mechanisch	Mech	mechanical
Medizin	Med	medicine
Meteorologie	Met	meteorology
Metallurgie, Hüttenkunde	Metal	metallurgy
militärisch	Mil	military
Bergbau	Min	mining
Mineralogie	Miner	mineralogy
Straßenverkehr	Mot	motoring and transport
Musik	Mus	music
Mythologie	Myth	mythology
Substantiv, Hauptwort	n	noun
nautisch, Seefahrt	Naut	nautical, naval
verneint	neg	negative
nordenglisch	N Engl	Northern English
norddeutsch	N Ger	North German
Substantiv im Plural	npl	plural noun
Nationalsozialismus	NS	Nazism
Neutrum	nt	neuter
Zahlwort	num	numeral
Objekt	obj	object
obsolet, ausgestorben	obs	obsolete
veraltet	old	
Optik	Opt	optics
Ornithologie, Vogelkunde	Orn	ornithology
Parlament	Parl	parliament
Passiv	pass	passive
pejorativ, abschätzig	pej	pejorative
persönlich/Person	pers	personal/person
Pharmazie	Pharm	pharmacy
Philosophie	Philos	philosophy
Phonetik, Phonologie	Phon	phonetics, phonology
Photographie	Phot	photography
Physik	Phys	physics
Physiologie	Physiol	physiology
Plural, Mehrzahl	pl	plural
poetisch	poet	
Dichtung	Poet	pertaining to poetry
Politik	Pol	politics
Possessiv-, besitzanzeigend	poss	possessive
prädikativ	pred	predicative
Präfix, Vorsilbe	pref	prefix
Präposition	prep	preposition
Präsens	pres	present
Presse	Press	
Präteritum, Imperfekt	pret	preterite
Pronomen, Fürwort	pron	pronoun
sprichwörtlich	prov	proverbial
Sprichwort	Prov	proverb
Partizip Präsens	prp	present participle
Psychologie, Psychiatrie	Psych	psychology, psychiatry
Partizip Perfekt	ptp	past participle
Warenzeichen	®	registered trade mark
Rundfunk	Rad	radio
Eisenbahn	Rail	railways
selten	rare	
regelmäßig	reg	regular
Relativ-	rel	relative
Religion	Rel	religion
	sb	somebody, someone
Schulwesen	Sch	school
Naturwissenschaften	Sci	science
schottisch	Scot	Scottish
Bildhauerei	Sculpt	sculpture
trennbar, veränderbare Folge	sep	separable
Handarbeit	Sew	sewing
süddeutsch	S Ger	South German
Singular, Einzahl	sing	singular
Skisport	Ski	skiing
Slang	sl	slang
Sozialwissenschaften	Sociol	social sciences
Raumfahrt	Space	space flight
Fachausdruck	spec	specialist term
Börse	St Ex	Stock Exchange
	sth	something
Konjunktiv	subjunc	subjunctive
Suffix, Nachsilbe	suf	suffix
Superlativ	superl	superlative
Landvermessung	Surv	surveying
schweizerisch	Sw	Swiss
Technik	Tech	technology
Nachrichtentechnik	Telec	telecommunications
Textilien	Tex	textiles
Theater	Theat	theatre
Fernsehen	TV	television
Typographie, Buchdruck	Typ	typography and printing
Hochschulwesen	Univ	university
(nord)amerikanisch	US	(North) American
gewöhnlich	usu	usually
Verb	vb	verb
Tiermedizin	Vet	veterinary medicine
intransitives Verb	vi	intransitive verb
reflexives Verb	vr	reflexive verb
transitives Verb	vt	transitive verb
transitives und intransitives Verb	vti	transitive and intransitive verb
transitives, intransitives und reflexives Verb	vtir	transitive, intransitive and reflexive verb
transitives und reflexives Verb	vtr	transitive and reflexive verb
vulgär	vulg	vulgar
Zoologie	Zool	zoology
ptp ohne ge-	*	*ptp* without ge-

GROSS WÖRTERBUCH
DEUTSCH-ENGLISCH
ENGLISCH-DEUTSCH
GERMAN-ENGLISH
ENGLISH-GERMAN
DICTIONARY

COLLINS

GERMAN–ENGLISH
ENGLISH–GERMAN
DICTIONARY

by
Peter Terrell
Veronika Calderwood-Schnorr   **Wendy V. A. Morris**
Roland Breitsprecher

Collins
London & Glasgow

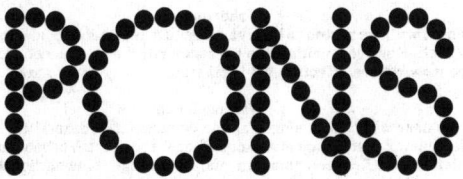

COLLINS
DEUTSCH-ENGLISCH
ENGLISCH-DEUTSCH

von
Peter Terrell
Veronika Calderwood-Schnorr   **Wendy V. A. Morris**
Roland Breitsprecher

Großwörterbuch
Klett

CIP-Kurztitelaufnahme der Deutschen Bibliothek

Pons-Großwörterbuch. – Stuttgart: Klett
→ Collins deutsch-englisch, englisch-deutsch

Collins deutsch-englisch, englisch-deutsch/
von Peter Terrell ...
1. Auflage – Stuttgart: Klett, 1981
(Pons-Großwörterbuch)
ISBN 3-12-517150-4
NE: Terrell, Peter [Mitverf.]

Computer typeset by G. A. Pindar & Son Ltd, Scarborough, England
with
Data capture and manipulation by Morton Word Processing Ltd, Scarborough, England
Einbandkonzeption: Erwin Poell, Heidelberg

First published 1980
© Copyright 1980 William Collins Sons & Co. Ltd.
7th Reprint 1987

ISBN 0 00 433480 9
with thumb index ISBN 0 00 433481 7

Printed and bound in Great Britain
by William Collins Sons & Co. Ltd.
P.O. Box, Glasgow G4 0NB

Lizenzausgabe für Ernst Klett, Stuttgart 1981

1. Auflage 1981 – Nachdruck 1987

Ernst Klett Verlage GmbH u. Co. KG
Stuttgart

ISBN 3-12-517150-4

CONTENTS INHALT

SENIOR EDITORS   LEITENDE REDAKTEURE
Peter Terrell
Veronika Calderwood-Schnorr   Wendy V. A. Morris
Roland Breitsprecher

EDITORS   REDAKTEURE
Dr Kathryn Rooney   Ingrid Schumacher   Dr Lorna A. Sinclair
Dorothee Ziegler   Ulrike Seeberger   Petra Schlupp

COMPILERS   MITARBEITER

Dr Christine R. Barker
Alexa H. Barnes
Michael Clark
Francis J. Flaherty
Susanne Flatauer
Ian Graham
Barbara Hellmann
Birgit Kahl
Christian Kay

Angelika Moeller
Günter Ohnemus
Dr John Pheby
Irmgard Rieder
Hanns Schumacher
Olaf Thyen
Karin Wiese
Renate Zenker-Callum

COLLINS STAFF   VERLAGSANGESTELLTE
Richard Thomas
Anne Dickinson   Irene Lakhani
Susan Lester   Valerie McNulty   Alice Truten
Elspeth Anderson

PREFACE

VORWORT

A dictionary is like a map, and like a map it can portray its subject in varying ways, with varying degrees of detail and of observation. This new dictionary is a map of the German and English languages and of the correspondences between the two. It has taken the most important and pervasive areas of language – the language of everyday communication, of newspapers, radio, television, the language of business, politics, the language of technology as it spreads into the layman's vocabulary, the language of literature and the arts – and has drawn a detailed picture. But where, as is the case with language (and in particular with the documented correlation of two languages) the terrain to be mapped is endless, subject to change and everything in it capable of being viewed from a multiplicity of angles, a wealth of details can easily become an inextricable maze. Detail needs clarity. And clarity has been made the principal criterion by reference to which the entries in this dictionary have been built up. Detail is never shown out of context, out of relation to the whole picture. Separate areas of meaning are clearly marked off, levels and types of language are pinpointed, dangers signalled, safe paths of idiomatic modes of expression are indicated. This dictionary is presented in the hope that the observations and distinctions that the editors have made in finding their way through two languages will enable the user to find his way too. And it is hoped too that the use of this book will be a source not only of understanding but of pleasure.

PMT
Glasgow
February 1980

Ein Wörterbuch ist wie eine Landkarte, und wie eine Landkarte kann es seinen Gegenstand auf verschiedene Weise, nach verschiedenen Graden der Genauigkeit und Detailliertheit, abbilden. Dieses neue Wörterbuch ist eine Landkarte der deutschen und der englischen Sprache und deren Beziehung zueinander. Es beschäftigt sich mit den wichtigsten Bereichen der Sprache, die von größter allgemeiner Bedeutung sind, der Sprache, wie sie uns im täglichen Umgang miteinander, in Presse, Rundfunk und Fernsehen, im Geschäftsleben und in der Politik begegnet, mit der Sprache der Technik, soweit der Laie sie in seinen Wortschatz aufgenommen hat, mit der Sprache von Literatur und Kunst – und versucht, sie in ihren Einzelaspekten abzubilden. Wo aber, wie in der Sprache, und ganz besonders in der dokumentarischen Gegenüberstellung zweier Sprachen, das Feld unendlich, Wandel permanent und Betrachtung aus den verschiedensten Blickwinkeln möglich ist, kann aus einer Fülle von Einzelheiten leicht ein Labyrinth werden. Zum Detail muß Klarheit treten, und Klarheit ist das grundlegende Kriterium für den Artikelaufbau in diesem Wörterbuch. Kein Detail ohne Kontext, in beziehungsloser Isolation. Bedeutungsunterschiede sind klar bezeichnet, Schattierungen beschrieben, Sprachebenen und -formen deutlich herausgehoben. Wo nötig, werden Gefahrensignale gesetzt, während Anwendungsbeispiele den Weg zum sicheren idiomatischen Ausdruck weisen. Wir legen dieses Wörterbuch in der Hoffnung vor, daß die Beobachtungen und Unterscheidungen, die die Verfasser bei ihrem Versuch gemacht haben, sich einen Weg durch zwei Sprachen zu bahnen, es dem Benutzer ermöglichen, sich seinerseits zurechtzufinden. Wir hoffen außerdem, daß die Benutzung dieses Wörterbuchs nicht nur die Verständigung erleichtert, sondern auch Spaß macht.

INTRODUCTION

This dictionary aims to provide the user with a detailed, accurate and thoroughly up-to-date source of reference for the study and use of the English and German languages. It is the conviction of the editors that the fundamental conception of this dictionary is such that it can justifiably claim to furnish the user not simply with a new and more modern reference book but with one that has such a significant difference in approach as to make it stand apart from existing German-English dictionaries. The character of this dictionary can best be described by an account of three aspects: scope; method; and treatment of entries.

Scope

The main emphasis of this dictionary is placed firmly on the contemporary English and German languages, with particular attention paid to the language of everyday communication. The total number of headwords and compounds (135,000) and of illustrative phrases (95,000) is greater than that contained in any comparable dictionary of single-volume format. And a brief look through a selection of these headwords and phrases will readily show that this fullness is not attained by the inclusion of rare or marginal words or expressions. In fact, on the contrary, a conscious effort has been made throughout all stages of the compilation of this dictionary to avoid the deadwood, the defunct term.

Nor is fullness attained simply by the inclusion of neologisms, although, of course, new words do figure largely in the text of this dictionary, along with newly coined idioms.

The fullness derives quite simply from an in-depth treatment of the ordinary English and German languages. There is an underlying central core of English and of German, the nuts and bolts of the languages, that often does not find expression in other bilingual (or indeed monolingual) dictionaries and that this dictionary has made its main concern. A huge range of quite ordinary words and expressions, the essential elements of communication (often quite complex to translate) are treated here in depth.

This, however, is not to say that older or more technical language does not figure at all in this dictionary. It most certainly does. If one were to define the range of the dictionary's wordlist in a slogan as 'the vocabulary of the educated layman' then where technical and old expressions have a place in this vocabulary they will have a place in the dictionary. Thus for example the language of computer technology and the micro-chip, which is fast impinging on the modern consciousness, is recorded in this book along with the more traditional technical areas.

The geographical spread of language is not neglected either. A wide coverage of American English is given. Swiss, Austrian and East German usages are treated. And regionalisms from within the main body of British English and German are covered.

In short then the aim of this dictionary as far as scope is concerned is to provide a range of words that will be genuinely useful in the modern world.

Method

It has been axiomatic throughout the compilation of this dictionary that English text was to be written only by lexicographers whose mother tongue was English and that German text was to be written by lexicographers of German mother tongue. This is the guarantee of authenticity of idiom both as regards source language and target language.

English and German lexicographers have worked together as a team, and at every stage of the six-year compilation period there has been discussion between English-speaker and German-speaker. The whole text, that is, compiled by lexicographers writing solely in their own native language, is vetted bilingually. This is the surest way to achieve the most accurate slotting-together of the two languages.

Treatment of entries

The distinguishing characteristic of the treatment of entries in this dictionary is the systematic use of indicators and collocators (see p ix) to identify and mark out varying areas of meaning and usage so that translations are only given with specific reference to the context or type of context in which they are valid. The user is not confronted by an undifferentiated barrage of possible but different translations; rather he is given context-specific translations. This applies both to translations where different *meanings* of a source language word have to be distinguished as well as to words where *usage* varies with context as, for example, in the combination (collocation) of nouns with an adjective.

The phrases which form a main part of this dictionary can be divided into two broad types. First there are the fixed expressions of the German and English languages: the proverbs, sayings and indeed the clichés. Secondly there are the phrases which serve to show the structural correspondence between the two languages, how, for example, a particular general translation, which is a noun, might have to be re-expressed as a verbal construction in a particular context if idiomaticity (and even, at times, intelligibility) is to be preserved.

To complete this detailed presentation of entries a sophisticated system of style labels is used to give the user information on the appropriateness of any particular translation or on the status of any headword he might look up from the point of view of register. The user, that is, is told, warned, if a word is informal, poetic, formal, old, dated, euphemistic etc. He is told if a word is likely to give offence, cause amusement, sound pompous, quaint, donnish or disgusting.

Further information on the structure of entries is given in the pages that follow. But, of course, the text itself is its own best exponent.

EINLEITUNG

Dieses Wörterbuch will dem Benutzer zum Studium und Gebrauch der deutschen und englischen Sprache ein ausführliches und zuverlässiges Nachschlagewerk an die Hand geben, das gründlich durchdacht und auf dem neuesten Stand ist. Die Verfasser sind der Überzeugung, daß das Wörterbuch in seiner Grundkonzeption so angelegt ist, daß es mit Recht den Anspruch erheben kann, dem Benutzer ein Nachschlagewerk zu bieten, das nicht einfach neuer und zeitgemäßer als andere ist. Es unterscheidet sich darüber hinaus schon in seinem Ansatz so beträchtlich von vorliegenden deutsch-englischen Wörterbüchern, daß ihm eine Sonderstellung zukommt. Die Eigenart dieses Wörterbuches läßt sich am besten durch die Darstellung folgender drei Aspekte beschreiben: Inhalt und Umfang; Methodik; Artikelaufbau.

Inhalt und Umfang

Bei diesem Wörterbuch liegt das Schwergewicht eindeutig auf der englischen und deutschen Gegenwartssprache, wobei der Sprache des Alltags besondere Aufmerksamkeit gilt. Die Gesamtzahl der Stichwörter und Zusammensetzungen (135.000) sowie der Anwendungsbeispiele (95.000) ist höher als in jedem anderen vergleichbaren einbändigen Wörterbuch. Schon ein kurzer Blick auf eine Auswahl von Stichwörtern und Wendungen zeigt deutlich, daß der Grund für diese Vollständigkeit nicht in der Aufnahme von seltenen Wörtern oder Redewendungen an der Peripherie der Sprache zu suchen ist. Ganz im Gegenteil ist in allen Arbeitsphasen bewußt Wert darauf gelegt worden, Abgelebtes und Ausgestorbenes aus diesem Wörterbuch zu verbannen. Auch ist die Vollständigkeit nicht einfach auf die Aufnahme von Neologismen zurückzuführen, obwohl freilich neue Wörter ebenso wie neugeprägte Redensarten einen breiten Raum in diesem Buch einnehmen.

Die Vollständigkeit beruht ganz einfach auf der Gründlichkeit und Ausführlichkeit, mit der die deutsche und englische Alltagssprache behandelt werden. Diesen eigentlichen Kern, den Baustoff der deutschen und englischen Sprache, der in anderen zweisprachigen (oder sogar einsprachigen) Wörterbüchern oft keinen Ausdruck findet, hat dieses Wörterbuch zu seinem Hauptanliegen gemacht. Es behandelt ein enormes Spektrum ganz gewöhnlicher Wörter und Redewendungen, die unentbehrlichen – oft recht schwierig zu übersetzenden – Elemente der sprachlichen Kommunikation, in aller Gründlichkeit. Damit soll jedoch nicht gesagt sein, daß älteres oder sondersprachliches Wortgut schlechthin in diesem Wörterbuch unberücksichtigt bleibt. Ganz im Gegenteil. Wenn man den Umfang des Wörterverzeichnisses schlagwortartig als den „Wortschatz des gebildeten Laien" beschreibt, heißt das gleichzeitig, daß ältere und sondersprachliche Ausdrücke, die in diesen Wortschatz eingegangen sind, auch in das Wörterbuch aufgenommen wurden. So ist zum Beispiel die Sprache der Computertechnik und der Mikrochips, die sich dem modernen Bewußtsein immer mehr aufprägt, ebenso wie die der traditionelleren Fachgebiete dokumentiert.

Auch die Verbreitung beider Sprachen in geographischer Hinsicht wird nicht vernachlässigt. Amerikanisches Englisch ist weitgehend berücksichtigt worden, und außer dem Sprachgebrauch in der Bundesrepublik Deutschland und der Deutschen Demokratischen Republik wird dem in Österreich und der Schweiz gesprochenen Deutsch ausführlich Rechnung getragen. Das gleiche gilt für den regionalen Sprachgebrauch in Deutschland und Großbritannien.

Kurzgefaßt läßt sich also sagen, daß dieses Wörterbuch nach Inhalt und Umfang das Ziel verfolgt, ein Spektrum von Wörtern anzubieten, die von echtem Nutzen in der heutigen Zeit sind.

Methodik

Für die Verfasser dieses Wörterbuches ist es von Anfang an eine Selbstverständlichkeit gewesen, daß der deutsche Text ausschließlich von Lexikographen mit Deutsch als Muttersprache und der englische Text ausschließlich von Lexikographen mit Englisch als Muttersprache verfaßt werden mußte. Damit ist die idiomatische Authentizität sowohl in der Ausgangssprache als auch in der Zielsprache gewährleistet. Deutsche und englische Lexikographen haben im Team gearbeitet, und während der sechsjährigen Redaktionsarbeit haben in allen Arbeitsphasen Diskussionen zwischen deutschen und englischen Muttersprachlern stattgefunden. Das heißt, daß der gesamte Text von Redakteuren ausschließlich in ihrer eigenen Sprache verfaßt wurde und aus zweisprachiger Sicht geprüft worden ist. Dies ist die sicherste und zuverlässigste Methode, beide Sprachen miteinander zu verzahnen.

Artikelaufbau

Der Artikelaufbau in diesem Wörterbuch zeichnet sich vor allem durch die systematische Verwendung von Indikatoren und Kollokatoren (siehe Seite ix) aus, die verschiedene Bedeutungs- und Anwendungsbereiche bezeichnen, so daß die angegebenen Übersetzungen sich immer auf den Kontext oder Kontextbereich beziehen, für den sie gelten. Der Benutzer wird nicht mit zwar möglichen, aber dennoch unterschiedlichen beziehungslosen Übersetzungen bombardiert. Statt dessen werden ihm kontextspezifische Übersetzungen geboten. Dies gilt sowohl für Übersetzungen, wo die unterschiedlichen *Bedeutungen* eines Wortes in der Ausgangssprache zu zeigen sind, als auch für Wörter, deren *Gebrauch* sich nach dem Kontext richtet, was z.B. bei der Verbindung (Kollokation) von Substantiv und Adjektiv der Fall ist.

Die Phraseologie bildet einen der wichtigsten Teile des Wörterbuchs und läßt sich grob in zwei Bereiche gliedern. Da sind zunächst die festen Wendungen im Deutschen und Englischen: die Sprichwörter, Redensarten und auch die Klischees; dann die Anwendungsbeispiele, mit denen die strukturelle Entsprechung beider Sprachen illustriert werden soll. So wird z.B. gezeigt, wie eine bestimmte allgemeine Übersetzung, sagen wir ein Substantiv, unter Umständen in einem bestimmten Kontext in eine Verbkonstruktion verwandelt werden muß, um die idiomatische Korrektheit – gelegentlich sogar die Verständlichkeit – zu wahren.

Zur Vervollständigung dieses detaillierten Artikelaufbaus wird ein hochentwickeltes System von Stilschichtbezeichnungen verwendet, damit der Benutzer erkennt, ob eine bestimmte Übersetzung angemessen ist oder welchen Stellenwert ein Stichwort, das er nachschlagen möchte, aus stilistischer Sicht hat. Es wird dem Benutzer mitgeteilt, ja er wird gewarnt, wenn ein Wort umgangssprachlich, dichterisch, förmlich, veraltet, altmodisch, verhüllend o.ä. ist, und es wird ihm gesagt, ob ein Ausdruck möglicherweise Anstoß erregt, Heiterkeit hervorruft, schwülstig, betulich, professoral oder abstoßend klingt. Weitere Erläuterungen zum Artikelaufbau werden auf den folgenden Seiten gegeben. Jedoch ist der Text selbst sein bester Interpret.

How to use the dictionary

Hinweise zur Benutzung des Wörterbuchs

Hinweise zur Benutzung des Wörterbuchs

Layout and order / Aufbau und Anordnung der Einträge

1.1 Alphabetical order is followed throughout. If two variant spellings are not alphabetically adjacent each is treated as a separate headword and there is a cross-reference to the form treated in depth. Where a letter occurs in brackets in a headword, this letter is counted for the alphabetical order, eg **Beamte(r)** will be found in the place of **Beamter, vierte(r, s)** in the place of **vierter**.

1.1 Die alphabetische Anordnung der Einträge ist durchweg gewahrt. Wo zwei verschiedene Schreibweisen alphabetisch nicht unmittelbar benachbart sind, wird jede als eigenes Stichwort behandelt. Es erfolgt ein Querverweis zu der ausführlich dargestellten Variante. In Klammern stehende Buchstaben in einem Stichwort unterliegen ebenfalls der Alphabetisierung, so findet man z.B. **Beamte(r)** an der Stelle von **Beamter, vierte(r, s)** unter **vierter**.

1.2 Abbreviations, acronyms and proper nouns will be found in their alphabetical place in the word list.

1.2 Abkürzungen, Akronyme und Eigennamen sind in alphabetischer Ordnung im Wörterverzeichnis zu finden.

1.3 Superior numbers are used to differentiate between words of like spelling.

1.3 Hochgestellte Ziffern werden verwendet, um zwischen Wörtern gleicher Schreibung zu unterscheiden.

rowing[1], rowing[2]; durchsetzen[1], durchsetzen[2].

1.4 Nouns which are always used in the plural are entered in the plural form.

1.4 Substantive, die stets im Plural verwendet werden, sind in der Pluralform angegeben.

trousers *npl*, **Ferien** *pl*.

1.5 Compounds will be found in their alphabetical place in the word list. The term "compound" is taken to cover not only solid and hyphenated compounds (eg **Bettwäsche, large-scale**) but also attributive uses of English nouns (eg **defence mechanism**) and other set collocations (eg **long jump**) which function in a similar way. Where the alphabetical order permits, compounds are run on in blocks with the first element printed in boldface type at the beginning of each block. Where possible a general translation has been given for the compound element.

1.5 Zusammengesetzte Wörter stehen an ihrer Stelle im Alphabet. Der Begriff „zusammengesetzte Wörter" bezeichnet nicht nur zusammengeschriebene oder durch Bindestrich verbundene Komposita (z.B. **Bettwäsche, large-scale**), sondern auch die attributive Verwendung englischer Substantive (z.B. **defence mechanism**) und andere feste Verbindungen (z.B. **long jump**), die eine ähnliche Funktion haben. Wo die alphabetische Ordnung es gestattet, werden die Zusammensetzungen in Blöcken angeordnet, wobei der erste Bestandteil am Kopf jedes Blocks in Fettdruck erscheint. Wo immer möglich, ist für das erste Element eine allgemeine Übersetzung angegeben.

Silber- *in cpds* silver.

From this the user can derive the translation for compounds not given in the word list. In the case of German compounds of the form **Brennessel, schnellebig** where the spelling changes if the word is split at the end of a line, this change is indicated.

Daraus kann der Benutzer die Übersetzung hier nicht angegebener Zusammensetzungen erschließen. Bei deutschen Komposita des Typs **Brennessel, schnellebig**, bei denen sich die Schreibweise bei Silbentrennung ändert, ist die getrennte Schreibweise angegeben.

Brennessel *f getrennt:* **Brenn-nessel.**

In a compound block the split form is given in its alphabetical place with a cross-reference to the standard form.

In einem Block von Komposita ist die getrennte Form an der entsprechenden Stelle in der alphabetischen Reihenfolge aufgeführt und auf die einfache Form verwiesen.

1.6 Phrasal verbs (marked ♦) will be found immediately after the main headword entry.

1.6 *Phrasal verbs* (durch ♦ bezeichnet) folgen unmittelbar auf das Hauptstichwort.

1.7 Idioms and set phrases will normally be found under the first meaningful element or the first word in the phrase which remains constant despite minor variations in the phrase itself. Thus 'to breast the tape' is included under 'breast' whereas 'to lend sb a hand' is treated under 'hand' because it is equally possible to say 'to give sb a hand'.
Certain very common English and German verbs such as be, get, have, make, put, bringen, haben, geben, machen, tun, which form the basis of a great many phrases eg to make sense, to make a mistake, etw in Ordnung bringen, etw in Gang bringen, have been considered as having a diminished meaning and in such cases the set phrase will be found under the most significant element in the phrase.

1.7 Redensarten und feste Wendungen sind im allgemeinen unter dem ersten bedeutungstragenden Element oder dem ersten Wort der Wendung, das trotz leichter Abwandlungen in der Wendung selbst unverändert bleibt, zu finden. So ist 'to breast the tape' unter 'breast' aufgenommen, 'to lend sb a hand' dagegen wird unter 'hand' abgehandelt, weil es ebenfalls möglich ist, 'to give sb a hand' zu sagen.
Bei als Funktionsverben gebrauchten Verben wie be, get, have, make, put, bringen, haben, geben, machen, tun, werden die meisten festen Wendungen, wie z.B. to make sense, to make a mistake, etw in Ordnung bringen, etw in Gang bringen, unter dem bedeutungstragenden Bestandteil der Wendung behandelt.

Indicating material / Erklärende Zusätze

General indicating material in the dictionary is printed in italics and takes the following forms:

Allgemeine erklärende Zusätze im Wörterbuch sind kursiv gedruckt und erscheinen in folgender Form:

2.1 Indicators in parentheses:

2.1 Indikatoren, in Klammern stehend:

2.1.1 synonyms and partial definitions

2.1.1 Synonyme und Teildefinitionen

gefühlvoll *adj* **(a)** *(empfindsam)* sensitive; *(ausdrucksvoll)* expressive. **(b)** *(liebevoll)* loving.

2.1.2 within verb entries, typical subjects of the headword

2.1.2 typische Substantiv-Ergänzungen in Verb-Einträgen

peel 3 *vi (wallpaper)* sich lösen; *(paint)* abblättern; *(skin, person)* sich schälen *or* pellen *(inf)*.

2.1.3 within noun entries, typical noun complements of the headword

2.1.3 typische Substantiv-Ergänzungen des Stichworts in Substantiv-Einträgen

gaggle 1 *n (of geese)* Herde *f*; *(hum: of girls, women)* Schar, Horde *f*.

2.2 Collocators, not in parentheses:

2.2 Kollokatoren, ohne Klammern stehend:

2.2.1 within transitive verb entries, typical objects of the headword

2.2.1 typische Objekte des Stichworts bei transitiven Verb-Einträgen

dent 2 *vt hat, car, wing* einbeulen, verbeulen; *wood, table* eine Delle machen in (+ *acc*); *(inf) pride* anknacksen *(inf)*.

2.2.2 within adjective entries, typical nouns modified by the headword

2.2.2 typische, durch das Stichwort näher bestimmte Substantive in Adjektiv-Einträgen

lilting *adj accent* singend; *ballad, tune, melody* beschwingt, munter.

2.2.3 within adverb entries, typical verbs or adjectives modified by the headword

2.2.3 typische, durch das Stichwort näher bestimmte Verben oder Adjektive bei Adverb-Einträgen

cumbersomely *adv move, write* schwerfällig; *phrased also* umständlich; *dressed* hinderlich.

2.3 Field labels are used:

2.3.1 to differentiate various meanings of the headword

2.3 Sachbereichsangaben werden verwendet:

2.3.1 um die verschiedenen Bedeutungen des Stichworts zu unterscheiden

Jungfrau *f* virgin; (*Astron, Astrol*) Virgo.

2.3.2 when the meaning in the source language is clear but may be ambiguous in the target language.

2.3.2 wenn die Bedeutung in der Ausgangssprache klar ist, jedoch in der Zielsprache mehrdeutig sein könnte.

Virgo *n* (*Astrol*) Jungfrau *f*.

A full list of field labels is given on the end-papers.

Eine vollständige Liste dieser Sachbereichsangaben befindet sich auf den Umschlag-Innenseiten.

2.4 Style labels are used to mark all words and phrases which are not neutral in style level or which are no longer current in the language. This labelling is given for both source and target languages and serves primarily as an aid to the non-native speaker.
When a style label is given at the beginning of an entry or category it covers all meanings and phrases in that entry or category.

2.4 Stilangaben werden verwendet zur Kennzeichnung aller Wörter und Wendungen, die keiner neutralen Stilebene oder nicht mehr dem modernen Sprachgebrauch angehören. Die Angaben erfolgen sowohl in der Ausgangs- als auch in der Zielsprache und sollen in erster Linie dem Nicht-Muttersprachler helfen.
Stilangaben zu Beginn eines Eintrages oder einer Kategorie beziehen sich auf alle Bedeutungen und Wendungen innerhalb dieses Eintrages oder dieser Kategorie.

(*inf*) denotes colloquial language typically used in an informal conversational context or a chatty letter, but which would be inappropriate in more formal speech or writing.

(*inf*) bezeichnet umgangssprachlichen Gebrauch, wie er für eine formlose Unterhaltung oder einen zwanglosen Brief typisch ist, in förmlicherer Rede oder förmlicherem Schriftverkehr jedoch unangebracht wäre.

(*sl*) indicates that the word or phrase is highly informal and is only appropriate in very restricted contexts, for example among members of a particular age group. When combined with a field label eg (*Mil sl*), (*Sch sl*) it denotes that the expression belongs to the jargon of that group.

(*sl*) soll anzeigen, daß das Wort oder die Wendung äußerst salopp ist und nur unter ganz bestimmten Umständen, z.B. unter Mitgliedern einer besonderen Altersgruppe, verwendet wird. In Verbindung mit einer Sachbereichsangabe, z.B. (*Mil sl*), (*Sch sl*), wird auf die Zugehörigkeit des Ausdrucks zum Jargon dieser Gruppe hingewiesen.

(*vulg*) denotes words generally regarded as taboo which are likely to cause offence.

(*vulg*) bezeichnet Wörter, die allgemein als tabu gelten und an denen vielfach Anstoß genommen wird.

(*geh*) denotes an elevated style of spoken or written German such as might be used by an educated speaker choosing his words with care.

(*geh*) bezeichnet einen gehobenen Stil sowohl im gesprochenen wie geschriebenen Deutsch, wie er von gebildeten, sich gewählt ausdrückenden Sprechern verwendet werden kann.

(*form*) denotes formal language such as that used on official forms, for official communications and in formal speeches.

(*form*) bezeichnet förmlichen Sprachgebrauch, wie er uns auf Formularen, im amtlichen Schriftverkehr oder in förmlichen Ansprachen begegnet.

(*spec*) indicates that the expression is a technical term restricted to the vocabulary of specialists.

(*spec*) gibt an, daß es sich um einen Fachausdruck handelt, der ausschließlich dem Wortschatz des Fachmanns angehört.

(*dated*) indicates that the word or phrase, while still occasionally being used especially by older speakers, now sounds somewhat old-fashioned.

(*dated*) weist darauf hin, daß das Wort bzw. die Wendung heute recht altmodisch klingt, obwohl sie besonders von älteren Sprechern noch gelegentlich benutzt werden.

(*old*) denotes language no longer in current use but which the user will find in reading.

(*old*) bezeichnet nicht mehr geläufiges Wortgut, das dem Benutzer jedoch noch beim Lesen begegnet.

(*obs*) denotes obsolete words which the user will normally only find in classical literature.

(*obs*) bezeichnet veraltete Wörter, die der Benutzer im allgemeinen nur in der klassischen Literatur antreffen wird.

(*liter*) denotes language of a literary style level. It should not be confused with the field label (*Liter*) which indicates that the expression belongs to the field of literary studies, or with the abbreviation (*lit*) which indicates the literal as opposed to the figurative meaning of a word.

(*liter*) bezeichnet literarischen Sprachgebrauch. Es sollte nicht mit der Sachbereichsangabe (*Liter*) verwechselt werden, die angibt, daß der betreffende Ausdruck dem Gebiet der Literaturwissenschaft angehört, und ebensowenig mit der Abkürzung (*lit*), die die wörtliche im Gegensatz zur übertragenen Bedeutung eines Wortes bezeichnet.

A full list of style labels is given on the end-papers.

Eine vollständige Liste der Stilangaben und ihrer Bedeutungen befindet sich auf den Umschlag-Innenseiten.

Grammatical Information

Gender
3.1 All German nouns are marked for gender in both sections of the dictionary.

3.2 Where two or more German nouns of the same gender are given consecutively as interchangeable translations, the gender is given only after the last translation in the series.

Grammatische Angaben

Geschlecht
3.1 Alle deutschen Substantive sind in beiden Teilen des Wörterbuches mit der Geschlechtsangabe versehen.

3.2 Wo zwei oder mehr deutsche Substantive gleichen Geschlechts als austauschbare Übersetzungen hintereinander stehen, wird das Geschlecht nur nach der letzten Übersetzung in der Folge angegeben.

trickster *n* Schwindler, Betrüger *m*.

3.3 Where a German translation consists of an adjective plus a noun, the adjective is given in the indefinite form which shows gender and therefore no gender is given for the noun.

3.3 Wenn eine deutsche Übersetzung aus einem Adjektiv und einem Substantiv besteht, wird das Adjektiv in der unbestimmten Form angegeben, die das Geschlecht erkennen läßt. Für das Substantiv erfolgt daher keine Geschlechtsangabe.

große Pause; zweites Frühstück.

3.4 Nouns of the form Reisende(r) *mf decl as adj* can be either masculine or feminine and take the same declensional endings as adjectives.

3.4 Substantive nach dem Muster Reisende(r) *mf decl as adj* können sowohl männlich wie weiblich sein und haben die gleichen Deklinationsendungen wie Adjektive.

m der Reisende, ein Reisender, die Reisenden *pl*
f die Reisende, eine Reisende, die Reisenden *pl*

3.5 Nouns of the form Beamte(r) *m decl as adj* take the same declensional endings as adjectives.

3.5 Substantive nach dem Muster Beamte(r) *m decl as adj* haben die gleichen Deklinationsendungen wie Adjektive.

der Beamte, ein Beamter, die Beamten *pl*

3.6 Adjectives of the form letzte(r, s) do not exist in an undeclined form and are only used attributively.

3.6 Adjektive nach dem Muster letzte(r, s) haben keine unflektierte Form und werden nur attributiv verwendet.

der letzte Mann, ein letzter Mann
die letzte Frau, eine letzte Frau
das letzte Kind, ein letztes Kind

3.7 Nouns of the form Schüler(in f) m are only used in the bracketed form in the feminine.

3.7 Substantive nach dem Muster Schüler(in f) m werden nur im Femininum in der eingeklammerten Form benutzt.

der/ein Schüler
die/eine Schülerin

3.8 The feminine forms are shown, where relevant, for all German noun headwords; unless otherwise indicated, the English translation will be the same as for the masculine form.
Where the feminine form is separated alphabetically from the masculine form but has the same translation it is given as a separate headword with a cross-reference to the masculine form.
Where the feminine form requires a different translation in English it is given as a separate headword.
Where there is no distinction between the translations given for the masculine and feminine forms and yet the context calls for a distinction, the user should prefix the translation with 'male/female or woman or lady . . .'

3.8 Für alle deutschen Substantive, die ein natürliches Geschlecht haben, wird die weibliche neben der männlichen Form angegeben. Wenn nicht anders angegeben, lautet die englische Form für beide gleich.
Wo die weibliche Form in der alphabetischen Reihenfolge nicht unmittelbar auf die männliche folgt, aber die gleiche Übersetzung hat, wird sie als eigenes Stichwort angegeben, wobei ein Querverweis auf die männliche Form erfolgt.
Wenn die weibliche Form im Englischen eine andere Übersetzung hat, wird sie als eigenes Stichwort angegeben.
Wo die für die männliche und die für die weibliche Form angegebene Übersetzung dieselbe ist, im entsprechenden Zusammenhang aber betont werden soll, daß es sich um einen Mann bzw. eine Frau handelt, sollte der Benutzer der Übersetzung 'male/female or woman or lady' voranstellen.

male teacher, female or woman or lady teacher

For German compound nouns the feminine forms have only been given where the English calls for a different translation.

Die weiblichen Formen der deutschen zusammengesetzten Substantive sind nur angegeben, wenn im Englischen eine eigene Übersetzung erforderlich ist.

Nouns
4.1 Nouns marked no pl are not normally used in the plural or with an indefinite article or with numerals. no pl is used:

(a) to give a warning to the non-native speaker who might otherwise use the word wrongly;
(b) as an indicator to distinguish the uncountable meanings of a headword in the source language.

Substantive
4.1 Substantive mit der Angabe no pl werden im allgemeinen nicht im Plural, mit dem unbestimmten Artikel oder mit Zahlwörtern verwendet. no pl dient:

(a) als Warnung an den Nicht-Muttersprachler, der das Wort sonst falsch benutzen könnte;
(b) zur Unterscheidung der unzählbaren und zählbaren Bedeutungen in der Ausgangssprache.

4.2 Nouns marked no art are not normally used with either a definite or an indefinite article except when followed by a relative clause.

4.2 Mit no art bezeichnete Substantive stehen im allgemeinen weder mit dem unbestimmten noch mit dem bestimmten Artikel, außer wenn ein Relativsatz von ihnen abhängig ist.

4.3 The genitive and plural endings are given for all German noun headwords except for certain regular noun endings. A complete list of these is given on page xvii.
The genitive and plural endings for German compound nouns are only given where the final element does not exist as a headword in its own right.

4.3 Bei allen deutschen Substantiv-Stichwörtern sind Genitivendung und Plural angegeben, mit Ausnahme bestimmter regelmäßiger Endungen. Diese sind in einer vollständigen Liste auf S. xvii erfaßt.
Die Genitivendung und der Plural sind bei zusammengesetzten Substantiven nur angegeben, wenn das letzte Element der Zusammensetzung nicht als Einzelwort vorkommt.

4.4 Irregular plural forms of English nouns are given on the English-German side.

4.4 Unregelmäßige Pluralformen englischer Substantive sind im englisch-deutschen Teil angegeben.

4.4.1 Most English nouns take -s in the plural.

4.4.1 Die meisten englischen Substantive bilden den Plural durch Anhängen von -s.

bed -s, site -s, key -s, roof -s

4.4.2 Nouns ending in -s, -z, -x, -sh, -ch take -es.

4.4.2 Substantive, die auf -s, -z, -x, -sh, -ch enden, erhalten die Endung -es.

gas -es, box -es, patch -es

4.4.3 Nouns ending in -y preceded by a consonant change the -y to -ie and add -s in the plural, except in the case of proper nouns.

4.4.3 Substantive, die auf Konsonant + -y enden, verwandeln im Plural das auslautende -y in -ie, auf das die Pluralendung -s folgt. Ausnahmen bilden Eigennamen.

lady – ladies, berry – berries
Germany – the two Germanys

Nouns ending in -quy also change the -y to -ie and add -s in the plural.

Auf -quy auslautende Substantive verwandeln bei der Pluralbildung ihr -y ebenfalls in -ie, worauf -s folgt.

soliloquy – soliloquies

Adjectives and adverbs
5.1 As a general rule, adjective translations of more than one word should be used postnominally or adverbially, but not before the noun.

Adjektive und Adverbien
5.1 Grundsätzlich sollten Übersetzungen von Adjektiven, die aus mehreren Wörtern bestehen, nur nachgestellt oder adverbial gebraucht und nicht dem Substantiv vorangestellt werden.

nacheifernswert adj worth emulating, worthy of emulation.

5.2 On the German-English side of the dictionary adverbs have only been treated as separate grammatical entries distinct from adjective entries:
(a) when their use is purely adverbial

5.2 Im deutsch-englischen Teil des Wörterbuches sind Adverbien als selbständige grammatische Einträge von Adjektiven nur dann unterschieden worden:
(a) wenn es sich um echte Adverbien handelt

höchst, wohl, sehr

(b) when the adverbial use is as common as the adjective use

(b) wenn der adverbiale Gebrauch genauso häufig ist wie der adjektivische

ordentlich

(c) when the English translation of the adverbial use cannot be derived from the adjectival translations by the rules of adverb formation.

(c) wenn die englische Übersetzung eines adverbial verwendeten Adjektivs nicht mit Hilfe der Regeln erschlossen werden kann, nach denen im Englischen Adverbien aus Adjektiven gebildet werden.

gut, schnell

Where no separate entry is given for the adverbial use of a German adjective, the user should form the English adverb from the translations given according to the rules given on page xiv.

Wo für den adverbialen Gebrauch eines deutschen Adjektivs kein gesonderter Eintrag vorliegt, ist es dem Benutzer selbst überlassen, aus den angegebenen Übersetzungen die englischen Adverbien nach den in Paragraph auf S. xiv angeführten Regeln zu bilden.

5.3 On the English-German side of the dictionary adverbs have been accorded the status of headwords in their own right.

In cases where an adverb is cross-referred to its related adjective, the German translations given under the adjective apply to the adverb too.

> **moodily** adv see adj.
> **moody** adj launisch, launenhaft; (bad-tempered) schlechtgelaunt attr, schlecht gelaunt pred; look, answer verdrossen, übellaunig.

In cases where the adverb and its related adjective occur consecutively in the alphabetical order and where the same translations apply to both, the entries have been conflated.

> **maladroit** adj, ~ly adv ungeschickt.

Verbs

6.1 All German verbs which form the past participle without ge- are marked with an asterisk in the text.

> **umarmen*** vt insep ptp **umarmt**
> **manövrieren*** vi ptp **manövriert**

6.2 All German verbs beginning with a prefix which can allow separability are marked sep or insep as appropriate.

> **überrieseln** vt insep ein Schauer überrieselte ihn
> **umschmeißen** vt sep das schmeißt alle meine Pläne um

Verbs beginning with the prefixes be-, er-, ver-, zer- are always inseparable.

6.3 All German verbs which take 'sein' as the auxiliary are marked aux sein.

> **gehen** pret **ging**, ptp **gegangen** aux sein

Where the auxiliary is not stated, 'haben' is used.

6.4 German irregular verbs composed of prefix and verb are marked irreg, and the forms can be found under the simple verb.

6.5 If the present or past participle of a verb has adjectival value it is treated as a separate headword in its alphabetical place.

> **gereift** 1 ptp of **reifen**. 2 adj (fig) mature.
> **struggling** adj artist etc am Hungertuch nagend.

Phrasal verbs

7.1 Phrasal verbs are covered in separate entries marked ♦ following the main headword.

7.2 Verb + adverb and verb + preposition combinations have been treated as phrasal verbs:
(a) where either the meaning or the translation is not simply derivable from the individual constituents;
(b) for clarity in the case of the longer verb entries.

Where a combination consists simply of a verb plus an adverb or preposition of direction it will frequently be covered under the main headword.

> **dash** . . . 3 vi (a) (rush) . . . to ~ away/back/up fort-/zurück-/hinaufstürzen.

7.3 Irregular preterites and past participles are only given in phrasal verb entries in the rare cases where they differ from those given in the main entry.

7.4 Phrasal verbs are treated in four grammatical categories:

7.4.1 vi

> **grow apart** vi (fig) sich auseinanderentwickeln.

7.4.2 vi +prep obj
This indicates that the verbal element is intransitive but that the particle requires an object.

> **hold with** vi +prep obj (inf) I don't ~ ~ that ich bin gegen so was (inf).

7.4.3 vt
This indicates that the verbal element is transitive. In most cases the object can be placed either before or after the particle; these cases are marked sep.

> **hand in** vt sep abgeben; forms, thesis also, resignation einreichen.

In some cases the object must precede the particle; these cases are marked always separate.

> **get over with** vt always separate hinter sich (acc) bringen.
> let's ~ this job ~ ~ bringen wir's hinter uns.

Occasionally the object must come after the particle; these cases are marked insep.

> **put forth** vt insep (liter) buds, shoots hervorbringen.

7.4.4 vt +prep obj
This indicates that both the verbal element and the particle require an object.

> **take upon** vt +prep obj he took that job ~ himself er hat das völlig ungebeten getan.

5.3 Im englisch-deutschen Teil des Wörterbuches sind die Adverbien als selbständige Stichwörter aufgeführt.

In Fällen, wo ein Adverb auf sein Adjektiv-Äquivalent verwiesen wird, gelten die für das Adjektiv angegebenen Übersetzungen auch für das Adverb.

In Fällen, wo Adjektiv und dazugehöriges Adverb in der alphabetischen Anordnung aufeinanderfolgen und wo die gleichen Übersetzungen für beide gelten, sind die Einträge zusammengefaßt worden.

Verben

6.1 Alle Verben im Deutschen, die das 2. Partizip ohne ge- bilden, sind im Text durch Sternchen gekennzeichnet.

6.2 Alle deutschen Verben, die mit einer oft trennbaren Vorsilbe beginnen, werden durch sep oder insep (= trennbar/untrennbar) bezeichnet.

Verben mit den Vorsilben be-, er-, ver-, zer- sind immer untrennbar.

6.3 Alle deutschen Verben, die die zusammengesetzten Zeiten mit „sein" bilden, sind durch aux sein gekennzeichnet.

Erfolgt keine Angabe, ist „haben" zu verwenden.

6.4 Zusammengesetzte unregelmäßige Verben im Deutschen sind durch irreg bezeichnet, ihre Stammformen sind beim Simplex angegeben.

6.5 Wenn 1. oder 2. Partizip eines Verbs den Status eines Adjektivs haben, werden sie wie eigenständige Stichwörter in alphabetischer Reihenfolge aufgeführt.

Phrasal verbs

7.1 Phrasal verbs sind in eigenen Einträgen abgehandelt. Sie sind durch ♦ bezeichnet und folgen dem Stichworteintrag für das Simplex.

7.2 Die Zusammensetzungen Verb + Adverb und Verb + Präposition werden als phrasal verbs abgehandelt:
(a) wo entweder die Bedeutung oder die Übersetzung sich nicht aus den Einzelbestandteilen ergibt;
(b) aus Gründen der Übersichtlichkeit bei längeren Verbeinträgen.

Bei einfachen Kombinationen von Verb + Adverb oder Präposition der Richtung ist unter dem Haupteintrag zu suchen.

7.3 Unregelmäßige Formen des Präteritums und des 2. Partizips werden in Einträgen, die phrasal verbs behandeln, nur in den seltenen Fällen angegeben, wo sie von den im Haupteintrag angegebenen abweichen.

7.4 Phrasal verbs werden unter vier grammatischen Kategorien abgehandelt:

7.4.1 vi

7.4.2 vi +prep obj
Hiermit soll gezeigt werden, daß das Verbelement intransitiv ist, daß aber die Partikel ein Objekt erfordert.

7.4.3 vt
Dies gibt an, daß das Verbelement transitiv ist. In den meisten Fällen kann das Objekt vor oder hinter der Partikel stehen; diese Fälle sind mit sep bezeichnet.

In einigen Fällen muß das Objekt der Partikel vorangehen; solche Fälle sind durch always separate bezeichnet.

Gelegentlich muß das Objekt der Partikel nachgestellt werden; solche Fälle sind durch insep bezeichnet.

7.4.4 vt +prep obj
Hiermit wird gezeigt, daß sowohl das Verbelement wie die Partikel ein Objekt verlangen.

In cases where a prepositional object is optional its translation is covered under *vi* or *vt*.

In Fällen, wo ein Präpositionalobjekt möglich, aber nicht nötig ist, findet man die entsprechende Übersetzung unter *vi* oder *vt*.

get off *vi* (*from bus, train*) aussteigen (*prep obj* aus);
(*from bicycle, horse*) absteigen (*prep obj* von).

8.1 Cross references are used in the following instances:

8.1.1 to refer the user to the most common term or to the spelling variant treated in depth;

8.1.2 to refer the user to the headword where a particular construction or idiom has been treated;

8.1.3 to avoid the repetition of indicating material where one word has been treated in depth and derivatives of that word have corresponding semantic divisions;

8.1.4 to refer the user from an English adverb to the related adjective in cases where the general translations given there also apply to the adverb;

8.1.5 to draw the user's attention to the full treatment of such words as numerals, languages, days of the week and months of the year under certain key words.

9.1 Punctuation and Symbols

, between translations indicates that the translations are interchangeable;
between source language phrases indicates that the phrases have the same meaning.

; between translations indicates a difference in meaning which is clarified by indicating material unless:

(a) the distinction has already been made within the same entry;
(b) in the case of some compounds the distinction is made under the simple form;
(c) the distinction is self-evident.

: between a headword and a phrase indicates that the headword is normally only used in that phrase.

/ between translations indicates parallel structure but different meanings, eg to feel good/bad.

(a) in a source language phrase it will normally be paralleled in the translation; where this is not the case, the translation covers both meanings;

(b) in a target language phrase where it is not paralleled by an oblique in the source language the distinction will either be made clear earlier in the entry or will be self-evident;

(c) in compounds it may be used to reflect a distinction made under the simple form.

~ is used within an entry to represent the headword whenever it occurs in an unchanged form.
In German headwords of the form Reisende(r) *mf decl as adj*, and höchste(r, s) *adj* it only replaces the element outside the brackets.
In German compound blocks it represents the compound element exactly as given at the beginning of the block. If it is given with a capital, any occurrence in a compound or phrase where it requires a small letter is clearly shown eg **Wochen-:** ...; **w~lang** *adj, adv* ...

— separates two speakers.

≈ indicates that the translation is the cultural equivalent of the term and may not be exactly the same in every detail.

* after a German verb indicates that the past participle is formed without *ge-*.

or is used to separate parts of a word or phrase which are semantically interchangeable.

also, auch used after indicating material denotes that the translations following it can be used in addition to the first translation or set of interchangeable translations given in the respective entry, category or phrase.

bold italics in a source language phrase indicate that the word is stressed.

italics in the translation of a phrase indicate that the word is stressed.

8.1 Querverweise sind in folgenden Fällen verwendet worden:

8.1.1 um den Benutzer auf den gebräuchlichsten Ausdruck oder auf die geläufigste Schreibweise zu verweisen, wo die ausführliche Darstellung des Stichworts zu finden ist;

8.1.2 um den Benutzer auf das Stichwort zu verweisen, wo eine bestimmte Konstruktion oder Wendung abgehandelt wird;

8.1.3 um die Wiederholung erklärender Zusätze zu vermeiden, wenn ein Wort bereits ausführlich behandelt worden ist und seine Ableitungen semantisch analog gegliedert sind;

8.1.4 um den Benutzer von einem englischen Adverb auf das entsprechende Adjektiv zu verweisen, wo die dort angegebenen allgemeinen Übersetzungen auch für das Adverb gelten;

8.1.5 um die Aufmerksamkeit des Benutzers auf die ausführliche Behandlung solcher Wortklassen wie Zahlwörter, Sprachbezeichnungen, Wochentage und Monate unter bestimmten Schlüsselwörtern zu lenken.

9.1 Satzzeichen und Symbole

, zwischen Übersetzungen zeigt an, daß die Übersetzungen gleichwertig sind;
zwischen Wendungen in der Ausgangssprache zeigt an, daß die Wendungen die gleiche Bedeutung haben.

; zwischen Übersetzungen zeigt einen Bedeutungsunterschied an, der durch erklärende Zusätze erläutert ist, außer:

(a) wenn die Unterscheidung innerhalb desselben Eintrags schon gemacht worden ist;
(b) bei Komposita, wo die Unterscheidung schon unter dem Simplex getroffen wurde;
(c) wenn die Unterscheidung offensichtlich ist.

: zwischen Stichwort und Wendung gibt an, daß das Stichwort im allgemeinen nur in der aufgeführten Wendung vorkommt.

/ zwischen Übersetzungen zeigt an, daß es sich um analoge Strukturen, aber verschiedene Übersetzungen handelt, z.B. to feel good/bad.

(a) der Schrägstrich in einer ausgangssprachlichen Wendung wird im allgemeinen seine Entsprechung in der Übersetzung finden; wo das nicht der Fall ist, gilt die Übersetzung für beide Bedeutungen;

(b) hat ein Schrägstrich in der Zielsprache kein Äquivalent in der Ausgangssprache, geht die getroffene Unterscheidung entweder aus in dem Eintrag bereits Gesagtem hervor, oder sie ist offensichtlich;

(c) bei Zusammensetzungen kann der Schrägstrich verwendet werden, um an eine für das Simplex getroffene Unterscheidung anzuknüpfen.

~ wird innerhalb von Einträgen verwendet, um das unveränderte Stichwort zu ersetzen.
Bei deutschen Substantiven des Typs Reisende(r) *mf decl as adj* und höchste(r, s) *adj* ersetzt der Strich den außerhalb der Klammer stehenden Teil des Wortes.
In deutschen Komposita-Blöcken ersetzt der Strich den Bestandteil der Zusammensetzung genau, wie er am Kopf des Blocks erscheint. Soll von Großschreibung auf Kleinschreibung übergegangen werden, ist dies angegeben, z.B. **Wochen-:** ...; **w~lang** *adj, adv* ...

— unterscheidet zwischen zwei Sprechern.

≈ soll darauf hinweisen, daß es sich bei der Übersetzung zwar um eine Entsprechung handelt, daß aber auf Grund kultureller Unterschiede Deckungsgleichheit nicht in allen Aspekten gegeben ist.

* nach einem deutschen Verb gibt an, daß das 2. Partizip ohne ge- gebildet wird.

or wird verwendet, um Bestandteile einer Wendung zu unterscheiden, die semantisch austauschbar sind.

also, auch nach erklärenden Zusätzen gibt an, daß die folgende(n) Übersetzung(en) zusätzlich zu der ersten Übersetzung oder Folge von austauschbaren Übersetzungen, die in dem Eintrag oder der Kategorie angegeben sind, benutzt werden kann/können.

Halbfette kursiv in ausgangssprachlichen Wendungen bezeichnet betonte Wörter oder Silben.

Kursivdruck in der Übersetzung einer Wendung gibt an, daß das Wort betont ist.

Adjectives and Adverbs

Declension of German adjectives
Adjectives ending in *-abel, -ibel, -el* drop the *-e-* when declined.

miserabel	ein miserabler Stil
	eine miserable Handschrift
	ein miserables Leben
heikel	ein heikler Fall
	eine heikle Frage
	ein heikles Problem

Adjectives ending in *-er, -en* usually keep the *-e-* when declined, except:
(a) in language of an elevated style level

finster   seine finstren Züge

(b) in adjectives of foreign origin

makaber	eine makabre Geschichte
integer	ein integrer Beamter

Adjectives ending in *-auer, -euer* usually drop the *-e-* when declined.

teuer	ein teures Geschenk
sauer	saure Gurken

Comparison of German adjectives and adverbs
Irregular comparative and superlative forms are given in the text, including those of adjectives and adverbs with the vowels *-a-, -o-, -u-* which take an umlaut.

hoch *adj comp* höher, *superl* höchste(r, s)

Where no forms are given in the text, the comparative and superlative are formed according to the following rules:
(a) Both adjectives and adverbs add *-er* for the comparative before the declensional endings.

schön – schöner

eine schöne Frau – eine schönere Frau
(b) Most adjectives add *-ste(r, s)* for the superlative.

schön – schönste(r, s)

ein schöner Tag – der schönste Tag
(c) Most adverbs form the superlative according to the following pattern.

schön – am schönsten

schnell – am schnellsten
(d) Adjectives and adverbs of one syllable or with the stress on the final syllable add *-e* before the superlative ending:
(i) always if they end in *-s, -ß, -st, -tz, -x, -z*
(ii) usually if they end in *-d, -t, -sch*

spitz *adj* spitzeste(r, s)

adv am spitzesten

gerecht *adj* gerechteste(r, s)

adv am gerechtesten
The same applies if they are used with a prefix or in compounds, regardless of where the stress falls.

unsanft *adj* unsanfteste(r, s)

adv am unsanftesten

Adjektive und Adverbien

Adverbialbildung im Englischen
(a) Die meisten Adjektive bilden das Adverb durch Anhängen von *-ly:*

strange *-ly*, odd *-ly*, beautiful *-ly*
(b) Adjektive, die auf Konsonant +*y* enden, wandeln das auslautende *-y* in *-i* um und erhalten dann die Endung *-ly:*

happy – happily

merry – merrily
(c) Adjektive, die auf *-ic* enden, bilden normalerweise das Adverb durch Anhängen von *-ally:*

scenic *-ally*

linguistic *-ally*

Steigerung der englischen Adjektive und Adverbien
Adjektive und Adverbien, deren Komparativ und Superlativ im allgemeinen durch Flexionsendungen gebildet werden, sind im Text durch (+*er*) bezeichnet, z.B.

young *adj* (+*er*)

Komparativ und Superlativ aller nicht durch (+*er*) bezeichneten Adjektive und Adverbien sind mit *more* und *most* zu bilden. Das gilt auch für alle auf *-ly* endenden Adverbien.
Unregelmäßige Formen des Komparativs und Superlativs sind im Text angegeben, z.B.

bad *adj comp* worst, *superl* worst

well *adj comp* better, *superl* best

Die flektierten Formen des Komparativs und Superlativs werden nach folgenden Regeln gebildet:
(a) Die meisten Adjektive und Adverbien fügen *-er* zur Bildung des Komparativs und *-est* zur Bildung des Superlativs an:

small smaller smallest
(b) Bei auf Konsonant +*y* endenden Adjektiven und Adverbien wird das auslautende *-y* in *-i* umgewandelt, bevor die Endung *-er* bzw. *-est* angefügt wird:

happy happier happiest
(c) Mehrsilbige Adjektive auf *-ey* wandeln diese Endsilbe in *-ier*, *-iest* um:

homey homier homiest
(d) Bei Adjektiven und Adverbien, die auf stummes *-e* enden, entfällt dieser Auslaut:

brave braver bravest
(e) Bei Adjektiven und Adverbien, die auf *-ee* enden, entfällt das zweite *-e:*

free freer freest
(f) Adjektive und Adverbien, die auf einen Konsonanten nach einfachem betontem Vokal enden, verdoppeln den Konsonanten im Auslaut:

sad sadder saddest
Nach Doppelvokal wird der auslautende Konsonant nicht verdoppelt:

loud louder loudest

German pronunciation is largely regular, and a knowledge of the basic patterns is assumed.
A full list of the IPA symbols used is given on page xvi.

Stress

1. The stress and the length of the stressed vowel are shown for every German headword.
2. The stressed vowel is usually marked in the headword, either with a dot if it is a short vowel
   eg sofo̦rt, Ao̦rta
or a dash if it is a long vowel or diphthong
   eg ho̲chmütig, alge̲braisch, ka̲u̲fen

Glottal Stop

1. A glottal stop (*Knacklaut*) occurs at the beginning of any word starting with a vowel.
2. A glottal stop always occurs in compounds between the first and second elements when the second element begins with a vowel.
3. When a glottal stop occurs elsewhere it is marked by a hairline before the vowel
   eg Be|amte(r)

Vowels

Vowel length

1. When phonetics are given for the headword a long vowel is indicated in the transcription by the length mark after it
   eg Chemie [çe'miː]
2. Where no phonetics are given a short stressed vowel is marked with a dot in the headword
   eg Mu̦tter
and a long stressed vowel is marked with a dash
   eg Va̲ter
3. Unstressed vowels are usually short; where this is not the case, phonetics are given for that vowel
   eg Almosen [-oː-]

Diphthongs and double vowels

1. Where phonetics are not given, vowel combinations which represent a stressed diphthong or a stressed long vowel are marked with an unbroken dash in the headword
   eg be̲iderlei, Ha̲ar, sie̲ben
2. *ie*
Stressed *ie* pronounced [iː] is marked by an unbroken line
   eg sie̲ben
When the plural ending -*n* is added, the pronunciation changes to [-iːən]
   eg Allego̲rie̲, *pl* Allego̲rien [-iːən]
When *ie* occurs in an unstressed syllable the pronunciation of that syllable is given
   eg Horte̦nsie [-iə]
3. *ee* is pronounced [eː].
When the plural ending -*n* is added, the change in pronunciation is shown
   eg Alle̲e *f* -, -n [-eːən]

Consonants

Where a consonant is capable of more than one pronunciation the following rules have been assumed:

1. *v*
(i) *v* is generally pronounced [f]
   eg Vater ['faːtɐ]
Where this is not the case phonetics are given
   eg Alkoven [al'koːvn, 'alkoːvn]

(ii) Words ending in -*iv* are pronounced [iːf] when undeclined, but when an ending is added the pronunciation changes to [iːv]
   eg aktiv [ak'tiːf]
      aktive (as in 'der aktive Sportler') [ak'tiːvə]
2. *ng*
(i) *ng* is generally pronounced [ŋ]
   eg Finger ['fɪŋɐ]
Where this is not the case phonetics are given
   eg Angora [aŋ'goːra]
(ii) In compound words where the first element ends in -*n* and the second element begins with g- the two sounds are pronounced individually
   eg Eingang ['aingaŋ]
      ungeheuer ['ʊngəhɔyɐ]
3. *tion* is always pronounced [-tsioːn] at the end of a word and [-tsion-] in the middle of a word
   eg Nation [na'tsioːn]
      national [natsio'naːl]
4. *st*, *sp*
(i) Where *st* or *sp* occurs in the middle or at the end of a word the pronunciation is [st], [sp]
   eg Fest [fest], Wespe ['vespə]
(ii) At the beginning of a word or at the beginning of the second element of a compound word the standard pronunciation is [ʃt] [ʃp].
   eg Stand [ʃtant], sperren ['ʃperən]
      Abstand ['ap-ʃtant], absperren ['ap-ʃperən]
5. *ch*
(i) *ch* is pronounced [ç] after *ä-, e-, i-, ö-, ü-, y-, ai-, ei-, äu,* *eu-* and after consonants
   eg ich [ɪç],
      Milch [mɪlç]
(ii) *ch* is pronounced [x] after *a-, o-, u-, au-*
   eg doch [dɔx], Bauch [baux]
Phonetics are given for all words beginning with *ch*.
6. *ig* is pronounced [ɪç] at the end of a word.
   eg König ['køːnɪç]
When an ending beginning with a vowel is added, it is pronounced [ɪg]
   eg Könige ['køːnɪgə]
7. *h* is pronounced [h]
   (i) at the beginning of a word
   (ii) between vowels in interjections
      eg oho [o'hoː]
   (iii) in words such as Ahorn ['aːhɔrn] and Uhu ['uːhu].
It is mute in the middle and at the end of non-foreign words
   eg leihen ['laiən], weh [veː]
Where *h* is pronounced in words of foreign origin, this is shown in the text.
8. *th* is pronounced [t].
9. *qu* is pronounced [kv].
10. *z* is pronounced [ts].
Phonetics are given where these rules do not apply and for foreign words which do not follow the German pronunciation patterns.

Where more than one pronunciation is possible this is also shown.

Partial phonetics are given where only part of a word presents a pronunciation difficulty.

Where the pronunciation of a compound or derivative can be deduced from the simplex no phonetics are given.

Die Zeichen der im Text verwendeten Lautschrift entsprechen denen der *International Phonetic Association*. Die angegebene Aussprache basiert auf dem weltweit als maßgebend anerkannten „English Pronouncing Dictionary" von Daniel Jones (vierzehnte Auflage, ausführlich überarbeitet und herausgegeben von A. C. Gimson).

Die Lautschrift gibt die Aussprache für das in Südengland gesprochene britische Englisch (Received Pronunciation) an, das in der gesamten Englisch sprechenden Welt akzeptiert und verstanden wird. Nordamerikanische Formen werden angegeben, wenn die Aussprache des betreffenden Wortes im amerikanischen Englisch erheblich abweicht (z.B. lever), nicht aber, wenn die Abweichung nur im „Akzent" besteht, wenn also Verständigungsschwierigkeiten nicht zu befürchten sind.

Jedes Stichwort im englischen Teil ist mit der Lautschrift versehen. Ausnahmen dazu bilden folgende Fälle:

(I) zusammengesetzte Stichwörter (*Komposita*), die getrennt geschrieben werden (z.B. **buffet car, buffalo grass**). Die Aussprache der einzelnen Teile ist unter dem entsprechenden Stichwort angegeben.

(II) *phrasal verbs* (z.B. **bring back, bring down, bring round**), wo ebenfalls die Einzelbestandteile an anderer Stelle behandelt sind.

(III) gleichlautende Stichwörter mit hochgestellten Ziffern (z.B. **bore²**, **bore³**, **bore⁴**), wo die Aussprache nur einmal beim ersten Eintrag in der Reihe (d.h. bei **bore¹**) angeführt ist.

(IV) wenn ein Stichwort auf eine andere Schreibweise verwiesen wird, die Aussprache aber gleich lautet (z.B. **checkered ... *see* chequered**). In diesem Falle wird die Aussprache nur unter dem Wort, auf das verwiesen wird (**chequered**), angegeben.

Sonstiges

(a) Die Aussprache von Abkürzungen, die als Kurzwörter (*Akronyme*) gebraucht werden, ist angegeben (z.B. NATO ['neɪtəʊ], ASLEF ['æzlef]). Wenn jeder Buchstabe einzeln ausgesprochen wird (z.B. MOT, RIP), erfolgt keine Ausspracheangabe.

(b) Stammformen unregelmäßiger Verben: Präteritum und 1. Partizip sind gesondert an der entsprechenden Stelle in der alphabetischen Reihenfolge angeführt und dort mit der Lautschrift versehen. Die Ausspracheangabe wird bei der Grundform des Verbs nicht wiederholt. So findet man z.B. die phonetische Umschrift für **bought, sold** usw. unter diesen Einträgen, nicht aber unter **buy, sell** usw.

Phonetic Symbols / Zeichen der Lautschrift

Vowels/Vokale

matt	[a]	
Fahne	[a:]	
Vater	[ɐ]	
	[ɑ:]	calm, part
	[æ]	sat
	[ɒ]	cot
Chanson	[ã]	
Gourmand	[ã:]	
	[ã:]	double *entendre*
Etage	[e]	egg
Seele, Mehl	[e:]	
Wäsche, Bett	[ɛ]	
zählen	[ɛ:]	
timbrieren	[ɛ̃]	
Timbre, Teint	[ɛ̃:]	
mache	[ə]	above
	[ɜ:]	burn, earn
Kiste	[ɪ]	pit, awfully
Vitamin	[i]	
Ziel	[i:]	peat
Oase	[o]	
oben	[o:]	
Fondue	[õ]	
Chanson	[õ:]	
Most	[ɔ]	
	[ɔ:]	born
ökonomisch	[ø]	
blöd	[ø:]	
Götter	[œ]	
Parfum	[œ̃:]	
	[ʌ]	cup, come
zuletzt	[u]	
Mut	[u:]	fool
Mutter	[ʊ]	put
Typ	[y]	
Kübel	[y:]	
Sünde	[ʏ]	

Diphthongs/Diphthonge

weit	[ai]	
	[aɪ]	buy, die, my
Haus	[au]	
	[aʊ]	house, now
	[eɪ]	pay, mate
	[ɛə]	pair, mare
	[əʊ]	no, boat
	[ɪə]	mere, shear
Heu, Häuser	[ɔy]	
	[ɔɪ]	boy, coin
	[ʊə]	tour, poor

Consonants/Konsonanten

Ball	[b]	ball
mich	[ç]	
denn	[d]	den
fern	[f]	field
gern	[g]	good
Hand	[h]	hand
ja, Million	[j]	yet, million
Kind	[k]	kind
links, Pult	[l]	left, little
matt	[m]	mat
Nest	[n]	nest
lang	[ŋ]	long
Paar	[p]	put
rennen	[r]	run
fassen	[s]	sit
Stein, Schlag	[ʃ]	shall
Tafel	[t]	tab
	[θ]	thing
	[ð]	this
wer	[v]	very
	[w]	wet
Loch	[x]	loch
singen	[z]	pods, zip
genieren	[ʒ]	measure

Other signs/Andere Zeichen

ǀ		glottal stop/Knacklaut
[ʳ]		[r] pronounced before a vowel/vor Vokal ausgesprochenes [r]
[ˈ]		main stress/Hauptton
[ˌ]		secondary stress/Nebenton

Regular German Noun Endings

nom		gen	pl
-ade	f	-ade	-aden
-ant	m	-anten	-anten
-anz	f	-anz	-anzen
-ar	m	-ars	-are
-är	m	-ärs	-äre
-at	nt	-at(e)s	-ate
-atte	f	-atte	-atten
-chen	nt	-chens	-chen
-ei	f	-ei	-eien
-elle	f	-elle	-ellen
-ent	m	-enten	-enten
-enz	f	-enz	-enzen
-esse	f	-esse	-essen
-ette	f	-ette	-etten
-eur	m	-eurs	-eure
-eurin	f	-eurin	-eurinnen
-euse	f	-euse	-eusen
-graph	m	-graphen	-graphen
-heit	f	-heit	-heiten
-ie	f	-ie	-ien
-ik	f	-ik	-iken
-in	f	-in	-innen
-ine	f	-ine	-inen
-ion	f	-ion	-ionen
-ist	m	-isten	-isten
-ium	nt	-iums	-ien
-ius	m	-ius	-iusse
-ive	f	-ive	-iven
-ivum	nt	-ivums	-iva
-keit	f	-keit	-keiten
-lein	nt	-leins	-lein
-ling	m	-lings	-linge
-ment	nt	-ments	-mente
-mus	m	-mus	-men
-nis	f	-nis	-nisse
-nis	nt	-nisses	-nisse
-nom	m	-nomen	-nomen
-oge	m	-ogen	-ogen
-or	m	-ors	-oren
-rich	m	-richs	-riche
-schaft	f	-schaft	-schaften
-sel	nt	-sels	-sel
-tät	f	-tät	-täten
-tiv	nt, m	-tivs	-tive
-tum	nt	-tums	-tümer
-ung	f	-ung	-ungen
-ur	f	-ur	-uren

The Genitive of Proper Names

The genitive of the proper names of people, cities, countries etc takes two forms. 1. When used with an article the word remains unchanged, e.g. des Aristoteles, der Bertha, des schönen Berlin. 2. When used without an article an 's' is added to the noun, e.g. die Straßen Berlins, Marias Hut, Olafs Auto. When the noun ends in s, ß, tz, x or z an apostrophe is added, e.g. Aristoteles' Schriften, die Straßen Calais'.

In most cases in this dictionary the genitive form given for the proper names of people is that which is correct for use with an article. For the proper names of countries and cities the form for use without an article is given.

Acknowledgements

The editors would like to express their thanks to Mr Peter P. Hasler and Dr Kurt-Michael Pätzold for their help in the initial stages of the work on this book.

Die Redaktion möchte Herrn Peter P. Hasler und Herrn Dr. Kurt-Michael Pätzold für ihre Mithilfe während der Anfangsstadien der Arbeit an diesem Buch ihren Dank aussprechen.

A, a [aː] *nt* -, - *or* (*inf*) -s, -s A, a. **das A und (das) O** (*fig*) the essential thing(s), the be-all and end-all; (*eines Wissensgebietes*) the basics *pl*; **sich (drehen und) winden wie ein ~** (*aus Verlegenheit*) von A bis Z (*fig inf*) from beginning to end, from A to Z; **sie/ihr alle, von A bis Z** them/you, the whole lot of them/you; **wer A sagt, muß auch B sagen** (*prov*) in for a penny, in for a pound (*prov*); (*moralisch*) if you start something, you should see it through.

à [a] *prep* (*esp Comm*) at.

Ä, ä [ɛː] *nt* -, - *or* (*inf*) -s, -s Ae, ae, A/a umlaut.

Aa [aˈa] *nt* -, *no pl* (*baby-talk*) **~ machen** to do big job (*baby-talk*) *or* number two (*baby-talk*).

AA [aːˈaː] *nt* -s, *no pl abbr of* **Auswärtiges Amt** FO (*Brit*).

Aal *m* -(e)s, -e eel. **sich (drehen und) winden wie ein ~** (*aus Verlegenheit*) to wriggle like an eel; (*aus Unaufrichtigkeit*) to try and wriggle out of it; **glatt wie ein ~** (*fig*) (as) slippery as an eel.

aalen *vr* (*inf*) to stretch out. **sich in der Sonne ~** to bask in the sun.

Aal-: **a~glatt** *adj* (*pej*) slippery (as an eel), slick; **er verstand es meisterhaft, sich a~glatt herauszureden** he very slickly *or* smoothly managed to talk himself out of it; **~suppe** *f* eel soup.

a.a.O. *abbr of* **am angegebenen** *or* **angeführten Ort** loc cit.

Aar *m* -(e)s, -e (*obs liter*) eagle, lord of the skies (*liter*).

Aas *nt* -es, -e (a) (*Tierleiche*) carrion, rotting carcass. (b) *pl* **Äser** (*inf: Luder*) bugger (*sl*), sod (*sl*), devil (*inf*). **kein ~** not a single bloody person (*inf*); **sie ist ein kleines ~** she's a little devil (*inf*).

Aasbande *f* (*pej inf*) bunch of hooligans (*inf*).

aasen *vi* (*inf*) to be wasteful. **mit etw ~** to waste sth; **mit Geld, Gütern auch** to squander sth, to be extravagant *or* wasteful with sth; **mit Gesundheit** to ruin sth.

Aas-: **~fresser** *m* scavenger, carrion-eater; **~geier** *m* (*lit, fig*) vulture.

aasig 1 *adj attr* abominable, horrible, disgusting. 2 *adv* (*inf: sehr*) horribly, abominably (*inf*).

Aas-: **~käfer** *m* burying *or* sexton beetle; **~seite** *f* flesh side (of a/the hide).

ab [ap] 1 *adv* off, away; (*Theat*) exit *sing*, exeunt *pl*. **die nächste Straße rechts ~** the next street (off) to *or* on the right; **~ Zoologischer Garten** from Zoological Gardens; **~ Hamburg** after Hamburg; **München ~ 12²⁰ Uhr** (*Rail*) leaving Munich 12.20; **~ wann?** from when?, as of when?; **~ nach Hause** go *or* off you go home; **~ ins Bett mit euch!** off to bed with you *or* you go; **Mütze/Helm ~!** caps/hats off; **Tell ~** exit Tell; **N und M ~** (*Theat*) exeunt N and M; **~ durch die Mitte** (*inf*) beat it! (*inf*), hop it! (*inf*); **kommt jetzt, ~ durch die Mitte!** come on, let's beat *or* hop it! (*inf*); **~ und zu** *or* (*N Ger*) **an** from time to time, now and again, now and then; *siehe* **von**.

2 *prep* +*dat* (*räumlich*) from; (*zeitlich*) from, as of, as from. **Kinder ~ 14 Jahren** children from (the age of) 14 up; **alle ~ Gehaltsstufe 4** everybody from grade 4 up; **Soldaten ~ Gefreiten** soldiers from private up; **~ Werk** (*Comm*) ex works; **~ sofort** as of now/then.

aba [ˈabɒ] *adv* (*Aus inf*) = **herunter; hinunter.**

Abakus *m* -, - abacus.

abänderbar, abänderlich (*old*) *adj* amendable.

abändern *vt sep* to alter (*in* +*acc* to); (*überarbeiten auch*) to revise; *Gesetzentwurf* to amend (*in* +*acc* to); *Strafe, Urteil* to revise (*in* +*acc* to).

Abänderung *f siehe vt* alteration (*gen* to); revision; amendment; revision. **in ~** (*Parl, Jur*) in amendment.

Abänderungs-: **~antrag** *m* (*Parl*) proposed amendment; **einen ~antrag einbringen** to submit an amendment; **~vorschlag** *m* proposed amendment; **einen ~vorschlag machen** to propose an amendment.

abarbeiten *sep* 1 *vt Schuld* to work off; *Überfahrt* to work; (*hinter sich bringen*) *Vertragszeit* to work. 2 *vr* to slave (away), to work like a slave; *siehe* **abgearbeitet.**

Abart *f* variety (*auch Biol*); (*Variation*) variation (*gen* on).

abartig *adj* abnormal, deviant.

Abartigkeit *f* abnormality, deviancy.

Abbau *m* -(e)s, *no pl* (a) (*Förderung*) (*über Tage*) quarrying; (*unter Tage*) mining.
(b) (*lit, fig: Demontage*) dismantling.
(c) (*Chem*) decomposition; (*im Körper auch*) breakdown; (*fig: Verfall*) decline; (*der Persönlichkeit*) disintegration.
(d) (*Verringerung*) (*von Personal, Produktion etc*) reduction (*gen* in, of), cutback (*gen* in); (*von überflüssigen Vorräten*) gradual elimination (*gen* of); (*von Preisen*) cut (*gen* in), reduction (*gen* in, of); (*von Privilegien*) reduction (*gen* of), stripping

away (*gen* of); (*von Vorurteilen*) gradual collapse (*gen* of). **der ~ von Beamtenstellen** the reduction in the number of civil service posts.

abbauen *sep* 1 *vt* (a) (*fördern*) (*über Tage*) to quarry; (*unter Tage*) to mine.
(b) (*demontieren*) *Gerüst, System* to dismantle; *Maschine auch* to strip down; *Gerüst auch* to take down; *Kulissen* to take down, to strike; *Zelt* to strike; *Lager* to break, to strike. **ein System allmählich ~** to phase out a system.
(c) (*Chem*) to break down, to decompose.
(d) (*verringern*) *Produktion, Personal, Bürokratie* to cut back, to reduce, to cut down on; *Preise* to reduce, to cut back; *Arbeitsplätze, -kräfte* to reduce the number of; *Privilegien* to cut back, to strip away.
2 *vi* (*inf*) (*Sportler etc*) to go downhill; (*erlahmen*) to flag, to wilt; (*abschalten*) to switch off.

Abbauprodukt *nt* (*Chem*) by-product.

abbehalten* *vt sep irreg den Hut* ~ to keep one's hat off.

abbeißen *sep irreg* 1 *vt* to bite off. **eine Zigarre ~** to bite the end off a cigar; **sich** (*dat*) **die Zunge ~** to bite one's tongue off. 2 *vi* to take a bite. **nun beiß doch mal richtig ab!** now bite it off properly!

abbekommen* *vt sep irreg* (a) to get. **etwas ~** to get some (of it); (*beschädigt werden*) to get damaged; (*verletzt werden*) to get hurt; (*Prügel ~*) to catch *or* cop it (*inf*); **das Auto/er hat dabei ganz schön was ~** (*inf*) the car/he really copped it (*inf*); **nichts ~** not to get any (of it); (*nicht beschädigt werden*) not to get damaged; (*nicht verletzt werden*) to come off unscathed; **sein(en) Teil ~** (*lit, fig*) to get one's fair share.
(b) (*abmachen können*) to get off (*von etw* sth).

abberufen* *vt sep irreg Diplomaten, Minister* to recall. (**von Gott**) **~ werden** (*euph*) to be called to one's maker.

Abberufung *f* recall; (*euph: Tod*) departure from this life.

abbestellen* *vt sep* to cancel; *jdn auch* to tell not to call *or* come; *Telefon* to have disconnected.

Abbestellung *f siehe vt* cancellation; disconnection.

abbetteln *vt sep jdm etw* ~ to scrounge sth off *or* from sb (*inf*).

abbeuteln *vt sep* (*Aus*) *siehe* **abschütteln.**

abbezahlen* *sep* 1 *vt Raten, Auto etc* to pay off. 2 *vi* (*auf Raten*) to pay in instalments; (*Raten ~*) to pay sth off.

abbiegen *sep irreg* 1 *vt* (a) to bend; (*abbrechen*) to bend off.
(b) (*inf: verhindern*) *Frage, Thema* to head off, to avoid; *Frage* to deflect; (*inf*) *das Gespräch ~* to change the subject; **zum Glück konnte ich das ~** luckily I managed to stop that; **diesen Vorschlag hat die Gewerkschaft abgebogen** the union put a stop to this proposal; **ich sollte tanzen/eine Rede halten, aber zum Glück konnte ich das ~** I was supposed to dance/make a speech but luckily I managed to get out of it.
2 *vi aux sein* to turn off (*in* +*acc* into); (*bei Gabelungen auch*) to fork off; (*Straße*) to bend. **nach rechts ~** to turn (off to the) right; to fork right; to bend (to the) right.

Abbild *nt* (*Nachahmung, Kopie*) copy, reproduction; (*Spiegelbild*) reflection; (*Wiedergabe*) picture, portrayal, representation; (*von Mensch*) image, likeness. **er ist das genaue ~ seines Vaters** he's the spitting image of his father.

abbilden *vt sep* (*lit, fig*) to depict, to portray, to show; *Verhältnisse etc auch* to reflect; (*wiedergeben*) to reproduce. **auf der Titelseite ist ein Teddybär abgebildet** there's a picture of a teddy bear on the front page; **auf dem Foto ist eine Schulklasse abgebildet** there's a school class (shown) in the photo.

Abbildung *f* (a) (*das Abbilden*) depiction, portrayal; (*Wiedergabe*) reproduction. (b) (*Illustration*) illustration; (*Schaubild*) diagram. *siehe* **~ S.12** see the illustration on p12; **das Buch ist mit zahlreichen ~en versehen** the book is copiously illustrated *or* has numerous illustrations.

abbinden *sep irreg* 1 *vt* (a) to undo, to untie; (*Med*) *Arm, Bein etc* to ligature. **sich** (*dat*) **die Schürze ~** to take off one's apron.
(b) (*Cook*) to bind. 2 *vi* (*Beton, Mörtel*) to set; (*Cook*) to bind.

Abbitte *f* apology. (**bei jdm wegen etw**) **~ tun** *or* **leisten** to make *or* offer one's apologies *or* to apologize (to sb for sth).

abbitten *vt sep irreg* (*liter*) **jdm etw ~** to beg sb's pardon for sth, to make *or* offer one's apologies to sb for sth.

abblasen *sep irreg* 1 *vt Staub, Schmutz* to blow off (*von etw* sth); *Tisch, Buch* to blow the dust *etc* off, to blow clean; *Gas* to release, to let off. **eine Hauswand mit Sandstrahl ~** to sandblast a house wall. (b) (*Tech*) *Hochofen* to let burn down. (c) (*inf*) *Veranstaltung, Feier, Streik* to call off.
2 *vi* (*Tech: Hochofen*) to burn down.

abblassen *vi sep aux sein* (*geh*) (*Mensch*) to blanch, to (go *or* grow) pale; (*Farbe*) to fade (*auch fig*).

abblättern vi sep aux sein (Putz, Farbe) to flake or peel (off).

abbleiben vi sep irreg aux sein (N Ger inf) to get to (inf). **wo ist er abgeblieben?** where has he got to?; **irgendwo muß er/es abgeblieben sein** he/it must be somewhere.

abblendbar adj Rückspiegel anti-dazzle.

Abblende f (Film) fade(-out).

abblenden sep 1 vt Lampe to shade, to screen; Scheinwerfer to dip (Brit), to dim (US). 2 vi (Phot) to stop down; (Film) to fade out. **dann wurde abgeblendet** the scene (was) faded out.

Abblendlicht nt (Aut) dipped (Brit) or dimmed (US) headlights pl. **mit ~ fahren** to drive on dipped or dimmed headlights.

abblitzen vi sep aux sein (inf) to be sent packing (bei by) (inf). **jdn ~ lassen** to send sb packing (inf), to send sb off with a flea in his/her ear (inf).

abblocken vt sep (Sport, fig) to block.

abblühen vi sep aux sein (rare) siehe **verblühen**.

Abbrand m (a) (Verbrennen) combustion. (b) (Kernenergie) burn-up.

Abbrändler m -s, - (S Ger, Aus) sb whose house has been destroyed by fire, fire victim.

abbrausen sep 1 vt to give a shower; Körperteil to wash under the shower. **sich ~** to have or take a shower, to shower. 2 vi aux sein (inf) to roar off or away.

abbrechen sep irreg 1 vt (a) to break off; Zweig, Ast auch to snap off; Bleistift to break, to snap. **etw von etw ~** to break sth off sth; **(nun) brich dir (mal) keine Verzierung(en)** (inf) or **keinen** (sl) **ab!** don't make such a palaver (inf) or song and dance (inf); **sich** (dat) **einen ~** (sl) (Umstände machen) to make heavy weather of it (inf); (sich sehr anstrengen) to go to a lot of bother, to bust one's arse (vulg).
   (b) (abbauen) Zelt to strike; Lager auch to break; (niederreißen) to demolish; Gebäude to demolish, to pull or tear down; siehe **Zelt**.
   (c) (unterbrechen) to break off; Sportveranstaltung to stop; Streik to call off; siehe **abgebrochen**.
   2 vi (a) aux sein to break off; (Ast, Zweig auch) to snap off; (Bleistift, Fingernagel) to break.
   (b) (aufhören) to break off, to stop.

abbremsen sep 1 vt Motor to brake; (fig) to curb. **auf 30 ~** to brake down to 30. 2 vi siehe **bremsen**.

abbrennen sep irreg 1 vt Wiesen to burn off or away the stubble in; Böschung to burn off or away the scrub on; Gehöft, Dorf to burn down; Feuerwerk, Rakete to let off; Kerze etc to burn; (wegbrennen) Lack to burn off; (Tech: abbeizen) to pickle, to scour; Stahl to blaze off. **ein Feuerwerk ~** to have fireworks or a firework display.
   2 vi aux sein to burn down. **unser Gehöft ist/wir sind abgebrannt** our farm was/we were burnt down; **dreimal umgezogen ist einmal abgebrannt** (prov) by the time you've moved house three times, you've lost as much as if the place had been burnt out; siehe **abgebrannt**.

Abbreviatur [abrevia'tuːɐ] f (Typ, Mus) abbreviation.

abbringen vt sep irreg (a) jdn davon ~, etw zu tun to stop sb doing sth; (abraten auch) to persuade sb not to do sth, to dissuade sb from doing sth; **jdn von etw ~** to make sb change his/her mind about sth; **ich lasse mich von meiner Meinung nicht ~** you won't get me to change my mind, nothing will make me change my mind; **jdn vom Thema ~** to get sb off the subject; **jdn vom Rauchen/Trinken ~** to get sb to stop smoking/drinking, to stop sb smoking/drinking; **jdn/einen Hund von der Spur ~** to throw or put sb/a dog off the scent; **jdn/etw vom Kurs ~** to throw or put sb/sth off course.
   (b) (inf: esp S Ger) Deckel etc to get off.

abbröckeln vi sep aux sein to crumble away; (fig) to fall off (auch St Ex), to drop off. **die Aktienkurse sind am A~** the share prices are falling (off); **die Familie/der Ruf der Firma ist am A~** the family/firm's reputation is gradually declining.

Abbruch m, no pl (a) (das Niederreißen) demolition; (von Gebäuden auch) pulling down. **auf ~ verkaufen** to sell for demolition; **auf ~ stehen** to be scheduled or due for demolition, to be condemned.
   (b) (Beendigung) (von Beziehungen, Verhandlungen, Reise) breaking off; (von Sportveranstaltung) stopping. **einem Land mit ~ der diplomatischen Beziehungen drohen** to threaten to break off diplomatic relations with a country; **es kam zum ~ des Kampfes** the fight had to be stopped.
   (c) (Schaden) harm, damage. **einer Sache** (dat) **~ tun** to harm or damage sth, to do (some) harm or damage to sth; **das tut der Liebe keinen ~** it doesn't harm their/our relationship; **das tut unseren Interessen ~** that is detrimental to our interests; **das hat der Fröhlichkeit keinen ~ getan** it didn't spoil the happy mood.

Abbruch-: ~**arbeiten** pl demolition work; ~**firma** f demolition firm; ~**liste** f siehe **Abrißliste**; **a~reif** adj only fit for demolition; (zum ~ freigegeben) condemned.

abbrühen vt sep to scald; Mandeln to blanch; siehe **abgebrüht**.

abbrummen sep 1 vt (inf) Zeit to do (inf). **eine Strafe ~** to do time (inf). 2 vi aux sein (inf) to roar off or away.

abbuchen vt sep (im Einzelfall) to debit (von to, against); (durch Dauerauftrag) to pay by standing order (von from); (fig: abschreiben) to write off. **für das A~ erhebt die Bank Gebühren** the bank makes a charge for each debit/for a standing order.

Abbuchung f siehe vt debit; (payment by) standing order; writing off. **etw durch ~ erledigen** to settle sth by standing order.

abbummeln vt sep (inf) Stunden to take off. **Überstunden ~** to take time off for overtime done.

abbürsten vt sep Staub to brush off (von etw sth); Kleid,

Mantel, Jacke to brush (down); Schuhe to brush.

abbusseln vt sep (Aus inf) siehe **abküssen**.

abbüßen vt sep Strafe to serve.

Abbüßung f serving. **nach ~ der Strafe** after serving or having served the sentence.

Abc [abe'tseː, aːbe'tseː] nt -, - (lit, fig) ABC. **Wörter/Namen nach dem ~ ordnen** to arrange words/names in alphabetical order or alphabetically.

ABC- in cpds (Mil) atomic, biological and chemical, Abc.

Abc-Buch nt (old) siehe **Fibel**[1].

abchecken ['æptʃɛkn] vt sep to check; (abhaken) to check off (US), to tick off (Brit).

Abc-Schütze m (hum) school-beginner. **dies Bild zeigt mich als ~n** this picture shows me when I was starting school.

abdachen vt sep to slope.

Abdachung f (a) (Geog) declivity, downward slope. (b) (Build) camber, cambering.

abdämmen vt sep Fluß to dam (up); (fig) to curb, to check.

Abdampf m exhaust steam.

abdampfen sep 1 vi aux sein (a) (Speisen) to dry off. (b) (Chem: verdunsten) to evaporate. (c) (Zug) to steam off; (fig inf: losgehen, -fahren) to hit the trail (inf) or road (inf), to push off (inf). 2 vt (Chem: verdunsten lassen) to evaporate.

abdämpfen vt sep siehe **dämpfen**.

abdanken sep 1 vi to resign; (König etc) to abdicate. 2 vt (old) siehe **abgedankt**.

Abdankung f (a) (Thronverzicht) abdication; (Rücktritt) resignation. **jdn zur ~ zwingen** to force sb to abdicate/resign. (b) (Dienstentlassung) retirement. (c) (Sw: Trauerfeier) funeral service.

abdecken vt sep (a) (herunternehmen) Bettdecke to turn back or down.
   (b) (freilegen) Tisch to clear; Bett to turn down; Haus to tear the roof off.
   (c) (old: Fell abziehen) Tierkadaver to flay, to skin.
   (d) (zudecken) Grab, Loch to cover (over); (verdecken auch) to hide.
   (e) (schützen, ausgleichen, einschließen) to cover; (Ftbl auch) to mark.

Abdecker(in f) m -s, - knacker.

Abdeckerei f knacker's yard.

Abdeckung f (a) cover. (b) no pl (Vorgang) covering.

abdichten vt sep (isolieren) to insulate; (verschließen) Loch, Leck, Rohr to seal (up); Ritzen to fill, to stop up. **gegen Luft/Wasser ~** to make airtight/watertight; **gegen Feuchtigkeit/Zugluft ~** to damp-proof/(make) draughtproof; **gegen Lärm/Geräusch/Schall ~** to soundproof.

Abdichtung f (Isolierung) insulation; (das Isolieren auch) insulating; (Verschluß, Dichtung) seal; (das Verschließen) sealing; (von Ritzen) filling, stopping up. ~ **gegen Zugluft/Feuchtigkeit/Wasser** draughtproofing/damp-proofing/waterproofing; ~ **gegen Lärm/Geräusch/Schall** soundproofing.

abdienen vt sep (old: abarbeiten) to work off; (Mil: ableisten) to serve.

Abdikation f (old) abdication.

abdingbar adj (Jur) capable of alteration subject to mutual agreement.

abdingen, pret **dingte ab**, ptp **abgedungen** vt sep (rare) **jdm etw ~** Zugeständnis to strike a deal with sb for sth; **diese Rechte lassen wir uns nicht ~** we shall not cede these rights.

abdizieren* vi insep (old) siehe **abdanken**.

abdorren vi sep aux sein (Zweig) to dry up, to wither.

abdrängen vt sep to push away (von from) or out of the way (von of); (fig) Bettler etc to shake off. **einen Spieler vom Ball ~** to push or barge a player off the ball; **vom Winde abgedrängt werden** to be blown off course (by the wind).

abdrehen sep 1 vt (a) Gas, Wasser, Hahn to turn off; Licht, Radio auch to switch off.
   (b) Film to shoot, to film.
   (c) Hals to wring. **er drehte dem Huhn/der Blume den Kopf ab** he wrung the chicken's neck/he twisted the head off the flower; **jdm den Hals** or **die Gurgel ~** to wring sb's neck (inf); (sl: ruinieren) to strangle sb, to bankrupt sb.
   2 vi aux sein or haben (Richtung ändern) to change course; (zur Seite auch) to veer off or away. **nach Osten ~** to turn east.

abdreschen vt sep siehe **abgedroschen**.

Abdrift f -, -en (Naut, Aviat) drift.

abdriften vi sep aux sein to drift (away).

abdrosseln vt sep Motor to throttle back or (gänzlich auch) down; (fig) Produktion to cut back, to cut down on.

Abdrosselung, Abdroßlung f throttling back/down; (fig) cutback (gen in).

Abdruck[1] m -(e)s, **Abdrücke** imprint, impression; (Stempel~) stamp; (von Schlüssel) impression, mould; (Finger~, Fuß~) print; (Gebiß~) mould, cast, impression; (Gesteins~) imprint, impression, cast. **einen ~ abnehmen** or **machen** (inf) to take or make an impression; **auf diesem Leder sieht man jeden ~** you can see every mark on this leather.

Abdruck[2] m -(e)s, -e (das Nachdrucken) reprinting; (das Kopieren) copying; (Kopie) copy; (Nachdruck) reprint. **der ~ dieses Romans wurde verboten** it was forbidden to reprint this novel; **ich habe den ~ des Interviews im SPIEGEL gelesen** I read the text or printed version of the interview in Spiegel; **dieser Roman erschien auch als ~ in ...** this novel was also printed in ...

abdrucken vt sep to print. **wieder ~** to reprint.

abdrücken sep 1 vt (a) Gewehr to fire.
   (b) (inf) jdn to squeeze, to hug.
   (c) (nachbilden) to make an impression of.

(d) *Vene* to constrict. **jdm fast die Finger/Hand ~** to almost squeeze sb's fingers/hand off; **jdm die Luft ~** (*inf*) (*lit*) to squeeze all the breath out of sb; (*fig*) to force sb into bankruptcy, to squeeze the lifeblood out of sb.

2 *vi* to pull *or* squeeze the trigger.

3 *vr* to leave an imprint *or* impression. **sich (durch etw) ~ to** show through (*sth*).

abducken *vi sep* (*Boxen*) to duck.

abdunkeln *vt sep Lampe* to dim; *Zimmer auch* to darken; *Farbe* to darken, to make darker.

abduschen *vt sep siehe* **abbrausen 1.**

ab|ebben *vi sep aux sein* to die *or* fade away; (*Zorn, Lärm auch*) to abate.

abend *adv* **heute/gestern/morgen/Mittwoch ~** this/yesterday/ tomorrow/Wednesday evening, tonight/last/tomorrow/Wednesday night.

-abend *m* **der Mittwoch~** Wednesday evening *or* night.

Abend *m* **-s, -e (a)** evening. **am ~** in the evening; (*jeden ~*) in the evening(s); **am ~ des 4. April** on the evening *or* night of April 4th; **die Vorstellung wird zweimal pro ~ gegeben** there are two performances every night *or* evening; **jeden ~** every evening *or* night; **gegen ~** towards (the) evening; **~ für *or* um** (*geh*) ~ every evening *or* night, night after night; **am nächsten *or* den nächsten ~** the next evening; **eines ~s** one evening; **den ganzen ~ über** the whole evening; **es wird ~** it's getting late, evening is drawing on; **es wurde ~** evening came; **jdm guten ~ sagen** to say good evening to sb, to bid sb good evening (*form*); **guten ~** good evening; **'n ~** [na:mt] (*inf*) evening (*inf*); **letzten ~** yesterday evening, last night; **der ~ kommt** (*geh*) *or* **naht** (*liter*) evening is drawing nigh (*liter*) *or* on; **des ~s** (*geh*) in the evening(s), of an evening; **du kannst mich am ~ besuchen!** (*euph inf*) you can take a running jump (*inf*); **zu ~ essen** (*geh*) to have supper *or* dinner, to dine (*form*); **je später der ~, desto schöner *or* netter die Gäste** (*prov*) the best guests always come late; **es ist noch nicht aller Tage ~** it's early days still *or* yet; **man soll den Tag nicht vor dem ~ loben** (*Prov*) don't count your chickens before they're hatched (*Prov*).

(b) (*~unterhaltung*) evening.

(c) (*Vor~*) eve. **am ~ vor der Schlacht** on the eve of the battle.

(d) (*liter: Ende*) close. **am ~ des Lebens** in the twilight *or* evening of one's life (*liter*), in one's twilight years (*liter*); **am ~ des Jahrhunderts** towards the close of the century.

(e) (*liter: Westen*) west. **gen ~** (*liter*) to(wards) the west, westward(s).

Abend- *in cpds* **~andacht** *f* evening service; **~anzug** *m* dinner jacket *or* suit, DJ (*inf*), tuxedo (*US*); **im ~anzug erscheinen** to come in a dinner jacket/dinner jackets *etc*; **~blatt** *nt* evening (news)paper; **~brot** *nt* supper, tea (*Scot, N Engl*); **~brot essen** to have (one's) supper/tea; **~dämmerung** *f* dusk, twilight.

abendelang *adj attr* night after *or* upon night, evening after *or* upon evening. **unsere ~en Diskussionen** our discussions night after *or* upon night.

Abend-: **~essen** *nt* supper, evening meal, dinner; **mit dem ~essen auf jdn warten** to wait with supper *or* dinner *or* one's evening meal for sb; **~friede(n)** *m* (*liter*) still *or* quiet of the evening; **a~füllend** *adj* taking up the whole evening; *Film, Stück* full-length; **a~füllend sein** to take up *or* fill the whole evening; **~gesellschaft** *f* soirée; **~gymnasium** *nt* night school (*where one can study for the Abitur*); **~kasse** *f* (*Theat*) box office; **~kleid** *nt* evening dress *or* gown; **~kleidung** *f* evening dress *no pl*; **~kurs(us)** *m* evening course, evening classes *pl* (*für in*); **~land** *nt, no pl* (*geh*) West, western world, Occident (*liter*); **das christliche ~land** the Christian West; **~länder(in** *f*) *m* **-s, -** (*geh*) westerner, Occidental (*liter*); **a~ländisch** *adj* **1** *adj* western, occidental (*liter*); **2** *adv* in a western way *or* fashion.

abendlich *adj no pred* evening *attr*. **~ stattfindende Veranstaltungen** evening events, events taking place in the evening; **die ~e Stille** the quiet *or* still of evening; **die ~e Kühle** the cool of the evening; **es war schon um drei Uhr ~ kühl** at three it was already as cool as (in the) evening.

Abendmahl *nt* **(a)** (*Eccl*) Communion, Lord's Supper. **das ~ nehmen** *or* **empfangen** to take *or* receive Communion, to communicate (*form*); **unter denen, die das ~ empfangen ...** amongst the communicants; **das ~ spenden** *or* **reichen** *or* **erteilen** to administer (Holy) Communion, to communicate (*form*); **zum ~ gehen** to go to (Holy) Communion.

(b) **das (Letzte) ~** the Last Supper.

Abendmahls-: **~gottesdienst** *m* (Holy) Communion, Communion service; **~wein** *m* Communion wine.

Abend-: **~mahlzeit** *f* evening meal; **~oberschule** *f siehe* **~gymnasium**; **~programm** *nt* (*Rad, TV*) evening('s) programmes *pl*; **damit ist unser heutiges ~programm beendet** and that ends our programmes for this evening; **~rot** *nt*, **~röte** *f* (*liter*) sunset; **die Felder lagen im ~rot** the fields lay bathed in the glow of the sunset *or* the light of the setting sun.

abends *adv* in the evening; (*jeden Abend*) in the evening(s). **spät ~** late in the evening; **~ um neun** at nine in the evening; **was machst du ~ immer?** what do you do in the evenings *or* of an evening *or* at night?

Abend-: **~schule** *f* night school; **~schüler** *m* night-school student; **~stern** *m* evening star; **~stille** *f* still *or* quiet of the evening; **~stunde** *f* evening (hour); **zu dieser späten ~stunde** at this late hour of the evening; **die frühen/schönen ~stunden** the early hours of the evening/the beautiful evening hours; **sich bis in die ~stunden hinziehen** to go on (late) into the evening; **~vorstellung** *f* evening performance; (*Film auch*) evening showing; **~zeit** *f* **zur ~zeit** in the evening.

Abenteuer *nt* **-s, -** adventure; (*Liebes~ auch*) affair. **ein militärisches/politisches/verbrecherisches ~** a military/ political/criminal venture; **auf ~ ausgehen/aussein** to go out in search of adventure/to be looking for adventure; **ein ~ mit jdm haben** to have an affair with sb; **die ~ des Geistes** (*liter*) intellectual adventure.

Abenteuer- *in cpds* adventure.

abenteuerlich *adj* **(a)** adventurous; (*erlebnishungrig auch*) adventuresome. **(b)** (*phantastisch*) bizarre; *Gestalten, Verkleidung auch*) eccentric; *Erzählung auch* fantastic.

Abenteuerlichkeit *f siehe adj* adventurousness; bizarreness, eccentricity; (*Unwahrscheinlichkeit*) improbability, unlikeliness.

Abenteuer-: **~lust** *f* thirst for adventure; **von der ~lust gepackt werden** to be seized with a thirst for adventure; **~roman** *m* adventure story; **~spielplatz** *m* adventure playground.

Abenteurer *m* **-s, -** adventurer (*auch pej*).

Abenteurer- *in cpds siehe* **Abenteuer-.**

Abenteu(r)erin *f* adventuress.

Abenteurernatur *f* adventurous person, adventurer.

aber 1 *conj* **(a)** but. **~ dennoch** *or* **trotzdem** but still; **es regnete, ~ dennoch haben wir uns köstlich amüsiert** it was raining, but we still had a great time *or* but we had a great time though *or* all the same; **schönes Wetter heute, was?** — **ja, ~ etwas kalt** nice weather, eh? — yes, a bit cold though *or* yes but it's a bit cold; **...**, **~ ich wünschte, sie hätte es mir gesagt** (al)though *or* but I wished she had told me; **komm doch mit!** — **~ ich habe keine Zeit** *or* **ich habe ~ keine Zeit!** come with us! — but I haven't got the time!; **da er ~ nicht wußte ...** but since he didn't know ..., since, however, he didn't know ..., however, since he didn't know ...; **oder ~** *or* else.

(b) (*zur Verstärkung*) **~ ja!** oh, yes!; (*sicher*) but of course; **~ selbstverständlich** *or* **gewiß (doch)!** but of course; **~ nein!** oh, no!; (*selbstverständlich nicht*) of course not!; **~ Renate!** but Renate!; **~, ~!** now, now!, tut, tut!, come, come!; **~ ich kann nichts dafür!** but I can't help it!; **~ das wollte ich doch gar nicht!** but I didn't want that!; **das ist ~ schrecklich!** but that's awful!; **das mach' ich ~ nicht!** I will *not* do that!; **dann ist er ~ wütend geworden** then he really got mad, (God), did he get mad!; **das ist ~ heiß/schön!** that's really hot/nice; **da haben wir uns ~ gefreut** we were really pleased; **du hast ~ einen schönen Ball** you've got a nice ball, haven't you?; **bist du ~ braun!** aren't you brown!; **das geht ~ zu weit!** that's just *or* really going too far!; **ein Bier, ~'n bißchen dalli!** (*inf*) a beer, and make it snappy!; **schreib das nochmal ab, ~ sauber!** write it out again, and make it tidy!

2 *adv* (*liter*) **~ und ~mals** again and again, time and again; **tausend und ~ tausend** *or* (*Aus*) **~tausend** thousands and *or* upon thousands.

Aber *nt* **-s, -** *or* (*inf*) **-s** but. **kein ~!** no buts (about it); **die Sache hat ein ~** there's just one problem *or* snag; **dagegen habe ich ein ~** there's something I don't like about it.

Aberglaube(n) *m* superstition; (*fig auch*) myth. **zum ~n neigen** to be superstitious.

abergläubisch *adj* superstitious. **er hängt ~ an .../er fürchtet sich ~ vor ...** he has a superstitious attachment to .../fear of ...

Aber-: **a~hundert** *num* (*esp Aus*) hundreds upon hundreds of; **~hunderte** (*esp Aus*) hundreds upon hundreds *pl*.

ab|erkennen* *vt sep or* (*rare*) *insep irreg* **jdm etw ~** to deprive *or* strip sb of sth; **jdm den Sieg ~** (*Sport*) to disallow sb's victory.

Ab|erkennung *f* deprivation, stripping; (*von Sieg*) disallowing, disallowance.

aber-: **~malig** *adj attr* repeated; **~mals** *adv* once again *or* more.

ab|ernten *vti sep* to harvest.

Ab|erration *f* (*Astron*) aberration.

Aber-: **a~tausend** *num* (*esp Aus*) thousands upon thousands of; **~tausende** *pl* (*esp Aus*) thousands upon thousands *pl*.

Aberwitz *m* (*liter*) *siehe* **Wahnwitz.**

aberwitzig *adj* (*liter*) *siehe* **wahnwitzig.**

ab|essen *sep irreg* **1** *vt* (*a*) (*herunteressen*) to eat. **sie aß nur die Erdbeeren von der Torte ab** she just ate the strawberries off the tart. **(b)** (*leer essen*) to eat *or* finish up; *Teller* to finish. **(c)** (*inf*) (*aufbrauchen*) to use up; (*ausnützen*) to get one's money's worth for. **2** *vi* to eat up.

Abessinien [-iən] *nt* **-s (a)** Abyssinia. **(b)** (*dated hum: Nacktbadestrand*) nudist beach.

Abessinier(in *f*) [-iɐ, -iɐrɪn] *m* **-s, -** Abyssinian.

abessinisch *adj* Abyssinian.

Abf. *abbr of* **Abfahrt** departure, dep.

abfackeln *vt Erdgas* to burn off.

abfahrbereit *adj siehe* **abfahrtbereit.**

abfahren *sep irreg aux sein* **1** *vi* **(a)** to leave, to depart (*form*); (*Schiff auch*) to sail; (*Ski: zu Tal fahren*) to ski down. **~!** (*Rail*) order given to a train driver to pull out; **der Zug fährt um 8⁰⁰ in** *or* **von Bremen ab** the train leaves Bremen *or* departs from Bremen at 8 o'clock; **der Zug fährt in Kürze ab** the train will be leaving *or* will depart shortly; **der Zug ist abgefahren** (*lit*) the train has left *or* gone; (*fig*) we've/you've *etc* missed the boat; **wir müssen schon um 7⁰⁰ ~** we must set off *or* leave *or* start (out) at 7 o'clock.

(b) (*sl: sterben*) to kick the bucket (*sl*), to croak *or* snuff it (*sl*). **(c)** (*inf: abgewiesen werden*) **jdn ~ lassen** to tell sb to push off (*inf*) *or* get lost (*inf*); **er ist bei ihr abgefahren** she told him to push off (*inf*) *or* get lost (*inf*).

2 *vt* **(a)** *Güter* to take away, to remove, to cart off (*inf*). **(b)** *Körperteil* to cut off, to sever; *Stück von Mauer etc* to knock off. **der Trecker hat ihm ein Bein abgefahren** the tractor cut off *or* severed his leg.

(c) *aux sein or haben* Strecke (*bereisen*) to cover, to do (*inf*); (*überprüfen, ausprobieren*) to go over. **er hat ganz Belgien abgefahren** he travelled *or* went all over Belgium; **wir mußten die ganze Strecke noch einmal ~, um ... zu suchen** we had to go over the whole stretch again to look for ...

(d) (*abnutzen*) Schienen, Skier to wear out; Reifen *auch* to wear down; (*benutzen*) Fahrkarte to use; (*ausnutzen*) Zeitkarte, Fahrkarte to get one's money's worth for. **abgefahrene Reifen/Schienen** worn tyres/rails; **das Geld fährst du doch allemal ab** you'll certainly get your money's worth.

(e) (*Film, TV: beginnen*) Kamera to roll; Film to start. **bitte ~! roll 'em!**

3 *vr* (*Reifen etc*) to wear out *or* down.

Abfahrt f (a) (*von Zug, Bus etc*) departure. **bis zur ~ sind es noch fünf Minuten** there's still five minutes before the train/bus leaves *or* goes; **Vorsicht bei der ~ des Zuges!** stand clear, the train is about to leave! (b) (*Ski*) (*Talfahrt*) descent; (~*sstrecke*) (ski-)run. (c) (*inf: Autobahn~*) exit. **die ~ Gießen** the Gießen exit, the exit for Gießen.

abfahrtbereit adj ready to leave.

Abfahrts-: ~lauf m (*Ski*) downhill; ~zeit f departure time.

Abfall m -s, **Abfälle** (a) *no pl* (*Müll*) waste; (*Haus~*) rubbish, garbage (*esp US*); (*Straßen~*) litter (*Brit*), trash (*US*). **in den ~ kommen** to be thrown away *or* out, to go into the dustbin *or* trashcan (*US*); (*Fleisch-/Stoff*)**abfälle** scraps (of meat/material).

(b) (*Rückstand*) waste *no pl*.

(c) *no pl* (*Lossagung*) break (*von* with); (*von Partei*) breaking away (*von* from). **seit ihrem ~ von der Kirche/Partei** ... since they broke with *or* since their break with the Church/since they broke away from the party; **seit dem ~ der Niederlande von Spanien** since the Netherlands broke with Spain.

(d) *no pl* (*Rückgang*) drop (*gen* in), fall (*gen* in), falling off; (*Verschlechterung auch*) deterioration.

(e) *no pl* (*Hang*) drop. **die Wiese zieht sich in sanftem ~ hinunter** the meadow falls gently away.

Abfall-: ~beseitigung f refuse *or* garbage (*US*) disposal; ~eimer m rubbish bin, waste bin, garbage *or* trashcan (*US*); (*auf öffentlichen Plätzen*) litterbin (*Brit*), trashcan (*US*).

abfallen vi sep irreg aux sein (a) (*herunterfallen*) to fall *or* drop off; (*Blätter, Blüten etc*) to fall. **von etw ~** to fall *or* drop off (from) sth.

(b) (*inf: herausspringen*) **wieviel fällt bei dem Geschäft für mich ab?** how much do I get out of the deal?; **es fällt immer ziemlich viel Trinkgeld ab** you/they *etc* always get quite a lot of tips (out of it).

(c) (*fig: übrigbleiben*) to be left (over). **das, was in der Küche abfällt** the kitchen leftovers; **der Stoff, der beim Schneidern abfällt** the leftover scraps of material.

(d) (*schlechter werden*) to fall *or* drop off, to go downhill; (*Sport: zurückbleiben*) to drop back. **gegen etw ~** to compare badly with sth.

(e) (*fig: sich lösen*) to melt away. **alle Scheu/Unsicherheit/Furcht fiel von ihm ab** all his shyness/uncertainty/fear left him, all his shyness/uncertainty/fear melted away (from him) *or* dissolved.

(f) (*von einer Partei*) to break (*von* with), to drop out (*von* of); (*Fraktion*) to break away (*von* from). **vom Glauben ~** to break with *or* leave the faith.

(g) (*sich senken: Gelände*) to fall *or* drop away; (*sich vermindern: Druck, Temperatur*) to fall, to drop. **die steil zum Meer ~de Bergkette** the mountain range falling *or* dropping steeply away to the sea; **der Weg talwärts verläuft sacht ~d** the path down to the valley slopes gently *or* falls calmly away.

Abfall-: ~erzeugnis nt siehe ~produkt; ~grube f rubbish pit; ~haufen m rubbish *or* refuse dump *or* tip.

abfällig adj Bemerkung, Kritik disparaging, derisive; Lächeln derisive; Urteil adverse. **über jdn ~ reden/sprechen** to be disparaging of *or* about sb, to speak disparagingly of *or* about sb; **darüber wurde ~ geurteilt** a very dim view was taken of this; **über jdn ~ urteilen** to be disparaging about sb; **etw ~ beurteilen** to be disparaging about sth.

Abfall-: ~produkt nt (*lit, fig*) waste-product; ~schacht m waste *or* (*US*) garbage disposal chute; ~verwertung f waste utilization.

abfälschen vti sep (*Sport*) to deflect.

abfangen vt sep irreg (a) Flugzeug, Funkspruch, Brief, Ball to intercept; Menschen *auch* to catch (*inf*); Schlag to block; (*inf: anlocken*) Kunden to catch (*inf*), to lure *or* draw away.

(b) (*abstützen*) Gebäude to prop up, to support.

(c) (*bremsen*) Fahrzeug to bring under control; Flugzeug *auch* to pull out; Aufprall to absorb; Trend to check.

Abfangjäger m (*Mil*) interceptor.

abfärben vi sep (a) (*Wäsche*) to run. **paß auf, die Wand färbt ab!** be careful, the paint comes off the wall; **das rote Handtuch hat auf die weißen Tischdecken abgefärbt** the colour has come out of the red towel onto the white tablecloths. (b) (*fig*) **auf jdn ~** to rub off on sb.

abfassen vt sep (a) (*verfassen*) to write; Erstentwurf to draft.

(b) (*inf: abtasten*) to touch up (*inf*).

Abfassung f siehe vt (a) writing; drafting.

abfaulen vi sep aux sein to rot away *or* off.

abfedern sep 1 vt Sprung, Stoß to cushion. 2 vi to absorb the shock; (*Sport*) (*beim Abspringen*) to push off; (*beim Aufkommen*) to bend at the knees. **er ist *or* hat schlecht abgefedert** he landed stiffly.

abfegen vt sep Schmutz to sweep away *or* off; Balkon, Hof to sweep. **den Schnee vom Dach ~** to sweep the snow off the roof.

abfeiern vt sep (*inf*) Stunden, Tage to take off.

abfeilen vt sep to file off *or* (*glättend*) down.

abferkeln vi sep to have a litter.

abfertigen sep 1 vt (a) (*versandfertig machen*) Pakete, Waren to prepare *or* make ready *or* get ready for dispatch, to process (*form*); Gepäck to check (in); (*be- und entladen*) Flugzeug to service, to make ready for take-off; Schiff to make ready to sail. **die Schauerleute fertigen keine Schiffe aus Chile mehr ab** the dockers won't handle any more ships from Chile.

(b) (*bedienen*) Kunden, Antragsteller to attend to, to deal with; (*inf: Sport*) Gegner to deal with. **jdn kurz *or* schroff ~** (*inf*) to snub sb; **ich lasse mich doch nicht mit 10 Mark ~** I'm not going to be fobbed off with 10 marks.

2 vti (*kontrollieren*) Waren, Reisende to clear. **beim Zoll/an der Grenze abgefertigt werden** to be cleared by customs/at the border; **die Zöllner fertigten (die Reisenden) sehr zügig ab** the customs officers dealt with the travellers very quickly; **die Zollbeamten hatten den Zug fast abgefertigt, als ... the customs officials had almost finished checking the train when ...

Abfertigung f (a) siehe vt (a) making ready for dispatch, processing (*form*); checking; servicing, making ready for take-off; making ready to sail.

(b) (~*sstelle*) dispatch office.

(c) (*Bedienung*) (*von Kunden*) service; (*von Antragstellern*) dealing with; (*fig: Abweisung*) rebuff, snub. **die geschickte ~ des Gegners** (*Sport*) the skilful way of dealing with his opponent; **eine so unfreundliche ~ habe ich bisher noch nie erlebt** I've never been attended to *or* dealt with in such an unfriendly way before.

(d) (*von Waren, Reisenden*) clearance. **die ~ an der Grenze** customs clearance; **zollamtliche ~** customs clearance.

Abfertigungsschalter m dispatch counter; (*von Zollamt*) customs clearance.

abfeuern vt sep to fire; (*Ftbl inf*) to let fire with.

abfinden sep irreg 1 vt to pay off; Gläubiger *auch* to settle with; (*entschädigen*) to compensate. **er wurde von der Versicherung mit 20.000 DM abgefunden** he was paid 20,000 DM (in) compensation by the insurance company; **einen Fürst/König mit einer Apanage ~** to endow a prince/king with an appanage; **jdn mit leeren Versprechungen ~** to fob sb off with empty promises.

2 vr **sich mit jdm/etw ~** to come to terms with sb/sth; **sich mit jdm/etw nicht ~ können** to be unable to accept sb/sth *or* to come to terms with sb/sth; **er konnte sich nie damit ~, daß ... he could never accept the fact that ...; **sich mit jdm/etw schwer ~** to find it hard to accept sb/sth; **mit allem kann ich mich ~, aber nicht ...** I can put up with most things, but not ...

Abfindung f (a) (*von Gläubigern*) paying off; (*Entschädigung*) compensation. (b) siehe **Abfindungssumme**.

Abfindungssumme f payment, (sum in) settlement; (*Entschädigung*) compensation *no pl*, indemnity. **eine/keine ~ für einen Unfall bekommen** to receive a sum in compensation *or* an indemnity/no compensation *or* no indemnity for an accident.

abfischen vt sep to fish dry.

abflachen sep 1 vt to level (off), to flatten (out). 2 vr (*Land*) to flatten out, to grow *or* get flatter; (*fig: sinken*) to drop *or* fall (off). 3 vi (*fig: sinken*) to drop *or* fall (off), to decline.

Abflachung f flattening out; (*fig*) dropping off, falling off.

abflauen vi sep aux sein (a) (*Wind*) to drop, to die away *or* down, to abate. **nach (dem) A~ des Windes** when the wind had dropped *or* died down *or* abated.

(b) (*fig*) (*Empörung, Erregung*) to fade, to die away; (*Interesse auch*) to flag, to wane; (*Börsenkurse*) to fall, to drop; (*Geschäfte*) to fall *or* drop off.

abfliegen sep irreg 1 vi aux sein (*Aviat*) to take off (*nach* for); (*Zugvögel*) to migrate, to fly off *or* away; (*inf: sich lösen*) to fly off. **sie sind gestern nach München/von Hamburg abgeflogen** they flew to Munich/from Hamburg yesterday.

2 vt Gelände to fly over; Verwundete to fly out (*aus* of).

abfließen vi sep irreg aux sein (*wegfließen*) to drain *or* run *or* flow away; (*durch ein Leck*) to leak away; (*Verkehr*) to flow. **ins Ausland ~** (*Geld*) to flow out of the country; (*der Auguß/die Wanne fließt nicht/schlecht ab** the water isn't running *or* draining out of the sink/bath (at all)/very well; **sie ließ das Badewasser ~** she let the bath water run away, she emptied the bath water; **den Verkehr ~ lassen** to get the traffic flowing.

Abflug m take-off; (*von Zugvögeln*) migration; (*inf: ~stelle*) departure point. **~ Glasgow 8⁰⁰** departure Glasgow 8.00 a.m.

Abflug-: a~bereit adj ready for take-off; ~hafen m departure airport.

Abfluß m (a) (*Abfließen*) draining away; (*durch ein Leck*) leaking away; (*fig: von Geld*) draining away; (*von Verkehr*) flow. **den ~ des Wassers verhindern** to prevent the water (from) draining *or* running *or* flowing away; **eine Regenrinne dient dem ~ des Regenwassers** a drainpipe allows the rainwater to drain away; **durch die Verstopfung kam kein ~ zustande** because of the blockage the water couldn't drain away; **der ~ der Zuschauermassen aus dem Stadion verlief reibungslos** the crowds of spectators emptied the stadium without incident; **dem ~ von Kapital ins Ausland Schranken setzen** to impose limits on the (out)flow of capital out of the country.

(b) (~*stelle*) drain; (*von Teich etc*) outlet; (~*rohr*) drainpipe; (*von sanitären Anlagen auch*) wastepipe.

Abfluß-: ~graben m drainage ditch; ~hahn m tap, drain-cock; ~rinne f gutter; ~rohr nt outlet; (*im Gebäude*) waste pipe; (*außen am Gebäude*) drainpipe; (*unterirdisch*) drain, sewer.

abfohlen vi sep (*Zool*) to foal.

Abfolge f (*geh*) sequence, succession.

abfordern vt sep **jdm etw ~** to demand sth from sb; **jdm den Ausweis ~** to ask to see sb's papers.

abformen vt sep to model, to copy.

abfotografieren* vt sep to photograph.

abfragen vt sep (esp Sch) jdn or jdm etw ~ to question sb on sth; (Lehrer) to test sb orally on sth; **die Klasse wurde abgefragt** the class was questioned or tested orally; **eine Lektion ~** to give an oral test on a lesson.

abfressen vt sep irreg Blätter to eat; Gras auch to crop; Metall, Schicht to eat away, to corrode. **das Aas bis auf die Knochen ~** to strip the carcass to the bones; **die Giraffe frißt die Blätter von den Bäumen ab** the giraffe strips the leaves off the trees.

abfretten vr sep (Aus inf) to struggle along.

abfrieren sep irreg 1 vi aux sein to get frostbitten. **ihm sind die Füße abgefroren** his feet got frostbite; **abgefroren sein** (Körperteil) to be frostbitten. **2** vr sich (dat) etw ~ to get frostbite in sth; **sich (dat) einen ~ (sl)** to freeze to death (inf).

abfrottieren* vt sep to towel down or dry.

Abfuhr f -, -en (a) no pl (Abtransport) removal. **(b)** (inf: Zurückweisung) snub, rebuff. **jdm eine ~ erteilen** to snub or rebuff sb, to give sb a snub or rebuff; (Sport) to thrash sb (inf), to give sb a thrashing (inf); **sich (dat) eine ~ holen** to meet with a snub or a rebuff, to be snubbed; **sich (dat) (gegen jdn) eine ~ holen** (Sport) to be given a thrashing or be thrashed (by sb) (inf).

abführen sep 1 vt (a) (wegführen) to lead or take away; (ableiten) Gase etc to draw off. **~! away with him/her etc**, take him/her etc away!; **das führt uns vom Thema ab** that will take us away or divert us from our subject.

(b) (abgeben) Betrag to pay (an + acc to). **Stuhl(gang) ~** to evacuate or move one's bowels, to have a bowel movement.

2 vi **(a)** (wegführen) **der Weg führt hier (von der Straße) ab** the path leaves the road here; **das würde vom Thema ~** that would take us off the subject.

(b) (den Darm anregen) to have a laxative effect.

(c) (Stuhlgang haben) to move or evacuate one's bowels, to have a bowel movement.

abführend adj laxative no adv, aperient no adv (form). **~ wirken** to have a laxative effect.

Abführ- in cpds laxative; **~mittel** nt laxative, aperient (form).

Abführung f closing quotation marks pl.

Abfüll-: **~anlage** f bottling plant; **~betrieb** m bottling factory.

abfüllen vt sep **(a)** (abschöpfen) to ladle off. **(b)** (abziehen) Wein etc to draw off (in + acc into); (in Flaschen) to bottle; Flasche to fill. **Wein in Flaschen ~** to bottle wine. **(c)** jdn ~ (inf) to get sb pickled (inf) or sloshed (inf).

abfüttern¹ vt sep Vieh, (hum) Menschen to feed.

abfüttern² vt sep (Sew) to line.

Abfütterung f feeding no pl; (hum Mahlzeit) meal (inf).

Abgabe f **(a)** no pl (Abliefern) handing or giving in; (von Gepäck auch) depositing; (Übergabe: von Brief etc) delivery, handing over. **zur ~ von etw aufgefordert werden** to be told to hand sth in.

(b) no pl (Verkauf) sale. **~ (von Prospekten) kostenlos** leaflets given away free.

(c) no pl (von Wärme etc) giving off, emission.

(d) no pl (von Schuß, Salve) firing. **nach ~ von vier Schüssen** after firing four shots.

(e) no pl (von Erklärung, Urteil, Meinungsäußerung etc) giving; (von Gutachten) submission, submitting; (von Stimme) casting.

(f) (Sport) (Abspiel) pass. **nach ~ von zwei Punkten ...** after conceding two points.

(g) (Steuer) tax; (auf Tabak etc auch) duty; (soziale ~) contribution.

Abgabe(n)-: **a~frei** adj, adv tax-free, exempt from tax; **~ordnung** f (Jur) tax law; **a~pflichtig** adj liable to taxation.

Abgabetermin m closing date; (für Dissertation etc) submission date.

Abgang m **(a)** no pl (Absendung) dispatch. **vor ~ der Post** before the post goes.

(b) no pl (Abfahrt) departure.

(c) no pl (Ausscheiden) (aus einem Amt) leaving, departure; (Schul~) leaving. **seit seinem ~ vom Gymnasium** since he left the grammar school.

(d) no pl (Theat, fig) exit. **sich (dat) einen guten/glänzenden ~ verschaffen** to make a grand exit.

(e) (Sport) dismount. **einen guten/schwierigen ~ turnen** to do a good/difficult dismount from the apparatus.

(f) (Med: Ausscheidung) passing; (von Eiter) discharging; (Fehlgeburt) miscarriage, abortion (form); (Fötus) aborted foetus.

(g) (Person) (Schul~) leaver; (Med Mil sl) death.

(h) (sl: Ejakulation) ejaculation.

(i) (Comm) want; (Aus: Fehlbetrag) missing amount.

Abgänger(in f) m -s, - (Sch) (school) leaver.

abgängig adj (Aus Admin) missing (aus from). **ein A~er a** missing person.

Abgängigkeitsanzeige f (Aus Admin) notification to the authorities that a person is missing. **~ erstatten** to report a person missing.

Abgangs-: **~prüfung** f leaving examination; **~zeugnis** nt leaving certificate.

Abgas nt exhaust no pl, exhaust fumes, waste gas (esp Tech).

Abgas-: **a~frei** adj Motor, Fahrzeug exhaust-free; **a~frei verbrennen** to burn without producing exhaust; **a~freie Produktionsverfahren** production methods which produce no waste gases; **~wolke** f cloud of exhaust.

abgaunern vt sep (inf) jdm etw ~ to con or trick sb out of sth (inf).

ABGB ['a:be:ge:'be:] nt - (Aus) abbr of **Allgemeines Bürgerliches Gesetzbuch.**

abgearbeitet adj (verbraucht) workworn; (erschöpft) worn out, exhausted.

abgeben sep irreg 1 vt **(a)** (abliefern) to hand or give in; (hinterlassen) to leave; Gepäck, Koffer to leave, to deposit; (übergeben) to hand over, to deliver.

(b) (weggeben) to give away; (gegen Gebühr) to sell; (an einen anderen Inhaber) to hand over. **Kinderwagen preisgünstig abzugeben** pram for sale at (a) bargain price.

(c) (verschenken) to give away. **jdm etw ~** to give sth to sb; **jdm etw von seinem Kuchen ~** to give sb some of one's cake.

(d) (überlassen) Auftrag to hand or pass on (an + acc to); (abtreten) Posten to relinquish, to hand over (an + acc to).

(e) (Sport) Punkte, Rang to concede; (abspielen) to pass.

(f) (ausströmen) Wärme, Sauerstoff to give off, to emit.

(g) (abfeuern) Schuß, Salve to fire.

(h) (äußern) Erklärung to give; Gutachten to submit; Meinungsäußerung auch to express; Stimmen to cast.

(i) (darstellen) Rahmen, Hintergrund, (liefern) Stoff, Material etc to give, to provide, to furnish. **den Vermittler ~ (inf)** to act as mediator.

(j) (verkörpern) to make.

2 vr sich mit jdm/etw ~ (sich beschäftigen) to bother or concern oneself with sb/sth; (sich einlassen) to associate with sb/sth.

3 vi (Sport) to pass.

abgebrannt 1 ptp of abbrennen. **2** adj pred (inf) broke (inf). **völlig ~ sein** to be flat or stony broke (inf).

abgebrochen 1 ptp of abbrechen. **2** adj (nicht beendet) Studium uncompleted; Worte disjointed. **mit einem ~en Studium kommt man nicht sehr weit** you don't get very far if you haven't finished university or your university course; **er ist ~er Mediziner** (inf) he broke off his medical studies; **ein ~er Riese** (hum) a stunted giant.

abgebrüht adj (inf) (skrupellos) hard-boiled (inf), hardened; (frech) cool.

abgedankt adj Offizier, Dienstbote discharged.

abgedreht adj (Aus inf) hardened, tough.

abgedroschen adj (inf) hackneyed, well-worn; Witz auch corny (inf). **eine ~e Phrase/Redensart** a cliché/a hackneyed saying.

abgefeimt adj cunning, wily.

Abgefeimtheit f cunning, wiliness.

abgegriffen 1 ptp of abgreifen. **2** adj Buch (well-)worn; (fig) Klischees, Phrasen etc well-worn, hackneyed.

abgehackt 1 ptp of abhacken. **2** adj clipped. **~ sprechen** to clip one's words, to speak in a clipped manner.

abgehangen 1 ptp of abhängen. **2** adj (gut) ~ well-hung.

abgehärmt 1 ptp of abhärmen. **2** adj careworn.

abgehärtet 1 ptp of abhärten. **2** adj tough, hardy; (fig) hardened. **gegen Erkältungen ~ sein** to be immune to colds.

abgehen sep irreg aux sein 1 vi **(a)** (abfahren) to leave, to depart (nach for); (Schiff auch) to sail (nach for). **der Zug ging in or von Frankfurt ab** the train left from Frankfurt; **der Zug ging in or von Frankfurt pünktlich ab** the train left Frankfurt on time.

(b) (Sport: abspringen) to jump down. **er ging gekonnt mit einem Doppelsalto vom Barren ab** he did a skilful double somersault down from or off the bars.

(c) (Theat: abtreten) to exit, to make one's exit. **Othello geht ab** exit Othello.

(d) (ausscheiden) (von der Schule, old: aus einem Amt) to leave. **von der Schule ~** to leave school; **mit dem Tode or mit Tod ~** (old form) to die in office.

(e) (Med sl: sterben) to die.

(f) (sich lösen) to come off; (herausgehen: Farbe etc auch) to come out. **an meiner Jacke ist ein Knopf abgegangen** a button has come off my jacket; **mir ist ein Fingernagel abgegangen** one of my fingernails has come off.

(g) (abgesondert werden) to pass out; (Eiter etc) to be discharged; (Fötus) to be aborted. **dem Kranken ging viel Blut ab** the invalid lost a lot of blood; **ihm ist einer abgegangen** (vulg) he shot or came off (vulg).

(h) (losgehen: Schuß) to be fired, to be loosed off.

(i) (abgesandt werden) to be sent or dispatched; (Funkspruch) to be sent. **etw ~ lassen** to send or dispatch sth.

(j) (inf: fehlen) **sie geht ihm sehr ab** he misses her a lot; **jdm geht Verständnis/Taktgefühl ab** sb lacks understanding/tact.

(k) (abgezogen werden) (vom Preis) to be taken off; (von Verdienst auch) to be deducted; (vom Gewicht) to come off. **(von etw) ~** (vom Preis) to be taken off (sth); (von Verdienst auch) to be deducted (from sth); (von Gewicht) to be taken off (sth); **davon gehen 5% ab** 5% is taken off that.

(l) (abzweigen) to branch off; (bei Gabelung auch) to fork off.

(m) (abweichen) von einem Plan/einer Forderung ~ to give up or drop a plan/demand; **von seiner Meinung ~** to change or alter one's opinion; **von einem Thema ~** to digress (from a subject); **davon kann ich nicht ~** I must insist on that; (bei Versprechungen etc) I can't go back on that.

(n) (verlaufen) to go. **gut/glatt/friedlich ~** to go well/smoothly/peacefully; **es ging nicht ohne Streit ab** there was an argument.

2 vt sep **(a)** (entlanggehen) to go or walk along; (hin und zurück) to walk up or go up and down; (Mil) Gebäudekomplex, Gelände to patrol; (inspizieren) to inspect.

(b) (messen) to pace out.

(c) (Sch inf: verweisen) **abgegangen werden** to be thrown or chucked (inf) out.

abgehend adj Post outgoing; Zug, Schiff departing. **die morgen ~e Post** the post which will go out tomorrow.

abgehetzt 1 *ptp of* **abhetzen. 2** *adj* out of breath.
abgekämpft 1 *ptp of* **abkämpfen. 2** *adj* exhausted, shattered (*inf*), worn-out.
abgeklärt 1 *ptp of* **abklären. 2** *adj* serene, tranquil.
Abgeklärtheit *f* serenity, tranquillity.
abgelagert 1 *ptp of* **ablagern. 2** *adj Wein* mature; *Holz, Tabak* seasoned.
abgeleben 1 *ptp of* **ableben. 2** *adj* (**a**) (*verbraucht*) decrepit. (**b**) (*altmodisch*) *Tradition, Vorstellung* antiquated.
abgelegen *adj* (*entfernt*) *Dorf, Land* remote; (*einsam*) isolated.
Abgelegenheit *f siehe adj* remoteness; isolation.
abgeleiert 1 *ptp of* **ableiern. 2** *adj* (*pej*) *Melodie etc* banal, trite; *Redensart etc auch* hackneyed.
abgelten *vt sep irreg Ansprüche* to satisfy; *Verlust* to make up, to compensate for; *Schuld* to wipe out. **sein Urlaub wurde durch Bezahlung abgegolten** he was given payment in lieu of holiday.
abgemacht 1 *ptp of* **abmachen. 2** *interj* OK, that's settled; (*bei Kauf*) it's a deal, done. **3** *adj* **eine ~e Sache** a fix (*inf*); **das war doch schon vorher eine ~e Sache, wer mit wem gehen würde** it was all fixed up *or* arranged beforehand who was to go with whom.
abgemagert 1 *ptp of* **abmagern. 2** *adj* (*sehr dünn*) thin; (*ausgemergelt*) emaciated.
abgemergelt *adj* emaciated. **er war bis zum Skelett ~** he was nothing but skin and bones, he was a walking skeleton.
abgemessen 1 *ptp of* **abmessen. 2** *adj Schritt, Takt, Worte* measured, deliberate. **~ gehen/sprechen** to walk with measured steps/speak in measured tones.
Abgemessenheit *f* measuredness, deliberateness.
abgeneigt *adj* adverse *pred* (*dat to*). **ich wäre gar nicht ~** (*inf*) actually I wouldn't mind; **der allem Neuen ~e Direktor** the headmaster, who objected to anything new; **jdm ~ sein** to dislike sb.
Abgeneigtheit *f* aversion; (*Unlust*) disinclination.
abgenutzt 1 *ptp of* **abnutzen. 2** *adj* worn, shabby; *Bürste, Besen* worn-out; *Reifen* worn-down; (*fig*) *Klischees, Phrasen* hackneyed, well-worn.
Abge|ordneten-: **~bank** *f* bench; **~haus** *nt* parliament; (*in West-Berlin*) House of Representatives.
Abge|ordnete(r) *mf decl as adj* (elected) representative; (*von Nationalversammlung*) member of parliament. **Herr ~r/Frau ~!** sir/madam.
abgeraten *vi sep irreg aux sein* (*geh*) **vom Weg ~** to lose one's way.
abgerissen 1 *ptp of* **abreißen. 2** *adj* (**a**) (*zerlumpt*) *Kleidung, Eindruck* ragged, tattered. (**b**) (*unzusammenhängend*) *Worte, Gedanken* disjointed, incoherent.
Abgesandte(r) *mf decl as adj* envoy.
Abgesang *m* (*Poet*) abgesang, *concluding section of the final strophe of the minnesang;* (*fig liter*) swan song, farewell.
abgeschabt 1 *ptp of* **abschaben. 2** *adj* (*abgewetzt*) *Kleider* threadbare.
abgeschieden 1 *ptp of* **abscheiden. 2** *adj* (**a**) (*geh: einsam*) secluded. **~ leben/wohnen** to live a secluded life/in seclusion. (**b**) (*liter: tot*) departed. **der A~e/die A~en** the departed.
Abgeschiedenheit *f* seclusion.
abgeschlagen 1 *ptp of* **abschlagen. 2** *adj* washed out (*inf*), shattered (*inf*).
Abgeschlagenheit *f* (feeling of) exhaustion.
abgeschliffen 1 *ptp of* **abschleifen. 2** *adj Manieren* polished, refined, cultivated.
abgeschlossen 1 *ptp of* **abschließen. 2** *adj* (*einsam*) isolated; (*attr: geschlossen*) *Wohnung* self-contained; *Grundstück, Hof* enclosed. **~ leben** to live in isolation.
Abgeschlossenheit *f* isolation.
abgeschmackt *adj* (*geh*) fatuous; *Witz auch* corny.
Abgeschmacktheit *f* (*geh*) fatuousness; (*von Witz auch*) corniness; (*Bemerkung*) platitude. **alberne Witze und ähnliche ~en** stupid jokes and similar corny things.
abgesehen 1 *ptp of* **absehen. es auf jdn ~ haben** to have it in for sb (*inf*); **es auf jdn/etw ~ haben** (*interessiert sein*) to have one's eye on sb/sth; **du hast es nur darauf ~, mich zu ärgern** you're only trying to annoy me. **2** *adv*: **~ von jdm/etw** apart from sb/sth; **~ davon, daß ...** apart from the fact that ...
abgesondert 1 *ptp of* **absondern. 2** *adj* isolated.
abgespannt 1 *ptp of* **abspannen. 2** *adj* weary, tired.
Abgespanntheit *f, no pl* weariness, tiredness.
abgespielt 1 *ptp of* **abspielen. 2** *adj Schallplatte* worn.
abgestanden 1 *ptp of* **abstehen. 2** *adj Luft, Wasser* stale; *Bier, Limonade etc* flat; (*fig*) *Witz, Redensart* hackneyed.
abgestorben 1 *ptp of* **absterben. 2** *adj Glieder* numb; *Pflanze, Ast, Gewebe* dead. **von der Kälte war mein Arm wie ~** my arm was numb with cold.
abgestraft 1 *ptp of* **abstrafen. 2** *adj* (*Aus*) *siehe* **vorbestraft**.
abgestumpft 1 *ptp of* **abstumpfen. 2** *adj* (*gefühllos*) *Person* insensitive; *Gefühle, Gewissen* dulled, blunted. **sie war in ihren Gefühlen so ~, daß ...** her feelings had been dulled *or* blunted so much that ...
Abgestumpftheit *f siehe adj* insensitivity; dullness, bluntedness.
abgetakelt 1 *ptp of* **abtakeln. 2** *adj* (*pej inf*) worn out, shagged out (*sl*).
abgetan 1 *ptp of* **abtun. 2** *adj pred* finished *or* done with. **damit ist die Sache ~** that settles the matter, that's the matter done with; **damit ist es (noch) nicht ~** that's not the end of the matter.
abgetragen 1 *ptp of* **abtragen. 2** *adj* worn. **~e Kleider** old clothes; **jds ~e Kleider anhaben** to have sb's cast-off clothes *or* cast-offs on.

abgewinnen *vt sep irreg* (**a**) (*lit*) **jdm etw ~** to win sth from sb. (**b**) (*fig*) **jdm Achtung ~** to win respect from sb *or* sb's respect; **jdm ein Lächeln ~** to persuade sb to smile; **dem Meer Land ~** to reclaim land from the sea; **jdm/einer Sache Reiz ~** können to be unable to see anything attractive in sb/sth; **einer Sache** (*dat*) **Geschmack ~** to acquire a taste for sth.
abgewirtschaftet 1 *ptp of* **abwirtschaften. 2** *adj* (*pej*) rotten; *Firma auch* run-down. **einen total ~en Eindruck machen** to be on its last legs.
abgewogen 1 *ptp of* **abwägen. 2** *adj Urteil, Worte* balanced.
Abgewogenheit *f* balance.
abgewöhnen *vt sep* **jdm etw ~** *Gewohnheiten, schlechte Manieren* to cure sb of sth; *das Rauchen, Trinken* to get sb to give up *or* stop sth; **sich** (*dat*) **etw/das Trinken ~** to give sth up/give up *or* stop drinking; **noch eins/einen zum A~** (*hum*) one last one; (*von Alkohol auch*) one for the road; **das/die ist ja zum A~** (*sl*) that/she is enough to put anyone off.
abgewrackt 1 *ptp of* **abwracken. 2** *adj* (*pej*) rotten; (*abgetakelt*) *Mensch* worn-out.
abgezehrt 1 *ptp of* **abzehren. 2** *adj* emaciated.
abgießen *vt sep irreg* (**a**) *Flüssigkeit* to pour off *or* away; *Kartoffeln, Gemüse* to strain. **du mußt den Eimer etwas ~** you must pour some of the water *etc* out of the bucket; **gieß dir/ich gieße dir einen Schluck ab** help yourself to/I'll give you a drop; **er goß einen Schluck in mein Glas ab** he poured a drop into my glass. (**b**) (*Art, Metal*) to cast.
Abglanz *m* reflection (*auch fig*). **nur ein schwacher** *or* **matter ~** (*fig*) a pale reflection.
abgleiten *vi sep irreg aux sein* (*geh*) (**a**) (*abrutschen*) to slip; (*Gedanken*) to wander; (*Fin: Kurs*) to drop, to fall. **von etw ~** to slip off sth; **in Nebensächlichkeiten ~** to wander off *or* go off into side issues; **in Anarchie ~** to descend into anarchy; **er gleitet in Gedanken immer ab** his thoughts always wander; **von der rechten Bahn** *or* **dem rechten Weg ~** to wander *or* stray from the straight and narrow.
(**b**) (*fig: abprallen*) **an/von jdm ~** to bounce off sb.
abglitschen *vi sep aux sein* (*inf*) to slip. **er glitschte mit den Händen ab** his hands slipped.
Abgott *m,* **Abgöttin** *f* idol. **Abgöttern dienen** to worship false gods; **jdn zum ~ machen** to idolize sb.
abgöttisch *adj* idolatrous. **~e Liebe** blind adoration; **jdn ~ lieben** to idolize sb; (*Eltern, Ehepartner auch*) to dote on sb; **jdn ~ verehren** to idolize sb, to worship sb (like a god); **jdm ~ lauschen** to listen adoringly to sb.
abgraben *vt sep irreg Erdreich* to dig away. **jdm das Wasser ~** (*fig inf*) to take the bread from sb's mouth, to take away sb's livelihood.
abgrasen *vt sep Feld* to graze; (*fig inf*) *Ort, Geschäfte* to scour, to comb; *Gebiet, Thema* to do to death (*inf*).
abgrätschen *vi sep aux sein* (*Sport*) to straddle off.
abgreifen *sep irreg* **1** *vt* (**a**) *Strecke, Entfernung* to measure off. (**b**) *Buch, Heft* to wear; *siehe* **abgegriffen.** (**c**) *siehe* **abtasten. 2** *vr* to wear *or* become worn.
abgrenzen *sep* **1** *vt Grundstück, Gelände* to fence off; (*fig*) *Rechte, Pflichten, Einflußbereich, Befugnisse, Begriff* to delimit (*gegen, von* from). **etw durch einen Zaun/ein Seil/eine Mauer/Hecke ~** to fence/rope/wall/hedge sth off; **diese Begriffe lassen sich nur schwer (gegeneinander) ~** it is hard to distinguish (between) these two concepts.
2 *vr* to dis(as)sociate oneself (*gegen* from).
Abgrenzung *f* (**a**) *no pl siehe vt* fencing/roping/walling/hedging off; (*fig*) delimitation; distinguishing. (**b**) *siehe vr* dis(as)sociation (*gegen* from). **Politik der ~** politics of separation. (**c**) (*Umzäunung, Zaun*) fencing *no pl*.
Abgrund *m* precipice; (*Schlucht, fig*) abyss, chasm. **sich am Rande eines ~es befinden** (*fig*) to be on the edge of a precipice; **erst am Rande des ~es ...** (*fig*) only when on the brink *or* edge of disaster ...; **diese Politik bedeutet ein Wandeln am Rande des ~es** this policy is an exercise in brinkmanship; **in einen ~ von Verrat/Gemeinheit blicken** (*fig*) to stare into a bottomless pit of treason/baseness; **die menschlichen Abgründe, der ~ der menschlichen Seele** the blackest depths of the human soul.
abgrundhäßlich *adj* loathsome, incredibly hideous.
abgründig *adj Humor, Ironie* cryptic.
abgrundtief *adj Haß, Verachtung* profound.
abgucken *vti sep* to copy. **jdm etw ~** to copy sth from sb; **bei jdm (etw) ~** (*Sch*) to copy (sth) from *or* off (*inf*) sb; **ich guck' dir nichts ab!** (*inf*) don't worry, I've seen it all before.
Abgunst *f* -, *no pl* (*old*) *siehe* **Mißgunst.**
abgünstig *adj* (*old*) *siehe* **mißgünstig.**
Abguß *m* (**a**) (*Art, Metal*) (*Vorgang*) casting; (*Form*) cast. (**b**) (*dial: Ausguß*) sink.
abhaben *vt sep irreg* (*inf*) (**a**) (*abgenommen haben*) *Brille, Hut* to have off; (*abgemacht haben*) to have got off; (*abgerissen haben*) to have off. (**b**) (*abbekommen*) to have. **willst du ein Stück/etwas (davon) ~?** do you want a bit/some (of it)?
abhacken *vt sep* to chop off, to hack off; *siehe* **Rübe, abgehackt.**
abhaken *vt sep* (**a**) (*abnehmen*) to unhook. (**b**) (*markieren*) to tick *or* (*esp US*) check off; (*fig*) to cross off.
abhalftern *vt sep Pferd* to take the halter off; (*fig inf: entlassen*) to get rid of; *esp Politiker* to oust.
Abhalfterung *f* (*fig inf*) *siehe vt* getting rid of; ousting.
abhalten *vt sep irreg* (**a**) (*fernhalten*) *Kälte, Hitze* to keep off; *Mücken, Fliegen auch* to keep off *or* away; (*draußen halten*) to keep out.
(**b**) (*hindern*) to stop, to prevent. **jdn von etw/vom Trinken/von der Arbeit ~** to keep sb from sth/drinking/working; **jdn davon ~, etw zu tun** to stop sb doing sth, to prevent sb from doing sth; **laß dich nicht ~!** don't let me/us *etc* stop you.

(c) ein Kind auf der Toilette/Straße ~ to hold a child over the toilet/on the street (*while it goes to the toilet*).
(d) (*veranstalten*) *Versammlung, Wahlen, Gottesdienst* to hold.

Abhaltung *f, no pl* (*Durchführung*) holding. **während der ~ der Konferenz/des Gottesdienstes** ... during the conference/service; **nach ~ der Wahlen** after the elections (were held).

abhandeln *vt sep* (a) *Thema* to treat, to deal with.
(b) (*abkaufen*) **jdm etw ~** to do *or* strike a deal with sb for sth; **sie wollte sich** (*dat*) **das Armband nicht ~ lassen** she didn't want to let her bracelet go.
(c) (*vom Preis ~*) **jdm 8 Mark/etwas ~** to beat sb down 8 marks/a bit, to get sb to knock 8 marks/a bit off (the price); **er ließ sich von seinen Bedingungen nichts ~** he wouldn't give up any of his conditions.

abhanden *adv* **~ kommen** to get lost; **jdm ist etw ~ gekommen** sb has lost sth.

Abhandenkommen *nt -s, no pl* loss.

Abhandlung *f* (a) treatise, discourse (*über +acc* (up)on). **~en** (*einer Akademie etc*) transactions. (b) (*das Abhandeln*) treatment.

Abhang *m* slope, incline.

abhängen *sep* 1 *vt* (a) (*herunternehmen*) *Bild* to take down; (*abkuppeln*) *Schlafwagen, Kurswagen* to uncouple; *Wohnwagen, Anhänger* to unhitch.
(b) (*sl: hinter sich lassen*) **jdn** to shake off (*inf*).
2 *vi* (a) *irreg* (*Fleisch etc*) to hang; *siehe* **abgehangen**.
(b) *irreg aux haben or* (*S Ger, Aus*) *sein* **von etw ~** to depend (up)on sth, to be dependent (up)on sth; **das hängt ganz davon ab** it all depends; **davon hängt viel/zuviel ab** a lot/too much depends on it; **von jdm (finanziell) ~** to be (financially) dependent on sb.
(c) (*inf: Telefon auflegen*) to hang up (*inf*). **er hat abgehängt** he hung up (on me *etc*).

abhängig *adj* (a) (*bedingt durch*) dependent (*auch Math*); *Satz auch* subordinate; *Rede* indirect; *Kasus* oblique. **von etw ~ sein** (*Gram*) to be governed by sth.
(b) (*angewiesen auf, euph: süchtig*) dependent (*von* on). **gegenseitig or voneinander ~ sein** to be dependent on each other *or* mutually dependent *or* interdependent.

Abhängige(r) *mf decl as adj* dependent, dependant; *siehe* **Unzucht**.

-abhängige(r) *mf decl as adj* (*-süchtiger*) addict; *siehe* **Drogen-, Lohn-** *etc*.

Abhängigkeit *f* (a) *no pl* (*Bedingtheit*) dependency *no pl* (*von* on); (*Gram: von Sätzen*) subordination (*von* to).
(b) (*Angewiesensein, euph: Sucht*) dependence (*von* on). **er wollte alle ~en loswerden** he wanted to be rid of all his ties; **gegenseitige ~** mutual dependence, interdependence.

Abhängigkeitsverhältnis *nt* dependent relationship; (*gegenseitig*) interdependence. **in einem ~ mit jdm stehen** to be dependent on sb; **zwischen den beiden besteht ein ~** the two of them are dependent on each other *or* mutually dependent *or* interdependent.

abhärmen *vr sep* to pine away (*um* for); *siehe* **abgehärmt**.

abhärten *sep* 1 *vt* to toughen up. 2 *vi* ... **das härtet (gegen Erkältung) ab** ... that toughens you up (and stops you catching cold).
3 *vr* to toughen oneself up. **sich gegen etw ~** to toughen oneself against sth; (*fig*) to harden oneself to sth; *siehe* **abgehärtet**.

Abhärtung *f siehe vb* toughening up; hardening.

abhaspeln *vt sep Garn, Wolle* to unwind; (*fig*) *Rede, Gedicht* to reel *or* rattle off.

abhauen *sep* 1 *ptp* **abgehauen** *vi aux sein* (*inf*) to clear out; (*verschwinden auch*) to push off; (*aus einem Land auch*) to get away. **hau ab!** beat it (*inf*), get lost (*inf*).
2 *vt* (a) *pret* **hieb** *or* (*inf*) **haute ab**, *ptp* **abgehauen** *Kopf* to chop *or* cut off; *Baum auch* to chop *or* cut down.
(b) *pret* **haute ab**, *ptp* **abgehauen** (*wegschlagen*) *Verputz, Schicht* to knock off.

abhäuten *vt sep siehe* **häuten**.

abheben *sep irreg* 1 *vti* (a) (*anheben*) to lift (up), to raise; (*abnehmen*) to take off; *Telefonhörer* to pick up, to lift (up); *Telefon* to answer; (*beim Stricken*) *Masche* to slip. **laß es doch klingeln, du brauchst nicht abzuheben** let it ring, you don't have to answer (it).
(b) *vt only* (*Cards*) to take, to pick up.
(c) *Geld* to withdraw. **du kannst nicht dauernd (Geld) ~!** you can't keep on withdrawing money *or* drawing money out; **wenn Sie ~ wollen** ... if you wish to make a withdrawal.
2 *vi* (a) (*Flugzeug*) to take off; (*Rakete*) to lift off.
(b) **auf etw** (*acc*) **~** (*form, Jur*) to emphasize sth.
(c) (*Cards*) (*vor Spielbeginn etc*) to cut; (*Karte nehmen*) to take a card.
3 *vr* **sich von jdm/etw** *or* **gegen jdn/etw ~** to stand out from/against sb/sth; **nur um sich von anderen** *or* **gegen andere abzuheben** just to be different (from other people), just to make oneself stand out; **sich wohltuend gegen etw ~** to make a pleasant contrast *or* to contrast pleasantly with sth.

abheften *vt sep* (a) *Rechnungen, Schriftverkehr* to file away.
(b) (*Sew*) to tack, to baste.

abheilen *vi sep aux sein* to heal (up).

abhelfen *vi sep irreg +dat* to remedy; *einem Fehler auch* to rectify, to correct. **dem ist leicht abzuhelfen** that can be *or* is easily remedied *etc*.

abhetzen *sep* 1 *vt Tiere* to exhaust, to tire out. **hetz' mich nicht so ab!** (*inf*) stop hustling me like that! (*inf*). 2 *vt* to wear *or* tire oneself out; *siehe* **abgehetzt**.

abheuern *sep* (*Naut*) 1 *vi* to be paid off. 2 *vt* to pay off.

Abhilfe *f -, no pl* remedy, cure. **~ schaffen** to take remedial action; **in einer Angelegenheit ~ schaffen** to remedy a matter.

abhin *adv* (*Sw*) **vom 18.9.78 ~** from 18.9.78 onwards.

Abhitze *f siehe* **Abwärme**.

abhobeln *vt sep Holz* to plane down. **wir müssen noch 2 cm ~** we need to plane another 2 cms off.

abhold *adj +dat* (*old liter*) **jdm/einer Sache ~ sein** to be averse *or* ill-disposed to(wards) sb/averse to sth; **jdm/einer Sache nicht ~ sein** (*iro*) not to be averse to sb/sth.

abholen *vt sep* to collect (*bei* from); *Bestelltes auch* to call for (*bei* at); *Fundsache* to claim (*bei* from); *jdn* to call for; (*mit dem Wagen auch*) to pick up; (*euph: verhaften*) to take away. **jdn am Bahnhof/Flughafen ~** to collect sb from *or* meet sb at the station/airport; (*mit dem Wagen auch*) to pick sb up from the station/airport; **ich hole dich heute abend ab** I'll call for you *or* pick you up this evening; **jdn zu einem Spaziergang ~** to call for sb to go for a walk; **er kam und wollte mich zu einem Spaziergang ~** he called and asked me to go for a walk; **etw ~ lassen** to have sth collected; ,,**Geldbörse gefunden, abzuholen bei ...**" "purse found, claim from ..."

Abholer *m -s, - (Comm)* **~ sein** to collect one's post from the post office/parcels from the station etc.

Abholung *f* collection. **zur ~ bereit** ready for *or* awaiting collection.

abholzen *vt sep Wald* to clear, to deforest; *Baumreihe* to fell, to cut down.

Abholzung *f siehe vt* clearing, deforesting; felling, cutting down.

Abhör-: **~anlage**, **~einrichtung** *f* bugging system.

abhorchen *sep* 1 *vt* to sound, to listen to; *Patienten auch* to auscultate (*form*); *Boden* to put one's ear to. 2 *vi* to auscultate (*form*).

abhören *vt sep* (a) (*auch vi: überwachen*) *Gespräch* to bug; (*mithören*) to listen in on; *Telefon* to tap. **abgehört werden** (*inf*) to be bugged; **der Geheimdienst darf (Telefone) ~** the Secret Service are allowed to tap telephones.
(b) (*zuhören*) *Sender, Schallplatte etc* to listen to.
(c) (*Med*) to sound, to listen to. **jdm das Herz ~** to listen to *or* sound sb's heart.
(d) (*Sch: abfragen*) **einen** *or* **einem Schüler etw ~** to test a pupil orally on sth; **einen** *or* **einem Schüler ein Gedicht ~** to hear a pupil recite a poem.

Abhörgerät *nt* bugging device.

Abhub *m -(e)s, no pl* (*liter*) *siehe* **Abschaum**.

abhungern *vr sep* **sich** (*dat*) **jeden Pfennig ~** to starve oneself by scrimping and saving every penny; **er mußte sich** (*dat*) **sein Studium ~** he had to starve himself to pay for his studies, he had to starve his way through college *etc*; **sich** (*dat*) **Gewicht/10 Kilo ~** to lose weight/10 kilos by going on a starvation diet; **abgehungerte Gestalten** emaciated figures.

abhusten *vi sep* to have a good cough.

abi (*Aus inf*) = **hinab**.

Abi *nt -s, -s* (*Sch inf*) *abbr of* **Abitur**.

abirren *vi sep aux sein* (*geh*) to lose one's way; (*fig: abschweifen*) (*Gedanken*) to wander. **vom Weg(e) ~** to wander off the path, to stray from the path; **vom rechten Weg ~** (*fig*) to stray *or* wander *or* err from the straight and narrow; **vom Thema ~** to wander off the subject, to digress.

Abirrung *f* (*geh*) (a) (*Verirrung*) lapse, aberration. (b) (*Astron*) aberration.

Abitur *nt -s, (rare) -e school-leaving exam and university entrance qualification*, = A-levels *pl* (*Brit*), Highers *pl* (*Scot*). (**sein** *or* **das**) **~ machen** to do *or* take (one's) school-leaving exam *or* A-levels *or* Highers; **sein** *or* **das ~ ablegen** (*form*) to obtain one's school-leaving exam *or* A-levels *or* Highers, = to graduate from high school (*US*).

Abiturfeier *f* school-leaver's party, graduation ball (*US*).

Abiturient(in *f*) *m person who is doing/has done the Abitur*.

Abitur-: **~klasse** *f final year class at school who will take the Abitur*, ≈ sixth form (*Brit*), senior grade (*US*); **~zeitung** *f light-hearted newspaper produced by Abitur candidates, lampooning teachers, school etc*; **~zeugnis** *nt certificate of having passed the Abitur*, = A-level (*Brit*) *or* Highers (*Scot*) certificate.

abjagen *sep* 1 *vt* (a) *siehe* **abhetzen** 1. (b) **jdm etw ~** to get sth off sb. 2 *vr* (*inf*) to wear oneself out.

Abk. *abbr of* **Abkürzung** abbreviation, abbr.

abkalben *vi sep* (*Agr*) to calve.

abkämmen *vt sep* (*fig*) to comb, to scour.

abkämpfen *sep* 1 *vt* (*geh*) **jdm etw ~** to wring sth out of sb. 2 *vr* to fight hard; *siehe* **abgekämpft**.

abkanzeln *vt sep* (*inf*) **jdn ~** to give sb a dressing-down.

Abkanz(e)lung *f* dressing-down.

abkappen *vt sep siehe* **kappen**.

abkapseln *vr sep* (*lit*) to become encapsulated; (*fig*) to shut *or* cut oneself off, to isolate oneself.

Abkaps(e)lung *f* (*lit*) encapsulation; (*fig*) isolation.

abkarren *vt sep* to cart away; (*fig*) *Menschen* to cart off.

abkarten *vt sep* to rig (*inf*), to fix. **die Sache war von vornherein abgekartet** the whole thing was a put-up job (*inf*).

abkassieren* *vti sep* (*inf*) to cash up (*inf*). **jdn** *or* **bei jdm ~** to get sb to pay; **darf ich mal (bei Ihnen) ~?** could I ask you to pay now?

abkauen *vt sep* (a) *Fingernägel* to bite; *Bleistift* to chew. (b) (*vulg*) **jdm einen ~** to suck sb off (*vulg*).

abkaufen *vt sep* **jdm etw ~** to buy sth from *or* off (*inf*) sb; (*inf: glauben*) to buy sth (*inf*); **diese Geschichte kauft uns keiner ab!** nobody will buy that story (*inf*).

Abkehr *f -, no pl* turning away (*von* from); (*von Glauben, von der Welt etc*) renunciation (*von* of); (*von der Familie*) estrangement (*von* from). **die ~ vom Materialismus** turning away from *or* rejecting materialism.

abkehren¹ vt sep (abfegen) Schmutz to sweep up; Hof, Dach to sweep.

abkehren² sep 1 vt (geh) (abwenden) Blick, Gesicht to avert, to turn away. **sie mußte den Blick (davon)** ~ she had to look away (from it); **den Sinn vom Irdischen** ~ to turn one's mind away from earthly things.

2 vr (fig) to turn away (von from); (von Gott etc auch) to renounce; (von einer Politik) to give up. **die von uns abgekehrte Seite des Mondes** the side of the moon away from us, the far side of the moon.

abkippen sep 1 vt (abladen) Abfälle, Baustoffe to tip; (herunterklappen) to let down. 2 vi aux sein to tilt; (Flugzeug) to nosedive.

abklappern vt sep (inf) Läden, Gegend, Straße to scour, to comb (nach for); Kunden, Museum to do (inf).

abklären sep 1 vt (a) (sich setzen lassen) Flüssigkeit to clarify. (b) (klarstellen) Angelegenheit to clear up, to clarify. 2 vr (a) (sich setzen) to clarify. (b) (sich beruhigen) to calm down; siehe abgeklärt.

Abklärung f (a) (von Flüssigkeit) clarification, clarifying. (b) (von Angelegenheit) clearing up.

Abklatsch m -(e)s, -e (Art) cast, casting; (fig pej) poor imitation or copy.

abklatschen sep 1 vt er klatschte sie ab he got to dance with her during the excuse-me; **es wird abgeklatscht** it's an excuse-me. 2 vi beim A~ during the excuse-me.

Abklatscher m -s, - (Ftbl sl) rebound.

abklemmen vt sep Nabelschnur, Leitung, Adern to clamp. **er hat sich (dat) in der Maschine den Finger abgeklemmt** he lost his finger in the machine.

abklingeln vi sep (bei Straßenbahn) to ring the bell.

abklingen vi sep irreg aux sein (a) (leiser werden) to die or fade away. (b) (nachlassen) to wear off, to abate; (Erregung, Fieber auch) to subside.

abklopfen sep 1 vt (a) (herunterklopfen) to knock off; (klopfend säubern) to brush down; Staub etc to brush off; Teppich, Polstermöbel to beat. **er klopfte die Asche von der Zigarre ab** he tapped or knocked the ash off his cigar; **sich (dat) die Schuhe** ~ to knock the mud etc off one's shoes; **den Staub nicht abbürsten sondern** ~ do not brush the dust off, pat it off. (b) (beklopfen) to tap; (Med) to sound, to percuss (form). (c) (fig inf: untersuchen) to go into.

2 vi (Mus) der Dirigent klopfte ab the conductor stopped the orchestra by rapping his baton).

abknabbern vt sep (inf) to nibble off; Knochen to gnaw at.

abknallen vt sep (sl) to shoot down (inf).

abknappen, **abknapsen** vt sep (inf) sich (dat) etw ~ to scrape together sth; sich (dat) jeden Pfennig ~ müssen to have to scrimp and save; **er hat mir 20 Mark abgeknapst** he got 20 marks off me; **die Hälfte wurde uns abgeknapst** we never even saw half of it (inf).

abkneifen vt sep irreg to nip off; (mit Zange auch) to clip off.

abknicken sep 1 vt (abbrechen) to break or snap off; (einknicken) to break. 2 vi aux sein (abzweigen) to fork or branch off. **~de Vorfahrt** traffic turning left/right has priority; **in den Knien** ~ to bend at the knees.

abknipsen vt sep (inf) to snip off; Film to finish.

abknöpfen vt sep (a) (abnehmen) to unbutton. (b) (inf: ablisten) jdm etw ~ to get sth off sb; jdm Geld ~ to get money out of sb.

abknutschen vt sep (sl) to canoodle with (inf). **sich** ~ to canoodle (inf); **ich laß mich doch nicht von jedem** ~! I don't let just anyone kiss me.

abkochen sep 1 vt (gar kochen) to boil; (durch Kochen keimfrei machen) to sterilize (by boiling); Milch auch to scald. **jdn** ~ (sl) to rook or fleece sb (inf). 2 vi to cook a meal in the open air, to have a cookout (US).

abkommandieren* vt sep (Mil) (zu anderer Einheit) to post; (zu bestimmtem Dienst) to detail (zu for). **jdn ins Ausland** ~ to post sb abroad.

Abkomme m -n, -n (liter) siehe **Nachkomme**.

abkommen vi sep irreg aux sein (a) (Sport: wegkommen) to get away; (zielen) to aim; (Flugzeug) to take off. **schlecht/gut** ~ (wegkommen) to get away to or to make a bad/good start; **wie ist der Schütze abgekommen?** how well did he shoot?, how was his shot?

(b) **von etw** ~ (abweichen) to leave sth; (abirren) to wander off sth, to stray from sth; **vom Kurs** ~ to deviate from or leave one's course; (vom Thema) to digress, to get off the subject, to digress; **vom rechten Weg** ~ (fig) to stray or wander from the straight and narrow.

(c) (aufgeben) **von etw** ~ to drop sth, to give sth up; (von Angewohnheit) to give sth up; (von Idee, Plan) to abandon or drop sth; **von einer Meinung** ~ to revise one's opinion, to change one's mind; **von diesem alten Brauch kommt man immer mehr ab** this old custom is dying out more and more.

(d) (aus der Mode kommen) to go out of fashion to become outdated. **abgekommen sein** to have gone out (of fashion), to be out of fashion; **das kommt immer mehr ab** that's going more and more out of fashion.

Abkommen nt -s, - agreement (auch Pol).

Abkommenschaft f (liter) siehe **Nachkommenschaft**.

abkömmlich adj available. **nicht** ~ sein to be unavailable.

Abkömmling m (a) (Nachkomme) descendant; (fig) adherent. **~e pl** (Jur) issue no pl; **er war (der)** ~ **einer Bankiersfamilie** he came from a banking family. (b) (Chem) derivative.

abkönnen vt sep irreg (sl) (a) (trinken) **der kann ganz schön was ab** he can knock it back (inf) or put it away (inf); **kann nicht viel ab** he can't take much (drink). (b) (mögen) **das kann ich überhaupt nicht ab** I can't stand or abide it.

abkoppeln vt sep (Rail) to uncouple; Pferd to untie; Degen, Pistole to unbuckle, to take off.

abkratzen sep 1 vt Schmutz etc to scratch off; (mit einem Werkzeug) to scrape off; Wand, Gegenstand to scratch; to scrape. **die Schuhe** ~ to scrape the mud/snow etc off one's shoes. 2 vi aux sein (a) (sl: sterben) to kick the bucket (sl), to croak (sl). (b) (dated inf: weglaufen) to scram (inf), to scarper (inf), to beat it (inf).

Abkratzer m -s, - shoe scraper.

abkriegen vt sep (inf) siehe **abbekommen**.

abkucken vti = **abgucken**.

abkühlen sep 1 vt to cool; Speise auch to cool down; (fig) Freundschaft, Zuneigung to cool; Zorn, Leidenschaft to cool, to calm.

2 vi aux sein to cool down; (fig: Freundschaft etc) to cool off; (Begeisterung) to cool.

3 vr to cool down or off; (Wetter) to become cool(er); (fig) to cool; (Beziehungen auch) to become cool(er).

Abkühlung f cooling.

Abkunft f -, no pl (liter) descent, origin; (Nationalität auch) extraction. **französischer** ~ **sein** of French descent etc.

abkuppeln vt sep siehe **abkoppeln**.

abkürzen sep 1 vt (a) (abschneiden) **den Weg** ~ to take a short cut.

(b) (verkürzen) to cut short; Verfahren to shorten; Aufenthalt, Urlaub auch to curtail.

(c) (verkürzt schreiben) Namen to abbreviate. **Millimeter wird mm abgekürzt** millimetres is abbreviated as mm, mm is the abbreviation for millimetres.

2 vi (a) (abschneiden) to take a short cut; (Weg) to be a short cut.

(b) (verkürzt schreiben) to abbreviate, to use abbreviations.

Abkürzung f (a) (Weg) short cut. **durch die** ~ **haben wir eine Stunde gespart** we've saved an hour by taking the short cut, taking the short cut has saved us an hour.

(b) (von Aufenthalt) curtailment, cutting short; (von Verfahren) shortening; (von Vortrag) shortening, cutting short. **gibt es keine** ~ **dieses Verfahrens?** isn't there any way of shortening this process?

(c) (von Wort) abbreviation.

Abkürzungsverzeichnis nt list of abbreviations.

abküssen vt sep to smother with kisses. **sie küßten sich stundenlang ab** they kissed away for hours.

abladen vti sep irreg Last, Wagen to unload; Schutt to dump; (esp Comm) Passagiere, Ware to off-load; (fig inf) Kummer, Ärger auch to vent (bei jdm on sb); Verantwortung to off-load, to shove (inf) (auf +acc onto). **seine Kinder/Arbeit auf jdn** ~ (fig inf) to unload or dump (inf) one's children/work on sb; **sie lud ihren ganzen Kummer bei ihrem Mann ab** she unburdened herself or all her worries to her husband.

Abladeplatz m unloading area; (für Schrott, Müll etc) dump, dumping ground.

Ablage f -, -n (a) (Gestell) place to keep/put sth. **wir brauchen eine** ~ **für die Akten** we need somewhere for our files or where we can keep our files; **der Tisch dient als** ~ **für ihre Bücher** her books are kept on the table; **etw als** ~ **benutzen** (für Akten, Bücher etc) to use sth for storage; **sie haben das Bett als** ~ **benutzt** they put everything on the bed; **gibt es hier irgendeine** ~ **für Taschen und Schirme?** is there anywhere here where bags and umbrellas can be left or for bags and umbrellas?

(b) (Aktenordnung) filing.

(c) (Sw) siehe **Annahmestelle**, **Zweigstelle**.

ablagern sep 1 vt (a) (anhäufen) to deposit.

(b) (deponieren) to leave, to store.

2 vi aux sein or haben (ausreifen) to mature; (Holz auch) to season. ~ **lassen** to allow to mature; Holz auch to (allow to) season; siehe **abgelagert**.

3 vr to be deposited. **in einem Wasserkessel lagert sich Kalk ab** a chalk deposit forms or builds up in a kettle.

Ablagerung f (Vorgang) depositing, deposition; (von Wein) maturing, maturation; (von Holz) maturing, seasoning; (abgelagerter Stoff) deposit.

ablandig adj (Naut) Wind offshore.

Ablaß m -sses, Ablässe (a) (Eccl) indulgence. (b) no pl (das Ablassen) letting out; (von Dampf) letting off; (Entleerung) drainage, draining. (c) (Vorrichtung) outlet.

Ablaßbrief m (Eccl) letter of indulgence.

ablassen sep irreg 1 vt (a) (herauslaufen lassen) Wasser, Luft to let out; Motoröl auch to drain off; Dampf to let off; (Zug, Kessel) to give or let off. **die Luft aus den Reifen** ~ to let the air out of the tyres, to let the tyres down.

(b) (leerlaufen lassen) Teich, Schwimmbecken to drain, to empty.

(c) Brieftaube to let off; Zug to start.

(d) (verkaufen, geben) jdm etw ~ to let sb have sth.

(e) (ermäßigen) to knock off (inf). **er hat mir 20 Mark (vom Preis) abgelassen** he knocked 20 marks off (the price) for me (inf), he reduced the price by 20 marks for me; **etwas vom Preis** ~ to knock something off the price (inf), to bring the price down.

(f) (inf: nicht befestigen, anziehen) to leave off.

2 vi (liter) (a) (mit etw aufhören) to desist. **von einem Vorhaben etc** ~ to abandon a plan etc.

(b) (jdn in Ruhe lassen) **von jdm** ~ to leave sb alone.

Ablaß-: ~**handel** m (Eccl) selling of indulgences; ~**ventil** nt outlet valve.

Ablativ m ablative (case).

ablatschen sep (sl) 1 vt Schuhe to wear out. **abgelatscht** (fig) worn-out, down at heel. 2 vi aux sein to wander off (inf), to push off (inf).

Ablauf m (a) (*Abfluß*) drain; (~*stelle*) outlet; (~*rohr*) drain-(pipe); (*im Haus*) wastepipe; (*Rinne*) drainage channel.
 (b) (*Ablaufen*) draining or running away.
 (c) (*Verlauf*) course; (*von Empfang, Staatsbesuch*) order of events (*gen* in); (*von Verbrechen*) sequence of events (*gen* in); (*von Handlung im Buch etc*) development. er sprach mit uns den ~ der Prüfung durch he took us through the exam; er hat den ~ des Unglücks geschildert he described the way the accident happened; der ~ der Ereignisse vollzog sich wie geplant the course of events was as planned; nach ~ der Vorstellung ... after the performance (was over) ...; es gab keinerlei Störungen im ~ des Programms the programme went off without any disturbances; der friedliche ~ der Veranstaltung hat alle überrascht the fact that the event went off peacefully surprised everybody.
 (d) (*von Frist etc*) expiry. nach ~ der Frist after the deadline had passed or expired.
 (e) (*von Zeitraum*) passing. nach ~ von 4 Stunden after 4 hours (have/had passed or gone by); nach ~ des Jahres/dieser Zeit at the end of the year/this time.
 (f) (*Start*) start.
ablaufen sep irreg 1 vt (a) (*abnützen*) Schuhsohlen, Schuhe to wear out; Absätze to wear down. sich (*dat*) die Beine or Hacken or Absätze or Schuhsohlen nach etw ~ (*inf*) to walk one's legs off looking for sth; das habe ich mir schon an den Schuhsohlen abgelaufen! (*inf*) I've been through all that; siehe Horn.
 (b) aux sein or haben (*entlanglaufen*) Strecke to go or walk over; (*hin und zurück*) to go or walk up and down; Stadt, Straßen, Geschäfte to comb, to scour (*round*).
 2 vi aux sein (a) (*abfließen: Flüssigkeit*) to drain or run away or off; (*sich leeren: Behälter*) to drain (off), to empty (itself); (*trocken werden: Geschirr*) to dry off. aus der Badewanne ~ to run or drain out of the bath; bei ~dem Wasser (*Naut*) with an outgoing tide; an ihm läuft alles ab (*fig*) he just shrugs everything off; jede Kritik läuft an ihm ab (*fig*) with him criticism is just like water off a duck's back; jdn ~ lassen (*inf*) to cut or snub sb.
 (b) (*vonstatten gehen*) to go off. wie ist das bei der Prüfung abgelaufen? how did the exam go (off)?; zuerst sah es sehr gefährlich aus, aber dann ist die Sache doch glimpflich abgelaufen at first things looked pretty dangerous but it was all right in the end.
 (c) (*sich abwickeln: Seil, Kabel*) to wind out, to unwind; (*sich abspulen: Film, Tonband*) to run; (*Schallplatte*) to play. eine Platte/einen Film/Tonband ~ lassen to play a record/to run or show a film/to run or play a tape; abgelaufen sein (*Film etc*) to have finished, to have come to an end.
 (d) (*ungültig werden: Paß, Visum etc*) to expire, to run out; (*enden: Frist, Vertrag etc auch*) to run out, to be up. die Frist ist abgelaufen the period has run out or is up.
 (e) (*vergehen: Zeitraum*) to pass, to go by.
 (f) (*Sport: starten*) to start.
ablauschen vt sep (*geh*) to learn (*dat* from). dem Leben abgelauscht (*fig liter*) taken or culled (*liter*) from life.
Ablaut m (*Gram*) ablaut.
ablauten vi sep (*Gram*) to undergo ablaut, to change by ablaut.
ableben sep (*old*) 1 vi aux sein to pass away, to decease (*form*).
 2 vt Zeit to live out; siehe abgelebt.
Ableben nt -s, no pl (*form*) demise (*form*), decease (*form*).
ablecken vt sep to lick; Teller, Löffel, Finger to lick (clean); Blut, Marmelade to lick off. sich (*dat*) etw von der Hand ~ to lick sth off one's hand.
abledern vt sep Fenster, Auto to leather (off), to polish with a leather.
ablegen sep 1 vt (a) (*niederlegen*) to put down; Last, Waffen auch to lay down; (*Zool*) Eier to lay.
 (b) (*abheften*) Schriftwechsel to file (away).
 (c) (*ausziehen*) Hut, Mantel, Kleider to take off, to remove (*form*).
 (d) (*nicht mehr tragen*) Anzug, Kleid to discard, to cast off; Trauerkleidung, Ehering to take off; Orden, Auszeichnungen to renounce. abgelegte Kleider cast-off or discarded clothes.
 (e) (*aufgeben*) Mißtrauen, Scheu, Stolz to lose, to shed; to cast off (*liter*); schlechte Gewohnheit to give up, to get rid of; kindische Angewohnheit to put aside; Namen to give up.
 (f) (*ableisten, machen*) Schwur, Eid to swear; Gelübde auch to make; Zeugnis to give; Bekenntnis, Beichte, Geständnis to make; Prüfung to take, to sit; (*erfolgreich*) to pass. alle abgelegten Prüfungen all exams taken.
 (g) (*Cards*) to discard, to throw down.
 2 vi (a) (*abfahren*) (Schiff) to cast off; (Space auch) to separate.
 (b) (*Schriftwechsel* ~) to file.
 (c) (*Garderobe* ~) to take one's things off. wenn Sie ~ möchten ... if you would like to take your things or hats and coats off ...
 (d) (*Cards*) to discard.
 3 vt impers (*geh: absehen*) es darauf ~, etw zu tun to be out to do sth; es auf etw (*acc*) ~ to be out for sth; er legte es auf eine Kränkung seines Gegners ab he was out to insult his opponent.
Ableger m -s, - (*Bot*) layer; (*fig: Zweigunternehmen*) branch, subsidiary; (*iro: Sohn*) son, offspring no pl. durch ~ by layering.
ablehnen vt sep (a) auch vi (*zurückweisen, nein sagen*) to decline, to refuse; Antrag, Angebot, Vorschlag, Bewerber, Stelle to turn down, to reject; (*Parl*) Gesetzentwurf to throw out. eine ~de Antwort a negative answer; ein ~der Bescheid a rejection; es ~, etw zu tun to decline or refuse to do sth; dankend ~ to decline with thanks. (b) (*mißbilligen*) to disapprove of. ich lehne es ab, wie er ... I disapprove of the way he ...

Ablehnung f (a) (*Zurückweisung*) refusal; (*von Antrag, Bewerber etc*) rejection. niemand hatte mit seiner ~ gerechnet nobody had expected him to refuse/reject it or turn it down; auf ~ stoßen to be refused/rejected, to meet with a refusal/a rejection.
 (b) (*Mißbilligung*) disapproval. auf ~ stoßen to meet with disapproval.
ableiern vt sep Melodie to churn out; (*inf*) Gedicht etc to reel off; siehe abgeleiert.
ableisten vt sep (*form*) Zeit to complete.
ableitbar adj (a) (*herleitbar*) derivable, deducible; Wort derivable (*aus* from). (b) siehe vt (b) able to be diverted/drawn off or out/conducted.
ableiten sep 1 vt (a) (*herleiten*) to derive; (*logisch folgern auch*) to deduce (*aus* from); (*Math*) Gleichung to differentiate.
 (b) (*umleiten*) Bach, Fluß to divert; (*herausleiten*) Rauch, Dampf, Flüssigkeit to draw off or out; (*ablenken*) Blitz to conduct.
 2 vr (*sich herleiten*) to be derived (*aus* from); (*logisch folgen auch*) to be deduced (*aus* from).
Ableitung f (a) siehe vt derivation; deduction; differentiation; diversion; drawing off or out; conduction. (b) (*Wort, Math*) derivative.
Ableitungssilbe f derivative affix.
ablenken sep 1 vt (a) (*ab-, wegleiten*) to deflect (*auch Phys*), to turn aside or away; Wellen, Licht to refract; Schlag to parry; Katastrophe to avert.
 (b) (*zerstreuen*) to distract. er ließ sich durch nichts ~ he wouldn't let anything distract him; wir mußten die Kinder ~ we had to find something to take the children's minds off things; jdn von seinem Schmerz/seinen Sorgen ~ to make sb forget his pain/worries, to take sb's mind off his pain/worries.
 (c) (*abbringen*) to divert; Verdacht to avert. jdn von der Arbeit ~ to distract sb from his work.
 2 vi (a) (*ausweichen*) (vom Thema) ~ to change the subject; (*bei einem Gespräch auch*) to turn the conversation.
 (b) (*zerstreuen*) to create a distraction. sie geht jede Woche ins Kino, das lenkt ab she goes to the cinema every week, which takes her mind off things.
 3 vr to take one's mind off things.
Ablenkung f (a) (*Ab-, Wegleitung*) deflection (*auch Phys*); (*von Wellen, Licht*) refraction.
 (b) (*Zerstreuung*) diversion, distraction. ~ brauchen to need something to take one's mind off things; sich (*dat*) ~ verschaffen to provide oneself with a distraction or with something to take one's mind off things.
 (c) (*Störung*) distraction.
 (d) (*von Plan, jds Interesse*) diversion; (*von Verdacht*) aversion, averting.
 (e) (*von Thema*) changing of the subject.
Ablenkungsmanöver nt diversionary tactic; (*um vom Thema, Problem abzulenken auch*) red herring.
ablesbar adj Rede, Meßgerät readable. seine Rede war nicht leicht ~ his speech couldn't be easily read out; die Erregung war von seinem Gesicht noch deutlich ~ excitement was still written all over his face; daraus ist ohne weiteres ~, daß ... it can be clearly seen from this that ...
ablesen sep vt irreg 1 vt (a) (*auch vi: vom Blatt*) to read. er muß (alles/seine Rede) ~ he has to read everything/his speech (from notes etc); (jdm) etw von den Lippen ~ to lip-read sth (that sb says).
 (b) (*auch vi: registrieren*) Meßgeräte, Barometer, Strom to read; Barometerstand to take. nächste Woche wird abgelesen the meter(s) will be read next week.
 (c) (*herausfinden, erkennen, folgern*) to see. jdm etw vom Gesicht/von der Stirn ~ to see or tell sth from sb's face, to read sth in sb's face; das konnte man ihr vom Gesicht ~ it was written all over her face; aus der Reaktion der Presse war die Stimmung im Volke deutlich abzulesen the mood of the people could be clearly gauged or read from the press reaction; jdm jeden Wunsch an or von den Augen ~ to anticipate sb's every wish; daraus kann man ~, daß ... it can be seen from this that ..., this shows that ...
 (d) (*wegnehmen*) Beeren, Raupen etc to pick off (*von etw* sth); (*leer machen*) Acker, Strauch etc to pick clean.
Ableser(in f) m meter-reader, meter-man.
ableuchten vt sep to light up, to illuminate.
ableugnen vt sep (a) Schuld, Tat to deny; Verantwortung auch to disclaim; Glauben to renounce. 2 vi er hat weiter abgeleugnet he continued to deny it; A~ hilft nichts denying it won't do any good.
Ableugnung f denial; (*von Glauben*) renunciation.
ablichten vt sep (*form*) to photocopy; (*fotografieren*) to photograph.
Ablichtung f (*form*) siehe vt photocopy; photograph; (*Vorgang*) photocopying; photographing.
abliefern vt sep (*bei einer Person*) to hand over (*bei* to); Examensarbeit etc to hand in; (*bei einer Dienststelle*) to hand in (*bei* to); (*liefern*) to deliver (*bei* to); (*inf*) Kinder, Freundin to deposit (*inf*); (*nach Hause bringen*) to take home. ich habe die Kinder bei Tante Moni abgeliefert I deposited or parked the kids with Aunty Moni (*inf*).
Ablieferung f siehe vt handing-over no pl; handing-in no pl; delivery.
abliegen vi sep irreg (a) (*entfernt sein*) to be at a distance; (*fig*) to be removed. das Haus liegt weit ab the house is a long way off or away or is quite a distance away; das liegt sehr weit ab von unserem Thema that is very far removed from or is a long way from the topic we are dealing with; siehe abgelegen.
 (b) (S Ger: lagern) (Obst) to ripen; (Fleisch) to hang.

ablisten vt sep jdm etw ~ to trick sb out of sth; **jdm die Erlaubnis ~, etw zu tun** to trick sb into giving one permission to do sth.

ablocken vt sep jdm etw ~ to get sth out of sb; **diese Äußerung lockte ihm nur ein müdes Lächeln ab** this statement only drew a tired smile from him or got a tired smile out of him; **er lockte seiner Geige süße Töne ab** he coaxed sweet sounds from his violin.

ablösbar adj (a) (abtrennbar) removable, detachable. **die Etiketten sind nur schwer ~** the labels are difficult to remove. (b) (ersetzbar) replaceable. (c) (tilgbar) redeemable.

ablöschen vt sep (a) (mit dem Löschblatt) to blot. (b) Tafel to wipe, to clean; Geschriebenes to wipe or clean off. (c) (Cook) to add water to.

Ablöse f -, -n (Aus) (a) (Abstand) key money. (b) (Ablösungssumme) transfer fee.

ablösen sep 1 vt (a) (abmachen) to take off, to remove; Etikett, Briefmarke etc auch to detach; Pflaster etc auch to peel off. (b) (Fin) (kapitalisieren) Rente to get paid in a lump sum; (auszahlen) to pay (off) in a lump sum; (tilgen) Schuld, Hypothek to pay off, to redeem. (c) (ersetzen) Wache to relieve; Kollegen auch to take over from. **drei Minister wurden abgelöst** (euph) three ministers were relieved of their duties. (d) (fig: an Stelle treten von) to take the place of; (Methode, System) to supersede. **Regen hat jetzt das schöne Wetter abgelöst** the fine weather has now given way to rain.
2 vr (a) (abgehen) to come off; (Lack etc auch) to peel off; (Netzhaut) to become detached. (b) (auch einander ~) to take turns; (Fahrer, Kollegen auch, Wachen) to relieve each other. **wir lösen uns alle drei Stunden beim Babysitten ab** we each do three-hour shifts of babysitting, we take turns at babysitting, doing three hours each. (c) (auch einander ~: alternieren) to alternate. **bei ihr lösen sich Fröhlichkeit und Trauer ständig ab** she constantly alternates between being happy and being miserable.

Ablöse-: ~spiel nt match of which the proceeds go to the club from which a player has been transferred; ~summe f (Sport) transfer fee.

Ablösung f (a) (Fin) (von Rente) lump payment; (von Hypothek, Schuld) paying off, redemption. (b) (Wachwechsel) relieving; (Wache) relief; (Entlassung) replacement. **wann findet die ~ der Wache statt?** when will the guard be relieved?; **er kam als ~** he came as a replacement; **bei dieser Arbeit braucht man alle zwei Stunden eine ~** you need relieving every two hours in this work; **die ~ des Vorsitzenden erfolgte auf eigenen Wunsch** the chairman was relieved of his duties at his own request. (c) (das Ablösen) removal, detachment; (von Pflaster etc auch) peeling off; (das Sichablösen) separation; (von Lack etc) peeling off; (von Netzhaut) detachment.

Ablösungssumme f (Sport) transfer fee.

ablotsen, abluchsen vt sep (inf) jdm etw ~ to get or wangle (inf) sth out of sb.

Abluft f -, no pl (Tech) used air.

ablutschen vt sep to lick. **das Blut/den Honig (von etw) ~** to lick the blood/honey off (sth); **sich (dat) die Finger ~** to lick one's fingers (clean); **jdm einen ~** (vulg) to suck sb off (vulg), to give sb a blow-job (sl).

abmachen vt sep (inf) (a) (entfernen) to take off; Schnur, Kette etc auch to undo; (herunternehmen) to take down. **er machte dem Hund die Leine ab** he took the dog's lead off. (b) (vereinbaren) Termin, Erkennungszeichen to agree (on). **wir haben abgemacht, daß wir das tun werden** we've agreed to do it, we've agreed on doing it; **es ist noch nichts abgemacht worden** nothing's been agreed (on) yet; siehe abgemacht. (c) (besprechen) to sort out, to settle. **etw mit sich allein ~** to sort sth out for oneself, to come to terms with sth oneself. (d) (ableisten) Zeit to do.

Abmachung f agreement.

abmagern vi sep aux sein to get thinner, to lose weight. **sehr ~** to lose a lot of weight; siehe abgemagert.

Abmagerung f, no pl (Auszehrung) emaciation; (Gewichtsverlust) slimming.

Abmagerungskur f diet. **eine ~ machen** to be on a diet, to be dieting; (anfangen) to go on a diet, to diet.

abmähen vt sep to mow.

abmalen vt sep (abzeichnen) to paint.

abmarkten vt sep **davon lassen wir uns nichts ~** we will cede nothing on this point; **er ließ sich seine Rechte nicht ~** he would not bargain away his rights.

Abmarsch m departure; (von Soldaten auch) march-off; (von Demonstranten etc auch) moving off. **ich sah dem ~ der Bergsteiger/Wanderer zu** I watched the climbers setting out or off; **zum ~ antreten** (Mil) to fall in (ready) for the march-off.

abmarschbereit adj ready to set out or off or move off; (Mil) ready to move off or march.

abmarschieren* vi sep aux sein to set out or off, to move off; (Mil) to march or move off.

abmartern vr sep to torment oneself.

abmatten vt sep (geh) to exhaust.

Abmelde-: ~bestätigung f document confirming that one has cancelled one's registration with the local police; ~formular nt form to be filled in when one cancels one's registration with the local police.

abmelden sep 1 vt (a) Zeitungen etc to cancel; Telefon to have disconnected; (bei Verein) jdn to cancel the membership of. **sein Auto ~** to take one's car off the road; **seinen Fernsehapparat ~** to cancel one's television licence; **ein Kind von einer Schule ~** to take a child away from or remove a child from a school; **seine Familie polizeilich ~** to inform or notify the police that one's family is moving away. (b) (inf) **abgemeldet sein** (Sport) to be outplayed/outboxed/outdriven etc; **jd/etw ist bei jdm abgemeldet** sb has lost interest in sb/sth; **er/sie ist bei mir abgemeldet** I don't want anything to do with him/her.
2 vr to ask for permission to be absent; (vor Abreise) to say one is leaving, to announce one's departure; (im Hotel) to check out. **sich bei jdm ~** to tell sb that one is leaving; **sich polizeilich or bei der Polizei ~** to inform or notify the police that one is moving away, to cancel one's registration with the police; **sich bei einem Verein ~** to cancel one's membership of a club.

Abmeldung f (von Zeitungen etc) cancellation; (von Telefon) disconnection; (bei der Polizei) cancellation of one's registration; (inf: Formular) form to be filled in so that one's registration with the police is cancelled. **seit der ~ meines Autos** since I took my car off the road; **die ~ meines Fernsehapparats** the cancellation of my television licence; **die ~ eines Kindes von einer Schule** the removal of a child from a school; **nach seiner ~ bei dem Verein** after he had cancelled his membership of the club.

abmergeln vi sep siehe abgemergelt.

abmessen vt sep irreg (a) (ausmessen) to measure; (genaue Maße feststellen von) to measure up; (fig) Worte to weigh; (abschätzen) Verlust, Schaden to measure. **er maß seine Schritte genau ab** (fig) he walked with great deliberation or very deliberately or with measured tread (liter); **seine Bewegungen ~** (fig) to make studied or deliberate movements; siehe abgemessen. (b) (abteilen) to measure off.

Abmessung f usu pl measurement; (Ausmaß) dimension.

abmildern vt sep Geschmack to tone down; Äußerung auch to moderate; Aufprall to cushion, to soften; Schock to lessen.

abmontieren* vt sep Räder, Teile to take off (von etw sth); Maschine to dismantle.

abmühen vr sep to struggle (away). **sich mit jdm/etw ~** to struggle or slave away with sb/sth.

abmurksen vt sep (dated sl) jdn to bump off (sl), to do in (inf); (schlachten) to kill; Motor to stall.

abmustern sep (Naut) 1 vt Besatzung to pay off. 2 vi to sign off, to leave the ship.

abnabeln vt sep ein Kind ~ to cut a baby's umbilical cord.

abnagen vt sep to gnaw off; Knochen to gnaw. **Fleisch vom Knochen ~** to gnaw meat off a bone, to gnaw off meat from a bone.

abnähen vt sep to take in.

Abnäher m -s, - dart.

Abnahme f -, -n (a) (Wegnahme) removal; (Herunternahme) taking down. **die ~ vom Kreuz(e)** the Descent from the Cross, the Deposition (form). (b) (Verringerung) decrease (gen in); (bei Anzahl, Menge auch) drop (gen in); (von Niveau auch) decline (gen in); (von Kräften, Energie) decline (gen in); (von Interesse, Nachfrage) falling off, decline; (von Aufmerksamkeit) falling off, flagging, waning; (Verlust) loss. **eine ~ des Niveaus** a drop in or dropping off of the level. (c) (von Prüfung) holding; (von Neubau, Fahrzeug etc) inspection; (von TÜV) carrying out; (von Eid) administering. **die ~ der Parade** the taking of the parade, the review of the troops; **die ~ der Prüfung kann erst erfolgen, wenn ...** the exam can only be held if ... (d) (Comm) purchase. **bei ~ von 50 Exemplaren** if you/we etc purchase or take 50 copies; **keine/gute ~ finden** to find no market, not to sell/to sell well.

abnehmbar adj (rare) removable, detachable.

abnehmen sep irreg 1 vt (a) (herunternehmen) to take off, to remove; Hörer to lift, to pick up; Obst to pick; (lüften) Hut to raise; Vorhang, Bild, Wäsche to take down; Maschen to decrease; (abrasieren) Bart to take or shave off; (Cards) Karte to take from the pile. **das Telefon ~** to answer the telephone; **den Deckel von der Kiste ~** to take the lid off the box, to take off the lid from the box. (b) (an sich nehmen) jdm etw ~ to take sth from sb, to relieve sb of sth (form); (fig) Arbeit, Sorgen to take sth off sb's shoulders, to relieve sb of sth; **darf ich Ihnen den Mantel/die Tasche ~?** can I take your coat/bag?; **kann ich dir etwas ~?** (tragen) can I take something for you?; (helfen) can I do anything for you?; **jdm die Beichte ~** to hear confession from sb; **jdm einen Eid ~** to administer an oath to sb; **jdm ein Versprechen ~** to make sb promise sth; **jdm einen Weg ~** to save sb a journey; **jdm eine Besorgung ~** to do some shopping for sb. (c) (wegnehmen) to take away (jdm from sb); (rauben, abgewinnen) to take (jdm off sb); (inf: abverlangen) to take (jdm off sb). **diese Schweine haben mir alles abgenommen** the bastards have taken everything (I had); **diese Strolche haben ihr die ganze Rente abgenommen** the rogues robbed her of her entire pension or took her entire pension. (d) (begutachten) Gebäude, Wohnung to inspect; (abhalten) Prüfung to hold; TÜV to carry out. (e) (abkaufen) to take (dat off), to buy (dat from, off); (fig inf: glauben) to buy (inf). **dieses Märchen nimmt dir keiner ab!** (inf) nobody'll buy that tale! (f) Fingerabdrücke to take; Totenmaske to make (dat of).
2 vi (a) (sich verringern) to decrease; (Vorräte auch) to go down, to diminish; (zahlenmäßig, mengenmäßig auch) to drop; (Unfälle, Diebstähle etc) to decrease (in number); (Niveau) to go down, to decline; (Kräfte, Energie) to fail, to decline; (Fieber) to lessen, to go down; (Interesse, Nachfrage) to fall off, to decline; (Aufmerksamkeit) to fall off, to flag, to wane;

(*Mond*) to wane; (*Tage*) to grow or get shorter; (*beim Stricken*) to decrease. (**an Gewicht**) ~ to lose weight; **in letzter Zeit hast du im Gesicht abgenommen** your face has got thinner recently. (**b**) (*Hörer, Telefon* ~) to answer.

Abnehmer *m* -s, - (*Comm*) buyer, purchaser, customer. **keine/viele/wenige** ~ **finden** not to sell/to sell well/badly.

Abnehmerkreis *m* buyers *pl*, customers *pl*, market.

Abneigung *f* dislike (*gegen* of); (*Widerstreben*) aversion (*gegen* to).

abnorm, abnormal (*Aus, Sw*) *adj* abnormal.

Abnormität *f* abnorm(al)ity; (*Monstrum auch*) freak.

abnötigen *vt sep* (*geh*) **jdm etw** ~ to wring or force sth from sb; **jdm Bewunderung** ~ to win or gain sb's admiration; **jdm Respekt** ~ to gain sb's respect.

abnutzen, abnützen *sep* 1 *vt* to wear out. **dieser Begriff ist schon sehr abgenutzt worden** this idea is pretty well-worn or has become hackneyed; *siehe* **abgenutzt.** 2 *vr* to wear out, to get worn out.

Abnutzung, Abnützung *f* wear (and tear). **die jahrelange** ~ **der Reifen** the years of wear (and tear) on the tyres; **die normale** ~ **ist im Mietpreis berücksichtigt** general wear and tear is included in the rent.

Abonnement [abɔnə'mã:] *nt* -s, -s *or* -e (**a**) (*Zeitungs*~) subscription. **eine Zeitung im** ~ **beziehen** to subscribe to a newspaper, to have a subscription for a newspaper. (**b**) (*Theater*~) season ticket. **ein** ~ **im Theater haben** to have a season ticket or subscription for the theatre or a theatre season ticket.

Abonnent(in *f*) *m* (*Zeitungs*~) subscriber; (*Theater*~) season-ticket holder.

abonnieren* 1 *vt* **Zeitung** to subscribe to, to have a subscription for; **Konzertreihe, Theater** to have a season ticket or subscription for.
2 *vi* **auf eine Zeitung abonniert sein** to subscribe to or to have a subscription for a newspaper; **auf eine Konzertreihe abonniert sein** to have a season ticket or subscription for a concert series.

ab|ordnen *vt sep* to delegate. **jdn zu einer Versammlung** ~ to send sb as a delegate to a meeting.

Ab|ordnung *f* delegation; (*Delegation auch*) deputation.

Abort[1] *m* -s, -e (*form, S Ger*) lavatory, toilet.

Abort[2] *m* -s, -e, **Ab|ortus** *m* -, - (*spec*) (*Fehlgeburt*) miscarriage, abortion (*form*); (*Abtreibung*) abortion. **einen** ~ **beibringen** to perform an abortion.

Abortgrube *f* (*form*) cesspool.

abpacken *vt sep* to pack. **ein abgepacktes Brot** a wrapped loaf.

abpassen *vt sep* (**a**) (*abwarten*) **Gelegenheit, Zeitpunkt** to wait for; (*ergreifen*) to seize. **den richtigen Augenblick** *or* **Zeitpunkt** ~ (*abwarten*) to bide one's time, to wait for the right time; (*ergreifen*) to move at the right time; **ich habe den Zeitpunkt nicht richtig abgepaßt** I mistimed it; **etw gut** ~ to manage or arrange sth well; (*zeitlich auch*) to time sth well. (**b**) (*auf jdn warten*) to catch; (*jdm auflauern*) to waylay. (**c**) (*dated: abmessen*) **Kleid, Vorhang** to fit, to adjust or alter the length of.

abpausen *vt sep* to trace, to make a tracing of.

abperlen *vi sep aux sein* to drip off (*von etw* sth); (*Tautropfen*) to fall.

abpfeifen *sep irreg* (*Sport*) 1 *vi* (*Schiedsrichter*) to blow one's whistle. 2 *vt* **das Spiel/die erste Halbzeit** ~ to blow the whistle for the end of the game/for half-time.

Abpfiff *m* (*Sport*) final whistle. ~ **zur Halbzeit** half-time whistle, whistle for half-time.

abpflücken *vt sep* to pick.

abplacken (*inf*), **abplagen** *vr sep* to struggle (away). **sich sein ganzes Leben lang (mit etw)** ~ to slave away one's whole life (at sth).

abplatten *vt sep* to flatten (out).

abplatzen *vi sep aux sein* (*Lack, Ölfarbe*) to flake or crack off; (*Knopf*) to fly or burst off. **drei Knöpfe platzten ihm ab** three of his buttons flew off.

abprägen *vr sep* (*Muster*) to leave an imprint or mark. **die Sorgen haben sich in seinem Gesicht abgeprägt** his worries have left their mark on his face; **der Charakter eines Menschen prägt sich in seinem Gesicht ab** a person's character shows clearly in his face.

Abprall *m* (*von Ball*) rebound; (*von Geschoß, Kugel*) ricochet (*von off*).

abprallen *vi sep aux sein* (*Ball*) to bounce off; (*Kugel*) to ricochet (*off*). **von** *or* **an etw** (*dat*) ~ to bounce/ricochet off sth; **an jdm** ~ (*fig*) to make no impression on sb; (*Beleidigungen*) to bounce off sb.

Abpraller *m* -s, - (*Sport*) rebound. **er hat den** ~ **eingeköpft** he headed it in on the rebound.

abpressen *vt sep* **jdm etw** ~ to wring sth from sb; **Geld** to extort sth from sb; **die Angst preßte ihm den Atem/das Herz ab** he could scarcely breathe for fear/fear ate into his heart.

abprotzen *sep* 1 *vti* (*Mil*) *Geschütz* to unlimber. 2 *vi* (*Mil sl*) to crap (*sl*), to have a crap (*sl*).

abpumpen *vt sep* **Teich, Schwimmbecken** to pump dry, to pump the water out of; **Wasser, Öl** to pump off; **Muttermilch** to express.

abputzen *sep* 1 *vt* to clean; **Schmutz** to clean off or up. **sich** (*dat*) **die Nase/den Mund/die Hände/den Hintern** ~ to wipe one's nose/mouth/hands/to wipe or clean one's bottom; **putz dir die Schuhe ab, bevor du ins Haus kommst** wipe your feet before you come into the house. 2 *vr* (*S Ger, Aus, Sw*) to clean oneself.

abquälen *sep* 1 *vr* to struggle (away).
2 *vt* **sich** (*dat*) **ein Lächeln** ~ to force (out) a smile; **sich** (*dat*) **eine Erklärung/Antwort** ~ to finally manage to produce an

explanation/answer; **ich muß mir noch diesen Aufsatz** ~ I still have to produce this essay; **er quält sich immer noch mit seiner Doktorarbeit ab** he's still struggling with or sweating away over (*inf*) his PhD.

abqualifizieren* *vt sep* to dismiss, to write off.

abquetschen *vt sep* to crush. **sich** (*dat*) **den Arm** ~ to get one's arm crushed; **sich** (*dat*) **ein paar Tränen** ~ to force or squeeze out a couple of tears; **sich** (*dat*) **ein Gedicht/eine Rede** ~ to deliver oneself of a poem/speech (*iro*).

abrackern *vr sep* (*inf*) to struggle. **sich für jdn** ~ to slave away for sb; **warum sollen wir uns hier** ~? why should we break our backs here? (*inf*); **sich im Garten** ~ to sweat away in the garden (*inf*).

Abraham *m* -s Abraham. **in** ~**s Schoß** in the bosom of Abraham; **sicher wie in** ~**s Schoß** safe and secure.

abrahmen *vt sep* **Milch** to skim.

Abrakadabra *nt* -s, *no pl* (*Zauberwort*) abracadabra; (*Unsinn*) double dutch.

abrasieren* *vt sep* to shave off (*inf*); *Gebäude* to flatten, to raze to the ground.

abraten *vti sep irreg* **jdm (von) etw** ~ to warn sb against sth, to advise sb against sth; **jdm davon** ~, **etw zu tun** to warn or advise sb against doing sth; **es wird dringend abgeraten, hier zu baden** you are strongly advised not to swim here.

Abraum *m* (*Min*) overburden, overlay shelf.

abräumen *vti sep* (**a**) to clear up or away. **den Tisch** ~ to clear the table. (**b**) (*Min*) to clear.

Abraumhalde *f* (*Min*) slag heap.

abrauschen *vi sep aux sein* (*inf*) to roar away or off; (*Aufmerksamkeit erregend*) to sweep away; (*aus Zimmer*) to sweep out.

abreagieren* *sep* 1 *vt* **Spannung, Wut** to work off, to get rid of, to abreact (*Psych*). **seinen Ärger an der Katze** ~ to take it out on the cat.
2 *vr* to work it off. **er war ganz wütend, aber jetzt hat er sich abreagiert** he was furious, but he's simmered down or cooled down now; **sich an der Katze** ~ to take it out on the cat.

abrechnen *sep* 1 *vi* (**a**) (*Kasse machen*) to cash up. **der Kellner wollte** ~ the waiter was wanting us/them to pay our/their bill (*Brit*) or check (*US*); **darf ich** ~? would you like to settle your bill or check now? (**b**) **mit jdm** ~ to settle up with sb; (*fig*) to settle (the score with) sb, to get even with sb.
2 *vt* (*abziehen*) to deduct, to take off; (*berücksichtigen*) to allow for, to make allowance(s) for. (**b**) **die Kasse** ~ to cash up.

Abrechnung *f* (**a**) (*Aufstellung*) statement (*über* +acc for); (*Rechnung*) bill, invoice; (*Bilanz*) balancing, reckoning up; (*das Kassemachen*) cashing up; (*fig: Rache*) revenge. **wieviel mußten Sie ausgeben? — ich bin gerade dabei, die** ~ **zu machen** or **ich bin gerade bei der** ~ how much did you have to spend? — I'm just working it out now; **bei der** ~ **der Konten** when the accounts are/were being balanced; **er muß noch die ganzen** ~**en machen** he still has to do all the accounts or the bookwork; **der Tag der** ~ (*fig*) the day of reckoning. (**b**) (*Abzug*) deduction. **nach** ~ **von** after the deduction of; **in** ~ **bringen** or **stellen** (*form*) to deduct; **folgende Beträge kommen in** ~ (*form*) the following sums are to be deducted.

Abrechnungs-: ~**termin** *m* accounting date; ~**verfahren** *nt* clearing procedure; ~**verkehr** *m* clearing business.

Abrede *f* (*form*) agreement. **etw in** ~ **stellen** to deny or dispute sth.

abreden *vi sep* (*old*) **jdm von etw** ~ to dissuade sb from sth.

abregen *vr sep* (*inf*) to calm or cool down. **reg dich ab!** relax!, cool it! (*inf*).

abreiben *vt sep irreg* **Schmutz, Rost** to clean or rub off; (*säubern*) **Fenster, Schuhe** to wipe; (*trocknen*) to rub down, to give a rub-down; (*Cook*) to grate.

Abreibung *f* (*Med*) rub-down; (*inf: Prügel*) hiding, beating, thrashing.

Abreise *f* departure (*nach* for). **bei der/meiner** ~ when I left/leave, on my departure.

abreisen *vi sep aux sein* to leave (*nach* for). **wann reisen Sie ab?** when will you be leaving?

abreißen *sep irreg* 1 *vt* (**a**) (*abtrennen*) to tear or rip off; **Tapete, Blätter auch** to strip off; **Pflanzen** to tear out. **er hat sich** (*dat*) **den Knopf abgerissen** he's torn his button off; **er wird dir nicht (gleich) den Kopf** ~ (*inf*) he won't bite your head off (*inf*); *siehe* **abgerissen.** (**b**) (*niederreißen*) **Gebäude** to pull down, to demolish. **das A**~ **von Gebäuden** the demolition of buildings. (**c**) (*sl: absitzen*) **Haftstrafe** to do.
2 *vi aux sein* (*Knopf etc*) to tear or come off; (*Schnürsenkel*) to break (off); (*fig: unterbrochen werden*) to break off. **das reißt nicht ab** (*fig*) there is no end to it; **den Kontakt etc nicht** ~ **lassen** to stay in touch.

Abreißkalender *m* tear-off calendar.

abreiten *sep irreg* 1 *vi aux sein* to ride off or away. 2 *vt* (**a**) *aux sein or haben* (*inspizieren*) *Front* to ride along; (*hin und zurück*) to ride up and down; *Strecke* to ride over; *Gelände* to patrol (on horseback). (**b**) (*Naut*) *Sturm* to ride out.

abrennen *sep irreg* (*inf*) 1 *vt* (**a**) *aux sein or haben Stadt, Geschäfte* to scour (round), to run round (*much looking for*). (**b**) **sich** (*dat*) **die Hacken** *or* **Beine (nach etw)** ~ to run one's legs off (looking for sth). 2 *vr* to run oneself off one's feet.

abrichten *vt sep* (**a**) (*dressieren*) **Tier, Menschen** to train. **der Hund ist nur auf Einbrecher abgerichtet** the dog is trained to go only for burglars; **darauf abgerichtet sein, etw zu tun** to be trained to do sth. (**b**) (*Tech*) **Werkstück, Brett** to true off or up.

Abrichter *m* -s, - trainer.

Abrichtung f siehe vt (a) training. (b) truing.

abriegeln vt sep (verschließen) Tür to bolt; (absperren) Straße, Gebiet to seal or cordon or block off.

Abrieg(e)lung f siehe vt bolting; sealing or cordoning or blocking off.

abringen vt sep irreg jdm etw ~ to wring or force sth from or out of sb, to wrest sth from sb (liter); **sich** (dat) **ein Lächeln** ~ to force a smile; **sich** (dat) **eine Entscheidung/ein paar Worte** ~ to force oneself into (making) a decision/to manage to produce a few words; **dem Meer Land** ~ (liter) to wrest land away from the sea (liter).

Abriß m (a) (Abbruch) demolition. (b) (Übersicht) outline, summary. (c) (von Eintrittskarte etc) tear-off part.

Abriß-: ~**arbeiten** pl demolition work; ~**liste** f (inf) demolition list; **auf der** ~**liste stehen** to be condemned; **a**~**reif** adj only fit for demolition; (zum Abriß freigegeben) condemned.

abrollen sep 1 vt (a) (abwickeln) Papier, Stoff to unroll; Film, Bindfaden to unwind, to unreel; Kabel, Tau to uncoil, to unwind.
(b) (abfahren) Frachtgut to fetch.
2 vi aux sein (a) (Papier, Stoff) to unroll, to come unrolled; (Film, Bindfaden) to unwind, to come unwound; (Kabel, Tau) to uncoil, to come uncoiled.
(b) (Sport) to roll.
(c) (abfahren) (Züge, Waggons) to roll off or away; (Flugzeug) to taxi off.
(d) (inf) (vonstatten gehen) (Programm) to run; (Veranstaltung) to go off; (Ereignisse) to unfold. **etw rollt vor jds Augen ab** sth unfolds or unfurls before sb's (very) eyes; **mein ganzes Leben rollte noch einmal vor meinen Augen ab** my whole life passed before me again.
3 vr (Papier, Stoff) to unroll itself, to come unrolled; (Film, Bindfaden) to unwind itself, to come unwound; (Kabel, Tau) to uncoil itself, to come uncoiled.

abrücken sep 1 vt (wegschieben) to move away. **etw von der Wand** ~ to move sth away from or out from the wall. 2 vi aux sein (a) (wegrücken) to move away; (fig: sich distanzieren) to dissociate oneself (von from). (b) (abmarschieren) to move out.

Abruf m (a) **sich auf** ~ **bereit halten** to be ready to be called (for); **Ihr Wagen steht jederzeit auf** ~ **bereit** your car will be ready at any time; **auf** ~ **zur Verfügung stehen** to be available on call.
(b) (Comm) **etw auf** ~ **bestellen/kaufen** to order/buy sth (to be delivered) on call.
(c) (Datenverarbeitung) retrieval. **auf** ~ **bereit** readily retrievable; **der Computer hat diese Daten auf** ~ **bereit** this data is readily retrievable from the computer.

abruf-: ~**bar** adj Daten retrievable; ~**bereit** adj (a) Mensch ready to be called (for); (einsatzbereit) ready (and waiting); (abholbereit) ready to be called for; (b) (Comm, Fin) ready on call.

abrufen vt sep irreg (a) (wegrufen) to call away. **jdn aus dem Leben** ~ (euph) to gather sb to his fathers (euph). (b) (Comm) to request delivery of; (Fin: abheben) to withdraw. (c) Daten, Informationen to retrieve.

abrunden vt sep (lit, fig) to round off. **eine Zahl nach oben/unten** ~ to round a number up/down; **wir haben die Summe abgerundet** we made it a round sum, we rounded it up/down; **DM 13,12, also abgerundet DM 13,10** 13 marks 12, so call it 13 marks 10; **die abgerundete, endgültige Form einer Sonate/eines Gedichts** the final polished or rounded form of a sonata/poem.

Abrundung f (lit, fig) rounding off. **zur** ~ **von etw** to round sth off.

abrupfen vt sep Gras, Blumen to rip or pull out; Laub to strip off; Blätter to pull or strip off.

abrupt adj abrupt.

Abruptheit f abruptness.

abrüsten sep 1 vi (a) (Mil, Pol) to disarm. (b) (Build) to take down or remove the scaffolding. 2 vt (a) (Mil, Pol) to disarm. (b) Gebäude to take down or remove the scaffolding from or on.

Abrüstung f, no pl (a) (Mil, Pol) disarmament. (b) (Build) removal of the scaffolding.

Abrüstungs-: ~**abkommen** nt disarmament treaty; ~**gespräche** pl disarmament talks pl; ~**konferenz** f disarmament conference.

abrutschen vi sep aux sein (abgleiten) to slip; (nach unten) to slip down; (Wagen) to skid; (Aviat) to sideslip; (fig) (Mannschaft, Schüler) to drop (down) (auf +acc to); (Leistungen) to drop off, to go downhill; (moralisch) to let oneself go, to go downhill.

Abs. abbr of Absatz; Absender.

absäbeln vt sep (inf) to hack or chop off.

absacken sep 1 vi aux sein (sinken) to sink; (Boden, Gebäude auch) to subside; (Flugzeug, Blutdruck) to drop, to fall; (fig inf: nachlassen) to fall or drop off; (Schüler) to go down; (verkommen) to go to pot (inf). **sie ist in ihren Leistungen sehr abgesackt** her performance has dropped off a lot.
2 vt (rare) to sack.

Absage f -, -n refusal; (auf Einladung auch) negative reply. **das ist eine** ~ **an die Demokratie** that's a denial of democracy; **jdm/einer Sache eine** ~ **erteilen** to reject sb/sth.

absagen sep 1 vt (rückgängig machen) Veranstaltung, Besuch to cancel, to call off; (ablehnen) Einladung to decline, to turn down, to refuse. **er hat seine Teilnahme abgesagt** he decided against taking part. 2 vi to cry off. **jdm** ~ to tell sb that one can't come; **wenn ich ihn einlade, sagt er jedesmal ab** whenever I invite him he says no.

absägen vt sep (a) (abtrennen) to saw off. (b) (fig inf) to chuck or sling out (inf); Minister, Beamten to oust; Schüler to make fail.

absahnen sep 1 vt Milch to skim; (fig) Geld to rake in; (sich verschaffen) to cream off; das Beste to take. **den Markt** ~ to take the cream, to take the pick of the bunch. 2 vi to skim milk; (fig) to take the best; (in bezug auf Menschen auch) to take the cream.

absatteln vti sep to unsaddle.

Absatz m -es, Absätze (a) (Unterbrechung) pause; (Abschnitt) paragraph; (Typ) indention; (Jur) section. **einen** ~ **machen** to pause or make a pause/to start a new paragraph/to indent.
(b) (Treppen~) half-landing; (Mauer~) overhang; (herausragend) ledge.
(c) (Schuh~) heel. **spitze Absätze** stilettos, stiletto heels; **sich auf dem** ~ **(her)umdrehen, auf dem** ~ **kehrtmachen** to turn on one's heel.
(d) (Ablagerung) deposit.
(e) (Verkauf) sales pl. **um den/unseren** ~ **zu steigern** to increase sales/our sales; ~ **finden** or **haben** to sell; **guten/begeisterten** or **starken** or **reißenden** ~ **finden** to sell well/like hot cakes.

Absatz-: ~**chance** f sales potential no pl; **a**~**fähig** adj marketable, saleable; ~**flaute** f slump in sales or in the market; ~**forschung** f sales research; ~**gebiet** nt sales area; ~**genossenschaft** f marketing cooperative; ~**kosten** pl sales costs pl; ~**krise** f sales crisis; ~**land** nt customer, buyer; ~**markt** m market; ~**planung** f sales planning; ~**schwierigkeiten** pl sales problems pl; **auf** ~**schwierigkeiten stoßen** to meet with sales resistance; ~**steigerung** f increase in sales, sales increase; ~**strategie** f sales strategy; **a**~**weise** adj in paragraphs.

absaufen vi sep irreg aux sein (sl: ertrinken) to drown; (inf: Motor, Min: Grube) to flood; (sl: Schiff etc) to go down.

absaugen vt sep Flüssigkeit, Gas, Staub to suck out or off; (mit Staubsauger) to hoover (Brit ®) or vacuum up; Teppich, Sofa to hoover ®, to vacuum.

abschaben vt sep to scrape off; (säubern) to scrape (clean); Stoff to wear thin; siehe abgeschabt.

abschaffen sep 1 vt (a) (außer Kraft setzen) to abolish, to do away with. (b) (nicht länger halten) to get rid of; Auto etc auch to give up. 2 vr (S Ger inf: sich abarbeiten) to slave away (inf), to work like a slave.

Abschaffung f siehe vt (a) abolition. (b) getting rid of; giving up.

abschälen sep 1 vt Haut, Rinde to peel off; Baumstamm to strip. **die Rinde eines Baumes** ~ to strip or peel the bark off a tree.
2 vr to peel off.

abschalten 1 vti sep (lit, fig inf) to switch off; Kontakt to break. 2 vr to switch itself off.

Abschaltung f switching off; (von Kontakt) breaking.

abschatten, abschattieren* vt sep (lit) to shade; (fig) to give a slight nuance to.

Abschattung, Abschattierung f (lit) shading; (fig) nuance.

abschätzen vt sep to estimate, to assess; Menschen, Fähigkeiten to assess, to appraise. **seine Lage** ~ to take stock of or assess one's position; **jdn nach seiner Kleidung** ~ to judge sb from his clothes; **ein** ~**der Blick** an appraising look; **jdn mit einer** ~**den Miene betrachten** to look at sb appraisingly.

abschätzig 1 adj disparaging; Bemerkung auch derogatory. 2 adv disparagingly. **sich** ~ **über jdn äußern** to make disparaging or derogatory remarks about sb.

Abschätzung f siehe **Schätzung.**

Abschaum m, no pl scum. **der** ~ **der Menschheit** or **der menschlichen Gesellschaft** the scum of the earth.

abscheiden sep irreg 1 vt (a) (ausscheiden) to give off, to produce; (Biol auch) to secrete; (Chem) to precipitate.
(b) (rare: absondern, trennen) to separate off; siehe abgeschieden.
2 vr (Flüssigkeit etc) to be given off or produced; (Biol auch) to be secreted; (Chem) to be precipitated.
3 vi aux sein (euph liter: sterben) to depart this life (liter), to pass away. **sein A**~ his passing; siehe abgeschieden.

abscheren vt sep Haare, Wolle to shear off; Bart to shave off; Kopf, Kinn to shave; Schafe to shear.

Abscheu m -(e)s, no pl or f -, no pl repugnance, repulsion, abhorrence (vor + dat at). **vor jdm/etw** ~ **haben** or **empfinden** to loathe or detest or abhor sb/sth; ~ **in jdm erregen** to repulse sb; **jdm** ~ **einflößen** to fill sb with loathing or horror or abhorrence.

abscheuern sep 1 vt (a) (reinigen) Fußboden, Wand to scrub (down); Schmutz to scrub off. (b) (abschürfen) Haut to rub or scrape off. (c) (abwetzen) Kleidung, Stoff to rub or wear thin; Ellbogen to wear out or through. **ein abgescheuerter Kragen** a worn collar. 2 vr (Stoff) to wear thin; (Tierfell) to get rubbed or scraped off.

abscheuerregend adj repulsive, loathsome, abhorrent.

abscheulich adj abominable, atrocious, loathsome; Verbrechen auch heinous; Anblick auch repulsive; (inf) awful, terrible (inf). **wie** ~! how ghastly or awful or terrible!; **es ist** ~ **kalt** it's hideously cold.

Abscheulichkeit f (Untat) atrocity, abomination; (no pl: Widerwärtigkeit) loathsomeness, atrociousness; (von Verbrechen auch) heinousness; (von Geschmack, Anblick) repulsiveness.

abschicken vt sep to send; Paket, Brief to send off, to dispatch; (mit der Post auch) to mail or post; (US auch) to mail (esp US).

Abschiebehaft f (Jur) remand pending deportation. **jdn in** ~ **nehmen** to put sb on remand pending deportation.

abschieben sep irreg 1 vt (a) (wegschieben) Schrank etc to push out or away (von from); (fig) Verantwortung, Schuld to push or shift (auf +acc onto). **er versucht immer, die Verantwortung auf andere abzuschieben** he always tries to pass the buck.
(b) (ausweisen) Ausländer, Häftling to deport.
(c) (inf: loswerden) to get rid of. **jdn in eine andere Abteilung ~** to shunt sb off to another department.
2 vi aux sein (sl) to push or clear off (inf). **schieb ab!** shove off! (inf).

Abschiebung f, no pl (Ausweisung) deportation.

Abschied m -(e)s, (rare) -e (a) (Trennung) farewell, parting. **von jdm/etw ~ nehmen** to say goodbye to sb/sth, to take one's leave of sb/sth; **ein Kuß zum ~** a farewell or goodbye kiss; **zum ~ überreichte er ihr einen Blumenstrauß** on parting, he presented her with a bunch of flowers; **ein trauriger ~** a sad farewell; **es war für beide ein schwerer ~** parting was hard for both of them; **ich hasse ~e** I hate farewells or goodbyes; **es war ein ~ für immer** or **fürs Leben** it was goodbye for ever; **beim ~ meinte er, ...** as he was leaving he said ...; **beim ~ auf Bahnhöfen ...** saying goodbye at stations ...; **der ~ von der Heimat fiel ihm schwer** it was hard for him to say goodbye to the land of his birth; **ihr ~ von der Bühne/vom Film** her farewell from the stage/from films; (letzte Vorstellung) her farewell performance; **ihre Heirat bedeutete für sie den ~ von der Kindheit** her marriage marked the end of her childhood; **sein ~ vom bisherigen Leben/von alten Gewohnheiten** breaking with his previous way of life/with his old habits; **der ~ von der Vergangenheit** breaking or the break with the past; **er bereitete sich auf den ~ vom Leben vor** (euph) he prepared himself to take his leave of the world; siehe französisch.
(b) (Rücktritt) (von Beamten) resignation; (von Offizieren) discharge. **seinen ~ nehmen** or **einreichen** to tender or hand in one's resignation/to apply for a discharge; **seinen ~ erhalten** or **bekommen** to be dismissed/discharged.

Abschieds- in cpds farewell; **~besuch** m farewell or goodbye visit; **~brief** m letter of farewell, farewell letter; **~feier** f farewell or going-away or leaving party; **~geschenk** nt (für Kollegen etc) leaving present; (für Freund) parting present; **~gesuch** nt (Pol) letter of resignation; **sein ~gesuch einreichen** to tender one's resignation; **~gruß** m farewell; (Wort zum ~) word of farewell; **~kuß** m farewell or parting or goodbye kiss; **~rede** f farewell speech, valedictory (speech) (form); **~schmerz** m pain of parting; **~stimmung** f mood of parting or farewell; **~stunde** f time or hour of parting, time to say goodbye; **~szene** f farewell scene; **~träne** f tear at parting.

abschießen sep irreg 1 vt (a) (losschießen) Geschoß, Gewehr, Kanone to fire; Pfeil to shoot (off), to loose off; Rakete to launch; (auf ein Ziel) to fire; (fig) Blick to shoot; Fragen, Befehle, Bemerkung to fire (auf +acc at).
(b) (außer Gefecht setzen) Flugzeug, Pilot to shoot down; Panzer to knock out; (wegschießen) Bein etc to shoot off.
(c) (sl: kennenlernen) Frau to pick up (inf).
(d) (totschießen) Wild to shoot; (sl: Menschen) to shoot down; (fig inf: abschieben) to get rid of; siehe Vogel.
2 vi (Sport) to kick off.

abschilfern vi sep aux sein to peel off.

abschinden vr sep irreg (inf) to knacker oneself (sl); (schwer arbeiten) to work one's fingers to the bone. **sich mit Gartenarbeiten/einem schweren Koffer ~** to knacker oneself gardening/carrying a heavy suitcase.

abschirmen sep 1 vt to shield; (schützen auch) to protect; (vor Licht auch) to screen; Lampe to cover. **jdn vor etw (dat) ~** to shield or protect sb from sth; **etw gegen die Sonne ~** to screen or shield sth from the sun.
2 vr to shield oneself (gegen from); (sich schützen) to protect oneself (gegen from or against); (sich isolieren) to isolate oneself, to cut oneself off (gegen from).

Abschirmung f, no pl (a) siehe vt shielding; protection; screening; covering. (b) (fig) (Selbstschutz, Pol) protection; (Isolierung) isolation.

abschirren vt sep to unharness; Ochsen to unyoke.

abschlachten vt sep to slaughter; Menschen auch to butcher.

Abschlachtung f siehe vt slaughter; butchering no pl.

abschlaffen sep (inf) 1 vi aux sein to flag. 2 vt to whack (inf).

Abschlag m (a) (Preisnachlaß) reduction; (Abzug) deduction. (b) (Zahlung) part payment (auf +acc of). (c) (Ftbl) kick-out, punt; (Hockey) bully(-off); (Golf) tee-off; (~fläche) tee. (d) (Abholzung) felling.

abschlagen sep irreg 1 vt (a) (mit Hammer etc) to knock off; (mit Schwert etc) to cut off; (mit Beil) to cut or chop off; Baum, Wald to cut or chop down; (herunterschlagen) to knock down. **etw vom Preis ~** to knock sth off the price.
(b) Gerüst etc to take down.
(c) (ablehnen) to refuse; Einladung, Bitte auch, Antrag to turn down. **jdm etw ~** to refuse sb sth; **sie/er kann niemandem etwas ~** she/he can never refuse anybody anything.
(d) (zurückschlagen) Angriff, Feind to beat or drive off; siehe abgeschlagen.
(e) auch vi (Ftbl) to punt; (Hockey) to bully off; (Golf) to tee off.
(f) sein Wasser ~ (inf) to relieve oneself.
2 vr (Dampf etc) to condense.

abschlägig adj negative. **jdn/etw ~ bescheiden** (form) to reject sb/sth, to turn sb/sth down.

Abschlag(s)zahlung f part payment.

abschlecken vt sep (S Ger, Aus) siehe ablecken.

abschleifen sep irreg 1 vt Kanten, Ecken, Unebenheiten to grind down; Rost to polish off; Messer to grind; Holzboden to sand (down).

2 vr to get worn off, to wear down; (fig) (Angewohnheit etc) to wear off; (Mensch) to have the rough edges taken off. **das schleift sich (noch) ab** (fig) that'll wear off; siehe abgeschliffen.

Abschleppdienst m breakdown service, (vehicle) recovery service.

abschleppen sep 1 vt (a) (wegziehen) to drag or haul off or away; Fahrzeug, Schiff to tow, to take in tow; (Behörde) to tow away.
(b) (inf) Menschen to drag along; (sich aneignen) to get one's hands on (inf); (aufgabeln) to pick up (inf).
2 vr sich mit etw ~ (inf) to struggle with sth.

Abschlepp-: **~fahrzeug** nt breakdown or recovery vehicle; **~kosten** pl recovery costs pl; **~seil** nt towrope.

abschließen sep irreg 1 vt (a) (zuschließen) to lock; Auto, Raum, Schrank to lock (up). **etw luftdicht ~** to put an airtight seal on sth.
(b) (beenden) Sitzung, Vortrag etc to conclude, to bring to a close; (mit Verzierung) to finish off. **sein Studium ~** to take one's degree, to graduate; **mit abgeschlossenem Studium** with a degree.
(c) (vereinbaren) Geschäft to conclude, to transact; Versicherung to take out; Wette to place. **einen Vertrag ~** (Pol) to conclude a treaty; (Jur, Comm) to complete a contract.
(d) (Comm: abrechnen) Bücher to balance; Konto auch to settle; Geschäftsjahr to close; Inventur to complete; Rechnung to make up.
2 vr (sich isolieren) to cut oneself off, to shut oneself away. **sich von der Außenwelt ~** to cut or shut oneself off from the outside world; siehe abgeschlossen.
3 vi (a) (zuschließen) to lock up. **sieh mal nach, ob auch abgeschlossen ist** will you see if everything's locked?
(b) (enden) to close, to come to a close, to conclude; (mit Verzierung) to be finished off.
(c) (Comm) (Vertrag schließen) to conclude the deal; (Endabrechnung machen) to do the books.
(d) (Schluß machen) to finish, to end. **mit allem/dem Leben ~** to finish with everything/life; **mit der Vergangenheit ~** to break with the past.

abschließend 1 adj concluding. 2 adv in conclusion, finally.

Abschluß m (a) (Beendigung) end; (inf: ~prüfung) final examination; (Univ) degree. **zum ~ von etw** at the close or end of sth; **zum ~ möchte ich ...** finally or to conclude I would like ...; **seinen ~ finden** (geh) **zum ~ kommen** to come to an end; **etw zum ~ bringen** to finish sth; **zum ~ unseres Programms hören Sie ...** to conclude or end our programmes for today ...; **ein Wort zum ~** a final word; **kurz vor dem ~ stehen** to be in the final stages; **der Kaiserwalzer bildete den ~ des Konzertabends** the Emperor Waltz brought the concert evening to a close or concluded the concert evening; **sie hat die Universität ohne ~ verlassen** she left the university without taking her degree; siehe krönen.
(b) no pl (Vereinbarung) conclusion; (von Wette) placing; (von Versicherung) taking out. **bei ~ des Vertrages** on completion of the contract.
(c) (Comm: Geschäft) business deal. **zum ~ kommen** to make a deal.
(d) no pl (Comm: der Bücher) balancing; (von Konto) settlement; (von Geschäftsjahr) close; (von Inventur) completion.
(e) (Rand, abschließender Teil) border.

Abschluß-: **~ball** m (von Tanzkurs) final ball; **~feier** f (Sch) speech or prizegiving day; **~klasse** f (Sch) final class or year; **~kommuniqué** nt final communiqué; **~prüfung** f (a) (Sch) final examination; (Univ auch) finals pl; (b) (Comm) audit; **~rechnung** f final account; **~zeugnis** nt (Sch) leaving certificate, diploma (US).

abschmälzen, abschmalzen (Aus) vt sep to gratinate.

abschmatzen vt sep (inf) to slobber over (inf).

abschmecken sep 1 vt (kosten) to taste, to sample; (würzen) to season. 2 vi (kosten) to taste; (nachwürzen) to add some seasoning.

abschmeicheln vt sep jdm etw ~ to wheedle or coax sth out of sb.

abschmelzen vti sep irreg (vi: aux sein) to melt (away); (Tech) to melt down. **die Sonne schmolz den Schnee vom Dach ab** the sun melted the snow off the roof.

abschmettern vt sep (inf) (Sport) to smash; (fig inf: zurückweisen) to throw out. **mit seinem Antrag wurde er abgeschmettert** his application was thrown or flung out; **er wurde abgeschmettert** he was shot down (inf).

abschmieren vt sep (a) (Tech) Auto to grease, to lubricate. (b) (inf: abschreiben) to crib (inf); (unordentlich schreiben) to scribble down.

abschminken vt sep (a) Gesicht, Haut to remove the make-up from. **sich ~** to take off or remove one's make-up. (b) (sl: aufgeben) sich (dat) etw ~ to get sth out of one's head.

abschmirgeln vt sep to sand down.

Abschn. abbr of **Abschnitt** para.

abschnacken vt sep (N Ger inf) jdm etw ~ to wheedle or coax sth out of sb.

abschnallen sep 1 vt to unfasten, to undo. 2 vr to unfasten one's seat belt. 3 vi (sl) (a) (nicht mehr folgen können) to give up. (b) (fassungslos sein) to be staggered (inf). **wenn man sich das überlegt, schnallt man ab** it's staggering if you think about it; **da schnallte ab!** it's unbelievable!

abschneiden sep irreg 1 vt (lit, fig) to cut off; Flucht, Ausweg auch to block off; Blumen, Scheibe to cut (off); Zigarre to cut the end off; Fingernägel, Haar to cut; Rock, Kleid to cut the seam off. **jdm die Rede/das Wort ~** to cut sb short; **jdm den Atem ~** to take sb's breath away; siehe Scheibe.

2 *vi* (a) bei etw gut/schlecht ~ (*inf*) to come off well/badly in sth.

(b) (*abkürzen*) to take a short cut; (*Weg, Straße*) to be a short cut.

abschnippeln *vt sep* (*inf*) etw von etw ~ to cut a bit off sth; (*mit Schere auch*) to snip sth off sth.

Abschnitt *m* (a) section; (*Math*) segment; (*Mil*) sector, zone; (*Geschichts~, Zeit~*) period. (b) (*Kontroll~*) (*von Scheck etc*) counterfoil; (*von Karte*) section; (*von Papier*) slip.

abschnitt(s)weise *adv* in sections. der Lehrer nahm das Buch ~ durch the teacher went through the book section by section.

abschnüren *vt sep* to cut off (*von from*); (*Med*) Glied to put a tourniquet on. jdm das Blut ~ to cut off sb's circulation; jdm die Luft ~ (*lit*) to stop sb breathing; (*fig*) to bankrupt or ruin sb; die Angst schnürte ihr das Herz ab (*liter*) she was paralyzed by fear.

abschöpfen *vt sep* to skim off; (*fig*) Dank, Ruhm to reap; (*für sich gewinnen*) to cream off. den Rahm or das Fett ~ (*fig*) to cream off the best part; den Gewinn ~ to siphon off the profits.

abschotten *vt sep* (*Naut*) to separate with a bulkhead, to bulkhead off. sich gegen etw ~ (*fig*) to cut oneself off from sth.

abschrägen *vt sep* to slope; Holz, Brett to bevel. ein abgeschrägtes Dach a sloping roof; er schrägte das Brett an den Kanten ab he bevelled the edges of the board.

Abschrägung *f* slope; (*von Brett*) bevel.

abschrauben *vt sep* to unscrew.

abschrecken *sep* 1 *vt* (a) (*fernhalten*) to deter, to put off; (*verjagen*) Hund, Vogelscheuche) to scare off. jdn von etw ~ to deter sb from sth, to put sb off sth; ich lasse mich dadurch nicht ~ that won't deter me, I won't be deterred by that. (b) (*abkühlen*) Stahl to quench; (*Cook*) to rinse with cold water. 2 *vi* (*Strafe*) to act as a deterrent.

abschreckend *adj* (a) (*warnend*) deterrent. ein ~es Beispiel a warning; eine ~e Wirkung haben, ~ wirken to act as a deterrent. (b) (*abstoßend*) Häßlichkeit repulsive.

Abschreckung *f* (a) (*das Fernhalten*) deterrence; (*das Verjagen*) scaring off; (*~smittel*) deterrent. (b) (*Abkühlung*) (*von Stahl*) quenching; (*Cook*) rinsing with cold water.

Abschreckungs-: ~maßnahme *f* deterrent; ~mittel *nt* deterrent; ~theorie *f* (*Jur*) theory of deterrence; ~waffe *f* deterrent weapon.

abschreiben *sep irreg* 1 *vt* (a) (*kopieren*) to copy out; (*Sch: abgucken*) to copy, to crib (*inf*); (*plagiieren*) to copy (*bei, von* from).

(b) (*schreibend abnutzen*) to use up; siehe **Finger**.

(c) (*Comm: absetzen, abziehen*) to deduct.

(d) (*verlorengeben*) to write off. er ist bei mir abgeschrieben I'm through or finished with him.

2 *vi* (a) (*Sch*) to copy, to crib (*inf*).

(b) jdm ~ to write to sb to tell him that one cannot come etc.

3 *vr* (*Bleistift, Farbband*) to get used up; (*Kugelschreiber, Filzstift auch*) to run out.

Abschreiber *m* (*pej*) plagiarist; (*Sch*) cribber.

Abschreibung *f* (*Comm*) deduction; (*Wertverminderung*) depreciation.

abschreiten *vt sep irreg* (a) (*entlanggehen*) to walk along; (*hin und zurück*) to walk up and down; Gelände to patrol; (*inspizieren*) to inspect. (b) (*messen*) to pace out.

Abschrift *f* copy.

abschriftlich *adv* (*form*) as a copy. etw ~ beilegen to enclose a copy of sth.

abschrubben *vt sep* (*inf*) (a) Schmutz to scrub off or away; Rücken, Kleid, Fußboden to scrub (down). schrubb euch richtig ab! give yourselves a good scrub! (b) (*zurücklegen*) to do; (*Aut auch*) to clock up (*inf*).

abschuften *vr sep* (*inf*) to slog one's guts out (*inf*).

abschuppen *sep* 1 *vt* Fisch to scale. 2 *vr* to flake off.

abschürfen *vt sep* to graze.

Abschürfung *f* (*Wunde*) graze.

Abschuß *m* (a) (*das Abfeuern*) firing, shooting; (*von Pfeil auch*) loosing off; (*von Rakete*) launch(ing); (*auf ein Ziel*) firing.

(b) (*das Außer-Gefecht-Setzen*) shooting down; (*von Panzer*) knocking out. die Luftwaffe erzielte zwölf Abschüsse the airforce shot or brought down twelve planes.

(c) (*von Wild*) shooting. Fasanen/Elefanten sind jetzt zum ~ freigegeben pheasant-shooting/the hunting of elephants is now permitted; die Zahl der Abschüsse the number of kills; durch ~ des Ministers (*fig inf*) by getting rid of the minister.

(d) (*Sport*) (goal) kick.

Abschußbasis *f* launching base.

abschüssig *adj* sloping. eine sehr ~e Straße a steep road, a steeply sloping road; auf die ~e Bahn geraten (*fig*) to go downhill.

Abschüssigkeit *f* slope.

Abschuß-: ~liste *f* er steht auf der ~liste (*inf*) his days are numbered; ~rampe *f* launching pad.

abschütteln *vt sep* Staub, Schnee to shake off; Decke, Tuch to shake (out); (*fig*) lästigen Menschen, Verfolger to shake off, to lose (*inf*); Gedanken, Ärger etc to get rid of. das Joch der Knechtschaft ~ to throw off the yoke of slavery.

abschütten *vt sep* Flüssigkeit, Mehl, Sand etc to pour off; (*Cook*) Flüssigkeit to drain off; Kartoffeln etc to drain; Eimer to empty.

abschwächen *sep* 1 *vt* to weaken; Behauptung, Formulierung, Foto to tone down; Schock, Aufprall to lessen; Wirkung, Einfluß auch to lessen; Stoß, Eindruck to soften.

2 *vr* to drop or fall off, to diminish; (*Lärm*) to decrease; (*Met: Hoch, Tief*) to disperse; (*Preisauftrieb, Andrang*) to ease off; (*St Ex: Kurse*) to weaken.

Abschwächung *f siehe vb* weakening; toning down; lessening; softening; decrease; dispersal; easing off; weakening; reduction.

abschwatzen, abschwätzen (*S Ger*) *vt sep* (*inf*) jdm etw ~ to talk sb into giving one sth; das habe ich mir von meinem Bruder ~ lassen I let my brother talk me into giving it to him.

abschweifen *vi sep aux sein* (*lit, fig*) to stray, to wander (off or away); (*Redner auch*) to digress. er schweifte vom Thema ab he deviated from the subject.

Abschweifung *f siehe vi* digression; deviation.

abschwellen *vi sep irreg aux sein* (*Entzündung, Fluß*) to go down; (*Lärm*) to die or fade or ebb away. der geschwollene Fuß ist wieder abgeschwollen the swelling in his foot has gone down.

abschwemmen *vt sep* (a) (*abtreiben*) to wash away. (b) (*reinigen*) to wash; Schmutz to wash away.

abschwenken *sep* 1 *vi aux sein* to turn away; (*Kamera*) to swing round, to pan. (von der Straße) ~ to turn off (the road); er ist nach links abgeschwenkt (*lit*) he turned off to the left; (*fig*) he swung (over) to the left; (nach rechts) ~ (*Mil*) to wheel (right); er schwenkte zur Medizin ab he changed over to medicine.

2 *vt* (a) (*abspülen*) Gläser etc to rinse; (*abschütteln*) Tropfen to shake off.

(b) (*Cook*) Kartoffeln, Gemüse to drain (off).

abschwimmen *sep irreg* 1 *vi aux sein* (*losschwimmen*) to swim off or away. 2 *vt* (a) *aux sein or haben* Strecke to swim; Gewässer to swim along. (b) (*verlieren*) (*sich dat*) überflüssige Pfunde ~ to swim off those extra pounds. (c) Zeit to do.

abschwindeln *vt sep* jdm etw ~ to swindle sb out of sth.

abschwirren *vi sep aux sein* to whirr off; (*fig inf: weggehen*) to buzz off (*inf*). die Vögel schwirrten plötzlich ab with a flutter of wings the birds suddenly flew off.

abschwitzen *vt sep* to sweat off. sich (*dat*) einen ~ (*sl*) to sweat like mad (*inf*) or crazy (*inf*).

abschwören *sep irreg aux sein* 1 *vi* (*old, liter*) to renounce (*dat* sth). dem Glauben/Teufel ~ to renounce one's faith/the devil; seinen Ketzereien ~ to recant one's heresies. 2 *vt* (*old: ableugnen*) Schuld, Mittäterschaft to deny, to repudiate; Glauben to renounce.

Abschwung *m* (*Sport*) dismount; (*Comm*) downward trend, recession.

absegeln *sep* 1 *vi* (a) *aux sein* (*lossegeln*) to sail off or away, to set sail; (*inf: weggehen*) to sail off. der Schoner segelte von Bremen ab the schooner sailed from Bremen or set sail from Bremen. (b) (*Sport: die Saison beenden*) to have one's last sail. 2 *vt* Strecke to sail; Küste to sail along.

absegnen *vt sep* (*inf*) Vorschlag, Plan to give one's blessing to. von jdm abgesegnet sein to have sb's blessing.

absehbar *adj* foreseeable. in ~er/auf ~e Zeit in/for the foreseeable future; das Ende seines Studiums ist noch nicht ~ the end of his studies is not yet in sight; die Folgen sind noch gar nicht ~ there's no telling what the consequences will be.

absehen *sep irreg* 1 *vt* (a) (*abgucken*) (bei) jdm etw ~ to pick sth up from sb; (*abschreiben*) to copy sth from sb.

(b) (*voraussehen*) to foresee. es ist noch gar nicht abzusehen, wie lange die Arbeit dauern wird there's no telling yet how long the work will last; es ist ganz klar abzusehen, daß ... it's easy to see that ...; das Ende läßt sich noch nicht ~ the end is not yet in sight; siehe abgesehen 1.

2 *vi* von etw ~ (*verzichten*) to refrain from sth; (*nicht berücksichtigen*) to disregard sth, to leave sth out of account or consideration; davon ~, etw zu tun to dispense with or to refrain from doing sth; siehe abgesehen 2.

abseifen *vt sep* to soap down; Gegenstand auch to wash down. jdm den Rücken ~ to soap sb's back.

abseilen *sep* 1 *vt* to let or lower down on a rope. 2 *vr* to let or lower oneself down on a rope; (*Bergsteiger*) to abseil (down); (*fig inf*) to skedaddle (*inf*).

absein *vi sep irreg aux sein* (*inf*) (a) (*weg sein*) to be off. die Farbe/der Knopf ist ab the paint/button has come off. (b) (*erschöpft sein*) to be knackered (*sl*) or shattered (*inf*). (c) (*abgelegen sein*) to be far away.

abseitig *adj* (a) (*geh: abseits liegend*) remote. (b) (*ausgefallen*) esoteric. (c) (*pervers*) perverse.

abseits 1 *adv* to one side; (*abgelegen*) out of the way, remote; (*Sport*) offside. ~ liegen to be out of the way or remote; ~ vom Wege off the beaten track; ~ von der Straße away from the road; etwas ~ von der Stadt some way out of the town; ~ stehen (*fig*) to be on the outside; (*Sport*) to be offside; ~ bleiben, sich ~ halten (*fig*) to hold or keep to oneself.

2 *prep* +*gen* away from. ~ des Weges off the beaten track.

Abseits *nt* -, - (*Sport*) offside. im ~ stehen to be offside; ein Leben im ~ führen, im ~ leben (*fig*) to live in the shadows.

Abseits-: ~position, ~stellung *f* offside position; ~tor *nt* offside goal.

absenden *vt sep* to send; Brief, Paket to send off, to dispatch; (*mit der Post auch*) to mail (*esp US*).

Absender(in *f*) *m* -s, - sender; (*Adresse*) (sender's) address.

Absendung *f* dispatch, sending off.

absengen *vt sep* to singe off.

absenken *sep* 1 *vt* (a) (*Build*) Grundwasserstand to lower; Fundamente to sink. (b) (*Agr*) Weinstöcke etc to layer. 2 *vr* to subside. das Gelände senkt sich zum Seeufer ab the terrain slopes down towards the shore.

Absenker *m* -s, - (*Hort*) siehe **Ableger**.

absentieren* *vr sep* (*old, hum*) to absent oneself.

Absenz *f* (*old, Sch: Aus, Sw*) absence.

abservieren* *sep* 1 *vi* to clear the table. 2 *vt* (a) Geschirr, Tisch to clear. (b) (*inf: absetzen*) jdn ~ to push sb out, to get rid of sb. **(c)** (*sl: umbringen*) to do in (*inf*). **(d)** (*Sport sl: besiegen*) to thrash (*inf*).

absetzbar *adj Ware* saleable; *Betrag* deductible; *Mensch* dismissible.

absetzen *sep* 1 *vt* **(a)** (*abnehmen*) *Hut, Brille* to take off, to remove; (*hinstellen*) *Gepäck, Glas* to set *or* put down; *Geigenbogen, Feder* to lift; *Gewehr* to unshoulder.
(b) (*aussteigen lassen*) *Mitfahrer, Fahrgast* to set down, to drop; *Fallschirmjäger* to drop. **wo kann ich dich ~?** where can I drop you?
(c) (*Naut*) to push off.
(d) *Theaterstück, Oper* to take off; *Fußballspiel, Turnier, Versammlung, Termin* to cancel; *Punkt von der Tagesordnung* to delete. **etw vom Spielplan ~** to take sth off the programme.
(e) (*entlassen*) to dismiss; *Minister, Vorsitzenden auch* to remove from office; *König, Kaiser* to depose.
(f) (*entwöhnen*) *Jungtier* to wean; (*Med*) *Medikament, Tabletten* to come off, to stop taking; *Behandlung* to break off, to discontinue; (*Mil*) *Ration etc* to stop. **die Tabletten mußten abgesetzt werden** I/she *etc* had to stop taking the tablets *or* come off the tablets.
(g) (*Comm: verkaufen*) *Waren* to sell. **sich gut ~ lassen** to sell well.
(h) (*abziehen*) *Betrag, Summe* to deduct. **das kann man ~** that is tax deductible.
(i) (*ablagern*) *Geröll* deposit.
(j) (*Sew*) to trim.
(k) (*kontrastieren*) to contrast. **etw gegen etw ~** to set sth off against sth.
(l) (*Typ*) *Manuskript* to (type)set, to compose. **(eine Zeile) ~** to start a new line.
2 *vr* **(a)** (*Chem, Geol*) to be deposited; (*Feuchtigkeit, Staub etc*) to collect.
(b) (*inf: weggehen*) to get *or* clear out (*aus* of) (*inf*); (*Sport: Abstand vergrößern*) to pull ahead. **sich nach Brasilien ~** to clear off to Brazil.
(c) **sich gegen jdn/etw ~** to stand out against sb/sth; **sich vorteilhaft gegen jdn/etw ~** to contrast favourably with sb/sth; **das macht er, nur um sich gegen die anderen abzusetzen** he only does that to be different from the others *or* to make himself stand out from the crowd.
3 *vi* to put one's glass down. **er trank das Glas aus, ohne abzusetzen** he emptied his glass in one.
4 *vt impers* **es setzt etwas ab** (*inf*) there'll be trouble.

Absetzung *f* **(a)** (*Entlassung*) (*von Beamten*) dismissal; (*von Minister, Vorsitzenden auch*) removal from office; (*von König*) deposing, deposition.
(b) (*Fin: Abschreibung*) deduction.
(c) (*von Theaterstück etc*) withdrawal; (*von Fußballspiel, Termin etc*) cancellation; (*von Punkt auf der Tagesordnung*) deletion.
(d) (*von Jungtier*) weaning; (*Med*) discontinuation.

absichern *sep* 1 *vt* to safeguard; (*garantieren*) to cover; *Bauplatz, Gefahrenstelle* to make safe; *Dach* to support. **jdn über die Landesliste ~** (*Pol*) ≈ to give sb a safe seat.
2 *vr* (*sich schützen*) to protect oneself; (*sich versichern*) to cover oneself.

Absicht *f* -, -en (*Vorsatz*) intention; (*Zweck*) purpose; (*Jur*) intent. **in der besten ~** with the best of intentions; **in der ~, etw zu tun** with the idea *or* object of doing sth, with a view to doing sth, with the intention of doing sth; **die ~ haben, etw zu tun** to intend to do sth; **eine ~ mit etw verfolgen** to have something in mind with sth; **~en auf jdn haben** (*inf*) to have designs on sb; **ernste ~en haben** (*inf*) to have serious intentions; **das war nicht meine ~!** I didn't intend that; **das war doch keine ~!** (*inf*) it wasn't deliberate *or* intentional; **etw mit/ohne ~ tun** to do/not to do sth on purpose *or* deliberately.

absichtlich *adj* deliberate, intentional. **etw ~ tun** to do sth on purpose *or* deliberately *or* intentionally.

Absichts-: **a~los** *adj* unintentional; **~satz** *m* (*Gram*) *siehe* **Finalsatz**; **a~voll** *adj siehe* **absichtlich**.

absingen *vt sep irreg* **(a)** (*vom Blatt*) to sight-read. **(b)** (*bis zu Ende*) to sing (right) through. **unter A~ der Nationalhymne/Internationale** with the singing of the national anthem/ Internationale; **unter A~ schmutziger Lieder** ... while singing dirty songs ...

absinken *vi sep irreg aux sein* (*Schiff*) to sink; (*Boden auch*) to subside; (*Temperatur, Wasserspiegel, Kurs*) to fall, to go down; (*Interesse, Leistungen*) to fall *or* drop off; (*fig: moralisch ~*) to go downhill.

Absinth *m* -(e)s, -e absinth.

absitzen *sep irreg* 1 *vt* **(a)** (*verbringen*) *Zeit* to sit out; (*verbüßen*) *Strafe* to serve.
(b) (*abnutzen*) *Hose etc* to wear thin (at the seat); *Sessel, Polster* to wear (thin).
2 *vi* **(a)** *aux sein* (*vom Pferd*) ~ to dismount (from a horse); **abgesessen!** dismount!
(b) **weit ~** to sit far away.
3 *vr* (*Hose etc*) to wear thin (at the seat); (*Sessel, Polster*) to wear (thin).

absolut *adj* (*alle Bedeutungen*) absolute; (*völlig auch*) complete, total. **~ nicht/nichts** absolutely not/nothing; **das ist ~ unmöglich** that's quite *or* absolutely impossible; **~ genommen** *or* **betrachtet** considered in the absolute.

Absolute(s) *nt decl as adj* (*Philos*) Absolute, absolute.

Absolutheit *f, no pl* absoluteness.

Absolutheits|anspruch *m* claim to absolute right. **einen ~ vertreten** to claim absoluteness.

Absolution *f* (*Eccl*) absolution. **jdm die ~ erteilen** to grant *or* give sb absolution.

Absolutismus *m, no pl* absolutism.

absolutistisch *adj* absolutistic.

Absolvent(in *f*) [apzɔl'vɛnt(ɪn)] *m* (*Univ*) graduate. **die ~en eines Lehrgangs** the students who have completed a course.

absolvieren* [apzɔl'viːrən] *vt insep* **(a)** (*Eccl*) to absolve. **(b)** (*durchlaufen*) *Studium, Probezeit* to complete; *Schule* to finish, to graduate from (*US*); *Prüfung* to pass. **er hat die technische Fachschule absolviert** he completed a course at technical college. **(c)** (*ableisten*) to complete.

Absolvierung *f siehe vt* (*b, c*) completion; finishing; graduation (*gen* from); passing; completion.

absonderlich *adj* peculiar, strange.

Absonderlichkeit *f* **(a)** *no pl* strangeness. **(b)** (*Eigenart*) peculiarity.

absondern *sep* 1 *vt* **(a)** (*trennen*) to separate; (*isolieren*) to isolate. **(b)** (*ausscheiden*) to secrete. 2 *vr* **(a)** (*Mensch*) to cut oneself off. **sie sondert sich immer sehr ab** she always keeps herself very much to herself; *siehe auch* **abgesondert**. **(b)** (*ausgeschieden werden*) to be secreted.

Absonderung *f* **(a)** *siehe vt* separation; isolation; secretion. **(b)** *siehe vr* segregation; secretion. **(c)** (*abgeschiedener Stoff*) secretion.

Absorber [ap'zɔrbɐ] *m* -s, - (*Tech*) absorber.

absorbieren* *vt insep* (*lit, fig*) to absorb.

Absorption *f* absorption.

abspalten *vtr sep* to split off; (*Chem*) to separate (off).

abspannen *sep* 1 *vt* **(a)** (*ausspannen*) *Pferd, Wagen* to unhitch; *Ochsen* to unyoke. **(b)** (*Build*) to anchor. 2 *vi* **(a)** to unhitch (the) horses *etc*; (*Ochsen ~*) to unyoke (the) oxen. **(b)** (*fig: entspannen*) to relax; *siehe auch* **abgespannt**.

Abspannung *f* **(a)** (*Erschöpfung*) *siehe* **Abgespanntheit**. **(b)** (*Build*) anchoring; (*Spannseil*) anchor (cable).

absparen *vt sep* **sich** (*dat*) **Geld von etw ~** to save money from sth; **sich** (*dat*) **ein Auto vom Lohn ~** to save up for a car from one's wages; **sich** (*dat*) **etw vom** *or* **am Munde** *or* **am eigenen Leib ~** to scrimp and save for sth.

abspecken *vt sep* (*inf*) to shed.

abspeichern *vt sep Daten* to store (away).

abspeisen *vt sep* **(a)** (*inf: beköstigen*) to feed. **(b)** (*fig: abfertigen*) **jdn mit etw ~** to fob sb off with sth.

abspenstig *adj* **jdm jdn/etw ~ machen** to lure sb/sth away from sb; **jdm die Freundin ~ machen** to pinch sb's girlfriend (*inf*); **jdm seine Kunden ~ machen** to lure *or* draw sb's customers away from him.

absperren *sep* 1 *vt* **(a)** (*versperren*) to block *or* close off. **(b)** (*abdrehen*) *Wasser, Strom, Gas etc* to turn *or* shut off. **(c)** (*S Ger: zuschließen*) to lock. 2 *vi* (*S Ger*) to lock up.

Absperr-: **~gitter** *nt* barrier; **~graben** *m* moat; **~hahn** *m* stopcock; **~kette** *f* chain.

Absperrung *f* **(a)** (*Abriegelung*) blocking *or* closing off. **(b)** (*Sperre*) barrier; (*Kordon*) cordon.

abspiegeln *vtr sep siehe* **widerspiegeln**.

Abspiel *nt* (*das Abspielen*) passing; (*Schuß*) pass.

abspielen *sep* 1 *vt* **(a)** *Schallplatte, Tonband* to play (through); *Nationalhymne* to play; (*vom Blatt*) *Musik* to sight-read; *siehe auch* **abgespielt**. **(b)** (*Sport*) *Ball* to pass; (*beim Billard*) to play. 2 *vr* (*sich ereignen*) to happen; (*stattfinden*) to take place. **wie mein Leben sich abspielt** what my life is like; **da spielt sich (bei mir) nichts ab!** (*inf*) nothing doing! (*inf*).

absplittern *sep* 1 *vti* (*vi: aux sein*) to chip off; *Holz auch* to splinter off. 2 *vr* to split *or* splinter off.

Absplitterung *f siehe vb* chipping off; splintering off; splitting off.

Absprache *f* arrangement. **eine ~ treffen** to make *or* come to an arrangement; **ohne vorherige ~** without prior consultation.

absprachegemäß *adv* as arranged.

absprechen *sep irreg* 1 *vt* **(a)** **jdm etw ~** (*verweigern*) *Recht* to deny *or* refuse sb sth; (*in Abrede stellen*) *Begabung* to deny *or* dispute sb's sth; **er ist wirklich sehr klug, das kann man ihm nicht ~** there's no denying that he's very clever.
(b) (*verabreden*) *Termin* to arrange. **die Zeugen hatten ihre Aussagen vorher abgesprochen** the witnesses had agreed on what to say in advance.
2 *vr* **sich mit jdm ~** to make an arrangement with sb; **die beiden hatten sich vorher abgesprochen** they had agreed on what to do/say *etc* in advance; **ich werde mich mit ihr ~** I'll arrange *or* fix things with her; **sich ~, etw zu tun** to arrange to do sth.

abspreizen *vt sep* to extend; (*Build*) to brace.

abspringen *vi sep irreg aux sein* **(a)** (*herunterspringen*) to jump down (*von* from); (*herausspringen*) to jump out (*von* of); (*Aviat*) to jump (*von* from); (*bei Gefahr*) to bale out; (*Sport*) to dismount; (*losspringen*) to take off; (*sl: Koitus interruptus praktizieren*) to pull out (*inf*). **A~ während der Fahrt verboten!** passengers are forbidden to alight while the vehicle/train *etc* is in motion; **mit dem rechten Bein ~** to take off on the right leg.
(b) (*sich lösen*) to come off; (*Farbe, Lack auch*) to flake *or* peel off; (*abprallen*) to bounce off (*von etw* sth).
(c) (*fig inf: sich zurückziehen*) to get out; (*von Partei, Kurs etc*) to back out. **von etw ~** to get *or* back out of sth.

abspritzen *sep* 1 *vt* **(a)** **etw/jdn/sich ~** to spray sth/sb/oneself down; *Schmutz* to spray off (*von etw* sth); (*Cook*) to sprinkle. **(b)** (*NS euph sl: töten*) to give a lethal injection to. 2 *vi aux sein* to spray off; (*vulg: ejakulieren*) to spunk (*vulg*); (*dated inf: wegeilen*) to race off.

Absprung *m* jump (*auch Aviat*), leap; (*Sport*) take-off; (*Abgang*) dismount. **den ~ schaffen** (*fig*) to make the break (*inf*), to make it (*inf*); **er hat den ~ gewagt** (*fig*) he took the jump; **den ~ (ins Berufsleben) verpassen** (*fig*) to miss the boat *or* bus.

abspulen vt sep Kabel, Garn to unwind; (inf) (filmen) to shoot; (vorführen) to show; (fig) to reel off.

abspülen sep 1 vt Hände, Geschirr to rinse; Fett etc to rinse off. 2 vi to wash up, to do the washing up.

abstammen vi sep no ptp to be descended (von from); (Ling) to be derived (von from).

Abstammung f descent; (Abkunft auch) origin; (Ling) origin, derivation. ehelicher/unehelicher ~ (Jur) of legitimate/ illegitimate birth; französischer ~ of French extraction or descent.

Abstammungs-: ~lehre, ~theorie f theory of evolution.

Abstand m (a) (Zwischenraum) distance; (kürzerer ~) gap, space; (Zeit~) interval; (Punkte~) gap; (fig) (Distanz) distance; (Unterschied) difference. mit ~ by far, far and away; ~ von etw gewinnen (fig) to distance oneself from sth; in regelmäßigen Abständen/Abständen von 10 Minuten at regular/10 minute intervals; ~ halten to keep one's distance; mit großem ~ führen/gewinnen to lead/win by a wide margin.
    (b) (form: Verzicht) von etw ~ nehmen to dispense with sth; davon ~ nehmen, etw zu tun to refrain from doing sth, to forbear to do sth (old, form).
    (c) (Abfindung) indemnity.

Abstandssumme f (form) indemnity.

abstatten vt sep (form) jdm einen Bericht ~ to make a report to sb; jdm Bericht ~ to report to sb; jdm einen Besuch ~ to pay sb a visit; jdm seinen Dank ~ to give thanks to sb.

Abstattung f siehe vt making; reporting; paying; giving.

abstauben vti sep (a) Möbel etc to dust. (b) (inf) (wegnehmen) to pick up; (schnorren) to cadge (von, bei, dat off, from). er will immer nur ~ he's always on the scrounge. (c) (Ftbl inf) (ein Tor or den Ball) ~ to put the ball into the net, to tuck the ball away.

Abstauber m -s, - (Ftbl inf) (a) (auch ~tor) easy goal. (b) (Spieler) goal-hanger (inf).

abstechen sep irreg 1 vt (a) ein Tier ~ to cut an animal's throat.
    (b) (abtrennen) Torf to cut; Rasen to trim (the edges of).
    (c) (ablaufen lassen) Hochofen, Metall to tap; Gewässer to drain; Wein to rack.
    2 vi (a) gegen jdn/etw ~, von jdm/etw ~ to stand out against sb/sth.
    (b) aux sein vom Ufer ~ to push off from the shore.

Abstecher m -s, - (Ausflug) excursion, trip; (Umweg) detour; (fig) sortie.

abstecken vt sep (a) Gelände, Grenze, Trasse to mark out; (mit Pflöcken auch) to peg or stake out; (fig) Verhandlungsposition, Programm to work out. (b) Kleid, Naht to pin. (c) (abnehmen) Plakette, Abzeichen to take off; Nadel auch to unpin.

abstehen sep irreg 1 vi (a) (entfernt stehen) to stand away; (nicht anliegen) to stick out. ~de Ohren ears that stick out.
    (b) (old form: verzichten) von etw ~ to abandon sth; davon ~, etw zu tun to refrain from doing sth, to forbear to do sth (old, form).
    (c) siehe abgestanden.
    2 vt (inf) sich (dat) die Beine ~ to stand for hours and hours.

absteifen vt sep (Build) to shore up.

Absteige f -, -n (inf) dosshouse (inf), flophouse (US inf); cheap hotel.

absteigen vi sep irreg aux sein (a) (heruntersteigen) to get off (von etw sth); (vom Pferd, Rad auch) to dismount. von einem Pferd/Rad etc ~ to dismount, to get off a horse/bicycle etc; Radfahrer ~! no cycling, cycling prohibited.
    (b) (abwärts gehen) to make one's way down; (Bergsteiger auch) to climb down. in ~der or der ~den Linie in the line of descent; ~der Ast der Flugbahn descending branch of the trajectory; auf dem ~den Ast sein, sich auf dem ~den Ast befinden (inf) to be going downhill, to be on the decline; gesellschaftlich ~ to go down in society.
    (c) (einkehren) to stay; (im Hotel auch) to put up (in + dat at).
    (d) (Sport: Mannschaft) to go down, to be relegated. aus der ersten Liga ~ to be relegated from the first division.

Absteigequartier nt siehe Absteige.

Absteiger m -s, - (Sport) relegated team; team facing relegation. gesellschaftlicher ~ (fig) someone who has come down in the world.

Abstellbahnhof m railway yard.

abstellen sep 1 vt (a) (hinstellen) to put down.
    (b) (unterbringen) to put; (Aut: parken auch) to park.
    (c) (abrücken, entfernt stellen) to put away from. das Klavier von der Wand ~ to leave the piano out from or away from the wall.
    (d) (abkommandieren) to order off, to detail; Offizier auch to second; (fig: abordnen) to assign; (Sport) Spieler to release.
    (e) (ausrichten auf) etw auf jdn/etw ~ to gear sth to sb/sth.
    (f) (abdrehen) to turn off; Geräte, Licht auch to switch off; (Zufuhr unterbrechen) Gas, Strom to cut off; Telefon to disconnect. den Haupthahn für das Gas ~ to turn the gas off at the mains.
    (g) (sich abgewöhnen) to give up, to stop.
    (h) (unterbinden) Mangel, Unsitte etc to bring to an end. das läßt sich nicht/läßt sich ~ nothing/something can be done about that; läßt sich das nicht ~? couldn't that be changed?
    2 vi auf etw (acc) ~ to be geared to sth; (etw berücksichtigen) to take sth into account.

Abstell-: ~gleis nt siding; jdn aufs ~gleis schieben (fig) to push or cast sb aside; auf dem ~gleis sein or stehen (fig) to have been pushed or cast aside; ~kammer f boxroom; ~raum m storeroom.

abstempeln vt sep to stamp; Post to postmark; (fig) to stamp, to brand (zu, als as).

Abstemp(e)lung f siehe vt stamping; postmarking; branding.

absteppen vt sep to stitch, to sew; Wattiertes, Daunendecke to quilt; Kragen etc to topstitch.

absterben vi sep irreg aux sein (eingehen, Med) to die; (gefühllos werden: Glieder) to go or grow numb; (fig) (Gefühle) to die; (Sitten) to die out. mir sind die Zehen abgestorben my toes have gone or grown numb; siehe abgestorben.

Abstich m -(e)s, -e (von Wein) racking; (von Metall, Hochofen) tapping; (Öffnung des Hochofens) taphole.

Abstieg m -(e)s, -e (das Absteigen) way down, descent; (Weg) descent; (Niedergang) decline; (Sport) relegation. einen alten Pfad als ~ benutzen to come down (on) an old path; vom ~ bedroht (Sport) threatened by relegation, in danger of being relegated.

abstillen sep 1 vt Kind to wean, to stop breastfeeding. 2 vi to stop breastfeeding.

abstimmen sep 1 vi to take a vote. über etw (acc) ~ to vote or take a vote on sth; über etw (acc) ~ lassen to put sth to the vote; geheim ~ to have a secret ballot.
    2 vt (harmonisieren) Instrumente to tune (auf + acc to); Radio to tune (in) (auf + acc to); (in Einklang bringen) Farben, Kleidung to match (auf + acc with); Termine to coordinate (auf + acc with); (anpassen) to suit (auf + acc to); (Comm) Bücher to balance. gut auf etw (acc)/aufeinander abgestimmt sein (Instrumente) to be in tune with sth/with each other; (Farben, Speisen etc) to go well with sth/with each other or together; (Termine) to fit in well with sth/with each other; (einander angepaßt sein) to be well-suited to sth/(to each other); bei Teamarbeit müssen alle aufeinander abgestimmt sein in teamwork everyone has to fit in with everyone else; etw miteinander ~ (vereinbaren) to settle sth amongst ourselves/themselves etc.
    3 vr sich ~ (mit jdm/miteinander) to come to an agreement (with sb/amongst ourselves/themselves etc).

Abstimmung f (a) (Stimmabgabe) vote; (geheime ~) ballot; (das Abstimmen) voting. zur ~ kommen or schreiten (form) to come to the vote; eine ~ durchführen or vornehmen to take a vote/to hold a ballot; zur ~ bringen (form) to put to the vote. (b) siehe vt tuning; matching; coordination; suiting; balancing. (c) (Vereinbarung) agreement.

Abstimmungs-: a~berechtigt adj siehe stimmberechtigt; ~ergebnis nt result of the vote; ~niederlage f eine ~niederlage erleiden to be defeated in a/the vote; ~sieg m einen ~sieg erringen to win a/the vote; „~sieg der Opposition" "opposition win vote".

abstinent adj teetotal; (geschlechtlich) abstinent, continent, not indulging in sex. ~ leben to live a life of abstinence.

Abstinenz f, no pl teetotalism, abstinence; (geschlechtlich) abstinence.

Abstinenz-: ~erscheinung f (Med) withdrawal symptom; ~gebot nt (Eccl) requirement of abstinence.

Abstinenzler(in f) m -s, - teetotaller.

Abstinenztag m (Eccl) day of abstinence.

abstoppen sep 1 vt (a) Auto, Maschine, Verkehr to stop, to bring to a standstill or halt; (drosseln) to halt. (b) (Sport) Ball to stop; (mit Stoppuhr) to time. jds Zeit ~ to time sb. 2 vi to stop, to come to a halt.

Abstoß m (a) (Ftbl) goal kick; (nach Fangen des Balls) clearance. (b) der ~ vom Ufer war so kräftig, daß ... the boat was pushed away or out from the shore so forcefully that ...

abstoßen sep irreg 1 vt (a) (wegstoßen) Boot to push off or away or out; (abschlagen) Ecken to knock off; Möbel to batter; (abschaben) Ärmel to wear thin. sich (dat) die Ecken und Kanten ~ (fig) to have the rough edges knocked off one; siehe Horn.
    (b) (zurückstoßen) to repel; (Comm) Ware, Aktien to get rid of, to sell off; (fig: anwidern) to repulse, to repel. dieser Stoff stößt Wasser ab this material is water-repellent; gleiche Pole stoßen sich or einander ab like poles repel (each other).
    (c) (Ftbl) den Ball ~ to take the goal kick; (nach Fangen) to clear (the ball).
    2 vr (a) (abgeschlagen werden) to get broken; (Möbel) to get battered.
    (b) (esp Sport: Mensch) to push oneself off. sich mit den Füßen vom Boden ~ to push oneself off.
    3 vi (a) aux sein or haben (weggestoßen werden) to push off.
    (b) (anwidern) to be repulsive. sich von etw abgestoßen fühlen to be repelled by sth, to find sth repulsive.
    (c) (Ftbl) to take a goal kick; (nach Fangen) to clear (the ball).

abstoßend adj Aussehen, Äußeres repulsive. sein Wesen hat etwas A~es there's something repulsive about him.

Abstoßung f (Phys) repulsion.

abstottern vt sep (inf) to pay off.

abstrafen vt sep siehe bestrafen.

abstrahieren* [apstra'hi:rən] vti insep to abstract (aus from).

abstrakt [ap'strakt] adj abstract. etw zu ~ ausdrücken to express sth too abstractly or too much in the abstract.

Abstraktheit [-st-] f abstractness.

Abstraktion [-st-] f abstraction.

Abstraktionsvermögen [-st-] nt ability to abstract.

Abstraktum [-st-] nt -s, Abstrakta (Begriff) abstract (concept); (Ling: Substantiv) abstract noun.

abstrampeln vr sep (inf) to kick the bedclothes off; (fig) to sweat (away) (inf), to flog one's guts out (sl).

abstreichen sep irreg 1 vt (a) (wegstreichen) to wipe off or away; Asche to knock or tap off; (säubern) to wipe. den Hals/die Zunge ~ (Med) to take a throat/tongue swab.
    (b) (abziehen) Betrag to knock off, to deduct; (fig) to discount. davon kann/muß man die Hälfte ~ (fig) you have to take it with a pinch of salt.

(c) (*Hunt*) *Feld* to beat; (*Mil*) *Gebiet, Himmel* to sweep.
2 *vi aux sein* (*Hunt*) to fly off or away.

abstreifen *vt sep* **(a)** (*abtreten*) *Schuhe, Füße* to wipe; *Schmutz* to wipe off. **(b)** (*abziehen*) *Kleidung, Schmuck* to take off, to remove, to slip off; (*entfernen*) *Haut* to cast, to shed; (*fig*) *Gewohnheit, Fehler* to get rid of. **(c)** (*absuchen*) to search, to scour.

abstreiten *vt sep irreg* (*streitig machen*) to dispute; (*leugnen*) to deny. **das kann man ihm nicht** ~ you can't deny it; **er wollte sich nicht das Recht** ~ **lassen, seine Meinung zu sagen** he refused to allow his right to express his own opinion to be disputed *or* to come under dispute.

Abstrich *m* **(a)** (*Kürzung*) cutback. ~**e machen** to cut back (*an* +*dat* on), to make cuts (*an* +*dat* in); (*weniger erwarten etc*) to lower one's sights.
(b) (*Med*) swab; (*Gebärmutter*~) smear. **einen** ~ **machen** to take a swab/smear.
(c) (*Mus, beim Schreiben*) downstroke. **zu dicke** ~**e machen** to make one's downstrokes too thick.

abströmen *vi sep aux sein* to flow away *or* off; (*Wasser auch*) to run away *or* off; (*Menschenmassen*) to stream out.

abstrus [ap'stru:s] *adj* (*geh*) abstruse.

abstufen *sep* **1** *vt Gelände* to terrace; *Haare* to layer; *Farben* to shade; *Gehälter, Steuern, Preise* to grade. **2** *vr* to be terraced. **der Weinberg stuft sich zum Fluß hin ab** the vineyard goes down in terraces to the river.

Abstufung *f siehe vt* terracing; layering; (*Nuancierung*) shading; (*Nuance*) shade; (*Staffelung*) grading; (*Stufe*) grade.

abstumpfen *sep* **1** *vt* **(a)** (*lit rare*) *Ecken, Kanten* to blunt; *Messer, Schneide auch* to take the edge off, to dull.
(b) *Mensch* to dull; *Sinne auch* to deaden; *Gerechtigkeitssinn, Gewissen, Urteilsvermögen auch* to blunt; *siehe* **abgestumpft.**
2 *vi aux sein* (*fig: Geschmack etc*) to become dulled. **wenn man ewig dasselbe machen muß, stumpft man nach und nach ab** always having to do the same thing dulls the mind; **er ist als Kritiker abgestumpft** his critical sensibilities have become blunted; **gegen etw** ~ to become inured to sth.

Abstumpfung *f siehe vt* **(b)** dulling; deadening; blunting.

Absturz *m siehe vi* crash; fall. **ein Flugzeug zum** ~ **bringen** to bring a plane down.

abstürzen *vi sep aux sein* **(a)** (*Flugzeug*) to crash; (*Bergsteiger*) to fall. **(b)** (*schroff abfallen*) to fall *or* drop away.

Absturzstelle *f* location of a/the crash; (*beim Bergsteigen*) location of a/the fall. **die Rettungsarbeiten an der** ~ the rescue work at the scene of the crash.

abstützen *sep* **1** *vt* to support (*auch fig*), to prop up; *Haus, Mauer auch* to shore up. **2** *vr* to support oneself, to prop oneself up; (*bei Bewegung*) to support oneself.

absuchen *vt sep* **(a)** to search; *Gegend auch* to comb, to scour; *Himmel, Horizont* to scan; (*Scheinwerfer*) to sweep. **wir haben den ganzen Garten abgesucht** we searched all over the garden.
(b) (*suchend absammeln*) *Raupen etc* to pick off; *Strauch etc* to pick clean. **die Sträucher nach Schädlingen** ~ to examine the bush for pests.

Absud ['apzu:t] *m* -(e)s, -e (*old*) decoction.

absurd *adj* absurd, preposterous. ~**es Drama** *or* **Theater** theatre of the absurd; **das A**~**e** the absurd.

Absurdität *f* absurdity (*auch Philos*), preposterousness.

Abszeß *m* -sses, -sse abscess.

Abszisse *f* -, -n abscissa.

Abt *m* -(e)s, -e abbot.

Abt. *abbr of* **Abteilung** dept.

abtakeln *vt sep Schiff* to unrig; (*außer Dienst stellen*) to lay up; *siehe* **abgetakelt.**

Abtak(e)lung *f siehe vt* unrigging; laying up.

abtasten *vt sep* **(a)** to feel; (*Med auch*) to palpate; (*Elec*) to scan; (*bei Durchsuchung*) to frisk (*auf* +*acc* for); (*fig: erproben*) *jdn* to sound out, to suss out (*sl*); (*Sport*) to get the measure of, to size up, to suss out (*sl*).

Abtastung *f* (*TV*) scanning.

abtauen *sep* **1** *vt* to thaw out; *Kühlschrank* to defrost. **2** *vi aux sein* to thaw. **der Schnee ist vom Dach abgetaut** the snow has thawed off the roof.

Abtausch *m* -(e)s, -e (*Chess, Sw: Tausch*) exchange.

abtauschen *vt sep* (*Chess, Sw: tauschen*) to exchange. **das habe ich ihm abgetauscht** I swopped him for it (*inf*).

Abtei *f* abbey.

Abteikirche *f* abbey (church).

Abteil *nt* -(e)s, -e compartment. ~ **erster Klasse** first-class compartment; ~ **für Mutter und Kind** *compartment reserved for mothers with young children*; ~ **für Raucher/Nichtraucher** smoker/non-smoker, no smoking compartment.

abteilen *vt sep* **(a)** (*einteilen*) to divide up. **fünf Stücke** ~ to cut off five pieces. **(b)** (*abtrennen*) to divide off; (*mit Wand auch*) to partition off.

Abteilung¹ *f, no pl siehe vt* dividing up; cutting off; dividing off; partitioning off.

Abteilung² *f* **(a)** (*in Firma, Kaufhaus, Hochschule*) department; (*in Krankenhaus, Jur*) section; (*Mil*) unit, section. **er arbeitet in der** ~ **Verkauf** he works in the sales department. **(b)** (*old: Abschnitt*) section.

Abteilungsleiter *m* head of department; (*in Kaufhaus*) department manager.

abtelefonieren* *vi sep* to telephone *or* ring *or* call to say one can't make it *or* come.

abtelegraphieren* *vi sep* to cable *or* send a telegram to say one can't make it *or* come.

abteufen *vt sep Schacht* to sink.

abtippen *vt sep* (*inf*) to type out.

Äbtissin *f* abbess.

abtönen *vt sep Farbe* to tone down. **zwei Farben gegeneinander** ~ to tone two colours in with each other.

Abtönung *f* (*von Farbe*) toning down; (*Farbton*) tone, shade.

abtöten *vt sep* (*lit, fig*) to destroy, to kill (off); *Nerv* to deaden; *sinnliche Begierde* to mortify. **in mir ist jedes Gefühl abgetötet** I am dead to all feeling.

Abtötung *f siehe vt* destruction, killing (off); deadening; mortification.

Abtrag *m* -(e)s, *no pl* (*old*) harm. **einer Sache** (*dat*) ~ **tun** to harm sth; **das tut der Sache keinen** ~ that will do no ill (*old*) *or* harm (*old*).

abtragen *vt sep irreg* **(a)** (*auch vi: abräumen*) *Geschirr, Speisen* to clear away.
(b) (*einebnen*) *Boden, Gelände* to level down.
(c) (*abbauen*) *Gebäude, Mauer* to dismantle, to take down; (*Fluß*) *Ufer* to erode, to wear away.
(d) (*abbezahlen*) *Schulden* to pay off.
(e) (*abnutzen*) *Kleider, Schuhe* to wear out; *siehe* **abgetragen.**

abträgig (*Sw*), **abträglich** *adj* detrimental, harmful, injurious; *Bemerkung, Kritik etc* adverse, unfavourable.

Abträglichkeit *f* harmfulness, injuriousness; (*von Bemerkung etc*) adverseness.

Abtragung *f* **(a)** (*Geol*) erosion. **(b)** (*Abbau*) dismantling, taking down. **(c)** (*Tilgung*) paying off.

Abtransport *m* transportation; (*aus Katastrophengebiet*) evacuation. **beim** ~ **der Gefangenen** when the prisoners were being taken away *or* transported.

abtransportieren* *vt sep Waren* to transport; *Personen auch* to take off *or* away; (*aus Katastrophengebiet*) to evacuate.

abtreiben *sep irreg* **1** *vt* **(a) vom Kurs** ~ *Flugzeug* to send *or* drive off course; *Boot auch, Schwimmer* to carry off course.
(b) (*zu Tal treiben*) *Vieh* to bring down.
(c) *Kind, Leibesfrucht* to abort. **sie hat das Kind abgetrieben** *or* ~ **lassen** she had an abortion.
(d) (*Aus, S Ger: Cook*) to whisk.
2 *vi* **(a)** *aux sein* (*vom Kurs*) ~ (*Flugzeug*) to be sent *or* driven off course; (*Boot auch, Schwimmer*) to be carried off course.
(b) (*Abort vornehmen*) to carry out an abortion; (*generell*) to carry out *or* do abortions; (*Abort vornehmen lassen*) to have an abortion.

Abtreibung *f* abortion. **eine** ~ **vornehmen lassen/vornehmen** to have/carry out an abortion.

Abtreibungs-: ~**paragraph** *m* abortion laws *pl*; ~**versuch** *m* attempt at an abortion; **einen** ~**versuch vornehmen** to try to give oneself an abortion, to attempt an abortion; **jährlich finden viele** ~**versuche statt** there is a large number of attempted abortions every year.

abtrennbar *adj* (*lostrennbar*) detachable; *Knöpfe, Besatz etc auch* removable; (*abteilbar*) separable; *Verfahren* severable (*form*).

abtrennen *vt sep* **(a)** (*lostrennen*) to detach; *Knöpfe, Besatz etc* to remove, to take off; (*abschneiden*) to cut off; *Bein, Finger etc* (*durch Unfall*) to sever, to cut off. „**hier** ~" "detach here"; **den Spitzenbesatz von einem Kleid** ~ to take the lace trimming off a dress, to remove the lace trimming from a dress.
(b) (*abteilen*) to separate off; (*räumlich auch*) to divide off; (*mit Zwischenwand etc auch*) to partition off. **diese Zeit läßt sich nicht einfach von der Geschichte des Landes** ~ this period cannot simply be set aside from the history of the country.

Abtrennung *f siehe vt* **(b)** separation; division; partitioning.

abtretbar *adj* (*Jur*) *Ansprüche* transferable, cedable (*form*).

abtreten *sep irreg* **1** *vt* **(a)** *Teppich* to wear; (*völlig*) to wear out; *Schnee, Schmutz* to stamp off. **sich** (*dat*) **die Füße** *or* **Schuhe** ~ to wipe one's feet.
(b) (*überlassen*) (*jdm* *or* *an jdn* to sb) to hand over; *Gebiet, Land auch* to cede (*form*); *Rechte, Ansprüche* to transfer, to cede (*form*); *Haus, Geldsumme* to transfer, to assign (*form*).
(c) (*inf*) **jdm etw** ~ (*verborgen*) to lend sth to sb; (*borgen*) to borrow sth from sb.
2 *vr* (*Teppich etc*) to wear, to get worn; (*völlig*) to wear out.
3 *vi aux sein* (*Theat*) to go off (stage), to make one's exit; (*Mil*) to dismiss; (*inf: zurücktreten*) *Politiker* to step down (*inf*), to resign; (*Monarch*) to abdicate, to step down (*inf*); (*euph: sterben*) to make one's last exit. ~**!** (*Mil*) dismiss!; **aus dem Leben** ~ (*euph*) to quit this life.

Abtreter *m* -s, - (*Fuß*~) doormat.

Abtretung *f* (*an* +*acc* to) transfer; (*von Rechten, Ansprüchen auch, von Gebiet*) ceding, cession (*form*); (*von Haus, Geldsumme auch*) assignment (*form*). **durch** ~ **aller Ansprüche an seinen Teilhaber** by transferring all rights to his partner.

Abtrieb *m* -(e)s, -e **(a)** (*Vieh*~) **im Herbst beginnt der** ~ **des Viehs von den Bergweiden** in autumn they start to bring the cattle down from the mountain pastures. **(b)** (*Tech*) output. **(c)** (*Aus*) mixture.

Abtrift *f* -, -en *siehe* **Abdrift.**

abtrinken *vt sep irreg* to drink. **einen Schluck** ~ to have *or* take a sip.

Abtritt *m* **(a)** (*Theat*) exit; (*Rücktritt*) (*von Minister*) resignation; (*von Monarch*) abdication. **(b)** (*old: Klosett*) privy (*old*).

Abtrockentuch *nt* tea *or* dish (*US*) towel.

abtrocknen *sep* **1** *vt* to dry (off); *Geschirr* to dry, to wipe. **2** *vi* to dry up, to do the drying-up.

abtropfen *vi sep aux sein* to drip; (*Geschirr*) to drain. **etw** ~ **lassen** *Wäsche etc* to let sth drip; *Salat* to drain sth; *Geschirr* to let sth drain.

abtrotzen *vt sep* **jdm etw** ~ (*geh*) to wring sth out of sb.

abtrünnig *adj* renegade, apostate (*form, esp Eccl*); (*rebellisch*) rebel; (*treulos auch*) disloyal. **jdm/einer Gruppe** *etc* ~ **werden**

to desert sb/a group; (*sich erheben gegen*) to rebel against sb/a group; **er ist dem Glauben ~ geworden** he has left *or* deserted the faith, he has apostatized (*form*); **weil der General schon ~ geworden war** because the general had already left the cause/gone over to the other side, because of the general's apostasy (*form*).

Abtrünnigkeit *f* apostasy (*form*); (*Treulosigkeit auch*) disloyalty; (*rebellische Gesinnung*) rebelliousness. **die ~ einer der Mitverschwörer** the desertion *or* apostasy (*form*) of one of the plotters.

abtun *vt sep irreg* (a) (*fig: beiseite schieben*) to dismiss. **etw mit einem Achselzucken/einem Lachen ~** to shrug/laugh sth off; **etw mit einer Handbewegung/einem arroganten Lachen ~** to dismiss sth with a wave of one's hand/an arrogant laugh; **etw kurz ~** to brush sth aside; *siehe* abgetan.
(b) (*dial: ablegen*) to take off.

abtupfen *vt sep* *Tränen, Blut* to dab away; *Gesicht, Mundwinkel* to dab; *Wunde* to swab, to dab.

ab|urteilen *vt sep* to pass sentence *or* judgement on; (*fig: verdammen*) to condemn. **Verbrecher, die noch nicht abgeurteilt worden sind** criminals upon whom sentence has not yet been passed.

Ab|urteilung *f* sentencing; (*fig*) condemnation. **bei der ~ des Täters** when sentence was/is being passed on the accused.

Abverkauf *m* (*Aus*) sale.

abverkaufen* *vt sep* (*Aus*) to sell off cheaply.

abverlangen* *vt sep* *siehe* abfordern.

abvermieten* *vt sep* (*form*) to let (*dat, an* +*acc* to).

abwägen *vt sep irreg* to weigh up; *Worte* to weigh. **er wog beide Möglichkeiten gegeneinander ab** he weighed up the two possibilities; *siehe* abgewogen.

Abwägung *f* weighing up; (*von Worten*) weighing.

Abwahl *f* voting out. **es kam zur ~ des gesamten Vorstands** the whole committee was voted out.

abwählbar *adj* **der Präsident ist nicht ~** the president cannot be voted out (of office).

abwählen *vt sep* to vote out (of office); (*Sch*) *Fach* to give up.

abwälzen *vt sep* *Schuld, Verantwortung* to shift (*auf* +*acc* onto); *Arbeit* to unload (*auf* +*acc* onto); *Kosten* to pass on (*auf* +*acc* to). **die Schuld von sich ~** to shift the blame onto somebody else.

abwandelbar *adj siehe vt* adaptable; modifiable.

abwandeln *vt sep* *Melodie* to adapt; *Thema auch* to modify.

Abwand(e)lung *f siehe vi* Abwandlung.

abwandern *sep* **1** *vi aux sein* to move (away) (*aus* from); (*Bevölkerung: zu einem anderen Ort auch*) to migrate (*aus* from); (*Kapital*) to be transferred (*aus* out of); (*inf: aus einer Veranstaltung etc*) to wander away *or* off (*inf*). **viele Spieler/Abonnenten etc wandern ab** a lot of players/subscribers *etc* are transferring.
2 *vt aux sein or haben* to hike over.

Abwanderung *f siehe vi* moving away; migration; transference.

Abwanderungsverlust *m* (*Sociol*) population drain.

Abwandlung *f* adaptation, variation; (*von Thema etc auch*) modification.

Abwärme *f* waste heat.

Abwart(in *f*) *m* (*Sw*) concierge, janitor/janitress.

abwarten *sep* **1** *vt* to wait for. **das Gewitter ~** to wait till the storm is over, to wait the storm out; **er kann es nicht mehr ~** he can't wait any longer; **das bleibt abzuwarten** that remains to be seen.
2 *vi* to wait. **warten Sie ab!** just wait a bit!; **~ und Tee trinken** (*inf*) to wait and see; **im Moment können wir gar nichts tun, wir müssen ~** we can't do anything at the moment, we'll have to bide our time; **eine ~de Haltung einnehmen** to play a waiting game, to adopt a policy of wait-and-see.

abwärts *adv* down; (*nach unten auch*) downwards. **den Fluß/Berg ~** down the river/mountain; **„~!"** (*im Fahrstuhl*) "going down!"; **Kinder von fünf Jahren ~** children of five and under; **vom Abteilungsleiter ~** from the head of department down(wards).

Abwärts-: **~entwicklung** *f* downwards *or* downhill trend; **~fahrt** *f* journey down; **bei der ~fahrt ist der Lift plötzlich stehengeblieben** the lift suddenly stopped on its *or* the way down.

abwärtsgehen *vi impers sep* (*fig*) **mit ihm/dem Land geht es ~ abwärts** he/the country is going downhill.

Abwärtstrend *m* downwards *or* downhill trend.

Abwasch[1] *m* -s, *no pl* washing-up. **den ~ machen** to do the washing-up, to wash up; ... **dann kannst du das auch machen, das ist (dann) ein ~** (*inf*) ... then you could do that as well and kill two birds with one stone (*prov*).

Abwasch[2] *f* -, **-en** (*Aus*) sink.

abwaschbar *adj* *Tapete* washable.

abwaschen *sep irreg* **1** *vt Geschirr* to wash (up); *Farbe, Schmutz* to wash off; *Pferd, Auto* to wash down; (*fig liter*) *Schande, Schmach* to wipe out. **den Schmutz (vom Gesicht) ~** to wash the dirt off (one's face). **2** *vi* to wash up, to do the washing-up.

Abwasch-: **~becken** *nt* sink; **~lappen** *m* dishcloth, washing-up cloth; **~mittel** *nt* washing-up liquid; **~tisch** *m* sink unit; **~wasser** *nt* washing-up water, dishwater; (*fig inf*) dishwater (*inf*).

Abwasser *nt* sewage *no pl*. **industrielle Abwässer** industrial effluents *pl or* waste *sing*.

Abwasser-: **~aufbereitung** *f* reprocessing of sewage/effluents; **~kanal** *m* sewer; **~reinigung** *f* purification of sewage/effluents.

abwechseln *vir sep* to alternate. **sich** *or* **einander ~** to alter-

nate; (*Menschen auch*) to take turns; **sich mit jdm ~** to take turns with sb; (*sich*) **miteinander ~** to alternate (with each other *or* one another); to take turns; **Regen und Schnee wechselten (sich) miteinander ab** first it rained and then it snowed; **ihre Launen wechseln oft blitzschnell miteinander ab** her moods often change *or* vary from one minute to the next.

abwechselnd *adv* alternately. **wir haben ~ Klavier gespielt** we took turns playing the piano; **er war ~ fröhlich und traurig** he alternated between being happy and sad, he was by turns happy and sad.

Abwechs(e)lung *f* change; (*Zerstreuung*) diversion. **eine angenehme/schöne ~** a pleasant/nice change; **zur ~ for a change; für ~ sorgen** to provide entertainment; **dort ist reichlich für ~ gesorgt** there's quite a variety of things going on there; **hier haben wir wenig ~** there's not much variety in life here; **da gibt es mehr ~** there's more going on there; **das war eine ~ im Einerlei des Dorfalltags** that relieved the monotony of village life, that brought a little variety into village life; **die ~ lieben** (*euph*) to enjoy (a little) variety.

abwechslungs-: **~halber** *adv* for a change, to make a change; **~los** *adj* monotonous; **~reich** *adj* varied.

Abweg ['apveːk] *m* (*fig*) mistake, error. **jdn auf ~e führen** to mislead sb, to lead sb astray (*auch moralisch*); **auf ~e geraten** *or* **kommen** to go astray; (*moralisch auch*) to stray from the straight and narrow; **die ~e seines Denkens** the eccentricities of his thought.

abwegig ['apveːgıç] *adj* (*geh*) erroneous; (*bizarr*) eccentric, off-beat; *Verdacht* unfounded, groundless.

Abwegigkeit *f* (*geh*) *siehe adj* erroneousness; eccentricity, off-beat nature; groundlessness.

Abwehr *f, no pl* (a) (*Psych, Med*) defence (*gen* against); (*Schutz*) protection (*gen* against). **Mechanismen der ~** defence mechanisms; **der ~ von etw dienen** to provide *or* give protection against sth.
(b) (*Zurückweisung*) repulse; (*Abweisung*) rejection; (*Spionage~*) counter-intelligence (service). **die ~ des Feindes** the repulsing *or* repelling of the enemy; **bei der ~ sein** to be with *or* in counter-intelligence; **auf ~ stoßen** to be repulsed, to meet with a repulse.
(c) (*Sport*) defence; (*~aktion*) piece of defence (work); (*abgewehrter Ball*) clearance; (*gefangen auch*) save. **er ist besser in der ~** he's better in *or* at defence.

Abwehr-: **a~bereit** *adj* (*Mil*) ready for defence; **~bereitschaft** *f* defence readiness; **~dienst** *m* counter-intelligence service.

abwehren *sep* **1** *vt* (a) *Gegner* to fend *or* ward off; *Angriff, Feind auch* to repulse, to repel; *Ball* to clear; *Schlag* to parry, to ward off. **hervorragend, wie der Torwart den Ball abwehrte** that was a really good save the goalkeeper made there.
(b) (*fernhalten*) to keep away; *Krankheitserreger* to protect against; *Gefahr, üble Folgen* to avert.
(c) (*abweisen*) *Anschuldigung* to dismiss. **eine ~de Geste** a dismissive wave of the hand.
2 *vi* (a) (*Sport*) to clear; (*Torwart auch*) to make a save. **mit dem Kopf ~** to head clear; **zur Ecke ~** to clear a corner.
(b) (*ablehnen*) to refuse. **nein, wehrte sie ab** no, she said in refusal.

Abwehr-: **~handlung** *f* defence reaction; **~kampf** *m* (*Mil, Sport*) defence; **ein ~kampf** a defensive action; **sich auf den ~kampf konzentrieren** to concentrate on defence; **~mechanismus** *m* (*Psych*) defence mechanism; **~reaktion** *f* (*Psych*) defence reaction.

abweichen[1] *vi sep irreg aux sein* (*sich entfernen*) to deviate; (*sich unterscheiden*) to differ; (*zwei Theorien, Auffassungen etc*) to differ, to diverge. **vom Kurs ~** to deviate *or* depart from one's course; **vom Thema ~** to digress, to go off the point; **vom rechten Weg ~** (*fig*) to wander *or* err from the straight and narrow; **ich weiche erheblich von seiner Meinung ab** I hold quite a different view from him; **~des Verhalten** (*Psych, Sociol*) deviant behaviour.

abweichen[2] *vti sep* *Briefmarke etc* to soak off.

Abweichler(in *f*) *m* -s, - (*Pol*) deviant.

abweichlerisch *adj* (*Pol*) deviant.

Abweichlertum *nt* (*Pol*) deviancy.

Abweichung *f siehe* abweichen[1] deviation; difference; divergence; (*von Magnetnadel*) declination. **~ von der Wahrheit** departure from the truth; **~ von der Parteilinie** failure to toe the party line, deviation from the party line; **zulässige ~** (*Tech*) tolerance; (*zeitlich, zahlenmäßig*) allowance.

abweiden *vt sep* (*rare*) *Wiese* to graze.

abweisen *vt sep irreg* to turn down, to reject; (*wegschicken*) to turn away; *Bitte auch* to refuse; (*Jur*) *Klage* to dismiss. **er läßt sich nicht ~** he won't take no for an answer.

abweisend *adj* *Ton, Blick* cold, chilly.

Abweisung *f siehe vt* rejection; turning away; refusal; dismissal.

abwendbar *adj* avoidable.

abwenden *sep reg or irreg* **1** *vt* (a) (*zur Seite wenden*) to turn away; *Blick* to avert; *Kopf* to turn. **er wandte das Gesicht ab** he looked away. (b) (*verhindern*) *Unheil, Folgen* to avert. **2** *vr* to turn away.

abwerben *vt sep irreg* to woo away (*dat* from).

Abwerbung *f* wooing away.

abwerfen *sep irreg* **1** *vt* to throw off; *Reiter* to throw; *Bomben, Flugblätter etc* to drop; *Ballast* to jettison; *Geweih* to shed, to cast; *Blätter, Nadeln* to shed; (*Cards*) to discard, to throw away; (*Comm*) *Gewinn* to yield, to return, to show; *Zinsen* to bear, to yield; (*fig liter*) *Joch, Fesseln* to cast *or* throw off.
2 *vti* (*Sport*) (*Ftbl*) *Ball* to throw out; *Speer etc* to throw; *Latte* to knock off *or* down.

abwerten *vt sep* (a) *auch vi Währung* to devalue. (b) (*fig*)

Ideale to debase, to cheapen. **diese Tugend ist heute vollkommen abgewertet** this virtue is no longer valued today; **er muß immer alles ~** he always has to run everything down.

abwertend *adj* pejorative.

Abwertung *f siehe vt* (a) devaluation. **eine ~ vornehmen** to devalue (the currency). (b) *(fig)* debasement, cheapening. **solche Ideale erfahren eine immer stärkere ~** such ideals are valued less and less *or* are constantly losing their value.

abwesend *adj (form)* absent; *(von Hause auch)* away *pred*; *(iro: zerstreut auch)* far away. **die A~en** the absentees.

Abwesenheit *f* absence; *(fig: Geistes~)* abstraction. **in ~** *(Jur)* in absence; **durch ~ glänzen** *(iro)* to be conspicuous by one's absence.

Abwetter *pl (Min)* used air.

abwetzen *sep* 1 *vt (abschaben)* to wear smooth. 2 *vi aux sein (inf)* to hare off *(inf)*, to bolt *(inf)*.

abwichsen *vt sep:* **sich/jdm einen ~** *(vulg)* to jerk *or* wank off *(sl)*/jerk sb off *(sl)*.

abwickeln *sep* 1 *vt* (a) *(abspulen)* to unwind; *Verband auch* to take off, to remove.
(b) *(fig: erledigen)* to deal with; *ein Geschäft* to complete, to conclude; *Kontrolle* to carry out; *Veranstaltung* to run; *(Comm: liquidieren)* to wind up. **die Versammlung wurde in aller Ruhe abgewickelt** the meeting went off peacefully.
2 *vr* to unwind; *(vonstatten gehen)* to go *or* pass off.

Abwicklung *f siehe vt* (a) unwinding; taking off, removal. (b) completion, conclusion; carrying out; running; winding up. **die Polizei sorgte für eine reibungslose ~ der Veranstaltung** the police made sure that the event went *or* passed off smoothly.

abwiegeln *sep* 1 *vt* to appease; *wütende Menge etc auch* to calm down. 2 *vi* to calm things down. **das A~** appeasement.

abwiegen *vt sep irreg* to weigh out.

Abwiegler(in *f)* *m* -s, - appeaser, conciliator.

abwimmeln *vt sep (inf)* jdn to get rid of *(inf)*; *Auftrag* to get out of *(inf)*. **die Sekretärin hat mich abgewimmelt** his secretary turned me away; **laß dich nicht ~** don't let them get rid of you.

Abwind *m (Aviat)* downwash; *(Met)* down current.

abwinkeln *vt sep Arm* to bend. **mit abgewinkelten Armen** *(in den Hüften)* with arms akimbo.

abwinken *sep* 1 *vi (inf) (abwehrend)* to wave it/him *etc* aside; *(resignierend)* to groan; *(fig: ablehnen)* to say no. **als er merkte, wovon ich reden wollte, winkte er gleich ab** when he realised what I wanted to talk about he immediately put me off *or* stopped me; **der Chef winkt bei so einem Vorschlag bestimmt gleich ab** the boss is bound to say no to *or* turn down a suggestion like that; **wenn Bonn abwinkt ...** if the (German) government turns us/them *etc* down *or* says no ...; **sie winkte schnell ab, damit er keine Bemerkung darüber machte** she signed *or* indicated to him not to say anything about it; *siehe* **müde**.
2 *vti (bei Zug)* to give the "go" signal. **ein Rennen ~** to wave the chequered flag; *(nach Unfall etc)* to stop the race; **einen Rennfahrer ~** to wave a driver down.

abwirtschaften *vi sep (inf)* to go downhill. **endgültig abgewirtschaftet haben** to have eventually reached rock bottom; *siehe* **abgewirtschaftet**.

abwischen *vt sep Staub, Schmutz etc* to wipe off *or* away; *Hände, Nase etc* to wipe; *Augen, Tränen* to dry. **er wischte sich** *(dat)* **den Schweiß/die Stirn ab** he mopped (the sweat from) his brow.

abwohnen *vt sep* (a) *Möbel* to wear out; *Haus, Zimmer* to make shabby. (b) *Baukostenzuschuß* to pay off with the rent. **die Miete voll ~** to stay for the time for which rent has been paid.

abwracken *vt sep Schiff, Auto* to break (up); *siehe* **abgewrackt**.

Abwurf *m* throwing off; *(von Reiter)* throw; *(von Bomben etc)* dropping; *(von Ballast)* jettisoning; *(von Geweih)* casting; *(Comm: von Zinsen, Gewinn)* yield; *(Sport) (der Latte)* knocking down *or* off; *(des Speers)* throwing. **ein ~ vom Tor** a goal-throw, a throw-out.

Abwurflinie *f (Sport)* (scratch) line.

abwürgen *vt sep (inf)* to scotch; *Motor* to stall. **etw von vornherein ~** to nip sth in the bud.

abzahlen *vt sep* to pay off.

abzählen *sep* 1 *vt* to count. **er zählte zwanzig Hundertmarkscheine ab** he counted out twenty hundred-mark notes; **das läßt sich an den (zehn *or* fünf) Fingern ~** *(fig)* that's plain to see, any fool can see that *(inf)*; **bitte das Fahrgeld abgezählt bereithalten** please tender exact *or* correct fare *(form)*.
2 *vi* to number off.

Abzählreim, Abzählvers *m* counting-out rhyme *(such as "eeny meeny miney mo", for choosing a person)*.

Abzahlung *f* (a) *(Rückzahlung)* repayment, paying off. (b) *(Ratenzahlung)* hire purchase *(Brit)*, HP *(Brit)*, instalment plan *(US)*; *(Rate)* (re)payment, instalment. **etw auf ~ kaufen** to buy sth on HP *(Brit)* or on hire purchase *(Brit)* or on the instalment plan *(US)*.

abzapfen *vt sep* to draw off. **jdm Blut ~** *(inf)* to take blood from sb; **jdm Geld ~** to get some money out of sb.

abzappeln *vr sep (inf)* to wear oneself out.

abzäumen *vt sep Pferd etc* to unbridle.

abzäunen *vt sep* to fence off.

Abzäunung *f* fencing.

abzehren *sep* 1 *vt (liter)* to emaciate. **der Kummer zehrt ihn ab** he is pining away with grief; *siehe* **abgezehrt**. 2 *vr* to waste *or* pine away.

Abzehrung *f* (a) *(Abmagerung)* emaciation. (b) *(obs: Schwindsucht)* consumption *(old)*.

Abzeichen *nt* badge; *(Mil)* insignia *pl*; *(Orden, Auszeichnung)* decoration.

abzeichnen *sep* 1 *vt* (a) to draw. (b) *(signieren)* to initial. 2 *vr* to stand out; *(Unterwäsche)* to show; *(fig: deutlich werden)* to

emerge, to become apparent; *(drohend bevorstehen)* to loom (on the horizon).

abzgl. *abbr of* **abzüglich.**

Abziehbild *nt* transfer.

abziehen *sep irreg* 1 *vt* (a) to skin; *Fell, Haut* to remove, to take off; *grüne Bohnen* to string.
(b) *Bett* to strip; *Bettzeug* to strip off.
(c) *Mantel, Schürze, Ring etc* to take off; *Hut* to raise.
(d) *Schlüssel* to take out, to remove; *Abzugshahn* to press, to squeeze; *Pistole* to fire.
(e) *(zurückziehen) Truppen, Kapital* to withdraw; *(subtrahieren) Zahlen* to take away, to subtract; *Steuern* to deduct. **DM 20 vom Preis ~** to take DM 20 off the price; **man hatte mir zuviel abgezogen** they'd deducted *or* taken off too much, I'd had too much deducted.
(f) *(abfüllen) Wein* to bottle. **Wein auf Flaschen ~** to bottle wine.
(g) *(Typ: vervielfältigen)* to run off; *Korrekturfahnen auch* to pull; *(Phot) Bilder* to make prints of. **etw zwanzigmal ~** to run off twenty copies of sth.
(h) *(schleifen)* to sharpen; *Rasiermesser auch* to strop; *Parkett* to sand (down).
(i) *(Cook) Suppe, Sauce* to thicken. **die Suppe mit einem Ei ~** to beat an egg into the soup.
(j) *(sl) Fest, Veranstaltung* to put on; *siehe* **Nummer, Schau.**
2 *vi* (a) *aux sein (sich verflüchtigen) (Rauch, Dampf)* to escape, to go away; *(Sturmtief etc)* to move away.
(b) *aux sein (Soldaten)* to pull out *(aus von)*, to withdraw *(aus from)*; *(inf: weggehen)* to go off *or* away. **an die Front ~** to leave for the front; **zieh ab!** *(inf)* clear off! *(inf)*, beat it! *(inf)*.
(c) *(abdrücken)* to pull *or* squeeze the trigger, to fire.

Abzieher *m* -s, - *(Typ)* proof puller.

Abziehpresse *f* proof press.

abzielen *vi sep* **auf etw** *(acc)* **~** *(Mensch)* to aim at sth; *(in Rede)* to get at sth; *(Bemerkung, Maßnahme etc)* to be aimed *or* directed at sth; **ich merkte sofort, worauf sie mit dieser Anspielung abzielte** I saw immediately what she was driving *or* getting at with that allusion.

abzirkeln *vt sep (rare: mit Zirkel abmessen)* to measure (off) with compasses; *(fig: vorausplanen)* to calculate very carefully; *Worte, Bewegungen* to measure.

abzittern *vi sep aux sein (dated sl)* to push off *(inf)*.

abzotteln *vi sep aux sein (inf)* to toddle off *(inf)*.

Abzug ['aptsuːk] *m* (a) *no pl (Weggang)* departure; *(Met: von Tief)* moving away; *(Wegnahme: von Truppen, Kapital etc)* withdrawal. **jdm freien ~ gewähren** to give *or* grant sb a safe conduct.
(b) *(usu pl: vom Lohn etc)* deduction; *(Rabatt)* discount. **ohne ~** *(Comm)* net terms only; **er verdient ohne Abzüge ...** before deductions *or* stoppages he earns ...; **etw in ~ bringen** *(form)* to deduct sth.
(c) *(Typ)* copy; *(Korrekturfahne)* proof; *(Phot)* print.
(d) *(Öffnung für Rauch, Gas)* flue. **es muß für hinreichenden ~ gesorgt werden** there must be sufficient means for the gas/smoke to escape *or* to be drawn off.
(e) *(am Gewehr)* trigger.

abzüglich *prep +gen (Comm)* minus, less.

Abzugs-: a~fähig *adj (Fin)* (tax-)deductible; **a~frei** *adj* tax-free; **~rohr** *nt* flue (pipe).

abzupfen *vt sep* to pull *or* pluck off *(von etw* sth); *(S Ger: pflücken)* to pick.

abzwacken *vt sep (dial)* (a) *(abkneifen)* to pinch off. (b) *siehe* **abknapsen.**

abzwecken *vi sep* **auf etw** *(acc)* **~** to be aimed at sth.

Abzweig *m (form)* junction. **der ~ nach Saarbrücken** the turn-off to *or* for Saarbrücken.

Abzweigdose *f* junction box.

abzweigen *sep* 1 *vi aux sein* to branch off. 2 *vt (inf)* to set *or* put on one side.

Abzweigung *f* junction, turn-off; *(Nebenstrecke)* turn-off; *(Gabelung)* fork; *(Rail: Nebenlinie)* branch line; *(Elec)* junction.

abzwicken *vt sep* to pinch *or* nip off.

abzwingen *vt sep irreg jdm Respekt etc* **~** to gain sb's respect *etc*; **er zwang sich** *(dat)* **ein Lächeln ab** he forced a smile.

abzwitschern *vi sep aux sein (inf)* to go off, to take oneself off.

Accessoires [aksɛˈsoaːɐ(s)] *pl (geh)* accessories *pl.*

Acetat [atseˈtaːt] *nt* -s, -e acetate.

Aceton [atseˈtoːn] *nt* -s, -e acetone.

Acetylen [atsetyˈleːn] *nt* -s, *no pl* acetylene.

Acetylen(sauerstoff)brenner *m* oxyacetylene burner.

ach [ax] 1 *interj* oh; *(poet auch)* O; *(bedauernd auch)* alas *(old, liter)*. **~ nein!** oh no!; *(überrascht)* no!, really!; *(ablehnend)* no, no!; **~ nein, ausgerechnet der!** well, well, him of all people; **~ so!** I see!, aha!; *(ja richtig)* of course!; **~ was** *or* **wo!** of course not; **~ was** *or* **wo, das ist doch nicht so schlimm!** come on now, it's not that bad; **~ was** *or* **wo, das ist nicht nötig!** no, no that's not necessary; **~ wirklich?** oh really?, do you/does he *etc* really?; **~ je!** oh dear!, oh dear(ie) me!; **~ und weh schreien** to scream blue murder *(inf)*.
2 *adv (geh)* **~ so schnell/schön** *etc* oh so quickly/lovely *etc.*

Ach *nt:* **mit ~ und Krach** *(inf)* by the skin of one's teeth *(inf)*; **eine Prüfung mit ~ und Krach bestehen** to scrape through an exam (by the skin of one's teeth); **ich habe die Behandlung überstanden, aber nur mit ~ und Weh** I had the treatment but I screamed blue murder *(inf)*.

Achäer(in *f)* [aˈxɛːɐ, -ɛːərɪn] *m* -s, - *(Hist)* Achaean.

Achat *m* -(e)s, -e agate.

achaten *adj attr* agate.

Achill(es) *m* Achilles.

Achillesferse f Achilles heel.
Ach-Laut m voiceless velar fricative (the sound "ch" in the Scottish "loch").
Achs-: ~abstand m wheelbase; ~bruch m siehe Achsenbruch; ~druck m axle weight.
Achse ['aksə] f -, -n (a) axis. die ~ (Rom-Berlin) (Hist) the (Rome-Berlin) Axis. (b) (Tech) axle; (Propeller~) shaft. auf (der) ~ sein (inf) to be out (and about); (Kraftfahrer, Vertreter etc) to be on the road.
Achsel ['aksl] f -, -n (a) shoulder. die ~n or mit den ~n zucken to shrug (one's shoulders). (b) (~höhle) armpit.
Achsel-: ~griff m underarm grip; ~haare pl die ~haare underarm hair, the hair under one's arms; ~höhle f armpit; ~klappe f, ~stück nt siehe Schulterklappe; ~polster nt shoulder pad or padding no pl; ~zucken nt shrug; mit einem ~zucken with a shrug (of one's shoulders); a~zuckend adj shrugging; er stand a~zuckend da he stood there shrugging his shoulders.
Achsen-: ~bruch m broken axle; ~kreuz nt siehe Koordinatenkreuz; ~mächte pl (Hist) Axis powers pl.
Achs-: ~lager nt axle bearing; ~last f siehe ~druck; ~schenkel m stub axle, steering knuckle (US); ~stand m wheelbase; ~welle f axle shaft.
acht num eight. für or auf ~ Tage for a week; in ~ Tagen in a week or a week's time; heute/morgen in ~ Tagen a week today/tomorrow, today/tomorrow week; heute vor ~ Tagen war ich ... a week ago today I was ...; vor ~ Tagen werden sie wohl nicht fertig sein they won't be ready for a week at least; siehe auch vier.
Acht¹ f -, -en eight; (bei Fahrrad) buckled wheel; (beim Eislaufen etc) figure (of) eight; siehe auch Vier.
Acht² f: sich in a~ nehmen to be careful, to take care, to watch or look out; etw außer a~ lassen to leave sth out of consideration, to disregard sth; etw außer aller ~ lassen (geh) to pay no attention or heed whatsoever to sth, not to heed sth; siehe achtgeben.
Acht³ f -, no pl (Hist) outlawry, proscription. jdn in die ~ tun, über jdn die ~ verhängen to outlaw or proscribe sb; jdn in ~ und Bann tun to outlaw or proscribe sb; (Eccl) to place sb under the ban; (fig) to ostracize sb.
achtbar adj (geh) Gesinnung, Eltern worthy.
Achtbarkeit f worthiness.
Acht|eck nt octagon.
acht|eckig adj octagonal, eight-sided.
achtel adj eighth; siehe auch viertel.
Achtel nt -s, - eighth; siehe auch Viertel¹ (a).
Achtel-: ~note f quaver or eighth note (US); ~pause f quaver or eighth note (US) rest.
achten 1 vt (a) (schätzen) to respect, to think highly of, to hold in high regard. geachtete Leute respected people.
  (b) (respektieren) Gesetze, Bräuche, jds Gesinnung to respect.
  (c) (geh: betrachten) to regard; (berücksichtigen) Gefahr, Kälte to pay heed to, to heed. etw (für) gering ~ to have scant regard for sth.
  2 vi auf etw (acc) ~ to pay attention to sth; auf die Kinder ~ to keep an eye on the children; darauf ~, daß ... to be careful or to see or to take care that ...
ächten vt (Hist) to outlaw, to proscribe; (fig) to ostracize.
achtens adv eighthly, in the eighth place.
achtenswert adj Person worthy; Bemühungen, Handlung auch commendable.
achte(r, s) adj eighth; siehe auch vierte(r, s).
Achte(r) mf decl as adj eighth; siehe auch Vierte(r).
Achter m -s, - eight; (Eislauf etc) figure (of) eight; siehe auch Vierer.
Achter-: a~aus adv (Naut) astern; ~bahn f big dipper (Brit), roller coaster (US), switchback; ~deck nt (Naut) afterdeck; a~lastig adj (Naut) Schiff stern-heavy.
achtern adv aft, astern. nach ~ gehen/abdrehen to go aft/to turn astern; von ~ from astern.
Acht-: a~fach 1 adj eightfold; in a~facher Ausfertigung with seven copies; siehe auch vierfach; 2 adv eightfold, eight times; ~füßer m -s, - (Zool) octopod.
achtgeben vi sep irreg to take care, to be careful (auf + acc of); (aufmerksam sein) to pay attention (auf + acc to). auf jdn/etw ~ (beaufsichtigen) to keep an eye on or to look after sb/sth; wenn man im Straßenverkehr nur einen Augenblick nicht achtgibt, ... if your attention wanders for just a second in traffic ...; "O Mensch, gib acht!" "O man, take heed".
achthaben vi sep irreg (geh) siehe achtgeben.
Acht-: a~hundert num eight hundred; siehe auch vierhundert; ~kampf m gymnastic competition with eight events; a~kantig adj (lit) eight-sided; a~kantig rausfliegen (sl) to be flung out on one's ear (inf) or arse over tit (sl); jdn a~kantig rausschmeißen (sl) to fling sb out on his/her ear (inf) or arse over tit (sl).
achtlos adj careless, thoughtless. er hat meinen Aufsatz nur ~ durchgeblättert he just casually leafed through my essay; viele gehen ~ daran vorbei many people just pass by without noticing them; werfen Sie dieses Flugblatt nicht ~ weg! don't just throw this pamphlet away without looking at it properly.
Achtlosigkeit f carelessness, thoughtlessness.
achtmal adv eight times.
achtsam adj (geh) attentive; (sorgfältig) careful. auf etw (acc) ~ sein to pay attention to/be careful of sth; darauf ~ sein, daß ... to be careful that ..., to take care that ...; mit etw ~ umgehen to be careful with sth.
Achtsamkeit f attentiveness; (Sorgfalt) care.
Acht-: ~stundentag m eight hour day; a~tägig adj lasting a week, week-long; mit a~tägiger Verspätung a week late; der a~tägige Streik ist ... the week-old or week-long strike is ...;

a~täglich adj weekly; a~tausend num eight thousand; ein ~tausender a mountain eight thousand metres in height; siehe auch viertausend.
Achtung f, no pl (a) ~! watch or look out!; (Mil: Befehl) attention!; ~, ~! (your) attention please!; ~, ~, präsentiert das Gewehr! present arms!; „~ Hochspannung!" "danger, high voltage"; „~ Lebensgefahr!" "danger"; „~ Stufe!" "mind the step"; ~, fertig, los! ready, steady or get set, go!
  (b) (Wertschätzung) respect (vor + dat for). die ~ vor sich selbst one's self-respect or self-esteem; bei aller ~ vor jdm/etw with all due respect to sb/sth; in hoher ~ bei jdm stehen to be held in high esteem or be highly esteemed by sb; jdm ~ einflößen to command or gain sb's respect; sich (dat) ~ verschaffen to make oneself respected, to gain respect for oneself; jdm die nötige ~ entgegenbringen to give sb the respect due to him/her etc; alle ~! good for you/him etc!
Achtung f, no pl (Hist, des Krieges etc) proscription, outlawing; (fig: gesellschaftlich) ostracism.
achtunggebietend adj (geh) awe-inspiring.
Achtungs-: ~applaus m polite applause; ~erfolg m succès d'estime; a~voll adj (rare) respectful.
achtzehn num eighteen; siehe auch vierzehn.
achtzig num eighty. jdn auf ~ bringen (inf) to make sb's blood boil (inf); auf ~ sein (inf) to be livid, to be hopping mad (inf); da war er gleich auf ~ (inf) then he got livid; mit ~ Sachen (sl) at fifty (miles an hour), at eighty kilometres an hour; (fig: rasend schnell) flat out (inf); siehe auch vierzig.
Achtziger(in f) m -s, - (Mensch) eighty-year-old, octogenarian; siehe auch Vierziger.
ächzen vi to groan (vor + dat with); (Brücke, Baum etc auch) to creak. ~ und stöhnen to moan and groan.
Ächzer m -s, - groan.
Acker m -s, ¨ (a) (Feld) field. den ~/die ~ bestellen to till the soil/plough the fields; einen ~ bebauen or bewirtschaften to work the land. (b) (old: Feldmaß) ≈ acre.
Acker-: ~bau m agriculture, farming; ~bau betreiben to farm the land; ~bau und Viehzucht farming; ~bauer m husbandman (old, liter), farmer; a~bautreibend adj attr farming; ~bürger m (Hist) townsman who farms a smallholding; ~fläche f area of arable land; ~furche f furrow; ~gaul m (pej) farm horse, old nag (pej); siehe Rennpferd; ~gerät nt farm or agricultural implement; ~krume f topsoil; ~land nt arable land; ~mann m siehe Ackersmann.
ackern 1 vi (a) (inf) to slog away (inf). (b) (old) to till the soil. 2 vt (old: pflügen) to till.
Ackerscholle f (liter) soil.
Ackersmann m (old, liter) husbandman (old, liter).
Acker-: ~walze f (land) roller; ~winde f (Bot) field bindweed.
a conto adv (Comm) on account.
Action ['ækʃən] f -, no pl action.
A.D. abbr of Anno Domini AD.
a.D. [a:'de:] abbr of außer Dienst.
Adabei ['a:dabai] m -s, -s (Aus inf) limelighter (inf).
ad absurdum adv ~ ~ führen to make a nonsense of; Argument etc to reduce to absurdity or absurdum.
ADAC [a:de:|a:'tse:] abbr of Allgemeiner Deutscher Automobil-Club ≈ AA (Brit), RAC (Brit), AAA (US).
ad acta adv: etw ~ ~ legen (fig) to consider sth finished; Frage, Problem to consider sth closed.
Adam m -s, -s Adam. seit ~s Zeiten (inf) since the year dot (inf); das stammt noch von ~ und Eva (inf) it's out of the ark (inf); bei ~ und Eva anfangen (inf) to start right from scratch (inf) or from square one (inf); der alte ~ the old Adam; siehe Riese.
Adams-: ~apfel m (inf) Adam's apple; ~kostüm nt (inf) birthday suit; im ~kostüm in one's birthday suit, as nature made one.
Adap(ta)tion f adaptation.
Adapter m -s, - adapter, adaptor.
adaptieren* vt (a) to adapt. (b) (Aus: herrichten) to fix up.
Adaptierung, Adaption f (a) siehe Adap(ta)tion. (b) (Aus: Herrichtung) fixing up.
adaptiv adj adaptive.
adäquat adj (geh) Bemühung, Belohnung, Übersetzung adequate; Stellung, Verhalten suitable; Kritik valid. einer Sache (dat) ~ sein to be adequate to sth.
Adäquatheit f (geh) siehe adj adequacy; suitability; validity.
addieren* 1 vt to add (up). 2 vi to add.
Addiermaschine f adding machine.
Addis Abeba nt - -s Addis Ababa.
Addition f addition; (fig) agglomeration.
Additionsmaschine f adding machine.
ade interj (old, S Ger) farewell (old, liter), adieu (old, liter). jdm ~ sagen to bid sb farewell; einer Sache (dat) ~ sagen to say farewell to sth.
Adebar m -s, -e (N Ger) stork.
Adel m -s, no pl (a) (Adelsgeschlecht, -stand) nobility; (Brit auch) peerage; (hoher auch) aristocracy. von ~ sein to be a member of the nobility, to be of noble birth; eine Familie von ~ an aristocratic family; er stammt aus altem ~ he comes of an old aristocratic family; der niedere ~ the lesser nobility, the gentry; der hohe ~ the higher nobility, the aristocracy; das ist verarmter ~ they are impoverished nobility; ~ verpflichtet noblesse oblige.
  (b) (~stitel) title; (des hohen Adels auch) peerage. jdm einen ~ verleihen to bestow a title on sb; to bestow a peerage on sb, to ennoble sb; erblicher/persönlicher ~ hereditary/nonhereditary title; hereditary/life peerage; den ~ ablegen to renounce one's title; einen ~ haben (inf) to have a title, to be titled.
  (c) (liter: edle Gesinnung) nobility. ~ der Seele/des Her-

zens/des Geistes nobility of the soul/of the heart/of mind.

adelig *adj siehe* **adlig.**

Adelige(r) *mf decl as adj siehe* **Adlige(r).**

adeln 1 *vt* to bestow a peerage on, to make a (life) peer (*Brit*), to ennoble; (*den Titel „Sir" verleihen*) to knight; (*niedrigen Adel verleihen*) to bestow a title on; (*fig liter: auszeichnen*) to ennoble. 2 *vi etw adelt* (*geh*) sth ennobles the soul.

Adels-: ~**bezeichnung** *f* title; ~**brief** *m* patent of nobility; ~**prädikat** *nt* mark of nobility (*in a name*); ~**stand** *m* nobility; (*Brit auch*) peerage; (*hoher auch*) aristocracy; a~**stolz** *adj* (*liter*) proud of one's noble birth; ~**stolz** *m* pride in one's noble birth; ~**titel** *m* title.

Adelung *f siehe vt* raising to the peerage; ennoblement; knighting; bestowing a title (*gen on*).

Adept(in *f)* *m* -en, -en (*old: der Geheimwissenschaften*) initiate; (*iro geh*) disciple.

Ader *f* -, -n (*Bot, Geol*) vein; (*Physiol*) blood vessel; (*Elec: Leitungsdraht*) core; (*fig: Veranlagung*) bent. **das spricht seine künstlerische/musikalische** ~ an that appeals to the artist/musician in him; **eine/keine** ~ **für etw haben** to have feeling/no feeling for sth; **eine poetische/musikalische** ~ **haben** to have a feeling for poetry/music, to be of *or* have a poetic/musical bent; **sich** (*dat*) **die** ~**n öffen** (*geh*) to slash one's wrists; **jdn zur** ~ **lassen** (*old, fig inf*) to bleed sb.

Äderchen *nt dim of* **Ader.**

Aderlaß *m* -lasses, -lässe (*old Med*) blood-letting (*auch fig*), bleeding. **bei jdm einen** ~ **machen** to bleed sb; **die Abwanderung der Akademiker ist ein** ~, **den sich das Land nicht länger leisten kann** the country can no longer afford the bleeding of its resources through the exodus of its academics.

ädern *vt* to make geädert.

Äderung *f* veining.

Adhäsion *f* (*Phys*) adhesion.

Adhäsions-: ~**kraft** *f* adhesive power, power of adhesion; ~**verschluß** *m* adhesive seal.

ad hoc *adv* (*geh*) ad hoc. ~ ~ **wurde ein Komitee gebildet** an ad hoc committee was set up.

Ad-Hoc-Maßnahme *f* ad hoc measure.

adieu [adiˈøː] *interj* (*old, dial*) adieu (*obs*), farewell (*old*). **jdm** ~ **sagen** to bid sb farewell (*old*), to say farewell *or* adieu to sb.

Adjektiv *nt* adjective.

adjektivisch *adj* adjectival.

Adjektivum *nt* -s, **Adjektiva** *siehe* **Adjektiv.**

Adjunkt *m* -en, -en (*Aus, Sw*) junior civil servant.

adjustieren* *vt* (a) (*Tech*) *Werkstück* to adjust; *Meßgerät* to set. (b) (*Aus*) to issue with uniforms/a uniform.

Adjustierung *f* (a) *siehe vt* adjustment; setting; issue of uniforms. (b) uniform.

Adjutant *m* adjutant; (*von General*) aide(-de-camp).

Adlatus *m* -, **Adlaten** *or* **Adlati** (*old, iro*) assistant.

Adler *m* -s, - eagle.

Adler-: ~**auge** *nt* (*fig*) eagle eye; ~**augen haben** to have eyes like a hawk, to be eagle-eyed; ~**blick** *m* (*fig*) eagle eye; ~**farn** *m* bracken; ~**horst** *m* (eagle's) eyrie; ~**nase** *f* aquiline nose.

adlig *adj* (*lit, fig*) noble. ~ **sein** to be of noble birth.

Adlige(r) *mf decl as adj* member of the nobility, nobleman/woman; (*Brit auch*) peer/peeress; (*hoher auch*) aristocrat.

Administration *f* administration.

administrativ *adj* administrative.

Administrator *m* administrator.

administrieren* *vi* (*geh: verwalten*) to administrate.

Admiral *m* -s, -e *or* **Admiräle** (a) admiral. (b) (*Zool*) red admiral.

Admiralität *f* (a) (*die Admirale*) admirals *pl*. (b) (*Marineleitung*) admiralty.

Admiralsrang *m* rank of admiral.

Adoleszenz *f* (*form*) adolescence.

Adonis *m* -, -se (*geh*) Adonis.

Adonisröschen *nt* pheasant's-eye.

adoptieren* *vt* to adopt.

Adoption *f* adoption.

Adoptiv-: ~**eltern** *pl* adoptive parents *pl*; ~**kind** *nt* adopted child.

Adr. *abbr of* **Addresse.**

Adrema ® *f* -, -s *abbr of* **Adressiermaschine.**

Adrenalin *nt* -s, *no pl* adrenalin.

Adressant *m* (*geh*) sender; (*Comm auch*) consignor (*form*).

Adressat *m* -en, -en (*geh*) addressee; (*Comm auch*) consignee (*form*). ~**en** (*fig*) target group.

Adressatengruppe *f* target group.

Adreßbuch *nt* directory; (*privat*) address book.

Adresse *f* -, -n (a) (*Anschrift, Datenverarbeitung*) address. **eine Warnung an jds** ~ (*acc*) **richten** (*fig*) to address a warning to sb; **dieser Vorwurf geht an Ihre eigene** ~ this reproach is directed at *or* addressed to you (personally); **sich an die richtige** ~ **wenden** (*inf*) to go/come to the right place *or* person/people; **an die falsche** *or* **verkehrte** ~ **kommen** *or* **geraten** (*all inf*) to go/come to the wrong person (*inf*); **an der falschen** ~ **sein** (*inf*) to have gone/come to the wrong person, to be knocking at the wrong door (*inf*).
(b) (*form: Botschaft*) address.

adressieren* *vt* to address (*an* +*acc* to).

Adressiermaschine *f* addressograph.

adrett *adj* (*dated*) neat.

Adria *f* - Adriatic (Sea).

Adriatisches Meer *nt* (*form*) Adriatic Sea.

Adstringens [atˈstrɪŋɡəns] *nt* -, -**genzien** astringent.

Advantage [adˈvaːntɪdʒ] *m*-s, -s (*Sport*) advantage.

Advent [atˈvɛnt] *m* -s, -e Advent. **im** ~ in Advent; **erster/vierter** ~ first/fourth Sunday in Advent.

Adventist [-vɛn-] *m* (*Rel*) (Second) Adventist.

Advents-: ~**kalender** *m* Advent calendar; ~**kranz** *m* Advent wreath; ~**sonntag** *m* Sunday in Advent; ~**zeit** *f* (season of) Advent.

Adverb [atˈvɛrp] *nt* -s, -(i)en adverb.

adverbial *adj* adverbial.

Adverbial-: ~**bestimmung** *f* adverbial qualification; **mit** ~**bestimmung** qualified adverbially; ~**satz** *m* adverbial clause.

adversativ [atvɛrzaˈtiːf] *adj* (*Gram*) adversative.

Adversativsatz *m* adversative clause.

Advocatus diaboli *m* - -, **Advocati** - (*geh*) devil's advocate.

Advokat [atvoˈkaːt] *m* -en, -en (*old Jur, fig*) advocate; (*Aus, Sw, auch pej*) lawyer.

Advokatur [-vo-] *f* (a) legal profession. (b) (*Büro*) lawyer's office.

Advokaturbüro *nt* (*Sw*), **Advokaturskanzlei** *f* (*Aus*) lawyer's office.

Aero- [aero] *in cpds* aero; ~**dynamik** *f* aerodynamics; a~**dynamisch** *adj* aerodynamic; ~**gramm** *nt* air-letter, aerogramme; ~**nautik** *f* aeronautics *sing*; a~**nautisch** *adj* aeronautic(al); ~**sol** *nt* -s, -e aerosol.

Affäre *f* -, -n (a) (*Angelegenheit*) affair, business *no pl*; (*Liebesabenteuer*) affair. **in eine** ~ **verwickelt sein** to be mixed up *or* involved in an affair; **sich aus der** ~ **ziehen** (*inf*) to get (oneself) out of it (*inf*). (b) (*Zwischenfall*) incident, episode.

Äffchen *nt dim of* **Affe.**

Affe *m* -n, -n (a) monkey; (*Menschen~*) ape. **der Mensch stammt vom** ~**n ab** man is descended from the apes; **der nackte** ~ the naked ape; **klettern wie ein** ~ to climb like a monkey; **du bist wohl vom wilden** ~**n gebissen!** (*sl*) you must be out of your tiny mind! (*inf*) *or* off your rocker! (*sl*); **einen** ~**n haben** (*sl*) to have had one over the eight (*inf*); *siehe* **lausen, Schleifstein.**
(b) (*sl: Kerl*) clown (*inf*), berk (*Brit sl*), twit (*Brit sl*). **ein eingebildeter** ~ a conceited ass (*inf*); **du (alter)** ~**!** (*sl*) you (great) berk *or* twit (*sl*).
(c) (*Mil inf*) knapsack.

Affekt *m* -(e)s, -e emotion, affect (*form*). **ein im** ~ **begangenes Verbrechen** a crime committed under the effect of emotion *or* in the heat of the moment; **im** ~ **handeln** to act in the heat of the moment.

Affekt-: a~**geladen** *adj* (*geh*) impassioned, passionate; ~**handlung** *f* act committed under the influence of emotion.

affektiert *adj* (*pej*) affected. **sich** ~ **benehmen** to be affected, to behave affectedly.

Affektiertheit *f* affectation, affectedness.

affektiv *adj* (*Psych*) affective.

Affektstau *m* (*Psych*) emotional block.

äffen *vt* (*liter, dial*) to make a fool of, to deceive.

Affen-: ~**arsch** *m* (*sl*) berk (*Brit sl*), stupid bum (*sl*); a~**artig** *adj* like a monkey; (*menschen~*) apelike; a~**artig klettern** to climb like a monkey; **mit a~artiger Geschwindigkeit** (*inf*) like greased lightning (*inf*), like *or* in a flash (*inf*); ~**brotbaum** *m* monkey-bread (tree), baobab; ~**geschwindigkeit** *f* (*inf*) *siehe* ~**tempo**; ~**haus** *nt* ape house; ~**hitze** *f* (*inf*) sweltering heat (*inf*); **gestern war eine** ~**hitze** yesterday was a scorcher (*inf*) *or* it was sweltering (*inf*); **dort ist zur Zeit eine** ~**hitze** it's boiling hot there at the moment; ~**jäckchen** *nt*, ~**jacke** *f* (*Mil inf*) monkey jacket; ~**käfig** *m* monkey's/ape's cage; **hier stinkt es/geht es zu wie in einem** ~**käfig** (*inf*) it smells like a sewer *or* stinks to high heaven in here (*inf*)/it's absolute pandemonium *or* bedlam here (*inf*); ~**liebe** *f* blind adoration (zuof); ~**mensch** *m* (*inf*) ape-man; ~**pinscher** *m* griffon (terrier); ~**schande** *f* (*inf*) crying shame (*inf*); ~**schaukel** *f* (*inf*) (*Mil*) fourragère; (*usu pl: Frisur*) looped plait; ~**schwein** *nt*: **ein** ~**schwein haben** (*sl*) to be hellish (*inf*) *or* bloody (*sl*) lucky; ~**spektakel** *nt* (*inf*) hullabaloo (*inf*), uproar; ~**stall** *m* (*sl*) (a) *siehe* ~**käfig**; (b) (*schlechte Unterkunft*) hole (*inf*); ~**tanz** *m* (*inf*) *siehe* ~**theater**; ~**tempo** *nt* (*inf*) breakneck speed (*inf*); **in** *or* **mit einem** ~**tempo** at breakneck speed (*inf*); (*laufen auch*) like the clappers (*sl*); ~**theater** *nt* (*inf*) to-do (*inf*), carry-on (*inf*), fuss; **ein** ~**theater aufführen** to make a fuss; ~**weibchen** *nt* female monkey/ape; ~**zahn** *m* (*sl*) *siehe* ~**tempo**.

affig *adj* (*inf*) (*eitel*) stuck-up (*inf*), conceited; (*geziert*) affected; (*lächerlich*) ridiculous, ludicrous. **sein** ~**arrogantes Benehmen** his stuck-up and arrogant behaviour; **sich** ~ **anstellen** *or* **haben** to be stuck-up (*inf*)/affected/ridiculous *or* ludicrous.

Affigkeit *f* (*inf*) (*Geziertheit*) affectedness; (*Lächerlichkeit*) ridiculousness, ludicrousness. **die** ~ **seines arroganten Benehmens** his being so stuck-up (*inf*) and acting so arrogantly.

Äffin *f* female monkey/ape.

Affinität *f* affinity.

Affirmation *f* (*geh*) affirmation.

affirmativ *adj* (*geh*) affirmative.

Affix *nt* -es, -e (*Ling*) affix.

affizieren* *vt* (*rare*) to affect.

Affrikata *f* -, **Affrikaten** (*Ling*) affricate.

Affront [aˈfrõː] *m* -s, -s (*geh*) affront, insult (*gegen* to).

Afghane *m* -n, -n, **Afghanin** *f* Afghan.

afghanisch *adj* Afghan. ~**er Windhund** Afghan (hound).

Afghanistan *nt* -s Afghanistan.

Afrika *nt* -s Africa.

Afrikaans *nt* - Afrikaans.

Afrikaner(in *f)* *m* -s, - African.

afrikanisch *adj* African.

Afrikanistik *f* African studies *pl*.

Afro-: ~-**Amerikaner** *m* Afro-American; ~-**Asiat** *m* Afro-Asian; ~-**Look** *m* -s Afro-look.

After m -s, - (form) anus.
After- (old pej): ~**kunst** f pseudo-art; ~**philosophie** f pseudo-philosophy; ~**rede** f calumny; ~**reden führen** to speak calumniously (form) or maliciously; a~**reden** vi insep to calumniate; **jdm a~reden** to calumniate sb, to speak ill of sb (old); ~**wissenschaft** f pseudo-science.
AG [aː'geː] f -, -s abbr of **Aktiengesellschaft** (public) limited company, Ltd (Brit), corporation, inc. (US).
Ägäis f - - Aegean (Sea).
ägäisch [ɛ'gɛːɪʃ] adj Aegean. Ä~**es Meer** Aegean Sea.
Agave f -, -n agave.
Agende f -, -n (Eccl) liturgy.
Agens nt -, **Agenzien** (Philos, Med, Ling) agent.
Agent m agent; (Spion) secret or foreign agent.
Agenten-: ~**netz** nt spy network; ~**ring** m spy ring; ~**tätigkeit** f espionage; **ihre ~tätigkeit** her activity as a secret or foreign agent.
Agentin f secret or foreign agent.
Agent provocateur [a'ʒãːprovoka'tøːɐ] m - -, -s -s agent provocateur.
Agentur f agency.
Agenturbericht m (news) agency report.
Agglomerat nt (Tech, Geol) agglomerate; (fig geh auch) agglomeration, conglomeration.
Agglutination f (Ling) agglutination.
agglutinieren* vi (Ling) to agglutinate. ~**d** agglutinative; **Sprache auch** agglutinating.
Aggregat nt (Geol) aggregate; (Tech) unit, set of machines.
Aggregatzustand m state. **die drei Aggregatzustände** the three states of matter.
Aggression f aggression (gegen towards). ~**en gegen jdn empfinden** to feel aggressive or aggression towards sb.
Aggressions-: a~**geladen** adj charged with aggression; a~**lüstern** adj (pej) belligerent, bellicose; ~**trieb** m (Psych) aggressive impulse.
aggressiv adj aggressive.
Aggressivität f aggression, aggressiveness.
Aggressor m aggressor.
Ägide f -, no pl (liter): **unter jds ~** (dat) (Schutz) under the aegis of sb; (Schirmherrschaft auch) under sb's patronage.
agieren* vi to operate, to act; (Theat) to act. **als Spekulant ~** to operate or act as a speculator; **als jd ~** (Theat) to act or play the part of sb.
agil adj (körperlich) agile, nimble. (geistig) ~ sharp, nimble-minded, mentally agile.
Agilität f siehe adj agility, nimbleness; sharpness, nimble-mindedness.
Agio ['aːdʒo] nt -s -, **Agien** ['aːdʒən] (Fin) (von Wertpapier) premium; (von Geldsorte) agio.
Agiopapiere pl (Fin) securities redeemable at a premium.
Agitation f (Pol) agitation. ~ **treiben** to agitate.
Agitator(in f) [-'toːrɪn] m (Pol) agitator.
agitatorisch adj (Pol) agitative; **Rede** inflammatory, agitating **attr.** ~ **argumentieren** to argue in an inflammatory style.
agitieren* vi to agitate.
Agitprop f -, no pl agitprop.
Agnostiker(in f) m -s, - agnostic.
agnostisch adj agnostic.
Agnostizismus m agnosticism.
Agonie f (lit, fig geh) throes pl of death, death pangs pl. **in (der) ~ liegen** to be in the throes of death; **das Land liegt in tiefer ~** the country is in the final throes of death.
Agrar- in cpds agrarian; ~**gesellschaft** f agrarian society.
Agrarier [-iɐ] m -s, - landowner; (hum, pej) country squire.
agrarisch adj agrarian.
Agrar-: ~**land** nt agrarian country; ~**markt** m agricultural commodities market; ~**politik** f agricultural policy; ~**zoll** m import tariff (on produce).
Agrément [agre'mãː] nt -s, -s (Pol) agrément. **einem Botschafter das ~ erteilen** to grant agrément to an ambassador.
Agrikultur f (form) agriculture.
Agrikulturchemie, Agrochemie f agricultural chemistry.
Agronom(in f) m (DDR) agronomist.
Agronomie f (DDR) agronomy.
Agrotechik f (DDR) agricultural technology.
Ägypten nt -s Egypt.
Ägypter(in f) m -s, - Egyptian.
ägyptisch adj Egyptian. ~**e Finsternis** (liter) Stygian darkness (liter).
Ägyptologie f Egyptology.
ah [aː] interj (genießerisch) ooh, ah, mmm; (überrascht, bewundernd, verstehend) ah, oh.
Ah nt -s, -s oh, ah.
äh [ɛː] interj (beim Sprechen) er, um; (Ausdruck des Ekels) ugh.
aha interj aha; (verstehend auch) I see.
Aha-Erlebnis nt sudden insight, aha-experience (Psych).
Ahle f -, -n awl; (Typ) bodkin.
Ahn m -(e)s or -en, -en (geh) ancestor, for(e)father (liter); (fig) for(e)bear (liter).
ahnden vt (liter) **Freveltat, Verbrechen** to avenge; (form) **Übertretung, Verstoß** to punish.
Ahn(d)l f -, -n or nt -s, -n (Aus) grandmother; (Urgroßmutter) great-grandmother.
Ahndung f siehe vt avengement; punishment.
Ahne¹ m -n, -n (liter) siehe **Ahn**.
Ahne² f -, -n (a) (geh) (weiblicher Vorfahr) ancestress; (fig) for(e)bear (liter).
(b) siehe **Ahn(d)l**.
ähneln vi +dat to be like, to be similar to, to resemble. **sich or**

einander (geh) ~ to be alike, to be similar, to resemble one another; **in diesem Punkt ähnelt sie sehr ihrem Vater** she's very like her father or very similar to her father or she greatly resembles her father in this respect; **diese Erklärung ähnelt seiner früheren Aussage überhaupt nicht mehr** this explanation bears no resemblance whatsoever to his earlier statement; **die beiden Systeme ~ einander nicht sehr/~ sich wenig** the two systems are not very similar or alike/have little in common.
ahnen 1 vt (voraussehen) to foresee, to know; **Gefahr, Tod** etc to have a presentiment or premonition or foreboding of; (vermuten) to suspect; (erraten) to guess. **das kann ich doch nicht ~!** I couldn't be expected to know that!; **nichts Böses ~** to have no sense of foreboding, to be unsuspecting; **nichts Böses ~d** unsuspectingly; **da sitzt man friedlich an seinem Schreibtisch, nichts Böses ~d ...** (hum) there I was sitting peacefully at my desk minding my own business ... (hum); **ohne zu ~, daß ...** without dreaming or suspecting (for one minute) that ...; **ohne es zu ~** without suspecting, without having the slightest idea; **davon habe ich nichts geahnt** I didn't have the slightest inkling of it, I didn't suspect it for one moment; **so etwas habe ich doch geahnt** I did suspect something like that; (ach), **du ahnst es nicht!** (inf) would you believe it! (inf); **du ahnst es nicht, wen ich gestern getroffen habe!** you'll never guess or believe who I met yesterday!; **die Umrisse waren/der Nußgeschmack war nur zu ~** the contours could only be guessed at/there was only the merest hint or suspicion of a nutty flavour.
2 vi (geh) **mir ahnt etwas Schreckliches** I have a dreadful foreboding; **mir ahnt nichts Gutes** I have a premonition that all is not well; **die Kinder im Nebenzimmer sind zu ruhig, mir ahnt nichts Gutes** (hum) the children are too quiet next door – it sounds rather suspicious or ominous!
Ahnen-: ~**bild** nt ancestral portrait; (auch ~**figur**) ancestral figure; ~**forschung** f genealogy; ~**galerie** f ancestral portrait gallery; ~**kult** m ancestor worship or cult; ~**paß** m (im Dritten Reich) proof of ancestry, pedigree; ~**reihe** f ancestral line; ~**tafel** f genealogical tree or table, genealogy, pedigree; ~**verehrung** f ancestor worship.
Ahn-: ~**frau** f (liter) ancestress; (Stammmutter) progenitrix (form, liter); ~**herr** m (liter) ancestor; (Stammvater) progenitor (form, liter).
ähnlich 1 adj similar (+ dat to). **ein dem Rokoko ~er Stil** a style similar to rococo, a similar style to rococo; **das dem Vater ~e Kind** the child that resembles his father or that is like his father; ~ **wie er/sie** like him/her; ~ **wie damals/vor 10 Jahren** as then/10 years ago; **sie sind sich ~** they are similar or alike; **ein ~ aussehender Gegenstand** a similar-looking object; **eine ~ komplizierte Sachlage** a similarly complicated state of affairs; **ich denke ~** my thinking is similar, I think likewise; **jdm ~ sehen** to be like sb, to resemble sb; **das sieht ihm (ganz) ~!** (inf) that's just like him!, that's him all over! (inf); (etwas) Ä~es something similar, something like it/that.
2 prep + dat similar to, like.
Ähnlichkeit f (mit to) (Vergleichbarkeit) similarity; (ähnliches Aussehen) similarity, resemblance. **mit jdm/etw ~ haben** to resemble sb/sth, to be like sb/sth.
Ahnung f (a) (Vorgefühl) hunch, presentiment; (düster) foreboding, premonition.
(b) (Vorstellung, Wissen) idea; (Vermutung) suspicion, hunch. **keine ~!** (inf) no idea! (inf), I haven't a clue! (inf); **er hat keine blasse or nicht die geringste ~** he hasn't a clue or the foggiest, he hasn't the faintest idea (all inf); **er redet zwar viel darüber, hat aber keine ~ davon** he talks a lot (about it) but he hasn't a clue or the slightest idea (inf) about it; **ich hatte keine ~, daß ...** I had no idea that ...; **hast du eine ~, wo er sein könnte?** have you any or an idea where he could be?; **du hast keine ~, wie schwierig das ist** you have no idea how difficult it is; **hast du eine ~!** (iro inf) a (fat) lot you know (about it)! (inf), that's what you know (about it)!
Ahnungs-: a~**los 1** adj (nichts ahnend) unsuspecting; (unwissend) clueless (inf); **2** adv unsuspectingly, innocently; ~**losigkeit** f (Unwissenheit) cluelessness (inf), ignorance; **er bewies seine völlige ~losigkeit darüber, daß ...** he showed how totally unsuspecting he was of the fact that ...; a~**voll** adj (geh) full of presentiment or (Böses ahnend) foreboding.
ahoi [a'hɔy] interj (Naut) **Schiff ~!** ship ahoy!
Ahorn m -s, -e maple.
Ahornblatt nt maple leaf.
Ähre f -, -n (Getreide~) ear; (allgemeiner, Gras~) head. ~**n lesen** to glean (corn).
Ähren-: ~**feld** nt field of (ripe) corn; ~**kranz** m garland of corn; ~**lese** f gleaning; ~**leser** m gleaner.
Aide-mémoire ['ɛːtme'moaːɐ] nt -, - aide-mémoire.
Air [ɛːɐ] nt -(s), -s (geh) air, aura.
Airbus ['ɛːɐbʊs] m (Aviat) airbus.
ais, Ais ['aːɪs] nt -, - A sharp.
Aischylos ['aɪsçylɔs] m - Aeschylus.
Akademie f academy; (Berg~, Forst~) college, school.
Akademiker(in f) m -s, - person with a university education; (Student) (university) student; (Hochschulabsolvent) (university) graduate; (Universitätslehrkraft) academic; (rare: Akademiemitglied) academician.
akademisch adj (lit, fig) academic. **die ~e Jugend** (the) students pl; **das ~e Proletariat** (the) jobless graduates pl; **das ~e Viertel** (Univ) the quarter of an hour allowed between the announced start of a lecture etc and the actual start; ~ **gebildet sein** to have (had) a university education, to be a graduate.
Akademisierung f **die ~ des öffentlichen Dienstes** turning the Civil Service into a graduate profession.
Akanthus m -, -, **Akanthusblatt** nt acanthus (leaf).
Akazie [-iə] f acacia.

Akelei f aquilegia, columbine.
Akklamation f (form, Aus) acclaim, acclamation. **Wahl per** or **durch** ~ election by acclamation.
akklamieren* (form, Aus) 1 vi to applaud (jdm sb). 2 vt Schauspieler, Szene to acclaim, to applaud; (wählen) to elect by acclamation.
Akklimatisation f (form) acclimatization.
akklimatisieren* 1 vr (lit, fig) (in +dat to) to become acclimatized, to acclimatize oneself/itself. 2 vt to acclimatize.
Akklimatisierung f acclimatization.
Akkolade f (a) (Typ) brace; (Mus) accolade. (b) (Hist) accolade.
Akkord m -(e)s, -e (a) (Mus) chord. (b) (Stücklohn) piece rate. **im** or **in** or **auf** ~ **arbeiten** to do piecework; **den** ~ **kaputtmachen** (inf) to sabotage the piece rate, to send the piece rate plummeting. (c) (Jur) settlement.
Akkord-: ~**arbeit** f piecework; ~**arbeiter** m piece-worker.
Akkordeon [-ɛɔn] nt -s, -s accordion.
Akkordeonist(in f), **Akkordeonspieler(in** f) m accordionist.
Akkord-: ~**lohn** m piece wages pl, piece rate; ~**satz** m piece rate; ~**zuschlag** m piece rate bonus.
akkreditieren* vt (a) (Pol) to accredit (bei to, at).
(b) (Fin) jdn ~ to give sb credit facilities; **akkreditiert sein** to have credit facilities; **jdn für einen Betrag** ~ to credit an amount to sb or sb's account, to credit sb or sb's account with an amount.
Akkreditierung f (a) (Pol) accrediting, accreditation (bei to, at). (b) (Fin) provision of credit facilities (gen to); (von Betrag) crediting.
Akkreditiv nt (a) (Pol) credentials pl. (b) (Fin) letter of credit. **jdm ein** ~ **eröffnen** to open a credit in favour of sb.
Akku ['aku] m -s, -s (inf) abbr of **Akkumulator** accumulator.
Akkumulation f accumulation.
Akkumulator m accumulator.
akkumulieren* vtir to accumulate.
akkurat 1 adj (dated, Aus, S Ger) precise; (sorgfältig auch) meticulous. 2 adv (esp Aus) precisely, exactly; (tatsächlich) naturally, of course.
Akkuratesse f, no pl (dated) siehe adj precision; meticulousness.
Akkusativ m accusative. **im** ~ **stehen** to be in the accusative.
Akkusativobjekt nt accusative object.
Akne f -, -n acne.
Akolyth, Akolyth m -en, -en (Eccl) acolyte.
Akonto nt -s, -s or **Akonten** (Aus) deposit.
Akontozahlung f payment on account.
akquirieren* [akvi'ri:rən] 1 vt (old) to acquire. 2 vi (Comm) to canvass for custom.
Akquisiteur [akvizi'tø:n] m agent, canvasser.
Akquisition [akvizitsi'o:n] f (old) acquisition; (Comm) (customer) canvassing.
Akribie f, no pl (geh) meticulousness, (meticulous) precision.
akribisch adj (geh) meticulous, precise.
Akrobat(in f) m -en, -en acrobat.
Akrobatik f, no pl acrobatics pl; (Geschicklichkeit) acrobatic abilities pl or skill.
akrobatisch adj acrobatic.
Akronym nt -s, -e acronym.
Akt[1] m -(e)s, -e (a) (Tat) act; (Zeremonie) ceremony, ceremonial act. (b) (Theat, Zirkus~) act. (c) (Art: ~bild) nude. (d) (Geschlechts~) sexual act, coitus no art (form).
Akt[2] m -(e)s, -en (Aus) siehe **Akte**.
Akt-: ~**aufnahme** f nude (photograph); ~**bild** nt nude (picture or portrait).
Akte f -, -n file, record. **die** ~ **Schmidt** the Schmidt file; **das kommt in die** ~**n** this goes on file or record; **etw zu den** ~**n legen** to file sth away, to put sth on file; (fig) Fall etc to drop.
Akten-: a~**bekannt** adj siehe a~**kundig**; ~**berg** m (inf) mountain of files or records (inf); ~**deckel** m folder; ~**einsicht** f (form) inspection of records or files; ~**koffer** m attaché case, executive case; a~**kundig** adj on record; a~**kundig werden** to be put on record; ~**mappe** f (a) (Tasche) briefcase, portfolio; (b) (Umschlag) folder, file; ~**notiz** f memo(randum); ~**ordner** m file; ~**schrank** m filing cabinet; ~**stoß** m pile of records or files; ~**tasche** f siehe ~**mappe** (a); ~**vermerk** m memo(randum); ~**wolf** m paper shredder; ~**zeichen** nt reference.
Akteur [ak'tø:n] m (geh) participant, protagonist.
Akt-: ~**foto** nt nude (photograph); ~**fotograf** m nude photographer, photographer of nudes; ~**fotografie** f nude photography; (Bild) nude (photograph); ~**gemälde** nt nude (painting).
Aktie ['aktsiə] f share; (~nschein) share certificate. **in** ~**n anlegen** to invest in (stocks and) shares; **die** ~**n fallen/steigen** share prices are falling/rising; **die** ~**n stehen gut** share prices are looking good, shares are buoyant; (fig) things or the prospects are looking good; **wie stehen die** ~**n?** (hum inf) how are things?; (wie sind die Aussichten) what are the prospects?
Aktien-: ~**besitz** m shareholdings pl, shares pl held; ~**besitzer** m shareholder, stockholder (esp US); ~**börse** f stock exchange; ~**gesellschaft** f joint-stock company; ~**index** m (Fin) share index; ~**kapital** nt share capital; (von Gesellschaft auch) (capital) stock; ~**kurs** m share price; ~**markt** m stock market; ~**mehrheit** f majority shareholding or interest.
Aktion f (Handlung) action (auch Mil); (Kampagne) campaign; (geplantes Unternehmen, Einsatz) operation (auch Mil). **in** ~ in action; **sie muß ständig in** ~ **sein** she always has to be active or on the go (inf); **in voller** ~ in action; **in** ~ **treten** to go into action.
Aktionär(in f) m shareholder, stockholder (esp US).

Aktionärsversammlung f shareholders' meeting.
Aktionismus m, no pl (Pol) actionism.
aktionistisch adj (Pol) actionist(ic).
Aktions-: ~**art** f (Gram) aspect; ~**ausschuß** m action committee; ~**einheit** f (Pol) unity in action, working unity; a~**fähig** adj capable of action; ~**komitee** nt action committee; ~**radius** m (Aviat, Naut) range, radius; (fig: Wirkungsbereich) scope (for action); a~**unfähig** adj incapable of action.
aktiv adj active; (Econ) Bilanz positive, favourable; (Mil) Soldat etc on active service. **sich** ~ **an etw** (dat) **beteiligen** to take an active part in sth; ~ **dienen** (Mil) to be on active duty or service; ~ **sein** (Univ) to be a full member of a/the students' association; siehe **Wahlrecht**.
Aktiv[1] nt (Gram) active.
Aktiv[2] nt -s, -s or -e (esp DDR) work team.
Aktiva pl assets. ~ **und Passiva** assets and liabilities.
Aktive f -n, -n (sl) fag (esp Brit sl), butt (US sl).
Aktive(r) mf decl as adj (Sport) active participant; (Univ) full member (of a/the students' association).
aktivieren* [akti'vi:rən] vt (Sci) to activate; (fig) Arbeit, Kampagne to step up; Mitarbeiter to get moving; (Comm) to enter on the assets side.
aktivisch adj (Gram) active.
Aktivismus m, no pl activism.
Aktivist m (DDR) activist.
Aktivität f activity.
Aktiv-: ~**posten** m (lit, fig) asset; ~**saldo** m credit balance; ~**seite** f assets side; ~**vermögen** nt realizable assets pl; ~**zinsen** pl interest receivable sing.
Akt-: ~**malerei** f nude painting; ~**modell** nt nude model.
Aktrice [ak'tri:sə] f -, -n (dated) actress.
aktsbekannt adj (Aus) siehe **aktenkundig**.
Aktstudie f nude study.
aktualisieren* vt to make topical.
Aktualität f relevance (to the present or current situation), topicality. ~**en** pl (geh: neueste Ereignisse) current events.
Aktuar m (a) (old) siehe **Gerichtsschreiber**. (b) (Sw) siehe **Schriftführer**.
aktuell adj relevant (to the current situation); Frage auch topical; Buch, Film auch of topical interest; Thema topical; (gegenwärtig) Problem, Theorie, Thema current; (Fashion: modern) Mode latest attr, current; Stil auch the (latest or current) fashion pred, fashionable; (Econ) Bedarf, Kaufkraft actual. **von** ~**em Interesse** or ~**er Bedeutung** of topical interest/of relevance to the present situation; **dieses Problem ist nicht mehr** ~ this is no longer a (current) problem; **das Buch ist wieder** ~ **geworden** the book has become relevant again or has regained topicality; **die Frage, ob ich das machen soll, ist doch nicht mehr** ~ the question as to whether I do it is no longer relevant; **eine** ~**e Sendung** (Rad, TV) a current-affairs programme.
Aktzeichnung f nude (drawing), drawing of a nude.
Akupunkteur [-'tø:n] m acupuncturist.
akupunktieren* 1 vt to acupuncture. 2 vi to perform acupuncture.
Akupunktur f acupuncture.
Akustik f, no pl (von Gebäude etc) acoustics pl; (Phys: Lehre) acoustics sing.
akustisch adj acoustic. **ich habe dich rein** ~ **nicht verstanden** I simply didn't catch what you said (properly).
akut adj (Med, fig) acute; Frage auch pressing, urgent.
Akut m -(e)s, -e acute (accent).
Akzent m -(e)s, -e (Zeichen, Aussprache) accent; (Betonung auch) stress; (fig auch) emphasis, stress. **den** ~ **auf etw** (acc) **legen** (lit) to stress sth, to put the stress or accent on sth; (fig auch) to emphasize sth; **dieses Jahr liegen die (modischen)** ~**e bei ...** this year the accent or emphasis is on ...; ~**e setzen** (fig) (Wichtiges hervorheben) to bring out or emphasize the main points or features; (Hinweise geben) to give the main points; **wo sollen wir die** ~ **setzen?** (fig) where are we to lay the stress or emphasis?; **dieses Jahr hat neue** ~**e gesetzt** this year has seen the introduction of new trends.
Akzent-: ~**buchstabe** m accented letter; a~**frei** adj without any or an accent.
akzentuieren* vt to articulate, to enunciate; (betonen) to stress; (fig: hervorheben) to accentuate.
Akzentverschiebung f (Ling) stress shift; (fig) shift of emphasis.
akzeptabel adj acceptable.
akzeptierbar adj acceptable.
akzeptieren* vt to accept.
Akzeptierung f acceptance.
Akzidens nt -, **Akzidenzien** [-iən] (Philos) accident; (Mus) accidental.
akzident(i)ell [-'tɛl, -tsi'ɛl] adj accidental.
Akzidenz f (Typ) job. ~**en** job printing.
Akzidenz-: ~**druck** m job printing; ~**druckerei** f jobbing printer's.
à la [a la] adv à la.
alaaf interj (dial) Kölle ~! up Cologne! (used in carnival procession).
Alabaster m -s, - (a) alabaster. (b) (dial: Murmel) marble.
Alarm m -(e)s, -e (Warnung) alarm; (Flieger~) air-raid warning; (Zustand) alert. **bei** ~ following an alarm/air-raid warning; (während) ~ during an alert; ~**!** fire!/air-raid! etc; ~ **schlagen** to give or raise or sound the alarm.
Alarm-: ~**anlage** f alarm system; a~**bereit** adj on the alert; Feuerwehr, Polizei auch standing by; **sich a~bereit halten** to be on the alert/standing by; ~**bereitschaft** f siehe adj alert; stand-by; **in** ~**bereitschaft sein** or **stehen** to be on the alert/standing

by; in ~bereitschaft versetzen to put on the alert, to alert; ~glocke f alarm bell.

alarmieren* vt Polizei etc to alert; (fig: beunruhigen) to alarm. ~d (fig) alarming; aufs höchste alarmiert (fig) highly alarmed.

Alarm-: ~ruf, ~schrei m warning cry; ~signal nt alarm signal; ~stufe f alert stage; ~übung f practice exercise or drill; ~vorrichtung f alarm; ~zustand m alert; im ~zustand sein to be on the alert; in den ~zustand versetzen to put on the alert.

Alaska nt -s Alaska.

Alaun m -s, -e alum.

Alaun-: ~stein, ~stift m styptic pencil.

Alb¹ m -(e)s, -en (Myth) elf.

Alb² f -, no pl (Geog) mountain region. die ~ the Swabian mountains pl.

Albaner(in f) m -s, - Albanian.

Albanien [-iən] nt -s Albania.

albanisch adj Albanian.

Albatros m -, -se albatross.

Albdruck m siehe Alpdruck.

Albe f -, -n (Eccl) alb.

Alben pl of Alb¹, Albe, Album.

Alberei f silliness; (das Spaßmachen) fooling about or around; (Tat) silly prank; (Bemerkung) inanity.

albern 1 adj silly, stupid, foolish; (inf: lächerlich) stupid, silly, ridiculous. sich ~ benehmen to act silly; (Quatsch machen) to fool about or around; ~es Zeug (silly) nonsense.

2 vi to fool about or around. ich weiß, ich bin unwiderstehlich, alberte er I know I'm irresistible he said jokingly.

Albernheit f (a) no pl (albernes Wesen) silliness, foolishness; (Lächerlichkeit) ridiculousness. (b) (Tat) silly prank; (Bemerkung) inanity.

Albinismus m, no pl albinism, albinoism.

Albino m -s, -s albino.

Albion ['albiən] nt -s (liter) Albion (poet).

Albtraum m siehe Alptraum.

Album nt -s, Alben album.

Alchemie (esp Aus), **Alchimie** f alchemy.

Alchemist(in f) (esp Aus), **Alchimist(in** f) m alchemist.

alchemistisch (esp Aus), **alchimistisch** adj alchemic(al).

Alemanne m -n, -n, **Alemannin** f Alemannic.

alemannisch adj Alemannic.

alert adj (geh) vivacious, lively.

Aleuten pl (Geog) die ~ the Aleutians.

Alexander m -s Alexander.

Alexandria f, **Alexandrien** [-iən] nt Alexandria.

Alexandriner m -s, - (Poet) alexandrine.

Alexandrit m -s, -e alexandrite.

Alge f -, -n alga.

Algebra f -, no pl algebra.

algebraisch adj algebraic(al).

Algerien [-iən] nt -s Algeria.

Algerier(in f) [-iɐ, -iɐrɪn] m -s, - Algerian.

algerisch adj Algerian.

Algier ['alʒiɐ] nt -s Algiers.

Algol nt -(s), no pl Algol.

Algorithmus m algorithm.

alias adv alias, also or otherwise known as.

Alibi nt -s, -s (Jur, fig) alibi.

Alibi-: ~beweis m (proof of one's) alibi; ~funktion f (fig) ~funktion haben to be used as an alibi.

Alimente pl maintenance sing.

alimentieren* vt (geh) to maintain, to support.

Alk m -(e)s, -en (Orn) auk.

Alkali nt -s, **Alkalien** [-iən] alkali. mit ~ düngen to fertilize with an alkali.

alkalisch adj alkaline.

Alkaloid nt -(e)s, -e alkaloid.

Alkohol ['alkoho:l, alko'ho:l] m -s, -e alcohol; (alkoholische Getränke auch) drink. seinen Kummer im ~ ertränken to drown one's sorrows; jdn unter ~ setzen to get sb drunk; unter ~ stehen to be under the influence (of alcohol or drink).

Alkohol-: a~arm adj low in alcohol (content); ~ausschank m sale of alcohol(ic drinks); ~einfluß m, ~einwirkung f influence of alcohol or drink; unter ~einfluß under the influence of alcohol or drink; ~fahne f (inf) smell of alcohol; eine ~fahne haben to smell of alcohol or drink; a~fest adj able to hold one's liquor or drink; a~frei adj non-alcoholic; Getränk auch soft; Gegend, Stadt dry; ein a~freies Café a café serving no alcohol, = an unlicensed café; ein a~freier Tag a day without drink or alcohol; ~gegner m opponent of alcohol; (selbst abstinent) teetotaller; (Befürworter des ~verbots) prohibitionist; ~gehalt m alcohol(ic) content; ~genuß m taking of alcohol; a~haltig adj alcoholic, containing alcohol.

Alkoholika pl alcoholic drinks pl, liquor sing.

Alkoholiker(in f) m -s, - alcoholic.

alkoholisch adj alcoholic.

alkoholisieren* vt Wein to fortify. jdn ~ (hum) to get sb drunk.

alkoholisiert adj (betrunken) inebriated. in ~em Zustand in a state of inebriation.

Alkoholismus m alcoholism.

Alkohol-: ~konsum m consumption of alcohol; ~pegel (hum), ~spiegel m jds ~pegel or ~spiegel the level of alcohol in sb's blood; a~süchtig adj addicted to alcohol, suffering from alcoholism; ~steuer f duty or tax on alcohol; ~sünder m (inf) drunk(en) driver; ~verbot nt prohibition (on alcohol); ~vergiftung f alcohol(ic) poisoning.

Alkoven [al'ko:vn, 'alko:vn] m -s, - alcove.

all indef pron ~ das/mein ... etc all the/my etc; siehe alle(r, s).

All nt -s, no pl (Sci, Space) space no art; (außerhalb unseres Sternsystems) outer space; (liter, geh) universe. **Spaziergang** im ~ space walk, walk in space; das weite ~ the immense universe.

all-: ~abendlich 1 adj (which takes place) every evening; der ~abendliche Spaziergang the regular evening walk; 2 adv every evening; ~bekannt adj known to all or everybody, universally known; ~da adv (old) in that (very) place; (relativisch) where; ~dem pron siehe alledem; ~dieweil (old, hum) 1 adv (währenddessen) all the while; 2 conj (weil) because.

alle 1 pron siehe alle(r, s). 2 adj pred (inf) all gone. die Milch ist ~ the milk's all gone, there's no milk left; etw ~ machen to finish sth off; ich bin ganz ~ I'm all in; ~ werden to be finished; (Vorräte auch) to run out.

alledem pron bei/trotz etc ~ with/in spite of etc all that; von ~ stimmt kein Wort there's no truth in any of that or it; zu ~ moreover.

Allee f -, -n [-e:ən] avenue.

Allegorie f allegory.

Allegorik f allegory. in der griechischen ~ in Greek allegory.

allegorisch adj allegorical.

Allegretto nt -s, -s or **Allegretti** allegretto.

Allegro nt -s, -s or **Allegri** allegro.

allein 1 adj pred (esp inf auch alleine) alone; Gegenstand, Wort auch by itself, on its own; (ohne Gesellschaft, Begleitung, Hilfe auch) by oneself, on one's own; (einsam) lonely, lonesome. für sich ~ by oneself, on one's own, alone; sie waren endlich ~ they were alone (together) or on their own at last; von ~ by oneself/itself; ich tue es schon von ~e I'll do that in any case; das weiß ich von ~(e) you don't have to tell me (that); ganz ~ (einsam) quite or all alone; (ohne Begleitung, Hilfe) all by oneself, all on one's own; jdm ganz ~ gehören to belong to sb alone, to belong completely to sb; auf sich (acc) ~ angewiesen sein to be left to cope on one's own, to be left to one's own devices.

2 adv (nur) alone. das ist ~ seine Verantwortung that is his responsibility alone, that is exclusively or solely his responsibility; nicht ~, ... sondern auch not only ... but also; ~ schon der Gedanke, (schon) der Gedanke ~ ... the very or mere thought ..., the thought alone ...; das Porto ~ kostet ... the postage alone costs ..., just the postage is ...

3 conj (old: jedoch) however, but.

Allein-: ~erbe m sole or only heir; ~flug m solo flight; im ~flug solo; ~gang m (inf) solo run; (von Bergsteiger) solo climb; (fig: Tat) solo effort; etw im ~gang machen (fig) to do sth on one's own; ~heit f (Philos) (universal) unity or oneness; ~herrschaft f autocratic rule, absolute dictatorship; (fig) monopoly; ~herrscher m autocrat, absolute dictator; der ~herrscher in der Familie sein (fig) to reign supreme in the family.

alleinig adj attr sole, only; (Aus, S Ger) (alleinstehend) single; (ohne Begleitung) unaccompanied.

Allein-: ~sein nt being on one's own no def art, solitude; (Einsamkeit) loneliness; a~seligmachend adj die a~seligmachende Kirche the only true church; er betrachtet sein Lehre als die a~seligmachende he considers his doctrine to be the only true one; a~stehend adj living on one's own, living alone; ~stehende(r) mf decl as adj single person; ~unterhalter m solo entertainer; ~untermiete f (Aus) subletting (where main tenant lives elsewhere); in ~untermiete wohnen = to live in a furnished flat; ~verkauf m sole or exclusive right of sale (+gen, von for); ~vertreter m (Comm) sole agent.

Alleinvertretung f (Comm) sole agency; (Pol) sole representation.

Alleinvertretungs-: ~anmaßung f (DDR Pol) unjustified claim to sole representation; ~anspruch m (Pol) claim to sole representation.

Alleinvertrieb m sole or exclusive marketing or distribution rights pl.

alleluja interj siehe halleluja.

allemal adv every or each time; (ohne Schwierigkeit) without any problem or trouble. was er kann, kann ich noch ~ anything he can do I can do too; ~! no problem or trouble! (inf); ein für ~ once and for all.

allenfalls adv (nötigenfalls) if need be, should the need arise; (höchstens) at most, at the outside; (bestenfalls) at best. es waren ~ 40 Leute da there were at most 40 people there, there were 40 people there at the outside; das schaffen wir ~ in 3 Stunden/bis übermorgen we'll do it in 3 hours/by the day after tomorrow at best.

allenthalben adv (liter) everywhere, on all sides.

alle(r, s) 1 indef pron (a) attr all; (bestimmte Menge, Anzahl) all the; (auf eine Person bezüglich: all sein) Geld, Liebe, Freunde, Erfahrungen all one's. ~ Kinder unter 10 Jahren all children under 10; ~ Kinder dieser Stadt all the children in this town; die Eltern fuhren mit ~n Kindern weg the parents went off with all their children; ~s Brot wird gebacken all bread is baked; im Geschäft war ~s Brot ausverkauft all the bread in the shop was sold out; er hat ~s Geld verloren he's lost all his money; ~ meine Kinder all (of) my children; ~ Liebe, die ich ihm entgegenbracht habe all the love I've shown him; wir haben ~n Haß vergessen we have forgotten all (our or the) hatred; ~ Anwesenden/Beteiligten/Betroffenen all those present/taking part/affected; ~s erforderliche Material all the required material; mit ~m Nachdruck with every emphasis; trotz ~r Mühe in spite of every effort; ohne ~n Grund without any reason, with no reason at all; mit ~r Deutlichkeit quite distinctly; in ~r Unschuld in all innocence; ohne ~n Zweifel without any doubt; siehe auch all.

(b) (substantivisch) ~s sing everything; (inf: alle Menschen) everybody, everyone; ~s, was ... all or everything that/everybody or everyone who ...; das ~s all that; ~s Schöne everything beautiful, all that is beautiful; „~s für das Baby/den Heimwerker" "everything for baby/the handyman"; (ich wünsche Dir) ~s Gute (I wish you) all the best; ~s und jedes anything and everything; in ~m (in jeder Beziehung) in everything; ~s in ~m all in all; trotz ~m in spite of everything; über ~s above all else; (mehr als alles andere) more than anything else; vor ~m above all; du bist mein ein und (mein) ~s you are everything to me, you are my everything or all; das ist ~s, das wäre ~s that's all, that's it (inf); das ist ~s Unsinn that's all nonsense; das ist ~s andere, als ... that's anything but ...; er ist ~s, nur kein Kaufmann he's anything but a salesman; das geht dich doch ~s nichts an! none of (all) that has anything to do with you!; das ist mir ~s gleich it's all the same to me; was soll das ~s? what's all this supposed to mean!; ~s schon mal dagewesen! (inf) it's all been done before!; es hat ~s keinen Sinn mehr nothing makes sense any more, it has all become meaningless; was habt ihr ~s gemacht? what did you get up to?; wer war ~s da? who was there?; was er (nicht) ~s weiß/kann! the things he knows/can do!; was es nicht ~s gibt! well (now) I've seen everything!, well I never ... (inf).

(c) (substantivisch) ~ pl all; (alle Menschen auch) everybody, everyone; sie sind ~ alt they're all old; die haben mir ~ nicht gefallen I didn't like any of them; ich habe (sie) ~ verschenkt I've given them all or all of them away; ~ beide/drei both of them/all three of them; ~ drei/die/diejenigen, die ... all three/(those) who ...; diese ~ all (of) these; der Kampf ~r gegen ~ the free-for-all; ~ für einen und einer für ~ all for one and one for all; sie kamen ~ they all came, all of them came; sie haben ~ kein Geld mehr none of them has any money left; redet nicht ~ auf einmal! don't all talk at once!

(d) (mit Zeit-, Maßangaben) usu pl every. ~ fünf Minuten/fünf Meter/halbe Stunde every five minutes/five metres/half-hour; ~ Jahre wieder year after year.

2 adj siehe **alle**.

aller- in cpds mit superl (zur Verstärkung) by far; das ~größte/die ~hübscheste by far the biggest/prettiest, the biggest/prettiest by far.

aller│aller- in cpds mit superl (inf: zur Verstärkung) far and away; das ~größte/die ~hübscheste far and away the biggest/prettiest.

aller-: ~art adj attr inv (dated) all sorts or kinds of; ~beste(r, s) adj very best, best of all, best ... of all; (exquisit) Waren, Qualität very best; ich wünsche Dir das A~beste (I wish you) all the best; der/die/das A~beste the very best/the best of all; du bist mein A~bester you're my (own) darling; es ist das ~beste or am ~besten, zu .../wenn ... the best thing would be to .../if ...; ~dings adv (a) (einschränkend) though, mind you; ich komme mit, ich muß ~dings erst zur Bank I'm coming but I must go to the bank first though, I'm coming though I must go to the bank first; das ist ~dings wahr, aber ... that may be true, but ...; (al)though that's true ...; (b) (bekräftigend) certainly; ~dings! (most) certainly!; ~erste(r, s) adj very first; ~frühestens adv at the very earliest.

Allergie f (Med) allergy; (fig) aversion (gegen to). eine ~ gegen etw haben to be allergic to sth (auch fig hum); (fig auch) to have an aversion to sth.

Allergiker(in f) m -s, - person suffering from an allergy.

allergisch adj (Med, fig) allergic (gegen to). auf etw (acc) ~ reagieren to have an allergic reaction to sth.

Aller-: a~hand adj inv (substantivisch) (allerlei) all kinds of things; (ziemlich viel) rather a lot; (attributiv) all kinds or sorts of; rather a lot of; das ist a~hand! (zustimmend) that's quite something!, not bad at all! (inf); das ist ja or doch a~hand! (empört) that's too much!, that's the limit!; ~heiligen nt -s All Saints' Day, All Hallows (Day); ~heiligste(s) nt decl as adj (Rel) inner sanctum; (jüdisch, fig) Holy of Holies; (katholisch) Blessed Sacrament; a~höchste(r, s) adj Berg etc highest of all, highest ... of all, very highest; Betrag, Belastung, Geschwindigkeit maximum; Funktionäre highest, top attr; Instanz, Kreise very highest; von a~höchster Stelle from the very highest authority; es wird a~höchste Zeit, daß ... it's really high time that ...; der ~höchste (Gott) the Most High (God); a~höchstens adv at the very most; a~lei adj inv (substantivisch) all sorts or kinds of things; (attributiv) all sorts or kinds of; ~lei nt -s, no pl (Durcheinander) farrago, pot pourri, welter; Leipziger ~lei (Cook) Leipzig mixed vegetables pl; a~letzte(r, s) adj very last; (a~neueste) very latest; (inf: unmöglich) most awful attr (inf); in a~letzter Zeit very recently; der/die/das ~letzte the very last (person)/thing; der/das ist (ja) das ~letzte (inf) he's/it's the absolute end! (inf); a~liebst adj (old: reizend) enchanting, delightful; a~liebste(r, s) adj (Lieblings-) most favourite attr; sie ist mir die ~liebste she's my absolute favourite; es wäre mir das a~liebste or am a~liebsten, wenn ... I would much prefer it if ...; am a~liebsten geh ich ins Kino I like going to the cinema most or best of all; ~liebste(r, s) mf decl as adj (old, hum) beloved, love of one's life; (Frau auch) ladylove; a~meiste(r, s) adj most of all, most ... of all; (weitaus beste) by far the most; die a~meiste Zeit the greatest part of the time by far, by far the greatest part of the time; am a~meisten most of all; das ~meiste ist schon geschafft by far the greatest part is already done; die ~meisten the vast majority; a~nächste(r, s) adj (in Folge) very next; (räumlich) nearest of all; Verwandte very closest; Route very shortest; in a~nächster Nähe right nearby, right close by; in a~nächster Zeit or Zukunft in the very near future; a~neu(e)ste(r, s) adj very latest; a~orten, a~orts adv (old) everywhere; ~seelen nt -s All Souls' Day; a~seits adv on all sides, on every side; guten Abend a~seits! good evening everybody or everyone or all;

vielen Dank a~seits thank you all or everybody or everyone; a~spätestens adv at the very latest.

Allerwelts- in cpds (Durchschnitts-) common; (nichtssagend) commonplace; ~kerl m Jack of all trades.

Aller-: a~wenigstens adv at the very least; a~wenigste(r, s) adj least of all, least ... of all; (pl) fewest of all, fewest ... of all; (äußerst wenig) very little; (pl) very few; (geringste) Mühe least possible; die a~wenigsten Menschen wissen das very (very) few people know that; das ist noch das a~wenigste Problem that's the (very) least of our problems; das ist noch das ~wenigste! that's the very least of it; das ist doch das ~wenigste, was man erwarten könnte but that's the very least one could expect; am a~wenigsten arbeiten/mögen to work/like least; (bei Vergleichen) to work/like least of all; er hat von uns allen das a~wenigste or am a~wenigsten Geld he has the least money of any of us; sie hat von uns allen die a~wenigsten or am a~wenigsten Sorgen she has the fewest worries of any of us; am a~wenigsten schön the least attractive; das am a~wenigsten! least of all that!; ~werteste(r) m decl as adj (hum) posterior (hum).

alles indef pron siehe **alle(r, s) (b)**.

allesamt adv all (of them/us etc), to a man. ihr seid ~ Betrüger! you're all cheats!, you're cheats, all or the lot of you!

Alles-: ~fresser m omnivore; ~kleber m all-purpose adhesive or glue; ~wisser m -s, - (iro) know-all (inf), know-it-all (US inf).

allewege adv (old) everywhere.

allezeit adv (liter) siehe **allzeit**.

All-: a~fällig adv (Aus, Sw) where applicable; zuzüglich a~fällig anfallende Portokosten, wenn ... plus relevant postal charges if or when ...; ~fällige(s) nt decl as adj (Aus, Sw) miscellaneous; ~gegenwart f omnipresence, ubiquity; a~gegenwärtig adj omnipresent, ubiquitous.

allgemein 1 adj general; Ablehnung, Zustimmung auch common; Feiertag public; Regelungen, Wahlrecht, Wehrpflicht universal; (öffentlich auch) public. im ~en in general, generally; im ~en Interesse in the common interest; in the public interest; von ~em Interesse of general interest; ~e Redensarten (idiomatische Ausdrücke) set expressions; (Phrasen) commonplaces; auf ~en Wunsch by popular or general request; die ~e Meinung the general opinion, the generally held opinion; public opinion; das ~e Wohl the common good; (the) public welfare, the public good; zur ~en Überraschung to the surprise of everyone, to everyone's surprise; die Diskussion darüber wurde ~ a general discussion developed; wir sind ganz ~ geblieben (inf) we stayed on a general level; das A~e und das Besondere the general and the particular.

2 adv (überall, bei allen, von allen) generally; (ausnahmslos von allen) universally; (generell auch) in the main, for the most part; (nicht spezifisch) in general terms. seine Thesen sind so ~ abgefaßt, daß ... his theses are worded in such general terms that ...; du kannst doch nicht so ~ behaupten, daß ... you can't make such a generalization and say that ..., you can't generalize like that and say that ...; es ist ~ bekannt it's common knowledge; es ist ~ üblich, etw zu tun it's the general rule that we/they etc do sth, it's commonly or generally the practice to do sth; ~ verbreitet widespread; ~ zugänglich open to all, open to the general public.

Allgemein-: ~befinden nt general condition, general state of being; a~bildend adj providing (a) general or all-round education; Studium auch with general educational value; eine Schule, die a~bildend ist a school that provides (a) general or all-round education; ~bildung f general or all-round education; a~gültig adj attr general, universal, universally or generally applicable or valid; ~gültigkeit f universal or general validity, universality; ~gut nt (fig) common property; ~heit f (a) (no pl: Öffentlichkeit) general public, public at large; (alle) everyone, everybody; (b) (no pl: Unbestimmtheit), (Unspezifisches) generality; ~medizin f general medicine; Arzt für ~medizin general practitioner, GP; ~platz m (pej) commonplace, platitude; a~verbindlich adj attr generally binding; a~verständlich adj no pred generally intelligible, intelligible to all; ~wissen nt general knowledge; ~wohl nt public good or welfare.

All-: ~gewalt f (liter) omnipotence; a~gewaltig adj omnipotent, all-powerful; a~gütig adj (liter) all-bountiful (liter); ~heilmittel nt universal remedy, cure-all, panacea (esp fig); a~hier adv (obs, liter) here.

Allianz f alliance.

Alligator m alligator.

alliieren* vr (geh) to form an alliance. sich mit jdm ~ to ally (oneself) with sb.

alliiert adj attr allied; (im 2. Weltkrieg) Allied.

Alliierte(r) mf decl as adj ally. die ~n (im 2. Weltkrieg) the Allies.

Alliteration f (Poet) alliteration.

alliterierend adj (Poet) alliterative.

alljähr. abbr of **alljährlich**.

All-: a~jährlich 1 adj annual, yearly; 2 adv annually, yearly, every year; ~macht f (esp von Gott) omnipotence; (von Konzern etc) all-pervading power; a~mächtig adj all-powerful, omnipotent; Gott auch almighty; ~mächtige(r) m decl as adj (Gott) der ~mächtige Almighty God, God (the) Almighty, the Almighty; ~mächtiger! good Lord!, heavens above!

allmählich 1 adj attr gradual.

2 adv gradually; (schrittweise auch) bit by bit, step by step; (inf: endlich) at last. es wird ~ Zeit (inf) it's about time; ~ verstand er, daß ... it gradually dawned on him that ..., he realized gradually that ...; ich werde (ganz) ~ müde (inf) I'm beginning to get tired; hoffentlich kommst du ~! (inf) are you coming at

last?; **wir sollten ~ gehen** (*inf*) shall we think about going?
Allmende *f* -, -n common land.
All-: a~**monatlich** 1 *adj* monthly; 2 *adv* every month, monthly; a~**morgendlich** 1 *adj* which takes place every morning; die a~**morgendliche Eile** the regular morning rush; 2 *adv* every morning; ~**mutter** *f* (*liter*) Mother of all; **die ~mutter Natur** Mother Nature; a~**nächtlich** 1 *adj* nightly; 2 *adv* nightly, every night.
Allongeperücke [a'lõ:ʒə-] *f* full-bottomed wig.
Allopath *m* -en, -en allopath(ist).
Allopathie *f* allopathy.
allopathisch *adj* allopathic.
Allotria *nt* -(s), *no pl* (*inf*) (*Unfug*) monkey business (*inf*) *no indef art*; (*ausgelassen, freudig*) skylarking (*inf*) *no indef art*, fooling around *or* about (*inf*) *no indef art*; (*Lärm*) racket (*inf*), din. ~ **treiben** (*inf*) to lark about (*inf*), to fool around *or* about (*inf*).
Allradantrieb *m* all-wheel drive.
Allround- ['ɔːl'raʊnd] *in cpds* all-round ...; ~**sportler**/ ~**künstler**/~**wissenschaftler** *m* all-round sportsman/artist/ scientist, all-rounder; ~**man** *m* -s, -men all-rounder.
allseitig *adj* (*allgemein*) general; (*ausnahmslos*) universal; (*vielseitig*) all-round *attr*. ~ **begabt sein** to have all-round talents, to be an all-rounder; **jdn** ~ **ausbilden** to provide sb with a general *or* an all-round education; **zur** ~**en Zufriedenheit** to the satisfaction of all *or* everyone; ~ **interessiert sein** to have all-round interests.
allseits *adv* (*überall*) everywhere, on all sides; (*in jeder Beziehung*) in every respect.
Allstrom-: ~**empfänger** *m* (*Rad*) all-mains *or* AC-DC receiver; ~**gerät** *nt* (*Rad*) all-mains *or* AC-DC appliance.
allstündlich (*geh*) 1 *adj* hourly. 2 *adv* hourly, every hour.
Alltag *m* (a) (*Werktag*) weekday. **am ~, an ~en** on weekdays; **Kleidung, die man am ~** trägt clothes for everyday wear; **mitten im ~** in the middle of the week. (b) (*fig*) everyday life. **der ~ der Ehe** the mundane side of married life.
alltäglich *adj* (a) (*tagtäglich*) daily. **er ging ~ in die Kirche** he went to church daily *or* every day.
(b) (*üblich*) everyday *attr*, ordinary, mundane (*pej*); *Gesicht, Mensch* ordinary; *Bemerkung* commonplace. **es ist ganz ~** it's nothing unusual *or* out of the ordinary; **das ist nichts A~es, daß/wenn ...** it doesn't happen every day that ..., it's not every day that ...; **was ich suche, ist nicht das A~e** I'm looking for something a bit out of the ordinary.
Alltäglichkeit *f* (a) *no pl siehe adj* (b) ordinariness; commonplaceness. **er sucht Abenteuer jenseits der grauen ~** he's looking for adventure beyond the mundane world of everyday life. (b) (*Gemeinplatz*) commonplace.
alltags *adv* on weekdays. **etw ~ tragen** to wear sth for every day.
Alltags- *in cpds* everyday; ~**beispiel** *nt* example (taken) from everyday life; ~**ehe** *f* mundane marriage; ~**leben** *nt* everyday life; **danach begann wieder das ~leben** after that life got back to normal again; ~**mensch** *m* ordinary person; ~**rhythmus** *m* daily rhythm; ~**trott** *m* (*inf*) daily round, treadmill of everyday life; ~**wort** *nt* everyday *or* household word.
allüber|all *adv* (*old, poet*) everywhere.
all|umfassend *adj* all-embracing, global.
Allüren *pl* behaviour; (*geziertes Verhalten*) affectations *pl*; (*eines Stars etc*) airs and graces *pl*.
Alluvium [a'lu:viʊm] *nt* -s, *no pl* diluvial *or* holocene epoch.
All-: ~**vater** *m* (*liter*) Father of all; a~**verehrt** *adj attr* universally revered; a~**weg** *adv* (*dial*) anyway, in any case; a~**weil** *adv* (*dial*) always; a~**wissend** *adj* omniscient; (*Gott*) **der** ~**wissende** God the Omniscient; **sie tut immer so** a~**wissend** she acts as though she knows everything; **ich bin nicht** a~**wissend!** I don't know everything!, I'm not omniscient!; ~**wissenheit** *f* omniscience; a~**wöchentlich** 1 *adj* weekly; 2 *adv* every week; a~**zeit** *adv* (*geh*) always; a~**zeit bereit!** be prepared!
allzu *adv* all too; (+*neg*) too. ~ **viele Fehler** far too many mistakes; **nur ~** only *or* all too.
allzu-: ~**früh** *adv* far too early; (+*neg*) too early; ~**gern** *adv* **mögen** only too much; (*bereitwillig*) only too willingly; (+*neg*) all that much/willingly, too much/willingly; **etw (nur)** ~**gern/nicht** ~**gern machen** to like doing sth only too much/not like doing sth all that much *or* too much *or* overmuch; **er ißt Muscheln nur** ~**gern** he's only too fond of mussels; ~**gleich** *adv* (*poet*) *siehe* zugleich; ~**hauf** *adv* (*obs*) *siehe* zuhauf; ~**mal** *adv* (*old, liter*) (a) (*zusammen*) all; (b) (*besonders weil*) especially as *or* since; (*überhaupt*) by far; ~**sehr** *adv* too much; **mögen** all too much; (+*neg*) too much, all that much, overmuch; **sich freuen, erfreut sein** only too; (+*neg*) too; **versuchen** too hard; **sich ärgern, enttäuscht sein** too; **... — nicht** ~**sehr ...** — not too much *or* all that much; **sie war** ~**sehr/nicht** ~**sehr in ihn verliebt** she was too much/wasn't too in love with him; ~**viel** *adv* too much; (+*neg*) too much; ~**viel ist ungesund** (*Prov*) you can have too much of a good thing (*prov*).
Allzweck- *in cpds* general purpose; ~**halle** *f* multi-purpose hall.
Alm *f* -, -en alpine pasture.
Alm|abtrieb *m* driving cattle down from the alpine pastures.
Alma mater *f* - -, *no pl* alma mater.
Almanach *m* -s, -e almanac.
Alm-: ~**auftrieb** *m* driving cattle up to the alpine pastures; ~**hütte** *f* alpine hut.
Almosen [-oː-] *nt* -s, - (a) (*geh: Spende*) alms *pl* (*old*). ~ *pl* (*fig*) charity. (b) (*geringer Lohn*) pittance.
Almrausch *m*, **Almrose** *f siehe* Alpenrose.
Aloe ['aːloe] *f* -, -n aloe.

alogisch *adj* (*geh*) illogical.
Alp¹ *f* -, -en *siehe* Alm.
Alp² *m* -(e)s, -e (*old: Nachtmahr*) demon believed to cause nightmares; (*fig geh: Bedrückung*) nightmare. **ihn drückte der** ~ (*old*) he had a nightmare; **jdm wie ein** ~ **auf der Brust liegen** (*fig geh*), **wie ein** ~ **auf jdm lasten** (*fig geh*) to lie or weigh heavily (up)on sb.
Alpaka *nt* -s, -s (a) (*Lamaart*) alpaca. (b) (*auch* ~**wolle**) alpaca (wool). (c) *no pl* (*Neusilber*) German *or* nickel silver.
Alp-: ~**druck** *m* (*lit, fig*) nightmare; **wie ein** ~**druck auf jdm lasten** to weigh sb down, to oppress sb; ~**drücken** *nt* -s, *no pl* nightmares *pl*.
Alpen *pl* Alps *pl*.
Alpen- *in cpds* alpine; ~**dollar** *m* (*hum*) Austrian schilling; ~**glühen** *nt* -s, - alpenglow; ~**jäger** *m* (*Mil*) mountain infantryman; *pl* mountain troops *pl or* infantry; ~**kette** *f* alpine chain; ~**land** *nt* alpine country; a~**ländisch** *adj* alpine; ~**paß** *m* alpine pass; ~**republik** *f* (*hum*) **die** ~**republiken** Austria and Switzerland; ~**rose** *f* Alpine rose *or* rhododendron; ~**rot** *nt* -s, *no pl* red snow; ~**veilchen** *nt* cyclamen; ~**vorland** *nt* foothills *pl* of the Alps.
alph. *abbr of* alphabetisch.
Alpha *nt* -(s), -s alpha.
Alphabet *nt* -(e)s, -e alphabet. **nach dem** ~ alphabetically, in alphabetical order; **das** ~ **lernen/aufsagen** to learn/say the *or* one's alphabet.
alphabetisch *adj* alphabetical. ~ **geordnet** arranged in alphabetical order *or* alphabetically.
alphabetisieren* *vt* to make literate.
Alphabetisierung *f* **ein Programm zur** ~ **Indiens** a programme against illiteracy in India; **die** ~ **Kubas ist abgeschlossen** the population of Cuba is now largely literate; **die fortschreitende** ~ **der Länder der Dritten Welt** the increasing literacy rate in the Third World countries.
Alpha-: ~**strahlen** *pl* alpha rays *pl*; ~**teilchen** *nt* alpha particle.
Alp-: ~**horn** *nt* alp(en)horn; ~**hütte** *f siehe* Almhütte.
alpin *adj* alpine.
Alpinist(in *f*) *m* alpinist.
Alpinistik *f* alpinism.
Älpler(in *f*) *m* -s, - alpine farmer.
älplerisch *adj* Tyrolean *no adv*.
Alp-: ~**traum** *m* (*lit, fig*) nightmare; a~**traumartig** *adj* nightmarish.
Alraun *m* -(e)s, -e, **Alraune** *f* -, -n mandrake.
als 1 *conj* (a) (*nach comp*) than. **ich kam später** ~ **er** I came later than he (did) *or* him; **Hans ist größer** ~ *or* ~ **wie** (*strictly incorrect*) **sein Bruder** Hans is taller than his brother; **mehr** ~ **arbeiten kann ich nicht** I can't do more than work.
(b) (*bei Vergleichen*) so ... ~ ... as ... as ...; **soviel/soweit** ~ **möglich** as much/far as possible; ~ **wie** as; **nichts/niemand/ nirgend anders** ~ nothing/nobody/nowhere but; **eher** *or* **lieber ...** ~ rather ... than; **ich würde eher sterben** ~ **das zu tun** I would rather die than do that *or* die rather than do that; **anders sein** ~ to be different from; **das machen wir anders** ~ **ihr** we do it differently to you; **alles andere** ~ anything but.
(c) (*in Modalsätzen*) as if *or* though. **es sieht aus, ~ würde es bald schneien** it looks as if *or* though it will snow soon; **sie sah aus,** ~ **ob** *or* **wenn sie schliefe** she looked as if *or* though she were asleep; ~ **ob ich das nicht wüßte!** as if I didn't know!; *siehe auch* ob.
(d) (*in Aufzählung*) ~ (**da sind**): ... that is to say, ..., to wit, ... (*old, form*).
(e) (*in Konsekutivsätzen*) **sie ist zu alt,** ~ **daß sie das noch verstehen könnte** she is too old to understand that; **die Zeit war zu knapp,** ~ **daß wir ...** the time was too short for us to ...; **das ist um so trauriger,** ~ **es nicht das erste Mal war** that's all the sadder in that it wasn't the first time.
(f) (*in Temporalsätzen*) when; (*gleichzeitig*) as. **gleich,** ~ **as** soon as; **damals,** ~ (*in the days*) when; **gerade,** ~ just as.
(g) (*in der Eigenschaft*) as. ~ **Beweis** as proof; ~ **Antwort/Warnung** as an answer/a warning; **sich** ~ **wahr/falsch erweisen** to prove to be true/false; ~ **Held/Revolutionär** as a hero/revolutionary; ~ **Kind/Mädchen** *etc* as a child/girl *etc*; ~ **Rentner** will **er ein Buch schreiben** when he retires he is going to write a book; *siehe* sowohl, insofern, insoweit.
2 *adv* (*dial inf*) (a) (*immer*) **etw** ~ (*nochmal*) **tun** to keep on (and on) doing sth; **er hat ihn geschlagen und** ~ **nochmal** he hit him time after time; **gehen Sie** ~ **geradeaus** keep going straight ahead.
(b) (*manchmal*) sometimes.
als-: ~**bald** *adv* (*old, liter*) directly, straightway (*old*); ~**baldig** *adj* (*form*) immediate; „**zum** ~**baldigen Verbrauch bestimmt**" "do not keep", "for immediate use only"; ~**dann** *adv* (a) (*old liter: dann*) then; (b) (*dial*) well then, well ... then.
also 1 *conj* (a) (*folglich*) so, therefore. **er war Künstler, ein hochsensibler Mensch** ~ he was an artist, (and) therefore a highly sensitive person.
(b) (*old: so, folgendermaßen*) thus.
2 *adv* so; (*nach Unterbrechung anknüpfend*) well; (*zusammenfassend, erklärend*) that is. ~ **doch** so ... after all; **du machst es** ~? so you'll do it then?; ~ **wie ich schon sagte** well (then), as I said before.
3 *interj* (*verwundert, entrüstet, auffordernd*) well; (*drohend*) just. ~, **daß du dich ordentlich benimmst!** (you) just see that you behave yourself!; ~ **doch!** so he/they did!; **na** ~! there you are!, you see?; ~, **ich hab's doch gewußt!** I knew it!; ~ **nein!** (oh) no!; ~ **nein, daß sie sich das gefallen läßt** my God, she can't put up with that!; ~ **gut** *or* **schön** well all right then; ~ **dann!** right then!; ~ **so was/so eine Frechheit!** well (I never)/what a cheek!

Als-|ob nt -, no pl fiction. **die Philosophie des** ~ the philosophy of "as-if".

alt adj, comp ¨er, superl ¨este(r, s) or adv am ¨esten **(a)** old; (betagt) Mensch auch aged (liter); (sehr ~) Mythos, Sage, Aberglaube auch, Griechen, Geschichte ancient; Sprachen classical. **das** ~e **Rom** ancient Rome; **das A**~e **Testament** the Old Testament; **die A**~ **Welt** the Old World; **A**~er **Herr** (Univ) graduate member of a fraternity; **der** ~e **Herr** (inf: Vater) the or one's old man (inf); **die** ~e **Dame** (inf: Mutter) the old lady (inf); ~er **Junge** or **Freund** or **Schwede** (dated inf) old boy (dated) or fellow (dated); ~ **und jung** (everybody) old and young; **ein drei Jahre** ~es **Kind** a three-year-old child, a child of three years of age; **wie** ~ **bist du?** how old are you?; **etw** ~ **kaufen** to buy sth second-hand; **man ist so** ~, **wie man sich fühlt** you're only as old as you feel (prov); **ich werde heute nicht** ~ **(werden)** (inf) I won't last long today/tonight etc (inf); **hier werde ich nicht** ~ (inf) this isn't my scene (inf); **aus** ~ **mach neu** (Prov inf) make do and mend (Prov); siehe **Eisen, Hase, Haus.**

(b) (dieselbe, gewohnt) same old. **sie ist ganz die** ~e **(Ingrid)** she's the same old Ingrid, she hasn't changed a bit; **jetzt ist sie wieder ganz die** ~e **lustige** or **die** ~e **Veronika** she's the old happy/old Veronika again; **wir bleiben die** ~en, **auch wenn sich alle andern verändern** we stay the same even when everybody else changes; **er ist nicht mehr der** ~e he's not what he was or the man he was; **es ist nicht mehr das** ~e **(Glasgow)** it's not the (same old) Glasgow I/we etc knew; **alles bleibt beim** ~en everything stays as it was; **alles beim** ~en **lassen** to leave everything as it was.

(c) (lange bestehend) old. ~e **Liebe rostet nicht** (Prov) true love never dies (prov); **in** ~er **Freundschaft, dein ...** yours as ever ...

Alt¹ m -s, -e (Mus) alto; (von Frau auch) contralto; (Gesamtheit der Stimmen) altos pl; contraltos pl.

Alt² nt -s, - siehe **Altbier.**

alt-: ~**adelig** adj belonging to the old nobility; ~**amerikanisch** adj old American.

Altan m -(e)s, -e balcony.

alt-: ~**angesehen** adj Familie old and respected; Firma old-established; ~**angesessen,** ~**ansässig** adj old-established.

Altar m -s, **Altäre** altar. **eine Frau zum** ~ **führen** to lead a woman to the altar; **jdn/etw auf dem** ~ **des Vaterlandes opfern** to sacrifice sb/sth for one's country.

Altar- in cpds altar; ~**bild** nt altarpiece, reredos; ~**gemälde** nt altarpiece; ~**gerät** nt altar furniture; ~**raum** m chancel.

Alt-: **a**~**backen** adj **(a)** stale; **(b)** (fig) Mensch old-fashioned; Kleidung, Ansichten auch outdated, out of date; ~**bau** m old building; ~**bauwohnung** f old flat, flat in an old building; **a**~**bekannt** adj well-known; **a**~**bewährt** adj Mittel, Methode etc well-tried; Sitte, Tradition, Freundschaft etc long-standing usu attr, of long standing; ~**bier** nt top-fermented German dark beer; ~**bundeskanzler** m former German Chancellor; ~**bürger(in** f) m senior citizen; **a**~**christlich** adj early Christian; **a**~**deutsch** adj old German; Möbel, Stil German Renaissance.

Alte siehe **Alte(r), Alte(s).**

Alt-: **a**~**ehrwürdig** adj venerable; Bräuche time-honoured; **a**~**eingeführt** adj introduced long ago; **a**~**eingesessen** siehe **a**~**angesessen;** ~**eisen** nt scrap metal; **a**~**englisch** adj old English; ~**englisch(e)** nt Old English, Anglo-Saxon.

Alten-: ~**heim** nt siehe **Altersheim;** ~**herrschaft** f gerontocracy; ~**hilfe** f old people's welfare; ~**pfleger** m old people's nurse; ~**tagesstätte** f old people's day centre; ~**teil** nt cottage or part of a farm reserved for the farmer when he hands the estate over to his son; **sich aufs** ~**teil setzen** or **zurückziehen** (fig) to retire or withdraw from public life.

Alte(r) mf decl as adj (alter Mann, inf: Ehemann, Vater) old man; (alte Frau, inf: Ehefrau, Mutter) old woman; (inf: Vorgesetzter) boss. **die** ~**n** (Eltern) the folk(s) pl (inf); (Tiereltern) the parents pl; (ältere Generation) the old people or folk pl; (aus klassischer Zeit) the ancients pl; **wie die** ~**n singen, so zwitschern auch die Jungen** (prov) like father like son (prov); **komischer** ~**r** (Theat) comic old man.

Alter nt -s, - age; (letzter Lebensabschnitt, hohes ~) old age. **im** ~ **in one's old age; im** ~ **wird man weiser** one grows wiser with age; **in deinem** ~ **at your age; er ist in deinem** ~ **he's your age; im** ~ **von 18 Jahren** at the age of 18; **von mittlerem** ~ **middle-aged; 45, das ist doch kein** ~ (inf) 45, that's no age at all; **er hat keinen Respekt vor dem** ~ **he has no respect for his elders;** ~ **schützt vor Torheit nicht** (Prov) there's no fool like an old fool (prov).

älter adj (a) comp of **alt** older; Bruder, Tochter etc auch elder. **werden Frauen** ~ **als Männer?** do women live longer than men? **(b)** attr (nicht ganz jung) elderly. **die** ~**en Herrschaften** the older members of the party.

Älterchen nt (inf) Grandad (inf).

Ältere(r) mf decl as adj **(a)** (älterer Mensch) older man/woman etc. **die** ~**n** the older ones. **(b)** (bei Namen) elder.

alt|erfahren adj experienced, of long experience.

altern 1 vi aux sein or (rare) haben to age; (Mensch auch) to get older; (Wein) to mature. **vorzeitig** ~ to grow old before one's time; ~**d** ageing. **2** vt to age; Wein to mature; Metall to age-harden.

alternativ adj (geh) alternative.

Alternativ- in cpds alternative.

Alternative f alternative (etw zu tun of doing sth).

alternieren* vi to alternate.

alternierend adj alternate; Strom, Verse alternating; Fieber intermittent.

alt|erprobt adj well-tried.

alters adv (geh) von or seit ~ (her) from time immemorial; **vor** ~ in olden days or times, in days of yore (old, liter).

Alters-: ~**abbau** m senile decay; ~**abstand** m age difference; ~**asyl** nt (Sw) siehe ~**heim;** ~**aufbau** m siehe ~**gliederung; a**~**bedingt** adj related to a particular age; related to or caused by old age; ~**beschwerden** pl complaints pl of old age, geriatric complaints pl; ~**blödsinn** m senile dementia (form); ~**erscheinung** f sign of old age; ~**forschung** f gerontology; ~**fürsorge** f care of the elderly; ~**genosse** m contemporary; (Kind) child of the same age; (Psych, Sociol) peer; **seine** ~**genossen** children/people the same age as him; **wir sind ja** ~**genossen** we are the same age; ~**gliederung** f age structure; ~**grenze** f age limit; (Rentenalter) retirement age; ~**gründe** pl reasons of age pl; ~**gruppe** f age-group; **a**~**halber** adv because of or on account of one's age; ~**heilkunde** f geriatrics sing; ~**heim** nt old people's home; ~**klasse** f (Sport) age-group; ~**krankheit** f geriatric illness; ~**präsident** m president by seniority; ~**prozeß** m ageing process, senescence (form); ~**pyramide** f age pyramid or diagram; ~**rente** f old age pension; ~**ruhegeld** nt retirement benefit; **a**~**schwach** adj Mensch old and infirm; Tier old and weak; Auto, Möbel decrepit; ~**schwäche** f siehe adj infirmity; weakness; decrepitude; ~**sicherung** f provision for one's old age; **a**~**sichtig** adj presbyopic (form); ~**sitz** m sein ~**sitz war München** he spent his retirement in Munich; ~**soziologie** f sociology of old age; ~**sport** m sport for the elderly; ~**starrsinn** m senile stubbornness; ~**stil** m later style; ~**stufe** f age-group; (Lebensabschnitt) age, stage in life; ~**versicherung** f retirement insurance; ~**versorgung** f provision for (one's) old age; ~**werk** nt later works pl; ~**zulage** f increment for age.

Altertum nt, no pl antiquity no art. **das deutsche** ~ early German history.

Altertümelei f antiquarianism.

altertümeln vi to antiquarianize.

Altertümer pl antiquities pl.

altertümlich adj (aus dem Altertum) ancient; (altehrwürdig) old-world; (altmodisch) old-fashioned no adv; (veraltet) antiquated.

Altertümlichkeit f siehe adj ancientness; old-world quality; old-fashionedness; antiquated nature.

Altertums-: ~**forscher** m archeologist; ~**forschung** f archeology, archeological research; ~**kunde** f archeology; ~**wert** m: **das hat schon** ~**wert** (hum) it has antique value (hum).

Alterung f (a) siehe **altern 1** ageing; maturation. **(b)** siehe **altern 2** ageing; maturation; age-hardening.

Alte(s) nt decl as adj **das** ~ (das Gewohnte, Traditionelle) the old; (alte Dinge) old things pl; **er hängt sehr am** ~**n** he clings to the past; **das** ~ **und das Neue** the old and the new, old and new; **sie hat Freude an allem** ~**n** she gets a lot of pleasure from anything old.

Ältestenrat m council of elders; (BRD Pol) all-party parliamentary advisory committee, ≈ think-tank (Brit).

Älteste(r) mf decl as adj oldest; (Sohn, Tochter auch) eldest; (Eccl) elder.

älteste(r, s) adj superl of **alt** oldest; Bruder etc auch eldest. **der** ~ **Junge** (Skat) the jack of clubs.

Alt-: ~**flöte** f treble recorder; (Querflöte) bass or alto flute; **a**~**fränkisch** adj quaint; Stadt etc auch olde-worlde (inf); ~**französisch(e)** nt Old French; ~**gold** nt old gold; (Goldart) artificially darkened gold; **a**~**griechisch** adj ancient Greek; (Ling) classical Greek; ~**griechisch(e)** nt classical Greek; **a**~**hergebracht,** **a**~**herkömmlich** adj (old) traditional; ~**herrenmannschaft** f (Sport) team of players over thirty; **a**~**hochdeutsch** adj, ~**hochdeutsch(e)** nt Old High German.

Altist(in f) m (Mus) alto.

Altjahrs(s)-: ~**abend** m (dial) New Year's Eve, Hogmanay (esp Scot); ~**tag** m (dial) New Year's Eve, Hogmanay (esp Scot).

Alt-: **a**~**jüngferlich** adj old-maidish, spinsterish; ~**kanzler** m former chancellor; ~**katholik** m, **a**~**katholisch** adj Old Catholic; ~**kleiderhändler** m second-hand clothes dealer; ~**kleidersammlung** f collection of old clothes; **a**~**klug** adj precocious; ~**klugheit** f precociousness; ~**lage** f (Mus) alto range.

ältlich adj oldish.

Alt-: ~**material** nt scrap; ~**meister** m doyen; (Sport) ex-champion; ~**metall** nt scrap metal; **a**~**modisch** adj old-fashioned; (rückständig) outmoded; ~**neubau** m prewar building; ~**papier** nt wastepaper; ~**partie** f (Mus) alto part; ~**philologe** m classical philologist; ~**philologie** f classical philology; **a**~**philologisch** adj Abteilung of classical philology; Bücher, Artikel on classical philology; **a**~**renommiert** adj old-established; **a**~**rosa** adj old rose.

Altruismus m, no pl (geh) altruism.

Altruist(in f) m (geh) altruist.

altruistisch adj (geh) altruistic.

Alt-: **a**~**sächsisch** adj old Saxon; ~**sängerin** f contralto (singer); ~**schlüssel** m (Mus) alto clef; ~**schnee** m old snow; ~**sein** nt being old no art; ~**silber** nt old silver; (Silberart) artificially darkened silver; ~**sprachler** m -s, - classicist; (Sprachwissenschaftler) classical philologist; **a**~**sprachlich** adj Zweig classical; Abteilung of classical languages; **a**~**sprachliches Gymnasium** grammar school (Brit), school teaching classical languages; ~**stadt** f old (part of a/the) town; **die Ulmer** ~**stadt** the old part of Ulm; ~**stadtsanierung** f renovation of the old part of a/the town; ~**steinzeit** f Palaeolithic Age, Old Stone Age; **a**~**steinzeitlich** adj Palaeolithic; ~**stimme** f (Mus) alto or (von Frau auch) contralto, contralto voice; (Partie) alto/contralto part; **a**~**testa-**

mentarisch, a~testamentlich *adj* Old Testament *attr*;
a~überkommen, a~überliefert *adj* traditional; a~väterisch,
a~väterlich *adj Bräuche, Geister* ancestral; (*altmodisch*) old-
fashioned *no adv*; *Erscheinung etc* patriarchal; ~waren *pl*
second-hand goods *pl*; ~warenhändler *m* second-hand dealer.
Altweiber-: ~geschwätz *nt* old woman's talk; ~knoten *m*
granny (knot); ~märchen *nt* old wives' tale; ~sommer *m* (a)
(*Nachsommer*) Indian summer; (b) (*Spinnfäden*) gossamer.
altweltlich *adj* old-world.
Alu *nt* -s, *no pl siehe* **Aluminium.**
Alufolie *f* tin *or* kitchen foil.
Aluminium *nt* -s, *no pl* aluminium, aluminum (*US*).
Aluminium-: ~folie *f* tin foil; ~(staub)lunge *f* (*Med*)
aluminosis (*form*).
Alumnat *nt* (*old*) boarding school; (*Aus*) seminary.
Alveolar [alveoˈlaːɐ] *m* (*Phon*) alveolar (sound).
Alzerl *nt* -s, - (*Aus*) little bit.
am *prep* (a) *contr of* **an dem.**
  (b) (*zur Bildung des Superlativs*) er war ~ tapfersten he was
(the) bravest; er hat ~ tapfersten gekämpft he fought (the)
most bravely; sie war ~ schönsten she was (the) most beautiful; sie hat es ~ schönsten gemalt she painted it (the) most
beautifully; ~ besten machen wir das morgen we'd do best to
do it tomorrow, the best thing would be for us to do it tomorrow;
~ seltsamsten war ... the strangest thing was ...
  (c) (*als Zeitangabe*) on. ~ letzten Sonntag last Sunday; ~ 8.
Mai on the eighth of May, on May (the *Brit*) eighth; (*geschrieben*) on May 8th; ~ Morgen/Abend in the morning/
evening; ~ Tag darauf/zuvor (on) the following/previous day.
  (d) (*als Ortsangabe*) on the; (*bei Gebirgen*) at the foot of the.
  (e) (*inf: als Verlaufsform*) ich war gerade ~ Weggehen I was
just leaving.
  (f) (*Aus: auf dem*) on the.
  (g) (*Comm*) ~ Lager in stock.
  (h) *in Verbindung mit n siehe auch dort* du bist ~ Zug it's
your turn; ~ Ball sein/bleiben to be/keep on the ball.
Amalgam *nt* -s, -e amalgam.
amalgamieren* *vtr* (*lit, fig*) to amalgamate.
Amaryllis *f* -, **Amaryllen** amaryllis.
Amateur [-ˈtøːɐ] *m* amateur.
Amateur-: amateur; a~haft *adj* amateurish.
Amazonas *m* - Amazon.
Amazone *f* -, -n (a) (*Myth*) Amazon; (*fig*) amazon. (b) (*Sport*)
woman show-jumper.
Amber *m* -s, -(n) ambergris.
Ambiente *nt* -, *no pl* (*geh*) ambience.
Ambition *f* (*geh*) ambition. ~en auf etw (*acc*) haben to have
ambitions of getting sth.
ambivalent [-vaˈlɛnt] *adj* ambivalent.
Ambivalenz [-vaˈlɛnts] *f* ambivalence.
Amboß *m* -sses, -sse anvil; (*Anat auch*) incus.
Ambra *f* -, **Ambren** *siehe* **Amber.**
Ambrosia *f* -, *no pl* ambrosia.
ambrosianisch *adj* Ambrosian.
ambrosisch *adj* (*geh, dated*) ambrosial (*liter*).
ambulant *adj* (a) (*Med*) *Versorgung, Behandlung* out-patient
attr. ~e Patienten out-patients; ~ behandelt werden (*Patient*)
to receive out-patient treatment; (*Fall*) to be treated in the out-
patient department.
  (b) (*wandernd*) itinerant.
Ambulanz *f* (a) (*Klinikstation*) out-patient department, outpatients *sing* (*inf*).
  (b) (~*wagen*) ambulance.
Ambulanz-: ~hubschrauber *m* ambulance helicopter;
~wagen *m* ambulance.
Ambulatorium *nt* (*esp DDR*) out-patient department, outpatients *sing* (*inf*).
Ameise *f* -, -n ant.
Ameisen-: ~bär *m* anteater; (*größer*) ant-bear, great anteater;
~fleiß *m* (*inf*) beaver-like industry; a~haft *adj* ant-like; Getriebe *etc* beaver-like; ~haufen *m* anthill; ~säure *f* formic
acid; ~staat *m* ant colony.
amen *interj* amen; *siehe* **ja.**
Amen *nt* -s, - amen. sein ~ zu etw geben to give one's blessing to
sth; das ist so sicher wie das ~ in der Kirche (*inf*) you can bet
your bottom dollar on that (*inf*).
Amerikaner(in *f*) *m* -s, - (a) American. (b) (*Gebäck*) *flat iced
cake.*
amerikanisch *adj* American.
amerikanisieren* *vt* to Americanize.
Amerikanisierung *f* Americanization.
Amerikanismus *m* Americanism.
Amerikanist(in *f*) *m* specialist in American studies.
Amerikanistik *f* American studies *pl.*
Amethyst *m* -s, -e amethyst.
Ami *m* -s, -s (*inf*) Yank (*inf*); (*sl: Soldat*) GI (*inf*).
Aminosäure *f* amino acid.
Ammann *m* (*Sw*) (a) mayor.
  (b) (*Jur*) local magistrate.
Amme *f* -, -n (*old*) foster-mother; (*Nährmutter*) wet nurse.
Ammenmärchen *nt* fairy tale *or* story.
Ammer *f* -, -n (*Orn*) bunting.
Ammoniak *nt* -s, *no pl* ammonia.
Ammonit *m* -en, -en (*Archeol*) ammonite.
Ammonshorn *nt* (a) (*Anat*) hippocampus major (*form*). (b)
(*Archeol*) ammonite.
Amnesie *f* (*Med*) amnesia.
Amnestie *f* amnesty.
amnestieren* *vt* to grant an amnesty to.
Amöbe *f* -, -n (*Biol*) amoeba.

Amöbenruhr *f* (*Med*) amoebic dysentery.
Amok [ˈaːmɔk, aˈmɔk] *m*: ~ laufen to run amok *or* amuck; ~
fahren to drive like a madman *or* lunatic.
Amok-: ~fahrer *m* mad *or* lunatic driver; ~fahrt *f* mad *or* crazy
ride; ~lauf *m* einen ~lauf aufführen to run amok *or* amuck;
~läufer *m* madman; ~schütze *m* crazed gunman.
Amor *m* - Cupid.
amoralisch *adj* (a) (*unmoralisch*) immoral. (b) (*wertfrei*)
amoral.
Amoralität *f* immorality.
Amorette *f* little cupid, amoretto.
amorph *adj* (*geh*) amorphous.
Amortisation *f* (a) (*Econ: von Investition*) amortization. (b)
(*DDR Econ: Abschreibung*) depreciation.
Amortisationsdauer *f* length of amortization period.
amortisieren* **1** *vt* eine ~ Investition ~ to ensure that an
investment pays for itself. **2** *vr* to pay for itself.
Amouren [aˈmuːrən] *pl* (*old, hum*) amours *pl* (*old, hum*).
amourös [amuˈrøːs] *adj* (*geh*) amorous.
Ampel *f* -, -n (a) (*Verkehrs~*) (traffic) lights *pl*. er hat eine ~
umgefahren he knocked a traffic light over; halte an der
nächsten ~ stop at the next (set of) (traffic) lights. (b) (*geh*)
(*Hängelampe*) hanging lamp; (*Hängeblumentopf*) hanging
flowerpot.
Ampel-: ~anlage *f* (set of) traffic lights; ~kreuzung *f* (*inf*)
junction controlled by traffic lights; ~phase *f* traffic light
sequence; die langen ~phasen an dieser Kreuzung the length
of time the lights take to change at this junction.
Ampere [amˈpɛːɐ, amˈpeːɐ] *nt* -(s), - amp, ampere (*form*).
Ampere-: ~meter *nt* ammeter; ~sekunde *f* ampere-second;
~stunde *f* ampere-hour.
Ampfer *m* -s, - (*Bot*) dock; (*Sauer~*) sorrel.
Amphibie [-iə] *f* (*Zool*) amphibian.
Amphibienfahrzeug *nt* amphibious vehicle.
amphibisch *adj* amphibious.
Amphitheater *nt* amphitheatre.
amphitheatralisch *adj* (*geh*) in the style of an amphitheatre.
Amphora *f* -, **Amphoren** amphora.
Amplitude *f* -, -n (*Phys*) amplitude.
Ampulle *f* -, -n (a) (*Behälter*) ampoule. (b) (*Anat*) ampulla.
Amputation *f* amputation.
amputieren* *vt* to amputate. jdm den Arm ~ to amputate sb's
arm; jdn ~ to carry out an amputation on sb; amputiert werden
(*Mensch*) to have an amputation.
Amputierte(r) *mf decl as adj* amputee, person who has had a
limb amputated.
Amsel *f* -, -n blackbird.
Amt *nt* -(e)s, ⁻er (a) (*Stellung*) office; (*Posten*) post. im ~ sein
to be in *or* hold office; jdm aus einem ~ entfernen to remove sb
from office; in ~ und Würden in an exalted position; von ~s
wegen (*aufgrund von jds Beruf*) because of one's job; kraft
seines ~es (*geh*) by virtue of one's office.
  (b) (*Aufgabe*) duty, task. seines ~es walten (*geh*) to carry out
or discharge (*form*) one's duties.
  (c) (*Behörde*) (*Friedhofs~, Fürsorge~, Sozial~ etc*)
cemeteries/welfare department *etc*/department of social security; (*Einwohnermelde~, Paß~, Finanz~*) registration/pass-
port/tax office; (*Stadtverwaltung*) council offices *pl*;
(*Oberschul~*) secondary school authority. zum zuständigen ~
gehen to go to the relevant authority; die ~er der Stadt the
town authorities; der Ärger mit den ~ern the bother with the
authorities; von ~s wegen (*auf behördliche Anordnung hin*)
officially.
  (d) (*Telefon~*) operator; (*Zentrale*) exchange.
  (e) (*Eccl: Messe*) High Mass.
Ämtchen *nt* (*pej*) duty.
Ämter-: ~jagd *f* position-hunting; ~kauf *m* buying one's way
into office; ~patronage *f* autocratic distribution of offices.
amtieren* *vi* (a) (*Amt innehaben*) to be in office. ~d incumbent; als Minister/Lehrer/Bürgermeister ~ to hold the post of
minister/to have a position as a teacher/to hold the office of
mayor.
  (b) (*Amt vorübergehend wahrnehmen*) to act. er amtiert als
Bürgermeister he is acting mayor.
  (c) (*fungieren*) als ... ~ to act as ...
amtl. *abbr of* **amtlich.**
amtlich *adj* official; (*wichtig*) *Miene, Gebaren* officious; (*inf:
sicher*) certain. ~es Kennzeichen registration (number),
license number (*US*).
amtlicherseits *adv* officially.
Amtlichkeit *f* officialdom *no pl.*
Amtmann *m, pl* -leute, **Amtmännin** *f* (a) (*Admin*) senior civil
servant. (b) (*Jur*) local magistrate.
Amts-: ~adel *m* (*Hist*) non-hereditary nobility who were
created peers because of their office; ~anmaßung *f* unauthorized assumption of authority; (*Ausübung eines Amtes*)
fraudulent exercise of a public office; das ist ja ~anmaßung!
he *etc* has overstepped his authority there; ~antritt *m* assumption of office/one's post; ~anwalt *m* prosecuting counsel in
relatively minor cases; ~apparat *m* official machinery; ~arzt
m medical officer; a~ärztlich *adj Zeugnis* from the medical
officer; *Untersuchung* by the medical officer; a~ärztlich
untersucht werden to have an official medical examination;
~befugnis *f*, ~bereich *m* area of competence; ~bezirk *m* area
of jurisdiction; ~blatt *nt* gazette; ~bote *m* official messenger;
~bruder *m* (*Eccl*) fellow clergyman; ~dauer *f* term of office;
~deutsch(e) *nt* officialese; ~diener *m* clerk; (*Bote*) messenger; ~eid *m* oath of office; den ~eid ablegen to be sworn in,
to take the oath of office; ~einführung, ~einsetzung *f* instalment, inauguration; ~enthebung, ~entsetzung (*Sw, Aus*) *f* dis-

missal *or* removal from office; ~**erschleichung** *f* obtaining office by devious means; ~**geheimnis** *nt* (a) *(geheime Sache)* official secret; **(b)** *(Schweigepflicht)* official secrecy; ~**gericht** *nt* = county *(Brit) or* district *(US)* court; ~**gerichtsrat** *m* = county *(Brit) or* district *(US)* court judge; ~**geschäfte** *pl* official duties *pl*; ~**gewalt** *f* authority; a~**handeln** *vi insep (Aus)* to take official action, to act officially; ~**handlung** *f* official duty; ~**hilfe** *f* cooperation between authorities; ~**kanzlei** *f (Aus)* office; ~**kette** *f* chain of office; ~**kleidung** *f* robes *pl* of office; ~**leitung** *f (Telec)* exchange line; ~**miene** *f* official air; **seine** ~**miene aufsetzen** to get *or* go all official *(inf)*; ~**mißbrauch** *m* abuse of one's position; ~**niederlegung** *f* resignation; ~**periode** *f* term of office; ~**person** *f* official; ~**pflicht** *f* official duty; ~**richter** *m* = county *(Brit) or* district *(US)* court judge; ~**schimmel** *m (hum)* officialism; **den** ~**schimmel reiten** to do everything by the book; **der** ~**schimmel wiehert** officialdom rears its ugly head; ~**sprache** *f* official language; ~**stube** *f (dated)* office; ~**stunden** *pl* hours *pl* open to the public; ~**tracht** *f* robes *pl* of office; *(Eccl)* vestments *pl*; ~**träger** *m* office bearer; ~**übergabe** *f* handing-over of office; ~**übernahme** *f* assumption of office/a post; ~**vergehen** *nt* malfeasance *(form)*; ~**vermittlung** *f (Telec)* connection by the operator; ~**verwalter**, ~**verweser** *(old) m* deputy; ~**vormund** *m (Jur)* public guardian; ~**vormundschaft** *f (Jur)* public guardianship; ~**vorstand**, ~**vorsteher** *m* head *or* chief of a/the department *etc*; ~**weg** *m* official channels *pl*; **den** ~**weg beschreiten** to go through the official channels; ~**zeichen** *nt (Telec)* dialling tone *(Brit)*, dial tone *(US)*; ~**zeit** *f* period of office; ~**zimmer** *nt* office.

Amulett *nt* -(e)s, -e amulet, charm, talisman.
amüsant *adj* amusing; *Film, Geschichte auch* funny. ~ **plaudern** to talk in an amusing way.
Amüsement [amyzə'mã:] *nt* -s, -s *(geh)* amusement, entertainment.
Amüsierbetrieb *m (inf)* nightclub; *(Spielhalle etc)* amusement arcade. **der** ~ **in Las Vegas** the pleasure industry in Las Vegas.
amüsieren* **1** *vt* to amuse. **was amüsiert dich denn so?** what do you find so amusing *or* funny?; **lassen Sie sich ein bißchen** ~ have some fun; **amüsiert zuschauen** to look on amused *or* with amusement. **2** *vr (sich vergnügen)* to enjoy oneself, to have a good time, to have fun. **sich mit etw** ~ to amuse oneself with sth; *(iro)* to keep oneself amused with sth; **sich über etw** *(acc)* ~ to find sth funny; *(über etw lachen)* to laugh at sth; *(unfreundlich)* to make fun of sth; **sich darüber** ~, **daß** ... to find it funny that ...; **sich mit jdm** ~ to have a good time with sb; **amüsiert euch gut** have fun, enjoy yourselves.
Amüsier-: ~**lokal** *nt* nightclub; ~**viertel** *nt* nightclub district.
amusisch *adj* unartistic.
an 1 *prep* +*dat* (a) *(räumlich: wo?)* at; *(~ etw dran)* on. **am Haus/Bahnhof** at the house/station; ~ **dieser Schule** at this school; ~ **der Wand stehen** to stand by the wall; **am Fenster sitzen** to sit at *or* by the window; **am Tatort** at the scene of the crime; ~ **der Tür/Wand** on the door/wall; ~ **der Donau/Autobahn/am Ufer/am Rhein** by *or (direkt* ~ *gelegen)* on the Danube/motorway/bank/Rhine; **Frankfurt** ~ **der Oder** Frankfurt on (the) Oder; **ein Fleck am Kleid** a spot on the dress; ~ **etw hängen** *(lit)* to hang from *or* on sth; **zu nahe** ~ **etw stehen** to be too near to sth; **etw** ~ **etw festmachen** to fasten sth to sth; ~ **der gleichen Stelle** at *or* on the same spot; **jdn** ~ **der Hand nehmen** to take sb by the hand; **oben am Berg** up the mountain; **unten am Fluß** down by the river; **sie wohnen Tür** ~ **Tür** they live next door to one another, they are next-door neighbours; **Haus** ~ **Haus/Laden** ~ **Laden** one house/shop after the other; ~ **etw vorbeigehen** to go past sth, to pass sth; ~ **jdm vorbeischauen** to look past sb; **sich** *(dat)* **die Hand am Tuch abwischen** to wipe one's hand on the cloth; **am Rücken liegen/fallen** *(dial)* to lie/fall on one's back; *siehe* **am, Bord, Land** *etc*.
(b) *(zeitlich)* on. ~ **diesem Abend** *(on)* that evening; **am Tag zuvor** the day before, the previous day; ~ **dem Abend, als ich** ... the evening I ...; ~ **Ostern/Weihnachten** *(dial)* at Easter/Christmas; *siehe* **am.**
(c) *(fig) siehe auch Substantive, Adjektive, Verben* **jung** ~ **Jahren sein** to be young in years; **fünf** ~ **der Zahl** five in number; **jdn** ~ **etw erkennen** to recognize sb by sth; **das Schönste/Schlimmste** ~ **der Sache war** ... the nicest/worst thing about it was ...; **der Mangel/das Angebot** ~ **Waren** the lack/choice of goods; ~ **etw arbeiten/schreiben/kauen** to be working on/writing/chewing sth; ~ **etw sterben/leiden** to die of/suffer from sth; **arm** ~ **Fett/reich** ~ **Kalorien** low in fat/high in calories; **was haben Sie** ~ **Weinen da?** what wines do you have?; **unübertroffen** ~ **Qualität** unsurpassed in quality; ~ **etw schuld sein** to be to blame for sth; ~ **dem Buch ist nicht viel** there is not much in that book; ~ **der ganzen Sache ist nichts** there is nothing in it; **es** ~ **der Leber** *etc* **haben** *(inf)* to have trouble with one's liver *etc*, to have liver *etc* trouble; **was findet sie** ~ **dem Mann?** what does she see in that man?; **das gefällt mir nicht** ~ **ihm** that's what I don't like about him; **es ist** ~ **dem** *(es stimmt)* that's right; **sie hat etwas** ~ **sich, das** ... there is something about her that ...; **es ist** ~ **ihm, etwas zu tun** *(geh)* it's up to him to do something.
2 *prep* +*acc* (a) *(räumlich: wohin?)* to; *(gegen)* on, against. **etw** ~ **die Wand/Tafel schreiben** to write sth on the wall/blackboard; **die Zweige reichten (bis)** ~ **den Boden/mein Fenster** the branches reached down to the ground/up to my window; **etw** ~ **etw hängen** to hang sth on sth; **er ging** ~**s Fenster** he went (over) to the window; **A~ den Vorsitzenden** ... *(bei Anschrift)* The Chairman ...; ~**s Telefon gehen** to answer the phone; *siehe* **bis, Bord, Land.**

(b) *(zeitlich: woran?)* ~ **die Zukunft/Vergangenheit denken** to think of the future/past; **bis** ~ **mein Lebensende** to the end of my days.
(c) *(fig) siehe auch Substantive, Adjektive, Verben* ~ **die Arbeit gehen** to get down to work; ~ **jdn/etw glauben** to believe in sb/sth; **ich habe eine Bitte/Frage** ~ **Sie** I have a request to make of you/question to ask you; **ein Gruß/eine Frage** ~ **jdn** greetings/a question to sb; ~ **(und für) sich** actually; **eine** ~ **(und für) sich gute Idee** actually quite a good idea; **dagegen ist** ~ **(und für) sich nichts einzuwenden** there are really no objections to that; **wie war es?** — ~ **(und für) sich ganz schön** how was it? — on the whole it was quite nice; *siehe* **ab.**
3 *adv* (a) *(ungefähr)* about. ~ **(die) hundert** about a hundred.
(b) *(Ankunftszeit)* **Frankfurt** ~: 18.30 *(Rail)* arriving Frankfurt 18.30.
(c) von diesem Ort ~ from here onwards; **von diesem Tag/heute** ~ from this day on(wards)/from today onwards.
(d) *(inf: angeschaltet, angezogen)* on. **Licht** ~! lights on!; **ohne etwas** ~ with nothing on, without anything on; *siehe* **ansein.**
Anabaptismus *m* anabaptism.
Anabaptist(in *f) m* anabaptist.
Anachronismus [-kr-] *m (geh)* anachronism.
anachronistisch [-kr-] *adj (geh)* anachronistic.
anaerob [anǀaeˈroːp] *adj attr* anaerobic.
Anagramm *nt (Liter)* anagram.
Anakoluth *nt* -s, -e anacoluthon.
Anakonda *f* -, -s anaconda.
anakreontisch *adj* anacreontic.
anal *adj (Psych, Anat)* anal.
Anal-: ~**erotik** *f* anal eroticism; ~**öffnung** *f (form)* anal orifice *(form)*.
analog *adj* (a) analogous (+*dat, zu* to). **(b)** *(Datenverarbeitung)* analogue *attr*.
Analogie *f* analogy.
Analogie-: ~**bildung** *f (Ling)* analogy; ~**schluß** *m (Philos, Jur)* argument by analogy.
analogisch *adj* analogous.
Analogrechner *m* analogue computer.
Analphabet(in *f) m* -en, -en (a) illiterate (person). **(b)** *(pej: Unwissender)* ignoramus, dunce.
Analphabetentum *nt*, **Analphabetismus** *m* illiteracy.
analphabetisch *adj* illiterate.
Analverkehr *m* anal intercourse.
Analyse *f* -, -n analysis *(auch Psych inf)*.
analysieren* *vt* to analyze.
Analysis *f* -, *no pl (Math)* analysis.
Analytiker(in *f) m* -s, - analyst; *(analytisch Denkender)* analytical thinker.
analytisch *adj* analytical.
Anämie *f* anaemia.
anämisch *adj* anaemic.
Anamnese *f* -, -n case history.
Ananas *f* -, - *or* -se pineapple.
Anapäst *m* -(e)s, -e *(Poet)* anapest.
Anarchie *f* anarchy.
anarchisch *adj* anarchic. ~ **leben** to live an anarchic life.
Anarchismus *m* anarchism.
Anarchist(in *f) m* anarchist.
anarchistisch *adj* anarchistic; *(den Anarchismus vertretend auch)* anarchist *attr*.
Anarcho- *in cpds* anarcho-.
Anästhesie *f* ana(e)sthesia.
anästhesieren* *vt* to an(a)esthetize.
Anästhetikum *nt* -s, **Anästhetika** an(a)esthetic.
anästhetisch *adj* an(a)esthetic; *(unempfindlich auch)* an(a)esthetized.
Anästhetist(in *f) m* an(a)esthetist.
Anatolien [-iən] *nt* -s Anatolia.
Anatolier(in *f)* [-ir, -iərin] *m* -s, - Anatolian.
anatolisch *adj* Anatolian.
Anatom(in *f) m* -en, -en anatomist.
Anatomie *f* (a) *(Wissenschaft, Körperbau)* anatomy. **(b)** *(Institut)* anatomical institute.
Anatomiesaal *m* anatomical *or* anatomy lecture theatre.
anatomisch *adj* anatomical.
anbacken *sep* **1** *vt (Cook)* to start baking. **2** *vi aux sein* (a) *(kurz gebacken werden)* to bake for a short time. **(b)** *(sich festsetzen)* to bake on *(an* +*dat* -to); *(dial: Lehm, Schnee etc)* to stick *(an* +*dat* to).
anbahnen *sep* **1** *vt* to initiate. **2** *vr (sich andeuten)* to be in the offing; *(Unangenehmes)* to be looming; *(Möglichkeiten, Zukunft etc)* to be opening up. **zwischen den beiden bahnt sich etwas an** *(Liebesverhältnis)* there is something going on between those two.
Anbahnung *f* initiation *(von, gen* of).
anbandeln *(S Ger, Aus)*, **anbandeln** *vi sep* (a) *(Bekanntschaft schließen)* to take up *(mit* with). **(b)** *(Streit anfangen)* to start an argument *(mit* with).
Anbau¹ *m* -(e)s, *no pl* (a) *(Anpflanzung)* cultivation, growing. **(b)** *(von Gebäuden)* building. **den** ~ **einer Garage planen** to plan to build on a garage.
Anbau² *m* -(e)s, -ten *(Nebengebäude)* extension; *(freistehend)* annexe; *(Stallungen etc)* outhouse, outbuilding.
anbauen *sep* **1** *vt* (a) to cultivate, to grow; *(anpflanzen)* to plant; *(säen)* to sow. **(b)** *(Build)* to add, to build on. **etw ans Haus** ~ to build sth onto the house. **2** *vi* to build an extension. **Möbel zum A~** unit furniture.
Anbau-: a~**fähig** *adj* (a) *Boden* cultivable; *Gemüse* growable; **(b)** *(Build)* extendible; ~**fläche** *f* (area of) cultivable land;

(bebaute Ackerfläche) area under cultivation; ~gebiet nt cultivable area; ein gutes ~gebiet für etw a good area for cultivating sth; ~grenze f limit of cultivation; ~möbel pl unit furniture; ~plan m (DDR) plan for land cultivation; ~schrank m cupboard unit; ~technik f, ~verfahren nt (Agr) growing methods pl.

anbefehlen* vt sep irreg (liter) (a) (befehlen) to urge (jdm etw sth on sb). (b) (anvertrauen) to commend (jdm etw sth to sb).

Anbeginn m (geh) beginning. von ~ (an) from the (very) beginning; seit ~ der Welt since the world began.

anbehalten* vt sep irreg to keep on.

anbei adv (form) enclosed. ~ schicken wir Ihnen ... please find enclosed ...

anbeißen sep irreg 1 vi (Fisch) to bite; (fig) to take the bait.
  2 vt Apfel etc to bite into. sie hat den Apfel nur angebissen she only took one bite of the apple; ein angebissener Apfel a half-eaten apple; sie sieht zum A~ aus (inf) she looks nice enough to eat.

anbekommen* vt sep irreg (inf) to (manage to) get on; Feuer to (manage to) get going.

anbelangen* vt sep to concern. was das/mich anbelangt ... as far as that is/I am concerned ...

anbellen vt sep to bark at.

anbequemen* vr sep (geh) sich einer Sache (dat) ~ to adapt (oneself) to sth.

anberaumen* vt sep or (rare) insep (form) to arrange, to fix; Termin, Tag auch to set; Treffen auch to call.

Anberaumung f siehe vt arrangement, fixing; setting; calling.

anbeten vt sep to worship; Menschen auch to adore; siehe Angebetete(r).

Anbeter m -s, - (Verehrer) admirer.

Anbetracht m: in ~ (+gen) in consideration or view of; in ~ dessen, daß ... in consideration or view of the fact that ...

anbetreffen* vt sep irreg siehe anbelangen.

anbetteln vt sep jdn ~ to beg from sb; jdn um etw ~ to beg sth from sb.

Anbetung f siehe vt worship; adoration.

anbetungswürdig adj admirable; Schönheit adorable.

anbezahlen* vt sep siehe anzahlen.

anbiedern vr sep (pej) sich (bei jdm) ~ to curry favour (with sb); (anbändeln) to chat sb up.

Anbiederung f siehe vr currying favour (gen with); chatting-up.

Anbiederungsversuch m attempt to curry favour with sb/chat sb up.

anbieten sep irreg 1 vt to offer (jdm etw sb sth); (Comm) Waren to offer for sale; seinen Rücktritt to tender. haben wir etwas zum A~ da? have we anything to offer our guests?; jdm das Du ~ to suggest sb uses the familiar form of address.
  2 vr (a) (Mensch) sich (als etw) ~ to offer one's services (as sth); sich für die Arbeit ~, sich ~, die Arbeit zu tun to offer to do the work; sich zur Unzucht ~ to solicit; du darfst dich den Männern nicht so ~ you shouldn't make yourself so available; ein Politiker, der sich als nächster Kanzler anbietet a politician who is the obvious choice as next chancellor; der Ort bietet sich für die Konferenz an that is the obvious place for the conference; das Fahrrad bietet sich geradezu zum Mitnehmen an that bicycle is just asking to be taken.
  (b) (in Betracht kommen: Gelegenheit) to present itself. das bietet sich als Lösung an that would provide a solution; es bieten sich mehrere Lösungsmöglichkeiten an there are several possible solutions, several possible solutions present themselves; es bietet sich an, das Museum zu besuchen the thing to do would be to visit the museum.

Anbieter m -s, - supplier.

anbinden sep irreg 1 vt (an +acc or dat to) to tie (up); Pferd auch to tether; Boot auch to moor. jdn ~ (fig) to tie sb down; siehe angebunden. 2 vi siehe anbändeln.

anblaffen vt sep (inf) (lit, fig) to bark at.

anblasen vt sep irreg (a) (blasen gegen) to blow at; (anfachen) to blow on. jdn mit Rauch ~ to blow smoke at sb. (b) (Mus) Instrument to blow; Ton to sound. (c) (durch Blassignal ankündigen) die Jagd ~ to sound the horn for the start of the hunt.

anblättern vt sep to start flicking or flipping through.

anblecken vt sep (lit, fig) to bare one's teeth at.

anblenden vt sep to flash at; (fig: kurz erwähnen) to touch on.

Anblick m sight. beim ersten ~ at first sight; beim ~ des Hundes when he etc saw the dog; in den ~ von etw versunken sein to be absorbed in looking at sth; in dem Hut bist du ein ~ für die Götter you really look a sight in that hat.

anblicken vt sep to look at. jdn lange/feindselig ~ to gaze/glare at sb.

anblinken vt sep jdn ~ (Fahrer, Fahrzeug) to flash (at) sb; (Lampe) to flash in sb's eyes; (Gold) to shine before sb's very eyes.

anblinzeln vt sep (a) (blinzelnd ansehen) to squint at. (b) (zublinzeln) to wink at.

anbohren vt sep (a) (teilweise durchbohren) to bore into; (mit Bohrmaschine auch) to drill into. jdn um Geld etc ~ to pump sb for money etc. (b) (zugänglich machen) Quellen etc to open up (by boring/drilling).

anborgen vt sep (dated) jdn (um etw) ~ to borrow (sth) from sb.

Anbot ['anbo:t] nt -(e)s, -e (Aus) siehe Angebot.

anbranden vi sep aux sein to surge.

anbraten vt sep irreg to brown; Steak etc to sear. etw zu scharf ~ to brown sth too much.

anbrauchen vt sep to start using; Kleidungsstück to start wearing; Schachtel, Flasche to open. eine angebrauchte Schachtel/Flasche an opened box/bottle; das ist schon ange-

braucht that has already been used/worn/opened.

anbräunen vt sep (Cook) to brown (lightly).

anbrausen vi sep aux sein to roar up. angebraust kommen to come roaring up.

anbrechen sep irreg 1 vt (a) Packung, Flasche etc to open; Vorrat to broach; Ersparnisse, Geldsumme, Geldschein to break into; siehe angebrochen.
  (b) (teilweise brechen) Brett, Gefäß, Knochen etc to crack. angebrochen sein to be cracked.
  2 vi aux sein (Epoche etc) to dawn; (Tag auch) to break; (Nacht) to fall; (Jahreszeit) to begin; (Winter) to close in.

anbremsen vti sep (den Wagen) ~ to brake, to apply the brakes.

anbrennen sep irreg 1 vi aux sein to start burning, to catch fire; (Holz, Kohle etc) to catch light; (Essen) to burn, to get burnt; (Stoff) to scorch, to get scorched. gut ~ to catch fire easily; mir ist das Essen angebrannt I burnt the food, I let the food get burnt; der Torwart ließ nichts ~ (Sport sl) the goalkeeper didn't let a single goal in; siehe angebrannt.
  2 vt to light.

anbringen vt sep irreg (a) (hierherbringen) to bring (with one); (nach Hause) to bring home (with one).
  (b) (befestigen) to fix, to fasten (an +dat (on)to); (aufstellen, aufhängen) to put up; Telefon, Feuermelder etc to put in, to install; Stiel an Besen to put on; Beschläge, Hufeisen to mount; Komma to insert. sich (dat) Tätowierungen ~ lassen to have oneself tattooed; „Plakate ~ verboten" "post no bills", "billposters will be prosecuted".
  (c) (äußern) Bemerkung, Bitte, Gesuch, Beschwerde to make (bei to); Kenntnisse, Wissen to display; Argument to use. es ~, daß ... to make it known that ...; er konnte seine Kritik/seinen Antrag nicht mehr ~ he couldn't get his criticism/motion in; siehe angebracht.
  (d) (inf: loswerden) Ware to get rid of (inf).
  (e) (inf) siehe anbekommen.

Anbringung f siehe vt (b) fixing, fastening; putting up; putting in, installing; putting on; mounting; insertion.

Anbruch m, no pl (a) (geh: Anfang) beginning; (von Zeitalter, Epoche) dawn(ing). bei ~ des Tages/Morgens at daybreak, at break of day; bei ~ der Nacht/Dunkelheit at nightfall. (b) (Min) seam. (c) (Hunt) rotting game. (d) (Forest) decayed or rotten wood.

anbrühen vt sep to scald.

anbrüllen sep 1 vt (Löwe etc) to roar at; (Kuh, Stier) to bellow at; (inf: Mensch) to shout or bellow at. 2 vi gegen etw ~ to shout above (the noise of) sth.

anbrummen sep 1 vt to growl at; (fig) to grumble at. 2 vi aux sein angebrummt kommen to come roaring along or (auf einen zu) up.

anbrüten vt sep to begin to sit on.

Anchovis [an'ço:vɪs, an'ʃo:vɪs] f -, - siehe Anschovis.

Andacht f -, -en (a) no pl (das Beten) (silent) prayer or worship. ~ halten to be at one's devotions; in tiefer ~ versunken sein to be sunk in deep devotion.
  (b) (Gottesdienst) prayers pl.
  (c) (Versenkung) rapt interest; (Ehrfurcht) reverence. in tiefe(r) ~ versunken sein to be completely absorbed; er trank den Wein mit ~ (hum) he drank the wine reverently; etw voller ~ tun to do sth reverently.

andächtig adj (a) (im Gebet) in prayer. die ~en Gläubigen the worshippers at their devotions or prayers. (b) (versunken) rapt; (ehrfürchtig) reverent.

Andachts-: ~bild nt devotional picture; a~voll adj siehe andächtig (b).

Andalusien [-iən] nt -s Andalusia.

Andalusier(in f) [-iɐ, -iərɪn] m -s, - Andalusian.

andampfen vi sep aux sein (inf) angedampft kommen (lit, fig) to steam or come steaming along or (auf einen zu) up; (Mensch) to charge or come charging along or (auf einen zu) up.

andauen vt sep to begin to digest. angedaute Speisen partially digested food.

Andauer f, no pl bei langer ~ des Fiebers if the fever continues for a long time.

andauern vi sep to continue; (anhalten) to last. das dauert noch an that is still going on or is continuing; der Regen dauert noch an the rain hasn't stopped; das schöne Wetter wird nicht ~ the fine weather won't last.

andauernd adj (ständig) continuous; (anhaltend) continual. die bis in den frühen Morgen ~en Verhandlungen the negotiations which went on or continued till early morning; wenn du mich ~ unterbrichst ... if you keep on interrupting me ...

Anden pl Andes.

Andenken nt -s, no pl (a) memory. das ~ von etw feiern to commemorate sth; jdm ein ehrendes ~ bewahren (geh) to honour the memory of sb; jdn in freundlichem ~ behalten to have fond memories of sb; zum ~ an jdn/etw (an Verstorbenen etc) in memory or remembrance of sb/sth; (an Freunde/Urlaub etc) to remind you/us etc of sb/sth.
  (b) (Reise~) souvenir (an +acc of); (Erinnerungsstück) memento, keepsake (an +acc from).

änderbar adj alterable, changeable. eine nicht mehr ~e Entscheidung a decision which can no longer be changed; der Entwurf ist jederzeit ~ the draft can be altered or changed at any time.

Änderbarkeit f alterability, changeability.

ander(e)n-: ~falls adv otherwise; ~orts adv (geh) elsewhere; ~tags adv (geh) (on) the next or following day; ~teils adv (geh) siehe ein(er)seits.

andere(r, s) indef pron 1 (adjektivisch) (a) different; (weiterer) other. ein ~r Mann/ ~s Auto/eine ~ Frau a different man/car/woman; (*ein weiterer etc*) another man/car/woman; **jede ~ Frau hätte** ... any other woman would have ...; **haben Sie noch ~ Fragen?** do you have any more questions?; **ich habe eine ~ Auffassung als sie** my view is different from hers, I take a different view from her; **das machen wir ein ~s Mal** we'll do that another time; **seine ~n Dramen** his other plays; **das ~ Geschlecht** the other sex; **er ist ein ~r Mensch geworden** he is a changed man; **~ Länder, ~ Sitten** different countries have different customs; **daran habe ich mich gewöhnt, ~ Länder, ~ Sitten** I've got used to it, when in Rome do as the Romans do.

(b) (*folgend*) next, following. **am ~n Tag, ~n Tags** (*liter*) (on) the next *or* following day.

2 (*substantivisch*) (a) (*Ding*) **ein ~r** a different one; (*noch einer*) another one; **etwas ~s** something *or* (*jedes, in Fragen*) anything else; **alle ~n all the others;** es **war noch drei ~s** he has three others *or* (*von demselben*) more; **ja, das ist etwas ~s** yes, that's a different matter; **das ist etwas ganz ~s** that's something quite different; **das gefällt mir, das ist ganz was ~s** (*inf*) I like it, it's different; **hast du etwas ~s gedacht?** did you think otherwise?; **ich muß mir etwas ~s anziehen** I must put on something else *or* different; **einen Tag um den ~n/ein Mal ums ~** every single day/time; **ich habe ~s zu tun** I've other things to do; **ich habe ~s gehört** I heard differently; **nichts ~s** nothing else; **nichts ~s als ...** nothing but ...; **es blieb mir nichts ~s übrig, als selbst hinzugehen** I had no alternative but to go myself; **und vieles ~ mehr** and much more besides; **alles ~ als zufrieden** anything but pleased, far from pleased; **bist du müde? — nein, alles ~ als** are you tired? — no, far from it *or* anything but; **unter ~m** among other things; **und ~s mehr** and more besides; **es kam eins zum ~n** one thing led to another; ... **man kann doch eines tun, ohne das ~ zu lassen** ... but you can have the best of both worlds; **ich habe ihn eines ~n belehrt** I taught him otherwise *or* (*eines besseren*) a lesson; **sie hat sich eines ~n besonnen** she changed her mind; **von einem Tag zum ~n** overnight; **von etwas ~m sprechen** to change the subject; **eines besser als das ~** each one better than the next.

(b) (*Person*) **ein ~r/eine ~** a different person; (*noch einer*) another person; **jeder ~/kein ~** anyone/no-one else; **es war kein ~r als** ... it was none other than ...; **niemand ~s** no-one else; **das haben mir ~ auch schon gesagt** other people *or* others have told me that too; **die ~n** the others; **alle ~n** all the others, everyone else; **jemand ~s or ~r** (*S Ger*) somebody or (*jeder, in Fragen*) anybody else; **wer ~s?** who else?; **wir/ihr ~n** the rest of us/you; **sie hat einen ~n** she has someone else; **der eine oder der ~ von unseren Kollegen** one or other of our colleagues; **es gibt immer den einen oder den ~n, der faulenzt** there is always someone who is lazy; **der eine ..., der ~ ...** this person ..., that person...; **einer nach dem ~n** one after the other; **eine schöner als die ~** each one more beautiful than the next; **der eine kommt, der ~ geht** as one person comes another goes; (*man geht ein und aus*) people are coming and going; **das kannst du ~n erzählen!** (*inf*) go tell it to the marines (*inf*).

and(e)rerseits *adv* on the other hand.

anderlei *adj inv* (*geh*) other. **ich habe ~ zu tun** I am otherwise engaged *or* occupied.

andermal *adv:* **ein ~** some other time.

ändern 1 *vt* to change, to alter; *Meinung, Richtung* to change; *Kleidungsstück* to alter. **das ändert die Sache** that changes things, that puts a different complexion on things; **ich kann es nicht ~** I can't do anything about it; **das ist nicht zu ~, das läßt sich nicht (mehr) ~** nothing can be done about it; **das ändert nichts an der Tatsache, daß** ... that doesn't alter the fact that ...

2 *vr* (a) to change, to alter; *Meinung, Richtung* to change. **hier ändert sich das Wetter oft** the weather here is very changeable; **es hat sich nichts/viel geändert** nothing/a lot has changed.

(b) (*Mensch*) to change; (*sich bessern*) to change for the better. **wenn sich das nicht ändert** ... if things don't improve ...

ändern- *in cpds siehe* **ander(e)n-**.

anders *adv* (a) (*sonst*) else. **jemand/niemand ~** somebody *or* anybody/nobody else; **wer/wo ~?** who/where else?; **irgendwo ~** somewhere else; **wie ~ hätte ich es machen sollen?** how else should I have done it?

(b) (*verschieden, besser, schöner*) differently; (*andersartig*) different (*als* to). **~ als jd sein, aussehen, klingen, schmecken** different (*als* to). **~ als jd denken/reagieren/aussehen** to think/react differently/look different from sb; **~ als jd** (*geh: im Gegensatz zu*) unlike sb; **es** *or* **die Sache verhält sich ganz ~** things *or* matters are quite different; **~ geartet sein als jd** to be different from *or* to sb; **~ ausgedrückt** to put it another way, in other words; **das machen wir so und nicht ~** we'll do it this way and no other; **das hat sie nicht ~ erwartet** she expected nothing else; **wie nicht ~ zu erwarten** as was to be expected; **sie ist ~ geworden** she has changed; **wie könnte es ~ sein?** how could it be otherwise?; ... **und, wie könnte es ~** (*iro*) ... and, surprise surprise, she came too late; **es geht nicht ~** there's no other way; **ich kann nicht ~** (*kann es nicht lassen*) I can't help it; (*muß leider*) I have no choice; **es sich** (*dat*) **~ überlegen** to change one's mind; **da wird mir ganz ~** I start to feel funny *or* (*übel auch*) peculiar; **ich kann auch ~** (*inf*) you'd/he'd *etc* better watch it (*inf*); **das klingt schon ~** (*inf*) now that's more like it.

(c) (*inf: anderenfalls*) otherwise, or else.

Anders-: **a~artig** *adj, no comp* different; **~artigkeit** *f* (*des Lebens*) different quality; **jdn wegen seiner ~artigkeit nicht verstehen** not to understand sb because he/she is different; **a~denkend** *adj attr* dissident, dissenting; **~denkende(r)** *mf decl as adj* peculiar; **ich kann auch ~** dissident, dissenter; **die Freiheit des ~denkenden** the freedom to dissent.

anderseits *adv siehe* **and(e)rserseits.**

Anders-: **a~farbig** *adj* different-coloured, of a different colour; **~farbige** *pl* people of a different colour; **a~geartet** *adj siehe* **a~artig;** **a~geschlechtlich** *adj* of the other *or* opposite sex; **a~gesinnt** *adj* of a different opinion; **a~gesinnt sein** to have a different opinion, to disagree (*in + dat* on); **~gesinnte(r)** *mf decl as adj* person of a different opinion; **er unterhält sich gern mit ~gesinnten** he likes talking to people who think differently; **a~gläubig** *adj* of a different faith *or* religion *or* creed; **a~gläubig sein** to be of *or* have a different faith *etc;* **~gläubige(r)** *mf decl as adj* person of a different faith *or* religion *or* creed; **a~(he)rum** 1 *adv* the other way round; **a~(he)rum gehen** to go the other way round; **dreh die Schraube mal a~(he)rum** turn the screw the other way; 2 *adj* (*sl: homosexuell*) **a~(he)rum sein** to be bent (*inf*); **a~lautend** *adj attr* (*form*) contrary; **a~lautende Berichte** contrary reports, reports to the contrary; **a~rum** (*inf*) *adv, adj siehe* **a~(he)rum;** **~sein** *nt* (*geh*) (a) *siehe* **~artigkeit** (b) (*euph: Homosexualität*) homosexuality; **a~sprachig** *adj Literatur* foreign(-language); **die a~sprachige Minderheit** the minority who speak a different language; **a~sprachiger Unterricht** teaching in a different language; **a~wie** *adv* (*inf*) (*auf andere Weise*) some other way; (*unterschiedlich*) differently; **a~wo** *adv* elsewhere; **das gibt es nicht a~wo** you can't get that anywhere else; **a~woher** *adv* from elsewhere; **a~wohin** *adv* elsewhere; **ich gehe nicht gerne a~wohin** I don't like going anywhere else.

anderthalb *num* one and a half. **~ Pfund Kaffee** a pound and a half of coffee; **~ Stunden** an hour and a half; **das Kind ist ~ Jahre alt** the child is eighteen months old *or* one and a half.

anderthalb-: **~fach** *adj* one and a half times; **nimm die ~fache Menge/das A~fache** use half as much again; *siehe auch* **vierfach;** **~mal** *adv* one and a half times; **~mal soviel/soviele** half as much/many again.

Änderung *f* change, alteration (*an + dat, gen* in, to); (*in jdm*) change (*in + dat* in); (*an Kleidungsstück, Gebäude*) alteration (*an + dat* to); (*der Gesellschaft, der Politik etc*) change (*gen* in).

Änderungs-: **~antrag** *m* (*Parl*) amendment; **~schneider** *m* tailor (who does alterations); **~vorschlag** *m* suggested change or alteration; **einen ~vorschlag machen** to suggest a change *or* an alteration; **~wunsch** *m* wish to make changes *or* alterations; **haben Sie ~wünsche?** are there any changes *or* alterations you would like made?

ander-: **~wärtig** *adj attr* (*geh*) *siehe* **~weitig** 1; **~wärts** *adv* elsewhere, somewhere else; **~weit** *adv* (*geh*) *siehe* **~weitig** 2; **~weitig** 1 *adj attr* (*andere, weitere*) other; **~weitige Ölvorkommen** (*an anderer Stelle*) other oil strikes, oil strikes elsewhere; 2 *adv* (*anders*) otherwise; (*an anderer Stelle*) elsewhere; **~weitig vergeben/besetzt werden** to be given to/filled by someone else; **etw ~weitig verwenden** to use sth for a different purpose.

andeuten *sep* 1 *vt* (*zu verstehen geben*) to hint, to intimate (*jdm etw* sth to sb); (*kurz erwähnen*) *Problem* to mention briefly; (*Art, Mus*) to suggest; (*erkennen lassen*) to indicate. **der Wald war nur mit ein paar Strichen angedeutet** a few strokes gave a suggestion of the wood.

2 *vr* to be indicated; (*Melodie etc*) to be suggested; (*Gewitter*) to be in the offing.

Andeutung *f* (*Anspielung, Anzeichen*) hint; (*flüchtiger Hinweis*) short *or* brief mention; (*Art, Mus*) suggestion *no pl;* (*Spur*) sign, trace; (*Anflug eines Lächelns etc*) faint suggestion. **eine ~ machen** to hint (*über + acc* at), to drop a hint (*über + acc* about); **versteckte ~en machen** to drop veiled hints; **eine Besserung zeichnet sich in ~en ab** there are vague signs of an improvement.

andeutungsweise 1 *adv* (*als Anspielung, Anzeichen*) by way of a hint; (*als flüchtiger Hinweis*) in passing. **jdm ~ zu verstehen geben, daß** ... to hint to sb that ...; **man kann die Mauern noch ~ erkennen** you can still see traces of the walls; **sein nur noch ~ vorhandenes Haar** his few remaining traces of hair.

2 *adj attr* (*rare*) faint.

andichten *vt sep* (a) **jdm etw ~** (*inf*) to impute sth to sb; *Fähigkeiten* to credit sb with sth; **alles kann man ihm ~, aber** ... you can say what you like about him but ... (b) **jdn ~** to write a poem/poems to sb; **jdn in Sonetten ~** to write sonnets to sb.

andicken *vt sep Suppe, Soße* to thicken.

andienen *sep* (*pej*) 1 *vt* **jdm etw ~** to press sth on sb; **man diente ihm einen hohen Posten im Ausland an, um ihn loszuwerden** they tried to get rid of him by palming him off with a high position abroad. 2 *vr* **sich jdm ~** to offer sb one's services (*als* as).

Andienungsstraße *f* (*Mot*) service road.

andiskutieren* *vt sep* to discuss briefly, to touch on.

andocken *vti sep* (*Space*) to dock.

andonnern *sep* (*inf*) 1 *vi aux sein* (*usu angedonnert kommen*) to come thundering *or* roaring along. 2 *vt jdn* to shout or bellow at.

Andrang *m* -(e)s, *no pl* (a) (*Zustrom, Gedränge*) crowd, crush. **es herrschte großer ~** there was a great crowd *or* crush. (b) (*von Blut*) rush; (*von Wassermassen*) onrush.

andrängen *vi sep aux sein* to push forward; (*Menschenmenge*) to surge forward; (*Wassermassen*) to surge. **die ~de Menschenmenge** the surging crowd.

Andreas *m* - Andrew.

Andreaskreuz *nt* diagonal cross; (*Rel*) St Andrew's cross.

andrehen *vt sep* (a) (*anstellen*) to turn on. (b) (*festdrehen*) to screw on; *Schraube* to screw in. (c) **jdm etw ~** (*inf*) to palm sth off on sb.

andren- *in cpds siehe* **ander(e)n-**.

andre(r, s) *adj siehe* **andere(r, s).**

andrerseits *adv siehe* **and(e)rserseits.**

andringen vi sep irreg aux sein (geh) (Menschen etc) to push forward, to press (gegen towards); (Wasser) to press, to push (gegen against). die ~de Flut von Pornographie the rising flood of pornography.

Androgen nt -s, -e androgen.

androhen vt sep to threaten (jdm etw sb with sth).

Androhung f threat. unter ~ der or von Gewalt with the threat of violence; unter der ~, etw zu tun with the threat of doing sth; unter ~ (Jur) under penalty (von, gen of).

Android(e) m -en, -en android.

Andruck m (a) (Typ) proof. (b) no pl (Space) g-force, gravitational force.

andrucken sep (Typ) 1 vt to pull a proof of. 2 vi to pull proofs; (mit dem Druck beginnen) to start or begin printing.

andrücken vt sep (a) Pflaster to press on (an + acc to). als ich kräftiger andrückte when I pressed or pushed harder. (b) (beschädigen) Obst etc to bruise. (c) (durch Druck einschalten) Licht etc to switch on (by pressing a button).

Andruckexemplar nt (Typ) proof copy.

andudeln vr sep sich (dat) einen ~ (sl) to get merry or tipsy (inf).

andünsten vti sep (Cook) to braise briefly; (beginnen zu dünsten) to start braising.

Äneas m - Aeneas.

anlecken vi sep aux sein (inf) (bei jdm/allen) ~ to rub sb/everyone up the wrong way; mit seinen or wegen seiner Bemerkungen ist er schon oft angeeckt his remarks have often rubbed people up the wrong way.

anleifern vt sep (S Ger, Aus) to spur on, to encourage; Mannschaft to cheer on. Kinder zum Lernen ~ to encourage children to learn.

anleignen vr sep sich (dat) etw ~ (etw erwerben) to acquire sth; (etw wegnehmen) to appropriate sth; (sich mit etw vertraut machen) to learn sth; (sich etw angewöhnen) to pick sth up.

Anleignung f siehe vr acquisition; appropriation; learning; picking up. widerrechtliche ~ (Jur) misappropriation.

anleinander adv (a) (gegenseitig, an sich) ~ denken to think of each other; sich ~ gewöhnen to get used to each other; sich ~ halten to hold on to each other; sich ~ ärgern (geh) to annoy each other; sich ~ stoßen (lit) to knock into each other; Freude ~ haben to enjoy each other's company. (b) (mit Richtungsangabe) ~ vorüber-/vorbeigehen to go past each other; ~ vorbeireden to talk or be at cross-purposes. (c) (einer am anderen, zusammen) befestigen together. die Häuser stehen zu dicht ~ the houses are built too close together.

anleinander- in cpds together; ~bauen vt sep to build together; die Häuser waren ganz dicht ~gebaut the houses were built very close together; ~fügen sep 1 vt to put together; 2 vr to join together; ~geraten* vi sep irreg to come to blows (mit with); (streiten) to have words (mit with); ~grenzen vi sep to border on each other; in Istanbul grenzen Orient und Okzident ~ in Istanbul East and West meet; ~halten vt sep irreg to hold against each other; ~hängen sep irreg 1 vi (a) (zusammenhängen) to be linked (together); (b) (fig: Menschen) to be attached to each other; 2 vt to link together; ~kleben sep 1 vt to stick together; 2 vi to be stuck together; (inf: unzertrennlich sein) to be glued together (inf); ~koppeln vt sep to couple; Raumschiffe to link up; ~lehnen vr sep to lean on or against each other; ~liegen vi sep irreg to be adjacent (to each other), to be next to each other; ~prallen vi sep aux sein to collide; (fig) to clash; ~reihen sep 1 vt to string together; 2 vr to be strung together; (zeitlich: Tage etc) to run together; A~reihung f stringing together; ~schmieden vt sep siehe zusammenschmieden; ~schmiegen vr sep to snuggle up; ~setzen vt sep to put together; ~stellen vt sep to put together; ~stoßen sep irreg 1 vt to bang together; 2 vi aux sein to collide; (Fahrzeuge, Köpfe auch, Menschen) to bump into each other; (~grenzen) to meet.

Äneis [ε'neːɪs] f - Aeneid.

Anekdötchen nt (hum) little story or anecdote.

Anekdote f -, -n anecdote.

anekdotenhaft adj anecdotal.

anekdotisch adj (Liter) anecdotic. sein Vortrag war ~ aufgelockert his lecture was lightened by anecdotes.

anlekeln vt sep (a) (anwidern) to disgust, to nauseate. die beiden ekeln sich nur noch an they just find each other nauseating or make each other sick. (b) (inf: beleidigen) to be offensive to. ..., ekelte er mich an ..., he spat at me.

Anemone f -, -n anemone.

anlempfehlen vt sep or insep irreg (geh) to recommend.

anlempfunden adj (geh) artificial, spurious, false. nicht echt, sondern nur ~ not genuine.

Anlerbe m (old) siehe Hoferbe.

Anlerbieten nt -s, - (geh) offer.

anlerbieten* vr sep or insep irreg (geh) to offer one's services. sich ~, etw zu tun to offer to do sth.

anlerkannt 1 ptp of anerkennen. 2 adj recognized; Tatsache auch established; Werk standard; Bedeutung accepted; Experte acknowledged.

anlerkanntermaßen adv diese Mannschaft ist ~ besser it is generally recognized or accepted or acknowledged that this team is better, this team is generally recognized etc to be better.

anlerkennen* vt sep or insep irreg Staat, König, Rekord to recognize; Forderung auch, Rechnung to accept; Vaterschaft to accept, to acknowledge; (würdigen) Leistung, Bemühung to appreciate; Meinung to respect; (loben) to praise. ..., das muß man ~ (zugeben) admittedly, ..., ... you can't argue with that; (würdigen) ... one has to appreciate that; als gleichwertiger

Partner anerkannt sein to be accepted as an equal partner; ihr ~der Blick her appreciative look.

anlerkennenswert adj commendable.

Anlerkenntnis nt (Jur) acknowledgement.

Anlerkennung f siehe vt recognition; acceptance; acknowledgement; appreciation; respect; praise.

Anlerkennungsschreiben nt letter of appreciation or commendation.

anlerziehen* vt insep irreg: jdm etw ~ (Kindern) to instil sth into sb; (neuen Angestellten etc auch) to drum sth into sb; sich (dat) etw ~ to train oneself to do sth.

anlerzogen adj acquired. das ist alles ~ she etc has just been trained to be like that.

Anf. abbr of Anfang.

anfachen vt sep (geh) (a) Glut, Feuer to fan. (b) (fig) to arouse; Leidenschaft auch to inflame, to fan the flames of; Haß auch to inspire.

anfahren sep irreg 1 vi aux sein (a) (losfahren) to start (up). angefahren kommen (herbeifahren) (Wagen, Fahrer) to drive up; (Zug) to pull up; (ankommen) to arrive; beim A~ when starting (up); das A~ am Berg üben to practise a hill start. (b) (inf) laß mal noch eine Runde ~ let's have another round. 2 vt (a) (liefern) Kohlen, Kartoffeln to deliver. (b) (inf: spendieren) to lay on. (c) (ansteuern) Ort to stop or call at; Hafen auch to put in at; (Aut) Kurve to approach. die Insel wird zweimal wöchentlich von der Fähre angefahren the ferry calls twice a week at the island. (d) (anstoßen) Passanten, Baum etc to run into, to hit; (fig: ausschelten) to shout at.

Anfahrt f (~sweg, ~szeit) journey; (Zufahrt) approach; (Einfahrt) drive. „nur ~ zum Krankenhaus" "access to hospital only".

Anfall m (a) (attack; (Wut~, epileptischer) fit. einen ~ haben/bekommen (lit) to have an attack or fit; (fig inf) to have or throw a fit (inf); da könnte man Anfälle kriegen (inf) it's enough to send or drive you round the bend (inf); in einem ~ von (fig) in a fit of. (b) (Ertrag, Nebenprodukte) yield (an + dat of); (von Zinsen auch) accrual. (c) (von Reparaturen, Kosten) amount (an + dat of); (form: Anhäufung) accumulation. bei ~ von Reparaturen in case of necessary repair; es ist mit einem hohen ~ an Reparaturen zu rechnen a high rate of repairs can be expected.

anfallen sep irreg 1 vt (a) (überfallen) to attack; (Sittenstrolch etc) to assault. (b) (liter) Heimweh/Sehnsucht fiel ihn an he was assailed by homesickness/filled with longing. 2 vi aux sein (sich ergeben) to arise; (Zinsen) to accrue; (Nebenprodukte) to be obtained; (sich anhäufen) to accumulate. die ~den Kosten/Reparaturen/Probleme the costs/repairs/problems incurred; die ~de Arbeit the work which comes up.

anfällig adj (nicht widerstandsfähig) delicate; Motor, Maschine temperamental. gegen or für etw/eine Krankheit ~ sein to be susceptible to sth/prone to an illness.

Anfälligkeit f siehe adj delicateness; temperamental nature; susceptibility; proneness.

Anfang m -(e)s, Anfänge (Beginn) beginning, start; (erster Teil) beginning; (Ursprung) beginnings pl, origin. zu or am ~ to start with; (anfänglich) at first; gleich zu ~ darauf hinweisen, daß ... to mention right at the beginning or outset that ...; am ~ schuf Gott Himmel und Erde in the beginning God created the heaven(s) and the earth; im ~ war das Wort (Bibl) in the beginning was the Word; ~ Fünfzig in one's early fifties; ~ Juni/1978 etc at the beginning of June/1978 etc; von ~ an (right) from the beginning or start; von ~ bis Ende from start to finish; den ~ machen to start or begin; (den ersten Schritt tun) to make the first move; einen neuen ~ machen to make a new start; (im Leben) to turn over a new leaf; ein ~ ist gemacht it's a start; seinen ~ nehmen (geh) to commence; das ist erst der ~ that's only the beginning; den richtigen ~ finden to know how to begin; aller ~ ist schwer (Prov) the first step is always the most difficult; aus kleinen/bescheidenen Anfängen from small/humble beginnings; der ~ vom Ende the beginning of the end.

anfangen sep irreg 1 vt (a) (beginnen) Arbeit, Brief, Gespräch, (inf: anbrauchen) neue Tube etc to start, to begin; Streit, Verhältnis, Fabrik to start. (b) (anstellen, machen) to do. das mußt du anders ~ you'll have to go about it differently; was soll ich damit ~? what am I supposed to do with that?; (was nützt mir das?) what's the use of that?; damit kann ich nichts ~ (nützt mir nichts) that's no good to me; (verstehe ich nicht) it doesn't mean a thing to me; was fangen wir jetzt an? what shall we do now?; nichts mit sich/jdm anzufangen wissen not to know what to do with oneself/sb; mit dir ist heute (aber) gar nichts anzufangen! you're no fun at all today! 2 vi to begin, to start. wer fängt an? who's going to start or begin?; fang (du) an! (you) begin or start!; ich habe schon angefangen I've already started; du hast angefangen! you started!; (bei Streit) you started it!; es fing zu regnen an or an zu regnen it started raining or to rain; das fängt ja schön or heiter an! (iro) that's a good start!; er fängt an, alt zu werden he's beginning to get old; jetzt fängt das Leben erst an life is only just beginning; fang nicht wieder davon or damit an! don't start all that again!, don't bring all that up again!; mit etw ~ to start sth; klein/unten ~ to start small/at the bottom; er hat als kleiner Handwerker angefangen he started out as a small-time tradesman; bei einer Firma ~ to start with a firm or working for a firm.

Anfänger(in f) m -s, - beginner; (Neuling) novice; (Aut) learner; (inf: Nichtskönner) amateur (pej). du ~! (inf) you amateur; sie ist keine ~in mehr (hum) she's certainly no beginner.

Anfänger-: ~kurs(us) m beginners' course; ~übung f (Univ) introductory course.

anfänglich 1 adj attr initial. **2** adv at first, initially.

anfangs 1 adv at first, initially. **wie ich schon ~ erwähnte** as I mentioned at the beginning; **gleich ~ auf etw (acc) hinweisen** to mention sth right at the beginning or outset.
2 prep +gen = **der zwanziger Jahre/des Monats** in the early twenties/at the beginning of the month.

Anfangs- in cpds initial; ~**buchstabe** m first letter; **kleine/große ~buchstaben** small/large or capital initials; ~**gehalt** nt initial or starting salary; ~**geschwindigkeit** f starting speed; (esp Phys) initial velocity; ~**gründe** pl rudiments pl, elements pl; ~**kapital** nt starting capital; ~**silbe** f first or initial syllable; ~**stadium** nt initial stage; **im ~stadium dieser Krankheit/dieses Projekts** in the initial stages of this illness/project; **meine Versuche sind schon im ~stadium steckengeblieben** my attempts never really got off the ground; ~**unterricht** m first lessons pl; ~**zeile** f first line; ~**zeit** f starting time.

anfassen sep **1** vt **(a)** (berühren) to touch. **faß mal meinen Kopf an** just feel my head.
(b) (bei der Hand nehmen) **jdn ~** to take sb's hand or sb by the hand; **sich er einander (geh) ~** to take each other by the hand; **faßt euch an!** hold hands!; **angefaßt gehen** to walk holding hands.
(c) (fig) (anpacken) Problem to tackle, to go about; (behandeln) Menschen to treat.
(d) (geh: befallen) to seize.
2 vi **(a)** (berühren) to feel. **nicht ~!** don't touch!
(b) (mithelfen) **mit ~, (mit) ~ helfen** to give a hand.
3 vr (sich anfühlen) to feel. **es faßt sich weich an** it feels or is soft (to the touch).

anfauchen vt sep (Katze) to spit at; (fig inf) to snap at.

anfaulen vi sep aux sein to begin to go bad; (Holz) to start rotting. **angefault** half-rotten.

anfechtbar adj contestable.

Anfechtbarkeit f contestability. **wegen der ~ seiner Argumentation** because his argument is/was contestable.

anfechten vt sep irreg **(a)** (nicht anerkennen) to contest; Meinung, Aussage auch to challenge; Urteil, Entscheidung to appeal against; Vertrag to dispute; Ehe to contest the validity of. **(b)** (beunruhigen) to trouble; (in Versuchung bringen) to tempt, to lead into temptation. **was ficht dich an?** (old) what ails you? (old); **das ficht mich gar nicht an** that doesn't concern me in the slightest. **(c)** (obs: einfallen, überkommen) **was ficht/focht dich an, das zu tun?** what possessed you to do that?

Anfechtung f **(a)** siehe vt **(a)** contesting; challenging; appeal (gen against); disputing; (von Ehe) action for nullification or annulment. **(b)** (Versuchung) temptation; (Selbstzweifel) doubt.

Anfechtungsklage f (Jur) (zu Ehescheidung) action for nullification or annulment; (zu Testament) action to set aside a/the will; (zu Patent) opposition proceedings.

anfegen vi sep aux sein (inf) **angefegt kommen** to come belting along or (auf einen zu) up (inf).

anfeilen vt sep to start to file.

anfeinden vt sep to treat with hostility.

Anfeindung f hostility. **trotz aller ~en** although he had aroused so much animosity.

anfertigen vt sep to make; Arznei to make up; Schriftstück, Hausaufgaben, Protokoll to do. **jdm etw ~** to make sth for sb; **sich (dat) einen Anzug etc ~ lassen** to have a suit etc made.

Anfertigung f siehe vt making; making up; doing. **die ~ dieser Übersetzung/der Arznei hat eine halbe Stunde gedauert** it took half an hour to do the translation/to make up the prescription; **die ~ des Protokolls ist Aufgabe der Sekretärin** it's the secretary's job to do the minutes, doing the minutes is the secretary's job.

Anfertigungskosten pl production costs pl. **die ~ eines Smokings** the cost of making a dinner jacket/having a dinner jacket made.

anfeuchten vt sep to moisten; Schwamm, Lippen auch to wet; Bügelwäsche auch to damp.

anfeuern vt sep Ofen to light; (Ind) to fire; (fig: ermutigen) to spur on.

Anfeuerung f (fig) spurring on.

Anfeuerungsruf m cheer; (esp Pol) chant; (Anfeuerungswort) shout of encouragement.

anfinden vr sep irreg to be found, to turn up (again).

anflachsen vt sep (sl) to make wise-cracks/a wise-crack to (inf); Mädchen etc to give the line (sl). **... flachste er mich an ...** he wisecracked.

anflegeln vt sep (inf) to speak rudely to. **ich lasse mich doch nicht von dir ~!** I'm not prepared to have you swearing at me!

anflehen vt sep to beseech, to implore (um for). **ich flehe dich an, tu das nicht!** I beg you, don't!

Anflehung f beseeching.

anfletschen vt sep to bare one's teeth at.

anfliegen sep irreg **1** vi aux sein (auch **angeflogen kommen**) (Flugzeug) to come in to land; (Vogel, Geschoß, fig geh: Pferd, Fuhrwerk, Reiter) to come flying up.
2 vt **(a)** (Flugzeug) Flughafen, Piste, (Mil) Stellung to approach; (landen) to land (in/auf in/on). **diese Fluggesellschaft fliegt Bali an** this airline flies or operates a service to Bali.
(b) (geh: befallen) to overcome.

anflitzen vi sep aux sein (inf) (usu **angeflitzt kommen**) to come racing along or (auf einen zu) up (inf).

Anflug m **(a)** (Flugweg) flight; (das Heranfliegen) approach. **wir befinden uns im ~ auf Paris** we are now approaching Paris. **(b)** (Spur) trace; (fig: Hauch auch) hint.

Anflug-: ~**weg** m landing path; ~**zeit** f (Zeitraum) descent; (Zeitpunkt) time of starting a/the descent.

anflunkern vt sep (inf) to tell fibs/a fib to.

anfluten vi sep aux sein to flood in. **angeflutet kommen** to come flooding in.

anfordern vt sep to request, to ask for.

Anforderung f **(a)** no pl (das Anfordern) request (gen, von for). **bei der ~ von Ersatzteilen** when requesting spare parts. **(b)** (Anspruch) requirement; (Belastung) demand. **große ~en an jdn/etw stellen** to make great demands on sb/sth; **hohe/zu hohe ~en stellen** to demand a lot/too much (an +acc of); **den ~en im Beruf/in der Schule gewachsen sein** to be able to meet the demands of one's job/of school. **(c)** ~**en** pl (Niveau) standards pl.

Anfrage f inquiry; (Parl) question. **kleine ~** (written) Parliamentary question; **große ~** Parliamentary question dealt with at a meeting of the Lower House.

anfragen vi sep to inquire (bei jdm of sb), to ask (bei jdm sb). **um Erlaubnis/Genehmigung ~** to ask for permission/approval.

anfressen vt sep irreg **(a)** (Maus) to nibble at; (Vogel) to peck (at). **sich (dat) einen Bauch ~** (sl) to get a paunch through overeating. **(b)** (zersetzen) to eat away, to erode.

anfreunden vr sep to make or become friends. **sich mit etw ~** (fig) to get to like sth; **mit Pop-Musik** etc to acquire a taste for sth.

anfrieren sep irreg **1** vi aux sein (leicht gefrieren) to start to freeze; (Pflanze) to get a touch of frost; (haften bleiben) to freeze on (an +acc -to); (fig: Mensch) to freeze stiff. **2** vr ich **habe mir die Hände angefroren** my hands are frozen.

anfrotzeln vt sep siehe **anflachsen**.

anfügen vt sep to add.

Anfügung f addition; (zu einem Buch) addendum.

anfühlen sep **1** vt to feel. **2** vr to feel. **sich glatt/weich etc ~** to feel smooth/soft etc, to be smooth/soft etc to the touch.

Anfuhr f -, -en transport(ation).

anführbar adj quotable.

anführen vt sep **(a)** (vorangehen, befehligen) to lead. **(b)** (zitieren) to quote, to cite; Tatsachen, Beispiel, Einzelheiten auch to give; Umstand to cite, to refer to; Grund, Beweis to give, to offer; (benennen) jdn to name, to cite. **(c)** (Typ) to indicate or mark with (opening) quotation marks or inverted commas. **(d)** jdn ~ (inf) to have sb on (inf), to take sb for a ride (inf); **der läßt sich leicht ~** he's easily taken in or had on (inf).

Anführer m (Führer) leader; (pej: Anstifter) ringleader.

Anführung f **(a)** (das Vorangehen) leadership; (Befehligung auch) command. **unter ~ von ...** under the leadership of ..., led by ... **(b)** (das Anführen) siehe vt **(b)** quotation, citation; giving; citing, referring to; giving, offering; naming; citing; (Zitat) quotation. **die ~ von Zitaten/Einzelheiten** giving quotations/details.

Anführungs-: ~**strich** m, ~**zeichen** nt quotation or quote mark, inverted comma; **in ~strichen** or ~**zeichen** in inverted commas, in quotation marks, in quotes; ~**striche** or ~**zeichen unten/oben quote/unquote; **ein Wort mit ~zeichen versehen** to put a word in inverted commas; **das habe ich in ~zeichen gesagt** I was saying that in inverted commas.

anfüllen vt sep to fill (up). **mit etw angefüllt sein** to be full of or filled with sth.

anfunkeln vt sep to flash at.

anfuttern vr sep (inf) **sich (dat) einen Bauch ~** to acquire or develop a paunch.

Angabe ['anga:-] f -, -n **(a)** usu pl (Aussage) statement; (Anweisung) instruction; (Zahl, Detail) detail. ~**n über jdn/etw (acc) machen** to give details about sth; **laut ~n (+gen)** according to; **nach ~n der Zeugen** according to (the testimony of) the witness; ~**n zur Person** (form) personal details or particulars.
(b) (Nennung) giving. **wir bitten um ~ der Einzelheiten/Preise** please give or quote details/prices; **er ist ohne ~ seiner neuen Adresse verzogen** he moved without informing anyone of or telling anyone his new address; **ohne ~ von Gründen** without giving any reasons; **vergessen Sie nicht die ~ des Datums auf dem Brief** don't forget to give or put the date on the letter.
(c) no pl (inf: Prahlerei) showing off; (Reden auch) bragging, boasting.
(d) (Sport: Aufschlag) service, serve. **wer hat ~?** whose service or serve is it?, whose turn is it to serve?

angaffen ['anga-] vt sep (pej) to gape at.

angähnen ['ange:-] vt sep to yawn at.

angaloppieren* ['anga-] vi sep aux sein to gallop up. **angaloppiert kommen** to come galloping up.

angängig ['angɛ-] adj (form) feasible; (erlaubt auch) permissible.

angeben ['ange:-] sep irreg **1** vt **(a)** (nennen) to give; (als Zeugen) to name, to cite; (schriftlich) to indicate; (erklären) to explain; (beim Zoll) to declare; (anzeigen) Preis, Temperatur etc to indicate; (aussagen) to state; (behaupten) to maintain. **(b)** (bestimmen) Tempo, Kurs to set; (Mus) Tempo, Note to give. **den Takt ~** (klopfen) to beat time; siehe **Ton²**. **(c)** (dated: anzeigen) to report (bei to).
2 vi **(a)** (prahlen) to show off; (durch Reden auch) to boast, to brag (mit about).
(b) (Tennis etc) to serve.

(c) (*Cards*) to deal.
Angeber ['ange:-] *m* -s, - (a) (*Prahler*) show-off; (*durch Reden auch*) boaster. (b) (*dated: Denunziant*) informer.
Angeberei [ange:-] *f* (*inf*) *no pl* (*Prahlerei*) showing-off (*mit about*); (*verbal auch*) boasting, bragging (*mit about*). (b) *usu pl* (*Äußerung*) boast.
Angeberin *f siehe* **Angeber (a).**
angeberisch ['ange:-] *adj Reden* boastful; *Aussehen, Benehmen, Tonfall* pretentious, showy, ostentatious.
Angebertum ['ange:-] *nt, no pl* (*in äußerer Erscheinung*) ostentation; (*durch Reden*) boastfulness; (*in Benehmen*) pretention.
Angebetete(r) ['angə-] *mf decl as adj* (*hum, geh*) (*verehrter Mensch*) idol; (*Geliebte(r)*) beloved.
Angebinde ['angə-] *nt* -s, - (*dated geh*) gift, present.
angeblich ['angə-] **1** *adj attr* so-called, alleged. **2** *adv* supposedly, allegedly. er ist ~ Musiker he says he's a musician.
angeboren ['angə-] *adj* innate, inherent; (*Med, fig inf*) congenital (*bei* to). an seine Faulheit mußt du dich gewöhnen, die ist ~ (*inf*) you'll have to get used to his laziness, he was born that way.
Angebot ['angə-] *nt* (a) (*Anerbieten, angebotener Preis*) offer; (*bei Auktion*) bid; (*Comm: Offerte auch*) tender (*über + acc, für* for). (b) *no pl* (*Comm, Fin*) supply (*an + dat, von* of); (*inf: Sonder~*) special offer. ~ und Nachfrage supply and demand.
Angebots- ['angə-]: ~lücke *f* gap in the market; ~preis *m* asking price; ~überhang *m* surplus, supply.
angebracht ['angə-] **1** *ptp of* **anbringen. 2** *adj* appropriate; (*sinnvoll*) reasonable. schlecht ~ uncalled-for.
angebrannt ['angə-] **1** *ptp of* **anbrennen. 2** *adj* burnt. ~ riechen/schmecken to smell/taste burnt; es riecht hier so ~ there's a smell of burning here.
angebrochen ['angə-] **1** *ptp of* **anbrechen.**
2 *adj Packung, Flasche* open(ed). wieviel ist von den ~en hundert Mark übrig? how much is left from the 100 marks we'd started using?; ein ~er Abend/Nachmittag/Urlaub (*hum*) the rest of an evening/afternoon/a holiday; das Parken kostet für jede ~e Stunde eine Mark parking costs one mark for every hour or part of an hour; für mich ist das erst ein ~er Abend as far as I'm concerned, the evening's just starting.
angebunden ['angə-] **1** *ptp of* **anbinden. 2** *adj* (*beschäftigt*) tied (down). kurz ~ sein (*inf*) to be abrupt or curt or brusque.
angedeihen* ['angə-] *vt sep irreg* jdm etw ~ lassen (*geh*) to provide sb with sth.
Angedenken ['angə-] *nt* -s, *no pl* (*geh*) remembrance. mein Großvater seligen ~s my late lamented grandfather; der Massenmörder Braun unseligen ~s the late notorious mass-murderer Braun.
angeduselt ['angə-] *adj* (*inf*) tipsy, merry (*inf*).
angeekelt ['angə-] **1** *ptp of* **anekeln. 2** *adj* disgusted.
angeführt ['angə-] **1** *ptp of* **anführen. 2** *adj siehe* **angegeben 2.**
angegangen ['angə-] **1** *ptp of* **angehen. 2** *adj* (*inf*) ~ sein to have gone off; ~e Lebensmittel food which has gone off.
angegeben ['angə-] **1** *ptp of* **angeben. 2** *adj* am ~en Ort loco citato.
angegilbt ['angə-] *adj* yellowed.
angegossen ['angə-] *adj* wie ~ sitzen or passen to fit like a glove.
angegraut ['angə-] *adj* grey; *Schläfen, Haar auch* greying.
angegriffen ['angə-] **1** *ptp of* **angreifen. 2** *adj Gesundheit* weakened; *Mensch, Aussehen* frail; (*erschöpft*) exhausted; (*nervlich*) strained. sie ist nervlich/gesundheitlich immer noch ~ her nerves are still strained/health is still weakened.
angehalten ['angə-] **1** *ptp of* **anhalten. 2** *adj* ~ sein, etw zu tun/unterlassen to be required or obliged to do/refrain from doing sth; zu Pünktlichkeit ~ sein to be required to be punctual.
angehaucht ['angə-] **1** *ptp of* **anhauchen. 2** *adj* links/rechts ~ sein to have or show left-/right-wing tendencies or leanings; links ~e Kreise circles with left-wing tendencies or leanings.
angeheiratet ['angə-] *adj* related by marriage. ein ~er Cousin a cousin by marriage.
angeheitert ['angə-] *adj* (*inf*) merry (*inf*), tipsy.
angehen ['ange:-] *sep irreg* **1** *vi* (a) (*dial: beginnen*) (*Schule, Theater etc*) to start; (*Feuer*) to start burning, to catch; (*Radio*) to come on; (*Licht*) to come or go on.
(b) (*entgegentreten*) gegen jdn ~ to fight sb, to tackle sb; gegen etw ~ to fight sth; gegen *Flammen, Hochwasser* to fight sth back, to combat sth; gegen *Mißstände, Zustände* to take measures against sth; dagegen muß man ~ something must be done about it.
(c) *siehe* **angegangen.**
2 *vt* (a) (*anpacken*) *Aufgabe, Schwierigkeiten, Hindernis* to tackle; *Gegner auch* to attack; *Kurve* to take.
(b) (*bitten*) to ask (jdm um etw sb for sth).
(c) (*betreffen*) to concern. was mich angeht for my part; was geht das ihn an? (*inf*) what's that got to do with him?; das geht ihn gar nichts or einen Dreck or einen feuchten Staub an (*inf*) that's none of his business, that's got nothing or damn all (*inf*) to do with him.
3 *vi impers* das geht nicht/keinesfalls an that won't do, that's not on, that's quite out of the question; es geht nicht/keinesfalls an, daß wir uns unsere Politik von der Kirche vorschreiben lassen we can't/can't possibly allow the Church to dictate our politics.
angehend ['angə-] *adj Musiker, Künstler* budding; *Lehrer, Ehemann, Vater* prospective. mit 16 ist sie jetzt schon eine ~e junge Dame at 16 she's rapidly becoming or is almost a young lady; er ist ein ~er Sechziger he's approaching sixty.

angehoben *ptp of* **anheben.**
angehören* ['angə-] *vi sep +dat* to belong to; (*einer Partei, einer Familie auch*) to be a member of. jdm/einander ~ (*liter*) to belong to sb/one another or each other.
angehörig ['angə-] *adj* belonging (*dat* to). keiner Partei ~e Bürger citizens who do not belong to any party.
Angehörige(r) ['angə-] *mf decl as adj* (a) (*Mitglied*) member. (b) (*Familien~*) relative, relation. der nächste ~ the next of kin.
angejahrt ['angə-] *adj* advanced in years.
Angeklagte(r) ['angə-] *mf decl as adj* accused, defendant.
angeknackst ['angə-] **1** *ptp of* **anknacksen. 2** *adj* (*inf*) *Mensch* (*seelisch*) uptight (*inf*); *Selbstvertrauen, Selbstbewußtsein* weakened. er/seine Gesundheit ist ~ he is in bad shape or a bad way; sie ist noch immer etwas ~ she still hasn't got over it yet.
angekränkelt ['angə-] *adj* (*geh*) sickly, frail, ailing. vom Geist ~ afflicted by or suffering from overintellectualizing.
angekratzt ['angə-] **1** *ptp of* **ankratzen. 2** *adj* (*inf*) seedy (*inf*), the worse for wear.
Angel *f* -, -n (*Tür~, Fenster~*) hinge. etw aus den ~n heben (*lit*) to lift sth off its hinges; (*fig*) to revolutionize sth completely; die Welt aus den ~n heben (*fig*) to turn the world upside down. (b) (*Fischfanggerät*) (fishing) rod and line, fishing pole (*US*); (*zum Schwimmenlernen*) swimming harness. die ~ auswerfen to cast (the line); jdm an die ~ gehen (*fig*) to fall for or swallow sb's line.
angelegen ['angə-] *adj* sich (*dat*) etw ~ sein lassen (*form*) to concern oneself with sth.
Angelegenheit ['angə-] *f* matter; (*politisch, persönlich*) affair; (*Aufgabe*) concern. das ist meine/nicht meine ~ that's my/not my concern or business; sich um seine eigenen ~en kümmern to mind one's own business; in einer dienstlichen ~ on official business; in eigener ~ on a private or personal matter.
angelegentlich ['angə-] *adj* (*geh*) *Bitte, Frage* pressing, insistent; (*drindend*) pressing, urgent; *Bemühung* enthusiastic; *Empfehlung* warm, eager. sich ~ über jdn erkundigen to ask particularly about sb.
angelegt ['angə-] **1** *ptp of* **anlegen. 2** *adj* calculated (*auf + acc* for).
angelernt ['angə-] **1** *ptp of* **anlernen. 2** *adj Arbeiter* semi-skilled. der Lohn für A~e the wage for semi-skilled workers.
Angel-: ~gerät *nt* fishing tackle *no pl*; ~haken *m* fish-hook; ~leine *f* fishing line.
angeln ['angə-] **1** *vi* (a) to angle, to fish. ~ gehen to go angling or fishing; nach etw or auf etw (*acc*) ~ (*lit*) to fish for sth; nach Komplimenten/Lob *etc* ~ to fish or angle for compliments/praise.
(b) (*zu greifen versuchen, hervorziehen*) to fish. nach etw ~ to fish (around) for sth.
2 *vt Fisch* to fish for; (*fangen*) to catch. sich (*dat*) einen Mann ~ (*inf*) to catch (oneself) a man; den werde ich mir ~ (*inf: vornehmen*) I'll give him a piece of my mind.
Angeln *pl* (*Hist*) Angles *pl*.
angeloben* ['angə-] *vt sep* (a) (*liter*) jdm etw ~ to swear sth to sb. (b) (*Aus: vereidigen*) to swear in.
Angelobung ['angə-] *f* (*Aus*) swearing in.
Angel-: ~punkt *m* crucial or central point; (*Frage*) key or central issue; ~rute *f* fishing rod.
Angelsachse *m decl as adj* Anglo-Saxon.
angelsächsisch ['angə-] *adj* Anglo-Saxon.
Angel-: ~schein *m* fishing permit; ~schnur *f* fishing line; ~sport *m* angling, fishing; a~weit *adv siehe* sperrangelweit.
angemessen ['angə-] *adj* (*passend, entsprechend*) appropriate (*dat* to, for); (*adäquat*) adequate (*dat* for); *Preis* reasonable, fair. eine der Leistung ~e Bezahlung payment commensurate with the effort; sie reagierte sehr empört, aber das war der Beleidigung auch ~ she reacted very angrily, but that was commensurate or in keeping with the insult.
Angemessenheit ['angə-] *f siehe adj* appropriateness; adequacy; fairness, reasonableness.
angenehm ['angə-] *adj* pleasant, agreeable. das wäre mir sehr ~ I should be very or most grateful, I should greatly appreciate it; es ist mir gar nicht ~, wenn ich früh aufstehen muß/daß er mich besuchen will I don't like getting up early/the fact that he wants to visit me; ist es Ihnen so ~? is that all right for you?, is it all right like that for you?; wenn Ihnen das ~er ist if you prefer; ~e Ruhe/Reise! *etc* have a good or pleasant rest/journey *etc*; (sehr) ~! (*form*) delighted (to meet you); das A~e mit dem Nützlichen verbinden to combine business with pleasure.
angenommen ['angə-] **1** *ptp of* **annehmen. 2** *adj* assumed; *Name auch, Kind* adopted. **3** *conj* assuming.
angepaßt ['angə-] **1** *ptp of* **anpassen. 2** *adj* conformist.
Angepaßtheit ['angə-] *f* conformism.
Anger *m* -s, - (*dial*) (a) (*Dorf~*) village green; (*old: Wiese*) pasture, meadow. (b) (*Schind~*) knacker's yard.
Anger-: ~blümchen *nt* daisy; ~dorf *nt* village built around a village green.
angeregt ['angə-] **1** *ptp of* **anregen. 2** *adj* lively, animated. ~ diskutieren to have a lively or an animated discussion.
Angeregtheit ['angə-] *f* liveliness, animation.
angereichert ['angə-] **1** *ptp of* **anreichern. 2** *adj* enriched.
angesäuselt ['angə-] *adj* (*inf*) tipsy, merry (*inf*).
angeschissen ['angə-] (*sl*) **1** *ptp of* **anscheißen. 2** *adj* buggered (*sl*). ~ sein to be buggered (*sl*) or in dead shtuck (*sl*).
angeschlagen ['angə-] **1** *ptp of* **anschlagen. 2** *adj* (*inf*) *Mensch, Aussehen, Nerven* shattered (*inf*); *Gesundheit* groggy (*inf*); (*betrunken*) sloshed (*inf*). von etw ~ sein to be shattered by sth (*inf*).

angeschlossen [ˈangə-] 1 *ptp of* **anschließen**. 2 *adj* affiliated (*dat* to *or* (*US*) with), associated (*dat* with).

angeschmiert [ˈangə-] 1 *ptp of* **anschmieren**. 2 *adj pred* (*inf*) in trouble, in dead shtuck (*sl*). **mit dem/der Waschmaschine bist du ganz schön ~** he/the washing machine is not all he/it is cracked up to be (*inf*); **der/die A~e sein** to have been had (*inf*).

angeschmutzt [ˈangə-] *adj* soiled; (*Comm*) shop-soiled.

angeschossen [ˈangə-] 1 *ptp of* **anschießen**. 2 *adj* (*inf*) **wie ein A~er** like a scalded cat (*inf*); **wie ~** like a chicken with no head (*inf*).

angeschrieben [ˈangə-] 1 *ptp of* **anschreiben**. 2 *adj* (*inf*) **bei jdm gut/schlecht ~ sein** to be in sb's good/bad books, to be well in/not very well in with sb (*inf*); **diese Partei ist bei den Wählern schlecht ~** this party is out of favour with the voters.

Angeschuldigte(r) [ˈangə-] *mf decl as adj* suspect.

angesehen [ˈangə-] 1 *ptp of* **ansehen**. 2 *adj* respected.

angesessen [ˈangə-] *adj siehe* **eingesessen**.

Angesicht [ˈangə-] *nt* -(e)s, -er *or* (*Aus*) -e (*geh*) face, countenance (*form*). **von ~ zu ~** face to face; **jdn von ~ sehen** to see sb face to face; **jdn von ~ kennen** to know sb by sight; **im ~ +gen** (*fig*) in the face of.

angesichts [ˈangə-] *prep +gen* in the face of; (*im Hinblick auf*) in view of. **~ des Todes** in the face of death; **~ des Sternenhimmels kommt sich der Mensch winzig und nichtig vor** in contrast to the starry sky man seems minute and insignificant.

angesoffen [ˈangə-] (*sl*) 1 *adj of* **ansaufen**. 2 *adj* pissed (*sl*), sloshed (*inf*). **~ or in ~em Zustand Auto fahren** to drive (a car) (when) sloshed (*inf*).

angespannt [ˈangə-] 1 *ptp of* **anspannen**.
2 *adj* (a) (*angestrengt*) *Nerven* tense, strained; *Aufmerksamkeit* close, keen. **aufs höchste ~ sein** to be very *or* highly tense; **~ zuhören** to listen attentively *or* closely.
(b) (*bedrohlich*) *politische Lage* tense, strained; (*Comm*) *Markt, Lage* tight, overstretched.

Angest. *abbr of* **Angestellte(r)**.

angestammt [ˈangə-] *adj* (*überkommen*) traditional; (*ererbt*) *Rechte* hereditary, ancestral; *Besitz* inherited.

angestellt [ˈangə-] 1 *ptp of* **anstellen**. 2 *adj pred* **~ sein** to be an employee *or* on the staff (*bei of*); **er ist bei Collins ~** he works for Collins; **fest ~ sein** to be on the permanent staff; **ich bin nicht beamtet, sondern nur ~** I don't have permanent tenure in my job.

Angestellte(r) [ˈangə-] *mf decl as adj* (*salaried*) employee; (*Büro-*) office-worker, white-collar worker; (*Behörden~*) public employee (without tenure).

Angestellten- [ˈangə-]: **~gewerkschaft** *f* white-collar union; **~verhältnis** *nt* employment (without permanent tenure); **im ~verhältnis** in non-tenured employment; **~versicherung** *f* (salaried) employees' insurance.

angestochen [ˈangə-] 1 *ptp of* **anstechen**. 2 *adj* (*inf*) **wie ~** like a stuck pig (*inf*).

angestrengt [ˈangə-] 1 *ptp of* **anstrengen**. 2 *adj* *Gesicht* strained; *Arbeiten, Denken* hard. **~ diskutieren** to have an intense discussion.

angetan [ˈangətan] 1 *ptp of* **antun**.
2 *adj pred* (a) **von jdm/etw ~ sein** to be taken with sb/sth; **es jdm ~ haben** to have made quite an impression on sb; **das Mädchen hat es ihm ~** he has fallen for that girl.
(b) **danach *or* dazu ~ sein, etw zu tun** (*geh*) to be suitable for doing sth; (*Wesen, Atmosphäre, Benehmen etc*) to be apt *or* calculated to do sth.
(c) **mit etw ~ sein** to be attired in sth.

Angetraute(r) [ˈangə-] *mf decl as adj* (*hum*) spouse, better half (*hum*).

angetrunken [ˈangə-] 1 *ptp of* **antrinken**. 2 *adj* *Mensch, Zustand* inebriated, intoxicated.

angewachsen [ˈangə-] 1 *ptp of* **anwachsen**. 2 *adj* **~e Ohrläppchen sind ein Zeichen von ...** not having ear-lobes is a sign of ...; **auf etw** (*acc*) **~ sein** (*inf*) to be stuck *or* lumbered with sth (*inf*).

angewandt [ˈangə-] 1 *ptp of* **anwenden**. 2 *adj attr* *Wissenschaft etc* applied.

angewidert [ˈangə-] 1 *ptp of* **anwidern**. 2 *adj* nauseated, disgusted. **vom Leben ~** sick of life.

angewiesen [ˈangə-] 1 *ptp of* **anweisen**.
2 *adj* **auf jdn/etw ~ sein** to have to rely on sb/sth, to be dependent on sb/sth; **auf sich selbst ~ sein** to have to fend for oneself; (*Kind*) to be left to one's own devices; **in dieser Arbeit war er auf sich selbst und sein eigenes Wissen ~** in this work he had to rely on himself and his own knowledge; **darauf bin ich nicht ~** I can get along without it, I don't need it; **ich bin selbst auf jede Mark ~** I need every mark myself.

angewöhnen [ˈangə-] *vt sep* **jdm etw ~** to get sb used to sth, to accustom sb to sth; **sich** (*dat*) **etw ~ /es sich** (*dat*) **~, etw zu tun** to get into the habit of sth/of doing sth.

Angewohnheit [ˈangə-] *f* habit.

angezecht [ˈangə-] *adj* (*inf*) tight (*inf*), pickled (*inf*).

angezeigt [ˈangə-] 1 *ptp of* **anzeigen**. 2 *adj* (*form*) advisable; (*angebracht*) appropriate.

angezogen [ˈangə-] 1 *ptp of* **anziehen**. 2 *adj* dressed. **dieser Mantel sieht ~er aus** this coat looks dressier *or* more dressy; **erscheinen Sie das nächste Mal bitte etwas ~er** please make sure that next time you are less scantily dressed.

angiften [ˈangi-] *vt sep* (*pej inf*) to snap at, to let fly at.

Angina [anˈgiːna] *f* -, **Anginen** (*Med*) angina. **~ pectoris** angina (pectoris).

Anglaise [ãˈglɛːzə] *f* -, -n anglaise.

angleichen [ˈangl-] *sep irreg* 1 *vt* to bring into line, to align (*dat, an +acc* with).
2 *vr* (*gegenseitig: Kulturen, Geschlechter, Methoden*) to grow

---

closer together. **sich jdm/einer Sache ~** (*einseitig*) to become like sb/sth; **die beiden haben sich (aneinander) angeglichen** the two of them have become more alike.

Angleichung *f* (a) *siehe vt* alignment (*an +acc* with). (b) *siehe vr* **die zunehmende ~ der Kulturen** the increasing similarity between the cultures; **die ~ Deutschlands an Amerika** Germany's growing similarity with America.

Angler(in *f*) *m* -s, - angler.

angliedern [ˈangl-] *vt sep* (*Verein, Partei*) to affiliate (*dat, an +acc* to *or* (*US*) with); *Land* to annexe (*dat, an +acc* to).

Angliederung *f siehe vt* affiliation; annexation.

anglikanisch [angli-] *adj* Anglican. **die A~e Kirche** the Anglican Church, the Church of England.

Anglikanismus [angli-] *m* anglicanism.

anglisieren* [angli-] *vt* to anglicize.

Anglisierung [angli-] *f* anglicizing.

Anglist(in *f*) [anˈglɪ-] *m* English specialist, Anglicist; (*Student*) English student; (*Professor etc*) English lecturer/professor.

Anglistik [anˈglɪ-] *f* English (language and literature).

Anglizismus [angli-] *m* anglicism.

Anglo- [-ŋg-] *in cpds* Anglo; **~-Amerikaner** *m* Anglo-Saxon, member of the English-speaking world; **~amerikaner** *m* Anglo-American; **~mane** *m decl as adj* anglomaniac; **~manie** *f* anglomania; **a~phil** *adj* anglophil(e); **~philie** *f* anglophilia; **a~phob** *adj* anglophobe, anglophobic; **~phobie** *f* anglophobia.

anglotzen [ˈangl-] *vt sep* (*inf*) to gawp *or* gape at (*inf*).

anglühen [ˈangl-] *vt sep* (*lit*) to heat red-hot; (*fig*) to glow at.

Angola [anˈgoːla] *nt* -s Angola.

Angolaner(in *f*) [angoˈla-] *m*, -s, - Angolan.

angolanisch [angoˈla-] *adj* Angolan.

Angora- [anˈgoːra] *in cpds* Angora; **~kaninchen** *nt* Angora rabbit; **~katze** *f* Angora cat; **~wolle** *f* Angora (wool).

Angostura [angoˈstuːra] *m* -s, -s Angostura (bitters *pl*).

angreifbar [ˈangr-] *adj* *Behauptung, Politiker* open to attack.

angreifen [ˈangr-] *sep irreg* 1 *vt* (a) (*überfallen, Sport, kritisieren*) to attack.
(b) (*schwächen*) *Organismus, Organ, Nerven* to weaken; *Gesundheit, Pflanzen* to affect; (*ermüden, anstrengen*) to strain; (*schädlich sein für, zersetzen*) *Lack, Farbe* to attack. **seine Krankheit hat ihn sehr angegriffen** his illness weakened him greatly; **das hat ihn sehr angegriffen** that affected him greatly; *siehe* **angegriffen**.
(c) (*anbrechen*) *Vorräte, Geld* to break into, to draw on.
(d) (*dial: anfassen*) to touch; (*fig: unternehmen, anpacken*) to attack, to tackle.
2 *vi* (a) (*Mil, Sport, fig*) to attack.
(b) (*geh: ansetzen*) to proceed *or* start (*an +dat* from).
(c) (*dial: anfassen*) to touch.
3 *vr* (*dial: sich anfühlen*) to feel.

Angreifer [ˈangr-] *m* -s, - attacker (*auch Sport, fig*).

angrenzen [ˈangr-] *vi sep* **an etw** (*acc*) **~** to border on sth, to adjoin sth.

angrenzend *adj attr* adjacent (*an +acc* to), adjoining (*an etw* (*acc*) sth).

Angriff [ˈangr-] *m* (*Mil, Sport, fig*) attack (*gegen, auf +acc* on); (*Luft~*) (air) raid. **~ ist die beste Verteidigung** (*prov*) attack is the best means of defence; **zum ~ übergehen** to go over to the attack, to take the offensive; **zum ~ blasen** (*Mil, fig*) to sound the charge; **etw in ~ nehmen** to tackle sth.

angriffig [ˈangr-] *adj* (*Sw*) aggressive.

Angriffs-: **~fläche** *f* target; **jdm/einer Sache eine ~fläche bieten** (*lit, fig*) to provide sb/sth with a target; **~krieg** *m* war of aggression; **~lust** *f* aggressiveness, aggression; **a~lustig** *adj* aggressive; **~punkt** *m* target; **~spiel** *nt* (*Sport*) aggressive *or* attacking game; **~spieler** *m* (*Sport*) attacking player; (*Ftbl*) forward; **~taktik** *f* attacking tactics *pl*; **~waffe** *f* offensive weapon.

angrinsen [ˈangr-] *vt sep* to grin at.

Angst *f* -, -̈e (*innere Unruhe, Psych*) anxiety (*um* about); (*Sorge*) worry (*um* about); (*Befürchtung*) fear (*um* for, *vor +dat* of); (*stärker: Furcht, Grauen*) fear, dread (*vor +dat* of); (*Existenz~*) angst. **~ haben** to be afraid *or* scared; **~ vor Spinnen/vorm Fliegen haben** to be afraid *or* scared of spiders/flying; **~ um jdn/etw haben** to be anxious *or* worried about sb/sth; **~ bekommen *or* kriegen** to get *or* become afraid *or* scared; (*erschrecken*) to take fright; **aus ~, etw zu tun** for fear of doing sth; **keine ~!** don't be afraid; **keine ~, ich sage ihm schon, was ich davon halte** (*inf*) don't you worry, I'll tell him what I think of that; **jdm ~ einflößen *or* einjagen** to frighten sb; **in tausend ~en schweben** to be terribly worried *or* anxious.

angst *adj pred* afraid. **ihr wurde ~ (und bange)** she became worried *or* anxious; **das machte ihn ~** that worried him *or* made him anxious; **mir ist um deine Gesundheit ~** I'm worried about your health.

Angst-: **a~erfüllt** *adj* frightened; **~gefühl** *nt* feeling of anxiety; **~gegner** *m* (*Sport*) formidable opponent; **~hase** *m* (*inf*) scaredy-cat (*inf*).

ängstigen 1 *vt* to frighten; (*unruhig machen*) to worry. 2 *vr* to be afraid; (*sich sorgen*) to worry. **sich vor etw** (*dat*) **~** to be afraid of sth; **sich wegen etw ~** to worry about sth.

Angst-: **~kauf** *m* panic buying *no pl*; **~laut** *m* alarm cry.

ängstlich *adj* (a) (*verängstigt*) anxious, apprehensive; (*schüchtern*) timid, timorous.
(b) (*übertrieben genau*) scrupulous, fastidious. **~ darauf bedacht sein, etw zu tun** to be at pains to do sth; **mit etw sehr ~ sein** to be very particular about sth; **ein ~ gehütetes Geheimnis** a closely guarded secret.

Ängstlichkeit *f siehe adj* (a) anxiety, apprehension; timidity, timorousness. (b) particularity, scrupulousness, fastidiousness.

Angst-: ~lust f (Psych) enjoyment and excitement combined with fear; ~mache f (inf) scaremongering no pl; ~macher m (inf) scaremonger; ~neurose f anxiety neurosis; ~neurotiker m neurotic; ~parole f (inf) scaremongering no pl; ~parolen verbreiten to spread alarm, to scaremonger; ~psychose f anxiety psychosis; ~röhre f (hum inf) topper (inf); ~schrei m cry of fear; ~schweiß m cold sweat; mir brach der ~schweiß aus I broke out in a cold sweat; ~traum m nightmare; a~verzerrt adj petrified, terror-struck; a~voll adj apprehensive, fearful; ~vorstellung f (Psych) imaginary fear; ~zustand m state of panic; ~zustände bekommen to get into a state of panic.

angucken ['angu-] vt sep to look at.

angurten ['angu-] vt sep siehe anschnallen.

anhaben vt sep irreg (a) (angezogen haben) to have on, to wear.
(b) (zuleide tun) to do harm. jdm etwas ~ wollen to want to harm sb; die Kälte kann mir nichts ~ the cold doesn't worry or bother me.
(c) (am Zeuge flicken) Sie können/die Polizei kann mir nichts ~! (inf) you/the police can't touch me.

anhaften vi sep (a) (lit) to stick (an + dat to), to cling (an + dat to). ~de Farbreste bits of paint left sticking on. (b) (fig) + dat to stick to, to stay with; (zugehören: Risiko etc) to be attached to.

Anhalt m -(e)s, (rare) -e (Hinweis) clue (für about); (für Verdacht) grounds pl (für for); (Hilfe) hint, indication (für of, about). ich habe keinerlei ~, wo er sich zur Zeit aufhält I have no idea where he is at the moment.

anhalten sep irreg 1 vi (a) (stehenbleiben) to stop. mit dem Sprechen ~ to stop talking.
(b) (fortdauern) to last.
(c) (werben) (bei jdm) um ein Mädchen or um die Hand eines Mädchens ~ to ask (sb) for a girl's hand in marriage.
2 vt (a) (stoppen) to stop; siehe Atem, Luft.
(b) (anlegen) Lineal to use. sie hielt mir/sich das Kleid an she held the dress up against me/herself.
(c) (anleiten) to urge, to encourage; siehe angehalten.

anhaltend adj continuous, incessant.

Anhalter(in f) m -s, - hitch-hiker, hitcher (inf). per ~ fahren to hitch-hike, to hitch (inf).

Anhaltspunkt m (Vermutung) clue (für about); (für Verdacht) grounds pl. ich habe keinerlei ~e I haven't a clue (inf), I have no idea.

anhand, an Hand prep + gen siehe Hand.

Anhang m -(e)s, **Anhänge** (a) (Nachtrag) appendix; (von Testament) codicil. (b) no pl (Gefolgschaft) following; (Angehörige) family. Witwe, 62, ohne ~ widow, 62, no family; mit etw ~/keinen ~ gewinnen to gain support or a following/no support or no following.

anhängen sep 1 vt (a) (ankuppeln) to attach (an + acc to); (Rail auch) to couple on (an + acc -to); Anhänger to hitch up (an + acc to); (fig: anfügen) to add (dat, an + acc to).
(b) Mantel, Telefonhörer to hang up.
(c) (inf) jdm etw ~ (verkaufen) to palm sth off on sb; (andrehen) to foist sth on sb; Krankheit, alte Kleider to pass sth on to sb; (nachsagen, anlasten) to blame sb for sth, to blame sth on sb; schlechten Ruf, Spitznamen to give sb sth; Verdacht, Schuld to pin sth on sb; ich weiß nicht, warum er mir unbedingt etwas ~ will I don't know why he always wants to give me a bad name.
2 vr (lit) to hang on (dat, an + acc to); (fig) to tag along (dat, an + acc with); (jdm hinterherfahren) to follow (dat, an + acc sth).
3 vi irreg (fig) (a) (anhaften) jdm ~ to stay with sb; (schlechter Ruf, Gefängnisstrafe auch) to stick with sb.
(b) (sich zugehörig fühlen) + dat to adhere to, to subscribe to.
(c) aux sein (dial Cook: am Topf) to stick.

Anhänger m -s, - (a) (Befürworter) supporter; (von Sportart auch) fan; (von Partei auch) follower; (von Verein) member. (b) (Wagen) trailer; (Straßenbahn~) second car. die Straßenbahn hatte zwei ~ the tram had two extra cars. (c) (Schmuckstück) pendant. (d) (Koffer~ etc) tag, label.

Anhängerin f siehe Anhänger (a).

Anhänger-: ~schaft f siehe Anhänger (a) supporters pl; fans pl; following, followers pl; membership, members pl; ~zahl f siehe Anhänger (a) number of supporters/fans/followers/members.

Anhänge-: ~schild nt tag, label; ~schloß nt padlock; ~vorrichtung f coupling device; (an Auto etc) tow bar.

anhängig adj (Jur) sub judice; Zivilverfahren pending. etw ~ machen to start legal proceedings over sth.

anhänglich adj Kind, Freundin clinging; Haustier devoted. mein Sohn/Hund ist sehr ~ my son/dog hardly leaves my side; seine Freundin war ihm zu ~ his girlfriend was too clinging.

Anhänglichkeit f tendency to cling to one; devotion.

Anhängsel nt (a) (Überflüssiges, Mensch) appendage (an + dat to); (von Gruppe, Partei) hanger-on. das ist ein ~ am Wort that is added onto the word.
(b) (Schildchen) tag; (rare: Schmuckstück) pendant; (an Armband) charm; (an Uhrenkette) fob. die ~ am Weihnachtsbaum the things hanging on the Christmas tree.
(c) (Zusatz) addition; (Nachtrag) appendix.

Anhauch m (geh) aura; (in Stimme) trace, tinge.

anhauchen vt sep to breathe on; siehe angehaucht.

anhauen vt sep (a) (auch irreg) Baum to cut a notch in. (b) (sl: ansprechen) to accost (um for). jdn um etw ~ to be on the scrounge for sth from sb (inf); um Geld auch to touch sb for sth (inf).

anhäufen sep 1 vt to accumulate, to amass; Vorräte, Geld to hoard. 2 vr to pile up, to accumulate; (Zinsen) to accumulate, to accrue.

Anhäufung f siehe vt accumulation, amassing; hoarding.

anheben¹ sep irreg 1 vt (a) (hochheben) to lift (up); Glas to raise. (b) (erhöhen) to raise. 2 vi to lift.

anheben² pret hob or (obs) hub an, ptp angehoben vi sep irreg (old) to commence, to begin. zu singen ~ to begin singing; ..., hub er an (obs) ..., quoth he (old).

Anhebung f increase (gen, von in); (das Anheben auch) raising (gen, von of); (Betrag, Größe auch) rise (gen, von in). eine ~ der Gehälter um 15% an increase or a rise of 15% in salaries.

anheften vt sep (an + acc or dat to) to fasten (on), to attach. jdm einen Orden ~ to pin a medal on sb; etw mit Reißzwecken/Heftklammern/Büroklammern/Stichen ~ to pin/staple/paperclip/tack sth on (an + acc or dat to).

anheilen vi sep aux sein to heal (up); (Knochen) to set, to mend.

anheimeln vt sep (geh) to remind of home.

anheimelnd adj (geh) homely; Klänge familiar.

anheim-: ~fallen vi sep irreg aux sein + dat (liter) to pass or fall to; einer Krankheit to fall prey to; einem Betrug to fall victim to; der Vergessenheit ~fallen to sink into oblivion; ~geben vt sep irreg + dat (liter) to commit or entrust to; etw den Flammen ~geben to commit sth to the flames; etw der Entscheidung eines anderen ~geben to entrust the decision about sth to somebody else; ~stellen vt sep + dat (geh) jdm etw ~stellen to leave sth to sb's discretion; das ist allein Gott ~gestellt that is in God's hands alone.

anheiraten vt sep siehe angeheiratet.

anheischig adv sich ~ machen, etw tun zu können (form) to assert that one can do sth; niemand kann sich ~ machen zu behaupten, alles zu wissen no-one can claim to know or allege that they know everything.

anheizen vt sep (a) Ofen to light. (b) (fig inf) (ankurbeln) Wirtschaft, Wachstum to stimulate; (verschlimmern) Krise to aggravate.

anherrschen vt sep to bark at.

anhetzen vi sep aux sein angehetzt kommen to come rushing along or (auf einen zu) up.

anheuern vti sep (Naut, fig) to sign on or up.

Anhieb m: auf (den ersten) ~ (inf) straight or right away, straight off (inf), first go (inf); das kann ich nicht auf ~ sagen I can't say offhand.

Anhimmelei f (inf) adulation, idolization; (schwärmerische Blicke) adoring gaze.

anhimmeln vt sep (inf) to idolize, to worship; (schwärmerisch ansehen) to gaze adoringly at.

Anhöhe f hill.

anhören sep 1 vt (a) (Gehör schenken) to hear; Schallplatten, Konzert to listen to. jdn ganz ~ to hear sb out.
(b) (zufällig mithören) to overhear. ich kann das nicht mehr mit ~ I can't listen to that any longer.
(c) (anmerken) man konnte ihr/ihrer Stimme die Verzweiflung ~ one could hear the despair in her voice; das hört man ihm aber nicht an! you can't tell that from his accent or from hearing him speak; man hört ihm sofort den Ausländer an you can hear at once that he's a foreigner.
2 vr (a) sich (dat) etw ~ to listen to sth; das höre ich mir nicht mehr länger mit an I'm not going to listen to that any longer; können Sie sich mal einen Moment ~, was ich zu sagen habe? can you just listen for a moment to what I have to say?
(b) (klingen) to sound. das hört sich ja gut an (inf) that sounds good.

Anhörtermin m date for a hearing.

Anhörung f hearing.

Anhörungsverfahren nt hearing.

anhupen vt sep to hoot at, to sound one's horn at.

anhusten vt sep to cough at; jdn to cough in sb's face.

Änigma nt -s, -ta or Änigmen (liter) enigma.

änigmatisch adj (liter) enigmatic.

Anilin nt -s, no pl aniline.

Anilinfarbe f siehe Teerfarben.

Anima f -, -s (Psych) anima.

animalisch adj animal; (pej auch) bestial, brutish.

Animateur(in f) [-'tø:ɐ] m host/hostess.

Animation f (Film) animation.

Animationsfilm m (animated) cartoon (film).

Animator, Animatorin mf (Film) animator.

Animierdame f nightclub or bar hostess.

animieren* vt sep (a) (anregen) to encourage. jdn zu einem Streich ~ to put sb up to a trick; sich animiert fühlen, etw zu tun to feel prompted to do sth; durch das schöne Wetter animiert encouraged or prompted by the good weather. (b) (Film) to animate.

animierend adj (geh) stimulating.

Animier-: ~lokal nt hostess bar, clipjoint (pej); ~mädchen nt siehe Animierdame.

Animo nt -s, no pl (Aus) (a) (Vorliebe) liking. (b) (Schwung) mit ~ mitmachen to join in with gusto.

animos adj (geh) hostile. ~e Gefühle gegen jdn haben to feel hostile towards sb.

Animosität f (geh) (gegen towards) (Feindseligkeit) animosity, hostility; (Abneigung) hostility; (Äußerung) hostile remark.

Animus m -, no pl (a) (Psych) animus. (b) (inf) hunch (inf), feeling. ich habe da so einen ~ I've got a hunch or feeling about it.

Anion ['anjo:n] nt -s, -en (Chem) anion.

Anis [a'ni:s, (S Ger, Aus) 'a:nıs] m -es, -e (Gewürz) aniseed; (Schnaps) aniseed brandy; (Pflanze) anise.

Anisett m -s, -s, **Anislikör** m anisette, aniseed liqueur.

Ank. abbr of Ankunft arr.

ankämpfen vi sep gegen etw ~ gegen die Elemente, Strömung to battle with sth; gegen Gefühle, Neigungen, Versuchungen, Müdigkeit to fight sth; gegen Inflation, Mißbrauch, Korruption,

Ideen to fight (against) sth; **gegen jdn ~** to fight (against) sb, to (do) battle with sb; **gegen die Tränen ~** to fight back one's tears.

ankarren vt sep (inf) to cart along.

ankarriolen* vi sep aux sein (inf) **ankarriolt kommen** to come rattling along.

Ankauf m purchase, purchasing. **durch den ~ einer Sache** (gen) through the purchase of sth, by purchasing sth; **An- und Verkauf von ...** we buy and sell ...; **An- und Verkaufs-Geschäft** = second-hand shop; **er hat ein An- und Verkaufs-Geschäft für ...** he has a shop that buys and sells ...

ankaufen sep 1 vti to purchase, to buy. 2 vr **sich (an einem Ort) ~** to buy oneself a place (somewhere).

Ankäufer m purchaser, buyer.

Ankaufsrecht nt (Jur) option, right of purchase.

ankeifen vt sep (inf) to scream or holler (inf) at.

Anker m -s, - (Naut, Archit, fig) anchor; (Elec) armature; (von Uhr) anchor. **~ werfen** to drop anchor; **vor ~ gehen** to drop anchor; (fig) (hum: heiraten) to settle down (bei with); (inf: Rast machen) to stop over; **sich vor ~ legen** to drop anchor; **vor ~ liegen** or **treiben** to lie or ride or be at anchor; **ein Schiff vor ~ legen** to bring a ship to anchor; **den/die ~ hieven** or **lichten** to weigh anchor.

Anker-: **~boje** f anchor buoy; **~grund** m anchorage; **~kette** f anchor cable; **~klüse** f (Naut) hawsehole.

ankern vi (Anker werfen) to anchor; (vor Anker liegen) to be anchored.

Anker-: **~platz** m anchorage; **~tau** nt anchor hawser or rope; **~winde** f capstan.

anketten vt sep to chain up (an +acc or dat to). **angekettet sein** (fig) to be tied up.

ankeuchen vi sep aux sein (inf) **angekeucht kommen** to come panting along or (auf einen zu) up.

ankieken vt sep (N Ger inf) siehe **angucken**.

ankitten vt sep to stick on (with putty) (an +acc -to).

ankläffen vt sep (pej) to bark at; (kleiner Hund) to yap at.

Anklage f (a) (Jur) charge; (~vertretung) prosecution. **gegen jdn ~ erheben** to bring or prefer charges against sb; **jdn unter ~ stellen** to charge sb (wegen with); **(wegen etw) unter ~ stehen** to have been charged (with sth); **als Vertreter der ~ fragte Herr Stein ...** acting for the prosecution Mr Stein asked ..., Mr Stein, prosecuting or for the prosecution, asked ...
(b) (Verurteilung) condemnation (gegen, gen of); (Beschuldigung) accusation; (Anprangerung) indictment (an +acc of). **ihr Blick war voller ~** her eyes were full of reproach.

Anklage-: **~bank** f dock; **auf der ~bank (sitzen)** (lit, fig) (to be) in the dock; **jdn auf die ~bank bringen** to put sb in the dock; **~behörde** f prosecution; **~erhebung** f preferral of charges.

anklagen sep 1 vt (a) (Jur) to charge, to accuse. **jdn einer Sache** (gen) or **wegen etw ~** to charge sb with sth, to accuse sb of sth. (b) (fig) (verurteilen) to condemn; (Buch, Rede) to be a condemnation of; (anprangern) to be an indictment of. **jdn einer Sache** (gen) **~** (beschuldigen) to accuse sb of sth; **jdn ~, etw getan zu haben** to accuse sb of having done sth. 2 vi to cry out in protest or accusation; (Buch, Bilder etc) to cry out in condemnation.

anklagend adj Ton accusing, accusatory; Blick reproachful; Buch, Bild etc that cries out in condemnation.

Ankläger m -s, - (Jur) prosecutor. **öffentlicher ~** (fig geh) (self-styled) public prosecutor.

anklägerisch adj siehe **anklagend**.

Anklage-: **~schrift** f indictment; **~vertreter** m (public) prosecutor, counsel for the prosecution.

anklammern sep 1 vt (mit Büroklammer) to clip (an +acc or dat on/to); (mit Heftmaschine) to staple (an +acc or dat on/to), to); Wäsche to peg (an +acc or dat on). 2 vr **sich an etw** (acc or dat) **~** to cling (on)to sth, to hang onto sth.

Anklang m (a) no pl (Beifall) approval. **~ (bei jdm) finden** to meet with (sb's) approval, to be well received (by sb); **großen/wenig/keinen ~ finden** to be very well/poorly/badly received.
(b) (Reminiszenz) **die Anklänge an Mozart sind unverkennbar** the echoes of Mozart are unmistakable; **ich konnte in seinem Buch einen deutlichen ~ an Thomas Mann erkennen** I found his book (to be) distinctly reminiscent of Thomas Mann; **Anklänge an etw** (acc) **enthalten** to be reminiscent of sth.

anklatschen sep (inf) 1 vt Plakat etc to slap or hang (inf). 2 vi aux sein **seine Kleider/Haare klatschen an** or **sind angeklatscht** his clothes are clinging to him/his hair is plastered down.

ankleben sep 1 vt to stick up (an +acc or dat on). 2 vi aux sein to stick.

ankleckern vi sep aux sein (inf) **angekleckert kommen** to come drifting along or (auf einen zu) up; (nach und nach eintreffen) to come in dribs and drabs (inf).

Ankleidekabine f changing cubicle.

ankleiden vtr sep (geh) to dress.

Ankleidepuppe f siehe **Schaufensterpuppe**.

Ankleider(in f) m -s, - (Theat) dresser.

Ankleideraum m, **Ankleidezimmer** nt dressing-room; (im Schwimmbad, Geschäft) changing room.

anklingeln vti sep (inf) Plakat etc to ring (up), to phone (up), to call (up). **jdn ~** to give sb a ring or a buzz (inf), to ring or phone or call sb (up).

anklingen vi sep aux sein (erinnern) to be reminiscent (an +acc of); (angeschnitten werden) to be touched (up)on; (spürbar werden) to be discernible. **in diesem Lied klingt etwas von Sehnsucht an** there is a suggestion or hint or note of longing (discernible) in this song.

anklopfen vi sep to knock (an +acc or dat at, on). **bei jdm wegen etw ~** (fig inf) to go/come knocking at sb's door for sth.

anknabbern vt sep (inf) (annagen) to gnaw or nibble (at); (fig) Ersparnisse etc to gnaw away at, to nibble away. **zum A~ (aussehen)** (fig) (to look) good enough to eat.

anknacksen vt sep (inf) (a) Knochen to crack; Fuß, Gelenk etc to crack a bone in. (b) (fig) Gesundheit to affect; Stolz to injure, to deal a blow to. **sein Selbstvertrauen/Stolz wurde dadurch angeknackst** that was a blow to his self-confidence/pride; siehe **angeknackst**.

anknattern vi sep aux sein (inf) **angeknattert kommen** to come roaring along or (auf einen zu) up.

anknipsen vt sep to switch or put on; Schalter to flick.

anknöpfen vt sep to button on (an +acc or dat -to).

anknoten vt sep to tie on (an +acc or dat -to).

anknüpfen sep 1 vt to tie on (an +acc or dat -to); Beziehungen to establish; Verhältnis to form, to start up; Gespräch to start up, to enter into. 2 vi **an etw** (acc) **~** to take sth up.

Anknüpfung f (fig) siehe vt establishing; forming; starting up. **die ~ an etw** (acc) taking sth up.

Anknüpfungspunkt m link.

anknurren vt sep (lit, fig) to growl at.

ankohlen vt sep (a) Holz to char. (b) (inf: belügen) to kid (inf).

ankommen sep irreg aux sein 1 vi (a) to arrive, (Brief, Paket auch) to come; (Zug, Bus etc auch) to get in, to arrive. **bist du gut angekommen?** did you arrive safely or get there all right?; **bei etw angekommen sein** to have reached sth, to have got to sth; **wir sind schon beim Sekt/Dessert angekommen** we've already reached the champagne/dessert stage; **das Kind soll in 6 Wochen ~** the baby is due (to arrive) in 6 weeks.
(b) (sich nähern) to approach.
(c) (Anklang, Resonanz finden) (bei with) to go down well; (Mode, Neuerungen) to catch on. **dieser Witz kam gut an** the joke went down very well; **mit deinem dummen Gerede kommst du bei ihm nicht an!** you won't get anywhere with him with your stupid talk!; **ein Lehrer, der bei seinen Schülern ausgezeichnet ankommt** a teacher who is a great success or who hits it off marvellously with his pupils; **es ist erstaunlich, wie er bei Mädchen ankommt** it's amazing what a success he is with the girls.
(d) (eine Stellung finden) to be taken on (bei by).
(e) (inf) (auftreten, erscheinen) to come along; (wiederholt erwähnen) to come up (mit with). **jdm mit etw ~** to come to sb with sth; **komm mir nachher nicht an, und verlange, daß ich ...** don't come running to me afterwards wanting me to ...; **komm mir nur nicht wieder damit an, daß du Astronaut werden willst** don't start up again with this business about (your) wanting to be an astronaut.
(f) (sich durchsetzen) **gegen etw ~** gegen Gewohnheit, Sucht etc to be able to fight sth; **gegen diese Konkurrenz kommen wir nicht an** we can't fight this competition; **er ist zu stark, ich komme gegen ihn nicht an** he's too strong, I'm no match for him; **die Mutter kommt gegen den Jungen nicht mehr an** the boy's mother can't cope or deal with him any longer.

2 vi impers (a) (wichtig sein) **es kommt auf etw** (acc) **an** sth matters; **darauf kommt es (uns) an** that is what matters (to us); **es kommt darauf an, daß wir ...** what matters is that we ...; **auf eine halbe Stunde kommt es jetzt nicht mehr an** it doesn't matter about the odd half-hour, an extra half-hour is neither here nor there (inf); **darauf soll es mir nicht ~** that's not the problem.
(b) (abhängig sein) to depend (auf +acc on). **es kommt darauf an** it (all) depends; **es käme auf einen Versuch an** we'd have to give it a try; **es kommt (ganz) darauf an, in welcher Laune er ist** it (all) depends (on) what mood he's in.
(c) (inf) **es darauf ~ lassen** to take a chance, to chance it; **laß es nicht drauf ~!** don't push your luck! (inf); **lassen wir's darauf ~** let's chance it; **er ließ es in der Prüfung darauf ~** he took a chance in the exam; **er ließ es auf einen Streit/einen Versuch ~** he was prepared to argue about it/to give it a try; **laß es doch nicht deswegen auf einen Prozeß ~** for goodness sake don't let it get as far as the courts.

3 vt (a) (geh: Gefühl etc) to come over. **Angst kam ihn an** fear crept or stole over him.
(b) (sein, erscheinen) **etw kommt jdn schwer/hart an** sth is difficult/hard for sb; **das Rauchen aufzugeben kommt ihn sauer an** he's finding it difficult to give up smoking.

Ankömmling m (new) arrival.

ankoppeln vt sep to hitch up (an +acc to) or on (an +acc -to); (Rail) to couple up (an +acc to) or on (an +acc -to); (Space) to link up (an +acc with, to).

ankotzen vt sep (sl) (a) (lit) to be sick over, to puke (up) over (sl). (b) (anwidern) to make sick (inf).

ankrallen vr sep to clutch (an +dat at).

ankratzen sep 1 vt to scratch; (fig) jds Ruf etc to damage; siehe **angekratzt**. 2 vr (fig inf) **sich bei jdm ~** to suck up to sb (inf).

ankrausen vt sep (Sew) to gather.

ankreiden vt sep (a) (obs: Schulden aufschreiben) to chalk up.
(b) (fig) **jdm etw (dick** or **übel) ~** to hold sth against sb; **jdm sein Benehmen als Frechheit/Schwäche ~** to regard sb's behaviour as an impertinence/as weakness.

Ankreis m (Math) escribed circle.

ankreuzen vt sep (a) to mark with a cross, to put a cross beside.
(b) aux sein or haben (Naut) **gegen den Wind ~** to sail against or into the wind.

ankünden vtr sep (old) siehe **ankündigen**.

ankündigen sep 1 vt (a) (ansagen, anmelden) to announce; (auf Plakat, in Zeitung etc) to advertize. **heute kam endlich der angekündigte Brief** today the letter I/we had been expecting arrived; **er besucht uns nie, ohne sich (nicht) vorher anzukün-**

digen he never visits us without letting us know in advance *or* without giving us advance notice.

(b) *(auf etw hindeuten)* to be a sign of.

2 *vr (fig)* to be heralded *(durch* by). **der Frühling kündigt sich an** spring is in the air; **diese Krankheit kündigt sich durch ... an** this illness is preceded by ...

Ankündigung *f* announcement; *(vorherige Benachrichtigung)* advance notice. **Preisänderungen nur nach vorheriger ~** price changes will be announced in advance, advance notice will be given of price changes.

Ankunft *f* -, **Ankünfte** arrival. **bei** *or* **nach ~** on arrival.

Ankunfts-: **~halle** *f* arrivals lounge; **~ort** *m* place of arrival; **~tafel** *f* arrivals (indicator) board; **~zeit** *f* time of arrival.

ankuppeln *vt sep siehe* **ankoppeln.**

ankurbeln *vt sep Maschine* to wind up; *(Aut)* to crank; *(fig) Wirtschaft, Konjunktur* to boost, to reflate.

Ankurbelung *f (fig)* reflation.

ankuscheln *vr sep sich bei jdm or an jdn ~* to snuggle up to sb.

Anl. *abbr of* **Anlage** encl.

anlabern *vt sep (sl) siehe* **anquatschen.**

anlächeln *vt sep* to smile at; *(fig: Schicksal, Glück etc)* to smile (up)on. **jdn ~** to smile at sb, to give sb a smile; **der Kuchen lächelte mich förmlich an** *(hum)* the cake sat there just asking to be eaten.

anlachen *vt sep* to smile at; *(fig: Himmel, Sonne)* to smile (up)on. **sich** *(dat)* **jdn ~** *(inf)* to pick sb up *(inf).*

Anlage *f* -, **-n (a)** *(Fabrik~)* plant.

(b) *(Grün~, Park~)* (public) park; *(um ein Gebäude herum)* grounds *pl.*

(c) *(Einrichtung) (Mil, Elec)* installation(s); *(sanitäre ~n)* bathroom *or* sanitary *(form)* installations *pl*; *(Sport~ etc)* facilities *pl.*

(d) *(inf: Stereo~)* (stereo) system *or* equipment.

(e) *(Plan, Grundidee)* conception; *(eines Dramas etc)* structure.

(f) *(Veranlagung) usu pl* aptitude, gift, talent *(zu* for); *(Neigung)* predisposition, tendency *(zu* to).

(g) *(das Anlegen) (von Park)* laying out; *(von Stausee etc)* construction, building. **die ~ einer Kartei veranlassen** to start a file; **die Stadt hat die ~ von weiteren Grünflächen beschlossen** the town has decided to provide more parks.

(h) *(Kapital~)* investment.

(i) *(Beilage zu einem Schreiben)* enclosure. **als ~ or in der ~ erhalten Sie ...** please find enclosed ...

anlagebedingt *adj* inherent. **Krampfadern sind ~** some people have an inherent tendency *or* a predisposition to varicose veins.

Anlage-: **~berater** *m* advisor on investments; **~kapital** *nt* investment capital.

anlagern *sep* **1** *vt* to take up. **2** *vr (Chem)* to be taken up *(an +acc* by).

Anlagevermögen *nt* fixed assets *pl.*

anlanden *sep* **1** *vi* **(a)** *aux sein (Naut)* to land. **(b)** *aux sein or haben (Geol)* to accrete. **2** *vt* to land.

Anlandung *f (Geol)* accretion.

anlangen *sep* **1** *vi aux sein (an einem Ort)* to arrive. **in der Stadt/am Gipfel angelangt sein** to have reached the town/summit, to have arrived in *or* at the town/at the summit.

2 *vt* **(a)** *(betreffen)* to concern. **was mich/diese Frage anlangt** as for me/this question, so *or* as far as I am/this question is concerned.

(b) *(S Ger: anfassen)* to touch.

Anlaß *m* -sses, **Anlässe** *(a) (Veranlassung)* (immediate) cause *(zu* for). **zum ~ von etw werden** to bring sth about, to trigger sth off; **das war zwar nicht der Grund, aber der ~** that wasn't the real reason but that's what finally brought it about *or* triggered it off; **welchen ~ hatte er, das zu tun?** what prompted him to do that?; **er hat keinen ~ zur Freude** he has no cause *or* reason *or* grounds for rejoicing; **es besteht kein ~ ...** there is no reason ...; **das ist kein ~ zu feiern** that doesn't call for a celebration; **beim geringsten/bei jedem ~** for the slightest reason/at every opportunity; **jdm ~ zu Beschwerden geben, jdm ~ geben, sich zu beschweren** to give sb reason *or* cause *or* grounds for complaint *or* for complaining; **das gibt ~ zur Sorge** this gives cause for concern.

(b) *(Gelegenheit)* occasion. **aus ~** *(+gen)* on the occasion of; **aus diesem ~** on this occasion; **dem ~ entsprechend** as befits the occasion, as is befitting to the occasion.

(c) *(Sw: Lustbarkeit)* social.

anlassen *sep irreg* **1** *vt* **(a)** *(in Gang setzen) Motor, Wagen* to start (up).

(b) *(inf) Schuhe, Mantel* to keep on; *Wasserhahn, Motor* to leave running *or* on; *Licht, Radio* to leave on; *Kerze* to leave burning; *Feuer* to leave in *or* burning.

(c) *(anreden) jdn hart ~ (dated)* to scold sb soundly.

2 *vr* **sich gut/schlecht ~** to get off to a good/bad start; *(Lehrling, Student, Geschäft etc auch)* to make a good/bad start *or* beginning; **das Wetter läßt sich gut an** the weather looks promising; **wie läßt er sich in der Sache denn an?** what sort of start has he made on it?

Anlasser *m* -s, - *(Aut)* starter.

anläßlich *prep* +*gen* on the occasion of.

anlasten *vt sep* **(a) jdm etw ~** to blame sb for sth, to lay the blame for sth on sb; **jdm die Schuld für etw ~** to lay the blame for sth at sb's door *or* on sb; **jdm etw als Schwäche ~** to regard *or* see sth as a weakness on sb's part. **(b)** *(dated) Kosten* to charge *(jdm* to sb).

anlatschen *vi sep aux sein (usu angelatscht kommen) (inf)* to come slouching along *or (auf einen zu)* up.

Anlauf *m* -(e)s, **Anläufe (a)** *(Sport)* run-up; *(Ski)* approach run; *(Mil: Ansturm)* onset, attack. **mit/ohne ~** with a run-up/from standing; **Sprung mit/ohne ~** running/standing jump; **~ nehmen** to take a run-up; **~ zu etw nehmen** *(fig)* to pluck up courage to do sth.

(b) *(fig: Versuch)* attempt, try. **beim ersten/zweiten ~** at the first/second attempt, first/second go *(inf)*; **noch einen ~ nehmen** *or* **machen** to have another go *(inf) or* try, to make another attempt.

(c) *(Beginn)* start.

anlaufen *sep irreg* **1** *vi aux sein* **(a)** *(beginnen)* to begin, to start; *(Saison auch, Film)* to open; *(Motor)* to start.

(b) *(usu angelaufen kommen)* to come running along *or (auf einen zu)* up.

(c) *(sich ansammeln)* to mount up *(auf +acc* to); *(Zinsen auch)* to accrue; *(dial: auch dick ~)* to swell (up).

(d) *(beschlagen) (Brille, Spiegel etc)* to steam *or* mist up; *(Metall)* to tarnish. **rot/blau ~** to turn *or* go red/blue.

(e) *(Sport) (zu laufen beginnen)* to start off; *(Anlauf nehmen)* to take a run-up.

(f) bei jdm schlecht ~ *(dated inf)* not to get on very well with sb; **gegen etw ~** *(sich stoßen)* to run into sth; *(fig)* to stand up to sth; **er kann kaum gegen so einen starken Wind ~** he can hardly walk against such a strong wind.

2 *vt* **(a)** *(Naut) Hafen etc* to put into, to call at.

(b) *(Sport) Rennen* to start off; *Strecke* to run.

Anlauf-: **~turm** *m (Ski)* ski-jump; **~zeit** *f (Aut)* warming-up time *or* period; *(fig)* time to get going *or* started; *(Film, Theat)* (time of the) first few performances; **ein paar Wochen ~zeit** a few weeks to get going *or* started.

Anlaut *m (Phon)* initial sound. **im ~ stehen** to be in initial position.

anlauten *vi sep* to begin.

anläuten *vt sep* **(a)** *Spiel, Pause* to ring the bell for. **eben wird die Pause angeläutet** there goes *or* there's the bell for break. **(b)** *auch vi (dial: anrufen)* **jdn** *or* **bei jdm ~** to ring sb (up), to phone *or* call sb.

anlautend *adj attr* initial.

anlecken *vt sep* to lick.

Anlegebrücke *f* landing stage, jetty.

anlegen *sep* **1** *vt* **(a)** *Leiter* to put up *(an +acc* against); *Brett, Karte, Dominostein* to lay (down) *(an +acc* next to, beside); *Holz, Kohle* to put *or* lay on; *Lineal* to position, to set. **das Gewehr ~** to raise the gun to one's shoulder; **das Gewehr auf jdn/etw ~** to aim the gun at sb/sth; **den Säugling ~** to put the baby to one's breast; **strengere Maßstäbe ~** to impose *or* lay down stricter standards *(bei* in).

(b) *(geh: anziehen)* to don *(form).*

(c) *(anbringen)* **jdm etw ~** to put sth on sb; **jdm/einer Sache Zügel ~** to take sb in hand/to contain *or* control sth.

(d) *Kartei, Akte* to start; *Vorräte* to lay in; *Garten, Gelände, Aufsatz, Bericht, Schaubild* to lay out; *Liste, Plan, Statistiken* to draw up; *Roman, Drama* to structure.

(e) *(investieren) Geld, Kapital* to invest; *(ausgeben)* to spend *(für* on).

(f) es darauf ~, daß ... to be determined that ...; **du legst es wohl auf einen Streit mit mir an** you're determined to have a fight with me, aren't you?

(g) *siehe* **angelegt.**

2 *vi* **(a)** *(Naut)* to berth.

(b) *(Cards)* to lay down cards/a card *(bei jdm* on sb's hand).

(c) *(Gewehr ~)* to aim *(auf +acc* at).

3 *vr* **sich mit jdm ~** to pick an argument *or* quarrel *or* fight with sb.

Anlegeplatz *m* berth.

Anleger *m* -s, - *(Fin)* investor.

Anlege-: **~steg** *m* jetty, landing stage; **~stelle** *f* mooring.

anlehnen *sep* **1** *vt* to lean *or* rest *(an +acc* against); *Tür, Fenster* to leave ajar *or* slightly open. **angelehnt sein** *(Tür, Fenster)* to be ajar *or* slightly open. **2** *vr (lit)* to lean *(an +acc* against). **sich an etw** *(acc)* **~** *(fig)* to follow sth.

Anlehnung *f* **(a)** *(Stütze)* support *(an +acc* of); *(Anschluß)* dependence *(an +acc* on). **~ an jdn suchen** to seek sb's support. **(b)** *(Imitation)* following *(an jdn/etw* sb/sth). **in ~ an jdn/etw** following sb/sth.

Anlehnungs-: **~bedürfnis** *nt* need of loving care; **a~bedürftig** *adj* needing loving care.

Anleihe *f* -, **-n, Anleihen** *nt* -s, - *(Sw)* **(a)** *(Fin) (Geldaufnahme)* loan; *(Wertpapier)* bond. **eine ~ aufnehmen** to take out a loan; **bei jdm eine ~ machen** to borrow (money) from sb. **(b)** *(von geistigem Eigentum)* borrowing. **bei jdm eine ~ machen** *(hum inf)* to borrow from sb.

anleinen *vt sep* to stick on *(an +acc or dat* -to). **jdn ~** *(inf) (foppen)* to pull sb's leg; *(betrügen)* to do sb *(inf).*

anleinen *vt sep (festmachen)* to tie up; *(fig)* to keep tied to one's apron-strings. **den Hund ~** to put the dog's lead on, to put the dog on the lead; **den Hund an etw** *(acc or dat)* **~** to tie the dog to sth.

anleiten *vt sep* **(a)** *(unterweisen)* to show, to teach, to instruct. **jdn bei einer Arbeit ~** to teach sb a job, to show sb how to do a job.

(b) *(erziehen)* **jdn zu etw ~** to teach sb sth; **jdn zu selbständigem Denken ~** to teach sb to think for himself/herself; **jdn zu Sauberkeit/Ehrlichkeit ~** to teach sb to be clean/honest, to teach sb cleanliness/honesty.

Anleitung *f (Erklärung, Hilfe)* instructions *pl.* **unter der ~ seines Vaters** under his father's guidance *or* direction.

Anlernberuf *m* semi-skilled job.

anlernen *vt sep* **(a)** *(ausbilden)* to train; *siehe* **angelernt. (b)** *(oberflächlich lernen)* **sich** *(dat)* **etw ~** to learn sth up;

angelerntes Wissen superficially acquired knowledge.

Anlernling *m* trainee.

anlesen *vt sep irreg* **(a)** *Buch, Aufsatz* to begin *or* start reading. **das angelesene Buch** the book I have/he/she has started reading. **(b)** *(aneignen)* **sich** *(dat)* **etw** ~ to learn sth by reading; **angelesenes Wissen** knowledge which comes straight out of books.

anleuchten *vt sep* **jdn** ~ to shine a light/lamp *etc* at sb; **jdn mit etw** ~ to shine sth at sb.

anliefern *vt sep* to deliver.

Anlieferung *f* delivery.

Anliegen *nt* **-s, -** **(a)** *(Bitte)* request. **(b)** *(wichtige Angelegenheit)* matter of concern.

anliegen *sep irreg* **1** *vi* **(a)** *(anstehen, vorliegen)* to be on. **(b)** *(Kleidung)* to fit closely *or* tightly *(an etw (dat)* sth); *(Haar)* to lie flat *(an +dat* against, on). **(c)** *(liter: belästigen)* **jdm mit etw** ~ to importune sb with sth *(liter)*. **(d)** *(geh: bewegen)* to be a matter of concern *(dat* to). **(e)** *(Naut)* **an den richtigen Kurs** ~ to be (headed) on the right course. **2** *vt (Naut) (zusteuern)* to be headed for; *Kurs* to be (headed) on.

anliegend *adj* **(a)** *Ohren* flat. (eng) ~ *Kleidung* tight- *or* close-fitting. **(b)** *(in Briefen)* enclosed. **(c)** *Grundstück* adjacent.

Anlieger *m* **-s, -** neighbour; *(Anwohner)* (local) resident. **die** ~ **der Nordsee** the countries bordering (on) the North Sea; ~ **frei**, **frei für** ~ no thoroughfare – residents only.

Anlieger-: ~**staat** *m* **die** ~**staaten des Schwarzen Meers** the countries bordering (on) the Black Sea; ~**verkehr** *m* (local) residents' vehicles; „~**verkehr frei**" "residents only".

anlinsen *vt sep (inf)* to take a sly look at. **jdn aus den Augenwinkeln** ~ to look at sb out of the corner of one's eye.

anlocken *vt sep Touristen* to attract; *Vögel, Tiere auch* to lure.

Anlockung *f* attraction.

anlöten *vt sep* to solder on *(an +acc or dat* -to).

anlügen *vt sep irreg* to lie *or* tell lies to.

anluven *vt sep (Naut)* to luff.

Anm. *abbr of* **Anmerkung.**

anmachen *vt sep* **(a)** *(inf: befestigen)* to put up *(an +acc or dat* on). **(b)** *(zubereiten)* to mix; *Salat* to dress. **(c)** *(anstellen) Radio, Licht, Heizung etc* to put *or* turn on; *Feuer* to light. **(d)** *(sl: aufreizen)* to give the come-on to *(sl)*. **das Publikum** ~ to get the audience going *(inf)*. **(e)** *(sl: kritisieren)* to slam *(inf)*.

anmahnen *vt sep* to send a reminder about.

anmalen *sep* **1** *vt* **(a)** *(bemalen) Wand, Gegenstand* to paint; *(ausmalen)* to colour in. **(b)** *(anzeichnen)* to paint *(an +acc* on). **(c)** *(schminken)* **sich** *(dat)* **die Lippen/Lider etc** ~ to paint one's lips/eyelids *etc*; **sich** *(dat)* **einen Schnurrbart/Sommersprossen** ~ to paint a moustache/freckles on one's face *or* on oneself. **2** *vr (pej: schminken)* to paint one's face *or* oneself.

Anmarsch *m, no pl (Weg)* walk (there); *(Mil)* advance. **im** ~ **sein** to be advancing *(auf +acc* on); *(hum inf)* to be on the way.

anmarschieren* *vi sep aux sein (Mil)* to advance. **anmarschiert kommen** to come marching along *or (auf einen zu)* up.

Anmarschweg *m* walk.

anmaßen *vr sep* **sich** *(dat)* **etw** ~ *Befugnis, Recht* to claim sth (for oneself); *Kritik* to take sth upon oneself; *Titel, Amt, Autorität* to assume sth; **sich** *(dat)* **ein Urteil/eine Meinung über etw** *(acc)* ~ to presume to pass judgement on/have an opinion about sth; **sich** *(dat)* ~, **etw zu tun** to presume to do sth.

anmaßend *adj* presumptuous.

Anmaßung *f* presumption, presumptuousness. **mit seinen ständigen** ~**en machte er sich viele Feinde** he made a lot of enemies with his presumptuous behaviour; **es ist eine** ~ **zu meinen, ...** it is presumptuous to maintain that ...

anmeckern *vt sep (inf)* to keep on at *(inf)*.

Anmelde-: ~**formular** *nt* application form; ~**frist** *f* registration period; ~**gebühr** *f* registration fee.

anmelden *sep* **1** *vt* **(a)** *(ankündigen) Besuch* to announce. **einen Freund bei jdm** ~ to let sb know that a friend is coming to visit. **(b)** *(bei Schule, Kurs etc)* to enrol *(bei* at, *zu* for). **(c)** *(eintragen lassen) Patent* to register; *(für neuen Wohnsitz, Auto, Untermieter* to register *(bei* at); *Fernseher* to get a licence for. **Konkurs** ~ to declare oneself bankrupt. **(d)** *(vormerken lassen)* to make an appointment for. **(e)** *(Telec)* **ein Gespräch nach Deutschland** ~ to book a call to Germany. **(f)** *(geltend machen) Recht, Ansprüche, (zu Steuerzwecken)* to declare; *Bedenken, Zweifel, Protest* to register; *Wünsche, Bedürfnisse* to make known. **ich melde starke Bedenken an** I have serious doubts about that, I'm rather doubtful *or* dubious about that. **2** *vr* **(a)** *(ankündigen) (Besucher)* to announce one's arrival; *(im Hotel)* to book (in); *(fig) (Baby)* to be on the way; *(Probleme, Zweifel etc)* to appear on the horizon. **sich bei jdm** ~ to tell sb one is coming. **(b)** *(an Schule, zu Kurs etc)* to enrol (oneself) *(an +dat* at, *zu* for). **sich polizeilich** ~ to register with the police. **(c)** *(sich einen Termin geben lassen)* to make an appointment. **sich beim Arzt etc** ~ to make an appointment at the doctor's *etc or* with the doctor *etc*.

Anmelde-: ~**pflicht** *f siehe adj* compulsory licensing/

registration/notification; **a**~**pflichtig** *adj* **a**~**pflichtig sein** *(Fernsehgerät, Hund)* to have to be licensed; *(Auto, Untermieter, Ausländer)* to have to be registered; *(Einfuhr, Waffenbesitz etc)* to be notifiable; ~**schein** *m* registration form.

Anmeldung *f* **(a)** *siehe vt* announcement; declaration; registration; making known *(von etw* sth); enrolment; application *(von, gen* for); registration; licensing; making an appointment *(gen* for); *(Konkurs~)* bankruptcy petition. **die** ~ **eines Gespräches** booking a call; **die erneute** ~ **seines Protestes** his renewed protest ... **(b)** *(Ankündigung)* announcement of one's arrival; *(im Hotel)* booking; *(an Schule, zu Kurs etc)* enrolment *(an +dat* at, *zu* for); *(bei Polizei)* registration; *(beim Arzt etc)* making an appointment. **nur nach vorheriger** ~ by appointment only. **(c)** *(Anmelderaum)* reception.

anmerken *vt sep (sagen)* to say; *(anstreichen)* to mark; *(als Fußnote)* to note. **sich** *(dat)* **etw** ~ to make a note of sth, to note sth down; **jdm seine Verlegenheit etc** ~ to notice sb's embarrassment *etc or* that sb is embarrassed *etc*; **sich** *(dat)* **etw** ~ **lassen** to let sth show; **man merkt ihm nicht an, daß ...** you wouldn't know *or* can't tell that ...

Anmerkung *f (Erläuterung)* note; *(Fußnote)* (foot)note; *(iro: Kommentar)* remark, comment.

anmessen *vt sep irreg* **(a)** **jdm etw** ~ *(geh)* to measure sb for sth. **(b)** *(Phot) Objekt* to take a reading off *or* from.

anmieten *vt sep* to rent; *Auto etc auch* to hire.

anmit *adv (Sw)* herewith.

anmontieren* *vt sep* to fix on *(an +acc or dat* -to).

anmustern *vti (Naut)* to sign on.

Anmut *f* **-, *no pl* grace; *(Grazie auch)* gracefulness; *(Schönheit)* beauty, loveliness; *(von Landschaft, Gegenständen)* charm, beauty.

anmuten *sep* **1** *vt (geh)* to appear, to seem *(jdn* to sb). **jdn seltsam** ~ to appear *or* seem odd to sb; **es mutete ihn wie ein Traum an** it seemed like a dream to him. **2** *vi* **es mutet sonderbar an** it *or* seems curious; **eine eigenartig** ~**de Geschichte** a story that strikes one as odd.

anmutig *adj (geh) (geschmeidig, behende) Bewegung* graceful; *(hübsch anzusehen)* lovely, charming.

Anmut(s)- *(geh)*: **a**~**los** *adj* graceless, lacking grace; *(nicht hübsch)* lacking charm; ~**losigkeit** *f siehe adj* lack of grace/charm; **a**~**voll** *adj Lächeln* lovely, charming; *(geschmeidig, behende)* graceful.

annageln *vt sep* to nail on *(an +acc or dat* -to). **er stand wie angenagelt da** he stood there rooted to the spot.

annagen *vt sep* to gnaw (at); *(fig) Ersparnisse etc* to gnaw away at, to nibble away.

annähen *vt sep* to sew on *(an +acc or dat* -to); *Saum* to sew up.

annähern *sep* **1** *vt* to bring closer *(dat, an +acc* to); *(in größere Übereinstimmung bringen auch)* to bring more into line *(dat, an +acc* with). **zwei Länder/Standpunkte soweit als möglich** ~ to bring two nations as close (to each other)/two points of view as much into line (with each other) as possible; **wir nähern unseren Lebensstil immer mehr dem der Amerikaner an** our way of life is becoming more and more similar to that of the Americans. **2** *vr* **(a)** *(lit, fig: sich nähern)* to approach *(einer Sache (dat)* sth). **(b)** *(sich angleichen, näherkommen)* to come closer *(dat, an +acc* to).

annähernd **1** *adj (ungefähr)* approximate, rough. **2** *adv (etwa)* roughly; *(fast)* almost. **können Sie mir den Betrag** ~ **nennen?** can you give me an approximate *or* a rough idea of the amount?; **nicht** ~ not nearly, nothing like; **nur** ~ **soviel** only about this/that much; **nicht** ~ **soviel** not nearly as much, nothing like as much.

Annäherung *f (lit: Näherkommen, fig: Angleichung)* approach *(an +acc* towards); *(von Standpunkten)* convergence *(dat, an +acc* with). **eine** ~ **an die Wirklichkeit** an approximation of reality; **eine** ~ **unserer Arbeitsweisen zeichnete sich ab** it became apparent that our ways of working had become more similar; **die** ~ **zwischen Ost und West** the rapprochement of East and West; **die** ~ **von zwei Menschen** when two people come close (together); **die** ~ **an den Partner** coming closer to one's partner.

Annäherungs-: ~**politik** *f* policy of rapprochement; ~**versuch** *m* overtures *pl*; **siehe plump**; **a**~**weise** *adv* approximately; ~**wert** *m siehe* **Näherungswert.**

Annahme *f* **-, -n (a)** *(Vermutung, Voraussetzung)* assumption. **in der** ~, **daß ...** on the assumption that ...; **gehe ich recht in der** ~, **daß ...?** am I right in assuming *or* in the assumption that ...?; **der** ~ **sein, daß ...** to assume that ...; **von einer** ~ **ausgehen** to work on *or* from an assumption. **(b)** *siehe vt (a-e, g, h)* acceptance; taking; taking on; taking up; approval; passing; adoption; acceptance; adoption; picking up; taking on; acquisition; adoption; assuming; acceptance; adoption; taking up; taking. ~ **an Kindes Statt** (child) adoption. **(c)** *siehe* **Annahmestelle.**

Annahme-: ~**frist** *f* **eine** ~**frist von vier Wochen** a period of four weeks during which applications/bets *etc* can be accepted; ~**frist bis zum 17. Juli** closing date 17th July; **die** ~**frist einhalten** to meet the deadline for applications/bets *etc*; **die** ~**frist für die Bewerbung ist schon vorbei** applications can no longer be accepted; ~**stelle** *f (für Pakete, Telegramme)* counter; *(für Wetten, Lotto, Toto etc)* place where bets *etc* are accepted; *(für Reparaturen)* reception; *(für Material)* delivery point; **die** ~**stelle für das Altmaterial ist ...** please bring your jumble to ..., jumble will be taken at ...; ~**verweigerung** *f* refusal; **bei** ~**verweigerung** when delivery *or* when a parcel/letter *etc* is refused.

Annalen pl annals pl. in die ~ eingehen (fig) to go down in the annals or in history.

annehmbar 1 adj acceptable; (nicht schlecht) reasonable, not bad. **sein altes Auto hat noch einen ~en Preis erzielt** he didn't get a bad price or he got a reasonable price for his old car. **2** adv reasonably well.

Annehmbarkeit f acceptability.

annehmen sep irreg **1** vt **(a)** (entgegennehmen, akzeptieren) to accept; Geld auch, Nahrung, einen Rat, Telegramm, Lottoschein, Reparaturen to take; Arbeit, Auftrag, Wette auch to take on; Herausforderung, Angebot auch to take up. **(b)** (billigen) to approve; Gesetz to pass; Resolution to adopt; Antrag to accept. **(c)** (sich aneignen) to adopt; Gewohnheit etc auch to pick up; Staatsangehörigkeit auch to take on; Akzent, Tonfall to acquire, to take on; (imitieren) to adopt; Gestalt, Namen to assume, to take on. **ein angenommener Name** an assumed name; siehe Wahl, Vernunft. **(d)** (zulassen) Patienten, Bewerber to accept, to take on. **(e)** (adoptieren) to adopt. **jdn an Kindes Statt ~** to adopt sb. **(f)** (aufnehmen) Farbe to take. **dieser Stoff/das Gefieder nimmt kein Wasser an** this material is/the feathers are water-repellent. **(g)** (Hunt) Fährte to take up; (angreifen) to attack, to go for. **(h)** (Sport) to take. **(i)** (vermuten) to presume, to assume. **von jdm etw ~** (erwarten) to expect sth of sb; (glauben) to believe sth of sb; **er ist nicht so dumm, wie man es von ihm ~ könnte** he's not as stupid as you might think or suppose; **was nehmen Sie denn von mir an!** what do you think I am?, what do you take me for? (inf). **(j)** (voraussetzen) to assume. **wir wollen ~, daß ...** let us assume that ...; **etw als gegeben** or **Tatsache ~** to take sth as read or for granted; **das kann man wohl ~** you can take that as read; siehe angenommen.
2 vr **sich jds/einer Sache ~** to look after a person/to see to or look after a matter.

Annehmlichkeit f (Bequemlichkeit) convenience; (Vorteil) advantage. **~en** pl comforts pl.

annektieren* vt to annex.

Annektierung f siehe **Annexion.**

Annex m -es, -e (Archit) annex(e); (Jur) annex, appendix.

Annexion f annexation.

annexionistisch adj annexationist.

anniesen vt sep to sneeze over or on.

annieten vt sep to rivet on (an +acc or dat -to).

Anno, anno (Aus) adv in. **der härteste Winter seit ~ zwölf** the coldest winter since 1912; **ein harter Winter, wie ~ 61** a cold winter, like the winter of '61; **von ~ dazumal** or **dunnemals** or **Tobak** (all inf) from the year dot (inf); **das war im Deutschland von ~ dazumal so üblich** that was the custom in Germany in olden days; **ein Überbleibsel von ~ dazumal** or **dunnemals** or **Tobak** (all inf) a hangover from the olden days; **~ dazumal** or **dunnemals war alles viel billiger** in those days everything was much cheaper.

Anno Domini adv in the year of Our Lord.

Annonce [a'nõ:sə] f -, -n advertisement, advert (Brit inf), ad (inf).

Annoncenteil m classified (advertisement) section.

annoncieren* [anõ'si:rən] **1** vi to advertise. **2** vt to advertise; (geh: ankündigen) Veröffentlichung, Heirat etc to announce.

annullieren* vt (Jur) to annul.

Annullierung f annulment.

Anode f -, -n anode.

an|öden vt sep (inf) (langweilen) to bore stiff (inf) or to tears (inf).

anomal adj (regelwidrig) unusual, abnormal; (nicht normal) strange, odd.

Anomalie f anomaly; (Med: Mißbildung) abnormality.

anonym adj anonymous.

Anonymität f anonymity. **er wollte die ~ wahren** he wanted to preserve his anonymity.

Anonymus m -, **Anonymi** or **Anonymen** anonym (rare), anonymous artist/author etc.

Anorak m -s, -s anorak.

an|ordnen vt sep **(a)** (befehlen, festsetzen) to order. **(b)** (nach Plan ordnen, aufstellen) to arrange; (systematisch) to order.

An|ordnung f **(a)** (Befehl) order. **laut (polizeilicher) ~ by** order (of the police); **auf ~ des Arztes** on doctor's orders; **~en treffen** to give orders. **(b)** (Aufstellung) arrangement; (systematische ~) order; (Formation) formation. **in welcher ~ wollen Sie die Tische für die Konferenz?** how do you want the tables arranged for the conference?

an|organisch adj **(a)** (Chem) inorganic. **(b)** (rare) haphazard; Wachstum random attr. **die Stadt ist ~ gewachsen** the town has grown in a haphazard way.

anormal adj (inf) siehe **anomal.**

anpacken sep (inf) **1** vt **(a)** (anfassen) to take hold of, to grab; (angreifen: Hund) to grab. **(b)** (handhaben, beginnen) to tackle, to set about. **(c)** (umgehen mit) jdn to treat. **2** vi (helfen) (auch mit ~) to lend a hand.

anpappen sep (inf) **1** vt to stick on (an +dat -to). **2** vi aux sein to stick (an +dat to).

anpassen sep **1** vt **(a)** Kleidung to fit (dat on); Bauelemente to fit (dat on). **(b)** (abstimmen) etw einer Sache (dat) ~ to suit sth to sth. **(c)** (angleichen) etw einer Sache (dat) ~ to bring sth into line with sth.
2 vr to adapt (oneself) (dat to). **Kinder passen sich leichter an als Erwachsene** children adapt (themselves) more easily or are

more adaptable than adults; **wir mußten uns (ihren Wünschen) ~** we had to fit in with their wishes or them; siehe **angepaßt.**

Anpassung f (an +acc to) adaptation; (von Gehalt etc) adjustment; (an Gesellschaft, Normen etc) conformity.

Anpassungs-: **a~fähig** adj adaptable; **~fähigkeit** f adaptability; **~mechanismus** m (Sociol) adaptation mechanism; **~schwierigkeiten** pl difficulties pl in adapting; **~vermögen** nt (Sociol) adaptability.

anpeilen vt sep (ansteuern) to steer or head for; (mit Radar, Funk etc) to take a bearing on. **etw ~** (fig inf) to set or have one's sights on sth; **jdn ~** (inf) to eye sb.

anpeitschen vt sep to urge on.

Anpeitscher m -s, - slavedriver, slavemaster; (fig) rabble-rouser.

anpesen vi sep aux sein (inf) (usu **angepest kommen**) to come belting along or (auf einen zu) up (inf).

anpfeifen sep irreg **1** vi (Sport) to blow the whistle. **2** vt **(a)** (Sport) **das Spiel ~** to start the game (by blowing one's whistle). **(b)** (inf) to bawl out (inf).

Anpfiff m **(a)** (Sport) (starting) whistle; (Spielbeginn) kick-off. **(b)** (inf) bawling out (inf).

anpflanzen vt sep (bepflanzen) to plant; (anbauen) to grow.

Anpflanzung f **(a)** siehe vt planting; growing. **(b)** (Fläche) cultivated area. **eine ~ anlegen** to lay out an area for cultivation.

anpflaumen vt sep (inf) to poke fun at.

anpflocken vt sep to tie up; Tier auch to tether.

anpinkeln vt sep (inf) to pee on (inf).

anpinnen vt sep (N Ger inf) to pin up (an +acc or dat on).

anpinseln vt sep to paint; Parolen etc to paint (up).

anpirschen sep **1** vt to stalk. **2** vr to creep up (an +acc on).

anpissen vt sep (sl) to piss on (sl).

Anpöbelei f pestering no pl. **wie soll man auf ~en reagieren?** how should you react when people pester you?

anpöbeln vt sep (inf) to pester.

anpochen vi sep to knock (an +acc on, at). **bei jdm ~, ob ...** (inf) to sound sb out (as to) whether ...

anpopeln vt sep (sl) to keep having a dig at (inf).

Anprall m impact. **beim ~ gegen** on impact with.

anprallen vi sep aux sein to crash (an or gegen jdn/etw into sb/against sth).

anprangern vt sep to denounce. **jdn als Betrüger/etw als Korruption ~** to denounce sb as a fraud/sth as corrupt.

Anprangerung f denunciation.

anpreisen vt sep irreg to extol (jdm etw sth to sb). **sich (als etw) ~** to sell oneself as sth.

Anpreisung f siehe vt extolling.

anpreschen vi sep aux sein (usu **angeprescht kommen**) to come hurrying along or (auf einen zu) up.

anpressen vt sep to press on (an +acc -to). **das Ohr an die Tür ~** to press or put one's ear to the door.

Anprobe f **(a)** fitting. **(b)** (Raum) (im Kaufhaus) changing room; (beim Schneider) fitting room.

anprobieren* sep **1** vt to try on. **jdm etw ~** (inf) to try sth on sb. **2** vi (beim Schneider) to have a fitting. **kann ich mal ~?** can I try this/it etc on?; **ich muß noch ~** I'll have to try it on.

anpumpen vt sep (inf) to borrow from. **jdn um 50 Mark ~** to touch sb for 50 marks (inf), to borrow 50 marks from sb.

anpusten vt sep (inf) to blow at; Feuer to blow on.

anquasseln vt sep (inf) to speak to.

anquatschen vt sep (inf) to speak to; Mädchen to chat up (inf).

Anrainer m -s, - **(a)** neighbour. **die ~ der Nordsee** the countries bordering (on) the North Sea. **(b)** (esp Aus) siehe **Anlieger.**

anranzen vt sep (inf) to bawl out (inf).

Anranzer m -s, - (inf) bawling-out (inf).

anrasen vi sep aux sein (usu **angerast kommen**) to come tearing or rushing along or (auf einen zu) up.

anraten vt sep irreg jdm etw ~ to recommend sth to sb; **auf A~ des Arztes etc** on the doctor's etc advice or recommendation.

anrattern vi sep aux sein (usu **angerattert kommen**) to come clattering or rattling along or (auf einen zu) up.

anrauchen vt sep **(a)** Zigarre etc to light (up). **eine angerauchte Zigarette** a partly or half-smoked cigarette. **(b)** Menschen to blow smoke at.

anräuchern vt sep to smoke lightly.

anrauhen vt sep to roughen; Stimme to make hoarse. **angerauht sein** to be rough.

anraunzen vt sep (inf) to tell or tick off (inf).

Anraunzer m -s, - (inf) telling or ticking off (inf).

anrauschen vi sep aux sein (usu **angerauscht kommen**) to come rushing or hurrying along or (auf einen zu) up.

anrechenbar adj countable. **auf etw (acc) ~ sein** to count towards sth.

anrechnen vt sep **(a)** (in Rechnung stellen) to charge for (jdm sb). **das wird Ihnen später angerechnet** you'll be charged for that later, that will be charged to you later. **(b)** (gutschreiben) to count, to take into account (jdm for sb). **das Auslandssemester wird Ihnen nicht auf die gesamte Studienzeit angerechnet** the term abroad will not count towards your total study time; **das alte Auto rechnen wir (Ihnen) mit DM 500 an** we'll allow (you) DM 500 for the old car; **den alten Fernseher ~** to allow something on the old television. **(c)** (bewerten) **dem Schüler wird die schlechte Arbeit nicht angerechnet** the pupil's bad piece of work is not being taken into account; **jdm etw hoch ~** to think highly of sb for sth; **jdm etw als Fehler ~** (Lehrer) to count sth as a mistake (for sb); (fig) to consider sth as a fault on sb's part; **ich rechne es ihm als Verdienst an, daß ...** I think it is greatly to his credit that ..., I think it says a lot for him that ...; **ich rechne es mir zur Ehre an**

(form) I consider it an honour, I consider myself honoured.

Anrechnung f allowance; *(fig: Berücksichtigung)* counting, taking into account *(auf +acc* towards). **jdm etw in ~ bringen** or **stellen** *(form)* to charge sb for sth.

anrechnungsfähig adj siehe **anrechenbar**.

Anrecht nt **(a)** *(Anspruch)* right, entitlement *(auf +acc* to). **ein ~ auf etw** *(acc)* **haben** or **besitzen** *auf Respekt, Ruhe etc* to be entitled to sth; *auf Geld, Land etc* to have a right to sth; **sein ~ (auf etw) geltend machen** to enforce one's right (to sth). **(b)** *(Abonnement)* subscription.

Anrede f form of address; *(Brief~ auch)* salutation *(form)*.

Anredefall, Anredekasus m *(Gram)* vocative (case).

anreden sep 1 vt to address. **jdn mit „du" ~** to address sb as "du", to use the "du" form (of address) to sb; **jdn mit seinem Titel ~** to address sb by his title. 2 vi **gegen jdn/etw ~** to argue against sb/to make oneself heard against sth.

anregen vt sep **(a)** *(ermuntern)* to prompt *(zu* to). **jdn zum Denken ~** to make sb think. **(b)** *(geh: vorschlagen)* Verbesserung to propose, to suggest. **(c)** *(beleben)* to stimulate; *Appetit auch* to whet, to sharpen. **Kaffee** etc **regt an** coffee etc is a stimulant or has a stimulating effect; siehe **angeregt**. **(d)** *(Phys)* to activate.

anregend adj stimulating. **ein ~es Mittel** a stimulant; **die Verdauung/den Kreislauf ~e Mittel** stimulants to the digestion/circulation.

Anregung f **(a)** *(Antrieb, Impuls)* stimulus. **jdm eine ~ zum Denken geben** to make sb think. **(b)** *(Vorschlag)* idea. **auf ~ von** or *+gen* **at** or **on the suggestion of. (c)** *(Belebung)* stimulation.

Anregungsmittel nt stimulant.

anreichen vt sep to pass, to hand.

anreichern sep 1 vt *(gehaltvoller machen)* to enrich; *(vergrößern)* Sammlung to enlarge, to increase. **das Gemisch mit Sauerstoff ~** *(zufügen)* to add oxygen to the mixture; **angereichert werden** *(Chem: gespeichert werden)* to be accumulated; **mit Rauch angereicherte Luft** smoky air; siehe **angereichert**. 2 vr *(Chem)* to accumulate.

Anreicherung f *(Bereicherung)* enrichment; *(Vergrößerung)* enlargement; *(Speicherung)* accumulation.

anreihen sep 1 vt **(a)** *(einer Reihe anfügen)* to add *(an +acc* to). **(b)** *(anheften)* to tack on; *Saum* to tack (up). 2 vr to follow *(einer Sache (dat)* sth). **reihen Sie sich bitte hinten an!** join the end of the queue, please.

Anreise f **(a)** *(Anfahrt)* journey there/here. **die ~ zu diesem abgelegenen Ort ist sehr mühsam** it is very difficult to get to this remote place. **(b)** *(Ankunft)* arrival. **Tag der ~ war Sonntag** the day of arrival was Sunday.

anreisen vi sep aux sein **(a)** *(ein Ziel anfahren)* to make a/the journey or trip (there/here). **über welche Strecke wollen Sie ~?** which route do you want to take (there/here)? **(b)** *(eintreffen)* *(auch* **angereist kommen)** to come.

anreißen vt sep irreg **(a)** *(einreißen)* to tear, to rip. **(b)** *(inf: anbrechen)* to start, to open. **(c)** *Außenbordmotor etc* to start (up). **(d)** *(Tech)* to mark (out). **(e)** *(kurz zur Sprache bringen)* to touch on. **(f)** *(pej inf)* Kunden to draw, to attract. **(g)** *Streichholz* to strike.

Anreißer m -s, - *(pej inf)* *(Kundenfänger)* tout; *(Gegenstand)* bait.

Anreißerei f *(pej inf)* touting.

anreißerisch adj *(pej inf)* attention-grabbing attr.

Anreißschablone f *(Tech)* template.

anreiten sep irreg 1 vi aux sein *(usu* **angeritten kommen)** to come riding along or *(auf einen zu)* up. 2 vt **(a)** *Ziel etc* to ride towards. **(b) gegen etw ~** *(Mil)* to charge sth. **(c)** *Pferd* to break in.

Anreiz m incentive. **ein ~ zum Lernen** etc an incentive to learn etc or for learning etc; **jdm den ~ nehmen, etw zu tun** to take away sb's incentive for doing sth.

anreizen sep 1 vt **(a)** *(anspornen)* to encourage. **jdn zum Kauf/zu großen Leistungen ~** to encourage sb to buy/to perform great feats. **(b)** *(erregen)* to stimulate, to excite. 2 vi to act as an incentive *(zu* to). **dazu ~, daß jd etw tut** to act as an incentive for sb to do sth.

anrempeln sep 1 vt **(a)** *(anstoßen)* to bump into; *(absichtlich)* Menschen to jostle. **(b)** *(fig: beschimpfen)* to insult. 2 vi aux sein **gegen** or **an etw** *(acc)* ~ to bump into sth.

anrennen sep irreg 1 vi aux sein **(a) gegen etw ~** *gegen Wind* etc to run against sth; *(Mil)* to storm sth; *(Sport)* to attack sth; *(sich stoßen)* to run into sth; *(fig: bekämpfen)* to fight against sth.

(b) **angerannt kommen** *(inf)* to come running.

2 vr **sich** *(dat)* **den Kopf ~** to bump one's head *(an +dat* against).

Anrichte f -, -n **(a)** *(Schrank)* dresser; *(Büfett)* sideboard. **(b)** *(Raum)* pantry.

anrichten vt sep **(a)** *(zubereiten)* Speisen to prepare; *(servieren)* to serve; *Salat* to dress. **es ist angerichtet** *(form)* dinner etc is served *(form)*. **(b)** *(fig: verursachen)* Schaden, Unheil to cause, to bring about. **etwas ~** *(inf: anstellen)* to get up to something *(inf)*; **da hast du aber etwas angerichtet!** *(inf)* *(verursachen)* you've started something there all right; *(anstellen)* you've really made a mess there.

anriechen vt sep irreg to sniff at. **jdm/einer Sache etw ~** to be able to tell sth by smelling sb/sth; **ich rieche dir doch an, daß du geraucht hast** I can smell that you've been smoking.

Anriß m *(Tech)* scribing, marking.

Anritt m *(old)* approach (on horseback); *(auf +acc* towards); *(Angriff)* charge *(gegen* on, against).

anritzen vt sep to slit (slightly).

anrollen sep 1 vi aux sein *(zu rollen beginnen)* to start to roll; *(heranrollen)* to roll up; *(Aviat)* to taxi. **gegen etw/jdn ~** *(fig: in feindlicher Absicht)* to move against sth/sb; **angerollt kommen** to roll along or *(auf einen zu)* up. 2 vt to roll; *(heranrollen)* to roll up.

anrosten vi sep aux sein to get (a bit) rusty.

anrösten vt sep to brown lightly.

anrotzen vt sep *(vulg)* to gob at *(sl)*. **jdn ~** *(fig: beschimpfen)* to give sb a bollocking *(sl)*.

anrüchig adj **(a)** *(von üblem Ruf)* of ill repute; *(berüchtigt)* Lokal etc notorious. **(b)** *(anstößig)* offensive; *(unanständig)* indecent.

Anrüchigkeit f siehe adj ill repute; notoriety; offensiveness; indecency.

anrücken sep 1 vi aux sein **(a)** *(Truppen)* to advance; *(Polizei* etc) to move in; *(hum: Essen, Besuch)* to turn up. **die Verwandten kamen angerückt** the relations turned up. **(b)** *(weiter heranrücken)* to move up or closer. 2 vt to move up. **etw an etw** *(acc)* ~ to push sth against sth.

Anruf m call; *(Mil: eines Wachtpostens)* challenge. **etw auf ~ tun** to do sth when called; **ohne ~ schießen** to shoot without warning.

Anrufbe|antworter m (telephone) answering machine, answerphone.

anrufen sep irreg 1 vt **(a)** to shout to; *(Telec auch)* to ring, to phone; *(Mil: Posten)* to challenge. **darf ich dich ~?** can I give you a ring?, can I call you? **(b)** *(fig: appellieren an)* *(um* for) to appeal to; *Gott* to call on. 2 vi *(inf: telefonieren)* to phone, to make a (phone) call/phone calls. **bei jdm ~** to phone sb; **kann man hier bei Ihnen ~?** can I make a (phone) call from here?; **kann man Sie** or **bei Ihnen ~?** are you on the phone?; **ins Ausland/nach Amerika ~** to phone abroad/America.

Anrufer m caller.

Anrufung f *(Gottes, der Heiligen* etc) invocation; *(Jur)* appeal *(gen* to). **nach ~ des Gerichts** after an appeal to the court.

anrühren vt sep **(a)** *(berühren, sich befassen)* to touch; *(fig)* Thema to touch upon. **er rührt kein Fleisch/keinen Alkohol an** he doesn't touch meat/alcohol; **sie konnte nichts ~** *(inf)* she couldn't touch food, she couldn't eat anything. **(b)** *(fig liter: rühren)* to move, to touch. **(c)** *(mischen)* Farben to mix; *Sauce* to blend; *(verrühren)* to stir.

anrußen vt sep to blacken.

ans contr of **an das. sich ~ Arbeiten machen** or **begeben** to set to work; **wenn es ~ Sterben geht** when it comes to dying.

ansäen vt sep to sow.

Ansage f -, -n announcement; *(Diktat)* dictation; *(Cards)* bid. **er übernimmt bei diesem Programm die ~** he is doing the announcements for this programme; **einen Brief nach ~ schreiben** to take a letter down (on dictation); **er hat die ~** *(Cards)* it's his bid.

ansagen sep 1 vt **(a)** to announce. **jdm den Kampf ~** to declare war on sb; siehe **Bankrott**. **(b)** *(diktieren)* to dictate. **(c)** *(Cards)* *(Bridge)* to bid; *(Skat)* to declare. 2 vr *(Besuch ankündigen)* to say that one is coming; *(Termin vereinbaren)* to make an appointment; *(Zeit, Frühling)* to announce oneself *(liter)*. **sich für Sonntag/fürs Wochenende/zum Mittagessen/bei jdm ~** to say that one is coming on Sunday/for the weekend/for lunch/to visit sb.

3 vi **(a)** *(old, liter)* **sag an, Fremdling ...** pray tell, stranger *(old, liter)* ... **(b) sie sagt im Radio an** she's an announcer on the radio.

ansagen vt sep to saw into.

Ansager(in f) m -s, - *(Radio* etc) announcer; *(im Kabarett)* compère.

ansammeln sep 1 vt **(a)** *(anhäufen)* to accumulate; *Reichtümer* to amass; *Vorräte* to build up; *Zinsen* to build up, to accrue *(form)*. **(b)** *(zusammenkommen lassen)* to gather together; *Truppen* to concentrate. 2 vr **(a)** *(sich versammeln)* to gather, to collect. **(b)** *(aufspeichern, aufhäufen)* to accumulate; *(Staub, Wasser auch, Fragen)* to collect; *(Druck, Stau, fig: Wut)* to build up; *(Zinsen)* to build up, to accrue *(form)*.

Ansammlung f **(a)** *(Anhäufung)* accumulation; *(Sammlung)* collection; *(von Druck, Stau, Wut)* build-up; *(Haufen)* pile. **(b)** *(Auflauf)* gathering, crowd; *(von Truppen)* concentration.

ansässig adj *(form)* resident. **sich in London ~ machen** to settle or take up residence *(form)* in London; **alle in diesem Ort A~en** all local residents.

Ansässigkeit f residence.

Ansatz m **(a)** *(von Hals, Arm, Henkel* etc) base; *(an Stirn)* hairline; *(Haarwurzeln)* roots pl. **(b)** *(Tech)* *(Zusatzstück)* attachment; *(zur Verlängerung)* extension; *(Naht)* join. **(c)** *(das Ansetzen: von Rost, Kalk* etc) formation, deposition; *(Schicht)* coating, layer. **(d)** *(erstes Anzeichen, Beginn)* first sign(s pl), beginning(s pl); *(Versuch)* attempt *(zu etw* at sth); *(Ausgangspunkt)* starting-point. **den ~ zu etw zeigen** to show the first signs or the beginnings of sth; **einen neuen ~ zu etw machen** to make a fresh attempt at sth; **die ersten Ansätze** the initial stages; **im ~** basically. **(e)** *(esp Philos, Liter* etc) approach. **(f)** *(Sport: Anlauf)* run-up; *(zum Sprung)* take-off. **(g)** *(Math)* formulation. **(h)** *(Mus)* intonation; *(Lippenstellung)* embouchure. **(i)** *(Econ form)* estimate; *(Fonds für Sonderzwecke)* appropriation. **außer** ~ **bleiben** to be excluded, to be left out of account; **etw für etw in** ~ **bringen** to appropriate sth for sth; **jdm etw in** ~ **bringen** to charge sb for sth.

Ansatz-: ~**punkt** *m* starting-point; ~**stück** *nt* (*Tech*) attachment; (*zur Verlängerung*) extension.

ansäuern *sep* 1 *vt* to make sour; *Brotteig* to leaven; (*Chem*) to acidify. 2 *vi aux sein* to start to go sour.

ansaufen *vr sep irreg* (*sl*) **sich** (*dat*) **einen** (**Rausch**) ~ to get plastered *or* sloshed (*sl*); **sich** (*dat*) **einen Bauch** ~ to get a beer-belly; *siehe* **angesoffen, antrinken.**

ansaugen *sep* 1 *vt* to suck *or* draw in; (*anfangen zu saugen*) to start to suck. 2 *vr* to attach itself (*by suction*).

ansäuseln *vr sep* **sich** (*dat*) **einen** ~ (*hum*) to have a tipple (*inf*); *siehe* **angesäuselt.**

anschaffen *sep* 1 *vt* (**a**) (**sich** *dat*) **etw** ~ to get oneself sth; (*kaufen*) to buy sth; **sich** (*dat*) **Kinder** ~ (*inf*) to have children. (**b**) (*sl: stehlen*) to pick up. 2 *vi* (**a**) (*Aus, S Ger*) to give orders. **jdm** ~ to order sb about, to give sb orders. (**b**) (*sl: durch Prostitution*) ~ **gehen** to be on the game; **für jdn** ~ **gehen** to work on the game for sb.

Anschaffer *m* **-s,** **-** (*sl*) thief, crook (*inf*).

Anschaffung *f* (**a**) *no pl* acquisition; (*das Kaufen auch*) buying. **ich habe mich zur** ~ **eines Autos entschlossen** I have decided to get *or* buy a new car. (**b**) (*angeschaffter Gegenstand*) acquisition; (*gekaufter Gegenstand auch*) purchase, buy. ~**en machen** to acquire things; (*kaufen*) to make purchases.

Anschaffungs-: ~**kosten** *pl* cost *sing* of purchase; ~**kredit** *m* (personal) loan; ~**preis** *m* purchase price; ~**wert** *m* value at the time of purchase.

anschalten *vt sep* to switch on.

anschauen *vt sep* (*esp dial*) to look at; (*prüfend*) to examine. **sich** (*dat*) **etw** ~ to have a look at sth; (*sich dat*) **eine Stadt/ Wohnung** ~ to have a look at a town/flat; (**da**) **schau einer an!** (*inf*) well I never!

anschaulich *adj* clear; (*lebendig, bildhaft*) vivid; *Beschreibung* graphic; *Beispiel* concrete. **etw** ~ **machen** to illustrate sth; **den Unterricht sehr** ~ **machen** to make teaching come alive.

Anschaulichkeit *f siehe adj* clearness; vividness; graphicness; concreteness.

Anschauung *f* (*Ansicht, Auffassung*) view; (*Meinung*) opinion; (*Vorstellung*) idea, notion; (*innere Versenkung*) contemplation; (~*svermögen*) ability to visualize things. **nach neuerer** ~ according to the current way of thinking; **in** ~ +*gen* (*geh*) in view of; **aus eigener** ~ from one's own experience.

Anschauungs-: ~**material** *nt* illustrative material, visual aids *pl*; ~**unterricht** *m* visual instruction; ~**vermögen** *nt* ability to visualize things; ~**weise** *f* (*geh*) view.

Anschein *m* appearance; (*Eindruck*) impression. **allem** ~ **nach** to all appearances, apparently; **den** ~ **erwecken, als ... zu** give the impression that ...; **sich** (*dat*) **den** ~ **geben, als ob man informiert sei** to pretend to be informed; **es hat den** ~, **als ob ...** it appears that *or* seems as if ...

anscheinen *vt sep irreg* to shine (up)on.

anscheinend *adj* apparent.

anscheißen *vt sep irreg* (*fig sl*) (**a**) (*betrügen*) **jdn** ~ to do the dirty on sb (*sl*); **da hast du dich aber** ~ **lassen** you were really done there; *siehe* **angeschissen.** (**b**) (*beschimpfen*) **jdn** ~ to give sb a bollocking (*sl*). (**c**) **und dann kam er angeschissen** and then the bugger came along (*sl*).

anschesen *vi sep aux sein* **angeschest kommen** (*N Ger inf*) to come tearing (*inf*) along *or* (*auf einen zu*) up.

anschicken *vr sep* **sich** ~, **etw zu tun** (*geh*) (*sich bereit machen*) to get ready *or* prepare to do sth; (*im Begriff sein, etw zu tun*) to be on the point of doing sth, to be about to do sth.

anschieben *vt sep irreg Fahrzeug* to push. **können Sie mich mal** ~? can you give me a push?

anschießen *sep irreg* 1 *vt* (**a**) (*verletzen*) to shoot (and wound); *Vogel* (*in Flügel*) to wing; *siehe* **angeschossen.** (**b**) *Gewehr* to test-fire. (**c**) (*Sport*) *Rennen* to start. (**d**) *Tor* to shoot at; *Latte, Pfosten, Spieler* to hit. (**e**) (*inf: kritisieren*) to hit out at (*inf*). 2 *vi aux sein* (*inf*) (*heranrasen*) to shoot up. **angeschossen kommen** to come shooting along *or* (*auf einen zu*) up.

anschimmeln *vi sep aux sein* to (start to) go mouldy.

anschirren *vt sep* to harness.

Anschiß *m* **-sses, -sse** (*sl*) bollocking (*sl*).

Anschlag *m* (**a**) (*Plakat*) poster, bill, placard; (*Bekanntmachung*) notice. **einen** ~ **machen** to put up a poster/ notice. (**b**) (*Überfall*) attack (*auf +acc* on); (*Attentat*) attempt on sb's life; (*Verschwörung*) plot (*auf +acc* against). **einen** ~ **auf jdn verüben** to make an attempt on sb's life; **einem** ~ **zum Opfer fallen** to be assassinated. (**c**) (*Kosten*~) estimate. **etw in** ~ **bringen** (*form*) to take sth into account; **eine Summe in** ~ **bringen** (*form*) to calculate an amount. (**d**) (*Aufprall*) impact; (*von Wellen auch*) beating. (**e**) (*Sport*) (*beim Schwimmen*) touch; (*beim Versteckspiel*) home. (**f**) (*von Klavier(spieler), Schreibmaschine*) touch. **200 Anschläge in der Minute** ≈ 40 words per minute. (**g**) (*in Strickanleitung*) ~ **von 20 Maschen** cast on 20 stitches. (**h**) (*von Hund*) bark. (**i**) (*bei Hebel, Knopf etc*) stop. **etw bis zum** ~ **durchdrücken/ drehen** to push sth right down/to turn sth as far as it will go.

(**j**) (*Mil*) aiming *or* firing position. **ein Gewehr in** ~ **heben** to present a rifle.

Anschlagbrett *nt* notice-board, bulletin board (*US*).

anschlagen *sep irreg* 1 *vt* (**a**) (*befestigen*) to fix on (*an +acc* -to); (*mit Nägeln*) to nail on (*an +acc* -to); (*aushängen*) *Plakat* to put up, to post (*an +acc* on). (**b**) *Stunde, Taste, Akkord* to strike; (*anstimmen*) *Melodie* to strike up; *Gelächter* to burst into; (*Mus*) to play. **eine schnellere Gangart** ~ (*fig*) to strike up a faster pace, to speed up; **ein anderes Thema/einen anderen Ton** ~ (*fig*) to change the subject/one's tune; **einen weinerlichen/frechen Ton** ~ to adopt a tearful tone/cheeky attitude. (**c**) (*beschädigen, verletzen*) *Geschirr* to chip. **sich** (*dat*) **den Kopf etc** ~ to knock one's head *etc*; *siehe* **angeschlagen.** (**d**) (*Sport*) *Ball* to hit. **den Ball seitlich** ~ to chip the ball. (**e**) (*Aus: anzapfen*) *Faß* to tap. (**f**) (*vormarkieren*) *Baum* to mark (for felling). (**g**) *Gewehr* to aim, to level (*auf +acc* at). (**h**) (*aufnehmen*) *Maschen* to cast on. (**i**) (*Naut*) to fasten; *Segel, Tau* to bend. (**j**) (*geh*) *Kosten etc* to estimate. 2 *vi* (**a**) (*Welle*) to beat (*an +acc* against). **mit etw gegen/an etw** (*acc*) ~ to strike *or* knock sth against/on sth. (**b**) (*Sport*) (*Tennis etc*) to serve; (*beim Schwimmen*) to touch. (**c**) (*Glocke*) to ring. (**d**) (*Taste betätigen*) to strike the keys. (**e**) (*Laut geben*) (*Hund*) to give a bark; (*Vogel*) to give a screech. (**f**) (*wirken: Arznei etc*) to work, to take effect. (**g**) (*inf: dick machen*) **bei jdm** ~ to make sb put on weight.

Anschlag-: ~**säule** *f* advertising pillar; ~**zettel** *m* notice.

anschleichen *sep irreg* 1 *vi aux sein* to creep along *or* (*auf einen zu*) up. **angeschlichen kommen** (*inf*) to come creeping along/up. 2 *vr* **sich an jdn/etw** ~ to creep up on sb/sth; (*sich anpirschen*) to stalk sth.

anschleifen *vt sep* (**a**) *irreg Schere* to grind, to sharpen. (**b**) (*inf: herbeischleppen*) to drag along. **was schleifst du denn da für einen Plunder an?** what's that junk you're carting up? (*inf*).

anschlendern *vi sep aux sein* to stroll *or* saunter along *or* (*auf einen zu*) up.

anschleppen *vt sep* (**a**) *Auto* to tow-start. (**b**) (*inf*) (*unerwünscht mitbringen*) to bring along; (*nach Hause*) to bring home; *Freund etc auch* to drag along; (*mühsam herbeibringen*) to drag along; (*hum: hervorholen, anbieten*) to bring out. **mit etw angeschleppt kommen** to bring/drag sth along; to drag sth along; (*hum*) to bring sth out.

anschließen *sep irreg* 1 *vt* (**a**) (*an +acc* to) to lock; (*mit Schnappschloß*) to padlock; (*anketten*) to chain (up). (**b**) (*an +acc* to) *Tech, Elec, Telec etc: verbinden*) to connect; (*in Steckdose*) to plug in. (**c**) (*fig: hinzufügen*) to add; *siehe* **angeschlossen.** 2 *vr* **sich jdm** *or* **an jdn** ~ (*folgen*) to follow sb; (*zugesellen*) to join sb; (*beipflichten*) to side with sb; **sich einer Sache** (*dat*) *or* **an etw** (*acc*) ~ (*folgen*) to follow sth; (*beitreten, sich beteiligen*) to join sth; (*beipflichten*) to endorse sth; (*angrenzen*) to adjoin sth; **sich leicht an andere** ~ to make friends easily, to be sociable; **dem Vortrag** *or* **an den Vortrag schloß sich ein Film an** the lecture was followed by a film. 3 *vi* **an etw** (*acc*) ~ to follow sth.

anschließend 1 *adv* afterwards. 2 *adj* following; *Ereignis, Diskussion auch* ensuing. **Essen mit** ~**em Tanz** dinner with a dance afterwards.

Anschluß *m* (**a**) (*Verbindung*) connection; (*Beitritt*) entry (*an +acc* into); (*an Klub*) joining (*an +acc* of); (*Hist euph*) Anschluss. ~ **haben nach** (*Rail*) to have a connection to; **den** ~ **verpassen** (*Rail etc*) to miss one's connection; (*fig*) to miss the boat *or* bus; (*alte Jungfer*) to be left on the shelf; **ihm gelang der** ~ **an die Spitze** (*Sport*) he managed to catch up with the leaders; **wir verloren den** ~ **an die Vordersten** we lost contact with the leaders. (**b**) (*Telec*) connection; (*Anlage*) telephone (connection); (*weiterer Apparat*) extension. **einen** ~ **beantragen** to apply for a telephone to be connected; ~ **bekommen** to get through; **der** ~ **ist besetzt** the line is engaged *or* busy (*esp US*); **kein** ~ **unter dieser Nummer** number unobtainable. (**c**) **im** ~ **an** (*+acc*) (*nach*) subsequent to, following; (*mit Bezug auf*) in connection with, further to; (*in Anlehnung an*) following, after. (**d**) (*fig*) (*Kontakt*) contact (*an +acc* with); (*Bekanntschaft*) friendship, companionship; (*Aufnahme*) integration. ~ **finden** to make friends (*an +acc* with); **er sucht** ~ he wants to make friends.

Anschluß-: ~**bahn** *f* (*Rail*) branch line; ~**dose** *f* (**a**) (*Elec*) junction box; (*Steckdose*) socket; (**b**) (*Telec*) connection box; **a**~**fertig** *adj* fully wired; ~**flug** *m* connecting flight; ~**nummer** *f* extension; ~**rohr** *nt* connecting pipe; ~**schnur** *f* extension lead; ~**stelle** *f* (*Mot*) junction; ~**zug** *m* (*Rail*) connecting train, connection.

anschmachten *vt sep* **jdn** ~ to gaze lovingly at sb.

anschmeißen *sep irreg* (*sl*) 1 *vt* (*in Gang setzen*) to turn on. 2 *vr* **sich jdm** *or* **an jdn** ~ (*pej*) to be all over sb (*inf*).

anschmieden *vt sep* to forge on (*an +acc* -to); (*anketten*) to chain (*an +acc* to); (*fig inf: fesseln*) to rivet (*an +acc* to).

anschmiegen *sep* 1 *vt* to nestle (*an +acc* against). 2 *vr* **sich an jdn/etw** ~ (*Kind, Hund*) to snuggle *or* nestle up to *or* against sb/sth; (*Kleidung*) to cling to sb/sth; (*geh: Dorf an Berg etc*) to nestle against sth.

anschmiegsam *adj Wesen* affectionate; *Material* smooth.

anschmieren *sep* 1 *vt* (**a**) (*bemalen*) to smear. (**b**) **jdn/sich mit etw** ~ (*inf*) (*beschmutzen*) to get sth all over

sb/oneself; (pej: schminken) to smear sth over sb's/one's lips/
face etc.
   (c) (inf) (betrügen) to con (inf), to take for a ride (inf);
(Streiche spielen) to play tricks on; siehe angeschmiert.
   2 vr sich bei jdm ~ (inf) to make up to sb (inf), to be all over sb
(inf).

anschmoren vt sep (Cook) to braise lightly.

anschnallen sep 1 vt (a) Rucksack to strap on; Skier to clip on.
   (b) jdn to strap up; (in etw) to strap in; (Aviat, Aut) to fasten
sb's seat belt.
   2 vr (Aviat, Aut) to fasten one's seat belt. bitte ~! fasten your
seat belts, please!; hast du dich or bist du angeschnallt? have
you fastened your seat belt?, are you strapped in?

anschnauben sep 1 vt to snort at; (fig inf: anschnauzen) to
bawl out (inf). 2 vi aux sein (usu: angeschnaubt kommen) (inf)
to come along huffing and puffing.

anschnaufen vi sep aux sein: angeschnauft kommen to come
panting along or (auf einen zu) up.

anschnauzen vt sep (inf) to yell at (inf).

Anschnauzer m -s, - (inf) sich (dat) einen ~ holen, einen ~
kriegen to get yelled at (inf).

anschneiden vt sep irreg (a) Brot etc to (start to) cut. (b) (fig)
Frage, Thema to touch on. (c) (Aut) Kurve, (Sport) Ball to cut.
(d) (Archeol) to come across.

Anschnitt m (Schnittfläche) cut part; (erstes Stück) first slice;
(Ende) cut end.

anschnorren vt sep (pej) to (try to) tap (inf). jdn um etw ~
to cadge sth from sb (inf), to tap sb for sth (inf).

Anschovis [an'ʃoːvɪs] f -, - anchovy.

anschrauben vt sep to screw on (an +acc -to); (festschrauben)
to screw tight or up.

anschreiben sep irreg 1 vt (a) (aufschreiben) to write up (an
+acc on). etw mit Kreide ~ to chalk sth up; angeschrieben
stehen to be written up; siehe angeschrieben.
   (b) (inf: in Rechnung stellen) to chalk up.
   (c) Kugelschreiber etc to break in.
   (d) Behörde, Versandhaus etc to write to. es antworteten nur
20% der Angeschriebenen only 20% of the people written to
replied.
   2 vi (inf) unser Kaufmann schreibt nicht an our grocer
doesn't give anything on tick (inf); sie läßt immer ~ she always
buys on tick (inf).

anschreien vt sep irreg to shout or yell at.

Anschrift f address. ein Brief ohne ~ an unaddressed letter.

anschuldigen vt sep to accuse (gen of).

Anschuldigung f accusation.

anschüren vt sep to stoke up; (fig) Streit to stir up, to kindle.

anschwanken vi sep aux sein (usu: angeschwankt kommen) to
come staggering along or (auf einen zu) up.

anschwärmen sep 1 vt (inf: verehren) to idolize, to have a
crush on (inf). 2 vi aux sein (auch angeschwärmt kommen) to
come in swarms.

anschwärzen vt sep (a) (lit) to blacken; (beschmutzen) to get
dirty. (b) (fig inf) jdn ~ to blacken sb's name (bei with);
(denunzieren) to run sb down (bei to).

anschweben vi sep aux sein (a) (Aviat) to come in to land. (b)
(fig) sie kam angeschwebt she came floating along or (auf
einen zu) up.

anschweigen vt sep irreg to say nothing to; (demonstrativ) to
refuse to speak to.

anschweißen vt sep (a) to weld on (an +acc -to). (b) (Hunt) to
wound, to draw blood from.

anschwellen vi sep irreg aux sein to swell (up); (Wasser auch,
Lärm) to rise. dick angeschwollen very swollen.

Anschwellung f swelling.

anschwemmen 1 vt sep to wash up or ashore. ange-
schwemmtes Land alluvial land. 2 vi aux sein to be washed up
or ashore.

Anschwemmung f (in Fluß, Hafen) silting up.

anschwimmen sep irreg 1 vt Ziel to swim towards.
   2 vi (a) aux sein angeschwommen kommen (Schwimmer,
Wasservogel) to come swimming along or (auf einen zu) up;
(Leiche, Brett) to come drifting along or (auf einen zu) up;
(Flasche) to come floating along or (auf einen zu) up.
   (b) aux sein gegen etw ~ to swim against sth.
   (c) (Saison eröffnen) to have the first swim.

anschwindeln vt sep (inf) jdn ~ to tell sb fibs (inf).

anschwirren vi sep aux sein (usu angeschwirrt kommen) to
come swarming along or (auf einen zu) up; (Insekt auch) to
come buzzing along or (auf einen zu) up.

ansegeln sep 1 vt (zusegeln auf) to sail for or towards, to make
for; (anlegen in) Hafen to put into. 2 vi (a) aux sein angesegelt
kommen (inf, fig) to come sailing along or (auf einen zu) up.
   (b) (Saison eröffnen) to start sailing, to start the sailing
season.

ansehen sep irreg 1 vt (a) (betrachten) to look at. er sah mich
ganz verwundert/groß/böse an he looked at me with great
surprise/stared at me/gave me an angry look; hübsch/schreck-
lich etc anzusehen pretty/terrible etc to look at; jdn nicht mehr
~ (fig inf) not to want to know sb any more; sieh mal einer an!
an! just look at that!; sieh mal einer an! (inf) well, I never! (inf).
   (b) (fig) to regard, to look upon (als, für as). ich sehe es als
meine Pflicht an I consider it to be my duty; sie sieht ihn nicht
für voll an she doesn't take him seriously; siehe angesehen.
   (c) (sich dat) etw ~ (besichtigen) to (have a) look at sth;
Fernsehsendung to watch sth; Film, Stück, Sportveranstaltung
to see sth; sich (dat) jdn/etw gründlich ~ (lit, fig) to take a close
look at sb/sth; sich (dat) die Welt ~ to see something of the
world.
   (d) das sieht man ihm an/nicht an he looks it/doesn't look it;

das sieht man ihm an der Gesichtsfarbe an you can tell (that) by
the colour of his face; man kann ihm die Strapazen der letzten
Woche ~ he's showing the strain of the last week; man sieht
ihm sein Alter nicht an he doesn't look his age; jdm etw (an den
Augen or an der Nasenspitze hum) ~ to tell or guess sth by
looking at sb; jeder konnte ihm sein Glück ~ everyone could
see that he was happy.
   (e) etw (mit) ~ to watch sth, to see sth happening; das kann
man doch nicht mit ~ you can't stand by and watch that; ich
kann das nicht länger mit ~ I can't stand it any more; das habe
ich (mir) lange genug (mit) angesehen! I've had enough of that!
   2 vr sich hübsch etc ~ to look pretty etc; es sieht sich an, als
hätte es ... it looks as if it ...

Ansehen nt -s, no pl (a) (Aussehen) appearance. ein anderes ~
gewinnen to take on a different appearance or (fig) aspect; jdn
vom ~ kennen to know sb by sight; dem ~ nach urteilen (geh)
to judge by appearances.
   (b) (guter Ruf) (high) reputation, standing; (Prestige) prestige. jdn zu ~ bringen to bring sb standing or a high reputation;
großes ~ genießen to enjoy a high reputation, to have a lot of
standing; zu ~ kommen to acquire standing or a high reputation; (bei jdm) in hohem ~ stehen to be held in high regard or
esteem (by sb); an ~ verlieren to lose credit or standing.
   (c) (Jur) ohne ~ der Person without respect of person.

ansehnlich adj (beträchtlich) considerable; Leistung impressive; (dated: gut aussehend, stattlich) handsome. ein ~es
Sümmchen/~er Bauch (hum) a pretty or tidy little sum/quite a
stomach.

Ansehung f: in ~ +gen (form) in view of.

anseilen vt sep jdn/sich ~ to rope sb/oneself up; etw ~ und
herunterlassen to fasten sth with a rope and let it down.

ansein vi sep irreg aux sein (Zusammenschreibung nur bei infin
und ptp) (inf) to be on.

ansengen vti sep (vi: aux sein) to singe. es riecht angesengt
there's a smell of singeing.

ansetzen sep 1 vt (a) (anfügen) to attach (an +acc to), to add
(an +acc to), to put on (an +acc -to); (annähen) to sew on.
   (b) (in Ausgangsstellung bringen) to place in position. eine
Leiter an etw (acc) ~ to put a ladder up against sth; den Blei-
stift/die Feder ~ to put pencil/pen to paper; die Flöte/Trompete
etc ~ to raise the flute/trumpet to one's mouth; das Glas ~ to
raise the glass to one's lips; an welcher Stelle muß man den
Wagenheber ~? where should the jack be put or placed?
   (c) (mit, auf +acc at) (festlegen) Kosten, Termin to fix; (veranschlagen) Kosten, Zeitspanne to estimate, to calculate.
   (d) (Sport) Spurt, Absprung to start.
   (e) (einsetzen) jdn auf jdn/etw ~ to put sb on(to) sb/sth;
Hunde (auf jdn/jds Spur) ~ to put dogs on sb/sb's trail.
   (f) (entstehen lassen) Blätter etc to put out; Frucht to form, to
produce. Fett ~ to put on weight; Rost ~ to get rusty.
   (g) (Cook) (vorbereiten) to prepare; Bowle to start; (auf den
Herd setzen) to put on.
   (h) (Math) to formulate.
   2 vr (Rost) to form; (Kalk etc) to be deposited; (Gekochtes) to
stick.
   3 vi (a) (beginnen) to start, to begin. mit der Arbeit ~ to start
or begin work; zur Landung ~ (Aviat) to come in to land; zum
Trinken/Sprechen ~ to start to drink/speak; er setzte immer
wieder an, aber ... he kept opening his mouth to say something
but ...; zum Sprung/Spurt ~ to prepare or get ready to jump/to
start one's spurt.
   (b) (Nase, Brust, Haare etc) to start.
   (c) (hervorkommen) (Knospen) to come forth; (Früchte) to
set; (Bäume) to sprout.
   (d) (Cook: sich festsetzen) to stick.
   (e) angesetzt kommen (Hund) to come bounding along or (auf
einen zu) up.

Ansicht f -, -en (a) view. ~ von hinten/vorn rear/front view; ~
von oben/unten view from above/below, top/bottom view
(Tech).
   (b) (das Betrachten, Prüfen) inspection. bei ~ (von unten etc)
on inspection (from below etc); zur ~ (Comm) for (your/our
etc) inspection; jdm Waren zur ~ anschicken (Comm) to send
sb goods on approval.
   (c) (Meinung) opinion, view. nach ~ +gen in the opinion of;
meiner ~ nach in my opinion or view; ich bin der ~, daß ... I am
of the opinion that ...; anderer/der gleichen ~ sein to be of a
different/the same opinion, to disagree/agree; über etw (acc)
anderer ~ sein to take a different view of sth, to have a different opinion about sth; anderer ~ werden to change one's
opinion; ich bin ganz Ihrer ~ I entirely agree with you; die ~en
sind geteilt or verschieden opinions differ, opinion is divided.

ansichtig adj jds/einer Sache ~ werden (dated, geh) to set eyes
on sb/sth.

Ansichts-: ~(post)karte f picture postcard; ~sache f das ist
~sache that is a matter of opinion; ~sendung f article(s pl) sent
on approval; jdm eine ~sendung schicken to send sb
articles/an article on approval.

ansiedeln sep 1 vt to settle; Tierart to introduce; Vogelkolonie,
Industrie to establish. dieser Begriff ist in der Literaturkritik
angesiedelt this term belongs to the field of literary criticism.
   2 vr to settle; (Industrie etc) to get established; (Bakterien
etc) to establish themselves.

Ansiedler m settler.

Ansiedlung f (a) settlement. (b) (das Ansiedeln) settling;
(Kolonisierung von Tieren) colonization; (von Betrieben)
establishing.

Ansinnen nt (dated, geh) (Gedanke) notion, idea; (Vorschlag)
suggestion. ein seltsames ~ an jdn stellen to make an
unreasonable suggestion to sb.

Ansitz m (Hunt) raised hide; (Aus) residence. „~ Claudia" "Claudia House".

ansonsten adv (im anderen Fall, inf: im übrigen) otherwise. ~ gibt's nichts Neues (inf) there's nothing new apart from that; ~ hast du nichts auszusetzen? (iro) have you any more complaints?

anspannen sep 1 vt (a) (straffer spannen) to tauten, to tighten; Muskeln to tense.

(b) (anstrengen) to strain, to tax; Geduld, Mittel auch to stretch. jdn zu sehr ~ to overtax sb; alle seine Kräfte ~ to strain every nerve, to exert all one's energy; das spannt meine Nerven/Kräfte zu sehr an! that's too much of a strain on my nerves/for me!; siehe angespannt.

(c) Wagen to hitch up; Pferd auch to harness; Ochsen auch to yoke up (zu for). jdn (zu einer Arbeit) ~ (inf) to get sb to do a job.

2 vi (Pferde/Wagen ~) to hitch up. ~ lassen to get a/the carriage ready; es ist angespannt! the carriage is ready.

Anspannung f (fig) strain; (körperliche Anstrengung auch) effort. unter ~ aller Kräfte by exerting all one's energies.

anspazieren* vi sep aux sein (usu anspaziert kommen) to come strolling along or (auf einen zu) up.

anspeien vt sep irreg to spit at.

Anspiel nt (Sport) start of play; (Cards) lead; (Chess) first move.

anspielen sep 1 vt (a) (Sport) to play the ball etc to; Spieler to pass to.

(b) (Mus) Stück to play part of; Instrument to try out (for the first time).

2 vi (a) (Spiel beginnen) to start; (Ftbl) to kick off; (Cards) to lead, to open; (Chess) to open.

(b) auf jdn/etw ~ to allude to sb/sth; worauf wollen Sie ~? what are you driving at?, what are you insinuating?; spielst du damit auf mich an? are you getting at me?

Anspielung f allusion (auf +acc to); (böse) insinuation, innuendo (auf +acc regarding).

anspießen vt sep Schmetterlinge to mount; Zettel to pin up; (prüfend) Braten to prick.

anspinnen sep irreg 1 vt Faden to join; (fig) Verhältnis, Thema to develop, to enter into. 2 vr (fig) to develop, to start up. da spinnt sich doch etwas an! (inf) something is going on there!

anspitzen vt sep Bleistift etc to sharpen. (b) (inf: antreiben) to have a go at. jdn ~, daß er etw tut to have a go at sb to do sth. (c) (sl: erotisch erregen) to get worked up (inf).

Ansporn m -(e)s, no pl incentive. ihm fehlt der innere ~ he has no motivation.

anspornen vt sep Pferd to spur (on); (fig auch) to encourage (zu to).

Ansprache f (a) (Rede) address, speech. eine ~ halten to hold an address, to make a speech. (b) (Beachtung) attention. wenn man tagelang keine ~ hat if you have no one to talk to for days on end.

ansprechbar adj (bereit, jdn anzuhören) open to conversation; (gut gelaunt) amenable; Patient responsive. er ist beschäftigt/ wütend und zur Zeit nicht ~ he's so busy/angry that you can't talk to him just now; auf etw (acc) ~ sein to respond to sth.

ansprechen sep irreg 1 vt (a) (anreden) to speak to; (die Sprache an jdn richten, mit Titel, Vornamen etc) to address; (belästigend) to accost. jdn auf etw (acc)/um etw ~ to ask or approach sb about/for sth; es kommt darauf an, wie man die Leute anspricht it depends on how you talk to people; damit sind Sie alle angesprochen this is directed at all of you.

(b) (gefallen) to appeal to; (Eindruck machen auf) to make an impression on.

(c) (fig geh) etw als ... ~ (ansehen) to declare sth to be ...; (beschreiben) to describe sth as ...

(d) (erwähnen) to mention.

2 vi (auf +acc to) (reagieren) (Patient, Gaspedal etc) to respond; (Meßgerät auch) to react. diese Tabletten sprechen bei ihr nicht an these tablets don't have any effect on her; leicht ~de Bremsen very responsive brakes; das Klavier etc spricht leicht an the piano etc plays easily.

(b) (Anklang finden) to go down well, to meet with a good response.

ansprechend adj (reizvoll) Äußeres, Verpackung etc attractive, appealing; (angenehm) Umgebung etc pleasant.

Ansprechzeit f (Aut, Tech) response or operating time.

anspringen sep irreg 1 vt (a) (anfallen) to jump; (Raubtier) to pounce (up)on; (Hund: hochspringen) to jump up at.

(b) (Sport) Gerät, Latte to jump at; Rolle, Überschlag to dive into.

2 vi aux sein (a) angesprungen kommen to come bounding along or (auf einen zu) up; auf etw (acc) ~ (fig inf) to jump at sth (inf); gegen etw ~ to jump against sth.

(b) (Sport) to jump.

(c) (Motor) to start.

anspritzen sep 1 vt (bespritzen) to splash; (mit Spritzpistole, -düse etc) to spray. 2 vi aux sein angespritzt kommen (inf) to come tearing (inf) along or (auf einen zu) up.

Anspruch m -(e)s, Ansprüche (a) (esp Jur) claim; (Recht) right (auf +acc to). ~ auf Schadenersatz erheben/haben to make a claim for damages/to be entitled to damages; ~ auf etw (acc) haben to be entitled to sth, to have a right to sth.

(b) (Anforderung) demand; (Standard) standard, requirement. an jdn dauernd Ansprüche stellen to make constant demands on sb; große or hohe Ansprüche stellen to be very demanding; (hohes Niveau verlangen) to demand high standards; den erforderlichen Ansprüchen gerecht werden to meet the necessary requirements.

(c) (Behauptung) claim, pretension. diese Theorie erhebt keinen ~ auf Unwiderlegbarkeit this theory does not claim to be irrefutable, this theory lays no claim to irrefutability.

(d) etw in ~ nehmen Recht to claim sth; jds Hilfe, Dienste to enlist sth; Möglichkeiten, Kantine etc to take advantage of sth; Zeit, Aufmerksamkeit, Kräfte to take up sth; jdn völlig in ~ nehmen to take up all of sb's time; (jds Aufmerksamkeit, Gedanken) to engross or preoccupy sb completely; sehr in ~ genommen very busy/preoccupied; darf ich Ihre Aufmerksamkeit in ~ nehmen? may I have your attention?

anspruchslos adj (ohne große Ansprüche) unpretentious; (bescheiden) modest, unassuming; (schlicht) plain, simple; (geistig nicht hochstehend) lowbrow; Roman etc light; (wenig Pflege, Geschick etc erfordernd) undemanding.

Anspruchslosigkeit f siehe adj unpretentiousness; modesty, unassuming nature; plainness, simplicity; lowbrow character; lightness; undemanding nature.

anspruchsvoll adj (viel verlangend) demanding; (übertrieben ~) hard to please, fastidious; (wählerisch) discriminating; (kritisch) critical; (hohe Ansprüche stellend) Stil, Buch ambitious; (kultiviert) sophisticated; (hochwertig) high-quality, superior. eine Zeitung/der Füllhalter für A~e a newspaper for the discriminating reader/the pen for people with discrimination; ~ gekleidet sein to dress with style.

anspucken vt sep to spit at or on.

anspülen vt sep to wash up or ashore.

anspüren vt sep siehe anmerken.

anstacheln vt sep to spur (on); (antreiben) to drive or goad on.

Anstalt f -, -en (a) institution (auch euph); (Institut) institute. eine ~ öffentlichen Rechts a public institution.

(b) ~en pl (Maßnahmen) measures pl; (Vorbereitungen) preparations pl; für or zu etw ~en treffen to take measures/ make preparations for sth; ~en/keine ~en machen, etw zu tun to make a/no move to do sth.

Anstalts-: ~arzt m resident physician; ~geistliche(r) m resident chaplain; ~kleidung f institutional clothing; (in Gefängnis) prison clothing; ~zögling m (in Erziehungsanstalt) child from an institution; (in Internat) boarding-school pupil; (in Fürsorgeheim) child from a home.

Anstand¹ m (a) no pl (Schicklichkeit) decency, propriety; (Manieren) (good) manners pl. keinen ~ haben to have no sense of decency/no manners; den ~ verletzen to offend against decency; das kann man mit ~/nicht mit ~ tun it's quite in order to do that/you can't in all decency do that; sich mit ~ zurückziehen to withdraw with good grace.

(b) (geh: Einwand) demur ~ ohne without demur (form) or hesitation; ~/keinen ~ an etw (dat) nehmen to object/not to object to sth, to demur/not to demur at sth (form); keinen ~ nehmen, etw zu tun not to hesitate to do sth.

(c) (esp S Ger: Ärger) trouble no pl.

Anstand² m (Hunt) raised hide. auf den ~ gehen to sit on the raised hide.

anständig 1 adj decent; Witz auch clean; (ehrbar) respectable; (inf: beträchtlich) sizeable, large. das war nicht ~ von ihm that was pretty bad of him; bleib ~! behave yourself!; eine ~e Tracht Prügel (inf) a good hiding.

2 adv decently. sich ~ benehmen to behave oneself; sich ~ hinsetzen to sit properly; jdn ~ bezahlen (inf) to pay sb well; ~ essen/ausschlafen (inf) to have a decent meal/sleep; es regnet ganz ~ (inf) it's raining pretty hard; sie hat sich ~ gestoßen (inf) she really took a knock (inf).

anständigerweise adv out of decency. du könntest ihm die zerbrochene Vase ~ bezahlen you could in all decency pay him for the broken vase.

Anständigkeit f decency; (Ehrbarkeit) respectability.

Anstands-: ~besuch m formal call; (aus Pflichtgefühl) duty visit; ~dame f chaperon(e); ~formen pl manners pl; a~halber adv out of politeness; ~happen m (inf) einen ~happen übriglassen to leave something for manners; a~los adv without difficulty; ~unterricht m lessons pl in deportment; ~wauwau m (hum inf) chaperon(e); den ~wauwau spielen to play gooseberry.

anstänkern vt sep (sl) jdn ~ to lay into sb (sl).

anstarren vt sep to stare at.

anstatt 1 prep +gen instead of. 2 conj ~ zu arbeiten instead of working; ~, daß er das tut, ... instead of doing that ...

anstauben vi sep aux sein to become or get dusty.

anstauen sep 1 vt Wasser to dam up; Gefühle to bottle up. 2 vr to accumulate; (Blut in Adern etc) to congest; (fig auch: Gefühle) to build up. angestaute Wut pent-up rage.

anstaunen vt sep to gaze or stare at in wonder, to marvel at; (bewundern) to admire. was staunst du mich so an? what are you staring at me like that for?

Anstauung f (von Wasser) accumulation; (von Blut) congestion; (fig: von Gefühlen) build-up.

anstechen vt sep irreg to make a hole in, to pierce; Kartoffeln, Fleisch to prick; Reifen to puncture; Blase to lance, to pierce; Faß to tap, to broach; (Archeol) to open up; (zufällig ~) to stumble (up)on. das Obst ist von Insekten angestochen the fruit is full of insect holes; siehe angestochen.

anstecken sep 1 vt (a) (befestigen) to pin on; Ring to put or slip on.

(b) (anzünden) to light; (in Brand stecken) to set fire to, to set alight.

(c) (Med, fig) to infect. ich will dich nicht ~ I don't want to give it to you.

2 vr sich (mit etw) ~ to catch sth (bei from).

3 vi (Med, fig) to be infectious or catching; (durch Berührung, fig) to be contagious.

ansteckend adj (Med, fig) infectious, catching pred (inf).

(durch Berührung, fig) contagious.

Anstecknadel *f* pin, badge.

Ansteckung *f (Med)* infection; *(durch Berührung)* contagion.

Ansteckungsherd *m* centre of infection.

anstehen *vi sep irreg aux haben or (S Ger etc) sein* **(a)** *(in Schlange)* to queue (up) *(Brit)*, to stand in line *(nach for)*.

  (b) *(auf Erledigung warten)* to be due to be dealt with; *(Verhandlungspunkt)* to be on the agenda. **anstehende Probleme** problems facing us/them *etc;* **etw ~ lassen** to put off or delay or defer sth; **eine Schuld ~ lassen** to put off paying a debt, to defer payment of a debt *(form)*.

  (c) *(Jur: Termin etc)* to be fixed or set *(für for)*.

  (d) *(geh: zögern)* **nicht ~, etw zu tun** not to hesitate to do sth.

  (e) *(geh: geziemen)* **jdm ~** to become or befit sb *(form, old)*; **das steht ihm schlecht an** that ill becomes or befits him.

  (f) *(Geol)* to be exposed, to crop out *(Geol)*. **~des Gestein** outcrop.

ansteigen *vi sep irreg aux sein* to rise; *(Weg auch, Mensch)* to ascend; *(Temperatur, Preis, Zahl auch)* to go up, to increase.

anstelle *prep +gen* instead of, in place of.

anstellen *sep* 1 *vt* **(a)** *(anlehnen)* to place; *(anlehnen)* to lean *(an +acc* against). **stell den Stuhl an!** put the chair right!

  (b) *(dazustellen)* to add *(an +acc* to).

  (c) *(beschäftigen)* to employ, to take on. **jdn zu etw ~** *(inf)* to get sb to do sth; *siehe* **angestellt**.

  (d) *(anmachen, andrehen)* to turn on; *(in Gang setzen auch)* to start.

  (e) *Betrachtung, Vermutung etc* to make; *Vergleich auch* to draw; *Verhör, Experiment* to conduct. **(neue) Überlegungen ~(, wie ...)** to (re)consider (how ...).

  (f) *(machen, unternehmen)* to do; *(fertigbringen)* to manage. **ich weiß nicht, wie ich es ~ soll** or **kann** I don't know how to do or manage it; **wie kann ich es nur ~, daß sie nichts merkt?** how can I get her not to notice anything?, how can I prevent her from noticing anything?

  (g) *(inf: Unfug treiben)* to get up to, to do. **etwas ~** to get up to mischief; **was hast du da wieder angestellt!** what have you done now?, what have you been up to now?

  2 *vr* **(a)** *(Schlange stehen)* to queue (up) *(Brit)*, to stand in line.

  (b) *(inf: sich verhalten)* to act, to behave. **sich dumm/ungeschickt ~** to act stupid/clumsily, to be stupid/clumsy; **sich geschickt ~** to go about sth well.

  (c) *(inf: sich zieren)* to make a fuss, to act up *(inf)*. **stell dich nicht so an!** don't make such a fuss!; *(sich dumm ~)* don't act so stupid!

Anstellerei *f (inf)* **(a)** *(Ziererei)* fuss. **laß diese ~!** don't make such a fuss! **(b)** *(Schlangestehen)* queueing *(Brit)*, standing in line.

anstellig *adj (dated)* able, clever.

Anstelligkeit *f (dated)* ability, skill.

Anstellung *f* employment; *(Stelle)* position, employment.

Anstellungsverhältnis *nt* contractual relationship between employer and employee; *(Vertrag)* contract. **im ~ or mit ~** under or with a contract (of employment); **im ~ sein** to have a contract, to be under contract.

ansteuern *vt sep* to make or steer or head *(auch hum)* for; *(lit, fig) Kurs* to head on, to follow; *(fig) Thema* to steer onwards.

Anstich *m (von Faß)* tapping, broaching; *(erster Glas)* first draught; *(erster Spatenstich)* digging the first sod; *(Archeol)* opening.

anstiefeln *vi sep aux sein* **angestiefelt kommen** *(inf)* to come marching along or *(auf einen zu)* up.

Anstieg *m -(e)s, -e* **(a)** *(Aufstieg)* climb, ascent; *(Weg)* ascent.

  (b) *(von Straße)* incline; *(von Temperatur, Kosten, Preisen etc)* rise, increase *(+gen* in).

anstieren *vt sep (pej)* to stare at.

anstiften *vt sep (anzetteln)* to instigate; *(verursachen)* to bring about, to cause. **jdn zu etw ~** to put sb up to, to put sb up to sth *(inf)*; **jdn zu einem Verbrechen ~** to incite sb to commit a crime.

Anstifter *m* instigator *(+gen, zu* of); *(Anführer)* ringleader.

Anstiftung *f (von Mensch)* incitement *(zu* to); *(von Tat)* instigation.

anstimmen *sep* 1 *vt* **(a)** *(singen)* to begin singing; *(Chorleiter) Grundton* to give; *(spielen)* to start playing; *(Kapelle)* to strike up, to start playing.

  (b) *(fig)* **ein Geheul/Geschrei/Proteste** *etc* **~** to start whining/crying/protesting *etc*; **ein Gelächter ~** to burst out laughing.

  2 *vi* to give the key-note.

anstinken *sep irreg (inf)* 1 *vt* **stink mich nicht mit deiner Zigarre an!** take that cigar away, it stinks!; **das stinkt mich an** *(fig)* I'm sick of that. 2 *vi* **dagegen/gegen ihn kannst du nicht ~** you can't do anything about it/him.

anstolzieren* *vi sep aux sein* **anstolziert kommen** to come strutting or swaggering along or *(auf einen zu)* up; *(Pfau etc)* to come strutting along/up.

Anstoß *m* **(a)** **den (ersten) ~ zu etw geben** to initiate sth, to get sth going; **den ~ zu weiteren Forschungen geben** to give the impetus to or to stimulate further research; **jdm den ~ geben, etw zu tun** to give sb the inducement or to induce sb to do sth; **der ~ zu diesem Plan/der ~ ging von ihr aus** she originally got this plan/things going; **den ~ zu etw bekommen, den ~ bekommen, etw zu tun** to be prompted or encouraged to do sth; **es bedurfte eines neuen ~es** new impetus or a new impulse was needed.

  (b) *(Sport)* kick-off; *(Hockey)* bully-off.

  (c) *(Ärgernis)* annoyance *(für* to). **~ erregen** to cause offence *(bei* to); **ein Stein des ~es** *(umstrittene Sache)* a bone of contention; **die ungenaue Formulierung des Vertrags war ein stän-**

diger Stein des ~es the inexact formulation of the contract was a constant obstacle or stumbling block; **das ist mir ein Stein des ~es** or **ein Stein des ~es für mich** that really annoys me.

  (d) *(Hindernis)* difficulty. **ohne jeden ~** without a hitch or any difficulty.

anstoßen *sep irreg* 1 *vi* **(a)** *aux sein* **(an etw acc) ~** to bump into sth; **paß auf, daß du nicht anstößt** take care that you don't bump into anything; **mit dem Kopf an etw** *(acc)* **~** to bump or knock one's head on sth; **das Auto darf nicht (am Randstein) ~** the car must not touch the kerb; **mit der Zunge ~** to lisp.

  (b) *(mit den Gläsern)* **~** to touch or clink glasses; **auf jdn/etw ~** to drink to sb/sth.

  (c) *(Sport)* to kick off; *(Hockey)* to bully off.

  (d) *aux sein (Anstoß erregen)* to cause offence. **bei jdm ~** to offend sb.

  (e) *(angrenzen)* **an etw** *(acc)* **~** to adjoin sth; *(Land auch)* to border on sth.

  2 *vt* **jdn** to knock (into); *(mit dem Fuß)* to kick; *(in Bewegung setzen)* to give a push; *Kugel, Ball* to hit. **sich** *(dat)* **den Kopf/Fuß** *etc* **~** to bang or knock one's head/foot.

anstoßend *adj siehe* **angrenzend**.

anstößig *adj* offensive; *Kleidung* indecent.

Anstößigkeit *f siehe adj* offensiveness; indecency.

anstrahlen *vt sep* to floodlight; *(im Theater)* to spotlight; *(strahlend ansehen)* to beam at. **das Gebäude wird rot/von Scheinwerfern angestrahlt** the building is lit with a red light/is floodlit; **sie strahlte/ihre Augen strahlten mich an** she beamed at me.

anstreben *sep* 1 *vt* to strive for. 2 *vi* **gegen etw ~** *(geh)* to struggle against sth, to resist sth.

anstrebenswert *adj* worth striving for.

anstreichen *vt sep irreg* **(a)** *(mit Farbe etc)* to paint. **(b)** *(markieren)* to mark. **jdm etw als Fehler ~** to mark sth wrong *(for sb)*; **er hat das/nichts angestrichen** he marked it wrong/didn't mark anything wrong; **das werde ich ihm ~** *(dial inf)* I'll remember that. **(c)** *(Mus) Saite* to bow. **(d)** *(streichen) Zündholz* to strike, to light.

Anstreicher *m -s, -* (house) painter.

anstreifen *vt sep* **(a)** *(überstreifen) Schuhe, Ring etc* to slip on.

  (b) *(streifen)* to brush against.

anstrengen *sep* 1 *vt* **(a)** *to strain; Muskel, Geist* to exert; *(strapazieren) jdn* to tire out; *esp Patienten* to fatigue. **das viele Lesen strengt meine Augen/mich an** all this reading is or puts a strain on my eyes/is a strain (for me); **alle Kräfte ~** to use all one's strength or *(geistig)* faculties; **sein Gedächtnis ~** to rack one's brains; **streng doch mal deinen Verstand ein bißchen an** think hard; *siehe* **angestrengt**.

  (b) *(Jur)* **eine Klage ~** to initiate or institute proceedings *(gegen* against).

  2 *vr* to make an effort; *(körperlich auch)* to exert oneself. **sich mehr/sehr ~** to make more of an effort/a big effort; **sich übermäßig ~** to make too much of an effort; to overexert oneself; **sich ~, etw zu tun** to make an effort or try hard to do sth; **unsere Gastgeberin hatte sich sehr angestrengt** our hostess had gone to or taken a lot of trouble.

anstrengend *adj (körperlich)* strenuous; *(geistig)* demanding, taxing; *Zeit* taxing, exhausting; *(erschöpfend)* exhausting, tiring. **das ist ~ für die Augen** it's a strain on the eyes.

Anstrengung *f* effort; *(Strapaze)* strain. **große ~en machen** to make every effort; **~en machen, etw zu tun** to make an effort to do sth; **mit äußerster/letzter ~** with very great/one last effort.

Anstrich *m* **(a)** *(das Anmalen, Tünchen)* painting; *(Farbüberzug)* paint; *(fig) (Anflug)* touch; *(fig: von Wissenschaftlichkeit etc)* veneer; *(Anschein)* air. **ein zweiter ~** a second coat of paint; **sich** *(dat)* **den ~ einer Dame von Welt geben** to give oneself the air of being a great lady.

  (b) *(Mus)* first touch.

  (c) *(beim Schreiben)* upstroke.

anstricken *vt sep* to knit on *(an +acc* -to); *Strumpf* to knit a piece onto.

anströmen *vi sep aux sein* to stream along. **angeströmt kommen** to come streaming or rushing along or *(auf einen zu)* up; **~de Kaltluft** a stream of cold air.

anstückeln, anstücken *vt sep Stück* to attach *(an +acc* to). **etw (an etw** *acc*) **~** to add sth (onto sth).

Ansturm *m* onslaught; *(Andrang) (auf Kaufhaus etc)* rush; *(auf Bank)* run; *(Menschenmenge)* crowd.

anstürmen *vi sep aux sein* **gegen etw ~** *(Mil)* to attack or storm sth; *(Wellen, Wind)* to pound sth; *(fig: ankämpfen)* to attack sth; **angestürmt kommen** to come storming along or *(auf einen zu)* up.

anstürzen *vi sep aux sein* **angestürzt kommen** to charge along or *(auf einen zu)* up.

ansuchen *vi sep (dated, Aus)* **bei jdm um etw ~** *(bitten um)* to ask sb for sth; *(beantragen)* to apply to sb for sth.

Ansuchen *nt -s, -* *(dated, Aus)* request; *(Gesuch)* application. **auf jds ~** *(acc)* at sb's request.

Antagonismus *m* antagonism.

Antagonist(in *f)* *m* antagonist.

antagonistisch *adj* antagonistic.

antaillieren* *vt sep* to shape (at the waist).

antanzen *vi sep aux sein* **(a)** *(fig inf)* to turn or show up *(inf)*. **er kommt jeden Tag angetanzt** *(inf)* he turns up here every day.

  (b) *(lit)* to come dancing along.

Antarktis *f -, no pl* Antarctic.

antarktisch *adj* antarctic.

antasten *vt sep* **(a)** *(verletzen) Ehre, Würde* to offend; *Rechte* to infringe, to encroach upon; *(anbrechen) Vorräte, Ersparnisse etc* to break into. **(b)** *(berühren)* to touch; *(fig) Thema, Frage* to touch on, to mention.

antauen vti sep (vi: aux sein) to begin to defrost.

antäuschen vi sep to feint; (Ftbl etc auch) to dummy; (Tennis) to disguise one's shot. **links** ~ to feint/dummy to the left.

antedatieren* vi sep (old) (a) (vorausdatieren) to postdate. **(b)** (zurückdatieren) to backdate.

Anteil m -(e)s, -e **(a)** share; (von Erbe auch) portion; (Fin) share, interest. **er hat bei dem Unternehmen** ~e **von 30%** he has a 30% interest or share in the company.

(b) (Beteiligung) ~ **an etw** (dat) **haben** (beitragen) to contribute to sth, to make a contribution to sth; (teilnehmen) to take part in sth; **an dieser Sache will ich keinen** ~ **haben** I want no part in this.

(c) (Teilnahme: an Leid etc) sympathy (an + dat with). **an etw** (dat) ~ **nehmen** an Leid etc to be deeply sympathetic over sth; an Freude etc to share in sth; **sie nahmen alle an dem Tod seiner Frau/an seinem Leid** ~ they all felt deeply for him when his wife died/felt for him in his sorrow.

(d) (Interesse) interest (an + dat in), concern (an + dat about). **regen** ~ **an etw** (dat) **nehmen/zeigen** or **bekunden** (geh) to take/show a lively interest in sth.

anteilig, anteilmäßig adj proportionate, proportional.

Anteil-: ~**nahme** f -, no pl **(a)** (Beileid) sympathy (an + dat with); **mit** ~**nahme zuhören** to listen sympathetically; **(b)** (Beteiligung) participation (an + dat in); ~**schein** m (Fin) share certificate.

antelefonieren* vti sep (inf) to phone. **bei jdm** ~ to phone sb up.

Antenne f -, -n (Rad) aerial; (Zool) feeler, antenna (form). **eine/keine** ~ **für etw haben** (fig inf) to have a/no feeling for sth.

Anthologie f anthology.

Anthrazit m -s, (rare) -e anthracite.

anthrazit(farben, -farbig) adj charcoal-grey, charcoal.

Anthropologe m, **Anthropologin** f anthropologist.

Anthropologie f anthropology.

anthropologisch adj anthropological.

anthropomorph adj anthropomorphous.

Anthropomorphismus m anthropomorphism.

Anthroposoph(in f**)** m -en, -en anthroposophist.

Anthroposophie f anthroposophy.

anthroposophisch adj anthroposophic.

anthropozentrisch adj anthropocentric.

Anti- pref anti; ~**alkoholiker** m teetota(l)ler; **a**~**autoritär** adj antiauthoritarian; ~**babypille**, ~-**Baby-Pille** f (inf) contraceptive pill; **a**~**bakteriell** adj antibacterial; ~**biotikum** nt -s, ~**biotika** antibiotic; **a**~**chambieren*** vi insep **bei jdm a**~**chambieren** to lobby sb (wegen about); (pej: kriechen) to grovel to sb; ~**christ** m **(a)** -(s) Antichrist; **(b)** -en, -en opponent of Christianity, antichristian; **a**~**christlich** adj antichristian; **a**~**demokratisch** adj antidemocratic; ~**faschismus** m antifascism; ~**faschist** m antifascist; **a**~**faschistisch** adj antifascist.

Antigen nt -s, -e (Med, Biol) antigen.

antigern vi sep aux sein siehe **tigern**.

Anti-: ~**held** m antihero; ~**heldin** f antiheroine.

antik adj **(a)** (Hist) ancient. **der** ~**e Mensch** man in the ancient world. **(b)** (Comm, inf) antique.

Antike f -, -n no pl antiquity. **die Kunst der** ~ the art of the ancient world. **(b)** (Kunstwerk) antiquity.

antikisieren* vi to imitate the classical style. ~**de Dichtung** poetry in the classical style.

Anti-: **a**~**klerikal** adj anticlerical; ~**klerikalismus** m anticlericalism; ~**klopfmittel** nt (Tech) antiknock (mixture); ~**kommunismus** m anticommunism; ~**kommunist** m anticommunist; **a**~**kommunistisch** adj anticommunist; ~**körper** m (Med) antibody.

Antilope f -, -n antelope.

Anti-: ~**militarismus** m antimilitarism; ~**militarist** m antimilitarist; **a**~**militaristisch** adj antimilitaristic.

Antimon nt -s, no pl antimony.

Anti-: **a**~**monarchisch** adj antimonarchist; ~**pathie** f antipathy (gegen to); ~**pode** m -n, -n antipodean; **die Engländer sind die** ~**poden Australiens** the English live on the opposite side of the world from Australia; **politsch sind wir** ~**poden** we have diametrically opposed political views.

antippen vt sep to tap; Pedal, Bremse to touch; (fig) Thema to touch on. **jdn** ~ to tab sb on the shoulder/arm etc; **bei jdm** ~, **(ob ...)** (inf) to sound sb out (as to whether ...).

Antiqua f -, no pl (Typ) roman (type).

Antiquar(in f**)** m antiquarian or (von moderneren Büchern) second-hand bookseller.

Antiquariat nt (Laden) antiquarian or (modernerer Bücher) second-hand bookshop; (Abteilung) antiquarian/second-hand department; (Handel) antiquarian/second-hand book trade; **modernes** ~ remainder bookshop/department.

antiquarisch adj antiquarian; (von moderneren Büchern) second-hand. **ein Buch** ~ **kaufen** to buy a book second-hand.

antiquiert adj (pej) antiquated.

Antiquität f usu pl antique.

Antiquitäten-: ~**geschäft** nt antique shop; ~**handel** m antique business or trade; ~**händler** m antique dealer; ~**laden** m antique shop; ~**sammler** m antique collector.

Anti-: ~**(raketen)rakete** f anti(-missile)-missile; ~**semit** m antisemite; **a**~**semitisch** adj antisemitic; ~**semitismus** m antisemitism; **a**~**septisch** adj antiseptic.

Antistatik- in cpds antistatic.

Anti-: **a**~**statisch** adj antistatic; ~**teilchen** nt (Phys) antiparticle; ~**these** f antithesis; **a**~**thetisch** adj antithetical; ~**transpirant** nt -s, -e or -s (form) antiperspirant.

Antizipation f (geh) anticipation no pl.

antizipieren* vt insep to anticipate.

antizyklisch adj anticyclical.

Antlitz nt -es, -e (poet) countenance (liter), face.

antoben vi sep **(a) gegen jdn/etw** ~ to rail at sb/sth. **(b) angetobt kommen** to come storming along or (auf einen zu) up.

Antonym nt -s, -e antonym.

antörnen vt sep siehe **anturnen²**.

antraben vi sep aux sein to start trotting, to go into a trot. **angetrabt kommen** to come trotting along or (auf einen zu) up.

Antrag m -(e)s, **Anträge** **(a)** (auf +acc for) application; (Gesuch auch) request; (Formular) application form. **einen** ~ **auf etw** (acc) **stellen** to make an application for sth; **auf** ~ + gen at the request of.

(b) (Jur) petition; (Forderung bei Gericht) claim. **einen** ~ **auf etw** (acc) **stellen** to file a petition/claim for sth.

(c) (Parl) motion. **einen** ~ **auf etw** (acc) **stellen** to propose a motion for sth.

(d) (dated: Angebot) proposal. **jdm unzüchtige Anträge machen** to make improper suggestions to sb.

antragen vt sep irreg (geh) to offer (jdm etw sb sth).

Antrags-: ~**formular** nt application form; ~**steller** m -s, - applicant.

antrainieren* vt sep **jdm/sich schnelle Reaktion/Tricks/gute Manieren** ~ to train sb/oneself to have fast reactions/to do tricks/to be well-mannered.

antrauen vt sep (old) **jdn jdm** ~ to marry sb to sb; **mein angetrauter Ehemann** my lawful wedded husband.

antreffen vt sep irreg to find; Situation auch to meet; (zufällig auch) to come across. **er ist schwer anzutreffen** it's difficult to catch him in; **ich habe ihn in guter Laune angetroffen** I found him in a good mood.

antreiben sep irreg **1** vt **(a)** (vorwärtstreiben) Tiere, Gefangene, Kolonne to drive; (fig) to urge; (veranlassen: Neugier, Liebe, Wunsch etc) to drive on. **jdn zur Eile/Arbeit** ~ to urge sb to hurry up/to work; **jdn zu größerer Leistung** ~ to urge sb to achieve more; **ich lasse mich nicht** ~ I won't be pushed.

(b) (bewegen) Rad, Fahrzeug etc to drive; (mit Motor auch) to power.

(c) (anschwemmen) to wash up or (an Strand auch) ashore. **etw ans Ufer** ~ to wash sth (up) onto the bank.

(d) (Hort) Pflanze to force.

2 vi aux sein to wash up or (an Strand auch) ashore.

Antreiber m (pej) slave-driver (pej).

antreten sep irreg **1** vt **(a)** Reise, Strafe to begin; Stellung to take up; Amt to take up, to assume; Erbe, Erbschaft to come into. **den Beweis** ~ to offer proof; **den Beweis** ~, **daß ...** to prove that ...; **seine Lehrzeit** ~ to start one's apprenticeship; **seine Amtszeit** ~ to take office; **die Regierung** ~ to come to power; **sein 30. Lebensjahr** ~ to have one's 30th birthday.

(b) Motorrad to kickstart.

(c) (festtreten) Erde to press or tread down firmly.

2 vi aux sein **(a)** (sich aufstellen) to line up; (Mil) to fall in. **(b)** (erscheinen) to assemble; (bei einer Stellung) to start; (zum Dienst) to report.

(c) (zum Wettkampf) to compete; (spurten) to put on a spurt; (Radfahrer) to sprint.

(d) (Ling) to be added (an + acc to).

Antrieb m **(a)** impetus no pl; (innerer) drive. **jdm** ~**/neuen** ~ **geben, etw zu tun** to give sb the/a new impetus to do sth; **aus eigenem** ~ on one's own initiative, off one's own bat (inf).

(b) (Triebkraft) drive. **Auto mit elektrischem** ~ electrically driven or powered car; **welchen** ~ **hat das Auto?** how is the car driven or powered?

Antriebs-: ~**achse** f (Aut) propeller shaft; **a**~**arm** adj siehe **a**~**schwach**; ~**kraft** f (Tech) power; ~**rad** nt drive wheel; **a**~**schwach** adj (Psych) lacking in drive; **a**~**stark** adj (Psych) full of drive; ~**welle** f driveshaft, half-shaft.

antrinken vt sep irreg (inf) to start drinking. **sie hat ihren Kaffee nur angetrunken** she only drank some of her coffee; **sich** (dat) **einen** or **einen Rausch/Schwips** ~ to get (oneself) drunk/tipsy; **sich** (dat) **Mut** ~ to give oneself Dutch courage; **eine angetrunkene Flasche** an opened bottle; **siehe angetrunken**.

Antritt m -(e)s, no pl **(a)** (Beginn) beginning, commencement (form). **bei** ~ **der Reise** on beginning one's journey; **nach** ~ **der Stellung/des Amtes/der Erbschaft/der Regierung** after taking up the post/taking up or assuming office/coming into the inheritance/coming to power.

(b) (Sport: Spurt) acceleration no indef art.

Antritts-: ~**rede** f inaugural speech; (Parl) maiden speech; ~**vorlesung** f inaugural lecture.

antrocknen vi sep aux sein to dry on (an, in + dat -to); (trocken werden) to begin or start to dry.

antuckern vi sep aux sein (inf) (usu angetuckert kommen) to chug along or (auf einen zu) up.

antun vt sep irreg **(a)** (erweisen) **jdm etw** ~ to do sth for sb; **jdm etwas Gutes** ~ to do sb a good turn; **tun Sie mir die Ehre an, und speisen Sie mit mir** (geh) do me the honour of dining with me; **tun mir die Liebe an und komm mit** be a dear or an angel and come with me; **jdm (große) Ehre** ~ to pay (great) tribute to sb.

(b) (zufügen) **jdm etw** ~ to do sth to sb; **das könnte ich ihr nicht** ~ I couldn't do that to her; **sich** (dat) **ein Leid** ~ to injure oneself; **sich** (dat) **etwas** ~ (euph) to do away with oneself; **jdm Schaden/Unrecht** ~ to do sb an injury/injustice; **tu mir keine Schande an!** don't bring shame upon me; **tun Sie sich** (dat) **keinen Zwang an!** (inf) don't stand on ceremony; **darf ich rauchen?— tu dir keinen Zwang an!** may I smoke?— feel free or please yourself.

(c) (Sympathie erregen) **es jdm** ~ to appeal to sb; **siehe angetan**.

(d) (Aus) **sich** (dat) **etwas** ~ (sich aufregen) to get excited or het-up (*inf*); (*sich Mühe geben*) to take a lot of trouble. (e) *Kleid etc* to put on; *siehe* **angetan**.

anturnen[1] *vi sep* (a) *aux sein* (*inf*) (*usu angeturnt kommen*) to come romping along *or* (*auf einen zu*) up. (b) (*Sport*) to open the season with a gymnastic event.

anturnen[2] ['antœrnan] *sep* (*sl*) **1** *vt* (*Drogen, Musik*) to turn on (*sl*). **2** *vi* to turn you on (*sl*). **3** *vr* to turn oneself on (*sl*). **sich angeturnt haben** to be turned on (*sl*); **sich** (*dat*) **einen ~ to get** stoned (*sl*).

Antw. *abbr of* **Antwort**.

Antwort *f* -, -en (a) (*auf Frage*) answer, reply; (*auf Brief*) reply, answer; (*Lösung, bei Examen, auf Fragebogen*) answer. **sie gab mir keine ~** she didn't reply (to me) *or* answer (me); **sie gab mir keine ~ auf die Frage** she didn't reply to *or* answer my question; **das ist doch keine ~** that's no answer; **in ~ auf etw** (*acc*) (*form*) in reply to sth; **um umgehende ~ wird gebeten** please reply at your earliest convenience; **um ~ wird gebeten** (*auf Einladungen*) RSVP; **keine ~ ist auch eine ~** (*Prov*) your silence is answer enough; *siehe* **Rede**.
  (b) (*Reaktion*) response. **als ~ auf etw** (*acc*) in response to sth.

Antwortbrief *m* reply, answer.

antworten *vi* (a) (*auf Frage*) to answer, to reply; (*auf Brief*) to reply, to answer. **jdm ~** to answer sb, to reply to sb; **auf etw** (*acc*) **~** to answer sth, to reply to sth; **was soll ich ihm ~?** what answer should I give him?, what should I tell him?; **jdm auf eine Frage ~** to reply to *or* answer sb's question; **mit Ja/Nein ~** to answer yes/no *or* in the affirmative/negative.
  (b) (*reagieren*) to respond (*auf +acc* to, *mit* with).

Antwort-: **~karte** *f* reply card; **a~lich** *prep +gen* (*old*) in reply to; **~schein** *m* (international) reply coupon; **~schreiben** *nt* reply, answer.

anvertrauen* *sep* **1** *vt* (a) (*übergeben, anheimstellen*) **jdm etw ~** to entrust sth to sb *or* sb with sth.
  (b) (*vertraulich erzählen*) **jdm etw ~** to confide sth to sb; **etw seinem Tagebuch ~** to confide sth to one's diary.
  2 *vr* **sich jdm ~** (*sich mitteilen*) to confide in sb; (*sich in jds Schutz begeben*) to entrust oneself to sb; **sich jds Führung** (*dat*)**/Schutz** (*dat*) **~** to entrust oneself to sb's leadership/protection.

anverwandt *adj* (*geh*) related.

Anverwandte(r) *mf decl as adj* (*geh*) relative, relation.

anvisieren* ['anvi-] *vt sep* (*lit*) to sight; (*fig*) to set one's sights on; *Entwicklung, Zukunft etc* to envisage.

anwachsen *vi sep irreg aux sein* (a) (*festwachsen*) to grow on; (*Haut*) to take; (*Nagel*) to grow; (*Pflanze etc*) to take root. **auf etw** (*dat*) **~** to grow onto sth; **bei ihr sind die Ohrläppchen angewachsen** her ear lobes are attached to the side of her head; *siehe* **angewachsen**.
  (b) (*zunehmen*) (*auf +acc* to) to increase; (*Lärm auch*) to grow.

Anwachsen *nt siehe vi* (a) growing on; taking; growing; taking root. (b) increase; growth. **im ~** (**begriffen**) **sein** to be on the increase, to be growing.

anwackeln *vi sep aux sein* (*usu angewackelt kommen*) to come waddling along *or* (*auf einen zu*) up; (*fig inf*) to come wandering up.

anwählen *vt sep* to dial; *jdn* to call.

Anwalt *m* -(e)s, **Anwälte** (a) *siehe* **Rechtsanwalt**. (b) (*fig: Fürsprecher*) advocate; (*der Armen etc auch*) champion.

Anwalts-: **~büro** *nt* (a) lawyer's office; (b) (*Firma*) firm of solicitors.

Anwaltschaft *f* (a) (*Vertretung*) **eine ~ übernehmen** to take over a case; **die ~ für jdn übernehmen** to accept sb's brief, to take over sb's case. (b) (*Gesamtheit der Anwälte*) solicitors *pl*, legal profession.

Anwalts-: **~gebühr** *f* lawyer's fees *pl*; **~kammer** *f* professional association of lawyers ~ Law Society (*Brit*); **~kosten** *pl* legal expenses *pl*; **~praxis** *f* legal practice; (*Räume*) lawyer's office; **~zwang** *m* obligation to be represented in court.

anwalzen *vi sep aux sein* (*usu angewalzt kommen*) to come rolling along *or* (*auf einen zu*) up.

anwandeln *vt sep* (*geh*) to come over. **jdn wandelt die Lust an, etw zu tun** sb feels the desire to do sth; **was wandelt dich an?** what are you thinking of?

Anwandlung *f* (*von Furcht etc*) feeling; (*Laune*) mood; (*Drang*) impulse. **aus einer ~ heraus** on (an) impulse; **in einer ~ von Freigebigkeit** in a fit of generosity *etc*; **dann bekam er wieder seine ~en** (*inf*) then he had one of his fits again; **merkwürdige etc ~en haben** to have strange *etc* moods.

anwärmen *vt sep* to warm up.

Anwärter(in *f*) *m* (*Kandidat*) candidate (*auf +acc* for); (*Sport*) contender (*auf +acc* for); (*Thron~*) heir (*auf +acc* to). **der ~ auf den Thron** the pretender *or* (*Thronerbe*) heir to the throne.

Anwartschaft *f*, *no pl* candidature; (*Sport*) contention. **seine ~ auf die Titel anmelden** to say one is in contention for the title; **~ auf den Thron** claim to the throne.

anwatscheln *vi sep aux sein* (*inf*) (*usu angewatschelt kommen*) to come waddling along *or* (*auf einen zu*) up.

anwehen *sep* **1** *vt Sand* to blow; *Schnee* to drift; (*fig geh: Gefühl*) to come over. **etw gegen etw ~** to blow sth against sth; **warme Luft wehte ihm/sein Gesicht an** warm air blew over him/his face. **2** *vi aux sein* to drift.

anweisen *vt sep irreg* (a) (*anleiten*) *Schüler, Lehrling etc* to instruct; (*beauftragen, befehlen auch*) to order. (b) (*zuweisen*) (*jdm etw sb* sth) to allocate; *Zimmer auch* to give. **jdm einen Platz ~** to show sb to a seat. (c) *Geld* to transfer. (d) *siehe* **angewiesen**.

Anweisung *f* (a) (*Fin*) payment; (*auf Konto etc*) transfer; (*Formular*) payment slip; (*Post~*) postal order.

(b) (*Anordnung*) instruction, order. **eine ~ befolgen** to follow an instruction, to obey an order; **~ haben, etw zu tun** to have instructions to do sth; **auf ~ der Schulbehörde** on the instructions of *or* on instruction from the school authorities.
  (c) (*Zuweisung*) allocation.
  (d) (*Anleitung*) instructions *pl*; (*Gebrauchs~ auch*) set of instructions.

anwendbar *adj Theorie, Regel* applicable (*auf +acc* to). **die Methode ist auch hier ~** the method can also be applied *or* used here; **das ist in der Praxis nicht ~** that is not practicable.

Anwendbarkeit *f* applicability (*auf +acc* to).

anwenden *vt sep auch irreg* (a) (*gebrauchen*) *Methode, Mittel, Technik, Gewalt* to use (*auf +acc* on); *Regel* to apply; *Sorgfalt, Mühe* to take (*auf +acc* over). **etw gut *or* nützlich ~** to make good use of sth.
  (b) *Theorie, Prinzipien* to apply (*auf +acc* to); *Erfahrung, Einfluß* to use, to bring to bear (*auf +acc* on). **sich auf etw** (*acc*) **~ lassen** to be applicable to sth; *siehe* **angewandt**.

Anwendung *f siehe vt* (a) use (*auf +acc* on); application; taking. **etw in ~** (*acc*) *or* **zur ~ bringen** (*form*) to use/apply sth; **zur ~ gelangen** *or* **kommen, ~ finden** (*all form*) to be used/applied. (b) application (*auf +acc* to); using, bringing to bear (*auf +acc* on).

Anwendungs-: **~bereich** *m*, **~gebiet** *nt* area of application; **~möglichkeit** *f* possible application; **~vorschrift** *f* instructions *pl* for use.

anwerben *vt sep irreg* to recruit (*für* to); (*Mil auch*) to enlist (*für* in). **sich ~ lassen** to enlist.

Anwerbung *f siehe vt* recruitment; enlistment.

anwerfen *sep irreg* **1** *vt* (a) *Wand* to roughcast. **Kalk *etc* an eine Wand ~** to roughcast a wall (with lime *etc*). (b) (*Tech*) to start up; *Propeller* to swing; (*inf*) *Gerät* to switch on. **2** *vi* (*Sport*) to take the first throw.

Anwesen *nt* -s, - (*geh*) estate.

anwesend *adj* present. **die nicht ~en Mitglieder** the members who are not present; **~ sein** to be present (*bei, auf +dat* at); **ich war nicht ganz ~** (*hum inf*) my thoughts were elsewhere, I was thinking of something else.

Anwesende(r) *mf decl as adj* person present. **die ~n** those present; **jeder ~/alle ~n** everyone/all those present.

Anwesenheit *f* presence. **in ~ +gen *or* von** in the presence of.

Anwesenheits-: **~liste** *f* attendance list; **~pflicht** *f* obligation to attend.

anwettern *vt sep* (*inf*) *jdn* to bawl at.

anwichsen *vt sep* (*sl*) (*ansprechen*) to accost; (*herausfordern*) to provoke.

anwidern *vt sep jdn ~* (*Essen, Anblick*) to make sb feel sick; **es/er widert mich an** I can't stand *or* I detest it/him; *siehe* **angewidert**.

anwinkeln *vt sep* to bend.

anwinseln *vt sep* to whimper at.

Anwohner *m* -s, - resident. **die ~ des Rheins** the people who live on the Rhine.

Anwohnerschaft *f*, *no pl* residents *pl*.

Anwurf *m* (a) (*Sport*) first throw; (*fig: Schmähung*) reproof, rebuke. (b) (*dated Build*) roughcast.

anwurzeln *vi sep aux sein* to take root. **wie angewurzelt dastehen/stehenbleiben** to stand rooted to the spot.

Anzahl *f*, *no pl* number. **die Parteien waren in ungleicher ~ vertreten** the parties were not represented in equal numbers; **eine ganze ~** quite a number.

anzahlen *vt sep Ware* to pay a deposit on, to make a down payment on. **einen Betrag/100 DM ~** to pay an amount/100 DM as a deposit.

anzählen *vt sep* (*Sport*) *jdn ~* to start giving sb the count.

Anzahlung *f* deposit, down payment (*für, auf +acc* on); (*erste Rate*) first instalment. **eine ~ machen *or* leisten** (*form*) to pay a deposit.

anzapfen *vt sep Faß* to broach; *Fluß* to breach; *Baum, Telefon* to tap; *elektrische Leitung* to tap. **jdn** (**um Geld**) **~** (*inf*) to touch sb (for money); **jdn ~** (*inf*) (*ausfragen*) to pump sb; (*Telec*) to tap sb's phone.

Anzeichen *nt* sign; (*Med auch*) symptom. **alle ~ deuten darauf hin, daß ...** all the signs are that ...; **wenn nicht alle ~ trügen** if all the signs are to be believed.

anzeichnen *vt sep* to mark; (*zeichnen*) to draw (*an +acc* on).

Anzeige *f* (a) (*bei Behörde*) report (*wegen of*); (*bei Gericht*) legal proceedings *pl*. **wegen einer Sache** (**eine**) **~ bei der Polizei erstatten *or* machen** to report sth to the police; **wegen einer Sache** (**eine**) **~ bei Gericht erstatten *or* machen** to institute legal proceedings over sth; **jdn/etw zur ~ bringen** (*form*) (*bei Polizei*) to report sb/sth to the police; (*bei Gericht*) to take sb/bring sth to court.
  (b) (*Bekanntgabe*) (*Karte, Brief*) announcement; (*in Zeitung auch*) notice; (*Inserat, Reklame*) advertisement.
  (c) (*das Anzeigen: von Temperatur, Geschwindigkeit etc*) indication; (*Instrument*) indicator; (*Meßwerte*) reading; (*auf Informationstafel*) information. **auf die ~ des Spielstands warten** to wait for the score to be shown *or* indicated.

anzeigen *vt sep* (a) *jdn ~* (*bei der Polizei*) to report sb (to the police); (*bei Gericht*) to institute legal proceedings against sb; **sich selbst ~** to give oneself up.
  (b) (*bekanntgeben*) *Heirat, Verlobung etc* to announce; (*ausschreiben auch, Reklame machen für*) to advertise.
  (c) (*mitteilen*) to announce; *Richtung* to indicate. **jdm etw ~** (*durch Zeichen*) to signal sth to sb.
  (d) (*angeben*) *Spielstand, Temperatur, Zeit, Wetterlage, Geschwindigkeit etc* to show, to indicate; *Datum* to show; (*fig: deuten auf*) to indicate, to show.
  (e) *siehe* **angezeigt**.

Anzeigen-: ~blatt nt advertiser; ~teil m advertisement section; ~werbung f newspaper and magazine advertising.
Anzeigepflicht f, no pl obligation to notify or report an event, illness etc. der ~ unterliegen (form) (Krankheit) to be notifiable.
anzeigepflichtig adj notifiable.
Anzeiger m (a) (bei Polizei) person reporting offence etc to the police. (b) (Tech) indicator. (c) (Zeitung) advertiser, gazette.
Anzeigetafel f indicator board.
anzetteln vt sep to instigate; Unsinn to cause.
anziehen sep irreg 1 vt (a) Kleidung to put on. sich (dat) etw ~ to put sth on; (fig inf) to take sth personally; siehe angezogen.
(b) (straffen) to pull (tight); Bremse (betätigen) to apply, to put on; (härter einstellen) to adjust; Zügel to pull; Saite, Schraube to tighten; (dial) Tür to pull to.
(c) (an den Körper ziehen) to draw up.
(d) (lit) Geruch, Feuchtigkeit to absorb; (Magnet, fig) to attract; Besucher to attract, to draw. sich von etw angezogen fühlen to feel attracted to or drawn by sth.
(e) (obs: zitieren) to quote, to cite.
2 vi (a) (sich in Bewegung setzen) (Pferde) to start pulling or moving; (Zug, Auto) to start moving; (beschleunigen) to accelerate.
(b) (Chess etc) to make the first move.
(c) (Fin: Preise, Aktien) to rise.
(d) aux sein (heranziehen) to approach. aus vielen Ländern angezogen kommen to come from far and near.
3 vr (a) (sich kleiden) to get dressed.
(b) (fig) (Menschen) to be attracted to each other; (Gegensätze) to attract.
anziehend adj (ansprechend) attractive; (sympathisch) pleasant.
Anziehung f attraction. die Stadt hat eine große ~ für sie she is very attracted to the town.
Anziehungskraft f (Phys) force of attraction; (fig) attraction, appeal. eine große ~ auf jdn ausüben to attract sb strongly.
anzischen sep 1 vt (inf, fig inf) to hiss at. 2 vi aux sein angezischt kommen to come whizzing along or (auf einen zu) up.
anzockeln vi sep aux sein (usu angezockelt kommen) (inf) to dawdle along or (auf einen zu) up; (Pferd) to plod along/up.
Anzug m -(e)s, Anzüge (a) (Herren~) suit. jdn aus dem ~ stoßen/boxen (inf) to beat the living daylights out of sb (inf); aus dem ~ kippen (inf) to be bowled over (inf) or flabbergasted (inf); (ohnmächtig werden) to pass out; siehe hauen.
(b) (das Heranrücken) approach. im ~ sein to be coming; (Mil) to be advancing; (fig) (Gewitter, Gefahr) to be in the offing; (Krankheit) to be coming on.
(c) (Chess etc) opening move. Weiß ist als erster im ~ white has first move.
(d) (von Auto etc) acceleration.
anzüglich adj lewd, suggestive. ~ werden to get personal; er ist mir gegenüber immer so ~ he always makes lewd etc remarks to me.
Anzüglichkeit f lewdness, suggestiveness. ~en personal or lewd or suggestive remarks.
Anzugskraft f, **Anzugsvermögen** nt acceleration.
anzünden vt sep Feuer to light. das Haus etc ~ to set fire to the house etc, to set the house etc on fire.
Anzünder m lighter.
anzweifeln vt sep to question, to doubt.
anzwinkern vt sep to wink at.
anzwitschern sep (inf) 1 vr sich (dat) einen ~ to get tipsy. 2 vi aux sein (usu angezwitschert kommen) to come strolling along or (auf einen zu) up.
AOK [a:o:'ka:] f -, -s abbr of **Allgemeine Ortskrankenkasse**.
Äolsharfe ['ɛːɔls-] f aeolian harp.
Äon [ɛ'ɔːn, 'ɛːɔn] m -s, -en usu pl (geh) (a)eon.
äonenlang adj (geh) eternal.
Aorta f -, **Aorten** aorta.
Apanage [-'naːʒə] f -, -n appanage (obs), (large) allowance (auch fig).
apart 1 adj distinctive, unusual; Mensch, Aussehen, Kleidungsstück auch striking. 2 adv (old) separately, individually.
Apartheid [a'paːɐthait] f -, no pl apartheid.
Apartheidpolitik f policy of apartheid, apartheid policy.
Apartheit f siehe adj distinctiveness, unusualness; strikingness.
Apartment [a'partmənt] nt -s, -s flat (Brit), apartment (esp US).
Apartment-: ~haus nt block of flats (Brit), apartment house (esp US); ~wohnung f siehe **Apartment**.
Apathie f apathy; (von Patienten) listlessness.
apathisch adj apathetic; Patient listless.
aper adj (Sw, Aus, S Ger) snowless.
Aperçu [aper'syː] nt -s, -s (geh) witty remark, bon mot.
Aperitif m -s, -s or -e aperitif.
apern vi (Sw, Aus, S Ger) es apert/die Hänge ~ the snow/the snow on the slopes is going.
Apex m -, **Apizes** (a) (Astron) apex. (b) (Phon) (Längezeichen) length mark; (Akzentzeichen) stress mark.
Apfel m -s, ¨ apple. in den sauren ~ beißen (fig inf) to swallow the bitter pill; etw für einen ~ (und ein Ei) kaufen (inf) to buy sth dirt cheap (inf) or for a song (inf); der ~ fällt nicht weit vom Stamm (Prov) it's in the blood, an apple doesn't fall far from the tree (US).
Apfel- in cpds apple; ~baum m apple tree; ~blüte f (a) apple blossom; (b) (das Blühen) blossoming of the apple trees; zur Zeit der ~blüte when the apples were born when the apple trees were in blossom; ~brei m apple puree.
Äpfelchen nt dim of **Apfel**.

Apfel-: ~griebs -(es), -e, ~grutzen -, - m (dial) apple core; ~klare(r) m clear apple schnapps; ~kompott nt stewed apple; ~kuchen m apple cake; ~most m apple juice; ~mus nt apple puree or (als Beilage) sauce; jdn zu ~mus hauen (inf) to beat sb to a pulp; ~saft m apple juice; ~säure f malic acid; ~schimmel m dapple-grey (horse).
Apfelsine f (a) orange. (b) (Baum) orange tree.
Apfel-: ~strudel m apfelstrudel; ~tasche f apple turnover; ~wein m cider; ~wickler m -s, - (Zool) codlin moth.
Aphasie f (Psych) aphasia.
Aphorismus m aphorism.
aphoristisch adj aphoristic.
Aphrodisiakum nt -s, **Aphrodisiaka** aphrodisiac.
Aplomb [a'plɔ:] m -s, no pl (geh) aplomb.
Apo, APO ['a:po] f -, no pl abbr of **außerparlamentarische Opposition**.
apodiktisch adj apod(e)ictic.
Apokalypse f -, -n apocalypse.
apokalyptisch adj apocalyptic. die A~en Reiter the Four Horsemen of the Apocalypse.
apokryph adj (Rel) apocryphal. die A~en pl the Apocrypha.
apolitisch adj non-political, apolitical.
Apoll m -s, (rare) -s (a) (Myth) siehe **Apollo**. (b) (fig geh: schöner Mann) er ist nicht gerade ein ~ he doesn't exactly look like a Greek god.
apollinisch adj (geh) apollonian.
Apollo m -s **Apollo**.
Apologet(in f) m -en, -en (geh) apologist.
Apologetik f (geh) (a) siehe **Apologie**. (b) (Theol) apologetics.
Apologie f apologia.
Aporie f (geh) aporia (rare), problem.
Apostel m -s, - apostle.
Apostel-: ~brief m epistle; ~geschichte f Acts of the Apostles pl.
a posteriori adv (Philos, geh) a posteriori.
aposteriorisch adj (Philos) a posteriori.
apostolisch adj apostolic. der A~e Stuhl the Holy See; das A~e Glaubensbekenntnis the Apostles' Creed.
Apostroph m -s, -e apostrophe.
apostrophieren* vt (a) (Gram) to apostrophize. (b) (bezeichnen) jdn als etw (acc) ~ to call sb sth, to refer to sb as sth.
Apotheke f -, -n (a) chemist's shop, pharmacy (old, US). (b) (Haus~) medicine chest or cupboard; (Reise~, Auto~) first-aid box. (c) (pej inf) expensive shop. das ist eine ~ that shop charges fancy prices.
apothekenpflichtig adj available only at a chemist's shop or pharmacy.
Apotheker(in f) m -s, - pharmacist, (dispensing) chemist, apothecary (old Brit, US).
Apotheker-: ~gewicht nt apothecaries' weight; ~preis m (pej inf) fancy price; ~waage f (set of) precision scales.
Apotheose f -, -n apotheosis.
Apparat m -(e)s, -e (a) apparatus no pl, appliance; (kleineres, technisches, mechanisches Gerät auch) gadget; (Röntgen~ etc) machine.
(b) (Radio) radio; (Fernseher) set; (Rasier~) razor; (Foto~) camera.
(c) (Telefon) (tele)phone; (Anschluß) extension. am ~ on the phone; (als Antwort) speaking; wer war am ~? who did you speak to?; jdn am ~ verlangen to ask to speak to sb; bleiben Sie am ~! hold the line.
(d) (sl) (nicht bestimmter Gegenstand) thing; (großer Gegenstand) whopper. der Mann/die Frau/das Kind ist ein ganz schöner ~ the man/woman/child is a real heavyweight.
(e) (Personen und Hilfsmittel) set-up; (Verwaltungs~, Partei~) machinery, apparatus; (technischer etc) equipment, apparatus.
(f) (Zusammenstellung von Büchern) collection of books to be used in conjunction with a particular course.
(g) (Liter) (text)kritischer ~ critical apparatus.
Apparatebau m instrument-making, machine-making.
apparativ adj ~e Einrichtungen (technical) appliances or equipment; ~e Neuerungen new ideas in technical equipment; ~e Untersuchung/~er Versuch examination/experiment using technical equipment; ~e Lernhilfen technical teaching aids.
Apparatschik m -s, -s (pej) apparatchik.
Apparatur f (a) equipment no pl, apparatus no pl. ~en/eine ~ pieces/a piece of equipment. (b) (fig Pol) machinery, apparatus.
Apparillo m -s, -s (hum inf) contraption.
Appartement [aparta'mãː] nt -s, -s siehe **Apartment**. (b) (Zimmerflucht) suite.
Appeal [ə'piːl] m -s, no pl appeal.
Appell m -s, -e (a) (Aufruf) appeal (an + acc to, zu for). einen ~ an jdn richten to make an appeal to sb. (b) (Mil) roll call. zum ~ antreten to line up for roll call. (c) (Hunt) obedience. der Hund hat guten/keinen ~ the dog is/is not obedient. (d) (rare) siehe **Appeal**.
Appellation f (Jur: obs, Sw) appeal.
Appellativ, Appellativum [-'tiːvʊm] nt -s, **Appellativa** [-'tiːva] (Ling) appellative.
appellieren* vi to appeal (an + acc to).
Appendix m -, **Appendizes** appendix; (fig: Anhängsel) appendage.
Apperzeption f (Philos, Psych) apperception.
Appetit m -(e)s, no pl (lit, fig) appetite. ~ auf etw (acc) haben (lit, fig) to feel like sth; das kann man mit ~ essen that's some-

thing you can really enjoy or tuck into; guten ~! bon appetit, enjoy your meal (usu nothing said); jdm den ~ verderben to spoil sb's appetite; (inf: Witz etc) to make sb feel sick; jdm den ~ an etw (dat) verderben (fig) to put sb off sth; der ~ kommt beim or mit dem Essen (prov) appetite grows with the eating (prov).

Appetit-: a~anregend adj Speise etc appetizing; a~anregendes Mittel appetite stimulant; ~bissen, ~happen m canapé; a~hemmend adj appetite suppressant; a~hemmendes Mittel appetite suppressant; ~hemmer m -s, - appetite suppressant; a~lich adj (lecker) appetizing; (verlockend aussehend, riechend) tempting; (hygienisch) hygienic, savoury, (fig) Mädchen attractive; a~lich verpackt hygienically packed; a~los adj without any appetite; a~los sein to have lost one's appetite; ~losigkeit f lack of appetite; ~zügler m -s, - appetite suppressant.

Appetizer ['apətaɪzɐ] m -s, -s (Pharm) appetite stimulant.

applaudieren* vti to applaud. jdm/einer Sache ~ to applaud sb/sth.

Applaus m -es, no pl applause.

applikabel adj (geh) applicable.

Applikation f (geh, Med) (Anwendung) application; (von Heilmethode) administering.

applizieren* vt (a) (geh: anwenden) to apply. (b) (Sew: aufbügeln) to apply; (aufnähen auch) to appliqué. (c) (Med) Heilmethode to administer.

apport interj (Hunt) fetch.

Apport m -s, -e (a) (Hunt) retrieving, fetching. (b) (Parapsychologie) apport.

apportieren* vti to retrieve, to fetch.

Apportierhund m retriever.

Apposition f apposition.

appretieren* vt (Tex) to starch; (imprägnieren) to waterproof; Holz to dress, to finish; Paper to glaze.

Appretur f (a) (Mittel) finish; (Tex) starch; (Wasserundurchlässigkeit) waterproofing; (für Papier auch) glaze. (b) siehe appretieren starching; waterproofing; dressing, finishing; glazing.

Approbation f (von Arzt, Apotheker) certificate (enabling a doctor etc to practise). einem Arzt die ~ entziehen to take away a doctor's licence to practise, to strike a doctor off (the register) (Brit).

approbieren* vt (old: genehmigen) to approve.

approbiert adj Arzt, Apotheker registered, certified.

Approximation f (Math) approximation, approximate value.

Après-Ski [aprɛ'ʃiː] nt -, -s après-ski; (Kleidung) après-ski clothes.

Aprikose f -, -n apricot. Wangen wie ~n soft rosy cheeks.

Aprikosen-: ~likör m apricot brandy; ~marmelade f apricot jam.

April m -s, no pl April. ~! ~! April fool!; der erste ~ April or All Fools' Day; jdn in den ~ schicken to make an April fool of sb; siehe März.

April-: ~scherz m April fool's trick; das ist doch wohl ein ~scherz (fig) you/they etc must be joking; ~wetter nt April weather.

a priori adv (Philos, geh) a priori.

apriorisch adj (Philos) a priori.

apropos [apro'poː] adv by the way, that reminds me. ~ Afrika talking about Africa.

Apside f -, -n (Astron) apsis.

Apsis f -, **Apsiden** (a) (Archit) apse. (b) (von Zelt) bell.

Aquädukt m -(e)s, -e aqueduct.

Aqua-: ~marin nt -s, -e aquamarine; a~marinblau adj aquamarine; ~naut m -en, -en aquanaut; ~planing nt -s, no pl (Aut) aquaplaning.

Aquarell nt -s, -e watercolour (painting). ~ malen to paint in watercolours.

Aquarellfarbe f watercolour.

aquarellieren* vi to paint in watercolours.

Aquarell-: ~maler m watercolourist; ~malerei f (a) (Bild) watercolour (painting); (b) (Vorgang) painting in watercolours, watercolour painting.

Aquarien- [-ən] in cpds aquarium; ~fisch m aquarium fish; ~tier nt aquarium animal.

Aquarium nt aquarium.

Aquatinta f -, **Aquatinten** aquatint.

Äquator m -s, no pl equator.

äquatorial adj equatorial.

Äquatortaufe f (Naut) crossing-the-line ceremony.

Aquavit [akva'viːt] m -s, -e aquavit.

Äquilibrist m juggler; (Seiltänzer) tight-rope walker.

Äquinoktium nt equinox.

Aquitanien [-iən] nt -s Aquitaine.

Äquivalent [-va'lɛnt] nt -s, -e equivalent; (Ausgleich) compensation.

äquivalent [-va'lɛnt] adj equivalent.

Äquivalenz [-va'lɛnts] f equivalence.

Ar nt or m -s, -e (Measure) are (100 m²).

Ära f -, **Ären** era. die ~ Adenauer the Adenauer era.

Araber [auch 'aː-] m -s, - (auch Pferd), **Araberin** f Arab.

Arabeske f -, -n arabesque; (Verzierung) flourish.

Arabien [-iən] nt -s Arabia.

arabisch adj Arab; Ziffer, Sprache, Schrift etc Arabic. die A~e Halbinsel (Geog) the Arabian Peninsula, Arabia.

Arabisch(e) nt Arabic.

Arabist(in f) m Arabist.

Arabistik f, no pl Arabic studies pl.

Aragon, Aragonien [-iən] nt -s Aragon.

aragonisch adj Aragonese.

Aralsee m Aral Sea, Lake Aral.

aramäisch adj Aramaic.

Arbeit f (a) (Tätigkeit, Phys, Sport) work; (das Arbeiten auch) working; (Pol, Econ, Lohn für ~) labour. ~ und Kapital capital and labour; Tag der ~ Labour Day; die ~en an der Autobahn the work on the motorway; es kann mit den ~en begonnen werden work can begin; bei der ~ mit Kindern when working with children; viel ~ machen to be a lot of work (jdm für sb); das ist/kostet viel ~ it's a lot of work or a big job; an or bei der ~ sein to be working; sich an die ~ machen, an die ~ gehen to get down to work, to start working; an die ~! to work!; jdm bei der ~ zusehen to watch sb working; etw ist in ~ work on sth has started or is in progress; etw in ~ haben to be working on sth; etw in ~ nehmen to undertake to do or (manuelle Arbeit) make sth; etw in ~ geben to have sth done/made; jdm etw in ~ geben to get sb to do/make sth; die ~ läuft dir nicht davon (hum) the work will still be there when you get back; erst die ~, dann ... work first and then ...; erst die ~, dann das Vergnügen (prov) business before pleasure (prov); ~ schändet nicht (Prov) work is no disgrace.

(b) no pl (Ausführung) work. ganze or gründliche ~ leisten (lit, fig iro) to do a good job.

(c) no pl (Mühe) trouble, bother. jdm ~ machen to put sb to trouble; machen Sie sich keine ~! don't go to any trouble or bother; das war vielleicht eine ~! what hard work or what a job that was!; die ~ zahlt sich nicht aus it's not worth the trouble or effort.

(d) (Berufstätigkeit, inf: Arbeitsplatz, -stelle, -zeit) work no indef art; (Arbeitsverhältnis auch) employment; (Position) job. eine ~ als etw work or a job as sth; (eine) ~ suchen/finden to look for/find work or a job; einer (geregelten) ~ nachgehen to have a (steady) job; ohne ~ sein to be out of work or unemployed; bei jdm/einer Firma in ~ stehen or sein to be employed by sb/with a firm; zur or auf (inf) ~ gehen/von der ~ kommen to go to/come back from work.

(e) (Aufgabe) job. seine ~ besteht darin, zu ... his job is to ...

(f) (Produkt) work; (handwerkliche) piece of work; (Prüfungs~) (examination) paper; (wissenschaftliche) paper; (Buch) work.

(g) (Sch) test. ~en korrigieren to mark test papers; eine ~ schreiben/schreiben lassen to do/set a test.

arbeiten 1 vi (a) to work (an +dat on); (sich anstrengen auch) to labour (old, liter), to toil (liter). der Sänger hat viel an sich (dat) gearbeitet the singer has worked hard or has done a lot of work; ~ wie ein Pferd/Wilder (inf) to work like a Trojan or horse/like mad (inf); die Zeit arbeitet für/gegen uns we have time on our side, time is on our side/against us; er arbeitet für zwei (inf) he does the work of two or enough work for two; er arbeitet über Schiller he's working on Schiller; er arbeitet mit Wasserfarben he works in or uses watercolours.

(b) (funktionieren) (Organ) to function, to work; (Maschine, Anlage etc auch) to operate. die Anlage arbeitet automatisch the plant is automatic; die Anlage arbeitet elektrisch/mit Kohle the plant runs or operates on electricity/coal.

(c) (berufstätig sein) to work. seine Frau arbeitet auch his wife works or is working or goes out to work too; für eine/bei einer Firma/Zeitung ~ to work for a firm/newspaper; das Büro arbeitet von ... bis ... the office hours are from ... to ...; die ~de Bevölkerung/Jugend the working population/youth.

(d) (in Bewegung sein) to work; (Most etc auch) to ferment; (Holz) to warp. in meinem Magen arbeitet es my stomach's rumbling; in seinem Kopf arbeitet es his mind is at work; in ihm begann es zu ~ he started to react, it began to work on him; die Beleidigung arbeitet heftig in ihm he's still smarting from the insult.

(e) (schneidern) wo/bei wem lassen Sie ~? where do you have your clothes made/who makes your clothes?

2 vr (a) sich krank/müde/krüpplig ~ to make oneself ill/tire oneself out with work/to work oneself silly (inf); sich zu Tode ~ to work oneself to death; sich (dat) die Hände wund ~ to work one's fingers to the bone.

(b) (sich fortbewegen) to work oneself (in +acc into, durch through, zu to). sich in die Höhe or nach oben/an die Spitze ~ (fig) to work one's way up/(up) to the top.

(c) impers es arbeitet sich gut/schlecht you can/can't work well; es arbeitet sich hier auch nicht besser it's no better working here either; mit ihr arbeitet es sich angenehm it's nice working with her.

3 vt (a) (herstellen) to make; (aus Ton etc auch) to work, to fashion.

(b) (tun) to do. was arbeitest du dort? what are you doing there?; (beruflich) what do you do there?; ich habe heute noch nichts gearbeitet I haven't done anything or any work today; du kannst auch ruhig mal was ~! (inf) it wouldn't hurt you to do something or a bit of work either!

Arbeiter m -s, - worker; (im Gegensatz zum Angestellten) blue-collar worker; (auf Bau, Bauernhof) labourer; (bei Straßenbau, im Haus) workman. der 22jährige ~ Horst Kuhn the 22-year-old factory worker/labourer/workman Horst Kuhn; die ~ (Proletariat, Arbeitskräfte) the workers; ~ und Arbeiterinnen male and female workers; ~ und Arbeiterinnen gesucht für unser neues Werk we are looking for men and women to work in our new factory; er ist ein guter/langsamer ~ he is a good/slow worker.

Arbeiter-: ~ameise f worker (ant); ~aufstand m workers' revolt; ~bevölkerung f labouring classes pl; ~bewegung f labour movement; ~biene f worker (bee); ~demonstration f workers' demonstration ~denkmal nt (a) (lit) monument erected to the labouring or working classes. (b) (hum) statue/monument to inactivity (hum); ~dichter m poet of the working class; ~familie f working-class family; a~feindlich *adj* anti-working-class; **a~freundlich** *adj* pro-working-class; **~führer** *m* (*Pol*) leader of the working classes; **~gewerkschaft** *f* blue-collar (trade) union, labor union (*US*).

Arbeiterin *f* **(a)** *siehe* **Arbeiter. (b)** (*Zool*) worker.

Arbeiter-: **~jugend** *f* young workers *pl*; **~kampfgruß** *m* clenched-fist salute; **~kampflied** *nt* socialist workers' song; **~kind** *nt* child from a working-class family *or* background; **~klasse** *f* working class(es *pl*); **~kneipe** *f* workers' pub; **~kontrolle** *f* (*DDR*) *system of watchdog committees set up to check production etc*; **~lied** *nt* workers' song; **~massen** *pl* working masses *pl*; **~milieu** *nt* working-class environment; **im ~milieu** in a working-class environment; **der Roman schildert das ~milieu sehr lebendig** the novel gives a vivid portrayal of working-class life; **~organisation** *f* association of workers, labour organization; **~partei** *f* workers' party; **~priester** *m* worker-priest; **~rat** *m* workers' council; **~schaft** *f* work force; **~schriftsteller** *m* working-class writer; **~selbstverwaltung** *f* workers' control; **~siedlung** *f* workers' housing estate; **~sohn** *m* son of a working-class family; **~stadt** *f* working-class town; **~student(in** *f***)** *m* (*DDR*) *mature student who was previously a factory worker*; **~-und-Bauern-Fakultät** *f* (*DDR*) *university department responsible for preparing young factory and agricultural workers for university*; **~-und-Bauern-Inspektion** *f* (*DDR*) *public body set up to check implementation of government policy in production, trading standards and consumer protection*; **~-und-Bauern-Macht** *f* (*DDR*) *power of the workers*; **~-und-Bauern-Staat** *m* (*DDR*) *workers' and peasants' state*; **~-und-Soldaten-Rat** *m* *workers' and soldiers' council*; **~unruhen** *pl* worker unrest, unrest among the workers; **~verein** *m* working men's association; **~verräter(in** *f***)** *m* traitor to the labour movement; **~veteran** *m* (*DDR*) veteran of the labour movement; **~viertel** *nt* working-class area; **~wohlfahrt** *f* workers' welfare association; **~zeitung** *f* paper of the labour movement.

Arbeitgeber *m* employer.

Arbeitgeber-: **~anteil** *m* employer's contribution; **~seite** *f* employers' side; **~verband** *m* employers' federation.

Arbeitnehmer *m* employee.

Arbeitnehmer-: **~anteil** *m* employee's contribution; **~schaft** *f* employees *pl*; **~seite** *f* employees' side.

Arbeitsablauf *m* work routine; (*von Fabrik*) production *no art*.

arbeitsam *adj* industrious, hard-working.

Arbeits|ameise *f* worker (ant).

Arbeitsamkeit *f* industriousness.

Arbeits-: **~amt** *nt* employment exchange, job centre (*Brit*), labour exchange (*dated Brit*); **~anfall** *m* workload; **~anleitung** *f* instructions *pl*; **~antritt** *m* commencement of work (*form*); **beim ~antritt** when starting *or* commencing (*form*) work; **~anzug** *m* working suit; **~atmosphäre** *f* work(ing) atmosphere, work climate; **~auffassung** *f* attitude to work; **~aufwand** *m* expenditure of energy; (*Ind*) expenditure of labour; **mit geringem/großem ~aufwand** with little/a lot of work; **der ~aufwand für etw** the labour required for sth; **a~aufwendig** *adj* energy-consuming; (*Ind*) expensive in labour; **a~aufwendig/nicht sehr a~aufwendig sein** to involve a lot of/not much work/labour; **~ausfall** *m* loss of working hours; **ein ~ausfall von fünf Stunden** a loss of five working hours; **um weitere ~ausfälle zu vermeiden** to avoid further working hours being lost; **~ausschuß** *m* working party; **~bedingungen** *pl* working conditions *pl*; **~beginn** *m* start of work; **bei ~beginn** when one starts work; **~belastung** *f* workload; **~bereich** *m* **(a)** (**~gebiet**) field of work; (*Aufgabenbereich*) area of work; **das gehört nicht in meinen ~bereich** that's not my job; **(b)** (*Umkreis*) field of operations; (*von Kran etc*) operating radius; **~bericht** *m* work report; **~beschaffung** *f* **(a)** (*Arbeitsplatzbeschaffung*) job creation; **(b)** (*Auftragsbeschaffung*) getting *or* bringing work in *no art*; **~bescheinigung** *f* certificate of employment; **~besuch** *m* working visit; **~biene** *f* worker (bee); (*fig*) busy bee; **~dienst** *m* (*NS*) labour service; **~disziplin** *f* discipline at work *no art*; **~eifer** *m* enthusiasm for one's work; **~einheit** *f* **(a)** (*DDR*) work unit; **(b)** (*Phys*) system of units; **~einkommen** *nt* earned income; **~einstellung** *f* **(a)** *siehe* **~auffassung**; **(b)** (**~niederlegung**) walkout; **die Belegschaft reagierte mit ~einstellung** the work force reacted by downing tools *or* walking out; **~emigrant** *m* immigrant worker; **~ende** *nt* *siehe* **~schluß**; **~erlaubnis** *f* (*Recht*) permission to work; (*Bescheinigung*) work permit; **~erleichterung** *f* **das bedeutet eine große ~erleichterung** that makes the work much easier; **~essen** *nt* (*esp Pol*) working lunch/dinner; **~ethos** *nt* work ethic; **~exemplar** *nt* desk copy; **a~fähig** *adj* Person able to work; (*gesund*) fit for *or* to work; *Regierung etc* viable; **~fähigkeit** *f* *siehe adj* ability to work; fitness for work; viability; **~feld** *nt* (*geh*) field of work; **~fieber** *nt* work mania; **~freude** *f* willingness to work; **~friede(n)** *m* peaceful labour relations *pl*, *no art*; **~gang** *m* **(a)** (*Abschnitt*) operation; **(b)** *siehe* **~ablauf**; **~gebiet** *nt* field of work; **~gemeinschaft** *f* team; (*Sch, Univ*) study-group; (*in Namen*) association; **~genehmigung** *f* *siehe* **~erlaubnis**; **~gerät** *nt* **(a)** *no pl* tools *pl*, equipment *no pl*; **~gericht** *nt* industrial tribunal; **~gruppe** *f* team; **~haus** *nt* (*old*) workhouse; **~hilfe** *f* aid; **~hypothese** *f* working hypothesis; **~inspektion** *f* (*Aus, Sw*) factory supervision; **a~intensiv** *adj* labour-intensive; **~kampf** *m* industrial action; **~kampfmaßnahme** *f* form of industrial action; **~kampfmaßnahmen** *pl* industrial action *sing*; **~kleidung** *f* working clothes *pl*; **~klima** *nt* work climate, work(ing) atmosphere; **~kollege** *m* (*bei Angestellten etc*) colleague; (*bei Arbeitern*) workmate; **~kollektiv** *nt* (*DDR*) team; **~konflikt** *m* industrial dispute; **~kosten** *pl* labour costs *pl*; **~kraft** *f* **(a)** *no pl* capacity for work; **die menschliche ~kraft ersetzen** to replace human labour; **seine ~kraft verkaufen** to

sell one's labour; **(b)** (*Arbeiter*) worker; **~kreis** *m* *siehe* **~gemeinschaft**; **~lager** *nt* labour *or* work camp; **~lärm** *m* industrial noise; **~last** *f* burden of work; **~leben** *nt* working life; **~leistung** *f* (*quantitativ*) output, performance; (*qualitativ*) performance; **~lenkung** *f* direction of labour; **~lohn** *m* wages *pl*, earnings *pl*.

arbeitslos *adj* **(a)** unemployed, out of work. **(b)** *Einkommen* unearned.

Arbeitslosen-: **~geld** *nt* earnings-related benefit; **~heer** *nt* army of unemployed; **~hilfe** *f* unemployment benefit; **~unterstützung** *f* (*dated*) unemployment benefit, dole money (*Brit inf*); **~versicherung** *f* **(a)** ≈ National Insurance (*Brit*), social insurance (*US*); **(b)** (*Amt*) ≈ Department of Health and Social Security (*Brit*), social insurance office (*US*); **~zahlen** *pl*, **~ziffer** *f* unemployment figures *pl*.

Arbeitslose(r) *mf decl as adj* unemployed person/man/woma n *etc.* **die ~n** the unemployed; **die Zahl der ~n** the number of unemployed *or* of people out of work.

Arbeitslosigkeit *f* unemployment.

Arbeits-: **~lust** *f* enthusiasm for work; **~mangel** *m* lack of work; **~mann** *m* (*dated*) worker; (*im Baugewerbe, in der Landwirtschaft*) labourer; **~markt** *m* labour market; **a~mäßig** *adj* with respect to work; **~material** *nt* material for one's work; (*Sch*) teaching aids *pl*; **~medizin** *f* industrial medicine; **~mensch** *m* (hard) worker; **~methode** *f* method of working; **~minister** *m* Employment Secretary (*Brit*), Labor Secretary (*US*); **~mittel** *nt* *siehe* **~material**; **~möglichkeit** *f* possibility of getting a job; **~moral** *f* *siehe* **~ethos**; **~nachweis** *m* **(a)** employment agency; (*amtlich*) employment exchange; **(b)** (*Bescheinigung*) certificate of employment; **~niederlegung** *f* walkout; **~norm** *f* **(a)** average work rate; **(b)** (*DDR*) time per unit of production; **~ordnung** *f* statement of conditions of employment; **~organisation** *f* organization of the/one's work; **~ort** *m* place of work; **~papier** *nt* working paper; **~papiere** *pl* cards, employment papers (*form*) *pl*.

arbeitsparend *adj* labour-saving.

Arbeits-: **~pause** *f* break; **~pensum** *nt* quota of work; **~pferd** *nt* (*lit*) workhorse; (*fig*) slogger (*inf*), hard worker; **~pflicht** *f* requirement to work; **~plan** *m* work schedule; (*in Fabrik*) production schedule.

Arbeitsplatz *m* **(a)** (**~stätte**) place of work. **am ~** at work; (*in Büro auch*) in the office; (*in Fabrik auch*) on the shop floor; **Demokratie am ~** industrial democracy.

(b) (*in Büro, Fabrik*) work station. **die Bibliothek hat 75 Arbeitsplätze** the library has room for 75 people to work *or* has working space for 75 people; **das Kind braucht einen richtigen ~** the child needs a proper place to work.

(c) (*Stelle*) job. **freie Arbeitsplätze** vacancies.

Arbeitsplatz-: **~sicherung** *f* safeguarding of jobs; **~wechsel** *m* change of jobs *or* employment (*form*).

Arbeits-: **~probe** *f* sample of one's work; **~produktivität** *f* productivity per man-hour worked; **~prozeß** *m* work process; **~psychologie** *f* industrial psychology; **~raum** *m* workroom; (*für geistige Arbeit*) study; **~recht** *nt* industrial law; **a~rechtlich** *adj* Streitfall, Angelegenheit concerning industrial law; *Literatur* on industrial law; **a~reich** *adj* full of *or* filled with work, busy; **~reserven** *pl* labour reserves *pl*; **~rhythmus** *m* work rhythm; **~richter** *m* judge in an industrial tribunal; **~ruhe** *f* (*kurze Zeit*) break from work; **gestern herrschte ~ruhe** the factories and offices were closed yesterday; **~sachen** *pl* (*inf*) working clothes *pl* *or* things *pl* (*inf*); **a~scheu** *adj* workshy; **~schluß** *m* end of work; **~schluß ist um 17⁰⁰** work finishes at 5 p.m.; **nach ~schluß** after work; **~schutz** *m* maintenance of industrial health and safety standards; **~schutzgesetz** *nt* act laying down industrial health and safety standards, ≈ Factories Act (*Brit*); **~schutzgesetzgebung** *f* legislation concerning health and safety at work; **~sitzung** *f* working session; **~sklave** *m* (*fig*) slave to one's job; **~sklaven** *pl* slave labour *sing*; **~soziologie** *f* industrial sociology; **a~sparend** *adj* *siehe* **arbeitsparend**; **~sprache** *f* language in which one works; **~stab** *m* planning staff; **~stätte** *f* place of work; **Goethes ~stätte** the place where Goethe worked; **~stelle** *f* **(a)** place of work; **(b)** (*Stellung*) job; **(c)** (*Abteilung*) section; **~stil** *m* work-style, style of working; **~stimmung** *f* **in der richtigen ~stimmung sein** to be in the (right) mood for work; **~studie** *f* time and motion study; **~stunde** *f* man-hour; **~stunden werden extra berechnet** labour will be charged separately; **vier ~stunden kosten …** four hours' labour costs …; **~suche** *f* search for work *or* employment *or* a job; **auf ~suche sein** to be looking for a job *or* be job-hunting; **~tag** *m* working day; **ein harter ~tag** a hard day; **~tagung** *f* conference, symposium; **~takt** *m* (*Tech*) **(a)** (*von Motor*) power stroke; **(b)** (*bei Fließbandarbeit*) time for an/the operation, phase time; **~tätigkeit** *f* work; **~team** *nt* team; **~technik** *f* technique of working; **a~teilig 1** *adj* based on the division of labour; **2** *adv* on the principle of the division of labour; **~teilung** *f* division of labour; **~tempo** *f* rate of work; **~therapie** *f* work therapy; **~tier** *nt* **(a)** (*lit*) working animal; **(b)** (*fig*) glutton for work; (*Geistesarbeiter auch*) workaholic (*inf*); **~tisch** *m* work-table; (*für geistige Arbeit*) desk; (*für handwerkliche Arbeit*) workbench; **~titel** *m* provisional *or* draft title; **~überlastung** *f* (*von Mensch*) overworking; (*von Maschine*) overloading.

Arbeit-: **~suche** *f* *siehe* **Arbeitssuche**; **a~suchend** *adj* after looking for work *or* a job, seeking employment; **~suchende(r)** *mf decl as adj* person *etc* looking for a job.

Arbeits-: **a~unfähig** *adj* unable to work; (*krank*) unfit for *or* to work; *Regierung etc* non-viable; **~unfähigkeit** *f* *siehe adj* inability to work; unfitness for work; non-viability; **~unfall** *m* industrial accident; **~unlust** *f* disinclination to work; **~unterlage** *f* work paper; (*Buch etc*) source for one's work;

a~unwillig *adj* reluctant *or* unwilling to work; ~urlaub *m* working holiday; (*Mil*) *leave from the forces to carry on one's usual employment*; ~verdienst *m* earned income; ~vereinfachung *f* simplification of the/one's work; ~verfahren *nt* process; ~verhältnis *nt* employee-employer relationship; ein ~verhältnis eingehen to enter employment; ~verhältnisse *pl* working conditions *pl*; ~verlust *m* loss of working hours; ein ~verlust von drei Stunden the loss of three working hours; ~vermittlung *f* (a) (*Vorgang*) arranging employment; (b) (*Amt*) employment exchange; (*privat*) employment agency; ~vertrag *m* contract of employment; ~verweigerung *f* refusal to work; ~vorbereitung *f* (a) preparation for the/one's work; (b) (*Ind*) production planning; ~vorgang *m* work process; ~vorhaben *nt* project; ~vorlage *f* sketch/plan/model to work from; jds ~vorlage the sketch *etc* sb works/worked from; ~weise *f* (*Praxis*) way *or* method of working, working method; (*von Maschine*) mode of operation (*form*); die ~weise dieser Maschine the way this machine works; ~welt *f* working world; die industrielle ~welt the world of industry; ~wille *m* willingness to work; a~willig *adj* willing to work; ~willige(r) *mf decl as adj* person willing to work; ~wissenschaft *f* industrial science, manpower studies *sing* (*US*); ~woche *f* working week; ~wut *f* work mania; a~wütig *adj* work-happy (*inf*); ~zeit *f* (a) working hours *pl*; während der ~zeit in *or* during working hours; (b) (*benötigte Zeit*) die ~zeit für etw the time spent on sth; (*in Fabrik*) the production time for sth; er ließ sich die ~zeit bezahlen he wanted to be paid for his time; ~zeitverkürzung *f* reduction in working hours; ~zeug *nt* (*inf*) (a) siehe ~kleidung; (b) (*Werkzeug*) tools *pl*; ~zeugnis *nt* reference from one's employer; ~zimmer *nt* study; ~zwang *m* requirement to work.

Arbitrage [-a:ʒə] *f* -, -n (*St Ex*) arbitrage *no art*; (~geschäft) arbitrage business.

arbiträr *adj* (*geh*) arbitrary.

Arboretum *nt* -s, **Arboreten** arboretum.

Archaikum, Archäikum *nt* (*Geol*) arch(a)ean period.

archaisch *adj* archaic.

archaisieren* *vi* (*Liter*) to archaize. ~d archaic, archaistic (*rare*).

Archaismus *m* archaism.

Archäologe *m*, **Archäologin** *f* archaeologist.

Archäologie *f* archaeology.

archäologisch *adj* archaeological.

Arche *f* -, -n die ~ Noah Noah's Ark.

Archetyp *m* -s, -en archetype.

archetypisch *adj* archetypal.

Archetypus *m siehe* **Archetyp**.

Archimedes *m* - Archimedes.

archimedisch *adj* Archimedean. ~es Axiom (*Math*) Archimedes' theorem; ~e Schraube (*Tech*) Archimedes' screw.

Archimedisch *adj* Archimedes' *attr*.

Archipel *m* -s, -e archipelago.

Architekt(in *f*) *m* -en, -en (*lit, fig*) architect.

Architekten-: ~büro *nt* architect's office; ~kollektiv *nt* team of architects.

Architektonik *f* architecture; (*geh: Aufbau von Kunstwerk*) structure, architectonics *sing* (*form*).

architektonisch *adj siehe* n architectural; structural, architectonic (*form*).

Architektur *f* architecture; (*Bau*) piece of architecture.

Architrav [-a:f] *m* -s, -e [-a:və] architrave.

Archiv *nt* archives *pl*.

Archivalien [-'va:liən] *pl* records *pl*.

Archivar(in *f*) [-'va:ɐ, -'va:rɪn] *m* archivist.

Archiv-: ~bild *nt* photo from the archives; ~exemplar *nt* file copy.

archivieren* [-'vi:rən] *vt* to put into the archives.

Archivmaterial *nt* records *pl*.

Arcus *m siehe* **Arkus**.

ARD ['a:ʔɛr'de:] *f* -, *no pl abbr of* **Arbeitsgemeinschaft der Rundfunkanstalten Deutschlands**.

Are *f* -, -n (*Sw*) siehe **Ar**.

Areal *nt* -s, -e area.

areligiös *adj* areligious.

Ären *pl of* **Ära**.

Arena *f* -, **Arenen** (*lit, fig*) arena; (*Zirkus~, Stierkampf~*) ring.

Areopag *m* -s, *no pl* (*Hist*) Areopagus.

arg 1 *adj, comp* ¨er, *superl* ¨ste(r, s) (*esp S Ger*) (a) (*old: böse*) evil, wicked. ~ denken to think evil thoughts; es ist nichts A~es an ihm there is no evil *or* malice in him.

    (b) (*schlimm*) bad; *Wetter auch, Gestank, Katastrophe, Verlust, Blamage, Verlegenheit, Schicksal* terrible; *Enttäuschung, Feind* bitter; *Säufer, Raucher* confirmed, inveterate. sein ¨ster Feind his worst enemy; etw noch ¨er machen to make sth worse; das Ä~ste befürchten to fear the worst; ich habe an nichts A~es gedacht I didn't think anything of it; etw liegt im ~en sth is at sixes and sevens; das ist mir ~ (*dial*) I'm very sorry about that.

    (c) *attr* (*stark, groß*) terrible; (*dial*) *Freude, Liebenswürdigkeit etc* tremendous.

2 *adv, comp* ¨er, *superl* am ¨sten (*schlimm*) badly; (*dial inf: sehr*) terribly (*inf*). es geht ihr ~ schlecht (*inf*) she's in a really bad way; er hat sich ~ vertan (*inf*) he's made a bad mistake; sie ist ~ verliebt (*inf*) she is very much *or* terribly in love; hast du Lust? — nicht so ~ (*inf*) do you feel like it? — not much *or* not terribly (*inf*); es zu ~ treiben to go too far, to take things too far.

Arg *nt* -s, *no pl* (*old*) malice.

Arge *m* -n, *no pl* (*old*) der ~ Satan, the devil.

Argentinien [-iən] *nt* -s Argentina, the Argentine.

Argentinier(in *f*) [-iɐ, iərɪn] *m* Argentine, Argentinean.

argentinisch *adj* Argentine, Argentinean.

ärger *comp of* **arg.**

Ärger *m* -s, *no pl* (a) annoyance; (*stärker*) anger. wenn ihn der ~ packt when he gets annoyed/angry; ~ über etw (*acc*) empfinden to feel annoyed about sth; zu jds ~ *or* jdm zum ~ to sb's annoyance.

    (b) (*Unannehmlichkeiten, Streitigkeiten*) trouble; (*ärgerliche Erlebnisse auch*) bother; (*Sorgen*) worry. jdm ~ machen *or* bereiten to cause sb a lot of trouble *or* bother; der tägliche ~ im Büro the hassle (*inf*) in the office every day; ~ bekommen *or* kriegen (*inf*) to get into trouble; ~ mit jdm haben to be having trouble with sb; mach keinen ~! (*inf*) don't make *or* cause any trouble!, cool it (*sl*); mach mir keinen ~ (*inf*) don't make any trouble for me; so ein ~! (*inf*) how annoying!, what a nuisance!; es gibt ~ (*inf*) there'll be trouble.

ärgerlich *adj* (a) (*verärgert*) annoyed, cross. ~ über *or* auf jdn/über etw (*acc*) sein to be annoyed *or* cross with sb/about sth, to be angry *or* infuriated with *or* mad (*inf*) at sb/about sth.

    (b) (*unangenehm*) annoying; (*stärker*) maddening, infuriating. eine ~e Tatsache an unpleasant fact.

Ärgerlichkeit *f* (a) *no pl* (*Verärgertsein*) annoyance, crossness. die ~ seines Tons the annoyance in *or* crossness of his voice. (b) (*Unerquicklichkeit, ärgerlicher Vorfall*) nuisance, annoyance.

ärgern 1 *vt* (a) to annoy, to irritate; (*stärker*) to make angry. jdn krank/zu Tode ~ to drive sb mad; sich krank/zu Tode ~ to drive oneself to distraction; über so etwas könnte ich mich krank/zu Tode ~ that sort of thing drives me mad; das ärgert einen doch! but it's so annoying!

    (b) (*necken*) to torment.

2 *vr* (*ärgerlich sein/werden*) to be/get annoyed; (*stärker*) to be/get angry *or* infuriated (*über jdn/etw* with sb/about sth). du darfst dich darüber nicht so ~ you shouldn't let it annoy you so much; nicht ~, nur wundern! (*inf*) that's life.

Ärgernis *nt* (a) *no pl* (*Anstoß*) offence, outrage. ~ erregen to cause offence; ~ an etw (*dat*) nehmen (*old*) to be offended by sth; bei jdm ~ erregen to offend sb; wegen Erregung öffentlichen ~ses angeklagt werden to be charged with offending public decency.

    (b) (*etwas Anstößiges*) outrage; (*etwas Ärgerliches*) terrible nuisance. es ist ein ~ für sie, wenn ... it annoys her (terribly) when ...; um ~se zu vermeiden to avoid upsetting anybody.

    (c) (*Ärgerlichkeit, Unannehmlichkeit*) trouble.

Arglist *f* -, *no pl* (*Hinterlist*) cunning, guile, craftiness; (*Boshaftigkeit*) malice; (*Jur*) fraud.

arglistig *adj* cunning, crafty; (*böswillig*) malicious. ~e Täuschung fraud.

Arglistigkeit *f siehe adj* cunning, craftiness; maliciousness.

arglos *adj* innocent; (*ohne Täuschungsabsicht*) guileless.

Arglosigkeit *f siehe adj* innocence; guilelessness.

Argon *nt* -s, *no pl* argon.

Argonaut *m* -en, -en (*Myth*) Argonaut.

Argot [ar'goː] *m or nt* -s, -s argot.

ärgste(r, s) *superl of* **arg.**

Argument *nt* argument. das ist kein ~ that's no argument; (*wäre unsinnig*) that's no way to go about things; (*keine Entschuldigung*) that's no excuse.

Argumentation *f* (a) argument; (*Darlegung*) argumentation *no pl*. (b) (*Sch: Aufsatz*) critical analysis.

argumentativ (*geh*), **argumentatorisch** (*rare*) *adj* ~ ist er sehr schwach his argumentation is weak; ~e Werbung betreiben to use persuasive advertising; etw ~ erreichen/bekämpfen to achieve sth by (force of) argument/to fight sth with arguments.

argumentieren* *vi* to argue. mit etw ~ to use sth as an argument.

Argus *m* -, -se Argus.

Argus-: ~auge *nt* (*geh*) Argus eye; mit ~augen Argus-eyed; ~blick *m* (*geh*) Argus eyes *pl*.

Argwohn *m* -s, *no pl* suspicion. jds ~ erregen/zerstreuen to arouse/allay sb's suspicions; ~ gegen jdn hegen/schöpfen (*geh*) to have/form doubts about sb, to be/become suspicious of sb; mit *or* voller ~ suspiciously.

argwöhnen *vt insep* (*geh*) to suspect.

argwöhnisch *adj* suspicious.

Ari *f* -, -s (*Mil sl*) artillery.

arid *adj* (*Geog*) arid.

Aridität *f* (*Geog*) aridity.

Arie [-iə] *f* (*Mus*) aria.

Arier(in *f*) [-iɐ, -iərɪn] *m* -s, - Aryan.

Arierparagraph *m* (*NS*) law precluding non-Aryans from becoming public servants.

Aries ['aːriɛs] *m* (*Astron*) Aries.

arisch *adj* (a) (*Ling*) Indo-European, Indo-Germanic. (b) (*NS*) Aryan.

arisieren* *vt* (*NS sl*) to Aryanize.

Aristokrat(in *f*) *m* -en, -en aristocrat.

Aristokratie *f* aristocracy.

aristokratisch *adj* aristocratic.

Aristoteles *m* - Aristotle.

Aristoteliker(in *f*) *m* -s, - Aristotelian.

aristotelisch *adj* Aristotelian.

Aristotelismus *m* Aristotelianism.

Arithmetik *f* -, *no pl* arithmetic.

Arithmetiker(in *f*) *m* -s, - arithmetician.

arithmetisch *adj* arithmetic(al).

Arkade *f* (*Bogen*) arch(way). ~n *pl* (*Bogengang*) arcade.

Arkadien [-iən] *nt* Arcadia.

arkadisch *adj* (*geh*) Arcadian.

Arktis f -, no pl Arctic.
arktisch adj arctic.
Arkus m -, - (Math) arc.
arm adj, comp ̈er, superl ̈ste(r, s) or adv am ̈sten (lit, fig) poor; (gering) Vegetation, Wachstum sparse. ~ und reich rich and poor; die A~en the poor pl; du'ißt mich noch mal ~! (inf) you'll eat me out of house and home!; du machst mich noch mal ~ (inf) you'll ruin me yet; ~ an etw (dat) sein to be somewhat lacking in sth; die Landschaft hier ist ~ an Bäumen the countryside around here doesn't have many trees; der Boden ist ~ an Nährstoffen the soil is poor in nutrients; ~ an Vitaminen low in vitamins; um jdn/etw ̈er werden/sein to lose/have lost sb/sth; um 55 Mark ̈er sein to be 55 marks poorer or worse off; ach, du/Sie A~er! (iro) you poor thing!, poor you!; ich A~er! (poet) woe is me! (poet); ~e Seelen (Rel) holy souls; ~ dran sein (inf) to have a hard time of it; ~es Schwein (inf) poor so-and-so (inf); ~er Irrer (sl) mad fool (inf); (bedauernswert) poor fool.
-arm adj suf lacking in.
Arm m -(e)s, -e (a) (Anat, Tech, fig) arm; (Fluß~ auch, Baum~) branch; (Waage~) beam; (Ärmel) sleeve. ~ in ~ arm in arm; über/unter den ~ over/under one's arm; die ~e voll haben to have one's arms full; jds ~ nehmen to take sb's arm or sb by the arm; jdm den ~ bieten (geh) or reichen to offer sb one's arm; jdn im ~ or in den ~en halten to hold sb in one's arms; jdn am ~ führen to lead sb by the arm; jdn in die ~e nehmen to take sb in one's arms; jdn in die ~e schließen to take or clasp sb in an embrace; sich in den ~en liegen to lie in each other's arms; jdm/sich in die ~e fallen or sinken to fall into sb's/each other's arms; sich aus jds ~en lösen (geh) to free oneself from sb's embrace; jdn auf den ~ nehmen to take sb onto one's arm; (fig inf) to pull sb's leg (inf); jdm unter die ~e greifen (fig) to help sb out; jdm in die ~e laufen (fig inf) to run or bump (inf) into sb; jdn mit offenen ~en empfangen (fig) to welcome sb with open arms; jdm in den ~ fallen (fig) to put a spoke in sb's wheel, to spike sb's guns; die Beine unter die ~e or den ~ nehmen (inf) to run for dear life or as fast as one's legs can carry one; sich jdm/einer Sache in die ~e werfen (fig) to throw oneself at sb/into sth; jdn jdm/einer Sache in die ~e treiben (fig) to drive sb into sb's arms/to sth; jdn am steifen ~ verhungern lassen (lit hum) to get sb in an armlock; (fig) to put the screws on sb (inf); der ~ des Gesetzes the long arm of the law; der ~ der Gerechtigkeit (fig) justice; einen langen/den längeren ~ haben (fig) to have a lot of/more pull (inf) or influence; jds verlängerter ~ an extension of sb.
(b) (euph ham) siehe **Arsch**.
Armada f -, -s or **Armaden** (lit, fig) armada.
Arm- in cpds arm; a~amputiert adj with an arm amputated; a~amputiert sein to have had an arm amputated; ~arbeit f (Boxen) fist work.
Armatur f, usu pl (Tech) (Hahn, Leitung etc) fitting; (Instrument) instrument.
Armaturen-: ~beleuchtung f (Aut) dash light; ~brett nt instrument panel; (Aut) dashboard.
Arm-: ~band nt bracelet; (von Uhr) (watch)strap; ~banduhr f wristwatch; ~beuge f (a) inside of one's elbow; (b) (Sport) arm bend; ~binde f armband; (Med) sling; ~bruch m (Med) broken or fractured arm; ~brust f crossbow.
Ärmchen nt dim of **Arm**.
armdick adj as thick as one's arm.
Armee f -, -n [-e:ən] (Mil, fig) army; (Gesamtheit der Streitkräfte) (armed) forces pl. bei der ~ in the army/forces.
Armee-: ~corps army; ~befehl m army order.
Ärmel m -s, - sleeve. sich (dat) die ~ hoch- or aufkrempeln (lit, fig) to roll up one's sleeves; etw aus dem ~ schütteln to produce sth just like that.
Armeleute-: ~essen nt poor man's food; ~geruch m smell of poverty; ~viertel nt poor district.
Ärmelhalter m sleeve band.
-ärm(e)lig adj suf -sleeved.
Ärmelkanal m (English) Channel.
ärmellos adj sleeveless.
Armen-: ~anwalt m lawyer who acts for poor people without charging them; ~arzt m doctor who gives free treatment to the poor; ~haus nt (old) poorhouse.
Armenien [-iən] nt Armenia.
Armenier(in f) [-iɐ, -iərin] m Armenian.
armenisch adj Armenian.
Armen-: ~kasse f (Hist) poor box; ~recht nt (Jur) legal aid.
Armensünder- in cpds (Aus) siehe **Armsünder-**.
Armenviertel nt poor district or quarter.
ärmer comp of **arm**.
Armeslänge f arm's length. um zwei ~n by two arms' length.
Armesünder m **Armesünders, Armesünder** (obs) condemned man.
Armesünder- in cpds siehe **Armsünder-**.
Arm-: ~flor m black armband; ~gelenk nt elbow joint; ~hebel m (Sport) arm lever.
armieren* vt (a) (old Mil) to arm. (b) (Tech) Kabel to sheathe; Beton to reinforce.
-armig adj suf -armed.
Arm-: a~lang adj arm-length; ~länge f arm length; ~lehne f armrest; (von Stuhl etc auch) arm; ~leuchter m (a) chandelier; (b) (pej inf: Mensch) twit (Brit inf), fool, twirp (inf).
ärmlich adj (lit, fig) poor; Kleidung, Wohnung shabby; Essen meagre; Verhältnisse humble. einen ~en Eindruck machen to look poor/shabby; aus ~en Verhältnissen from a poor family.
Ärmlichkeit f siehe adj poorness, shabbiness; meagreness; humbleness.

-ärmlig adj suf siehe **-ärm(e)lig**.
Ärmling m oversleeve.
Arm-: ~loch nt (a) armhole; (b) (euph: Arschloch) bum (sl); ~muskel m biceps; ~polster nt (a) (an Kleidung) shoulder padding; (b) (~lehne) padded armrest; ~prothese f artificial arm; ~reif(en) m bangle; ~schlüssel m (Sport) armlock, hammerlock (US); ~schutz m (Sport) arm guard.
armselig adj (dürftig) miserable; (mitleiderregend) pathetic, pitiful, piteous; (Summe, Ausrede) paltry. für ~e zwei Mark for a paltry two marks, for two paltry marks.
Armseligkeit f siehe adj miserableness; pitifulness, piteousness; wretchedness.
Armsessel, Armstuhl (old) m armchair.
ärmste(r, s) superl of **arm**.
Arm-: ~stummel (inf), ~stumpf m stump of one's arm; ~stütze f armrest.
Armsünder-: ~bank f, ~bänkchen nt (hum) (beim Essen) small table at which children sit; (bei Prüfung, Quiz etc) hot seat; dasitzen wie auf dem ~bänkchen to be sitting there looking as though the world were about to end; ~gesicht nt (hum) siehe ~miene; ~glocke f knell tolled during an execution; ~miene f (hum) hangdog expression.
Armut f -, no pl (a) (lit, fig) poverty. ~ an etw (dat) lack of sth; charakterliche ~ lack of character; geistige ~ intellectual poverty; (von Mensch) lack of intellect. (b) (obs: die Armen) die ~ the poor pl.
-armut f in cpds lack of.
Armutszeugnis nt (fig) jdm/sich (selbst) ein ~ ausstellen to show or prove sb's/one's (own) shortcomings; das ist ein ~ für ihn that shows him up.
Armvoll m -, - armful. zwei ~ Holz two armfuls of wood.
Arnika f -, -s arnica.
Arom nt -s, -e (poet) fragrance, scent.
Aroma nt -s, **Aromen** or -s or (dated) -ta (a) (Geruch) aroma. (b) (Geschmack) flavour, taste. (c) no pl flavouring.
aromatisch adj (a) (wohlriechend) aromatic. (b) (wohlschmeckend) savoury.
aromatisieren* vt to give aroma to. **aromatisiert** aromatic; zu stark aromatisiert sein to have too strong an aroma.
Aronsstab m arum.
Arrak m -s, -s or -e arrack.
Arrangement [arãʒə'mãː] nt -s, -s (alle Bedeutungen) arrangement.
Arrangeur [arã'ʒøːr] m (geh) organizer; (Mus) arranger. er war der ~ dieses Abkommens he arranged this agreement.
arrangieren* vt (alle Bedeutungen) to arrange (jdm for sb). **2** vr sich mit jdm ~ to come to an arrangement with sb; sich mit etw ~ to come to terms with sth.
Arrest m -(e)s, -s (a) (Sch, Mil, Jur: Jugend~) detention. seine Eltern bestraften ihn mit ~ his parents punished him by not letting him go out or by keeping him in.
(b) (Econ, Jur) (auch persönlicher ~) attachment; (auch dinglicher ~) distress (form), distraint. ~ in jds Vermögen distress upon sb's property.
Arrestant m (dated Jur) detainee.
Arrest-: ~lokal nt (dated) detention room; (Mil) guardroom; ~zelle f detention cell.
arretieren* vt (a) (dated) jdn to take into custody. (b) (Tech) to lock (in place).
Arretierung f (a) siehe vt taking into custody; locking. (b) (Vorrichtung) locking mechanism.
Arrhythmie f (Med) arrhythmia.
arrivieren* [-'viː-] vi aux sein to make it (inf), to become a success. zu etw ~ to rise to become sth.
arriviert [-'viːrt] adj successful; (pej) upstart. er ist jetzt ~ he has arrived, he has made it (inf).
Arrivierte(r) mf decl as adj arrivé; (pej) parvenu.
arrogant adj arrogant.
Arroganz f -, no pl arrogance.
arrondieren* vt (geh) (a) Grenze to realign, to adjust; Grundstück to realign or adjust the boundaries of. (b) Kanten etc to round off.
Arsch m -(e)s, ̈e (a) (vulg) arse (vulg), ass (sl), bum (sl), fanny (US sl), butt (US sl). jdm or jdn in den ~ treten to give sb a kick up the arse (vulg) or ass (sl); auf den ~ fallen (fig: schweiz'n) to fall flat on one's face; den ~ voll kriegen to get a bloody good hiding (sl); leck mich am ~! (laß mich in Ruhe) get stuffed! (inf), fuck off! (vulg); (verdammt noch mal) bugger! (sl), fuck it! (vulg); (überrascht) bugger me! (sl), fuck me! (vulg); er kann mich (mal) am ~ lecken he can get stuffed (inf) or fuck off (vulg); jdm in den ~ kriechen to lick sb's arse (vulg) or ass (sl); du hast wohl den ~ offen! (sl) you're out of your tiny mind (inf); ~ mit Ohren (sl) silly bugger (sl); aussehen wie ein ~ mit Ohren (sl) to be shit-faced (vulg); am ~ der Welt (sl) in the back of beyond; im or am ~ sein/in den ~ gehen (sl) to be/get fucked up (vulg); jdn am ~ haben/kriegen (sl) to have/get sb by the short and curlies (inf); einen kalten ~ kriegen/haben (sl) to kick/have kicked the bucket (inf); den ~ zukneifen (sl) to snuff it (inf); jdm den ~ aufreißen (esp Mil) to work the shit out of sb (sl); ihm geht der ~ mit Grundeis (sl) he's got the shits (inf), he's shit-scared (inf); ein ganzer ~ voll (sl) a whole lot; Schütze ~ (Mil) simple private; sich auf den ~ setzen ~ setzen (inf) to park one's arse (vulg) or fanny (US sl); (fig sl) (sich Mühe geben) to get one's arse in gear (vulg), to get one's finger out (sl); (aus Überraschung) to be knocked out (inf).
(b) (sl: Mensch) bastard, bugger, sod (all sl); (Dummkopf) stupid bastard etc (sl).
Arsch-: ~backe f (vulg) buttock, cheek; ~ficken nt (vulg) bumfucking (vulg); ~ficker m (a) (lit vulg) bum-fucker (vulg);

(b) *(fig sl)* slimy bastard *(sl)*; ~**geige** f *(sl) siehe* **Arsch** (b); a~**klar** *adj (sl)* bloody obvious *(sl)*; ~**kriecher** m *(sl)* ass-kisser *(sl)*; ~**kriecherei** f *(sl)* ass-kissing *(sl)*; ~**lecker** m -s, - *(sl)* ass-kisser *(sl)*.

ärschlings *adv (old)* backwards, arse first *(vulg)*.

Arsch-: ~**loch** nt *(vulg)* (a) *(lit)* arse-hole *(vulg)*, ass-hole *(sl)*; (b) *siehe* **Arsch** (b); ~**pauker** m *(Sch sl)* bloody teacher *(sl)*; ~**tritt** m *(sl)* kick up the arse *(vulg)* or behind *(inf)*; ~**-und-Titten-Presse** f *(sl)* tit-and-bum press *(inf)*; ~**wisch** m -(e)s, -e *(sl)* useless bumph *(inf)*, bum fodder *(sl)*.

Arsen nt -s, *no pl* arsenic.

Arsenal nt -s, -e *(lit, fig)* arsenal.

arsenhaltig *adj* arsenic.

Arsenik nt -s, *no pl* arsenic, arsenic trioxide *(form)*.

Art. *abbr of* **Artikel.**

Art f -, -en (a) kind, sort, type; *(von Pflanze, Insekt etc auch)* variety. **diese ~ Leute/Bücher** people/books like that, that kind or sort of person/book; **jede ~ (von) Buch/Terror** any kind etc of book/terrorism, a book of any kind etc/terrorism in any form; **alle möglichen ~en von Büchern, Bücher aller ~** all kinds or sorts of books, books of all kinds or sorts; **ein Heuchler schlimmster ~** the worst type or kind of hypocrite, a hypocrite of the worst type or kind; **einzig in seiner ~ sein** to be the only one of its kind, to be unique; **aus der ~ schlagen** not to take after anyone in the family.
(b) *(Biol)* species.
(c) *(Methode)* way. **auf die ~** in that way or manner; **auf die ~ geht es am schnellsten** that is the quickest way; **auf merkwürdige/grausame** etc **~** in a strange/cruel etc way; **die einfachste ~, etw zu tun** the simplest way to do sth or of doing sth; **auf diese ~ und Weise** in this way.
(d) *(Wesen)* nature; *(übliche Verhaltensweise)* way. **es entspricht nicht meiner ~** it's not my nature; **das ist eigentlich nicht seine ~** it's not like him; **von lebhafter ~ sein** to have a lively nature; to have a lively way (with one).
(e) *(Stil)* style. **Schnitzel nach ~ des Hauses** schnitzel à la maison.
(f) *(Benehmen)* behaviour. **daß es (nur so) eine ~ hat** *(old)* with a vengeance; **das ist doch keine ~!** that's no way to behave!; **was ist das (denn) für eine ~?** what sort of a way to behave is that?; **ist das vielleicht or etwa eine ~!** that's no way to behave!

Art-: ~**angabe** f *(Gram)* adverb of manner; *(Adverbialbestimmung)* adverbial phrase of manner; ~**bildung** f speciation *(form)*.

Artefakt nt -(e)s, -e *(geh)* artefact.

art|eigen *adj* characteristic (of the species).

arten vi aux sein *(geh)* **nach jdm ~** to take after sb; *siehe auch* **geartet.**

Arten-: a~**reich** *adj* with a large number of species; **diese Tierklasse ist sehr a~reich** this class of animal contains a large number of species; ~**reichtum** m *(Biol)* large number of species.

Art-: a~**erhaltend** *adj* survival *attr*; **das wirkte sich a~erhaltend aus** that contributed to the survival of the species; ~**erhaltung** f survival of the species.

Arterie [-iə] f artery.

arteriell *adj* arterial.

Arterienverkalkung [-iən-] f *(inf)* hardening of the arteries. **~ haben** *(fig)* to be senile.

Arteriosklerose f arteriosclerosis.

artesisch *adj* ~**er Brunnen** artesian well.

Art-: a~**fremd** *adj* foreign; ~**genosse** m animal/plant of the same species; *(Mensch)* person of the same type; a~**gleich** *adj* of the same species; *Mensch* of the same type.

Arthritis f -, **Arthritiden** arthritis.

arthritisch *adj* arthritic.

Arthrose f -, -n arthrosis.

artifiziell *adj (geh)* artificial.

artig *adj* (a) *Kind, Hund etc* good, well-behaved *no adv.* **sei schön ~** be a good boy/dog! etc, be good! (b) *(old: galant)* courteous, civil. (c) *(old: anmutig)* charming.

-artig *adj suf* -like.

Artigkeit f (a) *siehe adj (Wohlerzogenheit)* good behaviour; courtesy, courteousness, civility; charm. (b) *(old) (Kompliment)* compliment; *(höfliche Bemerkung)* pleasantry. **jdm einige ~en sagen** to pay sb compliments/make a few civil remarks to sb.

-artigkeit f *in cpds* -like quality.

Artikel m -s, - *(alle Bedeutungen)* article; *(Lexikon~ auch)* entry; *(Comm auch)* item.

-artikel pl *in cpds (Ausrüstungen)* equipment; *(Kleidung)* wear.

Artikulation f articulation; *(deutliche Aussprache auch)* enunciation; *(Mus)* phrasing.

Artikulations-: a~**fähig** *adj* articulate; *(Phon)* able to articulate; ~**fähigkeit** f *siehe adj* articulateness; ability to articulate; ~**organe** pl organs of speech pl; ~**vermögen** nt *siehe* ~**fähigkeit.**

artikulatorisch *adj (Phon)* articulatory.

artikulieren* 1 vti to articulate; *(deutlich aussprechen auch)* to enunciate; *(Mus)* to phrase. **sich artikuliert ausdrücken** to be articulate. 2 vr *(fig geh)* to express oneself.

Artikulierung f *siehe vb* articulation; enunciation; phrasing; expression.

Artillerie f artillery.

Artillerie- *in cpds* artillery; ~**beschuß** m artillery fire.

Artillerist m artilleryman.

artilleristisch *adj* artillery *attr.*

Artischocke f -, -n *(globe)* artichoke.

Artischockenboden m, *usu pl* artichoke heart.

Artist m (a) *(circus/variety)* artiste or performer. (b) *(obs, geh: Meister)* artist *(gen at).* (c) *(inf: Mensch)* joker *(inf).*

Artistenfakultät f *(Hist)* Faculty of Arts.

Artistik f artistry; *(Zirkus-, Varietékunst)* circus/variety performing.

Artistin f *siehe* **Artist.**

artistisch *adj* (a) **sein ~es Können** his ability as a performer; **eine ~e Glanzleistung/ ~ einmalige Leistung** a miracle/unique feat of circus etc artistry; **eine ~e Sensation** a sensational performance. (b) *(geschickt)* masterly *no adv.* (c) *(formalkünstlerisch)* artistic.

Artothek f -, -en picture (lending) library.

Artung f *(rare)* nature, character.

Artur m -s Arthur.

Artus m - *(Hist, Myth)* (King) Arthur.

Art-: a~**verschieden** *adj* of different species; a~**verwandt** *adj* generically related; ~**wort** nt *(Gram)* adjective.

Arznei f *(lit, fig)* medicine. **das war für ihn eine bittere/heilsame ~** *(fig)* that was a painful/useful lesson for him.

Arznei-: ~**buch** nt pharmacopoeia; ~**fläschchen** nt medicine bottle; ~**kunde, ~lehre** f pharmacology.

Arzneimittel nt drug.

Arzneimittel-: ~**forschung** f pharmacological research; ~**gesetz** nt law governing the manufacture and prescription of drugs; ~**hersteller** m drug manufacturer or company; ~**lehre** f pharmacology; ~**mißbrauch** m drug abuse; ~**versorgung** f provision of drugs *(gen* to).

Arznei-: ~**pflanze** f medicinal plant; ~**schränkchen** nt medicine cupboard.

Arzt m -es, -̈e doctor, physician *(old, form)*, medical practitioner *(form)*; *(Fach~)* specialist; *(Chirurg)* surgeon. **praktischer ~** general practitioner, GP *abbr.*

Arztberuf m medical profession.

Ärzte-: ~**besteck** nt set of surgical instruments; ~**kammer** f ≈ General Medical Council *(Brit)*, State Medical Board of Registration *(US)*; ~**kollegium** nt, ~**kommission** f medical advisory board; ~**mangel** m shortage of doctors; ~**schaft** f medical profession; ~**vertreter** m pharmaceutical consultant.

Arzt-: ~**frau** f doctor's wife; ~**helferin, ~hilfe** f *siehe* **Sprechstundenhilfe.**

Ärztin f woman doctor; *siehe auch* **Arzt.**

ärztlich *adj* medical. **er ließ sich ~ behandeln** he went to a doctor for treatment, he got medical treatment; **~ empfohlen** recommended by the medical profession.

Arzt-: ~**praxis** f doctor's practice; ~**rechnung** f doctor's bill; ~**wahl** f choice of doctor.

As¹ nt -ses, -se *(lit, fig)* ace. **alle vier ~se** *(lit)* all the aces.

As² nt *(Mus)* A flat.

Asbest nt -(e)s, -e *no pl* asbestos.

Asbest- *in cpds* asbestos; ~**beton** m asbestos cement.

Asbestose f -, -n asbestosis.

Asbestplatte f *(für Topf)* asbestos mat; *(für Bügeleisen)* asbestos stand.

Aschantinuß f *(Aus) siehe* **Erdnuß.**

Asch-: ~**becher** m *siehe* **Aschenbecher;** a~**blond** *adj* ash-blonde.

Asche f -, *no pl* ash(es pl); *(von Zigarette, Vulkan)* ash; *(fig) (sterbliche Überreste)* ashes pl; *(Trümmer)* ruins pl; *(nach Feuer)* ashes pl. **zu ~ werden** to turn to dust; **sich** *(dat)* **~ aufs Haupt streuen** *(fig geh)* to wear sackcloth and ashes.

Ascheimer m *(dial)* ash can *(esp US)* or ashbin.

Aschen-: ~**bahn** f cinder track; ~**becher** m ashtray; ~**brödel** nt -s, - *(Liter, fig)* Cinderella, Cinders *(inf)*; ~**brödeldasein** nt Cinderella existence; ~**eimer** m *siehe* **Ascheimer;** ~**kasten** m ash pan; ~**puttel** nt -s, - *siehe* ~**brödel;** ~**regen** m shower of ash.

Ascher m -s, - *(inf)* ashtray.

Aschermittwoch m Ash Wednesday.

Asch-: a~**fahl** *adj* ashen; a~**farben,** a~**farbig** *adj* ash-coloured; a~**grau** *adj* ash-grey; ~**kasten** m ash pan.

Ascorbinsäure [askɔr'biːn-] f ascorbic acid.

Asen pl *(Myth)* Aesir pl.

äsen *(Hunt)* **1** vir to graze, to browse. **2** vt to graze on.

aseptisch *adj* aseptic.

Aser¹ pl of **Aas.**

Äser² m -s, - *(Hunt)* mouth.

asexuell *adj* asexual.

Asiat(in f) m -en, -en Asian.

Asiatika pl Orientalia pl.

asiatisch *adj* Asian, Asiatic. **~e Grippe** Asian or Asiatic *(US)* flu.

Asien [-iən] nt -s Asia.

Askese f -, *no pl* asceticism.

Asket m -en, -en ascetic.

asketisch *adj* ascetic.

Askorbinsäure f ascorbic acid.

Äskulap-: ~**schlange** f snake of Aesculapius; ~**stab** m staff of Aesculapius.

Äsop m -s Aesop.

äsopisch *adj* Aesopic. **eine Ä~e Fabel** one of Aesop's Fables.

asozial *adj* antisocial.

Asoziale(r) mf decl as adj *(pej)* antisocial man/woman etc. **~ pl** antisocial elements.

Asozialität f antisocialness.

Aspekt m -(e)s, -e aspect. **unter diesem ~ betrachtet** looking at it from this point of view or aspect; **einen neuen ~ bekommen** to take on a different complexion.

Asphalt m -(e)s, -e asphalt.

Asphalt-: ~**beton** m asphalt; ~**decke** f asphalt surface.

asphaltieren* vt to asphalt.

asphaltiert adj asphalt.

Asphalt-: ~literat m (NS pej) hack (writer) (propounding liberal views); ~presse f (NS pej) yellow or gutter press (propounding liberal views); ~straße f asphalt road.

Aspik m or (Aus) nt -s, -e aspic.

Aspirant(in f) m (a) (geh) candidate (für, auf +acc for). (b) (DDR Univ) research assistant.

Aspirantur f (esp DDR) research assistantship.

Aspirata f -, (Phon) aspirate.

Aspiration f (a) usu pl (geh) aspiration. ~en auf etw (acc) or nach etw haben to have aspirations towards sth, to aspire to sth. (b) (Phon) aspiration.

aspirieren* 1 vi (geh) to aspire (auf +acc to); (Aus) to apply (auf +acc for). 2 vt (Phon) to aspirate.

aß pret of essen.

Aß nt (Aus) siehe As¹.

Assekuranz f (old) assurance; (Gesellschaft) assurance company.

Assel f -, -n isopod (form); (Roll~, Keller~, Land~ auch) woodlouse.

Assertion f (Philos) assertion.

Asservat [-'va:t] nt (court) exhibit.

Asservaten-: ~kammer f, ~raum m room where court exhibits are kept.

Assessor(in f) m graduate civil servant who has completed his/her traineeship.

Assimilation f assimilation; (Anpassung) adjustment (an +acc to).

assimilatorisch adj assimilatory, assimilative.

assimilieren* 1 vti to assimilate. 2 vr to become assimilated. sich an etw (acc) ~ (Mensch) to adjust to sth.

Assistent(in f) m assistant.

Assistenz f assistance. unter ~ von ... with the assistance of ...

Assistenz-: ~arzt m houseman (Brit), intern (US); ~professor m assistant professor.

assistieren* vi to assist (jdm sb).

Assonanz f (Poet) assonance.

Assoziation f association.

Assoziations-: ~freiheit f siehe Vereinigungsfreiheit; ~kette f chain of associations.

assoziativ adj (Psych, geh) associative.

assoziieren* (geh) 1 vt mit Grün assoziiere ich Ruhe I associate green with peace; ich assoziiere Schönes dabei or damit I associate it with something pleasant, it has pleasant associations for me; die Musik assoziierte bei mir Unangenehmes the music suggested something unpleasant to me.
2 vi to make associations. frei ~ to make free associations. 3 vr (a) (Vorstellungen etc) to have associations (in +dat, bei for). beim Anblick des Hauses ~ sich in or bei mir Kindheitserinnerungen when I see the house I think of my childhood. (b) (an-, zusammenschließen) sich mit jdm ~ to join with sb; sich an jdn/etw ~ to become associated to sb/sth.

assoziiert adj associated.

Assuan(stau)damm m Aswan (High) Dam.

Assyrer(in f) m -s, - Assyrian.

Assyrien [-iən] nt -s Assyria.

Assyrier(in f) [-iɐ, -iəriɐ] m -s, - siehe Assyrer(in).

Assyriologie f Assyriology.

assyrisch adj Assyrian.

Ast m -(e)s, "e (a) branch, bough; (fig: von Nerv) branch. sich in ~e teilen to branch; den ~ absägen, auf dem man sitzt (fig) to dig one's own grave; einen ~ durchsägen (hum) to snore like a grampus (inf), to saw wood (US inf); siehe absteigen (b). (b) (im Holz) knot. (c) (inf) (Rücken) back; (Buckel) hump(back), hunchback. sich einen ~ lachen (inf) to double up (with laughter).

AStA ['asta] m -s, Asten (Univ) abbr of Allgemeiner Studentenausschuß.

Ästchen nt dim of Ast.

asten (inf) 1 vi (a) (sich anstrengen) to slog (inf). (b) (büffeln) to swot. (c) aux sein (sich fortbewegen) to drag oneself. 2 vt to hump (inf), to lug (Brit inf).

Aster f -, -n aster, Michaelmas daisy.

Astgabel f fork (in a branch). eine ~ the fork of a branch.

Astheniker(in f) m -s, - asthenic.

Asthet m -en, -en aesthete.

Ästhetik f (a) (Wissenschaft) aesthetics sing. (b) (Schönheit) aesthetics pl. (c) (Schönheitssinn) aesthetic sense.

Ästhetiker(in f) m -s, - aesthetician.

Ästhetin f siehe Ästhet.

ästhetisch adj aesthetic.

ästhetisieren* (usu pej, geh) 1 vt to aestheticize. 2 vi to talk about aesthetics.

Ästhetizismus m (pej geh) aestheticism.

Ästhetizist(in f) m aestheticist.

ästhetizistisch adj (pej geh) aestheticist(ic).

Asthma nt -s, no pl asthma.

Asthmatiker(in f) m -s, - asthmatic.

asthmatisch adj asthmatic.

astig adj Holz knotty, gnarled.

Astloch nt knothole.

astral adj astral.

Astral-: ~körper, ~leib m (Philos) astral body; (iro inf) beautiful or heavenly body.

astrein adj (a) Holz, Brett free of knots. (b) (fig inf: moralisch einwandfrei) above board, on the level (inf). (c) (fig inf: echt) genuine. (d) (sl: prima) fantastic.

Astro-: ~loge m, ~login f astrologer; ~logie f astrology;

a~logisch adj astrological; ~naut(in f) m -en, -en astronaut; ~nautik f astronautics sing; a~nautisch adj astronautic(al); ~nom(in f) m astronomer; ~nomie f astronomy; a~nomisch adj (lit) astronomical; (fig auch) astronomic; a~nomische Navigation astronavigation.

astrophisch adj (Poet) not divided into strophes.

Astro-: ~physik f astrophysics sing; a~physikalisch adj astrophysical; ~physiker(in f) m astrophysicist.

Astwerk nt branches pl.

Äsung f (Hunt) grazing.

Asyl nt -s, -e (a) (Schutz) sanctuary no art (liter); (politisches ~) (political) asylum no art. jdm ~ gewähren to grant sb sanctuary (liter)/(political) asylum; um ~ bitten or nachsuchen (form) to ask or apply (form) for (political) asylum. (b) (old: Heim) home, asylum.

Asyl-: ~recht nt (Pol) right of (political) asylum; ~suchende(r) mf decl as adj, ~werber(in f) m (Aus) person seeking (political) asylum.

Asymmetrie f lack of symmetry, asymmetry.

asymmetrisch adj asymmetric(al); (fig) Gespräch one-sided.

Asymptote f -, -n asymptote.

asymptotisch adj asymptotic.

asynchron [-kro:n] adj asynchronous (form), out of synchronism.

asyndetisch adj (Ling) paratactic(al).

Asyndeton nt -s, Asyndeta (Ling) parataxis.

Aszendent m (a) (Astrol) ascendant. (b) (Vorfahr) ancestor, ascendant (form).

aszendieren* vi (a) aux sein (Astron) to be in the ascendant. (b) aux sein or haben (obs) to be promoted (zu to).

Aszese f -, no pl siehe Askese.

at ['a:'te:] abbr of Atmosphäre (Tech).

A.T. abbr of Altes Testament OT.

ata adv (baby-talk) ~ (~) gehen to go walkies (baby-talk).

ataktisch adj unco-ordinated.

Atavismus m atavism.

atavistisch adj atavistic.

Atelier [-'lie:] nt -s, -s studio. das Filmprojekt ging letzte Woche ins ~ shooting (on the film) started last week.

Atelier-: ~aufnahme f (a) (Produkt) studio shot; (b) usu pl (Vorgang) studio work no pl; ~fenster nt studio window; ~fest nt studio party; ~wohnung f studio apartment.

Atem m -s, no pl (a) (das Atmen) breathing. den ~ anhalten (lit, fig) to hold one's breath; mit angehaltenem ~ (lit) holding one's breath; (fig) with bated breath; einen kurzen ~ haben to be short-winded; wieder zu ~ kommen to get one's breath back; einen langen/den längeren ~ haben (fig) to have a lot of/more staying power; jdn in ~ halten to keep sb in suspense or on tenterhooks; das verschlug mir den ~ that took my breath away; siehe ausgehen.
(b) (lit, fig: ~luft) breath. ~ holen or schöpfen (lit) to take or draw a breath; (fig) to get one's breath back.
(c) (fig geh: Augenblick) in einem/im selben ~ in one/the same breath.

Atem-: ~beklemmung f difficulty in breathing; a~beraubend adj breathtaking; ~beschwerden pl trouble in breathing; unter ~beschwerden leiden to have trouble in breathing; ~gerät nt breathing apparatus; (Med) respirator; ~geräusch nt respiratory sounds pl; ~gymnastik f breathing exercises pl; ~holen nt -s, no pl breathing; man kommt nicht mehr zum ~holen (fig) you hardly have time to breathe; zum ~holen auftauchen to come up for air; ~lähmung f respiratory paralysis; a~los adj (lit, fig) breathless; ~losigkeit f breathlessness; ~luft f unsere ~luft the air we breathe; die ~luft anderer the air other people breathe; ~maske f breathing mask; not f difficulty in breathing; ~pause f (fig) breathing time no art, breathing space; eine ~pause einlegen/brauchen to take/need a breather; ~technik f breathing technique; ~übung f (Med) breathing exercise; ~wege pl (Anat) respiratory tracts pl; ~zentrum nt (Anat) respiratory centre; ~zug m breath; in einem/im selben ~zug (fig) in one/the same breath.

Atheismus m atheism.

Atheist m -en, -en atheist.

atheistisch adj atheist(ic).

Athen nt -s Athens.

Athener adj Athenian.

Athener(in f) m -s, - Athenian.

athenisch adj Athenian.

Äther m -s, no pl (a) ether. (b) (poet) (a)ether (poet); (Rad) air. etw in den ~ schicken to put sth on the air; über den ~ over the air.

ätherisch adj (Liter, Chem) ethereal.

ätherisieren* vt to etherize.

Äther-: ~krieg m (Press sl) radio propaganda war; ~maske f ether mask; ~narkose f etherization; ~rausch m rausch narcosis, etherrausch; ~wellen pl (Rad) radio waves pl.

Äthiopien [ɛ'tio:piən] nt -s Ethiopia, Abyssinia.

Äthiopier(in f) [-piɐ, -iəriɐ] -s, - Ethiopian, Abyssinian.

Athlet m -en, -en (a) athlete. (b) (inf: kräftig) he-man (inf).

Athletik f -, no pl athletics sing.

Athletiker(in f) m -s, - athletic type.

athletisch adj athletic.

Äthyl alkohol m ethyl alcohol.

Äthyl äther m ethyl ether.

Atlant m -en, -en atlas.

Atlanten pl of Atlas¹.

Atlantik m -s Atlantic.

Atlantikwall m (Mil Hist) Atlantic Wall.

atlantisch adj Atlantic. ein ~es Hoch a high-pressure area

over/from the Atlantic; **der A~e Ozean** the Atlantic Ocean.
Atlas[1] *m* - *or* **-ses, Atlanten** *or* **-se** atlas.
Atlas[2] *m* -, *no pl* (*Myth*) Atlas.
Atlas[3] *m* **-ses, -se** (*Seiden~*) satin; (*Baumwolle*) sateen.
Atlasseide *f* satin.
atmen 1 *vt* (*lit, fig geh*) to breathe. 2 *vi* to breathe, to respire (*form*). **frei ~** (*fig*) to breathe freely.
Atmosphäre *f* -, **-n** (*Phys, fig*) atmosphere.
Atmosphären-: **~druck** *m* atmospheric pressure; **~überdruck** *m* (a) atmospheric excess pressure; (b) (*Maßeinheit*) atmosphere (of pressure) above atmospheric pressure.
atmosphärisch *adj* atmospheric. **~e Störungen** atmospherics.
Atmung *f* -, *no pl* breathing; (*Eccl, Med*) respiration.
Atmungs-: **~apparat** *m siehe* **Atemgerät; ~organe** *pl* respiratory organs *pl*; **~zentrum** *nt siehe* **Atemzentrum.**
Atoll *nt* **-s, -e** atoll.
Atom *nt* **-s, -e** atom.
Atom- *in cpds* atomic; **~abfall** *m* nuclear *or* radioactive *or* atomic waste; **~angriff** *m* nuclear attack; **~antrieb** *m* nuclear *or* atomic propulsion; **ein U-Boot mit ~antrieb** a nuclear-powered submarine.
atomar *adj* atomic, nuclear; *Struktur* atomic; *Drohung* nuclear.
Atom-: **~basis** *f* nuclear base; **~behörde** *f* Atomic Energy Authority (*Brit*) *or* Commission (*US*); **a~betrieben** *adj* nuclear-powered; **~bombe** *f* atomic *or* atom bomb; **~bombenexplosion** *f* atomic *or* nuclear explosion; **a~bombensicher** *adj* atomic *or* nuclear blast-proof; **~bombenversuch** *m* atomic *or* nuclear test; **~bomber** *m* nuclear bomber; **~bunker** *m* nuclear *or* nuclear blast-proof bunker; **~busen** *m* (*dated inf*) big bust *or* boobs *pl* (*inf*); **~ei** *nt* (*inf*) dome-shaped reactor, reactor dome; **~energie** *f siehe* **Kernenergie; ~explosion** *f* atomic *or* nuclear explosion; **~forscher** *m* nuclear scientist; **~forschung** *f* atomic *or* nuclear research; **~gefahr** *f* danger from radiation; **a~getrieben** *adj* nuclear-powered; **~gewicht** *nt* atomic weight.
atomisch *adj* (*Sw*) *siehe* **atomar.**
atomisieren* *vt* to atomize; (*fig*) to smash to pieces *or* smithereens.
Atomismus *m* atomism.
Atom-: **~kern** *m* atomic nucleus; **~klub** *m* (*Press sl*) nuclear club; **~kraft** *f* atomic *or* nuclear power; **~kraftwerk** *nt* atomic *or* nuclear power station; **~krieg** *m* atomic *or* nuclear war; **~macht** *f* nuclear power; **~meiler** *m siehe* **Kernreaktor; ~modell** *nt* model of the atom; **~müll** *m* atomic *or* nuclear *or* radioactive waste; **~physik** *f* atomic *or* nuclear physics *sing*; **~physiker** *m* nuclear physicist; **~pilz** *m* mushroom cloud; **~rakete** *f* nuclear-powered rocket; (*Waffe*) nuclear missile; **~reaktor** *m* atomic *or* nuclear reactor; **~rüstung** *f* nuclear armament; **~schwelle** *f* nuclear threshold; **~spaltung** *f* nuclear fission; **die erste ~spaltung** the first splitting of the atom; **~sperrvertrag** *m siehe* **~waffensperrvertrag; ~sprengkopf** *m* atomic *or* nuclear warhead; **~stopp** *m* nuclear ban; **~strahlung** *f* nuclear radiation; **~streitmacht** *f* nuclear capability; **~strom** *m* (*inf*) electricity generated by nuclear power; **~technik** *f* nuclear technology, nucleonics *sing*; **~test** *m* nuclear test; **~teststoppabkommen** *nt* nuclear test ban treaty; **~tod** *m* (*Press sl*) nuclear death; **~triebwerk** *nt* nuclear engine; **~uhr** *f* atomic clock; **~versuch** *m* nuclear test; **~versuchsstopp** *m* nuclear test ban; **~waffe** *f* nuclear *or* atomic weapon; **a~waffenfrei** *adj* nuclear-free; **~waffensperrvertrag** *m* nuclear *or* atomic weapons non-proliferation treaty; **~waffenversuch** *m* nuclear test; **~wissenschaft** *f* nuclear *or* atomic science; **~wissenschaftler** *m* nuclear *or* atomic scientist; **~zeit** *f* nuclear time; **~zeitalter** *nt* atomic *or* nuclear age; **~zerfall** *m* atomic disintegration *or* decay; **~zertrümmerung** *f* splitting of the atom.
atonal *adj* atonal.
Atonalität *f* atonality.
atoxisch *adj* (*form*) non-toxic.
Atrium *nt* (*Archit, Anat*) atrium.
Atriumhaus *nt* house built around an atrium *or* open court.
Atrophie *f* (*Med*) atrophy.
atrophisch *adj* atrophied.
ätsch *interj* (*inf*) ha-ha.
Attaché [ata'ʃeː] *m* **-s, -s** attaché.
Attacke *f* -, **-n** (*Angriff*) attack; (*Mil Hist*) (cavalry) charge. **eine ~ gegen jdn/etw reiten** (*lit*) to charge sb/sth; (*fig*) to attack sb/sth.
attackieren* *vt* (*angreifen*) to attack; (*Mil Hist*) to charge.
Attentat [-taːt] *nt* **-(e)s, -e** assassination; (*~sversuch*) assassination attempt. **ein ~ auf jdn verüben** to assassinate sb; to make an attempt on sb's life; **ich habe ein ~ auf dich vor** (*hum*) listen, I've got a great idea.
Attentäter(in *f***)** *m* **-s, -** assassin; (*bei gescheitertem Versuch*) would-be assassin.
Attest *nt* **-(e)s, -e** certificate.
attestieren* *vt* (*form*) to certify. **jdm seine Dienstuntauglichkeit** *etc* ~ to certify sb as unfit for duty *etc.*
Ätti *m* **-s, -s** (*Sw inf*) granddad (*inf*).
Attika *nt* **-s** (*Geog*) Attica.
attisch *adj* Attic.
Attitüde *f* -, **-n** (*geh*) (a) attitude. (b) (*Geste*) gesture.
Attraktion *f* attraction.
attraktiv *adj* attractive.
Attraktivität *f* attractiveness.
Attrappe *f* -, **-n** dummy; (*fig: Schein*) sham. **die ~ eines ... a** dummy ...; **ihr Busen ist nur/bei ihr ist alles ~ her** bosom/everything about her is false.
Attribut *nt* **-(e)s, -e** (*geh, Gram*) attribute.

Attributivsatz *m* (*Gram*) relative clause.
atü [a'tyː] *abbr of* **Atmosphärenüberdruck.**
Atü *nt* **-s, -** atmospheric excess pressure.
atypisch *adj* (*geh*) atypical.
Ätze *m* **-s** (*dial, inf*) (a) *abbr of* **Arthur.** (b) (*Anrede*) mate (*inf*), mac (*US inf*), Jimmy (*Scot*).
ätzen *vt* (*Hunt*) to feed.
ätzen *vti* (a) to etch. (b) (*Säure*) to corrode. (c) (*Med*) to cauterize.
ätzend *adj* (a) (*lit*) *Säure* corrosive; (*Med*) caustic. (b) *Geruch* pungent; *Rauch* choking; *Spott* caustic.
Ätz-: **~mittel** *nt* (*Chem*) corrosive; (*Med*) cautery, caustic; **~natron** *nt* caustic soda; **~stift** *m* (*Med*) cautery; (*bei Friseur*) styptic pencil.
Atzung *f* (*Hunt, hum*) (*Vorgang*) feeding; (*Futter*) food, fodder. **wann gibt es ~?** (*hum*) when is it feeding time?
Ätzung *f, no pl siehe vti* etching; corrosion; cauterization, cautery.
Au *f* -, **-en** (*S Ger, Aus*) *siehe* **Aue.**
au *interj* (a) ow, ouch. **~, das war knapp!** oh *or* God, that was close! (b) (*Ausdruck der Begeisterung*) oh.
aua *interj* ow, ouch.
aubergine [ober'ʒiːnə] *adj pred,* **auberginefarben** *adj* aubergine.
Aubergine [ober'ʒiːnə] *f* aubergine, eggplant.
auch *adv* (a) (*zusätzlich, gleichfalls*) also, too, as well. **die Engländer müssen ~ zugeben, daß** ... the English must admit too *or* as well *or* must also admit that ...; **~ die Engländer müssen ...** the English too must ...; **das kann ich ~ I** can do that too *or* as well; **das ist ~ möglich** that's possible too *or* as well, that's also possible; **ja, das ~ yes, that too; ~ gut** that's OK too; **du ~?** you too?, you as well?; **~ nicht** not ... either; **~ der Vater war nicht ...** the father wasn't ... either; **das ist ~ nicht richtig** that's not right either; **er kommt — ich ~** he's coming — so am I *or* me too; **ich will eins — ich ~ I** want one — so do I *or* me too; **er kommt nicht — ich ~ nicht** he's not coming — nor *or* neither am I *or* I'm not either *or* me neither; **ich mag das nicht — ich ~** nicht I don't like that — nor *or* neither do I *or* I don't either *or* me neither; **nicht nur ..., sondern ~** not only ... but also ..., not only ... but ... too *or* as well; **~ das noch!** that's all I needed!
 (b) (*tatsächlich*) too, as well. **und das tue/meine ich ~** and I'll do it/I mean it too *or* as well; **wenn sie sagt, sie geht, dann geht sie ~** if she says she's going then she'll go; **Frechheit! — ja, das ist es ~** what a cheek! — you can say that again; **du siehst müde aus — das bin ich ~** you look tired — (so) I am; **das ist er ja ~** (and so) he is; **das müßt ihr aber ~ tun** but you have to do it; **so ist es ~** (so) it is.
 (c) (*sogar*) even. **~ wenn du Vorfahrt hast** even if you (do) have right of way; **ohne ~ nur zu fragen** without even asking.
 (d) (*emph*) **den Teufel ~!** damn it (all)!; **zum Donnerwetter ~!** blast it!; **so ein Dummkopf ~!** what an absolute blockhead!; **so was Ärgerliches aber ~!** it's really too annoying!; **wozu ~?** what on earth *or* whatever for?
 (e) (**~** *immer*) **wie dem ~ sei** be that as it may; **was er ~ sagen** mag whatever he might say; **und mag er ~ noch so klug sein, wenn er ~ noch so klug ist** however clever he may be; **so schnell er ~ laufen mag** however fast he runs *or* may run, no matter how fast he runs; *siehe* **immer.**
Auch- *in cpds* (*iro*) would-be; **~dichter** *m* would-be poet; **~maler** *m* would-be painter.
Audienz *f* (*bei Papst, König etc*) audience.
Audienzsaal *m* audience chamber.
Audimax *nt* -, *no pl* (*Univ sl*) main lecture hall.
audiovisuell *adj* audiovisual.
auditiv *adj* auditory.
Auditorium *nt* (a) (*Hörsaal*) lecture hall. **~ Maximum** (*Univ*) main lecture hall. (b) (*geh: Zuhörerschaft*) audience.
Aue *f* -, **-n** (a) (*dial, poet*) meadow, pasture, lea (*poet*), mead (*poet*). (b) (*dial: Insel*) island.
Auerbachsprung *m* (*Sport*) backward *or* reverse somersault.
Auerhahn *m* **-(e)s, Auerhähne** *or* (*Hunt*) **-en** capercaillie.
Auerhenne *f,* **Auerhuhn** *nt* capercaillie (hen).
Auer\|ochse *m* aurochs.
Auf *nt inv:* **das ~ und Ab** *or* **Nieder** the up and down; (*fig*) the ups and downs; **das ~ und Ab des Kolbens** the up(ward) and down-(ward) movement of the piston.
auf 1 *prep siehe auch* **Substantive, Verben** *etc* (a) + *dat* on; (*esp Schriftsprache auch*) upon. **~** (*der Insel*) **Skye** on the island of Skye; **~ den Orkney-Inseln** on *or* in the Orkney Islands; **~ See** at sea; **~ meinem Zimmer** in my room; **~ der Bank/Post/dem Rathaus** at the bank/post office/town hall; **mein Geld ist ~ der Bank** my money is in the bank; **~ der Straße** on *or* in the street.
 (b) **~ der Geige spielen** to play the violin; **etw ~ der Geige spielen** to play sth on the violin; **~ einem Ohr taub/einem Auge kurzsichtig sein** to be deaf in one ear/short-sighted in one eye; **das hat nichts ~ sich** (*inf*) it does not mean anything; **was hat es damit ~ sich?** what does it mean?; **die Tachonadel steht ~ 105** the speedometer is at *or* on 105; **~ der Fahrt/dem Weg** *etc* on the journey/way *etc*; **Greenwich liegt ~ 0 Grad** Greenwich lies at 0 degrees.
 (c) + *acc* on, onto. **etw ~ etw heben** to lift sth onto sth; **etw ~ etw stellen** to put sth on(to) *or* on top of sth; **sich ~ etw setzen/legen** to sit/lie (down) on sth; **sich ~ die Straße setzen** to sit down on *or* in the road; **das Wrack ist ~ den Meeresgrund gesunken** the wreck sank to the bottom of the sea; **jdm ~ den Rücken klopfen** to slap sb on the back; **er fiel ~ den Rücken** he fell on(to) his back; **etw ~ einen Zettel schreiben** to write sth on a piece of paper; **etw ~ einen Zettel abschreiben** to copy sth on(to) a piece of paper; **er ist ~ die Orkney-Inseln gefahren** he has gone to the Orkney Islands; **ich bringe dich ~ den Flugplatz**

I'll take you to the airport; jdn ~ **den Mond schießen** to send sb to the moon; **er segelt ~ das Meer hinaus** he is sailing out to sea; **man konnte nicht weiter als ~ 10 m herankommen** you couldn't get any nearer than 10 m; **geh mal ~ die Seite** go to the side; **Geld ~ die Bank bringen** to take money to the bank; (*einzahlen*) to put money in the bank; ~ **sein Zimmer/die Post/die Polizei** *etc* **gehen** to go to one's room/the post office/the police *etc*; ~s **Gymnasium gehen** to go to (the) grammar school; **die Uhr ~ 10 stellen** to put *or* set the clock to 10; **Heiligabend fällt ~ einen Dienstag** Christmas Eve falls on a Tuesday; **die Sitzung ~ morgen legen/verschieben** to arrange the meeting for tomorrow/to postpone the meeting until tomorrow; ~ **eine Party/ein Bankett** *etc* **gehen** to go to a party/banquet *etc*; ~ **ihn!** at him!, get him!

(d) +*acc* ~ **10 km/drei Tage** for 10 km/three days; ~ **eine Tasse Kaffee/eine Zigarette(nlänge)** for a cup of coffee/a smoke.

(e) +*acc* (*Häufung*) **Niederlage ~ Niederlage** defeat after *or* upon defeat; **Beleidigung ~ Beleidigung** insult upon insult; **einer ~ den anderen** one after another.

(f) +*acc* (*im Hinblick auf*) for. **ein Manuskript ~ Fehler prüfen** to check a manuscript for errors.

(g) +*acc* (*als Reaktion, auch:* **auf ... hin**) at. ~ **seinen Vorschlag (hin)** at his suggestion; ~ **meinen Brief hin** because of *or* on account of my letter; ~ **seine Bitte (hin)** at *or* upon his request.

(h) (*sl: in einer bestimmten Art*) ~ **die Elegante/Ehrliche** *etc* elegantly/honestly *etc*; ~ **die Billige** on the cheap; **komm mir bloß nicht ~ die wehleidige Tour!** just don't try the sad approach with me.

(i) (*sonstige Anwendungen*) **es geht ~ Weihnachten zu** Christmas is approaching; **er kam ~ mich zu und sagte ...** he came up to me and said ...; **ich war die halbe Nacht ~ mich zukam as** he was coming towards me; **die Nacht (von Montag) ~ Dienstag** Monday night; **die Hausaufgaben habt ihr ~ Freitag** (*inf*) the homework is for Friday, you have until Friday for the homework; **das Bier geht ~ mich** (*inf*) the beer's on me; ~ **wen geht das Bier?** (*inf*) who's paying for the beer?; ~ **das** *or* ~**s schändlichste/liebenswürdigste** *etc* (*geh*) most shamefully/kindly *etc*; ~ **einen Polizisten kommen 1.000 Bürger** there is one policeman for *or* to every 1,000 citizens; ~ **jeden kamen zwei Flaschen Bier** there were two bottles of beer (for) each; ~ **den Millimeter/die Sekunde genau** precise to the *or* to within one millimetre/second; ~ **unseren lieben Onkel Egon/ein glückliches Gelingen** *etc* here's to dear Uncle Egon/a great success; ~ **deine Gesundheit** (your very) good health; ~ **morgen/bald** till tomorrow/soon; **zwanzig ~ sieben** (*dial*) twenty to seven; **die Dauer ~ ein Jahr reduzieren** to reduce the duration to one year; **ein Brett ~ einen Meter absägen** to saw a plank down to one metre.

2 *adv* (a) (*offen*) open. **Mund/Fenster ~!** open your mouth/the window.

(b) (*hinauf*) up. ~ **und ab** *or* **nieder** (*geh*) up and down.

(c) (*sonstige Anwendungen*) **Helm/Brille ~!** helmets/glasses on; **ich war die halbe Nacht ~** I've been up half the night; **kaum drei Wochen ~, muß er nun schon wieder ins Krankenhaus** he's hardly been out of bed three weeks and he's already got to go back into hospital; **nachmittags Unterricht, und dann noch soviel ~!** (*inf*) school in the afternoon, and all that homework too!; **Handschuhe an, Wollmütze ~, so wird er sich nicht erkälten** with his gloves and woollen hat on he won't catch cold; **er konnte nicht/wollte ~** (*inf*) he could not/wanted to get up; ~**!** (*aufstehen*) (get) up!; ~**, laßt uns beginnen!** (*old*) come, let us start; ~ **nach Chicago!** let's go to Chicago; ~ **geht's!** let's go!; ~ **und davon** up and away, off; ~**, an die Arbeit!** come on, let's get on with it!; **Sprung ~! marsch, marsch!** (*Mil*) jump to it!, at the double!; *siehe* **aufsein**.

3 *conj* (*old, liter*) ~ **daß** that (*old, liter*); ~ **daß wir niemals vergessen mögen** lest we should ever forget, that we might never forget.

auf|addieren* *vtr sep* to add up.

auf|arbeiten *vt sep* (a) (*erneuern*) to refurbish, to do up; *Möbel etc auch* to recondition. (b) (*auswerten*) *Literatur etc* to incorporate critically; *Vergangenheit* to reappraise. (c) (*erledigen*) *Korrespondenz, Liegengebliebenes* to catch up with *or* on, to clear.

Auf|arbeitung *f siehe vt* refurbishing; reconditioning; critical incorporation; reappraisal; catching up. **die ~ des Liegengebliebenen dauerte einige Zeit** it took some time to catch up with *or* clear the backlog.

auf|atmen *vi sep* (*lit, fig*) to breathe *or* heave a sigh of relief. **ein A~** a sigh of relief.

aufbacken *vt sep* to warm *or* crisp up.

aufbahren *vt sep Sarg* to lay on the bier; *Leiche* to lay out. **einen Toten feierlich ~** to put a person's body to lie in state.

Aufbahrung *f* laying out; (*feierlich*) lying in state.

Aufbahrungshalle *f* funeral parlour, chapel of rest.

Aufbau *m* (a) *no pl* (*das Aufbauen*) construction, building; (*von neuem Staat*) building; (*das Wiederaufbauen*) reconstruction. **der wirtschaftliche ~** the building up of the economy. (b) *pl* **-ten** (*Aufgebautes, Aufgesetztes*) top; (*von Auto, LKW*) coachwork *no pl*, body. (c) *no pl* (*Struktur*) structure.

Aufbau|arbeit *f* construction (work); (*Wiederaufbau*) reconstruction (work).

aufbauen *sep* **1** *vt* (a) (*errichten*) to put up; *zusammensetzbare Möbel, Lautsprecheranlage auch* to fix up; (*hinstellen*) *Ausstellungsstücke, kaltes Buffet, Brettspiel etc* to set *or* lay out; (*inf*) *Posten, Ordnungspersonal etc* to post; (*zusammenbauen*) *Motor, elektrische Schaltung etc* to put together, to assemble.

(b) (*daraufbauen*) *Stockwerk* to add (on), to build on; *Karosserie* to mount.

(c) (*fig: gestalten*) *Organisation, Land, Armee, Geschäft, Angriff, Druck, Spannung, Verbindung, Eiweiß* to build up; *Zerstörtes* to rebuild; *Theorie, Plan, System* to construct. **sich** (*dat*) **eine (neue) Existenz** *or* **ein Leben ~** to build (up) a new life for oneself.

(d) (*fig: fördern, weiterentwickeln*) *Gesundheit, Kraft* to build up; *Star, Politiker auch* to promote. **jdn/etw zu etw ~** to build sb/sth up into sth.

(e) (*fig: gründen*) **etw auf etw** (*dat or acc*) ~ to base *or* found sth on sth.

(f) (*strukturieren, konstruieren*) to construct; *Maschine auch* to build; *Aufsatz, Rede, Organisation auch, Komposition* to structure.

2 *vi* (a) (*sich gründen*) to be based *or* founded (*auf* +*dat or acc* on).

(b) **wir wollen ~ und nicht zerstören** we want to build and not destroy.

3 *vr* (a) (*inf: sich postieren*) to take up position. **sie bauten sich in einer Reihe auf** they formed (themselves) up into a line; **er baute sich vor dem Feldwebel/Lehrer auf und ...** he stood up in front of the sergeant/teacher and ...; **sich vor jdm drohend ~** to plant oneself in front of sb (*inf*); **sie bewegte sich auf uns zu, baute sich auf und ...** she approached us, drew herself up (to her full height) and ...

(b) (*sich bilden*) *Wolken, Hochdruckgebiet* to build up.

(c) (*bestehen aus*) **sich aus etw ~** to be built up *or* composed of sth.

(d) (*sich gründen*) **sich auf etw** (*dat or acc*) ~ to be based *or* founded on sth.

aufbäumen *vr sep* (*Tier*) to rear. **sich gegen jdn/etw ~** (*fig*) to rebel *or* revolt against sb/sth; **sich vor Schmerz ~** to writhe with pain.

Aufbauprinzip *nt* structural principle. **die Motoren sind alle nach demselben ~ konstruiert** the engines are all constructed on the same principle; **diese Krimis folgen alle demselben ~** these thrillers are all structured on the same lines.

aufbauschen *sep* **1** *vt* to blow out; *Segel auch* to (make) billow out, to belly out; (*fig*) to blow up, to exaggerate. **2** *vr* to blow out; (*Segel auch*) to billow (out), to belly (out); (*fig*) to blow up (*zu* into).

Aufbau-: ~**studium** *nt* (*Univ*) research studies *pl*; ~**stufe** *f*, ~**zug** *m* (*Sch*) school class leading to university entrance, ≈ sixth form (*Brit*).

Aufbauten *pl* (*Naut*) superstructure.

aufbeben *vi sep* (*geh*) to shudder.

aufbegehren *vi sep* (*geh*) to rebel, to revolt (*gegen* against).

aufbehalten* *vt sep irreg Hut, Brille etc* to keep on; *Tür, Schrank etc* to leave *or* keep open; *Knopf* to leave *or* keep undone.

aufbeißen *vt sep irreg Verpackung etc* to bite open; *Nuß etc* to crack with one's teeth. **sich** (*dat*) **die Lippe ~** to bite one's lip (and make it bleed).

aufkommen* *vi sep irreg* (*inf*) (a) (*öffnen*) to get open. (b) *Aufgabe* to get as homework. **habt ihr keine Hausarbeiten ~?** didn't you get any homework? (c) *Essen* to (manage to) eat up. **ich habe nur die halbe Portion ~** I could only manage (to eat) half a portion.

aufbereiten* *vt sep* to process; *Erze, Kohlen* to prepare, to dress; *Trinkwasser auch* to purify; *Text etc* to work up. **etw literarisch/dramaturgisch ~** to turn sth into literature/to adapt sth for the theatre.

Aufbereitung *f siehe vt* processing; preparation, dressing; purification; working up; adaptation.

Aufbereitungs|anlage *f* processing plant.

aufbessern *vt sep* to improve; *Gehalt etc auch* to increase.

Aufbesserung, Aufbeßrung *f siehe vt* improvement; increase.

aufbewahren* *vt sep* to keep; *Lebensmittel auch* to store; (*behalten*) *alte Zeitungen etc auch* to save; *Wertsachen etc* to look after. **ein Dokument gut/Medikamente kühl ~** to keep a document in a safe place/medicines in a cool place; **jds Dokumente ~** to be looking after sb's documents, to have sb's documents in one's keeping; **kann ich hier mein Gepäck ~ lassen?** can I leave my luggage here?

Aufbewahrung *f* (a) *siehe vt* keeping; storage; saving. **jdm etw zur ~ übergeben** to give sth to sb for safekeeping, to put sth in(to) sb's safekeeping; **jdm etw zur ~ anvertrauen** to entrust sth to sb's safekeeping; **einen Koffer in ~ geben** to deposit a suitcase (at the left-luggage).

(b) (*Stelle*) left-luggage (office) (*Brit*), check room (*US*).

Aufbewahrungs|ort *m place where sth is kept, home* (*inf*). **etw an einen sicheren ~ bringen** to put sth in a safe place; **das ist kein geeigneter ~ für Medikamente** that is not the right place to keep medicines.

Aufbewahrungsschein *m* left-luggage receipt *or* ticket (*Brit*), check room ticket (*US*).

aufbiegen *sep irreg* **1** *vt* to bend open. **2** *vr* (*Ring etc*) to bend open; (*sich hochbiegen: Zweig etc*) to bend itself upright.

aufbieten *vt sep irreg* (a) *Menschen, Mittel* to muster; *Kräfte, Fähigkeiten auch* to summon (up); *Militär, Polizei* to call in; (*old*) *Soldaten* to levy (*old*).

(b) *Brautpaar* to call the banns of. **die beiden werden morgen aufgeboten** their banns will be called *or* read tomorrow.

(c) (*bei Auktionen*) to put up.

Aufbietung *f siehe vt* (a) mustering; summoning (up); calling in; levy. **unter** *or* **bei ~ aller Kräfte ...** summoning (up) all his/her *etc* strength ...

aufbinden *vt sep irreg* (a) (*öffnen*) *Schuh etc* to undo, to untie.

(b) (*hochbinden*) *Haare* to put up *or* tie; *Pflanzen, Zweige etc* to tie (up) straight.

(c) (*befestigen*) to tie on. **etw auf etw** (*acc*) ~ to tie sth on(to) sth.

(d) **laß dir doch so etwas nicht** ~ (*fig*) don't fall for that; **jdm eine Lüge** ~ to take sb in, to tell sb a lie.

(e) (*Typ*) *Buch* to bind.

aufblähen *sep* **1** *vt* to blow out; *Segel auch* to fill, to billow out, to belly out; (*Med*) to distend, to swell; (*fig*) to inflate.

2 *vr* to blow out; (*Segel auch*) to billow *or* belly out; (*Med*) to become distended *or* swollen; (*fig pej*) to puff oneself up. **so ein aufgeblähter Affe!** (*pej*) what a puffed-up idiot!

Aufblähung *f* (*Med*) distension.

aufblasbar *adj* inflatable.

aufblasen *sep irreg* **1** *vt* **(a)** to blow up; *Reifen etc auch* to inflate; *Backen* to puff out, to blow out. **(b)** (*hochblasen*) to blow up. **2** *vr* (*fig pej*) to puff oneself up; *siehe* **aufgeblasen**.

aufbleiben *vi sep irreg aux sein* **(a)** to stay up. **wegen jdm** ~ to wait *or* stay up for sb. **(b)** (*geöffnet bleiben*) to stay open.

Aufblende *f* (*Film*) fade-in.

aufblenden *sep* **1** *vi* (*Phot*) to open up the lens, to increase the aperture; (*Film*) to fade in; (*Aut*) to turn the headlights on full (beam). **er fährt aufgeblendet** he drives on full beam. **2** *vt* (*Aut*) *Scheinwerfer* to turn on full (beam); (*Film*) *Einstellung* to fade in.

aufblicken *vi sep* to look up. **zu jdm/etw** ~ (*lit, fig*) to look up to sb/sth.

aufblinken *vi sep* (*lit, fig*) to flash; (*Aut inf: kurz aufblenden*) to flash (one's headlights).

aufblitzen *vi sep* **(a)** to flash. **(b)** *aux sein* (*fig*) (*Emotion, Haß etc*) to flare up; (*Gedanke, Erinnerung*) to flash through one's mind. **etw blitzt in jdm auf** sth flares up in(side) sb/flashes through sb's mind.

aufblühen *vi sep aux sein* **(a)** (*Knospe*) to blossom (out); (*Blume auch*) to bloom. **(b)** (*fig*) (*Mensch*) to blossom out; (*Wissenschaft, Kultur auch*) to (begin to) flourish; (*Gesicht*) to take on a rosy bloom.

aufbocken *vt sep Auto* to jack up; *Motorrad* to put on its stand.

aufbohren *vt sep* to bore *or* drill a hole in; *Zahn auch* to drill.

aufbranden *vi sep aux sein* (*geh*) to surge; (*fig: Beifall*) to burst forth. **Beifall brandete immer wieder auf** there was wave upon wave of applause.

aufbraten *vt sep irreg Essen* to warm up; (*in der Pfanne auch*) to fry up.

aufbrauchen *sep* **1** *vt* to use up. **seine Geduld ist aufgebraucht** his patience is exhausted. **2** *vr* (*sich verbrauchen*) to get used up; (*Reifen: sich abnutzen*) to get worn out, to wear out.

aufbrausen *vi sep aux sein* **(a)** (*Brandung etc*) to surge; (*Brausetablette, Brause etc*) to fizz up; (*fig: Beifall, Jubel*) to break out, to burst forth. **(b)** (*fig: Mensch*) to flare up, to fly off the handle (*inf*).

aufbrausend *adj Temperament* irascible; *Mensch auch* quick-tempered, liable to flare up.

aufbrechen *sep irreg* **1** *vt* to break *or* force open; *Deckel* to prise off; *Tresor auch, Auto* to break into; *Boden, Asphalt, Oberfläche* to break up; (*geh*) *Brief* to break open; (*fig*) *System, soziale Struktur etc* to break down.

2 *vi aux sein* **(a)** (*sich öffnen*) (*Straßenbelag etc*) to break up; (*Knospen*) to (burst) open; (*Wunde*) to open.

(b) (*fig: Konflikte, Haß etc*) to break out.

(c) (*sich auf den Weg machen*) to start *or* set out *or* off.

aufbrennen *sep irreg* **1** *vt* **(a)** **einem Tier ein Zeichen** ~ to brand an animal; **jdm eins** ~ (*inf*) (*schlagen*) to wallop *or* clout sb (one) (*inf*); (*anschießen*) to shoot sb, to put a slug into sb (*sl*).

(b) (*verbrennen*) *Kerze, Kohlen etc* to burn up.

2 *vi aux sein* (*lit, fig*) (*Baum etc*) to go up in flames; (*Kerze*) to burn out; (*Feuer, Leidenschaft*) to flare up.

aufbringen *sep irreg* **1** *vt* **(a)** (*beschaffen*) to find; *Geld auch* to raise; *Kraft, Mut, Energie auch* to summon up.

(b) (*erzürnen*) to make angry, to irritate. **jdn gegen jdn/etw** ~ to set sb against sb/sth; *siehe* **aufgebracht**.

(c) (*ins Leben rufen*) to start; *Gerücht auch* to set going, to put about.

(d) (*Naut*) *Schiff* to seize; (*in Hafen zwingen*) to bring in.

(e) (*auftragen*) *Farbe etc* to put on, to apply. **etw auf etw** (*acc*) ~ to put sth on, to apply sth to sth.

(f) (*dial: aufbekommen*) *Tür etc* to get open.

Aufbruch *m* **(a)** *no pl* (*Abreise, das Losgehen*) departure. **das Zeichen zum** ~ **geben** to give the signal to set out *or* off; **der** ~ **ins 20. Jahrhundert** the emergence into the 20th century; **jdn zum** ~ **mahnen** to remind sb that it is time to set out *or* off; **eine Zeit des** ~**s** a time of new departures.

(b) (*aufgebrochene Stelle*) crack.

Aufbruchs-: **a**~**bereit** *adj* ready to set off *or* go *or* depart; ~**signal** *nt* signal to set off; **hast du das** ~**signal gehört?** did you hear the off?; ~**stimmung** *f* **hier herrscht schon** ~**stimmung** (*bei Party etc*) it's all breaking up; (*in Gastwirtschaft*) they're packing up; **es herrschte allgemeine** ~**stimmung (unter den Gästen)** the party was breaking up; **bist du schon in** ~**stimmung?** are you wanting *or* ready to go already?

aufbrühen *vt sep* to brew up (*inf*).

aufbrüllen *vi sep* to shout *or* yell out; (*Tier*) to bellow.

aufbrummen *sep* **1** *vt* (*inf*) **jdm etw** ~ to give sb sth; **jdm die Kosten** ~ to land sb with the costs (*inf*). **2** *vi* **(a)** to roar out. **(b)** *aux sein* (*Aut inf*) to bang *or* prang (*inf*) (*auf* +*acc* into); (*Naut sl*) to run aground, to hit the bottom.

aufbuddeln *vt sep* (*N Ger*) *siehe* **aufgraben**.

aufbügeln *vt sep* **(a)** *Kleidungsstück* to iron out; (*fig inf*) to vamp up (*inf*). **(b)** *Flicken, Bild etc* to iron on. **Flicken zum A**~ iron-on patches.

aufbumsen *vi sep* (*inf*) **(a)** *aux sein* to bang. **etw auf etw** (*dat*) ~ **lassen** to plump *or* plonk (*inf*) sth down on sth; **mit dem Hinterkopf** ~ to bump *or* bang the back of one's head. **(b)** **mit den Schuhen** ~ to stamp about.

aufbürden *vt sep* (*geh*) **jdm etw** ~ (*lit*) to load sth onto sb; (*fig*) to encumber sb with sth; **jdm die Schuld für etw** ~ to put the blame for sth on sb.

aufbürsten *vt sep etw* ~ to give sth a brush, to brush sth up.

aufdämmern *vi sep aux sein* (*geh*) (*Morgen, Tag*) to dawn, to break; (*fig: Verdacht*) to arise. **der Gedanke/die Einsicht dämmerte in ihm auf** the idea/realization dawned on him; **ein Funken Hoffnung dämmerte auf** a ray of hope glimmered.

auf daß *conj siehe* **daß 3**.

aufdecken *sep* **1** *vt* **(a)** *jdn* to uncover; *Bett(decke)* to turn down; *Gefäß* to open; *Spielkarten* to show.

(b) (*fig*) *Wahrheit, Verschwörung, Zusammenhänge* to discover, to uncover; *Verbrechen auch* to expose; *Schwäche* to lay bare; *Geheimnis, Rätsel* to solve; *wahren Charakter* to disclose, to lay bare, to expose.

(c) (*auf den Eßtisch stellen*) to put on the table. **das Geschirr** ~ to lay (*Brit*) *or* set the table.

2 *vi* to lay (*Brit*) *or* set the table.

Aufdeckung *f siehe* *vt* **(b)** uncovering; exposing; exposure; laying bare; solving; disclosing, disclosure.

aufdonnern *vr sep* (*pej inf*) to tart oneself up (*pej inf*), to get dolled up (*inf*) *or* tarted up (*pej inf*); *siehe* **aufgedonnert**.

aufdrängeln *vt sep* (*inf*) *siehe* **aufdrängen 1**.

aufdrängen *sep irreg* **1** *vt* **jdm etw** ~ to impose *or* force *or* push sth on sb.

2 *vr* to impose. **sich jdm** ~ (*Mensch*) to impose oneself *or* one's company on sb; (*fig: Erinnerung*) to come involuntarily to sb's mind; **dieser Gedanke/Verdacht drängte sich mir auf** I couldn't help thinking/suspecting that; **das drängt sich einem ja förmlich auf** it's perfectly obvious, the conclusion is irresistible.

aufdrehen *sep* **1** *vt* **(a)** *Wasserhahn, Wasser etc* to turn on; *Ventil* to open; *Schraubverschluß* to unscrew; *Schraube* to loosen, to unscrew; *Radio etc* to turn up; (*Aus: einschalten*) *Licht, Radio etc* to turn *or* switch on.

(b) (*inf: aufziehen*) *Uhr, Federtrieb etc* to wind up.

(c) (*aufrollen*) *Haar* to put in rollers; *Schnurrbart* to turn *or* twist up.

2 *vi* (*inf*) (*beschleunigen*) to put one's foot down hard, to open up; (*fig*) to get going, to start going like the clappers (*Brit inf*); (*fig: ausgelassen werden*) to get going, to let it all hang out (*sl*); *siehe* **aufgedreht**.

aufdringen *vtr sep irreg siehe* **aufdrängen**.

aufdringlich *adj Benehmen, Tapete* obtrusive; *Geruch, Parfüm* powerful; *Farbe auch* loud, insistent; *Mensch* insistent, pushing, pushy (*inf*), importunate (*liter*). **die** ~**e Art meines Mitreisenden** the way my fellow-passenger forced himself *or* his company upon me; **dieser** ~**e Kerl kam einfach auf mich zu** this chap just forced himself *or* his company on me; **beim Tanzen wurde er** ~ when we/they were dancing he kept trying to get fresh (*inf*).

Aufdringlichkeit *f siehe adj* obtrusiveness; powerfulness; loudness, insistence; insistence, pushiness, importunateness (*liter*); (*aufdringliche Art*) pushy way *or* nature. **die** ~ **meiner Nachbarin** the way my neighbour forces herself *or* her company on you.

aufdröseln *vt sep* (*lit, fig*) to unravel; *Strickarbeit* to undo.

Aufdruck *m* **(a)** (*Aufgedrucktes*) imprint; (*auf Briefmarke*) overprint. **(b)** (*Phys*) upward pressure.

aufdrucken *vt sep etw auf etw* (*acc*) ~ to print sth on sth; *Postwertstempel auf Briefe* to stamp letters.

aufdrücken *sep* **1** *vt* **(a)** *etw* (*auf etw acc*) ~ to press sth on (sth); **den Bleistift nicht so fest** ~! don't press (on) your pencil so hard.

(b) (*aufdrucken*) *etw auf etw* (*acc*) ~ to stamp sth on sth; **ein Siegel auf einen Brief** ~ to impress a seal on a letter; **jdm einen** ~ (*inf*) to give sb a kiss *or* a quick peck (*inf*); *siehe* **Stempel**.

(c) (*öffnen*) *Tür etc* to push open; *Ventil auch* to force open; *Pickel etc* to squeeze.

(d) (*inf: durch Knopfdruck öffnen*) *Tür* to open (by pressing the button). **er drückte die Tür auf** he pressed *or* pushed the button and the door opened.

(e) (*aufsetzen*) *Kranz, Hut etc* to press on.

2 *vi* **(a)** to press.

(b) (*inf: die Tür elektrisch öffnen*) to open the door (by pressing a button).

3 *vr* leave an impression (*auf* +*acc* on).

auf|einander *adv* **(a)** on (top of) each other *or* one another. **(b)** **sich** ~ **verlassen können** to be able to rely on each other *or* one another; ~ **zufahren** to drive towards each other.

auf|einander-: ~**beißen** *vt sep irreg Zähne* to clench, to bite together; ~**drücken** *vt sep* to press together; ~**fahren** *vi sep irreg aux sein* to drive *or* crash into each other; **A**~**folge** *f, no pl* sequence; (*zeitlich auch*) succession; **in schneller A**~**folge** in quick succession; ~**folgen** *vi sep aux sein* to follow each other *or* one another, to come after each other *or* one another; **die beiden Söhne/Termine folgten unmittelbar** ~ the two sons/appointments followed *or* came one immediately after the other, one son/appointment came immediately after the other; ~**folgend** *adj* successive; **drei schnell** ~**folgende Tore** three goals in quick succession; ~**hängen** *sep* **1** *vi irreg* (*fig: Leute*) to hang around together (*inf*); **die beiden Autos hängen zu nah** ~ the two cars are sticking too close (together); **in einer kleinen Wohnung hängt man immer zu eng** ~ in a small flat you're always too much on top of each other (*inf*); **(b)** (*übereinanderhängen*) to hang one over the other; **2** *vt* to hang on top of each other; ~**hetzen** vt sep to set on or at each other; ~**hocken** vi sep (inf) siehe ~**hängen 1 (a)**; ~**knallen** sep (inf) 1 vi aux sein (lit, fig) to collide; 2 vt to bang together; ~**legen** sep 1 vt to lay on top of each other, to lay one on top of the other; 2 vr to lie on top of each other; ~**liegen** vi sep irreg aux sein or haben to lie on top of each other; ~**passen** vi sep to fit on top of each other; ~**prallen** vi sep aux sein (Autos etc) to collide; (Truppen etc) to clash; ~**pressen** vt sep to press together; ~**rasen** vi sep aux sein to hurtle into each other; ~**schichten** vt sep to put in layers one on top of the other; ~**schlagen** sep irreg 1 vi aux sein to knock or strike against each other; 2 vt to knock or strike together; ~**setzen** sep 1 vt to put on top of each other; 2 vr (Gegenstände) to be placed one on top of the other or on top of each other; (Bienen etc) to settle on each other; ~**sitzen** vi sep irreg aux sein or haben (a) (Gegenstände) to lie on top of each other; (b) (inf) **die Autos sitzen zu dicht** ~ the cars are too close together; (c) (inf: Menschen) to sit on top of each other (inf); (eng wohnen) to live on top of each other (inf); ~**stellen** sep 1 vt to put or place on top of each other; 2 vr to pile on top of each other; ~**stoßen** vi sep irreg aux sein to bump into each other, to collide; (fig: Meinungen, Farben) to clash; ~**treffen** vi sep irreg aux sein (Mannschaften, Gruppen etc) to meet; (Meinungen) to clash, to come into conflict; (Kugeln, Gegenstände etc) to hit each other; ~**türmen** vt sep to pile on top of each other.

Auf|enthalt m -(e)s, -e (a) (das Sich-Aufhalten) stay; (das Wohnen) residence. **man muß der Polizei den** ~ **anzeigen** you have to report to the police that you're staying here; **der** ~ **im Aktionsbereich des Krans ist verboten** do not stand within the radius of the crane, keep well clear of the crane. (b) (Aufenthaltszeit) stay, sojourn (liter). (c) (esp Rail) stop; (bei Anschluß) wait. **der Zug hat 20 Minuten** ~ the train stops for 20 minutes; **wie lange haben wir** ~? how long do we stop for or do we have to wait? (d) (geh: Verzögerung) delay, wait. (e) (geh: Aufenthaltsort) abode (form), domicile, place of residence. ~ **nehmen** to take up residence.

Auf|enthalter(in f) m -s, - (Sw) foreign resident, resident alien (form).

Auf|enthalts-: ~**berechtigung** f right of residence; ~**bewilligung** f siehe ~**erlaubnis**; ~**dauer** f length or duration of stay; ~**erlaubnis**, ~**genehmigung** f residence permit; ~**ort** m whereabouts sing or pl; (Jur) abode, residence; **man weiß nicht, was sein augenblicklicher** ~**ort ist** his present whereabouts is or are not known; ~**raum** m day room; (in Betrieb) recreation room; ~**verbot** nt jdm ~**verbot erteilen** to ban sb from staying (in a country etc); **er hat** ~**verbot** he is not allowed to stay (in the country etc), he is banned.

aufer adv (Aus) siehe **herauf**.

auf|erlegen* vt sep or insep (geh) to impose (jdm etw sth on sb); Strafe auch to inflict. **jdm eine Pilgerfahrt** ~ to instruct sb to make a pilgrimage.

Auf|erstandene(r) m decl as adj (Rel) risen Christ.

auf|erstehen* vi sep or insep irreg aux sein to rise from the dead, to rise again (esp Rel). **Christus ist auferstanden** Christ is (a)risen.

Auf|erstehung f resurrection. **(fröhliche)** ~ **feiern** (hum) to have been resurrected.

Auf|erstehungsfest nt (geh) Feast of the Resurrection.

Auf|erstehungsglaube m (Rel) belief in the Resurrection.

auf|erwecken* vt sep or insep (geh) to raise from the dead; (fig) to reawaken.

Auf|erweckung f raising from the dead.

auf|essen sep irreg 1 vt to eat up. 2 vi to eat (everything) up.

auffächern sep 1 vt to fan out; (fig) to arrange or order neatly. 2 vr to fan out.

Auffächerung f fanning out; (fig) neat or orderly arrangement.

auffädeln vt sep to thread or string (together).

auffahren sep irreg 1 vi aux sein (a) (aufprallen) **auf jdn/etw** ~ to run or drive into sb/sth; **auf eine Sandbank** ~ to run onto or run aground on a sandbank. (b) (näher heranfahren) to drive up, to move up. **zu dicht** ~ to drive too close behind (the car in front); **mein Hintermann fährt dauernd so dicht auf** the car behind me is right on my tail all the time. (c) (in Position fahren) to draw up. **die Taxis sind in Zweierreihen vor dem Bahnhof aufgefahren** the taxis were drawn up in a double line outside the station. (d) (nach oben fahren) (Bergleute) to go up; (Rel) to ascend. (e) (hinauffahren) **auf etw** (acc) ~ to drive onto sth; (auf Autobahn) to enter sth. (f) (aufschrecken) to start. **aus dem Schlaf** ~ to awake with a start. (g) (aufbrausen) to flare up, to fly into a rage. 2 vt (a) (herbeischaffen) Truppen etc to bring up; Sand, Erde, Torf etc to put down; (inf) Getränke etc to serve up; Speisen, Argumente etc to dish (inf) or serve up. **laß mal eine Runde** ~ (inf) how about buying us a round? (inf). (b) (aufwühlen) to churn or dig up.

auffahrend adj Temperament irascible, hasty; Mensch auch quick-tempered.

Auffahrt f (a) (das Hinauffahren) climb, ascent. (b) (Zufahrt) approach (road); (bei Haus etc) drive; (Rampe) ramp. (c) (von Fahrzeugen) driving up. (d) (Sw) siehe **Himmelfahrt**.

Auffahrtstag m (Sw) siehe **Himmelfahrtstag**.

Auffahr|unfall m collision.

auffallen sep irreg 1 vi aux sein (a) (sich abheben) to stand out; (unangenehm) ~ to attract attention; (sich hervortun) to be remarkable (durch for). **er fällt durch seine roten Haare auf** his red hair makes him stand out; **er ist schon früher als**

unzuverlässig/Extremist aufgefallen it has been noticed before that he is unreliable/an extremist; **angenehm/unangenehm** ~ to make a good/bad impression; **man soll möglichst nicht** ~ you should try to be as inconspicuous as possible, you should keep a low profile, you should try to avoid being noticed; **nur nicht** ~! just don't be conspicuous, just don't make yourself noticed.

(b) (bemerkt werden) **jdm fällt etw auf** sb notices sth, sth strikes sb; **so etwas fällt doch sofort/nicht auf** that will be noticed immediately/that will never be noticed; **der Fehler fällt nicht besonders auf** the mistake is not all that noticeable or does not show all that much; **fällt es/der Fleck auf?** does it/the stain show?, is it/the stain noticeable?; **was fällt dir an dem Satz auf?** what do you notice or what strikes you about this sentence?; **das muß dir doch aufgefallen sein!** surely you must have noticed (it).

(c) (auftreffen: Regen, Licht etc) **auf etw** (acc) ~ to fall onto sth, to strike sth; **er fiel mit dem Knie (auf einen Stein) auf** he fell and hurt his knee (on a stone).

2 vr (rare) **sich** (dat) **etw** ~ to fall and hurt sth, to fall on sth.

auffallend adj conspicuous, noticeable; Schönheit, Ähnlichkeit, Farbe, Kleider striking. **das A~ste an ihr sind die roten Haare** her most striking feature or the most striking thing about her is her red hair; **er ist** ~ **intelligent** he is strikingly or remarkably intelligent; **stimmt** ~! (hum) too true!, how right you are!

auffällig adj conspicuous; Farbe, Kleidung loud. **er hat sich** ~ **genau erkundigt** he made a point of inquiring precisely; **er hat** ~ **wenig mit ihr geredet** it was conspicuous how little he talked with her; ~**er geht's nicht mehr** they/he etc couldn't make it more obvious or conspicuous if they/he etc tried.

Auffälligkeit f siehe adj conspicuousness; loudness.

auffalten vtr sep to unfold; (Fallschirm) to open; (Geol) to fold upward.

Auffangbecken nt collecting tank; (fig) gathering place.

auffangen vt sep irreg (a) Ball, Gesprächsfetzen to catch; Wagen, Flugzeug to get or bring under control; Flugzeug to pull out; (Telec) Nachricht to pick up. **jds Blick** ~ to catch sb's eye. (b) (abfangen) Aufprall etc to cushion, to absorb; Faustschlag to block; (fig) Preissteigerung etc to offset, to counterbalance. (c) (sammeln) Regenwasser etc to collect, to catch; (fig) Flüchtlinge etc to assemble.

Auffanglager nt reception camp or centre.

auffassen sep 1 vt (a) to interpret, to understand. **etw als etw** (acc) ~ to take sth as sth; **die Planeten als Götter** ~ to conceive of the planets as gods; **das Herz als (eine Art) Pumpe** ~ to think or conceive of the heart as a (kind of) pump; **etw falsch/richtig** ~ to take sth the wrong way/in the right way. (b) (geistig aufnehmen) to take in, to grasp. 2 vi to understand.

Auffassung f (a) (Meinung, Verständnis) opinion, view; (Begriff) conception, view. **nach meiner** ~ in my opinion, to my mind; **nach christlicher** ~ according to Christian belief. (b) (Auffassungsgabe) perception.

Auffassungs-: a~**fähig** adj intelligent; ~**fähigkeit**, ~**gabe** f intelligence, grasp; **er hat eine große** ~**fähigkeit** or ~**gabe** he has tremendous mental grasp; ~**kraft** f intellectual or mental powers pl; ~**sache** f (inf) question of interpretation; (Ansichtssache) matter of opinion; ~**vermögen** nt siehe ~**fähigkeit**; ~**weise** f interpretation; **es hängt von der** ~**weise ab** it depends (on) how you interpret it.

auffegen sep 1 vt to sweep up. 2 vi siehe **fegen**.

auffi adv (Aus) siehe **herauf, hinauf**.

auffindbar adj **es ist nicht/ist** ~ it isn't/is to be found, it can't/can be found.

auffinden vt sep irreg to find, to discover.

auffischen vt sep (a) to fish up; (inf) Schiffbrüchige to fish out. (b) (fig inf) to find; Menschen auch to dig up (inf).

aufflackern vi sep aux sein (lit, fig) to flare up.

aufflammen vi sep aux sein (lit, fig: Feuer, Unruhen etc) to flare up. **in seinen Augen flammte Empörung auf** his eyes flashed in indignation.

auffliegen vi sep irreg aux sein (a) (hochfliegen) to fly up. (b) (sich öffnen) to fly open. (c) (fig inf: jäh enden) (Konferenz etc) to break up; (Rauschgiftring, Verbrecher etc) to be busted (inf). **einen Schmugglerring/eine Konferenz** ~ **lassen** to bust a ring of smugglers/to bust or break up a meeting (inf).

auffordern vt sep (a) to ask. **wir fordern Sie auf, ...** you are required to ... (b) (bitten) to ask, to invite; (zum Wettkampf etc) to challenge. **jdm zum Sitzen/Sprechen** ~ to ask or invite sb to sit down/to speak. (c) (zum Tanz bitten) to ask to dance.

auffordernd adj inviting.

Aufforderung f request; (nachdrücklicher) demand; (Einladung) invitation; (Jur) incitement. **eine** ~ **zum Tanz** (fig) a challenge.

Aufforderungs-: ~**charakter** m (Psych) stimulative nature; **den** ~**charakter einer Äußerung nachweisen** (Jur) to prove that a statement constitutes incitement; ~**satz** m (Gram) (Hauptsatz) imperative sentence, command (sentence); (Teilsatz) imperative clause.

aufforsten sep 1 vt Gebiet to reafforest; Wald to retimber, to restock. 2 vi **man ist dabei, aufzuforsten** they are doing some reafforesting/retimbering.

Aufforstung f siehe vt reafforestation; retimbering, restocking.

auffressen sep irreg 1 vt (lit, fig) to eat up. **ich könnte dich** ~ (inf) I could eat you; **er wird dich deswegen nicht gleich** ~ (inf) he's not going to eat you (inf). 2 vi (Tier) to eat all its food up; (inf: aufessen) to finish eating.

auffrischen *sep* **1** *vt* to freshen (up); *Anstrich, Farbe* to brighten up; *Möbel etc* to renovate, to refurbish; *(ergänzen) Vorräte* to replenish; *(fig) Erinnerungen* to refresh; *Kenntnisse* to polish up; *Sprachkenntnisse* to brush up; *persönliche Beziehungen* to renew; *Impfung* to boost.
2 *vi aux sein or haben (Wind)* to freshen.
3 *vi impers aux sein* to get fresher *or* cooler.
Auffrischung *f siehe vt* freshening (up); brightening up; renovation, refurbishment; replenishment; refreshing; polishing up; brushing up; renewal; boosting.
Auffrischungslimpfung *f* booster. **eine** ~ **vornehmen lassen** to have a booster.
aufführbar *adj (Mus)* performable; *(Theat auch)* stageable. **Faust II ist praktisch gar nicht** ~ it is practically impossible to perform *or* stage Faust II.
aufführen *vt sep* **1** *vt* **(a)** to put on; *Drama, Oper auch* to stage, to perform; *Musikwerk, Komponist* to perform. **ein Theater** ~ *(fig)* to make a scene; **sie führte einen wahren Freudentanz auf** she danced with joy.
(b) *(auflisten)* to list; *(nennen) Zeugen, Beispiel* to cite; *Beispiel* to give, to quote, to cite. **einzeln** ~ to itemize.
2 *vr* to behave. **sich wie ein Betrunkener** ~ to act like a drunkard; **wie er sich wieder aufgeführt hat!** what a performance!
Aufführung *f* **(a)** *siehe vt (a)* putting on; staging, performance; performance. **etw zur** ~ **bringen** *(form)* to perform sth; **zur** ~ **kommen** *or* **gelangen** *(form)* to be performed. **(b)** *(Auflistung)* listing; *(Liste)* list. **einzelne** ~ itemization.
Aufführungs-: ~**recht** *nt* performing rights *pl*; **a**~**reif** *adj* ready to be performed.
auffüllen *vt sep* **(a)** *(vollständig füllen)* to fill up; *(nachfüllen)* to top up; *Mulde etc* auch to fill in.
(b) *(ergänzen) Flüssigkeit* to dilute; *Vorräte* to replenish; *Öl* to top up. **Benzin** ~ to tank up, to fill up with petrol *(Brit) or* gas *(US)*; **unsere Mannschaft muß (mit zwei neuen Leuten) aufgefüllt werden** we need (two new people) to make up our team *or* to bring our team up to strength.
(c) *auch vi Suppe, Essen* to serve. **soll ich dir noch mal** ~**?** can I give you some more?; *(Glas* ~*)* can I top you up?
auffuttern *vt sep (inf)* to eat up, to polish off.
auffüttern *vt* to rear *(mit on)*.
Aufgabe *f* **(a)** *(Arbeit, Pflicht)* job, task. **es ist deine** ~, ... it is your job *or* task *or* responsibility to ...; **es ist nicht** ~ **der Regierung,** ... it is not the job *or* task *or* responsibility of the government to ...; **sich** *(dat)* **etw zur** ~ **machen** to make sth one's job *or* business.
(b) *(Zweck, Funktion)* purpose, job.
(c) *(esp Sch) (Problem)* question; *(Math auch)* problem; *(zur Übung)* exercise; *(usu pl: Haus~)* homework *no pl*.
(d) *(Abgabe, Übergabe) (von Koffer, Gepäck)* registering, registration; *(Aviat)* checking(-in); *(von Brief, Postsendung)* handing in; *(von Anzeige)* placing *no pl*, insertion.
(e) *(Verzicht auf weiteren Kampf, weitere Anstrengungen) (Sport)* retirement; *(Mil etc)* surrender. **er hat das Spiel durch** ~ **verloren** he lost the game by retiring; **die Polizei forderte die Geiselnehmer zur** ~ **auf** the police appealed to the kidnappers to give themselves up *or* to surrender.
(f) *(von Gewohnheit, Geschäft)* giving up; *(von Plänen, Forderungen auch)* dropping; *(von Hoffnung, Studium)* abandoning, abandonment. **unter** ~ **all ihrer Habe** ... abandoning all their property; **er riet ihm zur** ~ **seines Studiums** he advised him to give up *or* abandon *or* drop his studies.
(g) *(das Verlorengeben)* giving up for lost.
(h) *(Volleyball, Tennis etc)* service, serve.
aufgabeln *vt sep Heu, Mist etc* to fork up; *(fig inf) jdn* to pick up *(inf); Sache* to get hold of; *Schnupfen* to catch. **wo hat er denn die aufgegabelt?** *(inf)* where did he dig her up?
Aufgaben-: ~**bereich** *m*, ~**gebiet** *nt* area of responsibility; ~**heft** *nt (Sch)* homework book; ~**kreis** *m (geh) siehe* ~**bereich;** ~**sammlung** *f* set of exercises *or* problems; maths *(Brit)* or math *(US)* question book; ~**stellung** *f* **(a)** *(Formulierung)* formulation; **(b)** *(Aufgabe)* type of problem; ~**verteilung** *f* allocation of responsibilities *or* tasks.
Aufgabe-: ~**ort** *m* place where a letter *etc* was posted; ~**stempel** *m* postmark.
aufgagen [-gɛ(:)gn] *vt sep (Press sl)* to pep *(inf)* or zap *(sl)* up.
Aufgang *m* **(a)** *(von Sonne, Mond)* rising; *(von Stern auch)* ascent; *(fig: von Stern)* appearance, emergence. **(b)** *(Treppen~)* stairs *pl*, staircase. **im** ~ on the stairs *or* staircase.
(c) *(Aufstieg)* ascent. **(d)** *(Sport)* opening, beginning, start.
Aufgangspunkt *m (Astron)* **der** ~ **eines Sterns** the point at which a star rises.
aufgeben *sep irreg* **1** *vt* **(a)** *Hausaufgaben* to give, to set; *schwierige Frage, Problem* to pose *(jdm* for sb). **jdm viel/nichts** ~ *(Sch)* to give *or* set sb a lot of/no homework.
(b) *(übergeben, abgeben) Koffer, Gepäck* to register; *Luftgepäck* to check in; *Brief* to post; *Anzeige* to put in, to place; *Bestellung* to place.
(c) *Kampf, Hoffnung, Arbeitsstelle, Freund etc* to give up. **gib's auf!** why don't you give up?
(d) *(verloren geben) Patienten* to give up; *(fig) Sohn, Schüler* to give up (with *or* on).
(e) *(inf) Essen* to serve. **jdm etw** ~ to give sb sth.
2 *vi* **(a)** *(sich geschlagen geben)* to give up *or* in.
(b) *(inf: bei Tisch)* to serve *(jdm* sb). **kann ich dir noch mal** ~**?** can I give you some more?
aufgeblasen **1** *ptp of* **aufblasen.** **2** *adj (fig)* puffed-up, self-important.
Aufgeblasenheit *f (fig)* self-importance.
Aufgebot *nt* **(a)** *(Jur)* public notice.
(b) *(zur Eheschließung)* notice of intended marriage; *(Eccl*

banns *pl*. **das** ~ **bestellen** to give notice of one's intended marriage; *(Eccl)* to put up the banns; **das** ~ **veröffentlichen** to publish the announcement of one's intended marriage; *(Eccl)* to call the banns.
(c) *(Ansammlung) (von Menschen)* contingent; *(von Material etc)* array.
(d) *(Aufbietung)* unter *or* mit dem ~ aller Kräfte ... summoning all his strength ...
aufgebracht **1** *ptp of* **aufbringen.** **2** *adj* outraged, incensed.
aufgedonnert **1** *ptp of* **aufdonnern.** **2** *adj (pej inf)* tarted up *(pej inf).*
aufgedreht **1** *ptp of* **aufdrehen.** **2** *adj (inf)* in high spirits.
aufgedunsen *adj* swollen, bloated; *Gesicht auch* puffy.
Aufgedunsenheit *f* bloatedness; *(von Gesicht)* puffiness.
aufgehen *vi sep irreg aux sein* **(a)** *(Sonne, Mond, Sterne)* to come up, to rise; *(Tag)* to break, to dawn.
(b) *(sich öffnen)* to open; *(Theat: Vorhang)* to go up; *(Knopf, Knoten etc)* to come undone.
(c) *(aufkeimen, Med: Pocken)* to come up.
(d) *(Cook)* to rise; *(Hefeteig auch)* to prove.
(e) *(klarwerden)* **jdm geht etw auf** sb realizes sth, sth dawns on sb, sth becomes apparent to sb.
(f) *(Math) (Rechnung etc)* to work out, to come out; *(fig)* to come off, to work (out). **wenn man 20 durch 6 teilt, geht das nicht auf** 20 divided by 6 doesn't go; **im Kriminalroman muß alles sauber** ~ in a detective story everything has to work out *or* be resolved neatly.
(g) *(seine Erfüllung finden)* **in etw** *(dat)* ~ to be wrapped up in sth, to be taken up with sth; **er geht ganz in der Familie auf** his whole life revolves around his family.
(h) *(sich auflösen)* **in Flammen etc** ~ to go up in flames *etc*; **in der Masse** ~ to disappear *or* merge into the crowd.
(i) *(Hunt: Jagdzeit)* to begin.
aufgehoben **1** *ptp of* **aufheben.** **2** *adj:* **(bei jdm) gut/schlecht** ~ **sein** to be/not to be in good keeping *or* hands (with sb).
aufgeilen *vt sep (sl)* to get worked up *(inf)*.
aufgeklärt **1** *ptp of* **aufklären.** **2** *adj* **(a)** enlightened *(auch Philos)*. **der** ~**e Absolutismus** *(Hist)* Benevolent Despotism.
(b) *(sexualkundlich)* ~ **sein** to know the facts of life.
Aufgeklärtheit *f* enlightenment; *(sexualkundlich)* knowledge of the facts of life.
aufgeknöpft **1** *ptp of* **aufknöpfen.** **2** *adj (inf)* chatty *(inf).*
aufgekratzt **1** *ptp of* **aufkratzen.** **2** *adj (inf)* in high spirits, full of beans *(inf)*, boisterous.
Aufgekratztheit *f, no pl* high spirits *pl*, boisterousness.
Aufgeld *nt (dial: Zuschlag)* extra charge; *(old: Anzahlung)* deposit, earnest (money) *(old)*.
aufgelegt **1** *ptp of* **auflegen.**
2 *adj* **(a)** **gut/schlecht** *etc* ~ in a good/bad *etc* mood; **(dazu)** ~ **sein, etw zu tun** to feel like doing sth; **zum Musikhören** ~ **sein** to be in the mood for *or* to feel like listening to music.
(b) *attr (offensichtlich)* blatant; *Unsinn auch* arrant; *Lüge auch* barefaced.
aufgelöst **1** *ptp of* **auflösen.** **2** *adj* **(a)** *(außer sich)* beside oneself *(vor + dat* with), distraught; *(bestürzt)* upset. **in Tränen** ~ in tears. **(b)** *(erschöpft)* exhausted, drained, shattered *(inf).*
aufgeräumt **1** *ptp of* **aufräumen.** **2** *adj (geh)* blithe, light-hearted.
aufgeregt **1** *ptp of* **aufregen.** **2** *adj (erregt)* excited; *(sexuell auch)* aroused; *(nervös)* nervous; *(durcheinander)* flustered.
Aufgeregtheit *f, no pl siehe adj* excitement; arousal; nervousness; flustered state.
aufgeschlossen **1** *ptp of* **aufschließen.**
2 *adj (nicht engstirnig)* open-minded *(für, gegenüber* about, as regards); *(empfänglich)* receptive, open *(für, gegenüber* to). **ich bin Vorschlägen gegenüber** *or* **für Vorschläge jederzeit** ~ I'm always open to suggestion(s); **einer Sache** *(dat)* ~ **gegenüberstehen** to be open-minded about *or* as regards sth.
Aufgeschlossenheit *f, no pl siehe adj* open-mindedness; receptiveness, openness.
aufgeschmissen **1** *ptp of* **aufschmeißen.** **2** *adj pred (inf)* in a fix *(inf)*, stuck *(inf).*
aufgeschossen **1** *ptp of* **aufschießen.** **2** *adj* **(hoch** *or* **lang)** ~ who/that has shot up; **ein lang** ~**er Junge** a tall lanky lad.
aufgeschreckt *ptp of* **aufschrecken.**
aufgeschwemmt **1** *ptp of* **aufschwemmen.** **2** *adj* bloated, swollen; *Mensch* bloated.
Aufgeschwemmtheit *f, no pl* bloatedness.
aufgetakelt **1** *ptp of* **auftakeln.** **2** *adj (pej)* dressed up to the nines *(inf).*
aufgewandt *ptp of* **aufwenden.**
aufgeweckt **1** *ptp of* **aufwecken.** **2** *adj* bright, quick, sharp.
Aufgewecktheit *f* intelligence, quickness, sharpness.
aufgewendet *ptp of* **aufwenden.**
aufgewühlt **1** *ptp of* **aufwühlen.** **2** *adj (geh)* agitated, in a turmoil *pred; Gefühle auch* turbulent; *Wasser, Meer* churning, turbulent. **völlig** ~ *(fig)* in a complete turmoil.
aufgießen *vt sep irreg* **(a)** **etw (auf etw** *acc)* ~ to pour sth on (sth); **das angebräunte Mehl mit Brühe** ~ to pour stock on(to) the browned flour. **(b)** *Kaffee,* to make; *Tee auch* to brew.
aufglänzen *vi sep aux sein (lit, fig)* to light up; *(Mond, Sonne, Sterne)* to come out; *(Strahlen reflektierend)* to (begin to) gleam.
aufgleisen *vt sep* to put on (the) rails; *(wieder~)* to re-rail.
aufgliedern *sep* **1** *vt (in + acc* into) to split up, to (sub)divide; *(analysieren auch)* to break down, to analyse; *(in Kategorien auch)* to categorize, to break down. **2** *vr (in + acc* into) to (sub)divide, to break down.
Aufgliederung *f siehe vt* division; breakdown, analysis; categorization, breakdown.

aufglimmen *vi sep irreg aux sein* to light up, to begin to glow; *(fig)* to glimmer.

aufglühen *vi sep aux sein or haben* to light up, to begin to glow; *(fig) (Gesicht)* to light up, to glow; *(Haß, Neid)* to (begin to) gleam; *(Leidenschaft, Liebe)* to awaken.

aufgraben *vt sep irreg* to dig up.

aufgrätschen *vi sep aux sein or haben (Sport)* **auf etw** *(acc)* ~ to straddle sth.

aufgreifen *vt sep irreg* **(a)** *(festnehmen)* to pick up, to apprehend *(form)*. **(b)** *(weiterverfolgen) Thema, Gedanken* to take up, to pick up; *(fortsetzen) Gespräch* to continue, to take up again.

aufgrund *prep +gen*, **auf Grund** *siehe* **Grund.**

aufgucken *vi sep (inf)* to look up *(von* from).

Aufguß *m* brew, infusion *(auch Sci)*; *(fig pej)* rehash.

Aufgußbeutel *m* sachet (containing coffee/herbs *etc*) for brewing; *(Teebeutel)* tea bag.

aufhaben *sep irreg* 1 *vt* **(a)** *Hut, Brille* to have on, to wear. **sie hat ihre Brille nicht aufgehabt** she didn't have her glasses on, she wasn't wearing her glasses.
    (b) *Tür, Augen, Laden, Jacke* to have open.
    (c) *(Sch: als Hausaufgabe)* **etw** ~ to have sth (to do); **ich habe heute viel auf** I've got a lot of homework today.
    (d) *(inf: aufgemacht haben)* to have got *or* gotten *(US)* open.
    (e) *(inf: aufgegessen haben)* to have eaten up.
    2 *vi (Laden etc)* to be open.

aufhacken *vt sep Straße* to break up; *(Vogel)* to break *or* peck open.

aufhalsen *vt sep (inf)* **jdm/sich etw** ~ to saddle *or* land sb/oneself with sth *(inf)*, to land sth on sb/oneself *(inf)*; **sich** *(dat)* **etw** ~ **lassen** to get oneself saddled *or* landed with sth *(inf)*.

aufhalten *sep irreg* 1 *vt* **(a)** *(zum Halten bringen) Fahrzeug, Entwicklung* to stop, to halt; *Vormarsch auch, Inflation etc* to check, to arrest; *(verlangsamen)* to hold up, to delay; *(abhalten, stören) (bei* from) to hold back, to keep back. **ich will dich nicht länger** ~ I don't want to keep *or* hold you back any longer.
    (b) *(inf: offenhalten)* to keep open. **die Hand** ~ to hold one's hand out.
    2 *vr* **(a)** *(an einem Ort bleiben)* to stay.
    (b) *(sich verzögern)* to stay on, to linger; *(bei der Arbeit etc)* to take a long time *(bei* over).
    (c) *(sich befassen)* **sich bei etw** ~ to dwell on sth, to linger over sth; **sich mit jdm/etw** ~ to spend time dealing with sb/sth.
    (d) *(sich entrüsten)* **sich über etw** *(acc)* ~ to rail against sth.

aufhängen *sep* 1 *vt* **(a)** to hang up; *(Aut) Rad* to suspend.
    (b) *(töten)* to hang *(an +dat* from).
    (c) *(inf)* **jdm etw** ~ *(aufschwatzen)* to palm sth off on sb; *(glauben machen)* to talk sb into believing sth; *(aufbürden)* to land *or* saddle sb with sth *(inf)*.
    (d) **etw an einer Frage/einem Thema** ~ *(fig: entwickeln)* to use a question/theme as a peg to hang sth on.
    2 *vr (sich töten)* to hang oneself *(an +dat* from); *(hum: seine Kleider* ~) to hang one's things up.

Aufhänger *m* tab, loop. **ein** ~ **(für etw)** *(fig inf)* a peg to hang sth on *(fig)*.

Aufhängung *f (Tech)* suspension.

aufharken *vt sep* to rake up.

aufhauen *sep* 1 *vt reg or (geh) irreg (öffnen)* to knock open, to hew open *(liter)*; *Eis* to open up, to hew open *(liter)*. **sich** *(dat)* **den Kopf** *etc* ~ to gash one's head *etc* open.
    2 *vi aux sein (inf: auftreffen)* **mit dem Kopf** *etc* **auf etw** *(acc or dat)* ~ to bash *(inf)* or bump one's head *etc* against *or* on sth.

aufhäufen *sep* 1 *vt* to pile up, to accumulate; *(fig auch)* to amass. 2 *vr* to accumulate, to pile up.

Aufhäufung *f* **(a)** *siehe vb* piling up, accumulation; amassing.
    (b) *(Haufen)* pile, heap, accumulation.

aufhebbar *adj* revocable, voidable *(form)*.

aufheben *sep irreg* 1 *vt* **(a)** *(vom Boden)* to pick up; *größeren Gegenstand auch* to lift up; *(in die Höhe heben)* to raise, to lift (up); *Deckel* to lift off.
    (b) *(nicht wegwerfen)* to keep. **jdm etw** ~ to put sth aside for sb, to keep sth (back) for sb; *siehe* **aufgehoben.**
    (c) *(ungültig machen)* to abolish, to do away with; *Gesetz auch* to repeal, to rescind; *Vertrag* to cancel, to annul, to revoke; *Parlament* to dissolve; *Urteil* to reverse, to quash; *Verlobung* to break off. **dieses Gesetz hebt das andere auf** this law supersedes the other.
    (d) *(beenden) Blockade, Belagerung* to raise, to lift; *Beschränkung* to remove, to lift; *Sitzung* to close; *siehe* **Tafel.**
    (e) *(ausgleichen)* to offset, to make up for; *Widerspruch* to resolve; *Schwerkraft* to neutralize, to cancel out.
    (f) *(obs: festnehmen)* to capture, to seize.
    2 *vr* **(a)** *(old: aufstehen)* to rise *(old, form)*.
    (b) *(sich ausgleichen)* to cancel each other out, to offset each other; *(Math)* to cancel (each other) out.

Aufheben *nt* **-s, no pl** fuss. **viel** ~**(s) (von etw) machen** to make a lot of fuss (about *or* over sth); **viel** ~**(s) von jdm machen** to make a lot of fuss about sb; **ohne (jedes)** ~**/ohne viel** *or* **großes** ~ without any/much *or* a big fuss.

Aufhebung *f* **(a)** *siehe vt (c)* abolition; repeal, rescinding; cancellation, annulment, revocation; dissolving; reversal, quashing; breaking off.
    (b) *siehe vt (d)* raising, lifting; removal, lifting; closing.
    (c) *(von Widerspruch)* resolving, resolution; *(von Schwerkraft)* neutralization, cancelling out.
    (d) *(obs: Festnahme)* capture, seizure.

aufheitern *sep* 1 *vt jdn* to cheer up; *Rede, Leben* to brighten up *(jdm* for sb). 2 *vr (Himmel)* to clear, to brighten (up); *(Wetter)* to clear up, to brighten up.

aufheiternd *adj (Met)* becoming brighter, brightening up.

Aufheiterung *f siehe vt* cheering up; brightening up; *(Met)* brighter period. **zunehmende** ~ gradually brightening up.

Aufheiterungsgebiet *nt (Met)* brighter area.

aufheizen *sep* 1 *vt* to heat (up); *(fig) Zuhörer* to inflame, to stir up. **die Stimmung** ~ to whip *or* stir up feelings. 2 *vr* to heat up; *(fig)* to hot up *(inf)*, to intensify, to build up.

aufhelfen *vi sep irreg (lit: beim Aufstehen)* to help up *(jdm* sb). **einer Sache** *(dat)* ~ *(aufbessern)* to help sth (to) improve; *(stärker)* to help strengthen sth.

aufhellen *sep* 1 *vt* to brighten (up); *Haare* to lighten; *(fig: klären)* to throw *or* shed light upon. **das hellte ihr die Zukunft auf** it made her future seem brighter (to her).
    2 *vr (Himmel, Wetter, fig: Miene)* to brighten (up); *(fig: Sinn)* to become clear. **das Rätsel/Geheimnis hellte sich auf** light was shed on the mystery/secret.

Aufheller *m* **-s, -** *(in Reinigungsmitteln)* colour-brightener; *(für Haare)* lightener.

Aufhellung *f siehe vb* brightening; lightening; clarification. **es kam zu zeitweisen** ~**en** from time to time the weather brightened up.

aufhetzen *vt sep* to stir up, to incite. **jdn gegen jdn/etw** ~ to stir up sb's animosity against sb/sth; **jdn zu etw** ~ to incite sb to (do) sth.

Aufhetzerei *f (inf)* agitation; *(esp durch Reden)* rabble-rousing.

aufhetzerisch *adj* inflammatory, rabble-rousing.

Aufhetzung *f* incitement, agitation.

aufheulen *vi sep* to give a howl *(vor* of), to howl *(vor* with); *(Sirene)* to (start to) wail; *(Motor, Menge)* to (give a) roar; *(weinen)* to start to howl.

aufhissen *vt sep* to hoist (up), to raise.

aufhocken *sep* 1 *vi aux sein or haben* **(a)** *(Sport)* to crouch-jump *(auf + acc* onto). **(b)** *(dial)* **auf etw** *(acc)* ~ to sit on sth. 2 *vr (dial)* to get up, to climb up.

aufholen *sep* 1 *vt* **(a)** *Zeit, Verspätung, Vorsprung* to make up; *Lernstoff* to catch up on; *Strecke* to make up, to catch up. **Versäumtes** ~ to make up for lost time.
    (b) *(Naut)* to haul up, to raise.
    2 *vi (Wanderer, Mannschaft, Schüler, Arbeiter)* to catch up; *(Läufer, Rennfahrer etc auch)* to make up ground; *(Zug)* to make up time; *(Versäumtes* ~) to make up for lost time.

aufholzen *vt sep* to afforest *(form)*, to plant with trees.

aufhorchen *vi sep* to prick up one's ears, to sit up (and take notice). **das ließ** ~ that made people sit up (and take notice).

aufhören *vi sep* to stop; *(bei Stellung)* to finish; *(Musik, Lärm, Straße auch, Freundschaft, Korrespondenz)* to (come to an) end. **nicht** ~/~, **etw zu tun** to keep on/stop doing sth; **hör doch endlich auf!** (will you) stop it!; **mit etw** ~ to stop sth; **da hört sich doch alles auf!** *(inf)* that's the (absolute) limit!; **da hört bei ihm der Spaß auf** *(inf)* he's not amused by that.

aufhüpfen *vi sep aux sein (Mensch)* to jump *or* leap up; *(Vogel)* to hop; *(Ball etc)* to bounce. **vor Angst/Freude** ~ to jump with fear/joy.

aufjagen *vt sep (lit)* to disturb; *(fig)* to chase away. **sein aufgejagtes Gehirn** *(fig)* his feverish brain; **die aufgejagten Gemüter der Zuhörer** the excited audience.

aufjauchzen *vi sep* to shout (out) *(vor* with).

aufjaulen *vi sep* to give a howl *(vor* of), to howl *(vor* with).

aufjubeln *vi sep* to shout (out) with joy, to cheer.

aufjuchzen *vi sep* to whoop with joy, to give a whoop of joy.

Aufkauf *m* buying up.

aufkaufen *vt sep* to buy up.

Aufkäufer *m* buyer.

aufkehren *vti sep (esp S Ger) siehe* **auffegen.**

aufkeimen *vi sep aux sein* to germinate, to sprout; *(fig) (Hoffnung, Liebe, Sympathie)* to bud, to burgeon *(liter)*; *(Zweifel)* to (begin to) take root. ~**d** *(fig)* budding, burgeoning *(liter)*, nascent *(liter)*; *Zweifel* growing, nascent *(liter)*.

aufklaffen *vi sep aux sein or haben* to gape; *(Abgrund auch)* to yawn. ~**d** *(lit, fig)* gaping.

aufklappbar *adj Fenster* hinged; *Truhe* which opens up; *Klappe* which lets down; *Verdeck* which folds back, fold-back.

aufklappen *sep* 1 *vt* to open up; *Klappe* to let down; *Verdeck* to fold back; *Messer* to unclasp; *Fenster, Buch* to open; *(hochschlagen) Kragen* to turn up. 2 *vi aux sein* to open.

aufklaren *sep (Met)* 1 *vi impers* to clear (up), to brighten (up) *(auch fig)*. 2 *vi (Wetter)* to clear *or* brighten (up); *(Himmel)* to clear, to brighten (up).

aufklären *sep* 1 *vt* **(a)** *Mißverständnis, Irrtum* to clear up, to resolve; *Verbrechen, Rätsel auch* to solve; *Ereignis, Vorgang* to throw *or* shed light upon, to elucidate.
    (b) *jdn* to enlighten. **Kinder** ~ *(sexualkundlich)* to explain the facts of life to children, to tell children the facts of life; *(in der Schule)* to give children sex education; **jdn über etw** *(acc)* ~ to inform sb about sth; **wir müssen die Bevölkerung darüber** ~, **wie gefährlich** ... we must inform the public how dangerous ...; **klär mich mal auf, wie** ... *(inf)* (can you) enlighten me as to how ...; *siehe* **aufgeklärt.**
    (c) *(Mil)* to reconnoitre.
    2 *vr (Irrtum, Geheimnis etc)* to resolve itself, to be cleared up; *(Himmel)* to clear, to brighten (up); *(fig: Miene, Gesicht)* to brighten (up).

Aufklärer *m* **-s, -** **(a)** *(Philos)* philosopher of the Enlightenment. **(b)** *(Mil)* reconnaissance plane; *(klein)* scout (plane). **(c)** *(DDR: Agitator)* political educator *or* propagandist.

aufklärerisch *adj (Philos)* (of the) Enlightenment; *(freigeistig)* progressive, striving to enlighten the people; *(erzieherisch, unterrichtend)* informative; *(Pol)* educational.

Aufklärung *f* **(a)** *(Philos)* **die** ~ the Enlightenment.
    (b) *siehe vt (a)* clearing up, resolution; solution; elucidation.

(c) *(Information)* enlightenment; *(von offizieller Stelle)* informing *(über +acc* about); *(Pol)* instruction.

(d) (sexuelle) ~ *(in Schulen)* sex education; **die ~von Kindern** explaining the facts of life to children.

(e) *(DDR: Agitation)* (political) education *or* propaganda.

(f) *(Mil)* reconnaissance.

Aufklärungs-: ~**arbeit** *f* instructional *or* educational work; ~**broschüre** *f* informative pamphlet; *(sexualkundlich)* sex education pamphlet; ~**buch** *nt* sex education book; ~**film** *m* sex education film; ~**flugzeug** *nt* reconnaissance plane; *(klein)* scout (plane); ~**kampagne** *f* information campaign; ~**literatur** *f* informative literature; *(Pol)* educational literature; *(sexualkundlich)* sex education literature; *(Philos)* literature of the Enlightenment; ~**material** *nt* informational material; ~**pflicht** *f (Jur) judge's duty to ensure that all the relevant facts of a case are clearly presented;* *(Med) duty to inform the patient of the possible dangers of an operation/a course of treatment etc;* ~**quote** *f (in Kriminalstatistik)* success rate (in solving cases), percentage of cases solved; ~**schiff** *nt (Mil)* reconnaissance ship; ~**schrift** *f* information pamphlet; *(Pol)* educational pamphlet; *(sexualkundlich)* sex education pamphlet; ~**tätigkeit** *f* informational activity; ~**zeit** *f,* ~**zeitalter** *nt* Age of Enlightenment; ~**ziel** *nt (Mil)* reconnaissance object, object of reconnaissance.

aufklatschen *vi sep aux sein (auf +acc* on) to land with a smack; *(auf Wasser auch)* to land with a splash.

aufklauben *vt sep (dial)* (lit, fig) to pick up.

Aufklebe|adresse adhesive address label.

aufkleben *vt sep (auf +acc* -to) to stick on; *(mit Leim, Klebstoff)* to glue on; *(mit Kleister)* to paste on; *Briefmarke auch* to affix *(form) (auf +acc* to), to put on.

Aufkleber *m* sticker.

aufklingen *vi sep irreg aux sein* to ring out; *(fig)* to echo.

aufklopfen sep **1** *vt (öffnen)* to crack open; *(aufschütteln) Kissen* to fluff up. **2** *vi* to (give a) knock *(auf +acc* on).

aufknabbern *vt sep (inf)* to gobble up *(inf)*.

aufknacken *vt sep Nüsse etc* to crack (open); *(inf) Tresor* to break into, to break open, to crack *(inf)*; *Auto* to break into.

aufknallen sep *(inf)* **1** *vt* **(a)** *(öffnen)* to bang (open).

(b) *(als Strafe)* to give.

2 *vi aux sein (Auto)* to crash; *(Gegenstand, Mensch)* to crash down. **auf etw** *(acc)* ~ *(gegen etw knallen)* to crash into sth; *(auf etw fallen)* to crash (down) onto sth; **mit dem Kopf (auf etw** *acc)* ~ to bang *or* hit one's head on sth.

aufknien sep **1** *vi aux sein* to kneel *(auf +acc* on). **2** *vr* to kneel *(auf +acc* (up)on).

aufknöpfen *vt sep (öffnen)* to unbutton, to undo. **etw auf etw** *(acc)* ~ to button sth to sth; **knöpf (dir) die Ohren auf!** *(hum)* wash your ears out! *(hum inf)*; *siehe* **aufgeknöpft.**

aufknoten *vt sep* to untie, to undo.

aufknüpfen sep **1** *vt* **(a)** *(aufhängen)* to hang *(an +dat* from), to string up *(inf) (an +dat* on).

(b) *(aufknoten)* to untie, to undo.

2 *vr* to hang oneself *(an +dat* from).

aufkochen sep **1** *vt* **(a)** *(zum Kochen bringen)* to bring to the boil. **(b)** *(erneut kochen lassen)* to boil up again. **2** *vi* **(a)** *aux sein* to come to the boil; *(fig)* to begin to boil *or* seethe. **etw** ~ **lassen** to bring sth to the boil; **das Pulver in die aufkochende Milch schütten** sprinkle the powder in the milk as it comes to the boil. **(b)** *(Aus)* to prepare a fine spread.

aufkommen *vi sep irreg aux sein* **(a)** (lit, fig: *entstehen)* to arise; *(Nebel)* to come down; *(Wind)* to spring *or* get up; *(aufbrausen: Mode etc auch)* to appear (on the scene). **etw** ~ **lassen** *(fig) Zweifel, Kritik* to give rise to sth; *üble Stimmung* to allow to develop.

(b) ~ **für** *(Kosten tragen)* to bear the costs of, to pay for; *(Verantwortung tragen)* to carry the responsibility for, to be responsible for; *(Haftung tragen)* to be liable for; **für die Kinder** ~ *(finanziell)* to pay for the children's upkeep; **für die Kosten** ~ to bear *or* defray *(form)* the costs; **für den Schaden** ~ to make good *or* pay for the damage.

(c) gegen jdn/etw ~ to prevail against sb/sth; **gegen jdn nicht** ~ **können** to be no match for sb.

(d) er läßt niemanden neben sich *(dat)* ~ he won't allow anyone to rival him.

(e) *(aufsetzen, auftreffen)* to land *(auf +dat* on).

(f) *(dated) (sich erheben)* to rise, to get up; *(sich erholen)* to recover.

(g) *(Naut: herankommen)* to come up; *(Sport: Rückstand aufholen) (bei Match)* to come back; *(bei Wettlauf, -rennen)* to catch up, to make up ground.

(h) *(dial: Schwindel, Diebstahl etc)* to come out, to be discovered.

Aufkommen *nt* -s, - **(a)** *no pl (das Auftreten)* appearance; *(von Methode, Mode etc auch)* advent, emergence. ~ **frischer Wind gegen Abend** a fresh wind will get up towards evening.

(b) *(Fin) (Summe, Menge)* amount; *(von Steuern)* revenue *(aus,* +gen from).

(c) *(DDR: Plansoll)* target.

(d) *no pl (von Flugzeug)* landing. **beim** ~ on touchdown.

(e) *no pl (dated: Genesung)* recovery.

aufkorken *vt sep* to uncork. .

aufkratzen sep **1** *vt (zerkratzen)* to scratch; *(öffnen) Wunde* to scratch open; *(hum: rauh machen) Kehle* to make rough *or* raw; *(fig inf: aufheitern)* to liven up; *siehe* **aufgekratzt. 2** *vr* to scratch oneself sore.

aufkreischen *vi sep (Mensch)* to (give a) scream *or* shriek; *(Bremsen, Maschine)* to (give a) screech.

aufkrempeln *vt sep* **(jdm/sich) die Ärmel/Hose** ~ to roll up sb's/one's sleeves/trousers.

aufkreuzen *vi sep* **(a)** *aux sein (inf: erscheinen)* to turn *or* show up *(inf)*. **(b)** *aux sein or haben gegen den Wind* ~ *(Naut)* to tack; **gegen die allgemeine Meinung** ~ *(fig)* to go against the general feeling.

aufkriegen *vt sep (inf) siehe* **aufbekommen.**

aufkünden *(geh),* **aufkündigen** *vt sep Vertrag etc* to revoke, to terminate. **jdm den Dienst** ~ to hand in one's notice to sb, to give notice to sb that one is leaving (one's employment); **jdm die Freundschaft** ~ *(geh)* to terminate one's friendship with sb; **jdm den Gehorsam** ~ to refuse obedience to sb.

Aufkündigung *f* termination, revocation; *(von Freundschaft)* termination. ~ **des Gehorsams** *(geh)* refusal to obey.

Aufl. *abbr of* **Auflage.**

auflachen *vi sep* to (give a) laugh; *(schallend)* to burst out laughing.

aufladbar *adj* chargeable; *(neu* ~) rechargeable.

aufladen sep *irreg* **1** *vt* **(a) etw (auf etw** *acc)* ~ to load sth on(to) sth; **jdm/sich etw** ~ to load sb/oneself down with sth, to burden sb/oneself with sth; *(fig)* to saddle sb/oneself with sth.

(b) *(elektrisch)* to charge; *(neu* ~) to recharge. **emotional aufgeladen** *(fig)* emotionally charged.

(c) *(Aut)* Motor to supercharge, to boost.

2 *vr (Batterie etc)* to be charged; *(neu)* to be recharged; *(elektrisch/elektrostatisch geladen werden)* to become charged.

Aufladung *f (Elec) (das Aufladen)* charging; *(Ladung)* charge.

Auflage *f* **(a)** *(Ausgabe)* edition; *(Druck)* impression; ~**(höhe)** number of copies; *(von Zeitung)* circulation. **das Buch/die Zeitung hat hohe** ~**n** erreicht a large number of copies of this book have been published/this paper has attained a large circulation; **die Zeitung will ihre** ~ **erhöhen** the newspaper is wanting to improve its circulation figures.

(b) *(Econ: Fertigungsmenge)* production.

(c) *(Bedingung)* condition. **jdm etw zur** ~ **machen** to impose sth on sb as a condition; **jdm zur** ~ **machen, etw zu tun** to make it a condition for sb to do sth, to impose a condition on sb that he do sth; **er bekam die Genehmigung nur mit der** ~**, das zu tun** he obtained permission only on condition that he do that; **die** ~ **haben, etw zu tun** to be obliged to do sth.

(d) *(Stütze)* support, rest.

(e) *(Überzug)* plating *no pl,* coating; *(Polsterung)* pad, padding *no pl.* **eine** ~ **aus Silber** silver plating *or* coating.

(f) *(DDR: Plansoll)* target.

Auflage-: ~**fläche** *f* supporting surface; ~**(n)höhe** *f (von Buch)* number of copies published; *(von Zeitung)* circulation; **das Buch/die Zeitung hatte eine** ~**höhe von 12.000** 12,000 copies of the book were published/the paper had a circulation of 12,000; ~**punkt** *m* point of support; **a~schwach** *adj* low-circulation *attr;* **a~stark** *adj* high-circulation *attr;* ~**ziffer** *f* circulation (figures *pl*); *(von Buch)* number of copies published.

auflandig *adj (Naut)* landward, coastward; *Wind auch* onshore *attr.*

auflassen *vt sep irreg* **(a)** *(inf) (offenlassen)* to leave open; *(aufbehalten) Hut* to keep *or* leave on. **das Kind länger** ~ to let the child stay up (longer).

(b) *(schließen) (Min) Grube, (Aus, S Ger) Betrieb* to close *or* shut down. **eine aufgelassene Grube** a closed-down *or* an abandoned mine.

(c) *(Jur) Grundstück* to convey *(form),* to transfer, to make over *(form).*

Auflassung *f* **(a)** *(Min, Aus, S Ger: von Geschäft)* closing down, shut-down. **(b)** *(Jur)* conveyancing *(form),* conveyance *(form),* transference.

auflasten *vt sep siehe* **aufbürden.**

auflauern *vi sep +dat* to lie in wait for; *(und angreifen, ansprechen)* to waylay.

Auflauf *m* **(a)** *(Menschen~)* crowd. **rechtswidriger** ~ *(Jur)* unlawful assembly. **(b)** *(Cook)* (baked) pudding *(sweet or savoury)*.

auflaufen sep *irreg* **1** *vi aux sein* **(a)** *(auf Grund laufen: Schiff)* to run aground *(auf +acc or dat* on).

(b) *(aufprallen)* **auf jdn/etw** ~ to run into sb/sth, to collide with sb/sth; **jdn** ~ **lassen** *(Ftbl)* to bodycheck sb.

(c) *(sich ansammeln)* to accumulate, to mount up.

(d) *(Wasser: ansteigen)* to rise. ~**des Wasser** flood tide, rising tide.

(e) *(dial: anschwellen)* to swell (up).

2 *vr sich (dat)* **die Füße** ~ *(inf)* to get sore feet.

Auflaufform *f (Cook)* ovenproof dish.

aufleben *vi sep aux sein* to revive; *(munter, lebendig werden)* to liven up, to come to life again; *(neuen Lebensmut bekommen)* to find a new lease of life. **Erinnerungen wieder** ~ **lassen** to revive memories.

auflecken *vt sep* to lick up; *Wunde* to lick open.

auflegen sep **1** *vt* **(a)** to put on; *Gedeck* to lay; *Kompresse auch* to apply; *Hörer* to put down, to replace. **jdm die Hand** ~ *(Rel)* to lay hands on sb.

(b) *(herausgeben) Buch* to bring out, to publish, to print. **ein Buch neu** ~ to reprint a book; *(neu bearbeitet)* to bring out a new edition of a book.

(c) *(zur Einsichtnahme)* to display, to put up.

(d) *(Econ)* Serie to launch.

(e) *(Fin)* Aktien to issue, to float.

(f) *(Naut) Schiff* to lay up.

(g) *siehe* **aufgelegt 2.**

2 *vi* **(a)** *(Telefonhörer* ~) to hang up, to ring off *(Brit)*.

(b) *(Feuerholz etc* ~) to put on more firewood/coal *etc.*

3 *vr (rare) sich (dat) Entbehrungen etc* ~ to impose sacrifices *etc* on oneself, to suffer self-imposed privations *etc.*

auflehnen sep **1** *vr* **sich gegen jdn/etw** ~ to revolt *or* rebel

against sb/sth. **2** *vt* (*dial*) **den Arm** ~ to lean on one's arm; **die Arme auf etw** (*acc or dat*) ~ to lean one's arms on sth.
Auflehnung *f* revolt, rebellion.
aufleimen *vt sep* to glue on (*auf* +*acc* -to).
auflesen *vt sep irreg* (*lit, fig inf*) to pick up. **jdn/etw von der Straße** ~ to pick sb/sth up off the street.
aufleuchten *vi sep aux sein or haben* (*lit, fig*) to light up.
auflichten *sep* **1** *vt* (a) *Wald, Gebüsch* to thin out. (b) (*aufhellen*) *Bild, Raum* to brighten up; (*fig*) *Hintergründe, Geheimnis* to clear up, to get to the bottom of. **2** *vr* (*Himmel*) to clear; (*fig: Hintergründe*) to be cleared up, to become clear.
Auflichtung *f siehe vb* thinning out; brightening up; clearing up; clearing.
Auflieferer *m* (*form*) sender; (*von Fracht*) consignor.
aufliefern *vt sep* (*form*) to dispatch; *Fracht* to consign (for delivery).
Auflieferung *f siehe vt* (*form*) dispatch; consignment (for delivery).
aufliegen *sep irreg* **1** *vi* (a) to lie *or* rest on top; (*Schallplatte*) to be on the turntable; (*Hörer*) to be on; (*Tischdecke*) to be on (the table). **auf etw** (*dat*) ~ to lie *or* rest/be on sth.
  (b) (*ausliegen*) (*zur Ansicht*) to be displayed; (*zur Benutzung*) to be available.
  (c) (*erschienen sein: Buch*) to be published.
  (d) (*Naut*) to be laid up.
2 *vr* (*inf*) (*Patient*) to get bedsores. **sich** (*dat*) **den Rücken** *etc* ~ to get bedsores on one's back; **er hat sich sehr aufgelegen** he has bad bedsores.
auflisten *vr sep* to list.
Auflistung *f* listing; (*Liste*) list.
auflockern *sep* **1** *vt* (a) *Boden* to break up, to loosen (up).
  (b) **die Muskeln** ~ to loosen up (one's muscles); (*durch Bewegung auch*) to limber up.
  (c) (*abwechslungsreicher machen*) *Unterricht, Stoff, Vortrag* to make less monotonous, to give relief to (*durch* with); (*weniger streng machen*) to make less severe; *Frisur, Muster* to soften, to make less severe.
  (d) (*entspannen, zwangloser machen*) to make more relaxed; *Verhältnis, Atmosphäre auch* to ease. **in aufgelockerter Stimmung** in a relaxed mood; **er war sehr aufgelockert** he was in a very relaxed mood.
2 *vr* (a) (*Sport*) to limber *or* loosen up.
  (b) (*Bewölkung*) to break up, to disperse.
Auflockerung *f* (a) (*von Boden*) breaking up, loosening (up); (*von Muskeln*) loosening up. **... trägt zur** ~ **des Stoffes/des strengen Musters bei** ... helps to make the material less monotonous/the pattern less severe; **ihm gelang die** ~ **einer gespannten Atmosphäre** he succeeded in easing a tense atmosphere.
  (b) *siehe vr* limbering *or* loosening up; breaking up, dispersal, dispersing.
auflodern *vi sep aux sein* (*Flammen*) to flare up; (*in Flammen aufgehen*) to go up in flames; (*lodernd brennen*) to blaze; (*fig: Kämpfe, Haß, Leidenschaft*) to flare up.
auflösbar *adj* soluble; *Gleichung auch* solvable; *Ehe* dissolvable; *Verlobung* that can be broken off; *Vertrag* revocable, able to be cancelled.
auflösen *sep* **1** *vt* (a) (*in Flüssigkeit*) to dissolve; (*in Bestandteile zerlegen, Phot*) to resolve (*in* +*acc* into); (*Math*) *Klammern* to eliminate; *Gleichung* to (re)solve; (*Mus*) *Vorzeichen* to cancel; *Dissonanz* to resolve (*in* +*acc* into); *siehe* **aufgelöst 2**.
  (b) (*aufklären*) *Widerspruch, Mißverständnis* to clear up, to resolve; *Rätsel auch* to solve.
  (c) (*zerstreuen*) *Wolken, Versammlung* to disperse, to break up.
  (d) (*aufheben*) to dissolve (*auch Parl*); *Einheit, Gruppe* to disband; *Verlobung* to break off; *Vertrag* to cancel; *Konto* to close; *Haushalt* to break up.
  (e) (*geh*) *Haar* to let down; *geflochtenes Haar* to let loose; *Knoten* to undo. **mit aufgelösten Haaren** with one's hair loose.
2 *vr* (a) (*in Flüssigkeit*) to dissolve; (*sich zersetzen: Zellen, Reich, Ordnung*) to disintegrate; (*Zweifel, Probleme*) to disappear. **all ihre Probleme haben sich in nichts aufgelöst** all her problems have dissolved into thin air *or* have disappeared.
  (b) (*sich zerstreuen*) to disperse; (*Wolken auch*) to break up; (*Nebel auch*) to lift.
  (c) (*auseinandergehen*) (*Verband*) to disband; (*sich formell* ~ : *esp Parl*) to dissolve itself.
  (d) (*sich aufklären*) (*Mißverständnis, Problem*) to resolve itself, to be resolved; (*Rätsel auch*) to be solved.
  (e) **sich in etw** (*acc*) ~ (*verwandeln*) to turn into sth; (*undeutlich werden*) to dissolve into sth.
  (f) (*geh: Schleife, Haar*) to become undone.
  (g) (*Phot*) to be resolved.
Auflösung *f siehe vt* (a-d) (a) dissolving; resolution; elimination; (re)solving; cancellation, resolution.
  (b) clearing up, resolving; solving.
  (c) dispersal.
  (d) dissolving; disbanding; breaking off; cancellation; closing; breaking up.
  (e) *siehe vr* dissolving; disintegration; disappearance; dispersal; disbandment; dissolution; resolution; solution (*gen, von* to).
  (f) (*Verstörtheit*) distraction.
Auflösungszeichen *nt* (*Mus*) natural.
aufmachen *sep* **1** *vt* (a) (*öffnen*) to open; (*lösen, aufknöpfen, aufschnallen*) to undo; *Haar* to loosen; (*inf: operieren*) to open up (*inf*), to cut open (*inf*).
  (b) (*eröffnen, gründen*) *Geschäft, Unternehmen* to open (up).
  (c) (*gestalten*) *Buch, Zeitung* to make *or* get up;

(*zurechtmachen*) *jdn* to dress, to get up (*pej*); (*in Presse*) *Ereignis, Prozeß etc* to feature. **der Prozeß wurde groß aufgemacht** the trial was given a big spread *or* was played up (in the press).
  (d) (*dial: anbringen*) *Plakat, Vorhänge* to put up, to hang (up).
2 *vi* (*Tür öffnen*) to open up, to open the door; (*Geschäft*) (*er*)*öffnen*) to open (up).
3 *vr* (a) (*sich zurechtmachen*) to get oneself up.
  (b) (*sich anschicken*) to get ready, to make preparations; (*aufbrechen*) to set out, to start (out). **sich zu einem Spaziergang** ~ to set out on a walk.
  (c) (*liter: Wind*) to rise (*liter*), to get up.
Aufmacher *m* (*Press*) lead.
Aufmachung *f* (a) (*Kleidung*) turn-out, rig-out (*inf*). **in großer** ~ **erscheinen** to turn up in full dress.
  (b) (*Gestaltung*) presentation, style; (*von Buch*) presentation, make-up; (*von Seite, Zeitschrift*) layout. **der Artikel erschien in großer** ~ the article was given a big spread *or* was featured prominently.
  (c) (*Press: Artikel etc auf Titelseite*) lead feature.
aufmalen *vt sep* to paint on (*auf etw* (*acc*) sth); (*inf*) to scrawl (*auf* +*acc* on).
Aufmarsch *m* (a) (*Mil*) (*das Aufmarschieren*) marching up; (*in Stellung, Kampflinie*) deployment. (b) (*Sw*) attendance.
Aufmarschgebiet *nt* deployment zone.
aufmarschieren* *vi sep aux sein* (*heranmarschieren*) to march up; (*Mil: in Stellung gehen*) to deploy; (*vorbeimarschieren*) to march past. ~ **lassen** (*Mil: an Kampflinie etc*) to deploy; (*fig hum*) to have march up/past.
aufmeißeln *vt sep* (*Med*) to trephine.
aufmerken *vi sep* (*aufhorchen*) to sit up and take notice; (*geh: achtgeben*) to pay heed *or* attention (*auf* +*acc* to).
aufmerksam *adj* (a) *Zuhörer, Beobachter, Schüler* attentive; *Blicke auch, Augen* keen; (*scharf beobachtend*) observant. **jdn auf etw** (*acc*) ~ **machen** to draw sb's attention to sth; **jdn darauf** ~ **machen, daß ...** to draw sb's attention to the fact that ...; **auf etw** (*acc*) ~ **werden** to become aware of sth; ~ **werden** to sit up and take notice.
  (b) (*zuvorkommend*) attentive. **(das ist) sehr** ~ **von Ihnen** (that's) most kind of you.
Aufmerksamkeit *f* (a) *no pl* attention, attentiveness. **das ist meiner** ~ **entgangen** I failed to notice that, that slipped my notice *or* escaped my attention.
  (b) *no pl* (*Zuvorkommenheit*) attentiveness.
  (c) (*Geschenk*) token (gift). **(nur) eine kleine** ~ (just) a little something *or* gift; **kleine** ~**en** little gifts.
aufmöbeln *vt sep* (*inf*) *Gegenstand* to do up (*inf*); *Kenntnisse* to polish up (*inf*); *jdn* (*beleben*) to buck up (*inf*), to pep up (*inf*); (*aufmuntern*) to buck up (*inf*), to cheer up.
aufmontieren* *vt sep* to mount, to fit (on). **etw auf etw** (*acc*) ~ to mount sth on sth, to fit sth on *or* to sth.
aufmotzen *vt sep* (*inf*) *Theaterstück* to revamp (*inf*).
aufmucken, aufmucksen *vi sep* (*inf*) to protest (*gegen at, against*).
aufmuntern *vt sep* (*aufheitern*) to cheer up; (*beleben*) to liven up, to ginger up (*inf*); (*ermutigen*) to encourage. **jdn zu etw** ~ to encourage sb to do sth; **ein** ~**des Lächeln** an encouraging smile.
Aufmunterung *f siehe vt* cheering up; livening up, gingering up (*inf*); encouragement.
aufmüpfig *adj* (*inf*) rebellious.
Aufmüpfigkeit *f* (*inf*) rebelliousness.
aufnageln *vt sep* to nail on (*auf* +*acc* -to).
aufnähen *vt sep* to sew on (*auf* +*acc* -to).
Aufnahme *f* -, -n (a) (*Empfang, fig: Reaktion*) reception; (*Empfangsraum*) reception (area). **bei jdm freundliche** ~ **finden** (*lit, fig*) to meet with a warm reception from sb; **jdm eine freundliche** ~ **bereiten** to give sb a warm welcome; **die** ~ **in ein Krankenhaus** admission (in)to hospital; **wie war die** ~ **beim Publikum?** how did the audience receive it *or* react?
  (b) (*in Verein, Orden etc*) admission (*in* +*acc* to); (*Aufgenommener*) recruit.
  (c) *no pl* (*lit, fig: Absorption*) absorption; (*Nahrungs*~) taking, ingestion (*form*).
  (d) *no pl* (*Einbeziehung*) inclusion, incorporation; (*in Liste, Bibliographie*) inclusion.
  (e) *no pl* (*von Geldern, Kapital, Hypothek*) raising.
  (f) *no pl* (*Aufzeichnung: von Protokoll, Diktat*) taking down; (*von Personalien*) taking (down); (*von Telegramm*) taking. **die** ~ **eines Unfalls** taking down details of an accident.
  (g) *no pl* (*Beginn*) (*von Gespräch etc*) start, commencement; (*von Tätigkeit auch*) taking up; (*von Beziehung, Verbindung auch*) establishment.
  (h) *no pl* (*das Fotografieren*) taking, photographing; (*das Filmen*) filming, shooting. **Achtung,** ~! action!
  (i) (*Fotografie*) photo(graph), shot (*inf*); (*Schnappschuß, Amateur*~) snap (*inf*). **eine** ~ **machen** to take a photo(graph) etc.
  (j) (*auf Tonband*) recording.
Aufnahme-: ~**antrag** *m* application for membership *or* admission; ~**bedingung** *f* condition of admission; a~**bereit** *adj Boden* ready for planting; *Kamera* ready to shoot; (*fig*) receptive, open (*für* to); ~**bereitschaft** *f* (*fig*) receptiveness, receptivity; a~**fähig** *adj* (a) **für etw** a~**fähig sein** to be able to take sth in; **ich bin nicht mehr** a~**fähig** I can't take anything else in; (b) *Markt* active; ~**fähigkeit** *f* ability to take things in; ~**fähigkeit für etw** ability to take sth in; activeness; ~**gebühr** *f* enrolment fee; (*in Verein*) admission fee; ~**gerät** *nt* (*Film*) (film) camera; (*Tonband*~) recorder; ~**land** *nt* host country (*für* to); ~**leiter** *m* (*Film*) production manager; (*Rad*) producer; ~**prüfung** *f* entrance examination; ~**studio** *nt* (film/recording) studio;

~**vermögen** nt (a) (~fähigkeit) receptiveness, receptivity (für to); (b) (Fassungsvermögen) capacity; ~**wagen** m (Rad) recording van; **a~würdig** adj (für Verein) worthy of admittance; (für Wörterbuch etc) worth including.

Aufnahmsprüfung f (Aus) siehe **Aufnahmeprüfung**.

aufnehmen vt sep irreg (a) (vom Boden) to pick up; (heben) to lift up.
(b) (lit: empfangen, fig: reagieren auf) to receive.
(c) (unterbringen) to take (in); (fassen) to take, to hold; Arbeitskräfte, Einwanderer to absorb.
(d) (in Verein, Orden etc) to admit (in + acc to); (Schule auch, Aus: anstellen) to take on.
(e) (absorbieren) to absorb, to take up; (im Körper ~) to take; (fig: eindringen lassen) Eindrücke to take in; (begreifen auch) to grasp. etw in sich (dat) ~ to take sth in; er nimmt (alles) schnell auf he takes things in or grasps things quickly, he's quick on the uptake.
(f) (mit einbeziehen) to include, to incorporate; (in Liste, Bibliographie) to include; (fig: aufgreifen) to take up.
(g) (esp Ftbl) Ball to take, to receive.
(h) (dial) (aufwischen) to wipe up; (mit Stück Brot auch) to mop or soak up.
(i) (beginnen) to begin, to commence; Verbindung, Beziehung to establish; Tätigkeit, Studium auch to take up. den Kampf ~ to commence battle; (fig auch) to take up the struggle; Kontakt or Fühlung mit jdm ~ to contact sb.
(j) Kapital, Summe, Gelder, Hypothek to raise; Kredit auch to get.
(k) (niederschreiben) Protokoll, Diktat to take down; Personalien to take (down); Telegramm to take.
(l) (fotografieren) to take (a photograph or picture of), to photograph; (filmen) to film, to shoot (inf).
(m) (auf Tonband) to record.
(n) (beim Stricken) Maschen to increase, to make.
(o) es mit jdm/etw ~ können to be a match for sb/sth, to be able to match sb/sth; es mit jdm/etw nicht ~ können to be no match for sb/sth; an Naivität kann es keiner mit ihm ~ where naïveté is concerned there's no-one to beat him.

aufnehmenswert adj siehe **aufnahmewürdig**.

Aufnehmer m (dial) (a) (N. Ger: Scheuertuch) cloth. (b) (dial: Müllschaufel) shovel.

äufnen vt (Sw) Geld etc to accumulate.

aufnesteln vt sep (inf) Knoten, Schnur to undo; Bluse, Haken auch to unfasten.

aufnorden vt sep (a) (Pol) to arianize. (b) (dated hum: verbessern) to tart up (inf), to improve; Image to brush up.

aufnotieren* vt sep (sich dat) etw ~ to note sth down, to make a note of sth.

aufnötigen vt sep jdm etw ~ Geld, Essen to force or press sth on sb; Entscheidung, Meinung to force or impose sth on sb; die Lage nötigt (uns) Vorsicht auf the situation requires or demands that we be cautious or requires caution (on our part).

auf|oktroyieren* vt sep jdm etw ~ (geh) to impose or force sth on sb.

auf|opfern sep 1 vr to sacrifice oneself. 2 vt to sacrifice, to give up.

auf|opfernd adj Mensch self-sacrificing; Liebe, Tätigkeit, Arbeit devoted. ein ~es Leben a life of self-sacrifice.

Auf|opferung f (a) (Aufgabe) sacrifice. durch ~ einer Sache (gen) by sacrificing sth; unter ~ einer Sache (gen) at the cost of sth. (b) (Selbst~) self-sacrifice. mit ~ with devotion.

Auf|opferungs-: a~bereit adj self-sacrificing; ~bereitschaft f self-sacrifice; a~voll adj self-sacrificing.

aufpacken vt sep jdm/einem Tier etw ~ to load sth onto sb/an animal, to load sb/an animal with sth; jdm etw ~ (fig) to burden or saddle (inf) sb with sth; er packte sich (dat) den Rucksack auf he put on his rucksack.

aufpäppeln vt sep (inf) (mit Nahrung) to feed up (inf); (durch Pflege) to nurse back to health.

aufpappen vt sep (inf) (jdm) etw ~ to stick sth on (sb); etw (auf etw acc) ~ to stick sth on (sth); sich (dat) etw ~ to stick sth on.

aufpassen vi sep (a) (beaufsichtigen) auf jdn/etw ~ to watch sb/sth, to keep an eye on sb/sth; (hüten) to look after or to mind sb/sth; (Aufsicht führen) to supervise sb/sth; (bei Examen) to invigilate sb.
(b) (aufmerksam sein, achtgeben) to pay attention. paß auf!, aufgepaßt! look, watch; (sei aufmerksam) pay attention; (Vorsicht) watch out, mind (out).

Aufpasser(in f) m -s, - (pej: Aufseher, Spitzel) spy (pej), watchdog (inf); (Beobachter) supervisor; (bei Examen) invigilator; (Wächter) guard.

aufpeitschen vt sep Meer, Wellen to whip up; (fig) Sinne to inflame, to fire; Menschen to inflame, to work up; (stärker) to whip up into a frenzy. eine ~de Rede a rabble-rousing (pej) or inflammatory speech; drei Tassen starken Kaffee, um ihn aufzupeitschen (inf) three cups of strong coffee to pep him up (inf).

aufpflanzen sep 1 vt to plant; (Mil) Bajonett to fix. 2 vr sich vor jdm ~ to plant oneself in front of sb.

aufpflügen vt sep to plough up. das Meer ~ (liter: Schiff) to plough through the sea.

aufpfropfen vt sep (lit) to graft on (+ dat -to); (fig) to superimpose (+ dat on).

aufpicken vt sep (a) to peck up; (fig) to glean, to pick up. (b) (öffnen) to peck open.

aufpinseln vt sep (inf) (hinschreiben) to scrawl (auf + acc on); (auftragen) Lack to slap on (inf) (auf etw (acc)) sth).

aufplätten vt sep (N Ger) siehe **aufbügeln**.

aufplatzen vi sep aux sein to burst open; (Wunde) to open up, to rupture; (Knopf) to pop open.

aufplustern sep 1 vt Federn to ruffle up; (fig) Vorfall, Ereignis to blow up, to exaggerate. 2 vr (Vogel) to ruffle (up) its feathers, to puff itself up; (Mensch) to puff oneself up.

aufpolieren* vt sep (lit, fig) to polish up.

aufprägen vt sep to emboss, to stamp. einen Stempel auf etw (acc) ~ to emboss sth with a stamp; jdm/einer Sache seinen/einen gewissen Stempel ~ (fig) to leave one's/its mark on sb/sth.

Aufprall m -(e)s, (rare) -e impact.

aufprallen vi sep aux sein auf etw (acc) ~ to strike or hit sth; (Fahrzeug auch) to collide with sth, to run into sth.

Aufpreis m extra or additional charge. gegen ~ for an extra or additional charge.

aufpressen vt sep to press on (auf + acc -to); (öffnen) to press open.

aufprobieren* vt sep to try (on).

aufpulvern vt sep (inf) to pep or buck up (inf); Moral to lift, to boost. der Kaffee pulvert (dich) auf coffee peps or bucks you up (inf) or is a good pick-me-up.

Aufpulverungsmittel nt (inf) pick-me-up (inf), stimulant.

aufpumpen vt sep 1 vt Reifen, Ballon to pump up, to inflate; Fahrrad to pump up or inflate the tyres of. 2 vr (Vogel, fig: sich aufspielen) to puff oneself up; (fig: wütend werden) to work oneself up (inf).

aufpusten vt sep (inf) siehe **aufblasen**.

aufputschen sep 1 vt (a) (aufwiegeln) to rouse; Gefühle, öffentliche Meinung auch to whip or stir up (gegen against). jdn zu etw ~ to incite sb to do sth. (b) (durch Reizmittel) to stimulate. ~de Mittel stimulants. 2 vr to pep oneself up (inf), to dope oneself (Sport inf).

Aufputschmittel nt stimulant.

Aufputz m get-up (inf), rig-out (inf); (festlich geschmückt) finery (iro), attire (iro).

aufputzen vt sep (a) (schmücken) Haus, Buch etc to decorate; (schön machen) jdn to dress up, to deck out; (fig: aufpolieren) Gegenstand to do up; Image to polish or brush up; Zahlen to dress up. (b) (dial: aufwischen) Boden to clean (up); Flüssigkeit to mop or wipe up.

aufquellen vi sep irreg aux sein (a) (anschwellen) to swell (up). aufgequollen swollen; Gesicht auch puffy, bloated; Mensch bloated(-looking); etw ~ lassen to soak sth (to allow it to swell up).
(b) (geh: aufsteigen) (Rauch) to rise; (Flüssigkeit auch, fig: Gefühle auch) to well or spring up.

aufraffen sep 1 vr to pull oneself up; (vom Boden auch) to pick oneself up. sich ~, etw zu tun, sich zu etw ~ (inf) to rouse oneself to do sth. 2 vt Rock, Papiere, Eigentum to gather up; (schnell aufheben) to snatch up.

aufragen vi sep aux sein or haben (in die Höhe ~) to rise; (sehr hoch, groß auch) to tower (up) (über + dat above, over). die hoch ~den Türme the soaring towers; die hoch ~den Fabrikkamine/Tannen the towering factory chimneys/fir trees.

aufrappeln vr sep (inf) (a) siehe **aufraffen 1**. (b) (wieder zu Kräften kommen) to recover, to get over it. er hat sich nach seiner Krankheit endlich wieder aufgerappelt he at last recovered from or got over his illness.

aufrauchen vt sep (zu Ende rauchen) to finish (smoking); (aufbrauchen) to smoke, to get through.

aufrauhen vt sep to roughen (up); (Tex) Stoff to nap; Haut, Hände to roughen, to make rough.

aufräumen sep 1 vt to tidy or clear up; (wegräumen auch) to clear or put away.
2 vi (a) mit etw ~ to do away with sth.
(b) (pej: dezimieren) unter der Bevölkerung (gründlich) ~ (Seuche etc) to decimate the population, to wreak havoc among the population; (Tyrann etc) to slaughter the population wholesale.
(c) siehe **aufgeräumt 2**.

Aufräumungs|arbeiten pl clear(ing)-up operation sing.

aufrechnen vt sep (a) jdm etw ~ to charge sth to sb or to sb's account; (fig: vorwerfen) to throw sth in sb's face. (b) etw gegen etw ~ to set sth off or offset sth against sth.

aufrecht adj (lit, fig) upright; Körperhaltung, Gangart auch erect. ~ gehen/stehen to walk/stand upright or erect; ~ sitzen to sit up(right); etw ~ hinstellen to place sth upright or in an upright position; sie kann sich kaum noch ~ halten she's fit or ready to drop, she can hardly keep (herself) upright.

aufrecht|erhalten* vt sep irreg to maintain; Kontakt, Bräuche auch to keep up; Behauptung auch to stick to; Entschluß, Glauben auch to keep or adhere to, to uphold; Verein to keep going; (moralisch stützen) jdn to keep going, to sustain.

Aufrecht|erhaltung f siehe vt maintenance, maintaining; keeping up; sticking (gen to); adherence (gen to), upholding; keeping going.

aufrecken sep 1 vt to stretch up; Hals to crane. 2 vr to stretch up.

aufreden vt sep siehe **aufschwatzen**.

aufregen sep 1 vt (ärgerlich machen) to irritate, to annoy; (nervös machen) to make nervous or edgy (inf); (beunruhigen) to agitate, to disturb; (bestürzen) to upset; (erregen) to excite. du regst mich auf! you're getting on my nerves; er regt mich auf he drives me mad (inf).
2 vr to get worked up (inf) or excited (über + acc about); siehe **aufgeregt**.

aufregend adj exciting.

Aufregung f excitement no pl; (Beunruhigung) agitation no pl. nur keine ~! don't get excited, don't get worked up (inf) or into a state (inf)!; die Nachricht hat das ganze Land in ~ versetzt the news caused a great stir throughout the country; jdn in ~ ver-

setzen to put sb in a flurry, to get sb in a state (*inf*); **alles war in heller** ~ everything was in utter confusion, there was complete bedlam.

aufreiben¹ *sep irreg* 1 *vt* (a) (*wundreiben*) *Haut etc* to chafe, to rub sore. **sich** (*dat*) **die Hände/Haut** ~ to chafe one's hands/oneself, to rub one's hands/oneself sore.
  (b) (*fig: zermürben*) to wear down *or* out.
  (c) (*Mil: völlig vernichten*) to wipe out, to annihilate.
  2 *vr* (*durch Sorgen etc*) to wear oneself out; (*durch Arbeit auch*) to work oneself into the ground.

aufreibend *adj* (*fig*) wearing, trying; (*stärker*) stressful. **nervlich** ~ stressful.

aufreihen *sep* 1 *vt* (*in Linie*) to line up, to put in a line/lines *or* a row/rows; *Perlen* to string; (*fig*) (*aufzählen*) to list, to enumerate. 2 *vr* to line up, to get in a line/lines *or* a row/rows.

aufreißen¹ *sep irreg* 1 *vt* (a) (*durch Reißen öffnen, aufbrechen*) to tear *or* rip open; *Straße* to tear *or* rip up.
  (b) *Tür, Fenster* to fling open; *Augen, Mund* to open wide.
  (c) (*beschädigen*) *Kleidung* to tear, to rip; *Haut* to gash (open).
  (d) (*Sport inf*) *Deckung, Abwehr* to open up.
  (e) (*in großen Zügen darstellen*) *Thema* to outline.
  (f) (*sl*) *Mädchen* to pick up (*inf*); (*sich verschaffen*) *Job, Angebot* to land (oneself) (*inf*), to get.
  2 *vi aux sein* (*Naht*) to split, to burst; (*Hose*) to tear, to rip; (*Wunde*) to tear open; (*Wolkendecke*) to break up.

aufreißen² *vt sep irreg* (*Tech*) to draw the/an elevation of.

aufreiten *sep irreg* 1 *vi aux sein* (*Reiterverband*) to ride up. 2 *vr* to get riding sores.

aufreizen *vt sep* (a) (*herausfordern*) to provoke; (*aufwiegeln*) to incite. **jdn zum Widerstand/zur Opposition** ~ to induce/incite sb to resist/stand in opposition. (b) (*erregen*) to excite; (*stärker*) to inflame.

aufreizend *adj* provocative.

aufribbeln *vt sep* (*inf*) to unpick.

Aufrichte *f* -, -n (*Sw*) *siehe* **Richtfest**.

aufrichten *sep* 1 *vt* (a) (*in aufrechte Lage bringen*) *Gegenstand* to put *or* set upright; *jdn* to help up; *Oberkörper* to raise (up), to straighten (up).
  (b) (*aufstellen*) to erect, to put up; (*fig*) to set up.
  (c) (*fig: moralisch*) to put new heart into, to give fresh heart to, to lift.
  2 *vr* (*gerade stehen*) to stand up (straight); (*gerade sitzen*) to sit up (straight); (*aus gebückter Haltung*) to straighten up; (*fig: moralisch*) to pick oneself up, to get back on one's feet. **sich im Bett** ~ to sit up in bed; **sich an jdm** ~ (*fig*) to find new strength in sb, to take heart from sb; **ein guter Freund, an dessen Stärke man sich in schweren Zeiten** ~ **kann** a good friend whose strength can bear one up in times of trouble.

aufrichtig *adj* sincere (*zu, gegen* towards); (*ehrlich auch*) honest.

Aufrichtigkeit *f siehe adj* sincerity; honesty.

aufriegeln *vt sep* to unbolt.

aufringeln *vr sep* to uncoil; (*zusammenringeln*) to coil itself up.

Aufriß *m* (a) elevation. **etw im** ~ **zeichnen** to draw the side/front elevation of sth. (b) (*fig: Abriß*) outline, sketch.

Aufrißzeichnung *f* (*Tech, Archit*) elevation.

aufritzen *vt sep* (*öffnen*) to slit open; (*verletzen*) to cut (open).

aufrollen *sep* 1 *vt* (a) (*zusammenrollen*) *Teppich, Ärmel* to roll up; *Kabel* to coil *or* wind up; (*auf Rolle*) to wind up.
  (b) (*entrollen*) to unroll; *Fahne* to unfurl; *Kabel* to uncoil, to unwind; (*von Rolle*) to unwind, to reel off.
  (c) (*fig*) *Problem* to go into. **einen Fall/Prozeß wieder** ~ to reopen a case/trial.
  2 *vr* (*sich zusammenrollen*) to roll up.

aufrücken *vi sep aux sein* (a) (*weiterrücken, aufschließen*) to move up *or* along. (b) (*befördert werden*) to move up, to be promoted; (*Schüler*) to move *or* go up. **zum Geschäftsleiter** ~ to be promoted to manager.

Aufruf *m* (a) appeal (*an* +*acc* to). (b) (*von Namen*) **seinen** ~ **abwarten** to wait for one's name to be called, to wait to be called; **nach** ~ on being called, when called. (c) (*Datenverarbeitung*) call. (d) (*Fin: von Banknoten*) calling in.

aufrufen *sep irreg* 1 *vt* (a) *Namen* to call; *Wartenden* to call (the name of). **Sie werden aufgerufen** your name *or* you will be called; **einen Schüler** ~ to ask a pupil (to answer) a question.
  (b) (*auffordern*) *jdn zu etw* ~ (*zu Mithilfe, Unterstützung etc*) to appeal to *or* call upon sb for sth; *jdn, etw zu tun* to appeal to *or* call upon sb to do sth; *Arbeiter zu einer Demonstration/zum Streik* ~ to call upon workers to attend a demonstration/to strike.
  (c) (*geh: mobilisieren*) *Hilfsbereitschaft, Spendenfreudigkeit, Gerechtigkeitsempfinden* to appeal to, to call upon.
  (d) (*Jur*) *Zeugen* to summon; *Erben* to give notice to.
  (e) (*Datenverarbeitung*) to call.
  (f) (*Fin: einziehen*) *Banknoten* to call in.
  2 *vi* **zum Widerstand/Streik etc** ~ to call for resistance/a strike etc, to call upon people to resist/strike etc.

Aufruhr *m* -(e)s, -e (a) (*Auflehnung*) revolt, rebellion, uprising.
  (b) (*Bewegtheit, fig: Erregung*) tumult, turmoil; (*in Stadt, Publikum auch*) pandemonium (*gen* in). **ihr innerlicher** ~ the tumult *or* turmoil within her; **in** ~ **sein** to be in a tumult *or* turmoil; (*Gefühle, Stadt auch*) to be in a tumult; **in** ~ **geraten** to be in a turmoil; **jdn in** ~ **versetzen** to throw sb into a turmoil; **das versetzte die ganze Stadt in** ~ this threw the whole town into a turmoil, this caused pandemonium throughout the whole town.

aufrühren *vt sep* to stir up; (*fig auch*) *Gefühle* to rouse. **alte Geschichten wieder** ~ to rake *or* stir up old stories; **das rührt nichts in mir auf** (*geh*) that leaves me unmoved.

Aufrührer(in *f*) *m* -s, - rabble-rouser.

aufrührerisch *adj* (a) (*aufwiegelnd*) *Rede, Pamphlet* rabble-rousing, inflammatory. (b) *attr* (*in Aufruhr*) rebellious; (*meuternd*) mutinous.

aufrunden *vt sep Betrag, Zahl etc* to round up (*auf* +*acc* to).

aufrüsten *vti sep* to arm. **ein Land atomar** ~ to give a country nuclear arms; **wieder** ~ to rearm.

Aufrüstung *f* arming. **atomare** ~ acquiring nuclear armaments.

aufrütteln *vt sep* to rouse (*aus* from); (*aus Lethargie etc auch*) to shake up (*aus* out of). **jdn/jds Gewissen** ~ to stir sb/sb's conscience; **jdn zum Handeln** ~ to rouse sb to action.

Aufrütt(e)lung *f* (*fig*) (*das Aufrütteln*) rousing; (*aus Lethargie etc auch*) shaking up; (*Zustand*) excitement.

aufs *contr of* **auf das**.

aufsagen *vt sep* (a) *Gedicht etc* to recite, to say. (b) (*geh: für beendet erklären*) **jdm die Freundschaft** ~ to break off one's friendship with sb; **jdm den Dienst/Gehorsam** ~ to refuse to serve/obey sb.

aufsammeln *vt sep* (*lit, fig*) to pick up.

aufsässig *adj* rebellious; *esp Kind auch* recalcitrant, obstreperous.

Aufsässigkeit *f siehe adj* rebelliousness; recalcitrance, obstreperousness.

aufsatteln *vt sep* (a) *Pferd* to saddle (up). (b) (*Tech*) *Anhänger* to hitch (up), to couple (on) (*an* +*acc* to).

Aufsatz *m* (a) (*Abhandlung*) essay; (*Schul~ auch*) composition. (b) (*oberer Teil*) top *or* upper part; (*zur Verzierung*) bit on top; (*von Kamera etc*) attachment. **ein Schrank mit abnehmbarem** ~ a cupboard with a removable top part *or* section. (c) (*Mil: von Geschütz*) (gun) sight.

Aufsatz-: ~**heft** *nt* essay *or* composition book; ~**sammlung** *f* collection of essays; ~**thema** *nt* essay subject.

aufsaugen *vt sep irreg Flüssigkeit* to soak up; (*Sonne auch*) to absorb; (*fig*) to absorb. **etw mit dem Staubsauger** ~ to vacuum sth up; **etw in sich** (*dat*) ~ (*Mensch*) to absorb sth, to soak sth in.

aufschauen *vi sep* (*dial*) *siehe* **aufblicken**.

aufschaufeln *vt sep* (a) (*aufhäufen*) to pile up. (b) (*aufgraben*) to dig up.

aufschaukeln *vr sep* (*Fahrzeug*) to bump up and down; (*fig inf: Haß, Emotionen*) to build up.

aufschäumen *vi sep aux sein* (*Meer*) to foam; (*Getränke*) to foam *or* froth up. **vor Zorn** ~ to boil with anger.

aufscheinen *vi sep irreg aux sein* (a) (*geh: aufleuchten*) to light up; (*Licht*) to appear; (*fig liter*) to shine out. (b) (*Aus: erscheinen*) to appear.

aufscheuchen *vt sep* to startle; (*inf*) *Öffentlichkeit* to startle, to shock. **jdn aus etw** ~ to jolt sb out of sth; **jdn von seiner Arbeit/Lektüre** ~ to disturb sb when he is working/reading.

aufscheuern *sep* 1 *vt Fuß etc* to rub sore; *Haut* to chafe. 2 *vr* to rub oneself sore. **meine Ellbogen/Knie haben sich aufgescheuert** I've rubbed my elbows/knees sore; **sich** (*dat*) **die Hände/Füße** ~ to take the skin off one's hands/feet.

aufschichten *vt sep* to stack, to pile up; *Stapel* to build up.

Aufschichtung *f siehe vt* stacking, piling up; building.

aufschieben *vt sep irreg Fenster, Tür* to slide open; *Riegel* to push *or* slide back; (*fig: verschieben*) to put off. **aufgeschoben ist nicht aufgehoben** (*prov*) putting something off does not mean it's solved.

aufschießen *sep irreg* 1 *vi aux sein* (a) (*Saat, Jugendlicher*) to shoot up; (*Flammen, Fontäne etc auch*) to leap up. **wie Pilze** ~ (*Hochhäuser etc*) to mushroom; *siehe* **aufgeschossen**. (b) (*emporschnellen, hochfahren*) to shoot *or* leap up. 2 *vt* (*Naut*) *Tau* to coil.

aufschimmern *vi sep aux sein or haben* (*geh*) to flash. **in etw** (*dat*) ~ (*fig*) to illuminate sth.

aufschlabbern *vt sep* (*N Ger inf*) *siehe* **auflecken**.

Aufschlag *m* (a) (*das Aufschlagen*) impact; (*Geräusch*) crash.
  (b) (*Tennis etc*) service, serve. **wer hat** ~? whose service *or* serve (is it)?; **sie hat** ~ she's serving, it's her service *or* serve.
  (c) (*Preis~*) surcharge, extra charge.
  (d) (*Ärmel~*) cuff; (*Hosen~*) turn-up (*Brit*), cuff (*US*); (*Mantel~ etc*) lapel.

Aufschlag- *in cpds* (*Sport*) service; ~**ball** *m* (*Tennis*) service, serve.

aufschlagen *sep irreg* 1 *vi* (a) *aux sein* (*auftreffen*) **auf etw** (*dat*) ~ to hit sth; **das Flugzeug schlug in einem Waldstück auf** the plane crashed into a wood; **mit dem Kopf etc auf etw** (*acc or dat*) ~ to hit one's head etc on sth; **dumpf** ~ to thud (*auf* +*acc* onto); **sie fühlte, wie ihr Kopf hart aufschlug** she felt the hard crack on her head.
  (b) *aux sein* (*sich öffnen*) to open.
  (c) *aux sein* (*Flammen*) to leap *or* blaze up (*aus* out of).
  (d) *aux haben or* (*rare*) *sein* (*Waren, Preise*) to rise, to go up (*um* by).
  (e) (*Tennis etc*) to serve. **du mußt** ~ it's your service *or* serve.
  2 *vt* (a) (*durch Schlagen öffnen*) *Nuß* to crack (open); *Eis* to crack a hole in. **jdm/sich den Kopf/die Augenbraue** ~ to crack *or* cut open sb's/one's head/cut open sb's/one's eyebrow.
  (b) (*aufklappen*) to open; (*zurückschlagen*) *Bett, Bettdecke* to turn back; (*hochschlagen*) *Kragen etc* to turn up; *Schleier* to lift up, to raise. **schlagt Seite 111 auf** open your books at page 111.
  (c) *Augen* to open.
  (d) (*aufbauen*) *Bett, Liegestuhl* to put up; *Zelt auch* to pitch; (*Nacht*)*lager* to set up, to pitch. **er hat seinen Wohnsitz in Wien/einem alten Bauernhaus aufgeschlagen** he has taken up residence in Vienna/an old farmhouse.

(e) (*Comm*) *Preise* to put up, to raise. **10% auf etw** (*acc*) ~ to put 10% on sth.

Aufschläger *m* (*Tennis etc*) server.

Aufschlagfehler *m* service fault.

Aufschlagzünder *m* (*Mil*) percussion fuse.

aufschlecken *vt sep* (*S Ger*) *siehe* **auflecken**.

aufschließen *sep irreg* 1 *vt* **(a)** (*öffnen*) to unlock; (*geh: erklären*) to elucidate (*jdm* to sb). **jdm die Tür** *etc* ~ to unlock the door *etc* for sb.
(b) (*geh: offenbaren*) **jdm sein Herz/Innerstes** ~ to open one's heart to sb/tell sb one's innermost thoughts.
(c) (*Chem, Biol*) to break down.
(d) *Rohstoffvorkommen, Bauland* to develop. **etw (für die Bebauung)** ~ to open sth up for development.
2 *vr* (*geh*) **sich leicht** ~ to find it easy to be open *or* frank; **sich jdm** ~ to be open *or* frank with sb; *siehe* **aufgeschlossen**.
3 *vi* **(a)** (*öffnen*) (**jdm**) ~ to unlock the door (for sb).
(b) (*heranrücken*) to close up; (*Sport*) to catch up (*zu* with).

aufschlitzen *vt sep* to rip (open); (*mit Messer auch*) to slit (open); *Gesicht* to slash; *Bauch* to slash open.

aufschluchzen *vi sep* (*geh*) to sob convulsively.

aufschlucken *vt sep Schall etc* to absorb; (*fig*) *Gelder etc* to swallow up.

Aufschluß *m* **(a)** (*Aufklärung*) information *no pl.* (**jdm**) ~ **über etw** (*acc*) **geben** to give (sb) information about sth; ~ **über etw** (*acc*) **verlangen** to demand an explanation of sth. **(b)** (*Chem, Biol*) breaking down. **(c)** (*Min: Erschließung*) development.

aufschlüsseln *vt sep* to break down (*nach* into); (*klassifizieren*) to classify (*nach* according to).

Aufschlüsselung, Aufschlüßlung (*rare*) *f siehe vt* breakdown; classification.

aufschlußreich *adj* informative, instructive.

aufschmeißen *vt sep irreg* **(a)** (*Aus inf*) *jdn* to send up (*inf*). **(b)** *siehe* **aufgeschmissen**.

aufschmieren *vt sep* (*inf*) to spread on; *Farbe* to smear on.

aufschnallen *vt sep* **(a)** (*festschnallen*) to buckle *or* strap on (*auf etw* (*acc*) *(-to)* sth). **(b)** (*losschnallen*) to unbuckle, to unstrap.

aufschnappen *sep* 1 *vt* to catch; (*inf*) *Wort etc* to pick up. 2 *vi aux sein* to snap *or* spring open.

aufschneiden *sep irreg* 1 *vt* **(a)** to cut open; (*tranchieren*) *Braten* to carve; *Buch* to cut; (*Med*) *Geschwür* to lance; *siehe* **Pulsader**. **(b)** (*in Scheiben schneiden*) to slice. 2 *vi* (*inf: prahlen*) to brag, to boast.

Aufschneider *m* (*inf*) braggart, boaster.

Aufschneiderei *f* (*inf*) bragging *no pl*, boasting *no pl.*

aufschneiderisch *adj* (*inf*) boastful.

aufschnellen *vi sep aux sein* **(a)** (*hochschnellen*) to leap *or* jump up; (*Schlange*) to rear up. **(b)** (*rare: sich plötzlich öffnen*) to fly *or* spring open.

Aufschnitt *m, no pl* (assorted) sliced cold meat *or* (*rare: Käse*) cheese. **kalter** ~ (assorted) sliced cold meat, cold cuts (*US*).

aufschnüren *vt sep* **(a)** (*lösen*) to untie, to undo; *Schuh auch* to unlace. **(b)** (*rare: befestigen*) to tie on (*auf* +*acc* -to).

aufschrammen *vt sep siehe* **aufschürfen**.

aufschrauben *vt sep* **(a)** *Schraube etc* to unscrew; *Flasche etc* to take the top off. **(b)** (*festschrauben*) to screw on (*auf* + *acc* -to).

aufschrecken *sep pret* **schreckte** *auf*, *ptp* **aufgeschreckt** 1 *vt* to startle; (*aus Gleichgültigkeit*) to rouse (*aus* from), to jolt (*aus* out of). **jdn aus dem Schlaf** ~ to rouse sb from sleep.
2 *vi pret auch* **schrak auf** *aux sein* to start (up), to be startled. **aus dem Schlaf** ~ to wake up with a start; **aus seinen Gedanken** ~ to start.

Aufschrei *m* yell; (*schriller* ~) scream, shriek. **ein** ~ **der Empörung/Entrüstung** (*fig*) an outcry.

aufschreiben *vt sep irreg* **(a)** (*niederschreiben*) **etw** ~ to write *or* note sth down.
(b) (*notieren*) **sich** (*dat*) **etw** ~ to make a note of sth.
(c) (*als Schulden anschreiben*) to put on the slate (*inf*), to chalk up (*inf*).
(d) (*inf: verordnen*) to prescribe.
(e) (*inf: polizeilich* ~) **jdn** ~ to take sb's particulars; **das Auto** ~ to take the car's number.

aufschreien *vi sep irreg* to yell out; (*schrill*) to scream *or* shriek out.

Aufschrift *f* (*Beschriftung*) inscription; (*Etikett*) label. **eine Flasche mit der „Vorsicht Gift" versehen** to label a bottle "Danger – Poison".

Aufschub *m* (*Verzögerung*) delay; (*Vertagung*) postponement. **die Sache duldet** *or* **leidet** (*old*) **keinen** ~ (*geh*) the matter brooks no delay (*liter*); **jdm** ~ **gewähren** (*Zahlungs*~) to allow sb grace; **jdn um** ~ **bitten** to ask sb for a delay *etc.*

aufschürfen *vt sep* **sich** (*dat*) **die Haut/das Knie** ~ to graze *or* scrape oneself/one's knee.

aufschürzen *vt sep siehe* **schürzen**.

aufschütteln *vt sep Kissen etc* to shake *or* plump up.

aufschütten *vt sep* **(a)** *Flüssigkeit* to pour on. **Wasser auf etw** (*acc*) ~ to pour water on *or* over sth. **(b)** (*nachfüllen*) *Kohle* to put on (the fire). **(c)** *Stroh, Steine* to spread; *Damm, Deich* to throw up; *Straße* to raise. **(d)** (*Geol*) to deposit.

Aufschüttung *f* **(a)** (*Damm*) bank of earth. **(b)** (*Geol*) deposit.

aufschwatzen, aufschwätzen (*dial*) *vt sep* (*inf*) **jdm etw** ~ to talk sb into taking sth; **sie hat ihr ihren Sohn aufgeschwatzt** she talked her into marrying her son.

aufschweben *vi sep aux sein* to float up.

aufschweißen *vt sep* to cut open (with an oxyacetylene torch).

aufschwellen *sep* 1 *vi irreg aux sein* to swell (up). **das Herz** *or* **die Brust schwoll ihm auf** (*geh*) his heart swelled. 2 *vt reg* to swell; (*fig*) *Satz, Buch* to pad out (*inf*).

aufschwemmen *vti sep* (**jdn**) ~ to make sb bloated; **jds Gesicht** ~ to make sb's face bloated *or* puffy; *siehe* **aufgeschwemmt**.

aufschwingen *vr sep irreg* to swing oneself up; (*Vogel*) to soar (up); (*fig: Gedanken*) to rise to higher realms. **sich zu etw** ~ (*sich aufraffen*) to bring oneself to do sth; (*sich aufwerfen*) to set oneself up to be sth; (*sich hocharbeiten*) to work one's way up to be(come) sth; (*hum: etw kaufen*) to bring oneself to get sth.

Aufschwung *m* **(a)** (*Antrieb*) lift; (*der Phantasie*) upswing; (*der Seele*) uplift; (*der Wirtschaft etc*) upturn, upswing (*gen* in). **das gab ihr (einen) neuen** ~ that gave her a lift; **durch diese Erfindung hat die Firma einen** ~ **genommen** the firm received *or* got a boost from this invention. **(b)** (*Turnen*) swing-up.

aufsehen *vi sep irreg siehe* **aufblicken**.

Aufsehen *nt* -s, *no pl* sensation. **großes** ~ **erregen** to cause a sensation *or* stir; **um etw viel** ~ **machen** to make a lot of fuss about sth; **ohne großes** ~ without any to-do (*inf*) *or* fuss; **ich möchte jedes** ~ **vermeiden** I want to avoid any fuss; **bitte kein** ~, **meine Herren** no fuss please, gentlemen.

aufsehenerregend *adj* sensational.

Aufseher(in *f*) *m* (*allgemein*) supervisor; (*bei Prüfung*) invigilator; (*Sklaven*~) overseer; (*Gefängnis*~) warder; (*Park*~, *Museums*~ etc) attendant.

aufsein *vi sep irreg aux sein* (*Zusammenschreibung nur bei infin und ptp*) **(a)** (*aufgestanden sein*) to be up. **(b)** (*geöffnet sein*) to be open.

aufsetzen *sep* 1 *vt* **(a)** (*auf etw setzen*) *Brille, Topf, Essen etc* to put on; *Kegel* to set up; *Knöpfe, Flicken etc* to put on; *Steine* to lay; *Tonarm* to lower; *Fuß* to put on the ground *or* down; (*fig*) *Lächeln, Miene etc* to put on. **ein Stockwerk (auf ein Haus)** ~ to add a storey (to a house); **einen Knopf auf die Jacke** ~ to put a button on the jacket; **ich kann den Fuß nicht richtig** ~ I can't put any weight on my foot; **sich** (*dat*) **den Hut** ~ to put on one's hat; *siehe* **Dämpfer, Horn** *etc.*
(b) *Flugzeug* to land, to bring down; *Boot* to pull up, to beach; (*unabsichtlich*) to ground, to run aground.
(c) (*aufrichten*) *Kranken etc* to sit up.
(d) (*verfassen*) to draft; (*ein Konzept machen für auch*) to make a draft of.
2 *vr* to sit up.
3 *vi* (*Flugzeug*) to touch down, to land; (*Tonarm*) to come down.

Aufsetzer *m* -s, - (*Sport*) bouncing ball.

aufseufzen *vi sep* (*tief/laut*) ~ to heave a (deep/loud) sigh.

Aufsicht *f* -, -en (a) *no pl* (*Überwachung*) supervision (*über* + *acc* of); (*Obhut*) charge. **unter jds** ~ (*dat*) under the supervision of sb; **in the charge of sb; unter polizeilicher/ärztlicher** ~ under police/medical supervision; ~ **über jdn/etw führen** to be in charge of sb/sth; **bei einer Prüfung** ~ **führen** to invigilate an exam; **im Pausenhof** ~ **führen** to be on duty during break; **jdn ohne** ~ **lassen** to leave sb unsupervised *or* without supervision; **der Kranke darf niemals ohne** ~ **sein** the patient must be kept under constant supervision; **jdm obliegt die** ~ **über etw** (*acc*) (*form*) sb is in charge of *or* responsible for sth.
(b) (~*führender*) person in charge; (*Aufseher*) supervisor. **die** ~ **fragen** (~*sschalter*) to ask at the office.
(c) (*Math: Draufsicht*) top view.

Aufsicht-: a~**führend** *adj attr Behörde* supervisory; *Beamter* supervising; ~**führende(r)** *mf decl as adj siehe* **Aufsicht (b)**.

Aufsichts-: ~**beamte(r)** *m* (*in Museum, Zoo etc*) attendant; ~**behörde** *f* supervisory authority *or* body; ~**personal** *nt* supervisory staff; ~**pflicht** (*Jur*) *legal responsibility to care for sb esp children*; **die elterliche** ~**pflicht, die** ~**pflicht der Eltern** (legal) parental responsibility; ~**rat** *m* board (of directors); (*Mitglied*) member of the board (of directors); **im** ~**rat einer Firma sitzen** to be *or* sit on the board of a firm; ~**ratsvorsitzende(r)** *m* chairman of the board (of directors).

aufsitzen *vi sep irreg* **(a)** (*aufgerichtet sitzen, aufbleiben*) to sit up.
(b) *aux sein* (*auf Reittier*) to mount; (*auf Fahrzeug*) to get on. **aufs Pferd** ~ to mount the horse; **aufgesessen!** (*Mil*) mount!
(c) (*ruhen auf*) to sit on (*auf etw* (*acc*) sth).
(d) (*Naut*) to run aground (*auf* + *dat* on).
(e) *aux sein* (*inf: hereinfallen*) **jdm/einer Sache** ~ to be taken in by sb/sth.
(f) *aux sein* (*inf*) **jdn** ~ **lassen** (*im Stich lassen*) to leave sb in the lurch, to let sb down; (*Verabredung nicht einhalten*) to stand sb up (*inf*).

aufspalten *vtr sep* to split; (*fig auch*) to split up. **eine Klasse in drei Gruppen** ~ to split up *or* divide up a class into three groups.

Aufspaltung *f* splitting; (*fig auch*) splitting-up. **seit der** ~ **der Partei** since the party split up.

aufspannen *vt sep* **(a)** *Netz, Sprungtuch* to stretch *or* spread out; *Schirm* to put up, to open. **(b)** (*aufziehen*) *Leinwand* to stretch (*auf* + *acc* onto); *Saite* to put on (*auf etw* (*acc*) sth).

aufsparen *vt sep* to save (up), to keep. **sich** (*dat*) **eine Bemerkung** ~ to save *or* keep a remark.

aufspeichern *vt sep* to store (up); *Waren auch* to accumulate; (*fig*) *Zorn etc* to build up.

Aufspeicherung *f* storage; (*von Energie auch*) accumulation.

aufsperren *vt sep* **(a)** (*S Ger, Aus: aufschließen*) *Tür etc* to unlock. **(b)** (*aufreißen*) *Tür, Schnabel* to open wide. **die Ohren** ~ to prick up one's ears.

aufspielen *sep* 1 *vi* (*dated*) to play; (*anfangen*) to strike up. **die Mannschaft spielte glänzend auf** the team began playing brilliantly. 2 *vr* (*inf*) **(a)** (*sich wichtig tun*) to give oneself airs. **(b)** (*sich ausgeben als*) **sich als etw** ~ to set oneself up as sth; **sich als Boß** ~ to play the boss.

aufspießen vt sep to spear; (durchbohren) to run through; (mit Hörnern) to gore; Schmetterlinge to pin; Fleisch (mit Spieß) to skewer; (mit Gabel) to prong. **sie schien mich mit Blicken ~ zu wollen** she looked daggers at me.

aufsplittern sep 1 vti (vi: aux sein) (Holz) to splinter; (Gruppe) to split (up). 2 vr (Gruppe etc) to split (up).

aufsprengen vt sep to force open; (mit Sprengstoff) to blow open.

aufsprießen vi sep irreg aux sein (geh) to burst forth, to sprout.

aufspringen vi sep irreg aux sein (a) (hochspringen) to jump or leap to one's feet or up. **auf etw** (acc) **~** to jump onto sth. (b) (auftreffen) to bounce; (Ski) to land. (c) (sich öffnen) (Tür) to burst or fly open; (platzen) to burst; (Rinde, Lack) to crack; (Haut, Lippen etc) to crack, to chap; (liter: Knospen) to burst open.

aufspritzen sep 1 vt etw (auf etw acc) **~** to spray sth on (sth). 2 vi aux sein to spurt (up).

aufsprudeln vi sep aux sein to bubble up.

aufsprühen sep 1 vt etw (auf etw acc) **~** to spray sth on (sth). 2 vi aux sein to spray up.

Aufsprung m (Sport) landing; (von Ball) bounce.

aufspulen vt sep to wind on a spool; Angelschnur, Garn auch to wind on a reel.

aufspülen vt sep (a) (anspülen) Sand, Schlick etc to wash up. (b) (aufwirbeln) Sand, Schlamm etc to whirl up.

aufspüren vt sep (lit, fig) to track down.

aufstacheln vt sep siehe anstacheln. **jdn ~, etw zu tun** (aufwiegeln) to goad or urge sb on to do sth or into doing sth.

aufstampfen vi sep to stamp. **mit dem Fuß ~** to stamp one's foot.

Aufstand m rebellion, revolt. **im ~** in rebellion or revolt.

aufständisch adj rebellious, insurgent.

Aufständische(r) mf decl as adj rebel, insurgent.

aufstapeln vt sep to stack or pile up.

aufstauen sep 1 vt Wasser to dam. **etw in sich** (dat) **~** (fig) to bottle sth up inside (oneself). 2 vr to accumulate, to collect; (fig: Ärger) to be/become bottled up.

aufstechen vt sep irreg to puncture; (Med) to lance; (dial: aufdecken) to bring into the open.

aufstecken sep 1 vt (a) (auf etw stecken) to put on (auf + acc -to); Fahne, Gardinen to put up (auf + acc on). **sich/jdm einen Ring ~** to put on a ring/put a ring on sb's finger; **Kerzen auf einen Leuchter/den Baum ~** to put candles in a candlestick/on the tree. (b) (mit Nadeln) to pin up; Haar auch to put up. (c) (inf: aufgeben) to pack in (inf). 2 vi (inf: aufgeben) to pack it in (inf); (bei Rennen etc auch) to retire.

aufstehen vi sep irreg aux sein (a) (sich erheben) to get or stand up; (morgens aus dem Bett) to get up; (fig: Persönlichkeit) to arise. **aus dem Sessel/Bett ~** to get up out of the chair/to get out of bed; **vor jdm/für jdn ~** to stand up for sb; **~ dürfen** (Kranker) to be allowed (to get) up; **er steht nicht mehr or wieder auf** (fig inf) he's a goner (inf); **da mußt du früher or eher ~!** (fig inf) you'll have to do better than that! (b) (inf: offen sein) to be open. (c) (sich auflehnen) to rise (in arms). (d) aux haben (auf dem Boden etc stehen) to stand (auf + dat on). **der Tisch steht nur mit drei Beinen/nicht richtig auf** the table is only standing on three legs/is not standing firmly; **das eine Tischbein steht nicht auf** one of the table legs is not touching the ground.

aufsteigen vi sep irreg aux sein (a) (auf Berg, Leiter) to climb (up); (Vogel, Drachen) to soar (up); (Flugzeug) to climb; (Stern, Sonne, Nebel) to rise; (Gewitter, Wolken) to gather; (Gefühl) to rise; (geh: aufragen) to tower, to rise up; (drohend) to loom. **zum Gipfel ~** to climb (up) to the summit; **einen Ballon ~ lassen** to release a balloon; **in einem Ballon ~** to go up in a balloon; **an die Oberfläche ~** to rise to the surface; **~de Linie** ascending line; **in jdm ~** (Haß, Verdacht, Erinnerung etc) to well up in sb. (b) (auf Fahrrad etc) to get on (auf etw acc (-to) on); (auf Pferd auch) to mount (auf etw acc) sth. (c) (fig: im Rang etc) to rise (zu to); (beruflich auch) to be promoted; (Sport) to go up, to be promoted (in + acc to). **zum Abteilungsleiter ~** to rise to be head of department; **das ~de Bürgertum** the rising middle classes.

Aufsteiger m (a) (Sport) league climber; (in höhere Liga) promoted team. (b) (sozialer) **~** social climber.

aufstellen sep 1 vt (a) (aufrichten, aufbauen) to put up (auf + dat on); etw Liegendes to stand up; Zelt auch to pitch; Mast, Denkmal auch to erect; Kegel to set up; Verkehrsampel auch to install; Maschine to put in, to install; Falle to set; (Mil) to deploy; (postieren) Wachposten to post, to station; Wagen to line up; (hochstellen) Kragen etc to put up; (aufrichten) Ohren, Stacheln to prick up. (b) Essen etc (auf Herd) to put on. (c) (fig: zusammenstellen) Truppe to raise; (Sport) Spieler to select, to pick; Mannschaft to draw up. (d) (benennen) Kandidaten to nominate; (erzielen) Rekord to set (up). (e) Forderung, Behauptung, Vermutung to put forward; System to establish; Programm, Satzungen to draw up. (f) Rechnung to draw up; Liste auch to make. (g) (dial) siehe anstellen 1 (g). 2 vr (a) (sich postieren) to stand; (hintereinander) to line up; (Soldaten) to fall into line. **sich im Karree/Kreis etc ~** to form a square/circle etc. (b) (Ohren etc) to prick up.

Aufstellung f (a) no pl (das Aufstellen) putting up; (von Zelt)

pitching; (von Schild, Mast, Denkmal auch) erection; (von Verkehrsampel) installation; (von Maschine) putting in, installation; (von Falle) setting; (Mil) deployment; (von Wachposten) posting, stationing; (von Wagen) lining up. **~ nehmen** (Mil) to take up position. (b) no pl (das Aufstellen) (von Truppen) raising; (von Spielern) selecting, picking; (von Mannschaft) drawing up; (Mannschaft) line-up (inf), team. (c) siehe vt (d) nominating; setting. (d) no pl siehe vt (e) putting forward; establishing; drawing up. (e) no pl siehe vt (f) drawing up. (f) (Liste) list; (Tabelle) table; (Inventar) inventory.

aufstemmen vt sep to force or prise open (with a chisel etc); (mit der Schulter) to force open.

aufstempeln vt sep to stamp on. **etw auf etw** (acc) **~** to stamp sth on sth; **jdm ein Etikett ~** (fig) to put a label on sb.

aufsteppen vt sep to sew or stitch on (auf etw (acc) (-to) sth).

aufstieben vi sep irreg aux sein to fly up.

Aufstieg m -(e)s, -e (a) no pl (auf Berg) climb, ascent; (von Flugzeug, Rakete) climb; (von Ballon) ascent. (b) (fig) (Aufschwung) rise; (beruflich, politisch, sozial) advancement; (Sport: von Mannschaft) climb, rise; (in höhere Liga) promotion (in + acc to). **den ~ zu etw/ins Management schaffen** to rise to (become) sth/to work one's way up into the management. (c) (Weg) way up (auf etw (acc) sth), ascent (auf + acc of).

Aufstiegs-: ~chance, ~möglichkeit f prospect of promotion; ~runde f (Sport) round deciding promotion; ~spiel nt (Sport) match deciding promotion.

aufstöbern vt sep Wild to start, to flush; Rebhühner etc auch to put up; (fig: stören) to disturb; (inf: entdecken) to run to earth.

aufstocken sep 1 vt (a) Haus to build another storey onto. (b) Kapital, Kredit, Armee to increase (um by); Vorräte to build or stock up. 2 vi to build another storey.

aufstöhnen vi sep to groan loudly, to give a loud groan. **erleichtert ~** to give a loud sigh of relief.

aufstören vt sep to disturb; Wild to start. **jdn aus dem or im Schlaf ~** to disturb sb while he is sleeping; **jdn aus seiner Lethargie ~** to prod sb out of his lethargy.

aufstoßen sep irreg 1 vt (a) (öffnen) to push open; (mit einem Fuß) to kick open. **als die Kolonialmächte die Tür nach Afrika aufstießen** when the colonial powers opened the door to Africa. (b) (rare) etw auf etw (acc) **~** to strike sth on sth, to hit sth against sth; **er stieß den Stock (auf den Boden) auf** he tapped his stick on the ground. 2 vi aux sein (a) auf etw (acc) **~** to hit (on or against) sth; **ich bin mit dem Ellbogen auf die Bordsteinkante aufgestoßen** I hit my elbow on or against the kerb; **er stieß mit dem Stock auf den Boden auf** he tapped his stick on the ground. (b) (rülpsen) to burp. (c) aux sein or haben (Speisen) to repeat. **Radieschen stoßen mir auf** radishes repeat on me; **das könnte dir noch sauer or übel ~** (fig inf) you might have to pay for that; **das ist mir sauer aufgestoßen** (fig inf) it left a nasty taste in my mouth. (d) (fig: auffallen) to strike (jdm sb). **beim Lesen ist mir nur ein Fehler aufgestoßen** I only noticed one mistake while I was reading. 3 vr to graze oneself. **sich** (dat) **das Knie ~** to graze one's knee.

Aufstoßen nt -s, no pl burping, flatulence (form).

aufstreben vi sep aux sein (geh: aufragen) to soar, to tower. **hoch ~de Türme/Berge** high soaring towers/mountains.

aufstrebend adj (fig) Land, Volk striving for progress; Stadt up-and-coming, striving; junger Mann ambitious; Bürgertum rising.

aufstreichen vt sep irreg to put on (auf etw (acc) sth); Butter etc to spread (auf + acc on).

aufstreifen vt sep jdm/sich etw **~** to slip sth on sb/to slip sth on; (sich dat) die Ärmel **~** to pull up one's sleeves.

aufstreuen vt sep to sprinkle on. **etw auf etw** (acc) **~** to sprinkle sth on(to) or over sth; **Splitt/Salz auf die Straßen ~** to grit/salt the roads.

Aufstrich m -(e)s, -e (a) (auf Brot) spread. **was möchten Sie als ~?** what would you like on your bread/toast etc? (b) (Mus) up-bow. (c) (beim Schreiben) upstroke.

aufstülpen vt sep (a) (draufstülpen) to put on. **etw auf etw** (acc) **~** to put sth on sth; **sich** (dat) **den Hut ~** to put or pull on one's hat. (b) (umstülpen) Ärmel, Kragen etc to turn up. **die Lippen ~** (schmollend) to pout; **aufgestülpte Lippen** thick lips; (schmollend) a pouting mouth; **eine aufgestülpte Nase** a snub or turned-up nose.

aufstützen sep 1 vt Kranken etc to prop up; Ellbogen, Arme to rest (auf + acc or dat on). **den Kopf ~** to rest one's head on one's hand. 2 vr to support oneself; (im Bett, beim Essen) to prop oneself up. **sich auf die or der Hand ~** to support oneself with one's hand.

aufsuchen vt sep (a) Bekannten to call on; Arzt, Ort, Toilette to go to. **das Bett ~** (geh) to retire to bed; **den Boden ~** (Boxen) to go down, to hit the canvas. (b) (aufsammeln) to pick up; (auf Landkarte, in Buch) to find.

aufsummen, aufsummieren* vtr sep to add up.

auftafeln vti sep to serve (up).

auftakeln vt sep (Naut) to rig up. **sich ~** (pej inf) to tart oneself up (inf); siehe aufgetakelt.

Auftakt m -(e)s, -e (a) (Beginn) start; (Vorbereitung) prelude. **den ~ von or zu etw bilden** to mark the beginning or start of sth/to form a prelude to sth. (b) (Mus) upbeat; (Poet) arsis (form).

auftanken vti sep to fill up; (Aviat) to refuel; **500 Liter** to refuel with, to take on; *10 Liter* to put in. **Benzin** ~ to fill up with petrol (*Brit*) *or* gas (*US*).

auftauchen *vi sep aux* sein (a) (*aus dem Wasser*) to surface; (*Taucher etc auch*) to come up.
   (b) (*fig*) (*sichtbar werden*) to appear; (*aus Nebel etc auch*) to emerge.
   (c) (*gefunden werden, sich zeigen, kommen*) to turn up.
   (d) (*sich ergeben*) to arise. **allmählich tauchten Zweifel in ihr auf** doubts slowly crept into *or* arose in her mind.

auftauen *sep* 1 *vi aux* sein to thaw; (*fig auch*) to unbend. 2 *vt Eis* to thaw; *Tiefkühlkost, Wasserleitung* to thaw (out).

aufteilen *vt sep* (a) (*aufgliedern*) to divide *or* split up (*in + acc* into). (b) (*verteilen*) to share out (*unter + acc* between).

Aufteilung *f* siehe *vt* division; sharing out.

auftippen *vi sep aux* sein to bounce.

auftischen *vt sep* to serve up; (*fig inf*) to come up with. **jdm etw** ~ (*lit*) to give sb sth, to serve sb (with) sth; **jdm Lügen etc** ~ (*inf*) to give sb a lot of lies *etc*.

Auftrag *m* -(e)s, **Aufträge** (a) *no pl* (*Anweisung*) orders *pl*, instructions *pl*; (*zugeteilte Arbeit*) job, task; (*Jur*) brief. **jdm den** ~ **geben, etw zu tun** to give sb the job of doing sth, to instruct sb to do sth; **einen** ~ **ausführen** to carry out an order; **ich habe den** ~, **Ihnen mitzuteilen ...** I have been instructed to tell you ...; **in jds** ~ (*dat*) (*für jdn*) on sb's behalf; (*auf jds Anweisung*) on sb's instructions; **die Oper wurde im** ~ **des Königs komponiert** the opera was commissioned by the king; **diese Modelle werden im** ~ **des Königs angefertigt** these models have been ordered by the king; **im** ~ *or* **i.A.: G. W. Kurz** *pp* G. W. Kurz.
   (b) (*Comm*) order (*über + acc* for); (*bei Künstlern, Freischaffenden etc*) commission (*über + acc* for). **etw in** ~ **geben** to order/commission sth (*bei* from); **im** ~ **und auf Rechnung von** by order and for account of.
   (c) *no pl* (*geh: Mission, Aufgabe*) task.
   (d) (*von Farbe etc*) application.

auftragen *sep irreg* 1 *vt* (a) (*servieren*) to serve. **es ist aufgetragen!** (*geh*) lunch/dinner *etc* is served!
   (b) *Farbe, Salbe, Schminke* to apply, to put on. **etw auf etw** (*acc*) ~ to apply sth to sth, to put sth on sth.
   (c) **jdm etw** ~ (*form*) to instruct sb to do sth; **er hat mir Grüße an Sie aufgetragen** he has asked me to give you his regards.
   (d) *Kleider* to wear out.
   2 *vi* (a) (*Kleider*) to make sb look fat. **die Jacke trägt auf** the jacket is not very flattering to your/her figure.
   (b) (*übertreiben*) **dick** *or* **stark** ~ (*inf*) to lay it on thick (*inf*) *or* with a trowel (*inf*).

Auftrag-: ~**geber(in** *f*) *m* client; (*von Firma, Freischaffenden*) customer; ~**nehmer(in** *f*) *m* (*Comm*) firm accepting the order; (*Build*) contractor.

Auftrags-: ~**bestätigung** *f* confirmation of order; **a~gemäß** *adj, adv* as instructed; (*Comm*) as per order; ~**lage** *f* order situation, situation concerning orders; ~**polster** *nt* **wir haben ein dickes** ~**polster** our order books are well-filled; ~**rückgang** *m* drop in orders; ~**walze** *f* (*Typ*) inking roller.

auftreffen *vi sep irreg aux* sein **auf etw** (*dat or acc*) ~ to hit *or* strike sth; (*Rakete*) to land on sth; **er traf mit dem Kopf auf der Kante auf** he hit his head on the edge; ~**de Strahlen** incident rays.

auftreiben *sep irreg* 1 *vt* (a) (*geh: hochtreiben*) *Staub etc* to raise.
   (b) *Teig* to make rise; *Leib* to distend, to bloat.
   (c) (*inf: ausfindig machen*) to find, to get hold of (*inf*).
   (d) *Vieh* (*zum Verkauf*) to drive to market; (*auf die Alm*) to drive up to the (Alpine) pastures.
   2 *vi aux* sein (*Teig*) to rise; (*Bauch etc*) to become distended *or* bloated. **sein aufgetriebener Bauch** his swollen *or* distended stomach.

auftrennen *vt sep* to undo.

auftreten *sep irreg* 1 *vi aux* sein (a) (*lit*) to tread. **der Fuß tut so weh, daß ich (mit ihm) nicht mehr** ~ **kann** my foot hurts so much that I can't walk on it *or* put my weight on it.
   (b) (*erscheinen*) to appear. **als Zeuge/Kläger** ~ to appear as a witness/as plantiff; **zum ersten Mal (im Theater)** ~ to make one's début *or* first (stage) appearance; **er tritt zum ersten Mal in Köln auf** he is appearing in Cologne for the first time; **gegen jdn/etw** ~ to stand up *or* speak out against sb/sth; **geschlossen** ~ to put up a united front.
   (c) (*fig: eintreten*) to occur; (*Schwierigkeiten etc*) to arise.
   (d) (*sich benehmen*) to behave. **bescheiden/arrogant** ~ to have a modest/arrogant manner; **vorsichtig** ~ to tread warily.
   (e) (*handeln*) to act. **als Vermittler/Friedensstifter etc** ~ to act as intermediary/peacemaker *etc*.
   2 *vt Tür etc* to kick open.

Auftreten *nt* -s, *no pl* (a) (*Erscheinen*) appearance. (b) (*Benehmen*) manner. (c) (*Vorkommen*) occurrence. **bei** ~ **von Schwellungen ...** in case swelling occurs ..., in the event of swelling ...

Auftrieb *m, no pl* (a) (*Phys*) buoyancy (force); (*Aviat*) lift.
   (b) (*fig: Aufschwung*) impetus; (*Preis*~) upward trend (*gen* in); (*Ermunterung*) lift. **das wird ihm** ~ **geben** that will give him a lift.
   (c) *no pl* (*des Alpenviehs*) **der** ~ **findet Anfang Mai statt** the cattle are driven up to the (Alpine) pastures at the beginning of May.
   (d) *no pl* (*von Marktvieh*) **der** ~ **an Vieh/Kälbern** the number of cattle/calves (at the market).

Auftriebskraft *f* buoyancy force; (*Aviat*) lift.

Auftritt *m* (a) (*Erscheinen*) entrance. **ich habe meinen** ~ **erst im zweiten Akt** I don't go *or* come on until the second act. (b) (*Theat: Szene*) scene. (c) (*Streit*) row.

Auftrittsverbot *nt* stage ban. ~ **bekommen/haben** to be banned from making a public appearance; ~ **über jdn verhängen** (*inf*) to ban sb from appearing.

auftrumpfen *vi sep* to be full of oneself (*inf*); (*sich schadenfroh äußern*) to crow; (*seine Leistungsstärke zeigen*) to show how good one is. **ich kann seine ~de Art nicht leiden** I can't stand the way he's so full of himself; ~**d sagte er ... ...,** he crowed.

auftun *sep irreg* 1 *vt* (a) (*dated: öffnen*) to open. **tu den Mund auf, wenn du was willst** say when you want something.
   (b) (*dial: eröffnen*) to open (up); *Verein* to start.
   (c) (*inf: servieren*) **jdm/sich etw** ~ to put sth on sb's/one's plate, to help sb/oneself to sth.
   (d) (*inf: ausfindig machen*) to find.
   (e) (*dial: aufsetzen*) to put on.
   2 *vi* (*inf*) **jdm/sich** ~ to help sb (*inf*)/oneself (*von* to).
   3 *vr* (a) (*sich öffnen*) to open (up).
   (b) (*dial: eröffnet werden*) to open (up); (*Verein*) to start.

auftürmen *sep* 1 *vt* to pile *or* stack up; (*Geol*) to build up (in layers). 2 *vr* (*Gebirge etc*) to tower *or* loom up; (*Schwierigkeiten*) to pile *or* mount up. **hoch aufgetürmte Felsen** towering cliffs.

aufwachen *vi sep aux* sein (*lit, fig*) to wake up. **aus seiner Lethargie/einer Narkose** ~ to snap out of one's lethargy/to come out of an anaesthetic.

aufwachsen *vi sep irreg aux* sein to grow up.

aufwallen *vi sep aux* sein to bubble up; (*Cook*) to boil up; (*Leidenschaft etc*) to surge up. **die Soße einmal** ~ **lassen** bring the sauce to the boil; **seine ~de Wut/Leidenschaft** his seething rage/the passion surging up in him.

Aufwallung *f* (*fig*) (*von Leidenschaft*) surge; (*Wut*) outburst, fit (of rage). **das brachte ihn zur** ~ that made him seethe.

Aufwand *m* -(e)s, *no pl* (a) (*von Geld*) expenditure (*an + dat* of). **das erfordert einen** ~ **von 10 Millionen Mark** that will cost *or* take 10 million marks; **das erfordert einen großen** ~ **an Zeit/Energie/Geld** that requires a lot of time/energy/money; **der** ~ **war umsonst, das war ein unnützer** ~ that was a waste of money/time/energy *etc*; **das hätte er auch ohne einen so großen** ~ **an Worten sagen können** he could have said that without using quite so many words; **der dazu nötige** ~ **an Konzentration/Zeit** the concentration/time needed.
   (b) (*Luxus, Prunk*) extravagance. (**großen**) ~ **treiben** to be (very) extravagant; **was da für** ~ **getrieben wurde!** the extravagance!

Aufwands|entschädigung *f* expense allowance.

Aufwand(s)steuer *f* tax on non-essentials.

aufwärmen *sep* 1 *vt* to heat *or* warm up; (*inf: wieder erwähnen*) to bring up, to drag up (*inf*). 2 *vr* to warm oneself up; (*Sport*) to warm *or* limber up.

Aufwartefrau *f* char(woman).

aufwarten *vi sep* (a) (*geh: bedienen*) to serve (*jdm* sb). (**bei Tisch**) ~ to wait at table; **uns wurde mit Sekt aufgewartet** we were served champagne.
   (b) (*zu bieten haben*) **mit etw** ~ to offer sth; **er hat viel Geld, damit kann ich nicht** ~ he's very rich, I can't compete with that.
   (c) (*dated: besuchen*) **jdm** ~ to wait on sb (*old*), to visit sb.

aufwärts *adv* up, upward(s); (*bergauf*) uphill. **die Ecken haben sich** ~ **gebogen** the corners have curled up; **den Fluß** ~ upstream; **von einer Million** ~ from a million up(wards); **vom Feldwebel** ~ from sergeant up; siehe **aufwärtsgehen.**

Aufwärts-: ~**bewegung** *f* upward movement; (*Tech*) upstroke; ~**entwicklung** *f* upward trend (*gen* in); **a~gehen** *vi impers sep irreg aux* sein **mit dem Staat/der Firma geht es a~** things are looking up *or* getting better *or* improving for the country/firm; **mit ihm geht es a~** (*finanziell, beruflich*) things are looking up for him; (*in der Schule, gesundheitlich*) he's doing *or* getting better; **mit seinen Leistungen geht es a~** he's doing better; ~**haken** *m* (*Boxen*) uppercut; ~**trend** *m* upward trend.

Aufwartung *f* (a) *no pl* (*dated: Bedienung*) waiting at table; (*Reinemachen*) cleaning. (b) (*geh: Besuch*) **jdm seine** ~ **machen** to wait (up)on sb (*old*), to visit sb. (c) (*dial: Aufwartefrau etc*) char(woman).

Aufwasch *m* -(e)s, *no pl* (*dial*) siehe **Abwasch**[1].

aufwaschen *vt sep irreg* (*dial*) siehe **abwaschen.**

aufwecken *vt sep* to wake (up), to waken; (*fig*) to rouse; siehe **aufgeweckt.**

aufwehen *sep* 1 *vt* (a) (*in die Höhe wehen*) to blow up; (*auftürmen*) to pile up. **der Wind hat Dünen aufgeweht** the wind has blown the sand into dunes. (b) (*öffnen*) to blow open. 2 *vi aux* sein to blow up.

aufweichen *sep* 1 *vt* to make soft; *Weg, Boden* to make sodden; *Brot* to soak; (*durch Wärme*) to soften; (*fig: lockern*) to weaken; *Doktrin* to water down. 2 *vi aux* sein to become *or* get soft; (*Weg, Boden*) to become *or* get sodden; (*fig: sich lockern*) to be weakened; (*Doktrin*) to become *or* get watered down.

Aufweis *m* -es, *no pl* **durch den** ~ **von einzelnen Fehlern** by pointing out isolated mistakes.

aufweisen *vt sep irreg* to show. **die Leiche wies keinerlei Verletzungen auf** the body showed no signs of injury; **das Buch weist einige Fehler auf** the book contains some mistakes *or* has some mistakes in it; **etw aufzuweisen haben** to have sth to show for oneself; **man muß schon einiges an Veröffentlichungen aufzuweisen haben** you have to have something to show in the way of publications.

aufwenden *vt sep irreg* to use; *Zeit, Energie* to expend; *Mühe* to take; *Geld* to spend. **viel Mühe/Zeit** ~, **etw zu tun** to take a lot of trouble/spend a lot of time doing sth; **das wäre unnütz aufgewandte Zeit/Energie** that would be a waste of time/energy.

aufwendig *adj* costly; (*üppig*) lavish.

Aufwendung f **(a)** no pl siehe vt using; expenditure; taking; spending. **unter ~ von ...** by using/expending/taking/spending ... **(b)** **~en** pl expenditure.

aufwerfen sep irreg 1 vt **(a)** (nach oben werfen) to throw up; (aufhäufen) to pile up; Damm etc to build (up). **(b)** Kopf to toss; Lippen to purse. **ein aufgeworfener Mund** pursed lips; **eine aufgeworfene Nase** a turned-up nose. **(c)** (auf etw werfen) to throw on; Karten to put down (auf +acc (on)to). **etw auf etw** (acc) **~** to throw sth on(to) sth. **(d)** Tür to throw open. **(e)** (zur Sprache bringen) Frage, Probleme to raise, to bring up.
2 vr **sich zu etw ~** to set oneself up as sth; **sich zum Richter ~** to set oneself up as judge.

aufwerten vt sep **(a)** (auch vi) Währung to revalue. **(b)** (fig) to increase the value of; Menschen, Ideal auch to enhance the status of.

Aufwertung f (von Währung) revaluation; (fig) increase in value. **das kommt einer ~ des Terrorismus gleich** that is tantamount to enhancing the status of terrorism.

aufwickeln vt sep **(a)** (aufrollen) to roll up; (inf) Haar to put in curlers. **(b)** (lösen) to untie; Windeln, Verband to take off. **ein Baby ~** to take off a baby's nappy or diaper (US).

Auf Wiedersehen, Auf Wiederschauen (geh, S Ger, Aus, Sw) interj goodbye.

Aufwiegelei f siehe **Aufwiegelung.**

aufwiegeln vt sep to stir up. **jdn zum Streik/Widerstand ~** to incite sb to strike/resist.

Aufwiegelung f incitement.

aufwiegen vt sep irreg (fig) to offset. **das ist nicht mit Geld aufzuwiegen** that can't be measured in terms of money.

Aufwiegler(in) f) m -s, - agitator; (Anstifter) instigator.

aufwieglerisch adj seditious; Rede, Artikel auch inflammatory.

Aufwind m (Aviat) upcurrent; (Met) upwind. **guter ~** good upcurrents pl; **(durch etw) neuen ~ bekommen** (fig) to get new impetus (from sth); **einer Sache** (dat) **~ geben** (fig) to give sth impetus.

aufwirbeln sep 1 vi aux sein (Staub, Schnee) to swirl or whirl up. 2 vt to swirl or whirl up; Staub auch to raise. **(viel) Staub ~** (fig) to cause a (big) stir.

aufwischen 1 vt Wasser etc to wipe or mop up; Fußboden to wipe. **die Küche (feucht) ~** to wash the kitchen floor; **das Bier vom Boden ~** to mop the beer up off the floor. 2 vi to wipe the floor(s). **feucht ~** to wash the floor(s).

aufwogen vi sep aux sein (liter) to heave.

aufwölben vr sep to curve up.

aufwühlen vt sep **(a)** (lit) Erde, Meer to churn (up). **(b)** (geh) to stir; (schmerzhaft) to churn up; Leidenschaften to rouse. **das hat seine Seele zutiefst aufgewühlt** that stirred him to the depths of his soul; **~d** stirring; siehe **aufgewühlt.**

aufzahlen vt sep (S Ger, Aus) **100 Schilling/einen Zuschlag ~** to pay an additional 100 schillings/a surcharge (on top).

aufzählen vt sep (aufsagen) to list; Gründe, Namen etc auch to give (jdm sb); (aufführen auch) to enumerate; Geld to count out (jdm for sb). **jdm ein paar (Hiebe etc) ~** (inf) to give sb a thrashing; **er hat mir alle meine Fehler aufgezählt** he told me all my faults, he enumerated all my faults to me.

Aufzahlung f (S Ger, Aus) additional charge.

Aufzählung f list; (von Gründen, Fehlern etc auch) enumeration.

aufzäumen vt sep to bridle. **etw verkehrt ~** to go about sth the wrong way.

aufzehren sep 1 vt to exhaust; (fig) to sap. 2 vr to burn oneself out.

Aufzehrung f exhaustion; (fig) sapping.

aufzeichnen vt sep **(a)** Plan etc to draw, to sketch. **(b)** (notieren, Rad, TV) to record.

Aufzeichnung f **(a)** (Zeichnung) sketch. **(b)** usu pl (Notiz) note; (Niederschrift auch) record. **(c)** (Magnetband~, Film~) recording.

aufzeigen sep 1 vt to show; (nachweisen auch) to demonstrate. 2 vi (dated Sch: sich melden) to put one's hand up.

aufziehen sep irreg 1 vt **(a)** (hochziehen) to pull or draw up; schweren Gegenstand auch to haul up; (mit Flaschenzug etc) to hoist up; Schlagbaum, Zugbrücke to raise; Flagge, Segel to hoist; Jalousien to let up; (Med) Spritze to fill; Flüssigkeit to draw up.
(b) (öffnen) Reißverschluß to undo; Schleife etc auch to untie; Schublade to (pull) open; Flasche to uncork; Gardinen to draw (back).
(c) (aufspannen) Photo etc to mount; Leinwand, Stickerei to stretch; Landkarte etc to pull up; Saite, Reifen to fit, to put on. **Saiten/neue Saiten auf ein Instrument ~** to string/restring an instrument; siehe **Saite.**
(d) (spannen) Feder, Uhr etc to wind up.
(e) (großziehen) to raise; Kind auch to bring up; Tier auch to rear.
(f) (inf) (veranstalten) to set up; Fest to arrange; (gründen) Unternehmen to start up.
(g) (verspotten) jdn ~ (inf) to make fun of sb, to tease sb (mit about).
2 vi aux sein (dunkle Wolke) to come up; (Gewitter, Wolken auch) to gather; (aufmarschieren) to march up. **die Wache zog vor der Kaserne auf** the soldiers mounted guard in front of the barracks.
3 vr to wind. **sich von selbst ~** to be self-winding.

Aufzucht f **(a)** no pl (das Großziehen) rearing, raising. **(b)** (Nachwuchs) young family.

Aufzug m **(a)** (Fahrstuhl) lift (Brit), elevator (US); (Güter~ auch) hoist. **(b)** (Phot) wind-on. **(c)** (Marsch) parade; (Festzug auch) procession. **der ~ der Wache** the mounting of the guard. **(d)** (von Gewitter etc) gathering. **(e)** (Turnen) pull-up. **(f)** (Theat) act. **(g)** no pl (pej inf: Kleidung) get-up (inf).

Aufzug- in cpds lift (Brit), elevator (US); **~führer** m lift or elevator operator.

aufzwicken vr sep (Aus inf) **sich** (dat) **jdn ~** to chat sb up (inf).

aufzwingen sep irreg 1 vt **jdm etw/seinen Willen ~** to force sth on sb/impose one's will on sb. 2 vr to force itself on one. **sich jdm ~** to force itself on sb; (Gedanke) to strike sb forcibly; **das zwingt sich einem doch förmlich auf** the conclusion is unavoidable.

Auglapfel m eyeball. **jdn/etw wie seinen ~ hüten** to cherish sb/sth like life itself.

Auge nt -s, -n **(a)** (Sehorgan) eye. **gute/schlechte ~n haben** to have good/bad eyesight or eyes; **die ~n aufmachen** or **aufsperren** (inf) or **auftun** (inf) to open one's eyes; **mit den ~n zwinkern/blinzeln** to wink/blink; **jdm in die ~n sehen** to look sb in the eye(s); **jdn mit** or **aus großen ~n ansehen** to look at sb wide-eyed; **etw mit eigenen ~n gesehen haben** to have seen sth with one's own eyes; **die ~n schließen** (lit) to close one's eyes; (euph) to fall asleep; **mit bloßem** or **nacktem ~** with the naked eye; **~n rechts/links!** (Mil) eyes right/left!; **mit verbundenen ~n** (lit, fig) blindfold; **etw im ~ haben** (lit) to have sth in one's eye; (fig) to have one's eye on sth; **ein sicheres ~ für etw haben** to have a good eye for sth; **da muß man seine ~n überall** or **hinten und vorn** (inf) **haben** you need eyes in the back of your head; **ich kann doch meine ~n nicht überall haben** I can't look everywhere at once; **ich hab' doch hinten keine ~n!** I don't have eyes in the back of my head; **ich habe doch ~n im Kopf!** I do have eyes in my head; **haben Sie keine ~n im Kopf?** (inf) haven't you got any eyes in your head?, use your eyes!; **große ~n machen** to be wide-eyed; **jdm schöne** or **verliebte ~n machen** to make eyes at sb; **ich konnte kaum aus den ~n sehen** or **gucken** I could hardly see straight; **die ~n offen haben** or **offenhalten** to keep one's eyes open or skinned (inf) or peeled (inf); **wenn du mir noch einmal unter die ~n kommst, ...** if you let me see you or catch sight of you again ...; **geh mir aus den ~n!** get out of my sight!; **komm mir nicht unter die ~n!** keep out of my sight!; **schafft mir den Kerl aus den ~n!** get that man out of my sight!; **jdn/etw mit den ~n verschlingen** to devour sb/sth with one's eyes; **er guckte** or **schaute** (inf) **sich** (dat) **die ~n aus dem Kopf** (inf) his eyes were popping out of his head (inf) or coming out on stalks (inf); **dem fallen bald die ~n raus** (sl) his eyes will pop out of his head in a minute (inf); **unter jds ~n** (dat) (fig) before sb's very eyes; **vor aller ~n** in front of everybody; **jdn/etw mit anderen ~n (an)sehen** to see sb/sth in a different light; **etwas fürs ~ sein** to be a delight to the eyes, to be a treat to look at; **nur fürs ~ good** to look at but not much else (inf); **die ~n sind größer als der Magen** or **Bauch** (inf) his etc eyes are bigger than his etc stomach; **aus den ~n, aus dem Sinn** (Prov) out of sight, out of mind (Prov); **das ~ des Gesetzes** the law; **sich** (dat) **die ~n ausweinen** or **aus dem Kopf weinen** (inf) to cry one's eyes out; **soweit das ~ reicht** or **blicken kann** as far as the eye can see; **er hatte nur ~n für sie** he only had eyes for her; **ich habe kein ~ zugetan** I didn't sleep a wink; **da blieb kein ~ trocken** (hum) there wasn't a dry eye in the place; **ein ~ auf jdn/etw haben** (aufpassen) to keep an eye on sb/sth; **ein ~ auf jdn/etw (geworfen) haben** to have one's eye on sb/sth; **die ~n vor etw** (dat) **verschließen** to close one's eyes to sth; **ein ~/beide ~n zudrücken** (inf) to turn a blind eye; **er läßt kein ~ von ihr** he can't let her out of his sight for two minutes together; **jdn im ~ behalten** (beobachten) to keep an eye on sb; (vormerken) to keep or bear sb in mind; **etw im ~ behalten** to keep or bear sth in mind; **sein Ziel im ~ behalten** to keep one's goal in mind; **sie ließen ihn nicht aus den ~n** they didn't let him out of their sight; **jdn/etw aus den ~n verlieren** to lose sight of sb/sth; (fig) to lose touch with sb/sth; **jdm in die ~n stechen** (fig) to catch or take sb's eye; **ins ~ springen** or **fallen** to leap to the eye; **jdm etw vor ~n führen** (fig) to make sb aware of sth; **etw steht** or **schwebt jdm vor ~n** sb has sth in mind; **etw ins ~ fassen** to contemplate sth; **etw noch genau** or **lebhaft vor ~n haben** to remember sth clearly or vividly; **das muß man sich** (dat) **mal vor ~n führen!** just imagine it!; **es führt sich offenbar niemand richtig vor ~n, ...** obviously nobody is really aware ...; **jdm die ~n öffnen** (fig) to open sb's eyes; **ein ~ riskieren** (hum) to risk a glance; **das kann leicht ins ~ gehen** (fig inf) it might easily go wrong; **in den ~n der Leute/Öffentlichkeit** in the eyes of most people/the public; **in meinen ~n** in my opinion or view; **mit offenen ~n schlafen** (fig) to daydream; **ganz ~ und Ohr sein** to be all ears; **mit einem lachenden und einem weinenden ~** with mixed feelings; **~ in ~** face to face; **~ um ~, Zahn um Zahn** (Bibl) an eye for an eye and a tooth for a tooth; **vor meinem geistigen** or **inneren ~** in my mind's eye; **etw/den Tod vor ~n sehen** to face sth/death; **dem Tod ins ~ sehen** to look death in the face.
(b) (Knospenansatz) (bei Kartoffel) eye; (bei Zweig) axil.
(c) (Punkt, Tupfen) eye; (Fett~) globule of fat; (Punkt bei Spielen) point. **wieviel ~n hat der König?** how much is or how many points is the king worth?
(d) (Rad) **magisches ~** magic eye.

äugeln 1 vi nach jdm **~** to eye sb; **mit jdm ~** to make eyes at sb. 2 vi (Bot) to bud.

äugen vi to look.

Augen-: **~abstand** m interocular distance (form), distance between the eyes; ~**arzt** m eye specialist, ophthalmologist; a~**ärztlich** adj attr Gutachten etc ophthalmological; Behandlung eye attr, ophthalmic; ~**aufschlag** m look; ~**auswischerei** f, no pl (fig inf) siehe ~**wischerei**; a~**bad** nt eyebath; **ein** ~**bad nehmen** to bathe one's eye(s); ~**bank** f eyebank; ~**binde** f eye bandage; (~**klappe**) eye patch.

Augenblick m moment. **alle** ~**e** constantly, all the time; **jeden** ~ any time or minute or moment; **einen** ~, **bitte** one moment please!; ~ **mal!** (inf) just a minute or second or sec! (inf); **im** ~ at the moment; **im letzten/richtigen** etc ~ at the last/right etc moment; **im ersten** ~ for a moment; **im nächsten** ~ the (very) next moment; **er ist gerade im** ~ **gegangen** he just left this very moment; **es geschah in einem** ~ it happened in an instant; **er zögerte keinen** ~ he didn't hesitate for a moment.

augenblicklich 1 adj (a) (sofortig) immediate. (b) (gegenwärtig) present, current. **die** ~**e Lage** the present or current situation, the situation at the moment. (c) (vorübergehend) temporary; (einen Augenblick dauernd) momentary. **2** adv (a) (sofort) at once, immediately, instantly. (b) (zur Zeit) at the moment, presently.

augenblicks adv at once, immediately, instantly.

Augenblicks-: ~**bildung** f nonce word; ~**erfolg** m short-lived success; ~**idee** f idea thought up on the spur of the moment; ~**sache** f quick job; **das ist nur eine** ~**sache** it'll just take a moment; **das war eine** ~**sache** it was over in a flash.

Augen-: ~**blinzeln** nt ~**s**, no pl wink; ~**braue** f eyebrow; ~**brauenstift** m eyebrow pencil; ~**deckel** m siehe ~**lid**; ~**entzündung** f inflammation of the eyes; a~**fällig** adj conspicuous; (offensichtlich) obvious; ~**farbe** f colour of eyes; **Menschen mit einer dunklen** ~**farbe** people with dark eyes; ~**fehler** m eye defect; ~**flimmern** nt -**s**, no pl flickering before the eyes; ~**glas** nt (dated) monocle; ~**gläser** pl (esp Aus) glasses pl, spectacles pl; ~**gymnastik** f eye exercises pl; ~**heilkunde** f ophthalmology; ~**höhe** f: **in** ~**höhe** at eye level; ~**höhle** f eye socket, orbit (form); ~**klappe** f (a) eye patch; (b) (für Pferde) blinker, blinder (US); ~**klinik** f eye clinic or hospital; ~**krankheit** f eye disease; ~**leiden** nt eye complaint; ~**licht** nt, no pl (eyes)sight; ~**lid** nt eyelid; ~**maß** nt eye; (für Entfernungen) eye for distance(s); (fig) perceptiveness; **nach** ~**maß** by eye; ~**maß haben** (lit) to have a good eye (for distance(s); (fig) to be able to assess or gauge things or situations; **ein gutes/schlechtes** ~**maß haben** to have a good eye/no eye (for distance(s)); **ein** ~**maß für etw haben** (fig) to have an eye for sth; ~**mensch** m (inf) visual(ly oriented) person; ~**merk** nt -**s**, no pl (Aufmerksamkeit) attention; **jds/sein** ~**merk auf etw** (acc) **lenken** or **richten** to direct sb's/one's attention to sth; **einer Sache** (dat) **sein** ~**merk zuwenden** to turn one's attention to a matter; ~**nerv** m optic nerve; ~**operation** f eye operation; ~**optiker** m optician; ~**paar** nt pair of eyes; ~**prothese** f artificial eye; ~**ränder** pl rims of the/one's eyes; **er hatte rote** ~**ränder, seine** ~**ränder waren gerötet** the rims of his eyes were red; ~**ringe** pl rings round or under the/one's eyes; ~**salbe** f eye ointment; ~**schatten** pl shadows pl under or round the/one's eyes; ~**schein** m -(e)s, no pl (a) (Anschein) appearance; **dem** ~**schein nach** by all appearances, to judge by appearances; **der** ~**schein trügt** appearances are deceptive; **nach dem** ~**schein urteilen** to judge by appearances; (b) **jdn/etw in** ~**schein nehmen** to look closely at sb/sth, to have a close look at sb/sth; a~**scheinlich** adj obvious, evident; **die beiden sind a**~**scheinlich zerstritten** the two have obviously or clearly had a quarrel; ~**schirm** m eyeshade; ~**schmaus** m (hum) feast for the eyes; ~**spiegel** m ophthalmoscope; ~**spiegelung** f ophthalmoscopy; ~**stern** m (a) (Liter: Pupille) pupil, orb (poet); (b) (dated: Liebstes) apple of one's eye, darling; ~**täuschung** f optical illusion; ~**tropfen** pl eyedrops pl; ~**weide** f feast or treat for the eyes; **nicht gerade eine** ~**weide** (iro) a bit of an eyesore; ~**wimper** f eyelash; ~**winkel** m corner of the/one's eye; ~**wischerei** f (fig) eyewash; ~**zahl** f (Cards etc) number of points; ~**zahn** m eyetooth; ~**zeuge** m eyewitness (bei to); **ich war** ~**zeuge dieses Unfalls** or **bei diesem Unfall** I was an eyewitness to this accident; ~**zeugenbericht** m eyewitness account; ~**zwinkern** nt -**s**, no pl winking; a~**zwinkernd** adj winking attr; (fig) sly; **er grinste mich a**~**zwinkernd an** he grinned at me, winking; **jdm etw** a~**zwinkernd zu verstehen geben** to give sb to understand sth with a wink.

Augiasstall m (fig geh) dunghill, Augean stables pl (liter).

-**äugig** adj suf -eyed.

Augur m -**s** or -**en**, -**en** (Hist, fig geh) augur.

Augurenlächeln nt (pej geh) knowing smile.

August¹ m -(e)s, -e August; siehe **März**.

August² m -**s** Augustus. **der dumme** ~ (inf) the clown; **den dummen** ~ **spielen** to play or act the clown or fool.

Augustapfel m Laxton.

augusteisch adj Augustan.

Augustfeier f (Sw) August public holiday.

Augustiner(mönch) m -**s**, - Augustinian (monk).

Auktion f auction.

Auktionator(in f) [-'to:rm] m auctioneer.

Aula f -, **Aulen** (Sch, Univ etc) (assembly) hall; (Atrium) atrium.

Au-pair- [o'pɛːr]: ~-**Mädchen** nt au-pair (girl); **als** ~-**Mädchen arbeiten** to work (as an) au-pair; ~-**Stelle** f au-pair job.

Aura f -, no pl (Med, geh) aura.

Aureole f -, -**n** (Art) aureole, halo; (Met) corona, aureole; (fig rare) aura.

Aurikel f -, -**n** (Bot) auricula.

Aurora f -**s** (Myth, liter) Aurora.

aus 1 prep + dat (a) (räumlich) from; (aus dem Inneren von) out of. ~ **dem Fenster/der Tür** out of the window/door; ~ **unserer** Mitte from our midst; ~ **der Flasche trinken** to drink from or out of the bottle; **jdm** ~ **einer Verlegenheit helfen** to help sb out of a difficulty.

(b) (Herkunft, Quelle bezeichnend) from. ~ **dem Deutschen** from (the) German; ~ **ganz Frankreich** from all over France; ~ **guter Familie** from or of a good family; **er ist** ~ **Köln** he's from Cologne; **ein Wort** ~ **dem Zusammenhang herausgreifen** to take a word out of (its) context.

(c) (auf Ursache deutend) out of. ~ **Haß/Gehorsam/Mitleid** out of hatred/obedience/sympathy; ~ **Erfahrung** from experience; ~ **Furcht vor/Liebe zu** for fear/love of; ~ **dem Grunde, daß** ... for the reason that ...; ~ **einer Laune heraus** on (an) impulse; ~ **Spaß** for fun, for a laugh (inf); ~ **Unachtsamkeit** due to carelessness; ~ **Versehen** by mistake; ~ **sich heraus** of one's own accord, off one's own bat (inf); **ein Mord** ~ **Berechnung** a calculated murder; **ein Mord** or **ein Verbrechen** ~ **Leidenschaft** a crime of passion.

(d) (zeitlich) from. ~ **dem Barock** from the Baroque period; ~ **der Goethezeit** from the time of Goethe.

(e) (beschaffen ~) (made out) of. **ein Herz** ~ **Stein** a heart of stone.

(f) (Herstellungsart) out of, from; (fig: Ausgangspunkt) out of. **kann man** ~ **diesem Stoff noch etwas machen?** can something still be made out of or from this material?; **einen Soldaten/Pfarrer** ~ **jdm machen** to make a soldier/minister (out) of sb; **einen anständigen Menschen** ~ **jdm machen** to make sb into a decent person; **was ist** ~ **ihm/dieser Sache geworden?** what has become of him/this?; ~ **der Sache ist nichts geworden** nothing came of it; ~ **ihm wird einmal ein guter Arzt** he'll make a good doctor one day; ~ **mir ist nichts geworden** I never got anywhere (in life).

(g) ~ **dem Gleichgewicht** out of balance; Mensch, Gegenstand balance; ~ **der Mode** out of fashion.

(h) (Aus: in) in. **eine Prüfung** ~ **Geschichte** an examination in or on history.

(i) (Typ) **gesetzt** ~ ... set in ...

2 adv siehe auch **aussein** (a) (Sport) out; (Ftbl, Rugby auch) out of play, in touch.

(b) (inf: vorbei, zu Ende) over. ~ **jetzt!** that's enough!, that'll do now! (inf); ~ **und vorbei** over and done with.

(c) (gelöscht) out; (an Geräten) off. **Licht** ~! lights out!

(d) (in Verbindung mit von) **vom Fenster** ~ from the window; **von München** ~ from Munich; **von sich** (dat) ~ off one's own bat (inf), of one's own accord; **von ihm** ~ as far as he's concerned; siehe **ein**.

Aus nt -, - (Sport) (a) no pl (Ftbl, Rugby) touch no art. **ins** ~ **gehen** to go out of play; (seitlich) to go into touch. (b) no pl (Ausscheiden) exit (für etw).

aus|arbeiten sep **1** vt to work out; (errichten, entwerfen auch) System, Gedankengebäude to elaborate, to draw up; (vorbereiten) to prepare; (formulieren auch) to formulate, to compose. **2** vr to work until one is fit to drop; (Sport) to have a workout.

Aus|arbeitung f siehe vt working out; elaboration, drawing up; preparation; formulation, composition.

aus|arten vi sep aux sein (a) (Party etc) to get out of control. ~ **in** (+acc) or **zu** to degenerate into.

(b) (ungezogen etc werden) to get out of hand, to become unruly; (pöbelhaft, ordinär etc werden) to misbehave; to use bad language. **dann artete er ganz übel aus** then he really started to misbehave und bad language.

aus|atmen vti sep to breathe out, to exhale.

ausbacken vt sep irreg (a) (in Fett backen) to fry. (b) (zu Ende backen) to bake (for) long enough; (durchbacken) to bake (right) through.

ausbaden vt sep (inf) to carry the can for (inf), to pay for. **ich muß jetzt alles** ~ I have to carry the can (inf).

ausbaggern vt sep Graben to excavate; Fahrrinne, Schlamm to dredge (out).

ausbalancieren* sep (lit, fig) **1** vt to balance (out). **2** vr to balance (each other out).

Ausbalancierung f (lit, fig) balancing.

ausbaldowern* vt sep (inf) to scout or nose out (inf). ~, **ob** ... to scout or nose around to find out whether ... (inf).

Ausball m (Sport) bei ~ when the ball goes out of play.

Ausbau m -(e)s, -**ten** (a) siehe vt removal; extension (zu into); reinforcement; conversion (zu (in)to); fitting out; building up, cultivation; elaboration; consolidation, strengthening. (b) (am Haus) extension. (c) (Einzelgehöft) (small) farmstead (separated from main settlement).

ausbauchen vtr sep to bulge (out). **weit ausgebaucht** bulging.

ausbauen vt sep (a) (herausmontieren) to remove (aus from).

(b) (lit, fig: erweitern, vergrößern) to extend (zu into); Befestigungsanlagen to reinforce; (umbauen) to convert (zu (in)to); (innen ~) to fit out; Beziehungen, Freundschaft to build up, to cultivate; Plan to elaborate; (festigen) Position, Vorsprung to consolidate, to strengthen; siehe **ausgebaut**.

ausbaufähig adj Position with good prospects; Geschäft, Produktion, Markt that can be extended; Beziehungen that can be built up; Machtstellung that can be consolidated or strengthened; (inf) Schüler, Mitarbeiter promising.

ausbedingen vr sep irreg sich (dat) etw ~ to insist on sth, to make sth a condition; **sich** (dat) ~, **daß** ... to stipulate that ..., to make it a condition that ...; **ich bin dazu bereit, aber ich bedinge mir aus,** ... I'm prepared to do it but (only) on condition that ...; **sich** (dat) **das Recht** ~, **etw zu tun** to reserve the right to do sth.

ausbeißen vr sep irreg sich (dat) einen Zahn ~ to break or lose a tooth (when biting into sth); **sich** (dat) **an etw** (dat) **die Zähne** ~ (fig) to have a tough time of it with sth.

ausbekommen* vt sep irreg (inf) to get off.

ausbessern vt sep to repair; Gegenstand, Wäsche etc auch to mend; Roststelle etc to remove; Gemälde etc to restore; Fehler to correct.

Ausbesserung f siehe vt repair; mending; removal; restoration; correction.

Ausbesserungs-: ~arbeiten pl repair work sing; a~bedürftig adj in need of repair etc; ~werk nt (Rail) repair shop.

ausbetonieren* vt sep to concrete.

ausbeulen sep 1 vt (a) Kleidung to make baggy; Hut to make floppy; siehe ausgebeult. (b) (Beule entfernen) to remove a dent/dents in; (Tech: durch Hämmern) to beat out. 2 vr (Hose) to go baggy; (Hut) to go floppy.

Ausbeulung f (Tech: das Ausbeulen) beating (out).

Ausbeute f (Gewinn) profit, gain; (Ertrag einer Grube etc) yield (an + dat in); (fig) result(s); (Einnahmen) proceeds pl. die ~ an verwertbaren Erkenntnissen war gering the useful results (gleaned) were minimal.

ausbeuten vt sep (lit, fig) to exploit; (Min) eine Grube auch to work; (Agr) Boden to overwork, to deplete.

Ausbeuter(in f) m -s, - exploiter. ~ und Ausgebeutete the exploiters and the exploited.

Ausbeuterei f (pej) exploitation.

Ausbeutergesellschaft f society based on exploitation.

ausbeuterisch adj exploitative (form); Firma which exploits. die Arbeiter ~ zu Überstunden antreiben to exploit the workers by forcing them to work overtime.

Ausbeutung f siehe vt exploitation; working; overworking; depletion.

ausbezahlen* vt sep Geld to pay out; Arbeitnehmer to pay off; (abfinden) Erben etc to buy out, to pay off. in bar ausbezahlt paid in cash; wieviel kriegst du pro Woche ausbezahlt? what is your weekly take-home pay?

Ausbezahlung f payment; (von Erben etc) buying out, paying off.

ausbiegen vi sep irreg aux sein jdm/einer Sache ~ (lit, fig) to avoid sb/sth; nach links/rechts ~ to swerve to the left/right.

ausbieten vt sep irreg to put on offer, to offer (for sale). ausgeboten werden to be on offer; (bei Versteigerung auch) to be up for auction.

ausbilden sep 1 vt (a) (beruflich, Sport, Mil) to train; (unterrichten auch) to instruct; (akademisch) to educate. sich in etw (dat)/als or zu etw ~ lassen (esp Arbeiter, Lehrling) to train in sth/as sth; (studieren) to study sth/to study to be sth; (Qualifikation erwerben) to qualify in sth/as sth; sich am Klavier etc ~ lassen to have piano etc tuition; jdn als Sänger ~ lassen to have sb trained as a singer; ein ausgebildeter Übersetzer a trained/qualified translator.
(b) Fähigkeiten to develop, to cultivate; (Mus) Stimme to train.
(c) (formen) to form; (gestalten) to shape; (entwickeln) to develop. etw oval ~ to give sth an oval shape; (Designer etc) to design sth with an oval shape.
2 vr (a) (sich entwickeln) to develop; (sich bilden) to form.
(b) (sich schulen) sich in etw (dat) ~ (esp Arbeiter, Lehrling) to train in sth; (studieren) to study sth; (Qualifikation erwerben) to qualify in sth.

Ausbilder(in f) m -s, - instructor/instructress.

Ausbildner m -s, - (Aus Mil) instructor.

Ausbildung f siehe vt training; instruction; education; development, cultivation; training; formation; shaping/shape; development.

Ausbildungs-: ~beihilfe f (für Schüler) (education) grant; (für Lehrling) training allowance; ~beruf m occupation that requires training; ~förderung f promotion of training; ~gang m training; ~kompanie f training unit (for weapons training); ~kurs(us), ~lehrgang m training course; ~methode f training method, method of training; ~munition f blank ammunition (used in training); ~offizier m training officer; ~ordnung f training regulations pl; ~platz m place to train; (Stelle) training vacancy; ~stand m level of training; ~stätte f place of training; ~versicherung f education insurance; ~vertrag m articles pl of apprenticeship; ~zeit f period of training; nach zweijähriger ~zeit after a two-year period of training or training period; ~ziel nt aims of of education; die ~ziele der Schule the aims of school education or education at school.

ausbitten vr sep irreg sich (dat) (von jdm) etw ~ (geh) to ask (sb) for sth, to request sth (from sb) (form); das möchte ich mir (auch) ausgebeten haben! I should think so too!; ich bitte mir Ruhe aus! I must or will have silence!

ausblasen vt sep irreg to blow out; Hochofen to shut down, to extinguish; Ei to blow.

Ausbläser m (Mil) dud.

ausbleiben vi sep irreg aux sein (fortbleiben) to stay out; (nicht erscheinen) Gäste, Schüler, Schneefall) to fail to appear; (nicht eintreten: Erwartung, Befürchtung) to fail to materialize; (überfällig sein) to be overdue; (aufhören: Puls, Atmung etc) to stop. die Strafe/ein Krieg wird nicht ~ punishment/a war is inevitable; die Folgen solchen Handelns können nicht ~ you/he etc will reap the rewards of such behaviour; das blieb nicht lange aus that wasn't long in coming; es konnte nicht ~, daß ... it was inevitable that ...; bei manchen Patienten bleiben diese Symptome aus in some patients these symptoms are absent or do not appear.

Ausbleiben nt -s, no pl (Fehlen) absence; (Nichterscheinen) non-appearance. bei ~ von ... in the absence of ...; bei ~ der Periode if your period doesn't come.

ausbleichen vti sep irreg to fade, to bleach.

ausblenden sep 1 vti (TV etc) to fade out; (plötzlich) to cut out. 2 vr sich (aus einer Übertragung) ~ to leave a transmission.

Ausblendung f siehe vt fade-out; cutting-out, cut.

Ausblick m (a) view (auf + acc of), outlook (auf + acc over, onto). ein Zimmer mit ~ auf die Straße/aufs Meer a room overlooking the street/with a view of the sea or overlooking the sea.
(b) (fig) prospect, outlook (auf + acc, in + acc for). einen ~ auf etw (acc) geben to give the prospects for sth.

ausblicken vi sep (geh) nach jdm ~ to look for sb.

ausbluten sep 1 vi (a) (auch verbluten) to bleed to death; (fig) to be bled white. ein Schwein ~ lassen to bleed a pig dry. (b) (Wunde) to stop bleeding. 2 vt (fig) to bleed white.

ausbohren vt sep to bore; (mit Bohrgerät, Med) to drill; (herausbohren) to bore/drill out.

ausbomben vt sep to bomb out. die Ausgebombten people who have been bombed out (of their homes).

ausbooten sep 1 vt (a) (inf) jdn to kick or boot sb out (inf). (b) (Naut) to disembark (in boats); (abladen) to unload. 2 vi (Naut) to disembark (in boats).

ausborgen vt sep (inf) sich (dat) etw (von jdm) ~ to borrow sth (from sb); jdm etw ~ to lend sb sth, to lend sth (out) to sb.

ausbraten sep irreg 1 vt (a) (zu Ende braten) to roast/fry (for) long enough; (durchbraten) to roast/fry (right) through. (b) (auslassen) Speck to fry the fat out of. 2 vi aux sein (Fett) to run out (aus of). ausgebratenes Fett melted bacon etc fat.

ausbrechen sep irreg 1 vt (a) (herausbrechen) Steine to break off (aus from); Mauer to break up; Tür, Fenster to put in. sich (dat) einen Zahn ~ to break off a tooth.
(b) (erbrechen) to bring up, to vomit (up).
2 vi aux sein (a) (lit, fig: sich befreien) to break out (aus of) (auch Mil), to escape (aus from); (herausbrechen) to break or come away.
(b) (Richtung ändern: Pferd, Wagen) to swerve.
(c) (Krieg, Seuche, Feuer, Schweiß etc) to break out; (Jubel, Zorn etc) to erupt, to explode; (Vulkan) to erupt. in Gelächter/Tränen or Weinen ~ to burst into laughter/tears, to burst out laughing/crying; in Jubel ~ to erupt with jubilation; in den Ruf: „..." ~ to burst out with the cry: "..."; in Schweiß ~ to break out in a sweat; in Zorn ~ to explode with rage or anger; bei dir ist wohl der Wohlstand ausgebrochen (fig inf) have you struck it rich?

Ausbrecher(in f) m -s, - (a) (inf) (Gefangener) escaped prisoner, escapee; (notorischer ~) jail-breaker (inf); (Tier) escaped animal, runaway. (b) (Pferd) horse that swerves round jumps.

ausbreiten sep 1 vt Landkarte, Handtuch to spread (out); Flügel, Äste to spread (out), to extend; Arme to stretch out, to extend; (ausstellen, fig: zeigen) to display; Licht, Wärme to spread. einen Plan/sein Leben vor jdm ~ to unfold a plan to sb/to lay one's whole life before sb.
2 vr (a) (sich verbreiten) to spread.
(b) (sich erstrecken) to extend, to stretch (out), to spread out.
(c) (inf: sich breitmachen) to spread oneself out.
(d) sich über etw (acc) ~ (fig) to dwell on sth; sich in Einzelheiten ~ to go into great detail; darüber will ich mich jetzt nicht ~ I'd rather not go into that now.

Ausbreitung f (das Sich-Ausbreiten) spread; (das Ausbreiten) spreading.

Ausbreitungsdrang m expansionist drive.

ausbrennen sep irreg 1 vi aux sein (a) (zu Ende brennen) to burn out; (Vulkan) to become extinct. (b) (völlig verbrennen) to be burnt out, to be gutted. er ist ausgebrannt (fig) he's burnt out. 2 vt to burn out; (Sonne: ausdörren) to scorch; (Med) to cauterize.

ausbringen vt sep irreg (a) Trinkspruch to propose. (b) (Naut) Boot, Anker to lower. (c) (Typ) Zeile to space out.

Ausbruch m (a) (aus from) (aus Gefängnis) break-out (auch Mil), escape (auch fig). (b) (Beginn) outbreak; (von Vulkan) eruption. zum ~ kommen to break out. (c) (fig) (Gefühls~, Zorn~) outburst; (stärker) eruption, explosion. zum ~ kommen to erupt, to explode.

Ausbruchs-: ~herd m (Geol) focus (of an earthquake); ~versuch m (aus from) attempted break-out (auch Mil) or escape, break-out or escape attempt; (fig) attempt at escape.

ausbrüten vt sep to hatch; (esp in Brutkasten) to incubate; (fig inf) Plan etc to cook up (inf), to hatch (up).

ausbuchen vt sep siehe ausgebucht.

ausbuchten sep 1 vt Ufer to hollow out; Straße to make a curve in the side of; Wand to round out. 2 vr to bulge or curve out. eine ausgebuchtete Jacke a bulging jacket; ein ausgebuchteter Strand a beach with a (small) cove.

Ausbuchtung f bulge; (von Strand) (small) cove.

ausbuddeln vt sep (inf) to dig up (auch fig inf).

ausbügeln vt sep to iron out; (inf) Fehler, Verlust, Mängel to make good; Mißverständnis, Angelegenheit to iron out (inf).

ausbuhen vt sep (inf) to boo.

Ausbund m -(e)s, no pl (von Tugend, Schönheit) paragon, model, epitome. ein ~ von Tugend a paragon or model of virtue, the epitome of virtue; er ist ein ~ an or von Gemeinheit/Frechheit he is baseness/cheek itself or personified.

ausbürgern vt sep jdn ~ to expatriate sb.

Ausbürgerung f expatriation.

ausbürsten vt sep to brush out (aus of); Anzug to brush.

ausbüxen vi sep aux sein (hum inf) to run off, to scarper (sl). jdm ~ to run away from sb.

Ausdauer f -, no pl staying power, stamina; (im Ertragen) endurance; (Beharrlichkeit) perseverance, persistence, tenacity; (Hartnäckigkeit) persistence. beim Lernen/Lesen keine ~ haben to have no staying power when it comes to learning/reading; nebenan wurde mit großer ~ gefeiert (iro) there was an endless or a never-ending party next door.

ausdauernd adj (a) (Mensch) with staying power, with

stamina; (*im Ertragen*) with endurance; (*beharrlich*) persevering, tenacious; (*hartnäckig*) persistent; *Bemühungen, Anstrengungen* untiring. ~ **lernen** to apply oneself to learning. **(b)** (*Bot: Pflanze*) perennial.

Ausdauertraining *nt* stamina training.

ausdehnbar *adj* expandable; (*dehnbar*) *Gummi etc* elastic; (*fig*) extendable (*auf* + *acc*), extensible.

ausdehnen *sep 1 vt* **(a)** (*vergrößern*) to expand; (*dehnen*) to stretch, to extend; (*länger machen*) to elongate, to stretch. **(b)** (*fig*) to extend; (*zeitlich auch*) to prolong (*auf* + *acc* to). **2** *vr* **(a)** (*größer werden*) to expand; (*durch Dehnen*) to stretch; (*sich erstrecken*) to extend, to stretch (*bis* as far as). **die Seuche/der Krieg dehnte sich über das ganze Land aus** the epidemic/the war spread over the whole country. **(b)** (*fig*) to extend (*über* + *acc* over, *bis* as far as, *to*); (*zeitlich*) to go on (*bis* until), to extend (*bis* until); *siehe* **ausgedehnt**.

Ausdehnung *f* **(a)** (*das Ausdehnen*) *siehe vt* expansion; stretching, extension; elongation; extension; prolongation. **(b)** (*Umfang*) expanse; (*Math: von Raum*) extension. **eine ~ von 10.000 km² haben** to cover an area of 10,000 sq km.

Ausdehnungs-: ~**drang** *m* impetus to expand; (*fig*) drive towards expansion, urge to expand; **a~fähig** *adj* (*esp Phys*) capable of expansion, expansile, expansible; ~**fähigkeit** *f* ability to expand, expansibility; ~**vermögen** *nt* (*esp Phys*) capacity to expand, expansibility.

ausdenken *vt sep irreg sich* (*dat*) **etw** ~ (*erfinden*) to think sth up; *Idee, Plan auch* to devise sth; (*in Einzelheiten*) to think sth out, to devise sth; *Wunsch* to think of sth; *Entschuldigung auch* to contrive sth; *Überraschung* to plan sth; *Geschichte auch* to make sth up; (*sich vorstellen*) to imagine sth; (*durchdenken*) to think sth through; **eine ausgedachte Geschichte** a made-up story; **das ist nicht auszudenken** (*unvorstellbar*) it's inconceivable; (*zu schrecklich etc*) it doesn't bear thinking about; **da mußt du dir schon etwas anderes ~!** (*inf*) you'll have to think of something better than that!

ausdeuten *vt sep* to interpret; *Äußerung, Wort auch* to construe. **falsch** ~ to misinterpret; to misconstrue.

ausdeutschen *vt sep* (*Aus inf*) **jdm etw** ~ to explain sth to sb in words of one syllable *or* ≈ in plain English; **sich etw** ~ to make sth out.

Ausdeutung *f* interpretation.

ausdienen *vi sep* **ausgedient haben** (*Mil old*) to have finished one's military service; (*im Ruhestand sein*) to have been discharged; (*fig inf*) to have had its day; (*Kugelschreiber etc*) to be used up *or* finished; *siehe* **ausgedient**.

ausdiskutieren* *sep 1 vt Thema* to discuss fully. **2** *vi* (*zu Ende diskutieren*) to finish discussing *or* talking.

ausdorren *vi sep aux sein* to dry up; (*Boden auch*) to become parched; (*Pflanze auch*) to shrivel (up).

ausdörren *sep 1 vt* to dry up; *Kehle* to parch; *Pflanzen* to shrivel. **2** *vi aux sein* to dry up; (*Boden auch*) to become parched; (*Pflanze auch*) to shrivel up; *siehe* **ausgedörrt**.

ausdrehen *vt sep* (*ausschalten*) to turn *or* switch off; *Licht auch* to turn out; (*rare: herausdrehen*) *Glühbirne etc* to unscrew; (*Tech*) *Bohrloch* to drill, to bore; *Gelenk* to dislocate.

ausdreschen *sep irreg 1 vt* to thresh (fully). **2** *vi* (*das Dreschen beenden*) to finish (the) threshing.

Ausdruck[1] *m* **-(e)s, Ausdrücke (a)** *no pl* (*Gesichts~*) expression. **der ~ ihrer Gesichter** the expression(s) on their faces. **(b)** *no pl* **als ~ meiner Dankbarkeit** as an expression of my gratitude; **mit dem ~ des Bedauerns** (*form*) expressing regret, with an expression of regret; **mit dem ~ der Hochachtung** (*form*) respectfully, with respect; **sein ~ ist mangelhaft** he expresses himself poorly; **ohne jeden ~ singen/spielen** to sing/play without any expression; **etw zum ~ bringen, einer Sache** (*dat*) **~ geben** *or* **verleihen** (*form*) to express sth, to give expression to sth; **in seinen Worten/seinem Verhalten kam Mitleid zum ~** his words expressed/behaviour showed his sympathy. **(c)** (*Wort*) expression; (*Math, Fach~ auch*) term. **das ist gar kein ~!** that's not the word for it; **du sollst keine Ausdrücke gebrauchen** you shouldn't use words like that!, language!; **sich im ~ vergreifen** to use the wrong word.

Ausdruck[2] *m* **-(e)s, -e** (*von Computer etc*) print-out; (*Typ*) end of printing.

ausdrucken *sep 1 vt* **(a)** (*Typ*) (*fertig drucken*) to finish printing; (*ungekürzt drucken*) to print in full *or* out. **ausgedruckte Exemplare** fully printed copies. **(b)** (*Telec, Computers*) to print out. **2** *vi* (*Buchstaben etc*) to come out.

ausdrücken *sep 1 vt* **(a)** to press out, to squeeze out; *Pickel* to squeeze; (*ausmachen*) to put out; *Zigarette* to stub out. **den Saft einer Zitrone** ~ to press *or* squeeze juice out of a lemon, to squeeze a lemon.

(b) (*zum Ausdruck bringen*) to express (*jdm* to sb); (*Verhalten, Gesicht auch*) *Trauer etc* to reveal. **um es anders/gelinde auszudrücken** to put it another way/mildly; **anders ausgedrückt** in other words; **einfach ausgedrückt** put simply, in simple terms, in words of one syllable.

2 *vr* (*Mensch*) to express oneself; (*Emotion*) to be expressed *or* revealed. **in ihrem Gesicht/Verhalten drückte sich Verzweiflung aus** her face/behaviour showed her despair; **er kann sich gewandt** ~ he is very articulate.

ausdrücklich **1** *adj attr Wunsch, Genehmigung* express. **2** *adv* expressly; (*besonders*) particularly. **etw ~ betonen** to emphasize sth particularly *or* specifically.

Ausdrücklichkeit *f*: **in aller ~** expressly.

Ausdrucks-: ~**bedürfnis** *nt* need to express oneself; **a~fähig** *adj* expressive; (*gewandt*) articulate; ~**fähigkeit** *f siehe adj* expressiveness; articulateness; ~**form** *f* form of expression; ~**kraft** *f*, *no pl* expressiveness; (*von Schriftsteller*) articulate-

ness, word-power; **a~leer** *adj* expressionless; ~**leere** *f* expressionlessness; **a~los** *adj* inexpressive; *Gesicht, Blick auch* expressionless; ~**losigkeit** *f siehe adj* inexpressiveness; expressionlessness; ~**mittel** *nt* means of expression; ~**möglichkeit** *f* mode of expression; **a~schwach** *adj* inexpressive; **a~stark** *adj* expressive; ~**tanz** *m* free dance; **a~voll** *adj* expressive; ~**weise** *f* way of expressing oneself, mode of expression; **was ist denn das für eine ~weise!** what sort of language is that to use!

ausdünsten *sep 1 vt Geruch* to give off; (*Med, Bot auch*) to transpire. **2** *vi* (*Dunst/Geruch absondern*) to give off vapour/a smell; (*Bot, Med*) to transpire.

Ausdünstung *f* **(a)** (*das Ausdünsten*) evaporation; (*von Körper, Pflanze*) transpiration. **(b)** (*Dampf*) vapour; (*Geruch*) fume, smell; (*von Tier*) scent; (*von Mensch*) smell; (*fig*) emanation.

aus|einander *adv* **(a)** (*voneinander entfernt, getrennt*) apart. **weit ~** far apart; *Augen, Beine etc* wide apart; *Zähne* widely spaced; *Meinungen* very different; **die Ereignisse liegen (um) zwei Tage ~** the events are separated by two days *or* are two days apart; **etw ~ schreiben** to write sth as two words; **zwei Kinder ~ setzen** to separate two children; **sich ~ setzen** to sit apart; **die beiden sind (im Alter) ein Jahr ~** there is a year between the two of them; **sich ~** (*inf: Paar*) to have broken *or* split up; **die Verlobung ist ~** (*inf*) the engagement is off.

(b) (*jedes aus dem anderen*) from one another. **diese Begriffe kann man nur ~ erklären** one can only explain these concepts in relation to one another.

aus|einander-: ~**bekommen*** *vt sep irreg* to be able to get apart; ~**biegen** *vt sep irreg* to bend apart; ~**brechen** *sep irreg 1 vt* to break in two; **2** *vi aux sein* (*lit, fig*) to break up; ~**breiten** *vt sep siehe* ~**falten**; ~**bringen** *vt sep irreg* (*inf*) to manage *or* be able to get apart (*auch fig*); ~**entwickeln*** *vr sep* to grow apart (*from each other*); (*Partner*) to drift apart; ~**fallen** *vi sep irreg* (*fig: sich gliedern*) to divide up (*in* + *acc* into); ~**falten** *vt sep* to unfold; ~**fliegen** *vi sep irreg aux sein* to fly apart; (*nach allen Seiten*) to fly in all directions; ~**fließen** *vi sep irreg aux sein* (*nach allen Seiten*) to flow in all directions; (*zerfließen*) to melt; (*Farben*) to run; ~**gehen** *vi sep irreg aux sein* **(a)** (*lit, fig: sich trennen*) (*Menschen, Vorhang*) to part, to separate; (*Menge*) to disperse; (*Versammlung, Ehe etc*) to break up; (*auseinanderfallen: Schrank etc*) to fall apart; **(b)** (*sich verzweigen: Weg etc*) to divide, to branch, to fork; (*zwei Wege*) to diverge; (*fig: Ansichten etc*) to diverge, to differ; **(c)** (*inf: dick werden*) to get fat; *siehe* **Hefeteig**; ~**halten** *vt sep irreg* to keep apart; (*unterscheiden*) *Begriffe* to distinguish between; *esp Zwillinge etc* to tell apart; ~**jagen** *vt sep* to scatter; ~**kennen** *vt sep irreg* (*inf*) to tell apart; ~**klaffen** *vi sep aux sein* to gape open; (*fig: Meinungen*) to be far apart, to diverge (wildly); ~**klamüsern*** *vt sep* (*dial, hum*) to sort out; **jdm etw** ~**klamüsern** to spell sth out for sb; ~**klauben** *vt sep* (*esp S Ger, Aus, Sw*) to sort out; ~**kriegen** *vt sep* (*inf*) *siehe* ~**bekommen**; ~**laufen** *vi sep irreg aux sein* **(a)** (*zerlaufen*) to melt; (*Farbe*) to run; (*sich ausbreiten*) to spread; **(b)** (*inf: sich trennen*) to break up; (*Menge*) to disperse; (*sich ~entwickeln*) to go their separate ways; **(c)** (*Wege*) to divide, to fork, to diverge; ~**leben** *vr sep* to drift apart (*mit* from); ~**machen** *vt sep* (*inf*) **(a)** (~**nehmen**) to take apart; **(b)** (~**falten**) to unfold; **(c)** (*spreizen*) *Arme, Beine* to spread (apart), to open; ~**nehmen** *vt sep irreg* to take apart; *Maschine etc auch* to dismantle; (*kritisch*) to tear apart *or* to pieces; ~**pflücken** *vt sep siehe* **zerpflücken**; ~**reißen** *vt sep irreg* to tear *or* rip apart; (*fig*) *Familie* to tear apart; ~**schlagen** *vt sep irreg* (*zerschlagen*) to hack apart; (*öffnen*) *Mantel, Vorhang* to fling open; ~**schrauben** *vt sep* to unscrew; ~**setzen** *sep* **1** *vt* (*fig*) (*jdm* to sb) to explain; (*schriftlich auch*) to set out; **2** *vr* **sich mit etw ~setzen** (*sich befassen*) to have a good look at sth; **sich kritisch mit etw ~setzen** to have a critical look at sth; **mit dem Problem habe ich mich seit Jahren ~gesetzt** I've been working on this problem for years; **sich damit ~setzen, was/weshalb ...** to tackle the problem of what/why ...; **sich mit jdm ~setzen** to talk *or* (*sich streiten*) to argue with sb; **sich mit jdm gerichtlich ~setzen** to take sb to court.

Aus|einandersetzung *f* **(a)** (*Diskussion*) discussion, debate (*über* + *acc* about, on); (*Streit*) argument; (*feindlicher Zusammenstoß*) clash (*wegen* over). **(b)** (*das Befassen*) examination (*mit of*); (*kritisch*) analysis (*mit of*).

aus|einander-: ~**spreizen** *vt sep* to open, to spread apart; ~**sprengen** *sep 1 vt* **(a)** (*sprengen*) to blow up; (*zerbersten lassen*) to burst (apart); **(b)** (~**jagen**) to scatter; *Demonstranten auch* to disperse; **2** *vi aux sein* to scatter; ~**springen** *vi sep irreg aux sein* to shatter; ~**stieben** *vi sep irreg aux sein* to scatter; ~**streben** *vi sep aux sein* (*lit*) to splay; (*fig: Meinungen, Tendenzen*) to diverge; ~**treiben** *sep irreg 1 vt* (*trennen*) to drive apart; (~**jagen**) to scatter; *Demonstranten* to disperse; **2** *vi aux sein* to drift apart; ~**ziehen** *sep irreg 1 vt* **(a)** (*dehnen*) to stretch; **(b)** (*trennen*) to pull apart; *Gardinen auch* to pull open; **2** *vi aux sein* (*gemeinsame Wohnung aufgeben*) to separate (and live apart); **3** *vr* to spread out; (*Kolonne auch*) to string out.

aus|erkiesen* *vt sep irreg* (*liter*) (*Gott*) to ordain (*liter*). **zu etw auserkoren (worden) sein** to be chosen *or* selected for sth.

aus|erkoren *adj* (*liter*) chosen, selected. **jds A~e(r)** (*hum*) sb's intended (*inf*).

aus|erlesen 1 *adj* (*ausgesucht*) select; *Speisen, Weine auch* choice *attr*. **2** *ptp* **zu etw** ~ (**worden**) **sein** to be chosen *or* selected for sth. **3** *adv* (*verstärkend*) particularly, especially.

aus|ersehen* *vt sep irreg* (*geh*) to choose; (*für Amt auch*) to designate (*zu as*). **dazu ~ sein, etw zu tun** to be chosen to do sth.

aus|erwählen* *vt sep* (*geh*) to choose. **das auserwählte Volk** the Chosen People.

Aus|erwählte(r) *mf decl as adj (geh)* chosen one. **die** ~n **the elect**, the chosen (ones); **seine** ~/**ihr** ~r *(hum)* his/her intended *(inf)*.

aus|essen *sep irreg* **1** *vt Speise* to eat up, to finish (eating); *Schüssel* to empty, to clear; *Pampelmuse* to eat. **2** *vi* to finish eating.

ausfädeln *vr sep sich* ~ **aus** *(Aut)* to slip out of or from.

Ausfädelungsspur *f* slip road.

ausfahrbar *adj* extensible, extendable; *Antenne, Fahrgestell* retractable.

ausfahren *sep irreg* **1** *vt* **(a)** *jdn (im Kinderwagen/Rollstuhl)* to take for a walk (in the pushchair *(Brit)* or stroller *(US)*/wheelchair); *(im Auto)* to take for a drive or ride.
  (b) *(ausliefern) Waren* to deliver.
  (c) *(abnutzen) Weg* to rut, to wear out. **sich in ausgefahrenen Bahnen bewegen** *(fig)* to keep to well-trodden paths.
  (d) *(Aut) Kurve* to (drive) round; *(mit aux sein) Rennstrecke* to drive round.
  (e) *(austragen) Rennen* to hold.
  (f) ein Auto *etc* **(voll)** ~ to drive a car *etc* flat out.
  (g) *(Tech)* to extend; *Fahrgestell etc auch* to lower.
  2 *vi aux sein* **(a)** *(spazierenfahren)* to go for a ride or *(im Auto auch)* drive. **mit dem Baby** ~ to take the baby out in the pushchair *(Brit)* or stroller *(US)*.
  (b) *(abfahren) (Zug)* to pull out *(aus of)*, to leave; *(Schiff)* to put to sea, to sail. **aus dem Hafen** ~ to sail out of the harbour, to leave harbour.
  (c) *(Min: aus dem Schacht)* to come up.
  (d) *(Straße verlassen)* to turn off, to leave a road/motorway.
  (e) *(Tech: Fahrgestell, Gangway)* to come out.
  (f) *(eine heftige Bewegung machen)* to gesture. **mit** ~**den Bewegungen** with expansive gestures.
  (g) *(böser Geist)* to come out *(aus of)*.
  (h) *(dial: ausrutschen)* to slip.

Ausfahrer *m (Aus, S Ger)* delivery man.

Ausfahrt *f* **(a)** *no pl (Abfahrt)* departure; *(Min: aus Schacht)* ascent *(aus from)*. **der Zug hat keine** ~ the train has not been cleared for departure. **(b)** *(Spazierfahrt)* drive, ride. **eine** ~ **machen** to go for a drive or ride. **(c)** *(Ausgang, Autobahn*~*)* exit. ~ **Gütersloh** Gütersloh exit, exit for Gütersloh.

Ausfahrt(s)-: ~**schild** *nt* exit sign; ~**signal** *nt (Rail)* departure signal; ~**straße** *f* exit road.

Ausfall *m* **(a)** *no pl (das Herausfallen)* loss.
  (b) *(Verlust, Fehlbetrag, Mil)* loss; *(das Versagen) (Tech, Med)* failure; *(von Motor)* breakdown; *(Produktionsstörung)* stoppage. **bei** ~ **des Stroms ...** in case of a power failure.
  (c) *no pl (von Sitzung, Unterricht etc)* cancellation. **wir hatten einen hohen** ~ **an Schulstunden** a lot of school lessons were cancelled.
  (d) *no pl (das Ausscheiden)* dropping out; *(im Rennen)* retirement; *(Abwesenheit)* absence.
  (e) *(Ling)* dropping, omission.
  (f) *(Mil: Ausbruch)* sortie, sally.
  (g) *(Sport) (Fechten)* thrust, lunge; *(Gewichtheben)* jerk.
  (h) *(fig: Angriff)* attack.
  (i) *(Ergebnis)* result, outcome.

ausfallen *vi sep irreg aux sein* **(a)** *(herausfallen)* to fall out; *(Chem)* to be precipitated; *(Ling)* to be dropped or omitted. **mir fallen die Haare aus** my hair is falling out.
  (b) *(nicht stattfinden)* to be cancelled. **etw** ~ **lassen** to cancel sth; **die Schule/die erste Stunde fällt morgen aus** there's no school/first lesson tomorrow.
  (c) *(nicht funktionieren)* to fail; *(Motor)* to break down.
  (d) *(wegfallen: Verdienst)* to be lost.
  (e) *(ausscheiden)* to drop out; *(während Rennen auch)* to retire; *(fernbleiben)* to be absent.
  (f) gut/schlecht *etc* ~ to turn out well/badly *etc*; **die Rede ist zu lang ausgefallen** the speech was too long or turned out to be too long; **die Bluse fällt zu eng aus** the blouse is too tight.
  (g) *(Mil)* to fall, to be lost *(bei* in*)*; *(old: einen Ausfall machen)* to make a sortie.
  (h) *(Fechten)* to thrust, to lunge.
  (i) *siehe* **ausgefallen.**

ausfällen *vt sep (Chem)* to precipitate.

ausfallend, ausfällig *adj* abusive.

Ausfälligkeit *f* abusiveness; *(Bemerkung)* abusive remark.

Ausfallstraße *f* arterial road.

Ausfall(s)winkel *m (Phys)* angle of reflection.

Ausfallzeit *f (Insur)* time which counts towards pension although no payments were made.

ausfasern *vi sep aux sein or haben* to fray, to become frayed.

ausfechten *vt sep irreg (fig)* to fight (out).

ausfegen *vt sep Schmutz* to sweep up; *Zimmer* to sweep out.

ausfeilen *vt sep* to file (out); *(glätten)* to file down; *(fig)* to polish; *siehe* **ausgefeilt.**

ausfertigen *vt sep (form)* **(a)** *Dokument* to draw up; *Rechnung, Lieferschein* to make out; *Paß* to issue. **(b)** *(unterzeichnen)* to sign.

Ausfertigung *f (form)* **(a)** *no pl siehe vt* drawing up; making out; issuing; signing. **(b)** *(Abschrift)* copy. **die erste** ~ the top copy; **in doppelter/dreifacher** ~ in duplicate/triplicate; **Zeugnisse in vierfacher** *etc* ~ four *etc* copies of references.

Ausfertigungs-: ~**datum** *nt (von Paß, Urkunde)* date of issue; ~**gebühr** *f* issuing fee.

ausfetten *vt sep* to grease.

ausfinden *vr sep irreg* to find one's way *(in* +*dat* around).

ausfindig *adj:* ~ **machen** to find, to discover; *(Aufenthaltsort feststellen)* to locate; to trace.

ausfischen *vt sep Karpfen etc* to catch; *Teich* to fish dry or out.

ausflennen *vir sep (inf) siehe* **ausheulen.**

ausflicken *vt sep (inf)* to mend, to patch up.

ausfliegen *sep irreg* **1** *vi aux sein (wegfliegen)* to fly away or off; *(aus Gebiet etc)* to fly out *(aus of)*; *(flügge werden)* to leave the nest; *(fig inf: weggehen)* to go out. **ausgeflogen sein** *(fig inf)* to be out, to have gone out; **der Vogel ist ausgeflogen** *(fig inf)* the bird has or is flown.
  2 *vt (Aviat)* **(a)** *Verwundete etc* to evacuate (by air), to fly out *(aus from)*.
  (b) *Flugzeug* to fly full out.

ausfliesen *vt sep* to tile.

ausfließen *vi sep irreg aux sein (herausfließen)* to flow out *(aus of)*; *(auslaufen: Öl etc, Faß)* to leak *(aus out of)*; *(Eiter etc)* to be discharged.

ausflippen *vi sep aux sein (sl)* to freak out *(sl)*; *siehe* **ausgeflippt.**

Ausflucht *f* -, **Ausflüchte** excuse; *(geh: Flucht)* escape *(in* +*acc* into*)*. **Ausflüchte machen** to make excuses; **keine Ausflüchte!** (I want) no excuses!

Ausflug *m* **(a)** trip, outing; *(esp mit Reisebüro)* excursion; *(Betriebs*~, *Schul*~*)* outing; *(Wanderung)* walk, hike; *(fig)* excursion. **einen** ~ **machen** to go on or for a trip *etc*; **einen** ~ **in die Politik machen** to make an excursion into politics.
  (b) *(von Vögeln etc)* flight; *(von Bienen)* swarming.
  (c) *(am Bienenstock)* hive exit.

Ausflügler(in *f)* *m* -s, - tripper. **Fahrkarte für** ~ excursion ticket.

Ausflugschneise *f (Aviat)* take-off path.

Ausflugs-: ~**dampfer** *m* pleasure steamer; ~**fahrt** *f* pleasure trip, excursion; ~**lokal** *nt* tourist café; *(am Meer)* seaside café; ~**ort** *m* place to go for an outing; ~**verkehr** *m (an Feiertagen)* holiday traffic; *(am Wochenende)* weekend holiday traffic; ~**ziel** *nt* destination (of one's outing).

Ausfluß *m* **(a)** *(das Herausfließen)* outflow; *(das Auslaufen)* leaking. **(b)** *(*~*stelle)* outlet. **(c)** *(Med)* discharge. **(d)** *(fig Ergebnis)* product, result.

ausfolgen *vt sep (Aus form)* to hand over *(jdm* to sb*)*.

Ausfolgung *f (Aus form)* handing over.

ausformen *sep* **1** *vt* to mo(u)ld, to shape *(zu* into*)*; *Manuskript etc* to polish, to refine. **2** *vr* to take shape, to be formed.

ausformulieren* *vt sep* to formulate; *Rede* to tidy up.

Ausformulierung *f siehe vt* formulation; tidying up.

Ausformung *f* **(a)** *siehe vt* mo(u)lding, shaping; polishing; refining. **(b)** *(Form)* shape, form.

ausforschen *vt sep* **(a)** *Sache* to find out; *(erforschen)* to investigate. **(b)** *jdn* to question. **jdn über etw** *(acc)* ~ to ask or question sb about sth. **(c)** *(Aus) Täter* to apprehend.

Ausforschung *f siehe vt* **(a)** finding out; investigating. **(b)** questioning. **(c)** apprehension.

ausfragen *vt sep* to question, to quiz *(inf) (nach* about*)*; *(strenger)* to interrogate. **so fragt man die Leute aus** *(inf)* that would be telling *(inf)*.

ausfransen *sep* **1** *vir (vi: aux sein)* to fray, to become frayed. **2** *vt* to fray.

ausfratscheln *vt sep (Aus inf)* to quiz *(inf)*.

ausfressen *vt sep irreg* **(a)** *siehe* **auffressen. (b)** *(ausspülen: Wasser, Fluß)* to erode, to eat away. **(c)** *(inf: anstellen)* **etwas** ~ to do something wrong; **was hat er denn wieder ausgefressen?** what's he (gone and) done now? *(inf)*. **(d)** *(inf: ausbaden)* to take the blame or carry the can *(inf)* for.

Ausfuhr *f* -, -**en (a)** *no pl (das Ausführen)* export; *(*~*handel)* exports *pl*. **(b)** ~**en** *pl (*~*güter)* exports *pl*.

Ausfuhrartikel *m* export.

ausführbar *adj* **(a)** *Plan* feasible, practicable, workable. **schwer** ~ difficult to carry out. **(b)** *(Comm)* exportable.

Ausführbarkeit *f* feasibility, practicability.

Ausfuhr-: *in cpds siehe auch* Export- export; ~**bestimmungen** *pl* export regulations *pl*.

ausführen *vt sep* **(a)** *(zu Spaziergang, ins Theater etc)* to take out; *Hund* to take for a walk; *(hum) Kleid* to parade.
  (b) *(durchführen)* to carry out; *Aufgabe, (Med) Operation auch* to perform; *Auftrag, Plan, Befehl, Bewegung, (Mil) Operation auch* to execute; *Anweisung auch, Gesetz* to implement; *Bauarbeiten* to undertake; *(Sport) Freistoß etc* to take. **die** ~**de Gewalt** *(Pol)* the executive.
  (c) *(gestalten) Plan, Entwurf, Bild etc* to execute.
  (d) *(erklären)* to explain; *(darlegen)* to set out; *(argumentierend)* to argue; *(sagen)* to say.
  (e) *(Comm) Waren* to export.

Ausführende(r) *mf decl as adj* **(a)** *(Spieler)* performer. **(b)** *(Handelnder)* executive.

Ausfuhr-: ~**güter** *pl* export goods *pl*, exports *pl*; ~**hafen** *m* port of exportation; ~**handel** *m* export trade; ~**land** *nt* **(a)** *(Land, das ausführt)* exporting country; **ein** ~**land für** jute a jute-exporting country; **(b)** *(Land, in das ausgeführt wird)* export market.

ausführlich ['ausfyːɐlɪç, *(Aus)* aus'fyːɐlɪç] **1** *adj* detailed; *Informationen, Gespräche, Katalog auch* full. **2** *adv* in detail, in full. **sehr** ~ in great detail; ~**er** in more or greater detail.

Ausführlichkeit *f siehe adj* detail; fullness. **in aller** ~ in (great) detail, in full.

Ausfuhr-: ~**prämie** *f* export premium; ~**sperre** *f* export ban or embargo; ~**überschuß** *m* export surplus.

Ausführung *f* **(a)** *no pl siehe vt* **(b)** carrying out; performance; execution; implementation; undertaking; taking. **zur** ~ **gelangen** or **kommen** to be carried out.
  (b) *siehe vt* **(c)** execution.
  (c) *(Erklärung)* explanation; *(von Thema etc)* exposition; *(Bemerkung)* remark; *(usu pl: Bericht)* report.
  (d) *(von Waren)* design; *(Tech: äußere* ~*)* finish; *(Qualität)* quality; *(Modell)* model.

Ausfuhr-: ~**volumen** *nt* volume of exports; ~**waren** *pl* exports *pl*, export goods *pl*; ~**zoll** *m* export duty.

ausfüllen *vt sep* to fill; *Loch* to fill (up *or* out); *Ritze* to fill in; *Platz* to take up; *Formular* to fill in (*Brit*) *or* out; *Posten* to fill. **jdn (voll** *or* **ganz)** ~ (*befriedigen*) to give sb (complete) fulfilment, to satisfy sb (completely); (*Zeit in Anspruch nehmen*) to take (all) sb's time; **er füllt den Posten nicht/gut aus** he is not fitted/well-fitted for the post; **der Gedanke an dich füllt mich ganz aus** the thought of you occupies my every minute; **seine Zeit mit etw** ~ to pass one's time doing sth, to fill up one's time with sth; **ein ausgefülltes Leben** a full life.

ausfüttern *vt sep* (a) (*Sew*) to line. (b) *Tier* to feed.

Ausgabe *f* -, **-n** (a) *no pl* (*Austeilung*) (*von Proviant, Decken etc*) distribution, giving out; (*von Befehl, Fahrkarten, Dokumenten etc*) issuing; (*von Essen*) serving; (*Ausdruck*) print-out.
  (b) (*Schalter*) issuing counter; (*in Bibliothek*) issue desk; (*in Kantine*) serving counter; (*Stelle, Büro*) issuing office.
  (c) (*von Buch, Zeitung, Sendung*) edition; (*von Zeitschrift auch, Aktien*) issue.
  (d) (*Ausführung*) version; (*inf: Abklatsch auch*) edition.
  (e) (*Geldaufwand*) expense, expenditure *no pl*. ~**en** *pl* (*Geldverbrauch*) expenditure *sing* (*für* on); (*Kosten*) expenses *pl*, costs *pl*.
  (f) (*Datenverarbeitung*) print-out.

Ausgabekurs *m* (*Fin*) rate of issue.

Ausgabe(n)-: ~**beleg** *m* receipt for expenditure; ~**buch** *nt* cashbook.

Ausgaben-: ~**politik** *f* expenditure policy; ~**seite** *f* expenditure column.

Ausgabe-: ~**schalter** *m* issuing counter; (*in Bibliothek etc*) issue desk; ~**termin** *m* date of issue.

Ausgang *m* (a) (*Erlaubnis zum Ausgehen*) permission to go out; (*Mil*) pass. ~ **haben** to have the day off *or* (*am Abend*) the evening off; (*Mil*) to have a pass; **bis 10 Uhr** ~ **haben** to be allowed out/to have a pass till 10 o'clock.
  (b) (*Spaziergang*) walk (*under supervision*).
  (c) (*Auslaß, Weg nach draußen*) exit, way out (*gen, von* from); (*Dorf~*) end; (*von Wald*) edge; (*Med: von Organ*) opening (*gen* out *of*).
  (d) *no pl* (*Ende, von Epoche auch*) close; (*von Roman, Film auch*) ending; (*Ergebnis*) outcome, result. **ein Unfall mit tödlichem** ~ a fatal accident; **ein Ausflug mit tragischem** ~ **an** excursion with a tragic outcome.
  (e) *no pl* (*Ausgangspunkt*) starting point, point of departure; (*Anfang*) beginning. **von hier nahm diese weltweite Bewegung ihren** ~ this was where this worldwide movement started.
  (f) *no pl* (*Abschicken von Post*) mailing, sending off.
  (g) **Ausgänge** *pl* (*Post*) outgoing mail *sing*; (*Waren*) outgoing goods *pl*.

ausgangs *prep* +*gen* (*auch adv* ~ **von**) at the end of; (*der Schlußkurve etc*) coming out of. **eine Frau** ~ **der Siebziger** a woman in her late seventies.

Ausgangs-: ~**basis** *f* fundamental basis; ~**frage** *f* initial question; ~**lage**, ~**position** *f* initial *or* starting position; ~**punkt** *m* starting point; (*von Reise auch*) point of departure; ~**sperre** *f* ban on going out; (*esp bei Belagerungszustand*) curfew; (*für Soldaten*) confinement to barracks; ~**sperre haben** (*Soldat*) to be confined to barracks; (*Schüler*) to be banned from going out, to be gated (*Brit inf*); ~**sprache** *f* source language; ~**stellung** *f* (*Sport*) starting position; (*Mil*) initial position; ~**tür** *f* exit (door); ~**verbot** *nt siehe* ~**sperre**; ~**zeile** *f* (*Typ*) club-line, widow; ~**zustand** *m* initial *or* original condition *or* (*Lage*) position; (*Pol auch*) status quo.

ausgebaut 1 *ptp of* **ausbauen.** 2 *adj* *Schul-, Verkehrssystem etc* fully developed.

ausgeben *sep irreg* 1 *vt* (a) (*austeilen*) *Proviant, Decken etc* to distribute, to give out; (*aushändigen*) *Dokumente, Fahrkarten, Aktien etc* to issue; *Befehl* to issue, to give; *Essen* to serve; (*Cards*) to deal; (*ausdrucken*) *Text* to print out.
  (b) *Geld* to spend (*für* on). **eine Runde** ~ to stand a round (*inf*); **ich gebe heute abend einen aus** (*inf*) it's my treat this evening; **unser Chef hat einen ausgegeben** our boss treated us; **darf ich dir einen/einen Whisky** ~? may I buy you a drink/a whisky?; **er gibt nicht gern einen aus** he doesn't like buying people drinks.
  (c) (*dial: außer Haus geben*) to send out.
  (d) (*Acker, Ölquelle etc*) to yield. **das gibt fünf Tassen aus** that makes five cups; **viel/wenig** ~ to go a long way/not to go a long way.
  (e) **jdn/etw als** *or* **für jdn/etw** ~ to pass sb/sth off as sb/sth; **sich als jd/etw** ~ to pose as sb/sth, to pass oneself off as sb/sth.
  2 *vr* to exhaust oneself; (*sein Geld ganz* ~) to spend all one's money.

ausgebeult 1 *ptp of* **ausbeulen.** 2 *adj* *Kleidung* baggy; *Hut* battered.

Ausgebeutete(r) *mf decl as adj die* ~**n** the exploited *pl*.

ausgebucht *adj* *Reise etc*, (*inf*) *Person* booked up.

ausgebufft *adj* (*sl*) (a) (*erledigt*) washed-up (*inf*); (*erschöpft*) knackered (*sl*). **diese Mode ist total** ~ that fashion has had it (*inf*). (b) (*trickreich*) shrewd, fly (*sl*).

Ausgeburt *f* (*pej*) (*der Phantasie etc*) monstrous product *or* invention; (*Geschöpf, Kreatur, Institution*) monster. **eine** ~ **der Hölle** a fiend from hell, a fiendish monster; **sie ist eine** ~ **von Eitelkeit und Dummheit** she is a monstrous combination of vanity and stupidity.

ausgedehnt 1 *ptp of* **ausdehnen.** 2 *adj* *Gummiband* (over-)stretched; (*breit, groß, fig: weitreichend*) extensive; (*zeitlich*) lengthy, extended; *Spaziergang* long, extended.

ausgedient 1 *ptp of* **ausdienen.** 2 *adj* (a) (*dated*) **ein** ~**er**

Soldat a veteran, an ex-serviceman. (b) (*inf: unbrauchbar*) *Auto, Maschine* clapped-out (*inf*). **meine** ~**en Sachen/Bücher** *etc* the things/books *etc* I don't have any further use for.

Ausgedinge *nt* -**s**, - *siehe* **Altenteil.**

ausgedörrt 1 *ptp of* **ausdörren.** 2 *adj* dried up; *Boden, Kehle* parched; *Pflanzen* shrivelled; *Land, Gebiet* arid; (*fig*) *Hirn* ossified, dull. **mein Hirn ist völlig** ~ (*fig*) I can't think straight any more.

ausgefallen 1 *ptp of* **ausfallen.** 2 *adj* (*ungewöhnlich*) unusual; (*übertrieben*) extravagant; *Mensch* eccentric; (*überspannt*) odd, weird.

Ausgefallenheit *f siehe adj* unusualness; extravagance; eccentricity; oddness, weirdness.

ausgefeilt 1 *ptp of* **ausfeilen.** 2 *adj* (*fig*) polished; *Schrift* stylized.

Ausgefeiltheit *f* polish; (*von Schrift*) stylized character.

ausgefeimt *adj siehe* **abgefeimt.**

ausgeflippt 1 *ptp of* **ausflippen.** 2 *adj* (*sl*) freaky (*sl*), freaked-out (*sl*), flipped-out (*sl*); (*aus der Gesellschaft*) dropout (*inf*). **er ist ein richtig** ~**er Typ** he's really freaky (*sl*) *or* freaked out (*sl*)/a real drop-out (*inf*).

Ausgeflippte(r) *mf decl as adj* (*sl*) freak (*sl*); (*aus der Gesellschaft*) drop-out (*inf*).

ausgefuchst *adj* (*inf*) clever; (*listig*) crafty (*inf*); *Kartenspieler* cunning.

ausgeglichen 1 *ptp of* **ausgleichen.** 2 *adj* balanced; *Spiel, Klima* even; *Torverhältnis* equal; (*gleichbleibend*) consistent.

Ausgeglichenheit *f* balance; evenness; consistency. **ihre** ~ her balanced nature *or* character.

ausgegoren *adj* Most fully fermented; (*fig inf*) *Pläne* worked out. **wenig** ~ half-baked (*inf*).

ausgehen *sep irreg aux sein* 1 *vi* (a) (*weggehen, zum Vergnügen*) to go out; (*spazierengehen auch*) to go (out) for a walk. **er geht selten aus** he doesn't go out much; **wir gehen heute abend ganz groß aus** we're going out for a big celebration tonight.
  (b) (*ausfallen: Haare, Federn, Zähne*) to fall out; (*Farbe*) to run; (*dial: Stoff*) to fade. **ihm gehen die Haare/Zähne aus** his hair is falling out/he is losing his teeth.
  (c) (*seinen Ausgang nehmen*) to start (*von* at); (*herrühren: Idee, Anregung etc*) to come (*von* from). **von dem Platz gehen vier Straßen aus** four streets lead off (from) the square; **etw geht von jdm/etw aus** (*wird ausgestrahlt*) sb/sth radiates sth; **von der Rede des Ministers ging eine große Wirkung aus** the minister's speech had a great effect.
  (d) (*abgeschickt werden: Post*) to be sent off. **die** ~**de Post** the outgoing mail; **einen Befehl** ~ **lassen** (*old*) to decree; **er ließ** ~, **daß ...** (*obs*) he decreed that ...
  (e) (*zugrunde legen*) to start out (*von* from). **gehen wir einmal davon aus, daß ...** let us assume that, let us start from the assumption that ...; **wovon gehst du bei dieser Behauptung aus?** on what are you basing your statement?; **davon kann man nicht** ~ you can't go that far.
  (f) **auf etw** (*acc*) ~ to be intent on sth; **auf Gewinn** ~ to be intent on making a profit; **auf Eroberungen** ~ (*hum inf*) to be out to make a few conquests.
  (g) (*einen bestimmten Ausgang haben: esp Sport*) to end; (*ausfallen*) to turn out. **gut/schlecht** ~ to turn out well/badly; (*Film etc*) to end happily/unhappily; (*Abend, Spiel*) to end well/badly.
  (h) (*Ling: enden*) to end.
  (i) **straffrei** *or* **straflos** ~ to receive no punishment; to get off scot-free (*inf*); **leer** ~ (*inf*) to come away empty-handed.
  (j) (*zu Ende sein: Vorräte etc*) to run out; (*dial: Vorstellung, Schule etc*) to finish. **mir ging die Geduld/das Geld aus** I lost (my) patience/ran out of money; **ihm ist die Luft** *or* **die Puste** *or* **der Atem ausgegangen** (*inf*) (*lit*) he ran out of breath/puff (*inf*); (*fig*) he ran out of steam (*inf*); (*finanziell*) he ran out of funds.
  (k) (*aufhören zu brennen*) to go out.
  (l) (*inf: sich ausziehen lassen*) to come off. **die nassen Sachen gehen so schwer aus** these wet things are so hard to take off.
  2 *vr* (*Aus*) **es geht sich aus** it works out all right; (*Vorräte, Geld etc*) there is enough.

ausgehend *adj attr* **im** ~**en Mittelalter** towards the end of the Middle Ages; **das** ~**e 20. Jahrhundert** the end *or* close of the 20th century.

Ausgeh|erlaubnis *f* permission to go out; (*Mil*) pass.

ausgehungert 1 *ptp of* **aushungern.** 2 *adj* starved; (*abgezehrt*) *Mensch etc* emaciated. **wie** ~**e Wölfe** like starving wolves; **nach etw** ~ **sein** (*fig*) to be starved of sth.

Ausgeh-: ~**uniform** *f* walking-out uniform; ~**verbot** *nt* **jdm** ~**verbot erteilen** to forbid sb to go out; (*Mil*) to confine sb to barracks; ~**verbot haben/bekommen** to be forbidden to go out; (*Mil*) to be confined to barracks.

ausgeklügelt 1 *ptp of* **ausklügeln.** 2 *adj* (*inf*) *System* cleverly thought-out; (*genial*) ingenious.

ausgekocht 1 *ptp of* **auskochen.** 2 *adj* (*pej inf*) (*berechnend*) cunning. **er ist ein** ~**er Bursche** he's a thoroughly bad character.

ausgelassen 1 *ptp of* **auslassen.** 2 *adj* (*heiter*) lively; *Stimmung* happy; (*wild*) *Kinder* boisterous; *Stimmung, Party* mad.

Ausgelassenheit *f siehe adj* liveliness; happiness; boisterousness; madness.

ausgelastet 1 *ptp of* **auslasten.**
  2 *adj* *Mensch* fully occupied; *Maschine, Anlage* working to capacity. **mit dem Job ist er nicht (voll)** ~ he is not fully stretched in that job; **mit den vier Kindern ist sie voll** ~ **her** four children keep her fully occupied, she has her hands full with her four children.

ausgelatscht 1 *ptp of* **auslatschen.** 2 *adj* (*inf*) *Schuhe* worn.

meine Schuhe sind völlig ~ my shoes have gone completely out of shape.

ausgeleiert 1 *ptp of* **ausleiern.** 2 *adj Gummiband, Gewinde, Feder* worn; *Hosen, Pullover* baggy; *Redensart* hackneyed.

ausgelernt 1 *ptp of* **auslernen.** 2 *adj (inf)* qualified.

ausgelesen 1 *ptp of* **auslesen.** 2 *adj (fig geh) Ware* select, choice.

Ausgeliefertsein *nt* subjection (*an* +acc to). **unser ~ an die Gesellschaft** the fact that we are at the mercy of society.

ausgemacht 1 *ptp of* **ausmachen.** 2 *adj* (a) *(abgemacht)* agreed. **es ist eine ~e Sache, daß ...** it is agreed that ... (b) *attr (inf: vollkommen)* complete, utter.

ausgemergelt 1 *ptp of* **ausmergeln.** 2 *adj Körper, Gesicht* emaciated, gaunt.

ausgenommen 1 *ptp of* **ausnehmen.**
2 *conj* except, apart from. **niemand/alle, ~ du, niemand/alle, du** *or* **dich ~** no-one/everyone except (for) you *or* apart from *or* save yourself; **täglich ~ sonntags** daily except for *or* excluding Sundays; **Anwesende ~** present company excepted; **~ wenn/daß ...** except when/that ...

ausgepicht *adj (fig inf) (raffiniert) Mensch, Plan* cunning; *(verfeinert) Geschmack* refined.

ausgeprägt 1 *ptp of* **ausprägen.** 2 *adj Gesicht* distinctive; *Eigenschaft* distinct; *Charakter, Interesse* marked, pronounced. **ein (stark) ~er Sinn für alles Schöne** a well-developed sense for everything beautiful.

ausgepumpt 1 *ptp of* **auspumpen.** 2 *adj (inf)* whacked *(inf).*

ausgerechnet 1 *ptp of* **ausrechnen.** 2 *adv* **~ du/er** *etc* you/he *etc* of all people; **~ mir muß das passieren** why does it have to happen to me (of all people)?; **~ heute/gestern** today/yesterday of all days; **muß das ~ heute sein?** does it have to be today (of all days)?; **~ jetzt kommt er** he would have to come just now; **~ dann kam er** he would have to come just at that moment; **~, als wir spazierengehen wollten, ...** just when we wanted to go for a walk ...

ausgeruht 1 *ptp of* **ausruhen.** 2 *adj* (well) rested.

ausgeschämt *adj (dial)* siehe **unverschämt.**

ausgeschlossen 1 *ptp of* **ausschließen.**
2 *adj pred (unmöglich)* impossible; *(nicht in Frage kommend)* out of the question. **es ist nicht ~, daß ...** it's just possible that ...; **diese Möglichkeit ist nicht ~** it's not impossible; **jeder Irrtum ist ~** there is no possibility of a mistake.

ausgeschnitten 1 *ptp of* **ausschneiden.** 2 *adj Bluse, Kleid* low-cut. **sie geht heute tief ~** *(inf)* she's wearing a very low-cut dress/blouse *etc* today; **ein weit** *or* **tief ~es Kleid** a dress with a plunging neckline.

ausgeschrieben 1 *ptp of* **ausschreiben.** 2 *adj Schrift* bold.

ausgespielt 1 *ptp of* **ausspielen.** 2 *adj* **~ haben** to be finished; **er hat bei mir ~** *(inf)* he's had it as far as I am concerned *(inf),* I'm finished *or* through with him.

ausgesprochen 1 *ptp of* **aussprechen.**
2 *adj (besonders) Schönheit, Qualität, Vorliebe* definite; *(ausgeprägt) Trinkernase etc auch* pronounced; *Begabung* particular; *Ähnlichkeit auch* marked; *Geiz, Großzügigkeit* extreme; *(groß) Pech, Freundlichkeit, Hilfsbereitschaft etc* real. **eine ~e Frohnatur** a very sunny person; **~es Pech haben** to have really bad luck, to be really unlucky.
3 *adv* really; *schön, begabt, groß, hilfsbereit etc auch* extremely; *geizig, frech etc auch* terribly.

ausgesprochenermaßen *adv* siehe **ausgesprochen 3.**

ausgestalten* *vt sep (künstlerisch, musikalisch)* to arrange; *(planend gestalten)* to organize; *(dekorieren, einrichten)* to decorate; *(ausbauen) Theorie, Begriff, Methode* to build up. **Bücher künstlerisch ~** to do the art work for books.

Ausgestaltung *f* (a) siehe *vt* arranging; organizing; decorating; building up. (b) *(Gestalt, Form)* form.

ausgestellt 1 *ptp of* **ausstellen.** 2 *adj Rock etc* flared.

ausgestorben 1 *ptp of* **aussterben.** 2 *adj Tierart* extinct; *(fig)* deserted. **der Park war wie ~** the park was deserted.

Ausgestoßene(r) *mf decl as adj* outcast.

ausgesucht 1 *ptp of* **aussuchen.**
2 *adj* (a) *(besonders groß)* extreme, exceptional.
(b) *(erlesen) Wein* choice, select; *Gesellschaft* select; *Worte* well-chosen.
(c) **die Bademoden/Geschäfte sind ziemlich ~** the choice in swimwear/choice *or* selection in the shops is pretty limited.
3 *adv (überaus, sehr)* extremely, exceptionally.

ausgetreten 1 *ptp of* **austreten.** 2 *adj Schuhe* well-worn; *Pfad auch* well-trodden; *Stufe* worn down. **~e Wege gehen** *(fig)* to tread a beaten track.

ausgewachsen 1 *ptp of* **auswachsen.** 2 *adj* fully-grown; *(inf) Blödsinn* utter, complete; *Skandal* huge.

ausgewählt 1 *ptp of* **auswählen.** 2 *adj* select; *Satz etc* well-chosen; *Werke* selected.

Ausgewanderte(r) *mf decl as adj* emigrant.

Ausgewiesene(r) *mf decl as adj* expellee.

ausgewogen *adj* balanced; *Maß* equal. **ein ~es Kräfteverhältnis** a balance of powers.

Ausgewogenheit *f* balance.

ausgezeichnet 1 *ptp of* **auszeichnen.** 2 *adj* excellent. **sie kann ~ schwimmen/tanzen** she is an excellent swimmer/dancer; **es geht mir ~** I'm feeling marvellous.

ausgiebig 1 *adj* (a) *Mahlzeit etc* substantial, large; *Mittagsschlaf* long; *Gebrauch* extensive. **~en Gebrauch von etw machen** to make full *or* good use of sth.
(b) *(dated: ergiebig)* economical.
2 *adv* **~ frühstücken** to have a substantial breakfast; **~schlafen/schwimmen** to have a good (long) sleep/swim; **~ einkaufen** to buy a lot of things; **etw ~ gebrauchen** to use sth extensively; **~ verziert** abundantly decorated.

ausgießen *vt sep irreg* (a) *(aus einem Behälter)* to pour out; *(weggießen)* to pour away; *Behälter* to empty; *(verschütten)* to spill; *(über jdn/etw gießen)* to pour *(über* +acc over). **seinen Spott/Hohn über jdn ~** *(geh)* to pour scorn on/to mock sb; **jdm sein Herz ~** *(geh)* to pour out one's heart to sb.
(b) *(füllen) Gußform* to fill; *Ritzen, Fugen* to fill in.
(c) *(rare) Feuer* to put out *or* extinguish (with water).

Ausgleich *m* **-(e)s,** *(rare)* **-e,** (a) *(Gleichgewicht)* balance; *(von Konto)* balancing; *(von Schulden)* settling; *(von Verlust, Fehler, Mangel)* compensation; *(von Abweichung, Unterschieden)* balancing out; *(von Meinungsverschiedenheiten, Konflikten)* evening out. **zum/als ~ für etw** in order to compensate for sth; **er treibt zum ~ Sport** he does sport for exercise; **Tennisspielen ist für mich ein guter ~** I like playing tennis, it gives me a change; **ein Ingenieur, der zum ~ ins Theater geht** an engineer who goes to the theatre to get a change; **wenn er ins Ausland geht, bekommt sie zum ~ ein Auto** when he goes abroad, she gets a car to even things out; **dieses Jahr fährt er zum ~ ans Meer** this year he's going to the seaside for a change; **zum ~ Ihres Kontos** to balance your account.
(b) *no pl (Ballspiele)* equalizer; *(Tennis)* deuce.

ausgleichen *sep irreg* 1 *vt Ungleichheit, Unterschiede* to even out; *Unebenheit* to level out; *Konto* to balance; *Schulden* to settle; *Verlust, Fehler* to make good; *Verlust, Mangel* to compensate for; *Meinungsverschiedenheiten, Konflikte* to reconcile. **etw durch etw ~** to compensate for sth with sth/by doing sth; **~de Gerechtigkeit** poetic justice.
2 *vi* (a) *(Sport)* to equalize. **zum 1:1 ~** to equalize the score at 1 all.
(b) *(vermitteln)* to act as a mediator. **~des Wesen** conciliatory manner.
3 *vr* to balance out; *(Einnahmen und Ausgaben)* to balance. **das gleicht sich wieder aus** it balances itself out; **das gleicht sich dadurch aus, daß ...** it's balanced out by the fact that ...

Ausgleichs-: **~getriebe** *nt (Tech)* differential gear; **~gymnastik** *f* exercises *pl*; **~tor** *nt*, **~treffer** *m* equalizer, equalizing goal; **~zahlung** *f* compensation.

ausgleiten *vi sep irreg aux sein* (a) *(ausrutschen)* to slip *(auf* +dat on). **es ist ihm ausgeglitten** it slipped from his hands *or* grasp; **die Zunge ist ihm ausgeglitten** *(geh)* his tongue ran away with him. (b) *(Boot, Skifahrer)* to coast in.

ausgliedern *vt sep* to exclude.

ausglitschen *vi sep aux sein* siehe **ausgleiten** (a).

ausglühen *sep* 1 *vt* (a) *Metall* to anneal; *(Med)* to sterilize *(by heating).* (b) *(ausdörren) Land* to scorch. 2 *vi aux sein* to burn out.

ausgraben *vt sep irreg* to dig up; *Grube, Loch* to dig out; *Altertümer auch* to excavate; *(fig)* to dig up; *(hervorholen)* to dig out; *alte Geschichten* to bring up.

Ausgrabung *f (das Ausgraben)* excavation; *(Ort)* excavation site; *(Fund)* (archaeological) find.

ausgräten *vt sep* siehe **entgräten.**

ausgreifen *vi sep irreg (Pferd)* to lengthen its stride; *(beim Gehen)* to stride out; *(fig: Redner)* to go far afield. **weit ~d** *Schritte* long, lengthy; *Bewegung* striding.

ausgründen *vt sep (Econ)* to establish.

Ausguck *m* **-(e)s, -e** lookout. **~ halten** to keep a lookout.

ausgucken *sep (inf)* 1 *vi* (a) *(Ausschau halten)* to look out *(nach* for). (b) *(auskundschaften)* to have a look. 2 *vr sich (inf)* **die Augen nach jdm ~** *(inf)* to look everywhere for sb.

Ausguß *m* (a) *(Becken)* sink; *(Abfluß)* drain; *(dial: ausgegossene Flüssigkeit)* waste (water *etc);* *(Tülle)* spout. (b) *(Tech)* tap hole.

aushaben *sep irreg (inf)* 1 *vt (fertig sein mit) Buch, Essen etc* to have finished; *(ausgezogen haben)* to have taken off. 2 *vi (Arbeit, Schule etc beendet haben)* to finish.

aushacken *vt sep* (a) *Unkraut* to hoe; *Rüben etc* to hoe out. (b) *(Vogel) Augen* to peck out; *Federn* to tear out; siehe **Krähe.**

aushakbar *adj* siehe *Kette/dieser Reißverschluß ist* ~ this chain can be unhooked/this zip opens right through.

aushaken *sep* 1 *vt Fensterladen, Kette* to unhook; *Reißverschluß* to undo. 2 *vi (inf)* **es hat bei ihm ausgehakt** *(nicht begreifen)* he gave up *(inf);* *(wild werden)* something in him snapped *(inf).* 3 *vr (Reißverschluß)* to come undone.

aushalten *sep irreg* 1 *vt* (a) *(ertragen können)* to bear, to stand, to endure; *(standhalten) Gewicht etc* to bear; *Druck* to stand, to withstand; *jds Blick* to return. **den Vergleich mit etw ~** to bear comparison with sth; **es läßt sich ~** it's bearable; **hier läßt es sich ~** this is not a bad place; **das ist nicht auszuhalten** *or* **zum A~** it's unbearable; **mit ihr/ihm ist es nicht mehr auszuhalten** she/he has become quite unbearable; **ich halte es vor Hitze/zu Hause nicht mehr aus** I can't stand the heat/being at home any longer; **er hält es in keiner Stellung lange aus** he never stays in one job for long; **wie kann man es bei der Firma bloß ~?** how can anyone stand working for that firm?; **es bis zum Ende ~** *(auf Party etc)* to stay until the end; **hältst du's noch bis zur nächsten Tankstelle aus?** *(inf)* can you hold out till the next garage?; **er hält viel/nicht viel aus** he can take a lot/can't take much; **ein Stoff, der viel ~ muß** a material which has to take a lot of wear (and tear).
(b) *Ton* to hold.
(c) *(inf: unterhalten)* to keep. **sich von jdm ~ lassen** to be kept by sb.
2 *vi* (a) *(durchhalten)* to hold out. **hältst du noch aus?** can you hold out (any longer)?
(b) *auf einem Ton* ~ to hold a note.

aushämmern *vt sep Beule* to hammer out; *Gefäß* to beat out.

aushandeln *vt sep Vertrag, Lösung* to negotiate; *bessere Bedingungen, höhere Löhne* to negotiate for; *(erfolgreich)* to negotiate.

aushändigen *vt sep* jdm etw/einen Preis ~ to hand sth over to sb/give sb a prize; **wann können Sie mir die Ware** ~? when can you deliver (the goods)?

Aushändigung *f* handing over; (*von Gütern etc*) delivery. **nach** ~ **seiner Papiere** after his papers had been handed over to him; **die** ~ **der Preise nimmt der Direktor vor** the headmaster will be giving out the prizes.

Aushang *m* -(e)s, **Aushänge** (*Bekanntmachung*) notice, announcement; (*das Aushängen*) posting. **etw durch** ~ **bekanntgeben** to post notice of sth; **etw im** ~ **lesen** to read a notice of or about sth.

Aushängekasten *m* (glass-fronted) noticeboard.

aushängen *sep* 1 *vt* (a) (*bekanntmachen*) Nachricht etc to put up; *Plakat auch* to post; (*inf: ausstellen*) to show.
  (b) (*herausheben*) Tür to unhinge; *Haken* to unhook.
2 *vi irreg* (*Anzeige, Aufgebot*) to have been put up; (*inf: Brautleute*) to have the banns up. **am schwarzen Brett** ~ to be on the noticeboard.
3 *vr* (a) (*sich lösen*) (*Fenster, Tür etc*) to come off its hinges; (*Haken*) to come off.
  (b) (*sich glätten: Falten, Locken*) to drop out. **das Kleid wird sich** ~ the creases will drop or hang out of the dress.
  (c) (*inf*) **sie hat sich (bei ihm) ausgehängt** she took her arm away from his.

Aushängeschild *nt* (*lit: Reklametafel*) sign; (*fig: Reklame*) advertisement.

ausharren *vi sep* (*geh*) to wait. **auf seinem Posten** ~ to stand by one's post.

aushauchen *vt sep* (*geh*) Luft, Atem, Rauch to exhale; (*fig*) Worte, Seufzer to breathe; (*ausströmen*) Geruch, Dünste to emit. **sein Leben** ~ to breathe one's last.

aushauen *vt sep irreg* (a) Loch, Stufen to cut out; Weg, Durchgang to hew out; Statue to carve out. (b) (*roden*) Wald, Weinberg to clear; (*einzelne Bäume fällen*) to cut down; (*Zweige entfernen*) to prune. (c) (*dial: verprügeln*) to beat up, to give a good thrashing.

aushäusig *adj* (*außer Haus*) outside the home; (*unterwegs*) away from home. **du warst doch letzte Woche wieder** ~? you were out gallivanting again last week, weren't you?; **eine** ~**e Phase** a spell of being rarely at home.

ausheben *vt sep irreg* (a) Tür etc to take off its hinges. **sich** (*dat*) **die Schulter** ~ (*dial inf*) to put out one's shoulder (*inf*).
  (b) Erde to dig out; Graben, Grab to dig; Baum to dig up.
  (c) Vogelnest to rob; Vogeleier, Vogeljunge to steal; (*fig*) Diebesnest to raid; Bande to make a raid on; (*Aus: leeren*) Briefkasten to empty.
  (d) (*old*) Truppen to levy (*old*).

Aushebung *f* (*old: von Truppen*) levying.

aushecken *vt sep* (*inf*) Plan to cook up (*inf*), to hatch. **neue Streiche** ~ to think up new tricks; **sich** (*dat*) **etw** ~ to think sth up.

ausheilen *sep* 1 *vt* Krankheit to cure; Organ, Wunde to heal. 2 *vi aux sein* (*Krankheit, Patient*) to be cured; (*Organ, Wunde*) to heal. 3 *vr* to recover.

Ausheilung *f siehe vt* curing; healing. **nach völliger** ~ **der Krankheit/Wunde** after a complete recovery from the illness/after the wound is completely healed.

aushelfen *vi sep irreg* to help out (jdm sb).

ausheulen *sep* (*inf*) 1 *vi* (*aufhören*) to stop crying; (*Sirene*) to stop sounding. 2 *vr* to have a good cry. **sich bei jdm** ~ to have a good cry on sb's shoulder.

Aushilfe *f* (a) help, aid; (*Notbehelf*) temporary or makeshift substitute. **jdn zur** ~ **haben** to have sb to help out; **Stenotypistin zur** ~ **gesucht** shorthand typist wanted for temporary work.
  (b) (*Mensch*) temporary worker; (*esp im Büro auch*) temp (*inf*). **als** ~ **arbeiten** to help out; (*im Büro auch*) to temp (*inf*).

Aushilfs-: ~**kraft** *f* temporary worker; (*esp im Büro auch*) temp (*inf*); ~**lehrer** *m* supply teacher; ~**personal** *nt* temporary staff; a~**weise** *adv* on a temporary basis; (*vorübergehend*) temporarily; **sie kocht ab und zu a~weise** she sometimes cooks to help out.

aushöhlen *vt sep* to hollow out; Ufer, Steilküste to erode; (*fig*) (*untergraben*) to undermine; (*erschöpfen*) to weaken.

Aushöhlung *f* (a) (*ausgehöhlte Stelle*) hollow. (b) *no pl siehe vt* hollowing out; erosion; undermining; weakening.

ausholen *sep* 1 *vi* (a) (*zum Schlag*) to raise one's hand/arm etc; (*zum Wurf*) to reach back; (*mit Schläger, Boxer*) to take a swing. **weit** ~ (*zum Schlag, beim Tennis*) to take a big swing; (*zum Wurf*) to reach back a long way; (*fig: Redner*) to go far afield; **bei einer Erzählung weit** ~ to go a long way back in a story; **mit dem Arm/der Hand zum Wurf/Schlag** ~ to raise one's arm/hand ready to throw/strike; **zum Gegenschlag** ~ (*lit, fig*) to prepare for a counter-attack.
  (b) (*ausgreifen*) to stride out. **er ging mit weit** ~**den Schritten** he walked with long strides.
2 *vt* (*dial inf*) jdn to quiz (*inf*) (*über* +acc about).

ausholzen *vt sep* (a) (*lichten*) to thin (out). (b) (*abholzen*) Schneise to clear.

aushorchen *vt sep* (*inf*) jdn to sound out.

aushülsen *vt sep* Erbsen to shell, to pod.

aushungern *vt sep* to starve out; *siehe* **ausgehungert**.

aushusten *sep* 1 *vt* to cough up. 2 *vi* (*zu Ende husten*) to finish coughing; (*Schleim* ~) to cough up phlegm/blood. 3 *vr* to finish coughing. **er hustete sich aus, bis** ... he coughed and coughed until ...

aus|ixen *vt sep* (*inf*) to cross or ex out.

aus|jammern *sep* 1 *vi* to stop moaning. 2 *vr* to have a good moan.

aus|jäten *vt sep* Blumenbeet to weed. **im Garten Unkraut** ~ to weed the garden.

auskämmen *vt sep* (a) (*entfernen*) Staub, Haare to comb out. (b) (*frisieren*) to comb out. (c) (*fig*) (*heraussuchen*) to weed out; (*durchsuchen*) to comb.

auskauen *vti sep* to finish chewing.

auskaufen *vt sep* (*inf*) to buy up.

auskegeln *sep* 1 *vt* (a) den Pokal ~ to bowl for the cup. (b) (*dial*) sich (*dat*) den Arm/die Schulter ~ to put out one's arm/shoulder (*inf*). 2 *vi* to finish bowling.

auskehren *sep* 1 *vt* Schmutz to sweep away; Zimmer to sweep out. 2 *vi* to do the sweeping.

auskeilen *vi sep* (a) (*ausschlagen*) to kick out. (b) (*keilförmig auslaufen*) to taper off.

auskeimen *vi sep aux sein* (*Getreide*) to germinate; (*Kartoffeln*) to sprout.

auskennen *vr sep irreg* (*an einem Ort*) to know one's way around; (*auf einem Gebiet*) to know a lot (*auf or in* +dat about). **sich in der Stadt** ~ to know one's way around the town; **sich bei Männern/Frauen** (*gut*) ~ to know (a lot) about men/women; **man kennt sich bei ihm nie aus** you never know where you are with him.

auskernen *vt sep* Obst to stone.

auskippen *vt sep* (*inf*) to empty (out); Flüssigkeit to pour out.

ausklammern *vt sep* Problem to leave aside, to ignore; (*Math*) Zahl to put outside the brackets.

ausklamüsern* *vt sep* (*inf*) to work out.

Ausklang *m* (*geh*) conclusion, end; (*esp Mus*) finale. **zum** ~ **des Abends** ... to conclude the evening ...

ausklappbar *adj* folding. **dieser Tisch/diese Fußstütze ist** ~ this table can be opened out/this footrest can be pulled out.

ausklappen *vt sep* to open out; Fußstütze etc to pull out.

ausklauben *vt sep* (*dial*) to pick out.

auskleiden *sep* 1 *vt* (a) (*geh: entkleiden*) to undress. (b) (*beziehen*) to line. 2 *vr* (*geh*) to get undressed.

Auskleidung *f* lining.

ausklingen *vi sep irreg* (a) (*Glocken*) to finish ringing. (b) *aux sein* (*Lied*) to finish; (*Abend, Feier etc*) to end (*in* +dat with). **die Verhandlungen klangen in die hoffnungsvolle Note aus, daß** ... the negotiations ended on the hopeful note that ...; **das** ~**de Jahrhundert** (*geh*) the close of the century.

ausklinken *sep* 1 *vt* to release. 2 *vir* to release (itself).

ausklopfen *vt sep* Teppich to beat; Pfeife to knock out; Kleider to beat the dust out of. **jdn** ~ (*inf*) to spank sb or give sb a spanking.

Ausklopfer *m* carpet beater.

ausklügeln *vt sep* to work out; *siehe* **ausgeklügelt**.

auskneifen *vi sep irreg aux sein* (*inf*) to run away (*dat, von* from).

ausknipsen *vt sep* (*inf*) Licht, Lampe to turn out or off, to switch out or off.

ausknobeln *vt sep* (a) (*inf*) Plan to figure (*inf*) or work out. (b) (*durch Knobeln entscheiden*) ≈ to toss for.

ausknocken [-nɔkn] *vt sep* (*Boxen, fig*) to knock out.

ausknöpfbar *adj* Futter detachable.

auskochen *vt sep* (a) (*Cook*) Knochen to boil; (*dial: Fett, Speck*) to melt. (b) Wäsche to boil; (*Med*) Instrumente to sterilize (*in boiling water*); (*fig inf: sich ausdenken*) to cook up (*inf*); *siehe* **ausgekocht**.

auskommen *vi sep irreg aux sein* (a) (*genügend haben, zurechtkommen*) to get by (*mit* on), to manage (*mit* on, with). **das Auto kommt mit sieben Litern aus** the car only needs seven litres; **ohne jdn/etw** ~ to manage or do without sth/sb.
  (b) **mit jdm** (*gut*) ~ to get on or along well with sb; **mit ihm ist nicht auszukommen** he's impossible to get on or along with.
  (c) (*dial*) (*Feuer*) to break out; (*rare: Gerücht*) to come out; (*Aus: entkommen*) to escape, to get away. **aus dem Ei** ~ (*Aus*) to hatch.

Auskommen *nt* -s, *no pl* (*Einkommen*) livelihood. **sein** ~ **haben/finden** to get by; **mit ihr ist kein** ~ she's impossible to get on with.

auskömmlich *adj* Gehalt adequate; Verhältnisse comfortable. ~ **leben** to live comfortably.

auskosten *vt sep* (a) (*genießen*) to make the most of; Leben to enjoy to the full. (b) (*geh: erleiden*) etw ~ müssen (*geh*) to have to suffer sth.

auskotzen *sep* (*sl*) 1 *vt* to throw up (*inf*); (*fig*) Wissen to spew out (*inf*). **vor dem möchte ich** ~ (*inf*) he makes me want to throw up (*inf*). 2 *vr* to throw up (*inf*); (*fig: sich aussprechen*) to have a bloody good moan (*sl*).

auskramen *vt sep* (*inf*) (a) to dig out, to unearth; (*fig*) alte Geschichten etc to bring up; Schulkenntnisse to dig up. (b) (*leeren*) to turn out.

auskratzen *sep* 1 *vt* to scrape out; (*Med*) Gebärmutter to scrape; Patientin to give a scrape. **jdm die Augen** ~ to scratch sb's eyes out. 2 *vi aux sein* (*inf*) to run away (*vor* +dat from).

Auskratzung *f* (*Med*) scrape.

auskriechen *vi sep irreg aux sein* to hatch out.

auskriegen *vt sep* (*inf*) Buch to finish; Flasche etc to empty.

Auskristallisation *f* crystallization.

auskristallisieren* *sep vtir* (*vi: aux sein*) to crystallize.

Auskuck *m* -(e)s, -e (*N Ger*) siehe **Ausguck**.

auskucken *vti sep* (*N Ger*) *siehe* **ausgucken**.

auskugeln *vr sep* sich (*dat*) den Arm/die Schulter ~ to dislocate one's arm/shoulder.

auskühlen *sep* 1 *vt* Speise to cool; Ofen etc to cool down; Körper, Menschen to chill through. 2 *vi aux sein* (*abkühlen*) to cool down; (*Körper, Menschen*) to chill through. **etw** ~ **lassen** to leave sth to cool.

Auskühlung *f* cooling; (*von Mensch*) loss of body heat.

auskundschaften *sep* 1 *vt* Weg, Lage to find out; Versteck to spy out; Geheimnis to ferret out; (*esp Mil*) to reconnoitre, to scout. **2** *vi* to find out. **jdn zum A~ vorschicken** to send sb ahead to reconnoitre.

Auskunft *f* -, **Auskünfte** (a) (*Mitteilung*) information *no pl* (*über* +*acc* about). **nähere ~** more information, further details; **jdm eine ~ erteilen** *or* **geben** to give sb some information; **wo bekomme ich ~?** where can I get some information?; **eine ~** *or* **Auskünfte einholen** *or* **einziehen** to make (some) enquiries (*über* +*acc* about).
(b) (*Schalter*) information office/desk; (*am Bahnhof auch*) enquiry office/desk; (*Telefon~*) information *no art*; (*für Telefonnummern*) directory enquiries *no art*.
(c) (*inf: Auskunftsperson*) information man/woman (*inf*).

Auskunftei *f* credit enquiry agency.

Auskunfts-: **~beamte(r)** *m* information officer; (*am Bahnhof*) information clerk; **~büro** *nt* information office; **~dienst** *m* information service; **~person** *f* informer; (*Beamter*) information clerk; **~pflicht** *f* (*Jur*) obligation to give information; **die Bank hat gegenüber dem Finanzamt ~pflicht** the bank has a duty *or* is obliged to inform the inland revenue; **die ~pflicht des Arbeitgebers gegenüber der Polizei** the employer's duty to inform the police; **a~pflichtig** *adj* (*Jur*) required to give information; **~schalter** *m* information desk; (*am Bahnhof*) enquiry desk; **~stelle** *f* information office.

auskuppeln *vi sep* to disengage the clutch.

auskurieren* *sep* (*inf*) **1** *vt* to cure; *Krankheit auch* to get rid of (*inf*). **2** *vr* to get better.

auslachen *sep* **1** *vt* **jdn** to laugh at. **laß dich nicht ~** don't make a fool of yourself. **2** *vr* to have a good laugh. **3** *vi* to stop laughing.

ausladen *sep irreg* **1** *vt* (a) *Ware, Ladung* to unload; (*Naut auch*) to discharge. (b) (*inf*) **jdn ~** to tell sb not to come, to uninvite sb (*hum*). **2** *vi* (*Äste*) to spread; (*Dach, Balkon*) to protrude, to jut out; (*Gelände*) to extend.

ausladend *adj Kinn etc* protruding; *Dach* overhanging, projecting; *Gebärden, Bewegung* sweeping.

Ausladung *f* (a) unloading; (*Naut*) discharge. (b) (*Archit*) overhang, projection; (*Reichweite*) reach. (c) (*inf*) **die ~ unserer Gäste ist jetzt unmöglich** we can't possibly tell our guests not to come now.

Auslage *f* (a) (*von Waren*) display; (*Schaufenster*) (shop) window; (*Schaukasten*) showcase. (b) (*Sport*) basic stance; (*Fechten*) on guard position. (c) *usu pl* expense. **seine ~n für Verpflegung** his outlay for food.

auslagern *vt sep* to evacuate; (*aus dem Lager bringen*) to take out of store.

Auslagerung *f* evacuation; taking out of store.

Ausland *nt* -(e)s, *no pl* foreign countries *pl*; (*fig: die Ausländer*) foreigners *pl*. **ins/im ~** abroad; **aus dem** *or* **vom ~** from abroad; **wie hat das ~ darauf reagiert?** what was the reaction abroad?; **Handel mit dem ~** foreign trade, trade with other countries; **das feindliche/nichtkapitalistische ~** enemy/non-capitalist countries.

Ausländer(in *f*) *m* -s, - foreigner; (*Admin, Jur*) alien.

ausländerfeindlich *adj* hostile to foreigners.

ausländisch *adj* (a) *attr* foreign; *Erzeugnisse, Freunde etc auch* from abroad; (*Bot*) exotic. (b) (*fig: fremdländisch*) exotic.

Auslands- in *cpds* foreign; **~anleihe** *f* foreign loan; **~aufenthalt** *m* stay abroad; **~beziehungen** *pl* foreign relations *pl*; **~brief** *m* letter going/from abroad, overseas letter (*Brit*); **~deutsche(r)** *mf* expatriate German, German national (living abroad); **~gespräch** *nt* international call; **~investition** *f* foreign investment; **~korrespondent** *m* foreign correspondent; **~reise** *f* journey *or* trip abroad; **~schule** *f* British/German *etc* school (abroad); **die ~schulen in Brüssel** the foreign schools in Brussels; **~schutzbrief** *m* international travel cover; (*Dokument*) certificate of entitlement for international travel cover; **~vertretung** *f* agency abroad; (*von Firma*) foreign branch.

auslassen *sep irreg* **1** *vt* (a) (*weglassen, aussparen, übergehen*) to leave *or* miss out; (*versäumen*) *Chance, Gelegenheit* to miss. **er läßt kein Geschäft aus** he doesn't miss a chance to make a deal.
(b) (*abreagieren*) to vent (*an* +*dat* on). **seine Gefühle ~** to vent one's feelings, to let off steam (*inf*).
(c) *Butter, Fett* to melt; *Speck auch* to render (down).
(d) *Kleider etc* to let out; *Saum* to let down.
(e) (*inf*) *Radio, Motor, Ofen etc* to leave off; *Licht auch* to leave out; (*nicht anziehen*) *Kleidung* to leave off.
(f) *Hund* to let out.
(g) (*Aus*) (*los-, freilassen*) to let go; (*in Ruhe lassen*) to leave alone.
(h) *siehe* **ausgelassen.**
2 *vr* to talk (*über* +*acc* about). **sich über jdn/etw ~** (*pej*) to go on about sb/sth (*pej*); **er hat sich nicht näher darüber ausgelassen** he didn't say any more about it.
3 *vi* (*Aus*) (a) (*loslassen*) to let go.
(b) (*versagen*) to fail.

Auslassung *f* (a) (*Weglassen*) omission. (b) **~en** *pl* (*pej*: *Äußerungen*) remarks *pl*.

Auslassungs-: **~punkte** *pl* suspension points *pl*, ellipsis *sing*; **~zeichen** *nt* apostrophe.

auslasten *vt sep* (a) *Fahrzeug* to make full use of; *Maschine auch* to use to capacity. (b) **jdn** to occupy fully; *siehe* **ausgelastet.**

auslatschen *vt sep* (*inf*) to wear out of shape. **latsch deine Schuhe nicht so aus** don't walk on your shoes like that; *siehe* **ausgelatscht.**

Auslauf *m* -(e)s, **Ausläufe** (a) *no pl* (*Bewegungsfreiheit*) exercise; (*für Kinder*) room to run about.
(b) (*Gelände*) run.

(c) (*Sport*) (*Leichtathletik*) slowing down; (*Ski: Strecke*) out-run.
(d) *no pl* (*das Auslaufen*) discharge; (*das Lecken*) leakage.
(e) (*Stelle*) outlet.

auslaufen *sep irreg* **1** *vi aux sein* (a) (*Flüssigkeit*) to run out (*aus of*); (*Behälter*) to empty; (*undicht sein*) to leak; (*Wasserbett, Blase, Auge*) to drain; (*Eiter*) to drain, to discharge.
(b) (*Naut: Schiff, Besatzung*) to sail.
(c) (*nicht fortgeführt werden: Modell, Serie*) to be discontinued; (*ausgehen: Vorräte, Lager*) to run out.
(d) (*aufhören: Straße, Vertrag etc*) to run out.
(e) (*ein bestimmtes Ende nehmen*) to turn out.
(f) (*zum Stillstand kommen*) (*Motor, Förderband*) to come to a stop; (*Sport*) (*Läufer*) to ease off, to slow down; (*Skifahrer*) to coast to a stop.
(g) (*übergehen in*) to turn (*in* +*acc* into). **die Berge laufen in die Ebene/spitz aus** the mountains run into the plain/come to a point; **in eine Bucht ~** to open out into a bay.
(h) (*Farbe, Stoff*) to run.
2 *vr* to have some exercise. **sich ~ können** (*Kinder*) to have room to run about.

Ausläufer *m* (a) (*Bot*) runner. (b) (*Met*) (*von Hoch*) ridge; (*von Tief*) trough. (c) (*Vorberge*) foothill *usu pl*. (d) (*von Stadt*) suburb. (e) (*Sw: Bote*) delivery boy/man.

auslaugen *vt sep* (*lit*) *Boden* to exhaust; (*Regen*) to wash the goodness out of; *Haut* to dry out; (*fig*) to exhaust, to wear out.

Auslaut *m* (*Ling*) final position.

auslauten *vi sep* to end (*auf* +*dat* in). **~der Konsonant** final consonant.

ausläuten *sep* **1** *vt* to ring out; *Gottesdienst* to ring out the end of; (*old*) *Nachricht* to ring out, to proclaim. **2** *vi* to finish *or* cease ringing.

ausleben *sep* **1** *vr* (*Mensch*) to live it up; (*Phantasie etc*) to run free. **2** *vt* (*geh*) to realize.

auslecken *vt sep* to lick out.

ausleeren *vt sep Flüssigkeit* to pour out, to empty; *Gefäß* to empty; (*austrinken auch*) to drain.

auslegen *sep* **1** *vt* (a) (*ausbreiten*) to lay out; *Waren etc auch* to display; *Köder* to put down; *Reusen* to drop; *Kabel, Minen* to lay; *Saatgut* to sow; *Kartoffeln* to plant.
(b) (*bedecken*) to cover; (*auskleiden*) to line; (*mit Einlegearbeit*) to inlay. **den Boden/das Zimmer (mit Teppichen) ~** to carpet the floor/room; **das Gebiet mit Minen ~** to lay mines in *or* to mine the area.
(c) (*erklären*) to explain; (*deuten*) to interpret. **etw richtig/falsch ~** to interpret sth correctly/wrongly *or* misinterpret sth; **jds Scherz/Tat übel ~** to take sb's joke/action badly.
(d) *Geld* to lend (*jdm etw* sb sth). **sie hat die 5 Mark für mich ausgelegt** she paid the 5 marks for me.
(e) (*Tech*) to be designed (*auf* +*acc, für* for). **straff ausgelegt sein** (*Federung*) to be tightly set.
2 *vi* (*dial inf: dicklich werden*) to put (it) on a bit (*inf*).
3 *vr* (*Fechten*) to adopt the on guard position.

Ausleger *m* -s, - (a) (*von Kran etc*) jib, boom. (b) (*an Ruderboot*) rowlock; (*Kufe gegen Kentern*) outrigger. (c) (*Deuter*) interpreter.

Auslegung *f* (*Deutung*) interpretation; (*Erklärung*) explanation (*zu* of). **falsche ~** misinterpretation.

Auslegungs-: **~frage** *f* question *or* matter of interpretation; **~methode** *f* method of interpretation; **~sache** *f* matter of interpretation.

ausleiden *vi sep irreg* **sie hat ausgelitten** her suffering is at an end.

ausleiern *sep* **1** *vt* (*inf*) **etw ~** *Gummiband, Gewinde, Feder* to wear sth out; *Hosen, Pullover* to make sth go baggy. **2** *vi* to wear out; (*Pullover*) to go baggy; *siehe* **ausgeleiert.**

Ausleih-: **~bibliothek**, **~bücherei** *f* lending library.

Ausleihe *f* (*das Ausleihen*) lending; (*Schalter*) issue desk. **eine ~ ist nicht möglich** it is not possible to lend out anything.

ausleihen *vt sep irreg* (*verleihen*) to lend (*jdm, an jdn* to sb); (*von jdm leihen*) to borrow. **sich** (*dat*) **etw ~** to borrow sth (*bei, von* from).

auslernen *vi sep* (*Lehrling*) to finish one's apprenticeship; (*inf: Schüler, Student etc*) to finish school/college etc. **man lernt nie aus** (*prov*) you live and learn (*prov*); *siehe* **ausgelernt.**

Auslese *f* -, **-n** (a) *no pl* (*Auswahl*) selection; (*Liter: verschiedener Autoren*) anthology. **natürliche ~** natural selection; **eine ~ treffen** *or* **vornehmen** to make a selection. (b) **die ~** the élite. (c) (*Wein*) high-quality wine made from selected grapes.

auslesen *vt sep irreg* (a) (*auswählen*) to select; (*aussondern*) *Schlechtes etc* to pick out; *Erbsen, Linsen etc* to pick over; *siehe* **ausgelesen.**
(b) (*auch vi*) (*inf*) *Buch etc* to finish reading. **hast du bald ausgelesen?** will you finish (reading) it soon?; **er legte das ausgelesene Buch beiseite** he put away the book he had finished reading; **die ausgelesenen Bücher behalte ich nicht** I don't keep the books I have read *or* finished.

Auslese-: **~prozeß** *m* selection process; **~verfahren** *nt* selection procedure.

auslichten *vt sep* to thin out.

ausliefern *vt sep* (a) *Waren* to deliver.
(b) **jdn** to hand over (*an* +*acc* to); (*an anderen Staat*) to extradite (*an* +*acc* to); (*fig: preisgeben*) to leave (jdm in the hands of). **sich der Polizei/Justiz ~** to give oneself up *or* surrender oneself to the police/to justice; **jdm/einer Sache ausgeliefert sein** to be at sb's mercy/the mercy of sth.

Auslieferung *f siehe vt* (a) delivery. (b) handing over; extradition.

Auslieferungs-: ~antrag m (Jur) application for extradition; ~lager nt (Comm) distribution centre; ~vertrag m (Jur) extradition treaty.

ausliegen vi sep irreg (Waren) to be displayed; (Zeitschriften, Liste etc) to be available (to the public); (Schlinge, Netz etc) to be down.

Auslinie f (Sport) (Ftbl) touchline; (bei Tennis, Hockey etc) sideline. die ~n (Tennis) the tramlines pl.

ausloben vt sep (form) (als Belohnung aussetzen) Geldbetrag to offer as a reward; (als Preis aussetzen) to offer as a prize.

Auslobung f siehe vt offer of a reward/prize; (Belohnung) reward.

auslöffeln vt sep Suppe etc to eat up completely; Teller to empty. etw ~ müssen (inf) to have to take the consequences (of sth); ~ müssen, was man sich eingebrockt hat (inf) to have to take the consequences.

auslöschen vt sep (a) Feuer to put out, to extinguish; Kerze auch to snuff out; (geh) Licht to extinguish.
(b) (auswischen) Spuren to obliterate; (mit Schwamm etc) to wipe out; Schrift to erase (an +dat from); Erinnerung, Schmach to blot out. ein Menschenleben ~ (geh) to destroy or blot out a human life.

auslosen vt sep to draw lots for; Preis, Gewinner to draw. es wurde ausgelost, wer beginnt lots were drawn to see who would start.

auslösen vt sep (a) Mechanismus, Alarm, Reaktion to set or trigger off, to trigger; Kameraverschluß, Bombe to release; (fig) Wirkung to produce; Begeisterung, Mitgefühl, Überraschung to arouse; Aufstand, Beifall to trigger off.
(b) (dated: einlösen) Gefangene to release; (durch Geld) to ransom; Wechsel, Pfand to redeem.
(c) (dial) Knochen etc to take out.

Auslöser m -s, - (a) trigger; (für Bombe) release button; (Phot) shutter release. der ~ für etw sein to trigger sth off. (c) (Psych) trigger mechanism.

Auslosung f draw.

Auslösung f (a) siehe vt (a) setting or triggering off, triggering; release, releasing; producing; arousing; triggering off. (b) (von Gefangenen) release; (von Wechsel, Pfand) redemption; (Lösegeld) ransom. (c) (dial) taking out. (d) (Entschädigung) travel allowance.

ausloten vt sep (Naut) Fahrrinne to sound the depth of; Tiefe to sound; (Tech) Mauer to plumb; (fig geh) to plumb; jds Wesen, Charakter to plumb the depths of. die Sache muß ich doch mal ~ (fig inf) I'll have to try to get to the bottom of the matter or to fathom it out.

auslüften sep 1 vti to air. lüfte dein Gehirn ein bißchen aus (inf) get your thoughts or ideas straightened out. 2 vr (inf) to get some fresh air.

auslutschen vt sep (inf) Orange, Zitrone etc to suck; Saft to suck out.

ausmachen sep 1 vt (a) Feuer, Kerze, Zigarette to put out; elektrisches Licht auch, Radio, Gas to turn off.
(b) (ermitteln, sichten) to make out; (ausfindig machen) to locate; (feststellen) to determine. es läßt sich nicht mehr ~, warum ... it can no longer be determined why ...
(c) (vereinbaren) to agree; Streitigkeiten to settle. einen Termin ~ to agree (on) a time; wir müssen nur noch ~, wann wir uns treffen we only have to arrange when we should meet; etw mit sich selbst ~ (müssen) to (have to) sort sth out for oneself; siehe ausgemacht.
(d) (bewirken, darstellen) (to go) to make up. alles, was das Leben ausmacht everything that is a part of life; all der Luxus, der ein angenehmes Leben ausmacht all the luxuries which go to make up a pleasant life; ihm fehlt alles, was einen Musiker ausmacht he has none of the qualities which go to make up a musician; die Farben machen den Reiz an diesem Bild aus the colours make this picture attractive.
(e) (betragen) Summe to come to; Unterschied auch to make; (zeitlich) to make up.
(f) (bedeuten) viel/wenig or nicht viel ~ to make a big/not much difference; das macht nichts aus that doesn't matter; (ist egal auch) that doesn't make any difference.
(g) (stören) to matter (jdm to). macht es Ihnen etwas aus, wenn ...? would you mind if ...?; es macht mir nichts aus, den Platz zu wechseln I don't mind changing places.
(h) (dial) Kartoffeln, Rüben to dig up.
2 vr (sl) to do one's business (inf).

ausmahlen vt sep to grind (down).

ausmalen vr sep sich (dat) etw/sein Leben ~ to imagine sth/picture one's life.

ausmanövrieren* vt sep to outmanoeuvre.

ausmären vr sep (dial inf) (langsam arbeiten) to dawdle (inf); (viel erzählen) to rattle on (über +acc about) (inf). mär dich endlich aus! stop dawdling!

Ausmarsch m departure.

ausmarschieren* vi sep aux sein to march out.

Ausmaß nt (Größe: von Gegenstand, Fläche) size; (Umfang: von Katastrophe) extent; (Grad) degree, extent; (meiner Liebe etc) extent; (Größenordnung: von Änderungen, Verlust etc) scale. ~e pl proportions pl; ein Verlust in diesem ~ a loss on this scale; das Feuer war nur von geringem ~ the fire was only on a small scale.

ausmergeln vt sep Gesicht, Körper etc to emaciate; jdn auch to make waste away; Boden to exhaust; siehe ausgemergelt.

ausmerzen vt sep (ausrotten) Ungeziefer, Unkraut to eradicate; (aussondern) schwache Tiere to cull; (fig) schwache Teilnehmer to sort or weed out; Fehler, Mißstände to eradicate; Erinnerungen to obliterate.

ausmessen vt sep irreg Raum, Fläche etc to measure (out). das

Zimmer ~ (fig) to pace up and down the room.

Ausmessung f (a) siehe vt measuring (out). (b) (Maße) dimensions pl.

ausmisten sep 1 vt Stall to muck out; (fig inf) Schrank etc to tidy out; Zimmer to clean out. 2 vi (lit) to muck out; (fig) to have a clean-out.

ausmöblieren* vt sep to furnish.

ausmontieren* vt sep to take out.

ausmünden vi sep aux sein or haben (in +acc into) to open out; (Fluß) to flow; (Straße) to come out, to run; (fig) to turn.

ausmustern vt sep Maschine, Fahrzeug etc to take out of service; (Mil: entlassen) to invalid out.

Ausnahme f -, -n exception. mit ~ von ihm or seiner (geh) with the exception of him, except (for) him; ohne ~ without exception; ~n bestätigen die Regel (prov), keine Regel ohne ~ (prov) the exception proves the rule (prov).

Ausnahme-: ~bestimmung f special regulation; ~erscheinung f exception; ~fall m exception, exceptional case; ~preis m special price; ~situation f special or exceptional situation; ~stellung f special position; ~zustand m (Pol) state of emergency; den ~zustand verhängen to declare a state of emergency.

ausnahmslos 1 adv without exception. 2 adj Bewilligung, Zustimmung unanimous. das ~e Erscheinen der ganzen Belegschaft the appearance of all the staff without exception.

ausnahmsweise adv darf ich das machen? — ~ may I do that? — just this once; wenn er ~ auch mal einen Fehler macht when he makes a mistake too just for once; sie hat es mir ~ einmal erlaubt she let me do it once as a special exception; er darf heute ~ früher von der Arbeit weggehen as an exception he may leave work earlier today.

ausnehmen sep irreg 1 vt (a) Eier to remove; (fig) Verbrecherbande, Diebesnest etc to raid; (Mil) Stellung to take out. das Nest ~ to remove the eggs from the nest.
(b) Fisch, Kaninchen to gut, to dress; Geflügel to draw; Hammel, Rind etc to dress; Eingeweide, Herz etc to take out, to remove.
(c) (ausschließen) jdn to make an exception of; (befreien) to exempt. ich nehme keinen aus I'll make no exceptions; siehe ausgenommen.
(d) (inf) jdn to fleece; (beim Kartenspiel) to clean out.
(e) (inf: ausfragen) to pump (inf).
(f) (Aus: erkennen) to make out.
2 vr (geh: wirken) sich schön or gut/schlecht ~ to look good/bad.

ausnehmend adj (geh) exceptional. das gefällt mir ~ gut I like that very much indeed.

ausnüchtern vtir sep to sober up.

Ausnüchterung f sobering up.

Ausnüchterungszelle f drying-out cell.

ausnutzen, ausnützen (esp S Ger, Aus) vt sep to use, to make use of; (ausbeuten) to exploit; Gelegenheit to make the most of; jds Gutmütigkeit, Leichtgläubigkeit etc to take advantage of.

Ausnutzung, Ausnützung (esp S Ger, Aus) f use; (Ausbeutung) exploitation.

auspacken sep 1 vti Koffer to unpack; Geschenk to unwrap. 2 vi (inf: alles sagen) to talk (inf); (seine Meinung sagen) to speak one's mind.

auspeitschen vt sep to whip.

auspellen sep (inf) 1 vt to peel; Nuß, Erbsen to shell. 2 vr to strip off.

auspennen vir sep (inf) to have a (good) kip (inf).

auspfeifen vt sep irreg to boo or hiss at; Stück, Schauspieler to boo off the stage.

auspflanzen vt sep (Hort) to plant out.

Auspizium nt, usu pl (geh) auspice.

ausplappern vt sep (inf) to blurt out (inf).

ausplaudern sep 1 vt to let out. 2 vr (dial) to have a good chat.

ausplündern vt sep Dorf etc to plunder, to pillage; Kasse, Laden, (hum) Speisekammer etc to raid; jdn to plunder (inf), to clean out (inf).

auspolstern vt sep Mantel etc to pad (out); Kiste etc to line, to pad. sie ist gut ausgepolstert (fig hum) she's well-padded (hum).

ausposaunen* vt sep (inf) to broadcast (inf).

auspowern [-po:vɐn] vt sep to impoverish; (ausbeuten) Massen, Boden to exploit.

Auspowerung f siehe vt impoverishment; exploitation.

ausprägen sep 1 vt Münzen etc to mint. Metall zu Münzen ~ to stamp coins out of metal. 2 vr (Begabung, Charaktereigenschaft etc) to reveal or show itself. die Erziehung prägt sich im Charakter/Verhalten aus one's upbringing shapes or stamps one's character/behaviour or leaves its stamp on one's character/behaviour; siehe ausgeprägt.

Ausprägung f (a) no pl (von Charakter) shaping, moulding. (b) no pl (das Ausgeprägtsein) markedness. in einer derart starken ~ ist mir diese Krankheit noch nicht untergekommen I have never come across this illness to such a marked degree. (c) (Ausdruck) expression.

auspreisen vt sep Waren to price.

auspressen vt sep (a) (herauspressen) Saft, Schwamm etc to squeeze out; Zitrone etc to squeeze. (b) (fig: ausbeuten) to squeeze dry, to bleed white. (c) (fig: ausfragen) to press. jdn wie eine Zitrone ~ to squeeze sb like a lemon (for information).

ausprobieren* vt sep to try out; Auto auch to test-drive.

Auspuff m -(e)s, -e exhaust.

Auspuff-: ~gase pl exhaust fumes pl; ~rohr nt exhaust pipe; ~topf m silencer (Brit), muffler (US).

auspumpen vt sep (a) to pump out. (b) (inf: erschöpfen) to drain; siehe ausgepumpt.

auspunkten vt sep (Boxen) to outpoint, to beat on points.
auspusten vt sep (inf) to blow out. **die Luft kräftig** ~ to blow out hard; **jdm das Lebenslicht** ~ to snuff out sb's life.
ausputzen sep **1** vt (a) (esp S Ger, Aus: reinigen) to clean out; Kleider to clean; Flecken to get out. (b) (Ftbl) Ball to clear. (c) (dial: ausnutzen) to use. **2** vi (Ftbl) to clear (the ball); (Ausputzer sein) to act as or be the sweeper.
Ausputzer m -s, - (Ftbl) sweeper.
ausquartieren* vt sep to move out; (Mil) to billet out.
Ausquartierung f moving out; (Mil) billeting out.
ausquatschen sep (sl) **1** vt to blurt out (inf). **2** vr to have a heart-to-heart (bei jdm with sb), to get a load off one's chest. **3** vi to finish.
ausquetschen vt sep Saft etc to squeeze out; Zitrone etc to squeeze; (inf: ausfragen) (Polizei etc) to grill (inf); (aus Neugier) to pump (inf).
ausradieren* vt sep to rub out, to erase; (fig: vernichten) to wipe out. **etw aus dem Gedächtnis** ~ to erase sth from one's mind or memory.
ausrangieren* vt sep Kleider to throw out; Maschine, Auto to scrap. **ein altes ausrangiertes Auto** an old disused car.
ausrasieren* vt sep to shave; Koteletten to trim. **jdm/sich die Haare im Nacken** ~ to shave sb's/one's neck.
ausrasten sep **1** vi aux sein (a) (Tech) to come out. (b) (hum inf: zornig werden) to blow one's top (inf), to do one's nut (inf). **2** vr (Aus, S Ger: ausruhen) to have a rest. **3** vi impers (inf) **es rastet bei jdm aus** something snaps in sb (inf).
ausrauben vt sep to rob.
ausräubern vt sep (auch hum) to plunder, to raid. **jdn** ~ to clean sb out (inf).
ausrauchen sep **1** vt Zigarette etc to finish (smoking). **2** vi (a) (zu Ende rauchen) to finish smoking. (b) aux sein (Aus) (verdunsten) to evaporate; (Geschmack verlieren) to lose its taste.
ausräuchern vt sep Zimmer to fumigate; Tiere, (fig) Schlupfwinkel, Bande to smoke out.
ausraufen vt sep to tear or pull out. **ich könnte mir die Haare** ~ I could kick myself.
ausräumen vt sep to clear out; Möbel auch to move out; Magen, Darm to purge; (fig) Mißverständnisse, Konflikt to clear up; Vorurteile, Bedenken to dispel; (inf: ausrauben) to clean out (inf).
ausrechnen vt sep to work out; (ermitteln) Gewicht, Länge etc to calculate. **sich** (dat) **etw** ~ **können** (fig) to be able to work sth out (for oneself); **sich** (dat) **große Chancen/einen Vorteil** ~ to reckon or fancy that one has a good chance/an advantage; siehe **ausgerechnet.**
Ausrechnung f siehe vt working out; calculation.
ausrecken sep **1** vt to stretch (out). **sich** (dat) **den Hals** ~ to crane one's neck. **2** vr to stretch out. **ich muß mich ein wenig** ~ I need to have a stretch.
Ausrede f excuse.
ausreden sep **1** vi to finish speaking. **er hat mich gar nicht erst** ~ **lassen** he didn't even let me finish (speaking).
  2 vt **jdm etw** ~ to talk sb out of sth.
  3 vr (esp Aus) (sich aussprechen) to have a heart-to-heart; (Ausflüchte machen) to make excuses. **er versucht sich immer auf irgendwas auszureden** he is always trying to make some excuse; **er hat sich darauf ausgeredet, daß ...** he excused himself by saying that ...
ausregnen vir impers sep to stop raining.
ausreiben vt sep irreg Fleck to rub out; Topf etc to scour; Gläser to wipe out. **sich** (dat) **die Augen** ~ to rub one's eyes.
ausreichen vi sep to be sufficient or enough. **die Zeit reicht nicht aus** there is not sufficient time; **mit etw** ~ (inf) to manage on sth.
ausreichend 1 adj sufficient, enough; (Sch) satisfactory. **2** adv sufficiently.
ausreifen vi sep aux sein to ripen; (fig auch) to mature.
Ausreise f **bei der** ~ on leaving the country; (Grenzübertritt) on crossing the border; **jdm die** ~ **verweigern** to prohibit sb from leaving the country.
Ausreise-: ~erlaubnis, ~genehmigung f exit permit.
ausreisen vi sep aux sein to leave (the country). **ins Ausland/nach Frankreich** ~ to go abroad/to France.
Ausreise-: ~sperre f ban on leaving the country; ~visum nt exit visa.
ausreißen sep irreg **1** vt Haare, Blatt to tear out; Unkraut, Blumen, Zahn to pull out. **einem Käfer die Flügel/Beine** ~ to pull a beetle's wings/legs off; **er hat sich** (dat) **kein Bein ausgerissen** (inf) he didn't exactly overstrain himself or bust a gut (sl); **ich könnte Bäume** ~ (inf) I feel full of beans; siehe **Fliege.**
  2 vi aux sein (a) (sich lösen) (Ärmel etc) to come away; (Knopf, Griff) to come off; (einreißen) (Naht) to come out; (Knopfloch) to tear.
    (b) (+dat from) (inf: davonlaufen) to run away; (Sport) to break away.
Ausreißer(in f) m -s, - (inf) runaway; (Mil) stray bullet; (Sport) runner/cyclist who breaks away.
ausreiten sep irreg **1** vi aux sein to ride out, to go riding or for a ride. **2** vt Pferd to take out, to exercise. **ein Pferd voll** ~ to ride a horse to its limit.
ausreizen vt sep Karten to bid up to strength; Kontrahenten to outbid.
ausrenken vt sep to dislocate. **sich/jdm den Arm** ~ to dislocate one's/sb's arm; **sich (fast) den Hals** ~ (inf) to crane one's neck.
ausrichten sep **1** vt (a) (aufstellen) to line up, to get or bring into line; Arbeitsstück etc auch, Gewehre to align. **jdn/etw auf etw** (acc) ~ (einstellen) to orientate sb/sth to sth, to align sb/sth

with sth; (abstellen) to gear sb/sth to sth.
  (b) (veranstalten) to organize; Hochzeit, Fest to arrange.
  (c) (erreichen) to achieve. **ich konnte bei ihr nichts** ~ I couldn't get anywhere with her.
  (d) (übermitteln) to tell; Nachricht to pass on. **jdm** ~, **daß ...** to tell sb (that) ...; **jdm etwas** ~ to give sb a message; **kann ich etwas** ~? can I give him/her etc a message?; **bitte richten Sie ihm einen Gruß aus** please give him my regards.
  (e) (Aus: schlechtmachen) to run down.
  2 vr to line up in a straight row; (Mil) to dress ranks. **sich nach dem Nebenmann/Vordermann/Hintermann** ~ to line up (exactly) with the person next to/in front of/behind one; **ausgerichtet in einer Reihe stehen** to stand next to one another in a straight line; **sich an etw** (dat) ~ (fig) to orientate oneself to sth.
Ausrichtung f siehe vt (a) lining up; alignment. (b) organization; arrangement. (c) (fig) (auf Ideologie etc) orientation (auf +acc towards), alignment (auf +acc with); (auf Bedürfnisse etc) gearing (auf +acc to); (an einer Ideologie) orientation (an +dat to).
ausringen vt sep irreg (dial) siehe **auswringen.**
ausrinnen vi sep irreg aux sein (S Ger, Aus) to run out.
Ausritt m ride (out); (das Ausreiten) riding out.
ausroden vt sep Baum to uproot; Wald to clear.
ausrollen sep **1** vt Teig, Teppich to roll out; Kabel auch to run or pay out. **2** vi aux sein (Flugzeug) to taxi to a standstill or stop; (Fahrzeug) to coast to a stop.
ausrotten vt sep to wipe out; Wanzen etc to destroy; Tiere, Volk auch to exterminate; Religion, Ideen auch to stamp out, to eradicate.
Ausrottung f siehe vt wiping out; destruction; extermination; stamping out, eradication.
ausrücken sep **1** vi aux sein (a) (Mil) to move or set out; (Polizei, Feuerwehr) to turn out.
  (b) (inf: ausreißen) to make off; (von zu Hause) to run away; (aus Gefängnis) to run away, to get out.
  2 vt (a) (Tech) to disengage, to release.
  (b) (Typ) Zeilen etc to reverse-indent (spec), to move out.
Ausruf m (a) (Ruf) cry, shout. (b) (Bekanntmachung) proclamation. **etw durch** ~ **bekanntmachen** to proclaim sth.
ausrufen vt sep irreg to exclaim; Schlagzeilen to cry out; Waren to cry; (auf Auktion) to start; (verkünden) to call out; Haltestellen, Streik to call. **die Stunden** ~ (Hist) to call the hours; **jdn zum** or **als König** ~ to proclaim sb king; **jdn** or **jds Namen** ~ (lassen) (über Lautsprecher etc) to put out a call for sb; (im Hotel) to page sb.
Ausrufer m -s, - (Hist) (town) crier; (von Waren) crier.
Ausrufe-: ~satz m exclamation; ~wort nt exclamation, interjection; ~zeichen nt exclamation mark.
Ausrufung f proclamation. **die** ~ **eines Streiks** a strike call.
Ausrufungszeichen nt siehe **Ausrufezeichen.**
ausruhen vtir sep to rest; (Mensch auch) to take or have a rest. **meine Augen müssen (sich) ein wenig** ~ I shall have to rest my eyes a little; **seine Augen** ~ (lassen) to rest one's eyes; siehe **ausgeruht, Lorbeer.**
ausrupfen vt sep to pull out; Federn auch to pluck out.
ausrüsten vt sep (lit, fig) to equip; Fahrzeug, Schiff to fit out; Tuch to treat. **ein Fahrzeug mit etw** ~ to fit a car with sth.
Ausrüstung f (a) no pl (das Ausrüsten vt) equipping; fitting-out; treating.
  (b) (~sgegenstände) equipment; (esp Kleidung) outfit.
Ausrüstungs-: ~gegenstand m, ~stück nt piece of equipment.
ausrutschen vi sep aux sein to slip; (Fahrzeug) to skid; (fig inf) (sich schlecht benehmen) to drop a clanger (inf); (straffällig werden) to get into trouble. **das Messer/die Hand ist mir ausgerutscht** my knife/my hand slipped.
Ausrutscher m -s, - (inf) (lit, fig) slip; (schlechte Leistung auch) slip-up.
Aussaat f (a) no pl (das Säen) sowing. (b) (Saat) seed.
aussäen vt sep (lit, fig) to sow.
Aussage f -, -n statement; (Behauptung) opinion; (Bericht) report; (Jur) (eines Beschuldigten, Angeklagten) statement; (Zeugen~) evidence no pl, testimony; (fig: von Roman etc) message. **eine eidliche/schriftliche** ~ a sworn/written statement; **hier steht** ~ **gegen** ~ it's one person's word against another's; **der Angeklagte/Zeuge verweigerte die** ~ the accused refused to make a statement/the witness refused to give evidence or testify; **eine** ~ **machen** to make a statement; to give evidence; **nach** ~ **seines Chefs** according to his boss.
Aussage-: ~kraft f meaningfulness; a~kräftig adj meaningful.
aussagen sep **1** vt to say (über +acc about); (behaupten) to state; (unter Eid) to testify. **was will der Roman** ~? what message does this novel try to convey?; **etw über jdn** ~ (Jur) to give sth in evidence about sb.
  2 vi (Jur) (Zeuge) to give evidence; (Angeklagter, schriftlich) to make a statement; (unter Eid auch) to testify. **eidlich** or **unter Eid** ~ to give evidence under oath; **für/gegen jdn** ~ to give evidence or to testify for/against sb; **schriftlich** ~ to make a written statement.
aussägen vt sep to saw out.
aussagend adj (Gram) predicative.
Aussage-: ~satz m statement; a~stark adj powerful; ~verweigerung f (Jur) refusal to give evidence or to testify; **ein Recht auf** ~verweigerung haben to have a right to refuse to give evidence or to testify; ~weise f (Gram) mood.
Aussatz m -es, no pl (Med) leprosy; (fig) pestilence.
aussätzig adj (Med) leprous.
Aussätzige(r) mf decl as adj (lit, fig) leper.
aussaufen sep irreg **1** vt (Tier) Wasser to drink up; Napf to

empty; (sl: Mensch) Flüssigkeit to swill down (inf); Glas etc to empty. **wer hat mein Glas/meinen Whisky ausgesoffen?** who's drunk my drink/whisky? **2** vi (sl) **sauf endlich aus!** come on, get that down you!

aussaugen vt sep Saft etc to suck out; Frucht to suck (dry); Wunde to suck the poison out of; (leersaugen) Glasglocke etc to evacuate; (fig: ausbeuten) to drain dry. **jdn bis aufs Blut or Mark ~** to bleed sb white.

ausschaben vt sep to scrape out; (Med auch) to curette.

Ausschabung f (Med) curettage, scrape.

ausschachten vt sep to dig, to excavate; Erde to dig up; Brunnen to sink.

Ausschachtung f **(a)** no pl siehe vt digging, excavation; digging up; sinking. **(b)** (Grube etc) excavation.

Ausschachtungs|arbeiten pl excavation work.

ausschalen vt sep (Build) siehe **verschalen.**

ausschälen vt sep to remove, to cut out; Nüsse, Hülsenfrüchte to shell.

ausschalten vt sep **(a)** (abstellen) to switch off, to turn off. **sich (automatisch) ~** to switch or turn (itself) off (automatically). **(b)** (fig) to eliminate.

Ausschaltung f siehe vt **(a)** switching off, turning off. **(b)** elimination.

Ausschank m -(e)s, **Ausschänke,** f -, **Ausschänke** (Aus) **(a)** (Schankraum) bar, pub (Brit); (Schanktisch) bar, counter. **(b)** (no pl: Getränkeausgabe) serving of drinks. „~ von 9⁰⁰ bis 14⁰⁰" "open from 9.00 to 14.00"; **~ über die Straße** off-sales pl; „kein ~ an Jugendliche unter 16 Jahren" "drinks not sold to persons under the age of 16".

Ausschank|erlaubnis f licence (Brit), license (US).

Ausschau f, no pl: **~ halten** (nach for) to look out, to be on the or keep a look-out.

ausschauen vi sep **(a)** (geh) (nach for) to look out, to be on the or keep a look-out. **(b)** (dial) siehe **aussehen. wie schaut's aus?** (inf) how's things? (inf).

ausschaufeln vt sep Grube, Grab to dig; Erde to dig out; Leiche to dig up.

Ausscheid m -(e)s, -e (DDR) siehe **Ausscheidungskampf.**

ausscheiden sep irreg **1** vt (aussondern) to take out; esp Menschen to remove; (Physiol) to excrete. **2** vi aux sein **(a)** (aus einem Amt) to retire (aus from); (aus Club, Firma) to leave (aus etw sth); (Sport) to be eliminated; (in Wettkampf) to drop out. **wer unfair kämpft, muß ~** whoever cheats will be disqualified. **(b)** (nicht in Betracht kommen: Plan, Möglichkeit etc) to be ruled out. **das/er scheidet aus** that/he has to be ruled out.

Ausscheidung f **(a)** no pl (das Aussondern) removal; (Physiol) excretion. **(b)** (Med) **~en** pl excretions pl. **(c)** (Sport) elimination; (Vorkampf) qualifying contest.

Ausscheidungs- in cpds (Physiol) excretory; (Sport) qualifying; **~kampf** m (Sport) qualifying contest; (Leichtathletik, Schwimmen) heat; **~organ** nt excretory organ; **~produkt** nt excretory product; **~spiel** nt qualifying match or game.

ausscheißen sep irreg (vulg) **1** vt to shit out (vulg). **wie ausgeschissen aussehen** to look like something the cat brought in (inf), to look shitty (inf). **2** vi (a) to finish shitting (vulg). **(b)** siehe **verscheißen. 3** vr to have a good shit (vulg).

ausschelten vt sep irreg (geh) to scold.

ausschenken vti sep to pour (out); (am Ausschank) to serve.

ausscheren vi sep aux sein (aus Kolonne) (Soldat) to break rank; (Fahrzeug, Schiff) to leave the line or convoy; (Flugzeug) to break formation, to peel off; (zum Überholen) to pull out; (ausschwenken, von gerader Linie abweichen) to swing out; (fig) to step out of line. **aus der Parteilinie ~** to deviate from the party line.

ausschicken vt sep to send out.

ausschießen sep irreg **1** vt **(a)** to shoot out. **jdm ein Auge ~** to shoot out sb's eye. **(b)** (in Wettbewerb) to shoot for. **(c)** (old: aussondern) to reject, to throw out. **(d)** (Typ) to impose. **2** vi aux sein **(a)** (Pflanzen) to shoot up. **(b)** (S Ger, Aus: verbleichen) to fade.

ausschiffen sep **1** vt to disembark; Ladung, Waren to unload, to discharge. **2** vr to disembark.

Ausschiffung f siehe vb disembarkation; unloading, discharging.

ausschildern vt sep to signpost.

ausschimpfen vt sep to tell off.

ausschirren vt sep Pferd to unharness; Ochsen to unyoke.

ausschl. abbr of **ausschließlich** excl.

ausschlachten vt sep **(a)** to gut, to dress. **(b)** (fig) Fahrzeuge, Maschinen etc to cannibalize. **(c)** (fig inf: ausnutzen) Skandal, Ereignis to exploit; Buch, Werk etc to get everything out of.

ausschlafen sep irreg **1** vt Rausch etc to sleep off. **2** vir to have a good sleep.

Ausschlag m **(a)** (Med) rash. **(einen) ~ bekommen** to come out in a rash. **(b)** (von Zeiger etc) swing; (von Kompaßnadel) deflection. **(c)** (fig) decisive factor. **den ~ geben** (fig) to be the decisive factor; **die Stimme des Vorsitzenden gibt den ~** the chairman has the casting vote.

ausschlagen sep irreg **1** vt **(a)** (herausschlagen) to knock out; (dial: ausschütteln) Staubtuch etc to shake out. **jdm die Zähne ~** to knock sb's teeth out. **(b)** Feuer to beat out. **(c)** (breit schlagen) Metall to beat out. **(d)** (auskleiden) to line. **(e)** (ablehnen) to turn down; Erbschaft to waive. **jdm etw ~ to refuse sb sth. 2** vi **(a)** aux sein or haben (Baum, Strauch) to come out, to start to bud, to burgeon (out) (liter).

(b) (los-, zuschlagen) to hit or lash out; (mit Füßen) to kick (out); (Pferd) to kick. **(c)** aux sein or haben (Zeiger etc) to swing; (Kompaßnadel) to be deflected; (Wünschelrute etc) to dip. **(d)** ausgeschlagen haben (Turmuhr) to have finished striking; (liter: Herz) to have beat its last (liter). **(e)** aux sein günstig/nachteilig ~ to turn out well or favourably/badly; **zum Guten ~** to turn out all right. **(f)** aux haben (rare: Wand) to sweat.

ausschlaggebend adj decisive; Stimme auch deciding. **~ sein** to be the decisive factor; **das ist von ~er Bedeutung** that is of prime importance.

ausschlecken vt sep (S Ger) siehe **auslecken.**

ausschleifen vt sep irreg (Tech) to grind out.

ausschließen vt sep irreg **(a)** (aussperren) to lock out. **(b)** (ausnehmen) to exclude; (aus Gemeinschaft) to expel; (vorübergehend) to suspend; (Sport) to disqualify; (Typ) to justify; Panne, Fehler, Möglichkeit etc to rule out. **das eine schließt das andere nicht aus** the one does not exclude the other; **ich will nicht ~, daß er ein Dieb ist, aber ...** I don't want to rule out the possibility that he's a thief but ...; **die Öffentlichkeit ~** (Jur) to exclude the public; siehe **ausgeschlossen.**

ausschließlich 1 adj attr exclusive; Rechte auch sole. **2** adv exclusively. **3** prep +gen exclusive of, excluding.

Ausschließlichkeit f exclusiveness.

Ausschließlichkeits|anspruch m claim to sole rights.

Ausschließung f siehe **Ausschluß.**

Ausschlupf m way (to slip) out.

ausschlüpfen vi sep aux sein to slip out; (aus Ei, Puppe) to hatch out.

Ausschluß m siehe **ausschließen (b)** exclusion; expulsion; suspension; disqualification; (Typ) spacing material. **mit ~ von** (dated) with the exception of; **unter ~ der Öffentlichkeit stattfinden** to be closed to the public; siehe **Rechtsweg.**

ausschmücken vt sep to decorate; (fig) Erzählung to embroider, to embellish. **~de Details** embellishments.

Ausschmückung f siehe vt decorating, decoration; embroidery, embellishment.

ausschnauben vr sep to blow one's nose.

Ausschneidebogen m cut-out sheet.

ausschneiden vt sep irreg **(a)** (herausschneiden) to cut out; Zweige etc to cut away; siehe **ausgeschnitten. (b)** Baum etc to prune.

Ausschnitt m **(a)** (Zeitungs~) cutting, clipping. **ein runder ~ in der Tür** a round piece cut out of the door. **(b)** (Math) sector. **(c)** (Kleid~) neck. **ein tiefer ~** a low neckline; **er versuchte, ihr in den ~ zu schauen** he was trying to look down her dress. **(d)** (fig: Teil) part; (aus einem Bild) detail; (aus einem Roman) excerpt, extract; (aus einem Film) clip. **ich kenne das Buch/den Film nur in ~en** I only know parts of the book/film.

ausschnittweise adj partial; Veröffentlichung in extracts. **bei ~m Lesen** by reading sections.

ausschnitzen vt sep to carve out.

ausschnüffeln vt sep (inf) to ferret or nose out (inf).

ausschöpfen vt sep **(a)** (herausschöpfen) Wasser etc to ladle out (aus of); (aus Boot) to bale out (aus of). **(b)** (leeren) to empty; Faß etc auch to drain; Boot to bale out; (fig) to exhaust. **die Kompetenzen voll ~** to do everything within one's power.

ausschreiben vt sep irreg **(a)** to write out; (ungekürzt schreiben) to write (out) in full; siehe **ausgeschrieben. (b)** (ausstellen) Rechnung etc to make out; Formular to fill in (Brit) or out. **(c)** (bekanntmachen) to announce; Versammlung, Wahlen to call; Projekt to invite tenders for; Stellen to advertise; Steuern to impose.

Ausschreibung f siehe vt **(a)** no pl (rare: ungekürzte Schreibung) writing out. **(b)** making out; filling in (Brit) or out. **(c)** announcement; calling; invitation of tenders (gen for); advertising; imposition.

ausschreien sep irreg **1** vt **(a)** siehe **ausrufen. (b)** (ausbuhen) to shout down. **2** vr **(a)** (inf: zu Ende schreien) to finish shouting. **(b)** sich (dat) **die Kehle/Lunge ~** (inf) to shout one's head off (inf). **3** vi to finish shouting.

ausschreiten sep irreg **1** vi aux sein (geh) to stride out, to step out. **2** vt to pace.

Ausschreitung f usu pl (Aufruhr) riot, rioting no pl; (dated: Ausschweifung) excess.

ausschulen sep **1** vt (form) jdn **~** to pass or send sb out; **ausgeschult werden** to leave school. **2** vi aux sein (Aus) to leave school.

Ausschuß m **(a)** no pl (Comm) rejects pl; (fig inf) trash. **(b)** (Komitee) committee. **(c)** (eines Geschosses) exit point; (Wunde) exit wound.

Ausschuß-: **~mitglied** nt committee member; **~öffnung** f point of exit, exit point/wound; **~sitzung** f committee meeting; **~ware** f (Comm) rejects pl.

ausschütteln vt sep to shake out.

ausschütten sep **1** vt **(a)** (auskippen) to tip out; Eimer, Glas, Füllhorn to empty. **jdm sein Herz ~** (fig) to pour out one's heart to sb; siehe **Kind. (b)** (verschütten) to spill. **Geschenke über jdn ~** (geh) to shower sb with presents. **(c)** (Fin) Dividende etc to distribute. **2** vr sich **(vor Lachen) ~** (inf) to split one's sides laughing.

Ausschüttung f **(a)** (Fin) distribution; (Dividende) dividend. **(b)** (Phys) fall-out.

ausschwärmen vi sep aux sein (Bienen, Menschen) to swarm out; (Mil) to fan out.

ausschwefeln vt sep to sulphur, to fumigate (with sulphur); Ungeziefer to smoke out (with sulphur).

ausschweifen sep 1 vi aux sein (Redner) to digress; (Phantasie) to run riot; (in Lebensweise) to lead a dissipated life. 2 vt Möbelstück to curve.

ausschweifend adj Leben dissipated; Phantasie wild.

Ausschweifung f (Maßlosigkeit) excess; (in Lebensweise) dissipation.

ausschweigen vr sep irreg to remain silent (über +acc, zu about). sich eisern ~ to maintain a stony silence.

ausschwemmen vt sep to wash out; Giftstoffe to flush out (aus of); (aushöhlen) to hollow out.

Ausschwemmung f (a) no pl siehe vt washing out; flushing out; hollowing out. (b) (Stelle) hollow.

ausschwenken sep 1 vt (ausspülen) to rinse out. 2 vi aux sein (a) (Mil) to wheel. nach links/rechts ~ to wheel left/right. (b) (Kran, Boot) to swing out.

ausschwitzen sep 1 vt to sweat out; (Wände) to sweat. 2 vi aux sein to sweat.

aussegnen vt sep (Eccl) Toten to give the last blessing to.

Aussegnung f last blessing.

aussehen vi sep irreg (a) to look. gut ~ to look good; (hübsch) to be good looking; (gesund) to look well; gesund/elend ~ to look healthy/wretched; zum Fürchten ~ to look frightening; es sieht nach Regen aus it looks like rain or as if it's going to rain; wie jd/etw ~ to look like sb/sth; weißt du, wie ein Gnu aussieht? do you know what a gnu looks like?; wie sieht's aus? (inf: wie steht's) how's things? (inf); wie siehst du denn (bloß) aus? what do you look like!, just look at you!; ich habe (vielleicht) ausgesehen! you should have seen me!; er sieht nach nichts aus he doesn't look anything special; es sieht nach etwas ~ it's got to look good; es sieht danach or so aus, als ob ... it looks as if ...; ihr seht mir danach aus (inf) I bet!; seh' ich so or danach aus? (inf) what do you take me for?; so siehst du (gerade) aus! (inf) that's just like you!; er sieht ganz so or danach aus he looks it; es sieht nicht gut mit ihm aus things don't look good for him; bei mir sieht es gut aus I'm doing fine.
(b) (geh: Ausschau halten) to look out (nach for).

Aussehen nt -s, no pl appearance. dem ~ nach to go by appearances, by the looks of it; etw dem ~ nach beurteilen to judge sth by appearances.

aussein sep irreg aux sein (Zusammenschreibung nur bei infin und ptp) 1 vi (inf) (a) (zu Ende sein) (Schule) to be out, to have finished; (Krieg, Stück auch) to have ended; (nicht ansein) (Feuer, Ofen) to be out; (Radio, Fernseher etc) to be off; (Sport) (außerhalb sein: Ball) to be out (of play); (ausgeschieden sein: Spieler) to be out.
(b) auf etw (acc) ~ to be (only) after sth or interested in sth or out for sth; auf jdn ~ to be after sb (inf); nur auf Männer/auf eins ~ to be interested only in men/one thing; ich war gestern abend (mit ihr) aus I went out (with her) last night.
2 vi impers es ist aus (und vorbei) zwischen uns it's (all) over between us; es ist aus mit ihm he is finished, he has had it (inf); es ist aus (und vorbei) mit dem bequemen Leben the life of leisure is (all) over; daraus ist nichts geworden, damit ist es aus nothing came of it, it's finished or all over.

außen adv (a) die Tasse ist ~ bemalt the cup is painted on the outside; ~ an der Windschutzscheibe on the outside of the windscreen; von ~ sieht es gut aus outwardly or on the outside it looks good; er kennt das Gefängnis nicht nur von ~ he doesn't only know what prison is like from the outside; er läuft ~ he's running on the outside; er spielt ~ he's playing on the wing; das Fenster geht nach ~ auf the window opens outwards; nach ~ hin (fig) outwardly. (b) (Aus) siehe draußen.

Außen[1] m -, - (Sport) wing. ~ spielen to play on the wing.

Außen[2] nt -, no pl outside.

Außen-: ~abmessung f external dimensions pl; ~ansicht f exterior, view of the outside; ~antenne f outdoor aerial; ~arbeiten pl work on the exterior; ~aufnahme f outdoor shot, exterior; ~bahn f outside lane; ~beleuchtung f exterior lighting; ~bezirk m outlying district; ~border m (inf) outboard; ~bordmotor m outboard motor; ~bords adv (Naut) outboard; ~deich m outside dyke.

aussenden vt sep irreg to send out.

Außendienst m external duty. im ~ sein to work outside the office; ~ machen or haben to work outside the office.

Aussendung f (Aus form) announcement.

Außen-: ~fläche f outside, outside or exterior surface; (Flächeninhalt) external surface area; ~hafen m outer harbour; (Hafenstadt) port.

Außenhandel m foreign trade.

Außenhandels-: ~beziehungen pl foreign trade relations pl; ~bilanz f balance of trade; ~politik f foreign trade policy.

Außen-: ~haut f outer skin; ~kurve f outside bend; ~läufer m (dated Ftbl) wing half (dated); ~linie f (Sport) boundary (line); ~minister m foreign minister, foreign secretary (Brit), secretary of state (US); ~ministerium nt foreign ministry, foreign office (Brit), state department (US); ~politik f (Gebiet) foreign politics sing; (bestimmte) foreign policy/policies; ~politiker m foreign affairs politician; a~politisch adj Debatte etc foreign policy attr; Fehler as regards foreign affairs; Berichterstattung of foreign affairs; Schulung, Erfahrung in foreign affairs; Sprecher on foreign affairs; a~politische Angelegenheiten foreign affairs; a~politisch gesehen, aus a~politischer Sicht from the point of view of foreign affairs; ein Experte auf a~politischem Gebiet an expert on foreign affairs; a~politisch versagen to fail with one's foreign policy; a~politisch sinnvoll sein to be sensible foreign policy; a~politisch orientiert orientated towards foreign affairs; ~seite f outside; die vordere ~seite des Hauses the front exterior of the house.

Außenseiter(in f) m -s, - (Sport, fig) outsider.

Außenseiter-: ~rolle f role as an outsider; eine ~rolle spielen to play the role of an outsider; ~tum nt, no pl being an outsider; das ~tum als literarisches Thema the outsider as a literary theme.

Außen-: ~spiegel m (Aut) outside mirror; ~stände pl (esp Comm) outstanding debts pl, arrears pl; wir haben noch 2.000 Mark ~stände we still have or there are still 2,000 marks outstanding; ~stehende(r) mf decl as adj outsider; ~stelle f branch; ~stürmer m (Ftbl) wing; ~tasche f outside pocket; ~temperatur f outside temperature; (außerhalb Gebäude) outdoor temperature; die ~temperatur or temperatur the temperature outdoors is 20°; bei 20° ~temperatur when the temperature outdoors or the outdoor temperature is 20°, when it's 20° outdoors; ~toilette f outside toilet; (auf dem Flur) shared toilet; ~treppe f outside staircase; ~wand f outer wall; ~welt f outside world; ~winkel m (Math) exterior angle; ~wirtschaft f foreign trade; ~zoll m external tariff.

außer 1 prep +dat or (rare) gen (a) (räumlich) out of. ~ Sicht/Gefecht/Kurs etc out of sight/action/circulation etc; ~ sich (acc) geraten to go wild; ~ sich (dat) sein to be beside oneself; ~ Haus or Hauses sein/essen to be/eat out; ~ Atem out of breath; siehe acht, Betrieb, Land etc.
(b) (ausgenommen) except (for); (abgesehen von) apart from, aside from (esp US). alle ~ mir all except (for) me; ~ ihm habe ich keine Verwandten mehr I have no relatives left apart from him or but him.
(c) (zusätzlich zu) in addition to.
2 conj except. ~ daß ... except that ...; ~ wenn ... except when...; ~ sonntags except Sundays.

Außer-: ~achtlassen nt, ~achtlassung f disregard; unter ~achtlassung der Regeln in total disregard of or with total disregard for the rules; a~amtlich adj unofficial; a~beruflich adj private; er macht diese Arbeit a~beruflich he doesn't do this job professionally, it isn't his job; a~betrieblich adj Veranstaltung, Regelung private; Tätigkeiten outside; a~betrieblich an den Angestellten interessiert sein to take an interest in the private lives of the employees; sie treffen sich auch a~betrieblich they also meet outside work.

außerdem adv besides; (dazu) in addition, as well; (überdies) anyway. ich kann ihn nicht leiden, (und) ~ lügt er immer I can't stand him and besides or anyway he always tells lies; er ist Professor und ~ noch Gutachter he's a professor and a consultant besides or as well.

außerdienstlich adj (nicht dienstlich) Telefonat, Angelegenheit private; (außerhalb der Arbeitszeit) social. ich bin heute ~ unterwegs I'm not on business today.

außer|ehelich 1 adj extramarital; Kind illegitimate. 2 adv outside marriage. das Kind war ~ gezeugt worden the child had been conceived out of wedlock.

äußere(r, s) adj (außerhalb gelegen, Geog) outer; Durchmesser, Verletzung, (außenpolitisch) external; Schein, Eindruck outward.

Äußere(s) nt decl as adj exterior; (fig: Aussehen auch) outward appearance. das ~ täuscht oft appearances are often deceptive; Minister des ~n siehe Außenminister.

Außer-: ~europäisch adj attr non-European; Raum outside Europe; a~fahrplanmäßig adj non-scheduled; a~gerichtlich adj out of court; a~gesetzlich adj extralegal; (gesetzbrecherisch) illegal; a~gewöhnlich 1 adj unusual, out of the ordinary; (sehr groß auch) remarkable; ~gewöhnliches leisten to do some remarkable things; 2 adv (sehr) extremely.

außerhalb 1 prep +gen outside. ~ der Stadt outside the town, out of town; ~ der Dienststunden outside or out of office hours; ~ der Legalität outside the law.
2 adv (außen) outside; (~ der Stadt) out of town. ~ wohnen/arbeiten to live/work out of town; nach ~ outside/out of town; von ~ from outside/out of town; ~ stehen (fig) to be on the outside.

Außer-: a~irdisch adj extraterrestrial; a~kirchlich adj non-ecclesiastic(al); Trauung civil; a~kraftsetzung f repeal; ~kurssetzung f (von Währung) withdrawal (from circulation); (fig) rejection.

äußerlich adj (a) external. (b) (fig) (oberflächlich) superficial; (scheinbar) outward; (esp Philos) Wahrnehmung external. „nur ~!", „nur zur ~en Anwendung!" for external use only; rein ~ betrachtet on the face of it; einer Sache (dat) ~ sein (geh) to be extrinsic to sth.

Äußerlichkeit f (a) (fig) triviality; (Oberflächlichkeit) superficiality; (Formalität) formality. (b) (lit) external characteristic. ~en (outward) appearances pl.

äußerln vti infin only (Aus) einen Hund ~ (führen) to take a dog for a walk.

äußern 1 vt (sagen) to say; Wunsch etc to express; Worte to utter; Kritik to voice. seine Meinung ~ to give one's opinion or views. 2 vr (Mensch) to speak; (Krankheit, Symptom) to show or manifest itself. sich dahin gehend ~, daß ... to make a comment to the effect that ...; ich will mich dazu nicht ~ I don't want to say anything about that.

Außer-: a~ordentlich 1 adj extraordinary; (ungewöhnlich auch) exceptional; (bemerkenswert auch) remarkable, exceptional; ~ordentliches leisten to achieve some remarkable things; 2 adv (sehr) exceptionally, extremely, extraordinarily; a~orts adv (Sw, Aus) out of town; a~parlamentarisch adj extraparliamentary; a~planmäßig adj Besuch, Treffen unscheduled; Mahlzeit additional; Ausgaben non-budgetary; a~schulisch adj Aktivitäten, Interessen extracurricular.

äußerst 1 adv extremely, exceedingly. 2 adj siehe ~e(r, s).

außerstande adv (unfähig) incapable; (nicht in der Lage) unable. ~ sein, etw zu tun to be incapable of doing sth; to be unable to do sth.

äußerstenfalls adv at most.

äußerste(r, s) adj, superl of **äußere(r, s)** (räumlich) furthest; Planet, Schicht outermost; Norden etc extreme; (zeitlich) latest possible; (fig) utmost, extreme. der ~ Preis the last price; mein ~s Angebot my last offer; im ~n Falle if the worst comes to the worst; mit ~r Kraft with all one's strength; von ~r Dringlichkeit/Wichtigkeit of (the) utmost urgency/importance.

Äußerste(s) nt decl as adj bis zum ~n gehen to go to extremes; er geht bis zum ~ he would go to any extreme; er hat sein ~s gegeben he gave his all; das ~ wagen to risk everything; ich bin auf das ~ gefaßt I'm prepared for the worst.

außertourlich [-tu:r-] adj (Aus, S Ger) additional. ein ~er Bus a special; und ich mache ~ noch Überstunden and I do overtime as well or on top.

Äußerung f (Bemerkung) remark, comment; (Ling, Behauptung) statement; (Zeichen) expression. Tränen als ~ der Trauer tears as an expression of mourning.

Äußerungsform f manifestation.

aussetzen sep 1 vt (a) Kind, Haustier to abandon; Wild, Fische to release; Pflanzen to plant out; (Naut) Passagiere to maroon; Boot to lower.
  (b) (preisgeben) jdn/etw einer Sache (dat) ~ to expose sb/sth to sth; jdm/einer Sache ausgesetzt sein (ausgeliefert) to be at the mercy of sb/sth; jdn dem Gelächter ~ to expose sb to ridicule.
  (c) (festsetzen) Belohnung, Preis to offer; (in Testament) to bequeath, to leave. auf jds Kopf (acc) 1000 Dollar ~ to put 1,000 dollars on sb's head.
  (d) (unterbrechen) to interrupt; Debatte, Prozeß to adjourn; Zahlung to break off.
  (e) (vertagen) Strafvollstreckung, Verfahren to suspend; Urteilsverkündung to defer. eine Strafe zur Bewährung ~ to give a suspended sentence.
  (f) an jdm/etw auszusetzen haben to find fault with sb/sth; daran ist nichts auszusetzen there is nothing wrong with it; daran habe ich nur eines auszusetzen I've only one objection to make to that; was haben Sie daran auszusetzen? what don't you like about it?
  (g) Billardkugel to place.
  (h) (Eccl) to expose.
  2 vi (aufhören) to stop; (Mensch auch) to break off; (bei Spiel) to sit out; (Herz) to stop (beating); (Motor auch) to fail; (versagen) to give out. mit etw ~ to stop sth; mit der Pille/Behandlung ~ to stop taking the pill/to interrupt the treatment; zwei Wochen mit der Arbeit ~ to interrupt one's work for two weeks; ich setze besser mal aus I'd better have a break; (bei Spiel) I'd better sit this one out; einen Tag ~ to take a day off; ohne auszusetzen without a break.

Aussetzung f siehe vt (a) abandonment; releasing; planting out; marooning; lowering.
  (b) siehe vt (c) offer; bequest. durch ~ einer Belohnung by offering a reward, by the offer of a reward.
  (c) siehe vt (d) interruption; adjournment; breaking off.
  (d) (Jur) siehe vt (e) suspension; deferment. die ~ der Strafe zur Bewährung war in diesem Falle nicht möglich it was impossible to give a suspended sentence in this case.
  (e) (Eccl: des Allerheiligsten) exposition.

Aussicht f **(a)** (Blick) view (auf +acc of). ein Zimmer mit ~ auf den Park a room overlooking the park; von meinem Fenster aus habe ich bloß ~ auf den Hinterhof the only view I have from my window is the backyard; jdm die ~ nehmen/verbauen to block or obstruct sb's view.
  (b) (fig) prospect (auf +acc of). die ~, daß etw geschieht the chances of sth happening; gute ~en haben to have good prospects; unser Plan hat große ~en auf Erfolg our plan has every prospect or chance of succeeding; keine or nicht die geringste ~ no or not the slightest prospect or chance; etw in ~ haben to have good prospects of sth; jdn/etw in ~ nehmen (form) to take sb/sth into consideration; jdm etw in ~ stellen to promise sb sth; in ~ stehen to be expected; das sind ja schöne ~en! (iro inf) what a prospect!

Aussichts-: a~los adj hopeless; (zwecklos) pointless; (völlig hoffnungslos) desperate; eine a~lose Sache a lost cause; ~losigkeit f siehe adj hopelessness; pointlessness; desperateness; ~punkt m vantage point; a~reich adj promising; Stellung with good prospects; ~turm m observation or lookout tower; a~voll adj siehe a~reich; ~wagen m (Rail) observation car.

aussieben vt sep (lit, fig) to sift out; (Rad) Störungen to filter out.

aussiedeln vt sep to resettle; (evakuieren) to evacuate.

Aussiedler m (Auswanderer) emigrant; (Evakuierter) evacuee.

Aussiedlung f resettlement; (Evakuierung) evacuation.

aussinnen vt sep irreg siehe ersinnen.

aussöhnen sep 1 vt jdn mit jdm/etw ~ to reconcile sb with sb/to sth; jdn ~ to appease sb. 2 vr sich mit jdm/etw ~ to become reconciled with sb/to sth; wir haben uns wieder ausgesöhnt we have made it up again. 3 vi mit etw ~ to compensate for sth.

Aussöhnung f reconciliation (mit jdm with sb, mit etw to sth).

aussondern vt sep **(a)** to select; Schlechtes to pick out; (euph) Menschen auch to single out. die ausgesonderte Ware wird billig abgegeben the reject goods are sold cheaply. **(b)** (Physiol) siehe absondern.

Aussonderung f siehe vt **(a)** selection; picking out; singling out. **(b)** siehe Absonderung.

aussorgen vi sep: ausgesorgt haben to have no more money worries.

aussortieren vt sep to sort out.

ausspähen sep 1 vi nach jdm/etw ~ to look out for sb/sth. 2 vt to spy out; (Mil) to reconnoitre.

ausspannen sep 1 vt **(a)** Tuch, Netz to spread out; Schnur, Leine to put up.
  (b) (ausschirren) to unharness, to unhitch; Ochsen to unyoke; (aus Schreibmaschine) Bogen to take out.
  (c) (fig inf) jdm etw ~ to do sb out of sth (inf); jdm die Freundin etc ~ to pinch sb's girlfriend etc (inf).
  2 vi **(a)** (sich erholen) to have a break.
  (b) (Pferde ~) to unharness the horses; (Ochsen ~) to unyoke the oxen.

Ausspannung f, no pl (fig) relaxation. zur ~ for relaxation.

aussparen vt sep Fläche to leave blank; (fig) to omit.

Aussparung f (Lücke) gap; (unbeschriebene Stelle) blank space.

ausspeien sep irreg 1 vt (ausspucken) to spit out; (erbrechen) to bring up, to disgorge (form); (fig: herausschleudern) to spew out or forth. 2 vi to spit out. das A~ spitting.

Ausspeisung f (Aus) siehe Schulspeisung.

aussperren vt sep to lock out.

Aussperrung f (Ind) lockout. mit ~ drohen to threaten (the workers with) a lockout; die ~ sollte illegal sein lockouts should be made illegal.

ausspielen sep 1 vt **(a)** Karte to play; (am Spielanfang) to lead with. seinen letzten/einen Trumpf ~ (lit, fig) to play one's last card/a or one's last trump card.
  (b) Rolle, Szene to act out. er hat (seine Rolle) ausgespielt (fig) he's finished or through (inf), he's played out (fig).
  (c) (zu Ende spielen) to finish playing.
  (d) (fig: einsetzen) Überlegenheit etc to display.
  (e) (fig) jdn/etw gegen jdn/etw ~ to play sb/sth off against sb/sth.
  (f) (Sport) Pokal, Meisterschaft to play for; Gegner to outplay.
  (g) Gewinne to give as a prize/as prizes.
  2 vi **(a)** (Cards) to play a card; (als erster) to lead. wer spielt aus? whose lead is it?, who has the lead?
  (b) (zu Ende spielen) to finish playing; siehe ausgespielt.

Ausspielung f (im Lotto) pay-out.

ausspinnen vt sep irreg to spin out; (sich ausdenken) to think up.

ausspionieren* vt sep Pläne etc to spy out; Person to spy (up)on.

ausspotten vt sep (S Ger, Sw, Aus) siehe verspotten.

Aussprache f **(a)** pronunciation; (Art des Artikulierens auch) articulation; (Akzent) accent. **(b)** (Meinungsaustausch) discussion; (Gespräch auch) talk. es kam zu einer offenen ~ zwischen den beiden they talked things out; eine ~ herbeiführen to bring things out into the open.

Aussprache-: ~angabe, ~bezeichnung f (Ling) phonetic transcription; ~wörterbuch nt dictionary of pronunciation, pronouncing dictionary.

aussprechbar adj pronounceable. leicht/schwer/nicht ~ easy/difficult to pronounce/unpronounceable.

aussprechen sep irreg 1 vt Wörter, Urteil etc to pronounce; Scheidung to grant; (zu Ende sprechen) Satz to finish; (äußern) to express (jdm to sb); Verdächtigung to voice; Warnung to give, to deliver. jdm ein Lob ~ to give sb a word of praise; der Regierung sein Vertrauen ~ to pass a vote of confidence in the government.
  2 vr **(a)** (Partner) to talk things out; (sein Herz ausschütten, seine Meinung sagen) to say what's on one's mind. sich mit jdm (über etw acc) ~ to have a talk with sb (about sth); (jdm sein Herz ausschütten) to have a heart-to-heart with sb (about sth); sich für/gegen etw ~ to declare or pronounce oneself in favour of/against sth, to come out in favour of/against sth; sich lobend über jdn/etw ~ to speak highly of sb/sth.
  (b) (Wort) to be pronounced. dieses Wort spricht sich leicht/schwer aus this word is easy/difficult to pronounce.
  (c) (sich zeigen: Erregung, Verzweiflung etc) to be expressed. in seinem Gesicht sprach sich Trauer aus his face expressed sorrow.
  3 vi (zu Ende sprechen) to finish (speaking); siehe ausgesprochen.

aussprengen vt sep **(a)** Wasser to sprinkle. **(b)** (mit Sprengstoff) to blast out.

ausspringen sep irreg 1 vi aux sein (Feder, Kette) to jump out. 2 vt (Ski) eine Schanze voll ~ to jump the maximum length on a ski-jump.

ausspritzen vt sep **(a)** Flüssigkeit to squirt out; (sprühend) to spray out; (fig) Gift to pour out. **(b)** Bottich to flush (out); (Med) Zahn etc to rinse out; Ohr to syringe. **(c)** Feuer to put out.

Ausspruch m remark; (geflügeltes Wort) saying.

ausspucken sep 1 vt to spit out; (fig) Produkte to pour or spew out; (hum inf) Geld to cough up (inf); Gelerntes to regurgitate. 2 vi to spit. vor jdm ~ to spit at sb's feet; (fig) to spit upon sb.

ausspülen vt sep to rinse (out); (kräftiger) to swill (out); (Med, Geol) to wash out. sich (dat) den Mund ~ to rinse one's mouth (out).

Ausspülung f (Med) irrigation; (Geol) erosion.

ausstaffieren* vt sep (inf) to equip, to fit out; jdn to rig or kit out; (herausputzen) to dress up. sein Roman ist mit sämtlichen Klischees ausstaffiert his novel is peppered with all the clichés.

Ausstaffierung f (inf) equipment, fittings pl; (Kleidung) rig (-out) (inf), outfit.

Ausstand m **(a)** (Streik) strike. im ~ sein to be on strike; in den ~ treten to (go on) strike. **(b)** usu pl (Comm) outstanding debt. **(c)** seinen ~ geben to hold a leaving party.

ausständig *adj* (*esp Aus*) outstanding.

ausstanzen *vt sep* Metallteil to stamp out; *Loch* to punch (out).

ausstatten *vt sep* to equip; (*versorgen*) to provide, to furnish; (*mit Rechten*) to vest (*esp Jur*); (*möblieren*) to furnish; *Buch* to produce. **mit Humor/Intelligenz** *etc* **ausgestattet sein** to be endowed with humour/intelligence *etc*; **ein Zimmer neu ~** to refurbish a room.

Ausstattung *f* (**a**) *siehe vt* equipping; provision; vesting; furnishing; production. (**b**) (*Ausrüstung*) equipment; (*Tech auch*) fittings *pl*; (*Kapital*) provisions *pl*; (*von Zimmer etc*) furnishings *pl*; (*Theat*) décor and costumes; (*Mitgift*) dowry; (*von Buch*) production.

Ausstattungs-: **~film** *m* spectacular (film); **~stück** *nt* (**a**) (*Theat*) spectacular (show); (**b**) (*Möbelstück*) piece of furniture.

ausstechen *vt sep irreg* (**a**) *Pflanzen, Unkraut* to dig up; *Torf, Plätzchen* to cut out; *Apfel* to core; *Graben* to dig (out). (**b**) *Augen* (*esp als Strafe*) to gouge out, to put out. (**c**) (*fig*) *jdn* (*verdrängen*) to push out; (*übertreffen*) to outdo. **jdn bei einem Mädchen/beim Chef ~** to take sb's place in a girl's affections/push sb out of favour with the boss.

Ausstech-: **~form** *f*, **~förmchen** *nt* (*Cook*) cutter.

ausstehen *sep irreg* **1** *vt* (*ertragen*) to endure; (*erdulden auch*) to put up with; *Sorge, Angst* to go through, to suffer. **ich kann ihn/so etwas nicht ~** I can't bear or stand him/anything like that; **jetzt ist es ausgestanden** now it's all over; **mit jdm viel auszustehen haben** to have to go through a lot with sb or put up with a lot from sb.

2 *vi* (**a**) to be due; (*Antwort*) to be still to come; (*Buch*) to be still to appear; (*Entscheidung*) to be still to be taken; (*Lösung*) to be still to be found; (*noch zu erwarten sein*) to be still expected.

(**b**) (*Schulden*) to be owing. **Geld ~ haben** to have money owing; **~de Forderungen** outstanding demands.

(**c**) (*im Schaufenster etc*) to be on display or show.

aussteigen *vi sep irreg* (**a**) *aux sein* to get out (*aus* of); (*aus Bus, Zug etc auch*) to get off (*aus etw* sth); to alight (*aus* from) (*form*); (*Aviat sl*) to bale or bail out (*aus* of). **alles ~!** everybody out!; (*von Schaffner auch*) all change!; **das A~ während der Fahrt ist verboten** do not alight while train *etc* is in motion.

(**b**) (*Sport: aufgeben*) to give up, to retire (*aus* from); (*bei Wettrennen auch*) to drop out (*aus* of). **einen Gegenspieler ~ lassen** (*esp Ftbl*) to outplay an opponent.

(**c**) (*inf: aus Geschäft etc*) to get out (*aus* of).

ausstellen *sep* **1** *vt* (**a**) (*zur Schau stellen*) to display; (*auf Messe, in Museum etc*) to exhibit.

(**b**) (*ausschreiben*) to make out (*jdm* to sb), to write (out) (*jdm* sb); (*behördlich ausgeben*) to issue (*jdm etw* sb with sth, sth to sb). **einen Scheck auf jdn ~** to make out a cheque to sb, to make a cheque payable to sb; **eine Rechnung über DM 100 ~** to make out a bill for DM 100.

(**c**) (*ausschalten*) *Gerät* to turn or switch off; *siehe* **ausgestellt**.

2 *vi* to exhibit.

Aussteller(in *f*) *m* **-s, -** (**a**) (*auf Messe*) exhibitor. (**b**) (*von Dokument*) issuer; (*von Scheck*) drawer.

Ausstellfenster *nt* (*Aut*) quarterlight.

Ausstellung *f* (**a**) (*Kunst~, Messe*) exhibition; (*Blumen~, Hunde~ etc*) show. (**b**) *no pl* (*von Scheck, Rezept, Rechnung etc*) making out; (*behördlich*) issuing.

Ausstellungs-: **~datum** *nt* date of issue; **~fläche** *f* exhibition area; **~gelände** *nt* exhibition site or area; **~halle** *f* exhibition hall; **~katalog** *m* exhibition catalogue; **~raum** *m* exhibition room; **~stand** *m* exhibition stand; **~stück** *nt* (*in Ausstellung*) exhibit; (*in Schaufenster etc*) display item; **~tag** *m* day of issue.

Aussterbe|etat *m* (*hum*) **auf dem ~ stehen** or **sein** to be being phased out; **etw auf den ~ setzen** to phase sth out.

Aussterben *nt* **-s,** *no pl* extinction. **im ~ begriffen** dying out, becoming extinct; **vom ~ bedroht sein** to be threatened by extinction.

aussterben *vi sep irreg aux sein* to die out; (*esp Spezies, Geschlecht auch*) to become extinct. **die Dummen sterben nie aus** there's one born every minute; *siehe* **ausgestorben**.

Aussteuer *f* **-, -n** dowry.

aussteuern *vt sep* (**a**) *Tochter* to provide with a dowry. (**b**) (*Insur*) to disqualify. (**c**) *Auto* to steer out of trouble.

Aussteuerung *f* (*Insur*) disqualification.

Aussteuerversicherung *f* endowment insurance (*for one's daughter's wedding etc*).

Ausstich *m* **-s, -e** (**a**) *no pl* (*das Beste*) best. (**b**) (*Entscheidungskampf*) final.

Ausstieg *m* **-(e)s, -e** (**a**) *no pl* (*das Aussteigen*) climbing out (*aus* of); (*aus Bus, Zug etc*) getting out or off, alighting (*aus* from) (*form*). (**b**) (*Ausgang*) exit. (**c**) (*auch ~luke*) escape hatch.

ausstopfen *vt sep* *Kissen etc, Tiere* to stuff; *Ritzen* to fill. **sich** (*dat*) **den Bauch ~** to pad one's stomach.

Ausstoß *m* (**a**) (*esp Phys, Tech: das Ausstoßen*) expulsion, ejection, discharge; (*von Torpedo, Geschoß*) firing. (**b**) (*Ausschluß von Verein etc*) expulsion. (**c**) (*Produktion*) output, production.

ausstoßen *vt sep irreg* (**a**) (*herausstoßen*) to eject, to discharge; *Atem, Plazenta* to expel; *Gas etc* to give off, to emit; (*Naut*) *Torpedo* to fire; (*herstellen*) *Teile, Stückzahl* to put or turn out, to produce.

(**b**) **sich** (*dat*) **ein Auge/einen Zahn ~** to lose an eye/a tooth; **jdm ein Auge/einen Zahn ~** to put sb's eye out/to knock sb's tooth out.

(**c**) (*ausschließen*) *aus Verein, Armee etc*) to expel (*aus* from); (*verbannen*) to banish (*aus* from). **jdn aus der**

Gesellschaft ~ to banish sb or cast sb out from society; *siehe* **Ausgestoßene(r)**.

(**d**) (*äußern*) to utter; *Schrei* to give; *Seufzer* to heave.

(**e**) (*Ling*) *Laut* to drop.

Ausstoßrohr *nt* (*Naut*) torpedo tube.

Ausstoßung *f* **-,** *no pl* (**a**) (*aus from*) (*Ausschließung*) expulsion; (*aus der Gesellschaft*) banishment; (*aus einer Gemeinschaft auch*) exclusion. (**b**) (*Ling: eines Lautes*) dropping.

ausstrahlen *sep* **1** *vt* to radiate (*auch fig*); *esp Licht, Wärme auch* to give off; (*Rad*) to transmit, to broadcast.

2 *vi* to radiate; (*esp Licht, Wärme auch*) to be given off; (*Schmerz*) to extend, to spread (*bis in +acc* as far as). **seine Freude strahlte auf die Zuhörer aus** his joy was communicated to the listeners.

Ausstrahlung *f* radiation; (*Rad*) transmission, broadcast(ing); (*fig: von Mensch, Ort*) aura. **die Sonne hat eine starke ~** the sun gives off strong radiations.

ausstrecken *sep* **1** *vt* to extend (*nach* towards); *Fühler auch* to put out; *Hand auch, Beine etc* to stretch out; *Zunge* to stick out (*nach* at). **mit ausgestreckten Armen** with arms extended. **2** *vr* to stretch (oneself) out.

ausstreichen *vt sep irreg* (**a**) *Geschriebenes* to cross or strike out, to delete; (*tilgen auch*) to obliterate. **jds Namen auf einer Liste ~** to cross or strike sb's name off a list, to delete sb's name from a list.

(**b**) (*glätten*) *Falten* to smooth out.

(**c**) (*breit streichen*) *Teig* to spread out.

(**d**) *Backform* (*mit Fett*) to grease.

(**e**) (*ausfüllen*) *Risse* to fill, to smooth over.

(**f**) (*ausmalen*) to paint.

ausstreuen *vt sep* to scatter, to spread; (*fig*) *Gerücht* to spread, to put about. **etw mit etw ~** to cover sth with sth.

Ausstrich *m* **-s, -e** (*Med*) smear.

ausströmen *sep* **1** *vi aux sein* (**a**) (*herausfließen*) to stream or pour out (*aus* of); (*entweichen*) to escape (*aus* from).

(**b**) (*ausstrahlen*) **die Hitze, die vom Ofen ausströmt** the heat which is radiated from the stove; **etw strömt von jdm/etw aus** (*fig*) sb/sth radiates sth.

2 *vt* *Duft, Gas* to give off; (*ausstrahlen*) *Wärme, Ruhe etc* to radiate.

ausstudieren* *vi sep* (*inf*) to finish studying.

aussuchen *vt sep* (**a**) (*auswählen*) to choose; (*esp iro*) to pick. **such dir was aus!** choose or pick what you want, take your pick; *siehe* **ausgesucht**. (**b**) (*old: durchsuchen*) to search.

aussülzen *vr sep* (*sl*) to talk one's head off; (*zu Ende sprechen*) to finish.

austäfeln *vt sep* to panel.

austapezieren* *vt sep* to paper.

austarieren* *vt sep* (**a**) (*ins Gleichgewicht bringen*) to balance; (*fig auch*) to equalize, to share out equally. (**b**) (*Aus: Leergewicht feststellen*) to determine the tare weight of.

Austausch *m* exchange; (*von Gedanken etc auch*) interchange; (*Ersatz*) replacement; (*Sport*) substitution. **im ~ für** or **gegen** in exchange for.

austauschbar *adj* interchangeable.

austauschen *vt sep* (*lit, fig*) to exchange (*gegen* for); (*untereinander ~*) to interchange; (*ersetzen*) to replace (*gegen* with). **er ist wie ausgetauscht** (*fig*) he's (become) a different person, he's completely changed.

Austausch-: **~lehrer** *m* exchange teacher; **~motor** *m* replacement engine; **~schüler** *m* exchange student or pupil; **~student** *m* exchange student; **a~weise** *adv* as part of an exchange; (*bei Studenten etc*) on an exchange basis.

austeilen *vt sep* to distribute (*unter +dat, an +acc* among); (*aushändigen auch*) to hand out (*unter +dat, an +acc* to); *Spielkarten* to deal (out); *Essen* to serve; *Sakrament* to administer, to dispense; *Befehle* to give, to issue; *Prügel* to hand out, to administer.

Austeilung *f* distribution; (*Aushändigung auch*) handing out; (*von Essen etc*) serving; (*von Sakrament*) administration, dispensation.

Auster *f* **-, -n** oyster.

Austern-: **~bank** *f* oyster bed or bank; **~fischer** *m* (*Orn*) oyster catcher; **~park** *m* oyster farm or park; **~schale** *f* oyster shell; **~zucht** *f* oyster farm; (**~züchtung**) oyster farming.

austilgen *vt sep* to eradicate (*auch fig*); *Schädlinge auch, Menschen* to exterminate; *Erinnerung* to obliterate.

Austilgung *f siehe vt* eradication; extermination; obliteration.

austoben *sep* **1** *vt* to work off (*an +dat* on).

2 *vr* (**a**) (*Mensch*) to let off steam; (*sich müde machen*) to tire oneself out; (*ein wildes Leben führen*) to have one's fling. **ein Garten, wo sich die Kinder ~ können** a garden where the children can romp about; **hat sie sich jetzt ausgetobt?** has she cooled down now?

(**b**) (*abebben: Leidenschaft, Sturm, Fieber etc*) to die down.

austollen *vr sep* (*umherspringen etc*) to have a good romp; (*Energie loswerden*) to let off steam; (*sich amüsieren*) to let one's hair down.

Austrag *m* **-(e)s** *no pl* (**a**) settlement, resolution; (*Sport: von Wettkampf*) holding. **zum ~ kommen/gelangen** to be up for settlement/to be settled or decided. (**b**) (*S Ger, Aus*) *siehe* **Altenteil**.

austragen *sep irreg* **1** *vt* (**a**) *Problem, Frage* to deal with; *Duell, Wettkampf etc* to hold. **einen Streit mit jdm ~** to have it out with sb.

(**b**) *Waren, Post etc* to deliver.

(**c**) **ein Kind ~** to carry a child (through) to the full term; (*nicht abtreiben*) to have a child.

(**d**) (*abmelden*) to sign out; (*löschen*) *Zahlen, Daten* to take out; (*aus Liste, bei Buchung*) jdn to cancel sb's name. **2** *vr* to sign out.

Austräger(in *f*) *m* delivery man/boy *etc*; (*von Zeitungen*) newspaper man/boy *etc*. **wir suchen Studenten als** ~ we are looking for students to deliver newspapers.

Austragung *f* (*Sport*) holding.

Austragungslort *m* (*Sport*) venue.

austrainiert *adj* (*Sport*) well-prepared.

Australide(r) *mf decl as adj* Australoid.

Australien [-iən] *nt* -s Australia. ~ **und Ozeanien** Australasia.

Australier(in *f*) [-iɐ, -iərɪn] *m* -s, - Australian.

australisch *adj* Australian. **A~er Bund** the Commonwealth of Australia.

Australneger *m* (*dated*) *siehe* **Australide**.

austräumen *vt sep* to finish dreaming. **sein Traum von Reichtümern ist ausgeträumt** (*fig*) his dream of riches is over.

austreiben *sep irreg* **1** *vt* **(a)** *Vieh* to drive or turn out.
 (b) (*vertreiben*) to drive out; *Teufel etc auch* to exorcise, to cast out (*esp old, liter*). **..., daß es mir den Schweiß austrieb ...** until the sweat was pouring off me; **jdm etw** ~ to cure sb of sth; (*esp durch Schläge*) to knock sth out of sb.
 (c) (*Typ*) *Zeilen* to space out.
 (d) (*rare: hervorbringen*) *Blüten, Knospen* to put forth.
 2 *vi* (*sprießen*) to sprout.

Austreibung *f* expulsion; (*von Teufel etc*) exorcism, driving out, casting out (*esp old, liter*).

austreten *sep irreg* **1** *vi aux sein* **(a)** (*herauskommen*) to come out (*aus* of); (*Blut etc auch*) to issue (*aus* from); (*entweichen*) *Gas etc* to escape (*aus* from, through).
 (b) (*Med: bei Bruch*) to protrude.
 (c) (*inf: zur Toilette gehen*) to go to the loo or john (*US*) (*inf*); (*Sch*) to be excused (*euph*).
 (d) (*ausscheiden*) to leave (*aus etw* sth); (*formell*) to resign (*aus* from); (*aus politischer Gemeinschaft*) to withdraw (*aus* from).
 (e) (*Hunt*) to come out (into the open). **aus der Deckung** ~ to break cover.
 2 *vt Spur, Feuer etc* to tread out; *Schuhe* to wear out (of shape); *siehe* **ausgetreten**.

austricksen *vt sep* (*inf: Sport, fig*) to trick.

austrinken *vti sep irreg* to finish. **trink (deine Milch) aus!** drink (your milk) up.

Austritt *m* **(a)** *no pl* (*das Heraustreten*) (*von Flüssigkeit*) outflow; (*das Entweichen*) escape; (*von Kugel*) exit; (*esp von Eiter*) discharge; (*von Blut*) issue; (*Med: von Bruch*) protrusion.
 (b) (*das Ausscheiden*) leaving *no art* (*aus etw* sth); (*formell*) resignation (*aus* from); (*aus politischer Gemeinschaft*) withdrawal (*aus* from). **die ~e aus der Kirche häufen sich** there are more and more people leaving the church.
 (c) (*old: Balkon*) balcony.

Austritts|erklärung *f* (notice of) resignation.

Austro- *in cpds* Austro-.

austrocknen *sep* **1** *vi aux sein* to dry out; (*Fluß etc*) to dry up; (*Kehle*) to become parched. **2** *vt* to dry out; *Fluß etc* to dry up; *Kehle* to make parched; (*trockenlegen*) *Sumpf auch* to drain.

austrommeln *vt sep* (*Hist*) to announce on the drum; (*fig*) to shout from the rooftops.

austrompeten* *vt sep siehe* **ausposaunen**.

austrudeln *vt sep* (*dial*) *siehe* **auswürfeln**.

austüfteln *vt sep* (*inf*) to work out; (*ersinnen*) to think up.

aus|üben *vt sep* **(a)** *Beruf, Kunst* to practise; *Gewerbe auch* to carry on; *Aufgabe, Funktion, Amt* to perform; (*innehaben*) *Amt* to hold. **eine Praxis** ~ to have a practice, to be in practice.
 (b) *Druck, Einfluß* to exert (*auf + acc* on); *Macht, Recht* to exercise; *Wirkung* to have (*auf + acc* on). **einen Reiz auf jdn** ~ to have or hold an attraction for sb.

aus|übend *adj Arzt, Rechtsanwalt, Künstler* practising; *Gewalt* executive.

Aus|übung *f siehe vb* **(a)** practice; performance; holding. **die** ~ **einer Praxis** having a practice; **in** ~ **seines Dienstes/seiner Pflicht** (*form*) in the execution of his duty; **in** ~ **seines Berufs** (*form*) in pursuance of one's profession (*form*). **(b)** exertion; exercise.

aus|ufern *vi sep aux sein* (*lit rare: Fluß*) to burst or break its banks; (*fig*) to get out of hand; (*Konflikt etc*) to escalate (*zu* into).

Ausverkauf *m* (clearance) sale; (*wegen Geschäftsaufgabe*) closing-down sale; (*fig: Verrat*) sell-out. **etw im** ~ **kaufen** to buy sth at the sale(s).

ausverkaufen* *vt sep* to sell off, to clear.

ausverkauft *adj* sold out. **vor ~em Haus spielen** to play to a full house.

ausverschämt *adj* (*dial*) *siehe* **unverschämt**.

auswachsen *sep irreg* **1** *vi aux sein* **(a) das ist (ja) zum A~** (*inf*) it's enough to drive you mad or round the bend (*inf*); **zum A~ langweilig** (*inf*) incredibly boring; *siehe* **ausgewachsen**.
 (b) (*Getreide*) to sprout.
 (c) (*Narbe*) to grow over; (*Mißbildung auch*) to right itself.
 2 *vt* (*rare*) *Kleider* to grow out of, to outgrow.
 3 *vr* **(a)** (*verschwinden*) to disappear; (*Narbe auch*) to grow over; (*sich verbessern*) to right itself.
 (b) sich zu etw ~ (*fig: Streit etc*) to turn into sth.

Auswahl *f* -, *no pl* selection (*an + dat* of); (*Angebot auch*) range; (*Wahl*) choice; (*die Besten*) pick; (*Vielfalt*) variety; (*Sport*) representative team. **ohne** ~ indiscriminately; **viel/eine reiche** ~ **a** large/wide selection or range; **hier gibt es keine** ~ there is no choice; **viele Sachen zur** ~ **haben** to have many things to choose from; **drei Bewerber stehen zur** ~ there are three applicants to choose from, there is a choice of three applicants;

jdm drei Sachen zur ~ **vorlegen** to offer sb a choice of three things; **eine** ~ **treffen** (*eines auswählen*) to make a choice; (*einige auswählen*) to make a selection.

Auswahl-: ~**antwort** *f* answer (to a/the multiple choice question); ~**band** *m* selection.

auswählen *vt sep* to select, to choose (*unter + dat* from among). **sich** (*dat*) **etw** ~ to select or choose sth (for oneself); *siehe* **ausgewählt**.

Auswahl-: ~**mannschaft** *f* representative team; ~**möglichkeit** *f* choice; ~**prinzip** *nt* selection principle, criterion; ~**sendung** *f* (selection of) samples; ~**spieler** *m* representative player.

auswalzen *vt sep* **(a)** *Metall* to roll out. **(b)** (*fig*) to go to town on; *Thema auch* to drag out.

Auswanderer *m* emigrant.

Auswanderer-: ~**schiff** *nt* emigrant ship; ~**visum** *nt* emigration visa.

Auswanderin *f* emigrant.

auswandern *vi sep aux sein* to emigrate (*nach, in + acc* to); (*Volk*) to migrate.

Auswanderung *f* emigration; (*Massen~*) migration.

auswärtig *adj attr* **(a)** (*nicht ansässig*) non-local; *Schüler, Mitglied* from out of town. **eine ~e Filiale** a branch in another area. **(b)** (*Pol*) foreign. **der ~e Dienst** the foreign service; **das A~e Amt** the Foreign Office (*Brit*), the State Department (*US*); **der Minister des A~en** (*form*) the Foreign Minister (*Brit*), the Secretary of State (*US*).

auswärts *adv* **(a)** (*nach außen*) outwards. **(b)** (*außerhalb des Hauses*) away from home; (*außerhalb der Stadt*) out of town; (*Sport*) away. ~ **essen** to eat out; ~ **sprechen** (*hum inf*) to speak foreign (*hum inf*).

Auswärts-: **a~gebogen** *adj attr* bent outwards; ~**spiel** *nt* (*Sport*) away (game).

auswaschen *sep irreg* **1** *vt* to wash out; (*spülen*) to rinse (out); (*Geol auch*) to erode. **2** *vr* (*Farbe*) to wash out.

auswattieren* *vt sep* to pad (out).

auswechselbar *adj* (ex)changeable; (*untereinander* ~) interchangeable; (*ersetzbar*) replaceable.

auswechseln *sep* **1** *vt* to change; (*esp gegenseitig*) to exchange; (*ersetzen*) to replace; (*Sport*) to substitute (*gegen* for). **er ist wie ausgewechselt** (*fig*) he's a changed or different person. **2** *vi* (*Sport*) to bring on a substitute, to make a substitution.

Auswechselspieler(in *f*) *m* substitute.

Auswechs(e)lung *f* exchange; (*Ersatz*) replacement; (*Sport*) substitution.

Ausweg *m* way out; (*fig: Lösung auch*) solution. **der letzte** ~ **a** last resort; **er sieht keinen anderen** ~, **als ... zu** he can see no other way out but to ...; **ich weiß keinen** ~ **mehr** I don't know any way out (*aus* of); **sich** (*dat*) **einen** ~ **offenlassen** or **offenhalten** to leave oneself an escape route or a way out.

Ausweg-: **a~los** *adj* (*fig*) hopeless; ~**losigkeit** *f* (*fig*) hopelessness.

ausweichen *vi sep irreg aux sein* **(a)** (*Hindernis, Gefahr umgehen*) to get out of the way (+ *dat* of); (*Platz machen*) to make way (+ *dat* for). **nach rechts** ~ to get out of the way/to make way by going to the right.
 (b) (*zu entgehen versuchen*) (*lit*) to get out of the way; (*fig*) to evade the point/issue *etc.* **einer Sache** (*dat*) ~ (*lit*) to avoid sth; (*fig*) to evade or dodge (*inf*) sth; **jdm/einer Begegnung** ~ to avoid sb/a meeting; **dem Feind** ~ to avoid (contact with) the enemy; **eine ~de Antwort** an evasive answer.
 (c) **auf etw** (*acc*) ~ (*fig*) to switch to sth.

Ausweich-: ~**flughafen** *m* alternative airport; ~**gleis** *nt* (*Rail*) siding; ~**lager** *nt* reserve depot or store; ~**manöver** *nt* evasive action or manoeuvre; ~**möglichkeit** *f* (*fig*) alternative; (*lit*) possibility of getting out of the way; ~**stelle** *f* (*auf Straßen*) passing place.

ausweiden *vt sep* (*Hunt*) to break up; *Opfertier etc* to disembowel.

ausweinen *sep* **1** *vr* to have a (good) cry; (*zu Ende weinen*) to finish crying. **sich bei jdm** ~ to have a cry on sb's shoulder; **sich** (*dat*) **die Augen** ~ to cry one's eyes or heart out (*nach* over). **2** *vi* to finish crying. **3** *vt* **seinen Kummer etc** ~ to weep (*bei jdm* on sb's shoulder).

Ausweis *m* -es, -e **(a)** (*Mitglieds~/Leser~/Studenten~ etc*) (membership/library/student) card; (*Personal~*) identity card; (*Berechtigungsnachweis*) pass. ~, **bitte** your papers please; **ich habe sämtliche ~e verloren** I have lost all my papers.
 (b) (*Beleg*) proof; (*von Identität*) proof of identity, identification. **nach** ~ + *gen* (*form*) according to.
 (c) (*Bank~*) bank return.
 (d) (*dated Aus Sch: Zeugnis*) report.

ausweisen *sep irreg* **1** *vt* **(a)** (*aus dem Lande*) to expel, to deport; **die Ausgewiesene(r)**.
 (b) (*Identität nachweisen*) to identify.
 (c) (*zeigen*) to reveal.
 2 *vr* **(a)** to identify oneself. **können Sie sich** ~? do you have any means of identification?
 (b) sich als etw ~ (*sich erweisen*) to prove oneself to be sth.

Ausweis-: ~**karte** *f siehe* **Ausweis** (*a*); ~**kontrolle** *f* identity check; ~**papiere** *pl* identity papers *pl*; ~**pflicht** *f* obligation to carry an identity card.

ausweißen *vt sep* to whitewash.

Ausweisung *f* expulsion, deportation.

Ausweisungsbefehl *m* expulsion or deportation order.

ausweiten *sep* **1** *vt* to widen; *esp Dehnbares* to stretch; (*fig*) to expand (*zu* into). **2** *vr* to widen; (*esp Dehnbares*) to stretch; (*fig*) (*Thema, Bewegung*) to expand (*zu* into); (*sich verbreiten*) to spread.

Ausweitung f widening; (*Ausdehnung*) stretching; (*fig*) expansion; (*von Konflikt etc auch*) widening; (*Verbreitung*) spreading.

auswendig adv by heart, from memory. etw ~ können/lernen to know/learn sth (off) by heart; das kann ich schon ~ (*fig inf*) I know it backwards (*inf*) or by heart; ein Musikstück ~ spielen to play a piece (of music) from memory; siehe **inwendig**.

Auswendiglernen nt -s, no pl (*von Geschichtszahlen, Fakten*) learning by heart, memorizing. ein Gedicht zum ~ a poem to learn by heart.

auswerfen vt sep irreg (a) Anker, Netz, Leine to cast.
(b) (*hinausschleudern*) Lava, Asche to throw out, to eject; Geschoßhülsen to eject.
(c) (*ausspucken*) Schleim, Blut to cough up.
(d) (*herausschaufeln*) to shovel out; Graben to dig out.
(e) (*verteilen*) Dividende to pay out; (*zuteilen*) Mittel, Summen to allocate.
(f) (*Comm*) Posten to set out.
(g) (*produzieren*) to produce, to put or turn out.
(h) Fenster to break, to smash.
(i) jdm ein Auge ~ to put out sb's eye.

auswerten vt sep (a) (*bewerten*) to evaluate; (*analysieren*) to analyse. (b) (*nutzbar machen*) to utilize.

Auswertung f siehe vt (a) evaluation; analysis. (b) utilization.

auswetzen vt sep to grind out.

auswickeln vt sep Paket, Bonbon etc to unwrap. ein Kind ~ to take a child out of its blankets etc; (*Hist: Windeln entfernen*) to unswaddle a child.

auswiegen vt sep irreg to weigh (out); siehe **ausgewogen**.

auswinden vt sep irreg siehe **auswringen**.

auswirken sep 1 vr to have an effect (auf +acc on). sich günstig/negativ ~ to have a favourable/negative effect; sich in etw (*dat*) ~ to result in sth; sich zu jds Vorteil ~ to work or turn out to sb's advantage.
2 vt (*geh, old: erwirken*) to obtain (jdm etw sth for sb, bei jdm from sb).

Auswirkung f (*Folge*) consequence; (*Wirkung*) effect; (*Rückwirkung*) repercussion.

auswischen vt sep to wipe out; Glas etc, Wunde to wipe clean; Schrift etc to rub or wipe out. sich (*dat*) die Augen ~ to rub or wipe one's eyes; jdm eins ~ (*inf*) to get one over on sb (*inf*); (*aus Rache*) to get one's own back on sb.

auswringen vt sep irreg to wring out.

Auswuchs m (a) (out)growth; (*Med, Bot auch*) excrescence (*form*); (*Mißbildung*) deformity. (b) (*fig*) (*Erzeugnis*) product; (*Mißstand, Übersteigerung*) excess. extreme Gruppen, die Auswüchse unserer Zeit sind extreme groups that are morbid growths of our time.

auswuchten vt sep Räder to balance.

Auswurf m, no pl (a) (*von Lava etc*) ejection, eruption; (*ausgeworfene Lava etc auch*) ejecta pl (*Geol*).
(b) (*Med*) sputum. ~/blutigen ~ haben to bring up phlegm/be coughing up blood.
(c) (*pej: Abschaum*) scum; (*Schund*) trashy product. der ~ der Menschheit the dregs pl or scum of humanity.

auswürfeln sep 1 vt to throw dice; (*das Glück entscheiden lassen*) to draw lots. 2 vt to (throw) dice for.

auswüten vir sep: (sich) ausgewütet haben to have calmed down; (*Sturm*) to have abated.

auszacken vt sep to serrate.

auszahlen sep 1 vt Geld etc to pay out; Arbeiter, Gläubiger to pay off; Kompagnon to buy out. er bekommt DM 400 die Woche ausgezahlt his net pay is DM 400 a week. 2 vr (*sich lohnen*) to pay (off).

auszählen sep 1 vt Stimmen to count (up); (*durch Zählen wählen*) Person to choose or select (by counting); (*Boxen*) to count out. 2 vi (*bei Kinderspielen*) to count out.

Auszahlreim m siehe **Abzählreim**.

Auszahlung f siehe vt paying out; paying off; buying out. zur ~ kommen (*form*) or gelangen (*form*) to be paid out.

Auszählung f (*von Stimmen etc*) counting (up), count.

Auszahlungs-: ~anweisung f order to pay; ~stelle f payments office.

Auszählvers m siehe **Abzählvers**.

auszahnen vt sep (*Tech*) to tooth.

auszanken vt sep 1 vt (*inf: ausschelten*) to bawl out (*inf*). 2 vi (zu Ende zanken) to finish quarrelling.

auszehren vt sep to drain, to exhaust; Land to drain. ~de Krankheit wasting disease.

Auszehrung f (a) (*Kräfteverfall*) emaciation. (b) (*obs Med*) consumption (*old*).

auszeichnen sep 1 vt (a) (*mit Zeichen versehen*) to mark; Waren to label; (*Typ*) Manuskript to mark up; Überschrift to display. etw mit einem Preis(schild) ~ to price sth.
(b) (*ehren*) to honour. jdn mit einem Orden ~ to decorate sb (with a medal); jdn mit einem Preis/Titel ~ to award a prize/title to sb.
(c) (*hervorheben*) to distinguish (from all others); (*kennzeichnen*) to be a feature of.
2 vr to stand out (*durch* due to), to distinguish oneself (*durch* by) (*auch iro*). dieser Wagen zeichnet sich durch gute Straßenlage aus one of the remarkable features of this car is its good road-holding, what makes this car stand out is its good road-holding; siehe **ausgezeichnet**.

Auszeichnung f (a) (*no pl: das Auszeichnen*) (*von Baum etc*) marking; (*von Waren*) labelling; (*Typ: von Manuskript*) mark up.
(b) (*no pl: das Ehren*) honouring; (*mit Orden*) decoration. jds/seine ~ mit einem Preis etc the awarding of a prize etc to sb/his being awarded a prize etc.

(c) (*Markierung*) marking (+gen, an +dat on); (an Ware) ticket; (*Typ: auf Manuskript*) mark up.
(d) (*Ehrung*) honour, distinction; (*Orden*) decoration; (*Preis*) award, prize. mit ~ bestehen to pass with distinction.

Auszeit f (*Sport*) time out.

ausziehbar adj extendible, extensible; Antenne telescopic. ein ~er Tisch a pull-out table.

ausziehen sep irreg 1 vt (a) (*herausziehen*) to pull out; (*verlängern auch*) to extend; Metall (zu Draht) to draw out (zu into).
(b) Kleider to take off, to remove; jdn to undress. jdm die Jacke etc ~ to take off sb's jacket etc; sich (*dat*) etw ~ to take off sth; die Uniform ~ (*fig*) to retire from the services; das zieht einem ja die Schuhe or Socken or Stiefel aus! (*sl*) it's enough to make you cringe!
(c) (*dated rare*) (*exzerpieren*) to excerpt, to extract; (*zusammenfassen*) to summarize. einen Autor ~ to take excerpts from an author's work.
(d) Wirkstoffe (*aus Kräutern*) to extract; Kräuter to make an extract from.
(e) (*ausbleichen*) Farbe to bleach (out), to take out.
(f) (*nachzeichnen*) Linie to trace (mit Tusche in ink).
2 vr (sich entkleiden) to undress, to take off one's clothes.
3 vi aux sein (a) (*aufbrechen, abreisen*) to set out; (*demonstrativ*) to walk out; (*aus einer Wohnung*) to move (*aus* out of).
auf Abenteuer/Raub ~ to set off or out in search of adventure/to rob and steal; zur Jagd ~ to set off for the hunt; zum Kampf ~ to set off to battle.
(b) (*schwinden: Aroma*) to disappear, to go.

Auszieh-: ~feder f drawing pen; ~leiter f extension ladder; ~platte f (von Tisch) leaf; ~tisch m extending or pull-out table; ~tusche f drawing ink.

auszischen vt sep (*Theat*) to hiss (off).

Auszubildende(r) mf decl as adj trainee.

Auszug m (a) (*das Weggehen*) departure; (*demonstrativ*) walk-out; (*zeremoniell*) procession; (*aus der Wohnung*) move. der ~ der Kinder Israel (*Bibl*) the Exodus (of the Children of Israel).
(b) (*Ausschnitt, Exzerpt*) excerpt; (*aus Buch auch*) extract; (*Zusammenfassung*) abstract, summary; (*Konto~*) statement; (*Chem*) extract; (*Mus*) arrangement. etw in Auszügen drucken to print extracts of sth.
(c) (*ausziehbarer Teil*) extension.

Auszugs-: ~mehl nt super-fine flour; a~weise adv in extracts or excerpts; (*gekürzt*) in an/the abridged version; a~weise aus etw lesen to read extracts from sth.

autark adj self-sufficient (*auch fig*), autarkical (*Econ*).

Autarkie f self-sufficiency (*auch fig*), autarky (*Econ*).

authentisch adj authentic; (*Mus*) Kadenz perfect.

Authentizität f authenticity.

Autismus m autism.

autistisch adj autistic.

Auto nt -s, -s car, automobile. ~ fahren (*selbst*) to drive (a car); (*als Mitfahrer*) to go by car; mit dem ~ fahren to go by car; er guckt wie ein ~ (*inf*) his eyes are popping out of his head (*inf*).

Auto-: ~apotheke f first-aid kit (for the car); ~atlas m road atlas.

Autobahn f motorway (*Brit*), expressway (*US*).

Autobahn- in cpds motorway etc; ~ausfahrt f motorway etc exit; ~dreieck nt motorway etc merging point; ~gebühr f toll; ~kreuz nt motorway etc intersection; ~rasthof m, ~raststätte f motorway etc service area or services pl; ~ring m motorway ring road; ~zubringer m motorway etc approach road or feeder.

Auto-: ~batterie f car battery; ~biograph m autobiographer; ~biographie f autobiography; a~biographisch adj autobiographical.

Autobus m bus; (*Reiseomnibus*) coach (*Brit*), bus. einstöckiger/zweistöckiger ~ single-decker/double-decker (bus).

Auto-: ~camping nt driving and camping; ~car m -s, -s (*Sw*) coach (*Brit*), bus; a~chthon [autɔxˈtoːn] adj (*geh*) autochthonous (*form*); ~-Cross nt -, no pl autocross; ~dafé nt -s, -s (*geh*) auto-da-fé; ~didakt(in f) m -en, -en autodidact (*form*), self-educated person; ~didaktentum nt autodidacticism (*form*); a~didaktisch adj autodidactic (*form*), self taught no adv; sich a~didaktisch bilden to educate oneself; sein Wissen a~didaktisch erwerben to acquire one's knowledge by oneself; ~dieb m car thief; ~diebstahl m car theft; ~drom nt -s, -e (a) motor-racing circuit; ~e (b) (*Aus*) dodgems pl; ~droschke f (*dated*) taxi-cab; ~elektrik f (car) electrics pl; ~erotik f autoeroticism; a~erotisch adj autoerotic; ~fähre f car ferry; ~fahren nt driving (a car); (*als Mitfahrer*) driving in a car; ~fahrer m (car) driver; ~fahrergruß m (*no inf*) jdm den ~fahrergruß bieten ~ to give sb a V (*Brit*) or the finger (*US*) sign; ~fahrt f drive; ~falle f (*bei Überfällen*) road trap; (*Radarkontrolle*) speed or radar trap; ~friedhof m (*inf*) car dump.

autogen adj autogenous. ~es Training (*Psych*) relaxation through self-hypnosis.

Autogramm nt -s, -e autograph.

Autogramm-: ~jäger m autograph hunter; ~stunde f autograph(ing) session.

Auto-: ~graph nt -s, -en autograph; ~hilfe f breakdown service; ~hypnose f autohypnosis; ~industrie f car industry; ~karte f road map; ~kino nt drive-in (cinema); ~knacker m (*inf*) car burglar; ~kolonne f line of cars; ~krat m -en, -en autocrat; ~kratie f autocracy; a~kratisch adj autocratic; ~kunde m customer with a car; ~lenker m (*Sw*) (car) driver; ~marder m (*sl*) siehe ~knacker; ~marke f make (of car).

Automat m -en, -en (auch fig: Mensch) machine; (Verkaufs~) vending machine; (Roboter) automaton, robot; (Musik~) jukebox; (Spiel~) slot-machine; (Rechen~) calculator; (rare: Telefon~) pay-phone; (Elec: selbsttätige Sicherung) cut-out.
Automaten-: ~buffet nt (esp Aus) automat; ~knacker m (inf) vandal (who breaks into vending machines); ~restaurant nt siehe ~buffet; ~straße f vending machines pl.
Automatic, Automatik[1] m -s, -s (Aut) automatic.
Automatik[2] f automatic mechanism (auch fig); (Gesamtanlage) automatic system; (Rad) automatic frequency control, AFC; (Aut) automatic transmission.
Automatikwagen m automatic.
Automation f automation.
automatisch adj automatic.
automatisieren* vt to automate.
Automatisierung f automation.
Automatismus m automatism.
Auto-: ~mechaniker m car or motor mechanic; ~minute f minute by car, minute's drive.
Automobil nt -s, -e (dated, geh) motor-car, automobile (esp US, dated).
Automobil-: ~ausstellung f motor show; (ständige ~) car exhibition; ~bau m -s, no pl car or automobile (US) manufacture; ~club m automobile association.
Automobilist m (Sw, geh) (car) driver.
Automobil-: ~klub m siehe ~club; ~salon m motor show.
Auto-: ~modell nt (car) model; (Miniaturauto) model car; a~nom adj autonomous (auch fig); Nervensystem autonomic; ~nomie f autonomy (auch fig); ~nomist m autonomist; ~nummer f (car) number; ~öl nt motor oil; ~pilot m (Aviat) autopilot; vom ~piloten gesteuert werden to be on autopilot.
Autopsie f (Med) autopsy.
Autor m [au'toːrən] author.
Auto-: ~radio nt car radio; ~reifen m car tyre; ~reisezug m = motorail train; mit dem ~reisezug fahren to go by motorail.
Autorenkollektiv nt team of authors.
Auto-: ~rennbahn f motor-racing circuit; ~rennen nt (motor) race; (Rennsport) motor racing; ~rennsport m motor racing.
Autorenregister nt index of authors.
Autoreparaturwerkstatt f garage, car repair shop.
Autorin f authoress.
Autorisation f (geh) authorization.
autorisieren* vt to authorize.
autoritär adj authoritarian.
Autoritarismus m (geh) authoritarianism.
Autorität f (alle Bedeutungen) authority.
autoritativ adj (geh) authoritative.
Autoritäts-: a~gläubig adj trusting in authority; ~gläubigkeit f trust in authority; a~hörig adj slavishly following authority; a~hörig sein to be a slave to authority.
Autor-: ~korrektur f (Korrekturfahne) author's proof; (Änderung) author's correction; ~schaft f authorship.
Auto-: ~schalter m drive-in counter; ~schlange f queue (Brit) or line of cars; ~schlosser m panel beater; ~schlosserei f body shop; ~skooter m dodgem or bumper car; ~spengler m (S Ger, Aus, Sw) siehe ~schlosser; ~spenglerei f (S Ger, Aus, Sw) siehe ~schlosserei; ~ sport m motor sport; ~stop(p) m (esp S Ger) hitch-hiking, hitching; ~stop(p) machen, per ~stop(p) fahren to hitch(-hike); ~straße f main road, highway (esp US).

~strich m (sl) prostitution to car-drivers; (Gegend) area where prostitutes are available for car-drivers; ~stunde f hour's drive; ~suggestion f autosuggestion; ~telefon nt car telephone; ~typie f autotypy; ~unfall m car accident; ~verkehr m motor traffic; ~verleih m, ~vermietung f car hire or rental; (Firma) car hire or rental firm; ~versicherung f car or motor insurance; ~werkstatt f garage, car repair shop (US); ~wrack nt (car) wreck, wrecked car; ~zoom nt (Phot) automatic zoom (lens); ~zubehör nt car or motor accessories pl; ~zug m siehe ~reisezug.
autsch interj (inf) ouch, ow.
auweh, auwei(a) interj oh dear.
Avance [a'vãːsə] f -, -n jdm ~n machen (geh) to make approaches to sb.
Avancement [avãsə'mãː] nt -s, -s (old) advancement.
avancieren* [avã'siːrən] vi aux sein (dated, geh) to advance (zu to).
Avant- [avã]: ~garde f (geh) (Art) avant-garde; (Pol) vanguard (fig); ~gardismus m avant-gardism; ~gardist m member of the avant-garde, avant-gardist; a~gardistisch adj avant-garde.
AvD [aːfau'deː] abbr of **Automobilclub von Deutschland**.
Ave-Maria ['aːvema'riːa] nt -(s), -(s) Ave Maria; (Gebet auch) Hail Mary.
Avers [a'vɛrs] m -es, -e face, obverse.
Aversion [avɛr'zioːn] f aversion (gegen to).
Aviarium [a'viaːrium] nt aviary.
Avis [a'viː] m or nt -, -, **Avis** [a'viːs] m or nt -es, -e (Comm) advice (Comm); (schriftlich) advice-note.
avisieren* [avi'ziːrən] vt to send notification of, to advise of.
Aviso [a'viːzo] nt -s, -s (Aus) siehe Avis.
Avitaminose [aviːtami'noːzə] f -, -n (Med) avitaminosis.
Avocado, Avokato [avo'kaːdo, -to] f -, -s avocado.
Axel m -s, - (Sport) axel.
axial adj axial.
Axiallager nt (Tech) axial or thrust bearing.
Axiologie f (Philos) axiology.
Axiom nt -s, -e axiom.
Axiomatik f, no pl axiomatics sing.
axiomatisch adj axiomatic.
Axt f -, ¨e axe (Brit), ax (US). sich wie eine or die ~ im Wald benehmen (fig inf) to behave like a peasant or boor; die ~ im Haus erspart den Zimmermann (Prov) self-help is the best help; die ~ an etw/an die Wurzel einer Sache legen (fig) to tear up the very roots of sth.
Axthieb m blow of the/an axe.
Azalea, Azalie [-iə] f -, -n (Bot) azalea.
Azetat nt acetate.
Azetatseide f acetate silk.
Azeton nt -s, no pl (Chem) siehe Aceton.
Azetylen nt -s, no pl (Chem) siehe Acetylen.
Azoren pl (Geog) Azores pl.
Azteke m -n, -n Aztec.
Aztekenreich nt Aztec empire.
Aztekin f Aztec.
aztekisch adj Aztec.
Azur m -s, no pl (poet) azure sky; (Farbe) azure.
azurblau, azurn (poet) adj azure(-blue).
azyklisch adj acyclic.

B

B, b [beː] nt -, - B, b; (Mus) (Ton) B flat; (Versetzungszeichen) flat. B-dur/b-Moll (the key of) B flat major/minor.
Baas m -es, -e (Naut) boss.
babbeln vi (inf) to babble; (Schwätzer auch) to chatter.
Babel nt -s (Bibl) Babel; (fig) (Sünden~) sink of iniquity; (von Sprachen) melting pot.
Baby ['beːbi] nt -s, -s baby.
Baby- in cpds baby; ~ausstattung f layette; ~doll nt -(s), -s baby-dolls pl, baby-doll pyjamas pl; ~korb m bassinet.
Babylon ['baːbylon] nt -s Babylon.
babylonisch adj Babylonian. eine ~e Sprachverwirrung a Babel of languages; der B~e Turm the Tower of Babel; die B~e Gefangenschaft Babylonian captivity.
Baby-: b~sitten vi insep to babysit; ~sitter(in) f) m -s, - babysitter; ~speck m (inf) puppy fat; ~waage f scales pl for weighing babies.
Baccara nt -s, no pl (Cards) siehe Bakkarat.
Bacchanal [baxa'naːl] nt -s, -ien [-liən] (a) (in der Antike) Bacchanalia. (b) pl -e (geh) bacchanal, drunken orgy.
Bacchant(in f) [ba'xant(in)] m bacchant.
bacchantisch [ba'xantiʃ] adj bacchanalian.

bacchisch ['baxiʃ] adj (Myth) Bacchic.
Bacchus ['baxus] m - (Myth) Bacchus. dem ~ huldigen (geh) to imbibe (form).
Bach m -(e)s, ¨e stream (auch fig), brook; (Naut, Aviat sl: Gewässer) drink (inf).
bach|ab adv (Sw) downstream. etw ~ schicken (fig inf) to throw sth away; ~ gehen (fig inf) to go up the creek (inf) or spout (inf).
Bache f -, -n (wild) sow.
Bächelchen nt dim of Bach.
Bachforelle f brown trout.
Bächlein nt dim of Bach (small) stream, brooklet. ein ~ machen (baby-talk) to do a wee-wee (baby-talk).
Bachstelze f -, -n wagtail.
back adv (Naut) back.
Back[1] f -, -en (Naut) (a) (Deck) forecastle, fo'c'sle. (b) (Schüssel) dixie, mess-tin, mess kit (US); (Tafel) mess table; (Besatzung) mess.
Back[2] [bɛk] m -s, -s (Ftbl dated) back.
Backblech nt baking tray.
Backbord nt -(e)s, no pl (Naut) port (side). von ~ nach Steuerbord from port to starboard; über ~ over the port side.

backbord(s) adv (Naut) on the port side. (nach) ~ to port.

Bäckchen nt (little) cheek.

Backe f -, -n (a) (Wange) cheek. mit vollen ~n kauen to chew or eat with bulging cheeks; au ~! (dated inf) oh dear! (b) (inf: Hinter~) buttock, cheek. (c) (von Schraubstock) jaw; (Brems~) (bei Auto) shoe; (bei Fahrrad) block; (von Skibindung) toe-piece; (von Gewehr) cheek-piece.

backen¹ pret backte or (old) buk, ptp gebacken 1 vt to bake; Brot, Kuchen auch to make; (dial: braten) Fisch, Eier etc to fry; (dial: dörren) Obst to dry. **frisch/knusprig gebackenes Brot** fresh (baked)/crusty bread; **wir ~ alles selbst** we do all our own baking; **gebackener Fisch** fried fish; (im Ofen) baked fish; **ein frisch gebackener Ehemann** (inf) a newly-wed; **ein frisch gebackener Arzt** (inf) a newly-fledged doctor.

2 vi (Brot, Kuchen) to bake; (dial: braten) to fry; (dial: dörren) to dry. **der Kuchen muß noch 20 Minuten ~** the cake will have to be in the oven or will take another 20 minutes; **sie bäckt gern** she enjoys baking.

backen² (dial inf) 1 vi (kleben: Schnee etc) to stick (an + dat to), to cake (an + dat on, onto). 2 vt **etw an etw** (acc) ~ to stick sth onto sth.

Backen-: ~bart m sideboards pl, sideburns pl, (side) whiskers pl; ~bremse f (bei Auto) shoe brake; (bei Fahrrad) block brake; ~knochen m cheekbone; ~streich m (old) slap on the face; ~tasche f (Zool) cheek pouch; ~zahn m molar.

Bäcker m -s, - baker. ~ lernen to learn the baker's trade, to be an apprentice baker; ~ werden to be or become a baker; **beim ~** at the baker's; **zum ~ gehen** to go to the baker's.

Back|erbsen pl (Aus, S Ger: Cook) small round noodles eaten in soup.

Bäckerei f (a) (Bäckerladen) baker's (shop); (Backstube) bakery. (b) (Gewerbe) bakery, baking trade. (c) (inf: das Backen) baking. (d) (Aus) (Gebäck) pastries pl; (Kekse) biscuits pl.

Bäcker-: ~geselle m (journeyman) baker; ~junge m baker's boy; (Lehrling) baker's apprentice; ~laden m baker's (shop); ~meister m master baker.

Bäckersfrau f baker's wife.

Backfeige f (dial) siehe **Ohrfeige**.

Back-: b~fertig adj oven-ready; ~fett nt cooking fat; ~fisch m (a) fried fish; (b) (dated) teenager, teenage girl; ~form f baking tin; (für Kuchen auch) cake tin.

Background ['bɛkgraunt] m -s, -s background.

Back-: ~hähnchen, ~hendl (S Ger, Aus), ~huhn, ~hühnchen nt roast chicken.

Backhand ['bɛkhɛnt] f or m -, -s (Sport) backhand.

Back-: ~mulde f siehe ~trog; ~obst nt dried fruit; ~ofen m oven; **es ist heiß wie in einem ~ofen** it's like an oven; ~pfeife f (dial) slap on or round (inf) the face; ~pfeifengesicht nt (dial) siehe **Ohrfeigengesicht**; ~pflaume f prune; ~pulver nt baking powder; ~rohr nt (Aus), ~röhre f oven.

Backstein m brick.

Backstein-: ~bau m brick building; ~gotik f Gothic architecture built in brick.

Back-: ~stube f bakery; ~trog m kneading or dough trough, dough tray, hutch; ~vorschrift f baking instructions pl; ~waren pl bread, cakes and pastries pl; ~werk nt (old) cakes and pastries pl; ~zeit f baking time.

Bad nt -(e)s, ˝er (a) (Wannen~, Badewanne, Phot) bath; (das Baden) bathing. **ein ~ nehmen** to have or take a bath; (sich dat) **ein ~ einlaufen lassen** to run (oneself) a bath; **jdm ˝er verschreiben** (Med) to prescribe sb a course of (therapeutic) baths.

(b) (im Meer etc) bathe, swim; (das Baden) bathing, swimming.

(c) (Badezimmer) bathroom. **Zimmer mit ~** room with (private) bath.

(d) (Schwimm~) (swimming) pool or bath(s). **die städtischen ˝er** the public baths.

(e) (Heil~) spa; (See~) (seaside) resort. **ins ~ reisen** to go to a spa.

Bade-: ~anstalt f (public) swimming baths pl; ~anzug m swimming costume, swimsuit; ~arzt m spa doctor; ~gast m (a) (im Kurort) spa visitor; (b) (im Schwimmbad) bather, swimmer; ~gelegenheit f gibt es dort eine ~gelegenheit? can one swim or bathe there?; ~(hand)tuch nt bath towel; ~haube f (dated) siehe ~kappe; ~hose f (swimming or bathing) trunks pl; **eine ~hose** a pair of (swimming or bathing) trunks; ~kabine f changing cubicle; ~kappe f swimming cap or hat, bathing cap; ~kostüm nt (geh) swimming or bathing costume; ~laken nt bath sheet; ~mantel m beach robe; (Morgenmantel) bathrobe, towelling dressing gown; ~matte f bathmat; ~meister m (im Schwimmbad) (pool) attendant; (am Strand) lifeguard; ~mütze f siehe ~kappe.

baden 1 vi (a) to have a bath, to bath. **hast du schon gebadet?** have you had your bath already?; **warm/kalt ~** to have a hot/cold bath.

(b) (im Meer, Schwimmbad etc) to swim, to bathe. **sie hat im Meer gebadet** she swam or bathed or had a swim in the sea; **die B~den** the bathers; ~ **gehen** to go swimming or (einmal) for a swim.

(c) (inf) ~ **gehen** to come a cropper (inf); **wenn das passiert, gehe ich ~** I'll be for it if that happens (inf).

2 vt (a) Kind etc to bath. **er ist als Kind zu heiß gebadet worden** (hum) he was dropped on the head as a child (hum); **in Schweiß gebadet** bathed in sweat.

(b) Augen, Wunde etc to bathe.

3 vr to bathe, to have a bath.

Baden nt -s (Geog) Baden.

Badener(in f**), Badenser(in** f**)** (inf) m -s, - person or man/

woman from Baden. **er ist ~** he comes from Baden.

Badenixe f (hum) bathing beauty or belle.

Bade-: ~ofen m boiler; ~ort m (Kurort) spa; (Seebad) (seaside) resort; ~platz m place for bathing.

Bader m -s, - (old) barber (old); (dial: Arzt) village quack (hum).

Baderaum m bathroom.

Bäderbehandlung f medical treatment using therapeutic baths.

Badereise f (dated) trip to a spa.

Bäder-: ~kunde f balneology; ~kur f siehe ~behandlung.

Bade-: ~sachen pl swimming things pl; ~saison f swimming season; (in Kurort) spa season; ~salz nt bath salts pl; ~schaum m bubble bath; ~schuh m bathing shoe; ~schwamm m sponge; ~strand m (bathing) beach; ~stube f (N Ger) bathroom; ~trikot nt swimming or bathing costume; ~tuch nt siehe ~(hand)tuch; ~verbot nt ban on bathing; ~wanne f bath(tub); ~wärter m swimming pool attendant; ~wasser nt bath water; ~wetter nt weather warm enough for bathing or swimming; ~zeit f bathing or swimming season; ~zeug nt swimming gear, swimming or bathing things pl; ~zimmer nt bathroom; ~zusatz m bath salts, bubble bath etc.

badisch adj Baden attr; Wein etc auch from Baden; Dialekt auch of Baden; Landschaft auch around Baden. **das Dorf ist ~ or im B~en** the village is in Baden.

Badminton ['bɛtmɪntən] nt -, no pl badminton.

baff adj pred (inf) ~ **sein** to be flabbergasted.

BAFöG ['baːføk] nt -, no pl abbr (Univ sl) **er kriegt ~** he gets a grant.

Bagage [ba'gaːʒə] f -, no pl (a) (old, Sw, inf: Gepäck) luggage, baggage. **du bringst ja wieder eine ~ mit!** (inf) just look at the luggage you've got again!

(b) (dated inf) (Gesindel) crowd, crew (inf), gang (inf); (Familie) pack (inf). **die ganze ~** the whole bloody lot (sl).

Bagatell f -, -en (Aus inf) siehe **Bagatelle**.

Bagatelldelikt nt petty or minor offence.

Bagatelle f trifle, bagatelle; (Mus) bagatelle.

bagatellisieren* 1 vt to trivialize, to minimize. 2 vi to trivialize.

Bagatell-: ~sache f (Jur) petty or minor case; ~schaden m minor or superficial damage.

Bagdad ['bakdat, bak'daːt] nt -s Baghdad.

Bagger m -s, - excavator; (für Schlamm) dredger.

Baggerführer m driver of an/the excavator/dredger.

baggern vti Graben to excavate, to dig; Fahrrinne to dredge.

Bagger-: ~schaufel f excavator shovel; ~see m artificial lake in gravel pit etc.

bah, bäh interj (a) (aus Schadenfreude) hee-hee (inf); (vor Ekel) ugh. (b) ~ **machen** (baby-talk: Schaf) to baa, to go baa.

Bählamm nt (baby-talk) baa-lamb (baby-talk).

Bahn f -, -en (a) (Weg) path, track; (von Fluß) course; (fig) course; (Fahr~) carriageway. ~ **frei!** make way!, (get) out of the way!; **jdm/einer Sache die ~ frei machen/ebnen** (fig) to clear/pave the way for sb/sth; **die ~ ist frei** (fig) the way is clear; **sich** (dat) ~ **brechen** (lit) to force one's way; (fig) to make headway; (Mensch) to forge ahead; **einer Sache** (dat) ~ **brechen** to open or pave the way for sth, to blaze the trail for sth; **sich auf neuen ~en bewegen** to break new or fresh ground; **in gewohnten ~en verlaufen** (fig) to go on in the same old way, to continue as before; **von der rechten ~ abkommen** (geh) to stray from the straight and narrow; **jdn auf die rechte ~ bringen** (fig) to put sb on the straight and narrow; **etw in die richtige ~ or die richtigen ~en lenken** (fig) to channel sth properly; **jdn aus der ~ werfen or schleudern** (fig) to throw sb off the track; (fig) to shatter sb; siehe **schief**.

(b) (Eisen~) railway, railroad (US); (Straßen~) tram, streetcar (US); (Zug) (der Eisen~, U-~) train; (der Straßen~) tram, streetcar (US); (~hof) station; (Verkehrsnetz, Verwaltung) railway usu pl, railroad (US). **mit der** or **per ~** by train or rail/tram; **frei ~** (Comm) carriage free to station of destination; **er ist or arbeitet bei der ~** he's with the railways or railroad (US), he works for or on the railways.

(c) (Sport) track; (für Pferderennen auch) course; (in Schwimmbecken) pool; (Kegel~) (bowling) alley; (für einzelne Teilnehmer) lane; (Schlitten~, Bob~) run.

(d) (Astron) orbit, path; (Raketen~, Geschoß~) (flight) path, trajectory. **werden sich unsere ~en noch einmal kreuzen?** will our paths ever cross again?

(e) (Stoff~, Tapeten~) length, strip.

(f) (Tech: von Werkzeug) face.

Bahn-: b~amtlich adj Tarife etc official railway or railroad (US) attr; ~anschluß m railway or railroad (US) connection or link; ~anschluß haben to be connected or linked to the railway or railroad (US) (system); ~arbeiter m railwayman, railroader (US); ~beamte(r) m railway or railroad (US) official; ~betriebswerk nt railway or railroad (US) depot; b~brechend adj pioneering; ~brechendes leisten to pioneer new developments; b~brechend sein/wirken to be pioneering; (Erfinder etc) to be a pioneer; ~brecher(in f) m pioneer; ~bus m bus run by railway company.

Bähnchen nt dim of **Bahn**.

Bahndamm m (railway) embankment.

bahnen vt Pfad to clear; Fußpfad to carve or channel out. **jdm/einer Sache den/einen Weg ~** to clear the/a way for sb/sth; (fig) to pave or prepare the way for sb/sth; **sich** (dat) **einen Weg ~** to fight or (lit auch) force one's way.

bahnenweise adv in lengths or strips.

Bahner m -s, - (inf) railwayman (Brit), railroad employee (US).

Bahn-: ~fahrt f rail journey; ~fracht f rail freight; b~frei adj (Comm) carriage free to station of destination; ~gelände nt railway or railroad (US) area; ~**gleis** nt railway or railroad (US) line; (von Straßen~) tram or streetcar (US) line.

Bahnhof m (railway or railroad (US)/bus/tram or streetcar US) station; (dated: Straßen~) tram or streetcar (US) depot. **am** or **auf dem** ~ at the station; ~ **Schöneberg** Schöneberg station; **ich verstehe nur** ~ (hum inf) it's as clear as mud (to me) (inf), it's all Greek to me (inf); **er wurde mit großem** ~ **empfangen** he was given the red carpet treatment, they rolled the red carpet out for him; **es wurde auf einen großen** ~ **verzichtet** they didn't bother with the red carpet treatment.

Bahnhof- (esp S Ger, Aus, Sw), **Bahnhofs-** in cpds station; ~**buffet** nt (esp Aus, Sw) station buffet; ~**gaststätte** f station restaurant; ~**halle** f (station) concourse; **in der** ~**halle** in the station; ~**mission** f charitable organisation for helping needy rail travellers; ~**platz** m station square; ~**uhr** f station clock; ~**vorplatz** m station forecourt; **sich auf dem** ~**vorplatz versammeln** to meet in front of the station; ~**vorstand** (Aus, Sw), ~**vorsteher** m stationmaster; ~**wirtschaft** f station bar; (~restaurant) station restaurant.

Bahn-: ~**körper** m track; **b~lagernd** adj (Comm) to be collected from the station; ~**linie** f (railway or railroad US) line or track; ~**meisterei** f railway or railroad (US) board; ~**netz** nt rail(way) or railroad (US) network; ~**polizei** f railway or railroad (US) police; ~**post** f travelling post office; ~**schranke** f, ~**schranken** m (Aus) level or grade (US) crossing barrier or gate; ~**steig** m platform; ~**steigkarte** f platform ticket; ~**strecke** f railway or railroad (US) route or line; ~**transport** m rail transport; (Güter) consignment sent by rail; ~**überführung** f railway or railroad (US) footbridge; ~**übergang** m level or grade (US) crossing; **beschrankter/unbeschrankter** ~**übergang** level crossing with gates/unguarded level crossing; ~**unterführung** f railway or railroad (US) underpass; ~**wärter** m (an ~**übergängen**) gatekeeper, (level crossing) attendant; (Streckenwärter) platelayer, trackman (US); ~**wärterhäuschen** nt gatekeeper's hut.

Bahre f -, -n (Kranken~) stretcher; (Toten~) bier.

Bahrtuch nt pall.

Bähschaf nt (baby-talk) siehe **Bählamm**.

Bai f -, en bay.

bairisch adj (Hist, Ling) Bavarian.

Baiser [bɛˈzeː] nt -s, -s meringue.

Baisse [ˈbɛːs(ə)] f -, -n (St Ex) fall; (plötzliche) slump. **auf (die)** ~ **spekulieren** to bear.

Baissespekulant m, **Baissier** [bɛˈsieː] m -s, -s bear.

Bajadere f -, -n bayadere.

Bajazzo m -s, -s clown.

Bajonett nt -(e)s, -e bayonet; siehe **fällen**.

Bajonett-: ~**fassung** f (Elec) bayonet fitting; ~**verschluß** m (Elec) bayonet socket.

Bajuware m -n, -n, **Bajuwarin** f (old, hum) Bavarian.

bajuwarisch adj (old, hum) Bavarian.

Bake f -, -n (Naut) marker buoy; (Aviat) beacon; (Verkehrszeichen) distance warning signal; (vor Bahnübergang, an Autobahn auch) countdown marker; (Surv) marker pole.

Bakelit ® nt -(e)s, no pl Bakelite ®.

Bakentonne f (Naut) beacon buoy.

Bakkarat [ˈbakara(t)] nt -s, no pl (Cards) baccarat.

Bakken m -(s), - (Ski) ski-jump.

Bakschisch nt -s, -e or -s baksheesh; (Bestechungsgeld) bribe, backhander (inf). ~ **geben** to give baksheesh/a bribe or backhander.

Bakterie [-riə] f -, -n usu pl germ, bacterium (spec). ~**n** germs pl, bacteria pl.

bakteriell adj bacterial, bacteria attr. ~ **verursacht** caused by germs or bacteria.

Bakterien-: ~**filter** m bacteria filter; ~**krieg** m germ or biological warfare; ~**kultur** f bacteria culture; ~**träger** m carrier; ~**züchtung** f growing or culturing of bacteria.

Bakteriologe m, **Bakteriologin** f bacteriologist.

Bakteriologie f bacteriology.

bakteriologisch adj Forschung, Test bacteriological; Krieg biological.

Bakterium nt (form) siehe **Bakterie**.

bakterizid adj germicidal, bactericidal.

Bakterizid nt -s, -e germicide, bactericide.

Balalaika f -, -s or **Balalaiken** balalaika.

Balance [baˈlãːs(ə)] f -, -n balance, equilibrium. **die** ~ **halten/verlieren** to keep/lose one's balance.

Balance|akt [baˈlãːs(ə)-] m (lit) balancing or tightrope or high-wire act; (fig) balancing act.

balancieren* [balãˈsiːrən] 1 vi aux sein to balance; (fig) to achieve a balance (zwischen +dat between). **über etw** (acc) ~ to balance one's way across sth. 2 vt to balance.

Balancierstange f (balancing) pole.

balbieren* vt (inf): **jdn über den Löffel** ~ to pull the wool over sb's eyes, to lead sb by the nose (inf).

bald 1 adv, comp eher or ˜er (old, dial), superl am ehesten (a) (schnell, in Kürze) soon. **er kommt** ~ he'll be coming soon; ~ **ist Weihnachten/Winter** it will soon be Christmas/winter; ~ **darauf** soon afterwards, a little later; (allzu)~ (all) too soon; **so** ~ **wie** or **als möglich, möglichst** ~ as soon as possible; **nicht so** ~ not in the near future; **das gibt es so** ~ **nicht noch einmal** you won't find one of those again in a hurry; (besonderes Ereignis) that won't happen again in a hurry; **wirst du wohl** ~ **ruhig sein?** will you just be quiet!; **wird's** ~? get a move on; **bis** ~! see you soon.

(b) (fast) almost, nearly. **sie platzt** ~ **vor Neugier** she's almost bursting with curiosity; **das ist** ~ **nicht mehr schön** that is really beyond a joke; siehe **sobald**.

2 conj (geh) ~ ..., ~ ... one moment ..., the next ..., now ..., now ...; ~ **hier**, ~ **da** now here, now there; ~ **so**, ~ **so** now this way, now that.

Baldachin [-xiːn] m -s, -e canopy, baldachin; (Archit) baldachin, baldaquin.

Bälde f: **in** ~ in the near future.

baldig adj attr, no comp quick, speedy; Antwort, Wiedersehen early. **wir hoffen auf Ihr** ~**es Kommen** we hope you will come soon; **auf** ~**es Wiedersehen!** (hope) to see you soon!

baldigst adv superl of **baldig** (form) as soon as possible, without delay.

baldmöglichst adv as soon as possible.

baldowern* vti (inf) siehe **ausbaldowern**.

Baldrian m -s, -e valerian.

Baldriantropfen pl valerian (drops pl).

Baldur m -s (Myth) Balder.

Balearen pl die ~ the Balearic Islands pl.

Balg¹ m -(e)s, ˜e (a) (Tierhaut) pelt, skin; (von Vogel) skin; (inf: Bauch) belly (inf); (einer Puppe) body. **einem Tier den** ~ **abziehen** to skin an animal; **sich** (dat) **den** ~ **vollschlagen** or **vollstopfen** (inf) to stuff oneself (inf); **ich habe eine Wut im** ~ (inf) I'm mad or livid; siehe **rücken**.

(b) (Blase~, Phot, Rail) bellows pl. **die** ˜**e treten** to work the bellows.

Balg² m or nt -(e)s, ˜er (pej inf: Kind) brat (pej inf).

Balgen m -s, - (Phot) bellows pl.

balgen vr to scrap (um over).

Balgerei f scrap, tussle. **hört jetzt auf mit der** ~! stop scrapping!

Balkan m -s (a) (~**halbinsel**, ~**länder**) der ~ the Balkans pl; **auf dem** ~ in the Balkans; **dort herrschen Zustände wie auf dem** ~ (fig inf) things are in a terrible state there. (b) (~**gebirge**) Balkan Mountains pl.

Balkanhalb|insel f Balkan Peninsula.

balkanisch adj Balkan. **dort herrschen** ~**e Zustände** (fig) things are in a terrible state there.

balkanisieren* vt to Balkanize.

Balkanisierung f Balkanization.

Bälkchen nt dim of **Balken**.

Balken m -s, - (a) (Holz~, Schwebe~) beam; (Stütz~) prop, shore; (Quer~) joist, crossbeam; (Sport: bei Hürdenlauf) rail. **der** ~ **im eigenen Auge** (Bibl) the beam in one's own eye; **lügen, daß sich die** ~ **biegen** (inf) to lie in one's teeth, to tell a pack of lies; **Wasser hat keine** ~ (Prov) not everyone can walk on water.

(b) (Strich) bar; (Her auch) fess(e); (Uniformstreifen) stripe.

(c) (an Waage) beam.

Balken-: ~**brücke** f girder bridge; ~**decke** f ceiling with wooden beams; ~**holz** nt (piece of) (squared) timber; (~gerüst) timbers pl, beams pl; ~**konstruktion** f timber-frame construction; ~**überschrift** f (Press) banner headline; ~**waage** f (beam) balance; ~**werk** nt timbering, timbers pl, beams pl.

Balkon [balˈkɔŋ, (Aus) balˈkoːn] m -s, -s or -e balcony; (Theat) (dress) circle. ~ **sitzen** (Theat) to have seats in the (dress) circle.

Balkon-: ~**möbel** pl garden furniture sing; ~**tür** f French window(s); ~**zimmer** nt room with a balcony.

Ball¹ m -(e)s, ˜e ball. ~ **spielen** to play (with a) ball; **am** ~ **sein** (lit) to have the ball, to be in possession of the ball; **bei jdm am** ~ **sein** (fig) to be in with sb; **immer am** ~ **sein** (fig) to be on the ball; **am** ~ **bleiben** (lit) to keep (possession of) the ball; (fig: auf dem neuesten Stand bleiben) to stay on the ball; **bei jdm am** ~ **bleiben** (fig) to keep in with sb; **er bemüht sich, bei ihr am** ~ **zu bleiben** he is trying to keep in the running with her; **hart am** ~ **bleiben** to stick at it; **jdm den** ~ **zuspielen** (lit) to pass (the ball) to sb; **jdm/sich gegenseitig die** ˜**e zuspielen** or **zuwerfen** (fig) to feed sb/each other lines; **einen** ~ **machen** (Billard) to pocket a ball; **der glutrote** ~ **der Sonne** (poet) the sun's fiery orb (poet).

Ball² m -(e)s, ˜e (Tanzfest) ball. **auf dem** ~ at the ball.

balla-balla adj pred (sl) mad, crazy, nuts (inf).

Ballade f ballad.

balladenhaft, balladesk 1 adj balladic, ballad-like. 2 adv in a balladic or ballad-like way or manner.

Balladensänger m balladier, ballad-singer.

Ballast [or -ˈ-] m -(e)s, (rare) -e (Naut, Aviat) ballast; (fig) burden, encumbrance; (in Büchern) padding. ~ **abwerfen** or **über Bord werfen** (lit) to discharge or shed ballast; (fig) to get rid of a burden or an encumbrance; **mit** ~ **beladen** or **beschweren** to ballast, to load with ballast; **jdn/etw als** ~ **empfinden** to find sb/sth (to be) a burden or an encumbrance.

Ballaststoffe pl (Med) roughage sing.

Ballbub m (S Ger, Aus, Sw) siehe **Balljunge**.

Bällchen nt dim of **Ball¹**.

Ballen m -s, - (a) bale; (Kaffee~) sack. **in** ~ **verpacken** to bale. (b) (Anat: an Daumen, Zehen) ball; (an Pfote) pad. (c) (Med: am Fußknochen) bunion.

ballen 1 vt Faust to clench; Papier to crumple (into a ball); Lehm etc to press (into a ball); siehe **geballt, Faust**. 2 vr (Menschenmenge) to crowd; (Wolken) to gather, to build up; (Verkehr) to build up; (Faust) to clench.

ballenweise adv in bales.

Ballerei f (inf) shoot-out (inf), shoot-up (inf).

Ballerina, Ballerine (rare) f -, **Ballerinen** ballerina, ballet dancer.

Ballermann m -s, **Ballermänner** (sl) iron (sl), gun.

ballern 1 vi (inf) to shoot, to fire; (Schuß) to ring out. **gegen die Tür** ~ to hammer on the door. 2 vt Stein etc to hurl; Tür to slam. **jdm eine** ~ (sl) to sock sb one (inf); **du kriegst gleich eine geballert** (sl) I'll sock you one (inf).

Ballett nt -(e)s, -e ballet. beim ~ sein (inf) to be (a dancer) with the ballet, to be a ballet dancer; zum ~ gehen to become a ballet dancer.

Ballettänzer(in f) m ballet dancer.

Balletteuse [-'tø:zə] f (usu pej) ballet dancer.

Ballett- in cpds ballet; ~**meister** m ballet master, maître de ballet; ~**ratte** f (inf) ballet pupil; ~**röckchen** nt tutu; ~**truppe** f ballet (company).

Ball-: b~**förmig** adj ball-shaped, round; ~**führung** f (Sport) ball control; ~**gefühl** nt (Sport) feel for the ball; ~**haus** nt (old) real tennis court.

Ballistik f, no pl ballistics sing.

ballistisch adj ballistic.

Ball-: ~**junge** m (Tennis) ball boy; ~**kleid** nt ball dress or gown; ~**königin** f belle of the ball; ~**künstler** m (Ftbl) artist with the ball.

Ballon [ba'lɔŋ, (Aus, Sw) ba'lo:n] m -s, -s or -e **(a)** balloon. **(b)** (Chem) carboy, demijohn. **(c)** (sl: Kopf) nut (inf). jdm eins auf den ~ geben to hit sb on the nut (inf); einen roten ~ kriegen to go bright red.

Ballon- [ba'lo:n-]: ~**mütze** f baker's boy cap; ~**reifen** m balloon tyre.

Ball-: ~**saal** m ballroom; ~**schani** m -s, - (Aus inf) siehe ~**junge**; ~**schuh** m evening or dancing shoe; ~**spiel** nt ball game; ~**spielen** nt -s, no pl playing ball; „~**spielen verboten**" "no ball games"; ~**technik** f (Sport) technique with the ball; ~**toilette** f: in großer ~**toilette** in full evening dress; ~**treter** m -s, - (inf) footballer.

Ballung f concentration; (von Truppen auch) massing.

Ballungs-: ~**gebiet** nt, ~**raum** m conurbation; ~**zentrum** nt centre (of population, industry etc).

Ballwechsel m (Sport) rally.

Balneologie f balneology.

Bal paradox m - -, -s - ball at which women ask men to dance.

Bal paré m - -, -s -s grand ball.

Balsaholz nt balsa wood.

Balsam m -s, -e balsam, balm (liter); (fig) balm. ~ in jds Wunden (acc) träufeln (liter) to pour balm on sb's wounds; die Zeit ist ein heilender ~ (liter) time is a great healer.

balsamieren* vt siehe einbalsamieren.

balsamisch adj (liter) **(a)** (duftend) balmy (liter), fragrant. **(b)** (lindernd) soothing.

Balte m -n, -n, **Baltin** f person or man/woman from the Baltic. er ist ~ he comes from the Baltic.

Baltikum nt -s das ~ the Baltic.

baltisch adj Baltic attr.

Balustrade f balustrade.

Balz f -, -en **(a)** (Paarungsspiel) courtship display. **(b)** (Paarungszeit) mating season.

balzen vi to perform the courtship display; (pej: Sänger) to croon.

Balz-: ~**ruf** m mating call or cry; ~**zeit** f siehe Balz (b).

Bambi[1] nt -s, -s (inf: Rehkitz) bambi.

Bambi[2] m -s, -s Bambi (West German film award).

Bambino m -s, **Bambini** or (inf) -s (inf) bambino.

Bambule f -, -n (sl) ructions pl. ~ machen to go on the rampage.

Bambus m -ses or -, -se bamboo.

Bambus-: ~**rohr** nt bamboo cane; ~**sprossen** pl bamboo shoots pl; ~**stab** m (Sport) bamboo (vaulting) pole; ~**vorhang** m (Pol) bamboo curtain.

Bammel m -s, no pl (inf) **(einen)** ~ vor jdm/etw haben to be nervous or (stärker) scared of sb/sth.

bammeln vi (inf) to swing, to dangle (an +dat, von from).

banal adj banal, trite.

banalisieren* vt to trivialize.

Banalität f **(a)** no pl banality, triteness. **(b)** usu pl (Äußerung) platitude. ~**en** äußern to utter platitudes.

Banane f -, -n banana.

Bananen-: ~**dampfer** m banana boat; ~**republik** f (Pol pej) banana republic; ~**schale** f banana skin; ~**stecker** m jack plug.

Banause m -n, -n (pej) peasant (inf); (Kultur- auch) philistine.

Banausen-: b~**haft** adj philistine; ~**tum** nt, no pl (pej) philistinism.

banausisch adj philistine.

band pret of binden.

Band[1] nt -(e)s, ~er **(a)** (Seiden~ etc) ribbon; (Isolier~, Maß~, Ziel~) tape; (Haar~, Hut~) band; (Schürzen~) string; (Tech: zur Verpackung) (metal) band; (Faß~) hoop; (Art: Ornament) band. das Blaue ~ the Blue Riband; das silberne ~ des Nils (liter) the silver ribbon of the Nile. **(b)** (Ton~) (recording) tape. etw auf ~ aufnehmen to tape or (tape-)record sth; etw auf ~ sprechen/diktieren to record sth on tape/dictate sth onto tape. **(c)** (Fließ~) conveyor belt; (als Einrichtung) production line; (Montage~) assembly line; (in Autowerk) track (inf). am ~ arbeiten or stehen to work on the conveyor belt etc; vom ~ laufen to come off the conveyor belt etc; ein neues Auto auf ~ legen (Ind inf) to put a new car into production; am laufenden ~ (fig) non-stop, continuously; es gab Ärger am laufenden ~ there was non-stop or continuous trouble; etw am laufenden ~ tun to keep on doing sth. **(d)** (Rad) wavelength, frequency band. auf dem 44m-~ senden to broadcast on the 44m band. **(e)** (Anat) usu pl ligament. **(f)** (Baubeschlag) hinge.

Band[2] nt -(e)s, -e (liter) **(a)** das ~ der Freundschaft/Liebe etc the bonds or ties of friendship/love etc; familiäre ~e family ties; mit jdm freundschaftliche ~e anknüpfen to become or make friends with sb; zarte ~e knüpfen sich an Cupid is at work; zarte ~e knüpfen to start a romance.

(b) ~e pl (Fesseln) bonds pl, fetters pl; (fig auch) shackles pl; jdn in ~e schlagen to clap or put sb in irons.

Band[3] m -(e)s, ~e (Buch~) volume. ein gewaltiger ~ a mighty tome; darüber könnte man ~e schreiben/erzählen you could write volumes or a book about that; mit etw ~e füllen to write volumes about sth; das spricht ~e that speaks volumes.

Band[4] [bɛnt] f -, -s (Mus) band; (Beat~ auch) group.

Bandage [-'da:ʒə] f -, -n bandage. mit harten ~n kämpfen/verhandeln (fig inf) to fight/negotiate with no holds barred; das sind harte ~n (fig inf) that is really tough.

bandagieren* [-'ʒi:rən] vt to bandage (up).

Band-: ~**aufnahme** f tape-recording; ~**aufnahmegerät** nt tape-recorder; ~**breite** f (a) (Rad) waveband, frequency range; (b) (von Meinungen etc) range; (c) (Fin) (range of) fluctuation or variation.

Bändchen nt dim of Band[1] (a), Band[3].

Bande[1] f -, -n gang; (Schmuggler~) band; (inf: Gruppe) bunch (inf), crew (inf).

Bande[2] f -, -n (Sport) (von Eisbahn) barrier; (von Reitbahn auch) fence; (Billard) cushion; (von Kegelbahn) edge. die Kugel an die ~ spielen to play the ball off the cushion/edge.

Band|eisen nt metal hoop.

Bändel m or nt -s, - (esp Sw) siehe Bendel. jdn am ~ haben or führen (dated inf) to be able to twist sb round one's little finger (inf).

Banden-: ~**bekämpfung** f (Mil sl) guerilla warfare; ~**chef** (inf), ~**führer** m gang-leader; ~**diebstahl** m (Jur) gang robbery; ~**krieg** m gang war.

Banderole f -, -n tax or revenue seal.

Bänderzerrung f (Med) pulled ligament.

Band-: ~**filter** m or nt (Rad) band-pass filter; ~**förderer** m conveyor belt.

-bändig adj suf -volume. eine drei~e Ausgabe a three-volume edition, an edition in three volumes.

bändigen vt (zähmen) to tame; Brand to bring under control; (niederhalten) Menschen, Tobenden etc to (bring under) control, to subdue; (zügeln) Leidenschaften etc to (bring under) control, to master; Wut to control; Naturgewalten to harness; (hum) temperamentvolle Frau to tame; Kinder to (bring under) control. du mußt lernen, dich zu ~ you must learn to control yourself.

Bändiger m -s, - (animal) tamer.

Bändigung m, no pl siehe vt taming; controlling, subduing; mastering; harnessing; taming.

Bandit m -en, -en bandit, brigand; (fig pej) brigand. einarmiger ~ one-armed bandit.

Banditen-: ~**tum**, ~**(un)wesen** nt banditry.

Bandkeramik f (Archeol) ribbon ware, band ceramics pl.

Bändl nt -s, - (esp Aus) siehe Bendel.

Bandleader ['bɛntli:dɐ] m -s, - band leader.

Band-: ~**maß** nt tape measure; ~**nudeln** pl ribbon noodles pl.

Bandoneon, Bandonion nt -s, -s bandoneon, bandonion.

Band-: ~**säge** f band-saw; ~**scheibe** f (Anat) (intervertebral) disc; er hat's an or mit der ~**scheibe** (inf) he has slipped a disc or has a slipped disc; ~**scheibenschaden**, ~**scheibenvorfall** m slipped disc; ~**stahl** m strip or band steel; ~**werk** nt (Art) siehe Flechtwerk; ~**wurm** m tapeworm; ein ~**wurm** von einem Satz (hum) an endless or never-ending sentence; ~**wurmsatz** m (inf) long or lengthy sentence.

Bangbüx f -, -en (N Ger inf) scaredy-cat (inf).

bang(e) adj, comp -er or ~er, superl -ste(r, s) or ~ste(r, s) **(a)** attr (ängstlich) scared, frightened; (vor jdm auch) afraid. mir ist ~e vor ihm/der Prüfung I'm scared or frightened or afraid of him/scared or frightened of the exam; das wird schon klappen, da ist mir gar nicht ~(e) it will be all right, I am quite sure of it; jdm ~e machen to scare or frighten sb; ~e machen or B~emachen gilt nicht (inf) you can't scare me, you won't put the wind up me (inf); du bist gar nicht ~e you've got a nerve; siehe angst.

(b) (geh: beklommen) uneasy; Augenblicke, Stunden auch anxious, worried (um about). es wurde ihr ~ ums Herz her heart sank, she got a sinking feeling; ihr wurde ~ und ~er she became more and more afraid; eine ~e Ahnung a sense of foreboding.

(c) (S Ger) ihr war ~ nach dem Kinde she longed or yearned (liter) for the child or to be with the child.

Bange f -, no pl (esp N Ger) ~ haben to be scared or frightened (vor +dat of); nur keine ~! (inf) don't worry or be afraid.

bangen (geh) **1** vi **(a)** (Angst haben) to be afraid (vor +dat of). es bangt mir, mir bangt vor ihm I'm afraid or frightened of him, I fear him.

(b) (sich sorgen) to worry, to be worried (um about). um jds Leben ~ to fear for sb's life.

(c) (dial, liter) nach jdm/etw ~ to long or yearn (liter) for sb/sth.

2 vr to be worried or anxious (um about).

Bangigkeit f (Furcht) nervousness; (Sorge) anxiety; (Beklemmung) apprehension. nur keine ~! don't be nervous or worried.

Bangladesch nt -s Bangladesh.

bänglich adj (geh) nervous.

Bangnis f (geh) anxiety, anxiousness no pl.

Banjo ['banjo, 'bendʒo, 'bandʒo] nt -s, -s banjo.

Bank[1] f -, ~e **(a)** bench; (mit Lehne auch) seat; (Schul~, an langem Tisch auch) form; (Kirchen~) pew; (Parlaments~) bench; (Anklage~) dock. auf or in der ersten/letzten ~ on the front/back bench etc; er predigte vor leeren ~en he preached to an empty church; die Debatte fand vor leeren ~en statt the debate took place in an empty house; **(alle) durch die ~** (inf) every single or last one, the whole lot (of them) (inf); etw auf die lange ~ schieben (inf) to put sth off.

(b) (*Arbeitstisch*) (work) bench; (*Dreh~*) lathe.
(c) (*Sand~*) sandbank, sandbar; (*Nebel~, Wolken~*) bank; (*Austern~*) bed; (*Korallen~*) reef; (*Geol*) layer, bed.
(d) (*Wrestling*) crouch (position).

Bank² *f -, -en* (a) (*Comm*) bank. **Geld auf der ~ liegen haben** to have money in the bank; **bei der ~** at the bank; **ein Konto bei einer ~ eröffnen** to open an account with a bank; **bei der ~ arbeiten** *or* **sein** (*inf*) to work for the bank, to be with the bank.
(b) (*bei Glücksspielen*) bank. **(die) ~ halten** (*inf*) to hold *or* be the bank, to be banker; **die ~ sprengen** to break the bank.

Bank-: **~angestellte(r)** *mf,* **~beamte(r)** *m* (*dated*) bank employee; **~anweisung** *f* banker's order.

Bänkchen *nt dim of* **Bank¹(a).**

Bank-: **~direktor** *m* director of a/the bank; **~einbruch** *m* bank raid; **~einlage** *f* (*Comm*) bank deposit.

Bänkel-: **~lied** *nt* street ballad; **~sang** *m* ballad; **~sänger** *m* ballad-singer, minstrel.

Bankenviertel *nt* banking area.

Banker *m -s, -* (*inf*) banker.

Bankerott *m -(e)s, -e siehe* **Bankrott.**

bankerott *adj siehe* **bankrott.**

Bankert *m -s, -e* (*old pej*) bastard.

Bankett¹ *nt -(e)s, -e,* **Bankette** *f* (a) (*an Straßen*) verge, shoulder (*US*); (*an Autobahnen*) (hard) shoulder. „~e nicht befahrbar", „weiche ~e" "soft verges *or* shoulder (*US*)". (b) (*Build*) footing.

Bankett² *nt -(e)s, -e* (*Festessen*) banquet.

Bank-: **~fach** *nt* (a) (*Beruf*) banking, banking profession; **im ~fach** in banking *or* the banking profession; (b) (*Schließfach*) safe-deposit box; **~filiale** *f* branch of a bank; **~gebäude** *nt* bank; **~geheimnis** *nt* confidentiality in banking; **~geschäft** *nt* (a) banking transaction; (b) *no pl* (**~wesen**) banking world; **~guthaben** *nt* bank balance; **~halter** *m* (*bei Glücksspielen*) bank, banker; **~haus** *nt* **~haus Grün & Co** Grün & Co., Bankers.

Bankier *[-'kie:] m -s, -s* banker.

Bank-: **~kaufmann** *m* (qualified) bank clerk; **~konto** *nt* bank account; **~kredit** *m* bank loan; **~leitzahl** *f* bank code number; **~leute** *pl* (*inf*) bankers *pl*; **~nachbar** *m* (*Sch*) **sie ist mein ~nachbar** I sit next to her (at school); **~note** *f* banknote, bill (*US*); **~raub** *m* bank robbery; **~räuber** *m* bank robber.

bankrott *adj* bankrupt; *Mensch, Politik* discredited; *Kultur* debased; (*moralisch*) bankrupt. **~ gehen** *or* **machen** to go *or* become bankrupt; **jdn ~ machen** to make sb (go) bankrupt, to bankrupt sb; **er ist politisch/innerlich ~** he is a politically discredited/a broken man.

Bankrott *m -(e)s, -e* bankruptcy; (*fig*) breakdown, collapse; (*moralisch*) bankruptcy. **~ machen** to become *or* go bankrupt; **den ~ anmelden** *or* **ansagen** *or* **erklären** to declare oneself bankrupt.

Bankrott|erklärung *f* declaration of bankruptcy; (*fig*) sell-out (*inf*).

Bankrotteur(in *f)* *[-'tø:ɐ, -'tø:rɪn] m* (*lit, fig*) bankrupt; (*fig*) moral bankrupt.

Bank-: **~scheck** *m* cheque; **~überfall** *m* bank raid; **b~üblich** *adj* **es ist b~üblich** it is normal banking practice; **~verkehr** *m* bank transactions *pl*; **~wesen** *nt das* **~wesen** banking.

Bann *m -(e)s, -e* (a) *no pl* (*geh: magische Gewalt*) spell. **im ~ eines Menschen/einer Sache stehen** *or* **sein** to be under sb's spell/the spell of sth; **in jds ~ (acc) geraten** to fall under sb's spell; **jdn in seinen ~ schlagen** to captivate sb; **sie zog** *or* **zwang ihn in ihren ~** she cast her spell over him.
(b) (*Hist: Kirchen~*) excommunication. **jdn in den ~ tun, jdn mit dem ~ belegen, den ~ über jdn aussprechen** to excommunicate sb; **jdn vom ~ lösen** to absolve sb.

Bannbrief *m,* **Bannbulle** *f* (*Hist*) letter of excommunication.

bannen *vt* (a) (*geh: bezaubern*) to bewitch, to captivate, to entrance. (**wie) gebannt** fascinated, in fascination; (*stärker*) spellbound; **jdn/etw auf die Platte** (*inf*)/**die Leinwand ~** (*geh*) to capture sb/sth on film/canvas. (b) (*vertreiben*) *böse Geister, Teufel* to exorcize; (*abwenden*) *Gefahr* to avert, to ward off.
(c) (*Hist*) to excommunicate.

Banner *nt -s, -* (*geh*) banner; (*fig auch*) flag. **das ~ des Sozialismus hochhalten** to wave the banner *or* fly the flag of socialism.

Bannerträger *m* (*geh*) standard-bearer; (*fig*) vanguard *no pl.*

Bannfluch *m* excommunication. **den ~ gegen jdn schleudern** (*liter*) to excommunicate sb.

bannig *adv* (*N Ger inf*) terribly, really; (*mit adj auch*) ever so (*inf*). **das hat ~ Spaß gemacht** that was great fun.

Bann-: **~kreis** *m* (*fig*) **in jds ~kreis** (*dat*) **stehen** to be under sb's influence; **~meile** *f* inviolable precincts *pl* (*of city, Parliament etc*); **~spruch** *m* excommunication; **~strahl** *m* (*liter*) *siehe* **~fluch;** **~wald** *m* (*Aus, Sw*) *forest for protection against avalanches etc;* **~wart** *m* (*Sw*) forester.

Bantam-: **~gewicht** *nt* bantamweight; **~gewichtler** *m -s, -* bantamweight; **~(huhn)** *nt* bantam.

Bantu *m -(s), -(s)* Bantu.

Bantu-: **~frau** *f* Bantu woman; **~neger** *m* Bantu; **~sprache** *f* Bantu language.

Baptist(in *f) m* Baptist.

Baptisterium *nt* (*Eccl*) baptistry; (*Taufbecken*) font.

bar *adj, no comp* (a) cash. **~es Geld** cash; **wirf die Flasche nicht weg, das ist ~es Geld!** don't throw the bottle away, it's worth something *or* money; **eine Summe in ~** a sum in cash; **(in) ~ bezahlen** *or* **zahlen** to pay in cash; **(in) bar** cash on the nail; (*Verkauf*) **nur gegen ~** cash (sales) only; **etw für ~e Münze nehmen** (*fig*) to take sth at face value.
(b) *attr* (*rein*) *Zufall* pure; *Unsinn auch* utter, absolute.
(c) *pred + gen* (*liter*) devoid of, utterly *or* completely without. **~ aller Hoffnung, aller Hoffnung ~** devoid of hope, completely

or utterly without hope.
(d) (*liter: bloß*) bare. **~en Hauptes** bareheaded.

Bar¹ *f -, -s* (a) (*Nachtlokal*) nightclub, bar. (b) (*Theke*) bar.

Bar² *nt -s, -s* (*Met*) bar.

Bär *m -en, -en* (a) bear. **stark wie ein ~** (*inf*) (as) strong as an ox *or* a horse; **der Große/Kleine ~** (*Astron*) the Great/Little Bear, Ursa Major/Minor; **jdm einen ~en aufbinden** (*inf*) to have sb on (*inf*); *siehe* **schlafen.**
(b) (*inf: tolpatschiger Mensch*) lumbering oaf (*inf*).
(c) (*Tech*) (*Schlag~*) hammer; (*Ramm~*) rammer.

Baraber *m -s, -* (*Aus inf*) labourer; (*Straßenarbeiter*) navvy (*inf*).

barabern* *vi* (*Aus inf*) to labour.

Baracke *f -, -n* hut, shack; (*pej: kleines Haus*) hovel. **die ~** (*Pol inf*) *SPD headquarters in Bonn.*

Baracken-: **~lager** *nt,* **~siedlung** *f* camp (made of huts); (*für Flüchtlinge*) refugee camp.

Barbar(in *f) m -en, -en* (a) (*pej*) barbarian; (*Rohling auch*) brute. (b) (*Hist*) Barbarian.

Barbarei *f* (*pej*) (a) (*Unmenschlichkeit*) barbarity. (b) (*no pl: Kulturlosigkeit*) barbarism.

barbarisch *adj* (a) (*pej*) (*unmenschlich*) *Grausamkeit, Folter, Sitten* barbarous, savage, brutal; (*ungebildet*) *Geschmack, Benehmen* barbaric; *Mensch* barbaric, uncivilized. (b) (*Hist*) *Volk, Stamm* barbarian. (c) (*inf: fürchterlich*) terrible, frightful, horrific. **~ kalt** terribly *or* frightfully cold.

Barbarismus *m* (*Liter*) barbarism.

Barbe *f -, -n* (*Zool*) barbel.

Barbecue *['ba:bkju:] nt -(s), -s* barbecue.

bärbeißig *adj* (*inf*) *Gesicht, Miene, Mensch* grouchy (*inf*), grumpy; *Antwort etc auch* gruff.

Bar-: **~bestand** *m* (*Comm*) cash; (*Buchführung*) cash in hand; **~betrag** *m* cash sum *or* amount.

Barbier *m -s, -e* (*old hum*) barber.

barbieren* *vt* (*old, hum*) jdn ~ to shave sb; (*Bart beschneiden*) to trim sb's beard; (*die Haare schneiden*) to cut sb's hair; **sich** (*dat*) **~ lassen** to go to the barber's; *siehe* **balbieren.**

Barbiturat *nt* barbiturate.

Barbitursäure *f* barbituric acid.

barbrüstig, barbusig *adj* topless. **~ bedienen** to be a topless waitress.

Bardame *f* barmaid; (*euph: Prostituierte*) hostess (*euph*).

bardauz *interj siehe* **pardauz.**

Barde *m -n, -n* (*Liter*) bard; (*iro*) minstrel.

bardisch *adj* (*Liter*) bardic.

Bären-: **~dienst** *m* jdm/einer Sache einen **~dienst** erweisen to do sb/sth a bad turn *or* a disservice; **~dreck** *m* (*S Ger, Aus, Sw: inf*) liquorice; **~fang** *m* (*Likör*) = mead; **~führer** *m* bear trainer; (*hum*) (tourist) guide; **~hatz** *f siehe* **~jagd; ~haut** *f:* **auf der ~haut liegen, sich auf die ~haut legen** (*dated*) to laze *or* loaf about; **~hunger** *m* (*inf*) einen **~hunger haben** to be famished (*inf*) *or* ravenous (*inf*); **~jagd** *f* bear hunt/hunting; **~kräfte** *pl* the strength *sing* of an ox; **~mütze** *f* bearskin, busby; **~natur** *f* eine **~natur haben** (*inf*) to be (physically) tough; **b~stark** *adj* strapping, strong as an ox; **~zwinger** *m* bear cage.

Barett *nt -(e)s, -e* *or* **-s** cap; (*für Geistliche, Richter etc*) biretta; (*Univ*) mortarboard; (*Baskenmütze*) beret.

barfuß *adj pred* barefoot(ed). **~ gehen** to go/walk barefoot(ed); **ich bin ~** I've got nothing on my feet, I am barefoot(ed).

Barfüßer(in *f) m -s, -* (*Eccl*) barefoot monk/nun.

barfüßig *adj* barefooted.

barg *pret of* **bergen.**

Bar-: **~geld** *nt* cash; **b~geldlos** 1 *adj* cashless, without cash; **b~geldloser Zahlungsverkehr** payment by money transfer; **b~geldlos sein** (*hum*) to be broke (*inf*); 2 *adv* without using cash; **b~haupt** *adj pred* (*liter*), **b~häuptig** *adj* (*geh*) bareheaded; **~hocker** *m* (bar) stool.

bärig *adj* (*Aus inf*) tremendous, fantastic.

Bärin *f* (she-)bear.

Bariton *[-tɔn] m -s, -e* [-to:nə] baritone.

Baritonist *m* baritone.

Barium *nt, no pl* barium.

Bark *f -, -en* (*Naut*) barque.

Barkarole *f -, -n* (*Mus*) barcarol(l)e.

Barkasse *f -, -n* launch; (*Beiboot auch*) longboat.

Barkauf *m* cash purchase. **~ ist billiger** it is cheaper to pay (in) cash.

Barke *f -, -n* (*Naut*) skiff; (*liter*) barque (*liter*).

Barkeeper *['ba:ɛki:pɐ] m -s, -* barman.

Barkredit *m* cash loan.

Bärlapp *m -s, -e* (*Bot*) lycopod(ium).

Barmann *m* barman.

barmen 1 *vi* (*dial*) to moan, to grumble (*über +acc* about). 2 *vt* (*liter*) **er barmt mich** I feel pity for him.

barmherzig *adj* (*liter, Rel*) merciful; (*mitfühlend*) compassionate. **~er Himmel!** (*old, dial*) good heavens above!; **der ~e Samariter** (*lit, fig*) the good Samaritan; **B~e Schwestern** Sisters of Charity.

Barmherzigkeit *f* (*liter, Rel*) mercy, mercifulness; (*Mitgefühl*) compassion. **~** (**an jdm**) **üben** to show mercy (to sb)/compassion (towards sb); **Herr, übe ~ an mir!** Lord, have mercy on me!; *siehe* **Gnade.**

Barmittel *pl* cash (reserves *pl*).

Barmixer *m* barman.

barock *adj* baroque; (*fig*) (*überladen auch, verschnörkelt*) ornate; (*seltsam*) *Einfälle* bizarre, eccentric. **sie hat eine sehr ~e Figur** (*hum*) she has a very ample figure.

Barock *nt or m -(s), no pl* baroque. **das Zeitalter des ~** the baroque age.

Barock- in cpds baroque; ~zeit f baroque period.
Barometer nt -s, - (lit, fig) barometer. das ~ steht auf Sturm the barometer is on stormy; (fig) things look stormy.
Barometerstand m barometer reading.
barometrisch adj attr barometric.
Baron m -s, -e (a) baron. ~ (von) Schnapf Baron or Lord Schnapf; Herr ~ my lord. (b) (fig: Industrie~ etc) baron, magnate.
Baroneß f -, -ssen (dated), **Baronesse** f daughter of a baron. Fräulein ~ my lady.
Baronin f baroness. Frau ~ my lady.
Barras m -, no pl (sl) army. beim ~ in the army; zum ~ gehen to join up (inf); er muß nächstes Jahr zum ~ he's got to do his military service or he'll be drafted next year.
Barren m -s, - (a) (Metall~) bar; (esp Gold~) ingot. (b) (Sport) parallel bars pl. (c) (S Ger, Aus: Futtertrog) trough.
Barrengold nt gold bullion.
Barriere f -, -n (lit, fig) barrier.
Barrikade f barricade. auf die ~n gehen (lit, fig) to go to the barricades.
Barrikadenkampf m street battle; (das Kämpfen) street fighting no pl.
barrikadieren* vt siehe verbarrikadieren.
Barsch m -(e)s, -e perch.
barsch adj brusque, curt; Befehl auch peremptory. jdm eine ~e Abfuhr erteilen to give sb short shrift; jdn ~ anfahren to snap at sb.
Barschaft f, no pl cash. meine ganze ~ bestand aus 10 Mark all I had on me was 10 marks.
Barscheck m open or uncrossed cheque.
Barschheit f siehe adj brusqueness, curtness; peremptoriness.
Barsoi m -s, -s borzoi.
Barsortiment nt book wholesaler's.
barst pret of **bersten**.
Bart m -(e)s, ¨e (a) (von Mensch, Ziege, Vogel, Getreide) beard; (Schnurr~) moustache; (von Katze, Maus, Robbe etc) whiskers pl. sich (dat) einen ~ wachsen or stehen lassen to grow a beard; ein drei Tage alter ~ three days' growth (on one's chin).
 (b) (fig inf) (sich dat) etwas in den ~ murmeln or brumme(l)n to murmur or mutter sth in one's boots or beard (inf); jdm um den ~ gehen, jdm Honig um den ~ streichen or schmieren to butter sb up (inf), to soft-soap sb (inf); der Witz hat einen ~ that's a real oldie (inf) or an old chestnut; der ~ ist ab that's that!, that's the end of it or that.
 (c) (Schlüssel~) bit.
Bartbinde f device for keeping a moustache in shape.
Bärtchen nt (Kinn~) (small) beard; (Oberlippen~) toothbrush moustache; (Menjou~) pencil moustache.
Barteln pl siehe **Bartfäden**.
Bartenwal m whalebone or baleen whale.
Bart-: ~fäden pl (Zool) barbels pl; ~flechte f (a) (Med) sycosis, barber's itch; (b) (Bot) beard lichen or moss; ~haar nt facial hair; (Bart auch) beard.
Barthel m: wissen, wo ~ den Most holt (inf) to know what's what (inf), to know all the tricks in the book (inf).
Bartholomäus m - Bartholomew.
Bartholomäusnacht f (Hist) Massacre of St. Bartholomew.
bärtig adj bearded.
Bart-: b~los adj beardless; (glattrasiert) clean-shaven; Jüngling auch smooth-faced; ~losigkeit f beardlessness; ~scherer m -s, - (old, hum) barber; ~stoppel f piece of stubble; ~stoppeln pl stubble sing; ~tasse f moustache cup; ~tracht f beard/moustache style; ~wichse f (dated) wax (for moustache etc); ~wisch m -(e)s, -e (S Ger, Aus) hand brush; ~wuchs m beard; (esp weiblicher) facial hair no indef art; er hat starken ~wuchs he has a strong or heavy growth of beard; ~zotteln pl wispy beard sing.
Bar-: ~verkauf m cash sales pl; in ~verkauf a cash sale; ~vermögen nt cash or liquid assets pl; ~zahlung f payment by or in cash; (Verkauf) nur gegen ~zahlung cash (sales) only; bei ~zahlung 3% Skonto 3% discount for cash.
Basalt m -(e)s, -e basalt.
basalten, basaltig adj basaltic.
Basar m -s, -e (a) (orientalischer Markt) bazaar. auf dem ~ in the bazaar. (b) (Wohltätigkeits~) bazaar. (c) (DDR: Einkaufs-zentrum) department store.
Bäschen ['bɛːsçən] nt dim of **Base**[1].
Base[1] f -, -n (old, dial) cousin; (Tante) aunt.
Base[2] f -, -n (Chem) base.
Baseball ['beːsboːl] m -s, no pl baseball.
Basedow [-do] m -s, no pl (inf), **Basedowsche Krankheit** f (exophthalmic) goitre.
Basel nt -s Basle, Basel.
Baseler adj attr siehe **Basler**.
Basen pl of **Basis, Base**.
basieren* 1 vi (auf +dat on) to be based, to rest. 2 vt to base (auf +acc or (rare) dat on).
Basilika f -, **Basiliken** basilica.
Basilikum nt -s, no pl basil.
Basilisk m -en, -en basilisk.
Basiliskenblick m (liter) baleful glare.
Basis f -, **Basen** (a) (Archit, Mil, Math) base.
 (b) (fig) basis. auf breiter ~ on a broad basis; auf einer festen or soliden ~ ruhen to be firmly established; etw auf eine solide ~ stellen to put sth on a firm footing; auf gleicher ~ treffen to meet on an equal footing or on equal terms.
 (c) (Pol, Sociol) ~ und Überbau foundation and superstructure.
 (d) (Pol inf) die ~ the grass roots (level); (die Leute) (those at the) grass roots.

Basisarbeit f (Pol) groundwork.
basisch adj (Chem) basic.
Basisgruppe f action group.
Baske m -n, -n, **Baskin** f Basque.
Basken-: ~land nt Basque region; ~mütze f beret.
Basketball m -s, no pl basketball.
baskisch adj Basque.
Baskisch(e) nt decl as adj Basque; siehe **Deutsch(e)**.
Basler adj attr Basle attr.
Basler(in f) m -s, - native of Basle; (Einwohner) inhabitant of Basle.
Basrelief ['barelief] nt (Archit, Art) bas-relief.
Baß m -sses, ¨sse (a) (Stimme, Sänger) bass. hoher/tiefer ~ schwarzer ~ basso cantante/profundo; einen hohen/tiefen ~ haben to be a basso cantante/profundo. (b) (Instrument) double bass; (im Jazz auch) bass. (c) (~partie) bass (part).
baß adv (old, hum): ~ erstaunt much or uncommonly (old) amazed.
Baßbariton m bass baritone.
Bassetthorn nt basset horn.
Baßgeige f (inf) (double) bass.
Bassin [ba'sɛː] nt -s, -s (Schwimm~) pool; (Garten~) pond.
Bassist(in f) m (a) (Sänger) bass singer. (b) (im Orchester etc) (double) bass player. ~ sein to be a (double) bass player, to play the (double) bass.
Baß-: ~klarinette f bass clarinet; ~partie f bass part; ~sänger m bass (singer); ~schlüssel m bass clef; ~stimme f bass (voice); (Partie) bass (part).
Bast m -(e)s, (rare) -e (a) (zum Binden, Flechten) raffia; (Bot) bast, phloem. (b) (an Geweih) velvet.
basta interj (und damit) ~! (and) that's that.
Bastard m -(e)s, -e (a) (Hist: uneheliches Kind) bastard. (b) (Biol: Kreuzung) (Pflanze) hybrid; (Tier) cross-breed, cross; (Mensch) half-caste, half-breed.
bastardieren* vt Pflanzen to hybridize; Tiere, Arten to cross.
Bastardschrift f (Typ) bastard type.
Bastei f bastion.
Bastelarbeit f piece of handcraft; (das Basteln) (doing) handcraft or handicrafts. etw in langer ~ bauen to spend a long time making or building sth; sich viel mit ~en beschäftigen to do a lot of handcraft or handicrafts.
Bastelei f (inf) handcraft; (Stümperei) botched job (inf).
basteln 1 vi (a) (als Hobby) to make things with one's hands; (Handwerksarbeiten herstellen auch) to do handcraft or handicrafts. sie kann gut ~ she is good with her hands.
 (b) an etw (dat) ~ to make sth, to work on sth; (an Modellflugzeug etc) to build or make sth; (an etw herumbasteln) to mess around or tinker with sth; mit Pappe/Holz etc ~ to make things out of cardboard/wood etc.
 2 vt to make; Geräte etc auch to build. wer hat denn das gebastelt? (pej) who botched (inf) that together?
Basteln nt -s, no pl handicraft, handicrafts pl; (Schulfach auch) handwork.
Bastelraum m workroom; (in Schule etc) handicrafts room.
basten adj attr raffia.
Bast-: b~farben, b~farbig adj straw-coloured; ~faser f bast fibre.
Bastille [bas'tiːjə, -tɪljə] f - (Hist) der Sturm auf die ~ the storming of the Bastille.
Bastion f bastion, ramparts pl; (fig) bastion, bulwark.
Bastler(in f) m -s, - (von Modellen etc) modeller; (von Möbeln etc) do-it-yourselfer. ein guter ~ sein to be good or clever with one's hands, to be good at making things; (in der Schule etc) to be good at handicrafts or handwork.
Bastonade f bastinado.
Bastseide f wild silk, shantung (US).
BAT ['beːɑ'teː] abbr of **Bundesangestelltentarif**.
bat pret of **bitten**.
Bataille [ba'taːjə] f -, -n (old) battle.
Bataillon [batal'joːn] nt -s, -e (Mil, fig) battalion.
Bataillons-: ~führer, ~kommandeur m battalion commander.
Batate f -, -n sweet potato, yam (esp US), batata.
Batik f -, -en or m -s, -en batik.
batiken 1 vi to do batik. 2 vt to decorate with batik. eine gebatikte Bluse a batik blouse.
Batist m -(e)s, -e batiste, cambric.
batisten adj attr batiste, cambric.
Batterie f (Elec, Mil) battery; (Misch~ etc) regulator; (Reihe von Flaschen auch) row.
Batterie-: ~betrieb m das Radio ist für ~betrieb eingerichtet the radio takes batteries or can be battery-powered; bei ~betrieb ist der Empfang besser batteries give better reception; ~zündung f battery ignition (system).
Batzen m -s, - (a) (dated: Klumpen) clod, lump. (b) (obs: Münze) batz (silver coin). ein (schöner) ~ Geld (inf) a tidy sum (inf), a pretty penny (inf).
Bau m (a) -(e)s, no pl (das Bauen) building, construction. im or in ~ under construction; im ~ (begriffen) sein, sich im ~ befinden to be under construction; alle im ~ befindlichen Projekte all projects at present under construction or being built; der ~ des Hauses dauerte ein Jahr it took a year to build the house; mit dem ~ beginnen, an den ~ gehen to begin building or construction; den ~ beenden, mit dem ~ fertig sein to finish building, to complete construction.
 (b) -(e)s, no pl (Auf~) structure; (von Satz, Maschine, Apparat auch) construction. von kräftigem/schwächlichem ~ sein (Körper~) to be powerfully/slenderly built, to have a powerful/slender build or physique.
 (c) -s, no pl (~stelle) building site. auf dem ~ arbeiten, beim

~ **sein** to be a building worker, to work on a building site; **vom** ~ **sein** (fig inf) to know the ropes (inf).
(d) -(e)s, -ten (Gebäude) building; (~werk) construction. ~ten (Film) sets.
(e) -(e)s, -e (Erdhöhle) burrow, hole; (Biber~) lodge; (Fuchs~) den; (Dachs~) set(t); (inf: Wohnung) lair (inf), den (inf). **heute gehe ich nicht aus dem** ~(inf) I'm not sticking my nose out of doors today (inf); **zu** ~ **gehen** (Hunt) to go to earth.
(f) -(e)s, -e (Min) workings pl. **im** ~ **sein** to be down the pit or mine.
(g) -(e)s, no pl (Mil sl) guardhouse. **4 Tage** ~ 4 days in the guardhouse.
Bau-: ~**abnahme** f building inspection; ~**abschnitt** m stage or phase of construction; ~**amt** nt planning department and building control office; ~**arbeiten** pl building or construction work sing; (Straßen~) roadworks pl; **mit den** ~**arbeiten beginnen** to begin construction; ~**arbeiter** m building or construction worker, building labourer; ~**art** f construction, design; (Stil) style; ~**aufsicht** f supervision of building or construction; **die** ~**aufsicht liegt bei der Stadtverwaltung** the town council is supervising the construction; ~**ausführung** f construction, building; ~**ausführung Firma Meyer** builders or constructors Meyer and Co; ~**behörde** f planning department and building control office; ~**block** m, pl -s block; ~**boom** m building boom; ~**bude** f building workers' hut.
Bauch m -(e)s, **Bäuche** (a) (von Mensch) stomach, tummy (inf); (Anat) abdomen; (von Tier) stomach, belly; (Fett~) paunch, potbelly (inf). **ihm tat der** ~ **weh** he had stomach-ache or tummy-ache (inf); **sich** (dat) **den** ~ **vollschlagen** (sl) to stuff oneself (inf); **ein voller** ~ **studiert nicht gern** (Prov) you can't study on a full stomach; **sich** (dat) **(vor Lachen) den** ~ **halten** (inf) to split one's sides (laughing) (inf); **einen** ~ **ansetzen** or **kriegen** to get a stomach or tummy (inf); **einen dicken** ~ **haben** (sl: schwanger sein) to have a bun in the oven (inf); **er hat ihr einen dicken** ~ **gemacht** (sl) he knocked her up (sl), he got her into trouble (inf); **vor jdm auf dem** ~ **rutschen** (inf) or **kriechen** (inf) to grovel or kowtow to sb (inf), to lick sb's boots (inf); **mit etw auf den** ~ **fallen** (inf) to come a cropper with sth (inf); siehe **Wut, Loch, Bein** etc.
(b) (Wölbung, Hohlraum) belly; (Innerstes: von Schiff auch, von Erde) bowels pl.
Bauch-: ~**ansatz** m beginning(s) of a paunch; ~**binde** f (a) (für Frack) cummerbund; (Med) abdominal bandage or support; (b) (um Zigarre, Buch) band; ~**decke** f abdominal wall; ~**fell** nt (a) (Anat) peritoneum; (b) (Fell am Bauch) stomach or belly fur; ~**fellentzündung** f peritonitis; ~**fleck** m (Aus inf) siehe ~**klatscher**; ~**flosse** f ventral fin; ~**gegend** f abdominal region; ~**grimmen** nt ~s, no pl (inf) stomach- or tummy- (inf) ache; ~**höhle** f abdominal cavity, abdomen; ~**höhlenschwangerschaft** f ectopic pregnancy.
bauchig adj Gefäß bulbous.
Bauch-: ~**klatscher** m -s, - (inf) belly-flop (inf); ~**laden** m vendor's tray; ~**landung** f (Aviat) belly landing; (bei Sprung ins Wasser) belly-flop.
Bäuchlein nt tummy (inf); (hum: Fett~) bit of a stomach or tummy (inf).
bäuchlings adv on one's front, face down. ~ **fallen** to fall flat (on one's face); ~ **ins Wasser fallen** to (do a) belly-flop into the water.
Bauch-: ~**muskel** m stomach or abdominal muscle; ~**nabel** m navel, tummy-button (inf); **b~pinseln** vt (inf) siehe **gebauchpinselt; b~reden** vi sep infin, ptp only to ventriloquize; ~**redner** m ventriloquist; ~**schmerzen** pl stomach- or tummy- (inf) ache; ~**schuß** m shot in the stomach; (Verletzung) stomach wound; **einen** ~**schuß abbekommen** to be shot in the stomach; ~**speck** m (Cook) belly of pork; (hum) spare tyre (inf); ~**speicheldrüse** f pancreas; ~**tanz** m belly-dance/dancing; **b~tanzen** vi sep infin, ptp only to belly-dance; ~**tänzerin** f belly-dancer.
Bauchung f bulge.
Bauch-: ~**wand** f stomach or abdominal wall; ~**weh** nt siehe ~**schmerzen**; ~**welle** f (Sport) circle on the beam.
Baude f -, -n (dial) mountain hut.
Bau-: ~**denkmal** nt historical monument; ~**element** nt component part.
bauen 1 vt (a) to build, to construct; (anfertigen auch) to make; Satz to construct; Höhle to dig, to make. **sich** (dat) **ein Haus/Nest** ~ to build oneself a house/make or build oneself a nest (auch fig); **die Symphonie ist gut gebaut** the symphony is well constructed; **seine Hoffnung auf jdn/etw** ~ to build one's hopes on sb/sth; **die Betten** ~ (esp Mil) to make the beds; **sich** (dat) **einen Anzug** ~ **lassen** (hum inf) to have a suit made for oneself; siehe **gebaut**.
(b) (inf: verursachen) Unfall to cause. **da hast du Mist** (inf) or **Scheiße** (sl) **gebaut** you really messed (inf) or cocked (Brit sl) that up; **bleib ruhig, bau keine Scheiße** (sl) cool it, don't make trouble (inf).
(c) (inf: machen, ablegen) Prüfung etc to pass. **den Führerschein** ~ to pass one's driving test; **seinen Doktor** ~ to get one's doctorate.
(d) (rare: an~) Kartoffeln etc to grow; (liter: bestellen) Acker to cultivate.
2 vi (a) to build. **wir haben neu/auf Sylt gebaut** we built a new house/a house on Sylt; **nächstes Jahr wollen wir** ~ we're going to build or start building next year; **an etw** (dat) ~ **to be** working on sth, to be building sth (auch fig); **hier wird viel gebaut** there is a lot of building or development going on round here; **hoch** ~ to build high-rise buildings.
(b) (vertrauen) to rely, to count (auf +acc on).
Bauentwurf m building plans pl.

Bauer[1] m -n or (rare) -s, -n (a) (Landwirt) farmer; (als Vertreter einer Klasse) peasant; (pej: ungehobelter Mensch) (country) bumpkin, yokel. **die dümmsten** ~**n haben die größten** or **dicksten Kartoffeln** (prov inf) fortune favours fools (prov); **was der** ~ **nicht kennt, das frißt er nicht** (prov inf) you can't change the habits of a lifetime.
(b) (Chess) pawn; (Cards) jack, knave.
(c) (vulg: Samenerguß) **ein kalter** ~ a wet dream.
Bauer[2] nt or (rare) m -s, - (bird-)cage.
Bäuerchen nt dim of **Bauer**[1]. (b) (baby-talk) burp. **(ein)** ~ **machen** to (do a) burp.
Bäuerin f (a) (Frau des Bauern) farmer's wife. (b) (Landwirtin) farmer; (als Vertreterin einer Klasse) peasant (woman).
bäuerisch adj siehe **bäurisch**.
Bäuerlein nt (liter, hum) farmer.
bäuerlich adj rural; (ländlich) Fest, Bräuche, Sitten rustic, country attr. ~**e Klein- und Großbetriebe** small and large farms.
Bauern-: ~**aufstand** m peasants' revolt or uprising; ~**brot** nt coarse rye bread; ~**bub** (S Ger, Aus, Sw), ~**bursche** m country lad; ~**dirne** f (old) siehe ~**mädchen**; ~**dorf** nt farming or country village; ~**fang** m: **auf** ~**fang ausgehen** (inf) to play con tricks; ~**fänger** m (inf) con-man (inf), swindler; ~**fängerei** f (inf) con (inf), swindle; **das ist ja** ~**fängerei** that's a con or swindle; ~**frau** f siehe **Bauersfrau**; ~**frühstück** nt bacon and potato omelette; ~**gut** nt farm(stead); ~**haus** nt farmhouse; ~**hochzeit** f country wedding; ~**hof** m farm; ~**junge** m country lad; ~**kalender** m country almanac; ~**kriege** pl (Hist) Peasant War(s); ~**legen** nt -s, no pl (Hist, Pol pej) expropriation of peasants' land; ~**mädchen** nt country girl or lass (inf); ~**magd** f farmer's maid; ~**partei** f country party; ~**regel** f country saying; ~**schädel** m (large) head; (pej) thick skull (inf); ~**schaft** f, no pl farming community; (ärmlich) peasantry; **b~schlau** adj cunning, crafty, shrewd; ~**schläue** f native or low cunning, craftiness, shrewdness; ~**stand** m farming community, farmers pl; ~**stube** f farmhouse parlour; (in Gasthaus) ploughman's bar; **im Stil einer** ~**stube eingerichtet** decorated in country or rustic style; ~**theater** nt rural folk theatre; ~**tölpel** m (pej) country bumpkin, yokel; ~**tum** nt, no pl (~stand) farming community, farmers pl; **er ist stolz auf sein** ~**tum** he is proud of coming from farming stock; ~**verband** m farmers' organization.
Bauerschaft f (Admin) (scattered) farming community.
Bauers-: ~**frau** f farmer's wife; ~**leute** pl farm(ing) folk, farmers pl; ~**mann** m (old, liter) farmer.
Bau-: ~**erwartungsland** nt (Admin) land set aside for building; ~**fach** nt construction industry; **b~fällig** adj dilapidated; Decke, Gewölbe unsound, unsafe; ~**fälligkeit** f dilapidation; **wegen** ~**fälligkeit gesperrt** closed because building unsafe; ~**firma** f building contractor or firm; ~**flucht** f line; ~**form** f form or shape (of a building); ~**gelände** nt land for building; (~stelle) building site; ~**geld** nt building capital; ~**genehmigung** f planning and building permission; ~**genossenschaft** f housing association; ~**gerüst** nt scaffolding; ~**geschäft** nt building firm; ~**gesellschaft** f property company; ~**gewerbe** nt building and construction trade; ~**glied** nt (Archit) part of a building; ~**grube** f excavation; ~**grundstück** nt plot of land for building; ~**handwerk** nt building trade; ~**handwerker** m (trained) building worker; ~**haus** nt (Archit, Art) Bauhaus; ~**herr** m client (for whom sth is being built); **seitdem er** ~**herr ist** ... since he has been having a house built ...; **der** ~**herr ist die Stadt** the clients are the town authorities; ~**herr: Ministerium des Innern** under construction for Ministry of the Interior; ~**holz** nt building timber; ~**hütte** f (a) siehe ~**bude**; (b) (Hist, Archit) church masons' guild; ~**industrie** f building and construction industry; ~**ingenieur** m civil engineer.
Bauj. abbr of **Baujahr**.
Bau-: ~**jahr** nt year of construction; (von Gebäude auch) year of building; (von Auto) year of manufacture; **VW** ~**jahr 70 VW 1970 model, 1970 VW; mein Auto ist** ~**jahr 70** my car is a 1970 model; **welches** ~**jahr?** what year?; **das** ~**jahr des Hauses** the year the house was built; ~**kasten** m building or construction kit; (mit Holzklötzen) box of bricks; (Chemie~) set; ~**kastensystem** nt (Tech) modular or unit construction system; ~**klotz** m (building) brick or block; ~**klötze(r) staunen** (inf) to gape (in astonishment); ~**kolonne** f gang of building workers or (bei Straßenbau) navvies; ~**kosten** pl building or construction costs pl; ~**kostenzuschuß** m building subsidy or grant; ~**kunst** f (geh) architecture; ~**künstler** m (geh) architect; ~**land** nt building land; (für Stadtplanung) development area; **einen Acker als** ~**land verkaufen** to sell a field for building; ~**leiter** m (building) site manager; ~**leitung** f au (Aufsicht) site supervision; (Büro) site office; (b) (die ~**leiter**) (building) site supervisory staff; **b~lich** adj structural; **in gutem/schlechtem Zustand b~lichem Zustand** structurally sound/unsound; **einen Gedanken b~lich verwirklichen** to realize an idea in bricks and mortar; ~**lichkeit** f usu pl (form) building; ~**löwe** m building speculator; ~**lücke** f empty site.
Baum m -(e)s, **Bäume** tree. **auf dem** ~ **in the tree; der** ~ **der Erkenntnis** (Bibl) the tree of knowledge; **er ist stark wie ein** ~ he's as strong as a horse; **zwischen** ~ **und Borke stecken** or **stehen** to be in two minds; **die Bäume wachsen nicht in den Himmel** (prov) all good things come to an end; **einen alten** ~ or **alte Bäume soll man nicht verpflanzen** (prov) you can't teach an old dog new tricks (prov); siehe **ausreißen, Wald**.
Bau-: ~**markt** m property market; ~**maschine** f piece of building machinery; ~**maschinen** pl building machinery or plant sing; ~**material** nt building material.

Baum-: ~bestand *m* tree population *no pl*, stock of trees; ~blüte *f* blossom.

Bäumchen *nt* small tree; (*junger Baum auch*) sapling. ~, wechsle dich spielen to play tag; (*hum: Partnertausch*) to swap partners.

Baumeister *m* (a) master builder; (*Bauunternehmer*) building contractor; (*Architekt*) architect. (b) (*Erbauer*) builder.

baumeln *vi* to dangle (*an* +*dat* from). die Haarsträhnen baumelten ihm ins Gesicht the strands of hair hung in his face; jdn ~ lassen (*sl*) to let sb swing (*inf*).

bäumen *vr* (*Pferd*) to rear (up); (*Mensch*) to jerk (up). sich gegen etw ~ (*fig geh*) to buck at sth.

Baum-: ~farn *m* tree fern; ~frevel *m* (*form*) malicious damage to trees; ~grenze *f* tree *or* timber line; ~gruppe *f* coppice, cluster of trees; b~hoch *adj* tree-high; ~krone *f* treetop; ~kuchen *m* cake baked so that when cut it looks like the annual rings of a tree; b~lang *adj* ein b~langer Kerl (*inf*) a beanpole (*inf*); ~läufer *m* tree creeper; b~los *adj* treeless; b~reich *adj* wooded; ~riese *m* (*liter*) giant tree; ~rinde *f* tree bark; ~schere *f* (*tree*) pruning shears *pl*, secateurs *pl*; ~schule *f* tree nursery; ~stamm *m* tree-trunk; b~stark *adj* Arme massive; Mann beefy (*inf*), hefty; ~steppe *f* scrub; ~strunk, ~stumpf *m* tree stump; ~wipfel *m* treetop.

Baumwoll- in *cpds* cotton.

Baumwolle *f* cotton. ein Hemd aus ~ a cotton shirt.

baumwollen *adj attr* cotton.

Baumwuchs *m* tree growth.

baun *vti siehe* **bauen.**

Bau-: ~ordnung *f* building regulations *pl*; ~plan *m* building plan *or* (*Vorhaben auch*) project; wir haben ~plane we are planning to build ourselves a house; ~planung *f* planning (of a building); ~plastik *f* architectural sculpture; ~platz *m* site (for building); ~polizei *f* building control department; ~preis *m* building price; ~rat *m* head of the planning department and building control office; ~recht *nt* planning and building laws and regulations; b~reif *adj* Grundstück available for building.

bäurisch *adj* (*pej*) boorish, rough.

Bau-: ~ruine *f* (*inf*) unfinished building; ~saison *f* building season; ~satz *m* kit.

Bausch *m* -es, Bäusche *or* -e (a) (*Papier~, Wolle~*) ball; (*Med auch*) swab. (b) (*Krause*) (*an Vorhang*) pleat; (*an Kleid*) bustle; (*an Ärmel*) puff. (c) (*old Med*) compress. (d) in ~ und Bogen lock, stock and barrel.

Bauschaffende(r) *mf decl as adj* (*DDR*) person working in the construction industry.

Bäuschchen *nt dim of* **Bausch.**

bauschen 1 *vr* (a) (*sich aufblähen*) to billow (out). (b) (*Kleidungsstück*) to puff out; (*ungewollt*) to bunch (up). 2 *vt* (a) Segel, Vorhänge to fill, to swell. (b) (*raffen*) to gather. gebauschte Ärmel puffed sleeves. 3 *vi* (*Kleidungsstück*) to bunch (up), to become bunched.

Bauschen *m* -s, - (*S Ger, Aus*) *siehe* **Bausch (a).**

bauschig *adj* (*gebläht*) billowing. (b) Rock, Vorhänge full.

Bau-: ~schlosser *m* fitter on a building site; ~schule *f* (*dated*) school of civil engineering; ~schutt *m* building rubble.

bausparen *vi sep usu infin* to save with a building society (*Brit*) *or* building and loan association (*US*).

Bausparer *m* saver with a building society (*Brit*) *or* building and loan association (*US*).

Bauspar-: ~kasse *f* building society (*Brit*), building and loan association (*US*); ~vertrag *m* savings contract with a building society (*Brit*) *or* building and loan association (*US*).

Bau-: ~stahl *m* mild *or* structured steel; ~stein *m* stone (for building); (*fig: Bestandteil*) constituent, ingredient; ~stelle *f* building *or* construction site; (*bei Straßenbau*) roadworks *pl*; (*bei Gleisbau*) railway construction site; „Achtung, ~stelle!" "danger, men at work"; „Betreten der ~stelle verboten" "unauthorized entry prohibited", "trespassers will be prosecuted"; die Strecke ist wegen einer ~stelle gesperrt the road/line is closed because of roadworks/(railway) construction work; ~stellenverkehr *m* heavy traffic (from a building site); „Achtung, ~stellenverkehr!" "heavy plant crossing"; ~stil *m* architectural style; ~stoff *m siehe* ~material; ~stopp *m* einen ~stopp verordnen to impose a halt on building (projects); es besteht ein ~stopp all building has been halted; ~summe *f* total building cost; ~tätigkeit *f* building; eine rege ~tätigkeit a lot of building; ~techniker *m* site engineer; ~teil *m* part of a building.

Bauten *pl of* **Bau (b).**

Bau-: ~tischler *m* joiner; ~träger *m* builder, building contractor; ~unternehmen *nt* (a) (*Firma*) building contractor; (b) *siehe* ~vorhaben; ~unternehmer *m* building contractor, builder; ~unternehmung *f siehe* ~unternehmen (a); ~volumen *nt* volume of building; ~vorhaben *nt* building project *or* scheme; ~weise *f* type *or* method of construction; (*Stil*) style; in konventioneller ~weise built in the conventional way/style; offene/geschlossene ~weise detached/terraced houses; ~werk *nt* construction; (*Gebäude auch*) edifice, building; ~wesen *nt* building and construction industry; ein Ausdruck aus dem ~wesen a building term; ~wich *m* -(e)s, -e (*Archit*) space between two neighbouring buildings; ~wirtschaft *f* building and construction industry.

Bauxit *m* -s, -e bauxite.

bauz *interj* wham, crash, bang. ~ machen (*baby-talk*) to go (crash bang) wallop.

Bau-: ~zaun *m* hoarding, fence; ~zeichnung *f* building plan *usu pl*; ~zeit *f* time taken for building *or* construction; die ~zeit betrug drei Jahre it took three years to build.

b.a.w. *abbr of* **bis auf weiteres** until further notice.

Bayer(in *f*) ['baiɐ, -ərɪn] *m* -n, -n Bavarian.

bay(e)risch ['bai(ə)rɪʃ] *adj* Bavarian. der B~e Wald the Bavarian Forest.

Bay(e)risch(e) ['bai(ə)rɪʃ(ə)] *nt decl as adj* Bavarian (dialect).

Bayern ['baiɐn] *nt* -s Bavaria.

Bayer(n)land ['baiɐ(n)lant] *nt* (*liter*) Bavaria.

Bazar *m* -s, -e *siehe* **Basar.**

Bazi *m* -, - (*Aus inf*) blighter, scoundrel.

Bazille *f* -, -n (*incorrect*) *siehe* **Bazillus.**

Bazillen-: ~furcht *f* germ phobia; ~träger *m* carrier.

Bazillus *m* -, Bazillen (a) bacillus, microbe; (*Krankheitserreger auch*) germ. (b) (*fig*) cancer, growth.

Bazooka [ba'zu:ka] *f* -, -s bazooka.

Bd., Bde *abbr of* **Band, Bände.**

BDI ['be:de:'|i:] *m* -, *no pl abbr of* **Bundesverband der Deutschen Industrie** ≈ CBI (*Brit*).

BDM ['be:de:'|ɛm] *m* -, *no pl* (*NS*) *abbr of* **Bund Deutscher Mädel.**

be|absichtigen* *vti* to intend. eine Reise/Steuererhöhung ~ (*form*) to intend to go on a journey/to increase taxes; was ~ Sie damit? what do you mean by that?; das hatte ich nicht beabsichtigt I didn't mean it *or* intend that to happen; das war beabsichtigt that was deliberate *or* intentional; die beabsichtigte Wirkung the desired *or* intended effect; wie beabsichtigt as planned *or* intended.

be|achten* *vt* (a) (*befolgen*) to heed; Ratschlag auch to follow; Vorschrift, Verbot, Verkehrszeichen to observe, to comply with; Regel to observe, to follow; Gebrauchsanweisung to follow. etw besser ~ to pay more attention to sth; *siehe* **Vorfahrt.**

(b) (*berücksichtigen*) to take into consideration *or* account. es ist zu ~, daß ... it should be taken into consideration *or* account that ...

(c) (*Aufmerksamkeit schenken*) jdn to notice, to pay attention to; (*bei Bild*)erklärungen, Reiseführung etc) to observe. jdn nicht ~ to ignore sb, to take no notice of sb; von der Öffentlichkeit kaum beachtet scarcely noticed by the public; das Ereignis wurde in der Öffentlichkeit kaum/stark beachtet the incident aroused little/considerable public attention; „bitte Stufe ~!" "mind the step".

be|achtenswert *adj* noteworthy, remarkable.

be|achtlich 1 *adj* (a) (*beträchtlich*) considerable; Verbesserung, Zu- *or* Abnahme auch marked; Erfolg notable; Talent auch remarkable, notable.

(b) (*bedeutend*) Ereignis significant; (*lobenswert*) Leistung considerable, excellent; (*zu berücksichtigend*) relevant. ~! (*dated*) well done; er hat im Leben/Beruf B~es geleistet he has achieved a considerable amount in life/his job.

2 *adv* (*sehr*) significantly, considerably.

Be|achtung *f siehe vt* (a) heeding; following; observance, compliance (*gen* with). die ~ der Vorschriften observance of *or* compliance with the regulations; unter ~ der Vorschriften in accordance with the regulations.

(b) consideration. unter ~ aller Umstände considering *or* taking into consideration all the circumstances.

(c) notice, attention (*gen* to). „zur ~" please note; ~ finden to receive attention; jdm/einer Sache ~ schenken to pay attention to *or* take notice of sb/sth; jdm keine ~ schenken to ignore sb, to take no notice of sb.

be|ackern* *vt* (a) Feld to till, to work. (b) (*inf*) Thema, Wissensgebiet to go into, to examine. (c) (*inf: zu überreden versuchen*) jdn to work on (*inf*).

Be|amte *m siehe* **Beamte(r).**

Be|amten-: ~apparat *m* bureaucracy; ~beleidigung *f* insulting an official; ~bestechung *f* bribing an official; ~deutsch *nt siehe* Amtsdeutsch; ~herrschaft *f* bureaucracy; ~laufbahn *f* career in the civil service; die ~laufbahn einschlagen to enter *or* join the civil service; ~recht *nt* civil service law; ~schaft *f* civil servants *pl*, civil service; ~seele *f* (*pej*) petty official; ~stand *m* (*dated*) civil service; ~tum *nt, no pl* (a) civil service; (*schaft auch*) civil servants *pl*; (b) (*Wesen*) sein ~tum the civil servant in him; stolz auf sein ~tum proud to be a civil servant; es ist Kennzeichen des ~tums, daß ... it is the mark of civil servants that ...; ~verhältnis *nt* im ~verhältnis stehen/ins ~verhältnis übernommen werden to be/become a civil servant; ~willkür *f* arbitrariness of officials; das war ~willkür that was an arbitrary bureaucratic decision.

Be|amte(r) *m decl as adj* official; (*Staats~*) civil servant; (*Zoll~ auch*, *Polizei~*) officer; (*dated: Büro~, Schalter~*) clerk. politischer ~r politically-appointed civil servant; er ist ~r (*bei Land, Bund*) he is a civil servant *or* in the civil service; er ist ein typischer ~r he is a typical petty official *or* bureaucrat; ein kleiner ~r a minor *or* (*esp pej*) petty official.

be|amtet *adj* (*form*) established, appointed on a permanent basis (*by the state*).

Be|amtin *f siehe* **Beamte(r).**

be|ängstigen* *vt* (*geh*) to alarm, to frighten, to scare.

be|ängstigend *adj* alarming, frightening. sein Zustand ist ~ his condition is giving cause for concern.

Be|ängstigung *f* alarm, fear. in großer ~ in (a state of) great alarm.

be|anspruchen* *vt* (a) (*fordern*) to claim; Gebiet auch to lay claim to. etw ~ können to be entitled to sth.

(b) (*erfordern*) to take; Zeit auch to take up; Platz auch to take up, to occupy; Kräfte auch, Aufmerksamkeit to demand; (*benötigen*) to need.

(c) (*ausnützen*) to use; jds Gastfreundschaft to take advantage of; jds Geduld to demand; jds Hilfe to ask for. ich möchte Ihre Geduld nicht zu sehr ~ I don't want to try your patience.

(d) (*strapazieren*) Maschine etc to use; jdn to occupy, to keep busy. etw/jdn stark or sehr ~ to put sth under a lot of stress etc/keep sb very busy or occupied; **eine höchst beanspruchte Maschine** a heavily used machine; **ihr Beruf beansprucht sie ganz** her job is very demanding or takes up all her time and energy.

Be|anspruchung f (a) (Forderung) claim (gen to); (Anforderung) demand. (b) (Ausnutzung: von jds Geduld, Hilfe etc) demand (von on). (c) (Belastung, Abnutzung) use; (von Beruf auch) demands pl.

be|anstanden* vt to query, to complain about. **das ist beanstandet worden** there has been a query or complaint about that; **er hat an allem etwas zu ~** he has complaints about everything; **die beanstandete Ware** the goods complained about or queried.

Be|anstandung f complaint (gen about). **zu ~en Anlaß geben** (form) to give cause for complaint; **er hat jahrelang ohne jede ~ seine Pflicht getan** for years he did his duty without giving any cause for complaint.

be|antragen* vt to apply for (bei to); (Jur) Strafe to demand, to ask for; (vorschlagen: in Debatte etc) to move, to propose. **er beantragte, versetzt zu werden** he applied for a transfer or to be transferred; **etw bei der Behörde ~** to apply to the authorities for sth; **eine Summe in der beantragten Höhe** the amount applied for.

Be|antragung f siehe vt application (gen for); demand (gen for); proposal.

be|antworten* vt to answer; Anfrage, Brief auch to reply to; Gruß, Beleidigung, Herausforderung auch to respond to. **jdm eine Frage ~** to answer sb's question; **eine Frage mit Nein ~** to answer a question in the negative; **leicht zu ~** easily answered.

Be|antwortung f siehe vt (gen to) answer; reply; response.

be|arbeiten* vt (a) (behandeln) to work on; Stein, Holz to work, to dress; (inf: mit Chemikalien) to treat. **etw mit dem Hammer/Meißel ~** to hammer/chisel sth; **etw mit einer Bürste ~** to brush sth hard.
(b) (sich befassen mit) to deal with; Fall auch to handle; Bestellungen etc to process.
(c) (redigieren) to edit; (neu ~) to revise; (umändern) Roman etc to adapt; Musik to arrange. **etw für die Drucklegung ~** to prepare sth for press.
(d) (inf: einschlagen auf) jdn to work over, to beat up (inf); Klavier, Trommel etc to hammer or bash away at; Geige to saw away at. **jdn mit Fußtritten/Fäusten ~** to kick sb about/thump sb.
(e) (inf: einreden auf) jdn to work on.
(f) Land to cultivate.

Be|arbeiter(in f) m (a) siehe vt (b) person dealing with etc sth. **wer war der ~ der Akte?** who dealt with the file? (b) siehe vt (c) editor; reviser; adapter; arranger.

Be|arbeitung f siehe vt (a) working (on); dressing; treating. **die ~ von Granit ist schwierig** it is difficult to work or dress granite.
(b) dealing with; handling; processing. **die ~ meines Antrags hat lange gedauert** it took a long time to deal with my claim.
(c) editing; revising; adapting; arranging; (bearbeitete Ausgabe etc) edition; revision, revised edition; adaptation; arrangement. **neue ~** (von Film etc) new version; **die deutsche ~** the German version.

Be|arbeitungs-: ~**gebühr** f processing fee; ~**zeit** f (Admin) (time for) processing; **die ~zeit beträgt zwei Wochen** processing will take two weeks.

be|argwöhnen* vt to be suspicious of.

Beat [biːt] m -(s), no pl (a) (Musik) beat or pop music. (b) (Rhythmus) beat.

Beatband f beat or pop group.

beaten ['biːtn] vi to bop (inf); (Beat spielen) to play beat or pop music.

Beatgeneration f beat generation.

Beatifikation f (Eccl) beatification.

beatifizieren* vt (Eccl) to beatify.

Beatlokal nt beat club.

be|atmen* vt Ertrunkenen to give artificial respiration to. **jdn künstlich ~** to keep sb breathing artificially.

Be|atmung f artificial respiration.

Beatmusik f beat or pop music.

Beatnik ['biːtnɪk] m -s, -s beatnik.

Beatschuppen m (inf) beat club.

Beau [boː] m -, -s good looker (inf).

be|aufsichtigen* vt Arbeit, Bau to supervise; Klasse, Schüler, Häftling auch to keep under supervision; Kind to mind; Prüfung to invigilate at. **jdn bei einer Arbeit/beim Arbeiten ~** to supervise sb's work/sb working; **staatlich beaufsichtigt** state-controlled, under state control.

Be|aufsichtigung f siehe vt supervision, supervising; minding; invigilation.

be|auftragen* vt (a) (heranziehen) to engage; Firma auch to hire; Architekten, Künstler etc, Forschungsinstitut to commission; Ausschuß etc to appoint, to set up. **jdn mit etw ~** to engage etc sb to do sth; **mit der Wahrnehmung beauftragt** temporarily in charge. (b) (anweisen) Untergebene etc to instruct. **wir sind beauftragt, das zu tun** we have been instructed to do that.

Be|auftragte(r) mf decl as adj representative.

be|augapfeln* vt (hum) to eye.

be|äugeln* vt (hum) to make eyes at (inf), to ogle.

be|äugen* vt (inf) to gaze or look at.

be|augenscheinigen* vt (form, hum) to inspect.

Beaujolais [boʒo'le] m -, - beaujolais.

Beauté [bo'teː] f -, -s (geh), **Beauty** ['bjuːti] f -, -s (Press sl) stunner (inf), beauty.

be|bändern* vt usu ptp to decorate with ribbons, to beribbon (liter).

bebartet adj (usu hum) bearded.

bebaubar adj (a) Boden cultiv(at)able. (b) Grundstück suitable for building; (zum Bau freigegeben) available for building.

bebauen* vt (a) Grundstück to build on, to develop. **das Grundstück ist jetzt mit einer Schule bebaut** the piece of land has had a school built on it; **das Viertel war dicht bebaut** the area was heavily built-up; **ein Gelände mit etw ~** to build sth on a piece of land.
(b) (Agr) to cultivate; Land to farm.

Bebauung f, no pl (a) (Vorgang) building (gen on); (von Gelände) development; (Bauten) buildings pl. **Viertel mit dichter ~** densely built-up area. (b) (Agr) cultivation; (von Land) farming.

Bebauungs-: ~**dichte** f density of building or development; **für geringere ~dichte sorgen** to ensure development is less dense; ~**plan** m development plan or scheme.

Bébé [be'beː] nt -s, -s (Sw) baby.

beben vi to shake, to tremble; (Stimme auch) to quiver (vor + dat with). **am ganzen Leib or an allen Gliedern ~** to tremble or shake all over; **vor jdm ~** (liter) to be in fear and trembling of sb; **um jdn ~** (liter) to tremble for sb.

Beben nt -s, - (Zittern) shaking, trembling; (von Stimme auch) quivering; (Erd~) earthquake.

bebildern* vt Buch, Vortrag to illustrate.

Bebilderung f illustrations pl (gen in).

bebrillt adj (hum inf) bespectacled.

bebrüten* vt Eier to incubate. **die Lage ~** (fig inf) to brood over the situation.

Becher m -s, - (a) (old: Kelch auch) goblet; (Glas~) glass, tumbler; (esp Porzellan~, Ton~ auch) mug; (Plastik~ auch) beaker; (Joghurt~ etc) carton, tub; (Eis~) (aus Pappe) tub; (aus Metall) sundae dish. **ein ~ Eis** a tub of icecream/an ice-cream sundae; **der ~ der Freude/des Leidens** (liter) the cup of joy/sorrow. (b) (Bot: Eichel~) cup, cupule (spec).

Becher-: b~**förmig** adj cup-shaped; ~**glas** nt (a) (Trinkglas) glass, tumbler; (b) (Chem) glass, beaker; ~**klang** m (old, liter) clink(ing) of glasses.

bechern vi (hum inf) to have a few (inf).

becircen* [ba'tsɪrtsn] vt (inf) to bewitch.

Becken nt -s, - (a) (Brunnen~, Hafen~, Wasch~, Geol) basin; (Abwasch~) sink; (Toiletten~) bowl, pan; (Schwimm~) pool; (Stau~) reservoir; (Fisch~) pond; (Tauf~) font. (b) (Anat) pelvis, pelvic girdle. **ein breites ~** broad hips. (c) (Mus) cymbal.

Becken- (Anat, Med): ~**bruch** m fractured pelvis, pelvic fracture; ~**endlage** f breech position or presentation; ~**knochen** m hip-bone.

Beckmesser m -s, - (pej) caviller, carper.

Beckmesserei f (pej) cavilling, carping.

beckmessern vi (pej) to cavil, to carp.

bedachen* vt to roof.

bedacht¹ ptp of bedenken, bedachen.

bedacht² adj (a) (überlegt) prudent, careful, cautious. (b) auf etw (acc) ~ sein to be concerned about sth; **er ist nur auf sich ~** he only thinks about himself; **darauf ~ sein, etw zu tun** to be concerned about doing sth or to do sth.

Bedacht m -s, no pl (geh) mit ~ (vorsichtig) prudently, carefully, with care; (absichtlich) deliberately; voll ~ very prudently or carefully, with great care; ohne ~ without thinking, imprudently; **etw mit (gutem) ~ tun** to do sth (quite) deliberately; **auf etw (acc) ~ nehmen** to be mindful of sth, to take sth into consideration.

Bedachte(r) mf decl as adj (Jur) beneficiary.

bedächtig adj (gemessen) Schritt, Sprache measured no adv, deliberate; Wesen deliberate, steady; (besonnen) thoughtful, reflective. ~ or mit ~en Schritten or ~en Schrittes (liter) gehen to walk with measured or deliberate steps; langsam und ~ sprechen to speak in slow, measured tones.

Bedächtigkeit f, no pl siehe adj measuredness, deliberateness; steadiness; thoughtfulness, reflectiveness. **etw mit großer ~ tun** to do sth with great deliberation/very thoughtfully or reflectively.

bedachtsam adj (geh) careful, deliberate.

Bedachtsamkeit f, no pl (geh) care, deliberation.

Bedachung f roofing; (Dach auch) roof.

bedang pret of bedingen 2.

bedanken* 1 vr (a) to say thank-you, to express one's thanks (form). **sich bei jdm (für etw) ~** to thank sb (for sth), to say thank-you to sb (for sth); **ich bedanke mich** thank you; **ich bedanke mich herzlich** thank you very much, (very) many thanks; **dafür können Sie sich bei Herrn Weitz ~** (iro inf) you've got Mr Weitz to thank or you can thank Mr Weitz for that (iro).
(b) (iro inf) **ich bedanke mich, dafür bedanke ich mich (bestens)** no thank you (very much); **dafür/für dergleichen wird er sich ~** he refuses point-blank.
2 vt (form) **seien Sie (herzlich) bedankt!** please accept my/our (grateful or deepest) thanks (form).

Bedarf m -(e)s, no pl (an + dat) (Bedürfnis) need (an + dat for); (~smenge) requirements pl, requisites pl. **bei ~** as or when required; **bei dringendem ~** in cases of urgent need; **der Bus hält hier nur bei ~** the bus stops here only on request; **Dinge des täglichen ~s** basic or everyday necessities; **alles für den häuslichen ~** all household requirements or requisites; **alles für den ~ des Rauchers/der jungen Mutter** everything for the smoker/young mother, everything for the smoker/young mother needs; **seinen ~ an Wein/Lebensmitteln etc einkaufen** to buy one's supply of wine/food etc or the wine/food etc one needs; **einem ~ abhelfen** to meet a need; **an etw (dat) ~ haben** to need sth, to be in need of sth; **danke, kein** ~ (*iro inf*) no thank you, not on your life (*inf*); *siehe* **decken**.

(b) (*Comm: Nachfrage*) demand (*an* +*dat* for). **(je) nach** ~ according to demand; **den** ~ **übersteigen** to exceed demand; **über** ~ in excess of demand.

Bedarfs-: ~**artikel** *m* requisite; ~**befriedigung**, ~**deckung** *f* satisfaction of the/sb's needs; ~**fall** *m* (*form*) need; **im** ~**fall** if necessary; (*wenn gebraucht*) as necessary *or* required; **für den** ~**fall vorsorgen** to provide for a time of need; **wir wissen nicht, wann der** ~**fall eintritt** we don't know when the need will arise; **b**~**gerecht** *adj* **b**~**gerecht produzieren** to match production and demand; **ein b**~**gerechtes Warenangebot** a range of goods which meets consumer demands; ~**güter** *pl* consumer goods *pl*; ~**haltestelle** *f* request (bus/tram) stop; ~**träger** *m* (*Comm*) consumer.

bedauerlich *adj* regrettable, unfortunate. ~! how unfortunate.

bedauerlicherweise *adv* regrettably, unfortunately.

bedauern* *vt* (a) *etw* to regret. **einen Irrtum** ~ to regret one's mistake *or* having made a mistake; **wir** ~, **Ihnen mitteilen zu müssen,** ... we regret to have to inform you ...; **er hat sehr bedauert, daß** ... he was very sorry that ...; **er schüttelte** ~**d den Kopf** he shook his head regretfully; **(ich) bedau(e)re!** I am sorry.

(b) (*bemitleiden*) *jdn* to feel *or* be sorry for. **sich selbst** ~ to feel sorry for oneself; **er ist zu** ~ he is to be pitied, one *or* you should feel sorry for him; **er läßt sich gerne** ~, **er will immer bedauert sein** he always wants people to feel sorry for him.

Bedauern *nt* -s, *no pl* regret. **(sehr) zu meinem** ~ (much) to my regret; **zu meinem** ~ **kann ich nicht kommen** I regret that *or* to my regret I will not be able to come; **zu meinem größten** ~ **muß ich Ihnen mitteilen** ... it is with the deepest regret that I must inform you ...; **mit** ~ **habe ich** ... it is with regret that I ...

bedauerns-: ~**wert**, ~**würdig** (*geh*) *adj* Mensch pitiful; *Zustand* deplorable.

bedecken* **1** *vt* (a) to cover. **von etw bedeckt sein** to be covered in sth; **mit einem Tuch/mit Papieren/Pickeln/Staub bedeckt sein** to be covered with a cloth/with *or* in papers/spots/dust; **sie hat ihre Familie mit Schande bedeckt** (*liter*) she brought shame upon her family.

(b) (*Astron*) Stern to eclipse, to occult (*spec*).

2 *vr* (a) (*sich zudecken*) to cover oneself. **bitte** ~ **Sie sich doch!** (*dated*) please put your hat on.

(b) (*Himmel*) to become overcast, to cloud over. **der Himmel bedeckte sich mit Wolken** it *or* the sky clouded over *or* became overcast.

bedeckt *adj* (a) covered. ~**en Hauptes** (*old*) with one's head covered. **(b)** (*bewölkt*) overcast, cloudy. **bei** ~**em Himmel** when the sky *or* it is overcast *or* cloudy.

Bedecktsamer [-za:-] *m*, **Bedecktsamige** [-za:-] *pl* (*Bot*) angiospermae *pl*.

Bedeckung *f* (a) (*das Bedecken*) covering. **(b)** (*Deckendes*) cover, covering. **(c)** (*Mil*) (*Geleitschutz*) guard, escort; (*Leibwache*) guard. **der Konvoi hatte drei Fregatten zur** ~ **the** convoy was escorted by *or* had an escort of three frigates. **(d)** (*Astron: von Stern*) eclipse, occultation (*spec*).

bedenken* *irreg* **1** *vt* (a) (*überlegen*) Sache, Lage, Maßnahme *etc* to consider, to think about. **das will wohl bedacht sein** (*geh*) that calls for careful consideration; **wenn man es recht bedenkt,** ... if you think about it properly ...

(b) (*in Betracht ziehen*) Umstand, Folgen *etc* to consider, to take into consideration. **man muß** ~, **daß** ... one must take into consideration the fact that ...; **das hättest du früher** *or* **vorher** ~ **sollen** you should have thought about that sooner *or* before; **ich gebe (es) zu** ~, **daß** ... (*geh*) I would ask you to consider that ...; **bedenke, daß du sterben mußt** remember you are mortal.

(c) (*in Testament*) to remember. **jdn mit einem Geschenk** ~ (*geh*) to give sb a present; **jdn reich** ~ (*geh*) to be generous to sb; **mit etw bedacht werden** to receive sth; **auch ich wurde bedacht** I was not forgotten (either), there was something for me too; **ich wurde auch diesmal reich bedacht** (*geh*) I did very well this time; *siehe* **Bedachte(r)**.

2 *vr* (*geh*) to think (about it), to reflect. **bedenke dich gut, ehe du** ... think well before you ...; **ohne sich lange zu** ~ without stopping to think *or* reflect; *siehe* **bedacht²**.

Bedenken *nt* -s, - (a) *usu pl* (*Zweifel, Einwand*) doubt, reservation, misgiving. *moralische* ~ moral scruples; ~ **haben** *or* **tragen** (*geh*) to have one's doubts (*bei* about); **ihm kommen** ~ he is having second thoughts; **ohne** ~ **vorgehen** to act relentlessly *or* unrelentingly. **(b)** *no pl* (*das Überlegen*) consideration (*gen* of), reflection (*gen* (up)on). **nach langem** ~ after much thought; **ohne** ~ without thinking.

bedenkenlos *adj* (a) (*ohne Zögern*) Zustimmung unhesitating, prompt. **ich würde** ~ **hingehen** I would not hesitate to go *or* would have no hesitation in going; ~ **zustimmen** to agree without hesitation. **(b)** (*skrupellos*) heedless of others; (*unüberlegt*) thoughtless. **etw** ~ **tun** to do sth without thinking.

Bedenkenlosigkeit *f*, *no pl* (a) (*Bereitwilligkeit*) readiness, promptness. **(b)** (*Skrupellosigkeit*) unscrupulousness, lack of scruples; (*Unüberlegtheit*) thoughtlessness, lack of thought.

bedenkenswert *adj* worth thinking about *or* considering.

bedenklich *adj* (a) (*zweifelhaft*) Geschäfte, Mittel *etc* dubious, questionable.

(b) (*besorgniserregend*) Lage, Verschlimmerung *etc* serious, disturbing, alarming; Gesundheitszustand serious. **der Zustand des Kranken ist** ~ the patient's condition is giving cause for concern; **der Himmel sah** ~ **aus** the sky looked ominous.

(c) (*besorgt*) apprehensive, anxious. **ein** ~**es Gesicht machen** to look apprehensive; **jdn** ~ **stimmen** to make sb (feel) apprehensive.

Bedenklichkeit *f* *siehe adj* (a) dubiousness, questionable-

ness. **(b)** seriousness, disturbing *or* alarming nature. **(c)** apprehension, anxiety. **(d)** *usu pl* (*old: Bedenken*) doubt, reservation.

Bedenkzeit *f* jdm zwei Tage/bis Freitag ~ **geben** to give sb two days/until Friday to think about it; **sich** (*dat*) **(eine)** ~ **ausbitten** *or* **erbitten, um** ~ **bitten** to ask for time to think about it.

bedeppert *adj* (*inf*) (a) (*ratlos*) dazed, stunned. **(b)** (*trottelig*) dopey (*inf*), daft.

bedeuten* *vt* (a) (*gleichzusetzen sein mit, heißen, bezeichnen*) to mean; (*Math, Ling*) to stand for, to denote; (*versinnbildlichen*) to signify, to symbolize. **was bedeutet dieses Wort?** what does this word mean?, what's the meaning of this word?; **was soll das** ~? what does that mean?; **was soll denn das** ~! what's the meaning of that?; **das hat nichts zu** ~ it doesn't mean anything; (*macht nichts aus*) it doesn't matter; **das würde ein Wagnis** ~ that would be really daring; **das bedeutet einen Eingriff in die Menschenrechte** that amounts to an attack on human rights.

(b) (*ankündigen, zur Folge haben*) to mean. **diese Wolken** ~ **schlechtes Wetter** these clouds mean *or* spell bad weather; **das hat etwas zu** ~! that must mean something; **das bedeutet nichts Gutes** that spells trouble, that bodes ill.

(c) (*gelten*) to mean (*dat, für* to); (*sein, gelten als auch*) to be. **Geld bedeutet mir nichts** money doesn't mean anything *or* means nothing to me; **sein Name bedeutet etwas in der Medizin** his name means something *or* he is a name in the field of medicine.

(d) (*geh: einen Hinweis geben*) to indicate, to intimate; (*mit Geste*) to indicate, to gesture; (*Abneigung, Zustimmung auch* to signify. **ich bedeutete ihm, das zu tun** I indicated *or* intimated that he should do that; **man bedeutete mir, daß** ... I was given to understand that ...

bedeutend 1 *adj* (a) (*wichtig, bemerkenswert*) Persönlichkeit important, distinguished, eminent; Leistung, Rolle significant, important. **etwas B**~**es leisten** to achieve something important *or* significant. **(b)** (*groß*) Summe, Erfolg considerable, significant. **2** *adv* (*beträchtlich*) considerably.

bedeutsam *adj* (a) (*vielsagend*) meaningful, significant; Rede, Blick auch eloquent. **jdm** ~ **zulächeln** to smile meaning(ful)ly at sb. **(b)** (*wichtig*) Gespräch, Fortschritt *etc* important; (*folgenschwer*) significant (*für* for).

Bedeutsamkeit *f* *siehe adj* (a) meaningfulness, significance; eloquence. **(b)** importance; significance.

Bedeutung *f* (a) (*Sinn, Wortsinn*) meaning. **in wörtlicher/übertragener** ~ in the literal/figurative sense.

(b) (*Wichtigkeit*) importance, significance; (*Tragweite*) significance. **von** ~ **sein** to be important *or* significant *or* of significance; **von (großer** *or* **tiefer/geringer)** ~ **sein** to be of (great/little) importance *or* (very/not very) important; **ein Mann von** ~ an important figure; **nichts von** ~ nothing of any importance; **ohne** ~ of no importance; **große** ~ **besitzen** to be of great importance.

Bedeutungs-: ~**erweiterung** *f* (*Ling*) extension of meaning; ~**gehalt** *m* meaning; ~**lehre** *f* (*Ling*) semantics *sing*, science of meaning (*old*); **b**~**los** *adj* (a) (*unwichtig*) insignificant, unimportant; **(b)** (*nichts besagend*) meaningless; ~**losigkeit** *f* insignificance, unimportance; **zur** ~**losigkeit verurteilt sein** to be condemned to insignificance; **b**~**schwer** *adj* (*geh*) meaningful, laden *or* pregnant with meaning (*liter*); (*folgenschwer*) momentous; ~**vereng(er)ung** *f* (*Ling*) narrowing of meaning; ~**verschiebung** *f* (*Ling*) shift of meaning, sense *or* semantic shift; **b**~**verwandt** *adj* (*Ling*) semantically related; **b**~**voll** *adj* *siehe* **bedeutsam**; ~**wandel** *m* change in meaning, semantic change; ~**wörterbuch** *nt* (defining) dictionary.

bedienen* **1** *vt* (a) (*Verkäufer*) to serve, to attend to; (*Kellner auch*) to wait on; (*Handlanger*) to assist; (*Diener etc*) to serve, to wait on. **werden Sie schon bedient?** are you being attended to *or* served?; **jdn mit Fleisch etc** ~ to serve sb (with) meat *etc*; **hier wird man gut bedient** the service is good here; **er läßt sich gern** ~ he likes to be waited on; **mit diesem Ratschlag war ich schlecht bedient** I was ill-served by that advice; **mit dieser Ware/damit sind Sie sehr gut bedient** these goods/that should serve you very well; **ich bin bedient!** (*inf*) I've had enough, I've had all I can take.

(b) (*Verkehrsmittel*) to serve. **diese Flugroute wird von X bedient** X operate (on) this route; **Concorde soll demnächst New York** ~ Concorde is due to operate to New York soon. **(c)** (*handhaben*) Maschine, Geschütz *etc* to operate; Telefon to answer.

(d) (*Sport*) to pass *or* feed (the ball) to.

(e) (*Cards*) eine Farbe/Karo ~ to follow suit/to follow suit in diamonds.

2 *vi* (a) to serve; (*Kellner auch*) to wait (at table); (*als Beruf*) to wait, to be a waiter/waitress.

(b) (*Cards*) **du mußt** ~ you must follow suit; **falsch** ~ to revoke, to fail to follow suit.

3 *vr* (a) (*bei Tisch*) to help *or* serve oneself (*mit* to). **bitte** ~ **Sie sich** please help *or* serve yourself.

(b) (*geh: gebrauchen*) **sich jds/einer Sache** ~ to use sb/sth.

Bedienerin *f* (*Aus*) charwoman.

bedienstet *adj*: **bei jdm** ~ **sein** to be in service with sb; ~ **sein** (*Aus: im öffentlichen Dienst*) to be in the civil service.

Bedienstete(r) *mf decl as adj* (a) (*im öffentlichen Dienst*) public employee. **(b)** (*old: Diener*) servant.

Bediente(r) *mf decl as adj* (*old*) servant.

Bedienung *f* (a) *no pl* (*in Restaurant etc*) service; (*von Maschinen*) operation. **die** ~ **der Kunden** serving the customers; **zur freien** *or* **gefälligen** (*old*) ~ please take one *or* help yourself; **die** ~ **des Geräts erlernen** to learn how to operate the machine.

(b) (~*sgeld*) service (charge).

(c) (~*spersonal*) staff; (*Kellner etc*) waiter/waitress. **kommt denn hier keine ~?** isn't anyone serving here?; **hallo, ~!, ~ bitte!** waiter/waitress!

(d) (*Mil*: ~*smannschaft*) crew.

Bedienungs-: ~**anleitung,** ~**anweisung** f operating instructions pl or directions pl; ~**aufschlag** m, ~**geld** nt service charge; ~**fehler** m mistake in operating a/the machine; ~**hebel** m operating lever; ~**mannschaft** f (*Mil*) crew; ~**vorschrift** f operating instructions pl; ~**zuschlag** m service charge.

bedingen 1 pret **bedingte,** ptp **bedingt** vt (a) (*bewirken*) to cause; (*notwendig machen*) to necessitate; (*Psych, Physiol*) to condition; (*logisch voraussetzen*) to presuppose. **sich gegenseitig ~** to be mutually dependent; ~**de Konjunktion** conditional conjunction; siehe **bedingt.**

(b) (*voraussetzen, verlangen*) to call for, to demand.

2 pret **bedang** or **bedingte,** ptp **bedungen** vr **sich** (dat) **etw ~** (old) to stipulate sth, to make sth a condition.

bedingt adj (a) (*eingeschränkt*) limited; Lob auch qualified. (nur) **~ richtig** (only) partly or partially right; (nur) **~ gelten** to be (only) partly or partially valid; **~ tauglich** (Mil) fit for limited duties; **gefällt es Ihnen hier? — ~!** do you like it here? — with some reservations.

(b) (*an Bedingung geknüpft*) Annahme, Straferlaß, Strafaussetzung conditional.

(c) (*Physiol*) Reflex conditioned.

Bedingtheit f (a) (*von Lob, Anerkennung*) limitedness. (b) (*von Existenz etw*) determinedness. **der Unterschied zwischen kausaler und logischer ~** the difference between being causally and logically determined.

Bedingung f (a) (*Voraussetzung*) condition; (*Erfordernis*) requirement. **die erste ~ für etw** the basic requirement for sth; **mit or unter der ~, daß ...** on condition or with the proviso that ...; **unter keiner ~** in or under no circumstances, on no condition; **(nur) unter einer ~** (only) on one condition; **unter jeder anderen ~** in any other circumstances; **von einer ~ abhängen** or **abhängig sein** to be conditional on one thing; **~ (für meine Zustimmung) ist, daß** ... it is a condition (of my consent) that ...; **es zur ~ machen, daß** ... to stipulate that ...

(b) (*Forderung*) term, condition. **zu günstigen ~en** (Comm) on favourable terms.

(c) ~**en** pl (*Umstände*) conditions pl; **unter guten/harten ~en arbeiten** to work in good/under or in difficult conditions.

Bedingungs-: ~**form** f (*Gram*) conditional (form); **b~los** adj Kapitulation unconditional; Hingabe, Gehorsam, Gefolgschaft unquestioning; **b~los für etw eintreten** to support sth without reservation; ~**satz** m conditional clause.

bedrängen vt Feind to attack; gegnerische Mannschaft to put pressure on, to pressurize; (*beständigen*) to plague, to badger; Schuldner to press (for payment); Passanten, Mädchen to pester; (*bedrücken: Sorgen*) to beset; (*heimsuchen*) to haunt. **Zweifel bedrängten ihn** he was beset or haunted by doubts; **ein bedrängtes Herz** a troubled heart; **sich in einer bedrängten Lage/in bedrängten Verhältnissen finden** to be in dire or desperate straits; **die Bedrängten und Verzweifelten** people in distress and despair.

Bedrängnis f (geh) (*seelische ~*) distress, torment. **in arger or großer/einer argen or großen ~** in dire or desperate straits; **jdn/etw in ~ bringen** to get sb/sth into trouble; **in ~ geraten** to get into difficulties.

Bedrängung f (a) siehe vt attacking; pressurizing; plaguing; badgering; pressing; pestering; besetting; haunting. (b) siehe **Bedrängnis.**

bedripst adj (N Ger) stunned, dazed.

bedrohen* vt (a) to threaten.

(b) (*gefährden*) to endanger, to threaten; Gesundheit to endanger. **den Frieden ~** to be a threat to peace; **vom Tode/von Überschwemmung bedroht** in mortal danger/in danger of being flooded; **vom Aussterben bedroht** threatened with extinction, in danger of becoming extinct.

bedrohlich adj (*gefährlich*) dangerous, alarming; (*unheilverkündend*) ominous, menacing, threatening. **sich ~ verschlechtern** to deteriorate alarmingly; **in ~e Nähe rücken or kommen** to get dangerously or perilously close.

Bedrohung f threat (gen to); (*das Bedrohen auch*) threatening (gen of). **in ständiger ~ leben** to live under a constant threat.

bedrucken* vt to print on. **ein bedrucktes Kleid** a print dress; **bedruckter Stoff** print, printed fabric; **etw mit einem Muster ~** to print a pattern on sth.

bedrücken* vt (a) to depress. **jdn ~** to depress sb, to make sb feel depressed; **was bedrückt dich?** what is (weighing) on your mind?; **Sorgen bedrückten ihn** cares were weighing upon him.

(b) (*old: unterdrücken*) to oppress.

bedrückend adj Anblick, Nachrichten, Vorstellung depressing; (*lastend*) oppressive; Sorge, Not pressing.

Bedrücker m -s, - (old) oppressor.

bedrückt adj (a) (*niedergeschlagen*) depressed, dejected; Schweigen oppressive. (b) (*old*) Volk oppressed.

Bedrückung f siehe adj (a) depression, dejection; oppressiveness. (b) (*old*) oppression.

Beduine m -n, -n, **Beduinin** f Bedouin.

bedungen ptp of **bedingen** 2.

bedürfen pret **bedurfte,** ptp **bedurft** vi + gen (geh) to need, to require. **das bedarf keiner weiteren Erklärung** there's no need for any further explanation; **es hätte nur eines Wortes bedurft, um** ... it would only have taken a word to ...; **es bedarf nur eines Wortes von Ihnen** you only have to or need to say the word; **es bedarf einiger Mühe** some effort is called for or required; **ohne daß es eines Hinweises bedurft hätte,** ... without having to be asked ...

Bedürfnis nt (a) (*Notwendigkeit*) need; (no pl: Bedarf auch) necessity. **die ~se des täglichen Lebens** everyday needs; **dafür liegt kein ~ vor or besteht kein ~** there is no need or necessity for that.

(b) no pl (*Verlangen*) need; (form: Anliegen) wish, desire. **es war ihm ein ~,** ... it was his wish or desire to ..., he wished or desired to ...; **ich hatte das ~/das dringende ~, das zu tun** I felt the need/an urgent need to do that; **das ~ nach Schlaf haben or fühlen** to be or feel in need of sleep.

(c) (*old: Notdurft*) call of nature. **(s)ein ~ verrichten** to relieve oneself.

Bedürfnis-: ~**anstalt** f (form) öffentliche ~**anstalt** public convenience or restroom (US); ~**befriedigung** f satisfaction of one's/sb's needs; **b~los** adj Mensch etc undemanding, modest in one's needs; Leben humble, simple; **unsere Vorfahren waren wesentlich b~loser als wir** our ancestors were much more modest in their needs than we are; ~**losigkeit** f modesty of one's needs.

bedurft ptp of **bedürfen.**

bedurfte pret of **bedürfen.**

bedürftig adj (a) (*hilfs~*) needy, in need. **die B~en** the needy pl, those in need. (b) **einer Sache** (gen) **~ sein** (geh) to be or stand in need of sth, to have need of sth.

Bedürftigkeit f, no pl need. **jds ~** (*amtlich*) **feststellen** to give sb a means test.

beduseln* vr (inf) to get sozzled (inf) or tipsy (inf).

beduselt adj (inf) (*angetrunken*) sozzled (inf), tipsy (inf); (*benommen*) bemused, befuddled.

Beefsteak ['bi:fste:k] nt steak. **deutsches ~** hamburger, beefburger.

be|ehren* 1 vt (iro, geh) to honour. **wann ~ Sie uns (mit einem Besuch)?** when will you honour us with a visit?; **bitte ~ Sie uns bald wieder** (Kellner etc) I hope you'll do us the honour of coming again soon.

2 vr **sich ~, etw zu tun** (form) to have the honour or privilege of doing sth (form).

be|eiden* (old) vt (*beschwören*) Sache, Aussage to swear to. **be|eidigen*** vt (a) siehe **beeiden.** (b) (old) siehe **vereidigen.**

Be|eidigung f siehe **Vereidigung.**

be|eilen* vr to hurry (up), to get a move on (inf). **beeil dich, das fertigzukriegen** hurry up and finish that; **sich sehr or mächtig** (inf) **~ to get a real move on** (inf); **er beeilte sich hinzuzufügen** ... (form) he hastened to add ...

Be|eilung interj (inf) get a move on (inf), step on it (inf).

be|eindrucken* vt to impress; (*Eindruck hinterlassen auch*) to make an impression on. **davon lasse ich mich nicht ~** I won't be impressed by that.

be|eindruckend adj impressive.

be|einflußbar adj Mensch impressionable, suggestive. **er ist nur schwer ~** he is hard to influence or sway; **diese Vorgänge sind nicht ~** these events cannot be influenced or changed.

be|einflussen* vt jdn to influence; Urteil, Meinung, Aussage auch to sway; Ereignisse, Vorgänge auch to affect. **jdn günstig/nachhaltig ~** to have a favourable or good/lasting influence on sb; **er ist leicht/schwer zu ~** he is easily influenced/hard to influence; **kannst du deinen Freund nicht ~?** can't you persuade your friend?; **durch etw beeinflußt sein** to be or to have been influenced or affected by sth.

Be|einflussung f (das Beeinflussen) influencing; (Einfluß) influence (durch of). **~ der Rechtspflege** (Jur) prejudicing the outcome of a trial.

be|einträchtigen* vt (*stören*) to spoil; Vergnügen, Genuß auch to detract from; Konzentration auch to disturb; Rundfunkempfang to interfere with, to impair; (*schädigen*) jds Ruf to damage, to harm; (*vermindern*) Qualität, Wert, Absatz, Energie, Appetit to reduce; Sehvermögen etc to impair; Reaktionen, Leistung to reduce, to impair; (*hemmen*) Entscheidung to interfere with; Freiheit, Entschlußkraft to restrict, to interfere with, to curb. **dadurch wird der Wert erheblich beeinträchtigt** that reduces the value considerably; **sich (gegenseitig) ~** to have an adverse effect on one another; (*Empfangsgeräte*) to interfere with one another; **jdn in seiner Freiheit or jds Freiheit ~** to restrict or interfere with or curb sb's freedom.

Be|einträchtigung f siehe vt spoiling; detracting (gen from); disturbance; interference (gen with); impairment; damage, harm (gen to); reduction (gen of, in); impairment; interference (gen with); restriction, curbing. **ohne ~ seiner Rechte** without restricting his rights.

be|enden* vt (Sw) to upset, to distress.

Beelzebub [be'ɛltsəbuːp, 'beːl-] m -s (Bibl) Beelzebub; siehe **Teufel.**

be|enden*, be|endigen* (old) vt to end; Arbeit, Aufgabe etc to finish, to complete; Vortrag, Brief, Schulstunde, Versammlung auch to bring to an end, to conclude; Streik, Streit, Krieg, Verhältnis auch to bring to an end; Studium to complete. **der Abend wurde mit einer Diskussion beendet** the evening ended with or finished with a discussion; **etw vorzeitig ~** to cut sth short; **sein Leben ~** (geh) to end one's days; (*durch Selbstmord*) to take one's life; **damit ist unser Konzert/unser heutiges Programm beendet** that concludes or brings to an end our concert/our programmes for today.

Be|endigung, Be|endung (rare) f, no pl ending; (Ende) end; (*Fertigstellung*) completion; (Schluß) conclusion. **zur ~ dieser Arbeit** to finish this piece of work; **zur ~ des heutigen Abends** ... to round off this evening ...; **nach ~ des Unterrichts** after school (ends).

be|engen* vt (lit) Bewegung to restrict, to cramp; (Möbel etc) Zimmer to make cramped; (fig) to stifle, to inhibit. **das Zimmer/Kleid beengt mich** the room is too cramped/the dress

is too tight for me; ~de Kleidung tight or restricting clothing.
be|engt adj cramped, confined; (fig auch) stifled. ~ wohnen to live in cramped conditions; sich ~ fühlen to feel confined etc; ~e Verhältnisse (fig) restricted circumstances.
Be|engtheit f (Eingeschränktheit) restriction, confinement; (von Räumen) cramped feeling pl. ein Gefühl der ~ a restricted or confined or (fig auch) stifled feeling; ein Gefühl der ~ haben to feel restricted or confined or (fig auch) stifled.
be|erben* vt jdn ~ to inherit sb's estate, to be heir to sb.
be|erdigen* vt to bury. jdn kirchlich ~ to give sb a Christian burial.
Be|erdigung f burial; (~sfeier) funeral. auf der falschen ~ sein (hum sl) to have come to the wrong place.
Be|erdigungs- in cpds siehe auch Bestattungs- funeral; ~feier f funeral service.
Beere f -, -n berry; (Wein~) grape. ~n tragen to bear fruit; ~n sammeln, in die ~n gehen (dial) to go berry-picking; (Brom-beeren) to go blackberrying.
Beeren-: ~auslese f (Wein) wine made from specially selected grapes; ~frucht f berry; ~lese f fruit picking; ~obst nt soft fruit.
Beet nt -(e)s, -e (Blumen~, Spargel~) bed; (Gemüse~) patch; (Rabatte) border (mit of).
Beete f -, -n siehe Bete.
befähigen* vt to enable; (Ausbildung) to qualify, to equip. jdn zu etw ~ to enable sb to do sth; to qualify or equip sb to do sth.
befähigt adj (a) (durch Ausbildung) qualified. sie ist zum Richteramt ~ she is qualified to be or become a judge. (b) capable, competent. zu etw ~ sein to be capable of doing sth or competent to do sth.
Befähigung f, no pl (a) (durch Ausbildung, Voraussetzung) qualifications pl. die ~ zum Richteramt the qualifications to be or become a judge.
  (b) (Können, Eignung) capability, ability. er hat nicht die ~ dazu he does not have the ability to do that; ~ zu etw zeigen to show talent or a gift for sth.
Befähigungsnachweis m certificate of qualifications.
befahl pret of befehlen.
befahrbar adj Straße, Weg passable; Seeweg, Fluß navigable. ~ sein (Straße) to be open to traffic; manche Alpenstraßen sind nur im Sommer ~ some alpine roads are only open (to traffic) or passable in the summer; nicht ~ sein (Straße, Weg) to be closed (to traffic); (wegen Schnee etc auch) to be impassable; (Seeweg, Fluß) to be unnavigable or not navigable; siehe Bankette, Seitenstreifen.
befahren[1]* vt irreg (a) (Straße, Weg to use, to drive on or along; Paßstraße to drive over; Gegend, Land to drive or travel through; Kreuzung, Seitenstreifen to drive onto; Eisenbahn-strecke to travel on. der Paß kann nur im Sommer ~ werden the pass is only open to traffic or passable in summer; die Strecke darf nur in einer Richtung ~ werden this stretch of road is only open in one direction; dieser Weg kann nur mit dem Fahrrad ~ werden you can only use a bicycle on this path; die Straße darf nicht ~ werden/wird von Panzern ~ the road is closed/tanks use this road; diese Straße wird stark/wenig ~ this road is used a lot/isn't used much, there is a lot of/not much traffic on this road; diese Strecke wird nicht mehr von Zügen ~ trains no longer use this stretch of track.
  (b) (Schiff, Seemann) to sail; Fluß auch to sail up/down; Seeweg auch to navigate; Küste to sail along. der See wird von vielen Booten ~ many boats sail on or use this lake; diese Route wird nicht mehr von Schiffen ~ ships no longer sail this route.
  (c) (Min) Schacht to go down. die Grube wird nicht mehr ~ the mine is not worked any more.
  (d) (abladen auf) to spread. ein Feld mit Dung ~ to spread manure on a field.
befahren[2] adj (a) Straße, Seeweg, Kanal used. eine viel or stark/wenig ~e Straße etc a much/little used road etc. (b) (Naut: erprobt) seasoned attr, experienced. (ein) ~es Volk seasoned or experienced sailors pl or seamen pl. (c) (Hunt: bewohnt) inhabited.
Befahren nt -s, no pl use (gen of); (Vorgang) using. beim ~ der Brücke when using the bridge; „~ verboten" "road closed"; „~ der Brücke verboten" "bridge closed".
Befall m -(e)s, no pl attack; (mit Schädlingen) infestation. es kam zum ~ aller Organe all organs were affected; der ~ (des Kohls) mit Raupen the blight of caterpillars (on the cabbage).
befallen[1]* vt irreg (a) (geh: überkommen) to overcome; (Angst auch) to grip, to seize; (Durst, Hunger auch) to assail; (Fieber, Krankheit, Seuche) to attack, to strike; (Mißgeschick, Schicksal etc) to befall, to affect. Schlaf/(die) Reue befiel ihn he was overcome by sleep/with remorse, sleep/remorse over-came him; Angst befiel uns we were gripped by or seized with fear, fear gripped or seized us; eine Schwäche/eine Ohnmacht befiel sie she felt faint/she fainted.
  (b) (angreifen, infizieren) to affect; (Schädlinge, Ungeziefer) to infest.
befallen[2] adj affected (von by); (von Schädlingen) infested (von with).
befangen adj (a) Mensch, Lächeln bashful, diffident; Schweigen, Stille awkward.
  (b) (esp Jur: voreingenommen) Richter, Zeuge prejudiced, bias(s)ed. als ~ gelten to be considered (to be) prejudiced etc or (Jur auch) an interested party; sich für ~ erklären (Jur) to declare one's interest; jdn als ~ ablehnen (Jur) to object to sb on grounds of interest.
  (c) (geh: verstrickt) in der Vorstellung ~ sein, daß ... or ... zu ... to have the impression that ...; er ist in seinen eigenen Anschauungen ~ he can only see his own point of view; in einem Irrtum ~ sein to labour under a misapprehension.

Befangenheit f, no pl siehe adj (a) bashfulness, diffidence; awkwardness. (b) bias, prejudice; (Jur) interest. jdn wegen (Besorgnis der) ~ ablehnen (Jur) to object to sb on grounds of interest.
befassen* 1 vr (a) (sich beschäftigen) sich mit etw ~ to deal with sth; mit Problem, Frage auch to look into sth; mit Fall, Angelegenheit auch to attend to sth; mit Arbeit auch, Forschungsbereich etc to work on sth; sich mit jds Vorleben ~ to look into sb's past; damit haben wir uns jetzt lange genug befaßt we have spent long enough on or over that; er hat sich lange damit befaßt, alle Einzelheiten auszuarbeiten he spent a long time working out all the details; mit solchen Kleinigkeiten hat er sich nie befaßt he has never bothered with or concerned himself with such trivialities.
  (b) (sich annehmen) sich mit jdm ~ to deal with sb, to attend to sb; mit Kindern auch to see to sb; sich mit jdm sehr ~ to give sb a lot of attention.
  2 vt (a) (dial: anfassen) to touch.
  (b) (form) jdn mit etw ~ to get sb to deal with sth; mit etw befaßt sein to be dealing with sth; die mit diesem Fall befaßten Richter the judges engaged on this case.
befehden* 1 vt (Hist) to be feuding with; (fig) to attack. 2 vr to be feuding. sich mit Worten ~ to attack each other verbally.
Befehl m -(e)s, -e (a) (Anordnung) order, command (an + acc to, von from); (Physiol) command; (bei Computer) instruction. einen ~ verweigern to refuse to obey an order etc; er gab (uns) den ~, ... he ordered us to ...; wir hatten den ~, ... we had orders or were ordered to ...; wir haben ~, Sie festzunehmen we have orders or have been ordered to arrest you; auf seinen ~ (hin) on his orders, at his command; auf ~ to order; (sofort) at the drop of a hat (inf); auf ~ handeln to act under or according to orders; auf höheren ~ on orders from above; zu ~, Herr Hauptmann (Mil) yes, sir; (nach erhaltenem Befehl auch) very good, sir; zu ~, Herr Kapitän aye-aye, sir; ~ ausgeführt! mission accomplished; ~ ist ~ orders are orders; ~ vom Chef! boss's orders; dein Wunsch ist mir ~ (hum) your wish is my command.
  (b) (Befehlsgewalt) command. den ~ haben or führen to have command, to be in command (über + acc of); den ~ über-nehmen to take or assume command.
befehlen pret befahl, ptp befohlen vti (a) to order; (vi: Befehle erteilen) to give orders. er befahl Stillschweigen or zu schweigen he ordered them/us to be silent; sie befahl ihm Stillschweigen or zu schweigen she ordered him to keep quiet; schweigen Sie, befahl er be quiet, he ordered; er befahl, den Mann zu erschießen or die Erschießung des Mannes he ordered the man to be shot; sie befahl, daß ... she ordered or gave orders that ...; du hast mir gar nichts zu ~, von dir lasse ich mir nichts ~ I won't take orders from you; gnädige Frau ~?, was ~ gnädige Frau? (old form) yes, Madam?, what can I do for you, Madam?; ~ Sie sonst noch etwas, gnädige Frau? (form) will there be anything else, Madam?; er befiehlt gern he likes giving orders; hier habe nur ich zu ~ I give the orders around here; wie Sie ~ as you wish; wer ~ will, muß erst gehorchen lernen (prov) if you wish to command you must first learn to obey.
  (b) (beordern) (an die Front etc) to order, to send; (zu sich auch) to summon.
  (c) vi only (Mil: den Befehl haben) to be in command, to have command (über + acc of). über Leben und Tod ~ to be in absolute command.
  (d) (liter: anvertrauen) to entrust, to commend (liter). seine Seele Gott/in die Hände Gottes ~ to commend or entrust one's soul to God/into God's hands; Gott befohlen! (old) God be with you! (old).
befehlerisch adj Ton, Wesen imperious, dictatorial.
befehligen* vt (Mil) to command, to be in command of, to have command of or over.
Befehls-: ~ausgabe f (Mil) issuing of orders; um 15 Uhr ist ~ausgabe orders will be issued at 15⁰⁰ hours; ~bereich m (Mil) (area of) command; ~empfang m (Mil) receiving of orders; ~empfänger m recipient of an order; ~empfänger sein to follow orders (gen from); jdn zum ~empfänger degradieren (fig) to lower sb to the level of just following orders; ~form f (Gram) imperative; b~gemäß adj as ordered, in accordance with (sb's) orders; ~gewalt f (Mil) command; ~gewalt haben to be in or to have command (über + acc over); jds ~gewalt (dat) unterstehen to be under sb's command; ~haber m -s, - commander; b~haberisch adj dictatorial; ~notstand m (Jur) compulsion or necessity to obey orders; unter ~notstand handeln to be under orders to act (Jur); ~satz m (Gram) imperative, command; ~stab m (a) (Rail) signalling baton; ~ green flag (Brit); (b) (Leitung) siehe Kommandostab; ~ton m peremptory tone; ~verweigerung f (Mil) refusal to obey orders; b~widrig adj contrary to orders, against orders.
befeinden* vt (a) (geh) Land to be hostile towards; Ideologie, Schriften, Schriftsteller to attack. 2 vr to be hostile (towards each other).
befestigen* vt (a) (an + dat to) (anbringen) to fasten; (fest-machen auch) to secure; Boot to tie up. etw durch Nähen/Kleben etc ~ to sew/glue etc sth; etw an der Wand/Tür ~ to attach or fix sth to the wall/door; die beiden Enden/Teile werden (aneinander) befestigt the two ends/parts are fastened together; die Wäsche mit Klammern an der Leine ~ to peg the washing on the line; ein loses Brett ~ to fasten down or secure a loose board.
  (b) (fest, haltbar machen) Böschung, Deich to reinforce; Fahrbahn, Straße to make up; (fig: stärken) Herrschaft, Ruhm to consolidate. eine Straße gut ~ to make up a road with good foundations.
  (c) (Mil: mit Festungsanlagen versehen) to fortify.

Befestigung f (a) (das Befestigen) fastening; (das Festmachen auch) securing; (von Boot) tying up. **zur ~ des Plakats ...** in order to attach the poster ...
  (b) (Vorrichtung zum Befestigen) fastening, catch.
  (c) (das Haltbarmachen) reinforcement; (fig: Stärkung) consolidation. **zur ~ der Macht des ...** in order to consolidate the power of ...
  (d) (Mil) fortification.

Befestigungs-: ~anlage f, ~bau m, ~werk nt fortification, defence.

befeuchten* vt to moisten; Finger auch to wet; Wäsche to damp(en). **von Tränen befeuchtet** wet or moist with tears; **das vom Tau befeuchtete Gras** the grass moistened by the dew.

befeuern* vt (a) (beheizen) to fuel. (b) (Naut, Aviat) Wasserstraße, Untiefen to light or mark with beacons; Start- und Landebahn to light, to mark with lights. (c) (lit, fig: mit Geschossen) to bombard. (d) (geh: anspornen) to fire with enthusiasm.

Befeuerung f (Aviat, Naut) lights pl, beacons pl.

Beffchen nt Geneva band.

befiedert adj feathered.

befiedert adj feathered.

befiehl imper sing of befehlen.

befinden* irreg **1** vr (a) (sein) to be; (liegen auch) to be situated; (esp in Maschine, Körper etc auch) to be located. **sich auf Reisen ~** to be away; **unter ihnen befanden sich einige, die ...** there were some amongst them who ...; **die Abbildung befindet sich im Katalog** the illustration can be found or is in the catalogue; **sich in Verwirrung/guter Laune/im Irrtum ~** to be confused/in a good mood/mistaken; **sich auf dem Weg der Besserung ~** to be on the road to recovery; **wenn man sich in schlechter Gesellschaft befindet ...** if you find yourself in bad company ...
  (b) (form: sich fühlen) to feel. **wie ~ Sie sich heute?** how are you (feeling) or how do you feel today?
  2 vt (form: erachten) to deem (form), to find. **etw für nötig/angemessen/für or als gut ~** to deem or find sth (to be) necessary/appropriate/good; **Ihre Papiere wurden in Ordnung befunden** your papers were found to be in order; **jdn für schuldig ~** to find sb guilty; siehe wiegen².
  3 vi (geh: entscheiden) to come to or make a decision, to decide (über +acc about, in +dat on). **darüber hat der Arzt zu ~/habe ich nicht zu ~** that is for the doctor/not for me to decide; **über jdn/etw ~** to pass judgement or reach a verdict on sb/sth.

Befinden nt -s, no pl (form: Gesundheitszustand) (state of) health; (eines Kranken) condition. **seelisches ~** mental state or condition; **wie ist Ihr ~?** (form) how are you (feeling)?
  (b) (geh: das Dafürhalten) view, opinion. **nach meinem ~** in my view or opinion; **nach eigenem ~ entscheiden** to decide according to one's own judgement.

befindlich adj usu attr (form) (a) (an einem Ort) Gebäude, Park situated, located; (in Behälter) contained. **der hinter dem Hause ~e Garten** the garden (situated) behind the house; **der an der Tür ~e Haken** the hook on the door; **alle in der Bibliothek ~en Bücher** all the books in the library.
  (b) (in einem Zustand) **das im Umbau ~e Hotel** the hotel which is being renovated; **das unterwegs ~e Paket** the parcel which is in the post; **das im Umlauf ~e Geld** the money in circulation; **die in Kraft ~e Verordnung** the regulation which is in force.

befingern* vt (inf) (betasten) to finger. **eine Sache ~** (sl) to deal with a matter.

beflaggen* vt Häuser to (be)deck or decorate with flags; Schiff to dress. **die beflaggten Straßen** the flag-decked streets, the streets (be)decked or decorated with flags; **anläßlich seines Todes wurden alle öffentlichen Gebäude beflaggt** flags were flown on all public buildings to mark his death.

Beflaggung f (das Beflaggen) (von Gebäuden) decoration with flags; (von Schiffen) dressing. (b) (Fahnenschmuck) flags pl.

beflecken* vt (a) (lit) to stain. **er hat seinen Anzug mit Farbe befleckt** he got paint on his suit; **er hat sich or seine Hände mit Blut befleckt** (fig) he has blood on his hands.
  (b) (fig geh) Ruf, Ehre to cast a slur on, to besmirch, to sully; Heiligtum to defile, to desecrate.

befleckt adj stained. **sein mit Blut ~er Anzug** his bloodstained suit. (b) Ruf, Ehre sullied, besmirched.

Befleckung f siehe vt (a) staining. (b) besmirching, sullying; defilement, desecration.

befleißen* pret befliß, ptp beflissen vr (old) siehe befleißigen.

befleißigen* vr (geh) sich einer Sache (gen) ~ to cultivate sth; **sich ~, etw zu tun** to make a great effort to do sth; **sich größter or der größten Höflichkeit ~** to go out of one's way to be polite.

befliegen* vt irreg (Aviat) Strecke to fly, to operate (on); Gegend to fly over; Raum to fly through or in. **eine viel beflogene Strecke** a heavily used route.

befliß pret of befleißen.

beflissen 1 ptp of befleißen. **2** adj (geh) (bemüht) zealous, keen; (pej: unterwürfig) obsequious. **um etw ~ sein** to be concerned for sth; **er war sehr um die Zufriedenheit seiner Gäste ~** he was very anxious or concerned to please his guests; **~ sein, etw zu tun** to be concerned to do sth; **ängstlich ~** anxious.

Beflissenheit f siehe adj zeal, keenness; obsequiousness.

beflissentlich adv siehe geflissentlich.

beflügeln* vt (geh) to inspire, to fire. **die Angst beflügelte seine Schritte** (liter) fear winged his steps (liter); **der Gedanke an Erfolg beflügelte ihn** the thought of success spurred him on.

befluten* vt to flood.

befohlen ptp of befehlen.

befolgen* vt Vorschrift, Befehl etc to obey, to comply with;

grammatische Regel to follow, to obey; Rat(schlag) to follow, to take.

Befolgung f siehe vt obeying, compliance (gen with); following, obeying; following, taking. **~ der Regel** obeying the rules, compliance with the rules.

Beförderer m (a) (form) carrier. (b) (rare) siehe **Förderer** (a).

befördern* vt (a) Waren, Gepäck to transport, to carry; Personen to carry; Post to handle. **etw mit der Post/per Luftpost/Bahn/Schiff ~** to send sth by post/airmail/rail/ship; to ship sth; **jdn/etw von A nach B ~** to transport or convey sb/sth from A to B; **jdn an die (frische) Luft or zur Tür hinaus or ins Freie ~** (fig) to fling or chuck sb out (inf); **jdn ins Jenseits ~** (inf) to bump sb off (inf), to do sb in (inf).
  (b) (dienstlich aufrücken lassen) to promote. **er wurde zum Major befördert** he was promoted to (the rank of) major.
  (c) (rare: begünstigen) siehe **fördern.**

Beförderung f siehe vt (a) transportation, carriage; carriage; handling. **die ~ der Post/eines Briefes dauert drei Tage** the post/a letter takes three days (to arrive); **für die ~ von 35 Personen zugelassen** permitted to carry 35 persons; **für die ~ der Kursteilnehmer wird gesorgt** transport will be arranged for course participants; **~ zu Lande/zur Luft/per Bahn** land/air/rail transportation. (b) promotion.

Beförderungs-: ~bedingungen pl terms pl or conditions pl of carriage; ~dauer f delivery time; ~kosten pl cost sing of transportation or carriage; ~liste f promotion list; ~mittel nt means of transport; ~pflicht f obligation of taxis, buses etc to accept passengers; ~steuer f transport tax; ~tarif m transportation or (Post~) postage charge.

befrachten* vt Fahrzeug, Schiff to load; (fig geh auch) to burden. **ein schwer befrachtetes Schiff** a heavily laden ship; **seine übermäßig mit Emotionen befrachtete Rede** his speech, overladen with emotion.

Befrachter m -s, - shipper, freighter.

Befrachtung f loading.

befrackt adj in tails, tail-coated. **~ sein** to be wearing tails.

befragen* **1** vt (a) (über +acc, zu, nach about) to question; Zeugen auch to examine. **jdn im Kreuzverhör ~** to cross-question or (esp Jur) to cross-examine sb; **auf B~** when questioned.
  (b) (um Stellungnahme bitten) to consult (über +acc, nach about). **jdn um Rat/nach seiner Meinung ~** to ask sb for advice/his opinion, to ask sb's advice/opinion; **jdn in einer Angelegenheit ~** to consult sb about or on a matter.
  2 vr (dated) to consult; (sich erkundigen) to make enquiries. **sich bei jdm/etw ~** to consult sb/sth.

Befragte(r) mf decl as adj person asked; (in Umfrage auch) interviewee. **alle ~n** all those asked.

Befragung f siehe vt (a) questioning; examining, examination. (b) consultation (gen with or of). (c) (Umfrage) survey.

befranst adj fringed, with a fringe.

befreien* **1** vt (a) (frei machen) to free, to release; Volk, Land to liberate, to free; (freilassen) Gefangenen, Tier, Vogel to set free, to free. **jdn aus einer schwierigen Lage ~** to rescue sb from or get sb out of a tricky situation.
  (b) (freistellen) (von from) to excuse; (von Militärdienst, Steuern) to exempt; (von Eid etc) to absolve; (von Pflicht auch) to release. **sich vom Religionsunterricht ~ lassen** to be excused religious instruction.
  (c) (erlösen: von Schmerz etc) to release, to free. **jdn von einer Last ~** to take a weight off sb's mind.
  (d) (reinigen) (von of) (von Ungeziefer etc) to rid; (von Schnee, Eis) to free. **einen Aufsatz von Fehlern ~** to get rid of the mistakes in an essay, to remove the mistakes from an essay; **seine Schuhe von Schmutz ~** to remove the dirt from one's shoes; **ein ~des Lachen** a healthy or an unrepressed laugh.
  2 vr (a) (Volk, Land) to free oneself; (entkommen) to escape (von, aus from). **sich aus einer schwierigen Lage ~** to get oneself out of a difficult situation.
  (b) (erleichtern) to rid oneself (von of), to free oneself (von from).

Befreier(in f) m -s, - liberator.

befreit **1** ptp of befreien. **2** adj (erleichtert) relieved. **~ aufatmen** to heave or breathe a sigh of relief.

Befreiung f siehe vt (a) freeing, releasing; liberation, freeing; setting free, freeing. (b) excusing; exemption; absolving; releasing. **um ~ von etw bitten** to ask to be excused/exempted from sth. (c) releasing; (Erleichterung) relief. (d) ridding; freeing.

Befreiungs-: ~bewegung f liberation movement; ~front f liberation front; ~kampf m struggle for liberation; ~krieg m war of liberation; ~schlag m (Eishockey) clearance; ~versuch m escape attempt.

befremden* **1** vt to displease. **es befremdet mich, daß ...** I'm displeased that ..., I find it displeasing that ...; **das befremdet mich an ihr** that (side of her) displeases me. **2** vi to cause displeasure.

Befremden nt -s, no pl displeasure. **nicht ohne ~ ...** it is with some displeasure that ...

befremdend adj displeasing.

befremdet adj disconcerted, taken aback.

befremdlich adj (geh) siehe befremdend.

Befremdung f siehe Befremden.

befreunden* vr (a) (sich anfreunden) to make or become friends. **ich habe mich schnell mit ihm befreundet** I quickly made friends with him, he and I quickly became friends; **die beiden haben sich (miteinander) befreundet** the pair made or became friends.

(b) (fig: mit einem Gedanken etc) to get used to, to get or grow accustomed to.

befreundet adj wir/sie sind schon lange (miteinander) ~ we/they have been friends or friendly for a long time; gut or eng ~ sein to be good or close friends; alle ~en Familien all the families we etc are friendly with; ein uns ~er Staat a friendly nation; das ~e Ausland friendly (foreign) countries; ein uns ~er Arzt a doctor (who is a) friend of ours; ~e Zahlen (Math) amicable numbers.

befrieden* vt (geh) to pacify.

befriedigen* 1 vt to satisfy; Gläubiger auch to pay; Hunger, Durst, Appetit auch to assuage (form); Gelüste auch to gratify; Ansprüche, Forderungen, Verlangen auch to meet. jdn (sexuell) ~ to satisfy sb (sexually); er ist leicht/schwer zu ~ he's easily/not easily satisfied, he's easy/hard to satisfy.
2 vi to be satisfactory. Ihre Leistung hat nicht befriedigt your performance was unsatisfactory.
3 vr sich (selbst) ~ to masturbate.

befriedigend adj satisfactory; Verhältnisse, Leistung, Arbeit, Antwort auch adequate; Gefühl satisfying; Lösung auch acceptable; (Schulnote) fair. nicht ~ sein to be unsatisfactory/inadequate/unacceptable.

befriedigt adj satisfied, contented. bist du nun endlich ~? are you satisfied at last?; er lächelte ~ he smiled with satisfaction.

Befriedigung f **(a)** siehe vt satisfaction, satisfying; payment; assuagement (form); gratification; meeting. sexuelle ~ sexual satisfaction; zur ~ deiner Neugier ... to satisfy your curiosity ~. **(b)** (Genugtuung) satisfaction. seine ~ in etw (dat) suchen to look for or seek satisfaction in sth.

Befriedung f (geh) pacification.

befristen* vt to limit, to restrict (auf +acc to); Aufgabe, Projekt to put a time limit on.

befristet adj Genehmigung, Visum restricted, limited (auf +acc to); Arbeitsverhältnis, Anstellung temporary. mein Arbeitsverhältnis ist auf zwei Jahre ~ my appointment is limited or restricted to two years; ~ sein/auf zwei Jahre ~ sein (Paß etc) to be valid for a limited time/for two years.

Befristung f limitation, restriction (auf +acc to).

befruchten* vt **(a)** (lit) Eizelle to fertilize; (schwängern auch) to impregnate (form); Blüte to pollinate. künstlich ~ to inseminate artificially.
(b) (fig: fruchtbar machen) to make fertile.
(c) (fig: geistig anregen) to stimulate, to have a stimulating effect on. auf etw (acc) ~d wirken to have a stimulating effect on sth.

Befruchtung f **(a)** siehe vt **(a)** fertilization; impregnation; pollination. künstliche ~ artificial insemination. **(b)** (fig) stimulation.

befugen* vt (form) to authorize. wer hat Sie dazu befugt? who authorized you to do that?

Befugnis f (form) authority no pl; (Erlaubnis) authorization no pl. eine ~ erhalten/erteilen to receive/give authorization or authority; besondere ~se erhalten to receive or be given special authority; Zutritt ohne ~ nicht gestattet no entry to unauthorized persons.

befugt adj (form) ~ sein(, etw zu tun) to have the authority or (ermächtigt worden sein) be authorized (to do sth).

befühlen* vt to feel; (hinstreichen über auch) to run one's hands over.

befummeln* vt (inf) **(a)** (betasten) to paw (inf). **(b)** (bearbeiten) to fix (inf).

Befund m -(e)s, -e results pl, findings pl. der ~ war positiv/negativ (Med) the results were positive/negative; ohne ~ (Med) (results) negative.

befürchten* vt to fear, to be afraid of. ich befürchte das Schlimmste I fear the worst; es ist zu ~, daß ... it is (to be) feared that ...; dabei sind Komplikationen/ist gar nichts zu ~ it is feared there may be complications/there's nothing to fear with that; das ist nicht zu ~ there is no fear of that; da Lawinen zu ~ waren ... as there was a danger or risk of avalanches ...

Befürchtung f fear usu pl. ~en or die ~ haben, daß ... to fear or be afraid that ...; die schlimmsten ~en haben or hegen (geh) to fear the worst.

befürworten* vt to approve.

Befürworter(in f) m -s, - supporter; (von Idee auch) advocate.

Befürwortung f approval.

begab pret of begeben.

begaben* vt usu pass (liter) to endow. mit etw begabt sein to be endowed with sth.

begabt adj talented; (esp geistig, musisch auch) gifted. für etw ~ sein to be talented at sth; für Musik, Kunst etc auch to have a gift for sth.

Begabten-: ~auslese f selection of the most gifted or talented people; ~förderung f (educational) grant.

Begabte(r) mf decl as adj talented or gifted person/man/woman etc.

Begabung f **(a)** (Anlage) talent; (geistig, musisch auch) gift. er hat eine ~ dafür, immer das Falsche zu sagen he has a gift for or a knack of always saying the wrong thing; er hat ~ zum Lehrer he has a gift for teaching; mangelnde ~ a lack of talent, insufficient talent.
(b) (begabter Mensch) talented person. sie ist eine musikalische ~ she has a talent for music.

Begabungsreserve f reservoir of talent.

begaffen* vt (pej inf) to gape or goggle at (inf).

begangen ptp of begehen.

Begängnis nt (old liter) siehe Leichenbegängnis.

begann pret of beginnen.

begasen* vt (Agr) to gas.

begatten* (esp Zool) 1 vt to mate or copulate with; (geh, hum) to copulate with. 2 vr to mate, to copulate; (geh, hum) to copulate.

Begattung f (esp Zool) mating, copulation; (geh, hum) copulation.

Begattungs- in cpds mating; ~organe pl reproductive organs pl.

begaunern* vt to swindle, to cheat.

begeben pret begab, ptp ~ 1 vr **(a)** (liter: gehen) to betake oneself (liter), to go. sich nach Hause or auf den Heimweg ~ to wend (liter) or make one's way home; sich auf eine Reise ~ to undertake a journey; sich zu Bett/zur Ruhe ~ to repair to one's bed (liter)/to retire; sich zu jdm ~ to betake oneself to see sb (liter); sich an seinen Platz ~ to take one's place; sich in ärztliche Behandlung ~ to undergo medical treatment; sich an die Arbeit ~ to commence work.
(b) (sich einer Sache aussetzen) sich in Gefahr ~ to expose oneself to or put oneself in danger; sich in jds Schutz (acc) ~ to place oneself under sb's protection; siehe Gefahr.
(c) (old liter: geschehen) to come to pass (old liter). es begab sich aber zu der Zeit, daß ... (Bibl) and it came to pass at that time that ...; es hatte sich vieles ~ many things had happened.
(d) (geh: aufgeben) +gen to relinquish, to renounce.
2 vt (Fin) to issue.

Begebenheit f (geh), **Begebnis** nt (old) occurrence, event.

begegnen* vi aux sein +dat **(a)** (treffen) to meet. sich or einander (geh) ~ to meet; ihre Augen or Blicke begegneten sich their eyes met; unsere Wünsche ~ sich (liter) our wishes coincide (form); sie ~ sich in dem Wunsch/in der Ansicht, ... they are united in the wish/opinion ... (form).
(b) (stoßen auf) to encounter; Schwierigkeiten auch to run into. dieses Wort wird uns später noch einmal ~ we will encounter this word again later.
(c) (widerfahren) jdm ist etw begegnet sth has happened to sb; es war mir schon einmal begegnet, daß ... it had happened to me once already that ...
(d) (geh: behandeln) to treat. man begegnete mir nur mit Spott I only met with derision.
(e) (geh) (entgegentreten) einer Krankheit, Seuche, der Not to combat; einem Übel, Angriff, Unrecht auch to oppose, to resist; (überwinden) einer Gefahr, Schwierigkeiten, dem Schicksal to confront, to meet, to face; (reagieren auf) einem Wunsch, Vorschlag, einer Ansicht to meet, to respond to. man begegnete seinen Vorschlägen mit Zurückhaltung his suggestions met with reserve.
(f) (geh: einwenden gegen) Behauptungen etc to counter.

Begegnung f **(a)** (Treffen) meeting, encounter; (fig: mit Idee etc) encounter. bei der ersten/letzten ~ der beiden at the first/last meeting between the two; ein Ort internationaler ~ an international meeting place.
(b) (Sport) encounter, match. die ~ Spanien–Italien findet nächsten Monat statt Spain and Italy meet next month.

begehen* pret beging, ptp begangen vt **(a)** (verüben) Selbstmord, Ehebruch, Sünde to commit; Verbrechen auch to perpetrate (form); Fehler to make. eine Indiskretion (gegenüber jdm) ~ to be indiscreet (about sb); einen Mord an jdm ~ to murder sb; eine Dummheit/Taktlosigkeit/Unvorsichtigkeit ~ to do something stupid/tactless/careless; damit hast du eine große Dummheit begangen you did something really stupid there; die Dummheit/Taktlosigkeit/Unvorsichtigkeit ~, ... to be so stupid/tactless/careless as to ...; an jdm ein Unrecht ~ to wrong sb, to be unjust to sb; Verrat an jdm/etw ~ to betray sb/sth; ein oft begangener Fehler a frequent mistake.
(b) (entlanggehen) Weg to use. der Weg ist viel begangen the path is used a lot, it is a much-used path; „B~ der Brücke auf eigene Gefahr" "persons using this bridge do so at their own risk".
(c) (abschreiten) Bahnstrecke, Felder to inspect (on foot).
(d) (geh: feiern) to celebrate; (Eccl) Fest auch to observe.

Begehr m or nt -s, no pl (old) wish, desire. er fragte nach meinem ~ he inquired after my wishes.

begehren* vt **(a)** (liter: Verlangen haben nach) to desire, to crave; Frau to desire; Gegenstände, Besitz eines andern to covet. etw zu tun ~ to desire or crave or wish to do sth; ein Mädchen zur Frau ~ to desire a girl's hand in marriage; sie bekam die von ihr so begehrte Rolle she was given the role she desired so much; du sollst nicht ~ ... (Bibl) thou shalt not covet ...; siehe begehrt.
(b) (old: wollen) to desire.

Begehren nt -s, (rare) - **(a)** (geh: Verlangen) desire (nach for). das ~ fühlen or haben, etw zu tun to feel the or a desire to do sth; heißes ~ burning desire.
(b) (old: Wunsch, Forderung) wish. was ist Ihr ~? what is your wish?; nach jds ~ fragen to inquire after sb's wishes, to ask what sb wants; auf mein ~ (hin) at my request.

begehrenswert adj desirable, attractive; Frau desirable.

begehrlich adj (geh) covetous.

Begehrlichkeit f (geh) covetousness.

begehrt 1 ptp of begehren. 2 adj much or very sought-after; Partner etc auch, Ferienziel popular; Junggeselle eligible; Posten auch desirable.

Begehung f **(a)** (form) (einer Sünde) committing; (eines Verbrechens auch) perpetrating (form). nach ~ des Verbrechens after committing etc the crime; zur Zeit der ~ des Verbrechens at the time (when) the crime was committed. **(b)** (das Abschreiten) inspection (on foot).

begeifern* vt (fig pej) to run down, to slam (inf); (lit) to dribble on.

begeistern* 1 vt jdn to fill with enthusiasm; (inspirieren) to inspire. er begeistert alle durch sein or mit seinem Talent everybody is enthusiatic about his talent; **er ist für nichts zu ~** he's never enthusiastic about anything. **2** *vr* to be *or* feel enthusiastic (**an** +*dat*, **für** about).

begeisternd *adj* inspiring; *Rede auch* stirring.

begeistert *adj* enthusiastic (*von* about).

Begeisterung *f, no pl* enthusiasm (*über* +*acc* about, *für* for). **etw mit ~ tun** to do sth enthusiastically *or* with enthusiasm; **in ~ geraten** to become enthusiastic *or* be filled with enthusiasm; **sich in ~ reden** to get carried away with what one is saying.

Begeisterungs-: **b~fähig** *adj* able to get enthusiastic; *Publikum etc* quick to show one's enthusiasm; **sie ist zwar b~fähig, aber ...** her enthusiasm is easily aroused but ...; **~fähigkeit** *f* capacity for enthusiasm; **ein Pessimist, dem jegliche ~fähigkeit abgeht** a pessimist who never shows enthusiasm for anything; **~sturm** *m* storm of enthusiasm; **~taumel** *m* frenzy of enthusiasm.

Begier *f -, no pl* (*liter*), **Begierde** *f -, -n* (*geh*) desire (*nach* for); (*Sehnsucht*) longing, yearning. **vor ~ brennen, etw zu tun** to be longing *or* burning to do sth; **voll ~ lauschte sie seinen Worten** she hung on his every word.

begierig *adj* (*voll Verlangen*) hungry, greedy; (*gespannt*) eager, keen; *Leser* avid. **auf etw** (*acc*) **~ sein** to be eager for sth; **~ (darauf) sein, etw zu tun** to be eager *or* keen to do sth.

begießen* *vt irreg* (**a**) (*mit Wasser*) to pour water on; *Blumen, Beet* to water; (*mit Fett*) *Braten etc* to baste; *siehe* **begossen**. (**b**) (*fig inf*) *freudiges Ereignis, Vereinbarung* to celebrate. **das muß begossen werden!** that calls for a drink!

beging *pret of* **begehen**.

Beginn *m -(e)s, no pl* beginning, start. **am** *or* **bei** *or* **zu ~** at the beginning; **mit ~ der Ferien** at the beginning *or* start of the holidays, when the holidays begin *or* start; **gleich zu ~** right at the beginning *or* start, at the very beginning *or* start.

beginnen *pret* **begann,** *ptp* **begonnen 1** *vi* to start, to commence (*form*); (*in Beruf etc auch*) to start off. **mit einer Arbeit ~** to start *or* begin (to do) a job; **mit der Arbeit ~** to start *or* begin work; **es beginnt zu regnen** it's starting *or* beginning to rain; **er hat als Lehrling/mit nichts begonnen** he started (off) *or* began as an apprentice/with nothing.

2 *vt* (**a**) (*anfangen*) to start, to begin; *Gespräch, Verhandlungen, Rede auch* to open. **~, etw zu tun** to start *or* begin to do sth, to start doing sth.
(**b**) (*anpacken*) *Aufgabe etc* to tackle, to go *or* set about.
(**c**) (*geh: unternehmen*) to do. **er wußte damit/mit ihm nichts zu ~** he had no idea what to do with it/him; **ich wußte nicht, was ich ~ sollte** I didn't know what to do; **wißt ihr nichts Besseres zu ~?** can't you think of anything better to do?

Beginnen *nt -s, no pl* (*geh*) (*Vorhaben*) enterprise, plan, scheme.

beginnend *adj attr* incipient (*form*). **eine ~e Erkältung** the beginnings of a cold; **bei ~er Dämmerung/Nacht** at dusk/nightfall; **im ~en 19. Jahrhundert** in the early 19th century.

beglänzen* *vt* (*poet*) to light up, to illumine (*poet*). **vom Monde beglänzt** moonlit, illumined by the moon.

beglaubigen* *vt* (**a**) *Testament, Unterschrift* to witness; *Zeugnisabschrift* to authenticate; *Echtheit* to attest (to). **etw behördlich/notariell ~ lassen** to have sth witnessed *etc* officially/by a notary. (**b**) *Gesandten, Botschafter* to accredit (**bei** to).

Beglaubigung *f siehe vt* (**a**) witnessing; authentication; attestation. (**b**) accrediting, accreditation (*form*).

Beglaubigungsschreiben *nt* credentials *pl*.

begleichen* *vt irreg* (*lit: bezahlen*) *Rechnung, Zeche* to settle, to pay; *Schulden auch* to discharge (*form*); (*fig*) *Schuld* to pay (off), to discharge. **mit Ihnen habe ich noch eine Rechnung zu ~** (*fig*) I've a score to settle with you.

Begleichung *f siehe vt* settlement, payment; discharging; payment, discharging. **vollständige/teilweise ~** payment in full/part payment.

Begleit-: **~adresse** *f siehe* **~schein**; **~brief** *m* covering letter.

begleiten* *vt* (**a**) to accompany; (*zu Veranstaltung auch*) to go/come with; (*zum Schutz auch*) to escort; *esp Schiff auch* to escort, to convoy. **er wurde stets von seinem Hund begleitet** his dog always went everywhere with him.
(**b**) (*fig*) to accompany; (*Glück, Erfolg auch*) to attend. **ein paar ~de Worte** a few accompanying words; **meine Wünsche ~ Sie** my best wishes go with you; **~de Umstände** attendant *or* accompanying circumstances (*form*).
(**c**) (*Mus*) to accompany (**an** *or* **auf** +*dat* on).

Begleiter(in *f*) *m -s, - (***a**) companion; (*zum Schutz*) escort; (*von Reisenden*) courier. **ständiger ~** constant companion. (**b**) (*Mus*) accompanist.

Begleit-: **~erscheinung** *f* concomitant (*form*); (*Med*) side effect; **ist Jugendkriminalität eine ~erscheinung der Wohlstandsgesellschaft?** does juvenile delinquency go hand-in-hand with an affluent society?; **das ist eine ~erscheinung des Alters** that is a concomitant of old age (*form*), that goes with old age; **~flugzeug** *nt* escort plane; **~instrument** *nt* accompanying instrument; **~mannschaft** *f* (*Mil*) escort; **~musik** *f* accompaniment; (*in Film etc*) incidental music; **~papiere** *pl* (*Comm*) accompanying documents *pl*; **~person** *f* escort; **die ~person eines Jugendlichen** the person accompanying a minor; **~personal** *nt* escort; **~schein** *m* dispatch note; **~schiff** *nt* (*Mil*) escort (ship); **~schreiben** *nt* covering letter; (*für Waren auch*) advice note; **~text** *m* (accompanying) text; **~umstände** *pl* attendant circumstances *pl*.

Begleitung *f* (**a**) *no pl* company. **er bot ihr seine ~ an** he offered to accompany *or* (*zum Schutz auch*) escort her; **in ~ seines Vaters/in Peters ~** accompanied by his father/Peter; **ich bin in ~ hier** I'm here with someone; **ohne ~ eines ...** without being accompanied by a ...

(**b**) (*Begleiter*) companion; (*zum Schutz*) escort; (*Gefolge*) entourage, retinue. **ohne ~** unaccompanied.
(**c**) (*Mus*) (*Begleitmusik*) accompaniment; (*das Begleiten auch*) accompanying; (*Begleitstimme*) harmony. **ohne ~ spielen** to play unaccompanied.

beglotzen* *vt* (*inf*) to goggle *or* gawp *or* gape at (*all inf*).

beglücken* *vt jdn ~* to make sb happy; **er hat uns gestern mit seinem Besuch beglückt** (*iro*) he honoured us with a visit yesterday; **Casanova hat Tausende von Frauen beglückt** (*hum*) Casanova bestowed his favours upon thousands of women; **alle wollten von ihm beglückt werden** (*hum*) all of them wanted to enjoy his favours; **ein ~des Gefühl/Erlebnis** a cheering feeling/experience; **er ist sehr beglückt darüber** he's very happy *or* pleased about it; **beglückt lächeln** to smile happily.

Beglücker *m -s, - (liter, iro*) benefactor. **er fühlt sich als ~ aller Frauen** (*hum*) he thinks he's God's gift to women.

Beglückung *f* (*liter*) (*das Beglücken*) bringing of happiness (*gen* to); (*Glück*) joy, happiness.

beglückwünschen* *vt* to congratulate, to offer one's congratulations (*form*) (**zu** on). **laß dich ~!** congratulations!

begnaden* *vt* (*liter*) to bless; *Künstler/Musiker* a gifted artist/musician.

begnadigen* *vt* to reprieve; (*Strafe erlassen*) to pardon. **einen zum Tode Verurteilten zu lebenslänglicher Haft ~** to commute sb's death sentence to life imprisonment.

Begnadigung *f siehe vt* reprieve; pardon. **um (jds) ~ ersuchen** to seek a reprieve (for sb).

Begnadigungs-: **~gesuch** *nt* plea for (a) reprieve; **~recht** *nt* right of reprieve.

begnügen* *vr* sich mit etw ~ to be content *or* satisfied with sth, to content oneself with sth; **sich damit ~, etw zu tun** to be content *or* satisfied with doing sth *or* to do sth, to content oneself with doing sth; **damit begnüge ich mich nicht** that doesn't satisfy me, I'm not satisfied with that.

Begonie [-niə] *f* begonia.

begonnen *ptp of* **beginnen**.

begossen 1 *ptp of* **begießen**. **2** *adj* **er stand da wie ein ~er Pudel** (*inf*) he looked that small, he looked so sheepish.

begraben* *vt irreg* (**a**) (*beerdigen*) to bury. **dort möchte ich nicht ~ sein** (*inf*) I wouldn't like to be stuck in that hole (*inf*); **der kann sich ~ lassen** (*inf*) he is worse than useless; **damit kannst du dich ~ lassen** (*inf*) you can stuff that (*sl*); *siehe* **Hund**.
(**b**) (*verschütten*) to bury. **beim Einsturz begrub das Gebäude alle Bewohner unter sich** when the building collapsed all the residents were buried.
(**c**) (*aufgeben*) *Hoffnung, Wunsch* to abandon, to relinquish; (*beenden*) *Streit, Angelegenheit, Feindschaft* to end. **ein längst ~er Wunsch** a long-abandoned wish; **diese Angelegenheit ist längst ~** this matter was over (and done with) long ago.

Begräbnis *nt* burial; (*~feier*) funeral.

Begräbnis-: **~kosten** *pl* funeral costs *pl*; **~stätte** *f* (*geh*) burial place.

begradigen* *vt* to straighten.

Begradigung *f* straightening.

begrast *adj* grassy, grass-covered.

begreifbar *adj* conceivable.

begreifen *pret* **begriff,** *ptp* **begriffen 1** *vt* (**a**) (*verstehen*) to understand; *Aufgabe, Problem* (*geistig*), *Zusammenhang auch* to grasp, to comprehend; *jdn, jds Handlung or Haltung auch* to comprehend; *Sinn, Notwendigkeit, (Schwierigkeit einer) Lage auch* to see, to appreciate. **~, daß ...** (*einsehen*) to realize that ...; **er begriff nicht, worum es ging** he didn't understand *or* comprehend what it was about; **hast du meine begriffen?** did you understand what I said?; **es ist kaum zu ~** it's almost incomprehensible; **es läßt sich leicht ~, daß ...** it's easy to understand that ...; **wie kann man Gott/die Unendlichkeit ~?** how can one comprehend God/infinity?; **ich begreife mich selbst nicht** I don't understand myself.
(**b**) (*auffassen, interpretieren*) to view, to see.
(**c**) (*geh: einschließen*) **etw in sich** (*dat*) **~** to encompass *or* include sth; *siehe auch* **begriffen**.
(**d**) (*dial: anfassen*) to touch.

2 *vi* to understand, to comprehend. **leicht/schnell ~** to be quick on the uptake; **schwer/langsam ~** to be slow on the uptake.

3 *vr* to be understandable. **eine solche Tat läßt sich nicht leicht ~** such an action cannot be easily understood; **es begreift sich, daß ...** it is understandable that ...

begreiflich *adj* understandable. **es wird mir allmählich ~, warum ...** I'm beginning to understand why ...; **ich kann mich ihm nicht ~ machen** I can't make myself clear to him; **ich habe ihm das ~ gemacht** I've made it clear to him.

begreiflicherweise *adv* understandably.

begrenzen* *vt* (**a**) (*Grenze sein von*) to mark *or* form the boundary of *no pass*; *Horizont* to mark; *Straße etc* to line. **das Gebiet wird durch** *or* **von einem Wald begrenzt** a forest marks *or* forms the boundary of the area. (**b**) (*beschränken*) to restrict, to limit (*auf* +*acc* to).

begrenzt *adj* (*beschränkt*) restricted, limited; (*geistig beschränkt*) limited. **meine Aufenthaltsdauer ist nicht zeitlich ~** there's no time limit on (the length of) my stay; **eine genau ~e Aufgabe** a clearly defined task.

Begrenztheit *f, no pl* (*von Möglichkeiten, Talent etc*) limitedness; (*von Menschen*) limitations *pl*.

Begrenzung *f* (**a**) (*das Begrenzen*) (*von Gebiet, Straße etc*) demarcation; (*von Horizont*) marking; (*von Geschwindigkeit, Redezeit*) restriction. (**b**) (*Grenze*) boundary.

begriff *pret of* **begreifen**.

Begriff *m -(e)s, -e* (**a**) (*objektiv: Bedeutungsgehalt*) concept; (*Terminus*) term. **etw in ~en ausdrücken** *or* **in ~e fassen** to put sth into words; **in neuen ~en denken** to think in new terms; **sein Name ist mir ein/kein ~** his name means something/doesn't mean anything to me; **sein Name ist in aller Welt ein ~** his name is known all over the world; **ein ~ für Qualität!** a byword for quality.

(b) (*subjektiv: Vorstellung, Eindruck*) idea. **sein ~ von** *or* **der Freiheit** his idea *or* conception of freedom; **falsche ~e von etw haben** to have the wrong ideas about sth; **sich** (*dat*) **einen ~ von etw machen** to imagine sth; **du machst dir keinen ~ (davon)** (*inf*) you've no idea (about it) (*inf*); **das geht über meine ~e** that's beyond me; **es war über alle ~e schön** it was incredibly beautiful; **einen hohen ~ von jdm/etw haben** to have a high opinion of sb/sth; **nach unseren heutigen ~en** by today's standards; **nach menschlichen ~en** in human terms; **für meine ~e** in my opinion.

(c) im ~ sein *or* **stehen** (*form*), **etw zu tun** to be on the point of doing sth, to be about to do sth.

(d) schwer *or* **langsam/schnell von ~ sein** (*inf*) to be slow/quick on the uptake; **sei doch nicht so schwer von ~!** (*inf*) don't be so dense (*inf*).

begriffen 1 *ptp of* **begreifen**. 2 *adj*: **in etw** (*dat*) **~ sein** (*form*) to be in the process of doing sth; **ein noch in der Entwicklung ~er Plan** a plan still in the process of being developed.

begrifflich *adj* **(a)** *attr* (*bedeutungsmäßig*) conceptual. **~e Klärung** clarification of one's terms; **~ bestimmen** to define (in clear terms); **~ ordnen** to arrange according to conceptual groups. **(b)** (*gedanklich, abstrakt*) abstract. **etw ~ erfassen** to understand sth in the abstract.

Begriffs-: **~bestimmung** *f* definition; **~bildung** *f* formation of a concept/concepts; **~inhalt** *m* meaning; (*in der Logik*) connotation; **b~mäßig** *adj* conceptual; **b~stutzig, b~stützig** (*Aus*) *adj* (*inf*) dense (*inf*); **~stutzigkeit** *f* (*inf*) denseness; **~vermögen** *nt* understanding; **das ging über ihr ~vermögen** that was beyond her grasp *or* understanding; **~verwirrung** *f* confusion of concepts/terms.

begründen* *vt* **(a)** (*Gründe anführen für*) to give reasons for; (*rechtfertigend*) *Forderung, Meinung, Ansicht* to justify; *Verhalten* to account for; *Verdacht, Behauptung* to substantiate. **wie** *or* **womit begründete er seine Ablehnung?** how did he account for *or* justify his refusal?, what reason(s) did he give for his refusal?; **etw eingehend/näher ~** to give detailed/specific reasons for sth; **ein ~der Satz** (*Gram*) a causal clause; *siehe* **begründet.**

(b) (*beginnen, gründen*) to establish; *Schule, Verein, Geschäft auch* to found; *Hausstand* to set up.

Begründer *m* founder.

begründet *adj* well-founded; (*berechtigt*) justified; (*bewiesen*) *Tatsache etc* proven. **es besteht ~e/keine ~e Hoffnung, daß ...** there is reason/no reason to hope that ...; **das halte ich für nicht ~** I think that's unfounded/unjustified; **sachlich ~** founded on fact; **etw liegt** *or* **ist in etw** (*dat*) **~** sth has its roots in sth.

Begründung *f* **(a)** reason (*für, gen* for), grounds *pl* (*für, gen* for); (*von Anklage, Behauptung etc*) grounds *pl* (*gen* for). **etwas zur** *or* **als ~ sagen** to say something in explanation. **(b)** (*Gründung*) establishment; (*von Schule, Verein, Geschäft auch*) foundation; (*von Hausstand*) setting up.

Begründungssatz *m* (*Gram*) causal clause.

begrüßen* *vt* **(a)** to greet; (*als Gastgeber auch*) to welcome. **jdn herzlich ~** to greet sb heartily, to give sb a hearty welcome; **es ist mir eine große Ehre, Sie bei mir ~ zu dürfen** (*form*) it's a great honour to (be able to) welcome you here; **wir würden uns freuen, Sie bei uns ~ zu dürfen** (*form*) we would be delighted to have the pleasure of your company (*form*).

(b) (*gut finden*) *Kritik, Entschluß etc* to welcome; (*esp iro, form*) to appreciate. **es ist zu ~, daß ...** it's a good thing that ...

(c) (*Sw: um Erlaubnis fragen*) to ask (*um for, wegen* about).

begrüßenswert *adj* welcome. **es wäre ~, wenn ...** it would be desirable if ...

Begrüßung *f* greeting; (*der Gäste*) (*das Begrüßen*) welcoming; (*Zeremonie*) welcome. **er nickte zur ~ mit dem Kopf** he nodded his head in greeting; **jdm einen Blumenstrauß zur ~ überreichen** to welcome sb with a bouquet of flowers; **jdm die Hand zur ~ reichen** to hold out one's hand to sb in welcome; **mit freundlicher ~** (*in Geschäftsbrief*) with kind regards.

Begrüßungs-: **~ansprache** *f* welcoming speech; **~kuß** *m* welcoming kiss; **~trank** *m* welcoming drink.

begucken* *vt* (*inf*) to look at. **laß dich mal ~** let's (have *or* take a) look at you!

begünstigen* *vt* **(a)** (*förderlich sein für*) to favour; *Wachstum, Handel* to encourage; *Pläne, Beziehungen* to further; (*Jur*) to aid and abet. **vom Glück/von schönem Wetter begünstigt** blessed with good luck/fine weather; **vom Schicksal begünstigt** smiled upon by fate; **durch die Dunkelheit begünstigt** assisted by the darkness.

(b) (*bevorzugen*) **jdn ~** to favour sb; **von jdm begünstigt werden/sein** to be favoured *or* shown favour by sb.

Begünstigung *f* **(a)** (*Jur*) aiding and abetting. **~ aiding and abetting; sachliche ~** (*acting as an*) accessory; **~ im Amt** connivance.

(b) (*Bevorzugung*) preferential treatment; (*Vorteil*) advantage.

(c) (*Förderung*) favouring; (*von Wachstum, Handel*) encouragement; (*von Plänen, Beziehungen*) furthering.

begutachten* *vt* (*beurteilen, Gutachten abgeben*) to give expert advice about; *Kunstwerk, Stipendiaten* to examine; *Projekte, Leistung* to judge; *Gelände, Haus* to survey; (*inf: ansehen*) to have *or* take a look at. **etw ~ lassen** to get *or* obtain expert advice about sth.

Begutachter *m* **-s, -** expert; (*von Haus, Gelände*) surveyor.

Begutachtung *f* (expert) assessment; (*von Haus, Gelände*)

survey; (*das Begutachten*) surveying. **psychologische/graphologische** *etc* **~** (expert) psychological/graphological *etc* assessment.

begütert *adj* **(a)** (*dated: Landgüter besitzend*) landed *attr*, propertied. **(b)** (*reich*) wealthy, affluent. **die ~e Klasse/Schicht** the rich *pl*.

begütigen* *vt* to pacify, to placate, to appease.

begütigend *adj Worte etc* soothing. **~ auf jdn einreden** to calm sb down.

behaaren* *vr* to grow hair.

behaart *adj* hairy, hirsute. **stark/dicht/schwarz ~** very hairy/(thickly) covered with hair/covered with black hair.

Behaarung *f* covering of hair, hairs *pl* (+*gen, an* +*dat* on).

behäbig *adj* **(a)** *Mensch* portly; (*phlegmatisch, geruhsam*) stolid; (*fig*) *Leben, Möbel, Auto* comfortable; *Architektur* solid; *Sprache, Ton* complacent. **(breit und) ~ in der Ecke sitzen** to sit on one's fat backside (*inf*). **(b)** (*old liter, Sw: wohlhabend*) well-to-do, affluent.

Behäbigkeit *f, no pl siehe adj* **(a)** portliness; stolidity; comfortableness; solidness; complacency.

behacken* *vt* **(a)** (*mit der Hacke*) to hoe. **(b)** (*Vogel*) to peck at. **(c)** (*inf: betrügen*) to do (*um* out of) (*inf*).

behaften* *vt* (*Sw*) **jdn bei etw ~** to catch sb out in sth.

behaftet *adj*: **mit etw ~ sein** *mit Krankheit etc* to be afflicted with sth; *mit Fehlern/Vorurteilen etc* to be full of sth; *mit einer schweren Last/Sorgen/Schulden etc* to be encumbered with sth; *mit Makel* to be tainted with sth.

Behagen *nt* **-s, no pl** contentment. **mit sichtlichem ~** with visible *or* obvious pleasure; **mit ~ essen** to eat with relish; **er findet sein ~ daran** *or* **darin** it gives him pleasure.

behagen* *vi* **etw behagt jdm** sth pleases sb, sb likes sth; **etw behagt jdm nicht** (*nicht gefallen*) sth doesn't please sb, sb doesn't like sth; (*beunruhigen*) sb feels uneasy about sth; **etw behagt ihr nicht** she doesn't like him.

behaglich *adj* cosy; (*heimelig auch*) snug, homely; (*bequem*) comfortable; (*zufrieden*) contented. **~ warm** comfortably warm; **es sich** (*dat*) **~ machen** to make oneself comfortable; **~ in der Sonne sitzen** to sit comfortably in the sun.

Behaglichkeit *f, no pl siehe adj* cosiness; snugness, homeliness; comfortableness; contentment. **es stört meine ~** it disturbs my sense of comfort.

behalten *pret* **behielt,** *ptp* **~** *vt* **(a)** (*nicht weggeben, nicht zurückgeben*) to keep.

(b) (*lassen, wo es ist*) to keep. **~ Sie (doch) Platz!** please don't get up!; **den Hut auf dem Kopf ~** to keep one's hat on; **jdn an der Hand ~** to keep hold of sb's hand; **der Kranke kann nichts bei sich ~** the patient can't keep anything down; *siehe* **Auge.**

(c) (*nicht verlieren*) to keep; *Wert auch* to retain. **die Ruhe/Nerven ~** to keep one's cool/nerve; **wenn wir solches Wetter ~** if this weather lasts; *siehe* **Fassung, Kopf, Zügel** *etc.*

(d) (*nicht vergessen*) to remember. **im Gedächtnis/im Kopf ~** to remember, to keep in one's head; **er behielt die Melodie im Ohr** he kept the tune in his head; **ich habe die Zahl/seine Adresse nicht ~** I've forgotten the number/his address.

(e) (*nicht weitersagen*) **etw für sich ~** to keep sth to oneself.

(f) (*nicht weggehen lassen*) to keep; *Mitarbeiter auch* to keep on. **jdn bei sich ~** to keep sb with one; **einen Gast zum Abendbrot bei sich ~** to invite a guest to stay on to supper.

(g) (*nicht aufgeben*) *Stellung, Namen, Staatsangehörigkeit* to keep. **sie muß immer ihren Willen ~** she always has to have her own way; *siehe* **lieb.**

(h) (*aufbewahren, versorgen*) *Kinder, Katze, Gegenstand* to look after; (*nicht wegwerfen*) *Briefe etc* to keep. **jdn/etw in guter/schlechter Erinnerung ~** to have happy/unhappy memories of sb/sth; *siehe* **Andenken.**

(i) (*zurückbehalten, nicht loswerden*) to be left with; *Schock, Schaden* to suffer. **vom Unfall hat er ein steifes Knie ~** after the accident he was left with a stiff knee.

Behälter *m* **-s, -** **(a)** container, receptacle (*form*). **(b)** (*Container*) container.

Behälter-: **~schiff** *nt* container ship; **~verkehr** *m* container traffic.

behämmern* *vt* (*lit, fig*) to hammer.

behämmert *adj* (*sl*) screwy (*sl*).

behandeln* *vt* **(a)** *Material, Stoff, Materie* to treat.

(b) *Thema, Frage, Problem, Antrag* to deal with.

(c) (*in bestimmter Weise umgehen mit*) to treat; (*verfahren mit*) to handle. **jdn/etw gut/schlecht ~** to treat sb/sth well/badly; **er weiß, wie man Kinder/die Maschine ~ muß** he knows how to handle children/the machine; **eine Angelegenheit diskret ~** to treat *or* handle a matter with discretion; **jdn/etw ungeschickt ~** to handle sb/sth clumsily.

(d) (*ärztlich*) *Patienten, Krankheit* to treat; *Zähne* to attend to. **jdn/etw operativ ~** to operate on sb/sth; **der ~de Arzt** the doctor in attendance.

behändigen* *vt* (*geh*) to hand over (*jdm* to sb).

Behandlung *f siehe* **behandeln (a)** treatment.

(b) treatment. **wir sind jetzt bei der ~ dieses Themas** we are now dealing with this theme; **um schnelle ~ des Antrags wird gebeten** please deal with the application as quickly as possible.

(c) treatment; handling. **die schlechte ~ seiner Frau und Kinder** the ill-treatment *or* maltreatment of his wife and children.

(d) treatment; attention (*gen* to). **waren Sie deswegen schon früher in ~?** have you had treatment *or* been treated for this before?; **bei wem sind Sie in ~?** who's treating you?

Behandlungs-: **~art** *f* type of treatment; **b~bedürftig** *adj* in need of treatment; **~form** *f* form of treatment; **~kosten** *pl* cost *sing* of treatment; **~methode** *f* (method of) treatment; **~pflicht** *f* obligation to report for treatment for venereal disease;

~**raum** m treatment room; ~**stuhl** m doctor's/dentist's chair; ~**verfahren** nt therapy; ~**weise** f treatment.

behandschuht adj gloved.

Behang m -(e)s, -̈e (a) curtain; (Wand~) hanging; (Schmuck) decorations pl; (Fransen) fringe; (Rüschen) frill. **der Birnbaum hat einen guten** ~ the pear tree promises a good crop. **(b)** (Hunt: von Hund) lop-ears pl.

behangen adj laden.

behängen* 1 vt to decorate; Wände auch to hang. 2 vr (pej) to deck oneself out (mit in or with).

beharken* 1 vt (Mil sl) to rake with gunfire. 2 vr (inf) to go at one another or each other hammer and tongs (inf).

beharren vi (a) (hartnäckig sein) to insist (auf +dat on); (nicht aufgeben) to persist, to persevere (bei in). **(b)** (bleiben) in etw (dat) ~ (in Zustand) to persist in sth; (an Ort) to remain in sth.

Beharren nt -s, no pl siehe vi (a) insistence (auf on); persistence, perseverance (bei in). **(b)** (in +dat in) persistence, perseverance; remaining.

beharrlich adj (hartnäckig) insistent; (ausdauernd) persistent; Glaube, Liebe steadfast, unwavering. ~**er Fleiß** perseverance; ~ **fortfahren, etw zu tun** to persist in doing sth.

Beharrlichkeit f siehe adj insistence; persistence; steadfastness.

Beharrung f (Phys) inertia.

Beharrungsvermögen nt (Phys) inertia.

behauchen* vt to breathe on; (Ling) to aspirate. **behauchte Laute** aspirates.

behauen* vt Holz, Baumstämme to hew; Stein to cut; (mit dem Meißel) to carve.

behaupten* 1 vt (a) (sagen) to claim; (bestimmte Aussage aufstellen auch) to maintain; (Unerwiesenes ~ auch) to assert. **steif und fest** ~ to insist; **von jdm** ~, **daß** ... to say (of sb) that ...; **es wird behauptet, daß** ... it is said or claimed that ...
(b) (erfolgreich verteidigen) Stellung, Recht to maintain; Meinung to assert; Markt to keep one's share of; siehe Feld.
2 vr to assert oneself; (bei Diskussion) to hold one's own or one's ground (gegenüber, gegen against). **sich auf dem Markt** ~ to maintain one's hold on the market.

Behauptung f (a) claim; (esp unerwiesene ~) assertion. **(b)** (Aufrechterhaltung) assertion; (von Stellung) successful defence. **(c)** (das Sich-Behaupten) assertion. **die** ~ **der Firma auf dem Markt** the firm's ability to maintain its hold on the market.

behausen* vt (liter: unterbringen) to accommodate, to house.

behaust adj (ansässig) resident (in +dat in); (heimisch) native, indigenous (in +dat to).

Behausung f (a) no pl (liter: das Behausen) accommodation, housing. **(b)** (geh, hum: Wohnung) dwelling.

Behaviorismus [bihevia'rɪsmus] m, no pl behaviourism.

Behaviorist [bihevia'rɪst] m behaviourist.

behavioristisch [bihevia'rɪstɪʃ] adj behaviouristic.

beheben* vt irreg (a) (beseitigen) to remove; Mängel, Mißstände to rectify, to remedy; Schaden to repair, to put right; Störung to clear. **(b)** (Aus: abheben) Geld to withdraw.

Behebung f, no pl siehe vt (a) removal; rectification, remedying; repairing; putting right; clearing. **(b)** (Aus) withdrawal.

beheimaten* vt to find a home for.

beheimatet adj (ansässig) resident (in +dat in); (heimisch) indigenous, native (in +dat to). **wo sind Sie** ~? where is your home?

beheizbar adj heatable; Heckscheibe heated.

beheizen* vt to heat.

Behelf m -(e)s, -e (a) (Ersatz) substitute; (Notlösung) makeshift. **als** ~ **dienen** to serve or act as a substitute/makeshift. **(b)** (Jur: Rechtsbehelf) (legal) remedy.

behelfen* vr irreg (a) (Ersatz verwenden) to manage, to make do. **sich mit Ausreden/Ausflüchten** ~ to resort to excuses/to be evasive. **(b)** (auskommen) to manage, to get by. **er weiß sich allein nicht zu** ~ he can't manage or get by alone.

Behelfs- in cpds temporary; ~**heim** nt temporary accommodation; b~**mäßig** adj makeshift; (zeitlich begrenzt) Straßenbelag, Ausweis temporary; b~**weise** adv temporarily; **er hat sich b~weise eingerichtet** his furnishings are only makeshift.

behelligen* vt to bother.

Behelligung f bother no pl. **jds** ~ **mit Fragen** (das Behelligen) bothering sb with questions; (das Behelligtwerden) sb being bothered with questions.

behelmt adj helmeted.

behend(e) adj (geh) (flink) swift, quick; (gewandt) nimble, agile.

Behendigkeit f, no pl siehe adj swiftness, quickness; nimbleness, agility.

beherbergen* vt (lit, fig) to house; Gäste to accommodate; Flüchtlinge auch to give shelter to.

Beherbergung f housing; (Unterkunft) accommodation.

beherrschen* 1 vt (a) (herrschen über) to rule, to govern; (fig: Gefühle, Vorstellungen) to dominate.
(b) (fig: das Übergewicht haben) Stadtbild, Landschaft, Ebene, Markt to dominate; siehe Feld, Szene.
(c) (zügeln) to control; Zunge to curb.
(d) (gut können) Handwerk, Sprache, Instrument, Tricks, Spielregeln to master; (bewältigen) Fahrzeug, Situation to have control of.
2 vr to control oneself. **ich kann mich** ~! (iro inf) not likely! (inf).

Beherrscher m (liter) ruler.

beherrscht adj (fig) self-controlled.

Beherrschtheit f, no pl (fig) self-control.

Beherrschung f, no pl control; (Selbst~) self-control; (des Markts) domination; (eines Fachs) mastery.

beherzigen* vt to take to heart, to heed.

beherzigenswert adj worth heeding.

Beherzigung f heeding. **dies zur** ~! (old) heed this!, take heed!

beherzt adj (geh) courageous, brave.

Beherztheit f, no pl (geh) courage, bravery.

behexen* vt to bewitch.

behielt pret of **behalten**.

behilflich adj helpful. **jdm (bei etw)** ~ **sein** to help sb (with sth).

behindern* vt to hinder; Sicht to impede; (bei Sport, im Verkehr) to obstruct. **jdn bei etw** ~ to hinder sb in sth; **eine behinderte Person** a handicapped person.

Behinderte(r) mf decl as adj handicapped person. **die** ~**n** the handicapped pl.

Behinderung f hindrance; (im Sport, Verkehr) obstruction; (körperlich, Nachteil) handicap.

behorchen* vt (a) to listen in on. **(b)** (Med inf) to listen to.

Behörde f -, -n authority usu pl; (Amtsgebäude) office usu pl. **die** ~**n** the authorities; **die zuständige** ~ the appropriate or proper authorities.

Behörden- in cpds official; ~**unwesen** nt sprawling bureaucracy; ~**wesen** nt bureaucracy.

behördlich adj official.

behördlicherseits adv (form) by the authorities; (auf behördlicher Seite) on the part of the authorities.

behost adj (inf) in trousers, trousered; (Hunt) with feathered upper legs.

Behuf m -(e)s, -e (old form) **zu diesem** ~ to this end, for this purpose; **zum** or **zu dem** ~ (gen) with a view to.

behufs prep +gen (old form) with a view to.

behuft adj hoofed.

behum(p)sen* vt (dial inf) to diddle (inf).

behüten* vt (beschützen, bewachen) to look after; (esp Engel etc) to watch over; Geheimnis to keep. **jdn vor etw (dat)** ~ to save or protect sb from sth; **(Gott) behüte!** (inf) God or Heaven forbid!; **behüt' dich Gott!** (old, S Ger) (may) God be with you!

Behüter m -s, - (geh) protector.

behütet adj Mädchen carefully brought up; Jugend sheltered. ~ **aufwachsen** to have a sheltered upbringing.

behutsam adj cautious, careful; (zart auch) gentle. **man muß es ihr** ~ **beibringen** it will have to be broken to her gently.

Behutsamkeit f, no pl care(fulness), cautiousness; (Zartheit auch) gentleness; (Feingefühl) delicacy.

bei prep +dat (a) (räumlich) (in der Nähe von) near; (zum Aufenthalt) at, with; (Tätigkeitsbereich angebend, in Institutionen) at; (in Werken) in; (jdn betreffend) with; (Teilnahme bezeichnend) at; (unter, zwischen Menge) among; (Ort der Berührung bezeichnend) by. **die Schlacht** ~ **Leipzig** the Battle of Leipzig; **dicht** ~ **dem Ort, wo** ... very near the place where ...; **ich stand/saß** ~ **ihm** I stood/sat beside him or next to him; **der Wert liegt** ~ **tausend Mark** the value is around a thousand marks; ~ **seinen Eltern wohnen** to live with one's parents; **ich war** ~ **meiner Tante** I was at my aunt's; ~ **Müller** (auf Briefen) care of or c/o Müller; ~ **uns in Deutschland** in Germany; ~ **uns zu Hause** (im Haus) at our house; (im Land, in Familie) back or at home; ~ **Tisch** at table; **sie sind** ~ **uns eingeladen** they're invited to our house; **er ist** or **arbeitet** ~ **der Post** he works for the post office; ~ **jdm Unterricht haben/Vorlesungen hören** to have lessons with or from sb/lectures from sb; ~**m Militär** in the army; ~**m Fleischer** at the butcher's; **ein Konto** ~ **der Bank** an account at the bank; ~ **Shakespeare liest man** ... in Shakespeare it says ...; ~ **Collins erschienen** published by Collins; ~ **Kühen findet man das nicht** one doesn't find or get that with cows; ~ **den Franzosen ißt man** ... in France one eats ...; ~ **mir hast du damit kein Glück** you're wasting your time with me; ~ **ihm ist es 8 Uhr** he makes it or he has (esp US) 8 o'clock; ~ **mir ist Schluß für heute** I've had enough for today; **das war** ~ **ihm der Fall** that was the case with him; **man weiß nicht, woran man** ~ **ihm ist** (inf) one never knows where one is with him; ~ **mir kannst du so einen Mist nicht loswerden** you're not getting rid of that rubbish on me; ~ **einer Hochzeit sein** to be at a wedding; **er hat** ~ **der Aufführung der Elektra mitgewirkt** he took part in the performance of Elektra; **er nahm mich** ~ **der Hand** he took me by the hand; **ich habe kein Geld** ~ **mir** I have no money on me; **Kopf** ~ **Kopf/dicht** ~ **dicht** close together; siehe weit, Wort, Name.

(b) (zeitlich) (Zeitspanne: während) during; (Zeitpunkt) (up)on; (bestimmten Zeitpunkt betreffend) at. ~**m letzten Gewitter** during the last storm; ~ **meiner Ankunft** on my arrival; ~**m Erwachen** (up)on waking; ~**m Erscheinen der Königin** ... when the queen appeared ...; ~ **Beginn und Ende der Vorstellung** at the beginning and end of the performance; ~ **der ersten Gelegenheit** at the first opportunity; ~ **Gelegenheit** when I etc get the chance; ~ **Lebzeiten meines Großvaters** in my grandfather's lifetime; ~ **Tag/Nacht** by day/at night; ~ **Tag und Nacht** day and night.

(c) (Tätigkeit, Geschehen ausdrückend) in, during. ~ **reiflicher Überlegung** upon mature reflection; **ich habe ihm** ~**m Arbeiten/** ~ **der Arbeit geholfen** I helped him with the work; ~**m Arbeiten/** ~ **der Arbeit** when I'm etc working; ~**m Lesen (dieses Artikels)** ... when reading (this article) ...; ~ **dem Zugunglück starben viele Menschen** a lot of people died in the train crash; ~ **dieser Schlacht** in or during this battle; **er verliert** ~**m Kartenspiel immer** he always loses at cards; **er ist gerade** ~**m Anziehen seiner Schuhe** he's just putting his shoes on.

(d) (Zustand, Umstand bezeichnend) in. ~ **Kerzenlicht essen** to eat by candlelight; **etw** ~ **einer Flasche Wein bereden** to discuss sth over a bottle of wine; ~ **guter Gesundheit sein** to be in good health; ~ **zehn Grad unter Null** when it's ten degrees below zero; ~ **Regen** in the rain; **das Schönste ~ der Sache** the best thing about it; **nicht ~ sich sein** (inf) to be out of one's mind (inf); ~ **offenem Fenster schlafen** to sleep with the window open; ~ **alledem** ... in spite of everything, for all that; siehe **Bewußtsein, Kraft, Verstand** etc.

(e) (konditionaler Nebensinn) in case of. ~ **Feuer Scheibe einschlagen** in case of fire break glass; ~ **Nebel und Glatteis muß man vorsichtig fahren** when there is fog and ice one must drive carefully; ~ **einer Erkältung sollte man sich warm halten** when one has a cold one should keep warm.

(f) (kausaler Nebensinn) with. ~ **dieser Sturheit/so vielen Schwierigkeiten** with this stubbornness/so many difficulties; ~ **solcher Hitze/solchem Wind** in such heat/such a wind; ~ **seinem Talent** with his talent.

(g) (konzessiver Nebensinn) in spite of, despite. ~ **aller Vorsicht** in spite of or despite all one's caution; **es geht** ~**m besten Willen nicht** with the best will in the world it's not possible; ~ **all seinen Bemühungen hat er es trotzdem nicht geschafft** in spite of or despite or for all his efforts he still didn't manage it.

(h) (in Schwurformeln) by. ~ **Gott** by God; ~ **meiner Ehre** upon my honour.

beibehalten* vt sep irreg to keep; Bräuche, Regelung auch to retain; Leitsatz, Richtung to keep to; Gewohnheit to keep up.

Beibehaltung f, no pl siehe vt keeping; retention; keeping to; keeping up.

beibiegen vt sep irreg jdm etw ~ (inf) to get sth through to sb (inf).

Beibl. abbr of **Beiblatt.**

Beiblatt nt (Press) insert.

Beiboot nt (Naut) dinghy.

beibringen vt sep irreg (a) jdm etw ~ (mitteilen) to break sth to sb; (zu verstehen geben) to get sth across to sb, to get sb to understand sth.

(b) (unterweisen in) to teach (jdm etw sb sth).

(c) (zufügen) Verluste, Wunde, Niederlage, Schläge to inflict (jdm etw sb sth).

(d) (herbeischaffen) to produce; Dokumente, Beweis, Geld etc to furnish, to supply.

Beibringung f, no pl siehe vt (c, d) infliction; production; furnishing, supplying.

Beichte f -, -n confession. zur ~ gehen to go to confession; (bei jdm) die ~ ablegen to make one's confession (to sb); eine ~ ablegen (fig) to make a confession; jdm die ~ abnehmen to hear sb's confession; ~ hören or sitzen (inf) to hear or take confession.

beichten vti (lit, fig) to confess (jdm etw sth to sb). ~ gehen to go to confession.

Beicht-: ~formel f form of words used at confession; ~geheimnis nt seal of confession or of the confessional; b~hören vi sep (inf, Aus) to hear confession.

Beichtiger m -s, - (dated) siehe **Beichtvater.**

Beicht-: ~kind nt penitent; ~siegel nt siehe ~geheimnis; ~stuhl m confessional; ~vater m father confessor; ~zettel m (Aufstellung) list of sins; (Bescheinigung) absolution.

beid-: ~armig adj with both arms; Lähmung of or in both arms; ~beinig adj with both legs; Lähmung of or in both legs; Absprung double-footed; ~beinig abspringen to take off with both feet.

beide pron (a) (adjektivisch) (ohne Artikel) both; (mit Artikel) two. alle ~n **Teller** both plates; seine ~n **Brüder** both his brothers, his two brothers.

(b) (als Apposition) both. **ihr** ~(n)/**euch** ~ you two; **euch** ~n **herzlichen Dank** many thanks to both of you.

(c) (substantivisch) (ohne Artikel) both (of them); (mit Artikel) two (of them). **alle** ~ both (of them); **alle** ~ **wollten gleichzeitig Urlaub haben** both of them or they both wanted holidays at the same time; **keiner/keines** etc **von** ~n neither of them; **ich habe** ~ **nicht gesehen** I haven't seen either of them.

(d) ~s (substantivisch: zwei verschiedene Dinge) both; **(alles)** ~s **ist erlaubt** both are permitted.

beidemal adv both times.

beider-: ~halb adv (Sw) on both sides; ~lei adj attr inv both; **das Abendmahl in** or **unter** ~lei **Gestalt** Communion of bread and wine; ~seitig adj (auf beiden Seiten) on both sides; (gegenseitig) Abkommen, Vertrag etc bilateral; Versicherungen, Einverständnis etc mutual; ~seits 1 adv on both sides; **sie haben** ~seits **versichert** ... they have given mutual assurances or assurances on both sides ...; 2 prep +gen on both sides of.

Beiderwand f or nt -(e)s, no pl (Tex) linsey-woolsey.

Beid-: b~füßig adj two-footed; Absprung double-footed; b~füßig abspringen to take off with both feet; ~händig m -s, - (Mensch) ambidextrous person; (Schwert) two-handed sword; b~händig adj (mit beiden Händen gleich geschickt) ambidextrous; (mit beiden Händen zugleich) two-handed; b~händig schießen/schreiben können to be able to shoot/write with either hand or both hands.

beidrehen vi sep (Naut) to heave to.

beid-: ~seitig 1 adj (auf beiden Seiten) on both sides; (gegenseitig) mutual; ~seitige Zufriedenheit satisfaction on both sides/mutual satisfaction; 2 adv on both sides; ~seits prep +gen (Sw, S Ger) on both sides of.

beieinander adv together.

beieinander- pref together; ~haben vt sep irreg (inf) to have together; **du hast sie nicht richtig** or **alle** ~ you can't be all there (inf); ~halten vt sep irreg to keep together; ~sein vi sep irreg aux sein (inf) (gesundheitlich) to be in good shape (inf); (geistig) to be all there (inf); **gut** ~sein to be in good shape/to be all there; (S Ger: dick) to be a bit chubby (inf); B~sein nt siehe **Zusammensein.**

Beifahrer m (Aut) (front-seat) passenger; (bei einem Motorrad) (im Beiwagen) sidecar passenger; (auf dem Soziussitz) pillion rider or passenger; (berufsmäßiger Mitfahrer, Sport) co-driver; (bei einem LKW) co-driver, driver's mate.

Beifahrer-: ~platz m passenger seat; ~sitz m passenger seat; (auf Motorrad) pillion.

Beifall m -(e)s, no pl (Zustimmung) approval; (Händeklatschen) applause; (Zuruf) cheering, cheers pl. ~ **finden** to meet with approval; ~ **spenden/klatschen/klopfen** etc to applaud.

beifallen vi sep irreg aux sein (old) (a) (einfallen) jdm ~ to occur to sb. (b) (zustimmen) to agree (dat with).

beifallheischend adj looking for approval/applause.

beifällig adj approving. ~e **Worte/Laute** words/noises of approval; **er nickte** ~ **mit dem Kopf** he nodded his head approvingly or in approval; **dieser Vorschlag wurde** ~ **aufgenommen** this suggestion was favourably received or met with approval.

Beifalls-: ~äußerung f expression of (one's) approval; ~bekundung f show or demonstration of (one's) approval; ~bezeigung, ~kundgebung f applause no pl.

beifallspendend adj applauding.

Beifalls-: ~ruf m cheer; ~sturm m storm of applause.

Beifilm m supporting film, B-film.

beifolgend adj, adv (obs form) enclosed. **etw** ~ **schicken** (mit gleicher Post) to send sth in the same post.

beifügen vt sep (mitschicken) to enclose (dat with); (beiläufig sagen) to add.

Beifügung f (a) no pl (form) enclosure. **unter** ~ **eines Schecks** enclosing a cheque. (b) (Gram) attribute.

Beifügungssatz m (Gram) attributive clause.

Beifuß m -es, no pl (Bot) mugwort.

Beifutter nt supplementary fodder.

Beigabe f (a) (das Beigeben) addition. **eine** ~ **von etw empfehlen** to recommend adding sth or the addition of sth; **unter** ~ **eines Löffels Senf** adding a spoonful of mustard.

(b) (Beigefügtes, Begleiterscheinung) addition; (Beilage: Gemüse, Salat etc) side-dish; (Comm: Zugabe) free gift; (Grab~) burial gift.

beige [beːʃ, ˈbeːʒə, beːʒə] adj (geh: inv) beige.

Beige¹ [beːʃ, ˈbeːʒə, beːʒə] nt -, or (inf) -s beige.

Beige² f -, -n (S Ger, Aus, Sw) pile.

beigeben sep irreg 1 vt (zufügen) to add (dat to); (mitgeben) jdn to assign (jdm to sb). 2 vi: **klein** ~ (inf) to give in.

beigebunden adj (Typ) bound in.

beigefarben [ˈbeːʃ-, ˈbeːʒə-, beːʒə-] adj beige(-coloured).

beigehen vi sep irreg aux sein (dial) to start.

beigeordnet 1 ptp of **beiordnen.** 2 adj (Gram) Nebensatz co-ordinate.

Beigeordnete(r) mf decl as adj (town) councillor.

Beigeschmack m aftertaste; (fig: von Worten) flavour. **es hat einen unangenehmen** ~ (lit, fig) it has a nasty or an unpleasant taste (to it).

beigesellen* sep (geh) 1 vt **ihr wurde ein Beschützer beigesellt** she was provided with an escort. 2 vr sich jdm ~ to join sb.

Beignet [bɛnˈjeː] m -s, -s (Cook) fritter.

Beiheft nt supplement; (Lösungsheft) answer book.

beiheften vt sep to append, to attach.

Beihilfe f (a) (finanzielle Unterstützung) financial assistance no art; (Zuschuß, Kleidungs~) allowance; (für Arztkosten) contribution; (Studien~) grant; (Subvention) subsidy. (b) (Jur) abetment. **wegen** ~ **zum Mord** because of being an or acting as an accessory to the murder.

beihilfefähig adj (form) eligible for financial assistance/a contribution/contributions etc.

Beiklang m (lit) (accompanying) sound; (fig) overtone usu pl.

beikommen vi sep irreg aux sein (a) jdm ~ (zu fassen bekommen) to get hold of sb; (fertig werden mit) to get the better of sb; **einer Sache** (dat) ~ (bewältigen) to deal with sth. (b) (old inf: einfallen) jdm ~ to occur to sb; **laß dir das ja nicht** ~! don't even think of it!

(c) (dial: herkommen) to come.

(d) (dial) **ich komme da nicht bei** I can't reach it.

Beikost f supplementary diet.

Beil nt -(e)s, -e axe; (kleiner) hatchet; (Fleischer~) cleaver; (zum Hinrichten) axe; (Fall~) blade (of a/the guillotine).

beil. abbr of **beiliegend.**

beiladen vt sep irreg (a) to add (dat to). (b) (Jur) to call in.

Beiladung f (a) (das Beiladen) additional loading; (zusätzliche Ladung) extra or additional load. (b) (Jur) calling in. **notwendige** ~ subpoena.

Beilage f -, -n (a) (Gedrucktes) insert; (Beiheft) supplement. (b) (das Beilegen) enclosure; (in Buch) insertion; (Aus: Anlage zu Brief) enclosure.

(c) (Cook) side-dish; (Gemüse~) vegetables pl; (Salat~) side-salad. **Erbsen und Pommes frites als** ~ **zum Hähnchen** chicken with peas and chips.

Beilager nt (Hist) consummation; (obs: Beischlaf) sexual relations pl.

beiläufig adj (a) casual; Bemerkung, Erwähnung auch passing attr. **etw** ~ **erwähnen** to mention sth in passing or casually. (b) (Aus: ungefähr) approximate.

Beiläufigkeit f (von Bemerkung, in Benehmen etc) casualness; (Nebensächlichkeit) triviality. ~en trivia pl.

beilegen vt sep (a) (hinzulegen) to insert (dat in); (einem Brief, Paket) to enclose (dat with, in).

(b) (beimessen) to attribute, to ascribe (dat to). **einer Sache** (dat) **Bedeutung** or **Gewicht/Wert** ~ to attach importance/value to sth.

(c) (*Titel geben*) (*dat* on) to confer, to bestow. **sich** (*dat*) **einen Grafentitel ~** to assume *or* adopt the title of count. **(d)** (*schlichten*) to settle. **(e)** (*Naut: anlegen*) to moor.

Beilegung *f siehe* vt **(a)** insertion; enclosure. **(b)** attribution, ascription; (*von Bedeutung, Wert*) attaching. **(c)** (*das Verleihen*) conferment, bestowal; (*das Annehmen*) assumption, adoption. **(d)** settlement. **(e)** mooring.

beileibe *adv*: **~ nicht!** certainly not; **das darf ~ nicht passieren** that mustn't happen under any circumstances; **~ kein ...** by no means a ..., certainly no ...

Beileid *nt* **-(e)s**, *no pl* condolence(s), sympathy. **jdm sein ~ aussprechen** *or* **ausdrücken** *or* **bezeigen** to offer sb one's condolences, to express one's sympathy with sb; **mein ~!** (*iro*) you have my sympathy!

Beileids- *in cpds* of condolence *or* sympathy; **~besuch** *m* visit of condolence; **~bezeigung**, **~bezeugung** *f* expression of sympathy; (*Brief, Telegramm etc*) condolence; **~karte** *f* sympathy *or* condolence card.

Beilhieb *m* blow with *or* from an axe.

beilegen *vi sep irreg* **(a)** (*beigefügt sein*) to be enclosed (*dat* with, in); (*einer Zeitschrift etc*) to be inserted (*dat* in). **(b)** (*Naut*) to lie to. **(c)** (*obs*) **jdm ~** to lie with sb (*obs*).

beiliegend *adj* enclosed. **~ finden Sie...** please find enclosed ...

beim *contr of* **bei dem**.

beimachen *vr sep* (*dial*) to get down to it.

beimengen *vt sep* to add (*dat* to).

Beimengung *f* addition. **unter ~ des Mehls** while adding the flour.

beimessen *vt sep irreg* **jdm/einer Sache Bedeutung** *or* **Gewicht/Wert ~** to attach importance/value to sb/sth.

beimischen *vt sep* to add (*dat* to). **unserer Freude war eine leichte Traurigkeit beigemischt** our joy was tinged with sadness.

Beimischung *f* addition. **eine leichte ~ von...** (*fig*) a touch of ...; **Freude mit einer ~ von Trauer** joy tinged with sorrow.

Bein *nt* **-(e)s**, **-e (a)** leg. **mit übereinandergeschlagenen ~en** cross-legged; **von einem ~ aufs andere treten** to shift from one leg *or* foot to the other; **sich kaum auf den ~en halten können** to be hardly able to stay on one's feet; **er ist noch gut auf den ~en** he's still sprightly; **jdm ein ~ stellen** (*lit, fig*) to trip sb up; **jdm wieder auf die ~e helfen** (*lit, fig*) to help sb back on his feet; **alles, was ~e hatte, ging zum Fußballspiel** everything on two legs went to the football match; **auf den ~en sein** (*nicht krank, in Bewegung*) to be on one's feet; (*unterwegs sein*) to be out and about; **sich auf die ~e machen** (*inf*) to make tracks (*inf*); **jdm ~e machen** (*inf*) (*antreiben*) to make sb get a move on (*inf*); (*wegjagen*) to make sb clear off (*inf*); **die ~e unter den Arm** *or* **in die Hand nehmen** (*inf*) to take to one's heels; **mein Geldbeutel hat ~e bekommen** (*fig*) my purse has vanished into thin air *or* seems to have grown legs and walked; **sich** (*dat*) **die ~e in den Bauch** *or* **Leib stehen** (*inf*) to stand about until one is fit to drop (*inf*); **mit beiden ~en im Leben** *or* **auf der Erde stehen** (*fig*) to have both feet (firmly) on the ground; **mit einem ~ im Grab/im Gefängnis stehen** (*fig*) to have one foot in the grave/to be likely to end up in jail; **das steht auf schwachen ~en** (*fig*) that isn't very sound; **auf eigenen ~en stehen** (*fig*) to be able to stand on one's own two feet; **auf einem ~ kann man nicht stehen!** (*fig inf*) you can't stop at one!; **er fällt immer wieder auf die ~e** (*fig*) he always falls on his feet; **wieder auf die ~e kommen** (*fig*) to get back on one's feet again; **wie geht's?** — **immer auf zwei ~en!** (*inf*) how are things? — still bearing up! (*inf*) *or* struggling along! (*inf*); **jdn/etw wieder auf die ~e bringen** *or* **stellen** (*fig*) to get sb/sth back on his/its feet again; **etw auf die ~e stellen** (*fig*) to get sth off the ground; **sich** (*dat*) **etw ans ~ binden** (*fig*) to saddle oneself with sth; **jdn/etw am ~ haben** (*fig inf*) to have sb/sth round one's neck (*inf*); *siehe* **ausreißen, Knüppel, Lüge, Klotz** *etc*.

(b) (*Knochen*) bone. **der Schreck ist ihm in die ~e gefahren** the shock went right through him; **Fleisch am ~** (*old*) meat on the bone; *siehe* **Stein, Mark**[1].

(c) (*Elfenbein*) ivory. **(d)** (*dial: Fuß*) foot.

beinah(e) *adv* almost, nearly. **~ in allen Fällen, in ~ allen Fällen** in almost *or* nearly every case; **das kommt ~ auf dasselbe heraus** that comes to almost *or* nearly the same thing.

Beiname *m* epithet.

Bein-: **~amputation** *f* leg amputation; **b~amputiert** *adj* with an amputated leg/amputated legs; **b~amputiert sein** to have had a leg/both legs amputated; **~arbeit** *f* (*Sport*) footwork; (*beim Schwimmen*) legwork; **~bruch** *m* fracture of the leg; **das ist kein ~bruch** (*fig inf*) it could be worse (*inf*); *siehe* **Hals- und Beinbruch**.

beinern *adj* (*aus Knochen*) made of bone; (*aus Elfenbein*) ivory.

beinhalten *vt insep* (*form*) to comprise.

Bein-: **b~hart** *adj* (*Aus, S Ger*) **Mensch** hard as nails; **Erde, Piste, Kuchen** rock-hard; **~haus** *nt* charnel-house.

-beinig *adj suf* -legged.

Bein-: **~kleid** *nt usu pl* (*old*) breeches *pl* (*old*); **~ling** *m* leg; **~prothese** *f* artificial leg; **~raum** *m* leg room; **~schiene** *f* (*Hist*) greave; (*Sport*) shin pad; (*bei Cricket*) (leg)pad; (*Med*) splint; **~stumpf** *m* stump.

beiordnen *vt sep* **(a)** (*Gram*) *siehe* **nebenordnen**. **(b)** (*beigeben*) **jdm/einer Sache beigeordnet sein** to be assigned to sb/appointed to sth; **bei einer Prüfung beigeordnet sein** to sit in on an examination.

Beipack *m* additional consignment *or* order; (*Frachtgut*) part load (*zu* with).

beipacken *vt sep* to enclose; **Frachtgut** to add (*dat* to).

beipflichten *vi sep* **jdm/einer Sache in etw** (*dat*) **~** to agree with sb/sth on sth.

Beipflichtung *f*, *no pl* agreement.

Beiprogramm *nt* supporting programme.

Beirat *m* (*Person*) adviser; (*Körperschaft*) advisory council *or* committee *or* body.

Beiratschaft *f* (*Sw Jur*) (legal) care and protection.

beirren* *vt* (*verwirren*) to disconcert. **sich nicht in etw** (*dat*) **~ lassen** not to let oneself be shaken *or* swayed in sth; **sich** (*durch etw*) **~/nicht ~ lassen** to let/not to let oneself be put off (by sth); **er läßt sich nicht ~** he won't be put off; **nichts konnte ihn** (*in seinem Vorhaben*) **~** nothing could shake him (in his intentions).

beisammen *adv* together.

beisammen- *pref* together; **~haben** *vt sep irreg* (*inf*) **Geld, Leute** to have got together; **seine Gedanken ~haben** to have one's wits about one; **seinen Verstand** *or* **seine fünf Sinne ~haben** to have all one's wits about one; **(sie) nicht alle ~haben** not to be all there; **~sein** *vi sep irreg aux sein* (*Zusammenschreibung nur bei infin und ptp*) (*fig*) (*körperlich*) to be in good shape; (*geistig*) to be all there; **gut ~sein** to be in good shape; (*kräftig gebaut sein*) to be well built; **B~sein** *nt* gettogether.

Beisasse *m* **-n**, **-n** (*Hist*) citizen without full civic rights.

Beisatz *m* (*Gram*) appositive.

beischaffen *vt sep* (*dial*) to bring.

beischießen *vt sep irreg* (*inf*) to chip in with (*inf*).

Beischlaf *m* (*Jur*) sexual intercourse *or* relations *pl*. **außerehelicher** *or* **unehelicher ~** extramarital intercourse *or* relations *pl*.

beischlafen *vi sep irreg* (*form*) to have sexual intercourse *or* relations *pl* (*dat* with).

Beischläfer(in *f*) *m* (*form*) bedfellow.

beischließen *vt sep irreg* (*Aus*) to enclose (*dat* with).

Beischluß *m* (*Aus*) enclosure. **unter ~ von ...** enclosing ...

Beisegel *nt* studdingsail.

Beisein *nt* presence. **in/ohne jds ~** in sb's presence/without sb being present.

beiseite *adv* aside (*auch Theat*); **treten, gehen, stehen** *auch* to one side; **legen**, (*fig*) **lassen** *auch* on one side; **setzen**, (*fig*) **schieben** *auch* to *or* on one side. **Spaß** *or* **Scherz ~!** joking aside *or* apart!; **jdn/etw ~ schaffen** *or* **bringen** to get rid of sb/sth.

Beiseiteschaffung *f* removal.

Beis(e)l *nt* **-s**, **-n** (*Aus inf*) pub (*Brit*).

beisetzen *vt sep* **(a)** (*beerdigen*) to inter (*form*), to bury; **Urne** to install (in its resting place). **(b)** (*Naut*) **Segel** to set, to spread. **(c)** (*old*) *siehe* **zusetzen**.

Beisetzung *f* funeral; (*von Urne*) installing in its resting place.

Beisetzungsfeierlichkeit *f* funeral ceremony.

beisitzen *vi sep irreg* (in Versammlung) to attend; (*einem Ausschuß*) to have a seat (*dat* on), to sit (*dat* on); (*bei Prüfung*) to sit in (*bei* on).

Beisitzer(in *f*) *m* **-s**, **-** **(a)** (*Jur*) assessor. **(b)** (*Ausschußmitglied*) committee member; (*bei Prüfung*) observer.

Beispiel *nt* **-(e)s**, **-e** example. **zum ~** for example *or* instance; **wie zum ~** such as; **jdm als ~ dienen** to be an example to sb; **jdm ein ~ geben** to set sb an example; **sich** (*dat*) **ein ~ an jdm/etw nehmen** to take a leaf out of sb's book/to take sth as an example; **mit gutem ~ vorangehen** to set a good example; **schlechte ~e verderben gute Sitten** (*Prov*) you shouldn't set a bad example.

Beispiel-: **b~gebend** *adj* exemplary; **b~gebend für etw sein** to serve as an example for sth; **b~haft** *adj* exemplary; **b~halber** *adv* by way of example; **b~los** *adj* unprecedented; (*unerhört*) outrageous; **~satz** *m* example.

Beispiels-: **b~weise** *adv* for example *or* instance; **~wirkung** *f* exemplary effect.

beispringen *vi sep irreg aux sein* **jdm ~** to rush to sb's aid; (*mit Geldbeträgen*) to help sb out.

beißen *pret* **biß**, *ptp* **gebissen 1** *vti* to bite; (*brennen: Geschmack, Geruch, Schmerzen*) to sting; (*kauen*) to chew. **in den Apfel ~** to bite into *or* take a bite out of the apple; **die Lösung beißt auf der Zunge** the solution stings the tongue; **der Hund hat mich** *or* **mir ins Bein gebissen** the dog has bitten my leg *or* me in the leg; **der Rauch/Wind beißt in den Augen/mich in die Augen** (*inf*) the smoke/wind makes one's/my eyes sting; **er wird dich schon nicht ~** (*fig*) he won't eat *or* bite you; **etwas/nichts zu ~ ~** (*inf: essen*) something/nothing to eat; **an etw** (*dat*) **zu ~ haben** (*fig*) to have sth to chew over; *siehe* **Gras, sauer, letzte(r, s)**.

2 *vr* (*Farben*) to clash. **sich** (*acc or dat*) **auf die Zunge/Lippen ~** to bite one's tongue/lips; **sich in den Arsch** (*vulg*) *or* **Hintern** (*sl*) **~** to kick oneself (*inf*).

beißend *adj* (*lit, fig*) biting; **Wind** *auch*, **Bemerkung** cutting; **Geschmack, Geruch** pungent, sharp; **Schmerz** gnawing; **Ironie, Hohn, Spott** bitter.

Beißerchen *pl* (*baby-talk*) toothy-pegs *pl* (*baby-talk*).

Beiß-: **~ring** *m* teething ring; **~zange** *f* (pair of) pincers *or* pliers; (*pej inf*) shrew; **das würde ich nicht mit der ~zange anfassen** *or* **anpacken** (*inf*) I wouldn't touch that with a barge pole (*inf*).

Beistand *m* **-(e)s**, **-e (a)** (*Hilfe*) help, assistance; (*Unterstützung*) support; (*von Priester*) attendance, presence. **jdm ~ leisten** to give sb help *or* assistance/give *or* lend sb one's support/attend sb.

(b) (*Jur*) legal adviser *or* representative; (*in Duell*) aid, representative, second. **einen ~ stellen** (*Jur*) to appoint a legal adviser *or* representative.

beiständig *adj* (*old*) helpful. **jdm ~ sein** to be of help *or* assistance to sb.

Beistands-: ~abkommen nt, ~pakt m mutual assistance pact; ~vertrag m treaty of mutual assistance.
beistehen vi sep irreg jdm ~ to stand by sb.
beistellen vt sep (a) to put or place beside. (b) (Aus: zur Verfügung stellen) (dat for) to make available, to provide. (c) (Rail: bereitstellen) to put on.
Beistell- in cpds side; ~herd m auxiliary cooker; ~möbel pl occasional furniture sing.
beisteuern vt sep to contribute.
beistimmen vi sep siehe zustimmen.
Beistrich m (esp Aus) comma.
Beitel m -s, - chisel.
Beitrag m -(e)s, ‑e (a) (Anteil) contribution; (Aufsatz auch) article. einen ~ zu etw leisten to make a contribution to sth, to contribute to sth. (b) (Betrag) contribution; (Versicherungs~) premium; (Mitglieds~) fee.
beitragen vti sep irreg to contribute (zu to); (mithelfen auch) to help (zu to). das trägt nur dazu bei, die Lage zu verschlimmern that only helps to make the position worse.
Beiträger m contributor.
Beitrags-: b~frei adj non-contributory; ~gruppe, ~klasse f insurance group; (bei Verein etc) class of membership; ~marke f stamp; b~pflichtig adj Arbeitsentgelt contributory; b~pflichtig sein (Mensch) to have to pay contributions; ~rückstand m arrears pl; ~satz m membership rate; ~schlüssel m, ~system nt contributory system.
beitreiben vt sep irreg Steuern to collect; Schulden auch to recover; (esp Jur) to enforce (the) payment of.
Beitreibung f (Jur) collection.
beitreten vi sep irreg aux sein +dat to join; einem Pakt, Abkommen to enter into; einem Vertrag to accede to.
Beitritt m joining (zu etw sth); (zu einem Pakt, Abkommen) agreement (zu to); (zu einem Vertrag) accession (zu to). seinen ~ erklären to become a member.
Beitritts-: ~erklärung f confirmation of membership; ~gesuch nt application for membership.
Beiwagen m (a) (beim Motorrad) sidecar. (b) (dated: Anhänger) carriage.
Beiwagen-: ~fahrer m sidecar passenger; ~maschine f motorcycle combination.
Beiwerk nt additions pl; (bei Aufsatz etc) details pl; (modisch) accessories pl.
beiwilligen vi sep (Sw) siehe zustimmen.
beiwohnen vi sep +dat (geh) (a) (dabeisein) to be present at. (b) (dated euph) to have sexual relations with.
Beiwohnung f (a) (form: Anwesenheit) presence. (b) (Jur) intimacy no art.
Beiwort nt -(e)s, (rare) ‑er (a) (Adjektiv) adjective. (b) (beschreibendes Wort) epithet.
Beiz f -, (Sw, S Ger inf) pub (Brit).
Beizbrühe f siehe Beize¹ (a) corrosive fluid; pickling solution, pickle; lye; mordant; marinade.
Beize¹ f -, -n (a) (Beizmittel) corrosive fluid; (Metall~) pickling solution, pickle; (Holz~) stain; (zum Gerben) lye; (Tabak~) sauce; (Agr) disinfectant; (Färbemittel, Typ) mordant; (Cook) marinade. (b) (das Beizen) steeping in a/the corrosive fluid etc. (c) (Hunt) hawking.
Beize² f -, -n (dial) pub (Brit).
beizeiten adv in good time.
beizen vt (a) to steep in corrosive fluid; (Metal) to pickle; Holz to stain; Häute to bate, to master; Tabak to steep in sauce; Saatgut to disinfect, to treat; Kupfer to etch; (Cook) to marinate. (b) (Hunt) to hawk.
Beiz-: ~mittel nt siehe Beize¹ (a); ~vogel m falcon, hawk.
bejahen* vti to answer in the affirmative; (gutheißen) to approve of. das Leben ~ to have a positive attitude towards life.
bejahend adj positive, affirmative; Einstellung positive. etw ~ beantworten (form) to answer sth in the affirmative.
bejahendenfalls adv (form) in the event of an affirmative answer.
bejahrt adj elderly, advanced in years.
Bejahrtheit f elderliness, advanced age.
Bejahung f affirmative answer (gen to); (Gutheißung) approval.
Bejahungsfall m (form) im ~e in the event of an affirmative answer.
bejammern* vt to lament; Schicksal, Los auch to bewail (liter); jdn to lament for.
bejammerns-: ~wert, ~würdig (rare) adj deplorable, lamentable; Mensch pitiable; Schicksal pitiable, dreadful.
bejubeln* vt to cheer; Ereignis to rejoice at. sie wurden als Befreier bejubelt they were acclaimed as liberators.
bekacken* (vulg) 1 vt to shit on (sl); Kleidungsstück to shit. bekackte Unterhosen shitty pants (sl). 2 vr to shit oneself (sl).
bekakeln* vt (inf) to talk over, to discuss.
bekalmen* vt (Naut) to becalm.
bekam pret of bekommen.
bekämpfen* vt to fight; (fig auch) to combat; Ungeziefer to control. sich gegenseitig ~ to fight one another.
Bekämpfung f fight, battle (von, gen against); (von Ungeziefer) controlling. zur/bei ~ der Terroristen to fight or combat/in fighting or combatting the terrorists.
Bekämpfungsmittel nt (Insekten~) pesticide, insecticide; (Unkraut~) weed-killer.
bekannt 1 ptp of bekennen. 2 adj (a) (allgemein gekannt, gewußt) well-known (wegen for); Mensch auch famous. die ~eren/~esten Spieler the better-/best-known or more/most famous players; wie ist das/er ~ geworden? how did that come to be so well-known/how did he become famous?; sie ist in Wien

~ she is (well-) known in Vienna; er ist ~ dafür, daß er seine Schulden nicht bezahlt he is well-known for not paying his debts; das/sie ist mir ~ I know about that/I know her, she is known to me; es ist allgemein/durchaus ~, daß ... it is common knowledge/a known fact that ...; ich darf diese Tatsachen als ~ voraussetzen I assume that these facts are known.
(b) (nicht fremd) familiar. jdn mit etw ~ machen mit Aufgabe etc to show sb how to do sth; mit Gebiet, Fach etc to introduce sb to sth; mit Problem to familiarize sb with sth; sich etw ~ machen to familiarize or acquaint oneself with sth; jdn/sich (mit jdm) ~ machen to introduce sb/oneself (to sb); wir sind miteinander ~ we already know each other, we have already met.
bekannte pret of bekennen.
Bekanntenkreis m circle of acquaintances.
Bekannte(r) mf decl as adj acquaintance; (euph: Freund) friend.
bekanntermaßen adv (form) siehe bekanntlich.
Bekanntgabe f announcement; (in Zeitung etc) publication.
bekanntgeben vt sep irreg to announce; (in Zeitung etc) to publish. ihre Verlobung geben bekannt ... the engagement is announced between ...
Bekanntheit f fame; (von Fakten) knowledge.
Bekanntheitsgrad m degree of fame.
bekanntlich adv ~ gibt es ... it is known that there are ...; er hat ~ eine Schwäche für Frauen he is known to have a weakness for women; London ist ~ die Hauptstadt Englands London is known to be the capital of England.
bekanntmachen vt sep to announce; (der Allgemeinheit mitteilen) to publicize; (in Zeitung auch) to publish; (durch Rundfunk, Fernsehen auch) to broadcast; siehe auch bekannt (b).
Bekanntmachung f (a) (das Bekanntmachen) siehe vt announcement; publicizing; publication; broadcasting. (b) (Anschlag etc) announcement, notice.
Bekanntschaft f (a) (das Bekanntwerden) acquaintance; (mit Materie, Gebiet) knowledge (mit of). jds ~ machen to make sb's acquaintance; mit etw ~ machen to come into contact with sth; wenn du weiter so frech bist, machst du gleich mit dem Rohrstock ~ if you go on being so cheeky you'll feel my stick; bei näherer ~ on closer acquaintance.
(b) (inf: Bekannte) acquaintance. meine ganze ~ all my acquaintances; ich habe gestern eine nette ~ gemacht I met a nice person yesterday.
bekanntwerden vi sep irreg aux sein to become known; (Geheimnis) to leak out.
bekaufen* vr (dial) to make a bad buy.
bekehren* 1 vt to convert (zu to). 2 vr to be(come) converted (zu to). er hat sich endlich bekehrt (fig) he has finally turned over a new leaf or mended his ways.
Bekehrer(in f) m -s, - apostle (gen to); (Missionar) missionary (gen to); (fig) proselytizer.
Bekehrte(r) mf decl as adj convert, proselyte.
Bekehrung f conversion.
bekennen pret bekannte, ptp bekannt 1 vt to confess, to admit; Sünde to confess; Wahrheit to admit; (Rel) Glauben to bear witness to.
2 vr sich (als or für) schuldig ~ to admit or confess one's guilt; sich als Homosexueller ~ to declare oneself to be a homosexual; sich zum Christentum/zu einem Glauben/zu Jesus ~ to profess Christianity/a faith/one's faith in Jesus; sich zu jdm/etw ~ to declare oneself or one's support for sb/sth; sich nicht zu jdm ~ to deny sb; die B~de Kirche the (German) Confessional Church.
Bekenner(in f) m -s, - confessor.
Bekenner-: ~geist, ~mut m courage of one's convictions; er hat seinen ~geist or ~mut mit dem Tode bezahlt he paid for the strength of his convictions with death.
Bekenntnis nt (a) (Geständnis) confession (zu of); (zum religiösen Glauben auch) profession (zu of). ein ~ zu den Menschenrechten a declaration of belief in human rights; sein ~ zum Sozialismus his declared belief in socialism; ein ~ zur Demokratie/zum Christentum ablegen to declare one's belief in democracy/profess one's Christianity.
(b) (Rel: Konfession) denomination.
Bekenntnis-: ~christ m member of the Confessional Church; ~freiheit f freedom of religious belief; b~freudig adj eager to make confessions; ~kirche f (German) Confessional Church; b~los adj uncommitted to any religious denomination; ~schule f denominational school; b~treu adj true to one's faith.
bekieken* (N Ger inf) 1 vt to look at. 2 vr to (have a) look at oneself; (gegenseitig) to look at each other.
bekiest adj gravelled, gravel attr.
bekiffen* vr (sl) to get stoned (sl). bekifft sein to be stoned (sl).
bekindert adj (form) with children.
beklagen* 1 vt to lament; Los to bewail; Tod, Verlust to mourn. Menschenleben sind nicht zu ~ there are no casualties.
2 vr to complain (über +acc, wegen about). sich bei jdm über etw (acc) ~ to complain or make a complaint to sb about sth; ich kann mich nicht ~ I can't complain, I've nothing to complain about.
beklagenswert, beklagenswürdig (geh) adj Mensch pitiful; Zustand lamentable, deplorable; Mißerfolg, Vorfall, Scheitern regrettable, unfortunate; Unfall terrible.
beklagt ptp of beklagen. 2 adj (Jur) die ~e Partei the defendant; (bei Scheidung) the respondent; der ~e Ehegatte the respondent.
Beklagte(r) mf decl as adj (Jur) defendant; (bei Scheidung) respondent.
beklatschen* vt (a) (applaudieren) to clap, to applaud. (b)

(inf: Klatsch verbreiten über) to gossip about.

beklauen* vt *(inf)* jdn to rob.

bekleben* vt etw *(mit Papier/Plakaten etc)* ~ to stick paper/posters etc on(to) sth; etw mit Etiketten ~ to stick labels on(to) or to label sth.

bekleckern* *(inf)* 1 vt to stain. ich habe mir das Kleid bekleckert I've made a mess on my dress; einen Bekleckerten machen *(sl)* to give oneself airs and graces.

2 vr sich *(mit Saft etc)* ~ to spill juice etc all down or over oneself; er hat sich nicht gerade mit Ruhm bekleckert he didn't exactly cover himself with glory.

beklecksen* 1 vt *(inf)* to splatter *(mit* with*)*. etw *(mit Tinte/Farbe)* ~ to splatter ink/paint on sth; ein bekleckstes Heft an ink-/paint- etc besplattered exercise book; du bist ja von oben bis unten bekleckst! *(inf)* you're covered in ink/paint etc!

2 vr to splatter oneself with ink/paint etc.

bekleiden* *(geh)* 1 vt *(anziehen)* to dress *(mit* in*)*; *(Kleidung geben)* to clothe. er war nur mit einer Hose bekleidet he was only wearing a pair of trousers; etw mit etw ~ *(geh)* to cover sth in sth.

(b) *(innehaben)* Amt etc to occupy, to hold. jdn mit einem Amt/einer Würde ~ to bestow an office/a title on sb.

2 vr to get dressed.

bekleidet adj dressed, clad *(mit* in*)*. sie war nur leicht ~ she was only lightly or *(spärlich)* scantily dressed or clad; nur mit einer Hose ~ sein to be clad in or wearing only a pair of trousers.

Bekleidung f (a) *(Kleider)* clothes pl, clothing; *(Aufmachung)* dress, attire. ohne ~ without any clothes on. (b) *(form: eines Amtes)* tenure; *(rare: mit einem Amt)* honouring.

Bekleidungs-: ~amt nt *(Mil)* quartermaster's store; ~gegenstand m garment, article of clothing; ~gewerbe nt clothing or garment *(esp US)* trade; ~industrie f clothing or garment *(esp US)* industry, rag trade *(inf)*; ~stück nt garment, article of clothing; ~vorschriften pl clothing/uniform regulations.

bekleistern* vt (a) Tapete etc to paste. (b) *(bekleben)* eine Wand *(mit Plakaten)* ~ to stick posters all over a wall.

beklemmen* vt *(fig)* to oppress; *(Schuld auch)* to weigh upon.

beklemmend adj *(beengend)* oppressive, constricting; *(beängstigend)* tormenting, oppressive.

Beklemmnis f feeling of oppressiveness; *(Gefühl der Angst)* feeling of apprehension or trepidation.

Beklemmung f usu pl feeling of oppressiveness; *(Gefühl der Angst)* feeling of apprehension or trepidation. ~en bekommen/haben to start to feel/to feel oppressed/full of apprehension or trepidation; *(bei enger Kleidung)* to start to feel/to feel restricted.

beklommen adj apprehensive, anxious, Mensch auch full of trepidation.

Beklommenheit f trepidation, apprehensiveness.

beklönen* vt *(N Ger inf)* to talk over.

beklopfen* vt to tap; Brust auch to sound.

bekloppt adj *(sl)* loony, crazy, mad *(all inf)*.

beknackt adj *(sl)* lousy *(inf)*, crappy *(sl)*.

beknien* vt *(inf)* jdn to beg.

bekochen* vt *(inf)* to cook for.

beködern* vt to bait.

bekommen pret bekam, ptp ~ 1 vt (a) to get; Genehmigung, Stimmen, Nachricht auch to obtain; Geschenk, Brief, Lob, Belohnung auch to receive; Zug, Bus, Krankheit auch to catch; gutes Essen, Verpflegung auch, Schlaganfall, Junges, ein Kind, Besuch to have; Spritze, Tadel to be given. ein Jahr Gefängnis ~ to be given one year in prison; sie ~ sich *(in Kitschroman)* boy gets girl; wir ~ Kälte/anderes Wetter the weather is turning cold/is changing; wir ~ Regen/Schnee we're going to have rain/snow; einen Stein/Ball etc an den Kopf ~ to be hit on the head by a stone/ball etc; kann ich das schriftlich ~? can I have that in writing?; etw zu Papier/aufs Bild ~ to get sth down on paper/get sth into the picture; wir haben das große Bett nicht nach oben ~ we couldn't get the big bed upstairs; jdn ins/aus dem Bett ~ to get sb into/out of bed; was bekommt der Herr? what will you have, sir?; ich bekomme bitte ein Glas Wein I'll have a glass of wine, please; was ~ Sie dafür/von mir? how much is that/how much do I owe you for that?; jdn dazu ~, etw zu tun to get sb to do sth; er bekam es einfach nicht über sich, ... he just could not bring himself to ...; ich bekomme den Deckel nicht abgeschraubt *(inf)* I can't unscrew the lid.

(b) *(entwickeln)* Fieber, Schmerzen, Vorliebe, Komplexe to get, to develop; Zähne to cut; Übung, neue Hoffnung to gain. Rost/Flecken/Risse ~ to get or become rusty/spotty/cracked, to develop rust/spots/cracks; Heimweh ~ to get or become homesick; Sehnsucht ~ to develop a longing *(nach for)*; graue Haare/eine Glatze ~ to go grey/bald; Hunger/Durst ~ to get or become hungry/thirsty; Angst ~ to get or become afraid; einen roten Kopf ~ to go red.

(c) *mit Infinitivkonstruktion* to get. etw zu essen/sehen/hören ~ to get to eat/see/hear sth; was muß ich denn da zu hören ~? what's all this I've been hearing?; das bekommt man hier nicht zu kaufen you can't buy that here; es mit jdm zu tun ~ to get into trouble with sb; kann ich etwas anderes zu tun ~? can I have something else to do?; etw zu fassen ~ to catch hold of sth; wenn ich ihn zu fassen bekomme ... if I get my hands on him ...

(d) *mit ptp oder adj siehe auch dort* etw gemacht ~ to get or have sth done; seine Arbeit fertig or gemacht *(inf)* ~ to get one's work finished or done; etw geschenkt ~ to be given sth *(as a present)*; ich habe das Buch geliehen ~ I have been lent the book; etw bezahlt ~ to get paid for sth; einen Wunsch erfüllt ~ to have a wish fulfilled; das Haus sauber ~ to get the

house clean; etw satt or über *(inf)* ~ to have enough of sth.

(e) *in Verbindung mit n siehe auch dort* Lust ~, etw zu tun to feel like doing sth; es mit der Angst/Wut ~ to become afraid/angry; Ärger ~ to get into trouble; eine Ohrfeige or eine *(inf)* ~ to catch it *(inf)*; Prügel or sie *(inf)* or es *(inf)* ~ to be given or to get a hiding.

2 vi (a) aux sein + dat *(zuträglich sein)* jdm *(gut)* ~ to do sb good; *(Essen)* to agree with sb; jdm nicht or schlecht ~ not to do sb any good; *(Essen)* to disagree or not to agree with sb; wie ist Ihnen das Bad ~? how was your bath?; wie bekommt ihm die Ehe? how is he enjoying married life?; es ist ihm schlecht ~, daß er nicht gearbeitet hat not working did him no good; wohl bekomm's! your health!

(b) *(bedient werden)* ~ Sie schon? are you being attended to or served?

bekömmlich adj Mahlzeit, Speisen (easily) digestible; Luft, Klima beneficial. leicht/schwer/besser ~ sein to be easily digestible/difficult/easier to digest.

Bekömmlichkeit f siehe adj digestibility; beneficial quality.

beköstigen* vt to cater for.

Beköstigung f *(das Beköstigen)* catering *(gen* for*)*; *(Kost)* food.

bekotzen* *(vulg)* vt to spew or puke over *(sl)*. er hat sich/seinen Anzug von oben bis unten bekotzt he spewed or puked all down himself/his suit *(sl)*.

bekräftigen* vt to confirm; Vorschlag to support, to back up. etw nochmals ~ to reaffirm sth; seine Aussage mit einem Eid ~ to reinforce one's evidence by swearing an oath; eine Vereinbarung mit einem Handschlag ~ to seal an agreement by shaking hands; er nickte ~d he nodded in support.

Bekräftigung f confirmation; *(Versicherung)* assurance. zur ~ seiner Worte to reinforce his words.

bekränzen* vt to crown with a wreath; *(mit Blumen)* to garland.

bekreuzen* 1 vt *(Eccl)* to bless (with the sign of the cross). 2 vr siehe bekreuzigen.

bekreuzigen* vr to cross oneself.

bekriechen* vt irreg to crawl over; *(fig)* to creep over.

bekriegen* vt to wage war on; *(fig)* to fight. sie ~ sich *(gegenseitig)* schon seit Jahren they have been at war with one another for years; bekriegt werden to be attacked.

bekritteln* vt to criticize; Arbeit auch to find fault with.

bekritzeln* vt to scribble over. das Buch mit Bemerkungen ~ to scribble comments over the book.

bekrönen* vt to crown *(auch fig)*; *(Archit)* to surmount.

bekucken* vt *(N Ger)* siehe begucken.

bekümmern* 1 vt to worry. was bekümmert Sie das? what concern is it of yours?; das braucht dich nicht zu ~ there is no need for you to worry about that. 2 vr sich über etw *(acc)* ~ to worry about sth; sich um etw ~ to concern oneself with sth.

Bekümmernis f *(geh)* distress.

bekümmert 1 ptp of bekümmern. 2 adj worried *(über + acc* about*)*.

bekunden* 1 vt to show, to express; *(in Worten auch)* to state; *(Jur: bezeugen)* to testify to. ~, daß ... *(Jur)* to testify that ... 2 vr *(geh)* to manifest itself.

Bekundung f expression, manifestation; *(in Worten auch)* statement; *(Jur)* testimony.

belächeln* vt to smile at.

belachen* vt to laugh at.

beladen* irreg 1 vt Schiff, Zug to load (up); *(fig: mit Sorgen etc)* jdn to burden. etw mit Holz etc ~ to load sth with wood etc, to load wood etc onto sth; ein Tier mit einer schweren Last ~ to put a heavy load on an animal.

2 vr *(mit Gepäck etc)* to load oneself up. sich mit Verantwortung/Sorgen ~ to take on responsibilities/worries; sich mit Schuld ~ to incur guilt.

3 adj loaded; Mensch laden; *(mit Schuld)* laden, burdened. mit etw ~ sein to be loaded with sth; *(Mensch)* to be loaded down or laden with sth; *(mit Schuld etc)* to be weighed down or laden or burdened with sth.

Belag m -(e)s, =e coating; *(Schicht)* layer; *(Ölfilm etc)* film; *(auf Pizza, Brot)* topping; *(auf Tortenboden, zwischen zwei Brotscheiben)* filling; *(auf Zahn)* film; *(Zungen~)* fur; *(Brems~)* lining; *(Fußboden~)* covering; *(Straßen~)* surface. einen ~ auf der Zunge haben to have fur on one's tongue.

Belagerer m -s, - besieger.

belagern* vt *(Mil)* to besiege *(auch fig)*, to lay siege to.

Belagerung f siege.

Belagerungs-: ~krieg m siege warfare; ~maschine f siege machine; ~zustand m state of siege; den ~zustand ausrufen to declare a state of siege.

Belami m -(s), -s *(dated)* ladykiller *(inf)*.

belämmern* vt, **belämmert** adj siehe belemmern, belemmert.

Belang m -(e)s, -e (a) *(no pl: Wichtigkeit)* importance, significance. von/ohne ~ *(für jdn/etw)* sein to be of importance/of no importance *(to sb/for or to sth)*. (b) ~e pl interests. (c) *(form: Sache)* matter. in diesem ~ as regards this matter.

belangen* vt (a) *(Jur)* to prosecute *(wegen* for*)*; *(wegen Beleidigung, Verleumdung)* to sue. dafür kann man belangt werden you could be prosecuted for that. (b) *(dated: betreffen)* was mich belangt as far as I am concerned.

belanglos adj inconsequential, trivial. das ist für das Ergebnis ~ that is irrelevant to the result.

Belanglosigkeit f (a) no pl inconsequentiality, triviality. (b) *(Bemerkung)* triviality.

Belangung f prosecution; *(wegen Beleidigung, Verleumdung)* suing.

belangvoll adj relevant *(für* to*)*.

belassen* *vt irreg* to leave. **wir wollen es dabei ~** let's leave it at that; **jdn in dem Glauben ~, daß ...** to allow sb to go on believing that ...; **jdn in seinem Amt ~** to allow sb to remain in office; **etw an seinem Ort ~** to leave sth in its place; **das muß ihm ~ bleiben** that must be left up to him.

belastbar *adj* (a) *(mit Last, Gewicht)* **bis zu 500 Kilogramm ~ sein** to have a maximum load of *or* load-bearing capacity of 500 kilogrammes; **wie hoch ist diese Brücke ~?** what is the maximum load of this bridge?; **ein mit maximal 5 Personen ~er Aufzug** a lift with a maximum load of 5 persons.
(b) *(fig)* **daran habe ich bemerkt, wie ~ ein Mensch ist** that made me see how much a person can take; **ich glaube nicht, daß sie noch zusätzlich ~ ist** I don't think she can take any more *or* *(mit Arbeit etc)* take on any more; **das Gedächtnis ist nur bis zu einem gewissen Grad ~** the memory can only absorb a certain amount; **weiter waren seine Nerven nicht ~** his nerves could take no more *or* were at breaking point.
(c) *(beanspruchbar)* *(Med)* *Mensch, Körper, Organe, Kreislauf* resilient. **die Atmosphäre ist nicht unbegrenzt *(durch Schadstoffe)* ~** the atmosphere cannot stand an unlimited degree of contamination; **da wird sich zeigen, wie ~ das Stromnetz/unser Wasserhaushalt ist** that will show how much pressure our electricity/water supply will take.
(d) **wie hoch ist mein Konto ~?** what is the limit on my account?; **der Etat ist nicht unbegrenzt ~** the budget is not unlimited; **der Arbeiter ist auf keinen Fall steuerlich höher ~** the worker will be unable to stand any increase in taxes.

Belastbarkeit *f* (a) *(von Brücke, Aufzug)* load-bearing capacity.
(b) *(von Menschen, Nerven)* ability to take stress; *(von Gedächtnis)* capacity.
(c) *(von Stromnetz etc)* maximum capacity; *(von Menschen, Organ)* maximum resilience. **die höhere physische ~ eines Sportlers** an athlete's higher degree of physical resilience.
(d) *(von Haushalt)* (maximum) limit *(gen* of, on); *(steuerlich)* maximum level of possible taxation.

belasten* 1 *vt* (a) *(lit)* *(mit Gewicht)* *Brücke, Balken, Träger, Ski* to put weight on; *(mit Last)* *Fahrzeug, Fahrstuhl* to load. **etw mit 50 Tonnen ~** to put a 50 ton load on sth, to put a weight of 50 tons on sth; **den Träger gleichmäßig ~** to distribute weight evenly over the girder; **das darf nur mit maximal 5 Personen/Tonnen belastet werden** its maximum load is 5 people/tons; **die Brücke/das Fahrzeug** *etc* **zu sehr ~** to put too much weight on the bridge/to overload the vehicle.
(b) *(fig)* **jdn mit etw ~** *mit Arbeit* to load sb with sth; *mit Verantwortung, Sorgen, Wissen* to burden sb with sth; **das Gedächtnis mit unnützem Wissen ~** to burden one's memory with useless knowledge; **jdn ~** *(mit Arbeit, Verantwortung, Sorgen)* to burden sb; *(nervlich, körperlich anstrengen)* to put a strain on sb; **jdn mit zu viel Arbeit/Verantwortung** *etc* **~** to overload/overburden sb with work/responsibility; **einen Aufsatz durch Einzelheiten ~** to overload an essay with details; *siehe* **erblich**.
(c) *(fig: bedrücken)* **jdn/jds Gewissen/Seele mit etw ~** *(Mensch)* to burden sb/sb's conscience/soul with sth; **jdn/jds Gewissen** *etc* **~** *(Schuld etc)* to weigh upon sb *or* sb's mind/conscience *etc*; **es belastet mich sehr, daß ich ihn damals belogen habe** the fact that I lied to him then weighs heavily upon my mind; **das belastet ihn sehr** that is weighing heavily on his mind; **mit einer Schuld belastet sein** to be burdened (down) by guilt; **von Sorgen belastet** weighed down with cares.
(d) *(beanspruchen)* *Wasserhaushalt, Stromnetz, Leitung* to put pressure on, to stretch; *Atmosphäre* to pollute; *(Med)* *Kreislauf, Magen, Organe, Körper, Menschen* to put a strain on, to strain; *Nerven* to strain, to tax. **jdn/etw zu sehr** *or* **stark ~** to overstrain sb/sth; *Wasserhaushalt etc* to put too much pressure on *or* to overstretch sth.
(e) *(Jur)* *Angeklagten* to incriminate. **~des Material** incriminating evidence.
(f) *(Fin)* *Konto* to charge; *Etat* to be a burden on; *(steuerlich)* **jdn** to burden. **etw (mit einer Hypothek) ~** to mortgage sth; **das Konto mit einem Betrag ~** to debit a sum from the account; **jdn mit den Kosten ~** to charge the costs to sb; **dafür werden wir Sie mit DM 50 ~** we will charge you 50 marks for that.
2 *vr* (a) **sich mit etw ~** *mit Arbeit* to take sth on; *mit Verantwortung* to take sth upon oneself; *mit Sorgen* to burden oneself with sth; **sich mit Schuld ~** to incur guilt; **damit belaste ich mich nicht** *(mit Arbeit, Verantwortung)* I don't want to take that on; **ich will mich nicht ~** *(mit Wissen)* I don't want to know (about it).
(b) *(Jur)* to incriminate oneself.

belästigen* *vt (zur Last fallen)* to bother; *(zudringlich werden)* to pester; *(körperlich)* to molest; *(Licht, Geräusch, Geruch)* to irritate.

belästigend *adj* annoying, aggravating; *Licht etc* irritating.

Belästigung *f* annoyance; *(durch Lärm etc)* irritation; *(Zudringlichkeit auch)* pestering; *(körperlich)* molesting. **etw als eine ~ empfinden** to find sth an annoyance *or* a nuisance; **sie beklagte sich über die ~en durch ihren Chef** she complained about being pestered by her boss.

Belastung *f siehe vt* (a) *(das Belasten)* putting weight on; loading; *(Last, Gewicht)* weight; *(in Fahrzeug, Fahrstuhl etc)* load. **die erhöhte ~ der Brücke** the increased weight put on the bridge; **maximale ~ der Brücke/des Fahrstuhls** weight limit of the bridge/maximum load of the lift.
(b) *(fig)* *(das Belasten)* *(mit Arbeit)* loading; *(mit Verantwortung etc)* burdening; *(Anstrengung)* strain; *(Last, Bürde)* burden.
(c) burden *(gen* on).
(d) pressure *(gen* on); pollution *(gen* of); strain *(gen* on).

(e) incrimination.
(f) *(Fin)* charge *(gen* on); *(von Etat, steuerlich)* burden *(gen* on); *(mit Hypothek)* mortgage *(gen* on).

Belastungs-: **b~fähig** *adj siehe* **belastbar**; **~grenze** *f (von Brücke, Fahrzeug, Balken etc)* weight limit; *(von Atmosphäre, Wasserhaushalt)* maximum capacity; *(seelisch, physisch)* limit; *(Elec)* level of peak load; **ich habe meine ~grenze erreicht/überschritten** I've reached my limit *or* had enough/I've overdone it; **~material** *nt (Jur)* incriminating evidence; **~probe** *f* endurance test; **~spitze** *f (Elec)* peak load; **~zeuge** *m (Jur)* witness for the prosecution.

belatschern* *vt (dial inf)* to talk round, to persuade.

belauben* *vr* to come into leaf. **spärlich/dicht belaubt sein** to have sparse/thick foliage.

Belaubung *f, no pl (Laub)* leaves *pl*, foliage; *(das Sichbelauben)* coming into leaf.

belauern* *vt* to eye; *Wild* to observe secretly; *(fig: Gefahr etc)* to menace.

belaufen* *irreg* 1 *vr* **sich auf etw** *(acc)* **~** to come *or* amount to sth. 2 *vt (rare: begehen)* to walk. **ein viel ~er Weg** a well-trodden path. 3 *vi aux sein (dial: anlaufen)* to become covered in condensation; *(Fenster auch)* to steam up, to become steamed up.

belauschen* *vt* to eavesdrop on; *(genau beobachten)* to observe.

beleben* 1 *vt* (a) *(anregen)* to liven up; *(neu ~)* *Natur* to revive; *(aufmuntern auch)* to brighten up; *Absatz, Konjunktur, jds Hoffnungen* to stimulate. **eine kalte Dusche wird dich neu ~** a cold shower will refresh you.
(b) *(lebendiger gestalten)* to brighten up; *Unterhaltung auch* to animate.
(c) *(zum Leben erwecken)* to bring to life.
2 *vr* *(Konjunktur)* to be stimulated; *(Augen, Gesicht)* to light up; *(Natur, Stadt)* to come to life; *(geschäftiger werden)* to liven up.
3 *vi* **das belebt** that livens you up.

belebend *adj* invigorating.

belebt *adj* (a) *Straße, Stadt etc* busy. (b) *(lebendig)* living. **die ~e Natur** the living world; **~er Schlamm** activated sludge.

Belebtheit *f siehe adj* (a) bustle. (b) life.

Belebung *f* revival; *(der Wirtschaft, Konjunktur)* stimulation. **zur ~ trank er einen starken Kaffee** to revive himself he drank a cup of strong coffee.

Belebungsversuch *m (Med)* resuscitation attempt.

belecken* *vt* to lick.

Beleg *m* -(e)s, -e (a) *(Beweis)* instance, piece of evidence; *(Quellennachweis)* reference. **~e für den Gebrauch eines Wortes** instances of the use of a word. (b) *(Quittung)* receipt.

belegbar *adj* verifiable.

belegen* *vt* (a) *(bedecken)* to cover; *Brote, Tortenboden* to fill. **etw mit Fliesen/Teppich ~** to tile/carpet sth; **mit Beschuß/Bomben ~** to bombard/bomb *or* bombard; *siehe* **belegt**.
(b) *(besetzen)* *Wohnung, Hotelbett* to occupy; *(reservieren)* to reserve, to book; *(Univ)* *Fach* to take; *Seminar, Vorlesung* to enrol for. **ein Haus mit Soldaten ~** to billet soldiers in a house; **eine Stadt mit Truppen ~** to station troops in a town; **den fünften Platz ~** to take fifth place, to come fifth.
(c) *(beweisen)* to verify.
(d) *(auferlegen)* **jdn mit etw ~** to impose sth on sb; **jdn mit dem Bann ~** to proscribe sb; *(Eccl)* to excommunicate sb; **etw mit einem Namen ~** to give sth a name.

Beleg-: **~exemplar** *nt* specimen copy; **~frist** *f (Univ)* enrolment period; **~material** *nt* documentation.

Belegschaft *f* (a) *(Beschäftigte)* staff; *(esp in Fabriken etc)* workforce. (b) *(inf: die Anwesenden)* **die ganze ~** the whole mob *(inf)* *or* gang *(inf)*.

Belegschafts-: **~aktien** *pl* employees' shares; **~mitglied** *nt* employee; **~versammlung** *f* meeting of employees.

Beleg-: **~stelle** *f* reference; **~stück** *nt* piece of evidence.

belegt 1 *ptp of* **belegen.** 2 *adj* *Zunge* furred; *Stimme* hoarse; *Zimmer, Bett, Wohnung* occupied. **~e Brote** open sandwiches.

belehnen* *vt* (a) *(Hist)* to enfeoff. (b) *(Sw)* *Haus* to mortgage.

Belehnung *f* (a) *(Hist)* enfeoffment. (b) *(Sw)* mortgaging.

belehrbar *adj* teachable.

belehren* *vt (unterweisen)* to teach, to instruct; *(aufklären)* to inform, to advise *(form)* *(über +acc* of). **jdn eines anderen ~** to teach sb otherwise; **sich eines anderen ~ lassen** to learn *or* be taught otherwise; **da mußte ich mich ~ lassen** I realized I was wrong; **ich mußte mich ~ lassen, daß das nicht zutrifft** I was told that that was not correct; **er ist nicht zu** *or* **läßt sich nicht ~** he won't be told; **ich bin belehrt!** I've learned my lesson; *siehe* **besser**.

belehrend *adj* didactic.

Belehrung *f* explanation, lecture *(inf)*; *(Anweisung)* instruction *(über +acc* about); *(von Zeugen, Angeklagten)* caution. **deine ~en kannst du dir sparen** there's no need to lecture me.

beleibt *adj* stout, corpulent, portly.

Beleibtheit *f* corpulence, stoutness.

beleidigen* *vt jdn* to insult; *(Verhalten, Anblick, Geruch etc)* to offend; *(Jur)* *(mündlich)* to slander; *(schriftlich)* to libel.

beleidigt *adj* insulted; *(gekränkt)* offended; *Gesicht, Miene auch* hurt. **~ weggehen** to go off in a huff *(inf)*; **er fühlt sich in seiner Ehre ~** he feels his honour has been insulted; **die ~e Leberwurst spielen** *(inf)* to be in a huff *(inf)*; **bist du jetzt ~?** have I offended you?; **jetzt ist er ~** now he's in a huff *(inf)*.

Beleidigung *f* insult; *(Jur)* *(mündliche)* slander; *(schriftliche)* libel. **eine ~ für den Geschmack/das Auge** an insult to one's taste/an eyesore; **etw als ~ auffassen** to take sth as an insult, to take offence at sth.

Beleidigungs-: ~**klage** f (Jur) slander/libel action, action for slander/libel; ~**prozeß** m (Jur) slander/libel trial.

beleihen* vt irreg (a) (Comm) to lend money on; Haus, Grundstück auch to mortgage, to give a mortgage on. (b) (Hist) siehe **belehnen**.

belemmern* vt (N Ger inf: belästigen) to bother.

belemmert adj (inf) (betreten) sheepish; (niedergeschlagen) miserable; (scheußlich) Wetter, Angelegenheit lousy (inf).

belesen adj well-read.

Belesenheit f wide reading. **eine gewisse** ~ a certain degree of erudition.

Beletage [beleˈtaːʒə] f (old) first floor (Brit), second floor (US).

beleuchten* vt (Licht werfen auf) to light up, to illuminate; (mit Licht versehen) Straße, Bühne etc to light; (fig: betrachten) to examine. **ein parkendes Auto muß beleuchtet werden** or **sein** a parked car must have its lights on.

Beleuchter(in f) m -s, - lighting technician.

Beleuchterbrücke f lighting bridge.

Beleuchtung f (a) (das Beleuchten) lighting; (das Bestrahlen) illumination; (fig) examination, investigation. (b) (Licht) light; (das Beleuchtetsein) lighting; (Lichter) lights pl. **die ~ der Straßen/Fahrzeuge** street lighting/lights pl on vehicles.

Beleuchtungs-: ~**anlage** f lighting (installation); ~**stärke** f intensity of light; ~**technik** f lighting engineering.

beleumdet, beleumundet adj **gut/schlecht ~ sein** to have a good/bad reputation; **ein schlecht ~es Etablissement** an establishment with a bad reputation.

belfern vti to bark; (Kanone) to boom. **Worte durchs Telefon ~** to bark down the phone.

Belgien [-iən] nt -s Belgium.

Belgier(in f) [-iɐ, -iɐɪn] m -s, - Belgian.

belgisch adj Belgian.

belichten* vt (Phot) to expose. **wie lange muß ich das Bild ~?** what exposure should I give the shot?

Belichtung f (Phot) exposure.

Belichtungs-: ~**dauer** f siehe ~**zeit**; ~**messer** m light meter; ~**tabelle** f exposure chart or table; ~**zeit** f exposure (time).

Belieben nt -s, no pl **nach ~** just as you/they etc like, any way you etc want (to); **das steht** or **liegt in Ihrem ~** that is up to you or left to your discretion.

belieben* 1 vi impers (geh) **wie es Ihnen beliebt** as you like or wish; **was beliebt?** (old: wird gewünscht) what can I do for you?

    2 vt (old, iro) **es beliebt jdm, etw zu tun** (hat Lust) sb feels like doing sth; (iro) sb deigns or condescends to do sth; **jd beliebt, etw zu tun** (neigt dazu) sb likes doing sth; **was euch beliebt** as you wish or like; **er beliebt zu scherzen** (iro) he must be joking.

beliebig 1 adj any. (irgend)**eine/jede** ~**e Farbe** any colour at all or whatever or you like; **nicht jede** ~**e Farbe** not every colour; **jeder B**~ anyone at all; **eine ganz** ~**e Reihe von Beispielen** a quite arbitrary series of examples; **in** ~**er Reihenfolge** in any order whatever; **alles B**~**e** anything whatever; **die Auswahl ist** ~ the choice is open or free.

    2 adv as you etc like. **Sie können ~ lange bleiben** you can stay as long as you like; **die Farben können ~ ausgewählt werden** you can choose any colour you like.

beliebt adj popular (bei with). **sich bei jdm ~ machen** to make oneself popular with sb.

Beliebtheit f popularity.

beliefern* vt to supply. **jdn (mit etw) ~** to supply sb with sth.

Belieferung f supplying. **die ~ einer Firma einstellen** to stop supplying a firm.

Belladonna f -, **Belladonnen** deadly nightshade, belladonna; (Extrakt) belladonna.

bellen 1 vi to bark; (Kanonen) to boom; (Maschinengewehr) to crack; (Donner) to crash. 2 vt to bark; **Befehle** to bark out.

bellend adj Husten hacking; Stimme gruff; Maschinengewehre cracking; Kanonen booming.

Belletrist m (geh) belletrist.

Belletristik f fiction and poetry, belles lettres pl.

belletristisch adj Zeitschrift, Neigung literary. ~**e Literatur/Bücher** fiction and poetry/books of fiction and poetry; ~**er Verlag** publisher specializing in fiction and poetry; ~**e Abteilung** department for fiction and poetry.

belobigen* vt to commend, to praise.

Belobigung f (form) commendation.

Belobigungs-: ~**schreiben** nt commendation; ~**urkunde** f certificate of commendation.

belohnen*, belöhnen* (Sw) vt to reward; jds Treue, gute Tat auch to repay. **starker Beifall belohnte den Schauspieler** the actor received hearty applause.

Belohnung, Belöhnung (Sw) f reward; (das Belohnen) rewarding. **zur** or **als ~ (für)** as a reward (for); **eine ~ aussetzen** to offer a reward; **zur ~ der Kinder für ihr gutes Benehmen** in order to reward the children for their good behaviour.

Belt m -s, -e **der Große/Kleine ~** the Great/Little Belt.

belüften* vt to ventilate; Kleider to air.

Belüftung f (a) (das Belüften) ventilating; airing. (b) (inf: die Anlage) ventilation.

belügen* vt to lie or tell lies/a lie to. **sich selbst ~** to deceive oneself.

belustigen* 1 vt to amuse. 2 vr (geh) **sich ~ über jdn/etw** to make fun of sb/sth; **sich an etw** (dat) ~ to laugh at sth; **sich mit etw ~** to amuse oneself by (doing) sth.

belustigt 1 adj Gesichtsausdruck, Ton, Stimme amused. 2 adv in amusement.

Belustigung f (geh: Veranstaltung) entertainment; (das Belustigtsein) amusement.

Belzebub m siehe **Beelzebub**.

bemachen* vr (inf) (a) (sich beschmutzen) to make oneself dirty or filthy. (b) (sich aufregen) to get het-up (inf).

bemächtigen* vr (geh) (a) (in seine Gewalt bringen) **sich eines Menschen/einer Sache ~** to take or seize hold of sb/sth; **sich des Thrones ~** to seize or take the throne; (durch Intrige) to usurp the throne. (b) (Gefühl, Gedanke) **sich jds ~** to come over sb.

bemähnt adj Tier maned; (hum) Jugendliche shaggy-haired.

bemäkeln* vt to find fault with, to pick holes in.

Bemäkelung f criticizing, criticism.

bemalen* 1 vt to paint; (verzieren auch) to decorate. **etw mit Blumen ~** to paint flowers on sth; **bemalt sein** (pej) to be heavily made up. 2 vr to paint oneself; (pej: schminken) to put on one's war paint (inf).

Bemalung f siehe vt painting; decoration. **bist du mit der ~ fertig?** (inf) have you finished putting on your war paint? (inf).

bemängeln* vt to find fault with, to fault. **was die Kritiker an dem Buch ~, ist ...** the fault the critics find with the book is ...

Bemängelung f finding fault (gen with), faulting (gen of).

bemannen* vt U-Boot, Raumschiff to man. **sie ist seit neuestem wieder bemannt** (inf) she has just recently got herself a man again or a new boyfriend.

Bemannung f manning; (rare: Mannschaft) crew.

bemänteln* vt to cover up.

Bemäntelung f covering-up.

Bembel m -s, - (dial) pitcher.

bemeistern* (geh) 1 vt to master; Wut, Erregung auch to control 2 vr (a) to control oneself. (b) **sich einer Sache** (gen) ~ to take or seize hold of sth.

bemerkbar adj noticeable, perceptible. **sich ~ machen** (sich zeigen) to make itself felt, to become noticeable; (auf sich aufmerksam machen) to draw attention to oneself, to attract attention; **mach dich ~, wenn du etwas brauchst** let me know if you need anything.

Bemerken nt (form): **mit dem ~** with the observation.

bemerken* vt (a) (wahrnehmen) to notice; Schmerzen auch to feel. **er bemerkte rechtzeitig/zu spät, daß ...** he realized in time/too late that ...

    (b) (äußern) to remark, to comment. **hör auf, bemerkte sie** stop that, she said; **nebenbei bemerkt** by the way; **ich möchte dazu ~, daß ...** I would like to say or add, that ...; **er hatte einiges zu ~** he had a few comments or remarks to make.

bemerkenswert adj remarkable.

Bemerkung f (a) remark, comment. (b) (old: Wahrnehmung) observation.

bemessen* irreg 1 vt (zuteilen) to allocate; (einteilen) to calculate. **der Raum ist für eine kleine Gruppe ~** the room is designed for a small group of people; **reichlich/knapp ~** generous/not very generous; **meine Zeit ist kurz** or **knapp ~** my time is limited or restricted.

    2 vr (form) to be proportionate (nach to).

Bemessung f (a) siehe vt allocation; calculation. (b) (Build) building specification.

bemitleiden* vt to pity, to feel pity or feel sorry for. **er ist zu ~** he is to be pitied; **sich selbst ~** to feel sorry for oneself.

bemitleidenswert adj pitiable, pitiful.

Bemitleidung f pity (gen for).

bemittelt adj well-to-do, well-off.

Bemme f -, -n (dial) slice of buttered bread; (zusammengeklappt) sandwich.

bemogeln* vt (inf) to cheat.

bemoosen* vr to become overgrown with moss.

bemoost adj mossy. ~**es Haupt** (inf) old fogey; (Student) perpetual student.

Bemühen nt -s, no pl (geh) efforts pl, endeavours pl (um for).

bemühen* 1 vt to trouble, to bother; Rechtsanwalt etc to engage. **jdn zu sich ~** to call in sb, to call upon the services of sb; **die Bibel** or **Bibelstellen ~** to quote from the Bible.

    2 vr (a) (sich Mühe geben) to try hard, to endeavour. **sich um gute Beziehungen/eine Stelle ~** to try to get good relations/a job; **sich um jds Wohl/jds Vertrauen/jds Gunst ~** to take trouble over sb's well-being/try to win sb's trust/court sb's favour; **sich um eine Verbesserung der Lage ~** to try to improve the situation; **sich um jdn ~** (für eine Stelle) to try to get sb; (um Kranken etc) to look after sb; (um jds Gunst) to court sb; **bitte ~ Sie sich nicht** please don't trouble yourself or put yourself out; **sich redlich ~** to make a genuine effort.

    (b) (geh: gehen) to go, to proceed (form). **sich ins Nebenzimmer ~** to proceed to the next room (form); **sich zu jdm ~** to go to sb; **sich auf die Polizei ~** to go to the police.

bemüht adj (a) ~ **sein, etw zu tun** to try hard or endeavour to do sth; **um etw ~ sein, darum ~ sein, etw zu tun** to endeavour or be at pains to do sth. (b) (angestrengt) forced; Mensch constrained.

Bemühung f effort, endeavour. **vielen Dank für Ihre (freundlichen)** ~**en** (form) thank you for your efforts or trouble.

bemüßigen* vr (geh) **sich einer Sache** (gen) ~ to avail oneself of sth.

bemüßigt adj **sich ~ fühlen/sehen/finden** (geh, usu iro) to feel called upon or obliged.

bemuttern* vt to mother.

Bemutterung f mothering.

bemützt adj wearing a cap/hat. **weiß ~e Bergkuppen** snow-capped mountains.

benachbart adj neighbouring attr; Haus, Familie auch next door; Staat auch adjoining. **die Häuser sind ~** the houses adjoin one another or are next (door) to one another.

benachrichtigen* vt to inform (von of); (amtlich auch) to notify (von of).

Benachrichtigung f (Nachricht) notification; (Comm)

advice note. **die ~ der Eltern ist in solchen Fällen vorge-schrieben** the parents must be notified in such cases.
Benachrichtigungsschreiben *nt* letter of notification.
benachteiligen* *vt* to put at a disadvantage; (*wegen Geschlecht, Klasse, Rasse, Glauben etc auch*) to discriminate against; (*körperliches Leiden auch*) to handicap. **benachteiligt sein** to be at a disadvantage/discriminated against/handicapped.
Benachteiligte(r) *mf decl as adj* victim. **der/die ~ sein** to be at a disadvantage.
Benachteiligung *f siehe vt* (*das Benachteiligen*) disadvantaging; discrimination (*gen* against); (*Zustand*) disadvantage; discrimination *no pl*.
benageln* *vt* **eine Wand/das Dach** *etc* **mit etw ~** to nail sth onto a wall/the roof *etc*.
benagen* *vt* to gnaw at.
benähen* *vt* **das Kleid** *etc* **mit etw ~** to sew sth onto the dress; **jdn ~** (*inf*) to sew (clothes) for sb.
benässen* *vt* (*geh*) to moisten.
Bendel *m* or *nt* **-s, -** (*dial*) ribbon; (*Schnürsenkel*) shoelace. **jdn (fest) am ~ haben** (*inf*) to have sb on a string (*inf*).
benebeln* *vt* (*inf*) **jdn/jds Sinne/jds Kopf ~** to make sb's head swim or reel; (*Narkose, Sturz*) to daze sb, to make sb feel dazed; **benebelt sein** to be feeling dazed or (*von Alkohol auch*) muzzy (*inf*).
benedeien *vt* (*Eccl*) to bless; *Gott* to glorify. **Maria, du Gebenedeite unter den Weibern** Mary, thou most blessed among women.
Benediktiner *m* **-s, -** (a) (*Eccl auch* **~in** *f*) Benedictine (friar/nun). (b) (*Likör*) Benedictine.
Benediktiner- *in cpds* Benedictine.
Benediktus *nt* **-, -** (*Eccl*) Benedictus.
Benefiz *nt* **-es, -e** benefit.
Benefizium *nt* **-s, Benefizien. (b)** (*Hist*) fee, feoff.
Benefizvorstellung *f siehe* **Benefiz.**
Benehmen *nt* **-s,** *no pl* (a) behaviour. **kein ~ haben** to have no manners, to be bad-mannered. (b) **sich mit jdm ins ~ setzen** (*form*) to get in touch with sb.
benehmen* *irreg* 1 *vt* (*geh*) (a) (*rauben*) to take away. **jdm den Atem ~** to take sb's breath away; **jdm die Lust ~, etw zu tun** to deter sb from doing sth.
(b) (*rare: die Sinne trüben*) **jdn/jdm die Sinne** *or* **den Kopf ~** to make sb feel dazed; *siehe* **benommen.**
2 *vr* to behave; (*in Bezug auf Umgangsformen auch*) to behave oneself. **benimm dich!** behave yourself!; **sich gut ~** to behave oneself *or* well; **sich schlecht ~** to behave (oneself) badly, to misbehave.
beneiden* *vt* to envy. **jdn um etw ~** to envy sb sth; **er ist nicht zu ~** I don't envy him.
beneidenswert *adj* enviable. **sie ist nicht ~** I don't envy her; **~ naiv** (*iro*) amazingly naïve.
BENELUX *abbr of* **Belgien, Niederlande, Luxemburg.**
Benelux- [*auch - - ' -*]: **~länder, ~staaten** *pl* Benelux countries *pl*.
benennen* *vt irreg* to name; *jdn auch* to call. **jdn/etw nach jdm ~** to name *or* call sb/sth after or for (*US*) sb.
Benennung *f* (*das Benennen*) naming; (*von Mensch auch*) calling; (*Bezeichnung*) name, designation (*form*).
benetzen* *vt* (*geh*) to moisten; (*Tau, Tränen auch*) to cover.
Bengale *m* **-n, -n, Bengalin** *f* Bengalese, Bengali.
Bengalen *nt* **-s** Bengal.
bengalisch *adj* (a) Bengalese; *Mensch, Sprache auch* Bengali. (b) **~es Feuer** brightly coloured flames from burning certain substances, Bengal light; **~es Hölzchen** Bengal match; **~e Beleuchtung** subdued multicoloured lighting.
Bengel *m* **-s, -(s)** (a) boy, lad; (*frecher Junge*) rascal. **ein süßer ~** (*inf*) a dear little boy. (b) *dial: Knüppel* stick. **den ~ wegwerfen** (*dial*) to lose courage.
bengelhaft *adj* rascally, mischievous.
Benimm *m* **-s,** *no pl* (*inf*) manners *pl*.
Benimmregel *f, usu pl* etiquette *sing*. **eine ~ a rule of etiquette.**
Benjamin [-miːn] *m* **-s, -e** Benjamin. **er ist der ~** he is the baby of the family.
benommen 1 *ptp of* **benehmen.** 2 *adj* dazed; (*von Ereignissen auch*) bemused.
Benommenheit *f* daze, dazed state.
benoten* *vt* to mark. **etw mit "gut" ~** to mark sth "good".
benötigen* *vt* to need, to require. **das benötigte Geld** *etc* the necessary money *etc*, the money *etc* needed.
Benotung *f* mark; (*das Benoten*) marking.
benutzbar *adj* usable; *Weg* passable.
benutzen*, benützen* (*dial*) *vt* (*verwenden*) to use; *Literatur* to consult; *Gelegenheit auch* to make use of, to take advantage of. **etw als Schlafzimmer/Vorwand ~** to use sth as a bedroom/an excuse; **das benutzte Geschirr** the dirty dishes.
Benutzer, Benützer (*dial*) *m* **-s, -** user; (*von Leihbücherei*) borrower.
Benutzung, Benützung (*dial*) *f* use. **etw in ~ haben/nehmen** to be/start using sth; **jdm etw zur ~ überlassen** to put sth at sb's disposal; **etw zur ~ freigeben** *or* **bereitstellen** to open sth.
Benutzungsgebühr *f* charge; (*Leihgebühr*) hire charge.
benzen *vi* (*Aus inf*) (a) (*betteln*) to beg. (b) (*klagen*) to complain.
Benzin *nt* **-s, -e** (*für Auto*) petrol (*Brit*), gasoline (*US*), gas (*US*); (*Reinigungs~*) benzine; (*Feuerzeug~*) lighter fuel.
Benzin-: **~abscheider** *m* **-s, -** petrol separator; **~einspritzung** *f* fuel injection.
Benziner *m* **-s, -** (*inf*) car which runs on petrol (*Brit*) *or* gasoline (*US*).

Benzin-: **~feuerzeug** *nt* petrol/gasoline lighter; **~hahn** *m* fuel cock; **den ~hahn zudrehen** (*fig*) to stop the supply of petrol; **~kanister** *m* petrol/gasoline can; **~kutsche** *f* (*dated inf*) limousine; **~leitung** *f* fuel *or* petrol/gasoline pipe; **~motor** *m* petrol/gasoline engine; **~pumpe** *f* (*Aut*) fuel pump; (*an Tankstellen*) petrol/gasoline pump; **~uhr** *f* fuel gauge; **~verbrauch** *m* fuel *or* petrol/gasoline consumption.
Benzoe [-tsoe] *f* **-,** *no pl* benzoin.
Benzoesäure *f* benzoic acid.
Benzol *nt* **-s, -e** benzol(e).
beobachtbar *adj* observable.
beobachten* *vt* to observe; (*bemerken auch*) to notice, to see; (*genau verfolgen, betrachten auch*) to watch. **etw an jdm ~** to notice sth in sb; **jdn ~ lassen** (*Polizei etc*) to put sb under surveillance.
Beobachter(in *f*) *m* **-s, -** observer.
Beobachtung *f* observation; (*polizeilich*) surveillance. **die ~ habe ich oft gemacht** I've often noticed that; **bei der ~ der Vorgänge ...** as I *etc* observed *or* watched these developments ...
Beobachtungs-: **~ballon** *m* observation balloon; **~gabe** *f* talent for observation; **er hat eine gute ~gabe** he has a very observant eye; **~posten** *m* (*Mil*) observation post; (*Mensch*) lookout; **auf ~posten sein** to be on lookout duty; **~station** *f* (a) (*Med*) observation ward; (*nach Operation*) post-operative ward; (b) (*Met*) weather station.
beölen* *vr* (*sl*) to piss (*sl*) *or* wet (*inf*) oneself (laughing).
beordern* *vt* to order; (*kommen lassen*) to summon, to send for; (*an andern Ort*) to instruct *or* order to go. **jdn zu sich ~** to send for sb.
bepacken* 1 *vt* to load (up). **jdn/etw mit etw ~** to load sb/sth up with sth. 2 *vr* to load oneself up.
bepflanzen* *vt* to plant. **das Blumenbeet mit etw ~** to plant sth in the flower bed.
Bepflanzung *f* (a) (*das Bepflanzen*) planting. (b) (*Gesamtheit der Pflanzen*) plants *pl* (*gen* in).
bepflastern* *vt* (a) *Straße* to pave; (*fig: behängen*) to plaster. (b) (*inf*) *Wunde etc* to put a plaster on. (c) (*Mil sl: bombardieren*) to plaster (*inf*); (*fig: bewerfen*) to bombard.
bepinkeln* (*inf*) 1 *vt* to pee on (*inf*). 2 *vr* to wet oneself (*inf*).
bepinseln* *vt* to paint (*auch fig*); (*Cook, Med*) to brush; *Zahnfleisch* to paint; *Wand* to brush down; (*vollschreiben*) to scribble on. **ganze Bögen mit schlechten Versen ~** to cover sheets of paper with bad verse.
bepissen* (*vulg*) 1 *vt* to piss on (*sl*). 2 *vr* to piss oneself (*sl*).
Beplankung *f* (*Tech*) planking.
bepudern* *vt* to powder (*auch fig*).
bequasseln* *vt* (*inf*) to talk over.
bequatschen* *vt* (*sl*) (a) *etw* to talk over. (b) (*überreden*) *jdn* to persuade. **wir haben sie bequatscht, daß sie kommt** we talked her into coming.
bequem *adj* (*angenehm*) comfortable; *Gast, Schüler etc* (*leicht, mühelos*) *Weg, Methode* easy; *Ausrede* convenient; (*träge*) *Mensch* idle. **es ~ haben** to have an easy time of it; **es sich** (*dat*) **~ machen** to make oneself comfortable; **machen Sie es sich ~** make yourself at home.
bequemen* *vr* **sich zu etw ~, sich (dazu) ~, etw zu tun** to bring oneself to do sth; **endlich bequemten sie sich nach Hause** they finally forced themselves to go home.
bequemlich *adj* (*dated*) *siehe* **bequem.**
Bequemlichkeit *f* (a) *no pl* (*Behaglichkeit*) comfort; (*Trägheit*) idleness. (b) (*Einrichtung*) convenience.
berappen* *vti* (*inf*) to fork *or* shell out (*inf*); *Schulden* to pay off. **er mußte schwer ~** he had to fork out a lot.
beraten* *irreg* 1 *vt* (a) *jdn ~* to advise sb, to give sb advice; **gut/schlecht ~ sein** to be well-/ill-advised; **jdn gut/schlecht ~** to give sb good/bad advice; **sich von jdm ~ lassen(, wie ...)** to ask sb's advice (on how ...), to consult sb (about how ...). (b) (*besprechen*) to discuss.
2 *vi* to discuss. **mit jdm über etw** (*acc*) **~** to discuss sth with sb; **sie ~ noch** they are still in discussion, they are still discussing it.
3 *vr* (*gegenseitig Rat spenden*) to give each other advice; (*sich besprechen*) to discuss. **sich mit jdm ~** to consult (with) sb (*über* +*acc* about); **das Kabinett tritt heute zusammen, um sich zu ~** the cabinet meets today for talks.
beratend *adj* advisory, consultative; *Ingenieur* consultant. **jdm ~ zur Seite stehen** to act in an advisory capacity to sb; **er hat nur eine ~e Stimme** he is only in an advisory capacity; **~ an einer Konferenz teilnehmen** to attend a conference in a consultative *or* an advisory capacity.
Berater(in *f*) *m* **-s, -** adviser.
Beratervertrag *m* consultative contract.
beratschlagen* *vti insep* to discuss.
Beratschlagung *f* discussion.
Beratung *f* (a) (*das Beraten*) advice; (*bei Rechtsanwalt, Arzt etc*) consultation. (b) (*Besprechung*) discussion. **eine ~ haben/abhalten** to have *or* hold talks *or* discussions.
Beratungs-: **~dienst** *m* advice *or* advisory service; (*esp Comm, Fin auch*) consultancy; **~gebühr** *f* consultancy fee; **~stelle** *f* advice centre; **~zimmer** *nt* consultation room.
berauben* *vt* to rob. **jdn einer Sache** (*gen*) **~** to rob sb of sth; **seiner Freiheit, seines Rechtes** to deprive sb of sth; **aller Hoffnung beraubt** having lost all hope.
Beraubung *f* **sich vor ~ schützen** to protect oneself from being robbed; **ich wehre mich gegen diese ~ meiner Freiheit** I object to being deprived of my freedom.
berauschen* 1 *vt* (*trunken machen*) to intoxicate; (*Alkohol auch*) to inebriate; (*Droge auch*) to make euphoric; (*in Verzükkung versetzen*) to intoxicate, to enrapture (*liter*); (*Geschwindigkeit*) to exhilarate; (*Blut, Greueltat etc*) to put in

a frenzy. **der Erfolg hat ihn völlig berauscht** he was drunk *or* carried away with success; **von Glück/Leidenschaft berauscht ... in transports** of happiness/passion ...; **berauscht von den Wein/der Poesie/den Klängen** intoxicated by the wine/intoxicated *or* enraptured by the poetry/the sounds; **seine berauschte Prosa** his ecstatic prose.

2 *vr* **sich an etw** (*dat*) ~ **an Wein, Drogen** to become intoxicated with sth; (*in Ekstase geraten*) to be intoxicated *or* enraptured (*liter*) *or* **an Geschwindigkeit** exhilarated by sth; **an Blut, Greueltat** *etc* to be in a frenzy over sth.

berauschend *adj Getränke, Drogen* intoxicating. **das war nicht sehr** ~ (*iro*) that wasn't very enthralling *or* exciting.

Berber **m -s, - (a)** Berber. **(b)** (*auch* ~**teppich**) Berber carpet. **(c)** (*sl*) (*Obdachloser*) tramp; (*großer Mensch*) giant.

Berberitze *f* **-, -n** (*Bot*) berberis.

berechenbar *adj Kosten* calculable; *Verhalten etc* predictable.

Berechenbarkeit *f siehe adj* calculability; predictability.

berechnen* *vt* **(a)** (*ausrechnen*) to calculate; *Umfang auch* to estimate; *Worte, Gesten* to calculate the effect of. **ihre Worte waren genau berechnet** her words were exactly calculated; **alles, was sie tut, ist berechnet** everything she does is calculated.

(b) (*in Rechnung stellen*) to charge. **das** ~ **wir Ihnen nicht** we will not charge you for it; **das hat er mir mit DM 75 berechnet** he charged me 75 marks for it; **er hat mir das zu teuer berechnet** he charged me too much for it, he overcharged me.

(c) (*vorsehen*) to intend, to mean. **alle Rezepte sind für 4 Personen berechnet** all the recipes are (calculated) for 4 persons; **auf eine bestimmte Wirkung berechnet sein** to be intended *or* calculated to have a particular effect.

berechnend *adj* (*pej*) *Mensch* calculating.

Berechnung *f siehe vt* **(a)** calculation; estimation. **meiner** ~ **nach, nach meiner** ~ according to my calculations, by my reckoning; **aus** ~ **handeln** to act calculatingly *or* in a calculating manner; **mit kühler** ~ **vorgehen** to act in a cool and calculating manner; **es war alles genaue** ~ it was all calculated exactly.

(b) charge. **ohne** ~ without any charge.

berechtigen* *vti* **(a)** (*jdn*) **zu etw** ~ to entitle sb to sth; **diese Karte berechtigt nicht zum Eintritt** this ticket does not entitle the bearer to admittance; **er/seine Begabung berechtigt zu den größten Hoffnungen** he/his talent gives grounds for the greatest hopes; **das berechtigt zu der Annahme, daß ...** this justifies the assumption that ...

berechtigt *adj* justifiable; *Frage, Hoffnung* legitimate; *Anspruch* legitimate, rightful; *Vorwurf auch* just; *Forderung, Einwand auch* justified. ~ **sein, etw zu tun** to be entitled to do sth; **einen** ~**en Anspruch auf etw** (*acc*) **haben** to have a legitimate *or* rightful claim to sth, to be fully entitled to sth.

berechtigterweise *adv* legitimately; (*verständlicherweise*) justifiably.

Berechtigung *f* **(a)** (*Befugnis*) entitlement; (*Recht*) right. **die** ~**/keine** ~ **haben, etw zu tun** to be entitled/not to be entitled to do sth. **(b)** (*Rechtmäßigkeit*) legitimacy; (*Verständlichkeit*) justifiability. **zu dieser Behauptung hat er doch gar keine** ~ he has no justification for (making) such a claim.

Berechtigungsschein *m* authorization.

bereden* **1** *vt* **(a)** (*besprechen*) to discuss, to talk over.

(b) (*überreden*) **jdn zu etw** ~ to talk sb into sth; **jdn dazu** ~, **etw zu tun** to talk sb into doing sth; **bleib bei deiner Entscheidung, laß dich nicht** ~ stick to your decision, don't let anybody talk you out of it.

(c) (*inf: beklatschen*) to gossip about.

2 *vr* **sich mit jdm über etw** (*acc*) ~ to talk sth over with sb, to discuss sth with sb; **die beiden haben sich miteinander beredet** the two of them talked it over.

beredsam *adj* (*liter*) eloquent; (*iro: redefreudig*) talkative.

Beredsamkeit *f siehe adj* eloquence; talkativeness.

beredt *adj* (*geh*) eloquent. **mit** ~**en Worten** eloquently.

Beredtheit *f* eloquence.

beregnen* *vt* to water, to sprinkle; (*vom Flugzeug aus*) to spray (with water). **beregnet werden** to be watered *etc*; (*natürlich*) to get rain.

Beregnung *f siehe vt* watering, sprinkling; spraying (with water); (*natürliche*) rain(fall).

Beregnungslanlage *f* sprinkler.

Bereich **m -(e)s, -e (a)** area. **in nördlicheren** ~**en** in more northerly regions; **im** ~ **der Kaserne** inside the barracks; **im** ~ **des Domes** in the precincts of the cathedral; **im** ~ **der Innenstadt** in the town centre (area).

(b) (*Einfluß*~, *Aufgaben*~) sphere; (*Sach*~) area, sphere, field; (*Sektor*) sector. **im** ~ **des Möglichen liegen** to be within the realms *or* bounds of possibility; **Musik aus dem** ~ **der Oper** music from the realm of opera; **in jds** ~ (*acc*) **fallen** to be within sb's province.

bereichern* **1** *vt* (*lit, fig*) to enrich; *Sammlung etc auch* to enlarge. **das Gespräch hat mich sehr bereichert** I gained a great deal from the conversation. **2** *vr* to make a lot of money (*an* +*dat* out of). **sich auf Kosten anderer** ~ to feather one's nest at the expense of other people.

Bereicherung *f* **(a)** (*das Bereichern*) enrichment; (*von Sammlung auch*) enlargement.

(b) (*das Reichwerden*) moneymaking. **seine eigene** ~ making money for oneself.

(c) (*Gewinn*) boon. **das Gespräch mit Ihnen war mir eine** ~ I gained a lot from my conversation with you; **das ist eine wertvolle** ~ it is a valuable addition.

bereifen[1]*** *vt* (*Aut*) *Wagen* to put tyres on; *Rad* to put a tyre on; *Faß* to hoop. **gut/richtig bereift sein** (*Auto*) to have good/the right tyres.

bereifen[2]*** *vt* (*liter*) to cover with (hoar) frost. **bereift** frosty, frost-covered.

Bereifung *f* (*Aut*) set of tyres. **eine neue** ~ new tyres, a new set of tyres; **die** ~ **bei diesem Auto** the tyres on this car.

bereinigen* *vt* to clear up, to resolve; *Meinungsverschiedenheiten auch* to settle. **ich habe mit ihr noch etwas zu** ~ I have something to clear up with her; **die Sache hat sich von selbst bereinigt** the matter resolved itself *or* cleared itself up.

Bereinigung *f siehe vt* clearing up, resolving; settlement.

bereisen* *vt ein Land* to travel around; (*Comm*) *Gebiet* to travel, to cover. **die Welt/fremde Länder** ~ to travel the world/in foreign countries.

bereit *adj usu pred* **(a)** (*fertig*) ready; (*vorbereitet auch*) prepared. **es ist alles zum Essen/Aufbruch** ~ the meal is all ready *or* prepared/we're all ready to go; **zum Einsatz** ~ **Truppen** troops ready *or* prepared to go into action; **sich** ~ **halten** to be ready *or* prepared; **eine Antwort/Ausrede** ~ **haben** to have an answer/excuse ready *or* a ready answer/excuse.

(b) (*willens*) willing, prepared. **zu Zugeständnissen/Verhandlungen** ~ **sein** to be prepared to make concessions/to negotiate; ~ **sein, etw zu tun** to be willing *or* prepared to do sth; **ich bin nicht** ~, **das zu ändern** I'm not willing *or* prepared *or* about (*esp US*) to change that; **sich** ~ **zeigen, etw zu tun** to show oneself willing *or* prepared *or* ready to do sth; **sich** ~ **erklären, etw zu tun** to agree to do sth; **sich zu etw** ~ **finden** to be willing *or* prepared to do sth; **sich zur Ausführung einer Arbeit** ~ **finden, sich** ~ **finden, eine Arbeit auszuführen** to be willing *or* prepared to carry out a piece of work.

bereiten[1]*** **1** *vt* **(a)** (*zu*~) (*dat for*) to prepare; *Arznei* to make up; *Bett* to make (up). **alles ist zum Empfang bereitet** everything is prepared for the reception.

(b) (*verursachen*) to cause; *Überraschung, Empfang, Freude, Kopfschmerzen* to give. **jdm Kummer/Ärger** ~ to cause sb grief/trouble; **er hat mir Schwierigkeiten bereitet** he made difficulties for me; **das bereitet mir Schwierigkeiten** it causes me difficulties; **einer Sache** (*dat*) **ein Ende** ~ to put an end to sth; **es bereitet mir (viel *or* ein großes) Vergnügen** (*form*) it gives me (the greatest) pleasure.

2 *vr* **sich zu etw** ~ (*geh*) to prepare oneself for sth; **sich zum Sterben** ~ to prepare oneself to die *or* for death.

bereiten[2]*** *vt irreg* **(a)** (*rare: einreiten*) to break in. **(b)** *Gebiet* to ride over.

bereit-: ~**halten** *vt sep irreg Fahrkarten etc* to have ready; (*für den Notfall*) to keep ready; *Überraschung* to have in store; **wer weiß, was das Schicksal für uns** ~**hält?** who knows what fate has in store for us?; ~**legen** *vt sep* to lay out ready; ~**liegen** *vi sep irreg* to be ready; ~**machen** *vt sep* to get ready.

bereits *adv* already. ~ **vor drei Wochen/vor 100 Jahren/damals/damals, als ...** even three weeks/100 years ago/then/when ...; **das haben wir** ~ **gestern *or* gestern** ~ **gemacht** we did that yesterday; **er ist** ~ **vor zwei Stunden angekommen** he arrived two hours ago; **ich warte** ~ **seit einer Stunde** I've (already) been waiting for an hour; **der Bus ist** ~ **abgefahren** the bus has already left; **das hat man mir** ~ **gesagt** I've been told that already; ~ **am nächsten Tage** on the very next day.

Bereitschaft *f* **(a)** *no pl* readiness; (*Bereitwilligkeit auch*) willingness, preparedness. **in** ~ **sein** to be ready; (*Polizei, Feuerwehr, Soldaten etc*) to be on stand-by; (*Arzt*) to be on call *or* (*im Krankenhaus*) on duty; **etw in** ~ **haben** to have sth ready *or* in readiness.

(b) *no pl* (~**sdienst**) ~ **haben** (*Arzt etc*) to be on call *or* (*im Krankenhaus*) on duty; (*Apotheke*) to provide emergency *or* after-hours service; (*Polizei etc*) to be on stand-by.

(c) (*Mannschaft*) squad.

Bereitschafts-: ~**arzt** *m* doctor on call; (*im Krankenhaus*) duty doctor; ~**dienst** *m* emergency service; ~**dienst haben** *siehe* **Bereitschaft** (b); ~**polizei** *f* riot police.

Bereit-: **b**~**stehen** *vi sep irreg* to be ready; (*Flugzeug auch, Truppen*) to stand by; (*die* **Truppen stehen b**~ the troops are standing by; **etw b**~**stehen haben** to have sth ready; **Ihr Wagen steht b**~ your car is waiting; **zur Abfahrt b**~**stehen** to be ready to depart; **b**~**stellen** *vt sep* to get ready; *Material, Fahrzeug, Mittel* to provide, to supply; (*Rail*) to make available; *Truppen* to put on stand-by; ~**stellung** *f* preparation; (*von Auto, Material, Mitteln*) provision, supply; (*von Truppen*) putting on stand-by.

Bereitung *f* preparation.

Bereit-: **b**~**willig** *adj* (*entgegenkommend*) willing; (*eifrig*) eager; **b**~**willig** *or* **b**~**willige Auskunft erteilen** to give information willingly; ~**willigkeit** *f siehe adj* willingness; eagerness.

berennen* *vt irreg* (*Mil*) to charge, to assault; (*Sport*) to rush, to storm.

berenten* *vt* (*Admin sl*) **berentet werden** to retire and receive a pension; **sich** ~ **lassen** to retire with a pension.

bereuen* *vt* to regret; *Schuld, Sünden* to repent of. ~, **etw getan zu haben** to regret having done sth; **das wirst du noch** ~! you will be sorry (for that)!

Berg **m -(e)s, -e (a)** hill; (*größer*) mountain. **wenn der** ~ **nicht zum Propheten kommt, muß der Prophet zum** ~ **kommen** (*Prov*) if the mountain won't come to Mahomet, then Mahomet must go to the mountain (*Prov*); **jdm goldene** ~**e versprechen** to promise sb the moon; ~**e versetzen (können)** to (be able to) move mountains; **mit etw hinterm** ~ **halten** (*fig*) to keep sth to oneself, to keep quiet about sth; **mit seinem Alter** to be cagey about sth; **in die** ~**e fahren** to go to the hills etc; **über** ~ **und Tal** up hill and down dale; **über den** ~ **sein** (*inf*) to be out of the wood; **über alle** ~**e sein** (*inf*) to be long gone *or* miles away (*inf*); **die Haare standen ihm zu** ~**e** his hair stood on end; **da stehen**

bergab(wärts) ~e it's enough to make your hair stand on end; *siehe* kreißen, Ochse. (b) (*große Menge*) heap, pile; (*von Sorgen*) mass; (*von Papieren auch*) mountain. (c) (*inf:* ~werk) pit. im ~ **arbeiten** to work down the pit.

Berg- in *cpds* mountain; (*Bergbau-*) mining; b~ab(wärts) *adv* downhill; es geht mit ihm b~ab(wärts) (*fig*) he is going downhill; ~abhang *m* side of a mountain, mountainside; ~absatz *m* ledge; ~absturz *m* drop; ~ahorn *m* sycamore (tree); ~akademie *f* mining college.

Bergamotte *f* -, -n bergamot.

Berg-: ~amt *nt* mining authority; b~an *adv siehe* b~auf; ~arbeiter *m* miner; b~auf(wärts) *adv* uphill; es geht wieder b~auf (*fig*) things are getting better *or* looking up; es geht mit seinem Geschäft/seiner Gesundheit wieder b~auf his business/health is looking up; ~bahn *f* mountain railway; (*Seilbahn auch*) cable railway; ~bau *m* mining; ~bewohner *m* mountain dweller.

Berge-: b~hoch *adj siehe* berghoch; ~lohn *m* (*Naut*) salvage (money).

bergen *pret* barg, *ptp* geborgen *vt* (a) (*retten*) Menschen to save, to rescue; Leichen to recover; Ladung, Schiff, Fahrzeug to salvage; Ernte to get *or* gather (in); (*Naut*) Segel to furl. aus dem Wasser/brennenden Haus tot/lebend geborgen werden to be brought out of the water/burning house dead/alive.
(b) (*geh: enthalten*) to hold; Schätze auch to hide. das birgt viele Gefahren in sich it holds many dangers; diese Möglichkeit birgt die Gefahr/das Risiko in sich, daß ... this possibility involves the danger/risk that ...
(c) (*liter: verbergen*) Gesicht to hide; Verfolgten etc to shelter. sie barg ihren Kopf an seiner Schulter she buried her face on his shoulder; *siehe* geborgen.

berge-: ~versetzend *adj* Glaube colossal; ~weise *adv* by the ton.

Berg-: ~fach *nt* mining; ~fahrt *f* (a) mountaineering *or* climbing expedition; auf ~fahrt gehen to go mountaineering *etc or* on a mountaineering *etc* expedition; (b) (*auf Fluß*) upstream passage; (*von Seilbahn*) uphill *or* upward journey; ~fest *nt* (*inf*) party to celebrate the halfway stage; ~fex *m* (*inf*) mountaineering enthusiast *or* freak (*sl*); ~fried *m* keep; ~führer *m* mountain guide; ~geist *m* mountain troll; ~gipfel *m* mountain top/peak; ~grat *m* mountain ridge; ~hang *m* mountain slope; b~hoch *adj* Wellen, Haufen mountainous; b~hoher Müll mountains of rubbish; die Wellen stiegen b~hoch the waves reached mountainous heights; der Abfall türmte sich b~hoch the rubbish was piled up to mountainous heights; ~hütte *f* mountain hut *or* refuge, bothy (*Scot*).

bergig *adj* hilly; (*hoch*~) mountainous.

Berg-: ~ingenieur *m* mining engineer; ~kamm *m* mountain crest; ~kessel *m* cirque, corrie; ~kette *f* mountain range *or* chain, range *or* chain of mountains; ~knappe *m* (*dated*) collier, miner; b~krank *adj* affected by mountain sickness; ~krankheit *f* mountain sickness; ~kraxler *m* -s, - (*esp Aus, inf*) mountaineer; ~kristall *m* rock crystal; ~kuppe *f* (round) mountain top; ~land *nt* hilly *or* (*Gebirgsland*) mountainous country/region; (*Landschaft*) hilly *etc* scenery; das schottische ~land the Scottish mountains pl.

Bergler(in *f*) *m* -s, - *siehe* **Bergbewohner.**

Bergmann *m, pl* **Bergleute** miner.

bergmännisch *adj* miner's attr.

Bergmanns-: ~gruß *m* miner's greeting; ~sprache *f* mining terminology.

Berg-: ~not *f* in ~not sein/geraten to be in/get into difficulties while climbing; jdn aus ~not retten to rescue sb who was in difficulties while climbing; ~plateau *nt* mountain plateau; ~predigt *f* (*Bibl*) Sermon on the Mount; ~recht *nt* mining law; b~reich *adj* mountainous; ~rennen *nt* (*Sport*) hill climbing; ein ~rennen a hill climb; ~rettungsdienst *m* mountain rescue service; ~riese *m* gigantic mountain; ~rücken *m* mountain ridge *or* crest; ~rutsch *m* landslide (*auch fig*), landslip; ~sattel *m* (mountain) saddle, col; ~schrund *m* bergschrund (*spec*); ~schuh *m* climbing boot; b~seits *adv* on the mountain side; ~spitze *f* mountain peak; ~sport *m* mountaineering, mountain climbing; ~station *f* station at the top end of a cable railway; b~steigen *vi sep irreg aux sein or* haben to go mountain climbing *or* mountaineering, to mountaineer; b~steigen gehen to go mountain climbing *or* mountaineering; (*das*) ~steigen mountaineering, mountain climbing; ~steiger *m* mountaineer, mountain climber; ~steigerei *f* (*inf*) mountaineering, mountain climbing; b~steigerisch 1 *adj* mountaineering, mountain-climbing; 2 *adv* from a mountaineering point of view; ~stock *m* (a) alpenstock; (b) (*Geol*) massif; ~straße *f* mountain road; die ~straße (*Geog*) wine-producing area north of Heidelberg; ~sturz *m siehe* ~rutsch; ~tour *f* trip round the mountains; (~besteigung) (mountain) climb; ~-und-Tal-Bahn *f* big dipper, roller-coaster (*esp US*), switchback; ~-und-Tal-Fahrt *f* ride on the big dipper *etc*; das war die reinste ~-und-Tal-Fahrt (*fig*) it was like being on a switchback *or* big dipper.

Bergung *f, no pl* (a) saving, rescue; recovery; salvage, salvaging; gathering (in). (b) (*liter: von Verfolgten*) sheltering.

Bergungs-: ~arbeit *f* rescue work; (*bei Schiffen etc*) salvage work; ~dampfer *m* salvage vessel; ~kommando *nt* (*esp Mil*), ~mannschaft *f*, ~trupp *m* rescue team.

Berg-: ~volk *nt* (a) mountain race; (b) (*rare:* ~leute) miners pl; ~vorsprung *m* (mountain) ledge; ~wacht *f* mountain rescue service; ~wand *f* mountain face; ~wanderung *f* walk *or* hike in the mountains; b~wärts *adv* uphill; ~welt *f* mountains pl; ~werk *nt* mine; im ~werk arbeiten to work down the mine; ~wesen *nt* mining; ~wiese *f* mountain pasture; ~zinne *f* (*geh*) mountain pinnacle.

Beriberi *f* -, *no pl* (*Med*) beriberi.

Bericht *m* -(e)s, -e report (*über* +acc about, on, *von* on); (*Erzählung auch*) account; (*Zeitungs*~ auch) story; (*Sch: Aufsatzform*) commentary. der ~ eines Augenzeugen an eyewitness account; ~e zum Tagesgeschehen news reports; eigener ~ from our correspondent; (*über etw acc*) ~ erstatten to report *or* give a report (on sth); jdm über etw (*acc*) ~ erstatten to give sb a report (on sth).

berichten* *vti* to report; (*erzählen*) to tell. jdm über etw (*acc*) ~ to report to sb about sth; to tell sb about sth; mir ist (darüber) berichtet worden, daß ... I have received reports *or* been told that ...; uns wird soeben berichtet, daß ... (*Rad, TV*) news is just coming in that ...; wie unser Korrespondent berichtet according to our correspondent; wie soeben berichtet wird, sind die Verhandlungen abgebrochen worden we are just receiving reports that negotiations have been broken off; gibt es Neues zu ~? has anything new happened?; sie berichtete, daß ... she said *or* reported that ...; nun berichte mal von dir! now tell me/us *etc* about yourself; sie hat bestimmt vieles zu ~ she is sure to have a lot to tell us; er berichtete von der Reise he told us *etc* about his journey.

Bericht-: ~erstatter *m* reporter; (*Korrespondent*) correspondent; ~erstatter ist ... (*bei Jahresversammlung etc*) the report will be given by ...; ~erstattung *f* reporting; eine objektive ~erstattung objective reporting; ~erstattung durch Presse/Rundfunk press/radio reporting; die ~erstattung über diese Vorgänge in der Presse press coverage of these events; zur ~erstattung zurückgerufen werden to be called back to report *or* make a report.

berichtigen* *vt* to correct; Fehler auch, (*Jur*) to rectify; Text, Aussage auch to amend.

Berichtigung *f siehe* vt correction; rectification; amendment.

Berichts-: ~heft *nt* apprentice's record book; ~jahr *nt* (*Comm*) year under review *or* report.

beriechen* *vt irreg* to sniff at, to smell. sich (gegenseitig) ~ (*fig inf*) to size each other up.

berieseln* *vt* (a) to spray with water *etc*; (*durch Sprinkleranlage*) to sprinkle. (b) (*fig inf*) von etw berieselt werden (*fig*) to be exposed to a constant stream of sth; sich von Musik ~ lassen to have a (constant stream of) music going on in the background; sich von Propaganda *etc* ~ lassen to expose oneself to a constant stream of propaganda *etc*.

Berieselung *f* watering. die ständige ~ der Kunden mit Musik/Werbung exposing the customers to a constant stream of music/advertisements; die ~ mit *or* durch etw (*fig*) the constant stream of sth.

Berieselungs|anlage *f* sprinkler (system).

beringen* *vt* to put a ring on; Vogel auch to ring. mit Diamanten beringte Finger fingers ringed with diamonds.

Beringung *f siehe* vt putting a ring on; ringing; (*Ring*) ring.

beritten *adj* mounted, on horseback. ~e Polizei mounted police.

Berittene(r) *mf decl as adj* rider.

Berlin *nt* -s Berlin.

Berliner[1] *m* -s, - (dial: auch ~ **Pfannkuchen**) doughnut.

Berliner[2] *adj attr* Berlin. ~ Weiße (mit Schuß) light, fizzy beer (with fruit juice added).

Berliner(in *f*) *m* -s, - Berliner.

berlinerisch *adj* (*inf*) Dialekt Berlin attr. er spricht B~ he speaks the Berlin dialect.

berlinern* *vi* (*inf*) to speak in the Berlin dialect.

berlinisch *adj* Berlin attr.

Bermuda|inseln, Bermudas pl Bermuda sing, no def art. auf den ~ in Bermuda *or* the Bermudas.

Bermudas, Bermudashorts pl Bermuda shorts pl, Bermudas pl.

Bern *nt* -s Bern(e).

Berner *adj attr* Berne(se).

Berner(in *f*) *m* -s, - Bernese.

Bernhardiner *m* -s, - Saint Bernard (dog).

Bernstein *m, no pl* amber.

bernstein-: ~farben, ~gelb *adj* amber(-coloured).

berockt *adj* (*hum*) (dressed) in a skirt.

Berserker *m* -s, - (*Hist*) berserker. wie ein ~ arbeiten/kämpfen to work/fight like mad *or* fury; wie ein ~ toben to go berserk; auf jdn einschlagen wie ein ~ to go berserk and attack sb.

bersten *pret* barst, *ptp* geborsten *vi aux sein* (*geh*) to crack; (*auf*~, zerbrechen) to break; (*zerplatzen*) to burst; (*fig: vor Wut etc*) to burst (*vor* with). als wollte ihm das Herz in die Seele ~ as if his heart would burst; die Erde barst the earth broke asunder (*liter*); vor Ungeduld/Neugier/Zorn *etc* ~ to be bursting with impatience/curiosity/anger *etc*; sie barst vor Lachen she was helpless with laughter; zum B~ voll (auch inf) full to bursting.

berüchtigt *adj* notorious, infamous.

berücken* *vt* (*geh*) to charm, to enchant.

berückend *adj* charming, enchanting. das ist nicht gerade ~ (iro inf) it's not exactly stunning.

berücksichtigen* *vt* (*beachten, bedenken*) to take into account *or* consideration; Mangel, Alter, geringe Erfahrung, körperliches Leiden to make allowances for; (in Betracht ziehen) Antrag, Bewerbung, Bewerber to consider. das ist zu ~ that must be taken into account *or* consideration; meine Vorschläge wurden nicht berücksichtigt my suggestions were disregarded.

Berücksichtigung *f* consideration. in *or* unter ~ der Umstände/der Tatsache, daß ... in view of the circumstances/the fact that ...; eine ~ Ihres Antrags ist zur Zeit nicht möglich it is impossible for us to consider your application at present.

Beruf m -(e)s, -e **(a)** (*Tätigkeit*) occupation; (*akademischer auch*) profession; (*handwerklicher*) trade; (*Stellung*) job. **was sind Sie von ~?** what is your occupation *etc*?, what do you do for a living?; **von ~ Arzt/Bäcker/Hausfrau sein** to be a doctor by profession/baker by trade/housewife by occupation; **ihr stehen viele ~e offen** many careers are open to her; **einen ~ ausüben** to have an occupation/follow a profession/carry on a trade; **seinen ~ verfehlt haben** to have missed one's vocation; **im ~ stehen** to be working; **von ~s wegen** on account of one's job. **(b)** (*dated: Berufung*) calling, vocation.

berufen* irreg **1** vt **(a)** (*ernennen, einsetzen*) to appoint. **jdn auf einen Lehrstuhl/zu einem Amt ~** to appoint sb to a chair/an office.
(b) (*old: kommen lassen*) **jdn zu sich/an einen Ort ~** to call or summon sb to one/a place; **Gott hat ihn zu sich ~** he has been called to his Maker.
(c) (*inf: beschwören*) **ich will/wir wollen etc es nicht ~** touch wood (*inf*); **ich will es nicht ~, aber ...** I don't want to tempt fate, but ...
(d) (*dial: ermahnen*) to tell off, to reproach.
2 vr **sich auf jdn/etw ~** to refer to sb/sth.
3 vi (*Aus Jur: Berufung einlegen*) to appeal.
4 adj **(a)** (*befähigt*) *Kritiker* competent, capable. **von ~er Seite, aus ~em Mund** from an authoritative source; **zu etw ~ sein, ~ sein, etw zu tun** to be competent to do sth.
(b) (*ausersehen*) **zu etw ~ sein** to have a vocation for sth; (*esp Rel*) to be called to sth; **viele sind ~** (*Bibl*) many are called; **sich zu etw ~ fühlen** to feel one has a mission to be/do sth.

beruflich adj (*esp auf akademische Berufe bezüglich*) professional; *Weiterbildung auch* job or career orientated. **sein ~er Werdegang** his career; **~e Aussichten** job prospects; **verschiedene ~e Tätigkeiten** different jobs; **im ~en Leben** in my *etc* working life, in my *etc* career; **meine ~en Probleme** my problems at work or in my job; **was das B~e betrifft, bin ich zufrieden** as far as my job is concerned I am satisfied; **~ ist sie sehr erfolgreich** she is very successful in her career; **sich ~ weiterbilden** to undertake further job or career orientated or professional training; **er ist ~ viel unterwegs** he is away a lot on business.

Berufs-: **~ausbildung** f training (*for an occupation*); (*für Handwerk*) vocational training; **~aussichten** pl job prospects pl; **~beamtentum** nt civil service with tenure; **~beamte(r)** m civil servant with tenure; **b~bedingt** adj occupational, caused by one's occupation; **~berater** m careers adviser; **~beratung** f careers guidance; **~bezeichnung** f job title; **b~bezogen** adj relevant to one's job; *Unterricht* vocationally orientated; **~bild** nt job outline; **~boxen** nt professional boxing; **b~erfahren** adj (*professionally*) experienced; **~erfahrung** f (*professional*) experience; **~ethos** nt professional ethics pl; **~fachschule** f training college (*attended full-time*); **~feuerwehr** f fire service; **~freiheit** f freedom to choose and carry out one's career; **b~fremd** adj unconnected with one's occupation; **eine b~fremde Tätigkeit** a job outside one's profession/trade; **b~fremd arbeiten** to work outside one's profession/trade; **~fußball** m professional football; **~geheimnis** nt professional secret; (*Schweigepflicht*) professional secrecy, confidentiality; **das ~geheimnis wahren** to observe professional secrecy or confidentiality; **~genossenschaft** f professional/trade association; **~gruppe** f occupational group; **~heer** nt professional or regular army; **~kleidung** f working clothes pl; **~krankheit** f occupational disease; **~leben** nt working or professional life; **im ~leben stehen** to be working or in employment; **b~los** adj without a profession/trade; **b~mäßig** adj professional; **etw b~mäßig betreiben** to do sth professionally or on a professional basis; **~offizier** m regular officer; **~pflicht** f professional duty; **~revolutionär** m professional revolutionary; **~risiko** nt occupational hazard or risk; **~schule** f vocational school, = technical college (*Brit*); **~schüler** m student at vocational school *etc*; **~soldat** m regular or professional soldier; **~spieler** m professional player; **~sport** m professional sport; **~sportler** m professional sportsman; **~sprache** f professional jargon; **~stand** m profession, professional group; (*Gewerbe*) trade; **b~tätig** adj working; **b~tätig sein** to be working, to work; **halbtags b~tätig sein** to work part-time; **ich bin auch b~tätig** I go out to work too; **nicht mehr b~tätig sein** to have left work; **~tätige(r)** mf decl as adj working person; **b~unfähig** adj unable to work; **~unfähigkeit** f inability to work; **~verband** m professional/trade organization or association; **~verbot** nt exclusion from a civil service profession by government ruling; **jdm ~verbot erteilen** to ban sb from a profession; **unter das ~verbot fallen** to be banned from a profession; **~verbrecher** m professional criminal; **~verkehr** m rush-hour traffic; **~wahl** f choice of occupation/profession/trade; **~wechsel** m change of occupation; **~ziel** nt profession one is aiming for; **~zweig** m siehe **Beruf** branch of an occupation *etc*; (~*gruppe*) occupation/profession/trade.

Berufung f **(a)** (*Jur*) appeal. **in die ~ gehen/~ einlegen** to appeal (*bei* to).
(b) (*in ein Amt etc*) appointment (*auf or an* +acc to).
(c) (*innerer Auftrag*) vocation; (*Rel auch*) mission, calling. **die ~ zu etw in sich** (*dat*) **fühlen** to feel one has a vocation *etc* to be sth.
(d) (*old: Einberufung*) summoning.
(e) (*form*) **die ~ auf jdn/etw** reference to sb/sth; **unter ~ auf etw** (*acc*) with reference to sth.

Berufungs-: **~ausschuß** m appeal tribunal; **~frist** f period in which an appeal must be submitted; **~gericht** nt appeal court, court of appeal; **~instanz** f court of appeal; **~klage** f appeal; **~kläger** m appellant.

beruhen* vi to be based or founded (*auf* +dat on). **das beruht**

auf Gegenseitigkeit (*inf*) the feeling is mutual; **etw auf sich ~ lassen** to let sth rest.

beruhigen* **1** vt to calm (down); *Baby* to quieten; (*trösten*) to soothe, to comfort; (*versichern*) to reassure; *Magen* to settle; *Nerven auch* to soothe; *Gewissen* to soothe, to salve; *Schmerzen* to ease, to relieve. **na, dann bin ich ja beruhigt** well I must say I'm quite relieved. **na, dann kann ich ja beruhigt schlafen/nach Hause gehen** then I can go to sleep/go home with my mind at rest; **~d** (*körperlich, beschwichtigend*) soothing; (*tröstlich*) reassuring; **es ist ~d zu wissen, daß ...** it is reassuring to know that ...
2 vr to calm down; (*Krise auch*) to ease off, to lessen; (*Gewissen*) to be eased; (*Andrang, Verkehr, Kämpfe*) to subside, to lessen; (*Börse, Preise, Magen*) to settle down; (*Krämpfe, Schmerzen*) to lessen, to ease; (*Meer*) to become calm; (*Sturm*) to die down, to abate. **sie konnte sich gar nicht darüber ~, daß ...** she could not get over the fact that ...; **beruhige dich doch!** calm down!

Beruhigung f, no pl **(a)** *siehe* vt calming (down); quietening; soothing, comforting; reassuring; settling; placating, appeasing; soothing; soothing, salving; easing, relieving. **zu Ihrer ~ kann ich sagen ...** you'll be reassured to know that ...
(b) *siehe* vr calming down; easing off, lessening; easing; subsiding, lessening; settling down; settling; lessening, easing; calming; abatement. **ein Gefühl der ~** a reassuring feeling.

Beruhigungs-: **~mittel** nt sedative, tranquillizer; **~pille, ~tablette** f sedative (pill), tranquillizer; **~spritze** f sedative (injection).

berühmt adj famous. **wegen or für etw ~ sein** to be famous or renowned for sth; **das war nicht ~** (*inf*) it was nothing to write home about (*inf*).

berühmt-berüchtigt adj infamous, notorious.

Berühmtheit f **(a)** fame. **~ erlangen** to become famous; **zu trauriger ~ gelangen** to become notorious or infamous. **(b)** (*Mensch*) celebrity.

berühren* **1** vt **(a)** (*anfassen, streifen, Math*) to touch; (*grenzen an*) to border on; (*auf Reise streifen*) *Länder* to touch; *Hafen* to stop at, to put in or call at; (*erwähnen*) *Thema, Punkt* to touch on. **B~ verboten** do not touch; **das B~ der Figuren mit den Pfoten ist verboten** (*inf*) pretty things should be seen and not touched (*hum*).
(b) (*seelisch bewegen*) to move; (*auf jdn wirken*) to affect; (*betreffen*) to affect, to concern. **das berührt mich gar nicht!** that's nothing to do with me; **von etw peinlich/schmerzlich berührt sein** to be embarrassed/pained by sth; **es berührt mich angenehm/seltsam, daß ...** I am pleased/surprised that ...
2 vr to touch; (*Menschen auch*) to touch each other; (*Drähte etc auch*) to be in/come into contact; (*Ideen, Vorstellungen, Interessen*) to coincide.

Berührung f touch; (*zwischen Drähten etc, menschlicher Kontakt*) contact; (*Erwähnung*) mention. **mit jdm/etw in ~ kommen** to come into contact with sb/sth; **jdn mit jdm/etw in ~ bringen** to bring sb into contact with sb/sth; **körperliche ~** physical or bodily contact; **die ~ der Instrumente ist zu vermeiden** avoid touching the instruments; **bei ~ Lebensgefahr!** danger! do not touch!; **Ansteckung durch ~** contagion, infection by contact.

Berührungs-: **~gift** nt contact poison; **~punkt** m point of contact; (*Math auch*) tangential point; **unsere Interessen haben keinerlei ~punkte** there are no points of contact between our interests.

berußen* vt to cover with soot, to soot. **berußte Mauern** soot-covered or sooty walls.

bes. abbr of **besonders.**

besabbern* (*inf*) **1** vt to slobber on or all over. **2** vr to slobber all over oneself.

besäen* vt (*lit*) to sow; *siehe* **besät.**

besagen* vt to say; (*bedeuten*) to mean, to imply. **das besagt nichts/viel** that does not mean anything/that means a lot; **das besagt nicht, daß ...** that does not mean (to say) that ...

besagt adj attr (*form*) said (*form*), aforementioned (*form*).

besaiten* vt to string. **etw neu ~** to restring sth; *siehe* **zart.**

besamen* vt to fertilize; (*künstlich*) to inseminate; (*Bot*) to pollinate.

besammeln* vr (*esp Sw*) to assemble, to gather.

Besammlung f (*esp Sw*) assembly.

Besamung f siehe vt fertilization; insemination; pollination.

Besan m -s, -e (*Naut*) mizzen (sail/mast).

besänftigen* **1** vt to calm down, to soothe; *Menge auch* to pacify; *jds Zorn, Erregung, Gemüt* to soothe. **er war nicht zu ~** it was impossible to calm him down. **2** vr (*Mensch*) to calm down; (*Meer, Elemente*) to become calm.

Besänftigung f siehe vt calming (down), soothing; pacifying; soothing.

Besanmast m (*Naut*) mizzen mast.

besaß pret of **besitzen.**

besät **1** ptp of **besäen. 2** adj covered; (*mit Blättern etc*) strewn; (*iro: mit Orden*) studded. **der mit Sternen ~e Himmel** the star-spangled sky.

Besatz m -es, ⁀e **(a)** edging, trimming; (*an Tischtuch auch*) border. **einen ~ aus etw haben** to be trimmed with sth. **(b)** (*Bestand*) stock.

Besatzer m -s, - (*pej inf*) occupying forces pl.

Besatzung f **(a)** (*Mannschaft*) crew; (*Verteidigungstruppe*) garrison. **(b)** (*~armee*) occupying army or forces pl.

Besatzungs-: **~armee** f occupying army, army of occupation; **~kind** nt illegitimate child of member of the occupying forces; **~kosten** pl costs pl of occupying a country *etc*; **~macht** f occupying power; **~statut** nt statute of occupation; **~streitkräfte, ~truppen** pl occupying forces pl; **~zone** f occupation zone; **die amerikanische** ∼**zone** the American (-occupied) zone.

besaufen* vr irreg (sl) to get plastered (sl) or pissed (Brit sl).

Besäufnis nt (inf) booze-up (inf).

besäuseln* vr (inf) to get tipsy or merry. **besäuselt** tipsy, merry.

beschädigen* vt to damage. **beschädigt** damaged; Schiff auch disabled.

Beschädigte(r) mf decl as adj disabled person.

Beschädigung f damage (von to). **das Auto hat mehrere** ∼**en** the car is damaged in several places.

beschaffen* **1** vt to procure (form), to get (hold of), to obtain. **jdm etw** ∼ to get (hold of) or obtain sth for sb; **jdm/sich eine Stelle** ∼ to get sb/oneself a job; **das ist schwer zu** ∼ that is difficult to get (hold of).
  2 adj (form) **wie ist es mit seiner Gesundheit** ∼? what about his health?; **mit jdm/damit ist es gut/schlecht** ∼ sb/it is in a good/bad way; **so** ∼ **sein wie** ... to be the same as ...; **das ist so** ∼, **daß** ... that is such that ...; **sie ist nun einmal so** ∼ she's just made that way, that is the way she is; **das ist anders** ∼ **als** ... that is different from ...; **die Sache ist folgendermaßen** ∼ the situation is as follows.

Beschaffenheit f, no pl composition; (von Mensch) (körperlich) constitution; (seelisch) nature, qualities pl. **die glatte** ∼ **des Steins** the smoothness of the stone; **von sensibler seelischer** ∼ **sein** to be of a very sensitive nature or disposition; **er hat für diesen Beruf nicht die seelische/körperliche** ∼ he doesn't have the right sort of psychological make-up/physique for this job; **je nach** ∼ **der Lage** according to the situation.

Beschaffung f, no pl procuring, obtaining.

beschäftigen* **1** vr **sich mit etw** ∼ to occupy oneself with sth; (sich befassen, abhandeln) to deal with sth; **sich mit dem Tod** ∼ to think about death; **sich mit Literatur** ∼ to devote oneself to (the study of) literature; **sich mit der Frage** ∼, **ob** ... to consider the question of whether ...; **sich mit jdm** ∼ to devote one's attention to sb; **sie beschäftigt sich viel mit den Kindern** she devotes a lot of her time to the children; **sie beschäftigt sich gerade mit den Kindern** she is busy with the children just now.
  2 vt (a) (innerlich ∼) **jdn** ∼ to be on sb's mind; **die Frage beschäftigt sie sehr** she is very preoccupied with that question, that question has been on her mind a lot.
  (b) (anstellen) to employ.
  (c) (eine Tätigkeit geben) to occupy, to keep occupied. **jdn mit etw** ∼ to give sb sth to do.

beschäftigt adj (a) busy. **mit dem Nähen/jdm** ∼ **sein** to be busy sewing/with sb; **mit sich selbst/seinen Problemen** ∼ **sein** to be preoccupied with oneself/one's problems. **(b)** (angestellt) employed (bei by).

Beschäftigte(r) mf decl as adj employee.

Beschäftigung f (a) (berufliche Arbeit) work no indef art, job; (Anstellung, Angestelltsein) employment. **eine** ∼ **suchen** to be looking for work or a job, to seek employment (form); **einer** ∼ **nachgehen** (form) to be employed; **ohne** ∼ **sein** to be unemployed or out of work.
  (b) (Tätigkeit) activity, occupation. **jdm eine** ∼ **geben** to give sb something to do; ∼ **haben** to have something to do; **da ist für** ∼ **gesorgt** there are plenty of things to do.
  (c) (geistige ∼) preoccupation; (mit Frage) consideration; (mit Thema) treatment; (mit Literatur) study (mit of); (mit sich, seinen Problemen) preoccupation.
  (d) siehe vt (c) (von Kindern, Patienten etc) occupying, keeping occupied. **die** ∼ **der Patienten** keeping the patients occupied.

Beschäftigungs-: b∼**los** adj unoccupied; (arbeitslos) unemployed, out-of-work; ∼**therapeut** m occupational therapist; ∼**therapie** f occupational therapy.

beschälen* vt (form) to cover, to serve.

Beschäler m -s, - (form) stallion, stud.

Beschälung f (form) covering, service.

beschämen* vt to shame; (jds Großzügigkeit) to embarrass. **es beschämt mich, zu sagen** ... I feel ashamed to have to say ...

beschämend adj (a) (schändlich) shameful. **es war** ∼ **für seine ganze Familie** it brought shame on or to his whole family.
  (b) (vorbildlich) shaming; Großzügigkeit auch embarrassing.
  (c) (demütigend) humiliating, shaming.

beschämt adj ashamed, abashed. **ich fühle mich durch deine Großzügigkeit** ∼ I am embarrassed by your generosity.

Beschämung f shame; (Verlegenheit) embarrassment. **zu meiner** ∼ to my shame; **in tiefer** ∼ **ging er nach Hause** he went home feeling very ashamed; **seine Güte war eine** ∼ **für uns alle** his kindness put us all to shame.

beschatten* vt (a) (geh: Schatten geben) to shade; (fig: trüben) to overshadow. **(b)** (überwachen) to shadow, to tail. **jdn** ∼ **lassen** to have sb shadowed or tailed. **(c)** (Sport) to mark closely.

Beschatter m -s, - (a) (Polizist etc) shadow, tail. **(b)** (Sport) marker.

Beschattung f siehe vt (a) shading; overshadowing. **(b)** shadowing, tailing. **(c)** marking.

Beschau f -, no pl inspection.

beschauen* vt (a) Fleisch etc to inspect. **(b)** (dial: betrachten) to look at. **sich** (dat) **etw** ∼ to look at sth.

Beschauer m -s, - (a) inspector. **(b)** (Betrachter) spectator; (von Bild) viewer.

beschaulich adj (a) (geruhsam) Leben, Abend quiet, tranquil; Charakter, Mensch pensive, contemplative. ∼ **dasitzen** to sit contemplating. **(b)** (Rel) contemplative.

Beschaulichkeit f siehe adj (a) quietness, tranquillity; pensiveness, contemplation. **ein Leben in** ∼ a life of contemplation. **(b)** (Rel) contemplativeness.

Beschauung f inspection.

Bescheid m -(e)s, -e (a) (Auskunft) information; (Nachricht) notification; (Entscheidung auf Antrag etc) decision. **wir erwarten Ihren** ∼ we look forward to hearing from you; **bis warte noch auf** ∼ I am still waiting to hear, I still have not heard anything; **jdm** (über etw acc or von etw) ∼ **sagen/geben** to let sb know (about sth), to tell sb (about sth); **jdm ordentlich** ∼ **sagen** or **gründlich** ∼ **stoßen** (inf) to tell sb where to get off (inf); **jdm** (beim Trinken) ∼ **tun** (obs) to drink to sb; ∼ **hinterlassen** to leave word.
  (b) (über etw acc or in etw dat) ∼ **wissen** to know (about sth); **weißt du** ∼ **wegen Samstagabend?** do you know about Saturday evening?; **weißt du** ∼ **mit den Maschinen?** do you know how to deal with these machines?, do you know about these machines?; **ich weiß hier nicht** ∼ I don't know about things around here; **er weiß gut** ∼ he is well informed; **auf dem Gebiet weiß ich nicht** ∼ I don't know much about that sort of thing; **weißt du schon** ∼? do you know?, have you heard?; **sag ihr, Egon habe angerufen, dann weiß sie schon** ∼ if you tell her Egon phoned she'll understand.

bescheiden[1] pret **beschied**, ptp **beschieden 1** vt (a) (form: bestellen) to summon (form) (zu jdm to sb).
  (b) (form: entscheiden) Gesuch, Antrag to decide upon. **etw abschlägig** ∼ to turn sth down.
  (c) (form: informieren) **jdn** ∼**to** notify or inform sb of one's decision; **jdn dahingehend** ∼, **daß** ... to inform or notify sb that ...
  (d) (geh: zuteil werden lassen) **jdm etw** ∼ to grant sb sth; **es war ihr nicht beschieden, den Erfolg zu genießen** she was not granted the opportunity to or it was not given to her to (liter) enjoy the success.
  2 vr (geh) to be content. **sich mit wenigem** ∼ to be content or to content oneself with little.

bescheiden[2] adj (a) modest; Mensch, Verhalten auch unassuming. ∼ or **in** ∼**en Verhältnissen leben** to live modestly; **darf ich mal** ∼ **fragen, ob** ... may I venture to ask whether ...; **eine** ∼ **Frage** one small question; **aus** ∼**en Anfängen** from humble beginnings.
  (b) (euph: beschissen) awful, terrible; (inf: mäßig) mediocre.

Bescheidenheit f siehe adj (a) modesty; unassumingness. **nur keine falsche** ∼ no false modesty now; ∼ **ist eine Zier, doch weiter kommt man ohne ihr** (hum inf) modesty is fine but it doesn't get you very far.

bescheinen* vt irreg to shine on; (Feuer) to light up. **vom Mond/von der Sonne beschienen** moonlit/sunlit.

bescheinigen* vt to certify; Gesundheit, Tauglichkeit to confirm in writing; Empfang to confirm, to acknowledge; (durch Quittung) to sign or give a receipt for; (inf: mündlich bestätigen) to confirm. **sich** (dat) **die Arbeit/Überstunden** ∼ **lassen** to get written confirmation of having done the work/overtime; **können Sie mir** ∼, **daß** ... can you confirm in writing that ... or give me written confirmation that ...; **hiermit wird bescheinigt, daß** ... this is to certify that ...; **jdm äußerste Kompetenz** ∼ to confirm sb's extreme competence; **das kann ich ihm jederzeit** ∼ I can confirm that any time; **deine Dummheit kann ich dir jederzeit** ∼ you really are silly.

Bescheinigung f siehe vt (das Bescheinigen) certification; confirmation; (Schriftstück) certificate; written confirmation; (Quittung) receipt.

bescheißen* vt irreg **1** vt (sl) jdn to swindle, to cheat, to do (um out of). **2** vi (sl) to cheat. **3** vr (vulg) to shit oneself (vulg).

beschenken* vt jdn to give presents/a present to. **jdn mit etw** ∼ to give sb sth (as a present); **sich** (gegenseitig) ∼ to give each other presents; **jdn reich** ∼ to shower sb with presents; **du solltest sie nicht immer so** ∼ you shouldn't always give them so many presents; **damit bin ich reich beschenkt** that's very generous.

bescheren* vti (a) jdn ∼ to give sb a Christmas present/presents; **jdn mit etw** ∼ to give sb sth for Christmas; **um 5 Uhr wird beschert** the Christmas presents will be given out at 5 o'clock; **jdm etw** ∼ to give sb sth; **jdm eine Überraschung** ∼ to give sb a nice surprise.
  (b) (zuteil werden lassen) **jdm etw** ∼ to grant sb sth, to bestow sth upon sb; (Gott) to bless sb with sth.

Bescherung f (a) (Feier) giving out of Christmas presents. **(b)** (iro inf) **das ist ja eine schöne** ∼! this is a nice mess; **die** (ganze) ∼ the (whole) mess; **da haben wir die** ∼! I told you so, what did I tell you!

bescheuert adj (inf) stupid; Mensch auch dumb (inf).

beschichten* vt (Tech) to coat, to cover. **mit Kunststoff beschichtet** laminated; **PVC-beschichtet** PVC coated.

beschicken* vt (a) (Vertreter schicken auf) to send representatives to; (Exemplare schicken auf) to send exhibits to. **eine Ausstellung mit jdm/etw** ∼ to send sb/sth to an exhibition; **die Firma hat die Messe beschickt** the firm exhibited at the fair; **der Kongreß wurde von den meisten Ländern beschickt** most countries sent representatives to the congress.
  (b) (Tech) Hochofen to charge; Kessel to fire.

beschickert adj (inf) tipsy.

Beschickung f (Tech) (von Hochofen) charging; (von Kessel) firing; (Ladung) load.

beschied pret of **bescheiden**[1].

beschieden ptp of **bescheiden**[1].

beschießen* vt irreg (a) to shoot at, to fire on or at; (mit Geschützen) to bombard; (aus Flugzeug auch) to strafe; (fig: mit Fragen, Vorwürfen, Argumenten) to bombard. **sich gegenseitig** ∼ (fig) to have a battle of words. **(b)** (Phys) Atomkern to bombard.

Beschießung f siehe vt (a) shooting (gen at), firing (gen on, at); bombardment (gen of); strafing (gen of). **(b)** bombarding.

beschildern* vt to put a sign or notice/signs or notices on; (mit Schildchen) Ausstellungsgegenstand, Käfig etc to label; (mit Verkehrsschildern) to signpost.

Beschilderung f siehe vt putting a sign etc (von on); labelling; signposting; (Schilder) signs pl; labels pl; signposts pl.

beschimpfen* vt jdn to swear at, to abuse; Ruf, guten Namen to slander.

Beschimpfung f (a) (das Beschimpfen) abusing, swearing (gen at); (Jur) slander (gen on). (b) (Schimpfwort) insult.

beschirmen* vt (a) (geh: beschützen) to shield, to protect. (b) (geh: sich breiten über) to shade. (c) (mit Schirm versehen) Lampe to put a shade on. **ich werde dich ~** (hum inf) I'll let you share my umbrella; **ich bin beschirmt** (hum inf) I have my own umbrella.

Beschirmung f protection.

Beschiß m -sses, -sse (sl) swindle, rip off (sl). **das ist ~** it's a swindle or swizz (inf).

beschissen adj (sl) bloody awful (Brit inf), lousy (inf), shit-awful (sl).

beschlafen* vt irreg (inf) (a) Sache to sleep on. (b) Mädchen to sleep with.

Beschlag m -(e)s, =e (a) (an Koffer, Truhe, Buch) (ornamental) fitting; (an Tür, Fenster, Möbelstück, Sattel) (ornamental) mounting; (Scharnier/Schließe) ornamental hinge/clasp; (von Pferd) shoes pl. **ein schlechter ~** a bad set of shoes, bad shoes.
(b) (das Beschlagen: von Pferd) shoeing.
(c) (auf Metall) tarnish; (auf Speisen) layer of mould; (auf Glas, Spiegel etc) condensation. **der Löffel hat einen ~** the spoon is tarnished.
(d) jdn/etw mit ~ belegen, jdn/etw in ~ nehmen to monopolize sb/sth; **mit ~ belegt sein** to be being used; (Mensch) to be occupied.

Beschläg nt -s, -e (Sw) siehe **Beschlag**.

beschlagen* irreg 1 vt (a) (mit Beschlägen versehen) Truhen, Möbel, Türen to provide or fit with (metal) furnishings; Huftiere to shoe; Schuhe to put metal tips on; (mit Ziernägeln) to stud. **ein Faß mit Reifen ~** to put hoops on a barrel, to hoop a barrel; **ist das Pferd ~?** is the horse shod?
(b) (Hunt) Wild to cover, to serve.
(c) (anlaufen lassen) (Dampf) to steam up; (Rost) to cover; (Patina) to tarnish; (Pilz) to cover, to grow over or on.
(d) (Sw: betreffen) to concern.
2 vir (vi: aux sein) (Brille, Glas, Fenster) to steam up, to get steamed up, to mist up or over; (Wand) to get covered in condensation, to get steamed up; (Silber etc) to tarnish; (einen Pilzbelag bekommen) to go mouldy. **eine ~e Wurst** a mouldy or mildewy sausage; **würden Sie bitte die ~en Scheiben abwischen?** the windows are getting steamed up etc, could you give them a wipe?
3 adj (erfahren) well-versed. **in etw** (dat) (gut) ~ **sein** to be (well-)versed in sth; **auf einem Gebiet ~ sein** to be well-versed in a subject.

Beschlagenheit f, no pl sound knowledge or grasp (auf +dat of).

Beschlagnahme f -, -n confiscation, seizure, impounding.

beschlagnahmen* vt insep (a) to confiscate, to seize, to impound. (b) (inf: in Anspruch nehmen) (Mensch) to monopolize, to hog (inf); (Arbeit) Zeit to take up.

Beschlagnahmung f siehe **Beschlagnahme**.

beschleichen* vt irreg to creep or steal up to or up on; Wild to stalk; (fig) to creep over.

beschleunigen* 1 vt (a) to accelerate, to speed up; Arbeit, Lieferung etc auch to expedite; Tempo auch to increase; Atem, Puls auch to quicken; Verfall, wirtschaftlichen Zusammenbruch etc to precipitate, to hasten, to accelerate. **die Angst beschleunigte ihre Schritte** fear quickened or hastened her steps.
2 vr siehe vt to accelerate, to speed up; to increase; to quicken; to be precipitated or hastened.
3 vi (Fahrzeug, Fahrer) to accelerate.

Beschleuniger m -s, - (Phys, Chem) accelerator.

beschleunigt adj faster. **~es Verfahren** (Jur) summary proceedings pl.

Beschleunigung f (a) acceleration (auch Aut, Phys), speeding up; (von Tempo auch) increase; (von Atem, Puls auch) quickening; (von Verfall etc) precipitation, hastening. **wir tun alles, was zur ~ der Arbeit führen könnte** we are doing everything we can towards speeding up or in order to speed up the work. (b) (Eile) speed.

Beschleunigungs-: **~anlage**, **~maschine** f accelerator; **~vermögen** nt accelerating power, acceleration; **~wert** m (Aut) acceleration ratio.

beschließen* irreg 1 vt (a) (Entschluß fassen) to decide on; Gesetz to pass; Statuten to establish. **~, etw zu tun** to decide or resolve to do sth. (b) (beenden) to end; Brief, Abend, Programm auch to conclude, to wind up. 2 vi **über etw** (acc) ~ to decide on sth.

beschlossen 1 ptp of **beschließen**. 2 adj (a) (entschieden) decided, agreed. (b) **in etw** (dat) ~ **liegen** or **sein** to be contained in sth.

Beschluß m -sses, =sse (a) (Entschluß) decision, resolution. **einen ~ fassen** to pass a resolution; **auf ~ des Gerichts** by order of the court; **wie lautete der ~ des Gerichts?** what was the court's decision? (b) (obs: Schluß) conclusion, end.

Beschluß-: **b~fähig** adj **b~fähig sein** to have a quorum; **b~fähige Anzahl** quorum; **~fähigkeit** f, no pl quorum; **wenn die ~fähigkeit des Gremiums nicht gewährleistet ist** if the committee does not have a quorum; **~fassung** f (passing of a) resolution; **~recht** nt competence (to pass or make a resolution); **b~reif** adj Gesetz ready to be voted on, ready for

the vote; **b~unfähig** adj **b~unfähig sein** not to have a quorum.

beschmeißen* vt irreg (inf) to pelt, to bombard; (mit Vorwürfen etc) to bombard. **jdn mit Dreck ~** (fig) to sling mud at sb.

beschmieren* 1 vt (a) (bestreichen) Brot to spread; Körperteil, Maschinenteil to smear, to cover. **Brot mit Butter/Käse ~** to butter bread/to spread cheese on the bread.
(b) Kleidung to (be)smear; Wand auch to bedaub; Tafel to scribble or scrawl all over. **ein Buch mit Bemerkungen ~** to scrawl comments all over a book.
2 vr to get (all) dirty, to get oneself in a mess. **sich von oben bis unten mit etw ~** to get sth all over oneself, to cover oneself with sth.

beschmunzeln* vt to smile (quietly) at. **der alte Scherz wird immer noch beschmunzelt** the old joke still raises a smile.

beschmutzen* 1 vt to (make or get) dirty, to soil; (fig) Ruf, Namen to besmirch, to sully; Ehre to stain; siehe Nest. 2 vr to make or get oneself dirty.

Beschmutzung f siehe vt dirtying, soiling; besmirching, sullying; staining.

beschneiden* vt irreg (a) (zurechtschneiden, stutzen) to trim; Sträucher, Reben to prune; Bäume auch to lop; Flügel to clip; Fingernägel auch to cut, to pare. (b) (Med, Rel) to circumcise. (c) (fig: beschränken) to cut back, to curtail.

Beschneidung f, no pl siehe vt (a) trimming; pruning; lopping; clipping; cutting, paring. (b) circumcision. (c) (von Unterstützung etc) cut-back; (von Rechten) curtailing, curtailment.

beschneien* vt to cover with artificial snow.

beschneit adj snow-covered; Berge auch snow-capped.

beschnüffeln* 1 vt to sniff at; (fig) (vorsichtig untersuchen) to sniff out, to suss out (sl); jdn to size up; (bespitzeln) to spy out. 2 vr (Hunde) to have a sniff at each other, to sniff each other; (fig) to size each other up.

beschnuppern* vtr siehe **beschnüffeln**.

bescholten adj Ruf bad, evil; Charakter notorious; Mensch of evil repute, with a bad reputation.

beschönigen* vt to gloss over. **~der Ausdruck** euphemism; ... **sagte er ~d** ... he said, trying to make things seem better.

Beschönigung f glossing over. **was er zur ~ angeführt hat,** ... what he said to make things seem better ...

beschottern* vt Straße to macadamize, to metal; (Rail) to ballast.

beschranken* vt Bahnübergang to provide with gates, to put gates on.

beschränken* 1 vt (auf +acc to) to limit, to restrict; Anzahl, Ausgaben, Bedeutung eines Wortes etc auch to confine.
2 vr (auf +acc to) to limit or restrict; (esp Jur, Rede, Aufsatz etc auch) to confine oneself; (sich einschränken) to restrict oneself. **das Wort beschränkt sich auf regionalen Gebrauch** the word is limited or restricted or confined to regional usage.

beschrankt adj siehe **Bahnübergang**.

beschränkt adj (a) (eingeschränkt, knapp) limited; Gebrauch auch restricted. **wir sind räumlich/zeitlich/finanziell ~** we have only a limited amount of space/time/money; **~e Haftung** limited liability; **Gesellschaft mit ~er Haftung** limited company (Brit), corporation (US).
(b) (pej) (geistig) Mensch, Intelligenz limited; (engstirnig auch) narrow. **wie kann man nur so ~ sein?** how can anyone be so dim or stupid?

Beschränktheit f siehe adj (a) limitedness; restriction. **die ~ der Plätze/Zeit** the limited number of seats (available)/the limited (amount of) time (available). (b) limitedness, limited intelligence; (Engstirnigkeit) narrowness, limitedness. **er konnte in seiner ~ nicht begreifen** ... his simple mind could not grasp ...

Beschränkung f siehe vt limitation, restriction; confinement. **eine ~ der Teilnehmerzahl scheint unvermeidbar zu sein** it seems unavoidable that the number of participants will have to be limited or restricted.
(b) siehe vr (auf +acc to) limitation, restriction; confinement.
(c) (Maßnahme) restriction, limitation. **jdm ~en auferlegen** to impose restrictions on sb; **trotz der mir auferlegten ~ auf drei wesentliche Punkte** in spite of being confined to three essential points.

beschreiben* vt irreg (a) (darstellen) to describe, to give a description of. **sein Glück/Schmerz war nicht zu ~** his happiness/pain was indescribable or beyond (all) description; **ich kann dir nicht ~, wie erleichtert ich war** I can't tell you how relieved I was; **~de Psychologie/Pädagogik** descriptive psychology/theory of education; **~de Grammatik** descriptive grammar.
(b) (vollschreiben) to write on. **ein eng beschriebenes Blatt Papier** a closely written piece of paper.
(c) Kreis, Bahn to describe.

Beschreibung f (a) description. (b) (Gebrauchsanweisung) instructions pl.

beschreien* vt irreg (inf) siehe **berufen** 1 (c).

beschreiten* vt irreg (lit geh) Pfad to walk or step along; Brücke to walk or step across; (fig) neue Wege to follow, to pursue, to take; neue Methode to follow, to pursue.

beschriften* vt to write on; Grabstein, Sockel etc to inscribe; (mit Aufschrift) to label; Umschlag to address; Karikatur to give a caption (to). **etw mit seinem Namen ~** to write one's name on sth; **die Funde waren mit Tusche beschriftet** the finds were marked with ink.

Beschriftung f siehe vt (a) (das Beschriften) inscribing; labelling; addressing; giving a caption to; marking. **bei der ~ der Etiketten** while filling in the labels. (b) (Aufschrift) writing; inscription; label; caption.

beschuhen* vt to shoe; (Tech) Pfahl, Spitze etc to tip with metal.

beschuht adj wearing shoes, shod.

beschuldigen* vt to accuse; (esp Jur auch, liter) to charge. **jdn einer Sache** (gen) ~ to accuse sb of sth; to charge sb with sth.

Beschuldigte(r) mf decl as adj accused.

Beschuldigung f accusation; (esp Jur auch, liter) charge.

beschulen* vt (form) to provide with school(ing) facilities.

Beschulung f, no pl provision of school(ing) facilities (gen for).

beschummeln*, **beschuppen*** vti (inf) to cheat. **jdn um etw** ~ to cheat or diddle (inf) sb out of sth.

beschuppt adj scaly. **dick** ~ thick-scaled, with thick scales.

beschupsen* vti (inf) siehe **beschummeln**.

Beschuß m -sses, no pl (Mil) fire; (mit Granaten auch) shelling, bombardment; (Phys) bombardment, bombarding. **jdn/etw unter** ~ **nehmen** (Mil) to (start to) bombard or shell sb/sth; **Stellung auch** to fire on sth; (fig) to attack sb/sth, to launch an attack on sb/sth; **unter** ~ **hängen** or **stehen** (Mil) to be under fire; **unter** ~ **geraten** (Mil, fig) to come under fire.

beschütten* vt (mit Sand etc) to cover. **jdn/etw** (mit Wasser etc) ~ to pour water etc on or over sb/sth; **die Straße mit Sand** ~ to throw or put sand on the road; **eine Feld mit Jauche** ~ to put liquid manure on a field; **wenn du den Salat so übermäßig beschüttest,** ... if you soak the lettuce like that ...; **sie hat sich von oben bis unten (mit Wasser) beschüttet** she's poured or got water all down herself.

beschützen* vt to protect, to shield, to shelter (vor + dat from); **Werkstatt** to shelter. **beschütze mich!** protect me; ~d protective.

Beschützer(in f) m -s, - protector/protectress.

beschwatzen*, **beschwätzen*** (dial) vt (inf) (a) (überreden) to talk over. **jdn zu etw** ~ to talk sb into sth; **sich zu etw** ~ **lassen** to get talked into sth; **versuch doch, ihn zu** ~ try and chat him up (inf). (b) (bereden) to chat about, to have a chat about.

Beschwer f - or nt -s, no pl (obs) hardship. **jdm** ~ **machen** to cause sb hardship.

Beschwerde f -, -n (a) (Mühe) hardship.

(b) ~**n** pl (Leiden) trouble; **das macht mir immer noch** ~**n** it's still causing or giving me trouble; **mit etw** ~**n haben** to have trouble with sth; **wenn Sie wieder ganz ohne** ~**n sind** when the trouble's cleared up completely.

(c) (Klage) complaint; (Jur) appeal. **eine** ~ **gegen jdn** a complaint about sb; **wenn Sie eine** ~ **haben** if you have a complaint or grievance; ~ **führen** or **einlegen** or **erheben** (form) to lodge a complaint; **jdm Grund zur** ~ **geben** to give sb grounds or cause for complaint.

Beschwerde-: ~**buch** nt complaints book; b~**frei** adj (Med) recovered; **er war nie wieder ganz** b~**frei** the symptoms never completely disappeared; **fünfzig** b~**freie Jahre** fifty years without any complaints; ~**frist** f (Jur) period of time during which an appeal may be lodged or filed; ~**führende(r)** mf decl as adj, ~**führer** m (form) person who lodges a complaint, complainant; (Jur) appellant; ~**schrift** f written (or formal) complaint, petition; ~**weg** m (form) possibility of lodging a complaint with sb (in authority); **auf dem** ~**weg** by (means of) lodging or making a complaint; **den** ~**weg beschreiten** to lodge a complaint.

beschweren* 1 vt (mit Gewicht) to weigh(t) down; (fig: belasten) (Problem, Kummer) to weigh on; (Mensch) to burden. **von Kummer beschwert** weighed down with sorrow. 2 vr (a) (sich belasten) (lit) to weigh oneself down; (fig) to encumber oneself. (b) (sich beklagen) to complain.

beschwerlich adj laborious, arduous; Reise arduous. **jdm** ~ **fallen** (old)/**werden** to be/become a burden to sb; **ihm fällt die Hitze** ~ (old) he finds the heat troublesome; **das Gehen/Atmen ist für ihn** ~ he finds walking/breathing hard work.

Beschwerlichkeit f difficulty; (von Reise, Aufgabe auch) laboriousness no pl, arduousness no pl.

Beschwernis f or nt (geh) (Mühsal) hardship; (Kümmernis) tribulation, vexation.

Beschwerung f (a) (das Beschweren) weigh(t)ing down. (b) (Gegenstand) weight.

beschwichtigen* vt jdn to appease, to pacify; Kinder to calm down, to soothe; jds Zorn, Gewissen to soothe, to appease, to calm.

Beschwichtigung f siehe vt appeasement, pacification; calming down, soothing; soothing, appeasement, calming; (beschwichtigende Worte) calming or soothing words pl.

Beschwichtigungspolitik f policy of appeasement.

beschwindeln* vt (inf) (a) (belügen) **jdn** ~ to tell sb a lie or a fib (inf). (b) (betrügen) to cheat, to swindle, to do (inf).

beschwingen* vt to exhilarate, to elate.

beschwingt adj elated, exhilarated; Musik, Mensch vibrant. **sich** ~ **fühlen** to walk on air; **ein** ~**es Gefühl** a feeling of elation or exhilaration; ~**en Schrittes** (geh) or **Fußes** (liter) with a spring or bounce in one's step, lightly tripping (liter).

Beschwingtheit f siehe adj elation, exhilaration; vibrancy.

beschwipsen* (inf) 1 vt to make tipsy, to go to sb's head. 2 vr to get tipsy.

beschwipst adj (inf) tipsy.

beschwören* vt irreg (a) (beeiden) to swear to; (Jur auch) to swear on oath.

(b) (flehen) to implore, to beseech. **sie hob** ~**d die Hände** she raised her hands imploringly or beseechingly.

(c) (erscheinen lassen) to conjure up; Verstorbene auch to raise, to call up; (bannen) böse Geister to exorcise, to lay; Schlangen to charm.

(d) (geh: hervorrufen) Erinnerung etc to conjure up. **das be-**

schwor Erinnerungen in mir that conjured up memories.

Beschwörung f (a) (das Flehen) entreaty. (b) siehe vt (c) conjuring up, conjuration; raising, calling up; exorcising, exorcism, laying; charming. (c) (auch ~sformel) incantation.

beseelen* vt (a) (lit: mit Seele versehen) to give a soul to Natur, Kunstwerk to breathe life into. **das beseelte Spiel des Pianisten** (geh) the pianist's inspired playing.

(b) (erfüllen) to fill. **neuer Mut beseelte ihn** he was filled or imbued with fresh courage; **ein Hochgefühl beseelte ihn** a feeling of joy filled his soul; **ein neuer Geist beseelt unser Jahrhundert** a new spirit pervades or informs (liter) our century.

besehen* irreg 1 vt (auch: sich dat ~) to take a look at, to look at. 2 vr to (take a) look at oneself.

beseibeln*, **beseibern*** vt (dial) to dribble all over, to slobber all over.

beseitigen* vt (a) (entfernen) to remove, to get rid of; Abfall, Schnee auch to clear (away); Schwierigkeiten auch to sort or smooth out; Fehler auch to eliminate; Mißstände to get rid of, to do away with. (b) (euph: umbringen) to get rid of, to eliminate.

Beseitigung f, no pl siehe vt (a) removal, getting rid of clearing (away); sorting or smoothing out; elimination; getting rid of, doing away with. (b) getting rid of, elimination.

beseligen* vt to make blissfully happy. ~**d/beselgt** blissful.

Besen m -s, - (a) (Kehr~) broom; (Reisig~) besom; (zum Rühren) whisk; (von Hexe) broomstick. **jdn auf den** ~ **laden** (inf) to pull sb's leg (inf), to have sb on (inf); **ich fresse einen** ~ **wenn das stimmt** (inf) if that's right, I'll eat my hat (inf); **neue** ~ **kehren gut** (Prov) a new broom sweeps clean (Prov).

(b) (pej inf: Frau) old bag (inf), old boot (inf).

(c) (vulg: Penis) prick (vulg).

Besen-: ~**binder** m broom-maker; ~**kammer** f broom cupboard; ~**macher** m siehe ~**binder**; b~**rein** adj well-swept; **eine Wohnung** b~**rein verlassen** to leave a flat in a clean and tidy condition (for the next tenant); ~**schrank** m broom cupboard; ~**stiel** m broom-stick, broom-handle; **steif wie ein** ~**stiel** as stiff as a poker; **er sitzt da/tanzt als hätte er einen** ~**stiel verschluckt** (inf) he's sitting there as stiff as a poker/he dances so stiffly; **hast du einen** ~**stiel verschluckt?** is your back too stiff to make a bow?

besessen 1 ptp of besitzen. 2 adj (von bösen Geistern) possessed (von by); (von einer Idee, Leidenschaft etc) obsessed (von with). **wie** ~ like a thing or one possessed.

Besessene(r) mf decl as adj one possessed no art. **die** ~**n** the possessed; **ein** ~**r wurde zu Jesus gebracht** a man possessed of an evil spirit was brought to Jesus; **wie ein** ~**r** like one possessed.

Besessenheit f, no pl siehe adj possession; obsession.

besetzen* vt (a) (dekorieren) to trim; (mit Edelsteinen) to stud. (b) (belegen) to occupy; (reservieren) to reserve; (füllen) Plätze, Stühle to fill. **ist hier or dieser Platz besetzt?** is this place taken?; **irgend jemand hat die (Telefon)leitung stundenlang besetzt** somebody was on the line for hours, somebody was keeping the line busy for hours; **viele Autos besetzten den Parkplatz** there were a lot of cars in the car-park; siehe auch besetzt.

(c) (esp Mil: eingenommen haben) to occupy.

(d) (mit Person) Stelle, Amt, Posten to fill; (Theat) Rolle to cast; (mit Tieren) to stock. **eine Stelle etc neu** ~ to find a new person to fill a job.

besetzt 1 ptp of besetzen.

2 adj (belegt) Telefon, Nummer, Leitung engaged (Brit), busy (esp US); (in Gebrauch) Spielautomat, Waschmaschinen etc taken; Hörsaal being used; (vorgebucht) booked; (voll) Bus, Wagen, Abteil etc full (up); (anderweitig beschäftigt, verplant) Mensch busy. **Freitag ist schon** ~ Friday I'm/he's etc busy, Friday's out.

Besetztton m, **Besetztzeichen** nt (Telec) engaged (Brit) or busy (esp US) tone.

Besetzung f (a) (das Besetzen) (von Stelle) filling; (von Rolle) casting; (mit Tieren) stocking; (Theat: Schauspieler) cast; (Sport: Mannschaft) team, side. **die Nationalelf in der neuen** ~ the new line-up for the international side; **das Stück in der neuen** ~ the play with the new cast. (b) (esp Mil) occupation.

Besetzungs- in cpds (Sw Mil) siehe Besatzungs-; ~**liste** f (Theat, Film) cast list.

besichtigen* vt (ansehen) Stadt, Kirche to have a look at, to visit; Betrieb to tour, to have a look over or round; (zur Prüfung) Haus to view, to have a look at, to look over; Ware to have a look at, to inspect; Schule auch to inspect; (inspizieren) Truppen to inspect, to review; (hum) Baby, zukünftigen Schwiegersohn etc to inspect.

Besichtigung f (von Sehenswürdigkeiten) sight-seeing tour; (von Museum, Kirche, Betrieb) tour; (zur Prüfung) (von Haus) viewing; (von Waren, Schule, Baby) inspection; (von Truppen) inspection, review. **nach einer kurzen** ~ **der Kirche/des Museums/Betriebs** etc after a short look round the church/museum/factory etc; **die Waren liegen zur** ~ **aus** the goods are on display.

Besichtigungs-: ~**reise** f (zum Vergnügen) sight-seeing tour or trip; (zur Überprüfung) tour of inspection; ~**zeiten** pl hours pl of opening.

besiedeln* vt (ansiedeln) to populate, to settle (mit with); (sich niederlassen in) to settle; (kolonisieren) to colonize; (Tiere) to populate, to inhabit; (Pflanzen) to be found in, to inhabit. **dicht/dünn/schwach besiedelt** densely/thinly/sparsely populated.

Besied(e)lung f, no pl siehe vt settlement; colonization. **dichte/dünne/schwache** ~ dense/thin/sparse population.

Besiedlungsdichte f population density.

besiegeln* vt to seal.

Besiegelung f sealing.

besiegen* vt (schlagen) to defeat, to beat; Feind auch to conquer, to vanquish (liter); (überwinden) to overcome, to conquer. **sich selbst ~** to overcome one's fears/doubts etc (seine Triebe ~) to repress the urge.

Besiegte(r) mf decl as adj defeated or vanquished person, loser.

Besiegung f, no pl siehe vt defeat; conquest, vanquishing; overcoming, conquest.

besingen* vt irreg (a) (rühmen) to sing of, to sing (poet). **jdn/etw ~** to sing the praises of sb/sth. (b) Schallplatte, Tonband to record.

besinnen* irreg 1 vr (überlegen) to reflect, to think; (erinnern) to remember (auf jdn/etw sb/sth); (es sich anders überlegen) to have second thoughts. **besinne dich, mein Kind!** take thought, my child; **sich anders** or **eines anderen/eines Besseren ~** to change one's mind/to think better of sth; **er hat sich besonnen** he has seen the light; **ohne sich (viel) zu ~, ohne langes B~** without a moment's thought or hesitation; **wenn ich mich recht besinne** if I remember correctly.

    2 vt (geh: bedenken) to reflect on, to ponder, to consider.

besinnlich adj contemplative. **eine ~e Zeit** a time of contemplation; **~ werden** to become thoughtful or pensive.

Besinnlichkeit f, no pl contemplativeness, thoughtfulness.

Besinnung f, no pl (a) (Bewußtsein) consciousness. **bei/ohne ~ sein** to be conscious/unconscious; **die ~ verlieren** to lose consciousness; (fig) to lose one's head; **wieder zur ~ kommen** to regain consciousness, to come to; (fig) to come to one's senses; **jdn zur ~ bringen** to bring sb round; (fig) to bring sb to his senses.

    (b) (das Sich-Besinnen) contemplation (auf +acc of), reflection (auf +acc upon).

    (c) (das Nachdenken) reflection. **ich brauche Zeit, zur ~ zu kommen** I need time to reflect or for reflection.

Besinnungs-: ~aufsatz m discursive essay; b~los adj unconscious, insensible; (fig) blind; Wut blind, insensate; b~los werden to lose consciousness; ~losigkeit f, no pl (lit) unconsciousness.

Besitz m -es, no pl (a) (das Besitzen) possession. **im ~ von etw sein** to be in possession of sth; **ich bin im ~ Ihres Schreibens** I am in receipt of your letter; **sich in den ~ von etw setzen** to take possession of sth; **etw in ~ nehmen** to take possession of; **von etw ~ ergreifen** to seize possession of sth; **von jdm ~ ergreifen** to take or seize hold of sb; (Zweifel, Wahnsinn etc) to take possession of sb's mind; **in privatem ~** in private ownership; **jdm den ~ an etw** (dat) **streitig machen** to dispute sb's ownership of sth.

    (b) (Eigentum) property; (Landgut) estate.

Besitz-: ~anspruch m claim of ownership; (Jur) title; **einen ~anspruch auf etw** (acc) **haben** to have a claim to sth; **seine ~ansprüche** (auf etw acc) **anmelden** to make one's claims (to sth), to lay claim to sth; b~anzeigend adj (Gram) possessive; ~bürgertum nt middle-class property owners pl, property-owning bourgeoisie.

besitzen pret besaß, ptp besessen vt to have, to possess; käufliche Güter auch to own; Vermögen to possess, to own; Wertpapiere auch to hold; Narbe, grüne Augen to have; Rechte, jds Zuneigung etc auch to enjoy. **das Zimmer besaß große Fenster** the room had big windows; **eine Frau ~** (euph) to possess or have a woman; **große Schönheit/Fähigkeiten etc ~** to be possessed of great beauty/abilities etc; **die ~den Klassen** the propertied classes.

Besitzer(in f) m -s, - owner; (von Wertpapieren auch, von Führerschein auch) holder; (Inhaber auch) proprietor. **den ~ wechseln** to change hands.

Besitz|ergreifung f seizure.

Besitzer-: ~stolz m pride of possession; voller ~stolz proudly; ~wechsel m change of ownership.

Besitz-: ~gier f acquisitive greed, acquisitiveness; b~los adj having no possessions; **sie ist nicht völlig b~los** she is not completely without possessions; ~nahme f, no pl seizure; ~stand m (form) assets pl; ~tum nt (Eigentum) possession, property no pl; (Grundbesitz) estate(s pl), property; **dieser Kunstgegenstand ist ein ~tum der Kirche** this work of art is the property of the Church.

Besitzung f possession; (privater Land- und Grundbesitz) estate(s).

Besitz-: ~verhältnisse pl property situation or conditions pl; ~verteilung f distribution of property.

besoffen adj (sl) (betrunken) pissed (Brit), stoned, smashed (all sl); (verrückt) out of one's mind, nuts (inf).

Besoffene(r) mf decl as adj (inf) drunk.

besohlen* vt to sole; (neu ~) to resole.

Besohlung f siehe vt soling no pl; resoling.

besolden* vt to pay.

Besoldung f pay.

Besoldungs-: ~dienstalter nt pay seniority; ~gruppe f pay or salary group; ~ordnung f pay or salary regulations pl.

besondere(r, s) adj (a) (ungewöhnlich, eine Ausnahme bildend) special; (hervorragend) Qualität, Schönheit etc exceptional. **für mich bist du ein ~r Mensch** you're a very special person for me; **er ist ein ganz ~r Freund** he is a very special friend; **es ist eine ~ Freude** it is a special or particular pleasure; **das sind ~ Umstände** those are special circumstances; **sie hat einen ~n Geschmack, was Kleidung betrifft** she has a very special or individual taste in clothes; **das ist eine ganz ~ Augenfarbe** that is a very unusual eye colour; **eine ganz ~ Anstrengung** a quite exceptional effort.

    (b) (speziell) special, particular; (bestimmt) particular.

unser ~s Interesse gilt ... we are particularly or (e)specially interested in ...; **wir legen ~n Wert auf ...** we place particular or special emphasis on ...; **ohne ~ Begeisterung** without any particular enthusiasm; **er hat sich mit ~m Eifer darangemacht** he set about it with particular enthusiasm; **es ist mein ganz ~r Wunsch, daß ...** it is my very special wish that ..., I particularly wish that ...; **in diesem ~n Fall** in this particular case; **keine ~n Vorlieben** no special or particular preferences; **das ist von ~r Bedeutung** it is of (e)special or particular importance.

    (c) (zusätzlich, separat, gesondert) special, separate.

Besondere(s) nt decl as adj (a) **das ~ und das Allgemeine** the particular and the general; **im b~n** (im einzelnen) in particular cases; (vor allem) in particular.

    (b) **etwas/nichts ~s** something/nothing special; **er möchte etwas ~s sein** he thinks he's something special; **das ist doch nichts ~s!** that's nothing special or out of the ordinary, what's special about that?; **das ~ daran** the special thing about it.

Besonderheit f exceptional or unusual quality or feature; (besondere Eigenschaft) peculiarity.

besonders adv gut, hübsch, teuer etc particularly, (e)specially; (ausdrücklich, vor allem) particularly, in particular, (e)specially; (gesondert) separately, individually; (speziell) anfertigen etc specially. **~ du müßtest das wissen** you particularly or in particular or especially should know that; **nicht ~ (lustig/kalt)** not particularly or not (e)specially (funny/cold); **nicht ~ viel Geld** not a particularly or not a(n) (e)specially large amount of money; **ich habe nicht ~ wenig Geld** I'm not particularly badly off; **das Essen/der Film war nicht ~** (inf) the food/film was nothing special or nothing to write home about (inf); **wie geht's dir? — nicht ~** (inf) how are you? — not too hot (inf); **~ wenig Fehler** an exceptionally or a particularly low number of mistakes; **er hat ~ viel/wenig gearbeitet/gegessen** he did a particularly large/small amount of work/he ate a particularly large amount of food/he ate particularly little.

besonnen 1 ptp of besinnen. 2 adj considered, level-headed. **die Polizei ist ~ vorgegangen** the police proceeded in a careful and thoughtful way; **ihre ruhige, ~e Art** her calm and collected way.

Besonnenheit f, no pl level-headedness. **durch seine ~ hat er eine Katastrophe verhindert** by staying calm and collected he avoided a disaster.

besonnt adj sunny.

besorgen* vt (a) (kaufen, beschaffen etc) to get; (euph inf: stehlen) to acquire (euph inf). **jdm/sich etw ~** to get sth for sb/oneself, to get sb/oneself sth; **jdm eine Stelle/einen neuen Anzug ~** to get or find a job for sb or to fix sb up with a job/new suit.

    (b) (erledigen) to attend or see to. **was du heute kannst ~, das verschiebe nicht auf morgen** (Prov) never put off until tomorrow what you can do today.

    (c) (versorgen) to take care of, to look after.

    (d) (inf) **es jdm ~** to sort sb out (inf), to fix sb (inf).

    (e) (sl) **es jdm ~** (Mann: mit jdm schlafen) to have it off with sb (sl); (Frau: jdn fellieren) to suck sb off (vulg), to give sb a blow-job (sl).

besorglich adj (rare) (besorgt) anxious, worried; (Sorge erregend) worrying.

Besorgnis f anxiety, worry, apprehension.

besorgnis|erregend adj alarming, disquieting, worrying.

besorgt 1 ptp of besorgen. 2 adj (voller Sorge) anxious, worried (wegen about). (b) **um jdn/etw ~ sein** to be concerned about sb/sth.

Besorgtheit f, no pl concern, solicitude.

Besorgung f (a) (das Kaufen) purchase. **er wurde mit der ~ von ... beauftragt** he was asked to get ... (b) (Erledigung) **jdn mit der ~ seiner Geschäfte betrauen** to entrust sb with looking after one's affairs; **die ~ des Haushaltes** looking after the house. (c) (Einkauf) errand (dial). **~en machen** to do some shopping.

bespannen* vt (a) (überziehen) (mit Material) to cover; (mit Saiten, Fäden etc) to string. (b) (mit Zugtieren) Wagen to harness up. **den Wagen mit zwei Pferden ~** to harness two horses to the cart.

Bespannung f (a) no pl (das Bespannen) covering; (mit Saiten etc) stringing; (mit Pferden) harnessing. (b) (Material) covering; (Saiten, Fäden etc) strings pl.

bespeien* vt irreg (geh) to spit at or (up)on; (mit Erbrochenem) to spew over.

bespicken* vt (mit Fett) to lard; (mit Nägeln) to stud, to spike; (fig: dicht bestecken) to cover. **seine mit Orden bespickte Brust** his chest bristling with medals; **seine Reden mit Fremdwörtern ~** to pepper or lard one's speeches with loan words.

bespiegeln* 1 vr (lit: im Spiegel) to look at oneself in a/the mirror; (fig: Selbstbetrachtung machen) to contemplate oneself or one's own navel (hum). 2 vt (geh) das eigene Ich ~ to contemplate; (darstellen, verarbeiten) Vergangenheit, Gefühle, Nöte to portray, to give a picture of.

bespiegelt adj (mit Spiegel versehen) mirrored, covered with mirrors.

bespielbar adj Rasen etc playable; Kassette capable of being recorded on.

bespielen* vt (a) Schallplatte, Tonband to record on, to make a recording on. **das Band ist mit klassischer Musik bespielt** the tape has a recording of classical music on it. (b) (Theat) Ort to play on. (c) (Sport) to play on.

bespitzeln* vt to spy on.

Bespitz(e)lung f spying.

bespötteln* vt to mock (at), to scoff at, to ridicule.

besprechen* irreg 1 vt (a) (über etw sprechen) to discuss, to

talk about. **wie besprochen** as arranged.
(b) (*rezensieren*) to review.
(c) *Schallplatte, Tonband* to make a recording on. **ein besprochenes Band** a tape of sb's voice *or* of sb talking; **eine von X mit Gedichten besprochene Platte** a record of X reading poems.
(d) (*beschwören*) to (attempt a) cure by magic *or* incantation.
2 *vr* **sich mit jdm** ~ to confer with sb, to consult (with) sb (*über + acc* about); **sich über etw** (*acc*) ~ to discuss sth.
Besprechung *f* **(a)** (*Unterredung*) discussion, talk; (*Konferenz*) meeting. **nach** ~ **mit** ... after discussion with ..., after talking with ...; **er ist bei einer** ~, **er hat eine** ~ he's in a meeting.
(b) (*Rezension*) review, notice. **(c)** (*von Tonbändern, Schallplatten*) recording. **(d)** (*Beschwörung*) conjuring away.
Besprechungs|exemplar *nt* review copy.
besprengen* *vt* to sprinkle.
besprenkeln* *vt* (*mit Farbe, Schmutz*) to speckle; (*fig: übersäen*) to stud.
bespringen* *vt irreg* (*Tier*) to mount, to cover.
bespritzen* **1** *vt* to spray; (*beschmutzen*) to (be)spatter, to splash. **2** *vr* to spray oneself; (*sich beschmutzen*) to (be)spatter oneself, to splash oneself.
besprühen* **1** *vt* to spray. **2** *vr* to spray oneself.
bespucken* *vt* to spit at *or* (up)on.
bespülen* *vt* (*Wellen*) to wash against.
besser *adj, adv, comp of* **gut, wohl (a)** better. ~**e Kreise/Gegend** better circles/neighbourhood; ~**e Leute** better class of people; **er hat** ~**e Tage or Zeiten gesehen** (*iro*) he has seen better days; **du willst wohl etwas B~es sein!** (*inf*) I suppose you think you're better than other people *or* think yourself superior; **soll es etwas B~es sein?** did you have something of rather better quality in mind?; ~ **ist** ~ (it is) better to be on the safe side; **um so** ~! (*inf*) so much the better!; ~ (**gesagt**) *or* rather, *or* better; ~ **werden** to improve, to get better; **sie will immer alles** ~ **wissen** she always thinks she knows better; **das ist auch** ~ **so** it's better that way; **das macht nichts** ~ that doesn't improve matters, that doesn't make things any (the) better; **es kommt noch** ~ there's worse or more to come *or* follow; **das wäre noch** ~ (*iro*) no way; **es** ~ **haben** to have a better life; **ich möchte, daß meine Kinder es** ~ **haben** I want something better for my children; **B~es zu tun haben** (*inf*) to have better things to do; **eine Wendung zum B~en nehmen** to take a turn for the better; **jdn eines B~en belehren** to teach sb otherwise *or* better; *siehe* **besinnen.**
(b) **laß das** ~ **bleiben** you had better leave well alone; **das solltest du** ~ **nicht tun** you had better not do that; **geh** ~ **zum Arzt** you had better go to see a doctor; **du tätest** ~ **daran** ... you would do better to ..., you had better ...; **dann geh ich** ~ **then** I'd better go.
(c) **das Essen war nur ein** ~**er Imbiß** the meal was just a glorified snack.
Besser-: **b~gehen** *vi impers sep irreg aux sein* **es geht jdm b~** sb is feeling better; **jetzt geht's der Firma wieder b~** the firm is doing better again now, things are going better again for the firm now; **b~gestellt** *adj* better-off; ~**gestellte** *pl* better off *pl.*
bessern **1** *vt* **(a)** to improve, to (make) better; *Verbrecher etc* to reform. **(b)** (*old*) (*ausbessern*) to mend; (*verbessern*) to improve. **2** *vr* (*moralisch, im Benehmen*) to mend one's ways. **bessere dich** (*hum inf*) mend your ways!
besser-: ~**stehen** *vr sep irreg* (*inf*) to be better off; ~**stellen** *sep* **1** *vt* **jdn** ~**stellen** to improve sb's financial position; **2** *vr* to be better off.
Besserung *f, no pl* improvement; (*von Verbrecher etc*) reformation; (*Genesung*) recovery. (**ich wünsche dir) gute** ~! I wish you a speedy recovery, I hope you get better soon; **auf dem Wege der** ~ **sein** to be getting better, to be improving; (*Patient auch*) to be on the road to recovery.
Besserungs-: ~**anstalt** *f* (*dated*) reformatory, approved school; **b~fähig** *adj* improvable; *Verbrecher* capable of being reformed, reformable; ~**maßnahme** *f* (*Jur*) corrective measure; **b~willig** *adj* willing to reform (oneself).
Besser-: ~**wisser** *m -s, -* (*inf*) know-all, know-it-all (*US*), smartaleck (*inf*), smart-ass (*esp US inf*); ~**wisserei** *f* (*inf*) know-all *etc* manner; **b~wisserisch** *adj* (*inf*) Einstellung, Art know-all *etc attr*; **er tut immer so b~wisserisch** he's such a know-all *etc.*
best- *in cpds mit adj* best.
bestach *pret of* **bestechen.**
bestallen* *vt* (*form*) to install, to appoint (*zu* as).
Bestallung *f* (*form*) installation, appointment.
Bestallungs|urkunde *f* certificate of appointment.
bestand *pret of* **bestehen.**
Bestand *m -(e)s, ⁻e* **(a)** (*Fortdauer*) continued existence, continuance. **von** ~ **sein/**~ **haben** to be permanent, to endure; **das Gesetz hat noch immer** ~ the law still continues to exist; **zum 100-jährigen** ~ **des Vereins** (*Aus*) on the (occasion of the) 100th anniversary of the society. **(b)** (*vorhandene Menge, Tiere*) stock (*an + dat* of); (*Forst~ auch*) forest *or* timber stand (*US*). ~ **aufnehmen** to take stock. **(c)** (*Aus: Pacht*) lease, tenure. **in** ~ **geben** to let (out) *or* put out on lease.
bestanden 1 *ptp of* **bestehen.**
2 *adj* **(a)** (*bewachsen*) covered with trees; *Allee* lined with trees. **die mit Bäumen** ~**en Alleen/Abhänge** the tree-lined avenues/tree-covered slopes; **der Wald ist gut** ~ the forest is well stocked.
(b) **nach** ~**er/„sehr gut"** ~**er Prüfung** after passing the/an exam/after getting a "very good" in the exam; **bei nicht** ~**er Prüfung** if you *etc* don't pass the exam; **sie feiert die** ~**e Prüfung** she's celebrating passing her exam.
(c) (*Sw: alt*) advanced (in years).

beständig *adj* **(a)** *no pred* (*dauernd*) constant, continual. **ich mache mir** ~ **Sorgen** I am constantly *or* continually worried. **(b)** (*gleichbleibend*) constant; *Mitarbeiter* steady; *Wetter* settled. **(c)** *no adv* (*widerstandsfähig*) resistant (*gegen* to); *Farbe* fast; (*dauerhaft*) *Freundschaft, Beziehung* lasting, durable.
-beständig *adj suf* -resistant.
Beständigkeit *f, no pl siehe adj* **(a)** continualness. **er fragt mit einer** ~ ... he asks so constantly ... **(b)** constancy; steadiness; settledness. **(c)** resistance; fastness; lastingness, durability.
Bestands-: ~**aufnahme** *f* stock-taking; ~**jubiläum** *nt* (*Aus*) anniversary (*of the foundation of a firm, society etc*).
Bestandteil *m* component, part, element; (*fig*) essential *or* integral part. **sich in seine** ~**e auflösen** to fall to pieces, to come apart; **etw in seine** ~**e zerlegen** to take sth apart *or* to pieces.
Best|arbeiter *m* (*DDR*) worker with the highest output.
bestärken* *vt* to confirm; *Verdacht auch* to reinforce. **jdn in seinem Vorsatz/Wunsch** ~ to confirm sb in his intention/desire, to make sb's intention/desire firmer *or* stronger; **das hat mich nur darin bestärkt, es zu tun** that merely made me all the more determined to do it.
Bestärkung *f* confirmation; (*von Verdacht auch*) reinforcement.
bestätigen* **1** *vt* to confirm; *Theorie, Beweise, Alibi etc* to bear out, to corroborate; (*Jur*) *Urteil* to uphold. **sich in etw** (*dat*) **bestätigt finden** to be confirmed in sth; **ich hatte angenommen, daß ... und fand mich darin bestätigt** I had assumed that ... and my assumption was confirmed *or* borne out; ~**d** confirmative, confirmatory; **ein** ~**des Kopfnicken** a nod of confirmation; ... **sagte er** ~**d** ... he said in confirmation.
(b) (*Comm*) *Empfang, Brief* to acknowledge (receipt of).
(c) (*beurkunden*) to confirm, to certify, to attest. **hiermit wird bestätigt, daß ...** this is to confirm *or* certify that ...
(d) (*anerkennen*) to acknowledge, to recognize. **jdn (im Amt)** ~ to confirm sb's appointment.
2 *vr* to be confirmed, to prove true, to be proved true.
Bestätigung *f siehe vt* **(a)** confirmation (*auch Dokument*); bearing out, corroboration; upholding. **(b)** (*auch Dokument*) acknowledgement (of receipt). **(c)** (*auch Dokument*) confirmation, certification, attestation. **(d)** recognition; confirmation of appointment.
Bestätigungsschreiben *nt* letter of confirmation.
bestatten* *vt* to bury. **bestattet liegen** to be *or* lie buried (*in + dat* in); **wo liegt er bestattet?** where is he buried?; **wann wird er bestattet?** when is the funeral (service)?
Bestatter *m -s, -* undertaker, mortician (*US*).
Bestattung *f* burial; (*Feuer~*) cremation; (*Feier auch*) funeral. **kirchliche/weltliche** ~ Christian/secular burial.
Bestattungs-: ~**institut**, ~**unternehmen** *nt* undertaker's, mortician's (*US*); ~**unternehmer** *m* undertaker, funeral director, mortician (*US*).
bestäuben* *vt* to dust (*auch Cook*), to sprinkle; (*Bot*) to pollinate; (*Agr*) to dust, to spray.
Bestäubung *f* dusting, sprinkling; (*Bot*) pollination; (*Agr*) dusting, spraying.
bestaunen* *vt* to marvel at, to gaze at in wonder *or* admiration; (*verblüfft*) to gape at, to stare at in astonishment. **laß dich** ~ let's have a good look at you; **sie wurde von allen bestaunt** they all gazed at her in admiration/gaped at her.
best-: ~**bekannt** *adj attr* best-known; ~**beleumdet**, ~**beleumundet** *adj* highly reputed; ~**bemittelt** *adj* (*Aus*) extremely well-off; ~**bewährt** *adj attr* well-proven; ~**bezahlt** *adj attr* best-paid.
beste *siehe* **beste(r, s).**
bestechen *pret* **bestach,** *ptp* **bestochen 1** *vt* **(a)** (*mit Geld, Geschenken etc*) to bribe; *Beamte auch* to corrupt. **ich lasse mich nicht** ~ I'm not open to bribery; (*mit Geld etc auch*) I don't take bribes.
(b) (*beeindrucken*) to captivate.
2 *vi* (*Eindruck machen*) to be impressive (*durch* because of). **ein Mädchen, das durch Schönheit besticht** a girl of captivating beauty.
bestechend *adj* *Schönheit, Eindruck* captivating; *Angebot* tempting, enticing; *Klarheit* irresistible; *Geist, Kondition* winning. **das ist so** ~ **einfach** it's so beautifully simple.
bestechlich *adj* bribable, corruptible, venal.
Bestechlichkeit *f, no pl* corruptibility, venality.
Bestechung *f* bribery; (*von Beamten etc auch*) corruption. **aktive** ~ (*Jur*) offering of bribes/a bribe (to an official); **passive** ~ (*Jur*) taking of bribes/a bribe (by an official).
Bestechungs-: ~**geld** *nt usu pl* bribe; ~**skandal** *m* bribery scandal; ~**summe** *f* bribe; ~**versuch** *m* attempted bribery.
Besteck *nt -(e)s, -e* **(a)** (*Eß~*) knives and forks *pl*, cutlery *sing* (*esp Brit*), flatware *sing* (*US*); (*Set, für ein Gedeck*) set of cutlery/flatware. **ein silbernes** ~ a set of silver cutlery/flatware; **Herr Ober, ich habe kein** ~ waiter, I haven't any cutlery/flatware.
(b) (*Instrumentensatz*) set of instruments; (*Raucher~*) pipe-cleaning implements *pl*, smoker's set. **chirurgisches** ~ (set of) surgical instruments.
(c) (*Naut*) reckoning, ship's position.
bestecken* *vt* to decorate.
Besteck-: ~**kasten** *m* cutlery tray; (*mit Deckel*) cutlery canteen, flatware chest (*US*); ~**(schub)fach** *nt* cutlery drawer.
bestehen *pret* **bestand,** *ptp* **bestanden 1** *vt* **(a)** *Examen, Probe* to pass. **eine Prüfung mit Auszeichnung/„sehr gut"** ~ to get a distinction/"very good" (in an exam), to pass an exam with distinction/"very good"; *siehe auch* **bestanden.**
(b) (*durchstehen*) *Schicksalsschläge* to withstand; *schwere Zeit* to come through, to pull through; *Gefahr* to overcome; *Kampf* to win.

2 vi **(a)** (existieren) to exist, to be in existence; (Zweifel, Hoffnung, Aussicht, Gefahr, Probleme etc) to exist; (Brauch auch) to be extant. ~ **bleiben** (Frage, Hoffnung etc) to remain; **die Universität/Firma besteht seit hundert Jahren** the university/firm has been in existence or has existed for a hundred years; **es besteht die Hoffnung/die Aussicht/der Verdacht, daß ...** there is a hope/a prospect/a suspicion that ...

(b) (Bestand haben) to continue to exist; (Zweifel, Problem etc auch) to persist.

(c) (sich zusammensetzen) to consist (aus of). **in etw** (dat) ~ to consist in sth; (Aufgabe) to involve sth; **seine einzige Chance besteht darin, ...** his only chance is to ...; **die Schwierigkeit/das Problem besteht darin, daß ...** the difficulty/problem consists or lies in the fact that ...; **das Problem besteht darin, zu zeigen ...** the problem consists in showing ...

(d) (standhalten, sich bewähren) to hold one's own (in +dat in). **vor etw** (dat) ~ to stand up to or against sth; **wie soll meine Arbeit neben seinen Glanzleistungen noch ~?** how will my work ever match up to or hold up against his performance?

(e) (durchkommen) to pass. **(in einer Prüfung) mit „sehr gut" ~** to get a "very good" (in an exam).

(f) auf etw (dat) ~ to insist on sth; **ich bestehe darauf** I insist.

Bestehen nt -s, no pl **(a)** (Vorhandensein, Dauer) existence. **seit ~ der Firma/des Staates** ever since the firm/state came into existence or has existed; **das 100-jährige ~ von etw feiern** to celebrate the hundredth anniversary or first hundred years of (the existence of) sth.

(b) (Beharren) insistence (auf +dat von).

(c) siehe vt (a, b) passing; withstanding; coming or pulling through; overcoming. **bei ~ der Prüfung** on passing the exam.

bestehenbleiben vi sep irreg aux sein to last, to endure; (Hoffnung) to remain; (Versprechen, Vereinbarungen) to hold good.

bestehend adj existing; Gesetze auch present, current; Preise current; Umstände, Verhältnisse auch prevailing. **die seit 1887 ~en Gesetze** the laws which have existed since 1887.

bestehenlassen vt sep irreg to keep, to retain; Freundschaft to keep alive, to sustain.

bestehlen* vt irreg to rob. **jdn (um etw) ~** (lit, fig) to rob sb of sth.

besteigen* vt irreg **(a)** Berg, Turm, Leiter to climb (up), to ascend (liter); Fahrrad, Pferd to mount, to get or climb on(to); Bus, Flugzeug to get on, to enter; Auto, Segelflugzeug, Hubschrauber to get into; Schiff to go on or aboard; Thron to ascend. **(b)** siehe **bespringen.**

Besteigung f (von Berg) climbing, ascent; (von Thron) accession (gen to).

Bestell-: ~**block** m order pad, pad of order forms; ~**buch** nt order book.

bestellen* 1 vt **(a)** (anfordern, in Restaurant) to order; (abonnieren auch) to subscribe to. **sich** (dat) **etw ~** to order sth; **das Material ist bestellt** the material has been ordered or is on order; **wie bestellt und nicht abgeholt** (hum inf) like orphan Annie (inf).

(b) (reservieren) to book, to reserve.

(c) (ausrichten) **bestell ihm (von mir), daß ...** tell him (from me) that ...; **soll ich irgend etwas ~?** can I take a message?, can I give him/her a message?; **sie läßt ~, daß ...** she told me to tell you that ...; ~ **Sie ihm schöne Grüße von mir** give him my regards; **er hat nicht viel/nichts zu ~** he doesn't have much/any say here.

(d) (kommen lassen) jdn to send for, to summon. **jdn zu jdm/an einen Ort ~** to summon sb to sb/a place, to ask sb to go/come to sb/a place; **ich bin um** or **für 10 Uhr bestellt** I have an appointment for or at 10 o'clock; **(für) wann sind Sie beim Arzt bestellt?** when is your appointment with the doctor?

(e) (einsetzen, ernennen) to nominate, to appoint.

(f) (bearbeiten) Land to till; (old) Haus to set in order.

(g) (fig) **es ist schlecht um ihn/mit seinen Finanzen bestellt** he is/his finances are in a bad way; **damit ist es schlecht bestellt** that's rather difficult.

(h) (dated: zustellen) Post to deliver.

2 vi (in Restaurant) to order.

Besteller m -s, - customer; (Abonnent) subscriber. **Hinweise für den ~** ordering instructions, instructions on how to order.

Bestellgeld nt price including postage and packing; (für Zeitungen etc) subscription rate or charge.

Bestelliste f getrennt **Bestell-liste** order list.

Bestell-: ~**karte** f order form; ~**liste** f siehe **Bestelliste;** ~**nummer** f order number or code; ~**schein** m order form or slip.

Bestellung f siehe vt (a–c, e, f) **(a)** (Anforderung, das Angeforderte) order; (das Bestellen) ordering; subscription. **(b)** booking, reservation. **(c)** message. **(d)** nomination, appointment. **(e)** tilling.

Bestellzettel m siehe **Bestellschein.**

besten adv: **am ~** siehe **beste(r, s) 2.**

bestenfalls adv at best.

bestens adv (sehr gut) very well; (herzlich) **danken** very warmly. **sie läßt ~ grüßen** she sends her best regards.

beste(r, s) 1 adj, superl of **gut, wohl (a)** attr best. **im ~n Fall** at (the) best; **im ~n Alter, in den ~n Jahren** in the prime of (one's) life; **mit (den) ~n Grüßen/Wünschen** with best wishes; **in ~n Händen** in the best of hands; **aus ~m Hause sein** to come from the very best of homes; **das kommt in den ~n Familien vor** (hum) that can happen in the best of families.

(b) der/die/das erste or **nächste ~** the first (person/job etc) that comes along; **der first (hotel/cinema etc)** one comes to; **ich hielte es für das ~, wenn ...** I thought it (would be) best if ...; **das ~ wäre, wir ...** the best thing would be for us to ..., it would be best for us to ...; **aufs** or **auf das ~** very well; **zum ~n** for the best; **es steht nicht zum ~n** it does not look too promising or good or hopeful; **jdn zum ~n haben** or **halten** to pull sb's leg, to have sb on (inf); **etw zum ~n geben** (erzählen) to tell sth; **jdm eine Geschichte/ein Liedchen zum ~n geben** to entertain sb with a story/song.

(c) der/die/das B~ the best; **der/die B~ sein** to be the best; (in der Klasse auch) to be top (of the class); **meine B~/mein B~r!** (dated inf) (my) dear lady/my dear fellow; **zu deinem B~n für** your good; **ich will nur dein B~s** I've your best interests at heart; **sein B~s tun** to do one's best; **sein B~s geben** to give or do one's best; **wir wollen das B~ hoffen** let's hope for the best.

2 adv **am ~n** best; **ich hielt es für am ~n, wenn ...** I thought it (would be) best if ...; **am ~n würden wir gleich gehen** we'd be best to go immediately; **am ~n gehe ich jetzt** I'd or I had best go or be going now.

besternt adj (geh) star-studded, starry.

Beste(s) nt siehe **beste(r, s) 1 (c).**

besteuern* vt to tax. **Luxusartikel sind sehr hoch besteuert** there is a high tax on luxury goods, luxury goods are heavily taxed.

Besteuerung f taxation; (Steuersatz) tax.

Best-: ~**form** f (esp Sport) top or best form; **in ~form sein** to be in top form or on one's best form; **b~gehaßt** adj attr (iro) most hated.

bestialisch adj bestial; (inf) awful, beastly (inf). ~ **kalt** beastly cold; ~ **stinken** to stink to high heaven (inf); ~ **weh tun** to hurt like billy-o (inf).

Bestialität f bestiality.

besticken* vt to embroider.

Bestie [-tiə] f beast; (fig) animal.

bestimmbar adj determinable.

bestimmen* 1 vt **(a)** (festsetzen) to determine; Grenze, Ort, Zeit etc auch to fix, to set; (entscheiden auch) to decide. **sie will immer alles ~** she always wants to decide the way things are to be done.

(b) (prägen) Stadtbild, Landschaft to characterize; (beeinflussen) Preis, Anzahl to determine; Entwicklung, Werk, Stil etc to have a determining influence on; (Gram) Kasus, Tempus to determine. **näher ~** (Gram: Adverb) to qualify.

(c) (wissenschaftlich feststellen) Alter, Standort to determine, to ascertain; Pflanze, Funde to classify; (definieren) Wort, Bedeutung to define.

(d) (vorsehen) to intend, to mean (für for). **jdn zu etw ~** to choose or designate sb as sth; **er ist zu Höherem bestimmt** he is destined for higher things; **wir waren füreinander bestimmt** we were meant for each other.

(e) (veranlassen: Situation) to determine. **jdn zu etw ~** to induce sb to do sth.

2 vi **(a)** to decide (über +acc on). **du hast hier nicht zu ~** you don't make the decisions here.

(b) (verfügen) **er kann über sein Geld allein ~** it is up to him what he does with his money; **du kannst nicht über ihn/seine Zeit/sein Geld ~** it's not up to you to decide what he's going to do/how his time is to be spent/you can't spend his money for him.

3 vr **sich nach etw ~** to be determined by sth.

bestimmend adj (entscheidend) Faktor, Einfluß determining, decisive, determinant. **an etw** (dat) ~ **mitwirken** to play a determining or decisive part in sth; **für etw ~ sein** to be characteristic of sth; (entscheidend) to have a determining influence on sth.

bestimmt 1 adj **(a)** (gewiß, nicht genau genannt) Leute, Dinge, Vorstellungen, Aussagen etc certain; (speziell, genau genannt) particular, definite; (festgesetzt) Preis, Tag set, fixed; (klar, deutlich) Angaben, Ausdruck definite, precise; (Gram) Artikel, Zahlwort definite. **ich will ein ~es Buch** I want a particular or definite or certain book; **suchen Sie etwas B~es?** are you looking for anything in particular?; **den ganz ~en Eindruck gewinnen, daß ...** to get or have a definite or the distinct impression that ...

(b) (entschieden) Auftreten, Ton, Mensch firm, resolute, decisive. **höflich, aber ~** polite but firm.

2 adv **(a)** (sicher) definitely, certainly. **ich weiß ganz ~, daß ...** I know for sure or for certain that ...; **kommst du? — ja — ~?** are you coming? — yes — definitely?; **ich komme ganz ~** I'll very definitely come; **ich schaffe es ~** I'll manage it all right; **er schafft es ~ nicht** he definitely won't manage it.

(b) (wahrscheinlich) no doubt. **das hat er ~ verloren** he's bound to have lost it; **er kommt ~ wieder zu spät** he's bound to be late again.

Bestimmtheit f **(a)** (Sicherheit) certainty. **ich kann mit ~ sagen, daß ...** I can say with certainty or definitely that ...; **ich weiß aber mit ~, daß ...** but I know for sure or for certain that ...

(b) (Entschiedenheit) firmness. **in** or **mit aller ~** quite categorically.

Bestimmung f **(a)** (Vorschrift) regulation. **gesetzliche ~en** legal requirements.

(b) no pl (Zweck) purpose. **eine Brücke/Straße/Anlage ihrer ~ übergeben** to open a new bridge/road/plant officially.

(c) (Schicksal) destiny.

(d) (old: Ort) destination.

(e) (Gram) modifier.

(f) (das Bestimmen) determination, determining; (von Grenze, Zeit etc) fixing, setting; (Gram, von Preis, Anzahl) determining, determination; (von Alter, Standort) determining, determination, ascertaining, ascertainment; (von Pflanze, Funden) classification; (Definition) definition. **seine ~ zu dieser Aufgabe** choosing him for this task; **nähere ~**

(durch Adverb) qualifying, qualification.
Bestimmungs-: ~**bahnhof** *m* (station of) destination; **b~gemäß** *adj* as agreed; ~**gleichung** *f* (*Math*) conditional equation; ~**hafen** *m* (port of) destination; ~**ort** *m* (place of) destination; ~**wort** *nt* (*Gram*) modifier.
bestirnt *adj* (*poet*) starry, star-studded.
Best-: ~**leistung** *f* (*esp Sport*) best performance; **seine persönliche** ~**leistung** his personal best; ~**marke** *f* record; **b~möglich** *adj no pred* best possible; **wir haben unser** ~**mögliches getan** we did our (level) best.
Best. Nr. *abbr of* **Bestellnummer.**
bestochen *ptp of* **bestechen.**
bestocken* *vt* to stock. **der Wald ist gut bestockt** the forest is well timbered.
Bestockung *f* (*das Bestocken*) stocking; (*Bestand*) stock.
bestrafen* *vt* to punish; (*Jur*) *jdn* to sentence (*mit by*); (*Sport*) *Spieler, Foul* to penalize. **der Schiedsrichter bestrafte das Foul mit einem Elfmeter** the referee awarded *or* gave a penalty for the foul.
Bestrafung *f siehe vt* punishment; sentencing; penalization. **wir fordern eine strengere** ~ **von ...** we demand more severe punishments *or* (*Jur auch*) sentences for ...
bestrahlen* *vt* to shine on; (*beleuchten*) *Gebäude, Bühne* to light up, to illuminate; (*Med*) to give ray *or* radiation treatment *or* radiotherapy to. **er ließ sich von der Sonne** ~ he was soaking up the sun.
Bestrahlung *f* illumination; (*Med*) ray *or* radiation treatment, radiotherapy. **Pflanzen der direkten** ~ **der Sonne aussetzen** to expose plants to direct sunlight *or* directly to the sun's rays; **15** ~**en verordnen** to prescribe (a course of) 15 doses of ray treatment *etc*.
Bestrahlungslampe *f* radiation *or* ray lamp.
bestreben* *vr* (*geh*) *siehe* **bestrebt.**
Bestreben *nt* -s, *no pl* endeavour. **im** *or* **in seinem** ~, **dem Fußgänger auszuweichen** in his efforts *or* attempts *or* endeavours to avoid the pedestrian.
bestrebt *adj* ~ **sein, etw zu tun** to endeavour to do sth; **wir waren immer** ~, ... we have always endeavoured ..., it has always been our endeavour ...
Bestrebung *f usu pl* endeavour, attempt, effort.
bestreichen* *vt irreg* **(a)** to spread; (*Cook*) (*mit Milch etc*) to coat; (*mit Butter auch*) to butter; (*mit Farbe*) to paint. **etw mit Butter/Fett/Öl** ~ to butter/grease/oil sth; **etw mit Butter/Salbe/Klebstoff** ~ to spread butter/ointment/glue on sth; **etw mit Farbe** ~ to put a coat of paint on sth.
(b) (*Mil*) to rake, to sweep.
(c) (*Scheinwerfer, Strahl*) to sweep (over); (*in der Elektronik: abtasten*) to scan.
bestreiken* *vt* to black. **bestreikt** strikebound; **die Fabrik wird zur Zeit bestreikt** there's a strike on in the factory at the moment; **ein Betrieb, der noch nie bestreikt worden ist** a firm which has never yet had a strike; „**dieser Betrieb wird bestreikt**" "please do not cross the picket line".
Bestreikung *f* blacking. **die** ~ **einer Fabrik beschließen** to decide to take strike action against *or* to black a factory.
bestreitbar *adj* disputable, contestable.
bestreiten* *vt irreg* **(a)** (*abstreiten*) to dispute, to contest, to challenge; (*leugnen*) to deny. **jdm das Recht auf ...** ~ to dispute *etc* sb's right to ...; **das möchte ich nicht** ~ I'm not disputing *or* denying it.
(b) (*finanzieren*) to pay for, to finance; *Kosten* to carry, to defray (*form*).
(c) (*tragen, gestalten*) to provide for, to carry. **er hat das ganze Gespräch allein bestritten** he did all the talking.
Bestreitung *f siehe vt* **(a)** contestation, challenge; denial. **(b)** financing; carrying, defrayal (*form*).
bestrenommiert ['best-] *adj attr* most renowned.
bestreuen* *vt* to cover (*mit* with); (*Cook*) to sprinkle.
bestricken* *vt* **(a)** (*fig*) to charm, to captivate. ~**der Charme** alluring charms. **(b)** (*hum inf*) to knit things for.
Bestrickung *f* charm.
bestrumpft *adj* in stockings; *Beine* stockinged.
Bestseller ['best-] *m* -s, - best-seller.
Bestseller-: ~**autor** *m* best-selling author, best-seller; ~**liste** *f* best-seller list; (*von Schallplatten*) charts *pl*.
bestsituiert ['best-] *adj attr* (*esp Aus*) well-to-do, well-off.
bestücken* *vt* to fit, to equip; (*Mil*) to arm; *Lager* to stock. **sie ist gut bestückt** (*hum inf*) she's pretty well stacked (*inf*).
Bestückung *f* **(a)** *siehe vt* fitting, equipping, arming; stocking. **(b)** (*Ausstattung*) equipment; (*Geschütze*) guns *pl*, armaments *pl*.
Bestuhlung *f* seating *no indef art*.
bestürmen* *vt* to storm; (*mit Fragen, Bitten*) to bombard; (*mit Anfragen, Briefen, Anrufen*) to inundate. **er wurde um Autogramme bestürmt** he was besieged with requests for autographs.
Bestürmung *f siehe vt* storming; bombardment; inundation.
bestürzend *adj* alarming. **ich finde es** ~, **wie wenig die Schüler wissen** it fills me with consternation to see how little the children know.
bestürzt *adj* filled with consternation. **sie machte ein** ~**es Gesicht** a look of consternation came over her face; **sie sah mich** ~ **an** he looked at me in consternation.
Bestürzung *f* consternation.
bestußt *adj* (*sl*) *Kerl, Ausrede, Behauptung* crazy.
Best-: ~**wert** *m* (*Fin*) top value; (*Tech, Sport*) best performance; ~**zeit** *f* (*esp Sport*) best time; ~**zustand** *m* perfect condition.
Besuch *m* -(e)s, -e **(a)** (*das Besuchen*) visit (*des Museums etc*

to the museum *etc*); (*von Schule, Veranstaltung*) attendance (*gen* at). **ein** ~ (**von**) **meiner Tante** a visit from my aunt; **zu seinen Aufgaben gehört auch der** ~ **der Klienten** his jobs include visiting clients; **bei jdm auf** *or* **zu** ~ **sein** to be visiting sb; (**von jdm**) ~ **erhalten** to have *or* get a visit (from sb); **jdm einen** ~ **abstatten** to pay sb a visit.
(b) (*Besucher*) visitor; visitors *pl*. **ist dein** ~ **wieder abgefahren?** have your visitors/has your visitor gone?; **er hat** ~ he has company *or* visitors/a visitor; **er bekommt viel** ~ he has a lot of visitors, he often has visitors.
besuchen* *vt jdn* to visit, to pay a visit to; (*Arzt*) *Patienten* to visit; *Vortrag, Schule, Seminar, Gottesdienst* to attend, to go to; *Kino, Theater, Lokal* to go to; *Bordell, Museum* to go to, to visit. **du kannst mich mal am Abend/im Mondschein** ~ (*euph inf*) you know what you can do (*inf*).
Besucher(in *f*) *m* -s, - visitor; (*von Kino, Theater*) patron (*form*). **etwa 1.000** ~ **waren zu der Veranstaltung/dem Vortrag/der Ausstellung gekommen** about 1,000 people attended *or* went to the function/lecture/visited the exhibition; **ein regelmäßiger** ~ **der Oper** a regular opera-goer, an habitué of the opera; **die** ~ **werden gebeten, sich auf ihre Plätze zu begeben** would you please take your seats now; (*Theat*) the audience are requested to take their seats; **die** ~ **warten schon auf Einlaß** there are people already waiting to come/go in.
Besucher-: ~**ritze** *f* (*hum inf*) crack between the two mattresses of twin beds; ~**zahl** *f* attendance figures *pl*; (*bei Schloß, Museum, Ausstellung etc*) number of visitors.
Besuchs-: ~**erlaubnis** *f* visitor's card; (*für Land*) visitor's visa; ~**erlaubnis haben/bekommen** to be allowed to receive visitors/to obtain permission to visit sb; ~**tag** *m* visiting day; **b~weise** *adv* on a visit; ~**zeit** *f* visiting time; **jetzt ist keine** ~**zeit** it's not visiting time; ~**zimmer** *nt* visitor's room.
besucht *adj* **gut/schlecht/schwach** ~ **sein** to be well/badly/poorly attended (*Schloß etc*) to get a lot of/not many/only a handful of visitors.
besudeln* *vt* **(geh)** *Wände* to besmear; *Kleidung, Hände* to soil; (*fig*) *Andenken, Namen, Ehre* to besmirch, to sully. **2** *vr* **sich mit Blut** ~ to get blood on one's hands.
Beta *nt* -(s), -s beta.
betagt *adj* (*geh*) aged, well advanced in years.
Betagtheit *f, no pl* (*geh*) old age, advancing years *pl*.
betakeln* *vt* (*Aus: betrügen*) to swindle.
betanken* *vt Fahrzeug* to tank up; *Flugzeug* to refuel.
betasten* *vt* to feel; (*Med auch*) to palpate (*form*). **die Waren bitte nicht** ~ please do not touch.
Beta-: ~**strahlen** *pl* beta rays *pl*; ~**strahlung** *f* beta radiation; ~**teilchen** *nt* beta particle.
betätigen* **1** *vt* **(a)** (*in Betrieb setzen*) to operate, to work; *Muskeln, Gehirn, Darm* to activate; *Bremse auch* to apply, to put on; *Mechanismus auch* to activate, to actuate (*form*); *Knopf auch* to press; (*drehen*) to turn; *Schalter auch* to turn on; *Hebel* to move, to operate; *Sirene* to operate, to sound.
(b) (*liter: bewirken*) to bring about, to effect.
(c) (*liter: einsetzen*) to put into effect.
2 *vr* to busy oneself; (*körperlich*) to get some exercise. **sich politisch** ~ to be active in politics; **sich wissenschaftlich/literarisch/künstlerisch** ~ to do (some) scientific work/some writing/painting; **sich geistig und körperlich** ~ to stay active in body and mind; **wenn man sich längere Zeit nicht geistig betätigt hat** if you haven't used your mind for months; **wenn er sich als Köchin/Kindermädchen betätigt** when he acts as cook/nanny.
Betätigung *f* **(a)** (*Tätigkeit*) activity. **an** ~ **fehlt es mir nicht** I've no lack of things to do.
(b) *siehe vt* **(a)** operation; activation; applying, application; activation, actuation; pressing; turning; turning; moving, operation; operation, sounding. **etw zur** ~ **der Muskeln tun** to do sth to exercise one's muscles; **die** ~ **des Mechanismus erfolgt durch Knopfdruck** pressing the button activates the mechanism *or* sets the mechanism in motion.
Betätigungs-: ~**drang** *m* need for activity; ~**feld** *nt* sphere *or* field of activity.
Betatron *nt* -s, -e betatron.
betatschen* *vt* (*inf*) to paw (*inf*).
betäuben* *vt* (*unempfindlich machen*) *Körperteil* to (be)numb, to deaden; *Nerv, Schmerzen* to deaden; *Schmerzen* to kill; (*durch Narkose*) to anaesthetize; (*mit einem Schlag*) to stun, to daze; (*fig*) *Kummer, Gewissen* to ease; (*fig: benommen machen*) to stun. **er versuchte, seinen Kummer mit Alkohol zu** ~ he tried to drown his sorrows with alcohol; ~**der Lärm** deafening noise; **ein** ~**der Duft an overpowering smell; der Duft betäubte mich fast** I was almost overcome by the smell.
Betäubung *f* **(a)** *siehe vt* (be)numbing, deadening; deadening; killing; anaesthetization; stunning, dazing; easing; stunning. **(b)** (*Narkose*) anaesthetic. **örtliche** *or* **lokale** ~ local anaesthetic.
Betäubungsmittel *nt* anaesthetic.
betaut *adj* dewy, bedewed.
Bet-: ~**bank** *f* kneeler; ~**bruder** *m* (*pej inf*) churchy type, holy Joe (*pej inf*).
Bete *f* -, (*rare*) -n beet. **rote** ~ beetroot.
beteilen* *vt* (*Aus*) to give presents to; *Flüchtlinge etc* to give gifts to. **jdn mit etw** ~ to give sb sth.
beteiligen* **1** *vt* **jdn an etw** (*dat*) ~ to let sb take part in sth, to involve sb in sth; (*finanziell*) to give sb a share in sth.
2 *vr* to take part, to participate (*an* + *dat* in); (*finanziell*) to have a share (*an* + *dat* in). **sich an den Unkosten** ~ to contribute to the expenses; **ich möchte mich bei** *or* **an dem Geschenk** ~ I would like to put something towards the present.
beteiligt *adj* **an etw** (*dat*) ~ **sein/werden** to be involved in sth, to

have a part in sth; *(finanziell)* to have a share in sth; *am Gewinn auch* to have a slice of sth; **an einem Unfall/einer Schlägerei ~ sein** to be involved in an accident/a fight; **an einer Tat/Sache ~ sein** to be party to a deed/cause; **er war an dem Gelingen der Aktion maßgeblich ~** he made a major contribution to the success of the campaign; **er ist an dem Geschäft (mit 500.000 Mark) ~** he has a (500,000-mark) share in the business.

Beteiligte(r) *mf decl as adj* person involved; *(Teilhaber)* partner; *(Jur)* party. **die an der Diskussion ~n** those taking part in *or* involved in the discussion; **die am Unfall ~n** those involved in the accident; **an alle ~n** to all concerned.

Beteiligung *f, no pl* **(a)** *(Teilnahme)* *(an + dat* in) participation; *(finanziell)* share; *(an Unfall)* involvement. **(b)** *(das Beteiligen)* involvement *(an + dat* in). **die ~ der Arbeiter am Gewinn** giving the workers a share in the profits.

Beteilung *f (Aus)* giving. **die ~ der Armen mit ...** the giving of ... to the poor.

Betel *m -s, no pl* betel.

Betelnuß *f* betel nut.

beten 1 *vi* to pray *(um, für* for, *zu* to), to say one's prayers; *(bei Tisch)* to say grace. **2** *vt* to say.

Beter(in *f)* *m -s, -* prayer.

beteuern* *vt* to declare, to aver, to asseverate *(liter)*; *Unschuld auch* to protest, to affirm. **er beteuerte mir seine Liebe** he declared his love to me, he professed his love for me.

Beteuerung *f siehe vt* declaration, averment, asseveration *(liter)*; protestation.

Beteuerungsformel *f* solemn declaration.

betexten* *vt Bild* to write a caption for; *Lied* to write the words or lyric(s) for.

Bet-: **~glocke** *f* church bell; **er hörte die ~glocke läuten** he heard the church bell ringing for prayer; **~haus** *nt* temple.

betiteln* *vt* to entitle; *(anreden)* jdn to address as, to call; *(beschimpfen)* to call. **die Sendung ist betitelt ...** the broadcast is entitled ...; **wie ist das Buch betitelt?** what is the book called?, what's the book's title?; **er betitelte seinen Beitrag ...** he called his article *or* gave his article the title ... *or* entitled his article ...

Betitelung *f* **(a)** *no pl (das Betiteln)* **eine andere ~ des Films wäre besser** it would be better to call the film something else *or* to find a different title for the film.

(b) *(Titel)* title; *(Anrede)* form of address; *(Benennung)* name. **ich verbitte mir eine solche ~** I refuse to be called names like that.

Beton [be'tɔŋ, be'tõ:, *esp Aus*] be'tɔːn] *m -s, (rare) -s* concrete.

Beton- in *cpds* concrete; **~bau** *m* **(a)** concrete building *or* structure; **(b)** *no pl (Bauweise)* concrete construction; **~decke** *f* concrete ceiling; *(von Straße)* concrete surface.

betonen* *vt* **(a)** *(hervorheben)* to emphasize; *Hüften, Augen auch* to accentuate; *(Gewicht legen auf auch)* to stress. **ich möchte noch einmal ~, daß ...** I want to stress *or* emphasize once again that ...; *siehe auch* **betont.**

(b) *(Ling, Mus: einen Akzent legen auf)* to stress; *(Tonfall gebrauchen)* to intonate *(form)*. **ein Wort falsch ~** to give a word the wrong stress, to stress a word wrongly; **du mußt den Satz anders ~** you must stress the sentence differently; *(mit Tonfall)* you must say the sentence with a different intonation.

betonieren* **1** *vt* **(a)** to concrete. **betoniert** concrete. **(b)** *(fig: festlegen)* to firm up. **2** *vi* **(a)** to concrete. **(b)** *(Sport sl)* to block the goal (area).

Betonierung *f (das Betonieren)* concreting; *(Betondecke auch)* concrete surface.

Beton-: **~klotz** *m (lit)* block of concrete, concrete block; *(fig pej)* concrete block; **~mischmaschine** *f* concrete-mixer; **~silo** *m (pej inf)* high-rise block, concrete block *(pej)*.

betont **1** *ptp of* **betonen.** **2** *adj* Höflichkeit emphatic, deliberate; *Kühle, Sachlichkeit* pointed; *Eleganz* pronounced. **sich ~ einfach kleiden** to dress with marked *or* pronounced simplicity.

Betonung *f* **(a)** *no pl siehe vt* emphasis; accentuation; stressing; intonation. **(b)** *(Akzent)* stress; *(fig: Gewicht)* emphasis, stress, accent. **die ~ liegt auf der ersten Silbe** the stress is on the first syllable; **er legte die ~ auf selbständiges Arbeiten** he laid great emphasis *or* stress on independent work.

Betonungszeichen *nt* stress mark.

Betonwüste *f (pej)* concrete jungle.

betören* *vt* to bewitch, to beguile.

Betörer(in *f)* *m -s, - (geh)* bewitcher, beguiler.

Betörung *f* bewitchment.

Betpult *nt* prie-dieu, kneeler.

Betr. *abbr of* Betreff, betrifft.

betr. *abbr of* betreffend, betrifft, betreffs.

Betracht *m -(e)s, no pl* **(a)** **außer ~ bleiben** to be left out of consideration, to be disregarded; **etw außer ~ lassen** to leave sth out of consideration, to disregard sth; **in ~ kommen** to be considered; **nicht in ~ kommen** to be out of the question; **jdn in ~ ziehen** to take sb into consideration, to consider sb; **etw in ~ ziehen** to take sth into account *or* consideration.

(b) *(dated: Hinsicht)* **in diesem ~** in this respect; **in gewissem ~** in certain respects.

betrachten* *vt* **(a)** *(sehen, beurteilen)* to look at; *Verhältnisse, Situation etc auch* to view. **sich** *(dat)* **etw ~** to have a look at sth; **bei näherem B~** on closer examination.

(b) *(halten für)* **als jd** *or* **jdn/etw ~** to regard *or* look upon *or* consider as sb/sth; **ich betrachte ihn als Freund** I regard *etc* him as a friend.

Betrachter *m -s, - (von Anblick)* beholder *(liter)*; *(von Situation)* observer. **der aufmerksame ~ wird bei diesem Bild festgestellt haben ...** to the alert eye it will have become apparent that in this picture ...

beträchtlich *adj* considerable. **um ein ~es** considerably.

Betrachtung *f* **(a)** *(das Betrachten)* contemplation. **bei näherer ~** on closer examination, when you look more closely; **eine neuartige ~ des Problems** a new way of looking at the problem.

(b) *(Überlegung, Untersuchung)* reflection. **über etw** *(acc)* **~en anstellen** to reflect on *or* contemplate sth; **in ~en versunken** lost in thought *or* meditation.

Betrachtungsweise *f* **verschiedene ~n der Lage** different ways of looking at the situation; **er hat eine völlig andere ~** he has a completely different way of looking at things.

Betrag *m -(e)s, -̈e* amount, sum. **der gesamte ~** the total (amount); **~ dankend erhalten** (payment) received with thanks.

betragen *pret* **betrug,** *ptp* **~ 1** *vi* to come; *(Kosten, Rechnung auch)* to amount to. **die Entfernung betrug 25 km** the distance was 25 km; **der Unterschied beträgt 100 DM** the difference is *or* amounts to 100 DM.

2 *vr* to behave. **sich gut/schlecht/unhöflich ~** to behave (oneself) well/badly/to behave impolitely.

Betragen *nt -s, no pl* behaviour; *(esp im Zeugnis)* conduct.

Betragensnote *f* mark for conduct.

betrauen* *vt* **jdn mit etw ~** to entrust sb with sth; **jdn damit ~, etw zu tun** to give sb the task of doing sth; **jdn mit einem öffentlichen Amt ~** to appoint sb to public office.

betrauern* *vt* to mourn; **jdn auch** to mourn for.

beträufeln* *vt* **den Fisch mit Zitrone ~** to squeeze lemon juice over the fish; **die Wunde mit der Lösung ~** to put drops of the solution on the wound.

Betrauung *f* entrustment, entrusting. **die ~ meines Rechtsanwalts mit dieser Angelegenheit** the entrustment *or* entrusting of the matter to my lawyer.

Betreff *m -(e)s, -e (form)* **~: Ihr Schreiben vom ...** re your letter of ...; **den ~ angeben** to state the reference *or* subject matter; **in ~ dieser Frage** with respect *or* regard to this question; **in diesem ~** *(old)* in this regard *(old)* *or* respect.

betreffen* *vt irreg* **(a)** *(angehen)* to concern. **das betrifft dich** it concerns you; **von dieser Regelung werde ich nicht betroffen** this rule does not concern *or* affect me; **was mich betrifft ...** as far as I'm concerned ...; **was das betrifft ...** as far as that goes *or* is concerned ...; **betrifft re;** *siehe auch* **betreffend, betroffen.**

(b) *(geh: widerfahren)* to befall.

(c) *(geh: seelisch treffen)* to affect, to touch. **jdn schwer ~** to affect sb deeply; *siehe auch* **betroffen.**

(d) *(rare: ertappen)* to catch.

betreffend *adj attr (erwähnt)* in question; *(zuständig, für etw relevant)* relevant. **das ~e Wort richtig einsetzen** to insert the appropriate word in the right place; **ich habe den ~en Artikel gelesen** I've read the article concerned *or* in question; **alle (mein Fach) ~en Artikel** all the articles relevant to my subject, all the relevant articles.

Betreffende(r) *mf decl as adj* person concerned. **die ~n** those concerned.

betreffs *prep + gen (form)* concerning, re *(esp Comm)*.

betreiben* *vt irreg* **(a)** *(vorantreiben)* to push ahead *or* forward; *Geschäft, Untersuchung, Angelegenheit auch* to prosecute. **auf jds B~** *(acc)* **hin** at sb's instigation.

(b) *(ausüben)* Gewerbe, Handwerk to carry on; *Geschäft auch* to conduct; *Handel auch, Sport* to do; *Studium, Politik* to pursue.

(c) *(Tech)* to operate.

(d) *(Sw)* to obtain a writ of account against.

Betreibung *f siehe vt* **(b)** carrying on; conduct; pursuit. **bei der ~ einer Klage** in the pursuit of a legal action.

betreßt *adj* braided.

betreten¹* *vt irreg (hineingehen in)* to enter, to go/come into; *(auf .w treten)* Rasen, Spielfeld etc to walk on; *feuchten Zementboden* to step *or* walk on; *Bühne, Brücke* to walk *or* step onto; *Podium* to step (up) onto; *(fig)* Zeitalter etc to enter. **wir ~ damit ein noch unerforschtes Gebiet** we are here entering unknown *or* unexplored territory; **„B~ (des Rasens) verboten!"** "keep off (the grass)"; **„B~ für Unbefugte verboten"** "no entry to unauthorized persons".

betreten² *adj* embarrassed.

Betretenheit *f* embarrassment.

betreuen* *vt* to look after; *Reisegruppe, Abteilung auch* to be in charge of ...

Betreuer(in *f)* *m -s, -* person who is in charge of *or* looking after sb; *(Kinder~)* child-minder; *(von alten Leuten, Kranken)* nurse. **wir suchen noch ~ für ...** we are still looking for people to look after *or* take charge of ...; **der medizinische ~ der Nationalelf** the doctor who looks after the international team.

Betreuung *f* looking after; *(von Patienten, Tieren etc)* care. **er wurde mit der ~ der Gruppe beauftragt** he was put in charge of the group, the group was put in his care.

Betrieb *m -(e)s, -e* **(a)** *(Firma)* business, concern; *(DDR auch)* enterprise; *(Fabrik)* factory, works sing *or* pl; *(Arbeitsstelle)* place of work. **wir kommen um 5 Uhr aus dem ~** we leave work at 5 o'clock; **ich esse im ~** I have lunch at work; **der Direktor ist heute nicht im ~** the director isn't at work *or* in (the office) today.

(b) *(Tätigkeit)* work; *(von Maschine, Fabrik)* working, operation; *(von Eisenbahn)* running; *(von Bergwerk)* working. **den ~ stören** to be disruptive, to cause disruption; **er hält den ganzen ~ auf** he's holding everything up; **der ganze ~ stand still** everything stopped *or* came to a stop; **außer ~** out of order; **die Maschinen sind in ~** the machines are running; **eine Maschine in/außer ~ setzen** to start a machine up/to stop a machine; **eine Fabrik außer ~ setzen** to put a factory out of operation; **eine Maschine/Fabrik in ~ nehmen** to put a machine/factory into operation, to start operating a machine/in a factory; **einen Bus in ~ nehmen** to put a bus into service; **etw dem ~ übergeben** to open sth.

(c) (*Betriebsamkeit*) bustle. **in den Geschäften herrscht großer ~** the shops are very busy; **auf den Straßen ist noch kein ~** there is nobody about in the streets yet; **bei dem ~ soll sich ein Mensch konzentrieren können!** how can anybody concentrate with all that (bustle) going on?

(d) (*inf*) **ich habe den ganzen ~ satt!** I'm fed up with the whole business! (*inf*); **ich schmeiß den ganzen ~ hin!** I'm going to chuck it all up! (*inf*), I'm going to chuck the whole business in (*inf*).

betrieblich *adj attr* internal company *attr*; *Nutzungsdauer etc* operational. **eine Sache ~ regeln** to settle a matter within the company.

Betriebs- in *cpds* (*Fabrik-*) factory, works; (*Firmen-*) company.

betriebsam *adj* busy, bustling *no adv.* **seine Assistenten huschten ~ herum** his assistants bustled around.

Betriebsamkeit *f* bustle; (*von Mensch*) active nature. **wegen der ständigen ~ meiner Mutter ...** because my mother is a very busy or active person ...

Betriebs-: ~**angehörige(r)** *mf* employee; ~**anleitung** *f* operating instructions *pl*; ~**begehung** *f* (*DDR*) round of inspection; **b~bereit** *adj* operational; **b~blind** *adj* blind to the shortcomings of one's company; ~**blindheit** *f* organizational blindness or myopia; **b~eigen** *adj* company *attr*, (*DDR*) employees' *attr*; ~**ergebnis** *nt* (*DDR*) annual figures *pl*; **b~fähig** *adj* in working condition, operational; ~**ferien** *pl* (annual) holiday; **wegen ~ferien geschlossen** closed for holidays; **b~fremd** *adj* outside; **b~fremde Personen** non-company employees; ~**frieden** *m* industrial peace; ~**führung** *f* management; ~**geheimnis** *nt* trade secret; ~**gemeinschaft** *f* staff and management *pl*; ~**gewerkschaftsleitung** *f* (*DDR*) company trade union committee; (*in Industrie*) works trade union committee; ~**ingenieur** *m* production engineer; **b~intern** *adj* internal company *attr*; **etw b~intern regeln** to settle sth within the company; ~**kampfgruppe** *f* (*DDR*) workers' militia branch; ~**kapital** *nt* (*laufendes Kapital*) working capital; (*Anfangskapital*) initial capital; ~**klima** *nt* atmosphere at work, working atmosphere; ~**kollektivvertrag** *m* (*DDR*) union agreement; ~**kosten** *pl* (*von Firma etc*) overheads *pl*, overhead expenses *pl*; (*von Maschine*) running costs *pl*; ~**leiter** *m* (works or factory) manager; ~**leitung** *f* management; ~**mittel** *nt siehe* **Produktionsmittel**; ~**nudel** *f* (*inf*) live wire (*inf*) (*Frau auch*) busy Lizzie (*inf*); (*Witzbold*) office/club *etc* clown; ~**prüfung** *f* (government) audit; ~**psychologie** *f* industrial psychology; ~**rat** *m* (a) (*Gremium*) works or factory committee; (b) (*inf: Person*) works or factory committee member; ~**ruhe** *f* shutdown; ~**schluß** *m* (*von Firma*) end of business hours; (*von Fabrik*) end of factory hours; **nach ~schluß** after business/factory hours; **was macht der Durchschnittsbürger nach ~schluß?** what does the average citizen do after work?; ~**schutz** *m* (*von Anlagen*) factory or works security; (*Arbeitsschutz*) industrial safety; **b~sicher** *adj* safe (to operate); ~**sicherheit** *f* (a) (operational) safety; (b) (*von Betrieb*) factory or works security; ~**soziologie** *f* industrial sociology; ~**stockung** *f* hold-up (in production); ~**stoff** *m* (a) (*Treibstoff etc*) fuel; (b) (*Rohstoff*) raw or working materials *pl*; ~**störung** *f* breakdown; ~**treue** *f* faithful service to the company; ~**unfall** *m* industrial accident; (*hum sl*) accident; ~**verfassung** *f* regulations governing industrial relations; ~**versammlung** *f* company meeting; ~**wirt** *m* management expert; ~**wirtschaft** *f* business management; **b~wirtschaftlich** *adj* business management *attr.*

betrinken* *vr irreg* to get drunk; *siehe* **betrunken.**

betroffen 1 *ptp of* **betreffen.** 2 *adj* (a) affected (*von* by). (b) (*bestürzt*) full of consternation; *Schweigen* embarrassed, awkward. **jdn ~ ansehen** to look at sb in consternation.

Betroffene(r) *mf decl as adj* person affected. **schließlich sind wir die ~n** after all we are the ones who are affected or on the receiving end (*inf*).

Betroffenheit *f* consternation. **stumme ~** embarrassed or awkward silence.

betrog *pret of* **betrügen.**

betrogen *ptp of* **betrügen.**

betrüben* 1 *vt* to sadden, to distress. **es betrübt mich sehr ...** it grieves or saddens me greatly ... 2 *vr* (*dated, hum*) to grieve (*über* + *acc* over). **da muß ich mich aber sehr ~** it grieves or saddens me more than somewhat; *siehe* **betrübt.**

betrüblich *adj* sad, distressing; *Zustände, Unwissenheit, Unfähigkeit* deplorable. **die Lage sieht ~ aus** things look bad.

betrüblicherweise *adv* lamentably.

Betrübnis *f* (*geh*) grief, sadness *no pl*, distress *no pl.* ~**se** sorrows.

betrübt 1 *ptp of* **betrüben.** 2 *adj* saddened, distressed.

Betrübtheit *f* sadness, distress, grief.

betrug *pret of* **betragen.**

Betrug *m* -(e)s, *no pl* deceit, deception; (*Jur*) fraud. **das ist ja (alles) ~** it's (all) a cheat or fraud; **das ist ja ~, du hast geguckt!** that's cheating, you looked!; *siehe* **fromm.**

betrügen *pret* **betrog,** *ptp* **betrogen** 1 *vt* to deceive; (*geschäftlich auch*) to cheat; *Freund(in), Ehepartner auch* to be unfaithful to, to cheat (on); (*Jur*) to defraud. **wenn ich ihr untreu werden sollte, hieße das sie ~** if I were unfaithful to her that would mean betraying her; **jdn um etw ~** to cheat or swindle sb out of sth; (*Jur*) to defraud sb of sth; **ich fühle mich betrogen** I feel betrayed; **sich um etw betrogen sehen** to feel deprived of or done out of sth; **ich sah mich in ihm betrogen** he disappointed me, he let me down, I was deceived in him; **sich in**

seinen Hoffnungen/seinem Vertrauen betrogen sehen to be disappointed in one's hopes/to be proved wrong in trusting sb. 2 *vr* to deceive oneself.

Betrüger(in *f*) *m* -s, - (*beim Spiel*) cheat; (*geschäftlich*) swindler; (*Jur*) defrauder; (*Hochstapler*) confidence trickster, con-man.

Betrügerei *f* deceit; (*geschäftlich*) cheating *no pl*, swindling *no pl*; (*von Ehepartner*) deceiving *no pl*; (*Jur*) fraud. **seine Frau ist nie hinter seine ~en gekommen** (*inf*) his wife never found out that he was deceiving her or being unfaithful to her.

betrügerisch *adj* deceitful; (*Jur*) fraudulent. **in ~er Absicht** with intent to defraud.

betrunken 1 *ptp of* **betrinken.** 2 *adj* drunk *no adv*, drunken *attr.* **er torkelte ~ nach Hause** he staggered home drunk; **he staggered drunkenly home; Fahren in ~em Zustand** driving while under the influence of drink or alcohol (*form*), drunken driving.

Betrunkene(r) *mf decl as adj* drunk.

Betrunkenheit *f* drunkenness.

Bet-: ~**saal** *m* (prayer) hall; (*in Gebäude*) prayer room, oratory (*form*); ~**schemel** *m siehe* ~**bank;** ~**schwester** *f* (*pej*) churchy type; ~**stuhl** *m siehe* ~**pult;** ~**stunde** *f* prayer meeting.

Bett *nt* -(e)s, -en (*alle Bedeutungen*) bed; (*Feder~*) (continental) quilt, duvet. **Frühstück ans ~** breakfast in bed; **an jds ~** (*dat*) **sitzen** to sit at sb's bedside or by sb's bed; **an jds ~** (*acc*) **gehen** to go to sb's bedside; **im ~** in bed; **jdn ins** or **zu ~ bringen** to put sb to bed; **mit jdm ins ~ gehen/steigen** (*euph*) to go to/jump into bed with sb; **mit jdm das ~ teilen** to share sb's bed; **er hat sich ins gemachte ~ gelegt** (*fig*) he had everything handed to him on a plate; *siehe* **französisch.**

Bettag ['be:tta:k] *m siehe* **Buß-** und **Bettag.**

Bett-: ~**anzug** *m* (*Sw*) *siehe* ~**bezug;** ~**bank** *f* (*Aus*) *siehe* ~**couch;** ~**bezug** *m* duvet or (continental) quilt cover; ~**couch** *f* bed settee; ~**decke** *f* blanket; (*gesteppt*) (continental) quilt, duvet; **sich unter der ~decke verstecken** to hide under the bedclothes.

Bettel *m* -s, *no pl* (a) (*obs: das Betteln*) begging.

(b) (*dial*) (*Gerümpel*) rubbish, lumber, junk. **der ganze ~** the whole rotten business; **jdm den (ganzen) ~ vor die Füße werfen** to throw the whole lot in sb's face; **er soll doch seinen ~ allein machen!** he can damn well do it by himself (*inf*)!

Bettel-: **b~arm** *adj* destitute; ~**brief** *m* begging letter; ~**bruder** *m* (a) (~*mönch*) mendicant or begging friar; (b) (*pej*) beggar, panhandler (*US inf*).

Bettelei *f* begging.

Bettel-: ~**frau** *f* (*dated*) beggarwoman (*dated*); ~**geld** *nt* (*pej*) pittance; ~**kram** *m siehe* **Bettel** (b); ~**leute** *pl* (*old*) beggars *pl*, beggary (*old*); ~**lohn** *m* (*pej*) pittance; ~**mann** *m* (*dated*) beggarman (*dated*); ~**mönch** *m* mendicant or begging monk; ~**musikant** *m* (*dated*) street musician.

betteln *vi* to beg. **um ein Almosen ~** to beg (for) alms; „**B**~ **verboten**" "no begging"; (**bei jdm**) **um etw ~** to beg (sb) for sth.

Bettel-: ~**orden** *m* mendicant order; ~**sack** *m* (a) beggar's sack; (b) (*pej: Mensch*) scrounger; ~**stab** *m*: **an den ~stab kommen** to be reduced to beggary; **jdn an den ~stab bringen** to reduce sb to beggary; ~**volk** *nt* (*pej*) beggars *pl*; ~**weib** *nt* (*old*) beggarwoman (*dated*).

betten 1 *vt* (a) (*legen*) to make a bed for, to bed down; *Unfallopfer* to lay or bed down; *Kopf* to lay. **jdn weich/flach ~** to put sb on a soft bed/to lay sb down flat; **die Patienten werden zweimal am Tag gebettet** the patients have their beds made up twice a day; **das Dorf liegt ins** or **im Tal gebettet** (*liter*) the village nestles or is nestling in the valley; *siehe* **Rose.**

(b) (*rare*) (*einlassen*) *Steine* to bed; (*einpflanzen*) to bed. 2 *vr* to make a bed for oneself, to bed oneself down. **wie man sich bettet, so liegt man** (*Prov*) as you make your bed so you must lie on it (*Prov*); **sich weich ~** to sleep on a soft mattress; **er hat sich schön weich gebettet** (*mit Heirat*) he's feathered his nest very nicely; (*in Stellung*) he's got a nice cushy little number for himself (*inf*).

Bett-: ~**feder** *f* bedspring; (*Daune*) feather from a/the duvet; ~**flasche** *f* hot-water bottle; ~**genosse** *m* (*dated, iro*) bedfellow; ~**geschichte** *f* (love) affair; ~**geschichten** bedroom antics; ~**gestell** *nt* bedstead; ~**häschen** *nt*, ~**hase** *m* (*inf*) sexy piece (*inf*); **ein richtiger ~hase** a very beddable little piece (*inf*); ~**himmel** *m* canopy; ~**hupferl** *nt* -s, - (*S Ger*) late-night snack; ~**jacke** *f* bed jacket; ~**kante** *f* edge of the bed; ~**kasten** *m* ottoman; ~**lade** *f* (*S Ger, Aus*) bedstead; **b~lägerig** *adj* bedridden, confined to bed; ~**lägerigkeit** *f, no pl* confinement to bed; ~**laken** *nt* sheet; ~**lektüre** *f* bedtime reading.

Bettler(in *f*) *m* -s, - beggar, mendicant (*form*).

Bett-: ~**nachbar** *m* neighbour, person in the next bed; ~**nässen** *nt* -s, *no pl* bed-wetting; ~**nässer** *m* -s, - bed-wetter; ~**pfanne** *f* bedpan; ~**pfosten** *m* bedpost; ~**platz** *m* (*Rail*) sleeping berth; ~**rand** *m* edge of the bed; **b~reif** *adj* ready for bed; ~**rost** *m* (bed) base; ~**ruhe** *f* confinement to bed, bed rest; **der Arzt hat eine Woche ~ruhe verordnet** the doctor ordered him *etc* to stay in bed for one week; ~**schüssel** *f* bedpan; ~**schwere** *f* (*inf*) **die nötige ~schwere haben/bekommen** to be/get tired enough to sleep; ~**statt** *f*, ~**stelle** *f* bed; ~**szene** *f* bedroom scene; ~**tuch** *nt siehe* **Bettuch;** ~**überwurf** *m* bedspread, counterpane; ~**überzug** *m siehe* ~**bezug.**

Bettuch *nt getrennt:* **Bett-tuch** sheet.

Bettumrandung *f* bed surround.

Bettung *f* (*Tech*) bed(ding); (*Rail*) ballast; (*Mil: Geschütze~*) platform.

Bett-: ~**vorlage** *f* (*dial*), ~**vorleger** *m* bedside rug; ~**wanze** *f* bedbug; ~**wärme** *f* warmth of one's bed; ~**wäsche** *f* bed linen; ~**zeug** *nt* bedding; ~**zipfel** *m* corner of the bed cover; **nach dem ~zipfel schielen** (*hum*) to be longing for one's bed; **der**

~**zipfel winkt** (hum) it's time for bed.
betucht adj (inf) well-to-do.
betulich adj (a) (übertrieben besorgt) fussing attr; Redeweise twee. **sei doch nicht so** ~ don't be such an old mother hen (inf). (b) (beschaulich) leisurely no adv.
Betulichkeit f siehe adj (a) fussing nature; tweeness. (b) leisureliness.
betun* vr irreg (inf) (a) (sich zieren) to make a song and dance (inf). (b) (übertrieben besorgt sein) to make a fuss, to fuss about.
betupfen* vt to dab; (Med) to swab.
betuppen* vt (dial inf) to cheat, to trick.
betütern* (N Ger inf) 1 vt to mollycoddle. 2 vr to get tipsy.
betütert adj (N Ger inf) (betrunken) tipsy; (verwirrt) dazed.
beugbar adj (Gram) Substantiv, Adjektiv etc declinable; Verb conjugable.
Beuge f -, -n bend; (von Arm auch) crook; (Rumpf~) forward bend; (seitlich) sideways bend; (Knie~) knee-bend. **in die** ~ **gehen** to bend.
Beugehaft f (Jur) coercive detention.
Beugel m -s, - (Aus) croissant.
Beuge-: ~**mann** m (hum) bow; ~**muskel** m flexor.
beugen 1 vt (a) (krümmen) to bend; (Phys) Wellen to diffract; Strahlen, Licht to deflect; (fig) Stolz, Starrsinn to break. **das Recht** ~ to pervert the course of justice; **vom Alter gebeugt** bent or bowed by age; **von der Last gebeugt** bowed down with the weight; **von Kummer/Gram gebeugt** bowed down with grief/sorrow; siehe auch **gebeugt**.
(b) (Gram) Substantiv, Adjektiv etc to decline; Verb to conjugate. **ein stark/schwach gebeugtes Substantiv/Verb** a strong/weak noun/verb.
2 vr to bend; (fig) to submit, to bow (dat to). **sich nach vorn** ~ to bend or lean forward; **sich aus dem Fenster** ~ to lean out of the window; **er beugte sich zu mir herüber** he leant across to me; **über seine Bücher/seinen Teller gebeugt** hunched over his books/his plate; **sich der Mehrheit** ~ to bow or submit to the will of the majority.
Beuger m -s, - (Anat) flexor.
Beugestellung f bent position.
Beugung f siehe vt (a) (Krümmung) bending; diffraction; deflection; breaking. **eine** ~ **des Rechts** a perversion of (the course of) justice. (b) (Gram) declension; conjugation.
Beule f -, -n (von Stoß etc) bump; (eiternd) boil; (Delle) dent.
beulen vi to bag.
Beulenpest f bubonic plague.
be|unruhigen* 1 vt to worry; (Nachricht etc auch) to disquiet, to disturb; (Mil) to harass. **über etw** (acc) **beunruhigt sein** to be worried or disturbed about sth; **es ist** ~**d** it's worrying or disturbing, it gives cause for concern. 2 vr to worry (oneself) (über +acc, um, wegen about).
Be|unruhigung f concern, disquiet; (Mil) harassment.
be|urkunden* vt (a) to certify; Vertrag to record; Geschäft to document. (b) (old: bezeugen) Gefühle, Gesinnung, Haltung to give evidence of.
Be|urkundung f (a) siehe vt (a) certification; recording; documentation. (b) (Dokument) documentary proof or evidence no indef art no pl.
be|urlauben* 1 vt to give or grant leave (of absence); (Univ) Studenten to give time off; Lehrpersonal auch to give or grant sabbatical leave; (von Pflichten befreien) to excuse (von from). **beurlaubt sein** to be on leave, to have leave of absence; to have time off; to be on sabbatical leave; (suspendiert sein) to have been relieved of one's duties; **sich** ~ **lassen** to take leave (of absence)/time off/sabbatical leave.
2 vr (dated: sich zurückziehen) to excuse oneself.
Be|urlaubung f siehe vt (gen to) granting of leave (of absence); giving time off; granting of sabbatical leave; (Beurlaubtsein) leave (of absence); time off; sabbatical leave. **seine** ~ **vom Dienst** (Befreiung) his being excused (from) his duties; (Suspendierung) his being relieved of his duties.
be|urteilen* vt to judge (nach by, from); Leistung, Wert to assess; Buch, Bild etc auch to give an opinion of. **etw richtig/falsch** ~ to judge sth correctly/to misjudge sth; **du kannst das doch gar nicht** ~ you are not in a position to judge.
Be|urteiler m -s, - judge.
Be|urteilung f (das Beurteilen) judging, judgement; assessing, assessment; (Urteil) assessment; (Kritik: von Stück etc) review.
Be|urteilungsmaßstab m criterion.
Beuschel nt -s, - (Aus) (a) (dish made of offal). (b) (sl) lungs pl; (Eingeweide) entrails pl.
Beute[1] f -, no pl (a) (Kriegs~, fig hum) spoils pl, booty, loot no indef art; (Diebes~) haul, loot (inf); (von Raubtieren etc) prey; (getötete) kill; (Jagd~) bag; (beim Fischen) catch. ~ **machen** to capture booty/make a haul/kill/get a bag/catch; **ohne** ~/**mit reicher** ~ (Hunt) empty-handed/with a good bag.
(b) (liter: Opfer) prey. **eine** ~ **einer Sache** (gen) **sein/werden** to have fallen (a) prey to/to fall prey to sth; **eine leichte** ~ **easy prey**; **jdm/einer Sache zur** ~ **fallen** (liter) to fall (a) prey to sb/sth.
Beute[2] f -, -n (Bienenkasten) (bee)hive.
beutegierig adj Tier eager for the kill, ravening attr; (fig) eager for booty or a haul.
Beutel m -s, - (a) (Behälter) bag; (Tasche) (draw-string) bag or purse; (Tragetasche) carrier bag; (Tabaks~, Zool) pouch; (dial) (Tüte) paper bag; (Päckchen) packet.
(b) (inf: Geld~) (von Frau) purse; (von Mann) wallet. **tief in den** ~ **greifen** to put one's hand in one's pocket, to dig deep into one's pocket(s); **jds** ~ **ist leer** sb has no money or is broke (inf); (von Staat etc) sb's coffers are empty; **das geht an den** ~ that

costs money!; **die Hand auf dem** ~ **haben, den** ~ **zuhalten** (dated) to be tight-fisted; siehe **Loch**.
beuteln 1 vt (a) (old) Mehl to sieve. (b) (dial) to shake; (fig) to shake about. **mich hat's gebeutelt!** (inf) (bin gefallen) I fell, I came a cropper (inf); (bin krank geworden) I've come down with it/with flu etc. 2 vi (sich bauschen) to bag.
Beutel-: ~**ratte** f opossum; ~**schneider** m (obs: Gauner) cutpurse (obs), pickpocket; (dated geh: Wucherer) swindler; ~**schneiderei** f (obs) theft, thievery (old); (geh: Nepp) swindling; ~**tier** nt marsupial.
Beute-: ~**recht** nt right of plunder; ~**stück** nt booty; ~**zug** m raid (auch fig); **auf** ~**zug durch die Geschäfte gehen** (fig) to go on a foray of the shops.
Beutler m -s, - (Zool) marsupial.
bevölkern* 1 vt (a) (bewohnen) to inhabit; (beleben) to crowd, to fill. **schwach/stark or dicht bevölkert** thinly or sparsely/densely or thickly populated; **Tausende bevölkerten den Marktplatz** the marketplace was crowded with thousands of people. (b) (besiedeln) to populate. 2 vr to become inhabited; (fig) to fill up.
Bevölkerung f (a) (die Bewohner) population. (b) no pl (das Bevölkern) peopling, populating.
Bevölkerungs-: ~**abnahme** f fall or decrease in population; ~**dichte** f density of population, population density; ~**explosion** f population explosion; ~**gruppe** f section of the population; ~**politik** f population policy; ~**schicht** f class of society, social stratum or class; ~**statistik** f population statistics pl; ~**zahl** f (total) population; ~**zunahme** f rise or increase in population.
bevollmächtigen* vt to authorize (zu etw to do sth).
Bevollmächtigte(r) mf decl as adj authorized representative; (Pol) plenipotentiary.
Bevollmächtigung f authorization (durch from).
bevor conj before. ~ **Sie** (nicht) **die Rechnung bezahlt haben** until you pay or you have paid the bill.
bevormunden* vt insep to treat like a child. **jdn** ~ to make sb's decisions (for him/her), to make up sb's mind for him/her; **ich lasse mich von niemandem** ~ I shan't let anyone make my decisions (for me) or make up my mind for me.
Bevormundung f seine Schüler/Untergebenen etc wehren sich gegen die ständige ~ his pupils/subordinates etc object to his constantly making up their minds for them; **unsere** ~ **durch den Staat** the State's making up our minds for us.
bevorraten* vt insep (form) to stock up.
bevorrechten* (old), **bevorrechtigen*** vt insep to give preference or priority to.
bevorrechtigt adj (privilegiert) privileged; (wichtig) high-priority.
Bevorrechtigung f preferential treatment no pl.
bevorschussen* vt insep (rare) to make an advance to. **jdm etw** ~ to advance sb sth.
bevorstehen vi sep irreg to be imminent; (Winter etc) to be near, to approach. **jdm** ~ to be in store for sb; **ihm steht eine Überraschung bevor** there's a surprise in store for him; **das Schlimmste steht uns noch bevor** the worst is yet or still to come; **die Prüfung stand ihm noch bevor** the exam was yet or still to come, the exam still lay ahead.
bevorstehend adj forthcoming; Gefahr, Krise imminent; Winter approaching.
bevorzugen* vt to prefer; (begünstigen) to favour, to give preference or preferential treatment to. **keines unserer Kinder wird bevorzugt** we don't give preference to any of our children; **hier wird niemand bevorzugt** there's no favouritism here.
bevorzugt 1 adj preferred; Behandlung preferential; (privilegiert) privileged. **die von mir** ~**en Bücher** the books I prefer. 2 adv **jdn** ~ **abfertigen/bedienen** etc to give sb preferential treatment; **etw** ~ **abfertigen/bedienen** etc to give sth priority.
Bevorzugung f preference (gen for); (vorrangige Behandlung) preferential treatment (bei in).
bewachen* vt to guard; (Sport) Tor to guard; Spieler to mark.
Bewacher m -s, - guard; (Sport: von Spieler) marker.
bewachsen* 1 vt irreg to grow over, to cover. 2 adj overgrown, covered (mit in).
Bewachung f guarding; (Wachmannschaft) guard; (Sport) marking. **jdn unter** ~ **halten/stellen** to keep/put sb under guard.
bewaffnen* 1 vt to arm. 2 vr (lit, fig) to arm oneself.
bewaffnet adj armed. **bis an die Zähne** ~ armed to the teeth; **mit** ~**em Auge** with a telescope etc; **mit** ~**er Hand** (geh) (with) arms at the ready; ~**e Organe** (DDR) armed forces.
Bewaffnete(r) mf decl as adj armed man/woman/person etc.
Bewaffnung f (a) no pl (das Bewaffnen) arming. **man hat die** ~ **der Polizei beschlossen** it was decided to arm the police. (b) (Waffen) weapons pl.
Bewahr|anstalt f (old) siehe **Kinderbewahranstalt**.
bewahren* vt (a) (beschützen) to protect (vor +dat from). **jdn vor etw** ~ to protect or save or preserve sb from sth; (**i or Gott**) **bewahre!** (inf) heaven or God forbid!, heaven or saints preserve us!
(b) (geh: auf~) to keep. **sich für jdn** ~ (liter) to keep oneself for sb; **jdn/etw in guter Erinnerung** ~ to have happy memories of sb/sth.
(c) (beibehalten) to keep, to retain, to preserve; Denkmal to conserve. **sich** (dat) **etw** ~ to keep or retain or preserve sth.
bewähren* 1 vt (dated) to prove.
2 vr to prove oneself/itself, to prove one's/its worth; (Methode, Plan, Investition, Sparsamkeit, Fleiß) to pay off, to prove (to be) worthwhile; (Auto, Gerät etc) to prove (to be) a

good investment. **sich im Leben**~ to make something of one's life; **wenn sich der Straftäter bewährt** if the offender proves he has reformed; **die Methode/das Gerät hat sich gut/schlecht bewährt** the method proved/didn't prove (to be) very worthwhile/the appliance proved/didn't prove (to be) a very good investment; **es bewährt sich immer, das zu tun** it's always worthwhile doing that; **ihre Freundschaft hat sich bewährt** their friendship stood the test of time; *siehe* **bewährt**.

Bewahrer *m* **-s, -** *(rare)* guardian, custodian, keeper.

bewahrheiten* *vr (Befürchtung, Hoffnung, Gerücht)* to prove (to be) well-founded; *(Prophezeiung)* to come true.

bewährt 1 *ptp of* **bewähren. 2** *adj* proven, tried and tested, reliable; *Geldanlage* worthwhile; *Rezept* tried and tested. **vielfach/seit langem** ~ tried and tested/well-established.

Bewährtheit *f, no pl* reliability.

Bewahrung *f siehe vt* **(a)** protection. **(b)** keeping. **(c)** keeping, retaining, preservation; conservation.

Bewährung *f* **(a)** *siehe vr* proving oneself/itself, proving one's/its worth; proving oneself/itself worthwhile. **bei** ~ **der Methode ...** if the method proves (to be) worthwhile ...; ~ **im Leben** making something of one's life.

(b) *(Jur)* probation. **eine Strafe zur** ~ **aussetzen** to impose a suspended sentence; **ein Jahr Gefängnis mit** ~ **a** suspended sentence of one year with probation; *siehe* **Bewährungsfrist.**

Bewährungs-: ~**auflage** *f (Jur)* probation order; ~**frist** *f (Jur)* probation(ary) period, (period of) probation; ~**heim** *nt* home for young offenders; ~**helfer** *m* probation officer; ~**hilfe** *f* probation service; ~**probe** *f* test; **etw einer** ~**probe** *(dat)* **unterziehen** to put sth to the test; **die** ~**probe bestehen** *or* **überstehen** to pass the test; ~**zeit** *f* time spent on probation.

bewalden* 1 *vt* to plant with trees, to afforest *(form)*. **2** *vr* **allmählich bewaldet sich das Gebiet** trees are gradually beginning to grow in the area.

bewaldet *adj* wooded.

Bewaldung *f (das Bewalden)* planting with trees, afforestation *(form)*; *(Baumbestand)* trees *pl*, woodlands *pl*. **spärliche/dichte** ~ few trees/dense woodlands.

bewältigen* *vt (meistern) Schwierigkeiten, Problem* to cope with; *Arbeit, Aufgabe auch, Strecke* to manage; *(überwinden) Vergangenheit, Erlebnis etc* to get over; *Schüchternheit auch* to overcome; *(erledigen, beenden)* to deal with; *(aufessen)* to manage.

Bewältigung *f siehe vt* **die** ~ **der Schwierigkeiten/der Arbeit/eines Erlebnisses** *etc* coping with the difficulties/ managing the work/getting over an experience *etc*.

bewandert *adj* experienced. **in etw** *(dat)***/auf einem Gebiet** ~ **sein** to be familiar with *or* well-versed in sth/to be experienced *or* well-versed in a field.

bewandt *adj (old)* **es ist so** ~, **daß ...** the situation *or* position is such that ...; **wie ist es damit** ~? how does the matter lie?

Bewandtnis *f* reason, explanation. **das hat** *or* **damit hat es eine andere** ~ there's another reason *or* explanation for that; **das hat** *or* **damit hat es seine eigene** ~ that's a long story; **mit der Liebe hat es seine eigene** ~ love is a strange thing; **das hat** *or* **damit hat es folgende** ~ the fact/facts of the matter is/are this/these.

bewässern* *vt* to irrigate; *(mit Sprühanlage)* to water.

Bewässerung *f siehe vt* irrigation; watering.

Bewässerungs-: ~**anlage** *f* irrigation plant; ~**graben** *m* irrigation channel, feeder; ~**kanal** *m* irrigation canal; ~**system** *nt* irrigation system.

bewegbar *adj siehe* **beweglich (a).**

bewegen¹ 1 *vt* **(a)** *(Lage verändern, regen)* to move; *Erdmassen, Möbelstück auch* to shift; *Hund, Pferd* to exercise.

(b) *(innerlich* ~*)* to move; *(beschäftigen, angehen)* to concern. **dieser Gedanke bewegt mich seit langem** this has been on my mind a long time; ~**d** moving; *siehe auch* **bewegt.**

2 *vr* **(a)** to move. **beide Reden bewegten sich in der gleichen Richtung** both speeches were along the same lines.

(b) *(Bewegung haben: Mensch)* to get some exercise; *(inf: spazierengehen)* to stretch one's legs, to take some exercise.

(c) *(fig) (variieren, schwanken)* to vary, to range *(zwischen* between*)*. **der Preis bewegt sich um die 50 Mark** the price is about 50 marks; **die Verluste** ~ **sich in den Tausenden** losses are in the thousands.

(d) *(auftreten, sich benehmen)* to behave, to act.

bewegen² ** *pret* **bewog, *ptp* **bewogen** *vt* **jdn zu etw** ~ to induce *or* persuade sb to do sth; **was hat dich dazu bewogen?** what induced you to do that?; **ich fühlte mich bewogen, etwas zu sagen** I felt I had to say something; **sich dazu** ~ **lassen, etw zu tun** to allow oneself to be persuaded to do sth.

Beweggrund *m* motive.

beweglich *adj* **(a)** *(bewegbar)* movable; *Hebel, Griff auch* mobile; *Truppe* mobile.

(b) *(wendig)* agile; *Fahrzeug* manoeuvrable; *(geistig* ~*)* agile-minded, nimble-minded; *(fig) Geist auch* nimble. **mit einem Kleinwagen ist man in der Stadt** ~**er** you're more mobile in town with a mini(car).

(c) *(dated: ergreifend)* moving.

Beweglichkeit *f, no pl siehe adj* **(a)** movability; mobility. **(b)** agility; manoeuvrability; agility *or* nimbleness of mind; nimbleness.

bewegt 1 *ptp of* **bewegen¹. 2** *adj* **(a)** *(unruhig) Wasser, See* choppy; *Zeiten, Vergangenheit, Leben* eventful; *Jugend* eventful, turbulent. **die See war stark** ~**/kaum** ~ the sea was rough/fairly calm. **(b)** *(gerührt) Stimme, Worte, Stille* emotional. ~ **sein** to be moved.

Bewegung *f* **(a)** movement; *(Hand*~ *auch)* gesture; *(Sci, Tech auch)* motion. **eine falsche** ~! one false move!; **keine** ~! freeze! *(inf)*, don't move!; **in** ~ **sein** *(Fahrzeug)* to be moving, to

be in motion; *(Menge)* to mill around; **sich in** ~ **setzen** to start moving, to begin to move; **etw in** ~ **setzen/bringen** to set sth in motion, to start sth moving; **jdn in** ~ **bringen** to get sb moving; **alle Hebel** *or* **Himmel und Hölle in** ~ **setzen** to move heaven and earth; **jdn in** ~ **halten** to keep sb moving, to keep sb on the go *(inf)*.

(b) *(körperliche* ~*)* exercise. **sich** *(dat)* ~ **verschaffen** *or* **machen** to get (some) exercise.

(c) *(Unruhe)* agitation. **in** ~ **geraten** to get into a state of agitation; **diese Nachricht ließ die ganze Stadt in** ~ **geraten** this news caused a commotion throughout the whole town *or* threw the whole town into a state of agitation.

(d) *(Ergriffenheit)* emotion. **bei jdm** ~ **bewirken** to move sb, to stir sb's emotions.

(e) *(Pol, Art etc)* movement.

Bewegungs-: ~**behandlung** *f siehe* ~**therapie;** ~**drang** *m* urge *or* impulse to be active; ~**energie** *f* kinetic energy; **b**~**fähig** *adj* mobile; ~**freiheit** *f* freedom of movement; *(fig)* freedom of action; ~**krieg** *m* mobile warfare; **b**~**los** *adj* motionless, immobile; ~**losigkeit** *f* motionlessness, immobility; ~**mangel** *m* lack of exercise; ~**nerv** *m* motor nerve; ~**spiel** *nt (Sport)* active game; ~**studie** *f* **(a)** *(Ind)* time and motion study; **(b)** *(Art)* study in movement; ~**therapie** *f (aktiv)* therapeutic exercise; *(passiv)* manipulation; ~**trieb** *m* urge *or* impulse to be active; **b**~**unfähig** *adj* unable to move; *(gehunfähig)* unable to move *or* get about; ~**unfähigkeit** *f siehe adj* inability to move; inability to move *or* get about; ~**unschärfe** *f (Phot)* camerashake; ~**zustand** *m* state of motion.

bewehren* *(old)* **1** *vt* to fortify; *(bewaffnen)* to arm. **2** *vr (auch iro)* to arm oneself.

Bewehrung *f* **(a)** *siehe vt* fortifying; arming. **(b)** *(Wehranlagen)* fortifications *pl*; *(Waffen)* arms *pl*.

beweiben* *vr (dated)* to take a wife *(dated)*, to wed *(dated)*; *(hum)* to get hitched *(inf)*.

beweibt *adj (dated)* wedded *(dated)*; *(hum)* hitched *pred (inf)*. **er kam** ~ *(hum)* he came along with a woman.

beweiden* *vt (Agr) Land* to pasture; *(Kühe)* to graze on.

beweihräuchern* *vt* to (in)cense; *(fig)* to praise to the skies. **sich (selbst)** ~ to indulge in self-adulation.

beweinen* *vt* to mourn (for), to weep for.

beweinenswert *adj (geh)* lamentable.

Beweinung *f* mourning. **die** ~ **Christi** *(Art)* the Mourning of Christ.

Beweis *m* **-es, -e** proof *(für* of*)*; *(Zeugnis)* evidence *no pl*. **als** *or* **zum** ~ as proof *or* evidence; **das ist kein** ~ **für das, was du behauptest** that doesn't prove *or* that's no proof of what you have been claiming; **ein eindeutiger** ~ clear evidence; **sein Schweigen ist ein** ~ **seines Schuldgefühls** his silence is proof *or* evidence of his feeling of guilt; **den** ~ **antreten** to offer evidence *or* proof; **einen/den** ~ **führen** to offer evidence *or* proof; **den** ~ **für etw/seiner Unschuld erbringen** to produce *or* supply evidence *or* proof of sth/one's innocence; ~ **erheben** *(Jur)* to hear *or* take evidence; **jdm einen** ~ **seiner Hochachtung geben** to give sb a token of one's respect.

Beweis-: ~**antrag** *m (Jur)* motion to take *or* hear evidence; ~**aufnahme** *f (Jur)* taking *or* hearing of evidence; **b**~**bar** *adj* provable, demonstrable, capable of being proved.

beweisen *pret* **bewies,** *ptp* **bewiesen 1** *vt* **(a)** *(nachweisen)* to prove. **was zu** ~ **war** QED, quod erat demonstrandum; **was noch zu** ~ **wäre** that remains to be seen. **(b)** *(erkennen lassen, dated: erweisen)* to show. **jdm Dank** ~ to show one's gratitude to sb. **2** *vr* to prove oneself/itself.

Beweis-: ~**erheblich** *adj* **b**~**erheblich** *adj (Jur)* evidentiary *(spec)*; ~**erhebung** *f (Jur) siehe* ~**aufnahme;** ~**führung** *f (Jur)* presentation of one's case; *(Math)* proof; *(Argumentation)* (line of) argumentation *or* reasoning; ~**gang** *m* argumentation *(in proving sth)*; ~**gegenstand** *m (esp Jur)* point at issue; ~**grund** *m* argument; ~**kette** *f* chain of proof; *(Jur auch)* chain of evidence; ~**kraft** *f* evidential value, value as evidence; **b**~**kräftig** *adj* evidential, probative *(form)*; ~**last** *f (Jur)* onus, burden of proof; ~**material** *nt* (body of) evidence; ~**mittel** *nt* evidence *no pl*; ~**not** *f (Jur)* lack of evidence; **in** ~**not sein** to be lacking evidence; ~**pflicht** *f (Jur)* onus, burden of proof; ~**stück** *nt* exhibit; ~**würdigung** *f (Jur)* assessment of the evidence.

bewenden *vt impers*: **es bei** *or* **mit etw** ~ **lassen** to be content with sth; **wir wollen es dabei** ~ **lassen** let's leave it at that.

Bewenden *nt*: **damit hatte es sein/die Angelegenheit ihr** ~ the matter rested there, that was the end of the matter.

Bewerb *m* **-(e)s, -e** *(Aus Sport) siehe* **Wettbewerb.**

bewerben* *vr irreg* to apply *(um* for, *als* for the post/job of*)*. **sich bei einer Firma** ~ to apply to a firm (for a job); **sich um jdn** ~ *(dated)* to ask for sb's hand in marriage.

Bewerber(in *f)* *m* **-s, -** applicant; *(dated: Freier)* suitor *(dated)*.

Bewerbung *f* application; *(dated: um Mädchen)* wooing *(dated)*, courting *(dated)*.

Bewerbungs-: ~**bogen** *m*, ~**formular** *nt* application form; ~**schreiben** *nt* (letter of) application; ~**unterlagen** *pl* application documents *pl*.

bewerfen* *vt irreg* **(a)** **jdn/etw mit etw** ~ to throw sth at sb/sth; **mit Steinen, Pfeilen etc auch** to pelt sb with sth; *(fig)* to hurl sth at sb/sth; **jdn/jds guten Namen mit Schmutz** *or* **Dreck** ~ to throw *or* sling mud at sb/sb's good name.

(b) *(Build)* to face, to cover; *(mit Rauhputz auch)* to roughcast; *(mit Gips auch)* to plaster; *(mit Zement auch)* to cement. **mit Kies beworfen** pebble-dashed.

bewerkstelligen* *vt* to manage; *Geschäft* to effect, to bring off. **es** ~, **daß jd etw tut** to manage *or* contrive to get sb to do sth.

Bewerkstelligung *f, no pl* managing.

bewerten* *vt* **jdn** to judge; *Gegenstand* to value, to put a value on; *Leistung auch, Schularbeit* to assess. **etw zu hoch/niedrig ~** to overvalue/undervalue sth; **jdn/etw nach einem Maßstab ~** to judge sb/measure sth against a yardstick; **etw mit der Note 5 ~** to give sb a mark of 5; **eine Arbeit mit (der Note) „gut" ~** to mark a piece of work "good", to give a "good" for a piece of work.

Bewertung *f siehe vt* judgement; valuation; assessment.

Bewertungs-: **~kriterium** *nt* criterion; **~maßstab** *m* set of criteria.

bewies *pret of* beweisen.

bewiesen *ptp of* beweisen.

bewiesenermaßen *adv* **was er sagt, ist ~ unwahr** it has been proved that *or* there is evidence to show that what he is saying is untrue; **er ist ~ ein Betrüger** he has been proved to be a fraud.

bewilligen* *vt* to allow; *Planstelle auch, Etat, Steuererhöhung etc* to approve; *Mittel, Geld, Darlehen etc auch* to grant; *Stipendium* to award. **jdm etw ~** to allow/grant/award sb sth.

Bewilligung *f siehe vt* allowing; approving, approval; granting; awarding; *(Genehmigung)* approval. **dafür brauchen Sie eine ~** you need approval for that; **die ~ für einen Kredit bekommen** to be allowed *or* granted credit.

Bewilligungs-: **~bescheid** *m* approval; **b~pflichtig** *adj* subject to approval.

bewillkommnen* *vt insep (geh)* to welcome.

Bewillkommnung *f (rare)* welcoming *no pl*, reception.

bewimpelt *adj* decked out with flags *or* bunting.

bewimpert *adj Auge* lashed; *(Zool)* ciliate(d) *(spec)*.

bewirken* *vt* (a) *(verursachen)* to cause, to bring about, to produce. **~, daß etw passiert** to cause sth to happen.
(b) *(erreichen)* to achieve. **mit so einem Auftreten kannst du bei ihm nichts ~** you won't get anywhere *or* achieve anything with him if you behave like that; **damit bewirkst du bei ihm nur das Gegenteil** that way you'll only achieve the opposite effect.

bewirten* *vt* **jdn ~** to feed sb; *(bei offiziellem Besuch etc)* to entertain sb to a meal; **wir wurden während der ganzen Zeit köstlich bewirtet** we were very well fed all the time, we were given excellent food all the time; **jdn mit Kaffee und Kuchen ~** to entertain sb to coffee and cakes; **wenn man so viele Leute zu ~ hat** if you have so many people to cater for *or* feed.

bewirtschaften* *vt* (a) *Betrieb etc* to manage, to run. **die Berghütte wird im Winter nicht/wird von Herrn und Frau X bewirtschaftet** the mountain hut is not serviced in the winter/is managed *or* run by Mr and Mrs X.
(b) *Land* to farm, to cultivate, to work.
(c) *(staatlich kontrollieren) Waren* to ration; *Devisen, Wohnraum* to control.

Bewirtschaftung *f siehe vt* (a) management, running; servicing. (b) farming, cultivation, working. (c) rationing, control.

Bewirtung *f (das Bewirten)* hospitality; *(im Hotel)* (food and) service; *(rare: Essen und Getränke)* food (and drink). **die ~ so vieler Gäste** catering for *or* feeding so many guests.

bewitzeln* *vt* to make fun of.

bewog *pret of* bewegen².

bewogen *ptp of* bewegen².

bewohnbar *adj* (a) *Gegend, Land etc* habitable. (b) *Haus, Wohnung etc* habitable, fit to live in; *(beziehbar)* habitable, ready to live in.

Bewohnbarkeit *f* habitability.

bewohnen* *vt* to live in; *Haus, Zimmer, Bau, Nest auch* to occupy; *(Volk)* to inhabit; *(Krankheit)* to be carried by. **die Höhle ist von einem Bären bewohnt** the cave is occupied *or* inhabited by a bear; **das Zimmer/das Haus war jahrelang nicht bewohnt** the room was unoccupied/the house was uninhabited *or* unoccupied for years; **die von der Schlafkrankheit bewohnte Tsetsefliege** the tsetse fly that carries sleeping sickness; *siehe auch* bewohnt.

Bewohner(in *f) m -s, -* *(von Land, Gebiet)* inhabitant; *(von Haus etc)* occupier. **dieser Vogel ist ein ~ der Wälder** this bird is a forest-dweller *or* a denizen of the forest *(liter)*.

Bewohnerschaft *f* occupants *pl*.

bewohnt *1 ptp of* bewohnen. **2** *adj Land, Gebiet* inhabited; *Haus auch* occupied.

bewölken* *vr (lit, fig)* to cloud over, to darken.

bewölkt *adj* cloudy. **~ bis bedeckt** *(Met)* cloudy, perhaps overcast.

Bewölkung *f (das Sich-Bewölken)* clouding over, darkening; *(das Bewölktsein)* cloud. **wechselnde bis zunehmende ~** *(Met)* variable amounts of cloud, becoming cloudier.

Bewölkungs-: **~auflockerung** *f* break-up of the cloud; **~zunahme** *f* increase in cloud.

bewuchern* *vt* to grow over, to cover.

Bewuchs *m, no pl* vegetation.

Bewund(e)rer(in *f) m -s, -* admirer.

bewundern* *vt* to admire *(wegen* for*)*. **~d** admiring; **ein überall bewunderter Künstler** a universally admired artist.

bewundernswert, bewundernswürdig *adj* admirable.

Bewunderung *f* admiration.

bewunderungswert, bewunderungswürdig *adj* admirable.

Bewundrer(in *f) m siehe* Bewund(e)rer(in).

Bewurf *m* (a) *(das Bewerfen) der ~ der Feinde/Mauern mit Steinen* throwing stones at the enemy/walls, pelting the enemy/walls with stones. (b) *(Build)* facing, covering; *(Rauhputz)* roughcast; *(Kies~)* pebble dash.

bewurzeln* *vr* to root, to grow roots.

bewußt 1 *adj* (a) *usu attr (Philos, Psych)* conscious.
(b) *attr (überlegt)* conscious; *Mensch* self-aware. **er führte ein sehr ~es Leben** he lived a life of total awareness.

(c) *pred* **sich** *(dat)* **einer Sache** *(gen)* **~ sein/werden** to be/become aware *or* conscious of sth, to realize sth; **etw ist jdm ~** sb is aware *or* conscious of sth; **es wurde ihm allmählich ~, daß ...** he gradually realized (that) ..., it gradually dawned on him (that) ...
(d) *attr (willentlich)* deliberate, intentional; *Lüge* deliberate.
(e) *attr (überzeugt)* convinced. **er ist ein ~er Kommunist** he is a convinced communist.
(f) *attr (bekannt, besagt)* in question; *Zeit* agreed. **die ~e Kreuzung** the crossroads in question.
2 *adv* (a) consciously; *leben* in total awareness.
(b) *(willentlich)* deliberately, intentionally.

Bewußtheit *f, no pl siehe adj (a, b, d, e)* (a) consciousness. (b) consciousness; self-awareness. (c) deliberate *or* intentional nature. (d) conviction.

Bewußt-: **b~los** *adj* (a) unconscious, senseless; **b~los werden** to lose consciousness, to become unconscious; **b~los zusammenbrechen** to fall senseless; (b) *(rare) siehe* unbewußt; **~lose(r)** *mf decl as adj* unconscious man/woman/person etc; **die ~losen** the unconscious; **~losigkeit** *f* unconsciousness; **bis zur ~losigkeit** *(inf)* ad nauseam; **b~machen** *vt sep* **jdm etw b~machen** to make sb aware *or* conscious of sth, to make sb realize sth; **sich** *(dat)* **etw b~machen** to realize sth; **sich die Gefühle anderer b~machen** to make oneself aware of other people's feelings; **das muß man sich mal b~machen** one must realize that.

Bewußtsein *nt -s, no pl* (a) *(Wissen)* awareness, consciousness. **etw kommt jdm zu(m) ~** sb becomes aware *or* conscious of sth *or* realizes sth; **jdm etw zu ~ bringen/ins ~ rufen** to make sb (fully) conscious *or* aware of sth; **etw tritt in jds** *(acc)* **~** sth occurs to sb; **das allgemeine ~** general awareness; **im ~ +gen/daß ...** in the knowledge of/that ...
(b) *(Philos, Psych, Med)* consciousness. **das ~ verlieren/wiedererlangen** to lose/regain consciousness; **bei ~ sein** to be conscious; **zu(m) ~ kommen** to regain consciousness; **bei vollem ~** fully conscious; **jdm schwindet das ~** *(geh)* sb faints *or* swoons *(liter)*.
(c) **er tat es mit (vollem)/ohne ~** he was (fully) aware/he was not aware of what he was doing.
(d) *(Anschauungen)* convictions *pl*.

Bewußtseins-: **~bildung** *f (Pol)* shaping of political ideas; **b~erweiternd** *adj* **b~erweiternde Drogen** mind-expanding drugs, drugs that heighten (one's) awareness; **~erweiterung** *f* heightening of (one's) awareness; **~inhalt** *m usu pl (Philos)* content of consciousness; **~kunst** *f (Liter)* stream-of-consciousness technique; **~lage** *f (Pol)* state of political awareness; **~lenkung** *f (Sociol)* manipulation of consciousness; **~schwelle** *f (Psych)* threshold of consciousness; **~spaltung** *f (Med, Psych)* splitting of the consciousness; **~störung** *f (Psych)* disturbance of consciousness; **~strom** *m (Liter)* stream of consciousness; **~trübung** *f (Psych)* dimming of consciousness; **b~verändernd** *adj (Psych)* **b~verändernde Drogen** drugs which alter one's (state of) awareness; **b~verändernde Erfahrungen** experiences which alter one's outlook; **das Erlebnis hatte b~verändernde Auswirkungen** the experience was to alter his/her *etc* (whole) outlook; **~veränderung** *f siehe adj* change in the state of mind; change in outlook; **(politische) ~veränderung** change in political outlook.

Bewußtwerdung *f* dawning of consciousness.

bez. *abbr of* (a) **bezahlt** paid. (b) **bezüglich** with reference to, re.

Bez. *abbr of* Bezirk.

bezahlbar *adj* payable. **das ist zwar recht teuer, aber für die meisten doch durchaus ~** although it's quite expensive most people can certainly afford it.

bezahlen* **1** *vt* (a) to pay; *Rechnung, Schuld auch* to pay off, to settle. **jdm 10 Mark ~** to pay sb 10 marks; **etw an jdn ~** to pay sb sth.
(b) *Sache, Leistung, Schaden* to pay for; *Zeche* to pay, to foot *(inf)*. **etw bezahlt bekommen** *or* **kriegen** *(inf)/***für etw nichts bezahlt bekommen** *or* **kriegen** *(inf)* to get/not to get paid for sth; **jdm etw ~** *(für jdn kaufen)* to pay for sth for sb; *(Geld geben für)* to pay sb for sth; **laß mal, ich bezahl' das** it's OK, I'll pay for that *or* I'll get that; **er hat seinen Fehler mit seinem Leben bezahlt** he paid for his mistake with his life; ... **das bezahlt bekäme** *(inf)* like mad *or* crazy *(inf)*, like hell *(sl)*; **Liebe ist nicht mit Geld zu ~** money can't buy love, love cannot be bought.
2 *vi* to pay. **Herr Ober, ~ bitte!** waiter, the bill *or* check *(esp US)* please!

bezahlt *adj* paid. **sich ~ machen** to be worth it, to pay off.

Bezahlung *f* (a) *siehe vt* payment; paying off, settlement; paying for *(einer Sache (gen))* sth. (b) *(Lohn, Gehalt)* pay; *(für Dienste)* payment. **ohne/gegen/für ~** without/for/for payment.

bezähmen* **1** *vt* (a) *(fig geh) Begierden, Leidenschaften* to master, to control, to curb. (b) *(lit obs) siehe* zähmen. **2** *vr* to control *or* restrain oneself.

bezastert *adj (sl)* loaded *(inf)*, rolling in money *or* it *(inf)*.

bezaubern* **1** *vt (fig)* to charm, to captivate. **2** *vi* to be bewitching *or* captivating.

bezaubernd *adj* enchanting, charming.

Bezauberung *f* bewitchment, captivation; *(Entzücken)* enchantment, delight.

bezechen* *vr* to get drunk.

bezecht *(inf) adj* drunk. **völlig ~** dead drunk *(inf)*.

bezeichnen* *vt* (a) *(kennzeichnen) (durch, mit* by) to mark; *Takt, Tonart* to indicate.
(b) *(genau beschreiben)* to describe. **er bezeichnete uns den Weg** he described the way to us.

(c) *(benennen)* to call, to describe. **ich weiß nicht, wie man das bezeichnet** I don't know what that's called; **das würde ich schlicht als eine Unverschämtheit ~** I would describe that as *or* call that sheer effrontery; **so kann man es natürlich auch ~** of course, you can call it that *or* describe it that way too; **jd/etw wird mit dem Wort ... bezeichnet** sb/sth is described by the word ..., the word ... describes sb/sth; **jdn/etw als Betrüger/Betrug ~** to describe sb/sth as a swindler/swindle, to call sb/sth a swindler/swindle; **er bezeichnet sich gern als Künstler** he likes to call himself an artist.

(d) *(bedeuten)* to mean, to denote.

(e) *(geh: typisch sein für)* to epitomize.

bezeichnend *adj (für of)* characteristic, typical. **es ist ~ für ihre Unfähigkeit, daß ... (ist ein Beweis für)** it's indicative of her incompetence that ...

bezeichnenderweise *adv* typically (enough). **die Regierung hat ~ die Wahlversprechen wieder nicht eingehalten** typically (enough), the government hasn't kept its election promises again.

Bezeichnung *f* **(a)** *siehe vt (a, b)* marking, indication; description. **(b)** *(Ausdruck)* expression, term.

Bezeichnungslehre *f (Ling) siehe* **Onomasiologie**.

bezeigen* *(geh)* **1** *vt* **(a) jdm etw ~** to show sth to sb. **(b)** *(rare) siehe* **zeigen**. **2** *vr* **sich dankbar** *etc* **~** to show one's gratitude *etc*.

bezeugen* *vt* **(a)** *(Sache)* to attest; *(Person auch)* to testify to. **~, daß ...** to attest the fact that ...; to testify that ... **(b)** *(geh)* **jdm etw ~** to show sb sth.

Bezeugung *f* attestation. **urkundliche ~** documentary proof *or* evidence.

bezichtigen* *vt* to accuse. **jdn einer Sache** *(gen)* **~** to accuse sb of sth, to charge sb with sth; **jdn ~, etw getan zu haben** to accuse sb of having done sth.

Bezichtigung *f* accusation, charge.

beziehbar *adj* **(a)** *(bezugsfertig) Wohnung etc* ready to move into. **(b)** *(erhältlich) Waren etc* obtainable. **(c)** relatable, referable. **das ist auf einen Vorfall in seiner Jugend ~** that can be related to an incident in his youth.

beziehen *pret* **bezog**, *ptp* **bezogen** **1** *vt* **(a)** *(überziehen) Polster, Regenschirm* to (re)cover; *Bettdecke, Kissen* to put a cover on; *(mit Saiten) Geige etc* to string. **die Betten frisch ~** to put clean sheets on *or* to change the beds.

(b) *(einziehen in) Wohnung* to move into.

(c) *(esp Mil: einnehmen) Posten, Position, Stellung* to take up; *(old) Universität* to enter, to go up to; *(fig) Standpunkt* to take up, to adopt. **ein Lager ~** to encamp; **Wache ~** to mount guard, to go on guard.

(d) *(sich beschaffen)* to get, to obtain; *Zeitungen etc* to take, to get.

(e) *(erhalten)* to get, to receive; *Einkommen, Rente auch* to draw; *Prügel etc* to get.

(f) *(in Beziehung setzen)* **etw auf jdn/etw ~** to apply sth to sb/sth; **warum bezieht er (bloß) immer alles auf sich?** why does he always take everything personally?; *siehe* **bezogen**.

(g) *(Sw: einfordern) Steuern* to collect.

2 *vr* **(a)** *(sich bedecken) (Himmel)* to cloud over, to darken. **(b)** *(betreffen)* **sich auf jdn/etw ~** to refer to sb/sth; **diese Bemerkung bezog sich nicht auf dich/auf den gestrigen Vorfall** this remark wasn't meant to refer to you *or* wasn't intended for you/wasn't meant to refer to what happened yesterday.

(c) *(sich berufen)* **sich ~ auf** *(+acc)* to refer to.

beziehentlich *prep +gen (form) siehe* **bezüglich**.

Bezieher(in *f)* *m* **-s, -** *(von Zeitung)* regular reader; *(Abonnent, von Aktien)* subscriber; *(von Waren)* purchaser; *(von Einkommen, Rente)* drawer.

Beziehung *f* **(a)** *(Verhältnis)* relationship; *(Philos, Math)* relation.

(b) *usu pl (Kontakt)* relations *pl.* **diplomatische ~en aufnehmen/abbrechen** to establish/break off diplomatic relations; **intime ~en zu jdm haben** to have intimate relations with sb; **menschliche ~en** human relations *or* intercourse.

(c) *(Zusammenhang)* connection *(zu* with), relation. **etw zu etw in ~ setzen** to relate sth to sth; **zwischen den beiden Dingen besteht keinerlei ~** there is absolutely no connection between the two (things), the two (things) are totally unconnected *or* unrelated; **etw hat keine ~ zu etw** sth has no bearing on sth *or* no relationship to sth; **ich habe die ~ zum Leben verloren** I've lost my grip on life; **jd verliert die ~ zur Wirklichkeit** sb feels cut off from reality.

(d) *usu pl (Verbindung)* connections *pl (zu* with). **er hat die Stelle durch ~en bekommen** he got the post through his connections *or* through knowing the right people; **seine ~en spielen lassen** to pull strings; **~en muß/müßte man haben** you need to know the right people, you need to be able to pull strings.

(e) *(Sympathie) (zu etw)* feeling *(zu* for); *(zu jdm)* affinity *(zu* for), rapport *(zu* with). **ich habe keine ~ zu abstrakter Malerei** I have no feeling for abstract art, abstract painting doesn't do anything for me; **er hat überhaupt keine ~ zu seinen Kindern** he just doesn't relate to his children, he has no affinity for his children.

(f) *(Bezug) siehe* **Bezug (g)**.

(g) *(Hinsicht)* **in einer/keiner ~** in one/no respect *or* way; **in jeder ~** in every respect, in all respects; **in mancher ~** in some *or* certain respects; **in dieser ~** in this respect.

Beziehungs-: **b~los** *adj* unrelated, unconnected; **~losigkeit** *f* unrelatedness, unconnectedness; **b~reich** *adj* having many associations; **b~voll** *adj* suggestive; **~wahn** *m (Psych)* paranoia.

beziehungsweise *conj* **(a)** *(oder aber)* or.

(b) *(im anderen Fall)* and ... respectively. **zwei Briefmarken, die 50 ~ 70 Pfennig kosten** two stamps costing 50 and 70 Pfennig respectively; **geben Sie in Ihrer Bestellung rot ~ blau als gewünschte Farbe an** state your choice of colour in your order: red or blue.

(c) *(genauer gesagt)* or rather, or that is to say.

Beziehungswort *nt (Gram)* antecedent.

beziffern* **1** *vt* **(a)** *(mit Ziffern versehen)* to number; *Baß* to figure.

(b) *(angeben)* to estimate *(auf +acc, mit* at). **man bezifferte den Schaden auf 750.000 Mark** the damage was estimated at *or* was put at 750,000 marks.

2 *vr* **sich ~ auf** *(+acc) (Verluste, Schaden, Gewinn)* to amount to, to come to; *(Teilnehmer, Besucher)* to number.

beziffert *adj (Mus) Baß* figured.

Bezifferung *f* **(a)** *(das Beziffern)* numbering; *(Mus)* figuring. **(b)** *(Zahlen)* numbers *pl*, figures *pl.*

Bezirk *m* **-(e)s, -e (a)** *(Gebiet)* district; *(fig: Bereich)* sphere, realm. **(b)** *(Verwaltungseinheit) (Stadt)* = district; *(von Land)* = region. **(c)** *(DDR inf: Bezirksdienststelle)* local government office.

Bezirks-: **~arzt** *m* district medical officer; **~beamte(r)** *m* local government officer; **~gericht** *nt* **(a)** *(DDR)* state court; **(b)** *(Aus, Sw)* district court; **~hauptmann** *m (Aus)* chief officer of local government; **~kabinett** *nt (DDR)* cabinet of a/the Bezirkstag; **~karte** *f (Rail)* season ticket; **~klasse** *f (Sport)* regional division; **~leiter** *m (DDR)* chief administration officer, chief officer of the state administration; **~liga** *f (Sport)* regional league; **~regierung** *f* regional administration; **~richter** *m* judge at a/the Bezirksgericht; **~spital** *nt (esp Sw)* district hospital; **~stadt** *f* = county town; **~tag** *m (DDR)* state parliament *(operating at regional level).*

bezirzen* *vt siehe* **becircen**.

bezog *pret of* **beziehen**.

bezogen **1** *ptp of* **beziehen**. **2** *adj* **auf jdn/etw ~** referring to sb/sth.

Bezogene(r) *mf decl as adj (Fin) (von Scheck)* drawee; *(von Wechsel)* acceptor.

bezug *siehe* **Bezug (h)**.

Bezug *m* **-(e)s, ⸚e** **(a)** *(Überzug) (für Kissen, Polster etc)* cover; *(für Kopfkissen)* pillow-case, pillow-slip.

(b) *(Bespannung)* strings *pl.*

(c) *(Erwerb) (von Waren etc)* buying, purchase; *(von Zeitung)* taking. **der ~ der diversen Magazine kostet uns ...** the various magazines we take cost (us) ...; **beim regelmäßigen ~ der Zeitung ...** if you take the newspaper on a regular basis ...

(d) *(Erhalt) (von Einkommen, Rente etc)* drawing.

(e) **~e** *pl (Einkünfte)* income, earnings *pl;* **~e aus Nebenerwerb** income *or* earnings from secondary sources.

(f) *(Zusammenhang) siehe* **Beziehung (c)**.

(g) *(form: Berufung)* reference. **~ nehmen auf** *(+acc)* to refer to, to make reference to; **~ nehmend auf** *(+acc)* referring to, with reference to; **mit** *or* **unter ~ auf** *(+acc)* with reference to.

(h) *(Hinsicht)* **in b~ auf** *(+acc)* regarding, with regard to, concerning; **in b~ darauf** regarding that.

Bezüger(in *f)* *m* **-s, -** *(Sw)* **(a)** *siehe* **Bezieher(in)**. **(b)** *(von Steuern)* collector.

bezüglich **1** *prep +gen (form)* regarding, with regard to, concerning, re *(Comm).* **2** *adj (sich beziehend)* **das ~e Fürwort** *(Gram)* the relative pronoun; **auf etw** *(acc)* **~** relating to sth; **alle darauf ~en Fragen** all questions relating to that.

Bezüglichkeit *f* relationship *(zu* to).

Bezugnahme *f* **-, -n** *(form)* reference. **unter ~ auf** *(+acc)* with reference to.

Bezugs-: **~bedingungen** *pl (von Zeitschriften)* terms of delivery *or* subscription; *(bei Katalogbestellungen etc)* conditions of purchase; **b~berechtigt** *adj* entitled to draw; **~berechtigte(r)** *mf (von Rente etc)* authorized drawer; *(von Versicherung)* beneficiary; **b~bereit, b~fertig** *adj Haus etc* ready to move into, ready for occupation.

Bezugschein *m siehe* **Bezugsschein**.

Bezugs-: **~person** *f* **die wichtigste ~person des Kleinkindes** the person to whom the small child relates most closely; **wenn die Großmutter die einzige ~person des Kindes** *or* **für das Kind ist** when the grandmother is the only person to whom the child relates; **der Professor für Geschichte war seine ~person** the history professor was the only person to whom he related; **~preis** *m (von Zeitungsabonnement etc)* subscription charge; **~punkt** *m (lit, fig)* point of reference; **~quelle** *f* source of supply; **~recht** *nt (Fin)* option (on a new share issue), subscription right; **~rechte erwerben/verkaufen** to acquire an/sell one's option on new share issues; **wieviel ~rechte haben Sie bekommen?** how many share issues did you get an option on?; **ich behalte zwei ~rechte** I'm keeping the *or* my option on two share issues; **~satz** *m (Gram) siehe* **Relativsatz**; **~schein** *m (ration)* coupon; **etw auf** *or* **durch ~schein bekommen** to get sth on coupons; **b~scheinpflichtig** *adj* rationed, available only on coupons; **~system** *nt* frame of reference; *(Statistics)* reference system; **~(wort)satz** *m siehe* **Relativsatz**.

bezuschussen* *vt* to subsidize.

Bezuschussung *f* subsidizing; *(Betrag)* subsidy.

bezwecken* *vt* to aim at; *(Regelung, Maßnahme auch)* to have as its object. **etw mit etw ~** *(Mensch)* to intend sth by sth; **bezweckt doch gar nichts** that doesn't get one/you anywhere (at all); **was soll das ~?** what's the point of that?

bezweifeln* *vt* to doubt, to question, to have one's doubts about. **das ist nicht zu ~** that's unquestionable *or* beyond question; **~, daß ...** to doubt that ..., to question whether ...

bezwingbar *adj siehe vt* conquerable; defeatable; beatable;

that can be conquered/defeated/overcome/beaten *etc*.
bezwingen* *irreg* **1** *vt* to conquer; *Feind auch* to defeat, to overcome, to vanquish (*liter*); (*Sport*) to beat, to defeat; *Festung* to capture; *Zorn, Gefühle* to master, to overcome; *Berg* to conquer, to vanquish (*liter*); *Strecke* to do. **2** *vr* to overcome *or* master one's emotions/desires *etc*.
bezwingend *adj* compelling.
Bezwinger(in *f)* *m* -s, - (*von Berg, Feind*) conqueror, vanquisher (*liter*); (*Sport*) winner (*gen* over); (*von Festung, Burg*) captor.
Bezwingung *f siehe* *vt* conquering, conquest; defeat(ing), overcoming; vanquishing (*liter*); beating, defeat(ing); capture, capturing; mastering, overcoming; conquering, vanquishing (*liter*).
Bf. *abbr of* **Bahnhof; Brief.**
BGB ['be:ge:'be:] *nt* -, *no pl abbr of* **Bürgerliches Gesetzbuch.**
BGBl ['be:ge:be:'ɛl] *nt* -, *no pl abbr of* **Bundesgesetzblatt.**
BGH [be:ge:'ha:] *m* -s *abbr of* **Bundesgerichtshof.**
BGS [be:ge:'|ɛs] *m* - *abbr of* **Bundesgrenzschutz.**
BH [be:'ha:] *m* -(s), -(s) *abbr of* **Büstenhalter** bra.
Bhf. *abbr of* **Bahnhof.**
bi [bi:] *adj pred* (*sl*) ac/dc (*sl*), bi (*sl*).
bi- *pref* bi-.
Bias *nt* -, - (*form*) bias.
Biathlon *nt* -s, -s (*Sport*) biathlon.
bibbern *vi* (*inf*) (*vor Angst*) to tremble, to shake; (*vor Kälte*) to shiver. **um jdn/etw ~** to fear for sb/sth.
Bibel *f* -, -n (*lit*) Bible; (*fig*) bible.
Bibel|auslegung *f* interpretation of the Bible.
Bibeleskäs(e) *m* (*dial*) *siehe* **Quark.**
Bibel-: **b~fest** *adj* well versed in the Bible; **~forscher** *m* (*dated*) Jehovah's witness; **~gesellschaft** *f* Bible Society; **~glaube(n)** *m* fundamentalism; **b~gläubig** *adj* fundamentalist(ic); **~sprache** *f* biblical language; **~spruch** *m* biblical saying, quotation from the Bible; **~stelle** *f* passage or text from the Bible; **~stunde** *f* Bible study *no pl*; **~text** *m* text of the Bible; (*Auszug*) text *or* passage from the Bible; **~vers** *m* verse from/of the Bible; **~wort** *nt*, *pl* **~worte** biblical saying.
Biber *m* -s, - (a) (*Tier, Pelz, Tuch*) beaver. (b) *auch nt* (*Tuch*) flannelette. (c) (*inf*) (*Vollbart*) full beard; (*Mensch*) man with a beard, bearded man.
Biber-: **~bau** *m*, *pl* **~baue**, **~burg** *f* beaver's lodge; **~geil** *nt* -(e)s, *no pl* castor(eum); **~pelz** *m* beaver (fur); **~schwanz** *m* (a) beaver's tail; (b) (*Build: Dachziegel*) flat tile, plain tile; **~tuch** *nt* flannelette.
Biblio-: **~graph(in** *f)* *m* bibliographer; **~graphie** *f* bibliography; **b~graphieren*** *insep* **1** *vt* (a) (*verzeichnen*) to record in a/the bibliography; (b) (*einordnen*) to take (the) bibliographical details of; **2** *vi* to take bibliographical details; **die Bibliothek ist geschlossen, weil b~graphiert wird** the library is closed for bibliographical work; **b~graphisch** *adj* bibliographic(al); **~man** *m* -s, -n bibliomaniac; **~manie** *f* bibliomania; **b~manisch** *adj* bibliomaniac(al) (*form*); **b~phil** *adj* *Mensch* bibliophilic (*form*), bibliophil(e) (*form*), book-loving *attr*; *Ausgabe* for bibliophil(e)s or book-lovers; **~phile(r)** *mf decl as adj* book-lover, lover of books, bibliophil(e); **~philie** *f* love of books, bibliophily (*form*).
Bibliothek *f* -, -en library.
Bibliothekar(in *f)* *m* librarian.
bibliothekarisch *adj* library attr. **~e Ausbildung** training in librarianship *or* as a librarian; **sich ~ betätigen** to work as a librarian.
Bibliotheks-: **~katalog** *m* library catalogue; **~kunde** *f* librarianship; **b~kundlich** *adj* library attr; **b~kundlich ausgebildet** trained in librarianship *or* as a librarian; **~lehre** *f* (practical aspects of) librarianship; **~wesen** *nt*, *no pl* libraries *pl*; (*als Fach*) librarianship; **~wissenschaft** *f* librarianship.
biblisch *adj* biblical. **ein ~es Alter** a great age, a ripe old age.
Bickbeere *f* (*N Ger*) *siehe* **Heidelbeere.**
Bidet [bi'de:] *nt* -s, -s bidet.
Bidonville [bidõ'vil] *nt* -s, -s (*geh*) slums *pl*; (*aus Wellblech etc*) shantytown.
bieder *adj* (a) (*rechtschaffen*) honest; *Mensch, Leben auch* upright. (b) (*pej*) conventional, conservative; *Miene* worthy (*iro*).
Biederkeit *f siehe adj* (a) honesty; uprightness. (b) conventionality, conservatism, conservativeness; worthiness.
Bieder-: **~mann** *m*, *pl* **~männer** (a) (*dated, iro*) honest man; (b) (*pej geh*) petty bourgeois; **b~männisch** *adj* (a) (*dated*) honest; **in b~männischen Kreisen ist das nicht üblich** honest people don't do that; (b) (*pej geh*) petty bourgeois; *Geschmack, Gesinnung auch* philistine.
Biedermeier *nt* -s, *no pl* Biedermeier period.
Biedermeier- *in cpds* Biedermeier; **~sträußchen** *nt* posy (with paper frill).
Bieder-: **~miene** *f* (*geh*) worthy air; **~sinn** *m* (*geh*) (a) (*dated*) honest mentality; (b) (*pej*) middle-class *or* petty-bourgeois mentality; **b~sinnig** (*geh*) *adj* (a) (*dated*) honest, upright; (b) (*pej*) petty bourgeois, middle-class.
biegbar *adj* *Lampenarm, Metall etc* flexible; *Material auch* pliable.
Biege *f* -, -n (*dial*) bend, curve. **eine ~ drehen/fahren/fliegen** (*inf*) to go for a walk/a short ride *or* a spin (*inf*)/a short flight *or* a spin (*inf*).
Biegefestigkeit *f* (*Tech*) bending strength.
biegen *pret* **bog**, *ptp* **gebogen 1** *vt* (a) to bend; *Glieder auch* to flex; (*fig: manipulieren*) to wangle (*inf*). **das Recht ~** (*fig dated*) to bend the law; **auf B~ oder Brechen** (*pej inf*) by hook or by

crook (*inf*), come hell or high water (*inf*); **es geht auf B~ oder Brechen** (*inf*) it's do or die; *siehe* **gebogen.**
(b) (*Aus Gram: flektieren*) to inflect.
2 *vi aux sein* (*Mensch, Wagen*) to turn; (*Weg, Straße auch*) to curve. **der Fahrer bog zur Seite** the driver turned; (*als Ausweichmanöver*) the driver pulled over to one side.
3 *vr* to bend; (*sich verziehen*) (*Schallplatte, Holz*) to warp; (*Metall*) to buckle. **seine Nase biegt sich leicht nach oben** his nose turns up slightly *or* is slightly turned-up; **sich vor Lachen ~** (*fig*) to double up *or* crease up (*inf*) with laughter; **die Tafel bog sich unter der Last der Speisen** (*fig*) the table was groaning beneath the weight of the food.
biegsam *adj* flexible; *Holz auch* pliable; *Stock, Gerte auch* pliant; *Metall auch* malleable, ductile; *Glieder, Körper* supple, lithe; *Einband* limp; (*fig*) pliable, pliant.
Biegsamkeit *f siehe adj* flexibility; pliability; pliancy; malleability, ductility; suppleness, litheness; pliability, pliancy.
Biegung *f* (a) bend; (*von Weg, Fluß auch, Wirbelsäule*) curve (*gen* in). **die ~en der Straße** (the twists and) turns *or* the curves in the road; **der Fluß/die Straße macht eine ~** the river/road curves *or* bends. (b) (*Aus Gram*) inflection.
Biene *f* -, -n (a) bee. (b) (*dated sl: Mädchen*) bird (*Brit sl*), chick (*esp US sl*).
Bienen-: **b~artig** *adj* *Insekt* bee-like; (*fig*) bustling *attr*; **~beute** (*dial*) *f siehe* **~stock**; **~fleiß** *m* bustling industriousness; **b~fleißig** *adj* industrious; **~gift** *nt* bee poison; **~haltung** *f* beekeeping; **~haube** *f* bee veil(s); **~haus** *nt* apiary; **~honig** *m* real or natural honey; **~kasten** *m* (bee)hive; **~königin** *f* queen bee; **~korb** *m* (bee)hive; **~schwarm** *m* swarm (of bees); **~sprache** *f* language of bees; **~staat** *m* bee colony; **~stich** *m* (a) bee sting; (b) (*Cook*) cake coated with sugar and almonds filled with custard or cream; **~stock** *m* (bee)hive; **~wachs** *nt* beeswax; **~weide** *f* honey-producing plants *pl*; **~weisel** *m siehe* **Weisel**; **~zucht** *f* beekeeping, apiculture; **~züchter** *m* beekeeper, apiarist.
Biennale [bie'na:lə] *f* -, -n biennial film/art festival.
Bier *nt* -(e)s, -e beer. **zwei ~, bitte!** two beers, please; **zwanzig verschiedene ~e** twenty different kinds of beer, twenty different beers; **das ist mein** *etc* **~** (*fig inf*) that's my *etc* business.
Bier- *in cpds* beer; **~arsch** *m* (*sl*) fat arse (*sl*); **~bankpolitiker** *m* (*inf*) *siehe* **Stammtischpolitiker**; **~baß** *m* (*inf*) deep bass voice; **~bauch** *m* (*inf*) beer gut (*inf*), beer belly (*inf*), pot-belly; **~brauerei** *f* (*das Brauen*) (beer-)brewing; (*Betrieb*) brewery.
Bierchen *nt* (glass of) beer.
Bier-: **~deckel** *m* beer mat; **~durst** *m* (*inf*) **~durst haben** to feel like a beer; **~eifer**, **~ernst** *m* (*inf*) deadly seriousness; **~filz** *m* beer mat; **~garten** *m* beer garden; **~keller** *m* (*Lager*) beer cellar; (*Gaststätte auch*) bierkeller; **~krug** *m* tankard, beer mug; (*aus Steingut*) (beer) stein; **b** (*inf*) beer-lorry (*Brit*) or -truck (*US*) driver; **~laune** *f* (*inf*) in einer ~laune, aus einer ~laune heraus after a few beers; **~leiche** *f* (*inf*) drunk; **es lagen noch einige ~leichen herum** there were still a few drunks lying around dead to the world; **~reise** *f* (*hum*) pub-crawl; **~ruhe** *f* (*inf*) cool (*inf*); **~schinken** *m* ham sausage; **~seidel** *nt* tankard; **b~selig** *adj* *Mensch* boozed up (*inf*); **er kam in einer b~seligen Stimmung nach Hause** he came home pretty merry; **~ulk** *m* (*inf*) drunken prank; **~verlag**, **~vertrieb** *m* beer wholesaler's; **~wärmer** *m* beer-warmer; **~zeitung** *f* (*inf*) comic newspaper; **~zelt** *nt* beer tent; **~zipfel** *m* (*Univ*) badge given by a member of one fraternity to a member of another as a sign of friendship.
Biese *f* -, -n (a) (*an Hose*) braid. (b) (*Sew*) tuck; (*an Schuh*) decorative seam.
Biest *nt* -(e)s, -er (*pej inf*) (a) (*Tier*) creature; (*Insekt auch*) bug. (b) (*Mensch*) (little) wretch; (*Frau*) bitch (*sl*), cow (*sl*). **sie ist ein süßes ~** she looks a sweet little thing but she can be a bitch at times (*sl*). (c) (*Sache*) beast (of a thing) (*inf*).
Biesterei *f* (*inf*) (a) (*Gemeinheit*) horrible thing. (b) (*Anstößendes*) obscenity. **es ist eine ~** it's obscene. (c) (*Schinderei*) beast of a job (*inf*).
biestig *adj* (*inf*) beastly (*inf*), horrible.
Biet *nt* -(e)s, -e (*Sw*) area.
bieten *pret* **bot**, *ptp* **geboten 1** *vt* (a) (*anbieten*) to offer (*jdm etw* sb sth, sth to sb); (*bei Auktion*) to bid (*auf* +*acc* for); *Möglichkeit, Gelegenheit auch* to give (*jdm etw* sb sth, sth to sb). **jdm die Hand ~** to hold out one's hand to sb, to offer sb one's hand; **jdm die Hand zur Versöhnung ~** (*fig*) to hold out the olive branch to sb; **jdm den Arm ~** to offer sb one's arm; **wer bietet mehr?** will anyone offer me *etc* more?; (*bei Auktion*) any more bids?; **mehr bietet dir niemand** no-one will give *or* offer you more *or* make you a higher offer; **diese Stadt/dieser Mann hat nichts zu ~** this town/man has nothing to offer.
(b) (*geben*) to give (*jdm etw* sb sth); *Gewähr, Sicherheit, Anlaß etc auch* to provide (*etw* sth, *jdm etw* sb with sth); *Asyl* to grant (*jdm etw* sb sth).
(c) (*haben, aufweisen*) to have; *Problem, Schwierigkeit* to present. **das Hochhaus bietet fünfzig Familien Wohnung/Wohnraum für fünfzig Familien** the tower block provides accommodation/flats for fifty families; **die Gesetzgebung bietet eine Lücke** there is a loophole in the law; **seine Argumentation bietet einige schwache Punkte** his argument has *or* contains some weak points.
(d) (*zeigen, darbieten*) *Anblick, Bild* to present; *Film* to show; *Leistung* to give. **die Mannschaft bot ein hervorragendes Spiel/hervorragende Leistungen** the team played an excellent game/played marvellously; **die Mannschaft bot den Zuschauern ein hervorragendes Spiel** the team put on an excellent game for the spectators; *siehe* **Blöße, Stirn, Trotz.**
(e) (*zumuten*) **sich** (*dat*) **etw ~ lassen** to stand for sth; **so**

etwas könnte man mir nicht ~ I wouldn't stand for that sort of thing; **ist dir so etwas schon einmal geboten worden?** have you ever known the like (*inf*) or anything like it?

(f) (*geh: sagen*) **jdm einen Gruß** ~ to greet sb; **jdm einen guten Morgen** ~ to bid sb good morning (*old, liter*); *siehe* **Paroli, geboten.**

2 *vi* (*Cards*) to bid; (*bei Auktion auch*) to make a bid (*auf + acc* for).

3 *vr* (*Gelegenheit, Lösung, Anblick etc*) to present itself (*jdm* to sb). **ein grauenhaftes Schauspiel bot sich unseren Augen** a terrible scene met our eyes.

Bieter(in *f*) *m* **-s,** - bidder.
Bigamie *f* bigamy.
Bigamist(in *f*) *m* bigamist.
bigamistisch *adj* bigamous.
bigott *adj* overly pious.
Bigotterie *f* (*pej*) **(a)** *no pl* excessive piousness. **(b)** (*Handlung*) overly pious behaviour *no pl*; (*Bemerkung*) overly pious remark.
Bijouterie [biʒutəˈriː] *f* **(a)** (*Schmuck*) jewellery. **(b)** (*Sw, obs: Geschäft*) jeweller's shop.
Bikarbonat *nt* bicarbonate.
Bikini *m* **-s, -s** bikini.
bikonkav *adj* biconcave.
bikonvex *adj* biconvex.
Bilanz *f* **(a)** (*Econ, Comm: Lage*) balance; (*Abrechnung*) balance sheet. **eine ~ aufstellen** to draw up a balance sheet; **~ machen** (*fig inf*) to check one's finances. **(b)** (*fig: Ergebnis*) end result. **(die) ~ ziehen** to take stock (*aus of*).
Bilanzbuchhalter *m* accountant.
bilanzieren* *vti* to balance; (*fig*) to assess.
Bilanz-: ~**prüfer** *m* auditor; ~**summe** *f* balance.
bilateral *adj* bilateral.
Bild *nt* **-(e)s, -er** **(a)** (*lit, fig*) picture; (*Fotografie auch*) photo; (*Film*) frame; (*Art: Zeichnung*) drawing; (*Gemälde*) painting; (*Cards*) court *or* face (*US*) card, picture card (*inf*). **~ oder Wappen** heads *or* tails; **ein ~ machen** to take a photo *or* picture; **etw im ~ festhalten** to photograph/paint/draw sth as a permanent record; **sie ist ein ~ von einer Frau** she's a fine specimen of a woman; **ein ~ des Elends** a picture of misery; **~: Hans Schwarz** (*TV, Film*) camera: Hans Schwarz; *siehe* **schwach.**
(b) (*Abbild*) image; (*Spiegel~ auch*) reflection. **sie ist ganz das ~ ihrer Mutter** she is the image of her mother; **Gott schuf den Menschen ihm zum ~e** (*Bibl*) God created man in His own image.
(c) (*Anblick, Ansicht*) sight. **das äußere ~ der Stadt** the appearance of the town.
(d) (*Opt*) image.
(e) (*Theat: Szene*) scene; *siehe* **lebend.**
(f) (*Metapher*) metaphor, image. **um mit einem** *or* **im ~ zu sprechen ...** to use a metaphor ...; **etw mit einem ~ sagen** to say *or* express sth metaphorically; **im ~ bleiben** to use the same metaphor.
(g) (*Erscheinungs~*) character. **sie gehören zum ~ dieser Stadt** they are part of the scene in this town.
(h) (*fig: Vorstellung*) image, picture. **im ~e sein** to be in the picture (*über + acc* about); **jdn ins ~ setzen** to put sb in the picture (*über + acc* about); **sich** (*dat*) **von jdm/etw ein ~ machen** to get an idea of sb/sth; **du machst dir kein ~ davon, wie schwer das war** you've no idea *or* conception how hard it was; **er beschwor das ~ seiner toten Geliebten** he conjured up the image of his dead sweetheart; **das ~ des Deutschen/Juden** the image of the German/Jew.
Bild-: ~**archiv** *nt* photo archives *pl*; ~**atlas** *m* pictorial atlas; ~**ausfall** *m* (*TV*) loss of vision; ~**autor** *m* photographer; ~**band** *m* coffee-table book.
bildbar *adj* (*lit, fig*) malleable. **der Charakter des Kindes ist noch ~** the child's character can still be shaped.
Bild-: ~**beilage** *f* colour supplement; ~**bericht** *m* photographic report; ~**beschreibung** *f* (*Sch*) description of a picture.
Bildchen *nt, pl auch* **Bilderchen** *dim of* **Bild.**
Bild-: ~**dokument** *nt* photograph/painting/drawing of documentary value; ~**ebene** *f* (*Phot*) focal plane; ~**empfänger** *m* (*Tech*) picture receiver.
bilden **1** *vt* **(a)** (*formen*) to form; *Figuren etc auch* to fashion; (*fig*) *Charakter auch* to shape, to mould; *Körper, Figur* to shape. **sich** (*dat*) **ein Urteil/eine Meinung ~** to form a judgement/an opinion.
(b) (*hervorbringen, Gram*) to form. **der Magen hat ein Geschwür gebildet** an ulcer formed in the stomach, the stomach developed an ulcer; **das Seifenwasser bildet Schaum** the soapy water produces lather.
(c) (*einrichten*) *Fond, Institution etc* to set up.
(d) (*zusammenstellen*) *Kabinett, Regierung* to form; *Ausschuß, Gruppe auch* to set up; *Vermögen* to acquire.
(e) (*ausmachen*) *Höhepunkt, Regel, Ausnahme, Problem, Gefahr etc* to constitute; *Dreieck, Kreis etc* to form. **die Teile ~ ein Ganzes** the parts make up *or* form a whole; **die drei ~ ein hervorragendes Team** the three of them make (up) an excellent team.
(f) (*erziehen*) to educate.
2 *vr* **(a)** (*entstehen*) to form, to develop. **damit sich keine Vorurteile ~ ...** so that no prejudices are allowed to form ...
(b) (*lernen*) to educate oneself; (*durch Lesen etc*) to improve one's mind; (*durch Reisen etc*) to broaden one's mind.
3 *vi siehe vr* (b) to be educated; to improve the *or* one's mind; to broaden the *or* one's mind.
bildend *adj*: **die ~e Kunst** art; **die ~en Künste** the fine arts; ~**er Künstler** artist.
Bilderbogen *m* illustrated broadsheet.

Bilderbuch *nt* **(a)** picture book. **eine Landschaft/Landung wie im ~** a picturesque landscape/a textbook landing. **(b)** (*rare*) *siehe* **Bildband.**
Bilderbuch- *in cpds* (*lit*) picture-book; (*fig*) perfect; ~**autor/-verlag** author/publisher of picture-books; **eine ~landung** *f* a textbook landing.
Bilder-: ~**geschichte** *f* picture story; (*in Comic, Zeitung*) strip cartoon; (*lustig*) comic strip; ~**kult** *m* (*Rel*) image-worship, iconolatry (*form*); ~**rahmen** *m* picture-frame; ~**rätsel** *nt* picture-puzzle; **b~reich** *adj Buch etc* full of pictures; (*fig*) *Sprache* rich in imagery; **b~reich sprechen** to use a lot of images; ~**reichtum** *m* (*lit*) wealth of illustrations (*gen* in); (*fig*) wealth of imagery (*gen* in); ~**schrift** *f* pictographic writing system; ~**sprache** *f* metaphorical language; ~**streit** *m* (*Eccl Hist*) controversy over image-worship, iconographic controversy; ~**sturm** *m* (*Eccl Hist*) iconoclasm; ~**stürmer** *m* (*lit, fig*) iconoclast; **b~stürmerisch** *adj* (*lit, fig*) iconoclastic; ~**verehrung** *f siehe* ~**kult.**
Bild-: ~**fernsprecher** *m* video-phone; ~**fläche** *f* **(a)** (*Leinwand*) projection surface; (*von Photoapparat*) film plane; **(b)** (*fig inf*) **auf der ~fläche erscheinen** to appear on the scene; **von der ~fläche verschwinden** to disappear (from the scene); ~**folge** *f* sequence of pictures; (*Film*) sequence of shots; ~**frequenz** *f* filming speed; ~**funk** *m* radio photography; **b~haft** *adj* pictorial; *Beschreibung, Vorstellung, Sprache* vivid; ~**haftigkeit** *f siehe adj* pictorial nature; vividness; ~**hauer** *m* sculptor; ~**hauerei** *f* sculpture; ~**hauerin** *f* sculptress; **b~hauerisch** *adj* sculptural; ~**hauerkunst** *f* sculpture; **b~hauern** *vti insep* (*inf*) to sculpt; **b~hübsch** *adj Mädchen* (*as*) pretty as a picture; *Kleid, Garten etc* really lovely; ~**journalist** *m* photojournalist; ~**karte** *f* court *or* face (*US*) card, picture card (*inf*); ~**konserve** *f* film recording; ~**kraft** *f* (*geh*) vividness; **b~kräftig** *adj* vivid.
bildlich *adj* pictorial; *Ausdruck etc* metaphorical, figurative. **sich** (*dat*) **etw ~ vorstellen** to picture sth in one's mind's eye; **stell dir das mal ~ vor!** just picture it.
Bildlichkeit *f* (*von Sprache*) figurativeness; (*von Beschreibung*) graphicness.
Bild-: ~**material** *nt* pictures *pl*; (*für Vortrag*) visual material, photographic and film material; (*für Buch*) pictorial material; (*Sch*) visual aids *pl*; ~**mischer** *m* **-s,** - (*TV*) vision mixer.
Bildner(in *f*) *m* **-s,** - *adj* (*geh: Schöpfer*) creator. **(b)** (*dated: Erzieher*) educator.
bildnerisch *adj Begabung, Fähigkeit, Wille* artistic; *Element, Mittel, Gestaltung* visual.
Bildnis *nt* (*liter*) portrait.
Bild-: ~**platte** *f* video disc; ~**plattenspieler** *m* video disc player; ~**qualität** *f* (*TV, Film*) picture quality; (*Phot*) print quality; ~**redakteur** *m* picture editor; ~**reporter** *m* photojournalist; ~**röhre** *f* (*TV*) cathode ray tube.
bildsam *adj* (*geh*) *siehe* **bildbar.**
Bildsamkeit *f* (*geh*) malleability. **bevor die Kinder ihre ~ verlieren** while the children's characters can still be shaped.
Bild-: ~**schärfe** *f* definition *no indef art*; ~**schirm** *m* (*TV*) screen; ~**schnitzer** *m* wood-carver; ~**schnitzerei** *f* (*wood*) carving; **b~schön** *adj* beautiful; ~**seite** *f* **(a)** face, obverse (*form*); **(b)** (*von Buch*) picture page; ~**stelle** *f* educational film hire service; ~**stock** *m* **(a)** wayside shrine; **(b)** (*Typ*) block; ~**störung** *f* (*TV*) interference (on vision *or* the picture); **b~synchron** *adj* (*Film, TV*) synchronized (with the picture); ~**tafel** *f* plate; ~**telefon** *nt siehe* ~**fernsprecher;** ~**telegramm** *nt* phototelegram; ~**text** *m* caption.
Bildung *f* **(a)** (*Erziehung*) education. **zu seiner ~ macht er Abendkurse/liest er viel/reist er** he does evening classes to try and educate himself/reads to improve his mind/travels to broaden his mind; **die allgemeine ~** general education; (*eines Menschen*) one's general education; **~ haben** to be educated.
(b) *no pl* (*das Formen*) formation, forming; (*von Figuren etc auch*) fashioning; (*fig: von Charakter etc auch*) shaping. **zur ~ des Passivs** to form the passive.
(c) (*Form: von Baum, Hand etc, Ling: Wort etc*) form.
(d) *no pl* (*Entstehung: von Rost etc*) formation.
(e) *no pl* (*Einrichtung*) setting-up.
(f) *no pl* (*Zusammenstellung*) (*von Kabinett, Regierung*) formation, forming; (*von Ausschuß, Gruppe auch*) setting-up; (*von Vermögen*) acquisition.
Bildungs-: ~**anstalt** *f* (*form*) educational establishment; ~**arbeit** *f* work in the field of education; **b~beflissen** *adj* eager to improve one's mind; ~**bürger** *m* member of the educated classes; ~**bürgertum** *nt* educated classes *pl*; ~**chancen** *pl* educational opportunities *pl*; ~**drang** *m* desire for education; ~**dünkel** *m* intellectual snobbery; ~**eifer** *m* desire to be educated; **b~eifrig** *adj* keen to be educated; ~**einrichtung** *f* educational institution; (*Kulturstätte*) cultural institution; ~**erlebnis** *nt* educational experience; **b~fähig** *adj* educable; **b~feindlich** *adj* anti-education; ~**gang** *m* school (and university/college) career; ~**grad** *m* level of education; ~**gut** *nt* established part of one's general education; **das gehört zum deutschen ~gut** that is part of the German cultural heritage; ~**hunger** *m* thirst for education; **b~hungrig** *adj* thirsting for education; ~**ideal** *nt* educational ideal; ~**institut** *nt siehe* ~**einrichtung;** ~**lücke** *f* gap in one's education; ~**monopol** *nt* monopoly on education; ~**niveau** *nt* standard *or* level of education; ~**notstand** *m* chronic shortage of educational facilities; ~**planung** *f* education(al) planning *no indef art*; ~**politik** *f* education policy; ~**politiker** *m* politician with a special interest in *or* responsibility for education; **b~politisch** *adj* politico-educational; ~**reform** *f* educational reform; ~**reise** *f* educational trip *or* journey; ~**roman** *m* (*Liter*) Bildungsroman (*form*), novel concerned with the intellectual *or* spiritual development of the main character; ~**schranke** *f usu pl* educational barrier;

~**stand** m level of education, educational level; ~**stätte** f (geh) place or seat of learning; ~**streben** nt striving after education; ~**stufe** f level of education; **eine hohe/niedrige ~stufe haben** to be highly/not very educated; ~**urlaub** m educational holiday; ~**weg** m jds ~**weg** the course of sb's education; **auf dem zweiten ~weg** through night school; **einen anderen ~weg einschlagen** to opt for a different type of education; ~**wesen** nt education system.

Bild-: ~**unterschrift** f caption; ~**wand** f projection wall; ~**werfer** m projector; ~**werk** nt (geh) sculpture; (aus Holz) carving; ~**winkel** m (Opt, Phot) angle of view; ~**wörterbuch** nt pictorial or picture dictionary; ~**zuschrift** f reply enclosing photograph.

Bilge f -, -n (Naut) bilge.

bilingual [bilɪŋ'guaːl], **bilinguisch** [bi'lɪŋguɪʃ] adj (form) bilingual.

Billard ['bɪljart] nt -s, -e or (Aus) -s (a) (Spiel) billiards sing. (b) (inf: Spieltisch) billiard table.

Billard- in cpds billiard; ~**ball** m, ~**kugel** f billiard ball; ~**queue** nt or (Aus inf) m, ~**stock** m billiard cue.

Billet(t) [bɪl'jet] nt -(e)s, -e or -s (a) (Sw, dated: Fahr~, Eintrittskarte) ticket. (b) (Aus, obs: Schreiben) note; (Briefkarte) letter-card.

Billet(t)eur [bɪljɛ'tøːɐ] m (a) (Aus: Platzanweiser) usher. (b) (Sw: Schaffner) conductor.

Billet(t)eurin [bɪljɛ'tøːrɪn] f (Aus) usherette.

Billet(t)euse [bɪljɛ'tøːzə] f (Sw) conductress.

Billettsteuer f (Sw) siehe **Vergnügungssteuer**.

Billiarde f -, -n thousand billion (Brit), thousand trillion (US).

billig adj (a) (preisgünstig) cheap; Preis low; (minderwertig auch) cheapjack attr. ~ **abzugeben** going cheap; ~ **davonkommen** to get off lightly.

(b) (pej: primitiv) cheap; Trick, Masche auch shabby; Ausrede feeble. **ein ~er Trost** cold comfort.

(c) (old) (angemessen) proper, meet (old); (gerecht, berechtigt) just, fair; siehe **recht**.

Billig- in cpds cheap; **b~denkend** adj attr (old) fair-minded; **alle ~- und Gerechtdenkenden** all fair and reasonably-minded people.

billigen vt to approve. **etw stillschweigend ~** to condone sth; **~, daß jd etw tut** to approve of sb's doing sth.

billigermaßen, billigerweise adv (old) (mit Recht) rightly; (gerechterweise) by rights.

Billigkeit f siehe adj (a) cheapness; lowness. (b) cheapness; shabbiness; feebleness; cheapjack nature. (c) (old) properness, meetness (old); justness, fairness.

Billigpreis m low price.

Billigung f approval. **jds ~ finden** to meet with sb's approval.

Billion f billion (Brit), trillion (US).

bim interj ding.

bimbam interj ding-dong.

Bimbam m: **ach, du heiliger ~!** (inf) hell's bells! (inf).

Bimbim f -, -s (baby-talk) tram.

Bimetall nt (Material) bimetal; (~streifen) bimetal strip.

Bimetallismus m bimetallism.

Bimmel f -, -n (inf) bell.

Bimmelbahn f (inf) small train with a warning bell.

Bimmelei f (pej) ringing.

bimmeln vi (inf) to ring.

Bims m -es, -e siehe **Bimsstein**.

Bimse f -, no pl (inf) ~ **kriegen** to get a walloping (inf); **dann gibt's aber ~** you'll etc get a walloping (inf).

bimsen vt (inf) (a) (drillen) to drill. (b) (einüben) Vokabeln etc to swot (inf), to cram (inf); Griffe etc to practise.

Bimsstein m (a) pumice stone. (b) (Build) breezeblock.

bin 1. pers sing present of **sein**.

binar, binär, binarisch adj binary.

Binde f -, -n (a) (Med) bandage; (Schlinge) sling. (b) (Band) strip of material; (Schnur) cord; (Arm~) armband; (Augen~) blindfold. (c) (Monats~) (sanitary) towel or napkin (US). (d) (dated: Krawatte) tie. **sich** (dat) **einen hinter die ~ gießen** or **kippen** (inf) to put a few drinks away.

Binde-: ~**gewebe** nt (Anat) connective tissue; ~**glied** nt (fig) link; ~**haut** f (Anat) conjunctiva; ~**hautentzündung** f conjunctivitis; ~**mittel** nt binder.

binden pret **band**, ptp **gebunden** 1 vt (a) (zusammen~) to tie; (fest~) to bind; (fig geh) to bind, to unite. **etw zu etw** or **in etw** (acc) ~ to tie or bind sth into sth.

(b) (durch Binden herstellen) to bind; Strauß, Kranz to make up; Knoten etc to tie; Faß to hoop.

(c) (zu~) Schal to tie; Krawatte to knot. **sich** (dat) **die Schuhe ~** to tie (up) one's shoelaces.

(d) (fesseln, befestigen) (an + acc to) to tie (up); Menschen auch to bind; Ziege, Pferd auch to tether; Boot auch to moor; (fig) Menschen to bind, tie; (an einen Ort) to bind; (Versprechen, Vertrag, Eid etc) to bind. **jdn an Händen und Füßen ~** to tie or bind sb hand and foot; **jdm die Hände auf den Rücken ~** to tie sb's hands behind his back; **mir sind die Hände gebunden** (fig) my hands are tied; **nichts bindet mich an Glasgow** I have no special ties to keep me in Glasgow; **sie versuchte, ihn an sich zu ~** she tried to tie him to her; siehe **gebunden, Nase**.

(e) (festhalten) Staub, Erdreich to bind; (Chem) (aufnehmen) to absorb; (sich verbinden mit) to combine with.

(f) (zusammenhalten, Cook) Farbe, Soße to bind.

(g) (verbinden) (Poet) to bind; (fig geh auch) to unite; (Mus) Töne to slur; gleiche Note to tie. **was Gott gebunden hat, soll der Mensch nicht trennen** what God has joined together let no man put asunder.

2 vi (Mehl, Zement, Soße etc) to bind; (Klebstoff) to bond; (fig) to be tying, to tie one down; (Erlebnisse) to create a bond.

3 vr (sich verpflichten) to commit oneself (an + acc to). **ich will mich nicht ~** I don't want to get involved.

bindend adj binding (für on); Zusage definite.

Binder m -s, - (a) (Krawatte) tie. (b) (Agr) (Bindemaschine) binder; (Mähbinder) reaper-binder. (c) (Build) (Stein) header; (Balken) truss beam. (d) (Bindemittel) binder. (e) (S Ger, Aus) siehe **Böttcher**.

Binderei f (Buch~) bindery; (Blumen~) wreath and bouquet department.

Binde-s ['bɪndə'|ɛs] nt -, - (Ling) siehe **Fugen-s**.

Binde-: ~**strich** m hyphen; ~**vokal** m thematic vowel; ~**wort** nt (Gram) conjunction.

Bindfaden m string. **ein (Stück) ~** a piece of string; **es regnet ~** (inf) it's sheeting down (inf).

-bindig adj suf **dieses Element ist vier~** this element has a valency of four.

Bindigkeit f valency.

Bindung f (a) (Beziehung zu einem Partner) relationship (an + acc with); (Verbundenheit mit einem Menschen, Ort) tie, bond (an + acc with); (Verpflichtung: an Beruf etc, durch Vertrag) commitment (an + acc to). **seine enge ~ an die Heimat** his close ties with his home country.

(b) (Ski~) binding.

(c) (Chem) bond.

(d) (Tex) weave.

Binkel m -s, -(n) (Aus inf) (a) siehe **Bündel**. (b) (Dummkopf) twit (inf). (c) siehe **Beule**.

binnen prep + dat or (geh) gen (form) within. ~ **kurzem** shortly.

Binnen-: **b~bords** adv (Naut) inboard; ~**deich** m inner dyke; **b~deutsch** adj Ausdruck, Wort used in Germany; Sprache, Dialekt spoken in Germany; ~**fischerei** f freshwater fishing; ~**gewässer** nt inland water; ~**hafen** m river port; ~**handel** m domestic trade; ~**land** nt (a) (Landesinnere) interior. (b) (N Ger: eingedeichtes Gebiet) dyked land; ~**länder** m -s, - inlander; **b~ländisch** adj inland; ~**markt** m home market; ~**meer** nt (a) inland sea; (b) siehe ~**see**; ~**reim** m (Poet) internal rhyme; ~**schiffahrt** f inland navigation; ~**schiffer** m sailor on inland waterways; (auf Schleppkahn) bargeman; ~**see** m lake, continental lake (form); ~**staat** m landlocked country or state; ~**verkehr** m inland traffic; ~**währung** f internal currency; ~**wanderung** f (Sociol) internal migration; ~**wasserstraße** f inland waterway; ~**wirtschaft** f domestic economy; ~**zoll** m internal duty.

Binom nt -s, -e binomial.

binomisch adj binomial.

Binse f -, -n usu pl rush. **in die ~n gehen** (fig inf) (mißlingen) to be a wash-out (inf); (verlorengehen) to go west (inf), to go for a burton (inf); (kaputtgehen) to give out (inf).

Binsenwahrheit, Binsenweisheit f truism.

Bio f -, no pl (Sch sl) biol (sl), bio (esp US sl), bilge (hum sl).

Bio- in cpds bio-; **b~aktiv** adj Waschmittel biological; ~**chemie** f biochemistry; **b~dynamisch** adj biodynamic; ~**genese** f biogenesis; **b~genetisch** adj biogenetic.

Biograph(in f) m biographer.

Biographie f biography.

biographisch adj biographical.

Biologe m, **Biologin** f biologist.

Biologie f biology.

biologisch adj biological.

Biophysik f biophysics sing.

Biopsie f (Med) biopsy.

Bio-: ~**rhythmus** m biorhythm; **das verlangt mein ~rhythmus** my internal clock tells me it's necessary; ~**top** nt -s, -e biotope; ~**wissenschaft** f biological science.

biquadratisch adj biquadratic.

Bircher-: ~**müesli** (Sw), ~**müsli** nt muesli (with fresh fruit).

birg imper sing of **bergen**.

Birke f -, -n birch; (Baum auch) birch tree.

birken adj (rare) birch.

Birken-: ~**pilz** m boletus (scaber); ~**wald** m birch wood or forest; ~**wasser** nt hair lotion (made from birch sap).

Birk-: ~**hahn** m black cock; ~**huhn** nt black grouse.

Birma nt -s Burma.

Birmane m -n, -n, **Birmanin** f Burmese.

birmanisch adj Burmese.

Birnbaum m (Baum) pear tree; (Holz) pear-wood.

Birne f -, -n (a) pear. (b) (Glühlampe) (light) bulb. (c) (inf: Kopf) nut (inf). **eine weiche ~ haben** (sl) to be soft in the head (inf).

birnenförmig adj pear-shaped.

bis[1] adv (Mus) bis, twice.

bis[2] **1** prep + acc (a) (zeitlich) until, till; (die ganze Zeit über bis zu einem bestimmtem Zeitpunkt auch) up to, up until, up till; (bis spätestens, nicht später als) by. **das muß ~ Ende Mai warten** that will have to wait until or till the end of May; ~ **Ende Mai bin ich noch in London** I'll be in London until etc or up to etc the end of May; ~ **Ende Mai bin ich wieder in Berlin/damit fertig** I'll be in Berlin again/I'll have finished it by the end of May; ~ **5 Uhr mache ich Hausaufgaben, und dann ...** I do my homework until 5 o'clock, and then ...; ~ **5 Uhr kann ich das unmöglich machen/gemacht haben, das ist viel zu früh** I can't possibly do it/get it done by 5 o'clock, that's much too early; ~ **jetzt hat er nichts gesagt** up to now or so far he has said nothing; **das hätte eigentlich ~ jetzt fertig sein müssen** that should really have been finished by now; ~ **dato** (form) to date; ~ **anhin** (Sw) hitherto; ~ **dahin** or **dann** until etc/up to etc/by then; ~ **dahin bin ich alt und grau/ist er längst weg** I'll be old and grey by then/he will have gone long before then; ~ **wann gilt der Fahrplan/ist das fertig/können Sie das machen?** when is the timetable valid till/will that be finished by/can you do that for me by?; ~ **wann?** when till/by?, till/by when?; ~ **wann bleibt ihr hier?** how long are you staying here?, when are you staying here till?; ~ **dann!** see you then!; ~ **bald/später/morgen** *etc!* see you soon/later/tomorrow *etc!*; **von ... ~ (einschließlich)** ... from ... to *or* till *or* through (*US*) *or* thru (*US*) ...; **von ... ~ ...** (*mit Uhrzeiten*) from ... till *or* to ...; **Montag ~ Freitag** Monday to *or* thru (*US*) Friday; ~ **einschließlich** *or* (*dial*) **mit/ausschließlich 5. Mai** up to and including/but not including 5th May; ~ **spätestens Montag brauche ich das Geld** I need the money by Monday at the latest; ~ **spätestens Montag darfst du es behalten** you can keep it until Monday at the latest; **die Wäsche ist frühestens** ~ **nächsten Montag fertig** the laundry won't be ready until *or* before next Monday at the earliest *or* will be ready by next Monday at the earliest; **es dauert mindestens/höchstens** ~ **nächste Woche** it will take until *etc* next week at the very least/most; **ich kann nur (noch)** ~ **nächste Woche warten** I can only wait until *etc* next week, no longer.

(b) (*zeitlich*) to; (*in Buch, Film etc auch*) up to. **ich fahre nur** ~ **München** I'm only going to *or* as far as Munich; **ich habe das Buch nur** ~ **Seite 35 gelesen** I've only read up to *or* as far as page 35; ~ **wo/wohin ...?** where ... to?; ~ **dort/dorthin/dahin** (to) there; ~ **dorthin sind es nur 5 km** it's only 5 km there; **höchstens** ~ **dahin stimme ich mit dir überein** I would only agree with you up to that point; ~ **hierher** (*lit*) (to) here; (*fig*) this *or* so *or* thus far; ~ **hierher und nicht weiter** (*lit, fig*) this far and no further; ~ **höchstens Carlisle** to Carlisle at the furthest; ~ **mindestens Carlisle** at least to *or* as far as Carlisle; ~ **einschließlich/ausschließlich** up to and including/but not including.

(c) (*bei Alters-, Maß-, Mengen-, Temperaturangaben*) (*bis zu einer oberen Grenze von*) up to; (*bis zu einer unteren Grenze von*) to. **Kinder** ~ **sechs Jahre,** ~ **sechs Jahre alte Kinder** children up to the age of six.

2 adv (a) (*zeitlich*) until, till; (*bis spätestens*) by. ~ **zu diesem Zeitpunkt war alles ...** up to this time everything was ...; **das sollte** ~ **zum nächsten Sommer fertig sein** that should be finished by next summer; **dieser Brauch hat sich** ~ **ins 19. Jh. gehalten** this custom continued until *or* till into the 19th century; ~ **in den Sommer/die Nacht hinein** (until *or* till) into the summer/night; **er ist** ~ **gegen 5 Uhr noch da** he'll be there (up) until *or* till about 5 o'clock; ~ **gegen 5 Uhr ist das bestimmt fertig** it'll certainly be ready by about 5 o'clock; ~ **auf weiteres** until further notice.

(b) (*räumlich*) to; *durch, über, unter* right. ~ **an unser Grundstück** (right *or* up) to our plot; ~ **vor den Baum** (up) to the tree; ~ **hinter den Baum** (to) beyond the tree; **es sind noch 10 km** ~ **nach Schlüchtern** it's another 10 km to Schlüchtern; ~ **unfern** *or* **unweit** (*geh*) **des Sees** almost to the lake, to within a short distance of the lake; ~ **ins letzte/kleinste** (right) down to the last/smallest detail.

(c) (*bei Alters-, Maß-, Mengen-, Temperaturangaben*) ~ **zu** (*bis zu einer oberen Grenze von*) up to; (*bis zu einer unteren Grenze von*) (down) to; **er ist genau** ~ **zur Haarspalterei** he is exact to the point of hair-splitting; **Gefängnis** ~ **zu 8 Jahren** a maximum of 8 years' imprisonment.

(d) ~ **auf** (*+ acc*) (*außer*) except (for); (*einschließlich*) (right) down to.

3 conj (a) (*beiordnend*) to. **zehn** ~ **zwanzig Stück** ten to twenty; **bewölkt** ~ **bedeckt** cloudy or overcast.

(b) (*unterordnend: zeitlich*) until, till; (*nicht später als*) by the time. **ich warte noch,** ~ **es dunkel wird,** I'll wait until *or* till it gets dark; ~ **es dunkel wird, möchte ich zu Hause sein** I want to get home by the time it's dark; ~ **daß der Tod euch scheide(t)** (*form*) until *or* till death you do part (*form*); ~ **das einer merkt!** it'll be ages before anyone realizes (*inf*); **ich gehe nicht eher los, als** ~ **es aufgehört hat/aufhört zu regnen** I'm not going until *or* till it has stopped/stops raining; **du gehst hier nicht weg,** ~ **das (nicht) gemacht ist** you're not leaving until *or* before that's done.

(c) (*Aus inf: sobald*) when. **gleich** ~ **er kommt** the moment (*inf*) *or* as soon as he comes.

Bisam m -s, -e *or* -s (a) (*Pelz*) musquash. (b) *no pl siehe* **Moschus.**

Bisamratte f muskrat (beaver).

Bischof m -s, ⸚e bishop.

bischöflich adj episcopal.

Bischofs- in cpds episcopal; ~**amt** nt episcopate; ~**mütze** f (a) (bishop's) mitre; (b) (*Kaktus*) bishop's mitre; ~**sitz** m diocesan town; ~**stab** m crosier, (bishop's) crook.

Bisexualität f bisexuality, bisexualism.

bisexuell adj bisexual.

bisher adv until *or* till now, hitherto; (*und immer noch*) up to now; ~ **nicht** not until *or* till now, not before; (*und immer noch nicht*) not as yet; **das wußte ich** ~ **nicht** I didn't know that before; ~ **habe ich es ihm nicht gesagt** I haven't told him as yet; **ein** ~ **unbekannter Stern** a hitherto *or* previously unknown star, a star unknown until *or* till now; **alle** ~ **bekannten Sterne** all the known stars; **ich habe** ~ **schon ein paar Briefe von ihm bekommen** I've already had a few letters from him up to now *or* the present.

bisherig adj attr (*vorherig*) previous; (*momentan*) present, up to now. **der** ~**e Außenminister ist jetzt Kanzler** the previous minister for foreign affairs is now chancellor; **der** ~**e Außenminister wird jetzt Kanzler** the present minister for foreign affairs *or* the person who was minister for foreign affairs up to now will become chancellor; **wegen unserer** ~**en Arbeitsweise war das unmöglich** because of our previous way of working *or* the way we worked before that wasn't possible; **wegen unserer** ~**en Arbeitsweise ist das unmöglich** because of our present way of working *or* the way we have worked up to now

that isn't possible; **wir müssen unsere** ~**en Anschauungen revidieren** we will have to revise our present views; **das ist mir in meiner** ~**en Karriere noch nicht vorgekommen** I've never known that in my career up to now; **die** ~**en Bestimmungen gelten seit letzter Woche/ab nächster Woche nicht mehr** the regulations previously/presently in force ceased to be valid last week/cease to be valid next week.

Biskaya [bɪs'kaːja] f **die** ~ (the) Biscay; **Golf von** ~ Bay of Biscay.

Biskuit [bɪs'kviːt, bɪs'kuiːt] nt *or* m -(e)s, -s *or* -e (fatless) sponge.

Biskuit-: ~**gebäck** nt sponge cake/cakes; ~**rolle** f Swiss roll; ~**teig** m sponge mixture.

bislang adv siehe **bisher**.

Bismarckhering m Bismarck herring (*filleted pickled herring*).

Bison m -s, -e bison.

biß pret of **beißen**.

Biß m -sses, -sse bite; (*Zahnmedizin auch*) occlusion. **mit einem** ~ **war das Törtchen verschwunden** the tart disappeared in one mouthful; **der nagende** ~ **der Zeit** the ravages of time; **die Mannschaft hatte heute keinen** ~ (*sl*) the team didn't play with much punch today.

Bißchen nt dim of **Biß, Bissen.**

bißchen 1 adj inv **ein** ~ **Geld/Liebe/Wärme** a bit of *or* a little money/love/warmth; **ein** ~ **Milch/Wasser** a drop *or* bit of milk/water, a little milk/water; **ein klein** ~ ... a little bit/drop of ...; **kein** ~ ... not one (little) bit/not a drop of ...; **das** ~ **Geld/Whisky** that little bit of money/drop of whisky; **ich habe kein** ~ **Hunger** I'm not a bit hungry.

2 adv **ein** ~ a bit, a little; **ein klein** ~ a little bit; **ein** ~ **wenig** not very much; **ein** ~ **mehr/viel/teuer** *etc* a bit more/much/expensive *etc*; **ein** ~ **zu wenig** not quite enough; **ein** ~ **zu viel/teuer** *etc* a bit too much/expensive *etc*; **ein** ~ **sehr** (*inf*) a little bit too much; **ein** ~ **sehr teuer** *etc* (*inf*) a (little) bit too expensive *etc*.

3 nt inv: **ein** ~ a bit, a little; (*Flüßigkeit*) a drop, a little; **ein ganz** ~ (*inf*) just a tiny bit/drop; *siehe* **lieb.**

bissel (*dial inf*) siehe **bißchen.**

Bissen m -s, - mouthful; (*Imbiß*) bite (to eat). **er will keinen** ~ **anrühren** he won't eat a thing; **einen** ~ **zu sich nehmen** to have a bite to eat; **sich** (*dat*) **den letzten/jeden** ~ **vom** *or* **am Munde absparen** to go short onself/to watch every penny one spends; **jdm die** ~ **in den Mund zählen** (*fig*) to watch everything sb eats.

bissenweise adv mouthful by mouthful; (*fig*) bit by bit.

Bisserl (*dial*) siehe **bißchen.**

Bißgurke f (*inf*), **Bißgurn** (*Aus inf*) f -, - bad-tempered bitch (*sl*).

bissig adj (a) (*lit, fig*) vicious. ~ **sein** to bite; „**Vorsicht,** ~**er Hund**" "beware of the dog". (b) (*übellaunig*) waspish. **du brauchst nicht gleich** ~ **zu werden** there's no need to bite my *etc* head off.

Bissigkeit f siehe adj (a) viciousness; (*Bemerkung*) vicious remark. **der Hund ist wegen seiner** ~ **berüchtigt** the dog is notorious for biting people. (b) waspishness; (*Bemerkung*) waspish remark.

bissl adj, adv, nt inv (*dial*) siehe **bißchen.**

Bißwunde f bite.

bist 2. pers sing present of **sein.**

biste (*inf*) 2. pers sing present of **sein.**

Bistro nt -s, -s bistro.

Bistum ['bɪstuːm] nt diocese, bishopric.

bisweilen adv (*geh*) from time to time, now and then.

Bit nt -(s), -(s) (*Computers*) bit.

Bitt-: ~**adresse** f appeal; ~**brief** m petition.

Bitte f -, -n request; (*inständig*) plea. **auf seine** ~ **hin** at his request; **ich habe eine große** ~ **an dich** I have a (great) favour to ask you; **ich habe nur die** ~, ... I have (just) one request, ...; **sich mit einer** ~ **an jdn wenden** to make a request to sb; **er kann ihr keine** ~ **ausschlagen** he can't refuse her anything; **er gab den** ~**n der Kinder nach** he gave in to the children's pleas.

bitte interj (a) (*bittend, auffordernd*) please. ~ **schön please;** **nun hör mir doch mal** ~ **zu** listen to me please; ~ **sei so gut und ruf mich an** would you phone me, please *or* please phone me; **wo ist** ~ **das nächste Telefon?** could you please tell me where the nearest telephone is?; ~ **nicht!** no, please!, please don't!; **ja** ~**!,** ~ **ja!** yes please; ~ ~ **machen** (*inf*) (*Kind*) = to say pretty please (*inf*); (*Hund*) to (sit up and) beg; ~ **zahlen, zahlen** ~**!** (could I/we have) the bill, please; ~ **nach Ihnen!** after you.

(b) (*bei höflicher Frage, Aufforderung*) meist nicht übersetzt ~ **schön?,** ~**(, was darf es sein)?** (*in Geschäft*) can I help you?; (*in Gaststätte*) what would you like?; ~**(, Sie wünschen)?** what can I do for you?; ~ (**schön** *or* **sehr**)**(, Ihr Bier/Kaffee)!** meist nicht übersetzt your beer/coffee, here you are (*inf*); **noch etwas Tee,** ~? (would you like some) more tea?; **ja** ~? yes?; ~**(, treten Sie ein)!** come in!, come!; ~**(, nehmen Sie doch Platz)!** (*form*) please *or* do sit down; ~ **hier, hier** ~! (over) here, please; **Entschuldigung!** — ~! I'm sorry! — that's all right; ~**(, gern)!/(selbstverständlich)!** yes, certainly/of course; ~**, mit (dem größten) Vergnügen!** (*form*) with pleasure; **aber** ~! sure; **(dem größten) Vergnügen!** (*form*) with pleasure; **aber** ~! sure; ~ (*inf*), go (right) ahead (*inf*), please do; (*aber*) ~, **keineswegs!** (*form*) (no,) not at all; ~, **nur zu!** help yourself; **na** ~! there you are!

(c) (*sarkastisch: nun gut*) all right. ~, **wie du willst** (all right,) just as you like; ~, **soll er doch kommen, mir ist das egal** (all right,) let him come, it's all the same to me; ~, **wenn du es besser weißt** if you know better.

(d) (*Dank erwidernd*) you're welcome, not at all (*Brit*), sure (*US inf*). ~ **sehr** *or* **schön** you're welcome, not at all (*Brit*), ~**(, gern geschehen)** (not at all,) my pleasure; ~, **keine Ursache** it was nothing; ~, **nichts zu danken** don't mention it; **aber** ~! there's no need to thank me.

(e) *(nachfragend)* **(wie)** ~? (I beg your) pardon? *(auch iro)*, sorry; what did you say?

bitten *pret* **bat,** *ptp* **gebeten 1** *vt* (a) to ask; *(inständig)* to beg; *(Eccl)* to beseech. **jdn um etw** ~ to ask/beg/beseech sb for sth; **jdn (darum)** ~, **etw zu tun** *or* **daß er etw tut** to ask *etc* sb to do sth; **jdn etw** *(acc)* ~ *(dated)* to ask sth of sb; **darf ich Sie um Ihren Namen** ~? might I ask your name?; **um Ruhe wird gebeten** silence is requested; *(auf Schild)* silence please; **darf ich Sie um den nächsten Tanz** ~? may I have the pleasure of the next dance?; **er wollte sie um den nächsten Tanz** ~ he wanted to ask her for the next dance; **es wird gebeten, keine Fahrräder abzustellen** no bicycles (by request); **wir** ~ **dich, erhöre uns!** *(Eccl)* we beseech Thee to hear us; *(katholisch)* Lord hear us; **ich bitte dich um alles in der Welt I** beg *or* implore you; **er läßt sich gerne** ~ he likes people to keep asking him; **er läßt sich nicht (lange)** ~ you don't have to ask him twice; **aber ich bitte dich!** not at all; **ich bitte dich, wie kann man nur so dumm sein?** I ask you, how can anyone be so stupid?; **wenn ich** ~ **darf** *(form)* if you please, if you wouldn't mind; **ich bitte darum** *(form)* I'd be glad if you would, if you wouldn't mind; **(keineswegs), ich bitte sogar darum** *(form)* (not at all,) I should be glad; **darum möchte ich doch sehr gebeten haben!** *(form)* I should hope so indeed; **ich muß doch (sehr)** ~! well I must say!

(b) *(einladen)* to ask, to invite. **jdn auf ein Glas Wein** ~ to invite sb to have a glass of wine; **jdn zum Abendessen (zu sich)** ~ to ask *or* invite sb to dinner; **jdn zu Tisch** ~ to ask sb to come to table; **jdn ins Zimmer** ~ to ask *or* invite sb to come in.

(c) *(bestellen)* **jdn an einen Ort** ~ to ask sb (to come) somewhere; **jdn zu sich** ~ to ask sb to come and see one.

2 *vi* (a) to ask; *(inständig)* to plead, to beg. **um etw** ~ to ask (for) *or* request sth; **to plead** *or* **beg for sth; bei jdm um etw** ~ to ask sb for sth; ~ **und betteln** to beg and plead; **du bittest vergeblich** pleading won't help you.

(b) *(einladen)* **der Herr Professor läßt** ~ the Professor will see you now; **ich lasse** ~ he/she can come in now, would you ask him/her to come in now?; **darf ich zu Tisch** ~? lunch/dinner is served; **darf ich (um den nächsten Tanz)** ~? may I have the pleasure of the next dance?

Bitten *nt* -s, *no pl* pleading. **sich aufs** ~ **verlegen** to resort to pleas *or* pleading; **auf** ~ **von** at the request of.

bittend *adj* pleading. **mit** ~**en Augen** with a look of appeal.

bitter *adj* (a) bitter; *Schokolade* plain; *(fig) Geschmack* nasty; *siehe* **Pille.**

(b) *(fig) Enttäuschung, Erfahrung, Ironie* bitter; *Wahrheit, Lehre, Verlust* hard, painful; *Zeit, Schicksal* hard; *Ernst, Feind* deadly; *Hohn, Spott* cruel. **ein** ~**es Gefühl** a feeling of bitterness; **bis zum** ~**en Ende** to the bitter end.

(c) *(fig: verbittert)* **bitter. jdn** ~ **machen** to embitter sb, to make sb bitter; ~**e Klagen führen** to complain bitterly.

(d) *(stark) Kälte, Frost, Reue, Tränen* bitter; *Not, Notwendigkeit* dire; *Leid, Unrecht* grievous. **jdn/etw** ~ **entbehren/vermissen** to miss sb/sth sadly; **etw** ~ **nötig haben** to be in dire need of sth; ~ **wenig Geld haben** to be desperately short of money; **solche Fehler rächen sich** ~ one pays dearly for mistakes like that.

Bitter *m* -s, - bitters *pl*.

bitterböse *adj* furious.

Bittere(r) *m decl as adj siehe* **Bitter.**

Bitter-: b~**ernst** *adj Situation etc* extremely serious; *Mensch* deadly serious; **damit ist es mir b~ernst** I am deadly serious *or* in deadly earnest; **b~kalt** *adj attr* bitterly cold, bitter; ~**keit** *f (lit, fig)* bitterness; **b~lich 1** *adj* bitter; **2** *adv* bitterly; ~**mandel** *f* bitter almond.

Bitternis *f (geh)* bitterness *no pl*; *(fig: von Mensch auch)* embitterment *no pl*; *(Leiden)* adversity, hardship. **in** ~ **schied sie aus dem Leben** embittered *or* filled with bitterness, she departed this life.

bittersüß *adj (lit, fig)* bitter-sweet.

Bitteschön *nt* -s, -s *(bittend, auffordernd)* please; *(Dank erwidernd)* not at all; *(anbietend) (von Verkäufer)* can I help you?; *(von Kellner)* what would you like? **mit einem artigen** ~ **überreichte er den Blumenstrauß** he presented the bouquet, saying politely 'this is for you'.

Bitt-: ~**gang** *m* (a) *(geh)* **einen** ~**gang zu jdm machen** to go to sb with a request; **das war ein schwerer** ~**gang** it was hard (for him *etc*) to ask that; (b) *(Eccl)* pilgrimage; *(~prozession)* rogation procession; ~**gebet** *nt* (prayer of) supplication; ~**gesuch** *nt* petition; ~**gottesdienst** *m* rogation service.

Bittre(r) *m decl as adj siehe* **Bitter.**

bittschön *interj* = **bitte schön.**

Bitt-: ~**schrift** *f (dated) siehe* ~**gesuch;** ~**steller(in** *f)* *m* -s, - petitioner, supplicant.

Bitumen *nt* -s, - *or* **Bitumina** bitumen.

bitzeln *(dial)* **1** *vi (prickeln)* to tingle; *(Bläschen bilden)* to sparkle, to bubble. **das bitzelt auf der Haut** it makes your skin tingle. **2** *vt (reizen)* **jdn** ~ to tickle *(inf) or* take sb's fancy.

Bitzelwasser *nt (dial inf)* sparkling mineral water.

bivalent [-va-] *adj* bivalent.

Biwak *nt* -s, -s *or* -e bivouac.

biwakieren* *vi* to bivouac.

bizarr *adj* bizarre; *Form, Gestalt etc auch* fantastic.

Bizarrerie *f (geh)* (a) *no pl* bizarreness. (b) *(Gedanke, Verhalten)* bizarre idea/behaviour *no pl*/comment *etc*. **er hält Science-fiction-Romane für** ~**n he** thinks that science fiction novels are completely bizarre.

Bizeps *m* -es, -e biceps.

Bj. *abbr of* **Baujahr.**

blabla *interj (inf)* blah blah blah *(inf)*.

Blabla *nt* -s, *no pl (inf)* blah *(inf)*.

Blachfeld *nt (poet)* battle-field.

Black box ['blæk'bɔks] *f - -, - -es* black box.

Blackout ['blɛkaut] *nt or m* -(s), -s *(form)* blackout.

blaffen, bläffen *vi* to yelp; *(schimpfen)* to snap.

Blaffer, Bläffer *m* -s, - *(inf) siehe* **Kläffer.**

Blag *nt* -s, -en, **Blage** *f* -, -n *(pej inf)* brat.

blähen 1 *vt* to swell; *Segel auch* to belly (out), to fill; *Anorak, Gardine, Windsack* to fill; *Nüstern* to dilate; *Bauch* to swell, to distend *(form)*. **voller Stolz blähte er seine Brust** his chest swelled with pride.

2 *vr* to swell; *(Segel auch)* to belly out, to billow; *(Anorak, Gardine)* to billow; *(Nüstern)* to dilate; *(fig: Mensch)* to puff oneself up *(inf)*.

3 *vi* to cause flatulence *or* wind.

blähend *adj (Med)* flatulent *(form)*.

Blähung *f usu pl (Med)* wind *no pl*, flatulence *no pl*. **eine** ~ **abgehen lassen** to break wind.

blakig *adj (verrußt)* sooty; *(rußend)* smoky.

blamabel *adj* shameful.

Blamage [bla'ma:ʒə] *f -, -n* disgrace.

blamieren* **1** *vt* to disgrace; *siehe* **Innung. 2** *vr* to make a fool of oneself; *(durch Benehmen)* to disgrace oneself.

blanchieren* [blã'ʃiːrən] *vt (Cook)* to blanch.

blank *adj* (a) *(glänzend, sauber)* shiny, shining; *(abgescheuert) Hosenboden etc* shiny. **etw** ~ **scheuern/polieren, etw scheuern/polieren, bis es** ~ **wird** to clean/polish sth till it shines; **der** ~**e Hans** *(poet)* the wild North Sea.

(b) *(poet: strahlend) Licht* bright; *Augen auch* shining. **der** ~**e Tag** broad daylight.

(c) *(nackt)* bare; *Schwert etc auch* naked; *(Aus: ohne Mantel)* coatless; *(inf: ohne Geld)* broke; *(Cards: einzeln)* single. **eine Karte** ~ **haben** to have only one card of a suit; **die Herz-Zehn habe ich** ~ the ten of hearts is the only heart I have; *siehe* **blankziehen.**

(d) *(rein)* pure, sheer; *Hohn* utter.

Blanke(r) *m decl as adj (dial inf)* bare bottom *or* behind *(inf)*.

Blankett *nt* -s, -e *(Fin)* blank form.

blankgewetzt *adj attr* shiny, worn shiny.

blanko *adj pred* (a) *Papier* plain. (b) *Scheck etc* blank.

Blanko- *in cpds* blank; ~**akzept** *nt (Fin)* blank acceptance; ~**kredit** *m* open *or* blank credit; ~**scheck** *m* blank cheque; ~**vollmacht** *f* carte blanche.

blankpoliert *adj attr* brightly polished.

Blankvers *m* blank verse.

blankziehen *sep irreg* **1** *vt* to draw. **2** *vi (sl)* to draw (one's gun).

Blasbalg *m siehe* **Blasebalg.**

Bläschen *nt* (a) *dim of* **Blase.** (b) *(Med)* vesicle *(form)*, small blister.

Bläschenausschlag *m* vesicular eruption *(form)*, blistery rash *(inf)*; *(von Pferden etc)* herpes *sing (form)*.

Blase *f* -, -n (a) *(Hohlraum)* bubble; *(Sprech~)* balloon. ~**n werfen** *or* **ziehen** *(Farbe)* to blister; *(Teig)* to become light and frothy; ~**n werfen** *(fig)* to cause a stir; ~**n ziehen** *(fig)* to cause trouble; **es regnet** ~**n** it's pelting.

(b) *(Med)* blister; *(Fieber~ auch)* vesicle *(form)*. **sich** *(dat)* ~**n laufen** *etc* to get blisters from walking *etc*.

(c) *(Anat)* bladder. **sich** *(dat)* **die** ~ **erkälten** to get a chill on the bladder.

(d) *(pej inf: Clique)* gang *(inf)*, mob *(inf)*.

Blasebalg *m* (pair of) bellows.

blasen *pret* **blies,** *ptp* **geblasen 1** *vi* (a) to blow; *(Posaunenbläser etc)* to play; *(auf Essen)* to blow on it; *(auf Wunde etc)* = to kiss it better. **zum Rückzug** ~ *(lit, fig)* to sound the retreat; **zum Aufbruch** ~ *(lit, fig)* to sound the departure; *(fig)* to say it's time to go; **auf dem Kamm** ~ to play a tune on one's comb; **es bläst** *(inf)* it's blowy *(inf) or* windy, there's a wind blowing; *siehe* **tuten, Horn.**

(b) *(sl: fellieren)* to suck *(sl)*.

2 *vt* (a) to blow; *Essen* to blow on; *Wunde etc* = to kiss better.

(b) *Melodie, Posaune etc* to play.

(c) *(inf)* **dir/ihm werd ich was** ~! I'll give you/him a piece of my mind; *siehe* **Marsch¹, Trübsal.**

(d) *(inf: mitteilen)* to tell. **jdm etw ins Ohr** ~ to whisper sth in sb's ear.

(e) *(sl: fellieren)* **jdn** ~ *(rare)*, **jdm einen** ~ to suck sb off *(sl)*, to do a blow job on sb *(sl)*.

Blasen-: ~**bildung** *f* formation of bubbles; *(bei Anstrich, an Fuß etc)* blistering; ~**entzündung** *f*, ~**katarrh** *m* cystitis; ~**leiden** *nt* bladder trouble *no art*; ~**stein** *m* bladder stone; ~**tang** *m* *(Bot)* bladder wrack; ~**tee** *m* herb tea beneficial in cases of bladder trouble.

Bläser(in *f)* *m* -s, - (a) *(Mus)* wind player. **die** ~ the wind (section). (b) *(vulg)* cock-sucker *(vulg)*.

Bläserquartett *nt* wind quartet.

blasiert *adj (pej geh)* blasé.

Blasiertheit *f (pej geh)* blasé character; *(von Mensch)* blasé attitude.

blasig *adj* full of troubles; *Flüssigkeit etc* aerated; *Teig* light and frothy; *(Med)* blistered.

Blas-: ~**instrument** *nt* wind instrument; ~**kapelle** *f* brass band.

Blasphemie *f* blasphemy.

blasphemisch *adj* blasphemous.

Blasrohr *nt* (a) *(Waffe)* blow-pipe. (b) *(Tech)* blast pipe.

blaß *adj (a) Gesicht, Haut etc* pale. ~ **werden** to go *or* grow pale, to pale; *(vor Schreck auch)* to blanch; ~ **wie der Tod** *(geh)* deathly pale; ~ **wie Kreide** white as chalk; ~ **vor Neid werden** to go green with envy; **etw macht jdn** ~ sth makes sb look pale.

(b) *Farbe, Schrift etc* pale.

(c) *(geh) Licht, Mond* pale, wan.

(d) (*fig*) faint; *Ahnung, Vorstellung auch* vague; *Erinnerung auch* dim, vague; *Ausdruck, Sprache, Schilderung* colourless. **ich habe keinen blassen Schimmer** *or* **Dunst** (**davon**) (*inf*) I haven't a clue *or* the faintest (idea) (about it) (*inf*).

(e) (*rare: pur*) sheer, pure.

blaß- *in cpds* pale.

Blässe *f* **-, -n** (a) paleness; (*von Haut, Gesicht etc auch*) pallor; (*von Licht auch*) wanness; (*fig: von Ausdruck, Schilderung etc*) colourlessness. (b) *siehe* **Blesse**.

Bläßhuhn *nt* coot.

bläßlich *adj* palish, rather pale.

Blaßschnabel *m* (*dated inf*) paleface (*hum*).

Blatt *nt* **-(e)s, ¨-er** (a) (*Bot*) leaf. **kein ~ vor den Mund nehmen** not to mince one's words.

(b) (*Papier etc*) sheet. **ein ~ Papier** a sheet of paper; **eine Packung mit 50 ~** a packet of 50 sheets; (**noch**) **ein unbeschriebenes ~ sein** (*unerfahren*) to be inexperienced; (*ohne Image*) to be an unknown quantity; **siehe fliegend**.

(c) (*Seite*) page. **das steht auf einem anderen ~** (*fig*) that's another story; **ein neues ~ in der Geschichte** *or* **im Buch der Geschichte** a new chapter of history.

(d) (*Noten~*) sheet. **vom ~ singen/spielen** to sight-read.

(e) (*Kunst~*) print; (*Reproduktion*) reproduction.

(f) (*bei Landkartenserien*) sheet.

(g) (*Zeitung*) paper.

(h) (*von Messer, Ruder, Propeller*) blade.

(i) (*Cards*) hand; (*Einzelkarte*) card. **das ~ hat sich gewendet** (*fig*) the tables have been turned.

(j) (*Hunt, Cook*) shoulder.

Blattader *f* (*Bot*) leaf vein.

Blättchen *nt dim of* **Blatt** (*pej: Zeitung*) rag (*inf*).

Blatter *f* **-, -n** (*dated Med*) (*Pocke*) pock, pustule. **~n** *pl* (*Krankheit*) smallpox.

blatt(e)rig *adj siehe* **blatternarbig**.

blätt(e)rig *adj Teig* flaky; *Farbe etc* flaking. **~ werden** (*Farbe etc*) to start flaking.

-blätt(e)rig *adj suf* -leaved.

Blättermagen *m* (*Zool*) omasum (*spec*).

blättern 1 *vi* (a) (*in Buch*) to leaf *or* (*schnell*) flick through it/them. **in etw** (*dat*) **~ to leaf** *or* flick through sth.

(b) *aux sein* (*rare*) (*in Schichten zerfallen*) to flake; (*abblättern*) to flake off.

2 *vt Geldscheine, Spielkarten* to put down one by one. **er blätterte mir die 100 Mark auf den Tisch** he put the 100 marks down note by note on the table for me.

Blatter-: **~narbe** *f* (*dated*) pockmark; **b~narbig** *adj* (*dated*) pockmarked.

Blätter-: **~pilz** *m* agaric; **~schmuck** *m* (*poet*) beautiful foliage; **~teig** *m* puff pastry *or* paste (*US*); **~teiggebäck** *nt* puff pastry; (*Backwaren*) puff pastries *pl*; **~wald** *m* (*Press hum*) press; **es rauscht im deutschen ~wald** there are murmurings in the German press; **b~weise** *adv siehe* **blattweise**; **~werk** *nt, no pl siehe* **Blattwerk**.

Blatt-: **~feder** *f* (*Tech*) leaf spring; **b~förmig** *adj* leaf-shaped, foliar (*form*); **~gemüse** *nt* greens *pl*, green *or* leaf (*form*) vegetables *pl*; **ein ~gemüse** a leaf vegetable; **~gewächs** *nt siehe* **~pflanze**; **~gold** *nt* gold leaf; **~grün** *nt* chlorophyll; **~knospe** *f* leafbud; **~laus** *f* greenfly, aphid; **b~los** *adj* leafless; **~pflanze** *f* foliage plant; **b~reich** *adj* leafy.

blattrig *adj siehe* **blatternarbig**.

blättrig *adj siehe* **blätt(e)rig**.

Blatt-: **~rippe** *f* (*Bot*) (leaf) rib *or* vein; **~salat** *m* green salad; **~schuß** *m* (*Hunt*) shot through the shoulder to the heart; **~silber** *nt* silver leaf; **~singen** *nt* sight-reading; **~spielen** *nt* sight-reading; **~stellung** *f* leaf arrangement; **~stengel, ~stiel** *m* petiole, leafstalk; **~trieb** *m* leaf shoot; **~vergoldung** *f* gilding; **b~weise** *adv* leaf by leaf; (*bei Papier*) sheet by sheet; **~werk** *nt, no pl* foliage.

Blätz *m* **-, -** (*Sw*) cloth.

Blätzli *nt* **-(s), -(s)** (*Sw*) cutlet.

blau *adj* (a) blue. **Forelle etc ~** (*Cook*) trout etc au bleu; **~er Anton** (*inf*) boilersuit; **ein ~es Auge** (*inf*) a black eye; **ich tu das nicht wegen deiner schönen ~n Augen** (*fig*) I'm not doing it for the sake of your bonny blue eyes; **mit einem ~en Auge davonkommen** (*fig*) to get off lightly; **die ~e Blume** (*Liter*) the Blue Flower; **~es Blut in den Adern haben** to have blue blood in one's veins; **ein ~er Brief** (*Sch*) letter informing parents that their child must repeat a year; (*von Hauswirt*) notice to quit; (*von der Firma*) one's cards; **ein ~er Fleck** a bruise; **~e Flecken haben** to be bruised; **die ~en Jungs** (*inf*) the boys in blue (*inf*), the navy; **~er Zappen** (*sl*) hundred mark note *or* bill (*US*), blue one (*inf*); **der B~e Nil** the Blue Nile; **der ~e Planet** the blue planet; **der B~e Reiter** (*Art*) the Blaue Reiter; **die ~e Stunde** (*poet*) the twilight hour; **er wird sein ~es Wunder erleben** (*inf*) he won't know what's hit him (*inf*); *siehe* **Dunst**.

(b) *usu pred* (*inf: betrunken*) drunk, tight (*inf*), canned (*inf*); *siehe* **Veilchen**.

(c) (*inf: geschwänzt*) **einen ~en Montag machen** to skip work on Monday (*inf*); **der letzte Freitag war für mich ~** I skipped work last Friday (*inf*).

Blau *nt* **-s, - or -(s) -s** blue; *siehe auch* **Blau²**.

Blau-: **~algen** *pl* blue-green algae *pl*; **b~äugig** *adj* blue-eyed; (*fig*) naïve; **~äugigkeit** *f* (*lit*) blue eyes *pl*; (*fig*) naïvety; **~bart** *m* (*pej*) Bluebeard; **~beere** *f siehe* Heidelbeere; **b~blütig** *adj* blue-blooded; **~blütigkeit** *f* blue blood; **~buch** *nt* bluebook.

Blaue¹ *m: der ~ siehe* **Blaue(r)**.

Blaue² *nt* **-n, no pl** (a) **das ~** (*Farbe*) the blue; **es spielt ins ~ it** has a touch of blue in it; **das ~ vom Himmel (herunter) lügen** (*inf*) to tell a pack of lies; **das ~ vom Himmel (herunter) reden**

(*inf*) to talk one's head off (*inf*), to prattle away nineteen to the dozen (*inf*); **jdm das ~ vom Himmel (herunter) versprechen** (*inf*) to promise sb the moon.

(b) (*ohne Ziel*) **ins ~ hinein** (*inf*) at random; **arbeiten** with no particular goal; **wir wollen ins ~ fahren** we'll just set off and see where we end up; **eine Fahrt ins ~** a trip to nowhere in particular; (*Veranstaltung*) a mystery tour.

Bläue *f* **-, no pl** blueness; (*des Himmels auch*) blue.

blauen *vi* (*liter*) (*Himmel*) to turn blue. **der Morgen** *or* **Tag blaute** it started to get light; **als wir erwachten, blaute es schon** when we woke up it was already getting light.

bläuen 1 *vt* (a) to dye blue; *Lackmuspapier etc* to turn blue. (b) *Wäsche* to blue. **2** *vr* to turn *or* go blue.

Blaue(r) *m decl as adj* (a) (*inf: Polizist*) cop (*inf*), copper (*inf*). (b) (*sl: Geldschein*) blue one (*inf*). **ein kleiner/großer ~r** a ten/hundred mark note.

Blau-: **~felchen** *m* whitefish, powan (*spec*); **~filter** *m or nt* (*Phot*) blue filter; **~fuchs** *m* arctic fox; **~gelbblindheit** *f* blue-yellow colour-blindness; **b~grau** *adj* blue-grey, bluish *or* bluey grey; **b~grün** *adj* blue-green, bluish *or* bluey green; **~hemd** *m* (*Press sl*) UN soldier; **~hemd** *nt* (*DDR*) (a) blue shirt (*worn by members of the Free German Youth*); (b) (*inf: Mensch*) member of the Free German Youth; **~jacke** *f* (*inf*) bluejacket (*inf*), sailor; **~kabis** *m* (*Sw*), **~kohl** *m* (*dial*), **~kraut** *nt* (*S Ger, Aus*) *siehe* Rotkohl; **~kreuz(l)er(in** *f*) *m* **-s, -** member of the Blue Cross Temperance League; **b~kreuz(l)erisch** *adj* puritanical.

bläulich *adj* bluish, bluey.

Blau-: **~licht** *nt* (*von Polizei etc*) flashing blue light; (*Lampe*) blue light; **mit ~licht** with its blue light flashing; **b~machen** *sep* (*inf*) **1** *vi* to skip work; **2** *vt* **den Freitag/zwei Tage b~machen** to skip work on Friday/for two days; **~mann** *m, pl* **~männer** (*inf*) boilersuit; **~meise** *f* bluetit; **~papier** *nt* carbon paper; **~pause** *f* blueprint; **b~rot** *adj* purple; **~säure** *f* prussic *or* hydrocyanic acid; **~schimmelkäse** *m* blue cheese; **b~schwarz** *adj* blue-black, bluey black; **~stich** *m* (*Phot*) blue cast; **b~stichig** *adj* (*Phot*) with a blue cast; **~stift** *m* (*zum Malen*) blue crayon; (b) *siehe* Tintenstift; **~strumpf** *m* bluestocking; **b~strümpfig** *adj* bluestocking *attr*; **~tanne** *f* blue *or* colorado spruce; **b~violett** *adj* (dark) bluish *or* bluey purple; **~wal** *m* blue whale.

Blazer ['ble:zɐ] *m* **-s, -**, **Blazerjacke** *f* blazer.

Blech *nt* **-(e)s, -e** (a) *no pl* (sheet) metal; (*von Auto*) body. **eine Dose aus ~** a tin (*Brit*), a metal container; **das ist doch nur ~** it's just ordinary metal.

(b) (*Blechstück*) metal plate.

(c) (*Backblech*) (baking) tray.

(d) *no pl* (*inf: Blechinstrumente*) brass.

(e) *no pl* (*pej inf: Orden etc*) gongs *pl* (*inf*), fruit salad (*US inf*).

(f) *no pl* (*inf: Unsinn*) rubbish *no art* (*inf*), trash *no art* (*inf*).

(g) *no pl* (*inf: Geld*) brass (*inf*), dough (*inf*).

Blech-: **~bläser** *m* brass player; **die ~bläser** the brass (section); **~blasinstrument** *nt* brass instrument; **~büchse** *f* (*Brit*), can; **~chaos** *nt* (*inf*) traffic chaos; **~dose** *f* tin container; (*esp für Konserven*) tin (*Brit*), can.

blechen *vti* (*inf*) to cough or pay up (*inf*), to fork out (*inf*).

blechern *adj* (a) *attr* metal. (b) *Geräusch, Stimme etc* tinny; (*fig: hohl*) hollow, empty.

Blech-: **~geschirr** *nt* metal pots and pans *pl* or utensils *pl* (*form*); **~instrument** *nt* brass instrument; **~kanister** *m* metal can; **~kiste** *f* (*pej inf*) (old) crate (*inf*); **~laden** *m* (*pej inf*) gongs *pl* (*inf*), fruit salad (*US inf*); **~lawine** *f* (*pej inf*) vast column of cars; **~lehre** *f* metal gauge; **~musik** *f* (*usu pej*) brass (band) music; **~napf** *m* metal bowl.

Blech-: **~schaden** *m* damage to the bodywork; **~schere** *f* (pair of) metal shears; (*Maschine*) metal shearer; **~schmied** *m* (*dial*) *siehe* Klempner; **~trommel** *f* tin drum; **~walzwerk** *nt* sheet (rolling) mill.

blecken **1** *vt* **die Zähne ~** to bare *or* show one's teeth. **2** *vi* (*rare*) to flash; (*Flammen*) to dart, to leap.

Blei¹ *nt* **-(e)s, -e** (a) *no pl* (*Metall*) lead. **jdm wie ~ in den Gliedern** *or* **Knochen liegen** (*Schreck*) to paralyse sb; (*Depression*) to weigh sb down; **die Müdigkeit/Anstrengung lag ihm wie ~ in den Gliedern** *or* **Knochen** his whole body ached with tiredness/the exertion; *siehe* Magen.

(b) (*Lot*) plumb, (plumb-)bob.

(c) (*Munition*) lead; (*Typ*) hot metal.

Blei² *m or nt* **-(e)s, -e** (*inf*) *siehe* **Bleistift**.

Blei- *in cpds* lead; **~ader** *f* lead vein.

Bleibe *f* **-, -n** (a) (*Unterkunft*) place to stay. **eine/keine ~ haben** to have somewhere/nowhere to stay. (b) (*Institution*) remand home.

bleiben *pret* **blieb**, *ptp* **geblieben** *vi aux sein* (a) (*sich nicht verändern*) to stay, to remain. **unbelohnt/unbestraft ~** to go unrewarded/unpunished; **unbeachtet ~** to go unnoticed, to escape notice; **unbeantwortet ~** to be left *or* to remain unanswered; **unvergessen ~** to continue to be remembered; **an Samstagen bleibt unser Geschäft geschlossen** this shop is closed on Saturdays; **in Verbindung ~** to keep *or* stay *or* remain in touch; **erfolglos** *or* **ohne Erfolg/Folgen ~** to remain unsuccessful/to have no consequences; **in Übung/Form ~** to keep in practice/form; **jdm in** *or* **in jds Erinnerung ~** to stay *or* remain in sb's mind; **ruhig/still ~** to keep calm/quiet; **wach ~** to stay *or* keep awake; **wenn das Wetter so bleibt** if this weather continues, if the weather stays *or* remains *or* keeps like this; **Freunde ~** to stay or remain friends, to go on being friends.

(b) (*sich nicht bewegen, zu Besuch ~*) to stay; (*nicht weggehen, nicht zurückkommen auch*) to remain. **sitzen/stehen ~** to stay sitting down/standing up, to remain seated/standing; **bitte, ~ Sie doch sitzen** please don't get up; **jdn zum B~ ein-**

laden *or* **auffordern** to invite sb to stay; **von etw ~** to stay *or* keep away from sth; **wo bleibst du so lange?** (*inf*) what's keeping you (all this time)?; **wo bleibt er so lange?** (*inf*) where has he got to?; **wo sind denn all die alten Häuser geblieben?** what (has) happened to all the old houses?, where have all the old houses gone (to)?; **bleibe im Lande und nähre dich redlich** (*Prov*) east, west, home's best (*prov*); **hier ist meines B~s nicht (mehr** *or* **länger)** (*geh*) I cannot remain here (any longer); *siehe* **Ball¹, Apparat.**

(c) (*fig*) **bei etw ~** to keep *or* stick (*inf*) to sth; **bleib du ruhig bei deiner Arbeit** you just carry *or* keep on with your work; **das bleibt unter uns** that's (just) between ourselves; **wir möchten für** *or* **unter uns ~** we want to keep ourselves to ourselves; *siehe* **dabei, Sache.**

(d) (*übrigbleiben*) to be left, to remain. **es blieb mir/es blieb keine andere Wahl/Möglichkeit** I had/there was no other choice/possibility; **es blieb mir keine Hoffnung** I lost all hope.

(e) (*sein*) **es bleibt abzuwarten** it remains to be seen; **es bleibt zu hoffen/wünschen, daß ...** I/we can only hope that ...

(f) (*inf: versorgt werden*) **sie können (selber) sehen, wo sie ~** they'll just have to look out for themselves (*inf*); **und wo bleibe ich?** and what about me?; **sieh zu, wo du bleibst!** you're on your own! (*inf*), you'd better look out for yourself! (*inf*).

(g) (*euph: umkommen*) **er ist auf See/im Krieg geblieben** he died at sea/didn't come back from the war; **er ist unter dem Messer geblieben** he died on the operating table.

bleibend *adj* **Wert, Erinnerung** *etc* lasting; **Schaden, Zähne** permanent.

bleibenlassen *vt sep irreg* (*inf*) (a) (*unterlassen*) **etw ~** to give sth a miss (*inf*); **das werde ich/wirst du ganz schön ~** I'll/you'll do nothing of the sort! (b) (*aufgeben*) to give up. **das Rauchen/Nägelkauen ~** to give up *or* stop smoking/chewing one's nails.

bleich *adj* pale; (*fig*) **Grauen, Entsetzen** sheer. **~ wie der Tod** deathly pale, pale as death.

Bleichart *m* **-s, -** *siehe* **Bleichert.**

Bleiche *f* **-, -n** (a) *no pl* paleness; (*von Mensch auch*) pallor. (b) (*Bleichplatz*) bleachery (*obs*), green *where sheets etc were laid out to be bleached by the sun.*

bleichen 1 *vt* to bleach. **2** *vi pret* **bleichte** *or* (*old*) **blich, ptp gebleicht** *or* (*old*) **geblicht** to be *or* become bleached. **in der Sonne ~** to be bleached by the sun.

Bleichert *m* **-s, -e** German rosé wine.

Bleich-: ~gesicht *nt* (a) (*inf: blasser Mensch*) pasty-face (*inf*), pale-faced person; (b) (*Weißer*) paleface; **b~gesichtig** *adj* (*inf*) pale-faced, pasty-faced (*inf*); **~mittel** *nt* bleach, bleaching agent; **~sucht** *f* (*old Med*) anaemia; **b~süchtig** *adj* (*old Med*) anaemic.

bleiern *adj* (a) *attr* (*aus Blei*) lead; (*fig*) **Farbe, Himmel** leaden. **wie eine ~e Ente schwimmen** (*hum*) to swim like a brick. (b) (*fig*) leaden; **Verantwortung** onerous. **die Verantwortung lastete ~ auf ihm/seiner Seele** the responsibility weighed heavily upon him/his mind; **es lag ihr ~ in den Gliedern** her limbs were like lead; *siehe* **Magen.**

Blei-: ~erz *nt* lead ore; **~farbe** *f* lead paint; **b~farbig, b~farben** *adj* lead-coloured, lead-grey; **Himmel** leaden; **b~frei** *adj* lead-free, which does not contain lead; **~fuß** *m:* **mit ~fuß fahren** (*inf*) to keep one's foot down; **~gehalt** *m* lead content; **~gewicht** *nt* lead weight; (*Angeln*) sinker; **~gießen** *nt* New Year's Eve custom of telling fortunes by the shapes made by molten lead dropped into cold water; **~glanz** *m* galena, galenite; **b~grau** *adj* lead-grey; **b~haltig** *adj* containing lead; **Erz, Gestein** plumbiferous (*spec*); **b~haltig/zu b~haltig sein** to contain lead/too much lead; **mir wird die Luft hier zu b~haltig** (*fig inf*) the air's a bit too thick with bullets for my liking, there's too much lead flying about here; **~hütte** *f* lead works *pl*; **~kristall** *nt* lead crystal; **~kugel** *f* lead bullet; lead ball; **~lot** *nt* plumbline; **~menninge** *f siehe* **Menninge; ~oxid, ~oxyd** *nt* lead oxide; **gelbes ~oxid** lead monoxide; **rotes ~oxid** red lead; **~rute** *f* came; **~ruten** leading; **~satz** *m* (*Typ*) hot-metal setting; **~schürze** *f* lead apron; **b~schwer** *adj siehe* **bleiern** (b); **~soldat** *m* = tin soldier.

Bleistift *m* pencil; (*zum Malen*) crayon. **mit/in ~** with a/in pencil.

Bleistift- *in cpds* pencil; **~absatz** *m* stiletto heel; **~spitzer** *m* pencil sharpener.

Blei-: ~vergiftung *f* lead poisoning; **b~verglast** *adj* leaded; **~verglasung** *f* lead glazing; **Fenster mit ~verglasung** leaded windows; **b~verseucht** *adj* lead-polluted; **~weiß** *nt* white lead.

Blendboden *m siehe* **Blindboden.**

Blende *f* **-, -n** (a) (*Lichtschutz*) shade, screen; (*Aut*) (sun) visor; (*an Fenster*) blind.

(b) (*Opt*) filter.

(c) (*Phot*) (*Öffnung*) aperture; (*Einstellungsposition*) f-stop; (*Vorrichtung*) diaphragm. **die ~ öffnen/schließen** to open up the aperture/to stop down; **bei** *or* **mit ~ 2.8 at** (an aperture setting of) f/2.8; **~ 4 einstellen** to set the aperture to f/4.

(d) (*Film, TV, Tontechnik: Aufblende, Abblende*) fade.

(e) (*Naut*) deadlight.

(f) (*Archit*) blind window/arch *etc.*

(g) (*Sew*) trim.

(h) (*Verkleidung*) cover.

(i) (*Geol*) blende.

Blendeinstellung *f* (*Phot*) aperture (setting); (*Vorrichtung*) aperture control.

blenden 1 *vt* (a) (*lit, fig: bezaubern*) to dazzle; (*fig: täuschen auch*) to blind. (b) (*blind machen*) to blind. **2** *vi* (a) to be dazzling. **~d weiß sein** to be shining *or* dazzling white. (b) (*fig: täuschen*) to dazzle.

Blendenautomatik *f* (*Phot*) automatic diaphragm.

blendend 1 *prp of* **blenden. 2** *adj* splendid; **Pianist, Schüler** *etc* brilliant; **Laune, Stimmung** sparkling. **es geht mir ~** I feel wonderful; **sich ~ amüsieren** to have a splendid *or* wonderful time; **er ist nicht gerade ~** he's not exactly brilliant, he doesn't exactly shine.

blendendweiß *adj attr* shining *or* dazzling white.

Blender(in *f*) *m* **-s, -** phoney (*inf*).

Blend-: b~frei *adj* dazzle-free; **Glas, Fernsehschirm** non-reflective; **~laterne** *f* signalling lantern.

Blendling *m* (*Zool*) *siehe* **Bastard.**

Blend-: ~öffnung *f* (*Phot*) aperture; **~rahmen** *m* (a) (*Art*) canvas-stretcher; (b) (*Build*) frame; **~schutz** *m* (a) protection against dazzle; (b) (*Vorrichtung*) anti-dazzle device; **~schutzgitter** *nt*, **~schutzzaun** *m* anti-dazzle barrier.

Blendung *f siehe vt* (a) dazzling; blinding. (b) blinding.

Blend-: ~werk *nt* (*liter*) illusion; (*Vortäuschung*) deception; **hinter einem ~werk schöner Worte** *or* **aus schönen Worten** behind a screen of pretty words; **ein ~werk des Teufels** *or* **der Hölle** a trap set by the devil; **~zaun** *m* anti-dazzle barrier.

Blesse *f* **-, -n** (a) (*Fleck*) blaze. (b) (*Tier*) horse *with a blaze.*

blessieren* *vt* (*old: verwunden*) to wound.

Blessur *f* (*old*) wound.

bleu [blø:] *adj inv* (*Fashion*) light blue.

bleuen *vti siehe* **prügeln.**

blich (*old*) *pret of* **bleichen 2.**

Blick *m* **-(e)s, -e** (a) (*das Blicken*) look; (*flüchtiger ~*) glance. **auf den ersten ~** at first glance; **Liebe auf den ersten ~** love at first sight; **auf den zweiten ~** when one looks (at it) again, the second time one looks (at it); **mit einem ~** at a glance; **jds ~** (*dat*) **ausweichen** to avoid sb's eye; **jds ~ erwidern** to return sb's gaze; **~e miteinander wechseln** to exchange glances; **jdn mit seinen ~en verschlingen** to devour sb with one's eyes; **er folgte ihr mit ~en** *or* **dem ~** his eyes followed her; **sie zog alle ~e auf sich** everybody's eyes were drawn to her; **einen ~ auf etw** (*acc*) **tun** *or* **werfen** to throw a glance at sth; **einen ~ hinter die Kulissen tun** *or* **werfen** (*fig*) to take a look behind the scenes; **sie würdigte ihn keines ~es** she did not deign to look at him; **jdm einen/keinen ~ schenken** to look at sb/not to spare sb a glance; **er hat keinen ~ für sie/dafür** he takes no notice of her/it; **wenn ~e töten könnten!** if looks could kill!; *siehe* **durchbohren.**

(b) (*~richtung*) eyes *pl.* **mein ~ fiel auf sein leeres Glas** my eye fell on his empty glass; **von hier aus fällt der ~ auf den Dom** from here one can see the cathedral; **den ~ heben** to raise one's eyes, to look up; **den ~ senken** to look down.

(c) (*Augenausdruck*) expression *or* look in one's eyes. **den bösen ~ haben** to have the evil eye; **in ihrem ~ lag Verzweiflung** there was a look of despair in her eyes; **er musterte sie mit durchdringendem/finsterem ~** he looked at her penetratingly/darkly.

(d) (*Ausblick*) view. **ein Zimmer mit ~ auf den Park** a room with a view of the park, a room overlooking the park; **dem ~ entschwinden** to disappear from view *or* sight, to go out of sight; **jdn aus dem ~ verlieren** to lose sight of sb; (*fig*) to lose trace of sb.

(e) (*Verständnis*) **jdm den ~ weiten** to broaden sb's outlook; **seinen ~ für etw schärfen** to increase one's awareness of sth; **einen klaren ~ haben** to see things clearly; **einen (guten) ~ für etw haben** to have an eye *or* a good eye for sth; **er hat keinen ~ dafür** he doesn't see *or* notice that sort of thing; **einen weiten ~ haben** to have a broad outlook; **die vielen Einzelheiten trüben** *or* **verstellen den ~ für den Zusammenhang** the welter of details makes it harder to see the connection.

blicken *vi* (*auf* + *acc* **at**) to look; (*flüchtig ~*) to glance; (*fig: hervorsehen*) to peep. **sich ~ lassen** to put in an appearance; **laß dich hier ja nicht mehr ~!** don't let me see you here again!, don't show your face here again!; **laß dich doch mal wieder ~!** why don't you drop in some time?; **danach hat er sich nie wieder ~ lassen** after that he was never seen again; **das läßt tief ~** that's very revealing.

Blick-: ~fang *m* eye-catcher; **als ~fang** to catch the eye; **~feld** *nt* field of vision; **ein enges ~feld haben** (*fig*) to have narrow horizons; **ins ~feld (der Öffentlichkeit) rücken** to become the focus of (public) attention; **~kontakt** *m* visual contact; **b~los** *adj* (*geh*) unseeing; **~punkt** *m* (a) (*Zentrum der Aufmerksamkeit*) centre of one's field of vision; (*fig*) limelight; **im ~punkt der Öffentlichkeit stehen** to be in the public eye; (b) (*fig: Standpunkt*) viewpoint, point of view; **~richtung** *f* line of vision *or* sight; (*fig*) outlook; **in ~richtung (nach)** links looking to the left; **~wechsel** *m* exchange of glances; (*fig*) change in one's viewpoint; **~winkel** *m* angle of vision; (*fig*) viewpoint.

blind *adj* (a) (*lit, fig*) blind (*für* to); **Zufall** pure, sheer; **Alarm** false. **~für etw** *or* **in bezug auf etw** (*acc*) **sein** (*fig*) to be blind to sth; **ich bin doch nicht ~!** (*fig*) I'm not blind; **jdn ~ machen** (*lit, fig*) to blind sb, to make sb blind; **ein ~es Huhn findet auch mal ein Korn** (*Prov*) anyone can be lucky now and again; **~ landen** (*Aviat*) to make a blind landing, to land blind; **~ (Schach) spielen** to play (chess) blind; **~er Fleck** (*Anat*) blind spot; **in ~er Liebe** blinded with love; **ihr Blick war von** *or* **vor Tränen ~** she was blinded with tears; **~e Gewalt** brute force; **~er Eifer** blind enthusiasm; **~er Eifer schadet nur** (*Prov*) it's not a good thing to be over-enthusiastic; **eine ~ endende Straße** (*lit, fig*) a blind alley; **ein ~er Schuß** (*nicht scharf*) a shot with a blank cartridge; (*nicht gezielt*) a blind shot; **~ schießen** (*nicht scharf*) to fire a blank/blanks; (*ziellos*) to fire blindly; **etw ~ herausgreifen** to take *or* pick sth at random; **~ in etw** (*acc*) **hineingreifen** to put one's hand in sth without looking.

(b) (*getrübt*) dull; **Spiegel, Glasscheibe** clouded; **Metall auch** tarnished; **Fleck** blind.

(c) (*verdeckt*) **Naht** *etc* invisible; (*vorgetäuscht*) (*Archit*)

false; *Fenster* blind, false. **ein ~er Passagier** a stowaway.
Blind-: ~**band** *m* (*Typ*) dummy; ~**boden** *m* (*Archit*) subfloor.
Blinddarm *m* (*Anat*) caecum; (*inf: Wurmfortsatz*) appendix.
Blinddarm-: ~**entzündung** *f* appendicitis; ~**operation** *f* append(ic)ectomy; ~**reizung** *f* grumbling appendix.
Blindekuh(spiel *nt*) *f no art* blind man's buff.
Blinden-: ~**anstalt** *f* home for the blind; ~**führer** *m* blind person's guide; ~**hund** *m* guide-dog; ~**schrift** *f* braille.
Blinde(r) *mf decl as adj* blind person/man/woman *etc.* **die ~n** the blind; **die ~n und die Lahmen** (*Bibl*) the lame and the blind; **das sieht doch ein ~r** (**mit dem Krückstock**) (*hum inf*) any fool can see that; **unter den ~n ist der Einäugige König** (*Prov*) in the country of the blind the one-eyed man is king; **der ~ verlacht den Lahmen** (*Prov*) the pot calling the kettle black; **von etw reden, wie der ~ von der Farbe** (*Prov*) to talk about sth when one knows nothing about it.
Blind-: ~**fenster** *nt* blind window; **b~fliegen** *vi sep irreg aux sein* to fly blind; ~**flug** *m* blind flight; (*das ~fliegen*) blind flying; ~**gänger** *m* (*Mil*) dud (shot); (*inf: Versager*) dud (*inf*), dead loss (*inf*); **b~geboren** *adj attr* blind from birth; ~**geborene(r)** *mf decl as adj* person blind from birth; **b~gläubig** *adj* credulous; ~**gläubigkeit** *f* credulousness; ~**heit** *f* (*lit, fig*) blindness; **jdn mit ~heit schlagen** (*Bibl, liter*) to strike sb blind; **wie mit ~heit geschlagen** (*fig*) as though blind; **mit ~heit geschlagen sein** (*fig*) to be blind; ~**landung** *f* blind landing; **b~lings** *adv* blindly; ~**material** *nt* (*Typ*) leads *pl*; ~**rahmen** *m* siehe **Blendrahmen**; ~**schleiche** *f* slow-worm; **b~schreiben** *vti sep irreg* to touch-type; ~**schreibverfahren** *nt* touch-typing; ~**spiel** *nt* (*Chess*) blind game; **b~spielen** *vi sep irreg* to play blind; ~**start** *m* (*Aviat*) blind take-off; **b~wütend**, **b~wütig** *adj* in a blind rage; ~**wütigkeit** *f* blind rage or fury.
blink *adj inv:* ~**und blank** (*inf*) gleaming.
blinken 1 *vi* (a) (*funkeln*) to gleam.
(b) (*Blinkzeichen geben*) (*Boje, Leuchtturm*) to flash; (*Aut*) to indicate.
2 *vt* **Signal** to flash. **SOS** ~ to flash an SOS (signal); **rechts/links** ~ to indicate right/left; **er hat mir geblinkt, daß ich überholen kann** he signalled for me to overtake.
Blinker *m* -s, - (a) (*Aut*) indicator, winker (*inf*). (b) (*Angeln*) spinner.
blinkern *vi* (a) (*inf: blinken*) to flash. **er blinkerte mit den Augen** he blinked. (b) (*Angeln*) to use a spinner.
Blink-: ~**feuer** *nt* flashing light; ~**leuchte** *f* indicator; ~**licht** *nt* flashing light; (*inf: ~leuchte*) indicator, winker (*inf*); ~**lichtanlage** *f* warning light system; ~**zeichen** *nt* signal.
blinzeln, **blinzen** (*dated*) *vi* to blink; (*zwinkern*) to wink; (*geblendet*) to squint.
Blitz *m* -es, -e (a) (*ein Blitzen*) lightning *no pl, no indef art*; (~**strahl**) flash of lightning; (*Lichtstrahl*) flash (of light). **vom ~ getroffen/erschlagen werden** to be struck by lightning; **wie vom ~ getroffen** (*fig*) thunderstruck; **aus ihren Augen schossen or sprühten ~e** her eyes flashed; **einschlagen wie ein ~** (*fig*) to be a bombshell; **die Nachricht schlug überall wie ein ~ ein** the news came as a bombshell to everyone; **wie ein ~ aus heiterem Himmel** (*fig*) like a bolt from the blue; **wie der ~** (*inf*) like lightning; **laufen wie ein geölter ~** (*inf*) to run like greased lightning; **die Antwort kam wie ein geölter ~** (*inf*) the answer came in a flash.
(b) (*Phot inf*) flash; (*Blitzlichtgerät auch*) flashgun.
Blitz- in *cpds* (*esp Mil: schnell*) lightning; ~**ableiter** *m* lightning conductor; **jdn als ~ableiter benutzen or mißbrauchen** to vent one's anger on sb; **er wurde zum ~ableiter für ihren Ärger** she vented her anger on him; ~**aktion** *f* lightning operation; ~**angriff** *m* (*Mil*) lightning attack; **der ~angriff auf London** the London Blitz; **b~artig** 1 *adj* lightning *attr*; 2 *adv* (*schnell*) **reagieren** like lightning; (*plötzlich*) **verschwinden** in a flash; **b~dumm** *adj* very stupid, dim; **b~(e)blank** *adj* (*inf*) spick and span.
blitzen 1 *vi impers* **es blitzt** there is lightning; (*mehrmals auch*) there are flashes of lightning; **es blitzt und donnert** there is thunder and lightning; **hat es eben geblitzt?** was that (a flash of) lightning?; **es fing an zu** ~ lightning began; **bei dir blitzt es** (*hum inf*) your slip is showing, Charlie's dead (*Brit inf*); **gleich blitzt es!** (*dial*) there'll be trouble.
2 *vi* (a) (*strahlen*) to flash; (*Gold, Zähne*) to sparkle. **vor Sauberkeit ~** to be sparkling clean; **Zorn blitzte aus seinen Augen** his eyes flashed with anger.
(b) (*inf: unbekleidet flitzen*) to streak.
(c) (*Phot inf*) to use (a) flash.
3 *vt* (*Phot inf*) to take a flash photograph of.
Blitzer(in *f*) *m* -s, (*inf*) streaker.
Blitzesschnelle *f* lightning speed. **mit ~** at lightning speed; **in ~** in a flash.
Blitz-: ~**gerät** *nt* (*Phot*) flash(gun); **b~gescheit** *adj* (*inf*) brilliant; ~**gespräch** *nt* special priority telephone call; ~**kaffee** *m* (*Sw*) instant coffee; ~**karriere** *f* rapid rise; **eine ~karriere machen** to rise rapidly; ~**krieg** *m* blitzkrieg; ~**licht** *nt* (*Phot*) flash(light); ~**lichtbirne**, ~**lichtlampe** *f* flashbulb; ~**mädel** *nt* (*Mil inf*) signals operator; ~**merker(in** *f*) *m* -s, - (*inf: usu iro*) bright spark (*inf*); ~**reise** *f* flying visit; **b~sauber** *adj* spick and span; ~**schaden** *m* damage caused by lightning; ~**schlag** *m* flash of lightning; **vom ~schlag getroffen** struck by lightning; **b~schnell** 1 *adj* lightning *attr*; 2 *adv* like lightning; (*plötzlich*) **verschwinden** in a flash; ~**schutzanlage** *f* lightning protection equipment; ~**sieg** *m* lightning victory; ~**strahl** *m* flash of lightning; ~**umfrage** *f* quick poll; ~**würfel** *m* (*Phot*) flashcube.
Blizzard ['blɪzɐt] *m* -s, -s blizzard.
Bloch *m or nt* -(e)s, -e or ⁻er (*S Ger, Aus*) log.
blochen *vt* (*dial*) to polish.
Blocher *m* -s, - (*dial*) floor polisher.

Block *m* -(e)s, ⁻e (a) block (*von, aus* of); (*von Seife, Schokolade*) bar.
(b) *pl auch* -s (*Häuser~, Haus*) block.
(c) *pl auch* -s (*Papier~*) pad; (*Briefmarken~*) block; (*von Fahrkarten*) book.
(d) *pl* -s (*Rail*) block.
(e) (*Zusammengefaßtes*) block. **etw im ~ kaufen** to buy sth in bulk.
(f) *pl auch* -s (*Pol*) (*Staaten~*) bloc; (*Fraktion*) faction.
(g) (*NS*) smallest organizational unit of Nazi party based on a block of houses.
(h) (*Sport*) wall.
(i) *pl auch* -s (*inf: Blockierung*) (mental) block.
(j) (*Folter~*) stocks *pl.*
Blockade *f* (*Absperrung*) blockade. **eine ~ brechen** to run or break a blockade.
Blockadebrecher *m* blockade runner.
Block-: ~**bau** *m* (a) (*Gebäude*) log cabin; (b) (*auch ~bauweise*) method of building houses from logs; ~**bildung** *f* (*Pol*) formation of blocs/factions; ~**buchstabe** *m* block letter or capital.
blocken *vti* (a) (*Rail*) to block. (b) (*Hunt*) to perch. (c) (*abfangen*) to block, to stop. (d) (*Sport: sperren*) to block. (e) (*dial: bohnern*) to polish.
Blocker *m* -s, - (*S Ger*) siehe **Blocher**.
Block-: ~**flöte** *f* recorder; **b~frei** *adj* non-aligned; ~**freiheit** *f* non-alignment; ~**haus** *nt*, ~**hütte** *f* log cabin.
blockieren* 1 *vt* (a) (*sperren, hemmen*) to block; *Verkehr, Verhandlung* to obstruct; *Flugverkehr* to halt; *Gesetz* to block the passage of; *Rad, Lenkung* to lock. (b) (*mit Blockade belegen*) to blockade. 2 *vi* to jam; (*Bremsen, Rad etc*) to lock.
Blockierung *f* siehe *vt* blocking; obstruction; locking; blockade.
Block-: ~**leiter** *m* (*NS*) block leader; ~**malz** *nt* type of cough sweet; ~**partei** *f* (*esp DDR*) party in a faction; ~**politik** *f* joint policy; ~**schokolade** *f*, *no pl* cooking chocolate; ~**schrift** *f* block capitals *pl* or letters *pl*; ~**staat** *m* aligned state; ~**station**, ~**stelle** *f* (*Rail*) block signal; ~**stunde** *f* (*Sch*) double period; ~**system** *nt* (a) (*Rail*) block system; (b) (*Pol*) system of factions; ~**unterricht** *m* (*Sch*) teaching by topics; ~**wart** *m* (*NS*) block leader; ~**werk** *nt* (*Rail*) block signal.
blöd(e) *adj* (*inf*) (a) (*dumm*) silly, stupid, idiotic; *Wetter* terrible; *Gefühl* funny. **das B~e daran ist, daß ...** the silly etc thing about it is that ... (b) (*Med: schwachsinnig*) imbecilic. (c) (*Sw: schüchtern*) shy. (d) (*S Ger: abgescheuert*) worn.
Blödel *m* -s, - (*inf*) stupid fool (*inf*) or idiot (*inf*); (*ungeschickter Mensch*) clumsy fool (*inf*) or idiot (*inf*).
Blödelei *f* (*inf*) (*Albernheit*) messing (*inf*) or fooling about or around; (*Witz*) joke; (*dumme Streiche*) pranks *pl*. **laß die ~** stop messing (*inf*) or fooling about.
blödeln *vi* (*inf*) to mess (*inf*) or fool about or around; (*Witze machen*) to make jokes. **mit jdm ~** to have fun with sb.
blöderweise *adv* (*inf*) stupidly.
Blödhammel *m* (*sl*) bloody fool (*Brit sl*), mother (*US sl*).
Blödheit *f* (a) (*Dummheit*) stupidity. (b) (*blödes Verhalten*) stupid thing; (*alberne Bemerkung*) silly or stupid remark. **es ist eine ~, das zu machen** it's stupid to do that. (c) (*Med: Schwachsinnigkeit*) imbecility. (d) (*Sw: Schüchternheit*) shyness.
Blödian *m* -(e)s, -e (*inf*) idiot.
Blödigkeit *f*, *no pl* (*obs*) shyness, bashfulness.
Blödling *m* (*inf*) fool, idiot.
Blödmann *m*, *pl* -männer (*inf*) stupid fool (*inf*).
Blödsinn *m*, *no pl* (a) (*Unsinn*) nonsense, rubbish; (*Unfug*) stupid tricks *pl*. **so ein ~** what nonsense or rubbish/how stupid; **das ist doch ~** that's nonsense or rubbish/stupid; ~ **machen** to fool or mess about; **wer hat diesen ~ hier gemacht?** what fool did this?; **mach keinen ~** don't fool or mess about.
(b)(*Schwachsinn*) imbecility.
blödsinnig *adj* (a) stupid, idiotic. (b) (*Med*) imbecilic.
Blödsinnigkeit *f* (*inf*) (a) (*Eigenschaft*) stupidity, idiocy. (b) (*Verhalten*) stupid thing. **laß diese ~en** stop being stupid.
blöken *vi* (*Schaf*) to bleat; (*geh: Rinder*) to low.
blond *adj* (a) (*blondhaarig*) fair(-haired); (*bei Frauen auch*) blonde; (*bei Männern, Menschenrasse auch*) blond. ~**es Gift** (*hum inf*) blonde bombshell (*inf*). (b) (*hum inf: hellfarbig*) light-coloured; *Bier* light, pale; *Kaffee* milky.
Blond *nt* -s, *no pl* blonde; blond.
Blonde(s) *nt decl as adj* (*inf: Bier*) lager.
Blond-: **b~gefärbt** *adj attr* dyed blonde/blond; **b~gelockt** *adj* with fair curly hair; *Haar* fair curly *attr*; **b~gelockt sein** to have fair curly hair; ~**haar** *nt* (*geh*) fair or blonde/blond hair; **b~haarig** *adj* fair-haired, blonde/blond.
blondieren* *vt* to bleach. **blondiert** *Haare* bleached; *Mensch* with bleached hair.
Blondierung *f* (a) (*Vorgang*) bleaching. (b) (*Zustand*) bleachedness.
Blondine *f* blonde.
Blond-: ~**kopf** *m* (a) (*Haare*) fair or blonde/blond hair or head; (b) (*Mensch*) fair-haired or blonde/blond person/girl/boy *etc*; **b~lockig** *adj* with fair or blonde/blond curly hair; ~**schopf** *m* siehe ~**kopf**.
bloß 1 *adj* (a) (*unbedeckt*) bare. **etw auf der ~en Haut tragen** to wear sth without anything on underneath; **mit ~en Füßen** barefooted, barefoot; **mit der ~en Hand** with one's bare hand; **mit ~em Kopf** bare-headed; **mit ~em Schwert** with bared sword; *siehe* **Oberkörper**.
(b) *attr* (*alleinig*) mere; *Neid, Dummheit* sheer; (*allein schon auch*) *Gedanke, Anblick* very. **im ~en Hemd dastehen** to stand there with nothing on over one's shirt/vest; **er kam mit dem ~en Schrecken davon** he got off with no more than a fright.

2 *adv* only. **ich möchte es schon machen,** ~ **weiß ich nicht wie** I'd like to but *or* only I don't know how; **wie kann so etwas** ~ **geschehen?** how on earth can something like that happen?; **was er** ~ **hat?** what on earth *or* whatever is wrong with him?; **tu das** ~ **nicht wieder!** don't you dare do that again; **geh mir** ~ **aus dem Weg** just get out of my way.

3 *conj:* **nicht** ~ **...,** **sondern auch ...** not only ... but also ...

Blöße *f* -, -n **(a)** (*geh*) (*Unbedecktheit*) bareness; (*Nacktheit*) nakedness. **(b)** (*im Wald*) clearing. **(c)** (*Sport*) opening. **jdm eine** ~ **bieten** (*lit*) to drop one's guard; (*fig*) to show sb one's ignorance; **sich** (*dat*) **eine** ~ **geben** (*fig*) to reveal *or* show one's ignorance.

Bloß-: b~füßig *adj* (*dated*) barefoot, bare-footed; **b~legen** *vt sep* to uncover; (*ausgraben auch, Med*) to expose; (*fig*) *Geheimnis* to reveal; *Hintergründe* to bring to light; **b~liegen** *vi sep* *irreg aux sein* to be *or* lie uncovered; (*Ausgegrabenes auch, Med*) to be exposed; (*fig geh: Geheimnis*) to be revealed; **b~stellen** *sep* 1 *vt* jdn to show up; *Lügner, Betrüger* to unmask, to expose; 2 *vr* to show oneself up; to expose oneself; ~**stellung** *f siehe* *vt* showing up; unmasking, exposing; **b~strampeln** *vr sep* to kick one's covers off.

Blouson [blu'zõː] *m or nt* -(s), -s blouson, bomber jacket.

blubbern *vi* (*inf*) to bubble; (*dial: undeutlich sprechen*) to gabble.

Blücher *m*: **er geht ran wie** ~ (*inf*) he doesn't hang about (*inf*).

Blue jeans ['bluːdʒiːns] *pl* (pair of) (blue) jeans *or* denims.

Blues [bluːs] *m* -, - blues *sing or pl.* **(einen)** ~ **tanzen** to smooch (*inf*).

Bluff [bluf, (*dated*) blœf] *m* -(e)s, -s bluff.

bluffen ['blufn, (*dated*) 'blœfn] *vti* to bluff.

blühen 1 *vi* **(a)** (*Blume*) to be in flower *or* bloom, to bloom, to flower; (*Bäume*) to be in blossom, to blossom; (*Garten, Wiese*) to be full of flowers; (*fig: gedeihen*) to flourish, to thrive. **weiß** ~ to have *or* bear white flowers; **ob mir dies Glück noch** ~ **wird?** will I ever see the happy day? **(b)** (*inf: bevorstehen*) to be in store (jdm for sb). **... dann blüht dir aber was** ... then you'll be in for it (*inf*); **das kann mir auch noch** ~ that may happen to me too.

2 *vi impers* **es blüht** there are flowers.

blühend *adj* *Baum* blossoming; *Pflanze, Frau, Aussehen* blooming; *Gesichtsfarbe, Gesundheit* glowing; *Garten, Wiese* full of flowers; (*fig*) *Geschäft, Stadt etc* flourishing, thriving; *Unsinn* absolute; *Phantasie* vivid, lively. **im** ~**en Alter** in one's prime, in the prime of life; **im** ~**en Alter von 18 Jahren** at the early age of 18; **wie das** ~**e Leben** *or* ~ **aussehen** to look the very picture of health.

Blümchen *nt dim of* **Blume.**

Blümchenkaffee *m* (*inf*) weak coffee.

Blume *f* -, -n **(a)** (*Blüte, Pflanze*) flower; (*Topfblume*) (flowering) pot plant; (*poet: Frau*) pearl. **vielen Dank für die** ~**n** (*iro*) thanks for nothing, thank you very much (*iro*); **jdm etw durch die** ~ **sagen/zu verstehen geben** to say/put sth in a roundabout way to sb. **(b)** (*von Wein, Weinbrand*) bouquet; (*von Bier*) head. **(c)** (*Hunt*) (*von Kaninchen, Hasen*) scut; (*von Fuchs*) tag.

Blumen- in *cpds* flower; ~**asch** *m* (*dial*) *siehe* ~**topf;** ~**ausstellung** *f* flower show; ~**bank** *f* (*am Fenster*) windowsill; (~**ständer**) flower stand; ~**beet** *nt* flowerbed; ~**binder(in** *f*) *m* florist; ~**blatt** *nt* petal; ~**bukett** *nt* (*old*) bouquet (of flowers); ~**draht** *m* florist's wire; ~**erde** *f* potting compost; ~**fenster** *nt* window full of flowers; (*Archit*) window for keeping and displaying flowers and pot plants; ~**flor** *m* (*liter*) abundance of flowers; ~**frau** *f* flower woman; ~**geschäft** *nt* florist's, flower shop; **b~geschmückt** *adj* adorned with flowers; ~**gruß** *m* jdm einen ~**gruß übermitteln** to send sb flowers; ~**händler** *m* florist; ~**igel** *m* pinholder; ~**kasten** *m* window box; ~**kind** *nt* (*inf*) flower child, hippie; ~**kinder** flower children *or* people, hippies; ~**kohl** *m* -s, *no pl* cauliflower; ~**kohlohr** *nt* (*inf*) cauliflower ear; ~**korso** *m* flower carnival; ~**kranz** *m* floral wreath; ~**mädchen** *nt* flower girl; ~**malerei** *f* flower painting; ~**meer** *nt* sea of flowers; ~**muster** *nt* floral pattern; ~**pracht** *f* brilliant display of flowers; ~**rabatte** *f* herbaceous border; **b~reich** *adj* full of flowers, flowery; (*fig*) *Stil, Sprache etc* flowery, ornate; ~**sprache** *f* language of flowers; ~**ständer** *m* flower stand; ~**stock** *m* flowering plant; ~**strauß** *m* bouquet *or* bunch of flowers; ~**stück** *nt* (*Art*) flower painting; ~**teppich** *m* carpet of flowers; ~**topf** *m* flowerpot; (*Pflanze*) flowering plant; **damit ist kein** ~**topf zu gewinnen** (*inf*) that's nothing to write home about (*inf*); ~**vase** *f* (flower) vase; ~**zucht** *f* growing of flowers, floriculture (*form*); ~**züchter** *m* flower-grower, floriculturist (*form*); ~**zwiebel** *f* bulb.

•lümerant *adj* *Gefühl* queer. **jdm wird es** ~ sb feels queer.

•lumig *adj* *Parfüm* flowery; *Wein* with a flowery bouquet; (*fig*) *Stil, Sprache auch* ornate.

•lüschen ['blyːsçən] *nt dim of* **Bluse.**

•luse *f* -, -n blouse. **eine pralle** ~ **haben** (*sl*) to be well stacked (*sl*); **ganz schön was in** *or* **unter der** ~ **haben** (*sl*) to have a nice pair (*sl*); **jdm an die** ~ **gehen** (*sl*) to touch sb up (*sl*).

•lüse *f* -, -n (*Naut*) flare.

•lusig *adj* bloused, blouse *attr*.

•lut *nt* -(e)s, *no pl* (*lit, fig*) blood. **er lag in seinem** ~ he lay in a pool of blood; **es ist viel** ~ **vergossen worden** *or* **geflossen** there was a lot of bloodshed; **im** ~ **waten** to have shed a lot of blood; **in jds** ~ **waten** to have sb's blood on one's hands; **nach** ~ **lechzen** *or* **dürsten** to thirst for blood; **er kann kein** ~ **sehen** he can't stand the sight of blood; ~ **lecken** (*lit: Hund*) to taste blood; (*fig*) to develop a taste *or* liking for it; **etw mit seinem** ~ **besiegeln** to lay down one's life for sth; **böses** ~ **machen** *or* **schaffen** *or* **geben** to cause bad *or* ill feeling; **jdm steigt das** ~ **in den Kopf** the blood rushes to sb's head; **ihnen gefror** *or* **stockte** *or* **gerann** *or* **erstarrte das** ~ **in den Adern** their blood froze; **vor Scham/Zorn schoß ihr das** ~ **ins Gesicht** she blushed with shame/went red with anger; **alles** ~ **wich aus ihrem Gesicht** she went deathly pale; **ihr kocht das** ~ **in den Adern** (*geh*) her blood is boiling; **heißes** *or* **feuriges** ~ **haben** to be hot-blooded; **kaltes** ~ **bewahren** to remain unmoved; **kalten** ~**es** cold-bloodedly; (*nur*) **ruhig** ~ keep your shirt on (*inf*); **jdn bis aufs** ~ **hassen** to loathe (and detest) sb; **jdn/sich bis aufs** ~ **bekämpfen** to fight sb/fight bitterly; **ein junges** ~ (*liter*) a young blood (*dated*) *or* (*Mädchen*) thing; **frisches** ~ (*fig*) new blood; ~ **und Eisen** blood and iron; ~ **und Boden** (*NS*) blood and soil, idea that political stability and power depend on unification of race and territory; ~ **und Wasser schwitzen** (*inf*) to sweat blood; **die Stimme des** ~**es** the call of the blood; **das ist das väterliche** ~ he/she *etc* gets that from his/her *etc* father; **das liegt mir/ihm** *etc* **im** ~ that's in my/his *etc* blood; **es geht (einem) ins** ~ it gets into your blood.

Blut-: ~**acker** *m* (*Bibl*) field of blood; ~**ader** *f* vein; ~**algen** *pl* red algae *pl*; ~**alkohol(gehalt)** *m* blood alcohol level *or* content; ~**andrang** *m* congestion; ~**apfelsine** *f* blood orange; **b~arm** *adj* **(a)** ['bluːt-] (*Med*) anaemic; (*fig auch*) colourless; **(b)** [-'arm] (*liter*) very poor, penniless; ~**armut** *f* (*Med*) anaemia; ~**auffrischung** *f* blood replacement; ~**austausch** *m* (*Med*) exchange transfusion; ~**bad** *nt* bloodbath; ~**bahn** *f* bloodstream; ~**bank** *f* blood bank; ~**bann** *m* power over life and death; **b~befleckt** *adj* bloodstained; **b~beschmiert** *adj* smeared with blood; ~**bild** *nt* blood picture; **b~bildend** *adj* haematinic (*spec*); *Nahrung* full of iron; ~**bildung** *f* formation of blood, blood formation; ~**blase** *f* blood blister; ~**buche** *f* copper beech; ~**druck** *m* blood pressure; **b~drucksenkend** *adj* hypotensive; *Mittel* anti-hypertensive; ~**durst** *m* (*geh*) blood lust; **b~dürstig** *adj* (*geh*) bloodthirsty.

Blüte *f* -, -n **(a)** (*Bot: Pflanzenteil*) (*von Blume*) flower, bloom; (*von Baum*) blossom. ~**n treiben** to be in flower *or* bloom, to be flowering *or* blooming; (*Baum*) to be blossoming *or* in blossom; **merkwürdige** ~**n treiben** to produce strange effects; (*Phantasie, Angst*) to produce strange fancies; **eine** ~ **seiner Phantasie** a figment of his imagination. **(b)** (*das Blühen, Blütezeit*) **zur** ~ **des Klees/der Kirschbäume** when the clover is in flower *or* bloom/cherry trees are blossoming *or* in blossom; **die** ~ **beginnt** the flowers/trees are coming into bloom/blossom; **die** ~ **der Apfelbäume ist vorüber** the apple trees are no longer blossoming *or* in blossom; **in (voller)** ~ **stehen** to be in (full) flower/blossom; (*Kultur, Geschäft*) to be flourishing; **sich zur vollen** ~ **entfalten** to come into full flower; (*Mädchen, Kultur*) to blossom; **seine** ~ **erreichen** *or* **erleben** (*Kultur etc*) to reach its peak; **ein Zeitalter kultureller** ~ an age of cultural ascendency; **in der** ~ **seiner Jahre** in his prime, in the prime of his life; **eine neue** ~ **erleben** to undergo a revival. **(c)** (*liter: Elite*) cream; (*der Jugend auch*) flower. **(d)** (*pej inf: Unfähiger*) duffer (*inf*). **(e)** (*Med: Ausschlag*) rash, efflorescence (*spec*). **(f)** (*inf: gefälschte Note*) dud (*inf*).

Blut|egel *m* leech.

bluten *vi* to bleed (*an* + *dat, aus* from). **mir blutet das Herz** my heart bleeds; ~**den Herzens** with heavy heart; **für etw (schwer)** ~ (*inf*) to cough up a lot of money for sth (*inf*).

Blüten-: ~**blatt** *nt* petal; ~**flor** *m* (*liter*) mass of flowers; ~**honig** *m* honey (*made from flowers*); ~**kelch** *m* calyx; ~**knospe** *f* flower bud; **b~los** *adj* non-flowering; ~**stand** *m* inflorescence; ~**staub** *m* pollen.

Blut|entnahme *f* taking of a blood sample. **eine weitere** ~ **war erforderlich** it was necessary to take another blood sample.

Blütenzweig *m* flowering twig.

Bluter *m* -s, - (*Med*) haemophiliac.

Blut|erguß *m* haemorrhage; (*blauer Fleck*) bruise.

Bluterkrankheit *f* haemophilia.

Blütezeit *f* **(a)** **während der** ~ **der Kirschbäume** while the cherries were in blossom; **die** ~ **der Obstbäume ist vorbei** the fruit trees are no longer in blossom. **(b)** (*fig*) heyday; (*von Mensch*) prime.

Blut-: ~**farbstoff** *m* haemoglobin; ~**faserstoff** *m* fibrin; ~**fehde** *f* blood feud; ~**fleck** *m* bloodstain; ~**flüssigkeit** *f siehe* ~**plasma;** ~**gefäß** *nt* blood vessel; ~**geld** *nt* blood money; ~**gerinnsel** *nt* blood clot; ~**gerinnung** *f* clotting of the blood; ~**gerüst** *nt* (*liter*) scaffold; **b~getränkt** *adj* blood-soaked, soaked in blood; ~**gier** *f* blood lust; **b~gierig** *adj* bloodthirsty.

Blutgruppe *f* blood group. **die** ~ **O haben** to be blood group O; **jds** ~ **bestimmen** to type *or* group sb's blood.

Blutgruppen-: ~**bestimmung** *f* blood-typing; ~**untersuchung** *f* (*Jur*) blood test (*to determine paternity*).

Blut-: ~**hochdruck** *m* high blood pressure; ~**hochzeit** *f siehe* **Bartholomäusnacht;** ~**hund** *m* (*lit, fig*) bloodhound; ~**husten** *m* haemoptysis (*spec*); **er hat** ~**husten** he is coughing (up) blood.

blutig *adj* **(a)** (*lit, fig*) bloody. **jdn** ~ **schlagen** to beat sb to a pulp; **sich** ~ **machen** to get blood on oneself; ~**e Tränen weinen** (*liter*) to shed bitter tears. **(b)** (*inf*) *Anfänger* absolute; *Ernst* deadly.

-blütig *adj suf* **(a)** (*Tier*) -blooded. **(b)** (*Pflanze*) -blossomed.

Blut-: b~jung *adj* very young; ~**konserve** *f* unit *or* pint of stored blood; ~**körperchen** *nt* blood corpuscle; ~**krankheit** *f* blood disease; ~**krebs** *m* leukaemia; ~**kreislauf** *m* blood circulation; ~**lache** *f* pool of blood; **b~leer** *adj* bloodless; ~**leere** *f, no pl* lack of blood; **b~los** *adj* bloodless; (*fig*) *Stil* colourless, anaemic; ~**opfer** *nt* **(a)** (*Opferung*) blood sacrifice; **(b)** (*Geopferter*) victim; (*fig*) casualty; ~**orange** *f* blood orange; ~**paß** *m* card giving blood group etc; ~**pfropf** *m* clot of blood; ~**plasma** *nt* blood plasma; ~**plättchen** *nt* platelet; ~**probe** *f* blood test; ~**rache** *f* blood feud; ~**rausch** *m* frenzy; **b~reinigend** *adj* blood-cleansing, depurative (spec); ~reinigung f cleansing of the blood; b~rot adj (liter) blood-red; b~rünstig adj bloodthirsty; ~sauger m (lit, fig) bloodsucker; (Vampir) vampire.

Bluts-: ~bande pl (geh) bonds or ties of blood pl; ~bruder m blood brother; ~brüderschaft f blood brotherhood.

Blut-: ~schande f incest; ~schänder m incestuous person; ~schuld f (liter) blood guilt; eine ~schuld auf sich (acc) laden to sully one's hands with blood (liter); ~schwamm m (Med) strawberry mark; ~senkung f (Med) sedimentation of the blood; eine ~senkung machen to test the sedimentation rate of the blood; ~serum nt blood serum; ~speien nt (geh) siehe ~husten; ~spende f unit or pint of blood (given by a donor); ~spenden nt giving blood no art; zum ~spenden aufrufen to appeal for blood donors; ~spender m blood donor; ~spucken nt siehe ~husten; ~spur f trail of blood; ~spuren traces of blood; ~stauung f congestion; ~stein m haematite; b~stillend adj styptic; ~strahl m stream of blood; ~strom m bloodstream; (aus Wunde) stream of blood.

Blutstropfen ['bluːts-] m drop of blood.

Blut-: ~stuhl m (Med) blood in the faeces; ~sturz m haemorrhage.

Bluts-: b~verwandt adj related by blood; ~verwandte(r) mf blood relation or relative; ~verwandtschaft f blood relationship.

blutt adj (Sw) (nackt) bare.

Blut-: ~tat f bloody deed; ~taufe f baptism of blood; ~transfusion f blood transfusion; b~triefend adj attr bloody, dripping with blood; b~überströmt adj streaming with blood; ~übertragung f blood transfusion.

Blutung f bleeding no pl; (starke) haemorrhage; (monatliche) period. eine/die ~ stillen to stop the bleeding.

Blut-: b~unterlaufen adj suffused with blood; Augen ~shot; ~untersuchung f blood test; ~vergießen nt -s, no pl bloodshed no indef art; ~vergiftung f blood-poisoning no indef art; ~verlust m loss of blood; b~verschmiert adj bloody, smeared with blood; b~voll adj vivid, lively; ~wallung f congestion; (bei Frau) hot flush; ~wäsche f (Med) detoxification of the blood; ~wasser nt siehe ~serum; b~wenig adj (inf) next to nothing; sich b~wenig um jdn kümmern not to give a damn about sb (inf); ~wurst f blutwurst (US), blood sausage; (zum Warmmachen) black pudding (Brit); ~zelle f blood corpuscle or cell; ~zeuge m (old) martyr; ~zirkulation f blood circulation; ~zoll m (geh) toll (of lives); ein ~zoll von 1000 Toten a toll of 1,000 lives; ~zucker m blood sugar; ~zuckerspiegel m blood sugar level; ~zufuhr f blood supply.

BND [beː|enˈdeː] m - s abbr of **Bundesnachrichtendienst**.

Bö f -, -en gust (of wind); (stärker, mit Regen) squall.

Boa f -, -s (Schlange, Schal) boa.

Bob m -s, -s bob(sleigh).

Bob-: ~bahn f bob(sleigh) run; ~fahrer m bobber.

Boccia ['bɔtʃa] nt -(s) or f -, no pl bowls sing.

Bock[1] m -(e)s, ̈e (a) (Reh~, Kaninchen~) buck; (Schafs~) ram; (Ziegen~) he-goat, billy-goat. alter ~ (inf) old goat (inf); sturer/geiler ~ (inf) stubborn old devil (inf)/randy (Brit) or horny old goat (inf); er ist ein steifer ~ (inf) or steif wie ein ~ (inf) he's not at all athletic, he's as stiff as a board (hum inf); wie ein ~ stinken to smell like a pig (inf), to stink to high heaven (inf); die ̈e von den Schafen scheiden or trennen (fig) to separate the sheep from the goats; den ~ zum Gärtner machen (fig) to be asking for trouble; ihn stößt der ~ (inf) he's (just) being awkward or difficult; einen ~ schießen (fig inf) to (make a) boob (inf); (Faux-pas auch) to drop a clanger (inf).
(b) (inf: Trotz) stubbornness. (s)einen ~ haben to be awkward or difficult, to play up (inf).
(c) (Gestell) stand; (Stützgerät) support; (für Auto) ramp; (aus Holzbalken, mit Beinen) trestle; (Säge~) sawhorse.
(d) (Sport) vaulting horse. den or einen ~ machen to bend over (for someone to vault over).
(e) (Schemel) (high) stool.
(f) (Kutsch~) box (seat).
(g) (Ramme) (battering) ram.
(h) (sl: Lust, Spaß) ̈e or einen ~ auf etw (acc) haben to fancy sth (inf); ̈e or einen ~ haben, etw zu tun to fancy doing sth; etw aus ~ tun to do sth for the hell of it (inf) or for a lark (Brit inf).

Bock[2] nt -s, - siehe **Bockbier.**

Bock-: b~beinig adj (inf) contrary, awkward; ~beinigkeit f (inf) contrariness, awkwardness; ~bier nt bock (beer) (type of strong beer).

bocken vi (a) (Zugtier etc) to refuse to move; (nicht springen wollen: Pferd) to refuse; (fig inf: Auto, Motor etc) to refuse to start/go properly. vor einer Hürde ~ to refuse a jump. (b) (inf: trotzen) to play or act up (inf). (c) (sl: koitieren) to have it off (sl), to have a screw (vulg).

bockig adj (inf) contrary, awkward.

Bock-: ~leiter f stepladder; ~mist m (inf) (dummes Gerede) bullshit (sl); ~mist machen to make a balls-up (sl).

Bocks-: ~bart m (a) (von Ziege) goat's beard; (b) (Bot) goatsbeard; ~beutel m wide, rounded bottle containing a particular type of wine; ~horn nt: jdn ins ~horn jagen to put the wind up sb (inf); sich von jdm ins ~horn jagen lassen to let sb upset one; sie ließ sich nicht ins ~horn jagen she didn't let herself get into a state.

Bock-: ~springen nt -s leapfrog; (Sport) vaulting; ~springen machen to play leapfrog; ~sprung m (a) (Sprung über Menschen) leap; (Sport) vault; (b) (ungeschickter Sprung) leap, bound; ~sprünge machen to leap up and down; ~wurst f bockwurst (type of sausage).

Boden m -s, - (a) (Erde, Grundfläche) ground; (Erdreich auch)

soil; (Fuß~) floor; (Grundbesitz) land; (no pl: Terrain) soil. auf spanischem ~ on Spanish soil; zu ~ fallen to fall to the ground; jdn zu ~ schlagen or strecken to knock sb down, to floor sb; festen ~ unter den Füßen haben, auf festem ~ sein to be or stand on firm ground, to be on terra firma; (fig) (finanziell abgesichert) to be secure; (fundierte Argumente haben) to be on firm ground; den ~ unter den Füßen verlieren (lit) to lose one's footing; (fig: in Diskussion) to get out of one's depth; als sie diese Nachricht erfuhr, verlor sie den ~ unter den Füßen when she learnt this news, the ground fell from beneath her feet; der ~ brannte ihm unter den Füßen, ihm wurde der ~ (unter den Füßen) zu heiß (fig) things were getting too hot for him; jdm den ~ unter den Füßen wegziehen (fig) to cut the ground from under sb's feet; ich hätte (vor Scham) im ~ versinken können (fig) I was so ashamed that I wished the ground would (open and) swallow me up; etw am ~ zerstören to destroy sth utterly or completely; (Feuer auch) to burn sth to the ground; am ~ zerstört sein (inf) to be shattered (fig inf); (an) ~ gewinnen/verlieren (fig) to gain/lose ground; ~ gutmachen or wettmachen (fig) to make up ground, to catch up; etw aus dem ~ stampfen (fig) to conjure sth up out of nothing; Häuser auch to build overnight; er stand wie aus dem ~ gewachsen vor mir he appeared in front of me as if by magic; auf fruchtbaren ~ fallen (fig) to fall on fertile ground; jdm/einer Sache den ~ bereiten (fig) to prepare the ground for sb/sth; siehe Faß, Grund, schießen.
(b) (unterste Fläche) (von Behälter) bottom; (von Meer auch) seabed; (von Hose) seat; (Torten~) base; siehe doppelt.
(c) (Raum) (Dach~, Heu~) loft; (Trocken~) (für Getreide) drying floor/room; (für Wäsche) drying room.
(d) (fig: Grundlage) auf dem ~ der Wissenschaft/Tatsachen/Wirklichkeit stehen to base oneself on scientific fact/on fact/on reality; (Behauptung) to be based or founded on scientific fact/on fact/on reality; sie wurde hart auf den ~ der Wirklichkeit zurückgeholt she was brought down to earth with a bump; auf dem ~ der Tatsachen bleiben to stick to the facts; den ~ der Tatsachen verlassen to go into the realm of fantasy; sich auf unsicherem ~ bewegen to be on shaky ground; er steht auf dem ~ des Gesetzes (nicht ungesetzlich) he is within the law, (hat Gesetz hinter sich) he has the backing of the law; einem Gerücht den ~ entziehen to knock the bottom out of a rumour, to show a rumour to be unfounded.

Boden-: ~abwehr f ground defence; ~belag m floor covering; ~beschaffenheit f condition of the ground; (von Acker etc) condition of the soil; ~erhebung f elevation; ~ertrag m (Agr) crop yield; ~feuchtigkeit f (Hort, Agr) soil or ground humidity (im Haus) rising damp; ~fläche f (Agr) area of land; (von Zimmer) floor space or area; ~frost m ground frost; ~gefecht nt ground fighting no pl; ~haftung f (Aut) road holding no indef art; ~heizung f underfloor (central) heating; ~kammer f attic; ~kampf m (a) (Mil) siehe ~gefecht; (b) (Sport) floorwork; ~kontrolle f (Space) ground control; ~kunde f soil science; ~leger m -s, - floor layer; b~los adj bottomless; (inf: unerhört) indescribable, incredible; ins ~lose fallen to fall into an abyss; ~nebel m ground mist; ~nutzung f land utilization; ~organisation f (Aviat) ground organization; ~personal nt (Aviat) ground personnel pl or staff pl; ~reform f land or agrarian reform; ~rente f ground rent; ~satz m sediment; (von Kaffee) grounds pl, dregs pl; ~schätze pl mineral resources pl; ~schicht f layer of soil; (Geol) stratum; ~see m: der ~see Lake Constance; ~senke f depression, hollow; ~sicht f (Aviat) ground visibility; ~spekulation f land speculation; b~ständig adj (einheimisch) native (in +dat to); (lang ansässig) long-established; (fig: mit dem Boden verwurzelt) rooted in the soil; ~station f (Space) ground station; ~streitkräfte pl ground forces pl; ~turnen nt floor exercises pl; ~übung f (Sport) floor exercise; ~vase f large vase (placed on the floor); ~welle f (a) bump; (b) (Rad) ground wave.

Bodmerei f (Naut) bottomry.

Bodybuilding ['bɔdibɪldɪŋ] nt -s, no pl bodybuilding. ~ machen to do bodybuilding exercises.

Bodycheck ['bɔdɪtʃɛk] m -s, -s (Sport) bodycheck.

Böe f -, -n siehe **Bö.**

bog pret of **biegen.**

Bogen m -s, - or ̈ (a) (gekrümmte Linie) curve; (Kurve) bend; (Umweg) detour; (Math) arc; (Mus) (zwischen zwei Noten gleicher Höhe) tie; (zur Bindung von verschiedenen Noten) slur (mark); (Ski) turn. einen ~ fahren (Ski) to do or execute a turn; den ~ heraushaben (inf) to have got the hang of it (inf); den ~ heraushaben, wie ... (inf) to have got the hang of how ... (inf); einen ~ machen (Fluß etc) to curve, to describe a curve (form); (einen Umweg machen) to make a detour; einen großen ~ um jdn/etw machen (meiden) to keep well clear of sb/sth, to give sb/sth a wide berth; jdn in hohem ~ hinauswerfen (inf) to send sb flying out.
(b) (Archit) arch.
(c) (Waffe, Mus: Geigen~ etc) bow. den ~ überspannen (fig) to overstep the mark, to go too far.
(d) (Papier~) sheet (of paper).

Bogen-: ~fenster nt bow window; b~förmig adj arched; ~führung f (Mus) bowing; ~gang m (a) (Archit) arcade; (b) (Anat: von Ohr) semicircular canal; ~lampe f arc lamp or light; ~pfeiler m pillar, column (supporting an arch); ~schießen nt archery; ~schütze m archer, bowman; ~sehne f bowstring; ~strich m (Mus) bowing.

Boheme [boˈeːm, boˈɛːm] f -, no pl bohemian world.

Bohemien [boeˈmiɛ̃ː, boheˈmiɛ̃ː] m -s, -s bohemian.

Bohle f -, -n (thick) board; (Rail) sleeper.

böhmakeln* vi (Aus inf) to speak with a dreadful accent.

Böhme m -n, -n, **Böhmin** f Bohemian (inhabitant of Bohemia).

Böhmerwald m Bohemian Forest.
böhmisch adj Bohemian. **das sind für mich** ~e **Dörfer** (inf) that's all Greek to me (inf); **das kommt mir** ~ **vor** (inf) that sounds a bit Irish to me (inf); ~ **einkaufen** (Aus inf) to shoplift; etw ~ einkaufen (Aus inf) to lift sth.
Böhnchen nt dim of **Bohne**.
Bohne f -, -n bean; (inf: Kot des Kaninchens, Rehs) droppings pl. **dicke/grüne/weiße** ~n broad/green or French or runner/haricot beans; **blaue** ~ (dated Mil sl) bullet; **nicht die** ~ (inf) not a scrap (inf), not one little bit; **ich habe nicht die** ~ **gemerkt** I didn't notice anything at all; **das kümmert mich nicht die** ~ I don't care a fig about that (inf); **du hast wohl** ~n **in den Ohren** (inf) are you deaf?; siehe scheren².
Bohnen-: ~**eintopf** m bean stew; ~**kaffee** m real coffee; **gemahlener** ~**kaffee** ground coffee; ~**kraut** nt savo(u)ry; ~**ranke** f tendril; ~**stange** f bean support; (fig inf) beanpole (inf); ~**stroh** nt: **dumm wie** ~**stroh** (inf) (as) thick as two (short) planks (inf), ~**suppe** f bean soup.
Bohner m -s, -, **Bohnerbesen** m, **Bohnerbürste** f floor-polishing brush.
bohnern vti to polish.
Bohnerwachs nt floor polish or wax.
Böhnlein nt dim of **Bohne**.
Bohr|arbeiten pl drillings pl.
bohren 1 vt to bore; (mit Bohrer, Bohrmaschine auch) to drill; Brunnen to sink; (hineindrücken) Stange, Pfahl, Schwert etc to sink (in + acc into). **ein Schiff in den Grund** ~ to send a ship to the bottom (of the sea).
2 vi **(a)** to bore (in + dat into); to drill (nach for). **in einem Zahn** ~ to drill a tooth; **in der Nase** ~ to pick one's nose.
(b) (drängen) to keep on; (peinigen: Schmerz, Zweifel etc) to gnaw. **er bohrte und bohrte, bekam aber keine Antwort** he kept on and on but got no reply; **der Schmerz bohrte ihm im Magen** he had a gnawing pain in his stomach.
3 vr **sich in/durch etw** (acc) ~ to bore its way into/through sth; **ein grelles Licht bohrte sich durchs Dunkel** a glaring light pierced the darkness.
bohrend adj (fig) Blick piercing; Schmerz, Zweifel, Hunger, Reue gnawing; Frage probing.
Bohrer m -s, - **(a)** (elektrisch, Drill~) drill; (Hand~) gimlet, auger. **(b)** (Arbeiter) driller.
Bohr-: ~**insel** f drilling rig; (für Öl auch) oilrig; ~**loch** nt borehole; (in Holz, Metall etc) drill-hole; ~**maschine** f drill; ~**probe** f drilling; ~**turm** m derrick.
Bohrung f **(a)** siehe vt boring; drilling; sinking. **(b)** (Loch) bore(-hole); (in Holz, Metall etc) drill-hole.
böig adj siehe **Bö** gusty; squally.
Boiler ['bɔylɐ] m -s, - (hot-water) tank. **den** ~ **anstellen** to put the water heater on.
Boje f -, -n buoy.
Bolero m -s, -s (Tanz, Jäckchen) bolero.
Bolivien [-iən] nt -s Bolivia.
Böller m -s, - (small) cannon (for ceremonial use). **jdn mit Schüssen aus einem** ~ **begrüßen** to greet sb with a gun or cannon salute.
böllern vi **(a)** aux sein (dial: poltern) to thud. **(b)** (Ftbl sl) to slam the ball blindly towards the goal.
böllern vi to fire. **es böllert** there is firing.
Böllerschuß m gun salute. **5 Böllerschüsse** 5 shots from the cannon.
Bollwerk nt (lit, fig) bulwark (usu fig), bastion, stronghold; (Kai) bulwark.
Bolschewik m -en, -en or -i Bolshevik.
bolschewikisch adj (pej) Bolshevik attr, bolshy (pej inf).
Bolschewismus m Bolshevism.
Bolschewist m Bolshevist.
bolschewistisch adj Bolshevist, Bolshevik attr.
Bolzen m -s, - **(a)** (Tech) pin; (esp mit Gewinde) bolt. **(b)** (Geschoß) bolt.
bolzen (inf) 1 vi to kick about. **es wurde mehr gebolzt als gespielt** they just kicked (the ball) about instead of playing football. 2 vt Ball to slam; Stein to chuck (inf), to fling.
Bombardement [bɔmbardə'māː, (Aus) bɔmbard'māː] nt -s, -s bombardment; (mit Bomben) bombing. **ein** ~ **von** (fig) a deluge or shower of.
bombardieren* vt (mit Bomben belegen) to bomb; (mit Granaten beschießen, fig) to bombard.
Bombardierung f (mit Bomben) bombing; (mit Granaten, fig) bombardment.
Bombast m -(e)s, no pl bombast.
bombastisch adj Sprache bombastic; Kleidung, Architektur, Hauseinrichtung overdone pred.
Bombe f -, -n bomb; (dated: Könner) ace (in + dat at); (Sport inf: Schuß) cracker (inf). **mit** ~n **belegen** to bomb; **wie eine** ~ **einschlagen** to come as a (real) bombshell; **eine/die** ~ **platzen lassen** (fig) to drop a/the bombshell; **die** ~ **ist geplatzt** (fig) the bombshell has been dropped.
bomben vt (Sport inf) Ball to smash (inf), to slam (inf). **(den Ball) ins Tor** ~ to smash or slam the ball into the back of the net (inf).
Bomben- in cpds (Mil) bomb; (inf: hervorragend) fantastic (inf), great (inf); ~**angriff** m bomb attack or raid; ~**anschlag** m bomb attack; ~**besetzung** f (inf) fantastic or great cast (inf); ~**erfolg** m (inf) smash hit (inf); b~**fest** adj **(a)** (Mil) bombproof; **(b)** (inf) Klebestelle, Naht absolutely secure; Entschluß unshakeable; **es steht b~fest, daß** ... it's absolutely certain or a dead cert (inf) that ...; ~**flugzeug** nt bomber; ~**geld** nt (inf) packet (inf), fantastic amount of money; ~**geschädigte(r)** mf decl as adj person who has been bombed out; ~**geschäft** nt (inf) **ein** ~**geschäft sein** to be a gold mine (fig

inf); **ein ~**geschäft machen** to do a roaring trade (inf) (mit in); ~**geschwader** nt bomber squadron; ~**hitze** f (inf) sweltering heat no indef art; ~**nacht** f night of bombing; ~**schaden** m bomb damage; ~**schuß** m (inf) unstoppable shot; b~**sicher** adj **(a)** (Mil) bombproof; **(b)** (inf) dead certain (inf); b~**sicher sein**, **eine b~sichere Sache sein** to be a dead cert (inf); ~**splitter** m bomb fragment; ~**stellung** f (inf) job in a million (inf), fantastic job (inf); ~**teppich** m **einen** ~**teppich legen** to blanket-bomb an/the area; ~**terror** m terror bombing; ~**trichter** m bomb crater.
Bomber m -s, - bomber.
bombig adj (dated inf) super (inf), smashing (inf).
Bommel f -, -n bobble.
Bon [bɔŋ] m -s, -s voucher, coupon; (Kassenzettel) receipt, (sales) slip.
Bonbon [bɔŋ'bɔŋ] nt or m -s, -s sweet (Brit), candy (US); (fig) treat.
bonbonfarben, bonbonfarbig adj candy-coloured.
Bonbonniere [bɔŋbo'nieːrə] f -, -n box of chocolates.
Bonbonpapier nt sweet or candy (US) wrapper.
bongen vt Betrag etc to ring up.
Bongo ['bɔŋgo] nt -(s), -s, f -, -s, **Bongotrommel** f bongo (drum).
Bonmot [bõ'moː] nt -s, -s bon mot.
Bonus m - or -ses, - or -se (Comm, bei Versicherung) bonus; (Univ, Sport: Punktvorteil) bonus points pl.
Bonze m -n, -n **(a)** (Rel) bonze. **(b)** (pej) bigwig (inf), big shot (inf).
Boogie(-Woogie) ['bugi('vugi)] m -(s), -s boogie-woogie.
Boom [buːm] m -s, -s boom.
Boot nt -(e)s, -e boat. ~ **fahren** to go out in a boat; (zum Vergnügen) to go boating; **wir sitzen alle in einem** or **im gleichen** ~ (fig) we're all in the same boat.
Boots-: ~**bauer** m boatbuilder; ~**deck** nt boat-deck; ~**fahrt** f boat trip; ~**haus** nt boathouse; ~**länge** f (Sport) (boat's) length; ~**mann** m (Naut) bo'sun, boatswain; (Dienstgrad) petty officer; ~**schuppen** m boathouse; ~**steg** m landing-stage; ~**verleih** m boat hire business; ~**verleiher** m boat hirer.
Bor nt -s, no pl boron.
Borax m -(es), no pl borax.
Bord¹ m -(e)s, no pl an ~ (eines Schiffes/der „Bremen") aboard or on board (a ship/the "Bremen"); **alle Mann an** ~! all aboard!; **frei an** ~ (Comm) free on board, f.o.b.; **an** ~ **gehen** to board or go aboard (the ship/plane), to go on board; **über** ~ overboard; **Mann über** ~! man overboard!; **über** ~ **gehen** to go overboard; (fig) to go by the board; **über** ~ **werfen** (lit, fig) to throw overboard, to jettison; **die Vorsicht über** ~ **werfen** to throw caution to the winds; **von** ~ **gehen** to leave (the) ship/the plane; (esp Passagiere am Ziel) to disembark.
Bord² nt -(e)s, -e (Wandbrett) shelf.
Bord³ nt -(e)s, -e (Sw) (Rand) ledge, raised edge; (Böschung) embankment, bank.
Bord-: ~**buch** nt log(book); ~**computer** m (Space) on-board computer; b~**eigen** adj ship's/plane's etc.
Bordell nt -s, -e brothel.
Bordellwirtin f brothel-keeper, madam.
Bord-: ~**funk** m (Naut) (ship's) radio; (Aviat) (aircraft) radio equipment; ~**funker** m (Naut, Aviat) radio operator.
bordieren* vt (Sew) to edge, to border.
Bord-: ~**kante** f kerb; ~**mechaniker** m ship's/aircraft mechanic; ~**stein** m kerb; **den** ~**stein mitnehmen** (inf) to hit the kerb; ~**steinkante** f, ~**steinrand** m kerb; ~**steinschwalbe** f (hum inf) street-walker, pro (inf).
Bordüre f -, -n edging, border.
Bord-: ~**waffen** pl (Mil) aircraft/tank/ship armaments pl; ~**wand** f (Naut) ship's side; (Aviat) side of the aircraft.
Boretsch m -(e)s, no pl siehe **Bor(r)etsch**.
Borg m (dated): **auf** ~ **on credit; etw auf** ~ **kaufen** to buy sth on credit or tick (inf).
borgen vti **(a)** (erhalten) to borrow (von from). **(b)** (geben) to lend, to loan (jdm etw sb sth, sth to sb).
Borke f -, -n bark.
Borken-: ~**flechte** f (Med) ringworm; ~**käfer** m bark beetle; ~**krepp** m (Tex) crepe.
Born m -(e)s, -e (old, liter) (Brunnen) well; (Quelle) spring; (fig) fountain, fount (liter).
borniert adj bigoted, narrow-minded.
Bor(r)etsch m -(e)s, no pl borage.
Borsalbe f boric acid ointment.
Börse f -, -n **(a)** (Geld~) (für Frauen) purse; (für Männer) wallet. **(b)** (Wertpapierhandel) stock market; (Ort) stock exchange.
Börsen-: ~**beginn** m opening of the stock market; **bei** ~**beginn** when the stock market opens/opened; ~**bericht** m stock market report; b~**fähig** adj negotiable on the stock exchange; ~**geschäft** nt (Wertpapierhandel) stockbroking; (Transaktion) stock market transaction; ~**krise** f crisis on the stock market; ~**kurs** m stock market price; ~**makler** m stockbroker; ~**notierung** f quotation (on the stock exchange); ~**schluß** m, no pl close of the stock market; **bei** ~**schluß** when the stock market closes/closed; ~**schwankungen** pl fluctuations on the stock market; ~**schwindel** m stock market swindle or fiddle (inf); ~**spekulant** m speculator on the stock market; ~**spekulation** f speculation on the stock market; ~**sturz** m collapse of the market; ~**tendenz** f stock market trend; ~**tip** m market tip; ~**verkehr** m stock market dealings pl or transactions pl; ~**wesen** nt stock market.
Börsianer m -s, - (inf) (Makler) broker; (Spekulant) speculator.
Borste f -, -n bristle.

Borsten-: ~tier nt pig, swine; ~vieh nt pigs pl, swine pl.
borstig adj bristly; (fig) snappish.
Borstigkeit f siehe adj bristliness; snappishness.
Borte f -, -n braid trimming.
Borwasser nt boric acid lotion.
bös adj siehe **böse**.
bös|artig adj malicious, nasty; Tier, (stärker) Mensch, Wesen vicious; (Med) Geschwür malignant.
Bös|artigkeit f siehe adj maliciousness, nastiness; viciousness; malignancy.
Böschung f (von Straße) bank, embankment; (von Bahndamm) embankment; (von Fluß) bank.
Böschungswinkel m gradient.
böse adj (a) (sittlich schlecht) bad; (stärker) evil, wicked; (inf: unartig auch) naughty. die ~ Fee/Stiefmutter the Wicked Fairy/Stepmother; ein ~r Geist an evil spirit; ~ Kräfte evil or malevolent forces; das war keine ~ Absicht there was no harm intended; das war nicht ~ gemeint I/he etc didn't mean it nastily; eine ~ Sieben (inf) a shrew, a vixen; (dominierend) a battleaxe (inf); eine ~ Zunge or ein ~s Mundwerk haben to have a malicious or wicked tongue; siehe Blick.
(b) no pred (unangenehm, übel) Traum, Angelegenheit, Krankheit bad; Überraschung, Streich, Geschichte nasty. ein ~s Erwachen a rude awakening; ~ Folgen dire consequences; ~ Zeiten bad times; er ist ~ dran life's not easy for him; (gesundheitlich) he's in a bad way; das/es sieht ~ aus things look/it looks bad; siehe Blut, Ende, Wetter².
(c) (verärgert) angry, cross (+ dat, auf + acc, mit with). ein ~s Gesicht machen to scowl; im ~n auseinandergehen to part on bad terms.
(d) (inf) (schmerzend, entzündet) bad attr, sore; (krank, schlimm) bad; Wunde, Husten nasty, bad.
(e) (inf: verstärkend) real (inf); Enttäuschung, Gewitter, Sturz bad, terrible. er hat ~ geschimpft he didn't half curse (Brit inf), he cursed like hell (inf).
Böse(r) mf decl as adj wicked or evil person; (Film, Theat) villain, baddy (inf). die ~n the wicked; der ~ (Teufel) the Evil One.
Böse(s) nt decl as adj (Schaden, Leid) harm. jdm ~s antun to do sb harm; ich habe damit nichts ~s beabsichtigt I didn't mean any harm (by that); ich will dir doch nichts ~s I don't mean you any harm; mir schwant ~s it sounds/looks ominous (to me); ich dachte an gar nichts ~s, als ... I was quite unsuspecting when ...; ich habe mir gar nichts ~s dabei gedacht, als ich das sagte I didn't mean any harm when I said that; siehe ahnen.
Bösewicht m -(e)s, -e or -er (old, hum) villain.
Bos-: b~haft adj malicious, spiteful, nasty; ~haftigkeit f maliciousness, spitefulness, nastiness; ~heit f malice, nastiness; (Bemerkung, Handlung) malicious or nasty remark/thing to do; er hat es mit konstanter ~heit getan maliciously he kept on doing it.
Boskop m -s, - ≈ russet.
Boß m Bosses, Bosse (inf) boss (inf).
Bossa Nova m - -, - -s bossanova.
Bosse f -, -n (Archit) boss.
bosseln (inf) 1 vi to tinker or fiddle about (inf) (an + dat with). 2 vt (zusammenbasteln) to rig up (inf) (jdm for sb).
böswillig adj malicious; (Jur auch) wilful. in ~er Absicht with malicious intent.
Böswilligkeit f malice, maliciousness.
bot pret of **bieten**.
Botanik f botany.
Botaniker(in f) m -s, - botanist.
botanisch adj botanic.
botanisieren* vi to collect and study plants, to botanize (rare).
Botanisiertrommel f (botanist's) specimen container.
Bötchen nt dim of Boot little boat.
Bote m -n, -n (a) (usu mit Nachricht) messenger; (Kurier) courier; (Post~) postman; (Zeitungs~) paperboy; (Laufbursche) errand boy; (Gerichts~) messenger-at-arms. (b) (fig: Anzeichen) herald, harbinger (liter).
Boten-: ~bericht m (Liter) report by messenger; ~dienst m errand; (Einrichtung) messenger service; ~gang m errand; einen ~gang machen to run an errand; ~lohn m delivery fee; (Bezahlung des Boten) messenger's/errand boy's fee; er kauft für sie ein, und bekommt dafür einen kleinen ~lohn he goes shopping for her and gets a small payment for running (her) errands.
Botin f siehe Bote (a) messenger; courier; postwoman; papergirl; errand girl.
botmäßig adj (old, geh) (untertänig) compliant, submissive; (gehorsam) obedient. jdm ~ sein to be at sb's command.
Botmäßigkeit f, no pl (old, geh) (a) (Herrschaft) dominion, rule. ein Volk unter seine ~ bringen to bring a people under one's sway or rule, to gain dominion over a people. (b) siehe adj compliance, submissiveness; obedience.
Botschaft f (a) (Mitteilung) message; (neuere) communication; (Neuigkeit) piece of news, news no indef art or pl. ein freudige ~ good news, glad tidings pl (liter, hum); die frohe ~ (Pol: Gesandtschaft) embassy.
Botschafter m -s, - ambassador.
Botschafter|ebene f: auf ~ at ambassadorial level.
Botschafterin f ambassador; (Ehefrau) ambassadress.
Botschaftssekretär m secretary (in the diplomatic service).
Böttcher m -s, - cooper.
Böttcherei f (no pl: Gewerbe) cooper's trade, cooperage; (Werkstatt) cooper's (work)shop, cooperage.
Bottich m -(e)s, -e tub.
Bouclé¹ [bu'kle:] nt -s, -s bouclé (yarn).

Bouclé² [bu'kle:] m -s, -s (a) (Gewebe) bouclé (fabric). (b) (Teppich) loop-pile carpeting.
Boudoir [bu'doa:ʀ] nt -s, -s (dated geh) boudoir.
Bouillon [bul'jɔn, bul'jõ:, (Aus) bu'jõ:] f -, -s stock, bouillon. (auf Speisekarte) bouillon, consommé.
Bouillonwürfel m stock or bouillon cube.
Boulevard [bulə'va:ʀ, (Aus) bul'va:ʀ] m -s, -s boulevard.
Boulevard-: ~blatt nt (inf) popular daily, tabloid; ~presse f (inf) popular press; ~stück nt light play/comedy; ~theater nt light theatre; ~zeitung f siehe ~blatt.
Bouquet [bu'ke:] nt -s, -s siehe Bukett.
Bourgeois [bur'ʒoa] m -, - (geh) bourgeois.
bourgeois [bur'ʒoa] adj (geh) bourgeois, middle-class.
Bourgeoisie [burʒoa'zi:] f (geh) bourgeoisie.
Boutique [bu'ti:k] f -, -n boutique.
Bovist m -s, -e (Bot) puffball, bovista (spec).
Bowle ['bo:lə] f -, -n (a) (Getränk) punch. eine ~ ansetzen to prepare a punch. (b) (Gefäß, Schüssel) punchbowl; (Garnitur) punch set (punchbowl and cups).
Bowlen-: ~schüssel f punchbowl; ~service nt punch set (punchbowl and cups); ~tasse f cup (for punch).
Bowling ['bo:lɪŋ] nt -s, -s (Spiel) (tenpin) bowling; (Ort) bowling alley. ~ spielen gehen to go bowling.
Bowlingkugel f bowl.
Box f (a) (abgeteilter Raum) compartment; (für Pferde) box; (in Großgarage) (partitioned-off) parking place; (für Rennwagen) pit; (bei Ausstellungen) stand. (b) (Kamera) box camera. (c) (Behälter) box. (d) (Musik~) jukebox; (Lautsprecher~) speaker (unit).
Boxen nt -s, no pl (Sport) boxing.
boxen 1 vi (Sport) to box; (zur Übung) to spar; (mit Fäusten zuschlagen) to hit out, to punch. um einen Titel ~ to fight for a title; gegen jdn ~ to fight sb.
2 vt (a) (schlagen) jdn to punch, to hit. ich box dir gleich eine (inf) I'll hit you one (inf).
(b) (Sport sl: antreten gegen) to fight.
(c) (mit der Faust) Ball to punch, to thump.
3 vr (a) (inf: sich schlagen) to have a punch-up (inf) or a fight.
(b) (sich einen Weg bahnen) to fight one's way. sich durchs Leben/nach oben ~ (fig inf) to fight one's way through life/up.
Boxer m -s, - (Sportler, Hund) boxer; (esp Aus: Schlag) punch.
Boxer-: ~aufstand m (Hist) Boxer Rebellion; ~motor m (Tech) opposed cylinder engine; ~nase f boxer's nose, broken nose; ~stellung f boxer's stance; in ~stellung gehen to put one's fists up, to square up.
Box-: ~handschuh m boxing glove; ~kalf nt -s, no pl box calf; ~kamera f box camera; ~kampf m (Disziplin) boxing no art; (Einzelkampf) fight, bout, (boxing) match; ~ring m boxing ring; ~sport m (sport of) boxing.
Boy [bɔy] m -s, -s pageboy (Brit), bellhop (esp US).
Boykott [bɔy'kɔt] m -(e)s, -e or -s boycott.
boykottieren* [bɔykɔ'tiːrən] vt to boycott.
BP abbr of Bundespost.
brabbeln vi (inf) to mumble, to mutter; (Baby) to babble.
brach¹ pret of brechen.
brach² adj attr (old) fallow.
Brache f -, -n (old) (Land) fallow (land); (Zeit) fallow period.
Brachet m -s, -e (obs) June.
Brachfeld nt fallow field.
Brachialgewalt f (inf) brute force.
Brach-: ~land nt fallow (land); b~legen vt sep to leave fallow; seine Talente b~gelegt his talents were left unexploited; b~liegen vi sep irreg to lie fallow; (fig) to be left unexploited; b~liegende Kenntnisse/Kräfte unexploited knowledge/powers; ~monat, ~mond m (obs) June.
brachte pret of bringen.
Brachvogel m curlew.
Brack nt -s, -s siehe Brackwasser.
brackig adj brackish.
Brackwasser nt brackish water.
Brahman nt -s, no pl Brahma.
Brahmane m -n, -n Brahman, Brahmin.
brahmanisch adj Brahminical, Brahman attr.
Brahmanismus m Brahmanism.
bramarbasieren* vi (geh) to brag (von about), to boast (von about), to swagger.
Bram-: ~rah(e) f topgallant yard; ~segel nt topgallant sail; ~stenge f topgallant stay.
Branche ['brã:ʃə] f -, -n (Fach) field, department; (Gewerbe) trade; (Geschäftszweig) area of business, trade; (Wirtschaftszweig) (branch of) industry. das gehört in seine ~ that's in his line or department or field.
Branchen-: ~adreßbuch nt classified directory; b~fremd adj Waren foreign to the trade/industry; Kollege not versed in the trade; die Firma hat sich b~fremd versucht the firm has branched out into a field in which it has no experience; ~kenntnis f knowledge of the trade/industry; b~kundig adj experienced or well-versed in the trade/industry; b~üblich adj usual in the trade/industry; b~unüblich adj not usual in the trade/industry; ~verzeichnis nt yellow pages.
Brand m -(e)s, ⁻e (a) (Feuer) fire; (lodernd auch) blaze, conflagration (liter). in ~ geraten to catch fire; (in Flammen aufgehen) to burst into flames; in ~ stehen to be on fire, to be ablaze; etw in ~ setzen or stecken to set fire to sth, to set sth alight or on fire.
(b) usu pl (brennendes Holz etc) firebrand.
(c) (fig geh: der Liebe, des Hasses) burning passion. der ~ der Leidenschaft a/the burning passion.
(d) (das Brennen, von Porzellan etc) firing.

(e) *(fig inf: großer Durst)* raging thirst.
(f) *(dial inf)* *(Brennstoff)* fuel; *(Holz auch)* firewood.
(g) *(Med)* gangrene *no art.*
(h) *(Pflanzenkrankheit)* blight.

Brand-: b~**aktuell** *adj (inf)* *Thema, Frage* red-hot *(inf)*; *Buch* hot from the presses; *Platte etc* the latest thing *(inf)*; ~**binde** f bandage for burns; ~**blase** f (burn) blister; ~**bombe** f firebomb, incendiary bomb *or* device; ~**brief** m *(inf)* *(Bettelbrief)* begging letter; *(Mahnbrief)* urgent reminder; ~**direktor** m = fire chief; b~**eilig** *adj (inf)* extremely urgent.

branden *vi* to surge *(auch fig)*. **an** *or* **gegen etw** *(acc)* ~ to break against sth; ~**der Beifall** thunderous applause.

Brand-: ~**fackel** f firebrand; ~**fleck** m burn; ~**gans** f shelduck; ~**gefahr** f danger of fire; **bei** ~**gefahr** when there is danger of fire; ~**geruch** m smell of burning; ~**herd** m source of the fire *or* blaze; *(fig)* source.

brandig *adj* (a) *(Bot)* suffering from blight; *(Med)* gangrenous. (b) ~ **riechen** to smell of burning; *(bei ausgegangenem Brand)* to have a burnt smell.

Brand-: ~**inspektor** m fire inspector; ~**kasse** f fire insurance company; ~**katastrophe** f fire disaster; ~**leger** m -s, - *(esp Aus)* siehe ~**stifter**; ~**legung** f *(esp Aus)* siehe ~**stiftung**; ~**loch** nt burn hole; ~**mal** nt -s, -e brand; *(fig auch)* stigma; ~**malerei** f pokerwork; *(Bild)* piece of pokerwork; b~**marken*** vt insep to brand; *(fig)* to denounce; **jdn als etw** b~**marken** *(fig)* to brand sb (as) sth; ~**markung** f siehe vt branding; denunciation; ~**mauer** f fire(proof) wall; ~**meister** m fire chief; b~**neu** *adj* (inf) brand-new, spanking new *(inf)*; ~**opfer** nt (a) *(Rel)* burnt offering; (b) *(Mensch)* fire victim; b~**rot** *adj* *Haare, Gesicht* bright red; ~**salbe** f ointment for burns; ~**satz** m incendiary compound; ~**schaden** m fire damage; b~**schatzen*** vt insep to sack, to lay waste to; *(Hist)* to lay under contribution; **die** b~**schatzenden Horden** the pillaging mob; ~**schatzung** f *(Hist)* contribution; ~**schutz** m protection against fire; ~**sohle** f insole; ~**stätte** f *(geh)* fire; *(grösser auch)* conflagration *(liter)*; ~**stelle** f *(Ort des Brandes)* fire, blaze; *(verbrannte Stelle)* burnt patch; ~**stifter** m fire-raiser, arsonist *(esp Jur)*; incendiary *(Jur)*; ~**stiftung** f arson *(auch Jur)*, fire-raising; ~**teig** m choux pastry.

Brandung f surf, breakers pl; *(fig geh)* surge.
Brandungswelle f breaker.

Brand-: ~**ursache** f cause of a/the fire *or* blaze; ~**versicherung** f fire insurance; *(Unternehmen)* fire insurance company; ~**wache** f (a) *(Überwachung der ~stelle)* firewatch; (b) *(Personen)* firewatch team; ~**wunde** f burn; *(durch Flüssigkeit)* scald; ~**zeichen** nt brand.

brannte *pret of* brennen.

Branntwein m spirits pl. **jede Art von** ~ all types *or* every type of spirit(s); **Whisky ist ein** ~ whisky is a (type of) spirit.

Branntwein-: ~**brenner** m distiller; ~**brennerei** f distillery; *(~brennen)* distilling *or* distillation of spirits; ~**schank** f -, -en *(Aus)* = public house *(Brit)*, bar; ~**steuer** f tax on spirits.

Brasil¹ f -, -(s) Brazil cigar.
Brasil² m -s, -e *or* -s *(Tabak)* Brazil(ian) tobacco.
Brasilholz nt brazilwood.
Brasilianer(in f) m -s, - Brazilian.
brasilianisch *adj* Brazilian.
Brasilien [-ian] nt -s Brazil.
Brasse f -, -n *(Naut)* brace.
brassen vt *(Naut)* to brace.
Brät nt -s, *no pl* sausage meat.
Bratapfel m baked apple.

braten *pret* **briet**, *ptp* **gebraten** 1 vti *(am Spieß, im Ofen: mit Fett)* to roast; *(im Ofen: ohne Fett)* to bake; *(in der Pfanne)* to fry. **etw braun/knusprig** ~ to roast/fry sth until it is brown/crispy. 2 vi *(inf: in der Sonne)* to roast *(inf)*. **sich** ~ **lassen** to roast oneself *(inf)*.

Braten m -s, - = pot-roast meat *no indef art, no pl;* *(im Ofen gebraten)* joint, roast, roast meat *no indef art, no pl*. **kalter** ~ cold meat; **ein fetter** ~ *(fig)* a prize catch; **wenn er das Auto zu dem Preis verkaufen kann, wird das ein fetter** ~ he'll make a killing if he can sell the car at that price *(inf)*; **den** ~ **riechen** *or* **schmecken** *(inf)* to smell a rat *(inf)*, to get wind of it/something.

Braten-: ~**fett** nt fat for frying/roasting; ~**fisch** m fried fish; ~**hähnchen** nt, ~**hendl** nt -s, - *(n)* *(Aus, S Ger)* roast chicken; ~**hering** m fried herring *(sold cold)*; ~**huhn, ~hühnchen** nt roast chicken; *(Huhn zum Braten)* roasting chicken; ~**kartoffeln** pl fried *or* sauté potatoes; ~**kartoffelverhältnis** nt *(hum)* er hat ein ~kartoffelverhältnis mit ihr he only sees her because she feeds and waters him *(hum)*; **er sucht ein** ~**kartoffelverhältnis** he's looking for a meal ticket; ~**ofen** m oven; ~**pfanne** f frying pan; ~**röhre** f oven; ~**rost** m grill; *(über offenem Feuer auch)* gridiron.

Bratsche f -, -n viola.
Bratscher m -s, -, **Bratschist(in** f) m violist, viola player.
Brat-: ~**spieß** m skewer; *(Teil des Grills)* spit; *(Gericht)* kebab; ~**wurst** f *(zum Braten)* (frying) sausage; *(gebraten)* (fried) sausage.

Bräu nt -(e)s, -e *(Biersorte)* brew, beer; *(Brauerei)* brewery; *(rare: Schenke)* inn *(old)*, pub *(Brit)*.

Brauch m -(e)s, **Bräuche** custom, tradition. **nach altem** ~ according to (established) custom *or* tradition; **etw ist** ~ sth is traditional, sth is the custom; **so ist es** ~, **so will es der** ~ that's the tradition *or* custom; **das ist bei uns so** ~ *(inf)* that's traditional with us; **außer** ~ **kommen** to die out.

brauchbar *adj* (a) *(benutzbar)* useable; *Plan* workable; *(nütz-*

lich) useful. (b) *(ordentlich)* *Schüler, Idee* decent, reasonable; *Arbeit, Arbeiter etc auch* useful *attr (inf)*.

Brauchbarkeit f (a) usefulness; *(von Plan)* workableness, workability. (b) **ich habe keine Zweifel an der** ~ **seiner Arbeit** I have no doubt that his work is quite reasonable.

brauchen 1 vt (a) *(nötig haben)* to need, to require *(form)* *(für, zu* for).
(b) *(bei Zeitangaben)* **Zeit/zwei Minuten** etc ~ to need time/two minutes etc; **normalerweise brauche ich zwei Stunden dafür** I normally take two hours to do it; **wenn 5 Männer 3 Stunden** ~, ... **if 5 men take 3 hours** ...; **es braucht alles seine Zeit** everything takes time; **wie lange braucht man, um** ...? how long does it take to ...?; **er hat zwei Tage dafür gebraucht** he took two days over it, he needed two days to do it.
(c) *(dated, geh: bedürfen)* **es braucht einer Sache** *(gen)* sth is necessary.
(d) *(inf: nützlich finden)* **das könnte ich** ~ I could do with *or* use that; **wir können das/ihn nicht** ~ we could *or* can do without that/him, we don't need that/him; **das kann ich gerade** ~! *(iro)* that's all I need!; **kannst du die Sachen** ~? have you any use for the things?, are the things of any use to you?; **er ist zu allem zu** ~ *(inf)* he's a really useful type (to have around) *(inf)*; **heute bin ich zu nichts zu** ~ *(inf)* I'm useless today *(inf)*.
(e) *(benutzen)* *Waffe, Verstand, Gerät* to use.
(f) *(inf: verbrauchen)* to use (up); *Strom etc* to use.

2 v aux to need. **du brauchst das nicht tun** you needn't do that, you've no need to do that, you don't have *or* need to do that; **du brauchst es ihm nicht (zu) sagen** you needn't tell *or* don't need to tell him that; *(er weiß das schon)* you don't need to tell him that; **du hättest das nicht (zu) tun** ~ you needn't have done that, you didn't need to *or* had no need to do that; **du brauchst nur an(zu)rufen** you only have *or* need to call, you need only call; **es braucht nicht besonders betont zu werden, daß** ... there's no need to stress the fact that ...; **es braucht nicht gleich zu sein** it doesn't need to be done immediately, there's no immediate need for that; **es hätte nicht zu sein** ~ there was no need for that; *(das hätte nicht geschehen müssen)* that needn't have happened.

Brauchtum nt customs pl, traditions pl. **zum** ~ **in diesem Land gehört** ... one of the customs in this country is ...
Braue f -, -n (eye)brow.
brauen 1 vti *Bier* to brew; *(inf: zubereiten)* *Tee* to brew up; *Kaffee* to make; *Zaubertrank, Punsch etc* to concoct. 2 vi *(old liter)* *(Nebel)* to build up.
Brauer m -s, - brewer.
Brauerei f (a) brewery. (b) *no pl (das Brauen)* brewing.
Brauereiwesen nt brewing trade *or* industry.
Brau-: ~**haus** nt brewery; ~**meister** m master brewer.
braun *adj* brown; *(von Sonne auch)* *Mensch, Haut* (sun-)tanned; *(inf: ~haarig)* brown-haired; *(pej: Nazi~)* Nazi. ~ **werden** *(Mensch)* to get a (sun-)tan, to go *or* get brown, to tan; **von der Sonne** ~ **gebrannt sein** to be tanned (by the sun); **die B~en** *(old: Pferde)* the brown *or* bay horses; *(Nazis)* the Brownshirts.
Braun nt -s, - brown.
Braun-: b~**äugig** *adj* brown-eyed; ~**bär** m brown bear.
Bräune f -, *no pl* (a) *(braune Färbung)* brown(ness); *(von Sonne)* (sun-)tan. (b) *(old inf: Krankheit)* *(Diphtherie)* diphtheria; *(Angina)* angina.
bräunen 1 vt *(Cook)* to brown; *(Sonne etc)* to tan. 2 vi *(Cook)* to go *or* turn brown; *(Mensch)* to tan, to go brown; *(Sonne)* to tan. **sich in der Sonne** ~ **lassen** to get a (sun-)tan. 3 vr *(Haut)* to brown; *(Mensch auch)* to tan.
Braun-: b~**gebrannt** *adj attr* (sun-)tanned, bronzed, brown; b~**haarig** *adj* brown-haired; *Frau auch* brunette; ~**kohl** m *(dial)* siehe Grünkohl; ~**kohle** f brown coal.
bräunlich *adj* brownish, browny.
braunrot *adj* reddish brown.
Braunschweig nt -s Brunswick.
Bräunung f browning; *(von Haut)* bronzing. **eine tiefe** ~ **der Haut** a deep (sun-)tan.
Braus m siehe Saus.
Brause f -, -n (a) *(Dusche, Duschvorrichtung)* shower. **sich unter die** ~ **stellen** to have a shower. (b) *(~aufsatz)* shower attachment; *(an Schlauch, Gießkanne)* rose, spray (attachment). (c) *(Getränk)* pop; *(Limonade)* (fizzy) lemonade; *(~pulver)* lemonade powder.
Brause-: ~**bad** nt shower(bath); ~**kopf** m *(dated)* hothead; ~**limonade** f fizzy lemonade.
brausen 1 vi (a) *(tosen)* to roar; *(Orgel, Beifall)* to thunder; *(Jubel)* to ring out; *(Ohren)* to ring, to buzz; *(sprudeln)* *(Wasser, Brandung)* to foam; *(geh: Blut)* to pound. **es brauste mir in den Ohren** *or* **meinen Ohren** my ears were ringing *or* buzzing; ~**der Beifall** thunderous applause.
(b) *aux sein (rasen, rennen, schnell fahren)* to race; *(Mensch auch)* to storm.
(c) *auch vr (duschen)* to (have a) shower.
2 vt *(abspülen)* *Gegenstände* to rinse (off); *(abduschen)* *Körperteil, Kinder* to put under the shower.
Brause-: ~**pulver** nt lemonade powder; ~**tablette** f lemonade tablet; ~**würfel** m tablet of lemonade powder.
Braut f -, **Bräute** bride; *(dated)* *(Verlobte)* fiancée, betrothed *(old)*, bride-to-be; *(Freundin)* girl(-friend). ~ **Christi** bride of Christ.
-braut f in cpds *(inf)* **Rocker~/Motorrad~** rocker/motor-cycle queen *(sl)*; **Fußball~/Tennis~** footballer's/tennis player's girl *or* moll *(hum sl)*.
Braut-: ~**bett** nt nuptial *or* marital bed; ~**führer** m person who gives away the bride; ~**gemach** nt *(Hist)* nuptial chamber.
Bräutigam m -s, -e (bride)groom; *(dated: Verlobter)* fiancé, betrothed *(old)*, husband-to-be.

Braut-: ~**jungfer** f bridesmaid; ~**kleid** nt wedding dress; ~**kranz** m headdress of myrtle leaves traditionally worn by a bride; ~**leute** pl siehe ~**paar**; ~**mutter** f bride's mother; ~**nacht** f (rare) wedding night; ~**paar** nt bride and (bride-) groom, bridal pair or couple; (dated: Verlobte) engaged couple; ~**schau** f: **auf (die) ~schau gehen/auf ~schau sein** to go looking/be looking for a bride or wife; (hum sl) to be out to make a kill (inf); ~**schleier** m wedding or bridal veil; ~**staat** m wedding finery; ~**stand** m, no pl (dated) engagement; **sich im ~stand befinden** to be engaged or betrothed (old); ~**unterricht** m in RC church, religious instruction of engaged couple prior to marriage; ~**vater** m bride's father; ~**werbung** f courtship, wooing; ~**zeit** f last few weeks before the wedding.

brav adj (a) (gehorsam) Kind good, well-behaved. **sei schön ~!** be a good boy/girl; ~ **(gemacht)!** (zu Tier) good boy!, well done; **iß das ~** leer be a good boy/girl and eat it up, eat it up like a good boy/girl.

(b) (rechtschaffen) upright, worthy, (good) honest; (bieder) Frisur, Kleid plain. **er soll ein ~es Mädchen heiraten** he should marry a good solid girl; ~ **seine Pflicht tun** to do one's duty worthily; **etw ~ spielen** to give an uninspired rendition of sth.

(c) (obs: tapfer) brave.

Bravheit f siehe adj (a) good behaviour. (b) uprightness, worthiness, honesty; plainness. (c) bravery.

bravo ['braːvo] interj well done; (für Künstler) bravo.

Bravoruf m cheer.

Bravour [braˈvuːr] f -, no pl (geh) bravura; (old: Kühnheit) bravery, daring. **mit ~** with style.

Bravourleistung f (geh) brilliant performance.

bravourös [bravuˈrøːs] adj (a) (meisterhaft) brilliant. (b) (forsch) **mit ~em Tempo** with verve; ~ **dahinbrausen** to surge along; **etw ~ in Angriff nehmen** to attack or tackle sth with verve or gusto.

Bravourstück nt (geh) brilliant coup; (Mus) bravura.

BRD [beːˈɛrˈdeː] f - (nicht offiziell) abbr of **Bundesrepublik Deutschland** FRG.

Brech-: b~**bar** adj breakable; ~**bohnen** pl French beans pl; ~**durchfall** m diarrhoea and sickness; ~**eisen** nt crowbar; (von Dieb) jemmy, jimmy (US).

brechen pret **brach**, ptp **gebrochen** 1 vt (a) to break; Schiefer, Stein, Marmor to cut; Widerstand, Trotz auch to overcome; Licht to refract; (geh: pflücken) Blumen to pluck, to pick. **sich/jdm den Arm ~** to break one's/sb's arm; **einer Flasche den Hals ~** to crack (open) a bottle; **das wird ihm das Genick or den Hals ~** (fig) that will bring about his downfall; **jdm die Treue ~** to break trust with sb; (Liebhaber etc) to be unfaithful to sb; siehe Bahn, Eis, Ehe.

(b) (erbrechen) to vomit up, to bring up.

2 vi (a) aux sein to break. **seine Augen brachen** (old, liter) he passed away; **mir bricht das Herz** it breaks my heart; **mit jdm/etw ~** to break with sb/sth; **zum B~ or ~d voll** sein to be full to bursting; **nichts zu ~ und beißen haben** to have not a bite to eat.

(b) (sich erbrechen) to be sick, to throw up. **das finde ich zum B~** (inf) it makes me sick (inf).

3 vir (Wellen) to break; (Lichtstrahl) to be refracted; (Schall) to rebound (an + dat off).

Brecher m -s, - (a) (Welle) breaker. (b) (Tech) crusher.

Brech-: ~**mittel** nt emetic; **er/das ist das reinste ~mittel (für mich)** he/it makes me feel ill; ~**reiz** m nausea; **ein leichter ~reiz** a slight touch of nausea; ~**stange** f crowbar.

Brechung f (a) (der Wellen) breaking; (des Lichts) refraction; (des Schalls) rebounding. (b) (Ling) mutation.

Brechungswinkel m angle of refraction.

Bredouille [breˈduljə] f **in der ~ sein or sitzen/in die ~ geraten or kommen** to be in/get into a scrape (inf).

Brei m -(e)s, -e mush, paste, goo (inf); (für Kinder, Kranke) mash, semi-solid food; (Hafer~) porridge; (Grieß~) semolina; (Reis~) rice pudding; (Papier~) pulp. **verrühren Sie die Zutaten zu einem dünnen ~** mix the ingredients to a thin paste; **die Lava fließt wie ein zäher ~** the lava flows like a sluggish pulp; **jdn zu ~ schlagen** (inf) to beat sb to a pulp (inf); **um den heißen ~ herumreden** (inf) to beat about the bush (inf); **jdm ~ um den Mund or ums Maul schmieren** (inf) to soft-soap sb (inf); siehe Katze, Koch.

breiig adj mushy. **eine ~e Masse** a paste, a paste-like substance.

breit 1 adj broad; (esp bei Maßangabe) wide; Bekanntenkreis, Publikum, Interessen auch wide; Schrift broadly spaced, sprawling. **etw ~er machen** to broaden or widen sth; **den Stoff ~ nehmen** to take the material widthways; ~**es Lachen** guffaw; **er hat ein ~es Lachen** he guffaws; **die ~e Masse** the masses pl, the broad mass of the population; **ein ~es Angebot** a broad or wide selection; ~**e Streuung des Eigentums** widespread distribution of property, distribution of property on a broad basis; **er hat einen ~en Rücken or Buckel** (fig inf) he has a broad back, his shoulders are broad.

2 adv ~ **lachen** to guffaw; ~ **sprechen** to speak with a broad accent; ~ **schreiben** to write big; ~ **gebaut** sturdily built; **die Schuhe ~ treten** to wear one's shoes out of shape; **der Stoff liegt doppelt ~** the material is double width; **sich ~ hinsetzen** to sit down squarely; **setz dich doch nicht so ~ hin** don't take up so much room; (mit gespreizten Beinen) don't sit like that (with your legs apart).

breit-: ~**beinig** 1 adj in ~**beiniger Stellung** with one's legs apart; ~**beiniger Gang** rolling gait; 2 adv with one's legs apart; ~**drücken** vt sep to press flat.

Breite f -, -n (a) breadth; (von Dialekt, Aussprache) broadness; (esp bei Maßangaben) width; (von Angebot) breadth; (von Interessen) breadth, wide range. **der ~ nach** widthways; **etw in aller ~ erklären** to explain sth in great detail; **in voller ~ vor**

jdm smack in front of sb; **in die ~ gehen** to go into detail; (inf: dick werden) to put on weight, to put it on a bit (inf).

(b) (Geog) latitude; (Gebiet) part of the world. **in südlichere ~n fahren** (inf) to travel to more southerly climes or parts; **es liegt (auf) 20° nördlicher ~** it lies 20° north.

breiten vt r to spread. **jdm etw über die Beine** etc ~ to spread sth across sb's legs etc; **sich über das Tal/jds Gesicht ~** to spread across the valley/across or over sb's face.

Breiten-: ~**arbeit** f broader or more general work; ~**grad** m (degree of) latitude; ~**kreis** m parallel; ~**sport** m popular sport; ~**wirkung** f (von Roman etc) large or widespread impact.

Breit-: b~**flächig** adj Gesicht wide; b~**flächig malen** to paint with broad strokes; b~**krempig** adj broad-brimmed; b~**machen** vr sep (inf) **wenn er sich auf dem Sofa b~macht ...** when he plants himself on the sofa ...; **mach dich doch nicht so b~!** don't take up so much room; **sie hat sich im Zimmer b~gemacht** she spread her things all over the room; **die Touristen haben sich im Hotel b~gemacht** the tourists in the hotel behaved as if they owned the place; b~**mäulig** adj Tierart broad-mouthed; (pej) Mensch with a wide mouth, mouthy (inf); b~**randig** adj Hut broadbrimmed; Bild having a wide edge or margin; Schwimmbecken, Gefäß, Brille broad-rimmed; b~**schlagen** vt sep irreg (inf) **jdn (zu etw) b~schlagen** to talk sb round (to sth); **sich b~schlagen lassen** to let oneself be talked round; b~**schult(e)rig** adj broad-shouldered; ~**schwanz** m, no pl caracul; ~**seite** f (Naut) broadside; (von Tisch) short end; **eine ~seite abgeben** to fire a broadside; ~**spurbahn** f broad-gauge railway; b~**spurig** adj broad-gauge attr; (fig) arrogant; b~**treten** vt sep irreg (inf) to go on about (inf); Thema, Witz to flog to death (inf); ~**wand** f wide screen; **etw in ~wand drehen** to film sth for the wide screen; ~**wandfilm** m film for the wide screen.

Brems-: ~**backe** f brake block; ~**belag** m brake lining.

Bremse¹ f -, -n (bei Fahrzeugen) brake. **auf die ~(n) treten/steigen** (inf) or **latschen** (sl) to put on or apply/slam on (inf) the brake(s).

Bremse² f -, -n (Insekt) horsefly.

bremsen 1 vi (a) to brake; (Vorrichtung) to function as a brake. **der Dynamo/Wind bremst** the dynamo acts as a brake/the wind slows you etc down.

(b) (inf: zurückstecken) to ease off, to put on the brakes (inf). **mit etw ~** to cut down (on) sth; **jetzt sollen wir mit den Ausgaben ~** it's time to apply the (financial) brakes.

2 vt (a) Fahrzeug to brake.

(b) (fig) to restrict, to limit; Entwicklung to slow down; Begeisterung to dampen; (inf) jdn to check. **er ist nicht zu ~** (inf) there's no stopping him.

3 vir (inf) **sich in seiner Ausdrucksweise ~** to moderate one's language; **ich kann or werd' mich ~** not likely!, no fear!

Bremser m -s, - (Rail, Sport) brakeman.

Brems-: ~**fallschirm** m brake parachute; ~**flüssigkeit** f brake fluid; ~**hebel** m brake lever; ~**klappe** f (Aviat) brake flap; ~**klotz** m brake chock; (anmontiert) brake block; ~**kraft** f braking power; ~**leistung** f braking efficiency; ~**leuchte** f, ~**licht** nt brake light; ~**pedal** nt brake pedal; ~**probe** f brake test; **eine ~probe machen** to test one's brakes; ~**rakete** f retrorocket; ~**schuh** m brake shoe; ~**spur** f skid mark usu pl.

Bremsung f braking.

Brems-: ~**vorrichtung** f brake mechanism; ~**weg** m braking distance.

Brenn-: b~**bar** adj combustible, inflammable; **leicht b~bar** highly combustible or inflammable; ~**dauer** f (von Glühbirnen) life.

brennen pret **brannte**, ptp **gebrannt** 1 vi to burn; (Haus, Wald auch) to be on fire; (elektrisches Gerät, Glühbirne etc) to be on; (Zigarette, Sparflamme) to be alight; (Stich) to sting; (Füße) to hurt, to be sore. **das Streichholz/Feuerzeug brennt nicht** the match/lighter won't light; **auf der Haut/in den Augen ~** to burn or sting the skin/eyes; **das Licht ~ lassen** to leave the light on; **im Zimmer brennt noch Licht** the light is still on in the room; **es brennt! fire, fire!**; (fig) it's urgent; **wo brennt's denn?** (inf) what's the panic?; **darauf ~, etw zu tun** to be dying to do sth; **vor Ungeduld ~** to burn with impatience; **das brennt mir auf der Seele** that is preying on my mind; **es brennt mir unter den Nägeln ...** (fig) I am itching or dying ...; siehe Boden.

2 vt to burn; Branntwein to distil; Mandeln, Kaffee to roast; Porzellan, Ton, Ziegel to fire, to bake; Tier to brand. **sich (dat) Locken ins Haar ~** to curl one's hair with curling tongs; **ein gebranntes Kind scheut das Feuer** (Prov) once bitten, twice shy (Prov).

3 vr (lit) to burn oneself (an + dat on); (inf: sich täuschen) to be very much mistaken.

brennend adj (lit, fig) burning; Zigarette lighted; Durst raging; Haß consuming. **das interessiert mich ~** (inf) I would be incredibly interested; **ich wüßte ja ~ gern ...** (inf) I'm dying or itching to know ... (inf).

Brenner m -s, - (a) (Tech) burner. (b) (Beruf) (Branntwein~) distiller; (Kaffee~) coffee-roaster; (Ziegel~) brick-firer.

Brennerei f distillery; (Kaffee~) coffee-roasting plant (Ziegel~) brickworks sing or pl.

Brennnessel f getrennt: **Brenn-nessel** stinging nettle.

Brenn-: ~**glas** nt burning glass; ~**holz** nt firewood; ~**material** nt fuel (for heating); ~**nessel** f siehe **Brennnessel**; ~**ofen** m kiln ~**punkt** m (Math, Opt) focus; **im ~punkt des Interesses stehen** to be the focus or focal point of attention; **etw in den ~punkt rücken** (fig) to focus attention on sth; ~**schere** f curling tongs pl; ~**spiegel** m burning glass; ~**spiritus** m methylated spirits sing or pl; ~**stoff** m fuel; ~**weite** f (Opt) focal length.

brenzlig adj (a) **ein ~er Geruch** a smell of burning; **e**

riecht/schmeckt ~ there is a smell of burning/there is a burnt taste. **(b)** (inf) *Situation, Angelegenheit* precarious, dicey (*Brit inf*). **die Sache/die Lage wurde ihm zu** ~ things got too hot for him.

Bresche f -, -n breach, gap. **in etw** (acc) **eine** ~ **schießen** to breach sth; **in die** ~ **springen** (fig) to step into or fill the breach; **für jdn/etw eine** ~ **schlagen** (fig) to stand up for sb/sth.

Bretagne [bre'tanjə] f - die ~ Brittany.

Bretone m -n, -n, **Bretonin** f Breton.

bretonisch adj Breton.

Brett nt -(e)s, -er **(a)** (*Holzplatte*) board; (*länger und dicker*) plank; (*Spiel*~, *Sprung*~) board; (*Bücher*~, *Gewürz*~) shelf; (*inf: Tablett*) tray; (*Frühstücks*~) platter, wooden plate. **schwarzes** ~ noticeboard; **etw mit** ~**ern vernageln** to board sth up; **hier ist die Welt mit** ~**ern vernagelt** this is a parochial little place; **ich habe heute ein** ~ **vor dem Kopf** (inf) I can't think straight today; **bei der Frage hatte ich ein** ~ **vorm Kopf** (inf) my mind went blank or I had a mental block (when he etc asked me that); *siehe* **Stein**.

(b) ~**er** pl (fig) (*Bühne*) stage, boards pl, planks pl (inf); (*Boden des Boxrings*) floor, canvas; (*Skier*) planks pl (sl); **über die** ~**er gehen** (*Theat*) to be put on; **die** ~**er, die die Welt bedeuten** the stage; **auf den** ~**ern (stehen)** (to be) on the stage; (*auf Skiern*) to ski; **jdn auf die** ~**er schicken** (*Sport*) to send sb to the canvas, to floor sb.

Brettchen nt (inf) platter, wooden plate; (*zum Schneiden*) board.

Bretter-: ~**boden** m wooden floor (*made from floorboards*); ~**bude** f booth; (pej) shack; ~**wand** f wooden wall; (*Trennwand*) wooden partition; (*Zaun, für Reklame*) hoarding; ~**zaun** m wooden fence; (*an Baustellen auch*) hoarding.

Brettspiel nt board game.

Brevier [bre'vi:ɐ] nt -s, -e **(a)** (*Eccl*) breviary. **(b)** (*Auswahl von Texten*) extracts pl; (*Leitfaden*) guide (gen to).

Brezel f -, -n pretzel. **das geht wie's** ~ **backen** it's no trouble at all.

brich imper sing of **brechen**.

Bridge [brɪtʃ] nt -, no pl (*Cards*) bridge.

Brief m -(e)s, -e letter; (*Bibl*) epistle. **aus seinen** ~**en** from his letters or correspondence; **etw als** ~ **schicken** to send sth (by) letter post; **etw unter** ~ **und Siegel versprechen** to promise faithfully; **jdm** ~ **und Siegel auf etw** (acc) **geben** to give sb one's word.

Brief- in cpds letter; ~**adel** m title conferred by letters patent; (*Leute*) non-hereditary nobility; ~**beschwerer** m -s, - paperweight; ~**block** m writing or letter pad; ~**bogen** m (sheet of) writing or letter or note paper.

Briefchen nt (a) note. **(b)** (*für Shampoo, Creme, Pulver*) sachet. **ein** ~ **Streichhölzer** a book of matches; **ein** ~ **Nadeln** a packet or paper of needles/pins.

Brief-: ~**drucksache** f circular; ~**einwurf** m (*in Tür*) letterbox; (*in Postamt etc*) post-box; ~**fach** nt pigeon-hole; ~**freund** m penfriend, pen-pal (inf); ~**freundschaft** f correspondence with a penfriend; **eine** ~**freundschaft mit jdm haben** to be penfriends with sb; **er interessiert sich für eine** ~**freundschaft mit einer Französin** he is interested in having a French penfriend; ~**geheimnis** nt privacy of the post; ~**karte** f correspondence card; ~**kasten** m (*am Haus*) letter box, mail box (US); (*im Post*) post- or pillar-box, mail box (US); (*in Zeitungen*) problem column, agony column; *siehe* **tot**.

Briefkasten-: ~**firma** f das ist nur eine ~**firma** that firm is just an accommodation address; ~**tante** f (inf) agony columnist.

Briefkopf m letterhead; (*handgeschrieben*) heading.

brieflich 1 adj by letter. **wir bitten um** ~**e Mitteilung** please inform us by letter; ~**er Verkehr** correspondence. 2 adv by letter. **mit jdm** ~ **verkehren** to correspond with sb.

Briefmarke f stamp.

Briefmarken- in cpds stamp; ~**bogen** m sheet of stamps; ~**kunde** f philately; ~**sammler** m stamp collector, philatelist; ~**sammlung** f stamp collection.

Brief-: ~**öffner** m letter opener, paper knife; ~**papier** nt letter or writing or note paper; ~**porto** nt postage; (*Gebühr*) postage rate for letters, letter rate; ~**post** f letter post; ~**roman** m epistolary novel, novel in letter form; ~**sendung** f letter, item sent by letter post; ~**steller** m -s, - (*dated*) (a) (*Buch*) letter-writing manual; **(b)** (*Person*) scribe; ~**tasche** f wallet, billfold (US); ~**taube** f carrier pigeon; ~**träger(in** f) m postman/-woman, mailman/-woman (US); ~**umschlag** m envelope; ~**verkehr** m correspondence; ~**waage** f letter scales pl; ~**wahl** f postal vote; **seine Stimme durch** ~**wahl abgeben** to use the postal vote, to vote by post; ~**wähler** m postal voter; ~**wechsel** m correspondence; **im** ~**wechsel mit jdm stehen, einen** ~**wechsel mit jdm führen** to be in correspondence or corresponding with sb; ~**zusteller** m (*form*) postman, mailman (US).

briet pret of **braten**.

Brigade f (a) (*Mil*) brigade. **(b)** (*DDR*) (work) team or group.

Brigadegeneral m brigadier, brigadier general (US).

Brigadier [-'die:] m -s, -e (*DDR*) (work) team leader.

Brigg f -, -s (*Naut: Schiff*) brig.

Brikett nt -s, -s or (*rare*) -e briquette.

brikettieren* vt to make into briquettes.

Brikettzange f fire tongs pl.

brillant [brɪl'jant] adj brilliant. ~ **aussehen** to look beautiful.

Brillant [brɪl'jant] m brilliant, diamond.

Brillant- in cpds diamond; ~**feuerwerk** nt cascade; ~**kollier** nt diamond necklace; ~**schmuck** m diamonds pl.

Brillanz [brɪl'jants] f brilliance.

Brille f -, -n **(a)** (*Opt*) glasses pl, spectacles pl, specs (inf) pl; (*Schutz*~) goggles pl; (*Sonnen*~) glasses pl. **eine** ~ a pair of glasses or spectacles; **eine** ~ **tragen** to wear glasses; *siehe* **rosa**. **(b)** (*Klosett*~) (toilet) seat.

Brillen-: ~**etui**, ~**futteral** nt glasses or spectacle case; ~**glas** nt lens; ~**schlange** f (pej) four-eyes (pej inf), woman who wears glasses; ~**träger(in** f) m person who wears glasses; **er ist** ~**träger** he wears glasses.

brillieren* [brɪl'ji:rən] vi (geh) to be brilliant. **sie brillierte mit ihrem Gesang** her singing was brilliant.

Brimborium nt (inf) fuss.

bringen pret **brachte**, ptp **gebracht** vt **(a)** (her~) to bring; (holen auch) to get (jdm for sb); (befördern) to take. **der Besuch hat mir Blumen gebracht** my visitors brought me flowers; **wir haben der Gastgeberin Blumen gebracht** we took our hostess flowers; **alle Gäste hatten Blumen gebracht** all the guests had taken or brought flowers; **sich** (dat) **etw** ~ **lassen** to have sth brought to one; **das Essen auf den Tisch** ~ to serve the food; **jdm eine Nachricht** ~ to give sb some news; **was für Nachricht** ~ **Sie?** what news have you got?; **der Briefträger hat mir/ihm schlechte Nachricht gebracht** the postman brought me/him bad news; **der letzte Sommer brachte uns viel Regen** last summer brought us a lot of rain; **jdn/etw unter or in seine Gewalt** ~ to gain control over or of sb/sth; **er bringt es nicht übers Herz or über sich** he can't bring himself to do it; **etw an sich** (acc) ~ to acquire sth; **etw mit sich** ~ to involve or imply or mean sth; **die Liebe bringt es mit sich, daß man leiden muß** love brings or involves suffering; **etw hinter sich** (acc) ~ to get sth over and done with, to get sth behind one; **endlich haben wir eine Woche ohne Krisen hinter uns gebracht** at last we've managed to get through a week without any crises; **diese Wolken** ~ **schönes Wetter** these clouds mean fine weather; **Unglück über jdn** ~ to bring unhappiness upon sb; **(jdm) Glück/Unglück** ~ to bring sb good/bad luck.

(b) (weg~, begleiten) to take; (im Auto mitnehmen auch) to give a lift. **bring das Auto in die Garage** put the car in the garage; **jdn ins Krankenhaus/zum Bahnhof/nach Hause** ~ to take sb to hospital/to the station/home; **die Kinder zu or ins Bett** ~ to put the children to bed.

(c) (inf: entfernen) to get. **ich bringe den Ring nicht vom Finger** I can't get the ring off my finger.

(d) (ein~) Geld, Gewinn to bring in, to make, to earn; (Boden, Mine etc) to produce; (Ärger) to cause; Freude to give, to bring; Vorteile to bring. **das Bild brachte DM 100** the picture went for or fetched 100 marks; **das bringt nichts** (fig inf) it's pointless.

(e) (lenken, bewirken) to bring. **etw in die richtige Form** ~ to get or put sth in the right form; **etw zum Stehen** ~ to bring sth to a stop; **das bringt dich vors Gericht/ins Gefängnis** you'll end up in court/prison if you do that; **das Gespräch/die Rede auf etw** (acc) ~ to bring the conversation/talk round to sth; **jdn auf die schiefe Bahn/auf den rechten Weg** ~ (fig) to lead sb astray/to bring or get sb back on the straight and narrow; **jdn in Gefahr** ~ to put sb in danger; **jdn zum Lachen/Weinen** ~ to make sb laugh/cry; **jdn zur Verzweiflung** ~ to drive sb to despair; **jdn zur Vernunft** ~ to bring sb to his senses; **jdn außer sich** (acc) ~ to upset sb; **jdn dazu** ~, **etw zu tun** to get sb to do sth; **jdn so weit or dahin** ~, **daß ...** to force sb to ...; **du wirst es noch so weit or dahin** ~, **daß man dich hinauswirft** you will make them throw you out.

(f) (leisten, erreichen) **es auf 80 Jahre** ~ to reach the age of 80; **der Motor hat es auf 180.000 km gebracht** the engine has kept going for 180,000 km; **das Auto bringt 180 km/h** the car can do 180 km/h; **er hat es auf 25 Punkte gebracht** he got or received 25 points; **es zu etwas/nichts** ~ to get somewhere/nowhere or achieve something/nothing; **es weit** (im Leben) ~ to do very well (for oneself), to get far; **es zu Ehren** etc ~ to achieve honours etc; **er hat es bis zum Hauptmann/ Direktor gebracht** he became a captain/director, he made it to captain/director.

(g) (darbieten) Opfer to offer. **welche Sprünge bringst du in deiner Übung?** what leaps are you doing in your exercise?

(h) (senden) Bericht etc to broadcast; Sonderbericht to present; (im Fernsehen auch) to show. **das Fernsehen brachte nichts darüber** there was nothing on television about it; **wir** ~ **Nachrichten!** here is the news; **um zehn Uhr** ~ **wir Nachrichten** at ten o'clock we have the news; **die nächsten Nachrichten** ~ **wir um ...** the next news will be at ...; **was bringt das Radio/Fernsehen heute abend?** what's on television/the radio tonight?; **was sie alles im Fernsehen** ~! the things they show or have on television!; **was bringt der Wetterbericht?** what does the weather forecast say?

(i) (veröffentlichen) (Verlag) to publish; (Zeitung) to print, to publish. **etw in die Zeitung** ~ to publish or put sth in the paper; Verlobung, Angebot to announce or put in the paper; **die Zeitung brachte nichts/einen Artikel darüber** there was nothing/an article in the paper about it, the paper had an article about it; **alle Zeitungen brachten es auf der ersten Seite** the papers had it on the front page.

(j) (aufführen) Stück to do.

(k) **jdn um etw** ~ to make sb lose sth, to do sb out of sth; **das bringt mich noch um den Verstand** it's driving me mad; **der Lärm hat mich um den Schlaf gebracht** the noise stopped me getting any sleep; **jdn ums Leben** ~ to kill sb.

(l) (sl: schaffen, können) **ich bringe diese Übung nicht** I can't do or manage this exercise; **das bringt er nicht** he's not up to it; **er bringt es nicht** he's got what it takes; **der Motor bringt's nicht mehr** the engine has had it (inf); **ihr Typ bringt's nicht mehr** her boyfriend can't make it or can't stand the pace any more (inf); **das bringt's doch nicht!** that's no damn use (inf)!; **das kannst du doch nicht** ~ that's not on (inf); **hat er das tatsächlich gebracht?** did he really do it?

brisạnt adj (lit, fig) explosive.

Brisạnz f explosive force; (fig) explosive nature. **ein Thema von äußerster ~** an extremely explosive subject.

Brise f -, -n breeze.

Britạnnien [-iən] nt -s (Hist) Britain, Britannia (Hist).

britạnnisch adj (Hist) Britannic.

Brite m -n, -n, **Britin** f Briton. **er ist ~** he is British; **die ~n** the British.

britisch adj British. **die B~en Inseln** the British Isles.

Bröckchen nt dim of Brocken.

bröckchenweise adv siehe brockenweise.

bröckelig adj crumbly; Mauer crumbling. **~ werden** to (start to) crumble.

bröckeln vti to crumble; (Gestein auch) to crumble away.

Brọcken m -s, - lump, chunk; (fig: Bruchstück) scrap; (Hunt) bait; (inf: Person) lump (inf). **das Baby ist ein richtiger ~** the baby's a regular little dumpling (inf); **ein paar ~ Spanisch/ Psychologie** a smattering of Spanish/psychology; **er schnappte den anderen die besten ~ weg** he snapped up all the best titbits; **das ist ein harter ~** that's a tough nut to crack.

brọcken vt Brot to break.

brọckenweise adv bit by bit.

brọdeln vi (Wasser, Suppe) to bubble; (in Krater auch) to seethe; (Dämpfe, liter: Nebel) to swirl, to seethe. **es brodelt** (fig) there is seething unrest.

Brọdem m -s, - (liter) foul-smelling vapour.

Brokạt m -(e)s, -e brocade.

Brọm nt -s, no pl bromine.

Brọmbeere f blackberry, bramble.

Brọmbeerstrauch m bramble or blackberry bush.

Brọmsilber nt silver bromide.

bronchịal adj bronchial.

Bronchịal-: **~asthma** nt bronchial asthma; **~katarrh** m bronchial catarrh.

Brọnchie [-iə] f usu pl bronchial tube, bronchus (form).

Bronchịtis f -, **Bronchitịden** bronchitis.

Brọnn m -s, -en, **Brọnnen** m -s, - (obs, liter) fount (liter).

Brontosaurus m -, -se, **Brontosaurier** m brontosaurus.

Brọnze ['brõ:sə] f -, -n bronze.

Brọnzemedaille f bronze medal.

brọnzen ['brõ:sn] adj bronze. **~ schimmern** to glint like bronze.

Brọsame f -, -n (liter) crumb.

Brọsche f -, -n brooch.

broschiẹrt adj Ausgabe paperback; (geheftet) sewn; (geklammert) wire-stitched. **jetzt auch ~ erhältlich** now also available in paperback; **~es Heftchen** booklet.

Broschüre f -, -n booklet.

Brösel m -s, - crumb.

brös(e)lig adj crumbly. **~ werden** to (start to) crumble.

bröseln vi (Kuchen, Stein) to crumble; (Mensch) to make crumbs.

Brọt nt -(e)s, -e bread; (Laib) loaf (of bread); (Scheibe) slice (of bread); (Stulle) sandwich; (fig: Unterhalt) daily bread (hum), living. **ein ~ mit Käse** a slice of bread and cheese; **das ist ein hartes or schweres ~** (fig) that's a hard way to earn one's living; **wes ~ ich ess', des Lied ich sing'** (Prov) he who pays the piper calls the tune (Prov); **der Mensch lebt nicht vom ~ allein** (Prov) Man does not live by bread alone; siehe Butterbrot, täglich.

Brọt-: **~aufstrich** m spread (for bread); **~belag** m topping (for bread); **~beutel** m haversack.

Brötchen nt roll. **(sich** dat**) seine ~ verdienen** (inf) to earn one's living or one's daily bread (hum); **kleine ~ backen** (inf) to set one's sights lower.

Brötchengeber m (inf) employer, provider (hum).

Brọt-: **~erwerb** m (way of earning one's) living; **etw zum ~erwerb betreiben** to do sth for a living; **~geber** (hum), **~herr** (obs) m employer, provider (hum); **~karte** f bread rationing card; **~kasten** m bread bin; **~korb** m bread basket; **jdm den ~korb höher hängen** (fig) to keep sb short; **~krume** f breadcrumb; **~kruste** f crust; **b~los** adj unemployed, out of work; **jdn b~los machen** to put sb out of work; siehe Kunst; **~marke** f bread (rationing) coupon; **~maschine** f bread slicer; **~messer** nt bread knife; **~neid** m envy of other people's incomes/jobs; **das ist der reine ~neid** he etc is just jealous of your salary/job; **~rinde** f crust; **~röster** m -s, - toaster; **~schneidemaschine** f bread slicer; **~schnitte** f sandwich; **~studium** nt career-orientated course of study; **~suppe** f soup made from bread, stock etc; **~teig** m bread dough; **~wunder** nt miracle of the loaves and fishes; **~zeit** f (a) (Pause) tea break; **~zeit machen** to have a tea break; (b) (Essen) sandwiches pl.

brr interj (Befehl an Zugtiere) whoa; (Zeichen des Ekels) ugh, yuck; (bei Kälte) brr.

Bruch[1] m -(e)s, ̈-e (a) (~stelle) break; (in Porzellan etc auch) crack; (im Damm) breach; (das Brechen) breaking; (von Fels) breaking-off; (von Damm) breaching. **das führte zu einem ~ an der Achse** it caused the axle to break; **zu ~ gehen** to get broken; **zu ~ fahren** to smash; **~ machen** (inf) (mit Flugzeug, Auto) to crash (mit etw sth); (beim Abwaschen) to break something; **da habe ich einen schrecklichen ~ gemacht** (inf) I made a terrible mess of that.
(b) (fig) (von Vertrag, Eid etc) breaking; (von Gesetz, Abkommen auch) violation, infringement; (mit Vergangenheit, Partei, in einer Entwicklung) break; (des Vertrauens) breach; (von Freundschaft) break-up; (im Stil) discontinuity, break; (von Verlöbnis) breaking-off. **in die ~e gehen** (Ehe, Freundschaft) to break up; **es kam zum ~ zwischen ihnen** they broke up.
(c) (zerbrochene Ware) broken biscuits/chocolate etc; (Porzellan) breakage.

(d) (Med) (Knochen~) fracture, break; (Eingeweide~) hernia, rupture. **sich** (dat) **einen ~ heben** to rupture oneself (by lifting something), to give oneself a hernia.
(e) (Stein~) quarry.
(f) (Geol) fault.
(g) (Knick) fold.
(h) (Math) fraction.
(i) (sl: Einbruch) break-in. **(einen) ~ in einem Geschäft machen** to break into a shop; **einen ~ machen** to do a break-in.

Bruch[2] m or nt -(e)s, ̈-e marsh(land), bog.

Bruch-: **~band** nt truss; **~bude** f (pej) hovel; **b~fest** adj unbreakable; **~fläche** f surface of the break; **die ~flächen zusammendrücken** press the two broken edges together.

brüchig adj brittle, fragile; Gestein, Mauerwerk crumbling; Leder cracked, split; (fig) Stimme cracked, rough; Verhältnisse, Ehe, Moral crumbling. **~ werden** (Gestein, Macht etc) to (begin to) crumble; (Ehe, Verhältnisse auch) to (begin to) break up; (Leder) to crack or split.

Brüchigkeit f brittleness, fragility; (von Gestein etc) crumbliness.

Bruch-: **~kante** f edge (of break/split etc); **~landung** f crash-landing; **eine ~landung machen** to crash-land; **b~rechnen** vi infin only to do fractions; **jdm b~rechnen beibringen** to teach sb how to do fractions; **~rechnen** nt fractions sing or pl; **~rechnung** f fractions sing or pl; (Aufgabe) sum with fractions; **~schreibweise** f (vulgar) fractions pl; **~schrift** f gothic script; **~stein** m rough, undressed stone; **~stelle** f break; (von Knochen auch) fracture; **~strich** m (Math) line (of a fraction); **~stück** nt fragment; (von Lied, Rede etc auch) snatch; **b~stückhaft** adj fragmentary; **ich kenne die Geschichte nur b~stückhaft** I only know parts or fragments of the story; **~teil** m fraction; **im ~teil einer Sekunde** in a split second; **~zahl** f (Math) fraction.

Brücke f -, -n (a) (lit, fig) bridge. **alle ~n hinter sich** (dat) **abbrechen** (fig) to burn one's bridges or boats behind one; **jdm eine ~ bauen** (fig) to give sb a helping hand; **jdm goldene ~n bauen** to make things easy for sb; **eine ~ schlagen** (liter) to build or throw (liter) a bridge (über + acc across); **~n schlagen** (fig) to forge links; **zwischen den Völkern ~n schlagen** to forge links between peoples, to bridge the gaps between peoples.
(b) (Turnen) crab; (Ringen) bridge.
(c) (Anat) pons Varolii.
(d) (Naut) bridge; (Landungs~) gangway, gangplank.
(e) (Zahn~) bridge.
(f) (Elec) bridge.
(g) (Teppich) rug.

Brücken-: **~bau** m (a) no pl bridge-building. (b) (Brücke) bridge; **~bogen** m arch (of a/the bridge); **~geländer** nt parapet; **~kopf** m (Mil, fig) bridgehead; **~pfeiler** m pier (of a/the bridge); **~schlag** m (fig) das war der erste **~schlag** that forged the first link; **möge dies als ~schlag zwischen ... dienen** may this serve to forge a link between ...; **~waage** f scale platform; **~zoll** m bridge toll.

Bruder m -s, ̈- (a) brother. **der große ~** (fig) Big Brother; **die ~ Müller/Grimm** the Müller brothers/the Brothers Grimm; ~ (Rel) brothers pl, brethren pl; **unter ~n** (inf) between friends; **~ im Geiste** (geh) spiritual brothers; **und willst du nicht mein ~ sein, so schlag' ich dir den Schädel ein** (prov) if you're not prepared to agree with me, then you'd better watch out!; **gleiche ~, gleiche Kappen** (dated) you're/they're all tarred with the same brush.
(b) (Mönch) friar, brother. **~ Franziskus** (als Anrede) Brother Francis; **die ~** the brothers pl, the brethren pl.
(c) (inf: Mann) guy (inf), bloke (Brit inf). **ein warmer ~** (dated) a poof (sl), a pansy (sl); **das sind alles ganz windige ~** (pej) they're a shady lot or crew (inf) or bunch (inf); **euch ~ kenn' ich** (pej) I know you lot.

Bruderbund m (geh, esp DDR) (link of) comradeship, fraternal or brotherly link.

Brüderchen nt little brother. **~, kannst du mir ...?** brother dear, could you ...?; **na ~!** (hum) well, brother!

Bruder-: **~hand** f (liter) hand of brotherhood; **~haß** m fraternal hatred, hatred between brothers; **~herz** nt (hum) dear brother; **na ~herz, wie geht's?** well, brother dear or dear brother, how are you?; **~hilfe** f (esp DDR) comradely or fraternal aid or assistance; **~krieg** m war between brothers, fratricidal war; **~kuß** m (fig) fraternal or brotherly kiss; **~land** nt (DDR) brother nation.

brüderlich adj fraternal, brotherly no adv. **~e Grüße** fraternal greetings; **~ teilen** to share and share alike; **mit jdm ~ teilen** to share generously with sb.

Brüderlichkeit f, no pl brotherliness.

Bruder-: **~liebe** f brotherly love; **~mord** m fratricide ~mörder m fratricide; **~partei** f (DDR) brother party.

Brüderschaft, Bruderschaft (esp Eccl) f (a) (Eccl) brotherhood. (b) (Freundschaft) close or intimate friendship (in which the familiar 'du' is used). **mit jdm ~ trinken** to agree to use the familiar 'du' (over a drink).

Bruder-: **~volk** nt (geh) sister people; **unser ~volk in Kuba** our Cuban brothers; **~zwist** m (liter) fraternal feud.

Brügge nt -s Bruges.

Brühe f -, -n (Suppe) (clear) soup; (als Suppengrundlage) stock; (dial: von Gemüse) vegetable water; (pej) (schmutzige Flüssigkeit) sludge; (Getränk) dishwater (inf), muck (inf).

brühen vt (a) to blanch; to pour boiling water over. (b) Tee to brew; Kaffee to make in the jug or pot. (c) (rare: ver~) to scald.

Brüh-: **b~heiß** adj scalding (hot), boiling hot; **~kartoffeln** pl potatoes boiled in meat stock; **b~warm** adj (inf) hot from the press (*inf*); **er hat das sofort b~warm weitererzählt** he promptly went straight off and spread it around; **~würfel** *m* stock cube; **~wurst** *f* sausage (*to be heated in water*).

Brüll|affe *m* howling monkey, howler; (*inf: Mensch*) loud-mouth (*inf*).

brüllen *vti* to shout, to roar; (*pej: laut weinen*) to yell, to bawl; (*Stier*) to bellow; (*Elefant*) to trumpet. **brüll doch nicht so!** don't shout; **er brüllte vor Schmerzen** he screamed with pain; **vor Lachen ~** to roar or howl or scream with laughter; **~des Gelächter** roars or howls or screams of laughter (*all pl*); **~ wie am Spieß** to cry or scream blue murder (*inf*); **das ist zum B~** (*inf*) it's a scream (*inf*).

Brumm-: **~bär** *m* (*inf*) (a) (*baby-talk*) teddy bear (*baby-talk*); (b) (*brummiger Mann*) crosspatch (*inf*), grouch (*inf*); **~bart** *m* (*inf*) siehe **~bär** (b); **~baß** *m* (*inf*) (*Baßgeige*) (double) bass; (*Baßstimme*) deep bass (voice).

brummeln *vti* (*inf*) to mumble, to mutter.

brummen *vti* (a) (*Insekt*) to buzz; (*Bär*) to growl; (*Motor, Baß*) to drone; (*Kreisel etc*) to hum. **mir brummt der Kopf** or **Schädel** my head is throbbing.
  (b) (*beim Singen*) to drone.
  (c) (*murren*) to grumble, to grouch (*inf*), to grouse (*inf*).
  (d) (*brummeln*) to mumble, to mutter.
  (e) (*inf*) (*in Haft sein*) to be locked up (*inf*); (*Sch: nachsitzen*) to be kept in. **vier Monate ~** to do four months (*inf*).

Brummer *m* -s, - (a) (*Schmeißfliege*) bluebottle; (*hum inf: Sänger*) droner. (b) (*inf*) (*etwas Großes*) whopper (*inf*); (*Last-wagen*) juggernaut.

brummig *adj* grumpy, grouchy (*inf*), sour-tempered.

Brummigkeit *f* grumpiness, grouchiness (*inf*).

Brumm-: **~kreisel** *m* (*inf*) humming-top; **~schädel** *m* (*inf*) thick head (*inf*).

brünett *adj* dark(-haired). **~es Mädchen** dark-haired girl, brunette; **sie ist ~** she is (a) brunette.

Brünette *f* brunette.

Brunft *f* -, ⁻e (*Hunt*) rut; (*~zeit auch*) rutting season. **in der ~ sein** to be rutting.

brunften *vi* (*Hunt*) to rut.

brunftig *adj* (*Hunt*) rutting.

Brunft-: **~platz** *m* rutting ground; **~schrei** *m* bell, mating or rutting call (*auch fig*); **~zeit** *f* rutting season, rut.

Brünn *nt* -s Brno.

Brunn *m* (e)s, -⁻e (*poet*) siehe **Brunnen**.

Brunnen *m* -s, - (a) well; (*fig liter*) fountain, fount (*liter*). **den ~ erst zudecken, wenn das Kind hineingefallen ist** (*fig*) to lock the stable door after the horse has bolted (*prov*); **erst, wenn das Kind in den ~ gefallen ist** (*fig*) but not until things had gone wrong.
  (b) (*Spring~*) fountain.
  (c) (*Heilquelle*) spring. **~ trinken** to take the waters.

Brunnen-: **~bauer(in** *f*) *m* -s, - well-digger or -borer; **~becken** *nt* basin (of a well/fountain); **~figur** *f* (decorative) sculpture on a fountain; **b~frisch** *adj* fresh from the well/spring; **~haus** *nt* pump room; **~kresse** *f* watercress; **~kur** *f* (course of) spa treatment, cure; **~schacht** *m* well shaft; **~vergifter(in** *f*) *m* -s, - (a) well-poisoner; (b) (*fig pej*) (political) trouble-maker; **~vergiftung** *f* well-poisoning; **politische ~vergiftung** political calumny; **~wasser** *nt* well water.

Brünnlein *nt dim of* **Brunnen**.

Brunst *f* -, ⁻e (*von männlichen Tieren*) rut; (*von weiblichen Tieren*) heat; (*~zeit*) rutting season/heat; (*hum: von Mensch*) lust, sexual appetite. **in der ~** rutting/on or in heat.

brunsten *vi* siehe **Brunst** to rut/to be on or in heat.

brünstig *adj* (a) siehe **Brunst** rutting/on or in heat; (*hum: von Mensch*) (feeling) sexy (*hum*). (b) (*liter: inbrünstig*) ardent, fervent.

Brunst-: **~schrei** *m* mating call; **~zeit** *f* siehe **Brunst**.

brunzen *vi* (*S Ger sl*) to (have a) piss (*sl*) or slash (*Brit sl*).

brüsk *adj* brusque, abrupt, curt. **sich ~ abwenden** to turn away abruptly or brusquely.

brüskieren* *vt* to snub.

Brüskierung *f* snub.

Brüssel *nt* -s Brussels.

Brüsseler, Brüßler *adj attr* Brussels. **~ Spitzen** Brussels lace; (*Sw: Chicorée*) chicory.

Brüsseler(in *f*)**, Brüßler(in** *f*) *m* -s, - inhabitant or (*gebür-tiger*) native of Brussels. **er ist ~** he lives in/comes from Brus-sels.

Brust *f* -, ⁻e (a) (*Körperteil*) chest; (*fig: Inneres*) breast, heart. **einen zur ~ nehmen** (*inf*) to have a quick drink or quick one or quickie (*inf*); **~ (he)raus!** chest out!; **~ an ~** face to face; **sich an jds ~ ausweinen** to weep on sb's shoulder; **sich** (*dat*) **an die ~ schlagen** (*fig*) to beat one's breast; **sich in die ~ werfen** (*fig*) to puff oneself up; **mit geschwellter ~** (*fig*) as proud as Punch or a peacock; **schwach auf der ~ sein** (*inf*) to have a weak chest; (*hum: an Geldmangel leiden*) to be a bit short (*inf*).
  (b) (*weibliche ~*) breast. **einem Kind die ~ geben, ein Kind an die ~ legen** to feed a baby (*at the breast*), to nurse a baby.
  (c) (*Cook*) breast.
  (d) (*~schwimmen*) breast-stroke.

Brust-: **~bein** *nt* (*Anat*) breastbone, sternum; **~beutel** *m* money bag (*worn around the neck*); **~bild** *nt* half-length por-trait; **~breite** *f* um **~breite** by a whisker.

Brüstchen *nt dim of* **Brust**.

Brustdrüse *f* mammary gland.

brüsten *vr* to boast, to brag (*mit* about). **deswegen brauchst du dich nicht zu ~!** that's nothing to be proud of or boast about or brag about!

Brust-: **~fell** *nt* (*Anat*) pleura; **~fellentzündung** *f* pleurisy; **~flosse** *f* pectoral fin; **~gegend** *f* thoracic region; **~haar** *nt*

hair on the chest, chest hair; **~harnisch** *m* breastplate; **b~hoch** *adj* chest-high; **~höhe** *f*: **in ~höhe** chest high; **~höhle** *f* thoracic cavity; **~kasten** *m* (*inf*) siehe **~korb**; **~kind** *nt* (*inf*) breast-fed baby; **~korb** *m* (*Anat*) thorax; **~krebs** *m* breast cancer, cancer of the breast; **~kreuz** *nt* (*Eccl*) pectoral cross; **~lage** *f* prone position; **in ~lage schwimmen** to swim in the prone position; **~muskel** *m* pectoral muscle; **~nahrung** *f* breast milk; **~panzer** *m* breastplate; **~plastik** *f* cosmetic breast surgery; **~schutz** *m* (*esp Fechten*) breast or chest protector, plastron; **~schwimmen** *nt* breast-stroke; **b~schwimmen** *vi infin only* to swim or do the breast-stroke; **~schwimmer** *m* breast-stroke swimmer; **~stimme** *f* chest-voice; **~stück** *nt* (*Cook*) breast; **~tasche** *f* breast pocket; (*Innentasche*) inside (breast) pocket; **~tee** *m* herbal tea (*for infections of the respiratory tract*); **b~tief** *adj* chest-deep, up to one's chest; **~ton** *m* (*Mus*) chest note; **im ~ton der Überzeugung, (daß ...)** in a tone of utter conviction (that ...); **~umfang** *m* chest measurement; (*von Frau*) bust measurement.

Brüstung *f* parapet; (*Balkon~ etc auch*) balustrade; (*Fenster~*) breast.

Brust-: **~wand** *f* (*Anat*) thoracic or chest wall; **~warze** *f* nipple; **~wehr** *f* (*Mil*) breastwork; (*Hist*) parapet; **~weite** *f* siehe **~umfang**; **~wickel** *m* chest compress; **~wirbel** *m* thoracic or dorsal vertebra.

Brut *f* -, -en (a) *no pl* (*das Brüten*) brooding, sitting, incubating. (b) (*die Jungen*) brood; (*pej*) lot, mob (*inf*). (c) (*bei Pflanzen*) offset, offshoot.

brutal *adj* brutal; (*gewalttätig auch*) violent. **jdm etw ganz ~ sagen** to be brutally or cruelly frank to sb about sth, to tell sb sth (quite) brutally.

brutalisieren* *vt* to brutalize.

Brutalisierung *f* brutalization.

Brutalität *f* (a) *no pl siehe adj* brutality; violence. (b) (*Gewalttat*) act of violence or brutality. **~en** brutalities, acts of violence or brutality.

Brut|apparat *m* incubator.

brüten 1 *vi* to brood, to sit, to incubate; (*fig*) to ponder (*über +dat* over). **~de Hitze** oppressive or stifling heat. **2** *vt* (a) (*künstlich*) to incubate; (*Tech*) to breed. (b) (*geh*) **Rache, Verrat** to plot.

brütendheiß *adj attr* sweltering, boiling (hot) (*inf*).

Brüter *m* -s, - (*Tech*) breeder (reactor). **schneller ~** fast-breeder (reactor).

Brut-: **~henne** *f* sitting hen; **~hitze** *f* (*inf*) stifling or sweltering heat; **~kasten** *m* (*Med*) incubator; **hier ist eine Hitze wie in einem ~kasten** (*inf*) it's like an oven or a furnace in here (*inf*); **~ofen** *m* (*fig*) furnace; **~pflege** *f* care of the brood; **~platz** *m* breeding ground; **~reaktor** *m* breeder (reactor); **~schrank** *m* incubator; **~stätte** *f* breeding ground (*gen* for); (*fig auch*) hotbed (*gen* of); **~teich** *m* spawning pond.

brutto *adv* gross. **~ 1000 DM, 1000 DM ~** DM 1000 gross.

Brutto-: **~einkommen** *nt* gross or before-tax income; **~ertrag** *m* gross or before-tax profit; **~gehalt** *nt* gross salary; **~gewinn** *m* gross or before-tax profit; **~lohn** *m* gross or before-tax wage(s); **~registertonne** *f* register ton; **~sozialprodukt** *nt* gross national product, GNP; **~verdienst** *m* gross or before-tax earnings *pl*.

Brutzeit *f* incubation (period).

brutzeln 1 *vi* to sizzle (away). **2** *vt* to fry (up).

Bruyère [bry'je:r] *nt* -s, *no pl*, **Bruyèreholz** *nt* briar or brier (wood).

Bruyère(pfeife) *f* -, -s briar or brier (pipe).

Bub *m* -en, -en (*S Ger, Aus, Sw*) boy, lad.

Bübchen *nt dim of* **Bub**.

Bube *m* -n, -n (a) (*old*) rogue, knave (*old*). (b) (*Cards*) jack, knave.

Bübel *nt* -s, -n (*Aus*) dim of **Bub**.

Bubenstreich *m*, **Bubenstück** *nt*, **Büberei** *f* (a) (*old*) piece of knavery (*old*) or villainy, knavish trick (*old*). (b) siehe **Dummejungenstreich**.

Bubi *m* -s, -s (*inf*) little boy or lad, laddie (*inf*); (*pej inf*) (school)boy; (*als Anrede*) laddie (*inf*).

Bubi-: **~kopf** *m* bobbed hair *no pl*, bob; **sich** (*dat*) **einen ~kopf machen lassen** to have one's hair bobbed or cut in a bob; **~kragen** *m* Peter Pan collar.

Bübin *f* (*old*) minx.

bübisch *adj* (a) (*old: schurkenhaft*) villainous, knavish (*old*). (b) (*verschmitzt*) roguish, mischievous.

Buch *nt* -(e)s, ⁻er (a) book; (*Band*) volume; (*Dreh~*) script. **über den ⁻ern sitzen** to pore over one's books; **reden wie ein ~** (*inf*) to talk like a book; **ein Gentleman, wie er im ⁻e steht** a perfect example of a gentleman; **ein Tor, wie es im ⁻e steht** a textbook or copybook goal; **das ~ der ⁻er** the Book of Books; **die ⁻er Mose** the Pentateuch; **das erste/zweite/dritte/vierte/fünfte ~ Mose** Genesis/Exodus/Leviticus/Numbers/Deuteronomy; **ein ~ mit sieben Siegeln** (*fig*) a closed book; **er ist für mich ein offenes** or **aufgeschlagenes ~** I can read him like a book; **das ~ der Natur** (*geh*) the book of nature; **sich ins ~ der Geschichte eintragen** (*geh*) to enter one's name in the annals or book of history; **~ machen** (*Pferderennen*) to make a book.
  (b) *usu pl* (*Comm: Geschäfts~*) books *pl*, accounts *pl*. **über etw** (*acc*) **~ führen** to keep a record of sth; **jdm die ⁻er führen** to keep sb's accounts or books; **zu ~(e) schlagen** to make a (sig-nificant) difference; **das schlägt mit 1000 DM zu ~(e)** that gives you DM 1000; **zu ~ stehen** mit to be valued at.

Buch-: **~besprechung** *f* book review; **~binder(in** *f*) *m* book-binder; **~binderei** *f* (*Betrieb*) bookbindery; (*Handwerk*) book-binding; **~block** *m* -s, -s book block; **~deckel** *m* book cover; **~druck** *m*, *no pl* letterpress (printing); **~drucker** *m* printer;

~druckerei f (Betrieb) printing works sing or pl; (Handwerk) printing; ~druckerkunst f art of printing.
Buche f -, -n beech (tree).
Buch|ecker f -, -n beechnut.
Buch|einband m binding, (book) cover.
buchen[1] vt (a) (Comm) to enter, to post (spec); (Kasse) to register; (fig: registrieren) to register, to record. **einen Erfolg für sich ~** to chalk (inf) or mark up a success (for oneself); **etw als Erfolg ~** to put sth down as a success. **(b)** (vorbestellen) to book, to reserve.
buchen[2] adj (rare) (made) of beech(wood), beech.
Buchen-: ~holz nt beech wood; ~wald m beech wood.
Bücher-: ~bord, ~brett nt bookshelf.
Bücherei f (lending) library.
Bücher-: ~freund m book-lover, bibliophile; ~gestell nt bookcase; ~narr m book-fan, book-freak (inf); **er ist ein richtiger ~narr** he's book mad or crazy about books, he's a real bookfreak (inf); ~reff nt case for transporting books; ~regal nt bookshelf; ~revision f audit; ~revisor m siehe Buchprüfer; ~schrank m bookcase; ~sendung f consignment of books; (im Postwesen) books (sent) at printed paper rate; ~stube f bookshop; ~stütze f book-end; ~verbot nt ban on books; ~verbrennung f burning of books; ~verzeichnis nt bibliography; ~wand f wall of book shelves; (als Möbelstück) (large) set of book shelves; ~weisheit f book learning; ~wurm m (lit, fig hum) bookworm; ~zensur f censorship of books.
Buchfink m chaffinch.
Buch-: ~form f: **in ~form** in book form; ~format nt format for a book; ~führung f book-keeping, accounting; **einfache/doppelte ~führung** single/double entry book-keeping; ~gelehrsamkeit f book-learning; ~gemeinschaft f book club; ~halter(in f) m book-keeper; b~halterisch adj book-keeping; **sich b~halterisch ausbilden lassen** to be trained in book-keeping or as a book-keeper; **ein Problem b~halterisch sehen** to see something as a book-keeping problem, to view a problem in terms of book-keeping; ~haltung f (a) siehe ~führung; **(b)** (Abteilung einer Firma) accounts department; ~handel m book trade; **im ~handel erhältlich** available or on sale in bookshops; ~händler m bookseller; b~händlerisch adj of or connected with the book trade; **eine b~händlerische Ausbildung haben** to be a trained book seller; **b~händlerisch interessiert sein** to be interested in the book trade; ~handlung f bookshop, bookstore (US); ~hülle f dust jacket or cover; ~kritik f (a) (das Rezensieren) book reviewing; (Rezension) book review; **(b)** no pl (die Rezensenten) book reviewers pl or critics pl.
Büchl nt -s, -n (Aus) dim of Buch.
Buch-: ~laden m bookshop, bookstore (US); ~macher m bookmaker, bookie (inf); ~malerei f illumination; ~messe f book fair; ~prüfer m auditor; ~prüfung f audit; ~rücken m spine.
Buchs ['buks] m -es, -e, **Buchsbaum** m box(tree).
Büchschen ['byksçǝn] nt dim of Büchse.
Buchse ['buksǝ] f -, -n (Elec) socket; (Tech) (von Zylinder) liner; (von Lager) bush.
Büchse ['byksǝ] f -, -n (a) tin; (Konserven~) can, tin (Brit); (Sammel~) collecting box. **die ~ der Pandora** (Myth, liter) Pandora's box. **(b)** (Gewehr) rifle, (shot)gun.
Büchsen-: ~fleisch nt canned or tinned (Brit) meat; ~gemüse nt canned or tinned (Brit) vegetables pl; ~macher m gunsmith; ~milch f tinned (Brit) or evaporated milk; ~öffner m can or tin (Brit) opener.
Buchstabe m -n(s), -n letter; (esp Druck~) character. **kleiner ~** small letter; **großer ~** capital (letter); **ein fetter ~** a bold character, a character in bold (face); **in fetten ~n** in bold (face); **dem ~n nach** (fig) literally; **auf den ~n genau** (fig), **bis auf den letzten ~n** (fig) to the letter; **nach dem ~n des Gesetzes ist das verboten, aber ...** according to the letter of the law that's illegal but ...; siehe vier.
Buchstaben-: b~getreu adj literal; **etw b~getreu befolgen** to follow sth to the letter; ~glaube m literalism; b~gläubig adj literalist(ic); ~kombination f combination (of letters); ~rätsel nt word-puzzle, anagram; ~rechnung f algebra; ~schloß nt combination lock (using letters); ~schrift f alphabetic script; ~treue f adherence to the letter; ~wort nt acronym.
buchstabieren* vt (a) to spell. **(b)** (mühsam lesen) to spell out.
Buchstabier-: ~methode f alphabetical method; ~tafel f word spelling alphabet.
buchstäblich adj literal.
Buchstütze f siehe Bücherstütze.
Bucht f -, -en (a) (im Meer) bay; (kleiner) cove. **(b)** (für Schweine etc) stall.
Buchteln pl (Aus Cook) jam-filled yeast dumplings.
buchtenreich, buchtig adj indented.
Buch-: ~titel m (book) title; ~umschlag m dust jacket or cover.
Buchung f (Comm) entry; (Reservierung) booking, reservation.
Buchungsmaschine f accounting machine.
Buchweizen m buckwheat.
Buch-: ~wesen nt book business, books pl no art; ~wissen nt (pej) book learning; ~zeichen nt bookmark(er).
Buckel m -s, - (a) hump(back), hunchback; (inf: Rücken) back. **einen ~ machen** (Katze) to arch its back; **steh gerade, mach nicht so einen ~!** stand up (straight), don't hunch your back or shoulders like that!; **einen krummen ~ machen** (fig inf) to bow and scrape, to kowtow; **den ~ voll kriegen** (inf) to get a good hiding; **jdm ~ voll geben** (inf), **jdm eins auf den ~ geben** (inf) to give sb a belting (inf); **er kann mir den ~ (he)runterrutschen** (inf) he can (go and) take a running jump, he can get lost or knotted (all inf); **viel/genug auf dem ~ haben** (inf) to have a lot/enough on one's plate (inf); **den ~ voll Schulden haben** (inf) to be up to one's neck or eyes in debt (inf); **den ~**

hinhalten (fig inf) to carry the can (inf); **sich (dat) den ~ freihalten** (inf) to keep one's options open; **seine 80 Jahre auf dem ~ haben** (inf) to be 80 (years old), to have seen 80 summers; siehe jucken, breit.
(b) (inf: Hügel) hummock, hillock.
(c) (inf: Auswölbung) bulge, hump.
(d) (von Schild) boss.
buck(e)lig adj hunchbacked, humpbacked; (inf) Straße bumpy; Landschaft undulating, hilly.
Buck(e)lige(r) mf decl as adj hunchback, humpback.
buckeln vi (pej) to bow and scrape, to kowtow. **nach oben ~ und nach unten treten** to bow to superiors and tread inferiors underfoot.
Buckelrind nt zebu.
bücken vr to bend (down), to stoop. **sich nach etw ~** to bend down or to stoop to pick sth up; siehe gebückt.
Buckerl nt -s, -(n) (Aus inf) siehe Bückling (b).
bucklig adj etc siehe buck(e)lig.
Bückling m (a) (Cook) smoked herring. **(b)** (hum inf: Verbeugung) bow.
Büdchen nt dim of Bude (a).
Buddel f -, -n (N Ger inf) bottle.
Buddelei f (im Sand) digging; (inf: Tiefbauarbeiten) constant digging (up) (of road etc).
Buddelkasten m (dial) sand-box.
buddeln 1 vi (inf) to dig. **in der Straße wird dauernd gebuddelt** they're always digging up the road. 2 vt (dial) (ausgraben) Kartoffeln to dig up; Loch to dig.
Buddha ['buda] m -s, -s Buddha.
Buddhismus m Buddhism.
Buddhist(in f) m Buddhist.
buddhistisch adj Buddhist(ic).
Bude f -, -n (a) (Bretterbau) hut; (Bau~) (workmen's) hut; (Markt~, Verkaufs~) stall, stand, booth; (Zeitungs~) kiosk. **(b)** (pej inf: Laden, Lokal etc) dump (inf). **(c)** (inf) (Zimmer) room; (von Untermieter auch) digs pl (inf); (Wohnung) pad (inf). **Leben in die ~ bringen** to liven or brighten up the place; **jdm die ~ einrennen** or **einlaufen** to pester or badger sb; **mir fällt die ~ auf den Kopf** I'm going mad shut up in here; **jdm auf die ~ rücken** (als Besucher) to drop in on sb, to land on sb (inf); (aus einem bestimmten Grund) to pay sb a visit, to go/come round to sb's place; **jdm die ~ auf den Kopf stellen** to turn sb's place upside down.
Budel f -, -n (Aus inf) (shop) counter.
Buden-: ~angst f (inf) claustrophobia; **~angst haben** to feel shut in, to have claustrophobia; ~besitzer m (market) stallholder; ~zauber m (dated inf) knees-up (dated sl), jamboree (dated inf).
Budget [by'dʒe:] nt -s, -s budget.
budgetär [bydʒe'tɛːr] adj budgetary.
Budget-: ~beratung f budget debate; ~entwurf m draft budget; ~vorlage f presentation of the budget.
Budike f -, -n (dial) bar, pub (Brit), saloon (US).
Budiker(in f) m -s, - (dial) bar keeper, landlord (Brit).
Büfett nt -(e)s, -e or -s (a) (Geschirrschrank) sideboard. **(b)** (Schanktisch) bar; (Verkaufstisch) counter. **(c)** kaltes ~ cold buffet. **(d)** (Sw: Bahnhofsgaststätte) (station) buffet.
Büfett-: ~dame f, ~fräulein nt, ~mamsell f (dated) (in Gastwirtschaft) barmaid; (in Konditorei) (counter) assistant.
Büfettier [byfɛ'tie:] m -s, -s barman.
Büffel m -s, - buffalo.
Büffel-: ~herde f herd of buffalo; ~leder nt buff (leather), buffalo skin.
Büffelei f (inf) swotting (inf), cramming (inf).
büffeln (inf) 1 vi to swot (inf), to cram (inf). 2 vt Lernstoff to swot up (inf).
Buffet, Büffet [by'fe:] (esp Aus) nt -s, -s siehe Büfett.
Buffo m -s, -s or Buffi buffo.
Buffo|oper f opera bouffe.
Bug m -(e)s, -e or -e (a) (Schiffs~) bow usu pl; (Flugzeug~) nose. **jdm eins vor den ~ knallen** (sl) to sock sb one (sl). **(b)** (Cook: Schultergegend) shoulder. **(c)** (Tech) brace, strut.
Bügel m -s, - (a) (Kleider~) (coat-)hanger. **(b)** (Steig~) stirrup. **(c)** (Stromabnehmer) bow (collector). **(d)** (von Säge) frame; (von Handtasche) frame; (Brillen~) side or ear-piece, bow; (von Gewehr) trigger-guard; (für Einweckgläser) clip, clamp.
Bügel-: ~automat m rotary iron; ~brett nt ironing board; **wie ein ~brett aussehen** (hum inf) to be as flat as a board (inf); b~echt adj ironable; ~eisen nt iron; ~falte f crease in one's trousers; b~fertig adj ready for ironing; b~frei adj non-iron; ~maschine f rotary iron.
bügeln 1 vt Wäsche to iron; Hose to press; (Sport sl) to lick, to hammer, to thrash (all inf); siehe gebügelt. 2 vi to iron.
Buggy ['bagi] m -s, -s buggy.
Bügler(in f) m -s, - ironer.
Bug-: ~mann m (Sport) bow(man); ~rad nt (Aviat) nose wheel; ~see f (Naut) siehe ~welle.
Bugsier- (Naut): ~dampfer, ~schlepper m tug(boat).
bugsieren* 1 vt (a) (Naut) to tow. **(b)** (inf) Möbelstück etc to manoeuvre, to edge. **jdn aus dem Zimmer ~** to steer or hustle sb out of the room. **(c)** (inf: lancieren) jdn in einen Posten ~ to wangle or fiddle a job for sb (inf). 2 vi (a) (Naut) to tow. **Schlepper, die im Hafen ~** tugs that do the towing in the port. **(b)** (inf: hantieren) **wir mußten umständlich ~, bis ...** we had to make all kinds of manoeuvres to ...
Bugsierer m -s, - (Naut) siehe Bugsierdampfer.
Bugsier- (Naut): ~tau nt, ~trosse f towline, towrope.

Bug- (Naut): ~ **spriet** nt bowsprit; ~**welle** f bow wave.
buh interj boo.
Buh nt -s, -s (inf) boo.
Bühel, Bühl m -s, - (S Ger, Aus, Sw) hill.
buhen vi (inf) to boo.
Buhle[1] m -n, -n (old liter) paramour (obs, liter), lover.
Buhle[2] f -, -n (old liter) paramour (obs, liter), mistress.
buhlen vi (a) (pej: werben) um jdn/Anerkennung ~ to woo sb/recognition; um jds Gunst ~ to woo or court sb's favour. (b) (obs) mit jdm ~ to have a love affair with sb.
Buhler(in f) m -s, - (a) (old liter) siehe **Buhle.** (b) (pej: Werbender) wooer.
Buhlerei f (pej) wooing (um jdn/etw of sb/sth).
buhlerisch adj (a) (old liter) amorous. (b) (pej) fawning attr. ~ um jdn werben to woo sb obsequiously.
Buhmann m, pl -männer (inf) bogeyman (inf).
Buhne f -, -n groyne, breakwater.
Bühne f -, -n (a) (lit, fig) stage; (von Konzertsaal, Aula etc auch) platform. über die ~ gehen (inf) to go or pass off; etw über die ~ bringen (inf) to stage sth; wie haben Sie Ihren ersten Elternabend/Ihre Antrittsvorlesung über die ~ gebracht? how did you manage your first parents' evening/your inaugural lecture?; hinter der ~ (lit, fig) behind the scenes; von der ~ abtreten or verschwinden (inf), die ~ verlassen to make one's exit, to leave the scene; von der ~ des Lebens abtreten (euph) to depart this (earthly) life.
   (b) (Theater) theatre; (als Beruf) stage. Städtische ~n Municipal Theatres; zur ~ gehen to go on the stage, to go into the theatre; an or bei der ~ sein to be on the stage, to be in the theatre; sie steht seit zwanzig Jahren auf der ~ she has been on the stage or in the theatre for twenty years; das Stück ging über alle ~n the play was put on or staged everywhere or in all the theatres.
   (c) (dial: Dachboden) loft.
   (d) (Tech: Hebe~) ramp.
Bühnen-: ~**anweisung** f stage direction; ~**arbeiter** m stagehand; ~**ausbildung** f dramatic training; ~**(aus)sprache** f standard or received pronunciation; ~**ausstattung** f stage property or props pl; ~**autor** m playwright, dramatist; ~**bearbeitung** f stage adaptation; ~**beleuchter** m lighting man; ~**beleuchtung** f stage lighting; ~**bild** nt (stage) set; ~**bildner** m set-designer; ~**dichter** m siehe ~**autor**; ~**dichtung** f dramatic verse; ~**effekt** m stage effect; ~**erfahrung** f stage experience; ~**erfolg** m success; (Stück auch) (stage) hit; ~**fassung** f stage adaptation; b~**gerecht** adj suitable for the stage; etw b~**gerecht bearbeiten** to adapt sth for the stage; ~**gestalt** f (dramatic) character; ~**haus** nt fly tower; ~**himmel** m cyclorama; ~**kunst** f siehe **Schauspielkunst**; ~**künstler(in** f) m (geh) stage actor/actress or artist; ~**maler** m scene painter; ~**malerei** f scene painting; ~**manuskript** nt script; ~**meister** m stage manager; ~**musik** f incidental music; ~**personal** nt theatre staff; ~**raum** m stage and backstage area; b~**reif** adj ready for the stage; ~**schaffende(r)** mf decl as adj (geh) dramatic artist; ~**sprache** f siehe ~**(aus)sprache**; ~**stück** nt (stage) play; ~**technik** f stage technique; ~**techniker** m stage-technician; ~**werk** nt stage entertainment, dramatic work; b~**wirksam** adj effective on the stage; läßt sich dieser Stoff b~**wirksam** gestalten? would this material be effective on the stage?; ~**wirksamkeit** f theatrical effectiveness, theatricality; ~**wirkung** f dramatic effect.
Buh-: ~**ruf** m boo, catcall; ~**rufer** m der Redner wurde von ~**rufern** empfangen the speaker was booed or greeted by boos or booing; die ~**rufer** wurden aus dem Saal entfernt those who had booed were removed from the auditorium.
buk (old) pret of **backen.**
Bukarest nt -s Bucharest.
Bukett nt -s, -s or -e (geh) (a) (Blumen~) bouquet. (b) (von Wein) bouquet, nose.
Bukolik f (Liter) bucolic or pastoral poetry.
Bukoliker(in f) m -s, - (Liter) bucolic or pastoral poet.
bukolisch adj (Liter) bucolic, pastoral.
Bulette f (dial) meat ball. ran an die ~n (inf) go right ahead!
Bulgare m -n, -n, **Bulgarin** f Bulgarian.
Bulgarien [-iən] nt -s Bulgaria.
bulgarisch adj Bulgarian.
Bulgarisch(e) nt decl as adj Bulgarian; siehe **Deutsch(e).**
Bulkladung f (Naut) bulk cargo.
Bull|auge nt (Naut) porthole.
Bulldogge f bulldog.
Bulldozer ['buldozɐ] m -s, - bulldozer.
Bulle[1] m -n, -n (a) bull. (b) (inf: starker Mann) great ox of a man. (c) (pej sl: Polizist) cop (inf). die ~n the fuzz (pej sl), the cops (inf).
Bulle[2] f -, -n (Hist, Eccl) bull.
Bullen-: ~**beißer** m -s, - (a) (fig pej) cantankerous or sour-tempered character; (b) (lit: Bulldogge) bulldog; ~**hitze** f (inf) sweltering or boiling (inf) heat; ~**kloster** nt (hum sl) (men's) hostel; b~**stark** adj (inf) beefy (inf), brawny, strong as an ox.
bull(e)rig adj (dial) sour-tempered, cantankerous.
bullern vi (inf) (a) (poltern) to thud, to rumble; (Wasser, Flüssigkeit) to bubble; (Ofen) to roar. (b) (dial: schimpfen) to bellyache (inf), to moan and groan (inf).
Bulletin [byl'tɛ̃] nt -s, -s bulletin.
bullig adj (inf) (a) brawny, beefy (inf). (b) Hitze sweltering, boiling (inf).
Bullterrier m bull-terrier.
bum interj bang; (tiefer) boom.
Bumerang m -s, -s or -e (lit, fig) boomerang.
Bumerang|effekt m boomerang effect.
Bummel m -s, - stroll; (durch Lokale) wander (durch around),

---

tour (durch of). einen ~ **machen, auf einen ~ gehen** to go for or take a stroll; einen ~**durch die Stadt/Nachtlokale machen** to go for or take a stroll round (the) town, to (go for a) wander round (the) town/to take in a few nightclubs.
Bummelant m (inf) (a) (Trödler) slowcoach (Brit inf), slowpoke (US inf), dawdler. (b) (Faulenzer) loafer (inf), idler.
Bummelantentum nt (pej) absenteeism.
Bummelei f (inf) (Trödelei) dawdling; (Faulenzerei) loafing about (inf), idling.
Bummelfritze m (inf) loafer (inf), idler.
bumm(e)lig adj (trödelnd) slow; (faul) idle.
Bummeligkeit f (inf) (Trödelei) slowness, dawdling; (Faulenzerei) idleness.
Bummelleben nt (inf) life of idleness.
bummeln vi (a) aux sein (spazierengehen) to stroll; (Lokale besuchen) to go round the pubs/bars etc; (ausgehen) to go out on the town. im Park ~ gehen to go for or take a stroll in the park. (b) (trödeln) to dawdle, to hang about (inf). (c) (faulenzen) to idle or fritter one's time away, to take it easy.
Bummel-: ~**streik** m go-slow; ~**zug** m (inf) slow or stopping train.
Bummerl nt -s, -(n) (Aus inf) point against.
bummern vi (dial) to hammer, to bang.
Bummler(in f) m -s, - (a) (Spaziergänger) stroller. (b) siehe **Bummelant.**
Bummlerei f (Aus) siehe **Bummelei.**
bummlig adj (inf) siehe **bumm(e)lig.**
bums interj thump, thud. ~, da fiel der Kleine hin bang! down went the little one.
Bums m -es, -e (inf) (a) (Schlag) bang, thump; (Ftbl sl) kick. (b) (sl) (Tanzvergnügen) hop (inf); (Tanzlokal) dance hall.
bumsen 1 vi impers (inf: dröhnen) ..., daß es bumste ... with a bang; er schlug gegen die Tür, daß es bumste he hammered or thumped on the door; es bumste, als ... there was a thump or thud when ...; es hat gebumst (von Fahrzeugen) there's been a smash-up (inf) or crash; gleich bumst es! you'll catch it (inf), you'll get clobbered (sl).
   2 vi (a) (schlagen) to thump, to hammer; (Ftbl sl) to kick. (b) aux sein (prallen, stoßen) to bump, to bang, to clout (inf); (fallen) to fall with a bang or bump. mit dem Kopf gegen etw ~ to bump or bang or clout (inf) one's head on sth.
   (c) (inf: koitieren) to have it off (Brit sl) or away (Brit sl), to have sex or nookie (hum inf). ich habe Lust zu ~ I fancy a bit (of the other) (inf).
   3 vt (a) (Ftbl sl) Ball to thump, to bang, to hammer.
   (b) (inf) jdn ~ to lay sb, to have it off or away with sb (Brit sl), to have sex or a bit of nookie (hum inf) with sb; gebumst werden to get laid (sl).
Bums-: ~**kneipe** f (pej inf), ~**lokal** nt (pej inf) (low) dive; ~**musik** f (inf) loud (vulgar) music; b~**voll** adj (inf) full to bursting.
Bund[1] m -(e)s, ̈-e (a) (Vereinigung, Gemeinschaft) bond; (Bündnis) alliance. der Alte/Neue ~ (Bibl) the Old/New Testament or Covenant; mit jdm im ~e stehen or sein to be in league with sb; sich (dat) die Hand zum ~e reichen (geh) to enter into a bond of friendship; den ~ der Ehe eingehen to enter (into) the bond of marriage; ein ~ der Freundschaft a bond of friendship; den ~ fürs Leben schließen to take the marriage vows; siehe australisch.
   (b) (Organisation) association, (con)federation; (Staaten~) league, alliance.
   (c) (Pol: Bundesstaat) Federal Government. ~ und Länder the Federal Government and the/its Länder.
   (d) (BRD inf: Bundeswehr) der ~ the army, the services pl.
   (e) (an Kleidern) waist-band.
   (f) (Mus: bei Saiteninstrumenten) fret.
Bund[2] nt -(e)s, -e (von Stroh, Flachs, Reisig etc) bundle; (von Radieschen, Spargel etc) bunch.
Bündchen nt neck- or sleeve-band.
Bündel nt -s, - bundle, sheaf; (Stroh~) sheaf; (von Banknoten auch) wad; (von Karotten, Radieschen etc) bunch; (Opt: Strahlen~) pencil; (Math) sheaf; (fig) (von Fragen, Problemen etc) cluster; (von Vorschlägen etc) set. ein hilfloses/schreiendes ~ a helpless/howling (little) bundle; sein ~ schnüren or packen (dated) to pack one's bags; jeder hat sein ~ zu tragen everybody has his cross to bear.
bündeln vt Zeitungen etc to bundle up, to tie into bundles/a bundle; Garben, Stroh to sheave; Karotten etc to tie into bunches/a bunch; (Opt) Strahlen to focus, to concentrate.
bündelweise adv by the bundle, in bundles. er holte ~ Banknoten aus der Tasche he pulled wads of banknotes out of his pocket.
Bünden nt -s siehe **Graubünden.**
Bundes- in cpds federal; ~**amt** nt Federal Office; ~**angestelltentarif** m (BRD) statutory salary scale; ~**anleihe** f government bond; ~**anstalt** f Federal Institute; ~**anwalt** m (a) (BRD) attorney of the Federal Supreme Court; (b) (Sw) ≈ Public Prosecutor; ~**anwaltschaft** f (BRD) Federal German bar; ~**anzeiger** m (BRD) federal legal gazette; ~**aufsicht** f (BRD) Government supervision; ~**autobahn** f (BRD, Aus) Federal autobahn (maintained by the Federal Government); ~**bahn** f (BRD, Aus, Sw) Federal Railway(s pl); ~**bahner** m (inf) railwayman (employed by the Bundesbahn); ~**bank** f Federal bank; Deutsche ~**bank** Federal Bank of Germany; ~**behörde** f Federal authority; ~**blatt** nt (Sw) Federal Law gazette; ~**bruder** m (Univ) fellow member of a/the student fraternity); ~**bürger** m West German, citizen of West Germany; b~**deutsch** adj West German; ~**deutsche(r)** mf West German; ~**ebene** f: auf ~**ebene** at a national level; b~**eigen** adj Federal(-owned), national; b~**einheitlich** adj Federal,

national; ~**fernstraße** f trunk road (*maintained by the Federal Government*); ~**gebiet** nt (*BRD*) federal territory; ~**genosse** m ally, confederate; ~**gericht** nt (a) Federal Court; (b) (*Sw*) Federal Appeal Court; ~**gerichtshof** m (*BRD*) Federal Supreme Court; ~**gesetzblatt** nt (*BRD, Aus*) Federal Law Gazette; ~**grenzschutz** m (*BRD*) Federal Border Guard; ~**hauptstadt** f federal capital; ~**haus** nt (*BRD, Sw*) Federal Houses of Parliament; ~**haushalt** m federal budget; ~**heer** nt (*Aus*) services pl, army, (federal) armed forces; ~**kabinett** nt Federal cabinet; ~**kanzlei** f (a) (*BRD*) Federal Chancellery; (b) (*Sw*) Federal Chancellery; ~**kanzler** m (a) (*BRD, Aus*) Federal or West German Chancellor; (b) (*Sw*) Head of the Federal Chancellery; ~**kanzleramt** nt (*BRD, Aus*) Federal Chancellery; ~**kriminalamt** nt (*BRD*) Federal Criminal Police Office; ~**lade** f (*Bibl*) Ark of the Covenant; ~**land** nt (a) state; (b) Land of the Federal Republic of Germany; ~**liga** f (*BRD Sport*) national league; ~**ligist** m (*BRD Sport*) national league team; ~**minister** m (*BRD, Aus*) Federal Minister; ~**ministerium** nt (*BRD, Aus*) Federal Ministry; ~**mittel** pl Federal funds pl; ~**nachrichtendienst** m (*BRD*) Federal Intelligence Service; ~**post** f: die (**Deutsche**) ~**post** the (German) Federal Post (Office); ~**präsident** m (*BRD, Aus*) (Federal) President; (*Sw*) President of the Federal Council; ~**presseamt** nt (*BRD*) Federal Government's Press and Information Office; ~**rat** m *Bundesrat* (*upper house of the West German Parliament*); ~**recht** nt Federal law; ~**regierung** f (*BRD, Aus*) Federal Government; ~**republik** f Federal Republic; ~**republik Deutschland** Federal Republic of Germany; ~**republikaner** m citizen of West Germany or of the Federal Republic of Germany; **b**~**republikanisch** adj West German; ~**staat** m (*Staatenbund, Gliedstaat*) federal state; ~**straße** f federal road (*maintained by the Federal Government*).

Bundestag m *Bundestag*, (lower house of the) West German Parliament; (*Hist*) Diet of the German Confederation.

Bundestags- (*BRD*): ~**abgeordnete(r)** m German member of Parliament, member of the *Bundestag*; ~**fraktion** f group or faction in the *Bundestag*; ~**präsident** m President of the *Bundestag* or West German Parliament; ~**wahl** f (federal) parliamentary elections pl.

Bundes-: ~**trainer** m (*BRD Sport*) national coach; ~**verdienstkreuz** nt (*BRD*) order of the Federal Republic of Germany, = OBE (*Brit*); ~**verfassung** f federal constitution; ~**verfassungsgericht** nt (*BRD*) Federal Constitutional Court; ~**versammlung** f (a) (*BRD*) Federal Convention; (b) (*Sw*) Federal Assembly; ~**verwaltungsgericht** nt (*BRD*) Supreme Administrative Court; ~**wehr** f (*BRD*) services pl, army, (West German) armed forces pl; **b**~**weit** adj nationwide.

Bundhose f knee breeches pl.

bündig adj (a) (*schlüssig*) conclusive; (*bestimmt*) concise, succinct, terse; siehe **kurz**. (b) (*in gleicher Ebene*) flush pred, level.

Bündigkeit f (*Schlüssigkeit*) conclusiveness; (*Bestimmtheit*) conciseness, succinctness, terseness.

bündisch adj: die ~e **Jugend** (*Hist*) members of the "free youth movement".

Bündner(in f) m -s, - siehe **Graubündner**.

Bündnis nt alliance.

Bündnis-: ~**block** m allied bloc; ~**politik** f policy vis-à-vis one's allies; ~**system** nt system of alliances; ~**treue** f loyalty to the alliance; **die** ~**treue der Ruritanier** the loyalty of the Ruritanians to the or their alliance; ~**verpflichtung** f commitment to one's allies; ~**vertrag** m pact of alliance.

Bund-: ~**schuh** m (*Hist*) emblem of peasant rebels during their insurrection; ~**weite** f waist measurement; ~**zeichen** nt jointing mark.

Bungalow ['bʊŋɡalo] m -s, -s bungalow.

Bunker m -s, - (a) (*Mil*) bunker; (*Luftschutz*~) air-raid shelter. (b) (*Sammelbehälter*) bin; (*Kohlen*~) bunker; (*Getreide*~) silo. (c) (*Golf*) bunker. (d) (*Mil sl: Gefängnis*) clink (sl), jankers (*Brit Mil* sl).

Bunkerkohle f bunker coal.

bunkern vti (a) *Kohle* to bunker; *Öl* to refuel. (b) (sl: verstecken) to stash (away) (sl).

Bunkeröl nt bunker oil or fuel.

Bunsenbrenner m Bunsen burner.

bunt adj (a) (*farbig*) coloured; (*mehrfarbig*) colourful; (*vielfarbig*) multi-coloured, many-coloured; (*gefleckt*) mottled, spotted. ~ **gestreift** pred colourfully striped; **zu** ~**e Kleidung** loud or gaudy clothing; **etw** ~ **anstreichen** to paint sth colourfully; ~**e Farben** bright or gay colours; ~**es Glas** stained glass; **etw** ~ **bekleben** to stick coloured paper on sth; ~ **gekleidet sein** to be colourfully or brightly dressed, to have colourful clothes on; **Abzüge in B**~, ~**e Abzüge** (*Phot*) colour prints; **ich sehe lieber Filme in B**~ I prefer seeing films in colour; ~ **fotografieren** (*inf*) to photograph in colour; siehe **Hund**.
(b) (fig: abwechslungsreich) varied. **eine** ~**e Menge** an assorted or a motley crowd; **ein** ~**es Bild** a colourful picture; **in** ~**er Reihenfolge** in a varied sequence; ~**e Reihe machen** to seat men and women/boys and girls alternately; **ein** ~**er Teller** a plate of cakes and sweets (*Brit*) or candy (*US*); **ein** ~**er Abend** a social; (*Rad, TV*) a variety programme.
(c) (fig: wirr) confused, higgledy-piggledy. **es geht hier** ~ **zu** (*inf*) it's lively here, this is some sort of mad-house (*pej inf*); **jetzt wird's mir aber zu** ~! (*inf*) that's going too far!, that's too much; **es zu** ~ **treiben** (*inf*) to carry things or go too far, to overstep the mark.

Bunt-: **b**~**bemalt** adj attr colourfully or brightly or gaily painted, painted in bright colours; ~**druck** m colour print; **b**~**farbig** adj colourful, brightly coloured; ~**film** m (*inf*) siehe **Farbfilm**; **b**~**geblümt** adj attr *Stoff* with a colourful flower

design or pattern; ~**gefärbt** adj attr multicoloured, many-coloured; **b**~**gefiedert** adj attr with multicoloured or bright feathers or plumage; **b**~**gefleckt** adj attr *Tier* spotted, mottled; **b**~**gemischt** adj attr *Programm* varied; **b**~**gestreift** adj attr with coloured stripes; ~**heit** f colourfulness, gay or bright colours pl; **b**~**kariert** adj attr with a coloured check (pattern); ~**metall** nt non-ferrous metal; ~**papier** nt coloured paper; ~**sandstein** m new red sandstone; **b**~**scheckig** adj spotted; *Pferd* dappled; **b**~**schillernd** adj attr (a) iridescent; (b) (fig) colourful; *Vergangenheit auch* chequered (*Brit*) or checkered (*US*); ~**specht** m spotted woodpecker; ~**stift** m coloured pencil; ~**wäsche** f coloureds pl.

Bürde f -, -n (*geh*) load, weight; (*fig*) burden. **jdm eine** ~ **aufladen** (*fig*) to impose a burden on sb.

bürden vt (dated geh) **etw auf jdn** ~ (lit, fig) to load sth upon sb.

Bure m -n, -n, **Burin** f Boer.

Burenkrieg m Boer War.

Burg f -, -en (a) castle; (*Strand*~) wall of sand (built on beach by holiday-maker to demarcate his chosen spot). (b) (*Biberbau*) (beaver's) lodge.

Burg-: ~**anlage** f castle buildings pl or complex; ~**berg** m castle hill or mound.

Bürge m -n, -n guarantor; (*fig*) guarantee (*für* of). **für jdn** ~ **sein** to be sb's guarantor, to stand surety for sb; **einen** ~**n stellen** (*Fin*) to offer surety.

bürgen vi **für etw** ~ to guarantee sth, to vouch for sth; (*fig*) to guarantee sth, to be a guarantee of sth; **für jdn** ~ (*Fin*) to stand surety for sb; (*fig*) to vouch for sb; **Sie** ~ **mir persönlich dafür, daß** ... you are personally responsible or answerable to me that ...

Bürger m -s, - (von Staat, Gemeinde) citizen, burgher (*Hist*); (*Sociol, pej*) bourgeois; (im Gegensatz zu Landbewohner) town/city-dweller. **die** ~ **von Ulm** the townsfolk of Ulm; **akademischer** ~ (dated) student.

Bürger-: ~**aktion** f siehe ~**initiative**; ~**beauftragte(r)** mf ombudsman; ~**begehren** nt (*BRD*) public petition; ~**brief** m patent of citizenship; ~**eid** m civic oath; ~**entscheid** m (*BRD*) citizen's or public decision; ~**familie** f merchant family; ~**forum** nt open or public debate; ~**haus** nt (a) town house or residence; (b) (dated: ~familie) merchant family; ~**initiative** f citizen's initiative; ~**komitee** nt citizen's committee; ~**krieg** m civil war.

bürgerlich adj (a) attr *Ehe, Recht etc* civil; *Pflicht* civic. **B**~**es Gesetzbuch** Civil Code.
(b) (dem Bürgerstand angehörend) middle-class (auch pej), bourgeois (esp pej); (*Hist*) bourgeois. **aus guter** ~**er Familie** from a good respectable or middle-class family; ~**es Essen/Küche** good plain food/cooking; ~ **essen** to eat good plain food; ~**es Trauerspiel** (*Liter*) domestic tragedy.

Bürgerliche(r) mf decl as adj commoner.

Bürgerlichkeit f (von Lebensstil) middle-class way of life; (von Denkweise) middle-class mentality.

Bürger-: ~**meister** m mayor; ~**meisteramt** nt (a) (Aufgabe) office of mayor; (b) (Behörde, Gebäude) town hall; ~**meisterei** f (old) (a) district council; (Gebäude) district council offices pl; (b) (dial) siehe ~**meisteramt** (b); ~**meisterin** f mayor(ess); (Frau eines ~meisters) mayoress; ~**pflicht** f civic duty; **Ruhe ist die erste** ~**pflicht** law and order is the citizen's first duty, the first duty of the citizen is law and order; ~**recht** nt usu pl civil rights pl; **jdm die** ~**rechte aberkennen** or **entziehen** to strip sb of his civil rights; ~**rechtler** m -s, - civil rights campaigner.

Bürgerrechts-: ~**bewegung** f civil rights movement; ~**kämpfer** m siehe **Bürgerrechtler**.

Bürger-: ~**schaft** f citizens pl; (Vertretung) City Parliament; ~**schreck** m bog(e)y of the middle classes.

Bürgersfrau f (old) middle-class woman, bourgeoise (*Hist*).

Bürgersinn m, no pl (Haltung) public spiritedness; (Auffassungen) middle-class mentality.

Bürgersmann m, pl -leute (old) citizen, bourgeois (*Hist*).

Bürger(s)sohn m (usu iro) son of the middle classes.

Bürgerstand m (old) middle class(es), bourgeoisie (*Hist*).

Bürgersteig m pavement (*Brit*), sidewalk (*US*).

Bürgerstochter f (usu iro) daughter of the middle classes.

Bürger-: ~**tum** nt, no pl (*Hist*) bourgeoisie (*Hist*); ~**wehr** f (*Hist*) militia.

Burg-: ~**fräulein** nt damsel of the/a castle (old); ~**fried** m -(e)s, -e keep; ~**friede(n)** m (a) (fig) truce; (b) (*Hist*) castle precincts pl, castellany; ~**herr** m lord of the/a castle.

Bürgin f siehe **Bürge**.

Bürgschaft f (*Jur*) (gegenüber Gläubigern) security, surety; (Haftungssumme) penalty; (old liter) pledge (old liter). ~ **für jdn leisten** to stand surety for sb, to act as guarantor for sb; (fig) to vouch for sb; **ich habe für ihn die** ~ **übernommen** I have agreed to stand surety or act as guarantor for him; **er verlangte eine** ~ he demanded (a) security or surety; he demanded that someone (should) vouch for him/her.

Bürgschafts-: ~**erklärung** f declaration of suretyship; ~**nehmer** m siehe **Gläubiger**.

Burgund nt -(e)s Burgundy.

Burgunder m -s, - (a) (Einwohner) Burgundian. (b) (auch: ~wein) burgundy.

burgundisch adj Burgundian. **die B**~**e Pforte** the Belfort Gap.

Burgverlies nt (castle) dungeon.

burlesk adj burlesque no adv.

Burleske f -, -n burlesque.

Burma nt - siehe **Birma**.

Burmese m -n, -n, **Burmesin** f siehe **Birmane**.

burmesisch adj siehe **birmanisch**.

Burnus m - or -ses, -se burnous(e).

Büro nt -s, -s office.

Büro- in cpds office; ~**angestellte(r)** mf office worker; ~**arbeit** f office work; ~**artikel** m item of office equipment; pl office supplies pl or equipment; ~**bedarf** m office supplies pl or equipment; ~**gehilfe** m (office) junior, office boy; ~**haus** nt office block; ~**hengst** m (pej inf) office worker; **all die** ~**hengste** all the office mob (inf); ~**kaufmann** m (office) buyer; ~**klammer** f paper clip; ~**kraft** f (office) clerk.

Bürokrat m -en, -en bureaucrat.

Bürokratie f bureaucracy.

bürokratisieren* vt to bureaucratize.

Bürokratismus m, no pl bureaucracy.

Büro-: ~**maschine** f office machine; ~**material** nt siehe ~**bedarf**; ~**mensch** m (inf) office worker, pen pusher (pej, inf); ~**schluß** m office closing time; **nach** ~**schluß** after office hours; ~**stunden** pl office hours pl; ~**tätigkeit** f office work; ~**vorsteher** m (dated) senior or chief clerk; ~**zeit** f siehe ~**stunden**.

Bursch m -en, -en (Univ, dial) siehe **Bursche**.

Bürschchen nt dim of **Bursche** little lad or fellow. **freches** ~ cheeky little devil; **mein** ~**!** laddie!

Bursche m -n, -n (a) (old, dial) boy, lad; (dial: Freund) young man. **ein toller** ~ quite a lad.

(b) (inf: Kerl) fellow, guy (inf), so-and-so (pej inf). **ein übler** ~ a bad lot.

(c) (Univ: Verbindungsmitglied) member of a student fraternity.

(d) (Lauf~) boy.

(e) (old Mil) batman (Brit), orderly.

(f) (inf: großes Exemplar) **das ist vielleicht ein** ~ what a whopper! (inf); **da haben wir den** ~**n** that's got it or him! (inf).

Burschen-: ~**herrlichkeit** f good old student days; ~**schaft** f student fraternity; ~**schaft(l)er** m -s, - member of a student fraternity; **b**~**schaftlich** adj attr of a/the (student) fraternity; **eine b**~**schaftliche Vereinigung** a student fraternity; **die b**~**schaftlich organisierten Studenten** the students belonging to fraternities.

burschikos adj (a) (jungenhaft) (tom)boyish. **benimm dich doch nicht so** ~ stop behaving like a tomboy. (b) (unbekümmert) casual.

Burschikosität f siehe adj (a) (tom)boyishness. (b) casualness.

Burse f -, -n hostel.

Bürste f -, -n brush; (inf: Bürstenfrisur) crew cut.

bürsten vt to brush; (vulg: koitieren) to screw (sl.).

Bürsten-: ~**binder** m (old) brushmaker; **wie ein** ~**binder** (inf) like mad (inf); siehe **saufen**; ~**frisur** f, ~**(haar)schnitt** m crew cut; ~**macher** m siehe ~**binder**; ~**massage** f brush massage.

Burundi nt -s Burundi.

Burundier(in f) [-iɐ, -iərɪn] m -s, - Burundian.

burundisch adj Burundian.

Bürzel m -s - (a) (Orn) rump. (b) (Hunt) tail. (c) (Cook) parson's nose.

Bus m -ses, -se bus; (Privat- und Überland~ auch) coach (Brit).

Busbahnhof m bus/coach (Brit) station.

Busch m -(e)s, ⸚e (a) (Strauch) bush, shrub. **etwas ist im** ~ (inf) there's something up; **mit etw hinter dem** ~ **halten** (inf) to keep sth quiet or to oneself; **auf den** ~ **klopfen** (inf) to fish (about) for information (inf); **bei jdm auf den** ~ **klopfen** (inf) to sound sb out; **sich (seitwärts) in die** ⸚**e schlagen** (inf) to slip away; (euph hum) to go behind a tree (euph hum).

(b) (Geog: in den Tropen) bush; (inf: Wildnis) jungle. **du kommst wohl aus dem** ~ (inf) have you just come down from the trees! (inf).

(c) (Strauß) bunch; (rare: Büschel) tuft.

Buschbohne f dwarf bean.

Büschel nt -s, - (von Gras, Haaren) tuft; (von Heu, Stroh) bundle; (von Blumen, Rettichen) bunch. **in** ⸚**n wachsen** to grow in tufts; (Blumen) to grow in clumps.

büsch(e)lig adj in tufts; (Blüten) in clusters.

büschelweise adv siehe n in tufts/bundles/bunches/clumps.

Buschen m -s, - (dial) bunch of leaves etc.

Buschenschenke f (Aus) inn.

Buschi nt -s, -s (Sw) baby.

buschig adj bushy.

Buschklepper m -s, - (dated) highwayman.

büschlig adj siehe **büsch(e)lig**.

Busch-: ~**mann** m, pl-männer bushman; ~**messer** nt machete; ~**neger** m maroon; ~**werk** nt bushes pl; ~**windröschen** nt (wood) anemone.

Busen m -s, - (von Frau) bust, bosom; (old: Oberteil des Kleides) bodice; (liter) (von Mann) breast (liter); (fig geh: Innerstes, von Natur) bosom (liter). **ein Geheimnis in seinem** ~ **wahren** to keep a secret deep in one's heart (liter).

Busen-: **b**~**frei** adj topless; ~**freund** m (iro) bosom friend; ~**nadel** f (dated) breastpin; ~**star** m (inf) busty filmstar (inf).

Buslinie f bus route. **welche** ~ **fährt zum Bahnhof?** which bus goes to the station?

Bussard m -s, -e buzzard.

Buße f -, -n (a) (Rel) (Reue) repentance, penitence; (Bußauflage) penance; (tätige ~) atonement. ~ **tun** to do penance; **jdm** ~ **als penance**; **zur** ~ **bereit sein** to be ready to do penance or to atone; **das Sakrament der** ~ the sacrament of penance.

(b) (Jur) (Schadenersatz) damages pl; (Geldstrafe) fine. **eine** ~ **von DM 100** a 100 mark fine; **jdn zu einer** ~ **verurteilen** to make sb pay (the) damages; to fine sb, to impose a fine on sb.

Bussel nt -s, -(n) (Aus) siehe **Busse(r)l**.

busseln, bussen vti (S Ger, Aus) siehe **busse(r)ln**.

---

büßen 1 vt to pay for; Sünden to atone for, to expiate. **das wirst or sollst du mir** ~ I'll make you or you'll pay for that. **2** vi für etw ~ (auch Rel) to atone for sth; (wiedergutmachen) to make amends for sth; für Leichtsinn etc to pay for sth; **schwer (für etw)** ~ müssen to have to pay dearly (for sth).

Büßer (in f) m -s, - penitent.

Büßer-: ~**gewand**, ~**hemd**, ~**kleid** nt penitential robe, hairshirt.

Busse(r)l nt -s, -(n) (S Ger, Aus) kiss.

busse(r)ln vti (S Ger, Aus) to kiss.

Büßerschnee m (spec) penitent snow (spec).

Buß-: **b**~**fertig** adj repentant, contrite; (Rel auch) penitent; ~**fertigkeit** f repentance, contrition; ~**gang** m penitential pilgrimage; **einen** ~**gang antreten** (fig) to don sackcloth and ashes; ~**gebet** nt prayer of repentance.

Bußgeld nt fine.

Bußgeld-: ~**bescheid** m notice of payment due (for traffic offence etc); ~**katalog** m list of offences punishable by fines; ~**verfahren** nt fining system.

Bußgesang m, **Bußlied** nt penitential hymn.

Bussole f -, -n compass; (Elec) galvanometer.

Buß-: ~**prediger** m preacher of repentance; ~**predigt** f sermon calling to repentance; ~**sakrament** nt sacrament of penance; ~**tag** m (a) day of repentance; (b) siehe ~**- und Bettag**; ~**übung** f act of penance; ~**- und Bettag** m day of prayer and repentance.

Büste f -, -n bust; (Schneider~) tailor's dummy; (weibliche) dressmaker's dummy.

Büsten-: ~**halter** m bra, brassière (dated); ~**weite** f siehe **Brustumfang**.

Busuki f -, -s bouzouki.

Busverbindung f bus connection.

Butan nt -s, -e, **Butangas** nt butane (gas).

Butt m -(e)s, -e flounder, butt. **die** ⸚**e** the bothidae (form), flounders.

Bütt f -, -en (dial) speaker's platform. **in die** ~ **steigen** to mount the platform.

Butte f -, -n (a) siehe **Bütte**. (b) grape container.

Bütte f -, -n vat; (dial: Wanne) tub.

Buttel f -, -n siehe **Buddel**.

Büttel m -s, - (old) bailiff; (pej) henchman (pej); (Polizist) cop(per) (inf). **die** ~ **the law** (inf), the cops (inf); **ich bin doch nicht dein** ~ (inf) I'm not going to do your dirty work (pej inf), I'm not your henchman.

Bütteldienst m dirty work (pej inf).

Bütten(papier) nt -s, no pl handmade paper (with deckle edge).

Bütten-: ~**rand** m deckle edge; ~**rede** f carnival speech.

Butter f -, no pl butter. **braune** ~ browned (melted) butter; **gute** ~ real butter; **es schmolz wie** ~ **in der Sonne** it vanished into thin air; **alles (ist) in** ~ (inf) everything is fine or OK or hunkydory (inf); **sein Herz ist weich wie** ~ his heart is as soft as butter; **ich hatte** ~ **in den Knien** (inf) my legs were like jelly; **jdm die** ~ **auf dem Brot nicht gönnen** (fig inf) to begrudge sb the very air he breathes; **ihm ist die** ~ **vom Brot gefallen** (fig inf) he's been let down with a bump (inf); **wir lassen uns nicht die** ~ **vom Brot nehmen** (inf) we're not going to let somebody put one over on us (inf), we're going to stick up for our rights.

Butter- in cpds butter; ~**bemme** f (dial) siehe ~**brot**; ~**berg** m butter mountain; ~**blume** f buttercup; ~**brot** nt bread and butter **no art**, no pl, slice or piece of bread and butter; (inf: Pausenbrot) sandwich; **für ein** ~**brot** (inf) for next to nothing; **kaufen, verkaufen auch** for a song; **das mußt du mir nicht ständig aufs** ~**brot streichen or schmieren** there's no need to keep rubbing it in; **das wird er mir noch lange aufs** ~**brot schmieren, daß ich** ... he'll keep on rubbing in the fact that I ...; ~**brotpapier** nt greaseproof paper; ~**creme** f butter cream; ~**dose** f butterdish; ~**faß** nt butter churn; ~**fett** nt butterfat; ~**flöckchen** nt (Cook) (small knob of) butter.

Butterfly(stil) ['bʌtəflaɪ-] m -s, - butterfly (stroke).

Butter-: ~**gelb** nt (a) (Farbe) butter yellow; (b) (Farbstoff) butter colour; **b**~**gelb** adj butter yellow.

Butter-: ~**gelb** nt (a) (Farbe) butter yellow; (b) (Farbstoff) butter colour; **b**~**gelb** adj butter yellow.

butterig adj buttery.

Butter-: ~**käse** m (full fat) cream cheese; ~**keks** m = morning coffee biscuit; ~**krem** f siehe ~**creme**; ~**milch** f buttermilk.

buttern 1 vt (a) Brot to butter; Gericht to add butter to. (b) Milch to make into butter. (c) (inf: investieren) to put (in + acc into). (d) (Sport sl) to slam (inf). **2** vi to make butter.

Butter-: ~**pilz** m boletus luteus (form), ~**säure** f butyric acid; ~**schmalz** nt clarified butter; ~**seite** f (lit) buttered side; **auf die** ~**seite fallen** (fig inf) to fall on one's feet (inf); **die** ~**seite betrachten** (fig inf) to look on the bright side; **b**~**weich** adj Frucht, Landung beautifully soft; (Sport) Abgabe, Paß, Aufschlag gentle.

Buttje(r) m -s, - (N Ger) kid (inf), child.

Büttner m -s, - (dial) siehe **Böttcher**.

buttrig adj siehe **butterig**.

Butz[1] m -en, -en (dial) (Zwerg) hobgoblin; (Schreckgestalt) bog(e)y(man).

Butz[2] m -en, -en (dial) (apple) core.

Butzemann m siehe **Butz**[1].

Butzen m -s, - (dial) (a) siehe **Butz**[2]. (b) (in ~**scheibe**) bulge (in a bull's-eye pane).

bützen vti (dial) to kiss.

Butzenscheibe f bull's-eye (window) pane.

Büx f -, -en, **Buxe** f -, -n (N Ger) trousers pl (Brit), pants pl. **fünf** ~**en** five pairs of trousers or pants.

Buxtehude nt (a) Buxtehude (town near Hamburg). (b) (inf): aus/nach ~ from/to the back of beyond (inf); in ~ leben to live in the back of beyond (inf); das macht man vielleicht noch in ~ perhaps they still do that in the provincial backwaters.
Bw abbr of **Bundeswehr**.
b.w. abbr of **bitte wenden** pto.
Byzantiner(in f) m -s, - (a) Byzantine. (b) (dated: Kriecher) sycophant.

byzantinisch adj (a) Byzantine. (b) (dated: kriecherisch) servile, sycophantic(al).
Byzantinismus m, no pl (dated fig) servility, sycophancy.
Byzantinist(in f) m Byzantine scholar.
Byzantinistik f Byzantine studies pl.
Byzanz nt -' Byzantium.
bzgl. abbr of **bezüglich**.
bzw. abbr of **beziehungsweise**.

C

(siehe auch K, Z; für CH siehe auch SCH)

C, c [tseː] nt -, - C, c. **C-Schlüssel** m alto or C clef.
C abbr of **Celsius**.
ca. abbr of **circa** approx.
Cabrio nt -s, -s siehe **Kabrio**.
Cabriolet [-leː] nt -s, -s siehe **Kabriolett**.
Cachou [kaˈfuː] nt -s, -s, **Cachoubonbon** nt cachou.
Caesar ['tseːzar] m -s siehe **Cäsar**[1].
Café [kaˈfeː] nt -s, -s café.
Cafeteria f -, -s cafeteria.
Cafetier [kafeˈtieː] m -s, -s (old, Aus) coffee-house proprietor.
cal abbr of **(Gramm)kalorie** (gramme-)calorie.
Calais [kaˈleː] nt -' Calais. die Straße von ~ the Straits of Dover.
Callboy ['koːlbɔy] m -s, -s male prostitute.
Callgirl ['koːlgøːɐl] nt -s, -s callgirl.
Calvados [kalvaˈdoːs] m -, - calvados.
calvinisch adj etc siehe **kalvinisch**.
Calypso m -(s), -s calypso.
Camembert ['kamɔmbeːɐ] m -s, -s Camembert.
Camion [kaˈmiõː] m -s, -s (Sw) siehe **Lastwagen**.
Camouflage [kamuˈflaːʒə] f -, -n (dated, geh) camouflage.
camouflieren* [kamuˈfliːrən] vtr (dated, geh) to camouflage.
Camp [kɛmp] nt -s, -s camp; (Gefangenenlager auch) compound.
campen ['kɛmpn] vi to camp.
Camper(in f) ['kɛmpɐ, -ərɪn] m -s, - camper.
campieren* [kam'piːrən] vi siehe **kampieren**. (b) (Aus, Sw) siehe **campen**.
Camping ['kɛmpɪŋ] nt -s, no pl camping no art. zum ~ fahren to go camping.
Camping- in cpds camping; ~artikel m piece or item of camping equipment; pl camping equipment sing; ~bus m dormobile ® (Brit), camper (US); ~führer m camping or camper's guide(book); ~platz m camping site; ~zubehör nt camping equipment.
Campus m -, - (Univ) campus. auf dem ~ on (the) campus.
Canasta nt -s, no pl canasta.
Cancan [kãˈkãː] m -s, -s cancan.
cand. abbr of **candidatus** siehe **Kandidat**. ~ phil./med. etc final year arts/medical etc student.
Cannabis m -, no pl cannabis.
Cañon ['kanjɔn] m -s, -s canyon.
Canossa nt -(s) siehe **Kanossa**.
Canto m -s, -s (Liter) canto.
Cape [keːp] nt -s, -s cape.
Capriccio [kaˈpritʃo] nt -s, -s (Mus) caprice, capriccio.
Capuccino [kapuˈtʃiːno] m -s, -s cappuccino.
Car m -s, -s (Sw) abbr of **Autocar**.
Caravan ['kaˑ(ː)ravan] m -s, -s (a) (Kombiwagen) estate car (Brit), station wagon. (b) (Wohnwagen) caravan (Brit), trailer (US).
CARE-Paket ['kɛə-] nt CARE packet or parcel.
carrarisch adj Marmor Carrara.
cartesianisch adj etc siehe **kartesianisch**.
Casanova [kazaˈnoːva] m -(s), -s (fig) Casanova.
Cäsar[1] ['tseːzar] m -s siehe Caesar.
Cäsar[2] ['tseːzar] m -en, -en [tseˈzaːrən] (Titel) Caesar.
Cäsaren-: ~herrschaft f autocratic rule, dictatorship; ~wahn(sinn) m megalomania.
cäsarisch [tseˈzaːrɪʃ] adj (geh) (a) (kaiserlich) Caesarean, Caesarian. (b) (fig: selbstherrlich) autocratic.
Cäsarismus [tsezaˈrɪsmus] m Caesarism, autocracy.
Cashewnuß ['kɛʃu-] f cashew (nut).
Casino nt -s, -s siehe **Kasino**.
Casus belli m -, - - (geh) casus belli (form).
Catch-as-catch-can ['kætʃ ɔz 'kætʃ 'kæn] nt -, no pl (lit) catch-as-catch-can, all-in wrestling; (fig) free-for-all.
catchen ['kɛtʃn] vi to do catch(-as-catch-can)-wrestling, to do all-in wrestling. er catcht gegen X he has an all-in or catch bout against X; er catcht gut he's a good all-in or catch wrestler.
Catcher(in f) ['kɛtʃɐ, -ərɪn] m -s, - all-in wrestler, catch(-as-

catch-can) wrestler.
Catull m -s Catullus.
Cause célèbre [kozseˈlɛbr] f - -, -s -s (geh) cause célèbre.
Causerie [kozəˈriː] f (old) causerie (old).
Causeur [koˈzøːɐ] m (old) conversationalist.
Cayennepfeffer [kaˈjen-] m cayenne (pepper).
cbm abbr of **Kubikmeter** cubic metre.
ccm abbr of **Kubikzentimeter** cc, cubic centimetre.
CDU ['tseːdeːˈluː] f - abbr of **Christlich-Demokratisch Union** Christian Democratic Union.
Cedille [seˈdiːj(ə)] f -, -n cedilla.
Celesta [tʃeˈlesta] f -, -s or **Celesten** celeste, celesta.
Cellist(in f) [tʃeˈlist(ɪn)] m cellist.
Cello ['tʃelo] nt -s, -s or **Celli** cello.
Cellophan ® [tseloˈfaːn] nt -s, no pl, **Cellophanpapier** nt (in cellophane (paper).
Celsius ['tselzius] no art, inv centigrade.
Celsiusskala f centigrade scale.
Cembalo ['tʃembalo] nt -s, -s cembalo, harpsichord.
Cent [tsent] m -s, -s cent.
Cercle ['serkl] m -s, -s (Aus) front stalls pl.
Cerclesitz m (Aus) seat in the (front) stalls.
cerise [səˈriːz] adj (Fashion) cerise, cherry.
Cervelat [tservəˈlaːt] m -s, -s (Sw) siehe **Zervelatwurst**.
ces, Ces [tses] nt -, - (Mus) C flat.
Ceylon ['tsailɔn] nt -s siehe Ceylon.
Ceylonese [tsai-] m -n, -n, **Ceylonesin** f Ceylonese, Sin(g)halese.
ceylonesisch [tsai-] adj Ceylonese, Sin(g)halese.
Cha-Cha-Cha ['tʃa'tʃa'tʃa] m -(s), -s cha-cha(-cha).
Chagrinleder [ʃaˈgrɛ̃-] nt shagreen.
Chaise ['ʃɛːzə] f -, -n (a) (old) (Kutsche) (post)chaise (old) (Stuhl) chair. (b) (inf) jaloppy (inf), banger (Brit inf).
Chaiselongue [ʃɛzəˈlɔŋ] f -, -s (old) chaise longue.
Chalet [ʃaˈleː] nt -s, -s Chalet.
Chamäleon [kaˈmeːleɔn] nt -s, -s (lit, fig) chameleon.
chamäleonartig 1 adj (lit, fig) chameleon-like. **2** adv like chameleon.
Chambre séparée [ʃãbrəsepaˈre] nt - -, -s -s (dated) private room.
Chamois [ʃaˈmoa] nt -, no pl (a) (Farbe) buff (colour), (light tan (colour). (b) (auch ~leder) chamois (leather).
Champagner [ʃamˈpanjɐ] m -s, - champagne.
Champignon ['ʃampinjɔŋ] m -s, -s mushroom.
Champignon-: [ʃampinjɔŋ-]: ~kultur f mushroom cultur ~zucht f mushroom cultivation or growing.
Champion ['tʃɛmpiɔn] m -s, -s champion; (Mannschaf champions pl.
Chance ['ʃãːsə, (Aus) 'ʃãːs] f -, -n (a) chance; (bei Wetten) odd pl. keine ~ haben not to have or stand a chance; nicht d geringste ~ haben not to have an earthly (chance) (inf); ic sehe keine ~, das noch rechtzeitig zu schaffen I don't see an chance of being able to do it in time; die ~n, von einem Au überfahren zu werden the chances of being run over by a ca jdm eine (letzte) ~ geben to give sb one (last) chance; die ~ stehen 100:1 the odds are a hundred to one; die ~n steige verringern sich the odds are shortening/lengthening; (f auch) the chances are improving/getting worse.
(b) ~n pl (Aussichten) prospects pl; im Beruf ~n haben have good career prospects; (bei jdm) ~n haben (inf) to stand chance (with sb) (inf).
changieren* [ʃãˈʒiːrən] vi (a) (schillern) to be iridescen changierende Seide shot silk. (b) (Pferd) to change step.
Chanson [ʃãˈsõː] nt -s, -s (political or satirical) song.
Chanson(n)ette [ʃãsoˈnetə] f, **Chansonnier** [ʃãsoˈnieː] m - -s political/satirical song-writer; singer of political/satiric songs.
Chaos ['kaːɔs] nt -, no pl chaos. einem ~ gleichen/ein einziges sein to be in utter chaos.
Chaot(in f) [kaˈoːt(ɪn)] m -en, -en (pej) anarchist (pej).

chaotisch [ka'o:tɪʃ] *adj* chaotic. **~e Zustände** a state of (utter) chaos; **es geht ~ zu** there is utter chaos.

Chapeau claque [ʃapo'klak] *m* **- -, -x -s** opera hat.

Chaplinade [tʃap-] *f* Chaplinesque scene/event.

chaplinesk [tʃa-] *adj* Chaplinesque.

Charakter [ka'raktɐ] *m* **-s, -e** [-'te:rə] **(a)** (*Wesen, Eigenart*) character. **er ist ein Mann von ~** he is a man of character; **etw prägt den ~** sth is character-forming; **keinen ~ haben** (*ohne Prägung*) to have no or to lack character; (*nicht ehrenhaft auch*) to have no principles; **die Party bekam immer mehr den ~ einer Orgie** the party became more and more like an orgy; **seine Warnung hatte mehr den ~ einer Drohung** his warning was more like a threat; **der vertrauliche ~ dieses Gespräches** the confidential nature of this conservation. **(b)** (*Person*) character, personality; (*Liter, Theat*) character. **sie sind ganz gegensätzliche ~e** their characters are entirely different, they have entirely different personalities; **er ist ein männlicher ~** he has a very masculine character or personality.
(c) *siehe* **Charakterkopf (b).**
(d) (*dated Typ*) *siehe* **Schriftzeichen.**

Charakter-: **~anlage** *f* characteristic, trait; **angeborene ~anlagen** innate characteristics; **jds gute ~anlagen fördern** to encourage sb's good (character) traits or qualities; **~bild** *nt* character (image); (*~schilderung*) character study; **c~bildend** *adj* character-forming; **~bildung** *f* character formation; **~darsteller** *m* character actor; **~eigenschaft** *f* character trait; **~fehler** *m* character defect; **c~fest** *adj* strong-minded, of firm or strong character; **ein c~fester Mann** a man of firm or strong character; **~festigkeit** *f* strength of character, strong-mindedness.

charakterisieren* [ka-] *vt* to characterize. **jdn als etw ~** to portray or characterize sb as sth.

Charakterisierung *f* characterization.

Charakteristik [ka-] *f* **(a)** description; (*typische Eigenschaften*) characteristics *pl*. **(b)** (*Tech*) characteristic curve.

Charakteristikum [ka-] *nt* **-s, Charakteristika** (*geh*) characteristic (feature).

charakteristisch [ka-] *adj* characteristic (*für of*).

charakteristischerweise *adv* characteristically.

Charakter-: **~kopf** *m* **(a)** (*Kopf*) distinctive or striking features *pl*; **(b)** (*Person*) **er ist ein ~kopf** he is a man of distinctive or striking appearance; **c~lich 1** *adj* (*of*) character, personal; **c~liche Stärke/Mängel/Qualitäten** strength of character/ character defects/personal qualities; **2** *adv* in character; **er ist c~lich schwierig** he has or is an awkward character; **sie hat sich c~lich sehr verändert** her character has changed a lot; **jdn c~lich stark prägen** to have a strong influence on sb's character; **c~los** *adj* (*niederträchtig*) *Mensch, Verhalten etc* unprincipled; **c~los handeln** to act in an unprincipled way; **(b)** (*ohne Prägung*) characterless; *Spiel, Vortrag* colourless, insipid; **~losigkeit** *f* **(a)** (*Niederträchtigkeit*) lack of principle; (*Handlung*) unprincipled behaviour *no pl*; **es ist eine ~losigkeit, das zu tun** it shows complete lack of principle to do that; **(b)** (*Prägungslosigkeit*) characterlessness; colourlessness; insipidity; **~merkmal** *nt* characteristic.

Charakterologe [ka-] *m*, **Charakterologin** *f* characterologist.

Charakterologie [karakterolo'gi:] *f* characterology.

charakterologisch [ka-] *adj* characterological.

Charakter-: **~rolle** *f* character part or role; **~sache** *f* (*inf*) **das ist ~sache** it's a matter of character; **~schauspieler** *m siehe* **~darsteller**; **c~schwach** *adj* weak, of weak character; **~schwäche** *f* weakness of character; **~schwein** *nt* (*inf*) unprincipled character; **c~stark** *adj* strong, of strong character; **~stärke** *f* strength of character; **~stück** *nt* (*Mus*) mood piece; **~studie** *f* character study; **c~voll** *adj* **(a)** (*anständig*) *Verhalten* which shows character; **dazu ist er zu c~voll** he has too much character for that; **er hat sich c~voll verhalten** his behaviour showed character; **(b)** (*ausgeprägt*) full of character; **eine c~volle Stadt** a town (full) of character; **~zug** *m* characteristic; (*von Menschen auch*) character trait; **es ist kein sehr schöner ~zug von ihm, ...** it is not very nice of him ...

Charge [ˈʃarʒə] *f* **-, -n** **(a)** (*Mil, fig: Dienstgrad, Person*) rank. **(b)** (*Theat*) minor character part.

chargieren* [ʃarˈʒiːrən] *vi* (*Theat*) (*übertreiben*) to overact, to ham (*inf*); (*eine Charge spielen*) to play a minor character part.

Charisma [ˈçaːrɪsma] *nt* **-s, Charismen** or **Charismata** (*Rel, fig*) charisma.

charismatisch [ça-] *adj* charismatic.

Charleston [ˈtʃarlstn] *m* **-, -s** charleston.

Charlottenburger [ʃa-] *m*: **einen ~ machen** (*dial sl*) to snot oneself with one's fingers (*sl*).

charmant [ʃarˈmant] *adj* charming.

Charme [ʃarm] *m* **-s, no pl** charm.

Charmeur [ʃarˈmøːɐ] *m* charmer; (*Schmeichler*) flatterer. **du alter ~!** you old smoothy! (*inf*).

Charmeuse [ʃarˈmøːz] *f*, *no pl* (*Tex*) charmeuse.

Charta [ˈkarta] *f* **-, -s** charter. **Magna ~** Magna Carta.

Charter [ˈtʃartɐ] *m* **-s, -** charter.

Charter-: **~flug** *m* charter flight; **~(flug)gesellschaft** *f* charter(flight) company; **~maschine** *f* charter plane.

chartern [ˈtʃartɐn] *vt Schiff, Flugzeug* to charter; (*fig inf*) *Taxi, Arbeitskräfte etc* to hire.

Chassis [ʃaˈsiː] *nt* **- -** [-iː(s), -iːs] (*Aut, Rad, TV*) chassis.

Chauffeur [ʃɔˈføːɐ] *m* chauffeur.

chauffieren* [ʃɔ-] *vti* (*dated*) to chauffeur, to drive.

Chaussee [ʃoˈseː] *f*, **-n** [-eːən] (*dated*) high road; (*in Straßennamen*) Avenue.

Chaussee-: **~baum** *m* (*dated*) roadside tree; **~graben** *m* (*dated*) *siehe* **Straßengraben.**

Chauvinismus [ʃovi-] *m* chauvinism; (*Benehmen, Äußerung*) chauvinist(ic) action/remark.

Chauvinist(in *f*) *m* chauvinist.

chauvinistisch [ʃovi-] *adj* chauvinist(ic).

checken [ˈtʃɛkn] **1** *vt* **(a)** (*überprüfen*) to check. **(b)** (*sl: verstehen*) to get (*inf*). **(c)** (*sl: merken*) to cotton on to (*inf*), to wise up to (*sl*). **er hat das nicht gecheckt** he didn't cotton on (*inf*), he didn't wise up to it (*sl*). **(d)** (*sl: schaffen*) to make (*inf*), to get. **2** *vti* (*Eishockey*) to block; (*anrempeln*) to barge.

Check- [ˈtʃɛk-]: **~liste** *f* check list; **~point** [-pɔynt] *m* **-s, -s** checkpoint.

Chef [ʃef, (*Aus*) ʃeːf] *m* **-s, -s** boss; (*von Bande, Delegation etc*) leader; (*von Organisation, inf: Schuldirektor*) head; (*der Polizei*) chief; (*Mil: von Kompanie*) commander. **~ des Stabes** Chief of Staff; **er ist der ~ vom ganzen** he's in charge or the boss here; **hallo ~!** (*inf*) hey, gov(ernor) or chief or squire (*all Brit inf*) or mac (*US inf*).

Chef-: **~arzt** *m* senior consultant; **~etage** *f* management or executive floor.

Chefeuse [ʃeˈføːzə] *f* (*hum*) boss's wife.

Chefideologe *m* (*inf*) chief ideologist.

Chefin [ˈʃefɪn, (*Aus*) ˈʃeːfɪn] *f* **(a)** boss; (*Sch*) head; (*von Delegation etc*) head. **(b)** (*inf: Frau des Chefs*) boss's wife. **Frau ~!** ma'am (*US*), ≈ excuse me.

Chef-: **~koch** *m* chef, head cook; **~redakteur** *m* editor-in-chief; **~redaktion** *f* **(a)** (*Aufgabe*) chief editorship; **(b)** (*Büro*) main editorial office; *siehe* **Redaktion**; **~sekretärin** *f* personal assistant/secretary; **~visite** *f* (*Med*) consultant's round.

chem. *abbr of* **chemisch.**

Chemie [çeˈmiː, (*esp S Ger*) keˈmiː] *f* **-, no pl** (*lit, fig*) chemistry; (*inf: Chemikalien*) chemicals *pl*. **was die so essen ist alles ~** they just eat synthetic food.

Chemie-: **~arbeiter** *m* chemical worker; **~beruf** *m* job in industrial chemistry; **~faser** *f* synthetic or man-made fibre; **~unterricht** *m* chemistry.

Chemikal [çe-] *nt* **-s, -ien** [-iən], **Chemikalie** [çemiˈkaːliə] *f* **-, -n** *usu pl* chemical.

Chemiker(in *f*) [ˈçe-, (*esp S Ger*) ˈke-] *m* **-s, -** chemist.

Cheminée [ˈʃmɪne] *nt* **-s, -s** (*Sw*) fireplace.

chemisch [ˈçe:-, (*esp S Ger*) ˈke:-] *adj* chemical; *siehe* **Reinigung.**

chemisieren* [çe-] *vti* (*DDR*) to make increasing use of chemistry (in).

Chemo- [çemo-]: **~technik** *f* chemical engineering, technochemistry; **~techniker** *m* chemical engineer.

-chen *suf dim* little.

Cherub [ˈçe:rup] *m* **-s, -im** [-biːm] or **-inen** [-ˈbiːnən] cherub.

cherubinisch [çe-] *adj* cherubic.

chevaleresk [ʃəvaləˈrɛsk] *adj* (*geh*) chivalrous.

Chiasmus [ˈçiasmos] *m* (*Ling*) chiasmus.

chiastisch [ˈçia-] *adj* (*Ling*) chiastic.

chic [ʃik] *adj siehe* **schick.**

Chicorée [ʃikoˈreː] *f* **- or -m -s, no pl** chicory.

Chiffon [ˈʃifo(:)] *m* **-s, -s** chiffon.

Chiffre [ˈʃifr, ˈʃifrə] *f* **-, -n** **(a)** cipher. **(b)** (*in Zeitung*) box number.

Chiffreschrift *f* cipher, code.

chiffrieren* [ʃɪf-] *vti* to encipher, to code. **chiffriert** coded.

Chile [ˈtʃiːle] *nt* **-s** Chile.

Chilene [tʃiˈleːnə] *m* **-n, -n**, **Chilenin** *f* Chilean.

chilenisch [tʃi-] *adj* Chilean.

Chilesalpeter *m* chile saltpetre, sodium nitrate.

Chili [ˈtʃiːli] *m* **-s, no pl** chil(l)i (pepper).

China [ˈçiːna, (*esp S Ger*) ˈkiːna] *nt* **-s** China.

China-: **~cracker** *m siehe* **~kracker**; **~kohl** *m* Chinese cabbage; **~kracker** [-krɛkɐ] *m* **-s, -** banger (*Brit*), firecracker (*US*); **~krepp** *m* crepe de Chine.

Chinchilla¹ [tʃɪnˈtʃɪla] *f* **-, -s** (*Tier*) chinchilla.

Chinchilla² [tʃɪnˈtʃɪla] *nt* **-s, -s (a)** (*Pelz*) chinchilla. **(b)** (*auch ~kaninchen*) chinchilla rabbit.

Chinese [çi-, (*esp S Ger*) ki-] *m* **-n, -n** Chinaman; (*heutig auch*) Chinese.

Chinesin [çi-, (*esp S Ger*) ki-] *f* Chinese woman; (*heutig auch*) Chinese.

chinesisch [çi-, (*esp S Ger*) ki-] *adj* Chinese. **die C~e Mauer** the Great Wall of China; **das ist ~ für mich** (*inf*) that's all Greek or Chinese to me (*inf*).

Chinesisch(e) [çi-, (*esp S Ger*) ki-] *nt decl as adj* Chinese; *siehe auch* **Deutsch(e).**

Chinin [çiˈniːn] *nt*, *no pl* quinine.

Chinoiserie [ʃinoazəˈriː] *f* chinoiserie.

Chip [tʃip] *m* **-s, -s (a)** (*Spiel~*) chip. **(b)** *usu pl* (*Kartoffel~*) (potato) crisp (*Brit*), potato chip (*US*).

Chiromant(in *f*) [çi-] *m* chiromancer.

Chiromantie [çiromanˈtiː] *f* chiromancy.

Chiro- [çiro-]: **~praktik** *f* chiropractic; **~praktiker** *m* chiropractor.

Chirurg(in *f*) [çiˈrʊrg(ɪn)] *m* **-en, -en** surgeon.

Chirurgie [çirʊrˈgiː] *f* surgery. **er liegt in der ~** he's in surgery.

chirurgisch [çi-] *adj* surgical. **ein ~er Eingriff** surgery.

Chitin [çiˈtiːn] *nt* **-s, no pl** chitin.

Chlor [kloːɐ] *nt* **-s, no pl** chlorine.

chloren, chlorieren* [klo-] *vt* to chlorinate.

chlorig [ˈkloː-] *adj* **(a)** (*Chem*) chlorous. **(b)** *Wasser* chlorinated.

Chloro- [kloro-]: ~**form** nt -s, no pl chloroform; c~**formieren*** vt insep to chloroform; ~**phyll** nt -s, no pl chlorophyll.

Chlorwasser nt (a) (Chem) chlorine water. (b) (im Hallenbad) chlorinated water.

Choke [tʃoːk] m -s, -s, **Choker** ['tʃoːkɐ] m -s, - choke.

Cholera ['koːlera] f -, no pl cholera.

Choleriker(in f) [ko-] m -s, - choleric person; (fig) irascible or hot-tempered person.

cholerisch [ko-] adj choleric.

Cholesterin [ço-] nt -s, no pl cholesterol.

Cholesterinspiegel m cholesterol level.

Chor[1] [koːɐ] m -(e)s, ̈-e (a) (Sänger~) choir; (Bläser~ etc) section. **im ~ singen** to sing in the choir; (zusammen singen) to sing in chorus, to chorus; **im ~ sprechen/rufen** to speak/shout in chorus; **ja, riefen sie im ~** yes, they chorused.
(b) (Theat) chorus.
(c) (Komposition) choral work or composition.
(d) (bei Orgel) rank.
(e) (bei Klavier, Laute etc) group of strings tuned in unison or to the same pitch.

Chor[2] [koːɐ] m or (rare) nt -(e)s, -e or ̈-e (Archit) (a) (Altarraum) chancel, choir. (b) (Chorempore) loft, gallery.

Choral [ko'raːl] m -s, **Choräle** (Mus) (a) (Gregorianischer) chant, plainsong. (b) (Kirchenlied) hymn.

Choreo- [koreo-]: ~**graph(in** f) m choreographer; ~**graphie** f choreography; c~**graphieren*** 1 vt to choreograph, to write or do the choreography for; 2 vi to write or do (the) choreography; c~**graphisch** adj choreographic(al).

Chor- [koːɐ]: ~**frau** f (Eccl) canoness; ~**gebet** nt Divine office; ~**gesang** m (Lied) choral music; (das Singen) choral singing; ~**gestühl** nt choir stalls pl; ~**herr** m (Eccl) siehe **Kanoniker**.

chorisch [koː-] adj choral.

Chorist(in f) [ko-] m siehe **Chorsänger(in)**.

Chor- [koːɐ]: ~**knabe** m choirboy; ~**leiter** m choirmaster; ~**sänger(in** f) m member of a choir; (im Kirchenchor) chorister; (im Opernchor etc) member of the chorus; ~**schranke** f choir or rood screen; ~**stuhl** m choirstall.

Chorus ['koːrus] m -, -se (Mus) (a) (obs) siehe **Chor**[1] (a). (b) (Jazz: Variationsthema) theme.

Chose ['ʃoːzə] f -, -n (inf) (a) (Angelegenheit) business, thing. (b) (Zeug) stuff. **die ganze ~** the whole lot.

Chow-Chow [tʃau'tʃau] m -s, -s chow.

Chr. abbr of **Christus**.

Christ[1] [krıst] m -s (old, geh) siehe **Christus**.

Christ[2] [krıst] m -en, -en Christian.

Christbaum m (a) Christmas tree; (Mil inf) flares pl.

Christbaum- in cpds siehe auch **Weihnachtsbaum-**; ~**kugel** f Christmas tree ball; ~**schmuck** m (a) Christmas tree decorations pl; (b) (iro: Orden) gongs pl (Brit inf), fruit salad (US inf).

Christ- ['krıst-]: ~**demokrat** m Christian Democrat; c~**demokratisch** adj Christian Democratic.

Christen- ['krıstn-]: ~**gemeinde** f Christian community; ~**glaube(n)** m Christian faith; ~**heit** f Christendom; ~**lehre** f siehe **Religionslehre**; ~**pflicht** f (one's) duty as a Christian, (one's) Christian duty; ~**seele** f (old) siehe **Menschenseele**; ~**tum** nt, no pl Christianity; ~**verfolgung** f persecution of the Christians.

Christfest nt (dated, dial) siehe **Weihnachtsfest**.

Christi gen of **Christus**.

christianisieren* [krı-] 1 vt to convert to Christianity, to christianize. 2 vi to convert people to Christianity.

Christianisierung f conversion to Christianity, Christianization.

Christin ['krıstın] f Christian.

Christ- ['krıst-]: ~**kind(chen)** nt, no pl baby or infant Jesus, Christ Child; (Sinnbild für Weihnachten) (das Geschenke bringt) Father Christmas; (fig inf: Dummerchen) little innocent; ~**kindl(e)** nt (dial) (a) siehe ~**kind(chen)**; (b) (dial: Geschenk) Christmas present; **zum ~kindl(e)** as a Christmas present, for Christmas.

christlich [krı-] 1 adj Christian. **er ist bei der ~en Seefahrt** (hum) he is a seafaring man; **C~er Verein Junger Männer** Young Men's Christian Association.
2 adv like or as a Christian. **~ leben** to live a Christian life; **~ handeln** to act like a Christian; **~ aufwachsen/jdn ~ erziehen** to grow up/bring sb up as a Christian; **eine ~ orientierte Moral** a Christian(-orientated) morality; **etw ~ teilen** to let the other person have the larger share.

Christlichkeit f Christianity.

Christ- ['krıst-]: ~**messe** f Midnight Mass; ~**mette** f (katholisch) Midnight Mass; (evangelisch) Midnight Service; ~**nacht** f (dial) Christmas Eve.

Christologie [krıstolo'giː] f Christology.

Christoph ['krı-] m -s Christopher.

Christophorus [krı-] m - Saint Christopher.

Christrose ['krıst-] f Christmas rose.

Christus ['krıstus] m **Christi**, dat - or (form) **Christo**, acc - or (form) **Christum** Christ; (~figur auch) figure of Christ. **vor Christi Geburt, vor Christo** (form) or ~ **before Christ, BC; nach Christi Geburt, nach Christo** (form) **AD, Anno Domini**, in the year of our Lord (liter); **Christi Himmelfahrt** the Ascension of Christ; (Himmelfahrtstag) Ascension Day.

Chrom [kroːm] nt -s, no pl chrome; (Chem) chromium.

Chromatik [kro-] f (a) (Mus) chromaticism. (b) (Opt) chromatics sing.

chromatisch [kro-] adj (Mus, Opt) chromatic.

chromblitzend adj gleaming with chrome.

Chromosom [kro-] nt -s, -en chromosome.

Chromosomen-: ~**paar** nt pair of chromosomes; ~**satz** m set of chromosomes.

Chronik ['kroː-] f chronicle. **etw in einer ~ aufzeichnen** to chronicle sth, to record sth in a chronicle.

chronisch ['kroː-] adj (Med, fig) chronic.

Chronist(in f) [kroː-] m chronicler.

Chronologie [kronolo'giː] f chronology.

chronologisch [kro-] adj chronological.

Chronometer [kro-] nt -s, - chronometer.

Chruschtschow [xru'ʃtʃof] m -s Khrushchev.

Chrysantheme [kryzan'teːmə] f -, -n chrysanthemum.

chthonisch ['çtoːnıʃ] adj (liter) chthonian (liter), chthonic (liter).

Chuzpe ['xutspə] f -, no pl (sl) chutzpa(h) (sl), audacity.

CIA ['siːai'ei] f or m -s CIA.

Cicero[1] ['tsiːtsero] m -s Cicero.

Cicero[2] ['tsiːtsero] f or m -, no pl (Typ) twelve-point type, pica.

Cicerone [tʃitʃe'roːnə] m -(s), -s or (geh) **Ciceroni** (a) (Mensch) cicerone (form), guide. (b) (Buch) (travel) guide(book).

ciceronisch [tsitse'roːnıʃ] adj Ciceronian.

Cie. abbr of **Kompanie**.

Cineast(in f) [sine'ast(ın)] m -en, -en cineast(e).

Cinemascope [sinema'skoːp] ® nt -s, no pl Cinemascope ®.

Cinemathek [sinema'teːk] f siehe **Kinemathek**.

circa ['tsırka] adv siehe **zirka**.

Circe ['tsırtsə] f -, -n (Myth) Circe; (fig geh) femme fatale.

circensisch [tsır'tsenzıʃ] adj siehe **zirzensisch**.

Circulus vitiosus ['tsırkulus vi'tsioːzus] m --, **Circuli vitiosi** (geh) (Teufelskreis) vicious circle; (Zirkelschluß auch) circular argument, petitio principii (form).

cis, Cis [tsıs] nt -, - (Mus) C sharp.

City ['sıtı] f -, -s city centre.

Clair-obscur [klerops'kyːɐ] nt -s, no pl (Art) chiaroscuro.

Clan [klaːn] m -s, -s or (rare) -e (lit, fig) clan.

Claque ['klakə] f -, no pl claque.

Claqueur [kla'køːɐ] m hired applauder, claqueur.

Clavicembalo [klavi'tʃembalo] nt -s, -s or **Clavicembali** clavicembalo, harpsichord.

clean [kliːn] adj pred (sl) off drugs. **~ werden** to kick (the habit) (sl).

Clearing ['kliːrıŋ] nt -s, -s (Econ) clearing.

Clementine f siehe **Klementine**.

clever ['klevɐ] adj (intelligent) clever, bright; (raffiniert) sharp, shrewd; (gerissen) crafty, cunning; (geschickt) clever.

Cleverness, Cleverneß ['klevɐnes] f, no pl siehe adj cleverness, brightness; sharpness, shrewdness; craftiness, cunning; cleverness.

Clinch [klıntʃ] m -(e)s, no pl (Boxen, fig) clinch. **in den ~ gehen** (lit, fig) to go into a clinch; (fig: Verhandlungspartner) to get stuck into each other (inf); **jdn in den ~ nehmen** (lit) to go into a clinch with sb; (fig) to get stuck into sb (inf); **sich aus dem ~ lösen, den ~ lösen** to break the clinch.

clinchen ['klıntʃn] 1 vi to clinch. 2 vt **jdn ~** to go into a clinch with sb.

Clip m -s, -s (Haar~, am Füller etc) clip; (Brosche) clip-on brooch; (Ohr~) (clip-on) earring.

Clips m -, -e siehe **Clip**.

Clique ['klıkə] f -, -n (a) (Freundeskreis) group, set. **wir fahren mit der ganzen ~ in Urlaub** the whole gang or crowd of us are going on holiday together; **Thomas und seine ~** Thomas and his set. (b) (pej) clique.

Cliquen-: ~**bildung** f forming of cliques; **da kam es natürlich zur ~bildung** then of course it started getting cliquey (inf) or people started forming cliques; ~**(un)wesen** nt (pej) cliquishness; ~**wirtschaft** f (pej inf) cliquey set-up (inf).

Clochard [klɔ'ʃaːɐ] m -s, -s tramp.

Clou [kluː] m -s, -s (von Geschichte) (whole) point; (von Show) highlight, high spot; (von Begebenheit) show-stopper; (Witz) real laugh (inf). **und jetzt kommt der ~ der Geschichte** and now, wait for it, ...; **das ist doch gerade der ~** but that's just it, but that's the whole point; **das wäre der ~** that'd be a real laugh (inf); **sein Auftritt war der ~ der Show** his act was the highlight or climax of the show.

Clown [klaun] m -s, -s (lit, fig) clown. **den ~ spielen** to clown around, to play the fool; **sich/jdn zum ~ machen** to make a clown of oneself/sb; **er macht sich zum ~ des Establishments/seiner Frau** he has taken on the role of the establishment's jester/his wife is making him act like a clown.

Clownerie [klaunə'riː] f clowning (around) no pl.

Club m -s, -s siehe **Klub**.

cm abbr of **Zentimeter** cm.

Co. abbr of **Kompagnon; Kompanie** Co.

Co-, co- in cpds co-.

Coach [koːtʃ] m -(s), -s (Sport) coach.

coachen ['koːtʃn] vti (Sport) to coach.

Coca f -, -s (inf) Coke ® (inf).

Cockerspaniel m cocker spaniel.

Cockpit nt -s, -s cockpit.

Cocktail ['kɔkteːl] m -s, -s (a) (Getränk) cocktail. (b) (DDR: Empfang) reception. (c) (~party) cocktail party. **jdn zum ~ einladen** to invite sb for cocktails, to invite sb to a cocktail party.

Cocktail-: ~**kleid** nt cocktail dress; ~**party** f cocktail party.

Code [koːt] m -s, -s siehe **Kode**.

Codex m -es or -, -e or **Codizes** ['koːditseːs] siehe **Kodex**.

Cognac ® ['kɔnjak] m -s, -s cognac.

Coiffeur [koa'føːɐ] m, **Coiffeuse** [koa'føːzə] f (Sw) hairdresser; (geh) hair stylist.

Coiffure [koa'fyːr] f -, -n (a) (geh) hairstyling. (b) (Sw) hairdressing salon.

Cola f -, -s (inf) Coke ® (inf).

Colanuß f cola nut.
Collage [kɔˈlaːʒə] f -, -n (Art, fig) collage; (Musik) medley.
Colli m -s, -s collie.
Collier [kɔˈlieː] nt -s, -s siehe **Kollier**.
Colloquium nt siehe **Kolloquium**.
Colonia-: ~kübel m (Aus) siehe **Koloniakübel**; ~wagen m (Aus) siehe **Koloniawagen**.
color adv (inf) in colour.
Color nt: in ~ in colour.
Color- in cpds colour.
Colt ® m -s, -s Colt.
Combo f -, -s combo.
Comeback [kamˈbɛk] nt -(s), -s comeback.
Comecon, COMECON [ˈkɔmɛkɔn] m or nt - Comecon.
Communiqué [kɔmyniˈkeː] nt -s, -s siehe **Kommuniqué**.
Computer [kɔmˈpjuːtɐ] m -s, - computer.
Computer- in cpds computer-; ~blitz m (Phot) siehe **Elektronenblitz**; ~diagnostik f (Med) computer diagnosis; ~generation f computer generation; c~gerecht adj (ready) for the computer; c~gesteuert adj controlled by computer, computer-controlled.
computerisieren* [kɔmpjutəriˈziːrən] vti to computerize.
Comtesse f countess.
Conditio sine qua non [kɔnˈdiːtsio] f - - - -, no pl (geh) sine qua non.
Conférencier [kõfɛrãˈsieː] m -s, -s compère, MC.
Confiserie [kõfizəˈriː] f siehe **Konditorei**.
Connaisseur [kɔnɛˈsøːɐ] m (geh) connoisseur.
Consensus m -, - (geh) siehe **Konsens**.
Consilium abeundi nt - -, no pl (Sch) final warning given to a pupil before being sent down.
Container [kɔnˈteːnɐ] m -s, - container.
Container- in cpds container; ~bahnhof m container depot; ~terminal m or nt -s, -s container terminal; ~verkehr m container traffic; auf ~verkehr umstellen to containerize.
Contenance [kõtəˈnãːs(ə)] f -, no pl (geh) composure.
Contergan ® nt -s thalidomide.
Contergankind nt (inf) thalidomide child/baby.
cool [ˈkuːl] adj (sl) (a) (gefaßt) cool. du mußt ~ bleiben you must keep your cool (inf) or stay cool (inf). (b) (angenehm) cool (sl). die Party war ~ the party was (real) cool (sl). (c) (ungefährlich) safe. (d) (fair) on the level (inf), fair. er ist ein ~er Dealer he is a fair dealer, as a dealer he is on the level.
Copilot, Co-Pilot m siehe **Kopilot**.
Copyright [ˈkɔpirait] nt -s, -s copyright.
coram publico adv (geh) publicly.
Cord m -s, no pl (Tex) cord, corduroy.
Cord- in cpds cord, corduroy; ~jeans pl cords pl.
Cordon bleu [kɔrdõˈbløː] nt - -, -s -s (Cook) veal cordon bleu.
Corner [ˈkɔːɐnɐ] m -s, - (Aus Sport) corner.
Corn-flakes, Corn Flakes ® [ˈkɔːɐnfleːks] pl cornflakes pl.
Cornichon [kɔrniˈfõː] nt -s, -s gherkin.
Corpora delicti pl of **Corpus delicti**.
Corps [kɔːɐ] nt -, - siehe **Korps**.
Corpus nt -, **Corpora** (Ling) siehe **Korpus**.
Corpus delicti nt - -, **Corpora** - corpus delicti; (hum) culprit (inf).
Corso m -s, -s siehe **Korso**.
cos. abbr of Kosinus cos.
Costa Rica nt -s Costa Rica.
Costaricaner(in f) m -s, - Costa Rican.
costaricanisch adj Costa Rican.
Couch [kautf] f or (Sw) m -, -es or -en couch.
Couch-: ~garnitur f three-piece suite; ~tisch m coffee table.
Couleur [kuˈløːɐ] f -, -s (a) (geh) kind, sort. Faschisten/Sozialisten jeder ~ Fascists/Socialists of every shade. (b)

(Univ) colours pl. ~ tragen to wear the colours of one's student society (Brit) or fraternity (US).
Countdown [ˈkauntˈdaun] m or nt -s, -s (Space, fig) countdown.
Coup [kuː] m -s, -s coup. einen ~ (gegen jdn/etw) landen to bring or pull (inf) off a coup (against sb/sth).
Coupé [kuˈpeː] nt -s, -s coupé.
Couplet [kuˈpleː] nt -s, -s political/cabaret/music-hall song.
Coupon [kuˈpõː] m -s, -s (a) (Zettel) coupon. (b) (Fin) (interest) coupon. (c) (Stoff~) length (of material).
Cour [kuːɐ] f (dated): einem Mädchen die ~ machen or schneiden to court a young lady (dated).
Courage [kuˈraːʒə] f -, no pl (geh) courage, pluck.
couragiert [kuraˈʒiːɐt] adj (geh) courageous, plucky.
Courtage [kurˈtaːʒə] f -, -n (Fin) commission.
Cousin [kuˈzɛ̃ː] m -s, -s, **Cousine** [kuˈziːnə] f cousin.
Couvert [kuˈveːɐ] nt -s, -s siehe **Kuvert**.
Cover [ˈkavɐ] nt -s, -s cover.
Cracker [ˈkrɛkɐ] m -s, -(s) (a) (Keks) cracker. (b) (Feuerwerkskörper) banger (Brit), fire-cracker (US).
Craquelé [krakəˈleː] nt -s, -s crackle.
Credo nt -s, -s siehe **Kredo**.
Creme [kreːm] f -, -s (Haut~, Cook, fig) cream. die ~ der Gesellschaft the cream of society, the crème de la crème (liter).
creme [kreːm] adj pred (Fashion) cream.
creme-: ~artig adj cream-like; ~farben adj cream-coloured.
cremen vt siehe **eincremen**.
Cremetorte f cream gateau.
cremig adj creamy.
Crêpe de Chine [krɛpdəˈʃin] m - - -, -s - - crepe de Chine.
Crescendo [kreˈʃendo] nt -s, -s or **Crescendi** (a) (Mus) crescendo. (b) (Sport) final spurt.
Crew [kruː] f -, -s crew; (Kadettenjahrgang) cadets of the same year/age.
Croissant [kroaˈsãː] nt -s, -s croissant.
Cromargan ® [kro-] nt -s, no pl stainless steel.
Croupier [kruˈpieː] m -s, -s croupier.
Croutonwecken [kruˈtõː-] m (Aus) siehe **Stangenbrot**.
Crux f -, no pl (a) (Last) nuisance. geduldig trägt sie ihre ~ she bears her cross patiently. (b) (Schwierigkeit) trouble, problem. die ~ bei der Sache ist, ... the trouble or problem (with that) is ...
CSU [tseːˈɛsˈʔuː] f - abbr of Christlich-Soziale Union Christian Social Union.
c.t. [ˈtseːˈteː] abbr of cum tempore adv within fifteen minutes of the time stated. 18.30 ~ 6.30 for 6.45.
cum grano salis adv (geh) with a pinch of salt.
cum laude adv (Univ) cum laude (form), with distinction.
Cunnilingus [-ˈlingus] m -, **Cunnilingi** [-ˈlingi] cunnilingus, cunnilinctus.
Cup [kap] m -s, -s (Sport) cup.
Cupido m -s Cupid.
Curling [ˈkøːɐliŋ] nt -s, no pl curling.
Curricula (geh) pl of **Curriculum**.
curricular adj attr (geh) curricular.
Curriculum nt -s, **Curricula** (geh) curriculum.
Curriculumforschung f curriculum development.
Curry [ˈkari] m or nt -s, no pl curry.
Currywurst f curried sausage.
Cut [kœt], **Cutaway** [ˈkœtəve] m -s, -s (dated) cutaway.
cutten [ˈkatn] vti (Film, Rad, TV) to cut, to edit.
Cutter(in f) [ˈkatɐ, -ərin] m -s, - (Film, Rad, TV) editor.
cuttern [ˈkatɐn] vi siehe **cutten**.
C.V.J.F. [tseːˈfaujɔtˈʔɛf] m -s abbr of Christlicher Verein Junger Frauen YWCA.
C.V.J.M. [tseːˈfaujɔtˈʔɛm] m -s abbr of Christlicher Verein Junger Männer YMCA.
Cypern [ˈtsyːpɐn] nt -s siehe **Zypern**.

D

D, d [deː] nt -, - D, d.
d.Ä. abbr of der Ältere sen.
da 1 adv (a) (örtlich) (dort) there; (hier) here. es liegt ~ draußen/drinnen/drüben/vorn it's out there/in there/over there/there in front; das liegt etwa ~ herum it's somewhere round about there or thereabouts; geh ~ herum go round there; ~ und ~ what's-its-name (inf); hier und ~, ~ und dort here and there; wer ~? who goes there?; he, Sie ~! hey, you there!; die Frau ~ that woman (over) there; ~ bin ich/sind wir here I am/we are; ~ bist du ja! there you are!; ~ kommt er ja here he comes; wir sind gleich ~ we'll soon be there, we're almost there; in einem kühlen Walde, ~ steht ein Mühlenrad

(liter) in a cool wood there stands a mill wheel; ~, wo ... where ...; wo die Straße über den Fluß geht, ~ fängt Schottland an Scotland begins where the road crosses the river, where the road crosses the river, that's where Scotland begins; ganz am Ende der Straße, ~ siehst du ein Schild at the end of the street you'll see a signpost; ach, ~ war der Brief! so that's where the letter was; ~ möchte ich auch einmal hinfahren (inf) I'd like to go there one day; geben Sie mir ein halbes Pfund von dem ~ give me half a pound of that one (there); ~ haben wir's or den Salat (inf) that had to happen; ~ hast du deinen Kram/dein Geld! (there you are,) there's your stuff/money; ~, nimm schon! here, take it!; siehe als.

(b) (*zeitlich: dann, damals*) then. **ich ging gerade aus dem Haus, ~ schlug es zwei** I was just going out of the house when the clock struck two; **vor vielen, vielen Jahren, ~ lebte ein König** (*liter*) long, long ago there lived a king *or* there once was a king; **~ werden wir uns den Schaden mal ansehen** (*inf*) let's have a look at the damage; **~ kommen Sie mal gleich mit** (*inf*) you just come along with me; **~ siehst du, was du angerichtet hast** now see what you've done.

(c) (*daraufhin*) **sagen/lachen** *at that.* **sie weinte, ~ ließ er sich erweichen** when she started to cry he softened, she started to cry, whereupon he softened (*liter*); **als er das Elend der Leute sah, ~ nahm er sich vor ...** when he saw the people's suffering he decided ...

(d) (*folglich*) so; (*dann*) then. **es war niemand im Zimmer, ~ habe ich ...** there was nobody in the room, so I ...; **wenn du keine Lust hast, ~ läßt du's eben bleiben** if you don't feel like it, then just leave it; **wenn ich schon gehen muß, ~ gehe ich lieber gleich** if I have to go, (then) I'd rather go straight away.

(e) (*inf: in diesem Fall*) there. **~ haben wir aber Glück gehabt!** we were lucky there!; **~ muß man vorsichtig sein** you've got to be careful there; **was gibt's denn ~ zu lachen/fragen?** what's funny about that?/what is there to ask?; **~ kann man nichts mehr machen** there's nothing more to be done (there *or* about it); **~ kann man sich nichts machen** nothing can be done about it; **~ könnte man aus der Haut fahren** it would drive you mad *or* crazy; **~ kann man nur lachen/sich nur fragen, warum/sich nur wundern** you can't help laughing/asking yourself why/being amazed; **~ kann man nur noch still sein/nur den Kopf schütteln** you can't say anything/you can only shake your head in despair/bewilderment *etc*; **und ~ fragst du noch?** and you still have to ask?; **und ~ soll einer** *or* **ein Mensch wissen, warum!** and you're meant to know why!; **~ fragt man sich (doch), ob der Mann noch normal ist** it makes you wonder if the man's normal; **~ hätte ich die Arbeit ja auch gleich selbst machen können** I might just as well have done it myself straight away; **~ hat doch jemand gelacht/alle Kekse gegessen** somebody laughed/has eaten all the biscuits.

(f) (*zur Hervorhebung*) **wir haben ~ eine neue Mitschülerin/Ausführung des Artikels** *etc* we've got this new girl in our school/this new model *etc*; **~ fällt mir gerade ein ...** it's just occurred to me ...

(g) (*N Ger*) *siehe* **dabei, dafür** *etc.*

2 *conj* **(a)** *weil*) as, since, seeing that.

(b) (*liter: als*) when. **die Stunde, ~ du ...** the hour when you ...; **nun** *or* **jetzt, ~** now that.

dabehalten* *vt sep irreg* to keep (here/there); (*in Haft auch*) to detain (there); **Schüler** to keep behind.

dabei *adv* **(a)** (*örtlich*) with it; (*bei Gruppe von Menschen, Dingen*) there. **ein Häuschen mit einem Garten ~** a little house with a garden (attached to it *or* attached); **ist die Lösung ~?** is the solution given (there)?; **nahe ~** nearby.

(b) (*zeitlich*) (*gleichzeitig*) at the same time; (*währenddessen, wodurch*) in the course of this. **er aß weiter und blätterte ~ in dem Buch** he went on eating, leafing through the book as he did so *or* at the same time; **warum arbeiten Sie im Stehen? Sie können doch auch ~ sitzen** why are you working standing up? you can sit down while you're doing it; **nach der Explosion entstand eine Panik; ~ wurden drei Kinder verletzt** there was a general panic after the explosion, in the course of which *or* during which three children were injured; **... orkanartige Winde; ~ kam es zu schweren Schäden** ... gale-force winds, which have resulted in serious damage; **als sich die beiden trafen, kam es ~ zu einer Schlägerei/zu einer Regelung der Frage** the meeting of the two of them resulted in a fight/in the question being resolved, when the two of them met there was a fight/the question was resolved.

(c) (*außerdem*) as well, into the bargain (*inf*), with it (*inf*). **sie ist schön und ~ auch noch klug** she's pretty, and clever as well *etc*.

(d) (*wenn, während man etw tut*) in the process; **ertappen, erwischen** at it. **er wollte helfen und wurde ~ selbst verletzt** he wanted to help and got injured in the process *or* (in) doing so *or* while he was about it (*inf*); **du warst bei einem Jugendtreffen? hast du denn ~ etwas gelernt?** you were at a youth meeting? did you learn anything there *or* from it?; **~ darf man nicht vergessen, daß ...** it shouldn't be forgotten that ...; (*Einschränkung eines Arguments*) it should not be forgotten here that ...; **die ~ entstehenden Kosten** the expenses arising from this/that; **als er das tat, hat er ~ ...** when he did that he ...; **wenn man das tut, muß man ~ ...** when you do that you have to ...; **wir haben ihn ~ ertappt, wie er über den Zaun stieg** we caught him in the act of climbing over the fence.

(e) (*in dieser Angelegenheit*) **das Schwierigste ~** the most difficult part of it; **wichtig ~ ist ...** the important thing here *or* about it is ...; **mir ist nicht ganz wohl ~** I don't really feel happy about it; **~ kann man viel Geld verdienen, da kann man viel Geld bei verdienen** (*N Ger*) there's a lot of money in that; **er hat ~ einen Fehler gemacht** he's made a mistake; **sie hat sich ~ sehr dumm benommen** she behaved very stupidly; **es kommt doch nichts ~ heraus** nothing will come of it.

(f) (*einräumend: doch*) (and) yet. **er hat mich geschlagen, ~ hatte ich gar nichts gemacht** he hit me and I hadn't even done anything *or* and yet I hadn't done anything; **ich habe fünf Stück gegessen, ~ hatte ich gar keinen Hunger** I've eaten five pieces, and I wasn't even hungry.

(g) **du gehst sofort nach Hause, und ~ bleibt es!** you're going straight home and that's that *or* that's the end of it!; **es bleibt ~, daß ihr morgen alle mitkommt** we'll stick to that *or* keep it like that, you're all coming tomorrow; **ich bleibe ~** I'm not

changing my mind; **er bleibt ~, daß er es nicht gewesen ist** he still insists *or* he's still sticking to his guns that he didn't do it; **aber ~ sollte es nicht bleiben** but it shouldn't stop there *or* at that; **lassen wir es ~** let's leave it at that!; **was ist schon ~?** so what? (*inf*), what of it? (*inf*); **was ist schon ~, wenn man das tut?** what harm is there in doing that?; **ich finde gar nichts ~** I don't see any harm in it; **es ist nichts ~** *or* (*N Ger*) **da ist nichts bei, wenn man das tut** (*schadet nichts*) there's no harm in doing that; (*will nichts bedeuten*) doing that doesn't mean anything; **nimm meine Bemerkung nicht so ernst, ich habe mir nichts ~ gedacht** don't take my remark so seriously, I didn't mean anything by it; **ich habe mir nichts ~ gedacht, als ich den Mann aus der Bank kommen sah** I didn't think anything of it when I saw the man coming out of the bank; **was hast du dir denn ~ gedacht?** what were you thinking of?; **~ kann er sich nicht viel gedacht haben, da kann er sich nicht viel bei gedacht haben** (*N Ger*) he can't have thought about it much.

dabeibleiben *vi sep irreg aux sein* to stay *or* stick (*inf*) with it; (*bei Firma, Stelle, Armee etc*) to stay on; *siehe auch* **dabei (g)**.

dabeihaben *vt sep irreg* (*Zusammenschreibung nur bei infin und ptp*) (*inf*) to have with one; **Geld, Paß, Schirm etc** auch to have on one.

dabeisein *vi sep irreg aux sein* (*Zusammenschreibung nur bei infin und ptp*) **(a)** to be there (*bei* at); (*mitmachen*) to be involved (*bei* in). **ich bin dabei!** count me in!; **er war bei der Flugzeugentführung dabei** he was there when the plane was hijacked, he was there at the hijacking; **ein wenig Furcht ist immer dabei** I'm/you're *etc* always a bit scared; **er will überall ~** he wants to be in on everything.

(b) (*im Begriff sein*) **~, etw zu tun** to be just doing sth; **ich bin (gerade) dabei** I'm just doing it.

dabeisitzen *vi sep irreg aux haben or sein* to sit there. **bei einer Besprechung ~** to sit in on a discussion.

dabeistehen *vi sep irreg aux haben or sein* to stand there.

dableiben *vi sep irreg aux sein* to stay (on); (*nachsitzen*) to stay behind. **(jetzt wird) dageblieben!** (you just) stay right there!

da capo *adv* da capo. **~ ~ rufen** to call for an encore.

Dach *nt* **-(e)s, ⁻er** **(a)** roof; (*Aut auch*) top. **das ~ der Welt** the roof of the world; **ein/kein ~ über dem Kopf haben** (*inf*) to have a/no roof over one's head; **mit jdm unter einem ~ wohnen** to live under the same roof as sb; **jdm das ~ überm Kopf anzünden** to burn down sb's house; **unterm ~ juchhe** (*inf*) right under the eaves; **unterm ~ wohnen** (*inf*) to live in an attic room/flat (*Brit*) *or* apartment; (*im obersten Stock*) to live right on the top floor; **unter ~ und Fach sein** (*abgeschlossen*) to be all wrapped up *or* in the bag (*inf*); (*Vertrag, Geschäft auch*) to be signed and sealed; (*in Sicherheit*) to be safely under cover; (*Ernte*) to be safely in; **etw unter ~ und Fach bringen** to get sth all wrapped up/signed and sealed/safely under cover/to bring sth in.

(b) (*fig inf*) **jdm eins aufs ~ geben** (*schlagen*) to smash sb on the head (*inf*); (*ausschimpfen*) to give sb a (good) talking-to; **eins aufs ~ bekommen** *or* **kriegen** (*geschlagen werden*) to get hit on the head; (*ausgeschimpft werden*) to be given a (good) talking-to; **jdm aufs ~ steigen** (*inf*) to get onto sb (*inf*).

Dach- *in cpds* roof; **~balken** *m* roof joist *or* beam; **~bedeckung** *f*, **~belag** *m* roofing; **~boden** *m* attic; **auf dem ~boden** in the attic; **~decker** *m* **-s, -** roofer; (*mit Ziegeln*) tiler; (*mit Schiefer*) slater; (*mit Stroh*) thatcher; **das kannst du halten wie ein ~decker** (*fig inf*) it doesn't matter two ha'pence (*Brit inf*) *or* one jot (*inf*); **~deckerarbeiten** *pl* roofing; tiling; slating; thatching.

dachen *vt* (*obs*) to roof.

Dach-: **~erker** *m* dormer window; **~fenster** *nt* skylight; (*ausgestellt*) dormer window; **~first** *m* ridge of the roof; **d~förmig** *adj* rooflike; **ein Felsenvorsprung ragte d~förmig vor** a piece of cliff jutted out like a roof; **~garten** *m* roof garden; **~gebälk** *nt* roof timbers *pl*; **~geschoß** *nt* attic storey; (*oberster Stock*) top floor *or* storey; **~gesellschaft** *f* parent company; **~gesims** *nt* (roof) cornice; **~gestühl** *nt* roof truss; **~giebel** *m* gable; **~gleiche(nfeier)** *f* **-, -n** (*Aus*) topping-out ceremony; **~hase** *m* (*hum*) cat; **~kammer** *f* attic room, garret (*dated*); **~latte** *f* tile *or* roof batten; **~luke** *f* skylight; **~neigung** *f* slope of the roof; **~organisation** *f* umbrella *or* (*Comm*) parent organization; **~pappe** *f* roofing felt; **~pfanne** *f* (roof) tile; **~reiter** *m* (*Archit*) roof *or* ridge turret; **~rinne** *f* gutter.

Dachs *m* **-es, -e** **(a)** (*Zool*) badger. **schlafen wie ein ~** (*inf*) to sleep like a log (*inf*). **(b)** (*inf: Mensch*) **ein frecher ~!** a cheeky devil!; **ein junger ~** a young whippersnapper.

Dachsbau *m* badger's sett.

Dach-: **~schaden** *m* **(a)** (*lit*) damage to the roof; **(b)** (*inf*) **einen (kleinen) ~schaden haben** to have a slate loose (*inf*); **der Boxer hat von seiner Karriere einen ~schaden zurückbehalten** his career as a boxer has done something to his brain; **~schiefer** *m* roofing slate; **~schindel** *f* (roof) shingle.

Dachshund *m* dachshund.

Dachsilhouette *f* outline of the roof.

Dächsin *f* female badger.

Dach-: **~sparren** *m* rafter; **~stein** *m* (cement) roofing slab; **~stroh** *nt* thatch; **~stube** *f*, **~stübchen** *nt* attic room, garret (*dated*); **~stuhl** *m* *siehe* **~gestühl**; **~stuhlbrand** *m* roof fire.

dachte *pret of* **denken**.

Dach-: **~terrasse** *f* sun roof; (*~garten*) roof garden; **~träger** *m* (*Aut*) roof rack; **~traufe** *f* rain spout; (*dial: ~rinne*) gutter; **~verband** *m* umbrella organization; **~wohnung** *f* attic flat (*Brit*) *or* apartment; **~ziegel** *m* roofing tile; **~zimmer** *nt* attic room, garret.

Dackel *m* **-s, -** dachshund, sausage dog (*inf*); (*inf: Person*) silly clot (*inf*).

Dackelbeine *pl* (*inf*) short stumpy legs *pl*.

Dadaismus *m* Dadaism, Dada.

Dadaist(in f) m Dadaist. **die ~en** the Dada group, the Dadaists.
dadaistisch adj dadaist.
dadurch adv (emph da̱durch) **(a)** (örtlich) through there; (wenn Bezugsobjekt vorher erwähnt) through it; (geh: in Relativsatz) through which.
    (b) (kausal) thereby (form); (mit Hilfe von, aus diesem Grund auch) because of this/that, through this/that; (durch diesen Umstand, diese Tat etc auch) by or with that; (auf diese Weise) in this/that way. **was willst du ~ gewinnen?** what do you hope to gain by or from that?; **meinst du, ~ wird alles wieder gut?** do you think that will make everything all right again?; **~ kam es, daß er nicht dabeisein konnte** that was why he couldn't be there.
    (c) ~, daß er das tat, hat er ... (durch diesen Umstand, diese Tat) by doing that he ...; (deswegen, weil) because he did that he ...; **~, daß ich das tat, hat er ...** by my doing that he ..., because I did that he ...; **~, daß er den zweiten Satz gewonnen hat, sind seine Chancen wieder gestiegen** his chances improved again with him or his winning the second set; **~, daß das Haus isoliert ist, ist es viel wärmer** the house is much warmer because it's insulated or for being insulated.
dafür adv (emph da̱für) **(a)** (für das, diese Tat etc) for that/it. **wir haben kein Geld ~** we've no money for that; **~ haben wir kein Geld, da haben wir kein Geld für** (N Ger inf) we've no money for that sort of thing; **der Grund ~ ist, daß ...** the reason for that is (that) ...; **warum ist er so böse? er hat doch keinen Grund ~** why is he so angry? there's no reason for it or he has no reason to be; **~ war er nicht zu haben** it wasn't his scene (inf); (erlaubte es nicht) he wouldn't have it; **~ ist er immer zu haben** he never says no to that; **ich bin nicht ~ verantwortlich, was mein Bruder macht** I'm not responsible for what my brother does; **~ bin ich ja hier** that's what I'm here for, that's why I'm here; **die Arbeit mußt du gut machen können, ~ wirst du auch besser bezahlt** you must be able to do the work well, that's why you're paid more; **er ist ~ bestraft worden, daß er frech zum Lehrer war** he was punished for being cheeky to the teacher.
    (b) (Zustimmung) for that/it, in favour (of that/it). **ich bin ganz ~** I'm all for it (inf), I'm all in favour; **ich bin (ganz) ~, daß wir/sie das machen** I'm (all) for or in favour of doing that/them doing that; **~ stimmen** to vote for it; **ich bin nicht ~, daß das so gemacht wird** I don't think it should be done like that, I'm not in favour of it being done that way.
    (c) (als Ersatz) instead, in its place; (als Bezahlung) for that/it; (bei Tausch) in exchange; (als Gegenleistung) in return. **... ich mache dir ~ deine Hausaufgaben** ... and I'll do your homework in return.
    (d) (zum Ausgleich) but ... to make up. **in Mathematik ist er schlecht, ~ kann er gut Fußball spielen** he's very bad at maths but he makes up for it at football or but he's good at football to make up; **ich hatte diesmal immer nur Kurzferien, ~ habe ich um so mehr gesehen** I've only had short holidays this time but I've seen a lot more for all that.
    (e) (im Hinblick darauf) **der Junge ist erst drei Jahre, ~ ist er sehr klug** the boy is only three, (so) considering that he's very clever; **~, daß er erst drei Jahre ist, ist er sehr klug** seeing or considering that he's only three he's very clever.
    (f) in Verbindung mit n, vb etc siehe auch dort **er interessiert sich nicht ~** he's not interested in that/it; **~ interessiert er sich nicht** he's not interested in that sort of thing; **er gibt sein ganzes Geld ~ aus** he spends all his money on that/it; **ein Beispiel ~ wäre ...** an example of that would be ...; **ich kann mich nicht ~ begeistern** I can't get enthusiastic about it, I can't rouse any enthusiasm for it; **sie ist dreißig/sehr intelligent — ~ hätte ich sie nicht gehalten** she's thirty/very intelligent — I would never have thought it or thought she was; **~ werde ich schon sorgen** I'll see to or take care of that; **ich werde ~ sorgen, daß ... I'll see** to it that ...
dafür-: **~halten** vi sep irreg (geh) to be of the opinion; **ich halte ~, daß wir zu Hause bleiben** I am of the opinion that we should stay at home; **nach meinem D~halten** in my opinion; **~können** vt sep irreg **er kann nichts ~** he can't help it, it's not his fault; **er kann nichts ~, daß er dumm ist** he can't help being stupid, it's not his fault that he's stupid; **er kann nichts/etwas ~, daß es kaputtgegangen ist** it's not/it was his fault that it broke, he couldn't help it breaking; **was kann ich ~, daß es heute regnet** it's not my fault (that) or I can't help that it's raining today; **als ob ich da was für könnte!** (N Ger inf) as if I could help it!, as if it were my fault!; **~stehen** vir sep irreg (Aus) to be worth it or worthwhile; **es steht sich ~, das zu tun** it's worth(while) doing it.
DAG [de:la:'ge:] f - abbr of **Deutsche Angestellten-Gewerkschaft** Trade Union of German Employees.
dagegen 1 adv (emph da̱gegen) **(a)** (örtlich) against it. **es stand ein Baum im Weg und der Vogel/Wagen prallte ~** there was a tree in the way and the bird/car crashed into it; **die Tür war verschlossen, also pochte er ~** the door was locked, so he hammered on it; **mache das Licht an und halte das Dia ~** put the light on and hold the slide up to it or against it.
    (b) (als Einwand, Ablehnung) against that/it. **~ sein** to be against it or opposed (to it); **etwas/nichts ~ haben** to object/not to object; **ich habe etwas ~, da habe ich was gegen** (N Ger inf) I object to that; **was hat er ~, daß wir früher anfangen?** what has he got against us starting earlier?, why does he object to us or our starting earlier?; **haben Sie was ~, wenn ich rauche?** do you mind if I smoke?, would you mind or object if I smoked?; **was hieltest du davon, wenn sie ins Ausland ginge? — ich habe/hätte nichts ~** what would you think of her going abroad? — I have nothing against it or no objection(s); **sollen wir ins Kino gehen? — ich hätte nichts ~ (einzuwenden)** shall we go to the cinema? — that's okay by me (inf); **ich hätte nichts ~, wenn** ...

nicht kommen würde I wouldn't mind at all if he didn't come; **ich werde ~ protestieren** I will protest against that/it; **ich werde ~ protestieren, daß das gemacht wird** I will protest against that being done.
    (c) (als Gegenmaßnahme) **tun, unternehmen** about it; (Medikamente einnehmen etc) for it. **~ läßt sich nichts machen** nothing can be done about it; **bei mir regnet es herein, aber ich kann nichts ~ machen** the rain comes in, but I can't do anything to stop it or about it.
    (d) (verglichen damit) compared with that/it/them, in comparison. **die Stürme letztes Jahr waren furchtbar, ~ sind die jetzigen nicht so schlimm** the gales last year were terrible, compared with them or those, these aren't so bad or these aren't so bad in comparison.
    (e) (als Ersatz, Gegenwert) for that/it/them.
    2 conj (im Gegensatz dazu) on the other hand, however. **er sprach fließend Französisch, ~ konnte er kein Deutsch** he spoke French fluently, but (on the other hand) he could not speak any German.
dagegen-: **~halten** vt sep irreg **(a)** (vergleichen) to compare it/them with; **wenn wir das Original ~halten ...** if we compare the original with it ...; **(b)** (einwenden) siehe **~setzen;** **~setzen** vt sep (fig) seine eigene Meinung **~setzen** to put forward one's own opinion in opposition; **das einzige, was Sie ~setzen könnten, wäre ...** the only objection you could put forward would be ...; **ich kann nichts ~setzen** I have no objections to put forward; **er setzte ~, daß ...** he put forward the objection that ...; **~sprechen** vi sep irreg to be against it; **was spricht ~?** what is there against it?; **was spricht ~, daß wir es so machen?** what is there against us doing it that way?, why shouldn't we do it that way?; **einige Gründe, die ~sprechen, so zu machen** several reasons for not doing it that way or which speak against doing it that way; **es spricht nichts ~, es so zu machen** there's no reason not to do it that way; **~stellen** vr sep to oppose it; **warum mußt du dich immer ~stellen?** why must you always oppose everything?; **~stemmen** vr sep to fight it, to oppose it bitterly; **~wirken** vi sep to act against it.
Daguerreotypie [dagero'ty'pi:] f daguerreotype.
dahaben vt sep irreg (Zusammenschreibung nur bei infin und ptp) **(a)** (vorrätig haben) to have here/there; (in Geschäft etc) to have in stock. **(b)** (zu Besuch haben) to have here/there; (zum Essen etc) to have in.
daheim adv at home; (nach prep) home. **bei uns ~** back home (where I/we come from); **das Buch liegt bei mir ~ or ~ bei mir** I've got the book at home; **wir haben bei mir ~ or ~ bei mir gefeiert** we had a celebration at my place; **~ sein** (lit, fig) to be at home; (nach Reise) to be home; **wo bist du ~?** where's your home?; **sie ist in Schwaben ~** her home is Swabia; **ich bin für niemanden ~** I'm not at home to anybody; **~ ist ~** (Prov) east, west, home's best (prov), there's no place like home (prov).
Daheim nt -s, no pl home.
Daheim-: **~gebliebene(r)** mf decl as adj person/friend/son etc (left) at home; **die/alle ~gebliebenen** those/all those at home; **~sein** nt das **~sein ist auch schön** being (at) home is nice too, it's nice being (at) home.
daher 1 adv (auch da̱her) **(a)** (von dort) from there. **von ~ from there;** **~ habe ich das** that's where I got it from.
    (b) (dial: hierher) here.
    (c) (durch diesen Umstand) that is why. **~ weiß ich das** that's how or why I know that; **~ die große Eile/all der Lärm** that's why there's or that's the reason for all this hurry/noise; **~ der Name X** that's why it's called X; **~ kommt es, daß ...** that is (the reason) why ...; **ich bin überzeugt, daß seine Krankheit ~ kommt** I'm sure that's why he's ill; **das kommt or rührt ~, daß ...** that is because ...
    2 conj (deshalb) that is why.
daher-: **~bringen** vt sep irreg (Aus) to produce, to bring along; **~fliegen** vi sep irreg aux sein to fly along; **da kam ein Vogel ~geflogen** a bird came flying along; **~gelaufen** adj jeder **D~gelaufene, jeder ~gelaufene Kerl** any Tom, Dick or Harry, any guy who comes/came along; **diese ~gelaufenen Kerle in der Politik** these jumped-up nobodies in politics; **sie hat so einen ~gelaufenen Kerl geheiratet** she married some fellow who just happened along (inf); **~kommen** vi sep irreg aux sein to come along; **da kommt so einer ~ ...** this guy comes along (inf); **wie kann man nur so geschminkt/schlampig ~kommen?** (inf) how can anybody go around with make-up like that/looking so scruffy?; **~laufen** vi sep irreg aux sein (gehen) to walk up; (laufen) to run up; **~gelaufen kommen** to come running up; **~reden** sep **1** vi to talk away; **red doch nicht so (dumm) ~!** don't talk such rubbish!; **2** vt to say without thinking; **was er alles/für ein blödes Zeug ~redet** the things/the rubbish he comes out with! (inf); **das war nur so ~geredet** I/he etc just said that; **~sagen** vt sep to say without thinking.
daherum adv round there.
dahier adv (old, Aus, Sw) here.
dahin 1 adv (emph da̱hin) **(a)** (räumlich) there; (hierhin) here. **kommst du auch ~?** are you coming too?; **~ und dorthin blicken** to look here and there; **~ gehe ich nie wieder, da gehe ich nie wieder hin** (inf) I'm never going there again; **bis ~** as far as there, up to that point; **ist es noch weit bis ~?** is it still a long way?; **bis ~ dauert es noch zwei Stunden** it'll take us another two hours to get there; **es steht mir bis ~** I've had it up to here (inf).
    (b) (fig: so weit) **~ kommen** to come to that, to reach such a pass; **es ist ~ gekommen, daß ...** things have got to the stage where or have reached such a pass that ...; **du wirst es ~ bringen, daß ...** you'll bring things to such a pass that ...
    (c) (in dem Sinne, in die Richtung) **er äußerte sich ~ gehend, daß ...** he said something to the effect that ...; **eine ~ gehende**

Aussage/Änderung *etc* a statement/change to that effect; ein ~ gehender Befehl, daß ... an order to the effect that ...; wir sind ~ gehend verblieben, daß ... we agreed that ...; er hat den Bericht ~ (gehend) interpretiert, daß ... he interpreted the report as saying ...; wir haben uns ~ geeinigt/abgesprochen, daß ... we have agreed that ...; alle meine Hoffnungen/Bemühungen gehen ~, daß ich dieses Ziel bald erreiche all my hopes/efforts are directed towards (my) reaching this goal soon; seine Meinung geht ~, daß ... he tends to feel that *or* to the opinion that ...

(d) (*zeitlich*) then; *siehe* bis².

2 *adj pred* ~ sein to have gone; sein Leben *or* er ist ~ (*geh*) his life is over; das Auto ist ~ (*hum inf*) the car has had it (*inf*).

da-: ~hinab *adv siehe* dorthinab; ~hinauf *adv siehe* dorthinauf; ~hinaus *adv* there; transportieren, bringen out that way; ~hinaus muß der Dieb entkommen sein that must be where the thief escaped; ~hinaus will er also! (*fig*) so that's what he's getting at!

dahin-: ~bewegen* *vr sep* to move on one's way; (*Fluß*) to flow on its way; ~dämmern *vi sep aux sein* to lie/sit there in a stupor; ~eilen *vi sep aux sein* (*liter*) to hurry along; (*Zeit*) to pass swiftly.

dahinein *adv siehe* dorthinein.

dahin-: ~fahren *vi sep irreg aux sein* (*liter: sterben*) to pass away *or* over; ~fliegen *vi sep irreg aux sein* (*liter*) (*wegfliegen*) to fly off; (*fig*) (*schnell fahren, vergehen*) to fly along *or* past; ~geben *vt sep irreg* (*liter*) Leben, Gut, Besitz to give up; D~gegangene(r) *mf decl as adj* (*liter*) departed.

dahingegen *adv* on the other hand.

dahingehen *vi sep irreg aux sein* (*geh*) (a) (*vergehen*) (*Zeit, Jahre*) to pass (*jdm* for sb). (b) (*vorbeigehen, entlanggehen*) to pass. (c) (*sterben*) to pass away *or* on.

dahingehend *adv siehe* dahin 1 (c).

dahin-: ~gestellt *adj* ~gestellt sein lassen, ob ... to leave it open whether ...; es bleibt *or* sei ~gestellt, ob ... it is an open question whether ...; ~leben *vi sep* to exist, to vegetate (*pej*); ~raffen *vt sep* (*liter*) to carry off; ~reden *vi sep* to say the first thing that comes into one's head; ~sagen *vt sep* to say without (really) thinking; das war nur so ~gesagt I/he *etc* just said that (without thinking); ~scheiden *vi sep irreg aux sein* (*geh*) to pass away; ~schleppen *vr sep* (*lit: sich fortbewegen*) to drag oneself along; (*fig: Verhandlungen, Zeit*) to drag on; ~schwinden *vi sep irreg aux sein* (*geh*) (*Vorräte, Geld, Kraft*) to dwindle (away); (*Interesse, Gefühle etc*) to dwindle; (*vergehen: Zeit*) to go past; ~siechen *vi sep aux sein* (*geh*) to waste away; von Kummer ~siechen to pine away; jahrelang siechte er in einem dunklen Keller ~ for years he languished in a dark cellar; ~stehen *vi sep irreg* to be debatable.

dahinten *adv* (*emph* dahinten) over there; (*hinter Sprecher*) back there. ganz weit ~ right *or* way (*inf*) over there.

dahinter *adv* (*emph* dahinter) (a) (*räumlich*) behind (it/that/him *etc*). was sich wohl ~ verbirgt? (*lit, fig*) I wonder what's behind that?; da ist schon etwas ~ (*fig*) there's something in that; (da ist) nichts ~ (*fig*) there's nothing behind it. (b) (*danach*) beyond.

dahinterher *adj*: ~ sein (*inf*) to push (*daß* to see that); die Polizei ist ~, die Jugendkriminalität einzudämmen the police are pretty hot on trying to keep juvenile delinquency under control (*inf*).

dahinter-: ~klemmen, ~knien *vr sep* (*inf*) to put one's back into it, to get *or* pull one's finger out (*sl*); klemm' *or* knie dich mal ein bißchen ~ make a bit of an effort; ~kommen *vi sep irreg aux sein* (*inf*) to find out; (*langsam verstehen*) to get it (*inf*); ~machen *vr sep* (*inf*) to get down to *or* on with it; ~setzen *vr sep siehe* ~klemmen; ~stecken *vi sep* (*inf*) to be behind it/that; da steckt doch etwas ~ there's something behind it; da steckt doch etwas ~, daß er jetzt gehen will there's something behind his *or* him wanting to go now; da werden die Eltern ~stecken, daß er nicht mehr kommen will his parents must be behind his *or* him not wanting to come any more; er redet viel, es steckt aber nichts ~ he talks a lot but there's nothing behind it; ~stehen *vi sep irreg* (a) (*unterstützen*) to back it/that, to be behind it/that; (b) (*zugrunde liegen*) to underlie it/that; man fühlt bei diesem Dichter, daß ein tiefes Mitgefühl für die leidende Kreatur ~steht one feels a deep underlying sympathy for the suffering of all beings in this poet's work.

dahinunter *adv siehe* dorthinunter.

Dahlie [-iə] *f* dahlia.

DAK [de:ʔaˈkaː] *f* - *abbr of* Deutsche Angestellten-Krankenkasse Employees' Health Insurance.

Dakapo *nt* -s, -s encore.

Dakaporuf *m* call for an encore.

daktylisch *adj* (*Poet*) dactylic.

Daktylo-: ~gramm *nt* (*von einem Finger*) fingerprint; (*von ganzer Hand*) fingerprints *pl*; ~graphie *f* (*Sw*) typing; ~graphin *f* (*Sw*) typist; ~skopie *f* fingerprinting; d~skopisch *adj* fingerprint *attr*.

Daktylus *m* -, Daktylen (*Poet*) dactyl.

da-: ~lassen *vt sep irreg* to leave (here/there); ~liegen *vi sep irreg* to lie there; ... sonst liegst du nachher ~ mit einer schweren Grippe (*inf*) otherwise you'll be in bed with a bad dose of flu.

Dalk *m* -(e)s, -e (*Aus inf*) (*Dummkopf*) fathead (*inf*); (*ungeschickter Mensch*) clumsy oaf (*inf*).

dalke(r)t *adj* (*Aus inf*) daft (*inf*).

Dalle *f* -, -n (*dial*) *siehe* Delle.

dalli *adv* (*inf*) ~, ~! on the double! (*inf*), look smart! (*inf*); mach ein bißchen ~! get a move on! (*inf*); verzieh dich, aber ~! beat it, go on, quick!

Dalmatiner *m* -s, - (*Hund*) dalmatian.

damalig *adj attr* at that *or* the time; Inhaber eines Amtes auch then *attr*; Sitten auch in those days.

damals *adv* at that time, then. seit ~ since then, since that time; von ~ of that time; ~, als ... at the time when ...; wenn ich daran denke, was ~ war when I think of that time *or* of what things were like then.

Damast *m* -(e)s, -e damask.

Damast- *in cpds* damask; d~artig *adj* damask.

damasten *adj attr* (*liter*) damask.

Damaszener-: ~klinge *f* damascene sword; ~stahl *m* Damascus steel.

Dambock *m siehe* Damhirsch.

Dämchen *nt* (*pej*) precocious young madam; (*Dirne*) tart (*inf*).

Dame *f* -, -n (a) lady. sehr verehrte (*form*) *or* meine ~n und Herren! ladies and gentlemen!; guten Abend, die ~n (*old, hum*) good evening, ladies; „~n" (*Toilette*) "Ladies"; die ~ wünscht? (*old*) can I be of assistance, madam? (*form*); ganz ~ sein to be the perfect lady *or* every inch a lady.

(b) (*allgemein gesehen: Tanzpartnerin, Begleiterin*) lady; (*auf einen bestimmten Herrn bezogen*) partner; (*bei Cocktailparty, Theaterbesuch etc*) (lady) companion. seine ~ ist eben mit einem anderen weggegangen the lady he came with has just left with someone else; bringen Sie ruhig Ihre ~n mit do by all means bring your wives and girlfriends.

(c) (*Sport*) woman, lady. Hundert-Meter-Staffel der ~n women's *or* ladies' hundred metre relay.

(d) (*Spiel*) draughts *sing*, checkers *sing* (*US*); (*Doppelstein*) king.

Damebrett *nt* draught(s)board, checkerboard (*US*).

Dämel *m* -s, - (*inf*) *siehe* Dämlack.

Dämelei *f* (*inf*) silliness, foolishness, nonsense.

Damen- *in cpds* ladies'; ~bart *m* facial hair; ~begleitung *f* ~begleitung erwünscht please bring a lady *or* (*bei Ball*) partner; in ~begleitung in the company of a lady; ~bekanntschaft *f* female acquaintance (*inf*); eine ~bekanntschaft machen to make the acquaintance of a lady/young lady; ~besuch *m* lady visitor/visitors; ~binde *f* sanitary towel; ~doppel *nt* (*Tennis etc*) ladies' doubles *sing*; ~einzel *nt* (*Tennis etc*) ladies' singles *sing*; ~gesellschaft *f* (a) *no pl* (*Begleitung von Dame*) company of ladies/a lady; (b) (*gesellige Runde*) ladies' gathering; d~haft *adj* ladylike *no adv*; sich d~haft benehmen/kleiden to behave/dress in a ladylike way; ~konfektion *f* ladies' wear (department); ~mangel *m* shortage of ladies; ~oberbekleidung *f* ladies' wear; ~rede *f* toast to the ladies; ~sattel *m* side-saddle; im ~sattel reiten to ride side-saddle; ~schneider *m* dressmaker; ~schneiderei *f* (a) dressmaking; (b) (*Werkstatt*) dressmaker's; ~sitz *m* side-saddle style of riding; im ~sitz side-saddle; ~stift *nt* home for gentlewomen run by nuns; ~toilette *f* (a) (*WC*) ladies, ladies' toilet *or* restroom (*US*); (b) (*Kleidung*) ladies' toilette; ~unterwäsche *f* ladies' underwear, lingerie; ~wahl *f* ladies' choice; ~welt *f* (*dated hum*) ladies *pl*; in *or* bei der ~welt beliebt popular with the ladies.

Dame-: ~spiel *nt* draughts *sing*, checkers *sing* (*US*); ~stein *m* draughtsman, checker (*US*).

Damhirsch *m* fallow deer.

damisch (*S Ger, Aus*) 1 *adj* (a) (*dämlich*) daft (*inf*). (b) (*pred: schwindelig*) dizzy, giddy. 2 *adv* (*sehr*) terribly (*inf*).

damit 1 *adv* (*emph auch* damit) *siehe auch* mit (a) (*mit diesem Gegenstand, dieser Tätigkeit, mit Hilfe davon*) with it/that. sie hatte zwei Koffer und stand ~ am Bahnhof she had two cases and was standing there with them in the station; sie hat Ärger mit der Waschmaschine — ~ habe ich auch Probleme she's got trouble with the washing machine — I've got problems with mine too; was will er ~? what does he want that for?, what does he want with that?; was soll ich ~? what am I meant to do with that?; ist Ihre Frage ~ beantwortet? does that answer your question?; ~ kann er mich ärgern, da kann er mich mit ärgern (*N Ger inf*) I get really annoyed when he does that.

(b) (*mit, in dieser Angelegenheit*) meint er mich ~? does he mean me?; weißt du, was er ~ meint? do you know what he means by that?; was ist ~? what about it?; wie wäre es ~? how about it?; er konnte mir nicht sagen, was es ~ auf sich hat he couldn't tell me what it was all about; wie sieht es ~ aus? what's happening about it?; muß er denn immer wieder ~ ankommen? (*davon reden*) must he keep on about it?; (*mit Bitten, Forderungen etc*) must he keep coming back about it?; das/er hat gar nichts ~ zu tun that/he has nothing to do with it; ~ ist nichts (*inf*) it's no go (*inf*); hör auf ~! (*inf*) lay off! (*inf*); ~ hat es noch Zeit there's no hurry for that.

(c) (*bei Verben*) *siehe vb* ~ was willst du ~ sagen? what's that supposed *or* meant to mean?; ~ will ich nicht sagen, daß ... I don't mean to say that ...; sind Sie ~ einverstanden? do you agree to that?; sind Sie ~ einverstanden, daß wir Ihr Gehalt kürzen? do you agree to our cutting your salary?; er hatte nicht ~ gerechnet he hadn't reckoned on *or* with that; er hatte nicht ~ gerechnet, daß sie mitkommen würde he hadn't reckoned on *or* with her coming along too; ~, daß du dich jetzt aufregst, machst du den Schaden auch nicht wieder gut you're not making anything better by getting excited; sie fangen schon ~ an they're already starting on it; sie fangen schon ~ an, das Haus abzureißen they're already starting to pull down the house; ~ fing der Streit an the argument started with that; Streit fing ~ an, daß er behauptete ... the argument started when he said ...; er fing ~ an, daß er ... sagte he began by saying that ...

(d) (*bei Befehlen*) with it. weg/heraus ~! away/out with it; her ~! give it here! (*inf*); Schluß/genug ~! that's enough (of that)!

(e) (*begründend*) because of that. **er verlor den zweiten Satz und ~ das Spiel** he lost the second set and because of that the match; **~ ist es klar, daß er es war** from that it's clear that it was he (*form*) or him.

(f) (*daraufhin, dann, jetzt*) with that. **~ schließe ich für heute** I'll close with that for today; **~ kommen wir zum Ende des Programms** that brings us to the end of our programmes.

2 *conj* so that. **~ er nicht fällt** so that he does not fall, lest he (should) fall (*old*).

Dämlack *m* -s, -e *or* -s (*inf*) sap (*sl*), jerk (*sl*).

damledern *adj attr* (*rare*) buckskin.

dämlich *adj* (*inf*) stupid, dumb (*inf*). **komm mir nicht so ~!** don't give me that! (*inf*), don't come that with me! (*inf*); **er ist mir vielleicht ~ gekommen** he acted really dumb (*inf*) *or* stupid; **~ fragen** to ask stupid *or* dumb (*inf*) questions/a stupid *or* dumb (*inf*) question.

Dämlichkeit *f* **(a)** stupidity, dumbness (*inf*). **(b)** (*dumme Handlung*) stupid *or* dumb (*inf*) thing.

Damm *m* -(e)s, ̈e **(a)** (*Deich*) dyke; (*Stau~*) dam; (*Hafen~*) wall; (*Ufer~*) embankment, levee (*esp US*); (*Verkehrsverbindung zu Insel*) causeway; (*fig*) barrier. **einen ~ gegen etw aufbauen, einer Sache** (*dat*) **einen ~ (entgegen) setzen** (*fig*) to check sth; **wenn wir das kleinste bißchen nachgeben, werden alle ̈~e brechen** if we give way at all, the floodgates will open wide.

(b) (*Bahn~, Straßen~*) embankment.

(c) (*dial: Fahr~*) road.

(d) (*Anat*) perineum.

(e) (*fig inf*) **wieder auf dem ~ sein** to be back to normal; **geistig auf dem ~ sein** to be with it (*inf*); **nicht recht auf dem ~ sein** not to be up to the mark (*inf*).

Dammbruch *m* breach in a/the dyke *etc*.

dämmen *vt* **(a)** (*geh*) (*lit*) to dam; (*fig*) to check; *Tränen, Gefühle* to (hold in) check; *Umtriebe, Gefühle, Seuche* to curb, to check. **(b)** (*Tech*) *Wärme* to keep in; *Schall* to absorb.

Dämmer *m* -s, *no pl* **(a)** (*poet*) siehe **Dämmerung**. **(b)** (*fig geh*) nebulousness.

dämmerhaft *adj* (*liter*) hazy, nebulous.

dämm(e)rig *adj Licht* dim, faint; *Stunden* twilight *attr*. **es wird ~** (*abends*) dusk is falling; (*morgens*) dawn is breaking.

Dämmerlicht *nt* twilight; (*abends auch*) dusk; (*Halbdunkel*) half-light, gloom.

dämmern 1 *vi* **(a)** (*Tag, Morgen*) to dawn; (*Abend*) to fall. **als der Tag** *or* **Morgen/Abend dämmerte ...** as dawn was breaking/dusk was falling; **die Erkenntnis/es dämmerte ihm, daß ...** (*inf*) he began to realize that ...

(b) (*im Halbschlaf sein*) to doze; (*Kranker*) to be dopey. **vor sich hin ~** (*im Halbschlaf sein*) to doze; (*nicht bei klarem Verstand sein*) to be dopey.

2 *vi impers* **es dämmert** (*morgens*) dawn is breaking; (*abends*) dusk is falling; **jetzt dämmert's (bei) mir!** (*inf*) now it's dawning (on me)!; **langsam dämmert's mir, warum ...** it's beginning to dawn on me why ...

Dämmer-: **~schein** *m* (*liter*) glow; **~schlaf** *m* doze; **ich war nur im ~schlaf** I was only dozing; **~schoppen** *m* early evening drink; **~stunde** *f* twilight, dusk.

Dämmerung *f* twilight; (*Abend~ auch*) dusk; (*Morgen~ auch*) dawn; (*Halbdunkel*) half-light. **in der ~ des Morgens** at dawn, when dawn came/comes; **bei** *or* **mit Anbruch der ~** when dusk began/begins to fall/dawn began/begins to break; **in der ~** at dusk/dawn.

Dämmerzustand *m* (*Halbschlaf*) dozy state; (*Bewußtseinstrübung*) dopey state.

dämmrig *adj* siehe **dämm(e)rig**.

Damm-: **~riß** *m* (*Med*) tear of the perineum; **~rutsch** *m* (*lit*) landslide which destroys a dyke *etc*; (*fig*) slump; **einen ~rutsch erleiden** (*fig*) to slump; **~schnitt** *m* (*Med*) episiotomy.

Dämmstoffe *pl* insulating materials *pl*.

Dämmung *f* insulation.

Dammweg *m* causeway.

Damoklesschwert *nt* (*lit, fig*) sword of Damocles.

Dämon *m* -s, **Dämonen** demon. **ein böser ~** an evil spirit, a demon.

Dämonie *f* demonic nature.

dämonisch *adj* demonic.

dämonisieren* *vt* to demonize.

Dämonismus *m* (*Rel*) demonism.

Dampf *m* -(e)s, ̈e **(a)** vapour; (*Wasser~*) steam. **~ ablassen** *or* **abblasen** (*lit, fig*) to let off steam; **unter ~ sein** *or* **stehen** to have (its) steam up; **aus dem Schornstein quoll der ~ in weißen Wolken** clouds of white smoke poured from the chimney.

(b) (*inf: Wucht, Schwung*) force. **jdm ~ machen** (*inf*) to make sb get a move on (*inf*); **~ dahinter machen** *or* **setzen** to get a move on (*inf*); **mit ~** (*inf*) at full tilt; **vorm Chef hat sie unheimlich ~** the boss really puts the wind up her (*inf*); **~ drauf haben** (*dated inf*) to be going at full steam.

Dampf- *in cpds* steam; **~antrieb** *m* steam drive; **Maschine mit ~antrieb** steam-driven engine; **~bad** *nt* (*Med*) steam *or* vapour bath; **~boot** *nt* steamboat; **~bügeleisen** *nt* steam iron; **~druck** *m* steam pressure.

dampfen *vi* **(a)** (*Dampf abgeben*) to steam; (*Badezimmer etc*) to be full of steam; (*Pferd*) to be in a lather. **ein ~des Bad/Essen** a steaming hot bath/meal.

(b) *aux sein* (*Zug, Schiff*) to steam.

(c) *aux sein* (*inf*) (*mit Dampfer fahren*) to sail, to steam; (*mit Zug fahren*) to go by (steam) train.

dämpfen *vt* **(a)** (*abschwächen*) to muffle; *Geräusch, Lärm, Schall auch* to deaden, to dampen; *Geige, Trompete, Farbe* to mute; *Licht, Stimme* to lower; *Wut* to calm; *Freude, Begeisterung, Stimmung* to dampen; *Aufprall* to deaden; (*fig*) *jdn* to

subdue; *Konjunktur* to depress; siehe auch **gedämpft**.

(b) (*Cook*) to steam.

(c) (*bügeln*) to press with a damp cloth/steam iron.

Dampfer *m* -s, - steamer, steamship. **auf dem falschen ~ sein** *or* **sitzen** (*fig inf*) to have got the wrong idea.

Dämpfer *m* -s, - **(a)** (*Mus: bei Klavier*) damper; (*bei Geige, Trompete*) mute. **dadurch hat er/sein Optimismus einen ~ bekommen** that dampened his spirits/optimism; **jdm einen ~ aufsetzen** to dampen sb's spirits; **einer Sache** (*dat*) **einen ~ aufsetzen** (*inf*) to put a damper on sth (*inf*).

(b) (*Cook: Dampfkochtopf*) steamer.

Dampfer-: **~anlegestelle** *f* steamer jetty; **~linie** *f* steamship line.

Dampf-: **d~förmig** *adj* vaporous; **~hammer** *m* steam hammer; **~heizung** *f* steam heating.

dampfig *adj* steamy.

dämpfig *adj* **(a)** (*Vet*) broken-winded. **(b)** (*dial: schwül*) muggy.

Dampf-: **~kessel** *m* (*Tech*) steam-boiler; (*Cook*) steamer; **~kocher**, **~(koch)topf** *m* pressure cooker; **~kraft** *f* steam power; **~kraftwerk** *nt* steam power station; **~lokomotive**, **~lok** (*inf*) *f* steam engine *or* locomotive; **~maschine** *f* steam(-driven) engine; **~nudel** *f* (*Cook*) sweet yeast dumpling cooked in milk and sugar; **aufgehen wie eine ~nudel** (*fig inf*) to blow up like a balloon (*inf*); **~pfeife** *f* steam whistle; (*von Schiff*) siren; **~schiff** *nt* steamship, steamer; **~schiffahrt** *f* steam navigation; **~schiffahrtsgesellschaft** *f* steamship company; **~turbine** *f* steam turbine.

Dämpfung *f* (*Mus*) damping; (*Phys, Rad, TV*) attenuation.

Dampfwalze *f* steamroller.

Damwild *nt* fallow deer.

danach *adv* (*emph auch* **danach**) **(a)** (*zeitlich*) after that/it; (*nachher auch*) afterwards, after (*inf*). **ich habe einen Whisky getrunken, ~ fühlte ich mich schon besser** I had a whisky and after that *or* afterwards felt better, I had a whisky and felt better after that *or* afterwards *or* after (*inf*); **ich las das Buch zu Ende, erst ~ konnte ich einschlafen** only when I had finished reading the book could I get to sleep; **zehn Minuten ~ war sie schon wieder da** ten minutes later she was back; **um die Zwanziger und ~** around the twenties and after.

(b) (*in der Reihenfolge*) (*örtlich*) behind (that/it/him/them *etc*); (*zeitlich*) after that/it/him/them *etc*. **als erster ging der Engländer durchs Ziel und gleich ~ der Russe** the Englishman finished first, immediately followed by the Russian *or* and the Russian immediately after him; **bei ihm kommt als erstes die Arbeit, ~ lange nichts und dann das Privatleben** work comes first with him, and then, a long long way behind, his private life.

(c) (*dementsprechend*) accordingly; (*laut diesem*) according to that; (*im Einklang damit*) in accordance with that/it. **wir haben hier einen Bericht; ~ war die Stimmung damals ganz anders** we have a report here, according to which the atmosphere at the time was quite different; **~ sein** (*Wetter, Bedingungen, Stimmung* etc) to be right; **er hat den Aufsatz in zehn Minuten geschrieben — ~ ist er auch** (*inf*) he wrote the essay in ten minutes — it looks like it too; **die Torte hat nur 2 Mark gekostet — ~ ist sie auch** the gateau only cost 2 marks — it tastes like it too; **sie sieht auch/nicht ~ aus** she looks/doesn't look (like) it; (*als ob sie so was getan hätte*) she looks/doesn't look the type; **~ siehst du gerade aus** (*iro*) I can just see that (*iro*); **lesen Sie Paragraph 218; ~ ist es verboten** read paragraph 218, under that it is illegal; **~ zu urteilen** judging by *or* from that; **mir war nicht ~** (*inf*) *or* **~ zumute** I didn't feel like it; **mir steht der Sinn nicht ~** (*geh*) I don't feel inclined to.

(d) (*in bestimmte Richtung*) towards it. **er griff schnell ~** he grabbed at it, he made a grab for it; **er sah den Vogel dasitzen und warf den Stein ~** he saw the bird perched there and threw the stone at it; **hinter ihm war etwas, aber er hat sich nicht ~ umgesehen** there was something behind him, but he didn't look round to see what it was.

(e) *in Verbindung mit n, vb etc siehe auch dort* **sie sehnte sich ~** she longed for that/it; **sie sehnte sich ~, ihren Sohn wiederzusehen** she longed to see her son again; **er hatte großes Verlangen ~** he felt a great desire for it; **er hatte großes Verlangen ~, wieder einmal die Heimat zu sehen** he felt a great desire to see his home again; **~ kann man nicht gehen** you can't go by that; **wenn es ~ ginge, was ich sage/was mir Spaß macht, dann ...** if it were a matter of what I say/enjoy then ...; **sich ~ erkundigen, ob ...** to enquire whether ...

Danaergeschenk ['da:nar-] *nt* (*fig*) two-edged gift.

Dandy ['dɛndi] *m* -s, -s dandy.

Däne *m* -n, -n Dane, Danish man/boy.

daneben *adv* (*emph auch* **daneben**) **(a)** (*räumlich*) (*in unmittelbarer Nähe von jdm/etw*) next to him/her/that/it *etc*; (*seitlich von jdm/etw auch, zum Vergleich*) beside him/her/that/it *etc*. **links/rechts ~** (*neben Sache*) to the left/right of it; (*neben Mensch*) to his/her *etc* left/right; **ich stand direkt ~, als die Bombe losging** the bomb went off right next to me; **wir wohnen im Haus ~** we live in the house next door; **die Limousine fuhr durch die Straßen, während zwei Polizisten ~ herfuhren** the limousine drove through the streets flanked by two policemen *or* with two policemen riding alongside (it) *or* next to it.

(b) (*verglichen damit*) compared with that/it/him/them *etc*, in comparison.

(c) (*außerdem*) besides that, as well as that, in addition (to that); (*gleichzeitig*) at the same time. **sie arbeitet bei uns in der Firma, ~ schreibt sie an einem Roman** she works in our firm, and besides that *etc* she's writing a novel.

daneben-: **~benehmen*** *vr sep irreg* (*inf*) to make an exhibition of oneself; **~fallen** *vi sep irreg aux sein* to miss (it *or* one's mark); ~**gehen** vi sep irreg aux sein **(a)** (verfehlen: Schuß etc) to miss; **(b)** (inf: scheitern) to go wrong; (Witz) to fall flat; ~**geraten*** vi sep irreg aux sein to go wrong; (Übersetzung) not to hit the mark; ~**greifen** vi sep irreg **(a)** (verfehlen) (auf dem Klavier etc) to play a wrong note/some wrong notes; (beim Fangen) to miss (the mark), to be wide of the mark; **(b)** (fig inf) (mit Schätzung, Prognose etc) to be wide of the mark or way out (inf); **im Ton** ~**greifen** to strike the wrong note; **im Ausdruck** ~**greifen** to put things the wrong way; **mit seiner Bemerkung hat er aber ganz schön** ~**gegriffen** he really put his foot in it with that remark (inf); ~**halten** sep irreg **1** vt **jdn/etw** ~**halten** to compare him/her/it etc with sb/sth; **man darf ihre Schwester nicht** ~**halten** you shouldn't compare her with her sister; **2** vi siehe ~**zielen**; ~**hauen** vi sep irreg **(a)** (beim Schlagen) to miss; (beim Klavierspielen) to play a wrong note/some wrong notes; **(b)** (inf: sich irren) to miss the mark, to be wide of the mark; (beim Berechnen, Raten, Schätzen auch) to be way out (inf); ~**liegen** vi sep irreg (inf: sich irren) to be quite wrong or way out (inf); ~**raten** vi sep irreg (inf) to guess wrong; ~**schießen** vi sep irreg **(a)** (verfehlen) to miss; **(b)** (absichtlich vorbeischießen) to shoot to miss; ~**sein** vi sep irreg aux sein (Zusammenschreibung nur bei infin und ptp) (inf) (verwirrt sein) to be completely confused; (sich nicht wohl fühlen) not to feel up to it (inf); ~**tippen** vi sep (inf) to guess wrong; ~**treffen** vi sep irreg siehe ~**schießen** (a); ~**zielen** vi sep to aim to miss.

Dänemark nt -s Denmark.

danieden adv (obs) down below. ~ **auf Erden** on earth below.

daniederliegen vi sep irreg **(a)** (old liter: krank sein) to be laid low, to be ill. **(b)** (fig geh: schwach sein) to be depressed.

Dänin f Dane, Danish woman/girl.

dänisch adj Danish.

Dänisch(e) nt decl as adj Danish; siehe auch **Deutsch(e)**.

Dank m -(e)s, no pl (ausgedrückt) thanks pl; (Gefühl der Dankbarkeit) gratitude. **besten** or **herzlichen** or **schönen** or **vielen** ~ many thanks, thank you very much, thanks a lot (inf); **vielen herzlichen/tausend** ~! many/very many thanks!, thanks a million! (inf); ~ **sei dem Herrn** (Eccl) thanks be to God; **haben Sie/hab** ~! (geh) thank you!; (für Hilfe auch) I'm much obliged to you; **nehmen Sie meinen (herzlichen)** ~ (form) please accept my (heartfelt) thanks (form); **jdm für etw** ~ **sagen** (liter) to express one's or give (esp Eccl) thanks to sb for sth; ~ **sagen** (Aus) to express one's thanks; (Eccl) to give thanks; **jdm** ~ **schulden** (form), **jdm zu** ~ **verpflichtet sein** (form) to owe sb a debt of gratitude; **jdm für etw** ~ **wissen** (form) to be indebted to sb for sth; **etw mit** ~ **annehmen** to accept sth with thanks; **mit bestem** ~ **zurück!** many thanks for lending it/them to me; (iro: Retourkutsche) thank you – the same to you!; **das war ein schlechter** ~ that was poor thanks; **das ist der (ganze)** ~ **dafür** that's all the thanks one gets; **als** ~ **für seine Dienste** in grateful recognition of his service; **zum** ~ **(dafür)** as a way of saying thank you; **das ist der** ~ **des Vaterlandes!** (iro) that's all the thanks one gets!; **der** ~ **des Vaterlandes ist dir gewiß** (iro) you'll get a medal for that.

dank prep + gen or dat thanks to.

Dank|adresse f official letter of thanks.

dankbar adj **(a)** (dankerfüllt) grateful; (erleichtert, froh) thankful; (Publikum, Zuhörer) appreciative. **jdm** ~ **sein** to be grateful to sb (für for); (für Rat, Hilfe etc auch) to be indebted to sb (für for); **sich** ~ **erweisen** or **zeigen** to show one's gratitude (gegenüber to); **ich wäre dir** ~, **wenn du ...** I would be grateful or I would appreciate it if you ... **(b)** (lohnend) Arbeit, Aufgabe, Rolle rewarding; Stoff easycare attr; (haltbar) hard-wearing. **eine** ~**e Pflanze** a plant which doesn't need much attention.

Dankbarkeit f gratitude (gegen, gegenüber to); (Gefühl der Erleichterung) thankfulness.

Dankbrief m thank-you letter.

danke interj **(a)** thank you, thanks (inf), ta (Brit inf); (ablehnend) no thank you. ~ **ja**, **ja**, ~ yes please, yes, thank you; ~ **nein**, **nein**, ~ no thank you; ~ **schön** or **sehr** thank you or thanks (inf) very much; (zu jdm) ~ **(schön) sagen** to say thank you (to sb); **ich soll dir von meiner Schwester** ~ **schön sagen** my sister sends (you) her thanks; ~ **vielmals** many thanks; (iro) thanks a million (inf); ~ **der Nachfrage** (form) thank you for your concern; **wie geht's?** — ~, **ich kann nicht klagen** how's it going? — (I can't complain; **soll ich helfen?** — ~, **ich glaube, ich komme allein zurecht** can I help? — thanks (all the same), but I think I can manage; siehe auch **danken**. **(b)** (inf) **mir geht's** ~ I'm OK (inf); **sonst geht's dir (wohl)** ~! (iro) are you feeling all right?

danken 1 vi **(a)** (Dankbarkeit zeigen) to express one's thanks. **jdm** ~ to thank sb (für for); **mit überschwenglichen Worten/einem Strauß Blumen** ~ to be effusive in one's thanks/to express one's thanks with a bunch of flowers; **mit einer Verbeugung** ~ to bow one's thanks; **ich danke dir für das Geschenk/die Gastfreundschaft etc** thank you for your or the present/your hospitality; **wir** ~ **für die Einladung** thank you for your or the invitation; **(ich) danke!** yes please; (ablehnend) no thank you, no thanks (inf); **(ich) danke bestens** (iro) thanks a million (inf), thanks for nothing (inf); **man dankt** (inf) thanks (inf), ta (Brit inf); **ich danke Ihnen (dafür), daß Sie mir den Betrag überwiesen haben** thank you for transferring the money (to me); **jdm** ~ **lassen** to send sb one's thanks; **bestellen Sie bitte Ihrem Vater, ich lasse herzlich** ~ please give your father my thanks; **nichts zu** ~ don't mention it, not at all; **dafür** or **für so was danke ich** (iro) not on your life!, not a chance! (inf); **na, ich danke** (iro) no thank you; **ich danke für Obst und Südfrüchte** (sl) no thank you very much (iro); ~**d erhalten/annehmen/ablehnen** to receive/accept/decline with thanks.

(b) (ablehnen) to decline.

(c) (Gruß erwidern) to return a/the greeting. **2** vt **(a)** (geh: verdanken) **jdm/einer Sache etw** ~ to owe sth to sb/sth; **ihm danke ich es, daß ...** I owe it to him that ...; **nur dem rechtzeitigen Erscheinen der Feuerwehr ist es zu** ~, **daß ...** it was only thanks to the prompt turn-out of the fire brigade that ...

(b) **jdm etw** ~ (jdm dankbar sein für) to thank sb for sth; (jdm etw lohnen) to repay sb for sth; **man wird es dir nicht** ~/**nicht zu** ~ **wissen** you won't be thanked for it/it won't be appreciated; **sie werden es mir später einmal** ~, **daß ich das getan habe** they'll thank me for doing that one day; **all meine Hilfe wurde mir mit keinem Wort/mit Beschimpfungen gedankt** I didn't get a single word of thanks for all my help/all my help was just repaid with insults; **man hat es mir schlecht gedankt, daß ich das getan habe** I got small thanks or I didn't get a lot of thanks for doing it; **wie kann ich Ihnen das jemals** ~? how can I ever thank you?

dankenswert adj Bemühung, Hingabe commendable; (Hilfe) kind; (lohnenswert) Aufgabe, Arbeit rewarding. **in** ~**er Weise** (löblich) (most) commendably; (freundlicherweise) very kindly.

dankenswerterweise adv generously.

dank|erfüllt adj (liter) grateful. ~ **möchte ich Ihnen meine Anerkennung aussprechen** I would like to express my grateful appreciation.

Dankesbezeigung f demonstration of one's gratitude or thanks.

Dankeschön nt -s, no pl thank-you.

Dankesworte pl words pl of thanks; (von Redner) vote sing of thanks.

Dank-: ~**gebet** nt prayer of thanksgiving; ~**gottesdienst** m service of thanksgiving; ~**opfer** nt thanks-offering; **d~sagen** pret **d~sagte**, ptp **d~gesagt**, infin auch **d~zusagen** vi (geh) to express one's thanks (jdm to sb); (Eccl) to give thanks (jdm to sb); ~**sagung** f **(a)** (Eccl) thanksgiving; **(b)** (Brief) note of thanks; ~**schreiben** nt letter of thanks.

dann adv **(a)** (Reihenfolge ausdrückend, später) then. ~ **und** ~ round about then; **von** ~ **bis** ~ for some time around then; ~ **und wann** now and then; **gerade** ~, **wenn ...** just when ...; **wenn das gemacht ist,** ~ **kannst du dann** when that's done you can go; **noch eine Woche,** ~ **ist Weihnachten** another week till Christmas, another week and (then) it's Christmas; siehe **bis²**. **(b)** (unter diesen Umständen) then. **wenn ...,** ~ **if ...,** (then); **wenn du was brauchst,** ~ **sagst du's mir, nicht?** just tell me if you need anything, if you need anything (then) just tell me; **ja, selbst** ~ yes, even then; **nein, selbst** ~ **nicht** no, not even then; **selbst** ~/**selbst** ~ **nicht, wenn ...** even/not even if ...; **erst** ~, **wenn ...** only when ...; **ja,** ~! (oh) well then!; **ich habe keine Lust mehr** — ~ **hör doch auf!** I'm not in the mood any more — well stop then!; **und wie es** ~ **so geht** or ist, **kommt natürlich Besuch** and as was bound to happen, I got visitors, but you know how it is, I got visitors; **wenn er seine Gedichte selbst nicht versteht, wer** ~? if he can't understand his own poems, who else could (understand them)?; **wenn man nicht einmal in Schottland echten Whisky bekommt, wo** ~? if you can't get real whisky in Scotland, where can you expect to find it?; **wenn ich nicht einmal das Einmaleins bei euch voraussetzen kann, was** ~? if I can't even assume you know your tables, what can I assume you know?; ~ **eben nicht** well, in that case (there's no more to be said); ~ **erst recht nicht!** in that case no way (sl) or not a chance (inf)!; ~ **ist ja alles in Ordnung** (oh well), everything's all right then, in that case everything's all right; ~ **will ich lieber gehen** well, I'd better be getting along (then); **ja** ~, **auf Wiedersehen** well then, good-bye; also ~ **bis morgen** right then, see you tomorrow, see you tomorrow then.

(c) (außerdem) ~ **... noch** on top of that; **strohdumm und** ~ **auch noch frech** as thick as they come and cheeky into the bargain; **kommandiert mich herum und meint** ~ **auch noch ...** orders me around and then on top of that thinks ...; **und** ~, **wer ist er denn überhaupt?** (and) anyway, who does he think he is then?

dannen adv: **von** ~ (obs: von woher) thence (old), from thence (Eccl); (liter: weg) away.

dantesk adj Dantesque.

dantisch adj Dantean.

daran adv (auch **dran**) **(a)** (räumlich: an dieser Stelle, diesem Ort, Gegenstand) on it/that; schieben, lehnen, stellen against it/that; legen next to it/that; kleben, befestigen, machen, gehen to it/that; sich setzen at it/that. **nahe** or **dicht** ~ right up against or up close against it; **nahe** ~ **sein** (fig) to be on the point of it, to be just about to; **nahe** ~ **sein, etw zu tun** to be on the point of doing sth or just about to do sth; **zu nahe** ~ too close (to it); ~ **vorbei** past it; **er hat dicht** ~ **vorbeigeschossen** his shot just missed it; ~ **kommen** or **fassen/riechen/schlagen** to touch/smell/hit it/that; **er hielt seine Hand** ~ he touched it with his hand; **das Telefon klingelte, er ging aber nicht** ~ the phone rang but he didn't answer it; **die Kinder sind wieder** ~ **gewesen** (inf) the children have been at it again.

(b) (zeitlich: danach anschließend) **im Anschluß** ~, ~ **anschließend** following that/this; **im Anschluß** ~ **findet eine Diskussion statt** it/this/that will be followed by a discussion; **erst fand ein Vortrag statt,** ~ **schloß sich eine Diskussion** first there was a lecture which was followed by a discussion or and after that a discussion.

(c) (inf) **er ist schlecht/gut** ~ (gesundheitlich, finanziell) he's in a bad way (inf)/he's OK (inf); **ich weiß nie, wie ich (bei ihm)** ~ **bin** I never know where I am with him; **sie sind sehr arm** ~ (haben wenig Geld) they're not at all well-off; (sind bedauernswert) they are poor creatures.

(d) in Verbindung mit n, adj, vb siehe auch dort; arbeiten on it/that; sterben, erinnern, Bedarf, Mangel of it/that; interessieren, sich beteiligen, arm, reich in it/that; sich klammern to it/that. ~ sticken/bauen to embroider/build it/that; was macht der Aufsatz? — ich bin zur Zeit ~ how's the essay doing? — I'm (working) on it now; er war ~ interessiert he was interested in it; er war ~ interessiert, es zu tun he was interested in doing it; ich zweifle nicht ~ I don't doubt it; ich zweifle nicht ~, daß ... I don't doubt that ...; erinnere mich ~ remind me about or of that; erinnere mich ~, daß ich das machen soll remind me to do that or that I must do that; ~ wird er zugrunde gehen that will be the ruin of him; wir haben großen Anteil ~ genommen we sympathized deeply; wird sich etwas ~ ändern? will that change at all?; wir können nichts ~ machen we can't do anything about it; ~ sieht man, wie ... there you (can) see how ...; Sie würden gut ~ tun, dieses Angebot anzunehmen you would do well or would be well-advised to accept this offer; das Beste/Schönste/Schlimmste etc ~ the best/nicest/worst etc thing about it; es ist kein wahres Wort ~ there isn't a word of truth in it, not a word of it is true; an den Gerüchten ist nichts ~ there's nothing in those rumours; es ist nichts ~ (ist nicht fundiert) there's nothing in it; (ist nichts Besonderes) it's nothing special; siehe auch dran.

Daran-: ~gabe f (geh) sacrifice; unter ~gabe seines Lebens by sacrificing his life; d~geben vt sep irreg (geh) to sacrifice; d~gehen vi sep irreg aux sein to set about it; d~gehen, etw zu tun to set about doing sth; d~machen vr sep (inf) to set about it; (endlich in Angriff nehmen) to get down to it; sich d~machen, etw zu tun to set about doing it/to get down to doing it; d~setzen sep 1 vt (einsetzen) to exert; (aufs Spiel setzen) to stake, to risk; seine ganzen Kräfte d~setzen, etw zu tun to spare no effort to do sth; 2 vr to sit down to it; d~wenden vt sep irreg (geh) to exert; seine ganzen Kräfte d~wenden, etw zu tun to spare no effort to do sth.

darauf adv (emph darauf) **(a)** (räumlich) on it/that/them etc; (in Richtung) towards it/that/them etc; schießen, zielen, losfahren at it/that/them etc; (fig) fußen, basieren, aufbauen on it/that; zurückführen, beziehen to it/that. da er es nicht wagte herunterzuklettern, mußte er ~ sitzen bleiben since he didn't dare climb down he just had to sit (up) there; er hielt den Nagel fest und schlug mit dem Hammer ~ he held the nail in place and hit it with the hammer; lege die Wäsche ~ put the washing on there; seine Behauptungen stützen sich ~, daß der Mensch von Natur aus gut ist his claims are based on the supposition that man is naturally good.

(b) (Reihenfolge: zeitlich, örtlich) after that. die Tage, die ~ folgten the days which followed; ~ folgte ... that was followed by ..., after that came ...; zuerst kam der Wagen des Premiers, ~ folgten Polizisten the prime minister's car came first, followed by policemen; am Tag/Abend/Jahr ~ the next day/evening/year, the day/evening/year after (that).

(c) (infolgedessen) because of that. er hat gestohlen und wurde ~ von der Schule verwiesen he was caught stealing and because of that was expelled.

(d) (als Reaktion) sagen, reagieren to that. ~ antworten to answer that; eine Antwort ~ an answer to that; er hat ein Gedicht ~ geschrieben that prompted him to write a poem; ~ wurde er ganz beschämt that made him feel quite ashamed; ~ haben sich viele Interessenten gemeldet a lot of people have shown an interest in it/that; nimm die Marke, ~ bekommst du ein Essen in der Kantine take this token, you'll get a meal in the canteen for or with it; ~ steht die Todesstrafe/stehen mindestens fünf Jahre Gefängnis that carries the death penalty/a minimum sentence of five years' imprisonment.

(e) in Verbindung mit n, adj, vb siehe auch dort; bestehen, verlassen, wetten, Zeit/Mühe verschwenden, Einfluß on that/it; hoffen, warten, sich vorbereiten, gefaßt sein, reinfallen for that/it; trinken to that/it; stolz sein of that/it. ich bin stolz ~, daß sie gewonnen hat I'm proud that she won or of her winning; ich bestehe ~, daß du kommst I insist that you come or on your coming; wir müssen ~ Rücksicht nehmen/Rücksicht ~ nehmen, daß ... we must take that into consideration/take into consideration that ...; ich möchte ~ hinweisen, daß ... I would like to point out that ...; gib mir die Hand ~ shake on it; ~ freuen wir uns schon we're looking forward to it already; wir freuen uns schon ~, daß du bald kommst we're looking forward to your or you coming; ~ kommen (auffinden) to come (up)on that/it; (sich erinnern) to think of that/it; wir kamen auch ~ zu sprechen we talked about that too; wie kommst du ~? what makes you think that?, how do you work that out? (inf); ~ willst du hinaus! that's what you're getting at!; er war nur ~ aus he was only after that or interested in that; er war nur ~ aus, möglichst viel Geld zu verdienen he was only interested in earning as much money as possible.

darauffolgend adj attr after him/it/that etc; Tag etc following; Wagen etc behind pred.

daraufhin adv **(a)** (aus diesem Anlaß, deshalb) as a result (of that/this); (danach) after that, thereupon. **(b)** (daraufhin) (im Hinblick darauf) with regard to that/this. wir müssen es ~ prüfen, ob es für unsere Zwecke geeignet ist we must test it with a view to whether it is suitable for our purposes.

daraus adv (emph auch daraus) **(a)** (räumlich) out of that/it/them. ~ kann man nicht trinken! you can't drink out of that/it!

(b) (aus diesem Material etc) from or out of that/it/them. ~ kann man Wein herstellen you can make wine from that.

(c) (aus dieser Sache, Angelegenheit) from that/it. in Verbindung mit n, vb siehe auch dort. ~ ergibt sich/folgt, daß ... it follows from that that ...; ~ sieht man ... from this it can be seen ...

darben vi (geh) (entbehren)) to live in want; (hungern) to starve.

darbieten sep irreg 1 vt (geh) **(a)** (vorführen) Tänze, Schauspiel to perform; (vortragen) Lehrstoff to present.

(b) (anbieten) to offer; Speisen to serve; (reichen) Hand, Geschenk etc auch to proffer.

2 vr to present itself; (Gelegenheit, Möglichkeit auch) to offer itself. dort bot sich (ihnen) ein schauerlicher Anblick dar a horrible sight met their eyes, they were faced with a horrible sight.

Darbietung f (das Darbieten) performance; (das Dargebotene) act.

darbringen vt sep irreg (geh) Opfer to offer.

Dardanellen pl die ~ the Dardanelles pl.

darein adv (emph auch darein) **(a)** (räumlich: hinein) in there; (wenn Bezugsobjekt vorher erwähnt) in it/them. hierein? — nein, ~! in here? — no, in there.

(b) (old: in diese Lage) einwilligen, sich ergeben to that. wir müssen uns ~ fügen we must accept that or bow to that.

darein- pref siehe auch drein-; ~finden vr sep irreg (geh) to come to terms with it, to learn to accept it; sich ~finden, etw zu tun to come to terms with or learn to accept doing sth; ~legen vt sep (fig geh) siehe ~setzen; ~mengen, ~mischen vr sep (geh) to interfere; ~reden vi sep (in Angelegenheiten) to interfere (jdm in sb's affairs); ~setzen vt sep (fig geh) Energie to put into it, to devote to it; seine ganze Energie ~setzen, etw zu tun to put all one's energy into or devote all one's energy to doing sth; er setzte seinen ganzen Stolz ~ it was a matter of pride with him.

darin adv (emph auch darin) **(a)** (räumlich) in there; (wenn Bezugsobjekt vorher erwähnt) in it/them; (fig) in that/it. ~ liegt ein Widerspruch there's a contradiction in that.

(b) (in dieser Beziehung) in that respect. ~ ist er ganz groß (inf) he's very good at that; ~ unterscheiden sich die beiden the two of them differ in that (respect); die beiden unterscheiden sich ~, daß ... the two of them differ in that ...; ~ liegt der Unterschied that is the difference, that is where the difference is; der Unterschied liegt ~, daß ... the difference is that ...; seine Schuld lag ~, daß er ... his crime was that he ...; wir stimmen ~ überein, daß ... we agree that ...; in Verbindung mit vb siehe auch dort.

(c) (old: worin) in which. das Haus, ~ er geboren the house in which he was born; siehe auch drin.

darinnen adv (old) therein (old).

darlegen vt sep to explain (jdm to sb); Theorie, Plan, Ansichten auch to expound (jdm to sb).

Darlegung f explanation.

Darleh(e)n nt -s, - loan. als ~ as a loan.

Darleh(e)ns-: ~bank f lending or credit bank; ~geber m lender; ~kasse f credit bank; ~konto nt loan account; ~nehmer m borrower; ~schuld f loan; ~summe f die ~summe the amount of the/a loan; eine ~summe a loan.

Darleiher m -s, - (Jur) lender.

Darling m -s, -s darling.

Darm m -(e)s, ~e intestine(s pl), bowel(s pl), gut(s pl); (für Wurst) (sausage) skin or case; (Material: für Saiten, Schläger etc) gut. Wurst in echtem/künstlichem ~ sausage in real/synthetic skin.

Darm- in cpds intestinal; ~ausgang m anus; ~bewegung f peristalsis no art, no pl, peristaltic movement; ~entleerung f evacuation of the bowels; ~grippe f gastric influenza or 'flu; ~katarrh m enteritis; ~krebs m cancer of the intestine; ~leiden nt intestinal trouble no art; ~saite f gut string; ~spülung f enema; ~tätigkeit f peristalsis no art; die ~tätigkeit fördern/regulieren to stimulate/regulate the movement of the bowels; ~trägheit f under-activity of the intestines; ~verschlingung f volvulus (form), twisting of the intestine; ~verschluß m obstruction of the bowels or intestines.

darnach adv (old) siehe danach.

darneben adv (old) siehe daneben.

darob adv (old) **(a)** siehe darüber. **(b)** (deswegen) er war ~ sehr erstaunt he was very surprised by that; er wurde ~ sehr bewundert he was much admired for that or on that account.

Darre f -, -n drying kiln or oven; (Hopfen~, Malz~) oast.

darreichen vt sep (liter) (anbieten) to offer (jdm etw sb sth, sth to sb); (reichen auch) to proffer (jdm etw sth to sb).

darren vt to (kiln-)dry; Malz, Hopfen to (oast-)dry.

Darr-: ~malz nt (oast-)dried malt; ~ofen m siehe Darre.

darstellbar adj (in Literaturwerk etc) portrayable; (in Bild etc auch) depictable; (durch Diagramm etc) representable; (beschreibbar) describable. schwer/leicht ~ hard/easy to portray/depict/show/describe; dieses Phänomen ist graphisch ~ this phenomenon can be shown on a graph.

darstellen sep 1 vt **(a)** to show; (ein Bild entwerfen von) to portray, to depict; (Theat) to portray; Rolle to play; (beschreiben) to describe. etw in einem möglichst günstigen Licht ~ to show sth in the best possible light; sie hat das Gretchen sehr überzeugend dargestellt she played (the role of) Gretchen most convincingly; etw kurz or knapp ~ to give a short description of sth; was sollen diese verworrenen Striche ~? what are these confused lines supposed to show or (in Zeichnung) be?; die ~den Künste (Theater) the dramatic or performing arts; (Malerei, Plastik) the visual arts; er stellt etwas/nichts dar (fig) he has a certain air/doesn't have much of an air about him.

(b) (Math) Funktion to plot; (Chem) to produce. ~de Geometrie projective geometry.

(c) (bedeuten) to constitute, to represent.

2 vr (Eindruck vermitteln) to appear (jdm to sb); (sich erweisen) to show oneself. die Sache stellte sich (als) sehr fragwürdig dar the matter appeared (to be) very dubious; bei dem

Talentwettbewerb stellte er sich als begabter Sänger dar at the talent competition he showed himself to be a gifted singer.

Darsteller *m* -s, - (*Theat*) actor. der ~ des Hamlet the actor playing Hamlet; ein hervorragender ~ tragischer Rollen an excellent actor in tragic roles.

Darstellerin *f* (*Theat*) actress; *siehe auch* Darsteller.

darstellerisch *adj* dramatic. ~ war die Weber der Klein weit überlegen as an actress Weber was much superior to Klein; eine ~e Höchstleistung a magnificent piece of acting.

Darstellung *f* (a) portrayal; (*in Buch, Bild auch*) depiction; (*durch Diagramm etc*) representation; (*Beschreibung*) description; (*Bericht*) account. an den Wänden fand man ~en der Heldentaten des Königs on the walls one could see the King's heroic deeds depicted; eine falsche ~ der Fakten a misrepresentation of the facts; er gab eine großartige ~ des Hamlet his performance as Hamlet was superb; der Stoff war in *or* durch ~en von Wanderbühnen bekannt geworden the material became known through being performed by travelling theatre groups.
(b) (*Math*) graphische ~ graph.
(c) (*Chem*) preparation.

Darstellungs-: ~form *f* form of representation (*gen* in); (*Theat*) dramatic art form; ~gabe *f* talent as a performer; (*Theat*) acting talent; ~kunst *f* stage technique; (*Theat*) acting technique; ~mittel *nt* technique (of representation).

dartun *vt sep* (*geh*) to set forth; Überlegenheit to demonstrate.

darüber *adv* (*emph* darüber) (a) (*räumlich*) over that/it/them; (*quer* ~) across *or* over there; (*wenn Bezugsobjekt vorher erwähnt*) across *or* over it/them; (*höher als etw*) above (there/it/them); (*direkt auf etw*) on top (of it/them). geh ~, nicht hierüber! go across *or* over there, not here!; die Aufgabe war sehr schwer, ich habe lange ~ gesessen the exercise was very difficult, I sat over it for a long time; ~ hinweg sein (*fig*) to have got over it; jetzt ist er ~ hinaus (*fig*) he is past that now.
(b) (*deswegen, in dieser Beziehung*) about that/it. sich ~ beschweren/beklagen *etc* to complain/moan *etc* about it; sich ~ beschweren/beklagen *etc*, daß ... to complain/moan *etc* that ...; wir wollen nicht ~ streiten, ob ... we don't want to argue *or* disagree about whether ...
(c) (*davon*) about that/it. Rechenschaft ~ ablegen to account for it; sie führt eine Liste ~ she keeps a list of it; in Verbindung mit *n*, *vb siehe auch* dort.
(d) (*währenddessen*) in the meantime. Wochen gingen ~ hin meanwhile *or* in the meantime weeks went past.
(e) (*mehr, höher*) above *or* over that. 21 Jahre/4 DM und ~ 21 years/4 DM and above *or* over; kein Pfennig ~ not a penny over (that) *or* more; ~ hinaus over and above that; es geht nichts ~ there is nothing to beat it.

darüber-: ~fahren *vi sep irreg aux sein* (*fig*) to run over it; wenn du mit der Hand ~fährst, ... if you run your hand over it ...; ~liegen *vi sep irreg* (*fig*) to be higher; ~machen *vr sep* (*inf*) to get to work on it (*inf*), to set about it (*inf*); ~schreiben *vt sep irreg* to write above it; ~stehen *vi sep irreg* (*fig*) to be above such things.

darum *adv* (*emph* darum) (a) (*räumlich*) round that/it/him/her/them. ~ herum round about (it/him/her/them); ~, wo ... round where ...
(b) (*um diese Angelegenheit*) in Verbindung mit *n*, *vb siehe auch* dort. es geht ~, daß ... the thing is that ...; ~ geht es gar nicht that isn't the point; ~ geht es that is what it is about, that's it; ~ geht es mir/geht es mir nicht that's my point/that's not the point for me; es geht mir ~, Ihnen das klarzumachen I'm trying to make it clear to you; wir kommen leider nicht ~ herum, die Preise heraufzusetzen unfortunately we cannot avoid raising prices; wir wollen nicht lange ~ herumreden we don't want to spend a long time talking around the subject; ich gäbe viel ~, die Wahrheit zu erfahren I would give a lot to learn the truth; ich habe ihn schon ein paarmal ~ gebeten, aber ... I've asked him a few times (for it/to to do it), but ...; könntest du ihn ~ bitten, zu mir zu kommen? could you ask him to to come to me?; sie haben sich ~ gestritten they argued over it; sie haben sich ~ gestritten, wer ... they argued over who ...
(c) (*liter: darüber, davon*) about that/it. nur wenige wissen ~, wie ... (*geh*) few people know how ...
(d) (*deshalb*) that's why, because of that. ~, daß *or* weil ... because of that; eben ~ that is exactly why; ach ~! so that's why!; ~? because of that?; warum willst du nicht mitkommen? — ~! (*inf*) why don't you want to come? — (just) 'cos! (*inf*); er ist faul aber ~ nicht dumm he's lazy but that doesn't mean he's stupid; *siehe auch* drum.

darum-: ~kommen *vi sep irreg aux sein* to lose it/them; ~kommen, etw zu tun to lose the opportunity of doing sth; ~legen *vt sep* to put around it/them; ~stehen *vi sep irreg aux haben or sein* to stand around; ~wickeln *vt sep* to wrap round it/them.

darunter *adv* (*emph auch* darunter) (a) (*räumlich*) under that/it/them, underneath *or* beneath (that/it/them); (*niedriger als etw auch*) below (that/it/them). ~ hervorkommen to appear from underneath; die Zimmerdecke ist so niedrig, daß man kaum ~ stehen kann the ceiling is so low that one can hardly stand up; als weitere Belastung kam der Tod seiner Mutter, ~ ist er dann zusammengebrochen his mother's death was an added burden and he broke down under this strain.
(b) (*weniger*) under that. Leute im Alter von 35 Jahren und ~ people aged 35 and under; der Preis beträgt 50 DM, ~ kann ich die Ware nicht abgeben the price is 50 marks, I can't sell for less; kein Pfennig ~ not a penny under that *or* less; ~ macht sie's nicht (*inf*) she won't do it for less.

(c) (*dabei*) among them. ~ waren viele Ausländer there were a lot of foreigners among them.
(d) (*unter dieser Angelegenheit*) in Verbindung mit *n*, *vb siehe auch* dort. was verstehen Sie ~? what do you understand by that/it?; ~ kann ich mir nichts vorstellen that doesn't mean anything to me; *siehe auch* drunter.

darunter-: ~bleiben *vi sep irreg aux sein* (*fig*) to be lower; Sie kennen die Anforderungen, wenn Sie mit *or* in Ihrer Leistung ~bleiben, werden Sie entlassen you are aware of the requirements, if you fail to meet them you will be dismissed; ~fallen *vi sep irreg aux sein* (*fig*) (*dazugerechnet werden*) to be included; (*davon betroffen werden*) to come *or* fall under it/them; ~gehen *vi sep irreg aux sein* (~*passen*) to fit underneath; ~liegen *vi sep irreg* (a) *aux haben or sein* (*lit*) to lie underneath; (b) (*fig*) *siehe* ~bleiben; ~mischen *sep* 1 *vt* Mehl *etc* to mix in; 2 *vr* (*Mensch*) to mingle (with) them; ~schreiben *vt sep irreg* to write underneath; Namen *auch* to sign at the bottom; ~setzen *vt sep* Unterschrift to put to it.

das *art etc siehe* der².

Dasein *nt* -s, *no pl* (*Leben, Existenz, Philos*) existence; (*Anwesendsein*) presence. der Kampf ums ~ the struggle for existence; etw ins ~ rufen (*liter*) to bring sth into existence, to call sth into being.

dasein *vi sep irreg aux sein* (*Zusammenschreibung nur bei infin und ptp*) (*lit, fig inf*) to be there. noch ~ to be still there; (*übrig sein auch*) to be left; wieder ~ to be back; ich bin gleich wieder da I'll be right *or* straight back; sind Sie schon lange da? have you been here/there long?; ist Post/sind Besucher für mich da? is there any mail/are there visitors for me?; war der Briefträger schon da? has the postman been yet?; ist die Milch schon da? has the milk come yet?; für jdn ~ to be there *or* available for sb; sie ist nur für ihren Mann da she lives for her husband; ein Arzt, der immer für seine Patienten da ist a doctor who always has time for his patients; voll ~ (*inf*) to be all there (*inf*); so etwas ist noch nie dagewesen it's quite unprecedented; das ist alles schon mal dagewesen it's all been done before; das übertrifft alles bisher Dagewesene that beats everything; ein dagewesener Erfolg an unprecedented success.

Daseins-: ~angst *f* (*Philos*) existential fear, angst; ~bedingungen *pl* living conditions *pl*; ~berechtigung *f siehe* Existenzberechtigung; ~form *f* form of life *or* existence; ~freude *f* zest for life, joie de vivre; ~kampf *m* struggle for existence; d~mäßig *adj* (*Philos*) *siehe* existentiell; ~weise *f* mode of being.

daselbst *adv* (*old*) in said place; (*bei Quellenangaben*) ibidem, ibid *abbr*. geboren 1714 zu Florenz, gestorben 1768 ~ born in Florence 1714, died there 1768.

dasitzen *vi sep irreg aux haben or sein* to sit there. wie die Kinder heutzutage ~! the way children sit nowadays!; ohne Hilfe/einen Pfennig ~ (*inf*) to be left without any help/without a penny.

dasjenige *dem pron siehe* derjenige.

daß *conj* (a) (*mit Subjektsatz*) that. ~ wir alle sterben müssen, ist sicher that we all must die is certain (*liter*), it is certain (that) we all must die.
(b) (*mit Objektsatz*) (that). ich bin überzeugt, ~ du das Richtige getan hast I'm sure (that) you have done the right thing; ich verstehe nicht, ~ man ihn als Bewerber abgelehnt hat I don't understand why he was turned down; ich sehe nicht ein, ~ wir hungern sollen I don't see why we should starve.
(c) (*mit Attributivsatz*) that. angenommen/vorausgesetzt, ~ ... given/provided that ...; ich bin dagegen, ~ ihr alle kommt I'm against you all coming; ich bin mir dessen bewußt, ~ ... I am aware (that) *or* of the fact that ...; unter der Bedingung, ~ ... on (the) condition that ...
(d) (*mit Kausalsatz*) that. ich war böse, ~ ... I was annoyed that ...; ich freue mich darüber, ~ ... I'm glad (that) ...; das kommt daher, ~ ... that comes because ...; das liegt daran, ~ ... that is because ...; das kommt davon, ~ er niemals aufpaßt that comes from him *or* his never paying attention.
(e) (*mit Konsekutivsatz*) that. er fuhr so schnell, ~ er sich überschlug he drove so fast that he overturned.
(f) (*geh: mit Finalsatz*) so that. ich gab ihm den Brief, ~ er ihn selbst lesen konnte I gave him the letter so that he could read it himself.
(g) (*als Einleitung eines Instrumentalsatzes*) er verbringt seine Freizeit damit, ~ er Rosen züchtet he spends his free time breeding roses.
(h) (*geh*) (*mit Wunschsatz*) if only, would that (*liter*); (*in Befehl*) see that. ~ er immer da wäre! would that he were always there (*liter*), if only he were always there; ~ es mir nur gelingt! if only I succeed; ~ du es mir nicht verlierst! see that you don't lose it!
(i) *siehe* als, auf, außer, ohne, so *etc*.

dasselbe, dasselbige *dem pron siehe* derselbe.

dastehen *vi sep irreg aux haben or sein* (a) to stand there. wie stehst denn du wieder da! what sort of a way do you call that to stand!; steh nicht so dumm da! don't just stand there looking stupid.
(b) (*fig*) anders/glänzend/gut/schlecht ~ to be in a different/splendid/good/bad position; die Firma/Regierung steht wieder gut da the company/government is doing all right again (*inf*) *or* is in a good position again; allein ~ to be on one's own; einzig ~ to be unique *or* unparalleled; jetzt stehe ich ohne Mittel/als Lügner da now I'm left with no money/looking like a liar; wenn die Sache schiefgeht, stehst du dumm da if things go wrong you'll be left looking stupid; wie stehe ich jetzt da! (*Selbstlob*) just look at me now!; (*Vorwurf*) what kind of fool do I look now!

Datei *f* data file.

Daten pl of **Datum**.
Daten-: ~**bank** f data bank; ~**erfassung** f data gathering; ~**schutz** m protection of the individual against infringement of his/her rights through storage of computerized data; ~**technik** f computer science; ~**träger** m data carrier; ~**typist(in** f) m terminal operator; ~**übertragung** f data transmission; ~**verarbeitung** f data processing; **elektronische** ~**verarbeitung** computer processing, electronic data processing; ~**verarbeitungsanlage** f data processor.

datieren* 1 vt Brief, Fund to date. **der Brief ist vom 20. April** datiert the letter is dated 20th April.
2 vi (stammen) to date (aus from). **dieser Brief datiert vom 1. Januar** this letter is dated January 1st; **unsere Freundschaft datiert seit einem Urlaub vor zehn Jahren** our friendship dates from or dates back to a holiday ten years ago.

Dativ m (Gram) dative (case).
Dativ|objekt nt (Gram) indirect object.
Dativus ethicus m - -, **Dativi ethici** [-vi -itsi] (Gram) ethical dative.
dato adv: **bis** ~ (Comm, inf) to date.
Datowechsel m (Comm) time bill.
Datscha f -, **Datschen**, **Datsche** f -, -n (esp DDR) country cottage. **auf seiner** ~ in his country cottage.
Dattel f -, -n date.
Dattel- in cpds date; ~**palme** f date palm.
Datterich m siehe **Tatterich**.
Datum nt -s, **Daten** (a) date. **was für ein** ~ **haben wir heute?** what is the date today?; **das heutige/gestrige/morgige** ~ today's/yesterday's/tomorrow's date; **sich im** ~ **irren** to get the date wrong; **ein Brief gleichen** ~**s** a letter of the same date; **gleichen** ~**s übersandten wir Ihnen ...** (form) on the same date we sent you ...; **etw mit dem** ~ **versehen** to date sth; **der Brief trägt das** ~ **vom 1. April** the letter is dated 1st April; **ein Brief ohne** ~ an undated letter; ~ **des Poststempels** date as postmark; **ein Nachschlagewerk neueren** ~**s** a recent reference work.
(b) usu pl (Faktum) fact; (statistische Zahlenangabe etc) datum (form), piece of data. **technische Daten** technical data pl.
Datums-: ~**grenze** f (Geog) (international) date line; ~**stempel** m date stamp.
Daube f -, -n stave; (beim Eisschießen) tee.
Dauer f -, no pl (das Andauern) duration; (Zeitspanne) period, term; (Länge: einer Sendung etc) length. **während der** ~ **des Vertrages/Krieges** for the duration of the contract/war; **für die** ~ **eines Monats** or **von einem Monat** for a period of one month; **ein Gefängnisaufenthalt von zehnjähriger** ~ a ten-year term of imprisonment; **von** ~ **sein** to be long-lasting; **seine Begeisterung war nicht von** ~ his enthusiasm was short-lived or wasn't long-lasting; **keine** ~ **haben** to be short-lived; **von langer/kurzer** ~ **sein** to last a long time/not to last long; **auf die** ~ in the long term; **auf die** ~ **wird das langweilig** it gets boring in the long run; **das kann man auf die** ~ **nicht ertragen** you can't stand it for any length of time; **das kann auf die** ~ **nicht so weitergehen** it can't go on like that indefinitely; **auf** ~ permanently; **auf** ~ **gearbeitet** made to last; **für die** ~ **Ihres Aufenthaltes in unserem Hause** as long as you stay with us, for the period or duration of your stay with us (form); **man konnte sich nicht über die** ~ **der Regelung einigen** they could not decide on the duration of the agreement.
Dauer- in cpds permanent; ~**auftrag** m (Fin) standing order; ~**ausweis** m (permanent) identity card; (Fahrkarte etc) season ticket; ~**belastung** f continual pressure no indef art; (von Maschine) constant load; **unter** ~**belastung** under continual pressure/a constant load; ~**beschäftigung** f (Stellung) permanent position; **er betreibt Briefmarkensammeln als** ~**beschäftigung** he spends all his time collecting stamps or in philately; ~**beziehung** f permanent relationship; ~**brandofen** m slow-burning stove; ~**brenner** m (a) siehe ~**brandofen**; (b) long runner; (hum: Kuß) long passionate kiss; ~**bügelfalte** f permanent crease; ~**einrichtung** f permanent institution; ~**erfolg** m long-running success; ~**festigkeit** f siehe ~(**schwing)festigkeit**; ~**feuer** nt (Mil) sustained fire; ~**flug** m (Aviat) long haul flight; ~**frostboden** m permafrost; ~**gast** m permanent guest; (häufiger Gast) regular visitor, permanent fixture (hum); **er scheint sich hier als** ~**gast einrichten zu wollen** (iro inf) he seems to be settling down for a long stay; ~**geschwindigkeit** f cruising speed.
dauerhaft adj Zustand, Einrichtung, Farbe permanent; Bündnis, Frieden, Beziehung lasting attr, long-lasting, durable. **durch eine Impfung sind Sie gegen diese Krankheit** ~ **geschützt** one vaccination gives you lasting immunity to this disease.
Dauerhaftigkeit f permanence; (von Material) durability.
Dauer-: ~**karte** f season ticket; ~**krause** f (dated) siehe ~**welle**; ~**lauf** m (Sport) jog; (das Laufen) jogging; **im** ~**lauf** at a jog or trot; **einen** ~**lauf machen** to jog, to go jogging or for a jog; ~**lauf** m (Phon) continuant; ~**lutscher** m lollipop; ~**marsch** m (Mil) forced march; **in** ~**märschen** by forced marches; ~**miete** f long lease or tenancy; **wir wohnen zur** ~**miete** we have a long lease (on the house/flat); **er hat das Haus in** ~**miete** he has the house on a long lease; ~**mieter** m long-term tenant; ~**milch** f long-life milk.
dauern[1] vi (a) (an~) to last, to go on. **das Gewitter dauerte zwei Stunden** the thunderstorm lasted (for) or went on for two hours; **die Verhandlungen** ~ **schon drei Wochen** the negotiations have already been going on for three weeks; **wie lange soll dieser Zustand noch** ~? how long will this situation last or go on (for) or continue?
(b) (Zeit benötigen) to take a while or some time; (lange) to

take a long time. **das dauert noch** (inf) it'll be a while or some time yet; **warum dauert das Anziehen bei dir immer so lange?** why do you always take so long to get dressed?; **es dauerte lange, bis er sich befreit hatte** it took him a long time to get free; **das dauert mir zu lange** it takes too long for me; **muß das so lange** ~? does it have to take so long?; **das dauert immer, bis er fertig ist** (inf) it always takes ages for him to get ready; **das dauert und dauert** (inf) it takes forever (inf); **es dauert jetzt nicht mehr lange** it won't take much longer; **das dauert heute vielleicht wieder einmal** (inf) it's taking ages again today.
(c) (geh: dauerhaft sein) to last.
dauern[2] vt (old, liter) **etw dauert jdn** sb regrets sth; **er/sie dauert mich** I feel sorry for him/her; **es dauert mich, daß ... I** regret or I'm sorry that ...; **es dauerte ihn im Alter, seine Jugend so vergeudet zu haben** in his old age he regretted having squandered his youth like that; **das arme Tier kann einen** ~ you can't help feeling sorry for the poor animal.
dauernd 1 adj (anhaltend) Frieden, Regelung lasting; (ständig) Wohnsitz, Ausstellung permanent; (fortwährend) Unterbrechung, Nörgelei, Sorge constant, perpetual.
2 adv **etw** ~ **tun** to keep doing sth; (stärker) to be always or forever (inf) doing sth, to do sth the whole time (inf); **sie mußte** ~ **auf die Toilette** she had to keep going to the toilet; **er beschwert sich** ~ **darüber** he's always or forever (inf) complaining about it, he complains about it the whole time (inf); **frag nicht** ~ **so dumm!** don't keep asking stupid questions.
Dauer-: ~**obst** nt fruit suitable for storing; ~**parker** m -s, - long-stay parker; **Parkplatz für** ~**parker** long-stay car park; ~**redner** m (pej) interminable speaker; ~**regen** m continuous rain; **ein mehrtägiger** ~**regen** several days of continuous rain; ~**rekord** m endurance record; ~**schlaf** m prolonged sleep; **ich fiel in einen 24-stündigen** ~**schlaf** I fell asleep for 24 hours solid; ~(**schwing)festigkeit** f (Tech) fatigue strength; ~**schwingung** f continuous oscillation; ~**sitzung** f prolonged or lengthy session; ~**sitzung halten** (hum inf) to spend hours in the loo (Brit inf) or john (US inf); ~**spannung** f (Elec) continuous voltage; ~**stellung** f permanent position; **in** ~**stellung beschäftigt** employed in a permanent capacity; ~**strom** m (Elec) constant current; ~**ton** m continuous tone; ~**wald** m permanent forest; ~**welle** f perm, permanent wave; ~**wirkung** f (long-)lasting effect; ~**wohnrecht** nt permanent right of tenure; ~**wurst** f salami; ~**zustand** m permanent state of affairs; **ich möchte das nicht zum** ~**zustand werden lassen** I don't want that to become permanent.
Däumchen nt (a) dim of **Daumen**. (b) (inf) ~ **drehen** to twiddle one's thumbs; **und da mußten wir** ~ **drehen** and we were left twiddling our thumbs.
Daumen m -s, - thumb. **am** ~ **lutschen** to suck one's thumb; **jdm** or **für jdn die Daumen drücken** or **halten** to keep one's fingers crossed for sb; **den** ~ **auf jdn halten** or **drücken** (inf) to breathe down sb's neck; **den** ~ **auf etw** (acc) **halten** (inf) to hold on to sth; siehe **peilen**.
Daumen-: ~**abdruck** m thumbprint; ~**ballen** m ball of the/one's thumb; **d**~**breit** adj as broad as your thumb; ~**breite** f thumb's width; ~**index** m siehe ~**register**; ~**lutscher** m thumb-sucker; ~**nagel** m thumbnail; ~**register** nt thumb index; ~**schraube** f (Hist) thumbscrew; **jdm die** ~**schrauben anlegen** (lit, fig inf) to put the (thumb)screws on sb; **die** ~**schrauben ansetzen** (fig) to put the screws on.
Däumling m (a) (im Märchen) ~ Tom Thumb. (b) (von Handschuh) thumb; (Med) thumbstall.
Daune f -, -n down feather. ~**n** down sing; **ich schlief dort wie auf** ~**n** it was like sleeping on air; **weich wie** ~**n** as soft as thistledown.
Daunen-: ~**bett** nt, ~**decke** f (down-filled) duvet or continental quilt; ~**feder** f down feather; ~**kissen** nt down-filled cushion; (Kopfkissen) down pillow; **d**~**weich** adj soft as down.
Dauphin [do'fɛ:] m -s, -s (Hist) dauphin.
Daus[1] m: **(ei) der** ~! (old), **was der** ~! (old) what the devil or deuce! (dated).
Daus[2] nt -es, **Däuse(r)** (a) (beim Würfel) deuce. (b) (Cards) ace (in German pack).
David(s)stern m star of David.
Davis- ['deɪvɪs]: ~**cup** [-kap], ~**pokal** m Davis cup.
davon adv (emph **davon**) (a) (räumlich) from there; (wenn Bezugsobjekt vorher erwähnt) from it/them; (mit Entfernungsangabe) away (from there/it/them). **weg** ~! (inf) get away from there/it/them; ~ **zweigt ein Weg ab** a path branches off it; siehe **auf**.
(b) (fig) in Verbindung mit n, vb siehe auch **dort es unterscheidet sich** ~ **nur in der Farbe** it only differs from it in the colour; **nein, weit** ~ **entfernt!** no, far from it!; **ich bin weit** ~ **entfernt, Ihnen Vorwürfe machen zu wollen** the last thing I want to do is reproach you; **wenn wir einmal** ~ **absehen, daß ...** if for once we overlook the fact that ...; **wir möchten in diesem Fall** ~ **absehen, Ihnen den Betrag zu berechnen** in this case we shall not invoice you; **in ihren Berechnungen sind sie** ~ **ausgegangen, daß ...** they made their calculations on the basis that ...
(c) (fig: dadurch) leben, abhängen on that/it/them; sterben of that/it; krank/braun werden from that/it/them. **... und** ~ **kommt die rote Farbe** ... and that's where the red colour comes from, ...; **and the red colour comes from that; die rote Farbe kommt** ~, **daß das Holz im Wasser gelegen hat** the red colour comes from the wood lying in the water; **das kommt** ~! I told you so!; **... und** ~ **hängt es ab** and it depends on that; **das hängt** ~ **ab, ob ...** that depends on whether ...; **der Erfolg hängt** ~ **ab, daß alle mitarbeiten** success depends on everyone doing their bit; ~ **hat man nur Ärger** you get nothing but trouble with it; ~ **wird man müde** that makes you tired; **er ißt keine Kartoffeln, weil man** ~

dick wird he doesn't eat potatoes because they make you fat; gib ihr ein bißchen mehr, ~ kann sie doch nicht satt werden give her a bit more, that won't fill her up; ~ stirbst du nicht it won't kill you; was habe ich denn ~? what do I get out of it?; was habe ich denn ~? why should I?; was hast du denn ~, daß du so schuftest? what do you get out of slaving away like that?

(d) (mit Passiv) by that/it/them. ~ betroffen werden or sein to be affected by it/them.

(e) (Anteil, Ausgangssatz) of that/it/them. ~ essen/trinken/nehmen to eat/drink/take some of that/it/them; nehmen Sie doch noch etwas ~! do have some more!; die Hälfte ~ half of that/it/them; das Doppelte ~ twice or double that; zwei/ein Viertelpfund ~, bitte! would you give me two of those/a quarter of a pound of that/those, please; er hat drei Schwestern, ~ sind zwei älter als er he has three sisters, two of whom are older than he is; früher war er sehr reich, aber nach dem Krieg ist ihm nichts ~ geblieben he used to be very rich but after the war nothing ~ was left of his earlier wealth.

(f) (darüber) hören, wissen, sprechen about that/it/them; verstehen, halten of that/it/them. genug ~! enough of this!; ich habe keine Ahnung ~ I've no idea about that/it; nichts mehr ~! no more of that!; nichts ~ halten not to think much of it; ich halte viel ~ I think it is quite good; was wissen Sie ~! what do you know about it anyway?; in Verbindung mit n, vb siehe auch dort.

davon-: ~bleiben vi sep irreg aux sein (inf) to keep away; (nicht anfassen) to keep one's hands off; ~eilen vi sep aux sein (geh) to hurry or hasten away; ~fahren vi sep irreg aux sein (a) (geh) to drive away; (auf Fahrrad etc) to ride away; (Zug) to pull away; (b) jdm ~fahren to pull away from sb; ~fliegen vi sep irreg aux sein (geh) to fly away; ~gehen vi sep irreg aux sein (geh) to walk away; ~jagen vt sep to chase off or away; ~kommen vi sep irreg aux sein (entkommen) to get away, to escape; (nicht bestraft werden) to get away with it; (freigesprochen werden) to get off; mit dem Schrecken/dem Leben/einer Geldstrafe ~kommen to escape with no more than a shock/with one's life/to get off with a fine; ~lassen vt sep irreg die Hände or Finger ~lassen (inf) to leave it/them well alone; du sollst die Hände or Finger ~lassen keep your hands or fingers off (it/them); ~laufen vi sep irreg aux sein (a) to run away (jdm/vor jdm from sb); (verlassen) to walk out (jdm on sb); den Eltern or von zu Hause ~laufen to run away from home; der Läufer ist dem ganzen übrigen Feld ~gelaufen the runner outstripped the whole of the rest of the field; das Hausmädchen/ihr Mann ist ihr ~gelaufen (inf) the maid/her husband walked out on her; es ist zum D~laufen! (inf) it's all too much!; (b) (außer Kontrolle geraten) to get out of hand; die Preise sind ~gelaufen prices have run away with themselves or have got out of hand; die Preise sind uns/den Löhnen ~gelaufen prices are beyond our control/have outstripped wages; ~machen vr sep to make off; ~rennen vi sep irreg aux sein (inf) siehe ~laufen; ~schleichen vir sep irreg (vi: aux sein) to creep or slink away or off; ~schwimmen vi sep irreg aux sein jdm ~schwimmen to outswim or outstrip sb; ~stehlen vr sep irreg (geh) to steal away; ~tragen vt sep irreg (a) (wegtragen) Gegenstände, Verletzte to carry away; Preis to carry off; Sieg, Ruhm to win; (b) (erleiden) Schaden, Verletzung to suffer; ~ziehen vi sep irreg aux sein (liter) to leave; (Prozession etc) to move off; (Sport inf) to pull away (jdm from sb).

davor adv (emph davor) (a) (räumlich) in front (of that/it/them); (wenn Bezugsobjekt vorher erwähnt) in front of it/them. ein Haus mit einem großen Rasen ~ a house with a big front lawn or with a big lawn in front.

(b) (zeitlich) (vor einem bestimmten Datum) before that; (bevor man etw tut) beforehand. ist er 1950 ausgewandert? — nein, schon ~ did he emigrate in 1950? — no, before that; wenn er ins Theater geht, trinkt er ~ meist ein Bier when he goes to the theatre he usually has a beer beforehand.

(c) in Verbindung mit n, vb siehe auch dort; bewahren, schützen from that/it; warnen of or about that/it; Angst haben of that/it; sich ekeln by that/it. ich habe Angst ~, das zu tun I'm afraid of doing that; ich habe Angst ~, daß der Hund beißen könnte I'm afraid that the dog might bite; sein Ekel ~ his disgust of it; er hat sie ~ bewahrt, in den sicheren Tod zu gehen he saved her from (a) certain death; ich warne Sie ~! I warn you!; ich habe ihn ~ gewarnt, sich in Gefahr zu begeben I warned him not to get into danger.

davor-: ~hängen vt sep to hang in front of it/them; sie hängte das Schloß ~ she put the lock on it; ~legen sep 1 vt to put in front of it/them; leg doch eine Kette ~ put a chain on it/them; 2 vr to lie down in front of it/them; ~liegen vi sep irreg aux haben or sein to lie in front of it/them; ~stehen vi sep irreg aux haben or sein to stand in front of it/them; ~stellen sep 1 vt to put in front of it/them; 2 vr to stand in front of it/them.

dawider adv (old) against it. dafür und ~ for and against.

dawiderreden vi sep (old) to contradict.

dazu adv (emph dazu) (a) (räumlich) there. wozu gehört das? — ~! where does that belong? — there!

(b) (dabei, damit) with it; (außerdem, obendrein auch) into the bargain (inf), at the same time. er ist dumm und ~ auch noch faul he's stupid and lazy with it or into the bargain (inf) or as well; sie ist hübsch und ~ nicht unintelligent she's pretty and not unintelligent either; noch ~ as well, too; noch ~, wo ... when ... too; er machte ein so lustiges Gesicht ~, daß ... he pulled such a funny face as he did/said it that ...; ~ reicht or serviert man am besten Reis it's best to serve rice with it; er singt und spielt Gitarre ~ he sings and accompanies himself on the guitar.

(c) (zu diesem Ergebnis) to that/it. auf dem besten Wege ~ sein, etw zu tun to be well on the way to doing sth; er ist auf dem

besten Wege ~ he's well on the way to it; das führt ~, daß weitere Forderungen gestellt werden that will lead to further demands being made; ~ führt das dann that's what it leads to; wie konnte es nur ~ kommen? how could that happen?; wer weiß, wie sie ~ gekommen ist (zu diesem Auto etc) who knows how she came by it; wer weiß, wie sie ~ gekommen ist, Alkoholikerin zu werden who knows how she came to be an alcoholic; wie komme ich ~? (empört) why on earth should I?; ... aber ich bin nicht ~ gekommen ... but I didn't get round to it; in Verbindung mit n, vb siehe auch dort.

(d) (dafür, zu diesem Zweck) for that/it. ~ bin ich zu alt I'm too old for that; ich bin zu alt ~, noch tanzen zu gehen I'm too old to go dancing; ~ habe ich dich nicht studieren lassen, daß du ... I didn't send you to university so that you could or for you to ...; ich habe ihm ~ geraten I advised him to (do that); Sie sind/die Maschine ist ~ wie geschaffen it's as if you were/the machine was made for it; ~ fähig/bereit sein, etw zu tun to be capable of sth/prepared to do sth; er war nicht ~ fähig/bereit he wasn't capable of it/prepared to; ~ gehört viel Geld that takes a lot of money; ~ ist er da that's what he's there for, that's why he's there; die Erlaubnis/die Mittel/das Recht ~ permission/the means/the right to do it; ich habe keine Lust ~ I don't feel like it; ich habe keine Lust ~, mitzugehen I don't feel like going along; ~ habe ich keine Zeit, da habe ich keine Zeit zu (N Ger inf) I haven't the time (for that); ich habe keine Zeit ~, die Fenster zu putzen I haven't (the) time to clean the windows; ich bin nicht ~ in der Lage I'm not in a position to; in Verbindung mit n, vb siehe auch dort.

(e) (darüber, zum Thema) about that/it. was sagst/meinst du ~? what do you say to/think about that?; meine Gedanken/Meinung ~ my thoughts about/opinion of that; ..., ~ hören Sie jetzt einen Kommentar ... we now bring you a commentary; das Hauptthema war die Inflation; ~ schreibt die Zeitung: ... the main subject was inflation – the paper has this to say about it ...; er hat sich nur kurz ~ geäußert he only commented briefly on that/it.

(f) (in Wendungen) im Gegensatz/Vergleich ~ in contrast to/comparison with that; früher war sie nicht so hysterisch, ~ hat sie ~ gemacht she never used to be so hysterical, he made her like that; früher war er nicht so aggressiv, er ist erst in der Haft ~ geworden he never used to be so aggressive, he only got or became like that in prison; er war nicht immer Lord, er wurde erst ~ gemacht he wasn't born a Lord, he was made or created one; ~ wird man nicht gewählt, sondern ernannt one is appointed rather than elected to that; in Verbindung mit n, vb siehe auch dort.

dazu-: ~geben vt sep irreg to add; siehe Senf; ~gehören vi sep to belong (to it/us etc); (als Ergänzung) to go with it/them; (eingeschlossen sein) to be included (in it/them); bei einer Familienfeier gehört Onkel Otto auch ~ Uncle Otto should be part of any family gathering too; das gehört mit ~ that belongs to/goes with/is included in it; (versteht sich von selbst) it's all part of it; es gehört schon einiges ~ that takes a lot; es gehört schon einiges ~, das zu tun it takes a lot to do that; ~gehörig adj attr which goes/go with it/them; Schlüssel etc belonging to it/them; (zu dieser Arbeit gehörend) Werkzeuge, Material necessary; (gebührlich) obligatory; ~kommen vi sep irreg aux sein (a) (ankommen) to arrive (on the scene); er kam zufällig ~ he happened to arrive on the scene; (b) (hinzugefügt werden) to be added; es kommen laufend neue Bücher ~ new books are always being added; es kamen noch mehrere Straftaten ~ there were several other offences; kommt noch etwas ~? is there or will there be anything else?; es kommt noch ~, daß er faul ist on top of that or in addition to that he's lazy; (c) (Aus Sw: Zeit dafür finden) to get round to it; ~legen sep 1 vt to add to it; jdm/sich noch ein Stückchen Fleisch ~legen to give sb/oneself another piece of meat; leg die Sachen ruhig ~ just put the things with it/them; 2 vr to lie down with him/them etc; ~lernen vt sep viel/nichts ~lernen to learn a lot more/nothing new; man kann immer was ~lernen there's always something to learn; schon wieder was ~gelernt! you learn something (new) every day!

dazumal adv (old) in those days; siehe Anno.

dazu-: ~rechnen vt sep (a) Kosten, Betrag, Zahl to add on; (b) (mit berücksichtigen) to consider also; ~schauen vi sep (Aus) siehe zusehen; ~schreiben vt sep irreg to add; schreiben Sie diesen Titel noch ~ add this title too; ~setzen sep 1 vt (a) können wir den Jungen hier noch ~setzen? could the boy sit here too?; (b) (~schreiben) to add; 2 vr to join him/us etc; komm, setz dich doch ~ come and sit with or join us; ~tun vt sep irreg (inf) to add.

Dazutun nt er hat es ohne dein ~ geschafft he managed it without your doing/saying anything; ohne dein ~ hätte er es nicht geschafft he wouldn't have managed it if you hadn't done/said something or without your doing/saying anything.

dazwischen adv (räumlich, zeitlich) in between; (in der betreffenden Menge, Gruppe) amongst them, in with them. die Betten standen dicht nebeneinander, es hing nur ein Vorhang ~ the beds were very close together, there was only a curtain between them.

dazwischen-: ~fahren vi sep irreg aux sein (a) (eingreifen) to step in and put a stop to things; (b) (unterbrechen) to break in, to interrupt; jdm ~fahren to interrupt sb; ~funken vi sep (Rad) to jam the signal; (inf: eingreifen) to put one's oar in (inf etw vereiteln) to put a spoke in it (inf); ~kommen vi sep irreg aux sein (a) mit der Hand/der Hose etc ~kommen to get one hand/trousers etc caught in it/them; (b) (störend erscheinen) to come along and spoil things; dann kam mir diese lästige Grippe ~ then I caught the wretched flu which spoilt things; ... wenn nichts ~kommt! ... if all goes well; leider ist or mir ist leider etwas ~gekommen, ich kann nicht dabeisein something has come or cropped up, I'm afraid I can't be there; ~legen vt sep to put in between; ~liegend adj attr die ~liegenden Seiten/Monate/Bahnhöfe etc the pages/months/stations in between; ~reden vi sep (a) (unterbrechen) to interrupt (jdm sb); (b) siehe dreinreden; ~rufen vti sep irreg to yell out; ~schlagen vi sep irreg to wade in, to lam in (esp US inf); ~stehen vi sep irreg aux haben or sein (a) (lit) to be amongst or (zwischen zweien) between them; (b) (zwischen den Parteien) to be neutral; (c) (geh: hindernd) to be in the way; ~treten vi sep irreg aux sein (a) (schlichtend) to intervene; sein D~treten his intervention; (b) (geh: störend) to come between them.

DB [de:'be:] f - abbr of **Deutsche Bundesbahn**.

DDR [de:de:'ɛr] f - abbr of **Deutsche Demokratische Republik** GDR, German Democratic Republic, East Germany.

DDR-Bürger m East German, citizen of the German Democratic Republic.

Dealer(in f) ['di:lɐ, -ərɪn] m -s, - (inf) pusher; (international) trafficker.

Debakel nt -s, - debacle. ein ~ erleiden (Stück etc) to be a debacle; damit hat die Regierung ein ~ erlitten that turned into something of a debacle for the government.

Debatte f -, -n debate. etw in die ~ werfen to throw sth into the discussion; etw zur ~ stellen to put sth up for discussion or (Parl) debate; was steht zur ~? what is being discussed or is under discussion?; (Parl) what is being debated?; das steht hier nicht zur ~ that's not the issue; sich in eine ~ (über etw acc) einlassen to enter into a discussion (about sth).

debattelos adj (Parl) without debate.

debattieren* vti to debate. über etw (acc) (mit jdm) ~ to discuss sth (with sb); mit ihm kann man schlecht ~ you can't have a good discussion with him.

Debattierklub m debating society.

Debet nt -s, -s (Fin) debits pl.

Debetseite f (Fin) debit side.

debil adj (Med) feeble-minded.

Debilität f (Med) feeble-mindedness.

debitieren* vt (Fin) to debit. jdn mit einem Betrag ~ to debit an amount to sb, to debit sb with an amount.

Debitor m (Fin) debtor.

Debüt [de'by:] nt -s, -s debut. sein ~ als etw geben to make one's debut as sth.

Debütant m person making his debut; (fig: Anfänger, Neuling) novice.

Debütantin f (a) siehe Debütant. (b) (in der Gesellschaft) debutante, deb.

Debütantinnenball m debutantes' ball.

debütieren* vi (Theat, fig) to make one's debut.

Dechanat nt -(e)s, -e (Eccl) deanery.

Dechanei f (Eccl) deanery, dean's residence.

Dechant m (Eccl) dean.

dechiffrieren* [deʃɪ'fri:rən] vt to decode; Text, Geheimschrift auch to decipher.

Dechiffrierung f siehe vt decoding; deciphering.

Deck nt -(e)s, -s deck; (in Parkhaus) level. auf ~ on deck; an ~ gehen to go on deck; alle Mann an ~! all hands on deck!; unter or von ~ gehen to go below deck; nicht ganz auf ~ sein (inf) to feel under the weather (inf); wieder auf ~ sein (inf) to be in the pink again (dated inf).

Deck-: ~adresse, ~anschrift f accommodation or cover (US) address; ~anstrich m top or final coat; ~aufbauten pl (Naut) superstructure sing; ~bett nt feather quilt; ~blatt nt (Bot) bract; (von Zigarre) wrapper; (Schutzblatt) cover; (Einlageblatt) overlay.

Deckchen nt mat; (auf Tablett) traycloth; (Torten~) doily; (auf Sessel etc) antimacassar; (für Lehne) arm-cover.

Deckdienst m (Naut) deck duty.

Decke f -, -n (a) cloth; (Woll~) blanket; (kleiner) rug; (Stepp~) quilt; (Bett~) cover; (fig: Schnee~, Staub~ etc) blanket. unter die ~ kriechen to pull the bedclothes up over one's head; sich nach der ~ strecken (fig) to cut one's coat according to one's cloth; mit jdm unter einer ~ stecken (fig) to be in league or in cahoots (inf) or hand in glove with sb.
(b) (Zimmer~) ceiling; (Min) roof. es tropft von der ~ there's water coming through the ceiling; an die ~ gehen (inf) to hit the roof (inf); vor Freude an die ~ springen (inf) to jump for joy; mir fällt die ~ auf den Kopf (fig inf) I feel really claustrophobic or shut in.
(c) (Schicht) layer; (Straßen~) surface; (Reifen~) outer tyre or cover or casing.
(d) (Buch~) cover.
(e) (Hunt) skin.

Deckel m -s, - lid; (von Schachtel, Glas auch, von Flasche) top; (Buch~, Uhr~) cover; (inf: Hut, Mütze) titfer (Brit inf), hat. eins auf den ~ kriegen (inf) (geschlagen werden) to get hit on the head; (ausgeschimpft werden) to be given a (good) talking-to (inf); jdm eins auf den ~ geben (inf) (schlagen) to smash sb on the head; (ausschimpfen) to give sb a (good) talking-to (inf); siehe Topf.

Deckel- in cpds with a lid.

deckeln 1 vt (a) (zu~) to cover. ein Dach mit Schiefer/Ziegeln ~ to roof a building with slate/tiles; ein Dach mit Stroh/Reet ~ to thatch a roof (with straw/reeds); gedeckter Gang/Wagen covered walk/hard-topped car; siehe auch gedeckt.
(b) (zurechtmachen) Tisch, Tafel to set, to lay. es ist für vier Personen gedeckt the table is laid or set for four (people); sich an einen gedeckten Tisch setzen (lit) to find one's meal ready and waiting; (fig) to be handed everything on a plate.
(c) (breiten) die Hand/ein Tuch über etw (acc) ~ to cover sth

with one's hand/a cloth, to put one's hand/a cloth over sth.
(d) (schützen) to cover; (Ftbl) Spieler auch to mark; Komplizen to cover up for.
(e) Kosten, Schulden, Bedarf to cover, to meet. mein Bedarf ist gedeckt I have all I need; (fig inf) I've had enough (to last me some time); damit ist unser Bedarf gedeckt that will meet or cover our needs; wir haben sofort unseren Bedarf gedeckt we immediately obtained enough to meet or cover our needs.
(f) (Comm, Fin: absichern) Scheck, Darlehen to cover; Defizit to offset. der Schaden wird voll durch die Versicherung gedeckt the cost of the damage will be fully met by the insurance.
(g) (begatten) Stute, Ziege to cover.
2 vi to cover; (Boxen) to guard; (Ftbl: Spieler ~ auch) to mark; (Tisch~) to lay a/the table. du mußt besser ~ (Ftbl) you must mark your opponent better; (Boxen) you must improve your guard; es ist gedeckt luncheon/dinner is served.
3 vr (a) (Standpunkte, Interessen, Begriffe) to coincide; (Aussagen) to correspond, to agree; (Math: Dreiecke, Figur) to be congruent. sich ~de Dreiecke congruent triangles; sich ~de Begriffe/Interessen concepts/interests which coincide.
(b) (sich schützen) to defend oneself; (mit Schild etc) to protect oneself; (Boxer etc) to cover oneself; (sich absichern) to cover oneself.

Decken-: ~balken m ceiling beam; ~beleuchtung f ceiling lighting; ~gemälde nt ceiling fresco; ~gewölbe nt (Archit) vaulting; ~heizung f overhead heating; ~konstruktion f roof construction; die gesamte ~konstruktion wurde zerstört the whole roof was destroyed; ~lampe f ceiling light; ~malerei f ceiling fresco; ~träger m ceiling girder.

Deck-: ~farbe f opaque water colour; ~flügel m (Zool) wing case; ~fracht f (Naut) deck cargo; ~geld nt (Agr) stud fee; ~glas nt (Opt) cover glass; ~haar nt top hair; ~haus nt (Naut) deckhouse; ~hengst m stud(horse), stallion; ~mantel m (fig) mask, blind; unter dem ~mantel von ... under the guise of ...; ~name m assumed name; (Mil) code name; ~offizier m (Naut) = warrant officer; ~passagier m (Naut) first-class passenger; ~plane f (Aut) tarpaulin; ~platte f (Build) slab; (von Mauer) coping stone; (von Grab) covering stone or slab; ~salon m (Naut) first-class lounge; ~schicht f surface layer; (von Straße) surface; (Geol) top layer or stratum; ~station f stud (farm); ~stein m (Build) coping stone; (von Grab) covering stone.

Deckung f (a) (Schutz) cover; (Ftbl, Chess) defence; (Boxen, Fechten) guard. in ~ gehen to take cover; ~ suchen to seek cover; volle ~! (Mil) take cover!; jdm ~ geben to cover sb; (Feuerschutz auch) to give sb cover.
(b) (Verheimlichung) die ~ von etw covering up for sth; er kann mit ~ durch den Minister rechnen he can count on the minister covering up for him.
(c) (Comm, Fin) (von Scheck, Wechsel) cover; (das Decken) covering; (von Darlehen) security; (das Begleichen) meeting. der Scheck ist ohne ~ the cheque is not covered; ein Darlehen ohne ~ an unsecured loan; zur ~ seiner Schulden to meet his debts; als ~ für seine Schulden as security or surety for his debts; dafür ist auf meinem Konto keine ~ there are no funds to cover that in my account; die Versicherung übernahm die ~ des Schadens the insurance company agreed to meet the cost of the damage.
(d) (Befriedigung) meeting. eine ~ der Nachfrage ist unmöglich demand cannot possibly be met.
(e) (Übereinstimmung) (Math) congruence. zur ~ bringen (Math) to make congruent; lassen sich diese Standpunkte/Interessen zur ~ bringen? can these points of view/interests be made to coincide?; diese beiden Zeugenaussagen lassen sich schwer zur ~ bringen these two statements can't be made to agree.
(f) (rare: Deckschicht) covering layer.

Deckungs-: ~auflage f (Typ) break-even quantity; ~fehler m (Ftbl) error by the defence; ~feuer nt (Mil) covering fire; im ~feuer der Kameraden under covering fire from their etc comrades; d~gleich adj (Math) congruent; d~gleich sein (fig) to coincide; (Aussagen) to agree; ~gleichheit f (Math) congruence; wegen der ~gleichheit der Ansichten/Aussagen because of the degree to which these views coincide/these statements agree; ~graben m (Mil) shelter trench; ~kapital nt (Insur) covering funds pl; ~loch nt (a) (Mil) foxhole; (b) (Fin) dafür hat der Haushalt ein ~loch no provision has been made for that in the Budget; ~lücke f (Fin) siehe ~loch (b).

Deck-: ~weiß nt opaque white; ~wort nt code word.

Decoder [de'ko:dɐ, dɪ'koʊdə] m -s, - decoder.

decodieren* vt to decode.

Decoding [dɪ'koʊdɪŋ] nt -s, -s decoding.

Décolleté [dekɔl'te:] nt -s, -s siehe Dekolleté.

decouragiert [dekura'ʒi:ɐt] adj (dated geh) disheartened, dispirited.

Decrescendo [dekre'ʃɛndo] nt -s, -s or Decrescendi (Mus) diminuendo.

Dedikation f (geh) (a) (Widmung) dedication. (b) (Schenkung) gift.

Dedikations|exemplar nt presentation copy.

dedizieren* vt (geh) (a) (widmen) to dedicate. (b) (schenken) jdm etw ~ to present sth to sb.

Deduktion f deduction.

deduktiv adj deductive.

deduzieren* vt to deduce (aus from).

Deern [de:ɐn] f -, -s (N Ger inf) lass(ie).

De|eskalation f (Mil) de-escalation.

Deez m -es, -e (hum inf) siehe Dez.

de facto adv de facto.

De-facto-Anerkennung f (Pol) de facto recognition.
Defäkation f (form) defecation.
defäkieren* vi (form) to defecate.
Defätismus m, no pl defeatism.
Defätist m defeatist.
defätistisch adj defeatist no adv.
defäzieren* vi (form) siehe **defäkieren**.
defekt adj Gerät etc faulty, defective. **geistig/moralisch ~ sein** to be mentally/morally deficient.
Defekt m -(e)s, -e fault, defect; (Med) deficiency. **körperlicher/geistiger ~** physical defect/mental deficiency; **einen ~ haben** to be faulty or defective; (inf: von Mensch) to be a bit lacking (inf).
defektiv adj (Gram) defective.
Defektivum nt -s, **Defektiva** (Gram) defective.
defensiv adj Maßnahmen, Taktik defensive; Fahrweise defensive (US), non-aggressive. **sich ~ verhalten** to be on the defensive.
Defensivbündnis nt defence alliance.
Defensive [-'zi:və] f, no pl defensive. **in der ~ bleiben** to remain on the defensive; **jdn in die ~ drängen** to force sb onto the defensive.
Defensivität [-vi'tɛːt] f defensiveness; (von Fahrweise) defensiveness (US) (gen of), lack of aggression (gen in).
Defensiv- in cpds defensive; **~krieg** m defensive warfare; **~spiel** nt defensive game; **~stellung** f defensive position, position of defence.
Defilee [defi'le:] nt -s, -s or -n [-e:ən] (Mil) march-past; (fig) parade.
defilieren* vi aux haben or sein (Mil) to march past; (fig) to parade past.
definierbar adj definable. **schwer/leicht ~** hard/easy to define.
definieren* vt to define.
Definition f definition.
definitiv adj definite.
definitorisch adj (geh) Frage, Problem of definition. **ein ~ schwieriges Problem** a problem which is hard to define.
defizient adj deficient.
Defizit nt -s, -e (Fehlbetrag) deficit; (Mangel) deficiency (an + dat of).
defizitär adj in deficit. **das Bahnwesen entwickelt sich immer ~er** the railways have a larger deficit every year; **die ~e Entwicklung der Organisation** the trend in the organization to run to a deficit; **eine ~e Haushaltspolitik führen** to follow an economic policy which can only lead to deficit.
Deflation f (Econ) deflation.
deflationär, deflationistisch adj deflationary no adv.
Deflationspolitik f deflationary policy.
deflatorisch adj (Econ) siehe **deflationär**.
Deflektor m deflector.
Defloration f defloration.
deflorieren* vt to deflower.
Deformation f deformation, distortion; (Mißbildung) deformity; (Entstellung) disfigurement.
deformieren* vt (Tech) to deform, to contort; (lit, fig: mißbilden) to deform; (entstellen) to disfigure. **in einer Schlägerei haben sie ihm die Nase deformiert** they flattened his nose (for him) in a fight; **eine deformierte Nase** a misshapen nose.
Deformierung f (a) (das Deformieren) deformation; (Entstellung) disfigurement. (b) siehe **Deformation**.
Deformität f (Med) deformity.
Defraudant m (old) defrauder.
Defroster m -s, - (Aut) heated windscreen; (Sprühmittel) deicer; (im Kühlschrank) defroster.
deftig adj (a) (derb, urwüchsig) Witz, Humor ribald. (b) (kräftig) Lüge whopping (inf), huge; Mahlzeit solid; Wurst etc substantial, good solid attr; Ohrfeige cracking (inf). **er hat sich ganz ~ ins Zeug gelegt** he really got going (inf); **dann langten die Kinder ~ zu** then the kids really got stuck in (inf).
Deftigkeit f, no pl siehe adj (a) ribaldry. (b) hugeness; solidness; substantialness; soundness.
degagieren* [dega'ʒiːrən] vt (Fechten) to disengage.
Degen¹ m -s, - rapier; (Sportfechten) épée. **mit bloßem or nacktem ~** with one's rapier drawn; siehe **kreuzen**.
Degen² m -s, - (old liter) knight.
Degeneration f degeneration.
Degenerationserscheinung f sign of degeneration.
degenerativ adj Schäden degenerative.
degenerieren* vi aux sein to degenerate (zu into).
degeneriert adj degenerate.
Degen-: **~fechten** nt épée fencing; **~klinge** f rapier blade; **~knauf** m pommel; **~korb** m guard; **~schlucker** m siehe Schwertschlucker; **~stoß** m thrust from one's/a rapier.
Degout [de'gu:] m -s, no pl (geh) distaste, disgust.
degoutant [degu'tant] adj (geh) distasteful, disgusting.
degoutieren* [degu'ti:rən] vt (geh) to disgust.
Degradation f (Phys) ~ **der Energie** degradation of energy.
degradieren* vt (Mil) to demote (zu to); (fig: herabwürdigen) to degrade. **jdn/etw zu etw ~** (fig) to lower sb/sth to the level of sth.
Degradierung f (Mil) demotion (zu to); (fig) degradation. **diese Behandlung empfand er als (eine) ~** he felt such treatment to be degrading.
Degression f (Fin) degression.
degressiv adj (Fin) degressive.
Degustation f (esp Sw) tasting.
degustieren* vti (esp Sw) Wein to taste.
dehnbar adj (lit) elastic; (fig auch) flexible; Stoff stretch attr,

stretchy (inf), elastic; Metall ductile. **ein ~er Vokal** a vowel which can be lengthened.
Dehnbarkeit f, no pl siehe adj elasticity; flexibility; stretchiness (inf), elasticity; ductility. **Eisen hat eine geringere ~ als Blei** iron is less ductile than lead; **die ~ der Vokale** the degree or extent to which the vowels can be lengthened.
dehnen 1 vt to stretch; (Med auch) to dilate; Laut, Silbe to lengthen. **er sprach das Wort „relax" sehr gedehnt aus** he really drawled the word "relax"; **seine gedehnte Sprechweise** his drawling way of speaking; **Vokale gedehnt aussprechen** to pronounce one's vowels long.
  2 vr to stretch. **er dehnte und streckte sich** he had a good stretch; **die Minuten dehnten sich zu Stunden** (geh) the minutes seemed like hours; **vor ihnen dehnte sich der Ozean** (geh) the ocean stretched out before them; **der Weg dehnte sich endlos** the road seemed to go on for ever.
Dehn- (Ling): **~strich** m length mark; **~stufe** f lengthened grade, dehnstufe (form).
Dehnung f siehe vt stretching; dilation; lengthening.
Dehnungs- (Ling): **~h** nt h with a lengthening effect on the preceding vowel; **~strich** m siehe Dehnstrich.
Dehors [de'o:r(s)] pl: **die ~ wahren** (dated geh) to preserve appearances.
dehydrieren* vt (Chem) to dehydrate.
Dehydrierung f (Chem) dehydration.
Deibel m -s, - (N Ger inf) siehe Teufel, pfui.
Deich m -(e)s, -e dyke, dike (esp US).
Deich-: **~bau** m dyke; (das Bauen) dyke building; **~bruch** m breach in the dyke; **~genossenschaft** f siehe **~verband**; **~graf**, **~hauptmann** m dyke reeve (old) or warden; **~krone** f dyke top.
Deichsel [-ks-] f -, -n shaft; (Doppel~) shafts pl. **ein Pferd in der ~** a horse in or between the shafts; **Ochsen an die ~ spannen** to yoke oxen into or between the shafts.
Deichsel-: **~bruch** m broken shaft/shafts; **~kreuz** nt handle; (b) (Rel) Y-shaped cross.
deichseln [-ks-] vt (inf) to wangle (inf). **das werden wir schon ~** we'll wangle it somehow.
Deich-: **~verband** m association of owners of dyked land; **~vogt** m (old) siehe **~graf**; **~vorland** nt land to the seaward side of a dyke.
Deifikation [deifika'tsio:n] f (Philos) deification.
deifizieren* [dei-] vt (Philos) to deify.
dein 1 poss pron (a) (adjektivisch) (in Briefen: D~) your, thy (obs, dial). **~ doofes/schönes Gesicht** that stupid/beautiful face of yours, your stupid/beautiful face; **rauchst du immer noch ~e 20 Zigaretten pro Tag?** are you still smoking your 20 cigarettes a day?; **herzliche Grüße, D~e Elke** with best wishes, yours or (herzlicher) love Elke; **stets or immer D~ Otto** yours ever, Otto; **D~ Wille geschehe** (Bibl) Thy will be done. (b) (old: substantivisch) yours. **behalte, was ~ ist** keep what is yours.
  2 pers pron gen of du (old, poet) **ich werde ewig ~ gedenken** I shall remember you forever.
deiner pers pron gen of du (geh) of you. **wir werden ~ gedenken** we will remember you.
deine(r, s) poss pron (substantivisch) yours. **der/die/das ~** (geh) yours; **tu du das D~** (geh) you do your bit; **stets or immer der D~** (form) yours ever; **die D~n** (geh) your family, your people; **du und die D~n** (geh: Familie) you and yours; **das D~** (geh: Besitz) what is yours.
deinerseits adv (auf deiner Seite) for your part; (von deiner Seite) on your part. **den Vorschlag hast du ~ gemacht** you made the suggestion yourself.
deinesgleichen pron inv people like you or yourself; (pej auch) your sort, the likes of you. **an Schönheit ist keine ~** (liter) in beauty there is none to equal you (liter); **ich will ~ werden** (liter) I want to be like you!
deinet-: **~halben** (dated), **~wegen** adv (wegen dir) because of you, on account of you, on your account; (dir zuliebe auch) for your sake; (um dich) about you; (für dich) on your behalf; **~willen** adv **um ~willen** for your sake.
deinige poss pron (old, geh) **der/die/das ~** yours; **die D~n** your family or people; **das D~** (Besitz) what is yours; **tu du das D~** you do your bit.
deins poss pron yours.
Deismus m, no pl (Philos) deism.
Deist m (Philos) deist.
deistisch adj (Philos) deistic.
Deiwel (N Ger), **Deixel** (S Ger) m -s, - siehe Teufel.
Déjà-vu-Erlebnis [deʒa'vy:-] nt (Psych) sense or feeling of déjà vu.
de jure adv de jure.
De-jure-Anerkennung f de jure recognition.
Deka nt -(s), - (Aus) siehe Dekagramm.
Dekade f (10 Tage) ten days, ten-day period; (10 Jahre) decade.
dekadent adj decadent.
Dekadenz f, no pl decadence.
dekadisch adj Zahlensystem decimal. **~er Logarithmus** common logarithm.
Deka-: **~eder** m -s, - decahedron; **~gon** nt -s, -e decagon; **~gramm** [(Aus) 'dɛka-] nt decagram(me); **10 ~gramm Schinken** (Aus) 100 grams of ham; **~liter** m decalitre.
Dekalog m -(e)s (Bibl) decalogue.
Dekameron [de'ka:merɔn] nt -s Decameron.
Dekameter m decametre.
Dekan m -s, -e (Univ, Eccl) dean.
Dekanat nt (a) (Univ, Eccl: Amt, Amtszeit) deanship. (b) (Amtssitz) (Univ) office of the dean; (Eccl) deanery.
Dekanei f (Eccl) deanery.
dekarbonisieren* vt to decarbonize; (Aut) to decoke.
dekartellieren*, **dekartellisieren*** vt to decartelize.

Deklamation f declamation. ~en (pej) (empty) rhetoric sing.
deklamatorisch adj declamatory, rhetorical.
deklamieren* vti to declaim.
Deklaration f (alle Bedeutungen) declaration.
deklarieren* vt (alle Bedeutungen) to declare.
Deklarierung f declaration.
deklassieren* vt (a) (Sociol, herabsetzen) to downgrade. (b) (Sport: weit übertreffen) to outclass.
Deklassierung f siehe vt downgrading; outclassing.
deklinabel adj (Gram) declinable.
Deklination f (a) (Gram) declension. (b) (Astron, Phys) declination.
deklinierbar adj (Gram) declinable.
deklinieren* vt (Gram) to decline.
dekodieren* vt siehe decodieren.
Dekolleté [dekɔl'te:] nt -s, -s low-cut or décolleté neckline, décolletage. ein Kleid mit einem tiefen/gewagten ~ a very/daringly low-cut or décolleté dress; ihr ~ war so tief, ... she was wearing such a low-cut or plunging neckline ...; ihr ~ ging fast bis zum Bauchnabel her neckline plunged almost to her navel.
dekolletieren* [dekɔl'ti:rən] vt to give a or cut with a low neckline.
dekolletiert [dekɔl'ti:rt] adj Kleid low-cut, décolleté. eine ~e Dame a woman in a low-cut dress.
Dekolonisation f decolonization.
dekolonisieren* vt to decolonize.
Dekolonisierung f decolonizing.
Dekomposition f decomposition.
Dekompositum nt -s, **Dekomposita** (Ling) (zusammengesetztes Wort) multiple compound, decomposite (form), decompound (form); (Ableitung) compound derivative.
Dekompression f decompression.
Dekompressionskammer f decompression chamber.
Dekontamination f decontamination.
dekontaminieren* vt to decontaminate.
Dekonzentration f deconcentration, decentralization.
Dekor m or nt -s, -s or -e (a) decoration; (von Raum auch) décor; (Muster) pattern. (b) (Theat, Film etc) décor.
Dekorateur(in f) [dekora'tø:n, -ø:rɪn] m (Schaufenster~) window-dresser; (von Innenräumen) interior designer.
Dekoration f (a) no pl (das Ausschmücken) decorating, decoration. (b) (Einrichtung) décor no pl; (Fenster~) window dressing or decoration; (Theat: Bühnenbild) set. zur ~ dienen to be decorative; zu Weihnachten haben viele Kaufhäuser schöne ~en many department stores have beautifully decorated windows for Christmas. (c) (Orden, Ordensverleihung) decoration.
Dekorations-: ~arbeiten pl decorating no pl; ~maler m (interior) decorator; (Theat) scene-painter; ~stoff m (Tex) furnishing fabric; ~stück nt piece of the décor; das ist nur ein ~stück that's just for decoration.
dekorativ adj decorative.
dekorieren* vt to decorate; Schaufenster to dress.
Dekorierung f siehe vt decoration; dressing.
Dekorum nt -s, no pl (liter) propriety, decorum. das ~ wahren to maintain or observe the proprieties; das ~ verletzen to go against or infringe the proprieties.
Dekostoff m siehe Dekorationsstoff.
Dekret nt -(e)s, -e decree.
dekretieren* vt to decree.
dekuvrieren* [deku'vri:rən] (geh) 1 vt Skandal, Machenschaften to expose, to uncover; Person, Betrüger etc to expose. 2 vr to reveal oneself. er hat sich als Spion dekuvriert he revealed himself to be a spy.
Deleatur(zeichen) nt -s, - (Typ) deletion mark.
Delegat m -en, -en delegate.
Delegation f (alle Bedeutungen) delegation.
Delegationschef m head of a delegation. der koreanische ~ the head of the Korean delegation.
delegieren* vt (alle Bedeutungen) to delegate (an + acc to).
Delegierten-: ~konferenz, ~versammlung f delegates' conference.
Delegierte(r) mf decl as adj delegate.
delektieren* (geh) 1 vt sich an etw (dat) ~ to delight in sth; an dem Obst könnt ihr euch ~ the fruit is there for your delectation (liter). 2 vt jdn mit etw ~ to delight sb with sth; sie delektierten den Sultan mit Tänzen they danced for the sultan's delectation (liter).
Delfter adj attr Porzellan etc Delft.
delikat adj (a) (wohlschmeckend) exquisite, delicious. (b) (behutsam) delicate; Andeutung auch gentle. (c) (heikel) Problem, Frage delicate, sensitive; (gewagt) risqué. (d) (geh: empfindlich) delicate.
Delikateß- in cpds top-quality.
Delikatesse f (a) (Leckerbissen, fig) delicacy. ein Geschäft für Obst und ~n a fruit shop and delicatessen sing. (b) no pl (Feinfühligkeit) delicacy, sensitivity.
Delikatessen-: ~geschäft nt, ~handlung f delicatessen sing.
Delikt nt -(e)s, -e (Jur) offence; (schwerer) crime.
delinquent [delɪŋ'kvɛnt] adj (Sociol, Psych) delinquent.
Delinquent(in f) [delɪŋ'kvɛnt] m (geh) offender.
Delinquenz [delɪŋ'kvɛnts] f (Sociol, Psych) delinquency.
Delir nt -s, -e (Med) siehe Delirium.
delirieren* vi (geh, Med) to be delirious. er delirierte im Fieber he was delirious with fever.
Delirium nt delirium. im ~ sein to be delirious or in a state of delirium; (betrunken) to be paralytic (inf); im ~ redete der Kranke wirr und konfus the sick man raved deliriously; in seinen Delirien whenever he was delirious or (betrunken)

paralytic (inf); ~ tremens delirium tremens, the DT's.
deliziös adj (liter) most delectable.
Delle f -, -n (a) (dial) dent. eine ~ bekommen to get a dent, to get or be dented. (b) (Boden~) hollow, dip.
delogieren* [delo'ʒi:rən] vt (Aus) Mieter to evict.
Delogierung f (Aus) eviction.
Delphi nt -s Delphi. das Orakel von ~ the Delphic oracle, the oracle of Delphi.
Delphin[1] m -s, -e (Zool) dolphin.
Delphin[2] nt -s, no pl siehe **Delphinschwimmen**.
Delphinarium nt dolphinarium.
Delphinschwimmen nt butterfly.
delphisch adj Delphic. das D~e Orakel the Delphic oracle.
Delta[1] nt -s, -s or **Delten** (Geog) delta.
Delta[2] nt -(s), -s (Buchstabe) delta.
Delta-: d~förmig adj delta-shaped, deltaic (rare); Muskel deltoid; ~mündung f delta estuary; ~muskel m deltoid; ~strahlen pl (Phys) delta rays pl.
de Luxe [də'lyks] adj (Comm) de luxe.
De-Luxe-Ausführung f (Comm) de-luxe version.
dem 1 dat of def art der, das (a) to the; (mit Präposition) the. (b) es ist nicht an ~ that is not the case or how it is; wenn ~ so ist if that is the way it is; wie ~ auch sei be that as it may. 2 dat of dem pron der, das (a) attr to that; (mit Präposition) that. (b) (substantivisch) to that one; that one; (Menschen) to him; him; (von mehreren) to that one; that one. 3 dat of rel pron der, das to whom, that or who(m) ... to; (mit Präposition) who(m); (von Sachen) to which, which or that ... to; which. ~ der Fehler unterlaufen ist, ... whoever made that mistake ...
Demagoge m demagogue.
Demagogentum nt, **Demagogie** f demagogy, demagoguery.
demagogisch adj Rede etc demagogic. er hat in seiner Rede die Tatsachen ~ verzerrt in his speech he twisted the facts to demagogic ends; leider lassen sich die Wähler immer noch ~ beeinflussen sadly voters can still be swayed by demagogues or by demagogic ploys.
Demant m -(e)s, -e (poet) diamond.
demanten adj (poet) siehe **diamanten**.
Demarche [de'marʃə] f -, -n (Pol) (diplomatic) representation, démarche. eine ~ unternehmen to lodge a diplomatic protest.
Demarkation f demarcation.
Demarkationslinie f (Pol, Mil) demarcation line. die ~ des Waffenstillstands the cease-fire line.
demarkieren* vt Grenze, Bereiche to demarcate.
demaskieren* 1 vt to unmask, to expose. jdn als etw ~ to expose sb as sth. 2 vr to unmask oneself, to take off one's mask. sich als etw ~ to show oneself to be sth.
Dementi nt -s, -s denial.
dementieren* 1 vt to deny. 2 vi to deny it.
Dementierung f denial, denying.
dementsprechend 1 adv correspondingly; (demnach) accordingly; bezahlt commensurately. 2 adj appropriate; Bemerkung auch apposite; Gehalt commensurate. er nennt sich Christ, aber sein Verhalten ist nicht ~ he says he is a Christian but he does not behave accordingly or correspondingly.
Demenz f (Med) dementia.
dem-: ~gegenüber adv (wohingegen) on the other hand; (im Vergleich dazu) in contrast; ~gemäß adv, adj siehe ~entsprechend.
demilitarisieren* vt to demilitarize.
Demilitarisierung f demilitarization.
Demimonde [dəmi'mõːd] f -, no pl (pej geh) demimonde.
Demission f (Pol) (Rücktritt) resignation; (Entlassung) dismissal. um seine ~ bitten to ask to be relieved of one's duties; er wurde zur ~ gezwungen he was forced to resign.
demissionieren* vi (Pol, Sw: kündigen) to resign.
Demissionsangebot nt offer of resignation or to resign.
Demiurg m -en or -s, no pl (Myth, liter) demiurge.
dem-: ~nach adv therefore; (~entsprechend) accordingly; ~nächst adv soon; ~nächst (in diesem Kino) coming soon.
Demo f -, -s (inf) demo (inf).
Demobilisation f (Mil) demobilization.
demobilisieren* 1 vt to demobilize; Soldaten auch to demob (Brit inf). 2 vi to demobilize; (Soldat auch) to get or be demobbed (Brit inf).
Demobilisierung f demobilization; (von Soldaten auch) demob (Brit inf).
démodé [de:mo'de:] adj attr (geh) outmoded.
Demograph(in f) m demographer.
Demographie f demography.
demographisch adj demographic.
Demokrat(in f) m -en, -en democrat.
Demokratie f democracy.
Demokratieverständnis nt understanding of (the meaning of) democracy.
demokratisch adj democratic.
demokratisieren* vt to democratize, to make democratic.
Demokratisierung f democratization.
Demokratismus m, no pl (pej) pseudo-democracy.
demolieren* vt to wreck, to smash up; (Rowdy auch) to vandalize. nach dem Unfall war das Auto total demoliert after the accident the car was a complete wreck; er sah ganz schön demoliert aus (inf) he was a real mess, he looked pretty badly bashed about.
Demolierung f siehe vt wrecking, smashing-up; vandalizing.
Demonstrant(in f) m demonstrator.
Demonstration f (alle Bedeutungen) demonstration. zur ~

seiner Friedfertigkeit ... as a demonstration of or to demonstrate his peaceful intentions ...; **eine ~ für/gegen etw** demonstration in support of/against sth.

Demonstrations-: ~**marsch** m march; ~**material** nt teaching material or aids pl; ~**objekt** nt teaching aid; ~**recht** nt right to demonstrate or hold demonstrations; ~**zug** m demonstration, (protest) march.

demonstrativ adj demonstrative (auch Gram); Beifall acclamatory; Protest, Fehlen pointed; Beispiel clear. **war seine Abwesenheit ~ oder reiner Zufall?** was his absence a deliberate or pointed gesture or pure chance?; **der Botschafter verließ während der Rede ~ den Saal** during the speech the ambassador pointedly left the room.

Demonstrativ- in cpds (Gram) demonstrative.

demonstrieren* vti (alle Bedeutungen) to demonstrate. **für/gegen etw ~** to demonstrate in support of/against sth; **die Regierung hat ihre Entschlossenheit demonstriert** the government gave a demonstration of or demonstrated its determination.

Demontage [-'ta:ʒə] f -, -n (lit, fig) dismantling.

demontieren* vt (lit, fig) to dismantle; Räder to take off.

Demoralisation f (Entmutigung) demoralization; (Sittenverfall) moral decline.

demoralisieren* vt (entmutigen) to demoralize; (korrumpieren) to corrupt. **die römische Gesellschaft war am Ende so demoralisiert, daß ...** ultimately Roman society had suffered such a moral decline that ...

Demoralisierung f siehe Demoralisation.

Demoskop(in f) m -en -en (opinion) pollster.

Demoskopie f, no pl (public) opinion research.

demoskopisch adj ~**es** Institut (public) opinion research institute; **alle ~en Voraussagen waren falsch** all the predictions in the opinion polls were wrong; **eine ~e Untersuchung** a (public) opinion poll; **das Institut hat die Wählermeinung ~ untersucht** the institute took an opinion poll of the electorate.

dem-: ~**selben** dat of derselbe, dasselbe; ~**unerachtet**, ~**ungeachtet** adv (old) siehe des(sen)ungeachtet.

Demut f -, no pl humility. **in ~** with humility.

demütig adj Bitte, Blick humble.

demütigen 1 vt Gefangenen, Besiegten, Volk to humiliate; (eine Lektion erteilen) stolzen Menschen etc to humble. **2** vr to humble oneself (vor +dat before).

Demütigung f humiliation. **jdm ~en/eine ~ zufügen** to humiliate sb.

Demuts-: ~**gebärde**, ~**haltung** f (esp Zool) submissive posture; **d~voll** adj humble.

demzufolge adv therefore.

den 1 (a) acc of def art **der** the. **(b)** dat pl of def art **der, die, das** the; to the. **2** acc of dem pron **der (a)** attr **der, die, das** that. **(b)** (substantivisch) that one; (Menschen) him; (von mehreren) that one. **3** acc of rel pron **der** who(m), that; (von Sachen) which, that.

Denaturalisation, Denaturalisierung f denaturalization.

denaturalisieren* vt to denaturalize.

denaturieren* 1 vt to denature. **2** vi zu etw ~ (fig geh) to degenerate into sth.

Dendrit m -en, -en (Geol, Med) dendrite.

Dendro-: ~**chronologie** f dendrochronology; ~**logie** f dendrology.

denen 1 dat pl of dem pron **der, die, das** to them; (mit Präposition) them. **2** dat pl of rel pron **der, die, das** to whom, that or who(m) ... to; (mit Präposition) whom; (von Sachen) to which, that or which ... to; which.

dengeln vt Sense to sharpen, to hone.

Denk-: ~**ansatz** m starting point; ~**anstoß** m something to start one thinking; **jdm ~anstöße geben** to give sb something to think about, to give sb food for thought; ~**art** f way of thinking; **eine edle/niedrige ~art** high-mindedness/low-mindedness; ~**aufgabe** f brain-teaser; **d~bar 1** adj conceivable; **es ist durchaus d~bar, daß er kommt** it's very possible or likely that he'll come; **2** adv extremely; (ziemlich) rather; **den d~bar schlechtesten/besten Eindruck machen** to make the worst/best possible impression; **sich im d~bar besten Einvernehmen trennen** to part on the very best of terms.

Denken nt -s, no pl **(a)** (Gedankenwelt) thought; (Denkweise) thinking. **ich kann seinem ~ nicht folgen** I can't follow his thinking or train of thought; **im ~ Goethes/der Aufklärung** in Goethe's thought/in the thinking of the Enlightenment; **abstraktes ~** abstract thought or thinking; **klares ~** clear thinking, clarity of thought. **(b)** (Gedanken) thoughts pl, thinking. **(c)** (Denkvermögen) mind.

denken pret **dachte**, ptp **gedacht 1** vi **(a)** (überlegen) to think. **bei sich ~** to think to oneself; **hin und her ~** to rack one's brains (über +acc over); **wo ~ Sie hin!** what an idea!; **ich denke, also bin ich** I think, therefore I am; **der Mensch denkt, (und) Gott lenkt** (Prov) man proposes, God disposes (Prov); **das gibt mir/einem zu ~** it starts you thinking, it makes you think; **langsam/schnell ~** to be a slow/quick thinker; **so darf man eben nicht ~** you shouldn't think like that. **(b)** (urteilen) to think (über +acc about, of). **wie ~ Sie darüber?** what do you think about it?; **schlecht von jdm** or **über jdn ~** to think badly of sb; **ich denke genauso** I think the same (way); **wieviel soll ich spenden? — wie Sie ~** how much should I donate? — it's up to you or as much as you think fit. **(c)** (gesinnt sein) to think. **edel ~** to be of a noble frame of mind, to be noble-minded; **kleinlich ~** to be petty-minded; **alle, die damals liberal gedacht haben, ...** all those who were thinking along liberal lines ...; **da muß man etwas großzügiger ~** one must be more liberally minded or liberal.

(d) (im Sinn haben) **an jdn/etw ~** to think of sb/sth, to have sb/sth in mind; **daran ist gar nicht zu ~** that's (quite) out of the question; **ich denke nicht daran!** no way! (inf), not on your life!; **ich denke nicht daran, das zu tun** there's no way I'm going to do that (inf), I wouldn't dream of doing that.

(e) (besorgt sein) **an jdn/etw ~** to think of or about sb/sth; **an die bevorstehende Prüfung denke ich mit gemischten Gefühlen** I'm looking ahead to the coming exam with mixed feelings.

(f) (sich erinnern) **an jdn/etw ~** to think of sb/sth; **solange ich ~ kann** (for) as long as I can remember or recall; **denk daran!** don't forget!; **an das Geld habe ich gar nicht mehr gedacht** I had forgotten about the money; **~ Sie zum Beispiel an England im 19. Jahrhundert** look at or think of England in the 19th century, for example; **wenn ich so an früher denke** when I cast my mind back, when I think back; **~ Sie mal an die Kriegsjahre** think of the war; **die viele Arbeit, ich darf gar nicht daran ~** all that work, it doesn't bear thinking about.

(g) (Einfall haben) **an etw** (acc) **~** to think of sth; **das erste, woran ich dachte** the first thing I thought of, the first thing that came or sprang to (my) mind.

2 vt **(a)** Gedanken to think; (sich vorstellen) to conceive of. **er war der erste, der diesen Gedanken gedacht hat** he was the first to conceive of this idea; **was denkst du jetzt?** what are you thinking (about)?; **ich denke gar nichts** I'm not thinking about anything; **... das wage ich kaum zu ~ ...** I hardly dare think; **wieviel Trinkgeld gibt man? — soviel, wie Sie ~** how big a tip does one give? — it's up to you or as much as you think fit; **sagen, was man denkt** to say what one thinks, to speak one's mind.

(b) (annehmen, glauben) to think. **(nur) Schlechtes/Gutes von jdm ~** to think ill/well of sb; **wer hätte das (von ihr) gedacht!** who'd have thought or believed it (of her)!; **was sollen bloß die Leute ~!** what will people think!; **ich dächte, ...** I would have thought ...; **ich denke schon** I think so; **ich denke nicht** I don't think so, I think not; **denkste!** (inf) that's what you think!

(c) (vorsehen) **für jdn/etw gedacht sein** to be intended or meant for sb/sth; **so war das nicht gedacht** that wasn't what I/he etc had in mind.

3 vr **(a)** (vorstellen) **sich** (dat) **etw ~** to imagine; **das kann ich mir ~** I can imagine; **wieviel soll ich Ihnen zahlen? — was Sie sich** (dat) **so gedacht haben** what shall I pay you? — whatever you had in mind; **ich könnte ihn mir gut als Direktor ~** I could just imagine him or see him as director; **wie denkst du dir das eigentlich?** (inf) what's the big idea? (inf); **ich habe mir das so gedacht: ...** this is what I had in mind: ..., this is what I'd thought: ...; **das habe ich mir gleich gedacht** I thought that from the first; **das habe ich mir gedacht** I thought so; **das habe ich mir beinahe gedacht** I thought as much; **dachte ich mir's doch!** I knew it!; **ich denke mir mein Teil** I have my own thoughts on the matter; **das läßt sich ~!** that's very likely; siehe **gedacht**.

(b) (beabsichtigen) **sich** (dat) **etw bei etw ~** to mean sth by sth; **ich habe mir nichts Böses dabei gedacht** I meant no harm (in it); **was hast du dir bei dieser Bemerkung bloß gedacht?** what were you thinking of when you made that remark?; **sie läuft zu Hause immer nackt herum und denkt sich nichts dabei** she runs around the house with nothing on and doesn't think anything of it.

Denker(in f) m -s, - thinker. **das Volk der Dichter und ~** the nation of poets and philosophers.

Denkerfalte f usu pl (hum) furrow on one's brow. **er zog seine Stirn in ~n** (acc) he furrowed his brow.

denkerisch adj intellectual.

Denkerstirn f lofty brow.

Denk-: **d~fähig** adj capable of thinking; **nicht mehr d~fähig** incapable of thinking (straight) (any more); **als d~fähiger Mensch** as an intelligent person; **d~fähigkeit** f ability to think; **d~faul** adj (mentally) lazy; **er ist d~faul** he can't be bothered to think; **sei nicht so d~faul!** get your brain working!; ~**faulheit** f (mental) laziness or sloth; ~**fehler** m mistake in the/one's logic, flaw in the/one's reasoning; **ein ~fehler in der Beurteilung der Lage** an error in the assessment of the situation; ~**form** f way of thinking, mode of thought; ~**gesetze** pl laws pl of thought; ~**gewohnheit** f usu pl thought habit, habitual way of thinking; ~**hilfe** f clue, hint; (Merkhilfe) reminder, ~**inhalt** m idea; ~**kategorie** f usu pl thought category; **in ~alten ~kategorien erzogen** brought up to think in outmoded categories; ~**kraft** f mental capacity.

Denkmal [-ma:l] nt -s, ¨-er or (liter) -e **(a)** (Gedenkstätte, monument, memorial (für to); (Standbild) statue. **die Stadt hat ihm ein ~ gesetzt** the town put up or erected a memorial/statue to him; **er hat sich** (dat) **ein ~ gesetzt** he has left a memorial (to himself). **(b)** (Zeugnis: literarisch etc) monument (gen to).

Denkmal(s)-: ~**kunde** f study of historical monuments; ~**pflege** f preservation of historical monuments; ~**pfleger** m curator of monuments; ~**schändung** f defacing a monument or art; ~**schändungen** defacing monuments; ~**schutz** m protection of historical monuments; **etw unter ~schutz stellen** to classify sth as a historical monument; **unter ~schutz stehen** to be under a preservation order or classified as a historical monument.

Denk-: ~**modell** nt (Entwurf) plan for further discussion; (wissenschaftlich) working hypothesis; (~muster) thought pattern; ~**muster** nt pattern of thought; **d~notwendig** ad (Philos) logically necessary; ~**pause** f break, adjournment **eine ~pause einlegen** to have a break or to adjourn to think things over; **Meier, hast du wieder ~pause?** (inf) asleep again Meier?; ~**prozeß** m thought-process; ~**psychologie** psychology of thought; ~**schablone** f (pej) (set or hackneyed thought pattern; ~**schema** nt thought pattern; ~**schrift** f memorandum; ~**schritt** m step (in one's/sb's/the thinking); ~**spiel** nt mental or mind game; ~**sport** m mental exercise; „~**sport**" "puzzle corner"; **er ist ein Liebhaber des ~sports** he loves doing puzzles and brain-teasers; ~**sportaufgabe** f brain-teaser; ~**spruch** m motto.

denkste interj siehe **denken 2 (b)**.

Denk-: ~**stil** m style of thinking or thought; ~**system** nt system of thought; ~**tätigkeit** f mental activity; ~**übung** f mental exercise.

Denk(ungs)-: ~**art**, ~**weise** f siehe **Denkart**.

Denk-: ~**vermögen** nt capacity for thought, intellectual capacity; ~**vers** m mnemonic (verse); ~**vorgang** m siehe ~**prozeß**; ~**weise** f siehe ~**art**; d~**würdig** adj memorable, notable; ~**würdigkeit** f (a) (von Ereignis) memorability, notability; (b) (liter: Ereignis) memorable or notable event; ~**würdigkeiten** memorabilia pl; ~**zentrum** nt thought centre; ~**zettel** m (inf) warning.

denn 1 conj (a) (kausal) because, for (esp liter).
(b) (geh: vergleichend) than. **schöner ~ je** more beautiful than ever.
(c) (konzessiv) **es sei ~, (daß)** unless; ..., **du segnest mich ~** (Bibl) ... except thou blessest me (obs, Bibl); **siehe geschweige**.
2 adv (a) (verstärkend) **wann/woran/wer/wie/wo ~?** when/why/who/how/where?; **ich habe ihn gestern gesehen — wo ~?** I saw him yesterday — oh, where?; **wieso ~?** why?, how come?; **warum ~ nicht?** why not?; **wie geht's ~?** how are you or things then?, how's it going then?; **wo bleibt er ~?** where has he got to?; **was soll das ~?** what's all this then?; **das ist ~ doch die Höhe!** (well,) that really is the limit!
(b) (N Ger inf: dann) then. **na, ~ man los!** right then, let's go!; **na, ~ prost!** well, cheers (then).

dennoch adv nevertheless, nonetheless, still. **~ liebte er sie** yet he still loved her or he loved her nevertheless; **er hat es ~ getan** (but or yet) he still did it, he did it nonetheless or nevertheless; **und ~, ...** and yet ...; **schön und ~ häßlich** beautiful and yet ugly.

Denominativ nt (Ling) denominative.
Denotat nt (Ling) denotation.
Denotation f (Ling) denotation.
denselben 1 acc of **derselbe**. **2** dat of **dieselben**.
dental adj (Med, Ling) dental.
Dentalisierung f (Ling) dentalization.
Dental(laut) m -s, -e (Ling) dental.
Dentist(in f) m (dated) dentist.
Denunziant(in f) m (pej) informer.
Denunziantentum nt system of informers.
Denunziation f informing no pl (von on, against); (Anzeige) denunciation (von of).
denunzieren* vt (pej) (a) (verraten) to inform on or against, to denounce (bei to). (b) (geh: verunglimpfen) to denounce, to condemn.
Deodorant nt -s, -s or -e deodorant.
Deodorantspray nt or m deodorant spray.
deodorierend adj deodorant.
Deospray nt or m siehe **Deodorantspray**.
Departement [departə'mãː] nt -s, -s (esp Sw) department.
Dependance [depã'dãːs] f -, -n (geh) branch. (b) (Hotel~) annexe.
Dependenz f (Philos) dependence.
Dependenzgrammatik f dependence grammar.
Depersonalisation f (Psych) depersonalization.
Depesche f -, -n (dated) dispatch.
depeschieren* vti (dated) to telegraph (dated).
deplaciert [depla'siːrt], **deplaziert** adj out of place.
Deponie f dump, disposal site.
deponieren* vt (geh) to deposit.
Deponierung f (geh) depository.
Deportation f deportation.
deportieren* vt to deport.
Deportierte(r) mf decl as adj deportee.
Depositar, Depositär m (Fin) depositary.
Depositen pl (Fin) deposits pl.
Depositen- (Fin): ~**bank** f deposit bank; ~**gelder** pl deposits pl, deposit(ed) money; ~**geschäft** nt deposit banking; ~**konto** nt deposit account.
Depot [de'poː] nt -s, -s depot; (Aufbewahrungsort auch) depository; (in Bank) strong room; (aufbewahrte Gegenstände) deposits pl; (Med) deposit.
Depot-: ~**behandlung** f (Med) depot treatment; ~**fett** nt (Med) adipose fat; ~**geschäft** nt (Fin) security deposit business.
Depp m -en or -s, -e(n) (S Ger, Aus, Sw pej) twit (inf).
deppert adj (S Ger, Aus; inf) dopey (inf).
Depravation [deprava'tsioːn] f (geh) depravity.
depraviert [depra'viːrt] adj (geh) depraved.
Depression f (alle Bedeutungen) depression.
depressiv adj depressive; (Econ) depressed.
Depressivität f depressiveness.
deprimieren* vt to depress.
deprimierend adj depressing.
deprimiert adj depressed.
Deprivation [depriva'tsioːn] f (Psych) deprivation.
deprivieren* ['-viːrən] vt (Psych) to deprive.
Deputat nt (a) (esp Agr) payment in kind. (b) (Sch) teaching load.
Deputation f deputation.
deputieren* vt to deputize.
Deputierte(r) mf decl as adj deputy.
Deputiertenkammer f (Pol) Chamber of Deputies.
der¹ 1 (a) gen of def art **die** sing, pl of the. **das Miauen ~ Katze** the miaowing of the cat, the cat's miaowing.
(b) dat of def art **die** sing to the; (mit Präposition) the.
2 dat of dem pron **die** sing (a) (adjektivisch) that; to that.
(b) (substantivisch) her; to her.
3 dat of rel pron **die** sing to whom, that or who(m) ... to; (mit Präposition) who(m); (von Sachen) to which, which ... to; which.
der², die, das, pl **die 1** def art gen des, der, des, pl der; dat dem, der, dem, pl den; acc den, die, das, pl die die. **der/die Arme!** the poor man/woman or girl!; **die Toten** the dead pl; **die Engländer** the English pl; **der Engländer** (dated inf: die Engländer) the Englishman; **der Hans** (inf)/**der Faust** Hans/Faust; **der kleine Hans** little Hans; **der Rhein** the Rhine; **der Michigansee** Lake Michigan; **die Domstraße** Cathedral Street; **die „Bismarck"** the "Bismarck"; **der Lehrer/die Frau** (im allgemeinen) teachers pl/women pl; **der Tod/die Liebe/das Leben** death/love/life; **der Tod des Sokrates** the death of Socrates; **das Viktorianische England** Victorian England; **in dem England, das ich kannte** in the England (that or which) I knew; **er liebt den Jazz/die Oper/das Kino** he likes jazz/(the) opera/the cinema; **das Singen macht ihm Freude** singing gives him pleasure; **das Singen meines Opas** my grandpa's singing; **mir fiel das Atmen schwer** I found breathing difficult; **das Herstellen von Waffen ist** ... manufacturing weapons is ..., the manufacturing of weapons is ...; **der Papa/die Mama** (baby-talk) Daddy/Mummy; **die Callas** Callas; **der spätere Wittgenstein** the later Wittgenstein; **er war nicht mehr der Hans, den** ... he was no longer the Hans, who ...; **er hat sich den Fuß verletzt** he has hurt his foot; **wascht euch** (dat) **mal das Gesicht!** wash your face!; **er nimmt den Hut ab** he takes his hat off; **das ist der Verlobte** that is her or the fiancé; **eine Mark das Stück** one mark apiece or each; **10 Mark die Stunde** 10 marks an or per hour; **der und der Wissenschaftler** such and such a scientist.
2 dem pron gen dessen or (old) des, deren, dessen, pl deren; dat dem, der, dem, pl denen; acc den, die, das, pl die (a) (attr) (jener, dieser) that; pl those, them (inf). **zu der und der Zeit** at such and such a time; **an dem und dem Ort** at such and such a place.
(b) (substantivisch) he/she/it; pl those, them (inf). **der/die war es** it was him/her; **die mit dem Holzbein** the one or her (inf) with the wooden leg; **der mit der großen Nase** the one or him (inf) with the big nose; **die** (pl) **mit den roten Haaren** those or them (inf) with red hair; **deine Schwester, die war nicht da** (inf) your sister, she wasn't there; **der und schwimmen?** him, swimming?, swimming?, (what) him?; **der/die hier/da** (von Menschen) he/she, this/that man/woman etc; (von Gegenständen) this/that (one); (von mehreren) this one/that one; **die hier/da** pl they, these/those men/women etc; these/those them (inf); **der, den ich meine** the one I mean; **der und der/die und die** so-and-so; **das und das** such and such.
3 rel pron (decl as 2) (Mensch) who, that; (Gegenstand, Tier) which, that.
4 rel + dem pron (decl as 2) **der/die dafür verantwortlich war,** ... the man/woman who was responsible for it; **die so etwas tun,** ... those or people who do that sort of thing ...
der|art adv (a) (Art und Weise) in such a way. **er hat sich ~ benommen, daß** ... he behaved so badly that ...; **sein Benehmen war ~, daß** ... his behaviour was so bad that ...; ~ **vorbereitet,** ... thus prepared ...
(b) (Ausmaß) (vor adj) so; (vor vb) so much, to such an extent. **ein ~ unzuverlässiger Mensch** such an unreliable person, so unreliable a person; **er hat mich ~ geärgert, daß** ... he annoyed me so much that ...; **es hat ~ geregnet, daß** ... it rained so much that ...
der|artig 1 adj such, of that kind. **bei ~en Versuchen** in such experiments, in experiments of that kind; **(etwas) D~es** something like that or of the kind. **2** adv siehe **derart**.
derb adj (a) (kräftig) strong; Stoff, Leder auch tough; Schuhe auch stout; Kost coarse. **jdn ~ anfassen** to manhandle sb; (fig) to be rough with sb.
(b) (grob) coarse; Manieren, Kerl auch uncouth; Witz, Sprache, Ausdrucksweise auch earthy, crude (pej). **um mich einmal ~ auszudrücken** ... to put it crudely ...
(c) (unfreundlich) gruff.
Derbheit f siehe adj (a) strength; toughness; stoutness; coarseness. (b) coarseness; uncouthness; earthiness, crudeness. ~**en** crudities. (c) gruffness.
derbknochig adj big-boned.
Derby ['dɛrbi] nt -s, -s horse-race for three-year-olds, derby (US); (fig: sportliche Begegnung) derby. **das (englische) ~** the Derby.
Derbyrennen nt siehe **Derby**.
der|einst adv (liter) (a) (in der Zukunft) one day. (b) (rare: früher) at one time, once.
der|einstig adj (liter) (a) (künftig) future, tomorrow's. **im ~en vereinten Europa** in tomorrow's united Europe, in the united Europe of tomorrow. (b) (damalig) of former times.
deren 1 gen pl of dem pron **der, die, das** their. **2 (a)** gen sing of rel pron **die** whose. (b) gen pl of rel pron **der, die, das** whose, of whom; (von Sachen) of which.
derent-: ~**halben** (dated), ~**wegen** adv (weswegen) because of whom, on whose account; (von Sachen) because of which, on account of which; (welcher zuliebe auch) for whose sake; for the sake of which; (um welche) about whom; (von Sachen) about which; (für welche) on whose behalf; ~**willen** adv um ~**willen (a)** (rel) for whose sake; (von Sachen) for the sake of which; (b) (dem) sing for her/its sake; pl for their sake.
derer gen pl of dem pron **der, die, das** of those. **das Geschlecht ~ von Hohenstein** (geh) the von Hohenstein family.
deret- in cpds siehe **derent-**.
dergestalt adv (geh) in such a way; (Ausmaß) so much; to such

an extent. ~ ausgerüstet, ... thus equipped ...; **dann gab er dem Pferde die Sporen ~, daß** ... then he spurred his horse on so forcefully that ...

dergleichen *inv* 1 *dem pron* (a) *(adjektivisch)* of that kind, such, like that. ~ **Dinge** things of that kind *or* like that, such things.

(b) *(substantivisch)* that sort of thing. **nichts ~** nothing of that kind *or* like it; **er tat nichts ~** he did nothing of the kind; **und ~ (mehr)** and suchlike.

2 *rel pron (old)* of the kind that. **Juwelen, ~ man selten sieht** jewels whose like *or* the like of which one rarely sees.

Derivat [-'va:t] *nt (Chem, Ling)* derivative.

Derivation [-va'tsio:n] *f (Ling)* derivation.

Derivativ *nt (Ling)* derivative.

derjenige, diejenige, dasjenige, *pl* **diejenigen** *dem pron* (a) *(substantivisch)* the one; *pl* those. **sie ist immer diejenige, welche** *(inf)* it's always her; **du warst also derjenige, welcher!** *(inf)* so it was you!, so you're the one! (b) *(form: adjektivisch)* the; *pl* those.

derlei *dem pron inv* (a) *(adjektivisch)* such, like that, that kind of. ~ **Probleme** problems like that, that kind of *or* such problems. (b) *(substantivisch)* that sort *or* kind of thing. **und ~ (mehr)** and suchlike.

dermaleinst *adv (old) siehe* **dereinst**.

dermalen *adv (old, Aus form)* presently, at present, now.

dermalig *adj (old, Aus form)* present, actual.

dermaßen *adv (mit adj)* so; *(mit vb)* so much. ~ **dumm** so stupid; **ein ~ dummer Kerl** such a stupid fellow; **sie hatte ~ Angst, daß** ... she was so afraid that ...; **er hat sich geärgert, und zwar ~, daß** ... he was angry, so much so that ...

Dermato-: ~**loge** *m*, ~**login** *f* dermatologist; ~**logie** *f* dermatology; ~**plastik** *f* plastic surgery, dermatoplasty *(spec)*.

Dernier cri [dɛrnje'kri] *m* - , -s -s dernier cri.

dero *poss pron (obs)* her; *pl* their. **D~ Gnaden** Your Grace.

derselbe, dieselbe, dasselbe, *pl* **dieselben** *dem pron* (a) *(substantivisch)* the same; *(old: er, sie, es)* he/she/it; *(inf: der, die, das gleiche)* the same. **er sagt in jeder Vorlesung dasselbe** he says the same (thing) in every lecture; **jedes Jahr kriegen dieselben mehr Geld** every year the same people get more money; **sie/er ist immer noch ganz dieselbe/derselbe** she/he is still exactly the same; **es sind immer dieselben** it's always the same ones *or* people; **noch mal dasselbe, bitte!** *(inf)* same again, please.

(b) *(adjektivisch)* the same. **ein und derselbe Mensch** one and the same person.

derselbige *etc dem pron (old) siehe* **derselbe** *etc.*

derweil(en) 1 *adv* in the meantime, meanwhile. 2 *conj (old)* whilst, while.

Derwisch *m* -es, -e dervish.

derzeit *adv* (a) *(jetzt)* at present, at the moment. (b) *(rare: damals)* at that *or* the time, then.

derzeitig *adj attr* (a) *(jetzig)* present, current. (b) *(rare: damalig)* of that *or* the time.

des¹ (a) *gen of def art* **der**, **das** of the. **das Bellen ~ Hundes** the barking of the dog, the dog's barking. (b) *(old) siehe* **dessen**.

des², Des *nt* -, *no pl (Mus)* D flat.

Desaster [de'zastɐ] *nt* -s, - disaster.

desavouieren* [dɛsavu'i:rən] *vt* (geh) to disavow; ~ **Bemühungen, Pläne** to compromise.

Desavouierung *f (geh) siehe vt* disavowal; compromising.

Desensibilisator *m (Phot)* desensitizer.

desensibilisieren* *vt (Phot, Med)* to desensitize.

Desensibilisierung *f (Phot, Med)* desensitization.

Deserteur(in *f)* [-'tø:ɐ, -'tø:ɔrin] *m (Mil, fig)* deserter.

desertieren* *vi aux sein or (rare) haben (Mil, fig)* to desert.

Desertion *f (Mil, fig)* desertion.

desgleichen 1 *adv (ebenso)* likewise, also. **er ist Vegetarier, ~ seine Frau** he is a vegetarian, as is his wife. 2 *dem pron inv (old: dasselbe)* the same. ~ **habe ich noch nie gehört** I have never heard the like. 3 *rel pron inv (old)* the like of which.

deshalb *adv, conj* therefore; *(aus diesem Grunde, darüber)* because of that; *(dafür)* for that. **es ist schon spät, ~ wollen wir anfangen** it is late, so let us start; **~ bin ich hergekommen** that is what I came here for, that is why I came here; **ich bin ~ hergekommen, weil ich dich sprechen wollte** what I came here for was to speak to you, the reason I came here was that I wanted to speak to you; **~ also!** so that's why *or* the reason!; **~ muß er nicht dumm sein** that does not (necessarily) mean (to say) he is stupid; **~ frage ich ja** that's exactly why I'm asking.

desiderabel *adj (geh)* desirable.

Desiderat *nt*, **Desideratum** *nt* -s, **Desiderata** desideratum; *(Anschaffungsvorschlag)* suggestion.

Desideratenbuch *nt* suggestions book.

Design [di'zaɪn] *nt* -s, -s design.

Designat [dezi'gna:t] *nt (Philos, Ling)* referendum.

Designation [dezigna'tsio:n] *f* designation.

Designator [dezi'gna:tɔr] *m (Philos, Ling)* referens.

Designer(in *f)* [di'zaɪnɐ, -ərɪn] *m* -s, - designer.

designieren* [dezi'gni:rən] *vt* to designate *(jdn zu etw* sb as sth).

designiert [dezɪ'gni:ɐt] *adj attr* **der ~e Vorsitzende** the chairman designate.

desillusionieren* *vt* to disillusion.

Desillusionierung *f* disillusionment.

Desinfektion *f* disinfection.

Desinfektions-: ~**lösung** *f* antiseptic solution; ~**mittel** *nt* disinfectant.

desinfizieren* *vt* **Zimmer, Bett** *etc* to disinfect; **Spritze, Gefäß** *etc* to sterilize.

Desinfizierung *f siehe vt* disinfection; sterilization.

Desinformation *f (Pol)* disinformation *no pl.*

Desintegration *f (Sociol, Psych)* disintegration.

Desinteresse *nt* lack of interest *(an +dat* in).

desinteressiert *adj* uninterested; **Gesicht** bored.

Deskription *f (geh)* description.

deskriptiv *adj* descriptive.

Desodorant *nt* -s, -s *or* -e *siehe* **Deodorant**.

desolat *adj (geh)* desolate; **Zustand, wirtschaftliche Lage** desperate.

Desorganisation *f* disorganization; *(Auflösung auch)* disruption. **auf der Tagung herrschte eine völlige ~** there was complete chaos at the conference.

desorganisieren* *vt* to disorganize.

desorientieren* *vt* to disorient(ate).

Desorientiertheit, Desorientierung *f* disorientation.

despektierlich [dɛspɛk'ti:ɐlɪç] *adj (old, hum)* disrespectful.

Desperado [dɛspe'ra:do] *m* -s, -s desperado.

desperat [dɛspe'ra:t] *adj (geh)* desperate.

Despot [dɛs'po:t] *m* -en, -en despot.

Despotie [dɛspo'ti:] *f* despotism.

despotisch [dɛs'po:tɪʃ] *adj* despotic.

Despotismus [dɛspo-] *m*, *no pl* despotism.

desselben *gen of* **derselbe, dasselbe**.

dessen 1 *gen of dem pron* **der²**, **das** his; *(von Sachen, Tieren)* its. 2 *gen of rel pron* **der²**, **das** whose; *(von Sachen)* of which, which ... of.

dessent-: ~**halben** *(dated)*, ~**wegen** *adv* gleiche Übersetzung wie für derenthalben *etc;* ~**willen** *adv:* **um ~willen** (a) *(rel)* for whose sake; (b) *(dem)* for his/its sake.

des(sen)ungeachtet *adv (geh)* nevertheless, notwithstanding (this).

Dessert [dɛ'se:ɐ] *nt* -s, -s dessert.

Dessert-: *in cpds* dessert.

Dessin [dɛ'sɛ̃] *nt* -s, -s *(Tex)* pattern, design.

Dessous [dɛ'su:] *nt* - , - [dɛ'su:s] *usu pl (dated)* undergarment, underwear *no pl.*

Destillat [dɛstɪ'la:t] *nt (Chem)* distillation, distillate; *(fig)* distillation.

Destillateur [dɛstɪla'tø:ɐ] *m* distiller.

Destillation [dɛstɪla'tsio:n] *f* (a) *(Chem)* distillation. (b) *(Branntweinbrennerei)* distillery. (c) *(dated dial: Großgaststätte)* drinking establishment, = gin palace *(old)*, brandy shop *(old)*.

Destillations-: ~**anlage** *f* distilling *or* distillation plant; ~**produkt** *nt* distillate.

Destille [dɛs'tɪlə] *f* -, -n (a) *(dial inf: Gaststätte)* (big) pub *(Brit)*, bar. (b) *(Brennerei)* distillery.

destillieren* [dɛstɪ'li:rən] *vt* to distil; *(fig)* to condense.

Destillierkolben [dɛstɪ'li:ɐ-] *m (Chem)* retort.

desto *conj* ~ **mehr/besser** all the more/better; ~ **grausamer/schneller** all the more cruel/all the faster; ~ **wahrscheinlicher ist es, daß wir** ... that makes it all the more probable that we ...; *siehe* **je**.

Destruktion [destruk'tsio:n] *f* destruction.

Destruktionstrieb *m (Psych)* destructive instinct.

destruktiv [destruk'ti:f] *adj* destructive.

Destruktivität *f* destructiveness.

desultorisch *adj (old, liter)* desultory.

desungeachtet *adv (old) siehe* **des(sen)ungeachtet**.

deswegen *adv siehe* **deshalb**.

deszendent *adj (Astron)* descendent *(spec)*, setting.

Deszendent *m* im ~**en sein** *(Astrol)* to be in the descendent.

Deszendenz *f* (a) *(Abstammung)* descent; *(Nachkommenschaft)* descendants *pl.* (b) *(Astron)* descendence *(spec)*, setting.

Deszendenztheorie *f (Biol)* theory of evolution.

deszendieren* *vi aux sein (Astron, liter)* to descend.

Detail [de'tai, de'tajl] *nt* -s, -s *(Filmeinstellung)* big close-up. **ins ~ gehen** to go into detail(s); **im ~** in detail; **bis ins kleinste ~** (right) down to the smallest *or* last detail; **in allen ~s** in the greatest detail; **etw mit allen ~s berichten** to report sth in full detail, to give a fully detailed account of sth; **die Schwierigkeiten liegen im ~** it is the details that are most difficult.

Detail-: ~**bericht** *m* detailed report; ~**frage** *f* question of detail; ~**handel** *m (dated) siehe* **Einzelhandel**; ~**händler** *m (dated) siehe* **Einzelhändler**; ~**kenntnisse** *pl* detailed knowledge *no pl.*

detaillieren* [deta'ji:rən] *vt (genau beschreiben)* to specify, to give full particulars of. **etw genauer ~** to specify sth more precisely.

detailliert [deta'ji:ɐt] *adj* detailed.

Detailliertheit *f* detail.

Detaillist [deta'jist] *m (dated Comm) siehe* **Einzelhändler**.

Detail-: ~**preis** *m (dated Comm)* retail price; **d~reich** *adj* fully detailed; **etw d~reich schildern** to describe sth in great detail; ~**schilderung** *f* detailed account; **die beiden Versionen unterscheiden sich in der ~schilderung** the two versions differ in their account of the details; ~**verkauf** *m (dated Comm) siehe* **Einzelverkauf**; ~**zeichnung** *f* detail drawing.

Detektei *f (private)* detective agency, firm of (private) investigators. „ ~ **R.B. von Halske**" "R.B. von Halske, private investigator".

Detektiv(in *f)* *m* private investigator *or* detective *or* eye *(inf)*.

Detektivbüro *nt siehe* **Detektei**.

detektivisch *adj* in ~**er Kleinarbeit** with detailed detection work; **bei etw ~ vorgehen** to go about sth like a detective.

Detektivroman *m* detective novel.

Detektor *m (Rad)* detector.

Detektorempfänger *m (Rad)* crystal set.

Détente [de'tã:t] *f* -, *no pl (rare) (Pol)* détente.

Determinante f -, -n (Math, Biol) determinant.
determinieren* vt to (pre)determine; (Gram) to govern.
Determiniertheit f (Philos) determinedness.
Determinismus m, no pl (Philos) determinism.
Determinist(in f) m (Philos) determinist.
deterministisch adj (Philos) deterministic.
Detonation f explosion, blast. etw (acc) zur ~ bringen to detonate sth.
detonieren* vi aux sein to explode, to go off.
Deubel m -s, - (dial) siehe **Teufel**.
deucht 3rd pers sing of **dünken**.
Deus ex machina ['de:ʊs ɛks 'maxina] m - - -, Dei - - (rare) deus ex machin..
Deut m um keinen ~ not one iota or jot; seine Ratschläge sind keinen ~ wert his advice is not worth tuppence; dafür gebe ich keinen ~ I don't give a rap for it(inf); er versteht nicht einen ~ davon he does not know the first thing about it; daran ist kein ~ wahr there is not a grain of truth in it; du bist keinen ~ besser you're not one jot or iota or whit better.
deutbar adj interpretable. ..., ob Nietzsche theologisch ~ ist ... whether Nietzsche can be interpreted or understood theologically; nicht/schwer ~ impossible/difficult to interpret; schwer ~e Beobachtungen observations (which are) difficult to explain; es ist nicht anders ~ it cannot be explained in any other way.
Deutelei f (pej geh) quibbling, quibbles pl, cavilling.
deuteln vi (geh) to quibble, to cavil. an jedem Wort ~ to quibble over every word; daran gibt es nichts zu ~! there are no ifs and buts about it!
deuten 1 vt (auslegen) to interpret; Zukunft auch to read. sich (dat) etw ~ (geh) to understand sth; etw falsch ~ to misinterpret sth.
2 vi (a) (zeigen) (mit dem Finger) auf etw (acc) ~ to point (one's finger) at sth.
(b) (fig: hinweisen) to indicate. alles deutet auf Regen/ Schnee all the signs are that it is going to rain/snow, everything points to rain/snow; alles deutet darauf, daß ... all the indications are that ..., everything indicates that ...
Deuter m -s, - (a) interpreter. (b) (Aus: Wink) sign.
deutlich adj (a) (klar) clear. ~ erkennbar/sichtbar/hörbar/ wahrnehmbar clearly or plainly recognizable/visible/audible/ perceptible; ~ sehen to see clearly; ~ fühlen to feel distinctly; ich fühle ~, daß ... I have the distinct feeling ...; ~ unterscheiden to distinguish clearly; ~ sprechen to speak clearly.
(b) (unmißverständlich) clear, plain. jdm etw ~ vor Augen führen to make sth perfectly clear or plain to sb; eine ~e Sprache mit jdm reden to speak plainly or bluntly with sb; sich ~ ausdrücken to make oneself clear or plain; das war ~! (taktlos) that was clear or plain enough; muß ich ~er werden? have I not made myself clear or plain enough?; ich muß es einmal ~ sagen let me make myself clear or plain; jdm ~ zu verstehen geben, daß to make it clear or plain to sb that.
Deutlichkeit f clarity. etw mit aller ~ sagen to make sth perfectly clear or plain; seine Antwort ließ an ~ nichts zu wünschen übrig his answer was perfectly clear or plain and left no possible doubt.
deutlichkeitshalber adv for the sake of clarity.
deutsch adj (a) German. ~e Schrift Gothic script; ~er Schäferhund Alsatian (Brit), German shepherd (US); ~e Gründlichkeit etc German or Teutonic efficiency etc; die D~e Bucht the German Bight; D~e Mark deutschmark, German mark; der D~e Orden (Hist) the Teutonic Order (of Knights).
(b) (in bezug auf Sprache) German. er hat ~, nicht englisch gesprochen he spoke German not English; sich (auf) ~ unterhalten to speak (in) German; auf or zu ~ heißt das ... in German it means ...; der Text ist (in) ~ geschrieben the text is written in German; der Vortrag wird in or auf ~ gehalten the lecture will be given in German; etw ~ aussprechen to pronounce sth in a German(ic) way, to give sth a German pronunciation; ~ denken to think in German; mit jdm ~ reden (fig inf: deutlich) to speak bluntly with sb; auf gut ~ (gesagt) (fig inf) in plain English.
Deutsch nt -(s), dat -, no pl German. das ~ Thomas Manns Thomas Mann's German; gut(es) ~ sprechen to speak good German; (Ausländer auch) to speak German well; ~ lernen/verstehen to learn/understand German; der Unterricht/die Schulnote in ~ German lessons pl/school mark in or for German; siehe auch **deutsch** (b).
Deutsch(e) nt -n, dat -n, no pl (a) (Sprache) German. aus dem ~en/ins ~e übersetzt translated from the/into (the) German; das ~ des Mittelalters medieval German, the German of the Middle Ages; die Aussprache des ~en the pronunciation of German, German pronunciation.
(b) (Charakteristik) Germanness. manchmal kommt noch das ~e in ihm durch sometimes the German in him or his Germanness shows through.
Deutschen-: ~feind, ~fresser (inf) m anti-German, Germanophobe; ~freund m Germanophile.
deutsch-|englisch adj (a) (Pol) Anglo-German. (b) (Ling) German-English.
Deutschen-: ~haß m Germanophobia; ~hasser m -s, - German-hater.
Deutsche(r) mf decl as adj er ist ~r he is (a) German; die ~n the Germans.
Deutsch-: d~feindlich adj anti-German, Germanophobic; ~feindlichkeit f Germanophobia; d~französisch adj (a) (Pol) Franco-German; der D~-Französische Krieg the Franco-Prussian war; (b) (Ling) German-French; d~freundlich

adj pro-German, Germanophile; ~freundlichkeit f Germanophilia; d~gesinnt adj d~gesinnt sein to feel oneself to be German, to think of oneself as being German; ~herren pl (Hist) Teutonic Knights pl; ~herrenorden m (Hist) Teutonic Order of Knights.
Deutschland nt -s Germany. die beiden ~(s) the two Germanys.
Deutschland-: ~frage f (Pol) German question; ~lied nt West German national anthem; ~politik f home or domestic policy; (von fremdem Staat) policy on or towards Germany; ~problem nt siehe ~frage.
Deutsch-: ~lehrer m German teacher; d~national adj (Hist) German National; ~ordensritter m (Hist) Teutonic Knight; ~ritterorden m (Hist) siehe ~herrenorden; ~schweizer m German Swiss; d~schweizerisch adj German-Swiss; d~sprachig adj Bevölkerung, Gebiete German-speaking; Zeitung, Ausgabe German language; Literatur German; d~sprachlich adj German(-language); ~sprechen nt speaking German; richtiges ~sprechen correct German; d~sprechend adj German-speaking; d~stämmig adj of German origin or stock; ~stämmige(r) mf decl as adj ethnic German; ~tum nt, no pl Germanness; (die ~en) Germans pl; ~tümelei f (pej) hyper-Germanness.
Deutung f interpretation. eine falsche ~ a misinterpretation.
Deutungsversuch m attempt at an interpretation. er unternimmt einen neuen ~ des ... he attempts a new interpretation of ...
Devise [de'vi:zə] f -, -n (a) (Wahlspruch) maxim, motto; (Her auch) device. (b) (Fin) ~n pl foreign exchange or currency.
Devisen-: ~abkommen nt foreign exchange agreement; ~ausgleich m foreign exchange offset; ~beschränkungen pl foreign exchange restrictions pl; ~bestimmungen pl foreign exchange control regulations pl; ~bewirtschaftung f foreign exchange control; ~bilanz f foreign exchange balance; ~börse f foreign exchange market; ~bringer m -s, - bringer or (Geschäft etc) earner of foreign exchange or currency; ~geschäft nt foreign exchange dealing; ~handel m foreign currency or exchange dealings pl, sale and purchase of currencies; ~knappheit f shortage of foreign exchange; ~kurs m exchange rate, rate of exchange; ~markt m foreign exchange market; ~politik f foreign exchange policy; ~schmuggel m currency smuggling; ~vergehen nt breach of exchange control regulations; ~vorschriften pl siehe ~bestimmungen.
devot [de'vo:t] adj (geh) (a) (pej: unterwürfig) obsequious. (b) (old: demütig) humble.
Devotion [devo'tsio:n] f siehe adj (geh) (a) obsequiousness. (b) humility.
Devotionalien [devotsio'na:liən] pl devotional objects pl.
Devotionalienhandlung f devotional objects shop.
Dextrose f -, no pl (Chem) dextrose.
Dez m -es, -e (dial inf) bonce (inf).
Dezember m -s, - December; siehe auch **März**.
Dezemvir [de'tsɛmvir] m -n or -s, -n decemvir.
Dezemvirat [detsɛmvi'ra:t] nt decemvirate.
Dezennium m (geh) decade, decennium (form).
dezent adj discreet.
dezentral adj decentralized.
Dezentralisation f decentralization.
dezentralisieren* vt to decentralize.
Dezentralisierung f siehe **Dezentralisation**.
Dezenz f, no pl (geh) (a) (old: Anstand) sense of decency. (b) (von Geschmack, Kleidung etc) discreetness; (von Benehmen auch) discretion.
Dezernat nt (Admin) department.
Dezernent(in f) m (Admin) head of department.
Dezibel ['de:tsibɛl, -'bɛl] nt -s, - (Phys) decibel.
dezidiert adj (geh) firm, determined.
Dezi- [(esp Aus) 'de:tsi-]: ~gramm nt decigram(me); ~liter m or nt decilitre.
dezimal adj decimal.
Dezimalbruch m decimal fraction.
dezimalisieren* vt to decimalize. als in Großbritannien dezimalisiert wurde when Great Britain went decimal.
Dezimalisierung f decimalization.
Dezimal-: ~klassifikation f decimal classification; ~maß nt decimal measure; ~rechnung f decimals pl; ~stelle f decimal place; auf zwei ~stellen genau correct to two decimal places; ~system nt decimal system; ~waage f decimal balance; ~zahl f decimal number.
Dezime f -, -n (Mus) tenth.
Dezimeter m or nt decimetre.
dezimieren* (fig) 1 vt to decimate. 2 vr to be decimated.
Dezimierung f (fig) decimation.
DGB [de:ge:'be:] m -s abbr of **Deutscher Gewerkschaftsbund** Federation of German Trade Unions.
dgl. abbr of **dergleichen, desgleichen** the like.
d. Gr. abbr of **der Große**.
d.h. abbr of **das heißt** i.e.
d.i. abbr of **das ist** i.e.
Dia nt -s, -s (Phot) slide, transparency.
Diabetes [dia'be:tes] m -, no pl diabetes.
Diabetiker- in cpds diabetic.
Diabetiker(in f) m -s, - diabetic.
diabetisch adj diabetic.
Diabetrachter m slide viewer.
Diabolik f (geh) diabolicalness, fiendishness.
diabolisch adj (geh) diabolical, fiendish.
Diachronie [diakro'ni:] f (Ling) diachrony.
diachron(isch) [-kr-] adj (Ling) diachronic.
Diadem nt -s, -e diadem.

Diadochen pl (Hist) diadochi pl; (fig) rivals pl in a power struggle.
Diadochenkämpfe pl (fig) power struggle.
Diagnose f -, -n diagnosis. eine ~ stellen to make a diagnosis.
Diagnose-: ~verfahren nt diagnostic method, method of diagnosis; ~zentrum nt diagnostic centre.
Diagnostik f diagnosis.
Diagnostiker(in f) m -s, - diagnostician.
diagnostisch adj diagnostic.
diagnostizieren* vti (Med, fig) to diagnose. (auf) etw (acc) ~ to diagnose sth.
diagonal adj diagonal. ein Buch ~ lesen (inf) to skim or flick through a book.
Diagonale f -, -n diagonal.
Diagonalreifen m (Aut) cross-ply (tyre).
Diagramm nt -s, -e diagram.
Diagramm-: ~form f in ~form diagrammatically; ~papier nt graph paper.
Diakon [dia'ko:n, (Aus) 'di:ako:n] m -s or -en, -e(n) (Eccl) deacon.
Diakonat nt (Eccl) (a) (Amt) deaconry, deaconship, diaconate. (b) (Wohnung) deacon's house.
Diakonie f (Eccl) social welfare work.
Diakonisse f -, -n, **Diakonissin** f (Eccl) deaconess.
diakritisch adj diacritic. ~e Zeichen diacritics, diacritic(al) marks or signs.
Dialekt m -(e)s, -e dialect.
dialektal adj dialectal.
Dialekt- in cpds dialect; ~färbung f accent, dialect features pl; ~forscher m dialectologist, dialectician; ~forschung f dialect research, dialectology; d~frei adj accent-free, without an accent, without a trace of dialect.
Dialektik f (Philos) dialectics sing or pl.
Dialektiker(in f) m -s, - (Philos) dialectician.
dialektisch adj (a) (Philos) dialectic(al). ~er Materialismus dialectical materialism. (b) (Ling) siehe **dialektal.**
Dialektismus m (Ling) dialecticism.
Dialog m -(e)s, -e dialogue.
Dialog-: ~autor m (Film) script-writer; ~form f dialogue form.
dialogisch adj dialogue antr.
Dialog-: ~regie f (Film) script supervision; ~stück nt (Theat) dialogue play.
Diamant¹ m -en, -en diamond.
Diamant² f -, no pl (Typ) four-point, diamond (4½ point).
diamantbesetzt adj attr diamond-studded.
diamanten adj attr diamond. von ~er Härte as hard as diamond; ~er Glanz adamantine lustre (liter).
Diamanten-, Diamant-: ~schleifer m diamond polisher; ~schliff m diamond polishing; ~schmuck m diamonds pl, diamond jewellery; ~stahl m diamond plate; ~staub m diamond dust.
DIAMAT, Diamat [dia'ma(:)t] m -, no pl abbr of **dialektischer Materialismus.**
Diameter m -s, - (Geom) diameter.
diametral adj diametral; (fig) Ansichten diametrically opposed. ~entgegengesetzt sein, sich ~ gegenüberliegen to be diametrically opposite; ~entgegengesetzt (fig) diametrically opposed.
Diana f -s (Myth) Diana.
Diaphragma [dia'fragma] nt -s, **Diaphragmen** (Tech, Med) diaphragm.
Dia- (Phot): ~positiv nt slide, transparency; ~projektor m slide projector; ~rahmen m slide frame.
Diärese f -, -n (Phon, Poet) dieresis.
Diarium nt (dated) journal.
Diarrhö(e) [dia'rø:] f -, -en (Med) diarrhoea.
Diaskop nt -s, -e siehe **Diaprojektor.**
Diaspora f -, no pl (Eccl) diaspora.
Diastole [di'astole, dia'sto:lə] f -, -n (Med) diastole.
diastolisch adj diastolic.
diät adv kochen, essen according to a diet; leben on a special diet.
Diät f -, -en (Med) diet. ~ halten to keep to or observe a strict diet; nach einer ~ leben to live on a diet or (wegen Krankheit) special diet; jdn auf ~ setzen (inf) to put sb on a diet.
Diät-: ~assistent(in f) m dietician; ~bier nt diabetic beer.
Diäten pl (Parl) parliamentary allowance.
Diätetik f dietetics sing.
diätetisch adj dietetic.
Diätfahrplan m (hum) dieting course or schedule.
Diathek f slide collection or library.
Diätist(in f) m dietician.
Diät-: ~kost f dietary preparations pl; ~kost bekommen to be on a special diet; ~kur f dietary or dietetic treatment.
Diatonik f (Mus) diatonicism.
diatonisch adj (Mus) diatonic.
Diatribe f -, -n (geh) diatribe.
dich 1 pers pron acc of **du** you; (obs, dial) thee. 2 refl pron yourself. wie fühlst du ~? how do you feel?
Dichotomie f dichotomy.
dicht 1 adj (a) Gefieder, Haar, Hecke thick; Laub, Nebel auch, Wald, (Menschen)menge, Gewühl dense; Verkehr auch heavy, dense; Gewebe close; Stoff closely-woven; (fig: konzentriert) Stil dense; Szene full, compact. in ~er Folge in rapid or quick succession; sie standen in ~en Reihen they were standing row upon row close together.
(b) (undurchlässig) watertight; airtight; Vorhänge thick, heavy; Rolladen heavy. ~ machen to make watertight/airtight; Fenster to seal; ~ halten to be watertight; ~ schließen to shut tightly; ~ verhängen to curtain heavily.

(c) (inf: zu) shut, closed.
2 adv (a) (nahe) closely. (~ an) ~ stehen to stand close together; ~ gefolgt von closely followed by.
(b) (sehr stark) bevölkert densely; bewaldet auch thickly. ~ mit Efeu bewachsen with ivy growing thickly over it; ~/~er behaart sein to be very hairy/have more hair.
(c) (mit Präpositionen) ~ an/bei close to; ~ dahinter/darüber/davor right behind/above/in front; ~ daneben right or close beside it; ~ bevor right before; ~ daran hard by it; ~ hintereinander close(ly) or right behind one another; ~ beieinander or beisammen close together; ~ am Winde halten (Naut) to sail close to or to hug the wind; ~ hinter jdm her sein to be right or hard or close behind sb.
dicht-: ~auf adv closely; ~auf folgen to follow close behind or closely; ~behaart adj attr (very) hairy; ~belaubt adj attr thick with leaves, densely foliated; ~bevölkert adj attr densely populated; ~bewachsen adj attr Baumstämme grown over with moss and lichen; Ufer thickly covered with vegetation; Landstriche rich in vegetation; ~bewölkt adj attr heavily overcast.
Dichte f -, -n (a) no pl siehe adj (a) thickness; denseness; heaviness, denseness, closeness; close weave; denseness; fullness, compactness. (b) (Phys) density.
Dichtemesser m -s, - (Phys) densimeter.
dichten¹ 1 vt to write, to compose. sein Glückwunsch war gedichtet his congratulations were (written) in verse. 2 vi to write poems/a poem. sein ganzes D~ und Trachten (dated geh) all his hopes and endeavours.
dichten² vt (undurchlässig machen) to seal, to make watertight/airtight; (Naut auch) to caulk.
Dichter m -s, - poet; (Schriftsteller) writer, author.
Dichterfürst m prince among poets.
Dichterin f siehe **Dichter** poet(ess); writer, author(ess).
dichterisch adj poetic; (schriftstellerisch) literary. ~e Freiheit poetic licence.
Dichter-: ~komponist m composer-librettist; ~kreis m circle of poets; ~lesung f reading (by a poet/writer from his own works); ~ling m (pej) rhymester (pej), poetaster (pej); ~schule f school of poets/writers; ~sprache f poetic language; ~wort nt (literary) quotation.
Dicht-: d~gedrängt adj attr closely packed; d~halten vi sep irreg (inf) to hold one's tongue (inf), to keep one's mouth shut (inf); ~heit f siehe **Dichte (a).**
Dichtigkeit f (Undurchlässigkeit) watertightness; airtightness.
Dichtkunst f art of poetry; (Schriftstellerei) creative writing.
dichtmachen vti sep (inf) to shut up, to close. (den Laden) ~ to shut up shop (and go home) (inf).
Dichtung¹ f (a) no pl (Dichtkunst, Gesamtwerk) literature; (in Versform) poetry. ~ und Wahrheit (Liter) poetry and truth; (fig) fact and fantasy or fiction. (b) (Dichtwerk) poem, poetic work; literary work. dramatische ~ dramatic poem.
Dichtung² f (Tech) seal; (in Wasserhahn etc) washer; (Aut: von Zylinder, Vergaser) gasket; (das Abdichten) sealing.
Dichtungs-: ~art, ~gattung f literary genre; ~manschette f seal; ~masse f sealant; ~material, ~mittel nt sealing compound; ~ring m, ~scheibe f seal, sealing ring; (in Wasserhahn) washer.
dick adj (a) thick; Mensch, Körperteil, Band, Buch, Brieftasche fat; Baum, Stamm big, large, thick; (inf) Gehalt, Belohnung, Rechnung, Gewinn fat, hefty; (inf) Tränen, Geschäft big. einen ~en Mercedes fahren (inf) to drive a big Mercedes; eine ~e Zigarre a big fat cigar; die ~e Berta Big Bertha; ein ~er Brocken (inf) a hard or tough nut (to crack); ~ machen (Speisen) to be fattening; ~ werden (Mensch: zunehmen) to get fat; sich/jdn ~ anziehen to wrap up/sb up warmly; ~(e) kommen (inf) to come thick and fast; etw ~ unterstreichen to underline sth heavily; ~e (inf: ausreichend) easily; er hat es ~(e) (inf) (satt) he's had enough of it; (viel) he's got enough and to spare.
(b) (nach Maßangaben) thick; Erdschicht deep. 3 m ~e Wände walls 3 metres thick, 3 metre thick walls.
(c) (inf: schwerwiegend) Fehler, Verweis big. das ist ein ~er Tadel/ein ~es Lob that's heavy criticism/high praise; ach, du ~es Ei! (sl) bloody hell! (Brit sl); das ist ein ~er Hund (sl) or ein ~es Ei (sl) that's a bit much (inf); das ~e Ende kommt noch (prov) the worst is yet to come.
(d) (geschwollen) Backe, Beine, Finger, Mandeln swollen; Beule big. ein ~er Kopf (inf) a thick head (inf); siehe **Bauch.**
(e) (zähflüssig, dicht) thick. eine ~e Suppe (inf: Nebel) a real pea-souper (inf); ~e Milch sour milk; durch ~ und dünn through thick and thin; siehe **Luft.**
(f) (inf: herzlich) Freundschaft, Freund close. mit jdm ~ befreundet or ~e sein to be thick with sb (inf).
Dick-: ~bauch m (inf) potbelly; d~bauchig adj Vase, Krug bulbous; Mann potbellied; d~bäuchig adj Mensch potbellied; (krankhaft auch) swollen-bellied; ~darm m (Anat) colon.
Dicke f -, -n (a) (Stärke, Durchmesser) thickness; (bei Maßangaben auch) depth. (b) (von Menschen, Körperteilen) fatness.
dicke adv (inf) siehe **dick (a, f).**
Dicken-: ~messer m -s, - thickness gauge; ~wachstum nt lateral growth.
Dicke(r) mf decl as adj (inf) fatty (inf), fatso (inf).
Dickerchen nt (inf) chubby chops (inf).
dicketun vr sep irreg siehe **dicktun.**
Dick-: d~fellig adj (inf) thick-skinned; ~felligkeit f (inf) insensitivity, rhinoceros hide (inf); d~flüssig adj thick, viscous; ~flüssigkeit f thickness, viscosity; ~häuter m -s, - pachyderm; (fig) thick-skinned person.
Dickicht nt -(e)s, -e (Gebüsch) thicket; (fig) jungle, maze.

Dick-: ~**kopf** m (a) (*Starrsinn*) obstinacy, stubbornness, mulishness; **einen** ~**kopf haben** to be obstinate or stubborn or mulish; **seinen** ~**kopf aufsetzen** to (decide to) be obstinate or stubborn or mulish; (b) (*Mensch*) mule (*inf*); **d**~**köpfig** adj (*fig*) stubborn; **d**~**leibig** adj Buch massive; Mensch corpulent; ~**leibigkeit** f siehe adj massiveness; corpulence; **d**~**lich** adj plump; Mensch auch plumpish, tubby (*inf*); ~**milch** f (*Cook*) sour milk; ~**schädel** m (*inf*) siehe ~**kopf**; **d**~**schalig** adj thick-skinned, with a thick skin or peel; ~**sein** nt fatness.

Dickte f -, -n (*Tech*) siehe **Dicke (a)**.

Dick-: ~**tuer(in** f) m -s, - (*inf*) swank; ~**tuerei** f (*inf*) swanking no pl; **d**~**tuerisch** adj swanky (*inf*); **d**~**tun** vir sep irreg (*inf*) to swank; (**sich**) **mit etw d**~**tun** to go swanking around (the place) with sth (*inf*); **d**~**wandig** adj Gebäude, Bunker, etc with thick walls, thick-walled; Gefäß, Schale with thick sides, thick; ~**wanst** m (*pej inf*) fatso (*inf*).

Didaktik f didactics (*form*), teaching methods pl.

Didaktiker(in f) m -s, - (*Univ*) lecturer in teaching methods. **er ist ein miserabler** ~ his teaching methods are terrible.

didaktisch adj didactic.

dideldum, dideldumdei interj tum-ti-tum.

die art etc siehe **der**[2].

Dieb m -(e)s, -e thief. **haltet den** ~! stop thief!; **sich wie ein** ~ **davonschleichen** to steal or slink away like a thief in the night.

Dieberei f thievery no pl, thieving no pl.

Diebes-: ~**bande** f band of thieves; ~**gesindel** nt siehe ~**pack**; ~**gut** nt stolen property or goods pl; ~**höhle** f thieves' den; ~**nest** nt den of thieves; ~**pack** nt (*pej*) thieving riff-raff (*pej*) or trash (*pej*); **d**~**sicher** adj thief-proof.

Diebin f thief.

diebisch adj (a) (*stehlend*) thieving attr. (b) (*inf: groß, verschmitzt*) Freude, Vergnügen impish, mischievous.

Diebstahl ['diːp-ʃtaːl] m -(e)s, ⸚e theft; (*Jur auch*) larceny. **einfacher/schwerer** ~ petty/grand larceny; **bewaffneter** ~ armed robbery; **geistiger** ~ plagiarism.

Diebstahlversicherung f insurance against theft.

diejenige dem pron siehe **derjenige**.

Diele f -, -n (a) (*Fußbodenbrett*) floorboard. (b) (*Vorraum*) hall, hallway; siehe **Eis**~, **Tanz**~. (c) (*N Ger*) siehe **Tenne**.

dielen vt Zimmer to lay floorboards in. **gedielter Fußboden** wooden floor.

Dielenbrett nt floorboard.

dienen vi (a) (*Dienste tun, sich einsetzen*) to serve (*jdm* sb); (*old: angestellt sein*) to be in service (*bei* with). **bei Hof** ~ to serve or wait at court; **bei der Messe** or **am Altar** ~ to serve at mass.

  (b) (*Mil*) (*beim Militär sein*) to serve; (*Militärdienst leisten*) to do (one's) military service. **bei der Kavallerie/unter jdm** ~ to serve in the cavalry/under sb; **ein gedienter Soldat** an ex-soldier; **18 Monate** ~ **to** or **bis zu 18 months'** (military) service, to serve 18 months; siehe **Pike**.

  (c) (*fördern*) (*einer Sache (dat)* sth) to serve; **dem Fortschritt, der Erforschung** to aid; **dem Verständnis** to promote; (*nützlich sein*) to be of use or service (*jdm* to sb). **es dient einem guten Zweck/einer guten Sache** it serves a useful purpose/it is in a good cause; **der Verbesserung der Arbeitsbedingungen** ~ to serve to improve working conditions; **das wird dir später** ~ that will be or come in useful to you later.

  (d) (*behilflich sein*) to help (*jdm* sb), to be of help or service (*jdm* to sb). **womit kann ich Ihnen** ~? what can I do for you?; (*im Geschäft auch*) can I help you?; **damit kann ich leider nicht** ~ I'm afraid I can't help you there; **damit ist mir wenig gedient** that's no use or good to me; **wäre Ihnen damit gedient?** would that be of any help to you?

  (e) (*verwendet werden*) **als/zu etw** ~ to serve or be used as/for sth; **laß dir das als Warnung** ~! let that serve as or be a warning to you!

Diener m -s, - (a) (*Mensch*) (*lit, fig*) servant; (*Lakai auch*) valet. ~ **Gottes** servant of God; **Ihr ergebenster** ~ (*old*) (*in Briefen*) your (most) obedient servant; siehe **stumm**. (b) (*inf: Verbeugung*) bow.

Dienerin f maid(-servant old).

dienern vi (*vor + dat* to) (*lit*) to bow; (*fig pej*) to bow and scrape.

Dienerschaft f servants pl, domestic staff.

dienlich adj useful, helpful; (*ratsam*) expedient, advisable. **jdm/einer Sache** ~ **sein** to help sb/sth, to be of use or help to sb/sth.

Dienst m -(e)s, -e (a) (*Arbeitsverhältnis, Tätigkeitsbereich*) service; (*Arbeitsstelle*) position. **diplomatischer/öffentlicher** ~ diplomatic/civil service; **bei jdm in** ~(en) or **in jds** ~(en) (*dat*) **sein** or **stehen** to be in sb's service; **jdn in (seinen)** ~ **nehmen** to engage sb; **in jds** ~(e) (*acc*) **treten** to enter sb's service; **Oberst etc außer** ~ (*abbr a.D.*) retired colonel etc, ex-colonel etc; **den** ~ **quittieren, aus dem** ~ (**aus**)**scheiden** to resign one's post; (*Mil*) to leave the service; **nicht mehr im** ~ **sein** to have left the service; **im** ~ **ergraut sein** to have many years of faithful service behind one.

  (b) (*Berufsausübung, Amtspflicht*) duty; (*Arbeit, Arbeitszeit*) work. **im** ~ **sein,** ~ **haben** (*Arzt, Feuerwehrmann etc*) to be on duty; (*Apotheke*) to be open; **im** ~ **sein** (*Angestellter etc*) to be working; **außer** ~ **sein** to be off duty; **nach** ~ after work; **zum** ~ **gehen** to go to work; ~ **tun** to serve (*bei in, als* as); **jdn vom** ~ **beurlauben** to grant sb leave of absence; **jdn vom** ~ **befreien** to exempt sb from his duties; ~ **ist** ~ **und Schnaps ist Schnaps** (*Prov inf*) you can't mix business with pleasure, there's a time for everything.

  (c) (*Tätigkeit, Leistung, Hilfe*) service. **im** ~(e) **einer Sache/der Menschheit** in the service of sth/humanity; **sich in den** ~ **der Sache stellen** to embrace the cause; **jdm einen** ~/**einen schlechten** ~ **erweisen** to do sb a good/bad turn or a

service/disservice; jdm gute ~**e leisten** or **tun** to serve sb well; **jdm den** ~ **verweigern** to refuse to work for sb; **die Stimme** etc **versagte ihr den** ~ her voice etc failed (her) or gave way; ~ **am Vaterland** service to one's country; ~ **am Kunden** customer service; **etw in** ~ **stellen** to put sth into commission or service; **jdm zu** ~**en** or **zu jds** ~**en stehen** to be at sb's disposal; (*Mensch auch*) to be at sb's service; (**ich stehe**) **zu** ~**en!** (*old*) at your service!; **was steht zu** ~**en?** (*old*) you wish, sir/madam?

  (d) (*Einrichtung: oft in cpds*) service.

  (e) (*Archit*) engaged column or shaft.

-dienst m in cpds service.

Dienst-: ~**abteil** nt (*Rail*) = guard's compartment, conductor's car (*US*); ~**adel** m (*Hist*) nobility whose titles derive from being in the king's service.

Dienstag m Tuesday. ~ **abend/morgen/nachmittag** (on) Tuesday evening/morning/afternoon; ~ **abends/nachts/vormittags** on Tuesday evenings/nights/mornings; **am** ~ on Tuesday; **hast du** ~ **Zeit?** have you time on Tuesday?; **heute ist** ~, **der 10. Juni** today is Tuesday the tenth of June or Tuesday June the tenth; **alle** ~**e** every Tuesday; **eines** ~**s** one Tuesday; **des** ~**s** (*geh*) on Tuesdays; **die Nacht von** ~ **auf** or **zum Mittwoch** the night of Tuesday to Wednesday; **den (ganzen)** ~ **über** all (day) Tuesday, the whole of Tuesday; **ab nächsten** or **nächstem** ~ from next Tuesday; ~ **in 8 Tagen** or **in einer Woche** a week on Tuesday, Tuesday week; **seit letzten** or **letztem** ~ since last Tuesday; ~ **vor einer Woche** or **acht Tagen** a week (ago) last Tuesday.

Dienstag-: ~**abend** m Tuesday evening; ~**nachmittag** m Tuesday afternoon.

dienstags adv on Tuesdays, on a Tuesday. ~ **abends** on Tuesday evenings, on a Tuesday evening.

dienstagsnachmittags adv on Tuesday afternoons.

Dienst-: ~**alter** nt length of service; ~**älteste(r)** mf (most) senior member of staff; ~**antritt** m assumption of one's duties; (*jeden Tag*) commencement of work; ~**antritt** on taking up one's duties/on commencing work; ~**anweisung** f instructions pl, regulations pl; ~**anzug** m (*Mil*) service uniform or dress; ~**auffassung** f conception of one's duties; **was ist denn das für eine** ~**auffassung?** have you no sense of duty!; ~**aufsicht** f supervision; **die** ~**aufsicht über etw** (*acc*) **haben** to be in charge of sth; **d**~**bar** adj (a) (*Hist*) subject; (b) (*fig: helfend*) **d**~**barer Geist** helpful soul; **d**~**bare Geister willing hands**; **sich** (*dat*) **etw d**~**bar machen** to utilize sth; ~**barkeit** f (a) (*Jur*) servitude; (b) (*Hist: Leibeigenschaft*) servitude; **etw in seine** ~**barkeit bringen** (*fig geh*) to utilize sth; (c) (*Gefälligkeit*) service; (d) (*rare: Tätigsein als Diener*) service; **d**~**beflissen** adj zealous, assiduous; ~**beflissenheit** f zealousness, assiduousness, assiduity; ~**befreiung** f (*Mil*) leave, furlough (*US*); **d**~**bereit** adj (a) (*geöffnet*) Apotheke open pred; Arzt on duty; (b) (*hilfsbereit*) willing to be of service, obliging; ~**bereitschaft** f (a) **in** ~**bereitschaft sein** to be on stand-by duty; **welche Apotheke hat dieses Wochenende** ~**bereitschaft?** which chemist is open this weekend?; (b) willingness to be of service; ~**beschädigung** f (*Mil*) injury sustained in the course of one's duties; ~**bezüge** pl salary sing; ~**bote** m servant; ~**boteneingang** m tradesmen's or service entrance; ~**eid** m oath of service; ~**eifer** m zeal; **d**~**eifrig** adj zealous, assiduous; ~**entlassung** f retirement from the service; (*Mil*) discharge; **Sparmaßnahmen führten zu** ~**entlassungen** economy measures led to redundancies; **d**~**fähig** adj (*Mil*) fit for duty; **d**~**fertig** adj siehe **d**~**beflissen**; **d**~**frei** adj free; **d**~**freier Tag** day off, free day; **d**~**frei haben/bekommen** to have/be given a day off; ~**gebrauch** m (*Mil, Admin*) **nur für den** ~**gebrauch** for official use only; ~**geheimnis** nt official secret; ~**gespräch** nt business call; (*von Beamten*) official call; ~**grad** m (*Mil*) (a) (*Rangstufe*) rank; (b) (*Mensch*) **ein höherer** ~**grad** a person of higher rank, a higher ranking person; ~**gradabzeichen** nt (*Mil*) insignia; **d**~**habend** adj attr Arzt, Offizier duty etc, on duty; **der** ~**habende** (*Mil*) the duty officer; ~**herr** m employer; ~**jahr** nt usu pl (*Mil, Admin*) year of service; ~**kleidung** f working dress; uniform; (*Mil*) service dress; ~**leistung** f service; ~**leistungsberuf** m job in the services sector; ~**leistungsbetrieb** m service industry; ~**leistungsgewerbe** nt services trade; **d**~**lich** 1 adj Angelegenheiten business attr; (*Schreiben, Befehl*) official; **d**~**lich werden** (*inf*) to become businesslike; 2 adv on business; **wir haben hier d**~**lich zu tun** we have business here; ~**mädchen** nt maid; ~**magd** f maid; farmgirl; ~**mann** m (a) pl -**männer** or -**leute** (*Gepäckträger*) porter; (b) pl -**mannen** or -**leute** (*Hist: Vasall*) liegeman, vassal; ~**mütze** f uniform cap; ~**ordnung** f (*Admin*) official regulations pl; (*Mil*) service regulations pl; ~**personal** nt staff, personnel; ~**pflicht** f compulsory service; **d**~**pflichtig** adj liable for compulsory service; ~**plan** m duty rota; ~**rang** m grade; (*Mil*) rank; ~**reise** f business trip; **auf** ~**reise** on a business trip; ~**sache** f (*Post*) **gebührenfreie** ~**sache** official matter sent postage paid; ~**schluß** m end of work; **nach** ~**schluß** (*von Arbeiter etc*) after work; (*von Büro, Firma etc auch*) after working hours; **wir haben jetzt** ~**schluß** we finish work now; ~**siegel** nt, ~**stempel** m official stamp; ~**stelle** f (*Admin*) department; (*Mil*) section; ~**stunden** pl working hours pl; **d**~**tauglich** adj (*Mil*) fit for service; **d**~**tuend** adj Arzt duty attr, on duty; **d**~**unfähig** adj unfit for work; (*Mil*) unfit for service; **d**~**untauglich** adj (*Mil*) unfit for service; ~**vergehen** nt breach of duty; ~**verhältnis** nt im ~**verhältnis stehen** to be a public employee; **ein** ~**verhältnis eingehen/ins** ~**verhältnis übernommen werden** to become a public employee; **d**~**verpflichten*** vt insep to call up or draft (*US*) for essential service; ~**vertrag** m contract of employment; ~**vorschrift** f official regulations pl; (*Mil*) service regulations pl; ~**wagen** m company car; (*von Beamten*) official car; (Mil) staff car; (Rail) = guard's carriage, conductor's car (US); ~weg m den ~weg einhalten to go through the proper or official channels pl; auf dem ~weg through the proper or official channels pl; d~willig adj willing to be of service; (Mil) willing to do one's duty; ~wohnung f police/army etc house, house provided by the police/army etc; ~zeit f (a) period of service; (b) (Arbeitszeit) working hours pl; (Mil) hours pl of duty; ~zeugnis nt testimonial.

dies dem pron inv this; pl these. ~ sind these are; siehe auch dieser.

diesbezüglich adj (form) relating to or regarding this. sich ~ äußern to give one's views regarding this or on this matter.

diese dem pron siehe dieser.

Diese f -, -n (Mus) sharp.

Diesel m -s, - (inf) diesel.

dieselbe, dieselbige dem pron siehe derselbe.

Diesel-: d~elektrisch adj diesel-electric; ~lok(omotive) f diesel locomotive; ~motor m diesel engine; ~öl nt diesel oil.

dieser, diese, dies(es), pl **diese** dem pron (a) (substantivisch) this; (~ dort, da) that; pl these; (~ dort, da) those. diese(r, s) hier this (one); diese(r, s) da that (one); wer hat es getan? — dieser! which one did it? — this/that one!; dieser ist es! this/that is the one!; dieser ..., jener ... the latter ..., the former ...; schließlich fragte ich einen Polizisten; dieser sagte mir ... in the end I asked a policeman, he told me ...; dies und das, dieses und jenes this and that; dieser und jener this person and that; dieser oder jener someone or other; ... oder dem Überbringer dieses (form) ... or to the bearer of this.

(b) attr this; (~ dort, da) that; pl these; (~ dort, da) those. gib mir dieses Buch give me that book; dies(es) Jahr/dieser Monat this year/month; Anfang dieses Jahres/Monats at the beginning of the or this or the current (form) year/month; in diesen Wochen/Jahren habe ich viel erlebt I experienced a lot in those weeks/years; ich fahre diese Woche/dieses Jahr noch weg I'm going away this week/year; am 5. dieses Monats on the 5th of this month; (in Briefen auch) on the 5th inst. (form); dieser Tage (vergangen) the other day; (zukünftig) one of these days; (nur) dieses eine Mal just this/that once; dies alles, alles dies all this/that; dieser Maier (inf) that or this Maier; siehe Nacht.

dieser-: ~art adv (Aus, old) thus, in this way; ~halb adv (old) siehe deshalb.

dieses dem pron siehe dieser.

diesig adj Wetter, Luft hazy, misty.

Diesigkeit f haziness, mistiness.

dies-: ~jährig adj attr this year's; die ~jährige Ernte this year's harvest; ~mal adv this time; ~malig adj attr der ~malige Preis the price this time; ~seitig adj (a) Ufer near(side) attr, (on) this side; (b) (irdisch) of this world; Leben in this world; ~seits prep + gen on this side of; D~seits nt -, no pl das D~seits this life; im D~seits in this life, on earth.

Dietrich m -s, -e picklock, skeleton key.

dieweil (obs) 1 adv meanwhile, in the meantime, the while (dial). 2 conj whilst, while.

Diffamation f siehe Diffamierung.

diffamatorisch adj (geh) defamatory.

diffamieren* vt to defame.

diffamierend adj defamatory.

Diffamierung f (das Diffamieren) defamation (of character); (Bemerkung etc) defamatory statement. die ~ seines Gegners the defamation of his opponent's character.

Differential [-'tsia:l] nt -s, -e (a) (Math) differential. (b) (Aut: auch ~getriebe nt) differential (gear).

Differential- in cpds (Tech, Math) differential; ~rechnung f (Math) differential calculus.

Differenz f (a) (Unterschied, fehlender Betrag, Math) difference; (Abweichung) discrepancy. (b) (usu pl: Meinungsverschiedenheit) difference (of opinion), disagreement.

Differenzbetrag m difference, balance.

differenzieren* 1 vt (a) to make distinctions/a distinction in; Behauptung, Urteil to be discriminating in; (abändern) to make changes/a change in, to modify. zwischen zwei Dingen ~ to differentiate between two things; dieser Eintrag ist zu subtil differenziert the distinctions made in this entry are too subtle; die Gesetze wurden immer stärker differenziert the laws became more and more sophisticated.

(b) (Math) to differentiate.

2 vi to make distinctions/a distinction (zwischen + dat between, bei in); (den Unterschied verstehen) to differentiate (zwischen + dat between, bei in); (bei Behauptung, Urteil) to be discriminating, to discriminate (bei in). ~de Methoden discriminative methods; genau ~ to make a precise distinction.

3 vr to become sophisticated; (sich auseinanderentwickeln) to become differentiated.

differenziert adj (fein unterscheidend) subtly differentiated; (verfeinert) sophisticated; Charakter, Mensch, Gefühlsleben complex; (verschiedenartig) Farbgebung, Anschauungen subtly diversified; Warenangebot diverse.

Differenzierung f (a) siehe vt (a) distinction; modification; differentiation. (b) (Math) differentiation. (c) siehe vr sophistication; differentiation.

differieren* vi to differ.

diffizil adj (geh) difficult, awkward; Mensch complicated.

diffus adj Licht diffuse; Gedanken, Ausdrucksweise confused.

Diffusion f diffusion.

Digest ['daidʒest] m or nt -(s), -s digest.

Digital- in cpds digital; ~rechner m digital calculator; ~uhr f digital clock.

Dikta (geh) pl of Diktum.

Diktaphon nt -s, -e dictaphone ®.

Diktat nt (a) dictation. etw nach ~ schreiben to write sth from dictation; Fräulein, bitte zum ~! take a letter, please; nach ~ verreist dictated by X and signed in his absence. (b) (fig: Gebot) dictate; (Pol auch) diktat.

Diktator m dictator.

diktatorisch adj dictatorial.

Diktatur f dictatorship.

diktieren* vt Brief, (fig) Bedingungen to dictate.

Diktiergerät nt, **Diktiermaschine** f dictating machine.

Diktion f style.

Diktionär [dɪktsio'nɛːɐ] nt or m -s, -e (old) dictionary.

Diktum nt -s, **Dikta** (geh) dictum, adage.

Dilemma nt -s, -s or (geh) -ta dilemma.

Dilettant m amateur; (pej auch) dilettante.

dilettantisch adj amateurish.

Dilettantismus m amateurism.

dilettieren* vi (geh) to dabble (in + dat in).

Dill m -(e)s, -e (Bot, Cook) dill.

diluvial [dilu'via:l] adj (Geol) diluvial.

Diluvium nt (Geol) glacial epoch, ice age.

Dimension f (Phys, Math, fig) dimension.

-dimensional adj suf -dimensional.

Diminuendo nt -s, -s (Mus) diminuendo.

diminutiv adj Form, Endung diminutive (zu, von of).

Diminutivform f diminutive form.

Diminutiv(um) nt diminutive (zu, von of).

DIN¹ ® [dɪn, di:n] f -, no pl abbr of **Deutsche Industrie-Norm** German Industrial Standard. ~ A4 A4; ~-Format German standard paper size.

DIN² [di:n] nt -(s), no pl (Phot) DIN. ~-Grad m DIN-speed.

dinarisch adj Rasse Dinaric. D~es Gebirge Dinaric Alps.

Diner [di'ne:] nt -s, -s (form) (Mittagessen) luncheon; (Abendessen) dinner.

Ding¹ nt -(e)s, -e or (inf) -er (a) (Sache, Gegenstand) thing. Gläser, Flaschen und ähnliche ~e glasses, bottles and that sort of thing or and things of that kind; die Welt der ~e (Philos) the world of material objects; das ~ an sich (Philos) the thing-in-itself; das ist ein ~ der Unmöglichkeit that is quite impossible; bei ihm ist kein ~ unmöglich nothing is impossible for him; guter ~e sein (old, liter) to be in good spirits or of good cheer (old); die ~e beim (rechten) Namen nennen to call a spade a spade (prov); jedes ~ hat zwei Seiten (Prov) there are two sides to everything; gut ~ will Weile haben (Prov) it takes time to do a thing well; siehe drei.

(b) (Gegebenheit) thing; (Angelegenheit, Thema auch) matter; (Ereignis auch) event. in diesen ~en about these things or matters; vergangene/berufliche ~e past events/professional matters; reden wir von andern ~en let's talk about something else; wir harrten der ~e, die da kommen sollten we waited to see what would happen; die ~e sind nun mal nicht so things aren't like that; so wie die ~e liegen as things are, as matters lie; wie ich die ~e sehe as I see things or matters; über den ~en stehen to be above things; die ~e stehen schlecht things are bad; nach Lage der ~e the way things are; das ist ein ander ~ (old) that is another matter; das ist ein eigen ~ (old, liter) that is a strange thing; vor allen ~en above all (things), first and foremost; es müßte nicht mit rechten ~en zugehen, wenn ... it would be more than a little strange if ...; siehe Lauf, Natur, unverrichtet etc.

(c) (inf) auch ~s (unbestimmtes Etwas) thing; (Vorrichtung auch) gadget; was ist das für ein ~? what's that thing?; das ~(s) da (inf) that thing (over) there; das ist ein ~! now there's a thing! (inf); ein tolles ~! great! (inf); das ~ ist gut! that's a good one! (inf).

(d) pl -er (sl: Verbrechen) job; sich (dat) ein ~ leisten to get up to something; da hast du dir aber ein ~ geleistet that was quite something you got up to (inf); ~er machen or schieben to get up to all sorts of tricks (inf); was macht ihr bloß für ~er? the things you do! (inf); das war vielleicht ein ~ (inf) that was quite something (inf); jdm ein ~ verpassen to get one's own back on sb; siehe drehen.

(e) (inf: Mädchen) thing, creature.

(f) (sl: Penis) tool (sl), dong (US sl).

Ding² nt -(e)s, -e (Hist) thing.

Dingelchen nt (inf) dear or sweet little thing.

dingen pret dingte, ptp gedungen vt (old) Diener to hire, to engage. gedungener Mörder hired assassin.

Dingens nt -, - (dial inf) siehe Ding¹.

dingfest adj jdn ~ machen to take sb into custody, to arrest sb.

Dinggedicht nt (Liter) poem dealing with a single object, animal etc.

Dingi ['dɪŋgi] nt -s, -s dinghy.

dinglich 1 adj material. ~er Anspruch/Klage (Jur) claim/action in rem. 2 adv (Fin) ~ gesicherte Forderungen claims covered by assets.

Dinglichkeit f materiality.

Dings, Dingsbums, Dingsda nt -, no pl (inf) (Sache) what'sit, doo-dah, thingummy(-bob or -jig) (all inf); (Person: auch der/die ~) what's-his-/-her-name (inf).

Dingsda nt -, no pl, **Dingskirchen** nt -s, no pl (inf) what's-its-name.

Dingwort nt -(e)s, ¨er (Gram) noun.

dinieren* vi (geh) to dine (form).

Dinner nt -s, - (geh) dinner.

Dinosaurier m dinosaur.

Diode f -, -n diode.

dionysisch adj Dionysian.

Diopter nt -s, - (old) (Phot) viewfinder; (am Gewehr) (peep) sight.

Dioskuren pl (Myth) heavenly twins (auch fig), Dioscuri (form).
Dioxyd nt -s, -e dioxide.
Diözesan m -en, -en diocesan.
Diözese f -, -n diocese. die ~ Münster the diocese of Münster.
Diphtherie [dɪfteˈriː] f diphtheria.
Diphtherie(schutz)impfung f diphtheria immunization; (eine Impfung) diphtheria injection.
diphtherisch [dɪfˈteːrɪʃ] adj diphtherial.
Diphthong [dɪfˈtɔŋ] m -s, -e diphthong.
diphthongieren* [dɪftɔŋˈgiːrən] vt to diphthongize.
Diphthongierung f diphthongization.
diphthongisch [dɪfˈtɔŋɪʃ] adj diphthongized. ~ aussprechen to pronounce as a diphthong.
Dipl. abbr of Diplom.
Dipl.-Ing. abbr of Diplomingenieur academically trained engineer.
Dipl.-Kfm. abbr of Diplomkaufmann person holding a diploma in commerce.
Diplom nt -s, -e diploma; (Zeugnis auch) certificate. ein ~ machen to take or do one's diploma.
Diplom- in cpds (vor Berufsbezeichnung) qualified.
Diplomand m -en, -en student about to take his diploma.
Diplom|arbeit f dissertation (submitted for a diploma).
Diplomat m -en, -en diplomat.
Diplomatenkoffer m executive case.
Diplomatie f (lit, fig) diplomacy.
diplomatisch adj (Pol, fig) diplomatic.
diplomieren* vt jdn ~ to award sb a diploma.
diplomiert adj qualified.
Dipol [ˈdiːpoːl] m -s, -e (a) (Phys) dipole. (b) (auch ~antenne) dipole (aerial or antenna).
dippen vt (Naut) Flagge to dip.
Dir. abbr of Direktion; Direktor; Dirigent.
dir pers pron dat of du to you; (obs, dial) to thee; (nach Präpositionen) you; (obs, dial) thou; siehe ihm.
direkt 1 adj (a) (unmittelbar, gerade) direct; Erledigung immediate. eine ~e Verbindung a through train/direct flight; ~e Rede direct speech.
   (b) (unverblümt) Mensch, Frage, Ausdrucksweise direct, blunt; (genau) Hinweis plain; Vorstellungen, Antwort, Auskunft clear.
   (c) (inf: ausgesprochen) perfect, sheer. es war keine ~e Katastrophe it wasn't exactly a catastrophe.
2 adv (a) (unmittelbar) directly; (geradewegs auch) straight. ~ aus or von/zu or nach straight or direct from/to; ~ an/neben/unter/über directly or right by/next to/under/over; ~ gegenüber right or directly or straight opposite; jdm ~ ins Gesicht/in die Augen sehen to look sb straight in the face/the eyes; ~ übertragen or senden to transmit live; ich kann von hier nicht ~ telefonieren I can't dial direct from here.
   (b) (unverblümt) bluntly. jdm etw ~ ins Gesicht sagen to tell sb sth (straight) to his face; ~ fragen to ask outright or straight out; ~ antworten to give sb a clear answer.
   (c) (inf: geradezu) really. nicht ~ not exactly or really.
Direkt- in cpds direct; (Rad, TV) live.
Direktion f (a) (Leitung) management, administration; (von Schule) headship (Brit), principalship (US). (b) (Direktoren, Vorstand) management. (c) (inf: Direktionsbüro) manager's office.
Direktive f (geh) directive.
Direktmandat nt (Pol) direct mandate.
Direktor m director; (von Gefängnis) governor, warden (US); (von Krankenhaus) = senior consultant; (von Hochschule) principal; (von Schule) head(master/mistress), principal (esp US). geschäftsführender ~ (Univ) head of department; ~ der Bank von England director of the Bank of England.
Direktorat nt (a) (Amt) directorship; (von Schule) headship, principalship (esp US); (von Gefängnis) governorship, wardenship (US).
   (b) (Diensträume) (von Firma, Museum) director's office; (von Hochschule etc) principal's office; (von Schule) head(master/mistress)'s or principal's (esp US) study or room; (von Gefängnis) governor's or warden's (US) office.
direktorial adj directorial.
Direktorin f siehe Direktor.
Direktorium nt (a) board of directors, directorate. (b) (Hist) Directory, Directoire.
Direktrice [dirɛkˈtriːsə] f -, -n manageress.
Direkt-: ~übertragung f (Rad, TV) live transmission; ~verbindung f (Rail) through train; (Aviat) direct flight.
Direx m -, -e (Sch sl) head, principal (esp US).
Dirigent m (Mus) conductor; (fig) leader.
Dirigenten-: ~stab, ~stock (inf) m (conductor's) bâton.
dirigieren* vt (a) (auch vi) (Mus) to conduct; (fig) to lead. (b) (leiten, einweisen) Verkehr etc to direct.
Dirigismus m (Pol) dirigism.
Dirn f -, -en (a) (S Ger, Aus: Magd) maid. (b) (N Ger: Mädchen) girl, lass (dial inf).
Dirndl nt -s, - (a) (auch ~kleid) dirndl. (b) (S Ger, Aus: Mädchen) girl, lass (dial inf).
Dirne f -, -n (a) (Prostituierte) prostitute, hooker (US inf). (b) (obs: Mädchen) lass (old, dial).
Dirnenviertel nt red light district.
dis, Dis nt -, - (Mus) D sharp.
Disco f -, -s disco.
Discount- [dɪsˈkaʊnt] in cpds discount.
Disharmonie f (Mus) discord, dissonance, disharmony; (fig: Unstimmigkeit) discord no pl, friction no pl, disagreement; (von Farben) clash.

disharmonieren* vi (geh) (Mus) to be discordant or dissonant; (Farben) to clash; (Menschen) to be at variance, to disaccord (form). die beiden ~ so offensichtlich the two of them are so obviously out of tune with one another.
disharmonisch adj Akkord discordant, dissonant, disharmonious; Farbzusammenstellung clashing; Ehe, Verbindung, Atmosphäre discordant.
Diskant m -s, -e (Stimmlage) treble; (Gegenstimme) descant.
Diskantschlüssel m soprano clef.
Diskjockey [ˈdɪskdʒɔke] m -s, -s disc jockey, deejay (inf), DJ (inf).
Diskont m -s, -e (Fin) discount.
Diskonten pl (Fin) discounted bills pl.
diskontieren* vt (Fin) to discount.
diskontinuierlich adj (geh) discontinuous.
Diskontinuität f (geh) discontinuity.
Diskontsatz m (Fin) discount rate.
Diskothek f -, -en (a) (Tanzbar) discotheque. (b) (Plattensammlung) record collection.
diskreditieren* vt (geh) to discredit.
Diskrepanz f discrepancy.
diskret adj (a) (taktvoll, unaufdringlich) discreet; (vertraulich) Angelegenheit, Gespräch confidential. er ist sehr ~ (verschwiegen) he's not one to betray a confidence; du mußt lernen, etwas ~er zu sein you must learn to be more discreet about confidential matters.
   (b) (Math) discrete.
Diskretion f discretion; (vertrauliche Behandlung) confidentiality. ~ üben to be discreet; strengste ~ wahren to preserve the strictest confidence; jdn um ~ in einer Angelegenheit bitten to ask sb to treat an affair as a matter of confidence; ~ ist Ehrensache! you can count on my discretion.
Diskriminante f -, -n (Math) discriminant.
diskriminieren* vt to discriminate against.
diskriminierend adj discriminatory.
Diskriminierung f discrimination.
Diskurs m -es, -e (geh) discourse.
diskursiv adj (Philos) discursive.
Diskus m -, -se or Disken discus.
Diskussion f discussion. zur ~ stehen to be under discussion; etw zur ~ stellen to put or bring sth up for discussion; sich mit jdm auf eine ~ einlassen to be drawn or to get into discussion with sb; da gibt's gar keine ~, du ... I'm not having any discussion about it, you ...
Diskussions-: ~beitrag m contribution to the discussion; ~redner m speaker (in a discussion); ~teilnehmer m participant (in a discussion).
Diskus-: ~werfen nt -s, no pl throwing the discus; ~werfer(in f) m discus-thrower.
diskutabel, diskutierbar adj worth discussing. das ist überhaupt nicht ~ that's not even worth talking about.
diskutieren* vti to discuss. über etw (acc) ~ to discuss sth; darüber läßt sich ~ that's debatable; er diskutiert gern he's a great one for discussing (everything); wir haben stundenlang diskutiert we've spent hours in discussion; was gibt's denn da zu ~? what is there to talk about or to discuss?
Dispens [dɪsˈpɛns] f -, -en or m -es, -e (Eccl) dispensation.
dispensieren* [dɪspɛnˈziːrən] vt (a) jdn to excuse (von from); (Eccl) to dispense. (b) (zubereiten) Arznei to dispense.
Dispersion [dɪspɛrˈzioːn] f (Chem, Opt) dispersion.
disponieren* [dɪspoˈniːrən] vi (geh) (a) (verfügen) über jdn ~ to command sb's services (form); willkürlich über jdn ~ to deal with sb high-handedly; ich kann nicht über sie ~ I can't tell her what to do; über etw (acc) (frei) ~ to do as one wishes or likes with sth; über etw (acc) ~ können (zur Verfügung haben) to have sth at one's disposal; ich kann über meine Zeit frei ~ my time is my own (to do with as I wish).
   (b) (planen) to make arrangements or plans.
disponiert [dɪspoˈniːrt] adj (geh) gut/schlecht ~ sein to be on/off form or in good/bad form; zu or für etw ~ sein (Med) to be prone to sth; so ~e Leute people with this kind of disposition; weil sie entsprechend ~ ist because she has the kind of disposition for this.
Disposition [dɪspoziˈtsioːn] f (geh) (a) (Verfügung) jdm zur or zu jds ~ stehen to be at sb's disposal; jdm etw zur ~ stellen to place sth at sb's disposal; jdn zur ~ stellen (old) to pension sb off.
   (b) (Anordnung) arrangement, provision. seine ~en treffen to make (one's) arrangements or plans.
   (c) (Gliederung) layout, plan.
   (d) (Med: Anlage) susceptibility, proneness (zu to).
disproportioniert [dɪsproportsioˈniːrt] adj ill-proportioned.
Disput [dɪsˈpuːt] m -(e)s, -e (geh) dispute.
disputabel [dɪspuˈtaːbl] adj (dated) disputable.
Disputant [dɪspuˈtant] m disputant.
Disputation [dɪsputaˈtsioːn] f (old) disputation.
disputieren* [dɪspuˈtiːrən] vi (geh) to dispute (über etw acc sth).
Disqualifikation f disqualification.
disqualifizieren* vt to disqualify.
Disqualifizierung f disqualification.
Dissens m -es, -e (Jur) dissent, disagreement no indef art.
Dissertation f dissertation; (Doktorarbeit) thesis.
dissertieren* vi to write a dissertation/thesis (über +acc on).
Dissident m dissident.
Dissimilation f (Ling) dissimilation; (Biol auch) catabolism.
dissimilieren* vt (Ling) Laut to dissimilate; (Biol) Stoffe to break down.
dissonant adj dissonant.
Dissonanz f (Mus) dissonance; (fig) (note of) discord.

Distanz f (a) (lit) distance; (fig) (Abstand, Entfernung) detachment; (Zurückhaltung) reserve. ~ halten or wahren (lit, fig) to keep one's distance; auf ~ gehen (fig) to become distant; die nötige ~ zu etw finden/haben to become/be sufficiently detached from sth. (b) (Sport) distance.
distanzieren* 1 vr sich von jdm/etw ~ to dissociate oneself from sb/sth. 2 vt (Sport) to outdistance.
distanziert adj Verhalten distant.
Distel f -, -n thistle.
Distelfink m goldfinch.
Distichon ['dɪstɪçɔn] nt -s, Distichen (Poet) distich.
distinguiert [dɪstɪŋ'giːɐt] adj (geh) distinguished.
distinkt adj (old) distinct, clear.
Distinktion f (geh) (a) (Auszeichnung) distinction. (b) (Rang) distinction; (Aus: Rangabzeichen) insignia pl.
Distribution f distribution.
distributiv adj (Gram, Math) distributive.
Distributivum nt, **Distributivzahl** f (Ling) distributive.
Distrikt m -(e)s, -e district.
Disziplin f -, -en (a) no pl (Zucht, Ordnung) discipline. ~ halten (Lehrer) to keep or maintain discipline; (Klasse) to behave in a disciplined manner. (b) (Fachrichtung, Sportart) discipline.
Disziplinar- in cpds disciplinary; ~gesetz nt disciplinary code; ~gewalt f disciplinary powers pl.
disziplinarisch adj disciplinary. jdn ~ bestrafen to take disciplinary action against sb; jdm ~ unterstellt sein to be answerable to sb.
Disziplinar-: ~strafe f punishment; mit einer ~strafe rechnen to expect disciplinary action; eine ~strafe bekommen to be disciplined; ~verfahren nt disciplinary proceedings pl.
disziplinieren* 1 vt to discipline. 2 vr to discipline oneself.
diszipliniert 1 adj disciplined. 2 adv in a disciplined manner.
Disziplin-: d~los 1 adj undisciplined; 2 adv in an undisciplined manner; ~losigkeit f lack no pl of discipline; ~verlust m loss of discipline.
dito adv (Comm, hum) ditto.
Diva ['diːva] f -, -s or Diven star; (Film) screen goddess.
divergent [diver'gent] adj divergent.
Divergenz [diver'gents] f (a) no pl divergence. (b) usu pl (Meinungsverschiedenheit) difference (of opinion).
divergieren* [diver'giːrən] vi to diverge.
divers [di'vers] adj attr various. die ~esten ... the most diverse ...; ~es Angebot von ... an assortment of ...; ~e (mehrere der gleichen Art) several; „D~es" "miscellaneous"; wir haben noch D~es zu erledigen we still have various or several things to see to.
Diversant [diver'zant] m (DDR) subversive.
Divertimento [diverti'mento] nt -s, -s or Divertimenti, **Divertissement** [divertɪsə'mãː] nt -s, -s (Mus) divertimento, divertissement.
Dividend [divi'dent] m -en, -en (Math) dividend.
Dividende [divi'dendə] f -, -n (Fin) dividend.
Dividendenausschüttung f (Fin) distribution of dividends.
dividieren* [divi'diːrən] vti to divide (durch by).
divinatorisch [divina'toːrɪʃ] adj (geh) divinatory.
Division [divi'zioːn] f (Math, Mil) division.
Divisionär [divizio'nɛːɐ] m (Sw) divisional commander.
Divisions- in cpds (Math) division; (Mil) divisional; ~stab m divisional headquarters pl.
Divisor [di'viːzɔr] m (Math) divisor.
Diwan m -s, -e divan.
d. J. abbr of (a) dieses Jahres of this year. (b) der Jüngere jun.
DJH [deːjɔt'haː] nt -(s) abbr of Deutsches Jugendherbergswerk German Youth Hostel Association.
DKP [deːkaː'peː] f - abbr of Deutsche Kommunistische Partei.
DM ['deː'ɛm] no art -, - abbr of Deutsche Mark.
d. M. abbr of dieses Monats inst.
D-Mark ['deː'mark] f -, - deutschmark, (West) German mark.
DNA [deː'ɛn'aː] abbr of Deutscher Normenausschuß German Committee of Standards.
do, Do nt -s, no pl (Mus) doh.
doch 1 conj (aber, allein) but; (jedoch, trotzdem) but still, yet. und ~ hat er es getan but he still or but still he did it.
2 adv (betont: dennoch) after all; (trotzdem) anyway, all the same; (sowieso) anyway. jetzt ist er ~ nicht gekommen now he hasn't come after all; ..., aber ich bin ~ hingegangen ... but I went anyway or all the same or after all; du weißt es ja ~ besser you always know better than I do anyway; das geht denn ~ zu weit! that really is going too far; und ~, ... and yet ...
(b) (betont: tatsächlich) really. ja ~! of course!, sure! (esp US); nein ~! of course or certainly not!; also ~! so it is/so he did! etc; er hat es gestohlen — also ~! he stole it — so it was him!; er hat es also ~ gesagt so he did say it; es ist ~ so, wie ich vermutet hatte so it (really) is as I thought; das ist er ~! (why, that is him!; das ist ~ interessant, was er da sagt what he's saying is really interesting; was es ~ alles für Leute gibt! the people you get!
(c) (als bejahende Antwort) yes I do/it does etc. hat es dir nicht gefallen? — (~,) ~! didn't you like it? — (oh) yes I did! or oh I did, I did!; will er nicht mitkommen? — ~! doesn't he want to come? — (oh) yes, he does; ~, schon, aber ... yes it is/well I do etc but ...
(d) (auffordernd) nicht übersetzt aber emphatisches „to do" wird oft gebraucht. komm ~ do come; kommen Sie ~ bitte morgen wieder won't you come back tomorrow?; gib ~ mal her (come on,) give it to me; seid ~ endlich still! do keep quiet!, keep quiet, can't you?; sei ~ nicht so frech! don't you be so cheeky!; laß ihn ~! just leave him!; soll er ~! well let him!, let

him then!; nicht ~! don't (do that)!
(e) (verstärkend) but; (Bestätigung erwartend) isn't it/ haven't you etc? sie ist ~ noch so jung but she's still so young; es wäre ~ schön, wenn ... (but) it would be nice if ...; daß sie ~ immer widersprechen muß! why must she always contradict everything?; das ist ~ die Höhe or das Letzte! well, that's the limit!, that really is the limit!; das ist ~ gar nicht wahr! (but) that's just not true!; das ist ~ wohl nicht wahr? that's not true, is it? du hast ~ nicht etwa ...? you haven't ..., have you?, surely you haven't or you haven't by any chance ...(, have you?)
(f) (eigentlich) really, actually. es war ~ ganz interessant it was really or actually quite interesting; ich habe ~ (aber) gefragt (but) I did ask.
(g) (als bekannt Angenommenes wiederholend) nicht übersetzt. Sie wissen ~, wie das so ist (well,) you know how it is, don't you?; du kennst dich ~ hier aus, wo ist denn ...? you know your way around here, where is ...?; wie war ~ Ihr Name? (I'm sorry,) what was your name?; hier darf man ~ nicht rauchen you can't smoke here(, you know).
(h) (in Wunschsätzen) wenn ~ if only; o wäre es ~ schon Frühling! oh if only it were spring!; daß dich ~ der Teufel holte! (oh) go to blazes!, the devil take you (old).
(i) (geh: begründet) but then. er sprach etwas verwirrt, war er ~ eben erst aus dem Bett aufgestanden he spoke in a somewhat confused manner, but then he had only just got out of bed.
Docht m -(e)s, -e wick.
Dochthalter m wick-holder.
Dock nt -s, -s or -e dock.
Docke f -, -n (a) (Korn) stook; (Wolle, Garn) hank, skein; (Tabak) bundle. (b) (dial: Puppe) doll.
docken[1] vti to dock.
docken[2] vt Korn etc to stook; Wolle etc to wind into a hank or skein; Tabak to bundle.
Docker m -s, - docker.
Dockhafen m port with docks.
Docking nt -s, -s (Space) docking.
Dodekaeder nt -s, - dodecahedron.
Doge ['doːʒə] m -n, -n (Hist) doge.
Dogenpalast m Doge's Palace.
Dogge f -, -n mastiff. englische ~ (English) mastiff; deutsche ~ great Dane.
Dogger[1] m -s, - (Naut) dogger.
Dogger[2] m -s (Geol) Middle Jurassic, Dogger; (Gestein) dogger.
Doggerbank f (Geog) die ~ the Dogger Bank.
Dogma nt -s, Dogmen dogma. etw zum ~ erheben to make sth into dogma.
Dogmatik f dogmatics sing; (fig: usu pej) dogmatism.
Dogmatiker(in f) m -s, - dogmatist.
dogmatisch adj (Rel, fig) dogmatic.
dogmatisieren* 1 vt to make into a dogma, to dogmatize. 2 vi (fig pej) to be dogmatic.
Dogmatismus m (pej) dogmatism.
Dogmengeschichte f (Eccl) history of dogmatic theology.
Dohle[1] f -, -n (Orn) jackdaw.
Dohle[2] f -, -n siehe Dole.
Döhnkes pl (N Ger) siehe Döntjes.
Doktor m (auch inf: Arzt) doctor. ja, Herr/Frau ~ yes, Doctor; er ist ~ der Philosophie/Theologie he is a doctor of philosophy/theology; sie hat den ~, sie ist ~ she has a doctorate or PhD, she has or is a PhD; den or seinen ~ machen or bauen (inf) to do a doctorate or PhD; zum ~ promoviert werden to receive one's doctorate or PhD; ~ spielen (inf) to play doctors and nurses.
Doktorand m -en, -en, **Doktorandin** f graduate student studying for a doctorate.
Doktorarbeit f doctoral or PhD thesis.
Doktorat nt (a) (dated) doctorate. (b) (Aus) siehe Doktorprüfung.
Doktor-: ~diplom nt doctor's diploma; ~examen nt siehe ~prüfung; ~frage f (inf) awkward or thorny problem, poser; ~grad m doctorate, doctor's degree, PhD; den ~grad erwerben to obtain one's doctorate; ~hut m doctor's cap; (fig) doctorate.
doktorieren* vi (rare) siehe promovieren.
Doktorin f doctor.
Doktor-: ~prüfung f examination for a/one's doctorate; ~schrift f (a) (inf: Handschrift) doctor's or illegible handwriting; (b) (rare) siehe Dissertation; ~spiele pl doctors and nurses sing; ~titel m doctorate; den ~titel führen to have the title of doctor; jdm den ~titel verleihen to confer a doctorate or the degree of doctor (up)on sb; ~vater m supervisor; ~würde f siehe ~titel.
Doktrin f -, -en doctrine.
doktrinär adj doctrinal; (pej: stur) doctrinaire.
Dokument nt document; (fig: Zeugnis) record.
Dokumentar(in f) m documentalist.
Dokumentar- in cpds documentary; ~film m documentary (film).
dokumentarisch 1 adj documentary. 2 adv (mit Dokumenten) with documents. etw ~ belegen/festhalten to provide documentary evidence for or of sth/to document sth.
Dokumentar-: ~literatur f documentary literature; ~sendung f documentary.
Dokumentation f documentation; (Sammlung auch) records pl.
Dokumenten-: d~echt, d~fest adj Tinte waterproof; d~echtes Papier, ~papier nt good quality paper used for documents, certificates etc.
dokumentieren* 1 vt to document; (fig: zu erkennen geben) to

reveal, to show. **2** *vr (fig)* to become evident.
Dolce vita [ˈdɔltʃə ˈviːta] *nt or f - -, no pl* life of ease, dolce vita.
~ ~ **machen** *(inf)* to live a life of ease.
Dolch *m* **-(e)s, -e** dagger; *(inf: Messer)* knife.
Dolchstich, Dolchstoß *(esp fig) m* stab *(auch fig)*, dagger thrust. **ein** ~ **(von hinten)** *(fig)* a stab in the back.
Dolchstoßlegende *f (Hist)* myth of the stab in the back *(betrayal of Germany in the first World War by its own politicians)*.
Dolde *f -, -n* umbel.
Dolden-: **d~blütig** *adj* umbelliferous; ~**blütler** *m* -s, - umbellifer, umbelliferous plant; **d~förmig** *adj* umbellate; ~**gewächs** *nt* umbellifer; **die** ~**gewächse** the umbelliferae.
Dole *f -, -n* drain.
doll *adj (dial, sl)* **(a)** *siehe* **toll. (b)** *(unerhört)* incredible. **das hat** ~ **weh getan** that hurt like hell *(inf)*.
Dollar *m* **-(s), -s** dollar. **hundert** ~ a hundred dollars.
Dollarzeichen *nt* dollar sign.
Dollbord *nt (Naut)* gunwale.
Dolle *f -, -n (Naut)* rowlock, oarlock *(US)*.
Dolly [ˈdɔli] *m* **-(s), -s** *(Film)* dolly.
Dolm *m* -s, - *(Aus)* idiot, clot *(inf)*.
Dolmen *m* -s, - *(Archeol)* dolmen.
Dolmetsch *m* **-(e)s, -e** **(a)** *(Aus, old)* interpreter. **(b)** *(geh: Fürsprecher)* spokesman *(gen, von* for).
dolmetschen *vti* to interpret.
Dolmetscher(in *f) m* -s, - interpreter.
Dolmetscher-: ~**institut** *nt*, ~**schule** *f* school *or* institute of interpreting.
Dolomit *m* -s, -e *(Geol, Chem)* dolomite.
Dolomiten *pl (Geog)* **die** ~ the Dolomites *pl*.
Dom *m* **-(e)s, -e** **(a)** cathedral. **(b)** *(fig poet)* vault *(poet)*, dome *(poet)*.
Domäne *f -, -n (Hist, Jur)* demesne; *(fig)* domain, province.
Dom-: ~**dechant**, ~**dekan** *m* dean of a/the cathedral.
Domestikation *f* domestication.
Domestik(e) *m* **-en, -en** *(pej old)* (domestic) servant, domestic; *(Sport)* pace-maker.
domestizieren* *vt* to domesticate; *(fig auch)* to tame.
Dom-: ~**freiheit** *f (Hist)* cathedral close *or* precincts *pl*; ~**herr** *m (Eccl)* canon.
dominant- *in cpds (Mus)* dominant.
Dominante *f -, -n (a)* *(Mus)* dominant. **(b)** *(wichtigster Faktor)* dominant *or* dominating feature.
Dominanz *f (Biol, Psych)* dominance.
dominieren* **1** *vi (vorherrschen)* to be (pre)dominant, to predominate; *(Mensch)* to dominate. **2** *vt* to dominate.
dominierend *adj* dominating, dominant.
Dominikaner(in *f) m* -s, - **(a)** *(Eccl)* Dominican. **(b)** *(Geog)* Dominican.
Dominikaner-: ~**kloster** *nt* Dominican monastery; ~**orden** *m* Order of St Dominic, Dominicans *pl*.
dominikanisch *adj* **(a)** *(Eccl)* Dominican. **(b)** *(Geog)* **die D~e Republik** the Dominican Republic.
Domino¹ *m* -s, -s domino.
Domino² *nt* -s, -s *(Spiel)* dominoes *sing*.
Dominospiel *nt* dominoes *sing*; *(Spielmaterial)* set of dominoes; *(Partie)* game of dominoes.
Dominostein *m* **(a)** domino. **(b)** *(Cook)* small chocolate cake with chocolate and vanilla icing.
Domizil *nt* -s, -e domicile *(form)*.
domizilieren* **1** *vi (iro, geh)* to reside, to dwell *(liter)*; *(form: Büro, Firma)* to be based. **2** *vt (Fin) Wechsel* to domicile.
Dom-: ~**kapitel** *nt* cathedral chapter; ~**kapitular** *m* canon; ~**pfaff** *m (Orn)* bullfinch; ~**prediger** *m* preacher in a/the cathedral; ~**propst** *m* dean of a/the cathedral.
Dompteur [dɔmpˈtøːr] *m*, **Dompteuse** [-ˈtøːzə] *f* trainer; *(von Raubtieren)* tamer.
Don *m* **-(s)** *(Geog)* Don.
Donar *m* -s Thor.
Donau *f* - **die** ~ the (river) Danube.
Donau- *in cpds* Danube *attr*, Danubian; ~**monarchie** *f (Hist)* Austria-Hungary, Austro-Hungarian Empire; ~**schwaben** *pl* Swabian settlers on the Danube in Hungary.
Donja *f -, -s (pej dated)* *(Dienstmädchen)* maid(servant); *(Geliebte)* ladylove.
Don Juan [dɔnˈxuan, dɔnˈjuːan] *m* - -s, - -s Don Juan.
Dönkes *pl (N Ger) siehe* **Döntjes**.
Donkosaken [ˈdɔn-] *pl* Don Cossacks *pl*.
Donna *f -, -s or* **Donnen** *(pej dated) siehe* **Donja**.
Donner *m* -s, *(rare)* - *(lit, fig)* thunder *no indef art, no pl*; *(~schlag)* peal or clap of thunder. **wie vom** ~ **gerührt** *(fig inf)* thunderstruck. ~ **und Doria** *or* **Blitz!** *(dated inf)* by thunder! *(dated inf)*, by Jove! *(dated inf)*.
Donner-: ~**balken** *m (Mil sl)* thunderbox *(old sl)*; ~**blech** *nt (Theat)* thunder sheet; ~**büchse** *f (hum dated)* shotgun.
Donnerer *m* -s, *no pl (liter)* **der** ~ the Thunderer, the god of thunder.
Donner-: ~**gepolter**, ~**getöse** *nt* thunderous *or* deafening crash; **mit** ~**getöse** with a thunderous *or* deafening crash; ~**gott** *m* god of thunder; ~**grollen** *nt* -s, *no pl* rolling thunder; ~**keil** *m (Geol)* thunderstone; *(Archeol)* flintstone; *(Myth, poet)* thunderbolt; ~**keil!** *(dated)*, ~**kiel!** *(dated)* my word!, heavens!, ~**maschine** *f (Theat)* thunder machine.
donnern **1** *vi impers* to thunder. **es donnerte in der Ferne** there was (the sound of) thunder in the distance.
2 *vi aux haben or (bei Bewegung) sein* to thunder. **gegen etw** ~ *(prallen)* to crash into sth; *(schlagen)* to hammer on sth; *(schimpfen)* to thunder against sth; **er hat furchtbar gedonnert** he really thundered on.

3 *vt (inf) (brüllen)* to thunder out; *(schleudern, schlagen)* to slam, to crash. **jdm eine** ~ to thump sb *(inf)*.
donnernd *adj (fig) Beifall* thunderous.
Donner-: ~**rollen** *nt* -s, *no pl* rolling of thunder; ~**schlag** *m* clap *or* peal of thunder, thunderclap; **die Nachricht traf mich wie ein** ~**schlag** the news left me thunderstruck, the news came like a thunderclap to me.
Donnerstag *m* Thursday; *siehe* **Dienstag**.
Donner-: ~**stimme** *f* thunderous voice; ~**wetter** *nt (lit old)* thunderstorm; *(fig inf: Schelte)* row; **das wird ein schönes** ~**wetter geben** *or* **setzen** *(inf)* all hell will be let loose *(inf)*; **wie ein** ~**wetter dreinfahren** *(inf)* to wade in; ~**wetter!** *(inf: anerkennend)* my word!; **(zum)** ~**wetter!** *(inf: zornig)* damn *or* blast (it)! *(inf)*; **wer, zum** ~**wetter, hat dir das gesagt?** *(inf)* who told you that for heaven's sake?
Don Quichotte [dɔnkiˈʃɔt] *m* - -s, - -s *siehe* **Don Quixote**.
Donquichot(t)erie [dɔnkiʃɔtəˈriː] *f (geh)* quixotism; *(Handlung)* quixotic gesture *or* act.
Don Quijote, Don Quixote [dɔnkiˈxoːtə] *m* - -s, - -s *(Liter, fig)* Don Quixote.
Döntjes *pl (N Ger)* story, anecdote.
doof *adj (inf)* stupid, dumb *(esp US inf)*.
Doofheit *f (inf)* stupidity, dumbness *(esp US inf)*.
Doofi *m* **-(s), -s** *(inf)* thicky, dummy, dumb-dumb *(all inf)*. **wie klein** ~ **mit Plüschohren aussehen** to look a proper charlie *(inf)*.
Doofkopp *(sl)*, **Doofmann** *(inf) m* thickhead *(inf)*, blockhead *(inf)*.
Dope [doːp] *nt* -s, -s *(sl)* dope *(sl)*.
dopen [ˈdɔpn, ˈdoːpn] *(Sport)* **1** *vt* to dope. **2** *vir* to take drugs.
Doping [ˈdɔpɪŋ, ˈdoːpɪŋ] *nt* -s, -s *(Sport)* doping.
Doppel *nt* -s, - **(a)** *(Duplikat)* duplicate (copy) *(gen, zu* of). **(b)** *(Tennis etc)* doubles *sing*; *(Mannschaft)* doubles pair.
Doppel- *in cpds* double; ~**adler** *m* double eagle; ~**agent** *m* double agent; ~**b** *nt (Mus)* double flat; ~**band** *m (von doppeltem Umfang)* double-sized volume; *(zwei Bände)* two volumes *pl*; ~**bauer** *m (Chess)* doubled pawn; ~**belastung** *f* double *or* dual load *or* burden *(gen* on); **steuerliche** ~**belastung** double taxation; ~**besteuerung** *f* double taxation; ~**bett** *nt* double bed; *(zwei Betten)* twin beds *pl*; ~**beziehung** *f* dual relationship; ~**bilder** *pl (Med)* ~**bilder wahrnehmen** *or* **sehen** to have double vision; ~**blindversuch** *m (Psych)* experiment using a double blind; ~**bock** *nt or m* double(-strength) bock beer; **d~bödig** *adj* Koffer etc false-bottomed; *(d~deutig)* ambiguous; ~**bödigkeit** *f (fig)* ambiguity; ~**bogen** *m* double sheet (of paper); ~**brief** *m* letter weighing over 20 g; ~**bruch** *m (Math)* compound fraction; ~**büchse** *f* double-barrelled gun *or* *(Schrotbüchse)* shotgun; ~**buchstabe** *m* double letter; ~**decker** *m* -s, - **(a)** *(Aviat)* biplane; **(b)** *(auch* ~**deckerbus)** double-decker (bus); **d~deutig** *adj* ambiguous; ~**deutigkeit** *f* ambiguity; ~**ehe** *f* bigamous marriage; *(Tatbestand)* bigamy *no pl*; **eine** ~**ehe führen** to live bigamously; ~**fehler** *m (Tennis)* double fault; *(Sch)* double mistake; **einen** ~**fehler machen** *(Tennis)* to (serve a) double-fault; ~**fenster** *nt* double window; ~**fenster haben** to have double-glazing; ~**flinte** *f siehe* ~**büchse**; ~**funktion** *f* dual *or* twin function; ~**gänger (in** *f) m* -s, - double, doppelgänger *(esp Liter)*; **d~geschlechtig** *adj (Bot)* hermaphrodite; ~**gesicht** *nt* two faces *pl; (fig)* two sides *pl*; **d~gesichtig** *adj* two-faced, having two faces; *(fig)* two-sided; ~**gestirn** *nt siehe* ~**stern**; **d~gleisig** *adj (Rail)* double-track, twin-track; *(fig)* double; **d~gleisig sein** *(lit)* to have two tracks; **d~gleisig fahren** *(fig)* to play a double game; ~**griff** *m (Mus)* double-stop; ~**haus** *nt* semi-detached house, semi *(Brit inf)*, duplex (house) *(US)*; **er bewohnt eine Hälfte eines** ~**hauses** he lives in a semi (-detached house); ~**heft** *nt (von Zeitschrift)* double number *or* edition; *(Sch)* exercise book of double thickness; ~**-Ich** *nt (Psych)* dual personality; ~**kabine** *f* double *or* twin cabin *or* *(von LKW)* cab; ~**kinn** *nt* double chin; ~**kolbenmotor** *m* two cylinder engine; ~**konsonant** *m* double *or* geminate *(spec)* consonant; ~**kopf** *m* German card game; **d~köpfig** *adj* two-headed, bicephalous *(form)*; ~**korn** *m* type of schnapps; ~**kreuz** *nt (Mus)* double sharp; *(Typ)* double dagger; ~**lauf** *m* double barrel; **d~läufig** *adj* double-barrelled; ~**laut** *m (Ling) (Konsonant)* double *or* geminate *(spec)* consonant; *(Vokal)* double vowel; *(Diphthong)* diphthong; ~**leben** *nt* double life; ~**moral** *f* double (moral) standard(s *pl*); ~**mord** *m* double murder.
doppeln *vt* **(a)** *siehe* **verdoppeln**. **(b)** *(Aus: besohlen)* to resole.
Doppel-: ~**naht** *f* double-stitched seam; ~**name** *m (Nachname)* double-barrelled name; *(Vorname)* double name; ~**natur** *f* dual nature; ~**nelson** *m (Ringen)* full nelson; ~**nummer** *f (von Zeitschrift)* double issue; ~**partner** *m (Sport)* doubles partner; ~**paß** *m (Ftbl)* one-two; ~**punkt** *m* colon; **d~reihig** *adj* in two rows; *Jacke* double-breasted; **d~reihige Perlenkette** double string of pearls; **d~reihige Nietung** two rows of rivets; **d~schläfrig** *adj Bett* double; ~**schlag** *m (Mus)* turn; ~**schnitte** *f* sandwich; **d~seitig** *adj* two-sided, double-sided; *Lungenentzündung* double; **d~seitige Anzeige** double page spread; **d~seitige Lähmung** diplegia; ~**sinn** *m* double meaning, ambiguity; **d~sinnig** *adj* ambiguous; ~**spiel** *nt* **(a)** *(Tennis)* (game of) doubles *sing*; **(b)** *(fig)* double game; ~**spielfeld** *nt (Tennis)* doubles court; **d~spurig** *adj siehe* **zweispurig**; ~**steckdose** *f* double socket; ~**stecker** *m* two-way adaptor; ~**stern** *m* double star; ~**stockbus** *m* double-decker (bus); **d~stöckig** *adj Haus* two-storey, twin-storey; *Bus* double-decker *attr; (hum inf) Schnaps* double; **ein d~stöckiges Bett** bunk beds *pl*; ~**strich** *m (Mus)* double bar; ~**studium** *nt* joint course (of study); ~**stunde** *f (esp Sch)* double period.
doppelt **1** *adj* double; *(verstärkt) Enthusiasmus* redoubled; *(mit zwei identischen Teilen)* twin *attr; (zweimal soviel*

twice; (*Comm*) *Buchführung* double-entry; *Staatsbürgerschaft* dual. **die ~e Freude/Länge/Menge** double *or* twice the pleasure/length/amount; **~e Negation *or* Verneinung** double negative; **~er Boden** (*von Koffer*) false bottom; (*von Boot*) double bottom; **~e Moral, eine Moral mit ~em Boden** double standards *pl*, a double standard; **in ~er Hinsicht** in two respects; **ein ~es Spiel spielen *or* treiben** to play a double game; *siehe* **Ausfertigung**.

2 *adv sehen, zählen* double; (*zweimal*) twice; (*direkt vor Adjektiv*) doubly. **~ so schön/soviel *etc*** twice as nice/much *etc*; **sie ist ~ so alt wie ich** she is twice as old as I am *or* twice my age; **dieser ist ~ so groß wie jener** this is twice as big *or* twice the size of that one; **das/die Karte haben ~** I have two of them/these cards; **das freut mich ~** that gives me double *or* twice the pleasure; **~ gemoppelt** (*inf*) tautologous, saying the same thing twice over; **sich ~ in acht nehmen** to be doubly careful; **~ und dreifach** *bereuen, leid tun* deeply; *sich entschuldigen* profusely; *prüfen* thoroughly; *versichern* absolutely; **seine Schuld ~ und dreifach bezahlen** to pay back one's debt with interest; **der Stoff liegt ~** the material is double width; **~ genäht hält besser** (*prov*) ~ better safe than sorry (*prov*).

Doppelte(r) *m decl as adj* (*inf*) double.
Doppelte(s) *nt decl as adj* double. **um das ~ größer** twice as large; (*Gegenstand auch*) double the size; **das ~ bezahlen** to pay twice as much *or* double the amount; **etw um das ~ erhöhen** to increase sth by double the amount.
Doppelt-: **d~kohlensauer** *adj* **d~kohlensaures Natron** sodium bicarbonate, bicarbonate of soda; **~sehen** *nt* double vision.
Doppelung *f* doubling.
Doppel-: **~verdiener** *m* person with two incomes; (*pl: Paar*) couple with two incomes; **~vergaser** *m* twin carburettors *pl or* carbs *pl*; **~versicherung** *f* double insurance; (*Police*) double insurance policy; **~vierer** *m* (*Sport*) quadruple skulls *pl*; **~vokal** *m* double vowel; **~währung** *f* bimetallism; **~zentner** *m* 100 kilos, (metric) quintal; **~zimmer** *nt* double room; **d~züngig** *adj* (*fig*) devious; (*stärker*) deceitful; *Mensch auch* two-faced; **d~züngig reden** to say one thing and mean another; **~züngigkeit** *f* (a) *no pl siehe adj* deviousness; deceitfulness; two-facedness; (b) (*Äußerung*) devious remark; **~zweier** *m* (*Sport*) double skulls *pl*.
Doppler|effekt *m* (*Phys*) Doppler effect.
Dorado *nt* -s, -s *siehe* **Eldorado**.
Dorf *nt* -(e)s, ¨er village; (*fig*) backwater. **auf dem ~(e)** (*in einem bestimmten Dorf*) in the village; (*auf dem Land*) in the country; **das Leben auf dem ~e** village life; **er ist vom ~(e)** he's from the/our village; (*vom Lande*) he's from the country; **nie aus seinem ~ herausgekommen sein** (*fig*) to be parochial *or* insular; **auf die ¨er gehen** (*inf*) (*umständlich sein*) to go all round the houses; (*Cards*) to lead the side suits; **aus jedem ~ einen Hund haben** (*Cards*) to have a mixed hand; *siehe* **böhmisch, Kirche**.
Dorf- *in cpds* village; **~akademie** *f* (*DDR*) *village college for adult further education through evening classes*; **~älteste(r)** *m* village elder; **~anger** *m* (*dated*) village green; **~bewohner** *m* villager.
Dörfchen *nt dim of* **Dorf** small village, hamlet.
Dorf-: **~gasthaus** *nt*, **~gasthof** *m* village inn; **~gemeinde** *f* village community; (*Admin*) rural district; (*Eccl*) village parish; **~geschichte** *f* (a) (*Liter: Erzählung*) story of village life; (b) *no pl* village history.
dörfisch *adj* rustic (*auch pej*).
Dorf-: **~jugend** *f* young people *pl* of the village, village youth *pl*; **~krug** *m* village inn *or* pub (*Brit*).
Dörflein *nt dim of* **Dorf**.
Dörfler(in *f*) *m* -s, - (*dated*) villager.
Dorfleute *pl* villagers *pl*.
dörflich *adj* village *attr*; (*ländlich*) rustic, rural.
Dorf-: **~platz** *m* village square; **~schaft** *f* (*Sw*) hamlet; **~schöne, ~schönheit** *f* (*iro*) village beauty; **~schulze** *m* (*Hist*) village mayor; **~trottel** *m* (*inf*) village idiot.
Doria *interj siehe* **Donner**.
dorisch *adj* (*Archit*) Doric; (*Hist auch, Mus*) Dorian.
Dorisch(e) *nt* -en, *no pl* Doric.
Dorn *m* -(e)s, -en *or* (*inf*) ¨er (a) (*Bot, fig*) thorn. **das ist mir ein ~ im Auge** (*fig*) that is a thorn in my flesh; (*Anblick*) I find that an eyesore. (b) *pl* -e (*poet*: **~busch**) briar, thornbush. (c) *pl* -e (*Sporn*) spike; (*von Schnalle*) tongue; (*von Scharnier*) pin; (*Tech; Werkzeug*) awl.
Dornbusch *m* briar, thornbush. **der brennende ~** (*Bibl*) the burning bush.
Dornen-: **d~gekrönt** *adj* (*Bibl*) wearing a crown of thorns, crowned with thorns; **der ~gekrönte Christ** Christ with the crown of thorns; **~gestrüpp** *nt* thorny bushes *pl or* undergrowth; **~hecke** *f* thorn(y) hedge; **~krone** *f* (*Bibl*) crown of thorns; **~pfad** *m* thorny path; (*fig*) path fraught with difficulties, path of tribulation; **d~reich** *adj* thorny; (*fig*) fraught with difficulty; **d~voll** *adj* (*fig*) fraught with difficulty.
Dornfortsatz *m* (*Anat*) spiny *or* spinous (*spec*) process.
dornig *adj* thorny; (*fig auch*) fraught with difficulty.
Dorn-: **~röschen** *nt* the Sleeping Beauty; **~röschenschlaf** *f* (*fig*) torpor, slumber; **~strauch** *m siehe* **~busch**.
Dörre *f* -, -n (*dial*) *siehe* **Darre**.
dorren *vi aux sein* (*geh*) *siehe* **dörren** 2.
dörren 1 *vt* to dry. 2 *vi aux sein* (*austrocknen*) to dry up.
Dörr- *in cpds* dried; **~fisch** *m* dried fish; **~fleisch** *nt* dried meat; **~obst** *nt* dried fruit; **~pflaume** *f* prune.
dorsal *adj* (*Zool, Ling*) dorsal; *Verkrümmung, Schwäche* spinal.
Dorsal *m* -s, -e, **Dorsallaut** *m* (*Ling*) dorsal (consonant).

Dorsch *m* -(e)s, -e fish of the cod group; (*Kabeljau*) cod(fish).
Dorschleber *f* cod liver.
dort *adv* there; *siehe* **da** 1 (a).
dort-: **~behalten*** *vt sep irreg* to keep there; **~bleiben** *vi sep irreg aux sein* to stay *or* remain there.
dorten *adv* (*old, Aus*) there.
dort-: **~her** *adv* **von ~her** from there, thence (*old, liter*); **~herum** *adv* around (there), thereabouts; **~hin** *adv* there, thither (*old, liter*); **bis ~hin** as far as there, up to that place; **wie komme ich ~hin?** how do I get there?; **~hin|ab** *adv* down there; **~hinauf** *adv* up there; **~hinaus** *adv* out there; **frech bis ~hinaus** (*inf*) really cheeky; **das ärgert mich bis ~hinaus** (*inf*) that really gets me (*inf*), that doesn't half annoy me (*Brit inf*); **~hinein** *adv* in there; **~hinunter** *adv* down there.
dortig *adj* there (*nachgestellt*). **die ~en Behörden** the authorities there.
dort-: **~selbst** *adv* (*geh*) *siehe* **daselbst**; **~zuland(e)** *adv* in that country, (over) there.
Döschen ['dø:sçən] *nt dim of* **Dose**.
Dose *f* -, -n (a) (*Blech~*) tin; (*Konserven~*) can, tin (*Brit*); (*Bier~*) can; (*esp aus Holz*) box; (*mit Deckel*) jar; (*Pillen~, für Schmuck*) box; (*Butter~*) dish; (*Zucker~*) bowl; (*für Gesichtspuder*) compact; (*Plastik~, Streu~*) pack (*inf*). **in ~n** (*Konserven*) canned, tinned (*Brit*).
(b) (*Elec*) socket.
(c) (*Pharm*) *siehe* **Dosis**.
(d) (*sl: Vaging*) hole (*sl*).
dösen *vi* (*inf*) to doze.
Dosen- *in cpds* canned, tinned (*Brit*); **~bier** *nt* canned beer; **~blech** *nt* tin for making cans *or* tins; **~öffner** *m* can-opener, tin-opener (*Brit*).
dosierbar *adj* **leichter ~ sein** to be more easily measured into exact doses; **etw in ~en Mengen verabreichen** to administer sth in exact doses.
dosieren* *vt* *Arznei* to measure into doses; *Menge* to measure out; (*fig*) *Rat, Liebe, Geschenke, Lob* to dispense, to measure *or* hand out; *Stoff, Hinweise* to dispense. **ein Medikament genau ~** to measure out an exact dose of a medicine; **etw dosiert verteilen** (*fig*) to dispense *etc* sth in small amounts *or* doses.
Dosierung *f* (a) (*Dosis*) dosage, dose. (b) *siehe vt* measuring into doses; measuring out; dispensing, handing out; dispensing.
dösig *adj* (*inf*) dozy (*inf*), drowsy.
Dosis *f* -, **Dosen** dose. **in kleinen Dosen** (*lit, fig*) in small doses; **eine große ~ Mut** *etc* a large amount of *or* quite a bit of courage *etc*.
Döskopp *m* (*N Ger inf*) dozy idiot (*inf*).
Dossier [dɔ'sie:] *nt or* (*dated*) *m* -s, -s dossier.
Dotation *f* endowment.
dotieren* *vt* *Posten* to remunerate (*mit* with); *Preis* to endow (*mit* with). **eine gut dotierte Stellung** a remunerative position.
Dotierung *f* endowment; (*von Posten*) remuneration.
Dotter *m or nt* -s, - yolk.
Dotter-: **~blume** *f* globe flower; (*Sumpf~*) marsh marigold; **d~gelb** *adj* golden yellow; **~sack** *m* (*Zool*) yolk sac.
doubeln ['du:bln] 1 *vt jdn* to stand in for; *Szene* to shoot with a stand-in; *Gesangsszene, Sänger* to dub. **er läßt sich nie ~** he never has a stand-in; **ein Stuntman hat die Szene für ihn gedoubelt** a stuntman doubled for him in the scene.
2 *vi* to stand in; (*als Double arbeiten*) to work as a stand-in.
Double ['du:bl] *nt* -s, -s (*Film etc*) stand-in; (*für Gesang*) dubber.
Doublé, Doublee [du'ble:] *nt* -s, -s *siehe* **Dublee**.
doublieren* [du'bli:rən] *vt siehe* **dublieren**.
Douglasie [du'gla:ziə], **Douglasfichte, Douglastanne** ['du:glas-] *f* Douglas fir *or* pine.
down [daʊn] *adj pred* (*sl*) **~ sein** to be (feeling) down *or* blue (*inf*).
Doyen [doa'jɛ̃:] *m* -s, -s (*lit, fig*) doyen.
Doyenne [doa'jɛn] *f* -, -n doyenne.
Doz. *abbr of* **Dozent**.
Dozent(in *f*) *m* lecturer (*für* in), (assistant) professor (*US*) (*für* of).
Dozentur *f* lectureship (*für* in), (assistant) professorship (*US*) (*für* of).
dozieren* (*Univ*) 1 *vi* to lecture (*über* + *acc* on, *an* + *dat* at); (*pej auch*) to hold forth (*über* + *acc* on), to pontificate (*über* + *acc* about). 2 *vt* to lecture in.
dozierend *adj* (*pej*) pontificating, lecturing.
Dozierton *m* (*pej*) pontificating tone.
dpa ['de:pe:'a:] *f* - *abbr of* **Deutsche Presse-Agentur**.
dpt *abbr of* **Dioptrie**.
Dr. ['dɔktɔr] *abbr of* **Doktor. Dr. rer. nat./rer. pol./phil.** PhD; **Dr. theol./jur.** DD/LLD; **Dr. med.** M.D.
Drache *m* -n, -n *siehe auch* **Drachen** (a) (*Myth*) dragon. (b) (*Astron*) Draco.
Drachen *m* -s, - (a) (*Papier~*) kite; (*Sport: Fluggerät*) hang-glider. **einen ~ steigen lassen** to fly a kite. (b) (*inf: zänkisches Weib*) dragon (*inf*), battleaxe (*inf*). (c) (*Wikingerschiff*) long-ship; (*Segelschiff*) dragon class yacht.
Drachen-: **~blut** *nt* (*Myth*) dragon's blood; **~brut** *f* (*pej old*) pack of cutthroats; **~fliegen** *nt* (*Sport*) hang-gliding; **~flieger** *m* (*Sport*) hang-glider; **~flug** *m* (*Sport*) flight; **~kampf** *m* (*Myth*) battle *or* fight with a/the dragon; **~saat** *f* (*pej geh*) seeds of discord *pl*; **~töter** *m* dragon-killer.
Drachme *f* -, -n drachma; (*Pharm old*) drachm.
Dragée, Dragee [dra'ʒe:] *nt* -s, -s (a) (*Bonbon*) sugar-coated chocolate sweet; (*Nuß~, Mandel~*) dragee. (b) (*Pharm*) dragee, sugar-coated pill *or* tablet.
Drageeform *f* **in ~** coated with sugar, in sugar-coated form.

dragieren* [dra'ʒiːrən] vt (Pharm) to sugar-coat, to coat with sugar.

Dragoman m -s, -e dragoman.

Dragoner m -s, - (Hist) dragoon; (pej: Frau) battleaxe, dragon. **fluchen wie ein** ~ (inf) to swear like a trooper (inf).

Draht m -(e)s, ¨e wire. **per** or **über** ~ by wire or (ins Ausland) cable; **eine Nachricht per** ~ **übermitteln** to wire a message; **auf** ~ **sein** (inf) to be on the ball (inf); (wissensmäßig auch) to know one's stuff; **du bist wohl heute nicht ganz auf** ~ (inf) you're not quite with it today (inf); **jdn auf** ~ **bringen** (inf) to bring sb up to scratch; siehe **heiß**.

Draht- in cpds wire; **~auslöser** m (Phot)) cable release; **~bürste** f wire brush.

drahten vt (dated) to wire, to cable.

Draht-: **~esel** m (dated hum) trusty bicycle; (alt auch) boneshaker (inf); **~fernsehen** nt cable television; **~funk** m wire or line broadcasting; **d~gebunden** adj wired, wireconnected; **~geflecht** nt wire mesh; **~gewebe** nt wire gauze; **~gitter** nt wire netting; **~haar(dackel)** m wire-haired dachshund; **d~haarig** adj wire-haired; **~haarterrier** m wirehaired terrier.

drahtig adj Haar, Mensch wiry.

Draht-: **d~los** adj Telegrafie wireless; **~puppe** f string puppet; **~saite** f (Mus) steel string; **~schneider** m -s, - wire cutters pl.

Drahtseil nt wire cable. **Nerven wie** ~e (inf) nerves of steel.

Drahtseil-: **~bahn** f cable railway; **~künstler** m (Seiltänzer) tightrope artist or walker.

Draht-: **~sieb** nt wire sieve; **~stift** m panel pin; **~telegrafie** f line telegraphy; **~verhau** m wire entanglement; (Käfig) wire enclosure; **~zaun** m wire fence; **~ziehen** nt -s, no pl wiredrawing; **~zieher(in** f) m -s, - wire-drawer; (fig) wire-puller.

Drainage [drɛ'naʒə, (Aus) drɛ'naː3] f -, -n drainage (auch Med etc).

drainieren* [drɛ'niːrən] vti to drain (auch Med).

Draisine [drai'ziːnə, drɛ'ziːnə] f (Rail) trolley; (Fahrrad) dandy horse.

drakonisch adj draconian.

drall adj Mädchen, Arme strapping, sturdy; Busen, Hintern ample; Backen rounded.

Drall m -(e)s, -e (a) (von Kugel, Ball) spin; (um Längsachse auch) twist; (Abweichung von Bahn) swerve; (inf: von Auto) pull. **einem Ball einen** ~ **geben** to give a ball (some) spin, to spin a ball; **einen** ~ **nach links haben** (Auto) to pull to the left.

(b) (fig: Hang) tendency, inclination. **sie hat einen** ~ **nach links/zum Moralisieren** she inclines or leans to the left/tends to moralize.

Drallheit f siehe adj strappingness, sturdiness; ampleness; roundedness.

Dralon ® nt -(s), no pl dralon.

Drama nt -s, Dramen (lit: Stück, Gattung, fig: dramatisches Geschehen) drama; (fig) (Katastrophe) disaster; (Aufheben) to-do (inf).

Dramatik f (lit, fig) drama.

Dramatiker(in f) m -s, - dramatist.

dramatisch adj (lit, fig) dramatic.

dramatisieren* vt (lit, fig) to dramatize.

Dramatisierung f dramatization.

Dramaturg(in f) m -en, -en dramaturge (form), literary manager.

Dramaturgie f dramaturgy; (Abteilung) drama department.

dramaturgisch adj dramatic, dramaturgical (rare); Abteilung drama attr.

dran adv (inf) siehe auch **daran** (a) (an der Reihe) **jetzt bist du** ~ it's your turn now; (beim Spielen auch) it's your go now; (wenn er erwischt wird,) **dann ist er** ~ or (hum) **am ~sten** (if he gets caught) he'll be for it or for the high jump (inf); **er war** ~ (mußte sterben) his time had come; **morgen ist Mathematik** ~ we've got maths tomorrow; siehe **drauf, drum, glauben**.

(b) **schlecht** ~ **sein** to be in a bad way; (unglücklich auch) to be unfortunate; **gut** ~ **sein** to be well-off; (glücklich) to be fortunate; (gesundheitlich) to be well; **früh/spät** ~ **sein** to be early/late.

(c) **an ihm ist nichts** ~ (sehr dünn) he's nothing but skin and bone; (nicht attraktiv, nicht interessant) there is nothing to him; **an dem Hühnchen ist nichts** ~ there is no meat on that chicken; **was ist an ihm** ~, **daß ...?** what is there about him that ...?; **da ist alles** ~! that's got everything; **da wird schon etwas (Wahres)** ~ **sein** there must be something or some truth in that; **an dem Auto ist irgendetwas** ~ there is something wrong or the matter with the car; **ich weiß nicht, wie ich (bei ihm)** ~ **bin** I don't know where I stand (with him).

Dränage [drɛ'naːʒə] f -, -n (esp Aus, Sw) siehe **Drainage**.

dranbleiben vi sep irreg aux sein (inf) (a) (sich nicht entfernen) to stay close; (am Apparat) to hang on; (an der Arbeit) to stick at it. **am Gegner/an der Arbeit** ~ to stick to one's opponent/at one's work.

(b) (sterben) to kick the bucket (inf). **er ist bei der Operation drangeblieben** the operation did for him (inf).

Drang m -(e)s, ¨e (a) (Antrieb) urge (auch Physiol), impulse; (Sehnsucht) yearning (nach for); (nach Wissen) thirst (nach for). ~ **nach Bewegung** urge or impulse to move; **ich habe einen** ~ (inf: zur Toilette) I'm dying to go (inf); siehe **Sturm**.

(b) **der** ~ **zum Tor** (Sport) the surge towards the goal; **der** ~ **nach Osten** the drive towards the East.

(c) (geh: Druck) pressure; (des Augenblicks auch) stress. **im** ~ **der Ereignisse** under the pressure of events.

drang pret von **dringen**.

drangeben vt sep irreg (inf) (a) (zufügen) to add (an + acc to). **ich geb' noch 10 Minuten dran** I'll wait another ten minutes, I'll give you/him etc another ten minutes. (b) (opfern) to give

up; Leben auch to sacrifice; Geld to fork out (inf). **sein Leben für etw** ~ to give one's life for sth.

drangehen vi sep irreg aux sein (inf) (a) (berühren, sich zu schaffen machen an) to touch (an etw (acc)) sth. **an etw** (acc) (zu nahe) ~ (sich nähern) to go too close to sth.

(b) (in Angriff nehmen) ~, **etw zu tun** to get down to doing sth; **es wird Zeit, daß ich drangehe** it's time I got down to it.

Drängelei f (inf) pushing, jostling; (Bettelei) pestering.

drängeln (inf) **1** vi to push, to jostle. **2** vti (betteln) to pester. **3** vr **sich nach vorne** etc ~ to push one's way to the front etc; **sich** ~, **etw zu tun** (fig) to fall over oneself to do sth (inf).

drängen 1 vi (a) (in Menge) to push, to press. **die Menge drängte zum Ausgang** the crowd pressed towards the exit.

(b) (Sport: offensiv spielen) to press or push forward.

(c) (fordern) to press (auf + acc for). **darauf** ~, **eine Antwort zu erhalten, auf Antwort** ~ to press for an answer; **darauf** ~, **daß jd etw tut/etw getan wird** to press for sb to do sth/for sth to be done; **zum Aufbruch/zur Eile** ~ to be insistent that one should leave/hurry.

(d) (zeitlich) to be pressing, to press. **die Zeit drängt** time is pressing or presses; **es drängt/drängt nicht** it's/it's not pressing or urgent.

2 vt (a) (mit Ortsangabe) to push.

(b) (auffordern) to press, to urge. **es drängt mich, das zu tun** I feel moved or the urge to do that.

3 vr (Menge) to throng or crowd; (fig: Termine etc) to mount up. **sich nach vorn/durch die Menge** ~ to push or force one's way to the front/through the crowd; siehe **gedrängt**.

Drängen nt -s, no pl urging; (Bitten) requests pl; (Bestehen) insistence.

drängend adj pressing, urgent.

Dränger m -s, - siehe **Stürmer**.

Drangsal ['draŋzaːl] f -, -e (old, liter) (Not) hardship; (Leiden) suffering, distress.

drangsalieren* vt (plagen) to pester, to plague; (unterdrücken) to oppress.

dranhalten sep irreg (inf) **1** vt to hold up (dat, an + acc to). **etw näher an etw** (acc) ~ to hold sth closer to sth.

2 vr (sich beeilen) to hurry up, to get a move on (inf); (sich anstrengen) to make an effort, to get one's finger out (sl); (nahe dranbleiben) to keep close to it.

dranhängen sep (inf) **1** vt **etw an etw** (acc) ~ to hang sth onto sth; **viel Zeit** etc ~, **etw zu tun** to put a lot of time etc into doing sth.

2 vi irreg **an etw** (dat) ~ to hang from sth; **es hing ein Zettel dran** a tag was attached (an + dat to).

3 vr to hang on; (verfolgen) to stay close behind, to stick to sb's tail (inf); (ständig begleiten) to latch on (bei to); (jds Beispiel folgen) to follow suit.

dränieren* vt siehe **drainieren**.

Drank m -(e)s, no pl swill, slops pl.

drankommen vi sep irreg aux sein (inf) (a) (berühren) to touch.

(b) (erreichen können) to be able to reach (an etw (acc) sth).

(c) (an die Reihe kommen) to have one's turn or (bei Spielen auch) go; (Sch: beim Melden) to be called; (Frage, Aufgabe etc) to come up. **jetzt kommst du dran** now it's your turn/go; **du kommst als erster/nächster dran** it's your turn/go first/next; **nun kommt das Schlafzimmer dran** it's the bedroom next, now it's the turn of the bedroom.

drankriegen vt sep (inf) **jdn** ~ to get sb (inf); (zu einer Arbeit) to get sb to do it/sth; mit Witz, Streich to catch sb out.

Dranktonne f (N Ger) swill bucket; (fig inf) walking dustbin (hum).

dranlassen vt sep irreg (inf) **etw (an etw** dat) ~ to leave sth on (sth).

dranmachen sep (inf) **1** vr siehe **daranmachen. 2** vt **etw (an etw** acc) ~ to put sth on (sth).

drannehmen vt sep irreg Schüler to ask, to question; Patienten to take, to see.

dransetzen sep (inf) **1** vt (a) (anfügen) **ein Stück/ein Teil** etc (an etw acc) ~ to add a piece/part (to sth).

(b) (einsetzen) seine Kraft/sein Vermögen etc ~ to put one's effort/money into it; **alles** ~ to make every effort; **jdn** ~ to put sb onto the job or it.

2 vr (a) (nahe an etw) **sich (an etw** acc) ~ to sit (down) next to sth.

(b) (Arbeit anfangen) to get down to work or it.

dransten adv (hum) superl of **dran**.

dranwollen vi sep (inf) (drankommen wollen) to want to have one's turn; (probieren wollen) to want to have a go.

Draperie [drapə'riː] f (old) drapery; (Faltenwurf) drapes pl.

drapieren* vt to drape; (fig) to cloak.

Drapierung f (a) (das Drapieren) siehe vt draping; cloaking. (b) (Schmuck, kunstvolle Falten) drape. **~en** (fig: beschönigende Worte) fine phrases.

Drastik f, no pl (Derbheit) drasticness; (Deutlichkeit) graphicness. **etw mit besonderer** ~ **beschreiben** to describe sth particularly graphically or in very extreme tones.

drastisch adj (derb) drastic; (deutlich) graphic.

dräuen vi (poet) siehe **drohen**.

drauf adv (inf) siehe auch **darauf. immer feste** ~! get stuck in there! (inf), let him have it! (inf); ~ **und dran sein, etw zu tun** to be on the point or verge of doing sth; **etw** ~ **haben** (sl) (können) to be able to do sth no bother (inf); Kenntnisse to be well up on sth (inf); Witze, Sprüche to have sth off pat (inf); **schwer was** ~ **haben** (sl) to know one's stuff or onions (inf); **160 Sachen** ~ **haben** (inf) to be doing 160.

Drauf-: **d~bekommen*** vt sep irreg (inf) **eins d~bekommen** to be given a smack; **~gabe** f (a) (Comm) deposit; (b) (Aus) siehe

Zugabe; ~**gänger** m -s, - daredevil, adventurous type; (bei Frauen) wolf; d~**gängerisch** adj daring, adventurous; (negativ) reckless; (bei Frauen) wolfish; d~**geben** vt irreg sep (a) jdm eins d~**geben** (inf) to give sb a smack; (b) (dazugeben) noch etwas d~**geben** to add some extra (inf); (c) (Aus: als Zugabe anfügen) to sing/play etc as an encore; d~**gehen** vi sep irreg aux sein (inf) (entzweigehen) to fall to bits or apart; (sterben) to bite the dust (inf); (Geld) to disappear; ~**geld** nt deposit; d~**halten** sep irreg (inf) 1 vt etw (auf etw acc) d~**halten** to hold sth on (sth); 2 vi (als Ziel angehen) to aim for it; d~**hauen** sep irreg 1 vi (inf: schlagen) to hit hard; 2 vt (sl) einen d~**hauen** to have a booze-up (inf); d~**kommen** vi sep irreg aux sein (inf) (sich erinnern) to remember; (begreifen) to catch on, to get it (inf); jdm d~**kommen** to get on to sb (inf); d~**kriegen** vt sep (inf) etw (auf etw acc) d~**kriegen** to get or fit sth on(to sth); eins d~**kriegen** to be given what-for (inf); (geschlagen werden) to be given a smack; (Schicksalsschlag erhalten) to receive a blow; (besiegt werden) to be given a thrashing; d~**lassen** vt sep irreg (inf) etw (auf etw dat) d~**lassen** to leave sth on (sth); d~**legen** vt sep (inf) (a) auch vi to lay out; 20 Mark d~**legen** to lay out an extra 20 marks; (b) etw (auf etw acc) d~**legen** to put or lay sth on(to sth).

drauflos adv (nur) immer feste or munter ~! (just) keep at it!, keep it up!

drauflos-: ~**arbeiten** vi sep (inf) to work away, to beaver away (inf); (anfangen) to start working; ~**gehen** vi sep irreg aux sein (inf) (auf ein Ziel) to make straight for it; (ohne Ziel) to set off; (nicht zögern) to set to work; ~**malen** vi sep (inf) to paint away; (anfangen) to start painting; ~**reden** vi sep (inf) to talk away; (anfangen) to start talking; ~**schießen** vi sep irreg (inf) to fire away; ~**schlagen** vi sep irreg (inf) to hit out, to let fly (inf).

drauf-: ~**machen** vt sep (inf) etw (auf etw acc) ~**machen** to put sth on(to sth); einen ~**machen** to make a night of it (inf); D~**sicht** f (inf) top view; ~**stehen** vi sep irreg (inf) aux haben or (dial) sein etw steht ~ sth is on it; auf etw (dat) ~**stehen** (Mensch, Sache) to stand on sth; (Aufschrift) to be on sth; (da) stehe ich nicht ~ (fig sl) it doesn't turn me on (sl); ~**stoßen** sep irreg (inf) 1 vi aux sein to come or hit upon it; (gegen etw stoßen) to bump or run into it; (finden) to come across it; wenn man geradeaus weitergeht, dann muß man ~**stoßen** if you go on straight ahead, you can't miss it; 2 vt jdn ~**stoßen** to point it out to sb; ~**stürzen** vr sep (inf) to swoop or pounce on it/them, to rush to get one's hands on it/them; ~**zahlen** vi sep (inf) (a) siehe ~**legen** (a); (b) (fig: Einbußen erleben) to pay the price.

draus adv siehe daraus.

draus-: ~**bringen** vt sep irreg (dial) jdn ~**bringen** (Konzentration stören) to make sb lose track, to distract sb; (irremachen) to put sb off; ~**kommen** vi sep irreg aux sein (a) (dial, Aus: aus dem Konzept kommen) to lose track; (b) (Sw: verstehen) to see, to get it (inf).

draußen adv outside; (im Freien auch) out of doors, outdoors; (da ~, weit weg von hier) out there; (im Ausland) abroad. ~ (an der Front) out there (on the front); ~ **auf dem Lande/dem Balkon/im Garten** out in the country/on the balcony/in the garden; ~ **(auf dem Meer)** out at sea; **da/hier** ~ out there/here; **ganz da** ~ way out there; ~ **(vor der Tür)** at the door; **nach** ~ outside; (ferner weg) out there; **weit/weiter** ~ far/further out; ~ **bleiben/lassen** to stay/leave out (auch fig inf) or outside; „Hunde müssen ~ **bleiben**" "no dogs (please)", "please leave your dog outside"; **etw** ~ **tragen** to wear sth outside.

Drechselbank f wood(-turning) lathe.

drechseln 1 vt to turn (on a wood lathe); (fig pej) to over-elaborate; Vers to turn; siehe auch gedrechselt. 2 vi to work the (wood) lathe.

Drechsler(in f) m -s, - (wood) turner.

Drechsler|arbeit f (wood) turning; (Gegenstand) piece turned on the lathe.

Drechslerei f (Werkstatt) (wood-)turner's workshop; (Handwerk) (wood) turning.

Dreck m -(e)s, no pl (a) dirt; (esp ekelhaft) filth; (Schlamm) mud; (Kot) muck; (fig) (Schund) rubbish; (Schmutz, Obszönes) dirt, muck; (stärker) filth; (inf: schlimme Lage) mess, jam (inf). ~ **machen** to make a mess; **in/mit** ~ **und Speck** (ungewaschen) unwashed; **er hat mir das Auto mit** ~ **und Speck verkauft** he sold me the car just as it was; **ich gehe in** ~ **und Speck dahin** I'll go just as I am; **im** ~ **sitzen** or **stecken** (inf) to be in a mess or jam (inf); **aus dem größten** or **gröbsten** ~ **heraus sein** (inf) to be through or past the worst; **jdn wie den letzten** ~ **behandeln** (inf) to treat sb like dirt; **der letzte** ~ **sein** to be the lowest of the low; ~ **am Stecken haben** (fig) to have a skeleton in the cupboard; **etw in den** ~ **ziehen** or **treten** (fig) to drag sth through the muck; siehe Karren, bewerfen.
(b) (inf) (Angelegenheit, Kram) business, stuff (inf); (Kleinigkeit) little thing. **sich einen** ~ **um jdn/etw kümmern** or **scheren** not to care or give a damn about sb/sth (inf); **mach deinen** ~ **alleine!** do it yourself; **die Nase in jeden** ~ **stecken** (inf) to poke one's nose into everyone's business or into everything; **das geht ihn einen** ~ **an** that's none of his business, that's got damn all to do with him (sl); **einen** ~ **wissen/verstehen/wert sein** to know/understand/be worth damn all (sl); **einen** ~ **ist er/hast du** like hell he is/you have (sl).

Dreck-: ~**arbeit** f (inf) (a) (lit, fig: schmutzige Arbeit) dirty work; (b) (pej: niedere Arbeit) drudgery no pl; ~**ding** nt (pej inf) dirty or filthy thing; (ärgerliche Sache) damn thing (inf); ~**eimer** m (inf) (im Haus) rubbish bin; (im Freien) dustbin, trash can (US); ~**finger** pl (inf) (lit, fig) dirty fingers pl; ~**fink** m (inf) siehe ~**spatz**.

dreckig adj (lit, fig) dirty; (stärker) filthy. ~ **lachen** to give or laugh a dirty laugh; **es geht mir** ~ (inf) I'm in a bad way; (finanziell) I'm badly off; **wenn man ihn erwischt, geht es ihm** ~ (inf)

---

if they catch him, he'll be sorry or in for it (inf).

Dreck-: ~**loch** nt (pej) hole (inf), hovel; ~**nest** nt (pej) dump (inf), hole (inf); ~**pfoten** pl (inf) (lit, fig) dirty or filthy paws pl; ~**sack** m (vulg) dirty bastard (sl); ~**sau** m (vulg) filthy swine (inf); ~**schleuder** f (pej) (Mundwerk) foul mouth; (Mensch) foul-mouthed person; ~**schwein** nt (inf) dirty pig (inf).

Dreckskerl m (inf) dirty swine (inf), louse (inf).

Dreckspatz m (inf) (Kind) mucky pup (inf); (Schimpfwort) filthy beggar (inf).

Dreck(s)zeug nt (inf) damn or blasted stuff (inf). **das ist doch ein** ~ damn this stuff (inf).

Dreckwetter nt (inf) filthy weather (inf).

Dreh m -s, -s or -e (List) dodge; (Kunstgriff) trick. **den** ~ **heraushaben, etw zu tun** to have got the knack of doing sth; **den (richtigen)** ~ **heraushaben** or **weghaben** (inf) to have got the hang of it.

Dreh-: ~**achse** f axis of rotation; ~**arbeit** f (a) (von Dreher) lathe work; (Gegenstand) piece turned on the lathe; (b) ~**arbeiten** pl (Film) shooting sing; ~**bank** f lathe; d~**bar** adj (rundum) rotating, revolving attr; (um einen Festpunkt) swivelling attr; (~gelagert) pivoted; d~**bar sein** to rotate or revolve/swivel; ~**beginn** m (Film) start of shooting; ~**bewegung** f turn(ing motion); (esp Tech) rotation, rotary motion; **eine** ~**bewegung machen** to turn/rotate/revolve once; ~**bleistift** m propelling (Brit) or mechanical (US) pencil; ~**brücke** f swing bridge; ~**buch** nt (Film) screenplay, (film) script; ~**buchautor** m scriptwriter, screenplay writer; ~**bühne** f revolving stage.

Drehe f -, no pl (inf) (so) **um die** ~ (zeitlich) or thereabouts, round about then; (so) **in der** ~ (örtlich) (there) or thereabouts, round about there.

drehen 1 vt to turn (auch Tech: auf Drehbank); (um eine Achse auch) to rotate; (um Mittelpunkt auch) to revolve, to rotate; Stuhl to swivel; Kreisel to spin; Kopf auch to twist; Zwirne to twist; Zigaretten, Pillen to roll; Film to shoot; (fig: verdrehen) to twist; (inf: schaffen) to fix (inf), to work (inf). **jdm den Rücken** ~ to turn one's back on sb; **das Gas hoch/auf klein** ~ to turn the gas up high/down low; **Fleisch durch den Wolf** ~ to put meat through the mincer; **ein Ding** ~ (sl) to play a or to pull off a prank; (Verbrecher) to pull a job (inf) or caper (sl); **wie man es auch dreht und wendet** no matter how you look at it; siehe Däumchen, Runde, Strick[1].

2 vi to turn; (Wind) to shift, to change; (Film) to shoot, to film; (Zigaretten ~) to roll one's own. **an etw** (dat) ~ to turn sth; **am Radio** ~ to turn a knob on the radio; **daran ist nichts zu** ~ **und deuteln** (fig) there are no two ways about it.

3 vr (a) to turn (um about); (um Mittelpunkt auch) to revolve, to rotate; (um Achse auch) to rotate; (sehr schnell: Kreisel) to spin; (Wind) to shift, to change. **sich auf den Rücken** ~ to turn on(to) one's back; **sich um etw** ~ to revolve or rotate around sth; **sich um sich (selbst)** ~ to rotate, to revolve on its own axis; (Mensch) to turn round; (Auto) to spin; **sich im Kreise** ~ to turn round and round; **sich im Tanze** ~ (liter) to spin around; **mir dreht sich alles** everything's spinning about me; **mir dreht sich alles im Kopf** my head is spinning or swimming; **sich** ~ **und winden** (fig) to twist and turn.

(b) **sich um etw** ~ (betreffen) to concern sth, to be about sth; (um zentrale Frage) to centre on sth; **alles dreht sich um sie** everything revolves around her; (steht im Mittelpunkt) she's the centre of attention or interest; **es dreht sich darum, daß ...** the point is that ...; **in meiner Frage dreht es sich darum, ob ...** my question is whether ...; **in dieser Sendung drehte es sich um ..., die Sendung drehte sich um ...** the broadcast was about ... or concerned ...

Dreher m -s, - (a) lathe operator; (Drechsler auch) (wood) turner.

(b) (Tanz) country waltz.

Dreherin f siehe Dreher (a).

Dreh-: ~**geschwindigkeit** f rotary or rotating speed; ~**gestell** nt (Rail) bogie; ~**impuls** m angular momentum; ~**knopf** m knob; ~**kolbenmotor** m siehe Kreiskolbenmotor; ~**kran** m slewing or rotary crane; ~**kreuz** nt turnstile; ~**leier** f barrel-organ, hurdy-gurdy; ~**maschine** f motorized (metal-turning) lathe; ~**moment** nt torque; ~**orgel** f barrel-organ, hurdy-gurdy; ~**orgelspieler** m organ-grinder, hurdy-gurdy man; ~**ort** m (Film) location; ~**pause** f (Film) break in shooting; ~**punkt** m pivot; ~**restaurant** nt revolving restaurant; ~**schalter** m rotary switch; ~**scheibe** f (a) (Rail) turntable; (b) siehe Töpferscheibe; ~**strom** m three-phase current; ~**stromlichtmaschine** f (esp Aut) three-phase (current) alternator; ~**stuhl** m swivel-chair; ~**tag** m (Film) day of shooting; ~**tür** f revolving door.

Drehung f (a) turn; (ganze ~ um eigene Achse auch) rotation; (um einen Punkt auch) revolution. **eine halbe/ganze** ~ a half/complete turn; **eine** ~ **um 180°** a 180° turn, a turn through 180°.

(b) (das Drehen) turning; (um eigene Achse auch) rotation; (um einen Punkt auch) revolving.

Drehwurm m (inf): **einen** or **den** ~ **kriegen/haben** to get giddy.

Drehzahl f number of revolutions or revs; (pro Minute) revolutions or revs pl per minute, rpm.

Drehzahl-: ~**bereich** m (Aut) engine speed range; **im niederen/hohen** ~**bereich** at low/high revs; ~**messer** m rev counter.

drei num three. **von uns** ~**en** from the three of us; **die (Heiligen) D~ Könige, die** ~ **Weisen aus dem Morgenland** the Three Kings or Wise Men (from the East), the Magi; **die** ~ **tollen Tage** the last three days of Fasching in Germany; **aller guten Dinge sind** ~! (prov) all good things/disasters come in threes!; (nach zwei mißglückten Versuchen) third time lucky!; **er arbeitet/ißt für** ~ (inf) he does the work of/eats enough for three; **etw in** ~

Worten erklären (*inf*) to explain sth briefly *or* in a few words; ehe man bis ~ zählen konnte (*inf*) in a trice, before you could say Jack Robinson (*inf*); **sie sieht aus, als ob sie nicht bis ~ zählen könnte** (*inf*) she looks pretty vacuous *or* empty-headed; (*unschuldig*) she looks as if butter wouldn't melt in her mouth; *siehe* **vier**.

Drei *f* -, -en three; *siehe auch* **Vier**.

Drei- *in cpds* three-, tri-; **~achttakt** *m* three-eight time; **d~ad(e)rig** *adj* (*Elec*) three-core; **~bein** *nt* (*inf*) three-legged stool; **d~beinig** *adj* three-legged; **~bund** *m* (*Hist*) Triple Alliance (*between Germany, Austria-Hungary and Italy in 1882*).

Drei-D- [drai'de:] *in cpds* 3-D.

Drei-: **~decker** *m* -s, - (*Aviat*) triplane; (*Naut*) three-decker; **d~dimensional** *adj* three-dimensional; **~dimensionalität** *f* three-dimensionality.

Drei|eck *nt* -(e)s, -e triangle; (*Zeichen~*) set-square; (*Sport: Winkel*) top left/right hand corner of the goal. **Südliches ~** Southern Triangle.

drei|eckig *adj* triangular, three-sided.

Drei|ecks-: **~tuch** *nt* triangular scarf; (*um die Schultern getragen*) triangular shawl; (*Med*) triangular bandage; **~verhältnis** *nt* (eternal) triangle; **ein ~verhältnis haben** to be involved in an eternal triangle.

drei|einig *adj* triune, three in one *pred*. **der ~e Gott** the Holy Trinity, the Triune God.

Drei|einigkeit *f* Trinity. **die ~ Gottes** the Holy Trinity.

Dreier *m* -s, - (a) (*Münze*) three pfennig piece, = thruppence (*Brit*). (b) (*Aus, S Ger: Ziffer, Note*) three. (c) (*Sport*) (*Eislauf etc*) three; (*Golf*) threesome.

Dreier- *in cpds siehe* **Vierer-, vierer-**.

dreifach 1 *adj* triple, threefold (*liter*). **die ~e Menge** triple *or* treble *or* three times the amount; **ein ~es Hoch!** three cheers!; *siehe* **Ausfertigung**. 2 *adv* three times. **~ abgesichert/verstärkt** trebly secure/reinforced; *siehe* **vierfach**.

Dreifache(s) *nt decl as adj* **das ~** triple *or* treble *or* three times the amount, three times as much; **9 ist das ~ von 3** 9 is *or* equals three times 3; **ein ~s kosten** to cost three times as much; **er verdient das ~ von dem, was ich bekomme** he earns three times as much as *or* treble the amount that I do; **etw um das ~ vermehren** to multiply sth three times *or* **Zahl** *auch* by three.

Dreifach- *in cpds siehe*: **~stecker** *m* three-way adapter.

Drei-: **d~faltig** *adj siehe* **d~einig**; **d~fältig** *adj siehe* **d~fach**; **~faltigkeit** *f* Trinity; **~faltigkeitsfest** *nt*, **~faltigkeitssonntag** *m* Trinity Sunday; **~farbendruck** *m* (a) (*Verfahren*) three-colour printing; (b) (*Gedrucktes*) three-colour print; **d~farbig**, **d~färbig** (*Aus*) *adj* three-colour *attr*, three-coloured, trichromatic (*form*); **~felderwirtschaft** *f* three-field system; **~fuß** *m* tripod; (*Gestell für Kessel*) trivet; (*Schemel*) three-legged stool; **d~füßig** *adj* Vers three-foot *attr*.

Dreigang *m* (*inf*) *siehe* **Dreigangschaltung**.

Dreigang-: **~getriebe** *nt* three-speed gear; **~rad** *nt* three-speed bike; **~schaltung** *f* three-speed gear; **ein Fahrrad mit ~schaltung** a three-speed bicycle.

Drei-: **~gespann** *nt* troika; (*fig*) threesome; (*an leitender Stelle*) triumvirate; **~gestirn** *nt* (*lit*) triple star; (*fig geh*) big three; **d~gestrichen** *adj* (*Mus*) **das d~gestrichene C/F** the C/F two octaves above middle C; **d~geteilt** *adj* divided into three (parts); **d~glied(e)rig** *adj* (*Math*) trinomial; **~gliederung** *f* (*Gegliedertsein*) three-part *or* tripartite structure; (*das Gliedern*) division into three (parts); **~groschenheft(chen)** *nt* (*pej*) penny-dreadful (*dated inf*).

Dreiheit *f* trinity.

Drei-: **d~hundert** *num* three hundred; *siehe* **vierhundert**; **~kaiserschlacht** *f* (*Hist*) Battle of Austerlitz; **~kampf** *m* three-part competition (*100 m sprint, long jump and shot-put*); **~kant** *nt* *or* *m* -(e)s, -e trihedron; **~käsehoch** *m* -s, -s (*inf*) tiny tot (*inf*); **~klang** *m* triad; **~klassenwahlsystem** *nt* (*Hist*) three-class electoral system (*in Prussia 1850–1918*); **~könige** *pl* Epiphany *sing*; **~königsfest** *nt* (feast of) Epiphany; **~königstag** *m* feast of Epiphany; **~ländereck** *nt* place where three countries meet; **~laut** *m* triphthong; **~mächtepakt** *m* (*Hist*) three-power *or* tripartite pact (*between Germany, Italy and Japan*), Axis pact.

dreimal *adv* three times, thrice (*old*); *siehe auch* **viermal**.

Drei-: **~master** *m* -s, - three-master; **~meilengrenze** *f* three-mile limit; **~meilenzone** *f* three-mile zone; **~meterbrett** *nt* three-metre board.

drein *adv* (*inf*) *siehe* **darein**.

drein- *in cpds siehe auch* **darein-:** **~blicken** *vi sep* traurig *etc* **~blicken** to look sad *etc*; **~fahren** *vi sep irreg aux sein* (*dial*) to intervene; **~fügen** *vr sep* to resign oneself (to it), to come to terms with it; **~reden** *vi sep* (*dial*) (*dazwischenreden*) to interrupt; (*sich einmischen*) to interfere (*bei* in, with); **ich lasse mir in dieser Angelegenheit von niemandem ~reden** I won't have anyone interfering (with this); **er ließ sich nirgends ~reden** he would never be told; **~schauen** *vi sep siehe* **~blicken**; **~schlagen** *vi sep irreg* (*dial*) to weigh in (*inf*).

Drei-: **~phasenstrom** *m* three-phase current; **d~polig** *adj* three-pole *attr*, with three poles; **Kabel** three-core; **Steckdose, Stecker** three-pin; **~punkt(sicherheits)gurt** *m* lap and diagonal seatbelt; **~rad** *nt* tricycle; (*inf: Auto*) three-wheeler; **d~räd(e)rig** *adj* three-wheeled; **~radwagen** *m* three-wheeled vehicle, three-wheeler.

Dreisatz *m* (*Math*) rule of three.

Dreisatz-: **~aufgabe** *f* problem using the rule of three; **~rechnung** *f* calculation using the rule of three.

Drei-: **d~schiffig** *adj* Kirche with three naves; **~sitzer** *m* (*Aut*) three-seater; **~spitz** *m* three-cornered hat, tricorn; **~springer** *m* triple-jumper; **~sprung** *m* triple jump, hop, step and jump.

dreißig *num* thirty; *siehe auch* **vierzig**.

dreißig- *in cpds siehe auch* **vierzig-;** **~jährig** *adj* (*dreißig Jahre dauernd*) thirty years' *attr*, lasting thirty years; (*dreißig Jahre alt*) thirty years old, thirty-year-old *attr*; **der D~jährige Krieg** the Thirty Years' War.

Dreißigstel¹ *nt* -s, - thirtieth; *siehe* **Viertel¹**.

Dreißigstel² *f* -, no pl (*Phot inf*) thirtieth (of a second).

dreißigste(r, s) *adj* thirtieth.

dreist *adj* bold; **Handlung** *auch* audacious.

Dreistigkeit *f* (a) no pl **eine adj** boldness; audacity. (b) (*Bemerkung*) bold remark; (*Handlung*) bold *or* audacious act.

Drei-: **~stufenrakete** *f* three-stage rocket; **d~stufig** *adj* Rakete three-stage *attr*, with three stages; Plan *auch* three-phase *attr*; **eine d~stufige Treppe** three steps; **d~teilig** *adj* (*aus 3 Teilen*) Kostüm *etc* three-piece *attr*; (*in 3 Teile geteilt*) three-part *attr*, tripartite (*form*); **~teilung** *f* division into three; **die ~teilung der Streitkräfte** dividing the armed forces into three.

dreiviertel ['drai'frtl] *siehe auch* **viertel** 1 *adj inv* three-quarter. **eine ~ Stunde** threequarters of an hour; **~ zwei** (*dial*) a quarter to two. 2 *adv* threequarters.

Dreiviertel ['drai'frtl] *nt* threequarters. **in einem ~ der Zeit in** threequarters of the time; **das Saal war zu einem ~ leer** the room was threequarters empty.

Dreiviertel-: **~arm** (*inf*), **~ärmel** *m* threequarter(-length) sleeve; **~jacke** *f* threequarter-length coat; **d~lang** *adj* threequarter-length; **~literflasche** *f* three-quarter litre bottle; **~mehrheit** *f* threequarters majority; **~spieler** *m* (*Rugby*) three-quarter; **~stunde** *f* threequarters of an hour no *indef art*; **~takt** *m* three-four time; **im ~takt** in three-four time.

Dreiweg- *in cpds* (*Elec*) three-way; **~(lautsprecher)box** *f* three-way loudspeaker system; **~schalter** *m* three-way switch; **~stecker** *m* three-way adapter.

Drei-: **d~wertig** *adj* (*Chem*) trivalent; (*Ling*) three-place; **d~wöchentlich** 1 *adj attr* three-weekly; 2 *adv* every three weeks, at three-weekly intervals; **d~wöchig** *adj attr* three-week; **~zack** *m* -s, -e trident; **d~zackig** *adj* three-pointed; **~zahl** *f* (*geh*) triplicity, triple character.

dreizehn *adj num* thirteen. **jetzt schlägt's aber ~** (*inf*) that's a bit much *or* thick (*inf*); *siehe auch* **vierzehn**.

Drell *m* -s, -e (*N Ger*) *siehe* **Drillich**.

Dresch-: **~boden** *m*, **~diele** *f* threshing floor.

Dresche *f* -, no pl (*inf*) thrashing. **~ kriegen** to get a thrashing.

dreschen *pret* **drosch**, *ptp* **gedroschen** 1 *vt* (a) Korn to thresh; (*inf*) Phrasen to bandy. **leeres Stroh ~** (*fig*) to talk a lot of hot air (*inf*), to talk/write a lot of claptrap (*inf*); **Skat ~** (*inf*) to play skat with enthusiasm.

(b) (*inf: prügeln*) to thrash. **jdn mit den Fäusten ~** to thump *or* pound sb with one's fists.

(c) (*Sport inf: treten, schlagen*) to slam (*inf*), to wallop (*inf*). 2 *vi* (a) to thresh.

(b) (*inf: schlagen, treten*) to hit violently. **auf die Tasten ~** to thump *or* pound the keys; **mit den Fäusten ~** to thump *or* pound one's fists.

3 *vr* (*inf: sich prügeln*) to have a fight.

Drescher *m* -s, - thresher.

Dresch-: **~flegel** *m* flail; **~maschine** *f* threshing machine; **~tenne** *f* threshing floor.

Dreß *m* -sses, -sse, (*Aus*) *f* -, -ssen (*Sport*) (sports) kit; (*für Fußball auch*) strip.

Dresseur [-'sø:r] *m* trainer.

dressierbar *adj* Tier trainable; (*pej*) Mensch *auch* susceptible to conditioning. **leicht/schwer ~** easy/difficult to train/condition.

dressieren* *vt* (a) Tier to train; (*pej*) Mensch *auch* to condition, to discipline. **auf jdn/etw dressiert sein** to be trained to respond to sb/sth; **auf den Mann dressiert sein** to be trained to attack people; **auf das Zusammentreiben von Tieren dressiert** trained to round up animals; **zu etw dressiert sein** to be trained *etc* to do sth.

(b) (*Cook*) Geflügel to dress; Braten to prepare; (*esp Aus*) Torte *etc* to decorate; Teig, Creme to pipe.

Dressman ['dresman] *m* -s, **Dressmen** male model.

Dressur f training; (*für ~reiten*) dressage; (*fig*) conditioning.

Dressur-: **~prüfung** *f* dressage test; **~reiten** *nt* dressage; **~reiter** *m* dressage rider.

dribbeln *vti* to dribble. **mit dem Ball ~** to dribble the ball.

Dribbling *nt* -s, -s dribbling. **ein ~** a piece of dribbling.

Drift f -, -en (*Naut*) drift.

driften *vi aux sein* (*Naut, fig*) to drift.

Drill *m* -(e)s, no pl (*Mil, fig*) drill; (*Sch auch*) drills pl.

Drillbohrer *m* drill.

drillen *vti* (a) (*Mil, fig*) to drill. **jdn auf etw** (*acc*) **~** to drill sb in sth; **auf etw** (*acc*) **gedrillt sein** (*fig inf*) to be practised at doing sth. (b) Loch to drill. (c) (*Agr*) to drill, to sow *or* plant in drills. (d) (*beim Angeln*) to play.

Drillich *m* -s, -e drill; (*für Matratzen etc*) ticking; (*für Markisen*) canvas.

Drillich-: **~anzug** *m* overalls pl, dungarees pl; **~zeug** *nt* overalls pl.

Drilling *m* (a) triplet. (b) (*Angelhaken*) three-pronged hook. (c) (*Jagdgewehr*) triple-barrelled shotgun.

Drillingsgeburt *f* triple birth.

Drill-: **~maschine** *f* (*Agr*) seed drill; **~übung** *f* drill.

drin *adv* (*inf*) *siehe* **darin** (a), **drinnen**.

(b) (*inf*) **da ~** *siehe* **darin** (b).

(c) in it. **er/es ist da ~** he/it is in there; **in der Flasche ist noch etwas ~** there's still something in the bottle; **hallo, ist da jemand ~?** hello, is (there) anyone in there?; *siehe* **~sitzen** *etc*.

(d) (*inf: in Redewendungen*) **das ist** *or* **liegt bei dem alles ~** anything's possible with him; **bis jetzt ist** *or* **liegt noch alles ~**

everything is still quite open; ~ **sein** (*in der Arbeit*) to be into it; **für sie ist doch (gegen ihn) nichts** ~ she hasn't a hope (against him); **für sie ist (bei der Weltmeisterschaft) schon was** ~ they have some chance (in the world championship); **das ist doch nicht** ~ (*geht nicht*) that's not on (*inf*).

dringen *pret* **drang**, *ptp* **gedrungen** *vi* (**a**) *aux sein* to penetrate, to come through; (*fig: Nachricht, Geheimnis*) to penetrate, to get through (*an or in* +*acc* to). (**durch etw**) ~ to come through (sth), to penetrate (sth); **jdm ans Herz** ~ to go to or touch sb's heart; **an or in die Öffentlichkeit** ~ to leak or get out, to become public knowledge; **der Pfeil drang ihm in die Brust** the arrow penetrated (into) his chest; **durch eine Menschenmenge** ~ to push (one's way) through a crowd of people; **hinter die Ursache/ein Rätsel** ~ to get to the bottom of this/a puzzle.
(**b**) *aux sein* **in jdn** ~ to press or urge sb; **mit Bitten/Fragen in jdn** ~ to ply or press sb with requests/questions; **sich gedrungen fühlen, etw zu tun** to feel obliged to do sth.
(**c**) **auf etw** (*acc*) ~ to insist on sth; **er drang darauf, einen Arzt zu holen** or **daß man einen Arzt holte** he insisted on fetching a doctor.

dringend *adj* (*eilig, wichtig*) urgent, pressing; (*nachdrücklich, zwingend*) strong; *Abraten, Anraten* strong, strenuous; *Gründe* compelling. **etw** ~ **machen** (*inf*) to treat sth as urgent; **ein** ~**er Fall** (*Med*) an emergency; **jdn** ~ **bitten, etw zu unterlassen** to ask sb in the strongest terms or to urge sb to stop doing sth; ~ **notwendig/erforderlich** urgently needed, essential; ~ **verdächtig** strongly suspected; ~ **empfehlen/abraten** to recommend/advise strongly.

dringlich *adj* urgent, pressing.

Dringlichkeit *f* urgency.

Dringlichkeits-: ~**anfrage** *f* (*Parl*) emergency question; ~**antrag** *m* (*Parl*) emergency motion; ~**stufe** *f* priority; ~**stufe 1** top priority.

drinhängen *vi sep irreg* (*inf*) *siehe* **drinstecken (b, c)**.

Drink *m* -s, -s drink.

drinnen *adv* (*in geschlossenem Raum*) inside; (*im Haus auch*) indoors; (*fig: im Inland*) internally, at home. ~ **und draußen** inside and outside; (*im Inland etc*) at home and abroad; **hier/dort** ~ in here/there; **ich gehe nach** ~ (*inf*) I'm going in(side).

drinsitzen *vi sep irreg* (*inf*) to be in trouble.

drinstecken *vi sep* (*inf*) (**a**) (*verborgen sein*) to be (contained). **auch bei ihm muß ein guter Kern** ~ there must be some good even in him.
(**b**) (*investiert sein*) **da steckt eine Menge Geld/Arbeit etc drin** a lot of money/work etc has gone into it.
(**c**) (*verwickelt sein*) to be involved in it. **er steckt bis über die Ohren drin** he's up to his ears in it.
(**d**) (*voraussehen können*) **da steckt man nicht drin** one never knows or can never tell (what will happen).

drinstehen *vi sep irreg aux haben or* (*dial*) *sein* (*inf*) to be in it.

drisch *imper sing of* **dreschen**.

dritt *adv* **wir kommen zu** ~ three of us are coming together; *siehe* **viert**.

dritt- *in cpds* third; ~**älteste(r, s)** *adj* third oldest.

Dritteil *nt* (*obs*) *siehe* **Drittel**.

Drittel *nt* -s, - third; *siehe* **Viertel**[1].

dritteln *vt* to divide into three (parts); *Zahl* to divide by three.

Drittelparität *f* equal say in decision-making for students/workers. **die** ~ **verlangen** to demand an equal say in decision-making.

Dritten|abschlagen *nt children's game,* ≈ tag.

drittens *adv* thirdly; *siehe* **viertens**.

Dritte(r) *mf decl as adj* third person, third man/woman etc; (*Unbeteiligter*) third party. **der lachende** ~ the third party who benefits from a division between two others; **in dieser Angelegenheit ist er der lachende** ~ he comes off best from this matter; **wenn zwei sich streiten, freut sich der** ~ (*prov*) when two people quarrel a third one rejoices; **der** ~ **im Bunde** the third in or of the trio; **im Beisein** ~**r** in the presence of a third party; *siehe* **Vierte(r)**.

dritte(r, s) *adj* third. **der** ~ **Fall** the dative case; **an einem** ~**n Ort** on neutral territory; **von** ~**r Seite** (*eine Neuigkeit erfahren*) (to learn a piece of news) from a third party; **Menschen** ~**r Klasse** third-class citizens; **ein D**~**s** a third thing; *siehe* **vierte(r, s)**.

Dritt-: **d**~**größte(r, s)** *adj* third-biggest or -largest; **d**~**höchste(r, s)** *adj* third highest; ~**interesse** *nt* interest of a third party; **d**~**klassig** *adj* third-rate (*pej*), third-class; ~**kläßler(in** *f*) *m* -s, - (*Sch*) third-former; **d**~**letzte(r, s)** *adj* third from last, last but two; **an d**~**letzter Stelle** third from last, last but two; ~**person** *f* third person or party; **d**~**rangig** *adj* third-rate; ~**schaden** *m* damage suffered by a third party.

Drive [draif] *m* -s, -s (*Mus, Sport*) drive.

DRK ['de:|er'ka:] *nt - abbr of* **Deutsches Rotes Kreuz**.

drob *adv* (*obs*) *siehe* **darob**.

droben *adv* (*old, dial*) up there. **dort** ~ up there.

Droge *f* -, -n drug.

dröge *adj* (*N Ger dial*) *siehe* **trocken**.

Drogen-: **d**~**abhängig** *adj* addicted to drugs; **er ist d**~**abhängig** he's a drug addict; **d**~**abhängige(r)** *mf decl as adj* drug addict; ~**abhängigkeit** *f* drug addiction *no art*; ~**geschäft** *nt* drug trade; ~**handel** *m* drug traffic; ~**mißbrauch** *m* drug abuse *no art*; ~**sucht** *f* drug addiction; **d**~**süchtig** *adj* addicted to drugs; ~**süchtige(r)** *mf* drug addict; ~**szene** *f* drug scene.

Drogerie *f* chemist's (shop), drugstore (*US*).

Drogist(in *f*) *m* chemist, druggist (*US*).

Drohbrief *m* threatening letter.

drohen 1 *vi* (**a**) to threaten (*jdm* sb). **er drohte dem Kind mit erhobenem Zeigefinger** he raised a warning finger to the child.
(**b**) (*jdm*) **mit etw** ~ to threaten (sb with) sth; **er droht mit**

Selbstmord he threatens to commit suicide; (**jdm**) ~, **etw zu tun** to threaten to do sth.
(**c**) (*bevorstehen*) (*Gefahr*) to threaten; (*Gewitter*) to be imminent or in the offing; (*Streik, Krieg*) to be imminent or looming. **jdm droht etw** sb is being threatened by sth; **jdm droht Gefahr/der Tod** sb is in danger/in danger of dying; **es droht Gefahr/ein Streik** there is the threat of danger/a strike.
2 *v aux* to threaten. **das Schiff drohte zu sinken** the ship was in danger of sinking.

drohend *adj* (**a**) *Handbewegung, Haltung, Blick, Wolken* threatening, menacing. (**b**) (*bevorstehend*) *Unheil, Gefahr, Krieg* imminent, impending.

Drohgebärde *f* threatening gesture.

Drohn *m* -en, -en (*form*), **Drohne** *f* -, -n drone; (*fig pej auch*) idler, parasite.

dröhnen *vi* (**a**) to roar; (*Donner*) to rumble; (*Lautsprecher, Musik, Stimme*) to boom. **etw dröhnt jdm in den Ohren/im Kopf** sth roars etc in sb's ears/head. (**b**) (*Raum etc*) to resound, to echo. **mir** ~ **die Ohren/dröhnt der Kopf** my ears are/head is ringing.

dröhnend *adj* *Lärm, Applaus* resounding, echoing; *Stimme* booming; *Gelächter* roaring.

Drohnen-: ~**dasein** *nt* (*fig pej*) idle or parasitic life; **d**~**haft** *adj* drone-like; (*fig auch*) idle, parasitic; ~**schlacht** *f* (*Zool*) slaughter of the drones.

Drohung *f* threat.

Droh-: ~**verhalten** *nt* threatening or aggressive behaviour; ~**wort** *nt* threat.

drollig *adj* (**a**) funny, comical, droll. (**b**) (*seltsam*) odd, strange. **werd' nicht** ~! don't be funny!; **ein** ~**er Kauz** an odd bod (*inf*), an oddball (*esp US inf*).

Drolligkeit *f* comicalness, drollness.

Dromedar *nt* -s, -e dromedary.

Dropout ['drɔp|aut] *m* -s, -s (**a**) (*Mensch*) dropout. (**b**) (*in Bandaufzeichnung*) fade.

Drops *m or nt* -, - or -e fruit drop.

drosch *pret of* **dreschen**.

Droschke *f* -, -n (*Pferde*~) (hackney) cab, hackney-carriage. (**b**) (*dated: Taxi*) (taxi-)cab.

Droschken-: ~(**halte)platz** *m* (*dated*) cab rank; ~**kutscher** *m* cab driver.

Drosophila [dro'zo:fila] *f* -, **Drosophilae** [dro'zo:filɛ] drosophila.

Drossel[1] *f* -, -n (*Orn*) thrush.

Drossel[2] *f* -, -n *siehe* **Drosselspule, Drosselventil.**

Drosselklappe *f* (*Tech*) throttle valve.

drosseln *vt* (**a**) *Motor, Dampf etc* to throttle, to choke; *Heizung, Wärme* to turn down; *Strom* to reduce; *Tempo, Produktion etc* to cut down. (**b**) (*dated: würgen*) to throttle, to strangle.

Drosselspule *f* (*Elec*) choking coil.

Drosselung, Droßlung *f siehe vt* (**a**) throttling, choking; turning down; reducing; cutting down.

Drosselventil *nt* throttle valve.

Drost *m* -(e)s or -en, -e or -en (*old*) bailiff.

Drostei *f* (*old*) bailiwick (*old*).

drüben *adv* over there; (*auf der anderen Seite, inf: auf die DDR bezogen*) on the other side; (*inf: auf Amerika bezogen*) over the water. **hier/dort or da** ~ over here/there; **nach** ~ over there; **bei der Nachbarin** ~ over at my neighbour's; ~ **über dem Rhein** on the other side of the Rhine; **nach/von** ~ over/from over there; *siehe* **hüben**.

Drüben *nt* -s, *no pl siehe* **Jenseits**.

drüber *adv* (*inf*) (**a**) *siehe* **darüber, hinüber**. (**b**) **da** ~ *siehe* **darüber**.

drübig *adj attr* (*inf*) over there.

Druck[1] *m* -(e)s, -̈e (**a**) (*Phys, fig*) pressure. **unter** ~ **stehen** (*lit, fig*) to be under pressure; **jdn unter** ~ **setzen** (*fig*) to put pressure on sb, to pressurize sb; (*fürchterlich*) **in** ~ **sein** (*fig*) to be under (terrible) pressure; ~ **auf jdn/etw ausüben** (*lit, fig*) to exert or put pressure on sb/sth; ~ **hinter etw** (*acc*) **machen** (*inf*) to put some pressure on sth; ~ **und Gegendruck** pressure and resistance; **ein** ~ **im Kopf/Magen** a feeling of pressure in one's head/stomach.
(**b**) (*das Drücken*) pressure (*gen* from) *no indef art.* **durch einen** ~ **auf den Knopf** by pressing the button.

Druck[2] *m* -(e)s, -e (**a**) (*das Drucken*) printing; (*Art des Drucks, Schriftart*) print; (*Druckwerk*) copy. ~ **und Satz** setting and printing; **das Buch ist im** ~ the book is in the press or is being printed; **im** ~ **erscheinen** to appear in print; **in** ~ **gehen** to go into print; **etw in** ~ **geben** to send sth to press or to be printed; ~ **und Verlag von ...** printed and published by ...
(**b**) (*Kunst*~) print.
(**c**) *pl* -s (*Tex*) print.

Druck-: ~**abfall** *m* drop or fall in pressure; ~**anstieg** *m* rise in pressure; ~**anzug** *m* pressure suit; ~**ausgleich** *m* pressure balance; ~**belastung** *f* pressure load; ~**bleistift** *m* retractable pencil; ~**bogen** *m* (*Typ*) printed sheet; ~**buchstabe** *m* printed character or letter; **den Bogen bitte in** ~**buchstaben ausfüllen** please fill out the form in block capitals or block letters; **in** ~**buchstaben schreiben** to print.

Drückeberger *m* -s, - (*pej inf*) (*fauler Mensch*) shirker, idle so-and-so (*inf*); (*in der Schule auch*) skiver (*Brit inf*); (*Feigling*) coward.

Drückebergerei *f, no pl* (*pej inf*) shirking; (*in der Schule auch*) skiving (*Brit inf*).

drückebergerisch *adj* (*pej inf*) *Mensch* idle. **sein** ~**es Verhalten** his idling or shirking.

druck|empfindlich *adj* sensitive (to pressure).

drucken *vti* (*Typ, Tex*) to print. **ein Buch** ~ **lassen** to have a book printed; **ein Buch in 1000 Exemplaren/einer hohen**

Auflage ~ to print 1000 copies/a large edition of a book; *siehe* **gedruckt.**

drücken, *(dial)* **drucken 1** *vt* **(a)** *Hand, Klinke, Hebel* to press; *Knopf auch* to push; *Obst, Saft, Eiter* to squeeze. **jdm etw in die Hand** ~ to press *or* slip sth into sb's hand; **jdn** ~ to squeeze sb; *(umarmen)* to hug sb; **jdn/etw an sich/ans Herz** ~ to press *or* clasp sb/sth to one/one's breast; **jdn zur Seite/nach hinten/in einen Stuhl** ~ to push sb aside/back/into a chair; **den Hut in die Stirn** ~ to pull one's hat down over one's brow *or* forehead. **(b)** *(fig: bedrücken)* to weigh heavily upon. **was drückt dich denn?** what's on your mind? **(c)** *(Druckgefühl erzeugen: Schuhe, Korsett etc)* to pinch, to nip. **jdn im Magen** ~ *(Essen)* to lie *or* weigh heavily on sb's stomach; **mich drückt der Magen** my stomach feels heavy. **(d)** *(verringern, herabsetzen)* to force down; *Rekord* to beat; *Leistung, Niveau* to lower. **(e)** *(inf: unterdrücken) jdn* to keep down; *Stimmung* to dampen. **(f)** *(Sport) Gewicht* to press; *Handstand* to press into. **(g)** *(Aviat)* to point down. **(h)** *(Cards)* to discard.

2 *vi* **(a)** to press; *(Wetter, Hitze)* to be oppressive; *(Brille, Schuhe, Korsett etc)* to weigh (on one's stomach). „**bitte** ~" "push"; **auf etw** *(acc)***/an etw** *(dat)* ~ to press sth; **der Kaffee drückt auf die Blase** coffee presses on the bladder; **aufs Gemüt** ~ to dampen *or* depress one's spirits, to get one down; **auf die Stimmung** ~ to dampen one's mood. **(b)** *(drängeln, stoßen)* to push. **(c)** *(bei Stuhlentleerung)* to strain, to push.

3 *vr* **(a)** *(mit Ortsangabe)* *(in +acc* into, *an +acc* against) *(sich quetschen)* to squeeze; *(schutzsuchend)* to huddle. **sich aus dem Zimmer** ~ to slip out of the room. **(b)** *(inf)* to shirk, to dodge; *(vor Militärdienst)* to dodge. **sich vor etw** *(dat)* ~ to shirk *or* dodge sth; **sich (um etw)** ~ to get out of (doing) sth; *(esp in Schule auch)* to skive off *or* out of (doing) sth *(Brit inf)*.

drückend *adj Last, Steuern* heavy; *Sorgen* serious; *Armut* grinding; *Wetter, Hitze* oppressive, close. **es ist** ~ **heiß** it's oppressively hot.

drückendheiß *adj attr* oppressively hot.

Drucker(in *f)* *m* -s, - printer.

Drücker *m* -s, - **(a)** *(Knopf)* (push) button; *(inf: von Pistole etc)* trigger; *(von Klingel)* push. **die Hand am** ~ **haben** *(fig inf)* to be ready to act; **am** ~ **sein** *or* **sitzen** *(fig inf)* *(in Machtposition)* to be in a key position; *(an der Quelle)* to be ideally placed *or* in an ideal position; **auf den letzten** ~ *(fig inf)* at the last minute. **(b)** *(Türklinke)* handle; *(von Schnappschloß)* latch.

Druckerei *f* **(a)** printing works *pl*, printery; *(Firma auch)* printer's. **(b)** *(Druckwesen)* printing *no art*.

Druck erlaubnis *f* imprimatur.

Drucker-: ~**presse** *f* printing press; ~**schwärze** *f* printer's ink; ~**zeichen** *nt* printer's mark.

Druck-: ~**erzeugnis** *nt* printed material; ~**fahne** *f* galley (-proof), proof; ~**farbe** *f* coloured printing ink; ~**fehler** *m* misprint, typographical *or* printer's error; ~**fehlerteufel** *m* *(inf)* gremlin *(which causes misprints)*; **d~fertig** *adj* ready to print *or* for the press; **d~fest** *adj* Werkstoff resistant to pressure; ~**form** *f* *(Typ)* printing forme, quoin; **d~frisch** *adj* hot from the press; ~**gefälle** *nt* *(Phys)* difference in pressure; ~**gefühl** *nt* feeling of pressure; ~**kabine** *f* pressurized cabin; ~**knopf** *m* **(a)** *(Sew)* press-stud, snap fastener; **(b)** *(Tech)* push-button; ~**kosten** *pl* printing costs *pl*; ~**legung** *f* printing; **mit der** ~**legung beginnen** to begin printing, to go to press.

Druckluft *f* compressed air.

Druckluft-: ~**bohrer** *m* pneumatic drill; ~**bremse** *f* air-brake.

Druck-: ~**maschine** *f* *(Typ)* printing press; ~**messer** *m* -s, - pressure gauge; ~**mittel** *nt* *(fig)* form of pressure, means of exerting pressure; **als politisches** ~**mittel** as a form of political pressure, as a means of exerting political pressure; ~**muster** *nt* print(ed pattern *or* design); **Stoffe mit** ~**muster** prints, printed materials; ~**ort** *m* place of printing; ~**papier** *nt* printing paper; ~**platte** *f* printing plate; ~**posten** *m* *(inf)* cushy job *or* number *(inf)*; ~**presse** *f* printing press; ~**pumpe** *f* pressure pump; **d~reif** *adj* ready for printing, passed for press; *(fig)* polished; **d~reif sprechen** to speak in a polished style; ~**sache** *f* **(a)** *(Post)* business letter; *(Werbematerial)* circular; *(als Portoklasse)* printed matter; „~**sache**" "printed matter"; **etw als** ~**sache schicken** ≈ to send sth at printed-paper rate; **(b)** *(Typ)* *(Auftrag)* stationery printing job; ~**sachen** *pl (Akzidenz)* stationery printing *sing*; ~**schalter** *m* push-button switch; ~**schrift** *f* **(a)** *(Schriftart)* printing; **in** ~**schrift schreiben** to print; **bitte das Formular in** *or* **mit** ~**schrift ausfüllen** please fill out the form in block capitals *or* block letters; **die** ~**schrift lernen** to learn printing, to learn to print; **(b)** *(gedrucktes Werk)* pamphlet; ~**seite** *f* printed page.

drucksen *vi (inf)* to hum and haw *(inf)*.

Druck-: ~**sorten** *pl (Aus)* printed forms *pl*; ~**stelle** *f* place *or* (*Mal*) mark *(where pressure has been applied)*; *(Fleck auf Pfirsich, Haut)* bruise; ~**stock** *m* *(Typ)* relief plate; ~**taste** *f* push-button; ~**technik** *f* printing technology *or* *(Verfahren)* technique; **d~technisch** *adj* typographical; *(in bezug auf mechanischen Vorgang)* printing *attr*; **d~technisch verfeinert** improved from the printing point of view; ~**type** *f* type; **d~unempfindlich** *adj* insensitive to pressure; ~**unterschied** *m* difference in pressure; ~**verband** *m* *(Med)* pressure bandage; ~**verbot** *nt* printing ban; ~**verfahren** *nt* printing process; ~**verlust** *m* *(Tech)* loss of pressure, reduction in pressure; ~**vermerk** *m* imprint; ~**vorlage** *f* *(Typ)* setting copy; ~**welle** *f* shock wave; ~**werk** *nt* printed work, publication; ~**wesen**

nt printing *no art;* ~**zeile** *f* line of print.

Drude *f* -, -n *(Myth)* witch.

Drudenfuß *m* *(Myth)* pentagram.

druff *adv (dial inf) siehe* **drauf.**

Druide *m* -n, -n Druid.

druidisch *adj* druidic(al), druid *attr.*

drum *adv (inf)* around, round *(Brit)*. ~ **rum** all around *or* round *(Brit)*; ~ **rumreden** to beat about the bush; **da wirst du nicht** ~ **rumkommen** there's no getting out of it; **sei's** ~! never mind; **das D~ und Dran** the paraphernalia; *(Begleiterscheinungen)* the fuss and bother; **mit allem D~ und Dran** with all the bits and pieces *(inf)* *or* *(Mahlzeit)* trimmings *pl; siehe* **darum.**

Drumherum *nt* -s *no pl* trappings *pl.*

drunten *adv (old, dial)* down there.

drunter *adv* under(neath). **da kann ich mir nichts** ~ **vorstellen** that means nothing to me; ~ **und drüber** upside down, topsy-turvy; **alles ging** *or* **es ging alles** ~ **und drüber** everything was upside down *or* topsy-turvy; **das D~ und Drüber** the confusion, the muddle; *siehe* **darunter.**

Drusch *m* -(e)s, -e *(Agr)* threshing; *(Produkt)* threshed corn.

Druse *f* -, -n *(Min, Geol)* druse.

Drüse *f* -, -n gland.

Drüsen-: **d~artig** *adj* glandular; ~**fieber** *nt* glandular fever, mono(nucleosis) *(US)*; ~**funktion** *f* glandular function; ~**krankheit** *f,* ~**leiden** *nt* glandular disorder; ~**schwellung** *f* glandular swelling, swollen glands *pl;* ~**überfunktion** *f* hyperactivity *or* overactivity of the glands; ~**unterfunktion** *f* underactivity of the glands.

DSB [de:|es'be:] *m* -s *abbr of* **Deutscher Sportbund** German Sports Association.

Dschungel *m* -s, - *(lit, fig)* jungle. **sich im** ~ **der Paragraphen zurechtfinden** to wade one's way through the verbiage.

Dschungel-: **d~artig** *adj Wald* jungle-like; ~**fieber** *nt* yellow fever; ~**gesetz** *nt* law of the jungle; ~**krieg** *m* jungle war/warfare.

Dschunke *f* -, -n junk.

DSG [de:|es'ge:] *f* - *abbr of* **Deutsche Schlafwagen- und Speisewagen-Gesellschaft.**

dt(sch). *abbr of* **deutsch.**

Dtzd. *abbr of* **Dutzend.**

du *pers pron gen* **deiner,** *dat* **dir,** *acc* **dich** you *(familiar form of address)*, thou *(obs, dial)*; *(man)* you. **D~** *(in Briefen)* you; **ich gehe heute ins Kino und** ~? I'm going to the cinema today, how about you? ~ *(zu jdm)* **sagen, jdn mit** ~ **anreden** to use the familiar form of address (with sb), to say "du" (to sb); ~, **der** ~ **es erlebt hast** you who have experienced it; **mit jdm auf** ~ **und** ~ **stehen** to be pals with sb; **mit jdm per** ~ **sein** to be on familiar *or* friendly terms with sb; ~ **bist es** it's you; **bist** ~ **es** *or* **das?** is it *or* that you?; **Vater unser, der** ~ **bist im Himmel** our Father, who *or* which art in heaven; **mach** ~ **das doch!** you do it!, do it yourself!; ~, **meine Heimat!** *(poet)* thou, my homeland!; ~ **Glücklicher!/Idiot!** lucky you *or* you lucky thing/ you idiot; ~ **Schlingel/Schuft(,** ~**)!** you rascal/scoundrel *etc,* (you)! **ach** ~ **lieber Gott** *or* **liebe Güte** good Lord!, good heavens!; ~ **(Mutti), kannst** ~ **mir mal helfen?** hey (mummy), can you help me?; ~, **ich muß jetzt aber gehen** listen, I have to go now; ~, ~! *(inf: drohend)* naughty, naughty; *siehe* **mir.**

Du *nt* -(s), -(s) "du", familiar form of address. **jdm das** ~ **anbieten** to suggest that sb uses "du" *or* the familiar form of address.

dual *adj* dual.

Dual *m* -s, -e, **Dualis** *m* -, **Duale** dual.

Dualismus *m* *(Philos, Pol, geh)* dualism.

Dualist(in *f)* *m* *(Philos)* dualist.

dualistisch *adj* *(Philos, Pol, geh)* dualistic.

Dualität *f* *(geh)* duality.

Dualsystem *nt* *(Math)* binary system.

Dübel *m* -s, - plug; *(Holz~)* dowel.

Dübelmasse *f* plugging compound, filler.

dübeln *vti* to plug.

dubios, dubiös *adj* *(geh)* dubious.

Dublee *nt* -s, -s rolled gold *no pl; (Gegenstand)* article made of rolled gold.

Dubleegold *nt* rolled gold.

Dublette *f* **(a)** *(doppelt vorhandenes Stück)* duplicate. **(b)** *(Hunt)* right and left. **(c)** *(Edelstein)* doublet. **(d)** *(Boxen)* one-two.

dublieren* *vt Metall* to coat with gold; *Garn* to twist.

ducken 1 *vr* to duck; *(fig)* to cringe, to cower; *(fig: Bäume, Häuser)* to nestle. **ich duckte mich vor dem Hieb** I ducked the blow; **sich in eine Ecke/hinter eine Deckung** ~ to duck *or* dodge into a corner/behind cover; *siehe* **geduckt. 2** *vt Kopf, Menschen* to duck; *(fig)* to humiliate. **3** *vi* *(fig pej)* to cower.

Duckmäuser *m* -s, - *(pej)* moral coward.

Duckmäuserei *f* - *(pej)* moral cowardice. **Erziehung zur** ~ bringing up to be moral cowards.

duckmäuserisch *adj (pej)* showing moral cowardice.

duckmäusern *vi insep (pej)* to be moral cowards/a moral coward.

Duckmäusertum *nt* *(pej)* chicken-heartedness. **jdn zum** ~ **erziehen** to bring sb up to be chicken-hearted.

Dudelei *f* *(pej inf)* humming; *(auf Flöte)* tootling.

Dudelkasten *m* *(pej inf)* noise-box.

dudeln *(pej inf)* **1** *vi* to hum; *(auf Flöte)* to tootle *(auf+dat* on). **2** *vt* **(a)** *Lied* to hum; *(auf Flöte)* to toot. **(b)** *(dial)* **einen** ~ to have a wee dram *(dial)*.

Dudelsack *m* bagpipes *pl.*

Dudelsack-: ~**pfeifer,** ~**spieler** *m* (bag)piper.

Duell *nt* -s, -e *(lit, fig)* duel *(um* over). **ein** ~ **auf Degen** a duel with swords; **ein** ~ **(mit jdm) austragen** to fight *or* have a duel (with sb); **jdn zum ~ (heraus)fordern/ins ~ fordern** to challenge sb to a duel.

Duellant [duɛ'lant] m dueller, duellist.

duellieren* [duɛ'liːrən] vr to (fight a) duel.

Duellpistole f duelling pistol.

Duett nt -(e)s, -e (a) (Mus, fig) duet. **im ~ singen** to sing a duet; **etw im ~ singen** to sing sth as a duet. (b) (fig inf: Paar) duo (inf).

duff adj (N Ger) matt; Glas, Fenster dull.

Dufflecoat ['daflko:t] m -s, -s dufflecoat.

Duft m -(e)s, -e (a) (pleasant) smell, scent; (von Blumen, Parfüm auch) fragrance, perfume; (von Essen, Kaffee etc) smell, aroma; (Absonderung von Tieren) scent; (fig) allure. **den ~ der großen weiten Welt verspüren** (usu iro) to get a taste of the big, wide world.
(b) (liter: Dunst) haze.
(c) (Sw) siehe **Rauhreif**.

Duftdrüse f scent gland.

dufte adj, adv (sl) smashing (inf), great (inf).

duften 1 vi to smell. **nach etw ~** to smell or have a smell of sth; **was duftet denn hier so (gut)?** what's that nice smell? 2 vi impers **hier duftet es nach Kaffee** there is a smell or it smells of coffee here; **hier duftet es (gut)** what a nice smell there is here.

duftend adj attr nice-smelling; Parfüm, Blumen etc fragrant. **sie kam ~ vom Friseur** she came back from the hairdresser's smelling nice.

Dufthauch m (poet) fragrance, aroma.

duftig adj (a) Kleid, Stoff gossamery; Spitzen frothy; Wolken fluffy; Kuchen, Klöße etc light. (b) (poet: zart dunstig) hazy.

Duftigkeit f siehe adj (a) gossamer lightness; frothiness; fluffiness; lightness.

Duft-: d~los adj odourless, unscented; **~marke** f scent mark; **~note** f (von Parfüm) scent; (von Mensch) smell; **~organ** nt scent gland; **~probe** f (a) (Vorgang) perfume test; (b) (Probeflasche) free sample of perfume; **~stoff** m scent; (für Parfüm, Waschmittel etc) fragrance; **~wasser** nt toilet water; (hum: Parfüm) perfume, scent; **~wolke** f (iro) fragrance (iro); (von Parfüm) cloud of perfume.

duhn adj (N Ger inf) sloshed (inf).

Dukaten m -s, - ducat.

Dukaten-: ~esel m (hum) siehe **~scheißer**; **~gold** nt fine gold; **~scheißer** m (inf) **einen ~scheißer haben, ein ~scheißer sein** to be a goldmine, to be made of money.

Duktus m -, no pl (geh) characteristic style; (von Handschrift) characteristics pl, flow.

dulden 1 vi (geh: leiden) to suffer.
2 vt (a) (zulassen) to tolerate; Widerspruch auch to countenance. **ich dulde das nicht** I won't tolerate that; **die Sache duldet keinen Aufschub** the matter cannot be delayed or postponed; **etw stillschweigend ~/stillschweigend ~, daß ...** to connive at sth.
(b) (nicht vertreiben) to tolerate. **er ist hier nur geduldet** he's only tolerated here, he's only here on sufferance.
(c) (geh: erdulden) Not, Schmerz to suffer. **es duldet mich hier nicht länger** I must away or hence (liter).

Dulder(in f) m -s, - silent sufferer.

Duldermiene f (iro) air of patient suffering. **mit ~** with an air of patient suffering.

duldsam adj tolerant (gegenüber of, jdm gegenüber towards sb).

Duldsamkeit f tolerance.

Duldung f toleration. **solche Zustände erlauben keine weitere ~** such conditions can be tolerated no longer; **unter** or **bei** or **mit stillschweigender ~ der Behörden** etc with the (tacit) connivance of the authorities etc.

Dulliäh[1] nt -, no pl (Aus inf) hoo-ha (inf).

Dulliäh[2] m -, no pl (Aus inf) tipsiness (inf). **im ~** (when one is/was) tipsy.

Dulzinea f -, Dulzineen (hum) ladylove.

Dumdum nt -(s), -(s), Dumdumgeschoß nt dumdum (bullet).

dumm adj comp "er, superl "-ste(r, s), adv am "-sten (a) stupid, dumb (esp US); Mensch auch thick (inf); (unklug, unvernünftig auch) silly, foolish. **der ~e August** (inf) the clown; **~e Gans** silly goose; **~es Zeug (reden)** (to talk) nonsense or rubbish; **ein ~es Gesicht machen, ~ gucken** to look stupid; **jdn wie einen ~en Jungen behandeln** (inf) to treat sb like a child; **jdn für ~ verkaufen** (inf) to think sb is stupid; **du willst mich wohl für ~ verkaufen** you must think I'm stupid; **ich lasse mich nicht für ~ verkaufen** I'm not so stupid (inf); **das ist gar nicht (so) ~** that's not a bad idea; **sich ~ anstellen** to behave stupidly; **sich ~ stellen** to act stupid or dumb (esp US); **~ fragen** to ask a silly question/silly questions; **~ dastehen** to look stupid or foolish; **sich ~ und dämlich reden** (inf) to talk till one is blue in the face (inf); **sich ~ und dämlich suchen** to search high and low; **sich ~ und dämlich verdienen** to earn the earth (inf); **~ geboren, nichts dazugelernt** (prov) he/she etc hasn't got the sense he/she etc was born with (prov); **jetzt wird's mir zu ~** I've had enough; **mir ist ganz ~ im Kopf/Magen** my head/stomach feels funny or peculiar; **der Krach macht mich ganz ~ (im Kopf)** the noise is making my head spin.
(b) (ärgerlich, unangenehm) annoying; Gefühl auch nagging; Sache, Geschichte, Angelegenheit auch silly. **es ist zu ~, daß er nicht kommen kann** it's too bad that he can't come; **jdm ~ kommen** to get funny with sb (inf); **etw D~es** a silly or stupid thing; **so etwas D~es** how silly or stupid; (wie ärgerlich) what a nuisance.

Dumm-: ~bach nt (inf) **ich bin doch nicht aus ~bach** you can't fool me that easily, I'm not stupid; **~bart, ~beutel** m (inf) fool (inf), dumbbell (US inf).

Dummchen nt (inf) silly-billy (inf).

dummdreist adj insolent.

Dummdreistigkeit f insolence.

Dummejungenstreich m silly or foolish or childish prank.

Dummenfang m **das ist der reinste ~** that's just a con (inf); **auf ~ ausgehen** to try to catch fools.

Dumme(r) mf decl as adj (inf) mug (inf), fool, sucker (inf). **der ~ sein** to be left to carry the can (inf), to be left holding the baby (inf); **einen ~n finden** to find a mug (inf) or a sucker (inf).

Dummerchen nt (inf) silly-billy (inf). **mein ~** you silly-billy.

Dummerjan m -s, -e (inf) silly dope (inf).

dummerweise adv unfortunately; (aus Dummheit) stupidly, foolishly.

dummfrech adj siehe **dummdreist**.

Dummheit f (a) no pl stupidity; (von Menschen auch) foolishness. (b) (dumme Handlung) stupid or foolish thing. **mach bloß keine ~en!** just don't do anything stupid or foolish.

Dummkopf m (inf) idiot, fool.

dümmlich adj silly, stupid; Mensch auch foolish, dumb (esp US). **eine ~e Blondine** a dumb blonde.

Dümmling m fool.

Dummrian m -s, -e (inf) silly dope (inf).

dümpeln vi (Naut) to bob up and down.

dumpf adj (a) Geräusch, Ton muffled. **~ aufprallen** to land with a thud. (b) Luft, Geruch, Keller, Geschmack etc musty; (fig) Atmosphäre stifling. (c) Gefühl, Ahnung, Erinnerung vague; Schmerz dull; (bedrückend) gloomy; (stumpfsinnig) dull; Mensch, Geist, Sinn dulled.

Dumpfheit f, no pl siehe adj (a) muffledness. (b) mustiness; stiflingness. (c) vagueness; dullness; gloominess; dullness; dulledness.

dumpfig adj (feucht) dank, damp; (muffig) musty; (moderig) mouldy.

Dumpfigkeit f, no pl siehe adj dankness, dampness; mustiness; mouldiness.

Dumping ['dampiŋ] nt -s, no pl (Econ) dumping.

Dumpingpreis m give-away price.

dun adj (N Ger inf) sloshed (inf).

Düne f -, -n (sand-)dune.

Dünen-: ~bildung f formation of dunes; **~gras** nt marram (grass); **~sand** m dune-sand; **sie lagen im ~sand** they lay in the dunes.

Dung m -(e)s, no pl dung, manure.

Düngemittel nt fertilizer.

düngen 1 vt to fertilize. 2 vi (Stoff) to act as a fertilizer; (Mensch) to apply fertilizer. **im Garten ~** to put fertilizer on the garden.

Dünger m -s, - fertilizer.

Dung-: ~fliege f dung fly; **~grube** f manure pit; **~haufen** m dung or manure heap.

Düngung f (a) (das Düngen) fertilizing. (b) siehe **Dünger**.

dunkel adj (a) (finster) dark; (fig auch) black. **im D~n** in the dark; **in dunkler Nacht** at dead of night; **im Zimmer ~ machen** (inf) to make the room dark, to darken the room.
(b) (farblich) dark. **~ gefärbt sein** to be a dark colour; **sich ~ kleiden** to dress in dark colours; **etw ~ anmalen** to paint sth a dark colour; **ein Dunkles, bitte!** = a brown ale (Brit) or dark beer, please.
(c) (tief) Stimme, Ton deep.
(d) (unbestimmt, unklar) vague; Erinnerung auch dim; Textstelle unclear. **in dunkler Vergangenheit/Vorzeit** in the dim and distant past; **im ~n tappen** (fig) to grope (about) in the dark; **jdn im ~n lassen** to leave sb in the dark; **das liegt noch im ~n** that remains to be seen.
(e) (zweifelhaft, zwielichtig) shady (inf), dubious.

Dunkel nt -s, no pl (lit, fig) darkness. **im ~ der Vergangenheit** in the dim and distant past; **das verliert sich im ~ der Geschichte** it is lost in the mists of history; **in ~ gehüllt sein** (fig) to be shrouded in mystery; **im ~ der Nacht** at dead of night.

Dünkel m -s, no pl conceit, arrogance.

dunkel-: in cpds dark; **~blau** adj dark blue; **~blond** adj dark blond, light brown; **~gekleidet** adj attr dressed in dark (-coloured) clothes; **~haarig** adj dark-haired.

dünkelhaft adj arrogant, conceited.

Dunkel-: d~häutig adj dark-skinned; **~heit** f (lit, fig) darkness; **bei Einbruch** or **Eintritt der ~heit** at nightfall; **~kammer** f (Phot) darkroom; **~kammerleuchte, ~kammerlampe** f safelight; **~mann** m, pl -männer (pej) (a) shady character; (b) (liter) obscurant(ist).

dunkeln 1 vi impers **es dunkelt** (geh) darkness is falling, it is growing dark. 2 vi (a) (poet: Nacht, Abend) to grow dark. **es** aux sein (dunkel werden) to become darker, to darken. 3 vt Holz, Leder, Haar to darken.

Dunkel-: d~rot adj dark red, maroon; **d~weiß** adj (hum) off-white; **~werden** nt nightfall; **~ziffer** f estimated number of unreported/undetected cases; **~zone** f twilight zone.

dünken (old, geh) irreg 1 vti impers **das dünkt mich gut, das dünkt mich** or **mir gut zu sein, mich dünkt, daß das gut ist** it seems good to me; **mich dünkt, er kommt nicht mehr** I think or methinks (obs) he will not come.
2 vi to seem, to appear.
3 vr to think or imagine (oneself). **sie dünkt sich sehr klug** she thinks herself very clever.

dünn adj thin; Suppe, Bier auch watery; Kaffee, Tee watery, weak; (fein) Schleier, Regen, Strümpfe fine; Haarwuchs, Besiedlung auch sparse. **~ gesät** (fig) thin on the ground, few and far between; **sich ~ machen** (hum) to breathe in; siehe **dick, dünnmachen**.

Dünn-: d~behaart adj attr Mensch with thin hair; Haupt thinly covered in hair; **d~besiedelt, d~bevölkert** adj attr sparsely populated; **~bier** nt weak beer; **~brettbohrer** m (pej inf)

chancer (inf); ~**darm** m small intestine; ~**druckausgabe** f
India paper edition; ~**druckpapier** nt India paper.
dünne adj pred (dial) siehe **dünn**.
Dünne f -, no pl siehe **Dünnheit**.
dünnemachen vr sep (dial, inf) siehe **dünnmachen**.
dunnemals adv (dated, hum) siehe **damals**.
Dünn-: d~**flüssig** adj Farbe, Öl thin; Teig runny; Stuhlgang
loose; ~**flüssigkeit** f siehe adj thinness; runniness; looseness;
d~**gesät** adj attr sparse; d~**häutig** adj thin-skinned; (fig auch)
sensitive; ~**heit** f siehe adj thinness; wateriness; weakness;
fineness; sparseness; d~**lippig** adj thin-lipped; d~**machen** vr
sep (inf) to make oneself scarce; ~**pfiff** m (inf) the runs (inf);
d~**schalig** adj Obst thin-skinned; Nüsse, Ei etc thin-shelled;
~**schiß** m (sl) siehe ~**pfiff**; d~**wandig** adj Haus thin-walled,
with thin walls; Behälter thin.
Dunst m -(e)s, ⁻e (leichter Nebel) mist, haze; (Dampf) steam;
(Smog) smog; (dumpfe Luft) fug; (Geruch) smell. **blauer** ~ (fig
inf) sheer invention; **jdm blauen** ~ **vormachen** (inf) to throw
dust in sb's eyes; **sich in** ~ **auflösen** to go up in smoke; siehe
blaß.
Dunst-: ~**abzugshaube** f extractor hood (over a cooker);
d~**artig** adj Rauch, Nebel vapoury, vaporous.
dunsten vi (a) (dampfen) to steam. **(b)** (Dunst ausströmen) to
give off a smell, to smell.
dünsten vt (Cook) Gemüse, Fisch, Fleisch to steam; Obst to
stew.
Dunst-: ~**glocke**, ~**haube** f haze; pall of smog.
dunstig adj (a) hazy, misty. **(b)** (schlecht belüftet) stuffy; (verräuchert) smoky.
Dunstkreis m atmosphere; (von Mensch) society.
Dunst|obst nt (Cook) stewed fruit.
Dunst-: ~**schicht** f layer of haze or mist; ~**schleier** m veil of
haze or mist; ~**schwaden** pl clouds pl of haze/steam; (Nebel)
haze sing; (Dampf) clouds pl of steam; (Rauch) clouds pl of
smoke; ~**wolke** f cloud of smog.
Dünung f (Naut) swell.
Duo nt -s, -s (a) (Mus) (Musikstück) duet, duo; (Ausführende)
duo. **(b)** (Paar) duo.
Duodez-: ~**ausgabe** f duodecimo edition; ~**band** m duodecimo
volume; ~**fürst** m (pej geh) princeling, minor or petty prince;
~**fürstentum** nt (pej geh) minor or petty princedom.
Duodezimalsystem nt duodecimal system.
Duodezstaat m (pej geh) miniature state.
düpieren* vt (geh) to dupe.
Duplikat nt duplicate (copy).
Duplikation f (geh) duplication.
duplizieren* vt (geh) to duplicate.
Duplizität f (geh) duplication.
Dur nt -, - (Mus) major. **ein Stück in** ~/**in G-**~ a piece in a major
key/in G major.
Dur|akkord m major chord.
durativ adj (Gram) durative.
durch 1 prep +acc **(a)** (räumlich: hindurch) through. **quer** ~
right across; **mitten** ~ **die Stadt** through the middle of the
town; ~ **den Fluß waten** to wade across the river; ~ **die ganze
Welt reisen** to travel all over the world or throughout the world.
(b) (mittels, vermöge) through, by (means of); (in Passivkonstruk-
tion: von) by; (über jdn/etw, mit jds Hilfe) through, via; (den
Grund, die Ursache nennend) through, because of. **Tod** ~
Ertrinken/den Strang death by drowning/hanging; **Tod** ~
Erfrieren/Herzschlag etc death from exposure/a heart attack
etc; ~ **Gottes Güte** by the grace of God; **neun (geteilt)** ~ **drei**
nine divided by three, three into nine; ~ **Zufall/das Los** by
chance/lot; ~ **die Post** by post; **etw** ~ **die Zeitung bekanntgeben**
to announce sth in the press; ~ **den Lautsprecher** through the
loudspeaker; **er ist** ~ **Rundfunk und Fernsehen bekannt
geworden** he became famous through radio and television.
(c) (aufgrund, infolge von) due or owing to.
(d) (Aus: zeitlich) for.
2 adv **(a)** (hin~) through. **die ganze Nacht** ~ all through the
night, throughout the night; **Sie dürfen hier nicht** ~ you can't
come through here; **da hilft alles nichts, da mußt du eben** ~
(fig) there's no help for it, you'll have to see it through; **es ist 4
Uhr** ~ it's past or gone 4 o'clock; ~ **und** ~ **kennen** through and
through; **verlogen, überzeugt** completely, utterly; ~ **und** ~ **ehrlich** honest through and through; ~ **und** ~ **naß** wet through; **das
geht mir** ~ **und** ~ that goes right through me.
(b) (Cook inf) Steak well-done. **das Fleisch ist noch nicht** ~
the meat isn't done yet.
durch- in Verbindung mit Verben through.
durch|abfertigen vt sep siehe **durchchecken (a)**.
durch|ackern sep (inf) **1** vt to plough through. **2** vr to plough
one's way through (durch etw sth).
durch|ädert adj veined.
durch|arbeiten sep **1** vt **(a)** Buch, Stoff etc to work or go
through. **(b)** (ausarbeiten) to work out (in detail). **(c)** (durchkneten) Teig, Knetmasse to work or knead thoroughly; Muskeln to massage or knead thoroughly. **2** vi to work through. **3** vr
sich durch etw ~ to work one's way through.
durch|arbeitet adj **nach fünf** ~**en Nächten** after being up
working five whole nights.
durch|atmen¹ vi sep to breathe deeply, to take deep breaths.
durch|atmen²* vt insep (poet) to pervade, to inform (liter).
durch|aus adv (emph auch durch**aus**) **(a)** (in bejahten
Sätzen: unbedingt) das muß ~ sein that definitely has to be; **sie
wollte** ~ **mitgehen** sie insisted on going; **er hat** ~ **einen neuen
Auto haben** she insisted on going too/having a new car; **wenn du das** ~ **willst** if you insist, if you
absolutely must; **das ist** ~ **nötig** that is absolutely necessary;
du mußt ~ **mitkommen** you really must come; **muß das sein?** —

ja ~ is that necessary? — yes, definitely or absolutely; **hat er
sich anständig benommen?** — **ja** ~ did he behave himself
properly? — yes, perfectly or absolutely; **es mußte** ~ **dieses
Kleid sein** it absolutely had to be this dress; **er will** ~ **recht
haben** he (absolutely) insists that he is right.
(b) (bekräftigend in bejahten Sätzen) quite; verständlich,
richtig, korrekt, möglich auch perfectly; passen, annehmen
perfectly well; sich freuen, gefallen really. **das könnte man** ~
machen, das läßt sich ~ **machen** that sounds feasible, I/we etc
could do that; **ich bin** ~ **Ihrer Meinung** I quite or absolutely
agree with you; **ich hätte** ~ **Lust/Zeit** ... I would like to/I would
have time; **es ist mir** ~ **ernst damit** I am quite or perfectly or
absolutely serious about it; **es ist** ~ **anzunehmen, daß sie
kommt** it's highly likely that she'll be coming; **das ist zwar** ~
möglich, aber ... that is quite or perfectly possible, but ...
(c) (in bejahten Sätzen: ganz und gar) ehrlich, zufrieden,
unerfreulich thoroughly, completely. **ein** ~ **gelungener Abend**
a thoroughly successful evening; **ein** ~ **beneidenswerter
Mensch** a thoroughly enviable person.
(d) (in verneinten Sätzen) ~ **nicht** (als Verstärkung) by no
means; (als Antwort) not at all; (stärker) absolutely not; ~
nicht reich/so klug by no means rich/as clever; **etw** ~ **nicht tun
wollen** to refuse absolutely to do sth; **das braucht** ~ **nicht
schlecht zu sein** that does not have to be bad; **das ist** ~ **kein Witz**
that's no joke at all; **er ist** ~ **kein schlechter Mensch** he is by no
means a bad person; **es ist** ~ **nicht so einfach wie** ... it is by no
means as easy as ...
durchbacken sep **1** vt Kuchen to bake through. **2** vi (Kuchen)
to bake thoroughly; (Mensch) to spend all day etc baking.
durchbeben* vt insep (geh) to run through.
durchbeißen¹ sep irreg **1** vt (in zwei Teile) to bite through. **2** vr
(inf) (durch etw sth) to struggle through; (mit Erfolg) to win
through.
durchbeißen²* vt insep irreg **jdm die Kehle** ~ to tear sb's
throat open.
durchbekommen* vt sep irreg (inf) to get through.
durchbetteln vr sep to beg one's way.
durchbeuteln vt sep (S Ger inf) to shake thoroughly (auch fig),
to give a good shaking.
durchbewegen* vr sep to get through (durch etw sth).
durchbiegen sep irreg **1** vt Knie to bend. **2** vr to sag.
durchblasen¹ sep irreg **1** vt **(a)** to blow through (durch etw
sth); Eileiter, Rohr, Ohren etc to clear (by blowing). **(b)** (Wind)
to blow. **2** vi to blow through (durch etw sth).
durchblasen²* vt insep irreg to blow (through).
durchblättern vt sep or **durchblättern*** insep Buch etc to
leaf or flick through.
durchbleuen vt sep (inf) to beat black and blue.
Durchblick m vista (auf +acc of); (Ausblick) view (auf +acc
of); (fig inf: Verständnis, Überblick) knowledge. **den** ~ **haben**
(inf) to know what's what (inf); **den** ~ **verlieren** to lose track
(bei of).
durchblicken vi sep **(a)** (lit) to look through (durch etw sth);
(zum Vorschein kommen) to shine through. **(b)** (fig) **etw** ~
lassen to hint at sth, to intimate sth. **(c)** (fig inf: verstehen) to
understand. **blickst du da durch?** do you get it? (inf).
durchblitzen¹* vt insep to flash through. **jdn** ~ to flash
through sb's mind.
durchblitzen² vt sep **etw** ~ **lassen** (geh) to display sth, to show
sth, to manifest sth.
durchbluten¹* vt insep to supply with blood.
durchbluten² vti sep **die Wunde hat** ~ (der Verband or durch den
Verband) durchgeblutet the wound has bled through (the bandage), blood from the wound has soaked through (the bandage);
es blutet durch the blood is soaking through.
durchblutet adj supplied with blood.
Durchblutung f circulation (of the blood) (gen to).
Durchblutungsstörung f circulatory disturbance, disturbance of the circulation.
durchbohren¹* vt insep Wand, Brett to drill through; (mit
Schwert etc) to run through; (Kugel) to go through. **jdn mit
Blicken** ~ (fig) to look piercingly at sb; (haßerfüllt) to look daggers at sb; **sie sah mich an, als wollte sie mich mit Blicken** ~
she looked daggers at me.
durchbohren² sep **1** vt **etw durch etw** ~ Loch, Tunnel to drill
sth through sth; Schwert etc to run sth through sth; Nagel to
pierce sth through sth. **2** vi to drill through (durch etw sth). **3** vr
(durch etw sth) to bore one's way through; (Speer) to go
through.
durchbohrend adj piercing; Blicke auch penetrating.
durchboxen sep (fig inf) (durch etw sth) **1** vt to push or force
through. **2** vr to fight one's way through.
durchbraten vti sep irreg to cook through. **durchgebraten** well
done.
durchbrausen¹ vi sep aux sein to tear or roar through (durch
etw sth).
durchbrausen²* vt insep to thunder or roar through.
durchbrechen¹ sep irreg **1** vt (in zwei Teile) to break (in two).
2 vi aux sein **(a)** (in zwei Teile) to break (in two).
(b) (einbrechen: Mensch) to fall through (durch etw sth).
(c) (hervorbrechen) (Knospen) to appear; (Zahn) to come
through; (Sonne auch) to break through (durch etw sth);
(Charakter) to reveal itself.
(d) (Med: Blinddarm etc) to burst, to perforate.
durchbrechen²* vt insep irreg Schallmauer to break; Mauer,
Blockade etc to break through; (fig) to break.
Durchbrechung f siehe vt insep breaking; breaking through;
breaking.
durchbrennen vi sep irreg **(a)** (nicht ausgehen: Ofen, Feuer,
Licht etc) to stay alight. **(b)** aux sein (Sicherung, Glühbirne)

to blow, to burn out; (*inf: davonlaufen*) to run off *or* away, to abscond. **jdm ~** (*inf*) to run away from sb. **(c)** *aux sein* (*vollständig brennen: Kohlen, Holz, Feuer*) to burn through.

Durchbrenner(in *f*) *m* (*inf*) siehe **Ausreißer(in).**

durchbringen *sep irreg* 1 *vt* **(a)** (*durch etw* sth) (*durchsetzen, durch Prüfung, Kontrolle*) to get through; (*durch Krankheit*) to pull through; (*für Unterhalt sorgen*) to provide for, to support. **(b)** *Geld* to get through, to blow (*inf*). **(c)** (*dial*) *siehe* **durchbekommen. 2** *vr* to get by. **sich kümmerlich ~** to scrape by.

durchbrochen 1 *ptp of* **durchbrechen²**. **2** *adj* open; *Stickerei etc* openwork *attr*. **~e Arbeit** openwork.

Durchbruch *m* **(a)** (*durch etw* sth) (*durch Eis*) falling through *no art*; (*von Knospen*) appearance; (*von Zahn*) coming through; (*von Sonne*) breaking through; (*von Charakter*) revelation; (*von Blinddarm*) perforation. **zum ~ kommen** (*fig*) (*Gewohnheit etc*) to assert *or* show itself; (*Natur*) to reveal itself; **der Patient wurde mit einem ~ (des Blinddarms) eingeliefert** the patient was admitted with a perforated appendix. **(b)** (*Mil*) breakthrough; (*Sport auch*) break; (*fig: Erfolg*) breakthrough. **eine Idee kommt zum ~** an idea comes to the fore *or* emerges; **jdm/etw zum ~ verhelfen** to help sb/sth on the road to success. **(c)** (*durchbrochene Stelle*) breach; (*Öffnung*) opening; (*Geog: von Fluß*) rise, resurgence.

Durchbruch|arbeit *f* openwork.

durchbuchstabieren* *vt sep* to spell out.

durchbummeln¹ *vi sep aux sein* (*inf*) (*durchschlendern*) to stroll through (*durch etw* sth). **die Nacht ~** to spend the night on the tiles (*inf*).

durchbummeln²* *vt insep Nacht* to spend on the tiles (*inf*).

durchbürsten *vt sep* to brush thoroughly.

durchchecken [-tʃɛkn] *vt sep* **(a)** *Gepäck* to check through. **(b)** (*inf: überprüfen*) to check through.

durchdacht *adj* thought-out. **gut/schlecht ~** well/badly thought-out.

durchdenken* *insep*, **durchdenken** *sep vt irreg* to think out *or* through.

durchdiskutieren* *vt sep* to discuss thoroughly, to talk through.

durchdrängeln (*inf*), **durchdrängen** *vr sep* to push *or* force one's way through (*durch etw* sth).

durchdrehen *sep* 1 *vt Fleisch etc* to mince; (*Aut*) *Motor* to turn over. **2** *vi* **(a)** (*Rad*) to spin; (*Motor*) to turn over. **(b)** (*inf*) to do one's nut (*sl*); to flip (*inf*); (*nervlich*) to crack up (*inf*). **ganz durchgedreht sein** (*inf*) to be really uptight (*inf*) *or* (*aus dem Gleichgewicht*) confused.

durchdringen¹ *vi sep irreg aux sein* **(a)** to penetrate (*durch etw* sth); (*Flüssigkeit, Kälte auch, Sonne*) to come through (*durch etw* sth); (*Stimme, Geräusch auch*) to be heard (*durch etw* through sth). **bis zu jdm ~** (*fig*) to go *or* get as far as sb. **(b)** (*sich durchsetzen, sich verständlich machen*) to get through. **zu jdm ~** to get through to sb; **mit einem Vorschlag ~** to get a suggestion accepted (*bei, in +dat* by).

durchdringen²* *vt insep irreg Materie, Dunkelheit etc* to penetrate; (*Gefühl, Idee, Gedanke*) to pervade; *siehe* **durchdrungen.**

durchdringend *adj* piercing; *Kälte, Wind auch* biting; *Stimme, Geräusch, Blick auch* penetrating; *Geruch* pungent, sharp.

Durchdringung *f* **(a)** penetration; (*Sättigung*) saturation; (*Verschmelzung*) fusion. **(b)** (*fig: Erfassen*) investigation, exploration.

durchdrucken *vi sep* to leave an imprint; (*ununterbrochen drucken*) to print non-stop.

durchdrücken *sep* 1 *vt* **(a)** (*durch Sieb*) to rub through; (*durch Presse*) to press through; *Knoblauch* to crush; *Creme, Teig* to pipe. **(b)** (*fig*) *Gesetz, Reformen, Neuerungen etc* to push *or* force through; *seinen Willen* to get. **es ~, daß ...** to get the decision that ... through. **(c)** *Knie, Ellbogen etc* to straighten. **(d)** *Wäsche* to wash through. **2** *vr* to squeeze *or* push (one's way) through (*durch etw* sth). **sich in der Menge ~** to squeeze *or* push (one's way) through the crowd.

durchdrungen 1 *ptp of* **durchdringen²**. **2** *adj pred* imbued (*von* with). **ganz von einer Idee ~ sein** to be taken with an idea; **von einem Gefühl der Freude ~ sein** to be full of *or* imbued with a feeling of joy.

durchdürfen *vi sep irreg* (*inf*) to be allowed through. **darf ich mal ~?** can I get through?

durch|einander 1 *adv* mixed *or* muddled up, in a muddle *or* mess. **alles ~ essen/trinken** to eat/drink indiscriminately. **2** *adj pred* **~ sein** (*inf*) (*Mensch*) to be confused *or* (*aufgeregt*) in a state (*inf*); (*Zimmer, Papier*) to be in a mess *or* muddle.

Durch|einander *nt* **-s**, *no pl* (*Unordnung*) mess, muddle; (*Wirrwarr*) confusion. **in dem Zimmer herrscht ein wüstes ~** the room is in a terrible mess *or* muddle.

durch|einander-: **~bringen** *vt sep irreg* to muddle *or* mix up; (*in Unordnung bringen auch*) to mess *or* muddle; (*verwirren*) *jdn* to confuse; **~gehen** *vi sep irreg aux sein* to get confused *or* into a muddle; **ihm geht alles ~** he's getting everything confused *or* mixed up; **~geraten*** *vi sep irreg aux sein* to get mixed *or* muddled up; **diese Begriffe geraten bei mir immer ~** I always get these concepts mixed *or* muddled up; **jetzt bin ich mit dem Datum völlig ~geraten** now I've got completely mixed *or* muddled up about the date; **~kommen** *vi sep irreg aux sein* **(a)** (*vermischt werden*) to get mixed *or* muddled up; **(b)** (*inf*) *siehe* **~geraten;** **~laufen** *vi sep irreg aux sein* to run about *or* around all over the place; **~liegen** *vi sep irreg aux haben or sein*

to be in a muddle, to be all over the place; **~mengen, ~mischen** *vt sep* to mix (up); **~reden** *vi sep* to all speak *or* talk at once *or* at the same time; **~rennen** *vi sep irreg aux sein siehe* **~laufen; ~rufen, ~schreien** *vi sep irreg* to all shout out at once *or* at the same time; **~werfen** *vt sep irreg* to muddle up; (*fig inf: verwechseln*) to mix up, to confuse.

durch|essen *vr sep irreg* **(a)** **sich bei jdm ~** to eat at sb's expense. **(b)** **sich durch etw ~** to eat one's way through sth.

durch|exerzieren* *vt sep* to rehearse, to run *or* go through.

durchfahren¹ *vi sep irreg aux sein* **(a)** to go through (*durch etw* sth). **(b)** (*nicht anhalten/umsteigen*) to go straight through (*without stopping/changing*). **er ist bei Rot durchgefahren** he jumped the lights; **die Nacht ~** to travel through the night.

durchfahren²* *vt insep irreg* to travel through; (*fig: Schreck, Zittern etc*) to shoot through. **ein Gedanke durchfuhr ihn blitzartig** a (sudden) thought flashed through his mind.

Durchfahrt *f* **(a)** (*Durchreise*) way through. **auf der ~ sein** to be passing through; **auf *or* bei der ~ sieht man ja nicht viel** one doesn't see much when one is just passing through. **(b)** (*Passage*) thoroughfare; (*Naut*) thoroughfare, channel. **~ bitte freihalten!** please keep access free. **(c)** (*das Durchfahren*) thoroughfare. **~ verboten!** no through road, no thoroughfare; **der Polizist gab endlich die ~ frei/gab das Zeichen zur ~** the policeman finally allowed/signalled the traffic through.

Durchfahrts-: **~höhe** *f* headroom, clearance; **~recht** *nt* right of way; **~straße** *f* through road; **~verbot** *nt* **seit wann besteht hier ~verbot?** since when has this been a no through road?; **die Anwohner haben das ~verbot durchgesetzt** the residents managed to get through traffic banned.

Durchfall *m* **(a)** (*Med*) diarrhoea, diarrhea (*US*) *no art*. **(b)** (*Mißerfolg*) failure; (*von Theaterstück auch*) flop.

durchfallen *vi sep irreg aux sein* **(a)** to fall through (*durch etw* sth). **(b)** (*inf: nicht bestehen*) to fail; (*Theaterstück etc auch*) to (be a) flop; (*Wahlkandidat*) to lose, to be defeated. **in der Prüfung ~** to fail the exam; **beim Publikum/bei der Kritik ~** to be a failure *or* flop with the public/critics; **bei der Wahl ~** to lose the election, to be defeated in the election.

durchfärben *sep* 1 *vt* to dye *or* colour (evenly). **2** *vi* to come *or* seep through (*durch etw* sth).

durchfaulen *vi sep aux sein* to rot through.

durchfechten *sep irreg* 1 *vt etw ~* to fight to get sth through. **2** *vr sich (im Leben) ~* to struggle through (in life).

durchfedern *vi sep* to bend one's knees.

durchfegen¹ *vt sep* 1 to sweep out. **2** *vi* to sweep up.

durchfegen²* *vt insep* to sweep through.

durchfeiern¹ *vi sep* to stay up all night celebrating.

durchfeiern²* *vt insep* **die Nacht ~** to stay up all night celebrating; **nach durchfeierter Nacht** after celebrating all night.

durchfeilen *sep or* **durchfeilen*** *insep vt* to file through; (*fig*) *Aufsatz* to polish up.

durchfeuchten* *vt insep* to soak. **von etw durchfeuchtet sein** to be soaked (through) with sth.

durchfinden *vir sep irreg* (*lit, fig*) to find one's way through (*durch etw* sth). **ich finde (hier) nicht mehr durch** (*fig*) I am simply lost; **ich kann mich bei diesem Kram nicht ~** (*fig*) I can't make head nor tail of this mess.

durchflammen* *vt insep* (*geh*) *etw durchflammt jdn, jd wird von etw durchflammt* sth burns (with)in sb, sth burns in sb's heart.

durchflechten¹ *vt sep irreg* to thread *or* weave through.

durchflechten²* *vt insep irreg etw mit etw ~* (*lit*) to thread *or* weave sth through sth, to intertwine sth with sth; (*fig*) to interweave sth with sth.

durchfliegen¹ *vi sep irreg aux sein* **(a)** to fly through (*durch etw* sth); (*ohne Landung*) to fly non-stop *or* direct. **(b)** (*inf*) (*durch Prüfung*) to fail, to flunk (*inf*) (*durch etw, in etw (dat)* in) sth).

durchfliegen²* *vt insep irreg Luft, Wolken* to fly through; *Land* to fly over; *Luftkorridor* to fly along; *Strecke* to cover; (*flüchtig lesen*) to skim through.

durchfließen¹ *vi sep irreg aux sein* to flow *or* run through (*durch etw* sth).

durchfließen²* *vt insep irreg* (*lit, fig*) to flow *or* run through.

Durchflug *m* flight through; (*das Durchfliegen*) flying through (*durch etw* sth). **auf dem ~ nach Amerika/durch Ostdeutschland** en route for America/flying through East Germany; **Passagiere auf dem ~** transit passengers, through-passengers.

Durchfluß *m* (*das Fließen, ~menge*) flow; (*Öffnung*) opening.

durchfluten¹ *vi sep aux sein* (*geh*) to flow through (*durch etw* sth).

durchfluten²* *vt insep* (*geh*) (*Fluß*) to flow through; (*Licht, Sonne*) to flood; (*Wärme, Gefühl*) to flow *or* flood through. **Licht durchflutete das Zimmer** the room was flooded with *or* bathed in light, light flooded the room.

durchformen *vt sep* to work out (down) to the last detail.

durchforschen* *vt insep Gegend* to search; *Land, Wissensgebiet* to explore; *Akten, Bücher* to search through.

durchforsten* *vt insep*, **durchforsten** *vt sep Wald* to thin out; (*fig*) *Bücher, Akten etc* to go through.

durchfragen *vr sep* to ask one's way.

durchfressen¹ *vt sep irreg* 1 *vr* (*durch etw* sth) (*Säure, Rost, Tier*) to eat (its way) through. **sich (bei jdm) ~** (*pej inf*) to live on sb's hospitality; **sich durch ein Buch ~** (*inf*) to plough *or* wade through a book. **2** *vt* (*Rost, Maus*) to eat (its way) through; (*Motten*) to eat holes in. **ein Loch durch etw ~** to eat a hole in sth.

durchfressen²* *vt insep irreg* to eat through; (*Motten*) to eat holes in. **ein von Motten ~er Pullover** a moth-eaten pullover.

durchfretten vr sep (Aus, S Ger) to eke out an existence.

durchfrieren vi sep irreg aux sein (See, Fluß) to freeze through, to freeze solid; (Mensch) to get frozen stiff, to get chilled to the bone.

durchfroren adj siehe **durchgefroren**.

Durchfuhr f transit, passage.

durchführbar adj practicable, feasible, workable.

Durchführbarkeit f feasibility, practicability, workability.

durchführen sep 1 vt (a) (durchleiten) (durch etw sth) jdn to lead through, to take through; Fluß to lead through; Leitung, Rohr to run through; Straße to build through, to lay through; Kanal, Tunnel to dig through. etw durch etw ~ to lead etc sth through sth; jdn durch eine Stadt/eine Wohnung ~ to show sb around a town/a flat.

(b) (verwirklichen) Vorhaben, Beschluß, Plan to carry out; Gesetz to implement, to enforce; (unternehmen, veranstalten) Experiment, Haussuchung, Sammlung, Untersuchung, Reform to carry out; Expedition, Reise to undertake; Messung to take; Kursus to run; Wahl, Prüfung to hold; Unterrichtsstunde to take, to give.

(c) (konsequent zu Ende bringen) to carry through; Gedankengang to carry through (to its conclusion).

2 vi (durch etw sth) to lead through; (Straße) to go through. zwischen/unter etw (dat) ~ to lead/go between/under sth.

Durchfuhr-: ~erlaubnis f transit permit; ~handel m transit trade; ~land nt country of transit.

Durchführung f siehe vt (a) leading (through); running (through); building (through); digging (through).

(b) (fig) carrying out; implementation, enforcement; carrying out; undertaking; taking; running; holding; taking, giving. zur ~ kommen (form) (Reform, Gesetz, Maßnahme) to come into force; zur ~ bringen (form) Reform, Gesetz, Maßnahme to bring into force.

(c) carrying through.

(d) (Mus) (von Sonate) development; (von Fuge) exposition.

Durchfuhr-: ~verbot nt transit embargo; ~zoll m transit duty.

durchfurchen* vt insep (geh) Land to plough; Wogen to plough through. ein durchfurchtes Gesicht a lined or furrowed face.

durchfüttern vt sep (inf) to feed. sich von jdm ~ lassen to live off sb.

Durchgabe f (a) (von Nachricht, Lottozahlen etc) announcement; (von Hinweis, Bericht) giving. bei der ~ der Zahlen übers Telefon kommen oft Fehler vor when numbers are given over the telephone mistakes are often made.

(b) (Nachricht, Ankündigung) announcement; (telefonisch) message (over the telephone). ich habe ihn um eine kurze ~ an meine Mutter gebeten I asked him to give my mother a short message over the telephone, I asked him to telephone a short message to my mother.

Durchgang m (a) (Weg, Passage) way; (schmaler auch) passage(way); (Torweg) gateway.

(b) (das Durchgehen) kein ~!, ~ verboten! no right of way; beim ~ durch das Tal going through the valley; der ~ zur Höhle/zum anderen Tal ist beschwerlich it's difficult to get through to the cave/other valley; er hat mir den ~ versperrt he blocked my passage.

(c) (von Experiment, bei Arbeit, Parl) stage.

(d) (bei Wettbewerb, von Wahl, Sport) round; (beim Rennen) heat.

(e) (Astron) transit.

Durchgänger m -s, - (Pferd) bolter; (dated: Ausreißer) runaway.

durchgängig adj universal, general. eine ~e Eigenschaft in seinen Romanen a constant feature in or of his novels.

Durchgangs-: ~bahnhof m through station; ~lager nt transit camp; ~stadium nt transition stage; ~station f (fig) stopping-off place; ~straße f through road, thoroughfare; ~verkehr m (Mot) through traffic; (Transitverkehr) transit traffic.

durchgaren sep 1 vt to cook thoroughly. 2 vi aux sein to cook through.

durchgeben vt sep irreg (a) to pass through (durch etw sth).

(b) (Rad, TV) Hinweis, Meldung, Wetter, Straßenzustandsbericht to give; Nachricht, Lottozahlen to announce. jdm etw telefonisch ~ to let sb know sth by telephone, to telephone sth to sb; ein Telegramm telefonisch ~ to telephone a telegram; jdm ~, daß ... to let sb know that ..., to tell sb that ...; es wurde im Radio durchgegeben it was announced on the radio; wir geben (Ihnen) nun den Wetterbericht durch and now we bring you the weather forecast.

durchgefroren adj Mensch frozen stiff, perishing (cold) (inf) pred.

durchgehen sep irreg aux sein 1 vi (a) (lit) (durch etw sth) to go through, to walk through; (durch Kontrolle, Zoll) to pass through; (weitergehen, inf: sich durchstecken lassen) to go through. bitte ~! (im Bus) pass right down (the bus) please!

(b) (Fluß, Weg, Linie etc) (durch etw sth) to run through, to go through; (fig: Thema) to run through.

(c) (durchdringen) to come through (durch etw sth).

(d) (nicht zurückgewiesen werden) (Gesetz) to be passed, to go through; (Antrag auch) to be carried; (Postsendung) to get through.

(e) (toleriert werden) to be allowed (to pass), to be tolerated. jdm etw ~ lassen to let sb get away with sth, to overlook sth; das lasse ich nochmal ~ I'll let it pass.

(f) (gehalten werden für) für etw ~ to pass for sth, to be taken for sth.

(g) (durchpassen) to go through (durch etw sth). zwischen/unter etw (dat) ~ to go (through) between/under sth.

(h) (ohne Unterbrechung) to go straight through; (Fußgänger auch) to walk straight through; (Flug) to be non-stop or direct; (zeitlich: Party, Unterricht; örtlich: Straße, Linie auch) to run (right) through. die ganze Nacht ~ (Mensch) to walk all night long, to walk through(out) the night.

(i) (Pferd etc) to bolt; (inf: sich davonmachen) to run off or away. mit jdm ~ to run or go off with sb, to elope with sb; jdm ~ to run away from sb; seine Frau ist ihm durchgegangen his wife has run off and left him; mit etw ~ to run or make off with sth.

(j) (außer Kontrolle geraten) mit jdm ~ (Temperament, Nerven) to get the better of sb; (Gefühle auch) to run away with sb.

2 vt auch aux haben (durchsehen, -sprechen etc) to go or run through, to go or run over.

3 vi impers es geht durch/nicht durch there's a/no way through; wo geht es durch? where's the way through?

durchgehend 1 adj Öffnungszeiten round-the-clock attr, continuous; Straße straight; Verkehrsverbindung direct; Zug nonstop, through attr, direct; Fahrkarte through attr; Muster continuous; Eigenschaft constant. ~e Güter goods in transit.

2 adv throughout, right through. ~ geöffnet open right through; open 24 hours; ~ gefüttert fully lined, lined throughout.

durchgeistigt adj cerebral.

durchgellen* vt insep (geh) to pierce.

durchgeschwitzt 1 ptp of **durchschwitzen**. 2 adj Mensch bathed in sweat; Kleidung soaked in sweat, sweat-soaked attr.

durchgestalten* vt sep to work out (down) to the last detail.

durchgießen vt sep irreg to pour through (durch etw sth). etw durch ein Sieb ~ to strain sth, to pour sth through a sieve.

durchgliedern vt sep to subdivide.

durchglühen[1] sep 1 vi aux sein to glow red-hot; (Lampe, Draht, Sicherung) to burn out. 2 vt Eisen to heat until red-hot or to red heat.

durchglühen[2]* vt insep (liter: Gefühl) to glow through. von Begeisterung durchglüht aglow with enthusiasm.

durchgraben sep irreg 1 vt to dig through (durch etw sth). 2 vr ┐to dig one's way through (durch etw sth).

durchgreifen vi sep irreg to reach through (durch etw sth); (fig) to take vigorous action, to resort to drastic measures. hier muß viel strenger durchgegriffen werden much more vigorous action is needed here.

durchgreifend adj Änderung, Maßnahme drastic; (weitreichend) Änderung far-reaching, radical, sweeping attr.

durchgucken vi sep (a) (durch etw sth) (Mensch) to look through, to peep through; (durchscheinen) to show through.

(b) (fig inf) siehe **durchblicken** (c).

durchhaben vt sep irreg (inf) etw ~ (hindurchbekommen haben) to have got sth through (durch etw sth); (durchgelesen etc haben) to have got through sth, to have finished sth; (zerteilt haben) to have got through sth, to be through sth.

durchhacken vt sep to chop or hack through.

Durchhalte|appell m appeal to hold out.

durchhalten sep irreg 1 vt (durchstehen) Zeit, Ehe, Kampf etc to survive; Streik to hold out till the end of, to see through; Belastung to (with)stand; (Sport) Strecke to stay; Tempo (beibehalten) to keep up; (aushalten) to stand. das Rennen ~ to stay the course.

2 vi to hold out, to stick it out (inf); (beharren) to persevere, to stick it out (inf); (bei Rennen auch) to stay the course. bis zum Äußersten ~ to hold out or stick it out (inf) to the last; eisern ~ to hold out grimly.

Durchhalte-: ~parole f exhortation to hold out; ~vermögen nt staying power, (powers pl of) endurance no indef art.

Durchhang m sag, slack.

durchhängen vi sep irreg aux haben or sein to sag.

durchhauen[1] sep irreg or (inf) reg 1 vt (a) to chop or hack in two; (spalten) to split, to cleave.

(b) (inf: verprügeln) jdn ~ to give sb a thrashing or walloping (inf), to thrash or wallop (inf) sb.

(c) (inf) Sicherung to blow.

2 vr (lit) to hack one's way through (durch etw sth); (fig: sich durchschlagen) to get by.

durchhauen[2]* vt insep irreg to chop or hack in two.

durchhecheln vt sep (a) Flachs etc to hackle. (b) (fig inf) to gossip about, to pull to pieces (inf). in allen Zeitungen durchgehechelt dragged through all the papers.

durchheizen sep 1 vt (gründlich heizen) to heat through; (ohne Unterbrechung heizen) to heat continuously, to heat day and night. 2 vi (ohne Unterbrechung) to keep the heating on. hier muß mal richtig durchgeheizt werden this place needs to be well heated.

durchhelfen sep irreg 1 vi jdm (durch etw) ~ to help sb through (sth). 2 vr to get by, to get along, to manage.

durchhören vt sep (a) etw (durch etw) ~ (lit) Lärm to hear sth (through sth); (fig) Gefühl, Enttäuschung auch to discern sth (through sth); ich konnte ~, daß ... I could hear or tell that ... (b) Schallplatte, Konzert etc to hear (all the way) through, to hear all of.

durchhungern vr sep to struggle along on the breadline, to scrape by.

durch|irren* vt insep to wander or rove or roam through.

durch|ixen vt sep (inf) to ex out.

durchjagen[1] sep 1 vt (a) to chase through (durch etw sth).

(b) (fig) Gesetz, Prozeß etc to rush or push through.

(c) (pej inf) Benzin/Geld durch den Auspuff ~ to burn a lot of juice (inf)/to burn money; Öl/Geld durch den Schornstein ~ to burn a lot of oil/to burn money; sein ganzes Geld durch die Kehle ~ to booze all one's money away (inf).

2 *vi aux sein* to race *or* tear through. **zwischen/unter etw** (*dat*) ~ to race *or* tear between/under sth.

durchjagen[2]* *vt insep Land etc* to race *or* tear through.

durchkämmen *vt sep* (a) *Haare* to comb out. (b) *auch* **durchkämmen*** *insep* (*absuchen*) to comb (through).

durchkämpfen *sep* 1 *vt* (*durchsetzen*) to push *or* force through.
2 *vr* (a) (*durch etw sth*) to fight *or* battle one's way through; (*fig*) to struggle through.
(b) siehe **durchringen**.
3 *vi* (*Kampf nicht aufgeben*) (*Soldaten*) to carry on fighting; (*Sportler, Bergsteiger*) to battle on, to carry on the battle *or* struggle. **es wurde selbst über die Weihnachtszeit durchgekämpft** the fighting continued even over Christmas.

durchkauen *vt sep Essen* to chew (thoroughly); (*inf: besprechen*) to go over *or* through.

durchklettern *vi sep aux sein* to climb through (*durch etw sth*).

durchklingen[1] *vi sep irreg aux haben or sein* (*durch etw sth*) to sound through; (*fig*) to come through (*durch etw sth*), to come across (*durch etw through sth*). **die Musik klang durch den Lärm** through the music could be heard above the noise.

durchklingen[2]* *vt insep irreg* to ring through.

durchkneifen *vt sep irreg Draht* to snip through.

durchkneten *vt sep Teig etc* to knead thoroughly; (*bei Massage*) to massage thoroughly. **sich ~ lassen** to have a thorough massage; **sich von jdm ~ lassen** to get sb to give one a thorough massage.

durchknöpfen *vt sep* to button all the way up. **ein durchgeknöpftes Kleid** a button-through dress.

durchkochen *vti sep* to boil thoroughly.

durchkommen *vi sep irreg aux sein* (a) (*durch etw sth*) (*durchfahren*) to come through; (*vorbeikommen, passieren auch*) to come past. **er ist durch diese Straße/Stadt/unter dieser Brücke durchgekommen** he came through this street/town/under *or* through this bridge.
(b) (*durch etw sth*) to get through; (*Sonne, Wasser etc*) to come through; (*Sender, Farbe*) to come through; (*Charakterzug*) to show through, to come out *or* through; (*sichtbar werden*) (*Sonne*) to come out; (*Blumen*) to come through. **kommst du durch?** can you get through?; **es kommt immer wieder durch, daß sie Ausländerin ist** the fact that she is a foreigner keeps showing *or* coming through.
(c) (*lit, fig: mit Erfolg* ~) to succeed (*durch etw in sth*), to get through (*durch etw sth*); (*sich durchsetzen*) (*telefonisch*) to get through; (*finanziell*) to get by. **ich komme mit meiner Hand nicht (durch das Loch) durch** I can't get my hand through (the hole); **mit etw ~** (*mit Forderungen etc*) to succeed with sth; (*mit Betrug, Schmeichelei etc*) to get away with sth; **er kam (bei dem Lärm) mit seiner Stimme nicht durch** he couldn't make his voice heard (above the noise); **damit kommt er bei mir nicht durch** he won't get away with that with me.
(d) (*Prüfung bestehen*) to get through, to pass.
(e) (*überleben*) to come through; (*Patient auch*) to pull through.
(f) (*im Radio*) to be announced.

durchkomponieren* *vt sep* (a) (*Mus*) *Libretto* to set to music; *Gedicht* to set to music (with a different setting for each stanza). (b) (*fig*) *Bild, Text* to work out in detail. (c) (*ohne Unterbrechung*) to compose right through. **die ganze Nacht ~** to compose right through the night.

durchkönnen *vi sep irreg* (*inf*) to be able to get through (*durch etw sth*).

durchkonstruieren* *vt sep* **ein Auto ~** to construct a car well throughout; **gut durchkonstruiert** well constructed throughout.

durchkosten *vt sep* (*geh*) to taste (one after the other); (*fig*) *Freuden* to taste; *Leiden* to endure, to experience.

durchkreuzen[1]* *vt insep* (a) *Land, Wüste, Ozean* to cross, to travel across. (b) (*fig*) *Pläne etc* to thwart, to foil, to frustrate.

durchkreuzen[2]* *vt sep* to cross out, to cross through.

Durchkreuzung *f* (a) (*von Land etc*) crossing. (b) (*von Plänen etc*) thwarting, foiling, frustrating.

durchkriechen *vi sep irreg aux sein* to crawl through, to creep through (*durch etw sth*).

durchkriegen *vt sep* (*inf*) siehe **durchbekommen**.

durchladen *vti sep irreg Gewehr* to reload.

durchlangen *sep* (*inf*) 1 *vi* (*durch etw sth*) to reach through, to put one's hand through. 2 *vt* (*durchreichen*) to pass through.

Durchlaß *m* -sses, **Durchlässe** (a) (*Durchgang*) passage, way through; (*für Wasser*) duct. (b) *no pl* (*geh*) permission to pass. **jdm/sich ~ verschaffen** to obtain permission for sb/to obtain permission to pass; (*mit Gewalt*) to force a way through for sb/to force one's way through.

durchlassen *vt sep irreg* (*durch etw sth*) (*passieren lassen*) to allow *or* let through; (*Licht, Wasser etc* (*durchdringen lassen*)) to let through; (*eindringen lassen*) to let in; (*inf: durch Prüfung*) to let through, to pass; (*inf: durchgehen lassen*) *Fehler etc* to let pass, to overlook.

durchlässig *adj Material* permeable; (*porös*) porous; *Zelt, Regenmantel, Schuh* that lets water in; *Zelt, Schuh* leaky; *Krug, Vase* that lets water out *or* through; *Grenze* open. **eine ~e Stelle** (*fig*) a leak; **die Bildungswege ~ machen** to make the elements of the education programme interchangeable.

Durchlässigkeit *f* permeability; (*Porosität*) porosity. **die ~ des Zelts/Krugs** the fact that the tent/jug leaks *or* lets water in/out *or* through; **die ~ der Bildungswege** the interchangeability of the elements of the education programme.

Durchlaucht *f* -, -en = member of the Royal Family. **Seine ~** His (Serene) Highness; (**Euer**) ~ Your Highness.

durchlauchtig *adj attr* (*old*) serene. **~ste Herren/Herrschaften** most Serene Highnesses.

Durchlauf *m* (a) (*das Durchlaufen*) flow. (b) (*Datenverarbeitung*) run. (c) (*TV, Rad*) run-through. (d) (*Ski*) heat.

durchlaufen[1] *sep irreg* 1 *vt Schuhe, Sohlen* to go *or* wear through.
2 *vi aux sein* (a) (*durch etw sth*) (*durch Straße/Öffnung etc gehen*) to go through; (*passieren auch*) to pass through; (*Straße, Rohr etc auch*) to run through; (*Flüssigkeit*) to run through.
(b) (*ohne Unterbrechung: Mensch*) to run without stopping. **8 Stunden lang ohne Pause ~** to run for 8 hours without stopping; **der Fries/das Geländer läuft von der einen Seite des Gebäudes zur anderen durch** the frieze/railing runs uninterrupted *or* without a break from one end of the building to the other.

durchlaufen[2]* *vt insep irreg* (a) *Gebiet* to run through; *Strecke* to cover, to run; (*Astron*) *Bahn* to describe; *Lehrzeit, Schule, Phase* to pass *or* go through. (b) (*erfassen, erfüllen*) (*Gerücht*) to spread through; (*Gefühl*) to run through. **es durchlief mich heiß** I felt hot all over.

durchlaufend *adj* continuous.

Durchlauf-: **~erhitzer** *m* -s, - continuous-flow water heater; **~zeit** *f* (*Datenverarbeitung*) length of the run.

durchlavieren* [-laviːrən] *vr sep* to steer *or* manoeuvre one's way through (*durch etw sth*).

durchleben* *vt insep Jugend, Gefühl* to go through, to experience; *Zeit* to go *or* live through.

durchleiden* *vt insep irreg* to suffer, to endure.

durchleiten *vt sep* to lead through (*durch etw sth*).

durchlesen *vt sep irreg* to read through. **etw ganz ~** to read sth all the way through; **etw flüchtig ~** to skim *or* glance through sth; **etw auf Fehler (hin) ~** to read sth through (looking) for mistakes; **sich** (*dat*) **etw ~** to read sth through.

durchleuchten[1]* *vt insep* (a) (*untersuchen*) *Patienten* to X-ray; *Eier* to candle; (*fig*) *Angelegenheit etc* to investigate, to probe. **jdn die Lunge ~** to X-ray sb's lungs; **sich ~ lassen** to have an X-ray; **sich** (*dat*) **die Lunge ~ lassen** to have one's lungs X-rayed.
(b) (*geh: Schein, Sonne etc*) to light up, to flood with light.

durchleuchten[2] *vi sep* to shine through (*durch etw sth*).

Durchleuchtung *f* (*Med: mit Röntgenstrahlen*) X-ray examination; (*fig: von Angelegenheit etc*) investigation. **zur ~ gehen** to go for an X-ray.

durchliegen *sep irreg* 1 *vt Matratze, Bett* to wear down (in the middle). 2 *vr* to get *or* develop bedsores.

durchlöchern* *vt insep* to make holes in; (*Motten auch, Rost*) to eat holes in; *Socken etc* to wear holes in; (*fig*) to undermine completely; *Argumente auch* to shoot down. (*mit Schüssen*) ~ to riddle with bullets; **eine völlig durchlöcherte Leiche** a corpse riddled with bullet holes; **er hatte völlig durchlöcherte Socken/Kleidung** an his socks/clothes were full of holes; **von Würmern durchlöchert** worm-eaten; **von Rost durchlöchert** eaten away with rust.

durchlotsen *vt sep* (*durch etw sth*) *Schiff* to pilot through; *Autofahrer* to guide through; (*fig*) to steer through. **jdn durch etw ~** to pilot *etc* sb through sth.

durchlüften[1] *vti sep* to air thoroughly; *Wäsche auch* to air through. **ich muß mich mal wieder ~ lassen** I must (go and) get some fresh air (in my lungs).

durchlüften[2]* *vt insep* to air thoroughly.

durchlügen *vr sep irreg* (*inf*) to lie one's way through (*durch etw sth*).

durchmachen *sep* 1 *vt* (a) (*erdulden*) to go through; *Krankheit* to have; *Operation* to undergo, to have. **er hat viel durchgemacht** he has been *or* gone through a lot.
(b) (*durchlaufen*) to go through; *Lehre* to serve; (*fig*) *Entwicklung* to undergo; *Wandlung* to undergo, to experience.
(c) (*inf: durchbewegen, durchstecken etc*) *Faden, Nadel, Stange etc* to put through (*durch etw sth*).
(d) (*inf: durchtrennen*) (**in der Mitte**) ~ to cut in half.
(e) (*inf*) (*durcharbeiten*) to work through. **eine ganze Nacht/Woche ~** (*durchfeiern*) to have an all-night/week-long party, to make a night/week of it (*inf*).
2 *vi* (*inf*) (*durcharbeiten*) to work right through; (*durchfeiern*) to keep going all night/day *etc*.

durchmanövrieren* *vt sep* to manoeuvre through (*durch etw sth*).

Durchmarsch *m* (a) march(ing) through. **der ~ durch die Stadt** the march through the town; **auf dem ~ when marching through.** (b) (*inf: Durchfall*) runs *pl* (*inf*). (c) (*Cards*) grand slam.

durchmarschieren* *vi sep aux sein* to march through (*durch etw sth*).

durchmengen *vt sep* siehe **durchmischen**[1].

durchmessen* *vt insep irreg* (*geh*) *Raum* to stride across; *Strecke* to cover.

Durchmesser *m* -s, - diameter. **120 cm im ~ 120 cm in diameter.**

durchmischen[1] *vt sep* to mix thoroughly.

durchmischen[2]* *vt insep* to (inter)mix. **etw mit etw ~** to mix sth with sth.

durchmogeln *sep* (*inf*) 1 *vr* to wangle *or* fiddle (*inf*) one's way through. 2 *vt* to fiddle through (*inf*) (*durch etw sth*).

durchmüssen *vi sep irreg* (*inf*) (*durch etw sth*) to have to go *or* get through; (*fig*) (*durch schwere Zeit*) to have to go through; (*durch Unangenehmes*) to have to go through with (*inf*).

durchnagen *sep* 1 *vt* to gnaw through. 2 *vr* to gnaw one's way through (*durch etw sth*).

Durchnahme *f* -, -n **die ~ des Konjunktivs** going through the subjunctive.

durchnässen[1]* vt insep to soak, to drench, to make wet through. **völlig durchnäßt** wet through, soaking wet, drenched.

durchnässen[2] vi sep (Flüßigkeit) to come or seep through (durch etw sth). **die Zeltplane/Wunde näßt durch** wet is coming or seeping through the canvas/moisture from the wound is coming or seeping through.

durchnehmen vt sep irreg (a) (Sch) to go through, to do (inf). (b) (pej inf) to gossip about.

durchnumerieren* vt sep to number consecutively (all the way through).

durchorganisieren* vt sep to organize down to the last detail.

durchpaginieren* vt sep to paginate.

durchpassieren* vt sep to (rub through a) sieve.

durchpauken vt sep (inf) (a) (Schüler) to cram (inf), to swot up (inf). **etw mit jdm ~** to drum sth into sb (inf). (b) (durchsetzen) Gesetz, Änderungen to force or push through. (c) (durch Schwierigkeiten bringen) Schüler to push through. **dein Anwalt wird dich schon irgendwie ~** your lawyer will get you off somehow.

durchpausen vt sep to trace.

durchpeitschen vt sep to flog; (fig) to rush through, to railroad through (inf).

durchpflügen[1] sep 1 vt to plough thoroughly. 2 vr to plough (one's/its way) through (durch etw sth).

durchpflügen[2]* vt insep to plough through.

durchplanen vt sep to plan (down) to the last detail.

durchplumpsen vi sep aux sein (inf) (lit) to fall through (durch etw sth); (bei Prüfung) to fail, to flunk (inf) (durch etw, in etw (dat) (in) sth).

durchpressen vt sep to press through, to squeeze through; Knoblauch to crush; Kartoffeln to mash (by pushing through a press); Teig to pipe.

durchproben vt sep to rehearse right through.

durchprobieren* vt sep to try one after the other.

durchprügeln vt sep to thrash, to beat.

durchpulsen* vt insep (geh) to pulsate through. **von etw durchpulst sein** to be pulsating or vibrating with sth; **von Leben durchpulst** pulsating or throbbing with life; **von Begeisterung durchpulst** vibrant with enthusiasm.

durchpusten vt sep (inf) Rohr, Düse to blow through. **etw (durch etw) ~** to blow sth through (sth); **der Wind hat uns kräftig durchgepustet** the wind blew right through us.

durchqueren* vt insep to cross; Land, Gebiet auch to pass through, to traverse (form).

durchquetschen sep (inf) 1 vt siehe **durchpressen**. 2 vr (inf) to squeeze (one's way) through.

durchrasen[1] vi sep aux sein (durch etw sth) to race or tear through; (inf: durchrennen auch) to dash through.

durchrasen[2]* vt insep to race through, to tear through; (liter: Schmerz) to shoot through.

durchrasseln vi sep aux sein (inf) to fail, to flunk (inf) (durch etw, in etw (dat) (in) sth).

durchrauschen[1] vi sep aux sein (inf) (durch etw sth) (a) to sweep through. (b) (bei Prüfung) siehe **durchrasseln**.

durchrauschen[2]* vt insep (poet) (Wind) to rustle through; (Wasser) to rush or gush through.

durchrechnen vt sep to calculate. **eine Rechnung noch einmal ~** to go over or through a calculation (again).

durchregnen sep 1 vi impers (a) (durchkommen) **hier regnet es durch** the rain is coming through here; **es regnet durchs Dach durch** the rain is coming through the roof. (b) (ununterbrochen regnen) to rain continuously. **während des ganzen Urlaubs hat es durchgeregnet** it rained throughout the whole holiday; **es hat die Nacht durchgeregnet** it rained all night long, it rained all through the night. 2 vt: **durchgeregnet sein** to be soaked to the skin or through.

durchreiben sep irreg 1 vt to rub through; Material to wear through. 2 vr (Material) to wear through.

Durchreiche f -, -n (serving) hatch, pass-through (US).

durchreichen vt sep to pass or hand through (durch etw sth).

Durchreise f journey through. **auf der ~ sein** to be on the way through, to be passing through.

Durchreise|erlaubnis f permission to travel through.

durchreisen[1] vi sep aux sein (durch etw sth) to travel through, to pass through. **wir reisen nur durch** we are just passing through, we are just on the way through.

durchreisen[2]* vt insep to travel through, to traverse (form).

Durchreisende(r) mf decl as adj traveller (passing through), transient (US). **~ nach München** through passengers to Munich.

Durchreisevisum nt transit visa.

durchreißen sep irreg 1 vt to tear in two or in half. **etw (in der Mitte) ~** to tear sth in two or in half or down the middle. 2 vi aux sein to tear in two or in half; (Seil) to snap (in two or in half).

durchreiten[1] sep irreg 1 vi aux sein to ride through (durch etw sth). **die Nacht ~** to ride through(out) the night, to ride all night long. 2 vt Hose to wear out (through riding). **ein Pferd durch etw ~** to ride a horse through sth. 3 vr to make oneself sore riding.

durchreiten[2]* vt insep irreg to ride through; Land auch to ride across.

durchrennen[1] vi sep irreg aux sein to run or race through (durch etw sth).

durchrennen[2]* vt insep irreg to run or race through.

durchrieseln[1] vi sep aux sein to trickle through (durch etw sth). **jdm zwischen den Fingern ~** to trickle between or through sb's fingers.

durchrieseln[2]* vt insep (fig: Gefühl, Schauer) to run through.

durchringen vr sep irreg to make up one's mind finally. **er hat**

sich endlich durchgerungen after much hesitation, he has finally made up his mind or come to a decision; **sich zu einem Entschluß ~** to force oneself to take a decision; **sich dazu ~, etw zu tun** to bring or force oneself to do sth.

durchrinnen[1] vi sep irreg aux sein to run through (durch etw sth); (durchsickern) to trickle through. **zwischen etw (dat) ~ to run between sth; das Geld rinnt mir nur so zwischen den Fingern durch** (fig inf) money just runs through my fingers or burns a hole in my pockets (inf).

durchrinnen[2]* vt insep irreg (Bach) to run through; (durchsickern) to trickle through; (fig: Gefühl, Schauder) to run through.

Durchritt m ride through. **beim ~, auf dem ~** on the ride through.

durchrosten vi sep aux sein to rust through.

durchrufen vi sep irreg (inf) to ring.

durchrühren vt sep to mix thoroughly.

durchrutschen vi sep aux sein (lit) to slip through (durch etw sth); (fig) (Fehler etc) to slip through; (bei Prüfung) to scrape through. **ein Brei, der einfach (durch die Speiseröhre) durchrutscht** a purée that simply slides or slips down the throat; **zwischen etw (dat) ~** to slip between sth; **einige Fehler sind ihm durchgerutscht** a few mistakes slipped past him, he let a few mistakes slip through.

durchrütteln vt sep to shake about.

durchs = **durch das**.

durchsäbeln vt sep (inf) to hack through.

durchsacken vi sep aux sein (a) (durchhängen) (Bett etc) to sag; (durchbrechen) (Dach, Sitz) to give way; (nach unten sinken) to sink. **durch etw ~** (Mensch) to fall (down) through sth. (b) (Aviat: Flugzeug) to pancake.

Durchsage f message; (im Radio) announcement. **eine ~ der Polizei** a police announcement.

durchsagen vt sep (a) siehe **durchgeben** (b). (b) Parole, Losung to pass on.

durchsägen vt sep to saw through.

durchsaufen[1] sep irreg (sl) 1 vi to booze the whole night/day long (inf). **die Nacht etc ~** to booze all the night etc long (inf). 2 vr to booze at somebody else's expense (inf). **sich durch etw ~** to booze one's way through sth (inf).

durchsaufen[2]* vt insep irreg (sl) siehe **durchsoffen**.

durchsausen vi sep aux sein (inf) (a) to rush or whizz (inf) through. (b) (inf: nicht bestehen) to fail, to flunk (inf) (durch etw, in etw (dat) (in) sth).

durchschalten sep 1 vt (Elec) to connect through. 2 vi (a) (Elec) to connect through. (b) (Aut) to change through the gears.

durchschaubar adj (fig) Hintergründe, Plan, Ereignisse clear; Lüge transparent. **gut/leicht ~** (verständlich) easily comprehensible or understood; (erkennbar, offensichtlich) perfectly clear. **eine leicht ~e Lüge** a lie that is easy to see through; **schwer ~er Charakter/Mensch** inscrutable or enigmatic character/person.

durchschauen[1]* vt insep (erkennen) Absichten, Lüge, jdn, Spiel to see through; Sachlage to see clearly; (begreifen) to understand, to comprehend. **du bist durchschaut!** I've/we've seen through you, I/we know what you're up to (inf) or what your little game is (inf).

durchschauen[2] vti sep siehe **durchsehen** 1 (a), 2 (a, b).

durchschauern* vt insep to run through. **es durchschauert mich** a shiver or shudder runs through me.

durchscheinen[1] vi sep irreg (durch etw sth) (Licht, Sonne) to shine through; (Farbe, Muster) to show through; (fig) to shine through.

durchscheinen[2]* vt insep irreg (Sonne) to flood with light.

durchscheinend adj transparent; Bluse etc see-through; Porzellan, Papier auch translucent; Stoff auch diaphanous.

durchscheuern sep 1 vt to wear through. **sich (dat) die Haut ~** to graze one's skin; **durchgescheuert sein** to be or have worn through. 2 vr to wear through.

durchschieben sep irreg 1 vt to push or shove (inf) through (durch etw sth). 2 vr to push or shove (inf) (one's way) through (durch etw sth).

durchschießen[1] vi sep irreg (a) **durch etw ~** to shoot through sth; **zwischen etw (dat) ~** to shoot between sth. (b) aux sein (schnell fahren, rennen) to shoot or flash through. **zwischen etw (dat) ~** to shoot between sth.

durchschießen[2]* vt insep irreg (a) (mit Kugeln) to shoot through; (fig) to shoot or flash through. **die Lunge/jdn ~** to shoot through the lung/to shoot sb through; **ein Gedanke durchschoß mich/mein Gehirn** a thought flashed through my mind. (b) (Typ: leere Seiten einfügen) to interleave. (c) auch vi (Typ: Zeilenabstand vergrößern) to set or space out; siehe **durchschossen**. (d) (Tex) Stoff to interweave.

durchschiffen* vt insep to sail across, to cross.

durchschimmern vi sep (durch etw sth) to shimmer through; (Farbe, fig) to show through.

durchschlafen vi sep irreg to sleep through.

Durchschlag m (a) (Kopie) carbon (copy), copy. (b) (Küchengerät) sieve, strainer. (c) (Lochgerät) punch. (d) (Loch) hole; (in Reifen auch) puncture. (e) (Elec) disruptive discharge.

durchschlagen[1] sep irreg 1 vt (a) **etw ~** (entzweischlagen) to chop through sth; (durchtreiben) to knock sth through (durch etw sth); (Cook) to rub sth through a sieve, to sieve sth. (b) (Elec) Sicherung to blow. 2 vi (a) aux sein (durchkommen) (durch etw sth) to come through; (fig: Charakter, Eigenschaft, Untugend) to show through. **bei ihm schlägt der Vater durch** you can see his father in him.

(b) *aux sein* (*Loch verursachen*) to come/go through (*durch etw* sth).

(c) *aux haben* (*abführen*) to have a laxative effect. **grüne Äpfel schlagen (bei mir/ihm) durch** (*inf*) green apples run or go straight through me/him.

(d) *aux sein* (*Wirkung haben*) to catch on. **auf etw** (*acc*) ~ to make one's/its mark on sth; **auf jdn** ~ to rub off on sb.

(e) *aux sein* (*Sicherung*) to blow, to go.

(f) (*Tech*) (*Federung, Stoßdämpfer*) to seize up. **das Auto schlug durch** the suspension went.

3 *vr* **(a)** (*sich durchbringen*) to fight one's way through; (*im Leben*) to struggle through or along.

(b) (*ein Ziel erreichen*) to fight one's way through.

4 *vt impers* (*Elec*) **es hat die Sicherung durchgeschlagen** the fuse has blown or gone.

durchschlagen²* *vt insep irreg* to blast a hole in.

durchschlagend *adj Sieg, Erfolg* sweeping; *Maßnahmen* effective, decisive; *Argument, Beweis* decisive, conclusive; *Grund* compelling, cogent. **eine ~e Wirkung haben** to be totally effective.

Durchschlagpapier *nt* copy paper; (*Kohlepapier*) carbon paper.

Durchschlags-: ~ **kraft** *f* (*von Geschoß*) penetration; (*fig*) (*von Argument*) decisiveness, conclusiveness; (*von Maßnahmen*) effectiveness; (*von Grund*) cogency; **d~kräftig** *adj* (*fig*) *Argument, Beweis* decisive, conclusive; *Grund* compelling, cogent; *Maßnahme* effective, decisive.

durchschlängeln *vr sep* (*durch etw* sth) (*Fluß*) to wind (its way) through, to meander through; (*Mensch*) to thread one's way through; (*fig*) to manoeuvre one's way through.

durchschleichen *vir sep irreg* (*vi: aux sein*) to slip through (*durch etw* sth).

durchschleppen *sep* **1** *vt* to drag or haul through (*durch etw* sth); (*fig*) *jdn* to drag along; *Kollegen, Mitglied etc* to carry (along) (with one). **2** *vr* (*lit: mühsam gehen*) to drag oneself along; (*fig*) to struggle through (*durch etw* sth).

durchschleusen *vt sep* **(a)** *ein Schiff* ~ to pass a ship through a lock. **(b)** (*fig*) (*durch etw* sth) (*durch schmale Stelle*) to guide or lead through; (*durchschmuggeln*) *Menschen, Gegenstand* to smuggle or get through.

Durchschlupf *m* -(e)s, **Durchschlüpfe** way through.

durchschlüpfen *vi sep aux sein* to slip through, to creep through (*durch etw* sth). **er ist der Polizei durchgeschlüpft** he slipped through the fingers of the police; **durch Lücken im Gesetz** ~ to slip through loopholes in the law.

durchschmecken *sep* **1** *vt* to taste. **man kann den Essig** ~ **one** can taste the vinegar through the other flavours. **2** *vi* to come through. **der Knoblauch schmeckt deutlich durch** the taste of the garlic comes through strongly.

durchschmuggeln *vt sep* to smuggle through (*durch etw* sth).

durchschneiden¹ *vt sep irreg* to cut through, to cut in two. **etw in der Mitte** ~ to cut sth (down) through the middle; **etw mitten** ~ to cut sth in two or in half.

durchschneiden²* *vt insep irreg* to cut through, to cut in two; (*Schiff*) *Wellen* to plough through; (*Straße, Weg*) to cut through; (*fig: Schrei*) to pierce. **Wasserwege** ~ **das Land** the country is criss-crossed by waterways.

Durchschnitt *m* **(a)** (*Mittelwert, Mittelmaß*) average; (*in Statistik*) mean; (*Math*) average, (arithmetic) mean. **der** ~ (*normale Menschen*) the average person; (*die Mehrheit*) the majority; **im** ~ **on** average; **im** ~ **100 km/h fahren/im** ~ **8 Stunden täglich arbeiten** to average 100 kmph/8 hours a day, to work on average 8 hours a day; **über/unter dem** ~ above/below average; ~ **sein** to be average; **guter** ~ **sein, zum guten** ~ **gehören** to be a good average.

(b) (*form: Querschnitt*) (cross-)section.

durchschnittlich **1** *adj* average; *Wert auch* mean *attr*; (*mittelmäßig auch*) ordinary. **2** *adv* (*im Durchschnitt*) verdienen, schlafen, essen etc on (an) average. ~ **begabt/groß etc** of average ability/height etc; ~ **gut** good on average; **die Mannschaft hat sehr** ~ **gespielt** the team played a very average game; **er arbeitet** ~ **fünf Stunden pro Tag** he works on average five hours a day, he averages five hours a day.

Durchschnitts- *in cpds* average; **~alter** *nt* average age; **~bildung** *f* average education; **~bürger** *m* average citizen; **~ehe** *f* average or normal marriage; **~einkommen** *nt* average income; **~geschwindigkeit** *f* average speed; **~gesicht** *nt* ordinary or nondescript (*pej*) face; **~leser** *m* average reader; **~mensch** *m* average person; **~schüler** *m* average pupil; **~temperatur** *f* average or mean (*spec*) temperature; **~wert** *m* average or mean (*Math*) value; **~zeichnung** *f* sectional drawing; **~zeit** *f* average time.

durchschnüffeln *sep or* **durchschnüffeln*** *insep vt* (*pej inf*) *Post, Tasche* to nose through (*inf*); *Wohnung* to sniff or nose around in (*inf*). **alle Winkel** ~ to poke one's nose into every corner (*inf*).

durchschossen **1** *ptp of* **durchschießen²**. **2** *adj* (*Typ*) *Buch* interleaved; *Satz* spaced.

Durchschreibeblock *m* duplicating pad.

durchschreiben *sep irreg* **1** *vt* to make a (carbon) copy of. **alles wird durchgeschrieben** copies are or a copy is made of everything. **2** *vi* **(a)** (*Kopie anfertigen*) to make a (carbon) copy. **(b)** (*Kopie liefern*) to print through, to produce a copy.

Durchschreibepapier *nt* copy paper.

durchschreiten¹ *vi sep irreg aux sein* (*geh*) to stride through.

durchschreiten²* *vt insep irreg* (*geh*) to stride through.

Durchschrift *f* (carbon) copy.

Durchschuß *m* **(a)** (*durchgehender Schuß*) shot passing right through. **bei einem** ~ ... when a shot passes right through ...

(b) (*Loch*) bullet hole; (*Wunde*) gunshot wound *where the*

bullet has passed right through. **ein** ~ **durch den Darm** a gunshot wound right through the intestine.

(c) (*Tex: Schußfaden*) weft.

(d) (*Typ: Zwischenraum*) space. **ohne** ~ unspaced, unleaded; **mit viel/wenig** ~ widely/lightly spaced.

durchschütteln *vt sep Mischung* to shake thoroughly; *jdn* (*zur Strafe*) to give a good shaking; (*in Auto, Bus etc*) to shake about. **er wurde von krampfhaften Gelächter durchgeschüttelt** he shook all over with convulsive laughter.

durchschwärmen* *vt insep* (*geh*) *Gebäude, Gelände* to swarm through. **die Nacht** ~ to make a merry night of it.

durchschweben¹ *vi sep aux sein* (*Vogel*) to glide through; (*Wolken auch, Ballon*) to float through.

durchschweben²* *vt insep* (*poet*) (*Vogel*) to glide through; (*Wolken auch*) to float through.

durchschweifen* *vt insep* (*liter*) to roam or wander through.

durchschweißen *vt sep* to through-weld.

durchschwimmen¹ *vi sep irreg aux sein* **(a)** (*durch etw* sth) to swim through; (*Dinge*) to float through. **unter/zwischen etw** (*dat*) ~ to swim/float under/between sth. **(b)** (*ohne Pause schwimmen*) to swim without stopping.

durchschwimmen²* *vt insep irreg* to swim through; *Strecke* to swim.

durchschwindeln *vr sep* to trick or cheat one's way through.

durchschwitzen *sep or* **durchschwitzen*** *insep vt* to soak with or in sweat; *siehe* **durchgeschwitzt**.

durchsegeln¹ *vi sep aux sein* **(a)** (*Schiff*) to sail through (*durch etw* sth). **unter/zwischen etw** (*dat*) ~ to sail under/between sth. **(b)** (*inf: nicht bestehen*) to fail, to flunk (*inf*) (*durch etw, bei etw* sth). **(c)** (*inf: durchlaufen*) to sail or sweep through (*durch etw* sth).

durchsegeln²* *vt insep Meer, See* to sail across. **die Meere** ~ to sail (across) the seas.

durchsehen *sep irreg* **1** *vi* **(a)** (*hindurchschauen*) to look through (*durch etw* sth). **ein Stoff, durch den man** ~ **kann** material one can see through.

(b) (*inf: verstehen, überblicken*) to see what's going on, to see what's what (*inf*). **ich sehe hier nicht durch** I can't make head nor tail of this (*inf*).

2 *vt* **(a)** (*nachsehen, überprüfen*) *etw* ~ to look or check sth through or over, to have a look through sth, to go or look or check through or over sth (*auf* +*acc* for); *etw* **flüchtig** ~ to glance or skim through sth.

(b) (*durch etw hindurch*) to see through (*durch etw* sth).

durchseihen *vt sep* (*Cook*) to strain.

durchsein *vi sep irreg aux sein* (*Zusammenschreibung nur bei infin und ptp*) (*inf*) **(a)** (*hindurchgekommen sein*) to be through (*durch etw* sth); (*vorbeigekommen sein*) to have gone.

(b) (*fertig sein*) to have finished, to be through (*esp US*). **durch etw** ~ to have got through sth, to have finished sth.

(c) (*durchgetrennt sein*) to be through, to be in half; (*durchgescheuert sein*) to have worn or gone through.

(d) (*Gesetz, Antrag*) to have gone or got through.

(e) (*eine Krankheit überstanden haben*) to have pulled through; (*eine Prüfung bestanden haben*) to be through, to have got through. **durch die Krise** ~ to be over the crisis.

(f) (*Cook*) (*Steak, Gemüse, Kuchen*) to be done; (*Käse*) to be ripe.

durchsetzen¹ *sep* **1** *vt Maßnahmen, Reformen* to put or carry through; *Anspruch, Forderung* to push through; *Vorschlag, Plan, Vorhaben* to carry through; *Ziel* to achieve, to accomplish. **etw bei jdm** ~ to get sb to agree to sth; **etw bei dem Aufsichtsrat** ~ to get sth through the board; **seinen Willen (bei jdm)** ~ to impose one's will (on sb), to get one's (own) way (with sb); **ich habe durchgesetzt, daß der Laden offenbleibt** I have succeeded in getting the shop to stay open; *siehe* **Kopf**.

2 *vr* **(a)** (*Mensch*) to assert oneself (*bei jdm* with sb); (*Partei etc*) to be successful, to win through. **sich gegen etw** ~ to win through against sth; **sich gegen jdn** ~ to assert oneself against sb, to have one's way despite sb; **sich mit etw** ~ to be successful with sth; **sich im Leben** ~ to make one's way in life, to be a success in life.

(b) (*Idee, Meinung, Neuheit*) to be (generally) accepted, to gain acceptance, to catch on.

durchsetzen²* *vt insep etw mit etw* ~ to intersperse sth with sth; **ein Land mit Spionen** ~ to infiltrate spies into a country; **von etw durchsetzt sein** to be interspersed with sth; **die Armee war von subversiven Elementen durchsetzt** the army was infiltrated by subversive elements.

Durchsetzung¹ *f siehe* **durchsetzen¹** 1 putting or carrying through; pushing through; carrying through; achievement, accomplishment.

Durchsetzung² *f* **die** ~ **des Laubwaldes mit Nadelbäumen** the fact that the deciduous forest is interspersed with conifers; ~ **mit Saboteuren** infiltration by saboteurs.

Durchsicht *f* examination, inspection, check; (*von Examensarbeiten*) checking through. **jdm etw zur** ~ **geben/vorlegen** to give sb sth to look through or over, to give sb sth to check (through) or to examine; **bei** ~ **der Bücher** on checking the books.

durchsichtig *adj Material* transparent; *Bluse etc auch* see-through; *Wasser, Luft* clear; (*fig*) transparent, obvious; *Stil* clear, lucid, transparent.

Durchsichtigkeit *f, no pl siehe adj* transparency; clarity; transparency, obviousness; clarity, lucidity, transparency.

durchsickern *vi sep aux sein* (*lit, fig*) to trickle through, to seep through; (*fig: trotz Geheimhaltung*) to leak out or through. **Informationen** ~ **lassen** to leak information.

durchsieben¹ *vt sep* to sieve, to sift; (*fig*) *Bewerber, Prüflinge* to sift through.

durchsieben[2*] *vt insep (inf)* etw (mit etw) ~ to riddle sth with sth.

durchsitzen *sep irreg* **1** *vt Sessel* to wear out (the seat of). **ich habe mir die Hose durchgesessen** I've worn out *or* through the seat of my trousers. **2** *vr (Sessel, Polster)* to wear out. **der neue Sessel hat sich schon durchgesessen** the seat of the new armchair is *or* has already worn out.

durchsoffen *adj attr (sl)* drunken. **eine ~e Nacht** a night of drinking, a drunken night.

durchsonnt *adj (poet)* sunny, sun-drenched, sun-soaked.

durchspielen *sep* **1** *vt Szene, Spiel, Stück* to play through; *Rolle* to act through; *(fig)* to go through. **2** *vi (zu Ende spielen)* to play through. **3** *vr (Sport)* to get through.

durchsprechen *sep irreg* **1** *vi* **(a)** to speak *or* talk through *(durch etw* sth). **(b)** *(durchgehend sprechen)* to speak without a break, to speak solidly. **2** *vt* **(a)** *Problem, Möglichkeiten, Taktik* to talk over *or* through, to go over *or* through. **(b)** *(Theat) Rolle* to read through.

durchsprengen *sep* **1** *vt Mauer etc* to blast through; *Tunnel, Schneise* to blast. **2** *vi aux sein (liter)* to gallop through. **unter/zwischen etw** *(dat)* ~ to gallop under/between sth.

durchspringen[1] *vi sep irreg aux sein* to jump *or* leap *or* spring through *(durch etw* sth).

durchspringen[2*] *vt insep irreg* to jump *or* leap *or* spring through.

durchspülen *vt sep* to rinse *or* flush *or* wash (out) thoroughly; *Mund, Wäsche* to rinse (out) thoroughly.

durchstarten *sep* **1** *vi (Aviat)* to pull up (out of a landing), to overshoot; *(Aut)* to accelerate off again; *(beim, vorm Anfahren)* to rev up. **2** *vt Flugzeug* to pull up; *Motor, Auto* to rev (up).

durchstechen[1] *sep irreg* **1** *vt Nadel, Spieß* to stick through *(durch etw* sth); *Ohren* to pierce; *Deich, Damm, Grassode* to cut through; *Kanal, Tunnel* to build *or* put through *(durch etw* sth).
2 *vi* to pierce; *(mit einer dünnen Nadel)* to prick. **die Nadel sticht durch** the needle is sticking through.

durchstechen[2*] *vt insep irreg* to pierce; *(mit Degen, Spieß etc)* to run through; *(mit Nadel)* to prick.

durchstecken *vt sep (durch etw* sth) to put *or* stick *(inf)* through; *Nadel etc* to stick through.

durchstehen *sep or* **durchstehen*** *insep vt irreg* Zeit, *Prüfung* to get through; *Krankheit* to pull *or* come through, to get over; *Tempo, Test, Qualen* to (with)stand; *Abenteuer* to have; *Schwierigkeiten, Situation* to get through.

Durchstehvermögen *nt* endurance, staying power.

durchsteigen[1] *vi sep irreg aux sein* to climb through *(durch etw* sth); *(fig sl)* to get *(inf)*, to see. **da steigt doch kein Mensch durch** *(fig sl)* you couldn't expect anyone to get that *(inf)*.

durchsteigen[2*] *vt insep irreg* to climb through.

durchstellen *vt sep* to put through; *(durchreichen auch)* to pass through. **einen Moment, ich stelle durch** one moment, I'll put you through.

Durchstich *m (Vorgang)* cut(ting); *(Öffnung)* cut.

Durchstieg *m* passage.

durchstöbern* *insep or* **durchstöbern** *sep vt* to hunt through *(nach* for), to rummage through *(nach* for); *Stadt, Gegend* to scour *(nach* for); *(durchwühlen)* to ransack *(nach* looking for, in search of).

Durchstoß *m* breakthrough.

durchstoßen[1*] *vt insep irreg* to break through; *(Mil auch)* to penetrate.

durchstoßen[2] *sep irreg* **1** *vi aux sein (zu einem Ziel gelangen)* to break through *(esp Mil)*. **wir sind im Urlaub bis nach Marseilles durchgestoßen** on holiday we pressed on as far as Marseilles.
2 *vt (durchbrechen)* to break through; *(abnutzen) Schuhe, Ärmel* to wear through. **etw (durch etw)** ~ to push sth through (sth); *Tunnel* to drive sth through sth.
3 *vr (Kragen, Manschetten, Schuhe)* to wear through.

durchstreichen[1] *vt sep irreg* to cross out *or* through, to strike out, to delete.

durchstreichen[2*] *vt insep irreg (liter)* to roam *or* wander *or* rove through.

durchstreifen* *vt insep (geh)* to roam *or* wander *or* rove through.

durchströmen[1] *vi sep aux sein* to flow *or* run through; *(fig: Menschenmenge)* to stream *or* pour through.

durchströmen[2*] *vt insep (lit, fig)* to flow *or* run through.

durchstrukturieren* *vt sep Aufsatz* to give a polished structure to; *Gesetzesvorlage* to work out in detail. **ein gut durchstrukturierter Aufsatz** a well-structured essay.

durchsuchen[1*] *vt insep (nach* for) to search (through); *jdn* to search, to frisk; *Stadt, Gegend auch* to scour.

durchsuchen[2] *vt sep* to search (through).

Durchsuchung *f* search *(auf* +dat for).

Durchsuchungsbefehl *m* search warrant. **richterlicher ~** official search warrant.

durchtanzen[1] *sep* **1** *vi* to dance through. **die Nacht ~** to dance through the night, to dance all night, to dance the night away. **2** *vt Schuhe* to wear out (by *or* with) dancing.

durchtanzen[2*] *vt insep* to dance through. **eine durchtanzte Nacht** a night of dancing.

durchtasten *vr sep* to feel *or* grope one's way through *(durch etw* sth).

durchtesten *vt sep* to test out.

durchtragen *vt sep irreg* to carry *or* take through *(durch etw* sth).

durchtrainieren* *sep* **1** *vt Sportler, Mannschaft, Körper, Muskeln* to get fit. **(gut) durchtrainiert** *Sportler* completely or

thoroughly fit; *Muskeln, Körper* in superb condition. **2** *vi (ohne Pause trainieren)* to train without a break, to train non-stop.

durchtränken* *vt insep* to soak *or* saturate (completely). **mit/von etw durchtränkt sein** *(fig geh)* to be imbued with sth.

durchtreiben *vt sep irreg* etw (durch etw) ~ to drive sth through (sth).

durchtrennen *sep or* **durchtrennen*** *insep vt Stoff, Papier* to tear (through), to tear in two; *(schneiden)* to cut (through), to cut in two; *Nerv, Sehne* to sever; *Nabelschnur* to cut (through).

durchtreten *sep irreg* **1** *vt* **(a)** *Pedal* to step on; *(am Fahrrad)* to press down; *Starter* to kick.
(b) *(abnutzen) Teppich, Schuh, Sohle* to go *or* wear through.
(c) *(durchkicken)* to kick through *(durch etw* sth).
2 *vi* **(a)** *(Aut: Pedal ~)* to step on the accelerator/brake/clutch; *(Radfahrer)* to pedal (hard).
(b) *(Ftbl)* to kick out.
(c) *aux sein (durchsickern, durchdringen)* to come through *(durch etw* sth).
(d) *aux sein (form: weitergehen)* to go *or* walk through.
3 *vr* to wear through.

durchtrieben *adj* cunning, crafty, sly.

Durchtriebenheit *f, no pl* cunning, craftiness, slyness.

Durchtritt *m (das Durchtreten)* passage; *(~sstelle)* place where the gas/water *etc* comes through.

durchtropfen *vi sep aux sein* to drip through *(durch etw* sth).

durchwachen[1] *vi sep* to stay awake. **die Nacht ~** to stay awake all night.

durchwachen[2*] *vt insep* **die Nacht ~** to watch through the night.

durchwachsen[1] *vi sep irreg aux sein* to grow through *(durch etw* sth).

durchwachsen[2] *adj* **(a)** *(lit) Speck* streaky; *Fleisch, Schinken* with fat running through (it). **der Rasen/die Hecke ist mit etw ~** the lawn/hedge is interspersed with sth *or* has sth growing in it.
(b) *pred (hum inf: mittelmäßig)* so-so *(inf)*, like the curate's egg *(hum)*, fair to middling. **ihm geht es ~** he's having his ups and downs.

durchwagen *vr sep* to venture through *(durch etw* sth).

Durchwahl *f (Telec)* direct dialling.

durchwählen *vi sep* to dial direct. **nach London ~** to dial London direct, to dial through to London (direct).

Durchwahlnummer *f* dialling code.

durchwalken *vt sep (inf)* **(a)** *(verprügeln) jdn* ~ to give sb a belting *(inf)* or hammering *(inf)*, to belt sb *(inf)*. **(b)** *(dated: durchkneten)* to knead thoroughly.

durchwalten* *vt insep (liter)* to rule (over), to reign over.

durchwandern[1] *vi sep aux sein (durch Gegend)* to hike through *(durch etw* sth); *(ohne Unterbrechung wandern)* to carry on *or* continue hiking. **den ganzen Tag ~** to hike all day (long).

durchwandern[2*] *vt insep Gegend* to walk through; *(hum) Zimmer, Straßen etc* to wander through. **die halbe Welt ~** to wander half way round the world; **ziellos die Welt ~** to wander aimlessly round the world.

durchwaschen *vt sep irreg* to wash through.

durchwaten[1] *vi sep aux sein* to wade through *(durch etw* sth).

durchwaten[2*] *vt insep* to wade through.

durchweben* *vt insep irreg (mit, von* with) to interweave; *(fig liter auch)* to intersperse.

durchweg, durchwegs *(esp Aus) adv (bei adj) (ausnahmslos)* without exception; *(in jeder Hinsicht)* in every way *or* respect; *(bei n)* without exception; *(bei vb) (völlig)* totally; *(ausnahmslos)* without exception. **~ gut** good without exception/in every way *or* respect.

durchwehen[1*] *vt insep (geh)* to waft through.

durchwehen[2] *vti sep* to blow through. **(etw) durch etw ~** to blow (sth) through sth; **hier weht's durch diese Ritzen durch** there's a draught (blowing) through these cracks.

durchweichen[1] *sep* **1** *vi aux sein (sehr naß werden)* to get wet through, to get soaked *or* drenched; *(weich werden: Karton, Boden)* to go soggy. **2** *vt Kleidung, jdn* to soak, to drench; *Boden, Karton* to make soggy.

durchweichen[2*] *vt insep (geh) Boden, Karton* to soften.

durchwerfen *sep irreg (durch etw* sth) **1** *vt* to throw through. **2** *vr* to throw oneself through.

durchwetzen *vt sep* to wear through.

durchwinden *vr sep irreg (Fluß)* to wind its way, to meander *(durch etw* through sth); *(Mensch)* to thread *or* worm one's way through *(durch etw* sth); *(fig)* to worm one's way through *(durch etw* sth). **sich zwischen etw** *(dat)* ~ to wind its way/to thread *or* worm one's way between sth.

durchwirken* *vt insep (geh) Gewebe* to interweave.

durchwitschen *vi sep aux sein (inf)* to slip through *(durch etw* sth).

durchwogen* *vt insep (fig geh)* to surge through.

durchwollen *vi sep (inf)* to want to go/come through *(durch etw* sth). **zwischen/unter etw** *(dat)* ~ to want to pass between/under sth; **der Bohrer/Faden will nicht (durch den Beton/das Öhr) durch** the drill/thread doesn't want to go through (the concrete/eye).

durchwühlen[1] *sep* **1** *vt* to rummage through, to rummage about in *(nach* for); *Zimmer, Haus auch* to ransack *(nach* looking for, in search of). **2** *vr (durch etw* sth) to burrow through; *(fig)* to work one's way through, to plough through.

durchwühlen[2*] *vt insep* to rummage through, to rummage about in *(nach* for); *Zimmer auch* to ransack *(nach* looking for, in search of); *Boden* to dig up.

durchwurschteln, durchwursteln *vr sep (inf)* to muddle through.

durchzählen sep 1 vt to count through or up. 2 vi to count or number off.

durchzechen[1] vi sep to carry on drinking.

durchzechen[2]* vt insep **die Nacht** ~ to drink through the night, to carry on drinking all night; **eine durchzechte Nacht** a night of drinking.

durchzeichnen vt sep siehe **durchpausen**.

durchziehen[1] sep irreg 1 vt **(a)** (durch etw hindurchziehen) to pull or draw through (durch etw sth).
  (b) (inf: erledigen, vollenden) to get through.
  (c) (sl: rauchen) Joint to smoke. **einen** ~ to have or smoke a joint (sl).
  (d) (durchbauen) (durch etw sth) Graben to dig through; Mauer to build through.
  2 vi aux sein **(a)** (durchkommen) (durch etw sth) to pass or go/come through; (Truppe auch) to march through; (Schmerz) to go through; (Kälte) to come through.
  (b) to soak. **etw in etw** (dat) ~ **lassen** to steep or soak sth in sth; (in Marinade) to marinate sth in sth.
  3 vr to run through (durch etw sth).

durchziehen[2]* vt insep irreg (durchwandern) to pass through, to go/come through; (Straße, Fluß, fig: Thema) to run through; (Geruch) to fill, to pervade; (Graben) to cut through. **sein Haar ist von grauen Fäden durchzogen** his hair is streaked with grey; **die Welt** ~ to travel (round) the world; **ein Feld mit Gräben** ~ to crisscross a field with ditches; **ein mit Goldfäden durchzogener Stoff** material with a gold thread running through it.

durchzittern* vt insep (geh) (lit, fig) to shake. **von Furcht** etc **durchzittert** (fig) shaking or quivering with fear etc.

durchzucken* vt insep (Blitz) to flash across; (fig: Gedanke) to flash through.

Durchzug m **(a)** no pl (Luftzug) draught. ~ **machen** to create a draught; (zur Lüftung) to get the air moving; ~ **bringen** (fig) to bring a breath of fresh air. **(b)** (durch ein Gebiet) passage; (von Truppen) march through. **auf dem/beim** ~ **durch ein Land** while passing through a country.

Durchzugsrecht nt right of passage.

durchzwängen sep (durch etw sth) 1 vt to force or squeeze through. 2 vr to force one's way through, to squeeze (one's way) through.

dürfen pret **durfte**, ptp **gedurft** or (modal aux vb) **dürfen** vi **(a)** (Erlaubnis haben) **etw tun** ~ to be allowed to do sth, to be permitted to do sth; **darf ich/man das tun?** may I/one do it?, am I/is one allowed to do it?; **darf ich?** — **ja, Sie** ~ **may I?** — yes, you may; **darf ich ins Kino?** may I go to the cinema?; **er hat nicht gedurft** he wasn't allowed to.
  (b) (verneint) **man darf etw nicht (tun)** (sollte, muß nicht) one must not or mustn't do sth; (hat keine Erlaubnis) one isn't allowed to do sth, one may not do sth; (kann nicht) one may not do sth; **hier darf man nicht rauchen/durchfahren** (ist verboten) smoking is prohibited here/driving through here is prohibited, it is prohibited to smoke/drive through here; **diesen Zug darf ich nicht verpassen** I must not miss this train; **du darfst ihm das nicht übelnehmen** you must not take offence at him; **man darf nicht vorschnell urteilen** one mustn't make hasty judgements; **die Kinder** ~ **hier nicht spielen** the children aren't allowed to or may not play here; **der Patient darf noch nicht transportiert werden** the patient may not be moved yet; **das darf doch nicht wahr sein!** that can't be true!; **da darf er sich nicht wundern** that shouldn't surprise him.
  (c) (in Höflichkeitsformeln) **darf ich das tun?** may I do that?; **Ruhe, wenn ich bitten darf!** quiet, (if you) please!, will you please be quiet!; **darf ich um den nächsten Tanz bitten?** may I have (the pleasure of) the next dance?; **darf ich Sie bitten, das zu tun?** may or could I ask you to do that?; **was darf es sein?** can I help you, what can I do for you?; (vom Gastgeber gesagt) what can I get you?, what'll you have?; **dürfte ich bitte Ihren Ausweis sehen** (als Aufforderung) may or might I see your identity card, please.
  (d) (Veranlassung haben, können) **wir freuen uns, Ihnen mitteilen zu** ~ we are pleased to be able to tell you; **ich darf wohl sagen, daß ...** I think I can say that ...; **wir** ~ **uns hier wirklich nicht beklagen** we shouldn't or can't really complain; **man darf doch wohl fragen** one can or may ask, surely?; **Sie** ~ **mir das ruhig glauben** you can or may take my word for it; **das darf schon mal vorkommen** that (sort of thing) can happen.
  (e) (im Konjunktiv) **das dürfte ... (als Annahme)** that must ...; (sollte) that should or ought to ...; (könnte) that could ...; **das dürfte Emil sein** that must be Emil; **das dürfte wohl das Beste sein** that is probably the best thing; **das dürfte reichen** that should be enough, that ought to be enough; **das Essen dürfte stärker gewürzt sein** the food could have been more highly spiced.

dürftig adj **(a)** (ärmlich) wretched, miserable; Essen auch meagre; Bekleidung poor.
  (b) (pej: unzureichend) miserable, pathetic (inf); Kenntnisse auch sketchy, scanty; Ausrede auch feeble, lame; Einkommen auch paltry; Ersatz poor attr; (spärlich) Haarwuchs, Pflanzenwuchs sparse; Bekleidung scanty, skimpy. **ein paar** ~**e Tannen** a few scrawny fir trees.

Dürftigkeit f -, no pl siehe adj **(a)** wretchedness, miserableness; meagreness; poorness. **(b)** (pej) miserableness, patheticness; sketchiness, scantiness; feebleness, lameness; paltriness; poorness; sparseness; scantiness, skimpiness.

dürr adj **(a)** (trocken) dry; (ausgetrocknet) Boden arid, barren; Ast, Strauch dried up, withered. **(b)** (pej: mager) skinny, scrawny, scraggy. **(c)** (fig) **mit** ~**en Worten** in plain terms, plainly, bluntly; **die** ~**en Jahre** (Bibl, fig) the lean years.

Dürre f -, -n **(a)** (Zeit der ~) drought. **(b)** siehe **Dürrheit**.

Dürre-: ~**jahr** nt year of drought; ~**katastrophe** f catastrophic or disastrous drought; ~**periode** f (period of) drought; (fig) barren period.

Dürrheit f, no pl (Trockenheit) dryness; (von Boden auch) aridity, barrenness; (pej: Magerkeit) skinniness, scrawniness, scragginess.

Durst m -(e)s, no pl (lit, fig) thirst (nach for). ~ **haben** to be thirsty; ~ **bekommen** to get or become thirsty; **den** ~ **löschen** or **stillen** to quench one's thirst; **das macht** ~ that makes you thirsty, that gives you a thirst; **einen** or **ein Glas über den** ~ **getrunken haben** (inf) to have had one too many or one over the eight (inf).

dursten 1 vi **(a)** (geh) to be thirsty, to thirst (liter). **er mußte** ~ he had to go thirsty. **(b)** (fig) siehe **dürsten 2**. 2 vt impers siehe **dürsten 1**.

dürsten 1 vt impers (liter) **es dürstet mich, mich dürstet** I thirst (liter); **es dürstet ihn nach Rache/Wissen/Wahrheit** he thirsts for revenge/knowledge/(the) truth; siehe **Blut**. 2 vi (fig) **er dürstet nach Rache/Wahrheit** he is thirsty for revenge/truth.

durstig adj thirsty. **jdn** ~ **machen** to make sb thirsty, to give sb a thirst; **diese Arbeit macht** ~ this is thirsty work (inf), this work makes you thirsty; **nach etw** ~ **sein** (fig geh) to be thirsty for sth, to thirst for sth (liter); **sie ist eine** ~**e Seele** (hum inf) she likes the bottle (hum).

Durstgefühl nt feeling of thirst.

-durstig adj suf (fig) thirsty for.

Durst-: **d**~**löschend, d**~**stillend** adj thirst-quenching; ~**strecke** f hard times pl; (Mangel an Inspiration) barren period; ~**streik** m thirst strike.

Dur-: ~**tonart** f major key; ~**tonleiter** f major scale.

Duschbad nt shower(-bath). **ein** ~ **nehmen** to have or take a shower(-bath).

Dusche f -, -n shower. **unter der** ~ **sein** or **stehen** to be in the shower, to be taking a shower; **eine** ~ **nehmen** to have or take a shower; **das war eine kalte** ~ (fig) that really brought him/her etc down with a bump; **bei ihrem Enthusiasmus wirkten seine Worte wie eine kalte** ~ (fig) his words poured cold water on her enthusiasm.

Dusch|ecke f shower (cubicle).

duschen 1 vir to have or take a shower, to shower. **(sich) kalt** ~ to have or take a cold shower. 2 vt **jdn** ~ to give sb a shower; **jdm/sich den Kopf/Rücken** ~ to spray sb's/one's head/back.

Dusch-: ~**gelegenheit** f shower facilities pl; ~**kabine** f shower (cubicle); ~**raum** m shower room, showers pl; ~**vorhang** m shower curtain.

Düse f -, -n nozzle; (Mech auch) jet; (von Flugzeug) jet.

Dusel m -s, no pl (inf) **(a)** (Glück) luck. ~ **haben** to be lucky; **da hat er (einen)** ~ **gehabt** his luck was in (inf), he was lucky; **so ein** ~! that was lucky!, that was a piece of luck! **(b)** (Trancezustand) daze, dream; (durch Alkohol) fuddle. **im** ~ in a daze or dream/in a fuddle.

duselig adj (schlaftrunken) drowsy; (benommen) dizzy, giddy; (esp durch Alkohol) fuddled. **mir ist ganz** ~ **(im Kopfe), ich habe ein** ~**es Gefühl** my head is swimming, I feel quite dizzy or giddy.

duseln vi (inf) to doze.

Düsen-: ~**antrieb** m jet propulsion; **mit** ~**antrieb** jet-propelled, with jet propulsion; ~**bomber** m jet bomber; ~**flugzeug** nt jet aircraft or plane, jet; **d**~**getrieben** adj jet-propelled, jet-powered; ~**jäger** m **(a)** (Mil) jet fighter; **(b)** (inf) siehe ~**flugzeug**; ~**klipper** m jet airliner; ~**maschine** f jet (aircraft or plane); ~**motor** m jet engine; ~**treibstoff** m jet fuel; ~**triebwerk** nt jet power-unit.

duslig adj (inf) siehe **duselig**.

Dussel m -s, - (inf) twit (Brit inf), twerp (inf), dope (inf).

dusselig, dußlig adj (inf) stupid.

Dusseligkeit, Dußligkeit f (inf) stupidity.

duster adj siehe **dunkel**.

düster adj gloomy; Nacht auch murky; Tag, Wetter auch dismal, murky; Musik auch funereal, lugubrious; Farbe, Gesicht auch sombre, dismal; Bild, Gedanken, Zukunftsvisionen sombre, dismal, dark; Miene, Stimmung auch dark, black; (unheimlich) Gestalten, Stadtteil sinister, (dark and) forbidding.

Düster nt -s, no pl (poet) siehe **Düsterkeit**.

Düstere(s) nt decl as adj gloom, dark(ness); (fig: von Gedanken, Stimmung) gloominess.

Düsterheit, Düsterkeit, Düsternis (geh) f gloominess; (Dunkelheit) gloom, dark(ness).

Dutt m -(e)s, -s or -e (dial) bun.

Dutte f -, -n (Aus) teat, nipple.

Duty-free-Shop ['dju:tɪ'fri:ʃɔp] m -s, -s duty-free shop.

Dutzend nt -s, -e dozen. **ein halbes** ~ half-a-dozen, a half-dozen; **zwei/drei** ~ two/three dozen; **ein** ~ **frische** or **frischer** (geh) **Eier kostet** or **kosten ...** a dozen fresh eggs cost(s) ...; **das** ~ **kostet 4 Mark** they cost 4 marks a dozen; ~**e** pl (inf) dozens pl; **sie kamen in** or **zu** ~**en** they came in (their) dozens; **im** ~ **billiger** (inf) (bei größerer Menge) the more you buy, the more you save; (bei mehr Leuten) the more you are, the more you save (inf); siehe **zwölf**.

dutzend(e)mal adv (inf) dozens of times.

Dutzend-: **d**~**fach** 1 adj dozens of; **in d**~**fachen Variationen** in dozens of variations; 2 adv in dozens of ways; ~**gesicht** nt (pej) nondescript or ordinary or run-of-the-mill face; ~**mensch** m (pej) ordinary or run-of-the-mill sort of person; ~**preis** m price per dozen; ~**typ** m siehe ~**mensch**; ~**ware** f (pej) (cheap) mass-produced item; ~**waren** (cheap) mass-produced goods; **d**~**weise** adv in dozens, by the dozen.

Duzbruder m good friend or pal (inf). **alte Duzbrüder** old

friends or pals (inf) or mates (inf).
duzen vt to address with the familiar "du"-form. **wir ~ uns** we use "du" or the "du"-form (to each other).
Duz-: **~freund** m good friend; **alte ~freunde** old friends; **~fuß** m: **mit jdm auf dem ~fuß stehen** (inf) to be on familiar terms with sb.
d. Verf. abbr of **der Verfasser.**
dwars adv (N Ger Naut) abeam.
Dynamik f, no pl (a) (Phys) dynamics sing. (b) (fig) dynamism. **Menschen mit einer solchen ~** people with such dynamism.
dynamisch adj (a) dynamic. **~e Gesetze** laws of dynamics. (b) (fig) dynamic; **Renten ~** index-linked.
dynamisieren* vt (geh) Politik to make dynamic; (vorantreiben) Prozeß, Reform to speed up; **Renten ~** to index-link.
Dynamisierung f (geh) (von Reform etc) speeding up; (von Renten) ~ index-linking. **sie streben eine ~ ihrer Politik an** they are seeking to make their policy more dynamic.
Dynamismus m, no pl (geh) dynamism.
Dynamit nt -s, no pl (lit, fig) dynamite.
Dynamo(maschine f) m -s, -s dynamo; (fig) powerhouse.
Dynast m -en, -en dynast.
Dynastie f dynasty.
dynastisch adj dynastic.
D-Zug ['de:tsu:k] m fast train; (hält nur in großen Städten) non-stop or through train. **ein alter Mann/eine alte Frau ist doch kein ~** (inf) I am going as fast as I can, I can't go any faster.
D-Zug-: **~-Tempo** nt (inf) fantastic speed (inf); **im ~-Tempo** like greased lightning (inf), in double-quick time (inf); **~-Zuschlag** m express travel supplement, supplement payable on fast trains; (inf: Karte) supplementary ticket.

E

E, e [e:] nt -, - E, e.
Eau de Cologne ['o: də ko'lɔnjə] nt - - -, no pl eau de Cologne.
Ebbe f -, -n (a) (ablaufendes Wasser) ebb tide; (Niedrigwasser) low tide. **~ und Flut** the tides, ebb and flow; **bei ~ baden/auslaufen** to swim when the tide is going out/to go out on the (ebb) tide; (bei Niedrigwasser) to swim/go out at low tide; **mit der ~** on or with the ebb tide; **die ~ tritt um 15³⁰ ein** the tide starts to go out or turns at 3.30 p.m.; **es ist ~** the tide is going out; (es ist Niedrigwasser) it's low tide, the tide is out.
(b) (fig) **bei mir** or **in meinem Geldbeutel ist or herrscht ~** I'm a bit hard up (inf) or my finances are at a pretty low ebb at the moment; **in den Beziehungen der beiden Staaten herrscht zur Zeit ~** or **ist eine ~ eingetreten** relations between the two countries are at a low ebb at the moment or have fallen off recently.
ebd. abbr of **ebenda.**
eben 1 adj (glatt) smooth; (gleichmäßig) even; (gleich hoch) level; (flach) flat; (Math) plane. **zu ~er Erde** at ground level; **auf ~er Strecke** on the flat.
2 adv (a) (zeitlich: so~) just; (schnell, kurz) for a minute or second. **das wollte ich ~ sagen** I was just about to say that; **mein Bleistift war doch ~ noch da** my pencil was there (just) a minute ago; **kommst du ~ mal mit?** will you come with me for a minute or second?; **ich gehe ~ zur Bank** I'll just pop to the bank (inf).
(b) (gerade or genau das) exactly, precisely. **(na) ~!** exactly!, quite!, precisely!; **das ist es ja ~!** that's just or precisely it!; **das ~ nicht!** no, not that!; **das ist es ~ nicht!** that's just or exactly what it isn't!; **~ das wollte ich sagen** that's just or exactly what I wanted to say; **nicht ~ billig/viel/angenehm** etc not exactly cheap/a lot/pleasant etc.
(c) (gerade noch) just. **das reicht so ~ or nur ~ aus** it's only just enough; **wir haben den Zug ~ noch erreicht** we just caught the train.
(d) (nun einmal, einfach) just, simply. **das ist ~ so** that's just the way it is or things are; **dann bleibst du ~ zu Hause** then you'll just have to stay at home; siehe **dann.**
Ebenbild nt image. **dein ~** the image of you; **das genaue ~ seines Vaters** the spitting image of his father.
ebenbürtig adj (a) (Hist: gleichrangig) of equal birth.
(b) (gleichwertig) equal; Gegner evenly matched. **jdm an Kraft/Ausdauer ~ sein** to be sb's equal in strength/endurance; **sie war ihm an Kenntnissen ~** her knowledge equalled his or was equal to his; **wir sind einander ~** we are equal(s).
Ebenbürtigkeit f (a) (Hist) equality of birth.
(b) (Gleichwertigkeit) equality. **ich bin von der ~ unserer Kenntnisse/Kräfte überzeugt** I am convinced that my knowledge/strength equals yours; **die ~ dieser beiden Gegner wurde deutlich** it became clear that the two opponents were evenly matched.
eben-: **~da** adv (a) (gerade dort) **~da will auch ich hin** that is exactly where I am bound too; (b) (in Büchern) ibid, ibidem; **~dahin** adv **~dahin zieht es auch mich** that is exactly where or whither (old) I am bound too; **~dann** adv **~dann soll ich zum Arzt** that is exactly when I have to go to the doctor; **~darum** adv that is why, for that reason; **~darum!** (zu Kind) because I say so!; **~das** pron siehe **~der;** **~daselbst** adv (old) siehe **~da;** **~der,** **~die,** **~das** pron he; she; it; **~der hat auch gesagt, daß ...** he was also the one who said that ..., it was he who also said that ...; **~deshalb,** **~deswegen** adv that is exactly why; **~die** pron siehe **~der;** **~diese(r, s) 1** pron (liter) he; she; it; **und ~dieser wurde später ermordet** and this same man was later murdered; **2** adj this very or same; **und ~diesen Mann hat sie geheiratet** and this was the very man she married; **~dort** adv (old) at that very or same place.
Ebene f -, -n (Tief~) plain; (Hoch~) plateau; (Math, Phys) plane; (fig) level. **auf höchster/der gleichen ~** (fig) at the highest/the same level; **seine Beleidigungen liegen auf der gleichen ~ wie ...** his insults are on a par with ...; siehe **eben 1**
eben-: **~erdig** adj at ground level; **~falls** adv as well, likewise; (bei Verneinungen) either; **er hat ~falls nichts davon gewußt** he knew nothing about it either; **danke, ~falls!** thank you, the same to you!
Ebenheit f siehe **eben 1** smoothness; evenness; levelness; flatness; planeness.
Ebenholz nt ebony.
Eben-: **e~jene(r,s)** (liter) **1** pron he; she; it; **e~jener wurde später Präsident** this same man later became president; **2** adj that very or same; **~maß** nt (von Gestalt, Gesichtszügen) elegant proportions pl; (von Zähnen) evenness; (von Versen) even flow; **e~mäßig** adj siehe **~maß** elegantly proportioned; even; evenly flowing; **e~mäßig geformt** elegantly proportioned; **~mäßigkeit** f siehe **~maß.**
ebenso adv (genauso) just as; (auch, ebenfalls) as well. **das kann doch ~ eine Frau machen** a woman can do that just as well; **die Geschäfte sind geschlossen, ~ alle Kinos** the shops are closed, as are all the cinemas; **viele Leute haben sich ~ wie wir beschwert** a lot of people complained just like or just as we did or just like us; **er freute sich ~ wie ich** he was just as pleased as I was; **er hat ein ~ großes Zimmer wie wir** he has just as big a room as we have.
ebenso-: **~gern** adv **ich mag sie ~gern** I like her just as much or equally well; **ich esse ~gern Reis** I like rice just as much, I'd just as soon eat rice; **ich komme ~gern morgen** I'd just as soon come tomorrow; **~gut** adv (just) as well; **ich kann ~gut Französisch wie Italienisch** I can speak French (just) as well as I can speak Italian, my French is (just) as good as my Italian; **~häufig** adv siehe **~oft;** **~lang(e)** adv just as long.
ebensolche(r,s) adj (exactly) the same.
ebenso-: **~oft** adv just as often or frequently; **~sehr** adv just as much; **~viel** adv just as much; **~wenig** adv just as little; **~wenig, wie man dies sagen kann, kann man behaupten, ...** there is just as little ground for saying this as for claiming ...
Eber m -s, - boar.
Eber|esche f rowan, mountain ash.
ebnen vt to level (off), to make level. **jdm/einer Sache den Weg ~** (fig) to smooth the way for sb/sth.
echauffieren* [eʃɔ'fiːrən] vr (dated) to get into a taking (dated), to get het-up.
Echo nt -s, -s echo; (fig) response (auf +acc to). **er war nur das ~ seines Chefs** (fig) he was only an echo of his boss; **ein starkes or lebhaftes ~ finden** (fig) to meet with or attract a lively or positive response (bei from).
echoen ['eçoən] vi (rare) to echo. **hallooo ...!,** **echote es hallooo ...!,** came the echo.
Echolot nt (Naut) echo-sounder, sonar; (Aviat) sonic altimeter.
Echse ['eksə] f -, -n (Zool) lizard.
echt 1 adj, adv (a) real, genuine; Gefühle auch sincere; Haar, Perlen, Gold real; Unterschrift, Geldschein, Gemälde genuine; Haarfarbe natural. **der Geldschein war nicht ~** the note was a forgery or was forged; **der Ring ist ~ golden** the ring is real gold.
(b) (typisch) typical. **ein ~er Bayer** a real or typical Bavarian; **~ englisch** typically English; **~ Shakespeare** typical of Shakespeare, typically Shakespearean; **~ Franz/Frau** typical of or just like Franz/a woman, Franz/a woman all over (inf).
(c) Farbe fast.
(d) (Math) **~er Bruch** proper fraction.
2 adv (inf) really. **meinst du das ~?** do you really or honestly

mean that?; **der spinnt doch ~** he must be cracked (*inf*) or round the bend (*inf*).

Echt-: e~**golden** *adj attr* real gold; ~**haarperücke** *f* real hair wig.

Echtheit *f* genuineness; (*von Unterschrift, Dokument auch*) authenticity; (*von Gefühlen, Glauben auch*) sincerity; (*von Haarfarbe*) naturalness; (*von Farbe*) fastness.

echtsilbern *adj attr* real silver.

Eck *nt* -(e)s, -e (a) (*esp Aus, S Ger*) *siehe* **Ecke.**
(b) (*Sport*) **das kurze/lange ~** the near/far corner of the goal.
(c) über ~ diagonally across *or* opposite; **die Schrauben über ~ anziehen** to tighten the nuts working diagonally across; **im ~ sein** (*Aus*) to be out of form; **da hat's ein ~** (*Aus inf*) you've/she's *etc* got problems there.

Eckart *m* -s **der getreue ~** (*liter*) the faithful Eckart *mythical figure in medieval German literature*; (*fig*) the old faithful.

Eck- *in cpds* corner; ~**ball** *m* (*Sport*) corner; **einen ~ball schießen** *or* **treten/geben** to take/give a corner; ~**bank** *f* corner seat.

Ecke *f* -, -n (a) corner; (*Kante*) edge; (*von Kragen*) point; (*Sport: Eckball*) corner. **Kantstraße ~ Goethestraße** at the corner of Kantstraße and Goethestraße; **ein Laden an der ~** a corner shop; **er wohnt gleich um die ~** he lives just round the corner; **ein Kind in die ~ stellen** to make a child stand in the corner; **etw in allen ~n und Winkeln suchen** to search *or* look high and low for sth; **jdn in die ~ drängen** (*fig*) to push sb into the background; **an allen ~n und Erden sparen** to pinch and scrape (*inf*); **jdn um die ~ bringen** (*inf*) to bump sb off (*inf*), to do away with sb (*inf*); **mit jdm um ein paar** *or* **sieben ~n herum verwandt sein** (*inf*) to be distantly related to sb, to be sb's second cousin twice removed (*hum inf*); **die neutrale ~** (*Boxen*) the neutral corner; *siehe* **fehlen.**
(b) (*Käse~, Kuchen~*) wedge.
(c) (*inf: Gegend*) corner, area; (*von Stadt auch*) quarter; (*Strecke*) way. **eine ganze ~ entfernt** quite a (long) way away, a fair way away; **ich komme noch eine ~ mit** I'll come with you for a (little) way; **aus welcher ~ kommst du?** what part of the world are you from?

Eckensteher *m* (*inf*) loafer (*inf*).

Ecker *f* -, -n (*Bot*) beechnut.

Eck-: ~**fahne** *f* (*Sport*) corner flag; ~**fenster** *nt* corner window; ~**haus** *nt* house at *or* on the corner; (*Reihen~*) end house.

eckig *adj* angular; *Tisch, Brot, Klammer* square; (*spitz*) sharp; (*fig*) *Bewegung, Gang* jerky.

-eckig *adj suf* -cornered.

Eck-: ~**kneipe** *f* (*inf*) pub on the corner (*Brit*); ~**laden** *m* shop on a corner, corner shop; ~**lohn** *m* basic wage; ~**pfeiler** *m* corner pillar; (*fig*) cornerstone; ~**pfosten** *m* corner post; ~**platz** *m* (*in Zug etc*) corner seat; (*in Theater etc*) end seat, seat at the end of a row; ~**schrank** *m* corner cupboard; ~**stein** *m* (a) (*lit, fig*) cornerstone; **(b)** (*Cards*) diamonds *pl*; ~**stoß** *m siehe* ~**ball**; ~**turm** *m* corner tower; ~**wurf** *m* (*beim Handball*) corner (throw); ~**zahn** *m* canine tooth.

Eclair [e'klɛːr] *nt* -s, -s (*Cook*) eclair.

Ecuador [ekua'doːr] *nt* -s Ecuador.

ecuadorianisch *adj* Ecuadorian.

Ed. *abbr of* **Edition.**

ed. *abbr of* **edidit = herausgegeben.**

Edamer (Käse) *m* -s, - Edam (cheese).

Edda *f* -, **Edden** (*Liter*) Edda.

edel *adj* (a) (*attr: vornehm, adlig*) noble. **(b)** (*hochwertig*) precious; *Hölzer auch, Rosen* fine; *Wein* noble, fine; *Pferd* thoroughbred. **(c)** (~ *geformt, harmonisch*) noble; *Nase* regal, aristocratic. **(d)** (*fig*) *Gesinnung, Mensch, Tat* noble; (*großherzig auch*) generous. **er denkt ~** he has noble thoughts; *siehe* **Spender(in).**

Edel-: ~**fäule** *f* (*bei Weintrauben*) noble rot; (*bei Käse*) (veins *pl* of) mould; ~**frau** *f* (*Hist*) noblewoman; ~**fräulein** *nt* (*Hist*) unmarried noblewoman; ~**gas** *nt* rare gas; ~**holz** *nt* precious wood.

Edeling *m* (*Hist*) (Germanic) nobleman.

Edel-: ~**kastanie** *f* sweet *or* Spanish chestnut; ~**kitsch** *m* (*iro*) pretentious rubbish *or* kitsch; ~**knappe** *m* (*Hist*) squire; ~**mann** *m, pl* -**leute** (*Hist*) noble(man); ~**metall** *nt* precious metal; ~**mut** *m* (*liter*) magnanimity; **e~mütig** *adj* (*liter*) magnanimous; ~**nutte** *f* (*iro*) high-class tart; ~**pilzkäse** *m* (vein) cheese, mould-ripened cheese (*spec*); ~**reife** *f* (*von Trauben*) noble rot; ~**reis** *nt* scion; ~**rost** *m* patina; ~**schulze** *f* (*iro*) sentimental ballad; ~**stahl** *m* high-grade steel; ~**stein** *m* precious stone; (*geschliffener auch*) jewel, gem; ~**tanne** *f* noble fir; ~**weiß** *nt* -(es), -e edelweiss.

Eden *nt* -s, *no pl* Eden. **der Garten ~** (*Bibl*) the Garden of Eden.

edieren* *vt* to edit.

Edikt *nt* -(e)s, -e (*Hist*) edict.

Edisonfassung *f* Edison screw fitting.

Edition *f* (*das Herausgeben*) editing; (*die Ausgabe*) edition.

Editor(in *f*) [-'toːrɪn] *m* editor.

editorisch *adj* editorial.

Edle(r) *mf decl as adj* (a) *siehe* **Edelfrau, Edelmann.** **(b)** (*in Namen*) Ulf **~ von Trautenau** Lord Ulf von Trautenau; **Johanna ~ von Fürstenberg** Lady Johanna von Fürstenberg.

Eduard *m* -s Edward.

EDV [eːdeːˈfau] *f* - *abbr of* **elektronische Datenverarbeitung.** ~-**Fachmann/-Lehrgang** specialist/training in data processing.

Efeu *m* -s, *no pl* ivy. **mit ~ bewachsen** covered in ivy, ivy-clad (*liter*), ivy-covered.

Eff|eff *nt* -, *no pl* (*inf*) **etw aus dem ~ können** to be able to do sth standing on one's head (*inf*), *or* just like that (*inf*); **etw aus dem ~ beherrschen/kennen** to know sth inside out.

Effekt *m* -(e)s, -e effect. **der ~ war gleich Null** it had absolutely nil effect *or* no effect whatsoever; **auf jdn/etw ~ ausüben** to make an impression on sb/sth.

Effektbeleuchtung *f* special lighting; (*Theat*) special effect lighting.

Effekten *pl* (*Fin*) stocks and bonds *pl*.

Effekten-: ~**börse** *f* stock exchange; ~**handel** *m* stock dealing; **im ~handel läßt sich viel Geld verdienen** there's a lot of money to be made in dealing on the stock exchange; ~**makler** *m* stockbroker; ~**markt** *m* stock market.

Effekthascherei *f* (*inf*) cheap showmanship.

effektiv *adj* effective. ~**e Verzinsung** *or* **Rendite** net yield; ~**nicht/kein** absolutely not/no.

Effektivgeschäft *nt* (*Comm*) spot transaction.

Effektivität *f* effectiveness.

Effektiv-: ~**lohn** *m* actual wage; ~**stand** *m* (*Mil*) actual strength.

effektvoll *adj* effective.

effeminiert *adj* (*geh*) effeminate.

Effet [ɛ'feː] *m or nt* -s, -s (*Billard*) side. **den Ball mit ~ schießen** to put side on a ball.

effizient *adj* efficient.

Effizienz *f* efficiency.

egal 1 *adj, adv* (a) *pred* (*gleichgültig*) **das ist ~** that doesn't matter, that doesn't make any difference; **das ist mir ganz ~** it's all the same to me; (*beides ist mir gleich*) I don't mind (either way), it doesn't make any difference to me; (*es kümmert mich nicht*) I don't care, I couldn't care less; **ob du willst oder nicht, das ist mir ganz ~** I don't care whether you want to or not; **~ ob/wo/wie** it doesn't matter whether/where/how, no matter whether/where/how; **ihm ist alles ~** he doesn't care about anything.
(b) (*inf*) (*gleichartig*) the same, identical; (*gleich groß*) the same size; (*gleichmäßig*) *Rocksaum* even. **~ gearbeitet sein** to be the same, to match; **die Bretter ~ schneiden** to cut the planks (to) the same size.
(c) (*inf: glatt*) *Holzfläche* smooth.
2 *adv* (*dial inf: ständig*) non-stop.

egalisieren* *vt* (*Sport*) *Rekord* to equal. **er egalisierte den Vorsprung des Gegners** he levelled with his opponent, he closed his opponent's lead.

egalitär *adj* (*geh*) egalitarian.

Egalität *f* (*liter*) equality.

egalweg *adv* (*dial inf*) *siehe* **egal 2.**

Egel *m* -s, - (*Zool*) leech.

Egge *f* -, -n (a) (*Agr*) harrow. **(b)** (*Tex*) selvedge.

eggen *vt* (*Agr*) to harrow.

Ego *nt* -s, -s (*Psych*) ego.

Egoismus *m* ego(t)ism.

Egoist(in *f*) *m* ego(t)ist.

egoistisch *adj* ego(t)istical.

Ego-: ~**schwäche** *f* (*Psych*) underdeveloped ego; ~**zentrik** *f, no pl* egocentricity; ~**zentriker(in** *f*) *m* -s, - egocentric; **e~zentrisch** *adj* egocentric.

e.h. *abbr of* **ehrenhalber.**

eh 1 *interj* hey.
2 *conj siehe* **ehe.**
3 *adv* (a) (*früher, damals*) **seit ~ und je** for ages, since the year dot (*inf*); **wie ~ und je** just as *or* like before; **es war alles wie ~ und je** everything was just as it always had been.
(b) (*esp S Ger, Aus: sowieso*) anyway. **ich komme ~ nicht dazu** I won't get round to it anyway.

ehe *conj* (*bevor*) before, ere (*old, liter*). **~ ich es vergesse ...** before I forget ...; **wir können nichts tun, ~ wir (nicht) Nachricht haben** we can't do anything until *or* before we get some news; **~ (daß) ich mich auf andere verlasse, mache ich lieber alles selbst** rather than rely on others, I would prefer to do everything myself.

Ehe *f* -, -n marriage. **er versprach ihr die ~** he promised to marry her; **in den Stand der ~ treten** (*form*), **die ~ eingehen** (*form*) to enter into matrimony (*form*) *or* the estate of matrimony (*form*); **mit jdm die ~ eingehen** *or* **schließen** (*form*) to marry sb, to enter into marriage with sb (*form*); **die ~ vollziehen** to consummate a/their/the marriage; **eine glückliche/unglückliche ~ führen** to have a happy/an unhappy marriage; **die ~ brechen** (*form*) to commit adultery; **~ zur linken Hand, morganatische ~** (*Hist*) morganatic *or* left-handed marriage; **sie hat drei Kinder aus erster ~** she has three children from her first marriage; **Kinder in die ~ mitbringen** to bring children into the marriage; **ein außerhalb der ~ geborenes Kind** a child born out of wedlock; **er ist in zweiter ~ mit einer Adligen verheiratet** his second wife is an aristocrat; **ihre ~ ist 1975 geschieden worden** they were divorced in 1975; **sie leben in wilder ~** (*dated*) they are living in sin; **~n werden im Himmel geschlossen** (*prov*) marriages are made in heaven; *siehe* **Hafen¹, Bund¹.**

Ehe-: **e~ähnlich** *adj* (*form*) similar to marriage; **in einer e~ähnlichen Gemeinschaft leben** to cohabit (*form*), to live together as man and wife; ~**anbahnung** *f* marriage-broking; (*Institut*) marriage bureau; ~**anbahnungsinstitut** *nt* marriage bureau; ~**berater(in** *f*) *m* marriage guidance counsellor; ~**beratung** *f* (*das Beraten*) marriage guidance (counselling); (*Stelle*) marriage guidance council; ~**bett** *nt* double bed; (*fig*) marital bed; **e~brechen** *vi* (*infin only*) to commit adultery; ~**brecher** *m* -s, - adulterer; ~**brecherin** *f* adulteress; **e~brecherisch** *adj* adulterous; ~**bruch** *m* adultery; ~**bund** *m*, ~**bündnis** *nt* (*form*) bond of matrimony.

ehedem *adv* (*old*) formerly. **seit ~** since time immemorial.

Ehe-: ~**fähigkeit** *f* (*Jur*) marriageability; ~**frau** *f* wife; ~**frauen**

haben es nicht leicht married women have a hard time; ~gatte m (form) husband, spouse (form); ~gattin f (form) wife, spouse (form); ~gemeinschaft f (form) wedlock (form), matrimony; ~gespons m or nt (hum) spouse (hum); ~glück nt married bliss or happiness; ~hafen m (hum): in den ~hafen einlaufen to plight one's troth (old, hum); ~hälfte f (hum) my better half ~hälfte my better half (inf); ~hindernis nt (Jur) impediment to marriage; ~joch nt (hum inf) yoke of marriage; unters ~joch kommen to get hitched (inf) or spliced (inf); die spannt dich noch ins ~joch ein! she'll drag you to the altar yet; ~komödie f marital comedy; ~krach m marital row; ~kreuz nt (hum inf) problems pl or troubles pl of married life; ~krise f marital crisis; ~krüppel m (hum inf) henpecked husband (inf); ~leben nt married life; ~leute pl (form) married couple; ich vermiete diese Wohnung an die ~leute A. und P. Meier I hereby let this flat to Mr and Mrs Meier; die jungen ~leute the young couple.

ehelich adj marital; Pflichten, Rechte auch conjugal; Kind legitimate. für ~ erklären to (declare or make) legitimate; das ~e Leben married life; die ~en Freuden the joys of marriage.
ehelichen vt (old, hum) to wed (old), to espouse (old, form).
Ehelichkeit f, no pl (von Kind) legitimacy.
Ehelichkeits|erklärung f (Jur) declaration of legitimacy.
ehelos adj unmarried, single.
Ehelosigkeit f, no pl unmarried state; (Rel) celibacy. ~ hat auch ihre Vorteile being single or unmarried also has its advantages.
ehem., ehm. abbr of ehemals.
ehemalig adj attr former. die E~en seiner/einer Schulklasse his former classmates/the ex-pupils or former pupils of a class; ein ~er Häftling an ex-convict; ein E~r (inf) an old lag (Brit sl), an ex-con (inf); mein E~er/meine E~e (hum inf) my ex (inf).
ehemals adv (form) formerly, previously. die ~ deutschen Ostgebiete the eastern territories which were formerly German.
Ehe-: ~mann m, pl -männer married man; (Partner) husband; seitdem er ~mann ist since he has been married; e~mündig adj (Jur) of marriageable age; ~mündigkeit f, no pl (Jur) marriageable age; die ~mündigkeit tritt im Alter von 18 Jahren ein a person becomes legally marriageable at the age of 18; ~paar nt (married) couple; ~partner m husband; wife; beide ~partner both partners (in the marriage).
eher adv (a) (früher) earlier, sooner. je ~, je or desto lieber the sooner the better; nicht ~ als bis/als not until/before.
(b) (lieber) rather, sooner; (wahrscheinlicher) more likely; (leichter) more easily. alles ~ als das! anything but that!; ~ verzichte ich or will ich verzichten, als daß ... I would rather or sooner do without than ...; um so ~, als the more so or all the more because or as; das läßt sich schon ~ hören that sounds more like it (inf) or better; das könnte man schon ~ sagen, das ist ~ möglich that is more likely or probable; diese Prüfung kannst du ~ bestehen this exam will be easier for you to pass.
(c) (vielmehr) more. er ist ~ faul als dumm he's more lazy than stupid, he's lazy rather than stupid; er ist alles ~ als das/ein Engel/dumm he's anything but that/an angel/stupid.
Ehe-: ~recht nt marriage law; ~ring m wedding ring.
ehern adj (liter) (lit) made of ore; (fig) iron. mit ~er Stirn boldly; (tollkühn auch) brazenly.
Ehe-: ~roman m novel about marriage; ~sache f (Jur) matrimonial matter; ~sakrament nt marriage sacrament, sacrament of marriage; ~scheidung f divorce; ~scheidungsklage f (Prozeß) divorce case; die ~scheidungsklage einreichen to file a divorce petition or a petition for divorce; e~scheu adj shy of marriage; er ist ein e~scheuer Junggeselle he is a confirmed bachelor; ~schließung f marriage ceremony, wedding.
ehest adv (Aus) as soon as possible.
Ehe-: ~stand m, no pl matrimony, marriage; ~standsdarlehen nt low interest bank loan given to newly married couples.
ehestens adv (a) (frühestens) ~ morgen tomorrow at the earliest; ich kann ~ heute abend kommen the earliest I can come is this evening.
(b) (Aus: baldigst) as soon as possible, at the earliest opportunity.
eheste(r, s) 1 adj bei ~r Gelegenheit at the earliest opportunity.
2 adv am ~n (am liebsten) best of all; (am wahrscheinlichsten) most likely; (am leichtesten) the easiest; (zuerst) first; am ~n würde ich mir ein Auto kaufen what I'd like best (of all) would be to buy myself a car; keins der Kleider gefällt mir so richtig, am ~n würde ich noch das rote nehmen I don't really like any of the dresses, but if I had to choose I'd take the red one; das geht wohl am ~n that's probably the best way; er ist am ~n gekommen he was the first (person) to come; die am ~n erschienenen Bände the first volumes to appear.
Ehe-: ~stifter m matchmaker; ~streit m marital row or argument; ~tragödie f marital tragedy; ~vermittlung f marriage-broking; (Büro) marriage bureau; ~versprechen nt (Jur) promise to marry; Bruch des ~versprechens breach of promise; ~vertrag m marriage contract; ~weib nt (old: ~frau) wife; (hum inf) old woman (inf); er nahm sie zum ~weib (obs) he took her to wife (old) or as his lawful wedded wife (form); e~widrig adj (form) Beziehungen extramarital, adulterous; Verhalten constituting a matrimonial offence.
Ehr|abschneider(in f) m -s, - calumniator (form).
ehrbar adj (achtenswert) respectable; (ehrenhaft) honourable; Beruf auch reputable.
Ehrbarkeit f, no pl siehe adj respectability; honourableness; reputability.
Ehr-: ~begriff m sense of honour; ~beleidigung f insult to one's honour.

Ehre f -, -n honour; (Ruhm) glory. etw in ~n halten to treasure or cherish sth; damit/mit ihm können Sie ~ einlegen that/he does you credit or is a credit to you; er wollte mit dieser Rede ~ einlegen he was wanting to gain kudos with this speech; für jdn/etw ~ einlegen to bring honour on sb/sth; bei jdm mit etw ~ einlegen to make a good impression on sb with sth; jdm ~/wenig ~ machen to do sb credit/not do sb any credit; auf ~!, bei meiner ~! (obs) by my troth! (obs), 'pon my oath! (obs); auf ~ und Gewissen on my/his etc honour; auf ~ und Gewissen? cross your heart? (inf), on your honour?; auf ~ und Gewissen: ich bin es nicht gewesen! cross my heart (inf) or I promise you, it wasn't me; zu seiner ~ muß ich sagen, daß ... in his favour I must say (that) ...; etw um der ~ willen tun to do sth for the honour of it; das mußt du schon um deiner ~ willen machen you should do that as a matter of honour; ein Mann von ~ a man of honour; keine ~ im Leib haben (dated) to have not a shred of self-respect; er ist in ~n ergraut (geh) or in ~n alt geworden he has had a long and honourable life; ein in ~n ergrauter Student (iro) a permanent student; sein Wort/seine Kenntnisse in allen ~n, aber ... I don't doubt his word/his knowledge, but ...; sich (dat) etw zur ~ anrechnen to count sth an honour; sich (dat) es zur ~ anrechnen, daß ... to feel honoured that ..., to count it an honour that ...; das rechne ich ihm zur ~ an I consider that a point in his honour or favour; mit wem habe ich die ~? (iro, form) with whom do I have the pleasure of speaking? (form); was verschafft mir die ~? (iro, form) to what do I owe the honour (of your visit)?; es ist mir eine besondere ~, ... (form) it is a great honour for me ...; um der Wahrheit die ~ zu geben ... (geh) to be perfectly honest ..., to tell you the truth ...; wir geben uns die ..., Sie zu ... einzuladen (form) we request the honour of your company at ... (form); zu ~n (+gen) in honour of; darf ich um die ~ bitten, Sie zu begleiten? (form) may I have the honour of accompanying you? (form), would you do me the honour of allowing me to accompany you? (form); habe die ~! (Aus, S Ger) hullo; goodbye; ~, wem ~ gebührt (prov) honour where honour is due (prov); ~ verloren, alles verloren (Prov) honour is all, a good name is better than riches; siehe Feld, letzte(r, s).
ehren vt (Achtung erweisen, würdigen) to honour. etw ehrt jdn sth does sb credit or honour; dein Besuch/Ihr Vertrauen ehrt mich I am honoured by your visit/trust; der Präsident ehrte den Preisträger in einer Rede the president made a speech in honour of the prizewinner; der Preisträger wurde in einer Rede geehrt a speech was made or there was a speech in honour of the prizewinner; jdm ein ~des Andenken bewahren to treasure sb's memory; du sollst Vater und Mutter ~ (Bibl) honour thy father and thy mother; siehe geehrt.
Ehren-: ~amt nt honorary office or post; e~amtlich 1 adj honorary; e~amtlicher Richter = member of the jury; 2 adv in an honorary capacity; ~bezeigung f (Mil) salute; jdm die ~bezeigung erweisen/verweigern to salute/refuse to salute sb, to give/refuse to give sb a salute.
Ehrenbürger m freeman. er wurde zum ~ der Stadt ernannt he was given the freedom of the city/town.
Ehrenbürger-: ~brief m document conferring the freedom of a city or town on sb; ~recht nt freedom; die Stadt verlieh ihm das ~recht he was given the freedom of the city/town.
Ehren-: ~doktor m honorary doctor; ~doktorwürde f honorary doctorate; ihm wurde die ~doktorwürde der Universität Wien verliehen he was made an honorary doctor of or given an honorary doctorate by the University of Vienna; ~erklärung f (von Beleidiger) (formal) apology; (von dritter Seite) statement in defence (of sb's honour); ich werde eine ~erklärung für Sie abgeben I will make a statement in your defence; (nach erfolgter Beleidigung) I will make (you) a formal apology; ~garde f guard of honour; ~gast m guest of honour; ~geleit nt guard of honour; ~gericht nt tribunal; ~haft adj honourable; ~haftigkeit f honourableness; e~halber adv er wurde e~halber zum Vorsitzenden auf Lebenszeit ernannt he was made honorary president for life; Doktor e~halber (abbr e.h.) Doctor honoris causa (form), honorary doctor; ~handel m, pl -händel (old) eine Form des ~handels war das Duell the duel was one way of settling an affair of honour; ~karte f complimentary ticket; ~kodex m code of honour; ~kompanie f (Mil) guard of honour; ~kränkung f insult, affront; ~kranz m (old) wreath, garland; (Brautkranz) garland, circlet; ~legion f legion of honour; ~loge f royal/VIP box; (in Stadion) directors' box; ~mal nt memorial; ~mann m, pl -männer man of honour; ein dunkler ~mann a man of doubtful integrity; ein sauberer ~mann (pej) a blackguard (pej); ~mitglied nt honorary member; ~mitgliedschaft f honorary membership; ~nadel f badge of honour; ~name m wir betrachten den Namen „Churchill" für unser Schiff als ~namen the name "Churchill" will lend honour to our ship; ~pflicht f bounden duty; ~platz m (lit) place or seat of honour; (fig) special place; ~preis m (a) (Auszeichnung) prize; (Anerkennung) consolation prize; (b) (Bot) speedwell, veronica; ~rechte pl (Jur) civil rights pl; Verlust/Aberkennung der bürgerlichen ~rechte loss/forfeiture of one's civil rights; ~rettung f retrieval of one's honour; eine ~rettung versuchen to attempt to retrieve one's honour; zu seiner ~rettung sei gesagt, daß ... in his favour it must be said that ...; e~rührig adj defamatory; etw als e~rührig empfinden to regard sth as an insult to one's honour; ~runde f (Sport) lap of honour; ~sache f matter of honour; ~sache! (inf) you can count on me; das ist für mich ~sache! that's a matter of honour for me; ~salut m, ~salve f salute; ~schuld f debt of honour; ~sold m honorarium; ~tafel f (a) (Tisch) top table; (b) (Gedenktafel) roll of honour; ~tag m (Geburtstag) birthday; (großer Tag) big or great day; zum heutigen ~tag on this special day; ~tanz m den ~tanz tanzen to lead off the dancing; ~titel m honorary title; ~tor nt, ~treffer m (Sport) consola-

tion goal; ~**tribüne** f VIP rostrum; ~**urkunde** f certificate (for outstanding performance in sport); **e~voll** adj Friede honourable; Aufgabe auch noble; ~**vorsitzende(r)** mf honorary chairman/chairwoman; ~**wache** f guard of honour; **e~wert** adj Mensch honourable, worthy; ~**wort** nt word of honour; ~**wort!** (inf) cross my heart! (inf); ~**wort?** (inf) cross your heart? (inf); **mein ~wort!** you have my word; **sein ~wort geben/halten/ brechen** to give/keep/break one's word; **Urlaub auf ~wort** parole; **e~wörtlich 1** adj Versprechen solemn, faithful; **2** adv on one's honour; ~**zeichen** nt decoration.

Ehr-: **e~erbietig** adj respectful, deferential; ~**erbietung** f respect, deference.

Ehrfurcht f, no pl great or deep respect (vor +dat for); (fromme Scheu) reverence (vor +dat for). **vor jdm/etw ~ haben** to respect/revere sb/sth, to have (great) respect for sb/sth; **von ~ ergriffen** overawed.

ehrfurchtgebietend adj Stimme, Geste authoritative. **er ist eine ~e Persönlichkeit** he's the kind of person who commands (one's) respect.

ehrfürchtig, ehrfurchtsvoll adj reverent.

ehrfurchtslos adj irreverent.

Ehrgefühl nt sense of honour; (Selbstachtung) self-respect. **etw aus falschem ~ heraus tun** to do sth out of a misplaced sense of honour.

Ehrgeiz m, no pl ambition.

ehrgeizig adj ambitious.

Ehrgeizling m (pej inf) pusher (inf).

ehrlich 1 adj, adv honest; Name good; Absicht, Zuneigung sincere. **der ~e Finder bekommt 100 Mark** a reward of 100 marks will be given to anyone finding and returning this; **eine ~e Haut** (inf) an honest soul; **ich hatte die ~e Absicht zu kommen** I honestly did intend to come; **er hat ~e Absichten** (inf) his intentions are honourable; ~ **verdientes Geld** hard-earned money; ~ **gesagt ...** quite frankly or honestly ..., to be quite frank ...; **er meint es ~ mit uns** he is being honest with us; ~ **spielen** (Cards) to play straight; ~ **währt am längsten** (Prov) honesty is the best policy (Prov).

2 adv (wirklich) honestly, really (and truly), truly. **ich bin ~ begeistert** I'm really thrilled; ~, **ich habe nichts damit zu tun** honestly, I've got nothing to do with it; ~! honestly!, really!

ehrlicherweise adv honestly, truly, in all honesty.

Ehrlichkeit f, no pl honesty; (von Absicht, Zuneigung) sincerity. **die ~ seines Namens** his good name; **sie zweifelte an der ~ seiner Absichten** she doubted the sincerity of his intentions; (in bezug auf Heirat) she doubted that his intentions were honourable; **mit großer ~** absolutely honestly, with great honesty.

Ehr-: **e~los** adj dishonourable; ~**losigkeit** f dishonourableness; (Schlechtigkeit) infamy; **die ~losigkeit seines Verhaltens** his dishonourable conduct; **e~pusselig, e~pußlig** adj (inf) sensitive about one's reputation; **e~sam** adj (old) siehe **e~bar**; ~**sucht** f (old) inordinate ambitiousness or ambition; **e~süchtig** adj (old) inordinately ambitious.

Ehrung f honour.

Ehr-: **e~vergessen** adj (old) lost to all sense of honour, shameless; **e~verletzend** adj (geh) insulting; ~**verletzung** f (geh) insult (to one's honour); ~**verlust** m loss of honour; (Jur) loss of one's civil rights.

Ehrwürden m -s, no pl Reverend. **Euer ~** Reverend Father/ Mother.

ehrwürdig adj venerable. ~**e Mutter/~er Vater** (Eccl) Reverend Mother/Father.

Ehrwürdigkeit f venerability, venerableness.

ei interj (zärtlich) there (there); (old) (spöttisch) well; (bekräftigend) oh. **(bei einem Kind/Tier) ~ ~ machen** to pet a child/ an animal; **komm, ich mache ~ ~, dann wird's gleich besser** come here and I'll kiss it better; ~ **freilich** or **gewiß!** (old) but of course!

Ei nt -(e)s, -er (a) (Vogel~, Schlangen~) egg; (Physiol auch) ovum (spec). **das ~ des Kolumbus finden** to come up with just the thing; **das ist das ~ des Kolumbus** that's just the thing or just what we want; **das ist ja auch nicht gerade das ~ des Kolumbus** (iro) that's not very inspired; **das ~ will klüger sein als die Henne** you're trying to teach your grandmother to suck eggs (prov); **jdn wie ein rohes ~ behandeln** (fig) to handle sb with kid gloves; **wie auf ~ern gehen** (inf) to teeter along; **wie aus dem ~ gepellt aussehen** (inf) to look spruce; **sie gleichen sich** or **einander wie ein ~ dem anderen** they are as alike as two peas (in a pod); **kümmere dich nicht um ungelegte ~er!** (inf) don't cross your bridges before you come to them! (prov); **das sind ungelegte ~er!** (inf) we'll cross that bridge when we come to it; ~**er** pl (sl: Hoden) balls pl (sl); **jdm die ~er polieren** (sl) to kick sb in the balls (sl); siehe **dick**.

(b) ~**er** pl (sl: Geld) marks; (in GB) quid (inf); (in US) bucks (inf); **das kostet seine 50** ~**er** that'll cost a good 50 marks.

(c) (Rugby sl) ball, pill (sl).

eiapopeia interj lullaby baby.

Eibe f -, -n (Bot) yew.

Eibisch m -(e)s, -e (Bot) marshmallow.

Eichamt nt = Weights and Measures Office (Brit).

Eichbaum m siehe **Eich(en)baum**.

Eiche f -, -n oak; (Baum auch) oak tree.

Eichel f -, -n (a) (Bot) acorn. **(b)** (Anat) glans. **(c)** (Cards) suit in German playing cards equivalent to clubs.

Eichelhäher m jay.

eichen[1] adj oak, oaken (old).

eichen[2] vt to calibrate; (prüfen auch) to check against official specifications. **darauf bin ich geeicht!** (inf) that's right up my street (inf).

Eich(en)baum m oak tree.

Eichen-: ~**holz** nt oak; **ein Tisch aus ~holz** an oak table; ~**laub** nt oak leaves pl; siehe **Ritterkreuz**; ~**sarg** m oak(en) coffin; ~**wald** m oakwood.

Eichhörnchen, Eichkätzchen nt squirrel. **mühsam nährt sich das Eichhörnchen** (inf) one struggles on and little by little.

Eich-: ~**maß** nt standard measure; (Gewicht) standard weight; ~**pfahl** m calibrated pole marking the maximum safe water level of a reservoir etc; ~**strich** m official calibration; (an Gläsern) line measure; **ein Glas mit ~strich** a lined glass.

Eichung f calibration; (Prüfung auch) official verification.

Eid m -(e)s, -e oath. **einen ~ ablegen** or **leisten** or **schwören** to take or swear an oath; **einen ~ auf die Bibel/Verfassung leisten** to swear an oath on the Bible/the constitution; **darauf kann ich einen ~ schwören** I can swear to that or take my oath on that; **ich nehme es auf meinen ~, daß ...** I would be prepared to swear that ...; **jdm den ~ abnehmen** to administer the oath to sb, to take the oath from sb; **unter ~** under or on oath; **eine Erklärung an ~es Statt abgeben** (Jur) to make a declaration in lieu of oath; **ich erkläre an ~es Statt, daß ...** I do solemnly declare that ...

Eidam m -(e)s, -e (obs) son-in-law.

Eid-: ~**bruch** m breach of one's oath; **einen ~bruch begehen** to break one's oath; **e~brüchig** adj **e~brüchig werden** to break one's oath; **du e~brüchiger Verräter!** (old) you faithless traitor!

Eidechse ['aideksə] f -, -n (Zool) lizard; (Astron auch) Lacerta; (inf: Hubwagen) fork-lift truck.

Eider-: ~**d(a)unen** pl eiderdown no pl; ~**ente** f eider (duck).

Eides-: ~**belehrung** f (Jur) caution as to the consequences of committing perjury; ~**formel** f wording of the oath; **die ~formel nachsprechen** to repeat the oath; ~**leistung** f swearing of the oath; **niemand kann zur ~leistung gezwungen werden** no-one can be forced to swear or take the oath; **e~stattlich** adj solemn; **etw e~stattlich erklären** to affirm sth; **eine e~stattliche Erklärung abgeben** to make a solemn declaration.

Eidetik f (Psych) eidetic ability.

Eidetiker(in) f m -s, - eidetic, eidetiker.

eidetisch adj eidetic.

Eidgenosse m confederate; (Schweizer ~) Swiss citizen.

Eidgenossenschaft f confederation. **Schweizerische ~** Swiss Confederation.

Eidgenossin f siehe **Eidgenosse**.

eidgenössisch adj confederate; (schweizerisch) Swiss.

eidlich 1 adj sworn attr, given on or under oath. **er gab eine ~e Erklärung ab** he made a declaration on or under oath; (schriftlich) he swore an affidavit. **2** adv on or under oath. ~ **gebunden** bound by (one's) oath.

Eidotter m or nt egg yolk.

Eier-: ~**becher** m eggcup; ~**brikett** nt ovoid (of coal); ~**farbe** f dye, paint etc used for colouring eggs at Easter; ~**handgranate** f (Mil) (pineapple) hand grenade, pineapple (sl); ~**kognak** m siehe ~**likör;** ~**kopf** m (inf) egghead (inf); (sl: Idiot) blockhead (inf), numbskull (inf); ~**kuchen** m pancake; (Omelette) omelette made with a mixture containing flour; ~**laufen** nt egg and spoon race; ~**laufen machen** to have an egg and spoon race; ~**likör** m advocaat; ~**löffel** m eggspoon.

eiern vi (inf) to wobble.

Eier-: ~**pflaume** f (large oval) plum; ~**schale** f eggshell; **er hat noch die ~schalen hinter den Ohren** (inf) he's still wet behind the ears (inf); **e~schalenfarben** adj cream, off-white; ~**schaum,** ~**schnee** m (Cook) beaten egg white; ~**schwamm** m (Bot: esp Aus) chanterelle; ~**speise** f (a) egg dish; (b) (Aus: Rührei) scrambled egg; ~**stock** m (Anat) ovary; ~**tanz** m **einen regelrechten ~tanz aufführen** (fig inf) to go through all kinds of contortions; ~**uhr** f egg timer.

Eifer m -s, no pl (Begeisterung) enthusiasm; (Eifrigkeit) eagerness, keenness. **mit ~** enthusiastically, eagerly, keenly; **mit ~ arbeiten** to work with a will or with great zeal; **in ~ geraten** to get agitated, to get into a state; **mit großem ~ bei der Sache sein** to put one's heart into it; **im ~ des Gefechts** (fig inf) in the heat of the moment; **er hat sich im ~ in diese Idee verrannt** his enthusiasm for this idea has run away with him.

Eiferer m -s, - (liter) fanatic; (Rel auch) zealot.

eifern vi (liter) (a) **gegen jdn/etw ~** to rail or inveigh against sb/sth; **für etw ~** to crusade or campaign for sth. **(b)** (streben) **nach etw ~** to strive for sth. **(c)** (wett~) **um etw ~** to compete or vie for sth.

Eifersucht f jealousy (auf +acc of). **aus/vor (lauter) ~** out of/for (pure) jealousy.

Eifersüchtelei f petty jealousy.

eifersüchtig adj jealous (auf +acc of).

Eifersuchts-: ~**szene** f **ihr Mann hat ihr wieder eine ~szene gemacht** her husband's jealousy caused another scene; **es gab häßliche ~szenen** his/her jealousy caused some horrible scenes; ~**tragödie** f „~**tragödie in München"** "jealousy causes tragedy in Munich".

eiförmig adj egg-shaped, oval.

eifrig adj eager; Befürworter auch keen; Leser, Sammler keen, avid; (begeistert) enthusiastic; (emsig) assiduous, industrious, zealous; (heftig) vehement. **er putzte gerade ~ sein Auto, als ich ankam** he was busy or busily cleaning his car when I arrived; **die E~en** the eager beavers (inf).

Eifrigkeit f siehe adj eagerness; keenness, avidity; enthusiasm; assiduity, industriousness, zeal; vehemence.

Eigelb nt -s, -e or (bei Zahlenangabe) - egg yolk. **vier ~ the** yolks of four eggs, four egg yolks.

eigen adj (a) own; (selbständig) separate. **seine ~e Wohnung/ Meinung haben** to have a flat/an opinion of one's own, to have one's own flat/opinion; **etw sein ~ nennen** (geh) to have sth to one's name, to have sth to call one's own; **er ist stolz, zwölf Kinder sein ~ nennen zu können** he is proud of being blessed with twelve children; **jdm etw zu ~ geben** (*liter*) to give sb sth; **meiner Mutter zu ~** (*liter*) for *or* (dedicated) to my mother; **~er Bericht** (*Press*) from *or* by our (own) correspondent; **Zimmer mit ~em Eingang** room with its own *or* a separate entrance; **San Marino ist ein ~er Staat** San Marino is an independent *or* a separate state; **sein ~ Fleisch und Blut** (*liter*) his own flesh and blood; **sich** (*dat*) **etw zu ~ machen** to adopt sth; (*zur Gewohnheit machen*) to make sth a habit, to make a habit of sth; **übergeben Sie diesen Brief dem Anwalt zu ~en Händen** (*form*) give this letter to the lawyer in person; **ich habe das Papier auf ~e Rechnung gekauft** I paid for the paper myself; **ich möchte kurz in ~er Sache sprechen** I would like to say something on my own account; *siehe* **Fuß, Nest, Tasche** *etc*.

  (b) (*typisch, kennzeichnend*) typical. **das ist ihm ~** that is typical of him; **er antwortete mit dem ihm ~en Zynismus** he answered with (his) characteristic cynicism; **ein Menschenschlag von ganz ~er Prägung** a race apart.

  (c) (*seltsam*) strange, peculiar. **es ist eine Landschaft von ganz ~em Reiz** the country is strangely attractive in its own way *or* has its own strange attractions; *siehe* **Ding[1]** (b).

  (d) (*ordentlich*) particular; (*übergenau*) fussy. **in Gelddingen** *or* **was Geld anbetrifft ist er sehr ~** he is very particular about money matters.

-eigen *adj suf* -owned.
Eigen|antrieb *m* **Fahrzeuge mit ~** self-propelled vehicles; **~ haben** to be self-propelled.
Eigen|art *f* (*Besonderheit*) peculiarity; (*Eigenschaft*) characteristic; (*Individualität*) individuality; (*Eigentümlichkeit von Personen*) idiosyncrasy. **das gehört zur ~ der Bayern** that's a typically Bavarian characteristic.
eigen|artig *adj* peculiar; (*sonderbar auch*) strange; (*persönlich kennzeichnend*) idiosyncratic.
Eigen-: ~**bau** *m, no pl* Tabak/Gemüse **im ~bau züchten** to grow one's own tobacco/vegetables; **er fährt ein Fahrrad/raucht Zigaretten Marke ~bau** (*hum inf*) he rides a home-made bike/smokes home-grown cigarettes (*hum*); ~**bedarf** *m* (*von Mensch*) personal use; (*von Staat*) domestic requirements *pl*; **zum ~bedarf** for (one's own) personal use/domestic requirements; **der Hausbesitzer machte ~bedarf geltend** the landlord showed that he needed the house/flat for himself; ~**bericht** *m* (*Press*) **diese Zeitung bringt kaum ~berichte** this paper rarely carries articles by its own journalists; ~**bewegung** *f* (*Astron*) proper motion; ~**brötelei** [aignbrøːtəˈlaɪ] *f* (*inf*) eccentricity; (*Einzelgängertum*) solitary ways *pl*; ~**brötelei stört hier nur** it's disruptive if people go off doing their own thing (*inf*); ~**brötler(in** *f*) *m* -s, - (*inf*) loner, lone wolf; (*komischer Kauz*) queer fish (*inf*), oddball (*esp US inf*); **e~brötlerisch** *adj* (*inf*) solitary; (*komisch*) eccentric; ~**dünkel** *m* sense of superiority; ~**dynamik** *f* momentum; **eine ~dynamik entwickeln** to gather momentum; ~**finanzierung** *f* self-financing; **wir bauen die neue Fabrik in ~finanzierung** we are financing the building of the new factory ourselves; **e~gesetzlich** *adj* autonomous; **jede Revolution entwickelt sich e~gesetzlich** every revolution develops according to laws of its own; **der Historiker zeigte den e~gesetzlichen Ablauf verschiedener geschichtlicher Prozesse auf** the historian pointed out the independent laws inherent in various historical processes; ~**gesetzlichkeit** *f* autonomous laws *pl*; **sein Handeln folgte einer geheimnisvollen ~gesetzlichkeit** his behaviour followed its own mysterious laws; ~**gewicht** *nt* (*von LKW etc*) unladen weight; (*Comm*) net weight; (*Sci*) dead weight; ~**goal** *nt* (*Aus Sport*) own goal; ~**gruppe** *f* (*Sociol*) in-group; **e~händig** *adj* Brief, Unterschrift **in one's own hand, handwritten;** Übergabe personal; **eine Arbeit e~händig machen** to do a job oneself *or* personally *or* with one's own hands; **e~händige Urkunde** holograph; ~**heim** *nt* one's own home; **sparen Sie für ein ~heim!** save for a home of your own!; ~**heit** *f siehe* ~**art;** ~**initiative** *f* initiative of one's own; **auf ~initiative** on one's own initiative; ~**kapital** *nt* (*von Person*) personal capital; (*von Firma*) company capital; **10.000 DM ~kapital** 10,000 DM of one's own capital; ~**leben** *nt, no pl* one's own life; (*selbständige Existenz*) independent existence; (*Privatleben*) private life; ~**liebe** *f* amour-propre; (*Selbstverliebtheit*) self-love, love of self; **jdn in seiner ~liebe kränken** to offend sb's amour-propre; ~**lob** *nt* self-importance, vaingloriousness; ~**lob stinkt!** (*inf*) don't blow your own trumpet! (*prov*); **e~mächtig 1** *adj* (*selbstherrlich*) high-handed; (*e~verantwortlich*) taken/done *etc* on one's own authority; (*unbefugt*) unauthorized; **e~mächtige Abwesenheit** (*Mil*) absence without leave; **2** *adv* high-handedly; (*entirely*) on one's own authority; without any authorization; **e~mächtigerweise** *adv* (*selbstherrlich*) high-handedly; (*unbefugt*) without any authorization; ~**mächtigkeit** *f* (*Selbstherrlichkeit*) high-handedness *no pl*; (*unbefugtes Handeln*) unauthorized behaviour *no pl*; **die ~mächtigkeit seines Vorgehens wurde von allen kritisiert** everyone criticized him for having acted high-handedly/without authorization; ~**mittel** *pl* (*form*) one's own resources; **die ~mittel der Körperschaft** the corporation's (own) resources; **man braucht nur 20% ~mittel** you only need to find 20% yourself *or* from your own resources; ~**name** *m* proper name; ~**nutz** *m, no pl* self-interest; **das habe ich ohne jeden ~nutz getan** I did that with no thought of myself *or* of furthering my own interests; **e~nützig** *adj* selfish; ~**nützigkeit** *f siehe* ~**nutz;** ~**produktion** *f* **das ist eine ~produktion** we/they *etc* made it ourselves/themselves *etc*; **etw in ~produktion herstellen** to make sth oneself, to make one's own sth; **aus ~produktion** (*hausgemacht*) home-made; Tabak *etc* home-grown; **das war eine ~produktion des Irischen Fernsehens** that was one of

Irish Television's own productions.
eigens *adv* (e)specially; (*ausdrücklich auch*) specifically.
Eigenschaft *f* (*Attribut*) quality; (*Chem, Phys etc*) property; (*Merkmal*) characteristic, feature; (*Funktion*) capacity.
Eigenschaftswort *nt* adjective.
Eigen-: ~**schwingung** *f* (*Sci*) free vibration; ~**sinn** *m, no pl* stubbornness, obstinacy; (*inf: Trotzkopf*) stubborn child; **e~sinnig** *adj* stubborn, obstinate; ~**sinnigkeit** *f* stubbornness, obstinacy; ~**sinnigkeiten** *pl* stubborn *or* obstinate behaviour; **e~staatlich** *adj* sovereign; ~**staatlichkeit** *f* sovereignty; **e~ständig** *adj* original; (*unabhängig*) independent; (e~*gesetzlich*) autonomous; ~**ständigkeit** *f siehe adj* originality; independence; autonomy; ~**sucht** *f, no pl* selfishness; (*Egotismus auch*) self-centredness; **e~süchtig** *adj siehe n* selfish; self-centred.
eigentlich 1 *adj* (*wirklich, tatsächlich*) real, actual; Wert true, real; (*ursprünglich*) original. **im ~en Sinne bedeutet das ... das** really means ...; **im ~en Sinne des Wortes ...** in the original meaning of the word ...
  2 *adv* actually; (*tatsächlich, wirklich auch*) really; (*überhaupt*) anyway. **~ wollte ich nur fünf Minuten bleiben** actually I was only *or* I was really only going to stay five minutes; **was willst du ~ hier?** what do you want here anyway?; **wissen Sie ~, wer ich bin?** do you know who I am?; **was ist ~ mit dir los?** what's the matter with you (anyway)?; **ich bin ~ froh, daß ...** really *or* actually I'm happy that ...; **~ müßtest du das wissen** you should really know that; **~ dürftest du das nicht tun** you shouldn't really do that.
Eigentlichkeit *f* (*Philos*) essentiality.
Eigentor *nt* (*Sport*) own goal. **ein ~ schießen** (*fig*) to score an own goal.
Eigentum *nt, no pl* property. **bewegliches ~** movables *pl*, movable property; **unbewegliches ~** immovables *pl*, real property; **~ an etw** (*dat*) **erwerben** to acquire possession of sth; **~ an den Produktionsmitteln** private ownership of the means of production; „**~ ist Diebstahl“** property is theft.
Eigentümer(in *f*) *m* -s, - owner.
eigentümlich *adj* (a) (*sonderbar, seltsam*) strange, curious, odd.
  (b) (*geh: typisch*) **jdm/einer Sache ~ sein** to be characteristic *or* typical of sb/sth.
eigentümlicherweise *adv* strangely *or* curiously *or* oddly enough.
Eigentümlichkeit *f* (a) (*Kennzeichen, Besonderheit*) characteristic. (b) (*Eigenheit*) peculiarity.
Eigentums-: ~**begriff** *m* concept of property; ~**bildung** *f* private acquisition of property; ~**delikt** *nt* (*Jur*) offence against property; ~**denken** *nt* (*Theorie*) property ethic; (*Gesinnung*) property-mindedness; ~**recht** *nt* right of ownership; (*Urheberrecht*) copyright; ~**streuung** *f* dispersal of property; ~**vergehen** *nt siehe* ~**delikt;** ~**verhältnisse** *pl* distribution *sing* of property; ~**vorbehalt** *m* (*Jur*) reservation of proprietary rights; ~**wohnung** *f* owner-occupied flat (*Brit*) *or* apartment; **er kaufte sich** (*dat*) **eine ~wohnung** he bought a flat (of his own); ~**wohnungen bauen** to build flats for owner-occupation.
Eigen-: **e~verantwortlich 1** *adj* autonomous; **2** *adv* on one's own authority; **e~verantwortlich für etw sorgen müssen** to be personally responsible for sth; **er hat e~verantwortlich dafür gesorgt** he saw to it personally *or* himself; ~**verantwortlichkeit** *f* autonomy; **jds ~verantwortlichkeit für etw** sb's personal responsibility for sth; ~**wärme** *f* body heat; ~**wert** *m* intrinsic value; **e~willig** *adj* with a mind of one's own; (e~*sinnig*) self-willed; (*unkonventionell*) unconventional, original; **sie ist in allem recht e~willig** she has a mind of her own in everything; ~**willigkeit** *f siehe adj* independence of mind; self-will; unconventionality, originality; ~**zeit** *f* (*Phys*) proper time.
eignen 1 *vr* to be suitable (*für, zu* for, *als* as). **er eignet sich nicht zum Lehrer** he's not suited to teaching, he doesn't/wouldn't make a good teacher; *siehe* **geeignet**.
  2 *vi* (*geh*) **ihm eignet der Charme des Österreichers** he has *or* possesses all the charm of an Austrian; **seinen Büchern eignet ein präziser Prosastil** his books are characterized by a precise narrative style; **ihm eignet viel Güte** (*old liter*) he is full of goodness.
Eigner(in *f*) *m* -s, - (*form*) owner.
Eignung *f* suitability; (*Befähigung*) aptitude.
Eignungs-: ~**prüfung** *f*, ~**test** *m* aptitude test.
eigtl. *abbr of* **eigentlich.**
Eiklar *nt* -s, - (*Aus, S Ger*) egg white.
Eiland *nt* -(e)s, -e (*liter*) isle (*liter*).
Eil-: ~**angebot** *nt* (*Comm*) express offer; ~**bote** *m* messenger; **per** *or* **durch ~boten** express; ~**brief** *m* express letter; **ich schicke diesen Brief als ~brief** I am sending this letter express.
Eile *f -, no pl* hurry. **in ~ sein** to be in a hurry; **~ haben** (*Mensch*) to be in a hurry *or* rush; (*Sache*) to be urgent; **damit hat es keine ~, das hat keine ~** there is no hurry *or* rush about it, it's not urgent; **er trieb uns zur ~ an** he hurried us up; **in aller ~** hurriedly, hastily; **in höchster ~ laufen/fahren** to rush/drive in a tremendous hurry; **mit ~/mit fieberhafter ~ arbeiten** to work very quickly/feverishly; **in der/meiner ~** in the hurry/my haste; **nur keine ~!** don't rush!
Eileiter *m* (*Anat*) Fallopian tube.
Eileiterschwangerschaft *f* ectopic pregnancy.
eilen 1 *vi* (a) *aux sein* to rush, to hasten (*liter*), to hurry. **er eilte dem Ertrinkenden zu Hilfe** he rushed *or* hastened to help the drowning man; **eile mit Weile** (*Prov*) more haste less speed (*Prov*).
  (b) (*dringlich sein*) to be urgent *or* pressing. **eilt!** (*auf Briefen*

etc) urgent; **die Sache eilt** it's urgent, it's an urgent matter.
2 *vr* (*inf*) to rush.
3 *vi impers* **es eilt** it's urgent *or* pressing; **damit eilt es nicht** there's no great hurry *or* rush about it; **mit dieser Arbeit eilt es sehr/nicht** this work is very/is not urgent.
eilends *adv* hurriedly, hastily.
Eil-: e~**fertig** *adj* (*geh*) zealous; ~**fertigkeit** *f* (*geh*) zeal, zealousness; ~**fracht** *f*, ~**gut** *nt* express freight; **etw als** ~**gut senden** to send sth express freight.
eilig *adj* **(a)** (*schnell, rasch*) quick, hurried, hasty. **es** ~ **haben** to be in a hurry *or* rush; **er bat den Arzt,** ~**st zu kommen** he asked the doctor to come as quickly as possible; **nur nicht so** ~! I don't be in such a hurry *or* rush!
　(b) (*dringend*) urgent. **er hatte nichts E~eres zu tun, als ...** (*iro*) he had nothing better to do than ... (*iro*).
Eil-: ~**marsch** *m* (*Mil*) fast march; ~**meldung** *f* (*Press*) flash; ~**paket** *nt* express parcel; ~**schrift** *f* speed writing; ~**sendung** *f* express delivery *or* letter/parcel; ~**sendungen** *pl* express mail *or* post; ~**tempo** *nt*: **etw im** ~**tempo machen** to do sth in a real rush; **er kam im** ~**tempo auf mich zugerannt** he came rushing *or* tearing up to me; ~**zug** *m* fast stopping train; ~**zustellung** *f* special delivery; **mit** ~**zustellung** (by) special delivery.
Eimer *m* **-s, -** **(a)** bucket, pail; (*Milch~*) pail; (*Müll~*) (rubbish) bin. **ein** ~ (**voll**) **Wasser** a bucket(ful) of water; **es gießt wie mit** *or* **aus** ~**n** (*inf*) it's bucketing down (*inf*), it's raining cats and dogs (*inf*). **(b)** **im** ~ **sein** (*sl*) to be up the spout (*sl*); (*kaputt auch*) to be bust (*inf*).
Eimer-: ~**kette** *f* bucket conveyor; **e~weise** *adv* in bucketfuls, by the bucket(ful).
ein¹ *adv* (*an Geräten*) **E~/Aus** on/off; ~ **und aus gehen** to come and go; **er geht bei uns** ~ **und aus** he is always round at our place; **ich weiß** (**mit ihm**) **nicht mehr** ~ **noch aus** I'm at my wit's end (with him).
ein², **eine**, **ein 1** *num* one. **das kostet nur** ~**e Mark** it only costs one mark; ~ **Uhr** one (o'clock); ~ **Uhr zwanzig** twenty past one; ~ **für allemal** once and for all; ~ **und derselbe/dieselbe/dasselbe** one and the same; **er ist ihr** ~ **und alles** he means everything to her; *siehe* **eins**.
　2 *indef art* **a**; (*vor Vokalen*) **an**. ~ **Mann/**~**e Frau/**~ **Kind** a man/woman/child; ~ **Europäer** a European; ~ **Hotel** a *or* an hotel; **der Sohn** ~**es Lehrers** the son of a teacher, a teacher's son; **nur** ~ **Hegel konnte das schreiben** only a Hegel could have written that; ~**e Hitze ist das hier!** the *or* some heat here!; ~ **Bier/**~**e Frau ist das!** that's some beer/she's some woman!; **was für** ~ **Wetter/Lärm!** some weather/noise, what a noise; **wir hatten** ~**en Durst!** (*inf*) we were parched!, were we thirsty!; *siehe auch* **eine(r, s)**.
ein|achsig *adj* two-wheeled, single-axle *attr*.
Ein|akter *m* **-s, -** (*Theat*) one-act play.
einander *pron* one another, each other. **zwei** ~ **widersprechende Zeugenberichte** two (mutually) contradictory eye-witness reports.
ein|arbeiten *sep* **1** *vr* to get used to the work. **sie muß sich in ihr neues Gebiet** ~ she has to get used to her new area of work. **2** *vt* **(a)** *jdn* to train. **(b)** (*einfügen*) to incorporate, to include. **(c)** (*einnähen*) to sew in; *Futter, Polster auch* to attach.
Ein|arbeitung *f siehe vt* **(a)** training. **(b)** incorporation, inclusion. **(c)** sewing in; attachment.
Ein|arbeitungszeit *f* training period.
ein|armig *adj* one-armed; *Turnübungen* single-arm.
ein|äschern *vt sep Leichnam* to cremate; *Stadt etc* to burn to the ground *or* down, to reduce to ashes.
Ein|äscherung *f siehe vt* cremation; burning down.
ein|atmen *vti sep* to breathe in.
ein|ätzen *vt sep* to etch (in).
ein|äugig *adj* one-eyed; *Spiegelreflexkamera* single-lens.
Einbahnstraße *f* one-way street.
einbalsamieren* *vt sep* to embalm.
Einbalsamierung *f* embalming, embalmment.
Einband *m* book cover, case (*spec*).
einbändig *adj* one-volume *attr*, in one volume.
einbasisch *adj* (*Chem*) monobasic.
Einbau *m* **-(e)s, -ten (a)** *no pl siehe vt* installation; fitting; working-in. **(b)** (*usu pl: Schrank etc*) fixture.
einbauen *vt sep* **(a)** to install, to put in; *Motor auch* to fit; (*inf: einfügen*) *Zitat etc* to work in. **eingebaute Möbel/eingebauter Belichtungsmesser** built-in furniture/exposure meter.
Einbauküche *f* (fully-)fitted kitchen.
Einbaum *m* dug-out (canoe).
Einbau-: ~**möbel** *pl* built-in *or* fitted furniture; (*Schränke*) fitted cupboards *pl*; ~**schrank** *m* built-in *or* fitted cupboard.
einbegriffen *adj* included.
einbehalten* *vt sep irreg* to keep back.
einbeinig *adj* one-legged.
einbekennen* *vt sep irreg* (*geh*) *Schuld* to admit.
Einbekenntnis *nt* (*geh*) admission.
einberechnen* *vt sep* to allow for (in one's calculations). ~, **daß ...** to allow for the fact that ...
einberufen* *vt sep irreg Parlament* to summon; *Versammlung* to convene, to call; (*Mil*) to call up, to conscript, to draft (*US*). **Leute zu einer Versammlung** ~ to summon *or* call people to a meeting.
Einberufene(r) *mf decl as adj* (*Mil*) conscript, draftee (*US*).
Einberufung *f* **(a)** (*einer Versammlung*) convention, calling; (*des Parlaments*) summoning. **(b)** (*Mil*) conscription; (~*sbescheid*) call-up.
Einberufungs-: ~**bescheid**, ~**befehl** *m* (*Mil*) call-up *or* draft (*US*) papers *pl*.
einbeschrieben *adj* (*Math*) *Kreis* inscribed.

einbetonieren* *vt sep* to cement in (*in* +*acc* -to).
einbetten *vt sep* to embed (*in* +*acc* in); *Rohr, Kabel* to lay (*in* +*acc* in); *siehe* **eingebettet**.
Einbettzimmer *nt* single room.
einbeulen *vt sep* to dent (in).
einbeziehen* *vt sep irreg* to include (*in* +*acc* in).
Einbeziehung *f* inclusion. **unter** ~ **von etw** including sth; **unter** ~ **sämtlicher Gesichtspunkte** having regard to all points.
einbiegen *sep irreg* **1** *vi aux sein* to turn (off) (*in* +*acc* into). **du mußt hier links** ~ you have to turn (off to the) left here; **diese Straße biegt in die Hauptstraße ein** this road joins the main road. **2** *vt* to bend in.
einbilden *vr sep* **(a)** **sich** (*dat*) **etw** ~ to imagine sth; **er bildet sich** (*dat*) **ein, daß ...** he's got hold of the idea that ...; **sich** (*dat*) **steif und fest** ~, **daß ...** (*inf*) to get it fixed in one's head that ... (*inf*); **das bildest du dir nur ein** that's just your imagination; **ich bilde mir nicht ein, ich sei ...** I don't have any illusions about being ...; I'm not pretending to be ...; **er bildet sich** (*dat*) **viel ein** he imagines a lot of things!; **bilde dir** (*doch*) **nicht ein!** don't kid (*inf*) *or* delude yourself!; **was bildest du dir eigentlich ein?** what's got into you?; **bilde dir bloß nicht ein, daß ich das glaube!** don't kid yourself (*inf*) *or* don't go thinking that I believe that!
　(b) (*stolz sein*) **sich** (*dat*) **viel auf etw** (*acc*) ~ to be conceited about *or* vain about sth; **er bildet sich viel darauf ein, daß seine Familie adlig ist** he gives himself all kinds of airs and graces because his family is aristocratic; **darauf kann ich mir etwas** ~ (*iro*) praise indeed!; **darauf können Sie sich etwas** ~! that's something to be proud of!, that's a feather in your cap!; **darauf brauchst du dir nichts einzubilden!** that's nothing to crow about (*inf*) *or* be proud of; **auf diesen bescheidenen Erfolg brauchst du dir nichts einzubilden** don't go getting any big ideas just because of this little success; *siehe* **eingebildet**.
Einbildung *f* **(a)** (*Vorstellung*) imagination; (*irrige Vorstellung*) illusion. **das sind** ~**en** that's pure imagination; **das ist alles nur** ~ it's all in the mind, it's just (your/his) imagination; **krank ist er bloß in seiner** ~ he just imagines *or* thinks he's ill.
　(b) (*Dünkel*) conceit. **an** ~**en leiden** (*hum inf*) to be (pretty) stuck on oneself (*inf*), to really fancy oneself (*inf*).
Einbildungs-: ~**kraft** *f*, ~**vermögen** *nt* (powers *pl* of) imagination.
einbimsen *vt sep* (*inf*) **jdm etw** ~ to drum *or* din sth into sb (*inf*).
einbinden *vt sep irreg Buch* to bind; (*in Schutzhülle*) to cover. **neu** ~ to rebind.
einblasen *vt sep irreg* to blow in (*in* +*acc* -to); *Kaltluft auch* to blast in (*in* +*acc* -to); (*Mus*) *Blasinstrument* to play *or* blow (*inf*) in. **Gott blies Adam den Lebenshauch ein** God breathed the breath of life into Adam; **jdm etw** ~ (*fig inf*) to whisper sth to sb.
einblenden *sep* (*Film, TV, Rad*) **1** *vt* to insert, to slot in; (*nachträglich*) *Musik etc* to dub on. **2** *vr* **sich in etw** (*acc*) ~ to link up with sth; **sich bei jdm/etw** ~ to go over to sb/sth.
Einblendung *f siehe vt* insert; (*das Einblenden*) insertion; dubbing on.
einbleuen *vt sep* (*inf*) **jdm etw** ~ (*durch Schläge*) to beat sth into sb; (*einschärfen*) to drum sth into sb, to ram sth into sb's head (*inf*); **ich habe ihm eingebleut, das ja nicht zu vergessen** I told him time and again not to forget it.
Einblick *m* **(a)** (*rare: Blick in etw hinein*) view (*in* +*acc* of). **(b)** (*fig: Kenntnis*) insight. ~ **in etw** (*acc*) **gewinnen** to gain an insight into sth; **einen ersten** ~ **in etw** (*acc*) **gewinnen** to gain a first impression of sth; ~ **in die Akten nehmen** to look at *or* examine the files; **jdm** ~ **in etw** (*acc*) **gewähren** to allow sb to look at sth; **er hat** ~ **in diese Vorgänge** he has some knowledge of these events.
einbrechen *sep irreg* **1** *vt Tür, Wand etc* to break down; *Eis* to break through.
　2 *vi* **(a)** *aux sein* (*einstürzen*) to fall *or* cave in. **er ist** (**auf dem Eis**) **eingebrochen** he went *or* fell through the ice.
　(b) *aux sein or haben* (*Einbruch verüben*) to break in. **in unser** *or* **unserem Haus sind Diebe eingebrochen** thieves broke into our house; **bei mir ist eingebrochen worden, man hat bei mir eingebrochen** I've had a break-in, I've been burgled *or* burglarized (*US*); **in ein Land** ~ (*Mil*) to invade a country; **in neue Absatzmärkte etc** ~ to make inroads into new markets *etc*.
　(c) *aux sein* (*Nacht, Dämmerung, Dunkelheit*) to fall; *Winter* to set in. **bei** ~**der Nacht** at nightfall.
Einbrecher(in *f*) *m* **-s, -** burglar.
einbrennen *sep irreg* **1** *vt Mal* to brand. **Buchstaben/Muster in Holz** ~ to burn letters/patterns into wood. **2** *vr* (*liter*) to engrave *or* etch itself.
einbringen *vt sep irreg* **(a)** (*Parl*) to introduce.
　(b) (*Ertrag bringen*) *Geld, Nutzen* to bring in; *Ruhm* to bring; *Zinsen* to earn. **jdm etw** ~ to bring/earn sb sth; **das bringt nichts ein** (*fig*) it's not worth it.
　(c) (*in die Ehe* ~) to bring sth into the marriage; **etw in die Firma** ~ to put sth into the firm.
　(d) (*hineinbringen, -schaffen*) to put in (*in* +*acc* -to); *Schiff* to bring in (*in* +*acc* -to); *Ernte* to bring *or* gather in; *Geflohene* to bring back.
　(e) (*wettmachen*) *Zeit, Verlust* to make up.
　(f) (*Typ*) *Zeilen* to take in.
einbrocken *vt sep* to crumble (*in* +*acc* into). **jdm/sich etwas** ~ (*inf*) to land sb/oneself in it (*inf*), to be in the soup (*inf*); **da hast du dir etwas Schönes eingebrockt!** (*inf*) you've really let yourself in for it there; **was man sich eingebrockt hat, das muß man auch auslöffeln** (*prov*) you've made your bed, now you must lie on it (*prov*); *siehe* **Suppe**.
Einbruch *m* **(a)** (~*diebstahl*) burglary (*in* +*acc* in), breaking and entering (*form*); (*Mil*) (*in Land*) invasion (*in* +*acc* of); (*in Front*) breakthrough (*in* +*acc* of). **ein** ~ a break-in *or* burg-

lary; der ~ in die Bank the bank break-in; dem Regiment gelang der ~ in die Front the regiment managed to break through the front-line.

(b) (von Wasser) penetration (form). ~ kühler Meeresluft (Met) a stream of cold air moving inland.

(c) (Einsturz: einer Mauer etc) collapse; (Geol) rift valley. ~ der Kurse (Fin) collapse of the stock exchange.

(d) (fig) (der Nacht) fall; (des Winters) onset. bei/vor ~ der Nacht/Dämmerung at/before nightfall/dusk.

Einbruch(s)-: ~diebstahl m (Jur) burglary, breaking and entering (form); e~sicher adj burglar-proof; ~stelle f (im Damm) breach; (im Eis) hole; ~tal nt (Geol) rift valley; ~versicherung f burglary insurance; ~werkzeug nt housebreaking tool.

einbuchten vt sep (lit) to indent; (inf) to put away (inf), to lock up.

Einbuchtung f indentation; (Bucht) inlet, bay.

einbuddeln sep (inf) 1 vt to bury (in +acc in). 2 vr sich (in den Sand) ~ to dig oneself in(to the sand).

einbürgern sep 1 vt Person to naturalize; Fremdwort, Gewohnheit, Pflanze to introduce. er ist in die or der Türkei eingebürgert worden he has become a naturalized Turk.

2 vr (Person) to become or be naturalized; (Brauch, Tier, Pflanze) to become established; (Fremdwort) to gain currency, to become established. er hat sich in Deutschland eingebürgert he has become a naturalized German; das hat sich so eingebürgert (Brauch) it's just the way we/they etc have come to do things; (Wort) it's been adopted into the language; es hat sich bei uns so eingebürgert, daß wir uns abwechseln we've got into the habit of taking turns.

Einbürgerung f siehe vt naturalization; introduction.

Einbuße f loss (an – dat to). der Skandal hat seinem Ansehen schwere ~ getan he lost a considerable amount of respect because of the scandal.

einbüßen sep 1 vt to lose; (durch eigene Schuld) to forfeit. 2 vi to lose something. an Klarheit (dat) ~ to lose some of its clarity.

eincremen vt sep to put cream on; Gesicht etc auch to cream.

eindämmen vt sep Fluß to dam; (fig: halten, vermindern) to check, to stem; (im Zaum halten) to contain.

Eindämmung f (a) (Damm) dam. (b) siehe vt damming; checking, stemming; containing.

eindampfen vt sep to evaporate.

eindecken sep 1 vr sich (mit etw) ~ to stock up (with sth); (für den Haushalt) to get in supplies (of sth); wir haben uns ausreichend mit Geld eingedeckt we've got enough money; ich bin gut eingedeckt, ich habe mich eingedeckt I am well supplied.

2 vt (a) (Build, Mil, fig) to cover. ein Dach mit Ziegeln/Stroh ~ to tile/thatch a roof.

(b) (inf: überhäufen) to inundate. mit Arbeit eingedeckt sein to be snowed under or inundated with work.

Eindecker m -s, - (Aviat) monoplane; (Autobus) single decker.

eindeichen vt sep to dyke; Fluß auch to embank.

eindellen vt sep (inf) to dent (in).

eindeutig adj clear; Beweis auch definite; (nicht zweideutig) unambiguous; Witz explicit. jdm etw ~ sagen to tell sb sth quite plainly or straight (inf); das ist ~ der Fall it's clearly or obviously the case.

Eindeutigkeit f siehe adj clearness; definiteness; unambiguity; explicitness.

eindeutschen vt sep Fremdwort to Germanize. Clips, ~d auch Klips Clips, sometimes Germanized as Klips.

Eindeutschung f Germanization.

eindicken vti sep (vi: aux sein) to thicken.

eindimensional adj one-dimensional, unidimensional.

eindosen vt sep to can, to tin (Brit).

eindösen vi sep aux sein (inf) to doze off, to drop off (inf).

eindrängen sep 1 vr to crowd in (in +acc -to); (fig) to intrude (in +acc upon); (sich einmischen) (in +acc in) to interfere, to meddle (inf). 2 vi aux sein (lit, fig) to crowd in (auf +acc on).

eindrecken vt sep (inf) to get dirty or muddy. etw/sich total or völlig ~ to get sth/(oneself) completely covered in mud.

eindrehen vt sep (a) (einschrauben) to screw in (in +acc -to).

(b) Haar to put in rollers.

eindreschen vi sep irreg (inf) auf jdn ~ to lay into (inf) or lambaste sb.

eindrillen vt sep (inf) jdm etw ~ to drill sb in sth; Verhalten, Manieren etc to din or drum sth into sb (inf).

eindringen vi sep irreg aux sein (a) (einbrechen) in etw (acc) ~ to force one's way into sth; (Dieb etc auch) to force an entry into sth; in unsere Linien/das Land ~ (Mil) to penetrate our lines/into the country.

(b) in etw (acc) ~ (Messer, Schwert) to go into or penetrate (into) sth; (Wasser, Gas auch) to get into or find its way into sth; (Fremdwörter, Amerikanismen) to find its way into sth; der Nagel drang tief ins Holz ein the nail went deep into the wood; ich bin noch nicht genügend in diese Materie eingedrungen I haven't yet gone into the subject deeply enough; eine Stimmung in sich ~ lassen to let oneself be carried away by a mood.

(c) (bestürmen) auf jdn ~ to go for or attack sb (mit with); (mit Fragen, Bitten etc) to besiege sb.

eindringlich adj (nachdrücklich) insistent; (dringend auch) urgent; Schilderung vivid. mit ~en Worten insistently, with insistence; vividly, in vivid words; ich habe ihn ~ gebeten, zu Hause zu bleiben I urged him to stay at home; jdm ~ nahelegen, etw zu tun to urge sb or advise sb most strongly to do sth.

Eindringlichkeit f siehe adj insistence; urgency; vividness.

Eindringling m intruder; (in Gesellschaft etc) interloper.

Eindruck m -(e)s, ⁻e (a) impression. den ~ erwecken, als ob or daß ... to give the impression that ...; die ⁻e, die wir gewonnen hatten our impressions; ich habe den ~, daß ..., ich kann mich des ~s nicht erwehren, daß ... (geh) I have the impression that ..., I can't help thinking that ... (inf); großen ~ auf jdn machen to make a great or big impression on sb; er macht einen heiteren ~/den ~ eines heiteren Menschen he gives the impression of being cheerful/a cheerful person; die Rede hat ihren ~ auf ihn nicht verfehlt the speech made a strong impression on him; er will ~ (bei ihr) machen or schinden (inf) he's out to impress (her); ich stehe noch ganz unter dem ~ der Ereignisse I'm still too close to it all; viele (neue) ⁻e sammeln to gain a whole host of new impressions; du solltest einmal neue ⁻e sammeln you should broaden your horizons.

(b) (rare: Spur) impression, imprint.

eindrücken sep 1 vt (a) to push in; Fenster to break; Tür, Mauer to push down; (Sturm, Explosion) to blow in/down; (einbeulen) to dent, to bash in (inf); Brustkorb to crush; Nase to flatten. die Wassermassen drückten den Damm ein the mass of the water made the dam collapse.

(b) Fußspuren etc to impress.

2 vr to make or leave an impression.

Eindrucks-: e~fähig adj receptive; ~fähigkeit f, no pl receptiveness; e~los adj unimpressive; e~voll adj impressive.

eind(r)useln vi sep aux sein (inf) to doze off, to drop off (inf).

eindübeln vt sep Haken to plug (in +acc into).

einduseln vi sep aux sein siehe **eind(r)useln**.

eine siehe **ein, eine(r, s)**.

einebnen vt sep (lit) to level (off); (fig) to level (out).

Einebnung f, no pl levelling.

Einehe f monogamy.

eineiig adj Zwillinge identical.

eineinhalb num one and a half; siehe **anderthalb**.

eineinhalbmal adv one and a half times.

einen vtr (geh) to unite.

einengen vt sep (lit) to constrict; (fig) Begriff to restrict, to narrow down; Freiheit to curb, to restrict. sich (in seiner Freiheit) eingeengt fühlen to feel cramped or restricted; jdn in seiner Freiheit ~ to curb sb's freedom; eingeengt sitzen/stehen/liegen to sit/stand/lie (all) squashed up.

einengend adj (lit) constricting; (fig) restricting. einen Begriff ~ interpretieren to interpret a concept narrowly.

Einengung f (lit) constriction; (fig) restriction.

einer adv (Aus) siehe **herein**.

eine(r, s) indef pron adj (a) one; (jemand) somebody, someone. der/die/das ~ the one; das ~ Buch habe ich schon gelesen I've already read one of the books or the one book; das ~ Gute war ... the one good thing was ...; sein ~r Sohn (inf) one of his sons; weder der ~ noch der andere neither (one) of them; die ~n sagen so, die anderen gerade das Gegenteil some (people) say one thing and others or some say just the opposite; jdm für alle, alle für ~n (Prov) all for one and one for all (Prov); dumm/geschickt etc wie nur ~r (dated) thick/skilful etc as they come (inf); das ist ~r! (inf) he's a (right) one! (inf); du bist mir vielleicht ~! (inf) you're a fine or right one (inf); sieh mal ~r an! (iro) well what do you know! (inf), surprise, surprise! (inf); alles in ~m abmachen to do everything in one go; in ~m fort, in ~r Tour (inf) non-stop; siehe **andere(r,s)**.

(b) (man) one (form), you. und das soll ~r glauben! (inf) and we're/you're meant to believe that!; wie kann ~r nur so unklug sein! how could anybody be so stupid!; wenn ~m so etwas gegeben wird if such a thing is given (to) one (form) or (to) you.

(c) ~s (auch eins) one thing; ~s gefällt mir nicht an ihm (there's) one thing I don't like about him; ~s sag' ich dir I'll tell you one thing; noch ~s! another one!; (Lied etc) more!; noch ~s, bevor ich's vergesse: (there's) something else or one other thing before I forget; es kam ~s nach dem or zum anderen it was (just) one thing after another; es läuft alles auf ~s hinaus, es kommt alles auf ~s heraus it all comes to the same (thing) in the end.

(d) (inf) sich (dat) ~n genehmigen to have a quick one (inf) or drink; jdm ~ kleben to thump sb one (inf); siehe **abbrechen**.

Einer m -s, - (a) (Math) unit. (b) (Ruderboot) single scull. Weltmeister im ~ world champion in the single sculls.

Einerkajak m single seater or one-man canoe or kayak; (Disziplin) single kayak or canoe.

einerlei adj inv (a) pred (gleichgültig) all the same. das ist mir ganz ~ it's all the same or all one to me; was du machst ist mir ~ it's all the same to me what you do; ~, ob er kommt no matter whether he comes or not; ~, was/wer ... it doesn't matter what/who ...

(b) Stoff von ~ Farbe self-coloured material; sie kocht immer nur ~ Essen she always cooks the same kind or sort of food; es gab für alle nur ~ zu essen everyone had to eat the same thing.

Einerlei nt -s, no pl monotony.

einerseits adv ~ ... andererseits ... on the one hand ... on the other hand ...

Einerstelle f (Math) unit (place).

einesteils adv ~ ... ander(e)nteils ... on the one hand ... on the other hand.

einexerzieren* vt sep (Mil, fig) to practise, to do drill in. jdm etw ~ to drill sb in sth.

einfach 1 adj (a) simple; Mensch ordinary; Essen plain.

(b) (nicht doppelt) Knoten, Schleife simple; Fahrkarte single; Fahrt one-way, single; Rockfalten knife; Buchführung single-entry. einmal ~! (im Bus etc) one (ordinary) single; das ist nicht so ~ zu verstehen that is not so easy to understand or so easily understood.

2 *adv* (a) simply. ~ **gefaltet** folded once.

(b) (*verstärkend: geradezu*) simply, just. ~ **gemein** downright mean; **das ist doch** ~ **dumm** that's (just) plain stupid.

Einfachheit *f siehe adj* simplicity; ordinariness; plainness. **der** ~ **halber** for the sake of simplicity.

einfädeln *sep* 1 *vt* (a) *Nadel, Faden* to thread (*in* +*acc* through); *Nähmaschine* to thread up. (b) (*inf*) *Intrige, Plan etc* to set up (*inf*). 2 *vr* **sich in eine Verkehrskolonne** ~ to filter into a stream of traffic.

einfahren *sep irreg* 1 *vi* (a) *aux sein* (*Zug, Schiff*) to come in (*in* +*acc* -to); (*Hunt: Fuchs, Dachs etc*) to go to earth. **in die Grube/den Schacht** ~ (*Min*) to go down (to the face); **auf Bahnsteig 2 fährt der Zug aus München ein** the train from Munich is arriving at *or* coming in at platform 2.

(b) (*inf: essen*) to tuck in.

2 *vt* (a) (*kaputtfahren*) *Mauer, Zaun* to knock down.

(b) *Ernte* to bring in.

(c) *Fahrgestell, Periskop* to retract.

(d) (*ans Fahren etc gewöhnen*) to break in; *Wagen* to run in (*Brit*), to break in (*US*). „**wird eingefahren**" "running in" (*Brit*), "being broken in" (*US*).

(e) *Verluste* to make; *Gewinne auch* to bring in.

3 *vr* to get used to driving. **ich muß mich erst mit dem neuen Auto** ~ I have to get used to (driving) the new car; **das hat sich so eingefahren** (*fig*) it has just become a habit; **die Sache hat sich gut eingefahren** (*fig*) things have settled down quite well; *siehe* **eingefahren**.

Einfahrsignal *nt* (*Rail*) home signal.

Einfahrt *f* (a) *no pl* (*das Einfahren*) entry (*in* +*acc* to); (*Min*) descent. **Vorsicht bei (der)** ~ **des Zuges!** stand well back, the train is arriving; **der Schnellzug hat** ~ **auf Gleis 3** the express is arriving at platform 3; **der Zug hat noch keine** ~ the train can't enter the station.

(b) (*Eingang*) entrance; (~*sstraße zu Autobahn*) sliproad; (*Tor~*) entry; (*Hunt*) tunnel.

Einfahrt(s)-: ~**gleis** *nt* entrance track; ~**signal** *nt siehe* **Einfahrsignal**.

Einfall *m* (a) (*fig*) (*plötzlicher Gedanke*) idea; (*Grille, Laune*) notion. **jdn auf den** ~ **bringen, etw zu tun** to give sb the idea of doing sth; **auf den** ~ **kommen, etw zu tun** to get the idea of doing sth; **es war ein bloßer** *or* **nur so ein** ~ it was just an idea; **er hat** ~**e wie ein altes Haus** (*hum inf*) he has some weird ideas.

(b) (*Mil*) invasion (*in* +*acc of*).

(c) (*des Lichts*) incidence (*spec*). **je nach (dem)** ~ **des Lichts** according to how the light falls.

(d) (*liter*) (*der Nacht*) fall; (*des Winters*) onset. **vor** ~ **der Nacht** before nightfall.

einfallen *vi sep irreg aux sein* (a) to collapse, to cave in; (*Gesicht, Wangen*) to become sunken *or* haggard; *siehe* **eingefallen**.

(b) (*eindringen*) **in ein Land** ~ to invade a country; **in die feindlichen Reihen** ~ to penetrate the enemy lines; **Wölfe sind in die Schafherde eingefallen** (*liter*) wolves fell upon the flock of sheep (*liter*).

(c) (*liter*) (*Nacht*) to fall; (*Winter*) to set in.

(d) (*Lichtstrahlen*) to fall, to be incident (*spec*); (*in ein Zimmer etc*) to come in (*in* +*acc* -to).

(e) (*Hunt: Federwild*) to come in, to settle.

(f) (*mitsingen, mitreden*) to join in; (*einsetzen: Chor, Stimmen*) to come in; (*dazwischenreden*) to break in (*in* +*acc* on).

(g) (*Gedanke*) **jdm** ~ to occur to sb; **das ist mir nicht eingefallen** I didn't think of that, that didn't occur to me; **mir fällt nichts ein, was ich schreiben kann** I can't think of anything to write; **jetzt fällt mir ein, wie/warum ...** I've just thought of how/why ..., it's just occurred to me how/why ...; **ihm fällt immer eine Ausrede ein** he can always think of an excuse; **das fällt mir nicht im Traum ein!** I wouldn't dream of it!; **es ist mir nie eingefallen zu glauben, daß ...** it would never have occurred to me to think that ..., I would never have dreamt of thinking that ...; **hast du dir etwas** ~ **lassen?** have you had any ideas?, have you thought of anything?; **da mußt du dir schon etwas anderes/Besseres** ~ **lassen!** you'll really have to think of something else/better; **wie es ihm gerade einfällt** just as he likes, just as the fancy *or* mood takes him; **was fällt Ihnen ein!** what are you thinking of!

(h) (*in Erinnerung kommen*) **jdm** ~ to come to sb; **dabei fällt mir mein Onkel ein, der ...** that reminds me of my uncle, who ...; **es fällt mir jetzt nicht ein** I can't think of it *or* it won't come to me at the moment; **es wird Ihnen schon wieder** ~ it will come back to you.

Einfalls-: **e~los** *adj* unimaginative; ~**losigkeit** *f* unimaginativeness; **e~reich** *adj* imaginative; ~**reichtum** *m* imaginativeness; ~**tor** *nt* gateway; ~**winkel** *m* (*Phys*) angle of incidence.

Einfalt *f -, no pl* (*Arglosigkeit*) simplicity, naivety; (*Dummheit*) simple-mindedness, simpleness.

einfältig *adj siehe* **Einfalt** simple, naive; simple(-minded).

Einfältigkeit *f* simple-mindedness, simpleness.

Einfaltspinsel *m* (*inf*) simpleton.

Einfamilienhaus *nt* detached family house.

einfangen *vt sep irreg* (*lit, fig*) to catch, to capture.

einfärben *vt sep* (a) *Stoff, Haar* to dye. (b) (*Typ*) *Druckwalze* to ink.

einfarbig, einfärbig (*Aus*) *adj* all one colour; (*Tex*) self-coloured.

einfassen *vt sep* (a) (*umsäumen*) *Beet, Grab* to border, to edge; *Kleid, Naht, Knopfloch* to trim.

(b) **ein Grundstück (mit einem Zaun/einer Mauer/Hecke)** ~ to put a fence/wall/hedge *etc* round a plot of land,

to fence/wall/hedge a plot of land round.

(c) *Edelstein* to set (*mit in*); *Bild* to mount; *Quelle* to put a wall round.

Einfassung *f siehe vt* (a) border, edging; trimming. (b) fence; wall; hedge. (c) setting; mount; wall.

einfetten *vt sep* to grease; *Leder, Schuhe* to dubbin; *Haut, Gesicht* to cream, to rub cream into.

einfeuern *vi sep* (*inf*) (*Feuer anmachen*) to get a fire going.

einfinden *vr sep irreg* to come; (*eintreffen*) to arrive; (*zu Prüfung etc*) to present oneself. **ich bitte alle, sich pünktlich in meinem Büro einzufinden** I would ask you all to be in my office punctually; **ich werde mich also um 10 Uhr bei euch** ~ I'll be *or* arrive at your place at 10 o'clock.

einflechten *vt sep irreg* *Band, Blumen* to twine; (*fig: ins Gespräch etc*) to work in (*in* +*acc* -to), to introduce (*in* +*acc* in, into). **darf ich an dieser Stelle kurz** ~, **daß ...** I would just like to say at this point that ...; **in das Buch sind viele witzige Anekdoten eingeflochten** many amusing anecdotes have been woven into the book.

einflicken *vt sep* *Stoff* to insert; (*fig: ins Gespräch etc*) to work or cobble (*inf*) in. **in eine Hose ein Stück** ~ to put a patch on *or* to patch a pair of trousers.

einfliegen *sep irreg* 1 *vt* (a) *Flugzeug* to test-fly. (b) *Proviant, Truppen* to fly in (*in* +*acc* -to). (c) *Verluste* to make; *Gewinne auch* to bring in. 2 *vi aux sein* to fly in (*in* +*acc* -to).

einfließen *vi sep irreg aux sein* to flow in; (*Gelder auch*) to pour in; (*Wasser auch*) to run in; (*fig*) to have some influence (*in* +*acc* on), to leave its mark (*in* +*acc* on). **er ließ nebenbei** ~, **daß er Professor sei** he let it drop that he was a professor.

einflößen *vt sep* **jdm etw** ~ to pour sth down sb's throat; *Medizin auch* to give sb sth; *Ehrfurcht, Mut etc* to instil sth into sb, to instil sb with a sense of sth.

Einflug *m* **er beobachtete das Flugzeug beim** ~ he watched the plane coming in; **er wurde beim** ~ **in Feindgebiet abgeschossen** he was shot down when flying into enemy territory.

Einflugschneise *f* (*Aviat*) flight *or* landing path.

Einfluß *m* (a) influence. **unter dem** ~ **von jdm/etw** under the influence of sb/sth; **unter dem** ~ **von Alkohol** under the influence (of alcohol); ~ **auf jdn haben/ausüben** to have/exert an influence on sb; ~ **nehmen** to bring an influence to bear; **das Wetter steht unter dem** ~ **eines atlantischen Tiefs** the weather is being affected *or* influenced by an Atlantic depression; **auf die Entscheidung hat es keinen** ~ it has no influence *or* bearing on the decision, it won't influence the decision; **darauf habe ich keinen** ~ I can't influence that, I've no influence over that.

(b) (*lit: das Einfließen*) (*von Luft, fig*) influx; (*von Gas, Abwässern*) inflow.

Einfluß-: ~**bereich** *m*, ~**gebiet** *nt* sphere of influence; **England liegt im** ~**bereich eines atlantischen Tiefs** England is being affected by an Atlantic depression; **e~los** *adj* uninfluential; ~**losigkeit** *f* lack of influence; ~**nahme** *f -, (rare)* ~ exertion of influence (*gen* by); **e~reich** *adj* influential; ~**sphäre** *f siehe* ~**bereich**.

einflüstern *vt sep* **jdm etw** ~ to whisper sth to sb; (*fig*) to insinuate sth to sb.

Einflüsterung *f* (*fig*) insinuation; (*liter: der Wollust etc*) dictate, prompting.

einfordern *vt sep Schulden* to demand payment of, to call (in).

einförmig *adj* uniform; (*eintönig*) monotonous.

Einförmigkeit *f siehe adj* uniformity; monotony.

einfressen *vr sep irreg* to eat in (*in* +*acc* -to). **der Haß hatte sich tief in ihn eingefressen** hate had eaten deep into his heart.

einfrieden *vt sep* (*geh*) to enclose.

Einfriedung *f* (*geh*) fence; wall; hedge.

einfrieren *sep irreg* 1 *vi aux sein* to freeze; (*Wasserleitung, Schiff*) to freeze up. **im Eis eingefroren** frozen into the ice; **die Beziehungen** ~ **lassen** to suspend relations. 2 *vt* (*lit, fig*) *Nahrungsmittel, Löhne etc* to freeze; (*Pol*) *Beziehungen* to suspend. **sich** ~ **lassen** to allow oneself to be put into deep-freeze.

Einfrierung *f* (*fig*) (*von Löhnen etc*) freezing; (*von Beziehungen*) suspension.

einfrosten *vt sep* *Gemüse, Fleisch* to freeze.

Einfrostung *f* freezing.

einfügen *sep* 1 *vt* *Steine, Maschinenteile* to fit (*in* +*acc* into); (*nachtragen*) to insert (*in* +*acc* in), to add (*in* +*acc* into). **darf ich an dieser Stelle** ~, **daß ...** may I add at this point that ...

2 *vr* to fit in (*in* +*acc* -to); (*sich anpassen*) to adapt (*in* +*acc* to); (*Haus in Umgebung etc*) to fit in (*in* +*acc* with).

Einfügung *f* insertion, addition.

einfühlen *vr sep* **sich in jdn** ~ to empathize with sb; (*Theat*) to feel oneself into (the role of) sb; **er kann sich gut in andere Leute** ~ he's good at putting himself in other people's shoes (*inf*) or places *or* at empathizing with other people; **sich in etw** (*acc*) ~ to understand sth; **sich in die Atmosphäre des 17. Jahrhunderts** ~ to get into *or* project oneself into the atmosphere of the 17th century; **sich in ein Gedicht** ~ to experience a poem.

einfühlsam *adj* *Interpretation* sensitive; *Mensch auch* understanding, empath(et)ic (*form*).

Einfühlung *f* understanding (*in* +*acc* of); (*in einen Menschen auch*) empathy (*in* +*acc* with); (*einer Interpretation*) sensitivity.

Einfühlungsvermögen *nt* capacity for understanding, empathy. **ein Buch mit großem** ~ **interpretieren** to interpret a book with a great deal of sensitivity.

Einfuhr *f -, -en* import; (*das Einführen auch*) importing.

Einfuhr- *in cpds* import; ~**artikel** *m* import; **ein** ~**artikel sein** to be imported.

einführen *sep* 1 *vt* (a) (*hineinstecken*) to insert, to introduce (*in* +*acc* into).

(b) *(bekannt machen)* to introduce *(in + acc* into*)*; *(Comm)* Firma, Artikel to establish. **jdn in sein Amt/seine Arbeit** ~ to install sb (in office)/introduce sb to his work; **jdn bei Hofe** ~ to present sb at court; **~de Worte** introductory words, words of introduction.

(c) *(als Neuerung)* to introduce, to bring in; *neue Mode* to set, to start; *Sitte* to start.

(d) *(Comm)* Waren, *Devisen* to import.

2 *vr* to introduce oneself. **sich gut/nicht gut** ~ to make a good/bad (initial) impression, to get off to a good/bad start *(inf)*.

Einfuhr-: ~**genehmigung** *f* import permit; ~**hafen** *m* port of importation; ~**kontingent** *nt* import quota; ~**land** *nt* importing country; ~**sperre** *f*, ~**stopp** *m* ban on imports; **eine ~sperre für etw a** ban on the import of sth.

Einführung *f* introduction *(in + acc* to*)*; *(Amts~)* installation; *(das Hineinstecken)* insertion *(in + acc* into*)*; *(bei Hof)* presentation.

Einführungs- in *cpds* introductory.

Einfuhr-: ~**verbot** *nt siehe* ~**sperre**; ~**zoll** *m* import duty.

einfüllen *vt sep* to pour in. **etw in Flaschen/Säcke/Fässer** ~ to put sth into bottles/sacks/barrels, to bottle/sack/barrel sth.

Einfüll-: ~**öffnung** *f* opening; ~**stutzen** *m* *(Aut)* filler pipe.

einfurchen *sep* **1** *vt* to furrow. **2** *vr* **sich in etw** *(acc)* ~ to carve itself deep into sth.

Eingabe *f* **(a)** *(form: Gesuch)* petition *(an + acc* to*)*. **(b)** *(von Medizin)* administration; *(in Computer)* input.

Eingabe-: ~**frist** *f* time limit for the filing of petitions; ~**termin** *m* final date for the filing of petitions.

Eingang *m* **(a)** entrance *(in + acc* to*)*; *(Zutritt, Aufnahme)* entry. „**kein ~!**" "no entrance"; **jdm/sich ~ in etw** *(acc)*/**zu etw verschaffen** to gain entry into/to sth; **einer Sache** *(dat)* ~ **verschaffen** to open the door for sth, to introduce sth; **in etw** *(acc)* ~ **finden** to find one's way into sth.

(b) *(Comm: Waren~, Post~)* delivery; *(Erhalt)* receipt. **wir bestätigen den** ~ **Ihres Schreibens vom ...** we acknowledge receipt of your communication of the ...; **die Waren werden beim** ~ **gezählt** the goods are counted on delivery; **den** ~ *or* **die** **~e bearbeiten** to deal with the in-coming post *or* mail.

(c) *(Beginn)* start, beginning. **zum** ~ **möchte ich bemerken ...** I would like to start by saying ...

eingängig *adj* Melodie, Spruch catchy; *Theorie* neat.

eingangs **1** *adv* at the start *or* beginning. **2** *prep + gen (form)* at the start *or* beginning of.

Eingangs-: ~**bestätigung** *f* *(Comm)* acknowledgement of receipt; ~**buch** *nt* *(Comm)* receipt book, book of receipts; ~**datum** *nt* date of delivery; ~**formel** *f* *(Jur)* preamble; *(in Brief)* opening phrase; ~**halle** *f* entrance hall; ~**pforte** *f* *(lit, fig)* gateway; ~**stempel** *m* *(Comm)* date stamp; **mit einem** ~**stempel versehen** stamped with the date of receipt; ~**tor** *nt* entrance, main gate; ~**tür** *f* entrance, door; ~**vermerk** *m* *(Comm)* notice of receipt; ~**zoll** *m siehe* Einfuhrzoll.

eingeben *vt sep irreg* **(a)** *(verabreichen)* to give. **jdm das Essen** ~ to feed sb.

(b) *(einspeichern)* **dem Computer etw** ~ to feed sth into the computer.

(c) *(dated: einreichen)* Gesuch *etc* to submit *(an + acc* to*)*. **jdn zur Beförderung** ~ to recommend sb for promotion.

(d) *(liter)* Gedanken *etc* **jdm etw** ~ to inspire sb with sth; **das hat uns Gott eingegeben** it comes from God.

eingebettet **1** *ptp of* einbetten. **2** *adj* **in** *or* **zwischen Wäldern/Hügeln** ~ nestling among the woods/hills.

eingebildet **1** *ptp of* einbilden. **2** *adj* **(a)** *(hochmütig)* conceited. **(b)** *(imaginär)* imaginary; *Schwangerschaft* false. **ein** ~**er Kranker** a hypochondriac.

Eingebildetheit *f* conceit.

eingeboren *adj* *(einheimisch)* native; *(angeboren)* innate, inborn *(dat* in*)*. **Gottes** ~**er Sohn** the only begotten Son of God.

Eingeborenensprache *f* native language.

Eingeborene(r) *mf decl as adj* native *(auch hum)*.

Eingebung *f* inspiration.

eingedenk *(old, liter)* **1** *prep + gen* bearing in mind, remembering. ~ **dessen, daß ...** bearing in mind *or* remembering that ... **2** *adj pred* **einer Sache** *(gen)* ~ **sein** to bear sth in mind, to be mindful of sth *(old, liter)*.

eingefahren **1** *ptp of* einfahren. **2** *adj* Verhaltensweise well-worn. **sein Leben bewegt sich in den ~en Gleisen bürgerlicher Tradition** his life is stuck in the rut of bourgeois tradition; **die Diskussion bewegte sich in ~en Gleisen** the discussion stayed in the same old groove *or* covered the same old well-worn topics.

eingefallen **1** *ptp of* einfallen. **2** *adj* Wangen hollow, sunken; *Augen* sunken, deep-set; *Gesicht* haggard, gaunt.

eingefleischt *adj* **(a)** *attr* *(überzeugt)* confirmed; *(unverbesserlich)* dyed-in-the-wool. ~**er Junggeselle** *(hum)* confirmed bachelor. **(b)** *(zur zweiten Natur geworden)* ingrained, deep-rooted.

eingefuchst *adj (inf)* ~ **sein** to have it all at one's fingertips; **die Kinder sind auf den Lehrer** ~ the children really know the teacher's little ways.

eingehen *sep irreg aux sein* **1** *vi* **(a)** *(old: eintreten)* to enter *(in + acc* into*)*; *(Aufnahme finden: Wort, Sitte)* to be adopted *(in + acc* in*)*. **in die Geschichte** ~ to go down in (the annals of) history; **in die Unsterblichkeit** ~ to attain immortality; **zur ewigen Ruhe** *or* **in den ewigen Frieden** ~ to go to (one's) rest.

(b) **etw geht jdm ein** *(wird verstanden)* sb grasps *or* understands sth; **wann wird es dir endlich ~, daß ...?** when will it finally sink in *or* when will you finally understand that ...?; **es will mir einfach nicht ~, wie ...** it's beyond me how ..., I just cannot understand how ...

(c) *(wirken)* **diese Musik geht einem leicht ein** this music is very catchy; **diese Worte gingen ihm glatt ein** these words were music to his ears.

(d) *(fig: einfließen)* to leave its mark, to have some influence *(in + acc* on*)*. **die verschiedensten Einflüsse sind in das Werk eingegangen** there have been the most diverse influences on his work.

(e) *(ankommen)* *(Briefe, Waren etc)* to arrive, to be received; *(Meldung, Spenden, Bewerbungen auch)* to come in. **~de Post/ Waren** incoming mail/goods; **eingegangene Post/Spenden** mail/donations received.

(f) *(einlaufen: Stoff)* to shrink.

(g) *(sterben: Tiere, Pflanze)* to die *(an + dat* of*)*; *(inf: Firma etc)* to fold. **bei dieser Hitze/Kälte geht man ja ein!** *(inf)* this heat/cold is just too much *(inf)* or is killing *(inf)*; **da/bei diesem Geschäft bist du ja schön eingegangen!** *(sl)* you really came unstuck there/with that deal, didn't you? *(inf)*; **bei dem Boxkampf ist er mächtig eingegangen** *(sl)* he got a clobbering in the fight *(inf)*.

(h) **auf etw** *(acc)* ~ *(behandeln)* Frage, Punkt *etc* to go into sth; **darauf gehe ich noch näher ein** I will go into that in more detail; **niemand ging auf meine Frage/mich ein** nobody took any notice of my question/me.

(i) *(sich widmen, einfühlen)* **auf jdn/etw** ~ to give (one's) time and attention to sb/sth; **wie die Mutter auf die Fragen des Kindes eingeht** the way the mother gives the child's questions her time and attention.

(j) *(zustimmen)* **auf einen Vorschlag/Plan** ~ to agree to *or* fall in with a suggestion/plan.

2 *vt* *(abmachen, abschließen)* to enter into; *Risiko* to take; *Wette* to make. **er gewinnt, darauf gehe ich jede Wette ein** I bet you anything he wins; **einen Vergleich** ~ *(Jur)* to reach a settlement.

eingehend *adj* *(ausführlich)* detailed; *(gründlich)* thorough; *Bericht, Studien, Untersuchungen auch* in-depth *attr*.

eingekeilt *adj* hemmed in; *Auto auch* boxed in; *(fig)* trapped.

Eingemachte(s) *nt decl as adj* bottled fruit and vegetables; *(Marmelade)* preserves *pl*.

eingemeinden* *vt sep* to incorporate *(in + acc, nach* into*)*.

Eingemeindung *f* incorporation.

eingenommen **1** *ptp of* einnehmen. **2** *adj* **für jdn/etw** ~ **sein** to be taken with sb/sth, to be enamoured of sb/sth; **gegen jdn/etw** ~ **sein** to be prejudiced *or* biased against sb/sth; **er ist sehr von sich** *(dat)* **selbst** ~ he thinks a lot of himself, he really fancies himself.

Eingenommenheit *f* partiality *(für, von* to*)*.

eingeschlechtig *adj* *(Bot)* unisexual, diclinous *(form)*.

eingeschlechtlich *adj* Gruppe single-sex.

eingeschnappt **1** *ptp of* einschnappen. **2** *adj (inf)* cross. ~ **sein** to be in a huff; **sie ist immer gleich** ~ she always gets into a huff.

eingeschossig ['aɪŋəʃɔsɪç] *adj* Haus single-storey.

eingeschränkt **1** *ptp of* einschränken. **2** *adj (eingeengt)* restricted, limited; *(sparsam)* careful. **in ~en Verhältnissen leben** to live in straitened circumstances.

Eingeschränktheit *f* restriction; *(finanziell)* straitened circumstances *pl*.

eingeschrieben **1** *ptp of* einschreiben. **2** *adj* Mitglied, Brief registered.

eingeschworen *adj* confirmed; *Gemeinschaft* close. **auf etw** *(acc)* ~ **sein** to swear by sth; **auf eine Politik** ~ **sein** to be committed to a policy; **er ist auf diese Art von Malerei** ~ he is a great fan of this type of painting; **die beiden sind aufeinander** ~ the two of them are very close (to one another).

eingesessen *adj* Einwohner, Familie old-established; *Firma auch* long-established. **die Firma/Familie ist dort seit Generationen** ~ the firm/family has been (established) there for generations; **die E~en** the old established inhabitants/families/firms.

Eingesottene(s) *nt decl as adj (Aus)* bottled fruit.

eingespannt **1** *ptp of* einspannen. **2** *adj* busy.

eingespielt **1** *ptp of* einspielen. **2** *adj* Mannschaft, Team (well-)adjusted to playing/working together. **aufeinander** ~ **sein** to be used to one another.

eingesprengt **1** *ptp of* einsprengen. **2** *adj (geh)* scattered.

eingestand(e)nermaßen *adv* admittedly.

Eingeständnis *nt* admission, confession.

eingestehen* *vt sep irreg* to admit, to confess. **sie hat den Diebstahl eingestanden** she admitted (to) *or* confessed to the theft; **sich** *(dat)* ~, **daß ...** to admit to oneself that ...

eingestellt **1** *ptp of* einstellen.

2 *adj* **materialistisch/fortschrittlich** ~ **sein** to be materialistically/progressively minded *or* materialistic/progressive; **links/rechts** ~ **sein** to have leanings to the left/right; **die links/rechts E~en** leftists, left-/right-wingers; **wer so** ~ **ist wie er** anyone who thinks as he does, anyone like him; **gegen jdn** ~ **sein** to be set against sb; **ich bin im Moment nicht auf Besuch** ~ I'm not prepared for visitors; **wir sind nur auf kleinere Reisegesellschaften** ~ we can only cater for small parties; **auf Export** ~ **sein** to be geared to exports *or* tailored to the export market.

eingestrichen *adj (Mus)*: **das ~e C/A** middle C/the A above middle C.

eingetragen **1** *ptp of* eintragen. **2** *adj* Mitglied, Warenzeichen, Verein registered.

Eingeweide *nt* **-s, -** *usu pl* entrails *pl*, innards *pl*. **der Schreck fuhr mir bis in die** ~ *(liter)* my blood froze.

Eingeweidebruch *m (Med)* hernia.

Eingeweihte(r) *mf decl as adj* initiate. **seine Lyrik ist nur ~n verständlich** his poetry can only be understood by the initiated; **ein paar** ~ a chosen few.

eingewöhnen* vr sep to settle down or in (**in** +dat in).

Eingewöhnung f settling down or in.

eingewurzelt 1 ptp of **einwurzeln. 2** adj deep-rooted, deep-seated. **tief bei jdm** ~ **sein** to be deeply ingrained in sb.

Eingezogene(r) mf decl as adj (Mil) conscript, draftee (US).

eingießen vt sep irreg (hineinschütten) to pour in (**in** +acc -to); (einschenken) to pour (out). **darf ich Ihnen noch Kaffee** ~? can I give you or pour you some more coffee?; **bitte gießen Sie sich** (dat) **noch ein!** do pour yourself some more.

eingipsen vt sep Arm, Bein to put in plaster; Dübel etc to plaster in (**in** +acc -to).

Einglas nt (dated) monocle.

eingleisig adj single-track. **der Zug/die Straßenbahn fährt hier nur** ~ the railway/tram-line is only single-track here; **er denkt sehr** ~ (fig) he's completely single-minded.

Eingleisigkeit f (fig) single-mindedness.

eingliedern sep 1 vt Firma, Gebiet to incorporate (dat into, with); jdn to integrate (**in** +acc into); (einordnen) to include (**unter** +acc under, in). **2** vr to fit in (dat, **in** +acc -to, in), to integrate oneself (dat, **in** +acc into) (form).

Eingliederung f (von Firma, Gebiet) incorporation; (von Behinderten, von Straffälligen) integration.

eingraben sep irreg **1** vt Pfahl, Pflanze, Krallen to dig in (**in** +acc -to); (vergraben) Schatz, Leiche to bury (**in** +acc in). **eine Inschrift in Granit** ~ (geh) to carve an inscription into granite.
2 vr to dig oneself in (auch Mil). **der Fluß hat sich ins Gestein eingegraben** the river carved itself a channel in the rock; **dieses Erlebnis hat sich seinem Gedächtnis eingegraben** this experience has carved itself on his memory; **die Krallen gruben sich ins Fleisch des Opfers ein** the claws dug into the victim's flesh.

eingravieren* vt sep to engrave (**in** +acc in).

eingreifen vi sep irreg (a) (Tech) to mesh (**in** +acc with). (b) (einschreiten, Mil) to intervene. **in jds Rechte** (acc) ~ to intrude (up)on sb's rights; **wenn nicht sofort ein Arzt eingreift,** ... without immediate medical intervention ...; **E~** intervention.

eingrenzen vt sep (lit) to enclose; (fig) Problem, Thema to delimit, to circumscribe; (verringern) to narrow or cut down.

Eingrenzung f siehe vt enclosure; delimitation, circumscription; narrowing down.

Eingriff m (a) (Med) operation. **ein verbotener** ~ an illegal abortion. (b) (Übergriff) intervention. **ein** ~ **in jds Rechte/Privatsphäre** an intrusion (up)on sb's rights/privacy.

Eingriffsmöglichkeit f possibility of intervention.

eingruppieren* vt sep to group (**in** +acc in).

Eingruppierung f grouping.

einhacken vi sep to peck (**auf** +acc at). **auf jdn** ~ (fig) to pick on sb.

einhaken sep 1 vt to hook in (**in** +acc -to). **2** vi (inf: Punkt aufgreifen) to intervene; (in Unterhaltung auch) to break in. **wenn ich an diesem Punkt vielleicht** ~ **darf** if I might just take up that point. **3** vr sie hakte sich bei ihm ein she put or slipped her arm through his; **eingehakt gehen** to walk arm in arm.

Einhalt m -(e)s, no pl jdm/einer Sache ~ **gebieten** to stop or halt sb/sth; einem Mißbrauch auch to put an end or a stop to sth.

einhalten sep irreg **1** vt (a) (beachten) to keep; Spielregeln auch to obey; Diät, Vertrag auch to keep to; Verpflichtungen to carry out. **die Zeit** ~ to keep to time or schedule; **den Kurs** ~ (Aviat) to maintain (its) course, to stay on course; **er hält seine Zahlungsverpflichtungen immer pünktlich ein** he's always prompt about payments.
(b) (old: aufhalten) Schwungrad to stop.
(c) (Sew) to gather.
2 vi (geh: aufhören) to stop or halt; (innehalten) to pause. **halt ein! stop!**
(b) (dial: Harn, Stuhlgang zurückhalten) to wait.

Einhaltung f siehe vt (a) keeping (gen of); obedience (gen to); keeping (gen to); carrying out (gen of). **ich werde ihn zur** ~ **des Vertrages zwingen** I will force him to keep (to) the contract.

einhämmern sep 1 vt Nagel etc to hammer in (**in** +acc -to); Inschrift etc to chisel in (**in** +acc -to), to engrave (**in** +acc into). **jdm etw** ~ (fig) to hammer or drum sth into sb.
2 vi **auf etw** (acc) ~to hammer on sth; **auf jdn** ~ (lit, fig) to pound sb; **die laute Musik hämmerte auf uns ein** the loud music pounded in our ears; **die Propaganda hämmerte auf das Volk ein** the people were pounded by propaganda.

einhamstern vt sep (inf) to collect.

einhandeln vt sep (a) (gegen, für for) to trade, to swop, to exchange. (b) (bekommen) sich (dat) **etw** ~ (inf) to get sth.

einhändig adj one-handed.

einhändigen vt sep (form) to hand in, to submit (form).

Einhändigung f (form) handing in, submission (form).

Einhandsegler m (a) single-handed yachtsman. **als** ~ **um die Welt fahren** to sail single-handed round the world. (b) (Boot) single-handed yacht, single-hander.

einhängen sep 1 vt Tür to hang; Fenster to put in; (Telec) Hörer to put down; Lampe, Girlande to hang up. **er hat eingehängt** he's hung up. **2** vr sich bei jdm ~ to slip or put one's arm through sb's; **sie gingen eingehängt** they walked arm in arm.

einhauchen vt sep (liter) jdm/einer Sache **etw** ~ to breathe sth into sb/sth; einer Sache (dat) **neues Leben** ~ to breathe new life into sth, to bring new life to sth.

einhauen sep irreg **1** vt (a) Nagel etc to knock or drive or bash (**inf**) in (**in** +acc -to).
(b) (zertrümmern) to smash or bash (inf) in.
(c) (einmeißeln) Kerbe to cut in (**in** +acc -to); Inschrift etc auch to carve in (**in** +acc -to).
2 vi (a) **auf jdn** ~ to lay into sb, to go for sb; **auf etw** (acc) ~ to go at sth.

(b) (inf: beim Essen) to tuck or pitch in (inf).

einheben vt sep irreg (a) (einhängen) Tür to hang. (b) (esp Aus) Steuern to levy; Geld to collect.

Einhebung f (esp Aus) (von Steuern) levying; (von Geldern) collection.

einheften vt sep (a) Buchseiten to stitch in; (mit Heftmaschine) to staple in; (Sew) Futter to tack in. (b) (einordnen) Akten etc to file.

einhegen vt sep to enclose.

einheimisch adj Mensch, Tier, Pflanze native, indigenous; Produkt, Industrie, Mannschaft local.

Einheimische(r) mf decl as adj local.

einheimsen vt sep (inf) to collect; Erfolg, Ruhm auch to walk off with; Geld auch to rake in (inf). **er hat den Ruhm für sich allein eingeheimst** he took the credit himself.

Einheirat f marriage (**in** +acc into).

einheiraten vi sep **in einen Betrieb** ~ to marry into a business.

Einheit f (a) (von Land etc, Einheitlichkeit) unity; (das Ganze) whole. **die drei** ~en (Liter) the three unities; **eine geschlossene** ~ **bilden** to form an integrated whole; ~ **von Forschung und Lehre** indivisibility of teaching and research. (b) (Mil, Sci) unit.

einheitlich adj (gleich) the same, uniform; (genormt) standard(ized); (in sich geschlossen) unified. ~ **gekleidet** dressed alike or the same; **wir müssen** ~ **vorgehen** we must act consistently with one another; **alle Spielplätze sind** ~ **gestaltet** all the playgrounds are built on the same lines; **die Pausenzeiten sind in allen Werken** ~ **geregelt** the times of breaks are laid down to be the same in all the works.

Einheitlichkeit f siehe adj uniformity; standardization; unity.

Einheits-: ~essen nt institution food; ~format nt standard format; ~front f (Pol) united front; (Volksfront) popular front; ~gewerkschaft f unified trade or labor (US) union; ~kleidung f uniform; ~kurzschrift f standard shorthand; ~liste f (Pol) single or unified list of candidates; ~partei f united party; **in einigen Staaten gibt es nur eine** ~partei in some countries there is only a single or only one political party; ~preis m standard price; ~schule f comprehensive (school); ~staat m (Pol) united state; ~tarif m standard tariff.

einheizen sep 1 vt to put the heating on. **bei dieser Kälte muß man tüchtig** ~ you have to have the heating going full blast in this cold weather; **jdm** (tüchtig) ~ (inf) (die Meinung sagen) to haul sb over the coals; (zu schaffen machen) to make things hot for sb; **er hat ganz schön eingeheizt** (fig inf) he's knocked back a few (inf).
2 vt Ofen to put on; Zimmer to heat (up).

einhelfen vi sep irreg (dial) to help out. **jdm** ~ to prompt sb, to help sb out.

einhellig adj unanimous.

Einhelligkeit f unanimity.

ein(h)er adv (Aus) siehe **herein.**

einher- pref (entlang) along; (hin und her) up and down. ~**reden** siehe **daherreden.**

einhin adv (Aus) siehe **hinein.**

einhöck(e)rig adj of Kamel one-humped.

einholen vt sep (a) (einziehen) Boot, Netz, Tau to pull or haul in; Fahne, Segel to lower, to take down.
(b) Rat, Gutachten, Erlaubnis to obtain. **bei jdm Rat** ~ to obtain sb's advice or advice from sb.
(c) (erreichen, nachholen) Laufenden to catch up; Vorsprung, Versäumtes, Zeit to make up; Verlust to make good.
(d) auch vi (dial) **einkaufen** to go shopping. **sie einkaufen.**

Einhol- (dial): ~netz nt string bag; ~tasche f shopping bag.

Einholung f (a) (von Fahne) lowering. (b) (von Rat, Gutachten etc) obtaining.

Einhorn nt (Myth, Astron) unicorn.

Einhufer m -s, - (Zool) solidungulate (spec).

einhufig adj solidungulate (spec).

einhüllen sep 1 vt Kind, Leichnam to wrap (up), to swathe (liter) (**in** +acc in). **in Nebel/Wolken eingehüllt** shrouded or enveloped in mist/clouds. **2** vr (geh) to wrap oneself up.

einhundert num (form) siehe **hundert.**

einhüten vi sep (N Ger) to keep house (bei for); (Kinder hüten) to babysit (bei for).

eini adv (Aus) siehe **hinein.**

einig adj (a) (geeint) united.
(b) (einer Meinung) agreed, in agreement (über +acc on, about, **in** +dat on). **ich weiß mich in dieser Sache mit ihm** ~ (geh) I know I am in agreement with him on this; **sich** (dat) **über etw** (acc) ~ **werden** to agree on sth; **darüber or darin sind wir uns** ~, **daß** ... we are agreed that ...; **wir werden schon miteinander** ~ **werden** we will manage to come to an agreement; **ich bin mir selbst noch nicht ganz** ~, **was** ... I am still somewhat undecided as to what ...; **Franz und Frieda sind sich** ~ (inf) Franz and Frieda have an understanding.

einige indef pron siehe **einige(r, s).**

einigeln vr sep (Mil) to take up a position of all-round defence; (fig) to hide (oneself) away.

einigemal adv a few times.

einigen 1 vt Volk etc to unite; Streitende to reconcile.
2 vr to reach (an) agreement (über +acc about). **sich über den Preis/eine gemeinsame Politik** ~ to reach agreement or to agree on the price/a common policy; **sich auf einen Kompromiß/Vergleich** ~ to agree to a compromise/settlement; **sich dahin** (gehend) ~, **daß** ... to agree that ...

Einiger m -s, - unifier.

einige(r, s) indef pron (a) sing (etwas) some; (ziemlich viel) (quite) some. **in** ~r **Entfernung** some distance away; **nach** ~r **Zeit** after a while or some time; **ich könnte dir** ~s **über ihn erzählen, was** ... I could tell you a thing or two about him that ...;

das wird ~s kosten that will cost something; **dazu ist noch ~s zu sagen** there are still one or two things to say about that; **dazu gehört schon ~s/~ Frechheit/~r Mut** that really takes something/that takes some cheek/some courage; **mit ~m guten Willen** (*mit Anstrengung*) with a bit of effort; **mit ~m guten Willen hätte der Richter ihn freisprechen können** the judge could have given him the benefit of the doubt and acquitted him; **mit ~m guten Willen kann man diese Pension als Hotel bezeichnen** if you're being generous about it you can call this guesthouse a hotel.

(b) *pl* some; (*mehrere auch*) several; (*ein paar auch*) a few. **mit ~n anderen** with several/a few others; **mit Ausnahme ~r weniger** with a few exceptions; **~ Male** several times; **~ hundert Menschen** a few hundred people; **~ Hunderte von Flaschen** hundreds of bottles, several hundred bottles; **an ~n Stellen** in some places; **in ~n Tagen** in a few days; **vor ~n Tagen** the other day, a few days ago.

einigermaßen 1 *adv* (*ziemlich*) rather, somewhat; (*vor adj*) fairly; (*ungefähr*) to some extent *or* degree. **ein ~ gutes Angebot** a fairly good offer, not a bad offer; **~ Bescheid wissen** to have a fair idea; **er hat die Prüfung so ~ geschafft** he did so-so in the exam; **wie geht's dir? — ~ how are you? — all right** *or* so-so *or* not too bad; **es ist ~ kalt heute** it's rather *or* a bit cold today.

2 *adj pred* (*inf: leidlich*) all right, fair, reasonable. **wie ist denn das Hotel? — na ja, ~ what's the hotel like? — oh, fair** *or* all right.

einiges *indef pron siehe* **einige(r, s).**

einiggehen *vi sep irreg aux sein* to agree, to be agreed (*in +dat* on). **ich gehe mit ihm darin einig, daß ...** I am agreed with him that ...; **wir gehen einig in der Überzeugung, daß ...** we are one in our conviction that ...

Einigkeit *f, no pl* (*Eintracht*) unity; (*Übereinstimmung*) agreement. **in diesem** *or* **über diesen Punkt herrschte** *or* **bestand ~** there was agreement on this point; **~ macht stark** (*Prov*) unity gives strength, strength through unity (*prov*).

Einigung *f* (a) (*Pol*) unification. (b) (*Übereinstimmung*) agreement; (*Jur: Vergleich*) settlement. **über etw** (*acc*) **~ erzielen** to come to *or* reach agreement on sth.

ein|impfen *vt sep jdm etw ~* (*lit*) to inject *or* inoculate sb with sth; **er hat seinen Kindern diese Ansichten eingeimpft** he dinned these ideas into his children.

einjagen *vt sep jdm Furcht/einen Schrecken ~** to frighten sb/to give sb a fright *or* a shock.

einjährig *adj Kind, Tier* one-year-old; *Pflanze* annual. **E~e** *pl* one-year-olds; **nach ~er Pause** after a break of one *or* a year; **~e Frist/Dauer** a period of one *or* a year.

Einjährige(r), **Einjährig-Freiwillige(r)** *m decl as adj* (*Mil Hist*) one-year army volunteer.

Einjährige(s) *nt decl as adj* (*old Sch*) = lower school certificate (*old*).

einkalkulieren* *vt sep* to reckon with *or* on; *Kosten* to include, to take into account.

Einkammersystem *nt* (*Pol*) single-chamber *or* unicameral (*form*) system.

einkapseln *sep* **1** *vt Tabletten* to encapsulate. **2** *vr* (*Med*) to encapsulate (*form*); (*fig*) to withdraw *or* go into one's shell.

einkassieren* *vt sep* (a) *Geld, Schulden* to collect. (b) (*inf: wegnehmen*) to take. **die Polizei hat den Dieb einkassiert** the police nabbed the criminal (*inf*); **er hat eine Ohrfeige einkassiert** he earned himself a clip on the ear.

einkasteln *vt sep* (*Aus, S Ger*) *Straftäter* to put away (*inf*), to lock up.

Einkauf *m* (a) (*das Einkaufen*) buying (*auch Comm*), purchase. **der Sommer ist die beste Zeit für den ~ von Kohlen** summer is the best time to buy *or* for buying (in) coal; **Einkäufe machen** to go shopping; **ich muß noch ein paar Einkäufe machen** I still have a few things to buy *or* a few purchases to make.

(b) (*Gekauftes*) purchase. **ein guter** *or* **vorteilhafter/ schlechter ~** a good/bad buy.

(c) *no pl* (*Comm: Abteilung*) buying (department).

(d) (*in Altersheim, Firma etc*) **durch den ~ in ein Seniorenheim** by buying oneself into an old people's home; **er versucht durch Einkäufe in diese Firma in Europa Fuß zu fassen** he is trying to get a foothold in Europe by buying up shares in this firm.

(e) (*Ftbl*) transfer.

einkaufen *sep* **1** *vt* to buy; *Vorräte* to buy (in). **2** *vi* to shop; (*Comm*) to buy, to do the buying. **~ gehen** to go shopping; **ich kaufe nur bei Müller ein** I only shop at Müllers. **3** *vr* to buy one's way (*in +acc* into).

Einkäufer *m* (*Comm*) buyer.

Einkaufs- *in cpds* shopping; **~bummel** *m* shopping spree; **einen ~bummel machen** to go on a shopping spree; **~genossenschaft** *f* consumers' co-operative society; **~leiter** *m* (*Comm*) chief buyer; **~netz** *nt* string bag, shopping net; **~preis** *m* wholesale price; **~quelle** *f* eine gute **~quelle für etw** a good place to buy sth; **~straße** *f* shopping street; **~tasche** *f* shopping bag; **~viertel** *nt* shopping area; **~wagen** *m* trolley; **~zentrum** *nt* shopping centre; **~zettel** *m* shopping list.

Einkehr *f -, no pl* (a) (*in Gasthaus*) stop. **in einem Gasthaus ~ halten** to (make a) stop at an inn. (b) (*geh: Besinnung*) self-examination, reflection. **bei sich ~ halten** to look into *or* search one's heart; **~ und Umkehr** (*geh*) reflection and renewal.

einkehren *vi sep aux sein* (a) (*in Gasthof*) to (make a) stop, to stop off (*in +dat* at); (*bei Freunden*) to call in (*bei* on). (b) (*Ruhe, Friede*) to come (*bei* to); (*Not, Sorge*) to come (*bei* upon, to). **wieder ~** to return (*bei* to).

einkeilen *vt sep siehe* **eingekeilt.**

einkellern *vt sep* to store in a cellar.

Einkellerungskartoffeln *pl* potatoes *pl* for storing over the winter.

einkerben *vt sep* to cut a notch/notches in, to notch; (*schnitzen*) to cut, to chip.

Einkerbung *f* notch.

einkerkern *vt sep* to incarcerate. **die Eingekerkerten** the (incarcerated) prisoners.

Einkerkerung *f* incarceration.

einkesseln *vt sep* to encircle, to surround.

Einkesselung *f* encirclement, surrounding.

einkitten *vt sep* to fix with putty (*in +acc* in).

einklagbar *adj Schulden* (legally) recoverable.

einklagen *vt sep Schulden* to sue for (the recovery of).

einklammern *vt sep* to put in brackets, to put brackets around; (*fig*) *Thema, Frage* to leave aside.

Einklang *m* (a) (*Mus*) unison.

(b) (*Übereinstimmung*) harmony. **in ~ bringen** to bring into accord; **in** *or* **im ~ mit etw stehen** to be in accord with sth; **seine Worte und Taten stehen nicht miteinander im** *or* **in ~** his words and deeds were at variance *or* not in accord with one another.

Einklassenschule *f* one-class school.

einklassig *adj Schule* one-class attr.

einkleben *vt sep* to stick in (*in +acc -to*).

einkleiden *vt sep Soldaten* to fit *or* kit out (with a uniform); *Novizen* to accept (as a novice); (*fig*) *Gedanken* to couch. **jdn/sich völlig neu ~** to buy sb/oneself a completely new wardrobe.

Einkleidung *f* (a) (*das Einkleiden*) fitting out; acceptance as a novice; (*von Gedanken*) couching. (b) (*Verhüllung*) veil. **in mystischer ~** veiled in mysticism.

einklemmen *vt sep* (a) (*quetschen*) to jam; *Finger etc* to catch, to get caught. **er hat sich/mir die Hand in der Tür eingeklemmt** he caught his/my hand in the door; **der Fahrer war hinter dem Steuer eingeklemmt** the driver was pinned behind the wheel.

(b) (*festdrücken*) to clamp. **der Hund klemmte den Schwanz ein** the dog put his tail between his legs; **eingeklemmter Bruch** (*Med*) strangulated hernia.

einklinken *sep* **1** *vt Tür etc* to latch; *Segelflugzeug, Leine* to hitch up. **die Tür ist eingeklinkt** the door is on the latch. **2** *vi* (*Verschluß, Sicherheitsgurt*) to click shut; (*Tech: einrasten*) to engage.

einklopfen *vt sep Nagel etc* to knock in (*in +acc -to*); *Hautcreme etc* to pat in (*in +acc -to*).

einkneifen *vt sep irreg Lippen* to press together; *Schwanz* (*lit*) to put between its legs. **mit eingekniffenem Schwanz** (*lit, fig inf*) with his *etc* tail between his *etc* legs.

einknicken *sep* **1** *vt Papier* to crease (over); *Streichholz, Äste* to snap.

2 *vi aux sein* (*Strohhalm*) to get bent; (*Äste*) to snap; (*Knie*) to give way, to buckle. **er knickt immer mit den Knien ein** his knees are always giving way; **mein Knöchel** *or* **Fuß knickt dauernd ein** I'm always going over on my ankle.

einknöpfbar *adj Futter* attachable.

einknöpfen *vt sep Futter* to button in.

einknüppeln *vi sep auf jdn ~to* beat sb (up) with cudgels; (*Polizei*) to beat sb (up) with batons *or* truncheons; (*fig*) to lash sb.

einkochen *sep* **1** *vt Gemüse* to preserve; *Obst auch, Marmelade* to bottle. **2** *vi aux sein* (*Marmelade etc*) to boil down; (*Wasser*) to boil away; (*Soße*) to thicken.

Einkochtopf *m* preserving pan.

einkommen *vi sep irreg aux sein* (*form*) (a) (*eingenommen werden: Geld*) to come in. (b) (*bei jdm*) **um etw ~** to apply (to sb) for sth. (c) (*Sport, Naut*) to come in.

Einkommen *nt -s, -* income.

Einkommens-: **~ausfall** *m* loss of income; **~grenze** *f* income limit; **e~los** *adj* (*form*) **e~los sein** to have no income, to be without an income; **e~schwach** *adj* low-income attr; **e~stark** *adj* high-income attr; **die ~starken** people in a high-income bracket.

Einkommen(s)steuer *f* income tax.

Einkommen(s)steuer-: **~erklärung** *f* income tax return; **e~pflichtig** *adj* liable to income tax; **~veranlagung** *f* income tax coding.

Einkommens-: **~verhältnisse** *pl* (level of) income; **~verteilung** *f* distribution of income; **~zuwachs** *m* increase in income.

einköpfen *vti sep* (*Ftbl*) to head in (*in +acc -to*). **Müller köpfte zum 1:0 ein** Müller's header made the score 1-0.

einkrachen *vi sep aux sein* (*inf*) to crash down.

einkreisen *vt sep Feind, Wild* to surround; (*fig*) *Frage, Problem* to consider from all sides; (*Pol*) to isolate.

Einkreisung *f* surrounding; (*von Frage, Problem*) systematic consideration; (*Pol*) isolation.

Einkreisungspolitik *f* policy of isolation.

einkremen *vt sep siehe* **eincremen.**

einkriegen *sep* (*inf*) **1** *vt* to catch up. **2** *vr* **sie konnte sich gar nicht mehr darüber ~, wie/daß ...** she couldn't get over how/the fact that ...; **krieg dich mal wieder ein!** control yourself!

Einkünfte *pl* income *sing*; (*einer Firma auch*) receipts.

einkuppeln *sep* **1** *vi* (*Aut*) to let the clutch in, to engage the clutch. **2** *vt Eisenbahnwaggon* to couple (up).

einladen *vt sep irreg* (a) *Waren* to load (*in +acc* into).

(b) to invite. **jdn zu einer Party/ins Kino ~** to invite *or* ask sb to a party/to ask sb to the cinema; **jdn auf ein Bier ~** to invite sb for a beer; **jdn für acht Tage ~** to invite sb (to stay) for a week; **laß mal, ich lade dich ein** let me treat you; **wir sind heute abend eingeladen** we've been invited out this evening; **er traut sich nicht, das Mädchen einzuladen** he doesn't dare ask the girl out;

dieses hübsche Plätzchen lädt zum Bleiben ein it's very tempting to linger in this pretty spot; **das lädt ja geradezu zum Stehlen/Einbrechen ein** that's inviting theft/a break-in, that's asking to be stolen/broken into.

   (c) (*Sw*) *siehe* **auffordern.**

einladend *adj* inviting; *Geste* of invitation; *Speisen* appetizing.

Einladung *f* (a) invitation. **einer ~ Folge leisten** (*form*) to accept an invitation. (b) (*Sw*) *siehe* **Aufforderung.**

Einladungs-: **~karte** *f* invitation (card); **~schreiben** *nt* (official) invitation.

Einlage *f* -, -n (a) (*Zahn~*) temporary filling.

   (b) (*Schuh~*) insole; (*zum Stützen*) (arch) support.

   (c) (*Sew*) padding; (*Versteifung*) interfacing.

   (d) (*in Brief, Paket*) enclosure. **einen Prospekt als ~ beilegen** to enclose a pamphlet.

   (e) (*Cook*) noodles, vegetables, egg etc added to a clear soup.

   (f) (*Zwischenspiel*) interlude.

   (g) (*Fin: Kapital~*) investment; (*Spar~ auch*) deposit; (*Spiel~*) stake.

Einlagebogen *m* supplementary form.

einlagern *sep* 1 *vt* to store. 2 *vr* to become deposited (*in +acc or dat* in); (*Met*) to settle.

Einlagerung *f* (a) storage. (b) (*Geol*) deposit.

einlangen *vi sep aux sein* (*Aus*) to arrive.

Einlaß *m* -sses, ⁻sse (a) *no pl* (*Zutritt*) admission. **sich** (*dat*) **~ in etw** (*acc*) **verschaffen** to gain entry *or* admission to sth. (b) (*Tech: Öffnung*) inlet, opening.

einlassen *sep irreg* 1 *vt* (a) (*eintreten lassen*) to let in, to admit.

   (b) (*einlaufen lassen*) *Wasser* to run (*in +acc* into). **er ließ sich** (*dat*) **ein Bad ein** he ran himself a bath.

   (c) (*einpassen, einfügen*) to let in (*in +acc* -to); (*in Holz, Metall auch*) to set in (*in +acc*-to). **ein eingelassener Schrank** a built-in cupboard, a cupboard let into the wall; **eingelassene Schraube** countersunk screw.

   (d) (*Aus*) *Boden, Möbel* to varnish.

   2 *vr* (a) **sich auf etw** (*acc*) **~** (*auf Angelegenheit, Abenteuer, Diskussion, Liebschaft*) to get involved in sth; (*auf Streit, zwielichtiges Unternehmen auch*) to get mixed up in sth, to get into sth; (*sich zu etw verpflichten*) to let oneself in for sth; **sich auf einen Kompromiß ~** to agree to a compromise; **sich in ein Gespräch ~** to get into (a) *or* get involved in a conversation; **ich lasse mich auf keine Erklärungen ein** I'm not going to give any explanations; **ich lasse mich auf keine Diskussion ein** I'm not having any discussion about it; **darauf lasse ich mich nicht ein!** (*bei Geschäft, Angelegenheit*) I don't want anything to do with it; (*bei Kompromiß, Handel etc*) I'm not agreeing to that; **lasse dich in keine Schlägerei ein!** don't you go getting mixed up in any rough stuff; **da habe ich mich aber auf etwas eingelassen!** I've let myself in for something there!

   (b) **sich mit jdm ~** (*pej: Umgang pflegen mit*) to get mixed up *or* involved with sb; **er ließ sich mit diesem Flittchen ein** he was carrying on with this tarty little bit (*pej inf*); **sie läßt sich mit jedem ein!** she'll go with anyone.

   (c) (*Jur: sich äußern*) to testify (*zu* on).

einläßlich *adj* (*Sw*) *siehe* **ausführlich.**

Einlassung *f* (*Jur*) testimony.

Einlauf *m* (a) *no pl* (*Sport*) (*am Ziel*) finish; (*ins Stadion etc*) entry. **beim ~ in die Zielgerade** ... coming into the finishing straight ...

   (b) (*Med*) enema. **jdm einen ~ machen** to give sb an enema.

   (c) (*Cook*) (*~suppe*) soup with egg and/or beurre manié added.

   (d) (*Comm: Post*) *siehe* **Eingang** (b).

   (e) (*rare: ~öffnung*) opening.

einlaufen *sep irreg* 1 *vi aux sein* (a) to come in (*in +acc* -to); (*ankommen auch*) to arrive (*in +acc* in); (*Sport*) (*ins Stadion*) to come *or* run in (*in +acc* -to), to enter (*in etw* (*acc*) sth); (*durchs Ziel*) to finish. **das Schiff läuft in den Hafen ein** the ship is coming into *or* entering the harbour; *siehe* **Zielgerade.**

   (b) (*hineinlaufen: Wasser*) to run in (*in +acc* -to).

   (c) (*eintreffen*) *Post* to arrive; *Bewerbungen, Spenden* to be received, to come in.

   (d) (*eingehen: Stoff*) to shrink. **garantiert kein E~** guaranteed non-shrink.

   2 *vt* *Schuhe* to wear in.

   3 *vr* (*Motor, Maschine*) to run in, to be broken in (*US*); (*Sport*) to warm *or* limber up; (*fig: Geschäfte*) to settle down.

Einlaufwette *f* (*Sport*) three-way bet.

einläuten *vt sep* *Sonntag etc* to ring in; (*Sport*) *Runde* to sound the bell for.

einleben *vr sep* to settle down (*in or an +dat* in); (*fig: sich hineinversetzen*) to immerse oneself (*in +acc* in).

Einlege|arbeit *f* inlay work *no pl.*

einlegen *vt sep* (a) (*in Holz etc*) to inlay. **eingelegte Arbeit** inlay work.

   (b) (*hineintun*) to insert (*in +acc* in), to put in (*in +acc* -to); *Film auch* to load (*in +acc* into); (*in Brief*) to enclose (*in +acc* in). **einen Pfeil (in den Bogen) ~** to fit an arrow (into the bow).

   (c) (*einfügen*) *Sonderschicht, Spurt, Sonderzug* to put on; *Lied, Kunststück, Pause* to have; (*Aut*) *Gang* to engage; (*Hist*) *Lanze* to couch.

   (d) (*Fin: einzahlen*) to pay in, to deposit.

   (e) (*fig: geltend machen*) *Protest* to register. **ein gutes Wort für jdn ~** to put in a good word for sb (*bei* with); **sein Veto ~** to exercise *or* use one's veto; *siehe* **Ehre, Berufung.**

   (f) (*Cook*) *Heringe, Gurken etc* to pickle.

   (g) *Haare* to set, to put in rollers.

Einleger(in *f*) *m* -s, - investor.

Einlege-: **~sohle** *f* insole; **~tisch** *m* inlaid table.

einleiten *sep* 1 *vt* (a) (*in Gang setzen*) to initiate; *Maßnahmen*

auch, *Schritte* to introduce, to take; *neues Zeitalter* to mark the start of, to inaugurate; (*Jur*) *Verfahren* to institute; (*Med*) *Geburt* to induce.

   (b) (*beginnen*) to start; (*eröffnen*) to open.

   (c) *Buch* (*durch Vorwort*) to write an introduction to, to introduce; (*Mus*) to prelude.

   (d) *Abwässer etc* to introduce (*in +acc* into).

   2 *vi* to give an introduction (*in +acc* to).

einleitend *adj* introductory; *Worte auch* of introduction. **er sagte ~, daß** ... he said by way of introduction that ...

Einleitung *f* (a) *siehe vt* (a) initiation; introduction; inauguration; institution; induction.

   (b) (*Vorwort*) introduction; (*Mus*) prelude.

   (c) (*von Abwässern*) introduction (*in +acc* into).

einlenken *sep* 1 *vi* (a) (*fig*) to yield, to give way. (b) (*einbiegen*) to turn in (*in +acc* -to). 2 *vt* *Rakete* to steer (*in +acc* onto).

einlernen *vt sep* (*pej inf*) **jdm etw ~** to teach sb sth; **sich** (*dat*) **etw ~** to memorize *or* learn sth.

einlesen *sep irreg* 1 *vr* **sich in ein Buch/Gebiet etc ~** to get into a book/subject *etc.* 2 *vt* *Daten* to feed (*in +acc* into).

einleuchten *vi sep* to be clear (*jdm* to sb). **der Grund seiner Abneigung leuchtet mir nicht ein** I don't see *or* understand *or* it's not clear to me why he doesn't like me; **ja, das leuchtet mir ein!** yes, I see that, yes, that's clear (to me); **das will mir nicht ~** I just don't understand *or* see that.

einleuchtend *adj* reasonable, plausible.

einliefern *vt sep* *Waren* to deliver. **jdn ins Krankenhaus ~** to admit sb to hospital; **jdn ins Gefängnis ~** to put sb in *or* commit sb to prison; **ein Paket bei der Post ~** to take a parcel to the post.

Einlieferung *f* (*von Waren*) delivery; (*ins Krankenhaus*) admission (*in +acc* to); (*ins Gefängnis*) committal (*in +acc* to); (*von Briefen etc*) sending. **die ~ von Paketen ist nur bis 17⁰⁰ möglich** parcels are not accepted after 5 pm.

Einlieferungsschein *m* certificate of posting.

einliegend *adj pred* (*form*) enclosed. **~ erhalten Sie** ... please find enclosed ...

einlochen *vt sep* (a) (*inf: einsperren*) to lock up, to put behind bars. (b) (*Golf*) to hole out.

einlogieren* [-loʒiˈrən] *sep* 1 *vt* to put up, to lodge. **wir haben immer zwei Studenten (bei uns) einlogiert** we always have two students lodging with us. 2 *vr* **sich (bei jdm) ~** to lodge (with sb); (*Mil*) to be billeted (with *or* on sb).

einlösbar *adj* redeemable.

einlösen *vt sep* *Pfand* to redeem; *Scheck, Wechsel* to cash (in); (*fig*) *Wort, Versprechen* to keep. **in der Praxis läßt sich das nicht problemlos ~** in practice that cannot easily be realized.

Einlösung *f* *siehe vt* redemption; cashing (in); keeping.

einlöten *vt sep* to solder in (*in +acc* -to).

einlullen *vt sep* *Kind* to lull to sleep; (*fig*) *Mißtrauen, Wachsamkeit* to allay, to quiet. **jdn mit Versprechungen/schönen Worten ~** to lull sb with (soothing) promises/soft words.

Einmach(e) [-max(ə)] *f* -, *no pl* (*Aus Cook*) roux.

einmachen *vt sep* *Obst, Gemüse* to preserve; (*in Gläser*) to bottle; (*in Dosen*) to can, to tin (*Brit*).

Einmach-: **~glas** *nt* bottling jar; **~topf** *m* preserving pan; **~zucker** *m* preserving sugar.

einmahnen *vt sep* (*form*) to demand payment of.

einmal *adv* (a) (*ein einziges Mal*) once; (*erstens*) first of all, firstly, for a start. **~ eins ist eins** once one *or* one times one is one; **~ sagt er dies, ~ das** sometimes he says one thing, sometimes another; **~ sagte sie, wir sollten bleiben, ~ wir sollten gehen** first of all she says that we should stay, then that we should go; **auf ~** (*plötzlich*) suddenly, all of a sudden, all at once; (*zugleich*) at once; **~ mehr** once again; **~ und nicht** *or* **nie wieder** once and never again; **noch ~** again; **versuch's noch ~** (*wieder*) try once more *or* again; **versuch's noch einmal** (*ein letztes Mal*) try one last time *or* just once again; **noch ~ so groß wie** as big again as; **wenn sie da ist, ist es noch ~ so schön** it's twice as beautiful when she's there; **~ ist keinmal** (*Prov*) (*schadet nicht*) once won't hurt *or* do any harm; (*zählt nicht*) once doesn't count.

   (b) (*früher, vorher*) once; (*später, in Zukunft*) one *or* some day. **waren Sie schon ~ in Rom?** have you ever been to Rome?; **er hat schon ~ bessere Zeiten gesehen** he has seen better days; **sie waren ~ glücklich, aber jetzt** ... they were happy once *or* at one time, but now ...; **du wirst noch ~ an meine Worte denken** you will think of my words some day; **es war ~** ... once upon a time there was ...; **das war ~!** that was then; **besuchen Sie mich doch ~!** come and visit me some time!; **das wird ~ anders werden** things will be different some *or* one day.

   (c) (*verstärkend, eingrenzend*) *meist nicht übersetzt.* **nicht ~** not even; **auch ~** also, too; **wieder ~** again; **ich bin/die Frauen sind nun ~ so** that's the way I am/women are, I'm just/women are like that; **wie die Lage nun ~ ist** with things as *or* the way they are; **wenn er nun ~ hier ist** ... seeing he's here ...; **alle ~ herhören!** listen everyone!; **sag ~, ist das wahr?** tell me, is it true?; *siehe* **erst** (a).

Einmal|eins *nt* -, *no pl* (multiplication) tables *pl*; (*fig*) ABC, basics *pl*. **das ~ lernen/aufsagen** to learn/say one's tables; **das kleine/große ~** (multiplication) tables up to/over ten.

Einmal-: **~flasche** *f* non-returnable bottle; **~handtuch** *nt* disposable towel.

einmalig *adj* (a) *Gelegenheit, Angebot, Fall* unique.

   (b) (*nur einmal erforderlich*) single; *Anschaffung, Zahlung* one-off *attr*. **beim ~en Durchlesen des Textes** on a single reading of the text, on reading the text through once.

   (c) (*inf: hervorragend*) fantastic, amazing. **dieser Film ist etwas E~es** this film is really something (*inf*); **der Bursche ist wirklich ~** that guy is really something (*inf*).

Einmaligkeit *f* uniqueness. **alle lobten die ~ dieses Films**

everyone said how fantastic the film was; **unübertroffen in ihrer** ~ completely unsurpassed.

Einmann-: ~**betrieb** *m* (a) one-man business; (b) **die Busse auf** ~**betrieb umstellen** to convert the buses for one-man operation; ~**bus** *m* one-man bus; ~**gesellschaft** *f* (*Comm*) one-man company; ~**wagen** *m* one-man tram.

Einmarkstück *nt* one-mark piece.

Einmarsch *m* entry (*in* +*acc* into); (*in ein Land*) invasion (*in* + *acc* of).

einmarschieren* *vi sep aux sein* to march in (*in* +*acc* -to).

einmassieren* *vt sep* to massage *or* rub in (*in* +*acc* -to).

Einmaster *m* -s, - (*Naut*) single-masted ship, single-master.

einmastig *adj* single-masted.

einmauern *vt sep* (a) (*ummauern*) to wall in, to immure (*liter*) (*in* +*acc* in). (b) (*einfügen*) to fix into the wall.

einmeißeln *vt sep* to chisel in (*in* +*acc* -to).

einmengen *sep* **1** *vt* to mix in (*in* +*acc* -to). **2** *vr siehe* **einmischen 1.**

Einmeterbrett *nt* one-metre (diving) board.

einmieten *sep* **1** *vt* (*Agr*) to clamp. **2** *vr* **sich bei jdm** ~ to take lodgings with sb; **er hat sich in der Wohnung unter uns eingemietet** he has taken the flat below us.

einmischen *sep* **1** *vr* to interfere (*in* +*acc* in), to stick one's oar in (*inf*). **sie muß sich bei allem** ~ she has to interfere *or* meddle in everything; **wenn ich mich kurz** ~ **darf ...** if I can butt in a moment ... **2** *vt siehe* **einmengen 1.**

Einmischung *f* interference, meddling (*in* +*acc* in).

einmonatig *adj attr* one-month.

einmonatlich *adj* monthly.

einmontieren* *vt sep* to slot in (*in* +*acc* -to); (*Tech*) to fit in (*in* +*acc* -to).

einmotorig *adj Flugzeug* single-engine(d).

einmotten *vt sep Kleider etc* to put in mothballs; *Schiff, Flugzeug* to mothball.

einmumme(l)n *vt sep* (*inf*) to muffle up.

einmünden *vi sep aux sein* (*Fluß*) to flow in (*in* +*acc* -to); (*Straße*) to run *or* lead in (*in* +*acc* -to). **in etw** (*acc*) ~ **auch** to join sth; (*fig*) to end up in sth; (*Elemente, Einflüsse*) to go into sth.

Einmündung *f* (*von Fluß*) confluence; (*von Straße*) junction. **die** ~ **der Isar in die Donau** the confluence of the Isar and the Danube.

einmütig *adj* unanimous. ~ **zusammenstehen** to stand together solidly *or* as a man.

Einmütigkeit *f* unanimity. **darüber besteht** ~ there is complete agreement on that.

einnachten *vi impers sep* (*Sw*) **es nachtet ein** it's getting dark.

einnageln *vt sep* to nail in (*in* +*acc* -to); (*einhämmern*) to hammer in (*in* +*acc* -to).

einnähen *vt sep* to sew in (*in* +*acc* -to); (*enger machen*) to take in.

Einnahme *f* -, -**n** (a) (*Mil*) seizure; (*einer Stellung, Stadt auch*) capture. (b) (*Ertrag*) receipt. ~**n** *pl* income *sing*; (*Geschäfts*~) takings *pl*; (*aus Einzelverkauf*) proceeds *pl*; (*Gewinn*) earnings *pl*; (*eines Staates*) revenue *sing*; ~**n und Ausgaben** income and expenditure. (c) (*das Einnehmen*) taking. **durch** ~ **von etw** by taking sth.

Einnahme-: ~**ausfall** *m* loss of income; (*von Geschäften*) loss of takings; ~**buch** *nt* (*Comm*) book of receipts, receipt book; ~**posten** *m* item of receipt; ~**quelle** *f* source of income; (*eines Staates*) source of revenue.

einnässen *sep* (*form*) **1** *vt* to wet. **2** *vr* to wet oneself; (*nachtsüber*) to wet the bed.

einnebeln *sep* **1** *vt* (*Mil*) to put up a smokescreen round; (*fig*) to befog, to obfuscate (*liter*). **2** *vr* (*Mil*) to put up a smokescreen (around oneself). **es nebelt sich ein** (*Met*) it's getting misty, there's a mist coming down.

einnehmen *vt sep irreg* (a) *Geld* (*Geschäft etc*) to take; (*Freiberufler*) to earn; *Steuern* to collect. **die eingenommenen Gelder** the takings. (b) (*Naut old*) *Kohle, Ladung* to take on. (c) (*Mil: erobern*) to take; *Stadt, Festung auch* to capture. (d) (*lit, fig*) *Platz etc* to take (up), to occupy; *Stelle* (*innehaben*) to have, to occupy (*form*); *Haltung, Standpunkt etc* to take up. **er nimmt vorübergehend die Stelle des Chefs ein** he is acting for the boss; **bitte, nehmen Sie Plätze ein!** (*form*) please take your seats!; **die Plätze** ~ (*Sport*) to take one's marks; **dieser Gedanke nahm ihn völlig ein** this idea was (pre)occupied *or* obsessed him completely. (e) (*zu sich nehmen*) *Mahlzeit, Arznei* to take. (f) **er nahm uns alle für sich ein** he won us all over; **er hat alle für seine Pläne eingenommen** he won everyone over to his plans; **jdn gegen sich/jdn/etw** ~ to set *or* put sb against oneself/sb/sth; **das nimmt mich sehr für sie ein** that makes me think highly of her; *siehe* **eingenommen.**

einnehmend *adj* likeable. **er hat etwas E~es** there is something likeable about him; **er hat ein ~es Wesen** (*gewinnend*) he's a likeable character; (*hum inf: habgierig*) he's a grabbing sort of person (*inf*).

Einnehmer *m* (*old*) collector.

einnicken *vi sep aux sein* (*inf*) to doze *or* nod off.

einnisten *vr sep* (*lit*) to nest; (*Parasiten, Ei*) to lodge; (*fig*) to park oneself (*bei on*). **in unserem Land haben sich so viele Kriminelle eingenistet** we have so many criminals settled in this country.

Einöd *f* -, -**en** (*Aus*) *siehe* **Einöde.**

Einödbauer *m* farmer of an isolated farm.

Einöde *f* **Moore/Wüsten und** ~ moors and wasteland/deserts and barren wastes *pl*; **die weiße** ~ **der Antarktis** the white

wastes of the Antarctic; **er lebt in der** ~ **des schottischen Hochlands** he lives in the wilds of the Scottish Highlands; **er verließ die** ~ **seines Schwarzwaldhofes** he left the isolation of his Black Forest farm.

Einödhof *m* ≈ croft.

einölen *sep* **1** *vt* to oil. **2** *vr* to rub oneself with oil, to oil oneself.

einordnen *sep* **1** *vt* (a) (*der Reihe nach*) *Bücher etc* to (put in) order; *Akten, Karteikarten* to file. (b) (*klassifizieren*) to classify; *Begriff, Theorie, Denker auch* to categorize. **2** *vr* (a) (*in Gemeinschaft etc*) to fit in (*in* +*acc* -to). (b) (*Aut*) to get in(to) lane. **sich links/rechts** ~ to get into the left/right lane; **„E~"** "get in lane".

einpacken *sep* **1** *vt* (a) (*einwickeln*) to wrap (up) (*in* +*acc* in). **jdn warm** ~ (*fig*) to wrap sb up warmly. (b) (*hineintun*) to pack (*in* +*acc* in). **laß dich damit** ~ (*inf*) forget it!; (*mit altem Witz etc*) cut it out! (*inf*); **mit deinen Witzen kannst du dich** ~ **lassen!** (*inf*) stuff you and your jokes! (*sl*). (c) (*packen*) *Paket* to pack up. **2** *vi* to pack, to do one's packing. **dann können wir** ~ (*inf*) in that case we may as well pack it all in (*inf*) *or* give up.

einparken *vti sep* to park. (**in eine Parklücke**) ~ to get into a parking space.

Einparteien- *in cpds* one-party.

einpassen *sep* **1** *vt* to fit in (*in* +*acc* -to). **2** *vr* to adjust, to adapt oneself (*in* +*acc* to).

einpauken *vt sep* (*inf*) to mug up (on) (*Brit inf*), to cram. **jdm etw** ~ to drum sth into sb.

Einpauker *m* (*inf*) crammer (*pej*).

Einpeitscher *m* -s, - (*Pol*) whip (*Brit*), floor leader (*US*); (*inf: Antreiber*) slave-driver (*inf*).

einpendeln *sep* **1** *vi* to commute in (*in* +*acc* -to). **2** *vr* (*fig*) to settle down; (*Währung, Preise etc*) to find its level, to level off.

Einpendler *m* commuter.

einpennen *vi sep aux sein* (*sl*) to doze off, to drop off (*inf*).

Einpersonen-: ~**haushalt** *m* single-person household; ~**stück** *nt* (*Theat*) one-man play.

Einpfennigstück *nt* one-pfennig piece.

einpferchen *vt sep Vieh* to pen in (*in* +*acc* -to); (*fig*) to coop up (*in* +*acc* in). **eingepfercht stehen** to be hemmed in.

einpflanzen *vt sep* to plant (*in* +*dat* in); (*Med*) to implant (*jdm* in(to) sb). **einem Patienten eine fremde Niere** ~ to give sb a kidney transplant; **jdm etw** ~ (*fig*) to imbue sb with a sense of sth, to instil (a sense of) sth into sb.

einpfropfen *vt sep* (a) *Korken* to put *or* bung in (*in* +*acc* -to). (b) (*fig inf*) *jdm Wissen* ~ to cram knowledge into sb.

Einphasenstrom, Einphasenwechselstrom *m* single-phase current.

einphasig *adj* single-phase.

einpinseln *vt sep Wunde, Mandeln* to paint; (*Cook*) to brush.

einplanen *vt sep* to plan (on), to include in one's plans; *Verzögerungen, Verluste* to allow for; *Baby* to plan.

einpökeln *vt sep Fisch, Fleisch* to salt. **eingepökeltes Rindfleisch** salt beef; **laß dich** ~**!** (*inf*) get stuffed! (*sl*) *or* knotted! (*inf*).

einpolig *adj* single-pole.

einprägen *sep* **1** *vt Muster, Spuren* to imprint, to impress; *Inschrift* to stamp. **ein Muster in Papier** ~ to emboss paper with a pattern; **jdm Pünktlichkeit** ~ (*fig*) to impress on sb the importance of being punctual; **sich** (*dat*) **etw** ~ to remember sth; (*auswendig lernen*) to memorize sth, to commit sth to memory. **2** *vr* **sich jdm ins Gedächtnis/sich jdm** ~ to make an impression on sb's mind/sb; **die Worte haben sich mir unauslöschlich eingeprägt** the words made an indelible impression on me.

einprägsam *adj* easily remembered; *Slogan, Melodie auch* catchy. **er kann sich** ~ **formulieren** he can put things in a way that is easy to remember.

einprasseln *vi sep aux sein* **auf jdn** ~ to rain down on sb, to come pouring down on sb; (*Fragen*) to be showered upon sb; **von allen Seiten prasselten Geschosse auf uns ein** we were caught in a hail of shots from all sides.

einpressen *vt sep* to press in (*in acc* -to).

einproben *vt sep* to rehearse.

einprogrammieren* *vt sep Daten* to feed in; (*fig*) to take into account. **jdm etw** ~ (*fig*) to inculcate sth in sb.

einprügeln *sep* (*inf*) **1** *vt* **jdm etw** ~ to din (*inf*) *or* drum sth into sb. **2** *vi* **auf jdn** ~ to lay into sb.

einpudern *sep* **1** *vr* to powder oneself. **2** *vt* to powder.

einpuppen *vr sep* (*Zool*) to pupate.

einquartieren* *sep* **1** *vt* to quarter; (*Mil auch*) to billet. **Gäste bei Freunden** ~ to put visitors up with friends. **2** *vr* to be quartered (*bei* with); (*Mil auch*) to be billeted (*bei* on); (*Gäste*) to stop (*bei* with) (*inf*). **er hat sich bei uns anscheinend für ewig einquartiert** he seems to have dumped himself on us for good (*inf*).

Einquartierung *f* (a) (*das Einquartieren*) quartering; (*Mil auch*) billeting. (b) **wir haben** ~ (*inf*) (*Soldaten*) we have soldiers billeted on us; (*Besuch*) we've got people staying *or* stopping (*inf*) (with us).

Einrad *nt* unicycle.

einräd(e)rig *adj* (*Schub*)*karren* one-wheeled.

einrahmen *vt sep* (*lit, fig*) to frame. **von zwei Schönen eingerahmt** with a beauty on either side; **das kannst du dir** ~ **lassen!** (*inf*) you ought to get that framed!

einrammen *vt sep Stadttor* to batter down *or* in; *Pfähle* to ram in (*in* +*acc* -to).

einrangieren* [ˈainʀaʒiːrən] *vt sep* (*inf*) *siehe* **einordnen 1.**

einrasten *vti sep* (*vi: aux sein*) to engage.

einräuchern *vt sep* (a) to envelop in smoke. **die Polizei**

räucherte die Demonstranten mit Tränengas ein the police used tear gas against the demonstrators. **(b)** (*inf*) *Zimmer* to fill with smoke, to smoke up; *Gardinen* to make reek of smoke.

einräumen *vt sep* **(a)** *Wäsche, Bücher etc* to put away; *Schrank, Regal etc* to fill; *Wohnung, Zimmer* to arrange; *Möbel* to move in (*in* +*acc* -to). **Bücher ins Regal/in einen Schrank ~** to put books on the shelf/in the cupboard; **er war mir beim E~ behilflich** he helped me sort things out; (*der Wohnung*) he helped me move in.

(b) (*zugestehen*) to concede, to admit; *Freiheiten etc* to allow; *Frist, Kredit* to give, to grant, to allow. **die Presse räumte diesem Skandal viel Platz ein** the press devoted a lot of space to this scandal; **jdm das Recht ~, etw zu tun** to give *or* grant sb the right to do sth, to allow sb to do sth; **~de Konjunktion** concessive conjunction.

Einräumungssatz *m* (*Gram*) concessive clause.

Einraumwohnung *f* one-room flat (*Brit*) *or* apartment (*US*).

einrechnen *vt sep* to include. **ihn (mit) eingerechnet** including him; **Mehrwertsteuer eingerechnet** including VAT, inclusive of VAT.

Einrede *f* (*form*) *siehe* **Einspruch.**

einreden *sep* **1** *vt* **jdm etw ~** to talk sb into believing sth, to persuade sb of sth; **sie hat ihm eingeredet, er sei dumm** she persuaded him that *or* talked him into believing that he was stupid; **das lasse ich mir nicht ~** you're not going to make me believe that; **wer hat dir denn diesen Unsinn eingeredet?** who put that rubbish into your head?; **er will mir ~, daß ... ** he'd have me believe *or* he wants me to believe that ...; **sich** (*dat*) **etw ~** to talk oneself into believing sth, to make oneself believe sth; **das redest du dir nur ein!** you're only imagining it.

2 *vi* **auf jdn ~** to keep on and on at sb.

einregnen *sep* **1** *vi aux sein* **(a)** to get soaked (through).

(b) (*fig*) (*Vorwürfe*) to rain down (*auf* +*acc* onto, on). **wilde Drohungen regneten auf uns ein** wild threats were hurled at us.

2 *vr* **es hat sich eingeregnet** the rain has set in.

einreiben *vt sep irreg* **er rieb sich** (*dat*) **das Gesicht mit Schnee/Creme ein** he rubbed snow over/cream into his face.

Einreibung *f* **~en verordnen** to prescribe embrocation.

einreichen *vt sep* **(a)** *Antrag, Unterlagen* to submit (*bei* to); (*Jur*) *Klage* to file; *siehe* **Abschied (b).**

(b) (*bitten um*) *Versetzung, Pensionierung* to apply for, to request.

(c) (*inf*) **jdn für/zu etw ~** to recommend sb for sth, to put sb up for sth (*inf*).

Einreichung *f, no pl siehe vt* (*a, b*) submission; filing; application, request.

einreihen *sep* **1** *vt* (*einordnen, einfügen*) to put in (*in* +*acc* -to); (*klassifizieren*) to class, to classify. **dieses Buch verdient, in die bedeutendste medizinische Fachliteratur eingereiht zu werden** this book deserves to be awarded a place amongst the most important works of medical literature; **er wurde in den Arbeitsprozeß eingereiht** he was fitted into *or* given a place in the work process.

2 *vr* **sich in etw** (*acc*) **~** to join sth.

Einreiher *m* **-s,** - single-breasted suit/jacket/coat.

einreihig *adj* *Anzug, Jackett, Mantel* single-breasted.

Einreise *f* entry (*in* +*acc* into, to). **bei der ~ in die DDR** when entering the GDR, on entry to the GDR.

Einreise-: **~erlaubnis, ~genehmigung** *f* entry permit.

einreisen *vi sep aux sein* to enter the country. **er reiste in die Schweiz ein** he entered Switzerland; **ein- und ausreisen** to enter and leave the country.

Einreise-: **~verbot** *nt* refusal of entry; **~verbot haben** to have been refused entry; **~visum** *nt* entry visa.

einreißen *sep irreg* **1** *vt* **(a)** *Papier, Stoff, Nagel* to tear. **ich habe mir einen Splitter in den Zeh eingerissen** I've got a splinter in my toe. **(b)** *Zaun, Barrikaden* to tear *or* pull down. **2** *vi aux sein* (*Papier*) to tear; (*fig inf: Unsitte etc*) to catch on (*inf*), to get to be a habit (*inf*).

einreiten *sep irreg* **1** *vt* *Pferd* to break in. **2** *vi aux sein* (*in die Manege etc*) to ride in (*in* +*acc* -to). **3** *vr* to warm up. **sich mit einem Pferd ~** to get used to riding a particular horse.

einrenken *sep* **1** *vt* *Gelenk, Knie* to reduce (*spec*); (*fig inf*) to sort out. **2** *vr* (*fig inf*) to sort itself out.

einrennen *vt sep irreg* (*inf*) *Mauer, Tür etc* to batter *or* break down. **sich** (*dat*) **den Kopf an der Wand ~** to bang *or* bash (*inf*) one's head against the wall; *siehe* **offen.**

einrichten *sep* **1** *vt* **(a)** (*möblieren*) *Wohnung, Zimmer* to furnish; (*ausstatten*) *Hobbyraum, Spielzimmer* to fit out; *Praxis, Labor* to equip, to fit out. **sich** (*dat*) **eine moderne Küche ~** to put in a modern kitchen; **eine Wohnung antik/modern ~** to furnish a flat in an old/modern style; **seine Wohnung neu ~** to refurnish one's flat; **Wohnungen im Dachgeschoß ~** to convert the attic into flats; **er hat ihr eine Wohnung eingerichtet** he has set her up in a flat.

(b) (*gründen, eröffnen*) to set up; *Lehrstuhl* to establish; *Konto* to open; *Katalog, Buslinie etc* to start.

(c) (*einstellen*) *Maschine* to set up; *Motor* to set (*auf* +*acc* for); (*Mil*) *Geschütz* to set (*auf* +*acc* at).

(d) (*bearbeiten*) *Musikstück* to arrange; *Theaterstück* to adapt.

(e) (*fig: arrangieren*) to arrange, to fix (*inf*). **kannst du es so ~, daß er nichts davon weiß?** can you arrange *or* fix things so that he doesn't know anything about it?; **ich werde es ~, daß wir um zwei Uhr da sind** I'll see to it that we're there at two; **das läßt sich ~** that can be arranged; **das Leben/die Welt ist nun einmal nicht so eingerichtet** life/the world isn't like that.

(f) (*Med*) *Arm, Knochen* to set.

2 *vr* **(a)** (*sich möblieren*) **sich ~/neu ~** to furnish/refurnish

one's flat/house; *siehe* **häuslich.**

(b) (*sich der Lage anpassen*) to get along *or* by, to manage; (*sparsam sein*) to cut down. **er hat sich im bürgerlichen Leben eingerichtet** he has settled down into middle-class life.

(c) **sich auf etw** (*acc*) **~** to prepare oneself for sth; **sich auf eine lange Wartezeit ~** to be prepared for a long wait; **auf Tourismus/warme Speisen eingerichtet sein** to be geared to tourism/equipped for hot meals; **da richtet man sich darauf ein, daß Gäste kommen, und dann sagen sie ab!** you get all ready for guests and then they cry off!

Einrichtung *f* **(a)** (*das Einrichten*) (*von Wohnung, Zimmer*) furnishing; (*von Hobbyraum, Spielzimmer*) fitting-out; (*von Labor, Praxis*) equipping; (*von Maschine*) setting-up; (*von Geschütz*) aiming; (*Med*) setting.

(b) (*Bearbeitung*) (*Mus*) arrangement; (*Theat*) adaptation.

(c) (*Wohnungs~*) furnishings *pl*; (*Geschäfts~ etc*) fittings *pl*; (*Labor~ etc*) equipment *no pl*.

(d) (*Gründung, Eröffnung*) setting-up; (*von Lehrstuhl*) establishment; (*von Konto*) opening; (*von Katalog, Busverkehr*) starting.

(e) (*behördlich, wohltätig*) institution; (*Schwimmbäder, Transportmittel etc*) facility.

Einrichtungs-: **~gegenstand** *m* item of furniture; (*Geschäfts~*) fitment; **~haus** *nt* furnishing house.

einriegeln *vtr sep* **jdn/sich ~** to lock sb/oneself in (*in* +*dat* -to).

Einritt *m* entry (*in* +*acc* into).

einritzen *vt sep* to carve in (*in* +*acc* -to).

einrollen *sep* **1** *vt* (*einwickeln*) to roll up (*in* +*acc* in); (*Hockey*) to roll on (*in* +*acc* -to). **sich** (*dat*) **das Haar ~** to put one's hair in rollers. **2** *vi aux sein* to roll in (*in* +*acc* -to). **3** *vr* to roll up; (*Tier etc auch*) to roll oneself up.

einrosten *vi sep aux sein* to rust up; (*fig: Glieder*) to stiffen up. **mein Latein ist ziemlich eingerostet** my Latin has got pretty rusty.

einrücken *sep* **1** *vt* *Zeile* to indent; *Anzeige* (*in Zeitung*) to insert. **2** *vi aux sein* (*Mil*) **(a)** (*in ein Land*) to move in (*in* +*acc* -to); (*wieder ~*) to return (*in* +*acc* to). **(b)** (*eingezogen werden*) to report for duty; (*nach Urlaub etc*) to report back.

einrühren *vt sep* to stir *or* mix in (*in* +*acc* -to); (*Cook*) *Ei* to beat in (*in* +*acc* -to).

einrüsten *vt sep* *Haus* to put scaffolding around.

eins *num* one. **es ist/schlägt ~** it's one/just striking one (o'clock); **~, zwei, drei** (*lit*) one, two, three; (*fig*) in a trice, in no time; **das ist ~, zwei, drei geschehen** (*fig*) it doesn't/won't take a second; **~ zu ~** (*Sport*) one all; **~ mit jdm/etw sein** to be one with sb; (*übereinstimmen*) to be in agreement with sb; **sich mit jdm ~ wissen** to know one is in agreement with sb; **das ist doch alles ~** (*inf*) it's all one *or* all the same; **es ist mir alles ~** (*inf*) it's all one *or* all the same to me; **sehen und handeln waren ~** to see was to act; **~ a** (*inf*) A 1 (*inf*), first-rate (*inf*); *siehe auch* **ein², eine(r, s),** **vier.**

Eins *f* **-, -en** one; (*Sch auch*) A, alpha. **er würfelte zwei ~en** he threw two ones; **eine ~ schreiben/bekommen** to get an A *or* alpha *or* a one; *siehe* **Vier.**

einsacken¹ *vt sep* **(a)** (*in Säcke füllen*) to put in sacks, to sack.

(b) (*inf*) (*erbeuten*) to grab (*inf*); *Geld, Gewinne* to rake in (*inf*).

einsacken² *vi sep aux sein* (*einsinken*) to sink; (*Bürgersteig, Boden etc auch*) to subside.

einsagen *sep* (*dial*) **1** *vi* **jdm ~** to prompt sb. **2** *vt* **jdm etw ~** to whisper sth to sb.

einsalben *vt sep* to rub with ointment; *Wunde, Hände auch* to rub ointment into.

einsalzen *vt sep* *Fisch, Fleisch* to salt. **laß dich ~!** (*inf*) get stuffed (*sl*) *or* knotted! (*inf*).

einsam *adj* **(a)** *Mensch, Leben, Gefühl* (*allein, verlassen*) lonely; (*einzeln*) solitary. **~ leben** to live a lonely/solitary life; **sich ~ fühlen** to feel lonely *or* lonesome (*esp US*); **ein ~es Boot/ein ~er Schwimmer** a lone *or* solitary boat/swimmer; **~ überragt dieser Gipfel die anderen** this peak towers over the others in solitary splendour.

(b) (*abgelegen*) *Haus, Insel* secluded; *Dorf* isolated; (*menschenleer*) empty; *Strände* lonely, empty. **~ liegen** to be secluded/isolated.

(c) (*inf: hervorragend*) **~e Klasse/Spitze** absolutely fantastic (*inf*), really great (*inf*).

Einsamkeit *f* *siehe adj* **(a)** loneliness; solitariness. **er liebt die ~** he likes solitude; **die ~ vieler alter Leute** the loneliness of many old people. **(b)** seclusion; isolation; emptiness; loneliness. **die ~ der Bergwelt** the solitude of the mountains.

Einsamkeitsgefühl *nt* feeling of loneliness.

einsammeln *vt sep* to collect (in); *Obst* to gather (in).

einsargen *vt sep* to put in a coffin. **laß dich (doch) ~!** (*inf*) go (*inf*) and) take a running jump! (*inf*), get stuffed! (*sl*).

Einsatz *m* **(a)** (*~teil*) inset; (*Schubladen~, Koffer~*) tray; (*Topf~*) compartment; (*Blusen~*) false blouse *etc* collar and neck to wear under pullover; (*Hemd~*) dicky (*dated*).

(b) (*Spiel~*) stake; (*Kapital~*) investment. **den ~ erhöhen** to raise the stakes; **mit dem ~ herauskommen, den ~ heraushaben** (*inf*) to recover one's stake.

(c) (*Mus*) entry; (*Theat*) entrance. **der Dirigent gab den ~** the conductor raised his bâton and brought in the orchestra; **der Dirigent gab den Geigern den ~** the conductor brought in the violins; **der ~ der Streicher war verfrüht** the strings came in too early.

(d) (*Verwendung*) use; (*esp Mil*) deployment; (*von Arbeitskräften*) employment. **im ~ sein** to be in use; **die Ersatzspieler kamen nicht zum ~** the reserves weren't put in *or* used; **unter ~ von Schlagstöcken** using truncheons; **unter ~ aller Kräfte** by making a supreme effort.

(e) (*Aktion*) (*Mil*) action; (*von Polizei*) intervention. **im ~ in**

action; **wo war er im ~?** where did he see action?; **zum ~ kommen** to go into action; **bei seinem ersten ~** the first time he saw action *or* went into action; **sich zum ~ melden** to report for duty; **die Pfadfinder halfen in freiwilligen ~en** the scouts helped on a voluntary basis.

(f) (*Hingabe*) commitment. **in selbstlosem ~ ihres Lebens** with a complete disregard for her own life; **etw unter ~ seines Lebens tun** to risk one's life to do sth, to do sth at the risk of one's life; **den ~ des eigenen Lebens nicht scheuen** (*geh*) not to hesitate to sacrifice one's own life.

Einsatz-: **~befehl** *m* order to go into action; **e~bereit** *adj* ready for use; (*Mil*) ready for action; **~bereitschaft** *f* readiness for use; (*Mil*) readiness for action; (*Bereitschaftsdienst*) stand-by (duty); **e~fähig** *adj* fit for use; (*Mil*) fit for action; *Sportler* fit; **~freude** *f* willing application; **e~freudig** *adj* eager (for action), enthusiastic; **~gruppe** *f*, **~kommando** (*Mil*) *nt* task force; **~leiter** *m* head of operations; **~plan** *m* plan of action; **~stück** *nt* (*Tech*) insert; (*Zubehörteil*) attachment; **~wagen** *m* police car; fire engine; ambulance; (*bei Straßenbahn, Bus*) extra tram/bus.

einsaugen *vt sep* (*lit, fig*) to soak up, to absorb; (*durch Strohhalm etc*) to suck; (*einatmen*) to breathe in; *frische Luft* to draw *or* suck in; *siehe* **Muttermilch**.

einsäumen *vt sep* (*Sew*) to hem; (*fig*) to edge, to line.

einschalten *sep* 1 *vt* **(a)** (*in Betrieb setzen*) to switch *or* turn *or* put on; *Sender* to tune in to.

(b) (*einfügen*) to interpolate; *Zitat, Erklärung etc auch* to include (*in +acc* in). **wir schalten in die Diskussion eine kurze Pause ein** we'll have a short break during the discussion.

(c) *jdn ~* to call sb in; *jdn in etw* (*acc*) *~* to bring sb into sth *or* in on sth.

2 *vr* to intervene; (*teilnehmen*) to join in. **wir schalten uns jetzt in die Sendungen von Radio Bremen ein** we now go over to *or* join Radio Bremen.

Einschalt-: **~hebel** *m* starting lever *or* handle; **~quote** *f* (*Rad, TV*) viewing figures *pl*.

Einschaltung *f* **(a)** (*von Licht, Motor etc*) switching *or* turning on. **(b)** (*von Nebensatz etc*) interpolation; (*von Zitat*) inclusion. **nach ~ einer kleinen Pause ging das Programm weiter** after a short break the programme continued. **(c)** (*von Person, Organisation*) calling *or* bringing in.

einschärfen *vt sep jdm etw ~* to impress sth (up)on sb; *Höflichkeit, Rücksichtnahme etc* to inculcate sth in sb; **er hat uns Vorsicht eingeschärft** he impressed on us the need for caution; **ich habe den Kindern eingeschärft, Fremden gegenüber vorsichtig zu sein** I have impressed upon the children to be careful of strangers; **schärf dir das ein!** get that firmly fixed in your mind.

einscharren *vt sep* to cover with earth.

einschätzen *vt sep* to assess (*auch Fin*), to evaluate; (*schätzen auch*) to estimate. *falsch ~* to misjudge; (*falsch schätzen*) to miscalculate; **wie ich die Lage einschätze** as I see the situation; **jdn sehr hoch/niedrig ~** to have a very high/low opinion of sb; **etw zu hoch/niedrig ~** to overestimate/underestimate sth; **jdn/sich zu hoch/niedrig ~** to overrate/underrate sb/oneself, to have too high/low an opinion of sb/oneself.

Einschätzung *f siehe vt* assessment, evaluation; estimation. *falsche ~* misjudgement; miscalculation; **nach meiner ~** in my estimation.

einschäumen *sep* 1 *vt* **(a)** to lather. **(b)** (*Tech*) to pack in plastic foam. 2 *vr* to lather oneself.

einschenken *vt sep* to pour (out). **darf ich Ihnen noch Wein ~?** can I give *or* pour you some more wine?

einscheren *sep* 1 *vi aux sein* to get back. 2 *vt Tau* to reeve.

einschichtig *adj* **(a)** single-layered. **(b)** *Arbeitstag* single-shift. **unsere Fabrik arbeitet ~** our factory works a single shift.

einschicken *vt sep* to send in (*an +acc* to).

einschieben *vt sep irreg* **(a)** (*hineinschieben*) to put in (*in +acc* -to). **lässig schob er zum 2:0 ein** (*Ftbl sl*) he casually put it away to make it 2-0 (*inf*).

(b) (*einfügen*) to put in; *Sonderzüge* to put on; (*dazwischenschieben*) *Diskussion, Schüler, Patienten* to fit *or* squeeze (*inf*) in (*in +acc* -to). **eine Pause ~** to have a break.

Einschiebsel *nt* insertion.

Einschienenbahn *f* monorail.

einschießen *sep irreg* 1 *vt* **(a)** (*zertrümmern*) *Fenster* to shoot in; (*mit Ball etc*) to smash (in). **(b)** *Gewehr* to try out and adjust. **(c)** (*Tech*) *Dübel etc* to insert. **(d)** *Fäden* to weave in. **ein Gewebe mit eingeschossenen Goldfäden** a cloth shot with gold (thread). **(e)** (*Typ*) *Seiten, Blätter* to interleave. **(f)** *Fußball* to kick in. **Müller schoß den Ball zum 2:0 ein** Müller scored to make it 2-0. **(g)** (*Comm*) *Geld* to inject (*in +acc* into). 2 *vr* to find one's range, to get one's eye in. **sich auf ein Ziel ~** to get the range of a target; **sich auf jdn ~** (*fig*) to line sb up for the kill. 3 *vi* **(a)** (*Sport*) to score. **er schoß zum 1:0 ein** he scored to make it 1-0. **(b)** (*Med*) **die Milch schießt in die Brust ein** the milk comes in. **(c)** *auf jdn ~* to shoot at sb.

einschiffen *sep* 1 *vt* to ship. 2 *vr* to embark. **er schiffte sich in London nach Amerika ein** he boarded a ship in London for America.

Einschiffung *f* (*von Personen*) boarding, embarkation; (*von Gütern*) loading.

einschirren *vt sep Pferd* to harness.

einschl. *abbr of* **einschließlich** incl.

einschlafen *vi sep irreg aux sein* to fall asleep, to go to sleep, to

---

drop off (*inf*); (*Bein, Arm*) to go to sleep; (*euph: sterben*) to pass away; (*fig: Gewohnheit, Freundschaft*) to peter out, to tail off. **ich kann nicht ~** I can't get to sleep; **bei *or* über seiner Arbeit ~** to fall asleep over one's work; **vor dem E~ zu nehmen** (*Medizin*) to be taken before retiring.

einschläferig *adj Bett* single.

einschläfern *vt sep* **(a)** (*zum Schlafen bringen*) to send to sleep; (*schläfrig machen*) to make sleepy *or* drowsy; (*fig*) *Gewissen* to soothe, to quiet. **das kann unsere Wachsamkeit nicht ~** that won't lull us into a false sense of security.

(b) (*narkotisieren*) to give a soporific.

(c) (*töten*) *Tier* to put to sleep, to put down, to destroy.

einschläfernd *adj* soporific; (*langweilig*) monotonous. **ein ~es Mittel** a soporific (drug).

einschläf(r)ig *adj Bett* single.

Einschlafstörung *f* problem in getting to sleep.

Einschlag *m* **(a)** (*von Geschoß*) impact; (*von Blitz*) striking. **dieses Loch ist der ~ eines Geschosses** this hole was made by a bullet; **der ~ der Granate war deutlich zu sehen** the place where the grenade had landed was clearly visible.

(b) (*Sew*) hem.

(c) (*Tex*) weft, woof.

(d) (*von Bäumen*) felling; (*gefällte Bäume*) timber.

(e) (*Aut: des Lenkrads*) lock. **das Lenkrad bis zum (vollen) ~ drehen** to put the wheel on full lock.

(f) (*Zusatz, Beimischung*) element. **einen stark(en) autoritären/südländischen ~ haben** to have more than a hint of authoritarianism/the Mediterranean about it/one *etc*.

einschlagen *sep irreg* 1 *vt* **(a)** *Nagel* to hammer *or* knock in; *Pfahl* to drive in; *Krallen* to sink in (*in +acc* -to).

(b) (*zertrümmern*) to smash (in); *Tür auch* to smash down; *Schädel auch* to bash in (*inf*); *Zähne* to knock out. **mit eingeschlagenem Schädel** with one's head bashed in; **Eier ~** (*inf*) to break eggs into the pan.

(c) *Bäume* to fell.

(d) (*einwickeln*) *Ware* to wrap up; *Buch* to cover.

(e) (*umlegen*) *Stoff, Decke* to turn up.

(f) (*Aut*) *Räder* to turn.

(g) (*wählen*) *Weg* to take; *Kurs* (*lit*) to follow; (*fig*) to pursue, to adopt; *Laufbahn etc* to enter on. **das Schiff änderte den eingeschlagenen Kurs** the ship changed from its previous course; **Peking schlägt einen weicheren/härteren Kurs ein** Peking is taking a softer/harder line.

2 *vi* **(a)** (*in etw acc*) *~* (*Blitz*) to strike (sth); (*Geschoß etc auch*) to hit (sth); **es muß irgendwo eingeschlagen haben** something must have been struck by lightning; **gut ~** (*inf*) to go down well, to be a big hit (*inf*); (*Schüler, Arbeiter*) to get on all right.

(b) **auf jdn/etw ~** to hit out at sb/sth.

(c) (*zur Bekräftigung*) to shake on it. **nachdem wir uns geeinigt hatten, schlug er ein** after we had reached an agreement, we shook on it.

einschlägig *adj* appropriate; *Literatur, Paragraph auch* relevant. **er ist ~ vorbestraft** (*Jur*) he has a previous conviction for a similar offence.

einschleichen *vr sep irreg* (*in +acc* -to) to creep in; (*lit auch*) to steal *or* sneak in (*inf*); (*fig: Fehler auch*) to slip in. **sich in jds Vertrauen ~** (*fig*) to worm one's way into sb's confidence.

einschleifen *vt sep irreg* to grind; (*eingravieren*) to cut in (*in +acc* -to). **eingeschliffene Reaktionen/Verhaltensweisen** (*Psych, geh*) established reactions/patterns of behaviour.

einschleppen *vt sep* (*Naut*) *Schiff* to tow in (*in +acc* -to); (*fig*) *Krankheit, Ungeziefer* to bring in.

Einschleppung *f* (*fig*) introduction, bringing-in.

einschleusen *vt sep* to smuggle in (*in +acc, nach* -to).

einschließen *vt sep irreg* **(a)** to lock up (*in +acc* in); (*Mil*) to confine to quarters. **er schloß sich/mich in dem *or* das Zimmer ein** he locked himself/me in the room.

(b) (*umgeben*) to surround; (*Mil*) *Stadt, Feind auch* to encircle. **einen Satz in Klammern ~** to put a sentence in brackets.

(c) (*fig: einbegreifen, beinhalten*) to include.

einschließlich 1 *prep +gen* including, inclusive of. **~ Porto** postage included; **Preis ~ Porto** price including postage *or* inclusive of postage.

2 *adv* **er hat das Buch bis S. 205 ~ gelesen** he has read up to and including p.205; **vom 1. bis ~ 31. Oktober *or* bis 31. Oktober ~ geschlossen** closed from 1st to 31st October inclusive.

Einschließung *f* (*esp Mil*) confinement.

einschlummern *vi sep aux sein* (*geh*) to fall asleep; (*euph: sterben*) to pass away.

Einschluß *m* **(a)** (*von Gefangenen*) locking of the cells. **(b)** **mit *or* unter ~ von** (*form*) with the inclusion of, including. **(c)** (*Geol*) inclusion.

einschmeicheln *vr sep* **sich bei jdm ~** to ingratiate oneself with sb, to insinuate oneself into sb's good graces; **~de Musik** enticing music; **~de Stimme** silky voice.

Einschmeich(e)lung *f* attempt to ingratiate oneself.

einschmeißen *vt sep irreg* (*inf*) *Fenster* to smash (in).

einschmelzen *sep irreg* 1 *vt* to melt down; (*fig: integrieren*) to put in the melting pot. **diese Unterschiede sind weitgehend eingeschmolzen** these differences have for the most part fused and coalesced. 2 *vi aux sein* to melt.

Einschmelzung *f* melting (down); (*fig*) coalescence.

einschmieren *vt sep* **(a)** (*mit Fett*) to grease; (*mit Öl*) to oil; *Gesicht* (*mit Creme*) to cream, to put cream on. **er schmierte mir den Rücken mit Heilsalbe/Sonnenöl ein** he rubbed my back with ointment/sun-tan lotion. **(b)** (*inf: beschmutzen*) to get dirty. **er hat sich ganz mit Dreck/Marmelade eingeschmiert** he has covered himself in dirt/jam.

einschmuggeln vt sep to smuggle in (in +acc -to). **er hat sich in den Saal eingeschmuggelt** he sneaked into the hall.

einschnappen vi sep aux sein (a) (Schloß, Tür) to click shut. **(b)** (inf: beleidigt sein) to take offence, to get into a huff (inf). **er schnappt wegen jeder Kleinigkeit ein** he takes offence at every little thing; siehe **eingeschnappt**.

einschneiden sep irreg **1** vt **(a)** Stoff, Papier to cut. **er schnitt das Papier an den Ecken einige Zentimeter ein** he cut a few centimetres into the corners of the paper; **die Fesseln schneiden mir die Handgelenke ein** the bonds are cutting into my wrists.
(b) (einkerben) Namen, Zeichen to carve (in +acc in, into). **der Fluß hat ein Tal in das Gestein eingeschnitten** the river has carved out or cut a valley in the rock; **tief eingeschnittene Felsen** steep cliffs; **eine tief eingeschnittene Schlucht** a deep ravine.
(c) (Cook) **Zwiebeln in die Suppe ~** to cut up some onions and put them in the soup.
(d) (Film) to cut in (in +acc -to).
2 vi to cut in (in +acc -to).

einschneidend adj (fig) drastic, radical; Maßnahmen auch trenchant; Bedeutung, Wirkung far-reaching.

einschneien vi sep aux sein to get snowed up; (Auto, Mensch auch) to get snowed in. **eingeschneit sein** to be snowed up/in.

Einschnitt m cut; (Med) incision; (im Tal, Gebirge) cleft; (Zäsur) break; (im Leben) decisive point.

einschnitzen vt sep to carve (in +acc into).

einschnüren sep **1** vt **(a)** (einengen) to cut into; Taille (mit Mieder) to lace in. **dieser Kragen schnürt mir den Hals ein** this collar is nearly choking or strangling me; **die Angst schnürte mir die Kehle ein** my throat was tight with fear.
(b) (zusammenbinden) Paket to tie up.
2 vr to lace oneself up or in.

einschöpfen vt sep to ladle out.

einschränken sep **1** vt to reduce, to cut back or down; Bewegungsfreiheit, Recht to limit, to restrict; Wünsche to moderate; Behauptung to qualify. **jdn in seinen Rechten ~** to limit or restrict sb's rights; **~d möchte ich sagen, daß ...** I'd like to qualify that by saying ...; **das Rauchen/Trinken/Essen ~** to cut down on smoking/on drinking/on what one eats.
2 vr (sparen) to economize. **sich im Essen/Trinken ~** to cut down on what one eats/on one's drinking; siehe **eingeschränkt**.

Einschränkung f **(a)** siehe vt reduction; limitation, restriction; moderation; qualification; (Vorbehalt) reservation. **ohne ~** without reservations, unreservedly. **(b)** (Sparmaßnahme) economy; (das Einsparen) economizing.

einschrauben vt sep to screw in (in +acc -to).

Einschreib(e)-: **~brief** m recorded delivery (Brit) or certified (US) letter; **~gebühr** f **(a)** (Post) charge for recorded delivery (Brit) or certified mail (US); **(b)** (Univ) membership fee; **(c)** (für Verein) membership fee.

einschreiben sep irreg **1** vt (eintragen) to enter; Post to send recorded delivery (Brit) or certified mail (US); siehe **eingeschrieben**. **2** vr (in Verein, für Abendkurse etc) to enrol; (Univ) to register. **er schrieb sich in die Liste ein** he put his name on the list.

Einschreiben nt recorded delivery (Brit) or certified (US) letter/parcel. **~ pl** recorded delivery (Brit) or certified (US) mail sing; **einen Brief als or per ~ schicken** to send a letter recorded delivery (Brit) or certified mail (US).

Einschreib(e)sendung f letter/parcel sent recorded delivery (Brit) or certified mail (US).

Einschreibung f enrolment; (Univ) registration.

einschreien vi sep irreg **auf jdn ~** to yell or bawl at sb.

einschreiten vi sep irreg aux sein to take action (gegen against); (dazwischentreten) to intervene, to step in.

Einschreiten nt -s, no pl intervention.

einschrumpeln (inf), **einschrumpfen** vi sep aux sein to shrivel (up).

Einschub m insertion.

einschüchtern vt sep to intimidate.

Einschüchterung f intimidation.

Einschüchterungsversuch m attempt at intimidation.

einschulen vti sep **eingeschult werden** (Kind) to start school; **wir müssen unseren Sohn dieses Jahr ~** our son has to start school this year; **wir schulen dieses Jahr weniger Kinder ein** we have fewer children starting school this year.

Einschulung f first day at school. **die ~ findet im Alter von 6 Jahren statt** children start school at the age of 6.

Einschulungsalter nt siehe **Schulalter**.

Einschuß m **(a)** (~stelle) bullet hole; (Med) point of entry. **Tod durch ~ in die Schläfe** death caused by a shot or a bullet through the side of the head; **der Arzt desinfizierte den ~ im Bein des Verletzten** the doctor disinfected the bullet wound in the injured man's leg.
(b) (Space) **nach ~ der Rakete in die Erdumlaufbahn** after the rocket had been shot into orbit round the earth.
(c) (Ftbl) shot into goal.
(d) (Tex) weft, woof.

Einschuß-: **~loch** nt bullet hole; **~stelle** f bullet hole; (Med) point of entry.

einschütten vt sep to tip in (in +acc -to); (inf) Flüssigkeiten to pour in (in +acc -to). **dem Pferd Futter ~** to give the horse some fodder; **er hat sich (dat) noch etwas Kaffee eingeschüttet** (inf) he poured himself (out) or gave himself some more coffee.

einschwärzen vt sep to blacken, to make black.

einschweben vi sep aux sein to glide in (in +acc -to).

einschweißen vt sep (Tech) (hineinschweißen) to weld in (in +acc -to); (zuschweißen) Buch, Schallplatte to seal, to heat-seal (spec).

einschwenken vi sep aux sein to turn or swing in (in +acc -to). **links/rechts ~** (Mil) to wheel left/right; **auf etw (acc) ~** (fig) to fall in with or go along with sth.

einschwören vt sep irreg **jdn auf etw (acc) ~** to swear sb to sth; siehe **eingeschworen**.

einsegnen vt sep **(a)** (konfirmieren) to confirm. **(b)** Altar, Kirche to consecrate; Feld, Haus, Gläubige to bless.

Einsegnung f siehe vt confirmation; consecration; blessing.

einsehen sep irreg **1** vt **(a)** Gelände to see; (Mil) to observe.
(b) (prüfen) Akte to see, to look at.
(c) (verstehen, begreifen) to see; Fehler, Schuld auch to recognize. **das sehe ich nicht ein** I don't see why; **verstehe ich nicht)** I don't see that.
2 vi **(a)** **in etw (acc) ~** to see sth; (Mil) to observe sth.
(b) (prüfen) Akte to look (in +acc at).

Einsehen nt: **ein ~ haben** to have some understanding (mit, für for); (Vernunft, Einsicht) to see reason or sense; **hab doch ein ~!** have a heart!; be reasonable!; **hast du kein ~?** have you no understanding?; can't you see sense?

einseifen vt sep to soap; (inf: betrügen) to con (inf), to take for a ride (inf); (inf: mit Schnee) to rub with snow.

einseitig adj **(a)** on one side; (Jur, Pol) Erklärung, Kündigung unilateral. **~e Lungenentzündung** single pneumonia; **~e Lähmung** hemiplegia (form), paralysis of one side of the body.
(b) Freundschaft, Zuneigung one-sided.
(c) (beschränkt) Ausbildung one-sided; (parteiisch) Bericht, Standpunkt, Zeitung auch biased; Ernährung unbalanced. **etw ~ schildern** to give a one-sided portrayal of sth, to portray sth one-sidedly.

Einseitigkeit f (fig) one-sidedness; (von Bericht, Zeitung etc auch) biasedness; (von Ernährung) imbalance.

einsenden vt sep irreg to send in, to submit (form) (an +acc to).

Einsender(in f) m sender; (bei Preisausschreiben) competitor. **wir bitten die ~ von Artikeln ...** we would ask those (people) who send in or submit articles ...

Einsendeschluß m last date for entries, closing date.

Einsendung f **(a)** no pl (das Einsenden) sending in, submission. **(b)** (das Eingesandte) letter/article/manuscript etc; (bei Preisausschreiben) entry.

einsenken sep **1** vt to sink in (in +acc -to). **2** vr (liter) **dieses Bild senkte sich tief in seine Seele ein** this image made a deep impression on him or his mind.

Einser m -s, - (esp S Ger) (Sch) A (grade), alpha, one; (Autobus) (number) one. **er hat einen ~ geschrieben** he got an A.

einsetzen sep **1** vt **(a)** (einfügen) to put in (in +acc -to); Maschinenteil auch to insert (in +acc into), to fit in (in +acc -to); Ärmel auch to set in (in +acc -to); Stück Stoff to let in (in +acc -to); (einschreiben auch) to enter (in +acc in); Stiftzahn to put on (in +acc -to); Gebiß to fit. **Fische in einen Teich ~** to stock a pond with fish; **jdm einen Goldzahn ~** to give sb a gold tooth; **eingesetzte Taschen** pockets let or set into the seams.
(b) (ernennen, bestimmen) to appoint; Ausschuß auch to set up; Erben, Nachfolger to name. **jdn in ein Amt ~** to appoint sb to an office; **jdn als or zum Richter ~** to appoint sb judge.
(c) (verwenden) to use (auch Sport), to employ; Truppen, Polizei, Feuerwehr to deploy, to bring into action; Schlagstöcke to use; Busse, Straßenbahn to put on; (Chess) König etc to bring into play. **etw als or zum Pfand ~** to give sth as a deposit.
(d) (beim Glücksspiel) to stake; (geh) Leben to risk. **seine ganze Energie or Kraft für etw ~** to devote all one's energies to sth.
2 vi (beginnen) to start, to begin; (Mus) to come in; (am Anfang) to start to play/sing. **die Ebbe/Flut setzt um 3 Uhr ein** the tide turns at 3 o'clock, the tide starts to go out/come in at 3 o'clock; **gegen Abend setzte stärkeres Fieber ein** the fever increased towards evening.
3 vr (sich (voll) ~** to show (complete) commitment (in +dat to); **die Mannschaft setzte sich bis an den Rand ihrer Kraft ein** the team did their absolute utmost.
(b) **sich für jdn ~** to fight for sb, to support sb's cause; (sich verwenden für) to give or lend sb one's support; **sie hat sich so sehr für ihn eingesetzt** she did so much for him; **sie hat sich voll für die Armen/Verwundeten eingesetzt** she lent her aid unreservedly to the poor/wounded; **sich für etw ~** to support sth; **ich werde mich dafür ~, daß ...** I will do what I can to see that ...; **er setzte sich für die Freilassung seines Bruders ein** he did what he could to secure the release of his brother.

Einsetzung f appointment (in +acc to). **die ~ des Bischofs in sein Amt** the Bishop's investiture; siehe auch **Einsatz**.

Einsicht f **(a)** (in Akten, Bücher) **~ in etw (acc) haben/nehmen/verlangen** to look/take a look/ask to look at sth; **jdm ~ in etw (acc) gewähren** to allow sb to look at or to see sth; **sie legte ihm die Akte zur ~ vor** she gave him the file to look at.
(b) (Vernunft) sense, reason; (Erkenntnis) insight; (Kenntnis) knowledge; (Verständnis) understanding; (euph: Reue) remorse. **zur ~ kommen** to come to one's senses; **ich bin zu der ~ gekommen, daß ...** I have come to the conclusion that ...; **~ ist der erste Schritt zur Besserung** a fault confessed is half redressed (Prov); **haben Sie doch ~!** have a heart!; (seien Sie vernünftig) be reasonable!; **jdn zur ~ bringen** to bring sb to his/her senses; **er hat durch diese Reise neue ~en gewonnen** this journey gave him new insights into the world; **er hat ~ in die internen Vorgänge der Firma** he has some knowledge of the internal affairs of the firm.

einsichtig adj **(a)** (vernünftig) reasonable; (verständnisvoll) understanding. **er war so ~, seinen Fehler zuzugeben** he was reasonable enough to admit his mistake.
(b) (verständlich, begreiflich) understandable, comprehensible. **etw ~ erklären** to explain sth clearly; **jdm etw ~ machen** to make sb understand or see sth.

Einsichtnahme f -, -n (form) perusal. **er bat um ~ in die Akten** he asked to see the files; **nach ~ in die Akten** after seeing the files; **„zur ~"** "for attention".

einsichts-: **~los** adj (unvernünftig) unreasonable; (verständnislos) lacking (in) understanding; **~voll** adj siehe **einsichtig (a)**.

einsickern vi sep aux sein to seep in (in +acc -to); (fig) to filter in (in +acc -to). **Spione sickerten in unser Land ein** spies infiltrated (into) our country.

Einsiedelei f hermitage; (fig hum: einsames Haus) country retreat or hideaway.

einsieden vt sep irreg (S Ger, Aus) Obst to bottle; Marmelade to make.

Einsiedler(in f) m hermit; (fig auch) recluse.

einsiedlerisch adj hermit-like no adv.

Einsiedlerkrebs m hermit crab.

Einsilber m -s, - siehe **Einsilb(l)er**.

einsilbig adj Wort monosyllabic; Reim masculine, single; (fig) Mensch uncommunicative; Antwort monosyllabic.

Einsilbigkeit f (lit) monosyllabism; (von Reim) masculinity; (fig: von Mensch) uncommunicativeness.

Einsilb(l)er m -s, - monosyllable.

einsingen vr sep irreg to get oneself into voice.

einsinken vi sep irreg aux sein (im Morast, Schnee) to sink in (in +acc or dat -to); (Boden etc) to subside, to cave in; (Knie) to give way. **er sank bis zu den Knien im Schlamm ein** he sank up to his knees in the mud; **ein Stück eingesunkenen Bodens** an area where the ground has subsided or caved in; **eingesunkene Schläfen/Wangen** sunken or hollow temples/cheeks.

einsitzen vi sep irreg (form) to serve a prison sentence. **drei Jahre ~** to serve three years or a three-year sentence.

Einsitzer m -s, - single-seater.

einsitzig adj Fahrzeug single-seater.

einsortieren* vt sep to sort and put away. **in Schachteln/Körbe ~** to sort into boxes/baskets.

einspaltig adj (Typ) single-column. **etw ~ setzen** to set sth in a single column/in single columns.

einspannen vt sep (a) (in Rahmen) Leinwand to fit or put in (in +acc -to). **Saiten in einen Schläger ~** to string a racket. **(b)** (in Schraubstock) to clamp in (in +acc -to). **(c)** (in Kamera) to put in (in +acc -to); (in Schreibmaschine auch) to insert (in +acc in, into). **(d)** Pferde to harness. **(e)** (fig: arbeiten lassen) to rope in (für etw to do sth). **jdn für seine Zwecke ~** to use sb for one's own ends; siehe **eingespannt**.

Einspänner m -s, - one-horse carriage; (hum: Junggeselle) bachelor; (Aus) black coffee in a glass served with whipped cream.

einspännig adj Wagen one-horse. **der Wagen ist/fährt ~** the carriage is pulled by one horse.

einsparen vt sep to save; Energie, Strom auch to save or economize on; Kosten, Ausgaben to cut down on, to reduce; Posten to dispense with, to eliminate.

Einsparung f economy; siehe vt (von of) saving; reduction; elimination.

einspeicheln vt sep to insalivate.

einspeichern vt sep Daten to feed in (in +acc -to).

einsperren vt sep to lock up (in +acc or dat in), to lock in (in +acc or dat -to); (versehentlich) to lock in (in +acc or dat in); (inf: ins Gefängnis) to put away (inf), to lock up.

einspielen sep 1 vr (Mus, Sport) to warm up; (nach Sommerpause etc) to get into practice; (Regelung, Arbeit) to work out. **... aber das spielt sich alles noch ein** ... but things should sort themselves out all right; **ich fahre jetzt mit dem Bus, das hat sich gut eingespielt** I come by bus now, it's working out well; **sich aufeinander ~** to become attuned to or to get used to one another; siehe **eingespielt**. 2 vt (a) (Mus, Sport) Instrument, Schläger to play in. **(b)** (Film, Theat) to bring in, to gross. **(c)** (aufnehmen) Lied to record; Schallplatte auch to cut.

Einspiel|ergebnis nt (von Film) box-office takings pl or receipts pl.

einspinnen sep irreg 1 vr (Spinne) to spin a web around itself; (Larve) to spin a cocoon around itself. **sich in seine Gedanken ~** to wrap oneself up in one's thoughts. 2 vt (Spinne) to spin a web around.

Einsprache f (Aus, Sw) siehe **Einspruch**.

einsprachig adj monolingual.

einsprechen sep irreg 1 vi auf jdn ~ to harangue sb. 2 vt Text to speak.

einsprengen vt sep (mit Wasser) to sprinkle with water, to dampen; siehe **eingesprengt**.

Einsprengsel nt (Geol) xenocryst (spec), embedded crystal. **ein Buch mit einigen lyrischen ~n** a book with the odd moment of lyricism.

einspringen sep irreg 1 vi aux sein (a) (Tech) to lock shut or into place; (Maschinenteile) to engage. **(b)** (inf: aushelfen) to stand in; (mit Geld etc) to help out. 2 vr (Sport) to do some practice jumps.

Einspritz- in cpds (Aut, Med) injection.

Einspritzdüse f (Aut) injector.

einspritzen vt sep (a) (Aut, Med) to inject. **er spritzte ihr/sich Insulin ein** he gave her/himself an insulin injection, he injected her/himself with insulin. **(b)** (einsprengen) Wäsche to dampen, to sprinkle with water. **(c)** (inf: mit Schmutz) to splash, to spray.

Einspritzung f injection.

Einspruch m objection (auch Jur). **~ einlegen** (Admin) to file an objection, to register a protest; **gegen etw ~ erheben** to

object to sth, to raise an objection to sth; **ich erhebe ~!** (Jur) objection!; **~ abgelehnt!** (Jur) objection overruled!; **dem ~ wird stattgegeben!** (Jur) objection sustained!

Einspruchs-: **~frist** f (Jur) period for filing an objection; **~recht** nt right to object or protest.

einspurig adj (Rail) single-track; (Aut) single-lane. **die Straße ist nur ~ befahrbar** only one lane of the road is open, it's single-lane traffic only; **er denkt sehr ~** his mind runs in well-worn grooves.

Einssein nt (liter) oneness.

einst adv (a) (früher, damals) once. **Preußen ~ und heute** Prussia past and present or yesterday and today or then and now; **das E~ und das Heute or Jetzt** the past and the present. **(b)** (geh: in ferner Zukunft) one or some day.

einstampfen vt sep Papier to pulp (down); Trauben, Kohl to tread.

Einstand m (a) **ein guter ~** a good start to a new job; **alles Gute zum ~!** best wishes for the first day in your new job; **er hat gestern seinen ~ gegeben or gefeiert** yesterday he celebrated starting his new job. **(b)** (beim Tennis) deuce.

Einstandspreis m (Comm) introductory price.

einstanzen vt sep to stamp in (in +acc -to).

einstauben sep 1 vi aux sein to get covered in dust. **eingestaubt sein** to be covered in dust. 2 vt (Aus) sich (dat) das Gesicht (mit Puder) ~ to powder one's face, to dust one's face with powder.

einstäuben vt sep (mit Puder) to dust with powder, to powder; (mit Parfüm etc) to spray.

einstechen sep irreg 1 vt to pierce; Gummi, Haut, Membran auch to puncture; Nadel to put or stick (inf) in (in +acc -to), to insert (in +acc in, into); (Cook) to prick; (eingravieren) to engrave. 2 vi auf jdn/etw ~ to stab at sb/sth.

Einsteck|album nt (stamp) stock book (spec), stamp album.

einstecken vt sep (a) (in etw stecken) to put in (in +acc -to); Stecker auch, Gerät to plug in; Schwert to sheathe. **(b)** (in die Tasche etc) (sich dat) etw ~ to take sth; **hast du deinen Paß/ein Taschentuch/deine Brieftasche eingesteckt?** have you got your passport/a handkerchief/your briefcase with you?; **er steckte (sich) die Zeitung ein und ging los** he put the paper in his briefcase/pocket etc or he took the paper and left; **warte mal, ich habe mir meine Zigaretten noch nicht eingesteckt** hang on, I haven't got my cigarettes yet; **ich habe kein Geld eingesteckt or (incorrect) ~** I haven't any money on me; **kannst du meinen Geldbeutel für mich ~?** can you take my purse for me?; **steck deine Pistole wieder ein** put away your pistol. **(c)** (in den Briefkasten) to post, to mail (esp US). **(d)** (inf) Kritik etc to take; Beleidigung auch to swallow; (verdienen) Geld, Profit to pocket (inf). **der Boxer mußte viel ~** the boxer had to take a lot of punishment; **er steckt sie alle ein** he beats the lot of them (inf).

Einsteck-: **~kamm** m (decorative) comb; **~tuch** nt breast pocket handkerchief.

einstehen vi sep irreg aux sein (a) (sich verbürgen) **für jdn/etw ~** to vouch for sb/sth; **ich stehe dafür ein, daß ...** I will vouch that ...; **er stand mit seinem Wort dafür ein** he vouched for it personally. **(b)** **für etw ~** (Ersatz leisten) to make good sth; (sich bekennen) to answer for sth, to take responsibility for sth; **für jdn ~** to assume liability or responsibility for sb; **ich habe das immer behauptet, und dafür stehe ich auch ein** I've always said that, and I'll stand by it.

einsteigen vi sep irreg aux sein (a) (in ein Fahrzeug etc) to get in (in +acc -to); (umständlich, mit viel Gepäck etc auch) to climb or clamber in (in +acc -to); (in Zug auch, in Bus) to get on (in +acc -to). **~! (Rail etc)** all aboard!; **in eine Felswand ~** to attack a rockface; **er ist in die Problematik dieses Buchs noch nicht so richtig eingestiegen** he hasn't really got to grips with the problems in this book. **(b)** (in ein Haus etc) to climb or get in (in +acc -to). **(c)** (Sport sl) hart ~ to go in hard. **(d)** (inf) **in die Politik/ins Verlagsgeschäft ~** to go into politics/publishing; **er ist mit einer Million in diese Firma/ins Börsengeschäft eingestiegen** he put a million into this firm/invested a million on the stock exchange; **er ist ganz groß in dieses Geschäft eingestiegen** he's (gone) into that business in a big way (inf); **der Verlag ist jetzt in Lexika eingestiegen** the publishing company has branched out into dictionaries or into the dictionary market.

einstellbar adj adjustable.

einstellen sep 1 vt (a) (hineinstellen) to put in. **das Auto in die or der Garage ~** to put the car in(to) the garage; **Bücher ins Regal ~** to put books in the bookcase or away on the shelves; **das Buch ist falsch eingestellt** the book has been put in the wrong place. **(b)** (anstellen) Arbeitskräfte to take on. **„wir stellen ein: Sekretärinnen"** "we have vacancies for or are looking for secretaries". **(c)** (beenden) to stop; (endgültig auch) to discontinue; Expedition, Suche to call off; (Mil) Feindseligkeiten, Feuer to cease; (Jur) Prozeß, Verfahren to abandon. **die Arbeit ist eingestellt worden** work has stopped; (vorübergehend auch) work has been halted; **die Zeitung hat ihr Erscheinen eingestellt** the paper has ceased publication; **die Arbeit ~** (in den Ausstand treten) to withdraw one's labour. **(d)** (regulieren) Gerät (auf +acc to); Kanone to aim (auf +acc at); Fernglas, Fotoapparat (auf Entfernung) to focus (auf +acc on); Wecker, Zünder to set (auf +acc for); Radio to tune (in) (auf +acc to); Sender to tune in to. **die Steuerung auf Automatik ~** to switch over to or put the plane on the automatic pilot; **den Hebel auf Start ~** to set the lever to start; **das Radio**

auf Zimmerlautstärke ~ to set the radio to normal listening volume.

  (e) (*fig: abstimmen*) to tailor (*auf +acc* to). **einen Vortrag auf das Publikum ~** to tailor a lecture for *or* gear a lecture to one's audience.

  (f) (*Sport*) *Rekord* to equal.

2 *vr* **(a)** (*Besucher etc*) to appear, to present oneself; (*Fieber, Regen*) to set in; (*Symptome*) to appear; (*Folgen*) to become apparent, to appear; (*Wort, Gedanke*) to come to mind; (*Jahreszeiten*) to come, to arrive. **wenn es kalt ist, stellen sich bei mir regelmäßig heftige Kopfschmerzen ein** I always suffer from bad headaches when it's cold.

  (b) sich auf jdn/etw ~ (*sich richten nach*) to adapt oneself to sb/sth; (*sich vorbereiten auf*) to prepare oneself for sb/sth; *siehe* eingestellt.

3 *vi* to take on staff/workers.

einstellig *adj Zahl* single-digit.

Einstell-: ~knopf *m* (*an Radio etc*) tuning knob; ~platz *m* (*auf Hof*) carport; (*in großer Garage*) (covered) parking accommodation *no indef art*; ~schraube *f* adjustment screw.

Einstellung *f* **(a)** (*Anstellung*) employment.
  (b) (*Beendigung*) *siehe vt* **(c)** stopping; discontinuation; calling-off; cessation; abandonment. **der Sturm zwang uns zur ~ der Suche/Bauarbeiten** the storm forced us to call off *or* abandon the search/to stop work on the building; **die Lackierer beschlossen die ~ der Arbeit** the paint-sprayers decided to withdraw their labour *or* to down tools.
  (c) (*Regulierung*) *siehe vt* **(d)** adjustment; aiming; focusing; setting; tuning (in); (*Film: Szene*) take.
  (d) (*Gesinnung, Haltung*) attitude; (*politisch, religiös etc*) views *pl*. **er hat eine falsche ~ zum Leben** he doesn't have the right attitude to *or* outlook on life; **das ist doch keine ~!** what kind of attitude is that!, that's not the right attitude!

Einstellungs-: ~gespräch *nt* interview; ~stopp *m* halt in recruitment; ~termin *m* starting date; ~untersuchung *f* medical examination when starting a new job.

einstens *adv* (*obs*) *siehe* einst.

Einstich *m* (~stelle) puncture, prick; (*Vorgang*) insertion.

Einstichstelle *f* puncture (mark).

Einstieg *m* -(e)s, -e **(a)** *no pl* (*das Einsteigen*) getting in; (*in Bus*) getting on; (*von Dieb: in Haus etc*) getting in; (*fig: zu einem Thema etc*) lead-in (*zu* to). **~ nur vorn!** enter only at the front; **kein ~** exit only; **er stürzte beim ~ in die Eigernordwand ab** he fell during the assault on the north face of the Eiger.
  (b) (*von Bahn*) door; (*von Bus auch*) entrance.

einstig *adj attr* former.

einstimmen *sep* **1** *vi* (*in ein Lied*) to join in; (*fig: beistimmen*) to agree (*in +acc* with); (*zustimmen*) to agree (*in +acc* to). **in den Gesang/die Buhrufe (mit) ~** to join in the singing/booing.
  2 *vt* (*Mus*) *Instrument* to tune. **jdn/sich auf etw (acc) ~** (*fig*) to get *or* put sb/oneself in the (right) mood for sth; **auf eine Atmosphäre etc** to attune sb/oneself to sth.

einstimmig *adj* **(a)** *Lied* for one voice. **~ singen** to sing in unison; **riefen sie ~** they called in unison. **(b)** (*einmütig*) unanimous.

Einstimmigkeit *f* unanimity.

Einstimmung *f* (*Mus: von Instrumenten*) tuning. **für die richtige ~ der Zuhörer sorgen** (*fig*) to get the audience in the right mood.

einstippen *vt sep* (*dial*) to dunk.

einstmals *adv siehe* einst.

einstöckig *adj Haus* two-storey (*Brit*), two-story (*US*). **~ (gebaut)** to have two storeys *or* stories.

einstöpseln *vt sep* (*Elec*) to plug in (*in +acc* -to).

einstoßen *vt sep irreg Tür, Mauer* to knock *or* break down; *Scheibe* to push in, to break.

einstrahlen *vi sep* to irradiate (*spec*), to shine.

Einstrahlung *f* (*Sonnen~*) irradiation (*spec*), shining.

einstreichen *vt sep irreg* **(a)** *eine Wunde (mit Salbe)* ~ to put ointment on a wound; *eine Kuchenform (mit Fett)* ~ to grease a baking tin. **(b)** (*inf*) *Geld, Gewinn* to pocket (*inf*).

einstreuen *vt sep* to sprinkle in (*in +acc* -to); (*fig*) *Bemerkung etc* to slip in (*in +acc* -to).

Einstrom *m* (*Met*) **der ~ milder Meeresluft** a stream of mild air moving in from the sea.

einströmen *vi sep aux sein* to pour *or* flood in (*in +acc* -to); (*Licht, fig auch*) to stream in (*in +acc* -to). **kältere Luftschichten strömen nach Bayern ein** a stream of cooler air is moving in towards Bavaria; **~de Kaltluft** a stream of cold air.

einstrophig *adj* one-verse *attr*.

einstudieren* *vt sep Lied, Theaterstück* to rehearse. **einstudierte Antworten** (*fig*) well-rehearsed answers.

Einstudierung *f* (*Theat*) production.

einstufen *vt sep* to classify. **in eine Klasse/Kategorie etc ~** to put into a class/category *etc*.

einstufig *adj Rakete* single-stage.

Einstufung *f* classification. **nach seiner ~ in eine höhere Gehaltsklasse** after he was put on a higher salary grade.

einstündig *adj attr* one-hour. **mehr als ~e Verspätungen** delays of more than an hour; **nach ~er Pause** after an hour's *or* a one-hour break, after a break of an hour.

einstürmen *vi sep aux sein* **auf jdn ~** (*Mil*) to storm sb; (*fig*) to assail sb; **mit Fragen auf jdn ~** to bombard *or* besiege sb with questions.

Einsturz *m* collapse; (*von Mauer, Boden, Decke auch*) caving-in.

einstürzen *vi sep aux sein* to collapse; (*Mauer, Boden, Decke auch*) to cave in; (*Theorie, Gedankengebäude auch*) to crumble. **auf jdn ~** (*fig*) to overwhelm sb; **es stürzte viel auf ihn ein** he was overwhelmed by events.

Einsturzgefahr *f* danger of collapse.

einstweilen *adv* in the meantime; (*vorläufig*) temporarily.

einstweilig *adj attr* temporary. **~e Verfügung/Anordnung** (*Jur*) temporary *or* interim injunction/order; **~ verfügen** (*Jur*) to issue a temporary *or* an interim injunction.

einsuggerieren* *vt sep* **jdm etw ~** to suggest sth to sb; (*inf*) to brainwash sb into believing sth.

Einswerden *nt* (*geh*) becoming one *no art*.

eintägig *adj attr* one-day; *siehe* viertägig.

Eintagsfliege *f* (*Zool*) mayfly; (*fig*) nine-day wonder; (*Mode, Idee*) passing craze.

eintanzen *vr sep* to get used to dancing with sb; (*vor Turnier etc*) to dance a few practice steps.

Eintänzer *m* gigolo.

eintätowieren* *vt sep* to tattoo (*in/auf +acc* on).

eintauchen *sep* **1** *vt* to dip (*in +acc* in, into); (*völlig*) to immerse (*in +acc* in); *Brot* (*in Kaffee etc*) to dunk (*in +acc* in). **2** *vi aux sein* (*Schwimmer*) to dive in; (*Springer*) to enter the water; (*U-Boot*) to dive. **das U-Boot ist jetzt ganz eingetaucht** the submarine is now completely submerged.

Eintausch *m* exchange, swap (*inf*). **im ~ gegen** *or* **für etw** in exchange for sth; **„~ von Gutscheinen"** "coupons exchanged here".

eintauschen *vt sep* to exchange, to swap (*inf*) (*gegen, für* for); (*umtauschen*) *Devisen* to change.

eintausend *num* (*form*) *siehe* tausend.

einteilen *sep* **1** *vt* **(a)** to divide (up) (*in +acc* into); (*aufgliedern auch*) to split (up) (*in +acc* into); (*in Grade*) *Thermometer* to graduate, to calibrate.
  (b) (*sinnvoll aufteilen*) *Zeit, Arbeit* to plan (out), to organize; *Geld auch* to budget. **wenn ich mir eine Flasche gut einteile, reicht sie eine Woche** if I plan it well a bottle lasts me a week.
  (c) (*dienstlich verpflichten*) to detail (*zu* for). **er ist heute als Aufseher/zur Aufsicht eingeteilt** he has been allocated the job of supervisor/detailed for *or* assigned supervisory duties today.
  2 *vi* (*inf: haushalten*) to budget.

einteilig *adj Badeanzug* one-piece *attr*.

Einteilung *f siehe vt* **(a)** division; splitting up; gradation, calibration. **(b)** planning, organization; budgeting. **(c)** detailment (*esp Mil*), assignment.

Eintel *nt* (*Sw auch m*) -s, - (*Math*) whole.

eintippen *vt sep* to type in (*in +acc* -to).

eintönig *adj* monotonous. **~ reden** to talk in a monotone.

Eintönigkeit *f* monotony; (*von Stimme*) monotonousness.

Eintopf *m, no pl*, **Eintopfgericht** *or* **-essen** *nt* stew.

Eintracht *f, no pl* harmony, concord. **er hat zwischen den beiden wieder ~ gestiftet** he restored peaceful relations between the two of them; **~ X** (*Sport*) = X United.

einträchtig *adj* peaceable.

Einträchtigkeit *f siehe* Eintracht.

Eintrag *m* -(e)s, ¨-e **(a)** (*schriftlich*) entry (*in +acc* in). **(b)** (*geh*) **das tut der Sache keinen ~** that does/will do no harm. **(c)** (*Tex*) weft, woof.

eintragen *sep irreg* **1** *vt* **(a)** (*in Liste, auf Konto etc*) to enter; (*amtlich registrieren*) to register. **sich ~ lassen** to have one's name put down; **siehe eingetragen**.
  (b) **jdm Haß/Undank/Gewinn ~** to bring sb hatred/ingratitude/profit; **das trägt nur Schaden ein** that will only do you harm.
  2 *vr* to sign; (*sich vormerken lassen*) to put one's name down. **er trug sich ins Gästebuch/in die Warteliste ein** he signed the guest book/put his name (down) on the waiting list.

einträglich *adj* profitable; *Geschäft, Arbeit auch* lucrative, remunerative.

Einträglichkeit *f* profitability, profitableness.

Eintragung *f siehe* Eintrag **(a)**.

eintrainieren* *vt sep* to practise.

einträufeln *vt sep* **jdm Medizin in die Nase/ins Ohr ~** to put drops up sb's nose/in sb's ear; **jdm Haß ~** (*geh*) to infuse sb with hatred.

eintreffen *vi sep irreg aux sein* **(a)** (*ankommen*) to arrive. **„Bananen frisch eingetroffen"** "bananas – just in". **(b)** (*fig: Wirklichkeit werden*) to come true; (*Prophezeiung auch*) to be fulfilled.

eintreibbar *adj Schulden* recoverable; *Steuern, Zinsen* exactable.

eintreiben *vt sep irreg* **(a)** *Vieh, Nagel, Pfahl* to drive in (*in +acc* -to). **(b)** (*einziehen*) *Geldbeträge* to collect; *Schulden auch* to recover.

Eintreibung *f* (*von Geldbeträgen*) collection; (*von Schulden auch*) recovery.

eintreten *sep irreg* **1** *vi* **(a)** *aux sein* (*hineingehen*) (*ins Zimmer etc*) to go/come in (*in +acc* -to); (*in Verein, Partei etc*) to join (*in etw (acc)* sth). **ins Haus ~** to go into *or* enter the house; **in eine Firma ~** to go into *or* join a firm; **in die Politik/den diplomatischen Dienst ~** to go into *or* enter politics/the diplomatic service; **ins Heer ~** to join the army, to join up; **in den Krieg ~** to enter the war; **in Verhandlungen ~** (*form*) to enter into negotiations; **ins 30. Lebensjahr ~** (*form*) to enter upon (*form*) *or* go into one's 30th year; **die Verhandlungen sind in eine kritische Phase eingetreten** the negotiations have entered a critical phase; **die Rakete trat in ihre Umlaufbahn ein** the rocket went into its orbit; **bitte treten Sie ein!** (*form*) (please) do come in.
  (b) **auf jdn ~** to boot *or* kick sb, to put the boot in on sb (*sl*).
  (c) *aux sein* (*sich ereignen*) (*Tod*) to occur; (*Zeitpunkt*) to come; (*beginnen*) (*Dunkelheit, Nacht*) to fall; (*Besserung, Tauwetter*) to set in. **bei E~ der Dunkelheit** at nightfall; **gegen Abend trat starkes Fieber ein** towards evening the patient started to run a high temperature; **die Ebbe/Flut tritt gegen 3**

Uhr ein the tide starts to go out/come in or starts to turn at about 3 o'clock; **es ist eine Besserung eingetreten** there has been an improvement; **wenn der Fall eintritt, daß** ... if it happens that ...; **es ist der Fall eingetreten, den wir befürchtet hatten** what we had feared has in fact happened.

  (d) *aux sein* **für jdn/etw** ~ to stand or speak up for sb/sth; **sein mutiges E~ für seine Überzeugung** his courageous defence of his conviction or belief.

  (e) *(Sw)* **auf etw** *(acc)* ~ to follow sth up.

  2 *vt* **(a)** *(zertrümmern)* to kick in; **Tür** *auch* to kick down.

  (b) *(hineintreten)* **Stein** *etc* to tread in (**in** +*acc* -to).

  (c) Schuhe to wear or break in.

  (d) *sich (dat)* **etw (in den Fuß)** ~ to run sth into one's foot.

eintrichtern, eintrimmen *vt sep (inf)* **jdm etw** ~ to drum sth into sb; **jdm** ~, **daß** ... to drum it into sb that ...

Eintritt *m* **(a)** *(das Eintreten)* entry (**in** +*acc* (in)to); *(ins Zimmer etc auch)* entrance; *(in Verein, Partei etc)* joining (**in** +*acc* of). **beim** ~ **ins Zimmer** when or on entering the room; „~ **im Sekretariat"** "entrance through the office"; **seine Beziehungen erleichterten ihm den** ~ **ins Geschäftsleben** his connections made it easier for him to get into the business world; **der** ~ **in den Staatsdienst** entry (in)to the civil service; **die Schule soll auf den** ~ **ins Leben vorbereiten** school should prepare you for going out into life; **der** ~ **in die EWG** entry to the EEC; **der** ~ **ins Gymnasium** starting at grammar school; **seit seinem** ~ **in die Armee** since joining the army or joining up.

  (b) *(~sgeld)* admission (**in** +*acc* to); *(Einlaß auch)* admittance (**in** +*acc* to). **was kostet der** ~? how much or what is the admission?; ~ **frei!** admission free; ~ **DM 1,50** admission DM 1.50; „~ **verboten"** "no admittance"; **jdm** ~ **in etw** *(acc)* **gewähren** *(form)* to allow or permit sb to enter sth, to grant sb admission to sth *(form)*.

  (c) *(von Winter, Dunkelheit)* onset. **bei** ~ **eines solchen Falles** in such an event; **der** ~ **des Todes** the moment when death occurs; **bei** ~ **der Dunkelheit** at nightfall, as darkness fell/falls.

Eintritts-: ~**geld** *nt* entrance money, admission charge; **die Zuschauer verlangten das** ~**geld zurück** the audience asked for their money back; ~**karte** *f* ticket (of admission), entrance ticket; ~**preis** *m* admission charge.

eintrocknen *vi sep aux sein (Fluß, Farbe)* to dry up; *(Wasser, Blut)* to dry.

eintrommeln *sep (inf)* **1** *vt siehe* **eintrichtern. 2** *vi* **auf jdn** ~ *(lit, fig)* to pound sb.

eintrüben *vr sep (Met)* to cloud over, to become overcast.

Eintrübung *f (Met)* cloudiness *no pl*.

eintrudeln *vi sep aux sein (inf)* to drift in (**in** *inf). ... bis alle eingetrudelt sind* ... until everyone has turned up.

eintunken *vt sep* **Brot** to dunk (**in** +*acc* in).

eintüten *vt sep (form)* to put into (paper) bags.

ein|üben *vt sep* to practise; **Theaterstück, Rolle** *etc* to rehearse; **Rücksichtnahme, Solidarität** to learn or acquire (through practice). **sich** *(dat)* **etw** ~ to practise sth.

Ein|übung *f* practice; *(Theat etc)* rehearsal.

Einung *f (geh) siehe* **Einigung.**

einverleiben* *vt sep and insep* **(a) Gebiet, Land** to annex (**dat** to); **Firma, Ministerium** to incorporate (**dat** into). **(b)** *(hum inf)* **sich** *(dat)* **etw** ~ *(essen, trinken)* to put sth away *(inf)*, to polish sth off *(inf)*; *(sich aneignen, begreifen)* to assimilate sth, to take sth in.

Einverleibung *f, no pl siehe vt (a)* annexation; incorporation.

Einvernahme *f* -, -**n** *(Jur: esp Aus, Sw) siehe* **Vernehmung.**

einvernehmen* *vt insep irreg (Jur: esp Aus, Sw) siehe* **vernehmen.**

Einvernehmen *nt* -**s**, *no pl (Eintracht)* amity, harmony; *(Übereinstimmung)* agreement. **in gutem** or **bestem** ~ **leben** to live in perfect amity or harmony; **wir arbeiten in gutem** ~ **(miteinander)** we work in perfect harmony (together); **im** ~ **mit jdm** in agreement with sb; **in gegenseitigem** or **beiderseitigem** ~ by mutual agreement; **sich mit jdm ins** ~ **setzen** *(form)* to come to or reach an agreement or understanding with sb.

einvernehmlich *(esp Aus form)* **1** *adj* **Regelung** conjoint. **2** *adv* in conjunction, conjointly.

Einvernehmung *f (Jur: esp Aus, Sw) siehe* **Vernehmung.**

einverstanden *adj* ~! okay! *(inf)*, agreed!; ~ **sein** to agree, to consent, to be agreed; **ich bin** ~ that's okay or all right by me *(inf)*, I'm agreed; **mit jdm/etw** ~ **sein** to agree to sb/sth; *(übereinstimmen)* to agree or be in agreement with sb/sth; **sie ist damit** ~, **daß sie nur 10% bekommt** she has agreed or consented to take only 10%, it's all right by or with her that she only gets 10% *(inf)*; **ich bin mit deinem Verhalten/mit dir gar nicht** ~ I don't approve of your behaviour; **sich mit etw** ~ **erklären** to give one's agreement to sth.

einverständlich *adj* mutually agreed; **Ehescheidung** by mutual consent. **diese Frage wurde** ~ **geklärt** this question was settled to the satisfaction of both parties.

Einverständnis *nt (Zustimmung)* consent. **wir haben uns in gegenseitigem** ~ **scheiden lassen** we were divorced by mutual consent; **er erklärte sein** ~ **mit dem Plan** he gave his agreement to the plan; **das geschieht mit meinem** ~ that has my consent or agreement; **im** ~ **mit jdm handeln** to act with sb's consent.

Einverständnis|erklärung *f* declaration of consent. **die schriftliche** ~ **der Eltern** the parents' written consent.

Einw. *abbr of* **Einwohner.**

Einwaage *f, no pl (Comm)* **(a)** *(Reingewicht)* weight of contents of can or jar excluding juice etc. **Frucht-~/Fleisch-~ 200 g** fruit/meat content 200g. **(b)** *(Comm: Gewichtsverlust)* weight loss.

einwachsen[1] *vt sep* **Boden, Skier** to wax.

einwachsen[2] *vi sep irreg aux sein (Baum, Staude)* to establish itself; *(Finger-, Zehennagel)* to become ingrown. **der Zehennagel ist mir eingewachsen** I have an ingrowing toenail.

Einwand *m* -(e)s, ¨e objection. **einen** ~ **erheben** or **vorbringen** or **geltend machen** *(form)* to put forward or raise an objection.

Einwanderer *m* immigrant.

einwandern *vi sep aux sein (nach, in* +*acc* to) to immigrate; *(Volk)* to migrate.

Einwanderung *f* immigration *(nach, in* +*acc* to). **vor seiner** ~ **in die USA** before he came or immigrated to the USA.

Einwanderungs- *in cpds* immigration.

einwandfrei *adj* **(a)** *(ohne Fehler)* perfect; **Sprache, Arbeit** *auch* faultless; **Benehmen, Leumund** irreproachable, impeccable; **Lebensmittel** perfectly fresh. **er arbeitet sehr genau und** ~ his work is very precise and absolutely faultless; **er spricht** ~ or **ein** ~**es Spanisch** he speaks perfect Spanish, he speaks Spanish perfectly.

  (b) *(unzweifelhaft)* indisputable; **Beweis** *auch* definite. **etw** ~ **beweisen** to prove sth beyond doubt, to give definite proof of sth; **es steht** ~ **fest, daß** ... it is beyond question or quite indisputable that ...; **das ist** ~ **Betrug/Unterschlagung** that is a clear case of fraud/embezzlement.

einwärts *adv* inwards.

einwärtsgebogen *adj attr* bent inwards.

einwässern *vt sep (Cook)* to steep.

einweben *vt sep irreg* to weave in (**in** +*acc* -to); *(fig auch)* to work in (**in** +*acc* -to).

einwechseln *vt sep* **Geld** to change (**in** +*acc, gegen** into). **jdm Geld** ~ to change money for sb.

einwecken *vt sep* to preserve; **Obst** *etc auch* to bottle; *(rare: in Büchsen)* to can, to tin *(Brit)*. **laß dich** ~! *(inf)* get stuffed! *(sl)*.

Einweck-: ~**glas** *nt* preserving jar; ~**gummi,** ~**ring** *m* rubber seal *(for preserving jar)*.

Einweg- [ˈainveːk]: ~**flasche** *f* non-returnable bottle; ~**scheibe** *f* one-way glass; ~**spiegel** *m* one-way mirror.

einweichen *vt sep* to soak.

einweihen *vt sep* **(a)** *(feierlich eröffnen)* to open (officially); *(fig)* to christen, to baptize. **(b) jdn in etw** *(acc)* ~ to initiate sb into sth; **er ist eingeweiht** he knows all about it; *siehe* **Eingeweihte(r).**

Einweihung(sfeier) *f* (official) opening.

einweisen *vt sep irreg* **(a)** *(in Wohnung, Haus)* to send, to assign (**in** +*acc* to).

  (b) *(in Krankenhaus, Heilanstalt)* to admit (**in** +*acc* to).

  (c) *(in Arbeit unterweisen)* **jdn** ~ to introduce sb to his job or work; **er wurde von seinem Vorgänger (in die Arbeit) eingewiesen** his predecessor showed him what the job involved.

  (d) *(in ein Amt)* to install (**in** +*acc* in).

  (e) *(Aut)* to guide in (**in** +*acc* -to).

Einweisung *f siehe vt* **(a)** accommodation (**in** +*acc* in). **(b)** admission (**in** +*acc* to). **die** ~ **der neuen Mitarbeiter übernehmen** to assume responsibility for introducing new employees to their jobs or work. **(d)** installation (**in** +*acc* in). **(e)** guiding in.

einwenden *vt sep irreg* **etwas/nichts gegen etw einzuwenden haben** to have an objection/no objection to sth, to object/not to object to sth; **dagegen läßt sich** ~, **daß** ... one objection to this is that ...; **dagegen läßt sich nichts** ~ there can be no objection to that; **er wandte ein, daß** ... he objected or raised the objection that ...; **er wandte gegen meinen Plan ein, daß** ... he had or raised the following objection to my plan, that ...; **er hat immer etwas einzuwenden** he always finds something to object to, he always has some objection to make.

Einwendung *f* objection *(auch Jur)*. **gegen etw** ~**en erheben** or **haben** or **vorbringen** to raise objections to sth.

einwerfen *sep irreg* **1** *vt* **(a) Fensterscheibe** *etc* to break, to smash.

  (b) *(Sport)* **Ball** to throw in.

  (c) Brief to post, to mail *(esp US)*.

  (d) *(fig)* **Bemerkung** to make, to throw in. **er warf ein, daß** ... he made the point that ...; **ja, warf er ein** yes, he interjected.

  2 *vi (Sport)* to throw in, to take the throw-in. **er hat falsch eingeworfen** he fouled when he was throwing in.

einwertig *adj (Chem)* monovalent; *(Ling)* one place.

einwickeln *vt sep* **(a)** to wrap (up). **er wickelte sich fest in seinen Mantel ein** he wrapped himself up well in his coat.

  (b) *(inf: übervorteilen, überlisten)* to fool *(inf)*, to take in; *(durch Schmeicheleien)* to butter up *(inf)*. **da hat er sich schön** ~ **lassen** he's really been taken for a ride *(inf)*.

Einwickelpapier *nt* wrapping paper.

einwiegen[1] *vt sep* **Kind** to rock to sleep.

einwiegen[2] *vt sep irreg (Comm)* **Mehl** *etc* to weigh out.

einwilligen *vi sep* (**in** +*acc* to) to consent, to agree.

Einwilligung *f (in* +*acc* to) consent, agreement.

einwinken *vt sep* to guide or direct in.

einwintern *vt sep* to winter.

einwirken *sep* **1** *vi* **auf jdn/etw** ~ to have an effect on sb/sth; *(beeinflussen)* to influence sb/sth; **diese Maßnahmen wirken günstig auf die Marktsituation ein** these measures are having a favourable effect on the market situation; **etw** ~ **lassen** *(Med)* to let sth work in; *(Chem)* to let sth react; **Beize** to let sth soak or work in.

  2 *vt* to work in (**in** +*acc* -to).

Einwirkung *f* influence; *(einer Sache auch)* effect; *(eines Katalysators)* effect. **die positive** ~ **dieser politischen Maßnahmen** the positive effect of these political measures; **Bayern steht unter** ~ **eines atlantischen Hochs** Bavaria is being affected by an anticyclone over the Atlantic; **unter (der)** ~ **von Drogen** *etc* under the influence of drugs *etc*; **unter (der)** ~ **eines Schocks stehen** to be suffering (from) the effects of shock; **nach ~ der Salbe** ... when the ointment has worked in ...

Einwirkungsmöglichkeit f influence. **da fehlt uns jede ~** we cannot bring any influence to bear in that matter; **dadurch haben wir eine gute ~** this has made it possible for us to have some influence or to bring some influence to bear.

einwöchig adj one-week attr.

Einwohner(in f) m -s, - inhabitant.

Einwohner-: ~meldeamt nt residents' registration office; **sich beim ~meldeamt (an)melden** ≈ to register with the police; ~schaft f, no pl population, inhabitants pl; ~verzeichnis nt list of inhabitants' names and addresses; ~zahl f population, number of inhabitants.

Einwurf m **(a)** (das Hineinwerfen) (von Münze) insertion; (von Brief) posting, mailing (esp US). **≈ 2 Mark** insert 2 marks. **(b)** (Sport) throw-in. **falscher ~** foul throw. **(c)** (Schlitz) slot; (von Briefkasten) slit. **(d)** (fig) interjection; (Einwand) objection.

einwurzeln vir sep (vi: aux sein) (Pflanzen) to take root; (fig auch) to become rooted (bei in); siehe eingewurzelt.

Einzahl f singular.

einzahlen vt sep to pay in. **Geld auf ein Konto ~** to pay money into an account.

Einzahlung f deposit.

Einzahlungs-: ~schalter m (Post) counter for paying in deposits at a post office; ~schein m (Beleg) = counterfoil; (Sw: Zahlkarte) pay(ing)-in slip, deposit slip (US).

einzäunen vt sep to fence in.

Einzäunung f (Zaun) fence, fencing; (das Umzäunen) fencing-in.

einzeichnen vt sep to draw or mark in. **ist der Ort eingezeichnet?** is the place marked?

Einzeichnung f **(a)** no pl (das Einzeichnen) drawing or marking in. **(b)** (Markierung) marking.

Einzeiler m -s, - (Liter) one-line poem, one-liner (inf), monostich (form).

einzeilig adj one-line attr.

Einzel nt -s, - (Tennis) singles sing.

Einzel-: ~aktion f independent action; (Sport) solo performance or effort; ~antrieb m (Tech) independent drive; ~aufhängung f (Aut) independent suspension; ~aufstellung f (Comm) itemized list; ~ausgabe f separate edition; ~behandlung f individual treatment; ~darstellung f individual treatment; **eine Geschichte unseres Jahrhunderts in ~darstellungen** a history of our century in individual portraits; ~erscheinung f isolated occurrence; ~fahrer m (Motorradrennen) solo rider.

Einzelfall m individual case; (Sonderfall) isolated case, exception.

Einzelfall-: ~hilfe f individual attention; ~studie f (Sociol, Psych) (individual) case study.

Einzel-: ~fertigung f special order; **in ~fertigung hergestellt** made to order, custom-made (esp US); ~feuer nt (Mil) independent fire; ~gänger m -s, - loner, lone wolf; (Elefant) rogue; ~haft f solitary confinement.

Einzelhandel m retail trade. **das ist im ~ teurer als im Großhandel** that is dearer (to buy) retail than wholesale; **im ~ erhältlich** available retail; **im ~ kostet das** ... it retails at ...

Einzelhandels-: ~geschäft nt retail shop; ~kaufmann m trained retail salesman; ~preis m retail price; ~spanne f retail profit margin.

Einzel-: ~händler m retailer, retail trader; ~haus nt detached house; ~heit f detail, particular; **auf ~heiten eingehen** to go into detail(s); **etw in allen/bis in die kleinsten ~heiten schildern** to describe sth in great detail/right down to the last detail; **sich in ~heiten verlieren** or **to get bogged down in details**; ~hof m isolated farm; ~kabine f (individual) cubicle; ~kampf m **(a)** (Mil) single combat; **(b)** (Sport) individual competition; ~kind nt only child.

Einzeller m -s, - (Biol) single-celled or unicellular organism.

einzellig adj single-cell(ed) attr, unicellular.

einzeln 1 adj **(a)** individual; (getrennt) separate; (von Paar) odd. **~e Teile des Bestecks kann man nicht kaufen** you cannot buy individual or separate or single pieces of this cutlery; **wir kamen ~** we came separately; **die Gäste kamen ~ herein** the guests came in separately or singly or one by one; **bitte ~ eintreten** please come in one (person) at a time; **Bände ~ verkaufen** to sell volumes separately or singly; **die ~en Städte, die wir besucht haben** the individual cities which we visited; **~ aufführen** to list separately or individually or singly; **im ~en Fall** in the particular case.

(b) Mensch individual.

(c) (alleinstehend) Baum, Haus single, solitary.

(d) (mit pl n: einige, vereinzelte) some; (Met) Schauer scattered. **~e Firmen haben ...** some firms have ..., the odd firm has ..., a few odd firms have ...; **~e Besucher kamen schon früher** a few or one or two visitors came earlier.

2 adj (substantivisch) **(a)** (Mensch) der/die ~e the individual; **ein ~er** an individual, a single person; (ein einziger Mensch) one single person; **~e** some (people), a few (people), one or two (people); **jeder ~e/jede ~e** each individual; **jeder ~e muß dabei helfen** (each and) every one of you/them etc must help; **als ~er kann man nichts machen** as an individual one can do nothing.

(b) ~es some; **~es hat mir gefallen** I liked parts or some of it; **~e haben mir gefallen** I liked some of them.

(c) das ~e the particular; **er kam vom E~en zum Allgemeinen** he went from the particular to the general; **jedes ~e** each one; **im ~en auf etw (acc) eingehen** to go into detail(s) or particulars about sth; **etw im ~en besprechen** to discuss sth in detail; **bis ins ~e** right down to the last detail.

einzelnstehend adj attr solitary. **ein paar ~e Bäume** a few

scattered trees, a few trees here and there; **ein ~er Baum** a tree (standing) all by itself, a solitary tree.

Einzel-: ~nummer f (von Zeitung) single issue; ~person f single person; **für eine ~person kochen** to cook for one (person) or a single person; ~personen haben es auf Reisen meist schwer, ein Hotelzimmer zu bekommen people travelling alone usually find it hard to get a hotel room; ~radaufhängung f (Aut) independent suspension; ~richter m judge sitting singly; ~sieger m individual winner; ~spiel nt (Tennis) singles sing; ~stehende(r) mf decl as adj siehe Alleinstehende(r); ~staat m individual state; ~stück nt ein schönes ~stück a beautiful piece; ~stücke verkaufen wir nicht we don't sell them singly; ~stunde f private or individual lesson; ~teil nt individual or separate part; (Ersatzteil) spare or replacement part; **etw in seine ~teile zerlegen** to take sth to pieces; ~unterricht m private lessons pl or tuition; ~verkauf m (Comm) retail sale; (das Verkaufen) retailing, retail selling; **Radios geben wir nicht im ~verkauf ab** we don't sell radios retail; ~verpackung f individual packing; ~wertung f (Sport) individual placings pl; (bei Kür) individual marks pl; ~wesen nt individual; ~wettbewerb m (Sport) individual competition; ~zelle f single cell (auch Biol); ~zimmer nt single room.

einzementieren* vt sep Stein to cement; Safe to build or set into (the) concrete; Kachel to cement on.

Einzieh-: **e~bar** adj retractable; Schulden recoverable; ~decke f duvet, continental quilt.

einziehen sep irreg 1 vt **(a)** (hineinziehen, einfügen) Gummiband, Faden to thread; (in einen Bezug etc) to put in; (Build: einbauen) Wand, Balken to put in. **sich (dat) einen Splitter ~** (dial) to get a splinter.

(b) (einsaugen) Flüssigkeit to soak up; (durch Strohhalm) to draw up; Duft to breathe in; Luft, Rauch to draw in.

(c) (zurückziehen) Fühler, Krallen, Fahrgestell to retract, to draw in; Bauch, Netz to pull or draw in; Antenne to retract; Schultern to hunch; Periskop, Flagge, Segel to lower, to take down; Ruder to ship, to take in. **den Kopf ~** to duck (one's head); **zieh den Bauch ein!** keep or tuck (inf) your tummy in; **der Hund zog den Schwanz ein** the dog put his tail between his legs; **mit eingezogenem Schwanz** (lit, fig) with its/his/her tail between its/his/her legs.

(d) (Mil) (zu into) Personen to conscript, to call up, to draft (esp US); Fahrzeuge etc to requisition.

(e) (kassieren) Steuern, Gelder to collect; (fig) Erkundigungen to make (über +acc about).

(f) (aus dem Verkehr ziehen) Banknoten, Münzen to withdraw (from circulation), to call in; (beschlagnahmen) Führerschein to take away, to withdraw; Vermögen to confiscate.

(g) (Typ) Wörter, Zeilen to indent.

2 vi aux sein **(a)** (in Wohnung, Haus) to move in. **wer ist im dritten Stock eingezogen?** who has moved into the third floor?; **er zog bei Bekannten ein** he moved in with friends; **ins Parlament ~** to take up one's seat in parliament).

(b) (auch Mil: einmarschieren) to march in (in +acc -to).

(c) (einkehren) to come (in +dat to). **mit ihm zog eine fröhliche Stimmung bei uns ein** he brought a happy atmosphere with him; **wenn der Friede im Lande einzieht** when peace comes to our country, when we have peace; **Ruhe und Ordnung zogen wieder ein** law and order returned; **bei uns müßte endlich einmal bessere Laune ~** it's time we had a better atmosphere here.

(d) (eindringen) to soak in (in +acc -to).

Einziehung f **(a)** (Mil) (von Personen) conscription, call-up, drafting (esp US); (von Fahrzeugen) requisitioning. **(b)** (Beschlagnahme) (von Vermögen, Publikationen) confiscation; (Rücknahme: von Banknoten, Führerschein etc) withdrawal. **(c)** (Eintreiben: von Steuern etc) collection.

einzig 1 adj **(a)** attr only, sole. **ich sehe nur eine ~e Möglichkeit** I can see only one (single) possibility; **ich habe nicht einen ~en Brief bekommen** I haven't had a single or solitary letter; **kein or nicht ein ~es Mal** not once, not one single time.

(b) (emphatisch) absolute, complete. **dieses Fußballspiel war eine ~e Schlammschlacht** this football match was just one big mudbath.

(c) pred (~artig) unique. **es ist ~ in seiner Art** it is quite unique; **sein Können steht ~ da** his skill is unmatched, his skill is second to none.

2 adj (substantivisch) der/die ~e the only one; das ~e the only thing; **das ist das ~e, was wir tun können** that's the only thing we can do; **ein ~er hat geantwortet** only one (person) answered; **kein ~er wußte es** nobody or not a single or solitary person knew; **die ~en, die es wußten** ... the only ones who knew ...; **er hat als ~er das Ziel erreicht** he was the one or the sole person to reach the finish; **Hans ist unser E~er** Hans is our only child or our one and only.

3 adv **(a)** (allein) only, solely. **seine Beförderung hat er ~ dir zu verdanken** he owes his promotion entirely to you; **die ~ mögliche Lösung** the only possible solution, the only solution possible; **~ und allein solely**; **~ und allein deshalb hat er gewonnen** he owes his victory solely or entirely to that, that's the only or sole reason he won; **das ~ Wahre or Senkrechte** (inf) the only thing; (das beste) the real McCoy; **jetzt Ferien machen/ein Bier trinken, das wäre das ~ Wahre** etc to take a holiday/have a beer, that's just what the doctor ordered (inf) or that would be just the job.

(b) (inf: außerordentlich) fantastically.

einzig|artig adj unique. **der Film war ~ schön** the film was astoundingly beautiful.

Einzig|artigkeit f uniqueness.

Einzigkeit f uniqueness.
Einzimmer- in cpds one-room.
Einzug m (a) (in Haus etc) move (in +acc into). **vor dem ~** before moving in or the move; **der ~ in das neue Haus** moving or the move into the new house; **der ~ ins Parlament** taking office; (Abgeordneter) taking up one's seat.
(b) (Einmarsch) entry (in +acc into).
(c) (fig: von Stimmung, Winter etc) advent. **der Winter hielt seinen ~ mit Schnee und Frost** winter arrived amid snow and frost; **der Frühling etc hält seinen ~** spring etc is coming; **in der Politik wirkt sich der ~ einer neuen Stimmung aus** a new mood is beginning to make itself felt in the world of politics, a new mood has entered the world of politics.
(d) (von Feuchtigkeit) penetration. **der ~ kühlerer Meeresluft ...** a low trough moving in from the sea ...
(e) (von Steuern, Geldern) collection; (von Banknoten) withdrawal, calling-in.
(f) (Typ) indentation.
Einzugs-: **~bereich** m catchment area; **~feier** f housewarming (party); **~gebiet** nt (lit, fig) catchment area.
einzwängen vt sep (lit) to squeeze or jam or wedge in; (fig) jdn to constrain, to constrict; Idee to force. **ich fühle mich eingezwängt** (in Kleidung, Ehe etc) I feel constricted.
Einzylindermotor m one- or single-cylinder engine.
Eipulver nt dried or powdered egg.
Eis nt -es, - (a) no pl (gefrorenes Wasser) ice. **zu ~ gefrieren** to freeze, to turn to ice; **vom ~ eingeschlossen sein** to be iced in or icebound; **ein Herz von ~** (fig) a heart of stone; **das ~ brechen** (fig) to break the ice; **jdn aufs ~ führen** (fig) to take sb for a ride (inf), to lead sb up the garden path; **etw auf ~ legen** (lit) to chill sth, to put sth on ice; (fig inf) to put sth on ice or into cold storage.
(b) (Speise~) ice(-cream). **er kaufte 3 ~** he bought 3 ice-creams or ices; **~ am Stiel** ice(d)-lolly (Brit), popsicle (US)®.
Eis-: **~bahn** f ice-rink; **~bär** m polar bear; **~becher** m (aus Pappe) ice-cream tub; (aus Metall) sundae dish; (Eis) sundae; **e~bedeckt** adj attr ice-covered, covered in ice; **~bein** nt (a) (Cook) knuckle of pork (boiled and served with sauerkraut); (b) (hum inf) wenn ich noch länger hier in dieser Kälte stehe, bekomme ich **~beine** if I stand around here in this cold any longer my feet will turn to ice; **~berg** m iceberg; **die Spitze des ~bergs** (fig) the tip of the iceberg; **~beutel** m ice pack; **~bildung** f es kam zur **~bildung auf den Flüssen** ice formed on the rivers; **zur Verhinderung der ~bildung auf Fahrbahndecken** to prevent icing on or ice forming on road surfaces; **e~blau** adj, **~blau** nt blue-white; **~block** m block of ice; **~blume** f usu pl frost pattern; **~bombe** f (Cook) bombe glacée; **~brecher** m icebreaker; **~bude** f ice-cream stall.
Eischnee m (Cook) beaten white of egg.
Eis-: **~creme** f ice(-cream); **~decke** f ice sheet, sheet of ice; **~diele** f ice-cream parlour.
eisen vt Tee, Wodka to ice, to chill; siehe geeist.
Eisen nt -s, - (a) (no pl: Metall) iron. **ein Mann aus ~** a man of iron; **mehrere/noch ein ~ im Feuer haben** (fig) to have more than one/another iron in the fire; **Muskeln von ~ haben** to have muscles of steel; **bei jdm auf ~ beißen** (fig) to get nowhere with sb; **zum alten ~ gehören** or **zählen** (fig) to be on the scrap heap; **jdn/etw zum alten ~ werfen** (fig) to throw sb/sth on the scrap heap; **man muß das ~ schmieden, solange es heiß** or **warm ist** (Prov) one must strike while the iron is hot (prov); siehe **Blut**, **heiß**.
(b) (Bügel~, Golf) iron; (~beschlag) iron fitting; (~band) iron band or.hoop; (Huf~) shoe; (Fang~) trap; (obs: Fesseln) fetters pl (obs), irons pl; (obs: Schwert) iron (obs). **jdn in ~ legen** (obs) to put or clap sb in irons; **durch das ~ sterben** (obs) to die by the sword.
(c) (no pl: Med) iron.
Eisen-: **~ader** f vein of iron ore; **e~artig** adj ironlike.
Eisenbahn f railway (Brit), railroad (US); (~wesen) railways pl, railroad (US); (inf: Zug) train; (Spielzeug~) train set. **ich fahre lieber (mit der) ~ als (mit dem) Bus** I prefer to travel by train or rail than by bus; **Onkel Alfred arbeitet bei der ~** uncle Alfred works for the railways/railroad; **es ist (aller)höchste ~** (inf) it's getting late.
Eisenbahn-: **~abteil** nt (railway/railroad) compartment; **~anlagen** pl railway/railroad installations pl; **~brücke** f railway/railroad bridge.
Eisenbahner(in) m -s, - railwayman (Brit), railway employee (Brit), railroader (US).
Eisenbahn-: **~fähre** f train ferry; **~fahrkarte** f rail ticket; **~fahrt** f train or rail journey or ride; **~gesellschaft** f railway/railroad company; **~gleis** nt railway/railroad track; **~knotenpunkt** m railway/railroad junction; **~netz** nt rail(way)/railroad network; **~schaffner** m (railway) guard, (railroad) conductor (US); **~schiene** f railway/railroad track; **~schwelle** f (railway/railroad) sleeper; **~signal** nt railway/railroad signal; **~station** f railway/railroad station; **~strecke** f railway line, railroad (US); **~überführung** f (railway/railroad) footbridge; **~unglück** nt railway/railroad accident, train crash; **~unterführung** f railway/railroad underpass; **~verbindung** f rail link; (Anschluß) connection; **~verkehr** m rail(way)/railroad traffic; **~wagen** m (Personen~) railway/railroad carriage; (Güter~) goods wagon or truck; **~wesen** nt railway/railroad system; **ein Begriff aus dem ~wesen** a concept from the railways/railroad; **~zug** m railway/railroad train.
Eisenbart(h) m: Doktor ~ (fig) quack, horse-doctor (inf).
Eisen-: **~bau** m steel girder construction; **~bereifung** f iron hooping; (Reif) iron hoop; **~bergwerk** nt iron mine; **~beschlag** m ironwork no pl; (zum Verstärken) iron band; **e~beschlagen**

adj with iron fittings; Stiefel steel-tipped; **~beton** m (dated) ferroconcrete, reinforced concrete; **~blech** nt sheet iron; **~block** m iron block, block of iron; **~bohrer** m (Tech) iron or steel drill; **~chlorid** nt (FeCl₂) ferrous chloride; (FeCl₃) ferric chloride; **~draht** m steel wire; **~erz** nt iron ore; **~feile** f iron file; **~feilspäne** pl iron filings pl; **~flecken** pl (in Kartoffeln) discoloured patches pl; **~garn** nt steel thread; **~gehalt** m iron content; **~gießerei** f (Vorgang) iron smelting; (Werkstatt) iron foundry; **~glanz**, **~glimmer** m ferric oxide, iron glance; **~guß** m iron casting; **e~haltig** adj Gestein iron-bearing, ferruginous (form); **das Wasser ist e~haltig** the water contains iron; **~hammer** m steam hammer; (Werkstatt) forge; **~handlung** f ironmonger's (shop); **e~hart** adj (lit) as hard as iron; **ein e~harter Mann/Wille** a man/will of iron; **~hut** m (a) (Bot) monk's hood, aconite; (b) (Hist) iron helmet; **~hütte** f ironworks pl or sing, iron foundry; **~hüttenkombinat** nt (DDR) iron processing combine; **~industrie** f iron industry; **~karbid** nt cementite; **~kern** m iron core; **~kies** m iron pyrites sing; **~kitt** m iron-cement; **~kur** f course of iron treatment; **~legierung** f iron alloy; **~mangel** m iron deficiency; **~oxyd** nt ferric oxide; **~präparat** nt (Med) iron tonic/tablets pl; **e~schaffend** adj attr iron and steel producing; **~schlacke** f iron slag; **e~schüssig** adj Boden iron-bearing, ferruginous (form); **~späne** pl iron filings pl; **~stange** f iron bar; **~sulphat** nt ferric sulphate; **~träger** m iron girder; **e~verarbeitend** adj attr iron processing; **~verbindung** f (Chem) iron compound; **~vitriol** nt iron or ferrous sulphate, green vitriol; **~waren** pl ironmongery sing; **~warenhändler** m ironmonger; **~warenhandlung** f ironmonger's (shop); **~werk** nt (a) (Art) ironwork; (b) siehe **~hütte**; **~zeit** f (Hist) Iron Age.
eisern adj (a) attr (aus Eisen) iron. **das E~e Kreuz** (Mil) the Iron Cross; **der E~e Kanzler** the Iron Chancellor; **der ~e Vorhang** (Theat) the safety curtain; **der E~e Vorhang** (Pol) the Iron Curtain; **~e Lunge** (Med) iron lung; **die E~e Jungfrau** (Hist) the Iron Maiden; **~e Hochzeit** 65th wedding anniversary.
(b) (fest, unnachgiebig) Disziplin iron attr, strict; Wille iron attr, of iron; Energie unflagging, indefatigable; Ruhe unshakeable. **~e Gesundheit** iron constitution; **sein Griff war ~** his grip was like iron; **er schwieg ~** he remained resolutely silent; **mit ~er Stirn** (unverschämt) brazenly; (unerschütterlich) resolutely; **er ist ~ bei seinem Entschluß geblieben** he stuck steadfastly or firmly to his decision; **mit ~er Faust** with an iron hand; **es ist ein ~es Gesetz, daß ...** it's a hard and fast rule that ...; **ein ~es Regiment führen** to rule with a rod of iron; **in etw** (dat) **~ sein/bleiben** to be/remain resolute about sth; **da bin or bleibe ich ~!** (inf) that's definite; (aber) **~!** (inf) (but) of course!, absolutely!; **mit ~em Besen auskehren** to make a clean sweep, to be ruthless in creating order; **~ trainieren/sparen** to train/save resolutely or with iron determination.
(c) attr (unantastbar) Reserve emergency; Ration auch iron.
Eiseskälte f icy cold.
Eis-: **~fischerei** f fishing through ice; **~fläche** f (surface of the) ice; **die ~fläche des Sees** the (sheet of) ice covering the lake; **e~frei** adj ice-free attr, free of ice pred; **~gang** m ice drift; **e~gekühlt** adj chilled; **~getränk** nt iced drink; **e~grau** adj (liter) steel(y) grey; **eine e~graue Alte** a hoary old woman; **~heiligen** pl: die drei **~heiligen** three Saints' Days, 12th-14th May, which are usually particularly cold and after which further frost is rare; **~hockey** nt ice hockey, hockey (US).
eisig adj (a) (kalt) Wasser, Wind icy (cold); Kälte icy. (b) (jäh) Schreck, Grauen chilling. **es durchzuckte mich ~** a cold shiver ran through me. (c) (fig: abweisend) icy, glacial; Schweigen auch frosty, chilly; Ablehnung cold; Blick icy, cold; Lächeln frosty.
Eis-: **~jacht** f ice-yacht; **~kaffee** m iced coffee; **e~kalt** adj (a) icy-cold; (b) siehe **eisig** (b); (c) (fig) (abweisend) icy, cold, frosty; (kalt und berechnend) cold-blooded, cold and calculating; (dreist) cool; **davor habe ich keine Angst, das mache ich e~kalt** I'm not afraid of that, I can do it without turning a hair; **machst du das? — ja! e~kalt** will you do it? — no problem; **~kappe** f icecap; **~kasten** m (S Ger, Aus) refrigerator, fridge (Brit), icebox (US); **~keller** m cold store, cold room; **unser Schlafzimmer ist ein ~keller** our bedroom is like an icebox; **~kraut** nt iceplant; **~kristall** m ice crystal; **~kunstlauf** m figure skating; **~kunstläufer** m figure skater; **~lauf** m ice-skating; **e~laufen** vi sep irreg aux sein to ice-skate; **sie läuft e~** she ice-skates; **~läufer** m ice-skater; **~männer** pl (S Ger, Aus) siehe **~heiligen**; **~maschine** f ice-cream machine; **~meer** nt polar sea; Nördliches/Südliches **~meer** Arctic/Antarctic Ocean; **~monat**, **~mond** m (obs) January; **~nadeln** pl ice needles pl; **~nebel** m freezing fog; **~palast** m ice rink; (hum inf) icebox; **~pickel** m ice axe, ice pick.
Eisprung m (Physiol) ovulation no art.
Eis-: **~pulver** nt (Cook) ice-cream mix; **~punkt** m (Phys) freezing point; **~regen** m sleet; **~revue** f ice revue, ice show; **~schießen** nt curling; **~schmelze** f thaw; **~schnellauf** m speed skating; **~schnelläufer** m speed skater; **~scholle** f ice floe; **~schrank** m refrigerator, fridge (Brit), icebox (US); **~segeln** nt ice-sailing; **~sport** m ice sports pl; **~(sport)stadion** nt ice rink; **~stock** m (Sport) curling stone; **~(stock)schießen** nt curling; **~tanz** nt ice-dancing; **~torte** f ice-cream cake; **~verkäufer** m ice-cream seller or man (inf); **~vogel** m (a) kingfisher; (b) (Schmetterling) white admiral; **~wasser** nt icy water; (Getränk) iced water; **~weln** m sweet wine made from grapes which have been exposed to frost; **~würfel** m ice cube; **~zapfen** m icicle; **~zeit** f Ice Age, glacial epoch (form); **e~zeitlich** adj ice-age, of the Ice Age.
eitel adj (a) Mensch vain; (eingebildet auch) conceited. **~ wie ein Pfau** vain as a peacock.

(b) (liter) *Hoffnung, Wahn, Versuch, Gerede* vain. **seine Hoffnungen erwiesen sich als ~** his hopes proved to be all in vain; **alles ist ~** all is vanity.

(c) inv (obs: rein) *Gold* pure. **es herrschte ~ Freude** (obs, hum) there was absolute joy; **er denkt, das ganze Leben sei ~ Freude und Sonnenschein** he thinks the whole of life is nothing but sweetness and light.

Eitelkeit f siehe adj (a, b) vanity; vainness.

Eiter m -s, no pl pus.

Eiter-: ~**beule** f boil; (fig) canker; ~**bläschen** nt, ~**blase** f pustule; ~**erreger** m pyogenic organism (spec); ~**herd** m suppurative focus (spec).

eit(e)rig adj *Ausfluß* purulent; *Wunde* festering, suppurating; *Binde* pus-covered.

eitern vi to fester, to discharge pus, to suppurate.

Eiter-: ~**pfropf** m core (of a boil); (von Pickel) head; ~**pickel** m pimple (containing pus).

Eiterung f discharge of pus, suppuration.

eitrig adj siehe eit(e)rig.

Eiweiß nt (egg-)white, white of egg, albumen (spec); (Chem) protein.

Eiweiß-: e~**arm** adj low in protein; **e~arme Kost** a low-protein diet; ~**bedarf** m protein requirement; ~**gehalt** m protein content; e~**haltig** adj protein-containing attr; **Fleisch ist sehr e~haltig** meat is high in protein or contains a lot of protein; ~**haushalt** m (Physiol) protein metabolism; ~**mangel** m protein deficiency; ~**präparat** nt protein preparation; ~**stoffwechsel** m protein metabolism.

Eizelle f (Biol) egg cell.

Ejakulat nt (Med) ejaculated semen, ejaculate (spec).

Ejakulation f ejaculation.

ejakulieren* vi to ejaculate.

EK [eː'kaː] nt -s, -s: EK I/II Iron Cross First/Second Class.

EKD [eːkaː'deː] f - abbr of **Evangelische Kirche in Deutschland**.

ekel adj attr (old) nauseating, revolting, loathsome.

Ekel[1] m -s, no pl disgust, revulsion, loathing; (Übelkeit) nausea. **vor jdm/etw einen ~ haben** or **empfinden** to have a loathing of sb/sth, to loathe sb/sth; **dabei empfinde ich ~** it gives me a feeling of disgust etc; **~ überkommt mich** a feeling of disgust etc overcomes me; **diese Heuchelei ist mir ein ~** this hypocrisy is just nauseating or disgusting, I find this hypocrisy nauseating or disgusting; **er hat das Essen vor ~ ausgespuckt** he spat out the food in disgust or revulsion; **er konnte es vor ~ nicht tun** he was too disgusted to do it; **er mußte sich vor ~ übergeben** he was so nauseated that he vomited.

Ekel[2] nt -s, - (inf) obnoxious person, horror (inf).

ekelerregend adj nauseating, revolting, disgusting.

ekelhaft, ek(e)lig adj disgusting, revolting; (inf) *Schmerzen, Problem, Chef* nasty (inf), horrible, vile. **sei nicht so ~ zu ihr!** don't be so nasty to her; **draußen ist es ~ windig** it's horribly windy outside.

ekeln 1 vt to disgust, to revolt, to nauseate.

2 vt impers **es ekelt mich vor diesem Geruch/Anblick, mich** or **mir ekelt vor diesem Geruch/Anblick** the smell/sight of it fills me with disgust or revulsion, this smell/sight is disgusting or revolting or nauseating.

3 vr to be or feel disgusted or revolted or nauseated. **sich vor etw** (dat) **~** to find sth disgusting or revolting or nauseating.

EKG, Ekg [eːkaː'geː] nt -s, -s ECG. **ein ~ machen lassen** to have an ECG.

Eklat [eˈklaː(ː)] m -s, -s (geh) (Aufsehen) sensation, stir; (Zusammenstoß) row, (major) altercation (form). **mit großem ~ causing** a great stir or sensation, spectacularly; **mit (großem) ~ durchfallen** to be a resounding flop or a spectacular failure.

eklatant adj (aufsehenerregend) *Fall* sensational, spectacular; (offenkundig) *Beispiel* striking; *Verletzung* flagrant.

Eklektiker(in f) m -s, - eclectic.

eklektisch adj eclectic.

Eklektizismus m eclecticism.

eklig adj siehe ek(e)lig.

Eklipse f -, -n eclipse.

Ekliptik f ecliptic.

ekliptisch adj ecliptical.

Ekstase f -, -n ecstasy. **in ~ geraten** to go into ecstasies; **jdn in ~ versetzen** to send sb into ecstasies.

Ekstatiker(in f) m -s, - ecstatic (rare).

ekstatisch adj ecstatic, full of ecstasy.

Ekzem nt -s, -e (Med) eczema.

Elaborat nt (pej) concoction (pej).

Elan [auch eˈlãː] m -s, no pl élan, zest, vigour.

Elast m -(e)s, -e (esp DDR) rubber, elastomer (spec).

elastisch adj elastic; *Gang auch* springy; *Metall, Holz* springy, flexible; *Stoff auch* stretchy; (fig) (spannkräftig) *Muskel, Mensch* strong and supple; (flexibel) flexible, elastic. **der Baum bog sich ~ im Wind** the tree bent supply in the wind; **er federte ~** he bent supply at the knees; **der Bügel schnellte ~ zurück** the bow sprang back.

Elastizität f siehe elastisch elasticity; springiness; flexibility; stretchiness; flexibility, elasticity. **die ~ seines Körpers** the supple strength of his body.

Elativ m (Gram) absolute superlative.

Elb-: ~**florenz** nt term used to describe Dresden; ~**kähne** pl (N Ger hum) beetle-crushers pl (inf), clodhoppers pl (inf).

Elch m -(e)s, -e elk.

Eldorado nt -s, -s (lit, fig) eldorado.

Elefant m elephant. **wie ein ~ im Porzellanladen** (inf) like a bull in a china shop (prov); **siehe Mücke**.

Elefanten-: ~**baby** nt (inf) baby elephant (auch fig hum);

~**bulle** m bull elephant; ~**kuh** f cow elephant; ~**robbe** f elephant seal; ~**rüssel** m elephant's trunk.

Elefantiasis f -, no pl (Med) elephantiasis.

elegant adj elegant. **die ~e Welt** (dated) high society.

Elegant [eleˈgãː] m -s, -s (dated) dandy (dated).

Eleganz f elegance.

Elegie f elegy.

Elegiendichter [-ˈgiːən-], **Elegiker(in** f) m -s, - elegist.

elegisch adj elegiac; (melancholisch auch) melancholy. **~ gestimmt** in a melancholy mood.

Eleison nt -s, -s (Eccl) Kyrie eleison.

Elektrakomplex m (Psych) Electra complex.

Elektrifikation f (Sw) siehe **Elektrifizierung**.

elektrifizieren* vt to electrify.

Elektrifizierung f electrification.

Elektrik f **(a)** (elektrische Anlagen) electrical equipment. **(b)** (inf: Elektrizitätslehre) electricity.

Elektriker(in f) m -s, - electrician.

elektrisch adj electric; *Entladung, Feld, Widerstand* electrical. **~e Geräte** electrical appliances; **~er Schlag/Strom** electric shock/current; **der ~e Stuhl** the electric chair; **~ betrieben** electrically driven, driven or run by electricity, electric; **wir kochen/heizen ~** we cook/heat by or with electricity; **bei uns ist alles ~** we're all electric; **das geht alles ~** (inf) it's all automatic.

Elektrische f -n, -n (dated) tram, streetcar (US).

elektrisieren* 1 vt (lit, fig) to electrify; (aufladen) to charge with electricity; (Med) to treat with electricity. **der Plattenspieler hat mich elektrisiert** the record-player gave me a shock or an electric shock; **ich habe mich elektrisiert** I gave myself or got an electric shock; **die elektrisierte Atmosphäre** the electrically-charged atmosphere; **wie elektrisiert** (as if) electrified. **2** vi to give an electric shock.

Elektrisiermaschine f electrostatic generator.

Elektrizität f electricity.

Elektrizitäts-: ~**gesellschaft** f electric power company; ~**lehre** f (science of) electricity; ~**versorgung** f (electric) power supply; ~**werk** nt (electric) power station; (Gesellschaft) electric power company; ~**zähler** m (form) electricity meter.

Elektro- [eˈlektro] in cpds electro- (auch Sci), electric; ~**analyse** f electroanalysis; ~**antrieb** m electric drive; ~**artikel** m electrical appliance; ~**chemie** f electrochemistry; e~**chemisch** adj electrochemical.

Elektrode f -, -n electrode.

Elektrodenspannung f electrode potential.

Elektro-: ~**diagnostik** f (Med) electrodiagnosis; ~**dynamik** f electrodynamics sing; e~**dynamisch** adj electrodynamic; ~**enzephalogramm** nt (Med) electroencephalogram, EEG; ~**fahrzeug** nt electric vehicle; ~**gerät** nt electrical appliance; ~**geschäft** nt electrical shop; ~**herd** m electric cooker; ~**industrie** f electrical industry; ~**ingenieur** m electrical engineer; ~**kardiogramm** nt (Med) electrocardiogram, ECG; ~**karren** m small electric truck; (des Milchmannes etc) electric float; ~**lyse** f -, -n electrolysis; ~**lyt** m -en, -en electrolyte; e~**lytisch** adj electrolytic; ~**magnet** m electromagnet; e~**lytisch** adj electrolytic; ~**magnet** m electromagnet; e~**magnetisch** adj electromagnetic; ~**mechaniker** m electrician; e~**mechanisch** adj electromechanical; ~**meister** m master electrician; ~**meter** nt electrometer; ~**mobil** nt -s, -e electric car; ~**motor** m electric motor.

Elektron [ˈeːlektrɔn, eˈlektrɔn, elekˈtroːn] nt -s, -en [elekˈtroːnən] electron.

Elektronen-: ~**blitz(gerät** nt) m (Phot) electronic flash; ~**(ge)hirn** nt electronic brain; ~**hülle** f (Phys) electron shell or cloud; ~**mikroskop** nt electron microscope; ~**orgel** f (Mus) electronic organ; ~**rechenmaschine** f, ~**rechner** m (electronic) computer; ~**röhre** f valve, electron tube (US); ~**schale** f electron shell; ~**schleuder** f (Phys) electron accelerator, betatron (spec); ~**strahlen** pl electron or cathode rays pl; ~**theorie** f electron theory.

Elektronik f electronics sing; (elektronische Teile) electronics pl.

elektronisch adj electronic.

Elektro-: ~**ofen** m (Metal) electric furnace; (Heizofen) electric heater; ~**rasierer** m electric shaver or razor; ~**schock** m (Med) electric shock, electroshock; ~**schweißung** f electric welding; ~**stahl** m (Metal) electrosteel, electric steel; ~**statik** f (Phys) electrostatics sing; e~**statisch** adj electrostatic; ~**technik** f electrical engineering; ~**techniker** m electrician; (Ingenieur) electrical engineer; e~**technisch** adj electrical, electrotechnical (rare); ~**therapie** f (Med) electrotherapy.

Elen m or nt (rare) -s, - siehe Elch.

elend adj **(a)** (unglücklich, jämmerlich, pej: gemein) wretched, miserable; (krank) wretched, awful (inf), ill pred. **~ aussehen/sich ~ fühlen** to look/feel awful (inf) or wretched; **mir ist ganz ~** I feel really awful (inf) or wretched; **mir wird ganz ~, wenn ich daran denke** I feel quite ill when I think about

it, thinking about it makes me feel quite ill.
(b) (inf) (sehr groß) Hunger, Hitze awful, dreadful; (sehr schlecht) Wetter, Kälte, Leistung wretched, dreadful, miserable. **ich habe** ~ **gefroren** I was miserably cold; **da bin ich** ~ **betrogen worden** I was cheated wretchedly; **ich habe mich** ~ **geschämt** I was dreadfully ashamed; **es war** ~ **heiß/kalt** it was awfully or dreadfully hot/miserably or dreadfully cold.

Elend nt -(e)s, no pl (Unglück, Not) misery, distress; (Verwahrlosung) squalor; (Armut) poverty, penury. **ein Bild des** ~**s** a picture of misery/squalor; **ins** ~ **geraten** to fall into poverty, to be reduced to penury, to become destitute; **im (tiefsten)** ~ **leben** to live in (abject) misery/squalor/poverty; **jdn/sich (selbst) ins** ~ **stürzen** to plunge sb/oneself into misery/poverty; **wie das leibhaftige** ~ **aussehen** (inf) to look really awful (inf) or terrible (inf); **(wie) ein Häufchen** ~ (inf) (looking) a picture of misery; **das heulende** ~ (inf) the blues pl (inf); **da kann man das heulende** ~ **kriegen** (inf) it's enough to make you scream (inf); **es ist ein** ~ **mit ihm** (inf) he makes you want to weep (inf), he's hopeless; **es ist ein** ~, ~... (inf) it's heart-breaking ...; siehe **lang**.

elendig(lich) adv miserably, wretchedly. ~ **zugrunde gehen** or **verrecken** (sl) to come to a wretched or miserable or dismal end.

Elends-: ~**gestalt** f (poor) wretch, wretched figure; ~**quartier** nt slum (dwelling), squalid dwelling; ~**viertel** nt slums pl, slum area.

Elephantiasis f (Med) siehe **Elefantiasis**.

Eleve [e'le:və] m -n, -n, **Elevin** [e'le:vɪn] f (Theat) student; (Agr) trainee, student; (old: Schüler) pupil.

elf num eleven; siehe auch **vier**.

Elf[1] f -, -en (Sport) team, eleven.

Elf[2] m -en, -en, **Elfe** f -, -n elf.

Elf-: ~**eck** nt undecagon, eleven-sided figure; **e**~**eckig** adj eleven-sided.

Elfenbein nt ivory.

Elfenbein|arbeit f ivory (carving).

elfenbeine(r)n 1 adj ivory, made of ivory. ~**er Turm** (Rel) Tower of Ivory. 2 adv ivory-like.

Elfenbein-: **e**~**farben**, **e**~**farbig** adj ivory-coloured; ~**küste** f Ivory Coast; ~**turm** m (fig) ivory tower.

Elfen-: **e**~**haft** adj (liter) elfish, elfin; ~**reich** nt fairyland.

Elfer m -s, - (Ftbl inf) siehe **Elfmeter**.

Elfer-: ~**probe** f (Math) casting out of elevens; ~**rat** m committee of eleven.

elf-: ~**fach** adj elevenfold; siehe **vierfach**; ~**mal** adv eleven times; siehe **viermal**.

Elfmeter m (Ftbl) penalty (kick) (für to, for). **einen** ~ **schießen** to take a penalty.

Elfmeter-: ~**marke** f, ~**punkt** m (Ftbl) penalty spot; ~**schießen** nt (Ftbl) sudden-death play-off; **durch** ~**schießen entschieden** decided on penalties; ~**schuß** m (Ftbl) penalty (kick); ~**schütze** m (Ftbl) penalty-taker.

Elftel nt -s, - eleventh; siehe **Viertel**[1].

elftens adv eleventh, in the eleventh place.

elfte(r, s) adj eleventh; siehe **vierte(r, s)**.

elidieren* vt (Gram) to elide.

Elimination f elimination (auch Math).

eliminieren* vt to eliminate (auch Math).

Eliminierung f elimination.

elisabethanisch adj Elizabethan.

Elision f (Gram) elision.

elitär 1 adj elitist. 2 adv in an elitist fashion.

Elite f -, -n elite.

Elite-: ~**denken** nt elitism; ~**truppe** f (Mil) crack or elite troops pl.

Elixier nt -s, -e elixir (liter), tonic.

Ellbogen m siehe **Ell(en)bogen**.

Elle f -, -n **(a)** (Anat) ulna. **(b)** (Hist) (Measure) cubit; (Maßstock) ≈ yardstick. **alles mit der gleichen** or **mit gleicher** ~ **messen** (fig) to measure everything by the same yardstick or standards.

Ell(en)bogen m -s, - elbow; (fig) push. **er bahnte sich seinen Weg mit den** ~ **durch die Menge** he elbowed his way through the crowd; **die** ~ **gebrauchen** (fig) to use one's elbows, to be ruthless; **er hat keine** ~ (fig) he's not ruthless enough, he has no push (inf).

Ell(en)bogen-: ~**freiheit** f (fig) elbow room; ~**mensch** m ruthless or pushy (inf) person, pusher (inf); ~**taktik** f pushiness (inf); ~**taktik anwenden** to be pushy (inf).

ellen-: ~**lang** adj (fig inf) incredibly long (inf); Liste, Weg auch mile-long or (inf), a mile long or (inf); Geschichte etc auch lengthy, interminable; Kerl incredibly tall (inf); ~**weise** adv ≈ by the yard.

Ellipse f -, -n (Math) ellipse; (Gram) ellipsis.

elliptisch adj (Math, Gram) elliptic(al).

Elmsfeuer nt (Met) St Elmo's fire, corposant.

Eloge [e'lo:ʒə] f -, -n eulogy.

E-Lok ['e:lɔk] f -, -s abbr of **elektrische Lokomotive** electric locomotive or engine.

eloquent adj (geh) eloquent.

Eloquenz f (geh) eloquence.

Elsaß nt - or -sses **das** ~ Alsace.

Elsässer(in f**)** m -s, - Alsatian, inhabitant of Alsace.

Elsässer, elsässisch adj Alsatian.

Elsaß-Lothringen nt Alsace-Lorraine.

elsaß-lothringisch adj Alsace-Lorraine attr, of Alsace-Lorraine.

Elster f -, -n magpie. **wie eine** ~ **stehlen** to be always stealing things, to have sticky fingers (inf); **eine diebische** ~ **sein** (fig) to be a thief or pilferer; **geschwätzig wie eine** ~ **sein** to chatter like a magpie.

Elter m or nt -s, -n (Sci, Statistics) parent.

elterlich adj parental.

Eltern pl parents pl. **nicht von schlechten** ~ **sein** (inf) to be quite something (inf), to be a good one (inf).

Eltern-: ~**abend** m (Sch) parents' evening; ~**beirat** m parents' council; ~**haus** nt (lit, fig) (parental) home; **aus gutem** ~**haus stammen** to come from a good home; ~**liebe** f parental love; **e**~**los** adj orphaned, parentless; ~**schaft** f parents pl; ~**sprechstunde** f (Sch) consultation hour (for parents); ~**sprechtag** m open or visiting day (for parents); ~**teil** m parent.

elysäisch, elysisch adj (Myth, fig) Elysian.

Elysium nt -s, no pl (Myth, fig) **das** ~ Elysium.

Email [e'mai, e'ma:j] nt -s, -s enamel.

Emaillack [e'mailak] m enamel paint.

Emaille [e'maljə, e'mai, e'ma:j] f -, -n siehe **Email**.

emaillieren* [ema'ji:rən, emal'ji:rən] vt to enamel.

Email-: ~**malerei** f enamel painting, enamelling; ~**schmuck** m enamel jewellery.

Emanation f (Philos, Chem) emanation.

Emanze f -, -n (sl) women's libber (inf).

Emanzipation f emancipation.

Emanzipationsbewegung f emancipation movement.

emanzipatorisch adj emancipatory.

emanzipieren* 1 vt to emancipate. 2 vr to emancipate oneself.

Emanzipierung f siehe **Emanzipation**.

Embargo nt -s, -s embargo. **etw mit einem** ~ **belegen, ein** ~ **über etw** (acc) **verhängen** to put or place an embargo on sth.

Emblem nt -(e)s, -e emblem.

emblematisch adj emblematic.

Embolie f (Med) embolism.

Embonpoint [ãbõ'poɛ̃] m or nt -s, -s (dated hum) embonpoint (liter), stoutness.

Embryo m (Aus auch nt) -s, -s or -nen [-'yo:nən] embryo.

Embryologie f embryology.

embryonal adj attr (Biol, fig) embryonic.

Emendation f (Liter) emendation.

emendieren* vt (Liter) to emend.

emeritieren* vt (Univ) to give emeritus status (to). **emeritierter Professor** emeritus professor.

Emeritus m -, **Emeriti** (Univ) emeritus.

Emigrant(in f**)** m emigrant; (politischer Flüchtling) émigré.

Emigration f emigration; (die Emigranten) emigrant/émigré community. **in der** ~ **leben** to live in (self-imposed) exile; **in die** ~ **gehen** to emigrate; siehe **innere(r, s)**.

emigrieren* vi aux sein to emigrate.

eminent adj (geh) Person eminent. ~ **wichtig** of the utmost importance; **von** ~**er Bedeutung** of the utmost significance; **er hat E**~**es geleistet** he is a man of eminent achievements.

Eminenz f (Eccl) (Seine/Eure) ~ (His/Your) Eminence; siehe **grau**.

Emir m -s, -e emir.

Emirat nt emirate.

Emissär m (old) emissary.

Emission f **(a)** (Fin) issue. **(b)** (Phys) emission. **(c)** (Sw: Radiosendung) (radio) broadcast.

Emissions-: ~**bank** f issuing bank; ~**kurs** m rate of issue, issuing price.

emittieren* vt **(a)** (Fin) to issue. **(b)** (Phys) to emit.

Emmchen nt (hum inf) mark, ≈ quid (Brit inf), buck (US inf).

Emmentaler m -s, - Emment(h)aler.

Emotion f emotion.

emotional adj emotional; Ausdrucksweise emotive.

emotionalisieren* vt to emotionalize.

emotionell adj siehe **emotional**.

emotions-: ~**arm** adj lacking in emotion, unfeeling; ~**geladen** adj emotion-laden, emotionally-charged; ~**los** adj free of emotion, unemotional.

Empf. abbr of **Empfänger**; **Empfohlen(er Preis)**.

empfahl pret of **empfehlen**.

empfand pret of **empfinden**.

Empfang m -(e)s, -̈e reception; (von Brief, Ware etc) receipt; (von Sakramenten) receiving. **jdm einen guten** ~ **bereiten** to give sb a good reception; **zu jds** ~ **kommen** (jdn begrüßen) to (come to) receive sb; **einen** ~ **geben** or **veranstalten** to give or hold a reception; **jdm/etw in** ~ **nehmen** to receive sb/sth; (Comm) to take delivery of sth; **(zahlbar) nach/bei** ~ (+ gen) (payable) on receipt (of); **auf** ~ **bleiben** (Rad) to stand by; **auf** ~ **schalten** (Rad) to switch over to "receive"; **wir wünschen Ihnen einen guten** ~ (TV, Rad) we wish you pleasant viewing/happy listening.

empfangen pret **empfing**, ptp **empfangen** 1 vt to receive; (begrüßen) to greet, to receive (form); (herzlich) to welcome; (abholen) Besuch to meet. **die gnädige Frau empfängt heute nicht** (form) milady is not receiving today (inf); **die Weihen** ~ (Eccl) to take Holy Orders; **die Polizisten wurden mit einem Steinhagel** ~ the police were greeted by a shower of stones.
2 vti (schwanger werden) to conceive.

Empfänger m -s, - recipient, receiver (auch Rad); (Adressat) addressee; (Waren~) consignee. ~ **unbekannt** (auf Briefen) not known at this address; ~ **verzogen** gone away.

Empfänger|abschnitt m receipt slip.

empfänglich adj (aufnahmebereit) receptive (für to); (beeinflußbar, anfällig) susceptible (für to).

Empfänglichkeit f siehe adj receptivity; susceptibility.

Empfängnis f conception; siehe **unbefleckt**.

Empfängnis-: **e**~**verhütend** adj contraceptive; **e**~**verhütende Mittel** pl contraceptives pl; ~**verhütung** f contraception.

Empfangs-: ~antenne *f* receiving aerial; e~**berechtigt** *adj* authorized to receive payment/goods *etc*; ~**berechtigte(r)** *mf* authorized recipient; ~**bereich** *m* (*Rad, TV*) reception area; ~**bescheinigung,** ~**bestätigung** *f* (acknowledgment of) receipt; ~**chef** *m* (*von Hotel*) head porter; ~**dame** *f* receptionist; ~**gerät** *nt* (*Rad, TV*) (radio/TV) set, receiver; ~**station** *f* (*Rad*) receiving station; (*Space*) tracking station; (*Comm*) destination; ~**störung** *f* (*Rad, TV*) interference *no pl*; ~**zimmer** *nt* reception room.

empfehlen *pret* **empfahl**, *ptp* **empfohlen** 1 *vt* to recommend; (*liter: anvertrauen*) to commend (*form*), to entrust. (**jdm**) **etw/jdn** ~ to recommend sth/sb (to sb); ~, **etw zu tun** to recommend *or* advise doing sth; **jdm** ~, **etw zu tun** to recommend *or* advise sb to do sth; **diese Methode/dieses Restaurant ist sehr zu** ~ I would recommend this method/restaurant, this method/restaurant is to be recommended; **ich würde dir Vorsicht/Geduld** ~ I would recommend caution/patience, I would advise *or* recommend you to be cautious/patient; **seinen Geist (dem Herrn)** ~ (*liter*) to commend one's soul to the Lord; **bitte,** ~ **Sie mich Ihrer Frau Gemahlin** (*form*) please convey my respects to your wife (*form*); *siehe* **empfohlen.**
  2 *vr* (**a**) to recommend itself/oneself. **sich für Reparaturen/als Experte** *etc* ~ to offer one's services for repairs/as an expert *etc*; **diese Ware empfiehlt sich von selbst** this product is its own recommendation; **es empfiehlt sich, das zu tun** it is advisable to do that.
  (**b**) (*dated, hum: sich verabschieden*) to take one's leave. **ich empfehle mich!** I'll take my leave; **ich empfehle mich Ihnen** (*am Briefende*) please be sure of my best wishes (*dated form*); *siehe* **französisch.**
empfehlenswert *adj* to be recommended, recommendable.
Empfehlung *f* recommendation; (*Referenz*) testimonial, reference; (*form: Gruß*) regards *pl*, respects *pl*. **auf** ~ **von** on the recommendation of; **mit freundlichen** *or* **den besten** ~**en** (*am Briefende*) with best regards; **meine** ~ **an Ihre Frau Gemahlin!** (*form*) my regards *or* respects to your wife (*form*).
Empfehlungsschreiben *nt* letter of recommendation, testimonial.
empfiehl *imper sing of* **empfehlen.**
empfinden *pret* **empfand**, *ptp* **empfunden** *vt* to feel. **etw als kränkend/Beleidigung** ~ to feel sth as an insult, to find sth insulting; **er hat noch nie Hunger empfunden** he has never experienced *or* known hunger; **er empfand einen solch starken Hunger, daß ...** his hunger was so great that ...; **bei Musik Freude** ~ to experience pleasure from music; **ich habe dabei viel Freude empfunden** it gave me great pleasure; **viel/nichts für jdn** ~ to feel a lot/nothing for sb; **sie hat den Verlust ihres Mannes tief empfunden** she felt the loss of her husband deeply; **jdn als (einen) Störenfried** ~ to think of sb as *or* feel sb to be a troublemaker.
Empfinden *nt* **-s,** *no pl* feeling. **meinem** ~ **nach** to my mind, the way I feel about it.
empfindlich *adj* (**a**) (*auch Phot, Tech*); *Gesundheit, Stoff, Glas, Keramik etc* delicate; (*leicht reizbar*) touchy (*inf*), (over)sensitive. ~ **reagieren** to be sensitive (*auf* +*acc* to); **wenn man ihren geschiedenen Mann erwähnt, reagiert sie sehr** ~ she is very sensitive to references to her ex-husband; ~**e Stelle** (*lit*) sensitive spot; (*fig auch*) sore point; **gegen etw** ~ **sein** to be sensitive to sth; **Kupfer ist sehr** ~ copper discolours/dents *etc* easily.
  (**b**) (*spürbar, schmerzlich*) *Verlust, Kälte, Strafe* severe; *Mangel* appreciable. **deine Kritik hat ihn** ~ **getroffen** your criticism cut him to the quick; **es ist** ~ **kalt** it is bitterly cold.
Empfindlichkeit *f siehe adj* (**a**) sensitivity (*auch Phot, Tech*), sensitiveness; delicateness, delicate nature; touchiness (*inf*), (over)sensitivity.
empfindsam *adj Mensch* sensitive; (*gefühlvoll, Liter*) sentimental.
Empfindsamkeit *f siehe adj* sensitivity; sentimentality. **das Zeitalter der** ~ (*Liter*) the age of sentimentalism.
Empfindsamkeitsdichtung *f* (*Liter*) sentimentalist poetry.
Empfindung *f* feeling; (*Sinnes-* *auch*) sensation; (*Eindruck, Ahnung auch*) impression.
Empfindungs-: e~**fähig** *adj* (*fig*) capable of feeling; e~**los** *adj* (*lit, fig*) insensitive (*für, gegen* to); *Glieder* numb, without sensation; ~**losigkeit** *f* (*lit, fig*) insensitivity; (*der Glieder*) numbness, loss of sensation; ~**nerven** *pl* (*Physiol*) sensory nerves *pl*; ~**vermögen** *nt* faculty of sensation; (*in Gliedern*) sensation; (*fig*) sensitivity, ability to feel; ~**vermögen für etw** ability to feel *or* sense sth; (*fig*) sensitivity to sth; ~**wort** *nt* (*Gram*) interjection.
empfing *pret of* **empfangen.**
empfohlen 1 *ptp of* **empfehlen.** 2 *adj* (**sehr** *or* **gut**) ~ (highly) recommended.
empfunden *ptp of* **empfinden.**
Emphase *f* **-,** **-n** emphasis.
emphatisch *adj* emphatic.
Empire[1] [ã'pi:ɐ] *nt* **-(s),** *no pl* (*Hist*) Empire; (~**stil**) Empire style.
Empire[2] ['ɛmpaɪɐ] *nt* **-(s),** *no pl* (*British*) Empire.
Empirestil *m* Empire style.
Empirik *f* **-,** *no pl* empirical experience.
Empiriker(in *f*) *m* **-s,** **-** empiricist.
empirisch *adj* empirical.
Empirismus *m* (*Philos, Sci*) empiricism.
Empirizismus *m* (*pej*) (narrow) empiricism.
empor *adv* (*liter*) upwards, up. **zum Licht** ~ up(wards) towards the light; ~ **die Herzen/Blicke!** lift up your hearts/eyes! (*liter*); *siehe auch* **hinauf.**
empor-: ~**arbeiten** *vr sep* (*geh*) to work one's way up; ~**blicken**

vi sep (*liter*) to raise one's eyes; (*fig*) to look up (*zu* to).
Empore *f* **-,** **-n** (*Archit*) gallery.
empören* 1 *vt* to fill with indignation, to outrage; (*stärker*) to incense; *siehe* **empört.**
  2 *vr* (**a**) (*über* +*acc* at) to be indignant *or* outraged; (*stärker*) to be incensed. **das ist unerhört! empörte sich der Schulmeister** that's scandalous!, said the schoolmaster indignantly.
  (**b**) (*liter: sich auflehnen*) to rise (up) *or* rebel (*gegen* against).
empörend *adj* outrageous, scandalous.
Empörer(in *f*) *m* **-s,** **-** (*liter*) rebel, insurrectionist.
empörerisch *adj* (*liter*) rebellious, insurrectionary.
empor-: ~**heben** *vt sep irreg* (*geh*) to raise, to lift up; **jdn über andere** ~**heben** (*fig*) to raise *or* elevate sb above others; ~**kommen** *vi sep irreg aux sein* (*geh*) to rise (up); (*fig*) (*aufkommen*) to come to the fore; (*vorankommen*) to rise *or* go up in the world, to get on; **nur an sein E~kommen denken** (*fig*) to think only of one's advancement; **E~kömmling** *m* upstart, parvenu; ~**lodern** *vi sep aux sein or haben* (*liter*) to blaze *or* flare upwards; ~**ragen** *vi sep aux haben or sein* (*geh: lit, fig*) to tower (*über* +*acc* above); ~**recken** *sep* 1 *vt* (*liter*) *Faust* to raise aloft; 2 *vr* to stretch upwards; ~**schauen** *vi sep* (*geh*) *siehe* ~**blicken**; ~**schweben** *vi sep aux sein* (*geh*) to float upwards *or* aloft (*liter*); ~**schwingen** *vr sep irreg* (*geh*) to soar upwards *or* aloft (*liter*); (*Turner*) to swing upwards; **sich zu etw** ~**schwingen** (*fig*) to (come to) achieve sth; **zu einer Stellung** ~**schwingen** (*fig*) to (come to) achieve sth; *zu einer Stellung* to reach sth; ~**steigen** *sep irreg aux sein* (*geh*) 1 *vt* to climb (up); 2 *vi* to climb (up); (*Mond, Angst etc*) to rise (up); (*fig: Karriere machen*) to climb, to rise; ~**streben** *vi sep aux sein* to soar upwards; (*fig*) *aux haben* to be ambitious.
empört 1 *ptp of* **empören.** 2 *adj* (**a**) (highly) indignant, outraged (*über* +*acc* at); (*schockiert*) outraged, scandalized. (**b**) (*liter: in Auflehnung*) rebellious.
emportreiben *vt sep irreg* (*geh*) to drive up.
Empörung *f* (**a**) *no pl* (*Entrüstung*) indignation (*über* +*acc* at). **über etw in** ~ **geraten** to become *or* get indignant about sth. (**b**) (*liter: Aufstand*) rebellion, uprising.
empor-: ~**ziehen** *sep irreg* (*geh*) 1 *vt* to draw *or* pull up; 2 *vi aux sein* to drift upwards; ~**züngeln** *vi sep aux sein* (*liter: Flammen*) to leap up(wards) *or* aloft (*liter*).
emsig *adj* busy, industrious; (*eifrig*) eager, keen; (*geschäftig*) bustling *attr*, busy.
Emsigkeit *f siehe adj* industry, industriousness; eagerness, zeal; bustle.
Emu *m* **-s,** **-s** emu.
emulgieren* *vti* to emulsify.
Emulsion *f* emulsion.
Emulsions-: ~**farbe** *f* emulsion (paint); ~**mittel** *nt* emulsifier.
en bloc [ã'blɔk] *adv* en bloc.
enchantiert [ãʃã'tiːɐt] *adj* (*dated*) delighted, charmed.
End- *in cpds* final; ~**abnehmer** *m* ultimate buyer; ~**abrechnung** *f* final account; ~**bahnhof** *m* terminus; e~**betont** *adj Wort* with final stress; ~**betrag** *m* final amount.
Endchen *nt* (*inf*) (small) piece, bit; (*eines Weges*) short distance, little way.
Ende *nt* **-s,** **-n** end; (*eines Jahrhunderts etc auch*) close; (*Ausgang, Ergebnis*) outcome, result; (*Ausgang eines Films, Romans etc*) ending; (*Hunt: Geweih-*) point; (*inf: Stückchen*) (small) piece; (*Strecke*) way, stretch; (*Naut: Tau*) (rope's) end. ~ **Mai/der Woche** at the end of May/the week; ~ **der zwanziger Jahre** in the late twenties; **er ist** ~ **vierzig** he is in his late forties; **das** ~ **der Welt** the end of the world; **er wohnt am** ~ **der Welt** (*inf*) he lives at the back of beyond *or* in the middle of nowhere; **bis ans** ~ **der Welt** to the ends of the earth; **ein** ~ **mit Schrecken** a terrible *or* dreadful end; **lieber ein** ~ **mit Schrecken als ein Schrecken ohne** ~ (*Prov*) it's best to get unpleasant things over and done with; **letzten** ~**es** when all is said and done, after all; (*am Ende*) in the end, at the end of the day; **einer Sache** (*dat*) **ein** ~ **machen** to put an end to sth; (*bei or mit etw*) **kein** ~ **finden** (*inf*) to be unable (to bring oneself) to stop (sth *or* telling/doing *etc* sth); **beim Erzählen kann er kein** ~ **finden** he really does go on a bit (*inf*), he can't seem to stop talking; **damit muß es jetzt ein** ~ **haben** there has to be an end to this now, this must stop now; **ein** ~ **nehmen** to come to an end; **das nimmt** *or* **findet gar kein** ~ (*inf*) there's no sign of it stopping, there's no end to it; **ein böses** ~ **nehmen** to come to a bad end; **kein** ~ **ist abzusehen** there's no end in sight; **da ist das** ~ **von weg!** (*N Ger inf*) it's incredible! (*inf*); **... und kein** ~ ... with no end in sight, ... without end; **es war des Staunens/Jubels** *etc* **kein** ~ (*old, liter*) there was no end to the surprise/celebrations *etc*; **es ist noch ein gutes** *or* **ganzes** ~ (*inf*) there's still quite a way to go (yet); **am** ~ at the end; (*schließlich*) in the end; (*inf: möglicherweise*) perhaps; (**am**) ~ **des Monats** at the end of the month; **am** ~ **sein** (*fig*) to be at the end of one's tether; **mit etw am** ~ **sein** to be at *or* have reached the end of sth; (*Vorrat*) to have run out of sth; **ich bin mit meiner Weisheit am** ~ I'm at my wits' end; **meine Geduld ist am** ~ my patience is at an end; **ein Problem am richtigen/falschen** *or* **verkehrten** ~ **anfassen** to tackle a problem from the right/wrong end; **Leiden ohne** ~ endless suffering, suffering without end; **das ist eine Kette** *or* **Schraube ohne** ~ (*fig*) it's an endless spiral; **zu** ~ finished, over, at an end; **etw zu** ~ **bringen** *or* **führen** to finish (off) sth; **ein Buch/einen Brief zu** ~ **lesen/schreiben** to finish (reading/writing) a book/letter; **etw zu einem guten** ~ **bringen** *or* **führen** to bring sth to a satisfactory conclusion; **zu** ~ **gehen** to come to an end; (*Vorräte*) to run out; **zu dem** ~, **daß** ... (*obs*) to the end that ... (*form*); **zu diesem** ~ (*obs*) to this end (*form*); ~ **gut, alles gut** (*Prov*) all's well that ends well (*Prov*); **es hat alles einmal** *or* **alles hat einmal ein** ~ (*Prov*) everything must come to an end sometime; (*angenehme Dinge*) all good things must come to an end (*Prov*); *siehe* **dick.**

End|effekt m: im ~ (inf) in the end, in the final analysis.
endeln vt (Aus) Saum to whip, to oversew.
Endemie f (Med) endemic disease.
enden vi to end, to finish; (Frist auch) to run out, to expire; (Zug) to terminate; (sterben) to meet one's end. **auf** (+acc) or **mit etw** ~ (Wort) to end with sth; **mit den Worten ...** ~ (bei Rede) to close with the words ...; **es endete damit, daß ...** the outcome was that ...; **der Streit endete vor Gericht** the quarrel ended up in court; **er endete im Gefängnis** he ended up in prison; **wie wird das noch mit ihm** ~? what will become of him?; **das wird böse** ~! no good will come of it!; **er wird schlimm** ~ he will come to a bad end; **nicht** ~ **wollend** unending.
-ender m suf **-s, -** (Hunt) -pointer.
End|ergebnis nt final result.
en detail [ãde'taj] adv (old) retail.
End-: ~**gehalt** nt final salary; ~**geschwindigkeit** f terminal velocity.
endgültig adj final; Beweis auch conclusive; Antwort definite; (geh: vorbildlich) definitive. **damit ist die Sache** ~ **entschieden** that settles the matter once and for all; **das ist** ~ **aus or vorbei** that's (all) over and done with; **sie haben sich jetzt** ~ **getrennt** they've separated for good; **jetzt ist** ~ **Schluß!** that's the end!, that's it!; **etwas E~es läßt sich noch nicht sagen** I/we etc cannot say anything definite at this stage.
Endgültigkeit f siehe adj finality; conclusiveness; definitiveness.
endigen vi (old) siehe enden.
Endivie [-viə] f endive.
End-: ~**kampf** m (Mil) final battle; (Sport) final; (~phase: Mil, Sport) final stages pl (of a battle/contest); ~**lauf** m final; ~**laufteilnehmer** m finalist.
endlich 1 adj (a) (Math, Philos) finite.
  (b) (rare: langerwartet, schließlich) eventual.
  2 adv finally, at last; (am Ende) eventually, in the end, finally. **na** ~! at (long) last!; **hör** ~ **damit auf!** will you stop that!; **komm doch** ~! come on, get a move on!; ~ **kam er doch** he eventually came after all, in the end he came (after all).
Endlichkeit f (Math, Philos) finiteness, finite nature.
endlos adj endless; (langwierig auch) interminable. **ich mußte** ~ **lange warten** I had to wait for an interminably long time, I had to wait for ages (inf); **(sich) bis ins E~e (erstrecken)** (to stretch) to infinity.
Endlosigkeit f endlessness, infinite nature; (Langwierigkeit) interminableness, interminable nature.
End-: ~**lösung** f: **die** ~**lösung** the Final Solution (extermination of the Jews by the Nazis); ~**moräne** f terminal moraine.
Endo- in cpds endo-; **e~gen** adj (Biol, Psych) endogenous; **e~krin** adj (Med) endocrine; ~**krinologie** f (Med) endocrinology; ~**skop** nt **-s, -e** (Med) endoscope.
End-: ~**phase** f final stage(s pl); ~**preis** m final price; ~**produkt** nt end or final product; ~**punkt** m (lit, fig) end; (von Buslinie etc auch) terminus; ~**reim** m (Liter) end rhyme; ~**resultat** nt final result.
Endrunde f (Sport) finals pl; (Leichtathletik, Autorennen) final lap; (Boxen, Fig) final round.
Endrunden-: ~**spiel** nt final (match); ~**teilnehmer** m finalist.
End-: ~**see** m (Geog) lake without an outlet; ~**sieg** m final or ultimate victory; ~**silbe** f final syllable; ~**spiel** nt (Sport) final; (Chess) end game; ~**spurt** m (Sport, fig) final spurt; ~**stadium** nt final or (Med) terminal stage; ~**station** f (Rail etc) terminus; (fig) end of the line; ~**stellung** f (Gram) final or end position; ~**stufe** f final stage; ~**summe** f (sum) total.
Endung f (Gram) ending.
endungslos adj (Gram) without an ending.
End-: ~**ursache** f ultimate cause; (Philos) final cause; ~**urteil** nt final verdict or judgement; ~**verbraucher** m consumer; ~**vierziger** m (inf) man in his late forties; ~**zeit** f last days pl; **e~zeitlich** adj attr Phase final; Stimmung, Prophezeiung apocalyptic; ~**ziel** nt ultimate goal or aim; ~**ziffer** f final number; ~**zustand** m final state; ~**zweck** m ultimate aim or purpose.
Energetik f (Phys) energetics sing.
energetisch adj (Phys) energetic.
Energie f (Sci, fig) energy; (Schwung auch) vigour, vitality. **seine ganze** ~ **für etw einsetzen or aufbieten** to devote all one's energies to sth; **mit aller or ganzer** ~ with all one's energy or energies.
Energie-: ~**bedarf** m energy requirement; ~**haushalt** m (Physiol) energy balance; **e~los** adj lacking in energy, weak; ~**losigkeit** f lack of energy; ~**politik** f energy policy/politics sing or pl; ~**prinzip** nt, ~**satz** m (Phys) principle of the conservation of energy; ~**verbrauch** m energy consumption; ~**versorgung** f supply of energy; ~**wirtschaft** f energy economy; (Wirtschaftszweige) energy industry; ~**zufuhr** f energy supply.
energisch adj (voller Energie) energetic; (entschlossen, streng) forceful, firm; Griff, Maßnahmen vigorous, firm; Worte forceful, strong; Protest energetic, strong. ~ **durchgreifen** to take vigorous or firm action, to act vigorously or firmly; ~ **werden** to assert oneself or one's authority; **wenn das nicht aufhört, werde ich** ~! if this doesn't stop I'll have to put my foot down!; **etw** ~ **sagen** to say sth forcefully; **etw** ~ **betonen** to stress or emphasize sth strongly; **etw** ~ **verteidigen** to defend sth vigorously; **etw** ~ **dementieren** to deny sth strongly or strenuously or emphatically.
enervieren* [enεr'vi:rən] vt (old) to enervate (form).
en famille [ãfa'mij] adv (geh) en famille.
Enfant terrible [ãfãte'ribl] nt **- -, -s -s** (geh) enfant terrible.
eng adj **(a)** (schmal) Straße etc narrow; (beengt) Raum cramped, confined; (~anliegend) Kleidung tight, close-fitting;

(ärmlich) Verhältnisse straitened, reduced; (beschränkt) Horizont, Moralbegriff narrow, limited, restricted. **ein Kleid** ~**er machen** to take a dress in; **im** ~**eren Sinne** in the narrow sense; **in dem Zimmer standen wir sehr** ~ we were very crowded in the room; ~ **zusammengedrängt sein** to be crowded together; **in die** ~**ere Wahl kommen** to be put on the short list, to be short-listed; **ein** ~**erer Ausschuß** a select committee.
  (b) (nah, dicht, vertraut) close. ~ **nebeneinander** or **zusammen** close together; **aufs** ~**ste befreundet sein** to be on the closest possible terms; **die Feier im** ~**sten Kreise** a small party for close friends; **die Hochzeit fand im** ~**sten Kreise der Familie statt** the wedding was celebrated with just the immediate family present; ~ **befreundet sein** to be close friends; **mit jdm** ~ **befreundet sein** to be a close friend of sb; **die** ~**ere Heimat** one's home area, the area (where) one comes from.
Engadin ['εŋgadi:n] nt **-s das** ~ the Engadine.
Engagement [ãgaʒə'mã:] nt **-s, -s (a)** (Theat) engagement. **(b)** (geh: Aktivität) involvement, engagement; (politisches ~) commitment (für to).
engagieren* [ãga'ʒi:rən] **1** vt to engage.
  2 vr to be/become committed (für to); (in einer Bekanntschaft) to become involved. **er hat sich sehr dafür engagiert, daß ...** he completely committed himself to ...; **engagierte Literatur** (politically/socially) committed literature; **er ist sehr engagiert** (politisch, sozial etc) he is very committed.
Engagiertheit [ãga'ʒi:ɐthait] f siehe vr commitment; involvement.
eng-: ~**anliegend** adj attr tight(-fitting), close-fitting; ~**bedruckt** adj attr close-printed; ~**befreundet** adj attr close; **die** ~**befreundeten Mädchen/Männer** etc the close friends; ~**begrenzt** adj attr restricted, narrow; ~**beschrieben** adj attr closely written; ~**brüstig** adj narrow-chested.
Enge f **-, -n (a)** no pl (von Straße etc) narrowness; (von Wohnung) confinement, crampedness; (Gedrängtheit) crush; (von Kleid etc) tightness; (fig) (Ärmlichkeit) straitened circumstances pl, poverty; (Beschränktheit) narrowness, limited or restricted nature. **(b)** (Meeres-) strait; (Engpaß) pass, defile. **jdn in die** ~ **treiben** (fig) to drive sb into a corner.
Engel m **-s, -** (lit, fig) angel. **ein rettender/guter** ~ (fig) a saviour/a guardian angel; **ich hörte die** ~ **im Himmel singen** (inf) it hurt like anything (inf), it was agony; **er ist auch nicht gerade ein** ~ (inf) he's no angel (inf); **wir sind alle keine** ~ (prov) none of us is perfect.
Engelaut m (Ling) fricative.
Engelchen, Eng(e)lein nt little angel.
Engel-: **e~gleich** adj siehe engel(s)gleich; ~**macher(in** f) m (euph inf) backstreet abortionist; ~**schar** f host of angels, angelic host.
Engel(s)-: ~**geduld** f saintly patience; **sie hat eine** ~**geduld** she has the patience of a saint; **e~gleich** adj angelic; ~**haar** nt angel's hair; **e~rein** adj pure as the driven snow; ~**zungen** pl: **(wie) mit** ~**zungen reden** to use all one's powers of persuasion.
Engelwurz f **-, -en** (Bot) angelica.
Engerling m (Zool) grub or larva of the May bug or cockchafer.
Eng-: **e~herzig** adj petty, hidebound; ~**herzigkeit** f pettiness.
engl. abbr of englisch.
England nt **-s** England.
Engländer m **-s, - (a)** Englishman; English boy. **die** ~ pl the English, the Britishers (US); **er ist** ~ he's English. **(b)** (Tech) adjustable spanner, monkey wrench.
Engländerin f Englishwoman; English girl.
England-: ~**feind** m Anglophobe; ~**freund** m Anglophile.
englisch¹ adj English. **die** ~**e Krankheit** (dated Med) rickets sing; (fig) the English disease or sickness; **die E~e Kirche** the Anglican Church, the Church of England; **die E~en Fräulein** (Eccl) institute of Catholic nuns for the education of girls; ~**e Broschur** case binding; siehe auch deutsch.
englisch² adj (Bibl) angelic. **der E~e Gruß** the Angelic Salutation, the Ave Maria or Hail Mary.
Englisch(e) nt decl as adj English; siehe auch Deutsch(e).
englisch-deutsch/-französisch etc adj Anglo-German/-French etc; Wörterbuch English-German/-French etc.
Englisch-: ~**horn** nt (Mus) cor anglais; ~**leder** nt (Tex) moleskin; **e~sprachig** adj Gebiet English-speaking; ~**traben** nt rising trot.
Eng-: **e~maschig** adj close-meshed; (fig, Sport) close; **e~maschig stricken** to knit to a fine tension; **e~maschig spielen** to play (it) close; ~**paß** m (narrow) pass, defile; (Fahrbahnverengung, fig) bottleneck.
Engramm [εn'gram] nt (Physiol) engram.
en gros [ã'gro] adv wholesale.
Engros- siehe Großhandels-.
Engrossist [ãgro'sist] m (Aus) wholesale dealer, wholesaler.
engstirnig adj narrow-minded, insular, parochial.
enharmonisch adj enharmonic.
enigmatisch adj (liter) siehe änigmatisch.
Enjambement [ãʒãbə'mã:] nt **-s, -s** (Poet) enjambement.
Enkel¹ m **-s, - (**~**kind) grandchild; (**~**sohn) grandson; (Nachfahr) descendant. **er ist** ~ **eines berühmten Geschlechts** (geh) he comes from a famous family or line.
Enkel² m **-s, -** (dial) ankle.
Enkelin f granddaughter.
Enkel-: ~**kind** nt grandchild; ~**sohn** m grandson; ~**tochter** f granddaughter.
Enklave [εn'kla:və] f **-, -n** enclave.
en masse [ã'mas] adv en masse.
en miniature [ãminja'ty:r] adv (geh) in miniature.
enorm adj (riesig) enormous; (inf: herrlich, kolossal) tre-

mendous (*inf*). **er verdient ~** *or* **~ viel (Geld)** (*inf*) he earns an enormous amount (of money); **~e Hitze/Kälte** tremendous heat/cold.

en passant [ãpɑ'sã] *adv* en passant, in passing.

Enquete [ã'keːt(ə), ãˈkeːt(ə)] *f* **-, -n** (*form*) survey; (*Aus auch: Arbeitstagung*) symposium.

Ensemble [ãˈsãbl] *nt* **-s, -s** ensemble; (*Besetzung*) cast.

Ensemblespiel *nt* (*Theat*) ensemble.

ent|arten* *vi aux sein* to degenerate (*zu* into).

ent|artet *adj* degenerate.

Ent|artung *f* degeneration.

Ent|artungs|erscheinung *f* symptom *or* sign of degeneration.

ent|äußern* *vr* **sich einer Sache** (*gen*) **~** (*geh*) to relinquish sth, to divest oneself of sth (*form*); **sich ~** (*Philos*) to be realized.

entbehren* **1** *vt* (*vermissen*) to miss; (*auch vi: verzichten*) to do *or* manage without; (*zur Verfügung stellen*) to spare. **wir haben jahrelang ~ müssen** for years we had/we have had to do *or* go without; **wir können ihn heute nicht ~** we cannot spare him/it today. **2** *vi* (*fehlen*) **einer Sache** (*gen*) **~** (*geh*) to lack sth, to be devoid of sth.

entbehrlich *adj* dispensable, unnecessary.

Entbehrlichkeit *f* dispensability, unnecessariness.

Entbehrung *f* privation, deprivation, want *no pl.* **~en auf sich** (*acc*) **nehmen** to make sacrifices.

entbehrungs-: ~reich, ~voll *adj* full of privation; **die ~reichen Kriegsjahre** the deprivation of the war years.

entbieten* *vt irreg* (*form*) (*jdm*) **seinen Gruß ~** (*old*) to present one's compliments (to sb) (*form*); **der Vorsitzende entbot der Delegation herzliche Willkommensgrüße** the Chairman welcomed the delegation cordially; **jdn zu sich ~** (*obs*) to summon sb (*form*).

entbinden* *irreg* **1** *vt* **(a)** (*Frau*) to deliver. **sie ist von einem Sohn entbunden worden** she has given birth to a son, she has been delivered of a son (*liter, old*). **(b)** (*befreien: von Versprechen, Amt etc*) to release (*von* from). **2** *vi* (*Frau*) to give birth.

Entbindung *f* delivery, birth; (*von Amt etc*) release.

Entbindungs-: ~anstalt *f* (*rare*), **~heim** *nt* maternity home *or* hospital; **~station** *f* maternity ward.

entblättern* **1** *vt* to strip (of leaves). **2** *vr* to shed its/their leaves; (*hum inf*) to strip, to shed one's clothes.

entblöden* *vr* **sich nicht ~, etw zu tun** to have the effrontery *or* audacity to do sth, to do sth unashamedly.

entblößen* *vt* (*form*) **(a)** to bare, to expose (*auch Mil*); **Kopf** to bare, to uncover; **Schwert** to draw, to unsheathe; (*fig*) **sein Innenleben** to lay bare, to reveal. **er hat sich entblößt** (*Exhibitionist*) he exposed himself; (*seinen wahren Charakter*) he showed his true colours.

(b) (*liter: des Schutzes berauben*) to divest, to denude (*form*). **jdn seiner Habe ~** to strip *or* divest sb of his possessions.

entblößt *adj* bare.

Entblößung *f siehe vt* **(a)** baring, exposing; (*Mil*) exposure; drawing; laying bare, revelation. **(b)** divesting, stripping.

entbrennen* *vi irreg aux sein* (*liter*) (*Kampf, Streit, Zorn*) to flare up, to erupt; (*Leidenschaft, Liebe*) to be (a)roused; (*Begeisterung*) to be fired. **in heißer Liebe zu jdm** *or* **für jdn ~** to fall passionately in love with sb; **in** *or* **von Leidenschaft/Wut ~** to become inflamed with passion/anger.

entbürokratisieren* *vt* to free of *or* from bureaucracy, to debureaucratize.

Entbürokratisierung *f* freeing from bureaucracy, debureaucratization.

Entchen *nt dim of* **Ente** duckling.

entdecken* **1** *vt* **(a)** to discover; *Fehler, Anzeichen, Lücke auch* to detect, to spot; (*in der Ferne*) to discern, to spot; (*in einer Menge*) to spot. **(b)** (*old: offenbaren*) **jdm etw ~** to reveal *or* discover (*obs*) sth to sb. **2** *vr* **sich jdm ~** (*old*) to reveal *or* discover (*obs*) oneself to sb (*form*).

Entdecker(in *f*) *m* **-s, -** discoverer.

Entdeckerfreude *f* joy(s) of discovery.

Entdeckung *f* discovery; (*von Fehler, Anzeichen auch*) detection, spotting; (*etw Entdecktes auch*) find.

Entdeckungs-: ~fahrt, ~reise *f* voyage of discovery; (*zu Lande*) expedition of discovery; **auf ~reise gehen** (*hum inf*) to go exploring.

Ente *f* **-, -n** duck; (*Press inf*) canard, hoax, false report; (*Med sl: Harngefäß*) (bed) urihal; (*Aut inf*) Citroën 2CV, deux-chevaux. **die ~ ist geplatzt** (*Press inf*) the story has turned out to be a hoax *or* canard *or* false report.

ent|ehren* *vt* to dishonour; (*entwürdigen*) to degrade; (*verleumden*) to defame; (*entjungfern*) to deflower. **~d** degrading; **sich ~** to degrade *or* disgrace oneself.

Ent|ehrung *f siehe vt* dishonouring; degradation; defamation; defloration.

ent|eignen* *vt* to expropriate; *Besitzer* to dispossess.

Ent|eignung *f siehe vt* expropriation; dispossession.

ent|eilen* *vi aux sein* (*old*) to hasten away (*liter*); (*liter: Zeit*) to fly by.

ent|eisen* *vt* to de-ice; *Kühlschrank* to defrost.

Ent|eisung *f siehe vt* de-icing; defrosting.

Ent|eisungs|anlage *f* de-icing unit.

Entelechie *f* (*Philos*) entelechy.

ent|emotionalisieren* *vt* to de-emotionalize.

Enten-: ~braten *m* roast duck; **~ei** *nt* duck's egg; **~flott** *nt*, **~grieß** *m*, **~grün** *nt*, **~grütze** *f* duckweed; **~küken** *nt* duckling.

Entente [ãˈtãt(ə)] *f* **-, -n** (*Pol*) entente.

Enterbeil *nt* boarding axe.

ent|erben* *vt* to disinherit.

Enterbrücke *f* boarding plank.

Ent|erbung *f* disinheriting.

Enterhaken *m* grappling iron *or* hook.

Enterich *m* drake.

entern (*Naut*) **1** *vti Schiff* to board. **2** *vi aux sein* to climb.

entfachen* *vt* (*geh*) *Feuer* to kindle; *Leidenschaft, Begierde* to arouse, to kindle (the flames of); *Krieg, Streit* to provoke.

entfahren* *vi irreg aux sein* **jdm ~** to slip out, to escape sb's lips; **Blödsinn! entfuhr es ihm** nonsense, he cried inadvertently; **ihr ist ein kleiner Furz entfahren** (*inf*) she accidentally broke wind *or* let off a little fart (*vulg*).

entfallen* *vi irreg aux sein* +*dat* **(a)** (*form: herunterfallen*) **jds Händen ~** to slip *or* fall *or* drop from sb's hands; **das Glas entfiel ihm** he dropped the glass.

(b) (*fig: aus dem Gedächtnis*) **jdm ~** to slip sb's mind, to escape sb; **der Name ist mir ~** the name has slipped my mind *or* escapes me.

(c) (*nicht in Betracht kommen*) not to apply, to be inapplicable; (*wegfallen*) to be dropped; (*erlöschen*) to lapse. **dieser Punkt der Tagesordnung entfällt** this point on the agenda has been dropped.

(d) auf jdn/etw ~ (*Geld, Kosten*) to be allotted *or* apportioned to sb/sth; **auf jeden ~ 100 Mark** each person will receive/pay 100 marks.

entfalten* **1** *vt* **(a)** (*auseinanderlegen*) to unfold, to open *or* spread out.

(b) (*fig*) (*entwickeln*) *Kräfte, Begabung, Theorie* to develop; (*beginnen*) *Tätigkeit* to launch into; (*darlegen*) *Plan, Gedankengänge* to set forth *or* out, to unfold, to expound. **seine Fähigkeiten voll ~** to develop one's abilities to the full.

(c) (*fig: zeigen*) *Pracht, Prunk* to display, to exhibit. **2** *vr* (*Knospe, Blüte*) to open, to unfold; (*fig*) to develop, to unfold, to blossom (out). **der Garten hat sich zu voller Pracht entfaltet** the garden blossomed (out) into its full magnificence; **hier kann ich mich nicht ~** I can't make full use of my abilities here, I'm held back here.

Entfaltung *f* unfolding; (*von Blüte auch*) opening; (*fig*) (*Entwicklung*) development; (*einer Tätigkeit*) launching into; (*Darstellung*) (*eines Planes, Gedankens*) exposition, setting out, unfolding; (*von Prunk, Tatkraft*) display. **zur ~ kommen** to develop, to blossom.

entfärben* **1** *vt* to take the colour out of, to decolour (*Tech*), to decolorize (*Tech*); (*bleichen*) to bleach. **das E~** the removal of colour, decolorization (*Tech*). **2** *vr* (*Stoff, Blätter*) to lose (its/their) colour; (*Mensch*) to turn *or* go pale.

Entfärber *m*, **Entfärbungsmittel** *nt* colour *or* dye remover, decolorant (*Tech*).

entfernen* **1** *vt* to remove (*von, aus* from). **jdn aus der Schule ~** to expel sb from school; **das entfernt uns (weit) vom Thema** that takes us a long way from our subject.

2 *vr* **(a) sich (von** *or* **aus etw) ~** (*weggehen*) to go away (from sth), to leave (sth); (*abfahren, abziehen*) to move off (from sth), to depart (from sth); **sich von seinem Posten/Arbeitsplatz ~** to leave one's post/position; **sich unerlaubt von der Truppe ~** (*Mil*) to go absent without leave; **sich unerlaubt von der Schule ~** to leave school *or* absent oneself from school (*form*) without permission; **sich zu weit ~** to go too far away.

(b) (*fig*) (*von* from) (*von jdm*) to become estranged; (*von Thema*) to depart, to digress; (*von Wahrheit*) to depart, to deviate. **er hat sich sehr weit von seinen früheren Ansichten entfernt** he has come a long way from his earlier views.

entfernt 1 *adj Ort, Verwandter* distant; (*abgelegen*) remote; (*gering*) *Ähnlichkeit* distant, remote, vague. **10 km ~ von** 10km (away) from; **das Haus liegt 2 km ~** the house is 2km away; **aus den ~esten Ländern** from the furthest corners of the globe; **ich hatte nicht den ~esten Verdacht** I didn't have the slightest *or* remotest suspicion; *siehe* **weit**.

2 *adv* remotely, slightly. **nicht einmal ~ (so gut/hübsch etc)** not even remotely (as good/pretty etc); **~ verwandt** distantly related; **er erinnert mich ~ an meinen Onkel** he reminds me slightly *or* vaguely of my uncle; **das hat nur ~ mit dieser Angelegenheit zu tun** that has only a distant bearing on this matter *or* is only vaguely related *or* has only a remote connection with this matter; **nicht im ~esten** not in the slightest *or* least!; **wenn ich auch nur im ~esten gedacht hätte ...** if I had had even the faintest suspicion ...

Entfernung *f* **(a)** distance; (*Mil: bei Waffen*) range. **man hört das Echo auf große ~ (hin)** you can hear the echo from a great distance *or* a long way away; **aus** *or* **in der ~** (*hörte er ...*) in the distance (he heard ...); **aus kurzer/großer ~ (schießen)** (to fire) at *or* from close/long range; **aus einiger ~** from a distance; **in einiger ~** at a distance; **in einer ~ von 20 Metern** at a distance of 20 metres; **etw auf eine ~ von 50 Meter treffen** to hit sth at a distance of 50 metres.

(b) (*das Entfernen*) removal; (*aus der Schule*) expulsion. **unerlaubte ~ (von der Truppe)** absence without leave; **unerlaubte ~ von der Schule/vom Posten** *etc* absence from school/one's post *etc* without permission.

Entfernungsmesser *m* **-s, -** (*Mil, Phot*) rangefinder.

entfesseln* *vt* (*fig*) to unleash.

entfesselt *adj* unleashed; *Leidenschaft, Trieb* unbridled, uncontrolled; *Mensch* wild; *Naturgewalten* raging. **vor Zorn/Begeisterung ~** wild with rage/enthusiasm; **der ~e** Prometheus Prometheus Unbound.

entfetten* *vt* to remove the grease from, to degrease (*Tech*); *Wolle* to scour.

Entfettung *f* **(a)** *siehe vt* removal of grease (from), degreasing; scouring. **(b)** (*Gewichtsabnahme*) losing fat.

Entfettungskur *f* weight-reducing course.

entflammbar *adj* inflammable.

entflammen* **1** *vt* (*fig*) to (a)rouse; *Leidenschaft, Haß auch* to inflame; *Begeisterung* to fire.

2 *vr* (*fig*) to be (a)roused *or* fired *or* inflamed.

3 *vi aux sein* to burst into flames, to catch fire, to ignite (*Chem etc*); (*fig*) (*Zorn, Streit*) to flare up; (*Leidenschaft, Liebe*) to be (a)roused *or* inflamed. **für etw entflammt sein** to be fired with enthusiasm for sth; **in Liebe ~/entflammt sein** to fall/be passionately in love.

entflechten* *vt irreg* (*Pol*) *Kartell etc* to break up.

Entflechtung *f* (*Pol*) breaking up.

entflecken* *vt* to remove the stain(s) from.

entfleuchen* *vi aux sein* (*obs: wegfliegen*) to fly away; (*hum: weggehen*) to be off (*inf*).

entfliegen* *vi irreg aux sein* to fly away, to escape (*dat or aus* from).

entfliehen* *vi irreg aux sein* (*geh*) **(a)** to escape, to flee (*dat or aus* from). **dem Lärm/der Unrast etc ~** to escape *or* flee (from) the noise/unrest *etc*. **(b)** (*vergehen: Zeit, Jugend etc*) to fly past.

entfremden* **1** *vt* to alienate (*auch Sociol, Philos*), to estrange. **jdn einer Person/Sache** (*dat*) **~, jdm eine Person/Sache ~** to alienate *or* estrange sb from sb/sth; **die lange Trennung hat die Freunde (einander) entfremdet** the long separation estranged the friends from each other *or* made the two friends strangers to each other; **entfremdete Arbeit** (*Sociol*) alienated work; **etw seinem Zweck ~** to use sth for the wrong purpose, not to use sth for its intended purpose.

2 *vr* to become alienated *or* estranged (*dat* from). **er hat sich seiner Frau ganz entfremdet** he has become completely alienated from his wife, he has become a complete stranger to his wife; **durch die lange Abwesenheit habe ich mich *or* bin ich der Stadt ganz entfremdet** my long absence has made me a stranger to the city.

Entfremdung *f* estrangement; (*Sociol, Philos*) alienation.

entfrosten* *vt* to defrost.

Entfroster *m* **-s, -** defroster.

entführen* *vt jdn* to abduct, to kidnap; *Beute etc* to carry off, to make off with; *LKW, Flugzeug* to hijack; *Mädchen* (*mit Zustimmung zur Heirat*) to elope with, to run off with; (*hum inf: wegnehmen*) to borrow (*often hum*). **sie ließ sich von ihrem Liebhaber ~** she eloped with her lover; **wer hat mir denn meinen Bleistift entführt?** (*inf*) who's made off with my pencil? (*inf*).

Entführer(in *f*) *m* **(a)** abductor, kidnapper. **(b)** (*Flugzeug~ etc*) hijacker; (*Flugzeug~ auch*) skyjacker (*inf*).

Entführung *f* (*Sache*) *vt* abduction, kidnapping; hijacking; elopement. **„Die ~ aus dem Serail"** "The Abduction from the Seraglio".

entgasen* *vt* (*Chem*) to degas.

entgegen **1** *adv* (*liter*) **dem Licht/der Zukunft etc ~!** on towards the light/future *etc!*; **dem Feind ~!** to the attack!; **neuen Ufern/Abenteuern ~!** on to new shores/adventures!; **dem Wind ~!** into the (teeth of the) wind!

2 *prep* +*dat* contrary to, against. **~ meiner Bitte** contrary to my request; **~ allen Erwartungen, allen Entwartungen ~** contrary to all *or* against all expectation(s).

entgegen|arbeiten *vi sep* +*dat* to oppose, to work against.

entgegenblicken *vi sep siehe* **entgegensehen.**

entgegenbringen *vt sep irreg* **jdm etw ~** to bring sth to sb; (*fig*) *Achtung, Freundschaft etc* to show *or* evince sth for sb.

entgegen|eilen *vi sep aux sein* +*dat* to rush towards; (*um jdn zu treffen*) to rush to meet.

entgegenfahren *vi sep aux sein* +*dat* to travel towards, to approach; (*um jdn zu treffen*) to travel to meet; (*mit dem Auto*) to drive towards/to meet.

entgegenführen *vt sep* +*dat* (*geh*) to lead to(wards).

entgegengehen *vi sep aux sein* +*dat* to go towards, to approach; (*um jdn zu treffen*) to go to meet; (*fig*) *einer Gefahr, dem Tode, der Zukunft* to face. **dem Ende ~** (*Leben, Krieg*) to draw to a close, to approach its end; **seinem Untergang/Schwierigkeiten ~** to be heading for disaster/difficulties; **seiner Vollendung ~** to near *or* approach completion.

entgegengesetzt *adj Richtung, Meinung* opposite; *Charakter auch* contrasting; (*fig: einander widersprechend*) *Interessen, Meinungen* opposing *attr*, opposed, conflicting *attr*. **einander ~e Interessen/Meinungen etc** opposing *or* conflicting interests/views *etc*; **genau ~ denken/handeln etc** to think/do *etc* exactly the opposite; **er reagierte genau ~** his reaction was exactly the opposite, he did exactly the opposite.

entgegenhalten *vt sep irreg* +*dat* **(a) jdm etw ~** to hold sth out towards sb. **(b)** (*fig*) **einer Sache ~, daß ...** to object to sth that ...; **dieser Ansicht muß man ~, daß ...** against this view it must be objected that ...

entgegenhandeln *vi sep siehe* **zuwiderhandeln.**

entgegenkommen *vi sep irreg aux sein* +*dat* to come towards, to approach; (*um jdn zu treffen*) to (come to) meet; (*fig*) to accommodate; *Wünschen, Bitten auch* to meet, to comply with. **jdm auf halbem Wege ~** (*lit, fig*) to meet sb halfway; **das kommt unseren Plänen/Vorstellungen etc sehr entgegen** that fits in very well with our plans/ideas *etc*; **Ihr Vorschlag kommt mir sehr entgegen** I find your suggestion very congenial.

Entgegenkommen *nt* (*Gefälligkeit*) kindness, obligingness; (*Zugeständnis*) concession, accommodation.

entgegenkommend *adj* (*fig*) obliging, accommodating.

entgegenkommenderweise *adv* obligingly, accommodatingly; (*als Zugeständnis*) as a concession.

entgegenlaufen *vi sep irreg aux sein* +*dat* to run towards; (*um jdn zu treffen*) to run to meet; (*fig*) to run contrary *or* counter to.

Entgegennahme *f* -, -n (*form*) (*Empfang*) receipt; (*Annahme*)

acceptance. **bei ~** on receipt/acceptance.

entgegennehmen *vt sep irreg* (*empfangen*) to receive; (*annehmen*) to accept. **nehmen Sie meinen Dank entgegen** (*form*) please accept my thanks.

entgegenschauen *vi sep siehe* **entgegensehen.**

entgegenschlagen *vi sep irreg aux sein* +*dat* (*Geruch, Haß*) to confront, to meet; (*Flammen auch*) to leap towards; (*Jubel, Begeisterung*) to meet, to greet. **ihm schlug Jubel/ein widerlicher Geruch entgegen** he was greeted with jubilation/confronted by a nauseating smell.

entgegensehen *vi sep irreg* **(a) jdm ~** to see sb coming. **(b)** (*fig*) *einer Sache* (*dat*) **~** to await sth; (*freudig*) to look forward to sth; *einer Sache* **~ müssen** to have to expect *or* face sth; **Ihrer baldigen Antwort ~d** (*form*) in anticipation of *or* looking forward to your early reply.

entgegensetzen *vt sep* +*dat* **etw einer Sache ~** to set sth against sth; **wir können diesen Forderungen nichts ~** we have nothing to counter these claims with; **einer Sache Alternativen ~** to put *or* pose alternatives to sth; **dem habe ich entgegenzusetzen, daß ...** against that I'd like to say that ...; **die Gewerkschaften hatten den Regierungsvorschlägen nichts entgegenzusetzen** the unions had nothing to offer in reply to the government's suggestions; **jdm/einer Sache Widerstand ~** to put up *or* offer resistance to sb/sth; **ihren Anklagen konnte er nichts ~** he could find no reply to her accusations; *siehe* **entgegengesetzt.**

entgegenstehen *vi sep irreg* +*dat* (*fig*) to stand in the way of, to be an obstacle to. **dem steht entgegen, daß ...** what stands in the way of that is that ...; **dem steht nichts entgegen** there's no obstacle to that, there's nothing against that; **was steht dem entgegen?** what obstacle is there to that?

entgegenstellen *vt sep* +*dat* **1** *vt siehe* **entgegensetzen.** **2** *vr* **sich jdm/einer Sache ~** to resist sb/sth, to oppose sb/sth.

entgegenstemmen *vr sep* **sich jdm/einer Sache ~** to pit oneself against sb/sth, to oppose sb/sth.

entgegenstrecken *vt sep* **jdm etw ~** to hold out sth to sb.

entgegenstürzen *vi sep aux sein* +*dat* to fall upon; (*zueilen auf*) to rush towards.

entgegentreten *vi sep irreg aux sein* +*dat* to step *or* walk up to; *dem Feind* to go into action against; *einer Politik, Forderungen* to oppose; *Behauptungen, Vorurteilen* to counter; *einer Gefahr, Unsitten* to take steps against, to act against.

entgegenwirken *vi sep* +*dat* to counteract.

entgegnen *vti* to reply; (*kurz, barsch*) to retort (*auf* +*acc* to). **er entgegnete nichts** he made no reply; **darauf wußte er nichts zu ~** he didn't know what to reply to that.

Entgegnung *f* reply; (*kurz, barsch*) retort.

entgehen* *vi irreg aux sein* +*dat* **(a)** (*entkommen*) *Verfolgern, dem Feind* to elude, to escape (from); *dem Schicksal, der Gefahr, Strafe* to escape, to avoid.

(b) (*fig: nicht bemerkt werden*) **dieser Fehler ist mir entgangen** I failed to notice *or* I missed this mistake, this mistake escaped my notice; **mir ist kein Wort entgangen** I didn't miss a word (of it); **es ist meiner Aufmerksamkeit nicht entgangen, daß ...** it has not escaped my attention that ...; **ihr entgeht nichts** she doesn't miss anything *or* a thing; **es ist ihm nicht entgangen, daß ...** he didn't fail to notice that ..., it didn't escape him that ...; **sich** (*dat*) **etw ~ lassen** to miss sth.

entgeistert *adj* dumbfounded, thunderstruck, flabbergasted (*inf*). **er starrte mich ganz ~ an** he stared at me quite dumbfounded *or* thunderstruck *or* flabbergasted (*inf*); **er reagierte ~** he reacted with complete astonishment.

Entgelt *nt* **-(e)s,** *no pl* (*form*) **(a)** (*Bezahlung*) remuneration (*form*); (*Entschädigung*) recompense (*form*), compensation; (*Anerkennung*) reward. **(b)** (*Gebühr*) fee, consideration. **gegen ~ for a fee** *or* consideration; **etw gegen ~ abgeben** to give sb sth for a consideration.

entgelten* *vt irreg* (*geh*) **(a)** (*büßen*) to pay for. **jdn etw ~ lassen** to make sb pay *or* suffer for sth. **(b)** (*vergüten*) **jdm etw ~** to repay sb for sth.

entgiften* *vt* to decontaminate; (*Med*) to detoxicate, to detoxify.

Entgiftung *f* decontamination; (*Med*) detoxication.

entgleisen* *vi aux sein* **(a)** (*Rail*) to be derailed; to leave *or* run off *or* jump the rails. **einen Zug zum E~ bringen** *or* **~ lassen** to derail a train. **(b)** (*fig: Mensch*) to misbehave; (*einen Fauxpas begehen*) to commit a faux pas, to drop a clanger (*inf*).

Entgleisung *f* derailment; (*fig*) faux pas, gaffe, clanger (*inf*).

entgleiten* *vi irreg aux sein* +*dat* to slip. **jdm *or* jds Hand ~** to slip from *or* out of sb's grasp; **jdm/einer Sache ~** (*fig*) to slip away from sb/sth.

entgotten*, entgöttern* *vt* (*liter*) to remove god(s) from. **die entgötterte Welt** the godless world, the world without god(s).

Entgötterung, Entgottung *f* (*liter*) removal of god(s) (*gen* from). **die ~ des Olymp** the banishing of the gods from Olympus.

entgräten* *vt Fisch* to fillet, to bone.

enthaaren* *vt* to remove unwanted hair from, to depilate (*form*).

Enthaarungsmittel *nt* depilatory.

enthalten* *irreg* **1** *vt* to contain. **~ sein in** (+*dat*) to be included in.

2 *vr* **(a)** (*geh*) **sich einer Sache** (*gen*) **~** to abstain from sth; **sich nicht ~ können, etw zu tun** to be unable to refrain from doing sth; **sich einer Bemerkung nicht ~ können** to be unable to refrain from making a remark.

(b) **sich (der Stimme) ~** to abstain.

enthaltsam *adj* abstemious; (*geschlechtlich*) abstinent, continent; (*mäßig*) moderate.

Enthaltsamkeit *f siehe adj* abstinence, abstemiousness; abstinence, continence; moderation.
Enthaltung *f* abstinence; *(Stimm~)* abstention.
enthärten* *vt Wasser* to soften; *Metall* to anneal.
Enthärter *m*, **Enthärtungsmittel** *nt* (water) softener.
Enthärtung *f siehe vt* softening; annealing.
enthaupten* *vt* to decapitate; *(als Hinrichtung auch)* to behead.
Enthauptung *f siehe vt* decapitation; beheading.
enthäuten* *vt* to skin; *(als Folter etc)* to flay.
entheben* *vt irreg jdn einer Sache (gen)* ~ to relieve sb of sth.
entheiligen* *vt* to desecrate, to profane.
Entheiligung *f* desecration, profanation.
enthemmen* *vti jdn* ~ to make sb lose his inhibitions, to free sb from his inhibitions; **Alkohol wirkt ~d** alcohol has a disinhibiting effect; **(moralisch etc)** **völlig enthemmt sein** to have no (moral etc) inhibitions whatsoever; **to have lost one's** (moral) inhibitions.
Enthemmtheit, **Enthemmung** *f* loss of inhibitions.
enthüllen* **1** *vt* to uncover, to reveal; *Skandal, Lüge auch* to expose; *Denkmal, Gesicht* to unveil; *Geheimnis, Plan, Hintergründe* to reveal. **2** *vr (lit, hum)* to reveal oneself. **er hat sich in seiner ganzen Gemeinheit enthüllt** he revealed himself for the villain he was.
Enthüllung *f siehe vt* uncovering, revealing; unveiling; revealing. **noch eine sensationelle** ~ another sensational revelation *or* disclosure.
enthülsen* *vt* to shell; *Getreide* to husk.
enthusiasmieren* *vt (dated, geh)* to fill with enthusiasm, to enthuse.
Enthusiasmus *m* enthusiasm.
Enthusiast(in *f)* *m* enthusiast.
enthusiastisch *adj* enthusiastic.
ent|ideologisieren* **1** *vt* to free from ideology. **2** *vr (Partei)* to dispense with one's ideology.
Ent|ideologisierung *f* freeing from ideology; *(das Entideologisiertwerden)* decreasing ideological commitment.
Entität *f (Philos)* entity.
entjungfern* *vt* to deflower.
Entjungferung *f* defloration.
entkalken* *vt* to decalcify.
entkeimen* **1** *vt* **(a)** *Kartoffeln* to remove the buds from. **(b)** *(keimfrei machen)* to sterilize. **2** *vi aux sein + dat (liter)* to burgeon forth from *(liter)*.
entkernen* *vt* **(a)** *Orangen etc* to remove the pips from; *Kernobst* to core; *Steinobst* to stone. **(b)** *Wohngebiet (Dichte reduzieren)* to reduce the density of; *(dezentralisieren)* to decentralize, to disperse.
Entkerner *m -s, -* *siehe vt* corer; stoner.
entkleiden* *(geh)* **1** *vt* to undress. **jdn einer Sache (gen)** ~ *(fig)* to strip *or* divest sb of sth. **2** *vr* to undress, to take one's clothes off.
Entkleidungsnummer *f* striptease act *or* number.
entknoten* *vt* to untie, to undo; *(fig: entwirren)* to unravel.
entkolonialisieren* *vt* to decolonialize.
Entkolonialisierung *f* decolonialization.
entkommen* *vi irreg aux sein* to escape, to get away *(+ dat, aus* from).
Entkommen *nt* escape.
entkorken* *vt Flasche* to uncork.
entkörperlicht *adj (liter)* incorporeal.
entkräften* *vt (schwächen)* to weaken, to debilitate, to enfeeble; *(erschöpfen)* to exhaust, to wear out; *(fig: widerlegen)* *Behauptung etc* to refute, to invalidate.
Entkräftung *f siehe vt* weakening, debilitation, enfeeblement; exhaustion; refutation, invalidation.
entkrampfen* *vt (fig)* to relax, to ease; *Lage* to ease. **eine entkrampfte Atmosphäre** a relaxed atmosphere.
Entkrampfung *f (fig)* relaxation, easing.
entkriechen* *vi irreg aux sein + dat (liter)* to crawl forth from *(liter)*.
entladen* *irreg* **1** *vt* to unload; *Batterie etc* to discharge. **2** *vr (Gewitter)* to break; *(Schußwaffe)* to go off, to discharge *(form)*; *(elektrische Spannung, Batterie etc)* to discharge; *(langsam)* to run down; *(Sprengladung)* to explode, to go off; *(fig: Emotion)* to vent itself/themselves. **sein Zorn entlud sich über mir** he vented his anger on me.
Entladung *f* **(a)** *(das Entladen)* unloading. **(b)** *siehe vr* breaking; discharge; discharge; running down; explosion; venting. **eine zur** ~ **bringen** *(Mil, fig)* to detonate sth.
entlang **1** *prep nach n + acc or (rare) + dat, vor n + dat or (rare) + gen* along. **den** *or (rare)* **dem Fluß** ~ along the river. **2** *adv* along. **am Bach** ~ along (by the side of) the stream; **am Haus** ~ along (by) the side of the house; **hier** ~ this way.
entlang- *pref* along; **~gehen** *vti sep irreg aux sein* to walk along, to go along *(auch fig)*; **am Haus ~gehen** to walk along by the side of the house.
entlarven* *vt (fig) Spion, Dieb etc* to unmask, to expose; *Pläne, Betrug etc* to uncover, to expose. **sich** ~ to reveal one's true colours *or* character; **sich als Schuft etc** ~ to reveal *or* show oneself to be a scoundrel etc.
Entlarvung *f siehe vt* unmasking, exposure; uncovering, exposure.
entlassen* *vt irreg (aus* from) *(gehen lassen, kündigen)* to dismiss; *(nach Streichungen)* to make redundant; *(aus dem Krankenhaus)* to discharge; *Soldaten* to discharge; *(in den Ruhestand versetzen)* to retire, to pension off; *(aus dem Gefängnis, aus Verpflichtungen)* to release, to discharge, to free; *(aus der Schule: als Strafe)* to expel. **aus der Schule** ~ **werden** to leave school; to be expelled from school; **jdn mit ein paar**

freundlichen Worten ~ to dismiss sb *or* send sb away with a few kind words; **jdn in den Ruhestand** ~ to retire sb, to pension sb off; **Soldaten ins Zivilleben** ~ to demobilize soldiers.
Entlassung *f siehe vt* dismissal; making redundant; discharge; discharge; retirement, pensioning off; release, discharge; expulsion. **um seine** ~ **einreichen** to tender one's resignation; **es gab 20** ~**en** there were 20 redundancies.
Entlassungs-: ~**gesuch** *nt* (letter of) resignation; *(Jur)* petition for release; **ein** ~**gesuch stellen** *or* **einreichen** to tender one's resignation; *(Jur)* to petition for one's/sb's release; ~**schein** *m* certificate of discharge; *(Mil auch)* discharge papers *pl*; ~**zeugnis** *nt (Sch)* school leaving certificate.
entlasten* *vt Achse, Telefonleitungen etc* to relieve the strain *or* load on; *Herz* to relieve the strain on; *(Mil, Rail), Gewissen* to relieve; *Verkehr* to ease; *Stadtzentrum* to relieve congestion in; *(Arbeit abnehmen) Chef, Hausfrau* to take some of the load off, to relieve; *(Jur) Angeklagten (völlig)* to exonerate; *(teilweise)* to support the case of; *(Comm: gutheißen) Vorstand* to approve the activities of; *(entlassen, Schulden) jdn* to discharge, to release. **jdn finanziell** ~ to ease sb's financial burden; **jdn** *or* **jds Konto um** *or* **für einen Betrag** ~ to credit sb *or* sb's account with a sum, to credit a sum to sb's account.
Entlastung *f* relief *(auch Mil, Rail etc)*; *(von Achse etc, Herz)* relief of the strain *(+ gen* on); *(Jur)* exoneration; *(Comm: des Vorstands)* approval; *(Fin)* credit; *(von Verpflichtungen etc)* release, discharge. **zu jds** ~ *(in order)* to take some of the load off sb; *(Mil)* *(in order)* to relieve sb ...; **eine Aussage zur** ~ **des Angeklagten** a statement supporting the case of the defendant; **zu seiner** ~ **führte der Angeklagte an, daß** ... in his defence the defendant stated that ...
Entlastungs-: ~**bogen** *m (Archit)* relieving arch; ~**material** *nt (Jur)* evidence for the defence; ~**zeuge** *m (Jur)* witness for the defence, defence witness; ~**zug** *m* relief train.
entlauben* *vt* to strip of leaves; *(Sci)* to defoliate.
Entlaubung *f* defoliation.
Entlaubungsmittel *nt* defoliant.
entlaufen* *vi irreg aux sein* to run away *(dat, von* from). **ein** ~**er Sklave**; ~**es Kind etc** a runaway slave/child etc; **ein** ~**er Sträfling** an escaped convict; **ein** ~**er Hund** a lost *or* missing dog; „**Hund** ~" "dog missing".
entlausen* *vt* to delouse.
Entlausung *f* delousing.
entledigen* *(form)* **1** *vr* **sich einer Person/Sache (gen)** ~ to rid oneself of sb/sth; **sich einer Pflicht** ~ to discharge a duty; **sich eines Komplizen** ~ *(euph)* to eliminate *or* dispose of an accomplice *(euph)*; **sich seiner Schulden** ~ to discharge *(form) or* pay off one's debts; **sich seiner Kleidung** ~ to remove one's clothes.
 2 *vt* **jdn einer Pflicht** *(gen)* ~ to release sb from a duty.
entleeren* *vt* to empty; *Darm*, *(Sci) Glasglocke* to evacuate.
Entleerung *f siehe vt* emptying; evacuation.
entlegen *adj Ort, Haus (abgelegen)* remote, out-of-the-way; *(weit weg)* far away *or* off, remote; *(fig) Gedanke etc* odd, out-of-the-way.
Entlegenheit *f* remoteness; *(fig)* oddness.
entlehnen* *vt (fig)* to borrow *(dat, von* from).
Entlehnung *f (fig)* borrowing.
entleiben* *vr (obs)* to take one's own life.
entleihen* *vt irreg* to borrow *(von, aus* from).
Entleiher *m -s, -* borrower.
Entleihung *f* borrowing.
Entlein *nt* duckling. **das häßliche** ~ the Ugly Duckling.
entloben* *vr* to break off one's engagement.
Entlobung *f* breaking off of one's engagement; broken engagement.
entlocken* *vt jdm/einer Sache etw* ~ to elicit sth from sb/sth; *(durch Überredung auch)* to coax sth out of sb; *(durch ständige Befragung auch)* to worm sth out of sb.
entlohnen*, **entlöhnen*** *(Sw)* *vt* to pay; *(fig)* to reward. **etw gegen** ~ tun to do sth for payment.
Entlohnung, **Entlöhnung** *(Sw)* *f* pay(ment); *(fig)* reward.
entlüften* *vt* to ventilate, to air; *Bremsen* to bleed.
Entlüfter *m -s, -* ventilator.
Entlüftung *f siehe vt* ventilation, airing; bleeding.
Entlüftungs|anlage *f* ventilation system.
entmachten* *vt* to deprive of power.
Entmachtung *f* deprivation of power.
entmagnetisieren* *vt* to demagnetize.
entmannen* *vt* to castrate; *(fig)* to emasculate, to unman.
Entmannung *f* castration; *(fig)* emasculation.
entmaterialisieren* *vt* to dematerialize.
entmenschlichen* *vt* to dehumanize.
entmenscht *adj* bestial, inhuman.
entmilitarisieren* *vt* to demilitarize.
Entmilitarisierung *f* demilitarization.
entminen* *vt (Mil)* to clear of mines.
entmündigen* *vt (Jur)* to (legally) incapacitate, to declare incapable of managing one's own affairs; *(wegen Geisteskrankheit auch)* to certify. **das Fernsehen entmündigt die Zuschauer, wenn** ... television takes away the viewer's right to form an independent opinion when ...
Entmündigung *f siehe vt (Jur)* (legal) incapacitation; certification.
entmutigen* *vt* to discourage, to dishearten. **sich nicht** ~ **lassen** not to be discouraged *or* disheartened.
Entmutigung *f* discouragement.
entmythologisieren* *vt* to demythologize.
Entmythologisierung *f* demythologization.
Entnahme *f -, -n (form)* removal, taking out; *(von Blut)* extraction; *(von Geld)* withdrawal. **vor etc** ~ **einer Sache** *(gen)* before

etc removing *or* extracting/withdrawing sth.
entnazifizieren* *vt* to denazify.
Entnazifizierung *f* denazification.
entnehmen* *vt irreg (aus, dat)* to take out (of), to take (from); *(aus Kasse)* Geld to withdraw (from); *(einem Buch etc)* Zitat to take (from); *(fig: erkennen, folgern)* to infer (from); to gather (from). **wie ich Ihren Worten entnehme, ...** I gather from what you say that ...
entnerven* *vt* to unnerve. ~d unnerving; *(nervtötend)* nerve-racking; **entnervt** unnerved, nervous.
Entoderm *nt* **-s, -e** *(Biol)* entoderm, endoderm.
entölen* *vt* Kakao to extract the oil from.
Entomologie *f* entomology.
entomologisch *adj* entomological.
entpersönlichen* *vt* to depersonalize.
Entpersönlichung *f* depersonalization.
entpflichten* *vt (form)* Pfarrer, Professor to retire.
entpolitisieren* *vt* to depoliticize.
Entpolitisierung *f* depoliticizing, depoliticization.
entpuppen* *vr (Schmetterling)* to emerge from its cocoon *or* chrysalis. **sich als Betrüger** ~ to turn out to be a cheat *etc*; **mal sehen, wie er sich entpuppt** we'll see how he turns out; **die hat sich aber ganz schön entpuppt!** *(inf)* she's really shown her true character!, she's really shown herself in her true colours!
entrahmen* *vt* Milch to remove the cream from, to skim; *(mit Zentrifuge)* to separate.
Entrahmung *f* skimming; *(mit Zentrifuge)* separation.
entraten* *vi irreg (geh, old)* einer Sache *(gen)* ~ to be devoid of sth; **einer Person/Sache** *(gen)* ~**/nicht** ~ **können** to be able/unable to dispense with sb/sth.
enträtseln* *vt* to solve; Sinn to work out; Schrift to decipher.
entrechten* *vt* jdn ~ to deprive sb of his rights; **die Entrechteten** those who have lost *or* been deprived of their rights.
Entrechtung *f* deprivation of rights. **die** ~ **des Parlaments** depriving parliament of its rights.
Entree [ã'tre:] *nt* **-s, -s** *(dated) (Eingang)* entrance; *(obs: Vorraum)* (entrance) hall; *(Eintrittsgeld)* entrance *or* admission fee; *(Mus: Vorspiel)* introduction; *(Cook: Vorspeise)* entrée; *(Theat: Auftritt)* solo entrance.
entreißen* *vt irreg* jdm etw ~ *(lit, fig liter)* to snatch sth (away) from sb; **jdn dem Tode** ~ *(liter)* to snatch sb from the jaws of death.
entrichten* *vt (form)* to pay.
Entrichtung *f (form)* payment.
entrinden* *vt* to remove the bark from, to decorticate *(form)*.
entringen* *irreg* **1** *vt (geh)* jdm etw ~ to wrench *or* wrest sth from sb; **jdm ein Geheimnis** *etc* ~ to wring a secret *etc* out of sb, to wrest a secret *etc* from sb. **2** *vr (liter)* sich jds Lippen *(dat)* ~ to escape from sb's lips; **ein Seufzer entrang sich seiner Brust** he heaved a sigh.
entrinnen* *vi irreg aux sein (geh)* **(a)** +dat to escape from; **dem Tod** to escape. **es gibt kein E~** there is no escape. **(b)** *(entfliehen: Zeit)* to fly by.
entrollen* **1** *vt* Landkarte etc to unroll; Fahne, Segel to unfurl. **ein Bild des Schreckens** ~ *(fig)* to reveal a picture of horror. **2** *vr* to unroll/unfurl. **ein Bild des Schreckens entrollte sich** *(fig)* a picture of horror unfolded. **3** *vi aux sein + dat (rare)* to roll out of.
Entropie *f (Phys)* entropy.
entrosten* *vt* to derust.
Entroster *m* **-s, -** deruster.
Entrostung *f* derusting.
Entrostungsmittel *nt siehe* **Entroster.**
entrücken* *vt (geh)* jdn jdm/einer Sache ~ *(lit, fig)* to carry *or* bear *(liter)* sb away from sb/sth, to transport sb (away) from sb/sth; **jdn (in den Himmel)** ~ *(Rel)* to translate sb (into heaven); **der Tod hat sie allen Sorgen entrückt** death has put her beyond all tribulation; **einer Sache weit entrückt sein** *(fig)* to be far removed from sth; **er ist dieser Welt jetzt weit entrückt** he is now quite removed *or* apart from this world; **jdn jds Blicken** ~ to remove sb from sb's sight; **jds Blicken entrückt (sein)** to be out of (sb's) sight.
entrückt *adj (geh) (verzückt)* enraptured, transported; *(versunken)* lost in reverie, rapt.
Entrückung *f (geh, Rel)* rapture, ecstasy; *(Versunkenheit)* rapt absorption; *(Rel: Versetzung)* translation.
entrümpeln* *vt* to clear out.
Entrümp(e)lung *f* clear-out; *(das Entrümpeln)* clearing out.
entrüsten* **1** *vt (empören)* to fill with indignation, to outrage; *(zornig machen)* to incense, to anger; *(schockieren)* to outrage, to scandalize.
2 *vr sich* ~ **über** *(+acc) (sich empören)* to be filled with indignation at, to be outraged at; *(zornig werden)* to be incensed at; *(schockiert sein)* to be outraged *or* scandalized at; **das ist unerhört!, entrüstete sich die alte Dame** that is scandalous!, said the old lady incensed.
entrüstet *adj siehe vt* (highly) indignant, outraged; incensed; outraged, scandalized.
Entrüstung *f (über +acc* at) indignation; *(Zorn)* anger. **ein Sturm der** ~ **brach los** a storm of indignation broke out.
entsaften* *vt* to extract the juice from.
Entsafter *m* **-s, -** juice extractor.
entsagen* *vi + dat (geh)* to renounce. **der Welt** ~ to renounce the world; **sie hat vielen Freuden** ~ **müssen** she had to forgo many pleasures; **dem muß ich** ~ **I** shall have to forgo that.
Entsagung *f (geh) (von der Welt etc)* renunciation. **Armut und** ~ **sind die Grundprinzipien des Klosterlebens** poverty and renunciation of worldly things are the basic principles of monastic life; ~**en (er)leiden** to suffer privation(s).

entsagungsvoll *adj (geh)* Leben (full) of privation; Blick, Geste resigned.
entsalzen* *vt* to desalinate.
Entsalzung *f* desalination.
Entsatz *m* **-es, no pl** *(Mil)* relief.
entschädigen* **1** *vt (für* for) *(lit, fig)* to compensate, to recompense, to indemnify *(form)*; *(für Dienste etc)* to reward; *(mit Geld auch)* to remunerate; *(Kosten erstatten)* to reimburse, to indemnify *(form)*. **das Theaterstück entschädigte uns für das lange Warten** the play made up for the long wait.
2 *vr sich (für etw)* ~ to compensate oneself for sth; **ihr Mann ist fremdgegangen, aber sie hat sich reichlich dafür entschädigt** her husband was unfaithful to her but she got her own back with a vengeance.
Entschädigung *f siehe vt* compensation, recompense, indemnification *(form)*; reward; remuneration; reimbursement. **jdm eine** ~ **zahlen** to pay sb compensation.
Entschädigungs-: ~**klage** *f* claim for compensation; ~**summe** *f* amount of compensation.
entschärfen* *vt* **(a)** Bombe etc to defuse, to de-activate. **(b)** *(fig)* Kurve to straighten out; Krise, Lage to defuse; Argument to neutralize; Buch, Film to tone down.
Entscheid *m* **-(e)s, -e** *(form) siehe* **Entscheidung.**
entscheiden* *pret* entschied, *ptp* entschieden **1** *vt* to decide. **das Gericht entschied, daß ...** the court decided *or* ruled that ...; ~ **Sie, wie es gemacht werden soll!** you decide how it is to be done; **das Spiel/die Wahl ist entschieden/schon entschieden** the game/election has been decided/is already decided; **den Kampf/Krieg (um etw) für sich** ~ to secure victory in the struggle/battle (for sth); **das hat das Spiel zu unseren Gunsten entschieden** that decided the game in our favour; **mit dem zweiten Tor hatten wir das Spiel für uns entschieden** our second goal was the decider; **es ist noch nichts entschieden** nothing has been decided (as) yet.
2 *vi (über +acc)* to decide (on); *(Jur auch)* to rule (on). **darüber habe ich nicht zu** ~ that is not for me to decide; **der Richter hat für/gegen den Kläger entschieden** the judge decided *or* ruled for/against the plaintiff.
3 *vr (Mensch)* to decide, to make up one's mind, to come to a decision; *(Angelegenheit)* to be decided. **sich für etw** ~ to decide in favour of sth, to decide on sth; **sich für jdn** ~ to decide in favour of sb; **sich gegen jdn/etw** ~ to decide against sb/sth; **jetzt wird es sich** ~, **wer der Schnellere ist** now we'll see *or* settle who is the quicker.
entscheidend *adj* decisive; Faktor auch deciding attr; Argument, Aussage auch conclusive; Augenblick auch crucial, critical; Fehler, Irrtum auch crucial. **die** ~**e Stimme** *(bei Wahlen etc)* the deciding *or* casting vote; **für jdn/etw** ~ **sein** to be decisive *or* crucial for sb/sth; **der alles** ~**e Augenblick** the all-decisive moment; **das E~e** the decisive *or* deciding factor.
Entscheidung *f* decision; *(Jur auch)* ruling; *(der Geschworenen auch)* verdict. **um die** ~ **spielen** *(Sport)* to play the deciding match *or* the decider; *(bei gleichem Tor-, Punktverhältnis auch)* to play off; **Spiel um die** ~ *(Sport)* deciding match, decider; play-off; **mit den finanziellen** ~**en habe ich nichts zu tun** I have nothing to do with the financial decision-making *or* decisions; **wie ist die** ~ **ausgefallen?** which way did the decision go?; **es geht um die** ~ it's going to be decisive, it's going to decide things; **es geht um die** ~, **ob ...** it's a question of deciding whether ...; **die Lage drängt zur** ~ the situation is coming to a head; **die Frage kommt heute zur** ~ the question will be decided today.
Entscheidungs-: ~**befugnis** *f* decision-making powers *pl*; ~**frage** *f (Gram)* yes-no question; ~**freiheit** *f* freedom of decision-making; **e~freudig** *adj* able to make decisions, decisive; ~**gremium** *nt* decision-making body; ~**kampf** *m* decisive encounter, show-down *(inf, auch fig)*; *(Sport)* decider; ~**schlacht** *f* decisive battle; *(fig)* show-down *(inf)*; ~**spiel** *nt* decider, deciding match; *(bei gleichem Punkt-, Torverhältnis auch)* play-off; ~**träger** *m* decision-maker.
entschieden *ptp of* **entscheiden.**
entschieden 1 *ptp of* **entscheiden.**
2 *adj* **(a)** *(entschlossen)* determined, resolute; Befürworter staunch; Ablehnung firm, uncompromising. **etw** ~ **ablehnen** to reject sth firmly.
(b) *no pred (eindeutig)* decided, distinct. **er ist ein** ~**er Könner in seinem Fach** he is unquestionably *or* decidedly an expert in his subject.
Entschiedenheit *f siehe adj* (a) determination, resolution; staunchness; firmness, uncompromising nature. **etw mit aller** ~ **dementieren/ablehnen** to deny sth categorically/reject sth flatly.
entschlacken* *vt (Metal)* to remove the slag from; *(Med)* Körper to purify.
Entschlackung *f (Metal)* removal of slag *(gen* from); *(Med)* purification.
entschlafen* *vi irreg aux sein (geh)* to fall asleep; *(euph auch: sterben)* to pass away. **der/die E~e/die E~en** the deceased, the departed.
entschlagen* *vr irreg sich einer Sache* *(gen)* ~ *(liter)* to relinquish sth *(liter)*.
entschleiern* **1** *vt* to unveil; *(fig auch)* to uncover, to reveal. **2** *vr* to unveil (oneself); *(hum)* to strip, to disrobe *(hum, form)*; *(fig: Geheimnis etc)* to be unveiled *or* revealed.
entschließen* *pret* entschloß, *ptp* entschlossen *vr* to decide *or* determine *or* resolve to do sth; **ich entschloß mich zum Kauf dieses Hauses** I decided to buy this house; **ich weiß nicht, wozu ich mich** ~ **soll** I don't know what to decide; **sich anders** ~ to change one's mind; **sich zu nichts** ~ **können** to be unable to make up one's mind; **ich bin**

fest entschlossen I am absolutely determined; **zu allem entschlossen sein** to be ready for anything; **er ist zum Schlimmsten entschlossen** he will stop at nothing, he's prepared to do anything; **kurz entschlossen** straight away, without further ado.

Entschließung f resolution.

entschloß pret of **entschließen**.

entschlossen 1 ptp of **entschließen**. 2 adj determined, resolute. ~ **handeln** to act resolutely or with determination.

Entschlossenheit f determination, resolution. **in wilder** ~ with fierce determination.

entschlummern* vi aux sein (liter, auch euph: sterben) to fall asleep.

entschlüpfen* vi aux sein (dat from), to slip away (dat from); (Küken) to be hatched; (fig: Wört etc) to slip out (dat from). **mir ist eine unüberlegte Bemerkung entschlüpft** I let slip an ill-considered remark.

Entschluß m (Entscheidung) decision; (Vorsatz) resolution, resolve. **zu keinem ~ kommen können** to be unable to make up one's mind or come to a decision; **mein ~ ist gefaßt** my decision is made, my mind is made up; **aus eigenem ~ handeln** to act on one's own initiative; **seinen ~ ändern** to change one's mind; **es ist mein fester ~ ...** it is my firm intention ..., I firmly intend ...; **ein Mann von schnellen ~ssen sein** to be good at decision-making, to be able to decide quickly.

entschlüsseln* vt to decipher; Funkspruch auch to decode.

Entschlüsselung f siehe vt deciphering; decoding.

Entschluß-: e~**freudig** adj decisive; ~**kraft** f decisiveness, determination; e~**los** adj indecisive, irresolute.

entschuldbar adj excusable, pardonable.

entschuldigen* 1 vt to excuse. **etw mit etw ~** to excuse sth as due to sth; **das ist durch nichts zu ~!**, **das läßt sich nicht ~!** that is inexcusable!; **der Lehrer entschuldigte das Kind** the teacher excused the child (from attendance); **das entschuldigt nicht, daß er sich so benimmt** that is no excuse for or doesn't excuse his behaving like that; **jdn bei jdm/einem Treffen ~** to make or present sb's excuses or apologies to sb/a meeting; **einen Schüler ~ lassen or ~** to ask for a pupil to be excused; **ich möchte meine Tochter für morgen ~** I would like to have my daughter excused for tomorrow; **ich möchte meinen Sohn wegen seines Fehlens ~** I would like to excuse my son for being absent; **ich bitte mich zu ~** I beg to be excused; **bitte entschuldigt die Störung, aber ...** please excuse or forgive the interruption, but ...

2 vi **entschuldige/~ Sie (bitte)!** (do or please) excuse me!, sorry!; (bei Bitte, Frage etc) excuse me (please), pardon me (US); (na) ~ **Sie/entschuldige mal!** excuse me!

3 vr **sich (bei jdm) ~** (sich abmelden, sich rechtfertigen) to excuse oneself, to make one's excuses (to sb); (sich bei Lehrer, Chef abmelden) to ask (sb) to be excused; **sich (bei jdm) (wegen etw) ~** (um Verzeihung bitten) to apologize (to sb) (for sth); **sich (von jdm) ~ lassen** to send or convey (form) one's excuses or apologies (via sb); **sich mit Krankheit ~** to excuse oneself on account of illness.

entschuldigend adj apologetic.

Entschuldigung f (Grund) excuse; (Bitte um ~) apology; (Sch: Brief) letter of excuse, note. ~**! excuse me!**; (Verzeihung auch) sorry!; **als or zur ~ für ...** as an excuse/apology for ..., in excuse of ... (form); **zu seiner ~ sagte er ...** he said in his defence that ...; **ohne ~ fehlen** to be absent without an excuse; (jdn) (wegen einer Sache) um ~ **bitten** to apologize (to sb) (for sth); **ich bitte vielmals um ~(, daß ich mich verspätet habe)!** I do apologize or beg your pardon (for being late)!

Entschuldigungs-: ~**brief** m letter of apology; (Sch) excuse note; ~**grund** m excuse.

entschweben* vi aux sein (geh, hum: weggehen) to float or waft away (dat from).

entschwefeln* vt to desulphurize.

entschwinden* vi irreg aux sein (geh: lit, fig) to vanish, to disappear (dat from, in +acc into). **dem Gedächtnis ~** to fade from one's memory; **die Tage entschwanden wie im Flug** the days flew or raced by.

entseelt adj (liter) lifeless, dead. ~ **zu Boden sinken** to sink lifeless to the ground.

entsenden* vt irreg or reg Abgeordnete etc to send; Boten auch to dispatch.

Entsendung f sending; dispatch.

entsetzen* 1 vt (a) (Mil) Festung, Truppen to relieve. (b) (in Grauen versetzen) to horrify, to appal. 2 vr **sich über jdn/etw ~** to be horrified or appalled at or by sb/sth; **sich vor etw** (dat) ~ to be horrified or appalled at sth; siehe **entsetzt**.

Entsetzen nt -s, no pl horror; (Bestürzung auch) dismay; (Erschrecken) terror. **von ~ erfaßt or ergriffen or gepackt werden** to be seized with horror/terror/dismay, to be horror-stricken; **zu meinem größten ~ bemerkte ich, daß ...** to my horror or great dismay I noticed that ...; **mit ~ sehen/hören, daß ...** to be horrified/terrified/dismayed to see/hear that ...

Entsetzensschrei m cry of horror.

entsetzlich adj dreadful, appalling, hideous; (inf: sehr unangenehm auch) terrible, awful. ~ **viel (Geld)** an awful lot (of money) (inf).

Entsetzlichkeit f dreadfulness, appallingness, hideousness.

entsetzt 1 ptp of **entsetzen**. 2 adj horrified, appalled (über +acc at, by). **ein ~er Schrei** a horrified scream, a cry or scream of horror.

Entsetzung f (Mil) relief.

entseuchen* vt (desinfizieren) to disinfect; (dekontaminieren) to decontaminate.

entsichern* vt eine Pistole ~ to release the safety catch of a

pistol; **eine entsicherte Pistole** a pistol with the safety catch off.

entsiegeln* vt Brief to unseal.

entsinnen* vr irreg (einer Sache (gen), an etw (acc)) sth) to remember, to recall, to recollect. **wenn ich mich recht entsinne** if my memory serves me correctly or right.

Entsittlichung f corruption, depravation.

entsorgen* 1 vt eine Stadt ~ to dispose of a town's refuse and sewage. 2 vi to dispose of refuse and sewage.

Entsorgung f waste management.

entspannen* 1 vt Muskeln, Nerven etc to relax; Bogen to unbend; Seil, Saite to slacken, to untighten; Wasser to reduce the surface tension of; (Tech) Feder to relax the tension of; (fig) Lage, Beziehungen to ease (up).

2 vr to relax (auch fig); (ausruhen) to rest; (nach der Arbeit etc) to unwind, to unbend; (Lage etc) to ease; (Feder etc) to lose tension; (Bogen) to unbend.

Entspannung f relaxation (auch fig); (von Lage, Fin: an der Börse) easing(-up); (Pol) easing or reduction of tension (+gen in), détente; (Tech: von Feder etc) reduction of tension (+gen on); (des Wassers) reduction of surface tension; (von Bogen) unbending; (von Seil etc) slackening, untightening. **nach der Arbeit sehe ich zur ~ etwas fern** after work I watch television for a bit to help me unwind.

Entspannungs-: ~**bemühungen** pl efforts aimed at easing (political) tension; ~**politik** f policy of détente; ~**übungen** pl (Med etc) relaxation exercises.

entspinnen* vr irreg to develop, to arise.

entspr. abbr of **entsprechend**.

entsprechen* vi irreg +dat to correspond to; der Wahrheit, den Tatsachen auch to be in accordance with; den Tatsachen auch to fit; (genügen) Anforderungen, Kriterien to fulfil, to meet; einem Anlaß to be in keeping with; Erwartungen to come or live up to; einer Beschreibung to answer, to fit; einer Bitte, einem Wunsch etc to meet, to comply with. **sich or einander ~** to correspond (with each other), to tally; **ihre Ausrüstung entsprach nicht den alpinen Bedingungen** her outfit wasn't suitable for the alpine conditions; **seinem Zweck ~** to fulfil its purpose.

entsprechend 1 adj corresponding; (zuständig) relevant; (angemessen) appropriate. **der Film war besonders geschmacklos, und die Kritiken waren dann auch ~** the film was particularly tasteless and the reviews of it were correspondingly harsh; **er hat die Arbeit auf eine meinem Vorschlag ~e Weise ausgeführt** he carried out the job along the lines I had suggested.

2 adv accordingly; (ähnlich, gleich) correspondingly. **er wurde ~ bestraft** he was suitably or appropriately punished; **etw ~ würdigen** to show suitable appreciation for sth.

3 prep +dat in accordance with, according to; (ähnlich, gleich) corresponding to. **er wird seiner Leistung ~ bezahlt** he is paid according to output; **er hat sich den Erwartungen ~ entwickelt** he has progressed as we had hoped; siehe **Umstand**.

Entsprechung f (Äquivalent) equivalent; (Gegenstück) counterpart; (Analogie) parallel; (Übereinstimmung) correspondence.

entsprießen* vi irreg aux sein (liter: lit, fig) einer Sache (dat) or aus etw ~ to spring forth from sth (liter); (old, hum) aus Ehe, Familie etc to issue from sth (old, form).

entspringen* vi irreg aux sein (a) (Fluß) to rise. (b) (entfliehen) to escape (dat, aus from). (c) (sich herleiten von) +dat to spring from, to arise from.

entstaatlichen* vt to denationalize.

Entstaatlichung f destalinization.

entstammen* vi aux sein +dat to stem or come from; einer Familie auch to be descended from; (fig auch) to originate in or from.

entstauben* vt to remove the dust from, to free from dust.

Entstaubungsanlage f dust extraction system.

entstehen* vi irreg aux sein (ins Dasein treten) to come into being; (seinen Ursprung haben) to originate; (sich entwickeln) to arise, to develop (aus, durch from); (hervorkommen) to emerge (aus, durch from); (verursacht werden) to result (aus, durch from); (Chem: Verbindungen) to be produced (aus, durch through, via); (Kunstwerk: geschrieben/gebaut etc werden) to be written/built etc. **das Feuer war durch Nachlässigkeit entstanden** the fire was caused by negligence; **bei E~ eines Feuers** in the event of (a) fire; **wir wollen nicht den Eindruck ~ lassen, ...** we don't want to give (rise to) the impression that ..., we don't want to let the impression emerge that ...; **im E~ begriffen sein** to be in the process of formation or development, to be emerging; **für ~den or entstandenen Schaden** for damages incurred.

Entstehung f (das Werden) genesis, coming into being; (das Hervorkommen) emergence; (Ursprung) origin; (Bildung) formation.

Entstehungs-: ~**geschichte** f genesis; (Bibl) Genesis; ~**ort** m place of origin; ~**ursache** f original cause; ~**zeit** f time of origin.

entsteigen* vi irreg aux sein +dat (geh) einem Wagen to alight from (form); dem Wasser, dem Bad to emerge from; (fig) Dampf etc) to rise from.

entsteinen* vt to stone.

entstellen* vt (verunstalten) Gesicht to disfigure; (verzerren) Gesicht(szüge) to distort, to contort; (fig) Bericht, Wahrheit etc to distort. **etw entstellt wiedergeben** to distort or misrepresent sth; **sein vor Haß/Schmerz entstelltes Gesicht** his face distorted or contorted with hate/pain.

Entstellung f disfigurement; (fig) distortion; (der Wahrheit) perversion, distortion.

entstempeln* vt (Aut) to cancel the registration of.
entstielen* vt Obst to remove the stalk(s) from.
entstofflichen* vt to dematerialize.
entstören* vt Radio, Telefon to free from interference; Auto, Staubsauger to fit a suppressor to, to suppress.
Entstörer m, **Entstörgerät** nt (für Auto etc) suppressor; (für Radio, Telefon) anti-interference device.
Entstörung f siehe vt freeing from interference, suppression of interference; fitting of a suppressor (gen to), suppressing.
Entstörungs-: ~dienst m, ~stelle f telephone maintenance service.
entströmen* vi aux sein to pour or gush out (+dat, aus of); (Gas, Geruch etc) to issue or escape (+dat, aus from).
Entsublimierung f (Psych, Sociol) repressive ~ repressive desublimation.
entsumpfen* vt Gebiet to drain.
enttabuisieren* [ɛnttabuiˈziːrən] vt to free from taboos, to remove the taboos from.
Enttabuisierung f removal of taboos (+gen from).
enttarnen* vt Spion to blow the cover of (inf).
enttäuschen* **1** vt to disappoint; Vertrauen to betray. **enttäuscht sein über** (+acc)/**von** to be disappointed at/by or in; **er ging enttäuscht nach Hause** he went home disappointed; **sie ist im Leben oft enttäuscht worden** she has had many disappointments in life; **du hast uns sehr enttäuscht** you have really let us down or disappointed us; **angenehm enttäuscht sein** to be pleasantly surprised.
2 vi **unsere Mannschaft hat sehr enttäuscht** our team were very disappointing or played very disappointingly; **der neue Wagen hat enttäuscht** the new car is a disappointment or let-down (inf).
Enttäuschung f disappointment. **das Theaterstück war eine große** ~ the play was a big disappointment or let-down (inf); **jdm eine** ~ **bereiten** to disappoint sb.
entthronen* vt (lit, fig) to dethrone.
Entthronung f (lit, fig) dethronement, dethroning.
enttrümmern* **1** vt to clear of rubble. **2** vi to clear the rubble (away).
Enttrümmerung f clearing of rubble (gen from).
entvölkern* vt to depopulate.
Entvölkerung f depopulation.
entw. abbr of **entweder**.
entwachsen* vi irreg aux sein +dat **(a)** (geh: herauswachsen aus) to spring from. **(b)** (zu groß werden für) to outgrow, to grow out of.
entwaffnen* vt (lit, fig) to disarm.
entwaffnend adj (fig) disarming.
Entwaffnung f disarming; (eines Landes) disarmament.
entwalden* vt to deforest.
entwarnen* vi to sound or give the all-clear.
Entwarnung f sounding of the all-clear; (Signal) all-clear.
entwässern* vt to drain; (Chem) to dehydrate.
Entwässerung f drainage; (Chem) dehydration.
Entwässerungs-: ~anlage f drainage system; ~graben m drainage ditch.
entweder [auch ˈɛntveːdɐ] conj ~ ... oder ... either ... or ...; ~ **oder!** make up your mind (one way or the other)!, yes or no; ~ **gleich oder gar nicht,** ~ **jetzt oder nie** it's now or never.
Entweder-Oder nt -, - **hier gibt es kein** ~ there is no alternative; **hier gibt es nur ein** ~ there has to be a definite decision one way or the other.
entweichen* vi irreg aux sein (geh: fliehen) to escape or run away (+dat, aus from); (sich verflüchtigen: Gas, Flüssigkeit) to leak or escape (+dat, aus from, out of).
entweihen* vt to violate (auch fig); (entheiligen) to profane, to desecrate.
Entweihung f siehe vt violation; profanation, desecration.
entwenden* vt (form) jdm etw/etw aus etw ~ to steal or purloin (hum, form) sth from sb/sth.
Entwendung f (form) theft, stealing, purloining (hum, form).
entwerfen* vt irreg **(a)** (zeichnen, gestalten) Zeichnung etc to sketch; Muster, Modell etc to design. **(b)** (ausarbeiten) Gesetz, Vortrag, Schreiben etc to draft, to draw up; Plan to devise, to draw up. **(c)** (fig) (darstellen, darlegen) Bild to depict, to draw; (in Umrissen darstellen) to outline.
Entwerfer(in f) m -s, - siehe **Designer(in).**
entwerten* vt **(a)** (in Wert mindern) to devalue, to depreciate; Zeugenaussage, Argument etc auch to undermine. **(b)** (ungültig machen) to make or render invalid; Münzen to demonetize; Briefmarke, Fahrschein to cancel.
Entwerter m -s, - (ticket-)cancelling machine.
Entwertung f siehe vt devaluation, depreciation; undermining; invalidation; demonetization; cancellation.
Entwesung f (form) disinfestation.
entwickeln* **1** vt to develop (auch Phot); (Phot) esp Diapositive to process; Methode, Verfahren auch to evolve; (Math auch) Formel to expand; (Chem) Gas etc to generate; erate; Mut, Energie to show, to display. **jdm etw** ~ to set out or expound sth to sb; **etw zu etw** ~ to develop sth into sth.
2 vr to develop (zu into); (Chem: Gase etc) to be produced or generated. **das Projekt/der neue Angestellte entwickelt sich gut** the project/the new employee is coming along or shaping up nicely; **das Kind entwickelt sich gut** the baby is coming along nicely; **er hat sich ganz schön entwickelt** (inf) he's turned out really nicely.
Entwickler m -s, - (Phot) developer.
Entwicklerbad nt (Phot) developing bath.
Entwicklung f development; (von Methoden, Verfahren, Gattung auch) evolution; (Math: von Formel auch) expansion;

(Erzeugung, Chem: von Gasen etc) production, generation; (von Mut, Energie) show, display; (Phot) developing; (esp von Diapositiven) processing. **das Flugzeug ist noch in der** ~ the plane is still being developed or is still in the development stage; **Jugendliche, die noch in der** ~ **sind** young people who are still in their adolescence or still developing; **das Flugzeug ist zur** ~ **höchster Geschwindigkeiten fähig** this plane is capable of reaching extremely high speeds.
Entwicklungs-: ~alter nt adolescence; ~arbeit f development (work); ~beschleunigung f (Physiol) acceleration (in development); ~dienst m voluntary service overseas (Brit), VSO (Brit), Peace Corps (US); e~fähig adj capable of development; **der Plan/die Idee ist durchaus e~fähig** this plan/idea is definitely worth following up or expanding; **diese Stelle ist e~fähig** this position has prospects; ~fähigkeit f capability of development, capacity for development; (einer Stelle) prospects pl; ~gang m development; ~gebiet nt development area; ~geschichte f developmental history, evolution; e~geschichtlich adj evolutionary attr, with respect to evolution or developmental history; ~gesetz nt developmental law; ~helfer m person doing Voluntary Service Overseas (Brit), VSO worker (Brit), Peace Corps worker (US); e~hemmend adj restricting or impeding development; ~hilfe f foreign aid; ~jahre pl adolescent or formative (auch fig) years, adolescence; ~land nt developing or third-world country; ~möglichkeit f possibility for development; ~phase f (Psych) developmental stage; ~psychologie f developmental psychology; ~roman m (Liter) novel showing the development of a character; ~stadium nt stage of development; (der Menschheit etc) evolutionary stage; ~störung f developmental disturbance, disturbance in development; ~stufe f stage of development; (der Menschheit etc) evolutionary stage; ~zeit f period of development; (Biol, Psych) developmental period; (Phot) developing time.
entwinden* vt irreg (geh) **jdm etw** ~ to wrest sth from sb.
entwirrbar adj (fig) extricable, soluble.
entwirren* vt (lit, fig) to disentangle, to unravel.
entwischen* vi aux sein (inf) to escape, to get away (dat, aus from).
entwöhnen* vt jdn ~ (einer Gewohnheit, Sucht) to break sb of the habit (+dat, von of), to cure sb (+dat, von of), to wean sb (+dat, von from); Säugling, Jungtier to wean; **sich einer Sache** (gen) ~ (geh) to lose the habit of doing sth, to disaccustom oneself from sth (form).
Entwöhnung f siehe vt cure, curing; weaning.
entwölken* vr (lit, fig liter) to clear.
entwürdigen* **1** vt to degrade; (Schande bringen über) to disgrace. **2** vr to degrade or abase oneself.
entwürdigend adj degrading.
Entwürdigung f degradation, abasement; (Entehrung) disgrace (gen to).
Entwurf m -s, ̈e **(a)** (Skizze, Abriß) outline, sketch; (Design) design; (Archit, fig) blueprint.
(b) (Vertrags~, von Plan, Gesetz etc, Konzept) draft (version), framework; (einer Theorie auch) outline; (Parl: Gesetz~) bill. **das Bild/die Doktorarbeit ist im** ~ **fertig** the sketch/the framework for the picture/PhD is finished.
Entwurfsstadium nt **sich im** ~ **befinden** to be in the planning stage, to be on the drawing board.
entwurzeln* vt (lit, fig) to uproot.
Entwurzelung f (lit, fig: das Entwurzeln) uprooting; (fig: das Entwurzeltsein) rootlessness.
entzaubern* vt jdn/etw ~ to break the spell on sb/sth; (fig auch) to deprive sb/sth of his/its mystique; **durch diese analytische Interpretation wird das Gedicht entzaubert** this analytic interpretation causes the poem to lose its magic; **ihre romantischen Vorstellungen wurden entzaubert** her romantic illusions were shattered.
Entzauberung f breaking of the/a spell (gen on); (fig auch) deprivation of mystique; (von Vorstellungen) shattering, destruction.
entzerren* vt to correct, to rectify.
Entzerrung f correction, rectification.
entziehen* irreg **1** vt (+dat) (wegnehmen) to withdraw, to take away; Gunst etc to withdraw; Flüssigkeit to draw, to extract; (Chem) to extract. **jdm Alkohol/Nikotin** ~ to deprive sb of alcohol/ nicotine; **die Ärzte versuchten ihn zu** ~ (inf) the doctors tried to cure him of his addiction; **jdm die Erlaubnis etc** ~ to withdraw or revoke sb's permit etc, to take sb's permit etc away; **jdm die Rente etc** ~ to cut off or stop sb's pension etc; **jdm sein Vertrauen** ~ to withdraw one's confidence or trust in sb; **dem Redner das Wort** ~ to ask the speaker to stop.
2 vr **sich jdm/einer Sache** ~ to evade or elude sb/sth; (entkommen auch) to escape (from) sb/sth; **sich seiner Verantwortung** ~ to shirk one's responsibilities; **sich jds Verständnis/Kontrolle** ~ to be beyond sb's understanding/control; **das entzieht sich meiner Kenntnis/Zuständigkeit** that is beyond my knowledge/authority; **das hat sich meiner Aufmerksamkeit entzogen** that escaped my attention; **diese Klänge** ~ **sich der Interpretierbarkeit** these sounds defy interpretation; **sich jds Blicken** ~ to be hidden from sight.
3 vi (inf) to undergo treatment for (drug) addiction; (Alkoholiker) to dry out (inf).
Entziehung f **(a)** (von Lizenz etc) withdrawal, revocation (form). **(b)** (von Rauschgift etc) (Wegnahme) withdrawal, deprivation; (Behandlung) treatment for drug addiction/ alcoholism.
Entziehungs-: ~anstalt f treatment centre for drug addicts/alcoholics; ~kur f cure for drug addiction/alcoholism cure.

entzifferbar *adj siehe* **vt** decipherable; decodable.
entziffern* *vt* to decipher; *Funkspruch etc* to decode.
Entzifferung *f siehe* **vt** deciphering; decoding.
entzücken* *vt* to delight. **von jdm/über etw** (*acc*) **entzückt sein** to be delighted by sb/at sth.
Entzücken *nt* -s, *no pl* delight, joy. **zu meinem (größten)** ~ to my (great) delight *or* joy; **in** ~ **geraten** to go into raptures; **jdn in (helles)** ~ **versetzen** to send sb into raptures.
entzückend *adj* delightful, charming. **das ist ja** ~! how delightful *or* charming!
Entzückung *f siehe* **Entzücken.**
Entzug *m* -(e)s, *no pl* (a) (*einer Lizenz etc*) withdrawal, revocation (*form*). (b) (*Med: von Rauschgift etc*) withdrawal; (*Behandlung*) cure for drug addiction/alcoholism. **er ist auf** ~ (*Med sl*) he is being treated for drug addiction; (*Alkoholiker*) he is being dried out (*inf*).
Entzugs-: ~**erscheinung** *f*, ~**symptom** *nt* withdrawal symptom.
entzündbar *adj* (*lit, fig*) inflammable. **leicht** ~ highly inflammable; (*fig*) easily roused or excited.
Entzündbarkeit *f* inflammability.
entzünden* **1** *vt* (a) *Feuer* to light; *Holz etc auch* to set light to, to ignite (*esp Sci, Tech*); *Streichholz auch* to strike; (*fig*) *Streit etc* to start, to spark off; *Haß* to inflame; *Phantasie* to fire; *Begeisterung* to fire, to kindle.
(b) (*Med*) to inflame.
2 *vr* (a) to catch fire, to ignite (*esp Sci, Tech*); (*fig*) (*Streit*) to be sparked off; (*Haß*) to be inflamed; (*Phantasie*) to be fired; (*Begeisterung*) to be kindled.
(b) (*Med*) to become inflamed. **entzündet** inflamed.
entzündlich *adj Gase, Brennstoff* inflammable; (*Med*) inflammatory. ~**e Haut** skin which easily becomes inflamed.
Entzündung *f* (a) (*Med*) inflammation. (b) ignition (*esp Sci, Tech*). **Funken führten zur** ~ **des Heus** sparks led to the hay catching fire.
Entzündungs- (*Med*): **e**~**hemmend** *adj* anti-inflammatory, antiphlogistic (*form*); ~**herd** *m* focus of inflammation.
entzwei *adj pred* in two (pieces), in half, asunder (*old, poet*); (*kaputt*) broken; (*zerrissen*) torn.
entzweibrechen *vti sep irreg* (*vi: aux sein*) to break in two; (*zerbrechen*) to break.
entzweien* **1** *vt* to turn against each other, to divide, to set at variance.
2 *vr* **sich (mit jdm)** ~ to fall out (with sb); (*sich streiten auch*) to quarrel (with sb).
entzwei-: ~**gehen** *vi sep irreg aux sein* to break (in two *or* half), to break asunder (*poet*); ~**reißen** *vt sep irreg* to tear *or* rend in two *or* in half *or* asunder (*poet*); (*zerreißen*) to tear to pieces; ~**schlagen** *vt sep irreg* to strike in half *or* in two *or* asunder (*poet*); (*zerschlagen*) to smash (to pieces); ~**schneiden** *vt sep irreg* to cut in two *or* half; (*zerschneiden*) to cut to pieces.
Entzweiung *f* (*fig*) (*Bruch*) split, rupture, break; (*Streit*) quarrel.
en vogue [ã'vo:k] *adj pred* (*geh*) in vogue *or* fashion.
Enzephalogramm *nt* -s, -e (*Med*) encephalogram.
Enzian ['entsia:n] *m* -s, -e gentian; (*Branntwein*) *spirit distilled from the roots of gentian.*
Enzyklika *f* -, **Enzykliken** (*Eccl*) encyclical.
Enzyklopädie *f* encyclop(a)edia.
enzyklopädisch *adj* encyclop(a)edic.
Enzyklopädist *m* Encyclop(a)edist.
Enzym *nt* -s, -e enzyme.
eo ipso *adv* (*geh*) ipso facto.
Epaulette [epo'lɛtə] *f* epaulette.
Epen *pl of* **Epos.**
Ephebe *m* -n, -n (*Hist*) ephebe, ephebus.
ephemer(isch) *adj* (*geh*) ephemeral.
Epheser *m* -s, - Ephesian.
Epheserbrief *m* Epistle to the Ephesians, Ephesians *sing.*
Epidemie *f* (*Med, fig*) epidemic.
epidemisch *adj* (*Med, fig*) epidemic.
Epidermis *f* -, **Epidermen** epidermis.
Epidiaskop *nt* -s, -e epidiascope.
Epigone *m* -n, -n epigone (*liter*); (*Nachahmer*) imitator.
epigonenhaft *adj* epigonic (*liter, rare*); (*nachahmend*) imitative.
Epigonentum *nt* epigonism (*liter, rare*); (*Nachahmung*) imitativeness.
Epigramm *nt* -s, -e epigram.
epigrammatisch *adj* epigrammatic.
Epigraph *nt* -s, -e epigraph.
Epik *f* epic poetry.
Epiker(in *f*) *m* -s, - epic poet.
Epikur *m* -s Epicurus.
Epikureer [epiku're:ɐ] *m* -s, - (*Philos*) Epicurean; (*fig*) epicure(an).
epikureisch [epiku're:ɪʃ] *adj* (*Philos*) Epicurean; (*fig*) epicurean.
Epilepsie *f* epilepsy.
Epileptiker(in *f*) *m* -s, - epileptic.
epileptisch *adj* epileptic.
Epilog *m* -s, -e epilogue.
Epiphänomen *nt* epiphenomenon.
episch *adj* (*lit, fig*) epic.
Episkop *nt* -s, -e episcope.
Episkopat *m or nt* episcopacy, episcopate.
Episode *f* -, -n episode.
episodenhaft, episodisch *adj* episodic.
Epistel *f* -, -n epistle (*auch inf*); (*old: Lesung*) lesson. **jdm die** ~ **lesen** (*old inf*) to read sb the riot act (*inf*).
Epistemologie *f* epistemology.

epistemologisch *adj* epistemological.
Epitaph *nt* -s, -e (*liter*) epitaph.
Epitheton [e'pi:teton] *nt* -s, **Epitheta** (*Poet*) epithet.
Epizentrum *nt* epicentre.
epochal *adj* (a) epochal. (b) *siehe* **epochemachend.**
Epoche *f* -, -n epoch. ~ **machen** to be epoch-making, to mark a new epoch.
epochemachend *adj* epoch-making.
Epos *nt* -, **Epen** epic (poem), epos.
Epoxydharz [epo'ksy:t-] *nt* epoxy resin.
Eprouvette [epru'vet] *f* (*Aus Chem*) test tube.
Equipage [ek(v)i'pa:3ə] *f* -, -n (*old*) equipage.
Equipe [e'kɪp] *f* -, -n team.
er *pers pron gen* **seiner**, *dat* **ihm**, *acc* **ihn** he; (*von Dingen*) it; (*von Hund etc*) it, he; (*vom Mond*) it, she (*poet*). **wenn ich** ~ **wäre** if I were him *or* he (*form*); ~ **ist es** it's him, it is he (*form*); **wer hat das gemacht/ist der Täter?** — ~/~ (**ist es**)**!** who did that/is the person responsible? — he did/is!, him (*inf*)!; ~ **war es nicht, ich war's** it wasn't he, it was me; **sie ist größer als** ~ she is taller than he is *or* him; **E**~ (*obs*) you; (*Bibl*) He; **ein E**~ **und eine Sie** (*hum inf*) a he and a she.
erachten* *vt* (*geh*) **jdn/etw für** *or* **als etw** ~ to consider *or* deem (*form*) sb/sth (to be) sth.
Erachten *nt* -s, *no pl*: **meines** ~**s**, **nach meinem** ~ in my opinion.
erahnen* *vt siehe* **ahnen 1.**
erarbeiten* *vt* (a) (*erwerben*) *Vermögen etc* to work for; *Wissen etc* to acquire. (b) (*erstellen*) *Entwurf etc* to work out, to elaborate.
Erb-: ~**adel** *m* hereditary nobility; ~**anlage** *f usu pl* hereditary factor(s *pl*); ~**anspruch** *m* claim to an/the inheritance; ~**anteil** *m* share *or* portion of an/the inheritance.
erbarmen* **1** *vt jdn* ~ to arouse sb's pity, to move sb to pity; **es kann einen** ~ it's pitiable; **er sieht zum E**~ **aus** he's a pitiful sight; **das ist zum E**~ it's pitiful; **sie singt zum E**~ she sings appallingly, she's an appalling singer; **es möchte einen Hund** ~ (*inf*) it would melt a heart of stone; ..., **daß (es) Gott erbarm'** (*old*) piteously (*esp liter*); **es war so schrecklich, daß es Gott erbarm'** (*old*) it was most piteous (*old*).
2 *vr* (+*gen*) to have *or* take pity (on) (*auch hum inf*); (*verzeihen, verschonen*) to have mercy (on). **Herr, erbarme dich (unser)!** Lord, have mercy (upon us)!
Erbarmen *nt* -s, *no pl* (*Mitleid*) pity, compassion (*mit on*); (*Gnade*) mercy (*mit on*). **aus** ~ out of pity; **ohne** ~ pitiless(ly), merciless(ly); **er kennt kein** ~ he knows no mercy; **kein** ~ **mit jdm kennen** to be merciless with sb, to show sb no mercy.
erbarmenswert *adj* pitiable, wretched, pitiful.
erbärmlich *adj* (*erbarmenswert, pej: dürftig*) pitiful, wretched; (*gemein, schlecht*) wretched, miserable; (*inf: furchtbar*) *Kälte* terrible, hideous. ~ **aussehen** to look wretched *or* terrible; **sich** ~ **verhalten** to behave abominably *or* wretchedly; **sie hat** ~ **gesungen** she sang wretchedly *or* appallingly.
Erbärmlichkeit *f* (*Elend*) wretchedness, misery; (*fig: Dürftigkeit, Gemeinheit etc*) wretchedness, miserableness.
Erbarmungs-: **e**~**los** *adj* (*lit, fig*) pitiless, merciless; ~**losigkeit** *f* (*lit, fig*) pitilessness, mercilessness; **e**~**voll** *adj* compassionate, full of pity; **e**~**würdig** *adj siehe* **erbarmenswert.**
erbauen* **1** *vt* (a) (*lit, fig: errichten*) to build.
(b) (*fig: seelisch bereichern*) to edify, to uplift. **wir waren von der Nachricht nicht gerade erbaut** (*inf*) we weren't exactly delighted by the news; **der Chef ist von meinem Plan nicht besonders erbaut** (*inf*) the boss isn't particularly enthusiastic about my plan.
2 *vr* **sich** ~ **an** (+*dat*) to be uplifted *or* edified by; **abends erbaut er sich an Bachschen Kantaten** in the evenings he finds uplift *or* spiritual edification in Bach's cantatas.
Erbauer(in *f*) *m* -s, - builder; (*fig auch*) architect.
erbaulich *adj* edifying (*auch iro*), uplifting; (*Rel*) *Buch, Schriften* devotional.
Erbauung *f siehe* **vt** building; edification. **zur** ~ for one's edification.
Erbauungs-: ~**buch** *nt* devotional book; ~**schrift** *f* devotional writing.
Erb-: ~**bauer** *m farmer with a hereditary right to his property*; ~**begräbnis** *nt* family grave *or* (*Gruft*) vault; **e**~**berechtigt** *adj* entitled to inherit; **die** ~**berechtigten** the legal heirs; **e**~**biologisch** *adj* (*Jur*) **e**~**biologisches Gutachten** blood test (*to establish paternity*).
Erbe[1] *m* -n, -n (*lit, fig*) heir (*einer Person* (*gen*) of *or* to sb, *einer Sache* (*gen*) to sth). **gesetzlicher** ~ legal heir, heir at law (*Jur*), **heir apparent** (*Jur*); **leiblicher** ~ blood-related heir, heir according to bloodright; **direkter** ~ direct *or* lineal heir, heir of the body (*Jur*); **mutmaßlicher** ~ presumptive heir, heir presumptive (*Jur*); **jdn zum** *or* **als** ~**n einsetzen** to appoint sb as *or* make sb one's/sb's heir.
Erbe[2] *nt* -s, *no pl* inheritance; (*fig*) heritage; (*esp Unerwünschtes*) legacy. **das** ~ **des Faschismus** the legacy of fascism.
erbeben* *vi aux sein* (*geh: Erde, Mensch etc*) to tremble, to shake, to shudder.
erbeigen *adj* (*geerbt, vererbt*) inherited; (*erblich*) hereditary.
erben **1** *vt* (*lit, fig*) to inherit (*von* from); *Vermögen auch* to come into; (*inf: geschenkt bekommen*) to get, to be given. **bei ihm ist nichts zu** *or* **kann man nichts** ~ (*inf*) you won't get anything *or* a sausage (*inf*) out of him. **2** *vi* to inherit.
Erbengemeinschaft *f* community of heirs.
erbetteln* *vt* to get by begging. **die Kinder müssen alles auf der Straße** ~ the children have to go begging on the streets for

everything; **seine Möbel hat er (sich** *dat***) alle bei seinen Bekannten erbettelt** he cadged all his furniture off his friends; **die Kinder erbettelten sich die Erlaubnis, ...** the children managed to wheedle permission ...

erbeuten* *vt (Tier) Opfer* to carry off; *(Dieb)* to get away with; *(im Krieg)* to capture, to take.

Erb-: e~**fähig** *adj* entitled to inherit, heritable *(spec);* ~**faktor** *m (Biol)* (hereditary) factor, gene; ~**fall** *m (Jur)* **im** ~**fall** in the case of inheritance; ~**fehler** *m (lit, fig)* hereditary defect; ~**feind** *m* traditional *or* arch enemy; **der** ~**feind** *(Teufel)* the Arch-Fiend; ~**folge** *f* (line of) succession; ~**folgekrieg** *m* war of succession; ~**gut** *nt* **(a)** *(Hof)* ancestral estate; **(b)** *(Nachlaß)* estate, inheritance; *(fig)* heritage; **(c)** *(Biol)* genotype, genetic make-up; ~**hof** *m* **siehe** ~**gut (a).**

erbieten* *vr irreg (geh)* **sich** ~, **etw zu tun** to offer *or* volunteer to do sth; **sich zu etw** ~ to offer one's services for sth.

Erbin *f* heiress.

erbitten* *vt irreg* to ask for, to request. **sich (nicht)** ~ **lassen** (not) to be prevailed upon.

erbittern* *vt* to enrage, to incense.

erbittert *adj Widerstand, Gegner etc* bitter.

Erbitterung *f* rage; *(rare: Heftigkeit)* fierceness, bitterness.

Erbkrankheit *f* hereditary disease.

erblassen* *vi aux sein* to (go *or* turn) pale, to blanch. **vor Neid** ~ to turn *or* go green with envy.

Erblasser(in *f) m* **-s, -** *(a)* person who leaves an inheritance. **(b)** *(Testator)* testator; testatrix.

erbleichen* *vi aux sein* **(a)** *(geh)* to (go *or* turn) pale, to blanch. **(b)** *pret* **erblich,** *ptp* **erblichen** *(obs, liter: sterben)* to expire.

erblich *adj* hereditary. **er ist** ~ **belastet, auch sein Vater ...** it's inherited, his father too ...; **er ist** ~ **schwer (vor)belastet** it runs in the family; **in der Beziehung bin ich** ~ **(vor)belastet** it runs in the family.

Erblichkeit *f* heritability, hereditability.

erblicken* *vt (geh)* to see, to perceive; *(erspähen)* to spot, to catch sight of. **in jdm/etw eine Gefahr** *etc* ~ to see sb/sth as a danger *etc,* to see a danger *etc* in sb/sth; **ich erblicke meine Aufgabe darin, ... zu ...** I see it as my task to ..., I see my task in (+*gerund*) ...; **siehe Licht.**

erblinden* *vi aux sein* to go blind, to lose one's sight.

Erblindung *f* loss of sight.

erblonden* *vi aux sein (hum)* to go blond(e).

erblühen* *vi aux sein (geh)* to bloom, to blossom. **zu voller Schönheit** ~ *(fig)* to blossom out.

Erb-: ~**masse** *f* estate, inheritance; *(Biol)* genotype, genetic make-up; ~**onkel** *m (inf)* rich uncle.

erbosen* *(geh)* **1** *vt* to infuriate, to anger. **erbost sein über** (+*acc*) to be furious *or* infuriated at. **2** *vr* **sich** ~ **über** (+*acc*) to get *or* become furious *or* infuriated at.

erbötig *adj* ~ **sein, etw zu tun** *(obs)* to be willing *or* prepared to do sth.

Erb-: ~**pacht** *f* hereditary lease(hold); ~**pächter** *m* hereditary leaseholder; ~**pflege** *f siehe* **Eugenik;** ~**prinz** *m* hereditary prince; *(Thronfolger)* heir to the throne.

erbrechen* *irreg* **1** *vt (liter) Schloß, Siegel* to break open; *Tür auch* to force (open). **2** *vr (sich)* ~ *(Med)* to vomit, to be sick *(not vt);* **etw bis zum E~ tun** *(fig)* to do sth ad nauseam; **etw zum E~ satt haben** *(fig)* to be absolutely sick of sth.

Erbrecht *nt* law of inheritance; *(Erbanspruch)* right of inheritance *(auf* +*acc* to).

erbringen* *vt irreg* to produce, to furnish, to adduce.

Erbrochene(s) *nt* **-n,** *no pl* vomit.

Erbschaden *m* hereditary defect.

Erbschaft *f* inheritance. **eine** ~ **machen** *or* **antreten** to come into an inheritance; **die** ~ **des Faschismus** the legacy of fascism.

Erbschafts-: ~**auseinandersetzung** *f* dispute over an inheritance; ~**klage** *f (Jur)* action for recovery of an/the inheritance; ~**steuer** *f* estate *or* death duty *or* duties *pl.*

Erb-: ~**schein** *m* certificate of inheritance; ~**schleicher(in** *f) m* legacy-hunter; ~**schleicherei** *f* legacy-hunting; ~**schuld** *f* inherited debt.

Erbse *f* **-, -n** pea. **gelbe** *or* **getrocknete** ~**n** dried peas.

Erbsen-: e~**groß** *adj* pea-size, the size of a pea; ~**püree** *nt* = pease pudding; ~**suppe** *f* pea soup.

Erb-: ~**stück** *nt* heirloom; ~**sünde** *f (Rel)* original sin.

Erbswurst *f* pea meal compressed into the form of a sausage.

Erb-: ~**tante** *f (inf)* rich aunt; ~**teil** *nt* **(a)** *(Jur: auch m)* (portion of an/the) inheritance; **(b)** *(Veranlagung)* inherited trait; ~**übel** *nt* age-old ill; ~**vertrag** *m* testamentary contract; ~**verzicht** *m* renunciation of one's claim to an inheritance.

Erd|achse *f* earth's axis.

erdacht **1** *pret* of **erdenken. 2** *adj Geschichte* made-up.

Erd-: ~**altertum** *nt (Geol)* Palaeozoic; ~**anziehung** *f* gravitational pull of the earth; ~**apfel** *m (Aus, S Ger)* potato; ~**arbeiten** *pl* excavation(s *pl*), earthwork sing; ~**arbeiter** *m* labourer; *(bei Kanälen, Straßen, Eisenbahn)* navvy *(Brit);* ~**atmosphäre** *f* earth's atmosphere; ~**bahn** *f* orbit of the earth, earth's orbit; ~**ball** *m (liter)* globe, world.

Erdbeben *nt* earthquake.

Erdbeben-: ~**gebiet** *nt* earthquake area; ~**herd** *m* seismic focus *or* centre; ~**messer** *m* seismograph; e~**sicher** *adj* earthquake-proof; ~**warte** *f* seismological station.

Erd-: ~**beere** *f* strawberry; e~**beerfarben** *adj* strawberry-colour(ed); ~**bestattung** *f* burial, interment; ~**bevölkerung** *f* population of the earth, earth's population; ~**bewohner** *m* inhabitant of the earth; *(gegenüber Marsbewohnern etc)* terrestrial, earthling *(pej);* ~**birne** *f (dial)* potato.

Erdboden *m* ground, earth. **etw dem** ~ **gleichmachen** to level sth, to raze sth to the ground; **vom** ~ **verschwinden** to disap-

pear from *or* off the face of the earth; **als hätte ihn der** ~ **verschluckt** as if the earth had swallowed him up.

Erde *f* **-, -n (a)** *(Welt)* earth, world. **unsere Mutter** ~ *(liter)* Mother Earth; **auf** ~**n** *(old, liter)* on earth; **auf der ganzen** ~ all over the world; **niemand auf der ganzen** ~ nobody in the whole world.

(b) *(Boden)* ground. **ihn deckt die kühle** ~ *(liter)* the cold earth covers him; **in fremder** ~ **ruhen** *(liter)* to lie *or* rest in foreign soil *(liter);* **unter der** ~ underground, below ground; *(fig)* beneath the soil; **du wirst mich noch unter die** ~ **bringen** *(inf)* you'll be the death of me yet *(inf);* **über der** ~ above ground; **auf die** ~ **fallen** to fall to the ground; **auf nackter** *or* **bloßer** ~ on the bare ground; **mit beiden Beinen** *or* **Füßen (fest) auf der** ~ **stehen** *(fig)* to have both feet firmly on the ground; **siehe eben.**

(c) *(Erdreich, Bodenart)* soil, earth *(auch Chem).* **fette/trockene** ~ rich/dry soil; **zu** ~ **werden** to turn to dust; ~ **zu** ~ *(Eccl)* dust to dust; **seltene** ~**n** *(Chem)* rare earths.

(d) *(Elec: Erdung)* earth, ground *(US).*

erden *vt (Elec)* to earth, to ground *(US).*

Erden-: ~**bürger** *m (geh)* mortal; **ein neuer** ~**bürger** a new addition to the human race; e~**fern** *adj (liter)* far from the earth; ~**glück** *nt (liter)* earthly happiness.

erdenken* *vt irreg* to devise, to think up.

Erdenkind *nt (geh)* child of the earth *(liter).*

erdenklich *adj attr* conceivable, imaginable. **alles** ~**(e) Gute** all the very best; **sich** *(dat)* **alle** ~**e Mühe geben** to take the greatest (possible) pains; **alles E~e tun** to do everything conceivable *or* imaginable.

Erden- *(liter):* ~**kreis** *m* world; ~**leben** *nt* earthly life, life on earth; ~**pilger** *m* earthly pilgrim; ~**rund** *nt* **-s,** *no pl* world.

Erd-: e~**farben,** e~**farbig** *adj* earth-coloured; e~**fern** *adj (Astron)* far from the earth; ~**ferne** *f (Astron)* apogee; ~**gas** *nt* natural gas; e~**geborene(r)** *mf (liter)* mortal; e~**gebunden** *adj (liter)* earthbound; ~**geist** *m* earth-spirit; ~**geruch** *m* earthy smell; ~**geschichte** *f* geological history, history of the earth; e~**geschichtlich** *adj no pred* geological; ~**geschoß** *nt* ground floor, first floor *(US);* **im** ~**geschoß** on the ground/first floor; e~**haft** *adj (fig)* earthy; e~**haltig** *adj* containing earth; ~**harz** *nt* bitumen; ~**haufen** *m* mound of earth.

erdichten* *vt* to invent, to fabricate, to make up. **das ist alles erdichtet und erlogen** it's all pure fabrication.

Erdichtung *f* invention, fabrication, fiction.

erdig *adj* earthy.

Erd-: ~**innere(s)** *nt* interior *or* bowels *pl* of the earth; ~**kabel** *nt* underground cable; ~**karte** *f* map of the earth; ~**kern** *m* earth's core; ~**klumpen** *m* clod of earth; ~**kreis** *m* globe, world; **auf dem ganzen** ~**kreis** all over the world; ~**kruste** *f* earth's crust; ~**kugel** *f* world, earth, globe; ~**kunde** *f* geography; e~**kundlich** *adj* geographical; ~**leitung** *f (Elec)* earth *or* ground *(US)* (connection); *(Kabel)* underground wire; ~**loch** *nt (Mil)* foxhole; e~**magnetisch** *adj* geomagnetic; ~**magnetismus** *m* geomagnetism; ~**mantel** *m* mantle; ~**metalle** *pl* earth metals *pl;* ~**mittelalter** *nt (Geol)* Mesozoic; e~**nah** *adj (Astron)* near to the earth; ~**nähe** *f (Astron)* perigee; ~**nuß** *f* peanut, groundnut; ~**oberfläche** *f* surface of the earth, earth's surface; ~**öl** *nt* (mineral) oil, petroleum.

erdolchen* *vt* to stab (to death). **jdn mit Blicken** ~ to look daggers at sb.

Erd-: ~**ölleitung** *f* oil pipeline; ~**pech** *nt* bitumen, asphalt, mineral pitch; ~**pol** *m (Geog)* (terrestrial) pole; ~**reich** *nt* soil, earth.

erdreisten* *vr* **sich** ~, **etw zu tun** to have the audacity to do sth; **wie können Sie sich** ~! how dare you!; **er hat sich zu dieser Eigenmächtigkeit erdreistet** he had the audacity to act in this high-handed way.

Erdrinde *f siehe* **Erdkruste.**

erdröhnen* *vi aux sein* to boom out, to thunder out; *(Kanonen auch)* to roar; *(Luft, Raum)* to resound *(von* with).

erdrosseln* *vt* to strangle, to throttle.

Erdrosselung *f* strangulation, throttling.

erdrücken* *vt* to crush (to death); *(fig: überwältigen)* to overwhelm. **ein** ~**des Gefühl** a stifling feeling; ~**de Übermacht/**~**des Beweismaterial** overwhelming superiority/evidence; **die Schuld erdrückte ihn beinahe** the sense of guilt oppressed him *or* weighed down on him.

Erd-: ~**rutsch** *m* landslide, landslip; **politischer** ~**rutsch** political upheaval; *(überwältigender Wahlsieg)* (political) landslide; ~**satellit** *m* earth satellite; ~**schatten** *m* shadow of the earth; ~**schicht** *f* layer (of the earth), stratum; ~**schluß** *m (Elec)* accidental earth *or* ground *(US);* ~**scholle** *f* clod of earth; ~**sicht** *f (Aviat)* ground visibility; ~**spalte** *f* crevice; ~**stoß** *m* (seismic) shock; ~**strich** *m* region, area; ~**teil** *m* continent; ~**trabant** *m* moon.

erdulden* *vt* to endure, to suffer.

Erd-: ~**umdrehung** *f* rotation *or* revolution of the earth; ~**umfang** *m* circumference of the earth; ~**umkreisung,** ~**umrundung** *f (durch Satelliten)* orbit(ing) of the earth; ~**umsegelung** *f* voyage around the world, circumnavigation of the globe; ~**umsegler** *m* round-the-world sailor, circumnavigator of the globe.

Erdung *f (Elec)* earth(ing), ground(ing) *(US).*

Erd-: e~**verbunden,** e~**verwachsen** *adj* earthy; ~**wall** *m* earthwork, earth bank *or* wall; e~**wärts** *adv* earthward(s); ~**zeitalter** *nt* geological era.

ereifern* *vr* to get excited *or* worked up *(über* +*acc* over).

Ereiferung *f* (over-)excitement, passion *(über* +*acc* at).

ereignen* *vr* to occur, to happen.

Ereignis *nt* event, occurrence; *(Vorfall)* incident, event; *(besonderes)* occasion, event; **siehe freudig.**

erǀeignis-: ~los *adj* uneventful; ~reich *adj* eventful.
erǀeilen* *vt (geh)* to overtake.
erektil *adj (Physiol)* erectile.
Erektion *f (Physiol)* erection.
Eremit *m* -en, -en hermit.
Eremitage [eremiˈtaːʒə] *f* -, -n hermitage.
Eren *m* -, - *(dial) siehe* Hausflur.
erǀerben* *vt* to inherit.
erfahren *pret* erfuhr, *ptp* erfahren 1 *vt* (a) *Nachricht etc* to learn, to find out; *(hören)* to hear *(von* about, of). wenn der Chef das erfährt, wird er wütend if the boss gets to hear about it *or* finds that out he'll be furious; etw zu ~ suchen to try to find out sth; darf man Ihre Absichten ~? might one inquire as to your intentions?
   (b) *(erleben)* to experience; *(erleiden auch) Rückschlag* to suffer; *(empfangen) Liebe, Verständnis* to receive; *Veränderungen etc* to undergo.
   2 *vi* to hear *(von* about, of).
   3 *adj* experienced.
Erfahrenheit *f* experience.
Erfahrung *f* experience; *(Übung auch)* practical knowledge; *(Philos auch)* empirical knowledge. aus *(eigener)* ~ from (one's own) experience; nach meiner ~ in my experience; ~en sammeln to gain experience; die ~ hat gezeigt, daß ... experience has shown that ...; etw in ~ bringen to learn *or* to find out sth; eine ~ machen to have an experience; seine ~en machen to learn (things) the hard way; jeder muß seine ~en selber machen everyone has to learn by experience; ich habe die ~ gemacht, daß ... I have found that ...; mit dieser neuen Maschine/Mitarbeiterin haben wir nur gute/schlechte ~en gemacht we have found this new machine/employee (to be) completely satisfactory/unsatisfactory; was für ~en haben Sie mit ihm/damit gemacht? how did you find him/it?; mit diesem Produkt haben wir sehr unerfreuliche ~en gemacht we've encountered a lot of difficulties with this new product; ich habe mit der Ehe nur schlechte ~en gemacht I've had a very bad experience of marriage; er hat mit Blonden nur gute ~en gemacht he's always had good experiences with blondes; durch ~ wird man klug *(Prov)* one learns by experience.
Erfahrungs-: ~austausch *m (Pol)* exchange of experiences; e~gemäß *adv* e~gemäß ist es ... experience shows ...; ~tatsache *f* empirical fact; ~wissenschaft *f* empirical science.
erfaßbar *adj* ascertainable.
erfassen* *vt* (a) *(rare: ergreifen)* to seize, to catch (hold of).
   (b) *(mitreißen: Auto, Strömung)* to catch.
   (c) *(Furcht, Verlangen etc)* to seize. Angst erfaßte sie she was seized by fear; Mitleid erfaßte sie she was filled with compassion.
   (d) *(begreifen)* to grasp, to comprehend, to understand. er hat's endlich erfaßt he's caught on at last.
   (e) *(einbeziehen)* to include; *(registrieren)* to record, to register. alle Fälle werden statistisch erfaßt statistics of all cases are being recorded; das ist noch nicht statistisch erfaßt worden there are no statistics on it yet.
Erfassung *f* registration, recording; *(Miteinbeziehung)* inclusion.
erfechten* *vt irreg Sieg* to gain; *Rechte* to fight for and win.
erfinden* *vt irreg* to invent; *(erdichten auch)* to make up, to fabricate. das hat sie glatt erfunden she made it all up; frei erfunden completely fictitious; er hat die Arbeit auch nicht erfunden *(inf)* he's not exactly crazy about work *(inf); siehe* Pulver.
Erfinder(in *f)* *m* -s, - inventor.
Erfindergeist *m* inventive genius.
erfinderisch *adj* inventive; *(phantasievoll auch)* imaginative; *(findig auch)* ingenious; *siehe* Not.
Erfinderschutz *m (Jur)* protection of inventors.
Erfindung *f* invention; *(Erdichtung, Lüge auch)* fiction, fabrication. eine ~ machen to invent something.
Erfindungs-: ~gabe *f* inventiveness, invention; e~reich *adj siehe* erfinderisch.
erflehen* *vt (geh)* to beg for. etw von jdm ~ to beg *or* beseech *(liter)* sb for sth, to beg sth of sb.
Erfolg *m* -(e)s, -e success; *(Ergebnis, Folge)* result, outcome. mit/ohne ~ successfully/without success *or* unsuccessfully; ~/keinen ~ haben to be successful/have no success *or* be unsuccessful; ohne ~ bleiben *or* sein to be unsuccessful; ein voller ~ a great success; *(Stück, Roman, Vorschlag etc auch)* a hit; ein kläglicher ~ not much of a success, a bit of a failure; ~(e) bei Frauen haben to be successful with women; und was war der ~? and what was the result *or* outcome?; sie wamte mich mit dem ~, daß ... the effect *or* result of her warning me was that ...
erfolgen* *vi aux sein (form) (folgen)* to follow, to ensue; *(sich ergeben)* to result; *(vollzogen werden)* to be effected *(form) or* carried out; *(stattfinden)* to take place, to occur; *(Zahlung)* to be effected *(form) or* made. nach erfolgter Zahlung after payment has been effected *(form) or* made; es erfolgte keine Antwort no answer was forthcoming.
Erfolg-: ~hascherei *f (pej)* striving *or* angling for success; e~los *adj* unsuccessful, without success; ~losigkeit *f* lack of success, unsuccessfulness; e~reich *adj* successful.
Erfolgs-: ~autor *m* successful author; ~buch *nt* bestseller, successful book; ~denken *nt* positive way of thinking; ~erlebnis *nt* feeling of success, sense of achievement; ~film *m* successful *or* hit film; ~leiter *f (fig)* ladder to success; ~meldung *f* news *sing* of success; endlich eine ~meldung! good news at last!; ~mensch *m* success, successful person; als einem ~menschen widerstrebt ihm so etwas being used to success *or* succeeding, he reacts against that sort of thing;

~roman *m* successful novel.
erfolgversprechend *adj* promising.
erforderlich *adj* necessary, required, requisite. es ist dringend ~, daß ... it is a matter of urgent necessity that ...; etw ~ machen to make sth necessary, to necessitate sth; unbedingt ~ (absolutely) essential *or* imperative.
erforderlichenfalls *adv (form)* if required, if necessary, if need be.
erfordern* *vt* to require, to demand, to call for.
Erfordernis *nt* requirement; *(Voraussetzung auch)* prerequisite.
erforschen* *vt* (a) *Land, Weltraum etc* to explore.
   (b) *Probleme etc* to explore, to investigate, to inquire into; *(in der Wissenschaft auch)* to research into; *Thema etc* to research; *Lage, Meinung, Wahrheit* to ascertain, to find out. sein Gewissen ~ to search *or* examine one's conscience.
Erforscher *m (eines Landes)* explorer; *(in Wissenschaft)* investigator, researcher.
Erforschung *f siehe vt* (a) examination, exploration. (b) investigation, inquiry *(+gen* into); research *(+gen* into); researching; ascertaining.
erfragen* *vt Weg* to ask, to inquire; *Einzelheiten etc* to obtain, to ascertain. Einzelheiten zu ~ bei ... for details apply to ..., details can be obtained from ...
erfrechen* *vr sich ~, etw zu tun* to have the audacity to do sth; wie können Sie sich zu so einer Behauptung ~? how dare you (have the audacity to) claim such a thing!
erfreuen* 1 *vt* to please, to delight; *Herz* to gladden. sehr erfreut! *(dated: bei Vorstellung)* pleased to meet you!, delighted! *(dated)*; er wollte damit die Menschen ~ he wanted to give people pleasure; ja, sagte er erfreut yes, he said delighted(ly); über jdn/etw erfreut sein to be pleased *or* delighted about *or* at sb/sth.
   2 *vr sich einer Sache (gen) ~ (geh)* to enjoy sth; sich an etw *(dat)* ~ to enjoy sth, to take pleasure in sth.
erfreulich *adj* pleasant; *Neuerung, Besserung etc* welcome; *(befriedigend)* gratifying. es ist wenig ~, daß wir ... it's not very satisfactory that we ...; es wäre ~, wenn die Regierung ... it would be good *or* nice if the government ...; ich habe diesmal keine Sechs in Latin — das ist ja sehr ~ I didn't get the lowest grade in Latin this time — that's good to hear *or* I'm so glad; sehr ~! very nice!; er hat sich ~ wenig beklagt it was pleasant *or* nice how little he complained; wir haben ~ viel geleistet it's very satisfactory *or* pleasing how much we've done.
erfreulicherweise *adv* happily. wir haben ~ einmal ein Spiel gewonnen I'm pleased *or* glad to say that we've won a game at last.
erfrieren* 1 *vi irreg aux sein* to freeze to death, to die of exposure; *(Pflanzen)* to be killed by frost. erfrorene Glieder frostbitten limbs. 2 *vt* sich *(dat)* die Füße/Finger ~ to suffer frostbite in one's feet/fingers.
Erfrierung *f usu pl* frostbite *no pl.* Tod durch ~ death from exposure.
erfrischen* 1 *vti* to refresh. 2 *vr* to refresh oneself; *(sich waschen)* to freshen up. ich erfrischte mich an ihrer heiteren Art I found her cheerful nature most refreshing.
erfrischend *adj (lit, fig)* refreshing.
Erfrischung *f* refreshment. es ist eine ~, das zu sehen it is refreshing to see it.
Erfrischungs-: ~getränk *nt* refreshment; ~raum *m* refreshment room, cafeteria, snack bar.
erfuhr *pret of* erfahren.
erfüllen* 1 *vt* (a) *Raum etc* to fill. Haß/Liebe/Ekel *etc* erfüllte ihn he was full of hate/love/disgust *etc*, he was filled with hate/love/disgust *etc*; Schmerz erfüllte ihn he was griefstricken; Freude erfüllte ihn his heart was full *of or* filled with joy; er/sein Leben war von einem starken Pflichtgefühl erfüllt he/his life was impregnated with a strong sense of duty; es erfüllt mich mit Genugtuung, daß ... it gives me great satisfaction to see that ...; ein erfülltes Leben a full life; als die Zeit erfüllt war *(liter)* in the fullness of time *(liter)*.
   (b) *(ausführen, einhalten)* to fulfil; *Bedingungen auch* to meet, to comply with; *Wunsch, Bitte auch* to carry out; *Pflicht, Aufgabe auch* to carry out, to perform; *Erwartungen auch* to come up to; *(Jur) Soll* to achieve; *Plan* to carry through; *Formalitäten* to comply with; *Zweck, Funktion* to serve. die Fee erfüllte ihm seinen Wunsch the fairy granted him his wish; ihr Wunsch nach einem Kind wurde erfüllt their wish for a child came true *or* was granted; erfüllst du mir einen Wunsch? will you do something for me?; *siehe* Tatbestand.
   2 *vr (Wunsch, Voraussagung)* to be fulfilled, to come true. als er diesen Titel bekam, hatte sich sein Leben erfüllt when he received this title his life had reached fulfilment.
   3 *vi (Jur)* to discharge one's debts.
Erfüllung *f* fulfilment; *(einer Bitte, eines Wunsches auch)* carrying out; *(einer Pflicht, Aufgabe, eines Vertrags auch)* performance; *(von Erwartungen)* realization; *(eines Solls)* achievement; *(eines Plans)* execution; *(Jur: Tilgung)* discharge. in ~ gehen to be fulfilled; in etw *(dat)* ~ finden to find fulfilment in sth.
Erfüllungs-: ~ort *m (Jur) (von Vertrag)* place where a contract is to be fulfilled; *(von Scheck)* place of payment; ~politik *f (Hist)* policy of fulfilment; *(pej)* (policy of) appeasement; ~politiker *m (Hist)* politician supporting the policy of fulfilment; *(pej)* appeaser.
erg. *abbr of* ergänze supply, add.
Erg *nt* -s, - *(Sci)* erg.
ergänzen* *vt* to supplement; *(vervollständigen)* to complete; *Fehlendes* to supply; *Lager, Vorräte* to replenish; *Bericht auch* to add (sth) to; *Ausführungen* to amplify; *Worte, Summe* to add·

Gesetz, Gesetzentwurf to amend. **seine Sammlung** ~ to add to *or* build up one's collection; **einander** *or* **sich** ~ to complement one another; **um das Team zu** ~ to make up the numbers of the team; **das Personal muß ergänzt werden** staff numbers have to be made up; **~d hinzufügen** *or* **bemerken** to make an additional remark (*zu* to).

ergänzt *adj Ausgabe* expanded.

Ergänzung *f* **(a)** (*das Ergänzen*) supplementing; (*Vervollständigung*) completion; (*von Fehlendem*) supply(ing); (*eines Berichts*) addition (+ *gen* to); (*von Summe*) addition; (*von Gesetz*) amendment; (*von Lager, Vorräten*) replenishment. **zur** ~ **meiner Sammlung** to add to *or* build up my collection; **zur** ~ **des vorher Gesagten möchte ich hinzufügen, daß** ... let me amplify the previous remarks by adding that ...; **zur** ~ **des Teams** to make up the numbers of the team.
(b) (*Zusatz, zu Buch etc*) supplement; (*Hinzugefügtes, Person*) addition; (*zu einem Gesetz*) amendment; (*Gram*) complement.

Ergänzungs-: **~antrag** *m* (*Parl*) amendment; **~band** *m* supplement(ary volume); **~bindestrich** *m* hyphen; **~satz** *m* (*Gram*) complementary clause.

ergattern* *vt* (*inf*) to get hold of.

ergaunern* *vt* (*inf*) (**sich** *dat*) **etw** ~ to get by dishonest means.

ergeben* *irreg* **1** *vt* to yield, to produce; (*zum Ergebnis haben*) to result in; (*zeigen*) to reveal; *Betrag, Summe* to amount to, to come to.
2 *vr* **(a)** (*kapitulieren*) (*dat* to) to surrender, to yield, to capitulate. **sich auf Gnade oder Ungnade** ~ to surrender unconditionally; **sich in etw** (*acc*) ~ to submit to sth.
(b) **sich einer Sache** (*dat*) ~ (*sich hingeben*) to take to sth, to give oneself up to sth; *der Schwermut* to sink into sth; *dem Dienst etc auch* to devote oneself to sth; **sich dem Trunk** *or* **Suff** (*sl*) ~ to take to drink *or* the bottle (*inf*).
(c) (*folgen*) to result, to arise, to ensue (*aus* from). **daraus können sich Nachteile** ~ this could turn out to be disadvantageous; **das eine ergibt sich aus dem anderen** the one (thing) follows from the other.
(d) (*sich herausstellen*) to come to light. **es ergab sich, daß unsere Befürchtungen** ... it turned out that our fears ...
3 *adj* (*hingegeben, treu*) devoted; (*demütig*) humble; (*unterwürfig*) submissive. **jdm treu** ~ **sein** to be loyally devoted to sb; **einem Laster** ~ **sein** to be addicted to a vice; **Ihr (sehr) ~er** ..., **Ihr ~ster** ... (*old form*) respectfully yours ... (*form*), your (most) obedient *or* humble servant ... (*old form*).

Ergebenheit *f* (*Hingabe, Treue*) devotion; (*Demut*) humility; (*Unterwürfigkeit*) submissiveness. **die** ~ **in sein hartes Schicksal** his submission to his cruel fate.

Ergebnis *nt* result; (*Auswirkung auch*) consequence, outcome. **die Verhandlungen führten zu keinem** ~ the negotiations led nowhere *or* were inconclusive; **die Verhandlungen führten zu dem ~, daß** ... the negotiations led to the conclusion that ...; **zu einem** ~ **kommen** to come to *or* reach a conclusion; **unsere Anstrengungen blieben ohne** ~ our efforts produced no results.

ergebnislos *adj* unsuccessful, without result, fruitless; *Verhandlungen auch* inconclusive. ~ **bleiben/verlaufen** to come to nothing; **Verhandlungen** ~ **abbrechen** to break off negotiations without having reached any conclusions.

Ergebung *f* (*Mil, fig*) surrender, capitulation; (*fig: Demut*) humility.

ergehen* *irreg* **1** *vi aux sein* **(a)** (*form*) (*an* + *acc* to) (*erteilt, erlassen werden*) to go out, to be issued; (*Einladung*) to go out, to be sent; (*Gesetz*) to be enacted. ~ **lassen** to issue, to send, to enact; **an Professor X ist ein Ruf an die Universität München ergangen** an offer of a chair at the University of Munich has been sent to Professor X.
(b) **sie ließ seine Vorwürfe/alles über sich** (*acc*) ~ she let his reproaches/everything simply wash over her; **sie ließ seine Zärtlichkeiten über sich** (*acc*) ~ she submitted to his intimacies.
2 *vi impers aux sein* **es ist ihm schlecht/gut ergangen** he fared badly/well; **es wird ihm schlecht** ~ he will suffer; **wie ist es ihm in der Prüfung ergangen?** how did he fare in the exam?
3 *vr* **(a)** (*geh*) to go for a walk *or* stroll, to take the air.
(b) (*fig*) **sich in etw** (*dat*) ~ to indulge in sth; **er erging sich in Lobreden** he indulged in lavish *or* profuse praise; **er erging sich in Schmähungen** he poured forth abuse; **sich (in langen Reden) über ein Thema** ~ to hold forth at length on sth, to expatiate on sth.

Ergehen *nt* -s, *no pl* (*geh*) (state of) health.

ergiebig *adj* (*lit, fig*) productive; *Geschäft* profitable, lucrative; (*fruchtbar*) fertile; (*sparsam im Verbrauch*) economic.

Ergiebigkeit *f siehe adj* productiveness, productivity; profitability; fertility; economicalness.

ergießen* *irreg* **1** *vt* (*liter*) to pour (*out* *or* *forth liter*). **2** *vr* (*geh*) to pour forth (*liter*) or out (*auch fig*).

erglänzen* *vi aux sein* to shine, to gleam; (*Licht auch*) to shine out.

erglühen* *vi aux sein* (*liter*) to glow; (*fig*) (*vor Scham, Zorn*) to burn; (*vor Freude*) to glow. **in Liebe für jdn** ~ (*liter*) to fall passionately in love with sb.

ergo *conj* therefore, ergo (*liter, hum*).

ergötzen* **1** *vt* to delight. **zum E~ aller** to everyone's delight. **2** *vr* **sich an etw** (*dat*) ~ to be amused by sth, to take delight in sth; (*schadenfroh auch, böswillig*) to gloat over sth.

ergötzlich *adj* delightful.

ergrauen* *vi aux sein* to turn *or* go grey; *siehe* **Dienst, Ehre**.

ergreifen* *vt irreg* **(a)** to seize; (*fassen auch*) to grasp, to grip; (*Krankheit*) to overcome; *Feder, Schwert auch* to take up; *Verbrecher* to seize, to apprehend. **Feuer ergriff ihren Rock** fire

caught her dress; **das Feuer ergriff den ganzen Wald** the fire engulfed the whole forest; *siehe* **Besitz**.
(b) (*fig*) *Gelegenheit, Macht* to seize; *Beruf* to take up; *Maßnahmen* to take, to resort to. **er ergriff das Wort** he began to speak; (*Parl, bei Versammlung etc*) he took the floor; *siehe* **Flucht, Partei**.
(c) (*fig*) *jdn* (*packen*) to seize, to grip; (*bewegen*) to move. **von Furcht/Sehnsucht** *etc* **ergriffen werden** to be seized with fear/longing *etc*; **wenn dich die Liebe ergreift** if love takes hold of you; **von Liebe ergriffen werden** to fall passionately in love.

ergreifend *adj* (*fig*) moving, stirring, touching (*auch iro*).

ergriffen *adj* (*fig*) moved, deeply stirred.

Ergriffenheit *f* emotion.

ergrimmen* (*old, liter*) **1** *vi aux sein* to become angry *or* furious. **2** *vt* to incense, to anger.

ergründen* *vt Sinn etc* to fathom; *Geheimnis auch* to penetrate; *Ursache, Motiv* to discover. **ich muß** ~, **ob** ... I have to discover whether ...

Ergründung *f siehe vt* fathoming; penetration; discovery.

Erguß *m* -sses, ¨-sse effusion; (*Blut~*) bruise, contusion (*form*); (*Samen~*) ejaculation, emission; (*fig*) outpouring, effusion.

erhaben *adj* **(a)** *Druck, Muster* raised, embossed.
(b) (*fig*) *Gedanken, Stil* lofty, elevated, exalted; *Schönheit, Anblick* sublime; *Augenblick* solemn; *Herrscher* illustrious, eminent. **vom E~en zum Lächerlichen ist nur ein Schritt** it is but a step from the sublime to the ridiculous.
(c) (*überlegen*) superior. ~ **lächeln** to smile in a superior way; **er dünkt sich über alles/alle** ~ he thinks himself to be above it all/superior to everybody; **über etw** (*acc*) ~ **(sein)** (to be) above sth; **über jeden Tadel/Verdacht** ~ **sein** to be above *or* beyond reproach/suspicion; ~ **tun** to act superior.

Erhabenheit *f siehe adj* **(a)** (*rare*) elevation, relief. **(b)** (*fig*) loftiness, elevation, sublimity; solemnity; illustriousness, eminence. **(c)** superiority.

Erhalt *m* -(e)s, *no pl* receipt.

erhalten* *irreg* **1** *vt* **(a)** to get, to receive; *Preis, Orden auch* to be awarded; *Strafe, neuen Namen, fünf Jahre Gefängnis auch* to be given; *Resultat, Produkt, Genehmigung* to obtain, to get. **der Aufsatz erhielt eine neue Fassung** the essay was given a new form; **das Wort** ~ to receive permission to speak; (*Betrag*) **dankend** ~ (*form*) received with thanks (the sum of...); *siehe* **Besuch, Kenntnis**.
(b) (*bewahren*) to preserve; *Gesundheit etc auch* to maintain. **jdn am Leben/bei guter Laune** ~ to keep sb alive/in a good mood; **ich hoffe, daß du uns noch lange** ~ **bleibst** I hope you'll be with us for a long time yet; (*nicht sterben*) I hope you'll have many more happy days; **erhalte dir deinen Frohsinn/Optimismus** stay cheerful/optimistic; **er hat sich** (*dat*) **seinen Frohsinn/Optimismus** ~ he kept up *or* retained his cheerfulness/optimism; **unser Kind ist uns** ~ **geblieben** our child was spared; **gut** ~ well preserved (*auch hum inf*), in good condition; **von der Altstadt sind nur noch ein paar Kirchen** ~ of the old town only a few churches remain *or* still stand.
(c) (*unterhalten*) *Familie* to support, to keep, to maintain.
2 *vr* **(a)** (*Brauch etc*) to be preserved, to remain. **sich frisch und gesund** ~ to keep *or* stay bright and healthy.

Erhalter(in *f*) *m* -s, - preserver, maintainer; (*der Familie*) breadwinner, supporter.

erhältlich *adj* obtainable, available. **schwer** ~ difficult to obtain, hard to come by.

Erhaltung *f* (*Bewahrung*) preservation; (*Unterhaltung*) support. **die** ~ **der Energie** (*Phys*) the conservation of energy.

erhandeln* *vt* to get by bargaining, to bargain for.

erhängen* *vt* to hang. **Tod durch E~** death by hanging; **sich** ~ to hang oneself.

erhärten* **1** *vt* to harden; (*fig*) *Behauptung etc* to substantiate, to corroborate; (*Verdacht*) to harden. **etw durch Eid** ~ to affirm sth on oath. **2** *vr* (*fig: Verdacht*) to harden.

Erhärtung *f* (*fig*) *siehe vt* substantiation, corroboration; hardening.

erhaschen* *vt* to catch (*auch fig*), to seize, to grab.

erheben* *irreg* **1** *vt* **(a)** to raise (*auch Math*), to lift (up); *Glas, Stimme* to raise. **die Hand zum Gruß** ~ to raise one's hand in greeting; **seinen** *or* **den Blick** ~ to look up; **jdn in den Adelsstand** ~ to raise *or* elevate sb to the peerage; **etw zu einem Prinzip/einer Regel etc** ~ to make sth into a principle/a rule *etc*, to raise *or* elevate sth to (the level of) a principle/rule *etc*; **jdn zum Herrscher** ~ to install sb as a/the ruler; *siehe* **Anklage, Anspruch, Einspruch, Geschrei, Potenz**.
(b) *Gebühren* to charge, to levy; *Steuern* (*einziehen*) to raise, to levy; (*auferlegen*) to impose.
(c) *Fakten, Daten* to ascertain.
(d) (*liter: loben*) to laud (*liter*), to extol (*liter*).
(e) **sich erhoben fühlen** to feel uplifted *or* edified.
2 *vr* **(a)** (*aufstehen*) to get up, to rise; (*Flugzeug, Vogel*) to rise.
(b) (*sich auflehnen*) to rise (up) (in revolt), to revolt.
(c) (*aufragen*) to rise (*über* + *dat* above).
(d) **sich über eine Schwierigkeit** ~ to overcome *or* rise above a difficulty; **sich über andere** ~ to elevate *or* place oneself above others.
(e) (*aufkommen*) (*Wind etc, form: Frage etc*) to arise.

erhebend *adj* elevating, uplifting; (*beeindruckend*) impressive; (*erbaulich*) edifying.

erheblich *adj* (*beträchtlich*) considerable; (*wichtig*) important; (*relevant*) relevant, pertinent; *Verletzung* serious, severe.

Erhebung *f* **(a)** (*Boden~*) elevation.
(b) (*Aufstand*) uprising, revolt; (*Meuterei*) mutiny.

(c) *(von Gebühren)* levying, imposition.
(d) *(amtliche Ermittlung)* investigation, inquiry. ~en machen *or* anstellen über *(+acc)* to make inquiries about *or* into.
(e) *(das Erheben)* raising; *(in den Adelsstand)* elevation; *(zum Herrscher)* installation *(zu* as). ~ ins Quadrat/in die dritte Potenz squaring/cubing, raising to the power of three.
(f) *(fig: Erbauung)* uplift, elevation.
erheischen* *vt (old, liter)* to require, to demand; *Achtung* to command.
erheitern* 1 *vt* to cheer (up); *(belustigen)* to entertain, to amuse. 2 *vr* to be amused *(über +acc* by); *(Gesicht)* to brighten, to cheer up.
Erheiterung *f* amusement. zür allgemeinen ~ to the general amusement.
erhellen* 1 *vt* to light up *(auch fig)*, to illuminate; *(fig: klären)* to elucidate, to illuminate; *Geheimnis* to shed light on.
2 *vr (lit, fig)* to brighten; *(plötzlich)* to light up.
3 *vi (geh: hervorgehen)* to be evident *or* manifest. daraus erhellt, daß ... from that it is evident *or* manifest that ...
Erhellung *f (fig)* elucidation, illumination.
erhitzen* 1 *vt* to heat (up) *(auf +acc* to). die Gemüter ~ to inflame passions, to whip up feeling.
2 *vr* to get hot, to heat up; *(fig: sich erregen)* to become heated *(an +dat* over); *(Phantasie etc)* to be inflamed *or* aroused *(an +dat* at). die Gemüter erhitzten sich feelings were running high; erhitzt aussehen to look hot; *(fig)* to look hot and bothered; vom Tanzen erhitzt hot from the dancing.
Erhitzung *f* heating up; *(fig) (Erregung)* excitement; *(der Gemüter, Phantasie)* inflammation.
erhoffen* *vt* to hope for. sich *(dat)* etw ~ to hope for sth *(von* from); was erhoffst du dir davon? what do you hope to gain from it?
erhöhen* 1 *vt* to raise; *Preise etc auch* to increase, to put up; *Zahl auch, Produktion, Kraft* to increase; *Wirkung, Schönheit* to increase, to heighten, to enhance; *Spannung* to increase, to heighten; *(Mus) Note* to sharpen. die Mauern wurden um zwei Meter erhöht the walls were made two metres higher *or* were raised (by) two metres; er hat sein Haus um ein Stockwerk erhöht he has added another storey to his house; etw um 10% ~ to raise *or* put up *or* increase sth by 10%; um das Doppelte ~ increase sth by twice as much again; jdn im Rang ~ to promote sb, to raise sb to a higher rank; erhöhte Temperatur haben to have a temperature; erhöhten Puls haben to have an accelerated pulse rate; erhöhte Wachsamkeit/Anstrengungen *etc* increased vigilance/efforts *etc*.
2 *vr* to rise, to increase; *(Spannung etc auch)* to heighten, to intensify. wer sich selbst erhöht, der wird erniedrigt (werden) *(Bibl)* whosoever shall exalt himself shall be abased.
Erhöhung *f* (a) *(das Erhöhen)* siehe *vt* raising; increase, heightening, enhancement; *(von Spannung)* heightening, intensification. (b) *(Lohn~)* rise *(Brit)*, raise *(US)*; *(Preis~)* increase. (c) *(Hügel)* hill, elevation.
Erhöhungszeichen *nt (Mus)* sharp (sign).
erholen* *vr (von* from) to recover; *(von Krankheit auch)* to recuperate; *(sich entspannen auch)* to relax, to have a rest; *(fig: Preise, Aktien)* to recover, to rally, to pick up. er hat sich von dem Schreck(en) noch nicht erholt he hasn't got over the shock yet; Sie müssen sich einmal gründlich ~ you must have a thorough rest; du siehst sehr erholt aus you look very rested.
erholsam *adj* restful, refreshing.
Erholung *f* siehe *vr* recovery; recuperation; relaxation, rest; *(der Wirtschaft)* recovery, rallying. der Direktor ist zur ~ in der Schweiz the director has gone to Switzerland for a holiday *(esp Brit)* or a vacation *(US)* and a rest; *(zur Genesung)* the director is convalescing in Switzerland; zur ~ an die See fahren to go to the seaside in order to recover *or* recuperate *or* convalesce; er braucht dringend ~ he badly needs a holiday *(esp Brit)* or a vacation *(US)* or a break; Urlaub ist zur ~ da holidays are for relaxation; gute ~! have a good rest; Gartenarbeit ist nicht gerade eine ~ gardening is not exactly a relaxation.
Erholungs-: ~aufenthalt *m* holiday *(esp Brit)*, vacation *(US)*; e~bedürftig *adj* in need of a rest, run-down; ~heim *nt* rest home; *(Ferienheim)* holiday home; *(Sanatorium)* convalescent home; ~kur *f* rest cure; ~ort *m* spa, health resort; ~pause *f* break; ~reise *f* holiday/vacation trip; ~urlaub *m* holiday/vacation; *(nach Krankheit)* convalescent leave *or* holiday.
erhören* *vt Gebet etc* to hear; *Bitte, Liebhaber* to yield to.
erhungern* *vt* er hat sich *(dat)* den Doktortitel erhungert he almost starved in order to get his PhD.
Eriesee *m* Lake Erie *no art*.
erigibel *adj (Physiol)* erectile.
erigieren* *vi* to become erect. erigiert erect.
Erika *f -, Eriken (Bot)* heather.
er|innerlich *adj pred* soviel mir ~ ist as far as I (can) remember *or* recall; es ist mir nicht ~, daß Sie das gesagt haben I don't remember *or* recall your having said that.
er|innern* 1 *vt* jdn an etw *(acc)* ~ to remind sb of sth; jdn daran ~, etw zu tun/daß ... to remind sb to do sth/that ...; etw ~ *(dial, sl)* to remember *or* recall sth.
2 *vr* sich an jdn/etw ~, sich einer Sache *(gen)* ~ *(old)* to remember *or* recall *or* recollect sb/sth; sich nur noch dunkel ~ an *(+acc)* to have only a faint *or* dim recollection *or* memory of; soweit *or* soviel ich mich ~ kann as far as I remember *etc*, to the best of my recollection; wenn ich mich recht erinnere, ... if my memory serves me right *or* correctly ..., if I remember rightly ...
3 *vi* (a) ~ an *(+acc)* to be reminiscent of, to call to mind, to

recall; sie erinnert sehr an ihre Mutter she reminds one very much of her mother.
(b) *(erwähnen)* daran ~, daß ... to point out that ...
Er|innerung *f (an +acc* of) memory, recollection; *(euph: Mahnung)* reminder; *(Andenken)* memento, remembrance, keepsake. ~en *pl (Lebens~)* reminiscences *pl*; *(Liter)* memoirs *pl*; ~en austauschen to reminisce; zur ~ an *(+acc)* in memory of; *(an Ereignis)* in commemoration of; *(als Andenken)* as a memento of; jdn/etw in guter/schlechter ~ haben *or* behalten to have pleasant/unpleasant memories of sb/sth; sich *(dat)* etw in die ~ zurückrufen to call sth to mind; wenn mich meine ~ nicht täuscht if my memory doesn't deceive me.
Er|innerungs-: ~bild *nt* visual memento *(an +acc* of); ~feier *f* commemoration; ~lücke *f* gap in one's memory; ~schreiben *nt (Comm)* reminder; ~stück *nt* keepsake *(an +acc* from); ~tafel *f* commemorative plaque; ~vermögen *nt* memory, powers *pl* of recollection; ~wert *m* sentimental value.
Erinnyen *pl (Myth)* Furies *pl*, Erin(n)yes *pl*.
erjagen* *vt* to bag, to catch; *(fig: ergattern)* to get hold of, to hunt down. um sich dort Reichtum zu ~ to make his fortune.
erkalten* *vi aux sein (lit, fig)* to cool (down *or* off), to go cold.
erkälten* *vr* to catch (a) cold; *(esp sich verkühlen)* to catch a chill. sich stark *or* sehr/leicht erkältet haben to have (caught) a heavy/slight cold/chill; sich *(dat)* die Blase ~ to catch a chill in one's bladder.
erkältet *adj* with a cold. (stark) ~ sein to have a (bad *or* heavy) cold; wir sind alle ~ we all have colds.
Erkältung *f* cold; *(leicht)* chill. sich *(dat)* eine ~ zuziehen to catch a cold/chill.
Erkältungskrankheiten *pl* coughs and sneezes *pl*.
erkämpfen* *vt* to win, to secure. sich *(dat)* etw ~ to win sth; hart erkämpft hard-won; er hat sich *(dat)* seine Position hart erkämpft he fought hard for his *or* to secure his position.
erkaufen* *vt* to buy. etw teuer ~ to pay dearly for sth; den Erfolg mit seiner Gesundheit ~ to pay for one's success with one's health, to buy success at the price of one's health; wahre Liebe läßt sich nicht ~ true love cannot be bought.
erkennbar *adj (wieder~)* recognizable; *(sichtbar)* visible; *(wahrnehmbar, ersichtlich)* discernible.
Erkennbarkeit *f* siehe *adj* recognizability; visibility; discernibility.
erkennen* *irreg* 1 *vt* (a) *(wieder~, an~, einsehen)* to recognize *(an +dat* by); *(wahrnehmen)* to see, to make out, to discern; *Unterschied* to see; *Situation* to see, to understand. ich erkannte die Lage sofort I immediately realized what the situation was; er hat erkannt, daß das nicht stimmte he realized that it wasn't right; kannst du ~, ob das da drüben X ist? can you see *or* tell if that's X over there?; jdn für schuldig ~ *(Jur)* to find sb guilty; (jdm) etw zu ~ geben to indicate sth (to sb); jdm zu ~ geben, daß ... to give sb to understand that ...; sich zu ~ geben to reveal oneself *(als* to be), to disclose one's identity; ~ lassen to show, to reveal; erkenne dich selbst! know thyself!; du bist erkannt! I see what you're after, I know your game.
(b) *(Bibl, obs)* to know *(Bibl)*.
2 *vi* ~ auf *(+acc) (Jur)* Freispruch to grant; *Strafe* to impose, to inflict; *(Sport)* Freistoß *etc* to give, to award; auf drei Jahre Haft ~ to impose a sentence of three years' imprisonment.
erkenntlich *adj* sich (für etw) ~ zeigen to show one's gratitude *or* appreciation (for sth). (b) *(rare)* siehe *erkennbar*.
Erkenntlichkeit *f (Dankbarkeit)* gratitude; *(Gegenleistung)* token of one's gratitude *or* appreciation.
Erkenntnis[1] *f (Wissen)* knowledge *no pl*; *(das Erkennen)* recognition, realization; *(Philos, Psych)* cognition *no pl*; *(Einsicht)* insight, realization; *(Entdeckung)* finding, discovery. zur ~ kommen to see the light; zu der ~ kommen *or* gelangen, daß ... to come to the realization that ..., to realize that ...
Erkenntnis[2] *nt (Jur)* decision, finding; *(der Geschworenen)* verdict.
Erkenntnis-: ~drang *m* thirst for knowledge; ~fähigkeit *f* cognitive faculty; ~gehalt *m* information content; e~hungrig *adj (geh)* thirsty *or* hungry for knowledge; ~lehre *f* siehe ~theorie; e~theoretisch *adj* epistemological; ~theorie *f* epistemology, theory of knowledge; ~vermögen *nt* cognitive capacity.
Erkennung *f* recognition, identification.
Erkennungs-: ~dienst *m* police records department; e~dienstlich adv jdn e~dienstlich behandeln to fingerprint and photograph sb; ~marke *f* identity disc *or* tag; ~melodie *f* signature tune; ~wort *nt* password; ~zeichen *nt* identification; *(Mil: Abzeichen)* badge; *(Aviat)* markings *pl*; *(Med)* sign *(für* of). das ist mein ~zeichen that's what you'll recognize me by.
Erker *m -s, -* bay; *(kleiner Vorbau)* oriel.
Erker-: ~fenster *nt* bay window; oriel window; ~zimmer *nt* room with a bay window; oriel window (recess).
erkiesen *pret* erkor, *ptp* erkoren *vt (obs, liter)* to choose, to elect *(zu* as, to be).
erklärbar *adj* explicable, explainable. leicht ~ easily explained; schwer ~ hard to explain; nicht ~ unexplained.
erklären* 1 *vt* (a) *(erläutern)* to explain *(jdm etw* sth to sb); *(begründen auch)* to account for. ich kann mir nicht ~, warum ... I can't understand why ...; wie erklärt ihr euch das? how can *or* do you explain that?, what do you make of that?; ich erkläre mir die Sache so: ... the way I see it, ...
(b) *(äußern, bekanntgeben)* to declare *(als* to be); *Rücktritt* to announce; *(Politiker, Pressesprecher etc)* to say. einem Staat den Krieg ~ to declare war on a country; er erklärte ihr seine Liebe he declared his love for her; eine Ausstellung *etc* für *or*

als eröffnet ~ to declare an exhibition *etc* open; **jdn für schuldig/tot/gesund** *etc* ~ to pronounce sb guilty/dead/healthy *etc*.

2 *vr* **(a)** *(Sache)* to be explained. **das erklärt sich daraus, daß** ... it can be explained by the fact that ...; **damit hat sich die Sache von selbst erklärt** the affair thereby explained itself; **das erklärt sich (von) selbst** that's self-explanatory.

(b) *(Mensch)* to declare oneself; *(Liebe gestehen auch)* to declare one's love. **sich für bankrott** *etc* ~ to declare oneself bankrupt *etc*; **sich für gesund/diensttauglich** ~ to pronounce or declare oneself healthy/fit for service; **sich für/gegen jdn/etw** ~ to declare oneself or come out for/against sb/sth.

3 *vi* to explain. **er kann sehr gut** ~ he's very good at explaining things.

erklärend *adj* explanatory. **einige** ~**e Worte** a few words of explanation; **er fügte** ~ **hinzu** ... he added in explanation ...

erklärlich *adj* **(a)** *siehe* **erklärbar**. **(b)** *(verständlich)* understandable. **ist Ihnen das** ~? can you find an explanation for that?; **mir ist einfach nicht** ~, **wie** ... I simply cannot understand how ...

erklärlicherweise *adv* understandably.

erklärt *adj attr Gegner etc* professed, avowed; *Favorit, Liebling* acknowledged.

erklärtermaßen *adv* avowedly.

Erklärung *f* **(a)** explanation. **(b)** *(Mitteilung, Bekanntgabe)* declaration; *(eines Politikers, Pressesprechers etc)* statement. **eine** ~ **(zu etw) abgeben** to make a statement (about or concerning sth).

erklecklich *adj* considerable.

erklettern* *vt* to climb (up); *Berg auch* to scale; *Alpengebiet* to climb.

erklimmen* *vt irreg (geh)* to scale; *(fig) Spitze, höchste Stufe* to climb to; *(fig) Leiter* to climb or ascend to the top of.

erklingen* *vi irreg (geh) aux sein* to ring out, to resound. **eine Harfe/ein Glöckchen/Stimmchen erklang** (the sound of) a harp/bell/voice was heard, I *etc* heard (the sound of) a harp/bell/voice; **ein Lied** ~ **lassen** to burst (forth) into song; **die Gläser** ~ **lassen** to clink glasses.

erkor *pret of* **erkiesen, erküren**.

erkoren *ptp of* **erkiesen, erküren**.

erkranken* *vi aux sein (krank werden)* to be taken ill, to fall ill *(an +dat* with); *(Organ, Pflanze, Tier)* to become diseased *(an +dat* with). **erkrankt sein** *(krank sein)* to be ill/diseased; **er ist am Magen erkrankt** he has contracted a stomach illness or disease; **die an Krebs erkrankten Menschen** people with or suffering from cancer; **die erkrankten Stellen** the diseased or affected areas.

Erkrankung *f* illness; *(von Organ, Pflanze, Tier)* disease. **wegen einer plötzlichen** ~ **des Viehbestandes** because the livestock suddenly became diseased.

Erkrankungsfall *m* case of illness. **im** ~ in case of illness.

erkühnen* *vr (old, liter)* **sich** ~ **zu** or *+gen* to dare or to make bold to do/say *etc* sth; **sich** ~, **etw zu tun** to dare to do sth, to make so bold as to do sth.

erkunden* *vt (esp Mil) Gelände, Stellungen* to reconnoitre, to scout; *(feststellen)* to find out, to establish, to ascertain.

erkundigen* *vr* **sich** *(nach etw/über jdn)* ~ to ask or inquire (about sth/sb); **sich nach jdm** ~ to ask after sb; **sich bei jdm (nach etw)** ~ to ask sb (about sth); **ich werde mich** ~ I'll find out.

Erkundigung *f* inquiry; *(Nachforschung auch)* investigation. ~**en einholen** or **einziehen** to make inquiries.

Erkundung *f (Mil)* reconnaissance.

Erkundungsgang *m (Mil, fig)* reconnaissance expedition.

erkünstelt *adj* affected.

erküren* *pret* **erkor**, *ptp* **erkoren** *vt (obs, liter) siehe* **erkiesen**.

Erlagschein *m (Aus) siehe* **Zahlkarte**.

erlahmen* *vi aux sein* to tire, to grow weary; *(Kräfte, fig: Interesse, Eifer)* to flag, to wane.

erlangen* *vt* to attain, to achieve; *Alter, Ziel auch* to reach; *Bedeutung, Eintritt* to gain.

Erlangung *f* attainment.

Erlaß *m* **-sses, -sse** or *(Aus)* **-sse** **(a)** *(Verfügung)* decree, edict; *(der Regierung)* enactment, edict. **(b)** *(Straf~, Schulden~, Sünden~ etc)* remission.

erlassen* *vt irreg* **(a)** *Verfügung* to pass; *Gesetz* to enact; *Dekret* to issue.

(b) *(von etw entbinden) Strafe, Schulden etc* to remit; *Gebühren* to waive. **jdm etw** ~ *Schulden etc* to release sb from sth; *Gebühren* to waive sth for sb; **bitte** ~ **Sie es mir, darüber zu sprechen** please don't ask me to talk about that; **jdm die Strafarbeit/eine Pflicht** ~ to let sb off a punishment/to release sb from a duty; **ich erlasse ihm den Rest (des Geldes)** I'll waive the rest or let him off paying the rest (of the money).

erlauben* **1** *vt (gestatten)* to allow, to permit. **jdm etw** ~ to allow or permit sb (to do) sth; **mein Vater erlaubt mir nicht, daß ich mit Mädchen ausgehe** my father doesn't or won't allow me to go out with girls; **es ist mir nicht erlaubt, das zu tun** I am not allowed or permitted to do that; **du erlaubst deinem Kind zuviel** you allow your child too much freedom; ~ **Sie?, Sie** ~? *(form)* may I?; ~ **Sie, daß ich das Fenster öffne?** do you mind if I open the window?; ~ **Sie, daß ich mich vorstelle** allow or permit me to introduce myself; ~ **Sie mal!** do you mind!; **soweit es meine Zeit/das Wetter erlaubt** *(form)* time/weather permitting; **seine Verhältnisse** ~ **ihm ein behagliches Leben** his circumstances allow or permit him to lead a comfortable life; **erlaubt ist, was gefällt** *(prov)* a little of what you fancy does you good *(prov)*; **erlaubt ist, was sich ziemt** *(prov)* you must only do what is proper.

2 *vr* **sich** *(dat)* **etw** ~ *(gestatten, sich gönnen)* to allow or permit oneself sth; *(wagen) Bemerkung, Vorschlag* to venture sth; *(sich leisten)* to afford sth; **sich** *(dat)* ~, **etw zu tun** *(so frei sein)* to take the liberty of doing sth; *(sich leisten)* to afford to do sth; **darf ich mir** ~, **nach Ihrem Namen zu fragen?** might I make so bold as to ask your name?; **darf ich mir** ~ ...? might I possibly...?; **wenn ich mir die folgende Bemerkung** ~ **darf** ... if I might venture or afford the following remark ...; **sich** *(dat)* **Frechheiten** ~ to take liberties, to be cheeky; **sich** *(dat)* **einen Scherz** ~ to have a joke; **was die Jugend sich heutzutage alles erlaubt!** the things young people get up to nowadays!; **was** ~ **Sie sich (eigentlich)!** how dare you!

Erlaubnis *f* permission; *(Schriftstück)* permit. **mit Ihrer (freundlichen)** ~ *(form)* with your (kind) permission, by your leave *(form)*; **du brauchst eine elterliche** ~ you need your parents' (written) permission; **(jdn) um** ~ **bitten** to ask (sb) (for) permission, to ask or beg leave (of sb) *(form)*; **jdm zu etw die** ~ **geben** or **erteilen** *(form)* to give sb permission or leave *(form)* for sth/to do sth.

Erlaubnisschein *m* permit.

erlaucht *adj (obs, iro)* illustrious.

Erlaucht *f* **-, -en** *(Hist)* Lordship.

erlauschen* *vt (rare)* to overhear.

erläutern* *vt* to explain, to elucidate; *(klarstellen auch)* to clarify; *Text* to comment on. ~**d explanatory**; ~**d fügte er hinzu** he added in explanation or clarification.

Erläuterung *f siehe vt* explanation, elucidation; clarification; comment, commentary. **zur** ~ in explanation.

Erle *f* **-, -n** alder.

erleben* *vt* to experience; *(noch lebend erreichen)* to live to see; *(durchmachen) schwere Zeiten, Sturm* to go through; *Aufstieg, Abenteuer, Enttäuschung* to have; *Erfolg* to have, to enjoy; *Mißerfolg, Niederlage* to have, to suffer; *Aufführung* to have, to receive; *Jahrhundertwende, erste Mondlandung* to see; *Schauspieler* to see (perform); *Musik, Gedicht, Fußballspiel, Landschaft* to experience. **im Urlaub habe ich viel erlebt** I had an eventful time on holiday; **was haben Sie im Ausland erlebt?** what sort of experiences did you have abroad?; **Deutschland, wie ich es erlebt habe, war** ... I remember Germany as being ...; **wir haben wunderschöne Tage in Spanien erlebt** we had a lovely time in Spain; **etwas Angenehmes etc** ~ to have a pleasant *etc* experience; **er hat schon viel Schlimmes erlebt** he's had a lot of bad times or experiences; **wir haben mit unseren Kindern viel Freude erlebt** our children have given us much pleasure; **das Buch hat viele Auflagen erlebt** the book has gone or been through a lot of editions; **ich habe es oft erlebt** ... I've often known or seen it happen ...; **so wütend habe ich ihn noch nie erlebt** I've never seen or known him so furious; **unser Land hat schon bessere Zeiten erlebt** our country has seen or known better times; **ich möchte mal** ~, **daß du rechtzeitig kommst** I'd like to see you come on time; **er hat gesagt, würde helfen — das möchte ich** ~! he said he'd like to help — that I'd like to see!; **das werde ich nicht mehr** ~ I shan't live to see that; **er möchte mal etwas** ~ he wants to have a good time; **er hat viel erlebt** he has been around *(inf)*, he has experienced a lot; **eine erlebte Geschichte** a true(-life) story; **das muß man erlebt haben** you've got to have experienced it (for) yourself; **erlebte Rede** *(Liter)* interior monologue; **na, der kann was** ~! *(inf)* he's going to be (in) for it! *(inf)*; **hat man so (etwas schon (mal) erlebt!** *(inf)* I've never heard anything like it!; **daß ich das** ~ **muß!** I never thought I'd see the day!; **so was Dummes habe ich noch nie erlebt!** I've never seen/heard anything so stupid in all my life!

Erlebensfall *m* **im** ~ in case of survival; **Versicherung auf den** ~ pure endowment insurance.

Erlebnis *nt* experience; *(Abenteuer)* adventure; *(Liebschaft)* affair. **(jdm) zu einem** ~ **werden** to be (quite) an experience (for sb).

Erlebnis-: ~**aufsatz** *m (Sch)* essay based on personal experience; ~**fähigkeit** *f* receptivity to experiences, ability to experience things (deeply); ~**lyrik** *f* poetry based on personal experience; **e~reich** *adj* eventful.

erledigen* **1** *vt* **(a)** to deal with, to take care of; *Akte etc* to process; *(ausführen) Auftrag* to carry out; *(beenden) Arbeit* to finish off, to deal with; *Sache* to settle. **Einkäufe** ~ to do the shopping; **ich habe noch einiges in der Stadt zu** ~ I've still got a few things to do in town; **ich muß noch schnell was** ~ I've just got something to do; **die Sache/er ist für mich erledigt** as far as I'm concerned the matter's closed/I'm finished with him; **erledigt!** *(Stempel)* dealt with, processed; **erledigt, reden wir nicht mehr darüber!** OK, let's say no more about it!; **das ist (damit) erledigt** that's settled or taken care of; **wird erledigt!** shall or will do! *(inf)*, right-ho! *(Brit inf)*, sure thing! *(US inf)*; **zu** ~ *(Vermerk auf Akten)* for attention; **schon erledigt!** I've already done it; *(mache ich sofort)* consider it done.

(b) *(inf: ermüden)* to wear or knock *(inf)* out; *(inf: ruinieren)* to finish, to ruin; *(sl: töten)* to do in *(sl)*; *(sl: k.o. schlagen)* to finish off, to knock out.

2 *vr* **damit erledigt sich das Problem** that disposes of or settles the problem; **das hat sich erledigt** that's all settled; **sich von selbst** ~ to take care of itself.

erledigt *adj* **(a)** *(obs) Stelle* vacant. **(b)** *(inf) (erschöpft)* shattered *(inf)*, done in *pred (inf)*; *(ruiniert)* finished, ruined. **wenn jetzt die Bullen kommen, sind wir** ~ if the cops come now, we've had it *(inf)*; **siehe auch vt (a)**.

Erledigung *f (Ausführung)* execution, carrying out; *(Durchführung, Beendung)* completion; *(einer Sache, eines Geschäfts)* settlement. **die** ~ **von Einkäufen** *(form)* shopping; **die** ~ **meiner Korrespondenz** dealing with my correspondence; **sie betraute ihn mit der** ~ **ihrer Geschäfte** she entrusted him with the execution of or with dealing with her business affairs; **einige ~en in der Stadt** a few things to do in town; **um rasche ~ wird gebeten** please give this your immediate attention; **in ~ Ihres Auftrages/Ihrer Anfrage** (form) in execution of your order/further to your inquiry (form).

Erledigungsvermerk m actioned stamp.

erlegen* vt (a) Wild to shoot, to bag (Hunt). (b) (Aus, Sw: bezahlen) to pay.

erleichtern* 1 vt (einfacher machen) to make easier; (fig) Last, Los to lighten; (beruhigen) to relieve; (lindern) Not, Schmerz etc to relieve, to alleviate. **sein Herz/Gewissen** or **sich** (dat) **das Gewissen ~** to unburden one's heart/conscience; **es würde mein Gewissen ~, wenn ...** it would ease my mind or conscience if ...; **jdm etw ~** to make sth easier for sb; **jdn um etw ~** (hum) to relieve sb of sth; **erleichtert aufatmen** to breathe a sigh of relief.
2 vr (old) to relieve oneself.

Erleichterung f (von Last etc) lightening; (Linderung) relief, alleviation; (Beruhigung) relief; (Zahlungs~) facility. **das trägt zur ~ meiner Aufgabe bei** it makes my work easier; **einem Kranken ~ verschaffen** to give relief to a sick person.

erleiden* vt irreg to suffer; Verluste, Schaden auch to sustain, to incur. **den Tod ~** (old) to suffer death (old); siehe **Schiffbruch**.

erlernbar adj learnable.

erlernen* vt to learn.

erlesen adj exquisite. **ein ~er Kreis** a select circle.

Erlesenheit f exquisiteness; (von Kreis) selectness.

erleuchten* vt to light (up), to illuminate; (fig) to enlighten, to inspire. **Herr, erleuchte uns!** Lord, let thy light shine upon us; **hell erleuchtet** brightly lit; Stadt brightly illuminated.

Erleuchtung f (Eingebung) inspiration; (religiöse auch) enlightenment no pl.

erliegen* vi irreg aux sein +dat (lit, fig) to succumb to; einem Irrtum to be the victim of. **zum E~ kommen/bringen** to come/bring to a standstill.

erlisch imper sing of **erlöschen**.

Erlös m -es, -e proceeds pl.

erlöschen pret **erlosch**, ptp **erloschen** vi aux sein (Feuer) to go out; (Gefühle, Interesse) to die; (Vulkan) to become extinct; (Leben) to come to an end; (Vertrag, Anspruch etc) to expire, to lapse; (Firma) to be dissolved; (Geschlecht, Name) to die out. **ein erloschener Vulkan** an extinct volcano; **mit ~der Stimme** (liter) in a dying voice; **seine Augen waren erloschen** (liter) his eyes were lifeless.

erlösen* vt (a) (retten) to save, to rescue (aus, von from); (Rel) to redeem, to save; (von Sünden, Qualen) to deliver (esp Bibl), to release. **erlöse uns von dem Bösen** (Rel) deliver us from evil. (b) (Comm: aus Verkauf) Geld to realize.

erlösend adj relieving, liberating. **sie sprach das ~e Wort** she spoke the word he/she/everybody etc was waiting for; **~ wirken** to come as a relief; **er empfand es beinahe ~, als ...** it was almost a relief for him when ...

Erlöser(in f) m -s, - (Rel) Redeemer; (Befreier) saviour.

Erlösung f release, deliverance; (Erleichterung) relief; (Rel) redemption. **der Tod war für sie eine ~** death was a release for her.

Erlösungswerk nt (Rel) (act of) redemption.

erlügen* vt irreg to fabricate, to make up, to invent. **eine erlogene Geschichte** a fabrication, a fiction.

ermächtigen* vt to authorize, to empower (zu etw to do sth).

ermächtigt adj authorized, empowered. **zur Unterschrift ~** authorized to sign.

Ermächtigung f authorization.

Ermächtigungsgesetz nt (Pol) Enabling Act (esp that of Nazis in 1933).

ermahnen* vt to exhort (form), to admonish, to urge; (warnend) to warn; (Jur) to caution. **jdn zum Fleiß/zur Aufmerksamkeit** etc **~** to exhort (form) or urge sb to work hard/to be attentive etc; **muß ich dich immer erst ~?** do I always have to remind or tell you first?; **jdn im Guten ~** to give sb a friendly warning.

Ermahnung f exhortation, admonition, urging; (warnend) warning; (Jur) caution.

ermangeln* vi einer Sache (gen) ~ (geh) to lack sth.

Ermang(e)lung f: **in ~ +gen** because of the lack of; **in ~ eines Besseren** for lack of something better.

ermannen* vr to pluck up courage.

ermäßigen* 1 vt to reduce. 2 vr to be reduced.

Ermäßigung f reduction; (Steuer~) relief.

Ermäßigungsfahrschein m concessionary ticket.

ermatten* (geh) 1 vt to tire, to exhaust. 2 vi aux sein to tire, to become exhausted.

ermattet adj (geh) exhausted, weary.

Ermattung f (geh) exhaustion, weariness, fatigue.

ermessen* vt irreg (einschätzen) Größe, Weite, Wert to gauge, to estimate; (erfassen, begreifen können) to appreciate, to realize.

Ermessen nt -s, no pl (Urteil) judgement, estimation; (Gutdünken) discretion. **nach meinem ~** in my estimation; **nach menschlichem ~** as far as anyone can judge; **nach bestem ~ handeln** to act according to one's best judgement; **nach freiem ~** at one's discretion; **nach eigenem ~ handeln** to act on one's own discretion; **etw in jds ~ (acc) stellen, etw jds ~ (dat) anheimstellen** to leave sth to sb's discretion; **in jds ~ (dat) liegen** or **stehen** to be within sb's discretion.

Ermessens-: **~entscheidung** f (Jur) discretionary decision; **~frage** f matter of discretion; **~mißbrauch** m abuse of (one's powers of) discretion; **~spielraum** m discretionary powers pl.

ermitteln* 1 vt to determine (auch Chem, Math), to ascertain;

Person to trace; Tatsache, Identität to establish. 2 vi to investigate. **gegen jdn ~** to investigate sb; **in einem Fall ~** to investigate a case.

Ermittlung f (a) no pl siehe vt determination, ascertaining; tracing; establishing, establishment. (b) (esp Jur: Erkundigung) investigation, inquiry. **~en anstellen** to make inquiries (über +acc about).

Ermittlungs-: **~ausschuß** m committee of inquiry; **~richter** m (Jur) examining magistrate; **~verfahren** nt (Jur) preliminary proceedings pl.

ermöglichen* vt to facilitate, to make possible. **es jdm ~, etw zu tun** to make it possible for sb or to enable sb to do sth; **um uns den freien Austausch von Informationen zu ~** to facilitate the free exchange of information, to make it possible for us or to enable us to exchange information freely; **jdm das Studium/eine Reise ~** to make it possible for sb to study/to go on a journey; **(nur,) wenn Sie es ~ können** (form) (only) if you are able (to); **können Sie es ~, morgen zu kommen?** (form) would it be possible for you to or are you able to come tomorrow?

ermorden* vt to murder; (esp aus politischen Gründen) to assassinate.

Ermordung f murder; (esp politisch) assassination.

ermüden* 1 vt to tire. 2 vi aux sein to tire, to become tired; (Tech) to fatigue.

ermüdend adj tiring.

Ermüdung f fatigue (auch Tech), tiredness, weariness.

Ermüdungs-: **~erscheinung** f sign or symptom of fatigue; **~zustand** m feeling of tiredness; **häufige ~zustände** a frequent feeling of tiredness.

ermuntern* 1 vt (ermutigen) to encourage (jdn zu etw sb to do sth); (beleben, erfrischen) to liven up, to stimulate, to invigorate; (aufmuntern) to cheer up. **seine Gegenwart wirkt ~d auf mich** his presence has an enlivening effect on me or stimulates me. 2 vr (rare) to wake up, to rouse oneself.

Ermunterung f siehe vt encouragement; enlivening, stimulation; cheering-up.

ermutigen* vt (ermuntern) to encourage; (Mut geben) to give courage, to embolden (form). **jdn zu etw ~** to encourage sb to do sth/give sb the courage or embolden (form) sb to do sth.

Ermutigung f encouragement.

Ern m -(e)s, -e (dial) siehe **Hausflur**.

ernähren* 1 vt to feed; (unterhalten) to support, to keep, to maintain. **schlecht/gut ernährt** undernourished/well-nourished or -fed; **dieser Beruf ernährt seinen Mann** you can make a good living in this profession.
2 vr to eat. **sich von etw ~** to live or subsist on sth; **sich von Übersetzungen ~** to earn one's living by doing translations; **sich selbst ~ müssen** to have to earn one's own living; **der Arzt klärte ihn auf, wie er sich ~ sollte** the doctor advised him on his diet.

Ernährer(in f) m -s, - breadwinner, provider.

Ernährung f (das Ernähren) feeding; (Nahrung) food, nourishment, nutrition (esp Med); (Unterhalt) maintenance. **auf vernünftige ~ achten** to eat sensibly; **die ~ einer großen Familie** feeding a big family; **falsche/richtige/pflanzliche ~** the wrong/a proper/a vegetarian diet.

Ernährungs- in cpds nutritional; **~forschung** f nutritional research; **~gewohnheiten** pl eating habits pl; **~krankheit** f nutritional disease; **~weise** f diet, form of nutrition; **~wissenschaft** f dietetics sing; **~wissenschaftler** m dietician, nutritionist.

ernennen* vt irreg to appoint. **jdn zu etw ~** to make or appoint sb sth.

Ernennung f appointment (zum as).

Ernennungs-: **~schreiben** nt letter of appointment; **~urkunde** f certificate of appointment.

Erneuerer m -s, -, **Erneuerin** f innovator.

erneuern* vt to renew; (renovieren) to renovate; (restaurieren) to restore; (auswechseln) Öl to change; Maschinenteile to replace; (wiederbeleben) to revive. **Reifen/Bettwäsche/Schnürsenkel** etc **~** to buy or get new tyres/sheets/shoelaces etc.

Erneuerung f siehe vt renewal; renovation; restoration; changing; replacing; revival.

erneut 1 adj attr renewed. **~e Verhandlung** (Jur) retrial. 2 adv (once) again, once more.

erniedrigen* 1 vt (demütigen) to humiliate; (herabsetzen) to degrade; (Mus) to flatten, to flat (US). 2 vr to humble oneself; (pej) to demean or lower oneself.

Erniedrigung f siehe vt humiliation; degradation, abasement; flattening, flatting (US).

Erniedrigungszeichen nt (Mus) flat (sign).

Ernst[1] m -s Ernest.

Ernst[2] m -(e)s, no pl seriousness; (Bedenklichkeit auch) gravity; (Dringlichkeit, Ernsthaftigkeit von Gesinnung) earnestness. **feierlicher ~** solemnity; **im ~** seriously; **allen ~es** in all seriousness, quite seriously; **meinen Sie das allen ~es?, ist das Ihr ~?** are you (really) serious?, you're not serious, are you?; **das kann doch nicht dein ~ sein!** you can't mean that seriously!, you can't be serious!; **das ist mein (völliger or voller) ~** I'm quite serious; **dieses Angebot ist im ~ gemeint** this offer is meant seriously; **es ist mir ~ damit** I'm serious about it, I'm in earnest; **mit etw ~ machen** to be serious about sth; **mit einer Drohung ~ machen** to carry out a threat; **der ~ des Lebens** the serious side of life, the real world; **damit wird es jetzt ~** now it's serious, now it's for real (inf); **mit ~ bei der Sache sein** to do sth seriously.

ernst adj serious; (bedenklich, bedrohlich, würdevoll auch) grave; (eifrig, ~haft) Mensch, Gesinnung earnest; (feier-

lich, elegisch) solemn.~e **Absichten haben** (*inf*) to have honourable intentions; **es** (**mit jdm/etw**) ~ **meinen** to be serious (about sb/sth); **jdn/etw** ~ **nehmen** to take sb/sth seriously; **es steht** ~ **um ihn/die Sache** things look bad for him/it; (*wegen Krankheit*) he's in a bad way; **es ist nichts E~es** it's nothing serious; ~ **bleiben** to remain *or* be serious; (*sich das Lachen verbeißen*) to keep a straight face.

Ernst-: ~**fall** *m* emergency; **im** ~**fall** in case of emergency; **e~gemeint** *adj attr* serious; **e~haft** *adj* serious; (*bedenklich, gewichtig auch*) grave; (*eindringlich, eifrig*) earnest; **etw e~haft tun** to do sth seriously *or* in earnest; ~**haftigkeit** *f siehe adj* seriousness; gravity; earnestness; **e~lich** *adj* serious; (*bedrohlich auch*) grave; (*attr: eindringlich*) earnest; **es ist mein e~licher Wille** it is my earnest desire; **e~lich besorgt um** seriously *or* gravely concerned about; **e~lich böse werden** to get really angry.

Ernte *f -, -n* (a) (*das Ernten*) (*von Getreide*) harvest(ing); (*von Kartoffeln*) digging; (*von Äpfeln etc*) picking.
(b) (*Ertrag*) harvest (*an* +*dat* of); (*von Kartoffeln etc auch, von Äpfeln, fig*) crop. **die** ~ **bergen** (*form*) *or* **einbringen** to bring in the harvest, to harvest the crop(s); **die** ~ **seines Fleißes** the fruits of his industry; **der Tod hielt grausige** ~ (*liter*) death took a heavy toll; **du siehst aus, als sei dir die ganze** ~ **verhagelt** (*fig inf*) you look as though you've lost a shilling and found sixpence.

Ernte-: ~**arbeiter** *m* (*von Getreide*) reaper, harvester; (*von Kartoffeln, Obst, Hopfen*) picker; ~**ausfall** *m* crop shortfall (*spec*) *or* failure; ~(**dank**)**fest** *nt* harvest festival; ~**maschine** *f* reaper, harvester.

ernten *vt* (a) *Getreide* to harvest, to reap; *Kartoffeln* to dig, to get in; *Äpfel, Erbsen* to pick. **ich muß jetzt meinen Apfelbaum** ~ it's time I picked my apples. (b) (*fig*) *Früchte, Lohn, Unfrieden* to reap; (*Un*)*dank, Applaus, Spott* to get.

ernüchtern* *vt* to sober up; (*fig*) to bring down to earth, to sober. ~**d** sobering; **ich war sehr ernüchtert** my illusions were shattered.

Ernüchterung *f* sobering-up; (*fig*) disillusionment.

Er|oberer *m -s, -* conqueror.

er|obern* *vt* to conquer; *Festung, Stadt* to take, to capture; (*fig*) *Sympathie etc* to win, to capture; *Herz, Mädchen* to conquer; (*inf: ergattern*) to get hold of. **im Sturm** ~ (*Mil, fig*) to take by storm.

Er|oberung *f* (*lit, fig*) conquest; (*einer Festung, Stadt*) capture, taking. **eine** ~ **machen** (*fig inf*) to make a conquest; **auf** ~**en ausgehen** (*fig inf*) to be out to make conquests.

Er|oberungs-: ~**krieg** *m* war of conquest; ~**zug** *m* campaign of conquest.

er|öffnen* **1** *vt* (a) to open (*auch Fin, Mil etc*); *Ausstellung auch* to inaugurate (*form*); *Konkursverfahren* to institute, to initiate; *Testament* to open. **etw für eröffnet erklären** to declare sth open.
(b) (*Med*) *Geschwür* to lance; (*rare*) *Geburt* to induce.
(c) (*hum, geh*) **jdm etw** ~ to disclose *or* reveal sth to sb; **ich habe dir etwas zu** ~ I have something to tell you.
2 *vr* (a) (*Aussichten etc*) to open up, to present itself/themselves.
(b) (*geh*) **sich jdm** ~ to open one's heart to sb.

Er|öffnung *f siehe vt* (a) opening; inauguration; institution; initiation; opening. (b) lancing; induction. (c) (*hum, geh*) disclosure, revelation. **jdm eine** ~ **machen** to disclose *or* reveal sth to sb; **ich habe dir eine** ~ **zu machen** I have something to tell you.

Er|öffnungs-: ~**ansprache** *f* inaugural *or* opening address; ~**kurs** *m* opening price; ~**periode** *f* (*Med*) first stage of labour; ~**wehen** *pl* (*Med*) labour pains *pl*.

erogen *adj* erogenous.

er|örtern* *vt* to discuss (in detail).

Er|örterung *f* discussion. **zur** ~ **stehen** (*form*) to be under discussion.

Eros *m -, no pl* (*esp Philos*) Eros.

Eros-Center [ˈeːrɔsˌsɛntɐ] *nt -s, -* eros centre.

Erosion *f* (*Geol, Med*) erosion.

Eroten *pl* (*Art*) Cupids *pl*.

Erotik *f* eroticism.

Erotika *pl* (*Liter*) erotica *sing*.

Erotiker(in *f*) *m -s, -* eroticist.

erotisch *adj* erotic.

Erotomanie *f* (*Psych*) erotomania (*spec*).

Erpel *m -s, -* drake.

erpicht *adj* **auf etw** (*acc*) ~ **sein** to be keen on sth; **er ist nur auf Geld** ~ **sein** he's only after money.

erpressen* *vt Geld etc* to extort (*von* from); *jdn* to blackmail. **die Kidnapper haben den Vater erpreßt** the kidnappers tried to extort money from the father.

Erpresser(in *f*) *m -s, -* blackmailer; (*bei Entführung*) kidnapper.

Erpresserbrief *m* blackmail letter; (*bei Entführung*) ransom note *or* demand.

erpresserisch *adj* blackmailing *attr*.

Erpressermethoden *pl* blackmail *sing*.

Erpressung *f* (*von Geld, Zugeständnissen*) extortion; (*eines Menschen*) blackmail. **die Kidnapper hatten keinen Erfolg mit ihrer** ~ the kidnappers failed to get their ransom money *or* failed in their ransom attempt.

Erpressungsversuch *m* blackmail attempt; (*durch Gewaltandrohung*) attempt at obtaining money by menaces; (*bei Entführung*) attempt at getting a ransom.

erproben* *vt* to test; (*fig*) to (put to the) test. **erprobt** tried and tested, proven; (*zuverlässig*) reliable; (*erfahren*) experienced.

erquicken* *vt* (*old, liter*) to refresh.

erquicklich *adj* (*angenehm*) pleasant; (*anregend*) stimulating.

Erquickung *f* (*old*) refreshment. **es ist eine** ~, **zu ...** it is refreshing to ...

Errata *pl* (*Typ*) errata *pl*.

erraten* *vt irreg* to guess; *Rätsel* to guess (the answer to). **du hast es** ~! how did you guess?, you guessed!

erratisch *adj* (*Geol*) erratic. **ein** ~**er Block** an erratic.

errechnen* *vt* to calculate, to work out.

erregbar *adj* excitable; (*sexuell*) easily aroused; (*empfindlich*) sensitive. **schwer** ~ not easily aroused.

Erregbarkeit *f siehe adj* excitability; ability to be aroused; sensitivity.

erregen* **1** *vt* (a) (*aufregen*) *jdn, Nerven etc* to excite; (*sexuell auch*) to arouse; (*fig*) *Wellen, Meer* to agitate; (*erzürnen*) to infuriate, to annoy. **er war vor Wut ganz erregt** he was in a rage *or* fury; **in der Debatte ging es erregt zu** feelings ran high in the debate, the debate was quite heated; **erregte Diskussionen** heated discussions; **erregt lief er hin und her** he paced to and fro in a state of agitation; **freudig erregt** excited; *siehe* **Gemüt**.
(b) (*hervorrufen, erzeugen*) to arouse; *Zorn auch* to provoke; *Leidenschaften auch* to excite; *Aufsehen, öffentliches Ärgernis, Heiterkeit* to cause, to create; *Aufmerksamkeit* to attract; *Zweifel* to raise; (*Elec*) *Strom* to produce, to generate.
2 *vr* to get worked up *or* excited (*über* +*acc* about, over); (*sich ärgern*) to get annoyed (*über* +*acc* at).

Erreger *m -s, -* (*Med*) cause, causative agent (*spec*); (*Bazillus etc*) pathogene (*spec*).

Erregtheit *f siehe* **Erregung** (**b**).

Erregung *f* (a) *no pl siehe vt* (*a*) excitation; arousal, arousing; agitation; infuriation, infuriating.
(b) *no pl siehe vt* (*b*) arousal, arousing; excitation; causing, creating; attracting; raising; generation; *siehe* **Ärgernis**.
(c) (*Zustand*) (*esp angenehm*) excitement; (*sexuell auch*) arousal; (*Beunruhigung*) agitation; (*Wut*) rage; (*liter: des Meeres, der Wellen*) turbulence. **in** ~ **geraten** to get excited/aroused/agitated/into a rage; **jdn in** ~ **versetzen** to get sb excited/aroused/agitated/put sb into a rage; **das Meer in** ~ **versetzen** to make the sea churn.

erreichbar *adj* able to be reached; (*nicht weit*) within reach; (*Telec*) obtainable; *Glück, Ziel* attainable. **leicht** ~ easily reached/within easy reach/easily attainable; **schwer** ~ **sein** (*Ort*) not to be very accessible; (*Mensch*) to be difficult to get hold of; (*Gegenstand*) to be difficult to reach; **zu Fuß** ~ able to be reached on foot; (*nicht weit*) within walking distance; **in** ~**er Nähe** near at hand (+*gen* to); **der Direktor ist nie** ~ the director is never available; (*telefonisch*) the director can never be reached; **sind Sie morgen zu Hause** ~? can I get in touch with you at home tomorrow?, are you contactable at home tomorrow?; *siehe* **telefonisch**.

erreichen* *vt* to reach; *Ort auch* to get to, to arrive at; *Festland, Hafen auch* to make; *Zug* to catch; *Alter, Geschwindigkeit auch* to attain; *Absicht, Zweck* to achieve, to attain; (*einholen*) to catch up with; (*sich in Verbindung setzen mit*) *jdn, Büro etc* to contact, to get, to reach. **ein hohes Alter** ~ to live to a great age; **vom Bahnhof leicht zu** ~ within easy reach of the station; **zu Fuß zu** ~ able to be reached on foot; (*nicht weit*) within walking distance; **wann kann ich Sie morgen** ~? when can I get in touch with you tomorrow?; **er hat es dann doch noch erreicht, daß ich ihm die Erlaubnis gegeben habe** he eventually managed to make me give him permission after all; **du erreichst damit nur, daß ...** all you'll achieve that way is that ...; **wir haben nichts erreicht** we achieved nothing; **bei ihm war nichts zu** ~ you couldn't get anywhere with him *or* anything out of him.

Erreichung *f* (*form*) attainment; (*eines Ziels auch*) achievement. **bei** ~ **des 60. Lebensjahres** on reaching the age of 60.

erretten* *vt* (*liter, esp Rel*) to save, to deliver (*liter*).

Erretter *m* (*liter, esp Rel*) saviour (*esp Rel*), deliverer (*liter*).

Errettung *f, no pl* (*liter*) rescue, deliverance (*liter*); (*Rel*) salvation.

errichten* *vt* to erect (*auch Math*), to put up; (*fig: gründen*) to establish, to set up.

Errichtung *f, no pl* erection, construction; (*fig: Gründung*) establishment, setting-up.

erringen* *vt irreg* to gain, to win; *den 3. Platz, Erfolg* to gain, to achieve; *Rekord* to set. **ein hart errungener Sieg** a hard-won victory.

Er-Roman *m* (*Liter*) third-person novel.

erröten* *vi aux sein* (*über* +*acc* at) to flush; (*esp aus Verlegenheit, Scham*) to blush; (*Gesicht*) to go *or* turn red, to redden. **jdn zum E~ bringen** to make sb flush/blush.

Errungenschaft *f* achievement; (*inf: Anschaffung*) acquisition.

Ersatz *m -es, no pl* substitute (*auch Sport*); (*für Altes, Zerbrochenes, Mitarbeiter*) replacement; (*inf: die* ~*spieler*) substitutes *pl*; (*Mil:* ~*truppen*) replacements *pl*; (*Reserveheer*) reserves *pl*; (*das Ersetzen*) replacement, substitution; (*durch Geld*) compensation; (*von Kosten*) reimbursement. **als** *or* **zum** ~ as a substitute/replacement; **zum** ~ **der beschädigten Ware verpflichtet** obliged to replace the damaged item; **für eine Mutter kann nie ein** ~ **gefunden werden** there can be no substitute for a mother; **als** ~ **für jdn einspringen** to stand in for sb; **für etw** ~ **leisten** (*Jur*) to pay *or* provide compensation *or* restitution for sth; ~ **schaffen für** to find replacements/a replacement for, to replace.

Ersatz-: ~**anspruch** *m* (*Jur*) entitlement to compensation; ~**anspruch haben** to be entitled to compensation; ~**befriedigung** *f* (*Psych*) vicarious satisfaction; **das Rauchen ist eine** ~**befriedigung** smoking is a substitute; ~**dehnung** *f* (*Ling*) compensatory lengthening; ~**dienst** *m* (*Mil*) alternative service; ~**handlung** *f* (*Psych*) substitute (act); ~**kaffee** *m siehe*

Kaffee-Ersatz; ~**kasse** f private health insurance; ~**mann** m, pl -**männer** or -**leute** replacement; (Sport) substitute; ~**mine** f refill; ~**objekt** nt (Psych) substitute, surrogate; ~**pflicht** f obligation to pay compensation; e~**pflichtig** adj liable to pay compensation; ~**rad** nt (Aut) spare wheel; ~**reifen** m (Aut) spare tyre; ~**spieler** m (Sport) substitute; ~**teil** nt spare (part); ~**truppen** pl replacements pl; (Reserveheer) reserve troops pl; e~**weise** adv as an alternative.

ersaufen* vi irreg aux sein (sl) (a) (ertrinken) to drown, to be drowned. (b) (überschwemmt werden, Aut) to be flooded, to flood.

ersäufen* vt to drown. **seinen Kummer im Alkohol** ~ (inf) to drown one's sorrows (in drink) (inf).

erschaffen pret **erschuf**, ptp **erschaffen** vt to create.
Erschaffer m -s, - creator.
Erschaffung f creation.

erschallen pret **erscholl** or **erschallte**, ptp **erschollen** or **erschallt** vi aux sein (geh) (Stimme, Lachen) to ring out; (Trompete) to sound.

erschaudern* vi aux sein (geh) to shudder (bei at).

erschauen* vt (liter) to see, to espy (liter).

erschauern* vi aux sein (geh) (vor Kälte) to shiver; (vor Erregung, Ehrfurcht) to tremble, to shudder.

erscheinen* vi irreg aux sein to appear; (vorkommen, wirken wie auch) to seem (dat to); (sich sehen lassen: auf Party etc auch) to put in an appearance (auf + dat at); (zur Arbeit auch) to turn up (zu for); (Buch auch) to come out. **in einem anderen Licht** ~ to appear in a different light; **es erscheint (mir) wünschenswert** it seems or appears desirable (to me); **das Buch ist in** or **bei einem anderen Verlag erschienen** the book was published by or brought out by another publisher; **das Buch erscheint nicht mehr** the book is no longer published.

Erscheinen nt -s, no pl appearance; (von Geist etc) apparition; (von Buch auch) publication. **um rechtzeitiges** ~ **wird gebeten** you are kindly requested to attend punctually; **er dankte den Besuchern für ihr (zahlreiches)** ~ he thanked his (many) guests for coming; **mit seinem** ~ **hatte ich nicht mehr gerechnet** I no longer reckoned on his turning up or appearing.

Erscheinung f (a) no pl (das Erscheinen) appearance. **das Fest der** ~ (Eccl) (the Feast of) the Epiphany; **in** ~ **treten** (Merkmale) to appear, to manifest themselves (form); (Gefühle) to show themselves, to become visible or obvious; **sie tritt (persönlich) fast nie in** ~ she hardly ever appears (in person). (b) (äußere) appearance; (Philos auch, Natur~, Vorkommnis) phenomenon; (Krankheits~, Alters~) symptom; (Zeichen) sign, manifestation. **es ist eine bekannte** ~, **daß** ... it is a well-known (phenomenon) that ... (c) (Gestalt) figure. **seiner äußeren** ~ **nach** judging by his appearance; **er ist eine stattliche** ~ he is a fine figure of a man; **eine elegante** ~ **sein** to cut an elegant figure. (d) (Geister~) apparition; (Traumbild) vision.

Erscheinungs-: ~**bild** nt (Biol) phenotype; ~**form** f manifestation; ~**jahr** nt (von Buch) year of publication; ~**ort** m (von Buch) place of publication; ~**weise** f (von Zeitschrift) publication dates pl; ~**weise: monatlich** appearing monthly.

erschießen* irreg 1 vt to shoot (dead). 2 vr to shoot oneself. **dann kannst du dich** ~ you might as well stick your head in a gas oven; siehe **erschossen.**

Erschießung f shooting; (Jur: als Todesstrafe) execution. **die Verurteilten wurden zur** ~ **abgeführt** the condemned were led off to be shot; **er drohte mit** ~ **der Geiseln** he threatened to shoot the hostages; **Tod durch** ~ (Jur) death by firing squad.

erschlaffen* 1 vi aux sein (ermüden) to tire, to grow weary; (schlaff werden) to go limp; (Seil) to slacken, to go slack; (Interesse, Eifer) to wane, to flag. 2 vt to tire; (Medikament) to relax.

Erschlaffung f siehe vi tiredness, weariness; limpness; slackness; waning, flagging.

erschlagen* 1 vt irreg to kill, to strike dead (liter). **vom Blitz** ~ **werden** to be struck (dead) by lightning. 2 adj ~ **sein** (inf) (todmüde) to be worn out or dead beat (inf); (erstaunt) to be thunderstruck or flabbergasted (inf).

erschleichen* vt irreg (sich dat) **etw** ~ to obtain sth by devious means or in an underhand way; **sich** (dat) **jds Gunst/Vertrauen** ~ to worm oneself into sb's favour or good graces/confidence.

Erschleichung f obtainment by devious or underhand means or by artifice.

erschließen* irreg 1 vt (a) Gebiet, Absatzmarkt, Baugelände to develop, to open up; Einnahmequelle to find, to acquire; Rohstoffquellen, Bodenschätze to tap. (b) (folgern) to deduce, to infer (aus from); Gedicht to decipher, to work out the meaning of. **daraus ist zu** ~, **daß** ... it can be deduced or inferred from this, that ... (c) (Ling, Liter) to reconstruct. 2 vr (liter) (Blüte) to open (out). **sich jdm** ~ (verständlich werden) to disclose itself to sb (liter); **sich** (dat) **etw** ~ to master sth.

erschlossen 1 ptp of **erschließen.** 2 adj Gebiet developed; (Ling, Liter) reconstructed.

erscholl pret of **erschallen.**

erschollen ptp of **erschallen.**

erschöpfbar adj exhaustible.

erschöpfen* 1 vt Mittel, Thema, Geduld to exhaust; (ermüden auch) to tire out. **in erschöpftem Zustand** in a state of exhaustion. 2 vr (a) (körperlich) to exhaust oneself. (b) (fig) **sich in etw** (dat) ~ to amount to nothing more than sth; **darin erschöpft sich seine Bildung** that's the sum total of his education; **ein Schriftsteller, der sich erschöpft hat** an

author who has run out of ideas or expended his talent.

erschöpfend adj (a) (ermüdend) exhausting. (b) (ausführlich) exhaustive.

Erschöpfung f (a) (völlige Ermüdung) exhaustion, fatigue. **bis zur** ~ **arbeiten** to work to the point of exhaustion. (b) (der Mittel, Vorräte etc) exhaustion.

Erschöpfungszustand m state of exhaustion no pl. **er ist in einem nervösen** ~ he is in a state of nervous exhaustion.

erschossen 1 ptp of **erschießen.** 2 adj (inf) (völlig) ~ **sein** to be whacked (inf), to be dead (beat) (inf).

erschrak pret of **erschrecken 2.**

erschrecken 1 pret **erschreckte**, ptp **erschreckt** vt to frighten, to scare; (bestürzen) to startle, to give a shock or a start; (zusammenzucken lassen) to make jump, to give a start, to startle. **es hat mich erschreckt, wie schlecht** or **aussah** it gave me a shock or a start or it startled me to see how bad he looked.
2 pret **erschreckte** or **erschrak**, ptp **erschreckt** or **erschrocken** vir (vi: aux sein) to be frightened (vor + dat by); (bestürzt sein) to be startled; (zusammenzucken) to jump, to start. **ich bin erschrocken, wie schlecht** er aussah it gave me a shock or a start or I was shocked or startled to see how bad he looked; **sie erschrak beim Gedanken, daß** ... the thought that ... gave her a start or a scare; **sie erschrak bei dem Knall** the bang made her jump; ~ **Sie nicht, ich bin's nur** don't be frightened or afraid, it's only me; ~ **Sie nicht, wenn Sie ihn sehen, er ist sehr alt geworden** don't be alarmed when you see him, he's grown very old; siehe **erschrocken.**

Erschrecken nt -s, no pl fright, shock.

erschreckend 1 prp of **erschrecken.** 2 adj alarming, frightening. ~ **aussehen** to look dreadful or terrible; ~ **wenig Leute** alarmingly few people; ~ **unwissend** alarmingly ignorant; ~ **viele** an alarmingly large number.

erschrick imper sing of **erschrecken.**

erschrocken 1 ptp of **erschrecken 2.** 2 adj frightened, scared; (bestürzt) startled. ~ **hochspringen/zusammenzucken** to jump, to (give a) start.

erschuf pret of **erschaffen.**

erschüttern* vt Boden, Gebäude, (fig) Vertrauen, Glauben etc to shake; (fig) Glaubwürdigkeit to cast doubt upon; (fig) Gesundheit to unsettle, to upset; (fig: bewegen, Schock versetzen) to shake severely. **jdn in seinem Glauben** ~ to shake or shatter sb's faith; **sie war von seinem Tod tief erschüttert** she was severely shaken by his death; **seine Geschichte hat mich erschüttert** I was shattered (inf) by his story; **über etw** (acc) **erschüttert sein** to be shaken or shattered (inf) by sth; **mich kann nichts mehr** ~ nothing surprises me any more; **er läßt sich durch nichts** ~, **ihn kann nichts** ~ he always keeps his cool (inf).

erschütternd adj shattering (inf); Nachricht auch distressing; Verhältnisse auch shocking. **das war nicht** ~ (iro) that was nothing startling.

Erschütterung f (des Bodens etc) tremor, vibration; (fig) (der Ruhe, Wirtschaftslage) disruption; (des Selbstvertrauens) blow (gen to); (seelische Ergriffenheit) emotion, shock. **bei der** ~ **des Gebäudes** when the building shook; **die Krise kann zu einer** ~ **des Staates führen** the crisis could rock the state; **ihr Tod löste allgemeine** ~ **aus** her death shocked everyone.

erschweren* vt to make more difficult; Sachlage auch to aggravate; Fortschritt etc auch to impede, to hinder. **jdm etw** ~ to make sth more difficult for sb; ~**de Umstände** (Jur) aggravating circumstances; **es kommt noch** ~**d hinzu, daß** ... to make matters worse, ...

Erschwernis f difficulty.

Erschwerung f impediment (gen to), obstruction (gen to). **das bedeutet eine** ~ **meiner Arbeit** that will make my job more difficult.

erschwindeln* vt to obtain by fraud. **sich** (dat) (von jdm) **etw** ~ to swindle or do (inf) sb out of sth.

erschwingen* vt irreg to afford.

erschwinglich adj Preise within one's means, reasonable. **das Haus ist für uns nicht** ~ the house is not within our means.

ersehen* vt irreg (form) **etw aus etw** ~ to see or gather sth from sth.

ersehnen* vt (geh) to long for.

ersehnt adj longed-for. **heiß** or **lang** ~ much-longed-for; **meine geliebte, heiß** ~**e Clara!** my beloved Clara, I long for you so much!

ersetzbar adj replaceable; Schaden reparable.

ersetzen* vt to replace; (als Ersatz dienen für, an die Stelle treten von auch) to take the place of. **niemand kann Kindern die Mutter** ~ no-one can take the place of or replace a child's mother; **diese Vase kannst du mir nie** ~ you'll never be able to replace that vase.

Ersetzung f, no pl replacing; (von Schaden, Verlust) compensation, reparation (gen for); (von Unkosten) reimbursement, repayment.

ersichtlich adj obvious, clear, apparent. **hieraus ist klar** ~, **daß** ... it is obvious etc from this that ..., this shows clearly that ...

ersinnen* vt irreg to devise, to think up; (erfinden) to invent.

ersitzen* vt irreg (Jur) Anspruch to acquire by prescription.

erspähen* vt irreg to catch sight of, to spot, to espy (liter).

ersparen* 1 vt Vermögen, Zeit, Kummer etc to save. **jdm/sich etw** ~ to spare or save sb/oneself sth; **ich kann mir jeglichen Kommentar** ~ I don't think I need to comment; **jdm eine Demütigung** ~ to spare sb a humiliation; ~ **Sie sich die Mühe!** save or spare yourself the trouble; **Sie können sich alles Weitere** ~ you don't need to say any more; **ihr blieb auch nichts erspart** she was spared nothing; **das Ersparte** the savings pl. 2 vr to be superfluous or unnecessary.

Ersparnis f or (Aus) nt (a) no pl (an Zeit etc) saving (an +dat of). (b) usu pl savings pl.

erspielen* vt (Sport) Punkte, Sieg to win, to gain.

ersprießlich adj (förderlich) beneficial, advantageous; (nützlich) fruitful, profitable; (angenehm) pleasant.

erst adv (a) first; (anfänglich) at first. **mach ~ (ein)mal die Arbeit fertig** finish your work first; **~ mal ist das gar nicht wahr** ... first or for one thing it's just not true...; **~ einmal mußt du an deine Pflicht denken** you should consider your duty first; **wenn du das ~ einmal hinter dir hast** once you've got that behind you; **~ wollte er, dann wieder nicht** first he wanted to, then he didn't; **siehe Arbeit.**

(b) (nicht früher als, nicht mehr als, bloß) only; (nicht früher als auch) not until. **eben or gerade ~** just; **~ gestern** only yesterday; **~ jetzt** (gerade eben) only just; **~ jetzt verstehe ich** ... I have only just understood ...; **~ jetzt wissen wir** ... it is only now that we know ...; **~ morgen** not until or before tomorrow; **~ vor kurzem** only a short time ago; **es ist ~ 6 Uhr** it is only 6 o'clock; **wir fahren ~ übermorgen/~ später** we're not going until the day after tomorrow/until later; **sie war ~ 6 Jahre** she was only 6; **~ als** only when, not until; **~ wenn** only if or when, not until.

(c) (emph: gar, nun gar) **da ging's ~ richtig los** then it really got going; **was wird Mutter ~ sagen!** whatever will mother say!; **was wird dann ~ passieren?** whatever will happen then?; **sie ist schon ziemlich blöd, aber ~ ihre Schwester!** she is fairly stupid, but you should see her sister!; **da fange ich ~ gar nicht an** I simply won't (bother to) begin; **wie wird er sich ~ ärgern, wenn er das noch erfährt** he really will be annoyed when he finds out about that; **jetzt ~ recht/recht nicht!** that just makes me all the more determined; **da tat er es ~ recht!** so he did it deliberately; **das macht es ~ recht schlimm** that makes it even worse or all the worse; **da habe ich mich ~ recht geärgert** then I really did get annoyed.

(d) **wäre er doch ~ zurück!** if only he were back!; **diese Gerüchte darf man gar nicht ~ aufkommen lassen** these rumours mustn't even be allowed to start.

erstarken* vi aux sein (geh) to gain strength, to become stronger.

erstarren* vi aux sein (geh) (Finger) to grow stiff or numb; (Flüssigkeit) to solidify; (Gips, Zement etc) to set, to solidify; (Blut, Fett etc) to congeal; (fig: Blut) to freeze, to run cold; (Lächeln) to freeze; (vor Schrecken, Entsetzen etc) to be paralyzed or petrified (vor +dat with); (Haltung, Meinung) to become rigid or fixed; (Ideen, Kunstform etc) to ossify, to become rigid. **erstarrte Formen** fossilized forms.

Erstarrung f, no pl siehe vi stiffness, numbness; solidification; congelation, congealment; freezing; paralysis, petrification; ossification; fossilization.

erstatten* vt (a) Unkosten to refund, to reimburse. (b) (form) (Straf)anzeige gegen jdn ~ to report sb; Meldung ~ to report; Bericht ~ to (give a) report (über +acc on).

Erstattung f, no pl (von Unkosten) refund, reimbursement.

Erst-: e~aufführen ptp e~aufgeführt vt infin, ptp only (Theat) to give the first public performance of; ~aufführung f (Theat) first performance or night, première; ~auflage f first printing.

erstaunen* 1 vt to astonish, to amaze; siehe erstaunt. 2 vi (a) aux sein (old: überrascht sein) to be astonished or amazed. (b) (Erstaunen erregen) to cause astonishment or amazement, to astonish or amaze (people). **seine Körperbeherrschung erstaunt immer wieder** his physical control never fails to amaze.

Erstaunen nt -s, no pl astonishment, amazement. **jdn in ~ (ver)setzen** to astonish or amaze sb.

erstaunlich adj astonishing, amazing.

erstaunt 1 ptp of erstaunen. 2 adj astonished, amazed (über +acc about). **er sah mich ~ an** he looked at me in astonishment or amazement.

Erst-: ~ausgabe f first edition; ~besteigung f first ascent; e~beste(r, s) adj attr siehe erste(r, s) (b); ~druck m first edition.

erstechen* vt irreg to stab to death.

erstehen* irreg 1 vt (inf) to buy, to get. 2 vi aux sein (form) to arise; (Städte) to rise up; (Bibl: auf~) to rise.

Erste-Hilfe-Leistung f administering first aid.

ersteigen* vt irreg to climb; Felswand auch, Stadtmauer to scale. **er hat den Gipfel des Ruhms erstiegen** he has risen to the heights of fame.

Ersteigung f siehe vt ascent; scaling.

erstellen* vt (a) (bauen) to construct, to erect. (b) (anfertigen) Liste etc to draw up, to make out.

Erstellung f siehe vt construction, erection; drawing up, making out.

erstemal adv **das ~** the first time; **das tue ich das ~** I'm doing this for the first time, it's the first time I've done this.

erstenmal adv **zum ~** for the first time.

erstens adv first(ly), in the first place.

erste(r, s) adj (a) first; (fig: führend auch) best, foremost. **Seite der Zeitung** front. **~r Stock, ~ Etage** first floor, second floor (US); **die ~ Klasse** (Rail) the first class (compartment); **~r Klasse fahren** to travel first class; **der ~ Rang** (Theat) the dress-circle, the (first) balcony (US); **~ Güte or Qualität** top quality; **E~ Hilfe** first aid; **die drei ~n/die ~n drei** the first three/the first three (from each group); **der E~ in der Klasse** the top of or best in the class; **die E~n werden die Letzten sein** (Bibl) the first shall be last; **E~r unter Gleichen** first among equals; **der E~ des Monats** the first (day) of the month; **vom nächsten E~n an** as of the first of next month; **das ist das ~, was ich höre** that's the first I've heard of it; **er kam als ~r** he was the first to come; **als ~s** first of all; **am ~n** first; **an ~r**

Stelle in the first place; **dieses Thema steht an ~r Stelle unserer Tagesordnung** this subject comes first on our agenda; **fürs ~** for the time being, for the present; **in ~r Linie** first and foremost; **zum ~n, zum zweiten, zum dritten** (bei Auktionen) going, going, gone!; **siehe Blick, Hand, Mal** etc, **siehe auch vierte(r, s).**

(b) **nimm das ~ beste!** take anything!; **er hat den ~n besten Kühlschrank gekauft** he bought the first fridge he saw, he bought any old fridge (inf); siehe beste(r, s).

ersterben* vi irreg aux sein (liter) to die; (Lärm, Wort) to die away. **ich ersterbe vor Ehrfurcht!** (iro) I am filled with awe, I am awestruck.

erstere(r, s) adj the former. **der/die/das ~** the former.

Erste(r)-Klasse- (Rail): **~-Abteil** nt first class compartment; **~-Wagen** m first class carriage (Brit) or car (US).

Erst-: ~gebärende f primigravida (spec); e~geboren adj attr first-born; ~geburt f (Kind) first-born (child); (Tier) first young; (Hist: auch ~geburtsrecht) birthright, right of primogeniture (Jur); e~genannt adj attr first-mentioned; (wichtigster) first to be mentioned.

ersticken* 1 vt jdn to suffocate, to smother; Feuer to smother; Geräusche to stifle, to smother; (fig: unterdrücken) Aufruhr etc to suppress. **mit erstickter Stimme** in a choked voice; **es war ~d heiß** it was stiflingly or suffocatingly hot; siehe Keim.

2 vi aux sein to suffocate; (Feuer) to die, to go out; (Stimme) to become choked. **an etw** (dat) **~** to be suffocated by sth; **an einer Gräte ~** to choke (to death) on a bone; **vor Lachen ~** to choke with laughter; **das Kind erstickt förmlich unter der Liebe der Mutter** the child is smothered by mother-love; **in der Arbeit ~** (inf) to be snowed under with work, to be up to one's neck in work (inf); **er erstickt im Geld** (inf) he's rolling in money (inf); **die Luft im Zimmer war zum E~** the air in the room was suffocating or stifling.

Erstickung f suffocation, asphyxiation.

Erstickungs-: ~gefahr f danger of suffocation; ~tod m death from or by suffocation, asphyxia.

erstkl. abbr of erstklassig.

Erst-: e~klassig adj first-class, first-rate; ~kläßler(in f) m (esp S Ger, Sw) pupil in the first class of primary school, first-grader (US); ~kommunion f first communion.

Erstling m (Kind) first (child); (Tier) first young; (Werk) first work or baby (inf).

Erstlingswerk nt first work.

erst-: ~malig 1 adj first; 2 adv for the first time; ~mals adv for the first time.

erstrahlen* vi aux sein (liter) to shine. **im Lichterglanz ~** to be aglitter (with lights).

erstrangig [ˈeːɐʃtraŋɪç] adj first-rate.

erstreben* vt to strive for or after, to aspire to.

erstrebenswert adj worthwhile, desirable; Beruf desirable.

erstrecken* vr to extend (auf, über +acc over); (räumlich auch) to reach, to stretch (auf, über +acc over); (zeitlich auch) to carry on, to last (auf, über +acc for). **sich auf jdn/etw ~** (betreffen) to apply to sb/sth.

Erst-: ~sendung f (Rad, TV) first broadcast; ~stimme f first vote; ~tagsbrief m first-day cover; ~tagsstempel m date stamp or postmark from a first-day cover.

erstunken adj: **das ist ~ und erlogen** (inf) that's a pack of lies.

erstürmen* vt (Mil) to (take by) storm; (liter) Gipfel to conquer.

Erstürmung f (Mil) storming.

Erst-: ~veröffentlichung f first publication; ~wähler m first-time voter.

ersuchen* vt (form) to request (jdn um etw sth of sb).

Ersuchen nt -s, - (form) request. **auf ~ von** at the request of; **ein ~ an jdn richten** or **stellen** to make a request of sb.

ertappen* vt to catch. **jdn/sich bei etw ~** to catch sb/oneself at or doing sth; **ich habe ihn dabei ertappt** I caught him at it or doing it; **ich habe ihn beim Stehlen ertappt** I caught him stealing.

ertasten* vt to feel, to make out by touch(ing); (um zu finden) to feel for.

erteilen* vt to give; Genehmigung auch to grant; Lizenz to issue; Auftrag auch to place (jdm with sb). **jdm einen Verweis ~** to reproach sb; Unterricht **~** to teach, to give lessons; siehe Wort.

Erteilung f siehe vt giving; granting; issue; placing. **für die ~ von Auskünften zuständig** responsible for giving information.

ertönen* vi aux sein (geh) to sound, to ring out. **von etw ~** to resound with sth; **~ lassen** to sound; **er ließ seine tiefe Baßstimme ~** his deep bass voice rang out.

Ertrag m -(e)s, ¨e (von Acker) yield; (Ergebnis einer Arbeit) return; (Einnahmen) proceeds pl, return. **~ abwerfen** or **bringen** to bring in a return; **vom ~ seiner Bücher/seines Kapitals leben** to live on the proceeds from one's books/the return on one's capital.

ertragen* vt irreg to bear; Schmerzen, Leiden, Schicksal auch to endure; Ungewißheit, Zweifel auch to tolerate; (esp in Frage, Verneinung auch) to stand. **das ist nicht mehr zu ~** it's unbearable or intolerable; **wie erträgst du nur seine Launen?** how do you put up with or stand his moods?

erträglich adj bearable, endurable; (leidlich) tolerable.

Erträglichkeit f bearableness, endurableness.

ertrag-: ~los adj Acker unproductive, infertile; Geschäft unprofitable; ~reich adj Acker productive, fertile; Geschäft profitable, lucrative.

Ertrags-: e~arm adj Boden poor, infertile; ~lage f returns pl, profits pl, profit situation; ~minderung f decrease in profit(s) or return(s); ~steigerung f increase in profit(s) or return(s); ~steuer f profit(s) tax, tax on profit(s); ~wert m

capitalized value of potential yield/return(s).
ertränken* 1 *vt* to drown. **seinen Kummer** *or* **seine Sorgen im Alkohol** ~ to drown one's sorrows. 2 *vr* to drown oneself.
erträumen* *vt* to dream of, to imagine. **eine erträumte Welt** an imaginary world; **das war alles nur erträumt** it was all in the mind; **sich (***dat***) etw** ~ to dream of sth, to imagine sth.
ertrinken* *vi irreg aux sein* to drown, to be drowned.
Ertrinken *nt* **-s**, *no pl* drowning.
ertrotzen* *vt (geh)* **(sich** *dat***) etw** ~ to obtain sth by sheer obstinacy *or* defiance.
ertüchtigen* *(geh)* 1 *vt* to get in (good) trim, to toughen up. 2 *vr* to keep fit, to train.
Ertüchtigung *f (geh)* getting in (good) trim, toughening up. **körperliche** ~ physical training.
er|übrigen* 1 *vt Zeit, Geld* to spare. 2 *vr* to be unnecessary *or* superfluous. **jedes weitere Wort erübrigt sich** there's nothing more to be said.
eruieren* *vt (form) Sachverhalt* to investigate, to find out; *(esp Aus) Person* to trace.
Eruption *f (Geol, Med, fig)* eruption.
Eruptivgestein *nt* volcanic rock.
erw. *abbr of* **erweitert** extended.
erwachen* *vi aux sein* to awake, to wake (up); *(aus Ohnmacht etc)* to come to *or* round *(aus* from); *(fig: Gefühle, Verdacht)* to be aroused; *(liter: Tag)* to dawn. **von etw** ~ to be awoken *or* woken up by sth; **ein böses E~** *(fig)* a rude awakening.
erwachsen* 1 *vi irreg aux sein (geh)* to arise, to develop; *(Vorteil, Kosten etc)* to result, to accrue; *(Stadt auch)* to grow. **daraus erwuchsen ihm Unannehmlichkeiten** that caused him some trouble; **daraus wird ihm kein Nutzen** ~ no advantage will accrue to him (from this); **in ihm erwuchs die Erkenntnis, daß ...** he came to the realization that ...; **mir sind Zweifel** ~ I have come to have doubts.
2 *adj* grown-up, adult. ~ **sein** *(Mensch)* to be grown-up *or* an adult.
Erwachsenen-: ~bildung *f* adult education; **~taufe** *f* adult baptism.
Erwachsene(r) *mf decl as adj* adult, grown-up.
erwägen* *vt irreg (überlegen)* to consider, to deliberate; *(prüfen)* to consider, to examine; *(in Betracht ziehen)* to consider, to take into consideration.
erwägenswert *adj* worthy of consideration, worth considering.
Erwägung *f* consideration. **aus folgenden ~en (heraus)** for the following reasons *or* considerations; **etw in** ~ **ziehen** to consider sth, to take sth into consideration.
erwählen* *vt* to choose.
erwähnen* *vt* to mention, to refer to, to make mention of *or* reference to. **ich möchte nur kurz erwähnt haben, daß ...** I would just briefly like to mention that ...; **davon hat er nichts erwähnt, das hat er mit keinem Wort erwähnt** he did not mention *or* refer to it at all, he made no mention of *or* reference to it; **beiläufig** *or* **nebenbei** ~ to mention in passing, to make a passing reference to.
erwähnenswert *adj* worth mentioning.
Erwähnung *f* mention *(gen* of), reference *(gen* to). ~ **finden** *(form)* to be mentioned, to be referred to.
erwandern* *vt* **er hat sich** *(dat)* **die ganze Insel erwandert** he's walked all over the island and knows its inside out; **ich möchte (mir) Arran** ~ I'd like to go walking on Arran and get to know it.
erwärmen* 1 *vt* to warm, to heat; *(fig)* to warm. 2 *vr* to warm up. **sich für jdn/etw** ~ *(fig)* to take to sb/sth; **ich kann mich für Goethe/Geometrie nicht** ~ Goethe/geometry leaves me cold.
erwarten* *vt Gäste, Ereignis* to expect. **etw von jdm/etw** ~ to expect sth from *or* of sb/sth; **ein Kind** *or* **Baby** ~ to be expecting a child *or* baby; **das war zu** ~ that was to be expected; **er erwartet, daß wir sofort gehorchen** he expects us to obey immediately; **etw sehnsüchtig** ~ to long for sth; **sie kann den Sommer kaum noch** ~ she can hardly wait for the summer, she's really looking forward to the summer; **sie kann es kaum** ~**, daß Vater heimkommt** she can hardly wait for father to come home, she's really looking forward to father coming home; **was mich da wohl erwartet?** I wonder what awaits me there; **von ihr ist nicht viel Gutes zu** ~ no good can come of her; **da hast du (et)was zu** ~**!** *(iro)* then you'll have something to think about!; **es steht zu** ~**, daß ...** *(form)* it is to be expected that ...; **über E~** beyond expectation; *siehe* **wider.**
Erwartung *f* expectation; *(Spannung, Ungeduld)* anticipation. **in** ~ **Ihrer baldigen Antwort** *(form)* in anticipation of *or* looking forward to *or* awaiting your early reply; **zu großen ~en berechtigen** to show great promise; **den ~en entsprechen** to come up to expectations; *(Voraussetzung erfüllen)* to meet the requirements.
erwartungs-: ~gemäß *adv* as expected; **~voll** *adj* expectant.
erwecken* *vt* (a) *(liter: aus Schlaf, Lethargie)* to wake, to rouse; *(Bibl: vom Tode)* to raise (from the dead). **etw zu neuem Leben** ~ to resurrect *or* revive sth.
(b) *(fig) Freude, Begeisterung etc* to arouse; *Hoffnungen, Zweifel* to raise; *Erinnerungen* to bring back. **(bei jdm) den Eindruck** ~**, als ob ...** to give (sb) the impression that ...
Erweckung *f, no pl (Bibl: vom Tode)* resurrection, raising (from the dead); *(Rel)* revival; *(fig)* arousal, awakening.
Erweckungsbewegung *f (Rel)* revivalist movement, revivalism.
erwehren* *vr (+gen) (geh)* to ward *or* fend off. **er konnte sich kaum der Tränen** ~ he could hardly keep *or* hold back his tears; **ich konnte mich des Lachens nicht** ~ I couldn't refrain from laughing; *siehe* **Eindruck.**
erweichen* *vt* to soften; *(fig: überreden auch)* to move. **jds Herz** ~ to touch sb's heart; **sich (durch Bitten) nicht** ~

lassen to be unmoved (by entreaties), not to give in *or* yield (to entreaties).
Erweis *m* **-es**, **-e** *(form)* proof.
erweisen* *irreg* 1 *vt* (a) *(nachweisen)* to prove. **eine erwiesene Tatsache** a proven fact; **es ist noch nicht erwiesen** it has not been proved yet.
(b) *(zuteil werden lassen)* to show. **jdm einen Gefallen/ Dienst** ~ to do sb a favour/service; **jdm Achtung** ~ to pay respect to sb; **jdm Gutes** ~ to be good to sb; **wir danken für die erwiesene Anteilnahme** we thank you for the sympathy you have shown.
2 *vr* **sich als etw** ~ to prove to be sth, to turn out to be sth; **sich als zuverlässig** ~ to prove to be reliable, to prove oneself reliable; **sich jdm gegenüber dankbar** ~ to show *or* prove one's gratitude to sb, to show *or* prove oneself grateful to sb; **es hat sich erwiesen, daß ...** it turned out that ...
erweislich *adj (geh)* provable, demonstrable. **das ist** ~ **falsch** that is demonstrably false.
erweitern* *vtr* to widen, to enlarge; *Absatzgebiet auch, Geschäft, Abteilung* to expand; *Kleid* to let out; *(Med)* to dilate; *(Math) Bruch* to reduce to the lowest common denominator; *(fig) Interessen, Kenntnisse, Horizont* to broaden; *Macht* to extend. **im erweiterten Sinn** in an extended sense.
Erweiterung *f siehe vtr* widening, enlargement; expansion; letting out; dilation; reduction to the lowest common denominator; broadening; extension.
Erweiterungsbau *m* extension.
Erwerb *m* **-(e)s**, **-e** *no pl* acquisition; *(Kauf)* purchase. **beim** ~ **eines Autos** when buying a car. (b) *(Brot~, Beruf)* living; *(Verdienst, Lohn)* earnings *pl*, income. **einem** ~ **nachgehen** to follow a profession.
erwerben* *vt irreg* to acquire; *Achtung, Ehre, Vertrauen* to earn, to gain, to win; *Pokal* to win; *(Sport) Titel* to win, to gain; *(käuflich)* to purchase. **sich** *(dat)* **etw** ~ to acquire *etc* sth; **sich** *(dat)* **sein Brot** ~ *(old)* to earn one's daily bread *(old)*; **er hat sich** *(dat)* **große Verdienste um die Firma erworben** he has done great service for the firm.
Erwerbs-: ~fähig *adj (form)* capable of gainful employment; **~fähigkeit** *f (form)* fitness for work; **e~gemindert** *adj* suffering a reduction in (one's) earning capacity; **~kampf** *m* rat-race; **e~los** *adj siehe* **arbeitslos**; **~minderung** *f* reduction in (one's) earning capacity; **~quelle** *f* source of income; **~sinn** *m* business sense *or* acumen; **e~tätig** *adj (gainfully)* employed; **~tätigkeit** *f* gainful employment; **~trieb** *m siehe* **~sinn**; **e~unfähig** *adj* unable to work, incapacitated; **~unfähigkeit** *f* inability to work, incapacitation; **~zweig** *m* line of business.
Erwerbung *f* acquisition.
erwidern* *vt* (a) *(antworten)* to reply *(auf +acc* to); *(schroff)* to retort. **darauf konnte er nichts** ~ he couldn't answer that, he had no answer to that; **auf meine Frage erwiderte sie, daß ...** in reply *or* answer to my question, she said that ...
(b) *(entgegnen, entgelten) Besuch, Grüße, Komplimente, Gefühle* to return, to reciprocate; *Blick, (Mil) Feuer* to return.
Erwiderung *f* (a) *(Antwort)* reply, answer; *(schroff)* retort, rejoinder. **in** ~ **Ihres Schreibens vom ...** *(form)* in reply *or* answer to your letter of the ... (b) return, reciprocation; *(von Gefühlen)* reciprocation; *(Mil: des Feuers)* return. **ihre Liebe fand bei ihm keine** ~ he did not return her love.
erwiesen *ptp of* **erweisen.**
erwiesenermaßen *adv* as has been proved *or* shown. **er hat dich** ~ **betrogen** it has been proved *or* shown that he has deceived you; **der Angeklagte ist** ~ **schuldig** the accused has been proved guilty.
erwirken* *vt (form)* to obtain.
erwirtschaften* *vt* to make *or* obtain through good *or* careful management. **seine Frau hat ein kleines Auto erwirtschaftet** his wife has bought a little car with her savings.
erwischen* *vt (inf) (erreichen, ertappen)* to catch; *(ergattern)* to get (hold of). **jdn beim Stehlen** ~ to catch sb stealing; **du darfst dich nicht** ~ **lassen** you mustn't get caught; **ihn hat's erwischt!** *(verliebt)* he's got it bad *(inf)*; *(krank)* he's got it, he's caught it; *(gestorben)* he's had it *(inf)*; **die Kugel/der Hund ihn am Bein erwischt** the bullet got *or* caught/the dog got him in the leg.
erworben 1 *ptp of* **erwerben.** 2 *adj* acquired *(auch Med, Jur)*.
erwünscht *adj Wirkung etc* desired; *Eigenschaft, Kenntnisse* desirable; *(willkommen) Gelegenheit, Anwesenheit* welcome. **persönliche Vorstellung** ~ applications should be made in person; **du bist hier nicht** ~**!** you're not welcome *or* wanted here!
erwürgen* *vt* to strangle, to throttle.
Erz *nt* **-es**, **-e** *ore; (Bronze)* bronze. **wie in** *or* **aus** ~ **gegossen dastehen** to stand there like a statue.
Erz- *in cpds (Geol)* mineral, ore; *(Rang bezeichnend)* arch-; **~ader** *f* mineral vein, vein of ore.
erzählen* 1 *vt* (a) *Geschichte, Witz etc* to tell; *(berichten) Traum, Vorfall, Erlebnis etc auch* to relate, to recount, to give an account of. **er hat seinen Traum/den Vorfall erzählt** he told *(us etc)* about his dream/the incident; **jdm etw** ~ to tell sth to sb; **man erzählt sich, daß ...** people say *or* it is said that ...; **erzähl mal, was/wie ...** tell me/us what/how ...; **Mutti, erzähl mir was** tell me a story, mummy; **erzähl mal was** *(inf)* say something; **wem** ~ **Sie das!** *(inf)* you're telling me!; **das kannst du einem anderen** ~ *(inf)* pull the other one *(inf) or* leg *(inf)*, tell that to the marines *(inf)*; **mir kannst du viel** *or* **nichts** ~ *(inf)* don't give *or* tell me that! *(inf)*; **davon kann ich etwas** ~**!** *(inf)* I can tell you a thing *or* two about it; **dem werd' ich was** ~**!** *(inf)* I'll have something to say to him, I'll give him a piece of my mind *(inf)*; *siehe* **Großmutter.**
(b) *(Liter)* to narrate. **~de Dichtung** narrative fiction;

Grundformen des E~s basic forms of narrative; **erzählte Zeit** narrated time.

2 *vi* **(a)** to tell (*von* about, *of* *liter*). **er kann gut** ~ he tells good stories, he's a good story-teller; **er hat die ganze Nacht erzählt** he told stories all night.

(b) (*Liter*) to narrate.

erzählenswert *adj* worth telling.

Erzähler(in *f*) *m* **-s,** - narrator (*auch Liter*); (*Geschichten*~) story-teller; (*Schriftsteller*) narrative writer.

erzählerisch *adj* narrative.

Erzählerstandpunkt *m* (*Liter*) point of view of the narrator.

Erzähl-: ~**formen** *pl* (*Liter*) narrative forms *pl*; ~**gedicht** *nt* (*Liter*) narrative poem.

Erzählung *f* (*Liter*) story, tale; (*das Erzählen*) narration, relation; (*Bericht, Schilderung*) account. **in Form einer** ~ in narrative form; **Dialog und** ~ **wechseln sich ab** dialogue alternates with narrative.

Erzählzeit *f* (*Liter*) narrative time.

Erz-: ~**bergbau** *m* ore mining; ~**bischof** *m* archbishop; **e**~**bischöflich** *adj attr* archiepiscopal; ~**bistum** *nt* archbishopric; **e**~**böswicht** *m* arrant rogue (*old*), arch-villain; ~**diözese** *f* archbishopric; **e**~**dumm** *adj* (*inf*) extremely stupid.

erzeigen* (*geh*) **1** *vt* **jdm etw** ~ to show sb sth, to show *or* display sth to sb; **das erzeigte Interesse** the interest shown. **2** *vr* **sich dankbar** ~ to show *or* prove oneself grateful.

erzen *adj* (*liter*) bronze.

Erz|engel *m* archangel.

erzeugen* *vt* (*Chem, Elec, Phys*) to generate, to produce; (*Comm*) *Produkt* to produce, to manufacture; *Wein, Butter etc* to produce; (*rare*) *Kinder* to beget (*old*); (*fig: bewirken*) to cause, to engender, to give rise to. **Mißtrauen/Angst etc in** *or* **bei jdm** ~ to give rise to *or* produce *or* engender a sense of mistrust/fear *etc* in sb; **der Autor versteht es, Spannung zu** ~ the author knows how to create *or* generate tension.

Erzeuger *m* **-s,** - (*form: Vater*) begetter (*old*), progenitor (*form*); (*Comm*) producer, manufacturer; (*von Natur-produkten*) producer.

Erzeuger-: ~**land** *nt* country of origin; ~**preis** *m* manufacturer's price.

Erzeugnis *nt* product; (*Industrieprodukt auch*) manufacture (*esp Comm*); (*Agr*) produce *no indef art, no pl*; (*fig: geistiges, künstlerisches auch*) creation. **deutsches** ~ made in Germany; ~ **seiner Phantasie** figment of his imagination.

Erzeugung *f, no pl* (*Chem, Elec, Phys*) generation, production; (*von Waren*) manufacture, production; (*eines Kindes*) procreation (*form*); (*geistige, künstlerische*) creation.

Erzeugungsgrammatik *f* (*Ling*) generative grammar.

Erz-: **e**~**faul** *adj* bone-idle; ~**feind** *m* arch-enemy; (*Theologie auch*) arch-fiend; ~**gang** *m* **siehe** ~**ader**; ~**gauner** *m* (*inf*) cunning *or* sly rascal (*inf*); ~**gießer** *m* brass-founder; ~**gießerei** *f* brass-foundry; ~**grube** *f* ore mine; **e**~**haltig** *adj* ore-bearing, metalliferous (*spec*); ~**halunke** *m* (*inf*) **siehe** ~**gauner**; ~**herzog** *m* archduke; ~**herzogin** *f* archduchess; **e**~**herzoglich** *adj attr* archducal; ~**herzogtum** *nt* archduchy; ~**hütte** *f* smelting works *sing or pl*.

erziehbar *adj Kind* educable; *Tier* trainable. **schwer** ~ *Kind* difficult; *Hund* difficult to train; **das Kind ist schwer** ~ he/she is a problem *or* a difficult child; **ein Heim für schwer** ~**e Kinder** a home for problem *or* difficult children.

erziehen* *vt irreg Kind* to bring up; *Tier, Körper, Gehör* to train; (*ausbilden*) to educate. **ein Tier/ein Kind zur Sauberkeit** *etc* ~ to train an animal/to teach *or* bring up a child to be clean *etc*; **jdn zu einem tüchtigen Menschen** ~ to bring sb up to be a fine, upstanding person; **ein gut/schlecht erzogenes Kind** a well-/badly-brought-up child, a well-/ill-bred child.

Erzieher *m* **-s,** - educator; (*Lehrer*) teacher; (*Privatlehrer*) tutor. **Unterschrift des** ~**s** signature of parent *or* legal guardian; **der Vater war ein strenger** ~ the father brought his children up strictly.

Erzieherin *f* educator; (*Lehrerin*) teacher; (*Gouvernante*) governess.

erzieherisch *adj* educational. **ein Vater mit wenig** ~**em Können** a father with little skill in bringing up children; **verschiedene** ~ **Methoden** different ways of bringing up children; **das ist** ~ **falsch** that is no way to bring up children.

Erziehung *f, no pl* upbringing; (*Ausbildung*) education; (*das Erziehen*) bringing up; (*von Tieren, Körper, Gehör*) training; (*Manieren*) upbringing, (*good*) breeding. **die** ~ **zu(r) Höflichkeit** teaching (sb) good manners *or* politeness; (*durch Eltern auch*) bringing (sb) up to be polite *or* well-mannered.

Erziehungs-: ~**anstalt** *f* approved school, borstal (*Brit*), reformatory (*US*); ~**beihilfe** *f* (*dated*) **siehe Ausbildungsbeihilfe**; ~**beratung** *f* educational guidance *or* counselling; **e**~**berechtigt** *adj* having parental authority; ~**berechtigte(r)** *mf* parent *or* (legal) guardian; ~**gewalt** *f* parental authority; ~**heim** *nt* **siehe** ~**anstalt**; ~**methode** *f* educational method; ~**mittel** *nt* aid to education; ~**wesen** *nt* educational system; ~**wissenschaft** *f* educational science; ~**wissenschaftler** *m* educationalist.

erzielen* *vt Erfolg, Ergebnis* to achieve, to attain, to obtain; *Kompromiß, Einigung* to reach, to arrive at; *Geschwindigkeit* to reach; *Gewinn* to make, to realize; *Preis* (*Mensch*) to secure; (*Gegenstand*) to fetch; (*Sport*) *Tor, Punkte* to score; *Rekord* to set. **was willst du damit** ~? what do you hope to achieve by that?

erzittern* *vi aux sein* (*liter*) to tremble, to shake, to quake.

Erz-: **e**~**konservativ** *adj* ultraconservative; (*Pol auch*) dyed-in-the-wool conservative; ~**lager** *nt* ore deposit; ~**lügner** *m* (*inf*) inveterate *or* unmitigated liar; ~**lump** *m* (*inf*) thorough *or* proper (*inf*) scoundrel; ~**reaktionär** *m* ultrareactionary.

erzürnen* (*geh*) **1** *vt* to anger, to incense. **2** *vr* to become *or* grow angry (*über* +*acc* about).

Erzvater *m* (*Bibl*) patriarch; (*fig*) forefather.

erzwingen* *vt irreg* to force; (*gerichtlich*) to enforce. **etw von jdm** ~ to force sth from *or* out of sb; **sie erzwangen den Zutritt zur Wohnung mit Gewalt** they forced entry into the flat.

es[1] *pers pron gen* **seiner,** *dat* **ihm,** *acc* **es (a)** (*auf Dinge bezogen*) it; (*auf männliches Wesen bezogen*) (*nom*) he; (*acc*) him; (*auf weibliches Wesen bezogen*) (*nom*) she; (*acc*) her.

(b) (*auf vorangehende Substantive, Adjektive bezüglich*) **wer ist da?** — **ich bin** ~ who's there? — it's me *or* I (*form*); **sie ist klug, er ist** ~ **auch** she is clever, so is he; **ich höre jemanden klopfen,** ~ **sind die Kinder** I can hear somebody knocking, it's the children; **wer ist die Dame?** — ~ **ist meine Frau** who's the lady? — it's *or* she's my wife.

(c) (*auf vorangehenden Satzinhalt bezüglich*) **das Glas wurde zerbrochen, keiner will** ~ **getan haben** the glass had been broken, but nobody will admit to doing it; **alle dachten, daß das ungerecht war, aber niemand sagte** ~ everyone thought it was unjust, but nobody said so.

(d) (*rein formales Subjekt*) ~ **ist kalt/8 Uhr/Sonntag** it's cold/8 o'clock/Sunday; ~ **friert mich** I am cold; ~ **freut mich, daß** ... I am pleased *or* glad that ...; ~ **sei denn, daß** ... unless ...

(e) (*rein formales Objekt*) **ich halte** ~ **für richtig, daß** ... I think it (is) right that ...; **ich hoffe** ~ I hope so; **ich habe** ~ **satt, zu** (+*infin*), **ich bin** ~ **müde, zu** (+*infin*) I've had enough of (+*prp*), I'm tired of (+*prp*).

(f) (*bei unpersönlichem Gebrauch des Verbs*) ~ **gefällt mir** I like it; ~ **klopft** there's a knock (at the door); ~ **regnet** it's raining; ~ **sich** (*dat*) **schön machen** to have a good time; **bei dem Licht liest** ~ **sich gut** this light is good for reading; ~ **sitzt sich bequem hier** it's comfortable sitting here; ~ **darf geraucht werden** smoking is permitted; ~ **wurde gesagt, daß** ... it was said that ...; ~ **wurde getanzt** there was dancing; **er läßt** ~ **nicht zu, daß ich länger bleibe** he won't allow me to stay any longer.

(g) (*Einleitewort mit folgendem Subjekt*) ~ **geschah ein Unglück** there was an accident; ~ **gibt viel Arbeit** there's a lot of work; ~ **gibt viele Leute, die** ... there are a lot of people who ...; ~ **kamen viele Leute** a lot of people came; ~ **lebe der König!** long live the king!; ~ **meldete sich niemand** nobody replied; ~ **war einmal eine Königin** once upon a time there was a queen.

es[2] *nt* **-,** - (*Mus*) E flat minor.

Es *nt* **-,** - **(a)** (*Mus: Dur*) E flat. **(b)** (*Psych*) id, Id.

Esche *f* **-, -n** ash-tree.

eschen *adj* (*rare*) ashen (*rare*).

Eschenholz *nt* ash.

Esel *m* **-s,** - donkey, ass (*old, esp Bibl*); (*inf: Dummkopf*) (silly) ass. **du alter** ~! you are an ass (*inf*) *or* a fool; **ich** ~! I am an ass *or* a fool!, silly (old) me!; **störrisch wie ein** ~ as stubborn as a mule; **der** ~ **nennt sich selbst zuerst** it's rude to put yourself first; **ein** ~ **schimpft den andern Langohr** (*prov*) (it's a case of) the pot calling the kettle black (*prov*); **wenn es dem** ~ **zu wohl wird, geht er aufs Eis (tanzen)** (*Prov*) complacency makes one *or* you reckless.

Eselei *f* (*inf*) stupidity; (*Streich*) silly prank.

Eselin *f* she-ass.

Esels-: ~**brücke** *f* (*Gedächtnishilfe*) mnemonic, aide-mémoire; (*gereimt*) jingle; (*Sch sl: Klatsche*) crib (*inf*), pony (*US*); ~**ohr** *nt* (*fig*) dog-ear, turned-down corner; **ein Buch mit** ~**ohren** a dog-eared book.

Eskalation *f* escalation.

eskalieren* *vti* (*vi: aux sein*) to escalate.

Eskalierung *f* escalation.

Eskamotage [eskamo'ta:ʒə] *f* **-, -n** sleight of hand.

eskamotieren* *vt* to spirit *or* conjure away.

Eskapade *f* (*von Pferd*) caper; (*fig*) escapade.

Eskapismus *m* (*Psych, Sociol*) escapism.

Eskimo *m* **-s, -s** Eskimo.

eskimotieren* *vi* (*Sport*) to roll.

Eskorte *f* **-, -n** (*Mil*) escort.

eskortieren* *vt* to escort.

Esoteriker(in *f*) *m* **-s,** - esoteric.

esoterisch *adj* esoteric.

Espe *f* **-, -n** aspen.

Espenlaub *nt* aspen leaves *pl*. **zittern wie** ~ to tremble like a leaf *or* an aspen.

Esperanto *nt* **-s,** *no pl* Esperanto.

Espresso[1] *m* **-(s), -s** *or* **Espressi** espresso.

Espresso[2] *nt* **-(s), -(s), Espressobar** *f* (*Café*) coffee *or* espresso bar.

Espressomaschine *f* espresso machine.

Esprit [ɛs'pri:] *m* **-s,** *no pl* wit. **ein Mann von** ~ a wit, a witty man.

Essai ['ɛse, ɛ'se:] *m or nt* **-s, -s siehe Essay.**

Eß|apfel *m* eating apple, eater.

Essay ['ɛse, ɛ'se:] *m or nt* **-s, -s** (*Liter*) essay.

Essayist(in *f*) *m* **-s** (*Liter*) essayist.

essayistisch [ɛse'ɪstɪʃ] *adj* (*Liter*) *Roman* essayistic. **das** ~**e Werk Thomas Manns** the essays of Thomas Mann.

Eß-: **e**~**bar** *adj* edible, eatable; *Pilz* edible; **habt ihr irgend etwas** ~**bares im Haus?** have you got anything to eat in the house?; **nicht e**~**bar** inedible, uneatable; ~**besteck** *nt* knife, fork and spoon, eating irons *pl* (*hum*).

Esse *f* **-, -n** (*dial: Schornstein*) chimney; (*Schmiede*~) hearth.

essen *pret* **aß,** *ptp* **gegessen** *vti* to eat. **gut/schlecht** ~ (*Appetit haben*) to have a good/poor appetite; **in dem Restaurant kann man gut** ~ that's a good restaurant; **die Franzosen** ~ **gut** the French eat well, French food is good; **da ißt es sich gut** the food is good there, you can eat well there, they do good food there;

warm/kalt ~ to have a hot/cold meal; **tüchtig** or **ordentlich** ~ to eat well or properly; **iß mal tüchtig!** tuck in!, eat up!; **sich satt** ~ to eat one's fill; **sich krank** ~ to overeat, to overindulge (in food); **jdn arm** ~ to eat sb out of house and home; **den Teller leer** ~ to eat everything up, to empty one's plate; **~ Sie gern Äpfel?** do you like apples?; **wer hat davon/von meinem Teller gegessen?** who has been eating that/who's been eating off my plate?; **gerade ~, beim E~ sein** to be in the middle of eating or a meal; **~ gehen** (auswärts) to eat out, to go out to eat; **wann gehst du ~?** when are you going to eat?; (normalerweise) **when do you eat?; ich bin ~** (inf) I've gone to eat; **nach dem Kino gingen wir noch ~** after the cinema we went for a meal; **wir waren gestern abend ~** we were out for a meal last night; **selber ~ macht fett** (prov) I'm all right, Jack (prov); **E~ und Trinken hält Leib und Seele zusammen** (prov) food and drink keep body and soul together; siehe **heiß, Tisch.**

Essen nt -s, - (Mahlzeit) meal; (Nahrung) food; (Küche) cooking; (Fest~) luncheon; dinner. **bleib doch zum** ~ stay for lunch/supper, stay for a meal; **das ~ kochen** or **machen** (inf) to cook or get the meal; **jdn zum ~ einladen** to invite sb for a meal; (bitte) **zum ~ lunch/dinner is ready;** siehe **ruhen.**

Essen(s)-: ~ausgabe f serving of meals; (Stelle) serving counter; **ab 12³⁰ ist in der Kantine** ~ausgabe meals are served in the canteen from 12.30; ~marke f meal voucher; ~zeit f mealtime; **bei uns ist um 12⁰⁰** ~zeit we have lunch at 12; **die Kinder müssen abends zur** ~zeit **zu Hause sein** the children have to be at home in time for their evening meal; ~zuschuß m meal subsidy.

essentiell [esɛnˈtsiɛl] adj (Philos) essential.

Essenz f (a) no pl (Philos) essence. (b) (Cook etc) essence.

Esser m -s, - diner; pl auch people eating. **ein guter** or **starker/schlechter** ~ **sein** to be a good or great/poor eater; **auf einen** ~ **mehr kommt es nicht** an one more person won't make any difference; **sie hat sieben** ~ **zu versorgen** she has seven mouths to feed.

Esserei f (inf) guzzling (inf); (Mahl) blow-out (inf), nosh-up (Brit sl). **die** ~ **im Stehen ist nicht gut** it's not good to eat standing up; **was ist denn das für eine** ~? what sort of way to eat is that!

Eß-: ~geschirr nt dinner service; (Mil) mess tin; ~gewohnheiten pl eating habits pl.

Essig m -s, -e vinegar. **damit ist es** ~ (inf) it's all off, it's up the spout (Brit sl).

Essig-: ~äther m siehe ~ester; ~baum m stag's horn sumac; ~essenz f vinegar concentrate; ~ester m ethyl acetate; ~gurke f (pickled) gherkin; ~mutter f mother of vinegar; e~sauer adj (Chem) acetic; e~saure Tonerde aluminium acetate; ~säure f acetic acid.

Eß-: ~kastanie f sweet chestnut; ~kultur f gastronomic culture; ~löffel m soup/dessert spoon; (in Rezept) tablespoon; e~löffelweise adv in tablespoonfuls; (inf) by the spoonful; ~lust f appetite; ~stäbchen pl chopsticks pl.

eßt imper pl of **essen.**

Eß-: ~tisch m dining table; ~unlust f loss of appetite; ~waren pl food, provisions pl; ~zimmer nt dining room; ~zwang m (Psych) compulsive eating; **an** ~zwang **leiden** to be a compulsive eater.

Establishment [ɪsˈtæblɪʃmənt] nt -s, -s (Sociol, Press) establishment.

Este m -n, -n, **Estin** f Est(h)onian.

Ester m -s, - (Chem) ester.

Estland nt Est(h)onia.

estländisch adj Est(h)onian.

Estnisch(e) nt decl as adj Est(h)onian.

Estrade f (esp DDR) (a) podium. (b) (auch ~nkonzert) concert of light music etc, especially performed out of doors.

Estragon m -s, no pl tarragon.

Estrich m -s, -e (a) stone or clay etc floor. (b) (Sw: Dachboden) attic.

Eszett nt -, - eszett, ß.

etablieren* 1 vt (dated) to establish. 2 vr to establish oneself; (als Geschäftsmann auch) to set up.

etabliert adj established. **er gehört jetzt zu den E~en** he is now part of the establishment; **die** ~e **Oberschicht** the upper echelons of the establishment.

Etablissement [etablisəˈmãː] nt -s, -s establishment.

Etage [eˈtaːʒə] f -, -n floor. **in** or **auf der 2.** ~ on the 2nd or 3rd (US) floor; **er bewohnt im 5. Stock die ganze** ~ he lives in or occupies the whole of the 5th or 6th (US) floor.

Etagen-: ~bett nt bunk bed; ~heizung f heating system which covers one floor of a building; ~wohnung f flat occupying the whole of one floor of a building.

Etagere [etaˈʒɛːrə] f -, -n (dated) étagère.

Etappe f -, -n (a) (Abschnitt, Stufe, beim Radrennen) stage; (einer Strecke auch) leg. (b) (Mil) communications zone. **in der** ~ **liegen/sein** to be behind the lines.

Etappen-: ~hengst m, ~schwein nt (Mil sl) base wallah (Mil sl); ~sieg m (Sport) stage-win; ~sieger m (Sport) stage-winner; e~weise 1 adj step-by-step, stage-by-stage; 2 adv step by step, stage by stage.

Etat [eˈtaː] m -s, -s budget.

Etat-: ~jahr nt financial year; e~mäßig adj (Admin) budgetary; **das Geld wurde e~mäßig ausgegeben** the money was spent as budgeted; **nicht e~mäßig erfaßt** not in the budget, not budgeted for; ~posten m item in the budget, budgetary item.

etc abbr of et cetera [ɛtˈtseːtera] etc, et cetera.

etc pp [ɛtˈtseːteraˈpeːˈpeː] adv (hum) and so on and so forth.

etepetete [eːtəpeˈteːtə] adj pred (inf) fussy, finicky (inf), pernickety (inf).

Eternit ® m or nt -s, no pl asbestos cement.

Ethik f ethics pl (als Fach sing). **die** ~ **Kants** Kantian ethics; **die christliche** ~ the Christian ethic, Christian ethics.

Ethiker m -s, - moral philosopher.

ethisch adj ethical.

ethnisch adj ethnic.

Ethnograph(in f) m ethnographer.

Ethnographie f ethnography.

Ethnologe m, **Ethnologin** f ethnologist.

Ethnologie f ethnology.

Ethologe m, **Ethologin** f ethologist.

Ethologie f ethology.

Ethos [ˈeːtɔs] nt -, no pl ethos; (Berufs~) professional ethics pl.

Etikett nt -(e)s, -e (lit, fig) label.

Etikette f (a) etiquette. **gegen die** ~ (bei Hofe) **verstoßen** to offend against (court) etiquette, to commit a breach of (court) etiquette. (b) (Aus: Etikett) label.

Etikettenschwindel m (Pol) terminological juggling. **es ist reinster** ~, **wenn ...** it is just playing or juggling with names if ...

etikettieren* vt (lit, fig) to label.

etlichemal adv quite a few times.

etliche(r, s) indef pron (a) sing attr quite a lot of. **nachdem** ~ **Zeit verstrichen war** after quite some time.

(b) **etliche** pl (substantivisch) quite a few, several people/things; (attr) several, quite a few.

(c) ~**s** sing (substantivisch) quite a lot; **ich habe** ~**s daran auszusetzen, aber im großen und ganzen ...** I have one or two objections to make but by and large ...; **um** ~**s älter als ich** quite a lot or considerably older than me.

Etrurien [-iən] nt -s (Hist) Etruria.

Etrusker(in f) m -s, - Etruscan.

etruskisch adj Etruscan.

Etsch f - Adige.

Etüde f -, -n (Mus) étude.

Etui [ɛtˈviː, eˈtyiː] nt -s, -s case.

etwa adv (a) (ungefähr, annähernd) about, approximately. **so** ~, ~ **so** roughly or more or less like this; **wann** ~ ...? about or approximately or roughly when ...?

(b) (zum Beispiel) for instance. **wenn man** ~ **behauptet, daß ...** for instance if one maintains that ...

(c) (entrüstet, erstaunt) **hast du** ~ **schon wieder kein Geld dabei?** don't tell me or you don't mean to say you haven't got any money again!; **soll das** ~ **heißen, daß ...** is that supposed to mean ...?; **willst du** ~ **schon gehen?** (surely) you don't want to go already!

(d) (zur Bestätigung) **Sie kommen doch, oder** ~ **nicht?** you are coming, aren't you?; **das haben Sie wohl nicht mit Absicht gesagt, oder** ~ **doch?** surely you didn't say that on purpose, you didn't say that on purpose — or did you?; **sind Sie** ~ **nicht einverstanden?** do you mean to say that you don't agree?; **ist das** ~ **wahr?** (surely) it's not true!, (surely) it can't be true!; **ist das** ~ **nicht wahr?** do you mean to say it's not true?; **können wir einen Termin festsetzen, nächsten Samstag** ~? could we fix a date, next Saturday perhaps? or how about next Saturday?

(e) (in Gegenüberstellung, einschränkend) **nicht** ~, **daß ...** (it's) not that ...; **er ist nicht** ~ **dumm, sondern nur faul** it's not that he's stupid, he's simply lazy; **das hat Fritz getan und nicht** ~ **sein Bruder Fritz** did it and not his brother; **sie soll nicht** ~ **meinen, das würde ich dulden** she shouldn't think or she's not to think that I will put up with it; **ich wollte dich nicht** ~ **beleidigen** I didn't intend to insult you.

etwaig [ˈɛtvaɪç, ɛtˈvaːɪç] adj attr possible. ~**e Einwände/Unkosten** any objections/costs arising or which might arise; **bei** ~**en Beschwerden/Schäden etc** in the event of (any) complaints/damage etc; **eine Liege für** ~**e Besucher** a campbed for possible visitors or in case there should be visitors.

etwas indef pron (a) (substantivisch) something; (fragend, bedingend auch, verneinend) anything; (unbestimmter Teil einer Menge) some; any. **kannst du mir** ~ (davon) **leihen?** can you lend me some (of it)?; **ohne** ~ **zu erwähnen** without saying anything; ~ **habe ich doch vergessen** there is something I've forgotten; ~ **anderes** something else; **das ist** ~ (ganz) **anderes** that's something (quite) different; ~ **sein** (inf) to be somebody (inf); ~ **werden** (inf), **es zu** ~ **bringen** (inf) to make something of oneself, to get somewhere (inf); **aus ihm wird nie** ~ (inf) he'll never become anything; **er kann** ~ he's good; **das ist immerhin** ~ at least that's something; **sein Wort gilt** ~ **beim Chef** what he says counts for something with the boss; **hast du** ~? is (there) something wrong or the matter (with you)?; **sie hat** ~ **mit ihm** (inf) she's got something going on with him; **das ist sicher, wie nur** ~ (inf) that's as sure as (sure) can be (inf); **schäm dich** ~! (inf) you should be ashamed of yourself!; **er hat** ~ **vom Schulmeister an sich** he has or there is something of the schoolmaster about him; **da ist** ~ **(Richtiges) dran** there's something in that; **da ist** ~ **Wahres dran** there is some truth in that.

(b) (adjektivisch) some; (fragend, bedingend auch) any. ~ **Salz?** some salt?; **kannst du mir vielleicht** ~ **Geld leihen?** could you possibly lend me some money?; ~ **Nettes** something nice; ~ **Schöneres habe ich noch nie gesehen** I have never seen anything more beautiful.

(c) (adverbial) somewhat, a little.

Etwas nt -, no pl something. **das gewisse** ~ that certain something; **ein winziges** ~ a tiny little thing.

Etymologe m, **Etymologin** f etymologist.

Etymologie f etymology.

etymologisch adj etymological.

Etymon [ˈeːtymɔn] nt -s, **Etyma** (Ling) root, etymon (form).

Et-Zeichen nt ampersand.

Etzel m -s Attila the Hun.

etzliche indef pron pl (obs, hum) siehe **etliche(r, s).**

euch *pers pron dat, acc of* **ihr** (*in Briefen:* E~) you; (*obs, dial*) thee; (*dat auch*) to/for you; to/for thee; (*refl*) yourselves. **wie ist das bei ~ (in Frankreich) mit den Ferien?** what are your holidays like in France?; **ein Freund von ~** a friend of yours; **wascht ~!** wash yourselves; **liebt ~!** love one another; **setzt ~!** sit (yourselves *inf*) down!; **vertragt ~!** stop quarrelling!

Eucharistie *f* (*Eccl*) Eucharist.

eucharistisch *adj* **Kongreß** Eucharistic.

euer **1** *poss pron* (**a**) (*adjektivisch*) (*in Briefen:* E~) your. **E~** (*Briefschluß*) yours; (*obs, dial*) thy; **viele Grüße, E~ Hans** best wishes, yours, Hans; **das sind ~e** *or* **eure Bücher** those are your books; **ist das ~ Haus?** is that your house?; **E~** *or* **Eure Gnaden/Exzellenz/Majestät** your Grace/Excellency/Majesty.
(**b**) (*old: substantivisch*) yours. **behaltet, was ~ ist** keep what is yours.

2 *pers pron gen of* **ihr**. **wir werden ~ gedenken** we will think of you; **~ beider gemeinsame Zukunft** your common future; **~ aller heimlicher Wunsch** the secret wish of all of you.

euere(r, s) *poss pron siehe* **eure(r, s)**.

euersgleichen *in cpds siehe* **euresgleichen**.

euert- *in cpds siehe* **euret-**.

Eugenik *f* (*Biol*) eugenics *sing*.

eugenisch *adj* (*Biol*) eugenic.

Eukalyptus *m* -, **Eukalypten** (*Baum*) eucalyptus (tree); (*Öl*) eucalyptus oil.

Eukalyptusbonbon *m or nt* eucalyptus sweet (*Brit*) *or* candy (*US*).

Euklid *m* -s Euclid.

euklidisch *adj* Euclidean.

Eule *f* -, -n owl; (*pej: häßliche Frau*) crow. **~n nach Athen tragen** (*prov*) to carry coals to Newcastle (*prov*).

Eulen-: **~spiegel** *m* Till **~spiegel** (*lit*) Till Eulenspiegel; **unser Sohn ist ein richtiger ~spiegel** (*fig*) our son is a real scamp (*inf*) *or* rascal (*inf*); **~spiegelei** *f*, **~spiegelstreich** *m* trick, caper.

Eunuch *m* -en, -en eunuch.

Euphemismus *m* euphemism.

euphemistisch *adj* euphemistic.

Euphorie *f* euphoria.

euphorisch *adj* euphoric.

Euphrat ['ɔyfrat] *m* -(s) Euphrates.

Eurasien [-iən] *nt* -s Eurasia.

Eurasier(in *f*) [-iɐ, -iərɪn] *m* -s, - Eurasian.

eurasisch *adj* Eurasian.

Euratom *abbr of* **Europäische Atomgemeinschaft** European Atomic Community, Euratom.

eure(r, s) *poss pron* (**a**) (*substantivisch*) yours. **der/die/das ~** (*geh*) yours; **tut ihr das E~** (*geh*) you do your bit; **stets** *or* **immer der E~** (*form*) yours ever; **die E~n** (*geh*) your family, your people; **ihr und die E~n** (*geh: Familie*) you and yours; **der/die E~** (*old: Ehepartner*) your spouse (*old*); **das E~** (*geh: Besitz*) what is yours. (**b**) (*adjektivisch*) *siehe* **euer 1** (**a**).

eurerseits *adv* (*auf eurer Seite*) for your part; (*von eurer Seite*) from *or* on your part. **den Vorschlag habt ihr ~ gemacht** you made the suggestion yourselves.

euresgleichen *pron inv* people like you *or* yourselves; (*pej auch*) the likes of you, your sort.

euret-: **~halben** (*dated*), **~wegen** *adv* (*wegen euch*) because of you, on account of you, on your account; (*euch zuliebe auch*) for your sake; (*um euch*) about you; (*für euch*) on your behalf *or* behalves.

Eur(h)ythmie *f* eurhythmics.

eurige *poss pron* (*old, geh*) **der/die/das ~** yours; **die E~n** your families; **das E~** (*Besitz*) what is yours; **tut ihr das E~** you do your bit.

Euro- *in cpds* Euro-; **~cheque** *m siehe* **~scheck**; **~dollar** *m* eurodollar; **~krat** *m* -en, -en (*Press sl*) Eurocrat.

Europa *nt* -s Europe.

Europäer(in *f*) *m* -s, - European.

europäisch *adj* European. **das E~e Parlament** the European Parliament; **E~e Wirtschaftsgemeinschaft** European Economic Community, Common Market; **die E~en Gemeinschaften** the European Community.

europäisieren* *vt* to Europeanize.

Europa-: **~meister** *m* (*Sport*) European champion; (*Team, Land*) European champions *pl*; **~meisterschaft** *f* European championship; **~pokal** *m* (*Sport*) European cup; **~rat** *m* Council of Europe; **~straße** *f* through route in Europe.

europid *adj* **Rasse** Caucasian.

Europide *mf* -n, -n Caucasian.

Euro-: **~scheck** *m* Eurocheque; **~vision** *f* Eurovision; **~visionssendung** *f* Eurovision broadcast *or* programme.

Eurythmie *f siehe* **Eur(h)ythmie**.

Eustachische Röhre *f* (*Anat*) Eustachian tube.

Euter *nt* -s, - udder.

Euthanasie *f* euthanasia.

ev. *abbr of* **evangelisch**.

e.V., E.V. *abbr of* **eingetragener Verein**.

Eva ['e:fa, 'e:va] *f* -s Eve. **sie ist eine echte ~** (*hum*) she is the archetypal woman.

evakuieren* [evaku'iːrən] *vt* to evacuate.

Evakuierte(r) [evaku'iːrtə] *mf decl as adj* evacuee.

Evakuierung [evaku'iːrʊŋ] *f* evacuation.

Evangelienbuch [evaŋ'geːliən-] *nt* book of the Gospels, Gospel.

Evangelisation [evaŋgeliza'tsioːn] *f* evangelization.

evangelisch [evaŋ'geːlɪʃ] *adj* Protestant.

Evangelist [evaŋe'lɪst] *m* evangelist.

Evangelium [evaŋ'geːliʊm] *nt* Gospel; (*fig*) gospel. **alles, was er sagt, ist für sie (ein) ~** (*fig*) everything he says is gospel to her.

evaporieren* [evapo'riːrən] *vi aux sein* to evaporate.

Eva(s)kostüm *nt* (*dated hum*) **im ~** in the altogether (*hum*), in her birthday suit (*hum*).

Evastochter ['eːfas-, 'eːvas-] *f* (*dated hum*) coquette.

Eventual- [evɛntu'aːl]: **~fall** *m* eventuality; **~haushalt** *m* (*Parl*) emergency *or* contingency budget.

Eventualität [evɛntuali'tɛːt] *f* eventuality, contingency.

eventuell [evɛntu'ɛl] **1** *adj attr* possible.
2 *adv* possibly, perhaps. **~ rufe ich Sie später an** I may possibly call you later; **das Modell kann auf Wunsch ~ geändert werden** the model can be changed to your requirements if necessary; **ich komme ~ ein bißchen später** I might (possibly) come a little later.

Evergreen ['ɛvɐgriːn] *m* -s, -s evergreen.

evident [evi'dɛnt] *adj* (*geh: offenbar*) obvious, clear.

Evidenz [evi'dɛnts] *f* (**a**) (*Philos*) evidence. (**b**) (*Aus*) **etw in ~ halten** to keep a current record of sth, to keep sth up-to-date.

Evidenzbüro *nt* (*Aus*) registry.

ev.-luth. *abbr of* **evangelisch-lutherisch** Lutheran Protestant.

Evolution [evolu'tsioːn] *f* evolution.

evolutionär, evolutionistisch [evolutsio-] *adj* evolutionary.

Evolutionstheorie *f* theory of evolution.

evtl. *abbr of* **eventuell**.

EWA [eːveː'laː] *nt* -s *abbr of* **Europäisches Währungsabkommen** European Monetary Agreement.

E-Werk ['eːvɛrk] *nt abbr of* **Elektrizitätswerk** generating *or* power station.

EWG [eːveː'geː] *f* - *abbr of* **Europäische Wirtschaftsgemeinschaft** EEC, Common Market.

ewig **1** *adj* eternal; **Leben** *auch* everlasting; **Eis, Schnee** perpetual; (*inf*) **Nörgelei** *etc auch* never-ending. **der E~e Jude** the Wandering Jew; **das E~e Licht, die E~e Lampe** (*Eccl*) the sanctuary lamp; **in den ~en Frieden** *or* **die ~e Ruhe eingehen** to find eternal peace; **die E~e Stadt** the Eternal City; **(Gott,) der E~e** God, the Eternal; *siehe* **Jagdgründe**.
2 *adv* for ever, eternally. **auf ~ for ever; das dauert ja ~** (**und drei Tage** *hum*) it goes on for ever (and a day); **das dauert ja ~, bis ...** it'll take ages until ...; **er muß sich ~ beklagen** he's eternally *or* for ever complaining; **es ist ~ schade, daß ...** (*inf*) it's an enormous pity *or* shame that ...; **~ dankbar** eternally grateful; **ich habe Sie ~ lange nicht gesehen** (*inf*) I haven't seen you for absolutely ages *or* for an eternity; *siehe* **immer**.

Ewigkeit *f* eternity; (*der Naturgesetze*) immutability; (*inf*) ages. **in die ~ eingehen** to go to eternal rest; **bis in alle ~** *or* **von ~ zu ~ amen** for ever and ever, amen; **bis in alle ~** for ever, for all eternity (*liter*); **eine ~** *or* **eine halbe ~** (*hum*) dauern (*inf*) to last an age *or* an eternity; **es dauert eine ~** *or* **eine halbe ~** (*hum*), **bis ...** it'll take absolutely ages until ...; **ich habe sie seit ~en** *or* **einer ~ nicht gesehen** (*inf*) I've not seen her for ages.

ewiglich (*liter*) **1** *adj attr* eternal, everlasting. **2** *adv* eternally, for ever, to the end of time (*liter*).

e.Wz. *abbr of* **eingetragenes Warenzeichen**.

ex *adv* (*inf*) **(a)** (*leer*) (trink) **~!** down the hatch! (*inf*); **etw ~ trinken** to drink sth down in one. (**b**) (*Schluß, vorbei*) (all) over, finished. **mit unserer Freundschaft ist es ~** our friendship is all over *or* finished.

Ex- *in cpds* ex-.

exakt *adj* exact. **eine ~e Wissenschaft** an exact science; **~ arbeiten** to work accurately.

Exaktheit *f* exactness, precision.

exaltiert *adj* exaggerated, effusive.

Exaltiertheit *f* exaggeratedness, effusiveness.

Examen *nt* -s, - *or* **Examina** exam, examination; (*Univ*) final examinations, finals *pl*. **~ machen** to do *or* take one's exams *or* finals; **das ~ mit Eins machen** to get top marks in an exam; (*Univ*) **=** to get a First; **das mündliche ~** oral examination; (*Univ*) viva (voce).

Examens-: **~angst** *f* exam nerves *pl*; **~kandidat** *m* candidate (for an examination), examinee.

examinieren* *vt* (*geh*) to examine. **jdn über etw** (*acc*) **~** (*lit, fig*) to question sb about sth.

Exegese *f* -, -n exegesis.

Exeget *m* -en, -en exegete.

exegetisch *adj* exegetic(al).

exekutieren* *vt* (*form*) to execute. **jdn ~** (*Aus: pfänden*) to seize *or* impound sb's possessions.

Exekution *f* execution; (*Aus: Pfändung*) seizing, impounding.

Exekutionskommando *nt* firing squad.

exekutiv *adj* executive.

Exekutivausschuß *m* executive committee.

Exekutive [-'tiːvə], **Exekutivgewalt** *f* executive; (*Aus*) forces *pl* of law and order.

Exekutor *m* (*Aus*) bailiff.

Exempel *nt* -s, - (*geh*) example; (*dated Math: Rechen~*) example (*dated*). **die Probe aufs ~ machen** to put it to the test; *siehe* **statuieren**.

Exemplar *nt* -s, -e specimen; (*Buch~, Zeitschriften~*) copy.

exemplarisch *adj* exemplary. **~es Lehren/Lernen** teaching/ learning by example; **etw ~ durcharbeiten** to work through sth as an example; **jdn ~ bestrafen** to punish sb as an example (to others); **das Urteil wurde ~ für alle folgenden Fälle** the verdict set a precedent for all subsequent cases.

Exemplifikation *f* (*geh*) exemplification.

exemplifizieren* *vt* (*geh*) to exemplify.

Exequatur *nt* -s, -en [-'tuːrən] (*Admin, Pol*) exequatur.

exerzieren* *vti* to drill; (*fig*) to practise.

Exerzierplatz *m* (*Mil*) parade ground.

Exerzitien [ɛksɐ'tsiːtsiən] *pl* (*Eccl*) spiritual exercises *pl*.

Exhibitionismus [ɛkshibitsio'nɪsmʊs] *m* exhibitionism.
Exhibitionist(in *f*) [ɛkshibitsio'nɪst(ɪn)] *m* exhibitionist.
exhibitionistisch [ɛkshibitsio'nɪstɪʃ] *adj* exhibitionist.
exhumieren* *vt* to exhume.
Exhumierung *f* exhumation.
Exil *nt* -s, -e exile. **im (amerikanischen)** ~ **leben** to live in exile (in America); **ins** ~ **gehen** to go into exile.
Exil-: ~**literatur** *f* literature written in exile (*esp by Germans exiled during the 3rd Reich*); ~**regierung** *f* government in exile.
existent *adj* (*geh*) existing, existent. **für ihn sind UFOs** ~ he believes in the existence of UFOs.
Existentialismus [ɛksɪstɛntsia'lɪsmʊs] *m* existentialism.
Existentialist(in *f*) [ɛksɪstɛntsia'lɪst(ɪn)] *m* existentialist.
existentialistisch [-tsia'lɪstɪʃ] *adj* existential(ist).
Existentialphilosophie [ɛksɪstɛn'tsia:l-] *f* existential(ist) philosophy.
existentiell [ɛksɪstɛn'tsiɛl] *adj* (*geh*) existential. **das Problem der Umweltverschmutzung ist** ~ the problem of environmental pollution is of vital significance; **von** ~**er Bedeutung** of vital significance.
Existenz *f* existence; (*Lebensgrundlage, Auskommen*) livelihood; (*pej inf: Person*) character, customer (*inf*). **eine gescheiterte** *or* **verkrachte** ~ (*inf*) a failure; **sich eine (neue)** ~ **aufbauen** to make a (new) life for oneself; **keine sichere** ~ **haben** to have no secure livelihood.
Existenz-: ~**angst** *f* (*Philos*) existential fear, angst; (*wirtschaftlich*) fear for one's livelihood *or* existence; ~**berechtigung** *f* right to exist; **hat die UNO noch eine** ~**berechtigung?** can the UN still justify its existence?; **e**~**fähig** *adj* able to exist; *Firma* viable; ~**fähigkeit** *f* ability to exist; (*von Firma*) viability; ~**grundlage** *f* basis of one's livelihood; ~**kampf** *m* struggle for existence; ~**minimum** *nt* subsistence level; (*Lohn*) minimal living wage *or* income; **das Gehalt liegt noch unter dem** ~**minimum** that salary is not enough to live on, that is not even a living wage; **er verdient nicht einmal das** ~**minimum** he does not even earn enough to live on *or* a living wage; **das gibt uns gerade das** ~**minimum** we just have enough to get by on; ~**philosophie** *f* existentialism.
existieren* [ɛksɪs'ti:rən] *vi* to exist; (*Gesetz, Schule etc auch*) to be in existence.
Exitus *m* -, *no pl* (*Med*) death.
exkl. *abbr of* **exklusive.**
Exklave [ɛks'kla:və] *f* -, -n (*Pol*) exclave.
exklusiv *adj* exclusive.
Exklusivbericht *m* (*Press*) exclusive (report).
exklusive [-'zi:və] **1** *prep* +*gen* exclusive of, excluding. **2** *adv* *Getränke* ~ excluding drinks; **bis zum 20.** ~ to the 20th exclusively.
Exklusivinterview *nt* (*Press*) exclusive interview.
Exklusivität [-zivi'tɛːt] *f* exclusiveness.
Exkommunikation *f* (*Eccl*) excommunication.
exkommunizieren* *vt* to excommunicate.
Exkrement *usu pl nt* (*geh*) excrement *no pl*, excreta *pl*.
Exkretion *f* (*Med*) excretion.
Exkurs *m* -es, -e digression.
Exkursion *f* (study) trip.
Exlibris *nt* -, - ex libris, bookplate.
Exmatrikulation *f* (*Univ*) being taken off the university register.
exmatrikulieren* *vt* (*Univ*) to take off the university register. **sich** ~ **lassen** to withdraw from the university register.
exmittieren* *vt* (*Admin*) *Mieter* to evict.
Exmittierung *f* (*Admin*) eviction.
Exodus *m* - (*Bibl, fig*) exodus.
exogen *adj* (*Biol, Geol*) exogenous.
exorbitant *adj* (*geh*) *Preise* exorbitant.
exorz(is)ieren* *vt* to exorcize.
Exorzismus *m* exorcism.
Exorzist *m* exorcist.
Exot(e) *m* -en, -en, **Exotin** *f* exotic *or* tropical animal/plant *etc*; (*Mensch*) exotic foreigner. **er hat eine schöne Exotin geheiratet** he married an exotic beauty.
exotisch *adj* exotic.
Expander *m* -s, - (*Sport*) chest-expander.
expandieren* *vi* to expand.
Expansion *f* (*Phys, Pol*) expansion.
Expansionspolitik *f* expansionism, expansionist policies *pl*.
expansiv *adj* *Politik* expansionist; *Wirtschaftszweige* expanding; *Gase* expansile, expansive.
expatriieren* *vt* to expatriate.
Expedient *m* (*Comm*) dispatch clerk.
expedieren* *vt* to dispatch, to send (off).
Expedition *f* (**a**) (*Forschungs*~, *Mil*) expedition. (**b**) (*Versendung*) dispatch; (*Versandabteilung*) dispatch office.
Experiment *nt* experiment. ~**e machen** *or* **anstellen** to carry out *or* do experiments.
Experimental- *in cpds* experimental.
experimentell *adj* experimental. **etw** ~ **nachweisen** to prove sth by experiment.
experimentieren* *vi* to experiment (*mit* with).
Experte *m* -n, -n, **Expertin** *f* expert (*für* in).
Expertise *f* -, -n (expert's) report.
Expl. *abbr of* **Exemplar.**
Explikation *f* (*geh*) explication (*form*).
explizieren* *vt* (*geh*) to explicate (*form*).
explizit *adj* explicit.
explizite *adv* explicitly.
explodieren* *vi aux sein* (*lit, fig*) to explode.

Exploration *f* (*eines Landes*) exploration; (*Psych*) examination.
Explosion *f* explosion. **etw zur** ~ **bringen** to detonate *or* explode sth.
Explosions-: ~**gefahr** *f* danger of explosion; ~**motor** *m* internal combustion engine.
explosiv *adj* (*lit, fig*) explosive.
Explosiv(laut) *m* -s, -e (*Ling*) plosive.
Explosivstoff *m* explosive.
Exponat *nt* exhibit.
Exponent *m* (*Math*) exponent; (*fig auch*) spokesman.
Exponential- [ɛkspon'tsia:l-]: ~**funktion** *f* (*Math*) exponential function; ~**gleichung** *f* (*Math*) exponential equation.
exponieren* **1** *vt* (*herausheben, dated Phot*) to expose. **jdn zu sehr** ~ to overexpose sb; **an exponierter Stelle stehen** to be in an exposed position.
2 *vr* (*sich auffällig benehmen*) to behave boisterously; (*in der Politik*) to take a prominent stance; (*in Diskussion*) to make one's presence felt, to come on strong (*inf*). **die Studenten wollen sich nicht mehr** ~ the students are keeping a low profile.
Export *m* -(e)s, -e export (*an* – *dat* of); (~*waren*) exports *pl*.
Export- *in cpds* export; ~**abteilung** *f* export department; ~**artikel** *m* export; ~**gut** *nt* (*ausführung*) export model.
Exporteur [ɛkspɔr'tøːr] *m* exporter.
Export-: ~**geschäft** *nt* (**a**) (*Firma*) export business; (**b**) (*Handel*) export business *or* trade; ~**handel** *m* export business *or* trade.
exportieren* *vti* to export.
Export-: ~**kaufmann** *m* exporter; ~**quote** *f* export ratio; ~**ware** *f* export.
Exposé [ɛkspo'zeː] *nt* -s, -s (*für Film, Buch etc*) outline, plan; (*Denkschrift*) memo(randum).
Exposition *f* (*Liter, Mus*) exposition; (*Gliederung eines Aufsatzes*) outline, plan.
Expositur *f* (*Aus*) (*Zweigstelle*) branch; (*Sch*) annexe.
expreß *adv* (*dated*) quickly, expeditiously (*form*); (*Post*) express.
Expreß *m* -sses, *pl* **Expreßzüge** (*old Rail, Aus*) express (train).
Expreß-: ~**brief** *m* express letter; ~**gut** *nt* express goods *pl*.
Expressionismus *m* expressionism.
Expressionist(in *f*) *m* expressionist.
expressionistisch *adj* expressionist *no adv*, expressionistic.
expressis verbis *adv* explicitly, expressly.
expressiv *adj* expressive.
Expressivität *f* expressiveness.
Expreß-: ~**reinigung** *f* express dry-cleaning service; ~**zug** *m* siehe **Expreß.**
Expropriation *f* expropriation.
exquisit *adj* exquisite.
extemporieren* *vti* (*geh*) to improvise, to extemporize.
extensiv *adj* (*auch Agr*) extensive.
extern *adj* (*Sch*) *Prüfung, Kandidat* external. **ein** ~**er Schüler** a day boy.
Externat *nt* (*Sch*) day school.
Externe(r) *mf decl as adj* (*Sch*) day boy/girl.
Externist *m* (*Aus*) (**a**) (*Schüler*) day boy. (**b**) pupil educated by private tuition, not at school.
exterritorial *adj* extraterritorial.
Exterritorialität *f* extraterritoriality.
extra 1 *adj inv* (*inf*) extra. **etwas E**~**es** (*inf*) something special.
2 *adv* (*besonders, außerordentlich*) extra, (e)specially; (*eigens, ausschließlich*) (e)specially, just; (*gesondert*) separately; (*zusätzlich*) extra, in addition; (*inf: absichtlich*) on purpose, deliberately. **etw** ~ **legen** to put sth in a separate place; **ich gebe Ihnen noch ein Exemplar** ~ I'll give you an extra copy; **jetzt tu ich's** ~! (*inf*) just for that I will do it!
Extra *nt* -s, -s extra.
Extra-: ~**ausgabe** *f* special edition; ~**blatt** *nt* special edition; (*zusätzlich zur Zeitung*) special supplement; **e**~**fein** *adj* superfine; **e**~**fein gemahlener Kaffee** extra finely ground coffee.
extrahieren* [ɛkstra'hiːrən] *vt* to extract.
Extrakt *m* -(e)s, -e (*Med, Pharm auch nt*) extract; (*von Buch etc*) synopsis. **etw im** ~ **wiedergeben** to summarize sth, to give a summary of sth.
Extra-: **e**~**ordinär** *adj* (*dated geh*) extraordinary; ~**ordinarius** *m* (*Univ*) ≈ reader (*Brit*), associate professor (*US*); ~**polation** *f* (*Math, fig*) extrapolation; **e**~**polieren*** *vti* (*Math, fig*) to extrapolate; ~**post** *f* (*old*) express postal service; (~*wagen*) post-chaise; ~**tour** *f* (*fig inf*) siehe ~**wurst.**
extravagant [-va'gant] *adj* extravagant; *Kleidung auch* flamboyant.
Extravaganz [-va'gants] *f* siehe *adj* extravagance; flamboyance.
extravertiert [-vɛrtiːɐt] *adj* (*Psych*) extrovert.
Extrawurst *f* (**a**) (*inf: Sonderwunsch*) special favour. **jdm eine** ~ **braten** to make an exception of *or* for sb; **er will immer eine** ~ (**gebraten haben**) he always wants something different *or* special. (**b**) (*Aus*) siehe **Lyoner.**
extrem *adj* extreme; *Belastung* excessive; (*sl*) way-out (*sl*). ~ **schlecht/gut** *etc* extremely badly/well *etc*; **die Lage hat sich** ~ **verschlechtert** the situation has deteriorated enormously; **ich habe mich** ~ **beeilt** I hurried as much as I could; **du bist immer so** ~ you always go to extremes; ~**e Zeit!** (*sl*) have a great time.
Extrem *nt* -s, -e extreme. **von einem** ~ **ins andere fallen** to go from one extreme to the other.
Extremfall *m* extreme (case).
Extremist(in *f*) *m* extremist.

extremistisch *adj* extremist.
Extremität *f usu pl* extremity *usu pl.*
Extremwert *m* extreme (value).
extrovertiert [-ver'tiːɐt] *adj siehe* **extravertiert.**
exzellent *adj* (*geh*) excellent.
Exzellenz *f* Excellency.
exzentrisch *adj* (*Math, fig*) eccentric.
Exzentrizität *f* (*Geometry, Tech, fig*) eccentricity.

exzerpieren* *vt* to select *or* extract (*aus* from).
Exzerpt *nt* -(e)s, -e excerpt.
Exzeß *m* -sses, -sse (a) excess. bis zum ~ excessively, to excess; etw bis zum ~ treiben to take sth to excess *or* extremes; bis zum ~ gesteigerter Haß excessive hate. (b) *usu pl* (*Ausschreitung*) excess.
exzessiv *adj* excessive.
E-Zug ['eːtsuːk] *m abbr of* **Eilzug.**

F

F, f [ɛf] *nt* -, - F, f. nach Schema F (*inf*) in the usual way.
F *abbr of* **Fahrenheit; Farad; Fernschnellzug.**
f. *abbr of* **und folgende(r, s).**
Fa. *abbr of* **Firma.**
fa *interj* (*Mus*) fa(h).
Fabel *f* -, -n (a) fable. (b) (*inf*) fantastic story. (c) (*Liter: Handlung*) plot.
Fabel-: ~**buch** *nt* book of fables; ~**dichter** *m* writer of fables, fabulist (*form*).
Fabelei *f* (a) (*das Fabeln*) romancing. (b) (*Geschichte*) fantastic story.
Fabel-: ~**geschöpf** *nt*, ~**gestalt** *f siehe* ~**wesen; f**~**haft** *adj* splendid, magnificent; **ein f**~**haft niedriger Preis** a fabulously *or* fantastically low price; ~**land** *nt* imaginary land.
fabeln 1 *vi* to romance. 2 *vt Unsinn* to concoct, to fabricate.
Fabel-: ~**tier** *nt* mythical creature; **der Fuchs als** ~**tier** the fox (as he appears) in fables; ~**welt** *f* world *or* realm of fantasy; ~**wesen** *nt* mythical creature.
Fabrik *f* -, -en factory; (*Papier*~) mill. **in die** ~ **gehen** (*inf*) to work in a factory.
Fabrik|anlage *f* (manufacturing) plant; (~**gelände**) factory premises *pl.*
Fabrikant(in *f*) *m* (a) (*Fabrikbesitzer*) industrialist. (b) (*Hersteller*) manufacturer.
Fabrik-: ~**arbeit** *f, no pl* factory work; **das ist** ~**arbeit** that is factory-made; ~**arbeiter** *m* factory worker.
Fabrikat *nt* (a) (*Marke*) make; (*von Nahrungs- und Genußmitteln*) brand. (b) (*Produkt*) product; (*Ausführung*) model.
Fabrikation *f* manufacture, production.
Fabrikations-: ~**fehler** *m* manufacturing fault; ~**stätte** *f* manufacturing *or* production plant.
Fabrik-: *in cpds* factory; ~**bau** *m, pl* **-ten** factory (building); ~**direktor** *m* managing director (of a factory); **f**~**frisch** *adj* straight from the factory; ~**gelände** *nt* factory site; ~**halle** *f* factory building.
Fabrikler(in *f*) *m* -s, - (*Sw*) factory worker.
fabrik-: ~**mäßig** *adj* ~**mäßige Herstellung** mass production; ~**mäßig hergestellt** mass-produced; ~**neu** *adj* straight from the factory; (*nagelneu*) brand-new; ~**neu aussehen** to be in mint condition.
Fabriks- *in cpds* (*Aus*) *siehe* **Fabrik-.**
Fabrikschiff *nt* factory ship.
fabrizieren* *vt* (a) (*dated*) (*industriell produzieren*) to manufacture, to produce, to fabricate (*dated*). (b) (*inf*) *Möbelstück etc* to make; (*geistiges Produkt* to produce; *Alibi, Lügengeschichte* to concoct, to fabricate. (c) (*inf: anstellen*) to get up to (*inf*).
Fabulant(in *f*) *m* (*geh*) (a) (*pej*) fabulist. (b) *siehe* **Fabulierer(in).**
fabulieren* *vi* (*geh*) (a) (*pej: schwätzen*) to romance. (b) (*phantasievoll erzählen*) to spin a yarn. **er fabulierte, wie ...** he spun some yarns about how ...
Fabulierer(in *f*) *m* -s, - (*geh*) romancer, storyteller.
fabulös *adj* (*geh*) fabulous (*liter*); (*unglaubwürdig, hum: großartig*) fantastic.
Facette [fa'setə] *f* facet.
Facetten-: **f**~**artig** 1 *adj* facet(t)ed; 2 *adv schleifen* in facets; ~**auge** *nt* compound eye; ~**schliff** *m* facet(t)ing; **ein Amethyst mit** ~**schliff** a facet(t)ed amethyst.
facettieren* [fasɛ'tiːrən] *vt* to facet. **facettiert** (*lit, fig*) facet(t)ed.
Fach *nt* -(e)s, -̈er (a) compartment; (*in Tasche, Brieftasche, Portemonnaie etc auch*) pocket; (*in Schrank, Regal etc*) shelf; (*für Briefe etc*) pigeonhole.
(b) (*Wissens-, Sachgebiet*) subject; (*Gebiet*) field; (*Handwerk*) trade. **ein Mann vom** ~ an expert; **er ist nicht gerade/ist vom** ~ it isn't exactly/it's his subject/trade; **sein** ~ **verstehen** to know one's stuff (*inf*) *or* one's subject/trade; **das** ~ **Medizin** *etc* medicine *etc.*
(c) (*Theat*) mode.
-fach *adj suf* -fold; (*-mal*) times; *siehe* **vier**~ *etc.*
Fach-: ~**arbeiter** *m* skilled worker; **Bau-/Brauerei-** *etc*

~**arbeiter** construction/brewery *etc* workers; ~**arbeiterbrief** *m* certificate of proficiency; ~**arzt** *m* specialist (*für* in); **f**~**ärztlich** *adj Behandlung* specialist *attr; Untersuchung* by a specialist; **ein f**~**ärztliches Attest/Gutachten** a certificate from *or* signed by a specialist/a specialist's opinion; ~**ausdruck** *m* technical *or* specialist term; ~**bereich** *m* (a) *siehe* ~**gebiet;** (b) (*Univ*) school, faculty; **f**~**bezogen** *adj* specifically related to one's/the subject; (*fachlich beschränkt*) specialized; **f**~**bezogen denken** to think in terms of one's own subject; ~**blatt** *nt* (specialist) journal; **ein medizinisches** ~**blatt** a medical journal; ~**buch** *nt* reference book; **wasserbautechnische** ~**bücher** specialist books on hydraulic engineering; ~**buchhandlung** *f* specialist bookshop; ~**buchhandlung für Medizin/Mathematik** *etc* bookshop specializing in medical/mathematical *etc* books; ~**buchverlag** *m* specialist publishing company; ~**buchverlag für Geographie/Fremdsprachen** *etc* publisher of geography/modern language *etc* books; ~**egoismus** *m* belief that one's own subject is more important than any other.
fächeln (*geh*) 1 *vt* to fan; *Blätter etc* to stir. 2 *vi* to stir.
fachen *vt* (*rare*) to blow (with bellows).
Fächer *m* -s, - fan; (*fig*) range, array.
Fächer-: **f**~**artig** 1 *adj* fanlike; 2 *adv* like a fan; ~**besen** *m* (*Hort*) wire rake; **f**~**förmig** 1 *adj* fan-shaped; 2 *adv* like a fan; ~**gewölbe** *nt* fan vaulting; **ein** ~**gewölbe** a fan vault.
fächern 1 *vt* to fan (out); (*fig*) to diversify. **gefächert** diverse; *Auswahl auch* varied; *Unterricht* diversified. 2 *vr* to fan out. 3 *vti* (*rare*) *siehe* **fächeln.**
Fächerpalme *f* fan palm.
Fächerung *f, no pl* variety, range, diversity.
Fach-: **f**~**fremd** *adj Lektüre, Aufgaben etc* unconnected with the/one's subject; *Mitarbeiter* with no background in the subject; *Methode* foreign to the subject; **ich bin f**~**fremd** *or* **ein** ~**fremder** I'm a stranger to this subject, this subject is foreign territory for me; ~**gebiet** *nt* (special) field; **f**~**gebunden** *adj* related (to the field/subject); ~**gelehrte(r)** *mf* specialist; **f**~**gemäß, f**~**gerecht** *adj* expert; *Ausbildung etc* expert; ~**geschäft** *nt* specialist shop *or* store (*esp US*); ~**geschäft für Lederwaren** leather shop, shop *or* store specializing in leather goods; ~**gespräch** *nt* professional *or* technical discussion; ~**größe** *f* authority; **die** ~**größen der Soziologie** the big names of sociology; ~**gruppe** *f* professional group; (*Univ*) study group; (*Gruppe von Experten*) team of specialists; ~**handel** *m* specialist shops *pl or* stores *pl* (*esp US*); ~**hochschule** *f* college; ~**idiot** *m* (*Univ sl*) crank who can think of nothing but his/her subject, philosophy/chemistry *etc* freak (*sl*); ~**jargon** *m* technical jargon; ~**kenntnisse** *pl* specialized knowledge; ~**kollege** *m* professional colleague; ~**kraft** *f* qualified employee; ~**kreise** *pl:* **in** ~**kreisen** among experts; **f**~**kundig** *adj* informed *no adv;* (*erfahren*) with a knowledge of the subject; (*fachmännisch*) proficient; **jdn f**~**kundig beraten** to give sb informed advice; ~**lehrer** *m* subject teacher.
fachlich *adj* technical; *Ausbildung* specialist *attr; Spezialisierung* in one aspect of a/the subject; (*beruflich*) professional. **ein** ~ **ausgezeichneter Lehrer** a teacher who is academically excellent; ~ **hochqualifizierte Mitarbeiter** staff members who are highly qualified in their field; **sich** ~ **qualifizieren** to gain qualifications in one's field; ~ **auf dem laufenden bleiben** to keep up to date in one's subject.
Fach-: ~**literatur** *f* specialist literature; ~**mann** *m, pl* **-leute** *or* (*rare*) **-männer** expert; **f**~**männisch** *adj* expert; ~**personal** *nt* specialist staff; ~**presse** *f* specialist publications *pl;* **die medizinische/philologische** *etc* ~**presse** the medical/philological *etc* publications *pl;* ~**redakteur** *m* (special) editor; ~**redakteur für Sport/Naturwissenschaft** *etc* sports/science *etc* editor; ~**richtung** *f* subject area; **die** ~**richtung Mathematik** mathematics; ~**schaft** *f* (*Univ*) students *pl* of the/a department; ~**schule** *f* technical college; ~**simpelei** *f* (*inf*) shop-talk; **f**~**simpeln** *vi insep* (*inf*) to talk shop; **f**~**spezifisch** *adj* technical, subject-specific; ~**sprache** *f* technical terminology; **f**~**sprachlich** 1 *adj* technical; 2 *adv* in technical terminology; ~**terminus** *m* technical term; **f**~**übergreifend** 1 *adj*

Problematik, Lernziel etc inter-disciplinary, which extends across the disciplines; **2** *adv* across the disciplines; ~**vokabular** *nt* technical vocabulary; ~**werk** *nt, no pl* half-timbering; ~**werkbauweise** *f* half-timbering; ~**werkhaus** *nt* half-timbered house; ~**wissen** *nt* (specialized) knowledge of the/one's subject; ~**wissenschaft** *f* specialists *pl* or experts *pl* (in a particular/the subject); **ein Experte der entsprechenden** ~**wissenschaft** an expert from the relevant field; ~**wissenschaftler** *m* specialist or expert (in a particular/the subject); **f**~**wissenschaftlich** *adj* technical; *Publikation auch* specialist; ~**wörterbuch** *nt* specialist dictionary; *(wissenschaftliches auch)* technical dictionary; ~**zeitschrift** *f* specialist journal; *(technisch)* technical journal; *(naturwissenschaftlich)* scientific journal; *(für Berufe)* trade journal.

Fackel *f* -, -**n** *(lit, fig)* torch; *(der Revolution auch, des Glaubens)* flame.

Fackellauf *m* torch race.

fackeln *vi (inf)* to shilly-shally *(inf)*. **nicht lange gefackelt!** no shilly-shallying!; **da wird nicht lange gefackelt** there won't be any shilly-shallying.

Fackel-: ~**schein** *m* torchlight; **im** ~**schein** by torchlight; **im** ~**schein sah man ...** you could see by the light of the torches ...; ~**zug** *m* torchlight procession; **einen** ~**zug bekommen** to be honoured with a torchlight procession; **jdm einen** ~**zug bringen** to hold a torchlight procession in sb's honour.

fad *adj pred* **(a)** *siehe* **fad(e) (a, b). (b)** *(Aus, S Ger)* *(zimperlich)* soft *(inf)*, wet *(inf)*, soppy *(inf)*.

Fädchen *nt* dim of **Faden**[1].

fad(e) *adj* **(a)** *Geschmack* insipid; *Essen auch* tasteless. **(b)** *(fig: langweilig)* dull. **(c)** *(Aus, S Ger)* *siehe* **fad (b).**

fädeln *vt* **(a)** to thread. **(b)** *(fig) siehe* **einfädeln 1(b).**

Faden[1] *m* -**s**, **ⁿ** **(a)** *(lit, fig)* thread; *(an Marionetten)* string; *(Med)* stitch. **der rote** ~ *(fig)* the leitmotif, the central theme; **den** ~ **verlieren** *(fig)* to lose the thread; **alle** ~ **laufen in seiner Hand/hier zusammen** he is at the hub of the whole business/this is the hub or the nerve centre of the whole business; **er hält alle** ~ **(fest) in der Hand** he holds the reins; **sein Leben hing an einem** *(dünnen or seidenen)* ~ his life was hanging by a thread; **keinen guten** ~ **an jdm/etw lassen** *(inf)* to tear sb/sth to shreds *(inf)* or pieces *(inf)*. **(b)** *(Spinnen~ etc)* thread; *(Bohnen~)* string. **der Klebstoff/Käse zieht** ~ the glue is tacky/the cheese has gone stringy; **die Bohnen haben** ~ the beans are stringy; **graue** ~ **im Haar haben** to have the odd grey hair.

Faden[2] *m* -**s**, - *(Naut)* fathom.

Faden-: ~**kreuz** *nt* crosshair; **jdn/etw im** ~**kreuz haben** to have sb/sth in one's sights; ~**nudeln** *pl* vermicelli *pl*; **f**~**scheinig** *adj* **(a)** threadbare; **(b)** *(fig)* flimsy; *Argument auch, Moral* threadbare *no adv*; *Ausrede auch* transparent; *Trost* poor; ~**schlag** *m* *(Sw Sew)* basted or tacked seam; ~**wurm** *m* threadworm.

Fadheit *f siehe* **fad(e) (a)** insipidness, insipidity; tastelessness. **(b)** *(fig)* dullness.

Fading ['fe:dɪŋ] *nt* -**s**, *no pl (Rad)* fading.

fadisieren* *vr (Aus) siehe* **langweilen 3.**

Fagott *nt* -**(e)s**, -**e** bassoon.

Fagottbläser(in *f***), Fagottist(in** *f***)** *m* bassoonist.

Fähe *f* -, -**n** *(Hunt)* *(Füchsin)* vixen; *(Dächsin)* sow.

fahen *vt (obs, poet) siehe* **fangen.**

fähig *adj* **(a)** *(tüchtig)* *Mensch, Mitarbeiter etc* capable, competent, able. **sie ist ein** ~**er Kopf** she has an able mind. **(b)** *(sl: gut)* great *(inf)*. **(c)** *pred (befähigt, bereit)* capable *(zu, gen* of). **(dazu)** ~ **sein, etw zu tun** to be capable of doing sth; **bei dem Lärm bin ich keines klaren Gedankens** ~ I can't think straight or hear myself think with all this noise; **zu allem** ~ **sein** to be capable of anything.

Fähigkeit *f (Begabung)* ability; *(Tüchtigkeit auch)* capability; *(Geschicklichkeit auch)* aptitude; *(praktisches Können)* skill. **die** ~ **haben, etw zu tun** to be capable of doing sth; **eine Frau von großen** ~**en** a woman of great ability; **bei deinen** ~**en ...** with your talents ...

fahl *adj (geh)* pale; *Mondlicht auch* wan *(liter)*.

Fahlheit *f siehe adj* paleness; wanness *(liter)*.

Fähnchen *nt* **(a)** *dim of* **Fahne;** *siehe* **Wind. (b)** *(Wimpel)* pennant. **(c)** *(usu pej, inf)* flimsy dress.

fahnden *vi* to search *(nach* for).

Fahndung *f* search.

Fahndungs-: ~**aktion** *f* search; ~**buch** *nt*, ~**liste** *f* wanted (persons) list.

Fahne *f* -, -**n** **(a)** flag; *(von Verein etc auch)* banner; *(Mil, von Pfadfinder etc auch)* colours *pl*. **die** ~ **hochhalten** *(fig)* to keep the flag flying; **die** ~ **des Glaubens etc hochhalten** *(fig geh)* to hold aloft the flag or banner of faith etc; **etw auf seine** ~ **schreiben** *(fig)* to take up the cause of sth; **mit fliegenden or wehenden** ~**n** with beat of drum and flourish of trumpets *(liter)*; **mit fliegenden or wehenden** ~**n untergehen** to go down with all flags flying; **zu den** ~**n eilen** *(old, geh)* to join the colours *(old)*; **jdn zu den** ~**n rufen** *(old, geh)* to call sb up (for military service); **unter der** ~ **stehen** *(old, geh)*, **der** ~ **folgen** *(old, geh)* to follow the flag *(old)*, to serve with the colours *(old)*; **unter jds** ~**n fechten or kämpfen** *(old, geh)* to fight under sb's flag; *siehe* **Wind.**
(b) *(inf)* **eine** ~ **haben** to reek of alcohol; **man konnte seine** ~ **schon aus drei Meter Entfernung riechen** you could smell the alcohol on his breath ten feet away.
(c) *(Typ)* galley (proof).

Fahnen-: ~**abzug** *m* *(Typ)* galley (proof); ~**eid** *m* oath of allegiance; ~**flucht** *f* *(Mil, fig)* desertion; **f**~**flüchtig** *adj* **f**~**flüchtig sein/werden** *(Mil, fig)* to be a deserter, to have deserted/to desert; **ein f**~**flüchtiger Soldat** a deserter;

~**flüchtige(r)** *mf* *(Mil, fig)* deserter; **f**~**geschmückt** *adj* beflagged, decorated with flags; ~**junker** *m* *(Mil, Hist)* officer cadet; ~**mast** *m* flagpole; ~**schmuck** *m* drapery of flags and bunting; **im** ~**schmuck** decked out with flags and bunting; ~**stange** *f* flagpole; ~**träger** *m* standard-bearer, colour-bearer; ~**tuch** *nt* **(a)** *(Tex)* bunting; **(b)** *(Fahne)* flag; ~**weihe** *f* consecration of the flag.

Fähnlein *nt* **(a)** *dim of* **Fahne. (b)** *(kleine Gruppe)* troop.

Fähnrich *m* *(Hist)* standard-bearer; *(Mil)* sergeant. ~ **zur See** petty officer.

Fahr-: ~**abteilung** *f (form)* convoy; ~**ausweis** *m* **(a)** *(Sw, form)* ticket; **(b)** *(Sw)* *siehe* **Führerschein;** ~**bahn** *f* carriageway *(Brit)*, highway *(US)*; *(Fahrspur)* lane; **Betreten der** ~**bahn verboten** pedestrians are not allowed on the road(way); ~**bahnmarkierung** *f* road marking; **f**~**bar** *adj* **(a)** on castors; *Kran* mobile; **f**~**barer Untersatz** *(hum)* wheels *pl (hum)*; **(b)** *(dated) siehe* **befahrbar; f**~**bereit** *adj* in running order; **etw f**~**bereit machen** to get sth in(to) running order.

Fähr-: ~**betrieb** *m* ferry service; **es herrschte reger** ~**betrieb** there were a lot of ferries running; ~**boot** *nt* ferry (boat).

Fahrbücherei *f* mobile or travelling library.

Fahrdamm *m* *(dial) siehe* **Fahrbahn.**

Fährde *f* -, -**n** *(poet) siehe* **Gefahr.**

Fahrdienst *m* **(a)** ~ **haben** to have crew duty. **(b)** *(Rail)* rail service.

Fährdienst *m* ferry service.

Fahrdienstleiter *m* area manager.

Fahrdraht *m* *(Rail etc)* overhead contact wire or line.

Fähre *f* -, -**n** ferry.

Fahr|eigenschaft *f usu pl* handling characteristic. **die** ~**en eines Wagens** the handling of a car; **der Wagen hat hervorragende** ~**en** the car handles excellently.

fahren *pret* **fuhr,** *ptp* **gefahren 1** *vi* **a** *aux sein (sich fortbewegen)* *(Fahrzeug, Fahrgast)* to go; *(Fahrer)* to drive; *(Schiff)* to sail; *(Kran, Kamera, Rolltreppe etc)* to move. **mit dem Auto/Rad** ~ to drive/cycle, to go by car/bike; **mit dem Zug/Motorrad/Bus/Taxi** ~ to go by train or rail/motorbike/bus/taxi; **mit dem Aufzug** ~ to take the lift, to ride the elevator *(US)*; **wollen wir** ~ **oder zu Fuß gehen?** shall we go by car/bus etc or walk?; **links/rechts** ~ to drive on the left/right; **wie lange fährt man von hier nach Basel?** how long does it take to get to Basle from here?; **wie fährt man von hier/am schnellsten zum Bahnhof?** how does one get to the station from here/what is the quickest way to the station (by car/bus etc)?; **ich fahre lieber auf der Autobahn** I'd rather go on or take the motorway; **zweiter Klasse** ~ to travel or go or ride *(US)* second class; **per Anhalter or Autostop** ~ to hitch(hike); **der Wagen/Fahrer ist mir über den Fuß gefahren** the car/driver went or ran or drove over my foot; **gegen einen Baum** ~ to drive or go into a tree; **über den See** ~ to cross the lake; **die Lok fährt elektrisch/mit Dampf** the engine is electric or powered by electricity/is steam-driven; **der Wagen fährt sehr ruhig** the car is very quiet or is a very quiet runner; **gen Himmel/zur Hölle** ~ *(old)* to ascend into heaven/descend into hell; **fahr zur Hölle** or **zum Teufel!** *(old)* the devil take you! *(old)*; *siehe* **fahrend, Grube** *etc*.
(b) *aux sein or haben (ein Fahrzeug lenken, Fahrer sein)* to drive.
(c) *aux sein (losfahren)* *(Verkehrsmittel, Fahrer, Mitfahrer)* to go, to leave. **einen** ~ **lassen** *(inf)* to let off *(inf)*, to fart *(vulg)*.
(d) *aux sein (verkehren)* to run. **es** ~ **täglich zwei Fähren** there are two ferries a day; ~ **da keine Züge?** don't any trains go there?; ~ **bis Walterplatz?** do you go as far as or all the way to Walterplatz?; **hier fährt alle 20 Minuten ein Bus** there's a bus every 20 minutes from here; **die U-Bahn fährt alle fünf Minuten** the underground goes or runs every five minutes.
(e) *aux sein (reisen)* to go. **ich fahre mit dem Auto nach Schweden** I'm taking the car to Sweden, I'm going to Sweden by car.
(f) *aux sein (sich rasch bewegen)* **blitzartig fuhr es ihm durch den Kopf, daß ...** the thought suddenly flashed through his mind that ...; **was ist (denn) in dich gefahren?** what's got into you?; **in den Mantel** ~ to fling on one's coat; **in seine Kleider** ~ to fling on or leap into one's clothes; **der Blitz fuhr in die Eiche** the lightning struck the oak; **die Katze fuhr ihm ins Gesicht** the cat leapt or sprang at his face; **der Hexenschuß fuhr ihm durch den Rücken** a twinge of lumbago shot down his back; *siehe* **Glied** *etc*.
(g) *aux sein or haben (streichen)* **er fuhr mit der Hand/einem Tuch/einer raschen Handbewegung über den Tisch** he ran his hand/a cloth over the table/he swept his hand over the table; **ihre Hand fuhr sanft über ...** she gently ran her hand over ...; **jdm/sich durchs Haar** ~ to run one's fingers through sb's/one's hair; **sich** *(dat)* **mit der Hand über die Stirn** ~ to pass one's hand over one's brow.
(h) *aux sein (zurechtkommen)* **(mit jdm/etw) gut/schlecht** ~ to get on all right/not very well (with sb/sth), not to fare very well (with sb/sth); **(bei etw) gut/schlecht** ~ to do well/badly (with sth); **du fährst besser, wenn ...** you would do or fare better if ...
(i) *(Film: eine Kamerafahrt machen)* to track.
2 *vt* **(a)** *(lenken)* *Auto, Bus, Zug etc* to drive; *Fahrrad, Motorrad* to ride.
(b) *aux sein (zum Fahren benutzen)* *Straße, Strecke, Buslinie etc* to take. **welche Strecke fährt der 59er?** which route does the 59 go?, which route does the 59 take?; **einen Umweg** ~ to go a long way round; **wir sind die Umleitung gefahren** we took or followed the diversion; **ich fahre lieber Autobahn als Landstraße** I prefer (driving on) motorways to ordinary roads; *siehe* **Eisenbahn, Karussell, Schlitten** *etc*.

(c) (benutzen) Kraftstoff etc to use; Reifen to drive on.
(d) (befördern) to take; (hierher~) to bring; (Lastwagen, Taxi: gewerbsmäßig) to carry; Personen auch to drive. **ich fahre dich nach Hause** I'll take or drive you or give you a lift home; **jdn in den Tod ~** (geh) to kill sb.
(e) schrottreif or **zu Schrott ~ Fahrzeug** (durch Unfall) to write off; (durch Verschleiß) to drive into the ground.
(f) aux sein Straße, Strecke to drive; Kurve, Gefälle etc to take.
(g) aux sein Geschwindigkeit to do.
(h) aux haben or sein (Sport) Rennen to take part in; Runde etc to do; Zeit, Rekord etc to clock up.
(i) (Tech) (steuern, betreiben) to run; (abspielen) Platten, Tonbandspulen etc to play; (senden) to broadcast; (durchführen) Sonderschicht to put on; Angriff to launch.
(j) (Film) Aufnahme to track.
3 vr **(a)** impers mit diesem Wagen/bei solchem Wetter/auf dieser Straße fährt es sich gut it's good driving this car/in that kind of weather/on this road.
(b) (Fahrzeug, Straße etc) der neue Wagen/die Autobahn fährt sich gut the new car is nice to drive/the motorway is nice to drive on.
fahrend adj itinerant; Musikant auch travelling. **~es Volk** travelling people; **~e Leute** itinerants; **ein ~er Sänger** a wandering minstrel; **~e Habe** (Jur) chattels pl, moveables pl.
Fahrenheit no art Fahrenheit.
fahrenlassen* vt sep irreg (lit) to let go of, to relinquish one's hold on; (fig) to abandon; siehe fahren 1 (c).
Fahrensmann m, pl -leute or -männer (dial) sailor, seafarer (liter).
Fahrer(in f) m -s, - **(a)** driver; (Chauffeur auch) chauffeur/chauffeuse. **(b)** (Sport inf) (Rad~) cyclist; (Motorrad~) motorcyclist.
Fahrerei f driving.
Fahrer-: **~flucht** f hit-and-run driving; **~flucht begehen** to fail to stop after being involved in an accident, to be involved in a hit-and-run; **seine Unfallflucht**; **f~flüchtig** adj (form) hit-and-run attr; **f~flüchtig sein** to have failed to stop after being involved in an accident, to have committed a hit-and-run offence; **~haus** nt (driver's) cab.
fahrerisch adj driving attr. **er ist mir ~ weit überlegen** he is a far better driver than I am.
Fahr-: **~erlaubnis** f (form) driving licence (Brit), driver's license (US); **~gastschiff** nt passenger boat; **~gefühl** nt unser neues Modell vermittelt Ihnen ein völlig neues **~gefühl** our new model offers you a completely new driving experience; **zu harte Reifen vermitteln/mit einem Wagen mit Automatik zu fahren vermittelt ein merkwürdiges ~gefühl** driving on over-inflated tyres/an automatic car is a very strange sensation; **~geld** nt fares pl; (für einzelne Fahrt) fare; **„das ~geld bitte passend** or **abgezählt bereithalten"** "please tender exact fare" (form), "please have the exact fare ready"; **~gelegenheit** f transport no indef art, means of transport; **~geschwindigkeit** f (form) speed; **~gestell** nt **(a)** (Aut) chassis; **(b)** siehe **~werk (a)**; **(c)** (hum inf) legs pl; **ein hohes ~gestell** long legs.
Fähr-: **~hafen** m ferry terminal; **~haus** nt ferry house.
fahrig adj nervous; (unkonzentriert) distracted.
Fahrigkeit f siehe fahrig nervousness; distractedness, distraction.
Fahrkarte f **(a)** ticket; (Zeit~, Streckenkarte) season ticket; (fig) passport (nach to). **mit diesem Sieg hatten sie die ~ zum Endspiel in der Tasche** this victory was their passport to the final. **(b)** (Schießsport) miss.
Fahrkarten-: **~ausgabe** f ticket office; **~automat** m ticket machine; **~schalter** m ticket office.
Fahr-: **~komfort** m (motoring) comfort; **~kosten** pl siehe Fahrtkosten; **~kunst** f driving skills pl; **f~lässig** adj negligent (auch Jur); **f~lässig handeln** to be guilty of negligence, to be negligent; siehe Körperverletzung, Tötung; **~lässigkeit** f negligence (auch Jur); **~lehrer** m driving instructor; **~leistung** f road performance.
Fährmann m, pl -männer or -leute ferryman.
Fahrnis f (Jur) chattels pl, moveables pl.
Fährnis f (obs) peril.
Fahr-: **~personal** nt drivers and conductors pl; (Rail) footplatemen pl (Brit), railroad crews pl (US); (von Einzelfahrzeug) bus/tram/train crew; **~plan** m timetable, schedule (US); (fig) schedule; **f~planmäßig** adj scheduled attr, pred; **f~planmäßig verkehren/ankommen** to run/arrive on schedule; **es verlief alles f~planmäßig** everything went according to schedule; **~praxis** f, no pl driving experience no indef art; **~preis** m fare; **~preisanzeiger** m taxi meter; **~prüfung** f driving test.
Fahrrad nt bicycle, cycle, bike (inf).
Fahrrad-: **~fahrer** m cyclist, bicyclist (form); **~händler** m bicycle dealer; (Geschäft) cycle shop; **~ständer** m (bi)cycle stand; **~weg** m cycle path, cycleway.
Fahrrinne f (Naut) shipping channel, fairway.
Fahrschein m ticket.
Fahrschein-: **~block** m, **~heft** nt book of tickets; **~entwerter** m automatic ticket stamping machine (in bus/trams etc).
Fährschiff nt ferry(boat).
Fahr-: **~schule** f driving school; **~schüler** m **(a)** (bei Fahrschule) learner driver, student driver (US); **(b)** pupil who has to travel some distance to and from school; **~sicherheit** f safe driving or motoring no art; **erhöhte ~sicherheit** safer driving or motoring; **~spur** f lane; **~steig** m moving walkway; **~stil** m style of driving/riding/skiing etc; **~straße** f road (for vehicular traffic form); **das ist eine reine ~straße** pedestrians aren't allowed on this road; **~streifen** m siehe **~spur**.

~stuhl m lift (Brit), elevator (US); **~stuhlschacht** m lift (Brit) or elevator (US) shaft; **~stunde** f driving lesson.
Fahrt f -, -en **(a)** (das Fahren) journey. **„während der ~ nicht hinauslehnen"** "do not lean out of the window while the train/bus etc is in motion"; **nach zwei Stunden ~** after travelling for two hours; (mit dem Auto auch) after two hours' drive; siehe frei.
(b) (Fahrgeschwindigkeit) speed. **volle/halbe ~ voraus!** (Naut) full/half speed ahead!; **30 Knoten ~ machen** to do 30 knots; **~ aufnehmen** to pick up speed; **jdn in ~ bringen** to get sb going; **in ~ kommen** or **geraten/sein** to get/have got going.
(c) (Reise) journey. **was kostet eine ~/eine einfache ~ nach London?** how much is it to London/how much is a single to London?, what is the fare/the single fare to London?; **gute ~!** bon voyage!, safe journey!; **auf ~ gehen** (dated) to take to the road.
(d) (Ausflug, Wanderung) trip. **eine ~ machen** to go on a trip.
(e) (Naut) voyage; (Über~) crossing. **für große/kleine ~ zugelassen sein** to be licensed for long/short voyages.
(f) (Film) tracking shot.
Fahr-: **f~tauglich** adj fit to drive; **~tauglichkeit** f fitness to drive; **jdm die ~tauglichkeit bescheinigen** to certify sb fit to drive.
Fahrtdauer f time for the journey. **bei einer ~ von fünf Stunden** on a five-hour journey; **man muß für diese Strecke mit einer ~ von drei Stunden rechnen** you have to allow three hours for this stretch.
Fährte f -, -n tracks pl; (Hunt auch) spoor; (Witterung) scent; (Spuren) trail. **auf der richtigen/falschen ~ sein** (fig) to be on the right/wrong track; **jdn auf die richtige ~ bringen** (fig) to put sb on the right track; **jdn auf eine falsche ~ locken** (fig) to put sb off the scent; **eine ~ verfolgen** (fig) to follow up a lead; **eine falsche ~ verfolgen** (fig) to be on the wrong track.
Fahr-: **~technik** f driving technique; **f~technisch** adj as regards the technicalities of driving; **eine gute f~technische Ausbildung bekommen** to learn to drive well; **eine f~technisch schwierige Strecke** a difficult stretch of road (to drive).
Fahrten-: **~buch** nt **(a)** (Kontrollbuch) driver's log; **(b)** (Wandertagebuch) diary of a trip; **~messer** nt sheath knife; **~schreiber** m siehe Fahrtschreiber; **~schwimmer** m person who has passed an advanced swimming test; **seinen ~schwimmer machen** (inf) to do one's advanced swimming test.
Fahrtest m road test.
Fahrtkosten pl travelling expenses pl.
Fahrtreppe f escalator.
Fahrt-: **~richtung** f direction in which one is travelling; (im Verkehr auch) direction of the traffic; **entgegen der/in ~richtung** (im Zug) with one's back to the engine/facing the engine; (im Bus etc) facing backwards/the front; **die Züge in ~richtung Norden/Süden** etc the northbound/southbound etc trains; **in ~richtung Norden sind Stauungen zu erwarten** long delays are affecting northbound traffic; **die Autobahn ist in ~richtung Norden gesperrt** the northbound carriageway of the motorway is closed; **~richtungsanzeiger** m (Aut) indicator; **~schreiber** m tachograph.
Fahr-: **f~tüchtig** adj fit to drive; Wagen etc roadworthy; **~tüchtigkeit** f driving ability; roadworthiness.
Fahrt-: **~unterbrechung** f break in the journey, stop; **~wind** m airstream.
Fahr-: **f~untauglich** adj unfit to drive; Wagen etc unroadworthy; **~untauglichkeit** f unfitness to drive; unroadworthiness; **~verbot** nt loss of one's licence, driving ban; **jdn mit ~verbot belegen** to ban sb from driving, to take sb's licence away; **~verhalten** nt (von Fahrer) behaviour behind the wheel; (von Wagen) road performance.
Fährverkehr m ferry traffic.
Fahr-: **~wasser** nt **(a)** (Naut) siehe **~rinne**; **(b)** (fig) in jds **~wasser geraten** to get in with sb; **in ein gefährliches/fragwürdiges ~wasser geraten** to get on to dangerous/questionable ground; **in ein politisches/kommunistisches ~wasser geraten** to get tied up with politics/communism; **in jds ~wasser segeln** or **schwimmen** to follow in sb's wake; **in seinem** or **im richtigen ~wasser sein** to be in one's element; **~weise** f sense **~weise** his driving, the way he drives; **~werk** nt **(a)** (Aviat) undercarriage, landing gear; **(b)** siehe **~gestell (a)**; **~wind** m **(a)** (Naut) wind; **(b)** siehe Fahrtwind; **~zeit** f siehe Fahrtdauer.
Fahrzeug nt vehicle; (Luft~) aircraft; (Wasser~) vessel.
Fahrzeug-: **~brief** m registration document, log book (Brit inf); **~führer** m (form) driver of a vehicle; **~halter** m vehicle owner; **~kolonne** f **(a)** (Schlange) queue (Brit) or line of vehicles etc; **(b)** (auch ~konvoi) convoy; (bei Staatsbesuchen etc) motorcade; **~lenker** m (form) siehe **~führer**; **~papiere** pl vehicle documents pl; **~park** m (form) fleet; **~verkehr** m (form) vehicular traffic (form).
Faible ['fɛːbl] nt -s, -s (geh) liking; (Schwäche auch) weakness; (Vorliebe auch) penchant.
fair [fɛːɐ] **1** adj fair (gegen to). **2** adv fairly. **~ spielen** (Sport) to play fairly; (fig) to play fair.
Faireß, Fairness ['fɛːɐnɛs] f -, no pl fairness.
Fair play ['fɛɐ 'pleɪ] nt - -, no pl fair play.
fäkal adj (geh) faecal.
Fäkaldünger m natural manure, dung.
Fäkalien [-iən] pl faeces pl.
Fakir m -s, -e fakir.
Faksimile [fak'ziːmile] nt -s, -s facsimile.
Faksimile-: **~ausgabe** f facsimile edition; **~druck** m **(a)** printed facsimile; **(b)** (Verfahren) autotype; **~stempel** m signature stamp; **~unterschrift** f facsimile signature.

faksimilieren* *vt* to make a facsimile of, to reproduce in facsimile, to facsimile.
Fakt *nt or m* -(e)s, -en *siehe* **Faktum.**
Fakten *pl of* **Fakt, Faktum.**
Fakten-: ~**material** *nt, no pl* facts *pl*; ~**sammlung** *f* collection of facts; ~**wissen** *nt* factual knowledge.
Faktion *f (old, Sw) siehe* **Fraktion.**
faktisch 1 *adj attr* actual, real. **2** *adv* (a) in reality or actuality *(form).* (b) *(esp Aus inf: praktisch)* more or less.
faktitiv *adj (Gram)* factitive.
Faktitiv(um) *nt (Gram)* factitive verb.
Faktizität *f (geh)* factuality.
Faktor *m* (a) factor *(auch Math).* (b) *(Typ)* caseroom/bookbindery *etc* supervisor.
Faktorei *f (Comm)* trading post.
Faktoren|analyse *f* factor analysis.
Faktotum *nt* -s, -s *or* **Faktoten** factotum.
Faktum *nt* -s, **Fakten** fact.
Faktur *f* (a) *(dated)* invoice. (b) *(Mus)* structure.
Faktura *f* -, **Fakturen** *(Aus, dated) siehe* **Faktur** (a).
fakturieren* *vt (Comm)* to invoice.
Fakturist(in *f) m (Comm)* (a) bookkeeper. (b) *(Aus: Rechnungsprüfer)* invoice clerk.
Fakultas *f* -, **Fakultäten:** die ~ für ein Fach haben to be qualified to teach a subject.
Fakultät *f* (a) *(Univ: Fachbereich)* faculty. (ein Kollege) von der anderen ~ sein *(hum inf) (homosexuell sein)* to be one of them *(inf),* to be the other way round *(inf); (rare: eine andere Weltanschauung haben)* to be of another school of thought. (b) *(obs: Begabung)* faculty. (c) *(Math)* factorial.
fakultativ *adj (geh)* optional.
Falange [fa'laŋgɛ] *f* -, *no pl (Pol)* Falange.
Falangist(in *f)* [falaŋ'gɪst(ɪn)] *m (Pol)* Falangist.
falb *adj (geh)* dun.
Falbe *m* -n, -n dun.
Falke *m* -n, -n falcon; *(fig)* hawk.
Falken-: ~**auge** *nt* (a) *(liter) siehe* **Adlerauge;** (b) *(Miner)* hawk's-eye; ~**beize** *f* falconry.
Falkenier *m* -s, -e *siehe* **Falkner(in).**
Falkenjagd *f siehe* **Falkenbeize.**
Falkner(in *f) m* -s, - falconer.
Falknerei *f* (a) falconry. (b) *(Anlage)* falcon house.
Fall¹ *m* -(e)s, ⁻e (a) *(das Hinunterfallen)* fall. im/beim ~ hat er ... when/as he fell he ...; *siehe* **frei.**
(b) *(das Zufallkommen)* fall; *(fig) (von Menschen, Regierung)* downfall; *(von Plänen, Gesetz etc)* failure. **zu ~ kommen** *(lit geh)* to fall; über die **Affäre ist er zu ~ gekommen** *(fig)* the affair was or caused his downfall; **zu ~ bringen** *(lit geh)* to make fall, to trip up; *(fig) Menschen* to cause the downfall of; *Regierung* to bring down; *Gesetz, Plan etc* to thwart; *Tabu* to break down; **der Baumstamm brachte ihn zu ~** *(geh)* he fell or tripped over the tree trunk.
(c) *(fig: Untergang, Sturz)* fall.
(d) *(von Kurs, Temperatur etc)* drop, fall *(gen* in).
(e) *(von Gardine etc)* hang, drape.
Fall² *m* -(e)s, ⁻e (a) *(Umstand)* gesetzt den ~ assuming or supposing (that); für den ~, daß ich ... in case I ...; für den ~ meines Todes/einer Reifenpanne in case I die/in case of a puncture; für alle ⁻e just in case; in jedem/keinem ~(e) always/never; auf jeden/keinen ~ at any rate, at all events/on no account; auf alle ⁻e in any case, anyway; für solche ⁻e for such occasions; im äußersten ~(e) if the worst comes to the worst; im anderen ~(e) if not, if that is not the case; im günstigsten/schlimmsten ~(e) at best/worst; im ⁻e eines ⁻es if it comes to it; wenn dieser ~ eintritt if this should be the case, if this should arise; auch mit diesem ~ sollten wir rechnen we should take this possibility into account as well.
(b) *(gegebener Sachverhalt)* case. in diesem ~ in this case or instance; ein ~ von ... a case or an instance of ...; von ~ zu ~ from case to case, from one case to the next; *(hin und wieder)* periodically; in diesem ~(e) will ich noch einmal von einer Bestrafung absehen, aber ... I won't punish you on this occasion either, but ...; jds ~ sein *(inf)* to be sb's cup of tea *(inf);* klarer ~! *(inf)* sure thing! *(esp US inf),* you bet! *(inf).*
(c) *(Jur, Med: Beispiel, Person)* case.
(d) *(Gram: Kasus)* case. der erste/zweite/dritte/vierte/fünfte/sechste ~ the nominative/genitive/dative/accusative/ablative/vocative case.
Fall³ *nt* -(e)s, -en *(Naut)* halyard.
Fallapfel *m* windfall.
fällbar *adj (Chem)* precipitable.
Fall-: ~**beil** *nt* guillotine; ~**beschleunigung** *f* gravitational acceleration, acceleration due to gravity; ~**bö** *f* down gust; ~**brücke** *f* drawbridge; *(Enterbrücke)* gangplank.
Falle *f* -, -n (a) *(lit, fig)* trap. in eine ~ geraten or gehen *(lit)* to get caught in a trap; *(fig)* to fall into a trap; jdm in die ~ gehen, in jds ~ geraten to walk or fall into sb's trap; in der ~ sitzen to be trapped; jdn in eine ~ locken *(fig)* to trick sb; jdm eine ~ stellen *(fig)* to set a trap for sb; dieses Angebot war nur eine ~ that offer was just a con *(inf).*
(b) *(Tech)* catch, latch.
(c) *(inf: Bett)* bed. in der ~ sein/liegen to be in bed; sich in die ~ hauen, in die ~ gehen to hit the hay *(inf),* to turn in; ab *(mit euch)* in die ~! off to beddy-byes *(baby-talk)* or bed!
fallen *pret* **fiel,** *ptp* **gefallen** *vi aux sein* (a) *(hinabfallen, umfallen)* to fall; *(Gegenstand, Wassermassen auch)* to drop; *(Theat, Vorhang auch)* to come down; *(Klappe auch)* to come down, to drop. etw ~ lassen to drop sth; über etw *(acc)* ~ to trip over sth; sich ~ lassen to drop; *(fig)* to give up; die ~de Sucht *(obs)* falling sickness *(old);* durch eine Prüfung *etc* ~ to fail an

exam *etc;* ein gefallenes Mädchen *(dated)* a fallen woman *(dated); siehe auch* **fallenlassen, Nase, Groschen** *etc.*
(b) *(hängen: Vorhang, Kleid etc)* to hang; *(reichen)* to come down *(bis auf + acc* to). die Haare ~ ihr bis auf die Schultern/über die Augen/ins Gesicht/in die Stirn her hair comes down to or reaches her shoulders/falls into her eyes/face/onto her forehead.
(c) *(abfallen, sinken)* to drop; *(Wasserstand, Preise, Fieber auch, Thermometer)* to go down; *(Fluß, Kurse, Wert, Aktien auch, Barometer)* to fall; *(Nachfrage, Ansehen)* to fall off, to decrease. im Preis/Wert ~ to go down or drop or fall in price/value; im Kurs ~ to go down, to drop.
(d) *(im Krieg ums Leben kommen)* to fall, to be killed. mein Mann ist gefallen my husband was killed in the war.
(e) *(erobert werden: Festung, Stadt etc)* to fall.
(f) *(fig) (Regierung)* to fall; *(Gesetz etc)* to be dropped; *(Tabu, Brauch etc)* to disappear. das Gesetz muß ~ that law will have to go.
(g) *(mit schneller Bewegung)* jdm ins Lenkrad ~ to grab the steering wheel from sb; einem Pferd in die Zügel ~ to grab a horse's reins; die Tür fällt ins Schloß the door clicks shut; die Tür ins Schloß ~ lassen to let the door shut; der Tiger fiel dem Elefanten in die Flanke the tiger pounced on the elephant's flank; *siehe* **Hals¹, Wort.**
(h) *(treffen)* to fall; *(Wahl, Verdacht auch)* to light *(form).* das Licht fällt durch die Luke the light comes in through the skylight; das Los, das zu tun, fiel auf ihn it fell to his lot to do that.
(i) *(stattfinden, sich ereignen: Weihnachten, Datum etc)* to fall *(auf + acc* on); *(gehören)* to come *(unter + acc* under, *in + acc* within, under). in eine Zeit ~ to belong to an era; unter einen Begriff ~ to be part of a concept; aus einer Gruppe/Kategorie etc ~ to come outside or be excluded from a group/category etc; aus der Besteuerung/Studienförderung ~ to become exempt from taxation/ineligible for a university grant.
(j) *(zufallen: Erbschaft etc)* to go *(an + acc* to). das Elsaß fiel an Frankreich Alsace fell to France; *(nach Verhandlungen)* Alsace went to France.
(k) *(gemacht, erzielt werden) (Entscheidung)* to be made; *(Urteil)* to be passed or pronounced; *(Schuß)* to be fired; *(Sport: Tor)* to be scored.
(l) *(Wort)* to be uttered or spoken; *(Name)* to be mentioned; *(Bemerkung)* to be made.
(m) *(geraten)* in Schlaf ~ to fall asleep; in Schrecken/Melancholie ~ to become frightened/melancholy; in eine andere Tonart ~ to speak in or *(absichtlich)* adopt a different tone (of voice); in eine andere Sprache ~ to lapse or drop into another language; in eine andere Gangart ~ to change one's pace; *siehe* **Opfer, Rahmen, Rolle** *etc.*
(n) *(sein)* das fällt ihm leicht/schwer he finds that easy/difficult; *siehe* **Last, lästig** *etc.*
fällen *vt* (a) *(umschlagen)* to fell.
(b) *(fig) Entscheidung* to make, to come to; *Urteil* to pass, to pronounce.
(c) *(zum Angriff senken) Lanze* to lower, to level. mit gefälltem Bajonett with bayonet(s) at the ready.
(d) *(Chem)* to precipitate.
(e) *(Math) siehe* **Lot¹** (d).
fallenlassen* *vt sep irreg* (a) *(aufgeben)* Plan, Mitarbeiter to drop. (b) *(äußern)* Bemerkung to let drop. hat er irgend etwas darüber ~? *(inf)* has he let anything drop about it?
Fallensteller *m* -s, - *(Hunt)* trapper.
Fall-: ~**gatter** *nt siehe* ~**gitter;** ~**geschwindigkeit** *f (Phys)* speed of fall; ~**gesetz** *nt (Phys)* law of falling bodies; ~**gitter** *nt* portcullis; ~**grube** *f (Hunt)* pit; *(fig rare)* pitfall; ~**hammer** *m* pile-driver; ~**höhe** *f (Phys)* (height or depth of) drop; *(beim Wasserkraftwerk)* head.
fallieren* *vi (Fin)* to fail, to go bankrupt.
fällig *adj* due *pred; (Fin)* Rechnung, Betrag etc auch payable; Wechsel mature(d). längst ~ long overdue; die ~en Zinsen the interest due; ~ werden to become or fall due; *(Wechsel)* to mature; am Wochenende ist endlich Rasenmähen/eine Party ~ the lawn is about due for a cut/a party is about due at the weekend; bei ihm or für ihn ist (et)was ~ *(inf)* he's got it coming to him *(inf),* he's asking for it *(inf);* der Kerl ist ~ *(inf)* he's for it *(inf).*
Fälligkeit *f (Fin)* settlement date; *(von Wechseln)* maturity. zahlbar bei ~ payable by settlement date; payable at or on maturity.
Fälligkeits-: ~**tag,** ~**termin** *m* settlement date; *(von Wechsel)* date of maturity.
Fall|obst *nt* windfalls *pl; (sl: Hängebrüste)* floppy boobs *(sl).* ein Stück ~ a windfall.
Fallout, Fall-out [fo'laut] *m* -s, -s fall-out.
Fall-: ~**reep** *nt (Naut)* rope ladder; *(Treppe)* gangway; ~**rohr** *nt* drainpipe, downpipe *(form);* ~**rückzieher** *m (Ftbl)* overhead kick, bicycle kick.
falls *conj (wenn)* if; *(für den Fall, daß)* in case. ~ möglich if possible; ~ du Lust hast if you (happen) to want to, if you should (happen to) want to; gib mir deine Telefonnummer, ~ ich mich verspäten sollte give me your phone number in case I'm late; ~ ich mich verspäten sollte, rufe ich vorher an if I'm late or in the event of my being late *(form)* I'll phone you first.
Fallschirm *m* parachute. mit dem ~ abspringen to parachute, to make a parachute jump; mit dem ~ über Frankreich abspringen to parachute out over France; *(in Kriegszeit)* to parachute into France; etw mit dem ~ abwerfen to drop sth by parachute.
Fallschirm-: ~**absprung** *m* parachute jump; ~**jäger** *m (Mil)*

paratrooper; **die ~jäger** (*Einheit*) the paratroop(er)s; **~springen** *nt* parachuting; **~springer** *m* parachutist; **~truppe** *f* (*Mil*) paratroops *pl*.

Fall-: **~strick** *m* (*fig*) trap, snare; **jdm ~stricke** *or* **einen ~strick legen** to set a trap *or* snare for sb (to walk into); **~studie** *f* case study; **~sucht** *f* (*old*) falling sickness (*old*); **f~süchtig** *adj* (*old*) epileptic; **~süchtige(r)** *mf* (*old*) epileptic; **~tür** *f* trapdoor.

Fällung *f*, *no pl* **(a)** (*von Bäumen etc*) felling. **(b)** (*Jur: eines Urteils*) pronouncement; (*einer Entscheidung*) reaching. **(c)** (*Chem*) precipitation.

Fällungsmittel *nt* (*Chem*) precipitant.

Fall-: **f~weise** *adv* **(a)** from case to case; **(b)** (*esp Aus: gelegentlich*) now and again, occasionally; **bei f~weisem Auftreten von** (*form*) with the occasional occurrence of; **~wind** *m* katabatic (*form*) *or* fall wind; **~wurf** *m* (*Sport*) diving throw.

falsch *adj* **(a)** (*verkehrt, fehlerhaft*) wrong (*in der Logik etc*) false. **richtig/wahr oder ~** right *or* wrong/true *or* false; **alles ~ machen** to do everything wrong; **wie man's macht, ist es ~** (*inf*) whatever I/you *etc* do it's bound to be wrong; **mach dir keine ~en Vorstellungen darüber/davon** don't get the wrong idea (*inf*) *or* any misconceptions about it; **du machst dir völlig ~e Vorstellungen** you have *or* you've got quite the wrong idea *or* some misconceptions; **~es Bewußtsein** (*Philos, Sociol*) false consciousness; **~er Alarm** (*lit, fig*) false alarm; **etw ~ verstehen** to misunderstand sth, to get sth wrong (*inf*); **etw ~ schreiben/aussprechen** to spell/pronounce sth wrongly, to misspell/mispronounce sth; **die Uhr geht ~** the clock is wrong; **Kinder ~ erziehen** to bring children up badly; **~ spielen** (*Mus*) to play the wrong note/notes; (*unrein*) to play off key *or* out of tune; (*Cards*) to cheat; **~ singen** to sing out of tune *or* off key; **Sie sind hier ~** you're in the wrong place; **bei jdm an den F~en geraten** *or* **kommen** to pick the wrong person in sb; **~ liegen** (*inf*) to be wrong (*bei, in + dat* about, *mit* in); *siehe* **Licht, Pferd** *etc*.

(b) (*unecht, nachgemacht*) *Zähne etc* false; *Perlen auch* fake; *Würfel* loaded; (*gefälscht*) *Paß etc* forged, fake; *Geld* counterfeit; (*betrügerisch*) bogus, fake. **~er Zopf** hairpiece, switch.

(c) (*unaufrichtig, unangebracht*) *Gefühl, Freund, Scham, Pathos etc* false. **ein ~er Hund, eine ~e Schlange** (*inf*) a snake-in-the-grass; **ein ~es Spiel (mit jdm) treiben** to play (sb) false; **~ lachen** to give a false laugh; **~ schwören** (*Jur*) to give false evidence; **unter ~er Flagge segeln** (*lit, fig*) to sail under false colours; *siehe* **Bescheidenheit.**

(d) (*dial: tückisch*) nasty.

Falsch *m* (*old*): **ohne ~** to be without guile *or* artifice; **es ist kein ~ an ihm** there is no guile in him.

Falsch|aussage *f* (*Jur*) (*uneidliche*) **~** false statement.

Falsch|eid *m* (*Jur*) (unintentional) false statement *or* oath.

fälschen *vt* to forge, to fake; *Geld, Briefmarken auch* to counterfeit; (*Comm*) *Bücher* to falsify; *Geschichte, Tatsachen* to falsify; *siehe* **gefälscht.**

Fälscher(in *f*) *m* **-s, -** forger; (*von Geld, Briefmarken auch*) counterfeiter.

Falsch-: **~fahrer** *m* person/car driving in the wrong direction/on the wrong side of the road *etc*; **~fahrt** *f* driving in the wrong direction *etc no art*; **~geld** *nt* counterfeit *or* forged money; **f~gläubig** *adj* (*old Rel*) heterodox; **~heit** *f*, *no pl* falsity, falseness; (*dial: von Menschen*) nastiness.

fälschlich 1 *adj* false; *Behauptung auch* erroneous; *Annahme, Glaube auch* mistaken, erroneous. **2** *adv* wrongly, falsely; *behaupten, annehmen, glauben auch* mistakenly, erroneously; (*versehentlich*) by mistake.

fälschlicherweise *adv* wrongly, falsely; *behaupten, annehmen, glauben auch* mistakenly, erroneously.

Falsch-: **~meldung** *f* (*Press*) false report; **~münzer(in** *f*) *m* **-s, -** forger, counterfeiter; **~münzerei** *f* forgery, counterfeiting; **f~spielen** *vi sep* (*Cards*) to cheat; **~spieler** *m* (*Cards*) cheat; (*professionell*) cardsharp(er).

Fälschung *f* **(a)** *no pl* (*das Fälschen*) forgery, forging, faking; (*von Geld, Briefmarken auch*) counterfeiting. **(b)** (*gefälschter Gegenstand*) forgery, fake.

Falsett *nt* **-(e)s, -e** falsetto. **~ singen, mit ~stimme singen** to sing falsetto.

Falsifikat *nt* forgery, fake.

Falsifikation *f* falsification.

falsifizieren* *vt* to falsify.

Falt-: **f~bar** *adj* foldable; (*zusammenklappbar*) collapsible; *Stuhl, Tisch, Fahrrad* folding *attr*, collapsible; **~blatt** *nt* leaflet; (*in Zeitschrift etc auch*) insert; **~boot** *nt* collapsible boat.

Fältchen *nt* dim of **Falte.**

Falte *f* **-, -n** **(a)** (*in Stoff, Papier*) fold; (*Knitter~, Bügel~*) crease. **in ~n legen** to fold; **~n schlagen** to get creased, to crease; **~n werfen** to fall in folds, to drape.

(b) (*in Haut*) wrinkle. **strenge ~n** harsh lines; **die Stirn in ~n ziehen** *or* **legen** to knit *or* furrow one's brow.

(c) (*Geol*) fold.

fälteln *vt* to pleat.

falten 1 *vt* to fold. **die Stirn ~** to knit one's brow. **2** *vr* to fold.

Falten-: **~gebirge** *nt* fold mountains *pl*; **f~los** *adj* *Gesicht* unlined; *Haut auch* smooth; **f~reich** *adj* *Haut* wrinkled; *Gesicht auch* lined; **~rock** *m* pleated skirt; **~wurf** *m* fall of the folds; **um bei den Gardinen einen eleganten ~wurf zu garantieren** to ensure that the curtains hang well.

Falter *m* **-s, -** (*Tag~*) butterfly; (*Nacht~*) moth.

faltig *adj* (*zerknittert*) creased; (*in Falten gelegt*) hanging in folds; *Gesicht, Haut* wrinkled. **~ fallen** to hang in folds; **~ gerafft sein** to be gathered into folds.

-fältig *adj suf* -fold.

Falt-: **~karte** *f* folding *or* fold-up map; **~karton** *m*, **~schachtel** *f* collapsible box; **~tür** *f* folding door.

Falz *m* **-es, -e** (*Kniff, Faltlinie*) fold; (*zwischen Buchrücken und -deckel*) joint; (*Tech*) rabbet; (*zwischen Blechrändern*) join, lock seam (*spec*); (*Briefmarken~*) hinge.

falzen *vt* *Papierbogen* to fold; *Holz* to rabbet; *Blechränder* to join with a lock seam.

Fam. *abbr of* **Familie.**

familiär *adj* **(a)** (*Familien~*) family *attr*. **(b)** (*zwanglos*) informal; (*freundschaftlich*) close; (*pej: plump-vertraulich*) familiar. **ein ~er Ausdruck** a colloquialism; **mit jdm ~ verkehren** to be on close terms with sb.

Familiarität *f siehe adj* (*b*) informality; closeness; familiarity.

Familie [fa'mi:liə] *f* family. **~ Müller** the Müller family; **~ Otto Francke** (*als Anschrift*) Mr. & Mrs. Otto Francke and family; **eine ~ gründen** to start a family; **~ haben** (*inf*) to have a family; **aus guter ~ sein** to come from a good family; **es liegt in der ~** it runs in the family; **zur ~ gehören** to be one of the family; **es bleibt in der ~** it'll stay in the family; *siehe* **beste(r, s).**

Familien- [-iən-] *in cpds* family; **~angehörige(r)** *mf* dependant; **~anschluß** *m*: **Unterkunft/Stellung mit ~anschluß** accommodation/job where one is treated as one of the family; **~anschluß suchen** to wish to be treated as one of the family; **~anzeigen** *pl* personal announcements *pl*; **~bad** *nt* family swimming/sauna; **~besitz** *m* family property; **in ~besitz sein** to be owned by the family; **~betrieb** *m* family concern *or* business; **~buch** *nt* book of family events with some legal documents, = family bible; **~feier** *f*, **~fest** *nt* family party; **~flasche** *f* family-size bottle; **~forschung** *f* genealogy; **~grab** *nt* family grave; **~gruft** *f* family vault; **~kreis** *m* family circle; **die Trauung fand im engsten ~kreis statt** only the immediate family were present at the wedding; **~leben** *nt* family life; **~mitglied** *nt* member of the family; **~nachrichten** *pl* births, marriages and deaths, personal announcements; **~name** *m* surname, family name (*US*); **~oberhaupt** *nt* head of the family; **~packung** *f* family(-size) pack; **~paß** *m* family passport; **~planung** *f* family planning; **~rat** *m* family council; **~recht** *nt* family law; **~roman** *m* (*family*) saga; **~serie** *f* (*TV*) family series; **~sinn** *m* sense of family; **~stand** *m* marital status; **~stück** *nt* family heirloom; **~unterhalt** *m* family upkeep *or* maintenance; **den ~unterhalt verdienen** to support the family; **~vater** *m* father of a family; **~verhältnisse** *pl* family circumstances *pl or* background *sing*; **aus was für ~verhältnissen kommt sie?** what is her family background?, what kind of family does she come from?; **~vorstand** *m* (*form*) head of the family; **~wappen** *nt* family arms *pl*; **~zulage** *f* dependants' allowance (*in unemployment benefit*); **~zusammenführung** *f* (*Pol*) principle of allowing families to be united; **~zuwachs** *m* addition to the family.

famos *adj* (*dated inf*) capital (*dated inf*), splendid.

famulieren* *vi* (*Med*) to do some practical work.

Famulus *m* **-, Famuli (a)** (*Med*) student doing practical work. **(b)** (*obs: Gehilfe*) servant.

Fan [fɛn] *m* **-s, -s** fan; (*Ftbl auch*) supporter.

Fanal *nt* **-s, -e** (*liter*) signal (*gen* for).

Fanatiker(in *f*) *m* **-s, -** fanatic.

-fanatiker(in *f*) *m in cpds* -fiend (*inf*), -fanatic, -maniac.

fanatisch *adj* fanatical.

fanatisiert *adj* (*geh*) rabid.

Fanatismus *m* fanaticism.

fand *pret of* **finden.**

Fanfare *f* **-, -n (a)** (*Mus*) fanfare. **(b)** (*Aut*) horn.

Fanfaren-: **~stoß** *m* flourish (of trumpets), fanfare; **~zug** *m* trumpeters *pl*.

Fang *m* **-(e)s, ⸚e (a)** *no pl* (*das Fangen*) hunting; (*mit Fallen*) trapping; (*Fischen*) fishing. **auf ~ gehen** to go hunting/trapping/fishing; **zum ~ auslaufen** to go fishing.

(b) *no pl* (*Beute*) (*lit, fig*) catch; (*von Wild auch*) bag; (*fig: von Gegenständen*) haul. **einen guten ~ machen** to make a good catch/get a good bag/haul.

(c) *no pl* (*Hunt: Todesstoß*) coup de grâce.

(d) *usu pl* (*Hunt*) (*Kralle*) talon; (*Reißzahn*) fang. **in den ⸚en + gen** (*fig*) in the clutches of; **wenn sie ihn in ihren ⸚en hat** when she's got her talons into him, when she's got him in her clutches.

Fang-: **~arm** *m* (*Zool*) tentacle; **~ball** *m* catch; **~eisen** *nt* (*Hunt*) gin trap.

fangen *pret* **fing** *ptp* **gefangen** **1** *vt* *Tier, Fisch, Verbrecher* to catch; *Wild auch* to bag; (*mit Fallen*) to trap; (*fig: überlisten*) (*durch geschickte Fragen*) to trap; (*durch Versprechungen etc*) to trick. **(sich** *dat*) **eine (Ohrfeige** *etc*) **~** (*inf*) to catch it (*inf*); *siehe* **gefangen.**

2 *vi* to catch. **F~ spielen** to play tag *or* it.

3 *vr* **(a)** (*in einer Falle*) to get caught. **er hat sich in der eigenen Schlinge** *or* **Falle gefangen** (*fig*) he was hoist with his own petard.

(b) (*das Gleichgewicht wiederfinden*) to steady oneself; (*beim Reden etc*) to recover oneself; (*Flugzeug*) to straighten out; (*seelisch*) to get on an even keel again.

(c) (*sich verfangen*) to get caught (up); (*Wind*) to get trapped. **ich fing mich mit dem Hosenbein in der Fahrradkette** I got my trouser leg caught (up) in the bicycle chain.

Fänger *m* **-s, - (a)** (*Tier~*) hunter; (*mit Fallen*) trapper; (*Wal~*) whaler; (*Robben~*) sealer.

(b) (*Sport*) catcher.

Fang-: **~frage** *f* catch *or* trick question; **~gründe** *pl* fishing grounds *pl*; **~korb** *m* lifeguard, cowcatcher (*inf*); **~leine** *f* **(a)** (*Naut*) hawser; **(b)** (*Aviat*) arresting gear cable; **(c)** (*von Fallschirm*) rigging line; **~messer** *nt* hunting knife; **~netz** *nt* **(a)** (*Hunt, Fischen*) net; **(b)** (*Aviat*) arresting gear; **~schiff** *nt* fishing boat; (*mit Netzen*) trawler; (*Walfangschiff*) whaler; **~schnur** *f* (*Mil*) aiguillette; **~schuß** *m* (*Hunt, fig*) coup de grâce (*with a gun*); f~**sicher** *adj* safe; f~**sicher sein** to be a good catch; ~**stoß** *m* coup de grâce (*with a knife*); ~**tuch** *nt* life-net (*US*), jumping-sheet, blanket (*inf*); f~**unsicher** *adj* butter-fingered; ~**vorrichtung** *f* arresting device; ~**zahn** *m* canine (tooth), fang; (*von Eber*) tusk.

Fant *m* -(e)s, -e (*old pej*) jackanapes (*old*).

Fantasie *f* (a) (*Mus*) fantasia. (b) *siehe* **Phantasie**.

Farad *nt* -(s), - farad.

Farb- *in cpds* colour; ~**abstimmung** *f* colour scheme; (*TV*) colour adjustment; ~**aufnahme** *f* colour photo(graph); ~**bad** *nt* dye-bath; ~**band**[1] *nt* (*von Schreibmaschine*) (typewriter) ribbon; ~**band**[2] *m* (*Buch*) book with colour illustrations.

färbbar *adj* colourable.

Farb-: ~**bericht** *m* (*Press, TV*) report in colour; (*in Zeitschriften auch*) colour feature; ~**bild** *nt* (*Phot*) colour photo(graph); ~**druck** *m* colour print.

Farbe *f* -, -n (a) (*Farbton, Tönung*) colour, color (*US*); (*Tönung auch*) shade. ~ **bekommen** to get a bit of colour, to catch the sun (*inf*); ~ **verlieren** to go pale; **in** ~ in colour; **einer Sache** (*dat*) **mehr** ~ **geben** (*fig*) to brighten sth up; **etw in den dunkelsten** *or* **schwärzesten/glänzendsten** ~**n schildern** *or* **ausmalen** to paint a black/rosy picture of sth, to paint sth in glowing colours. (b) (*Maler~, Anstrich~*) paint; (*für Farbbad*) dye; (*Druck~*) ink. (c) (*Fahne, Univ*) ~**n** *pl* colours *pl*. (d) (*Cards*) suit. ~ **bedienen** to follow suit; ~ **bekennen** (*fig*) (*alles zugeben*) to make a clean breast of it, to come clean; (*sich entscheiden*) to nail one's colours to the mast.

farb|echt *adj* colourfast.

Färbemittel *nt* dye.

farb|empfindlich *adj* (*Phot*) colour-sensitive.

färben 1 *vt* to colour; *Stoff, Haar* to dye; *siehe* **gefärbt**. 2 *vi* (*ab~*) to run (*inf*). 3 *vr* to change colour. **ihre Wangen färbten sich leicht** she coloured slightly; **sich grün/blau** *etc* ~ to turn green/blue *etc*.

Farben- *in cpds* colour; f~**blind** *adj* colour-blind; ~**druck** *m* (*Typ*) colour printing; f~**freudig** *adj* colourful; *Mensch* keen on bright colours; f~**froh** *adj* colourful; ~**kleckser** *m* -s, - (*pej*) dauber (*pej*); ~**lehre** *f* theory of colour; (*Fach auch*) chromatics *sing*; ~**pracht** *f* blaze of colour; **in seiner ganzen** ~**pracht** in all its glory; f~**prächtig** *adj* gloriously colourful; f~**reich** *adj* colourful; ~**reichtum** *m* wealth of colours; ~**sinn** *m* sense of colour (*auch Biol*), colour sense; ~**spiel** *nt* play *or* kaleidoscope of colours; f~**tragend** *adj* (*Univ*) f~**tragende Verbindung** society with traditional heraldic colours; ~**zusammenstellung** *f* colour combination.

Färber *m* -s, - dyer.

Färberei *f* (a) (*Betrieb*) dyeing works *sing or pl*. (b) *no pl* (*Verfahren*) dyeing.

Farb-: ~**fernsehen** *nt* colour television *or* TV; ~**film** *m* colour film; ~**filter** *m* (*Phot*) colour filter; ~**foto** *nt* colour photo-(graph); ~**fotografie** *f* (*Verfahren*) colour photography; (*Bild*) colour photo(graph); ~**gebung** *f* colouring, coloration.

farbig *adj* (a) coloured; (*fig*) *Schilderung* vivid, colourful. **ein** ~**er Druck/eine** ~**e Postkarte** a colour print/postcard; ~ **fotografieren** to take colour photographs. (b) *attr* (*Hautfarbe*) coloured.

färbig *adj* (*Aus*) *siehe* **farbig** (a).

Farbige(r) *mf decl as adj* coloured man/woman/person *etc*. **die** ~**n** the coloureds *pl*, coloured people *pl*.

Farb-: ~**kasten** *m* paintbox; ~**kissen** *nt* inkpad; ~**klecks** *m* blob of paint, paint spot; f~**los** *adj* (*lit, fig*) colourless; ~**losigkeit** *f* (*lit, fig*) colourlessness; ~**mine** *f* coloured-ink cartridge; ~**mischung** *f* (*gemischte Farbe*) mixture of colours; ~**sinn** *m* *siehe* **Farbensinn**; ~**stich** *m* (*Phot, TV*) colour fault; ~**stift** *m* coloured pen; (*Buntstift*) crayon, coloured pencil; ~**stoff** *m* (*Lebensmittel~*) (artificial) colouring; (*Haut~*) pigment; ~**tafel** *f* colour plate; (*Tabelle*) colour chart; ~**ton** *m* shade, hue; (*Tönung*) tint; f~**tüchtig** *adj* (*TV*) equipped for colour.

Färbung *f* (*das Färben, Farbgebung*) colouring; (*Tönung*) tinge, hue; (*fig*) slant, bias.

Farce [ˈfarsə] *f* -, -n (a) (*Theat, fig*) farce. (b) (*Cook*) stuffing; (*Fleisch auch*) forcemeat.

farcieren* [farˈsiːrən] *vt* (*Cook*) to stuff.

Farm *f* -, -en farm.

Farmer *m* -s, - farmer.

Farmhaus *nt* farmhouse.

Farn *m* -(e)s, -e, **Farnkraut** *nt* fern; (*Adler~*) bracken.

Färöer *pl* Faeroes *pl*, Faeroe Islands *pl*.

Färse *f* -, -n heifer.

Fasan *m* -s, -e *or* -en pheasant.

Fasanerie *f* pheasant-house; (*im Freien*) pheasant-run.

Fasche *f* -, -n (*Aus*) bandage.

faschen *vt* (*Aus*) to bandage.

faschieren* *vt* (*Aus Cook*) to mince. **Faschiertes** mince, minced meat.

Faschine *f* fascine.

Fasching *m* -s, -e *or* -s Shrovetide carnival, Fasching.

Faschings- *in cpds* carnival; ~**dienstag** *m* Shrove Tuesday, Pancake Day; ~**zeit** *f* carnival period.

Faschismus *m* fascism.

Faschist(in *f*) *m* fascist.

faschistisch *adj* fascist.

faschistoid *adj* fascistic.

Fase *f* -, -n bevel, chamfer.

Faselei *f* (*pej*) *siehe* **Gefasel**.

Fas(e)ler *m* -s, - (*pej*), **Faselhans** *m* -(e)s, **Faselhänse** (*pej*) drivelling idiot (*pej*).

faseln (*pej*) 1 *vi* to drivel (*inf*). 2 *vt* *Blödsinn etc* ~ to talk drivel; **das ist alles gefaselt** that's drivel (*inf*), that's just (so much)

twaddle (*inf*); **was hat er gefaselt?** what was he drivelling about?

Faser *f* -, -n fibre. **ein Pullover aus synthetischen** ~**n** a pullover made of synthetic fibre; **er hat keine trockene** ~ **am Leib** he's soaked through *or* drenched; **mit allen** ~**n des Herzens** (*liter*) with every fibre of one's being (*liter*).

Faser-: f~**artig** *adj* fibrous; ~**gewebe** *nt* (*Biol*) fibrous tissue.

fas(e)rig *adj* fibrous; *Fleisch, Spargel auch* stringy (*pej*); (*zerfasert*) frayed.

fasern *vi* to fray.

Faser-: f~**nackt** *adj* *siehe* **splitter(faser)nackt**; ~**pflanze** *f* fibre plant; ~**platte** *f* fibre-board; f~**schonend** *adj* gentle (*to fabrics*); ~**stoff** *m* fibrous material.

Fasler *m* -s, - *siehe* **Fas(e)ler**.

Fasnacht *f* *siehe* **Fastnacht**.

fasrig *adj* *siehe* **fas(e)rig**.

Faß *nt* Fasses, **Fässer** barrel; (*kleines Bier~*) keg; (*zum Gären, Einlegen*) vat; (*zum Buttern*) (barrel) churn; (*für Öl, Benzin, Chemikalien*) drum. **etw in Fässer füllen** to put sth into barrels/drums, to barrel sth; **drei Fässer/~ Bier** three barrels of beer; **vom** ~ on tap; *Bier auch* on draught (*esp Brit*); *Sherry, Wein auch* from the wood (*esp Brit*); **er trinkt nur Bier vom** ~ he only drinks draught beer; **ein** ~ **ohne Boden** (*fig*) a bottomless pit; **ein** ~ **aufmachen** (*fig inf*) to kick up a shindy (*inf*) *or* a dust (*inf*); **das schlägt dem** ~ **den Boden aus** (*inf*) that beats everything!, that takes the biscuit! (*inf*); **das brachte das** ~ **zum Überlaufen** (*fig*) that put the tin lid on it (*inf*).

Fassade *f* (*lit, fig*) façade; (*inf: Gesicht*) face. **das ist doch nur** ~ (*fig*) that's just a façade.

Fassaden-: ~**kletterer** *m* cat burglar; ~**reinigung** *f* exterior cleaning.

Faß-: ~**band** *nt* hoop (of a barrel); f~**bar** *adj* comprehensible, understandable; **das ist doch nicht f~bar!** that's incomprehensible!; ~**bier** *nt* draught beer; ~**binder** *m* (*old, Aus*) cooper.

Fäßchen *nt* *dim of* **Faß** cask.

Faßdaube *f* stave.

fassen 1 *vt* (a) (*ergreifen*) to take hold of; (*hastig, kräftig*) to grab, to seize; (*festnehmen*) *Einbrecher etc* to apprehend (*form*), to seize; (*Mil*) *Munition* to draw. **jdn beim** *or* **am Arm** ~ to take/grab sb by the arm; **er faßte ihre Hand** he took her hand; **Schauder/Grauen/Entsetzen faßte ihn** he was seized with horror; **faß! seize!** (b) (*fig*) *Beschluß, Entschluß* to make, to take; *Mut* to take. **Vertrauen zu jdm** ~ to come to trust sb; **den Gedanken** ~, **etw zu tun** to form *or* have the idea of doing sth; **den Vorsatz** ~, **etw zu tun** to make a resolution to do sth; *siehe* **Auge, Fuß, Herz** *etc*. (c) (*begreifen*) to grasp, to understand. **es ist nicht zu** ~ it's unbelievable *or* incredible. (d) (*enthalten*) to hold. (e) (*aufnehmen*) *Essen* to get; (*Rail, Naut*) *Wasser, Kohlen* to take on. **Essen** ~! come and get it! (f) (*ein~*) *Edelsteine* to set; *Bild* to frame; *Quelle* to surround; (*fig: ausdrücken*) to express. **in Verse/Worte** ~ to put into verse/words; **neu** ~ *Manuskript, Rede, Erzählung* to revise; **etw weit/eng** ~ to interpret sth broadly/narrowly.

2 *vi* (a) (*nicht abrutschen*) to grip; (*Zahnrad*) to bite. (b) (*greifen*) **an/in etw** (*acc*) ~ to feel sth; (*berühren*) to touch sth; **faß mal unter den Tisch** feel under the table; **da faßt man sich** (*dat*) **an den Kopf** (*inf*) you wouldn't believe it, would you?

3 *vr* (*sich beherrschen*) to compose oneself. **faß dich!** pull yourself together!; **sich vor Freude kaum** ~ **können** to be beside oneself with joy; **sich in Geduld** ~ to be patient, to possess one's soul in patience; **sich kurz** ~ to be brief; *siehe* **gefaßt**.

fässerweise *adv* (*in großen Mengen*) by the gallon; (*in Fässern*) by the barrel.

faßlich *adj* comprehensible, understandable.

Faßlichkeit *f*, *no pl* comprehensibility.

Fasson [faˈsõː] *f* -, -s *or* (*Sw, Aus*) -en (*von Kleidung*) style; (*von Frisur*) shape. **aus der** ~ **geraten** (*lit*) to go out of shape, to lose its shape; (*dated: dick werden*) to get a spare tyre (*inf*), to get (a bit) broad in the beam (*inf*); **jeder soll nach seiner** ~ **selig werden** (*prov*) everyone has to find his own salvation.

fassonieren* *vt* (*Aus*) *Haare* to (cut and) shape.

Fassonschnitt [faˈsõː-] *m* style in which the hair is shaped into the neck; (*für Herren*) short back and sides.

Faßreif(en) *m* hoop.

Fassung *f* (a) (*von Juwelen*) setting; (*von Bild*) frame; (*Elec*) holder. (b) (*Bearbeitung, Wortlaut*) version. **ein Film/Buch in ungekürzter** ~ the uncut/unabridged version of a film/book; **ein Film in deutscher** ~ a film with German dubbing; **das Lied hat noch eine andere** ~ there's another version of the song. (c) *no pl* (*Ruhe, Besonnenheit*) composure. **die** ~ **bewahren** *or* **behalten** to maintain one's composure; **etw mit** ~ **tragen** to take sth calmly *or* with equanimity; **die** ~ **verlieren** to lose one's composure; **völlig außer** ~ **geraten** to lose all self-control; **jdn aus der** ~ **bringen** to disconcert *or* throw (*inf*) sb; *Redner auch* to put sb off.

Fassungs-: ~**kraft** *f* (*liter*) (powers of) comprehension *or* understanding; **die menschliche** ~**kraft übersteigen** to be beyond human understanding; f~**los** *adj* aghast, stunned; ~**losigkeit** *f* complete bewilderment; ~**vermögen** *nt* (*lit, fig*) capacity; **das übersteigt mein** ~**vermögen** that is beyond me *or* beyond the limits of my comprehension.

Faß-: ~**wein** *m* wine from the wood; f~**weise** *adv* by the barrel; (*in Fässern*) in barrels.

fast *adv* almost, nearly. ~ **nie** hardly ever, almost never; ~ **nichts** hardly anything, almost nothing; **ich wäre** ~ **überfahren worden** I was almost *or* nearly run over.

Fastel|abend m (dial) siehe **Faschingsdienstag.**
fasten vi to fast.
Fasten-: ~kur f diet; eine ~kur machen/anfangen to be/go on a diet; ~zeit f period of fasting; (Eccl) Lent.
Fastnacht f, no pl (a) siehe **Faschingsdienstag.** (b) siehe **Fasching.**
Fastnachts-: ~narr m disguised figure in Shrove Tuesday celebrations; ~spiel nt (Liter) Shrovetide play; ~umzug m Shrove Tuesday procession.
Fasttag m day of fasting.
Faszikel m -s, - (old, form) section of manuscript, fascicle (spec).
Faszination f fascination. ~ ausstrahlen to radiate charm; jds ~ (dat) erlegen sein to succumb to sb's fascinating power.
faszinieren* vti to fascinate (an + dat about). ~d fascinating; mich fasziniert der Gedanke, das zu tun I'm very attracted by or to the idea of doing that.
fatal adj (geh) (verhängnisvoll) fatal, fateful, dire; (peinlich) embarrassing, awkward.
Fatalismus m fatalism.
Fatalist(in f) m fatalist.
fatalistisch adj fatalistic.
Fatalität f great misfortune.
Fata Morgana f - -, - **Morganen** or -s (lit, fig) Fata Morgana (liter), mirage.
Fatsche f -, -n (Aus) siehe **Fasche.**
fatschen vt (Aus) siehe **faschen.**
Fatzke m -n or -s, -n or -s (inf) stuck-up twit (inf).
fauchen vti to hiss.
faul adj (a) (verfault) bad; Lebensmittel auch off pred; Eier, Obst auch, Holz, Gesellschaftsordnung rotten; Geschmack, Geruch auch foul, putrid; Zahn auch decayed; Laub rotting; Wasser foul.
(b) (verdächtig) fishy (inf), suspicious, dubious; (Comm) Wechsel, Scheck dud (inf); (fadenscheinig) Ausreden flimsy, feeble; Kompromiß uneasy; Friede empty; (dumm) Witz bad. hier ist etwas ~ (inf) there's something fishy here (inf); etwas ist ~ daran, an der Sache ist etwas ~ (inf) there's something fishy about the whole business (inf); etwas ist ~ im Staate Dänemark (prov) there's something rotten in the State of Denmark (prov).
(c) (träge) lazy, idle. ~ wie die Sünde bone-idle; nicht ~ (reaktionsschnell) quick as you please; er hat seinen ~en Tag (müßiger Tag) he's having a lazy day; (~e Stimmung) he's in a lazy mood; siehe **Haut, Strick**[1].
Fäule f -, no pl (a) (Vet) (liver) rot. (b) siehe **Fäulnis.**
faulen vi aux sein or haben to rot; (Aas auch) to putrefy; (Zahn) to decay; (Lebensmittel) to go bad.
faulenzen vi to laze or load (esp pej inf) about.
Faulenzer m -s, - (a) layabout. (b) (Aus: Linienblatt) sheet of ruled paper.
Faulenzerei f lazing or loafing (esp pej inf) about.
Faulheit f laziness, idleness. er stinkt vor ~ (inf) he's bone-idle.
faulig adj going bad; Lebensmittel auch going off; Eier, Obst auch going rotten; Wasser stale; (in Teich, See etc) stagnating; Geruch, Geschmack foul, putrid. ~ riechen/schmecken to taste/smell bad; (Wasser) to taste/smell foul.
Fäulnis f, no pl rottenness; (von Fleisch auch) putrefaction; (von Zahn) decay; (fig) decadence, degeneracy. von ~ befallen rotting, decaying; in ~ übergehen to go rotten; (Lebensmittel auch) to go bad; (Fleisch auch) to putrefy; (Zahn auch) to decay.
Fäulnis-: f~erregend adj putrefactive; ~erreger m putrefier.
Faul-: ~pelz m (inf) lazybones sing (inf); ~schlamm m sapropel (spec), sludge; ~tier nt sloth; (inf: Mensch) lazybones sing (inf).
Faun m -(e)s, -e (Myth) faun.
Fauna f -, **Faunen** fauna.
Faust f -, **Fäuste** fist. die (Hand zur) ~ ballen to clench one's fist; jdm eine ~ machen (inf) to shake one's fist at sb; jdm mit der ~ ins Gesicht schlagen to punch sb in the face; jdm die ~ unter die Nase halten to shake one's fist in sb's face or under sb's nose; mit der ~ auf den Tisch schlagen (lit) to thump on the table (with one's fist); (fig) to take a hard line, to put one's foot down; etw aus der ~ essen to eat sth with one's hands; ein Butterbrot auf die ~ a sandwich in one's hand; die ~/Fäuste in der Tasche ballen (fig) to bottle up or choke back one's anger; mit geballten Fäusten zusehen müssen (fig) to watch in helpless anger; das paßt wie die ~ aufs Auge (paßt nicht) it's all wrong; (Farbe) it clashes horribly; (ist fehl am Platz) it's completely out of place; (paßt gut) it's just the thing (inf) or job (inf); jds ~ im Nacken spüren (fig) to have sb breathing down one's neck; auf eigene ~ (fig) off one's own bat (inf); reisen, fahren under one's own steam; siehe **eisern.**
Faust-: ~abwehr f (Sport) save using the fists; herrlich, diese ~abwehr des Torwarts! the goalkeeper punches the ball clear beautifully!; ~ball m form of volleyball.
Fäustchen nt dim of **Faust;** sich (dat) ins ~ lachen to laugh up one's sleeve; (bei finanziellem Vorteil) to laugh all the way to the bank (inf).
faustdick adj (inf) eine f~dicke Lüge a whopper (inf), a whopping (great) lie (inf); das ist f~dick gelogen that's a whopping lie (inf) or a whopper (inf); er hat es f~dick hinter den Ohren he's a fly or crafty one (inf); f~dick auftragen to lay it on thick.
Fäustel m or nt -s, - sledgehammer.
fausten vt Ball to punch; (Ftbl auch) to fist.
Faust-: ~feuerwaffe f handgun; f~groß adj as big as a fist, the size of a fist; ~handschuh m mitt(en).
faustisch adj Faustian.

Faust-: ~kampf m fist-fight; ~kämpfer m (old) pugilist (old); ~keil m hand-axe.
Fäustlein nt dim of **Faust.**
Fäustling m mitt(en).
Faust-: ~pfand nt security; ~recht nt, no pl law of the jungle; ~regel f rule of thumb; ~schlag m punch; ~skizze f rough sketch.
Fauteuil [fo'tø:j] m -s, -s (old, Aus) leather armchair.
Fauxpas [fo'pa] m -, - gaffe, faux pas.
favorisieren* [favori'zi:rən] vt to favour. die Wettbüros ~ X als Sieger the betting shops show X as favourite or have X to win; favorisiert werden to be favourite.
Favorit(in f) [favo'ri:t(in)] m -en, -en favourite.
Faxen pl (a) (Alberei) fooling about or around. ~ machen to fool about or around. (b) (Grimassen) ~ schneiden to pull faces.
Fayence [fa'jã:s] f -, -n faience.
Fazit nt -s, -s or -e das ~ der Untersuchungen war ... on balance the result of the investigations was ...; das ~ aus all seinen Reisen war ... on balance the conclusion he drew from all his travels was ...; wenn wir aus diesen vier Jahren das ~ ziehen if we take stock of these four years; wenn ich das ~ ziehen müßte, würde ich sagen ... on balance I would say ...
FDGB [efde:ge:'be:] m -(s) (DDR) abbr of **Freier Deutscher Gewerkschaftsbund.**
FDJ [efde:'jɔt] f - (DDR) abbr of **Freie Deutsche Jugend.**
FDJler(in f) m -s, - (DDR) member of the Free German Youth.
FDP [efde:'pe:] f - abbr of **Freie Demokratische Partei.**
FD-Zug [ef'de:-] m long-distance express (train).
Feature ['fi:tʃr] nt -s, -s (Rad, TV) feature programme.
Feber m -s, - (Aus) February.
Februar m -(s), -e February; siehe auch **März.**
Fecht-: ~bahn f (Sport) piste; ~bruder m (pej) beggar.
fechten pret focht, ptp gefochten 1 vi (a) (Sport) to fence; (geh: kämpfen) to fight. das F~ fencing. (b) (old: betteln) to beg. 2 vt (a) Degen/Säbel/Florett ~ to fence with épées/sabres/foils; einen Gang ~ to fence a bout. (b) (old: betteln) to beg.
Fechter(in f) m -s, - fencer.
Fechterstellung f fencing stance.
Fecht-: ~handschuh m fencing glove; ~hieb m (fencing) cut; ~kunst f art of fencing; (Geschick) skill in fencing; ~meister m fencing master; ~sport m fencing.
Feder f -, -n (a) (Vogel~) feather; (Gänse~ etc) quill; (lange Hut~) plume. leicht wie eine ~ as light as a feather; ~n lassen müssen (inf) not to escape unscathed; in den ~n stecken or liegen (inf) to be/stay in one's bed or pit (inf); jdn aus den ~n holen (inf) to drag or turf sb out of bed (inf); raus aus den ~n! (inf) rise and shine! (inf), show a leg! (inf); siehe fremd.
(b) (Schreib~) quill; (an ~halter) nib. ich greife zur ~ ... I take up my pen ...; aus jds ~ fließen to flow from sb's pen; eine scharfe or spitze ~ führen to wield a wicked or deadly pen; mit spitzer ~ with a deadly pen, with a pen dipped in vitriol (liter); ein Mann der ~ (dated geh) a man of letters.
(c) (Tech) spring.
(d) (in Holz) tongue.
Feder-: ~antrieb m clockwork; mit ~antrieb clockwork-driven, driven by clockwork; ~ball m (Ball) shuttlecock; (Spiel) badminton; ~bein nt (Tech) suspension strut; ~besen m feather duster; ~bett nt quilt; (in heutigen Zusammenhängen) continental quilt, duvet; ~blatt nt leaf of a spring; ~busch m (von Vögeln) crest; (von Hut, Helm) plume; ~decke f siehe ~bett; ~fuchser m -s, - (pej) petty-minded pedant (pej); (Schreiberling) pettifogging penpusher (pej); f~führend adj Behörde in overall charge (für of); ~führung f unter der ~führung + gen under the overall control of; die ~führung haben to be in or have overall charge; ~gewicht nt (Sport) featherweight (class); ~gewichtler m -s, - (Sport) featherweight; ~halter m (dip) pen; (Füll~) (fountain) pen; (ohne Feder) pen(holder); ~hut m plumed hat; ~kasten m (Sch) pencil box; ~kernmatratze f interior sprung mattress; ~kiel m quill; ~kissen nt feather cushion; (in Bett) feather pillow; ~kleid nt (liter) plumage; ~krieg m (fig) war of words; f~leicht adj light as a feather; ~lesen nt: nicht viel ~lesens mit jdm/etw machen to waste no time on sb/sth, to make short work of sb/sth; ohne langes ~lesen, ohne viel ~lesens without ceremony or any (further) ado; ~mäppchen nt, ~mappe f pencil case; ~messer nt penknife.
federn 1 vi (a) (Eigenschaft) to be springy.
(b) (hoch~, zurück~) to spring back; (Fahrzeug) to bounce (up and down); (Knie) to give; (Springer, Turner: hochgeschleudert werden) to bounce. (in den Knien) ~ (Sport) to bend or give at the knees.
(c) (Kissen etc) to shed (feathers); (Vogel) to moult, to shed its feathers.
2 vt to moult, to shed its feathers.
3 vt to spring; Auto, Räder auch to fit with suspension. ein Auto hydraulisch ~ to fit a car with hydraulic suspension; siehe gefedert.
federnd adj (Tech) sprung. ~e Radaufhängung spring suspension; einen ~en Gang haben to have a jaunty or springy step or gait; mit ~en Schritten with a spring in one's step.
Feder-: ~pennal nt (Aus) pencil case; ~ring m spring washer; ~schmuck m feather trimming; (von Indianern etc) headdress; (~busch) plume; (von Vogel) plumage; ~skizze f pen-and-ink sketch; ~spiel nt (Hist) lure; ~stiel m (Aus) siehe ~halter; ~strich m pen-stroke, stroke of the pen; mit einem or durch einen ~strich with a single stroke of the pen.
Federung f springs pl, springing; (Aut auch) suspension.
Feder-: ~vieh nt poultry; ~waage f spring balance; ~weiße(r) m decl as adj (dial) new wine; ~wild nt (Hunt) game birds pl;

~**wisch** m (old) feather duster; ~**wölkchen** nt, ~**wolke** f fleecy cloud; ~**zeichnung** f pen-and-ink drawing.
Fee f -, -n ['fe:ən] fairy.
Feedback ['fi:dbæk] nt -s, -s feedback.
feenhaft ['fe:ən-] adj (liter) fairylike.
Feez m -es, no pl (dated inf) siehe Fez².
Fegefeuer nt das ~ purgatory.
fegen 1 vt (a) to sweep; (auf~) to sweep up. den Schmutz von etw ~ to sweep sth (clean). (b) (Hunt) Geweih to fray. **2** vi (a) (ausfegen) to sweep (up). (b) aux sein (inf: jagen) to sweep; (Wind auch) to race.
Feger m -s, - (a) (inf) brush. (b) (sl: Mädchen) little tigress.
Fehde f -, -n (Hist) feud. mit jdm eine ~ ausfechten to feud or carry on a feud with sb; mit jdm in ~ liegen (lit, fig) to be feuding or in a state of feud with sb.
Fehdehandschuh m: jdm den ~ hinwerfen (lit, fig) to throw down the gauntlet (to sb); den ~ aufheben (lit, fig) to take up the gauntlet.
fehl adj: ~ am Platz(e) out of place.
Fehl m (old, liter): ohne ~ without (a) blemish.
Fehl-: ~**anpassung** f (a) (Psych) maladjustment; (b) (Elec) mismatch; ~**anzeige** f (inf) dead loss (inf); ~**anzeige!** no go (inf); ~**aufschlag** m (Sport) fault; einen ~**aufschlag machen** to serve a fault; f~**bar** adj fallible; (Sw) guilty; f~**besetzen*** vt sep to miscast; ~**besetzung** f miscasting; eine ~**besetzung** a piece or bit of miscasting; ~**betrag** m (form) deficit, shortfall; ~**bildung** f siehe **Mißbildung**; ~**bitte** f (form) vain request; eine ~**bitte tun** to make a vain request; ~**deutung** f misinterpretation; ~**diagnose** f wrong or false diagnosis; ~**disposition** f miscalculation; ~**druck** m (Typ) misprint; ~**einschätzung** f false estimation; (der Lage auch) misjudgement.
fehlen 1 vi (a) (mangeln) to be lacking; (nicht vorhanden sein) to be missing; (in der Schule etc) to be away or absent (in + dat from); (schmerzlich vermißt werden) to be missed. das Geld fehlt (ist nicht vorhanden) there is no money; (ist zuwenig vorhanden) there isn't enough money; etwas fehlt there's something missing; jdm fehlt etw sb lacks or doesn't have sth; (wird schmerzlich vermißt) sb misses sth; mir fehlt Geld I'm missing some money; mir ~ 20 Pfennig am Fahrgeld I'm 20 pfennigs short or I'm short of 20 pfennigs for my fare; mir ~ die Worte words fail me; meine Bibliothek fehlt/du fehlst mir sehr I miss my library/you a lot; der/das hat mir gerade noch gefehlt! (inf) he/that was all I needed (iro); das durfte nicht ~ that had to happen.
(b) (los sein) was fehlt dir? what's the matter or what's up (with you)?; fehlt dir (et)was? is something the matter (with you)?; mir fehlt nichts there's nothing the matter (with me); dem Hund scheint etwas zu ~ the dog seems to have something the matter with it, there seems to be something wrong or the matter with the dog.
(c) (old: etwas falsch machen) to err.
2 vi impers es fehlt etw or an etw (dat) there is a lack of sth; (völlig) there is no sth, sth is missing; an ~ drei Messer there are three knives missing; es fehlt jdm an etw (dat) sb lacks sth; es an etw (dat) ~ lassen to be lacking in sth, to lack sth; er ließ es uns an nichts ~ (geh) he let us want for nothing; es fehlt hinten und vorn(e) or an allen Ecken und Enden or Kanten we/they etc are short of everything; (bei Kenntnissen) he/she etc has a lot to learn or a long way to go; (bei Klassenarbeit etc) it's a long way from perfect; wo fehlt es? what's the trouble?, what's up? (inf); es fehlte nicht viel, und ich hätte ihn verprügelt I almost hit him; es fehlt(e) nur noch, daß wir sonntags arbeiten sollen working Sundays is all we need (iro).
3 vt (old Hunt) to miss. weit gefehlt! (fig) you're way out! (inf); (ganz im Gegenteil) far from it!
Fehl|entscheidung f wrong decision.
Fehler m -s, - (a) (Irrtum, Unrichtigkeit) mistake, error; (Sport) fault. einen ~ machen or begehen to make a mistake or error; ihr ist ein ~ unterlaufen she's made a mistake; ~! (Sport) fault!
(b) (Mangel) fault, defect; (Charakter~ auch) failing. einen ~ aufweisen to prove faulty; jeder hat seine ~ we all have our faults, nobody's perfect; das ist nicht mein ~ that's not my fault; einen ~ an sich (dat) haben to have a fault; er hat den ~ an sich, immer dazwischenzureden or daß er immer dazwischenredet the trouble with him is that he's always interrupting; in den ~ verfallen, etw zu tun to make the mistake of doing sth.
Fehler-: f~**frei** adj perfect; Arbeit, Übersetzung, Aussprache etc auch faultless, flawless; Messung, Rechnung correct; f~**freier** Lauf/Sprung (Sport) clear round/jump; ~**grenze** f margin of error; f~**haft** adj (Mech, Tech) faulty, defective; Ware substandard, imperfect; Messung, Rechnung incorrect; Arbeit, Übersetzung, Aussprache poor; f~**los** adj siehe f~**frei**; ~**quelle** f cause of the fault; (in Statistik) source of error; ~**verzeichnis** nt errata pl.
Fehl-: ~**farbe** f (Cards) missing suit; (Nicht-Trumpf) plain or side suit; (Zigarre) cigar with a discoloured wrapper; ~**geburt** f miscarriage.
fehlgehen vi sep irreg aux sein (a) (geh: sich verirren) to go wrong, to miss the way. (b) (sich irren) to be wrong or mistaken, to err (form). ich hoffe, ich gehe nicht fehl in der Annahme, daß ... I trust I am not mistaken in assuming that ...
Fehl-: ~**griff** m mistake; einen ~**griff tun** to make a mistake; ~**information** f incorrect information no pl; ~**interpretation** f misinterpretation; ~**investition** f bad investment; ~**konstruktion** f bad design; der Stuhl ist eine ~**konstruktion** this chair is badly designed; ~**landung** f bad landing; ~**leistung** f slip, mistake; Freudsche ~**leistung** Freudian slip; f~**leiten** vt

---

sep to misdirect; die Akte wurde f~**geleitet** the file was sent to the wrong place; ~**leitung** f misdirection; ~**paß** m (Ftbl) bad pass; ~**planung** f misplanning, bad planning; eine ~**planung** a piece of bad planning or misplanning; ~**prägung** f (einer Münze) mis-strike; ~**reaktion** f (eines Menschen) mistake made in the heat of the moment; es könnte bei dem Tier einmal zu einer ~**reaktion kommen** it's just possible the animal might react differently some time; f~**schießen** vi sep irreg to shoot wide; ~**schlag** m (fig) failure; f~**schlagen** vi sep irreg aux sein to go wrong; (Hoffnung) to be misplaced, to come to nothing; ~**schluß** m false conclusion; ~**schuß** m miss; f~**sichtig** adj (form) with defective vision; ~**sichtigkeit** f (form) defective vision; ~**spekulation** f bad speculation; ~**start** m false start; (Space) faulty launch; ~**stoß** m (Ftbl) miskick; (Billard) miscue; f~**stoßen** vi sep irreg (Ftbl, Billard) to miskick/miscue; f~**treten** vi sep irreg aux sein (geh) to miss one's footing; (fig) to err, to lapse; ~**tritt** m (geh) false step; (fig) (Vergehen) slip, lapse; (Affäre) indiscretion; ~**urteil** nt miscarriage of justice; ~**verhalten** nt (Psych) abnormal behaviour; ~**versuch** m unsuccessful or abortive attempt; ~**wurf** m (Sport) misthrow, bad throw; ~**zug** m (Chess) bad move; ~**zündung** f misfiring no pl; eine ~**zündung** a backfire; das war bei mir eine ~**zündung** (fig inf) I got hold of the wrong end of the stick (inf).
Fehn nt -(e)s, -e (N Ger) marsh, fen.
feien vt (old) to protect (gegen from), to make proof (gegen against); siehe **gefeit**.
Feier f -, -n celebration; (Party) party; (Zeremonie) ceremony; (Hochzeits~) reception. zur ~ von etw to celebrate sth; zur ~ des Tages in honour of the occasion.
Feier|abend m (a) (Arbeitsschluß) end of work; (Geschäftsschluß) closing time. ~ machen to finish work, to knock off (work) (inf); (Geschäfte) to close; ich mache jetzt ~ I think I'll call it a day (inf) or I'll knock off now (inf); ~! (in Gaststätte) time, please!; nach ~ after work; jetzt ist aber ~! (fig inf) enough is enough; damit ist jetzt ~ (fig inf) that's all over now; dann ist ~ (fig inf) then it's all over, then it's the end of the road; für mich ist ~ (fig inf) I've had enough.
(b) (Zeit nach Arbeitsschluß) evening. schönen ~! have a nice evening!
Feier|abendheim nt (DDR) old people's home.
feierlich adj (ernsthaft, würdig) solemn; (festlich) festive; (förmlich) ceremonial. einen Tag ~ begehen to celebrate a day; das ist ja nicht mehr ~ (inf) that's beyond a joke (inf).
Feierlichkeit f (a) siehe adj solemnity; festiveness; ceremony. (b) usu pl (Veranstaltungen) celebrations pl, festivities pl.
feiern 1 vt (a) to celebrate; Party, Fest, Orgie to hold. das muß gefeiert werden! that calls for a celebration; Triumphe ~ to achieve a great triumph, to make one's mark.
(b) (umjubeln) to fête.
2 vi (a) to celebrate. die ganze Nacht ~ to make a night of it.
(b) (nicht arbeiten) to stay off work. ~ müssen (inf: ohne Beschäftigung) to be laid off.
Feier-: ~**schicht** f cancelled shift; eine ~**schicht fahren/einlegen** to miss/cancel a shift; ~**stunde** f ceremony; ~**tag** m holiday; f~**täglich** adj holiday attr; f~**tägliche** Stimmung holiday mood; f~**täglich angezogen** in one's Sunday best.
feig(e) 1 adj cowardly. ~ wie er war like the coward he was. **2** adv in a cowardly way. er zog sich ~ zurück he retreated like a coward.
Feige f -, -n fig.
Feigen-: ~**baum** m fig tree; ~**blatt** nt fig leaf; ein ~**blatt für etw** (fig) a front to hide sth; als ~**blatt** (fig) for appearances' sake; als demokratisches ~**blatt** (fig) to give a veneer of democracy.
Feigheit f cowardice, cowardliness.
Feigling m coward.
feil adj (old, geh) (up) for sale. der Schmuck war ihr um or für nichts auf der Welt ~ not for all the world would she have sold the jewellery; eine ~e Dirne a harlot (old).
feilbieten vt sep irreg (old) to offer for sale.
Feile f -, -n file. die letzte ~ an eine Arbeit (an)legen (fig) to put the finishing touches to a piece of work.
feilen 1 vt to file. **2** vi to file; (fig) to make some improvements. an etw (dat) ~ (lit) to file (away at) sth; (fig) to hone sth, to polish sth up.
feilhalten vt sep irreg (old) to offer for sale; siehe **Maulaffen**.
Feilheit f, no pl (old, geh) saleability; (fig) venality.
feilschen vi (pej) to haggle (um over).
Feilsel nt filing.
Feil-: ~**span** m filing; ~**staub** m (fine) filings pl.
fein 1 adj (a) (nicht grob) fine; Humor, Ironie delicate; (fig: listig) cunning.
(b) (erlesen) excellent, choice attr; Geruch, Geschmack delicate; Gold, Silber refined; Mensch, Charakter thoroughly nice; (prima) great (inf), splendid, swell (esp US inf); (iro) fine. ~ säuberlich (nice and) neat; etw ~ machen to do sth beautifully; ein ~er Kerl a great guy (inf), a splendid person; das war von dir aber wieder ~ bemerkt you have such a nice way of putting things; ~! great! (inf), marvellous!; (in Ordnung) fine!; ~, daß ... great that ... (inf), (I'm) so glad that ...; das ist etwas F~es that's really something (inf) or nice; ~ (he)raussein to be sitting pretty.
(c) (scharf) sensitive, keen; Gehör, Gefühl auch acute. etw ~ einstellen to adjust sth accurately.
(d) (vornehm) refined, fine (esp iro), posh (inf). nicht ~ genug sein not to be good enough; er/sie hat sich ~ gemacht he's dressed to kill/she's all dolled up.
2 adv (baby-talk) just; (vor adj, adv) nice and ... du gehst jetzt

~ **nach Hause** now just you go straight home; **sei jetzt mal** ~ still now keep nice and quiet.

Fein- in cpds fine; ~**abstimmung** f (Rad, TV) fine tuning; ~**arbeit** f precision work; ~**bäckerei** f cake shop, patisserie; ~**blech** nt thin sheet metal.

feind adj pred (old) **jdm/einer Sache** ~ **sein** to be hostile to sb/sth.

Feind m -(e)s, -e enemy, foe (liter). **jdn zum** ~ **haben** to have sb as an enemy; **sich** (dat) **jdn zum** ~ **machen** to make an enemy of sb; **sich** (dat) ~**e schaffen** to make enemies; **er war ein** ~ **jeden Fortschritts** he was opposed to progress in any shape or form; **ran an den** ~ (inf) let's get stuck in (inf); **der böse** ~ (Bibl) the Evil One, the Enemy; **liebet eure** ~**e** (Bibl) love thine enemy (Bibl).

-**feind** m in cpds -hater.

Feind- in cpds enemy; ~**berührung** f contact with the enemy; ~**bild** nt concept of an/the enemy.

Feindes-: ~**hand** f (old, liter) the hands of the foe (liter); ~**land** nt (old, liter) enemy territory.

Feindfahrt f (naval) mission.

feindlich adj (a) (Mil: gegnerisch) enemy. **im** ~**en Lager** (lit, fig) in the enemy camp. (b) (feindselig) hostile. **jdm/etw** ~ **gegenüberstehen** to be hostile to sb/sth.

-**feindlich** adj suf anti-. **deutsch**~ anti-German; **russen**~ anti-Russian; **england**~ anti-English.

Feindmacht f enemy power. **eine** ~ **unseres Landes** an enemy of our country.

Feindschaft f enmity. **sich** (dat) **jds** ~ **zuziehen** to make an enemy of sb; **mit jdm in** ~ **leben** or **liegen** to be at daggers drawn or to live in enmity with sb; **eine** ~ **auf Leben und Tod** mortal enmity.

feindselig adj hostile.

Feindseligkeit f hostility.

Fein-: f~**fühlend**, f~**fühlig** adj sensitive; (taktvoll) tactful; ~**fühligkeit** f siehe ~**gefühl**; ~**gebäck** nt cakes and pastries pl; ~**gefühl** nt, no pl sensitivity; (Takt) delicacy, tact(fulness); **jds** ~**gefühl verletzen** to hurt sb's feelings; f~**gemahlen** adj attr finely ground; f~**glied(e)rig** adj delicate, slender; ~**gold** nt refined gold.

Feinheit f siehe adj (a) fineness; delicacy. (b) excellence; delicateness; refinement; niceness. (c) keenness; acuteness. (d) refinement, fineness, poshness (inf). (e) ~**en** pl niceties pl, finer points pl; (Nuancen) subtleties pl; **das sind eben die** ~**en** it's the little things that make the difference.

Fein-: ~**kohle** f slack; f~**körnig** adj fine-grain; Sand, Salz auch fine; ~**kost** f delicacies pl; „~**kost"** "Delicatessen"; ~**kosthandlung** f delicatessen; f~**maschig** adj with a fine mesh; Strickwaren finely knitted; ~**mechanik** f precision engineering; ~**mechaniker** m precision engineer; ~**meßgerät** nt precision instrument; ~**schliff** m fine finish(ing); ~**schmecker** m -s, - gourmet, epicure; (fig) connoisseur; ~**schnitt** m (Tabak) fine cut; (Film) final editing; ~**silber** nt refined silver; f~**sinnig** adj sensitive; ~**sinnigkeit** f sensitivity.

Feinsliebchen nt (poet) lady-love (poet), sweetheart.

Fein-: ~**struktur** f fine structure; ~**wäsche** f delicates pl; ~**waschmittel** nt mild(-action) detergent.

feist adj fat; Mensch auch gross, obese. **ein** ~**es Lachen** an obscene chuckle.

Feistheit, Feistigkeit f siehe adj fatness; grossness, obesity.

Feitel m -s, - (Aus) penknife.

feixen vi (inf) to smirk.

Felchen m -s, - whitefish.

Feld nt -(e)s, -er (a) (offenes Gelände) open country. **auf freiem** ~ in the open country; siehe Wald.

(b) (Acker) field.

(c) (Flächenstück: auf Spielbrett) square; (an Zielscheibe) ring; (Her) field.

(d) (Sport: Spiel~) field, pitch. **das** ~ **beherrschen** to be on top.

(e) (Kriegsschauplatz) (battle)field. **ins** ~ **ziehen** or **rücken** (old) to take the field, to march into battle; **im** ~ **stehen** (old) to be on the battlefield; **im** ~ **bleiben** (euph) to fall in action; **auf dem** ~**e der Ehre fallen** (euph old) to fall on the field of honour; **gegen jdn/etw zu** ~ **ziehen** (fig) to crusade against sb/sth; **Argumente ins** ~ **führen** to bring arguments to bear; **das** ~ **behaupten** (fig) to stand or stay one's ground; **das** ~ **räumen** (fig) to quit the field, to bow out; **jdm/einer Sache das** ~ **überlassen** or **räumen** to give way or yield to sb/sth; (freiwillig) to hand over to sb/sth.

(f) (fig: Bereich) field, area.

(g) (Ling, Min, Phys) field.

(h) (Sport: Gruppe) field. **er ließ das** ~ **hinter sich** he left the rest of the field behind (him); **das** ~ **ist geschlossen** the field is bunched (up).

Feld- in cpds field; ~**ahorn** m field maple; ~**arbeit** f (Agr) work in the fields; (Sci, Sociol) fieldwork; ~**arbeiter** m fieldworker; ~**arzt** m (old Mil) army doctor; ~**bau** m cultivation of the (fields); ~**besteck** nt field eating irons pl; ~**bett** nt campbed; ~**binde** f (a) (old: Schärfe) sash; (b) (Med Mil) Red Cross armband; ~**blume** f wild flower; ~**dienst** m (old Mil) active service; ~**elektronen** pl (Elec) field electrons pl; ~**energie** f (Phys) field energy.

Felderwirtschaft f (Agr) crop rotation.

Feld-: ~**flasche** f canteen (Mil), water bottle; ~**flugplatz** m (military) airstrip (near the front); ~**frucht** f (Agr) agricultural crop; ~**geistliche(r)** m (old Mil) army chaplain, padre; ~**gendarmerie** f (old Mil) military police; ~**gepäck** nt (Mil) kit; ~**geschrei** nt (Mil) battle cry; (Her) motto; ~**gleichung** f (Math) field equation; ~**gottesdienst** m (Mil) camp service;

~**graue(r)** m German soldier in battle dress; ~**handball** m European (outdoor) handball; ~**hase** m European hare; ~**haubitze** f (Mil) (field) howitzer; ~**heer** nt (Mil) army in the field; ~**herr** m (old) commander; ~**herrnkunst** f (old) strategy; ~**herrnstab** m (old) (general's) baton or swagger stick; ~**heuschrecke** f grasshopper; (schädlich) locust; ~**huhn** nt partridge; ~**hüter** m watchman (in charge of fields); ~**jäger** m (a) (old Mil) (Kurier) courier; (Infanterist) infantryman; (b) (Mil) military police; (bei der Marine) shore patrol; ~**konstante** f (Phys) space constant; ~**kraft** f (Phys) field intensity or strength; ~**krähe** f rook; ~**küche** f (Mil) field kitchen; ~**lager** nt (old Mil) camp, encampment; ~**lazarett** nt (Mil) field hospital; ~**lerche** f skylark; ~**linie** f (Phys) line of force; ~**mark** f (von Gemeinde) parish land; (von Gut) estate; ~**marschall** m (old) field marshal; f~**marschmäßig** adj in full marching order; ~**maus** f field mouse (loosely), common vole (spec); ~**messer** m -s, - (land) surveyor; ~**pflanze** f agricultural crop; ~**post** f (Mil) forces' postal service; ~**postamt** nt (Mil) forces' letter; ~**postnummer** f (Mil) forces' postal code; **der Kamerad von der anderen** ~**postnummer** (dated hum) our friend across the trenches; ~**prediger** m (old Mil) siehe ~**geistliche(r)**; ~**rain** m edge of the field; ~**salat** m siehe **Rapunzel.**

Feldscher m -s, -e (a) (old Mil) army doctor. (b) (DDR) senior medical orderly.

Feld-: ~**schlacht** f (old) battle; ~**schütz** m -es, -e (obs) siehe ~**hüter**; ~**spat** m (Geol) fel(d)spar; ~**spieler** m (Sport) player (on the field); ~**stärke** f (Phys) field strength or intensity; (Rad, TV) strength of the signal; ~**stecher** m -s, - (pair of) binoculars or field glasses; ~**stuhl** m folding stool; ~**telefon** nt (Mil) field telephone; ~**telegraph** m (Mil) field telegraph; ~**theorie** f (Ling, Phys, Psych) field theory; ~**verweis** m siehe **Platzverweis**; ~**wache** f (old Mil) outpost.

Feld-, Wald- und Wiesen- in cpds (inf) common-or-garden, run-of-the-mill.

Feld-: ~**webel** m sergeant; (fig inf) sergeant-major (type); ~**weg** m track across the fields; ~**weibel** m (Sw) sergeant; ~**wirtschaft** f agriculture, cultivation of the fields; ~**zeichen** nt (old Mil) standard, ensign; ~**zeugmeister** m (old Mil) (Befehlshaber der Artillerie) artillery commander; (Chef der Beschaffung) quartermaster; ~**zeugmeisterei** f (old Mil) quartermaster's stores; ~**zug** m (old, fig) campaign.

Felg|aufschwung m (Sport) upward circle forwards.

Felge f -, -n (a) (Tech) (wheel) rim. (b) (Sport) circle.

Felgenbremse f calliper brake.

Felg|umschwung m (Sport) circle.

Fell nt -(e)s, -e (a) fur; (von Schaf, Lamm) fleece; (von toten Tieren) skin, fell. **ein gesundes** ~ a healthy coat; **einem Tier das** ~ **abziehen** to skin an animal; **ihm sind alle** or **die** ~**e weggeschwommen** (fig) all his hopes were dashed.

(b) (fig inf: Menschenhaut) skin, hide (inf). **ein dickes** ~ **haben** to be thickskinned or have a thick skin; **jdm das** ~ **gerben** to tan sb's hide; **jdm das** ~ **über die Ohren ziehen** to dupe sb, to pull the wool over sb's eyes; **ihn** or **ihm juckt das** ~ he's asking for a good hiding; **das** ~ **versaufen** to hold the wake.

(c) (von Trommel) skin.

Fell- in cpds fur; (Ziegen~/Schaf~ etc) goatskin/sheepskin etc.

Fellache m -n, -n fellah.

Fellatio [fɛ'la:tsio] f -, no pl fellatio.

Fell-: ~**eisen** nt (obs) knapsack; ~**handel** m trade in skins.

Fels m -en, -en, **Felsen** m -s, - rock; (Klippe) cliff.

Fels-: ~**block** m boulder; ~**brocken** m (lump of) rock.

Fels(en)-: ~**bild** nt rock-scape; ~**burg** f mountain fortress.

Felsen-: f~**fest** adj firm; f~**fest überzeugt sein** to be absolutely or firmly convinced; **sich** f~**fest auf jdn verlassen** to put one's complete trust in sb; ~**gebirge** nt (a) rocky mountain range; (b) (Geog) Rocky Mountains pl, Rockies pl; ~**grab** nt rock tomb.

Fels(en)-: ~**grund** m rockbed; (poet: Tal) rocky vale (poet) or glen; ~**höhle** f rock cave; ~**klippe** f rocky cliff; (im Meer) stack; ~**nest** nt mountain lair or hideout; ~**riff** nt (rocky) reef; ~**schlucht** f rocky valley or glen.

Felsentor nt -(e)s, -e arch in the rock.

Fels-: ~**gestein** nt (Geol) (solid) rock; ~**glimmer** m (Geol) mica; ~**grat** m (rocky) ridge.

felsig adj rocky; (steilabfallend) Küste cliff-lined, cliffy.

Fels-: ~**kessel** m corrie; ~**malerei** f rock painting; ~**massiv** nt rock massif; ~**nase** f rock overhang or shelf; ~**spalte** f crevice; ~**vorsprung** m ledge; ~**wand** f rock face; ~**wüste** f rock desert; ~**zacke** f crag.

Feluke f -, -n felucca.

Feme f -, -n, **Fem(e)gericht** nt (Hist) Vehmgericht; (Bandengericht) kangaroo court.

Fememord m (Hist) killing ordered by a Vehmgericht; (fig) lynch-law killing; (bei Gangstern) underworld killing.

feminin adj (a) (Gram) feminine. (b) (fraulich) feminine; (pej) effeminate.

Femininum nt -s, **Feminina** (Gram) feminine noun.

Feminismus m feminism.

Feminist(in f) m feminist.

feministisch adj feminist.

Fenchel m -s, no pl fennel.

Fenchel- in cpds fennel; ~**holz** nt sassafras wood.

Fender m -s, - fender.

Fenn nt -(e)s, -e siehe **Fehn.**

Fenster nt -s, - window; siehe **Geld.**

Fenster- in cpds window; ~**bank** f, ~**brett** nt window-sill, window ledge; ~**briefumschlag** m window envelope; ~**flügel** m side of a window; ~**glas** nt window glass; (in Brille) plain glass; ~**griff** m window catch; ~**kitt** m (window) putty;

~**klappe** f fanlight; ~**kreuz** nt mullion and transom (of a cross window); ~**kurbel** f window handle (for winding car windows); ~**laden** m shutter; ~**leder** nt chamois, shammy (leather).

fensterln vi (S Ger, Aus) to climb through one's sweetheart's bedroom window.

Fenster-: f~**los** adj windowless; ~**pfosten** m mullion; ~**platz** m seat by the window, window seat; ~**putzer** m window cleaner; ~**rahmen** m window frame; ~**rose** f rose window; ~**scheibe** f window pane; ~**sims** m window ledge, windowsill; ~**stock** m window frame; ~**sturz** m (a) (Build) window lintel; (b) (Hist) **der Prager** ~**sturz** the Prague defenestration.

-**fenstrig** adj suf -windowed.

Ferge m -n, -n (poet) ferryman.

Ferial- in cpds (Aus) siehe **Ferien-**.

Ferien ['feːriən] pl holidays pl (Brit), vacation sing (US, Univ); (~**reise**) holiday sing (Brit), vacation sing (US); (Parlaments~, Jur) recess sing. **die großen** ~ the summer holidays (Brit) or long vacation (US, Univ); ~ **haben** to be on holiday or vacation; ~ **machen** to have or take a holiday or vacation; ~ **vom Ich machen** to get away from it all; **auf** ~ **sein** to be on holiday or vacation; **in die** ~ **gehen** or **fahren** to go on holiday or vacation.

Ferien- in cpds holiday (Brit), vacation (US); ~**gast** m holiday-maker; (Besuch) person staying on holiday; ~**kind** nt child from a town on a state-subsidized holiday; ~**kolonie** f children's holiday camp; ~**ordnung** f holiday dates pl; ~**ort** m holiday resort; ~**reise** f holiday (Brit), vacation (US); ~**tag** m day of one's holidays (Brit) or vacation (US); ~**zeit** f holiday period.

Ferkel nt -s, - piglet; (fig) (unsauber) pig, mucky pup (inf); (unanständig) dirty pig (inf).

Ferkelei f (inf) (Schmutz) mess; (Witz) dirty joke; (Handlung) dirty or filthy or disgusting thing to do. **der mit seinen** ~**en** the filthy thing.

ferkeln vi (a) (Zool) to litter. (b) (inf) siehe **Ferkelei** to make a mess; to tell dirty jokes; to be dirty or filthy or disgusting.

Fermate f -, -n (Mus) pause.

Ferment nt -s, -e enzyme.

Fermentation f fermentation.

fermentieren* vt to ferment.

Fermentmangel m enzyme deficiency.

fern 1 adj (a) (räumlich) distant, far-off, faraway. ~ **von hier** a long way (away) from or far away from here; **von** ~(**e**) **betrachtet** seen from a distance; **sich** ~ **sein** (fig) to be not at all close (to one another); **der F**~**e Osten** the Far East; **von** ~(**e**) **kennen** (fig) to know (only) slightly; **das sei** ~ **von mir** (fig) nothing is further from my thoughts, heaven forbid.

(b) (zeitlich entfernt) far-off. ~**e Vergangenheit** (dim and) distant past; **in nicht zu** ~**er Zeit** in the not-too-distant future; **der Tag ist nicht mehr** ~, **wo ...** the day is not far off when ...

2 prep +gen far (away) from. ~ **der Heimat** (liter) far from home; **unrasiert und** ~ **der Heimat** (hum inf) down on one's luck and a long way from home.

Fern-: f~**ab** adv far away; f~**ab gelegen** far away; ~**amt** nt (telephone) exchange; **das Gespräch wurde vom** ~**amt vermittelt** the call was connected by the operator; ~**aufnahme** f (Phot) long shot; ~**auge** nt (closed-circuit) TV camera; ~**auslöser** m (Phot) cable release; ~**bahn** f (Rail) main-line service; ~**beben** nt distant earthquake; ~**bedienung** f remote control; f~**bleiben** vi sep irreg aux sein to stay away (dat, von from); ~**blick** m good view; **ein herrlicher** ~**blick** a splendid view for miles around; ~-**D-Zug**, ~**durchgangszug** m long-distance express (train).

ferne adv (poet, geh) siehe **fern 2**.

Ferne f -, -n (a) (räumlich) distance; (old: ferne Länder) distant lands pl or shores pl (liter). **in der** ~ in the distance; **aus der** ~ from a distance; **in die** ~ **ziehen** (old) to seek out far-off shores or distant climes (liter). (b) (zeitlich) (Zukunft) future; (Vergangenheit) (distant) past. **in weiter** ~ **liegen** to be a long time off or in the distant future.

Fernempfang m (Rad, TV) long-distance reception.

ferner 1 adj comp of **fern** further. **Ihre** ~**en Aufträge** (Comm) your future or further orders; **des** ~(**e**)**n** in addition; **für die** ~**e Zukunft** for the long term.

2 adv (a) further. ~ **liefen** ... (Sport) also-rans ...; **unter** ~ **liefen rangieren** or **kommen** (inf) to be among the also-rans. (b) (künftig) in future. (auch) ~ **etw machen** to continue to do sth; **auch** ~ **im Amt bleiben** to continue in office.

fernerhin adv siehe **ferner 2**.

fernerliegen vi sep irreg (fig) **nichts läge mir ferner, als ...** nothing could be further from my thoughts or mind than ...; **kein Gedanke könnte** ~ **als ...** nothing could be further from my thoughts than ...

Fern-: ~**fahrer** m long-distance lorry (Brit) or truck driver; ~**flug** m long-distance flight; ~**gas** nt gas piped over a long distance; f~**gelenkt** adj remote-controlled; (fig) manipulated (von by); ~**geschütz** nt (Mil) long-range weapon; ~**gespräch** nt trunk (Brit) or long-distance call; f~**gesteuert** adj remote-controlled; (durch Funk auch) radio-controlled; ~**glas** nt (pair of) binoculars or field glasses.

fernhalten sep irreg 1 vt to keep away. 2 vr to keep or stay away.

Fern-: ~**heizung** f district heating (spec); f~**her** adv (old) (von) f~**her** from afar (old, liter); f~**hin** adv (old) far off or hence (old); ~**kurs(us)** m correspondence course; ~**laster** m (inf) long-distance lorry (Brit) or truck, juggernaut; ~**lastfahrer** m (inf) long-distance lorry driver (Brit) or trucker; ~**lastverkehr** m long-distance goods traffic; ~**lastzug** m siehe ~**laster**; ~**lehrgang** m correspondence course; ~**leitung** f (a) (Telec) trunk (Brit) or long-distance line(s); (b) (Röhren) pipeline; f~**lenken** vt sep to operate by remote control;

~**lenkung** f remote control; ~**lenkwaffen** pl (Mil) guided missiles; ~**licht** nt (Aut) full or main or high (esp US) beam; **mit** ~**licht fahren, (das)** ~**licht anhaben** to be or drive on full beam; f~**liegen** vi sep irreg (fig) (jdm) f~**liegen** to be far from sb's thoughts or mind; **es liegt mir f**~, **das zu tun** far be it from me to do that; **es hat mir f**~**gelegen, dich zu kränken** the last thing I wanted (to do) was to offend you.

Fernmelde- in cpds telecommunications; telephone; (Mil) signals; ~**amt** nt telephone exchange; ~**dienst** m telecommunications/telephone service; ~**geheimnis** nt (Jur) secrecy of telecommunications.

Fernmelder m -s, - (a) (Apparat) telephone. (b) (Mil inf) signaller.

Fernmelde-: ~**satellit** m communication satellite; ~**technik** f telecommunications/telephone engineering; ~**truppe** f (Mil) signals corps sing; ~**wesen** nt telecommunications pl.

Fern-: ~**messung** f telemetering; f~**mündlich 1** adj telephone attr; **2** adv by telephone.

Fernost no art aus/in/nach ~ from/in/to the Far East.

Fernost- in cpds Far East; ~**exporte** pl exports pl to the Far East; ~**handel** m trade with the Far East.

fernöstlich adj Far Eastern attr.

Fernostreise f journey to the Far East.

Fern-: ~**pendler** m long-distance commuter; ~**rakete** f long-range missile; ~**rohr** nt telescope; (Doppel~) (pair of) binoculars or field glasses; ~**ruf** m (form) telephone number; ~**ruf 68190** Tel. 68190; ~**schalter** m (Elec) remote-control switch; ~**schnellzug** m long-distance express (train); ~**schreiben** nt telex; ~**schreiber** m (a) teleprinter; (Comm) telex(-machine). (b) (Mensch) teleprinter/telex operator; ~**schreibnetz** nt telex network; f~**schriftlich** adj by telex.

Fernseh- in cpds television, TV; ~**ansager** m television announcer; ~**anstalt** f television organization; ~**apparat** m television or TV (set); ~**empfänger** m (form) television receiver.

fernsehen vi sep irreg to watch television or TV or telly (Brit inf).

Fernsehen nt -s, no pl television, TV, telly (Brit inf). ~ **haben** (Familie etc) to have a television; (Staat etc) to have television or TV; **beim** ~ **arbeiten** to work or be in television; **vom** ~ **übertragen werden** to be televised; **im** ~ on television or TV or (the) telly (Brit inf); **das** ~ **bringt etw** sth is on television, they're showing sth on television.

Fernseher m -s, - (inf) (a) (Gerät) television, TV, telly (Brit inf). (b) (Zuschauer) (television) viewer.

Fernseh-: ~**gebühr** f television licence fee; ~**genehmigung** f television licence; ~**gerät** nt television or TV set; f~**gerecht** adj suitable for television; etw f~**gerecht aufbereiten** to adapt sth for television; ~**journalist** m television or TV reporter; ~**kamera** f television or TV camera; **wir haben Herrn Schmidt vor die** ~**kamera gebeten** we've asked Herr Schmidt to speak to us; ~**kanal** m (television) channel; ~**konserve** f (tele)-recording; ~**norm** f television standard; ~**programm** nt (a) (Kanal) channel, station (US); (b) (Sendung) programme; (Sendefolge) programmes pl; (c) (~**zeitschrift**) (television) programme guide; ~**publikum** nt viewers pl, viewing public; ~**röhre** f (cathode ray) tube; ~**schirm** m television or TV screen; ~**sender** m television transmitter; ~**sendung** f television programme; ~**spiel** nt television play; ~**sprecher** m television announcer; ~**spot** m (a) (Werbespot) TV ad(vertisement); (b) (Kurzfilm) TV short; ~**teilnehmer** m (form) television licence holder; ~**truhe** f cabinet TV; ~**turm** m television tower; ~**übertragung** f television broadcast; (von außerhalb des Studios) outside broadcast; ~**übertragungswagen** m outside broadcast vehicle or van; ~**zuschauer** m (television) viewer.

Fern-: ~**sicht** f clear view; (eine) **gute** ~**sicht haben** to be able to see a long way; f~**sichtig** adj (Med) long-sighted; ~**sichtigkeit** f (Med) long-sightedness.

Fernsprech- in cpds (form) telephone; ~**anschluß** m telephone; **15** ~**anschlüsse haben** to have 15 lines; ~**apparat** m telephone; ~**auftragsdienst** m telephone services pl; ~**buch** nt telephone directory.

Fernsprecher m -s, - (form) (public) telephone.

Fernsprech-: ~**gebühr** f telephone charges pl; ~**geheimnis** nt siehe **Fernmeldegeheimnis**; ~**leitung** f (per Draht) (telephone) line; (per Radio, Satellit) telephone link; ~**netz** nt telephone system; ~**stelle** f (telephone) number; ~**teilnehmer** m (form) telephone subscriber; ~**verbindung** f telephone link; ~**verkehr** m telephone traffic; ~**verzeichnis** nt telephone directory; ~**wesen** nt telephone system; ~**zelle** f (tele)phone box or booth (US), callbox; ~**zentrale** f telephone exchange.

Fern-: ~**spruch** m telephone message; **laut** ~**spruch vom 2. März** as mentioned on the telephone on March 2nd; f~**stehen** vi sep irreg: **jdm/etw** f~**stehen** to have no connection with sb/sth; **ich stehe ihm ziemlich f**~ I'm not on very close terms with him; f~**steuern** vt sep to operate by remote control; (per Funk auch) to control by radio; ~**steuerung** f remote/radio control; ~**steuerung haben** to be remote-/radio-controlled; ~**straße** f trunk or major road, highway (US); ~**studium** nt correspondence degree course (also with radio, TV etc), ≈ Open University course (Brit); ~**trauung** f marriage by proxy; ~**überwachung** f remote monitoring; ~**universität** f ≈ Open University (Brit); ~**unterricht** m correspondence course also using radio, TV etc, multi-media course; ~**verkehr** m (a) (Transport) long-distance traffic; (b) (Telec) trunk (Brit) or long-distance traffic; ~**verkehrsstraße** f siehe ~**straße**; ~**vermittlung(sstelle)** f telephone exchange; ~**versorgung** f long-distance supply; ~**wärme** f district heating (spec); ~**weh** nt wanderlust; ~**wirkung** f (Phys) long-distance effect;

~ziel nt long-term goal; ~zug m long-distance train; ~zündung f long-range or remote ignition.

Ferrat nt (Chem) ferrate.

Ferrit m -s, -e (Chem) ferrite.

Ferro- in cpds ferro-.

Ferse f -, -n heel. jdm (dicht) auf den ~n sein or folgen/bleiben to be/stay hard or close on sb's heels; siehe heften.

Fersen-: ~automatik f (Ski) automatic heel release; ~bein nt (Anat) heel bone, calcaneus (spec); ~geld nt: ~geld geben to take to one's heels.

fertig adj (a) (abgeschlossen, vollendet) finished; (ausgebildet) qualified; (reif) Mensch, Charakter mature. etw ~ kaufen to buy sth ready-made; Essen to buy sth ready-prepared or ready to eat; ~ ausgebildet fully qualified; mit der Ausbildung ~ sein to have completed one's training; ~ ist die Laube (inf) or der Lack (inf) (and) there we are!, (and) Bob's your uncle! (inf).
(b) (zu Ende) finished. wird das/werden wir rechtzeitig ~ werden? will it/we be finished in time?; mit etw ~ sein, etw ~ haben to have finished sth; ~ essen/lesen to finish eating/reading; mit jdm ~ sein (fig) to be finished or through with sb; mit jdm/etw ~ werden to cope with sb/sth; ich werde damit nicht ~ I can't cope with it; du darfst nicht gehen, ~! you're not going and that's that or and that's the end of it!
(c) (bereit) ready. ~ zur Abfahrt ready to go or leave; bist du/ist das Essen ~? are you/is the meal ready?; siehe Achtung, Platz.
(d) (inf) shattered (inf), all in (inf); (ruiniert) finished; (erstaunt) knocked for six (inf). mit den Nerven ~ sein to be at the end of one's tether; da bin ich ~! (erstaunt) my God!, well I never!; siehe fix.

Fertig- in cpds finished; (Build) prefabricated; ~bau m (Build) (no pl: Bauweise) prefabricated building; (Gebäude auch) pl -bauten prefab; f~bekommen* vt sep irreg to finish, to get finished; f~bringen vt sep irreg (a) (vollenden) to get done; (b) (imstande sein) to manage; (iro) to be capable of; ich habe es nicht f~gebracht, ihr die Wahrheit zu sagen I couldn't bring myself to tell her the truth; er bringt das f~ (iro) I wouldn't put it past him; er bringt es f~, und sagt ihr das he's quite capable of saying that to her.

fertigen vt (form) to manufacture.

Fertig-: ~erzeugnis nt finished product; ~fabrikat nt finished product; ~gericht nt ready-to-serve meal; ~haus nt prefabricated house, prefab.

Fertigkeit f skill. wenig/eine große ~ in etw (dat) haben to be not very/to be very skilled at or in sth.

Fertig-: f~kriegen vt sep (inf) siehe f~bringen; f~machen vt sep (a) (vollenden) to finish; (b) (bereit machen) to get ready; sich f~machen to get ready; f~machen! get ready!; (Sport) get set!, steady!; (c) (inf) jdn f~machen (erledigen) to do for sb; (ermüden) to take it out of sb; (deprimieren) to get sb down; (abkanzeln) to tear sb off a strip, to lay into sb (inf); sich f~machen to do oneself in; ~produkt nt finished product; f~stellen vt sep to complete; ~stellung f completion; ~teil nt finished part.

Fertigung f production. in der ~ arbeiten to work in production or in the production department.

Fertigungs- in cpds production; ~straße f production line; ~technik f production engineering.

Fertigware f finished product.

Fes¹, fes nt -, no pl (Mus) F flat.

Fes² [feːs] m -(es), -(e) fez.

fesch adj (S Ger, Aus: inf) (modisch) smart; (hübsch) attractive. das ist ~ that's great (inf); sei ~! (Aus) (sei brav) be good; (sei kein Frosch) be a sport (inf).

Fessel f -, -n (a) (Bande) (lit, fig) bond, fetter, shackle; (Kette) chain. sich von den ~n befreien to free oneself, to loose one's bonds (liter); jdm ~n anlegen, jdn in ~n legen to fetter or shackle sb/put sb in chains; jdn in ~n schlagen (liter, fig) to put sb in fetters, to enchain sb (liter); die ~n der Ehe/Liebe the shackles of marriage/love.
(b) (Anat) (von Huftieren) pastern; (von Menschen) ankle.

Fessel-: ~ballon m captive balloon; ~gelenk nt postern; (von Menschen) ankle joint; ~griff m lock.

fesseln vt (a) (mit Tau etc) to tie (up), to bind; (Hist: mit Hand~, Fußschellen) to fetter, to shackle; (mit Handschellen) to handcuff; (mit Ketten) to chain (up). jdn (an Händen und Füßen) ~ to tie/fetter/chain sb (hand and foot); jdm die Hände auf dem Rücken ~ to tie sb's hands behind his back; der Gefangene wurde gefesselt vorgeführt the prisoner was brought in handcuffed/in chains; jdn ans Bett ~ (fig) to confine sb to (his) bed, to keep sb in bed; jdn ans Haus ~ (fig) to tie sb to the house; jdn an jdn/sich ~ (fig) to bind sb to sb/oneself.
(b) (faszinieren) to grip; Aufmerksamkeit to hold.

fesselnd adj gripping.

fest 1 adj (a) (hart) solid. ~e Nahrung solid food, solids pl; ~e Form or Gestalt annehmen (fig) to take shape.
(b) (stabil) solid; Gewebe, Schuhe tough, sturdy; (Comm, Fin) stable; Zuneigung strong. die Börse ist ~ the stock market is steady or stable; ~es Geld (Fin) money on time deposit; siehe Boden.
(c) (sicher, entschlossen) firm; Plan auch definite; Stimme steady. ~ versprechen to promise faithfully; ~ verankert (lit) firmly or securely anchored; (fig) firmly rooted; eine ~e Meinung von etw haben to have definite views on sth; etw ist ~ sth is definite; in etw (dat) ~ sein (können) to be sure of oneself in sth; ~ entschlossen sein to be absolutely determined.
(d) (kräftig) firm; Schlag hard, heavy. ~ zuschlagen to hit hard.
(e) (nicht locker) tight; Griff firm; (fig) Schlaf sound. ~ packen to grip tightly or firmly; etw ~ anziehen/zudrehen to

pull/screw sth tight; die Handbremse ~ anziehen to put the handbrake on firmly; die Tür ~ schließen to shut the door tight; ~ schlafen to sleep soundly; er hat schon ~ geschlafen he was sound asleep; jdn/etw ~ in der Hand haben to have sb under one's thumb/have sth firmly under control.
(f) (ständig) regular; Freund(in) steady; Stellung, Mitarbeiter permanent; Kosten, Tarif, Einkommen fixed; Redewendung set. ~ befreundet sein to be good friends; (Freund und Freundin) to be going steady; jdn ~ anstellen to employ sb as a regular member of staff; Geld ~ anlegen to tie up money; in ~en Händen sein or sich befinden (Besitz) to be in private hands; (inf: Mädchen) to be spoken for; sie hat keinen ~en Platz im Büro she doesn't have her own desk in the office; er hat einen ~en Platz in ihrem Herzen he has a special place in her affections; siehe auch Platz.
2 adv (inf: tüchtig, kräftig) helfen, arbeiten with a will. du mußt ~ essen you must eat properly; ich habe ihn ~ verhauen I gave him a sound or proper thrashing.

Fest nt -(e)s, -e (a) (Feier) celebration; (historische Begebenheit) celebrations pl; (Party) party; (Hochzeits~) reception; (Bankett) banquet, feast (old); (Ball~) ball; (Kinder~, Schützen~) carnival. ein ~ zum hundertjährigen Bestehen des Vereins the club's centenary celebrations, celebrations to mark the club's centenary; es ist mir ein ~, das zu machen (inf) I really enjoy doing that, I get a real kick out of doing that (inf); das war ein ~! (inf) it was great fun; man soll die ~e feiern, wie sie fallen (prov) make hay while the sun shines (Prov).
(b) (kirchlicher Feiertag) feast, festival; (Weihnachts~) Christmas. bewegliches/unbewegliches ~ movable/immovable feast; frohes ~! Merry or Happy Christmas!

Fest-: ~akt m ceremony; f~angestellt adj employed on a regular basis; ~angestellte(r) mf regular member of staff; ~ansprache f speech; ~aufführung f festival production; f~backen vi sep irreg aux sein (dial) siehe f~kleben; ~bankett nt ceremonial banquet; f~beißen vr sep irreg (Hund etc) to get a firm hold with its teeth (an +dat on); (Zecke etc) to attach itself firmly (an +dat to); (fig: nicht weiterkommen) to get bogged down (inf) (an +dat in); der Hund biß sich an ihrem Bein f~ the dog sank its teeth firmly into her leg; ~beleuchtung f festive lighting or lights pl; (inf: im Haus) blazing lights pl; was soll denn diese ~beleuchtung? (inf) why is the place lit up like a Christmas tree? (inf); f ~ besoldet adj on a regular salary; f~binden vt sep irreg to tie up; jdn/etw an etw (dat) f~binden to tie sb/sth to sth; f~bleiben vi sep irreg aux sein to stand firm, to remain resolute; f~drehen vt sep to screw up tightly; f~drücken vt sep to press in/down/together firmly.

feste adv (inf) siehe fest 2; immer ~ druff! let him/her etc have it! (inf), give it to him/her etc! (inf).

Feste f -, -n (old) (a) siehe Festung. (b) (Erde) dry land, terra firma. die ~ des Himmels (Bibl) the firmament.

Fest-: ~essen nt banquet; Christmas dinner; f~fahren vr sep irreg (fig) to get bogged down; (lit auch) to get stuck, to stick fast; f~fressen vr sep irreg to seize up; f~frieren vi sep irreg aux sein to freeze solid; ~gabe f (a) (Geschenk) presentation gift; (b) (~schrift) commemorative paper, festschrift; ~gedicht nt celebratory or occasional poem; ~gelage nt banquet; ~geläute nt festive peal of bells; ~geld nt (Fin) time deposit; ~gewand nt (liter) festive garb (liter); f~gewurzelt adj: wie f~gewurzelt rooted to the spot; ~gottesdienst m festival service; f~gurten sep 1 vr to strap oneself in; (in Auto, Flugzeug auch) to fasten one's seat belt; sich an etw (dat) f~gurten to strap oneself to sth; 2 vt to strap in; f~haken sep 1 vt to hook up (an +dat on); 2 vr to get caught (up) (an +dat on); ~halle f festival hall.

festhalten sep irreg 1 vt (a) to keep a firm hold on, to keep hold of, to hold on to. jdn am Arm/Rockzipfel ~ to hold on to sb's arm/the hem of sb's coat.
(b) (bemerken) to stress, to emphasize.
(c) (inhaftieren) to hold, to detain.
(d) (speichern) to record; Atmosphäre etc to capture. etw schriftlich/im Gedächtnis ~ to record sth/bear sth firmly in mind; etw in Wort und Bild ~ to record sth in words and pictures.
2 vi an etw (dat) ~ to hold or stick (inf) to sth; am Glauben ~ to hold to the faith.
3 vr to hold on (an +dat to). sich irgendwo ~ to hold on to something; halt dich fest! (lit) hold tight!; halt dich fest, und hör dir das an! (inf) brace yourself and listen to this!

festheften vt sep (mit Nadel) to pin (an +dat on/to); (mit Faden) to tack (an +dat on/to).

festigen 1 vt to strengthen; Freundschaft, Macht, Ruf auch to consolidate. ein gefestigter Charakter a firm or resolute character; jdn sittlich ~ to give sb a sense of moral responsibility; sittlich gefestigt sein to have a sense of moral responsibility.
2 vr to become stronger; (Freundschaft, Macht, Ruf auch) to consolidate.

Festigkeit f, no pl strength; (fig) steadfastness; (von Meinung) firmness. die ~ seines Charakters his moral strength, his strength of character.

Festigung f siehe vb strengthening; consolidation.

Festival ['festival, 'festɪval] nt -s, -s festival.

Festivität [festivi'tɛːt] f (old, hum inf) celebration, festivity.

Fest-: f~keilen vt sep to wedge; f~klammern sep 1 vt to clip on (an +dat to); Wäsche an or auf der Leine f~klammern to peg washing on the line; 2 vr to cling (an +dat to); f~kleben vti sep (vi: aux sein) to stick (firmly) (an +dat on/to); ~kleid nt formal dress; die Stadt legte ihr ~kleid an (liter) the town decked itself out in all its finery; **f~klemmen** *sep* 1 *vt* to wedge fast; (*mit Klammer, Klemme*) to clip; **f~geklemmt werden** (*aus Versehen*) to get stuck or jammed; 2 *vir* (*vi: aux sein*) to jam, to stick (fast); **f~klopfen** *vt sep* to pack down; **f~knoten** *vt sep siehe* **f~binden**; **~komma** *nt* fixed point; **~körper** *m* (*Phys*) solid; **~körperphysik** *f* solid-state physics *sing*; **f~krallen** *vr sep* (*Tier*) to dig one's claws in (*an +dat* -to); (*Mensch*) to dig one's nails in (*an +dat* -to); (*fig*) to cling (*an +dat* to).

Festland *nt* (*nicht Insel*) mainland; (*nicht Meer*) dry land; (*europäisches* ~) Continent, Europe.

festländisch *adj* mainland *attr*; Continental, European.

Festlands-: ~**masse** *f* continent; ~**sockel** *m* continental shelf.

festlaufen *sep irreg* 1 *vr* (*Schiff*) to run aground; (*fig*) (*Verhandlungen*) to founder. **die Stürmer liefen sich** (**an der Verteidigung**) **immer wieder fest** the forwards kept coming up against a solid line of defence. 2 *vi aux sein* (*Schiff*) to run aground.

festlegen *sep* 1 *vt* (a) (*festsetzen*) Reihenfolge, Termin, Kurs *etc* to fix; Grenze *auch* to establish; Sprachgebrauch to establish, to lay down; (*bestimmen*) Regelung, Arbeitszeiten to lay down; (*feststellen*) Geburtsdatum to determine. **etw schriftlich/testamentarisch** ~ to stipulate or specify sth in writing/in one's will.

(b) **jdn auf etw** (*acc*) ~**/darauf** ~, **etw zu tun** (*festnageln*) to tie sb (down) to sth/to doing sth; (*einschränken auch*) to restrict or limit sb to sth/to doing sth; (*verpflichten*) to commit sb to sth/to doing sth.

(c) Geld to put on time deposit, to tie up.

2 *vr* (a) to tie oneself down (*auf +acc* to); (*sich verpflichten*) to commit oneself (*auf +acc* to). **ich kann mich darauf nicht** ~, **ich kann mich auch irren** I can't swear to it, I might be wrong; **sich darauf** ~, **etw zu tun** to tie oneself down/commit oneself to doing sth.

(b) (*einen Entschluß fassen*) to decide (*auf +acc* on). **sich darauf** ~, **etw zu tun** to decide on doing sth or to do sth.

Festlegung *f siehe vt* (a, b) (a) fixing; establishing; laying-down; determining. (b) tying-down; restriction, limiting; commitment.

festlich *adj* festive; (*feierlich*) solemn; (*prächtig*) splendid, magnificent. **ein** ~**er Tag** a special or red-letter day; **etw** ~ **begehen** to celebrate sth.

Festlichkeit *f* celebration; (*Stimmung*) festiveness.

Fest-: **f~liegen** *vi sep irreg* (*f~gesetzt sein*) to have been fixed or definitely decided; (*Sprachgebrauch, Grenze*) to have been established; (*Arbeitszeiten, Regelung*) to have been laid down; **liegt das jetzt f~?** is that definite now?; (b) (*Fin: Geld*) to be on time deposit or tied up; (c) (*nicht weiterkönnen*) to be stuck; (*Naut*) to be aground; **f~machen** *sep* 1 *vt* (a) (*befestigen*) to fix on (*an +dat* -to); (*f~binden*) to fasten (*an +dat* (on)to); (*Naut*) to moor; (b) (*vereinbaren*) to arrange; **ein Geschäft f~machen** to clinch a deal; (c) (*Hunt: aufspüren*) to bring to bay; (d) (*beweisen, zeigen*) to demonstrate, to exemplify; 2 *vi* (*Naut*) to moor; ~**mahl** *nt* (*geh*) banquet, feast; ~**meter** *m or nt* cubic metre of solid timber; **f~nageln** *vt sep* (a) to nail (down/up/on); **etw an/auf etw** (*dat*) **f~nageln** to nail sth to sth; (b) (*fig inf*) **jdn f~nageln** to tie down (*auf +acc* to); ~**nähen** *vt sep* to sew up/on; ~**nahme** *f -, -n* arrest, apprehension; **vorläufige ~nahme** temporary detention; **f~nehmen** *vt sep irreg* to apprehend, to arrest; **vorläufig f~nehmen** to take into custody; ~**offerte** *f* (*Comm*) firm offer.

Feston [fɛsˈtõ] *nt -s, -s* festoon.

Fest-: ~**ordner** *m* steward; ~**platz** *m* festival ground; (*für Volksfest*) fairground; ~**predigt** *f* feast-day sermon; ~**preis** *m* (*Comm*) fixed price; ~**programm** *nt* festival programme; ~**punkt** *m* fixed point; ~**rede** *f* speech; **die ~rede halten** to give the main speech; **eine ~rede halten** to make a speech on a special occasion; **f~reden** *vr sep* to get involved in a conversation; ~**redner** *m* (main) speaker; **f~rennen** *vr sep irreg* (*inf*) to get bogged down (*inf*); **unsere Spieler rannten sich** (**an der gegnerischen Abwehr**) **f~** our players came up against the solid line of the opponents' defence; ~**saal** *m* hall; (*Speisesaal*) banqueting hall; (*Tanzsaal*) ballroom; **f~saufen** *vr sep* (*inf*) to get stuck in (*inf*), to make a night of it (*inf*); **f~saugen** *vr sep* to attach itself firmly (*an +dat* to); ~**schmaus** *m* (*old*) *siehe* ~**mahl**; ~**schmuck** *m* festive decorations *pl*; **im ~schmuck** festively decorated; **f~schnallen** *vtr sep siehe* **anschnallen**; **f~schnüren** *vt sep siehe* **f~binden**; **f~schrauben** *vt sep* to screw (in/on/down/up) tight; **f~schreiben** *vt sep irreg* (*fig*) to establish; ~**schrift** *f* commemorative publication; (*für Gelehrten*) festschrift.

festsetzen *sep* 1 *vt* (a) (*bestimmen*) Preis, Rente, Grenze to fix (*bei, auf +acc* at); Ort, Termin *auch* to arrange (*auf +acc*, *bei* for); Frist *auch* to set; Arbeitszeiten to lay down. **der Beginn der Veranstaltung wurde auf zwei Uhr festgesetzt** the event was scheduled to begin at 2 o'clock.

(b) (*inhaftieren*) to detain.

2 *vr* (*Staub, Schmutz*) to collect; (*Rost, Ungeziefer, unerwünschte Personen*) to get a foothold; (*Mil*) to take up one's position; (*fig: Gedanke*) to take root, to implant itself.

Festsetzung *f siehe vt* (a) fixing; arrangement; setting; laying-down. (b) (*Inhaftierung*) detention.

festsitzen *vi sep irreg* (a) (*klemmen, haften*) to be stuck; (*Schmutz*) to cling; (*in Zwischenräumen*) to be trapped. (b) (*steckengeblieben sein*) to be stuck (*bei* on); (*Naut*) to be aground.

Festspiel *nt* (*einzelnes Stück*) festival production. ~**e** *pl* (*Veranstaltung*) festival *sing*.

Festspiel-: ~**haus** *nt* festival theatre; ~**stadt** *f* festival city/town.

fest-: ~**stampfen** *vt sep* to pound down; (*mit den Füßen auch*) to

stamp or tread down; ~**stecken** *sep* 1 *vt* to pin (*an +dat* (on)to, **in** *+dat* in); Haare, Rocksaum to pin up; 2 *vi aux sein* (*steckengeblieben sein*) to be stuck; ~**stehen** *vi sep irreg* (*sicher sein*) to be certain; (*beschlossen sein*) to have been settled or fixed; (*unveränderlich sein*) to be definite; ~ **steht or eines steht** ~, **daß ...** one thing's (for) certain or sure and that is that ...; **soviel steht** ~ this or so much is certain; ~**stehend** *adj* (a) (*Mech*) fixed; (b) *attr* (*bestimmt, verbindlich*) definite; Redewendung, Reihenfolge set; Brauch (well-)established; ~**stellbar** *adj* (a) (*Mech: arretierbar*) **der Wagen der Schreibmaschine ist ~stellbar** the typewriter carriage can be locked in position; (b) (*herauszufinden*) ascertainable.

feststellen *vt sep* (a) (*Mech*) to lock (fast).

(b) (*ermitteln*) to ascertain, to find out; Personalien, Sachverhalt, Datum *etc auch* to establish; Ursache, Grund *auch* to establish, to determine; Schaden to assess; Krankheit to diagnose. **einen Totalschaden an einem Wagen** ~ to assess a car as a total write-off; **der Arzt konnte nur noch den Tod** ~ the doctor found him to be dead.

(c) (*erkennen*) to tell (*an +dat* from); Fehler, Unterschied to find, to detect; (*bemerken*) to discover; (*einsehen*) to realize. **wir mußten** ~, **daß wir uns geirrt hatten** we were forced to realize that we had made a mistake; **ich mußte entsetzt/überrascht** *etc* ~, **daß ...** I was horrified/surprised *etc* to find that ...

(d) (*aussprechen*) to stress, to emphasize.

Feststelltaste *f* shift lock.

Feststellung *f* (a) *siehe vt* (b) ascertainment; establishment; assessment; diagnosis.

(b) (*Erkenntnis*) conclusion. **zu der** ~ **kommen** or **gelangen**, **daß ...** to come to the conclusion that ...

(c) (*Wahrnehmung*) observation. **die** ~ **machen** or **treffen daß ...** to realize that ...; **wir mußten leider die** ~ **machen, daß ...** (*form*) it has come to our notice that ...; **ist das eine Frage oder eine ~?** is that a question or a statement (of fact)?

(d) (*Bemerkung*) remark, comment, observation. **die abschließende** ~ one's closing remarks; **die** ~ **machen, daß ...** to remark or observe that ...; **erlauben Sie mir die** ~, **daß ...** permit me to remark or observe that ...

Feststellungsklage *f* action for a declaratory judgement.

Fest-: ~**stimmung** *f* festive atmosphere; (~**laune**) festive mood; ~**stoffrakete** *f* solid-fuel rocket; ~**tafel** *f* banquet table; (*bei Familienlässen*) (dinner) table.

Festtag *m* (a) (*Ehrentag*) special or red-letter day. (b) (*Feiertag*) holiday, feast(day) (*Eccl*). **angenehme ~e!** happy Christmas/Easter *etc*!

festtäglich *adj* holiday *attr*. ~ **gestimmt sein** to be in a holiday mood; ~ **gekleidet** festively dressed.

Festtags-: ~**kleidung** *f* ~**kleidung tragen** to be festively dressed; ~**laune** *f* festive mood; **in ~laune sein** (*iro*) to have been celebrating; ~**stimmung** *f* festive atmosphere; **in ~stimmung** in a festive mood.

Fest-: **f~treten** *sep irreg* 1 *vt* to tread down; (*in Teppich etc*) to tread in (*in +acc* -to); 2 *vr* to get trodden down/in; **das tritt sich f~!** (*hum inf*) don't worry, it's good for the carpet (*hum*); **f~trocknen** *vi sep aux sein* to dry (on); **f~umrissen** *adj attr* clear-cut; ~**umzug** *m* procession.

Festung *f* (a) (*Befestigung*) fortress; (*Burgfeste*) castle. (b) *no pl* (*inf*) *siehe* **Festungshaft**.

Festungs-: ~**graben** *m* moat; ~**haft** *f* imprisonment in a fortress; ~**wall** *m* rampart.

Fest-: ~**veranstaltung** *f* function; ~**versammlung** *f* assembled company; **f~verwurzelt** *adj attr* deep-rooted, deep-seated; **f~verzinslich** *adj* fixed-interest *attr*; ~**vorstellung** *f* gala performance; ~**vortrag** *m* lecture, talk; **f~wachsen** *vi sep irreg aux sein siehe* **anwachsen** (*lit*); ~**wiese** *f* festival ground; (*für Volksfest*) fairground; ~**woche** *f* festival week; **die ~wochen** the festival *sing*; **f~wurzeln** *vi sep aux sein* to take root; *siehe* **f~gewurzelt**; ~**zeit** *f* holiday period; (~*spielzeit*) festival (period); ~**zelt** *nt* carnival marquee; **f~ziehen** *vt sep irreg* to pull tight; Schraube to tighten (up); ~**zug** *m* carnival procession; **f~zurren** *vt sep* (*Naut*) to lash up.

fetal *adj attr siehe* **fötal**.

Fete, Fête [ˈfeːtə, ˈfɛːtə] *f -, -n* party. **eine** ~ **feiern** (*als Gastgeber*) to have or give or throw a party; (*als Gast*) to go to a party.

Feten *pl of* **Fetus**.

Fetisch *m -(e)s, -e* fetish.

fetischisieren *vt* (*geh*) to make a fetish of.

Fetischismus *m* fetishism.

Fetischist *m* fetishist.

fett *adj* (a) (~*haltig*) Speisen, Kost fatty; (*fig inf: ölig*) Stimme fat. ~ **essen** to eat fatty food; ~ **kochen** to cook fatty food; (*viel Fett gebrauchen*) to use a lot of fat; ~**e Lache** guffaw; ~**e Lache** to guffaw; **ein** ~**er Bissen** or **Brocken** or **Happen** (*lit*) a juicy morsel; (*fig*) a lucrative deal.

(b) (*dick*) fat; (*Typ*) Überschrift, Schlagzeilen bold. ~ **gedruckt** (*Typ*) printed in bold(face); **sich dick und** ~ **fressen** (*sl*) to stuff oneself (*inf*) or one's face (*sl*); ~ **dasitzen** (*inf*)/**sich** ~ **hinsetzen** (*inf*) to sit there/plump oneself down like a sack of potatoes (*inf*); **setz dich nicht so** ~ **hin!** (*inf*) don't spread yourself so much! (*inf*).

(c) (*üppig*) Boden, Weide, Klee rich, luxuriant; (*fig inf*) rich; Beute, Gewinn fat; Geschäft lucrative. ~**e Jahre** fat years; **ein** ~**er Posten** (*inf*) a cushy job or number (*inf*); *siehe* **sieben**[2].

(d) (*dial inf: betrunken*) plastered *pred* (*inf*).

(e) (*Aut*) Gemisch rich.

Fett *nt -(e)s, -e* fat; (*zum Schmieren*) grease. ~ **ansetzen** to put on weight, to get fat; (*Tiere*) to fatten up; **mit heißem** ~ **übergießen** to baste (with hot fat); **in schwimmendem** ~ **backen** to deep-fry; **sein** ~ **bekommen** (*inf*) or **kriegen** (*inf*)/**weghaben**

(inf) to get/have got what was coming to one *(inf) or* one's come-uppance *(inf)*; **im eigenen ~ ersticken** to be a mountain of flesh; **~ schwimmt oben** *(prov)* *(hum: Dicke im Wasser)* fat floats; *siehe* **abschöpfen, schmoren.**

Fett-: **~ablagerung** *f, no pl* deposition of fat; **~ablagerungen** fatty deposits; **~ansatz** *m* layer of fat; **zu ~ansatz neigen** to tend to corpulence; **f~arm** *adj* low-fat, with a low fat content; **f~arm essen** to eat foods with a low fat content; **~auge** *nt* globule of fat; **~bauch** *m* paunch; *(inf: fetter Mann)* fatso *(inf)*; **f~bäuchig** *adj (inf)* paunchy, fat-bellied *(inf)*; **~bedarf** *m* fat requirements *pl*; **~creme** *f* skin cream with oil; **f~dicht** *adj* Papier greaseproof; **f~dicht verpacken** to wrap in greaseproof paper; **~druck** *m (Typ)* bold type.

Fette *f -, no pl (rare) siehe* **Fettheit.**
Fette Henne *f (Bot)* stonecrop.
Fett|embolie *f (Med)* fat-embolism.
fetten **1** *vt* to grease. **2** *vi* to be greasy; *(Fett absondern)* to get greasy.
Fett-: **~film** *m* greasy film; **~fleck(en)** *m* grease spot, greasy mark; **f~fleckig** *adj* covered in grease spots; **f~frei** *adj* fat-free; Milch non-fat; Kost non-fatty; Creme non-greasy; **f~füttern** *vt sep* to fatten up; **f~gedruckt** *adj attr (Typ)* bold, in bold face; **~gehalt** *m* fat content; **~geschwulst** *f (Med)* fatty tumour; **~gewebe** *nt (Anat)* fat(ty) tissue; **f~glänzend** *adj* die **f~glänzenden Ringer** the wrestlers with their oiled bodies glistening; **f~haltig, f~hältig** *(Aus)* *adj* fatty; **~haushalt** *m* fat balance; **ein gestörter ~haushalt** a fat imbalance.
Fettheit *f, no pl (inf: Dickheit)* fatness; *(Fetthaltigkeit)* fatti-ness.
Fett-: **~henne** *f (Bot)* stonecrop; **~herz** *nt* fatty heart.
fettig *adj* greasy; Haut auch oily.
Fettigkeit *f siehe adj* greasiness; oiliness.
Fett-: **~kloß** *m (pej)* fatty *(inf)*, dumpling *(inf)*; **~klumpen** *m* globule of fat; **~lebe** *f (inf)* **~lebe machen** to live the life of Riley *(inf)*; **~leber** *f* fatty liver; **f~leibig** *adj (geh)* obese, corpulent; **~leibigkeit** *f (geh)* obesity, corpulence; **f~los** *adj* fat-free; **völlig f~los essen** to eat no fats at all; **f~löslich** *adj* fat-soluble; **~massen** *pl (inf)* mass sing of fat; **~mops** *m (inf)* roly-poly *(inf)*, dumpling *(inf)*; **~näpfchen** *nt (inf):* **ins ~näpfchen treten** to put one's foot in it *(bei jdm with sb)*, to drop a clanger *(inf)*; **~polster** *nt (Anat)* (layer of) subcutaneous fat; *(hum inf)* flab no *pl*, padding no *pl*; **~polster haben** to be well-padded; **~pölsterchen** *nt* padding no *pl*; **f~reich** *adj* high-fat, with a high fat content; **f~reich essen** to eat foods with a high fat content; **~sack** *m (sl)* fatso *(inf)*; **~salbe** *f* fat-based ointment; **~sau** *f (vulg)* fat slob *(sl)*; **~säure** *f (Chem)* fatty acid; **~schicht** *f* layer of fat; **~steiß** *m (Anat)* steatopygia *(spec)*; *(hum)* fat bottom *(inf)*; **~stift** *m* grease pencil, lithographic crayon; **~sucht** *f, no pl (Med)* obesity; **f~süchtig** *adj (Med)* obese; **f~triefend** *adj* greasy, dripping with fat; **~wanst** *m (pej)* potbelly; *(Mensch)* paunchy man, fatso *(inf)*.
Fetus *m - or -sses, -sse or* **Feten** *siehe* **Fötus.**
Fetzen *m -s, -* **(a)** *(abgerissen)* shred; *(zerrissen auch)* tatter; *(Stoff~, Papier~, Gesprächs~)* scrap; *(Kleidung)* rag; *(Nebel~)* wisp. **in ~ sein, nur noch ~ sein** to be in tatters or shreds; **in ~ gekleidet** dressed in rags; **das Kleid ist in ~ gegangen** the dress has fallen to pieces; **etw in ~/in tausend ~ (zer)reißen** to tear sth to shreds/into a thousand pieces; **..., daß die ~ fliegen** *(inf)* ... like mad *(inf) or* crazy *(inf)*. **(b)** *(Aus) (Scheuertuch)* rag. **einen ~ haben** *(inf: Rausch)* to be sloshed *(inf)*.
fetzen **1** *vi (sl)* **(a)** *(mitreißen)* to be mind-blowing *(sl)*. **(b)** *aux sein (rasen)* to hare *(inf)*, to tear *(inf)*. **2** *vt* to rip.
Fetzenball *m (Aus) siehe* **Maskenball.**
Fetzer *m -s, - (sl)* wow *(sl)*.
feucht *adj* damp; *(schlüpfrig)* moist; *(feuchtheiß)* Klima humid; Hände sweaty; Tinte, Farbe not quite dry. **sich ins ~e Element stürzen** *(hum)* to plunge into the water; **sie kriegte/hatte ~e Augen** her eyes moistened/were moist; **ein ~er Abend** *(hum)* a convivial evening's drinking; **eine ~e Aussprache haben** *(hum inf)* to spatter one's audience when one speaks; **das geht dich einen ~en Kehricht** *(inf) or* Dreck *(sl) or* Schmutz *(sl)* an that's none of your goddamn *(sl) or* bloody *(Brit sl)* business; *siehe* **Ohr.**
Feuchte *f -, no pl siehe* **Feuchtigkeit.**
feucht-: **~fröhlich** *adj (hum)* merry, convivial; **ein ~fröhlicher Abend** an evening of convivial drinking; **~heiß** *adj* hot and damp, muggy.
Feuchtigkeit *f, no pl* **(a)** *siehe adj* dampness; moistness; humidity; sweatiness; wetness. **(b)** *(Flüssigkeit)* moisture; *(Luft~)* humidity.
Feuchtigkeits-: **~creme** *f* moisturizer, moisturizing cream; **~gehalt, ~grad** *m* moisture level or content; **~messer** *m* hygrometer.
feucht-: **~kalt** *adj* cold and damp; Höhle, Keller etc auch dank; **~warm** *adj* muggy, humid.
feudal *adj* **(a)** *(Pol, Hist)* feudal. **(b)** *(inf: prächtig)* plush *(inf)*.
Feudal- *in cpds* feudal; **~herrschaft** *f* feudalism.
Feudalismus *m* feudalism.
feudalistisch *adj* feudalistic.
Feudalität *f* **(a)** *(Hist)* feudality. **(b)** *(inf)* plushness *(inf)*.
Feudal-: **~system** *nt* feudalism, feudal system.
Feudel *m -s, - (N Ger)* (floor)cloth.
feudeln *vt (N Ger)* to wash, to wipe.
Feuer *nt -s, -* **(a)** *(Flamme, Kamin~)* fire; *(olympisches ~)* flame. **am ~** by the fire; **~ machen** to light a/the fire; **~ schlagen** to make fire, to strike a spark; **~ speien** to spew flames or fire; **das brennt wie ~** *(fig)* that burns; **~ hinter etw** *(acc)* **machen** *(fig)* to chase sth up; **jdm ~ unter den Hintern** *(inf) or* Arsch *(sl)* **machen** to put a bomb under sb; **mit dem ~**

spielen *(fig)* to play with fire; **sie sind wie ~ und Wasser** they're as different as chalk and cheese.
(b) *(Naut, Funk~)* beacon; *(von Leuchtturm)* light.
(c) *(Herd)* fire. **auf offenem ~ kochen** to cook on an open fire.
(d) *(für Zigarette etc)* light. **haben Sie ~?** have you got a light?; **jdm ~ geben** to give sb a light.
(e) *(Brand)* fire. **~!** fire!; **~ legen** to start a fire; **an etw** *(acc)* **/in etw** *(dat)* **~ legen** to set fire to sth; **~ fangen** to catch fire; **mit ~ und Schwert ausrotten/verheeren** *(old)* to destroy with fire and sword; **für jdn durchs ~ gehen** to go through fire and water for sb.
(f) *(Schwung) (von Frau)* passion; *(von Liebhaber auch)* ardour; *(von Pferd)* mettle; *(von Wein)* vigour. **~ haben** to be passionate/ardent/mettlesome/full of vigour; **das ~ der Jugend/Liebe** the fire of youth/love; **in ~ geraten** to become inflamed with passion; **sich in ~ reden** to become inflamed with passion; **~ fangen** to be really taken *(bei with)*; **bei jdm ~ fangen** to fall for sb; **~ und Flamme sein** *(inf)* to be as keen as mustard *(inf) (für on)*.
(g) *(liter: Glanz)* sparkle, glitter. **das ~ ihrer Augen** her flashing or fiery eyes.
(h) *(Schießen)* fire. **~!** fire!; **~ frei!** open fire!; **~ geben/das ~ eröffnen** to open fire; **das ~ einstellen** to cease fire or firing; **etw unter ~ nehmen** to open fire on sth; **unter ~** *(dat)* **liegen** to be under fire; **zwischen zwei ~** *(acc)* **geraten** *(fig)* to be caught between the Devil and the deep blue sea *(prov)*.
Feuer- *in cpds* fire; **~alarm** *m* fire alarm; **~anbeter** *m* fire-worshipper; **~anzünder** *m* firelighter; **~bake** *f (Naut)* light beacon; **~ball** *m* fireball; **~befehl** *m (Mil)* order to fire; **~bekämpfung** *f* fire-fighting; **~bereich** *m (Mil)* firing range; **f~bereit** *adj (Mil)* ready to fire; **f~beständig** *adj* fire-resistant; **~bestattung** *f* cremation; **~büchse** *f* **(a)** *(Rail)* firebox; **(b)** *(old: Gewehr)* musket; **~eifer** *m* zeal; **mit ~eifer spielen/diskutieren** to play/discuss with zest; **~eimer** *m* fire-bucket; **~einstellung** *f* cessation of fire; *(Waffenstillstand)* cease-fire; **f~farben, f~farbig** *adj* fiery, flame-coloured; **f~fest** *adj* fireproof; Geschirr heat-resistant; **f~fester Ton/ Ziegel** fireclay/firebrick; **f~flüssig** *adj* Lava molten; **~fresser** *m* fire-eater; **~garbe** *f siehe* **~stoß; ~gefahr** *f* fire hazard or risk; **bei ~gefahr** in the event of fire; **f~gefährlich** *adj* (highly) (in)flammable or combustible; **~gefährlichkeit** *f* (in)flamma-bility, combustibility; **~gefecht** *nt* gun fight, shoot-out *(inf)*; **~geist** *m (liter)* volatile young genius, fireball; **~glocke** *f* fire bell; **~gott** *m* god of fire; **~haken** *m* poker; **~herd** *m siehe* Brandherd; **~holz** *nt, no pl* firewood.
feuerjo *interj (old) siehe* **feurio.**
Feuer-: **~käfer** *m* cardinal beetle; **~kasse** *f siehe* **Brandkasse; ~katastrophe** *f siehe* **Brandkatastrophe; ~kopf** *m (geh)* fireball; **~kult** *m (Rel)* fire cult; **~land** *nt* Tierra del Fuego; **~länder** (in *f*) *m -s, -* Fuegian; **~leiter** *f (am Haus)* fire escape; *(bei ~wehrauto)* (fireman's) ladder; *(fahrbar)* turntable ladder; **~linie** *f (Mil)* firing line.
Feuerlösch-: **~apparat** *m siehe* **~gerät; ~boot** *nt* fireboat.
Feuerlöscher *m* fire extinguisher.
Feuerlösch-: **~gerät** *nt* fire-fighting appliance; **~teich** *m* emergency water reserve; **~zug** *m* convoy of fire engines, set of appliances *(form)*.
Feuer-: **~mal** *nt* strawberry mark, port-wine stain; **~mauer** *f siehe* **Brandmauer; ~meer** *nt* sea of flames, blazing inferno; **~melder** *m -s, -* fire alarm; **er hat ein Gesicht wie ein ~melder (, so schön zum Reinschlagen)** *(sl)* he's got the kind of face that just makes you want to hit it.
feuern **1** *vi* **(a)** *(heizen)* **mit Öl/Holz ~** to have oil heating/use wood for one's heating.
(b) *(Mil)* to fire.
2 *vt* **(a)** Zimmer to heat; Ofen to light. **Öl/Briketts ~** to have oil heating/use briquettes for one's heating.
(b) *(inf) (werfen)* to fling *(inf)*, to sling *(inf)*; *(Ftbl)* Ball to slam *(inf)*; *(ins Tor)* to slam home *(inf) or* in *(inf)*. **du kriegst gleich eine gefeuert!** *(sl)* I'll thump you one in a minute *(inf)*.
(c) *(inf: entlassen)* to fire *(inf)*, to sack *(inf)*. **gefeuert werden** to get the sack, to be fired or sacked.
Feuer-: **~ofen** *m (Bibl)* fiery furnace; **~patsche** *f* fire-beater; **~pause** *f* break in firing; **f~polizeilich** *adj* Bestimmungen laid down by the fire authorities; **f~polizeilich verboten** prohibited by order of the fire authorities; **~probe** *f (Hist: Gottesurteil)* ordeal by fire; **die ~probe bestehen** *(fig)* to pass the (acid) test; **das war seine ~probe** *(fig)* that was the acid test for him; **~quelle** *f* stinging jellyfish; **~rad** *nt* fire-wheel; **(~werkskörper)** catherine wheel; **~reiter** *m* phantom horseman who puts out a fire; **f~rot** *adj* fiery red; Haar auch flaming; Kleidung, Auto scarlet; *(vor Verlegenheit etc)* **~rot werden** *(vor Verlegenheit etc)* to turn crimson or scarlet; **~salamander** *m* fire or European salamander; **~säule** *f (Bibl)* pillar of fire.
Feuersbrunst *f (geh)* conflagration.
Feuer-: **~schaden** *m* fire damage no *pl*; **~schein** *m* glow of the fire; **~schiff** *nt* lightship; **~schlucker** *m -s, - siehe* **~fresser; f~schnaubend** *adj attr (poet)* fire-breathing; **~schneise** *f* fire break; **~schutz** *m* **(a)** *(Vorbeugung)* fire prevention; **(b)** *(Mil: Deckung)* covering fire; **~schutzhelm** *m* fireman's helmet; **~schweif** *m* fiery tail.
Feuergefahr *f siehe* **Feuergefahr.**
Feuer-: **f~sicher** *adj siehe* **f~fest; ~sirene** *f* fire siren.
Feuersnot *f (liter)* fiery peril *(poet)*.
Feuer-: **f~speiend** *adj attr* Drache fire-breathing; Berg spewing (forth) fire; **~spritze** *f* fire hose; **f~sprühend** *adj (liter) siehe* **funkensprühend; ~stätte** *f (form)* **(a)** *(Koch-, Heizstelle)* fireplace, hearth; **(b)** *(Brandstelle)* scene of the fire; **~stein** *m* flint; **~stelle** *f* campfire site; *(Spuren eines Feuers)* burnt spot, remains *pl* of a fire; *(Herd)* fireplace; **~stellung** *f*

(*Mil*) firing position; ~**stoß** *m* burst of fire; ~**strahl** *m* (*geh*) jet of flame *or* fire; (*poet: Blitz*) thunderbolt; ~**stuhl** *m* (*sl*) (motor)bike; ~**sturm** *m* fire storm; ~**taufe** *f* baptism of fire; **die** ~**taufe bestehen/erhalten** to go through/have one's baptism of fire; ~**tod** *m* (*Hist*) (death at) the stake; **den** ~**tod erleiden** to be burnt *or* to die at the stake; ~**treppe** *f* fire escape; ~**tür** *f* fire door; ~**überfall** *m* armed attack.

Feuerung *f* (a) (*das Beheizen*) heating. (b) (*Brennstoff*) fuel. (c) (*Heizanlage*) heating system.

Feuer-: ~**verhütung** *f* fire prevention; ~**versicherung** *f* fire insurance; **f**~**verzinkt** *adj* galvanized; ~**wache** *f* fire station; ~**waffe** *f* firearm; ~**wasser** *nt* (*inf*) firewater (*inf*); ~**wechsel** *m* exchange of fire.

Feuerwehr *f* fire brigade. **fahren wie die** ~ (*inf*) to drive like the clappers (*Brit inf*).

Feuerwehr-: ~**auto** *nt* fire engine; ~**ball** *m* firemen's ball; ~**mann** *m* fireman; ~**schlauch** *m* fire hose; ~**übung** *f* fire-fighting exercise; ~**wagen** *m* fire engine.

Feuer-: ~**werk** *nt* fireworks *pl*; (*Schauspiel auch*) firework display; (*fig*) cavalcade; **f**~**werken** *vi insep* to let off fireworks; ~**werker** *m* -s, - firework-maker; ~**werkskörper** *m* firework; ~**zange** *f* fire tongs *pl*; ~**zangenbowle** *f* red wine punch containing rum which has been flamed off; ~**zeichen** *nt* (a) (*Signal*) beacon; (b) (*Astrol*) fire sign; ~**zeug** *nt* (cigarette) lighter; ~**zeugbenzin** *nt* lighter fuel; ~**zone** *f* (*Mil*) firing zone; ~**zunge** *f* (*Bibl*) tongue of flame.

Feuilleton [fœjə'tõ, 'fœjətõ] *nt* -s, -s (*Press*) (a) (*Zeitungsteil*) feature pages *pl or* section. (b) (*Artikel*) feature (article). **das ist ja** ~! (*pej*) that's a facile piece of writing.

Feuilletonismus [fœjəto'nɪsmʊs] *m* style of writing used in feature articles, often regarded as facile.

Feuilletonist(in *f*) [fœjətó'nɪst(ɪn)] *m* feature writer.

feuilletonistisch [fœjətó'nɪstɪʃ] *adj* **dieser Journalist ist ein** ~**es Talent** this journalist has a natural flair for writing feature articles; **er hat den Stoff geistreich** ~ **aufgearbeitet** he wrote a witty and vivid article from this material; **dieser Aufsatz ist zu** ~ (*pej*) this essay is too glib *or* facile.

Feuilleton-: ~**schreiber** *m* siehe Feuilletonist(in); ~**stil** *m* style used in feature articles; (*pej*) facile *or* glib style.

feurig *adj* fiery; (*old: glühend*) glowing.

feurio *interj* (*old*) (fire,) fire.

Fex *m* -es *or* -en, -e *or* -en (*S Ger, Aus*) enthusiast.

Fez¹ [feːʦ] *m* -, - fez.

Fez² *m* -(e)s, *no pl* (*dated inf*) larking about (*inf*). ~ **machen** to lark about (*inf*).

ff [ɛf'|ɛf] *adj inv* first-class, top-grade; siehe **Effeff**.

ff. *abbr of* **folgende Seiten.**

Ffm. *abbr of* **Frankfurt am Main.**

Fiaker *m* -s, - (*Aus*) (a) (*Kutsche*) (hackney) cab. (b) (*Kutscher*) cab driver, cabby (*inf*).

Fiale *f* -, -n (*Archit*) pinnacle.

Fiasko *nt* -s, -s (*inf*) fiasco. **mit seinem Buch erlitt er ein** ~ his book was a complete failure *or* flop *or* fiasco; **dann gibt es ein** ~ it'll be disastrous *or* a fiasco.

Fibel¹ *f* -, -n (*Sch*) primer.

Fibel² *f* -, -n (*Archeol*) fibula (*spec*), clasp.

Fiber *f* -, -n fibre.

Fibrin *nt* -s, *no pl* (*Physiol*) fibrin.

Fibrom *nt* -s, -e (*Med*) fibroma (*spec*).

fibrös *adj* (*Med*) fibrous.

Fiche¹ [fiːʃ] *f* -, -s counter.

Fiche² [fiːʃ] *m* -(s), -s (micro)fiche.

Fichte *f* -, -n (*Bot*) spruce.

fichten *adj* spruce(wood).

Fichten- *in cpds* spruce; ~**apfel** *m* siehe ~zapfen; ~**baum** *m* spruce tree; ~**nadelextrakt** *m* pine essence; ~**zapfen** *m* spruce cone.

Fick *m* -s, -s (*vulg*) fuck (*vulg*).

ficken *vti* (*vulg*) to fuck (*vulg*). **mit jdm** ~ to fuck sb (*vulg*).

Fickerei *f* (*vulg*) (*no pl: das Koitieren*) fucking (*vulg*); (*Koitus*) fuck (*vulg*).

fick(e)rig *adj* (a) (*dial*) fidgety. (b) (*vulg: geil*) randy (*Brit inf*), horny (*inf*).

Fideikommiß [fideiko'mɪs, 'fiːdeɪkɔmɪs] *nt* -sses, -sse (*old Jur*) entail (*form*), entailed estate.

fidel *adj* jolly, merry.

Fidel *f* -, -n siehe **Fiedel**.

Fidibus *m* - *or* -ses, - *or* -se spill.

Fidschi ['fɪdʒi] *nt* -s Fiji.

Fidschianer(in *f*) *m* -s, - Fijian.

Fidschilinseln *pl* Fiji Islands.

Fiduz *nt* (*old inf*) **kein** ~ **zu etw haben** (*Lust*) not to feel like sth; (*Mut*) not to have the confidence for sth.

Fieber *nt* -s, - (a) temperature; (*sehr hoch, mit Phantasieren*) fever. ~ **haben** to have *or* be running a temperature; **to be feverish** *or* **running a fever; 40°** ~ **haben** to have a temperature of 40; (**jdm**) **das** ~ **messen** to take sb's temperature; **im** ~ **seiner Leidenschaft** in a fever of passion; **das** ~ **der Leidenschaft hat ihn gepackt** he was seized with passion. (b) (*Krankheit*) fever.

Fieber- *in cpds* feverish, febrile (*form*); ~**anfall** *m* attack *or* bout of fever; ~**flecken** *pl* fever spots *pl*; **f**~**frei** *adj* free of fever; ~**frost** *m* feverish shivering; **f**~**haft** *adj* (a) (*fiebrig*) feverish, febrile (*form*); (b) (*hektisch*) feverish.

fieb(e)rig *adj* feverish, febrile (*form*).

Fieber-: ~**kurve** *f* temperature curve; ~**messer** *m* -s, - (*dated, Sw*) thermometer; ~**mittel** *nt* anti-fever drug, antipyretic (*spec*); ~**mücke** *f* malarial mosquito.

fiebern *vi* (a) to have a fever *or* temperature; (*schwer*) to be feverish *or* febrile (*form*). (b) (*fig*) **nach etw** ~ to long fever-

ishly for sth; **vor Ungeduld/Erregung** (*dat*) ~ to be in a fever of impatience/excitement; **in Erwartung jds/einer Sache** ~ to await sb/sth with feverish excitement.

Fieber-: ~**phantasien** *pl* feverish *or* febrile (*form*) wanderings *pl or* ravings *pl*; ~**tabelle** *f* temperature chart; ~**thermometer** *nt* (clinical) thermometer; ~**wahn** *m* (feverish *or* febrile) delirium.

fiebrig *adj* siehe **fieb(e)rig**.

Fiedel *f* -, -n fiddle.

Fiedelbogen *m* fiddle bow. **gespannt sein wie ein** ~ (*inf*) to be on tenterhooks.

fiedeln (*hum, pej*) *vti* to fiddle. **ein Liedchen** ~ to play a song on the fiddle.

fiedern *vr* (*Orn*) to acquire its plumage; siehe **gefiedert**.

Fiederung *f* (a) (*Orn*) plumage. (b) (*Bot*) pinnation (*spec*).

Fiedler *m* -s, - (*hum, pej: Geiger*) fiddler.

fiel *pret of* **fallen.**

fiepen *vi* (*Reh*) to call; (*Hund, Mensch*) to whimper; (*Vogel*) to cheep.

fieren *vt* (*Naut*) *Segel, Last* to lower; *Tau* to pay out.

fies *adj* (*inf*) (*abstoßend, unangenehm*) *Mensch, Gesicht, Geruch, Arbeit* nasty, horrid, horrible; (*gemein*) *Charakter, Methoden auch* mean. **benimm dich nicht so** ~! don't be so horrid!; (*ordinär*) don't behave so horribly!; siehe **Möp.**

Fiesling *m* (*inf*) (*abstoßender Mensch*) slob (*sl*); (*gemeiner Mensch*) sod (*sl*), bastard (*sl*).

Fifa, FIFA *f* - FIFA.

fifty-fifty ['fɪftɪ'fɪftɪ] *adv* (*inf*) fifty-fifty (*inf*). ~ **machen** to go fifty-fifty; **die Sache steht** ~ there's a fifty-fifty chance; **die Sache ist** ~ **ausgegangen** things were fifty-fifty *or* pretty even.

Figaro *m* -s, -s (*hum*) hairdresser.

Fight [fait] *m* -s, -s fight.

fighten ['faitn] *vi* to fight.

Fighter ['faitɐ] *m* -s, - fighter.

Figur *f* (a) (*Bildwerk, Abbildung, Math*) figure; (*gedankenlos hingezeichnet*) doodle. (b) (*Gestalt, Persönlichkeit*) figure; (*Körperform*) (*von Frauen*) figure; (*von Männern*) physique; (*inf: Mensch*) character. **in ganzer** ~ (*Phot, Art*) full-figure; **auf seine** ~ **achten** to watch one's figure; **eine gute/schlechte/traurige** ~ **machen** *or* **abgeben** to cut a good/poor/sorry figure; **eine komische** *or* **ulkige** ~ (*inf*) a strange customer (*inf*) *or* character. (c) (*Roman~, Film~ etc*) character. (d) (*Sport, Mus*) figure; (*rhetorische* ~) figure of speech.

Figura *f*: **wie** ~ **zeigt** (*old*) as shown (above/under).

figural *adj* (*Art*) figured.

Figuralmusik *f* figural *or* florid music.

Figurant *m* figurant.

Figurantin *f* figurante.

Figuration *f* figuration.

figurativ *adj* figurative.

Figürchen *nt dim of* **Figur.**

Figurenlaufen *nt* figure skating.

Figurgedicht *nt* picture poem.

figurieren * 1 *vi* (*geh*) to figure. 2 *vt* (*Mus*) to figure.

Figurine *f* (*Art*) figure; (*kleine Statue*) figurine; (*Theat*) costume design *or* sketch.

figürlich *adj* (a) (*übertragen*) figurative. (b) (*figurmäßig*) as regards the/her figure; (*von Männern*) as regards physique.

Fiktion *f* fiction.

fiktiv *adj* fictitious.

Filet [fi'leː] *nt* -s, -s (a) (*Cook*) (*Schweine~, Geflügel~, Fisch~*) fillet; (*Rind~*) fillet steak; (*zum Braten*) piece of sirloin *or* tenderloin (*US*). (b) (*Tex*) siehe **Filetarbeit.**

Filetlarbeit [fi'leː-] *f* (*Tex*) netting.

filetieren * *vt* to fillet.

Filet- [fi'leː-]: ~**steak** *nt* fillet steak; ~**stück** *nt* piece of sirloin *or* tenderloin (*US*).

Filialbetrieb *m* branch.

Filiale *f* -, -n branch.

Filial-: ~**generation** *f* (*Biol*) (first) filial generation; ~**geschäft** *nt* branch; ~**kirche** *f* daughter church; ~**leiter** *m* branch manager; ~**netz** *nt* network of branches.

Filibuster¹ *m* -s, - siehe **Flibustier.**

Filibuster² [fili'bastɐ] *nt* -(s), - (*Pol*) filibuster.

Filigran *nt* -s, -e filigree.

Filigranlarbeit *f* filigree work; (*Schmuckstück*) piece of filigree work.

Filipino *m* -s, -s Filipino.

Filius *m* -, -se (*hum*) son, offspring (*hum*).

Film *m* -(e)s, -e (a) (*alle Bedeutungen*) film; (*Spiel~ auch*) movie (*esp US*), motion picture (*US*); (*Dokumentar~ auch*) documentary (film). **ein** ~ **nach dem Roman von E. Marlitt** a film of *or* based on the novel by E. Marlitt; **in einen** ~ **gehen** to go and see a film, to go to a film; **da ist bei mir der** ~ **gerissen** (*fig sl*) I had a mental blackout (*inf*). (b) (~*branche*) films *pl*, movie (*esp US*) *or* motion-picture (*esp US*) business. **zum** ~ **gehen/kommen** to go/get *or* break into films *or* movies (*esp US*); **beim** ~ **arbeiten** *or* **sein** (*inf*) to work in films *or* the movie business (*esp US*).

Film- *in cpds* film, movie (*esp US*); ~**amateur** *m* home-movie enthusiast *or* buff (*inf*); ~**archiv** *nt* film archives *pl*; ~**atelier** *nt* film studio; ~**autor** *m* scriptwriter, screen-writer; ~**ball** *m* film festival ball; ~**bauten** *pl* film sets *pl*; ~**bearbeitung** *f* (screen) adaptation; ~**bericht** *m* film report; ~**bewertungsstelle** *f* ≈ board of film censors; ~**bühne** *f* (*dated*) picture house (*dated*), movie house (*US*); ~**diva** *f* (*dated*) screen goddess; ~**drama** *nt* film drama.

Filmemacher(in *f*) *m* film-maker, writer-director.

Film|empfindlichkeit f film speed.
filmen vti to film. **jdn ~** (fig inf) to take sb for a ride (inf).
Film-: **~entwickler** m developer; **~epos** nt epic film.
Filmer m -s, - (inf) film or movie (esp US) director.
Filmerei f filming.
Film-: **~fan** m film or movie (esp US) fan; **~festival** nt, **~festspiele** pl film festival; **~förderungsgesetz** nt law on film subsidies; **~format** nt (für Fotoapparat) film size; (für **~kamera**) film gauge; **~foto** nt still (from a film); **~fritze** m -n, -n (inf) film or movie (esp US) guy (inf); **f~gerecht** adj filmable; der Roman muß **f~gerecht** bearbeitet werden the novel will have to be adapted for the cinema or for film; **~geschäft** nt film or movie (esp US) or motion-picture (US) industry; **~geschichte** f history of the cinema; **~geschichte machen** to make film history; **~gesellschaft** f film company; **~größe** f great star of the screen; **~held** m screen or movie (esp US) hero; **~hochschule** f film or movie (esp US) college.
filmisch adj cinematic.
Film-: **~kamera** f film or movie (esp US) camera; (Schmalfilm-**kamera**) cine-camera; **~kassette** f film cassette; **~komponist** m composer of film music; **~kritik** f film criticism or reviewing; (Artikel) film review; (Kritiker) film critics pl; **~kulisse** f setting for a film; **~kunst** f cinematic art; **~kunsttheater** nt film theatre; **~leitzahl** f film speed; **~material** nt film; **~musik** f film music; **die originale ~musik** the original soundtrack.
Filmothek f -, -en siehe **Kinemathek**.
Film-: **~palast** m picture or movie (esp US) palace; **~preis** m film or movie (esp US) award; **~produzent** m film or movie (esp US) producer; **~projektor** m film projector; **~prüfstelle** f film censorship office; **~publikum** nt filmgoing public; **~rechte** pl film rights pl; **~regie** f direction of a/the film; **~regisseur** m film or movie (esp US) director; **~reportage** f film report; **~riß** m (lit) tear in a film; (fig sl) mental blackout (inf); **~rolle** f (Spule) spool of film; (für Fotoapparat) roll of film; (Part) film part or role; **~salat** m (inf) camera buckle; **~satz** m (Typ) siehe **Lichtsatz**; **~schaffen** nt film making; **~schaffende(r)** mf decl as adj film-maker; **~schauplatz** m setting of a film; der **~schauplatz** liegt in Marokko the film is set in Morocco; **~schauspieler** m film or movie (esp US) actor; **~schauspielerin** f film or movie (esp US) actress; **~schönheit** f screen beauty; **~serie** f (esp TV) film series sing; **~spule** f film spool; **~star** m filmstar; **~statist** m film extra; **~sternchen** nt starlet; **~studio** nt film or movie (esp US) studio; **~szene** f scene of a film; **~theater** nt (form) cinema, movie theater (US); **~transport** m film transport; **~trick** m film stunt; **~- und Fernsehakademie**, **~- und Fernsehhochschule** f college of film and television technology; **~verleih** m film distributors pl; **~vorführer** m projectionist; **~vorführgerät** nt (film) projector; **~vorstellung** f film show; **~welt** f film or movie (esp US) world; **~werk** nt film work; **~wesen** nt film or motion-picture business; **~wissenschaft** f film studies pl; **~zensur** f film censorship; (Zensoren) film censors pl.
Filou [fiˈluː] m -s, -s (dated inf) devil (inf).
Filter nt or m -s, - filter. **eine Zigarette mit/ohne ~** a (filter-)tipped/plain cigarette.
Filter-: **f~fein** adj finely ground; **f~fein mahlen** to grind finely; **~glas** nt tinted glass; **~kaffee** m filter or drip (US) coffee; **~mundstück** nt filter-tip.
filtern vti to filter.
Filter-: **~papier** nt filter paper; **~rückstand** m residue (after filtering); **~tuch** nt filter cloth; **~tüte** f filter bag.
Filterung f filtering.
Filterzigarette f tipped or filter(-tipped) cigarette.
Filtrat nt filtrate.
Filtration f filtration.
filtrierbar adj filterable.
filtrieren* vt to filter.
Filtrierung f siehe **Filterung**.
Filz m -es, -e (a) (Tex) felt; (inf: ~hut) felt hat. (b) (inf: Bier-**deckel**) beermat. (c) (inf: Geizkragen) skinflint (inf), pennypincher (inf), miser. (d) (Pol pej) siehe **Filzokratie**.
filzen 1 vi (a) (Tex) to felt, to go felty. (b) (inf: fest schlafen) to sleep. (c) (inf: knausern) to be a skinflint (inf) or penny-pincher (inf). **mit jedem Pfennig ~** to be a real old penny-pincher (inf). 2 vt (inf) (durchsuchen) jdn to frisk, to search; Gepäck etc to search, to go through; (berauben) to do over (inf).
Filzhut m felt hat.
filzig adj (a) (wie Filz) felty, feltlike. (b) (inf: geizig) penny-pinching (inf), miserly.
Filz-: **~latschen** m (inf) carpet slipper; **~laus** f crablouse.
Filzokrat m -en, -en (Pol pej) corrupt nepotist.
Filzokratie f (Pol pej) corruption and nepotism.
filzokratisch adj (Pol pej) nepotically corrupt.
Filz-: **~pantoffel** m (carpet) slipper; **~schreiber** m felt(-tip) pen, felt-tip; **~sohle** f felt insole; **~stiefel** m felt boot; **~stift** m siehe **~schreiber**.
Fimmel m -s, - (inf) (a) (Tick) mania. **er hat diesen ~ mit dem Unkrautjäten** he's got this thing about weeding (inf). (b) (Spleen) obsession (mit about). **du hast wohl einen ~!** you're crazy (inf) or mad (inf).
final adj final.
Finale nt -s, -s or - (Mus) finale; (Sport) final, finals pl.
Finalist m finalist.
Finalität f (Philos) finality.
Finalsatz m final clause.
Financier [finãˈsieː] m -s, -s financier.
Finanz f, no pl financial world. **die hohe ~** the world of high finance; **Kreise der ~** financial circles.
Finanz- in cpds financial; **~adel** m plutocrats pl, plutocracy;

~amt nt tax office; **~aristokratie** f plutocrats pl, plutocracy; **~ausgleich** m redistribution of income between 'Bund', 'Länder' and 'Gemeinden'; **~ausschuß** m finance committee; **~autonomie** f siehe **~hoheit**; **~beamte(r)** m tax official; **~behörde** f tax authority; **~dinge** pl financial matters pl.
Finanzen pl finances pl. **das übersteigt meine ~** that's beyond my means.
Finanzer m -s, - (Aus) siehe **Zollbeamte(r)**.
Finanz-: **~frage** f question of finance; **~gebaren** nt management of public finances; **~genie** nt financial genius or wizard (inf); **~gericht** nt tribunal dealing with tax and other financial matters; **~gewaltige(r)** mf decl as adj (hum) financial mogul; **~hai** m (pej) (financial) shark; **~hoheit** f financial autonomy.
finanziell adj financial. **sich ~ an etw** (dat) **beteiligen** to take a (financial) stake in sth.
Finanzier [finanˈtsieː] m -s, -s financier.
finanzieren* vt to finance. **frei ~** to finance privately; **ich kann meinen Urlaub nicht ~** I can't afford a holiday.
Finanzierung f financing. **zur ~ von etw** to finance sth; **die ~ meines Urlaubs ist noch nicht gesichert** it isn't certain whether I will have the money for my holiday.
Finanz-: **~jahr** nt financial year; **f~kräftig** adj financially strong; **~minister** m minister of finance; **~plan** m financial plan; **~politik** f financial policy; (Wissenschaft, Disziplin) politics of finance; **f~politisch** adj Fragen, Probleme relating to financial policy; **~recht** nt financial law; **f~schwach** adj financially weak; **f~stark** adj financially strong; **~welt** f financial world; **~wesen** nt financial system; **ein Ausdruck aus dem ~wesen** a financial term.
finassieren* vi (pej) to machinate, to do some finagling (inf). **das F~** machinations pl, finagling (inf).
Findel-: **~haus** nt (old) foundling hospital (old); **~kind** nt (old) foundling (old).
finden pret **fand**, ptp **gefunden** 1 vt (a) (entdecken) to find. **ich finde es nicht** I can't find it; **es war nicht/nirgends zu ~ it** was not/nowhere to be found; **das muß zu ~ sein** it must be somewhere (to be found); **es ließ sich niemand ~** we/they etc couldn't find anybody, there was nobody to be found; **der Grund/die Ursache läßt sich nicht ~** we/they etc couldn't find the reason/cause; **er findet immer etwas zu bemängeln** or **beanstanden** or **kritisieren** he always finds something to criticize; **etwas an jdm ~** to see something in sb; **nichts dabei ~** to think nothing of it.
(b) (vor~) to find. **jdn schlafend/bei der Arbeit ~** to find sb asleep/working.
(c) in Verbindung **mit** n siehe auch dort. Trost, Hilfe, Ruhe, Schlaf etc to find; Anklang, Zustimmung auch to meet with; Beifall to meet or be met with; Berücksichtigung, Beachtung to receive. (den) Mut/(die) Kraft **~**, etw **zu tun** to find the courage/strength to do sth; (bei jdm) Anerkennung **~** to find recognition (with sb); Bestätigung **~** to be confirmed.
(d) (ansehen, betrachten) to think. **es kalt/warm/ganz erträg-lich** etc **~** to find it cold/warm/quite tolerable etc; **etw gut/zu teuer/eine Frechheit** etc **~** to think (that) sth is good/too expensive/a cheek etc; **jdn blöd/nett** etc **~** to think (that) sb is stupid/nice etc; **wie findest du das?** what do you think?; **wie finde ich denn das?** what do I think (of that)?
2 vi (lit, fig: den **Weg ~**) to find one's way. **er findet nicht nach Hause** (lit) he can't find his or the way home; (fig) he can't tear or drag himself away (inf); **zu sich selbst ~** to sort oneself out.
3 vti (meinen) to think. **~ Sie (das)?** do you think so?; **ich finde (das) nicht** I don't think so; **~ Sie (das) nicht auch?** don't you agree?, don't you think so too?; **ich finde, wir sollten/daß wir ...** I think we should/that we ...; **ich kann das** or **das kann ich nicht ~** I don't think so; **ich fände es besser, wenn ...** I think it would be better if ...
4 vr (a) (zum Vorschein kommen) to be found; (wieder-**auftauchen** auch) to turn up; (sich befinden auch) to be. **das wird sich (alles) ~** it will (all) turn up; (sich herausstellen) it'll all come out (inf); **es fand sich, daß ich recht hatte** I was found to be right, it was found that I was right; **es fand sich niemand, der sich freiwillig gemeldet hätte** there was nobody who volunteered.
(b) (in Ordnung kommen: Angelegenheit etc) to sort itself out; (Mensch: zu sich ~) to sort oneself out. **das wird sich alles ~** it'll all sort itself out.
(c) (sich fügen) **sich in etw** (acc) **~** to reconcile oneself or become reconciled to sth.
(d) (sich treffen) (lit) to find each other; (fig) to meet. **da haben sich aber zwei gefunden!** (iro) they'll make a fine pair.
Finder(in f) m -s, - finder.
Finderlohn m reward for the finder.
Fin de siècle [fɛˈdsjɛkl] nt - - -, no pl fin de siècle. **die Kunst des ~ ~ ~** fin de siècle art.
findig adj resourceful.
Findigkeit f resourcefulness.
Findling m (a) (Geol) erratic. (b) (Findelkind) foundling (old).
Findlings-: **~block** m erratic (boulder); **~heim** nt foundling hospital (old).
Finesse f (a) (Feinheit) refinement; (no pl: Kunstfertigkeit) finesse. **mit allen ~n** with every refinement. (b) (Trick) trick.
finessenreich adj artful.
fing pret of **fangen**.
Finger m -s, - finger. **der kleine ~** one's little finger, one's pinkie (US, Scot inf); **der elfte ~** (hum) one's third leg (inf); **mit dem ~ auf jdn/etw zeigen** or **weisen** (geh) to point to sb/sth; **mit ~n auf jdn zeigen** (fig) to look askance at sb; **jdm mit dem ~ drohen** to wag one's finger at sb; **jdm eins/was auf die ~ geben** to give sb a rap/to rap sb across the knuckles; **jdm**

auf die ~ schlagen or hauen (lit)/klopfen (fig) to rap sb's knuckles, to give sb a rap on the knuckles; zwei ~ breit the width of two fingers, two fingers wide; (nimm/laß die) ~ weg! (get/keep your) hands off!; sich (dat) nicht die ~ schmutzig machen (lit, fig) not to get one's hands dirty, not to dirty one's hands; das kann sich jeder an den (fünf or zehn) ~n abzählen (inf) it sticks out a mile (to anybody) (inf); das läßt er nicht mehr aus den ~n he won't let it out of his hands; jdn/etw in die ~ bekommen or kriegen (inf) to get one's hands on sb/sth, to get hold of sb/sth; bei etw die ~ drin haben (sl) to have a hand in sth; er hat überall seine ~ drin (sl) he has a finger in every pie (inf); sich (dat) die ~ abschreiben or wund schreiben/arbeiten etc to write/work etc one's fingers to the bone; wenn man ihm/dem Teufel den kleinen ~ gibt, (dann) nimmt er (gleich) die ganze Hand (prov) give him an inch and he'll take a mile (inf); lange ~ machen (hum inf) to be light-fingered; jdm in or zwischen die ~ geraten or fallen to fall into sb's hands or clutches; sich (dat) bei or an etw (dat) die ~ verbrennen to burn one's fingers or get one's fingers burnt over sth; jdm (scharf) auf die ~ sehen to keep an eye or a close eye on sb; sich (dat) etw aus den ~n saugen to make sth up off the top of one's head (inf), to dream sth up; sich (dat) die or alle ~ nach etw lecken (inf) to be panting or dying for sth (inf); für jdn keinen ~ rühren not to lift a finger to help sb; keinen ~ krumm machen (inf) not to lift a finger (inf); den ~ auf eine/die Wunde legen to touch on a sore point; mich or mir juckt es in den ~n(, etw zu tun) (inf) I'm itching or dying to (do sth); da hast du dich in den ~ geschnitten (inf) you've made a big mistake; er hat eine or zehn an jedem ~ he's got a woman for every day of the week; jdn um den kleinen ~ wickeln to twist sb round one's little finger; etw im kleinen ~ haben (perfekt beherrschen) to have sth at one's fingertips; (sicher im Gefühl haben) to have a feel for sth; man zeigt nicht mit nacktem ~ auf angezogene Leute (inf) it's rude to point.

Finger-: ~abdruck m fingerprint; jds ~abdrücke nehmen to take sb's fingerprints, to fingerprint sb; ~alphabet nt manual alphabet; ~beere f pad (of the finger); f~breit adj the width of a finger; ~breit m -, - finger's breadth, fingerbreadth; (fig) inch; keinen ~breit bekommen or weichen not to give an inch; wir sind keinen ~breit vorwärtsgekommen we haven't got any further forward at all; f~dick adj as thick as a finger; ~druck m touch of the finger; ~farbe f finger paint; f~fertig adj nimble-fingered, dexterous; ~fertigkeit f dexterity; ~gelenk nt finger joint; ~glied nt phalanx (of the finger) (form); ~hakeln nt finger-wrestling; ~haltung f finger position; ~handschuh m glove; ~hut m (a) (Sew) thimble; ein ~hut (voll) (fig) a thimbleful; (b) (Bot) foxglove; ~knochen, ~knöchel m knucklebone; ~kuppe f fingertip; f~lang adj Narbe etc the length of a finger; ~ling m fingerstall.

fingern 1 vi an or mit etw (dat) ~ to fiddle with sth; nach etw ~ to fumble (around) for sth; ... als eine Hand über die Decke fingerte ... as a hand moved over the bedclothes. 2 vt (hervorholen) to fumble around and produce; (sl: manipulieren) to fiddle (inf).

Finger-: ~nagel m fingernail; ~nägel kauen to bite one's (finger)nails; ~ring m ring (for one's finger); ~schale f fingerbowl; ~spitze f fingertip, tip of one's finger; er ist musikalisch bis in die ~spitzen he's musical right down to his fingertips or the tips of his fingers; das muß man in den ~spitzen haben you have to have a feel for it; mir juckt or kribbelt es in den ~spitzen, das zu tun I'm itching to do that; ~spitzengefühl nt, no pl (Einfühlungsgabe) instinctive feel or feeling; (im Umgang mit Menschen) tact and sensitivity, fine feeling; ~sprache f manual alphabet, sign language; ~übung f (Mus) finger exercise; (Übungsstück) étude; (fig) (erste Arbeit) first stage of one's apprenticeship; (Anfangswerk) apprentice piece; ~zeig m -s, -e hint; etw als ~zeig Gottes/des Schicksals empfinden to regard sth as a sign from God/as meant.

fingieren* [fɪŋˈgiːrən] vt (vortäuschen) to fake; (erdichten) to fabricate.

fingiert [fɪŋˈgiːrt] adj (vorgetäuscht) bogus; (erfunden) fictitious.

fini [ˈfiːni] adj pred (inf): jetzt/dann ist ~ that's it, finito (inf).

Finish [ˈfɪnɪʃ] nt -s, -s (a) (Endverarbeitung) finish; (Vorgang) finishing. (b) (Sport: Endspurt) final spurt.

finit adj (Gram) finite.

Fink m -en, -en finch.

Finkenschlag m, no pl finch's song.

Finne[1] f -, -n (a) (Zool: Stadium des Bandwurms) bladder worm, cysticercus (form). (b) (Med: Mitesser) pimple. (c) (Rückenflosse) fin. (d) (von Hammer) peen.

Finne[2] m -n, -n, **Finnin** f Finn, Finnish man/woman/boy/girl.

finnisch adj Finnish. der F~e Meerbusen the Gulf of Finland; siehe auch deutsch.

Finnisch(e) nt -n Finnish; siehe auch Deutsch(e).

finnisch-ugrisch adj siehe finnougrisch.

Finnland nt Finland.

Finnländer(in f) m -s, - Finn.

finnländisch adj Finnish.

finnlandisieren* vt (Pol sl) to Finlandize.

Finnlandisierung f (Pol sl) Finlandization.

Finnmark f (Währung) Finnish mark, markka (form).

finnougrisch, finno-ugrisch adj Finno-Ugric, Finno-Ugrian.

Finno-Ugristik f Finno-Ugric studies pl.

Finnwal m finback, finwhale.

finster adj (a) (ohne Licht) dark; Zimmer, Wald, Nacht dark (and gloomy). im F~n in the dark; im F~n liegen to be in darkness; ~ machen (inf) to plunge the place into darkness;

(zumachen) to put up the shutters; im ~n tappen (fig) to be groping in the dark; im ~n liegen (fig) to be obscure; es sieht ~ aus (fig) things look bleak.

(b) (dubios) shady.

(c) (mürrisch, verdrossen, düster) grim; Wolken dark, black. ~ entschlossen sein to be grimly determined; jdn ~ ansehen to give sb a black look.

(d) (fig: unaufgeklärt) dark. das ~(st)e Mittelalter the Dark Ages pl.

(e) (unheimlich) Gestalt, Blick, Gedanken sinister.

Finsterkeit f (Verdrossenheit) grimness; (Unheimlichkeit) sinisterness.

Finsterling m sinister character; (Dunkelmann) obscurantist.

Finsternis f (a) (Dunkelheit, Bibl: Hölle) darkness. (b) (Astron) eclipse.

Finte f -, -n (a) (Sport) feint; (im Rugby) dummy. (b) (List) ruse, subterfuge.

fintenreich adj artful, crafty.

finz(e)lig adj (N Ger inf) (a) (winzig) Schrift tiny, weeny (inf). (b) (knifflig) fiddly.

Fips m -es, -e (dial) little chap (Brit inf) or fellow (inf).

fipsig adj (dial) titchy (inf).

Firlefanz m -es, no pl (inf) (a) (Kram) frippery, trumpery. (b) (Albernheit) clowning or fooling around. ~ machen to play the fool, to clown or fool around.

firm adj pred ich bin noch nicht ~ I don't really know it yet; in einem Fachgebiet ~ sein to have a sound knowledge of sth, to be good at sth (inf).

Firma f -, **Firmen** (a) company, firm; (Kleinbetrieb) business. die ~ Wahlster/Lexomat Wahlster(s)/Lexomat; die ~ dankt (hum) much obliged (to you).

(b) (Geschäfts- or Handelsname) eine ~ löschen to strike a company's name/the name of a business from the register; eine ~ eintragen to register a company name/the name of a business; unter der ~ Smith under the name of Smith; unter eigener ~ under one's own name.

Firmament nt -s, no pl (liter) heavens pl (liter), firmament (Bibl).

firmen vt (Rel) to confirm.

Firmen pl of Firma.

Firmen-: ~aufdruck m company stamp; ~bücher pl siehe Geschäftsbücher; ~chef m head of the company or firm/business; f~eigen adj company attr; f~eigen sein to belong to the company; ~inhaber m owner of the company/business; f~intern adj internal company attr; f~intern geregelt decided internally by the company; f~intern sein to be an internal company matter; ~kopf m company/business letterhead; ~name m company name/name of a business; ~register nt register of companies/businesses; ~schild nt company/business plaque; ~stempel m company/business stamp; ~verzeichnis nt trade directory; ~wagen m company car; ~wert m (Comm) goodwill; ~zeichen nt trademark.

firmieren* vi: als or mit ... ~ (Comm, fig) to trade under the name of ...

Firmling m (Rel) candidate for confirmation.

Firm-: ~pate m, ~patin f sponsor.

Firmung f (Rel) confirmation. jdm die ~ erteilen to confirm sb.

firn adj Wein old.

Firn m -(e)s, -e névé, firn.

Firne f -, no pl well-seasoned taste.

firnig adj Schnee névé attr.

Firnis m -ses, -se (Öl~) oil; (Lack~) varnish.

firnissen vt to oil; to varnish.

Firnschnee m névé, firn.

First m -(e)s, -e (a) (Dach~) (roof) ridge. (b) (geh: Gebirgskamm) crest, ridge.

First-: ~feier f (Aus) topping-out ceremony; ~ziegel m ridge tile.

Fis nt -, - (Mus) F sharp. in ~/f~ in F sharp major/minor.

Fisch m -(e)s, -e (a) (Zool, Cook) fish. ~e/drei ~e fangen to catch fish/three fishes; das sind kleine ~e (fig inf) that's child's play (inf) (für to, for); ein großer or dicker ~ (fig inf) a big fish; ein paar kleine ~e ein kleiner ~ some of/one of the small fry; ein (kalter) ~ sein (fig) to be a cold fish; munter or gesund sein wie ein ~ im Wasser to be in fine fettle; sich wohl fühlen wie ein ~ im Wasser to be in one's element; stumm wie ein ~ sein to be as silent as a post; weder ~ noch Fleisch neither fish nor fowl; die ~e füttern (hum) to be sick; ~ will schwimmen (prov) fish gives you a thirst.

(b) (Astrol) Pisces. die ~e (Astron) Pisces sing, the Fish sing; ein ~ sein to be Pisces or a Piscean.

(c) (Typ) character from the wrong fount.

Fisch- in cpds fish; ~adler m osprey; f~ähnlich adj fish-like; f~arm adj low in fish; f~armut f scarcity of fish; f~artig adj (Zool) fish-like; Geschmack, Geruch fishy; ~auge nt (Phot) fish-eye lens; f~äugig adj fish-eyed; ~becken nt fishpond; ~behälter m fish tank; ~bein nt, no pl whalebone; ~bestand m fish population; ~blase f (Zool) air-bladder, swim bladder; (b) (Archit) foil; ~blut nt (fig): ~blut in den Adern haben to be a cold fish; ~boulette f fishcake; ~braterei, ~bratküche f fish and chip shop; ~brut f fry pl, young fish pl; ~bude f fish and chip stand; ~dampfer m trawler.

fischen vti (lit, fig) to fish. mit (dem) Netz ~ to trawl; (auf) Heringe ~ to fish for herring; siehe trüb(e).

Fischer m -s, - fisherman.

Fischer-: ~boot nt fishing boat; ~dorf nt fishing village.

Fischerei f (das Fangen) fishing. (b) (~gewerbe) fishing industry, fisheries pl (form).

Fischerei- in cpds fishing; ~frevel m (Jur) poaching; ~gerät nt fishing tackle; (einzelnes Stück) piece of fishing tackle;

~grenze f fishing limit; ~hafen m fishing port; ~recht nt, no pl (a) fishing rights pl; (b) (Jur) law on fishing; ~schutzboot nt fishery protection vessel; ~wesen nt fishing no art; Ministerium für ~wesen ministry of fisheries.

Fischer-: ~netz nt fishing net; ~ring m (Rel) Ring of the Fisherman.

Fischfang m, no pl vom ~ leben to live by fishing; zum ~ auslaufen to set off for the fishing grounds.

Fischfang-: ~flotte f fishing fleet; ~gebiet nt fishing grounds pl.

Fisch-: ~filet nt fish fillet; ~frevel m (Jur) poaching; ~frikadelle f fishcake; ~futter nt fish food; ~geruch m smell of fish, fishy smell; ~geschäft nt fishmonger's (shop) (Brit), fish shop (Brit) or dealer (US); ~gräte f fish bone; ~grätenmuster nt herringbone (pattern); ~gründe pl fishing grounds pl, fisheries pl; ~halle f fish market hall; ~händler m fishmonger (Brit), fish dealer (US) (Großhändler) fish merchant; ~köder m bait; ~konserve f canned or tinned (Brit) fish; ~kutter m fishing cutter; ~laden m fish shop (Brit) or dealer (US); ~leder nt shagreen; ~markt m fish market; ~mehl nt fish meal; ~milch f milt, soft roe; ~otter m otter; f~reich adj rich in fish; ~reichtum m richness in fish; ~reiher m grey heron; ~reuse f fish trap, weir basket; ~rogen m (hard) roe; ~schuppe f (fish) scale; ~schuppenkrankheit f ichthyosis (spec); ~schwarm nt shoal of fish; ~stäbchen nt fish finger; ~sterben nt death of fish; ~tran m train oil; ~trawler m trawler; f~verarbeitend adj attr fish-processing; ~verarbeitung f fish processing; ~waren pl fish products pl; ~wasser nt (Cook) fish stock; ~wehr nt fish weir; ~weib nt (dated) fish seller, fishwoman; (pej) fishwife; ~wilderei f poaching; ~wirtschaft f fishing industry; ~zaun m fish weir; ~zucht f fish-farming; (inf: auch ~zuchtanstalt) fish farm; ~zug m (a) (Bibl) der ~zug des Petrus, Petri ~zug the miraculous draught of fishes; (b) (fig: Beutezug) raid, foray.

Fisimatenten pl (inf) (Ausflüchte) excuses pl; (Umstände) fuss; (Albernheiten) nonsense. ~ machen to make excuses/a fuss/to get up to a lot of nonsense; mit jdm/etw ~ machen to mess about with sb/sth (inf).

fiskalisch adj fiscal.

Fiskal-: ~politik f, no pl fiscal politics sing/policy; f~politisch adj politico-economic.

Fiskus m -, -se or **Fisken** (Staatsvermögen) treasury, exchequer (Brit); (fig: Staat) Treasury.

Fisolen pl (Aus) green beans pl.

fisselig adj (dial) fine; (empfindlich zu handhaben) fiddly.

Fisselregen m (dial) siehe **Nieselregen**.

Fission f fission.

Fissur f (Anat) fissure; (Med) crack.

Fistel f -, -n (Med) fistula (spec).

fisteln vi to speak in a falsetto (voice) or piping voice.

Fistelstimme f (a) (Mus) falsetto. (b) (hohes Sprechstimmchen) falsetto (voice), piping voice.

fit adj pred, no comp fit. sich ~ halten/machen to keep/get fit.

Fitness, Fitneß f -, no pl physical fitness.

Fitness-: ~center nt health centre; ~training nt fitness training.

fitten vt (Tech) to fit.

Fittich m -(e)s, -e (liter) wing, pinion (liter). jdn unter seine ~e nehmen (hum) to take sb under one's wing (fig).

Fitting nt -s, -s (Tech) fitting.

Fitzchen nt (dial), **Fitzel** m or nt -s, -, **Fitzelchen** nt little bit.

fix adj (a) (inf) (flink) quick; (intelligent auch) bright, smart. in etw (dat) ~ sein to be quick at sth; mach ~! be quick!, look lively! (inf); das geht ganz ~ that doesn't/won't take long at all; geht das nicht ~er? does it have to take so long?

(b) (inf) ~ und fertig sein to be all finished; (bereit) to be all ready; (nervös) to be at the end of one's tether; (erschöpft) to be worn out or done in (inf) or all in (inf); (emotional, seelisch) to be shattered; (ruiniert) to be done for (inf); jdn ~ und fertig machen (fertig anziehen etc) to get sb all ready; (nervös machen) to drive sb mad; (erschöpfen) to wear sb out, to do sb in (inf); (emotional, seelisch) to shatter sb; (in Prüfung, Wettbewerb, Kampf etc) to give sb a thrashing (inf); (ruinieren) to do for sb (inf).

(c) (feststehend) fixed. ~e Idee obsession, idée fixe.

Fix m -(es), -e (sl) fix (sl).

Fixa pl of **Fixum**.

Fixe f -, -n (sl) needle (inf).

fixen vi (a) (sl: Drogen spritzen) to fix (sl), to shoot (sl). (b) (St Ex) to fix.

Fixer(in f) m -s, - (a) (sl) fixer (sl). (b) (St Ex) bear.

Fixgeschäft nt (Comm) transaction for delivery by a fixed date; (St Ex) time bargain.

Fixierbad nt fixer.

fixierbar adj specifiable, definable.

fixieren* vt (a) (anstarren) jdn/etw (mit seinem Blick/seinen Augen) ~ to fix one's gaze/eyes on sb/sth.

(b) (festlegen) to specify, to define; (Gehälter, Termin etc) to set (auf + acc for); (schriftlich niederlegen) to record. er ist zu stark auf seine Mutter fixiert (Psych) he has a mother fixation; seine Interessen sind auf Fußball fixiert he has a fixation about football.

(c) (haltbar machen) to fix.

(d) (Gewichtheben) to lock; (Ringen) to get in a lock. er fixierte seinen Gegner auf den Schultern he pinned his opponent/his opponent's shoulders to the canvas.

Fixier-: ~mittel nt fixer, fixative; ~natron, ~salz nt hypo.

Fixierung f (a) (Festlegung) siehe vt (b) specification, definition; setting; recording; (Psych) fixation. (b) (Anstarren) fixing of one's gaze (gen on).

Fixigkeit f (inf) speed.

Fix-: ~kosten pl fixed overheads pl; ~punkt m siehe Festpunkt; ~stern m fixed star.

Fixum nt -s, **Fixa** basic salary, basic.

Fixzeit f siehe **Kernzeit**.

Fjord m -(e)s, -e fiord.

FKK [εfka'ka:] no art abbr of **Freikörperkultur**. ~-Anhänger sein to be a nudist or naturist.

FKK-Strand [εfka'ka:-] m nudist beach.

Fla f -, no pl (Mil) abbr of **Flugabwehr**.

Flab f -, no pl (Sw) siehe **Flak**.

flach adj (a) (eben, platt, niedrig) flat; Gebäude low; Abhang gentle; Boot flat-bottomed. sich ~ hinlegen/~ liegen to lie down/lie flat; ~ schlafen to sleep without a pillow; die ~e Klinge/Hand the flat of the blade/one's hand; eine ~e Brust a hollow chest; (Busen) a flat chest; auf dem ~en Land in the middle of the country.

(b) (untief) shallow.

(c) (fig) flat; Geschmack insipid; (oberflächlich) shallow. ~ atmen to take shallow breaths.

Flach nt -(e)s, -e (Naut) shallows pl.

Flach-: ~bau m low building; ~bauweise f low style of building; f~brüstig adj flat-chested; ~dach nt flat roof; ~druck m (a) (Verfahren) planography; (b) (Produkt) planograph; ~drucker m planographic printer.

Fläche f -, -n (Ausdehnung, Flächeninhalt, Math) area; (Ober~) surface; (von Würfel) face; (Gelände, Land~, Wasser~) expanse (of ground/water).

Flach|eisen nt flat bar; (Werkzeug) flat-bladed chisel.

Flächen-: ~ausdehnung f surface area; ~brand m extensive fire; sich zu einem ~brand ausweiten (fig) to spread to epidemic proportions; ~ertrag m yield per acre/hectare etc; f~gleich adj equal in area; f~haft adj two-dimensional; (ausgedehnt) extensive; ~inhalt m area; ~maß nt unit of square measure; ~nutzung f land utilization; f~treu adj Projektion equal-area.

Flach-: f~fallen vi sep irreg aux sein (inf) not to come off; (Regelung) to end; ~feile f flat file; ~glas nt sheet-glass; ~hang m gentle slope.

Flachheit f siehe adj (a) flatness; lowness; gentleness. (b) shallowness. (c) flatness; insipidity, insipidness; shallowness.

flächig adj Gesicht flat; Aufforstungen extensive.

Flach-: ~kopf m (inf) dunderhead (inf), numskull (inf); f~köpfig adj (inf) dumb (inf); ~küste f flat coast; ~land nt lowland; (Tiefland) plains pl; ~länder(in f) m -s, - lowlander, plainsman; ~landtiroler m (inf) pseudo-Tyrolean type; f~legen sep (inf) 1 vt to lay out; 2 vt to lie down; f~liegen vi sep irreg (inf) to be laid up (inf); ~mann m, pl ~männer (inf) hip-flask; ~meißel m flat chisel; ~moor nt fen; ~paß m (Ftbl) low pass; ~relief nt bas-relief; ~rennen nt flat (race).

Flachs [flaks] m -es, no pl (a) (Bot, Tex) flax. (b) (inf: Neckerei, Witzelei) kidding (inf); (Bemerkung) joke. ~ machen to kid around (inf); das war nur ~ I/he etc was only kidding (inf); jetzt mal ganz ohne ~ joking or kidding (inf) apart.

Flachs-: ~bart m (inf) man with a flaxen beard; f~blond adj flaxen.

Flachschuß m (Ftbl) low shot.

Flachse ['flaksə] f -, -n (Aus) siehe **Flechse**.

flachsen ['flaksn] vi (inf) to kid around (inf). mit jdm ~ to kid sb (on) (inf).

Flachserei [flaksə'rai] f (inf) siehe **Flachs (b)**.

Flachs-: f~farben adj flaxen; ~haar nt flaxen hair; ~kopf m flaxen-haired child/youth.

Flachzange f flat-nosed pliers pl.

flackern vi (lit, fig) to flicker.

Flackerschein m flicker, flickering light.

Fladen m -s, - (a) (Cook) round flat dough-cake. (b) (inf: Kuh~) cowpat.

Fladenbrot nt round flat loaf.

Flader f -, -n grain no pl; (Jahresring) ring.

flad(e)rig adj grained.

fladern vti (Aus inf) to steal, to nick (Brit inf).

Flagellant m flagellant.

Flagellantentum nt (Rel) self-flagellation, flagellantism.

Flagellantismus m (Psych) flagellantism.

Flagellat m -en, -en (Biol) flagellate.

Flagellation f (Psych) flagellation.

Flagge f -, -n flag; die belgische ~ führen to fly the Belgian flag or colours; die ~ streichen (lit) to strike the flag; (fig) to capitulate, to show the white flag; ~ zeigen to nail one's colours to the mast.

flaggen vi to fly flags/a flag. geflaggt haben to fly flags/a flag; siehe halbmast, Topp.

Flaggen-: ~alphabet nt semaphore no art; ~gala f: in großer ~gala dressed overall; ~gruß m dipping of the flag; ~leine f siehe **Flaggleine**; ~mast m flagpole, flagstaff; ~parade f morning/evening colours sing; ~signal nt flag signal; ~tuch nt, no pl bunting.

Flagg-: ~leine f (flag) halyard; ~offizier m flag officer; ~schiff nt (lit, fig) flagship.

flagrant adj flagrant; siehe in flagranti.

Flair [flɛ:ɐ] nt or (rare) m -s, no pl (geh) atmosphere; (Nimbus) aura; (esp Sw: Gespür) flair.

Flak f -, - or -s abbr of **Flug(zeug)abwehrkanone** (a) anti-aircraft or ack-ack gun. (b) (Einheit) anti-aircraft or ack-ack unit.

Flak-: ~batterie f anti-aircraft or ack-ack battery; ~helfer(in f) m (Hist) anti-aircraft auxiliary.

Flakon [fla'kõ:] nt or m -s, -s bottle, flacon.

Flakstellung f anti-aircraft or ack-ack (inf) artillery position.

Flambeau [flã'bo:] *m* -s, -s (*geh*) chandelier.
flambieren* *vt* (*Cook*) to flambé.
flamboyant [flãboa'jã:] *adj* (*geh, Archit*) flamboyant.
Flamboyantstil [flãboa'jã:-] *m* flamboyant style.
Flame *m* -n, -n Fleming, Flemish man/boy.
Flamenco *m* -(s), -s flamenco.
Flamin, Flämin *f* Fleming, Flemish woman/girl.
Flamingo [fla'mɪŋ'go] *m* -s, -s flamingo.
flämisch *adj* Flemish.
Flämisch(e) *nt* -en Flemish; *siehe auch* **Deutsch(e)**.
Flämmchen *nt dim of* **Flamme**.
Flamme *f* -, -n (a) (*lit, fig*) flame. **mit ruhiger/flackernder ~ brennen** to burn with a steady/flickering flame; **in ~n aufgehen** to go up in flames; **in (hellen) ~n stehen** to be ablaze *or* in flames; **etw den ~n übergeben** (*liter*) to consign sth to the flames; **etw auf kleiner ~ kochen** (*lit*) to cook sth on a low flame; (*fig*) to let sth just tick over; **etw auf großer ~ kochen** to cook sth fast.
   (b) (*Brennstelle*) flame, burner.
   (c) (*dated inf: Geliebte*) flame (*inf*).
flammen *vi* (*old, fig*) to blaze; *siehe* **flammend**.
flammend *adj* fiery. **mit ~em Gesicht** blazing.
flammendrot *adj* (*geh*) flame red, blazing red.
Flammen-: **~meer** *nt* sea of flames; **~tod** *m* death by burning; **den ~tod erleiden** to be burnt to death; **jdn zum ~tod verurteilen** to sentence sb to be burnt to death; **~werfer** *m* flamethrower; **~zeichen** *nt* (*geh*) *siehe* **Feuerzeichen**.
Flandern *nt* -s Flanders *sing*.
flandrisch *adj* Flemish.
Flanell *m* -s, -e flannel.
flanellen *adj attr* flannel.
Flaneur [fla'nøːɐ] *m* -s, -e (*geh*) stroller.
flanieren* *vi* to stroll, to saunter.
Flanke *f* -, -n (a) (*Anat, Mil, Chess*) flank; (*von Bus, Lastzug etc*) side. **dem Feind in die ~n fallen** to attack the enemy on the flank. (b) (*Sport*) (*Turnen*) flank-vault; (*Ftbl*) centre pass; (*Spielfeldseite*) wing.
flanken *vi* (*Turnen*) to flank-vault; (*Ftbl*) to centre.
Flanken-: **~angriff** *m* (*Mil, Chess*) flank attack; **~ball** *m* (*Ftbl*) centre pass; **~deckung** *f* (*Mil*) flank defence; **~schutz** *m* (*Mil*) protection on the flank; **jdm ~schutz geben** (*fig*) to give sb added support; **~sicherung** *f* (*Mil*) *siehe* **~deckung**.
flankieren* *vt* (*Mil, Chess, fig*) to flank; (*fig: ergänzen*) to accompany. **~de Maßnahmen** supporting measures.
Flansch *m* -(e)s, -e flange.
Flappe *f* -, -n (*dial*) pout. **eine ~ ziehen** to look petulant, to pout.
flappen *vi* (*N Ger*) to flap.
Flaps *m* -es, -e (*dial inf*) *siehe* **Flegel**.
flapsig *adj* (*dial inf*) *siehe* **flegelhaft**.
Fläschchen *nt* bottle.
Flasche *f* -, -n (a) bottle. **einem Baby die ~ geben** to give a baby its bottle; **mit der ~ aufziehen** to bottle-feed; **das Kind bekommt die ~** (*momentan*) the child is having its bottle; (*generell*) the child is bottle-fed; **eine ~ Wein/Bier** *etc* a bottle of wine/beer *etc*; **aus der ~ trinken** to drink (straight) from *or* out of the bottle; **zur ~ greifen** (*fig*) to take to the bottle.
   (b) (*inf: Versager*) dead loss (*inf*). **du ~!** you're a dead loss! (*inf*).
Flaschen-: **~batterie** *f* array of bottles; **~bier** *nt* bottled beer; **~bürste** *f* bottle-brush; **~etikett** *nt* label on a/the bottle; **~fach** *nt* bottle compartment; **~gärung** *f* fermentation in the bottle; **~gestell** *nt* bottle rack; **f~grün** *adj* bottle-green; **~hals** *m* neck of a bottle; (*fig*) bottleneck; **~kind** *nt* bottle-fed baby; **er ist ein ~kind** (*hum*) he's a straight-from-the-bottle man (*inf*), he always drinks straight from the bottle; **~knacker** *m* bottle crusher; **~kürbis** *m* calabash, bottle gourd; **~milch** *f* bottled milk; **~nahrung** *f* baby milk; **~öffner** *m* bottle-opener; **~pfand** *nt* deposit on a/the bottle; **~post** *f* message in a bottle; **mit der ~post** in a bottle; **~regal** *nt* wine rack; **f~reif** *adj* *Wein* ready for bottling; **~verschluß** *m* bottle top; **~wein** *m* bottled wine; **f~weise** *adv* by the bottle; **~zug** *m* block and tackle.
flaschig *adj* (*inf*) lousy (*inf*). **so was F~es!** what a dead loss!
Flaschner *m* -s, - (*S Ger, Sw*) plumber.
Flash [fleʃ] *m* -s, -s (*Film*) flash, intercut scene (*form*); (*Rückblende*) flashback; (*sl*) flash (*sl*).
Flatter *f*: **die ~ machen** (*sl*) to beat it (*inf*).
Flatter-: **~geist** *m* butterfly; **f~haft** *adj* butterfly *attr*, fickle; **sie ist ziemlich ~haft** she's a bit of a butterfly; **~haftigkeit** *f* fickleness.
flatterig *adj* fluttery; *Puls* fluttering.
Flattermann *m, pl* -männer (*inf*) (a) **einen ~ haben** (*Zittern der Hände*) to have the shakes; (*Lampenfieber*) to have stagefright. (b) (*hum: Hähnchen*) chicken.
flattern *vi* (*lit, fig*) to flutter; (*mit den Flügeln schlagen*) to flap its wings; (*Fahne, Segel beim Sturm, Hose*) to flap; (*Haar*) to stream, to fly; (*Blick*) to flicker; (*inf: Mensch*) to be in a flap (*inf*); (*Lenkung, Autorad*) to wobble. **ein Brief flatterte mir auf den Schreibtisch** a letter turned up *or* arrived on my desk.
Flattersatz *m* (*Typ*) unjustified print.
Flatulenz *f* (*Med*) flatulence.
flau *adj* (a) *Brise, Wind* slack. (b) *Farbe* weak; *Geschmack* insipid; *Stimmung*, (*Phot inf*) *Negativ* flat. (c) (*übel*) queasy; (*vor Hunger*) faint. **mir ist ~ (im Magen)** I feel queasy. (d) (*Comm*) *Markt, Börse* slack. **in meiner Kasse sieht es ~ aus** (*inf*) my finances aren't too healthy (*inf*).
Flauheit *f siehe adj* (b-d) weakness; insipidity, insipidness; flatness; queasiness; faintness; slackness.
Flaum *m* -(e)s, *no pl* (a) (**~federn**, *Härchen, auf Obst*) down. (b) (*dial: Schweinebauchfett*) lard.

Flaumacher *m* -s, - (*inf*) *siehe* **Miesmacher**.
Flaum-: **~bart** *m* downy beard, bum-fluff (*sl*) *no indef art*; **~feder** *f* down feather, plumule (*spec*).
flaumig *adj* downy; (*Aus: flockig*) light and creamy.
flaumweich *adj* (*fig inf*) *Mensch* soft; *Haltung* milk-and-water *attr*, lukewarm.
Flausch *m* -(e)s, -e fleece.
flauschig *adj* fleecy; (*weich*) soft.
Flausen *pl* (*inf*) (a) (*Ausflüchte*) excuses *pl*. **das sind ~** that's just a pack of excuses (*inf*); **mach (mir) doch keine ~ (vor)** don't spin me any yarns (*inf*). (b) (*Unsinn*) nonsense; (*Illusionen*) fancy ideas *pl* (*inf*). **macht keine ~!** don't try anything! (*inf*).
Flaute *f* -, -n (a) (*Met*) calm. **das Schiff geriet in eine ~** the ship was becalmed. (b) (*fig*) (*Comm*) lull, slack period; (*der Stimmung*) fit of the doldrums (*inf*); (*der Leistung*) period of slackness.
Flaxe *f* -, -n (*Aus*) *siehe* **Flechse**.
Fläz *m* -es, -e (*dial inf*) lout, roughneck.
fläzen *vr* (*inf*) to sprawl (*in* +*acc* in).
Flebbe *f* -, -n (*sl*) ID (*inf*).
Flechse ['fleksə] *f* -, -n tendon.
flechsig ['fleksɪç] *adj* *Fleisch* stringy (*inf*), sinewy.
Flechtarbeit *f* wickerwork, basketwork; (*aus Rohr*) canework.
Flechte *f* -, -n (a) (*Bot, Med*) lichen. (b) (*geh: Zopf*) plait, braid (*dated*).
flechten *pret* **flocht**, *ptp* **geflochten** *vt* *Haar* to plait, to braid (*dated*); *Kranz, Korb, Matte* to weave, to make; *Seil* to make; *Stuhl* to cane. **sich/jdm das Haar zu Zöpfen** *or* **in Zöpfe ~** to plait *or* braid (*dated*) one's/sb's hair; **Blumen zu einem Kranz ~** to weave flowers into a wreath; **Zitate in eine Rede ~** to punctuate a speech with quotations; *siehe* **Rad**.
Flechtwerk *nt* (a) (*Art*) interlace. (b) *siehe* **Geflecht**.
Fleck *m* -(e)s, -e *or* -en (a) (*Schmutz~*) stain. **dieses Zeug macht ~en** this stuff stains (*in/auf etw* (*acc*) sth); **mach dir nur keinen ~ ins Hemd** (*sl*) don't be so ridiculous!; **einen ~ auf der (weißen) Weste haben** (*fig*) to have blotted one's copybook; **einen ~ auf der Ehre haben** to have a stain on one's honour *or* a blot on one's escutcheon.
   (b) (*Farb~*) splodge (*Brit*), splotch, blob; (*auf Arm etc*) blotch; (*auf Obst*) blemish. **ein grüner/gelber etc ~** a patch of green/yellow *etc*, a green/yellow *etc* patch; **weißer ~** white patch; (*auf Stirn von Pferd*) star, blaze; (*auf Landkarte*) blank area; *siehe* **blau**.
   (c) (*Stelle*) spot, place. **auf demselben ~** in the same place; **sich nicht vom ~ rühren** not to move *or* budge (*inf*); **nicht vom ~ kommen** not to get any further; **er hat das Herz auf dem rechten ~** (*fig*) his heart is in the right place; **am falschen ~** (*fig*) in the wrong way; *sparen* in the wrong places; **vom ~ weg** on the spot.
   (d) (*dial: Flicken*) patch.
   (e) *no pl* (*Cook dial*) *siehe* **Kaldaune**.
Fleckchen *nt* (a) *dim of* **Fleck**. (b) **ein schönes ~ (Erde)** a lovely little spot.
flecken *vi* (*dial*) to stain.
Flecken *m* -s, - (a) (*old: Markt~*) small town. (b) *siehe* **Fleck** (a, b, d).
fleckenlos *adj* (*lit, fig*) spotless.
Fleck-: **~entferner** *m*, **~entfernungsmittel** *nt* stain-remover.
Fleckenwasser *nt* stain-remover.
Fleckerlteppich *m* (*S Ger, Aus*) patchwork rug.
Fleckfieber *nt* (a) typhus fever. (b) (*inf: lästiger Mensch*) pest (*inf*).
fleckig *adj* marked; (*mit Flüssigkeit auch*) stained; *Obst* blemished; *Tierfell* speckled; *Gesichtshaut* blotchy.
Flecktyphus *m siehe* **Fleckfieber (a)**.
Fledderer *m* -s, - *siehe* **Leichenfledderer**.
fleddern *vt* *Leichen* to rob; (*inf: durchwühlen*) to rummage *or* ferret (*inf*) through.
Fleder-: **~maus** *f* bat; **~wisch** *m* feather duster.
Fleet [fleːt] *nt* -(e)s, -e (*N Ger*) canal.
Flegel *m* -s, - (a) (*Lümmel*) uncouth fellow; (*Kind*) brat (*inf*). (b) (*Dresch~, old: Kriegs~*) flail.
Flegelalter *nt* awkward adolescent phase.
Flegelei *f* uncouthness; *Benehmen, Bemerkung* uncouth behaviour *no pl*/remark; **so eine ~!** how rude *or* uncouth!
Flegel-: **f~haft** *adj* uncouth; **~haftigkeit** *f* uncouthness; **~jahre** *pl siehe* **~alter**.
flegeln *vr* to loll, to sprawl. **sich in die Bank/den Sessel ~** to loll *or* sprawl all over the bench/in the armchair.
flehen *vi* (*geh*) to plead (*um* +*acc* for, *zu* with). **..., flehte er zu Gott ...,** he beseeched *or* besought God (*liter, old*).
flehentlich *adj* imploring, pleading, beseeching (*liter, old*). **eine ~e Bitte** an earnest entreaty *or* plea; **jdn ~ bitten** to plead with sb; **jdn ~ bitten, etw zu tun** to entreat *or* implore sb to do sth.
Fleisch *nt* -(e)s, *no pl* (a) (*Gewebe, Muskel~*) flesh. **nacktes ~** (*lit, fig hum*) bare flesh; **vom ~ fallen** to lose (a lot of) weight; **sich (dat or acc) ins eigene ~ schneiden** to cut off one's nose to spite one's face; **den Weg allen ~es gehen** (*liter*) to go the way of all flesh; **Menschen von ~ und Blut** flesh and blood; **sein eigen ~ und Blut** (*liter*) his own flesh and blood; **jdm in ~ und Blut übergehen** to become second nature to sb; **und das Wort ward ~** (*Bibl*) and the Word was made flesh.
   (b) (*Nahrungsmittel*) meat; (*Frucht~*) flesh.
Fleisch- *in cpds* (*Cook*) meat; (*Anat*) flesh; **~abfälle** *pl* (meat) scraps *pl*; **f~arm** *adj* containing little meat; **f~arm sein** to contain little meat; **~berg** *m* (*pej inf*) mountain of flesh; **~beschau** *f* (a) meat inspection; (b) (*hum inf*) cattle market (*inf*); **~beschauer(in** *f*) *m* meat inspector; **~brocken** *m* lump of

meat; ~brühe f (Gericht) bouillon; (Fond) meat stock; ~brühwürfel m (meat) stock cube; ~einlage f meat; ~einwaage f meat content, weight of meat.
Fleischer m -s, - butcher; (pej inf: Chirurg) sawbones sing (inf).
Fleischerbeil nt meat cleaver.
Fleischerei f butcher's (shop).
Fleischer-: ~handwerk nt butcher's trade, butchery; ~hund m (lit) butcher's dog; (fig) brute of a dog; ein Gemüt wie ein ~hund haben (inf) to be a callous brute; ~innung f butchers' guild; ~laden nt siehe Fleischerei; ~messer nt butcher's knife.
fleischern adj (rare) siehe fleischig.
Fleischerne(s) nt decl as adj (S Ger) meat.
Fleischeslust f (old liter) carnal lust, lusts pl of the flesh.
Fleisch-: ~esser m meat-eater; ~extrakt m beef extract; ~farbe f flesh colour; f~farben, f~farbig adj flesh-coloured; ~fliege f flesh-fly; f~fressend adj (Biol) f~fressende Pflanzen carnivorous plants, carnivores; ~fressende pl (form), f~fressende Tiere carnivores, carnivorous animals; ~fresser m (Zool) carnivore; ~genuß m consumption of meat; f~geworden adj attr (liter) incarnate; der f~gewordene Sohn Gottes the Son of God incarnate; ~hauer m (Aus) butcher; ~hauerei f (Aus) butcher's (shop).
fleischig adj fleshy.
Fleisch-: ~käse m meat loaf; ~klopfer m steak hammer; ~kloß m, ~klößchen nt (a) meat ball; (b) (pej inf) mountain of flesh; ~koloß m (pej inf) hulking great creature; ~konserve f can or tin (Brit) of meat; (in Glas) pot or jar of meat; ~konserven pl (als Gattung) canned or tinned (Brit) meat; (in Glas) potted meat.
fleischlich adj attr Speisen, Kost meat; (old liter: Lüste, Genüsse, Begierden) carnal, of the flesh.
Fleisch-: f~los adj (a) (ohne Fleisch) meatless; Kost, Ernährung vegetarian; f~los essen/kochen to eat no meat/to cook without meat; (b) (mager) thin, lean; ~maschine f (Aus, S Ger) siehe ~wolf; ~pastete f meat vol-au-vent; ~reste pl left-over meat sing; ~saft m meat juices pl; ~salat m diced meat salad with mayonnaise; ~stück(chen) nt piece of meat; ~suppe f meat soup; ~ton m (Art) flesh-colour; ~topf m (a) (Cook) meat pan; (b) ~töpfe (Bibl) fleshpots pl; (fig) good life; f~verarbeitend adj attr meat-processing; ~vergiftung f food poisoning (from meat); ~vogel m (Sw) siehe Roulade; ~waren pl meat products pl; ~werdung f (Rel, liter) incarnation; ~wolf m mincer, meat grinder (esp US) Rekruten/Prüflinge durch den ~wolf drehen (inf) to put new recruits/exam candidates through the mill; ~wunde f flesh wound; ~wurst f pork sausage.
Fleiß m -(e)s, no pl diligence; (eifriges Tätigsein) industry; (Beharrlichkeit) application; (als Charaktereigenschaft) industriousness. ~ aufwenden to apply oneself; ihm fehlt der ~ he lacks application; mit ~ kann es jeder zu etwas bringen anybody can succeed if he works hard; er hat die Prüfung ausschließlich durch ~ geschafft he passed the exam by sheer hard work or simply by working hard; mit ~ bei der Sache sein to work hard; mit großem ~ machte er sich an die Arbeit he set about his work very industriously; er verwandte großen ~ auf die Arbeit he took great pains over the work; mit ~ (old, S Ger: absichtlich) deliberately, on purpose; ohne ~ kein Preis (Prov) success never comes easily.
Fleiß|arbeit f industrious piece of work; (nichts als Fleiß erfordernd) laborious task. eine (reine) ~ (pej) an industrious but uninspired piece of work.
fleißig adj (a) (arbeitsam) hard-working no adv, industrious, diligent. ~ studieren/arbeiten to study/work hard; ~ wie die Bienen sein to work like beavers; ~e Hände busy hands; ~es Lieschen (Bot) busy Lizzie.
(b) (Fleiß zeigend) diligent, painstaking.
(c) (inf: unverdrossen) assiduous, diligent; Theaterbesucher, Sammler etc keen. wir haben immer ~ getrunken bis 12 Uhr we were drinking away till 12 o'clock.
flektierbar adj (in)flectional (form); Verbum conjugable; Substantiv, Adjektiv declinable.
flektieren 1 vt to inflect (form); Substantiv, Adjektiv to decline; Verbum to conjugate. 2 vi to inflect; to be declined; to be conjugated. „schwimmen" flektiert stark "schwimmen" is (conjugated as) a strong verb; ~d siehe flektierbar.
flennen vi (pej inf) to blubb(er) (inf).
Flennerei f (pej inf) blubb(er)ing (inf).
Fleppe f -, -n (sl) siehe Flebbe.
fletschen vti die Zähne or mit den Zähnen ~ to bare or show one's teeth.
fleucht (obs, poet) 3. pers sing of fliegen; siehe kreucht.
Fleurist(in) f [flø'rɪst(ɪn)] m -en, -en florist.
Fleurop ® ['flɔyrɔp, 'flø:rɔp, flɔy'ro:p, flø'ro:p] f - Interflora ®.
fleußt obs 3. pers sing of fließen.
flexibel adj (lit, fig) flexible; Holz, Kunststoff auch pliable.
Flexibilität f siehe adj flexibility; pliability.
Flexion f (Gram) inflection.
Flexions-: ~endung f inflectional ending or suffix; f~fähig adj siehe flektierbar; f~los adj uninflected.
Flibustier [fli'bustiɐ] m -s, - (old, fig) buccaneer.
flicht imper sing and 3. pers sing present of flechten.
Flick|arbeit f (Sew) mending.
flicken vt to mend; Wäsche (stopfen auch) to darn; (mit Flicken) to patch; siehe Zeug.
Flicken m -s, - patch. eine Jacke mit ~ a patched jacket; (als Schmuck) a patchwork jacket.
Flick-: ~flack m (Sport) backflip; ~schneider m (dated) mender; (pej) bungler (inf); bungling tailor; ~schuster m (old)

cobbler; (fig pej) bungler (inf), botcher (inf); ~schusterei f cobbler's (shop); das ist ~schusterei (fig pej) that's a patch-up job; ~wäsche f mending; ~werk nt die Reform war reinstes ~werk the reform had been carried out piecemeal; ~wort nt filler; ~zeug nt (Nähzeug) sewing kit; (Reifen~) (puncture) repair outfit.
Flieder m -s, - (a) lilac; (dial: Holunder) elder. (b) (Aus inf: Geld) money.
Flieder-: ~beere f (dial) elderberry; ~busch m lilac; f~farben, f~farbig adj lilac; ~tee m elderflower tea.
Fliege f -, -n (a) fly. sie fielen um wie die ~n they went down like ninepins; sie starben wie die ~n they fell like flies; er tut keiner ~ etwas zuleide, er würde keiner ~ ein Bein ausreißen (fig) he wouldn't hurt a fly; zwei ~n mit einer Klappe schlagen to kill two birds with one stone; ihn stört die ~ an der Wand, er ärgert sich über die ~ an der Wand every little thing irritates him; die or 'ne ~ machen (sl) to beat it (inf).
(b) (Bärtchen) imperial.
(c) (Schlips) bow tie.
fliegen pret flog, ptp geflogen 1 vi aux sein (a) to fly; (Raumschiff, Raumfahrer) to go, to travel (form). mit General Air ~ to fly (with or by) General Air; in den Urlaub ~ to fly on holiday; nach Köln fliegt man zwei Stunden it takes two hours to fly to Cologne, it's a two-hour flight to Cologne; ich kann doch nicht ~! I haven't got wings (inf).
(b) (eilen) to fly. jdm/einander in die Arme ~ to fly into sb's/each other's arms; jdm an den Hals ~ to hurl oneself at sb; ein Lächeln flog über sein Gesicht a brief smile lit up his face; die Zeit fliegt time flies; auf jdn/etw ~ (inf) to be mad or wild about sb/sth (inf).
(c) (inf: fallen) to fall. von der Leiter ~ to fall off the ladder; ich bin von der Treppe geflogen I went flying down the stairs; durchs Examen ~ to fail or flunk (inf) one's exam.
(d) (sl: hinausgeworfen werden) to be chucked or slung or kicked out (inf) (aus, von of). aus der Firma ~ to get the sack or the boot (inf); auf die Straße ~ to be put out on the street(s), to find oneself on the street(s).
(e) (bewegt werden) (Fahne, Haare) to fly; (Puls) to race. das Tier flog am ganzen Körper the animal was quivering or trembling all over.
(f) (geworfen werden) to be thrown or flung (inf) or chucked (inf). geflogen kommen to come flying; in den Papierkorb ~ to go into the wastepaper basket, to be immediately consigned to the wastepaper basket; die Tür flog ins Schloß the door flew shut; ein Schuh flog ihm an den Kopf he had a shoe flung at him; der Hut flog ihm vom Kopf his hat flew off his head; aus der Kurve ~ to skid off the bend; siehe Luft.
2 vt Flugzeug, Güter, Personen, Route, Einsatz etc to fly.
3 vr in dieser Maschine/nachts fliegt es sich angenehm flying in this plane/at night is pleasant; das Flugzeug fliegt sich leicht/schwer this plane is easy/difficult to fly, flying this plane is easy/difficult; die Maschine fliegt sich gut/schlecht this aircraft flies well/badly; siehe auch fliegend.
Fliegen-: ~bein nt (lit) fly's leg; ~beine (fig) mascara-matted eyelashes; ~beinzählen nt (iro) head-counting (iro).
fliegend adj attr Fische, Untertasse, Start flying; Personal flight; Würstchenbuden mobile. ~er Hund flying fox; in ~er Eile or Hast in a tremendous hurry; ~er Händler travelling hawker; (mit Lieferwagen) mobile trader; ~e Brigade (DDR) mobile work brigade; Der F~e Holländer the Flying Dutchman; ~e Hitze hot flushes pl; ~e Blätter loose leaves or sheets; (Hist) broadsheets.
Fliegen-: ~draht m wire mesh; ~dreck m fly droppings pl; ~fänger m (Klebestreifen) fly-paper; ~fenster nt wire-mesh window; ~gewicht nt (Sport, fig) flyweight; ~gewichtler m -s, - (Sport) flyweight; ~gitter nt fly screen; ~klatsche f fly-swat; ~kopf m (Typ) turn; ~netz nt fly-net; ~papier nt flypaper; ~pilz m fly agaric.
Flieger m -s, - (a) (Pilot) airman, aviator (dated), flier (dated); (Mil: Rang) aircraftman (Brit), airman basic (US). er ist bei den ~n (dated) he's in the air force. (b) (inf: Flugzeug) plane. (c) (Vogel) flier. (d) (Sport) (Radrennen) sprinter; (Pferderennen) flier.
Flieger-: (Mil): ~abwehr f siehe Flugabwehr; ~abzeichen nt wings pl; ~alarm m air-raid warning; ~angriff m air-raid; ~bombe f aerial bomb.
Fliegerei f, no pl flying.
Fliegerhorst m (Mil) military airfield or aerodrome (Brit).
Fliegerin f siehe Flieger.
fliegerisch adj attr aeronautical.
Flieger-: ~karte f aviation chart; ~krankheit f die ~krankheit altitude sickness; ~offizier m (Mil, Aviat) air force officer; ~schule f flying school; ~sprache f pilots' jargon; ~staffel f (Mil) (air force) squadron; ~truppe f (Mil) air corps sing.
Fliehburg f refuge.
fliehen pret floh, ptp geflohen 1 vi aux sein (a) to flee; (entkommen) to escape (aus from). vor jdm/der Polizei/einem Gewitter ~ to flee from sb/the police/before a storm; die Zeit flieht time flies; die Jahre ~ the years fly by; aus dem Lande ~ to flee the country; siehe geflohen, fliehend.
2 vt (liter) (meiden) to shun; (entkommen) to flee from. jds Gegenwart ~ to shun/flee sb's presence.
fliehend adj Kinn receding; Stirn sloping.
Fliehende(r) mf decl as adj fugitive.
Flieh-: ~kraft f centrifugal force; ~kraftkupplung f centrifugal clutch.
Fliese f -, -n tile. ~n legen to lay tiles; etw mit ~n auslegen to tile sth.
fliesen vt to tile.
Fliesen-: ~(fuß)boden m tiled floor; ~leger m tiler.

Fließ-: ~arbeit f, no pl production-line or assembly-line work; ~band nt conveyor-belt; (als Einrichtung) assembly or production line; am ~band arbeiten or stehen (inf) to work on the assembly or production line; ~(band)fertigung f belt production.

fließen pret **floß**, ptp **geflossen** vi to flow; Verkehr, Luftmassen auch to move; Fluß, Bach auch to run. es ist genug Blut geflossen enough blood has been shed or spilled; der Schweiß floß ihm von der Stirn sweat was pouring off his forehead; die Steuergelder flossen in finstere Kanäle the taxes were diverted along rather dubious channels; die Mittel für Jugendarbeit ~ immer spärlicher less and less money is being made available for youth work; aus der Feder ~ (geh) to flow from the pen; Nachrichten ~ spärlich the flow of news is minimal; alles fließt (Philos) all is in a state of flux; siehe Strom.

fließend adj flowing; Leitungswasser, Gewässer running; Verkehr moving; Rede, Vortrag, Sprache fluent; Grenze, Übergang fluid. sie spricht ~ Französisch or ein ~es Französisch she speaks fluent French, she speaks French fluently.

Fließ-: ~fertigung f siehe ~(band)fertigung; ~heck nt fastback; ~komma nt floating point; ~laut m liquid; ~papier nt blotting paper; ~straße f (Tech) assembly or production line; ~wasser nt (esp Aus) running water.

Flimmer m -s, - (a) (Anat) cilium. (b) no pl (liter: zitternder Glanz) shimmer.

Flimmer-: f~frei adj (Opt, Phot) flicker-free; ~härchen nt cilium; ~kasten m, ~kiste f (inf) TV (inf), (goggle)box (Brit inf), telly (Brit inf).

flimmern 1 vi to shimmer; (Film, TV) to flicker. es flimmert mir vor den Augen everything is swimming or dancing in front of my eyes; über den Bildschirm ~ (inf) to be on the box (Brit inf) or on TV. 2 vt (dial: blank putzen) to polish, to shine (inf).

flink adj (geschickt) nimble; Bewegung, Finger auch deft; (schnell, dated: aufgeweckt) quick; Mundwerk, Zunge quick, ready; Augen sharp, bright. ein bißchen ~! (inf) get a move on!, make it snappy! (inf); mit etw ~ bei der Hand sein to be quick (off the mark) with sth.

Flinkheit f siehe adj nimbleness; deftness; quickness; readiness; sharpness, brightness.

Flint m -(e)s, -e (old) flint.

Flinte f -, -n (Schrot~) shotgun. jdn/etw vor die ~ bekommen (fig) to get hold of sb/sth; wenn der mir vor die ~ kommt ... (fig) just wait till I get hold of him ...; die ~ ins Korn werfen (fig) to throw in the sponge or towel.

Flinten-: ~lauf m (dial) gun barrel; ~weib nt (pej) gunwoman.

Flintglas nt flint glass.

Flipflopschaltung ['flɪpflɔp-] f flip-flop circuit.

flippen vti siehe **flippern.**

Flipper m -s, -, **Flipperautomat** m pinball machine.

flippern 1 vt to flip. eine heiße Kugel ~ (sl) to be a pinball wizard (inf). 2 vi to play pinball.

flirren vi to whirr; (Luft, Hitze) to shimmer.

Flirt [flɪrt, auch flø:ɛt, flœrt] m -s, -s (a) (Flirten) flirtation. (b) (dated) (Schwarm) flame (dated); (Mann auch) beau (dated).

flirten ['flɪrtn, auch 'flø:ɛtn, 'flœrtn] vi to flirt. mit einem Gedanken ~ (inf) to toy with an idea.

Flitscherl nt -s, -(n) (Aus), **Flittchen** nt (pej inf) slut.

Flitter m -s, - (a) (~schmuck) sequins pl, spangles pl. (b) no pl (pej: Tand) trumpery.

Flittergold nt gold foil.

flittern vi (a) to glitter, to sparkle. (b) (hum) to honeymoon.

Flitter-: ~werk nt siehe Flitter (b); ~wochen pl honeymoon sing; in die ~wochen fahren/in den ~wochen sein to go/be on one's honeymoon; ~wöchner m -s, - (hum) honeymooner.

Flitz(e)bogen m bow and arrow. ich bin gespannt wie ein ~ (inf) the suspense is killing me (inf); gespannt wie ein ~ sein, ob ... (inf) to be on tenterhooks waiting to see whether ...

flitzen vi aux sein (inf) to whizz (inf), to dash. (b) (nackt rennen) to streak. (das) F~ streaking.

Flitzer m -s, - (inf) (a) (Fahrzeug) sporty little job (inf); (Schnelläufer) streak of lightning (inf). (b) (Nacktrennender) streaker.

floaten ['flo:tn] vti (Fin) to float. ~ (lassen) to float.

Floating ['flo:tɪŋ] nt (Fin) floating.

F-Loch ['ɛflɔx] nt (Mus) f-hole.

flocht pret of flechten.

Flöckchen nt dim of Flocke.

Flocke f -, -n flake; (Woll~) piece of wool; (Schaum~) blob (of foam); (Staub~) ball (of fluff). Getreide zu ~n verarbeiten to flake cereals.

flockig adj fluffy.

flog pret of fliegen.

floh pret of fliehen.

Floh m -(e)s, -e (a) (Zool) flea. von ~en zerbissen or zerstochen flea-bitten attr, bitten by fleas; es ist leichter, einen Sack ~e zu hüten, als ... I'd as soon jump in the lake as ...; jdm einen ~ ins Ohr setzen (inf) to put an idea into sb's head; die ~e husten hören (inf) to imagine things. (b) (sl: Geld) ~e pl dough (sl), bread (sl).

Floh-: ~beißen nt: angenehmes ~beißen (hum inf) sleep tight, mind the fleas or bugs don't bite (hum); ~biß m fleabite.

flöhe pres subjunc of fliehen.

flöhen vt jdn/sich ~ to get rid of sb's/one's fleas, to debug sb/oneself (inf).

Floh-: ~hüpfen nt tiddl(e)ywinks sing, no art; ~kino nt (inf) local fleapit (inf); ~kiste f (inf) pit (sl), bed; ~markt m flea market; ~spiel nt siehe ~hüpfen; ~zirkus m flea circus.

Flom(en) m -s, no pl (Cook) siehe Flaum.

Flop m -s, -s flop (inf).

Flor[1] m -s, -e (liter) array of flowers. ein ~ duftenden Flieders an abundance of fragrant lilac; in ~ stehen to be in full bloom; ein ~ schöner Damen a bevy of fair ladies.

Flor[2] m -s, -e or (rare) -e (a) (dünnes Gewebe) gauze; (Trauer~) crêpe; (liter: Schleier) veil. (b) (Teppich~, Samt~) pile.

Flora f -, **Floren** flora.

Florentiner 1 m -s, - (a) (Geog, Cook) Florentine. (b) (auch ~hut) picture hat. 2 adj Florentine.

florentinisch adj Florentine.

Florenz nt -' or -ens Florence.

Florett nt -(e)s, -e (a) (Waffe) foil. ~ fechten to fence with a foil. (b) (auch ~fechten) foil-fencing.

Florfliege f lacewing.

florieren* vi to flourish, to bloom.

Florileg(ium) nt -s, **Florilegien** (old) anthology.

Florist(in f) m -en, -en florist.

Florpost f, **Florpostpapier** nt bank paper.

Floskel f -, -n set phrase. eine höfliche/abgedroschene ~ a polite but meaningless/a hackneyed phrase.

floskelhaft adj Stil cliché-ridden; Rede, Brief auch full of set phrases; Phrasen, Ausdrucksweise stereotyped.

floß pret of fließen.

Floß nt -es, -e raft; (Fishing) float.

flößbar adj navigable by raft.

Floßbrücke f floating bridge.

Flosse f -, -n (a) (Zool) (Fisch~) fin; (Wal~, Robben~) flipper. (b) (Aviat, Naut: Leitwerk) fin. (c) (Taucher~) flipper. (d) (sl: Hand) paw (inf), mauler (inf). reich mir die ~, Genosse! (hum) shake, pal! (inf).

flößen vti to raft.

Flößer(in f) m -s, - raftsman.

Flößerei f, no pl rafting.

Flöte f -, -n (a) pipe; (Quer~, in Zusammensetzungen) flute; (Block~) recorder; (Pikkolo~) piccolo; (des Pan) pipes pl; (Orgel~) flute; (dial: Pfeife) whistle. die ~ or auf der ~ spielen or blasen to play the pipe etc. (b) (Kelchglas) flute glass. (c) (Cards) flush. (d) (sl: Penis) cock (sl).

flöten 1 vt (Mus) to play on the flute. 2 vi a (Mus) to play the flute. (b) (sl: fellieren) to do a blow-job (sl). 3 vti (a) (Vogel) to warble; (dial: pfeifen) to whistle. (b) (hum inf: süß sprechen) to flute, to warble.

Flöten-: ~bläser m siehe ~spieler; f~gehen vi sep aux sein (sl) to go west (inf), to go for a burton (inf); ~register nt flute-stop; ~spiel nt pipe-/flute- etc playing; (~musik) pipe-/flute- etc music; ~spieler m piper; flautist; recorder/piccolo player; ~ton m (a) (lit) sound of flutes/a flute; (b) (inf) jdm die ~töne beibringen to teach sb what's what (inf); ~werk nt fluework.

Flötist(in f) m -en, -en flautist; piccolo player.

flott adj (a) (zügig) Fahrt quick; Tempo, Geschäft brisk; Arbeiter, Bedienung speedy (inf), quick and efficient; Tänzer good; (flüssig) Stil, Artikel racy (inf); (schwungvoll) Musik lively. aber ein bißchen ~! and look lively!, and make it snappy!; den ~en Otto or Heinrich haben (hum inf) to have the runs (inf); ~ auftreten to cut a dash.
(b) (schick) smart.
(c) (lebenslustig) fun-loving, fast-living. ~ leben, ein ~es Leben führen to be a fast liver.
(d) pred ~/wieder ~ werden (Schiff) to be floated off/refloated; (fig inf) (Auto etc) to be/get back on the road; (Flugzeug) to be working/working again; (Mensch) to be out of the woods/back on top; (Unternehmen) to be/get back on its feet; wieder ~ sein (Schiff) to be afloat again; (fig inf) (Auto etc) to be back on the road; (Flugzeug) to be working again; (Mensch) (gesundheitlich) to be in the pink again (inf); (finanziell) to be in funds again; (Unternehmen) to be back on its feet.

Flott nt -(e)s, no pl (a) (N Ger) skin of the milk. (b) (Enten~) duckweed.

flottbekommen* vt sep irreg Schiff to float off; (fig inf) Auto etc to get on the road; Flugzeug to get working; Unternehmen to get on its feet.

Flotte f -, -n (a) (Naut) fleet. (b) (Tex) (Färbebad) dye (solution); (Bleichlösung) bleach (solution); (Einweichlösung) soaking solution.

Flotten-: ~abkommen nt naval treaty; ~basis f naval base; ~chef m commander-in-chief of the fleet; ~kommando nt fleet command; ~parade f naval review; die ~parade abnehmen to review the fleet; ~stützpunkt m naval base; ~verband m naval unit.

Flottille [flɔtɪl(j)ə] f -, -n (Mil) flotilla; (Fischfang~) fleet.

Flottillenadmiral m (Mil) commodore.

flott-: ~kriegen, ~machen vt sep siehe ~bekommen; ~weg [-vɛk] adv (inf) non-stop; das geht immer ~weg there's no hanging about (inf).

Flöz nt -es, -e (Min) seam.

Fluch m -(e)s, -e curse; (Schimpfwort auch) oath. ein ~ liegt über or lastet auf diesem Haus there is a curse on this house, this house lies under a curse; ~ über dich! (old) a curse (up)on you! (old); ~ dem Alkohol! a curse on alcohol!; das (eben) ist der ~ der bösen Tat (prov) evil begets evil (Prov).

fluchbeladen adj (liter) accursed, cursed.

fluchen 1 vi (Flüche ausstoßen, schimpfen) to curse (and swear). auf or über jdn/etw ~ to curse sb/sth. 2 vt (old) jdm/etw ~ to curse sb/sth.

Flucht f -, -en (a) (Fliehen) flight; (geglückt auch) escape. ~ ergreifen to take flight, to flee; (erfolgreich auch) to (make one's) escape; ihm glückte die ~ he escaped, he succeeded in escaping; auf der ~ sein to be fleeing; (Gesetzesbrecher) to be on the run; jdn/etw in die ~ treiben or jagen or schlagen to put sb/sth to flight; sich durch die ~ retten to flee or escape to safety; **in wilder** or **heilloser ~ davonjagen** to stampede; **jdm zur ~ verhelfen** to help sb to escape; **auf der ~ erschossen werden** to be shot while attempting to escape; **sein Heil in der ~ suchen** (geh) to take refuge in flight; **die ~ nach vorn antreten** to take the bull by the horns; **die ~ in die Anonymität/die Krankheit/den Trotz/die Öffentlichkeit antreten** to take refuge in anonymity/illness/to resort to defiance/publicity; **die ~ vor der Verantwortung** the abdication of one's responsibilities; **die ~ nach Ägypten** (Bibl) the flight into Egypt.

(b) (Hunt) leap, bound. **eine ~ machen** to make a leap or bound.

(c) (Häuser~) row; (~linie) alignment.

(d) (Zimmer~) suite.

Flucht-: **f~artig** adj hasty, hurried, precipitate (form); **in f~artiger Eile** in great haste; **~auto** nt escape car; (von Gesetzesbrecher) getaway car; **~burg** f refuge.

fluchten (Archit) 1 vt to align. 2 vi to be aligned.

flüchten vi **(a)** aux sein (davonlaufen) to flee; (erfolgreich auch) to escape. **aus dem Land/Südafrika ~** to flee the country/from South Africa; **vor der Wirklichkeit ~** to escape reality.

(b) auch vr (vi: aux sein) (Schutz suchen) to take refuge.

Flucht-: **~fahrzeug** nt escape vehicle; (von Gesetzesbrecher) getaway vehicle; **~gefahr** f risk of escape or an escape attempt; **~geld** nt money which has been taken out of the country in order that no tax be paid on it; **~geschwindigkeit** f (Phys) escape velocity; **~helfer** m escape helper; **~hilfe** f escape aid; **~hilfe leisten** to aid an escape; **wegen ~hilfe angeklagt** charged with aiding an escape/aiding people to escape; **~hilfeorganisation** f escape organization.

flüchtig adj **(a)** (geflüchtet) fugitive. **~ sein** to be still at large; **ein ~er Verbrecher** a criminal who hasn't been caught.

(b) (kurz, schnell vorübergehend) fleeting, brief; Gruß brief. **~ erwähnen** to mention in passing.

(c) (oberflächlich) cursory, sketchy. **etw ~ lesen** to glance or skim through sth; **~ arbeiten** to work hurriedly or hastily; **jdn ~ kennen** to have met sb briefly.

(d) (Chem) volatile.

Flüchtige(r) mf decl as adj fugitive; (Ausbrecher) escaper.

Flüchtigkeit f **(a)** (Kürze) briefness, brevity. **(b)** (Oberflächlichkeit) cursoriness, sketchiness; (von Arbeit) hastiness; (~sfehler) careless mistake. **(c)** (Vergänglichkeit) fleetingness, briefness. **(d)** (Chem) volatility.

Flüchtigkeitsfehler m careless mistake; (beim Schreiben auch) slip of the pen.

Flüchtling m refugee.

Flüchtlings- in cpds refugee; siehe auch Vertriebenen-; **~ausweis** m refugee's identity card; **~hilfe** f aid to refugees; (inf: ~organisation) (refugee) relief agency; **~lager** nt refugee camp.

Flucht-: **~linie** f alignment; (einer Straße) building line; **~punkt** m vanishing point; **~verdacht** m bei **~verdacht** if an attempt to abscond is thought likely; **es besteht ~verdacht** there are grounds for suspecting that he/she etc will try to abscond; **f~verdächtig** adj suspected of planning to abscond; **~versuch** m escape attempt or bid; **~weg** m escape route.

fluchwürdig adj (liter) dastardly (old) no adv, execrable (liter).

Flug m -(e)s, :-e (alle Bedeutungen) flight; (Ski~) jump. **im ~(e)** in the air; (bei Vögeln auch) in flight, on the wing; **einen ~ antreten** to take off (nach for); **einen ~ stornieren** to cancel a booking; **der ~ zum Mond** (Fliegen) travel to the moon; (spezifische Fahrt) the moon flight or trip; **wie im ~(e)** (fig) in a twinkling or flash.

Flug-: **~abwehr** f air defence; **~abwehrkanone** f anti-aircraft gun; **~angst** f fear of flying; **~asche** f flying ashes pl; **~bahn** f (von Vogel, Flugzeug) flight path; (von Rakete, Satelliten auch, von Kugel) trajectory; (Kreisbahn) orbit; **~ball** m (Sport) high ball; (Tennis etc) volley; **~basis** f (Mil) air base; **~begleiter(in** f) m steward/stewardess or air hostess; **~benzin** nt aviation fuel; **~bereich** m operational range no pl; **f~bereit** adj ready for take-off; **~betrieb** m air traffic; **den ~betrieb auf einem Flughafen einstellen** to close an airport; **~bild** nt (Zool) flight silhouette; **~blatt** nt leaflet; (als Werbung auch) handbill; **~blattverteiler** m distributor of leaflets/handbills; **~boot** nt flying boat; **~buch** nt logbook; (von ~daten)schreiber m flight recorder; **~dauer** f flying time; **~deck** nt flight deck; **~dichte** f density of air traffic; **~dienst** m air traffic services pl; (~verkehr) air service; **~echse** f siehe **~saurier**; **~eigenschaft** f usu pl handling characteristic.

Flügel m -s, - **(a)** (Anat, Aviat) wing. **mit den ~ n schlagen** to beat or flap its wings; **einem Vogel/jdm die ~ stutzen** or **beschneiden** to clip a bird's/sb's wings; **die Hoffnung/der Gedanke verlieh ihm ~** (liter) hope/the thought lent him wings (liter).

(b) (von Hubschrauber, Ventilator) blade; (Propeller~ auch) vane; (Windmühlen~) sail, vane.

(c) (Altar~) sidepiece, wing; (Fenster~) casement (form), side; (Tür~) door (of double doors), leaf (form); (Lungen~) lung; (Nasen~) nostril.

(d) (Mil, Sport: Teil einer Truppe) wing. **über den/auf dem linken ~ angreifen** to attack up/on the left wing.

(e) (Gebäude~) wing.

(f) (Konzert~) grand piano, grand (inf). **auf dem ~ spielen** to play the piano; **am ~:** ... at or on the piano: ...

Flügel-: **~adjutant** m (Mil, Hist) aide-de-camp (often of the rank of general); **~altar** m winged altar; **~ärmel** m hanging sleeve; **~fenster** nt casement window; (Verandafenster) French window; **f~förmig** adj wing-shaped; **~haube** f pinner,

cap with upturned lappets; **~horn** nt (Mus) flugelhorn; **~klappe** f (Aviat) wing flap, aileron (spec); **f~lahm** adj with injured wings/an injured wing; (fig) Industrie etc ailing; Mensch feeble; **f~lahm sein** (lit) to have an injured wing/its wings injured; **einen Vogel f~lahm schießen** to wing a bird; **f~los** adj wingless; **~mann** m (Ftbl) wing forward, winger; (Mil) flank man; **~mutter** f wing or butterfly nut.

flügeln vt Vogel to wing.

Flügel-: **~rad** nt (Rail fig) winged wheel (symbol of the West German railways); **~roß** nt (Myth) winged horse; **~schlag** m (liter) beat of its wings; **den ~schlag der Zeit spüren** (liter) to feel the life-pulse of history; **f~schlagend** adj beating its wings; **~schraube** f (a) wing bolt; (b) siehe **~mutter**; **~spanne**, **~spannweite** f wing span; **~stürmer** m (Sport) wing forward; **~tür** f leaved door (form); (mit zwei Flügeln) double door; (Verandatür) French door.

Flug-: **~entfernung** f air or flying distance; **~erfahrung** f flying experience; **f~fähig** adj able to fly; Flugzeug (in Ordnung) airworthy; **~fähigkeit** f ability to fly; airworthiness; **~feld** nt airfield; **~frequenz** f frequency of flights; **~frosch** m flying frog; **~fuchs** m (Indian) flying fox; **~funk** m air radio; **~gast** m (airline) passenger; **~gastraum** m passenger cabin.

flügge adj fully-fledged; (fig) Jugendlicher independent. **~ werden** (lit) to be able to fly; (fig) to leave the nest.

Flug-: **~gelände** nt airfield; **~gepäck** nt baggage; **erlaubtes ~gepäck 15 Kilo** baggage allowance 15 kilos; **~gerät** nt, no pl aircraft; **~geschwindigkeit** f (von Vögeln, Insekten) speed of flight; (von Flugzeug) flying speed; (von Rakete, Geschoß, Ball) velocity; **~gesellschaft** f airline (company); **~gewicht** nt all-up weight.

Flughafen m airport; (Mil) aerodrome (Brit), airdrome (US). **der ~ Hamburg** Hamburg airport; **auf dem ~** at the airport.

Flughafen-: **~gebühr** f airport charges pl; **~gelände** nt airport grounds pl; **~steuer** f airport tax.

Flug-: **~höhe** f flying height (auch Orn); altitude; **unsere** or **die ~höhe beträgt 10.000 Meter** we are flying at an altitude of 10,000 metres; **die ~höhe erreichen** to reach one's cruising altitude or flying height; **~hörnchen** nt flying squirrel; **~hund** m flying fox; **~ingenieur** m flight engineer; **~kanzel** f cockpit; **~kapitän** m captain (of an/the aircraft); **~karte** f (a) (Luftfahrtkarte) flight or aviation chart; (b) (rare: ~schein) plane ticket; **~kilometer** m (air) kilometre; **~körper** m projectile; **ein unbekannter ~körper** an unidentified flying object, a UFO; **~korridor** m siehe Luftkorridor; **~kosten** pl flying costs pl; **~kunst** f airmanship, flying skill; **~künste** pl flying skills pl; (Kunststücke) aerobatic feats pl; **~lärm** m aircraft noise; **~lage** f flying position or attitude (spec); **~lehrer** m flying instructor; **~leitsystem** nt flight control system; **~leitung** f air-traffic or flight control; **~linie** f (a) (Strecke) airway, air route; (b) siehe **~gesellschaft**; **~loch** nt entrance hole; (bei Bienenstock) (hive) entrance; **~lotse** m air-traffic or flight controller; **~manöver** nt aerial manoeuvre; **~maschine** f (a) (Hist: ~zeug) flying machine; (b) (Theat) wires pl; **~meldedienst** m (Mil) enemy aircraft warning service; **~meteorologie** f aeronautical meteorology; **~minute** f nach fünf **~minuten** after flying for five minutes; **dreißig ~minuten von hier** thirty minutes by air from here; **~mission** f space mission; **~motor** m aircraft engine; **~netz** nt network of air routes; **~objekt** nt: **ein unbekanntes ~objekt** an unidentified flying object, a UFO; **~ordnung** f flight formation; **~passagier** m siehe **~gast**; **~personal** nt flight personnel pl; **~plan** m flight schedule; **~platz** m airfield; (größer) airport; **~post** f (dated) airmail; **~preis** m air fare; **~programm** nt schedule or programme of flights; **~prüfung** f examination for one's pilot's licence; **~reise** f flight; **eine ~reise machen** to travel by air; **ich ziehe ~reisen vor** I prefer to travel by air or to fly; **~reisende(r)** mf (airline) passenger; **~richtung** f direction of flight; **die ~richtung ändern** to change one's flight course; **~route** f air-route.

flugs [fluks] adv (dated) without delay, speedily.

Flug-: **~sand** m drifting sand; **~saurier** m pterodactyl; **die ~saurier** the pterosauria; **~schanze** f (Sport) ski-jump; **~schein** m (a) pilot's licence; (b) (~karte) plane or air ticket; **~schneise** f flight path; **~schreiber** m siehe **~(daten)schreiber**; **~schrift** f pamphlet; **~schüler** m trainee pilot; **~sicherheit** f air safety; **~sicherung** f air traffic control; **~simulator** m flight simulator; **~sport** m flying, aviation; **~staub** m flue dust; **~steig** m gate; **~strecke** f flying distance; **eine große ~strecke zurücklegen** to fly a long distance; **~stunde** f (a) flying hour; **zehn ~stunden entfernt** ten hours away by air; (b) (Unterricht) flying lesson; **f~tauglich** adj Pilot fit to fly; **~technik** f (a) aircraft engineering; (b) (~fertigkeit) flying technique; **f~technisch** adj aeronautical; Bedeutung, Entwicklung, Prinzipien auch aerotechnical; Erfahrung, Fehler flying attr; **eine f~technische Ausbildung haben** to have been trained in flying; **f~technisch ist er perfekt** his flying is perfect; **~ticket** nt plane ticket; **~touristik** f holiday air travel; **f~tüchtig** adj airworthy; **~tüchtigkeit** f airworthiness; **f~unfähig** adj unable to fly; Flugzeug (nicht in Ordnung) unairworthy; **~unterbrechung** f stop; (mit Übernachtung auch) stopover; **f~untüchtig** adj unairworthy; **~veranstaltung** f air display or show; **~verbindung** f air connection; **es gibt auch eine ~verbindung** there are flights there too; **~verbot** nt flying ban; **nachts besteht ~verbot auf dem Flughafen** the airport is closed to air traffic at night; **jdm ~verbot erlassen** to ground; (über bestimmten Gebieten) to ban from flying; **jdm ~verbot erteilen** to ground sb, to ban sb from flying; **~verkehr** m air traffic; **~versuch** m attempt to fly or at flight; **~warndienst** m siehe **~meldedienst**; **~wesen** nt, no pl aviation no art; (mit Ballons *etc*) aeronautics *sing no art*; ~**wetter** *nt* flying weather; ~**wild** *nt siehe* **Federwild**; ~**zeit** *f* flying time; ~**zettel** *m* (*Aus*) *siehe* ~**blatt**.

Flugzeug *nt* -(e)s, -e plane, aircraft, aeroplane (*Brit*), airplane (*US*); (*Düsen~ auch*) jet; (*Segel~*) glider. **im** *or* **mit dem** *or* **per ~** by air *or* plane; **ein ~ der Lufthansa** a Lufthansa plane/jet.

Flugzeug- *in cpds* aircraft; ~**abwehr** *f* (*Mil*) *siehe* **Flugabwehr**; ~**abwehrgeschütz** *nt*, ~**abwehrkanone** *f siehe* **Flugabwehrkanone**; ~**bau** *m* aircraft construction *no art*; ~**besatzung** *f* air *or* plane crew; ~**entführer** *m* (aircraft) hijacker, skyjacker (*esp US*); ~**entführung** *f* (aircraft) hijacking, skyjacking (*esp US*); ~**führer** *m* (aircraft) pilot; ~**führerschein** *m siehe* **Flugschein** (a); ~**halle** *f* (aircraft) hangar; ~**katastrophe** *f* air disaster; ~**modell** *nt* model plane; ~**park** *m* fleet of aircraft; ~**rumpf** *m* fuselage; ~**schleuder** *f* catapult; ~**start** *m* aeroplane *or* airplane (*US*) take-off; ~**träger** *m* aircraft carrier; ~**typ** *m* type of aircraft; ~**unglück** *nt* plane *or* air crash; ~**verband** *m* (*Mil*) aircraft formation; **im** ~**verband fliegen** to fly in formation; ~**wrack** *nt* **ein** ~**wrack/zwei** ~**wracks** the wreckage of a plane/two planes.

Flugziel *nt* destination.

Fluidum *nt* -s, **Fluida** (a) (*fig*) aura; (*von Städten, Orten*) atmosphere. **von ihr ging ein geheimnisvolles ~ aus** she was surrounded by an aura of mystery. (b) (*Chem*) fluid.

Fluktuation *f* fluctuation (*gen* in).

fluktuieren* *vi* to fluctuate.

Flunder *f* -, -n flounder. **da war ich platt wie eine ~** (*inf*) you could have knocked me down with a feather (*inf*).

Flunkerei *f* (*inf*) (a) (*no pl: Flunkern*) story-telling. (b) (*kleine Lüge*) story.

Flunkerer *m* -s, - (*inf*) story-teller.

flunkern (*inf*) **1** *vi* to tell stories. **2** *vt* to make up.

Flunsch *m or f* -(e)s, -e (*inf*) pout. **eine(n) ~ ziehen** *or* **machen** to pout.

Fluor[1] *nt* -s, *no pl* (*Chem*) fluorine; (~**verbindung**) fluoride.

Fluor[2] *m* -s, *no pl* (*Med*) (vaginal) discharge.

Fluoreszenz *f* fluorescence.

Fluoreszenzfarbe *f* luminous paint.

fluoreszieren* *vi* to be luminous, to fluoresce (*form*).

Fluorid *nt* -(e)s, -e (*Chem*) fluoride.

Fluorit *m* -s, -e *siehe* **Flußspat**.

Flur[1] *m* -(e)s, -e corridor; (*Haus~*) hall.

Flur[2] *f* -, -en (*liter*) (*unbewaldetes Land*) open fields *pl*; (*Wiese*) meadow, mead (*poet*); (*Agr*) agricultural land of a community. **durch Wald/Feld und ~** through woods/fields and meadows; **allein auf weiter ~ stehen** (*fig*) to be out on a limb.

Flurbeleuchtung *f* corridor/hall light/lights *pl*.

Flurbereinigung *f* reparcelling of the agricultural land of a community.

Flurfenster *nt* corridor/hall window.

Flur-: ~**form** *f* layout of the agricultural land of a community; ~**gang** *m siehe* ~**umgang**.

Flurgarderobe *f* hall-stand.

Flurhüter *m siehe* **Feldhüter**.

Flurlicht *nt* corridor/hall light.

Flur-: ~**name** *m* field-name; ~**schaden** *m* damage to an agricultural area; ~**toilette** *f* toilet on the landing; ~**tür** *f* door to the corridor; hall door.

Flur|umgang *m* (*Rel*) procession round the boundaries of a community to bless the fields and define the boundaries.

Fluse *f* -, -n (*N Ger*) bit of fluff; (*Woll~*) bobble. ~**n** fluff/bobbles.

Fluß *m* -sses, ⸚sse (a) (*Gewässer*) river. **am ~** by the river; **Stadt am ~** on the river; **unten am ~** down by the river(side); **den ~ aufwärts/abwärts fahren** to go upstream *or* upriver/downstream *or* downriver.

(b) *no pl* (*Tech: Schmelz~*) molten mass. **im ~ sein** to be molten.

(c) (*kontinuierlicher Verlauf: von Verkehr, Rede, Strom, Elektronen*) flow; (*von Verhandlungen auch*) continuity. **etw in ~** (*acc*) **bringen** to get sth moving *or* going; **etw kommt** *or* **gerät in ~** sth gets underway *or* going; (*sich verändern*) sth moves into a state of flux; **im ~ sein** (*sich verändern*) to be in a state of flux; (*im Gange sein*) to be in progress *or* going on.

Fluß- *in cpds* river; ~**aal** *m* common eel; **f~ab(wärts)** downstream, downriver; ~**arm** *m* arm of a/the river; **f~aufwärts** *adv* upstream, upriver; ~**bau** *m siehe* ~**regelung**.

Flüßchen *nt dim of* **Fluß** (a).

Fluß-: ~**diagramm** *nt* flow chart *or* diagram; ~**ebene** *f* fluvial plain; ~**eisen** *nt siehe* ~**stahl**; ~**gebiet** *nt* river basin; ~**gefälle** *nt* gradient of a/the river; ~**geschiebe** *nt, no pl* silt; ~**hafen** *m* river port.

flüssig *adj* (a) (*nicht fest*) liquid; Honig, Lack runny; (*geschmolzen*) Glas, Metall *auch* molten; Butter melted. ~**e Nahrung** *pl*, liquid food; ~ **ernährt werden** to be fed on liquids; ~ **machen** to liquefy; Glas, Metall, Wachs, Fett **to melt**; ~ **werden** to turn *or* become liquid, to liquefy; (*Lack*) to become runny; (*Glas, Metall*) to become molten; (*Wachs, Fett*) to melt.

(b) (*fließend*) Stil, Spiel flowing, fluid. ~ **lesen/schreiben/sprechen** to read/write/talk fluently; **die Polizei meldete** ~**en Verkehr** the police reported that the traffic was flowing smoothly; **den Verkehr ~ halten** to keep the traffic flowing.

(c) (*verfügbar*) Geld available. ~**es Vermögen** liquid assets *pl*; Wertpapiere ~ **machen** to convert *or* realize securities; **ich bin im Moment nicht ~** (*inf*) I haven't much money *or* I'm out of funds at the moment; **wenn ich wieder ~ bin** when I'm in funds again; **kein Geld ~ haben** to have no money available.

Flüssiggas *nt* liquid gas.

Flüssigkeit *f* (a) (*flüssiger Stoff*) liquid. (b) *no pl* (*von Metall*) liquidity; (*von Geldern*) availability; (*von Stil*) fluidity.

Flüssigkeits-: ~**aufnahme** *f* fluid *or* liquid intake; ~**bremse** *f* hydraulic brake; ~**kupplung** *f* hydraulic clutch; ~**maß** *nt* liquid measure; ~**menge** *f* quantity *or* amount of liquid; ~**presse** *f* hydraulic press.

flüssigmachen *vt sep* to realize; (*in Geld umwandeln auch*) to convert (into cash).

Fluß-: ~**krebs** *m* crayfish (*Brit*), crawfish (*US*); ~**landschaft** *f* countryside by a/the river; (*Art*) riverscape; ~**lauf** *m* course of a/the river; ~**mündung** *f* river mouth; (*Gezeiten~*) estuary; ~**niederung** *f* fluvial plain; ~**nixe** *f* river sprite; ~**pferd** *nt* hippopotamus; ~**regelung**, ~**regulierung** *f* river control *no art, no pl*; ~**sand** *m* river *or* fluvial sand; ~**schiff** *nt* river boat; ~**schiffahrt** *f, no pl* river navigation; (*Verkehr*) river traffic; ~**spat** *m* fluorspar, fluorite (*US*); ~**stahl** *m* ingot steel.

Flüster-: ~**galerie** *f*, ~**gewölbe** *nt* whispering gallery; ~**laut** *m* whisper.

flüstern *vti* to whisper; (*etwas lauter tuscheln*) to mutter. **jdm etw ins Ohr ~** to whisper sth in sb's ear; **sich ~d unterhalten** to talk in whispers; **miteinander ~** to whisper together; **es wurde viel geflüstert** there was a lot of whispering; **wer hat da geflüstert?** who was that whispering?; **das kann ich dir ~** (*inf*) take it from me (*inf*); (*Zustimmung heischend auch*) I can tell you (*inf*); **dem werde ich was ~** (*inf*) I'll tell him a thing or two (*inf*).

Flüster-: ~**parole** *f* rumour, whisper (*inf*); **die ~parole heißt: ...** the rumour *or* whisper is that ...; it's rumoured *or* whispered (that) ...; ~**propaganda** *f* underground rumours *pl*; ~**stimme** *f* whisper; **mit ~stimme sprechen** to talk in a whisper *or* in whispers; ~**ton** *m* whisper; **sich im ~ton unterhalten** to talk in whispers; **im ~ton sprechen** to talk in a whisper *or* in whispers; ~**tüte** *f* (*inf*) megaphone; ~**witz** *m* underground joke.

Flut *f* -, -en (a) (*ansteigender Wasserstand*) incoming *or* flood (*spec*) tide; (*angestiegener Wasserstand*) high tide. **es ist ~** the tide is coming in; **it's high tide, the tide's in; die ~ kommt** *or* **steigt** (*form*) the tide's coming in *or* rising; **bei ~ baden/einlaufen** to swim when the tide is coming in/to come in on the tide; **to swim/come in at high tide; mit der ~** with the tide *or* flood tide (*spec*); **die ~ tritt um 16³⁰ ein** the tide starts to come in *or* turns at 4.30 p.m.; **die ~ geht zurück** the tide has started to go out *or* has turned; *siehe* **Ebbe**.

(b) *usu pl* (*Wassermasse*) waters *pl*. **sich in die kühlen ~en stürzen** (*hum*) to plunge into the water.

(c) (*fig: Menge*) flood. **eine ~ von Tränen** floods of tears.

fluten 1 *vi aux sein* (*geh*) (*Wasser, Licht*) to flood, to stream, to pour; (*Verkehr*) to stream, to pour; (*Musik*) to flood, to pour. ~**des Licht** streaming light. **2** *vt* (*Naut*) to flood.

Flut-: ~**hafen** *m* tidal harbour; ~**katastrophe** *f* flood disaster; ~**kraftwerk** *nt siehe* **Gezeitenkraftwerk**; ~**licht** *nt* floodlight; ~**lichtspiel** *nt* match played by floodlight, floodlit match; ~**mündung** *f* estuary.

flutschen *vi* (*N Ger*) (a) *aux sein* (*rutschen*) to slide. (b) (*funktionieren*) to go smoothly *or* well *or* swimmingly (*dated inf*).

Flutwelle *f* tidal wave.

fl.W. *abbr of* **fließendes Wasser**.

focht *pret of* **fechten**.

Fock *f* -, -en (*Naut*) foresail.

Fock-: ~**mast** *m* foremast; ~**rah(e)** *f* foreyard; ~**segel** *nt siehe* **Fock**.

föderal *adj siehe* **föderativ**.

föderalisieren* *vt* to federate, to federalize.

Föderalismus *m* federalism.

Föderalist(in *f*) *m* -en, -en federalist.

föderalistisch *adj* federalist.

Föderation *f* federation.

föderativ *adj* federal.

föderieren* *vr* to federate. **föderierte Staaten** federated states.

fohlen *vi* to foal.

Fohlen *nt* -s, - foal; (*männliches Pferd auch*) colt; (*weibliches Pferd auch*) filly.

Föhn *m* -(e)s, -e foehn, föhn. **wir haben ~** the foehn is blowing.

föhnen *vi impers*: **es föhnt** the foehn is blowing.

föhnig *adj* foehn *attr*. **es ist ~** there's a foehn (wind).

Föhre *f* -, -n Scots pine (tree).

fokal *adj* focal.

Fokalinfektion *f* focal infection.

Fokus *m* -, -se focus.

fokussieren* *vti* to focus.

Folge *f* -, -n (a) (*Reihen~*) order; (*Aufeinander~*) succession; (*zusammengehörige Reihe, Math*) sequence; (*Cards*) run, sequence; (*Lieferung einer Zeitschrift*) issue; (*Fortsetzung*) instalment; (*TV, Rad*) episode; (*Serie*) series. **in chronologischer/zwangloser ~** in chronological/no particular order; **in rascher/dichter ~** in rapid *or* quick/close succession; **Musik in bunter ~** a musical potpourri; **in der** *or* **für die ~** (*form*) in future.

(b) (*Ergebnis*) consequence; (*unmittelbare ~*) result; (*Auswirkung*) effect. **als ~ davon** in consequence, as a result (of that); **dies hatte zur ~, daß ...** the consequence *or* result of this was that ...; **dies hatte seine Entlassung zur ~** this resulted in his dismissal *or* in his being dismissed; **bedenke die ~n!** think of the consequences!; **die ~n werden nicht ausbleiben** that won't be without (its) consequences; **die ~n für den Tourismus** the effect on *or* the consequences for tourism; **für die ~n aufkommen** to take the consequences; **an den ~n eines Unfalls/einer Krankheit sterben** to die as a result of an accident/illness; **das wird ~n haben** that will have serious consequences; **ohne ~n bleiben** to have no consequences; **ihr**

Verhältnis blieb nicht ohne ~n (*euph*) their relationship was not exactly unfruitful.
(c) (*form*) einem Befehl/einer Einladung ~ leisten to comply with *or* obey an order/to accept an invitation.

Folge-: ~einrichtung *f* facility *or* utility (*US*) for the community; ~erscheinung *f* result, consequence; ~lasten *pl* resultant costs *pl*.

folgen *vi aux sein* (a) to follow (*jdm/einer Sache* sb/sth). auf etw (*acc*) ~ to follow sth, to come after sth; auf jdn (im Rang) ~ to come *or* rank after sb; ~ Sie mir (bitte/unauffällig)! come with me please; es folgt nun *or* nun folgt ein Konzert we now have a concert, a concert now follows; ... dann ~ die Meldungen im einzelnen ... followed by the news in detail; dem (*liter*) *or* auf den Sommer folgt der Herbst summer is followed by autumn, autumn follows summer; Fortsetzung folgt (to be) continued; wie folgt as follows; *siehe* Tod.
(b) (*verstehen*) to follow (*jdm/einer Sache* sb/sth). können Sie mir ~? are you with me? (*inf*), do you follow (me)?
(c) (*gehorchen*) to do as *or* what one is told. einem Befehl/einer Anordnung~ to follow an order/instruction; jdm ~ (*inf*) to do what sb tells one.
(d) +*dat* (*sich richten nach*) einer Mode, einem Vorschlag to follow; jdm to agree with, to go along with (*inf*).
(e) (*hervorgehen*) to follow (*aus* from). was folgt daraus für die Zukunft? what are the consequences of this for the future?

folgend *adj* following. ~es the following; er schreibt ~es *or* das F~e he writes (as follows *or* the following); im ~en in the following; (*schriftlich auch*) below; es handelt sich um ~es the matter is this.

folgendermaßen, folgenderweise (*rare*) *adv* like this, as follows. wir werden das ~ machen we'll do it like this *or* in the following way.

Folgen-: f~los *adj* without consequences; (*wirkungslos*) ineffective; f~los bleiben not to have any consequences; to be ineffective; das konnte nicht f~los bleiben that was bound to have serious consequences/could not fail to be effective; f~reich *adj* (*bedeutsam*) momentous; (*f~schwer*) of serious consequences; (*wirkungsvoll*) effective; f~schwer *adj* of serious consequence; ~schwere *f* seriousness.

Folge-: ~problem *nt* resultant problem; die ~probleme einer Sache (*gen*) the problems arising from *or* out of sth; f~recht (*rare*), f~richtig *adj* (logically) consistent; die einzig ~richtige in dieser Situation the only logical *or* consistent thing to do in this situation; ~richtigkeit *f* logical consistency.

folgern 1 *vti* to conclude. aus diesem Brief läßt sich ~, daß ... it can be concluded *or* we can conclude from this letter that ... 2 *vi* to draw a/the conclusion. logisch ~ lernen to learn to think logically.

Folgerung *f* conclusion. daraus ergibt sich die ~, daß ... from this it can be concluded that ...

Folge-: ~satz *m* (*Gram*) consecutive clause; ~tonhorn *nt* (*Aus*) *siehe* Martinshorn; f~widrig *adj* (*geh*) logically inconsistent; ~widrigkeit *f* (*geh*) logical inconsistency; ~zeit *f* following period, period following.

folglich *adv, conj* consequently, therefore.

Folgsam *adj* obedient.

Folgsamkeit *f* obedience.

Foliant *m* folio (volume); (*dicker Band*) tome.

Folie ['foːliə] *f* (a) (*Plastik~*) film; (*Metall~, Typ*) foil; (*Schicht*) layer of film/foil. eine ~ aus Kupfer a thin layer of copper. (b) (*fig: Hintergrund*) background.

Folien ['foːliən] *pl of* Folie, Folio.

Folio *nt* -s, -s *or* **Folien** folio.

Folklore *f* -, *no pl* folklore; (*Volksmusik*) folk music.

Folklorist(in *f*) *m* folklorist.

folkloristisch *adj* folkloric; *Kleidung* ethnic.

Folksänger *m* folk singer.

Folksong *m* folk song.

Follikel *m* -s, - follicle.

Follikelsprung *m* ovulation.

Folter *f* -, -n (a) (*lit, fig*) torture; (*fig auch*) torment. die ~ anwenden to use torture; das ist die reinste ~ (*fig*) that's sheer torture. (b) (*old:* ~bank) rack. jdn auf die ~ spannen (*fig*) to keep sb on tenterhooks, to keep sb in an agony of suspense.

Folterbank *f* rack.

Folterer *m* -s, - torturer.

Folter-: ~gerät, ~instrument *nt* instrument of torture; ~kammer *f*, ~keller *m* torture chamber; ~knecht *m* torturer; ~methode *f* method of torture.

foltern 1 *vt* to torture; (*quälen auch*) to torment. jdn ~ lassen to have sb tortured. 2 *vi* to use torture.

Folterqual *f* (*lit*) agony of torture; (*fig*) agony of torment.

Folterung *f* torture.

Folterwerkzeug *nt* instrument of torture.

Fön ® *m* -(e)s, -e hair-dryer.

Fond [fõː] *m* -s, -s (a) (*geh: Wagen~*) back, rear. (b) (*Hintergrund*) (*Art*) background; (*Tex*) (back)ground. im ~ der Bühne (*Theat*) at the back of the stage. (c) (*geh: Basis*) foundation (*zu* for). (d) (*Cook: Fleischsaft*) meat juices *pl*.

Fondant [fõˈdãː] *m or* (*Aus*) *nt* -s, -s (*Cook*) fondant.

Fonds [fõː] *m* -, - (a) (*Geldreserve, fig geh*) fund. keinen ~ für etw haben to have no funds for sth. (b) (*Fin: Schuldverschreibung*) government bond.

Fonds-: [fõː]: (*Fin*) ~börse *f*, ~geschäft *nt* market of government bonds.

Fondue [fõˈdyː] *nt* -s, -s *or f* -, -s fondue.

fönen *vt* to dry.

Fono- *siehe* Phono-.

Fontäne *f* -, -n jet, fount (*poet*); (*geh: Springbrunnen*) fountain, fount (*poet*).

Fontanelle *f* -, -n (*Anat*) fontanelle.

foppen *vt* (*inf*) jdn ~ to make a fool of sb; (*necken*) to pull sb's leg (*inf*); er fühlte sich gefoppt he felt he'd been made a fool of.

Fopperei *f* (*inf*) leg-pulling *no pl* (*inf*).

Fora (*Hist*) *pl of* Forum.

forcieren* [forˈsiːrən] *vt* to push; *Entwicklung auch, Tempo* to force; *Konsum, Produktion* to push *or* force up. seine Anstrengungen ~ to increase one's efforts.

forciert [forˈsiːrt] *adj* forced.

Förde *f* -, -n firth (*esp Scot*), narrow coastal inlet.

Förder-: ~anlage *f* conveyor; ~band *nt* conveyor belt.

Förderbetrag *m* (*Univ*) grant.

Förderbetrieb *m* (*Min*) production. den ~ aufnehmen to start production.

Förderer *m* -s, -, **Förderin** *f* sponsor; (*Gönner*) patron.

Förderklasse *f* (*Sch*) special class.

Förder- (*Min*): ~kohle *f* run of mine (coal), through-and-through coal (*Brit*); ~korb *m* mine cage.

Förderkurs(us) *m* (*Sch*) special classes *pl*.

Förderleistung *f* (*Min*) output.

förderlich *adj* beneficial (*dat* to). guten Beziehungen/jds Gesundung/der Krebsbekämpfung ~ sein to be conducive to *or* to promote good relations/to aid sb's recovery/to contribute to *or* to help in the fight against cancer; ein der Weiterbildung ~er Kursus a course which contributes to one's further education.

Fördermaschine *f* winding engine.

fordern 1 *vt* (a) (*verlangen*) to demand; *Preis* to ask; (*in Appell, Aufrufen etc, erfordern*) to call for; (*Anspruch erheben auf*) *Entschädigung, Lohnerhöhung* to claim. viel/zuviel von jdm ~ to ask *or* demand a lot/too much of sb, to make too many demands on sb; haben Sie von mir noch etwas zu ~? have I any more claims to settle?; jdn vor Gericht ~ to summon sb to court; *siehe* Rechenschaft.
(b) (*fig: kosten*) Menschenleben, Opfer to claim.
(c) (*lit, fig: herausfordern*) to challenge. er ist noch nie im Leben richtig gefordert worden he has never been faced with a real challenge.
(d) (*Sport*) to make demands on; (*das Äußerste abverlangen*) to stretch.
2 *vi* to make demands. er fordert nur, ohne selbst zu geben he demands everything as a right, without giving anything himself.

fördern *vt* (a) (*unterstützen*) *Handel, Projekt, Entwicklung, Arbeit, Kunst, Wissenschaft* to support; (*propagieren*) to promote; (*finanziell*) *bestimmtes Projekt* to sponsor; *Nachwuchs, Künstler* to support, to help; *jds Talent, Kunstverständnis, Neigung* to encourage, to foster; (*voranbringen*) *Freundschaft, Frieden* to foster, to promote; *Verdauung* to aid; *Appetit* to stimulate; *Untersuchung, Wahrheitsfindung* to further. jdn beruflich ~ to help sb in his career.
(b) (*steigern*) *Wachstum* to promote; *Umsatz, Absatz, Produktion, Verbrauch auch* to boost, to increase.
(c) *Bodenschätze* to extract; *Kohle, Erz auch* to mine.

fordernd *adj* imperious.

Förder- (*Min*): ~schacht *m* winding shaft; ~seil *nt* winding rope; ~sohle *f* haulage level.

Förderstufe *f* (*Sch*) *mixed ability class(es) intended to foster the particular talents of each pupil.*

Förderturm *m* (*Min*) winding tower; (*auf Bohrstelle*) derrick.

Forderung *f* (a) (*Verlangen*) demand (*nach* for); (*Lohn~, Entschädigungs~ etc*) claim (*nach* for); (*in Appell, Aufrufen etc*) call (*nach* for). ~en/hohe ~en an jdn stellen to make demands on sb/to demand a lot of sb; die Kinder heutzutage stellen nur ~en children today demand everything as of right; eine ~ nach etw erheben to call for sth; jds ~ *or* jdm eine ~ erfüllen to meet sb's demands/claim.
(b) (*geh: Erfordernis*) requirement. die ~ des Tages sein to be the/our etc number one priority.
(c) (*Comm: Anspruch*) claim (*an* +*acc, gegen* on, against). eine ~ einklagen/eintreiben *or* einziehen to sue for payment of a debt/to collect a debt.
(d) (*Herausforderung*) challenge.

Förderung *f* (a) *siehe* fördern (a) support; promotion; sponsorship; support, help; encouragement, fostering; fostering; promotion; aid; stimulation; furtherance. Maßnahmen zur ~ des Fremdenverkehrs measures to promote tourism *or* for the promotion of tourism.
(b) (*inf: Förderungsbetrag*) grant.
(c) (*Gewinnung*) extraction; (*von Kohle, Erz auch*) mining.

Förderungs-: ~maßnahme *f* supportive measure; ~maßnahmen *pl* assistance *sing*; ~mittel *pl* aid *sing*; ~programm *nt* aid programme; f~würdig *adj* (*unterstützungswürdig*) deserving aid; (*f~berechtigt*) entitled to aid; (*Univ*) eligible for a grant.

Förder|unterricht *m* special instruction.

Förderwagen *m* (*Min*) tram, mine car.

Forehand ['foːhænd] *f* -, -s (*Sport*) forehand.

Forelle *f* trout; *siehe* blau.

Forellen-: ~teich *m* trout hatchery; ~zucht *f* trout farming; (*Anlage*) trout farm.

Foren *pl of* Forum.

forensisch *adj* *Medizin* forensic; (*old: rhetorisch*) oratorical.

Forke *f* -, -n (*N Ger*) pitch fork.

Form *f* -, -en (a) form; (*Gestalt, Umriß*) shape. in ~ von Regen/Steuerermäßigungen in the form of rain/tax reductions; in ~ von Dragees/Salbe in pill/cream form, in the form of pills/cream; in ~ eines Dreiecks shaped like *or* in the shape of a triangle; eine bestimmte ~ haben to be in a certain form; to be a certain shape; seine ~ verlieren/aus der ~ geraten to lose its

shape; (*Kleidung auch*) to go out of shape; **einer Sache** (*dat*) ~ **(und Gestalt) geben** (*lit*) to shape sth; (*fig*) to give sth a coherent shape; **Sie müssen Ihr Gesuch in die geeignete ~ kleiden** your application must be in the proper form; **feste ~ annehmen** (*fig*) to take shape; **häßliche/gewalttätige ~en annehmen** (*fig*) to become ugly/violent; **(weibliche) ~en** feminine figure; *siehe* **bringen.**
  (b) (*Gestaltung*) form. **~ und Inhalt** form and content.
  (c) (*Umgangs~en*) **~en** *pl* manners *pl*; **die ~ wahren** to observe the proprieties; **der ~ wegen** *or* **halber, um der ~ zu genügen** for form's sake, as a matter of form; **in aller ~** formally; **ein Mann mit/ohne ~en** a well-/ill-mannered gentleman.
  (d) (*Kondition*) form. **in bester ~ sein** to be in great form *or* shape; **in ~ bleiben/kommen** to keep/get (oneself) fit *or* in condition; (*Sportler*) to keep/get in form; **hoch in ~** in great form *or* shape; **außer ~** out of condition.
  (e) (*Gieß~*) mould; (*Kuchen~, Back~*) baking tin (*Brit*) or pan (*US*); (*Hut~, Schuh~*) block.
formal *adj* **(a)** formal. **~-ästhetisch** formal aesthetic. **(b)** (*äußerlich*) *Besitzer, Fehler, Grund* technical.
Formal|ausbildung *f* drill.
Formaldehyd *m* -s, *no pl* formaldehyde.
Formalie [-liə] *f usu pl* formality; (*Äußerlichkeit*) technicality.
Formalin ® *nt* -s formalin.
formalisieren* *vt* to formalize.
Formalismus *m* formalism *no pl*.
Formalist(in *f*) *m* formalist.
formalistisch *adj* formalistic.
Formalität *f* formality; (*Äußerlichkeit*) technicality. **alle ~en erledigen** to go through all the formalities.
formaliter *adv* (*geh*) in form; (*äußerlich*) technically.
formal-: **~juristisch, ~rechtlich** *adj* technical.
Formans *nt* -, **-manzien** [-tsiən] *or* **-zie** [-tsiə] (*Ling*) formative (element).
Format *nt* -(e)s, -e **(a)** (*Größenverhältnis*) size; (*von Zeitung, Papierbogen, Photographie, Buch, Film*) format. **im ~ Din A4** in A4 (format). **(b)** (*Rang, Persönlichkeit*) stature. **(c)** (*fig: Niveau*) class (*inf*), quality. **internationales ~ haben** to be of international quality.
Formation *f* formation; (*Gruppe*) group. **die Panzer schlossen zur ~ auf** the tanks closed into formation.
Formationsflug *m* (*Mil*) formation flying.
formativ *adj* formative.
Formativ *nt* -s, -e (*Ling*) syntactic morpheme; (*Formans*) formative (element).
Form-: **f~bar** *adj* (*lit, fig*) malleable; **~barkeit** *f* (*lit, fig*) malleability; **f~beständig** *adj* **(a)** **f~beständig sein** to hold *or* retain its shape; **(b)** (*Sport*) consistent in form; **~blatt** *nt* form; **~eisen** *nt* structural steel.
Formel *f* -, -n formula; (*von Eid etc*) wording; (*Floskel*) set phrase. **etw auf eine ~ bringen** to reduce sth to a formula.
Formel-1-Rennen ['fɔrmlʔains-] *nt* formula-one race/racing.
Form|element *nt* (*esp Art*) formal element, element of form.
Formel-: **f~haft** *adj* **(a)** (*floskelhaft*) *Sprache, Stil* stereotyped; **f~hafte Wendung** set phrase; **f~haft reden** to talk in set phrases; **(b)** (*als ~*) formulistic; **etw f~haft zusammenfassen** to summarize sth in a formula; **~haftigkeit** *f* **(a)** stereotyped nature; (*einer Wendung*) setness; **(b)** formulism; **~kram** *m* (*pej*) tiresome formulae *pl*.
formell *adj* müssen. **als Bürgermeister mußte er den Vorfall ~ verurteilen** as mayor he had to deplore the incident as a matter of form.
Formel-: **~sammlung** *f* (*Math*) formulary; **~sprache** *f* system of notation.
formen **1** *vt* to form, to shape; *Charakter auch, Eisen* to mould; *Wörter* to articulate. **schön geformte Glieder** beautifully shaped limbs; **der Krieg hat ihn geformt** the war shaped his character; **~de Kraft** formative power.
  2 *vr* (*lit*) to form *or* shape itself; (*fig*) to mature.
Formen-: **~fülle** *f* wealth of forms; **~lehre** *f* morphology; (*Mus*) theory of musical form; **f~reich** *adj* with a great variety *or* wealth of forms; **f~reich sein** to have a great variety *or* wealth of forms; **~reichtum** *m* wealth of forms; **~sinn** *m* sense of *or* feeling for form; **~sprache** *f* (*geh*) use of forms.
Former(in *f*) *m* moulder.
Formerei *f* moulding shop.
Form-: **~fehler** *m* irregularity; (*gesellschaftlich*) breach of etiquette; **~gebung** *f* (*geh*) design; **~gefühl** *nt* sense of form; **f~gerecht** *adj* (*lit, fig*) correct, proper; **~gestalter** *m* (*geh*) designer; **~gestaltung** *f* design; **f~gewandt** *adj* urbane, suave.
formidabel *adj* (*dated*) formidable.
formieren* **1** *vt Truppen* to draw up; *Kolonne, Zug* to form (into), to fall into; (*bilden*) to form. **formierte Gesellschaft** (*dated*) aligned society. **2** *vr* to form up.
Formierung *f* formation; (*Mil: von Truppen*) drawing-up.
-förmig *adj suf* -shaped.
Formkrise *f* (*esp Sport*) loss of form.
förmlich *adj* **(a)** (*formell*) formal. **(b)** (*regelrecht*) positive. **ich hätte ~ weinen können** I really could have cried.
Förmlichkeit *f* **(a)** *no pl* (*Benehmen*) formality. **(b)** *usu pl* (*Äußerlichkeit*) social convention. **bitte keine ~en!** please don't stand on ceremony.
formlos *adj* **(a)** (*ohne Form*) shapeless; *Vortrag, Aufsatz auch* unstructured. **(b)** (*zwanglos*) informal, casual. **(c)** (*Admin*) *Antrag* unaccompanied by a form/any forms.
Formlosigkeit *f* **(a)** (*Gestaltlosigkeit*) shapelessness, lack of shape; (*von Vortrag, Aufsatz auch*) lack of structure. **(b)** (*Zwanglosigkeit*) informality, casualness.
Form-: **~sache** *f* matter of form, formality; **f~schön** *adj* elegant, elegantly proportioned; **~schönheit** *f* elegant

proportions *pl*, elegance; **~strenge** *f* strict observance of form; **~tief** *nt* loss of form; **sich in einem ~tief befinden** to be badly off form; **f~treu** *adj siehe* **f~beständig.**
Formular *nt* -s, -e form.
formulieren* **1** *vt* to word, to phrase, to formulate. **... wenn ich es mal so ~ darf** ... if I might put it like that. **2** *vi* to use words skilfully. **..., wie der Kanzler formulierte** ... as the chancellor put it; **wenn ich mal so ~ darf** if I might put it like that.
Formulierung *f* **(a)** *no pl* wording, phrasing, formulation. **(b)** phraseology *no pl*. **eine bestimmte ~** a particular phrase.
Formung *f* **(a)** *no pl* (*Formen*) forming, shaping; (*von Eisen*) moulding; (*von Charakter auch*) moulding, formation; (*von Wörtern*) articulation. **zur ~ muß das Eisen erhitzt werden** the iron has to be heated before it can be moulded. **(b)** (*Form*) shape; (*von Felsen, Dünen etc auch*) formation.
Form-: **~veränderung** *f* change in the form; (*einer Sprache*) change in the forms; (*Gestaltveränderung*) change in the shape; **eine kleine ~veränderung am Protokoll** a change in protocol; **eine kleine ~veränderung vornehmen** to make a small modification; **~verstoß** *m* breach of form; **ein ~verstoß gegen das Protokoll** a breach of form *or* etiquette; **f~vollendet** *adj* perfect; *Vase etc* perfectly shaped; *Gedicht, Musikstück* perfectly structured; **er verabschiedete/verneigte sich f~vollendet** he took his leave/bowed with perfect elegance; **~vorschrift** *f* formal requirement; **f~widrig** *adj* incorrect; (*Admin, Jur*) irregular; *Urkunde* incorrectly drawn up; **~wille** *m* (*geh*) striving for form.
forsch *adj* brash; (*dated: schneidig*) dashing. **eine Sache ~ anpacken** to attack sth energetically *or* with vigour.
forschen **1** *vi* **(a)** (*suchen*) to search (*nach* for), to seek (*liter*) (*nach jdm/etw* sb/sth). **in alten Papieren ~** to search in old papers; **nach der Wahrheit ~** to seek *or* search after truth. **(b)** (*Forschung betreiben*) to research. **über etw** (*acc*) **~** to research on *or* into sth. **2** *vt* (*Sw*) *siehe* **erforschen (b).**
forschend *adj* inquiring; (*musternd*) searching.
Forscher *m* -s, - **(a)** (*Wissenschaftler*) researcher; (*in Medizin, Naturwissenschaften*) research scientist. **(b)** (*Forschungsreisender*) explorer.
Forscher-: **~arbeit** *f siehe* **Forschungsarbeit;** **~blick** *m, no pl* (*geh*) scientific eye; **~drang** *m* (*geh*) (*des Wissenschaftlers*) thirst for knowledge; (*des Forschungsreisenden*) urge to explore; **~geist** *m* (*geh*) inquiring mind; (*Entdeckungsreisender*) explorer; (*Entdeckergeist*) exploratory spirit; **der Mensch in seinem angeborenen ~geist ist bestrebt, ... man, with his inquiring mind, strives ...**
Forscherin *f siehe* **Forscher.**
forscherisch *adj* (*als Wissenschaftler*) research *attr*; (*als Forschungsreisender*) explorative, exploratory. **eine ~ Höchstleistung** a triumph for research/exploration; **sich ~ betätigen** to be engaged in research/exploration.
forscherlich *adj attr* scholarly.
Forschheit *f siehe* **forsch** brashness; dash.
Forschung *f* **(a)** *research no pl*. **eingehende ~en** intensive research; **ältere/verschiedene ~en** older/various studies; **~en betreiben** to research, to be engaged in research. **(b)** *no pl* (*Wissenschaft*) research *no art*. **~ und Lehre** research and teaching.
Forschungs- *in cpds* research; **~arbeit** *f, no pl* research; **~aufgabe** *f* research assignment; (*~auftrag eines Wissenschaftlers*) research duty; **~auftrag** *m* research assignment *or* contract; **~ballon** *m* observation balloon; **~bereich** *m siehe* **~gebiet;** **~bericht** *m* report of an/the inquiry; **~ergebnis** *nt* result of the research; **neueste ~ergebnisse** results of the latest research; **~gebiet** *nt* field of research; **ein/das ~gebiet der Medizin** a/the field of medical research; **~gegenstand** *m* object of research; **~gemeinschaft** *f* research council; **~methode** *f* method of research; **~ministerium** *nt* ministry of research and development; **~objekt** *nt siehe* **~gegenstand;** **~reise** *f* expedition; **~reisende(r)** *mf decl as adj* explorer; **~schiff** *nt* research vessel; **~semester** *nt* sabbatical term; **~station** *f* research station; **~tätigkeit** *f* research *no indef art*; **~vorhaben** *nt* research project; **~zentrum** *nt* research centre; **~zweig** *m* branch of research.
Forst *m* -(e)s, -(e)n forest.
Forst-: **~akademie** *f* school of forestry; **~amt** *nt* forestry office; **~assessor** *m graduate forestry official who has completed the probationary period*; **~beamte(r)** *m* forestry official.
forsten *vt* (*form*) to forest.
Förster(in *f*) *m* -s, - forest warden *or* ranger (*US*).
Försterei *f* forest warden's *or* ranger's (*US*) lodge.
Forst-: **~frevel** *m* (*Jur*) offence against the forest laws; **~haus** *nt* forester's lodge; **~meister** *m* forestry commissioner, chief (forest) ranger (*US*); **~recht** *nt* forest law; **~revier** *nt* forestry district; **~schaden** *m* forest damage *no pl*; **~schädling** *m* forest pest; **~schule** *f* school of forestry; **~verwaltung** *f* forestry commission; **~wesen** *nt* forestry *no art*; **~wirt** *m* graduate in forestry; **~wirtschaft** *f* forestry; **~wissenschaft** *f* forestry science.
Forsythie [fɔr'zy:tsiə, *Aus* fɔr'zy:tiə] *f* -, -n forsythia.
Fort [fɔrt] *nt* -s, -s fort.
fort *adv* **(a)** (*weg*) away; (*verschwunden*) gone. **~ mit ihm/damit!** away with him/it!, take him/it away!; **... und dann ~!** ... and then away with you/we'll get away; **etw ist ~** sth has gone *or* disappeared; **es war plötzlich ~** it suddenly disappeared; **die Katze ist schon seit gestern ~** the cat has been missing since yesterday; **er ist ~** he has left *or* gone; (*dial: ist nicht zu Hause*) he isn't here; **weit ~** far away, a long way away; **von zu Hause ~ away** from home; **wann sind Sie von zu Hause ~?** (*dial*) when did you leave home?; **nur ~ von hier!** (*geh*) let us begone (*old*)

~ **von hier!** (geh) begone! (old), hence! (old).
  (b) (weiter) on. **und so** ~ and so on, and so forth; **das ging immer so weiter und so** ~ **und so** ~ (inf) that went on and on and on; **in einem** ~, ~ **und** ~ (old) incessantly, continually.
fort- pref in cpd vbs (weg) away.
Fort-: f~**ab** (rare), f~**an** (geh) adv from this time on, henceforth (old, liter), henceforward (old); f~**begeben*** vr sep irreg (geh) to depart, to leave; **sich aus dem Schloß etc** f~**begeben** to depart from (form) or to leave the castle etc; ~**bestand** m, no pl continuance; (von Staat, Institution) continued existence; f~**bestehen*** vi sep irreg to continue; (Staat, Institution) to continue in existence; (Zustand) to continue (to exist); f~**bewegen*** sep 1 vt to move away; 2 vr to move; ~**bewegung** f, no pl locomotion; ~**bewegungsmittel** nt means of locomotion; f~**bilden** vt sep jdn/sich f~**bilden** to continue sb's/one's education; ~**bildung** f, no pl further education; **berufliche** ~**bildung** further vocational training; ~**bildungskurs(us)** m further education/vocational training course; f~**bleiben** vi sep irreg to stay away; ~**bleiben** nt -s, no pl absence; f~**bringen** vt sep irreg to take away; (zur Reparatur, Reinigung etc) to take in; **Brief, Paket etc** to post; (zurückbringen) to take back; (bewegen) to move; **sie war vom Fenster nicht** f~**zubringen** she wouldn't move from the window; ~**dauer** f continuance, continuation; f~**dauern** vi sep to continue; f~**dauernd** **1** adj continuing; (in der Vergangenheit) continued; **2** adv constantly, continuously.
forte adv (Mus, Pharm) forte.
Forte nt -s, -s or **Forti** forte.
Fort-: f~**eilen** vi sep (geh) to hurry or hasten away; f~**entwickeln*** sep 1 vt to develop; 2 vr to develop; ~**entwicklung** f, no pl development; f~**existieren*** vi sep siehe f~**bestehen**; f~**fahren** sep 1 vi aux sein **(a)** (wegfahren) to leave, to go; (einen Ausflug machen) to go away; (abfahren) to leave, to go; **(b)** (weitermachen) to continue; f~**fahren, etw zu tun** to continue doing sth or to do sth; **in einer Tätigkeit** f~**fahren** to continue with an activity; **ich fahre** f~ **...** as I was about to say ...; 2 vt (wegbringen) to take away; **Wagen** to drive away; ~**fall** m discontinuance; **in** ~**fall kommen** (form) to be discontinued; f~**fallen** vi sep irreg aux sein to cease to exist; (nicht mehr zutreffend sein) to cease to apply; (Zuschuß etc) to be discontinued or stopped; (abgeschafft werden) to be abolished; f~**fliegen** vi sep aux sein to fly away or off; f~**führen** sep 1 vt **(a)** (fortsetzen) to continue, to carry on; **(b)** (wegführen) to take away; (zu Fuß, fig) to lead away; 2 (fig) to lead away; ~**führung** f continuation; ~**gang** m, no pl **(a)** (Weggang) departure (aus from); **bei/nach seinem** ~**gang** when he left/after he had left, on/after his departure; **(b)** (Verlauf) progress; **seinen** ~**gang nehmen** to progress; f~**gehen** vi sep aux sein **(a)** to leave; **von zu Hause** f~**gehen** to leave home; **geh** ~**/nicht** ~**!** away/don't go (away)!; **(b)** siehe weitergehen; f~**geschritten** **1** ptp of f~**schreiten**; **2** adj advanced; **zu** f~**geschrittener Stunde wurden sie fröhlich** as the night wore on they got quite merry; **er kam zu** f~**geschrittener Stunde** he came at a late hour; ~**geschrittenenkurs(us)** m advanced course; ~**geschrittene(r)** mf decl as adj advanced student; f~**gesetzt** **1** ptp of f~**setzen**; **2** adj continual, constant, incessant; **Betrug, Steuerhinterziehung** repeated; f~**hin** adv (dated) from this time on, henceforth (old, liter), henceforward (old).
Forti pl of **Forte**.
Fortifikation f (old Mil) fortification.
fortissimo nt -s, -s or -**tissimi** fortissimo. **im** ~ **spielen** to play fortissimo.
Fort-: f~**jagen** sep 1 vt **Menschen** to throw out (aus, von of); **Tier, Kinder** to chase out (aus, von of); 2 vi aux sein to race or career off; f~**kommen** vi aux sein **(a)** (wegkommen) to get away; (weggebracht werden) to be taken away; **mach, daß du** f~**kommst!** begone! (old), be off!; **wie kommen wir hier bloß** f~**?** how on earth do we get away from here?; **(b)** (abhanden kommen) to disappear, to vanish; **mir ist schon wieder die Brille** f~**gekommen** my glasses have vanished or disappeared or gone again; **(c)** (vorankommen) to get on well; **im Leben** f~**kommen** to get on in life or the world; ~**kommen** nt **(a)** (lit, fig: Weiterkommen) progress; **jdn am** ~**kommen hindern** to hold sb back, to hinder sb's progress; **(b)** (Auskommen) **sein** ~**kommen finden** to find a means of earning one's living; f~**können** vi sep irreg to be able to get away; f~**lassen** vt sep (a) (weggehen lassen) **jdn** f~**lassen** to let sb go, to allow sb to go; **(b)** (auslassen) to leave out, to omit; f~**laufen** vi sep aux sein to run away; **der Hund/meine Freundin ist mir** f~**gelaufen** the dog has run away from me/my girlfriend has (gone off and) left me; f~**laufend** adj **Handlung** ongoing no adv; **Erscheinen** serial attr; **Zahlungen** regular; (andauernd) continual; **die Handlung geht** f~**laufend weiter** the storyline unfolds steadily; f~**laufend numeriert Geldscheine, Motoren** serially numbered; **Bücher, Zeitschriften** consecutively paginated; f~**leben** vi sep (liter) to live on; **ein** ~**leben nach dem Tode** a life after death, an after-life, a hereafter (liter); f~**locken** vt sep to lure away; f~**machen** sep (inf) **1** vr to clear out or off (inf); 2 vi aux sein (wegziehen) to move; **(b)** siehe weitermachen; f~**müssen** vi sep irreg to have to go or leave; (ausgehen müssen) to have to go out; **Brief** to have to go (off); f~**nehmen** vt sep irreg to take away (jdm from sb); **hat jemand meinen Ring** f~**genommen?** has somebody taken my ring?; f~**pflanzen** vr sep (Mensch) to reproduce; (Pflanzen auch) to propagate (itself); (Schall, Wellen, Licht) to travel, to be transmitted; (Gerücht) to spread.
Fortpflanzung f -, no pl reproduction; (von Pflanzen) propagation.
Fortpflanzungs-: f~**fähig** adj capable of reproduction; **Pflanze** capable of propagation; ~**geschwindigkeit** f (Phys) speed of propagation; ~**organ** nt reproductive organ; ~**trieb** m

reproductive instinct; f~**unfähig** adj incapable of reproduction; **Pflanze** incapable of propagation; ~**werkzeug** nt siehe ~**organ**.
Fort-: f~**räumen** vt sep (lit, fig) to clear away; f~**reisen** vi sep aux sein to go away; f~**reißen** vt sep irreg to snatch or tear away; (Menge, Flut, Strom) to sweep or carry away; (fig) to carry away; **jdn/etw mit sich** f~**reißen** (lit) to carry or sweep sb/sth along; (fig) to carry sb/sth away; **das Publikum zu heller Begeisterung** f~**reißen** to rouse the audience to a frenzy of enthusiasm; f~**rennen** vi sep irreg aux sein to race or tear (inf) off or away; f~**rücken** sep 1 vt to move away; 2 vi aux sein to move away; ~**satz** m (Anat) process; f~**schaffen** vt sep to remove; f~**scheren** vr sep (inf) to clear off (aus out of) or out (aus of) (inf); f~**schicken** vt sep to send away; **Brief etc** to send off; f~**schleppen** sep 1 vt to drag away; (fig) **Fehler, Traditionen** to perpetuate; 2 vr to drag oneself along; (fig) **Fehler, Traditionen** to be perpetuated; (Beziehung, Unterhaltung) to limp along; f~**schreiben** vt sep irreg **(a)** **Statistik etc** to extrapolate; **(b)** (weiterführend aktualisieren) **Programm etc** to continue; ~**schreibung** f siehe vt extrapolation; continuation; f~**schreiten** vi sep irreg aux sein (vorwärtsschreiten) to progress; (weitergehen) to continue; (Entwicklung, Sprache) to develop; (Wissenschaft) to advance; (Zeit) to go or march (liter) on; **die Ausbreitung der Epidemie schreitet weiter** f~ the epidemic is continuing to spread; **siehe auch** f~**geschritten;** f~**schreitend** adj progressive; **Alter, Wissenschaft** advancing.
Fortschritt m advance; (esp Pol) progress no pl. **gute** ~**e machen** to make good progress, to get on (inf) or progress well; ~**e erzielen** to make progress; ~**e in der Medizin** advances in medicine; **das ist ein wesentlicher** ~ that's a considerable step forward or improvement; **dem** ~ **dienen** to further progress.
fortschrittlich adj progressive (auch Pol); **Mensch, Ideen** auch forward-looking.
Fortschrittlichkeit f progressiveness.
Fortschritts-: ~**fanatiker** m fanatical progressive; f~**feindlich** adj anti-progressive; ~**feindlichkeit** f anti-progressiveness; ~**glaube** m belief in progress; f~**gläubig** adj f~**gläubig sein** to believe in progress; **das** f~**gläubige 19. Jh.** the 19th century with its belief in progress; ~**gläubigkeit** f naïve belief in progress; ~**optimismus** m belief in progress.
Fort-: f~**sehnen** vr sep to long or yearn to be away (aus from); f~**setzen** sep 1 vt to continue; (nach Unterbrechung auch) to resume; **den Weg zu Fuß** f~**setzen** to continue on foot; „**wird** f~**gesetzt**" "to be continued"; 2 vr (zeitlich) to continue; (räumlich) to extend; ~**setzung** f **(a)** no pl (Fortsetzen) continuation; (nach Unterbrechung auch) resumption; **(b)** (folgender Teil) (Rad, TV) episode; (eines Romans) instalment; **ein Film in drei** ~**setzungen** a film in three parts; „~**setzung folgt**" "to be continued"; **(c)** (anschließendes Stück) continuation; ~**setzungsroman** m serialized novel, novel in serial form; f~**stehlen** vr sep irreg (geh) to steal or slip away; **sich aus etw** f~**stehlen** to steal or slip out of sth; f~**streben** vi sep (geh) to attempt or try to get away (aus from); f~**stürzen** vi sep aux sein (geh) to rush off or away; (Pferd) to bolt; f~**treiben** sep irreg 1 vt **(a)** (verjagen) to drive away; **jdn aus dem Haus** f~**treiben** to drive sb out of the house; **(b)** (weitertragen) to carry away; (fig: weitermachen) to go or keep or carry on with; **wenn er es weiter so** f~**treibt wie bisher** ... if he goes or keeps or carries on as he has been (doing) ...; 2 vi aux sein to be carried away.
Fortuna f - (Myth) Fortuna; (fig) Fortune.
Fortune ['fɔ:tju:n] (geh), **Fortüne** f -, no pl good fortune. **politische** ~ **haben** to have good fortune in politics; **keine** ~ **haben** to have no luck.
fort-: ~**währen** vi sep (geh) to continue, to persist; ~**während** adj no pred constant, continual, incessant; ~**wälzen** sep 1 vt to roll away; **mit sich** ~**wälzen** to carry away (with it); 2 vr to roll on; ~**weg** [-vek] adv (rare) the whole time, all the time; **er hat** ~**weg geschwatzt** he was chattering the whole time or all the time; ~**wirken** vi sep to continue to have an effect; **das wirkt noch bis heute** ~ that still has an effect today; **das Gesehene wirkte noch lange in ihm** ~ what he had seen affected him or went on having an effect on him for a long time; **das** F~**wirken klassischer Ideale** the continued effect of classical ideals; ~**wollen** vi sep to want to get away (aus from); ~**zeugen** vi sep (liter) to continue to have an effect; ~**ziehen** sep irreg 1 vt **(a)** to pull away; (mit großer Anstrengung) to drag away; (Strom, Strudel) to carry away; **er zog den widerstrebenden Hund mit sich** ~ he dragged or pulled the unwilling dog along or off or away; 2 vi aux sein **(a)** (weiterziehen) to move on; (Vögel) to migrate; **(b)** (von einem Ort) to move away (aus from); (aus einer Wohnung) to move out (aus of).
Forum nt -s, **Foren** or (Hist) **Fora** forum. **etw vor das** ~ **der Öffentlichkeit bringen** to bring sth before the forum of public opinion.
Forums-: ~**diskussion** f, ~**gespräch** nt forum (discussion).
Forward ['fɔ:twəd] m -(s), -s (esp Aus Ftbl) forward.
Forz m -es, -e (dial inf) siehe **Furz**.
fossil adj attr fossil attr, fossilized.
Fossil nt -s, -ien [iən] fossil.
fötal adj foetal.
Föten pl of **Fötus**.
Foto[1] nt -s, -s photo(graph), snap(shot) (inf).
Foto[2] m -s, -s (dial inf) camera.
Foto- in cpds (Sci) photo; siehe auch Photo-; ~**ecke** f corner; ~**finish** nt (Sport) photo finish.
fotogen adj photogenic.
Fotograf m -en, -en photographer.
Fotografie f siehe **Photographie**.
fotografieren* vti siehe **photographieren**.

fotografisch *adj siehe* **photographisch**.

Foto-: ~**labor** *nt* darkroom; ~**material** *nt* photographic materials *pl*; ~**modell** *nt* photographic model; ~**papier** *nt* photographic paper; ~**satz** *m* (*Typ*) *siehe* **Lichtsatz**.

Fotothek *f* -, -en photographic collection.

Fötus *m* -, **Föten** *or* -ses, -se foetus.

Fotze *f* -, -n (a) (*vulg*) cunt (*vulg*). (b) (*sl: S Ger, Aus*) (*Maul*) cakehole (*sl*), gob (*sl*); (*Ohrfeige*) box on the ears, clip round the ear.

Fötzel *m* -s, - (*Sw*) scoundrel, rogue.

fotzen *vt* (*sl: S Ger, Aus: ohrfeigen*) jdn ~ to box sb's ears.

Fotzhobel *m* (*inf: S Ger, Aus*) mouth-organ.

foul [faul] *adj* (*Sport*): ~ **spielen** to foul; **das war aber** ~ (*inf*) that was a foul.

Foul [faul] *nt* -s, -s (*Sport*) foul.

Foulelfmeter [ˈfaul-] *m* (*Ftbl*) penalty (kick).

foulen [ˈfaulən] *vti* (*Sport*) to foul. **es wurde viel gefoult** there was a lot of fouling.

Foulspiel [ˈfaul-] *nt* (*Sport*) foul play.

Fourage [fuˈraːʒə] *f* -, *no pl siehe* **Furage**.

Fox *m* -(es), -e, **Foxterrier** *m* fox-terrier.

Foxtrott *m* -s, -e *or* -s foxtrot.

Foyer [foaˈjeː] *nt* -s, -s foyer; (*in Hotel auch*) lobby, entrance hall.

Fr. *abbr of* **Frau**.

Fracht *f* -, -en (a) (*Ladung*) freight *no pl*; (*von Flugzeug, Schiff auch*) cargo; (*Güter auch*) payload. **etw per** ~ **schicken** to send sth freight, to freight sth. (b) (~*preis*) freight *no pl*, freightage *no pl*; (*bei Lastwagen*) carriage *no pl*; (~*tarif*) freight/carriage rate.

Fracht-: ~**brief** *m* consignment note, waybill; ~**dampfer** *m* (*dated*) cargo *or* freight steamer.

frachten *vt* to freight; (*Schiff*) (*laden*) to load; (*befördern*) to carry.

Frachtenbahnhof *m* (*Aus*) *siehe* **Güterbahnhof**.

Frachter *m* -s, - freighter.

Fracht-: ~**flugzeug** *nt* cargo *or* freight plane, (air) freighter; f~**frei** *adj* carriage paid *or* free; ~**führer** *m* (*form*) carrier; ~**geld** *nt* freight, freightage; (*bei Lastwagen*) carriage; ~**gut** *nt* (ordinary) freight *no pl*; **etw als** ~**gut schicken** to send sth freight *or* as ordinary freight; ~**kosten** *pl* freight charges *pl*; ~**raum** *m* hold; (*Ladefähigkeit*) cargo space; ~**schiff** *nt* cargo ship, freighter; ~**schiffahrt** *f* cargo shipping; ~**sendung** *f* freight load; (*Aviat, Naut*) cargo *or* freight; **als** ~**sendung** (as) freight; ~**tarif** *m* freight rate *or* charge; ~**verkehr** *m* goods traffic; ~**zettel** *m siehe* **Frachtbrief**.

Frack *m* -(e)s, -s (*inf*) *or* ̈-e (a) tails *pl*, tail coat. **im** ~ in tails. (b) (*inf: Jacke*) jacket. **jdm den** ~ **vollhauen** (*inf*) to dust sb's jacket (*inf*).

Frack-: ~**hemd** *nt* dress shirt; ~**hose** *f* dress trousers *pl*; ~**jacke** *f* tails *pl*, tail coat; ~**sausen** *nt*: ~**sausen haben** (*inf*) to be in a funk (*inf*); ~**schoß** *m* coat-tail; ~**verleih** *m* dress hire (service); ~**weste** *f* waistcoat *or* vest (*US*) worn with tails; ~**zwang** *m* requirement to wear tails; (**es herrscht**) ~**zwang** tails are obligatory, you have to wear tails; „~**zwang**" "tails".

Frage *f* -, -n question; (*Rück~, Zwischen~ auch*) query; (*Problem auch*) problem; (*Angelegenheit auch*) matter, issue (*esp Pol*). **eine** ~ **zu etw a** question on sth; **jdm eine** ~ **stellen, an jdn eine** ~ **stellen** *or* **richten** to ask sb a question; **an jdn eine** ~ **haben** to have a question for sb; **gestatten Sie mir eine** ~? (*form*) might I ask a question?; (*in Diskussionen auch*) permit me to ask you a question (*form*); **auf eine** ~ **mit Ja oder Nein antworten** to answer a question with a straight yes or no; **sind noch** ~**n?, hat jemand noch eine** ~? does anyone have *or* are there any more *or* any further questions?; **auf eine dumme** ~ (**bekommt man**) **eine dumme Antwort** (*prov*) ask a silly question (get a silly answer) (*prov*); **die deutsche** ~ the German question *or* issue; **das ist** (**doch sehr**) **die** ~ that's (just *or* precisely) the question/problem, that's the whole question/problem; **das ist die große** ~ that's the big *or* sixty-four thousand dollar (*inf*) question; **das ist gar keine** ~, **das steht** *or* **ist außer** ~ there's no question *or* doubt about it; **daß ..., steht** *or* **ist außer** ~ that ... is beyond question, ..., there's no question *or* doubt about it; **ohne** ~ without question *or* doubt; **in** ~ **kommen** to be possible; **sollte er für diese Stelle in** ~ **kommen, ...** if he should be considered for this post ...; **für jdn/etw nicht in** ~ **kommen** to be out of the question for sb/sth; **das kommt** (**überhaupt**) **nicht in** ~! that's (quite) out of the question!; **in** ~ **kommend** possible; *Bewerber* worth considering; **eine** ~ **der Zeit/des Geldes** a question *or* matter of time/money.

-frage *f in cpds* question of; (*Problem auch*) problem of. **die ...** ~ the ... question/problem, the question/problem of ...; (*Angelegenheit auch*) the ... issue.

Frage-: ~**bogen** *m* questionnaire; (*Formular*) form; ~**fürwort** *nt* interrogative pronoun.

fragen 1 *vti* to ask. **nach** *or* **wegen** (*inf*) **jdm** ~ to ask after sb; (*in Hotel etc*) to ask for sb; **ich fragte sie nach den Kindern** I asked her how the children were doing; **nach jds Namen/Alter/dem Weg** ~ to ask sb's name/age/the way; **nach Arbeit/Post** ~ to ask whether there is/was any work/mail; **nach den Ursachen** ~ to inquire as to the causes; **ich fragte sie nach ihren Wünschen** I asked her what she wanted; **ich habe nicht nach Einzelheiten gefragt** I didn't ask any details; **nach den Folgen** ~ to bother *or* care about the consequences; **er fragte nicht danach, ob ...** he didn't bother *or* care whether ...; **wegen etw** ~ to ask about sth; **frag** (**mich/ihn**) **lieber nicht** I'd rather you didn't ask (that), you'd better not ask (him) that; **das frage ich dich!** I could ask you the same; **da fragst du noch?** you still have to ask?, you still don't know?; **frag nicht so dumm!** don't ask silly questions; **du fragst zuviel** you ask too many questions; **da fragst du mich**

zuviel (*inf*) I really couldn't say; **man wird ja wohl noch** ~ **dürfen** (*inf*) I was only asking (*inf*), there's no law against asking, is there? (*inf*); **wenn ich** (**mal**) ~ **darf?** if I may *or* might ask?; **ohne lange zu** ~ without asking a lot of questions.

2 *vr* to wonder. **das/da frage ich mich** I wonder; **das frage ich mich auch** that's just what I was wondering; **ja, das fragt man sich** yes, that's the question; **es/man fragt sich, ob ...** it's debatable *or* questionable/one wonders whether ...; **da muß man sich** ~, **ob ...** you can't help wondering if ...; **ich frage mich, wie/wo ...** I'd like to know how/where ..., I really wonder how/where ...

fragend *adj* questioning, inquiring; (*Gram*) interrogative.

Fragen-: ~**komplex, ~kreis** *m* complex of questions.

Frager(in *f*) *m* -s, - questioner. **wer ist denn der lästige** ~? who is this wretched person who keeps asking questions?

Fragerei *f* questions *pl*.

Frage-: ~**satz** *m* (*Gram*) interrogative sentence/clause; ~**steller(in** *f*) *m* -s, - questioner; (*Interviewer*) interviewer; ~**stellung** *f* (a) formulation of a question; **das ist eine falsche** ~**stellung** the question is wrongly put *or* stated *or* formulated; (b) (*Frage*) question; ~**stunde** *f* (*Parl*) question time; ~**und-Antwort-Spiel** *nt* question and answer game; ~**wort** *nt* interrogative (particle); ~**zeichen** *nt* question mark (*auch fig*), interrogation mark *or* point (*form*); **hinter diese Behauptung muß man ein dickes** *or* **großes** ~**zeichen setzen** (*fig*) this statement should be taken with a large pinch of salt; **dastehen/dasitzen wie ein** ~**zeichen** to slouch.

fragil *adj* (*geh*) fragile.

Fragilität *f, no pl* (*geh*) fragility.

fraglich *adj* (a) (*zweifelhaft*) uncertain; (*fragwürdig*) doubtful, questionable. (b) *attr* (*betreffend*) in question; *Angelegenheit* under discussion. **zu der** ~**en Zeit** at the time in question.

Fraglichkeit *f, no pl siehe adj* (a) uncertainty; doubtfulness.

fraglos *adv* undoubtedly, unquestionably.

Fragment *nt* fragment. ~ **bleiben** to remain a fragment.

fragmentarisch *adj* fragmentary. **die Manuskripte sind nur** ~ **erhalten** only fragments of the manuscript have been preserved.

fragwürdig *adj* (a) doubtful, dubious. (b) (*pej*) *Lokal, Mensch, Kreise* dubious.

Fragwürdigkeit *f siehe adj* doubtful *or* dubious nature, doubtfulness; dubiousness, dubious nature.

fraise [ˈfrɛːzə] *adj inv* (*Aus Fashion*) strawberry(-coloured).

Fraisen [ˈfraɪzən] *pl* (*Aus Med*) **die** ~ (infant) spasms *pl*.

Fraktion *f* (a) (*Pol*) = parliamentary *or* congressional (*US*) party; (*von mehreren Parteien*) = coalition party; (*Sondergruppe*) group, faction. (b) (*Aus: Ortsteil*) area. (c) (*Chem*) fraction.

fraktionell [fraktsioˈnɛl] *adj* (*Pol*) ~**entschieden** decided by the parliamentary *etc* party; ~**e Gruppen** factions within the parliamentary *etc* party.

fraktionieren* [fraktsioˈniːrən] *vt* (*Chem*) to fractionate.

Fraktions- *in cpds* (*Pol*) party; ~**bildung** *f* formation of factions/a faction; ~**führer** *m* party whip; f~**los** *adj* independent; ~**mitglied** *nt* member of a parliamentary *etc* party; ~**sitzung** *f* party meeting; ~**spaltung** *f* party split; (*auf Dauer*) split into two parties; ~**stärke** *f* (a) numerical strength of a/the parliamentary *etc* party; (b) (*erforderliche Mitgliederzahl*) numerical strength required for recognition of a parliamentary party; ~**vorsitzende(r)** *mf* party whip; ~**vorstand** *m* party executive; ~**zwang** *m* requirement to vote in accordance with party policy; **unter** ~**zwang stehen** to be under the whip.

Fraktur *f* (a) (*Typ*) Gothic print, Fraktur. (**mit jdm**) ~ **reden** (*inf*) to be blunt (with sb). (b) (*Med*) fracture.

Frakturschrift *f* Gothic script.

Franc [frãː] *m* -, -s franc.

frank *adv*: ~ **und frei** frankly, openly.

Frankatur *f* franking.

Franke *m* -n, -n (*Geog*) Franconian; (*Hist*) Frank.

Franken[1] *nt* -s Franconia.

Franken[2] *m* -s, - (**Schweizer**) ~ (Swiss) franc.

Frankfurt *nt* -s ~ (**am Main**) Frankfurt (on the Main); ~ (**Oder**) Frankfurt on the Oder.

Frankfurter *m* -s, - (a) (*Einwohner Frankfurts*) Frankfurter. (b) (*inf: Würstchen*) frankfurter.

frankfurterisch (*inf*), **frankfurtisch** *adj* Frankfurt *attr*. **er spricht F~** he speaks the Frankfurt dialect.

frankieren* *vt* to stamp; (*mit Maschine*) to frank.

Frankiermaschine *f* franking machine.

Frankierung *f* franking; (*Porto auch*) postage.

Fränkin *f* Franconian (woman).

fränkisch *adj* Franconian.

Fränkler *m* -s, -, **Fränkli** *nt* -s, - (*inf*) (*Sw*) franc (piece).

franko *adj inv* (*Comm*) carriage paid; (*von Postsendungen*) post-free, postpaid (*esp US*).

Franko-: ~**kanadier** *m* French-Canadian; f~**kanadisch** *adj* French-Canadian; ~**manie** *f* (*geh*) Francomania; f~**phil** *adj* (*geh*) Francophile; ~**philie** *f* Francophilia; f~**phob** *adj* (*geh*) Francophobe; ~**phobie** *f* Francophobia; f~**phon** *adj* francophone.

Frankreich *nt* France.

Franktireur [frãtiˈrøːɐ] *m* -s, -e (*old*) franc-tireur.

Fränschen [ˈfrɛnsçən] *nt dim of* **Franse**.

Franse *f* -, -n (*lose*) (loose) thread; (*von Haar*) strand of hair. ~**n** (*als Besatz, Pony*) fringe; **ein mit** ~**n besetzter Schal** a shawl with a fringe, a fringed shawl; **sich in** ~**n auflösen** to fray (out).

fransen *vi* to fray (out).

fransig *adj* (*Sew*) fringed *no adv*; *Haar* straggly *no adv*; (*ausgefasert*) frayed *no adv*.

Franz¹ m -' or -ens Francis; (bei Deutschen) Franz.
Franz² nt - (Sch inf) French.
Franz-: ~band m leather binding; ein ~band-Buchrücken a leather spine; ~branntwein m alcoholic liniment.
Franziskaner m -s, - (Eccl) Franciscan (friar).
Franziskanerin f (Eccl) Franciscan (nun).
Franziskaner|orden m (Eccl) Franciscan Order, Order of St. Francis.
Franzmann m, pl **Franzmänner** (dated sl) Frenchie (inf), frog (pej inf).
Franzose m -n, -n (a) Frenchman/French boy. er ist ~ he's French; die ~n the French. (b) (Werkzeug) adjustable spanner, monkey wrench.
Franzosen-: f~feindlich adj anti-French; ~krankheit f (old) French disease (old), syphilis.
Französin f (a) Frenchwoman/French girl. sie ist ~ she's French. (b) (euph) prostitute who does oral sex or blow-jobs (sl).
französisch adj French. die ~e Schweiz French-speaking Switzerland; die F~e Revolution the French Revolution; die ~e Krankheit (old) the French disease (old), syphilis; ~es Bett divan bed; ~e Spielkarten ordinary playing cards; ~ kochen to do French cooking; sich (auf) ~ empfehlen to leave without saying goodbye; sich (auf) ~ Abschied nehmen to leave without saying good-bye/paying; (sich unerlaubt entfernen) to take French leave; siehe auch deutsch.
Französisch(e) nt decl as adj French; siehe Deutsch(e).
französisieren* vt to Gallicize, to Frenchify.
frappant adj (geh) Schnelligkeit, Entdeckung remarkable, astounding; Verbesserung, Wirkung, Ähnlichkeit auch striking. auf jdn ~ wirken to astound sb.
frappieren* 1 vt (verblüffen) to astound, to astonish, to amaze. 2 vi (Sache) to be astounding or astonishing. er hat immer wieder frappiert he continually astounded or amazed us/them.
frappierend adj siehe frappant.
Fräse f -, -n (a) (Werkzeug) milling cutter; (für Holz) moulding cutter; (Boden~) rotary hoe. (b) (Bart) chinstrap (beard).
fräsen vt to mill, to mill-cut; Holz to mould.
Fräser m -s, - (a) (Beruf) milling cutter. (b) (Maschinenteil) milling cutter; (für Holz) moulding cutter.
Fräsmaschine f milling machine.
fraß pret of **fressen.**
Fraß m -es, -e (a) food; (pej inf) muck (inf) no indef art. etw einem Tier zum ~ vorwerfen to feed sth to an animal; jdn den Kritikern zum ~ vorwerfen to throw sb to the critics. (b) (Abfressen) vom ~ befallen eaten away.
Frater m -s, **Fratres** (Eccl) Brother.
Fraternisation f fraternization.
fraternisieren* vi to fraternize.
Fraternisierung f fraternization.
Fratz m -es, -e or (Aus) -en, -en (a) (pej) brat. (b) (schelmisches Mädchen) rascal, scallywag (inf).
Frätzchen nt dim of Fratz, Fratze.
Fratze f -, -n (a) grotesque face. (b) (Grimasse) grimace; (inf: Gesicht) face, phiz (dated inf); (fig: Zerrbild) caricature. jdm eine ~ schneiden to pull or make a face at sb; eine ~ ziehen, das Gesicht zu einer ~ verziehen to pull or make a face, to grimace.
fratzenhaft adj grotesque.
Frau f -, -en (a) (weiblicher Mensch) woman. zur ~ werden to become a woman; von ~ zu ~ woman to woman; Unsere Liebe ~ (Eccl) our blessed Lady, the blessed Virgin.
(b) (Ehe~) wife. sich (dat) eine ~ nehmen (dated) to marry, to take a wife (old); willst du meine ~ werden? will you marry me?, will you be my wife?; jdn zur ~ haben to be married to sb; seine zukünftige/geschiedene ~ his bride-to-be/ ex-wife; die junge ~ (dated) the son's wife/the daughter-in-law.
(c) (Anrede) madam; (mit Namen) Mrs; (für eine unverheiratete ~) Miss, Ms (feministisch). liebe ~! (dated) my dear lady!; ~ Doktor/Direktor doctor/headmistress; Ihre (liebe) ~ Mutter/Schwester your good mother/sister; ~ Nachbarin (old) neighbour (old).
Frauchen nt dim of Frau (inf) (a) (Koseform für eine Ehefrau) little woman. (b) (Herrin von Hund) mistress. geh zum ~ go to your mistress.
Frauen- in cpds women's; (einer bestimmten Frau) woman's; (Sport auch) ladies'; ~arbeit f (a) (Arbeit für Frauen, von Frauen) female or women's labour; das ist keine ~arbeit that's no job for a woman; niedrig bezahlte ~arbeit badly paid jobs for women; (b) (Arbeit zugunsten der Frau) work among women; in der ~arbeit tätig sein to be involved in work among women; ~art f: nach ~art (dated) as women do; ~arzt m gynaecologist; ~bad nt spa where the waters cure women's illnesses; ~beruf m career for women; ~beschäftigung f use of female labour; ~bewegung f women's (auch Hist) or feminist movement; ~chor m ladies' or female choir; ~emanzipation f female emancipation no art, emancipation of women; (in der heutigen Zeit auch) women's lib(eration); ~fachschule f domestic science college; ~feind m misogynist; f~feindlich adj anti-women pred; Mensch, Verhalten auch misogynous; ~frage f question of women's rights; f~freundlich adj pro-women pred; ~funk m woman's radio, = Woman's Hour (Brit); ~gefängnis nt women's prison; ~geschichte f affair with a woman; ~geschichten (Affären) womanizing; (Erlebnisse) sexploits pl (hum inf), experiences with women pl; ~gestalt f female figure; (Liter, Art) female character; ~haar nt (a) woman's hair; (b) (Bot) maidenhair (fern); f~haft adj womanly no adv; ~hand f: von (zarter) ~hand by a woman's fair hand; ~hasser m -s, - misogynist, woman-hater; ~heilkunde f gynaecology; ~held m lady-killer; ~herz nt heart of a woman; ~herzen (Frauen) the fair sex; ~kenner m connoisseur of

women; ~kleider pl women's clothes pl or clothing sing; ~klinik f gynaecological hospital or clinic; ~kloster nt convent, nunnery (old); ~krankheit f, ~leiden nt gynaecological disorder; **Facharzt für ~krankheiten und Geburtshilfe** gynaecologist and obstetrician; ~mantel m (Bot) lady's mantle; ~mörder m murderer of women/a woman; ~orden m (Eccl) women's order; ~rechtlerin f feminist; (in der heutigen Zeit auch) Women's Libber (inf); f~rechtlerisch adj feminist; sich f~rechtlerisch betätigen to be involved in women's rights or (in der heutigen Zeit auch) Women's Lib; ~schänder m -s, - rapist; ~schuh m no pl (Bot) lady's slipper no pl.
Frauens-: ~leute pl (hum inf) womenfolk pl; ~person f female person; (hum inf) female (inf), broad (US inf).
Frauen-: ~sport m women's sport; ~station f women's ward; ~stimme f women's voice; (Parl) woman's vote; ~stimmen women's voices/votes; ~stimmrecht nt siehe ~wahlrecht; ~tausch m wife-swapping; (Anthropologie) exchange of partners; ~tum nt, no pl (geh) womanhood, femininity; ~typ m (a) feminine type (of woman); mütterlicher ~typ motherly type of woman; (b) (inf) ladies' man; ~überschuß m surplus of women; ~verband, ~verein m women's association or society; ~wahlrecht nt vote for women, female suffrage no art; ~zeitschrift f women's magazine; ~zimmer nt (old, dated) woman; (hum) woman, female (inf), broad (US inf).
Fräulein nt -s, - or -s (a) (unverheiratete weibliche Person) young lady. ein altes or älteres ~ an elderly spinster.
(b) (Anrede) Miss. Ihr ~ Tochter/Braut your daughter/bride.
(c) (weibliche Angestellte) young lady; (Verkäuferin auch) assistant; (Kellnerin) waitress; (dated: Lehrerin) teacher, mistress. ~! Miss!; (Kellnerin auch) waitress!; das ~ vom Amt (dated) the operator, the switchboard girl.
fraulich adj feminine; (reif) womanly no adv.
Fraulichkeit f, no pl siehe adj femininity; womanliness.
frech adj (a) (unverschämt) cheeky (esp Brit), fresh pred (esp US), impudent; Lüge brazen, bare-faced no adv. ~ werden to get cheeky etc; werd' (mir) nicht ~ don't (you) get cheeky etc with me; jdm ~ kommen to get cheeky etc with sb; sich ~ benehmen to be cheeky etc; halt deinen ~en Mund! (you) shut up and stop being cheeky etc; ~ wie Oskar (inf) or wie ein Spatz sein (inf) to be a cheeky little devil (Brit inf), to be a little monkey.
(b) (herausfordernd) Kleidung etc saucy (inf), cheeky (Brit inf).
Frechdachs m (inf) cheeky monkey (Brit inf) or devil (Brit inf), monkey.
Frechheit f (a) no pl (Verhalten) impudence; (esp von Kindern auch) cheekiness (esp Brit). das ist der Gipfel der ~ that's the height of impudence; die ~ haben or besitzen, ... zu ... to have the cheek (esp Brit) or nerve (inf) or impudence to ...; die ~ zu weit treiben to be a bit too cheeky (esp Brit) or fresh (esp US).
(b) (Äußerung, Handlung) piece or bit of cheek (esp Brit) or impudence. sich (dat) einige ~en erlauben to be a bit cheeky (esp Brit) or fresh (esp US); solche ~en what cheek (esp Brit) or impudence.
Frechling m (dated inf) cheeky devil (Brit inf), little monkey.
Freesie ['fre:ziə] f freesia.
Fregatte f frigate.
Fregattenkapitän m commander.
Fregattvogel m frigate-bird.
frei adj (a) (uneingeschränkt, unbehindert) free; Blick clear. ~e Rhythmen free verse; ~e Hand haben to have a free hand; jdm ~e Hand lassen to give sb free rein or a free hand; aus ~er Hand or aus der ~en Hand or ~ Hand zeichnen to draw freehand; jdm zur ~en Verfügung stehen to be completely at sb's disposal; das ~e Spiel der Kräfte the free play of forces; aus ~en Stücken or ~em Willen of one's own free will; das Recht der ~en Rede the right of free speech or to freedom of speech; ~ schalten und walten to do what one wants or pleases; ~ nach ... based on ...; ~ nach Goethe (Zitat) as Goethe didn't say; ich bin so ~ (form) may I?; von Kiel nach Hamburg hatten wir ~e Fahrt we had a clear run from Kiel to Hamburg; einem Zug ~e Fahrt geben to give a train the "go" signal; der Polizist gab uns ~e Fahrt the policeman signalled us on; das Signal zeigte or stand auf „F~e Fahrt" the signal was at clear or "go"; für etw ~e Fahrt geben (fig) to give sth the go-ahead or green light; die Straße ~ machen to clear the road; der ~e Fall (Phys) free fall; ~er Durchgang thoroughfare; ~er Zutritt entry; ~er Zugang unlimited or unrestricted access; der Film ist ~ (für Jugendliche) ab 16 (Jahren) the film may be seen by people over (the age of) 16; ~es Geleit safe conduct; auf ~er Wildbahn in its natural surroundings or habitat; auf ~em Fuß sein, ~ herumlaufen (inf) to be free, to be running around free (inf); jdn auf ~en Fuß setzen to set sb free; sich von etw ~ machen to rid oneself of or free oneself from sth; ~ von etw free of sth; siehe frank, Lauf.
(b) (unabhängig) free; Schriftsteller etc freelance; (nicht staatlich) private. ~er Beruf independent profession; ~er Mitarbeiter sein to be freelance; als ~er Mitarbeiter arbeiten to work freelance; ~er Mitarbeiter freelance collaborator; ~er Markt open market; ~e Marktwirtschaft free-market or open market economy; die ~e Wirtschaft private enterprise; in die ~e Wirtschaft gehen to go into industry; ~ machen to have a liberating effect; Jesus macht ~ Jesus makes you free or gives you freedom; ~e Reichsstadt (Hist) free city of the Empire; F~e und Hansestadt Hamburg/F~e Hansestadt Bremen Free Hansa Town of Hamburg/Bremen; F~er Deutscher Gewerkschaftsbund (DDR) Free German Trades Union Congress; F~e Deutsche Jugend (DDR) Free German Youth; F~e Demokratische Partei (BRD) Free Democratic Party.

(c) (*ohne Hilfsmittel*) *Rede* extemporary. **das Kind kann ~ stehen** the child can stand on its own *or* without any help; **~ schwimmen** to swim unaided *or* on one's own; **~ in der Luft schweben** to hang in mid-air; **ein Vortrag in ~er Rede** a talk given without notes, an extempory talk; **~ sprechen** to speak extempore *or* without notes, to extemporize.

(d) (*verfügbar*) *Mittel, Geld* available; *Zeit, Mensch* free. **morgen/Mittwoch ist ~** tomorrow/Wednesday is a holiday; **einen Tag ~ nehmen/haben** to take/have a day off; **Herr Mayer ist jetzt ~** Mr Mayer is free now; **ich bin jetzt ~ für ihn** I can see him now; **Fräulein, sind Sie noch ~?** (*dated form*) are you still not spoken for? (*dated*); **fünf Minuten ~ haben** to have five minutes (free).

(e) (*unbesetzt*) *Zimmer, Toilette* vacant, empty; *Platz* free; *Stelle* vacant, free; *Taxi* for hire, free. **ist hier** *or* **ist dieser Platz noch ~?** is anyone sitting here?, is this anyone's seat?, is this seat taken *or* free?; **„~"** (*an Taxi*) "for hire"; (*an Toilettentür*) "vacant", **„Zimmer ~"** "vacancies"; **haben Sie noch etwas ~?** do you have anything?; (*in Hotel*) have you got any vacancies *or* any rooms left *or* free?; (*in Restaurant*) do you have a table (free)?; **eine Stelle wird ~** a position is becoming vacant, a vacancy is arising; **einen Platz ~ machen** (*aufstehen*) to vacate a seat; (*leerräumen*) to clear a seat; **für etw Platz ~ lassen/machen** to leave/make room *or* space for sth; **eine Wohnung ~ machen** to vacate a flat; **einen Platz für jdn ~ lassen** to leave a seat for sb; *siehe* **Bahn, Ring.**

(f) (*offen*) open. **unter ~em Himmel** in the open (air), out of doors, outdoors; **im ~en Raum** (*Astron*) in (outer) space; **eine Frage/Aussage im ~en Raum stehenlassen** to leave a question/statement hanging (in mid-air *or* in the air); **auf ~er Strecke** (*Rail*) between stations; (*Aut*) on the road; **~ stehen** (*Haus*) to stand by itself; **~ stehen** *or* **sein** (*Sport*) to be free *or* not marked; *siehe* **Freie.**

(g) (*kostenlos*) free. **Eintritt ~** admission free; **~ Grenze** free frontier; *siehe* **Haus.**

(h) (*unkonventionell*) free, liberal. **sie benimmt sich etwas zu ~** she's rather free in her behaviour.

(i) (*unbekleidet*) bare. **sich ~ machen** to take one's clothes off, to strip; **~ lassen** to leave bare.

(j) (*ungeschützt*) *Autor* out of copyright. **seit die Rechte an Karl May ~ geworden sind** since Karl May's books have been out of copyright.

Frei-: **~anlage** *f* (*im Zoo*) outdoor *or* open-air enclosure; (*Sport*) sports ground *pl*, playing fields *pl*; (*Park*) park grounds *pl*; **~bad** *nt* open-air (swimming) pool, lido; **~ballon** *m* free balloon; **~bank** *f* stall *or* shop selling substandard meat; **f~bekommen*** *vt sep irreg* (a) (*befreien*) **jdn f~bekommen** to get sb freed *or* released; **etw f~bekommen** to get sth free, to free sth; (b) **einen Tag/eine Woche f~bekommen** to get a day/a week off; **~berufler(in** *f*) *m* **-s, -** self-employed person; **f~beruflich** *adj* self-employed; **f~beruflich arbeiten** to be self-employed; **~betrag** *m* tax allowance; **~beuter** *m* **-s, -** pirate, buccaneer, freebooter (*old*); (*fig*) exploiter; **ein literarischer ~beuter** a literary pirate; **~beuterei** *f* piracy, buccaneering, freebooting (*old*); (*fig*) exploitation; **literarische ~beuterei** literary piracy; **f~beweglich** *adj* free-moving; **~bier** *nt* free beer; **f~bleibend** *adj* subject to alteration; **~bord** *m* (*Naut*) freeboard; **f~brief** *m* (a) (*Hist*) (*Privileg*) royal charter; (*~lassung*) letter of manumission; (b) (*fig*) licence; **~deck** *nt* uncovered level (*of multistorey car park*); **~denker** *m* freethinker; **f~denkerisch** *adj* freethinking; **~denkertum** *nt* freethinking *no art*.

Freie *nt* **-n, *no pl*** **das ~** the open (air); **im ~n** in the open (air); **ins ~ gehen** to go outside *or* into the open (air); **ins ~ gelangen** to get out; **im ~n übernachten** to sleep out in the open.

freien (*old*) **1** *vt* to wed (*old, liter*). **2** *vi* **um ein Mädchen ~** to woo (*old*) *or* court (*dated*) a girl; **jung gefreit hat nie gereut** (*Prov*) marry young and you'll never regret it.

Freie(r) *mf decl as adj* (*Hist*) freeman.

Freier *m* **-s, -** (a) (*dated, hum*) suitor. (b) (*inf: von Dirne*) (prostitute's) client, john (*US inf*).

Freiersfüße *pl*: **auf ~n gehen** (*hum*) to be courting (*dated*).

Frei-: **~exemplar** *nt* free copy; **~fahrschein** *m* free ticket; **~fahrt** *f* free journey; **~fahrt haben** to travel free; **~fläche** *f* open space; **~flug** *m* free flight; **~frau** *f* baroness (*by marriage*); **~fräulein** *nt* baroness (*in her own right*); **~gabe** *f siehe* *vt* release; decontrol, lifting of controls (*gen on*); opening; passing; putting back into play; **f~geben** *sep irreg* **1** *vt* to release (*an + acc* to); *Gefangene, Ehepartner auch* to set free; *Preise* to decontrol, to lift controls on; *Straße, Strecke, Flugbahn* to open; *Film* to pass; (*Ftbl*) *Ball* to put back into play; **etw zum Verkauf f~geben** to allow sth to be sold on the open market; **jdm den Weg f~geben** to let sb past *or* by; **2** *vi* **jdm f~geben** to give sb a holiday; **jdm zwei Tage f~geben** to give sb two days off; **f~gebig** *adj* generous; (*iro auch*) free, liberal; **~gebigkeit** *f* generosity; (*iro*) liberalness; **~gehege** *nt* open-air *or* outdoor enclosure; **~geist** *m* freethinker; **f~geistig** *adj* freethinking; **~gelände** *nt* open-air exhibition ground; **~gelassene(r)** *mf decl as adj* (*Hist*) freedman; freedwoman; **~gepäck** *nt* baggage allowance; **~gericht** *nt* (*Hist*) Vehmgericht; **~graf** *m* (*Hist*) Vehmic judge; **~grenze** *f* (*bei Steuer*) tax exemption limit; **f~haben** *vi sep irreg* to have a holiday; **ich habe heute/zwei Tage f~** I have today/two days off; **eine Stunde/die sechste Stunde f~haben** (*Sch*) to have a free period/have the sixth period free; **er hat mittags eine Stunde f~** he has an hour free at midday; **~hafen** *m* free port; **f~halten** *sep irreg* **1** *vt* (a) (*nicht besetzen*) to keep free *or* clear; (b) (*reservieren*) to keep, to save; (c) (*jds Zeche begleichen*) to pay for; **sich von jdm f~halten lassen** to let sb pay for one; **2** *vr* **sich von etw f~halten** to avoid sth; **von Vorurteilen etc** to be free of sth; **von Verpflich-**

tungen to keep oneself free of sth; **~handbücherei** *f* open-shelf library; **~handel** *m* free trade; **~handelszone** *f* free trade area; **die kleine ~handelszone** EFTA, the European Free Trade Area; **f~händig** *adj* *Zeichnung* freehand; *Radfahren* without hands, (with) no hands; *Schießen* offhand (*spec*), without support; **~handzeichnung** *f* freehand drawing; **f~hängend** *adj attr* suspended.

Freiheit *f* (a) *no pl* freedom. **die ~** freedom; (*persönliche ~ als politisches Ideal*) liberty; **~, Gleichheit, Brüderlichkeit** liberty, equality, fraternity; **persönliche ~** personal freedom; **in ~** (*dat*) **sein** to be free; (*Tier*) to be in the wild; **jdn in ~** (*acc*) **setzen** to set sb free; **jdm die ~ schenken** to give sb his/her *etc* freedom, to free sb; **der Weg in die ~** the path to freedom. (b) (*Vorrecht*) freedom *no pl*. **dichterische ~** poetic licence; **alle ~en haben** to have all the freedom possible; **die ~ haben** *or* **genießen** (*geh*), **etw zu tun** to be free *or* at liberty to do sth, to have *or* enjoy the freedom to do sth; **sich** (*dat*) **die ~ nehmen, etw zu tun** to take the liberty of doing sth; **sich** (*dat*) **zu viele ~en erlauben** to take too many liberties.

freiheitlich *adj* liberal; *Verfassung* based on the principle of liberty; *Demokratie* free. **die ~-demokratische Grundordnung** (*BRD*) the free democratic constitutional structure; **~ gesinnt** liberal.

Freiheits-: **~begriff** *m* concept of freedom; **~beraubung** *f* (*Jur*) wrongful deprivation of personal liberty; **~bewegung** *f* liberation movement; **~delikt** *nt* (*Jur*) offence against personal liberty; **~drang** *m*, *no pl* urge or desire for freedom; **~entzug** *m* imprisonment; **f~feindlich** *adj* operating against freedom; *Kräfte auch* anti-freedom *attr*; **~kampf** *m* fight for freedom; **~kämpfer** *m* freedom-fighter; **~krieg** *m* war of liberation; **f~liebend** *adj* freedom-loving; **~rechte** *pl* civil rights and liberties *pl*; **~statue** *f* Statue of Liberty; **~strafe** *f* prison sentence; **er erhielt eine ~strafe von zwei Jahren** he was sentenced to two years' imprisonment *or* given a two-year prison sentence.

Frei-: **f~heraus** *adv* candidly, frankly; **~herr** *m* baron; **f~herrlich** *adj attr* baronial.

Freiin *f siehe* **Freifräulein.**

Frei-: **f~kämpfen** **1** *vt sep* to get free; (*durch Gewaltanwendung*) to free by force; **2** *vr* to get free; to free oneself by force; **~karte** *f* free *or* complimentary ticket; **f~kaufen** *vt sep* **jdn/sich f~kaufen** to buy sb's/one's freedom; **~kirche** *f* Free Church; **f~kommen** *vi sep irreg aux sein* (a) (*entkommen*) to get out (*aus* of); (*befreit werden*) to be released *or* freed (*aus, von* from); (b) (*sich bewegen lassen: Boot*) to come free; **~konzert** *nt* (*Sw*) *siehe* Platzkonzert; **~körperkultur** *f, no pl* nudism, naturism; **~korps** *nt* (*Mil*) volunteer corps *sing*; **~ladebahnhof** *m* station with public loading facilities.

Freiland *nt* (*Hort*) open beds *pl*. **auf/im ~** outdoors.

Freiland-: **~gemüse** *nt* outdoor vegetables *pl*; **~kultur** *f* outdoor cultivation.

Frei-: **f~lassen** *vt sep irreg* to set free, to free; (*aus Haft, Gefangenschaft auch*) to release; *Hund* to let off the lead *or* leash; **~lassung** *f* release; (*von Sklaven*) setting free; **~lauf** *m* (*Aut*) neutral; (*bei Fahrrad*) freewheel; **im ~lauf fahren** to coast (in neutral); to freewheel; **f~laufen** *vr sep irreg* (*Sport*) to get free; **f~lebend** *adj* living free; **f~legen** *vt sep* to expose; *Ruinen, Trümmer* to uncover; (*fig auch*) to lay bare; **~legung** *f siehe* *vt* exposure; uncovering; laying bare; **~leitung** *f* overhead cable.

freilich *adv* (a) (*allerdings*) admittedly. **es scheint ~ nicht leicht zu sein** admittedly *or* certainly it doesn't seem easy. (b) (*esp S Ger: natürlich*) of course, certainly, sure (*esp US*). **aber ~!** of course!; **ja ~** yes of course.

Freilicht- *in cpds* open-air; **~bühne** *f* open-air theatre; **~kino** *nt* open-air cinema; (*Autokino*) drive-in cinema; **~malerei** *f* outdoor painting.

Frei-: **~los** *nt* free lottery ticket; (*Sport*) bye; **f~machen** *sep* **1** *vt* to stamp; (*mit Frankiermaschine*) to frank; **einen Brief mit 80 Pfennig f~machen** to put stamps to the value of 80 pfennigs on a letter; *siehe auch* **frei (a, d)**; **2** *vi* to take time/a day/a week *etc* off; **ich habe eine Woche/gestern f~gemacht** I took a week off/the day off yesterday; **3** *vr* to arrange to be free; *siehe* **frei (h)**; **~machung** *f, no pl siehe* *vt* stamping; franking; **~marke** *f* (*postage*) stamp; **~maurer** *m* Mason, Freemason; **~maurerei** *f* Freemasonry; **f~maurerisch** *adj* Masonic; **~maurerloge** *f* Masonic Lodge.

Freimut *m, no pl* frankness, honesty, openness. **mit allem ~** perfectly frankly *or* honestly *or* openly.

freimütig *adj* frank, honest, open.

Freimütigkeit *f* frankness, honesty, openness.

Frei-: **~platz** *m* (a) free *or* complimentary seat; (b) (*Univ*) scholarship; (*Sch auch*) free place; (c) (*Sport*) open-air court/pitch/ground; **f~pressen** *vt sep* **jdn f~pressen** to obtain sb's release, to get sb set free; **versuchen, jdn f~zupressen** to demand sb's release; **~pressung** *f* **die erfolgreiche ~pressung der Häftlinge verursachte einen Skandal** there was a scandal when the prisoners were released in response to the terrorists' demands; **~raum** *m* (*fig*) freedom *no art, no pl* (*zu* for); **~raum brauchen, in dem man sich entwickeln kann** to need freedom to develop *or* in which to develop; **die Universität ist kein gesellschaftlicher ~raum** university isn't a social vacuum; **f~religiös** *adj* non-denominational; **~saß** [-zas], **~sasse** *m*, **-sassen, -sassen** (*Hist*) yeoman; **f~schaffend** *adj attr* freelance; **~schaffende(r)** *mf decl as adj* freelance; **~schar** *f* (*Hist*) (irregular) volunteer corps *sing*; **~schärler** *m* **-s, -** guerrilla; (*Hist*) irregular (volunteer); **f~schaufeln** *vt sep* to clear, to dig clear; **f~schießen** *vt sep irreg sich* (*dat*) **den Weg f~schießen** to shoot one's way out; **jdn f~schießen** to shoot sb free; **~schuß** *m* free shot; **f~schwimmen** *vr sep irreg* (*Sport*) to pass a test by swimming for 15 minutes; (fig) to learn to stand on one's own two feet; ~schwimmen nt 15 minute swimming test; f~setzen vt sep to release; (euph) Arbeitskräfte to make redundant; (vorübergehend) to lay off; ~setzung f release; (euph) dismissal; (vorübergehend) laying off; ~sinn m, no pl (dated) liberalism; f~sinnig adj (dated) liberal; ~spiel nt free game; f~sprechen vt sep irreg (a) to acquit; jdn von einer Schuld/von einem Verdacht f~sprechen to acquit sb of guilt/clear sb of suspicion; jdn wegen erwiesener Unschuld f~sprechen to prove sb not guilty; (b) (Handwerk) Lehrling to qualify; ~spruch m acquittal; es ergeht ~spruch the verdict is "not guilty"; auf ~spruch plädieren to plead not guilty; ~staat m free state; der ~staat Bayern the Free State of Bavaria; ~statt, ~stätte f (liter) sanctuary; f~stehen vi sep irreg (a) (überlassen sein) es steht jdm f~, etw zu tun sb is free or at liberty to do sth; das steht Ihnen völlig f~ that is completely up to you; es steht Ihnen f~, ob ... it is up to you whether ...; (b) (leerstehen) to stand empty; f~stellen vt sep (a) (anheimstellen) jdm etw f~stellen to leave sth (up) to sb; wir haben ihm f~gestellt, ob er Musik studieren will oder nicht or Musik zu studieren we've left it (up) to him whether he studies music or not; (b) (zur Verfügung stellen) Mittel to make available; Personal to release; (c) (befreien) to exempt; einen Schüler vom Unterricht f~stellen to excuse a pupil from a lesson/his lessons; ~stempel m frank.

Freistil- in cpds freestyle; ~ringen nt all-in or freestyle wrestling.

Frei-: ~stoß m (Ftbl) free kick (für to, for); ~stück nt free copy; ~stunde f free hour; (Sch) free period.

Freitag m Friday. der Schwarze ~ the day of the Wall Street crash; ein schwarzer ~ a black day; der Stille ~ Good Friday; siehe auch Dienstag.

freitäglich adj after Friday.

freitags adv on Fridays, on a Friday.

Frei-: ~tisch m free meals pl; ~tod m suicide; den ~tod wählen or suchen to decide to put an end to one's life; f~tragend adj self-supporting; Konstruktion, Flügel cantilever attr; Treppe hanging, cantilever attr; ~treppe f (flight of) steps (gen leading up to); ~übung f exercise; ~übungen machen to do one's exercises; ~umschlag m stamped addressed envelope, s.a.e.

freiweg ['frai'vɛk] adv openly; (freiheraus) straight out, frankly. er fing an, ~ zu erzählen he started talking away.

Frei-: ~wild nt (fig) fair game; ich kam mir vor wie ~wild everyone seemed to consider me fair game; f~willig adj voluntary; (Jur) Gerichtsbarkeit auch non-contentious; (freigestellt) Versicherung, Unterricht optional; f~willige Feuerwehr voluntary fire brigade; sich f~willig melden to volunteer (zu, für for); etw f~willig machen to do sth voluntarily or of one's own free will; f~willig in den Tod gehen to take one's own life; ~willige(r) mf decl as adj volunteer; ~willige vor! volunteers, one pace forwards!; ~willigkeit f voluntary nature, voluntariness; ~wurf m free throw; ~zeichen nt ringing tone; ~zeichnungsklausel f (Jur, Comm) exemption from liability clause.

Freizeit f (a) (arbeitsfreie Zeit) free or spare or leisure time. (b) (Zusammenkunft) weekend/holiday course; (Eccl) retreat.

Freizeit-: ~bekleidung f siehe ~kleidung; ~gestaltung f organization of one's leisure time; das Problem der ~gestaltung the leisure problem; ~hemd nt sports shirt; ~industrie f leisure industry; ~kleidung f casual clothes pl; (Warengattung) leisurewear no pl; ~problem nt problem of leisure, leisure problem.

Frei-: f~zügig adj (a) (reichlich) Gebrauch, Anwendung liberal; f~zügig Geld ausgeben to spend money freely or liberally; (b) (in moralischer Hinsicht) permissive; ein f~zügiger Ausschnitt a (low) plunging neckline; (c) (den Wohnort frei wählen könnend) free to move; ~zügigkeit f siehe adj (a) liberalness; (b) permissiveness; die ~zügigkeit ihres Ausschnitts the revealing cut of her neckline; (c) freedom of movement.

fremd adj (a) (andern gehörig) someone else's; Bank, Bibliothek, Firma different; (Comm, Fin, Pol) outside attr. ohne ~e Hilfe without anyone else's/outside help, without help from anyone else/outside; ich schlafe nicht gern in ~en Betten I don't like sleeping in strange beds; ~es Eigentum someone else's property, not one's own (form); das ist nicht für ~e Ohren that is not for other people to hear; von ~er Hand geschrieben written in someone else's hand; unter ~em Namen under an assumed name; etw geht in ~e Hände über sth passes into the hands of strangers or into strange hands; sich mit ~en Federn schmücken to claim all the glory for oneself. (b) (~ländisch) foreign, alien (esp Admin, Pol). (c) (andersartig) strange; Planeten other; Welt different. (d) (unvertraut) strange. jdm ~ sein (unbekannt) to be unknown to sb; (unverständlich) to be foreign or alien to sb; (nicht in jds Art) to be foreign or alien to sb or to sb's nature; es ist mir ~, wie ... I don't understand how ...; das ist eine ~e/mir ~e Seite seines Wesens that is a side of his character which nobody has/I haven't seen before; ich bin hier/in London ~ I'm a stranger here/to London; meine Heimat ist mir ~ geworden I've become a stranger in my own country, my own country has become quite foreign or alien to me; sich or einander (dat) ~ werden to grow apart, to become strangers (to one another); sich ~ fühlen to feel alien, to feel like a stranger; ~ tun to be reserved.

Fremd-: ~arbeiter m (dated) foreign worker; f~artig adj strange; (exotisch) exotic; ~artigkeit f siehe adj strangeness; exoticism; ~bestäubung f cross-fertilization; f~bestimmt adj heteronomous; ~bestimmung f heteronomy.

Fremde f -, no pl (liter) die ~ foreign parts pl; in die ~ gehen/in der ~ sein to go to/be in foreign parts, to go/be abroad.

fremde(l)n vi (S Ger, Sw) to be scared of strangers.

Fremden-: ~bett nt spare or guest bed; (in Hotel) hotel bed; f~feindlich adj hostile to strangers; (ausländerfeindlich) hostile to foreigners, xenophobic (form); ~führer m (a) (Mensch) (tourist) guide; (b) (Buch) guide(book); ~heim nt guest house; ~industrie f tourist trade or industry, tourism no def art; ~legion f Foreign Legion; ~legionär m Foreign Legionnaire; ~paß m alien's passport; ~polizei f aliens branch (of the police); (Aviat) aliens office.

Fremdenverkehr m tourism no def art.

Fremdenverkehrs-: ~ort m tourist resort or centre; ~verein m tourist association.

Fremdenzimmer nt guest room.

Fremde(r) mf decl as adj (Unbekannter, Orts~) stranger; (Ausländer) foreigner; (Admin, Pol) alien; (Tourist) visitor.

Fremd-: ~finanzierung f outside financing; f~gehen vi sep irreg aux sein (inf) to be unfaithful; ~heit f, no pl (ausländische Natur) foreignness; (Unvertrautheit) strangeness; (Entfremdung) alienation; (zwischen Menschen) reserve; ~herrschaft f, no pl foreign rule; ~kapital nt outside capital; ~körper m foreign body; (fig) alien element; sich als ~körper fühlen to feel out of place; f~ländisch adj foreign no adv; (exotisch) exotic; ~ling m (liter) stranger.

Fremdsprache f foreign language. eine Begabung für ~n a gift for languages.

Fremdsprachen-: ~korrespondent m foreign correspondence clerk; ~unterricht m language teaching; ~unterricht haben/erteilen to have/give language classes.

Fremd-: f~sprachig adj in a foreign language; Fähigkeiten (foreign) language; Schulen für die f~sprachige Bevölkerung schools for non-English/non-German etc speakers; f~sprachlich adj foreign; f~sprachlicher Unterricht language teaching; f~stämmig adj of foreign origin; ~stoff m foreign matter no pl or substance; ~wort nt borrowed or foreign word, borrowing; Rücksichtnahme ist für ihn ein ~wort (fig) he's never heard of the word consideration; ~wörterbuch nt dictionary of borrowed or foreign words.

frenetisch adj frenetic, frenzied; Beifall auch wild.

frequentieren* vt (geh) to frequent.

Frequenz f (a) (Häufigkeit) frequency (auch Phys); (Med) (pulse) rate. (b) (Stärke) numbers pl; (Verkehrsdichte) volume of traffic.

Frequenz- in cpds frequency.

Freske f -, -n (rare), **Fresko** nt -s, **Fresken** fresco.

Fressalien [-ian] pl (inf) grub sing (inf), eats pl (inf).

Freßbeutel m (a) (dated inf) bag of grub (inf) or tucker (dated inf). (b) (für Pferd) nosebag.

Fresse f -, -n (sl) (Mund) trap (sl), gob (sl), cakehole (Brit sl); (Gesicht) mug (inf). die ~ halten to shut one's trap or gob or face (all sl); eine große ~ haben to be a loud-mouth (inf); jdn or jdm in die ~ hauen, jdm die ~ polieren to smash sb's face in (inf); ach du meine ~! bloody hell!; Jesus Christ! (sl).

fressen pret fraß, ptp gefressen 1 vi (a) to feed, to eat; (sl: Menschen) to eat; (gierig) to guzzle. jdm aus der Hand ~ (lit, fig inf) to eat out of sb's hand; für drei ~ to eat enough for a whole army (inf); er ißt nicht, er frißt (wie ein Schwein) he eats like a pig; siehe Vogel, Scheunendrescher.
(b) (zerstören) to eat away (an etw (dat) sth).
2 vt (a) (verzehren: Tier, sl: Mensch) to eat; (sich ernähren von) to feed or live on; (sl: gierig) to guzzle, to scoff. etwas zu ~ something to eat; den Napf leer ~ (Tiere) to lick the bowl clean; (Menschen) to polish everything off (inf); jdn arm ~, jdm die Haare vom Kopf ~ to eat sb out of house and home; siehe Bauer[1], Not.
(b) (in Wendungen) Kilometer ~ to burn up the kilometres; Löcher in etw (acc) ~ (lit) to eat holes in sth; ein Loch in den Geldbeutel ~ to make a big hole in one's pocket; ich habe dich zum F~ gern (inf) you're good enough to eat (inf); ich könnte dich ~ (inf) I could eat you (inf); sie sieht zum F~ aus (inf) she looks good enough to eat (inf); ich will dich doch nicht ~ (inf) I'm not going to eat you (inf); sie sah mich an, als ob sie mich ~ wollte (inf) she gave me a murderous look; ich fresse einen Besen or meinen Hut, wenn ... (inf) I'll eat my hat if ...; jdn/etw gefressen haben (inf) to have had one's fill or as much as one can take or sb/sth; jetzt hat er es endlich gefressen (inf) he's got it or got there at last (inf), at last the penny's dropped; einen Narren or Affen an jdm/etw gefressen haben to dote on sb/sth; siehe Weisheit.
(c) (verbrauchen) Benzin, Ersparnisse to eat or gobble up; Zeit to take up.
(d) (geh: Neid, Haß) to eat up.
3 vr (a) (sich bohren) to eat one's way (in +acc into, durch through).
(b) sich voll/satt ~ to gorge oneself/eat one's fill; (Mensch auch) to stuff oneself (inf); sich krank ~ to eat oneself sick.

Fressen nt -s, no pl food; (sl) grub (sl); siehe gefunden.

Fresser m -s, - (Tier) eater; (sl: gieriger Mensch) glutton, greedyguts (inf). wenn man fünf ~ im Haus hat (inf) when you have five hungry mouths to feed.

Fresserei f (inf) (a) no pl (übermäßiges Essen) guzzling; (Gefräßigkeit) piggishness (inf), gluttony. (b) (Schmaus) blow-out (inf), nosh-up (Brit sl).

Freß-: ~gier f voraciousness; (pej: von Menschen) gluttony, piggishness (inf); f~gierig adj Tier voracious; (pej: Mensch) gluttonous, piggish (inf); ~korb m (sl) (für Picknick) picnic hamper; (Geschenkkorb) food hamper; ~napf m feeding bowl; ~paket nt (inf) food parcel; ~sack m (sl) greedyguts (inf), glutton; ~sucht f (inf) gluttony; (krankhaft) craving for food.

freßt *imper pl of* **fressen**.

Freß-: ~**welle** *f* (*hum inf*) wave of gluttony; ~**werkzeuge** *pl* feeding equipment *no pl or* organs *pl*; (*von Insekten*) mouthpart.

Frettchen *nt* ferret.

Freude *f* -, -n (a) *no pl* pleasure; (*innig*) joy (*über* + *acc* at); (*Erfreutheit*) delight (*über* + *acc* at). ~ **an etw** (*dat*) **haben** to get *or* derive pleasure from sth; **er hat** ~ **an seinen Kindern** his children give him pleasure; ~ **am Leben haben** to enjoy life; **wenn man an der Arbeit keine** ~ **hat** if you don't get any pleasure out of *or* if you don't enjoy your work; **die** ~ **an der Natur** the joy one gets from nature; **daran hat er seine** ~ that gives him pleasure; (*iro*) he thinks that's fun; **es ist eine (wahre** *or* **reine)** ~, **zu** ... it's a (real) joy *or* pleasure to ...; **es war eine reine** ~, **das mit anzusehen** it was a joy to see; **es ist keine (reine)** ~, **das zu tun** (*iro*) it's not exactly fun doing that; **es ist mir eine** ~, **zu** ... it's a real pleasure for me to ...; **es macht mir** ~, **ihm zuzusehen** I really enjoy watching him, I get a lot of pleasure out of watching him; **das Kind macht seinen Eltern viel/nur** ~ the child gives his parents a lot of/nothing but joy; **er macht ihnen keine/wenig** ~ he's no joy/not much of a joy to them; **es macht ihnen keine/wenig** ~ they don't enjoy it (at all)/much; **jdm eine** ~ **machen** *or* **bereiten** to make sb happy; **jdm eine** ~ **machen wollen** to want to do something to please sb; **eine unerwartete** ~ an unexpected pleasure; **zu meiner großen** ~ to my great delight; **zu unserer größten** ~ **können wir Ihnen mitteilen** ... we are pleased to be able to inform you ...; **Sie hätten seine** ~ **sehen sollen** you should have seen how happy he was; **aus** ~ **an der Sache** for the love of it *or* the thing; **aus Spaß an der** ~ (*inf*) for the fun *or* hell (*inf*) of it *or* the thing; **in Freud' und Leid zu jdm halten** (*dated*) to stand by sb come rain, come shine.

(b) (*Vergnügung*) joy. **die kleinen** ~n **des Lebens** the pleasures of life; **herrlich und in** ~n **leben** to live a life of ease; **mit** ~n with pleasure.

Freuden-: **f**~**arm** *adj* joyless; ~**botschaft** *f* good news *sing*, glad tidings *pl* (*old, Bibl*); ~**fest** *nt* celebration; ~**feuer** *nt* bonfire; ~**geheul**, ~**geschrei** *nt* howls *pl or* shrieks *pl* of joy; ~**haus** *nt* (*dated, hum*) house of pleasure *or* ill-repute; ~**junge** *m* (*hum*) male prostitute; **f**~**leer** *adj* joyless, devoid of joy; **f**~**los** *adj siehe* **freudlos**; ~**mädchen** *nt* (*dated, hum*) lady of easy virtue; (*euph*), prostitute; ~**mahl** *nt* celebration meal, banquet (*old*), feast; **f**~**reich** *adj* (*geh*) joyful, joyous; ~**ruf**, ~**schrei** *m* joyful cry, cry of joy; ~**sprung** *m* joyful leap; **einen** ~**sprung machen** to jump for joy; ~**tag** *m* happy *or* joyful (*esp liter*) day; ~**tanz** *m* dance of joy; **einen** ~**tanz auf-** *or* **vollführen** to dance with joy; ~**taumel** *m* ecstasy (of joy); ~**tränen** *pl* tears *pl* of joy; **f**~**voll** *adj siehe* **freudvoll**.

freude-: ~**strahlend** *adj no pred* beaming with delight; *Gesicht auch* beaming; ~**trunken** *adj* (*liter*) delirious with joy.

Freudianer *m* -s, - Freudian.

freudig *adj* (a) (*frohgestimmt*) joyful; (*gern bereit*) willing; (*begeistert*) enthusiastic. **einen Vorschlag** ~ **begrüßen** to greet a suggestion with delight; **jdn** ~ **stimmen** to raise sb's spirits; **etw** ~ **erwarten** to look forward to sth with great pleasure; ~ **überrascht sein** to have a delightful surprise.

(b) (*beglückend*) happy, joyful (*liter*). **eine** ~**e Nachricht** some good *or* joyful (*liter*) news, some glad tidings *pl* (*old, Bibl*); **ein** ~**es Ereignis** (*euph*) a happy *or* blessed event (*euph*).

Freudigkeit *f, no pl siehe adj* (a) joyfulness; willingness; enthusiasm.

Freud-: **f**~**los** *adj* joyless, cheerless; **f**~**los dahinleben** to lead a joyless *or* cheerless existence; ~**losigkeit** *f, no pl* joylessness, cheerlessness.

Freudsch *adj* Freudian.

freudvoll *adj* (*geh*) joyful, joyous (*liter*); *Tage, Leben* filled with joy.

freuen 1 *vr* (a) to be glad *or* pleased (*über* + *acc*, (*geh*) + *gen* about). **sich über ein Geschenk** ~ to be pleased with a present; **sich sehr** *or* **riesig** (*inf*) ~ to be delighted *or* ever so pleased (*inf*) (*über* + *acc* about); **ich habe es bekommen, freute sie sich** I've got it, she said happily *or* (*stärker*) joyfully; **sich an etw** (*dat*) ~ to get *or* derive a lot of pleasure from sth; **er freut sich sehr an seinen Kindern** his children give him a lot of pleasure; **sich für jdn** ~ to be glad *or* pleased for sb *or* for sb's sake; **sich mit jdm** ~ to share sb's happiness; **sich seines Lebens** ~ to enjoy life; **ich freue mich, Ihnen mitteilen zu können,** ... I'm pleased to be able to tell you ...; *siehe* **Kind**.

(b) **sich auf jdn/etw** ~ to look forward to seeing sb/to sth; **sich auf das Kind** ~ to look forward to the child being born *or* to the child's birth; **sich zu früh** ~ to get one's hopes up too soon.

2 *vt impers* to please. **es freut mich/ihn, daß** ... I'm/he's pleased *or* glad that ...; **es freut ihn sehr, daß** ... I'm/he's delighted *or* very pleased *or* glad that ...; **das freut mich** I'm really pleased; **es freut mich sehr/es hat mich sehr gefreut, Ihre Bekanntschaft zu machen** (*form*) (I'm) pleased to meet/have met you.

freund *adj pred* (*old*) **jdm** ~ **sein/bleiben/werden** to be/remain/ become sb's friend.

Freund *m* -(e)s, -e (a) (*Kamerad*) friend. **wir sind schon seit 1924** ~**e** we've been friends since 1924; **mit jdm gut** ~ **sein** to be good friends with sb; **das habe ich mir unter** ~**en gesagt** that was just between ourselves; **10 Mark unter** ~**n** 10 marks to a friend; ~ **und Feind** friend and foe; **ein schöner** ~ (*iro inf*) a fine friend; **jdn zum** ~ **haben** to have sb for *or* as a friend; **guter** ~! (*liter*) my dear man; *siehe* **alt**.

(b) (*Liebhaber*) boyfriend; (*älter auch*) gentleman-friend.

(c) (*fig*) (*Anhänger*) lover; (*Förderer*) friend. **ein** ~ **der Kunst** an art-lover, a lover/friend of art; **ich bin kein** ~ **von Hunden** I'm no lover of dogs; **er ist kein** ~ **von vielen Worten** he's not one for talking much, he's a man of few words; **ich bin kein** ~ **von so etwas** I'm not one for that sort of thing; **ein** ~ **des Alkohols sein** to like one's drink.

-freund *m in cpds* (a) (*Kamerad*) friend. (b) (*fig: Liebhaber*) lover of.

Freundchen *nt* (*inf*) my friend (*iro*). ~! ~! watch it, mate (*Brit inf*) *or* my friend!

Freundes-: ~**hand** *f* (*geh*) **jdm die** ~**hand reichen** to extend the hand *or* arm of friendship to sb; **von** ~**hand** by the hand of a friend; ~**kreis** *m* circle of friends; **etw im engsten** ~**kreis feiern** to celebrate sth with one's closest friends; ~**land** *nt* (*esp DDR*) fellow socialist country; ~**treue** *f* (*geh*) loyal friendship.

Freund-Feind-Denken *nt* attitude that if you're not for us you're against us.

Freundin *f* (a) friend; (*Liebhaberin*) girlfriend; (*älter auch*) lady-friend. (b) (*fig: Anhänger, Förderer*) *siehe* **Freund (c)**.

freundlich *adj* (a) (*wohlgesinnt*) friendly *no adv*. **jdn** ~ **behandeln** to treat sb in a friendly way, to be friendly towards sb; **bitte recht** ~! say cheese! (*inf*), smile please!; **mit** ~**en Grüßen** *or* ~**em Gruß** (with) best wishes; **einem Vorschlag** ~ **gegenüberstehen** to be in favour of *or* be well-disposed to a suggestion.

(b) (*liebenswürdig*) kind (*zu* to). **würden Sie bitte so** ~ **sein und das tun?** would you be so kind *or* good as to do that?, would you be kind *or* good enough to do that?; **das ist sehr** ~ **von Ihnen** that's very kind *or* good of you.

(c) (*ansprechend*) *Aussehen, Landschaft, Wetter etc* pleasant; *Zimmer, Einrichtung, Farben* cheerful; *Atmosphäre* friendly, congenial; (*Fin, Comm: günstig*) favourable.

-freundlich *adj suf* (*wohlgesinnt*) pro-; (*liebend*) fond of; (*schonend*) kind to.

freundlicherweise *adv* kindly. **er trug uns** ~ **die Koffer** he was kind enough to carry our cases for us, he kindly carried our cases (for us).

Freundlichkeit *f* (a) *no pl siehe adj* (a-c) friendliness; kindness; kindliness; pleasantness; cheerfulness; friendliness; congeniality; favourableness. **würden Sie (wohl) die** ~ **haben, das zu tun?** would you be so kind *or* good as to *or* be kind *or* good enough to do that? (b) (*freundliche Handlung, Gefälligkeit*) kindness, favour; (*freundliche Bemerkung*) kind remark. **jdm** ~**en erweisen** to be kind to sb; **jdm ein paar** ~**en sagen** to say a few kind words *or* make a few kind remarks to sb.

Freundschaft *f* (a) (*freundschaftliches Verhältnis*) friendship. **mit jdm** ~ **schließen** to make *or* become friends with sb, to form a friendship with sb; **jdm die** ~ **anbieten** to offer sb one's friendship; **in aller** ~ in all friendliness; **da hört die** ~ **auf** (*inf*) friendship doesn't go that far; **in Geldsachen hört die** ~ **auf** friendship doesn't extend to money matters; ~! (*DDR*) greeting used by the Free German Youth; *siehe* **kündigen, Geschenk**.

(b) (*Freundeskreis*) friends *pl*.

(c) *no pl* (*dial: Verwandtschaft*) relatives *pl*, relations *pl*.

(d) (*DDR*) the Pioneer groups in one school.

freundschaftlich *adj* friendly *no adv*. **jdm** ~ **gesinnt sein** to feel friendly towards sb; **jdm** ~ **auf die Schulter klopfen** to give sb a friendly slap on the back; ~**e Gefühle** feelings of friendship.

Freundschafts-: ~**bande** *pl* (*liter*) ties *pl* of friendship; ~**besuch** *m* (*Pol*) goodwill visit; ~**bund** *m* friendly alliance; ~**dienst** *m* favour to a friend; **jdm einen** ~**dienst erweisen** to do sb a favour; ~**preis** *m* (special) price for a friend; **er überließ mir sein Auto zu einem** ~**preis/einem** ~**preis von 100 DM** he let me have his car cheaply/for 100 DM because we're friends; **ich mache dir einen** ~**preis** (*inf*) seeing we're friends I'll let you have it for a special price; ~**spiel** *nt* (*Sport*) friendly game *or* match, friendly (*inf*); ~**vertrag** *m* (*Pol*) treaty of friendship.

frevel *adj* (*obs liter*) *Tat* heinous (*liter*); *Verblendung, Mut, Vermessenheit* wanton.

Frevel *m* -s, - (*geh*) sin (*gegen* against); (*Tat auch*) heinous deed (*liter*); (*fig*) crime (*an* + *dat* against).

Frevel-: **f**~**haft** *adj* (*geh*) (*verwerflich*) sinful; *Leichtsinn, Verschwendung* wanton; ~**haftigkeit** *f* (*geh*) *siehe adj* sinfulness; wantonness; ~**mut** *m* (*obs liter*) wanton daring *or* boldness.

freveln *vi* (*liter*) to sin (*gegen, an* + *dat* against).

Freveltat *f* (*liter*) heinous deed (*liter*).

freventlich *adj* (*obs liter*) *siehe* **frevelhaft**.

Frevler(in *f*) *m* -s, - (*liter*) sinner. **die Strafe für den** ~ **an der Natur/gegen Gott** the punishment for someone who sins against nature/God.

frevlerisch *adj* (*liter*) *siehe* **frevelhaft**.

friderizianisch *adj* of Frederick the Great.

Friede *m* -ns, -n (*old*) peace. **der** ~ **der Natur** the tranquillity of nature; ~ **auf Erden** peace on earth; ~ **sei mit euch** peace be with you; ~ **seiner Asche** God rest his soul.

Frieden *m* -s, - (a) peace. **ein langer, ungestörter** ~ a long period of uninterrupted peace; **im** ~ in peacetime, in time of peace; **in** ~ **und Freiheit leben** to live at peace and in freedom; **im tiefsten** ~ (living) in perfect tranquillity; **seit letztem Jahr herrscht in dieser Gegend** ~ this region has been at peace since last year; ~ **schließen** to make one's peace; (*Pol*) to conclude (*form*) *or* make peace; ~**stiften** to make peace (*zwischen* + *dat* between).

(b) (*Friedensschluß*) peace; (*Vertrag*) peace treaty. **der Westfälische** ~ (*Hist*) the Peace of Westphalia; **den** ~ **diktieren** to dictate the peace terms; **über den** ~ **verhandeln** to hold peace negotiations; **den** ~ **einhalten** to keep the peace, to keep to the peace agreement.

(c) (*Harmonie*) peace, tranquillity. **der häusliche** ~ domestic harmony; **in** ~ **und Freundschaft** *or* **Eintracht leben** to live in peace and harmony *or* tranquillity.

(d) (*Ruhe*) peace. jdn in ~ lassen to leave sb in peace; um des lieben ~s willen (*inf*) for the sake of peace and quiet; sein schlechtes Gewissen ließ ihn keinen ~ mehr finden his guilty conscience gave him no peace; ich traue dem ~ nicht (*inf*) something (fishy) is going on (*inf*); (er) ruhe in ~ rest in peace.

Friedens- in cpds peace; **~bedingungen** *pl* peace terms *pl*; **~bemühung** *f usu pl* effort to achieve peace; (*~angebot*) peace move; **~bewegung** *f* peace movement; **~bruch** *m* violation of the peace; **~engel** *m* (*lit, fig*) angel of peace; **~fahrt** *f* (*DDR*) peace race, *international cycling race through East Germany, Czechoslovakia and Poland*; **~forscher** *m* peace researcher; **~forschung** *f* peace studies *sing*; **~fühler** *pl*: die **~fühler** ausstrecken (*inf*) to make a tentative move towards peace (*in Richtung* with); **~kämpfer** *m* pacifist; **~konferenz** *f* peace conference; **~kuß** *m* (*Eccl*) pax, kiss of peace; **~lager** *nt* (*DDR*) nations of the Socialist bloc; **~liebe** *f* love of peace; **~nobelpreis** *m* Nobel peace prize; **~pfeife** *f* peace-pipe; mit jdm/miteinander die **~pfeife** rauchen (*lit*) to smoke a peace-pipe with sb/together; (*fig*) to make (one's) peace with sb/to bury the hatchet; **~pflicht** *f* (*Ind*) obligation binding on employers and unions to avoid industrial action during wages negotiations; **~politik** *f* policy of peace; **~produktion** *f* peacetime production; **~richter** *m* justice of the peace, JP; **~schluß** *m* peace agreement; **~sicherung** *f* maintenance of peace; Maßnahmen zur **~sicherung** peacekeeping measures; **~stärke** *f* (*Mil*) peacetime strength; **~stifter** *m* peacemaker; **~taube** *f* dove of peace; **~truppen** *pl* peacekeeping forces *pl*; **~verhandlungen** *pl* peace negotiations *pl*; **~vertrag** *m* peace treaty; **~vorschlag** *m* peace proposal; **~wille** *m* desire or wish for peace; **~wirtschaft** *f* peacetime economy; **~zeit** *f* period of peace; in **~zeiten** in peacetime, in times of peace; **~zustand** *m* state of peace; im **~zustand** at peace.

friedfertig *adj* peaceable. selig sind die F**~en** (*Bibl*) blessed are the peacemakers.

Friedfertigkeit *f* peaceableness; (*von Hund*) placidness. in seiner **~/aus reiner ~** hat er ... peaceable as he is/because of his peaceable nature, he ...

Friedhof *m* (*Kirchhof*) graveyard; (*Stadt~ etc*) cemetery. auf dem **~** in the graveyard/cemetery.

Friedhofs-: **~atmosphäre** *f* gloomy atmosphere; es herrscht im Haus eine **~atmosphäre** the house is like a graveyard; **~gärtnerei** *f* cemetery flower shop; **~kapelle** *f* cemetery chapel; **~ruhe** *f* (*lit*) peace of the graveyard/cemetery; (*fig*) deathly quiet.

friedlich *adj* **(a)** (*nicht kriegerisch, ohne Gewalt*) Lösung, Demonstration, Volk, Zeiten peaceful; (*friedfertig, ohne Streit*) Mensch, Abschied peaceable; Hund placid. etw auf **~em** Wege lösen to find a peaceful solution to sth, to solve sth peacefully or by peaceful means; damit er endlich **~** ist (*inf*) to keep him happy; nun sei doch endlich **~**! (*fig inf*) give it a rest! (*inf*); sei **~**, ich will keinen Streit take it easy or calm down, I don't want any trouble.

(b) (*friedvoll*) peaceful. **~** sterben or einschlafen (*euph*) to die peacefully.

Friedlichkeit *f, no pl siehe adj* **(a)** peacefulness; peaceableness; placidness, placidity. **(b)** peacefulness.

fried-: **~liebend** *adj* peace-loving; **~los** *adj* (*a*) (*Hist*) Person outlawed; (*b*) (*liter: ruhelos*) Leben without peace; Mensch unable to find peace; **~sam** *adj* (*old*) siehe friedlich.

frieren *pret* fror, *ptp* gefroren 1 *vi* (*a*) auch *vt impers* (*sich kalt fühlen*) to be/get cold. ich friere, mich friert, es friert mich (*geh*) I'm cold; wie ein Schneider **~** (*inf*) to be/get frozen to the marrow (*inf*); mir or mich **~** die Zehen, mich friert es or ich friere an den Zehen my toes are/get cold.

(b) aux sein (*gefrieren*) to freeze; (*Fluß auch*) to freeze over. 2 *vi impers* to freeze. heute nacht hat es gefroren it was below freezing last night.

Fries *m -es, -e* (*Archit, Tex*) frieze.

Friese *m -n, -n*, **Friesin** *f* Fri(e)sian.

friesisch *adj* Fri(e)sian.

Friesland *nt* Friesland.

Friesländer(in *f*) *m -s, -* (*rare*) siehe Friese.

friesländisch *adj* (*rare*) siehe friesisch.

frigid(e) *adj* frigid.

Frigidität *f* frigidity.

Frika(n)delle *f* (*Cook*) rissole.

Frikassee *nt -s, -s* (*Cook*) fricassee.

frikassieren* *vt* (*Cook*) to fricassee.

Frikativ(laut) *m* (*Ling*) fricative.

Friktion *f* (*Tech, fig geh*) friction *no pl*.

frisch *adj* **(a)** fresh; (*feucht*) Farbe, Fleck wet. **~es** Obst fresh-picked fruit; **~e** Eier new-laid eggs; ein **~es** Faß Bier a fresh or new barrel of beer; Bier **~** vom Faß beer (straight) from the barrel; **~** gestrichen newly painted; (*auf Schild*) wet paint; **~** geschlachtet fresh(ly) slaughtered; Geflügel fresh(ly) killed; **~** gefallener Schnee freshly or newly fallen snow; **~** gewaschen Kind clean; Hemd etc auch freshly washed or laundered; das Bett **~** beziehen to change the bed, to make the bed up with fresh sheets; sich **~** machen to freshen up; mit **~en** Kräften with renewed vigour or strength; **~en** Mut fassen to gain new courage; **~e** Luft schöpfen to get some fresh air; jdn an die **~e** Luft setzen (*inf*) to show sb the door; das ist mir noch **~** in Erinnerung that is still fresh in my mind or memory; noch einmal **~** anfangen (*dial*) to make a fresh start, to start afresh; jdn auf **~er** Tat ertappen to catch sb in the act or red-handed; siehe backen[1].

(b) (*munter*) Wesen, Art bright, cheery; Erzählung bright; (*gesund*) Aussehen, Gesichtsfarbe fresh; Mädchen fresh-looking. **~** und munter sein (*inf*) to be bright and lively; **~**, fromm, fröhlich, frei (*prov*) *motto of a 19th century gymnastic*

movement; (*iro*) cheerfully, gaily; immer **~** drauflos! don't hold back!; er geht immer **~** drauflos he doesn't hang about; er redet/schreibt immer **~** drauflos he just talks/writes away; **~** begonnen, halb gewonnen (*Prov*), **~** gewagt ist halb gewonnen (*Prov*) a good start is half the battle.

(c) (*kühl*) cool, chilly; Luft, Wind auch fresh. es weht ein **~er** Wind (*lit*) there's a fresh wind; (*fig*) the wind of change is blowing.

frisch|auf *interj* (*old*) let us away (*old*).

Frische *f -, no pl* **(a)** freshness; (*Feuchtigkeit: von Farbe, Fleck*) wetness.

(b) (*Munterkeit: von Wesen, Erzählung*) brightness; (*gesundes Aussehen*) freshness. in voller körperlicher und geistiger **~** in perfect health both physically and mentally; in alter **~** (*inf*) as always.

(c) (*Kühle*) coolness, chilliness; (*von Luft, Wind auch*) freshness.

Frische-Datum *nt* sell-by date.

Frisch|ei *nt* new-laid egg.

frischen 1 *vt* Metall to refine. 2 *vi* (*Wildschwein*) to farrow.

Frisch-: **~fisch** *m* fresh fish; **~fleisch** *nt* fresh meat; **f~fröhlich** *adj* bright and cheerful; **~gemüse** *nt* fresh vegetables *pl*; **~haltebeutel** *m* airtight bag; **~haltepackung** *f* airtight pack; **~ling** *m* **(a)** (*Hunt*) young wild boar; **(b)** (*hum: Neuling*) raw beginner; **~luft** *f* fresh air; **~milch** *f* fresh milk; **~wasser** *nt* fresh water; **f~weg** *adv* (*ohne Hemmungen*) straight out (*inf*); die Kinder fingen **f~weg** an zu singen the children started to sing right off (*inf*); **~zelle** *f* (*Med*) live cell; **~zellentherapie** *f* (*Med*) cellular or live-cell therapy.

Friseur [fri'zøːɐ] *m* hairdresser; (*Herren~ auch*) barber; (*Geschäft*) hairdresser's; barber's.

Friseursalon *m* hairdresser's, hairdressing salon.

Friseuse [fri'zøːzə] *f* hairdresser.

Frisiercreme *f* haircream.

frisieren* 1 *vt* **(a)** (*kämmen*) jdn **~**, jdm das Haar **~** to do sb's hair; (*nach dem Legen*) to comb sb's hair or sb (*inf*) out; ihr elegant frisierter Kopf her elegant hairdo; ich bin heute morgen noch nicht frisiert I haven't done my hair yet this morning; sie ist stets gut frisiert her hair is always beautifully done; eine modisch frisierte Dame a lady with a fashionable hairstyle or hairdo.

(b) (*inf: abändern*) Abrechnung to fiddle; Bericht, Meldung to doctor (*inf*). die Bilanzen **~** to cook the books (*inf*).

(c) Auto to hot or soup up (*inf*); Motor auch to tweak (*sl*). 2 *vr* to do one's hair.

Frisier-: **~haube** *f* (*Trockner*) hairdryer hood; (*beim Friseur*) hairdryer; **~kommode** *f* dressing table; **~salon** *m* hairdressing salon; (*für Herren*) barber's shop; **~spiegel** *m* dressing (table) mirror; **~tisch** *m* dressing table; **~umhang** *m* hairdressing cape.

Frisör *m -s, -e*, **Frisöse** *f -, -n** siehe Friseur, Friseuse.

friß *imper sing of* fressen.

Frist *f -, -en* **(a)** (*Zeitraum*) period; (*Kündigungs~*) period of notice. eine **~** von vier Tagen/Wochen etc four days/weeks etc; eine **~** einhalten to meet a deadline; (*bei Rechnung*) to pay within the period stipulated; jds **~** verlängern/um zwei Tage verlängern to give sb more time/two more days; die Bibliothek hat mir die **~** für die Rückgabe der Bücher verlängert the library extended the loan-period on my books; eine **~** verstreichen lassen to let a deadline pass; (*bei Rechnung*) not to pay within the period stipulated; innerhalb kürzester **~** without delay; nur auf **~** only for a limited period.

(b) (*Zeitpunkt*) deadline (*zu* for); (*bei Rechnung*) last date for payment. eine **~** versäumen or verpassen to miss a deadline/the last date for payment.

(c) (*Aufschub*) extension, period of grace. jdm eine **~** von vier Tagen/Wochen geben to give sb four days/weeks grace.

Frist|ablauf *m* nach **~** after the deadline has/had expired; (*bei Rechnung*) after expiry of the stipulated period.

fristen *vt* sein Leben or Dasein **~/mit** etw **~** to eke out an existence/one's existence with sth; ein kümmerliches Dasein **~** to eke out a miserable existence; (*Partei, Institution*) to exist on the fringes; die Bauern mußten in Armut ihr Leben **~** the peasants barely managed to scrape a living.

Fristenlösung, **Fristenregelung** *f law allowing the termination of a pregnancy within the first three months.*

Frist-: **f~gerecht** *adj* within the period stipulated; **f~los** *adj* instant, without notice; Sie sind **f~los** entlassen you are dismissed without notice; **~verlängerung** *f* extension.

Frisur *f* hairstyle.

Friteuse [fri'tøːzə] *f* chip pan, deep fat fryer.

fritieren* *vt* to (deep-)fry.

Fritüre *f -, -n* **(a)** siehe Friteuse. **(b)** (*Fett*) fat. **(c)** (*Speise*) fried food.

-fritze *m* in cpds *-n, -n* (*inf*) chap (*Brit inf*), guy (*inf*).

frivol [fri'voːl] *adj* (*leichtfertig*) frivolous; (*anzüglich*) Witz, Bemerkung risqué, suggestive; (*verantwortungslos*) irresponsible.

Frivolität [frivoli'tɛːt] *f* **(a)** *no pl siehe adj* frivolity; suggestiveness; irresponsibility. **(b)** (*Bemerkung*) risqué remark.

Frivolitäten|arbeit *f* (*Sew*) tatting.

Frl. *abbr of* Fräulein.

froh *adj* **(a)** (*heiter*) happy; (*dankbar auch*) glad; (*erfreut auch*) glad, pleased. über etw (*acc*) **~** sein to be pleased with sth; (*darüber*) **~** sein, daß ... to be glad or pleased that ...; um etw **~** sein to be grateful for sth; **~en** Mutes or Sinnes sein (*old, geh*) to be cheerful, to be of good cheer (*old*); **~en** Mutes machte sie sich an die Arbeit (*old, geh*) cheerfully or with a light heart she set herself to work; seines Lebens nicht (mehr) **~** werden not to enjoy life any more; **da wird man seines Lebens nicht mehr ~!** it makes your life a misery.

(b) (*erfreulich*) happy, joyful; *Nachricht auch* good. **~e Ostern!** Happy Easter!; **~e Weihnachten!** Happy *or* Merry Christmas!; *siehe* Botschaft.

Froh-: **~botschaft** *f* (*geh*) Good News; **f~gelaunt** *adj* joyful (*liter*), cheerful, happy; **f~gemut** *adj* (*old*) with a cheerful heart; **f~gestimmt** *adj* (*geh*) happy, joyful (*liter*).

fröhlich 1 *adj* happy, cheerful, merry; *Lieder, Lachen, Stimme auch* gay. **~e Weihnachten!** Happy *or* Merry Christmas!; **~es Treiben** gaiety. **2** *adv* (*unbekümmert*) merrily, blithely, gaily. **er kam einfach so ~ ins Zimmer marschiert** he came waltzing into the room (*inf*).

Fröhlichkeit *f, no pl* happiness; (*fröhliches Wesen*) happy *or* cheerful nature; (*gesellige Stimmung*) merriment, gaiety.

frohlocken* *vi* (*geh*) to rejoice (*über* +*acc* over, at); (*vor Schadenfreude auch*) to gloat (*über* +*acc* over, *bei* at). **frohlocket dem Herrn!** (*Bibl*) praise to the Lord!, rejoice in the Lord!

Froh-: **~natur** *f* (*geh*) **(a)** (*Mensch*) happy *or* cheerful soul *or* person; **(b)** (*Wesensart*) happy *or* cheerful nature; **~sinn** *m, no pl* cheerfulness; (*fröhliches Wesen*) cheerful nature; **f~sinnig** *adj* cheerful.

fromm *adj, comp* **̈er** *or* **-er,** *superl* **̈ste(r, s)** *or* **-ste(r, s)** *or adv* **am -̈sten (a)** (*gläubig*) religious; *Christ* devout; *Werke* good; *Leben, Tun, Versenkung etc* godly, pious; (*scheinheilig*) pious, sanctimonious. **~ werden** to become religious, to turn to *or* get (*inf*) religion; **mit ~em Augenaufschlag/Blick** looking as if butter wouldn't melt in his/her mouth.

(b) (*old: rechtschaffen*) *Bürger, Leute, Denkungsart* god-fearing, upright. **es kann der F~ste nicht in Frieden leben, wenn es dem bösen Nachbarn nicht gefällt** (*Prov*) you can't be on good terms with a bad neighbour however hard you try.

(c) (*old: gehorsam*) meek, docile; *Tier* quiet, docile. **~ wie ein Lamm sein** to be as meek *or* (*Tier*) gentle as a lamb.

(d) (*fig*) **eine ~e Lüge, ein ~er Betrug** self-deception; **das ist ja wohl nur ein ~er Wunsch** that's just a pipe-dream.

Fromme *m siehe* Nutz.

Frömmelei *f* (*pej*) false piety.

frömmeln *vi* (*pej*) to act piously, to affect piety.

frommen *vi* (*old*) **jdm/nichts ~** to avail sb (*form*)/avail sb naught (*old*); **was frommt ihm das Geld?** of what avail is the money to him? (*form*); **was frommt es zu klagen?** of what avail is it to complain? (*form*).

Frömmigkeit *f siehe* fromm **(a, b)** religiousness; devoutness; goodness; godliness, piousness; piousness, sanctimony; uprightness.

Frömmler(in *f***)** *m* **-s, -** (*pej*) sanctimonious hypocrite.

frömmlerisch *adj* (*pej*) pious, sanctimonious.

Fron *f* **-, -en, Fronarbeit** *f* (*Hist*) socage *no pl*; (*fig*) drudgery *no pl*; (*Sklavenarbeit*) slavery.

Fronde ['frõːdə] *f* **-, -n** (*Pol*) faction.

Frondeur [frõdøːr] *m* factionist.

Frondienst *m* (*Hist*) socage *no pl*. **jdm ~e leisten** to do socage (work) for sb.

fronen *vi* (*Hist*) to labour for one's feudal lord; (*fig geh*) to labour.

frönen *vi* +*dat* (*geh*) to indulge in; *seiner Eitelkeit* to indulge.

Fronleichnam *no art* **-(e)s,** *no pl* (the Feast of) Corpus Christi. **zu** *or* **an ~** at the Feast of Corpus Christi, on Corpus Christi.

Fronleichnams-: **~fest** *nt* Feast of Corpus Christi; **~prozession** *f*, **~zug** *m* Corpus Christi procession.

Front *f* **-, -en (a)** (*Vorderseite*) front; (*Vorderansicht*) frontage. **die hintere/rückwärtige ~** the back/the rear; **der General schritt die ~ der wartenden Truppen ab** the general inspected the waiting troops; **er schritt die ~ der geparkten Wagen ab** he walked up and down in front of the parked cars.

(b) (*Kampflinie, -gebiet*) front. **in vorderster ~ stehen** to be in the front line; **auf breiter ~** along a wide front; **an der ~ at the front; **klare ~en schaffen** (*fig*) to clarify the/one's position.

(c) (*Met*) front.

(d) (*Einheit*) ranks *pl*; (*in Namen*) front. **sich einer geschlossenen ~ gegenübersehen** to be faced with a united front; **~ gegen jdn/etw machen** to make a stand against sb/sth.

(e) (*Sport: Führung*) **in ~ liegen/gehen** to be in/go into *or* take the lead.

Front|abschnitt *m* section of the front.

frontal 1 *adj no pred* frontal; *Zusammenstoß* head-on. **2** *adv* frontally; *zusammenstoßen* head-on.

Frontal-: **~angriff** *m* frontal attack; **~zusammenstoß** *m* head-on collision.

Front-: **~antrieb** *m* (*Aut*) front-wheel drive; **~begradigung** *f* straightening of the front; (*fig*) streamlining operation; **~bericht** *m* report from the front; **~dienst, ~einsatz** *m* service at the front; **er wurde zum ~dienst nach Rumänien abkommandiert** he was posted to serve on the Rumanian front.

Frontispiz *nt* **-es, -e** (*Archit, Typ*) frontispiece.

Front-: **~kämpfer** *m siehe* **~soldat; ~motor** *m* front-mounted engine; **~schwein** *nt* (*sl*), **~soldat** *m* front-line soldier; **~stadt** *f* frontier town/city; **die ~stadt (West-Berlin)** (*pej*) West Berlin; **~urlaub** *m* leave from the front; **~wand** *f* frontage; **~wechsel** *m* (*fig*) about-turn; **einen ~wechsel vornehmen** to do an about-turn; **~zulage** *f* supplement for service at the front.

Fronvogt *m* (*Hist*) (socage) overseer.

fror *pret of* **frieren.**

Frosch *m* **-(e)s, -̈e** frog; (*Feuerwerkskörper*) (fire)cracker, jumping jack (*Brit*). **einen ~ in der Kehle** *or* **im Hals haben** (*inf*) to have a frog in one's throat; **sei kein ~!** (*inf*) be a sport!

Frosch-: **~auge** *nt* (*fig inf*) pop eye; **er hat ~augen** he has pop eyes *or* is pop-eyed; **~biß** *m* (*Bot*) frogbit; **~hüpfen** *nt* leapfrog;

~könig *m* Frog Prince; **~konzert** *nt* (*hum*) frog chorus; **~laich** *m* frogspawn; **~lurch** *m* salientian (*form*), member of the frog family; **~mann** *m* frogman; **~maul** *nt* (*fig inf*) pout; **ein ~maul machen** *or* **ziehen** to pout; **~perspektive** *f* worm's-eye view; (*fig*) blinkered view; **etw aus der ~perspektive foto-grafieren/sehen** to take/get a worm's-eye view of sth; **etw aus der ~perspektive betrachten** (*fig*) to have a blinkered view of sth; **~schenkel** *m* frog's leg; **~test** *m* (*Med*) Bickenbach (pregnancy) test.

Frost *m* **-(e)s, -̈e (a)** frost. **es herrscht strenger/klirrender ~** there's a hard *or* heavy/crisp frost; **bei eisigem ~** in heavy frost; **~ (ab)bekommen** (*Hände, Ohren*) to get frostbitten; **~ vertragen (können)** to be able to stand the/(the) frost.

(b) (*Med: Schüttel~*) fit of shivering *or* the shivers (*inf*). **er wurde von einem heftigen ~ geschüttelt** he shivered violently.

Frost-: **~aufbruch** *m* frost damage; **f~beständig** *adj* frost-resistant; **~beule** *f* chilblain; **~boden** *m* frozen ground; (*ständig gefroren*) permafrost.

fröst(e)lig *adj* (*inf*) chilly. **er ist ein ~er Mensch** he's a chilly mortal (*inf*), he feels the cold.

frösteln 1 *vi* to shiver; (*vor Angst auch*) to tremble; (*vor Entsetzen auch*) to shudder. **im Fieber ~** to shiver feverishly. **2** *vt impers* **es fröstelte mich** I shivered/trembled/shuddered.

frosten *vt* to freeze.

Froster *m* **-s, -** (*im Kühlschrank*) icebox (*Brit*), freezer compartment; (*Gefriertruhe*) freezer, deep-freeze.

Frost-: **f~frei** *adj* frost-free, free from *or* of frost; **die Nacht war f~frei** there was no frost overnight; **~gefahr** *f* danger of frost.

frostig *adj* (*lit, fig*) frosty. **ein ~er Hauch** an icy draught.

Frostigkeit *f* (*fig*) frostiness.

Frost-: **f~klar** *adj* clear and frosty; **f~klirrend** *adj attr* (*liter*) crisp and frosty; **~schaden** *m* frost damage; **~schutz** *m* protection against frost; **~schutzmittel** *nt* (*Aut*) antifreeze; **~warnung** *f* frost warning; **~wetter** *nt* frosty weather.

Frottee [frɔteː] *nt or m* **-s, -s** terry towelling. **ein Kleid aus ~ a towelling dress.

Frottee-: **~(hand)tuch** *nt* (terry) towel; **~kleid** *nt* towelling dress.

frottieren* *vt Haut* to rub; *jdn, sich* to rub down.

Frottier(hand)tuch *nt siehe* **Frottee(hand)tuch.**

Frotzelei *f* (*inf*) teasing; (*Bemerkung*) teasing remark.

frotzeln *vti* (*inf*) to tease. **über jdn/etw ~** to make fun of sb/sth.

Frucht *f* **-, -̈e** (*Bot, fig*) fruit; (*Embryo*) foetus; (*no pl: Getreide*) crops *pl*. **~e** (*Obst*) fruit *sing*; **~e tragen** (*lit, fig*) to bear fruit; **die ~e des Feldes** (*liter*) the fruits of the earth (*liter*); **verbotene ~e** forbidden fruits; **eine ~ der Liebe** (*old euph*) a love child; **an ihren ~en sollt ihr sie erkennen** (*Bibl*) by their fruits ye shall know them (*Bibl*).

Frucht|ansatz *m* (*Bot*) fruit buds *pl*. **einen guten ~ haben** to have a lot of fruit buds.

fruchtbar *adj* **(a)** (*lit, fig: zeugungsfähig, reiche Frucht bringend*) fertile; *siehe* Boden. **(b)** (*lit, fig: viele Nachkommen zeugend, viel schaffend*) prolific; (*Bibl*) fruitful. **(c)** (*fig: nutzbringend*) fruitful, productive. **etw für jdn/etw ~ machen** to use sth for the good of sb/sth, to use sth to benefit sb/sth.

Fruchtbarkeit *f siehe adj* fertility; prolificness; fruitfulness, productiveness.

Fruchtbarkeits-: **~kult** *m* fertility cult; **~symbol** *nt* fertility symbol; **~zauber** *m* fertility rite.

Fruchtbarmachung *f* (*von Wüste*) reclamation.

Frucht-: **~becher** *m* fruit sundae; (*Bot*) cupule (*spec*), cup; **~blase** *f* amniotic sac; **~bonbon** *m or nt* fruit drop; **f~bringend** *adj* (*geh*) fruitful, productive.

Früchtchen *nt dim of* Frucht (*inf*) (*Tunichtgut*) good-for-nothing; (*Kind*) rascal (*inf*). **du bist mir ein sauberes** *or* **nettes ~** (*iro*) you're a right one (*inf*).

Früchtebrot *nt* fruit loaf.

fruchten *vi* to bear fruit. **nichts ~** to be fruitless.

Frucht-: **~fleisch** *nt* flesh (*of a fruit*); **~fliege** *f* fruit-fly; **~folge** *f* (*Agr*) rotation of crops.

fruchtig *adj* fruity.

Frucht-: **~kapsel** *f* (*Bot*) capsule; **~knoten** *m* (*Bot*) ovary; **f~los** *adj* (*fig*) fruitless; **~losigkeit** *f* fruitlessness; **~mark** *nt* (*Cook*) fruit pulp; **~presse** *f* fruit press *or* squeezer; **~saft** *m* fruit juice; **~säure** *f* fruit acid; **~stand** *m* (*Bot*) multiple fruit; **f~tragend** *adj attr* fruit-bearing; **~wasser** *nt* (*Physiol*) amniotic fluid; **das ~wasser ist vorzeitig abgegangen** the waters broke early; **~wechsel** *m* crop rotation; **~zucker** *m* fructose.

frugal *adj* (*geh*) frugal.

früh 1 *adj* early. **am ~en Morgen** early in the morning, in the early morning; **in ~er Jugend** in one's early youth; **in ~er/~ester Kindheit** in one's early childhood/very early in one's childhood; **der ~e Goethe** the young Goethe; **ein Werk des ~en Picasso** an early work by Picasso; **ein ~er Picasso** an early Picasso; **er war der F~ste bei der Party** he was the first (person) at the party.

2 *adv* **(a)** early; (*in jungen Jahren*) young, at an early age; (*in Entwicklung*) early on. **es ist noch ~ am Tag/im Jahr** it is still early in the day/year; **von ~ bis spät** from morning till night, from dawn to dusk; **er hat schon ~ erkannt, daß ...** he recognized early on that ...; **du hast dich nicht ~ genug angemeldet** you didn't apply early *or* soon enough; **zu ~ starten** to start too soon; **~ übt sich, was ein Meister werden will** (*Prov*) there's nothing like starting young.

(b) Freitag/morgen ~ Friday/tomorrow morning; **heute ~** this morning.

Früh- *in cpds* early; **~antike** *f* early classical period; **f~auf** *adv* **von f~auf** from an early age; **~aufsteher** *m* **-s, -** early riser, early bird (inf); ~beet nt cold frame; ~behandlung f early or prompt treatment no indef art; f~christlich adj early Christian; ~diagnose f early diagnosis; ~dienst m early duty; ~dienst haben to be on early duty.

Frühe f -, no pl (a) (liter: Frühzeit) dawn. in der ~ des Tages in the early morning. (b) (Morgen) in der ~ early in the morning; in aller or gleich in der ~ at break or (the) crack of dawn.

Frühehe f young marriage.

früher comp of früh 1 adj (a) earlier. in ~en Jahren/Zeiten in the past; in ~em Alter when he/she etc was younger; in meinem ~en Leben habe ich ~ when I was younger I ...; der Mangel an technischen Geräten in ~en Zeitaltern the lack of technical equipment in past ages.

(b) (ehemalig) former; (vorherig) Besitzer, Wohnsitz previous. der Kontakt zu seinen ~en Freunden ist abgebrochen he lost contact with his old friends.

2 adv (a) earlier. ~ als 6 Uhr/Freitag kann ich nicht kommen I can't come earlier than 6 o'clock/earlier or sooner than Friday; ~ geht's nicht it can't be done any/I etc can't make it earlier or sooner; ~ am Abend hat er gesagt ... earlier (on) in the evening he said ...; alle, die sich ~ angemeldet haben, werden zuerst berücksichtigt the first to apply will be the first to be considered; damit das Kind das ~ lernt so that the child learns that earlier or sooner or at an earlier age; das hättest du ~ sagen müssen/wissen sollen you should have said that before or sooner/known that before; ~ oder später sooner or later.

(b) (in jüngeren Jahren, in vergangenen Zeiten) Herr X, ~ Direktor eines Industriebetriebs Herr X, formerly director of an industrial concern; ich habe ihn ~ mal gekannt I used to know him; ~ habe ich so etwas nie gemacht I never used to do that kind of thing; ~ stand hier eine Kirche there used to be a church here; ~ war alles besser/war das alles anders things were better/different in the old days, things used to be better/different; genau wie ~ just as it/he etc used to be; Erzählungen von/Erinnerungen an ~ stories/memories of times gone by or of bygone days (liter); das habe ich noch von ~ I had it before; ich kannte/kenne ihn von ~ I knew him before/I've known him some time; wir kennen uns noch von ~ we got to know each other some time ago; die Beule am Auto ist or stammt noch von ~ that's an old dent on the car; meine Freunde von ~ my old friends.

frühestens adv at the earliest. ~ am Sonntag on Sunday at the earliest; wann kann das ~ fertig sein? what is the earliest that can be ready?

früheste(r, s) adj superl of früh.

frühestmöglich adj attr earliest possible.

Früh-: ~geburt f premature birth; (Kind) premature baby; sie hatte/meine Tochter war eine ~geburt her baby/my daughter was premature or born prematurely; ~geschichte f early history; ~gottesdienst m early service; ~herbst m early autumn or fall (US); f~herbstlich adj early autumn/fall attr; ~invalidität f early retirement due to ill health.

Frühjahr nt spring.

Frühjahrs-: ~bote m (liter) harbinger of spring (liter); ~müdigkeit f springtime lethargy; ~putz m spring-cleaning no indef art; ~putz machen, einen großen ~putz veranstalten to do the spring-cleaning, to spring-clean.

Früh-: ~kapitalismus m early capitalism; ~kartoffeln pl early potatoes pl; f~kindlich adj (Psych) of early childhood; Sexualität, Entwicklung in early childhood; Trauma, Erlebnisse from early childhood; ~konzert nt early morning concert; (von Vögeln) dawn chorus; ~kultur f (a) early culture; die griechische ~kultur the culture of the early Greeks, early Greek culture; (b) (Hort) propagated seedlings pl.

Frühling m spring. es wird ~ spring is coming; im ~ in spring; die Stadt des ewigen ~s (poet) the springtime city (liter); im ~ des Lebens stehen (poet) to be in the springtime of one's life (liter); einem neuen ~ entgegengehen (fig) to start to flourish again; seinen zweiten ~ erleben to go through one's second adolescence.

Frühlings- in cpds spring; ~anfang m first day of spring; am 21. März ist ~anfang March 21st is the first day of spring; ~fest nt spring festival; ~gefühle pl (hum inf) ~gefühle haben/bekommen to be/get frisky (hum inf); wenn sich ~gefühle (bei ihm) regen when he starts to feel frisky (hum inf), when the sap starts to rise (hum); f~haft adj springlike; ~zeit f springtime, springtide (liter).

Früh-: ~messe f early mass; f~morgens adv early in the morning; ~nebel m early morning mist; ~neuhochdeutsch nt Early New High German; f~reif adj precocious; (körperlich) mature at an early age; ~reif m (hoar) frost; ~reife f siehe adj precociousness; early maturity; ~rentner m person who has retired early; ~schicht f early shift; ich gehöre zur ~schicht (inf) I'm on the early shift; ~schoppen m morning/lunchtime drinking; zum ~schoppen gehen to go for a morning/lunchtime drink; ~sommer m early summer; f~sommerlich adj early summer attr; das Wetter ist schon f~sommerlich the weather is already quite summery; ~sport m early morning exercise; ~sport treiben to get some early morning exercise; ~stadium nt early stage; im ~stadium in the early stages; ~start m false start.

Frühstück nt -s, -e breakfast; (~spause) morning or coffee break. zweites ~ ≈ elevenses (Brit inf), midmorning snack; um 9 Uhr ist ~ breakfast is at 9 o'clock; was ißt du zum ~? what do you have for breakfast?; die ganze Familie saß beim ~ the whole family were having breakfast.

frühstücken insep 1 vi to have breakfast, to breakfast. 2 vt to breakfast on.

Frühstücks-: ~brett nt wooden platter; ~brot nt sandwich (for one's morning snack); ~fleisch nt luncheon meat; ~pause f

morning or coffee break; ~pause machen to have one's morning or coffee break; ~teller m dessert plate.

Früh-: f~vollendet adj attr (liter) ein f~vollendeter Maler/ Dichter, ein ~vollendeter a young artist/poet of genius whose life was soon over; ~warnsystem nt early warning system; ~werk nt early work; ~zeit f early days pl; die ~zeit des Christentums/der Menschheit early Christian times/the early days of mankind; f~zeitig 1 adj early; (vorzeitig auch) premature; Tod auch premature, untimely; 2 adv early; (vorzeitig) prematurely; (früh genug auch) in good time; (ziemlich am Anfang) early on; ~zug m early train; ~zündung f (Aut) pre-ignition.

Frust m -(e)s, no pl (sl) frustration no art. das ist der totale ~, wenn ... it's totally frustrating when ...

Frustration f frustration.

frustrieren* vt to frustrate; (inf: enttäuschen) to upset.

frz. abbr of französisch.

F-Schlüssel ['ɛfʃlʏsl] m (Mus) F or bass clef.

FU [ɛf'uː] f - abbr of **Freie Universität** (Berlin).

Fuchs [fʊks] m -es, -e (a) (Tier) fox; (fig auch) cunning devil (inf). er ist ein alter or schlauer ~ (inf) he's a cunning old devil (inf) or fox (inf); schlau wie ein ~ as cunning as a fox; wo sich die ~e or wo sich Hase und ~ gute Nacht sagen (hum) in the back of beyond or the middle of nowhere.

(b) (~pelz) fox (fur).

(c) (Pferd) chestnut; (mit hellerem Schwanz und Mähne) sorrel; (inf: Mensch) redhead.

(d) (Univ) siehe Fux.

Fuchs-: ~bau m fox's den; ~eisen nt (Hunt) fox trap.

fuchsen ['fʊksn] (inf) 1 vt to vex, to annoy. 2 vr to be annoyed or cross.

Fuchsie ['fʊksiə] f (Bot) fuchsia.

fuchsig ['fʊksɪç] adj (inf) (a) (rotblond) Haar ginger, carroty (inf). (b) (wütend) mad (inf).

Füchsin ['fʏksɪn] f vixen.

Fuchs-: ~jagd f fox-hunt/-hunting; ~loch nt foxhole; ~pelz m fox fur; f~rot adj Fell red; Pferd chestnut; Haar ginger, carroty (inf); ~schwanz m (a) fox's tail; (Hunt) (fox's) brush; (b) (Bot) love-lies-bleeding, amaranth, (c) (Tech: Säge) handsaw; f~teufelswild adj (inf) hopping mad (inf).

Fuchtel f -, -n (a) (Hist: Degen) broadsword; (fig inf: Knute) control. unter jds ~ under sb's thumb; er ist unter ihre ~ gekommen or geraten she's got or gotten (US) him under her thumb; er steht unter der ~ he's not his own master. (b) (Aus, S Ger inf: zänkische Frau) shrew, vixen.

fuchteln vi (inf) (mit den Händen) ~ to wave one's hands about (inf); mit etw ~ to wave sth about or around; (drohend) to brandish sth.

fuchtig adj (inf) (hopping) mad (inf).

Fuder nt -s, - (a) (Wagenladung) cartload. (b) (Hohlmaß für Wein) tun.

fuderweise adv by the cartload. ~ Salat essen (hum) to eat tons of salad (inf).

Fudschijama m -s Fujiyama.

Fuffzehn f -, -en (dial) fifteen; (sl: Pause) fifteen-minute break. 'ne ~ machen (sl) to take or have a break.

fuffzehn num (dial) fifteen. bei mir ist ~ (sl) I've had all I'm going to take (inf).

Fuffziger m -s, - (dial) fifty-pfennig piece. er ist ein falscher ~ (sl) he's a real crook (inf).

Fug m: mit ~ und Recht (geh) with complete justification; etw mit ~ und Recht tun to be completely justified in doing sth.

Fuge f -, -n (a) joint; (Ritze) gap, crack. in allen ~n krachen to creak at the joints; aus den ~n gehen or geraten (Auto etc) to come apart at the seams; die Menschheit/Welt ist/die Zeiten sind aus den ~n geraten (geh) mankind has gone awry (liter)/the world is/the times are out of joint (liter).

(b) (Mus) fugue.

fugen vt to joint.

fügen 1 vt (a) (setzen) to put, to place; (ein~ auch) to fix; (geh) Worte, Satz to formulate. Wort an Wort ~ to string words together.

(b) (geh: bewirken) to ordain; (Schicksal auch) to decree. der Zufall fügte es, daß ... fate decreed that ...

2 vr (a) (sich unterordnen) to be obedient, to obey. sich jdm/einer Sache or in etw (acc) (geh) ~ to bow to sb/sth; Anordnungen etc to obey sth; sich dem or in das Schicksal ~ to accept one's fate, to bow to one's fate.

(b) impers (geh: geschehen) es hat sich so gefügt it was decreed by fate; es fügte sich, daß ... it so happened that ...

Fugen-: f~los adj smooth; ~s nt (Ling) linking 's'; ~zeichen nt (Ling) linking letter.

füglich adv (geh) justifiably, reasonably.

fügsam adj Mensch obedient; Haar manageable.

Fügsamkeit f siehe adj obedience; manageability.

Fügung f (a) (Bestimmung) chance, stroke of fate. eine glückliche ~ a stroke of good fortune, a happy chance; göttliche ~ divine providence; eine ~ Gottes/des Schicksals an act of divine providence/of fate; eine seltsame ~ wollte es, daß er ... by some or a strange chance he ...

(b) (Ling: Wortgruppe) construction.

fühlbar adj (spürbar) perceptible; (beträchtlich auch) marked. bald wird die Krise auch bei uns ~ the crisis will soon be felt here too.

fühlen 1 vt (a) (spüren, empfinden) to feel. Mitleid mit jdm ~ to feel sympathy for sb.

(b) (ertasten) Beule, Erhebung to feel; Puls to take.

2 vi (a) (geh: empfinden) to feel.

(b) nach etw ~ to feel for sth.

3 vr (a) (empfinden, sich halten für) to feel. sich

krank/beleidigt/verantwortlich ~ to feel ill/insulted/responsible; **wie ~ Sie sich?** how are you feeling or do you feel?; **er fühlte sich als Held** he felt (like) a hero.

(b) (inf: stolz sein) to think one is so great (inf).

Fühler m **-s, -** (Zool) feeler, antenna; (von Schnecke) horn. **seine ~ ausstrecken** (fig inf) to put out feelers (nach towards).

fühllos adj (geh) siehe **gefühllos.**

Fühlung f contact. **mit jdm in ~ bleiben/stehen** to remain or stay/be in contact or touch with sb.

Fühlungnahme f **-, -n die erste ~ der beiden Parteien** the initial contact between the two parties.

fuhr pret of **fahren.**

Fuhr-: ~**amt** nt (form) cleansing department; ~**betrieb** m haulage business.

Fuhre f **-, -n** (Ladung) load; (Taxieinsatz) fare. **eine ~ Stroh** a (cart- or waggon-)load of straw; **wir müssen die Leute in zwei ~n zum Bahnhof bringen** we'll have to take the people to the station in two batches.

führen 1 vt **(a)** (geleiten) to take; (vorangehen, -fahren) to lead. **eine alte Dame über die Straße ~** to help an old lady over the road; **sie hat uns den richtigen Weg geführt** she showed us the right way; **er führte uns durch das Schloß/durch Italien** he showed us round the castle/he was our guide in Italy; **~ Sie mich zum Geschäftsführer!** take me to the manager!; **eine Klasse zum Abitur ~** to see a class through to A-levels; **jdn zum (Trau)altar ~** to lead sb to the altar.

(b) (leiten) Geschäft, Betrieb etc to run; Gruppe, Expedition etc to lead, to head; Schiff to captain; Armee etc to command.

(c) (in eine Situation bringen) to get (inf), to lead; (veranlassen zu kommen/gehen) to bring/take. **der Hinweis führte die Polizei auf die Spur des Diebes** that tip put the police on the trail of the thief; **das führt uns auf das Thema ...** that brings or leads us (on)to the subject ...; **was führt Sie zu mir?** (form) what brings you to me?; **ein Land ins Chaos ~** to reduce a country to chaos.

(d) (registriert haben) to have a record of. **wir ~ keinen Meier in unserer Kartei** we have no (record of a) Meier on our files.

(e) (handhaben) Pinsel, Bogen, Kamera etc to wield. **den Löffel zum Mund/das Glas an die Lippen ~** to raise one's spoon to one's mouth/one's glass to one's lips; **die Hand an die Mütze ~** to touch one's cap.

(f) (entlangführen) Leitung, Draht to carry.

(g) (form: steuern) Kraftfahrzeug to drive; Flugzeug to fly, to pilot; Kran, Fahrstuhl to operate; Schiff to sail.

(h) (transportieren) to carry; (haben) Autokennzeichen, Wappen, Namen to have, to bear. **Geld/seine Papiere bei sich ~** (form) to carry money/one's papers on one's person; **der Fluß führt Hochwasser** the river is running high.

(i) (im Angebot haben) to stock, to carry (spec), to keep. **etw ständig im Munde ~** to be always talking about sth; **er führt diesen Spruch ständig im Munde** he is always using that phrase.

2 vi **(a)** (in Führung liegen) to lead; (bei Wettkämpfen auch) to be in the lead. **die Mannschaft führt mit 10 Punkten Vorsprung** the team has a lead of 10 points or is in the lead by 10 points; **die Firma XY führt in Tonbandgeräten** XY is the leading firm for tape recorders.

(b) (verlaufen) (Straße) to go; (Kabel, Pipeline etc) to run; (Spur) to lead. **das Rennen führt über 10 Runden/durch ganz Frankreich** the race takes place over 10 laps/covers France; **der Fahrstuhl führt in die 81. Etage** the lift goes up to the 81st or 82nd (US) floor; **die Autobahn führt nach Kiel/am Rhein entlang** the motorway goes to Kiel/runs or goes along the Rhine; **die Brücke führt über die Elbe** the bridge crosses or spans the Elbe; **der Waldweg führt zu einem Gasthof** the forest path leads or goes to an inn; **wohin soll das alles nur ~?** where is it all leading (us)?

(c) (als Ergebnis haben) **zu etw ~** to lead to sth, to result in sth; **das führt zu nichts** that will come to nothing; **es führte zu dem Ergebnis, daß er entlassen wurde** it resulted in or led to his being dismissed.

3 vr (form: sich benehmen) to conduct oneself.

führend adj leading attr; Rolle, Persönlichkeit auch prominent. **diese Firma ist im Stahlbau ~** that is one of the leading firms in steel construction; **die Sowjets sind im Schach ~** the Soviets lead the world in chess.

Führer m **-s, -** **(a)** (Leiter) leader; (Oberhaupt) head. **der ~** (Hist) the Führer or Fuehrer. **(b)** (Fremden~, Berg~) guide. **(c)** (Buch) guide. **~ durch England** guide to England. **(d)** (form: Lenker) driver; (von Flugzeug) pilot; (von Kran, Fahrstuhl) operator; (von Schiff) person in charge.

Führerhaus nt cab; (von Kran auch) cabin.

Führerin f siehe **Führer (a-c).**

Führer-: **f~los** adj Gruppe, Partei leaderless no adv, without a leader; Wagen driverless no adv, without a driver; Flugzeug pilotless no adv, without a pilot; Schiff with no-one at the helm; ~**schaft** f leadership; (die Führer auch) leaders pl; (Oberhäupter) heads pl; ~**schein** m (für Auto) driving licence, driver's license (US); (für Flugzeug) pilot's licence; (für Motorboot) motorboat licence; **den ~schein machen** (Aut) to learn to drive; (die Prüfung ablegen) to take one's (driving) test; **jdm den ~schein entziehen** to take away sb's driving licence, to disqualify sb from driving; **ihm ist der ~schein abgenommen worden** he's lost his licence; ~**scheinentzug** m disqualification from driving; ~**stand** m (von Zug) cab; (von Kran auch) cabin.

Fuhr-: ~**geld** nt siehe ~**lohn;** ~**geschäft** nt siehe ~**unternehmen.**

führig adj Schnee good for skiing.

Fuhr-: ~**knecht** m (old) siehe ~**mann;** ~**leute** pl of ~**mann;**

~**lohn** m delivery charge; ~**mann** m, pl **-leute** carter; (Kutscher) coachman; **der ~mann** (Astron) Auriga, the Charioteer; ~**park** m fleet (of vehicles).

Führung f **(a)** no pl guidance, direction; (von Partei, Expedition etc) leadership; (Mil) command; (eines Unternehmens etc) management. **unter der ~ +gen** under the direction/leadership/command/management of, directed/led or headed/commanded/managed by; **wer hat hier die ~?** (Mil) who is in command here?

(b) no pl (die Führer) leaders pl, leadership sing; (Mil) commanders pl; (eines Unternehmens etc) directors pl.

(c) (Besichtigung) guided tour (durch of).

(d) no pl (Vorsprung) lead. **die klare ~ haben** to have a clear lead; **die Firma hat eine klare ~ auf diesem Gebiet** the firm clearly leads the field in this area; **in ~ gehen/liegen** to go into/be in the lead.

(e) no pl (Betragen) conduct.

(f) no pl (Handhabung) touch.

(g) (Mech) guide, guideway.

(h) (form: Lenken) **zur ~ eines Kraft-/Wasserfahrzeugs/Flugzeugs berechtigt sein** to be allowed to drive a motor vehicle/be in charge of a vessel/fly or pilot an aeroplane.

(i) no pl (Betreuung) running. **die ~ der Akten/Bücher** keeping the files/books.

Führungs-: ~**anspruch** m claims pl to leadership; **seinen ~anspruch anmelden** to make a bid for the leadership; ~**aufgabe** f executive duty; ~**kraft** f executive; ~**rolle** f role of leader; ~**schicht** f ruling classes pl; ~**schiene** f guide rail; ~**spitze** f highest echelon of the leadership; (eines Unternehmens etc) top management; ~**stab** m (Mil) command no pl; (Comm) top management; **die ~stäbe der Marine** naval command; ~**tor** nt (Ftbl) goal which gives/gave a/the team the lead; ~**zeugnis** nt siehe **polizeilich.**

Fuhr-: ~**unternehmen** nt haulage business; ~**unternehmer** m haulier, haulage contractor, carrier; ~**werk** nt wag(g)on; (Pferde~) horse and cart; (Ochsen~) oxcart; **f~werken** vi insep **(a)** (inf) in der Küche **f~werken** to bustle around in the kitchen; **mit den Armen f~werken** to wave one's arms about; **(b)** (S Ger, Aus) to drive a cart; ~**wesen** nt cartage business.

Fülle f **-,** no pl **(a)** (Körpermasse) corpulence, portliness.

(b) (Stärke) fullness; (von Stimme, Klang auch) richness; (von Wein auch) full-bodiedness. **aus der ~ des Herzens** (liter) from the fullness of one's heart.

(c) (Menge) wealth. **eine ~ von Fragen/Eindrücken** etc a whole host of questions/impressions etc; **in ~** in abundance; siehe **Hülle.**

füllen 1 vt **(a)** to fill; (Cook) to stuff. **etw in Flaschen ~** to bottle sth; **etw in Säcke ~** to put sth into sacks; siehe **gefüllt.** **(b)** (in Anspruch nehmen) to fill, to occupy; Regal auch to take up. **2** vr (Theater, Badewanne) to fill up. **ihre Augen füllten sich mit Tränen** her eyes filled with tears.

Füllen nt **-s, -** siehe **Fohlen.**

Füller m **-s, -** **(a)** (Füllfederhalter) fountain pen. **(b)** (Press) filler.

Füll-: ~**federhalter** m fountain pen; ~**gewicht** nt **(a)** (Comm) weight at time of packing; (auf Dosen) net weight; **(b)** (von Waschmaschine) maximum load, capacity; ~**horn** nt (liter) cornucopia; (fig auch) horn of plenty; **das ~horn seines Wissens** the endless wealth of his knowledge; **das ~horn der Natur** nature's infinite storehouse.

füllig adj Mensch corpulent, portly; Figur, Busen generous, ample; Frisur bouffant attr.

Füllmasse f filler, filling material; (Zahn~) filling compound.

Füllsel nt (in Paket etc) packing; (in Geschriebenem) (Wort) filler; (Floskel) padding.

Füllung f filling; (Geflügel~, Fleisch~, Stofftier~, Polster~) stuffing; (Tür~) panel; (von Pralinen) centre.

Füllwort nt filler.

fulminant adj (geh) sparkling, brilliant.

Fummel m **-s, -** (sl) rag.

Fummelei f (inf) fidgeting, fiddling; (sl: Petting) petting, groping (inf). **ich finde Häkeln eine furchtbare ~** I find crocheting terribly fiddly (inf).

Fummelkram m (inf) fiddle (inf), fiddly job (inf).

fummeln vi (inf) to fiddle; (hantieren) to fumble; (erotisch) to pet, to grope (inf). **an etw** (dat) or **mit etw ~** to fiddle (about)/fumble around with sth.

Fummeltrine f (sl) transvestite, drag queen (sl).

Fund m **-(e)s, -e** find; (das Entdecken) discovery, finding. **einen ~ machen** to make a find.

Fundament nt (lit, fig) foundation (usu pl). **das ~ zu etw legen** or **für etw schaffen** (fig) to lay the foundations for sth.

fundamental adj fundamental.

Fundamentalismus m fundamentalism.

fundamentieren* vi to lay the foundations.

Fund-: ~**amt,** ~**büro** nt lost property office; ~**grube** f (fig) treasure trove; **eine ~grube des Wissens** a treasury of knowledge.

fundieren* vt (fig) to back up.

fundiert adj sound. **schlecht ~** unsound.

fündig adj (Min) Sohle rich. **~ werden** to make a strike; (fig) to strike it lucky.

Fund-: ~**ort** m der ~**ort von etw** (the place) where sth is/was found; ~**sachen** pl lost property sing; ~**stätte,** ~**stelle** f die ~**stätte von etw** (the place) where sth is/was found.

Fundus m **-, -** (lit, fig) fund; (Theat) basic equipment. **der ~ seines reichen Wissens** his/the rich fund of knowledge.

fünf num five. **es ist ~ Minuten vor zwölf** (lit) it's five to twelve; (fig) it's almost too late; **sie warteten bis ~ Minuten vor zwölf** (fig) they waited till the eleventh hour; **seine ~ Sinne**

beieinander or **beisammen haben** to have all one's wits about one; **seine ~ Sinne zusammennehmen** to gather one's wits together; **man mußte seine ~ Sinne zusammennehmen** you had to have your wits about you; **~(e) gerade sein lassen** (inf) to turn a blind eye, to look the other way; **siehe auch Finger, vier.**

Fünf f -, **-en** five; **siehe auch Vier.**

Fünf- in cpds five; **siehe auch Vier-; ~eck** nt pentagon; **f~eckig** adj pentagonal, five-cornered.

Fünfer m -s, - (inf) five-pfennig piece; five-marks; **siehe auch Vierer.**

Fünf-: f~fach adj fivefold; **siehe auch vierfach; f~füßig** adj (Poet) pentametrical; **f~füßiger Jambus** iambic pentameter; **f~hundert** num five hundred; **siehe auch vierhundert; ~jahr(es)plan** m five-year plan; **f~jährig** adj Frist, Plan etc five-year, quinquennial (form); Kind five-year-old; **eine f~jährige Zeitspanne** a period of five years, a quinquennium (form); **siehe auch vierjährig; ~kampf** m (Sport) pentathlon; **~ling** m quintuplet; **f~mal** adv five times; **siehe auch viermal; ~markschein** m five-mark note; **~markstück** nt five-mark piece; **~pfennigstück** nt five-pfennig piece; **~prozentklausel** f (Parl) clause in the constitution of a country which debars parties with less than 5% of the vote from entering Parliament; **f~seitig** adj (Geom) five-sided; (Brief) five-page attr; **siehe auch vierseitig; ~stromland** nt (Geog) Punjab; **f~tägig** adj five-day attr; **f~tausend** num five thousand; **siehe auch viertausend.**

Fünftel nt -s, - fifth; **siehe auch Viertel**[1].

fünftens adv fifth(ly), in the fifth place.

fünfte(r, s) adj fifth. **die ~ Kolonne** the fifth column; **siehe auch vierte(r,s), Rad.**

Fünf-: ~uhrtee m afternoon tea; **f~undzwanzig** num twenty-five; **f~zehn** num fifteen.

fünfzig num fifty; **siehe auch vierzig.**

Fünfzig f -, **-en** fifties; **siehe auch Vierzig.**

Fünfziger m -s, - (inf) (Fünfzigjähriger) fifty-year-old; (Geld) fifty-pfennig piece; fifty-mark note; **siehe auch Fuffziger, Vierziger(in).**

Fünfzig-: f~jährig adj Person fifty-year-old attr; Zeitspanne fifty-year; **er ist f~jährig verstorben** he died at (the age of) fifty; **~markschein** m fifty-mark note; **~pfennigstück** nt fifty-pfennig piece.

fungieren* [fuŋ'giːrən] vi to function (als as a).

Funk m -s, no pl radio, wireless (dated). **über** or **per ~** by radio; **er arbeitet beim ~** he works in radio or broadcasting.

-funk in cpds broadcasts pl.

Funk-: ~amateur m radio ham, amateur radio enthusiast; **~anlage** f radio set or transceiver; **~aufklärung** f (Mil) radio intelligence; **~ausstellung** f radio and television exhibition; **~bake** f siehe **~feuer; ~bild** nt telephotograph (spec), radio picture.

Funkchen nt dim of Funke. **ein/kein ~ Wahrheit** a grain/not a particle or shred of truth.

Funkdienst m radio communication service.

Funke m -ns, -n, **Funken** m -s, - (a) (lit, fig) spark. **~n sprühen** to spark, to send out or emit sparks; **ihre Augen sprühten ~n** her eyes flashed; **der zündende ~** (fig) the vital spark; **der ~ der Begeisterung sprang auf die Zuschauer über** the audience was infected by his/her etc enthusiasm; **ein ~ des Verständnisses** a spark of understanding; **arbeiten, daß die ~n fliegen** or **sprühen** (inf) to work like mad (inf) or crazy (inf); **zwischen den beiden sprang der ~ über** (inf) something clicked between them (inf).
(b) (ein bißchen) scrap; (von Hoffnung auch) gleam, ray, glimmer; (von Anstand auch) spark.

Funk|einrichtung f radio (equipment). **mit ~ versehen** radio-equipped, equipped with radio.

funkeln vi to sparkle; (Sterne auch) to twinkle; (Augen) (vor Freude) to gleam, to twinkle; (vor Zorn auch) to glitter, to flash; (Edelsteine auch) to glitter; (Edelmetall) to gleam.

funkelnagelneu adj (inf) brand-new.

Funken m -s, - siehe Funke.

funken 1 vt Signal to radio. **SOS ~** to send out or radio an SOS. 2 vi (a) (senden) to radio. (b) (Funken sprühen) to give off or emit sparks, to spark; (fig inf: funktionieren) to work. 3 vi impers **endlich hat es bei ihm gefunkt** (inf) it finally clicked (with him) (inf), the light finally dawned (on him).

Funken-: ~entladung f spark discharge; **~flug** m der Brand wurde durch **~flug von einer Lokomotive** verursacht the fire was caused by sparks from a locomotive; **f~sprühend** adj giving off or emitting sparks; (fig) Diskussion lively; Augen flashing attr, fiery.

Funk|entstörung f suppression of interference.

Funker m -s, - radio or wireless operator.

Funk-: ~erzählung f (Rad) story written for radio; **~fernsteuerung** f radio control; (Anlage) radio-control equipment no pl; **~feuer** nt radio beacon; **~gerät** nt (a) no pl radio equipment; (b) (Sprechfunkgerät) radio set, walkie-talkie; **~haus** nt broadcasting centre, studios pl; **~kolleg** nt educational radio broadcasts pl; **~meßgerät** nt radar (equipment) no pl; **~navigation** f radio navigation; **~ortung** f radiolocation; **~peilung** f radio direction finding; **~sprechgerät** nt radio telephone; (tragbar) walkie-talkie; **~sprechverkehr** m radiotelephony; **~spruch** m radio signal; (Mitteilung) radio message; **~station** f radio station; **~stille** f radio silence; **~streife** f police radio patrol; **~streifenwagen** m police radio patrol or squad car; **~taxi** nt radio taxi; **~technik** f radio technology.

Funktion f (no pl: Tätigkeit) functioning; (Zweck, Aufgabe, Math) function; (Amt) office; (Stellung) position. **in ~ treten/sein** to come into/be in operation; (Organ, Maschine etc) to

---

start to function/be functioning; **etw außer ~ setzen** to stop sth functioning; **dieser Bolzen hat die ~, den Apparat senkrecht zu halten** the function of this bolt is to hold the machine upright.

funktional [fuŋktsio'naːl] adj siehe **funktionell.**

Funktionalismus [fuŋktsiona'lɪsmus] m functionalism.

Funktionär(in f) [fuŋktsio'nɛːɐ, -'nɛːərɪn] m functionary, official.

funktionell [fuŋktsio'nɛl] adj functional (auch Med), practical.

funktionieren* [fuŋktsio'niːrən] vi to work; (Maschine etc auch) to function, to operate; (inf: gehorchen) to obey.

Funktions-: f~fähig adj able to work/function or operate; **~störung** f (Med) malfunction, functional disorder; **f~tüchtig** adj in working order; Organ sound; **~verb** nt (Ling) empty verb.

Funk-: ~turm m radio tower; **~universität** f university of the air; **~verbindung** f radio contact; **~verkehr** m radio communication or traffic; **~wagen** m radio car; **~weg** m auf dem **~weg** by radio; **~werbung** f radio advertizing; **~wesen** nt radio; (Sendesystem) broadcasting system.

Funsel, Funzel f -, -n (inf) dim light, gloom.

Für nt: **das ~ und Wider** the pros and cons (pl).

für 1 prep +acc (a) for. **~ was ist denn dieses Werkzeug?** (inf) what is this tool (used) for?; **kann ich sonst noch etwas ~ Sie tun?** will there be anything else?; **~ mich** for me; (meiner Ansicht nach) in my opinion or view; **diese Frage muß jeder ~ sich (alleine) entscheiden** everyone has to decide this question for or by themselves; **das ist gut ~ Migräne** that's good for migraine; **~ zwei arbeiten** (fig) to do the work of two people; **~ einen Deutschen** ... for a German ...; **~s erste** for the moment; **~s nächstemal** next time.
(b) (Zustimmung) for, in favour of. **sich ~ etw entscheiden** to decide in favour of sth; **was Sie da sagen, hat etwas ~ sich** there's something in what you're saying; **er/das hat was ~ sich** he's not a bad person/it's not a bad thing.
(c) (Gegenleistung) (in exchange) for. **das hat er ~ zehn Pfund gekauft** he bought it for ten pounds.
(d) (Ersatz) for, instead of, in place of. **~ jdn einspringen** to stand in for sb; **er hat mir Mehl ~ Zucker verkauft** he gave me flour instead of sugar.
(e) (Aufeinanderfolge) **Tag ~ Tag** day after day; **Schritt ~ Schritt** step by step.
(f) in Verbindung mit vb, adj siehe auch dort **etw ~ sich behalten** to keep sth to oneself; **~ etw bekannt sein** to be famous or known for sth; **ich halte sie ~ intelligent** I think she is intelligent.
(g) was **~** siehe was.
2 adv (old poet): **~ und ~** for ever and ever.

Furage (fu'raːʒə] f -, no pl (Mil old) forage.

furagieren* [fura'ʒiːrən] vi (Mil old) to forage.

fürbaß adv (obs) onwards. **~ gehen/schreiten** to continue on one's way.

Fürbitte f (Eccl, fig) intercession. **er legte beim Kaiser ~ für die Gefangenen ein** he interceded with the Emperor on behalf of the prisoners.

Fürbitten nt (Eccl) prayers pl; (fig) pleading.

Fürbitter(in f) m -s, - intercessor, interceder.

Furche f -, -n (Acker~, Gesichtsfalte) furrow; (Wagenspur) rut. **ein von ~n durchzogenes Gesicht** a deeply furrowed or lined face.

furchen vt to furrow; (Gesicht etc auch) to line. **die Spuren des Traktors furchten den Weg** the tractor made ruts or furrows in the road; **eine gefurchte Stirn** a furrowed brow.

furchig adj furrowed; (durch Wagenspuren etc auch) rutted.

Furcht f -, no pl fear. **aus ~ vor jdm/etw** for fear of sb/sth; **ohne ~ sein** to be fearless or without fear; **~ vor jdm/etw haben** or **empfinden** to be afraid of sb/sth, to fear sb/sth; **~ ergriff** or **packte ihn** fear seized him, he was seized with fear; **jdn in ~ versetzen, jdm ~ einflößen** to frighten or scare sb.

furchtbar adj terrible, awful, dreadful. **ich habe einen ~en Hunger** I'm ever so or terribly hungry (inf).

furcht|einflößend adj terrifying, fearful.

fürchten 1 vt jdn/etw **~** to be afraid of sb/sth, to fear sb/sth; **das Schlimmste ~** to fear the worst; **~, daß** ... to be afraid or fear that ...; **es war schlimmer, als ich gefürchtet hatte** it was worse than I had feared; **Gott ~** to fear God; **siehe gefürchtet.**
2 vr to be afraid (vor +dat of). **sich im Dunkeln ~** to be afraid or scared of the dark.
3 vi für or um jdn/jds Leben/etw **~** to fear for sb/sb's life/sth; **zum F~ aussehen** to look frightening or terrifying; **da kannst du das F~ lernen** that will scare you stiff; **jdn das F~ lehren** to put the fear of God into sb.

fürchterlich adj siehe **furchtbar.**

Furcht-: f~erregend adj siehe **f~einflößend; f~los** adj fearless, intrepid, dauntless; **~losigkeit** f fearlessness, intrepidity, dauntlessness; **f~sam** adj timorous; **~samkeit** f timorousness.

Furchung f (Biol) cleavage.

fürder(hin) adv (obs) hereafter (old), in future.

für|einander adv for each other, for one another.

Furie ['fuːriə] f (Myth) fury; (fig) hellcat, termagant. **wie von ~n gejagt** or **gehetzt** (liter) as though the devil himself were after him/them etc; **sie gingen wie ~n aufeinander los** they went for each other like cats or wild things.

fürliebnehmen (old) vi sep irreg siehe **vorliebnehmen.**

Furnier nt -s, -e veneer.

furnieren* vt to veneer. **mit Mahagoni furniert** with a mahogany veneer.

Furore f - or nt -s, no pl sensation. **~ machen** (inf) to cause a sensation.

Fürsorge f, no pl (a) (Betreuung) care; (Sozial~) welfare.
(b) (inf: Sozialamt) welfare (inf), welfare services. **der ~ zur**

Last fallen to be a burden on the state.
(c) (*inf: Sozialunterstützung*) social security. ~ **bekommen** to get social security; **von der** ~ **leben** to live on social security.
Fürsorge-: ~**amt** *nt* (church) welfare office; ~**beruf** *m* job in one of the welfare services; ~**erziehung** *f* education in a special school; ~**pflicht** *f* (*Jur*) employer's obligation to provide for the welfare of his employees.
Fürsorger(in *f*) *m* -s, - (church) welfare worker.
fürsorgerisch *adj* welfare *attr*. **alte Menschen** ~ **betreuen** to look after the welfare of old people.
Fürsorge-: ~**satz** *m* rate of social security (benefit); ~**unterstützung** *f* social security benefit.
fürsorglich *adj* careful; *Mensch auch* solicitous. **jdn sehr** ~ **behandeln** to lavish care on sb.
Fürsorglichkeit *f siehe* **adj** care; solicitousness.
Fürsprache *f* recommendation. **für jdn** ~ **einlegen** to recommend sb (*bei* to), to put in a word for sb (*inf*) (*bei* with); **auf** ~ **von jdm on sb's recommendation.
Fürsprech *m* -s, -e (a) (*old: Rechtsbeistand*) counsel. (b) (*Sw: Rechtsanwalt*) barrister.
Fürsprecher(in *f*) *m* (a) advocate. (b) *siehe* **Fürsprech.**
Fürst *m* -en, -en prince; (*Herrscher*) ruler. **geistlicher** ~ prince-bishop; **wie ein** ~ **leben** to live like a lord *or* king; **der** ~ **der Finsternis** *or* **dieser Welt** (*liter*) the Prince of Darkness *or* of this world (*Bibl*); **gehe nie zu deinem** ~, **wenn du nicht gerufen wirst** (*Prov*) there's no point in looking for trouble.
Fürsten-: ~**geschlecht**, ~**haus** *nt* royal house; ~**stand** *m* royal rank; **jdn in den** ~**stand erheben** to create sb prince; ~**tum** *nt* principality, princedom (*old*); **das** ~**tum Monaco/Liechtenstein** the principality of Monaco/Liechtenstein.
Fürstin *f* princess; (*Herrscherin*) ruler.
fürstlich *adj* (*lit*) princely *no adv*; (*fig auch*) handsome, lavish. **jdn** ~ **bewirten** to entertain sb right royally; ~ **leben** to live like a lord.
Fürstlichkeit *f* (a) *no pl* princeliness, handsomeness, lavishness. (b) (*form: fürstl. Herrschaften*) royal personage (*form*).
Furt *f* -, -en ford.
Furunkel *nt or m* -s, - boil.
fürwahr *adv* (*old*) forsooth (*old*), in truth (*old*).
Fürwitz *m* (*old*) *siehe* **Vorwitz.**
Fürwort *nt* -(e)s, ⸚er (*Gram*) *siehe* **Pronomen.**
fürwörtlich *adj* (*Gram*) *siehe* **pronominal.**
Furz *m* -(e)s, ⸚e (*inf*) fart (*vulg*). **einen** ~ (**fahren**) **lassen** to let off a fart (*vulg*).
furzen *vi* (*inf*) to fart (*vulg*).
Fusel *m* -s, - (*pej*) rotgut (*inf*), hooch (*esp US inf*).
Fuselöl *nt* fusel oil.
füsilieren* *vt* (*old Mil*) to execute by firing squad.
Fusilier *m* -s, -e (*old Mil, Sw*) fusilier.
Fusion *f* amalgamation; (*von Unternehmen auch*) merger; (*von Atomkernen, Zellen*) fusion.
fusionieren* *vti* to amalgamate; (*Unternehmen auch*) to merge.
Fuß *m* -es, ⸚e (a) (*Körperteil*) foot; (*S Ger, Aus: Bein*) leg. **zu** ~ on foot; **zu** ~ **gehen/kommen** to walk, to go/come on foot; **er ist gut/schlecht zu** ~ he is steady/not so steady on his feet; **sich jdm zu** ~**en werfen** to prostrate oneself before sb; **jdm zu** ~**en fallen/liegen/sitzen/sinken** to fall/lie/sit at sb's feet/to sink to the ground at sb's feet; **jdm zu** ~**en fallen** *or* **sinken** (*fig: Bittsteller*) to go down on one's knees to *or* before sb; **das Publikum lag/sank ihm zu** ~**en** he had the audience at his feet; **den** ~ **in** *or* **zwischen die Tür stellen** to get *or* put one's foot in the door; **den** ~ **auf die Erde/den Mond setzen** to set foot on the earth/the moon; **über seine eigenen** ~**e stolpern** to trip over one's own feet; (*fig*) to get tied up in knots; **kalte** ~**e bekommen, sich** (*dat*) **kalte** ~**e holen** (*lit, fig*) to get cold feet; **so schnell/weit ihn seine** ~**e trugen** as fast/far as his legs would carry him; **bei** ~! heel!; **jdm zwischen die** ~**e geraten** *or* **kommen** to get under sb's feet; **jdm etw vor die** ~**e werfen** *or* **schmeißen** (*inf*) (*lit*) to throw sth at sb; (*fig*) to tell sb to keep *or* stuff (*sl*) sth; **jdn/etw mit** ~**en treten** (*lit*) to kick sb/sth about; (*fig*) to trample all over sb/sth; (**festen**) ~ **fassen** (*lit, fig*) to gain a foothold; (*sich niederlassen*) to settle down; **auf eigenen** ~**en stehen** (*lit*) to stand by oneself; (*fig*) to stand on one's own two feet; **jdn auf freien** ~ **setzen** to release sb, to set sb free; **auf großem** ~ **leben** to live the high life; **mit jdm auf gutem** ~ **stehen** to be on good terms with sb; **jdm/einer Sache auf dem** ~**e folgen** (*lit*) to be hot on the heels of sb/sth; (*fig*) to follow hard on sb/sth; **mit einem** ~ **im Grab stehen** to have one foot in the grave; *siehe* **Boden, Hand, Gewehr, frei.**
(b) (*von Gegenstand*) base; (*Tisch*~ *Stuhlbein*) leg; (*von Schrank, Gebirge*) foot. **auf schwachen/tönernen** ~**en stehen** to be built on sand.
(c) (*Poet*) foot.
(d) (*von Strumpf*) foot.
(e) *pl* - (*Längenmaß*) foot. **12** ~ **lang** 12 foot *or* feet long.
Fuß-: ~**abdruck** *m* footprint; ~**abstreicher,** ~**abstreifer** *m* -s, - footscraper; (*aus Gummi etc*) doormat; ~**abtreter** *m* -s, - doormat; ~**angel** *f* (*lit*) mantrap; (*fig*) catch, trap; ~**bad** *nt* foot bath.
Fußball *m* (a) (*no pl*: ~**spiel**) football; (*als Kampfsport auch*) soccer. (b) (*Ball*) football.

Fußballer *m* -s, - (*inf*) footballer.
Fußball-: ~**mannschaft** *f* football team; ~**match** *nt* (*Aus*) football *or* soccer match; ~**meisterschaft** *f* football league championship; ~**platz** *m* football *or* soccer pitch; ~**schuh** *m* football boot; ~**spiel** *nt* football *or* soccer match; (*Sportart*) football; ~**spieler** *m* football *or* soccer player; ~**toto** *m or nt* football pools *pl*.
Fuß-: ~**bank** *f* footstool; ~**boden** *m* floor; ~**bodenbelag** *m* floor covering; ~**breit** *m* -, *no pl* foot; **keinen** ~**breit weichen** (*lit, fig*) not to budge an inch (*inf*); f~**breit** *adj* a foot wide; **die Erde öffnete sich** f~**breit** a crack a foot wide appeared in the ground; ~**bremse** *f* footbrake; ~**eisen** *nt* mantrap.
Fussel *f* -, -n *or m* -s, - fluff *no pl*. **ein(e)** ~ some fluff, a bit of fluff.
fusselig *adj* fluffy. **sich** (*dat*) **den Mund** ~ **reden** (*inf*) to talk till one is blue in the face.
fusseln *vi* (*von Stoff, Kleid etc*) to go bobbly (*inf*), to pill (*spec*).
füßeln *vi* to play footsie (*inf*) (*mit* with).
fußen *vi* to rest, to be based (*auf* +*dat* on).
Fuß-: ~**ende** *nt* (*von Bett*) foot; ~**fall** *m siehe* **Kniefall;** f~**fällig** *adj siehe* **kniefällig;** ~**fesseln** *pl* shackles *pl*.
Fußgänger *m* -s, - pedestrian.
Fußgänger-: ~**brücke** *f* footbridge; ~**überweg** *m* pedestrian crossing; (*auch* ~**überführung**) pedestrian bridge; ~**unterführung** *f* pedestrian subway; ~**zone** *f* pedestrian precinct.
Fuß-: ~**gelenk** *nt* ankle; f~**hoch** *adj* ankle-deep.
-füßig *adj suf Mensch* -footed; *Tisch, Insekt* -legged; (*Poet*) -foot.
Fuß-: f~**kalt** *adj* **die Wohnung ist immer** f~**kalt** there's always a draught around your feet in that flat; f~**krank** *adj* f~**krank sein** to have trouble with one's feet; ~**lappen** *m* footcloth; ~**leiden** *nt* foot complaint; ~**leiste** *f* skirting (board) (*Brit*), baseboard (*US*).
fußlig *adj* fluffy.
Füßling *m* (*von Strumpf*) foot; (*Socke*) footlet.
Fuß-: ~**marsch** *m* walk; (*Mil*) march; ~**matte** *f* doormat; ~**note** *f* footnote; ~**pfad** *m* footpath; ~**pflege** *f* chiropody; **zur** ~**pflege gehen** to go to the chiropodist; ~**pfleger** *m* chiropodist; ~**pilz** *m* (*Med*) athlete's foot; (b) (*Math*) foot (*of a perpendicular*); ~**ring** *m* ring; ~**schemel** *m siehe* ~**bank;** ~**schweiß** *m* foot perspiration; ~**sohle** *f* sole of the foot; ~**soldat** *m* (*Mil old*) foot soldier; ~**spitze** *f* toes *pl*; **sich auf die** ~**spitzen stellen** to stand on tiptoe; **auf (den)** ~**spitzen gehen** to walk on) tiptoe; ~**sprung** *m* **einen** ~**sprung machen** to jump feet-first; ~**spur** *f* footprint; ~**stapfen** *m* footprint; **in jds** ~**stapfen treten** (*fig*) to follow in sb's footsteps; ~**steig** *m* (a) (*Weg*) footpath; (b) (*S Ger: Bürgersteig*) pavement (*Brit*), sidewalk (*US*); ~**stütze** *f* footrest; f~**tief** *adj* ankle-deep; ~**tritt** *m* (*Geräusch*) footstep; (*Spur auch*) footprint; (*Stoß*) kick; **jdm einen** ~**tritt geben** *or* **versetzen** to kick sb, to give sb a kick; **jdn mit einem** ~**tritt hinausbefördern** to kick sb out; **einen** ~**tritt bekommen** (*fig*) to be kicked out; ~**truppe** *f* infantry *no pl*; ~**volk** *nt* (a) (*Mil old*) footmen *pl*; (b) (*fig*) **das** ~**volk** the rank and file; ~**wanderung** *f* walk; ~**waschung** *f* foot-washing; **die** ~**waschung Christi** the washing of Christ's feet; ~**weg** *m* (a) (*Pfad*) footpath; (b) (*Entfernung*) **es sind nur 15 Minuten** ~**weg** it's only 15 minutes walk; ~**wurzel** *f* (*Anat*) tarsus.
futsch *adj pred* (*inf*) (*weg*) gone, vanished; (*S Ger: kaputt*) bust (*inf*), broken.
Futter *nt* -s, - (a) *no pl* (animal) food *or* feed; (*für Kühe, Pferde etc auch*) fodder. **gut im** ~ **sein** to be well-fed. (b) (*Auskleidung*) (*Kleider*~, *Briefumschlag*~) lining; (*Tür*~) casing. (c) (*Spann*~) chuck.
Futteral *nt* -s, -e case.
Futter-: ~**getreide** *nt* forage cereal; ~**krippe** *f* manger; **an der** ~**krippe sitzen** (*inf*) to be well-placed.
futtern 1 *vi* (*hum inf*) to stuff oneself (*inf*). 2 *vt* (*hum inf*) to scoff.
füttern *vt* (a) *Tier, Kind, Kranke* to feed. **ich füttere dem Papagei Reis** I feed the parrot rice; „**F~ verboten**" "do not feed the animals". (b) *Kleidungsstück* to line.
Futter-: ~**napf** *m* bowl; ~**neid** *m* (*fig*) green-eyed monster (*hum*); ~**pflanze** *f* forage plant; ~**rübe** *f* root vegetable used for forage; ~**sack** *m* nosebag; ~**stoff** *m* lining (material); ~**trog** *m* feeding trough.
Fütterung *f* feeding. **die** ~ **der Nilpferde findet um 17⁰⁰ Uhr statt** feeding time for the hippos is 5 p.m.
Futur *nt* -(e)s, -e (*Gram*) future (tense).
Futura *pl of* **Futurum.**
futurisch *adj* (*Gram*) future.
Futurismus *m* futurism.
Futurist *m* futurist.
futuristisch *adj* futurist(ic).
Futurologe *m* futurologist.
Futurologie *f* futurology.
futurologisch *adj* futurological.
Futurum *nt* -s, **Futura** (*Gram*) *siehe* **Futur.**
Fux *m* -es, ⸚e (*Univ*) new member of a student fraternity.
Fuxmajor *m* (*Univ*) student in charge of the new members of a fraternity.
fuzeln *vi* (*Aus*) to write small.

G

G, g [ge:] *nt* -, - G, g.
g *abbr of* **Gramm.**
gab *pret of* **geben.**
Gabardine ['gabardi:n, gabar'di:n(ə)] *m* -s, *no pl or f* -, *no pl* gaberdine, gabardine.
Gabe *f* -, -n **(a)** (*dated: Geschenk*) gift, present (*gen* of, from); (*Schenkung*) donation (*gen* from); (*Eccl: Opfer*) offering; *siehe* **mild(e). (b)** (*Begabung*) gift. **die ~ haben, etw zu tun** to have a natural *or* (*auch iro*) (great) gift for doing sth. **(c)** (*Med: Dosis*) dose.
Gabel *f* -, -n fork; (*Heu~, Mist~*) pitchfork; (*Deichsel*) shafts *pl*; (*Telec*) rest, cradle; (*Geweih mit zwei Enden*) two-pointed antler; (*zwei Enden des Geweihs*) branch, fork.
Gabel-: **~bissen** *m* canapé; **~bock** *m* (*Hunt: Rehbock*) two-pointer; (*~antilope*) pronghorn (antelope); **~deichsel** *f* shafts *pl*; **g~förmig** *adj* forked *no adv*; **sich g~förmig teilen** to fork; **~frühstück** *nt* buffet lunch, fork lunch; **~hirsch** *m* (*Hunt: Rothirsch*) two-pointer; (*Andenhirsch*) guemal.
gabelig *adj siehe* **gabelförmig.**
gabeln *vtr* to fork.
Gabelstapler *m* -s, - fork-lift truck.
Gabelung *f* fork.
Gabentisch *m* table for Christmas or birthday presents.
gackern *vi* (*lit, fig*) to cackle.
gacksen *vi* (*inf*) (*gackern*) to cackle; (*herumstottern*) to splutter.
Gaffel *f* -, -n (*Naut*) gaff.
Gaffel-: **~schoner** *m* (*Naut*) fore-and-aft schooner; **~segel** *nt* (*Naut*) gaffsail.
gaffen *vi* to gape, to gawp (*inf*), to stare (*nach* at). **gaff nicht, sondern hilf mir lieber!** don't just stand there gaping *etc*, come and help!
Gaffer(in *f*) *m* -s, - gaper, gawper (*inf*), starer. **die neugierigen ~ bei einem Unfall** the nosy people standing gaping at an accident.
Gafferei *f* gaping, gawping (*inf*), staring.
Gag [gɛ(:)k] *m* -s, -s (*Film~*) gag; (*Werbe~*) gimmick; (*Witz*) joke; (*inf: Spaß*) laugh.
Gagat *m* -(e)s, -e, **Gagatkohle** *f* jet.
Gage ['ga:ʒə] *f* -, -n (*esp Theat*) fee; (*regelmäßige ~*) salary.
gähnen *vi* (*lit, fig*) to yawn. **~de Leere** total emptiness; **im Kino herrschte ~de Leere** the cinema was (totally) deserted; **ein ~der Abgrund/~des Loch** a yawning abyss/gaping hole; **ein G~** a yawn; **das G~ unterdrücken** to stop oneself (from) yawning; **das G~ der Schüler** the pupils' yawning; **das war zum G~ (langweilig)** it was one big yawn (*inf*).
Gala *f* -, *no pl* formal *or* evening *or* gala dress; (*Mil*) full *or* ceremonial *or* gala dress. **sich in ~ werfen** to get all dressed up (to the nines *inf*), to put on one's best bib and tucker (*inf*).
Gala-: *in cpds* formal, evening; (*Mil*) full ceremonial, gala; (*Theat*) gala; **~anzug** *m* formal *or* evening dress; (*Mil*) full *or* ceremonial *or* gala dress; **~diner** *nt* formal dinner; **~empfang** *m* formal reception.
galaktisch *adj* galactic.
Galan *m* -s, -e (*old*) gallant; (*hum inf auch*) beau.
galant *adj* (*dated*) gallant. **die ~e Dichtung** galant poetry; **~es Abenteuer** affair of the heart, amatory adventure.
Galanterie *f* (*dated*) gallantry.
Galanteriewaren *pl* (*old*) fashion accessories *pl*.
Gala-: **~uniform** *f* (*Mil*) full dress *or* ceremonial *or* gala uniform; **~vorstellung** *f* (*Theat*) gala performance.
Gäle *m* -n, -n Gael.
Galeere *f* -, -n galley. **jdn zu fünf Jahren ~ verurteilen** to sentence sb to five years in the galleys.
Galeerensklave, Galeerensträfling *m* galley slave.
Galeone *f* -, -n (*Hist*) galleon.
Galerie *f* **(a)** (*Empore, Gang, Kunst~, Mil, Naut*) gallery. **auf der ~** in the gallery. **(b)** (*Geschäftspassage*) arcade.
Galerist(in *f*) *m* owner of a gallery.
Galgen *m* -s, - gallows *pl*, gibbet; (*Film*) boom; (*Tech*) crossbeam; (*Spiel*) hangman. **jdn an den ~ bringen** to bring sb to the gallows; **an den ~ mit ihm!** let him swing!, to the gallows with him!; **jdn am ~ hinrichten** to hang sb (from the gallows).
Galgen-: **~frist** *f* (*inf*) reprieve; **jdm eine ~frist geben** to give sb a reprieve, to reprieve sb; **~humor** *m* gallows humour; **sagte er mit ~humor** he said with a macabre sense of humour; **~strick, ~vogel** *m* (*inf*) gallows bird (*inf*).
Galiläa *nt* -s, *no pl* Galilee.
Galiläer(in *f*) *m* -s, - Galilean.
galiläisch *adj* Galilean.
Galion *nt* -s, -s (*Hist*) cutwater.
Galionsfigur *f* figurehead.
gälisch *adj* Gaelic.
Gallapfel *m* gallnut; (*an Eichen*) oak-apple, oak-gall.
Galle *f* -, -n (a) (*Anat: Organ*) gallbladder; (*Flüssigkeit*) bile, gall; (*Bot, Vet*) gall; (*fig: Bosheit*) virulence. **wie ~ schmecken** to taste like bile; **bitter wie ~** bitter as gall *or* wormwood; **seine ~ verspritzen** (*fig*) to pour out one's venom;

(*bei Rezension etc auch*) to dip one's pen in gall; **verspritz ruhig deine ~!** have your little bitch! (*inf*); **jdm kommt die ~ hoch** sb's blood begins to boil; **die ~ läuft ihm über** (*inf*) he's seething *or* livid; *siehe* **Gift.**
(b) (*Agr*) patch of waterlogged land, watergall (*old*).
galle(n)bitter *adj* bitter as gall; *Wein, Geschmack auch* acid, acrid; *Arznei auch* bitter; *Bemerkung* caustic.
Gallen- *in cpds* gall; **~blase** *f* gall-bladder; **~gang** *m* bile duct; **~grieß** *m* small gall-stones *pl*; **~kolik** *f* gall-stone colic; **~leiden** *nt* trouble with one's gall-bladder; **~stein** *m* gall-stone.
Gallert *nt* -(e)s, -e, **Gallerte** *f* -, -n jelly.
gallert|artig *adj* jelly-like, gelatinous.
gallig *adj* gall-like *attr*; (*fig*) *Mensch, Bemerkung, Humor* caustic, acerbic.
gallisch *adj* Gallic.
Gallium *nt*, *no pl* (*Chem*) gallium.
Gallizismus *m* (*Ling*) Gallicism.
Gallomane *m* -n, -n, **Gallomanin** *f* Francophile.
Gallomanie *f* Francophilia, Gallomania.
Gallone *f* -, -n gallon.
Galopp *m* -s, -s *or* -e gallop; (*Tanz*) galop. **im ~** (*lit*) at a gallop; (*fig*) at top *or* high speed; **langsamer ~** canter; **gestreckter/kurzer ~** full/checked gallop; **in den ~ verfallen** to break into a gallop; **das Pferd sprang in fliegendem ~ über die Mauer** the horse flew *or* soared over the wall in mid-gallop; **ein bißchen ~, bitte** (*inf*) get a move on please (*inf*).
galoppieren* *vi aux haben or sein* to gallop. **~de Inflation** galloping inflation.
Galosche *f* -, -n galosh *usu pl*, overshoe.
galt *pret of* **gelten.**
Galvanisation [galvaniza'tsio:n] *f* galvanization; (*Chem auch*) electroplating.
galvanisch [gal'va:nɪʃ] *adj* galvanic.
Galvaniseur [galvani'zø:r] *m* electroplater.
Galvanisier|anstalt *f* electroplating works *sing or pl*.
galvanisieren* [galvani'zi:rən] *vt* to electroplate; (*mit Zink auch*) to galvanize.
Galvanisierung *f* electroplating; (*mit Zink auch*) galvanization, galvanizing.
Galvanismus [galva'nɪsmus] *m* galvanism.
Galvano [gal'va:no] *nt* -s, -s (*Typ*) electrotype, electro (*inf*).
Galvano-: **~meter** *nt* galvanometer; **~plastik** *f* (*Tech*) electroforming, galvanoplasty (*form*); (*Typ*) electrotype.
Gamasche *f* -, -n gaiter; (*kurze ~*) spat; (*Wickel~*) puttee. **sie hat ~n vor ihm/davor** (*dated inf*) he/it makes her tremble in her boots (*inf*).
Gamaschenhose *f* (*pair sing of*) leggings *pl*.
Gambe *f* -, -n viola da gamba.
Gammastrahlen, Gamma-Strahlen *pl* gamma rays *pl*.
Gammel *m* -s, *no pl* (*dial*) junk (*inf*), rubbish.
Gammel-: **~bruder** *m siehe* **Gammler; ~dienst** *m* (*Mil sl*) lazy spell of duty.
gammelig *adj* (*inf*) *Lebensmittel* old, ancient (*inf*); *Kleidung* tatty (*inf*); *Auto auch* decrepit. **das Fleisch ist ja schon ganz ~** the meat has already gone bad *or* off.
Gammelleben *nt* (*inf*) loafing *or* bumming around (*inf*) *no art*.
gammeln *vi* (*inf*) to laze *or* loaf (*inf*) about, to bum around (*inf*); (*wie ein Gammler leben*) to live like a drop-out.
Gammler(in *f*) *m* -s, - drop-out.
Gammler-: **~leben** *nt* life of a drop-out; **~tum** *nt*, *no pl* dropping out *no art*.
Gams *f* -, -(en) (*Aus, S Ger, Hunt*) *siehe* **Gemse.**
Gams-: **~bart** *m* tuft of hair from a chamois worn as a hat decoration, shaving-brush (*hum inf*); **~bock** *m* chamois buck; **~leder** *nt* chamois (leather).
gang *adj*: **~ und gäbe sein** to be the thing, to be quite usual.
Gang¹ *m* -(e)s, ~e **(a)** (*no pl: ~art*) walk, way of walking, gait; (*eines Pferdes*) gait, pace. **einen leichten/schnellen ~ haben** to be light on one's feet, to walk lightly/to be a fast walker; **jdn an seinem *or* am ~ erkennen/am aufrechten ~ erkennen** to recognize sb's walk *or* sb from the way he walks/from his upright carriage; **seinen ~ verlangsamen/beschleunigen** to slow down/to speed up, to hasten one's step (*liter*).
(b) (*Besorgung*) errand; (*Spazier~*) walk. **einen ~ machen *or* tun** to go on an errand/to go for a walk; **einen ~zum Anwalt/zur Bank machen** to go to *or* pay a visit to one's lawyer/the bank; **einen schweren ~ tun** to do something difficult; **das war für ihn immer ein schwerer ~** it was always hard for him; **ich muß einen schweren ~ tun** I have a difficult thing to do; **sein erster ~ war ...** the first thing he did was ...; **den ~ nach Canossa antreten** (*fig*) to eat humble pie; **der ~ nach Canossa** (*Hist*) the pilgrimage to Canossa; **seinen letzten ~ tun** (*euph*) to go to one's last resting-place (*euph*), to go on one's last journey (*euph*).
(c) (*no pl: Bewegung eines Motors*) running; (*einer Maschine auch*) operation; (*Ablauf*) course; (*eines Dramas*) development. **der Motor hat einen leisen ~** the engine runs quietly; **der**

~ **der Ereignisse/der Dinge** the course of events/things; **seinen gewohnten** ~ **gehen** (*fig*) to run its usual course; **etw in** ~ **bringen** *or* **setzen** to get *or* set sth going; (*fig auch*) to get sth off the ground *or* under way; **etw in** ~ **halten** (*lit, fig*) to keep sth going; *Maschine, Motor auch* to keep sth running; **in** ~ **kommen** to get going; (*fig auch*) to get off the ground *or* under way; **in** ~ **sein** to be going; (*eine Maschine auch*) to be in operation, to be running; (*Motor auch*) to be running; (*fig*) to be off the ground *or* under way; (*los sein*) to be going on *or* happening; **in vollem** ~ in full swing; **es ist etwas im** ~**(e)** (*inf*) something's up (*inf*); **bei ihm/gegen ihn ist etwas im** ~**(e)** there's something up with him/there's a plot against him; *siehe* **tot.**

(**d**) (*Arbeits*~) operation; (*Speisenfolge*) course; (*Fechten, im Zweikampf*) bout; (*beim Rennen*) heat. **ein Essen von** *or* **mit vier** ~**en** a four-course meal.

(**e**) (*Verbindungs*~) passage(way); (*Rail, in Gebäuden*) corridor; (*Hausflur*) (*offen*) passage(way), close (*Scot*); (*hinter Eingangstür*) hallway; (*im oberen Stock*) landing; (*Theat, Aviat, in Kirche, in Geschäft, in Stadion*) aisle; (*Aviat, in Stadion*) gangway; (*Säulen*~) colonnade, passage; (*Bogen*~) arcade, passage; (*Wandel*~) walk; (*in einem Bergwerk*) tunnel, gallery; (*Durch*~ *zwischen Häusern*) passage(way); (*Anat*) duct; (*Gehör*~) meatus; (*Min: Erz*~) vein; (*Tech: eines Gewindes*) thread.

(**f**) (*Mech*) gear; (*bei Fahrrad auch*) speed. **den ersten** ~ **einschalten** *or* **einlegen** to engage first (gear); **auf** *or* **in den dritten** ~ **schalten** to change *or* shift (*US*) into third (gear).

Gang² [gɛŋ] *f* -, **-s gang.**

Gang|art *f* (**a**) walk, way of walking, gait; (*von Pferd*) gait, pace; (*Haltung*) carriage, bearing. **Menschen haben eine aufrechte** ~ **humans walk upright; eine leicht nach vorne gebeugte** ~ **haben** to walk with one's body bent slightly forward; **eine schnellere** ~ **vorlegen** to walk faster.

(**b**) (*Min*) gangue, matrix.

gangbar *adj* (*lit*) *Weg, Brücke etc* passable; (*fig*) *Lösung, Weg* practicable. **nicht** ~ impassable/impracticable.

Gängelband *nt:* **jdn am** ~ **führen** (*fig*) (*Lehrer etc*) to spoon-feed sb; (*Ehefrau, Mutter*) to keep sb tied to one's apron strings.

Gängelei *f* spoon-feeding. **warum wehrt er sich nicht gegen die** ~ **seiner Mutter/Frau?** why doesn't he fight against being tied to his mother's/wife's apron strings?

gängeln *vt* (*fig*) **jdn** ~ to spoon-feed sb, to treat sb like a child/children; (*Mutter, Ehefrau*) to keep sb tied to one's apron strings.

Ganghebel *m* (*Tech*) gear lever.

gängig *adj* (**a**) (*üblich*) common; (*aktuell*) current; *Münze* current; (*vertretbar*) possible.

(**b**) (*gut gehend*) *Waren* popular, in demand. **die** ~**ste Ausführung** the best-selling model.

(**c**) (*rare: gut laufend*) ~ **sein** (*Pferd*) to be a good goer; (*Hund*) to be well-trained; **ein** ~**es/schlecht** ~**es Gespann** a fast/slow team; **einen Hund** ~ **machen** (*Hunt*) to train a dog.

Ganglien [-iən] *pl* (*Anat*) ganglia *pl*.

Ganglien-: ~**system** *nt* gangliar *or* ganglionic system; ~**zelle** *f* gangliocyte, ganglion cell.

Gangräne *f* -, **-n** *or* **Gangrän** *nt* **-s, -e** (*Med*) gangrene.

gangränös *adj* (*Med*) gangrenous.

Gangschaltung *f* gears *pl.*

Gangster ['gɛnstɐ, 'gaŋstɐ] *m* **-s, -** gangster.

Gangster-: ~**boß** *m* gang boss; ~**braut** *f* (gang) moll (*sl*); ~**methode** *f* gangster method.

Gangway ['gɛŋweɪ] *f* -, **-s** (*Naut*) gangway; (*Aviat*) steps *pl.*

Ganove [ga'no:və] *m* **-n, -n** (*inf*) crook; (*hum: listiger Kerl*) sly old fox.

Ganoven-: ~**ehre** *f* honour among(st) thieves; **das verbietet mir meine** ~**ehre** even crooks have some honour; ~**sprache** *f* underworld slang.

Gans *f* -, **⁻e** goose. **wie die** ~**e schnattern** to cackle away, to cackle like a bunch of old hens (*inf*).

Gans- in *cpds* (*Aus*) *siehe* **Gänse-.**

Gänschen ['gɛnsçən] *nt* gosling; (*fig inf*) little goose (*inf*).

Gänse- in *cpds* (*Aus*) *siehe* **Gans. ~blümchen** *nt*, ~**blume** *f* daisy; ~**braten** *m* roast goose; ~**brust** *f* (*Cook*) breast of goose; ~**feder** *f* (goose-)quill; ~**fett** *nt* goose-fat; ~**füßchen** *pl* (*inf*) inverted commas *pl*, quotation marks *pl*, sixty-sixes and ninety-nines *pl* (*inf*); ~**haut** *f* (*fig*) goose-pimples *pl*, goose-flesh; **eine** ~**haut bekommen** *or* **kriegen** (*inf*) to get goose-pimples *or* goose-flesh, to go all goose-pimply (*inf*); ~**kiel** *m* (goose-)quill; ~**klein** *nt* **-s**, *no pl* goose pieces *pl*; (*Innereien*) goose giblets *pl*; ~**leberpastete** *f* pâté de foie gras; ~**marsch** *m:* **im** ~**marsch in single** *or* Indian file.

Gänserich *m* **-s, -e,** **Ganser** *m* **-s, -** (*Aus*) gander.

Gänse-: ~**schmalz** *nt* goose-dripping; ~**wein** *m* (*hum*) Adam's ale (*hum*), water.

Ganter *m* **-s, -** (*N Ger*) *siehe* **Gänserich.**

ganz 1 *adj* (**a**) whole, entire; (*vollständig*) complete; *Wahrheit* whole. **eine** ~**e Zahl** a whole number, an integer; **eine** ~**e Note/Pause** (*Mus*) a semi-breve (*Brit*), a whole note (*US*)/a semi-breve *or* whole note rest; **die** ~**e Mannschaft war ...** the whole *or* entire team was ..., all the team were ...; **wir haben keine** ~**e Mannschaft** we don't have a complete team; **die** ~**en Tassen/Kinder** (*inf*) all the cups/children; **der** ~**e Vordergrund** the whole *or* entire foreground, the whole of the foreground, all the foreground; ~ **England/London** the whole of England/London; **wir fuhren durch** ~ **England** we travelled all over England; **in** ~ **England/London** in the whole of *or* in all England/London; **die** ~**e Zeit** all the time, the whole time; **der** ~**e Kram** the whole lot; **eine** ~**e Menge** quite a lot; **sein** ~**es Geld/Vermögen** all his money/fortune, his entire *or* whole fortune; **seine** ~**en Sachen** all his things; **seine**

~**e Kraft** all his strength; **sie ist seine** ~**e Freude** (*inf*) she's the apple of his eye (*inf*); **du bist ja mein** ~**es Leben** you're my whole life; **du hast mir den** ~**en Spaß verdorben** you've spoilt all my fun; **sie ist die** ~**e Mutter** (*inf*) she's just like her mother; **ein** ~**er Mann** a real *or* proper man; **du bist ein** ~ **Schlauer** you're really a crafty one; **etwas** ~ **Intelligentes/Verrücktes** *etc* something really intelligent/mad *etc.*

(**b**) **Käse/eine Sammlung** ~ *or* **im** ~**en kaufen** to buy a whole cheese/a collection as a whole; **im** (**großen und**) ~**en** (**genommen**) on the whole, by and large, (taken) all in all.

(**c**) (*inf: unbeschädigt*) intact. **etw wieder** ~ **machen** to mend sth; **wieder** ~ **sein** to be mended; **die Familie ist wieder** ~ the family is intact again.

(**d**) (*inf: nicht mehr als*) all of. **ich verdiene im Monat** ~**e 200 DM** I earn all of 200 marks a month; **noch** ~**e zehn Minuten** all of ten minutes.

2 *adv* (**a**) (*völlig*) quite; (*vollständig, ausnahmslos*) completely; (*ziemlich, leidlich*) quite; (*sehr*) really; (*genau*) exactly, just. ~ **hinten/vorn** right at the back/front; **nicht** ~ not quite; ~ **gewiß!** most certainly, absolutely; **ein** ~ **gutes Buch** (*ziemlich*) quite a good book; (*sehr gut*) a very *or* really good book; **ich habe mich** ~ **riesig gefreut** I was really enormously pleased; **du hast ihn** ~ **fürchterlich beleidigt** you've really insulted him very badly; **ein** ~ **billiger Trick/böser Kerl** a really cheap trick/ evil character; **das war** ~ **lieb von dir** that was really nice of you; **das ist mir** ~ **gleich** it's all the same *or* all one to me; **er hat** ~ **recht** he's quite *or* absolutely right; ~ **mit Ruß bedeckt** all *or* completely covered with soot; ~ **allein all alone; du bist ja** ~ **naß** you're all wet; **so** ~ **vergnügt/traurig** *etc* so very happy/sad *etc*; ~ **Aufmerksamkeit/Demut etc** sein to be all attention/humility *etc*; **es ist** ~ **aus** it's all over; ~ **wie Sie meinen** just as you think (best); ~ **gleich wer** it doesn't matter who, no matter who; **eine Zeitschrift** ~ **lesen** to read a magazine right through *or* from cover to cover; **das habe ich nicht** ~ **gelesen** I haven't read it all yet, I haven't finished reading it yet; **ein** ~ ~ **hoher Berg** a very very *or* really really high mountain; ~ **und gar** completely, utterly; ~ **und gar nicht** not at all, not in the least; **noch nicht** ~ **zwei Uhr** not quite two o'clock yet; **ich habe** ~ **den Eindruck, daß ...** I've rather got the impression that ...; **ein** ~ **klein wenig** just a little *or* tiny bit; **das mag ich** ~ **besonders gerne** I'm particularly *or* especially fond of that; **sie ist** ~ **die Mutter** she's just *or* exactly like her mother; **etw** ~ **oder gar nicht machen** to do sth properly or not at all.

Ganz|aufnahme *f* (*Phot*) full-length photo(graph).

Gänze *f* -, *no pl* (*form, Aus*) entirety. **zur** ~ completely, fully, in its entirety.

Ganze(s) *nt decl as adj* whole; (*alle Sachen zusammen*) lot; (*ganzer Satz, ganze Ausrüstung*) complete set. **etw als** ~ **sehen** to see sth as a whole; **das** ~ **kostet ...** altogether it costs ...; **das** ~ **alleine machen** to do the whole thing *or* it all on one's own; **das** ~ **halt!** (*Mil*) parade, halt!; **das ist nichts** ~**s und nichts Halbes** that's neither one thing nor the other; **das** ~ **gefällt mir gar nicht** I don't like it at all, I don't like anything about it; **aufs** ~ **gehen** (*inf*) to go all out; **es geht ums** ~ everything's at stake.

Ganzheit *f* (*Einheit*) unity; (*Vollständigkeit*) entirety. **keine selbständige** ~ not an independent entity; **als** ~ as an integral whole; **in seiner** ~ in its entirety.

ganzheitlich *adj* (*umfassend einheitlich*) integral. **ein Problem** ~ **betrachten/darstellen** to view/present a problem in its entirety.

Ganzheits-: ~**medizin** *f* holistic medicine; ~**methode** *f* look-and-say method; ~**psychologie** *f* holism.

Ganz-: **g**~**jährig** *adj* non-seasonal, all the year round; ~**leder** *nt* **ein Buch in** ~**leder** a leather-bound book, a book with a leather binding; ~**lederband** *m* leather-bound volume; **g**~**ledern** *adj* leather-bound, bound in leather; ~**leinen** *nt* (**a**) (*Stoff*) pure linen; (**b**) (~**einband**) **ein Buch in** ~**leinen** a cloth-bound book, a book with a cloth binding; ~**leinenband** *m* cloth-bound volume.

gänzlich 1 *adv* completely, totally. **2** *adj* (*rare*) complete, total.

Ganz-: **g**~**seiden** *adj* pure silk; **g**~**tägig** *adj* all-day; *Arbeit, Stelle* full-time; **ein g**~**tägiger Ausflug** a day-trip; **g**~**tägig arbeiten** to work full-time; **sie ist jetzt g**~**tägig zu Hause** she's at home all day now; **das Schwimmbad ist g**~**tägig geöffnet** the swimming baths are open all day.

Ganztags-: ~**beschäftigung** *f* full-time occupation; ~**schule** *f* all-day schooling *no pl* *or* schools *pl*; (*Gebäude*) all-day school; ~**stelle** *f* full-time job.

Ganz-: ~**ton** *m* (*Mus*) (whole) tone; **g**~**wollen** *adj* all-wool; ~**wortmethode** *f* *siehe* **Ganzheitsmethode.**

gar 1 *adv* (**a**) (*überhaupt*) at all; (*ganz*) quite. ~ **keines** not a single one, none whatsoever *or* at all; ~ **kein Grund** no reason whatsoever *or* at all, not the slightest reason; ~ **niemand** not a soul, nobody at all *or* whatsoever; ~ **nichts** nothing at all *or* whatsoever; ~ **nicht schlecht** *or* **übel** not bad at all, not at all bad.

(**b**) (*old, S Ger, Aus: zur Verstärkung*) **es war** ~ **so kalt/warm** it was really *or* so cold/warm; **er wäre** ~ **zu gern noch länger geblieben** he would really *or* so have liked to stay longer; **war er davon begeistert?** — **nicht** ~ **zu sehr** did he like it? — not (all) that much; **es ist** ~ **zu dumm, daß er nicht gekommen ist** (*old, S Ger, Aus*) it's really *or* so *or* too stupid that he didn't come; *siehe* **ganz 2.**

(**c**) (*geh, S Ger, Aus: sogar*) even. **er wird doch nicht** ~ **verunglückt sein?** he hasn't had an accident, has he?; **du hast das doch nicht** ~ **meinem Mann erzählt?** you haven't told my husband, have you?; **warum nicht** ~! (and) why not?, why not indeed?; **und nun will sie** ~ **... und now she even wants ...; am Ende willst du** ~ **noch, daß ich deine Zigarette für dich rauche** (*iro*) you'll be wanting me to smoke your cigarette for you next; **hast du eine Wohnung, oder ~ ein eigenes Haus?** do you have a flat, or perhaps even a house of your own?

(d) (obs, Aus, S Ger: sehr) really, indeed. **ein ~ feiner Mensch** a really splendid person, a splendid person indeed; **~ schön** passing fair (obs); **er kommt ~ oft** he comes really frequently or very frequently indeed; **~ mancher** many a person; **~ manchmal** many a time, many a time and oft (old).

2 adj **(a)** Speise done pred, cooked. **das Steak ist ja nur halb ~** this steak is only half-cooked.

(b) (form) Leder tanned, dressed; (Agr) Boden well-prepared.

(c) (S Ger, Aus) (verbraucht) used up, finished; (zu Ende) at an end, over. **das Öl wird ja nie ~** we'll never use all this oil.

Garage [ga'ra:ʒə] f -, **-n** garage; (Hoch~, Tief~) car-park. **das Auto in einer ~ unterstellen** to garage one's car.

garagieren* [gara'ʒi:rən] vt (Aus, Sw) to park.

Garant m guarantor.

Garantie f (lit, fig) guarantee. **die Uhr hat ein Jahr ~** the watch is guaranteed for a year or has a year's guarantee; **das fällt noch unter die ~** or geht noch auf ~ that comes under or is covered by the guarantee; **ich gebe dir meine ~ darauf** (fig inf) I guarantee (you) that; **etw unter ~ machen** (fig inf) to be bound or guaranteed or certain to do sth.

Garantie-: **~anspruch** m right to claim under guarantee; **~frist** f guarantee period; **~lohn** m guaranteed minimum wage.

garantieren* **1** vt to guarantee (jdm etw sb sth). **der Name dieser Firma garantiert Qualität** the name of this firm is a guarantee of good quality or guarantees good quality; **er konnte mir nicht ~, daß ...** he couldn't give me any guarantee that ...; **ich kann dir ~, daß du eine Ohrfeige bekommst** (inf) you'll get a box on the ears, I can guarantee you that (inf).

2 vi to give a guarantee. **für etw ~** to guarantee sth; **diese Marke garantiert für Qualität** this brand is a guarantee of quality; **er konnte für nichts ~** he couldn't guarantee anything.

garantiert adv guaranteed; (inf) I bet (inf). **er kommt garantiert nicht** I bet he won't come (inf), he's bound not to come.

Garantieschein m guarantee, certificate of guarantee (form).

Garaus m: (inf) **jdm den ~ machen** to do sb in (inf), to bump sb off (inf); **einer Sache den ~ machen** to put an end or a stop to a matter.

Garbe f -, **-n** (Korn~) sheaf; (Licht~) beam; (Mil: Schuß~) burst of fire; (Metal) faggot. **das Getreide wurde in** or **zu ~n gebunden** the corn was bound into sheaves.

Garbenbindemaschine f (Agr) sheaf-binder, sheaf-binding machine.

Gärbottich m fermenting vat.

Garçonnière [garsɔ'niɛːrə] f -, **-n** (Aus) one-room flat (Brit) or apartment.

Garde f -, **-n** guard. **~ zu Fuß** (Hist) Foot Guards pl; **bei der ~** in the Guards; **die alte ~** (fig) the old guard.

Garde-: **~maß** nt height required for eligibility for the Guards; **~maß haben** (inf) to be as tall as a tree; **~offizier** m Guards officer; **~regiment** nt Guards regiment.

Garderobe f -, **-n (a)** (Kleiderbestand) wardrobe. **eine reiche ~ haben** to have a large wardrobe, to have a great many clothes.

(b) (Kleiderablage) hall-stand; (im Theater, Kino etc) cloakroom, checkroom (US). **seinen Mantel an der ~ abgeben** to leave one's coat in the cloakroom.

(c) (Theat: Umkleideraum) dressing-room.

Garderoben-: **~frau** f cloakroom or checkroom (US) attendant; **~haken** m coat hook; **~marke** f cloakroom or checkroom (US) number; **~schein** m cloakroom or checkroom (US) ticket; **~schrank** m hall cupboard; **~ständer** m hat-stand.

Garderobier [gardəro'biɛː] m -s, **-s (a)** (Theat: für Kostüme) wardrobe master; (im Umkleideraum) dresser. **(b)** (an der Abgabe) cloakroom or checkroom (US) attendant.

Garderobiere [-'biɛːrə] f -, **-n (a)** wardrobe mistress, dresser. **(b)** cloakroom or checkroom (US) attendant.

gardez [gar'deː] interj (Chess) gardez.

Gardine f curtain, drape (US); (Scheiben~) net curtain; siehe schwedisch.

Gardinen-: **~band** nt curtain tape; **~blende** f pelmet; **~leiste** f curtain rail; **~predigt** f (inf) dressing-down, talking-to; **jdm eine ~predigt halten** to give sb a dressing-down or a talking-to; **~rolle** f, **~röllchen** nt curtain runner; **~schnur** f curtain cord; **~stange** f curtain rail; (zum Ziehen) curtain rod.

Gardist m (Mil) guardsman.

garen (Cook) vti to cook; (auf kleiner Flamme) to simmer.

gären 1 vi aux haben or sein to ferment; (Hefe) to work; (fig: Gefühle etc) to seethe. **die Wut/das Unrecht gärte in ihm** he was seething with anger/a sense of injustice; **in ihm gärt es** he is in a state of inner turmoil. **2** vt to ferment.

Gären nt -s, no pl siehe **Gärung**.

Gärfutter nt (Agr) silage no pl.

Gar-: **~koch** m (old) cook at a hot food stall; **g~kochen** vt sep to cook/boil etc sth (until done); siehe **kochen**; **~küche** f (old) hot food stall.

Gärmittel nt ferment.

Garn nt -(e)s, **-e (a)** thread; (Baumwoll~ auch) cotton; (Häkel~, fig: Seemanns~) yarn. **ein ~ spinnen** (fig) to spin a yarn. **(b)** (Netz) net. **jdm ins ~ gehen** (fig) to fall into sb's snare, to fall or walk into sb's trap.

Garnele f -, **-n** (Zool) prawn; (Granat) shrimp.

garni adj siehe **Hotel ~**.

garnieren* vt Kuchen, Kleid to decorate; Gericht, (fig) Reden etc to garnish.

Garnierung f siehe vt **(a)** (das Garnieren) decoration; garnishing. **(b)** (Material zur ~) decoration; garnish. **Zitate als ~**

einer Rede quotations to garnish a speech.

Garnison f (Mil) garrison. **mit ~ belegen** to garrison; **in ~ liegen** to be garrisoned or in garrison.

Garnison(s)- in cpds garrison; **~kirche** f garrison church; **~stadt** f garrison town.

Garnitur f **(a)** (Satz) set; (Unterwäsche) set of (matching) underwear. **die erste ~** (fig) the pick of the bunch, the top-notches pl (inf); **erste/zweite ~ sein, zur ersten/zweiten ~ gehören** to be first-rate or first-class/second-rate. **(b)** (Besatz) trimming. **(c)** (Mil: Uniform) uniform. **erste ~** number one uniform or dress.

Garn-: **~knäuel** m or nt ball of thread or yarn; **~rolle** f spool; (von Baumwolle, Nähgarn) cotton reel; **~spinnerei** f spinning mill.

Garotte f -, **-n** garrotte.

garottieren* vt to garrotte.

garstig adj (dated) nasty, horrible.

Garstigkeit f (dated) nastiness.

Gärstoff m ferment.

Garten m -s, ⸚ garden; (Obst~) orchard. **öffentlicher/botanischer/zoologischer ~** public/botanic(al)/zoological gardens pl; **im ~ arbeiten** to work in the garden, to do some gardening; **das ist nicht in seinem ~ gewachsen** (fig inf) (Ideen) he didn't think of that himself, that's not his own idea; (Leistungen) he didn't do that by himself.

Garten- in cpds garden; **~arbeit** f gardening no pl; **~architekt** m landscape gardener; **~bau** m horticulture; **~bauausstellung** f horticultural exhibition; **~blume** f garden or cultivated flower; **~gerät** nt gardening tool or implement; **~haus** nt summer house; (für Geräte) garden shed; (Hinterhaus) back or rear building; **~kolonie** f allotments pl; **~laube** f (~häuschen) summer house; (aus Blattwerk) arbour, bower; (für Geräte) garden shed; **~lokal** nt beer garden; (Restaurant) garden café; **~möbel** pl garden furniture; **~schere** f secateurs pl (Brit), pruning-shears pl (Heckenschere) shears pl; **~schlauch** m garden hose; **~theater** nt open-air theatre; **~tür** f garden gate; **~wirtschaft** f siehe **~lokal**; **~zwerg** m garden gnome; (pej inf) squirt (inf); **~zwiebel** f flower bulb.

Gärtner m -s, - gardener; siehe **Bock¹**.

Gärtnerei f **(a)** (Baumschule, für Setzlinge) nursery; (für Obst, Gemüse, Schnittblumen) market-garden. **(b)** no pl (Gartenarbeit) gardening; (Gartenbau) horticulture.

Gärtnerin f gardener.

gärtnerisch 1 adj attr gardening; Ausbildung horticultural. **~e Gestaltung** landscaping; **die ~en Kosten** the cost of the landscaping. **2** adv **einen Park ~ gestalten** to landscape a park; **~begabt sein** to have green fingers, to have a gift for gardening; **~ ausgebildet** trained in horticulture.

gärtnern vi to garden.

Gärung f fermentation; (fig) ferment, turmoil. **in ~ kommen** to start fermenting; **in ~ sein** (fig) to be in ferment or in a turmoil.

Gärungs-: **~erreger** m ferment; **~prozeß** m process of fermentation.

Gas nt -es, **-e** gas; (Aut: ~pedal) accelerator, gas pedal (esp US). **~ geben** (Aut) to accelerate, to put one's foot down (inf), to step on the gas (inf); (auf höhere Touren bringen) to rev up; **~ wegnehmen** (Aut) to decelerate, to ease one's foot off the accelerator, to throttle back (US); **mit ~ vergiften** to gas.

Gas- in cpds gas; **~anstalt** f (dated) gasworks sing or pl; **~automat** m gas meter; **~badeofen** m gas(-fired) water heater; **~behälter** m gas-holder, gasometer; **g~beheizt** adj gas-heated; **~dichte** f (Phys) density of a/the gas; **~erzeugung** f generation of gas; (Ind) gas-production; **~fernversorgung** f (System) long-distance gas supply; **~flasche** f bottle of gas, gas canister; **g~förmig** adj gaseous, gasiform; **~geruch** m smell of gas; **~glühlicht** nt gaslight; (Vorrichtung) gas-lighting; **~hahn** m gas-tap; **den ~hahn aufdrehen** (fig) to put one's head in the gas oven; **~hebel** m (Aut) accelerator (pedal), gas pedal (esp US); (Hand~) (hand) throttle; **~hülle** f atmosphere; **~installateur** m gas fitter; **~kammer** f gas chamber; **~kocher** m camping stove; **~krieg** m chemical or gas war/warfare; **~laterne** f gas (street) lamp; **~leitung** f (Rohr) gas pipe; (Hauptrohr) gas main; **~licht** nt gaslight; (Beleuchtung) gas-lighting; **etw mit ~licht beleuchten** to light sth by gas; **~mann** m gasman; **~maske** f gasmask; **~ofen** m (Heizofen) gas fire or heater; (Heizungsofen) gas(-fired) boiler; (Backofen) gas oven; (Herd) gas cooker or stove.

Gasolin nt -s, no pl petroleum ether.

Gasometer m gasometer.

Gas-: **~pedal** nt (Aut) accelerator (pedal), gas pedal (esp US); **~pistole** f tear-gas gun; **~rohr** nt siehe **~leitung**.

Gäßchen nt alley(way).

Gasse f -, **-n** lane; (Durchgang) alley(way); (S Ger, Aus: Straße) street; (Rugby) line-out. **die schmalen ~n der Altstadt** the narrow streets and alleys of the old town; **eine ~ bilden** to make a passage; (Rugby) to form a line-out; **eine ~ für jdn bilden** to make way or clear a path for sb; **sich** (dat) **eine ~ bahnen** to force one's way; **auf der ~** (S Ger, Aus) on the street; **etw über die ~ verkaufen** (Aus) to sell sth to take away.

Gassen-: **~hauer** m (old, inf) popular melody; **~jargon** m gutter language; **einen furchtbaren ~jargon sprechen** to talk like a guttersnipe; **~junge** m street urchin or arab; **~schänke** f (S Ger) off-sales (Brit), package store (US).

Gassi adv (inf) **~ gehen** to go walkies (inf); **mit einem Hund ~ gehen** to take a dog (for) walkies (inf).

Gast¹ m -es, **-e** guest; (Besucher auch, Tourist) visitor; (in einer ~stätte) customer; (Theat) guest (star); (Univ: ~hörer) observer, auditor (US). **Vorstellung vor geladenen ~en** performance before an invited audience; **ungeladener ~** uninvited guest; (bei einer Party auch) gatecrasher; **jdn zu ~ bitten**

(form) to request the pleasure of sb's company (form); **wir haben heute abend ~e** we're having people round or company this evening; **bei jdm zu ~ sein** to be sb's guest(s); **in einem anderen Ort/bei einem anderen Sender zu ~ sein** (Rad) to visit another place/go over to another station.

Gast[2] m -(e)s, -en (Naut) (Signal~) signalman; (Radio~) operator.

Gast-: ~**arbeiter** m immigrant or foreign worker; ~**bett** nt spare or guest bed.

Gästebuch nt visitor's book.

Gastechnik f gas-engineering.

Gäste-: ~**haus** nt guest house; ~**heim** nt (dated) guest house, boarding house; ~**zimmer** nt guest room.

Gast-: g~**frei** adj siehe g~**freundlich**; ~**freiheit** f siehe ~**freundlichkeit**; ~**freund** m (old) guest; (~**geber**) host; g~**freundlich** adj hospitable; ~**freundlichkeit**, ~**freundschaft** f hospitality; g~**gebend** adj attr Land host; ~**geber** m host; ~**geberin** f hostess; ~**geschenk** nt present brought by a guest; ~**haus** nt, ~**hof** m inn; ~**hörer(in** f) m (Univ) observer, auditor (US).

gastieren* vi to guest, to make a guest appearance.

Gast-: ~**land** nt host country; g~**lich** adj siehe g~**freundlich**; ~**lichkeit** f siehe ~**freundlichkeit**; ~**mahl** nt (old) banquet; **Platos „~mahl"** Plato's "Symposium".

Gastod m death by gassing. **den ~ sterben** to be gassed.

Gast-: ~**professor** m visiting professor; ~**recht** nt right to hospitality.

gastrisch adj (Med) gastric.

Gastritis f -, **Gastritiden** gastritis.

Gastrolle f (Theat) guest role. **eine ~ geben** or **spielen** (lit) to make a guest appearance; (fig) to put in or make a fleeting appearance.

Gastronom m (Gastwirt) restaurateur; (Koch) cuisinier, cordon-bleu cook.

Gastronomie f (form: Gaststättengewerbe) catering trade; (geh: Kochkunst) gastronomy.

gastronomisch adj gastronomic.

Gastroskopie f (Med) gastroscopy.

Gast-: ~**spiel** nt (Theat) guest performance; (Sport) away match; **ein ~spiel geben** (lit) to give a guest performance; (fig inf) to make or put in a fleeting or brief appearance; ~**spielreise** f (Theat) tour; **auf ~spielreise** on tour; ~**stätte** f (Speise~) restaurant; (Trinklokal) pub (Brit), bar; ~**stättengewerbe** nt catering trade; ~**stube** f lounge; ~**tier** nt (Biol) parasite.

Gasturbine f gas turbine.

Gast-: ~**vorlesung** f (Univ) guest lecture; ~**vorstellung** f (Theat) siehe ~**spiel**; ~**vortrag** m guest lecture; ~**wirt(in** f) m (Besitzer) restaurant owner or proprietor/proprietress; (Pächter) restaurant manager(ess f); (von Trinklokal) landlord/landlady; ~**wirtschaft** f siehe ~**haus**; ~**zimmer** nt guest room.

Gas-: ~**uhr** f siehe ~**zähler**; ~**verbrauch** m gas consumption; ~**vergiftung** f gas poisoning; ~**versorgung** f (System) gas supply (gen to); ~**werk** nt gasworks sing or pl; (~**verwaltung**) gas board; ~**zähler** m gas meter; ~**zentralheizung** f gas-fired central heating.

Gatt nt -(e)s, -en or -s (Naut) (Spei~) scupper; (Heckform) stern; (kleiner Raum) locker; (Loch) clew; (enge Durchfahrt) strait.

Gatte m -n, -n (form) husband, spouse (form). **die (beiden) ~n** both partners, husband and wife.

Gatten-: ~**liebe** f (form) married or conjugal (form) love; ~**mord** m (form) murder of one's husband/wife; ~**wahl** f (Biol) choice of mate; **das Ritual der ~wahl** the complicated ritual of choosing a mate.

Gatter nt -s, - (a) (Tür) gate; (Zaun) fence; (Rost) grating, grid. (b) (Tech: auch ~**säge**) gangsaw, framesaw.

Gattin f (form) wife, spouse (form).

Gattung f (Biol) genus; (Liter, Mus, Aut) genre, form; (fig: Sorte) type, kind.

Gattungs-: ~**begriff** m generic concept; ~**name** m generic term.

Gau m or nt -(e)s, -e (a) (Hist) gau, a tribal district, later an administrative district under the Nazis. (b) (Bezirk) district, region, area. **aus allen ~en** (liter) from all quarters.

Gaudee f -, -n (Aus) fun no pl. **auf der ~ sein** to be out gallivanting (inf).

Gaudi nt -s or (S Ger, Aus) f -, no pl (inf) fun. **das war eine ~** that was great fun; **das war eine ~ auf der Party** the party was great fun; **etw zur ~ machen** to do sth for fun or for a laugh.

Gaudium nt, no pl (old) amusement, entertainment.

Gaukelei f trickery no pl. ~**en** tricks pl, trickery.

gaukeln 1 vi (liter: Schmetterling) to flutter; (fig liter) to flit. **2** vt siehe vor~.

Gaukelspiel nt (liter) illusion. **ein ~ mit jdm treiben** to play sb false (liter), to deceive sb.

Gaukler m -s, - (a) (liter) travelling entertainer; (fig) storyteller. (b) (Orn) bateleur eagle.

Gaul m -(e)s, **Gäule** (pej) nag, hack; (rare: Arbeitspferd) workhorse; siehe **Schwanz, schenken, scheu.**

Gauleiter m (Pol) Gauleiter, head of a Nazi administrative district.

Gaullismus [go'lɪsmʊs] m Gaullism.

Gaullist [go'lɪst] m Gaullist.

gaullistisch [go'lɪstɪʃ] adj Gaullist no adv.

Gaumen m -s, - palate (auch fig), roof of the/one's mouth. **die Zunge klebte ihm vor Durst am ~** his tongue was hanging out (with thirst); **einen feinen ~ haben** (fig) to be (something of) a gourmet, to enjoy good food; **das kitzelt mir den ~** (fig)

that tickles my taste-buds or my palate.

Gaumen-: ~**kitzel** m (inf) delight for the taste-buds; ~**laut** m palatal (sound); ~**platte** f (dental) plate; ~**segel** nt soft palate, velum (spec); ~**zäpfchen** nt uvula.

Gauner m -s, - rogue, rascal, scoundrel; (Betrüger) crook; (hum inf: Schelm auch) scamp, scallywag (inf); (inf: gerissener Kerl) cunning devil (inf), sly customer (inf). **kleine ~** (Kriminelle) small-time crooks.

Gaunerbande f bunch of rogues or rascals or scoundrels/crooks; (hum: Kinder auch) bunch of scamps or scallywags (inf).

Gaunerei f swindling no pl, cheating no pl. **das ist doch eine ~, wenn ...** that's a swindle or cheat if ...

gaunerhaft adj rascally no adv.

gaunern (inf) vi (a) (betrügen) to swindle, to cheat; (stehlen) to thieve. **er hat sich durchs Leben gegaunert** he cheated his way through life. (b) aux sein (sich herumtreiben) to bum around (inf), to mooch about (inf).

Gauner-: ~**sprache** f underworld jargon; ~**zinken** m tramp's or gypsy's sign written on wall etc.

Gavotte f -, -n (Mus) gavotte.

Gaze ['ga:zə] f -, -n gauze; (Draht~ auch) (wire) mesh.

Gazelle f gazelle.

Gazette f (old, pej) gazette (old), (news)paper, rag (pej inf).

Geächtete(r) mf decl as adj outlaw; (fig) outcast.

Geächze nt -s, no pl groaning no pl, groans pl.

geädert adj veined.

geartet adj gutmütig/freundlich ~ sein to be goodnatured/have a friendly nature; **er ist (eben) so ~(, daß ...)** it's (just) his nature (to ...); **sie ist ganz anders ~** she has a completely different nature, she's quite different; **so ~e Probleme** problems of this nature; **das Problem ist so ~, daß ...** the nature of the problem is such that ...

Geäst nt -(e)s, no pl branches pl, boughs pl (liter); (von Adern etc) branches pl.

geb. abbr of geboren née.

Gebabbel nt -s, no pl (inf) babbling.

Gebäck nt -(e)s, -e (Kekse) biscuits pl; (süße Teilchen) pastries pl; (rundes Hefe~) buns pl; (Törtchen) tarts pl, tartlets pl. **allerlei (Kuchen und) ~** all kinds of cakes and pastries.

gebacken ptp of backen[1].

Gebälk nt -(e)s, -e timberwork no pl, timbers pl; (Archit: Verbindung zu Säulen) entablature. **ein Partisan im ~** (inf) a nigger in the woodpile (inf); siehe **knistern.**

geballt 1 ptp of ballen. **2** adj (konzentriert) Energie, Kraft, Ladung, (fig) concentrated; Stil auch concise; Beschuß massed.

gebannt 1 ptp of bannen. **2** adj spellbound. **vor Schreck ~** rigid with fear; **wie ~** as if spellbound.

gebar pret of gebären.

Gebärde f -, -n gesture; (lebhafte auch) gesticulation.

gebärden* vr to behave, to conduct oneself (form).

Gebärden-: ~**spiel** nt, no pl gestures pl, gesticulation(s); **das ~spiel der Sänger** the singers' use of gesture; ~**sprache** f gestures pl; (Zeichensprache) sign language; (in Stummfilmen etc) gesturing; (unbewußte ~sprache) body language.

gebaren* vr (rare) siehe **gebärden.**

Gebaren nt -s, no pl (a) behaviour. (b) (Comm: Geschäfts~) conduct.

gebären pret gebar, ptp geboren **1** vt to give birth to; Kind auch to bear (old, form), to be delivered of (old); (fig liter: erzeugen) to breed. **jdm ein Kind ~** to bear or give sb a child; **geboren werden** to be born; **wo sind Sie geboren?** where were you born?; **aus der Not geborene Ideen** ideas springing or stemming from necessity; siehe **geboren.**

2 vi to give birth.

gebär-: ~**fähig** adj child-bearing; ~**freudig** adj: **ein ~freudiges Becken haben** (hum) to have good child-bearing hips.

Gebärmutter f (Anat) womb, uterus.

Gebärmutter-: ~**hals** m neck of the womb or uterus, cervix; ~**krebs** m cancer of the uterus; ~**mund** m mouth of the uterus.

Gebarung f (Aus Comm) siehe **Gebaren (b).**

Gebarungs- (Aus Comm): ~**bericht** m financial report; ~**jahr** nt financial year; ~**kontrolle** f siehe **Buchprüfung.**

Gebäu nt -s, -e (obs) siehe **Gebäude.**

gebauchpinselt adj (hum inf) **sich ~ fühlen** to be tickled pink (inf).

Gebäude nt -s, - building; (Pracht~) edifice; (fig: Gefüge) structure; (von Ideen) edifice; construct; (von Lügen) web.

Gebäude-: ~**komplex** m building complex; ~**reiniger** m cleaner; (Fensterputzer) window cleaner; (Fassadenreiniger) building cleaner; ~**reinigung** f (das Reinigen) commercial cleaning; (Firma) cleaning contractors pl; ~**teil** m part of the building.

gebaut 1 ptp of bauen. **2** adj built. **gut/stark ~ sein** to be wellbuilt/to have a broad frame; **... so, wie du ~ bist** (inf) ... a big man/woman like you; **ein gut ~es Stück** a well-constructed play.

gebefreudig adj generous, open-handed.

Gebefreudigkeit f generosity, open-handedness.

Gebein nt -(e)s, -e (a) skeleton. **der Schreck fuhr ihm ins ~** (old) his whole body trembled with fear. (b) ~**e** pl (geh) bones pl, mortal remains pl (liter); (von Heiligen etc auch) relics pl.

Gebelfer nt -s, no pl (inf) yapping (auch fig), yelping.

Gebell(e) nt -s, no pl barking; (von Jagdhunden) baying; (fig inf: Geschimpfe) bawling (inf).

geben pret gab, ptp gegeben **1** vt (a) (auch vi) to give; (reichen auch) to pass, to hand; (her~) Leben to give up; (fig) Schatten, Kühle to provide; (machen, zusprechen) Mut, Hoff-

nung to give. **wer hat dir das gegeben?** who gave you that?; **gib's mir!** give it to me!, give me it!; **jdm einen Tritt ~** to kick sb, to give sb a kick; (*fig*) to get rid of sb; **gib's ihm (tüchtig)!** (*inf*) let him have it! (*inf*); **sich** (*dat*) (**von jdm**) **etw ~ lassen** to ask sb for sth; **was darf ich Ihnen ~?** what can I get you?; **~ Sie mir bitte zwei Flaschen Bier** I'd like two bottles of beer, please; **ich gebe dir das Auto für 100 Mark/zwei Tage** I'll let you have *or* I'll give you the car for 100 marks/two days; **jdm etw zu verstehen ~** to let sb know sth; **ein gutes Beispiel ~** to set a good example; **jdn/etw verloren ~** to give sb/sth up for *or* as lost; **~ Sie mir bitte Herrn Braun** (*Telec*) can I speak to Mr Braun please?; **man kann nicht für alles ~** (*spenden*) you can't give to everything; **ich gäbe viel darum, zu ...** I'd give a lot to ...; **sie gaben ihr Leben fürs Vaterland** they gave *or* laid down their lives for their country; **~** *or* **G~ ist seliger denn nehmen** *or* **Nehmen** (*Bibl*) it is more blessed to give than to receive.

(b) (*stellen*) to give; *Thema, Aufgabe, Problem auch* to set; (*gewähren*) *Interview, Audienz auch* to grant; *Rabatt auch* to allow; (*vergönnen*) to grant; (*verleihen*) *Titel, Namen* to give; *Preis auch* to award; (*zusprechen*) *Verwarnung* to give; *Freistoß auch* to award. **Gott gebe, daß ...** God grant that ...; **Taktgefühl ist ihm nicht gegeben** he has not been endowed with tactfulness; **es war ihm nicht gegeben, seine Eltern lebend wiederzusehen** he was not to see his parents alive again.

(c) (*schicken*) to send; (*dial: tun*) to put. **in die Post ~** to post; **ein Auto in Reparatur/ein Manuskript in Druck ~** to have a car repaired/to send a manuscript to be printed; **ein Mädchen aufs Gymnasium ~** (*dated*) to send a girl to a grammar school; **ein Kind in Pflege ~** to put *or* place a child in care; **einen Jungen in die Lehre ~** (*dated*) to have a boy apprenticed; **Zucker über etw** (*acc*) **~** (*dial*) to sprinkle sugar over sth; **Milch in den Teig ~** (*dial*) to add milk to the dough; *siehe* **Bescheid, Nachricht.**

(d) (*ergeben, erzeugen*) to produce. **2 + 2 gibt 4** 2 + 2 makes 4; **fünf Manuskriptseiten ~ eine Druckseite** five pages of manuscript give *or* equal one page of print; **die Kuh gibt Milch** the cow produces *or* yields milk; **ein Pfund gibt fünf Klöße** you can get five dumplings from one pound; **ein Wort gab das andere** one word led to another; **das gibt keinen Sinn** that doesn't make sense; **Rotwein gibt Flecken** red wine leaves stains.

(e) (*veranstalten*) *Konzert, Fest* to give; *Theaterstück etc* to put on; (*erteilen*) *Schulfach etc* to teach. **was wird heute im Theater gegeben?** what's on at the theatre today?; **das Stück wurde sechs Monate lang gegeben** the play ran *or* was on for six months; **Unterricht ~** to teach; **er gibt Nachhilfeunterricht/Tanzstunden** he gives private coaching/dancing lessons.

(f) **viel/nicht viel auf etw** (*acc*) **~** to set great/not much store by sth; **auf die Meinung der Nachbarn brauchst du nichts zu ~** you shouldn't pay any attention to what the neighbours say; **ich gebe nicht viel auf seinen Rat** I don't think much of his advice; **das Buch hat mir viel gegeben** I got a lot out of the book; **der Mann kann ihr nichts ~** the man can't give her anything.

(g) **etw von sich ~** *Laut, Worte, Flüche* to utter; *Rede* to deliver; *Meinung* to express; *Lebenszeichen* to show, to give; *Essen* to bring up; **was ich gestern von mir gegeben habe, war völlig unverständlich** what I said yesterday was completely incomprehensible.

2 *vi* (*rare vt*) (*Cards*) to deal; (*Sport: Aufschlag haben*) to serve. **wer gibt?** whose deal/serve is it?

3 *vt impers* **es gibt** (+*acc*) there is/are; **was gibt's?** what's the matter?, what's up?, what is it?; **gibt es einen Gott?** is there a God?, does God exist?; **was gibt's zum Mittagessen?** what's (there) for lunch?; **wann gibt's was zu essen?** — **es gibt gleich was** when are we going to get something to eat? — in a minute; **freitags gibt es bei uns immer Fisch** we always have fish on Fridays; **heute gibt's noch Regen** we'll get some rain yet today; **es wird noch Ärger ~** there'll be trouble (yet); **was wird das noch ~?** what will it come to?; **dafür gibt es 10% Rabatt** you get 10% discount for it; **ein Mensch mit zwei Köpfen? das gibt's nicht!** a two-headed person? there's no such thing!; **das gibt's nicht, daß ein Analphabet Lexikograph wird** it's impossible for an illiterate to become a lexicographer; **das gibt's doch nicht!, das darf es noch nicht ~!** that's impossible!, that can't be true!; **das hat es ja noch nie gegeben/so was gibt's bei uns nicht!** that's just not on! (*inf*); **da gibt's nichts** (*inf*) there's no two ways about it (*inf*); **so was gibt's also!** (*inf*) who'd have thought it! (*inf*); **gleich gibt's was!** (*inf*) there'll be trouble in a minute!; **hat es sonst noch etwas gegeben?** was there anything else?; **was es sonst noch gegeben?** was there anything else?; **was es nicht alles gibt!** it's a strange *or* funny world.

4 *vr* **(a)** (*nachlassen*) to ease off, to let up; (*Schmerz auch*) to get less; (*Leidenschaft auch*) to cool.

(b) (*sich erledigen*) to sort itself out; (*aufhören*) to stop. **er gab sich in sein Schicksal** he gave himself up to his fate; **sich gefangen/verloren ~** to give oneself up/to give oneself up for lost; **das wird sich schon ~** it'll all work out; **gibt sich das bald!** (*inf*) cut it out! (*inf*); *siehe* **schlagen, erkennen etc.**

(c) (*sich benehmen, aufführen*) to behave. **sich als etw ~** to play sth; **sich von oben herab ~** to behave condescendingly; **sich von der besten Seite ~** to show one's best side; **nach außen gab er sich heiter** outwardly he seemed quite cheerful; **sie gibt sich, wie sie ist** she doesn't try to be anything she's not.

Gebenedeite *f -n, no pl* (*Eccl*) **die ~** the Blessed Virgin.
Geber *m -s, -* giver; (*Cards*) dealer; (*Rad: Sender*) transmitter.
Geberlaune *f* generous mood. **in ~ sein** to be feeling generous, to be in a generous mood.
Gebet *nt -(e)s, -e* prayer. **ein ~ sprechen** to say a prayer; **sein ~ sprechen** *or* **verrichten** to say one's prayers; **das ~ des Herrn** the Lord's Prayer; **die Hände zum ~ falten** to join one's hands in prayer; **jdn ins ~ nehmen** (*fig*) to take sb to task; (*iro: bei Polizeiverhör etc*) to put the pressure on sb.

Gebetbuch *nt* prayer-book.
gebeten *pret of* **bitten.**
Gebetläuten *nt* (*Aus*) angelus.
Gebets-: **~mantel** *m* prayer shawl, tallith; **~mühle** *f* prayer wheel; **~riemen** *m* phylactery; **~stätte** *f* place of prayer; **~teppich** *m* prayer mat *or* rug.
Gebettel *nt -s, no pl* begging.
gebeugt 1 *ptp of* **beugen. 2** *adj* **(a)** *Haltung* stooped; *Kopf* bowed; *Schultern* sloping. **~ sitzen/stehen** to sit/stand hunched up. **(b)** (*Gram*) *Verb, Substantiv* inflected.
gebeut (*obs*) *3. pers sing present of* **gebieten.**
gebier (*liter*) *imper sing of* **gebären.**
Gebiet *nt -(e)s, -e* **(a)** area, region; (*Fläche, Stadt~*) area; (*Staats~*) territory. **(b)** (*fig: Fach*) field; (*Teil~*) branch. **auf diesem ~** in this field.
gebieten *pret* **gebot,** *ptp* **geboten** (*geh*) **1** *vti* (*verlangen*) to demand; (*befehlen*) to command. **jdm etw ~** to command sb to do sth; **der Ernst der Lage gebietet** *or* **gebeut** (*obs*) **sofortiges Handeln** the seriousness of the situation demands immediate action; *siehe* **Einhalt, geboten, ehrfurchtgebietend.**
    2 *vi* **(a)** (*liter: herrschen*) to have command (*über* +*acc* over). **über ein Land/Volk ~** to have dominion over a country/nation. **(b)** (*geh: verfügen*) **über etw** (*acc*) **~** *Geld etc* to have sth at one's disposal; *Wissen etc* to have sth at one's command.
Gebieter *m -s, -* (*liter*) master, lord; (*über Heer*) commander (*über* +*acc* of). **(mein) Herr und ~** (*old*) (my) lord and master.
Gebieterin *f* (*liter, old*) mistress, lady; (*über Heer*) commander.
gebieterisch 1 *adj* (*geh*) imperious; (*herrisch*) domineering; *Ton* peremptory. **2** *adv* (*unbedingt*) absolutely.
Gebiets-: **~abtretung** *f* (*form*) cession of territory; **~anspruch** *m* territorial claim; **~erweiterung** *f* territorial expansion; **~hoheit** *f* territorial sovereignty; **~körperschaft** *f* regional administrative body; **~reform** *f* local government reform; **~teil** *m* area (of territory); **g~weise** *adv* locally.
Gebilde *nt -s, -* (*Ding*) thing; (*Gegenstand*) object; (*Bauwerk*) construction; (*Schöpfung*) creation; (*Muster*) pattern; (*Form*) shape; (*Einrichtung*) organization; (*der Phantasie*) figment.
gebildet *adj* educated; (*gelehrt*) learned, erudite; (*wohlerzogen*) well-bred; (*kultiviert*) cultured, cultivated; (*belesen*) well-read; *Manieren* refined. **sich ~ unterhalten** to have a cultured conversation.
Gebildete(r) *mf decl as adj* educated person. **die ~n** the intellectuals.
Gebimmel *nt -s, no pl* (*inf*) ting-a-ling (*inf*).
Gebinde *nt -s, -* **(a)** (*Blumen~*) arrangement; (*Sträußchen*) posy; (*Blumenkranz*) wreath; (*Getreidegarbe*) sheaf. **(b)** (*von Garn*) skein.
Gebirge *nt -s, -* **(a)** mountains *pl*, mountain range. **im/ins ~** in/into the mountains. **(b)** (*Min*) rock.
gebirgig *adj* mountainous.
Gebirgigkeit *f* hilliness. **die Schweiz ist wegen ihrer ~ ...** because of its mountains, Switzerland is ...
Gebirgler(in *f*) *m -s, -* mountain-dweller, highlander.
Gebirgs- *in cpds* mountain; **~bach** *m* mountain stream; **~bahn** *f* mountain railway *crossing a mountain range*; (*in Alpen*) transalpine railway; **~blume** *f* mountain flower, flower growing in the mountains; **~jäger** *m* (*Mil*) mountain soldier; *pl auch* mountain troops; **~landschaft** *f* (*Gegend*) mountainous region; (*Gemälde*) mountainscape; (*Ausblick*) mountain scenery; **~massiv** *nt* massif; **~rücken** *m* mountain ridge; **~stock** *m* massif; **~straße** *f* mountain road; **~truppen** *pl* mountain troops *pl*; **~wand** *f* mountain face; **~zug** *m* mountain range.
Gebiß *nt -sses, -sse* **(a)** (*die Zähne*) (set of) teeth; (*künstliches ~*) dentures *pl*. **ich habe noch mein ganzes ~** I still have all my teeth; **das scharfe ~ eines Wolfs** the sharp teeth of a wolf. **(b)** (*am Pferdezaum*) bit.
Gebiß-: **~abdruck** *m* impression; **~anomalie** *f* deformity of the teeth.
gebissen *ptp of* **beißen.**
Gebläse *nt -s, -* blower; (*Motor~*) supercharger; (*Verdichter*) compressor.
Gebläse-: **~luft** *f* air from a blower; **~motor** *m* supercharger (engine).
geblasen *ptp of* **blasen.**
geblichen *ptp of* **bleichen.**
geblieben *ptp of* **bleiben.**
Geblödel *nt -s, no pl* (*inf*) nonsense; (*blödes Gerede auch*) twaddle (*inf*), baloney (*inf*); (*von Komiker*) patter. **die Unterhaltung artete in allgemeines ~ aus** the conversation degenerated into silliness.
Geblök(e) *nt -(e)s, no pl* (*von Schaf, Kalb*) bleating; (*von Kuh*) lowing; (*inf: von Mensch*) bawling (*inf*).
geblümt, geblumt (*Aus*) *adj* flowered; (*Liter, fig*) *Stil* flowery. **er drückt sich sehr ~ aus** he has a very flowery way of expressing himself.
Geblüt *nt -(e)s, no pl* (*geh*) (*Abstammung*) descent, lineage; (*fig: Blut*) blood; (*liter: Geschlecht*) family. **von edlem ~** of noble blood; **ein Prinz von ~** a prince of the blood (royal).
gebogen 1 *ptp of* **biegen. 2** *adj* *Nase* Roman.
geboren 1 *ptp of* **gebären. 2** *adj* **sich ~ fühlen/~ sein** to have been born blind; **er ist blind ~** he was born blind; **~er Engländer/Londoner sein** to be English/a Londoner by birth; **er ist der ~e Erfinder** he's a born inventor; **Hanna Schmidt ~e** *or* **geb. Müller** Hanna Schmidt, née Müller; **sie ist eine ~e Müller** she was born Müller, her maiden name was Müller.
Geborenzeichen *nt asterisk used to denote "date of birth".*
geborgen 1 *ptp of* **bergen. 2** *adj* **sich ~ fühlen/~ sein** to feel/be secure *or* safe.

Geborgenheit f security.
geborsten ptp of **bersten**.
gebot pret of **gebieten**.
Gebot nt -(e)s, -e **(a)** (Gesetz) law; (Regel, Vorschrift) rule; (Bibl) commandment; (Grundsatz) precept; (old: Verordnung) decree; (old: Befehl) command.
(b) (geh: Erfordernis) requirement. **das ~ der Stunde** the needs of the moment; **das ~ der Vernunft** the dictates of reason; **das ~ der Vernunft verlangt, daß ...** reason dictates that ...
(c) (Verfügung) command. **jdm zu ~e stehen** to be at sb's command or (Geld etc) disposal.
(d) (Comm: bei Auktionen) bid.
geboten 1 ptp of **gebieten** and **bieten. 2** adj (geh) (ratsam, angebracht) advisable; (notwendig) necessary; (dringend ~) imperative. **bei aller ~en Achtung** with all due respect; **er hat es am ~en Respekt seiner Mutter gegenüber fehlen lassen** he failed to give his mother the respect due to her.
Gebotsschild nt sign giving orders.
Gebr. abbr of **Gebrüder** Bros.
Gebrabbel nt -s, no pl (inf) jabbering (inf), prattling (inf).
gebracht ptp of **bringen**.
gebrannt 1 ptp of **brennen. 2** adj **~er Kalk** quicklime; **~e Mandeln** pl burnt almonds pl; **ein ~es Kind scheut das Feuer** (Prov) once bitten twice shy (Prov).
gebraten ptp of **braten**.
Gebratene(s) nt decl as adj fried food.
Gebräu nt -(e)s, -e brew; (pej) strange concoction; (fig) concoction (aus of).
Gebrauch m -(e)s, **Gebräuche** (Benutzung) use; (eines Wortes) usage; (Anwendung) application; (Brauch, Gepflogenheit) custom. **falscher ~** misuse; abuse; misapplication; **von etw ~ machen** to make use of sth; **außer ~ kommen** to fall into disuse; (von Sitte etc) to become rare; **in ~ sein** to be used or in use; (Auto) to be running; **etw in ~ (dat) haben** to use sth; **Auto etc** to run sth; **allgemein in ~ (dat)** in general use; **etw in ~ nehmen** (form) to put sth into use; **zum äußeren/inneren ~** to be taken externally/internally; **vor ~ (gut) schütteln** shake (well) before use.
gebrauchen* vt (benutzen) to use; (anwenden) to apply. **sich zu etw ~ lassen** to be useful for sth; (mißbrauchen) to be used as sth; **nicht mehr zu ~ sein** to be no longer any use, to be useless; **er/das ist zu nichts zu ~** he's/that's (of) no use to anybody or absolutely useless; **das kann ich gut ~** I can make good use of that, I can really use that; **ich könnte ein neues Kleid/einen Whisky ~** I could use a new dress/a whisky; **Geld kann ich immer ~** money's always useful; **Mitarbeiter, die nicht mehr gebraucht werden, ...** employees who are no longer needed, ...; siehe **gebraucht**.
gebräuchlich adj (verbreitet) common; (gewöhnlich) usual, customary; (herkömmlich) conventional. **nicht mehr ~** (Ausdruck etc) no longer used.
Gebräuchlichkeit f siehe adj commonness; usualness, customariness; conventionality.
Gebrauchs-: ~anleitung f (form), **~anweisung** f (für Arznei) directions pl; (für Geräte etc) instructions pl; **~artikel** m article for everyday use; **~artikel** pl (esp Comm) basic consumer goods pl; **g~fähig** adj in working order, usable; **etw g~fähig machen** to put sth into working order; **g~fertig** adj ready for use; Nahrungsmittel instant; **~gegenstand** m -̈e necessary item, necessity, basic commodity; (Werkzeug, Küchengerät) utensil; **~graphik** f commercial art; **~graphiker** m commercial artist; **~gut** nt usu pl consumer item; **Konsum- und ~güter** consumer and utility goods; **~lyrik** f everyday poetry; **~möbel** pl utility furniture no pl; **~muster** nt registered pattern or design; **~musterschutz** m protection of patterns and designs; **~wert** m utility value.
gebraucht 1 ptp of **brauchen. 2** adj second-hand, used. **etw ~ kaufen** to buy sth second-hand.
Gebrauchtwagen m used or second-hand car.
Gebrauchtwaren pl second-hand goods pl.
Gebrauchtwaren-: ~händler m dealer in second-hand goods; **~handlung** f second-hand shop.
gebräunt 1 ptp of **bräunen. 2** adj (braungebrannt) (sun-)tanned.
Gebrechen nt -s, - (geh) affliction; (fig) weakness. **die ~ des Alters** the afflictions or infirmities of old age.
gebrechen* vi irreg (old liter) **es gebricht an etw** (dat) sth is lacking; **es gebricht ihm an Mut** he lacks courage.
gebrechlich adj frail; (altersschwach) infirm; (fig: unvollkommen) weak.
Gebrechlichkeit f siehe adj frailty; infirmness; weakness.
Gebresten nt -s, - (obs) ailment.
gebrochen 1 ptp of **brechen. 2** adj broken; Mensch auch crushed. **~e Zahl** (Math) fraction; **vor Kummer ~** (geh) griefstricken; **mit ~em Herzen, ~en Herzens** broken-hearted; **an ~em Herzen** of a broken heart; **~ Deutsch sprechen** to speak broken German.
Gebrüder pl (Comm) Brothers pl. **~ Müller** Müller Brothers.
Gebrüll nt -(e)s, no pl (von Rind) bellowing; (von Esel) braying; (von Löwe) roar; (in Todesangst) screaming; (von Mensch) yelling. **auf ihn mit ~!** (inf) go for him!, at him!
Gebrumm nt -es, no pl buzzing; (von Motor, von Baß, Singen) droning; (inf: Gebrummel) grumping (inf).
Gebrummel nt -s, no pl grumping.
gebückt 1 ptp of **bücken. 2** adj **eine ~e Haltung** a stoop; **~ gehen** to stoop.
gebügelt 1 pret of **bügeln. 2** adj (inf: perplex) knocked flat (inf); siehe **geschniegelt**.
Gebühr f -, -en **(a)** charge; (Post~) postage no pl; (Honorar,

Beitrag) fee; (Schul~, Studien~) fees pl; (Vermittlungs~) commission no pl; (Straßenbenutzungs~) toll. **~en erheben** to make or levy (form) a charge, to charge postage/a fee etc; **zu ermäßigter ~** at a reduced rate; **eine ~ von 50 DM** or **50 DM ~en bezahlen** to pay a fee/charge etc of DM 50; **~ (be)zahlt Empfänger** postage to be paid by addressee; **die ~en für Rundfunk/Fernsehen werden erhöht** radio/television licences are going up.
(b) (Angemessenheit) **nach ~** suitably, properly; **über ~** excessively.
gebühren* (geh) **1** vi to be due (dat to). **ihm gebührt Anerkennung/Achtung** he deserves or is due recognition/respect; **das gebührt ihm** (steht ihm zu) it is his (just) due; (gehört sich für ihn) it befits him.
2 vr to be proper or seemly or fitting. **wie es sich gebührt** as is proper; **es gebührt sich schlecht für fun**, zu it ill befits him to.
Gebühren|anhebung f augmentation in charges/fees etc.
gebührend adj (verdient) due; (angemessen) suitable; (geziemend) proper. **das ihm ~e Gehalt** the salary he deserves; **jdm die ~e Achtung erweisen/verweigern** to pay/deny sb the respect due to him.
Gebühren-: ~einheit f (Telec) (tariff) unit; **~erhöhung** f increase in charges/fees; **~erlaß** m remission of charges/fees; **g~frei** adj free of charge; Brief, Paket postfree; **~freiheit** f exemption from charges/fees/postage; **~marke** f revenue stamp; **~ordnung** f scale of charges, tariff; **g~pflichtig** adj subject or liable to a charge, chargeable; Autobahnbenutzung subject to a toll; **g~pflichtige Verwarnung** (Jur) fine; **jdn g~pflichtig verwarnen** to fine sb; **~satz** m rate (of charge); **~zähler** m meter.
gebührlich adj siehe **gebührend**.
Gebums(e) nt -es, no pl **(a)** (inf: Gepolter) thumping, thudding. **(b)** (sl: Koitieren) screwing (sl).
gebündelt 1 ptp of **bündeln. 2** adj Strahlen bundled; (fig) joint.
gebunden 1 ptp of **binden**.
2 adj tied (an +acc to sth); (durch Verpflichtungen etc) tied down; Kapital tied up; Preise controlled; (Ling, Phys, Buch) bound; Wärme latent; (Mus) legato. **in ~er Rede** in verse; **zeitlich/vertraglich ~ sein** to be restricted as regards time/to be bound by contract; **anderweitig ~ sein** to be otherwise engaged; **an einen Ort ~ sein** to be tied to a particular place.
Gebundenheit f restriction; (von Wärme) latency. **auf Grund der ~ unseres Kapitals** because our capital is tied up; **ein Gefühl der ~** a feeling of being tied; **~ ist ihr zuwider** she hates being tied down; **wegen ihrer ~ ans Elternhaus** because she is/was etc tied to her parents.
Geburt f -, -en (lit, fig) birth; (fig: Produkt) fruit, product. **von ~ by birth; von ~ an** from birth; **von hoher/adliger ~** of good/noble birth; **bei der ~ sterben** (Mutter) to die in childbirth; (Kind) to die at birth; **das war eine schwere ~!** (fig inf) that took some doing (inf).
Geburten-: ~beihilfe f maternity grant; **~beschränkung** f population control; **~buch** nt register of births; **~häufigkeit** f birth rate; **~kontrolle, ~regelung** f birth control; **~rückgang** m drop in the birth rate; **g~schwach** adj Jahrgang with a low birth rate; **g~stark** adj Jahrgang with a high birth rate; **~statistik** f birth statistics pl; **~überschuß** m excess of births over deaths; **~zahl, ~ziffer** f number of births; **~zuwachs** m increase in the birth rate.
gebürtig adj **~er Londoner** or **aus London ~ sein** to have been born in London, to be London-born, to be a native Londoner.
Geburts-: ~adel m hereditary nobility; **er stammt aus altem ~adel** he comes from a long line of nobility; **~anzeige** f birth announcement; **~datum** nt date of birth; **~fehler** m congenital defect; **~haus** nt **das ~haus Kleists** the house where Kleist was born; **~helfer(in** f) m (Arzt) obstetrician; (Laie) assistant at a birth; **~hilfe** f **(a)** assistance at a birth; **~hilfe leisten** to assist at a birth; (fig) to help sth see the light of day; **(b)** (als Fach) obstetrics; (von Hebamme auch) midwifery; **~jahr** nt year of birth; **~lage** f presentation; **~land** nt native country; **sein ~land Italien** his native Italy; **~mal** nt birth mark; **~ort** m birth place; **~stadt** f native town; **ihre ~stadt Wien** her native Vienna; **~stätte** f (geh) birthplace.
Geburtstag m birthday; (auf Formularen) date of birth. **herzlichen Glückwunsch zum ~!** happy birthday!, many happy returns (of the day)!; **jdm zum ~ gratulieren** to wish sb **(a)** happy birthday or many happy returns (of the day); **heute habe ich ~** it's my birthday today; **~ feiern** to celebrate one's/sb's birthday; **jdm etw zum ~ schenken** to give sb sth for his/her birthday.
Geburtstags- in cpds birthday; **~kind** nt birthday boy/girl.
Geburts-: ~urkunde f birth certificate; **~wehen** pl labour pains pl; (fig auch) birth pangs pl; **~zange** f (pair sing of) forceps pl.
Gebüsch nt -(e)s, -e bushes pl; (Unterholz) undergrowth, brush.
Geck m -en, -en (pej) fop, dandy.
geckenhaft adj (pej) foppish.
Geckenhaftigkeit f (pej) foppishness.
Gecko m -s, -s (Zool) gecko.
gedacht 1 ptp of **denken** and **gedenken. 2** adj Linie, Größe, Fall imaginary.
Gedächtnis nt memory; (Andenken auch) remembrance. **etw aus dem ~ hersagen** to recite sth from memory; **das ist seinem ~ entfallen** it went out of his mind; **sich** (dat) **etw ins ~ zurückrufen** to recall sth, to call sth to mind; **wenn mich mein ~ nicht trügt** if my memory serves me right; **noch frisch in jds ~ (dat) sein** to be still fresh in sb's mind; **zum ~ der** or **an die Toten** in memory or remembrance of the dead.

Gedächtnis-: ~ausstellung f commemorative exhibition; ~fehler m lapse of memory; ~feier f commemoration; (kirchliche) memorial or commemorative service; ~hilfe f memory aid, mnemonic; er machte sich ein paar Notizen als ~hilfe he made a few notes to aid his memory; ~kraft f (powers pl of) memory; ~lücke f gap in one's memory; (Psych) localized amnesia; da habe ich eine ~lücke I just don't remember anything about it; ~rede f commemorative speech; ~rennen nt memorial race; ~schulung f memory training; ~schwund m amnesia, loss of memory; ~störung f partial or (vorübergehend) temporary amnesia; ~stütze f siehe ~hilfe; ~übung f memory training exercise; ~verlust m loss of memory.

gedämpft 1 ptp of **dämpfen. 2** adj Geräusch muffled; Farben, Musikinstrument, Stimmung muted; Licht, Freude subdued; Wut suppressed; (Tech) Schwingung damped. mit ~er Stimme in a low voice.

Gedanke m -ns, -n thought (über + acc on, about); (Idee, Plan, Einfall) idea; (Konzept) concept; (Betrachtung) reflection (über + acc on). der bloße ~ an ... the mere thought of ...; da kam mir ein ~ then I had an idea, then something occurred to me; einen ~n fassen to formulate an idea; bei diesem Lärm kann man ja keinen ~n fassen you can't hear yourself think in this noise; seine ~n zusammennehmen to concentrate one's mind or thoughts; seine ~n beisammen haben to have one's mind or thoughts concentrated; in ~n vertieft or versunken/verloren sein to be deep or sunk/lost in thought; in ~n, Worten und Werken sündigen to sin in thought, word and deed; in ~n bin ich bei dir in thought I am with you, my thoughts are with you; jdn auf andere ~n bringen to make sb think of other things, to divert sb's thoughts; schwarzen ~n nachhängen to think gloomy or dismal thoughts; wo hat er nur seine ~n? whatever is he thinking about?; sich (dat) über etw (acc) ~n machen to think about sth; (sich sorgen) to worry or be worried about sth; mach dir keine ~n (darüber)! don't worry about it!; man macht sich (dat) so seine ~n (inf) I've got my ideas; kein ~ (daran)! (stimmt nicht) not a bit of it! (inf); (kommt nicht in Frage) (that's) out of the question; etw ganz in ~n (dat) tun to do sth (quite) without thinking; jds ~n lesen to read sb's mind or thoughts; ich kann doch nicht ~n lesen! I'm not a mind-reader!; seine ~n abschalten to make one's mind a blank; auf einen ~n kommen to have or get an idea; wie kommen Sie auf den ~n? what gives you that idea?, what makes you think that?; auf dumme ~n kommen (inf) to get up to mischief; jdn auf den ~n bringen, etw zu tun to give sb the idea of doing sth; sich mit dem ~n tragen, etw zu tun (geh) to consider or entertain the idea of doing sth; der Europa~ or europäische/olympische ~ the European/Olympic Idea; der Mitbestimmungs~ the concept or idea of co-determination; die ~n sind zollfrei (Prov) thoughts are free.

Gedanken-: ~arbeit f thought; ~armut f lack of thought; (Ideenarmut) lack of originality; ~austausch m (Pol) exchange of ideas; ~blitz m brainwave; ~flug m (geh) flight(s) of thought; ~folge f reasoning; ~freiheit f freedom of thought; ~fülle f wealth of ideas; ~gang m train of thought; ~gebäude nt edifice or construct of ideas; ~gut nt body of thought; ~kette f chain of thought; ~lesen nt mind-reading; g~los adj (unüberlegt) unthinking; (zerstreut) absent-minded; (rücksichtslos) thoughtless; etw g~los tun to do sth without thinking; ~losigkeit f siehe adj lack of thought; absent-mindedness; thoughtlessness; ~lyrik f reflective poetry; g~reich adj full of ideas; ~reichtum m wealth of ideas; ~reihe f siehe ~kette; ~splitter m aphorism; ~sprung m mental leap, jump from one idea to another; ~strich m dash; ~tiefe f depth of thought; ~übertragung f telepathy (auch fig), thought transference; ~verbindung f, ~verknüpfung f association of ideas; g~verloren adj lost in thought; g~voll adj (nachdenklich) thoughtful, pensive; ~welt f world of thought or (Ideenwelt) ideas; die römische ~welt (the world of) Roman thought; er lebt in seiner eigenen ~welt he lives in a world of his own.

gedanklich adj intellectual; (vorgestellt) imaginary. sich (dat) ~ or in ~er Hinsicht näherkommen to find a common way of thinking; in ~er Hinsicht übereinstimmen to have an affinity of mind; die große ~e Klarheit in seinem Werk the great clarity of thought in his work.

Gedärm(e) nt -(e)s, -e (old, liter) bowels pl, entrails pl.

Gedärme pl intestines pl. da drehen sich einem ja die ~ um! it's enough to make your insides or stomach turn over!

Gedeck nt -(e)s, -e (a) (Tisch~) cover. ein ~ auflegen to lay or set a place; ein ~ für drei Personen places or covers for three people; eine Tafel mit zehn ~en a table laid for ten (people). (b) (Menü) set meal, table d'hôte. (c) (im Nachtclub) cover charge; drink with cover charge.

gedeckt 1 pret of **decken. 2** adj Farben muted; Basar, Gang covered; Auto hard-top(ped).

Gedeih m: auf ~ und Verderb for better or (for) worse; jdm auf ~ und Verderb ausgeliefert sein to be completely and utterly at sb's mercy.

gedeihen pret **gedieh**, ptp **gediehen** vi aux sein to thrive; (wirtschaftlich auch) to prosper, to flourish; (geh: sich entwickeln) to develop; (fig: vorankommen) to make progress or headway, to progress. die Sache ist so weit gediehen, daß ... the matter has reached the point or stage where ...

Gedeihen nt -s, no pl siehe vi thriving; prospering, flourishing; (Gelingen) success. zum ~ dieses Vorhabens braucht es Geduld und Glück if this plan is to succeed patience and luck will be called for.

gedeihlich adj (geh) (vorteilhaft) beneficial, advantageous, salutary; (erfolgreich) successful.

Gedenk|ausstellung f commemorative exhibition.

Gedenken nt -s, no pl memory. zum or im ~ an jdn in memory or remembrance of sb; etw in gutem ~ behalten to treasure the memory of sth; jdm in ehrendes ~ bewahren to remember sb with honour; jdm etw zu treuem ~ geben to give sb sth as a token of remembrance.

gedenken* vi irreg + gen (a) (geh: denken an) to remember, to think of; (erwähnen) to recall. gedenke, daß ... (liter) remember or be mindful (old, liter) that ...; in seiner Rede gedachte er ... in his speech he recalled ... (b) (feiern) to commemorate, to remember. (c) ~, etw zu tun to propose to do sth.

Gedenk-: ~feier f commemoration; ~gottesdienst m memorial or commemorative service; ~marke f commemorative stamp; ~minute f minute's silence; ~münze f commemorative coin; ~rede f commemorative speech; ~stätte f memorial; ~stein m commemorative or memorial stone; ~stunde f hour of commemoration; ~tafel f plaque; ~tag m commemoration day.

gedeucht ptp of **dünken.**

Gedicht nt -(e)s, -e poem. die ~e Enzensbergers Enzensberger's poetry or poems; dieses Kleid/der Nachtisch ist ein ~ (fig inf) this dress/the dessert is sheer poetry.

Gedicht-: ~form f poetic form; in ~form in verse; ~sammlung f collection of poems; (von mehreren Dichtern auch) anthology.

gediegen adj (a) Metall pure, native (esp Min). (b) (von guter Qualität) high-quality; (geschmackvoll) tasteful; (rechtschaffen) upright; Verarbeitung solid; Kenntnisse sound. (c) (inf: wunderlich) peculiar.

Gediegenheit f siehe adj (a) purity, nativeness. (b) high quality; tastefulness; uprightness; solidity; soundness.

gedieh pret of **gedeihen.**

gediehen ptp of **gedeihen.**

gedient 1 ptp of **dienen. 2** adj: ein ~er Soldat someone who has completed his military service.

Gedinge nt -s, - (Miner): im ~ arbeiten to work on a piece-rate basis.

Gedöns nt -es, no pl (dial inf) fuss, hullabaloo (inf).

Gedränge nt -s, no pl (Menschenmenge) crowd, crush; (Drängeln) jostling; (Sport) bunching; (Rugby) scrum(mage). vor der Theaterkasse herrschte ~ there was a big crush at the ticket office; ein offenes ~ (Rugby) a loose scrum; ins ~ kommen or geraten (fig) to get into a fix.

Gedrängel nt -s, no pl (inf) (Menschenmenge) crush; (Drängeln) shoving (inf).

gedrängt 1 ptp of **drängen. 2** adj packed; (fig) Stil terse. ~ voll packed full, jam-packed (inf); ~e Übersicht synopsis; ~ stehen to be crowded together.

Gedrängtheit f (von Stil) terseness; (von Übersicht) conciseness.

gedrechselt 1 ptp of **drechseln. 2** adj (pej) Rede, Sätze, Stil stilted. wie ~ reden to speak in a stilted fashion or stiltedly; kunstvoll ~e Sätze nicely turned phrases.

Gedröhn(e) nt -es, no pl (von Motoren) droning; (von Kanonen, Lautsprecher, Hämmern etc) booming.

gedroschen ptp of **dreschen.**

gedruckt 1 ptp of **drucken. 2** adj lügen wie ~ (inf) to lie right, left and centre (inf).

gedrückt 1 ptp of **drücken. 2** adj depressed, dejected. ~er Stimmung sein to be in low spirits, to feel depressed.

Gedrücktheit f depression, dejection.

gedrungen 1 ptp of **dringen. 2** adj Gestalt sturdy, stocky.

Gedrungenheit f sturdiness, stockiness.

geduckt 1 ptp of **ducken. 2** adj Haltung, Mensch crouching; Kopf lowered. hinter einer Hecke ~ crouching down behind a hedge; ~ sitzen to sit hunched up.

Gedudel nt -s, no pl (inf) (von Klarinette etc) tootling; (von Dudelsack) droning, whining; (von Radio) noise.

Geduld f -, no pl patience. mit jdm/etw ~ haben to be patient or have patience with sb/sth; sich mit ~ wappnen to possess one's soul in patience; mir geht die ~ aus, mir reißt die ~, ich verliere die ~ my patience is wearing thin, I'm losing my patience; jds ~ auf eine harte Probe stellen to try sb's patience.

gedulden* vr to be patient.

geduldig adj patient. ~ wie ein Lamm meek as a lamb.

Gedulds-: ~arbeit f job calling for patience; ~faden m jetzt reißt mir aber der ~faden! (inf) I'm just about losing my patience; einen langen ~faden haben to have a lot of patience, to have the patience of Job; ~probe f trial of (one's) patience; das war eine harte ~probe it was enough to try anyone's patience or to try the patience of a saint; ~spiel nt puzzle.

gedungen ptp of **dingen.**

gedunsen adj bloated.

Gedunsenheit f bloatedness.

gedurft ptp of **dürfen.**

ge|ehrt 1 ptp of **ehren. 2** adj honoured, esteemed. sehr ~e Damen und Herren! Ladies and Gentlemen!; sehr ~er Herr Kurz! dear Mr Kurz!; sehr ~e Damen, sehr ~e Herren! (in Briefen) dear Sir or Madam.

ge|eicht 1 ptp of **eichen². 2** adj (inf) darauf ist er ~ that's right up his street (inf).

ge|eignet 1 ptp of **eignen. 2** adj (passend) suitable; (richtig) right. sie ist für diesen Posten nicht ~ she's not the right person for this job; er ist nicht der ~e Mann für meine Tochter he's not the right or a suitable man for my daughter; im ~en Augenblick at the right moment; er ist zu dieser Arbeit nicht ~ he's not suited to this work; er wäre zum Lehrer gut/schlecht ~ he would/wouldn't make a good teacher.

ge|eigneten|orts adv (form) in an appropriate place.

ge|eist 1 ptp of **eisen. 2** adj Früchte, Getränke iced.

Geest f -, -en, **Geestland** nt coastal moorlands of N.W. Germany.

Gefahr f -, -en (a) danger (für to, for); (Bedrohung) threat (für to, for). die ~en des Dschungels/Verkehrs/dieses Berufs the dangers or perils or hazards of the jungle/traffic/this job; in ~ sein/schweben to be in danger or jeopardy; (bedroht) to feel threatened; außer ~ (nicht gefährdet) not in danger; (nicht mehr gefährdet) out of danger; (Patienten) out of danger, off the danger list; sich ~en or einer ~ aussetzen to expose oneself to danger, to put oneself in danger; es besteht die ~, daß ... there's a risk or the danger that ...; ihm droht keine ~ von uns he's in no danger from us; er liebt die ~ he likes living dangerously; (nur) bei ~ (bedienen)! (to be used only) in case of emergency!; wer sich in ~ begibt, kommt darin um (Prov) if you play with fire, you must expect to get your fingers burned.
(b) (Wagnis, Risiko) risk (für to, for). auf eigene ~ at one's own risk or (stärker) peril; auf die ~ hin, etw zu tun/daß jd etw tut at the risk of doing sth/of sb doing sth; ~ laufen, etw zu tun to run the risk of doing sth; unter ~ seines eigenen Lebens at the risk of one's own life; auf eigene Rechnung und ~ (Comm) at one's own account and risk.

gefahrbringend adj dangerous.

gefährden* vt to endanger; Position, Wirtschaft, Chancen etc auch to jeopardize; (bedrohen) to threaten; (aufs Spiel setzen auch) to put at risk. Versetzung or Vorrücken gefährdet (Sch) comment on a school report indicating that the pupil may have to repeat a year.

gefährdet adj Tierart endangered; Ehe, Jugend at risk. G~e people at risk.

Gefährdung f no pl (a) siehe vt endangering; jeopardizing; risking. (b) (Gefahr) danger (gen to).

gefahren ptp of fahren.

Gefahren-: ~herd m danger area; ~moment[1] nt potential danger; ~moment[2] m (Schrecksekunde) moment of danger; ~quelle f source of danger; ~stelle f danger spot; ~zone f danger zone or area; ~zulage f danger money; eine ~zulage von 200 Mark 200 marks danger money.

gefährlich adj dangerous; (gewagt auch) risky; (lebens~ auch) perilous. das ~e Alter (fig) the dangerous age.

Gefährlichkeit f siehe adj dangerousness; riskiness; perilousness.

Gefahr-: g~los adj safe; (harmlos) harmless; ~losigkeit f safety; harmlessness.

Gefahrstelle f siehe Gefahrenstelle.

Gefährt nt -(e)s, -e (dated) wagon, carriage; (hum) jalopy (inf).

Gefährte m -n, -n, **Gefährtin** f (geh) (lit, fig) companion; (Lebens~ auch) partner (through life).

Gefahr-: g~voll adj dangerous, full of danger; ~zeichen nt danger sign.

Gefälle nt -s, - (a) (Neigung) (von Fluß) drop, fall; (von Land, Straße) slope; (Neigungsgrad) gradient. das Gelände/der Fluß hat ein starkes ~ the land slopes down steeply/the river drops sharply; ein ~ von 10% a gradient of 10%; starkes ~! steep hill.
(b) (fig: Unterschied) difference.

gefallen[1] pret **gefiel**, ptp ~ vi to please (jdm sb). es gefällt mir (gut) I like it (very much or a lot); es gefällt ihm, wie sie spricht he likes the way she talks; das gefällt mir gar nicht, das will mir gar nicht ~ (dated) I don't like it at all or one little bit; das Stück hat ~ (geh) the play was well received; das gefällt mir schon besser (inf) that's more like it (inf); er gefällt mir gar nicht (inf: gesundheitlich) I don't like the look of him (inf); sie gefällt sich (dat) in dem Hut she likes herself in that hat; sich (dat) in einer Rolle ~ to fancy oneself in a rôle; er gefällt sich in der Rolle des Leidenden he likes playing the martyr; sich (dat) etw ~ lassen (dulden) to put up with sth, to tolerate sth; er läßt sich alles ~ he'll put up with anything; das lasse ich mir (von Ihnen/denen) nicht ~! I won't stand for or put up with that (from you/them)!; das lasse ich mir ~! that's just the job (inf) or thing (inf), there's nothing I'd like better.

gefallen[2] 1 ptp of fallen and gefallen[1]. 2 adj Engel, (dated) Mädchen fallen; (Mil) killed in action. sie/er ist eine ~e Größe (geh) she/he has fallen from grace; er ist ~ he was killed in action.

Gefallen[1] nt -s, no pl (geh) pleasure. an etw (dat) ~ finden to derive or get pleasure from sth, to delight in sth; an jdm/aneinander (großes) ~ finden to take a (great) fancy to sb/each other; bei jdm ~ finden to appeal to sb; nach ~ (just) as one pleases, at one's discretion (form).

Gefallen[2] m -s, - favour. jdn um einen ~ bitten to ask a favour of sb; tun Sie mir den ~ und schreiben Sie would you do me a favour and write, would you do me the favour of writing; Sie würden mir einen ~ tun, wenn ... you'd be doing me a favour if ...; jdm etw zu ~ tun (geh) to do sth to please sb; jdm zu ~ reden (dated) to say what sb likes to hear; ihm zu ~ to please him.

Gefallenendenkmal nt war memorial.

Gefallene(r) mf decl as adj soldier killed in action. die ~n und die Toten des Krieges the soldiers and civilians who died in the war; ein Denkmal für die ~n des Krieges a memorial to those killed in the war.

Gefäll(e)strecke f incline.

gefällig adj (a) (hilfsbereit) helpful, obliging. sich ~ zeigen to show oneself willing to oblige; jdm ~ sein to oblige or help sb.
(b) (ansprechend) pleasing; (freundlich) pleasant.
(c) ist noch etwas ~? (dated) will there be anything else?; wenn es (Ihnen) ~ ist (iro, form) if that is all right (with you); Zigarette ~? (form) would you care for a cigarette?; siehe gefälligst.

Gefälligkeit f (a) (Gefallen) favour. jdm eine ~ erweisen to do sb a favour. (b) no pl (gefälliges Wesen) pleasantness; (Entgegenkommen) helpfulness. etw aus ~ tun to do sth out of the kindness of one's heart.

Gefälligkeits-: ~akzept nt, ~wechsel m (Fin) accommodation bill or paper; ~attest nt sick note on request; ~fahrt f (Aut) private trip.

gefälligst adv (inf) kindly. sei ~ still! kindly keep your mouth shut! (inf).

Gefällstrecke f siehe Gefäll(e)strecke.

Gefall-: ~sucht f craving for admiration; g~süchtig adj desperate to be liked.

gefälscht 1 ptp of fälschen. 2 adj forged.

gefangen 1 ptp of fangen. 2 adj (~genommen) captured; (fig) captivated. sich ~ geben to give oneself up, to surrender.

Gefangenen-: ~aufseher m guard; ~austausch m exchange of prisoners; ~befreiung f rescue of a prisoner/prisoners; (als Delikt) aiding and abetting the escape of a prisoner; ~fürsorge f prison welfare; (inf: Dienst) prison welfare service; ~haus nt (Aus) prison; ~lager nt prison camp; ~wärter m prison officer, (prison) warder, jailer (old, inf).

Gefangene(r) mf decl as adj captive; (Sträfling, Kriegs~, fig) prisoner. 500 ~ machen (Mil) to take 500 prisoners; keine ~n machen (Mil) to take no prisoners (alive).

Gefangen-: g~halten vt sep irreg to hold prisoner; Tiere to hold captive; (fig) to captivate; ~haus nt (form, Aus) siehe Gefangenenhaus; ~nahme f -, -n capture; (Verhaftung) arrest; bei der ~nahme on one's capture/arrest; g~nehmen vt sep irreg Mensch to take captive; Geiseln auch to capture; (verhaften) to arrest; (Mil) to take prisoner; (fig) to captivate; ~schaft f captivity; in ~schaft geraten to be taken prisoner; g~setzen vt sep to take into captivity; (verhaften) to imprison.

Gefängnis nt prison, jail, gaol (Brit); (~strafe) imprisonment. im ~ sein or sitzen (inf) to be in prison; ins ~ kommen to be sent to prison; zwei Jahre ~ bekommen to get two years' imprisonment or two years in prison; auf Meineid steht ~ perjury is punishable by imprisonment or by a prison sentence.

Gefängnis- in cpds prison; ~aufseher m warder, prison officer, jailer (old, inf); ~direktor m prison governor, prison warden (esp US); ~gebäude nt prison; ~geistlicher m prison chaplain; ~haft f imprisonment; ~insasse m inmate; ~strafe f prison sentence; eine ~strafe von zehn Jahren ten years' imprisonment; er wurde zu einer ~strafe verurteilt he was sent to prison, he was given a prison sentence; ~tor nt prison gate usu pl; für ihn öffneten sich die ~tore the prison gates were opened for him; ~wagen m prison van; ~wärter m siehe ~aufseher; ~zelle f prison cell.

gefärbt 1 ptp of färben. 2 adj dyed; Lebensmittel artificially coloured; (fig) Aussprache tinged; Bericht biased. ihre Sprache ist schottisch ~ her accent has a Scottish tinge or ring to it; konservativ ~ sein to have a conservative bias.

-gefärbt adj suf dyed; Lebensmittel coloured. rot~es Haar dyed red hair, hair dyed red; gelb~er Korn spirit with yellow colouring.

Gefasel nt -s, no pl (pej) twaddle (inf), drivel (inf).

Gefäß nt -es, -e vessel (auch Anat, Bot); (Behälter) receptacle; (Degenkorb) coquille.

Gefäß- (Med): g~erweiternd adj vasodilatory; ~erweiterung f vasodilation, vascular dilatation; ~leiden nt angiopathy, vascular disease.

gefaßt 1 ptp of fassen. 2 adj (ruhig) composed, calm. einen sehr ~en Eindruck machen to appear cool, calm and collected; auf etw (acc) ~ sein to be prepared or ready for sth; sich auf etw (acc) ~ machen to prepare oneself for sth; er kann sich auf etwas ~ machen (inf) I'll give him something to think about (inf).

Gefaßtheit f composure, calmness.

Gefäß-: g~verengend adj vasoconstrictive; ~verengung f vasoconstriction, vascular constriction; ~verschluß m, ~verstopfung f embolism; ~wand f vascular wall.

Gefecht nt -(e)s, -e (lit, fig) battle; (Mil) encounter, engagement; (Scharmützel) skirmish. ein hartes ~ fierce fighting; das ~ abbrechen/einleiten to cease/open combat; den Feind in ein ~ verwickeln to engage the enemy (in battle); jdn/etw außer ~ setzen (lit, fig) to put sb/sth out of action; mit diesen Argumenten setzte er seinen Gegner außer ~ he spiked his opponent's guns with these arguments; Argumente ins ~ führen to advance arguments; im Eifer or in der Hitze des ~s (fig) in the heat of the moment; klar zum ~! (Naut) clear for action!; (fig) clear the decks!

Gefechts-: ~abschnitt m battle zone; ~aufklärung f tactical reconnaissance; ~ausbildung f combat training; g~bereit adj ready for action or battle; (einsatzfähig) (fully) operational; ~bereitschaft f readiness for action or battle; in ~bereitschaft fully operational; g~klar adj (Naut) cleared for action; ein Schiff g~klar machen to clear a ship for action; ~lage f tactical situation; ~lärm m noise of battle; g~mäßig adj combat attr, under combat conditions; ~pause f break in the fighting; ~stand m command post; ~stärke f fighting strength; ~tätigkeit f combat activity; ~übung f field exercise, manoeuvres pl.

gefedert 1 ptp of federn. 2 adj (Matratze) sprung; (Karosserie) spring-suspended. ein gut ~es Auto/eine gut ~e Kutsche a car with good suspension/a well-sprung carriage.

gefeiert 1 ptp of feiern. 2 adj celebrated.

Gefeilsche nt -s, no pl (inf) haggling.

gefeit 1 ptp of feien. 2 adj gegen etw ~ sein to be immune to sth; gegen diesen Fehler bin ich jetzt ~ I have now learnt from my mistake; niemand ist gegen den Tod ~ nobody is immortal; dagegen ist keiner ~ that could happen to anyone.

gefestigt 1 ptp of festigen. 2 adj Tradition established; Charakter steadfast.

Gefiedel nt -s, no pl (inf) fiddling (inf), scraping (pej).

Gefieder nt -s, - plumage, feathers pl; (old: von Pfeil) flight.

gefiedert 1 *ptp of* **fiedern. 2** *adj* feathered; *Blatt* pinnate. **die** ~**en Sänger** (*poet*) the feathered songsters (*poet*); **unsere** ~**en Freunde** (*geh*) our feathered friends.

gefiel *pret of* **gefallen**[1].

Gefilde *nt* -s, - (*old, liter*) realm. **liebliche grüne** ~ delightful verdant landscape (*liter*); **die** ~ **der Seligen** the Elysian fields; **die heimatlichen** ~ (*hum*) home pastures.

gefinkelt *adj* (*esp Aus*) cunning, crafty.

Geflacker *nt* -s, *no pl* flickering.

geflammt 1 *ptp of* **flammen. 2** *adj Marmor* waved, rippled; *Holz* wavy-grained; *Stoff* watered.

Geflatter *nt* -s, *no pl* fluttering; (*von Fahne etc: bei starkem Wind*) flapping.

Geflecht *nt* -(e)s, -e (*lit, fig*) network; (*Gewebe*) weave; (*Rohr*~) wickerwork, basketwork; (*von Haaren*) plaiting.

gefleckt 1 *ptp of* **flecken. 2** *adj* spotted; *Blume, Vogel* speckled; *Haut* blotchy.

Geflenn(e) *nt* -s, *no pl* (*pej inf*) blubbering (*inf*).

Geflimmer *nt* -s, *no pl* shimmering; (*Film, TV*) flicker(ing); (*heiße Luft*) heat-haze; (*von Stern*) twinkling.

Geflissenheit *f siehe* **Beflissenheit.**

geflissentlich *adj* (*geh*) deliberate, intentional. **zur** ~**en Beachtung** (*form*) for your attention.

geflochten *ptp of* **flechten.**

geflogen *ptp of* **fliegen.**

geflohen *ptp of* **fliehen.**

geflossen *ptp of* **fließen.**

Geflügel *nt* -s, *no pl* (*Zool, Cook*) poultry *no pl*; (*Vögel auch*) fowl.

Geflügel- *in cpds* poultry; ~**cremesuppe** *f* cream of chicken/turkey *etc* soup; ~**fleisch** *nt* poultry; ~**händler** *m* poulterer, poultry dealer; ~**handlung** *f* poulterer's; ~**klein** *nt* giblets *pl*; ~**leber** *f* chicken/turkey *etc* liver; ~**salat** *m* chicken/turkey *etc* salad.

geflügelt *adj* winged. ~**e Worte** familiar *or* standard quotations; **er spricht immer in** ~**en Worten** he always speaks in quotations.

Geflunker *nt* -s, *no pl* (*inf*) fibbing (*inf*). **das ist alles** ~ it's all lies *or* fibs (*inf*).

Geflüster *nt* -s, *no pl* whispering; (*von Bäumen, Blättern auch*) rustling.

gefochten *ptp of* **fechten.**

Gefolge *nt* -s, - retinue, entourage; (*Trauer*~) cortege; (*fig*) wake. **im** ~ in the wake (+ *gen* of); **etw im** ~ **haben** (*fig*) to result in sth, to bring sth in its wake.

Gefolgschaft *f* (a) (*die Anhänger*) following; (*NS: Betriebs*~) workforce; (*Hist: Gefolge*) retinue, entourage. (b) (*Treue*) fealty (*Hist*), allegiance (*auch Hist*), loyalty.

Gefolgschaftstreue *f siehe* **Gefolgschaft** (b).

Gefolgsmann *m, pl* -**leute** follower; (*Hist*) liegeman.

Gefrage *nt* -s, *no pl* (*inf*) questions *pl*. **hör auf mit deinem** ~! stop pestering me with (your) questions!

gefragt 1 *ptp of* **fragen. 2** *adj* in demand *pred*.

gefräßig *adj* gluttonous; (*fig geh*) voracious. ~**e Stille** (*hum*) the silence of people who enjoy their food; *siehe* **dick.**

Gefräßigkeit *f* gluttony; (*fig geh*) voracity.

Gefreite(r) *mf decl as adj* (*Mil*) lance corporal (*Brit*), private first class (*US*); (*Naut*) able seaman (*Brit*), seaman apprentice (*US*); (*Aviat*) leading aircraftman (*Brit*), airman first class (*US*).

gefressen *ptp of* **fressen. jdn** ~ **haben** (*inf*) to be sick of sb (*inf*).

G(e)frett *nt* -s, *no pl* (*Aus*) worry.

Gefrier-: ~**anlage** *f* refrigeration plant; ~**apparat** *m* refrigeration *or* freezing unit, freezer (*inf*); ~**chirurgie** *f* cryosurgery.

gefrieren* *vi irreg aux* **sein** (*lit, fig*) to freeze; *siehe* **Blut.**

Gefrier-: ~**fach** *nt* freezing *or* ice compartment; ~**fleisch** *nt* frozen meat; ~**gemüse** *nt* frozen vegetables *pl*; **g**~**getrocknet** *adj* freeze-dried; ~**kette** *f siehe* **Kühlkette;** ~**kost** *f* frozen food; ~**punkt** *m* freezing point; (*von Thermometer*) zero; **auf dem** ~**punkt stehen** to be at freezing point/zero; **Temperaturen unter dem** ~**punkt** temperatures below zero *or* freezing (point); ~**raum** *m* deep-freeze room; ~**schutzmittel** *nt* (*Aut*) anti-freeze; ~**temperatur** *f* freezing temperature; ~**trocknung** *f* freeze-drying; ~**truhe** *f* freezer, deep freeze; ~**verfahren** *nt* freezing process.

gefroren *ptp of* **frieren, gefrieren.**

Gefror(e)ne(s) *nt decl as adj* (*dated: esp S Ger, Aus*) ice cream.

gefrühstückt *ptp of* **frühstücken.**

Gefuchtel *nt* -s, *no pl* gesticulating.

Gefüge *nt* -s, - (*lit, fig*) structure; (*Bau*~ *auch*) construction; (*Aufbau*) structure, make-up. **das** ~ **seiner Ideen** the framework of his ideas.

gefügig *adj* (*willfährig*) submissive; (*gehorsam*) obedient. **ein** ~**es Instrument** *or* **Werkzeug** a willing tool; **jdn** ~ **machen** to make sb bend to one's will.

Gefügigkeit *f siehe adj* submissiveness; obedience. **jdn zur** ~ **zwingen** to force sb to obey.

Gefühl *nt* -(e)s, -e (a) (*Sinneswahrnehmung*) feeling. **etw im** ~ **haben** to have a feel for sth; **sie hat mehr** ~ **in den Fingern als ich** she has a better sense of touch than I do; **er hat kein** ~ **für heiß und kalt/oben und unten** he can't feel the difference between hot and cold/tell the difference between above and below. (b) (*seelische Empfindung, Ahnung*) feeling; (*Emotionalität*) sentiment. **ich habe das** ~, **daß ...** I have the feeling that ...; **ich habe ein** ~, **als ob ...** I feel as though ...; **ein gutes/schlechtes/mein** ~ ... I don't like ...; **mein** ~ **täuscht mich nie** my instinct is never wrong; **jds** ~**e erwidern/verletzen** to return sb's affection/hurt sb's feelings; **ein Mensch ohne** ~ (*hartherzig*) a person without

any feelings; (*gefühlskalt*) a person without any emotions; **er ist zu keinem menschlichen** ~ **fähig** he is incapable of (feeling) any human emotion; ~ **und Verstand** emotion and reason; **die Romantik war das Zeitalter des** ~**s** romanticism was the age of sensibility; **das höchste der** ~**e** (*inf*) the ultimate. (c) (*Verständnis*) feeling; (*Sinn*) sense. **ein** ~ **für Zahlen/Musik** a feeling for figures/music; **ein** ~ **für Gerechtigkeit/Anstand/Proportionen/Rhythmus** a sense of justice/decency/proportion/rhythm; **Tiere haben ein** ~ **dafür, wer sie mag** animals can sense who likes them; **einen Apparat mit** ~ **behandeln** to treat an appliance sensitively.

gefühlig *adj* (*pej geh*) mawkish.

gefühllos *adj* (*unempfindlich, hartherzig*) insensitive; (*mitleidlos*) callous, unfeeling; *Glieder* numb, dead *pred*. **ich habe ganz** ~**e Finger** my fingers are quite numb *or* have gone dead.

Gefühllosigkeit *f siehe adj* insensitivity; callousness, unfeelingness; numbness, deadness. **die** ~ **haben, etw zu tun** to be so insensitive/callous *etc* as to do sth.

Gefühls-: **g**~**aktiv** *adj* supersensitive; ~**anwandlung** *f* (fit of) emotion; **g**~**arm** *adj* unemotional; ~**armut** *f* lack of emotion *or* feeling; ~**(auf)wallung** *f* emotional outburst; ~**ausbruch** *m* emotional outburst; ~**ausdruck** *m*, ~**äußerung** *f* expression of one's emotions; **g**~**bedingt**, **g**~**bestimmt** *adj* emotional; **g**~**betont** *adj* emotional; *Rede, Äußerung auch* emotive; ~**dinge** *pl* emotional matters *pl*; ~**duselei** *f* (*pej*) mawkishness; **g**~**kalt** *adj* cold; ~**kälte** *f* coldness; ~**lage** *f* emotional state; ~**leben** *nt* emotional life; **g**~**mäßig** *adj* instinctive; ~**mensch** *m* emotional person; ~**nerv** *m* sensory nerve; ~**regung** *f* stir of emotion; (*seelische Empfindung*) feeling; **g**~**roh** *adj* hardhearted; ~**sache** *f* (*Geschmackssache*) matter of feeling; **Kochen ist zum großen Teil** ~**sache** cooking is largely something you have a feel for; ~**schwelgerei** *f* wallowing in one's emotions *no pl*; **g**~**selig** *adj* sentimental; **g**~**tief** *adj* intense; ~**tiefe** *f* (emotional) intensity; ~**überschwang** *m* flood of emotions; ~**wallung** *f siehe* ~**(auf)wallung;** ~**wärme** *f* warmth (of feeling); ~**welt** *f* emotions *pl*; ~**wert** *m* sentimental value; ~**wirkung** *f* emotional effect.

gefühlvoll *adj* (a) (*empfindsam*) sensitive; (*ausdrucksvoll*) expressive. **sehr** ~ **singen** to sing with real feeling. (b) (*liebevoll*) loving.

gefüllt 1 *ptp of* **füllen. 2** *adj Paprikaschoten etc* stuffed; *Brieftasche* full. ~**e Pralinen** chocolates *or* candies (*US*) with soft centres.

Gefummel *nt* -s, *no pl* (*inf*) fiddling (*inf*); (*Hantieren*) fumbling (*inf*); (*erotisch*) groping (*inf*). **diese Arbeit ist ein furchtbares** ~ this work is a terrible fiddle.

gefunden 1 *ptp of* **finden. 2** *adj* **das war ein** ~**es Fressen für ihn** that was handing it to him on a plate.

Gefunkel *nt* -s, *no pl* (*von Sonne, Glas, Wein etc*) sparkling; (*von Sternen auch*) twinkling; (*von Augen*) (*vor Freude*) gleaming, twinkling; (*vor Zorn*) flashing; (*von Edelsteinen*) glittering; (*von Edelmetall*) gleaming.

gefurcht 1 *ptp of* **furchen. 2** *adj* furrowed. **eine von Sorgen** ~**e Stirn** a brow lined with cares.

gefürchtet 1 *ptp of* **fürchten. 2** *adj* dreaded *usu attr*. ~**sein** to be feared.

Gegacker *nt* -s, *no pl* (*lit, fig*) cackle, cackling.

gegangen *ptp of* **gehen.**

gegeben 1 *ptp of* **geben. 2** *adj* (a) (*bekannt*) given. (b) (*vorhanden*) given *attr*; (*Philos: real*) factual; *Bedingung, Voraussetzung* fulfilled *pred*. **im** ~**en Fall ...** should the situation arise ...; **bei den** ~**en Tatsachen/der** ~**en Situation** given these facts/this situation; **etw als** ~ **voraussetzen** to assume sth. (c) (*günstig*) **das ist das** ~**e** it is the obvious thing; **zu** ~**er Zeit** in due course.

gegebenenfalls *adv* should the situation arise; (*wenn nötig*) if need be, if necessary; (*eventuell*) possibly; (*Admin*) if applicable.

Gegebenheit *f* (*actual*) fact; (*Realität*) actuality; (*Zustand*) condition. **sich mit den** ~**en abfinden** to come to terms with the facts as they are.

gegen *prep* + *acc* (a) (*wider*) against. **X** ~ **Y** (*Sport, Jur*) X versus Y; **für oder** ~ for *or* against; ~ **seinen Befehl** contrary to *or* against his orders; **haben Sie ein Mittel** ~ **Schnupfen?** do you have anything for colds?; **etwas/nichts** ~ **jdn/etw haben** to have something/nothing against sb/sth; ~ **etw sein** to be against sth *or* opposed to sth; **10** ~ **1 wetten** to bet 10 to 1. (b) (*in Richtung auf*) towards, toward (*US*); (*nach*) to; (*an*) against. ~ **einen Baum rennen/prallen** to run/crash into a tree; **er pochte** ~ **das Tor** he hammered on the gate; **etw** ~ **das Licht halten** to hold sth to *or* against the light; ~ **Osten etc fahren** to travel eastwards *etc*, to travel to(wards) the east *etc*; **es wird** ~ **abend kühler** it grows cooler towards evening. (c) (*ungefähr*) round about, around; (*nicht mehr als*) getting on for; (*nicht später als*) towards. (d) (*gegenüber*) towards, to. (e) (*im Austausch für*) for. ~ **bar** for cash; ~ **Bezahlung/Quittung** against payment/a receipt. (f) (*verglichen mit*) compared with, in comparison with.

Gegen-: ~**aktion** *f* counteraction; ~**angebot** *nt* counteroffer; ~**angriff** *m* (*Mil, fig*) counterattack; ~**ansicht** *f* opposite opinion; ~**antrag** *m* countermotion; (*Jur*) counterclaim; ~**anzeige** *f* (*Med*) contraindication; ~**argument** *nt* counterargument; ~**aussage** *f* counterstatement; ~**bedingung** *f* countercondition, counterstipulation; ~**befehl** *m* (*Mil*) countermand, countercommand; ~**behauptung** *f* counterclaim; ~**beispiel** *nt* counterexample; ~**beschuldigung** *f* counteraccusation; ~**besuch** *m* return visit; **jdm einen** ~**besuch machen** to return sb's visit; ~**bewegung** *f* (*Tech, fig*) countermovement; (*Mus*) contramotion; ~**beweis** *m* counterevidence *no indef art, no pl;* den ~beweis zu etw erbringen *or* antreten to produce evidence to counter sth; bis zum ~beweis müssen wir ... until we have evidence to the contrary we must ...; ~buchung *f* cross entry.

Gegend *f* -, -en area; (*Wohn~ auch*) neighbourhood, district; (*geographisches Gebiet, Körper~*) region; (*Richtung*) direction; (*inf: Nähe*) area. die ~ von London, die Londoner ~ the London area; er wohnt in der ~ des Bahnhofs he lives in the area near the station; Neuwied liegt in einer schönen ~ Neuwied is in a beautiful area; eine schöne ~ Deutschlands a beautiful part of Germany; eine andere ~ der Stadt another part of the town; hier in der ~ (a)round here, in this area, hereabouts; ungefähr in dieser ~ somewhere (a)round here *or* in this area/region; die ganze ~ spricht davon it's the talk of the neighbourhood; ein bißchen durch die ~ laufen (*inf*) to have a stroll around; sie warfen die leeren Bierflaschen einfach in die ~ (*inf*) they just threw the empty beer bottles around anywhere; brüll nicht so durch die ~ (*inf*) don't scream your head off (*inf*).

Gegen-: ~darstellung *f* reply; ~demonstration *f* counterdemonstration; ~dienst *m* favour in return; jdm einen ~dienst leisten *or* erweisen to return the favour, to do sb a favour in return; ~dreier *m* (*Sport*) bracket; ~druck *m* (*Tech*) counterpressure; (*fig*) resistance; *siehe* Druck[1].

gegen|einander *adv* against each other *or* one another; (*zueinander*) to(wards) each other *or* one another; (*im Austausch*) for each other *or* one another. sich ~ aufheben to cancel each other *or* one another out; sie haben etwas ~ they've got something against each other.

Gegen|einander *nt* -s, *no pl* conflict.

gegen|einander-: ~halten *vt sep irreg* (*lit*) to hold side by side *or* together; (*fig*) to compare; ~prallen *vi sep aux sein* to collide; ~stehen *vi sep irreg* (*fig*) to be on opposite sides; (*Aussagen*) to conflict; ~stellen *vt sep* (*lit*) to put together; (*fig*) to compare; ~stoßen *vi sep irreg aux sein* to bump into each other; (*kollidieren*) to collide.

Gegen-: ~entwurf *m* alternative plan; ~erklärung *f* counterstatement; (*Dementi*) denial, disclaimer; ~fahrbahn *f* oncoming carriageway (*Brit*) *or* highway (*US*) *or* (*Spur*) lane; ~farbe *f* complementary colour; ~feuer *nt* backfire; ~forderung *f* counterdemand; (*Comm*) counterclaim; ~frage *f* counterquestion; darf ich mit einer ~frage antworten? may I answer your question with another (of my own)?; jdm eine ~frage stellen to ask sb a question in reply (to his); ~gabe *f* (*geh*) *siehe* ~geschenk; ~gerade *f* (*Sport*) back straight, backstretch (*US*); ~geschenk *nt* present *or* gift in return; jdm etw als ~geschenk überreichen to give sb sth in return; ~gewalt *f* counterviolence; Gewalt mit ~gewalt beantworten to counter violence with violence; ~gewicht *nt* counterbalance (*auch fig*), counterweight, counterpoise; als (ausgleichendes) ~gewicht zu etw wirken (*lit, fig*) to counterbalance sth; ~gift *nt* antidote (*gegen* to); ~gleis *nt* opposite track; ~grund *m* reason against; Gründe und ~gründe (für etw) reasons for and against (sth); ~gruß *m* greeting in return; ~hieb *m* counterstroke; ~kaiser *m* (*Hist*) anti-emperor; ~kandidat *m* rival candidate; als ~kandidat zu jdm aufgestellt werden to be put up as a candidate against sb; ~klage *f* (*Jur*) countercharge; ~klage gegen jdn erheben to put in a countercharge against sb, to countercharge sb; ~kläger *m* (*Jur*) bringer of a countercharge; ~könig *m* (*Hist*) anti-king; ~kraft *f* (*lit, fig*) counterforce; ~kultur *f* alternative culture; ~kurs *m* (*lit, fig*) opposite course; einen ~kurs steuern to take an opposing course of action; g~läufig *adj* (*Tech*) Bewegung contrarotating; (*fig*) Tendenz contrary, opposite; ~leistung *f* service in return; als ~leistung für etw in return for sth; ich erwarte keine ~leistung I don't expect anything in return; g~lenken *vi sep* (*Aut*) to steer in the opposite direction; g~lesen *vti sep irreg* countercheck.

Gegenlicht *nt* bei ~ Auto fahren to drive with the light in one's eyes; etw bei *or* im ~ aufnehmen (*Phot*) to take a contre-jour photo(graph) of sth.

Gegenlicht- (*Phot*): ~aufnahme *f* contre-jour photo(graph) *or* shot; ~blende *f* lens hood.

Gegen-: ~liebe *f* requited love; (*fig: Zustimmung*) approval; sie fand keine ~liebe (*lit*) her love was not returned *or* reciprocated; (*fig*) she met with no approval; auf ~liebe/wenig ~liebe stoßen (*fig*) to be welcomed/hardly welcomed with open arms; ~macht *f* hostile power; ~maßnahme *f* countermeasure; ~maßnahmen zur Bekämpfung der Inflation measures to counter inflation; ~meinung *f* opposite view *or* opinion; ~mittel *nt* (*Med*) antidote (*gegen* to); ~mutter *f* (*Tech*) locknut; ~offensive *f* (*lit, fig*) counteroffensive; ~papst *m* (*Hist*) antipope; ~partei *f* other side; (*Sport*) opposing side; (*Jur*) opposing party; ~pol *m* counterpole; (*fig*) antithesis (*zu* of, to); ~position *f* opposite standpoint; ~probe *f* crosscheck; die ~probe zu etw machen to carry out a crosscheck on sth, to crosscheck sth; ~propaganda *f* counterpropaganda; ~reaktion *f* counter-reaction; ~rechnung *f* (*a*) (*Math:* ~*probe*) crosscheck; (*b*) (*Comm*) set-off; (~*schuld*) offset; etw durch ~rechnung begleichen to offset sth; die ~rechnung aufmachen (*fig*) to present one's own reckoning; ~rede *f* (*Antwort*) reply; (*Widerrede*) contradiction; eine ~rede zu jds Rede halten to reply to sb's speech; (da gibt es) keine ~rede! no contradiction!; Rede und ~rede dialogue; eine Diskussion, in der Rede und ~rede einander abwechseln a discussion with a lively exchange between the speakers; ~reformation *f* (*Hist*) Counter-Reformation; ~regierung *f* rival government; ~revolution *f siehe* Konterrevolution; ~richtung *f* opposite direction; ~ruder *nt* opposed control surfaces.

Gegensatz *m* -es, -̈e (*konträrer* ~) contrast; (*kontradiktori-*

scher ~, Gegenteil) opposite; (*Unvereinbarkeit*) conflict; (*Unterschied*) difference; (*Philos*) antithesis; (*Mus*) countersubject. ~e (*Meinungsverschiedenheiten*) differences *pl;* im ~ zu unlike, in contrast to; Marx, im ~ zu ... Marx, as against ...; er, im ~ zu mir, ... unlike me, he ...; einen krassen ~ zu etw bilden to contrast sharply with sth; ~e ziehen einander *or* sich an (*prov*) opposites attract; im ~ zu etw stehen to conflict with sth; ~e ausgleichen to even out differences; unüberbrückbare ~e irreconcilable differences.

gegensätzlich *adj* (*konträr*) contrasting; (*widersprüchlich*) opposing; (*unterschiedlich*) different; (*unvereinbar*) conflicting. Schwarz und Weiß sind ~e Begriffe black and white are opposites; eine ~e Meinung a conflicting view; etw völlig ~ beurteilen to assess sth totally differently; sie verhalten sich völlig ~ they behave in totally different ways.

Gegensätzlichkeit *f* (*gen* between) (*der* adj contrast; opposition; difference; conflict. die ~ dieser beiden Systeme the contrast between *or* contrasting nature of these two systems; bei aller ~ ... in spite of all (the) differences ...

Gegensatzpaar *nt* pair of opposites.

Gegen-: ~schlag *m* (*Mil*) reprisal; (*fig*) retaliation *no pl;* einen ~schlag (gegen jdn) führen to strike back (at sb); zum ~schlag ausholen to prepare to retaliate; ~seite *f* (*lit, fig*) other side; (*gegenüberliegende Seite auch*) opposite side; g~seitig *adj* mutual; (*wechselseitig auch*) reciprocal; sie beschuldigten sich g~seitig they (each) accused one another *or* each other; sich g~seitig bedingen to be contingent (up)on one another *or* each other; sich g~seitig ausschließen to be mutually exclusive, to exclude one another; g~seitige Abhängigkeit mutual dependence, interdependence; in g~seitigem Einverständnis by mutual agreement; ~seitigkeit *f siehe* adj mutuality; reciprocity; ein Abkommen/Vertrag auf ~seitigkeit a reciprocal agreement/treaty; Versicherung auf ~seitigkeit mutual insurance; ~sinn *m* im ~sinn in the opposite direction; g~sinnig *adj* (*Tech*) in the opposite direction; ~spieler *m* opponent; (*Liter*) antagonist; (*bei Mannschaftsspielen auch*) opposite number; ~spionage *f* counterespionage; ~sprechanlage *f* (two-way) intercom; (*Telec*) duplex (system); ~sprechverkehr *m* two-way communication.

Gegenstand *m* -(e)s, -̈e (*Ding*) object, thing; (*Econ: Artikel*) article; (*Thema, Angelegenheit, Stoff*) subject; (*von Gespräch, Diskussion*) subject, topic; (*der Neugier, des Hasses etc, Philos*) object; (*Aus: Schulfach*) subject. ein harter ~ fiel ihm auf den Kopf something hard *or* a hard object fell on his head; sie wurde mit einem stumpfen ~ erschlagen she was killed by a blow from a blunt instrument; ~ des Gespötts laughingstock, object of ridicule; (*Mensch auch*) figure of fun.

gegenständlich *adj* concrete; (*Philos*) objective; (*Art*) representational; (*anschaulich*) graphical. die ~e Welt the world of objects.

Gegenständlichkeit *f siehe* adj concreteness; objectivity; representationalism; graphicalness.

Gegenstandpunkt *m* opposite point of view.

Gegenstands-: g~los *adj* (*überflüssig*) redundant, unnecessary; (*grundlos*) unfounded, groundless; (*hinfällig*) irrelevant; (*Art*) non-representational, abstract; bitte betrachten Sie dieses Schreiben als g~los, falls ... please disregard this notice if ...; ~wort *nt* concrete noun.

Gegen-: g~steuern *vi sep* (*Aut*) to steer in the opposite direction; (*fig*) to take countermeasures; ~stimme *f* (*Parl*) vote against; der Antrag wurde mit 250 Stimmen bei *or* und 30 ~stimmen/ohne ~stimmen angenommen the motion was carried by 250 votes to 30/unanimously; ~stoß *m* (*Mil, Sport*) counterattack; ~strömung *f* (*lit, fig*) countercurrent; ~stück *nt* opposite; (*passendes* ~*stück*) counterpart.

Gegenteil *nt* opposite (*von* of); (*Umkehrung*) reverse (*von* of). im ~! on the contrary!; ganz im ~ quite the reverse; das ~ bewirken to have the opposite effect; (*Mensch*) to achieve quite the opposite; ins ~ umschlagen to swing to the other extreme; eine Äußerung ins ~ um- *or* verkehren to twist a statement to mean just the opposite.

gegenteilig *adj* Ansicht, Wirkung opposite, contrary. eine ~e Meinung a different opinion; sich ~ entscheiden to come to a different decision; ~e Behauptungen statements to the contrary; ich habe nichts G~es gehört I've heard nothing to the contrary.

Gegenteilsbeweis *m* (*Jur*) evidence to the contrary.

Gegentor *nt* (*esp Ftbl*), **Gegentreffer** *m* (*Sport*) goal. sie konnten ein ~ verhindern they managed to stop any goals being scored against them; ein ~ hinnehmen müssen to concede a goal.

gegen|über **1** *prep* +dat (**a**) (*örtlich*) opposite. er wohnt mir ~ he lives opposite me *or* across from me; er saß mir genau schräg ~ he sat directly opposite *or* facing me/diagonally across from me.

(**b**) (*zu*) to; (*in bezug auf*) with regard *or* respect to, as regards; (*angesichts, vor*) in the face of; (*im Vergleich zu*) in comparison with, compared with. mir ~ hat er das nicht geäußert he didn't say that to me; allem Politischen ~ ist er mißtrauisch he's distrustful of anything political *or* as far as anything political is concerned; er ist allem Neuen ~ wenig aufgeschlossen he's not very open-minded about anything new *or* where anything new is concerned.

2 *adv* opposite. der Park ~ the park opposite; die Leute von ~ (*inf*) the people opposite *or* (from) across the way.

Gegen|über *nt* -s, - (*bei Kampf*) opponent; (*bei Diskussion*) opposite number. mein ~ im Zug/am Tisch the person (sitting) opposite me in the train/at (the) table; mein ~ war ein riesiger Bernhardiner I had an enormous St Bernard opposite me; wir haben einen freien Ausblick und kein ~ we've an open view with no building opposite.

gegen|über-: ~**gestellt** adj: **sich einer Sache** (dat) ~**gestellt sehen** to be faced or confronted with sth; ~**liegen** sep irreg **1** vi +dat to be opposite, to face; **2** vr **sich** (dat) ~**liegen** to face each other; ~**liegend** adj attr opposite; **das** ~**liegende Grundstück** the plot of land opposite; **der der Hypotenuse** ~**liegende Winkel** the angle opposite or facing the hypotenuse; ~**sehen** vr sep irreg +dat **sich einer Aufgabe** ~**sehen** to be faced or confronted with a task; ~**sitzen** vi sep irreg +dat to sit opposite or facing; ~**stehen** vi sep irreg +dat to be opposite, to face; jdm to stand opposite or facing; **jdm feindlich/freundlich/desinteressiert** ~**stehen** to have a hostile/friendly/disinterested attitude towards sb; **Ausländern steht er wohlwollend/kritisch** ~ he takes a favourable/critical view of foreigners; **einem Plan freundlich** ~**stehen** to be favourably disposed to a plan; **einer Gefahr** ~**stehen** to be faced with a danger; ~**stellen** vt sep (konfrontieren mit) to confront (dat with); (fig: vergleichen) to compare (dat with); **G**~**stellung** f confrontation; (fig: Vergleich) comparison; ~**treten** vi sep irreg aux sein jdm ~**treten** to face sb.

Gegen-: ~**verkehr** m oncoming traffic; ~**vorschlag** m counterproposal.

Gegenwart f, - no pl **(a)** (jetziger Augenblick) present; (heutiges Zeitalter) present (time or day); (Gram) present (tense). **in der** ~ **leben** to live in the present; (den Augenblick genießen) to live for the present or for today; **die Literatur/Musik der** ~ contemporary literature/music; **die Probleme der** ~ the problems of today, today's problems; **in der** ~ **stehen** (Gram) to be in the present (tense). **(b)** (Anwesenheit) presence. **in** ~ **des** in the presence of.

gegenwärtig 1 adj **(a)** attr (jetzig) present; (heutig auch) current, present-day. **der** ~ **Minister/Preis** the present minister/current price. **(b)** (geh: anwesend) present pred. **die** ~**en Gäste** the guests present; **bei einer Feier** ~ **sein** to attend a party, to be present at a party; **es ist mir im Moment nicht** ~ I can't recall it at the moment. **2** adv **(a)** (augenblicklich) at present, at the moment; (heutzutage auch) currently. **(b)** **sich** (dat) **etw** ~ **halten** (geh) to bear sth in mind.

Gegenwarts-: **g**~**bezogen** adj relevant to present times; **ein sehr g**~**bezogener Mensch** a person whose life revolves very much around the present; ~**deutsch** nt modern German; ~**form** f (Gram) present (tense); **g**~**fremd** adj out-of-touch (with reality); ~**kunde** f (Sch) siehe **Gemeinschaftskunde**; **g**~**nah(e)** adj relevant (to the present); ~**nähe** f relevance (to the present); ~**problem** nt current or topical problem; ~**roman** m contemporary novel; ~**schaffen** nt contemporary scene; ~**sprache** f present-day language; **die englische** ~**sprache** modern English.

Gegen-: ~**wehr** f resistance; ~**wert** m equivalent; ~**wind** m headwind; **wir hatten starken** ~**wind** there was a strong headwind; ~**winkel** m (Geom) opposite angle; (korrespondierend) corresponding angle; ~**wirkung** f reaction, counteraction; **diese Tabletten können eine** ~**wirkung haben** these tablets can have the opposite effect; **g**~**zeichnen** vt sep to countersign; ~**zeichnung** f (Unterschrift) countersignature; (das Unterschreiben) countersigning; ~**zeuge** m witness for the other side; ~**zug** m **(a)** countermove; **im** ~**zug zu etw** as a countermove to sth; **(b)** (Luftzug) cross-draught; **(c)** (Rail) corresponding train in the other direction; (entgegenkommender Zug) oncoming train.

gegessen ptp of **essen**.

Gegirre nt -s, no pl cooing.

geglichen ptp of **gleichen**.

gegliedert 1 ptp of **gliedern**. **2** adj jointed; (fig) structured; (organisiert) organized.

geglitten ptp of **gleiten**.

Geglitzer nt -s, no pl glitter(ing).

geglommen ptp of **glimmen**.

geglückt 1 ptp of **glücken**. **2** adj **Feier** successful; **Wahl** lucky; **Überraschung** real.

Gegner(in f**)** m -s, - opponent (auch Sport), adversary; (Rivale) rival; (Feind) enemy. **ein** ~ **der Todesstrafe sein** to be against or opposed to capital punishment.

gegnerisch adj attr opposing; (Mil: feindlich) enemy attr, hostile; **Übermacht** of the enemy.

Gegnerschaft f opposition.

gegolten ptp of **gelten**.

gegoren ptp of **gären**.

gegossen ptp of **gießen**.

gegr. abbr of **gegründet** established, est.

gegraben ptp of **graben**.

gegriffen ptp of **greifen**.

Gegrinse nt -s, no pl (inf) grin(ning).

Gegröle nt -s, no pl (inf) raucous bawling.

Gegrübel nt -s, no pl (inf) worrying.

Gegrunze nt -s, no pl grunting.

Gehabe nt -s, no pl (inf) affected behaviour.

gehaben* vr (old, Aus) to behave, to deport oneself (old, form). **gehab dich wohl!** (old, dial) farewell! (old).

gehabt ptp of **haben**.

Gehackte(s) nt decl as adj mince (Brit), minced or ground (US) meat.

Gehalt[1] m -(e)s, -e **(a)** (Anteil) content. **der** ~ **an Eiweiß/Kohlenhydraten** the protein/carbohydrate content; **ein hoher** ~ **an Kohlenmonoxyd** a high carbon monoxide content. **(b)** (fig: Inhalt) content; (Substanz) substance. ~ **und Gestalt** (liter) form and content.

Gehalt[2] nt or (Aus) m -(e)s, ⸚er salary; (esp Eccl) stipend.

gehalten 1 ptp of **halten**. **2** adj: ~ **sein, etw zu tun** (form) to be required to do sth.

Gehalt-: **g**~**los** adj **Nahrung** unnutritious; (fig) empty; (oberflächlich) shallow, empty; **dieses Brot ist ziemlich g**~**los** there's not much nourishment in this bread; **g**~**lose Münzen** coins with a low precious metal content; ~**losigkeit** f siehe adj (fig) lack of content/substance; emptiness; shallowness; **g**~**reich** adj **(a)** **Erz** high-yield; **g**~**reiche Münzen** coins with a high precious metal content; **(b)** siehe **g**~**voll**.

Gehalts-: ~**abrechnung** f salary statement; **die** ~**abrechnung ist abgeschlossen** the salaries have been worked out; ~**abzug** m salary deduction; ~**anspruch** m salary claim; ~**bescheinigung** f salary declaration; ~**empfänger** m salary-earner; ~**empfänger sein** to receive a salary, to be salaried; **die Firma hat 500** ~**empfänger** the firm has 500 salaried staff or employees; ~**erhöhung** f salary increase, rise in salary; (regelmäßig) increment; ~**forderung** f salary claim; ~**gruppe**, ~**klasse** f salary bracket; **er ist in der** ~**gruppe 6** he's on grade 6 on the salary scale; ~**konto** nt current account; ~**kürzung** f cut in salary; ~**nachzahlung** f back-payment; ~**pfändung** f deduction of salary (at source); ~**streifen** m salary slip; ~**stufe** f siehe ~**gruppe**; ~**vorrückung** f (Aus) siehe ~**erhöhung**; ~**vorstellung** f, ~**wunsch** m salary requirement; ~**zahlung** f salary payment; **der Tag der** ~**zahlung ist der 28.** salaries are paid on the 28th; ~**zulage** f (~**erhöhung**) salary increase, rise in salary; (regelmäßige) increment; (Extrazulage) salary bonus.

gehaltvoll adj **Speise** nutritious, nourishing; (fig) rich in content. **ein** ~**es Buch/eine** ~**e Rede** a book/speech which says a great deal.

Gehämmer nt -s, no pl hammering.

gehandikapt [gə'hendikept] adj handicapped (durch by).

Gehänge nt -s, - **(a)** garland; (Ohr~) drop, pendant. **(b)** (Wehr~) ammunition belt. **(c)** (Min: Abhang) declivity, incline. **(d)** (Build) system of fascines. **(e)** (sl) balls pl (sl).

gehangen ptp of **hängen**.

Gehängte(r) mf decl as adj hanged man/woman. **die** ~**n** the hanged.

Gehänsel nt -s, no pl (inf) mocking. **hört auf mit dem** ~! stop making fun of me/him etc!

geharnischt adj **(a)** (fig) **Antwort, Rede** sharp, forceful; **Brief** strong. **jdm eine** ~**e Abfuhr erteilen** to rebuff sb in no uncertain terms. **(b)** (Hist: gepanzert) armour-clad. **ein** ~**er Ritter** a knight in armour.

gehässig adj spiteful.

Gehässigkeit f spite, spitefulness. ~**en** spiteful things; **jdm** ~**en sagen** to be spiteful to sb.

Gehaue nt -s, no pl (inf) fisticuffs (inf). **Schluß mit dem ewigen** ~! stop fighting all the time!

gehauen ptp of **hauen**.

gehäuft 1 ptp of **häufen**. **2** adj **Löffel** heaped. **3** adv in large numbers.

Gehäuse nt -s, - **(a)** case; (Radio~, Kamera~, Uhr~, Kompaß~ auch) casing; (Lautsprecher~) box; (großes Lautsprecher~, Radio~) cabinet. **(b)** (Schnecken~) shell. **(c)** (Obst~) core. **(d)** (Ftbl sl) goal.

gehaut 1 ptp of **hauen**. **2** adj (Aus inf) tricky (inf), leery (dial inf), cunning.

gehbehindert adj disabled.

Gehege nt -s, - reserve; (im Zoo) enclosure, compound; (Wild~) preserve. **jdm ins** ~ **kommen** (fig inf) to get under sb's feet (inf); (ein Recht streitig machen) to poach on sb's preserves.

geheiligt 1 ptp of **heiligen**. **2** adj **Brauch, Tradition, Recht** sacred; **Räume** sacrosanct. **sein** ~**es Mittagsschläfchen** (inf) his precious afternoon nap.

geheim adj secret. **seine** ~**sten Gefühle/Wünsche/Gedanken** his innermost or most private feelings/wishes/thoughts; **streng** ~ top secret; „**die** ~**en Verführer**" "the hidden persuaders"; **G**~**er Rat** privy council; (Mitglied) privy councillor; ~ **bleiben** to remain (a) secret; ~ **abstimmen** to vote by secret ballot; **im** ~**en** in secret, secretly.

Geheim- in cpds secret; ~**bund** m secret society; ~**bündelei** f organization/membership of illegal secret societies; ~**dienst** m secret service; ~**dienstler** m -s, - (inf) man from the secret service; ~**fach** nt secret compartment; (Schublade) secret drawer; ~**favorit** m personal favourite; **g**~**halten** vt sep irreg **etw** (vor jdm) **g**~**halten** to keep sth a secret (from sb).

Geheimhaltung f secrecy. **zur** ~ **von etw verpflichtet sein** to be bound to keep sth secret.

Geheimhaltungs-: ~**pflicht** f obligation to maintain secrecy; ~**stufe** f security classification; **die** ~**stufe für etw aufheben** to declassify sth.

Geheim-: ~**konto** nt private or secret account; ~**lehre** f esoteric doctrine; ~**mittel** nt (lit) (Zaubertrank) secret potion; (Pulver) secret powder; (Heilmittel) secret remedy; (der Alchimisten) arcanum, elixir; (fig) secret something (inf).

Geheimnis nt -ses, -se; (rätselhaftes) ~ mystery. **das** ~ **der Schönheit/des Erfolgs** the secret of beauty/success; **das** ~ **der Auferstehung/des Lebens** the mystery of the Resurrection/of life; **ein offenes** or **öffentliches** (rare) ~ an open secret; **das ist das ganze** ~ (inf) that's all there is to it; **aus etw ein/kein** ~ **machen** to make a big secret about sth/no secret of sth; **sie hat ein süßes** ~ (inf) she's expecting a happy event.

Geheimnis-: ~**krämer** m (inf) mystery-monger (inf); ~**krämerei** f (inf) secretiveness; ~**träger** m bearer of secrets; ~**tuer(in** f**)** m -s, - mystery-monger (inf); ~**tuerei** f secretiveness; **g**~**tuerisch** adj secretive; **g**~**umwittert** adj (geh) shrouded in mystery (liter); ~**verrat** m offence under the Official Secrets Act; **g**~**voll** adj mysterious; **g**~**voll tun** to be mysterious; **mit etw g**~**voll tun** to make a big mystery of sth.

Geheim-: ~**nummer** f (Telefon) secret number; (Konto) secret account; ~**polizei** f secret police; ~**polizist** m member of the secret police; ~rat *m* privy councillor; ~ratsecken *pl* (*inf*) receding hairline *sing*; er hat ~ratsecken he is going bald at the temples; ~rezept *nt* secret recipe; ~schloß *nt* combination lock; ~schrift *f* code, secret writing; ~tinte *f* invisible ink; ~tip *m* (personal) tip; ~treppe *f* secret staircase; ~tuerei *f* secretiveness; g~tun *vi* *sep* *irreg* to be secretive; mit etw g~tun to be secretive about sth; was soll das ~tun? why all the secrecy?; ~tür *f* secret door; ~waffe *f* secret weapon; ~wissenschaft *f* secret *or* esoteric lore; aus seinem Wissen eine richtige ~wissenschaft machen to make a great mystery of one's knowledge; ~zeichen *nt* secret sign; (*Chiffre*) cipher.

Geheiß *nt* -es, *no pl* (*geh*) behest (*old, form*) *no pl*. auf jds ~ (*acc*) at sb's behest *or* bidding.

geheißen *ptp of* **heißen**.

gehemmt 1 *ptp of* **hemmen**. 2 *adj* Mensch inhibited; Benehmen self-conscious. ~ sprechen to have inhibitions in speaking.

gehen *pret* **ging**, *ptp* **gegangen** *aux sein* 1 *vi* (**a**) to go; (*zu Fuß*) to walk; (*Gerücht*) to go around. im Schritt/Trab ~ to walk/trot; über die Straße/Brücke ~ to cross the road/(over) the bridge; auf die andere Seite ~ to cross (over) to the other side; am Stock/auf Stelzen (*dat*) ~ to walk with a stick/on stilts; geh mal in die Küche go into the kitchen; zur Post/zum Fleischer ~ to go to the post office/the butcher; zur Schule ~ to go to school; zu jdm ~ to go to see sb; er ging im Zimmer auf und ab he walked *or* paced up and down the room; wie lange geht man bis zum Bus? how long a walk is it to the bus?; wie geht man dorthin? how do you get there?; er kam gegangen he came; das Kind lernt ~ the baby is learning to walk; wo er geht und steht wherever he goes *or* is; schwimmen/tanzen/spielen/schlafen ~ to go swimming/dancing/out to play/to bed; unter Menschen ~ to mix with people; bitte ~ Sie (*höflich*) please carry on; (*bestimmt*) please go; geh doch! go on (then)!; geh schon! go on!; ~ Sie (mir) nicht an meine Sachen! don't touch my things; gut/schlecht angezogen ~ to be well/badly dressed; ohne Hut/Schirm ~ not to wear a hat/take an umbrella; mit jdm ~ to go with sb; (*befreundet sein*) to go out with sb, to be with sb; mit der Zeit/Mode ~ to move with the times/follow the fashion; in sich (*acc*) ~ to think things over; (*bereuen*) to turn one's eyes inward; er geht ins siebzigste Jahr he's getting *or* going on for seventy; das Erbe ging an ihn the inheritance went to him; nach einer Regel ~ to follow a rule; das geht gegen meine Überzeugung that is contrary to *or* runs against my convictions; er ging so weit, zu behaupten ... (*fig*) he went so far as to claim ...; das geht zu weit (*fig*) that's going too far; wie geht das Lied/Gedicht? how does the song/poem go?; das Lied geht so/nach einer anderen Melodie the song goes like this/has a different tune; heute geht ein scharfer Wind there's a biting wind today; die See geht hoch there's a high sea, the sea is running high; der Schmerz ging sehr tief the pain went very deep.

(**b**) (*führen*) (*Weg, Straße*) to go; (*Tür*) to lead (*auf +acc, nach* onto); (*blicken*) (*Fenster*) to look out (*auf +acc, nach* onto), to give (*auf +acc, nach* onto). die Brücke geht dort über den Fluß the bridge crosses the river there; die Reise geht über Dresden we/they *etc* are going via Dresden; es ging schon auf den Winter (*geh*) winter was drawing near.

(**c**) (*weg~*) to go; (*abfahren auch*) to leave; (*ausscheiden*) to leave, to go; (*aus einem Amt*) to go, to quit. ich muß ~ I must go *or* be going *or* be off; ~ wir! let's go; das Schiff geht nach Harwich the boat is going to *or* is bound for Harwich; jdm aus dem Licht/Weg ~ to get *or* move out of sb's light/way; er ist gegangen worden (*hum inf*) he was given a gentle push (*hum inf*); er ist von uns gegangen (*euph*) he has gone from us (*euph*).

(**d**) (*funktionieren*) to work; (*Auto, Uhr*) to go. die Uhr geht gut the clock keeps good time; die Uhr geht falsch/richtig the clock is wrong/right.

(**e**) (*laufen*) (*Geschäft*) to go; (*verkauft werden auch*) to sell. wie ~ die Geschäfte? how's business?

(**f**) (*hineinpassen*) to go. wieviele Leute ~ in deinen Wagen? how many people can you get in your car?; in diese Schachtel ~ 20 Zigaretten this packet holds 20 cigarettes; das Klavier geht nicht durch die Tür the piano won't go through the door; 3 geht in 9 dreimal 3 into 9 goes 3; das geht mir nicht in den Kopf I just can't understand it.

(**g**) (*dauern*) to go on. wie lange geht das denn noch? how much longer is it going to go on?; es geht schon eine halbe Stunde it's been going (on) for half an hour; mein Urlaub geht vom 2. bis 28. Juni my holiday goes *or* runs from the 2nd to the 28th of June.

(**h**) (*reichen*) to go. das Wasser ging ihm bis zum Bauch the water went up to his waist; der Rock geht ihr bis zum Knie her skirt goes *or* is down to her knee; der Blick geht bis an den Horizont the view extends right to the horizon; in die Tausende ~ to run into (the) thousands.

(**i**) (*Teig*) to rise; (*vor dem Backen auch*) to prove.

(**j**) (*urteilen*) nach etw ~ to go by sth.

(**k**) (*sich kleiden*) in etw (*dat*) ~ to wear sth; als etw ~ (*sich verkleiden*) to go as sth.

(**l**) (*betreffen*) der Artikel ging gegen ... the article criticized ...; das Buch ging um ... the book was about ...; die Wette geht um 100 Mark the bet is for 100 marks; das geht auf Sie! it was Konto *or* auf ihn he's responsible for that; das ging auf Sie! that was aimed at you!; mein Vorschlag geht dahin, daß ... my suggestion is that ...

(**m**) (*sich bewegen*) ich hörte, wie die Tür ging I heard the door (go); diese Tür/Schublade geht schwer this door/drawer is very stiff; mein Rasenmäher geht schwer my lawnmower is very heavy to push.

(**n**) (*ertönen: Klingel, Glocke*) to ring.

(**o**) (*übertreffen*) das geht über meine Kräfte that's beyond my power; (*seelisch*) that's too much for me; sein Garten geht ihm über alles his garden means more to him than anything else; nichts geht über (+*acc*) ... there's nothing to beat ..., there's nothing better than ...

(**p**) (*inf*) (ach) geh (doch), das darf doch nicht wahr sein! get along *or* on with you, that can't be true (*inf*); geh, geh *or* (ach) geh, so schlimm ist das nicht! (oh) come on, it's not as bad as all that; ~ Sie (mir) doch mit Ihren Ausreden! none of your lame excuses!; geh mir mit deinem ständigen Selbstmitleid/Gejammere! stop feeling sorry for yourself/moaning all the time; geh! (*Aus: erstaunt*) get away! (*inf*).

(**q**) (*Beruf etc ergreifen*) ins Kloster ~ to go into *or* join a monastery/convent; zur See ~ to go to sea; zum Militär ~ to join the army; zum Theater/zur Universität ~ to go on the stage/become an academic; in die Industrie/Politik ~ to go into industry/politics; in die Gewerkschaft/Partei ~ to join the union/party; unter die Lexikographen/Künstler/Säufer ~ (*usu hum*) to join the ranks of lexicographers/artists/alcoholics.

(**r**) (*sich betätigen, arbeiten*) als etw ~ to earn one's living as sth; (*Beruf auch*) to get a job as sth.

(**s**) (*möglich, gut sein*) to be all right, to be OK (*inf*). das geht doch nicht that's not on; Dienstag geht auch nicht (*inf*) Tuesday's no good either.

(**t**) was geht hier vor sich? what's going on here?; ich weiß nicht, wie das vor sich geht I don't know the procedure.

2 *vi* *impers* (**a**) (*gesundheitlich*) wie geht es Ihnen? how are you?; (*zu Patient*) how are you feeling?; wie geht's denn (so)? (*inf*) how are things (with you)? (*inf*); (danke,) es geht (*inf*) all right *or* not too bad(, thanks) (*inf*); es geht ihm gut/schlecht he's quite well/not at all well; es geht mir (wieder) besser I'm better (again) now; nach einem Bad ging's mir gleich besser I soon felt better after a bath; sonst geht's dir gut? (*iro*) are you sure you're feeling all right? (*iro*).

(**b**) (*ergehen*) wie geht's? how are things?; (*bei Arbeit etc*) how's it going?; wie geht's sonst? (*inf*) how are things otherwise?; es geht not too bad, so-so; wie war denn die Prüfung? — ach, es ging ganz gut how was the exam? — oh, it went quite well; mir ist es genauso gegangen (ich habe dasselbe erlebt) it was just the same *or* just like that with me; (ich habe dasselbe empfunden) I felt the same way; laß es dir gut ~ look after yourself, take care of yourself.

(**c**) es geht (*läßt sich machen*) it's all right *or* OK (*inf*); (*funktioniert*) it works; solange es geht as long as possible; geht es? (*ohne Hilfe*) can you manage?; es geht nicht (*ist nicht möglich*) it can't be done, it's impossible; (*kommt nicht in Frage*) it's not on; (*funktioniert nicht*) it won't *or* doesn't work; es wird schon ~ I'll/he'll *etc* manage; (*wird sich machen lassen*) it'll be all right; wir müssen uns damit abfinden, es geht eben nicht anders there's nothing else for it, we'll just have to put up with it; so geht das, das geht so that/this is how it's done; so geht es *or* das, es *or* das geht so that's all right *or* OK (*inf*); so geht es *or* das (eben) (*so ist das Leben*) that's how it goes, that's the way things go; so geht es *or* das nicht that's not how it's done; (*entrüstet*) it just won't do; es ging anders, als ich erwartet hatte it didn't turn out as I had expected; morgen geht es nicht tomorrow's no good; paßt dir Dienstag? — nein, Dienstag geht's nicht is Tuesday all right for you? — no, I can't manage Tuesday.

(**d**) (*betreffen*) worum geht's denn? what's it about?; ich weiß nicht, worum es geht I don't know what this is about; es geht um seinen Vertrag it's about *or* it concerns his contract; worum geht es in diesem Film/bei eurem Streit? what is this film/your argument about?; es geht um Leben und Tod it's a matter of life and death; das geht gegen meine Prinzipien that goes against my principles; es geht um meine Ehre my honour is at stake; es geht ihm nur um eins he's only interested in one thing; bei diesem Job geht es mir nur ums Geld I'm just in this job for the money; darum geht es mir nicht that's not the point; (*spielt keine Rolle*) that's not important to me; es geht um 5 Millionen bei diesem Geschäft (*im Spiel sein*) the deal involves 5 million; (*auf dem Spiel stehen*) 5 million are at stake in the deal; wenn es ums Lügen geht, ist er unübertrefflich he is unbeatable when it comes to lying; wenn es nach mir ginge ... if it were *or* was up to me ..., if I had my way ...; es kann nicht immer alles nach dir ~ you can't expect to have your own way all the time.

(**e**) (*führen*) dann geht es immer geradeaus (*Richtung, in der jd geht*) then you keep going straight on; (*Straßenrichtung*) then it just goes straight on; dann ging es nach Süden/ins Gebirge (*Richtung, in der jd geht*) then we/they *etc* were off to the south/the mountains; (*Straßenrichtung*) then it went south/into the mountains; wohin geht es diesmal in Urlaub? where are you off to on holiday this time?

(**f**) es geht ein starker Wind there's a strong wind (blowing); es geht das Gerücht, daß ... there's a rumour going around that ...; es geht auf 9 Uhr it is approaching 9 o'clock.

3 *vt* er ging eine Meile he walked a mile; ich gehe immer diesen Weg/diese Straße I always walk *or* go this way/along this road.

4 *vr* es geht sich schlecht hier it's hard to walk here, it's bad for walking here; in diesen Schuhen geht es sich bequem these shoes are comfortable to walk in *or* for walking in.

Gehen *nt* -s, *no pl* (*Zu-Fuß-~*) walking; (*Abschied*) leaving; (*Sport*) (*Disziplin*) walking; (*Wettbewerb*) walk.

Gehenk *nt* -(e)s, -e (*Hist*) (*für Schwert*) sword-belt; (*für Degen*) knife-belt; (*für Pistolen*) gun-belt.

Gehenkte(r) *mf decl as adj* hanged man/woman. die ~n the hanged.

gehenlassen *sep irreg* 1 *vt* (*inf: in Ruhe lassen*) to leave alone.

2 *vr* (a) (*sich nicht beherrschen*) to lose one's self-control, to lose control of oneself. (b) (*nachlässig sein*) to let oneself go.

Geher(in *f*) *m* -s, - (*Sport*) walker. **er ist Weltmeister der ~** he's the world champion in walking.

Gehetze *nt* -s, *no pl* (*inf*) (a) (*Eile*) mad rush *or* dash. (b) (*pej: das Aufhetzen*) backbiting (*pej inf*).

gehetzt 1 *ptp of* **hetzen**. 2 *adj* harassed.

geheuer *adj* **nicht ~** (*beängstigend*) scary (*inf*); (*spukhaft*) eerie, creepy (*inf*), spooky; (*verdächtig*) dubious, fishy; (*unwohl*) uneasy; **es ist mir nicht ganz ~** it is scary (*inf*); it is eerie *etc or* gives me the creeps (*inf*); it seems a bit dubious *or* fishy to me; I feel uneasy about it; **mir ist es hier nicht ~** (*mir ist unheimlich*) this place gives me the creeps (*inf*); (*mir ist unwohl*) I have got an uneasy feeling about this place.

Geheul(e) *nt* -(e)s, *no pl* howling.

Gehilfe *m* -n, -n, **Gehilfin** *f* (a) (*dated: Helfer*) assistant, helper. **er ist mir ein guter ~ bei der Arbeit** he helps me a great deal with my work. (b) (*kaufmännischer* ~) trainee. (c) (*Jur*) accomplice.

Gehilfenbrief *m* diploma.

Gehilfenschaft *f* (*Sw*) aiding and abetting.

Gehilfin *f siehe* **Gehilfe**.

Gehirn *nt* -(e)s, -e brain; (*Geist*) mind. **das ist nicht seinem ~ entsprungen** (*inf*) he didn't think of that himself; **sich** (*dat*) **das ~ verrenken** (*inf*) to rack one's brains; **hast du denn kein ~ im Kopf?** (*inf*) haven't you got any brains? (*inf*).

Gehirn- *in cpds siehe auch* **Hirn-**; **~akrobatik** *f* (*inf*) mental acrobatics *pl*; **g~amputiert** *adj* (*pej sl*) dead from the neck up (*sl*); **~blutung** *f* brain *or* cerebral haemorrhage; **~chirurg** *m* brain surgeon; **~chirurgie** *f* brain surgery; **~erschütterung** *f* concussion; **~erweichung** *f* (*lit, fig inf*) softening of the brain; **~kasten** *m* (*inf*) thick skull; **~nerv** *m* cranial nerve; **~rinde** *f* cerebral cortex; **~schlag** *m* stroke; **~schwund** *m* atrophy of the brain; **~substanz** *f* brain matter; **graue ~substanz** grey matter; **~wäsche** *f* brainwashing *no pl*; **jdn einer ~wäsche unterziehen** to brainwash sb.

gehl *adj* (*dial*) yellow.

gehn *siehe* **gehen**.

gehoben 1 *ptp of* **heben**. 2 *adj Sprache, Ausdrucksweise* elevated, lofty; (*anspruchsvoll*) sophisticated; *Stellung* senior, high; *Stimmung* elated. **sich ~ ausdrücken** to use elevated language; **Güter des ~en Bedarfs** semi-luxuries; **~er Dienst** professional and executive levels of the civil service.

Gehöft *nt* -(e)s, -e farm(stead).

geholfen *ptp of* **helfen**.

Geholper(e) *nt* -s, *no pl* bumping.

Gehölz *nt* -es, -e (*geh*) copse, coppice, spinney; (*Dickicht*) undergrowth.

Geholze *nt* -s, *no pl* (*Sport inf*) bad play; (*unfair*) rough play.

Gehoppel(e) *nt* -s, *no pl* hopping.

Gehör *nt* -(e)s, (*rare*) -e (a) (*Hörvermögen*) hearing; (*Mus*) ear. **kein musikalisches ~ haben** to have no ear for music; **ein schlechtes ~ haben** to be hard of hearing, to have bad hearing; (*Mus*) to have a bad ear (for music); **nach dem ~ singen/spielen** to sing/play by ear; **absolutes ~** perfect pitch; **das ~ verlieren** to go *or* become deaf.
(b) (*geh: Anhörung*) **ein Musikstück zu ~ bringen** to perform a piece of music; **~ finden** to gain a hearing; **er fand kein ~** he was not given a hearing; **jdm ~/kein ~ schenken** to listen/not to listen to sb; **schenkt mir ~!** (*old*) lend me your ears (*old*); **um ~ bitten** to request a hearing; **der Vorsitzende bat das Publikum um ~ für den Redner** the chairman requested the audience's attention for the speaker; **sich** (*dat*) **~ verschaffen** to obtain a hearing; (*Aufmerksamkeit*) to gain attention.

Gehörbildung *f* aural training.

gehorchen* *vi* to obey (*jdm sb*); (*Wagen, Maschine etc*) to respond (*jdm/einer Sache* to sb/sth). **seine Stimme gehorchte ihm nicht mehr** he lost control over his voice; **der Junge gehorcht überhaupt nicht** the boy is completely disobedient *or* is never obedient; **siehe Wort**.

gehören* 1 *vi* (a) **jdm ~** (*jds Eigentum sein*) to belong to sb, to be sb's; **das Haus gehört ihm** he owns the house, the house belongs to him; **ihm gehört meine ganze Liebe** he is the only one I love, he has all my love; **ihr Herz gehört einem anderen** her heart belongs to another.
(b) (*den richtigen Platz haben*) to go ; (*Mensch*) to belong; (*gebühren*) to deserve. **das gehört nicht hierher** (*Gegenstand*) it doesn't go here; (*Vorschlag*) it is irrelevant here; **das Buch gehört ins Regal** the book belongs in *or* goes on the bookshelves; **das gehört nicht zur Sache/zum Thema** that is irrelevant to the matter/topic; **dieser Betrag gehört unter die Rubrik „Einnahmen"** this sum comes *or* belongs under the heading "credits"; **er gehört ins Bett** he should be in bed; **er gehört verprügelt** (*dial*) he needs a thrashing, he ought to be thrashed.
(c) (*zu ~ zu zählen zu*) to be amongst; to be one of; (*Bestandteil sein von*) to be part of; (*Mitglied sein von*) to belong to; **es gehört zu seiner Arbeit/zu seinen Pflichten** it's part of his work/one of his duties; **zur Familie ~** to be one of the family; **zu diesem Kleid gehört ein blauer Hut** (*ist Bestandteil von*) a blue hat goes with *or* belongs to this dress; (*würde dazu passen*) a blue hat would go with this dress; **zum Wild gehört einfach Rotwein** red wine is a must with venison.
(d) **~ zu** (*Voraussetzung, nötig sein*) to be called for by; **zu dieser Arbeit gehört viel Konzentration** this work calls for *or* takes a lot of concentration; **dazu gehört Mut** that takes courage; **dazu gehört nicht viel** it doesn't take much; **dazu gehört (schon) einiges or etwas** that takes some doing (*inf*); **dazu gehört mehr** there's more to it than that; **es gehört schon viel Frechheit dazu, seinen Lehrer zu bestehlen** it takes a lot of cheek to steal from your teacher.

2 *vr* to be (right and) proper. **das gehört sich einfach nicht** that's just not done; **wie es sich gehört** (*wie es sich schickt*) as is (right and) proper; (*wie es zünftig ist*) comme il faut; **benimm dich, wie es sich gehört!** behave yourself properly.

Gehör-: **~fehler** *m* **ein ~fehler** a hearing defect, defective hearing; **~gang** *m* auditory canal.

gehörig *adj* (a) (*geh*) **jdm/zu etw ~** belonging to sb/sth; **zu etw ~ sein** to belong to sth; **nicht zur Sache ~** irrelevant; **alle nicht zum Thema ~en Vorschläge** all suggestions not pertaining to *or* relevant to the topic.
(b) *attr, adv* (*gebührend*) proper; (*notwendig auch*) necessary, requisite. **er behandelt seinen Vater nicht mit dem ~en Respekt** he doesn't treat his father with proper respect *or* with the respect due to him.
(c) (*inf: beträchtlich, groß*) good *attr*, good and proper (*inf*) *adv*, well and truly *adv*. **eine ~e Achtung vor jdm haben** to have a healthy respect for sb; **eine ~e Tracht Prügel** a good *or* proper thrashing; **ich hab's ihm ~ gegeben** (*inf*) I showed him what's what (*inf*), I gave him what for (*inf*); (*verbal*) I gave him a piece of my mind (*inf*).

gehörlos *adj* (*form*) deaf. **~ sein** to have no hearing.

Gehörlosenschule *f* (*form*) school for the deaf.

Gehörlose(r) *mf decl as adj* (*form*) deaf person.

Gehörlosigkeit *f* (*form*) lack of hearing; (*Taubheit*) deafness.

Gehörn *nt* -(e)s, -e (*Hunt*) antlers *pl*, set of antlers.

Gehörnerv *m* auditory nerve.

gehörnt *adj* horned; (*mit Geweih*) antlered. **ein ~er Ehemann** (*hum inf*) a cuckold; **der G~e** Satan.

gehorsam *adj* obedient. **ich bitte ~st** (*old*) I respectfully beg; **Ihr ~ster Diener** (*old*) your most obedient servant (*old*), yours obediently (*old*); *siehe* **melden**.

Gehorsam *m* -s, *no pl* obedience. **jdm den ~ verweigern** to refuse to obey sb.

Gehorsamkeit *f* obedience.

Gehorsams-: **~pflicht** *f* duty to obey; **~verweigerung** *f* (*Mil*) insubordination, refusal to obey orders.

Gehörsinn *m* sense of hearing.

gehren *vti* (*Tech*) to mitre.

Gehrock *m* frock coat.

Gehrung *f* (*Tech*) (*das Gehren*) mitring; (*Eckfuge*) mitre joint.

Gehsteig *m* pavement (*Brit*), sidewalk (*US*).

Gehupe *nt* -s, *no pl* (*inf*) hooting, honking.

gehupft *ptp of* **hupfen**.

Gehuste *nt* -s, *no pl* (*inf*) coughing.

Geh-: **~verband** *m* (*Med*) plaster cast *allowing the patient to walk*; **~weg** *m* footpath; **~werkzeuge** *pl* locomotive organs *pl*.

Gei *f* -, -en (*Naut*) *siehe* **Geitau**.

Geier *m* -s, - (*lit, fig*) vulture. **hol dich der ~!** (*inf*) go to hell! (*inf*).

Geifer *m* -s, *no pl* slaver; (*Schaum vor dem Mund*) froth, foam; (*fig pej*) venom. **seinen ~ (gegen etw) verspritzen** to pour out one's venom (on sth).

Geiferer *m* -s, - (*fig pej*) venomous writer/speaker *etc*.

geifern *vi* to slaver; (*Schaum vor dem Mund haben*) to foam at the mouth; (*fig pej*) to be bursting with venom. **vor Wut/Neid ~** to be bursting with rage/envy; **gegen jdn/etw ~** to revile sb/sth.

Geige *f* -, -n violin, fiddle (*inf*). **die erste/zweite ~ spielen** (*lit*) to play first/second violin; (*fig*) to call the tune/play second fiddle; **nach jds ~ tanzen** (*fig*) to dance to sb's tune.

geigen 1 *vi* to play the violin, to (play the) fiddle (*inf*). 2 *vt Lied* to play on a/the violin *or* fiddle (*inf*). **jdm die Meinung ~** (*inf*) to give sb a piece of one's mind (*inf*).

Geigen-: **~bauer** *m* violin-maker; **~bogen** *m* violin bow; **~harz** *nt* rosin; **~kasten** *m* violin-case; (*hum inf*) clodhoppers *pl* (*inf*); **~saite** *f* violin string; **~strich** *m* stroke of the violin bow.

Geiger(in *f*) *m* -s, - violinist, fiddler (*inf*). **erster ~** first violin.

Geigerzähler *m* Geiger counter.

geil *adj* (*Brit*), horny; (*pej: lüstern*) lecherous. **auf jdn ~ sein** to be lusting after sb. (b) (*Agr*) *Boden* rich, fertile; (*üppig*) luxuriant; *Vegetation* rank.

Geilheit *f siehe adj* (a) randiness (*Brit*), horniness; lecherousness. (b) richness, fertility; luxuriance; rankness.

Geisel *f* -, -n hostage. **jdn als ~ nehmen** to take sb hostage; **~n stellen** to produce hostages.

Geisel-: **~gangster** *m* (*Press sl*) gangster who takes/took *etc* hostages; **~nahme** *f* -, -n taking of hostages *no pl*; **mit ~nahme der Besatzung** with the crew taken hostage; **~nehmer(in** *f*) *m* hostage-taker.

Geiser *m* -s, - *siehe* **Geysir**.

Geisha ['ge:ʃa] *f* -, -s geisha (girl).

Geiß *f* -, -en (a) (*S Ger, Aus, Sw: Ziege*) (nanny-)goat. (b) (*von Rehwild etc*) doe.

Geiß-: **~bart** *m* (*Bot*) goatsbeard; (*esp S Ger inf: Spitzbart*) goatee (beard); **~blatt** *nt* honeysuckle, woodbine; **~bock** *m* billy-goat.

Geißel *f* -, -n (a) (*lit, fig*) scourge; (*dial: Peitsche*) whip. (b) (*Biol*) flagellum.

Geißelbruder *m* (*Eccl*) *siehe* **Geißler**.

geißeln *vt* (a) to whip, to flagellate (*esp Rel*). (b) (*fig*) (*kasteien*) to chastise; (*anprangern*) to castigate; (*heimsuchen*) to scourge.

Geißeltierchen *nt* flagellate.

Geiß(e)lung *f siehe vt* (a) whipping, flagellation. (b) chastisement; castigation; scourging.

Geiß-: **~fuß** *m* (*Gehreisen*) parting tool; (*Brechstange*) crowbar; **~hirt** *m* goatherd; **~kitz** *nt* (female) kid; **~lein** *nt* kid.

Geißler *m* -s, - (*Rel*) flagellant.

Geißlung *f siehe* **Geiß(e)lung**.

Geist *m* -(e)s, -er (a) *no pl* (*Denken, Vernunft*) mind. **der**

menschliche ~, der ~ des Menschen the human mind; ~ und
Materie mind and matter; mit ~ begabt endowed with a mind;
„Phänomenologie des ~es" "Phenomenology of the Spirit".

(b) (Rel: Seele, außerirdisches Wesen) spirit; (Gespenst)
ghost. ~ und Körper mind and body; seinen ~ aufgeben or
aushauchen (liter, iro) to give up the ghost; der ~ ist willig,
aber das Fleisch ist schwach the spirit is willing, but the flesh is
weak; der Heilige ~ the Holy Ghost or Spirit; der ~ Gottes the
Spirit of God; der böse ~ the Evil One; der ~ der Finsternis the
Prince of Darkness; gute/böse ~er good/evil spirits; die Stunde
der ~er the witching hour; der gute ~ des Hauses (geh) the
moving spirit in the household; von allen guten ~ern verlassen
sein (inf) to have taken leave of one's senses (inf); in dem
Schloß gehen ~er um the castle is haunted, the castle is walked
by ghosts (liter); siehe empfehlen.

(c) (no pl: Intellekt) intellect, mind; (fig: Denker, Genie)
mind. ~ haben to have a good mind or intellect; (Witz) to show
wit; einen regen/lebhaften ~ haben to have an active/lively
mind; ein Mann von großem ~ a man of great intellect or with a
great mind; die Rede zeugte nicht von großem ~ the speech
was not particularly brilliant; das geht über meinen ~ (inf)
that's way over my head (inf), that's beyond me (inf); hier
scheiden sich die ~er this is the parting of the ways; seinen ~
anstrengen (inf) to use one's brains (inf); sie sind verwandte
~er they are kindred spirits; kleine ~er (iro: ungebildet)
people of limited intellect; (kleinmütig) small- or petty-minded
people; siehe unruhig.

(d) no pl (Wesen, Sinn, Gesinnung) spirit. in kameradschaft-
lichem ~ in a spirit of comradeship; in diesem Büro herrscht
ein kollegialer ~ this office has a friendly atmosphere; in
seinem/ihrem ~ in his/her spirit; in jds ~ handeln to act in the
spirit of sb; der ~ der Zeit/der russischen Sprache the spirit or
genius (liter) of the times/of the Russian language; nach dem ~
des Gesetzes, nicht nach seinem Buchstaben gehen to go by the
spirit rather than the letter of the law; daran zeigt sich, wes
~es Kind er ist that (just) shows what kind of person he is.

(e) no pl (Vorstellung) mind. etw im ~(e) vor sich sehen to see
sth in one's mind's eye; sich im ~(e) als etw/als jd/an einem
Ort sehen to see or picture oneself as sth/as sb/in a place; im
~e bin ich bei Euch I am with you in spirit, my thoughts are
with you.

Geister-: ~bahn f ghost train; ~beschwörer(in f) m -s, - (a) (der
Geister herbeiruft) necromancer; (b) (der Geister austreibt)
exorcist; ~beschwörung f (a) (Herbeirufung) necromancy; (b)
(Austreibung) exorcism; ~bild nt (TV) ghost image; ~bilder
ghosting no pl; ~erscheinung f (ghostly) apparition; (im
Traum etc) vision; eine ~erscheinung haben to see a ghost or
an apparition/to have a vision; ~fahrer m (inf) ghost-driver
(US inf), person driving in the wrong direction; ~geschichte f
ghost story; ~glaube m belief in the supernatural; g~haft adj
ghostly no adv, unearthly no adv; (übernatürlich) supernatural; ~hand f: wie von/durch ~hand as if by magic.

geistern vi aux sein to wander like a ghost. der Gedanke gei-
sterte in seinem Hirn/durch sein Hirn the thought haunted him
or his mind; Lichter geisterten hinter den Fenstern ghostly
lights shone through the windows; Schatten geisterten an der
Wand ghostly or ghostlike shadows played on the wall.

Geister-: ~seher(in f) m visionary; ~stadt f ghost town;
~stimme f ghostly voice; ~stunde f witching hour; ~welt f
spirit world.

Geistes-: g~abwesend adj absent-minded; ~abwesenheit f
absent-mindedness; ~arbeit f brainwork (inf); ~arbeiter m
brain-worker (inf); ~armut f dullness, intellectual poverty;
(von Mensch auch) poverty of mind; ~art f disposition; ~blitz
m brainwave; ~gabe f intellectual gift; ~gegenwart f presence
of mind; g~gegenwärtig adj quick-witted; g~gegenwärtig
duckte er sich unter das Steuer with great presence of mind he
ducked below the steering wheel; ~geschichte f history of
ideas; die ~geschichte der Goethezeit the intellectual history
of Goethe's time; g~gestört adj mentally disturbed or
(stärker) deranged; du bist wohl g~gestört! (inf) are you out of
your mind? (inf); ein ~gestörter a mentally disturbed/
deranged person; ~gestörtheit f mental instability or (stärker)
derangement; ~größe f (a) no pl (Genialität) greatness of
mind; (b) (genialer Mensch) great mind, genius; ~haltung f
attitude of mind; g~krank adj mentally ill; ~kranke(r) mf
mentally ill person; die ~kranken the mentally ill; ~krankheit
f mental illness; (Wahnsinn) insanity; ~störung f mental
disturbance or (stärker) derangement; ~verfassung f frame or
state of mind; g~verwandt adj mentally akin (mit to); die
beiden sind g~verwandt they are kindred spirits;
~verwandtschaft f spiritual affinity (mit to); ~verwirrung f
mental confusion; ~welt f (liter) world of thought;
~wissenschaft f arts subject; die ~wissenschaften the arts;
(als Studium) the humanities; ~wissenschaftler m arts
scholar; (Student) arts student; g~wissenschaftlich adj Fach
arts attr; g~wissenschaftliche Psychologie humanistic
psychology; er ist mehr g~wissenschaftlich orientiert he is
more orientated towards the arts; ~zustand m mental condition; jdn auf seinen ~zustand untersuchen to give sb a
psychiatric examination; du mußt dich mal auf deinen
~zustand untersuchen lassen (inf) you need your head
examined (inf).

Geist-: g~feindlich adj anti-intellectual; ~feindlichkeit f anti-
intellectualism.

geistig adj (a) (unkörperlich) Wesen, Liebe, Existenz spiritual.
ein ~es Band a spiritual bond; ~-seelisch mental and spiritual.
   (b) (intellektuell) intellectual; (Phys, Psych) mental. ~e
Arbeit intellectual work, brain-work (inf); ~e Nahrung
intellectual nourishment; ~ anspruchsvoll/anspruchslos

intellectually demanding/undemanding, highbrow/lowbrow
(inf); ~ nicht mehr folgen können to be unable to understand or
follow any more; ~er Diebstahl plagiarism no pl; ~es
Eigentum intellectual property; der ~e Vater the spiritual
father; ~ behindert/zurückgeblieben mentally handicapped or
deficient/retarded.
   (c) (imaginär) sein ~es Auge one's mind's eye; etw vor
seinem ~en Auge sehen to see sth in one's mind's eye.
   (d) attr (alkoholisch) spirituous.

Geistigkeit f intellectuality.

geistlich adj Angelegenheit, Einstellung, Führer, Beistand
spiritual; (religiös) Drama, Dichtung, Schrift religious; Musik
religious, sacred; (kirchlich) ecclesiastical; Gewand ecclesiastical, clerical. ~es Amt/~er Orden religious office/order; ~es
Recht canon law; der ~e Stand the clergy; die ~en Weihen
empfangen to take holy orders.

Geistliche f -n, -n woman priest; (von Freikirchen) woman
minister.

Geistliche(r) m decl as adj clergyman; (Priester) priest;
(Pastor, von Freikirchen) minister; (Gefängnis~, Militär~ etc)
chaplain. ~es Amt/~er Orden religious office/order; ~es

Geistlichkeit f siehe Geistliche(r) clergy; priesthood;
ministry. die ganze ~ des Bistums all the clergy or priests or
ministers of the diocese.

Geist-: g~los adj (dumm) stupid; (langweilig) dull; (einfallslos)
unimaginative; (trivial) inane; ~losigkeit f (a) no pl siehe adj
stupidity; dullness; unimaginativeness; inaneness; (b) (g~lose
Äußerung) dull/stupid etc remark; g~reich adj (witzig) witty;
(klug) intelligent; (einfallsreich) ingenious; Beschäftigung,
Gespräch, Unterhaltung intellectually stimulating; (schlagfertig) quick-witted; das war sehr g~reich (iro) that was bright
(iro); ~reichelei f (iro inf) (a) no pl (geistreiches Getue) wittiness, bons mots pl; (b) (Äußerung) witticism, bon mot;
g~reicheln vi insep (iro inf) to witticize; g~sprühend adj attr
(geh) scintillatingly or brilliantly witty; g~tötend adj soul-
destroying; g~voll adj Mensch, Äußerung wise, sage; Buch,
Gespräch, Beschäftigung intellectual.

Geitau nt (Naut) stay.

Geiz m -es, no pl meanness; (Sparsamkeit, Knauserei auch)
miserliness.

geizen vi to be mean; (sparsam, knausrig sein auch) to be miserly; (mit Worten, Zeit) to be sparing. mit etw ~ to be mean etc
with sth; sie geizt nicht mit ihren Reizen she doesn't mind
showing what she's got; nach etw ~ (old) to crave (for) sth.

Geiz-: ~hals m miser; ~hammel m (inf) skinflint.

geizig adj mean; (sparsam, knausrig auch) miserly; (mit Geld
auch) tight-fisted. „Der G~e" "The Miser".

Geizkragen m (inf) siehe Geizhammel.

Gejammer nt -s, no pl moaning (and groaning); (inf: Klagen
auch) bellyaching (inf), griping (inf).

Gejauchze nt -s, no pl jubilation, exultation (liter), rejoicing.

Gejaule nt -s, no pl howling; (von Tieren auch) yowling.

Gejohle nt -s, no pl howling; (von Betrinkenen etc) caterwauling.

gek. abbr of gekürzt abbreviated.

gekannt ptp of kennen.

Gekeife nt -s, no pl carping, nagging.

Gekicher nt -s, no pl giggling, tittering; (spöttisch) sniggering,
snickering.

Gekläff nt -(e)s, no pl yapping (auch fig pej), yelping. er
bezeichnete die Kritik seiner Gegner als ~ he described his
opponents' criticisms as bitching.

Geklapper nt -s, no pl clatter(ing).

Geklatsche nt -s, no pl (inf) (a) (von Händen) clapping. (b)
(pej: Tratscherei) gossiping, title-tattling.

gekleidet 1 ptp of kleiden. 2 adj dressed. gut/schlecht ~ sein
to be well/badly dressed; weiß/schwarz ~ sein to be dressed in
white/black.

Geklimper nt -s, no pl (inf) (Klavier~) tinkling; (stümperhaft)
plonking (inf); (Banjo~ etc) twanging; (von Geld) jingling;
(von Wimpern) fluttering.

Geklingel nt -s, no pl ringing; (von Motor) pinking, knocking.

Geklirr(e) nt -(e)s, no pl clinking; (von Gläsern auch) tinkling;
(von Fensterscheiben) rattling; (von Ketten etc) clanging,
clanking; (von Waffen) clashing; (von Lautsprecher, Mikrophon) crackling; (von Eis) crunching.

gekloben ptp of klieben.

geklobt ptp of klieben.

geklommen ptp of klimmen.

Geklön(e) nt -(e)s, no pl (inf) natter (inf).

Geklopfe nt -s, no pl knocking; (von Fleisch, Teppich) beating;
(des Spechts) tapping, hammering; (des Motors) knocking,
pinking.

geklungen ptp of klingen.

Geknall(e) nt -(e)s, no pl (inf) banging; (von Tür auch) slamming;
(von Schüssen) cracking, ringing out; (bei Feuerwerk)
banging; (von Pfropfen) popping; (von Peitsche) cracking.

Geknarr(e) nt -(e)s, no pl creaking; (von Stimme) rasping,
grating.

Geknatter nt -s, no pl (von Motorrad) roaring; (von Preßlufthammer) hammering; (von Maschinengewehr) rattling, chattering; (von Schüssen) rattling (out).

geknickt 1 ptp of knicken. 2 adj (inf) glum, dejected.

gekniffen ptp of kneifen.

Geknipse nt -(e)s, no pl (inf) snap-taking (inf).

Geknister nt -s, no pl crackling, crackle; (von Papier, Seide)
rustling.

geknüppelt 1 ptp of knüppeln. 2 adj ~ voll (inf) packed (out),
chock-a-block (inf).

gekommen ptp of kommen.

gekonnt 1 *ptp of* **können**. 2 *adj* neat; *(meisterhaft)* masterly.
Gekrächz(e) *nt* -es, *no pl* croaking; *(von Mensch auch)* rasping.
Gekrakel *nt* -s, *no pl* *(inf)* scrawl, scribble; *(Krakeln)* scrawling, scribbling.
Gekratze *nt* -s, *no pl* scratching.
gekräuselt 1 *ptp of* **kräuseln**. 2 *adj* ruffled.
Gekreisch(e) *nt* -s, *no pl* screeching; *(von Vogel auch)* squawking; *(von Reifen, Bremsen auch)* squealing; *(von Mensch auch)* shrieking, squealing.
Gekreuzigte(r) *m decl as adj* crucified (person). **Jesus der** ~ Jesus the Crucified.
Gekrieche *nt* -s, *no pl* *(inf)* crawling, creeping.
gekrischen *ptp of* **kreischen**.
Gekritzel *nt* -s, *no pl* (a) scribbling, scrawling; *(Männchenmalen)* doodling. (b) *(Gekritzeltes)* scribble, scrawl, doodle.
gekrochen *ptp of* **kriechen**.
Gekröse *nt* -s, - *(Anat)* mesentery; *(Kutteln)* tripe; *(eßbare Eingeweide)* chitterlings *pl*; *(von Geflügel)* giblets *pl*.
gekühlt 1 *ptp of* **kühlen**. 2 *adj* chilled.
gekünstelt *adj* artificial; *Sprache, Benehmen auch* affected. **er spricht sehr** ~ his speech is very affected.
Gekünsteltheit *f* artificiality; affectedness.
Gel *nt* -s, -e gel.
Gelaber(e) *nt* -s, *no pl* *(inf)* jabbering *(inf)*, prattling *(inf)*.
Gelache *nt* -s, *no pl* *(inf)* silly laughter.
Gelächter *nt* -s, - laughter. **in** ~ **ausbrechen** to burst into laughter, to burst out laughing; **sich dem** ~ **aussetzen** to make oneself a/the laughing-stock, to expose oneself to ridicule; **jdn dem** ~ **preisgeben** *(inf)* to make sb a/the laughing-stock.
gelackmeiert *adj (inf)* duped, conned *(inf)*. ~ **oder der G~e sein** *(hintergangen worden sein)* to have been duped *or* conned *(inf)*; *(dumm dastehen)* to look a right fool *(inf)*; **ich kam mir ziemlich** ~ **vor** I felt I'd been had *(inf)*; I felt a right fool *(inf)*.
geladen 1 *ptp of* **laden**[1], **laden**[2]. 2 *adj* (a) loaded; *(Phys)* charged; *(inf: wütend)* (hopping *inf*) mad. (b) ~ **haben** *(inf)* to be tanked up *(inf)*.
Gelage *nt* -s, - feast, banquet; *(Zech~)* carouse.
gelagert 1 *ptp of* **lagern**. 2 *adj* **in anders/ähnlich/besonders ~en Fällen** in different/similar/exceptional cases; **anders** ~ **sein** to be different.
gelähmt 1 *ptp of* **lähmen**. 2 *adj* paralyzed. **er ist seit seinem Unfall** ~ his accident left him paralyzed, he's been paralyzed since his accident; **er hat ~e Beine** his legs are paralyzed, he's paralyzed in the legs.
gelahrt *adj (obs) siehe* **gelehrt**.
Gelände *nt* -s, - (a) *(Land)* open country; *(Mil: Gebiet, Terrain)* ground. **offenes** ~ open country; **schwieriges** ~ difficult terrain *or* country; **das** ~ **erkunden** *(Mil)* to reconnoitre. (b) *(Gebiet)* area. (c) *(Grundstück)* *(Fabrik~, Schul~ etc)* grounds *pl*; *(Bau~)* site; *(Ausstellungs~)* exhibition centre.
Gelände-: ~**darstellung** *f* contour representation; ~**fahrt** *f* cross-country drive; **für ~fahrten gut geeignet** well-suited to cross-country driving *or* to driving cross-country; ~**fahrzeug** *nt* cross-country vehicle; **g~gängig** *adj* *Fahrzeug* suitable for cross-country work; ~**lauf** *m* cross-country run; *(Wettbewerb)* cross-country race; **er macht gerne ~lauf** he enjoys cross-country running; ~**marsch** *m* cross-country march; **einen ~marsch machen** to march cross-country.
Geländer *nt* -s, - railing(s *pl*); *(Treppen~)* banister(s *pl*).
Gelände-: ~**rennen** *nt* cross-country race; ~**ritt** *m* cross-country riding; **ein ~ritt** a cross-country ride; **für ~ritte ungeeignet** unsuitable for cross-country riding; ~**spiel** *nt* scouting game; *(Mil)* field exercise; ~**übung** *f* field exercise; ~**wagen** *m* cross-country *or* general-purpose vehicle.
gelang *pret of* **gelingen**.
gelangen* *vi aux sein* **an/auf etw** *(acc)*/**zu etw** ~ *(lit, fig)* to reach sth; *(fig: mit Mühe)* to attain sth; *(erwerben)* to acquire sth; **zum Ziel** ~ to reach one's goal; *(fig auch)* to attain one's end *or* goal; **in jds Besitz** ~ to come into sb's possession; **in die richtigen/falschen Hände** ~ to fall into the right/wrong hands; **zu Reichtum** ~ to come into a fortune; *(durch Arbeit)* to make a *or* one's fortune; **zu Ruhm** ~ to achieve *or* acquire fame; **zur Reife** ~ to reach *or* attain *(form)* maturity; **zur Blüte** ~ to come to flower; **zu einer Überzeugung** ~ to become convinced; **zum Abschluß/zur Abstimmung** ~ *(form)* to reach a conclusion/be put to the vote; **zur Durchführung/Aufführung** ~ *(form)* to be carried out/performed; **zur Auszahlung** ~ *(form)* to be paid out; **an die Macht** ~ to come to power.
gelangweilt 1 *ptp of* **langweilen**. 2 *adj* bored *no adv*. **die Zuschauer saßen ~ da** the audience sat there looking bored; **er hörte ihr ~ zu** he was bored listening to her.
gelappt *adj Blatt* lobate, lobed.
Gelärme *nt* -s, *no pl* *(inf) siehe* **Lärm**.
Gelaß *nt* -sses, -sse *(dated)* small, usually dark room, often in a cellar; *(Verlies)* dungeon.
gelassen 1 *ptp of* **lassen**. 2 *adj (ruhig)* calm; *(gefaßt auch)* cool, composed *no adv*. ~ **bleiben** to keep calm *or* cool; **etw** ~ **hinnehmen** to take sth calmly *or* with composure.
Gelassenheit *f siehe adj* calmness; coolness, composure.
Gelatine [ʒelaˈtiːnə] *f, no pl* gelatine.
gelatinieren* [ʒelatiˈniːrən] *vti* to gelatinize.
Geläuf *nt* -(e)s, -e (a) *(Hunt)* tracks *pl* *(of game birds)*. (b) *(von Pferderennbahn)* turf.
Gelaufe *nt* -s, *no pl* *(inf)* running about. **das war ein** ~ that was a real run round *(inf)*.
gelaufen *ptp of* **laufen**.
geläufig *adj (üblich)* common; *(vertraut)* familiar; *(dated: fließend)* fluent. **eine ~e Redensart** a common saying; **das ist mir nicht** ~ I'm not familiar with that, that isn't familiar to me;

~ **Spanisch sprechen** to speak Spanish fluently *or* fluent Spanish; ~ **Maschine schreiben** to type quickly.
Geläufigkeit *f (des Sprechens)* fluency; *(von Maschineschreiben)* speed.
gelaunt *adj pred* **gut/schlecht** ~ good-/bad-tempered, good-/ill-humoured; *(vorübergehend)* in a good/bad mood; **wie ist er** ~? what sort of mood is he in?
Geläut(e) *nt* -(e)s, *no pl* (a) *(Glockenläuten)* ringing; *(harmonisch auch)* chiming; *(Läutwerk)* chime. (b) *(Hunt)* baying.
gelb *adj* yellow; *(bei Verkehrsampel)* amber. **die Blätter werden** ~ the leaves are turning (yellow); ~**er Fleck** *(Anat)* yellow spot; **das ~e Fieber** yellow fever; ~**e Rübe** carrot; **die ~e Rasse** the yellow race, the Orientals *pl*; **die ~e Gefahr** *(Pol pej)* the yellow peril; **der G~e Fluß/das G~e Meer** the Yellow River/Sea; ~**e Gewerkschaften** *(Christian)* trade unions which tend to sympathize with the employers; ~ **vor Neid** green with envy; **Löwenzahn blüht** ~ the dandelion has a yellow flower.
Gelb *nt* -s, - *or (inf)* -s yellow; *(von Verkehrsampel)* amber. **die Ampel stand auf** ~ the lights were amber *or* had turned amber; **bei** ~ **stehenbleiben** to stop on amber.
Gelbe(r) *mf decl as adj* Oriental.
Gelbe(s) *nt decl as adj (vom Ei)* yolk.
Gelb-: ~**fieber** *nt* yellow fever; ~**filter** *m (Phot)* yellow filter; **g~grün** *adj* yellowish-green; ~**kreuz** *nt (Chem)* mustard gas.
gelblich *adj* yellowish, yellowy; *Gesichtsfarbe* sallow.
Gelbling *m (Bot)* chanterelle.
Gelb-: ~**sucht** *f* jaundice; **g~süchtig** *adj* jaundiced; **er ist g~süchtig** he has jaundice.
Geld *nt* -(e)s, -er (a) *no pl* *(Zahlungsmittel)* money. **bares/großes/kleines** ~ cash/notes *pl*/change; ~ **und Gut** wealth and possessions; **alles für unser** ~! and we're paying for it!; **knapp bei** ~ **sein** to be hard up, to be short of money; ~ **aufnehmen** to raise money; **aus etw** ~ **machen** to make money out of sth; **zu** ~ **machen** to sell off; *Aktien* to cash in; **(mit etw)** ~ **machen** *(inf)* to make money (from sth); **um** ~ **spielen** to play for money; **ins** ~ **gehen** *(inf)* *or* **laufen** *(inf)* to cost a pretty penny *(inf)*; **das kostet ein (wahnsinniges)** ~ *(inf)* that costs a fortune *or* a packet *(inf)*; **etw für teures** ~ **kaufen** to pay a lot for sth; **das habe ich für billiges** ~ **gekauft** I got it cheaply, I didn't pay much for it; **ich stand ohne** ~ **da** I was left penniless *or* without a penny; **wenn er wieder bei** ~ **ist** when he's got some *or* when he's in the *(inf)* money again; **in** *or* **im** ~ **schwimmen** *(inf)* to be rolling in it *(inf)*, to be loaded *(inf)*; **er hat** ~ **wie Heu** *(inf)* *or* **Dreck** *(sl)* *or* **Mist** *(sl)* he's got stacks of money *(inf)*, he's filthy *or* stinking rich *(inf)*; **das** ~ **auf die Straße werfen** *(inf)* *or* **zum Fenster hinauswerfen** *(inf)* to spend money like water *or* like it was going out of fashion *(inf)*; **da hast du das Geld zum Fenster hinausgeworfen** *(inf)* that's money down the drain *(inf)*; **mit** ~ **um sich werfen** *or* **schmeißen** *(inf)* to chuck one's money around *(inf)*; **jdm das** ~ **aus der Tasche ziehen** *or* **lotsen** *(inf)* to get *or* squeeze money out of sb; **am** ~ **hängen** *or* **kleben** to be tight with money; **hinterm** ~ **hersein** *(inf)* to be a money-grubber *(inf)*; **das ist nicht für** ~ **zu haben** *(inf)* that can't be bought; **sie/das ist nicht mit** ~ **zu bezahlen** *(inf)* she/that is priceless; **er kann sich für** ~ **sehen lassen** he could go on stage; **nicht für** ~ **und gute Worte** *(inf)* not for love nor money; ~ **allein macht nicht glücklich** *(, aber es beruhigt)* *(Prov)* money isn't everything *(, but it helps)* *(prov)*; ~ **oder Leben!** your money or your life!; ~ **stinkt nicht** *(Prov)* there's nothing wrong with money; ~ **regiert die Welt** *(Prov)* money makes the world go round *(prov)*.
(b) *(~summen)* ~**er** *pl* money; **tägliche ~er** day-to-day money *or* loans *pl*; **staatliche/öffentliche ~er** state/public funds *pl* or money.
Geld-: ~**abwertung** *f* currency devaluation; **der ~adel** the money aristocracy; *(hum: die Reichen)* the rich *pl*; **diese Familie ist ~adel** the family bought their way into the nobility; ~**angelegenheit** *f* financial matter; **jds ~angelegenheiten** sb's financial affairs; ~**anlage** *f* (financial) investment; ~**aristokratie** *f siehe* ~**adel**; ~**aufwertung** *f* currency revaluation; ~**ausgabe** *f* (financial) expenditure; ~**beutel** *m*, ~**börse** *f* purse; **tief in den ~beutel greifen** *(inf)* to dig deep (into one's pocket) *(inf)*; ~**brief** *m siehe* **Wertbrief**; ~**briefträger** *m* postman who delivers money orders; ~**buße** *f (Jur)* fine; **eine hohe ~buße** a heavy fine; ~**dinge** *pl* financial matters; ~**einlage** *f* capital invested *no pl*; ~**einwurf** *m* slot; **beim ~einwurf müssen Sie ...** when inserting the money you should ...; ~**entwertung** *f (Inflation)* currency depreciation; *(Abwertung)* currency devaluation; ~**erwerb** *m* zum ~**erwerb arbeiten** to work to earn money; **etw zum ~erwerb machen** to make money out of sth; ~**fälschung** *f* counterfeiting; ~**geber(in** *f)* *m* financial backer; *(esp Rad, TV)* sponsor; *(hum: Arbeitgeber)* employer; ~**geschäft** *nt* financial transaction; ~**geschenk** *nt* gift of money; ~**gier** *f* avarice; **g~gierig** *adj* avaricious; ~**heirat** *f* **das war eine reine ~heirat** she/he *etc* just got married for the money; ~**herrschaft** *f* plutocracy.
geldig *adj (esp Aus)* moneyed.
Geld-: ~**institut** *nt* financial institution; ~**kassette** *f* cash box; ~**katze** *f (Hist)* money pouch; *(Gürtel)* money-belt; ~**klemme** *f* *(inf)* financial difficulties *pl*; ~**knappheit** *f* shortage of money; ~**kurs** *m (St Ex)* buying rate.
geldlich *adj* financial.
Geld-: ~**mangel** *m* lack of money; ~**mann** *m*, *pl* ~**leute** *(inf)* financier; ~**markt** *m* money market; ~**menge** *f* money supply; ~**mittel** *pl* funds *pl*; ~**not** *f (~mangel)* lack of money; *(~schwierigkeiten)* financial difficulties *pl*; ~**politik** *f* financial policy; **etwas von ~politik verstehen** to know something about the politics of finance; ~**prämie** *f* bonus; *(als Auszeichnung)* (financial) award; *(als Belohnung)* (financial) reward; ~**preis** *m* cash prize; ~**quelle** *f* source of income;

~**rolle** f roll of money or coins; ~**sache** f money or financial matter; **in** ~**sachen hört die Gemütlichkeit auf** (prov) business is business (prov); ~**sack** m money bag; (pej inf: reicher Mann) moneybags sing; **auf dem** ~**sack sitzen** (inf) to be sitting on a pile of money (inf); ~**säckel** m (dial) money bag; (fig: von Kanton, Staat etc) coffers pl; ~**schein** m banknote, bill (US); ~**schneider** m (inf) moneygrabber (inf); ~**schneiderei** f (inf) moneygrabbing (inf); ~**schöpfung** f (Fin) money creation; ~**schrank** m safe; ~**schrankknacker** m (inf) safeblower; ~**schuld** f (financial) debt; ~**schwierigkeiten** pl financial difficulties pl; ~**sendung** f cash remittance; ~**sorgen** pl financial worries pl, money troubles pl; ~**sorgen haben, in** ~**sorgen sein** to have financial worries or money troubles; ~**sorte** f (Fin) (type of) currency; ~**spende** f donation, gift of money; ~**spritze** f (inf) injection of money; ~**strafe** f fine; **jdn zu einer** ~**strafe verurteilen** or **mit einer** ~**strafe belegen** to fine sb, to impose a fine on sb; ~**stück** nt coin; ~**summe** f sum of money; ~**tasche** f purse, wallet (US); (Herren~) wallet; (sackartig) money bag; ~**theorie** f money theory; ~**umlauf** m circulation of money; ~**umtausch** m siehe ~**wechsel**; ~**verdiener** m (inf) moneymaker (inf); ~**verkehr** m money transactions pl; ~**verlegenheit** f financial embarrassment no pl; **in** ~**verlegenheit sein** to be short of money; **jdm aus einer** ~**verlegenheit helfen** to help sb out of his financial difficulties; ~**verleiher** m moneylender; ~**verschwendung** f waste of money; ~**volumen** nt (Fin) siehe ~**menge**; ~**wechsel** m exchange of money; **beim** ~**wechsel muß man eine Gebühr bezahlen** there is a charge for changing money; „~**wechsel**" "bureau de change"; ~**wechselautomat** m change machine; ~**wechsler** m moneychanger; (Automat) change machine; ~**wert** m cash value; (Fin: Kaufkraft) (currency) value; **innerer/äußerer** ~**wert** an/the internal/external value of currency; ~**wertstabilität** f stability of a/the currency; ~**wesen** nt monetary system; ~**wirtschaft** f money economy; ~**zusteller** m (form) sb who delivers or deals with money orders; ~**zuwendungen** pl money sing; (~geschenk) gifts pl of money; (regelmäßiges ~**geschenk**) allowance sing; **private** ~**zuwendungen erhalten** to receive a private income.

geleckt 1 ptp of **lecken**. 2 adj **wie** ~ **aussehen** Mann to be spruced up; Zimmer, Boden etc to be spick and span.

Gelee [ʒeˈleː] nt or nt -s, -s jelly.

Gelege nt -s, - (Vogel~) clutch (of eggs); (Frosch~) spawn no pl; (von Reptilien) eggs pl.

gelegen 1 ptp of **liegen**.
   2 adj (a) (befindlich, liegend) Haus situated; Grundstück auch located. **ein herrlich** ~**er Ort** a place in a magnificent area.
   (b) (passend) opportune. **zu** ~**er Zeit** at a convenient time; **wenn ich nicht** ~ **komme, gehe ich gleich wieder** if it's not convenient, I'll go immediately; **du kommst mir gerade** ~ (iro) you do pick your time well; **es kommt mir sehr/nicht sehr** ~ it comes just at the right/wrong time.
   (c) pred (wichtig) **mir ist viel/nichts daran** ~ it matters a great deal/doesn't matter to me; **was ist (schon) daran** ~? what does it matter (after all)?

Gelegenheit f (a) (günstiger Umstand) opportunity. **bei** ~ some time (or other); **bei passender** ~ when the opportunity arises; **bei passender/der ersten (besten)** ~ **werde ich ...** when I get the opportunity or chance/at the first opportunity I'll ...; **(die)** ~ **haben** to get an or the opportunity or a or the chance (etw zu tun to do sth); **jdm (die)** ~ **geben** or **bieten** to give sb an or the opportunity or a or the chance (etw zu tun to do sth); ~ **macht Diebe** (Prov) opportunity makes a thief; siehe **wahrnehmen**.
   (b) (Anlaß) occasion. **bei dieser** ~ on this occasion; **ein Kleid für alle** ~**en** a dress suitable for all occasions; siehe **Schopf**.
   (c) (Comm) bargain.

Gelegenheits-: ~**arbeit** f (a) casual work no pl; (b) (eines Autors) minor work; ~**arbeiter** m casual labourer; ~**dichter** m occasional poet; ~**dichtung** f occasional poetry; (Gedicht) occasional poem; ~**gedicht** nt occasional poem; ~**kauf** m bargain; ~**raucher** m occasional smoker; ~**trinker** m occasional drinker.

gelegentlich 1 adj attr occasional. **von** ~**en Ausnahmen abgesehen** except for the odd occasion.
   2 adv (manchmal) occasionally, now and again; (bei Gelegenheit) some time (or other). **wenn Sie** ~ **dort sind** if you happen to be there; **lassen Sie** ~ **etwas von sich hören!** keep in touch.
   3 prep +gen (geh) ~ **seines 60. Geburtstags** on the occasion of his 60th birthday.

gelehrig adj quick to learn. **sich bei etw** ~ **anstellen** to be quick to grasp sth.

Gelehrigkeit f quickness to learn.

gelehrsam adj (a) (old) siehe **gelehrt 2**. (b) (rare) siehe **gelehrig**.

Gelehrsamkeit f (geh) learning, erudition.

gelehrt 1 ptp of **lehren**. 2 adj learned, erudite; (wissenschaftlich). ~**e Gesellschaft** (old) learned society.

Gelehrte(r) mf decl as adj scholar. **darüber sind sich die** ~**n noch nicht einig** that's a moot point.

Gelehrten-: ~**familie** f family of scholars; ~**kopf** m scholarly profile; ~**streit** m dispute amongst the scholars; ~**tum** nt learning; (die Gelehrten) scholars pl; ~**welt** f world of learning.

Gelehrtheit f learning, erudition.

Geleier nt -s, no pl droning.

Geleise nt -s, - (geh, Aus) siehe **Gleis**.

Geleit nt -(e)s, -e (Hist: Gefolge) retinue, entourage; (Be-

gleitung, Mil) escort; (Naut) convoy, escort; (Leichenzug) cortege. **freies** or **sicheres** ~ safe-conduct; **jdm das** ~ **geben** to escort or accompany sb; **er wurde mit großem** ~ **zum Palast gebracht** he was given a heavy escort to the palace; „**zum** ~" "preface"; siehe **letzte(r, s)**.

Geleit-: ~**boot** nt escort or convoy ship; ~**brief** m (Hist) letter of safe-conduct.

Geleite nt -s, - (old) siehe **Geleit**.

geleiten vt (geh) to escort; (begleiten auch) to accompany; (Naut) to convoy, to escort.

Geleiter(in f) m -s, - (liter) escort.

Geleit-: ~**schiff** nt siehe ~**boot**; ~**schutz** m escort (Naut auch) convoy; **jdm** ~**schutz gewähren** or **geben** to give sb an escort/a convoy; (persönlich) to escort/convoy sb; **im** ~**schutz (von Polizeifahrzeugen)** under (police) escort; ~**wort** nt (geh) preface; ~**zug** m (Mil, Naut) convoy; **im** ~**zug fahren** to drive in/sail under convoy.

Gelenk nt -(e)s, -e joint; (Hand~) wrist; (Fuß~) ankle; (Ketten~) link; (Scharnier~) hinge.

gelenk adj (old) siehe **gelenkig**.

Gelenk-, Gelenks- (Aus): ~**entzündung** f arthritis; ~**fahrzeug** nt articulated vehicle.

gelenkig adj supple; Mensch auch agile. ~ **verbunden sein** (Tech) to be jointed; (zusammengefügt) to be articulated; (mit Kettengelenk) to be linked; (mit Scharniergelenk) to be hinged.

Gelenkigkeit f suppleness; (von Mensch auch) agility.

Gelenk-, Gelenks- (Aus): ~**kopf** m, ~**kugel** f (Anat) head of a bone, condyle; ~**omnibus** m articulated bus; ~**pfanne** f (Anat) glenoid cavity; ~**plastik** f (Med) anthroplasty; ~**puppe** f siehe **Gliederpuppe**; ~**rheumatismus** m rheumatic fever; ~**schmiere** f (Anat) synovial fluid; ~**welle** f (Tech) cardan shaft; ~**zug** m articulated train.

gelernt 1 ptp of **lernen**. 2 adj trained; Arbeiter skilled.

gelesen ptp of **lesen**.

Gelichter nt -s, no pl (dated pej) rabble (inf), riff-raff (inf).

geliebt 1 ptp of **lieben**. 2 adj dear, beloved (liter, Eccl).

Geliebte f decl as adj sweetheart; (Mätresse) mistress; (liter: als Anrede) beloved (liter).

Geliebte(r) m decl as adj sweetheart, lover (old); (Liebhaber) lover; (liter: als Anrede) beloved (liter).

geliefert 1 ptp of **liefern**. 2 adj ~ **sein** (inf) to have had it (inf); **jetzt sind wir** ~ that's the end (inf).

geliehen ptp of **leihen**.

gelieren [ʒeˈliːrən] vi to gel.

Gelier- [ʒeˈliːɐ]: ~**mittel** nt gelling agent; ~**zucker** m preserving sugar.

gelind(e) adj (geh) (a) (mäßig, mild) mild; (schonend, vorsichtig) gentle; Wind, Frost, Regen light; Klima, Anhöhe gentle. ~ **gesagt** putting it mildly, to put it mildly. (b) (inf: heftig) awful (inf). **da packte mich** ~ **Wut** I got pretty angry.

gelingen pret **gelang**, ptp **gelungen** vi aux sein (glücken) to succeed; (erfolgreich sein) to be successful. **es gelang ihm, das zu tun** he succeeded in doing it; **es gelang ihm nicht, das zu tun** he failed to do it, he didn't succeed in doing it; **dem Häftling gelang die Flucht** the prisoner managed to escape or succeeded in escaping; **dein Plan wird dir nicht** ~ you won't succeed with your plan; **es will mir nicht** ~/~ ... **zu ...** I can't seem to manage it/manage to ...; **das Essen ist ihr gut/schlecht gelungen** her picture turned out well/badly; siehe **gelungen**.

Gelingen nt -s, no pl (geh) (Glück) success; (erfolgreiches Ergebnis) successful outcome. **gutes** ~ **für Ihren Plan!** good luck with your plan!; **auf gutes** ~! to success!; **auf gutes** ~ **hoffen** to hope for success/a successful outcome.

Gelispel nt -s, no pl (das Lispeln) lisping; (Geflüster) whispering.

gelitten ptp of **leiden**.

gell[1] adj shrill, piercing.

gell[2]**, gelle** interj (S Ger, Sw) siehe **gelt**.

gellen vi to shrill; (von lauten Tönen erfüllt sein) to ring. „**Hilfe!" gellte es laut** there was a shrill cry of "Help"; **der Lärm gellt mir in den Ohren** the noise makes my ears ring; **ein schriller Schrei gellte durch die Nacht** a shrill scream pierced the night.

gellend 1 prp of **gellen**. 2 adj shrill, piercing. ~ **um Hilfe schreien** to scream for help.

geloben* vt (geh) to vow, to swear. **die Fürsten gelobten dem König Treue** the princes pledged their loyalty or vowed loyalty to the king; **ich habe mir gelobt, das Rauchen aufzugeben** I've vowed or sworn or made a pledge to give up smoking; **das Gelobte Land** (Bibl) the Promised Land; **ich schwöre und gelobe, ...** I (do) solemnly swear and promise ...

Gelöbnis nt (geh) vow. **ein** or **das** ~ **ablegen** to take a vow.

gelockt 1 ptp of **locken**. 2 adj Haar curly; Mensch curlyhaired, curly-headed.

Gelöder nt -s, no pl (geh) blaze.

gelogen ptp of **lügen**.

gelöst 1 ptp of **lösen**. 2 adj relaxed. **danach war sie** ~ **und entspannt** afterwards she felt calm and relaxed.

Gelöstheit f feeling of relaxation; (gelöste Stimmung) relaxed mood. ~ **verspüren** to be or feel relaxed.

Gelse f -, -n (Aus) gnat, mosquito.

gelt interj (S Ger) right. **morgen kommst du wieder,** ~? you'll be back tomorrow, won't you or right?; **das habe ich nicht gemacht,** ~? I didn't do that, did I or right?; ~, **du leihst mir 5 Mark?** you'll lend me 5 marks, won't you or right?; **jetzt hör aber auf mit dem Blödsinn,** ~? now stop all this nonsense, (all) right or OK (inf)?; **ich werde es mal versuchen,** ~? well, I'll give it a try.

gelten pret **galt**, ptp **gegolten** 1 vi (a) (gültig sein) to be valid; (Gesetz) to be in force; (Preise) to be effective; (Münze) to be legal tender; (*erlaubt sein*) to be allowed *or* permitted; (*zählen*) to count. **die Wette gilt!** the bet's on!, it's a bet!; **was ich sage, gilt!** what I say goes!; **das gilt nicht!** that doesn't count!; (*nicht erlaubt*) that's not allowed!; **da gilt keine Ausrede** it's no good making excuses; **das Gesetz gilt für alle** the law is made for everyone; **diese Karte gilt nur für eine Person** this ticket only admits one; *siehe* **geltend.**

    (b) + *dat* (*bestimmt sein für*) to be meant for *or* aimed at.

    (c) + *dat* (*geh: sich beziehen auf*) to be for. **seine ganze Liebe galt der Musik** music was his only love; **sein letzter Gedanke galt seinem Volk** his last thought was for his people.

    (d) (*zutreffen*) **für jdn/etw** ~ to hold (good) for sb/sth, to go for sb/sth; **das gleiche gilt auch für ihn/von ihm** the same goes for him too/is true of him too.

    (e) ~ **als** *or* **für** (*rare*) to be regarded as; **es gilt als sicher, daß ...** it seems certain that ...

    (f) ~ **lassen** to accept; **das lasse ich** ~! I'll agree to that!, I accept that!; **für diesmal lasse ich es** ~ I'll let it go this time; **etw als etw** ~ **lassen** to accept sth as sth; **Tatsachen muß man** ~ **lassen** one has to accept the facts; **er läßt nur seine eigene Meinung** ~ he won't accept anybody's opinion but his own.

    2 *vti impers* (*geh*) **es gilt, ... zu ...** it is necessary to ...; **jetzt gilt es, Mut zu zeigen/zusammenzuhalten** it is now a question of courage/of sticking together; **jetzt gilt's!** this is it!; **was gilt's?** (*bei Wette*) what do you bet?; **es gilt!** done!, you're on!, it's a deal!; **es gilt Leben oder Tod** (*liter*) it's a matter of life or death.

    3 *vt* (*wert sein*) to be worth; (*zählen*) to count for. **was gilt die Wette?** what do you bet?

geltend *adj attr Preise, Tarife* current; *Gesetz, Regelung* currently operative *or* valid; (*vorherrschend*) *Meinung etc* currently accepted, prevailing. ~ **machen** (*form*) to assert; **einen Einwand** ~ **machen** to raise an objection.

Geltendmachung *f* (*form*) enforcement.

Geltung *f* (*Gültigkeit*) validity; (*von Münzen*) currency; (*Wert*) value, worth; (*Einfluß*) influence; (*Ansehen*) prestige. ~ **haben** to have validity; (*Münzen*) to be legal tender, to have currency; (*Gesetz*) to be in force; (*Preise*) to be effective; (*Auffassung etc*) to be prevalent; (*Einfluß haben*) to carry weight; (*angesehen sein*) to be recognized; **in** ~ **bleiben** to remain operative *or* in force; (*Auffassung*) to remain prevalent; **an** ~ **verlieren** to lose prestige; **einer Sache** (*dat*) ~ **verschaffen** to enforce sth; **sich** (*dat*) ~ **verschaffen** to establish one's position; **etw zur** ~ **bringen** to show sth (off) to advantage; (*durch Kontrast*) to set sth off; **ein Minirock bringt schöne Beine voll zur** ~ a mini-skirt shows good legs (off) to their best advantage; **zur** ~ **kommen** to show to advantage; (*durch Kontrast*) to be set off; **in diesem Konzertsaal kommt die Musik voll zur** ~ the music can be heard to its best advantage in this concert hall.

Geltungs-: ~**bedürfnis** *nt*, *no pl* need for admiration; **g**~**bedürftig** *adj* desperate for admiration; ~**bereich** *m* der ~**bereich einer Fahrkarte/eines Gesetzes** the area within which a ticket is valid/a law is operative; ~**dauer** *f* (*einer Fahrkarte etc*) period of validity; **die** ~**dauer eines Vertrages/einer Genehmigung** the period during which a contract is in force/a licence is valid; ~**drang** *m*, ~**streben** *nt* *siehe* ~**bedürfnis**; ~**sucht** *f* craving for admiration; **g**~**süchtig** *adj* craving (for) admiration; ~**trieb** *m* (~**bedürfnis**) need for admiration; (~**sucht**) craving for admiration.

Gelübde *nt* -s, - (*Rel, geh*) vow. **ein/das** ~ **ablegen** *or* **tun** to take a vow.

Gelump(e) *nt* -s, *no pl* (*inf: Plunder, Sachen*) junk, trash; (*pej: Gesindel*) trash.

gelungen **1** *ptp of* **gelingen.**

    2 *adj attr* (a) (*geglückt*) successful. **ein gut** ~**er Abend/Braten** a very successful evening/a roast that turned out very well; **eine nicht so recht** ~**e Überraschung** a surprise that didn't quite come off.

    (b) (*dial: drollig*) priceless. **du bist mir ein** ~**er Bursche** you're priceless, you *are* a funny chap.

Gelüst(e) *nt* -(e)s, -e (*geh*) desire; (*Sucht*) craving (*auf* + *acc*, *nach* for).

gelüsten* *vt impers* (*liter, iro*) **es gelüstet mich** *or* **mich gelüstet nach ...** I am overcome by desire for ...; (*süchtig nach*) I have a craving for ...; **es gelüstet mich, das zu tun** I'm more than tempted *or* I'm sorely tempted to do that.

Gelüsten *nt* -s, *no pl siehe* **Gelüst(e).**

gelüstig *adj* (*old, dial*) (a) *siehe* **lüstern.** (b) (*dial*) ~ **sein** to fancy something nice.

GEMA ['ge:ma] *f* -, *no pl abbr of* **Gesellschaft für musikalische Aufführungs- und mechanische Vervielfältigungsrechte.**

gemach *adv* (*old*) slowly. ~! not so fast!; (*nichts übereilen*) one mustn't rush things!

Gemach *nt* -(e)s, ~**er** (*geh*) chamber (*old, form*). **sich in seine** ~**er zurückziehen** to repair to one's chamber (*old, hum*).

gemächlich *adj* leisurely *no adv*; *Mensch* unhurried. **ein** ~ **fließender Strom** a gently flowing river; **er wanderte** ~ **durch die Wiesen** he strolled through the meadows, he took a leisurely stroll through the meadows; **ein** ~**es Leben führen** to lead a quiet life.

Gemächlichkeit *f* leisureliness; (*Ruhe*) peace. **die** ~, **mit der er sein Leben lebt** the leisurely pace at which he lives.

gemacht **1** *ptp of* **machen.** **2** *adj* (a) made. **für etw** ~ **sein** to be made for sth; **ein** ~**er Mann sein** to be made *or* a made man; *siehe* **Bett.** (b) (*gewollt, gekünstelt*) false, contrived. (c) (*ist*) ~! (*inf*) done! (*inf*).

Gemächt(e) *nt* -(e)s, *no pl* (*old, hum*) privy parts *pl* (*old*).

Gemahl[1] *m* -s, -e (*geh, form*) spouse (*old, form*), husband; (*Prinz*~) consort. **bitte grüßen Sie Ihren Herrn** ~ do give my regards to your husband.

Gemahl[2] *nt* - *or* -(e)s, -e (*obs*) spouse (*old, form*), wife.

Gemahlin *f* (*geh, form*) spouse (*old, form*), wife; (*von König auch*) consort. **bitte empfehlen Sie mich Ihrer Frau** ~ do give my regards to your lady wife (*form, hum*) *or* to your good lady.

gemahnen* *vt* (*geh*) **jdn an jdn/etw** ~ to remind sb of sb/sth, to put sb in mind of sb/sth.

Gemälde *nt* -s, - painting; (*fig: Schilderung*) portrayal.

Gemälde-: ~**ausstellung** *f* exhibition of paintings; ~**galerie** *f* picture gallery; ~**sammlung** *f* collection of paintings; (~**galerie**) art collection.

Gemansche *nt* -s, *no pl* (*dial*) mush. **hör auf mit dem** ~! stop messing about with it!

Gemarkung *f* (*dated, form*) (*Feldmark*) bounds *pl*; (*Gemeindegebiet*) district.

gemasert **1** *ptp of* **masern. 2** *adj Holz* grained.

gemäß **1** *prep* + *dat* in accordance with. **Ihren Anordnungen** ~ as per your instructions, in accordance with your instructions; ~ **den Bestimmungen** under the regulations; ~ **§ 209** under § 209.

    2 *adj appropriate* (*dat* to). **dieser Umgang ist seiner sozialen Stellung nicht** ~ the company he is keeping ill befits *or* does not befit his social position; **eine ihren Fähigkeiten** ~**e Arbeit** a job suited to her abilities; **das einzig G**~**e** the only fitting thing.

Gemäßheit *f* (*rare*) *siehe* **Angemessenheit.**

gemäßigt **1** *ptp of* **mäßigen. 2** *adj* moderate; *Klima, Zone* temperate; *Optimismus etc* qualified.

Gemäuer *nt* -s, *no pl* (*geh*) masonry, walls *pl*; (*Ruine*) ruins *pl*.

Gemauschel *nt* -s, *no pl* (*pej inf*) scheming.

Gemeck(e)re, Gemecker *nt* -s, *no pl* (*von Ziegen*) bleating; (*inf: Nörgelei*) moaning, belly-aching (*inf*); (*meckerndes Lachen*) cackling.

gemein *adj* (a) *pred, no comp* (*gemeinsam*) **etw** ~ **mit jdm/etw haben** to have sth in common with sb/sth; **Menschen/einer Sache** (*dat*) ~ **sein** (*geh*) to be common to people/sth; **nichts mit jdm** ~ **haben wollen** to want nothing to do with sb; **sich mit jdm** ~ **machen** to lower oneself to sb's level; **das ist beiden** ~ it is common to both of them.

    (b) *attr, no comp* (*Biol, old: üblich, verbreitet, öffentlich*) common. ~**er Bruch** (*Math*) vulgar fraction; ~**es Recht** common law; **ein** ~**er Soldat** a common soldier; **das** ~**e Volk/Wohl** the common people/good *or* weal (*old*); **der** ~**e Mann** the ordinary man.

    (c) (*niederträchtig*) mean; (*roh, unverschämt auch*) nasty; *Verräter, Lüge* base. **das war** ~ **von dir!** that was mean *or* nasty of you; **ein** ~**er Streich** a dirty *or* rotten trick; **alles ins G**~**e ziehen** to cheapen *or* debase everything.

    (d) (*ordinär*) vulgar; *Bemerkung, Witz auch* coarse.

    (e) (*inf: unangenehm*) horrible, awful. **die Prüfung war** ~ **schwer** the exam was horribly *or* awfully difficult.

Gemeinbesitz *m* common property.

Gemeinde *f* -, -n (a) (*Kommune*) municipality; (~**bewohner** *auch*) community; (*inf:* ~*amt*) local authority. **die** ~ **Burg** the municipality of Burg. (b) (*Pfarr*~) parish; (*Gläubige auch*) parishioners *pl*; (*beim Gottesdienst*) congregation. (c) (*Anhängerschaft*) (*von Theater etc*) patrons *pl*; (*von Schriftsteller etc*) following.

Gemeinde-: ~**abgaben** *pl* rates and local taxes *pl*; ~**ammann** *m* (*Sw*) (a) *siehe* ~**vorsteher**; (b) bailiff; ~**amt** *nt* local authority; (*Gebäude*) local administrative office; ~**bau** *m* (*Aus*) council house; ~**beamte(r)** *m* local government officer; ~**behörde** *f* local authority; ~**beschluß** *m* local government decision; ~**bezirk** *m* district; (*Aus*) ward; **im** ~**bezirk Dumfries** in the district of Dumfries; ~**diener** *m* (*dated*) beadle; **g**~**eigen** *adj* local authority *attr*; (*esp städtisch*) municipal; ~**eigentum** *nt* communal property; ~**glied** *nt* (*Eccl*) parishioner; ~**haus** *nt* (*Eccl*) parish rooms *pl*; (*von Freikirchen*) church rooms *pl*; (*katholisch*) parish house; ~**helfer(in** *f*) *m* (*Eccl*) parish worker; ~**mitglied** *nt* (*Eccl*) *siehe* ~**glied**; ~**ordnung** *f* bylaws *pl*, ordinances *pl* (*US*); ~**präsident** *m* (*Sw*) mayor; ~**rat** *m* district council; (*Mitglied*) district councillor; ~**saal** *m* (*Eccl*) church hall; ~**schwester** *f* district nurse; (*Eccl*) nun working in a parish as a nurse or social worker; ~**spital** *nt* (*Aus*) local hospital; ~**steuer** *f* local tax; (*Grundsteuer*) rates *pl* (*Brit*).

gemeindeutsch *adj* standard German.

Gemeinde-: ~**väter** *pl* (*hum*) venerable councillors *pl* (*hum*); ~**vertretung** *f* *siehe* ~**rat**; ~**vorstand** *m* = aldermen *pl*; ~**vorsteher** *m* head of the district council; (*Bürgermeister*) mayor; ~**wahl** *f* local election; ~**zentrum** *nt* community centre; (*Eccl*) parish rooms *pl*; (*von Freikirchen*) church rooms *pl*; (*katholisch*) parish house.

Gemeineigentum *nt* common property.

Gemeine(r) *m decl as adj* (a) (*dated: Soldat*) common soldier. **die** ~**n** the ranks. (b) (*Typ*) lower-case letter. **in** ~**n** in lower case.

Gemein-: **g**~**gefährlich** *adj* constituting a public danger; **ein g**~**gefährlicher Verbrecher** a dangerous criminal; **g**~**gefährlich handeln** to endanger the public safety; ~**gefährlichkeit** *f* danger to the public; ~**geist** *m* public spirit; **g**~**gültig** *adj siehe* **allgemeingültig**; ~**gut** *nt* (*lit, fig*) common property; **Schumanns Lieder gehören zum** ~**gut der Deutschen** Schumann's Lieder are part of the German heritage.

Gemeinheit *f* (a) *no pl* (*Niedertracht*) meanness; (*Roheit, Unverschämtheit auch*) nastiness. (b) *no pl* (*Vulgarität*) vulgarity; (*von Bemerkung, Witz auch*) coarseness. (c) (*Tat*) mean *or* dirty trick; (*Behandlung*) nasty treatment *no pl*; (*Worte*) mean thing. **das war eine** ~ that was a mean thing to do/say. (d) (*inf: ärgerlicher Umstand*) (blasted *inf*) nuisance.

Gemein-: **g**~**hin** *adv* generally; ~**kosten** *pl* overheads *pl*, overhead costs *pl*; ~**nutz** *m* public *or* common good; ~**nutz geht vor Eigennutz** (*dated prov*) service before self (*Prov*); **g~nützig** *adj* of benefit to the public *pred*; (*wohltätig*) charitable; **g~nütziger Verein** charitable *or* non-profit-making organization; **g~nützige Einrichtung** public utility; **Schulen und Parkanlagen sind g~nützige Einrichtungen** schools and parks are for the benefit of the public; **als g~nützig angesehene Spenden** gifts regarded as charitable donations; ~**nützigkeit** *f* benefit to the public; **die ~nützigkeit einer Organisation** the charitable status of an organization; ~**platz** *m* commonplace.

gemeinsam 1 *adj* (*mehreren gehörend*) *Eigenschaft, Interesse, Zwecke, Politik* common; *Konto* joint; *Freund* mutual; (*von mehreren unternommen*) *Aktion, Ausflug* joint. **sie haben vieles ~, ihnen ist vieles ~** they have a great deal in common; **die Firma ist ~es Eigentum** *or* **das ~e Eigentum der beiden Brüder** the firm belongs jointly to *or* is the joint property of the two brothers; **unser ~es Leben** our life together; **der G~e Markt** the Common Market; **mit jdm ~e Sache machen** to join up with *or* join forces with sb; **er betonte das G~e** he stressed all that we/they had in common.
2 *adv* together. **etw ~ haben** to have sth in common; **es gehört den beiden ~** it belongs jointly to the two of them.
Gemeinsamkeit *f* (**a**) (*gemeinsame Interessen, Eigenschaft etc*) common ground *no pl*. **die ~en zwischen ihnen sind sehr groß** they have a great deal in common.
(b) *no pl* (*gemeinsames Besitzen*) joint possession; (*von Freunden, Interessen*) mutuality. **uns verbindet die ~ unserer Interessen** we are united by many common interests.
Gemeinschaft *f* community; (*Gruppe*) group; (*Zusammensein*) company; (*Zusammengehörigkeitsgefühl*) sense of community. **die ~ der neun** (*Pol*) the nine; **eine ~ zu etw** an association for sth; **in ~ mit** jointly with, together with; **die ~ mit jdm** sb's companionship; **in ~ mit jdm leben** to live in close companionship with sb; **die ~ der Heiligen/der Gläubigen** the communion of saints/of the faithful; **eheliche ~** (*Jur*) matrimony.
gemeinschaftlich *adj siehe* **gemeinsam.**
Gemeinschafts-: ~**anschluß** *m* (*Telec*) party line; ~**antenne** *f* block *or* party aerial *or* antenna (*esp US*); ~**arbeit** *f* teamwork; **das Buch ist eine ~arbeit** the book is a team effort; (*von zwei Personen*) the book is a joint effort; ~**aufgabe** *f* joint task; (*BRD: Aufgabe des Bundes*) federal project; ~**beichte** *f* (*Eccl*) general confession; **g~bildend** *adj* community-building; (*einigend*) unifying; ~**ehe** *f* group *or* communal marriage; ~**erziehung** *f* coeducation; (*soziale Erziehung*) social education; ~**gefühl** *nt* sense of community; (*Uneigennützigkeit*) public-spiritedness; ~**geist** *m* community spirit, esprit de corps; ~**grab** *nt* communal grave; ~**haft** *f* group confinement; ~**küche** *f* (*Kantine*) canteen; (*gemeinsame Kochgelegenheit*) communal *or* (*kleiner*) shared kitchen; ~**kunde** *f* social studies *pl*; ~**leben** *nt* community life; ~**leistung** *f* collective achievement; ~**praxis** *f* joint practice; ~**produktion** *f* (**a**) *siehe* ~**arbeit**; (**b**) (*Rad, TV, Film*) co-production; ~**raum** *m* common room; **g~schädigend** *adj Verhalten* antisocial; ~**schule** *f* interdenominational school; ~**sendung** *f* simultaneous broadcast; ~**sinn** *m siehe* ~**geist**; ~**verpflegung** *f* canteen meals *pl*; ~**werbung** *f* joint advertising *no pl*; ~**werbung machen** to advertise jointly, to run a joint advertisement; ~**wohnung** *f* shared house/flat *etc*; ~**zelle** *f* communal cell.
Gemein-: ~**sinn** *m* public spirit; ~**sprache** *f* standard language; **g~verständlich** *adj* generally comprehensible *no adv*; **sich g~verständlich ausdrücken** to make oneself generally understood; **wissenschaftliche Probleme g~verständlich darstellen** to present scientific problems in such a way that they are intelligible *or* comprehensible to the layman; ~**verständlichkeit** *f* general comprehensibility; ~**werk** *nt* (*Sw*) voluntary work; ~**wesen** *nt* community; (*Staat*) polity; ~**wille** *m* collective will; ~**wirtschaft** *f* co-operative economy; **g~wirtschaftlich** *adj* co-operative; ~**wohl** *nt* public welfare; **etw zum ~wohl tun** to do sth for the common good; **das dient dem ~wohl** it is in the public interest.
Gemenge *nt* **-s, -** (**a**) (*Mischung*) mixture (*aus* of); (*Agr*) mixed crop; (*fig*) mixture; (*wirres Durcheinander*) jumble (*aus* of). (**b**) (*Gewühl*) bustle; (*Hand~*) scuffle. **mit jdm ins ~ kommen** to come to blows with sb.
Gemengsel *nt* mixture (*aus* of).
gemessen 1 *ptp of* **messen. 2** *adj* (**a**) (*würdevoll*) measured, studied. **~en Schrittes** with measured tread. (**b**) (*dated: zurückhaltend*) reticent. (**c**) *attr* (*angemessen*) *Abstand, Entfernung* respectful.
Gemessenheit *f siehe adj* (**a**) measuredness, studiedness. (**b**) reticence. (**c**) respectfulness.
Gemetzel *nt* **-s,** - bloodbath; (*Massaker auch*) slaughter, massacre.
gemieden *ptp of* **meiden.**
Gemisch *nt* **-(e)s, -e** (**a**) (*lit, fig*) mixture (*aus* of). (**b**) *no pl* (*Durcheinander*) jumble (*aus* of).
gemischt 1 *ptp of* **mischen. 2** *adj* mixed; (*inf: nicht sehr gut auch*) patchy. **mit ~en Gefühlen** with mixed feelings.
Gemischt-: **g~rassig** *adj* of mixed race; (*mit mehreren Rassen*) multi-racial; **g~sprachig** *adj* multilingual; ~**warenhandlung** *f* (*dated*) grocery and general store; **g~wirtschaftlich** *adj* mixed.
gemittelt *adj* standardized.
Gemme *f* **-, -n** (*erhaben*) cameo; (*vertieft*) intaglio.
gemocht *ptp of* **mögen.**
gemolken *ptp of* **melken.**
gemoppelt *adj siehe* **doppelt.**
Gemotze *nt* **-s,** *no pl* (*sl*) moaning, fault-finding.

Gems-: ~**bart** *m siehe* **Gamsbart**; ~**bock** *m* chamois buck.
Gemse *f* **-, -n** chamois.
Gemsleder *nt siehe* **Gamsleder.**
Gemunkel *nt* **-s,** *no pl* rumours; (*Klatsch*) gossip. **es geht das ~ daß ...** there's a rumour going round *or* the whisper is that ...
Gemurmel *nt* **-s,** *no pl* murmuring; (*unverständliches Reden auch*) mumbling. **zustimmendes ~ ging durch den Saal** a murmur of approval ran through the hall.
Gemurre *nt* **-s,** *no pl* (*inf*) grumbling (*inf*).
Gemüse *nt* **-s,** (*rare*) - vegetables *pl*. **frisches ~** fresh vegetables; **ein ~** a vegetable; **junges ~** (*hum inf*) whippersnappers *pl* (*inf*), green young things *pl* (*inf*).
Gemüse-: ~**(an)bau** *m* vegetable-growing; (*für den Handel*) market gardening (*Brit*), truck farming (*US*); ~**beet** *nt* vegetable bed *or* patch; ~**beilage** *f* vegetables *pl*; ~**beilage nach Wunsch** a choice of vegetables; ~**eintopf** *m* vegetable stew; ~**fach** *nt* vegetable compartment; ~**frau** *f* (*inf*) vegetable woman (*inf*); ~**fritze** *m* **-n, -n** (*inf*) vegetable seller; ~**garten** *m* vegetable *or* kitchen garden; **quer durch den ~garten** (*hum inf*) a real assortment; **in dem Geschäft dort gibt es alles quer durch den ~garten** they have everything but the kitchen sink in that shop there (*inf*); ~**händler** *m* greengrocer; (*Großhändler*) vegetable supplier; ~**handlung** *f* greengrocer's (shop); ~**konserve** *f* tinned (*Brit*) *or* canned vegetables *pl*; (*in Gläsern*) preserved vegetables *pl*; ~**laden** *m* greengrocer's (shop); ~**markt** *m* vegetable market; ~**paprika** *m* pepper, capsicum; ~**pflanze** *f* vegetable; ~**platte** *f* (*Cook*) eine ~platte assorted vegetables *pl*; ~**saft** *m* vegetable juice; ~**sorte** *f* kind *or* type of vegetable; ~**suppe** *f* vegetable soup.
gemüßigt *adv siehe* **bemüßigt.**
gemußt *ptp of* **müssen.**
gemustert 1 *ptp of* **mustern. 2** *adj* patterned.
Gemüt *nt* **-(e)s, -er** (**a**) (*Geist*) mind; (*Charakter*) nature, disposition; (*Seele*) soul; (*Gefühl*) feeling; (*Gutmütigkeit*) warm-heartedness. **ganz ~ sein, viel ~ haben** to be very warm-hearted; **die Menschen hatten damals mehr ~** people had more soul in those days; **das denkst du (dir) so einfach in deinem kindlichen ~!** that's what you think in your innocence; **etwas fürs ~** (*hum*) something for the soul; (*Film, Buch etc*) something sentimental; **jds ~ bewegen** (*liter*) *or* **erregen** (*liter*) to stir sb's heart *or* emotions; **sich** (*dat*) **etw zu ~e führen** (*beherzigen*) to take sth to heart; (*hum inf*) *Glas Wein, Speise, Buch etc* to indulge in sth; **das ist ihr aufs ~ geschlagen** that made her worry her heart out.
(b) (*fig: Mensch*) person; (*pl*) people. **sie ist ein ängstliches ~** she's a nervous soul, she has a nervous disposition; **die ~er erregen** to cause a stir; **wir müssen warten, bis sich die ~er abgekühlt** *or* **beruhigt haben** we must wait until feelings have cooled down.
gemütlich *adj* (**a**) (*bequem, behaglich*) comfortable, comfy (*inf*); (*freundlich*) friendly *no adv*; (*zwanglos*) informal; (*klein und intim*) cosy, snug; *Schwatz, Beisammensein etc* cosy. **wir verbrachten einen ~en Abend** we spent a very pleasant evening; **es sich/jdm ~ machen** to make oneself/sb comfortable. (**b**) *Mensch* good-natured, pleasant; (*leutselig*) approachable, friendly; (*gelassen*) easy-going *no adv*, relaxed *no adv*. (**c**) (*gemächlich*) unhurried, leisurely *no adv*. **in ~em Tempo** at a comfortable *or* leisurely speed; **er arbeitete ~ vor sich hin** he worked away at a leisurely pace *or* unhurriedly; **nur immer ~!** (*inf*) take it easy!
Gemütlichkeit *f siehe adj* (**a**) comfortableness; friendliness; informality; cosiness, snugness.
(b) good-naturedness, pleasantness; approachability, friendliness; easy-going nature. **da hört doch die ~ auf!** (*inf*) that's going too far; **da hört bei mir die ~ auf** I won't stand for that; **ein Prosit der ~.** happy days!
(c) unhurriedness, leisure. **in aller ~** at one's leisure; **ihr sitzt da in aller ~, und ich arbeite wie ein Verrückter** you sit there as though there were all the time in the world and I'm working like mad.
Gemüts-: **g~arm** *adj* emotionally impoverished; ~**armut** *f* emotional impoverishment; ~**art** *f* disposition, nature; **ein Mensch von heiterer ~art** a person of cheerful disposition *or* nature; ~**athlet** *m* (*iro*) emotional iceberg; ~**bewegung** *f* emotion; **bist du zu keiner ~bewegung fähig?** can't you show some emotion?; ~**fetzen** *m* (*inf*) tear-jerker; **g~kalt** *adj* cold; **g~krank** *adj* emotionally disturbed; ~**kranke(r)** *mf* emotionally disturbed person; ~**krankheit** *f* emotional disorder *or* disturbance; ~**krüppel** *m* (*inf*) emotional cripple; ~**lage** *f* mood; **je nach ~lage** as the mood takes me/him *etc*; ~**leben** *nt* emotional life; ~**leiden** *nt siehe* ~**krankheit**; ~**mensch** *m* good-natured, phlegmatic person; **du bist vielleicht ein ~mensch!** (*iro inf*) you're a fine one! (*inf*); (*das ist unmöglich*) you'll be lucky! (*inf*); ~**regung** *f siehe* ~**bewegung**; ~**ruhe** *f* calmness; (*Kaltblütigkeit*) sang-froid, composure, coolness; (*Phlegma*) placidness; **in aller ~ruhe** (*inf*) (as) cool as a cucumber (*inf*) *or* as you please (*inf*); (*gemächlich*) at a leisurely pace; (*aufreizend langsam*) as if there were all the time in the world; **du hast eine ~ruhe!** you take everything so calmly; **deine ~ruhe möchte ich haben!** (*iro*) I like your cool! (*inf*); ~**verfassung** *f*, ~**zustand** *m* frame *or* state of mind.
gemütvoll *adj* sentimental; (*warmherzig*) warm-hearted.
gen *prep* + *acc* (*old, liter*) towards, toward. **~ Norden/Osten** *etc* northwards/eastwards *etc*; **~ Himmel blicken** to look up to the sky, to look heavenwards; *siehe* **gegen.**
Gen *nt* **-s, -e** gene.
genannt *ptp of* **nennen.**
genant [ʒe'nant] *adj* (*dated*) (*schüchtern*) bashful, shy; (*peinlich*) embarrassing.
genarbt *adj Leder* grained.

genas pret of **genesen**.
genäschig adj siehe **naschhaft**.
Genäsel nt -s, no pl nasal voice.
genau 1 adj exact; (richtig auch) accurate; (präzis auch) precise; (sorgfältig auch) meticulous; (förmlich ~ auch) punctilious. **haben Sie die ~e Zeit?** have you got the right or exact time?; **G~eres** further details pl or particulars pl; **G~eres weiß ich nicht** I don't know any more than that; **man weiß nichts G~es über ihn** no-one knows anything definite about him.
2 adv ~! (inf) exactly!, precisely!, quite!; ~ **dasselbe** just or exactly the same; ~ **das Gegenteil** just or exactly the opposite; ~ **in der Mitte** right in the middle; ~ **das wollte ich sagen** that's just or exactly what I wanted to say; **ich kenne ihn** ~ I know just or exactly what he's like; **etw** ~ **wissen** to know sth for certain or for sure; **etw** ~ **nehmen** to take sth seriously; **er nimmt es sehr/nicht sehr** ~ he's very/not very particular (mit etw about sth); **einen Entschluß** ~ **überlegen** to think a decision over very carefully; **meine Uhr geht** ~ my watch keeps accurate time; **es stimmt auf den Millimeter** ~ it's right to the millimetre; **die Schuhe paßten mir** ~/**nicht ganz** ~ the shoes fitted me perfectly/didn't quite fit me; **das reicht** ~ that's just enough; ~**estens, aufs G~este** (right) down to the last (little) detail; ~ **entgegengesetzt** diametrically opposed; ~ **auf die Minute** dead (inf) or exactly on time; **so** ~ **wollte ich es** (nun auch wieder) **nicht wissen!** (iro) you can spare me the details; siehe **Wahrheit**.
genaugenommen adv strictly speaking.
Genauigkeit f siehe adj exactness, exactitude (form); accuracy; precision; meticulousness; punctiliousness.
genauso adv (vor Adjektiv) just as; (alleinstehend) just or exactly the same.
genauso- siehe **ebenso-**.
Gendarm [ʒanˈdarm, ʒãˈd-] m -en, -en (old, Aus) gendarme.
Gendarmerie [ʒandarməˈriː, ʒãd-] f (old, Aus) gendarmerie.
Genealoge m, **Genealogin** f genealogist.
Genealogie f genealogy.
genealogisch adj genealogical.
genehm adj (geh) suitable, acceptable. **jdm** ~ **sein** to suit sb; **ist es so** ~? is that agreeable or acceptable to you?; **wenn es** ~ **ist** if you are agreeable.
genehmigen* vt Baupläne, Antrag, Veränderungen to approve; (erlauben) to sanction; (Lizenz erteilen) to license; Durchreise, Aufenthalt to authorize; (zugestehen) to grant; Bitte auch to agree to, to assent to. **sich** (dat) **den Aufenthalt** ~ **lassen** to obtain authorization for one's stay; **wer kann mir den Urlaub** ~? from whom do I get permission for my holiday?; **sich** (dat) **etw** ~ to indulge in sth; (kaufen) to lash or splash out on sth; **sich** (dat) **einen** ~ (hum inf) to have a little drink.
Genehmigung f siehe vt (a) (das Genehmigen) approval; sanctioning; licensing; authorization; granting. (b) (Erlaubnis) approval; sanction; licence; authorization; agreement (gen to), assent (gen to); (Berechtigungsschein) permit. **mit freundlicher** ~ **von** by kind permission of.
Genehmigungs-: ~**pflicht** f (form) licence requirement; **g~pflichtig** adj (form) requiring official approval; (mit Visum, Stempel, Marke) requiring official authorization; (mit schriftlicher Genehmigung) requiring a licence; **Radiosender sind g~pflichtig** a licence is required for radio transmitters.
geneigt 1 ptp of **neigen**. 2 adj (geh) Zuhörer, Publikum willing; Aufmerksamkeit kind; (obs: huldvoll) gracious. ~**er Leser!** gentle reader; **jdm/einer Sache** ~ **sein** to be well-disposed or favourably disposed to sb/sth; **zu etw** ~ **sein/~ sein, etw zu tun** to be inclined to do sth; **nicht** ~ **sein, etw zu tun** not to be inclined to do sth; siehe **Ohr**.
Geneigtheit f (Bereitwilligkeit) inclination; (Wohlwollen) goodwill (gegenüber towards); (Huld) favour (gegenüber to). **bei aller** ~ **diesem Plan gegenüber, muß ich doch sagen ...** favourably disposed as I am to this plan, nevertheless I must say ...
Genera pl of **Genus**.
General m -(e)s, -e or ¨e (a) (Mil, Eccl) general. **Herr** ~ General. (b) (inf: ~direktor) head.
General-: ~**absolution** f general absolution; ~**agent** m general agent; ~**agentur** f general agency; ~**amnestie** f general amnesty; ~**angriff** m (Mil, fig) general attack; ~ **baß** m (basso) continuo; ~**beichte** f general confession; ~**bevollmächtigte(r)** mf plenipotentiary; (Comm) general representative; ~**bundesanwalt** m (BRD) Chief Federal Prosecutor; ~**direktion** f head office; ~**direktor** m chairman, president (US); ~**feldmarschall** m field marshal, general of the army (US); ~**gouverneur** m governor-general; ~**inspekteur** m (BRD) inspector general; ~**intendant** m (Theat, Mus) director.
Generalisation f generalization.
generalisieren* vi to generalize.
Generalisierung f generalization.
Generalissimus m -, **Generalissimi** or -se generalissimo.
Generalist m generalist.
Generalität f (Mil) generals pl.
General-: ~**klausel** f general or blanket clause; ~**konsul** m consul general; ~**konsulat** nt consulate general; ~**leutnant** m (BRD) lieutenant general; (Brit Aviat) air marshal; ~**major** m major general; ~**musikdirektor** m (chief) musical director; ~**nenner** m siehe **Hauptnenner**; ~**obere(r)** m (Eccl) general (of a religious order); ~**oberst** m (DDR) general; (Brit Aviat) air chief marshal; ~**prävention** f (Jur) general deterrence; ~**probe** f (Theat, fig) dress rehearsal; ~**repräsentanz** f (esp Aus) sole or exclusive agency or distribution; ~**sekretär** m secretary-general; ~**staatsanwalt** m public prosecutor for a provincial court, ≈ district attorney (US); ~**stab** m general

staff; ~**stäbler** m -s, - (inf) siehe ~**stabsoffizier**; ~**stabskarte** f Ordnance Survey map (on the scale 1:100,000); ~**stabsoffizier** m general staff officer; ~**streik** m general strike; ~**synode** f general synod; ~**überholen*** vt infin and ptp only etw **g~überholen** to give sth a general overhaul; **etw g~überholen lassen** to have sth generally overhauled; ~**überholung** f general overhaul; ~**versammlung** f general meeting; ~**vertreter** m general representative; ~**vertretung** f sole agency; ~**vikar** m vicar-general; ~**vollmacht** f general or full power of attorney.
Generation f generation.
Generationen-: ~**konflikt** m generation gap; **g~lang** 1 adj age-long; 2 adv for generations.
Generations-: ~**konflikt** m siehe **Generationenkonflikt**; ~**problem** nt problem of one generation; **ein** ~**problem der Jugend** a problem of the younger generation; ~**roman** m saga; ~**wechsel** m (Biol) alternation of generations; **wir brauchen einen** ~**wechsel in der Regierung** we need a new generation in government.
generativ adj generative. ~**e Zellen** reproductive cells; ~**e (Transformations)grammatik** (transformational) generative grammar.
Generator m generator; (Gas~ auch) producer.
Generatorgas nt producer gas.
generell adj general. ~ **kann man sagen, daß ...** generally or in general one can say that ...
generieren* vt (Ling, geh) to generate.
generös adj (geh) generous; (freigebig auch) munificent (liter).
Generosität f (geh) siehe adj generosity; munificence (liter).
Genese f -, -n (Biol, fig) genesis.
genesen pret **genas**, ptp ~ vi aux sein (a) (geh) to convalesce; (fig) to recuperate. (b) (obs: gebären) **sie genas eines Knaben** she was delivered of a boy child (obs liter).
Genesende(r) mf decl as adj convalescent.
Genesis f -, no pl genesis. **die** ~ (Bibl) (the Book of) Genesis.
Genesung f convalescence, recovery (auch fig). **auf dem Wege der** ~ on the road to recovery; **ich wünsche baldige** ~ I wish you a speedy recovery; **er fuhr zur** ~ **ins Sanatorium** he went into a sanatorium to convalesce.
Genesungs-: ~**heim** nt (dated) convalescent home; ~**prozeß** m convalescence; **der** ~**prozeß hat sich verzögert** his etc convalescence was protracted; ~**urlaub** m convalescent leave.
Genetik f genetics sing.
Genetiker(in f) m -s, - geneticist.
genetisch adj genetic.
Genezareth: **der See** ~ the Sea of Galilee.
Genf nt -s Geneva.
Genfer(in f) m -s, - Genevan, native or (Einwohner) inhabitant of Geneva.
Genfer adj attr Genevan. **der** ~ **See** Lake Geneva, Lake Leman; ~ **Konvention** f Geneva Convention.
genial adj Entdeckung, Einfall, Mensch brilliant; Künstler, Stil auch inspired; (erfinderisch) ingenious. **ein** ~**er Mensch, ein G~er** a genius; **ein** ~**es Werk** the work of a genius; **das war eine** ~**e Idee** that idea was or showed a stroke of genius.
genialisch adj (geh) brilliant; (unkonventionell) eccentric.
Genialität f genius; (Erfindungsreichtum) ingenuity.
Genick nt -(e)s, -e neck. **jdm am** ~ **packen** to grab sb by the scruff of the neck; **ein Schlag ins** ~ a blow on the back of the neck; **seinen Hut ins** ~ **schieben** to push one's hat back (on one's head); **sich** (dat) **das** ~ **brechen** to break one's neck; (fig) to kill oneself; **jdm/einer Sache das** ~ **brechen** (fig) to finish sb/sth.
Genick-: ~**schuß** m shot in the neck; ~**starre** f stiffness of the neck; (Med) (cerebral) meningitis; ~**starre haben** (inf) to have a stiff neck.
Genie¹ [ʒeˈniː] nt -s, -s genius. **er ist ein** ~ he's a (man of) genius; **er ist ein** ~ **im Taktieren** he's a genius when it comes to tactics, he has a genius for tactics.
Genie² f (Sw Mil) siehe **Genietruppe**.
Genien [ˈgeːniən] pl of **Genius**.
genieren* [ʒeˈniːrən] 1 vr to be embarrassed. **sich vor Fremden** ~ to be shy of or with strangers; **Sie sich nicht!** don't be shy!; **dabei geniere ich mich** I get embarrassed doing it; **ich geniere mich, das zu sagen** I don't like to say it; **er genierte sich (gar) nicht, das zu tun** it didn't bother him (at all) to do that.
2 vt jdn ~ (peinlich berühren) to embarrass sb; (old, dial: stören) to bother or disturb sb; **geniert es Sie, wenn ich rauche?** (old, dial) would it incommode you (old, form) or bother you if I smoke?; **das geniert mich wenig!** that doesn't bother or worry me.
genierlich [ʒeˈniːrlɪç] adj (a) (inf: lästig) bothersome; (genant) embarrassing. (b) (dated: schüchtern) shy, bashful.
geniert [ʒeˈniːrt] 1 ptp of **genieren**. 2 adj embarrassed. 3 adv with embarrassment.
genießbar adj (eßbar) edible; (trinkbar) drinkable; (fig: annehmbar) acceptable. **er ist heute nicht** ~ (fig inf) he is unbearable today.
genießen pret **genoß**, ptp **genossen** vt (a) (lit, fig: sich erfreuen an) to enjoy. **den Wein muß man** ~ you must savour the wine; **er ist heute nicht zu** ~ (inf) he is unbearable today. (b) (essen) to eat; (trinken) to drink. **das Essen/der Wein ist kaum zu** ~ the meal/wine is scarcely edible/drinkable; **ich habe noch nichts genossen** (geh) I have not yet partaken of anything (form); siehe **Vorsicht, Kavalier**.
Genießer(in f) m -s, - connoisseur; (des Lebens) pleasure-lover; (Feinschmecker) gourmet, epicure. **er ist ein richtiger/stiller** ~ he really knows how to enjoy life/he really knows how to enjoy life in his quiet way.
genießerisch 1 adj appreciative. **sein** ~**er Ausdruck** his

expression of pleasure. **2** *adv* appreciatively; (*mit Behagen*) pleasurably. ~ **schmatzte er mit den Lippen** he smacked his lips with relish; ~ **zog er an seiner Zigarre** he drew on his cigar with the utmost enjoyment.

Genie- [ʒe'niː]: ~**streich** *m* stroke of genius; ~**truppe** *f* (*Sw Mil*) engineer corps; ~**zeit** *f* Storm and Stress period.

genital *adj* genital.

Genital- *in cpds* genital.

Genitale *nt* **-s, Genitalien** [-iən] genital. **die Genitalien** the genitals *or* genitalia (*form*).

Genitiv *m* (*Fall*) genitive (case); (*Form*) genitive (form). **im** ~ in the genitive.

Genitivobjekt *nt* genitive object.

Genius *m* -, **Genien** ['geːniən] **(a)** (*Myth*) genius, guardian spirit. **(b)** (*Genie*) genius. ~ **loci** (*geh*) genius loci. **(c)** (*Art*) genius.

Genmutation *f* gene mutation.

Genom *nt* **-s, -e** genome.

genommen *ptp of* **nehmen**.

genoppt *adj* Teppich, Stoff, Wolle nubbly; Gummi pimpled.

Genörgel *nt* **-s**, *no pl* (*inf*) moaning, grumbling, carping.

genoß *pret of* **genießen**.

Genosse *m* **-n, -n** comrade; (*dated: Gefährte auch*) companion; (*Mitglied einer Genossenschaft*) member of a co-operative; (*pej: Kumpan*) mate (*Brit inf*), buddy (*US inf*), pal (*inf*). **X und ~n** (*Jur*) X and others; (*pej*) X and co (*inf*), X and his mates (*Brit inf*).

genossen *ptp of* **genießen**.

Genossen-: ~**schaft** *f* co-operative; ~**schaft(l)er** *m* **-s,** - member of a co-operative; **g~schaftlich** *adj* co-operative; **g~schaftlich organisiert** organized as a co-operative.

Genossenschafts-: ~**bank** *f* co-operative bank; ~**bauer** *m* co-operative farmer; ~**betrieb** *m* co-operative; ~**wesen** *nt* co-operative system.

Genossin *f siehe* **Genosse**.

genötigt 1 *ptp of* **nötigen**. **2** *adj* ~ **sein, etw zu tun** to be forced *or* obliged to do sth; **sich** ~ **sehen, etw zu tun** to feel (oneself) obliged to do sth.

Geno-: **g~typisch** *adj* genotypic; ~**typ(us)** *m* genotype; ~**zid** *m or nt* **-(e)s, -e** *or* **-ien** [-iən] (*geh*) genocide.

Genre [ʒãː, ʒãːrə] *nt* **-s, -s** genre.

Genre-: ~**bild** *nt* genre picture; ~**malerei** *f* genre painting.

Gent¹ *nt* **-s** Ghent.

Gent² [dʒɛnt] *m* **-s, -s** (*inf*) dandy.

Genua *nt* **-s** Genoa.

Genuese [genu'eːzə] *m* **-n, -n, Genueser(in** *f*) *m* **-s,** - Genoese.

genuesisch [genu'eːzɪʃ] *adj* Genoese.

genug *adj* enough. ~ **Platz, Platz** ~ enough *or* sufficient room; **groß/alt/reich** ~ big/old/rich enough; ~ **davon** enough of that; ~ **der vielen Worte!** enough of words!; **danke, das ist** ~ that's enough, thank you; **das ist wenig** ~ that's precious little; **und damit noch nicht** ~ and that's not/that wasn't all; **sie sind jetzt** ~, **um ...** there are enough of them now to ...; **sag, wenn's** ~ **ist!** (*beim Einschenken etc*) say when!; **jetzt ist('s) aber** ~! that's enough, that does it!; (*von etw*) ~ **haben** to have (got) enough (of sth); (*überdrüssig sein*) to have had enough (of sth); **er kann nicht** ~ **bekommen** *or* **kriegen** he can't get enough; **nicht** ~, **daß er sein ganzes Geld verspielt, außerdem ... er** ... not only does he gamble away all his money, he also ...; **er konnte sich nicht** ~ **darin tun, ihre Gastfreundschaft zu loben** (*geh*) he could not praise her hospitality enough *or* sufficiently; **sich** (*dat*) **selbst** ~ **sein** to be sufficient unto oneself; (*gern allein sein*) to be content with one's own company; **Manns** ~ **sein, um zu ...** to be man enough to ...

Genüge *f* -, *no pl* **zur** ~ enough; **das habe ich zur** ~ **getan/gehört/gesehen** I have done/heard/seen it often enough *or* (*stärker, abwertend*) quite often enough; **etw zur** ~ **kennen** to know sth well enough; (*abwertender*) to know sth only too well, to be only too familiar with sth; **wenn Sie sich zur** ~ **in der Bibliothek umgesehen haben, können Sie ...** if you have seen enough of the library you can ...; **jdm** ~ **tun** (*geh*) to satisfy sb; **jds Forderungen** ~ **tun** (*geh*) *or* **leisten** (*geh*) to satisfy *or* meet sb's demands; **jds Erwartungen** ~ **tun** (*geh*) *or* **leisten** (*geh*) to fulfil sb's expectations.

genügen* *vi* **(a)** (*ausreichen*) to be enough *or* sufficient (*dat* for). **das genügt (mir)** that's enough *or* sufficient (for me), that will do (for me); **diese Wohnung genügt uns/für uns** we're happy with this flat/this flat is enough for us.

(b) +*dat* (*befriedigen, gerecht werden*) **den Anforderungen** to satisfy; **jds Wünschen, Erwartungen, den Anforderungen** to fulfil.

genügend 1 *prp of* **genügen**. **2** *adj* **(a)** *inv* (*ausreichend*) enough, sufficient. **(b)** (*befriedigend*) satisfactory. **3** *adv* (*reichlich*) enough, sufficiently. **ich habe** ~ **oft versucht, zu ...** I have tried often enough *or* sufficiently often to ...

genugsam *adv* (*geh*) enough. **es ist** ~ **bekannt** it is sufficiently well-known; **es gibt noch** ~ **Menschen, die ...** there are still sufficient people who ...

genügsam *adj* (*anspruchslos*) Tier, Pflanze undemanding; Mensch *auch* modest. ~ **leben, ein** ~**es Leben führen** to live modestly.

Genügsamkeit *f siehe adj* simple needs *pl*; undemandingness, modesty. **die** ~ **einer Pflanze/eines Tieres** the modest requirements of a plant/an animal.

genugtun *vi sep irreg* +*dat* (*dated*) to satisfy. **er konnte sich** (*dat*) **nicht** ~, **ihre Schönheit zu preisen** he couldn't praise her beauty enough, he never tired of praising her beauty.

Genugtuung *f* satisfaction (*über* +*acc* at). **für etw** ~ **leisten** to make amends for sth; ~ **verlangen** *or* **fordern** to demand satisfaction; **ich hörte mit** ~, **daß ...** it gave me great satisfac-

---

tion to hear that ...; **das hat mir** ~ **verschafft** that gave me a sense of satisfaction.

Genus *nt* -, **Genera** **(a)** (*Biol*) genus. **(b)** (*Gram*) gender. ~ **verbi** voice of the verb.

Genuß *m* **-sses, ̈sse** **(a)** *no pl* (*das Zusichnehmen*) consumption; (*von Drogen*) taking, use; (*von Tabak*) smoking. **der** ~ **von Alkohol ist Kindern verboten** children are forbidden to drink *or* consume (*form*) alcohol; **der übermäßige** ~ **von Tabak ist gesundheitsschädlich** excessive smoking is injurious to one's health; **nach dem** ~ **der Pilze** after eating the mushrooms.

(b) (*Vergnügen*) pleasure. **die ̈sse des Lebens** the pleasures *or* joys of life; **etw mit** ~ **essen** to eat sth with relish; **den Wein hat er mit** ~ **getrunken** he really enjoyed the wine; **ich könnte ihn mit** ~ **verprügeln** I'd take great delight *or* pleasure in hitting him.

(c) *no pl* (*Nutznießung*) **in den** ~ **von etw kommen** (*von Vergünstigungen*) to enjoy sth; (*von Rente, Prämie etc*) to be in receipt of sth.

Genuß-: **g~freudig** *adj* (*geh*) pleasure-loving *no adv*; ~**gift** *nt* (*form*) social drug.

genüßlich *adj* pleasurable. **er grunzte** ~ he grunted with obvious enjoyment; **er schmatzte** ~ he smacked his lips with relish.

Genuß-: ~**mensch** *m* hedonist; (*auf Essen und Trinken bezogen*) bon-vivant; ~**mittel** *nt* semi-luxury foods and tobacco; **g~reich** *adj* enjoyable; ~**sucht** *f* hedonism; **g~süchtig** *adj* hedonistic; **g~voll** *adj* Aufenthalt, Urlaub, Erlebnis, Abend delightful; Schmatzen appreciative; Lächeln gratified; **g~voll rekelte er sich vor dem warmen Feuer** he sprawled in front of the fire with obvious enjoyment.

Geodäsie *f* geodesy, geodetics *sing*.

Geodät(in *f*) *m* **-en, -en** geodesist.

geodätisch *adj* geodesic.

Geo-Dreieck *nt* (*inf*) set square.

Geograph(in *f*) *m* geographer.

Geographie *f* geography.

geographisch *adj no pred* geographic(al).

Geologe *m*, **Geologin** *f* geologist.

Geologie *f* geology.

geologisch *adj no pred* geological.

Geometer *m* **-s,** - **(a)** surveyor. **(b)** (*old*) geometrician.

Geometrie *f* geometry.

geometrisch *adj* geometric. ~**er Ort** locus.

Geomorphologie *f* geomorphology.

Geophysik *f* geophysics *sing*.

Geopolitik *f* geopolitics *pl or* (*Fach*) *sing*.

geopolitisch *adj no pred* geopolitical.

geordnet 1 *ptp of* **ordnen**. **2** *adj* Leben, Zustände well-ordered. **in** ~**en Verhältnissen leben** to live a well-ordered life; **Kinder aus** ~**en Verhältnissen** children from well-ordered backgrounds; ~**e Verhältnisse schaffen** to put things on an orderly basis.

Georgette [ʒɔr'ʒɛt] *f* **-, -s,** *or nt* **-s, -s** georgette.

Georgien [ge'ɔrgiən] *nt* **-s** Georgia (*in Caucasia*).

Georgier(in *f*) [ge'ɔrgiɐ, -iərin] *m* **-s,** - Georgian.

georgisch *adj* Georgian.

geozentrisch *adj* geocentric.

Gepäck *nt* **-(e)s** *no pl* luggage *no pl* (*Brit*), baggage *no pl*; (*Mil: Marsch~*) baggage; (*von Soldat, Pfadfinder etc*) kit; (*von Bergsteiger*) pack. **mit leichtem** ~ **reisen** to travel light.

Gepäck-, Gepäcks- (*Aus*): ~**abfertigung** *f* (*Vorgang*) (*am Bahnhof*) luggage *or* baggage processing; (*am Flughafen*) checking-in of luggage *or* baggage; (*Stelle*) (*am Bahnhof*) luggage *or* baggage office; (*am Flughafen*) luggage *or* baggage check-in; ~**ablage** *f* luggage *or* baggage rack; ~**annahme** *f* (*Vorgang*) checking-in of luggage *or* baggage; (*auch* ~**annahmestelle**) (*am Bahnhof*) (*zur Beförderung*) (in-counter of the) luggage *or* baggage office; (*zur Aufbewahrung*) (in-counter of the) left-luggage office (*Brit*) *or* checkroom (*US*); (*am Flughafen*) luggage *or* baggage check-in; **die** ~**annahme dauert ... it takes ...** to check in the luggage; ~**aufbewahrung** *f* (*das Aufbewahren*) looking after left luggage *no art*; (*auch* ~**aufbewahrungsstelle**) left-luggage office (*Brit*), checkroom (*US*); ~**aufbewahrungsschein** *m* left-luggage ticket (*Brit*), check number (*US*); ~**ausgabe** *f* (*auch* ~**ausgabestelle**) (*am Bahnhof*) (*zur Beförderung*) (out-counter of the) luggage *or* baggage office; (*zur Aufbewahrung*) (out-counter of the) left-luggage office (*Brit*) *or* checkroom (*US*); (*am Flughafen*) luggage *or* baggage reclaim; (*Vorgang*) **die** ~**ausgabe dauert ... it takes ...** to give *or* hand the luggage *or* baggage out; **wir müssen noch zur** ~**ausgabe** we still have to collect our luggage; ~**karren** *m* luggage *or* baggage trolley; ~**kontrolle** *f* luggage *or* baggage control *or* check; ~**marder** *m* (*Press sl*) luggage *or* baggage pilferer; ~**marsch** *m* (*Mil*) pack march; ~**netz** *nt* luggage *or* baggage rack; ~**raum** *m* luggage *or* baggage hold; ~**schalter** *m siehe* ~**annahme**; ~**schein** *m* luggage *or* baggage ticket; ~**schließfach** *nt* luggage *or* baggage locker; ~**stück** *nt* piece *or* item of luggage *or* baggage; ~**träger** *m* **(a)** (*Person*) porter (*Brit*), baggage handler; **(b)** (*am Fahrrad*) carrier; ~**versicherung** *f* luggage *or* baggage insurance; ~**wagen** *m* luggage van, baggage car (*US*).

gepanzert *ptp of* **panzern**.

Gepard *m* **-s, -e** cheetah.

gepfeffert 1 *ptp of* **pfeffern**. **2** *adj* (*inf*) (*hoch*) Preise, Mieten steep; Preise *auch* fancy (*inf*); (*schwierig*) Fragen, Prüfung tough; (*hart*) Kritik biting; Strafpredigt tough; (*anzüglich*) Witz, Geschichte spicy.

Gepfeife *nt* **-s,** *no pl* whistling.

gepfiffen *ptp of* **pfeifen**.

gepflegt 1 *ptp of* **pflegen**.

2 adj (a) (nicht vernachlässigt) well looked after; Garten auch well-tended; Hände, Parkanlagen auch well-kept; Mensch, Äußeres, Hund well-groomed; Aussehen well-groomed, soigné (liter).
(b) (inf: kultiviert, niveauvoll) civilized; Atmosphäre, Restaurant sophisticated; Ausdrucksweise, Gespräche cultured; Sprache, Stil cultured, refined; (angenehm) Abend pleasant. ein ganz ~es Bad nehmen to have a nice long bath.
(c) (erstklassig) Speisen, Weine select; (inf: von guter Qualität) decent. „~e Küche" "excellent cuisine".
3 adv (a) (kultiviert) sich ~ unterhalten to have a civilized conversation; sich ~ ausdrücken to have a cultured way of speaking; drück dich gefälligst ein bißchen ~er aus don't be so crude; sehr ~ wohnen to live in style; so richtig ~ essen gehen (inf) to go to a really nice restaurant; ~ tanzen gehen (inf) to go out to a good old-fashioned dance.
(b) (inf: gut, gründlich) ganz ~ ausschlafen/sich ganz ~ ausruhen to have a good long sleep/rest.
Gepflegtheit f (a) well-looked-after state. die ~ seines Aussehens his well-groomed appearance.
(b) die ~ ihrer Aussprache/ihres Stils her refined or cultured accent/style.
gepflogen (old) ptp of **pflegen**.
Gepflogenheit f (geh) (Gewohnheit) habit; (Verfahrensweise) practice; (Brauch) custom, tradition.
Geplänkel nt -s, - skirmish; (fig) squabble.
Geplapper nt -s, no pl babbling; (fig: Geschwätz auch) chatter(ing).
Geplärr(e) nt -(e)s, no pl bawling; (von Radio) blaring.
Geplätscher nt -s, no pl splashing; (pej inf: Unterhaltung) babbling.
geplättet 1 ptp of **plätten**. 2 adj pred (sl) floored (inf). ich bin ganz ~ (inf) I'm flabbergasted (inf).
Geplauder nt -s, no pl (geh) chatting.
Gepolter nt -s, no pl (Krach) din; (an Tür etc) banging, thudding; (von Kutsche etc) clattering; (inf: Geschimpfe) ranting. die Fässer fielen mit ~ die Treppe hinunter the barrels went thudding down the stairs.
gepr. abbr of **geprüft**.
Gepräge nt -s, no pl (auf Münzen) strike; (fig: Eigentümlichkeit) character; (Aura) aura. das hat den 60er Jahren ihr ~ gegeben or verliehen it has left its mark or stamp on the sixties.
Geprahle nt -s, no pl (inf) boasting, bragging.
Gepränge nt -s, no pl (geh) splendour, magnificence. widersagst du dem Satan und all seinem ~? (Eccl) do you renounce the devil and all his works?
Geprassel nt -s, no pl clatter(ing), rattle, rattling; (von Regen, Hagel) drumming; (von Feuer) crackle, crackling.
gepriesen ptp of **preisen**.
gepunktet adj Linie dotted; Stoff, Kleid spotted; (regelmäßig) polka-dot.
Gequake nt -s, no pl croaking; (pej inf: Geschwätz) chatter.
Gequäke nt -s, no pl (inf) (von Kind) whining; (von Radio) blaring.
gequält 1 ptp of **quälen**. 2 adj Lächeln forced; Miene, Ausdruck pained; Gesang, Stimme strained.
Gequassel nt -s, no pl (pej inf) chattering.
Gequatsche nt -s, no pl (pej sl) gabbing (inf); (Blödsinn) twaddle (inf).
Gequengel(e), Gequengle nt -s, no pl whining.
Gequieke nt -s, no pl squealing.
Gequietsche nt -s, no pl squeaking; (von Reifen, Mensch) squealing.
gequollen ptp of **quellen**.
Ger m -(e)s, -e (old) javelin used by the ancient Germanic peoples.
gerade, grade (inf) 1 adj straight; Zahl even; (aufrecht) Haltung upright; (fig: aufrichtig) Charakter honest; Mensch upright, upstanding. ~ gewachsen sein (Mensch) to be clean-limbed; (Baum) to be straight; eine ~ Körperhaltung haben to hold oneself up straight; in ~r Linie von jdm abstammen to be directly descended from sb; seine ~ Linie haben (fig) to remain true to oneself; seinen ~n Weg gehen (fig) to maintain one's integrity; jdn mit ~m und offenem Blick ansehen to look sb straight in the face; das ~ Gegenteil the exact or very opposite, exactly or just the opposite; ~sitzen/stehen to sit up/stand up straight; siehe fünf.
2 adv (a) (im Augenblick, soeben) just. wenn Sie ~ Zeit haben if you have time just now; wo Sie ~ da sind just while you're here; er wollte ~ aufstehen he was just about to get up; der Zug war ~ weg the train had just gone; ~ erst only just; da wir ~ von Geld sprechen, ... talking of money ...; es macht uns ~ so viel Spaß we're just enjoying it so much.
(b) (knapp) just. ~ so viel, daß er davon leben kann just enough for him to live on; sie hat die Prüfung ~ so bestanden she just about passed the exam; ~ noch only just; ~ noch zur rechten Zeit just in time; das hat ~ noch gefehlt! (iro) that's all we wanted!
(c) (genau) just; (direkt) right. es ist ~ 8 Uhr it's just 8 o'clock; ~ zur rechten Zeit at just or exactly the right time, just at the right time; ~ heute hab' ich an dich gedacht I was thinking of you just or only today; jdm ~ in die Augen sehen to look sb straight or right in the eyes; ~ deshalb that's just or exactly why; ~ umgekehrt or das Gegenteil exactly or just the opposite; das ist es ja ~! that's just or exactly it!; so ist es ~ richtig that's just or exactly right.
(d) (speziell, besonders) especially. ~, weil ... just because ...; ~ du solltest dafür Verständnis haben you should be particu-

larly understanding; sie ist nicht ~ eine Schönheit she's not exactly a beauty; das war nicht ~ schön/interessant that wasn't particularly or exactly nice/interesting; du kannst dich ~ beklagen (iro) what are you complaining about?, you've got a lot to complain about (iro).
(e) (ausgerechnet) warum ~ das? why that of all things?; warum ~ heute/ich? why today of all days/me of all people?; warum ~ im Winter/in Venedig? why in winter of all times/in Venice of all places?; ~ diesem Trottel mußte ich begegnen of all people I would have to meet that idiot; warum hat er es ~ so gemacht? why on earth did he do it like that?
(f) (inf: erst recht) nun ~! you try and stop me now! (inf); jetzt or nun ~ nicht! I'll be damned if I will! (inf).
Gerade f -n, -n (a) (Math) straight line. (b) (Sport) (von Renn-, Laufbahn) straight; (beim Boxen) straight left/right. seine rechte ~ traf ihn genau am Kinn he hit him with a straight right to the chin.
gerade-: ~aus adv straight ahead; gehen, fahren auch straight on; ~biegen vt sep irreg to straighten out; (fig inf auch) to put straight, to sort out; ~halten sep irreg 1 vt to hold straight; 2 vr to hold oneself (up) straight; G~halter m (shoulder) brace; ~heraus (inf) 1 adj pred forthright, frank, plain-spoken; 2 adv frankly; ~heraus gesagt quite frankly; ~legen vt sep to put straight; ~machen vt sep to straighten (out); ~nwegs adv siehe ~(s)wegs; ~richten vt sep to straighten up; (horizontal) to straighten out.
gerädert 1 ptp of **rädern**. 2 adj (inf) wie ~ sein, sich wie ~ fühlen to be or feel (absolutely) whacked (inf).
gerade-: ~sitzen vi sep irreg aux haben or sein to sit up straight; ~so adv siehe ebenso; ~sogut adv siehe ebensogut; ~soviel adv just as much; ~stehen vi sep irreg aux haben or sein (a) (aufrecht stehen) to stand up straight; (b) für jdn/etw ~stehen (fig) to be answerable or to answer for sb/sth; ~(s)wegs adv to get straight down to sth; er nahm ~(s)wegs dazu Stellung he voiced his opinion about it straight away or immediately; ~zu 1 adv (a) (beinahe) virtually, almost; (wirklich, durchaus) really; das ist doch ~zu Selbstmord that's nothing short of suicide, that's absolute suicide; das ist ja ~zu verblüffend/lächerlich! that is absolutely amazing/ridiculous!; (b) (ohne Umschweife) frankly; er sagte mir ~zu, daß ... he told me straight out or frankly that ...; ~zu aufs Ziel zusteuern (fig) to go straight to the point; 2 adj pred (inf: ehrlich) frank, candid; (unverblümt) blunt.
Gerad-: ~führung f (Tech) guide; ~heit f (fig) (Aufrichtigkeit) rectitude; (Freimut) frankness, candidness; g~linig adj straight; Abkomme, Abstammung direct; Entwicklung etc linear; (fig: aufrichtig) straight; die Straße verläuft g~linig durch die Wiesen the road runs in a straight line through the meadows; eine Straße g~linig anlegen to build a road in a straight line; g~linig denken/handeln to be straight; ~linigkeit f (lit, fig) straightness; g~sinnig adj (geh) upright; ~sinnigkeit f uprightness, integrity.
G(e)raffel nt -s, no pl (Aus, S Ger) siehe **Gerümpel**.
gerammelt 1 ptp of **rammeln**. 2 adv: ~ voll (inf) (jam-)packed (inf), chock-a-block (inf).
Gerangel nt -s, no pl (Balgerei) scrapping; (fig: zäher Kampf) wrangling. ein kurzes ~ der beiden Spieler a short scrap between the two players; das ~ um die Sonderangebote the tussle over the bargains.
Geranie [-iə] f geranium.
gerann pret of **gerinnen**.
gerannt ptp of **rennen**.
Geraschel nt -s, no pl rustle, rustling.
Gerassel nt -s, no pl rattle, rattling.
Gerät nt -(e)s, -e (a) piece of equipment; (Vorrichtung) device; (Apparat) gadget; (landwirtschaftliches ~) implement; (elektrisches ~) appliance; (Radio~, Fernseh~, Telefon) set; (Meß~) instrument; (Küchen~) utensil; (Werkzeug, Garten~) tool; (Turn~) piece of apparatus.
(b) no pl (Ausrüstung) equipment no pl; (von Handwerker) tools pl.
geraten[1] pret **geriet**, ptp **geraten** 1 vi aux sein (a) (zufällig gelangen) to get (in +acc into). an jdn ~ (jdn kennenlernen) to come across sb; (jdn bekommen) to find sb, to dig sb up (pej); an etw (acc) ~ to get sth, to come by sth; an einen Ort ~ to come to a place; an den Richtigen/Falschen ~ to come to the right/wrong person; an einer im Fahrzeug ~ to fall under a vehicle; mit der Hand in eine Maschine ~ to get one's hand caught in a machine; in Gefangenschaft ~ to be taken prisoner; in eine Falle ~ to fall into a trap; das Schiff ist in einen Sturm ~ the boat got caught in a storm; in Bewegung ~ to begin to move; ins Stocken/Schleudern ~ to come to a halt/get into a skid; in Brand ~ to catch fire; in Angst/Begeisterung/Schwierigkeiten ~ to get scared/enthusiastic/into difficulties; in Vergessenheit ~ to fall into oblivion; aus der Bahn ~ (lit) to come off or leave the track; (fig) to go off the rails; auf krumme Wege or die schiefe Bahn ~ to stray from the straight and narrow; aus der Fassung/der Form ~ to lose one's composure/one's shape; außer sich (acc) ~ (vor etw) to be beside oneself (with sth); unter schlechten Einfluß ~ to come under a bad influence; siehe Abweg, Haar etc.
(b) (sich entwickeln, gelingen, ausfallen) to turn out. ihm gerät einfach alles everything he does turns out well or is a success, everything always goes right for him; mein Aufsatz ist mir zu lang ~ my essay turned out too long; das Essen/die Torte ist mir schlecht or nicht ~ the meal (I cooked)/my cake didn't turn out well or wasn't a success; der Junge/Kaktus ist gut ~ the boy/cactus turned out well; nach jdm ~ to take after sb; zu etw ~ (geh) to develop into sth.

2 *adj* (*geh: ratsam*) advisable.

geraten² *ptp of* **raten, geraten¹**.

Geräte-: ~**raum** *m* equipment room; ~**schuppen** *m* toolshed; ~**turnen** *nt* apparatus gymnastics *no pl*.

Geratewohl *nt*: **aufs** ~ on the off-chance; (*aussuchen, auswählen etc*) at random; **er hat die Prüfung einfach aufs** ~ **versucht** he decided to have a go at the exam just on the off-chance of passing; **er ist aufs** ~ **nach Amerika ausgewandert** he emigrated to America just like that; **wir schlugen aufs** ~ **diesen Weg ein** we decided to trust to luck and come this way.

Gerätschaften *pl* (*Ausrüstung*) equipment *sing*; (*Werkzeug*) tools *pl*.

Geratter *nt* -s, *no pl* clatter(ing), rattle, rattling; (*von Maschinengewehr*) chatter(ing).

Geräucherte(s) *nt*, *no pl decl as adj* smoked meat *especially* bacon and ham.

geraum *adj attr* **vor** ~**er Zeit** some time ago; **seit** ~**er Zeit** for some time; **es dauerte eine** ~**e Weile** it took some time.

geräumig *adj* Haus, Zimmer spacious, roomy; *Koffer, Kofferraum auch* capacious.

Geräumigkeit *f*, *no pl siehe adj* spaciousness, roominess; capaciousness.

Geraune *nt* -s, *no pl* (*liter*) whispering.

Geraunze *nt* -s, *no pl* (*inf: S Ger, Aus*) grousing (*inf*), grouching (*inf*).

Geräusch *nt* -(e)s, -e sound; (*esp unangenehm*) noise. **der Arzt horchte meine Brust auf** ~**e ab** the doctor listened to my chest for any unusual sounds; **die** ~**e des Verkehrs** the noise of the traffic; **aus dem Keller hörte man verdächtige** ~**e** suspicious noises came from the cellar; **mit einem dumpfen** ~ with a dull thud.

Geräusch-: ~**archiv** *nt* sound archive *usu pl*; **g**~**arm** *adj* quiet; ~**dämpfung** *f* sound damping; (*stärker*) deadening of sound; **g**~**empfindlich** *adj* sensitive to noise; (*Tech*) sound-sensitive; ~**kulisse** *f* background noise; (*Film, Rad, TV*) sound effects *pl*; **g**~**los** *adj* silent; **g**~**los öffnete er die Tür** without a sound *or* noiselessly *or* silently he opened the door; ~**losigkeit** *f*, *no pl* quietness, noiselessness, silence; ~**messer** *m* sound level recorder; ~**pegel** *m* sound level; **g**~**voll** *adj* (*laut*) loud; (*lärmend*) noisy.

Geräusper *nt* -s, *no pl* throat-clearing.

gerben *vt* to tan. **vom Wetter gegerbte Haut** weather-beaten skin; *siehe* Fell.

Gerber *m* -s, - tanner.

Gerbera *f* -, -(s) (*Bot*) gerbera.

Gerberei *f* (a) *no pl* (*Gerben*) tanning. (b) (*Werkstatt*) tannery.

Gerberlohe *f* tanbark.

Gerbung *f* tanning.

gerecht *adj* (a) (*rechtgemäß, verdient*) just; (*unparteiisch auch*) fair; (*rechtschaffen*) upright. ~ **gegen jdn sein** to be fair *or* just to sb; ~**er Lohn für alle Arbeiter!** fair wages for all workers!; **seinen** ~**en Lohn bekommen** (*fig*) to get one's just deserts *or* reward; **das ist nur** ~ that's only fair *or* just; ~**er Gott** *or* **Himmel!** (*inf*) good heavens (above)!; **die G**~**en die** just; **Gott, der G**~**e** God the righteous; **den G**~**en muß viel leiden** (*prov*) no peace for the wicked (*iro prov*); **den Schlaf des G**~**en schlafen** (*usu hum*) to sleep the sleep of the just.

(b) (*berechtigt*) just, legitimate. ~**er Zorn** righteous anger; **sich für eine** ~**e Sache einsetzen** to fight for a just cause.

(c) **jdm/einer Sache** ~ **werden** to do justice to sb/sth; **den Bedingungen** ~ **werden** to fulfil the conditions; **jds Erwartungen** (*dat*) ~ **werden** to come up to *or* fulfil sb's expectations; *siehe* Sattel.

-gerecht *adj suf* suitable for.

gerechterweise *adv* to be fair.

gerechtfertigt **1** *ptp of* **rechtfertigen**. **2** *adj* justified.

Gerechtigkeit *f* (a) justice; (*das Gerechtsein*) justness; (*Unparteilichkeit*) fairness; (*Rechtschaffenheit*) righteousness. **die** ~ **nahm ihren Lauf** justice took its course; **jdm/einer Sache** ~ **widerfahren lassen** to be just to sb/sth; (*fig*) to do justice to sb/sth. (b) (*geh: Gerichtsbarkeit*) justice. **jdn (den Händen) der** ~ **ausliefern** to bring sb to justice.

Gerechtigkeits-: ~**fimmel** *m* (*pej inf*) thing about justice (*inf*); ~**gefühl** *nt* sense of justice; ~**liebe** *f* love of justice; **g**~**liebend** *adj* **ein g**~**liebender Mensch** a lover of justice, a person with a love of justice; **g**~**liebend sein** to have a love of justice; ~**sinn** *m* sense of justice.

Gerechtsame *f* -, -**n** (*Hist*) rights *pl*. **eine** ~ **für die Jagd** hunting rights *pl*.

Gerede *nt* -s, *no pl* talk; (*Klatsch*) gossip(ing). **ins** ~ **kommen** *or* **geraten** to get oneself talked about; **jdn ins** ~ **bringen** to get sb talked about; **kümmere dich nicht um das** ~ **der Leute** don't worry about what people say.

geregelt **1** *ptp of* **regeln**. **2** *adj* Arbeit(szeiten), Mahlzeiten regular; Leben well-ordered.

gereichen* *vi* (*geh*) **jdm zur Ehre** ~ to do sb honour, to redound to sb's honour (*form*); **jdm zum Schaden/Nutzen** ~ to be damaging/beneficial to sb, to redound to sb's benefit (*form*); **jdm/einer Sache zum Vorteil** ~ to be an advantage to sb/sth, to redound to sb's advantage (*form*); (*vorteilhaft einzuschätzen lassen*) to be advantageous for sb/sth; **zur Zierde** ~ to be decorative.

gereift **1** *ptp of* **reifen**. **2** *adj* (*fig*) mature.

Gereiftheit *f* (*fig*) maturity.

gereizt **1** *ptp of* **reizen**. **2** *adj* (*verärgert*) irritated; (*reizbar*) irritable, touchy; (*nervös*) tetchy, edgy. **im Zimmer herrschte** ~**e Stimmung** there was a strained atmosphere in the room.

Gereiztheit *f siehe adj* irritation; irritability; tetchiness, edginess; strainedness; touchiness.

Gerenne *nt* -s, *no pl* (*inf*) running, racing; (*das Umherlaufen*) running *or* racing about *or* around.

gereuen* (*old, geh*) **1** *vt impers* **es gereut mich, daß ... I** regret that ..., I am sorry that ...; **es wird Sie nicht** ~ you will not regret it. **2** *vt* **meine Tat gereut mich** I regret my action.

Gerfalke *m* gyrfalcon, gerfalcon.

Geriater *m* -s, - geriatrician.

Geriatrie *f* geriatrics *sing*.

Geriatrikum *nt* -s, **Geriatrika** geriatric medicine.

geriatrisch *adj* geriatric.

Gericht¹ *nt* -(e)s, -e (*Speise*) dish. **leckere** ~**e** delicious meals.

Gericht² *nt* -(e)s, -e (a) (*Behörde*) court (of justice); (*Gebäude*) court(house), law courts *pl*; (*die Richter*) court, bench. **Hohes** ~! My Lord! (*Brit*), Your Honor! (*US*); **vor** ~ **erscheinen/aussagen** to appear/testify in court; **vor** ~ **kommen** (*Fall*) to come to court; (*Mensch*) to come *or* appear before a/the court; **vor** ~ **stehen** to stand trial; **jdn vor** ~ **laden** to summon *or* call sb to appear in court; **jdn/einen Fall vor** ~ **bringen** to take sb/sth to court; **mit etw vor** ~ **gehen** to go to court *or* take legal action about sth; **jdn bei** ~ **verklagen** to take sb to court; **jdn/einen Fall vor** ~ **vertreten** to represent sb/sth in court; **das** ~ **zieht sich zur Beratung zurück** the court will adjourn.

(b) **das Jüngste** *or* **Letzte** ~ the Last Judgement; **über jdn/etw** ~ **halten** to pronounce judgement on sb/sth; **über jdn zu** ~ **sitzen** (*fig*) to sit in judgement on sb; **mit jdm (scharf) ins** ~ **gehen** (*fig*) to judge sb harshly.

gerichtlich *adj attr* judicial; Bestimmung, Entscheidung etc court; Medizin, Psychologie forensic; Verhandlung legal. **laut** ~**em Beschluß** according to the decision of a/the court *or* a/the court decision; **ein** ~**es Nachspiel** a court sequel; **ein** ~**es Nachspiel haben** to finish up in court; ~**gegen jdn vorgehen** to take court proceedings against sb, to litigate against sb; **eine Sache** ~ **or auf** ~**em Weg klären** to settle a matter in court *or* by litigation; **Schulden** ~ **eintreiben** to recover debts through the courts; **jdn** ~ **für tot erklären lassen** to have sb legally declared dead; ~ **vereidigt** sworn.

Gerichts-: ~**akten** *pl* court records *pl*; ~**arzt** *m* court doctor; ~**assessor** *m* ≈ junior barrister (*Brit*) *or* lawyer.

Gerichtsbarkeit *f* jurisdiction.

Gerichts-: ~**berichterstatter** *m* legal correspondent; ~**beschluß** *m* decision of a/the court, court decision; ~**bezirk** *m* juridical district; ~**bote** *m* (*old*) messenger of the court; ~**diener** *m* (*old*) court usher; ~**entscheid** *m*, ~**entscheidung** *f* court decision; ~**ferien** *pl* court vacation, recess; ~**gebühren** *pl siehe* ~**kosten**; ~**herr** *m* (*Hist*) lord of the manor; ~**hof** *m* court (of justice), law court; **Oberster** ~**hof** Supreme Court (of Justice); **Hoher** ~**hof!** (*old*) may it please your lordships; **der Hohe** ~**hof** the high court; ~**hoheit** *f* jurisdiction; ~**kasse** *f* **den Betrag von DM 200 an die** ~**kasse zahlen** to pay the court DM 200; ~**kosten** *pl* court costs *pl*; **jdn zum Tragen der** ~**kosten verurteilen, jdm die** ~**kosten auferlegen** (*form*) to order sb to pay costs; **g**~**kundig** *adj siehe* **g**~**notorisch**; ~**medizin** *f* forensic medicine, medical jurisprudence; ~**mediziner** *m* forensic doctor; **g**~**medizinisch** *adj* forensic medical *attr*; **die Leiche wurde g**~**medizinisch untersucht** the body was examined by an expert in forensic medicine; **g**~**notorisch** *adj* known to the court; ~**ordnung** *f* rules *pl* of the court; ~**ort** *m* town etc with a court; ~**präsident** *m* president of the court; ~**referendar** *m* law student who has passed the first State Examination ≈ articled barrister (Brit); ~**reporter** *m* legal correspondent; ~**saal** *m* courtroom; ~**schreiber** *m* clerk of the court; ~**sprache** *f* language of the courts; ~**stand** *m* (*form*) court of jurisdiction; ~**tafel** *f* court notice board; (*für öffentliche Bekanntmachungen*) ≈ public notice board; ~**tag** *m* court day; **Montag ist** ~**tag** the court sits on Monday *or* is in session on Monday; ~**tag über sich selbst halten** (*fig*) to sit in judgement on oneself; ~**termin** *m* date of a/the trial; (*für Zivilsachen*) date of a/the hearing; **einen** ~**termin ansetzen** to fix a date for a/the trial/hearing; **der** ~**termin für diesen Prozeß** the date fixed for this trial/hearing; ~**verfahren** *nt* court *or* legal proceedings *pl*; **ein** ~**verfahren gegen jdn einleiten** to institute court proceedings against sb; (*zivil auch*) to litigate against sb; **er wurde ohne ordentliches** ~**verfahren verurteilt** he was sentenced without a proper trial; ~**verfassung** *f* legal constitution; ~**verhandlung** *f* trial; (*zivil*) hearing; ~**vollzieher** *m* bailiff; ~**weg** *m* **auf dem** ~**weg** through the courts; ~**wesen** *nt* judiciary, judicial system.

gerieben **1** *ptp of* **reiben**. **2** *adj* (*fig inf*) smart, sharp; (*verschlagen auch*) tricky, sly, fly (*inf*). **der ist verdammt** ~ (*inf*) there are no flies on him (*inf*).

Geriebenheit *f*, *no pl* smartness, sharpness; (*Verschlagenheit auch*) trickiness, slyness, flyness (*inf*).

Geriesel *nt* -s, *no pl* (*von Sand*) trickling; (*von Schnee*) floating down.

geriet *pret of* **geraten¹**.

gering *adj* (a) (*nicht sehr groß, niedrig*) Temperatur, Luftdruck, Leistung low; Gehalt, Preis low, modest; Menge, Vorrat, Betrag, Produktion, Entfernung, small; Wert little *attr*; (*kurz*) Zeit, Entfernung short. **mit** ~**en Ausnahmen** with few exceptions; **Berge von** ~**er Höhe** low hills; **etw in** ~**er Höhe anbringen** to fix sth fairly low down; ~ **gerechnet** at a conservative estimate; **seine Leistung erhielt eine zu** ~**e Bewertung** his achievement wasn't rated highly enough; **ein Mann von** ~**em Selbstbewußtsein** a man with very little self-confidence.

(b) (*unbedeutend, unerheblich*) slight; Chance *auch* small, slim; Bedeutung, Rolle minor. **die** ~**ste Kleinigkeit** the least *or* smallest *or* slightest little thing; **das ist meine** ~**ste Sorge** that's the least of my worries; **die Kosten sind nicht** ~ the costs are not inconsiderable; **nicht das G**~**ste** nothing at all; **nicht im** ~**sten** not in the least *or* slightest; **das G**~**ste** the least thing

nichts G~eres als ... nothing less than ...; **um ein G~es** (old) (für wenig Geld) for a small amount; (ein wenig) a little; (fast) very nearly.
(c) (unzulänglich) Qualität, Kenntnisse poor; (abschätzig) Meinung low, poor. ~ **von jdm sprechen/denken** to speak badly/ have a low opinion of sb.
(d) attr (fig geh) Familie, Herkunft humble. **(auch) der G~ste** even the most humble person; **kein G~erer als Freud** ... no less a person than Freud.
gering|achten vt sep siehe **geringschätzen.**
geringelt adj (a) Muster ringed; Socken hooped; siehe **ringeln.**
(b) (lockig) Haare curly.
Gering-: g~fügig adj (unwichtig) insignificant; Verbesserung, Unterschied slight; Vergehen, Verletzung minor; Einzelheiten minor, trivial; Betrag small; **sein Zustand hat sich g~fügig gebessert** his condition is marginally or slightly improved; ~fügigkeit f (a) insignificance; slightness; (von Vergehen, Einzelheiten) triviality; smallness; **ein Verfahren wegen ~fügigkeit einstellen** (Jur) to dismiss a case because of the trifling nature of the offence; (b) (Kleinigkeit) little or small thing, trifle; g~schätzen vt sep (verachten) Menschen, Leistung to think little of, to have a poor or low opinion of; Erfolg, Reichtum to set little store by, to place little value on; menschliches Leben to have scant regard for, to place little value on; (mißachten) Gefahr, Folgen to disregard; **eine Tugend, die man nicht g~schätzen sollte** a virtue not to be despised; g~schätzig adj contemptuous; Bemerkung auch disparaging; ~schätzigkeit f contemptuousness; disparagement; ~schätzung f, no pl (Ablehnung) disdain; (von Bemerkung) disparagement (für, gen of); (schlechte Meinung) poor or low opinion (für, gen of); (für Erfolg, Reichtum, menschliches Leben) low regard (für, gen for).
geringstenfalls adj (geh) at the (very) least.
geringwertig adj (rare) inferior; Nahrung low-value.
gerinnbar adj siehe **gerinnungsfähig.**
gerinnen pret **gerann,** ptp **geronnen** vi aux sein to coagulate; (Blut auch) to clot; (Milch auch) to curdle. **mir gerann (vor Schreck) das Blut in den Adern** (fig) my blood ran cold; **zu etw ~** (fig geh) to develop into sth.
Gerinnsel nt (a) (Blut~) clot, coagulum (spec). (b) (geh: Rinnsal) rivulet, trickle.
Gerinnung f siehe vi coagulation; clotting; curdling.
Gerinnungs-: g~fähig adj coagulable; ~fähigkeit f coagulability.
Gerippe nt -s, - skeleton; (von Schiff, Flugzeug auch, von Schirm, Gebäude) frame; (von Blatt auch) ribbing; (fig: Grundplan) framework. **er ist nur noch ein ~** he's nothing but skin and bones.
gerippt adj ribbed no adv; Säule fluted no adv.
G(e)riß nt -sses, no pl (Aus inf) crush.
gerissen 1 ptp of **reißen.** 2 adj crafty, cunning.
Gerissenheit f cunning.
geritten ptp of **reiten.**
geritzt 1 ptp of **ritzen.** 2 adj pred (inf) **die Sache ist ~** everything's fixed up or settled.
Germ m or f, no pl (Aus) baker's yeast.
Germane m -n, -n Teuton. **die alten ~n** the Teutons.
Germanentum nt Teutonicism; (Kultur) Teutonism; (Gesamtheit der Germanen) Teutonic world, Teutons pl.
Germania f - (Myth) Germania.
Germanien [-iən] nt -s Germania.
Germanin f Teuton.
germanisch adj Germanic. **G~es Seminar** Institute of Germanic Studies.
germanisieren* vt to Germanize.
Germanisierung f Germanization.
Germanismus m (Ling) Germanism.
Germanist(in f) m Germanist; (Student auch) German student; (Wissenschaftler auch) German specialist.
Germanistik f German (studies pl). ~ **studieren** to do German studies, to study German; **Professor der ~** professor of German studies or German.
germanistisch adj German; Zeitschrift on Germanic/German studies.
Germanium nt, no pl germanium.
Germano- (geh): g~phil adj Germanophile; ~philie f Germanophilia; g~phob adj Germanophobe; ~phobie f Germanophobia.
gern(e) adv, comp **lieber,** superl **am liebsten** (a) (freudig) with pleasure; (bereitwillig auch) willingly, readily. **(aber) ~!** of course!; **ja, ~!** (yes) please; **kommst du mit?** — **ja, ~** are you coming too? — oh yes, I'd like to; **darf ich das?** — **ja, ~** can I do that? — (yes,) of course; **~ geschehen!** you're welcome! (esp US), not at all!, my pleasure!; **„Witwer, 61, sucht Partnerin, ~ älter/mit Kindern"** "widower, aged 61, seeks partner, age not important/children not a problem"; **von mir aus kann er ja ~ älter sein** I don't mind if he's older; **etw ~ tun** to like doing sth or to do sth (esp US); **etw ~ essen/trinken** to like sth; **sie ißt am liebsten Spargel** asparagus is her favourite food; **~ ins Kino gehen** to like or enjoy going to the cinema; **das tue ich für mein Leben ~** I adore doing that; **etw ~ sehen** to like to see sth; **das sähe ich ~** I would welcome it; **das wird nicht ~ gesehen** that's frowned (up)on; **er sieht es nicht ~, wenn wir zu spät kommen** he doesn't like us coming too late; **ein ~ gesehener Gast** a welcome visitor; **das glaube ich ~** I can quite or well believe it, I'm quite willing to believe it; **das würde ich zu ~ tun** I'd really love to do that; **er macht seine Arbeit ~ und mit Freude** he does his work willingly and gets a lot of pleasure out of it; **ich stehe ~ zu Ihren Diensten** (old form) I am/would be happy or pleased to be of service to you; **ich bin ~ dazu bereit** I'm quite willing or

happy to do it; **jdn/etw ~ haben** or **mögen** to like or be fond of sb/sth; **jdn/etw am liebsten haben** or **mögen** to like sb/sth best or most; **das kannst du ~ haben** you're welcome to it, you can have it with pleasure; **er hat es ~,** wenn man ihm schmeichelt he likes being flattered, he likes it when you flatter him; **ich hätte or möchte ~ ...** I would like ...; **ich hätte ~ Herrn Kurtz gesprochen** could I speak to Mr Kurtz?, I would like to speak to Mr Kurtz, please; **wie hätten Sie's (denn) ~?** how would you like it?; **du kannst/er kann mich mal ~ haben!** (inf) (you can)/he can go to hell! (inf), stuff you/him! (sl); siehe **gut 2, lieber.**
(b) (gewöhnlich, oft) **etw ~ tun** to tend to do sth; **Weiden wachsen ~ an Flüssen** willows tend to grow by rivers; **morgens läßt er sich ~ viel Zeit** he likes to leave himself a lot of time in the mornings; **er ist ~ eingeschnappt** he gets upset easily.
Gernegroß m -, -e (hum) **er war schon immer ein kleiner ~** he always did like to act big (inf).
Geröchel nt -s, no pl groans pl; (von Sterbenden) (death-) rattle.
gerochen ptp of **riechen.**
Geröll nt -(e)s, -e, **Gerölle** (rare) nt -s, - detritus no pl; (im Gebirge auch) scree no pl; (größeres) boulders pl.
Geröll-: ~halde f scree (slope); ~schutt m rock debris.
geronnen ptp of **rinnen, gerinnen.**
Gerontokratie f (Pol) gerontocracy.
Gerontologe m, **Gerontologin** f (Med) gerontologist.
Gerontologie f (Med) gerontology.
gerontologisch adj (Med) gerontological.
Geröstete pl decl as adj (S Ger, Aus: Cook) sauté potatoes pl.
Gerste f -, -n barley.
Gersten- in cpds barley; ~graupen pl pearl barley sing; ~grütze f barley groats pl; (Brei) barley porridge; ~kaffee m coffee substitute made from malted barley; ~korn nt (a) barleycorn; (b) (Med) stye; ~saft m (hum) John Barleycorn (hum), beer; ~zucker m barley sugar.
Gerte f -, -n switch; (Reit~ auch) crop. **sie ist schlank wie eine ~** she is slim and willowy, she is as slender as a reed.
gertenschlank adj slim and willowy.
Geruch m -(e)s, -e (a) smell, odour (nach of); (Duft auch) fragrance, scent, perfume (nach of); (von Kuchen etc auch) aroma (nach of); (unangenehm auch) stench (nach of). **der starke ~ nach Alkohol/Knoblauch** the reek of alcohol/garlic.
(b) no pl (~ssinn) sense of smell.
(c) no pl (fig: Ruf) reputation. **in schlechtem ~ stehen** to be in bad odour (bei jdm with sb); **in den ~ von etw kommen** to get a reputation for sth; **er steht im ~, ein großer Gauner zu sein** he has the reputation of being a real rogue.
Geruch-: g~los adj odourless; (duftlos) scentless; g~los sein not to have a smell, to be odourless; (Blumen) not to smell; ~losigkeit f lack of smell.
Geruch(s)-: ~belästigung f **das ist eine ~belästigung** the smell is a real nuisance; g~bindend adj deodorizing no adv; ~empfindung f (a) (Riechempfindung) smell; (b) (~sinn) sense of smell; ~nerv m olfactory nerve; ~organ nt organ of smell, olfactory organ; ~sinn m sense of smell; ~verschluß m (Tech) odour trap; ~werkzeuge pl olfactory organs pl.
Gerücht nt -(e)s, -e rumour. **es geht das ~, daß ... there's a** rumour (going round) that ..., it's rumoured that ...; **das halte ich für ein ~** (inf) I have my doubts about that.
Gerüchte-: ~küche f (inf) gossip factory (inf); **die Pressestelle ist eine wahre ~küche** the press office is filled with rumourmongers; ~macher m rumour-monger.
geruchtilgend adj deodorizing no adv, deodorant attr.
gerüchteweise adv **etw ~ hören** to hear sth rumoured; **~ ist bekanntgeworden, daß ...** rumour has it that ...; **ich habe ~ erfahren, daß ...** I've heard or heard say that ...; **das ist mir ~ zu Ohren gekommen** I've heard it rumoured.
Geruckel nt -s, no pl jerking, jolting.
Gerufe nt -s, no pl calling.
gerufen ptp of **rufen.**
geruhen* vt ~, **etw zu tun** (dated form) to deign or condescend to do sth (auch iro), to be pleased to do sth.
geruhig adj (old) siehe **ruhig.**
geruhsam adj peaceful; Spaziergang etc leisurely no adv. ~ **essen** to eat in peace (and quiet); **jdm eine ~e Nacht wünschen** to wish sb a good night's rest.
Geruhsamkeit f siehe adj peacefulness; leisureliness.
Gerümpel nt -s, no pl rumbling, rumble.
Gerümpel nt -s, no pl junk.
Gerundium nt gerund.
gerundi(isch) adj gerundival.
Gerundiv(um) nt -s, -e gerundive.
gerungen ptp of **ringen.**
Gerüst nt -(e)s, -e scaffolding no pl; (Gestell) trestle; (Brücken~, Dach~) truss; (Hänge~) cradle; (fig: Gerippe) framework (zu of). **ein ~ aufstellen** to put up or erect scaffolding.
Gerüst-: ~bau m erection of scaffolding; „W. Friedrich GmbH, ~bau" "W. Friedrich Ltd, Scaffolders"; ~bauer m scaffolder; ~stange f scaffolding pole.
Gerüttel nt -s, no pl shaking (about); (im Zug, Wagen etc) jolting (about).
gerüttelt 1 ptp of **rütteln.** 2 adj ~ **voll** chock-a-block (inf), jam-packed (inf), chock-full; **ein ~es Maß von** or **an etw** (dat) a fair amount of sth; **er besitzt ein ~es Maß Unverschämtheit** he has more than his fair share of cheek.
ges, Ges nt -, - (Mus) G flat.
Gesalbte(r) m decl as adj (Rel) **der ~** the Lord's Anointed.
gesalzen 1 ptp of **salzen.** 2 adj (fig inf) Witz spicy; Preis, Rechnung steep, fancy (inf), stiff.
Gesalzene(s) nt decl as adj (Cook) salted meat.

gesammelt 1 *ptp of* **sammeln.** 2 *adj Aufmerksamkeit, Kraft* collective; *Werke* collected.

gesamt *adj attr* whole, entire. **die** ~**e Familie** all the family, the whole *or* entire family; **die** ~**en Lehrkräfte** all the teachers; **im** ~**en in** all; **die** ~**en Kosten** the total costs; **die** ~**en Werke Kleists** the complete works of Kleist.

Gesamt *nt* **-s,** *no pl* (*liter*) *siehe* **Gesamtheit.**

Gesamt-: ~**ansicht** *f* general *or* overall view; ~**auflage** *f* (*von Zeitung etc*) total circulation; (*von Buch*) total edition; **bisherige** ~**auflage: 300.000 Stück** sales totalling 300,000; ~**ausfuhr** *f* total exports *pl*; ~**ausgabe** *f* complete edition; ~**bedarf** *m* complete needs *pl*; ~**betrag** *m* total (amount); ~**bild** *nt* general *or* overall picture; **g~deutsch** *adj* all-German; **Ministerium für g~deutsche Fragen** (*Hist*) Ministry for all-German Affairs; ~**deutschland** *nt* all Germany; **ein** ~**deutschland hat nur von 1871 bis 1945 bestanden** there was one Germany *or* a united Germany only from 1871 to 1945; ~**eindruck** *m* general *or* overall impression; ~**einfuhr** *f* total imports *pl*; ~**einkommen** *nt* total income; ~**erbe** *m* sole heir (*gen* to); ~**ergebnis** *nt* overall result; ~**erlös** *m* total proceeds *pl*; ~**ertrag** *m* total yield; ~**fläche** *f* total area; ~**gesellschaft** *f* (*Sociol*) society as a whole; **g~gesellschaftlich** *adj* (*Sociol*) **Produktion** by society as a whole; ~**gewicht** *nt* total weight; (*eines LKW etc auch*) laden weight; ~**gläubiger** *pl* (*Jur*) joint creditors *pl*; **g~haft** (*esp Sw*) 1 *adj siehe* **gesamt;** 2 *adv siehe* **insgesamt;** ~**haftung** *f* (*Jur*) joint liability.

Gesamtheit *f* totality. **die** ~ **der ...** all the ...; (*die Summe*) the totality of ...; **die** ~ (**der Bevölkerung**) the population (as a whole); **die** ~ **der Studenten/Arbeiter** the entire student population/work-force, all the students/workers; **die** ~ **der Delegierten** all the delegates; **in seiner** ~ in its entirety; **das Volk in seiner** ~/**die Steuerzahler in ihrer** ~ the nation/taxpayers as a whole.

Gesamt-: ~**hochschule** *f* polytechnic, comprehensive university; ~**interesse** *nt* general interest; ~**kapital** *nt* total capital; ~**katalog** *m* union catalogue; ~**klassement** *nt* (*Sport*) overall placings *pl*; ~**kosten** *pl* total *or* overall costs *pl*; ~**kunstwerk** *nt* synthesis of the arts; ~**lage** *f* general situation; ~**masse** *f* (*Comm*) total assets *pl*; ~**note** *f* (*Sch*) overall mark; ~**planung** *f* overall planning; ~**schaden** *m* total damage; **ein** ~**schaden von 5.000 Mark** damage totalling 5,000 marks; ~**schau** *f* synopsis (*über + acc* of); ~**schuldner** *pl* (*Jur*) (joint) debtors *pl*; ~**schule** *f* comprehensive school; ~**sieger** *m* (*Sport*) overall winner; ~**stärke** *f* total strength; ~**stimmenzahl** *f* total number of votes cast; ~**strafe** *f* (*Jur*) overall sentence (*for a series of offences, longer than the maximum sentence for the most serious offence but less than the total sentences taken consecutively*); ~**summe** *f siehe* ~**betrag;** ~**übersicht** *f* general survey (*über + acc* of); ~**umsatz** *m* total turnover; ~**unterricht** *m* teaching which cuts across the traditional boundaries between subjects; ~**werk** *nt* complete works *pl*; ~**wert** *m* total value; **im** ~**wert von ...** totalling ... in value; ~**wertung** *f* (*Sport*) overall placings *pl*; **er liegt in der** ~**wertung vorn** he's leading overall, he has the overall lead; ~**wirkung** *f* general *or* overall effect; ~**wirtschaft** *f* national economy; **g~wirtschaftlich** *adj* national economic *attr*; **g~wirtschaftlich nicht vertretbar** not justifiable from the point of view of the national economy; ~**zahl** *f* total number; **eine** ~**zahl von 8.000 Punkten** a total of 8,000 points; ~**zusammenhang** *m* general view.

gesandt *ptp of* **senden**[1].

Gesandte(r) *m decl as adj,* **Gesandtin** *f* envoy, legate; (*inf: Botschafter*) ambassador. **päpstlicher** ~ (papal) nuncio.

Gesandtschaft *f* legation; (*inf: Botschaft*) embassy; (*päpstliche* ~) nunciature.

Gesang *m* **-(e)s,** ~**e** (**a**) (*Lied, Vogel*~) song; (*Preislied*) hymn; (*gregorianischer* ~ *etc*) chant. **erster** ~ **der Ilias/von Dantes Inferno** first book of the Iliad/first canto of Dante's Inferno; **geistliche** ~**e** religious hymns and chants. (**b**) *no pl* (*das Singen*) singing; (*von Mönchen etc*) chanting.

Gesang-, Gesangs- (*Aus*): ~**buch** *nt* (*Eccl*) hymnbook; **das richtige/falsche** ~**buch haben** (*inf*) to belong to the right/wrong denomination; ~**lehrer** *m* singing teacher.

gesanglich *adj* vocal; *Begabung* for singing. **die Opernaufführung war von hoher** ~**er Perfektion** the singing in the opera was superb.

Gesangskunst *f* singing technique.

Gesang-, Gesangs- (*Aus*): ~**stunde** *f* singing lesson; ~**unterricht** *m* singing lessons *pl*; ~**verein** *m* choral society; **mein lieber Herr** ~**verein!** (*hum*) ye gods and little fishes! (*hum*).

Gesäß *nt* **-es,** **-e** seat, bottom, posterior (*hum*).

Gesäß-: ~**backe** *f* buttock, cheek; ~**muskel** *m* gluteal muscle (*spec*); ~**spalte** *f* (*form*) cleft between the buttocks; ~**tasche** *f* back pocket.

gesättigt 1 *ptp of* **sättigen.** 2 *adj* (*Chem*) saturated.

Gesäusel *nt* **-s,** *no pl* (*von Blättern*) rustling, rustle, whisper; (*vom Wind*) murmur(ing), whisper(ing), sigh(ing); (*fig iro: von Menschen*) purring.

gesch. *abbr of* **geschieden** divorced.

Geschacher *nt* **-s,** *no pl* (*pej*) haggling (*um* about).

Geschädigte(r) *mf decl as adj* victim.

geschaffen *ptp of* **schaffen**[1].

Geschäft *nt* **-(e)s,** **-e** (**a**) (*Gewerbe, Handel*) business *no pl*; (~**sabschluß**) (business) deal *or* transaction. ~ **ist** ~ business is business; **wie geht das** ~?, **wie gehen die** ~**e?** how's business?; **mit jdm ins** ~ **kommen** to do business with sb; **mit jdm** ~**e machen** to do business *or* have business dealings with sb; **im** ~ **sein** to be in business; **für jdn die** ~**e führen** to act for sb; (*im Gewerbe, Handel*) to run the business for sb; **ein** ~ **tätigen** to do a deal, to make *or* carry out a transaction; **dunkle** ~**e treiben** to

be involved in some shady dealings *or* business; **ein gutes/schlechtes** ~ **machen** to make a good/bad deal; **dabei hat er ein** ~ **gemacht** he made a profit by it; **das war für mich ein/kein** ~ that was a good/bad bit of business for me; **~e mit etw machen** to make money out of sth; **viel in** ~**en unterwegs sein** to travel a lot on business; **das** ~ **mit der Lust** the sex industry; **Boulevardzeitungen leben von dem** ~ **mit der Angst** the popular press make their living by trading on people's fears.

(**b**) (*Aufgabe*) duty. **das gehört zu den** ~**en des Ministers** that is one of the minister's duties, that is part of the minister's work; **seinen** ~**en nachgehen** to go about one's business.

(**c**) (*Firma*) business (concern); (*Laden*) shop (*Brit*), store; (*inf: Büro*) office. **die** ~**e schließen um 17³⁰ Uhr** the shops *or* stores close at 5.30; **ich gehe um 8 Uhr ins** ~ I go to work *or* to the office at 8.00; **im** ~ at work, in the office; (*im Laden*) in the shop.

(**d**) (*baby-talk: Notdurft*) **kleines/großes** ~ little/big job (*baby-talk*), number one/two (*baby-talk*); **ein** ~ **machen** to do a job (*baby-talk*); **sein** ~ **verrichten** to do one's business (*euph*).

Geschäfte-: **g~halber** *adv* (*in Geschäften*) on business; (*wegen Geschäften*) because of business; ~**macher** *m* (*pej*) profiteer; ~**macherei** *f* (*pej*) profiteering *no indef art*.

geschäftig *adj* (*betriebsam*) busy; (*emsig, eifrig auch*) industrious, assiduous, zealous (*esp pej*). ~ **tun, sich** ~ **geben** to look busy; ~**es Treiben** *or* **Hin und Her** hustle and bustle, bustling activity; ~ **hin und her laufen** to bustle around (busily).

Geschäftigkeit *f* busyness; (*Emsigkeit, Eifer auch*) industriousness, assiduousness, zealousness (*esp pej*); (*geschäftiges Treiben auch*) (hustle and) bustle.

Geschäftlhuber *m* **-s,** - (*S Ger*) *siehe* **Gschaftlhuber.**

geschäftlich 1 *adj* (*das Geschäft betreffend*) business *attr*; (*sachlich*) *Ton* businesslike.

2 *adv* (*in Geschäften*) on business; (*wegen Geschäften*) because of business; (~ *gesehen*) from a business point of view. **er hat morgen** ~ **in Berlin zu tun** he has business in Berlin tomorrow *or* has to be in Berlin on business tomorrow; ~ **verhindert** prevented by business; ~ **verreist** away on business; ~ **mit jdm verkehren** to have business dealings with sb; **ich habe mit ihm etwas G~es zu besprechen** I have some business *or* business matters to discuss with him.

Geschäfts-: ~**ablauf** *m* course of business; ~**abschluß** *m* business deal *or* transaction; ~**angelegenheit** *f siehe* ~**sache;** ~**anteil** *m* share of a/the business; ~**aufgabe,** ~**auflösung** *f* closure of a/the business; **Räumungsverkauf wegen** ~**aufgabe** closing-down sale; **zur** ~**aufgabe gezwungen werden** to be forced to close down (one's business); ~**auslage** *f* window display; ~**auto** *nt* company car; ~**bank** *f* commercial bank; ~**bedingungen** *pl* terms of business *pl*; ~**bereich** *m* (*Parl*) responsibilities *pl*; **Minister ohne** ~**bereich** minister without portfolio; ~**bericht** *m* report; (*einer Gesellschaft*) company report; ~**besitzer** *m siehe* ~**inhaber;** ~**beziehungen** *pl* business connections *pl* (*zu* with); ~**brief** *m* business letter; ~**bücher** *pl* books *pl*, accounts *pl*; ~**eröffnung** *f* opening of a store *or* shop (*Brit*); **g~fähig** *adj* (*Jur*) capable of contracting (*form*), competent (*form*); **voll/beschränkt g~fähig sein** to have complete/limited competence; ~**fähigkeit** *f* (*Jur*) (legal) competence; ~**frau** *f* businesswoman; ~**freund** *m* business associate; **ein guter** ~**freund** a good business friend, a close business associate; **g~führend** *adj attr* executive; (*stellvertretend*) acting; *Regierung* caretaker; ~**führer** *m* (*von Laden*) manager; (*von GmbH*) managing director; (*von Verein*) secretary; (*von Partei*) whip; ~**führung** *f* management; **mit der** ~**führung beauftragt** (*abbr* **m.d.G.b.**) in charge of administration; ~**gang** *m* business *no art*; (*Besorgung*) errand; ~**gebaren** *nt* business methods *pl or* practices *pl*; ~**gegend** *f* shopping centre; ~**geheimnis** *nt* business secret; ~**geist** *m siehe* ~**sinn;** ~**haus** *nt* (**a**) (*Gebäude*) business premises *pl*; (*von Büros*) office block; (**b**) (*Firma*) house, firm; ~**herr** *m* (*Sw*) owner (of a business); ~**inhaber** *m* owner (of a business); (*von Laden, Restaurant*) proprietor, owner; ~**inhaberin** *f siehe* ~**inhaber** owner; proprietress; ~**interesse** *nt* business interest; ~**jahr** *nt* financial year; ~**kapital** *nt* working capital; ~**kosten** *pl* business expenses *pl*; **das geht alles auf** ~**kosten** it's all on expenses; ~**lage** *f* (**a**) (*Wirtschaftslage*) business situation; (**b**) **in erstklassiger** ~**lage** in a good business location; ~**leben** *nt* business life; **er steht noch im** ~**leben** he's still active in the world of business; ~**leitung** *f siehe* ~**führung;** ~**liste** *f* (*Sw*) *siehe* **Tagesordnung;** ~**mann** *m,* *pl* ~**leute** businessman; **g~mäßig** *adj* businesslike *no adv*; ~**methoden** *pl* business methods *pl*; ~**ordnung** *f* standing orders *pl*; **zur** ~**ordnung!** point of order!; **eine Frage zur** ~**ordnung** a question on a point of order; ~**papiere** *pl* business papers *pl*; ~**partner** *m* business partner; (~**freund**) business associate; **mein** ~**partner** my partner (in the business); ~**räume** *pl* (business) premises *pl*; (*Büroräume*) offices *pl*; **in den** ~**räumen** on the premises/in the offices; ~**reise** *f* business trip; **auf** ~**reise sein** to be on a business trip; ~**rückgang** *m* decline in business; ~**sache** *f* business matter *or* affair; **g~schädigend** *adj* bad for business; **g~schädigendes Verhalten,** ~**schädigung** *f* conduct *no art* injurious to the interests of the company (*form*); ~**schluß** *m* close of business; (*von Läden*) closing-time; **nach** ~**schluß** out of working hours/after closing-time; ~**sinn** *m* business sense; ~**sitz** *m* place of business; ~**stelle** *f* offices *pl*; (*von Gericht*) administrative office; ~**straße** *f* shopping street; ~**stunden** *pl* office *or* working hours *pl*; (*von Läden*) (shop) opening hours; „~**stunden**" "hours of opening"; ~**tätigkeit** *f* business activity; ~**träger** *m* (*Pol*) chargé d'affaires; **g~*tüchtig** *adj* business-minded; ~**übernahme** *f* takeover of a/the business/store; **g~unfähig** *adj* (*Jur*) not capable of contracting (*form*), (legally) incompetent (*form*); ~**unfähigkeit** *f* (*Jur*) (legal) incompetence; ~**verbindung** f business connection; in ~**verbindung mit jdm stehen** to have business connections with sb; ~**verkehr** m (a) business no art; **in regem** ~**verkehr mit einer Firma stehen** to do a considerable amount of business with a firm; (b) (Straßenverkehr) business traffic; ~**viertel** nt (a) siehe ~**gegend**; (b) (Banken- und Versicherungsviertel) business or commercial district; ~**wagen** m company car; ~**welt** f world of business, business world; ~**wert** m value of a/the business; ~**zimmer** nt office; ~**zweig** m branch of a/the business.

geschah pret of geschehen.

Geschäker nt -s, no pl (inf) flirting.

geschamig adj (esp Aus inf) siehe **gschamig**.

Geschaukel nt -s, no pl (im Schaukelstuhl) swinging; (in Bus, Wagen) lurching; (in Boot) pitching, rolling.

gescheckt adj spotted; Pferd skewbald, pinto (US).

geschehen pret **geschah**, ptp ~ vi aux sein to happen (jdm to sb); (vorkommen auch) to occur; (stattfinden auch) to take place; (ausgeführt werden) to be done; (Verbrechen) to be committed. **ihr Selbstmord geschah aus Verzweiflung** her despair led her to commit suicide; **es ist nun einmal** ~ what's done is done; **Dein Wille geschehe** (Bibl) Thy or Your will be done; **es wird ihm nichts** ~ nothing will happen to him; **das geschieht ihm (ganz) recht** it serves him (jolly well inf) right; **ihm ist ein Unrecht** ~ he has been wronged; **ihm ist ein Mißgeschick** ~ he had a mishap; **er wußte nicht, wie ihm geschah** he didn't know what was happening or going on; **was soll mit ihm/damit** ~? what is to be done with him/it?; **es ist um ihn** ~ it's all up with him; **als er sie sah, war es um ihn** ~ he was lost the moment he set eyes on her; **da war es um meine Seelenruhe** ~ that was an end to my peace of mind; **es kann** ~, **daß** ... it could happen that ...; **und so geschah es, daß** ... and so it happened or came about that ...; **es muß etwas** ~ something must be done; **so** ~ **am** ... such was the case on ...; **G~es ruhen lassen** (geh) to let bygones be bygones; siehe **gern**.

Geschehen nt -s, (rare) - events pl, happenings pl.

Geschehnis nt (geh) event; (Vorfall auch) incident.

gescheit adj (a) clever; Mensch, Idee auch bright; (vernünftig) sensible. **du bist wohl nicht recht** ~? you must be out of your mind or off your head; **sei** ~! be sensible; **es wäre** ~**er** ... it would be wiser or more sensible ...; **ich werde daraus nicht** ~ I can't make head nor tail of it; **jetzt bin ich so** ~ **wie vorher** I'm none the wiser now.
(b) (S Ger: tüchtig, ordentlich) proper, good. **ich habe ihm** ~ **die Meinung gesagt** (S Ger) I really gave him a piece of my mind; **wie** ~ (Aus inf) like mad (inf).

Gescheitheit f siehe adj (a) cleverness; brightness; sensibleness.

Geschenk nt -(e)s, -e present, gift; (Schenkung) gift. **jdm ein** ~ **machen** to give sb a present; **jdm etw zum** ~ **machen** to make sb a present of sth, to give sb sth (as a present); **ein** ~ **seiner Mutter** a present or gift from his mother; **ein** ~ **Gottes** a gift from or of God; **das war ein** ~ **des Himmels** it was a godsend; **kleine** ~**e erhalten die Freundschaft** (prov) little presents keep a friendship alive.

Geschenk-, Geschenks- (Aus) in cpds gift; ~**artikel** m gift; ~**packung** f gift pack or box; (von Pralinen) gift box; **Zigaretten in** ~**packung** a gift pack of cigarettes, cigarettes in a gift pack; ~**sendung** f gift parcel.

Gescherte(r) mf decl as adj (Aus inf) siehe **Gscherte(r)**.

Geschichtchen nt little story.

Geschichte f -, -n (a) no pl (Historie) history. ~ **des Altertums/der Neuzeit, Alte/Neuere** ~ ancient/modern history; **die** ~ **Spaniens/der Menschheit** the history of Spain/mankind; ~ **machen** to make history; **das ist längst** ~ that's past history.
(b) (Erzählung, Lügen) story; (Märchen, Fabel etc auch) tale; (Kurz~) short story. **das sind alles bloß** ~**n** that's all just made up, that's just a story; ~**n erzählen** to tell stories.
(c) (inf: Angelegenheit, Sache) affair, business no pl. **das sind alte** ~**n** that's old hat (inf); **das ist (wieder) die alte** ~ it's the same old or the old old story (all over again); **alte** ~**n wieder aufwärmen** to rake up the past; **die ganze** ~ the whole business; **eine schöne** ~! (iro) a fine how-do-you-do! (inf); **das sind ja nette** ~**n!** (iro) this is a fine thing; **die** ~ **mit seinem Magen** the trouble or business with his stomach; **als er damals diese** ~ **mit der Tänzerin hatte** when he was having that affair with the dancer; **mach keine** ~**n!** don't be silly! (inf); (Dummheiten) don't get up to anything silly!; **mach keine langen** ~**n** don't make a fuss.

Geschichten-: ~**buch** nt storybook; ~**erzähler** m (lit, fig) storyteller.

geschichtlich adj (historisch) historical; (bedeutungsvoll) historic. ~ **bedeutsam** historic; ~ **denken** to think in terms of history; **etw** ~ **betrachten** to consider sth from the historical point of view; ~ **belegt** or **nachgewiesen sein** to be a historical fact.

Geschichts-: ~**atlas** m historical atlas; ~**auffassung, ~betrachtung** f conception of history; ~**bewußtsein** nt awareness of history, historical awareness; ~**buch** nt history book; ~**deutung** f interpretation of history; ~**drama** nt historical drama; ~**epoche** f period of history; ~**fälschung** f falsification of history; ~**forscher** m historian; ~**forschung** f historical research; ~**kenntnis** f knowledge of history no pl, historical knowledge no pl; ~**klitterung** f historical misrepresentation; ~**lehrer** m history teacher; **g~los** adj Land, Stadt with no history; Zeit with no historical records; Volk with no sense of history; ~**losigkeit** f siehe adj lack of history; absence of historical records (gen for); historical unawareness; ahistoricity (form); **manche Volksstämme verharren noch heute im Dunkel der**

~**losigkeit** some tribes even today lead a life untouched by the flow of history; ~**maler** m historical painter; ~**malerei** f historical painting; ~**philosoph** m philosopher of history; ~**philosophie** f philosophy of history; **g~philosophisch** adj Schrift etc on the philosophy of history; Interesse, Studien in the philosophy of history; **ein Problem g~philosophisch interpretieren** to interpret a problem from the point of view of the philosophy of history; ~**schreiber** m historian, historiographer; ~**schreibung** f historiography; ~**werk** nt historical work; ~**wissenschaft** f (science of) history; ~**wissenschaftler** m historian; ~**zahl** f (historical) date.

Geschick[1] nt -(e)s, -e (geh) (Schicksal) fate; (politische etc Entwicklung, Situation) fortune. **ein gütiges** ~ good fortune, providence; **ein schlimmes/schweres/trauriges** ~ a sad fate.

Geschick[2] nt -s, no pl skill.

Geschicklichkeit f siehe geschickt skill, skilfulness; cleverness, adroitness; dexterity; agility. **für** or **zu etw** ~ **haben** or **zeigen** to be clever at sth.

Geschicklichkeits-: ~**fahren** nt (Sport) skill tests pl; (Aut) manoeuvring tests pl; ~**spiel** nt game of skill; ~**übung** f exercise in skill/agility.

geschickt 1 ptp of **schicken. 2** adj (a) skilful; (taktisch auch) clever, adroit; (fingerfertig auch) dexterous; (beweglich auch) agile.
(b) (S Ger) siehe **praktisch 1**.

Geschicktheit f siehe **Geschicklichkeit**.

Geschiebe nt -s, no pl (a) (Geol) debris; (in Flüssen) deposit.
(b) (Gedränge) pushing and shoving (inf).

geschieden ptp of **scheiden.**

Geschiedene f decl as adj divorcee. **seine** ~ (inf) his ex (inf).

Geschiedene(r) m decl as adj divorced man, divorcé. **ihr** ~**r** (inf) her ex (inf).

geschienen ptp of **scheinen.**

Geschimpfe nt -s, no pl (inf) cursing; (tadelnd) scolding.

Geschirr nt -(e)s, -e (a) no pl (Haushaltsgefäße) crockery (Brit), tableware; (Küchen~) pots and pans pl, kitchenware; (Teller etc) china; (zu einer Mahlzeit benutzt) dishes pl. **(das)** ~ **(ab)spülen** to wash or do the dishes, to wash up; **feuerfestes** ~ ovenware.
(b) (Service) (dinner/tea etc) service; (Glas~) set of glasses; (feuerfestes ~) set of ovenware. **das gute** ~ the best china.
(c) (old) (Gefäß) vessel, pot; (Nacht~) chamber-pot.
(d) (von Zugtieren) harness. **einem Pferd das** ~ **anlegen** to harness (up) a horse; **sich ins** ~ **legen** or **werfen** (Pferde, Ochsen) to pull hard; (fig) to put one's shoulder to the wheel, to put one's back into it.

Geschirr-: ~**aufzug** m dumb waiter; ~**handtuch** nt tea towel; ~**macher** m harness-maker; ~**schrank** m china cupboard; ~**spülen** nt washing-up; ~**spüler** m -s, -, (Mensch) ~**spülmaschine** f dishwasher; ~**tuch** nt tea towel.

Geschiß nt -sses, no pl (sl) fuss and bother.

geschissen ptp of **scheißen.**

Geschlabber nt -s, no pl (inf) slurping.

geschlafen ptp of **schlafen.**

geschlagen ptp of **schlagen.**

Geschlecht nt -(e)s, -er (a) sex; (Gram) gender. **Jugendliche beiderlei** ~**s** young people of both sexes; **das andere** ~ the opposite sex; **das schwache/schöne/starke** ~ the weaker/fair/stronger sex; **das dritte** ~ transvestites pl; (Homosexuelle) homosexuals pl.
(b) (geh: Geschlechtsteil) sex (liter).
(c) (liter) (Gattung) race; (Generation) generation; (Sippe) house; (Abstammung) lineage. **das menschliche** ~, **das** ~ **der Menschen** the human race; **das** ~ **der Götter** the gods; **er ist vornehmen** ~**s** he is of noble lineage.

Geschlechter-: ~**folge** f line; ~**kunde** f genealogy; ~**trennung** f segregation of the sexes.

geschlechtlich adj sexual. ~**e Erziehung** sex education; **die** ~**e Aufklärung ihrer Kinder ist für viele Eltern eine peinliche Angelegenheit** many parents find it most embarrassing to tell their children the facts of life; ~**en Verkehr mit jdm haben, mit jdm** ~ **verkehren** to have sexual intercourse with sb.

Geschlechtlichkeit f sexuality.

Geschlechts-: **g~abhängig** adj sexually determined; ~**akt** m sex(ual) act; ~**bestimmung** f sex determination; ~**chromosom** nt sex chromosome; ~**drang** m sex(ual) urge; ~**drüse** f sex gland; ~**erziehung** f sex(ual) education; **g~gebunden** adj siehe **g~abhängig**; ~**genosse** m person of the same sex; **jds** ~**genossen** those or people of the same sex as sb; ~**hormon** nt sex hormone; **g~krank** adj suffering from VD or a venereal disease; **g~krank sein** to have VD; **ein** ~**kranker** a person with VD; ~**krankheit** f venereal disease; **eine** ~**krankheit haben** to have VD or a venereal disease; ~**leben** nt sex life; ~**leiden** nt venereal disease; **g~los** adj asexual (auch Biol), sexless; ~**losigkeit** f asexuality (auch Biol), sexlessness; ~**lust** f (geh) lust; ~**merkmal** nt sex(ual) characteristic; ~**organ** nt sex(ual) organ; **g~reif** adj sexually mature; ~**reife** f sexual maturity; ~**rolle** f (Sociol) sex role; **g~spezifisch** adj (Sociol) sex-specific; ~**teil** nt genitals pl; ~**trieb** m sex(ual) urge; sex(ual) drive; ~**umwandlung** f sex change; ~**unterschied** m difference between the sexes; ~**verirrung** f sexual perversion; ~**verkehr** m sexual intercourse; ~**wort** nt (Gram) article; ~**zelle** f sexual cell.

geschlichen ptp of **schleichen.**

geschliffen 1 ptp of **schleifen[2]. 2** adj Manieren, Ausdrucksweise polished, refined; Sätze polished.

Geschliffenheit f siehe adj refinement; polish.

Geschling nt -(e)s, -e, **Geschlinge** nt -s, - innards pl, pluck (form).

geschlissen ptp of **schleißen.**

geschlossen 1 *ptp of* **schließen.**
  2 *adj* closed; (*vereint*) united, unified. **in sich** (*dat*) ~ self-contained; *Mensch, Charakter* well-rounded; *Buch, Handlung* well-knit; **es war eine ~e Wolkendecke vorhanden** the sky was completely overcast; **ein ~es Ganzes** a unified whole; **~e Gesellschaft** closed society; (*Fest*) private party; **in ~er Sitzung** in closed session; (*Jur*) in camera; **~e Gewässer** lakes, inland seas; **ein ~er Wagen** a saloon car; **~e Ortschaft** built-up area; **in ~er Formation** (*Aviat*) in close formation.
  3 *adv* ~ **für etw sein/stimmen** to be/vote unanimously in favour of sth; **wir protestierten ~ gegen das neue Gesetz** we were unanimous in our protest against the new law; **~ hinter jdm stehen** to stand solidly behind sb; **wir gingen ~ mit der ganzen Klasse ins Kino** the whole class went to the cinema en masse *or* as a body; **dieses zwölfbändige Lexikon wird nur ~ abgegeben** this twelve-volume encyclopaedia is only sold as a complete set; **dieser Vokal wird ~ ausgesprochen** this vowel has closed articulation.

Geschlossenheit *f* unity.
Geschluchz(e) *nt* -es, *no pl* sobbing.
geschlungen *ptp of* **schlingen**[1] *and* **schlingen**[2].
Geschlürfe *nt* -s, *no pl* (*inf*) slurping.
Geschmack *m* -(e)s, **-e** *or* (*hum, inf*) **-er** (*lit, fig*) taste; (*Aroma auch*) flavour; (*S Ger: Geruch*) smell; (*no pl:* ~*ssinn*) sense of taste. **je nach ~** to one's own taste; **Salz (je) nach ~ hinzufügen** add salt to taste; **seinen ~ bilden** *or* **entwickeln** (*lit*) to develop one's sense of taste; (*fig*) to acquire a sense of the aesthetic; **an etw** (*dat*) ~ **finden** to acquire a taste for sth; **auf den ~ kommen** to acquire a taste for it; **einen guten ~ haben** (*Essen*) to taste good; **er hat einen guten ~** (*fig*) he has good taste; **für meinen ~** for my taste; **das ist nicht mein/nach meinem ~** that's not my/to my taste; **hast du ~ für so etwas?** (*inf*) do you really like that kind of thing?; **die ~er sind verschieden** tastes differ; **über ~ läßt sich (nicht) streiten** (*Prov*) there's no accounting for taste(s) (*prov*).
geschmäcklerisch *adj* highly elaborate; *Aufführung auch* camp.
geschmacklich *adj* (*lit, fig*) as regards taste. **ausgezeichnete ~e Qualitäten** (*form*) exquisite flavour *or* taste.
geschmacklos *adj* (*lit, fig*) tasteless; (*taktlos auch*) in bad taste.
Geschmacklosigkeit *f* **(a)** *no pl* (*lit, fig*) tastelessness, lack of taste; (*Taktlosigkeit auch*) bad taste. **(b)** (*Beispiel der* ~) example of bad taste; (*Bemerkung*) remark in bad taste. **das ist eine ~!** that is the most appalling bad taste!
Geschmacks-: g~**bildend** *adj* aesthetically formative; ~**bildung** *f* formation of good taste; ~**empfindung** *f* sense of taste; **keine ~empfindung haben** to be unable to taste anything; ~**frage** *f* matter *or* question of (good) taste; ~**knospen** *pl* taste buds *pl*; g~**neutral** *adj* tasteless; ~**richtung** *f* taste; **das liegt genau in meiner ~richtung** that is exactly my taste; ~**sache** *f* matter of taste; **das ist ~sache** it's (all) a matter of taste; ~**sinn** *m* sense of taste; ~**verirrung** *f* unter ~**verirrung leiden** (*iro*) to have no taste; **der Hut ist eine ~verirrung** that hat is an aberration; **in einem Anfall von ~verirrung habe ich eine violette Hose gekauft** in a moment of aberration I bought a pair of purple trousers.
geschmackvoll *adj* tasteful; (*taktvoll auch*) in good taste. **~e Kleider tragen, sich ~ kleiden** to dress tastefully.
Geschmatze *nt* -s, *no pl* (*inf*) noisy eating.
Geschmeide *nt* -s, - (*geh*) jewellery *no pl*. **ein ~** a piece of jewellery.
geschmeidig *adj* **(a)** *Haar, Leder, Haut* supple; *Körper, Bewegung auch* lithe, lissom(e); *Fell* sleek; (*weich*) *Handtuch, Haar* soft; *Teig* workable; *Wachs* malleable; (*anschmiegsam*) soft and clinging. **er hat einen ~en Gang** he moves with supple grace; **~ glitt die Katze vom Stuhl** the cat slid off the chair with feline grace.
  (b) (*fig*) (*anpassungsfähig*) flexible; (*wendig*) adroit; *Zunge, Worte* glib, smooth.
Geschmeidigkeit *f, no pl siehe adj* **(a)** suppleness; litheness, lissomeness; sleekness; softness; malleability; clinging softness. **(b)** flexibility; adroitness; glibness.
Geschmeiß *nt* -es, *no pl* **(a)** (*old lit, fig*) vermin *pl*. **(b)** (*Hunt*) droppings *pl*.
Geschmetter *nt* -s, *no pl* flourish.
Geschmier(e) *nt* -s, *no pl* (*inf*) mess; (*Handschrift*) scrawl; (*Geschriebenes*) scribble; (*schlechtes Bild*) daub. **hör auf mit dem ~!** stop making that mess!
geschmissen *ptp of* **schmeißen.**
geschmolzen *ptp of* **schmelzen.**
Geschmorte(s) *nt decl as adj* (*Cook*) braised meat.
Geschmunzel *nt* -s, *no pl* smiling.
Geschmus(e) *nt* -s, *no pl* (*inf*) cuddling; (*von Pärchen auch*) canoodling (*inf*).
Geschnäbel *nt* -s, *no pl* billing; (*hum: Küsserei*) billing and cooing.
Geschnatter *nt* -s, *no pl* (*lit*) cackle, cackling; (*fig*) jabber, jabbering.
Geschnetzelte(s) *nt decl as adj* (*esp Sw Cook*) meat cut into strips stewed to produce a thick sauce.
geschniegelt 1 *ptp of* **schniegeln. 2** *adj* (*pej*) flashy. ~ **und gebügelt** *or* **gestriegelt** spruced up, all dressed up with one's hair smarmed down (*pej*).
geschnitten *ptp of* **schneiden.**
geschnoben *ptp of* **schnauben.**
Geschnüffel *nt* -s, *no pl* sniffing; (*fig*) nosing *or* sniffing about.
geschoben *ptp of* **schieben.**
geschollen (*old*) *ptp of* **schallen.**
gescholten *ptp of* **schelten.**

Geschöpf *nt* -(e)s, **-e** (*Geschaffenes*) creation; (*Lebewesen*) creature. **wir sind alle ~e Gottes** we are all God's creatures; **sie ist sein ~** (*geh*) she is his creature.
geschoren *ptp of* **scheren**[1].
Geschoß[1] *nt* -sses, **-sse** projectile (*form*); (*Wurf*~, *Rakete etc auch*) missile; (*Kugel auch*) bullet; (*fig inf: scharf geschossener Ball*) shot. **ferngelenktes ~** guided missile.
Geschoß[2] *nt* -sses, **sse** (*Stockwerk*) floor, storey (*Brit*), story (*US*). **im ersten ~ on the first** (*Brit*) *or* **second** (*US*) **floor; das Haus/Geschäft hat vier ~sse** the house has four storeys/the store has four floors.
Geschoßbahn *f* trajectory; (*einer Rakete auch*) flight path.
geschossen *ptp of* **schießen.**
Geschoß-: ~**garbe** *f* burst of fire; ~**hagel** *m* hail of bullets.
-geschossig *adj suf* -storey *attr* (*Brit*), -story *attr* (*US*), -storeyed (*Brit*), -storied (*US*). **mehr~** multistorey.
geschraubt 1 *ptp of* **schrauben. 2** *adj* (*pej*) *Stil, Redeweise* pretentious.
Geschraubtheit *f* pretentiousness *no pl*; (*Ausdruck*) pretentious phrase.
Geschrei *nt* -s, *no pl* shouts *pl*, shouting; (*von Kindern, Fußballfans, Streitenden auch*) yells *pl*, yelling; (*von Verletzten, Babys, Popfans*) screams *pl*, screaming; (*schrilles* ~) shrieks *pl*, shrieking; (*fig: Aufhebens*) fuss, to-do (*inf*). **viel ~ um etw machen** to kick up (*inf*) *or* make a big fuss about sth; **er wurde mit großem Hallo und ~ empfangen** he was given a noisy *or* vociferous welcome; **ein großes ~ erheben** to set up a cry *etc*; (*fig*) to raise an outcry.
Geschreibsel *nt, no pl* (*inf*) scribble; (*fig: Schreiberei*) scriblings *pl*.
geschrieben *ptp of* **schreiben.**
geschrie(e)n *ptp of* **schreien.**
geschritten *ptp of* **schreiten.**
geschrocken (*old*) *ptp of* **schrecken.**
geschunden *ptp of* **schinden.**
Geschütz *nt* -es, -e gun. **schweres ~** heavy artillery; **eine Kanone ist ein ~** a cannon is a piece of artillery; **ein ~ auffahren** to bring up a gun; **schweres** *or* **grobes ~ auffahren** (*fig*) to bring up one's big guns.
Geschütz-: ~**bedienung** *f* gunnery; (*Personal*) gun-crew; ~**donner** *m* roar *or* booming of (the) guns; ~**feuer** *nt* shell fire; **etw unter ~feuer nehmen** to (start to) shell sth, to open fire on sth; ~**rohr** *nt* gun barrel; ~**stand** *m*, ~**stellung** *f* gun emplacement.
geschützt 1 *ptp of* **schützen. 2** *adj* *Winkel, Ecke* sheltered; *Pflanze, Tier* protected.
Geschützturm *m* gun turret.
Geschw. *abbr of* **Geschwister.**
Geschwader *nt* -s, - squadron.
Geschwader-: ~**kommandeur** *m* (*Naut*) commodore; ~**kommodore** *m* (*Aviat*) squadron-leader (*Brit*), major (*US*).
Geschwafel *nt* -s, *no pl* (*pej inf*) waffle (*inf*).
geschwänzt 1 *ptp of* **schwänzen. 2** *adj Peitsche* with tails.
Geschwätz *nt* -es, *no pl* (*pej*) (*Klatsch*) tittle-tattle (*inf*), gossip.
Geschwatze, Geschwätze (*S Ger inf*) *nt* -s, *no pl* chattering, nattering (*inf*).
geschwätzig *adj* talkative, garrulous; (*klatschsüchtig*) gossipy.
Geschwätzigkeit *f, no pl siehe adj* talkativeness, garrulousness; gossipiness. **das haben wir deiner ~ zu verdanken** we've you and your eternal chattering/gossiping to thank for that.
geschweift 1 *ptp of* **schweifen. 2** *adj* **(a)** curved. **(b)** *Stern* with a tail.
geschweige *conj* ~ (**denn**) let *or* leave alone, never mind.
geschwiegen *ptp of* **schweigen.**
geschwind *adj* (*old, S Ger*) swift, quick, fast *no adv*. ~! quick(ly)!, hurry!; ~**en Schrittes** (*geh*) with rapid steps; ~ **wie der Wind** (*geh*) as swift as the wind.
Geschwindigkeit *f* speed; (*Schnelligkeit auch*) swiftness, quickness; (*Phys: von Masse*) velocity. **mit einer ~ von ... at a speed of ...; mit höchster ~** at top speed; **mit rasender ~ fahren** to belt *or* tear along (*inf*); **eine zu große ~ draufhaben** (*inf*) to be going too fast; **an ~ zunehmen** to gather *or* pick up speed; (*Phys: Masse*) to gain momentum; **die ~ steigern/verringern** to increase/decrease one's speed, to speed up/slow down; **die ~ eines Fahrzeugs steigern/verringern** to increase/reduce the speed of a vehicle.
Geschwindigkeits-: ~**abfall** *m* (*Phys*) loss of speed; ~**begrenzung**, ~**beschränkung** *f* speed limit; **gegen die ~begrenzung verstoßen** to exceed the speed limit; ~**kontrolle** *f* speed check; ~**messer** *m* tachometer; (*Aut auch*) speedometer, speedo (*Brit inf*); ~**überschreitung**, ~**übertretung** *f* exceeding the speed limit, speeding; ~**zunahme** *f* (*Phys*) increase in velocity.
Geschwirr *nt* -s, *no pl* (*von Insekten*) buzzing; (*von Pfeilen*) whizzing.
Geschwister 1 *pl* brothers and sisters *pl*. **wir sind drei ~ there** are three of us in my *or* our family; **haben Sie noch ~?** do you have any brothers or sisters?
  2 *nt* -s, - (*form*) sibling (*form*); (*Bruder*) brother; (*Schwester*) sister. **ist das andere ~ ein Junge oder ein Mädchen?** is the other child (in the family) a boy or a girl?
Geschwisterchen *nt* little brother/sister.
Geschwisterkind *nt* (*old*) **(a)** (*Neffe*) nephew; (*Nichte*) niece. **meine ~er** my nephews and nieces. **(b)** cousin.
geschwisterlich 1 *adj* brotherly/sisterly. **2** *adv* in a brotherly/sisterly way. **sie leben ~ zusammen** they live together as brother and sister.
Geschwister-: ~**liebe** *f* brotherly/sisterly love; (*gegenseitig*

love between a brother and a sister; **g~los** *adj* who have no brothers or sisters; **~paar** *nt* brother and sister *pl*; **die beiden sind ein reizendes ~paar** the children are a lovely pair.

geschwollen 1 *ptp of* **schwellen**. 2 *adj (pej)* turgid, pompous, bombastic.

geschwommen *ptp of* **schwimmen**.

geschworen 1 *ptp of* **schwören**. 2 *adj attr* sworn.

Geschworenen-: **~bank** *f* jury-box; *(die Geschworenen)* jury; **~gericht** *nt siehe* **Schwurgericht**; **~liste** *f* panel.

Geschworene(r), **Geschworne(r)** *(Aus) mf decl as adj* juror. **die ~n** the jury *sing or pl.*

Geschwulst *f -, -̈e* growth; *(Hirn~, Krebs~ etc auch)* tumour.

Geschwulst-: **g~artig** *adj* growth-like; tumorous; **~knoten** *m* growth.

geschwunden *ptp of* **schwinden**.

geschwungen 1 *ptp of* **schwingen**. 2 *adj* curved. **leicht/kühn ~e Nase** slightly curved nose/aquiline nose.

Geschwür *nt -s, -e* ulcer; *(Haut~ auch)* sore; *(Furunkel)* boil; *(fig)* running sore, ulcer.

geschwür|artig *adj* ulcerous. **sich ~ verändern** to go ulcerous, to ulcerate.

gesegnet 1 *ptp of* **segnen**. 2 *adj (geh)* **mit etw ~ sein** to be blessed with sth; **~en Leibes sein** *(old, Bibl)* to be great with child *(old, Bibl)*; **~es Neues Jahr/~e Mahlzeit!** Happy New Year/for what we are about to receive may the Lord make us truly thankful; **im ~en Alter von 84 Jahren** at the age of 84; **einen ~en Schlaf/Appetit haben** to be a sound sleeper/to have a healthy appetite.

gesehen *ptp of* **sehen**.

Geseich(e) *nt -(e)s, no pl (sl)* claptrap *(inf)*, drivel *(inf)*, crap *(sl)*. **die Vorlesung war ein einziges inhaltsloses ~** the lecture was a load of empty waffle *(inf)*.

Geseier, Geseire *nt -s, no pl*, **Geseires** *nt -, no pl (pej inf)* *(Gejammer)* moaning, bellyaching *(inf)*; *(Geschwafel)* claptrap *(inf)*.

Geselchte(s) *nt decl as adj (S Ger, Aus)* salted and smoked meat.

Gesell *m -en, -en (obs)*, **Geselle** *m -n, -n* **(a)** *(Handwerks~)* journeyman. **(b)** *(old inf: Bursche)* fellow. **(c)** *(dated: Kamerad)* companion.

gesellen* *vr* **sich zu jdm ~** to join sb; **dazu gesellte sich noch, daß ...** *(geh)* in addition to this was the fact that ..., this was accompanied by the fact that ...; **zu diesem Problem gesellt sich noch ein weiteres** *(geh)* a further problem arises in connection with this one; *siehe* **gleich**.

Gesellen-: **~brief** *m* articles *pl*; **~jahre** *pl* years *pl* as a journeyman; **~prüfung** *f* examination to become a journeyman; **~stück** *nt* journeyman's piece; **~zeit** *f* period as a journeyman.

gesellig *adj* sociable, convivial; *Tier* gregarious; *Verkehr* social. **der Mensch ist ein ~es Tier** man is a social creature *or* animal; **~es Beisammensein** social gathering, get-together *(inf)*; **sie saßen ~ bei einer Flasche Wein zusammen** they were sitting together over a friendly bottle of wine.

Geselligkeit *f* **(a)** *no pl* sociability, conviviality; *(von Tieren)* gregariousness; *(geselliges Leben)* social intercourse. **die ~ lieben** to be sociable, to enjoy company. **(b)** *(Veranstaltung)* social gathering.

Gesellschaft *f* **(a)** *(Sociol, fig: Oberschicht)* society. **die ~ verändern** to change society; **eine Dame der ~** a society lady; **die ~ der** the high society of the town; **jdn in die ~ einführen** to introduce sb into society; **sie ist noch nicht in die ~ eingeführt worden** she hasn't come out yet, she hasn't made her society debut yet.

(b) *(Vereinigung)* society; *(Comm)* company. **die ~ der Freunde** the Society of Friends; **~ des bürgerlichen Rechts** private company *or* corporation *(US)*.

(c) *(Abend~)* reception, party; *(Gäste)* guests *pl*, party. **geschlossene ~** private party; **eine erlesene ~ hatte sich eingefunden** a select group of people had gathered.

(d) *(in Restaurant etc)* function.

(e) *(Umgang, Begleitung)* company, society *(old, form)*. **zur ~ to be sociable**; **in schlechte ~ geraten** to get into bad company; **da befindest du dich in guter ~** then you're in good company; **jdm ~ leisten** to keep sb company; **darf ich Ihnen ~ leisten?** may I join you?

(f) *(Kreis von Menschen)* group of people; *(pej)* pack, bunch, crowd *(all inf)*. **diese Familie/Abteilung ist eine komische ~** that family/department are an odd lot; **wir waren eine bunte ~** we were a mixed bunch.

Gesellschafter(in) *m -s, -* **(a)** *(Unterhalter)* companion; *(euph: Prostituierte)* escort. **ein guter ~ sein** to be good company; **er ist der Typ des ~s** he's not good company; **mit einem so anregenden ~ ...** with somebody who is such good company ...

(b) *(Comm) (Teilhaber)* shareholder; *(Partner)* partner. **stiller ~** sleeping *(Brit) or* silent *(US)* partner.

gesellschaftlich *adj* social; *(Sociol auch)* societal. **~e Produktion** production by society; **er ist ~ erledigt** he's ruined socially; **sich ~ unmöglich machen** to disgrace oneself socially.

Gesellschafts-: **~abend** *m* social evening; **~anteil** *m (Comm)* share of the business; **~anzug** *m* formal dress; **~aufbau** *m* structure of society; **~bild** *m (Sociol)* view of society; **~dame** *f (old)* (lady's) companion; **g~fähig** *adj* *Verhalten* socially acceptable; *Mensch, Aussehen auch* presentable; **~fahrt** *f* group tour; **g~feindlich** *adj* hostile to society; **~form** *f* social system; **~formation** *f (Sociol)* development of society; **~kapital** *nt (Comm)* company's capital; **~klasse** *f (Sociol)* social class; **~klatsch** *m* society gossip; **~kleidung** *f* formal dress; **~kritik** *f* social criticism, criticism of society; **~kritiker**

m social critic; **g~kritisch** *adj* critical of society; **g~kritisch denken** to have a critical attitude towards society; **die g~kritische Funktion einer Zeitung** the function of a newspaper as a critic of society *or* social critic; **~lehre** *f (dated)* sociology; *(Sch)* social studies *pl*; **~löwe** *m (inf) siehe* Salonlöwe; **~ordnung** *f* social order; **~politik** *f siehe* Sozialpolitik; **~raum** *m* function room; **~reise** *f siehe* **~fahrt**; **~roman** *m* social novel; **~schicht** *f* stratum of society, social stratum; **~spiel** *nt* party game, parlour game; **~struktur** *f* structure of society; *(bestimmte auch)* social structure; **~stück** *nt (Theat)* comedy of manners; *(Art)* genre painting; **~system** *nt* social system; **~tanz** *m* ballroom dance; **~veränderung** *f* social change; **~vertrag** *m (Philos)* social contract; *(Comm)* articles *pl* of partnership, partnership agreement; **~wissenschaften** *pl* social sciences *pl*; **g~wissenschaftlich** *adj* sociological.

Gesenk *nt -(e)s, -e (Tech)* die. **(b)** *(Min)* blind shaft, winze.

Gesenkschmiede *f (Tech)* drop forge.

gesessen *ptp of* **sitzen**.

Gesetz *nt -es, -e (Jur, Natur~, Prinzip)* law; *(~buch)* statute book; *(Parl: Vorlage)* bill; *(Parl: nach der dritten Lesung)* act; *(Satzung, Regel)* rule. **das Miet-/Copyright-~** the Rent/Copyright Act; **(zum) ~ werden** to become law, to pass into law; **auf Grund des ~es, nach dem ~** under the law *(über +acc on)*; **vor dem ~** in (the eyes of the) law; **im Sinne des ~es** within the meaning of the act; **steht etwas davon im ~?** is there any law about it?; **ich kann nichts im ~ finden, wonach das verboten wäre** I can't find any law forbidding it; **das ~ der Schwerkraft** the law of gravity; **das erste *or* oberste ~** (der Wirtschaft *etc*) the golden rule (of industry *etc*); **das ~ Mose** *(Bibl)* the Law of Moses, the Mosaic Law; **ein ungeschriebenes ~** an unwritten rule; **das ~ des Handelns an sich reißen** to seize the initiative; **wenn uns das ~ des Handelns aufgezwungen wird** if we are forced to take the initiative *or* the first step.

Gesetz-: **~blatt** *nt* law gazette; **~buch** *nt* statute book; **Bürgerliches ~buch** Civil Code; **~entwurf** *m* (draft) bill.

Gesetzes-: **~brecher(in** *f)* *m -s, -* law-breaker; **~hüter** *m (iro)* guardian of the law; **~initiative** *f* legislative initiative; *(Sw: Volksbegehren)* petition for a referendum; **~kraft** *f* the force of law; **~kraft erlangen** to become law; **~kraft haben** to be law; **g~kundig** *adj* (well-)versed in the law; **~novelle** *f* amendment; **~sammlung** *f* compendium of laws *(zu on)*; **~tafeln** *pl (Bibl)* tablets on which the Ten Commandments were written; **~text** *m* wording of a/the law; **g~treu** *adj* law-abiding; **~treue** *f* law-abidingness; **~übertretung** *f* infringement of a/the law; **~vorlage** *f* (draft) bill; **~werk** *nt* corpus of laws.

Gesetz-: **g~gebend** *adj attr* legislative, law-making; **die g~gebende Gewalt** legislature; **~geber** *m* legislator, law-maker; *(Versammlung)* legislature, legislative body; **g~geberisch** *adj attr* legislative; **~gebung** *f* legislation *no pl.*

Gesetzgebungs-: **~hoheit** *f* legislative sovereignty; **~notstand** *m* legislative state of emergency.

gesetzkundig *adj siehe* **gesetzeskundig**.

gesetzlich 1 *adj* *Verpflichtung, Bestimmungen, Vertreter, Zahlungsmittel* legal; *Feiertag, Rücklage, Zinsen, Reglungen* statutory; *(rechtmäßig)* lawful, legitimate. **auf ~em Wege zur Macht gelangen** to come to power by legal means.

2 *adv* legally; *(durch Gesetze auch)* by law; *(rechtmäßig)* lawfully, legitimately. **~ zu etw verpflichtet sein** to be required by law *or* to be legally required to do sth; *siehe* **schützen**.

Gesetzlichkeit *f, no pl (Gesetzmäßigkeit)* legality; *(Rechtmäßigkeit)* lawfulness, legitimacy; *(Rechtsordnung)* law. **Ordnung und ~ garantieren** to guarantee law and order.

Gesetz-: **g~los** *adj* lawless; **~losigkeit** *f* lawlessness; **g~mäßig** *adj* **(a)** *(gesetzlich)* legal; *(rechtmäßig)* lawful, legitimate; **(b)** *(einem Natur~ folgend)* in accordance with a law (of nature); *(rare: regelmäßig)* regular; **Denkprozesse, die g~mäßig ablaufen** thought processes which are law-governed; **~mäßigkeit** *f siehe adj* legality; lawfulness, legitimacy; regularity; **unser Seelenleben folgt vielleicht uns unbekannten ~mäßigkeiten** perhaps the life of the mind runs in accordance with laws which are unknown to us.

gesetzt 1 *ptp of* **setzen**. 2 *adj (reif)* sedate, sober. **ein Herr im ~en Alter** a man of mature years. 3 *conj* **~ den Fall, ...** assuming (that) ...

Gesetztheit *f (Reife)* sedateness.

Gesetz-: **g~widrig** *adj* illegal; *(unrechtmäßig)* unlawful; **~widrigkeit** *f siehe adj* illegality; unlawfulness *no pl.*

Geseufze *nt -s, no pl* sighing.

ges. gesch. *abbr of* **gesetzlich geschützt** reg'd.

Gesicht[1] *nt -(e)s, -er* **(a)** face. **ein ~ machen *or* ziehen** *(inf)* to make *or* pull a face; **ein intelligentes/trauriges/böses/wütendes ~ machen** to look intelligent/sad/cross/angry; **ein langes ~ machen** to make *or* pull a long face; **was machst du denn heute für ein ~?** what's up with you today?; **jdm ein ~ schneiden** *(inf)* to make *or* pull a face at sb; **jdm ins ~ spucken** to spit in sb's face; **jdm ins ~ lachen/lügen/sehen** to laugh in sb's face/to lie to sb's face/to look sb in the face; **den Tatsachen ins ~ sehen** to face facts; **jdm etw ins ~ sagen** to tell sb sth to his face; **mir schien die Sonne ins ~** the sun was (shining) in my eyes; **es stand ihm im ~ geschrieben** it was written all over his face; **jdm ins ~ springen** *(fig inf)* to go for sb; **aufs ~ fallen** to fall on one's face; *(fig inf: Brot etc)* to fall sticky side down; **sein wahres ~ zeigen** to show (oneself in) one's true colours; **neue ~er sehen** to see some new faces; **das sieht man ihm am ~ an** you can see *or* tell (that) from his face; **da fiel mir fast das Essen aus dem ~** *(sl)* I almost threw up *(inf)*; **sich *(dat)* eine (Zigarette) ins ~ stecken** *(inf)* to stick a cigarette in one's mouth *or* face *(sl)*; **jdm wie aus dem ~ geschnitten sein** to be the spitting image of sb; **der Hut steht ihr gut zu ~** *(dated)* her hat is very becoming, her hat becomes her; **dieses Verhalten**

steht dir nicht zu ~ (dated) such behaviour ill becomes you, it
ill becomes you to behave like that; **das/sein ~ verlieren** to lose
face; **das ~ wahren** or **retten** to save face; **siehe Schlag.**
  (b) (fig) (Aussehen) look, appearance; (einer Stadt, Landschaft etc auch) face; (geh: Charakter) character. **ein
anderes/freundlicheres ~ bekommen** to look quite different/
more friendly; **die Sache bekommt ein anderes ~** the matter
takes on a different complexion; **so hat die Sache endlich ein ~**
now it's beginning to take shape or look like something; **das gibt
der Sache ein neues ~** that puts a different complexion on the
matter or on things.
  (c) no pl (old: Sehvermögen) sight. **das Zweite ~** second
sight; **jdn aus dem ~ verlieren** (lit) to lose sight of sb; (fig) to
lose touch with sb; **etw aus dem ~ verlieren** (lit, fig) to lose
sight of sth; **jdn/etw zu ~ bekommen** to set eyes on sb/sth, to
see sb/sth; **jdm zu ~ kommen** (geh) to be seen by sb.
Gesicht² nt -(e)s, -e: **~e haben** to have visions.
Gesichts-: **~ausdruck** m (facial) expression; (Mienenspiel
auch) face; **einen ängstlichen ~ausdruck haben** to look scared,
to have a scared look or expression on one's face; **~bildung** f
(geh) features pl; **eine feine ~bildung haben** to have delicately
cast or delicate features; **~creme** f face cream; **~erker** m
(hum inf) hooter (inf), conk (Brit inf); **~farbe** f complexion;
~feld nt field of vision, visual field; **~hälfte** f side or half of the
face; **seine linke ~hälfte** the left side or half of his face; **~haut** f
facial skin; **~kontrolle** f face check (carried out by bouncers);
~kreis m (dated) (Umkreis) field of vision; (Horizont)
horizon; **jds ~kreis** (dat) **entschwinden** to disappear from
(sb's) sight, to be lost to sight; **jdn aus dem/seinem ~kreis verlieren** to lose sight of sb; **(b)** (fig) horizons pl, outlook; **~lage** f
(Med) face presentation; **~lähmung** f facial paralysis; **~los**
adj (fig) faceless; **~maske** f face mask; (eines Chirurgen)
mask; **~massage** f facial massage, facial; **~milch** f face lotion;
~muskel m facial muscle; **~nerv** m facial nerve; **~operation** f
operation to one's face; **sich einer ~operation unterziehen** to
undergo facial surgery; **~packung** f face pack; **~partie** f part
of the/one's face; **~pflege** f care of one's face; **sie braucht eine
ganze Stunde zur ~pflege** she needs a whole hour for her face
or to do her face; **~plastik** f facial or cosmetic surgery; **~puder**
m face powder; **~punkt** m (Betrachtungsweise) point of view,
standpoint; (Einzelheit) point; **unter diesem ~punkt betrachtet**
looked at from this point of view or standpoint; **~rose** f (Med)
facial erysipelas (spec); **~schädel** m (Anat) facial bones pl;
~schnitt m features pl; **ein ovaler/feiner ~schnitt** an oval
face/delicate features pl; **~verlust** m loss of face; **~wasser** nt
face lotion; **~winkel** m visual angle; (fig) angle, point of view;
aus or **unter diesem ~winkel betrachtet** looked at from this
angle or point of view; **~züge** pl features pl.
Gesims nt -es, -e ledge.
Gesinde nt -s, - (old) servants pl; (Bauern~) (farm)hands pl.
Gesindel nt -s, no pl (pej) riff-raff pl.
Gesinde-: **~ordnung** f (Hist) rules governing relations between
servant and master; **~stube** f (old) servants' room.
Gesinge nt -es, no pl (inf) singing.
gesinnt adj usu pred **jdm gut/günstig/übel ~ sein** to be
well/favourably/ill disposed to(wards) sb; **jdm freund-
lich/feindlich ~ sein** to be friendly/hostile to(wards) sb;
sozial/fortschrittlich ~ sein to be socially/progressively
minded; **er ist anders ~ als wir** his views are different from
ours, he holds different views from us; **die so ~en Mitglieder**
the members holding or taking this view.
Gesinnung f (Charakter) cast of mind; (Ansichten) views pl,
basic convictions pl; (Einstellung) fundamental attitude;
(Denkart) way of thinking; (einer Gruppe) ethos. **eine
liberale/edle ~** liberal-/noble-mindedness; **anständige/knech-
tische** (geh) **~** decency/servility; **seiner ~ treu bleiben** to
remain loyal to one's basic convictions; **wegen seiner ~ verfolgt werden** to be persecuted because of one's views or basic
convictions or way of thinking; **seine wahre ~ zeigen** to show
(oneself in) one's true colours; **Meinungen kann man ändern,
nicht aber seine ~** opinions can be changed, but not one's
fundamental attitude or way of thinking.
Gesinnungs-: **~freund**, **~genosse** m like-minded person;
Herr Klein und seine ~genossen von der Opposition Mr. Klein
and people from the Opposition who think as he does or who
share his views; **g~los** adj (pej) unprincipled; **sich g~los verhalten** to behave in an unprincipled manner, to show a total lack
of character; **~losigkeit** f lack of principle, unprincipledness;
~lump m (pej) timeserver (pej inf); **~lumperei** f (pej)
timeserving (pej inf); **~schnüffelei** f (pej) **~schnüffelei betreiben** to snoop around and find out people's political convictions; **~täter** m person motivated by political/moral convictions; **g~treu** adj true to one's convictions; **~treue** f loyalty to
one's convictions; **~wandel**, **~wechsel** m conversion.
gesittet adj (a) (wohlerzogen) well-mannered, well-behaved.
die Kinder benahmen sich sehr ~ the children were very well-
behaved or well-mannered. **(b)** (zivilisiert, kultiviert)
civilized.
Gesittung f, no pl (geh) (zivilisiertes Verhalten) civilized
(mode of) behaviour; (Gesinnung) ethos.
Gesocks nt -es, no pl (pej sl) riff-raff pl.
Gesöff nt -(e)s, -e (sl) muck (inf), swill (inf); (Bier) piss (vulg).
gesoffen ptp of **saufen**.
gesogen ptp of **saugen**.
gesollt ptp of **sollen**.
gesondert 1 ptp of **sondern²**. 2 adj separate. **Ihre Frau wird ~
benachrichtigt** your wife will be informed separately.
gesonnen 1 ptp of **sinnen**. 2 adj (a) **~ sein, etw zu tun** to be of a
mind to do sth. **(b)** (incorrect) siehe **gesinnt.**
gesotten 1 ptp of **sieden**. 2 adj (dial) boiled. **G~es** boiled meat.

gespalten 1 ptp of **spalten**. 2 adj Bewußtsein split; Lippe,
Rachen cleft; Huf cloven; Zunge forked. **mit ~er Zunge reden**
(old, liter) to talk falsely; (esp in Indianergeschichten) to talk
with forked tongue.
Gespann nt -(e)s, -e (a) (Zugtiere) team; (zwei Ochsen) yoke.
  (b) (Wagen und Zugtier) (Ochsen~) oxcart, ox-drawn cart;
(Pferde~) horse and cart; (zur Personenbeförderung) horse
and carriage; (fig inf: Paar) pair. **ein gutes ~ abgeben** to make a
good team.
gespannt 1 ptp of **spannen**.
  2 adj (a) Seil, Schnur taut.
  (b) (fig) tense; Beziehungen auch strained. **seine Nerven
waren aufs äußerste ~** his nerves were at breaking point.
  (c) (neugierig) curious; (begierig) eager; Aufmerksamkeit
close. **in ~er Erwartung** in eager or keen anticipation; **ich bin
~, wie er darauf reagiert** I wonder how he'll react to that, I'd
like to see how he reacts to that; **ich bin sehr ~, was ich zu
Weihnachten bekomme** I'm longing or dying to know what I'm
getting for Christmas; **ich bin schon sehr auf diesen Film ~** I'm
dying to see this film; **ich bin auf seine Reaktion sehr ~** I'm
longing or dying to see how he reacts; **ich bin ~ wie ein
Regenschirm** (hum inf) or **Flitzbogen** (hum inf) I'm dying to
know/see/find out, I'm on tenterhooks; **da bin ich aber ~!** I'm
looking forward to that; (iro) oh really?, that I'd like to see!
Gespanntheit f, no pl siehe adj (a) tension. **(b)** tension; strain.
(c) curiosity; eagerness; closeness. **es herrscht große ~**
everyone is on tenterhooks.
gespaßig adj (S Ger, Aus) siehe **spaßig.**
Gespenst nt -(e)s, -e (a) ghost, spectre (liter); (fig: Gefahr)
spectre. **~er sehen** (fig inf) to imagine things; **er sieht wie ein ~
aus** (inf) he looks like a ghost.
Gespenster-: **~furcht** f fear of ghosts; **~geschichte** f ghost
story; **~glaube** m belief in ghosts; **g~haft** adj ghostly no adv;
(fig) eerie, eery; **er sah g~haft bleich aus** he was deadly or
deathly pale, he looked like a ghost; **das Licht flackerte g~haft**
the light flickered eerily.
gespenstern* vi (rare) siehe **geistern.**
Gespenster-: **~schiff** nt phantom ship; **~stunde** f witching
hour.
gespenstig (rare), **gespenstisch** adj (a) siehe **gespen-
sterhaft.** **(b)** (fig: bizarr, unheimlich) eerie, eery.
gespie(e)n ptp of **speien.**
Gespiele m -n, -n (old liter, hum), **Gespielin** f (old liter, hum)
playmate.
gespielt 1 ptp of **spielen**. 2 adj feigned. **mit ~em Interesse**
with a pretence of being interested.
gespiesen (hum) ptp of **speisen.**
Gespinst nt -(e)s, -e (a) (Tex) weave; (gedrehtes Garn) thread,
spun yarn; (von Spinne) gossamer; (von Raupe) cocoon. **(b)** (fig
geh) web; (von Lügen auch) tissue; (der Phantasie) product,
fabrication.
Gespinstfaser f (Tex) spinning fibre.
gesplissen ptp of **spleißen.**
gesponnen ptp of **spinnen.**
Gespons¹ m -es, -e (old, hum) spouse (hum, form).
Gespons² nt -es, -e (old, hum) spouse (hum, form).
gespornt adj siehe **gestiefelt.**
Gespött nt -(e)s, no pl mockery; (höhnisch auch) derision,
ridicule; (Gegenstand des Spotts) laughing-stock. **jdn/sich zum
~ der Leute machen** to make sb/oneself a laughing stock or an
object of ridicule; **zum ~ werden** to become a laughing stock;
zum ~ der ganzen Welt werden to become the laughing stock of
the whole world; **mit jdm sein ~ treiben** to poke fun at sb.
Gespöttel nt -s, no pl mocking, sneering.
Gespräch nt -(e)s, -e (a) (Unterhaltung) conversation;
(Diskussion) discussion; (Dialog) dialogue. **~e** (Pol) talks; **ich
habe ein sehr interessantes ~ mit ihm geführt** I had a very
interesting conversation or talk with him; **ein ~ unter vier
Augen** a confidential or private talk; **mit jdm ein ~ anknüpfen**
to start a or get into conversation with sb; **das ~ auf etw** (acc)
bringen to bring or steer the conversation etc round to sth; **im
~ sein** (lit) to be being discussed, to be being talked about; (in
der Schwebe) to be under discussion; **mit jdm ins ~ kommen** to
get into conversation with sb; (fig) to establish a dialogue with
sb.
  (b) (~sstoff) **das ~ des Tages** the topic of the hour; **das ~ der
Stadt** the talk of the town; **zum ~ werden** to become a talking-
point.
  (c) (Telec: Anruf) (telephone) call. **wir haben in unserem
gestrigen ~ vereinbart, daß ...** we agreed in our telephone
conversation yesterday that ...; **ein ~ für dich** a call for you;
stundenlange ~e führen to be on the telephone for hours.
gesprächig adj talkative, chatty (inf); (mitteilsam)
communicative. **~ von etw erzählen** to talk volubly about sth;
jdn ~ machen to make sb talk, to loosen sb's tongue.
Gesprächigkeit f, no pl talkativeness, chattiness (inf);
(Mitteilsamkeit) communicativeness. **von unglaublicher ~
sein** to be incredibly talkative or chatty (inf)/communicative.
Gesprächs-: **g~bereit** adj (esp Pol) ready to talk;
~bereitschaft f (esp Pol) readiness to talk; **~dauer** f (a) (Telec)
call time; **(b) nach vierstündiger ~dauer** after four hours of
talks; **~einheit** f (Telec) unit; **~fetzen** m scrap or snippet of
conversation; **~form** f in **~form** in dialogue form; **~gebühr** f
(Telec) charge for a/the call; **~gegenstand** m topic; **der
Skandal ist ~gegenstand Nummer eins** the scandal is the
number one topic; **damit die Leute endlich einen ~gegenstand
haben** so that people at last have something to talk about;
~partner m interlocutor (form); **~partner bei der Diskussion
sind die Herren X, Y und Z** taking part in the discussion are Mr
X, Mr Y and Mr Z; **mein ~partner bei den Verhandlungen** my

opposite number at the talks; **Carter und seine beiden ~partner Sadat und Begin** Carter and his two partners in the talks, Sadat and Begin; **er ist nicht gerade ein anregender ~partner** he's not exactly an exciting conversationalist; **wer war dein ~partner?** who did you talk with?; **mein ~partner heute abend ist ...** with me this evening is ...; **~pause** f break in a/the conversation/talks; **eine ~pause einlegen** to have a break, to break off (for a while); **~stoff** m topics pl; (*Diskussionsstoff*) topics to discuss; **~teilnehmer** m somebody taking part in (the) talks; participant in a/the discussion; (*bei Fernsehserien etc*) panellist; **~thema** nt siehe **~gegenstand**; **~weise** adv in conversation; **~zähler** m (*Telec*) telephone meter.

gespreizt 1 ptp of **spreizen**. 2 adj (fig) affected, unnatural.

Gespreiztheit f affectation, unnaturalness. **von unerträglicher ~** unbearably affected.

gesprenkelt 1 ptp of **sprenkeln**. 2 adj speckled.

Gespritzte(r) m decl as adj (S Ger, Aus) wine with soda water.

gesprochen ptp of **sprechen**.

gesprossen ptp of **sprießen, sprossen**.

gesprungen ptp of **springen**.

Gespür nt -s, no pl feel(ing).

gest. abbr of **gestorben**.

Gestade nt -s, - (liter) strand (poet).

gestaffelt ptp of **staffeln**.

Gestagen [gɛsta'geːn] nt -s, -e (Med) gestagen.

Gestalt f -, -en (a) (lit, fig) form; (*Umriß auch*) shape. **im Nebel zeichnete sich undeutlich eine ~ ab** a figure or form or shape loomed murkily out of the mist; **in ~ von** (fig) in the form of; **(feste) ~ annehmen** or **gewinnen** to take shape; **einer Sache** (dat) **~ geben** or **verleihen** to shape sth; **das Abendmahl in beiderlei ~** (Eccl) Communion under both kinds; **sich in seiner wahren ~ zeigen** (fig) to show (oneself in) one's true colours; **~ geworden** (liter) made flesh pred; siehe **Ritter**.

(b) (*Wuchs*) build.

(c) (*Person, Persönlichkeit, Traum~*) figure; (*in Literaturwerken auch, pej: Mensch*) character.

gestalten* 1 vt to shape, to form, to fashion (zu into); **Wohnung** to lay out; **Programm, Abend** to arrange; **Schaufenster** to dress; **Freizeit** to organize, to structure. **ich gestalte mein Leben so, wie ich will** I live or organize my life the way I want to; **etw interessanter/moderner etc ~** to make sth more interesting/modern etc; **der Umbau wurde nach den ursprünglichen Plänen gestaltet** the conversion was carried out in accordance with the original plans; **die Gastgeber haben den Abend sehr lebendig gestaltet** our hosts laid on a very lively evening; **etw schöpferisch ~** to give artistic form to sth; **schöpferisches G~** creative expression; **einen historischen Stoff zu einem Roman ~** to fashion or mould a historical subject into a novel; **einen Stoff literarisch ~** to give literary form to one's material.

2 vr (werden) to become; (sich entwickeln) to turn or develop (zu into). **sich zu einem Erfolg ~** to turn out to be a success.

Gestalter(in f) m -s, - creator; (Tech rare) designer.

gestalterisch adj formal, structural. **er hat eine große ~e Begabung** he has a great feeling for form.

Gestalt-: **~lehre** f (dated) morphology; **~los** adj formless, shapeless, amorphous; **~psychologie** f Gestalt psychology.

Gestaltung f (a) siehe vt shaping, forming, fashioning (zu into); lay-out; arrangement; dressing; structuring. **wir bemühen uns um eine möglichst interessante ~ des Sprachunterrichts** we are trying to make our language-teaching as interesting as possible or to structure our language-teaching as interestingly as possible.

(b) (liter: Gestaltetes) creation.

Gestaltungs-: **~form** f form; **~kraft** f creative power; **~prinzip** nt formal principle.

Gestammel nt -s, no pl stammering, stuttering.

gestand pret of **gestehen**.

gestanden 1 ptp of **stehen, gestehen**. 2 adj attr **ein ~er Mann, ein ~es Mannsbild** a (fully grown) man.

geständig adj **~ sein** to have confessed; **ein ~er Mörder** a murderer who confesses.

Geständnis nt confession. **ein ~ ablegen** to make a confession; **jdm ein ~ machen** to make a confession to sb; **jdn zu einem ~ zwingen** to force sb to make a confession.

Gestänge nt -s, - (von Gerüst) bars pl, struts pl; (von Maschine) linkage; (Min: Bohr~) drill stem.

Gestank m -(e)s, no pl stink, stench.

Gestänker nt -s, no pl (inf) trouble-making, stirring (inf).

Gestapo [ge'staːpo] f -, no pl gestapo.

gestärkt 1 ptp of **stärken**. 2 adj strengthened.

gestatten* vti to allow, to permit; (einwilligen in) to agree or consent to. **jdm etw ~** to allow sb sth; **jdm ~, etw zu tun** to allow or permit sb to do sth; **~ Sie?(, darf ich ...), ~ Sie, daß ich ...?** may I ...?, would you mind if I ...?; **wenn Sie ~ ...** with your permission ...; **wenn gnä' Frau ~** (dated) if madam would permit (form); **~ Sie eine Frage?** may I ask you something or a question?; **sich** (dat) **~, etw zu tun** (geh) to take the liberty of doing sth, to be or make so bold as to do sth (dated, hum); **sich** (dat) **etw ~** to permit or allow oneself sth; **wenn ich mir eine Frage/Bemerkung ~ darf ...** (geh) if I might be permitted a question/comment, if I may make or be so bold or free as to ask a question/make a remark ...; **mein Gehalt gestattet mir das nicht** (geh) my salary won't permit it; **mein Gehalt gestattet es mir nicht, nach Afrika zu fahren** (geh) my salary won't allow or permit me to go to Africa; **wenn es die Umstände ~ ...** (geh) circumstances permitting ...

Geste ['gɛstə, 'geːstə] f -, -n (lit, fig) gesture.

Gesteck nt -(e)s, -e flower arrangement.

gesteckt 1 ptp of **stecken**. 2 adv **~ voll** (dial) chock-a-block (inf).

gestehen pret **gestand**, ptp **gestanden** vti to confess (jdm etw sth to sb). **offen gestanden** to be frank, quite frankly.

Gestehungskosten pl (Comm) production costs pl.

Gestein nt -(e)s, -e rock(s); (Schicht) rock stratum.

Gesteins-: **~ader** f vein of rock; **~art** f type of rock; **~bohrer** m, **~bohrmaschine** f rock drill; **~brocken** m rock; **~kunde** f petrography; **~masse** f mass of rock; **~probe** f rock sample; **~schicht** f rock layer or stratum.

Gestell nt -(e)s, -e (a) stand; (Regal) shelf; (Ablage) rack; (Rahmen, Bett~, Brillen~, Tisch~) frame; (auf Böcken) trestle; (Wäsche~) clothes dryer; (Wäsche~ aus Holz) clothes horse; (Fahr~) chassis; (Flugzeug~) undercarriage, landing gear; (Tech: von Hochofen) hearth.

(b) (fig inf) (Beine) pins (inf) pl. **langes ~** beanpole (inf).

gestellt 1 ptp of **stellen**. 2 adj posed.

Gestellung f (a) (old Mil) muster. (b) (form) furnishing (form), making available. **er ordnete die ~ von fünf Fässern Sherry an** he ordered (the) delivery of five barrels of sherry; **ich bitte um ~ von zwei Lastwagen** I request that two lorries be made available.

Gestellungsbefehl m (Mil) call-up, draft papers pl (US).

gestelzt 1 ptp of **stelzen**. 2 adj stilted.

Gestelztheit f stiltedness.

gestern adv yesterday. **~ abend** (früh) yesterday evening; (spät) last night; **die Zeitung von ~** yesterday's paper; **Ansichten von ~** outdated views, opinions of yesteryear (liter); **er ist nicht von ~** (inf) he wasn't born yesterday; **~ vor acht Tagen** a week (ago) yesterday, yesterday week; **~ in acht Tagen** a week (from) yesterday.

Gestern nt -, no pl yesterday. **das ~** yesterday, yesteryear (liter); **im ~** in the past.

Gestichel nt -s, no pl snide remarks pl.

gestiefelt adj (a) wearing or in boots. **der G~e Kater** Puss-in-Boots; **~e Mädchen** girls in boots. (b) **~ und gespornt** (fig inf) ready and waiting, ready for the off (inf).

gestiegen ptp of **steigen**.

gestielt adj stemmed (auch Bot).

Gestik ['gɛstɪk] f -, no pl gestures pl.

Gestikulation [gɛstikulaʦioːn] f gesticulation(s).

gestikulieren* [gɛstiku'liːrən] vi to gesticulate.

Gestikulieren nt -s, no pl gesticulation(s), gesticulating.

gestimmt 1 ptp of **stimmen**. 2 adj **froh/düster ~** in a cheerful/sombre mood.

Gestimmtheit f siehe **Stimmung**.

Gestionsbericht [gɛs'tioːns-] m (Aus) siehe **Geschäftsbericht**.

Gestirn nt -(e)s, -e star, heavenly body.

gestirnt adj attr (geh) starry, star-studded (liter).

gestisch ['gɛstɪʃ] adj gesticulatory. **all seine Worte waren ~ untermalt** everything he said was underlined by gesture.

gestoben ptp of **stieben**.

Gestöber nt -s, - siehe **Schneegestöber**.

gestochen 1 ptp of **stechen**. 2 adj Handschrift clear, neat. **~ scharfe Fotos** needle-sharp photographs.

gestockt adj (S Ger) Milch soured.

gestohlen 1 ptp of **stehlen**. 2 adj **der/das kann mir ~ bleiben** (inf) he/it can go hang (inf).

Gestöhn(e) nt -s, no pl moaning, groaning.

gestopft 1 ptp of **stopfen**. 2 adv **~ voll** (inf) jam-packed (inf).

gestorben ptp of **sterben**.

gestört 1 ptp of **stören**.

2 adj disturbed; Schlaf auch broken; Verhältnis auch troubled; Rundfunkempfang poor, with a lot of interference; Einverständnis troubled, disrupted. **seelisch/geistig ~ sein** to be (psychologically/mentally) unbalanced or disturbed; **~er Kreislauf** circulation problems; **Kinder aus ~en Familien** children from problem families.

gestoßen ptp of **stoßen**.

Gestotter nt -s, no pl stuttering, stammering.

Gestrampel nt -s, no pl kicking about; (beim Radfahren) pedalling.

Gesträuch nt -(e)s, -e shrubbery, bushes pl; (Dickicht) thicket.

gestreckt 1 ptp of **strecken**. 2 adj Galopp full; Winkel, Flugbahn elongated.

gestreift adj striped. **eine rot-grün ~e Bluse** a red and green striped blouse; **sie zieht gern ~ an** (inf) she likes (wearing) stripes.

Gestreite nt -s, no pl (inf) bickering (inf), quarrelling.

gestreng adj (old) strict, stern. **~er Herr!** gracious master or Lord; **die G~en Herren** siehe **Eisheiligen**.

gestrichen 1 ptp of **streichen**.

2 adj (a) painted; Papier coated. **frisch ~!** wet paint.

(b) (genau voll) **ein ~es Maß** a level measure; **~ voll** level; (sehr voll) full to the brim; **ein ~er Teelöffel voll** a level teaspoon(ful); **er hat die Hosen ~ voll** (sl) he's wetting (inf) or shitting (vulg) himself; **ich habe die Nase ~ voll** (sl) I'm fed up to the back teeth with it (inf).

(c) Wort, Satz deleted.

gestriegelt adj: **~ und gebügelt** dressed up to the nines.

gestrig adj attr yesterday's. **unser ~es Gespräch/Schreiben** our conversation (of) yesterday/our letter of yesterday; **am ~en Abend** (geh) (früh) yesterday evening; (spät) last night; **am ~en Tage** (geh) yesterday; **die ewig G~en** the stick-in-the-muds.

gestritten ptp of **streiten**.

Gestrüpp nt -(e)s, -e undergrowth, brushwood; (fig) jungle.

gestuft ptp of **stufen** (in Stufen) terraced; (fig) (abgestuft) graded; (zeitlich) staggered.

Gestühl nt -(e)s, -e seating.

Gestümper nt -s, no pl (pej inf) bungling. **sein erbärmliches ~ auf dem Klavier** his pathetic plonking away on the piano (inf).

gestunken ptp of **stinken**.

Gestus ['gεstʊs] m -, no pl (geh) **(a)** siehe **Gestik**. **(b)** (fig: Ausdruck) air.

Gestüt nt -(e)s, -e stud; (Anlage auch) stud farm.

Gestütbuch nt stud book.

Gestüts-: ~**brand** m stud brand; ~**hengst** m stud (horse); ~**pferd** nt horse at stud; ~**zeichen** nt siehe ~**brand**.

Gesuch nt -(e)s, -e petition (auf, um +acc for); (Antrag) application (auf, um +acc for). **ein ~ einreichen** or **stellen** to make or lodge a petition/an application.

Gesuchsteller(in f) m -s, - (dated) petitioner; (Antragsteller) applicant.

gesucht 1 ptp of **suchen**. **2** adj **(a)** (begehrt) sought after. **sehr ~** (very) much sought after; **Ingenieure sind ~e Arbeitskräfte** engineers are much sought after. **(b)** (gekünstelt) contrived.

Gesudel nt -s, no pl (pej) siehe **Sudelei**.

Gesülze nt -s, no pl (sl) claptrap (inf).

Gesumm nt -(e)s, no pl humming, droning.

Gesums nt -es, no pl (sl) fuss.

gesund adj, comp ⁻er or -er, superl ⁻este(r, s) or -este(r, s) or adv am ⁻esten or -esten (allgemein) healthy; (arbeits-, leistungsfähig) fit; Unternehmen, Politik auch sound; (heilsam) Lehre salutary. **frisch und ~, ~ und munter, ~ wie ein Fisch** in the pink, hale and hearty, (as) sound as a bell; **ich fühle mich nicht ganz ~** I don't feel very or too well; **jdn ~ schreiben** to certify sb (as) fit; **sonst bist du ~?** (iro inf) are you feeling all right? (iro), you need your head examined (inf); **jdn ~ pflegen** to nurse sb back to health; **wieder ~ werden** to get better, to get well again, to recover; **Äpfel sind ~** apples are healthy or good for you or good for your health; **das ist ganz ~ für ihn!** (that) serves him right; **bleib (schön) ~!** look after yourself.

Gesund-: **g~beten** vt sep to heal through prayer; ~**beten** nt faith-healing; ~**beter** m faith-healer; ~**beterei** f (pej inf) praying; ~**brunnen** m (fig) **das ist ein wahrer ~brunnen** it's like a fountain of youth.

gesunden* vi aux sein to recover (auch fig), to regain one's health.

Gesunde(r) mf decl as adj healthy person.

Gesundheit f -, no pl (seelisches, körperliches Wohlbefinden) health; (Sportlichkeit) healthiness; (Arbeits-, Leistungsfähigkeit) fitness; (von Unternehmen, Politik) healthiness, soundness; (von Klima, Lebensweise etc) healthiness. **bei guter ~** in good health; **bei bester ~** in the best of health; **mit meiner ~ steht es nicht zum besten** I'm not in the best of health, my health is not all (that) it might be; **~!** bless you; **auf Ihre ~!** your (very good) health; **eine robuste/eiserne/zarte ~ haben** to have a robust/an iron/a delicate constitution.

gesundheitlich adj **~ geht es mir nicht besonders** my health is not particularly good; **vom ~en Standpunkt aus betrachtet** as regards health, healthwise; **sein ~er Zustand** (the state of) his health; **aus ~en Gründen** for health reasons; **wie geht es Ihnen ~?** how is your health?

Gesundheits-: ~**amt** nt public health department; ~**apostel** m (iro) health nut (inf) or freak (inf); ~**attest** nt health certificate; ~**behörde** f health authorities pl; ~**dienst** m siehe ~**wesen**; ~**fanatiker** m siehe ~**apostel**; **g~fördernd** adj healthy, good for the health; ~**fürsorge** f health care; **g~halber** adv for health reasons; ~**pflege** f hygiene; **Ratschläge zur ~pflege** health advice; **öffentliche ~pflege** public health (care); ~**rücksichten** pl **aus ~rücksichten** on health grounds, on grounds of health; ~**schaden** m health defect; ~**schäden** damage to one's health; **viele Arbeiter haben dabei einen ~schaden davongetragen** the health of many workers has suffered as a result; **g~schädigend, g~schädlich** adj unhealthy, damaging to (one's) health; **g~strotzend** adj bursting (inf) or glowing with health; ~**tee** m herbal tea; ~**wesen** nt health service; ~**zeugnis** nt certificate of health, health certificate; ~**zustand** m, no pl state of health.

gesund-: ~**machen** vr sep (fig inf) to grow fat (an +dat on); ~**schrumpfen** sep 1 vt (fig) to trim down, to streamline; 2 vi aux sein to be trimmed down or streamlined; **G~schrumpfung** f trimming down, streamlining; ~**stoßen** vr sep irreg (sl) to line one's pockets (inf).

Gesundung f, no pl (lit, fig) recovery; (Genesung) convalescence, recuperation. **seine ~ macht Fortschritte** he's progressing well.

gesungen ptp of **singen**.

gesunken ptp of **sinken**.

Gesurr(e) nt -s, no pl humming.

Getäfel, Getäfer (Sw) nt -s, no pl panelling.

getan ptp of **tun**. **nach ~er Arbeit** when the day's work is done.

Getändel nt -s, no pl (dated, geh) dalliance (old, liter).

Getier nt -s, no pl **(a)** (Tiere, esp Insekten) creatures pl. **(b)** (einzelnes) creature.

getigert 1 ptp of **tigern**. **2** adj (mit Streifen) striped; (mit Flecken) piebald.

Getobe nt -s, no pl (inf) chasing about.

Getose nt -s, no pl raging.

Getöse nt -s, no pl din, racket, row; (von Auto, Beifall etc) roar. **mit ~** with a din etc.

getragen 1 ptp of **tragen**. **2** adj **(a)** Kleidung, Schuhe second-hand. **(b)** (fig) Melodie, Tempo etc stately no adv.

Getragenheit f stateliness.

Geträller nt -s, no pl trilling.

Getrampel nt -s, no pl trampling; (Beifalls~, Protest~) stamping.

Getränk nt -(e)s, -e drink, beverage (form). **er gibt viel für ~e aus** he spends a lot on drink.

Getränke-: ~**automat** m drinks machine or dispenser; ~**karte** f (in Café) list of beverages; (in Restaurant) wine list; ~**kiosk**, ~**stand** m drinks stand; ~**steuer** f alcohol tax.

Getrappel nt -s, no pl patter; (Huf~) clop.

Getratsch(e) nt -(e)s, no pl (pej) gossip, gossiping.

getrauen* vr to dare. **getraust du dich** or **dir** (inf) **das?** do you dare do that?; **ich getraue mich nicht dorthin** I don't dare (to) or daren't go there; **ich getraue mich zu behaupten, daß ...** (geh), **ich getraue mir die Behauptung, daß ...** (geh) I would venture to say that ...

Getreide nt -s, (form) - grain, cereal. **in diesem Klima wächst kein ~** grain doesn't or cereals don't grow in this climate; **das ~ steht gut** the grain or cereal crop is doing well.

Getreide-: ~**(an)bau** m cultivation of grain or cereals; ~**art** f cereal; ~**börse** f grain or corn (Brit) exchange; ~**ernte** f grain harvest; ~**feld** nt grain field, cornfield (Brit); ~**garbe** f sheaf of grain; ~**handel** m grain trade; ~**händler** m grain or corn (Brit) merchant; ~**kammer** f siehe **Kornkammer**; ~**korn** nt grain; ~**land** nt **(a)** grain-growing land, cornland (Brit); **(b)** no pl (~**felder**) grain fields pl, cornfields pl (Brit); ~**pflanze** f cereal (plant); ~**produkt** nt cereal product; ~**silo** nt or m, ~**speicher** m silo; ~**wirtschaft** f grain cultivation; **Indiens ~wirtschaft ist fast autark** India is almost self-supporting in terms of grain cultivation.

getrennt 1 ptp of **trennen**. **2** adj separate. **~ leben** to be separated, to live apart; **sie führten ~e Kasse** they each paid for themselves; **~ schlafen** not to sleep together, to sleep in different rooms; siehe **Tisch**.

Getrenntschreibung f writing as two/three etc words. **zu beachten ist die ~ von „zu Hause"** remember that "zu Hause" is written as two (separate) words.

getreten ptp of **treten**.

getreu adj **(a)** (genau, entsprechend) faithful, true no adv. **(b)** pred +dat true to. **(c)** (liter, dated) faithful, loyal, trusty (old). **jdm/sich selbst/einer Sache ~ sein/bleiben** to be/remain true to sb/oneself/sth.

Getreue(r) mf decl as adj (faithful or trusty) follower.

getreulich adj siehe **getreu (a)**.

Getriebe nt -s, - **(a)** (Tech) gears pl; (~**kasten**) gearbox; (Antrieb) drive; (von Uhr) movement, works pl; siehe **Sand**. **(b)** (lebhaftes Treiben) bustle, hurly-burly.

Getriebe- in cpds (Tech) gear; ~**gehäuse** nt gear housing, gearbox.

getrieben ptp of **treiben**.

Getriebenheit f (geh) restlessness.

Getriebe-: ~**öl** nt gear(box) oil; ~**schaden** m gearbox trouble no indef art.

Getriller nt -s, no pl warbling.

Getrippel nt -s, no pl tripping along; (affektiert) mincing.

getroffen ptp of **treffen**.

getrogen ptp of **trügen**.

Getrommel nt -s, no pl drumming.

getrost 1 adj confident. **du kannst ~ sein, sei ~ rest** assured, never fear; **er war ~en Mutes** (old) his mind was reassured. **2** adv **(a)** (vertrauensvoll) confidently. **~ sterben** (geh) to die in peace. **(b)** (bedenkenlos) **wenn er ungezogen ist, darfst du ihm ~ eine runterhauen** if he's cheeky, feel free to or don't hesitate to clout him (one) (inf); **du kannst dich ~ auf ihn verlassen** you need have no fears about relying on him; **man kann ~ behaupten/annehmen, daß ...** one need have no hesitation in or about asserting/assuming that ...; **die Firma könnte ~ etwas mehr zahlen** the company could easily pay a little more.

getrunken ptp of **trinken**.

Getto nt -s, -s ghetto.

Getue [gə'tuːə] nt -s, no pl (pej) to-do (inf), fuss; (geheuchelte Höflichkeit) affectation. **ein ~ machen** to make a to-do (inf) or fuss; (überhöflich sein, sich wichtig machen) to put on airs.

Getümmel nt -s, no pl turmoil. **das ~ des Kampfes** the tumult of battle; **sich ins ~ stürzen** to plunge into the tumult or hurly-burly.

Getuschel nt -s, no pl whispering.

geübt 1 ptp of **üben**. **2** adj Auge, Ohr, Griff practised; Fahrer, Segler etc proficient. **im Schreiben/Reden ~ sein** to be a proficient writer/talker.

Gevatter m -s, or -n, -n (obs) (Pate) godfather; (fig) brother. **~ Tod** (Death) the Reaper (liter).

Gevatterin f (obs) godmother; (fig) sister (old).

Geviert [gə'fiːɐ̯t] nt -s, -e (old: Quadrat) square; (Min) crib; (Typ) quad(rat). **5 Meter im ~** (old) 5 metres square.

Geviertmeter m siehe **Quadratmeter**.

Gevögel nt -s, no pl **(a)** (obs: Vögel) birds pl. **(b)** (vulg: Koitieren) screwing (vulg).

Gewächs nt -es, -e **(a)** (Pflanze) plant. **er ist ein seltsames ~** (dated) he is an odd specimen (inf). **(b)** (Weinjahrgang) wine. **(c)** (Med) growth.

gewachsen 1 ptp of **wachsen**[1]. **2** adj **(a)** (von allein entstanden) evolved. **diese in Jahrtausenden ~en Traditionen** these traditions which have evolved over the millennia. **(b)** **jdm/einer Sache ~ sein** to be a match for sb/to be up to sth; **er ist seinem Bruder (an Stärke/Intelligenz) durchaus ~** he is his brother's equal in strength/intelligence.

Gewächshaus nt greenhouse; (Treibhaus) hothouse.

Gewackel nt -s, no pl (inf) (von Tisch, Stuhl etc) wobbling. **~ mit den Hüften/dem Schwanz** waggling one's hips/wagging its tail.

gewagt 1 ptp of **wagen**. **2** adj **(a)** (kühn) daring; (gefährlich) risky. **(b)** (moralisch bedenklich) risqué.

Gewagtheit f **(a)** no pl siehe adj daring; riskiness; risqué nature. (b) (*gewagte Äußerung*) daring remark.

gewählt 1 *ptp of* **wählen.** 2 *adj Sprache* refined *no adv*, elegant.

Gewähltheit *f* elegance.

gewahr *adj pred* = **werden** +*gen* (*geh*) *siehe* **gewahren.**

Gewähr *f* -, *no pl* guarantee. **jdm ~ dafür geben, daß ...** to guarantee (sb *or* to sb) that ...; **dadurch ist die ~ gegeben, daß ...** that guarantees that ...; **die ~ für jds Zahlungsfähigkeit übernehmen** to guarantee sb's ability to pay; **die Angabe erfolgt ohne ~** this information is supplied without liability; **„ohne ~"** (*auf Fahrplan, Preisliste*) "subject to change"; (*bei Lottozahlen, statistischen Angaben*) "no liability assumed"; **für etw ~ leisten** to guarantee sth.

gewahren* *vt* (*liter*) to become aware of.

gewähren* *vt* to grant; *Rabatt, Vorteile* to give; *Sicherheit, Trost, Schutz* to afford, to give. **jdm Unterstützung ~** to provide sb with support, to support sb; **jdn ~ lassen** (*geh*) not to stop sb.

gewährleisten* *vt insep* (*sicherstellen*) to ensure (*jdm etw* sb sth); (*garantieren*) to guarantee (*jdm etw* sb sth).

Gewährleistung *f* guarantee. **zur ~ der Sicherheit** to ensure safety.

Gewahrsam[1] *m* -s, *no pl* (a) (*Verwahrung*) safe-keeping. **etw in ~ nehmen/haben** to take sth into/have sth in safekeeping; **etw (jdm) in ~ geben** to hand sth over (to sb) for safekeeping; **der sichere ~ der Burg** the shelter of the castle. (b) (*Haft*) custody. **jdn in ~ nehmen** to take sb into custody; **in ~ sein, sich in ~ befinden** to be in custody.

Gewahrsam[2] *nt* -s, -e (*old: Gefängnis*) prison.

Gewährsmann *m, pl* -männer *or* -leute source.

Gewährung *f* -, *no pl siehe vt* granting; giving; affording.

Gewalt *f* -, -en (a) (*Machtbefugnis, Macht, Herrschaft*) power. **die drei ~en** (*Pol*) the three powers; **die ausübende *or* vollziehende/gesetzgebende/richterliche ~** the executive/legislature/judiciary; **elterliche ~** parental authority; **jdn in seiner ~ haben** to have sb in one's power; **~ über jdn haben *or* besitzen** to have power over sb; **etw in der ~ haben** (*übersehen*) to have control of sth; (*steuern können*) to have sth under control; (*entscheiden können*) to have sth in one's power; **sich in der ~ haben** to have oneself under control; **etw in/wieder in seine ~ bringen** to gain/regain control of sth; **in/unter jds ~ (dat) sein *or* stehen** to be in sb's power/under sb's control; **die ~ über etw (acc) verlieren** to lose control of sth; **~ über Leben und Tod (haben)** (to have) power over life and death.

(b) *no pl* (*Zwang*) force; (*~tätigkeit*) violence. **~ anwenden** to use force; **höhere ~** acts/an act of God; **nackte ~** brute force; **mit ~** by force; **mit aller ~** (*inf*) for all one is worth; **etw mit aller ~ wollen** (*inf*) to want sth desperately; **jdm/einer Sache ~ antun** to do violence to sb/sth; **einer Frau ~ antun** to violate a woman; **sich (*dat*) ~ antun** (*fig: sich überwinden*) to force oneself; **~ geht vor Recht** (*Prov*) might is right (*Prov*).

(c) (*geh: Natur~*) force. **die tobenden ~en der Natur** the raging forces of nature.

(d) *no pl* (*Heftigkeit, Wucht*) force; (*elementare Kraft auch*) power. **die ~ der Explosion/des Sturmes** the force of the explosion/storm; **er warf sich mit ~ gegen die Tür** he hurled himself violently against the door.

Gewalt-: **~akt** *m* act of violence; **~androhung** *f* threat of violence; **unter ~androhung** under threat of violence; **~anwendung** *f* use of force *or* violence; **~einwirkung** *f* violence.

Gewalten-: **~teilung, ~trennung** *f* separation of powers.

Gewalt-: **~friede(n)** *m* dictated peace; **~haber** *m* -s, - holder of power; **die ~haber** those in power; **~herrschaft** *f*, *no pl* tyranny; **~herrscher** *m* tyrant.

gewaltig *adj* (a) (*heftig*) *Sturm etc* violent. (b) (*groß, riesig*) colossal, immense; (*wuchtig auch*) massive; *Anblick* tremendous; *Stimme, Töne* powerful; (*inf: sehr groß*) *Unterschied, Hitze etc* tremendous, colossal (*inf*). **sich ~ irren** to be very much mistaken *or* very wrong, to be way out (*inf*); **du mußt dich ~ ändern** you'll have to change one hell of a lot (*inf*); **er hat sich ~ in meine Schwester verknallt** (*inf*) he's really got it bad for my sister (*inf*); **ich habe ihn ~ ausgeschimpft** (*inf*) I really told him off.

(c) (*geh: mächtig*) powerful. **die G~en der Erde** the mighty rulers of the world.

Gewaltigkeit *f*, *no pl siehe adj* (a) violence. (b) colossalness, immenseness; massiveness; tremendousness. (c) powerfulness.

Gewalt-: **~kur** *f* drastic measures *pl*; (*Hungerdiät*) crash diet; **das ist eine ~kur** that's pretty drastic; **~leistung** *f* feat of strength, tour de force; **g~los** 1 *adj* non-violent; 2 *adv* without force/violence; **~losigkeit** *f*, *no pl* non-violence; **~marsch** *m* forced march; **im ~marsch** at a cracking pace (*inf*); **~maßnahme** *f* (*fig*) drastic measure; **jdm mit ~maßnahmen drohen** to threaten to use force against sb; (*fig*) to threaten sb with drastic action; **auf ~maßnahmen verzichten** not to use force; **~mensch** *m* pusher (*inf*); (*brutaler Mensch*) brute; **g~sam** 1 *adj* forcible; *Tod* violent; 2 *adv* forcibly, by force; **~streich** *m* (*Mil*) storm; (*fig*) coup (de force); **im *or* in einem ~streich** by storm; **im ~streich** (*fig: ohne Zögern*) at a stroke; **~tat** *f* act of violence; **g~tätig** *adj* violent; **~tätigkeit** *f* (*no pl*: *Brutalität*) violence; (*Handlung*) act of violence; **~verbrechen** *nt* crime of violence; **~verbrecher** *m* violent criminal; **~verzicht** *m* non-aggression; **~verzichtsabkommen** *nt* non-aggression treaty.

Gewand *nt* -(e)s, ¨-er (a) (*geh: Kleidungsstück*) garment; (*weites, langes*) robe, gown; (*Eccl*) vestment, robe; (*old: Kleidung*) garb, garments *pl*, apparel (*old*); (*fig: Äußeres*) look;

(*fig: Maske*) guise. **ein altes Buch in neuem ~** an old book with a new look *or* appearance *or* livery, an old book dressed up; **sich in neuem ~ zeigen** (*fig*) to have a new look about it.

(b) (*obs: Tuch*) fabric, cloth.

gewandet *adj* (*old, hum*) clad, apparelled (*old*). **blau-/gelb- etc ~** clad in blue/yellow *etc*.

gewandt 1 *ptp of* **wenden.** 2 *adj* skilful; (*körperlich*) nimble; (*geschickt*) deft, dexterous; *Auftreten, Redner, Stil* elegant.

Gewandtheit *f*, *no pl siehe adj* skilfulness; nimbleness; deftness, dexterity; elegance.

Gewandung *f* (*old, hum*) garb, apparel (*old*), raiment (*obs*).

gewann *pret of* **gewinnen.**

gewärtig *adj pred* (*geh*) prepared (*gen* for). **~ sein, daß ...** to be prepared for the possibility that ...

gewärtigen* *vtr* (*geh*) to expect; (*sich einstellen auf auch*) to be prepared for. **~, daß ...** to expect that .../to be prepared for the possibility that ...; **etw ~ müssen** to have to be prepared for sth, to have to expect sth; **er hat eine hohe Strafe zu ~** he must expect a severe punishment.

Gewäsch *nt* -(e)s, *no pl* (*pej inf*) twaddle (*inf*), claptrap (*inf*).

gewaschen *ptp of* **waschen.**

Gewässer *nt* -s, - stretch of water. **~ pl** inshore waters *pl*, lakes, rivers and canals *pl*; **ein fließendes/stehendes ~** a stretch of running/standing water.

Gewässer-: **~kunde** *f* hydrography; **~schutz** *m* prevention of water pollution.

Gewebe *nt* -s, - (*Stoff*) fabric, material; (*~art*) weave; (*Biol*) tissue; (*fig*) web. **ein ~ von Lügen** a web *or* tissue of lies.

Gewebe-, Gewebs-: **~flüssigkeit** *f* (*Med*) lymph; **~probe** *f* (*Med*) tissue sample; **g~schonend** *adj* (*Comm*) kind to fabrics; **~transplantation** *f* (*Med*) tissue graft.

Gewehr *nt* -(e)s, -e (*Flinte*) rifle; (*Schrotbüchse*) shotgun. **~ ab!** (*Mil*) order arms!; **das ~ über!** (*Mil*) shoulder arms!; **an die ~e!** (*Mil*) to arms!; (*dated inf*) let's get cracking (*dated inf*) *or* started; **präsentiert das ~!** (*Mil*) present arms!; **das *or* mit dem ~ (auf jdn) anlegen** to aim (at sb); (*Mil*) to train a gun (on sb); **~ bei Fuß stehen** (*Mil*) to stand at order arms; (*fig auch*) to be at the ready.

Gewehr-: **~griff** *m* rifle position; **~griffe üben** to do rifle drill; **~kolben** *m* rifle butt/butt of a shotgun; **~kugel** *f* rifle bullet; **~lauf** *m* rifle barrel/barrel of a shotgun; **„die politische Macht kommt aus den ~läufen"** "political power grows out of the barrel of a gun"; **~mündung** *f* muzzle (of a rifle/shotgun); **~riemen** *m* rifle sling/gunsling.

Geweih *nt* -(e)s, -e (set of *sing*) antlers *pl*. **das/ein ~** the antlers/a set of antlers.

Geweih-: **~ende** *nt* point *or* tine (*spec*) of an antler; **~schaufel** *f* palm (of an antler).

Geweine *nt* -s, *no pl* (*inf*) crying.

Gewerbe *nt* -s, - (a) (*Frau*) trade and industry; **das älteste ~ der Welt** (*hum*) the oldest profession in the world (*hum*); **ein dunkles ~** a shady business; **einem dunklen/seinem ~ nachgehen** to be in a shady trade *or* have a shady occupation/to carry on *or* practise one's trade; **ein ~ (be)treiben *or* ausüben** to follow a *or* carry on a trade; **aus etw ein ~ machen** to make sth one's trade.

(b) (*Sw: Bauerngehöft*) farm.

Gewerbe-: **~amt** *nt siehe* **~aufsichtsamt; ~aufsicht** *f* = factory safety and health control; **~aufsichtsamt** *nt* = factory inspectorate; **~betrieb** *m* commercial enterprise; **~freiheit** *f* freedom of trade; **~lehrer** *m* teacher in a trade school; **~ordnung** *f* trading regulations *pl*; **~schein** *m* trading licence; **~schule** *f* trade school; **~steuer** *f* trade tax; **~tätigkeit** *f* commercial activity; **~treibende(r)** *mf decl as adj* trader; **~verein** *m* (*old*) trade association; **~zweig** *m* branch of a/the trade.

gewerblich *adj* commercial; *Lehrling, Genossenschaft* trade *attr*; (*industriell*) industrial. **~e Arbeiter** industrial workers; **die ~e Wirtschaft** industry; **~er Rechtsschutz** legal protection of industrial property; **die ~en Berufe** the trades; **diese Räume dürfen nicht ~ genutzt werden** these rooms are not to be used for commercial purposes.

Gewerbs-: **g~mäßig** 1 *adj* professional; **g~mäßige Unzucht** (*form*) prostitution; 2 *adv* professionally, for gain; **~unzucht** *f* (*form*) prostitution *no art*.

Gewerkschaft *f* (trade *or* trades *or* labor *US*) union.

Gewerkschaft(l)er(in *f*) *m* -s, - trade *or* labor (*US*) unionist.

gewerkschaftlich *adj* (trade *or* labor *US*) union *attr*. **~er Vertrauensmann** (*im Betrieb*) shop steward; **wir haben uns ~ organisiert** we organized ourselves into a union; **~ organisierter Arbeiter** unionized *or* organized worker; **~ engagiert** involved in the (trade *or* labor) union movement.

Gewerkschafts- *in cpds* (trade/labor) union; **~bank** *f* trade union bank/labor bank; **~bewegung** *f* (trade/labor) union movement; **~boß** *m* (*usu pej*) (trade/labor) union boss; **~bund** *m* federation of trade/labor unions, = Trades Union Congress (*Brit*), = Federation of Labor (*US*); **~eigen** *adj* owned by a (trade/labor) union; **~kongreß** *m siehe* **~tag; ~mitglied** *nt* member of a/the (trade/labor) union; **~tag** *m* trade/labor union conference; **~verband** *m* federation of trade/labor unions; **~vorsitzende(r)** *mf* (trade/labor) union president; **~wesen** *nt* (trade/labor) union movement.

Gewese *nt* -s, *no pl* (*inf*) fuss, to-do (*inf*).

gewesen 1 *ptp of* **sein**[1]. 2 *adj attr* former.

gewichen *ptp of* **weichen**[2].

gewichst [gə'vɪkst] 1 *ptp of* **wichsen.** 2 *adj* (*inf*) fly (*inf*), crafty.

Gewicht *nt* -(e)s, -e (a) *no pl* (*lit, fig*) weight. **dieser Stein hat ein großes ~/ein ~ von 100 kg** this rock is very heavy/weighs 100 kg; **er hat sein ~ gehalten** he has stayed the same weight;

er brachte zuviel ~ **auf die Waage** he weighed in too heavy; **er legte sein ganzes ~ in den Schlag** he put his whole weight behind or into the punch; **spezifisches ~** specific gravity; **das hat ein ~!** (*inf*) it isn't half heavy! (*inf*); **das hat sein ~** (*inf*) it's not exactly light, it's some weight; **etw nach ~ verkaufen** to sell sth by weight; **~ haben** (*lit*) to be heavy; (*fig*) to carry weight; **ins ~ fallen** to be crucial; **nicht ins ~ fallen** to be of no consequence; **auf etw** (*acc*) **~ legen, einer Sache** (*dat*) **~ beilegen** or **beimessen** to set (great) store by sth, to lay stress on sth.
(b) (*Metallstück zum Beschweren etc, Sport*) weight.
gewichten* *vt* (*Statistik*) to weight; (*fig*) to evaluate.
Gewicht-: **~heben** *nt* -s, *no pl* (*Sport*) weight-lifting; **~heber** *m* weight-lifter.
gewichtig *adj* (a) (*dated: schwer*) heavy, hefty (*inf*). **eine ~e Persönlichkeit** (*hum inf*) a personage of some weight. (b) (*fig*) (*wichtig*) weighty; (*wichtigtuerisch*) self-important; (*einflußreich*) influential.
Gewichtigkeit *f, no pl* (*fig*) weightiness; self-importance; influence.
Gewichts-: **~abnahme** *f* loss of weight; **~analyse** *f* (*Chem*) gravimetric analysis; **~angabe** *f* indication of weight; **die Hersteller von Konserven sind zur ~angabe verpflichtet** the manufacturers of canned food are obliged to show the weight; **~klasse** *f* (*Sport*) weight (category); **~kontrolle** *f* weight check; **g~los** *adj* weightless; (*fig*) lacking substance; **~satz** *m* set of weights; **~verlagerung** *f* shifting of weight; (*fig*) shift of or in emphasis; **~verlust** *m* loss of weight, weight loss; **~verschiebung** *f* siehe **~verlagerung**; **~zunahme** *f* increase in weight.
Gewichtung *f* (*Statistik*) weighting; (*fig*) evaluation.
gewieft *adj* (*inf*) fly (*inf*), crafty (*in* +*dat* at).
Gewieftheit *f* (*inf*) flyness (*inf*), craftiness.
gewiegt *adj* shrewd, slick (*inf*), canny (*esp Scot inf*).
Gewieher *nt* -s, *no pl* whinnying; (*fig*) guffawing, braying.
gewiesen *ptp of* **weisen.**
gewillt *adj* **~ sein, etw zu tun** to be willing to do sth; (*entschlossen*) to be determined to do sth; **bist du ~, diesen Mann zu ehelichen?** wilt thou take this man to be thy lawful wedded husband?
Gewimmel *nt* -s, *no pl* swarm, milling mass; (*Menge*) crush, throng.
Gewimmer *nt* -s, *no pl* whimpering.
Gewinde *nt* -s, - (*Tech*) thread.
Gewinde- (*Tech*): **~bohrer** *m* (screw) tap; **~bolzen** *m* threaded bolt; **~fräsen** *nt* thread milling; **~gang** *m* pitch (of screw thread); **~schneiden** *nt* thread cutting; (*für Innengewinde*) tapping.
gewinkelt *adj* angled.
Gewinn *m* -(e)s, -e (a) (*Ertrag*) profit. **~-und-Verlust-Rechnung** profit-and-loss account; **~ abwerfen** or **bringen** to make a profit; **~ erzielen** to make a profit; **aus etw ~ schlagen** (*inf*) to make a profit out of sth; **etw mit ~ verkaufen** to sell sth at a profit.
(b) (*Preis, Treffer*) prize; (*bei Wetten, Glücksspiel*) winnings *pl*. **einen großen ~ machen** to win a lot; **jedes Los ist ein ~** every ticket a winner; **er hat im Lotto einen ~ gehabt** he had a win on the lottery; **mit einem ~ herauskommen** (*inf*) to get a prize.
(c) *no pl* (*fig: Vorteil*) gain. **das ist ein großer ~ (für mich)** I have gained a lot from this, that is of great benefit (to me); **ein ~ für die Abteilung** a valuable addition to the department; **ein Buch mit ~ lesen** to gain something from reading a book.
Gewinn-: **~anteil** *m* (a) (*Comm*) dividend; (b) (*beim Wetten etc*) share; **~ausschüttung** *f* prize draw; **~beteiligung** *f* (a) (*Ind*) (*Prinzip*) profit-sharing; (*Summe*) (profit-sharing) bonus; (b) (*Dividende*) dividend; **g~bringend** *adj* (*lit, fig*) profitable; **~chance** *f* chance of winning; **~chancen** (*beim Wetten*) odds.
gewinnen *pret* **gewann**, *ptp* **gewonnen** 1 *vt* (a) (*siegen in*) to win; (*erwerben, bekommen auch*) to gain; **jds Herz ~** to win; **Preis** to win. **jdn (für etw) ~** to win sb over (to sth); **jdn für sich ~** to win sb over (to one's side); **jdn zum Freund ~** to win sb as a friend; **es gewinnt den Anschein, als ob ...** (*form*) it would appear that ...; **das Freie** or **Weite ~** to make good one's escape; **das Ufer ~** (*liter*) to reach or gain (*liter*) the bank; **Zeit ~** to gain time; **es über sich ~, etw zu tun** (*old*) to bring oneself to do sth; **was ist damit gewonnen?** what good is that?; **was ist damit gewonnen, wenn du das tust?** what is the good or use of you or your doing that?; **wie gewonnen, so zerronnen** (*prov*) easy come easy go (*prov*); **(bei jdm) gewonnenes Spiel haben** to be home and dry (with sb).
(b) (*als Profit*) to make (a profit of).
(c) (*erzeugen*) to produce, to obtain; *Erze etc* to mine, to extract, to win (*liter*); (*aus Altmaterial*) to reclaim, to recover.
2 *vi* (a) to win (*bei, an* +*dat* at).
(b) (*profitieren*) to gain; (*sich verbessern*) to gain something. **an Bedeutung ~** to gain (in) importance; **an Boden ~** (*fig*) to gain ground; **an Höhe/Geschwindigkeit ~** to gain height/to pick up or gain speed; **an Klarheit ~** to gain in clarity; **sie gewinnt durch ihre neue Frisur** her new hairstyle does something for her; **sie gewinnt bei näherer Bekanntschaft** she improves on closer acquaintance; *siehe* **wagen.**
gewinnend *adj* (*fig*) winning, winsome.
Gewinner(in *f*) *m* -s, - winner.
Gewinnerstraße *f* (*Sport sl*) **auf der ~ sein** to be headed for a win, to be on the way to victory.
Gewinn-: **~gemeinschaft** *f* (*Comm*) profit pool; **~klasse** *f* prize category.
Gewinnler(in *f*) *m* -s, - *siehe* **Kriegsgewinnler(in).**

Gewinn-: **~liste** *f* list of winners, winners list; **~los** *nt* winning ticket; **~maximierung** *f* siehe **Profitmaximierung**; **~nummer** *f* siehe **Gewinnnummer**; **~satz** *m* (*Tennis etc*) **mit drei ~sätzen spielen** to play the best of five sets; **der dritte Satz war sein ~satz** the third set was the winning set for him; **~spanne** *f* profit margin; **~streben** *nt* pursuit of profit; **~sucht** *f* profit-seeking; **aus ~sucht** for motives of (financial/material) gain; **g~süchtig** *adj* profit-seeking; **g~trächtig** *adj* profitable.
Gewinnnummer *getrennt* **Gewinn-nummer, Gewinnzahl** *f* winning number.
Gewinsel *nt* -s, *no pl* (*lit, fig*) whining.
Gewinst *m* -(e)s, -e (*old*) *siehe* **Gewinn.**
Gewirbel *nt* -s, *no pl* whirl(ing).
Gewirr *nt* -(e)s, *no pl* tangle; (*fig: Durcheinander*) jumble; (*von Paragraphen, Klauseln etc*) maze, confusion; (*von Gassen*) maze; (*von Stimmen*) confusion, babble.
Gewisper *nt* -s, *no pl* whispering.
gewiß 1 *adj* (a) (*sicher*) certain, sure (+*gen* of). (**ja**) **~!** certainly, sure (*esp US*); **ich bin dessen ~** (*geh*) I'm certain or sure of it; **das ist so ~, wie die Nacht dem Tag folgt** (*geh*) as night follows day; **darüber weiß man noch nichts Gewisses** nothing certain is known as yet.
(b) *attr* certain. **ein gewisser Herr Müller** a certain Herr Müller; **in gewissem Maße** to some or a certain extent; **in gewissem Sinne** in a (certain) sense; *siehe* **Etwas.**
2 *adv* (*geh*) certainly. **Sie denken ~, daß ...** no doubt you think that ...; **ich weiß es ganz ~** I'm certain or sure of it; **eins ist or weiß ich (ganz)** ~ one thing is certain or sure, there's one thing I know for certain or sure; (**aber**) **~ (doch)!** (but) of course; **darf ich ...? — (aber) ~ (doch)!** may I ...? — but, of course or by all means.
Gewissen *nt* -s, *no pl* conscience. **ein schlechtes ~** a guilty or bad conscience; **ich sage es Ihnen auf mein ~** (*dated*) I (can) say this in all conscience; **jdn/etw auf dem ~ haben** to have sb/sth on one's conscience; **das hast du auf dem ~** it's your fault; **sich** (*dat*) **kein ~ daraus machen, etw zu tun** to have no scruples about or hesitation in doing sth; **jdm ins ~ reden** to have a serious talk with sb; **jdm ins ~ reden, etw zu tun** to get or persuade sb to do sth; **das mußt du vor deinem ~ verantworten** you'll have to answer to your own conscience for that; **ein gutes ~ ist ein sanftes Ruhekissen** (*Prov*) I *etc* just want to have a clear conscience, I *etc* just want to be able to sleep nights (*esp US*); *siehe* **Ehre, Wissen.**
Gewissen-: **g~haft** *adj* conscientious; **~haftigkeit** *f, no pl* conscientiousness; **g~los** *adj* unprincipled, without conscience, unscrupulous; (*verantwortungslos*) irresponsible; **g~los sein** to have no conscience; **wie kann man so g~los sein und ...** how could anybody be so unscrupulous/irresponsible as to ...; **~losigkeit** *f* unscrupulousness, lack of principle; (*Verantwortungslosigkeit*) irresponsibility.
Gewissens-: **~angst** *f* pangs of conscience *pl*; **~bisse** *pl* pangs of conscience *pl*; **mach dir deswegen keine ~bisse!** there's nothing for you to feel guilty about; **~bisse bekommen** to get a guilty conscience; **ohne ~bisse** without compunction (*liter*), without feeling guilty; **~entscheidung** *f* question of conscience, matter for one's conscience to decide; **~erforschung** *f* examination of one's conscience; **~frage** *f* matter of conscience; **~freiheit** *f* freedom of conscience; **~gründe** *pl* conscientious reasons *pl*; **~konflikt** *m* moral conflict; **~not** *f* moral dilemma; **~pein** (*geh*), **~qual** (*geh*) *f* pangs of conscience *pl*; **~sache** *f* siehe **~frage**; **~skrupel** *pl* (moral) scruples *pl*; **~skrupel haben, etw zu tun** to have scruples about doing sth; **~zwang** *m, no pl* moral constraint(s); **~zweifel** *m* moral doubt.
gewissermaßen *adv* (*sozusagen*) so to speak, as it were; (*auf gewisse Weise*) in a way, to an extent.
Gewißheit *f* certainty. **mit ~** with certainty; **wissen** for certain or sure; **~ erlangen** to achieve certain knowledge; (**zur**) **~ werden** to become a certainty; *siehe* **verschaffen.**
gewißlich *adv* (*old, geh*) *siehe* **gewiß 2.**
Gewitter *nt* -s, - thunderstorm; (*fig*) storm.
Gewitter-: **~fliege** *f* thunder fly; **~front** *f* (*Met*) storm front; **~guß** *m* rainstorm; **~himmel** *m* stormy sky, thunderclouds *pl*.
gewitt(e)rig *adj* thundery. **~ schwül** thundery (and oppressive); **~e Schwüle** thundery (and oppressive) air.
Gewitterluft *f* thundery atmosphere. **es ist ~** there's thunder in the air or about.
gewittern* *vi impers* **es gewittert** it's thundering.
Gewitter-: **~neigung** *f* (*Met*) likelihood of thunder storms; **~regen, ~schauer** *m* thundery shower; **g~schwül** *adj* siehe **gewitt(e)rig**; **~schwüle** *f* thundery (and oppressive) atmosphere; **~stimmung** *f* (*fig*) stormy atmosphere; **~sturm** *m* thunderstorm; **~wand** *f* wall or mass of thunderclouds; **~wolke** *f* thundercloud; (*fig inf*) storm-cloud; **Vater hatte ~wolken auf der Stirn** Father's face was as black as thunder; **~ziege** *f* (*pej inf*) sour old hag.
gewitzig *adj* crafty, cunning.
Gewitzel *nt* -s, *no pl* joking, jokes *pl*.
Gewitzheit *f, no pl* craftiness, cunning.
gewitzigt *adj pred* (*made*) wiser. **ich bin jetzt ~** I've learned by (bitter) experience, I'm wiser now.
gewitzt *adj* crafty, cunning.
gewoben *ptp of* **weben.**
Gewoge *nt* -s, *no pl* surging; (*von Kornfeld auch*) waving; (*hum: von Busen*) surging.
gewogen[1] *ptp of* **wägen, wiegen**[2].
gewogen[2] *adj* (*geh*) well-disposed, favourably disposed (+*dat* towards).
Gewogenheit *f, no pl* (*geh*) favourable attitude. **bei aller ~ stand er ihm doch nicht unkritisch gegenüber** although favour-

ably disposed he was not altogether uncritical in his attitude towards him.

gewöhnen* 1 *vt* jdn an etw (*acc*) ~ to make sb used *or* accustomed to sth, to accustom sb to sth; **jdn an Höflichkeit** ~ to train *or* teach sb to be polite; **einen Hund an Sauberkeit** ~ to house-train a dog; **Sie werden sich noch daran** ~ **müssen, daß** ... you'll have to get used to *or* accept the fact that ...; **an jdn/etw gewöhnt sein, jdn/etw gewöhnt sein** (*inf*) to be used to sb/sth.

2 *vr* **sich an jdn/etw** ~ to get *or* become used to sb/sth, to accustom oneself to sb/sth; **du mußt dich an Ordnung/Pünktlichkeit** ~ you must get used to being *or* get into the habit of being orderly/punctual; **sich daran** ~, **etw zu tun** to get used *or* accustomed to doing sth; **das bin ich gewöhnt** I'm used to it.

Gewohnheit *f* habit. **aus (lauter)** ~ from (sheer) force of habit; **die** ~ **haben, etw zu tun** to have a habit of doing sth; **wie es seine** ~ **war, nach alter** ~ as was his wont *or* custom; **aus der** ~ **kommen** to get out of practice; **das ist ihm zur** ~ **geworden** it's become a habit with him; **sich** (*dat*) **etw zur** ~ **machen** to make a habit of sth.

Gewohnheits-: g~**gemäß,** g~**mäßig 1** *adj* habitual; **2** *adv* (*ohne nachzudenken*) automatically; ~**mensch** *m* creature of habit; ~**recht** *nt* (*Jur*) (a) (*im Einzelfall*) established *or* customary right; **(b)** (*als Rechtssystem*) common law; ~**sache** *f* question of habit; ~**tier** *nt*: **der Mensch ist ein** ~**tier** (*inf*) man is a creature of habit; ~**trinker** *m* habitual drinker; ~**verbrecher** *m* habitual criminal.

gewöhnlich 1 *adj* **(a)** *attr* (*allgemein, üblich*) usual, customary; (*normal*) normal; (*durchschnittlich*) ordinary; (*alltäglich*) everyday. **ein** ~**er Sterblicher** an ordinary mortal.
(b) (*pej: ordinär*) common. **sie zieht sich immer so** ~ **an** she always wears such common clothes.
2 *adv* normally, usually. **wie** ~ as usual, as per usual (*inf*).

Gewöhnlichkeit *f* (*pej*) commonness.

gewohnt *adj* usual. **etw** (*acc*) ~ **sein** to be used to sth; **ich bin es** ~, **früh aufzustehen** I am used to getting up early.

gewohntermaßen *adv* usually.

Gewöhnung *f*, *no pl* (*das Sich-Gewöhnen*) habituation (*an* +*acc* to); (*das Angewöhnen*) training (*an* +*acc* in); (*Sucht*) habit, addiction. **die** ~ **an den Kindergarten kann bei einigen Kindern ziemlich lange dauern** it can take a fairly long time for some children to get used to kindergarten.

Gewölbe *nt* -s, - (*Decken*~) vault; (*Keller*~ *auch*) vaults *pl*. **das** ~ **des Himmels** (*liter*) the vault of the heavens (*liter*).

Gewölbe-: ~**bogen** *m* arch (of a vault); ~**pfeiler** *m* pier (of a vault).

gewölbt *adj* Stirn domed; Himmel, Decke vaulted; Brust bulging; Nase aquiline.

Gewölk *nt* -(e)s, *no pl* clouds *pl*.

gewölkt *adj* (*liter*) Stirn o'erclouded (*poet*).

gewollt 1 *ptp of* wollen[2]. **2** *adj* forced, artificial.

gewonnen *ptp of* gewinnen.

geworben *ptp of* werben.

geworden *ptp of* werden.

geworfen *ptp of* werfen.

gewrungen *ptp of* wringen.

Gewühl *nt* -(e)s, *no pl* **(a)** (*pej: das Wühlen*) (*in Kisten, Schubladen etc*) rummaging around; (*im Schlamm etc*) wallowing (about); (*im Bett*) wriggling. **(b)** (*Gedränge*) crowd, throng; (*Verkehrs*~) chaos, snarl-up (*inf*).

gewunden 1 *ptp of* winden[1]. **2** *adj* Weg, Fluß etc winding; Erklärung roundabout *no adv*, tortuous.

gewund(e)rig *adj* (*Sw*) curious, inquisitive.

gewunken (*dial*) *ptp of* winken.

gewürfelt 1 *ptp of* würfeln. **2** *adj* check(ed).

Gewürge *nt* -s, *no pl* (*vor dem Erbrechen*) retching; (*fig: Kampf*) struggle.

Gewürm *nt* -(e)s, *no pl* worms *pl*; (*Kriechtiere*) creeping animals *pl*, creepy-crawlies *pl* (*inf*); (*fig*) vermin.

Gewürz *nt* -es, -e spice; (*Kräutersorte*) herb; (*Pfeffer, Salz*) condiment.

Gewürz-: ~**essig** *m* spiced/herb vinegar; ~**gurke** *f* pickled gherkin; ~**kraut** *nt* potherb; ~**mischung** *f* mixed herbs *pl*; (~*salz*) herbal salt; ~**nelke** *f* clove; ~**paprika** *m* paprika; ~**pflanze** *f* spice plant; (*Kräuterpflanze*) herb; ~**ständer** *m* spice rack.

Gewusel *nt* -s, *no pl* (*dial*) siehe Gewimmel.

gewußt *ptp of* wissen.

Geysir ['gaizɪr] *m* -s, -e geyser.

gez. *abbr. of* gezeichnet.

gezackt *adj* Fels jagged; Hahnenkamm toothed; Blatt serrated, dentate (*spec*).

gezahnt, gezähnt *adj* serrated; (*Bot*) serrated, dentate (*spec*); (*Tech*) cogged; Briefmarke perforated.

Gezänk, Gezanke (*inf*) *nt* -s, *no pl* quarrelling.

Gezappel *nt* -s, *no pl* (*inf*) wriggling.

gezeichnet 1 *ptp of* zeichnen. **2** *adj* marked; (*als Straffälliger auch*) branded. **vom Tode** ~ *or* **ein vom Tode** G~**er sein** to have the mark of death on one.

Gezeiten *pl* tides *pl*.

Gezeiten-: ~**kraftwerk** *nt* tidal power plant *or* station; ~**tafel** *f* table of (the) tides; ~**wechsel** *m* turn of the tide.

Gezerre *nt* -s, *no pl* tugging.

Gezeter *nt* -s, *no pl* (*inf*) (*lit*) nagging; (*fig*) clamour. **in** ~ (*acc*) **ausbrechen** (*fig*) to set up *or* raise a clamour.

Geziefer *nt* -s, *no pl* (*obs*) siehe Ungeziefer.

geziehen *ptp of* zeihen.

gezielt 1 *ptp of* zielen. **2** *adj* purposeful; Schuß well-aimed; Frage, Maßnahme, Forschung etc specific; Hilfe well-

directed; Indiskretion deliberate. ~ **schießen** to shoot to kill; **er hat sehr** ~ **gefragt** he was obviously getting at something specific with his questions.

geziemen* (*old, geh*) **1** *vi* +*dat* to befit. **dieses Verhalten geziemt ihm nicht** such behaviour ill befits him; **ihm geziemt eine bessere Behandlung** he is deserving of *or* he deserves better treatment.
2 *vr* to be proper. **wie es sich geziemt** as is proper; **wie es sich für ein artiges Kind geziemt** as befits a well-behaved child.

geziemend *adj* proper. **einen** ~**en Streifen trinken** (*dated*) to quaff a jar or two (*dated*).

geziert *adj* affected.

Geziertheit *f* affectedness.

Gezirp(e) *nt* -(e)s, *no pl* chirruping, chirping.

Gezisch(e) *nt* -es, *no pl* hiss(ing).

Gezischel *nt* -s, *no pl* (*fig: Klatsch*) gossip, tittle-tattle (*inf*).

gezogen 1 *ptp of* ziehen. **2** *adj* Gewehrlauf etc rifled; Soldat conscript(ed). **ein** G~**er** (*Mil inf*) a conscript.

Gezücht *nt* -(e)s, -e (*obs*) (*pej: Brut*) brood; (*inf: Gesindel*) riff-raff *pl*, rabble *pl*.

Gezüngel *nt* -s, *no pl* (*geh*) (*von Schlange*) darting *or* flicking of its tongue; (*von Flamme*) flickering.

Gezweig *nt* -(e)s, *no pl* (*geh*) branches *pl*.

Gezwinker *nt* -s, *no pl* winking.

Gezwitscher *nt* -s, *no pl* chirruping, twitter(ing).

gezwungen 1 *ptp of* zwingen. **2** *adj* (*nicht entspannt*) forced; Atmosphäre strained; Stil, Benehmen stiff.

gezwungenermaßen *adv* of necessity. **etw** ~ **tun** to be forced to do sth, to do sth of necessity.

Gezwungenheit *f*, *no pl* artificiality; (*von Atmosphäre*) constraint; (*von Stil, Benehmen*) stiffness.

Gfrast *nt* -es, -er (*Aus inf*) siehe Flegel.

ggf. *abbr of* gegebenenfalls.

Ghetto *nt* -s, -s ghetto.

Ghostwriter ['goustraɪtə] *m* -s, - ghostwriter. **er ist der** ~ **des Premiers** he ghosts *or* ghostwrites for the PM.

gib *imper sing of* geben.

Gibbon *m* -s, -s gibbon.

Gicht *f* -, -en **(a)** *no pl* (*Med, Bot*) gout. **(b)** (*Metal*) throat (of a/the furnace).

Gicht-: ~**anfall** *m* attack of gout; g~**brüchig** *adj* (*old*) gouty; **die** G~**brüchigen** (*Bibl*) the palsied, those stricken with the palsy; ~**gas** *nt* (*Metal*) top gas.

gichtisch *adj* gouty.

Gicht-: ~**knoten** *m* gouty deposit, tophus (*form*); g~**krank,** g~**leidend** *adj* gouty; ~**kranke(r)** *mf decl as adj* gout sufferer.

Gickel /*m* -s, - (*dial*) siehe Hahn.

gickeln, gickern *vi* (*dial*) to giggle.

gicks *adj*: **weder** ~ **noch gacks wissen/sagen** (*dial*) not to know/say a (single) thing.

gicksen (*dial*) **1** *vi* (*kichern*) to giggle; (*piepsen*) to squeak; (*Stimme*) to go squeaky. **2** *vt* to prod, to poke.

Giebel *m* -s, - gable; (*Tür*~, *Fenster*~) pediment.

Giebel-: ~**dach** *nt* gabled roof; ~**feld** *nt* tympanum (*spec*); ~**fenster** *nt* gable window; ~**haus** *nt* gabled house.

gieb(e)lig *adj* gabled.

Giebel-: ~**seite** *f* gable end; ~**wand** *f* gable end *or* wall; ~**zimmer** *nt* attic room.

Gieper *m* -s, *no pl* (*dial*) craving (*auf* +*acc* for).

Gier *f* -, *no pl* (*nach for*) greed; (*nach Geld auch*) avarice, lust; (*nach Macht, Ruhm auch*) craving, lust; (*Lüsternheit*) lust.

gieren[1] *vi* (*pej*) to lust (*nach* for).

gieren[2] *vi* (*Naut*) to yaw.

gierig *adj* greedy; (*nach Geld*) avaricious; (*lüstern*) lustful. ~ **nach etw sein** to be greedy for sth; (*nach Macht auch, sexuell*) to lust for sth; (*nach Vergnügen auch*) to crave sth; (*nach Wissen auch*) to be avid for sth; **etw** ~ **verschlingen** (*lit, fig*) to devour sth greedily.

Gierigkeit *f*, *no pl* siehe *adj* greediness; avariciousness; lustfulness.

Gießbach *m* (*mountain*) torrent.

gießen *pret* goß, *ptp* gegossen **1** *vt* **(a)** to pour; (*verschütten*) to spill; Pflanzen, Garten etc to water; (*liter*) Licht to shed. **gieß das Glas nicht so voll!** don't fill the glass so full!
(b) Glas to found (*zu in*)to; Metall auch to cast (*zu in*)to.
2 *vi impers* to pour. **es gießt in Strömen** *or* **wie aus Eimern** it's pouring down, it's chucking it down (*inf*).

Gießer *m* -s, - **(a)** (*Metal*) caster, founder. **(b)** (*an Kanne*) pourer.

Gießerei *f* **(a)** *no pl* (*Gießen*) casting, founding. **(b)** (*Werkstatt*) foundry.

Gießerei-: ~**arbeiter** *m* foundry worker; ~**betrieb** *m* foundry; ~**technik** *f* foundry practice.

Gieß-: ~**form** *f* siehe Gußform; ~**grube** *f* foundry pit; ~**kanne** *f* watering can; **sich** (*dat*) **die** ~**kanne verbiegen** (*hum sl*) to get (a dose of) the clap (*sl*); ~**kannenprinzip** *nt* (*inf*) principle of giving everyone a slice of the cake; ~**kelle** *f*, ~**löffel** *m* casting ladle; ~**ofen** *m* foundry furnace; ~**pfanne** *f* casting ladle.

gietzig *adj* (*Sw*) siehe geizig.

Gift *nt* -(e)s, -e (*lit, fig*) poison; (*Bakterien*~) toxin; (*Schlangen*~, *fig: Bosheit*) venom. ~ **nehmen** to poison oneself; **das ist (wie)** ~ **für ihn** (*inf*) that is very bad for him; **darauf kannst du** ~ **nehmen** (*inf*) you can bet your bottom dollar *or* your life on that (*inf*); **sein** ~ **verspritzen** to be venomous; ~ **und Galle spucken** (*inf*) *or* **speien** (*inf*) to be in a rage.

Gift-: ~**ampulle** *f* poison capsule; ~**becher** *m* cup of poison; ~**drüse** *f* venom gland.

giften (*inf*) **1** *vt impers* to rile. **2** *vi* to be nasty (*gegen* about).

Gift-: g~**frei** *adj* non-toxic, non-poisonous; ~**gas** *nt* poison gas; g~**grün** *adj* bilious green; g~**haltig,** g~**hältig** (*Aus*) *adj*

containing poison, poisonous, toxic; ~**hauch** *m* (*liter*) miasma (*liter*).
giftig *adj* (a) (*Gift enthaltend*) poisonous; *Stoff, Chemikalien etc auch* toxic. (b) (*fig*) (*boshaft, haßerfüllt*) venomous; (*zornig*) vitriolic; *siehe* **Zunge**. (c) (*grell*) bilious.
Gift-: ~**küche** *f* devil's workshop; ~**mischer**(**in** *f*) *m* -s, - preparer of poison; (*fig*) trouble-maker, stirrer (*inf*); (*hum: Apotheker*) chemist; ~**mord** *m* poisoning; ~**mörder** *m* poisoner; ~**müll** *m* toxic waste; ~**nudel** *f* (*hum inf*) (a) (*Zigarre, Zigarette*) cancer tube (*hum inf*); (b) (*gehässige Frau*) vixen, shrew; ~**pfeil** *m* poisoned arrow; ~**pflanze** *f* poisonous plant; ~**pilz** *m* poisonous toadstool; ~**schlange** *f* poisonous snake; ~**schrank** *m* poison cabinet; (*hum inf*) restricted access section of a library *etc*; ~**stoff** *m* poisonous or toxic substance; ~**wirkung** *f* effect of (the) poison; **die** ~**wirkung machte sich nach ein paar Sekunden bemerkbar** the poison took effect after a few seconds; ~**zahn** *m* fang; **jdm die** ~**zähne ausbrechen** (*fig inf*) to draw sb's fangs; ~**zwerg** *m* (*inf*) spiteful little devil (*inf*).
gigampfen* *vi* (*Sw*) to swing.
Gigant *m* giant; (*Myth*) Titan; (*fig auch*) colossus.
gigantesk *adj* (*geh*) Titanesque.
gigantisch *adj* gigantic, colossal.
Gigantismus *m* (*Med*) gigantism; (*fig*) giantism.
Gigantomanie *f, no pl* (*geh*) love of things big.
Gigerl *m or nt* -s, -(**n**) (*Aus inf*) dandy, peacock (*inf*).
Gigolo ['ʒiːgolo, 'ʒiɡ-] *m* -s, -s gigolo.
gilben *vi aux sein* (*liter*) to yellow.
Gilde *f* -, -n guild.
Gildehaus *nt* guildhall.
Gildensozialismus *m* (*Hist*) guild socialism.
Gilet [ʒiˈleː] *nt* -s, -s (*Aus, Sw*) waistcoat (*Brit*), vest (*US*).
gilt 3. pers present of **gelten**.
Gimpel *m* -s, - (*Orn*) bullfinch; (*inf: Einfaltspinsel*) ninny (*inf*).
Gin [dʒɪn] *m* -s, -s gin. ~ **tonic** gin and tonic.
Gin-Fizz ['dʒɪnfɪs] *m* -, - gin-fizz.
ging *pret* of **gehen**.
Ginseng ['ɡɪnzɛŋ, 'ʒɪnzɛŋ] *m* -s, -s (*Bot*) ginseng.
Ginster *m* -s, - (*Bot*) broom; (*Stech~*) gorse.
Gipfel *m* -s, - (a) (*Bergspitze*) peak; (*höchster Punkt eines Berges*) summit; (*old: Baum~*) top, tip. (b) (*fig: Höhepunkt*) height; (*des Ruhms, der Karriere auch*) peak; (*der Vollkommenheit*) epitome. **er hat den** ~ **seiner Wünsche/Träume erreicht** all his wishes/dreams have been fulfilled or have come true; **das ist der** ~! (*inf*) that's the limit, that takes the cake (*inf*). (c) (~**konferenz**) summit.
Gipfel-: ~**gespräch** *nt* (*Pol*) summit talks *pl*; ~**konferenz** *f* (*Pol*) summit conference; ~**kreuz** *nt* cross on the summit of a/the mountain; ~**leistung** *f* crowning achievement.
gipfeln *vi* to culminate (**in** + *dat* in).
Gipfel-: ~**punkt** *m* (*lit*) zenith; (*fig*) high point; ~**stürmer** *m* (*liter*) conqueror of a/the peak; ~**treffen** *nt* (*Pol*) summit (meeting).
Gips *m* -es, -e (a) plaster; (*gebrannter* ~, *Art auch*) plaster of Paris; (*Chem*) gypsum. (b) (~**verband**) plaster. **einen Arm in** ~ **legen** to put an arm in plaster; **er lag sechs Wochen in** ~ he was in plaster for six weeks.
Gips- *in cpds* plaster; ~**abdruck**, ~**abguß** *m* plaster cast, ~**bein** *nt* (*inf*) leg in plaster.
gipsen *vt* to plaster; *Arm, Bein* to put in plaster.
Gipser *m* -s, - plasterer.
gipsern *adj attr* plaster.
Gips-: ~**figur** *f* plaster (of Paris) figure; ~**form** *f* plaster (of Paris) mould; ~**kopf** *m* (*inf*) blockhead, dimwit, num(b)skull (*all inf*); ~**korsett** *nt* (*Med*) plaster jacket; ~**krawatte** *f* (*Med*) plaster collar; ~**mehl** *nt* powdered plaster; ~**verband** *m* (*Med*) plaster cast *or* bandage (*form*); **er trug den Arm im** ~**verband** he had his arm in plaster *or* in a plaster cast; **einem Arm einen** ~**verband anlegen** to put an arm in plaster *or* in a plaster cast.
Giraffe *f* -, -n giraffe.
Giri ['ʒiːri] (*Aus*) *pl* of **Giro**.
Girl [gøːrl, gœrl] *nt* -s, -s (*inf*) girl; (*Revue~ etc*) chorus girl.
Girlande *f* -, -n garland (*aus* of). **etw mit** ~**n schmücken** to garland sth, to decorate sth with garlands.
Girlitz *m* -es, -e (*Orn*) serin (finch).
Giro ['ʒiːro] *nt* -s, -s *or* (*Aus*) **Giri** ['ʒiːri] (*Fin*) (bank) giro; (*Indossament*) endorsement. **durch** ~ by giro.
Giro-: ~**bank** *f* clearing bank; ~**geschäft** *nt* (bank) giro transfer; ~**konto** *nt* current account; ~**verkehr** *m* giro system; (~**geschäft**) giro transfer (business); ~**zentrale** *f* clearing house.
girren *vi* (*lit, fig*) to coo.
Gis *nt* -, - (*Mus*) G sharp. ~**-Dur/g~-Moll** G sharp major/minor.
Gischt *m* -(e)s, -e *or* *f* -, -en spray.
Gitarre *f* -, -n guitar.
Gitarre(**n**)-: ~**spiel** *nt* guitar-playing; ~**spieler** *m* guitarist, guitar-player.
Gitarrist *m* guitarist.
Gitter *nt* -s, - bars *pl*; (*engstäbig, vor Türen, Schaufenstern*) grille; (*in Fußboden, Straßendecke*) grid, grating; (*für Gewächse etc*) lattice, trellis; (*feines Draht~*) (wire-)mesh; (*Kamin~*) fire-guard; (*Geländer*) railing *usu pl*; (*Phys, Chem: Kristall~*) lattice; (*Elec, Geog*) grid. **hinter** ~**n** (*fig inf*) behind bars.
Gitter-: ~**bett** *nt* cot (*Brit*), crib (*US*); ~**elektrode** *f* (*Elec*) grid (electrode); ~**fenster** *nt* barred window; ~**mast** *m* (*Elec*) (lattice) pylon; ~**netz** *nt* (*Geog*) grid; ~**rost** *m* grid, grating; ~**spannung** *f* (*Elec*) grid voltage; ~**stab** *m* bar; ~**struktur** *f* (*Chem*) lattice structure; ~**tor** *nt* (paled) gate; ~**tüll** *m* latticework tulle; ~**tür** *f* (paled) gate; ~**verschlag** *m* crate; ~**zaun** *m* paling; (*mit gekreuzten Stäben*) lattice fence.

Glace [glaːs] *f* -, -n (*Sw*) ice(cream).
Glacé- [glaˈseː]: ~**handschuh** *m* kid glove; **jdn mit** ~**handschuhen anfassen** (*fig*) to handle sb with kid gloves; ~**leder** *nt* glacé leather.
glacieren* [glaˈsiːrən] *vt* (*Cook*) to glaze.
Glacis [glaˈsiː] *nt* -, - (*Mil*) glacis.
Gladiator *m* gladiator.
Gladiole *f* -, -n (*Bot*) gladiolus.
Glamour ['glɛmɐ] *m or nt* -s, *no pl* (*Press sl*) glamour.
Glamourgirl *nt* glamour girl.
glamourös [glamuˈrøːs] *adj* glamorous.
Glanz *m* -es, *no pl* gleam; (*von Oberfläche auch*) shine; (*Funkeln*) sparkle, glitter; (*von Augen*) sparkle; (*von Haaren*) sheen, shine; (*von Seide, Perlen*) sheen, lustre; (*von Farbe*) gloss; (*blendender: von Sonne, Scheinwerfer etc*) glare; (*fig*) (*der Schönheit, Jugend*) radiance; (*von Ruhm, Erfolg*) glory; (*Gepränge, Pracht*) splendour. **mit** ~ **und Gloria** (*iro inf*) in grand style; **eine Prüfung mit** ~ **bestehen** (*inf*) to pass an exam with flying colours; **den** ~ **verlieren** *or* **einbüßen** (*Metall, Leder, Möbel*) to lose its shine; (*Diamanten, Augen, fig*) to lose its/one's sparkle; **etw auf** ~ **polieren** to polish sth till it shines; **welch** ~ **in dieser Hütte!** (*iro*) to what do I owe the honour (of this visit)? (*iro*).
Glanz-: ~**abzug** *m* (*Phot*) glossy *or* gloss print; ~**bürste** *f* polishing brush.
glänzen *vi* (*lit, fig*) to shine; (*polierte Oberfläche auch*) to gleam; (*glitzern*) to glisten; (*funkeln*) to sparkle; (*blenden*) to glare; (*Hosenboden, Ellbogen, Nase*) to be shiny. **vor jdm** ~ **wollen** to want to shine in front of sb; **ihr Gesicht glänzte vor Freude** her face shone with *or* was radiant with joy; *siehe* **Gold**.
glänzend *adj* shining; *Haar, Seide auch* lustrous; *Metall, Leder, Holz auch* gleaming; (*strahlend*) radiant; (*blendend*) dazzling; (*glitzernd*) glistening; (*funkelnd*) sparkling, glittering; *Papier* glossy, shiny; *Stoff, Nase, Hosenboden, Ellbogen* shiny; (*fig*) brilliant; *Aussehen, Fest* dazzling; *Gesellschaft* glittering; (*erstklassig*) marvellous, splendid. ~ **in Form** (*inf*) in splendid form; **ein** ~**er Reinfall** (*iro*) a glorious failure; **wir haben uns** ~ **amüsiert** we had a marvellous *or* great (*inf*) time; **mir geht es** ~ I'm just fine; **sie sieht heute wieder** ~ **aus** she looks stunning today as usual.
Glanz-: ~**form** *f, no pl* (*inf*) brilliant form; ~**gras** *nt* canary grass; ~**idee** *f* (*inf*) brilliant idea; ~**kohle** *f* glance coal; ~**lack** *m* gloss (paint); ~**leder** *nt* patent leather; ~**leinwand** *f* (*Tex*) glazed taffeta; ~**leistung** *f* brilliant achievement; **eine wissenschaftliche** ~**leistung** a brilliant scientific achievement; ~**licht** *nt* (a) (*Art, fig*) highlight; (b) (*Phys*) reflected light; **g~los** *adj* (*lit, fig*) dull; *Augen, Haar, Vorstellung auch* lacklustre; *Lack, Oberfläche* matt; ~**nummer** *f* big number, pièce de résistance; ~**papier** *nt* glossy paper; ~**periode** *f siehe* ~**zeit**; ~**politur** *f* gloss polish; ~**punkt** *m* (*fig*) highlight, high spot; ~**rolle** *f* star role; ~**stück** *nt* pièce de résistance; **g~voll** *adj* (*fig*) brilliant; *Darstellung, Unterhaltung auch* sparkling; (*prachtvoll*) glittering; ~**zeit** *f* heyday; **seine** ~**zeit ist vorüber** he has had his day.
Glas¹ *nt* -es, ~**er** *or* (*als Maßangabe*) - **a** - (*Stoff, Gefäß*) glass; (*Konserven~*) jar. **buntes** *or* **farbiges** *or* **gefärbtes** ~ stained glass; „**Vorsicht** ~!" "glass - handle with care"; **ein** ~ **Milch** a glass of milk; **ein** ~ **Marmelade/Gurken** a pot (*Brit*) *or* jar of jam/a jar of gherkins; **zwei** ~ **Wein** two glasses of wine; **zu tief ins** ~ **gucken** (*inf*) *or* **schauen** (*inf*), **ein** ~ **über den Durst trinken** (*inf*) to have one too many *or* one over the eight (*inf*); **unter** ~ behind glass; (*Gewächs*) under glass.
(**b**) (*Brillen~*) lens *sing*; (*Fern~*) binoculars *pl*, (field-) glasses *pl*; (*Opern~*) opera glasses *pl*. ~**er** (*old*) (*Brille*) spectacles *pl*, glasses *pl*.
Glas² *nt* -es, -en (*Naut: halbe Stunde*) bell. **es schlägt acht** ~**en** it's eight bells.
Glas- *in cpds* glass; ~**ballon** *m* carboy; ~**bau** *m, pl* -ten glass structure; ~**baustein** *m* glass block; **g~blasen** *vi sep irreg* to blow glass; ~**bläser** *m* glassblower; ~**bläserei** *f* (a) *no pl* (*Handwerk*) glass-blowing; (b) (*Werkstatt*) glassworks *sing or pl*; ~**bruch** *m* broken glass; ~**dach** *nt* glass roof.
Gläschen ['glɛːsçən] *nt dim of* **Glas¹** (*Getränk*) little drink. **darauf müssen wir ein** ~ **trinken** we must drink to that, that calls for a little drink.
Glaser *m* -s, - glazier.
Gläserbord *nt* glasses shelf, shelf for (the) glasses.
Glaserei *f* (a) *no pl* (*Handwerk*) glasswork. (b) (*Werkstatt*) glazier's workshop.
Glaser-: ~**handwerk** *nt* glazing; ~**kitt** *m* glazier's putty.
Gläserklang *m* (*dated*) the clink of glasses.
Glasermeister *m* master glazier.
gläsern *adj* glass; (*liter: starr*) glassy. **sich** ~ **anfühlen** to feel like glass.
Gläser-: ~**tuch** *nt* glasscloth; **g~weise** *adv* by the glassful.
Glas-: ~**fabrik** *f* glassworks *sing or pl*; ~**faser** *f* glass fibre; **g~faserverstärkt** *adj* glass-fibre reinforced; ~**fenster** *nt* glass window; ~**fiber** *f siehe* ~**faser**; ~**fiberstab** *m* (*Sport*) glass fibre pole; ~**flügler** *m* -s, - (*Zool*) clearwing; ~**form** *f* glass mould; (*Backform*) glass ® dish; ~**geschirr** *nt* glassware; ~**glocke** *f* glass cover *or* dome; (*als Lampenschirm*) glass ball; ~**harfe** *f* musical glasses *pl*; ~**harmonika** *f* musical glasses *pl*, glass harmonica; **g~hart** *adj* brittle; (*Sport sl*) cracking (*inf*); ~**haus** *nt* greenhouse; (*in botanischen Gärten etc*) glasshouse; **wer (selbst) im** ~**haus sitzt, soll nicht mit Steinen werfen** (*Prov*) people who live in glass houses shouldn't throw stones (*Prov*); ~**hütte** *f* glassworks *sing or pl*.
glasieren* *vt* to glaze; *Kuchen* to ice, to frost (*esp US*).
glasig *adj Blick* glassy; (*Cook*) *Kartoffeln* waxy; *Speck, Zwiebeln* transparent.

Glas-: ~industrie f glass industry; ~kasten m glass case; (in Fabrik, Büro) glass box; (Hort) cold frame; g~klar adj (lit) clear as glass; (fig) crystal-clear; ~kolben m glass flask; (von Glühlampe, Radioröhre etc) glass bulb; ~kugel f glass ball; (Murmel) marble; ~malerei f glass painting; ~masse f molten glass; ~papier nt glasspaper; ~perle f glass bead; ~platte f glass top; ~röhrchen nt small glass tube; ~röhre f glass tube; ~scheibe f sheet of glass; (Fenster~) pane of glass; ~scherbe f fragment of glass, piece of broken glass; ~scherben broken glass; ~schleifer m (Opt) glass grinder; (Art) glass cutter; ~schliff m (Opt) glass grinding; (Art) glass cutting; ~schmelze f glass melt; ~schneider m glass cutter; ~schrank m glass-fronted cupboard; ~splitter m splinter of glass.
Glast m -(e)s, no pl (poet) siehe Glanz.
Glasur f glaze; (Metal) enamel; (Zuckerguß) icing, frosting (esp US).
Glas-: ~veranda f glass veranda, sun parlor (US); ~versicherung f glass insurance; ~waren pl glassware sing; ~watte f glass wool; g~weise adj, adv by the glass; ~wolle f glass wool; ~zylinder m glass cylinder; (von Petroleumlampe) (glass) chimney.
glatt 1 adj, comp -er or ⁻er, superl -este(r, s) or ⁻este(r, s) or adv am -esten or ⁻esten (a) (eben) smooth; Meer auch unruffled; Haar straight; (Med) Bruch clean; Stoff (faltenlos) uncreased; (ungemustert) plain; (Aus) Mehl finely ground.
(b) (schlüpfrig) slippery.
(c) (fig) Landung, Ablauf smooth. eine ~e Eins (Sch) a straight A.
(d) attr (inf: klar, eindeutig) outright; Lüge, Unsinn etc auch downright. das kostet ~e 1000 Mark it costs a good 1,000 marks.
(e) (pej: allzu gewandt) smooth, slick.
2 adv (a) smoothly. er hat sich ~ aus der Affäre gezogen he wriggled neatly out of the whole affair.
(b) (ganz, völlig) completely; leugnen, ablehnen flatly; vergessen clean. jdm etw ~ ins Gesicht sagen to tell sb sth to his/her face; die Rechnung ist ~ aufgegangen the sum works out exactly; es kostete ~ DM 10.000 it cost a good DM 10,000.
(c) (inf: wirklich) really.
(d) ~ stricken to knit garter stitch.
glattbügeln vt sep to iron smooth.
Glätte f -, no pl (a) (Ebenheit) smoothness; (von Haar) sleekness. (b) (Schlüpfrigkeit) slipperiness. (c) (Politur) polish. (d) (fig) (des Auftretens) smoothness, slickness; (des Stils) polish.
Glatteis nt ice. „Vorsicht ~!" "danger, black ice"; sich auf ~ begeben (fig), aufs ~ geraten (fig) to skate on thin ice; jdn aufs ~ führen (fig) to take sb for a ride.
Glatteisbildung f formation of black ice.
Glatteisen nt (Sw) iron, smoothing iron (old).
Glatteisgefahr f danger of black ice.
glätten 1 vt (glattmachen) to smooth out; (glattstreichen) Haar, Tuch to smooth; (esp Sw: bügeln) to iron; (fig: stilistisch ~) to polish up.
2 vr to smooth out; (Wellen, Meer, fig) to subside.
Glätterin f (esp Sw) presser.
Glatt-: g~gehen vi sep irreg aux sein to go smoothly or OK (inf); ~hobel m smoothing plane; g~hobeln vt sep to plane smooth; g~kämmen vt sep to comb straight; (mit Haarpomade) to sleek down; g~legen vt sep to fold up carefully; g~machen vt sep (a) (g~streichen) to smooth out; Haare to smooth (down); (mit Kamm) to comb straight; (b) (inf: begleichen) to settle; g~polieren* vt sep to polish highly; g~rasieren* vt sep to shave; g~rasiert adj Mann, Kinn clean-shaven; Beine shaved; g~rühren vt sep to stir till smooth; g~schleifen vt sep irreg to rub smooth; Linsen, Diamanten etc to grind smooth; Felsen etc to wear smooth; g~schneiden vt sep irreg to cut straight; g~streichen vt sep irreg to smooth out; Haare to smooth (down); g~walzen vt sep to roll smooth; g~weg ['glatvɛk] adv (inf) simply, just, just like that (inf); er hat meinen Vorschlag g~weg abgelehnt he simply turned my suggestion down, he turned my suggestion down flat or just like that (inf); das ist g~weg erlogen that's a blatant lie; g~züngig adj (pej geh) glib, smooth-tongued; ~züngigkeit f, no pl (pej geh) glibness.
Glatze f -, -n bald head; (rare: kahle Stelle) bald patch or spot. eine ~ bekommen/haben to go/be bald; er zeigt Ansätze zu einer ~ he shows signs of going bald; ein Mann mit ~ bald(-headed) man, a man with a bald head; sich (dat) eine ~ schneiden lassen to have one's head shaved.
Glatz-: ~kopf m bald head; (inf: Mann mit Glatze) baldie (inf); g~köpfig adj bald(-headed); ~köpfigkeit f, no pl baldness.
Glaube m -ns, no pl (Vertrauen, religiöse Überzeugung, Konfession) faith (an +acc in); (Überzeugung, Meinung) belief (an +acc in). ~, Liebe, Hoffnung faith, hope and charity; im guten or in gutem ~n in good faith; (bei jdm) ~n finden to be believed (by sb); (Bericht, Aussage etc auch) to find credence (with sb); den ~n an jdn/etw verlieren to lose faith in sb/sth; jdm ~n schenken to believe sb, to give credence to sb; laß ihm bei seinem ~! let him keep his illusions; er ist katholischen ~ns he is of the Catholic faith; siehe Treue.
Glauben m -s, no pl siehe Glaube.
glauben vti (Glauben schenken, überzeugt sein, vertrauen) to believe (an +acc in); (meinen, annehmen, vermuten) to think. jdm ~ to believe sb; das glaube ich dir gerne/nicht I quite/don't believe you; glaube es mir believe me; diese Geschichte/das soll ich dir ~? do you expect me to believe that story/that?; er glaubte mir jedes Wort he believed every word I said; jdm (etw) aufs Wort ~ to take sb's word (for sth); d(a)ran ~ müssen (inf) to cop it (sl); (sterben auch) to buy it (sl); das glaubst du doch selbst nicht! you can't be serious; das will ich ~! (dated) (als Antwort) I'm sure!, I can well believe it; jdn etw ~ machen

wollen to try to make sb believe sth; das glaube ich nicht von ihm I can't believe that of him; ob du es glaubst oder nicht, ... believe it or not ...; wer's glaubt, wird selig (iro) a likely story (iro); wer hätte das je geglaubt? who would have thought it?; ich glaubte ihn zu kennen, doch ... I thought I knew him, but ...; ich glaubte ihn tot/in Sicherheit I thought he was or thought him dead/safe; ich glaubte ihn in Berlin I thought he was in Berlin; er glaubte sich unbeobachtet he thought nobody was watching him; man glaubte ihm den Fachmann one could well believe him to be an expert; es ist nicht or kaum zu ~ it's incredible or unbelievable; ich glaube dir (einen) Wort (einzeln) (iro) pull the other one (inf); ich glaube, ja I think so; ich glaube, nein I don't think so, I think not.
Glaubens-: ~artikel m article of faith; ~bekenntnis nt creed; ~bewegung f religious movement; ~bruder m co-religionist (form), brother in faith, fellow Buddhist/Christian/Jew etc; ~dinge pl matters of faith pl; ~eifer m religious zeal; ~frage f question of faith; ~freiheit f freedom of worship, religious freedom; ~gemeinschaft f religious sect; (christliche auch) denomination; ~genosse m co-religionist (form); ~kampf m religious battle; ~krieg m religious war; ~lehre f dogmatics sing; (pej: Doktrin) doctrine, dogma; g~los adj unbelieving, areligious; ~sache f matter of faith; ~satz m dogma, doctrine; ~spaltung f schism; ~streit m religious controversy; g~verwandt adj jdm g~verwandt sein to be of a similar faith to sb; die beiden Völker sind g~verwandt the two nations have a similar faith; ~wahrheit f religious truth; ~wechsel m change of faith or religion; zum ~wechsel bereit sein to be prepared to change one's faith or religion; ~zweifel m usu pl religious doubt; ~zwist m religious controversy.
Glaubersalz nt (Chem) Glauber('s) salt.
glaubhaft adj credible, believable; (einleuchtend) plausible. (jdm) etw (überzeugend) ~ machen to substantiate sth (to sb), to satisfy sb of sth.
Glaubhaftigkeit f, no pl credibility; (Evidenz) plausibility.
Glaubhaftmachung f, no pl (Jur) substantiation.
gläubig adj religious; (vertrauensvoll) trusting. ~ hörten sie meiner Geschichte zu they listened to and believed my story.
Gläubige(r) mf decl as adj believer. die ~n the faithful.
Gläubiger(in f) m -s, - (Comm) creditor.
Gläubiger-: ~ansprüche pl creditors' claims pl; ~ausschuß m committee or board of creditors; ~versammlung f meeting of creditors.
Gläubigkeit f, no pl siehe adj devoutness; trust.
glaublich adj: kaum ~ scarcely credible.
glaubwürdig adj credible. ~e Quellen reliable sources.
Glaubwürdigkeit f, no pl credibility.
Glaukom nt -s, -e (Med) glaucoma.
glazial adj (Geol) glacial.
Glazial nt -s, -e (Geol) glacial epoch or episode.
gleich 1 adj (identisch, ähnlich) same; (mit indef art) similar; (~wertig, ~berechtigt, Math) equal; (auf ~er Höhe) level. der/die/das ~e ... wie the same ... as; in ~em Abstand at an equal distance; wir sind in ~er Weise daran schuld we are equally to blame; zu ~en Teilen in equal parts; in ~er Weise in the same way; ~er Lohn für ~e Arbeit equal pay for equal work, the same pay for the same work; mit ~er Post with the same post; ~e Rechte, ~e Pflichten (prov) equal rights, equal responsibilities; zur ~en Zeit at the same time; die beiden haben ~es Gewicht they are both the same weight, they both weigh the same; ich habe den ~en Wagen wie Sie I have the same car as you; das ~e, aber nicht dasselbe Auto a similar car, but not the same one; das kommt or läuft aufs ~e hinaus it comes (down) or amounts to the same thing; wir wollten alle das ~e we all wanted the same thing; es ist genau das ~e it's exactly the same; es waren die ~en, die ... it was the same ones who/which ...; zwei mal zwei (ist) ~ vier two twos are four, two times two equals or is four; vier plus/durch/minus zwei ist ~ ... four plus/divided by/minus two equals or is ...; jdm an etw (dat) ~ sein to be sb's equal in sth; ihr Männer seid doch alle ~! you men are all the same!; alle Menschen sind ~, nur einige sind ~er (hum) all men are equal, but some are more equal than others; es ist mir (alles or ganz) ~ it's all the same to me; ganz ~ wer/was etc no matter who/what etc; das sieht ihm ~ that's just like him, that's just his style (inf); ein G~es tun (geh) to do the same; G~es mit G~em vergelten to pay like with like; mit jdm in einem Ton von ~ zu ~ reden (geh) to talk to sb as an equal; ~ und ~ gesellt sich gern (Prov) birds of a feather flock together (Prov); siehe Boot, Münze, Strang.
2 adv (a) (ebenso) equally; (auf ~e Weise) alike, the same. sie sind ~ groß/alt/schwer they are the same size/age/weight; der Lehrer behandelt alle Kinder ~ the teacher treats all the children equally or the same; ~ gekleidet dressed alike or the same.
(b) (räumlich) right, immediately, just.
(c) (zur selben Zeit) at once; (sofort auch) immediately, straight or right away; (bald) in a minute. ~ anfangs or am Anfang right at the beginning, at the very beginning; ~ danach immediately or straight or right after(wards); ich komme ~ I'm just coming, I'll be right there; ich komme ~ wieder I'll be right back or back in a moment; das mache ich ~ heute I'll do that today; es muß nicht ~ sein there's no hurry, it's not urgent; es ist ~ drei Uhr it's almost or very nearly three o'clock; ich werde ihn ~ morgen besuchen I'll go and see him tomorrow; ~ zu Beginn der Vorstellung ... right at the beginning of the performance ...; du kriegst ~ eine Ohrfeige you'll get a slap in a minute; habe ich es nicht ~ gesagt! what did I tell you?; das habe ich mir ~ gedacht I thought that straight away; warum nicht ~ so? why didn't you say/do that in the first place or

straight away?; **na komm schon!** — ~! come along — I'm just coming or I'll be right there; **wann machst du das?** — ~! when are you going to do it? — right away or in just a moment; ~ **als** or **nachdem er ... as soon as he ...; so wirkt das Bild** ~ **ganz anders** suddenly, the picture has changed completely; **wenn das stimmt, kann ich's ja** ~ **aufgeben** if that's true I might as well give up right now; **deswegen braucht man nicht** ~ **Hunderte auszugeben** you don't have to spend hundreds because of that; **er ging** ~ **in die Küche/vor Gericht** he went straight to the kitchen/to court; **sie hat sich** ~ **zwei Hüte gekauft** she bought two hats; **bis** ~! see you in a while, see you later.
(d) (in Fragesätzen) again. **wie war doch** ~ **die Nummer/Ihr Name?** what was the number/your name again?; **woher kenne ich ihn doch** ~ **wieder?** where have I seen him before?
3 prep +dat (liter) like. **einer Sintflut** ~ like a deluge.
4 conj (old, liter) **ob er** ~ ... although he ...; **wenn er** ~ ... even if he ...

Gleich-: g~altrig adj (of) the same age; **die beiden sind g~altrig** they are both the same age; **G~altrige** people/children (of) the same age; **g~armig** adj (Phys) **Hebel** equal-armed; **g~artig** 1 adj of the same kind (+dat as); (ähnlich) similar (+dat to); (homogen) homogeneous (+dat with); 2 adv in the same way; similarly; homogeneously; **~artigkeit** f similarity; (Homogenität) homogeneity; **g~auf** adv (esp Sport) equal; **g~auf liegen** to be lying or to be equal, to be level-pegging; **g~bedeutend** adj synonymous (mit with); (so gut wie) tantamount (mit to); **~behandlung** f equal treatment; **g~berechtigt** adj with equal or the same rights; **g~berechtigt sein** to have equal rights; **~berechtigung** f equal rights sing or pl, equality (+gen for); **g~bleiben** sep irreg aux sein 1 vi to stay or remain the same; (Temperaturen, Geschwindigkeit, Kurs auch) to remain constant; 2 vr **sich** (dat) **g~bleiben** (Mensch) to stay or remain the same; **das bleibt sich g~** it doesn't matter; **g~bleibend** adj Temperatur, Geschwindigkeit, Kurs constant, steady; **g~bleibend sein** to stay or remain the same; (Temperatur auch) to stay or remain steady or constant; **bei g~bleibendem Gehalt** when one's salary stays the same; **in g~bleibendem Abstand** always at the same distance; **es waren g~bleibend rund fünfzig Mitglieder** the membership remained steady at about fifty; **unter g~bleibenden Umständen** if things remain as they are; **er ist immer g~bleibend zuvorkommend** he is always equally helpful; **g~denkend** adj siehe **g~gesinnt**.

gleichen pret **glich**, ptp **geglichen** vi jdm/einer Sache ~ to be like sb/sth; **sich** ~ to be alike or similar; **jdm an Erfahrung/Schönheit** ~ to be sb's equal or to equal sb in experience/beauty.

gleicher-: ~gestalt (old), **~maßen**, **~weise** adv equally; **~weise ... und ... both ... and ...**

Gleich-: g~falls adv (ebenfalls) likewise; (auch) also; (zur gleichen Zeit) at the same time; **danke g~falls!** thank you, (and) the same to you; **g~farbig** adj (of) the same colour; **g~förmig** adj of the same shape; (einheitlich, fig: eintönig) uniform (auch Phys); (ähnlich) similar; **~förmigkeit** f siehe adj similarity of shape; uniformity; similarity; **g~geartet** adj siehe **g~artig**; **g~gelagert** adj parallel; **g~geschlechtig** adj (Biol, Zool) of the same sex, same-sex attr; (Bot) homogamous; **g~geschlechtlich** adj (a) homosexual. (b) **siehe g~geschlechtig**; **~geschlechtlichkeit** f homosexuality no def art; **g~gesinnt** adj like-minded; „**Ehepaar sucht g~gesinntes**" "married couple seeks couple of similar interests"; **g~gestellt** adj equal (+dat to, with), on a par (+dat with); **er spricht nur mit g~gestellten** he only speaks to his equals; **rechtlich g~gestellt** equal in law; **g~gestimmt** adj (Mus) in tune (+dat with); (fig) in harmony (+dat with).

Gleichgewicht nt, no pl (lit) balance, equilibrium (auch Phys, Chem); (fig) (Stabilität) balance; (seelisches ~) equilibrium. **im** ~ (lit) balanced, in equilibrium; **wieder im** ~ **sein** (fig) to become more balanced again; **to regain one's equilibrium; das** ~ **verlieren, aus dem** ~ **kommen** to lose one's balance or equilibrium (auch fig); **das** ~ **behalten** (lit) to keep one's balance or equilibrium; (fig) to retain one's equilibrium; **jdn aus dem** ~ **bringen** to throw sb off balance; (fig auch) to disturb sb's equilibrium; **das** ~ **einer Sache wiederherstellen** to get sth back into balance or equilibrium; **das** ~ **zwischen ... (dat) und ... halten** to maintain a proper balance between ... and ...; **diese Dinge müssen sich** (dat) **das** ~ **halten** (fig) these things should balance each other out.

gleichgewichtig adj (ausgeglichen) Verhältnis balanced; (gleich wichtig) equal in weight. **die Kommission ist nicht** ~ **zusammengesetzt** the commission is not properly balanced.

Gleichgewichts-: ~empfinden, **~gefühl** nt sense of balance; **~lage** f (fig) equilibrium; **~organ** nt organ of equilibrium; **~sinn** m sense of balance; **~störung** f impaired balance, disturbance of the sense of balance; **~übung** f (Sport) balancing exercise; **~zustand** m siehe **~lage**.

gleichgültig, **gleichgiltig** (old) adj indifferent (gegenüber, gegen to, towards); (uninteressiert) apathetic (gegenüber, gegen towards); (unwesentlich) trivial, immaterial, unimportant. **das ist mir** ~ it's a matter of (complete) indifference to me; **Politik ist ihm** ~ he doesn't care about politics; **wir müssen die G~en aufrütteln** we must jolt people out of their indifference; ~, **was er tut no matter what he does**, irrespective of what he does; **es ist mir** ~, **was er tut** I don't care what he does; **er war ihr nicht** ~ geblieben she had not remained indifferent to him; **bin ich dir gänzlich** ~ **geworden?** have I become a matter of complete indifference to you?, have you become quite indifferent towards me?

Gleichgültigkeit f indifference (gegenüber, gegen to, towards); (Desinteresse) apathy (gegenüber, gegen towards).

Gleichheit f (a) no pl (gleiche Stellung) equality; (Identität) identity; (Übereinstimmung) uniformity, correspondence; (Ind) parity. (b) (Ähnlichkeit) similarity.

Gleichheits-: ~grundsatz m, **~prinzip** nt principle of equality; **~zeichen** nt (Math) equals sign.

Gleich-: ~klang m (fig) harmony, accord; **g~kommen** vi sep irreg aux sein +dat (a) (die gleiche Leistung etc erreichen) to equal (an +dat for), to match (an +dat for, in); **niemand kommt ihm an Dummheit g~** no-one can equal or match him for stupidity; (b) (g~bedeutend sein mit) to be tantamount or equivalent to, to amount to; **~lauf** m, no pl (Tech) synchronization; **g~laufend** adj parallel (mit to); (Tech) synchronized; **g~lautend** adj identical; **g~lautende Abschrift** duplicate (copy); **g~lautende Wörter** homonyms; **g~machen** vt sep to make the same, to level out; siehe **Erdboden**; **~macher** m (pej) leveller (pej); **g~macherisch** adj egalitarian; **~macherei** f (pej) levelling down (pej), egalitarianism; **g~macherisch** adj levelling (pej), egalitarian; **~maß** nt (a) (Ebenmaß) evenness; (von Proportionen) symmetry; (b) (geh: Regelhaftigkeit) monotony (pej), regularity; **g~mäßig** adj even, regular; Puls auch steady; Abstände regular; (ausgeglichen) well-balanced, stable; Proportionen auch symmetrical; **er ist immer g~mäßig freundlich** he is always equally friendly; **sie hat die Bonbons g~mäßig unter die Kinder verteilt** she distributed the sweets equally among the children; **die Farbe g~mäßig auftragen** apply the paint evenly; **~mäßigkeit** f siehe adj evenness, regularity; steadiness; regularity; stability; symmetry; **mit** or **in schöner ~mäßigkeit** (iro) with monotonous regularity; **~mut** m equanimity, serenity, composure; **g~mütig** adj serene, composed; **~mütigkeit** f siehe **~mut**; **g~namig** adj of the same name; (Math) with a common denominator; **Brüche g~namig machen** (Math) to reduce fractions to a common denominator.

Gleichnis nt (a) (Liter) simile. (b) (Allegorie) allegory; (Bibl) parable.

gleichnishaft siehe n 1 adj as a simile; allegorical; parabolic. 2 adv in a simile; allegorically; in a parable.

Gleich-: g~rangig adj Beamte etc equal in rank (mit to); at the same level (mit as); Straßen etc of the same grade (mit as), similarly graded; Probleme etc equally important, of equal status; **das verdient eine g~rangige Behandlung** it merits equal treatment; **g~richten** vt sep (Elec) to rectify; **~richter** m (Elec) rectifier; **~richterröhre** f (Elec) rectifier tube (esp US) or valve; **~richtung** f (Elec) rectification.

gleichsam adv as it were, so to speak. ~, **als ob** just as if.

Gleich-: g~schalten sep (Pol: NS, pej) 1 vt to bring or force into line; 2 vr to conform, to step into line; **~schaltung** f (Pol: NS, pej) bringing or forcing into line; (unter Hitler auch) gleichschaltung; **er wehrte sich gegen eine ~schaltung** he refused to be brought or forced into line; **g~schenk(e)lig** adj Dreieck isosceles; **~schritt** m, no pl (Mil) marching in step; **im ~schritt** (lit, fig) in step; **im ~schritt, marsch!** forward march!; **im ~schritt marschieren** to march in step; (den) **~schritt üben** to practise marching in step; **~schritt halten** (lit, fig) to keep in step; **aus dem ~schritt kommen** (lit, fig) to get out of step; **jdn zum ~schritt zwingen** (fig) to force sb to keep in step or to toe the line; **g~sehen** vi sep irreg jdm/einer Sache **g~sehen** to look like sb/sth; **das sieht dir g~!** that's just like you; **g~seitig** adj Dreieck equilateral; **g~setzen** vt sep (als dasselbe ansehen) to equate (mit with); (als gleichwertig ansehen) to treat as equivalent (mit to); **nichts ist mit echter Wolle g~zusetzen** there's nothing to compare with pure wool; **~setzung** f die **~setzung der Arbeiter mit den Angestellten** treating workers as equivalent to office employees; **g~silbig** adj with the same number of syllables; **~stand** m, no pl (a) (Sport) in einem Spiel/in der Liga den **~stand herbeiführen** to make two teams even or level in a game/to give two teams the same number of points in the league, to put two teams at the same position in the league; **den ~stand erzielen** to draw level; **beim ~stand von 1:1** with the scores level at 1 all; **das Spiel wurde beim ~stand von 4:4 beendet** the game ended in or was a 4-all draw; (b) (Pol) equal stage of development; **g~stehen** vi sep irreg to be equal (+dat to or with), to be on a par (+dat with); (Sport auch) to be level (+dat with); **er steht im Rang einem Hauptmann g~** he is equal in rank to a captain; **g~stehende equals**, people on an equal footing; **g~stellen** vt sep (a) (rechtlich etc) to treat as equal, to give parity of treatment (to); **daß Frauen und Männer arbeitsrechtlich g~zustellen sind** that men and women should be treated as equals or equally or given parity of treatment as far as work is concerned; siehe **g~gestellt**; (b) siehe **g~setzen**; **~stellung** f, no pl (a) (rechtlich etc) equality (+gen of, for), equal status (+gen of, for), parity; siehe **~setzung**; **~strom** m (Elec) direct current, DC; **~tritt** m siehe **~schritt**; **g~tun** vt impers sep irreg **es jdm g~tun** to equal or match sb; **es jdm im Laufen etc g~tun** to equal or match sb at or in running etc.

Gleichung f equation. **eine** ~ **ersten/zweiten Grades** a simple or linear/quadratic equation, an equation of the first/second degree (form).

Gleich-: g~viel adv (geh) nonetheless; **g~viel ob** no matter whether; **g~viel wie** however; **g~viel wohin** no matter where; **g~wertig** adj of the same value; (gleich zu bewerten) Leistung Qualität equal (+dat to); Gegner equally or evenly matched; (Chem) equivalent; **~wertigkeit** f, no pl siehe adj equal value, equality, equivalence, equivalency; **an der ~wertigkeit der beiden Gegner/Armeen bestehen berechtigte Zweifel** justifiable doubts exist as to whether the two opponents/armies are equally or evenly matched; **g~wie** adv (old) (just) as; **g~wink(e)lig** adj (Geometry) equiangular (form), with (all) angles equal; **g~wohl** (geh) adv nevertheless nonetheless; **g~zeitig** 1 adj simultaneous; 2 adv simultaneously, at the same time; (*ebenso, sowohl*) at the same time; **ihr sollt nicht alle g~zēitig reden** you mustn't all speak at the same time; **~zeitigkeit** *f* simultaneity; **g~ziehen** *vi sep irreg* (*inf*) to catch up (*mit* with).

Gleis *nt* **-es, -e** (*Rail*) line, track, rails *pl*; (*einzelne Schiene*) rail; (*Bahnsteig*) platform; (*fig*) rut. ~ **6** platform *or* track (*US*) 6; "**Überschreiten der ~e verboten**" "passengers must not cross the line"; **ein totes ~** (*lit*) a siding; (*fig*) a dead end; **jdn/etw aufs tote ~ schieben** to put sb/sth on ice (*inf*); **aus dem ~ springen** to jump the rails; **aus dem ~ kommen** (*fig*) to go off the rails (*inf*); **etw ins (rechte) ~ bringen** (*fig*) to straighten *or* sort sth out; **jdn aus dem ~ bringen** (*fig*) to put sb off his stroke; (*verrückt machen*) to make sb go *or* send sb off the rails (*inf*); **wieder im richtigen ~ sein/wieder ins richtige ~ kommen** (*fig*) to be/get back on the rails (*inf*) *or* right lines (*inf*).

Gleis-: **~anlagen** *pl* railway (*Brit*) *or* railroad (*US*) lines *pl*; **~anschluß** *m* works siding; **~arbeiten** *pl* work on the line; line *or* track repairs; **~bau** *m, no pl* railway/railroad construction; **~baustelle** *f* place where work is being done on the line; **überall auf der Strecke waren ~baustellen** work was being done all along the line (*inf*); **~bettung** *f* ballast; **~bremse** *f* rail brake; **~dreieck** *nt* triangular junction.

-gleisig *adj suf* -track, -line.

Gleis-: **~kette** *f* caterpillar track; **~kettenfahrzeug** *nt* caterpillar vehicle; **~körper** *m* railway embankment.

Gleisner *m* **-s, -** (*old*) hypocrite, dissembler (*liter*).

gleisnerisch *adj* (*old*) dissembling (*liter*), hypocritical.

gleißen pret **gleißte** *or* (*dial*) **gliß**, ptp **gegleißt** *or* (*dial*) **geglissen** *vi* (*liter*) to gleam, to glisten.

Gleit-: **~boot** *nt* hydroplane; **~bügel** *m* (*Elec*) pantograph, current collector.

gleiten pret **glitt**, ptp **geglitten** *vi* (**a**) *aux sein* (*Vogel, Flugzeug, Tänzer, Boot, Skier, Schlange*) to glide; (*Blick*) to pass, to range; (*Hand auch*) to slide. **ein Lächeln glitt über ihr Gesicht** a smile flickered across her face; **sein Auge über etw** (*acc*) **~ lassen** to cast an eye over sth; **die Finger über etw** (*acc*) **~ lassen** to glide *or* slide one's fingers over *or* across sth.
(**b**) *aux sein* (*rutschen*) to slide; (*Auto*) to skid; (*ent~: Gegenstand*) to slip; (*geh: ausrutschen*) to slip. **zu Boden ~** to slip to the floor/ground; **ins Wasser ~** to slide *or* slip into the water; **aus dem Sattel ~** to slide out of the saddle; **ins G~ kommen** to start to slide *or* slip.
(**c**) (*Ind inf:* **~de Arbeitszeit haben**) to have flex(i)time.

gleitend *adj* **~e Löhne** *or* **Lohnskala** sliding wage scale; **~e Arbeitszeit** flexible working hours *pl*, flex(i)time.

Gleiter *m* **-s, -** (*Aviat*) glider.

Gleit-: **~flug** *m* glide; **im ~flug niedergehen** to glide *or* plane down; **~flugzeug** *nt* glider; **~klausel** *f* (*Comm*) escalator clause; **~komma** *nt* floating point; **~kufe** *f* (*Aviat*) landing skid; **~mittel** *nt* (*Med*) lubricant; **~schutz** *m* (*Aut*) anti-skid(ding) device; **~wachs** *nt* (*für Skier*) wax; **~winkel** *m* gliding angle; **~zeit** *f* flex(i)time.

Glencheck [ˈglɛntʃɛk] *m* **-(s), -s** glencheck.

Gletscher *m* **-s, -** glacier.

Gletscher-: **g~artig** *adj* glacial; **~bach** *m* glacial stream; **~brand** *m* glacial sunburn; **~brille** *f* sun glasses *pl*; **~eis** *nt* glacial ice; **~feld** *nt* glacier; **~forschung** *f* glaciology; **~kunde** *f* glaciology; **~milch** *f* glacier milk; **~mühle** *f* moulin, glacier mill; **~spalte** *f* crevasse; **~tor** *nt* mouth (of glacier); **~wasser** *nt* glacier water.

Glibber *m* **-s, no pl** (*N Ger inf*) slime.

glibberig *adj* (*N Ger inf*) slimy.

glich pret of **gleichen**.

Glied *nt* **-(e)s, -er** (**a**) (*Körperteil*) limb, member (*form*); (*Finger~, Zehen~*) joint. **seine ~er recken** to stretch (oneself); **an allen ~ern zittern** to be shaking all over; **der Schreck fuhr ihm in alle ~er** the shock made him shake all over; **der Schreck sitzt** *or* **steckt ihr noch in den ~ern** she is still shaking with the shock; **sich** (*dat*) **alle ~er brechen** to break every bone in one's body.
(**b**) (*Penis*) penis, organ, member (*form*).
(**c**) (*Ketten~, fig*) link.
(**d**) (*Teil*) section, part; (*von Grashalm*) segment.
(**e**) (*Mit~*) member; (*Mil etc*) rank; (*Bibl*) generation; (*Math*) term. **aus dem ~ treten** (*Mil*) to step forward (out of the ranks); **ins ~ zurücktreten** (*Mil*) to step back into the ranks.

Glieder-: **~armband** *nt* (*von Uhr*) expanding bracelet; **~bau** *m* limb structure; (*Körperbau*) build; **~füßer** *m* **-s, -** *usu pl* (*Zool*) arthropod; **g~lahm** *adj* heavy-limbed, weary; **ich bin ganz g~lahm** my limbs are so stiff.

gliedern 1 *vt* (**a**) (*ordnen*) to structure, to order, to organize. (**b**) (*unterteilen*) to (sub)divide (*in* + acc into). **2** *vr* (*zerfallen in*) **sich ~ in** (+ acc) to (sub)divide into; (*bestehen aus*) to consist of.

Glieder-: **~puppe** *f* jointed doll; (*Marionette*) (string) puppet, marionette; (*Art*) lay figure; **~reißen** *nt*, **~schmerz** *m* rheumatic pains *pl*; **~satz** *m* (*Ling*) period; **~schwere** *f* heaviness in one's limbs; **~tier** *nt* articulate.

Gliederung *f* (**a**) (*das Gliedern*) structuring, organization; (*das Unterteilen*) subdivision. (**b**) (*Aufbau*) structure; (*Unterteilung, von Organisation*) subdivision. (**c**) (*Aufstellung in Reihe etc*) formation.

Glieder-: **~zucken** *nt* twitching of the limbs; **~zug** *m* articulated train.

Glied-: **~kirche** *f* member church; **~maßen** *pl* limbs *pl*; **~satz** *m* (*Ling*) subordinate clause; **~staat** *m* member *or* constituent state; **g~weise** *adv* (*Mil*) in ranks.

glimmen pret **glomm** *or* (*rare*) **glimmte**, ptp **geglommen** *or* (*rare*) **geglimmt** *vi* to glow; (*Feuer, Asche auch*) to smoulder. **~der Haß** (*geh*) smouldering hatred; **noch glomm ein Funken**

Hoffnung in ihm (*geh*) a ray of hope still glimmered within him.

Glimmer *m* **-s, -** (**a**) (*Min*) mica. (**b**) (*rare: Schimmer*) gleam, glint.

glimmern *vi* to glimmer.

Glimmerschiefer *m* (*Min*) mica schist.

Glimm-: **~lampe** *f* glow lamp; **~stengel** *m* (*hum inf*) fag (*esp Brit inf*), cigarette, butt (*US inf*).

Glimpf *m*: **mit ~** (*old*) siehe **glimpflich**.

glimpflich *adj* (*mild*) mild, light, lenient. **wegen des ~en Ausgangs des Unfalls** because the accident wasn't too serious; **~ davonkommen** to get off lightly; **mit jdm ~ umgehen** *or* **verfahren** to treat sb mildly *or* leniently; **~ abgehen** *or* **ablaufen** *or* **verlaufen**, **einen ~en Ausgang nehmen** to pass off without serious consequences; **die Sache ist für sie ~ abgegangen** *or* **verlaufen** they got off lightly.

gliß (*dial*) pret of **gleißen**.

Glitschbahn *f* (*dial*) slide.

glitschen *vi aux sein* (*inf*) to slip (*aus* out of).

glitschig *adj* (*inf*) slippery, slippy (*inf*).

glitt pret of **gleiten**.

glitzern *vi* to glitter; (*Stern auch*) to twinkle.

global *adj* (**a**) (*weltweit*) global, worldwide. **~ verbreitet** global, worldwide. (**b**) (*ungefähr, pauschal*) general. **~ gerechnet** in round figures.

Globen *pl* of **Globus**.

Global-: **~steuerung** *f* overall control; **~strategie** *f* (*Pol*) global *or* worldwide strategy.

Globetrotter [ˈgloːbətrɔtɐ, ˌgloːpˈtrɔtɐ] *m* **-s, -** globetrotter.

Globus *m* **- or -ses, Globen** *or* **-se** globe; (*inf: Kopf*) nut (*inf*).

Glöckchen *nt* (*little*) bell.

Glocke *f* **-, -n** (*auch Blüte*) bell; (*Käse~ etc*) cover; (*Florett~*) coquille; (*in Labor*) bell jar; (*Taucher~*) (diving) bell; (*Damenhut*) cloche; (*inf: Herrenhut*) bowler. **nach den ~n von Big Ben** after the chimes from Big Ben, after Big Ben strikes; **etw an die große ~ hängen** (*inf*) to shout sth from the rooftops, to bandy sth about; **wissen, was die ~ geschlagen hat** (*inf*) to know what one is in for (*inf*) *or* what's in store for one; **über der Stadt wölbte sich eine dichte ~ von Rauch** a thick pall of smoke hung over the city.

Glocken-: **~balken** *m* (bell) yoke; **~blume** *f* bellflower, campanula; **~bronze** *f* bell metal; **g~förmig** *adj* bell-shaped; **~geläut(e)** *nt* (peal of) bells; **~gießer** *m* bell-founder; **~gießerei** *f* bell-foundry; **~guß** *m* bell-founding; **g~hell** *adj* (*geh*) bell-like; **Stimme auch** as clear as a bell; **~helm** *m* top of a/the bell; **~klang** *m* ringing *or* (*esp hell auch*) pealing (of bells); **g~klar** *adj* siehe **g~hell**; **~klöppel** *m* clapper, tongue (of a/the bell); **~läuten** *nt* siehe **~geläut(e)**; **~mantel** *m* cope (*for founding bell*); **~putzen** *nt* (*dial inf*) ringing doorbells and running away; **g~rein** *adj* (*geh*) bell-like; **Stimme auch** as clear as a bell; **~rock** *m* flared skirt; **~schlag** *m* stroke (of a/the bell); (*von Uhr auch*) chime; **es ist mit dem ~schlag 6 Uhr** on the stroke it will be 6 o'clock; **auf den** *or* **mit dem ~schlag** on the stroke of eight/nine etc; (*genau pünktlich*) on the dot; **~speise** *f* bell metal; **~spiel** *nt* (*in Turm*) carillon; (*automatisch auch*) chimes *pl*; (*Instrument*) glockenspiel; **~strang** *m* bell rope; **~stube** *f* belfry; **~stuhl** *m* bell cage; **~ton** *m* sound of a/the bell; **~turm** *m* belltower, belfry; **~weihe** *f* consecration of a/the bell; **~zeichen** *nt* ring of a/the bell; **auf ein ~zeichen erschien der Butler** a ring on the bell summoned the butler; **~zug** *m* (*~strang*) bell rope; (*Klingelschnur*) bellpull, bell cord.

glockig *adj* bell-shaped.

Glöckner *m* **-s, -** bellringer. **der ~ von Notre-Dame** the Hunchback of Notre Dame.

glomm pret of **glimmen**.

Gloria¹ *nt* **-s, -s** (*Eccl*) gloria, Gloria; siehe **Glanz**.

Gloria² *f* **- or nt -s, no pl** (*usu iro*) glory.

Glorie [-iə] *f* (**a**) *no pl* (*Ruhm*) glory, splendour. (**b**) (*Heiligenschein*) halo.

Glorienschein [-iən-] *m* halo; (*fig*) aura.

Glorifikation *f* siehe **Glorifizierung**.

glorifizieren *vt* to glorify.

Glorifizierung *f* glorification.

Gloriole *f* **-, -n** halo; (*fig*) aura.

glorios *adj* (*oft iro*) glorious, magnificent.

glorreich *adj* glorious. **seine Laufbahn ~ beenden** to bring one's career to a glorious conclusion; **der ~e Rosenkranz** (*Eccl*) the Glorious Mysteries *pl*.

glosen *vi* (*rare*) siehe **glimmen**.

Glossar *nt* **-s, -e** glossary.

Glosse *f* **-, -n** (**a**) (*Liter*) gloss (*zu* on). (**b**) (*Press, Rad etc*) commentary. (**c**) **~n** *pl* (*inf*) snide *or* sneering comments; **seine ~n über jdn/etw machen** (*inf*) to make snide comments about sb/sth.

Glossenschreiber *m* (*Press*) commentator.

glossieren *vt* (**a**) (*Liter*) to gloss, to write a gloss/glosses on. (**b**) (*bespötteln*) to sneer at. (**c**) (*Press, Rad etc*) to do a commentary on, to commentate on.

Glotz-: **~auge** *nt* (**a**) (*usu pl: inf*) staring *or* goggle (*inf*) eye; **~augen machen** to stare (goggle-eyed), to gawp; (**b**) (*Med*) exophthalmia (*spec*); **g~äugig** *adj, adv* (*inf*) goggle-eyed (*inf*).

Glotze *f* **-, -n** (*sl*) goggle-box (*inf*), one-eyed monster (*pej inf*).

glotzen *vi* (*inf*) to gape (*inf, auf, in* + acc at) to stare, to gawp, to gape.

Glotzkasten *m* (*sl*), **Glotzkiste** *f* (*sl*), **Glotzophon** *nt* **-s, -e** (*pej inf*) goggle-box (*inf*), one-eyed monster (*pej inf*).

Gloxinie [-iə] *f* (*Bot*) gloxinia.

Glubsch|auge *nt* (*inf*) siehe **Glotzauge (a)**.

gluck interj (**a**) (*von Huhn*) cluck. (**b**) (*von Flüssigkeit*) glug. **~ ~, weg war er** (*inf*) glug glug, and he'd gone.

Glück *nt* **-(e)s, (rare) -e** (**a**) luck. **ein seltenes ~** a funny stroke *or* piece of luck; **ein ~!** how lucky!, what a stroke *or* piece of luck!; ~/kein ~ haben to be lucky/unlucky; er hat das ~ gehabt, zu ... he was lucky enough to ..., he had the good fortune to ...; ~ gehabt! that was lucky; auf gut ~ (aufs Geratewohl) on the off-chance; (unvorbereitet) trusting to luck; (wahllos) at random; es ist ein wahres ~, daß ... it's really lucky that ...; du hast ~ im Unglück gehabt it could have been a great deal worse (for you); in ~ und Unglück in good times and in bad, through thick and thin; viel ~ (bei ...)! good luck or the best of luck (with ...)!; ~ bei Frauen haben to be successful with women; jdm ~ für etw wünschen to wish sb luck for sth; jdm ~ wünschen zu ... to congratulate sb on ...; er wünscht/ich wünsche dir ~ bei deiner Prüfung he wishes you (good) luck in your exam/good luck in your exam; jdm zum Neuen Jahr/zum Geburtstag ~ wünschen to wish sb (a) Happy New Year/happy birthday; zum ~ luckily, fortunately; zu seinem ~ luckily or fortunately for him; das ist dein ~! that's lucky for you!; ~ auf! (Min) good luck!; mehr ~ als Verstand haben to have more luck than brains; sie weiß noch nichts von ihrem ~ (iro) she doesn't know anything about it yet; damit wirst du bei ihr kein ~ haben you won't have any joy with her (with that) (inf), that won't work with her; sein ~ machen to make one's fortune; sein ~ probieren or versuchen to try one's luck; er kann von ~ reden or sagen, daß ... he can count himself lucky that ..., he can thank his lucky stars that ... (inf); sein ~ mit Füßen treten to turn one's back on fortune; ~ muß der Mensch haben (inf) my/your etc luck is/was in; das war das ~ des Tüchtigen (prov) he/she deserved the break (inf) or his/her good luck; das hat mir gerade noch zu meinem ~ gefehlt! (iro) that was all I wanted; man kann niemanden zu seinem ~ zwingen (prov) you can lead a horse to water but you can't make him drink (Prov); ein Kind/Stiefkind des ~s sein (geh) to have been born under a lucky star/to be a born loser; jeder ist seines ~es Schmied (Prov) life is what you make it (prov), everyone is the architect of his own future.

(b) (Freude) happiness. eheliches ~ wedded or marital bliss; er ist ihr ganzes ~ he is her whole life; das Streben nach ~ the pursuit of happiness; ~ und Glas, wie leicht bricht das! (prov) happiness is such a fragile thing.

Glück-: ~auf nt -s, no pl (cry of) "good luck"; ~bringend adj lucky, propitious (form); sie glaubt an die g~bringende Wirkung von Sternschnuppen she believes that shooting stars are lucky or bring luck.

Glucke f -, -n (Bruthenne) broody or sitting hen; (mit Jungen) mother hen. wie eine ~ ist sie ständig um ihre Kinder herum she fusses round her children like a mother hen.

glucken vi (a) (brüten) to brood; (brüten wollen) to go broody; (fig inf) to sit around. (b) (Küken rufen) to cluck.

glücken vi aux sein to be a success, to be successful. nicht ~ to be a failure, not to be a success; (Plan auch) to miscarry; ihm glückt alles/nichts everything/nothing he does is a success, he succeeds/fails at whatever he does; dieses Bild/die Torte ist dir gut geglückt your picture/cake has turned out very well; endlich ist es ihm geglückt at last he managed it; es ist ihm geglückt zu fliehen he succeeded in escaping, he managed to escape; es wollte nicht ~ it wouldn't go right.

gluckern vi to glug.

glückhaft adj (geh) happy.

Glückhenne f siehe Glucke.

glücklich 1 adj (a) (erfolgreich, vom Glück begünstigt) lucky, fortunate; (vorteilhaft, treffend, erfreulich) happy. ~e Reise! bon voyage!, pleasant journey!; er kann sich ~ schätzen(, daß) he can count or consider himself lucky (that); wer ist der/die G~e? who is the lucky man/woman/girl etc?

(b) (froh, selig) happy. ein ~es Ende, ein ~er Ausgang a happy ending; ~ machen to bring happiness; jdn ~ machen to make sb happy, to bring sb happiness.

2 adv (a) (mit Glück) by or through luck; (vorteilhaft, treffend, erfreulich) happily. ~ zurückkommen (in Sicherheit) to come back safely.

(b) (froh, selig) happily. die ~-heiteren Tage der Kindheit the bright and happy days of childhood.

(c) (inf: endlich, zu guter Letzt) finally, eventually.

glücklicherweise adv luckily, fortunately.

Glück-: g~los adj hapless, luckless; ~sache f siehe Glückssache.

Glücks-: ~automat m (fig) gaming machine; ~bote m bearer of (the) glad or good tidings; ~botschaft f glad or good tidings pl; ~bringer m -s, - bearer of (the) glad tidings; (Talisman) lucky charm; ~bude f try-your-luck stall.

glückselig adj blissfully happy, blissful; Lächeln, Gesichtsausdruck auch rapturous.

Glückseligkeit f bliss, rapture.

glucksen vi (a) (lachen) (Kleinkind) to gurgle; (Erwachsener) to chortle. (b) siehe gluckern.

Glücks-: ~fall m piece or stroke of luck; durch einen ~fall by a lucky chance; im ~fall kannst du mit einer Geldstrafe rechnen if you're lucky you'll get away with a fine; ~gefühl nt feeling of happiness; ~göttin f goddess of luck; die ~göttin ist mir nicht hold (hum, geh) (Dame) Fortune has deserted me; ~güter pl (geh) mit ~gütern gesegnet sein to have been blessed with the good things in life; ~hafen m (S Ger, Aus) siehe ~bude; ~kind nt child of Fortune; ~klee m four-leaf(ed) clover; ~linie f line of fortune or luck; ~pfennig m lucky penny, a new, shiny pfennig piece supposed to bring luck; ~pilz m lucky beggar (inf) or devil (inf); ~rad nt wheel of fortune; ~ritter m adventurer; ~sache f das ist ~sache it's a matter of luck; ich hab gedacht ... — Denken ist ~sache (inf) I thought ... — you thought?; ~schwein(chen) nt pig as a symbol of good luck; ~spiel nt game of chance; ~spieler m gambler; ~stern m lucky star; ~strähne f lucky streak; eine ~strähne haben to be

on a lucky streak; ~tag m lucky day.

glückstrahlend adj beaming or Kind, Frau auch radiant (with happiness).

Glücks-: ~treffer m stroke of luck; (beim Schießen, Ftbl) lucky shot, fluke (inf); ~umstand m fortunate circumstance; ~zahl f lucky number.

glückverheißend adj (liter) Religion, Gesichtsausdruck which holds out a promise of happiness; Zeichen etc propitious (form), auspicious.

Glückwunsch m -es, ~e congratulations pl (zu on). herzlichen ~ congratulations; herzlichen ~ zum Geburtstag! happy birthday, many happy returns of the day; ~e zur Verlobung/zur bestandenen Prüfung congratulations on your engagement/on passing your examination.

Glückwunsch-: ~adresse f message of congratulations, congratulatory message; ~brief m letter of congratulations, congratulatory letter; ~karte f greetings card; ~schreiben nt siehe ~brief; ~telegramm nt greetings telegram.

Glüh- (Elec): ~birne f (electric) light bulb; ~draht m filament.

glühen 1 vi to glow; (fig auch) to be aglow. der Ofen/die Sonne glüht, daß man es nicht aushalten kann the fire/sun is too hot to bear; vor Fieber/Scham ~ to be flushed with fever/shame; der Haß glühte in ihm he was burning with hatred; vor Verlangen etc ~ (liter) to burn with desire etc. 2 vt to heat until red-hot.

glühend adj glowing; (heiß~) Metall red-hot; Hitze blazing; (fig: leidenschaftlich) ardent; Haß burning; Wangen flushed, burning. ~ heiß scorching; Sonne auch blazing hot.

Glüh-: ~faden m (Elec) filament; ~kerze f (Aut) heater or incandescent plug; ~lampe f (form) electric light bulb; ~ofen m (Metal) annealing furnace; ~strumpf m (gas) mantle; ~wein m glühwein, mulled wine, glogg (US); ~würmchen nt glow-worm; (fliegend) firefly.

Glukose f -, -n glucose.

Glumse f -, no pl (dial) siehe Quark.

glupsch adj pred (N Ger inf) peeved (inf), miffed (inf).

Glupsch|auge nt (N Ger inf) siehe Glotzauge (a).

glupschen vi (N Ger inf) siehe glotzen.

Glut f -, -en (a) (glühende Masse, Kohle) embers pl; (Tabaks~) burning ash; (Hitze) heat. (b) (fig liter) (glühende Farbe, Hitze) glow; (auf Gesicht) flush, redness; (Leidenschaft) ardour. schamrote ~ stieg ihr ins Gesicht she blushed for shame, a flush of shame tinged her features.

Glutamat nt glutamate.

Glutamin nt -s, -e glutamine.

Glutaminsäure f glutamic acid.

Glut-: g~äugig adj (geh) with smouldering eyes; ~ball m (poet) fiery orb (poet); ~hauch m (liter) torrid or sweltering heat; g~heiß adj (geh) swelteringly hot; ~hitze f sweltering heat; g~rot adj (liter) fiery red; ~röte f (liter) fiery red; g~voll adj passionate; ~wind m (liter) torrid wind.

Glyzerin nt -s, no pl (Chem) glycerin(e).

GmbH [ge:|embe:'ha:] f -, -s abbr of **Gesellschaft mit beschränkter Haftung** limited company, Ltd.

Gnade f -, -n (Barmherzigkeit) mercy; (heiligmachende ~ grace; (Gunst) favour; (Verzeihung) pardon. um ~ bitten to ask for or crave (liter) mercy; jdn um ~ für seine Sünden bitten to ask sb to pardon (one for) one's sins; jds ~ finden, bei jdm or vor jdm or vor jds Augen (dat) ~ finden to find favour with sb or in sb's eyes; ~ vor or für Recht ergehen lassen to temper justice with mercy; etw aus ~ und Barmherzigkeit tun to do sth out of the kindness of one's heart; ohne ~ without mercy; ~ mercy!; bei jdm in (hohen) ~n stehen (old) to stand high in sb's favour; von jds ~n by the grace of sb; Fürst von Gottes ~n (Hist) by the Grace of God, Prince; jdn in ~n entlassen to allow sb to go unpunished; jdn in ~n wieder aufnehmen to restore sb to favour; sich (dat) eine ~ erbitten (geh) to ask or crave (liter) a favour; jdm eine ~ gewähren (geh) to grant sb a favour; Euer ~n! (Hist) Your Grace; die Jungfrau der ~n (Eccl) Our Lady of Mercy; die ~ haben, etw zu tun (iro) to graciously consent to do sth.

gnaden vi: (dann) gnade dir Gott! (then) God help you or heaven have mercy on you.

Gnaden-: ~akt m act of mercy; ~beweis m ein ~beweis von jdm a proof or token of sb's mercy/grace/favour; ~bezeigung siehe ~beweis; ~bild nt (Eccl) picture/statue with miraculous powers; ~brot nt, no pl jdm/einem Tier das ~brot geben to keep sb/an animal in his/her/its old age; einem Pferd das ~brot geben to put a horse out to grass; das ~brot bei jdm essen to be provided for by sb (in one's old age); ~erlaß m (Jur) general pardon; ~frist f (temporary) reprieve; eine ~frist von 2 Stunden a 24 hour(s') reprieve, 24 hours' grace; ~gesuch nt plea for clemency; ~instanz f (Jur) authority invested with the power to grant pardons; ~kraut nt hedge-hyssop; g~los adj merciless; ~losigkeit f mercilessness; ~mittel pl (Eccl) means pl of grace; g~reich adj (old, Eccl) gracious; Maria, die ~reiche Our Gracious Lady; ~schuß m coup de grâce (by shooting); ~stoß m coup de grâce (with sword etc, fig); ~tod m (geh) mercy killing, euthanasia; ~verheißung f promise or grace; g~voll adj siehe g~reich; ~weg m auf dem ~weg by pardon; jedem Häftling steht der ~weg offen every prisoner is at liberty to ask for a pardon.

gnädig adj (barmherzig) merciful; (gunstvoll, herablassend) gracious; Strafe lenient; (freundlich) kind. das ~e Fräulein (form) the young lady; die ~e Frau (form) the mistress madam; der ~e Herr (old) the master; darf ich das ~e Fräulein zum Tanz bitten? (form) may I have the pleasure of this dance (form); ~es Fräulein (form) madam; (jüngere Dame) miss; ~ Frau (form) madam, ma'am; ~er Herr (old) sir; meine G~ (dated) or G~ste (dated) my dear madam; ~er Gott! (inf) merciful heavens! (inf); Gott sei uns ~! (geh) (may the good

Lord preserve us; **sei doch so ~, und mach mal Platz!**(iro) would you be so good as to make some room?; **~ davonkommen** to get off lightly; **es ~ machen** to be lenient, to show leniency.

Gnatz m -es, -e (dial) (old) bear (inf), bad-tempered so-and-so (inf).

gnatzig adj (dial) bearish (inf), bad-tempered.

Gneis m -es, -e (Geol) gneiss.

Gnom m -en, -en gnome.

gnomenhaft adj gnomish.

Gnosis f -, no pl (Rel) gnosis.

Gnostik f -, no pl (Rel) gnosticism.

Gnostiker m -s, - (Rel) gnostic.

gnostisch adj (Rel) gnostic.

Gnostizismus m -, no pl (Rel) Gnosticism.

Gnu nt -s, -s (Zool) gnu, wildebeest.

Go nt -, no pl go (Japanese board game).

Goal nt -s, -s (Aus, Sw Sport) goal.

Goal- ['goːl-] (Aus, Sw): **~getter** m -s, - scorer; **~keeper** m -s, -, **~mann** m, pl -männer goalkeeper, goalie (inf); **~stange** f crossbar.

Gobelin [gobə'lɛ̃ː] m -s, -s tapestry, Gobelin; (Webart) tapestry weave.

Gockel m -s, - (esp S Ger, baby-talk) cock; (fig) old goat (inf).

Gockelhahn m (esp S Ger, baby-talk) cock.

Göd m -en, -en (Aus inf) godfather.

Göd(e)l f -, -n (Aus inf) godmother.

Godemiche [goːdmi'ʃeː] m -, -s dildo.

Goderl nt -s, -n: **jdm das ~ kratzen** (Aus inf) to butter sb up (inf).

Goethe m -s Goethe.

goethesch, goethisch adj Goethean.

Goethesch, Goethisch adj Goethean.

Gogo-Girl ['goːgogøːrl] nt go-go dancer or girl.

Goi ['goːi] m -(s), **Gojim** goy, Gentile.

Go-in [goː'ɪn] nt -s, -s **die Versammlung wurde durch ein ~ gestört** the meeting was disrupted (by demonstrators); **ein ~ veranstalten** to disrupt a/the meeting.

Go-Kart m -(s), -s kart, go-cart.

gokeln vi (dial) to play with matches.

Gold nt -(e)s, no pl (lit, fig) gold. **nicht mit ~ zu bezahlen** or **aufzuwiegen sein** to be worth one's weight in gold; **nicht für alles ~ der Welt** (liter) not for all the money in the world; **er hat ein Herz aus ~** he has a heart of gold; **er hat ~ in der Kehle** he has a golden voice; **zehnmal olympisches ~ holen** to win ten golds in the Olympics; **es ist nicht alles ~, was glänzt** (Prov) all that glitters or glisters is not gold (Prov); siehe **Morgenstunde, treu**.

Gold- in cpds gold; (von Farbe, Zool) golden; **~ader** f vein of gold; **~ammer** f yellowhammer; **~amsel** f golden oriole; **~arbeit** f goldwork; **~barren** m gold ingot; **~barsch** m (Rotbarsch) redfish; (Kaulbarsch) ruff; **~basis** f gold basis; **eine Währung auf ~basis** a gold-based currency; **g~bestickt** adj embroidered with gold (thread); **g~betreßt** adj trimmed with gold braid; **~blech** nt gold foil; **~borte** f gold edging no pl; **~broiler** m -s, - (DDR Cook) roast chicken; **~deckung** f (Fin) gold backing; **~doublé, ~dublée** nt gold-plated metal; **~druck** m gold print; (Schrift) gold lettering; **g~durchwirkt** adj shot with gold thread.

golden 1 adj attr (lit, fig) golden; (aus Gold) gold, golden (liter). **~e Schallplatte** gold disc; **~er Humor** irrepressible sense of humour; **~e Worte** wise words, words of wisdom; **ein ~es Herz haben** to have a heart of gold; **~e Berge versprechen** to promise the moon (and the stars); **die ~e Mitte** or **den ~en Mittelweg wählen** to strike a happy medium; **~e Hochzeit** golden wedding (anniversary); **G~er Schnitt** (Math, Art) golden section; **das G~e Buch** the visitors' book; **die G~e Stadt** (geh) Prague; **das G~e Horn** (Geog) the Golden Horn; **die ~e Horde** (Hist) the Golden Horde; **das G~e Zeitalter** (Myth, fig) the golden age; **das G~e Vlies** (Myth) the Golden Fleece; **das G~e Kalb** (Bibl) the golden calf; **der Tanz ums G~e Kalb** (fig) the worship of Mammon (fig); **das Auto war das G~e Kalb der sechziger Jahre** in the sixties everything was sacrificed to the altar of the motor car; siehe **Brücke**.

2 adv like gold. **~ schimmern** to shimmer like gold.

Gold-: **~esel** m (Liter) ass which rained gold coins; **leider habe ich keinen ~esel** (inf) money doesn't grow on trees, I'm afraid; **~faden** m gold thread; **g~farben, g~farbig** adj golden, gold-coloured; **~feder** f gold nib; **~fieber** nt (fig) gold fever; **~fisch** m goldfish; **sich (dat) einen ~fisch angeln** (hum inf) to make a rich catch, to marry money; **~fuchs** m (a) (Pferd) golden chestnut (horse); (b) (old inf) gold piece; **g~führend** adj gold-bearing; **g~gefaßt** adj Brille gold-rimmed; **g~gelockt** adj (dated) with golden locks; **g~gerändert** adj edged with gold; Brille gold-rimmed; **~gewicht** nt gold weight; = troy weight; **~gier** f greed for gold; **g~gierig** adj greedy for gold; **~glanz** m (liter) golden gleam; **g~glänzend** adj (liter) gleaming gold; **~gräber** m gold-digger; **~grube** f (lit, fig) goldmine; **~grund** m, no pl (Art) gold ground; **g~haltig, g~hältig** (Aus) adj gold-bearing, auriferous (spec); **~hamster** m (golden) hamster.

goldig adj (a) (fig inf: allerliebst) sweet, cute. **du bist vielleicht ~!** (iro) the ideas you get! (b) (poet: golden) golden.

Gold-: **~junge** m (inf) blue-eyed boy (inf), golden boy (inf); (Sport) gold medallist; **~käfer** m (inf: reiches Mädchen) rich girl; **~kehlchen** nt (inf) singer with a golden voice; **~kind** nt (inf) little treasure (inf), dear child; **mein ~kind** (als Anrede) (my) pet or precious; **~klumpen** m gold nugget; **~küste** f (Geog) Gold Coast; **~lack** m (a) (Bot) wallflower; (b) (Glanzlack) gold lacquer; **~land** nt land of gold; **~mädchen** nt (inf) blue-eyed girl (inf), golden girl (inf); (Sport) gold medallist; **~mark** f (Hist) gold mark.

Goldmedaille f gold medal.

Goldmedaillen-: **~gewinner, ~träger** m gold medallist.

Gold-: **~mine** f gold mine; **~mundstück** nt gold tip; **~papier** nt gold foil; **~probe** f assay (for gold); **~rahmen** m gilt frame; **~rand** m gold edge; **mit ~rand** with a gold edge; **~rausch** m gold fever; **~regen** m (Bot) laburnum; (Feuerwerkskörper) Roman candle; (fig) riches pl; **g~reich** adj rich in gold; **~reif** m (geh) circlet of gold; (Ring) gold ring; (Armband) gold bracelet; **~reserve** f (Fin) gold reserves pl; **g~richtig** adj (inf) absolutely or dead (inf) right; Mensch all right (inf); **~schatz** m golden treasure; (von Geld) hoard of gold; (Kosewort) treasure.

Goldschmied m goldsmith.

Goldschmiede-: **~arbeit** f (Handwerk) gold work; (Gegenstand) worked gold article; **~handwerk** nt, **~kunst** f gold work.

Gold-: **~schnitt** m, no pl gilt edging; **~schnittausgabe** f gilt-edged edition; **~schrift** f gold lettering; **~stück** nt piece of gold; (Münze) gold coin or piece, piece of gold (old); (fig inf) jewel, treasure; **~suche** f search for gold; **~sucher** m gold-hunter; **~taler** m golden coin; **~topas** m yellow topaz; **~tresse** f gold braid; **~überzug** m layer of gold plate; **~uhr** f gold watch; **g~umrändert, g~umrandet** adj siehe **g~gerändert**; **~vorkommen** nt gold deposit; **~waage** f gold or bullion balance; **jedes Wort** or **alles auf die ~waage legen** (sich vorsichtig ausdrücken) to weigh one's words; (überempfindlich sein) to be hypersensitive; **~währung** f gold standard; **eine ~währung a** currency on the gold standard; **~waren** pl gold articles pl; **~wäscher** m gold panner; **~wert** m, no pl value in gold; (Wert des ~es) value of gold.

Golem m -s golem.

Golf[1] m -(e)s, -e (Meerbusen) gulf. **der ~ von Biskaya** the Bay of Biscay; **der (Persische) ~** the (Persian) Gulf.

Golf[2] nt -s, no pl (Sport) golf.

Golfer(in f) m -s, - (inf) golfer.

Golf- in cpds golf; **~platz** m golf course; **~schläger** m golf club; **~spiel** nt das **~spiel** golf; **~spieler** m golfer; **~staaten** pl die **~staaten** the Gulf States pl; **~strom** m (Geog) Gulf Stream; **~tasche** f golf bag, caddie.

Golgatha ['gɔlgata] nt -s (Bibl) Golgotha.

Goliath ['goːliat] m -s, -s (Bibl, fig) Goliath.

Gomorrha [go'mɔra] nt -s (Bibl) Gomorrah; siehe **Sodom**.

Gonade f (Biol) gonad.

Gondel f -, -n gondola; (von Sessellift etc auch) (cable-)car.

Gondel-: **~bahn** f cable railway; (Sw) chairlift; **~fahrt** f trip in a gondola; **~führer** m gondolier.

gondeln vi aux sein to travel by gondola; (Gondelführer) to punt; (inf) (reisen) to travel around; (herumfahren) to drive around. **durch die Welt ~** to go globetrotting (inf).

Gondoliere [gɔndo'lieːrə] m -, **Gondolieri** gondolier.

Gong m -s, -s gong; (bei Boxkampf etc) bell. **der ~ zur dritten Runde** the bell for the third round.

gongen 1 vi impers **es hat gegongt** the gong has gone or sounded; **es gongte zum Essen** the gong went or sounded for dinner etc. 2 vi to ring or sound a/the gong.

Gongschlag m stroke of the gong.

gönnen vt **jdm etw ~** not to (be)grudge sb sth; (zuteil werden lassen) to grant or allow sb sth; **jdm etw nicht ~** to (be)grudge sb sth, not to grant or allow sb sth; **sich (dat) etw ~** to allow oneself sth; **jdm ~, daß ...** not to (be)grudge sb the fact that ...; **sie gönnt ihm kein gutes Wort** she never has a good word for him; **er gönnte mir keinen Blick** he didn't spare me a single glance; **er gönnt ihm nicht die Luft zum Atmen** he (be)grudges her the very air she breathes; **ich gönne ihm diesen Erfolg/ seine Frau von ganzem Herzen** I'm delighted for him that he's had this success/that he has such a nice wife; **das sei ihm gegönnt** I don't (be)grudge him that.

Gönner(in f) m -s, - patron.

Gönner-: **g~haft** adj (pej) patronizing; **g~haft tun** to play the big benefactor; **~haftigkeit** f (pej) patronizingness; **seine ~haftigkeit** his patronizing(ness); **~miene** f (pej) patronizing air; **~schaft** f (Förderung) patronage.

Gonokokkus m -, **Gonokokken** (usu pl) (Med) gonococcus.

Gonorrhö(e) [gono'røː] f -, -en (Med) gonorrhoea. **er hat die ~** he has gonorrhoea.

Goodwill ['gudwil] m -s, no pl (auch Econ) goodwill, good will; (guter Ruf) good name.

Goodwill-: **~reise, ~tour** f goodwill journey or trip.

gor pret of **gären**.

Gör nt -(e)s, -en (N Ger inf) (a) (kleines Kind) brat (pej inf), kid (inf). (b) siehe **Göre**.

gordisch adj **der G~e Knoten** (Myth) the Gordian knot; **ein ~er Knoten** (fig) a Gordian knot.

Göre f -, -n (N Ger inf) (a) (kleines Mädchen) (cheeky or saucy) little miss. (b) siehe **Gör** (a).

Gorilla m -s, -s gorilla; (sl: Leibwächter auch) heavy (sl).

Gorillapranke f gorilla's hand.

Gosche f -, -, **Goschen** f -, - (S Ger, Aus: pej) gob (sl), mouth. **eine freche ~ haben** to have the cheek of the devil (inf); **halt die ~!** shut your mouth or gob (sl) or trap (inf).

Gospel ['gɔspl] m or nt -s, -s, **Gospelsong** m gospel song.

goß pret of **gießen**.

Gosse f -, -n (a) (Rinnstein) gutter; (rare: Abfluß, Gully) drain. (b) (fig) gutter. **in der ~ enden** or **landen** to end up in the gutter; **jdn aus der ~ holen** or **ziehen** to take sb from or pull sb out of the gutter; **jdn** or **jds Namen durch die ~ ziehen** or **schleifen** to drag sb's name through the mud.

Gossen-: **~ausdruck** m vulgarity; **~jargon** m, **~sprache** f gutter language, language of the gutter.

Gote m -n, -n Goth.

Göteborg nt -s Gothenburg.

Gotha m -s, -s *directory of the German nobility*, ≈ Debrett's (Peerage) (*Brit*).

Gotik f -, *no pl* (*Art*) Gothic (style); (*gotische Epoche*) Gothic period. **ein Meisterwerk der** ~ a masterpiece of Gothic architecture *etc*; **typisch für die** ~ typical of Gothic.

Gotin f Goth.

gotisch *adj* Gothic. ~**e Schrift** (*Typ*) Gothic (script).

Gott m -es, ˵er (a) god; (*als Name*) God. ~ **der Herr** the Lord God; ~ **(der) Vater God the Father;** ~ **der Allmächtige** Almighty God, God (the) Almighty; **der liebe** ~ (*dated*) the good or dear Lord; **an** ~ **glauben** to believe in God; **zu** ~ **beten** or **flehen** (*liter*) to pray to God; **er ist ihr** ~ she worships him like a god; **bei** ~ **schwören** to swear by Almighty God.

(b) **in** ~ **entschlafen** (*liter*) to pass away *or* on; **dein Schicksal liegt in** ~**es Hand** you are *or* your fate is in God's hands; **dich hat** ~ **im Zorn erschaffen!** God left something out when he put you together! (*hum*); **dem lieben** ~ **den Tag stehlen** to laze the day(s) away; **den lieben** ~ **einen guten** or **frommen Mann sein lassen** (*inf*) to take things as they come; **er ist wohl (ganz und gar) von** ~ *or* **den** ˜**ern verlassen** (*inf*) he's (quite) taken leave of his senses; ~ **ist mein Zeuge** (*liter*) as God is my witness; **wie** ~ **ihn geschaffen hat** (*hum inf*) as naked as the day (that) he was born; **ein Anblick** or **Bild für die** ˜**er** (*hum inf*) a sight for sore eyes; **das wissen die** ˜**er** (*inf*) heaven *or* God (only) knows; ~ **weiß** (*inf*) heaven knows (*inf*), God knows (*inf*); **er hat** ~ **weiß was erzählt** (*inf*) he said God knows what (*inf*); **ich bin weiß** ~ **nicht prüde, aber ...** heaven or God knows I'm no prude but ...; **so** ~ **will** (*geh*) God willing, D.V.; **vor** ~ **und der Welt** before the whole world; ~ **und die Welt** (*fig*) everybody; **über** ~ **und die Welt reden** (*fig*) to talk about everything under the sun *or* anything and everything; **im Namen** ~**es** in the name of God; **leider** ~**es** unfortunately, alas; **bei** ~ **ist kein Ding unmöglich** with God all things are possible; **was** ~ **tut, das ist wohlgetan** God does all things well; ~**es Mühlen mahlen langsam** (*hum*) the mills of God grind slowly (but they grind exceeding fine); **ein Leben wie** ~ **in Frankreich führen, wie** ~ **in Frankreich leben** (*inf*) to be in clover *or* the lap of luxury, to live the life of Riley (*inf*); **was** ~ **zusammengefügt hat, soll der Mensch nicht scheiden** (*prov*) what God has joined together let no man put asunder.

(c) **grüß** ~! (*esp S Ger, Aus*) hello, good morning/afternoon/evening; ~ **zum Gruß!** (*old*) God be with you (*old*); ~ **sei mit dir!** (*old*) God be with you (*old*); **geh mit** ~! (*old*) (may) God go with you (*old*); ~ **mit dir!** (*old*) God bless you; **vergelt's** ~! (*dated*) God bless you, may you be rewarded; **wollte** or **gebe** ~, **daß ...** (*old*) (may) God grant that ...; ~ **soll mich strafen, wenn ...** (*old*) may God strike me dumb if ...; ~ **steh' mir bei!** God help me!; ~ **hab' ihn selig!** God have mercy on his soul; **in** ~**es Namen!** for heaven's *or* goodness sake!; **ach (du lieber)** ~! (*inf*) oh Lord! (*inf*), oh heavens! (*inf*); **mein** ~!, **ach** ~! (my) God!; (*als Leerformel in Antworten*) (oh) well, (oh) you know; **großer** ~! good Lord *or* God!; ~ **im Himmel!** (*dated*) heavens above!; **bei** ~! by God!; ~ **behüte** *or* **bewahre!, da sei** ~ **vor!** God *or* Heaven forbid!; **um** ~**es willen!** for heaven's *or* God's sake!; ~ **sei Dank!** thank God!

Gott-: **g~ähnlich 1** *adj* godlike; **2** *adv* **verehren** as a god; **~ähnlichkeit** f godlike nature; **g~begnadet** *adj* divinely gifted; **g~behüte** (*esp Aus*), **g~bewahre** *adv* heaven *or* God forbid.

Göttchen nt (ach) ~! (*inf*) gosh! (*inf*), golly! (*inf*).

Gott|erbarmen nt **zum** ~ (*inf*) pitiful(ly), pathetic(ally) (*inf*).

Götter-: ~**bild** nt idol; ~**bote** m (*Myth*) messenger of the gods; ~**dämmerung** f götterdämmerung, twilight of the gods; ~**epos** nt epic of the gods; ~**gatte** m (*dated hum*) lord and master (*hum*), better half (*inf*).

Gott-: **g~ergeben** *adj* (*demütig*) meek; (*fromm*) pious; ~**ergebenheit** f meekness.

Götter-: ~**gestalt** f god; **g~gleich** *adj* godlike; ~**sage** f myth about the gods/a god; (*als Literaturform*) mythology of the gods; ~**speise** f (*Myth*) food of the gods; (*Cook*) jelly (*Brit*), jello (*US*); ~**trank** m (*Myth*) drink of the gods; ~**vater** m (*Myth*) father of the gods.

Gottes-: ~**acker** m (*old*) God's acre; ~**anbeterin** f (*Zool*) praying mantis; ~**begriff** m conception of God; ~**beweis** m proof of the existence of God; **der ontologische** *etc* ~**beweis** the ontological *etc* argument.

Gottesdienst m (a) (*Gottesverehrung*) worship. (b) (*Eccl*) service. **zum** ~ **gehen** to go to church; **dem** ~ **beiwohnen** (*form*) to attend church.

Gottesdienstbesuch m church attendance.

Gottes-: ~**erkenntnis** f knowledge of God; ~**friede** m (*Hist*) (*Pax Dei*) Peace of God; (*Treuga Dei*) Truce of God; ~**furcht** f (*geh*) fear of God; **jdn zur** ~**furcht erziehen** to teach sb to fear God; **g~fürchtig** *adj* godfearing; ~**gabe** f gift of *or* from God; ~**gelehrte(r)** m *decl as adj* (*old*) theologian, divine (*old*); ~**gericht** nt (a) punishment of God; (b) (*Hist*) *siehe* ~**urteil**; ~**geschenk** nt *siehe* ~**gabe**; ~**gnadentum** nt, *no pl* (*Hist*) doctrine of divine right; ~**haus** nt place of worship; ~**lamm** nt (*Rel*) Lamb of God; ~**lästerer** m blasphemer; **g~lästerlich** *adj* blasphemous; ~**lästerung** f blasphemy; ~**leugner** m (*dated*) unbeliever; ~**lohn** m, *no pl* (*old*) reward from God; **das ist der** ~**lohn für deine guten Taten** that is God's reward for your good deeds; **etw für einen** ~**lohn tun** to do sth for love; ~**mann** m, *pl* -**männer** (*old, iro*) man of God; ~**mutter** f (*Rel*) Mother of God; **Maria, die** ~**mutter** Mary (the) Mother of God; ~**sohn** m (*Rel*) Son of God; ~**staat** m theocracy; **Augustins „**~**staat"** Augustine's "City of God"; ~**urteil** nt (*Hist*) trial by ordeal.

Gott-: **g~froh** *adj* (*esp Sw*) *siehe* **heilfroh**; **g~gefällig** *adj* (*old*) godly **no** *adv*, pleasing in the sight of God (*form*); **g~gefällig leben** to live in a manner pleasing in the sight of God

---

g~gegeben *adj* god-given; **g~gesandt** *adj* (*old, liter*) sent from God; **g~geweiht** *adj* (*liter*) dedicated to God; **g~gewollt** *adj* willed by God; **g~gläubig** *adj* religious; (*NS*) non-denominational.

Gotthardchinese m (*Sw pej*) eyetie (*pej sl*), Italian.

Gottheit f (a) *no pl* (*Göttlichkeit*) divinity, godhood, godship. **die** ~ (*Gott*) the Godhead. (b) (*esp heidnische Göttergestalt*) deity. **jdn wie eine** ~ **verehren** to worship sb like a god.

Göttin f goddess.

göttlich *adj* (*lit, fig*) divine. **wir haben uns** ~**amüsiert** (*lustig gemacht*) we were terribly amused; (*gut unterhalten*) we had a wonderful time; **du bist ja** ~! (*dated*) you (really) are a one (*dated inf*); **das G~e im Menschen** the divine in Man.

Göttlichkeit f, *no pl* divinity.

Gott-: **g~lob** *interj* thank God *or* heavens *or* goodness; **er ist g~lob wieder gesund** he has recovered now thank God *or* heavens *or* goodness; **g~los** *adj* godless; (*verwerflich*) ungodly; **halt dein g~loses Mundwerk!** don't be irreverent!; ~**losigkeit** f, *no pl* godlessness; ~**mensch** m God become Man; ~**seibeiuns** m (*euph*) **der** ~**seibeiuns** the Evil One, the Tempter.

Gotts-: **g~erbärmlich**, **g~jämmerlich** *adj* (*inf*) dreadful, godawful (*sl*); ~**öberste** m -n, -n (*Aus iro*) his lordship (*iro*), my noble lord (*iro*); **die** ~**öbersten** the noble lords.

Gott-: ~**suche** f search for God; ~**sucher** m seeker after God; ~**vater** m, *no pl* God the Father; **g~verdammnis interj** (*sl*) bloody hell (*Brit sl*), God Almighty (*sl*); **g~verdammt**, **g~verflucht** *adj attr* (*sl*) goddamn(ed) (*sl*), damn(ed) (*inf*), bloody (*Brit sl*); **g~vergessen** *adj* (*sl*) godless; (b) *siehe* **g~verlassen**; **g~verlassen** *adj* godforsaken; **g~verlassen allein** utterly alone; ~**vertrauen** nt trust *or* faith in God; **dein** ~**vertrauen möchte ich haben!** I wish I had your faith; **g~voll** *adj* (*fig inf*) divine; **du bist ja g~voll!** you (really) are a one! (*inf*); ~**wesen** nt (*liter*) god(head).

Götze m -n, -n (*lit, fig*) idol.

Götzen-: ~**anbeter** m divine ~**diener**; ~**bild** nt idol, graven image (*Bibl*); ~**diener** m idolater; (*fig*) worshipper; ~**dienerin** f idolatress; (*fig*) worshipper; ~**dienst**, ~**glaube** m, ~**verehrung** f idolatry.

Götz von Berlichingen m (*euph*) **er beschimpfte ihn mit** ~ ~ he used a few four-letter words to him.

Götzzitat nt **das** ~ ≈ the V-sign (*Brit*), the finger (*US*).

Gouache [ɡuaː(ː)ʃ] f -, -n (*Art*) gouache.

Goulache [ˈɡulaʃ] m *or* nt *siehe* **Gulasch**.

Gourmand [ɡurˈmãː] m -s, -s glutton, gourmand.

Gourmet [ɡurˈmɛ, -ˈmeː] m -s, -s gourmet.

goutieren* [ɡuˈtiːrən] *vt* (*geh*) (a) (*fig*) (*Gefallen finden an*) to appreciate; (*gutheißen*) to approve (of). (b) (*rare: kosten, genießen*) to taste, to partake of (*liter*).

Gouvernante [ɡuvɛrˈnantə] f -, -n governess; (*pej*) schoolmarm.

gouvernantenhaft [ɡuvɛrˈnantən-] *adj* schoolmarmish.

Gouvernement [ɡuvɛrnəˈmãː] nt -s, -s (a) (*Hist*) (*Regierung*) government; (*Verwaltung*) administration. (b) province.

Gouverneur [ɡuvɛrˈnøːr] m governor.

GPU [ɡeːpeːˈʔuː] f - GPU, Ogpu.

Grab nt -(e)s, ˵er grave; (*Gruft*) tomb, sepulchre; (*fig: Untergang*) end, ruination. **das Heilige** ~ the Holy Sepulchre; **jdn zu** ~**e tragen** to bear sb to his grave; **er hat erst letzten Monat seine Frau zu** ~**e getragen** it was only last month that his wife passed on; **ins** ~ **sinken** (*old liter*) to be laid in the earth (*liter*); **ein frühes** ~ **finden** (*geh*) to go to an early grave; **ein** ~ **in fremder Erde finden** (*geh*) to be buried in foreign soil; **ein feuchtes** *or* **nasses** ~ **finden**, **sein** ~ **in den Wellen finden** (*liter*) to go to a watery grave, to meet a watery end; **ein Geheimnis mit ins** ~ **nehmen** to take a secret with one to the grave; **treu bis ans** ~ **faithful to the end, faithful unto death** (*liter*); **(bis) über das** ~ **hinaus in death, beyond the grave; verschwiegen wie ein** or **das** ~ (as) silent as the grave; **er würde sich im** ~**e umdrehen, wenn ...** he would turn in his grave if ...; **du bringst mich noch ins** ~ *or* **an den Rand des** ~**es!** you'll be the death of me yet (*inf*), you'll send me to an early grave; **das bringt mich/dich noch ins** ~! it'll be the death of me/you yet (*inf*); **mit einem Bein** *or* **Fuß im** ~ **e stehen** (*fig*) to have one foot in the grave; **sich** (*dat*) **selbst sein** or **sich** (*dat*) **sein eigenes** ~ **graben** *or* **schaufeln** (*fig*) to dig one's own grave; **das** ~ **seiner Hoffnungen** (*geh*) the end *or* downfall of his hopes; **seine Hoffnungen** *etc* **zu** ~**e tragen** (*geh*) to abandon *or* bury one's hopes *etc*; *siehe* ~**mal**.

Grabbeigabe f (*Archeol*) burial object.

Grabbelei f (*inf*) groping *or* rummaging (about) (*inf*).

grabbeln *vi* (*inf*) to grope about, to rummage (about).

Grabbeltisch m (*inf*) cheap goods table *or* counter.

Gräbchen nt *dim of* **Grab**.

Grabdenkmal nt *siehe* **Grabmal**.

graben pret **grub**, ptp **gegraben 1** *vti* (a) to dig; *Torf* to cut; *Kohle etc* to mine. **seine Zähne in etw** (*acc*) ~ to sink or bury one's teeth into sth; **nach Gold/Erz** ~ to dig for gold/ore.

(b) (*geh: gravieren, einkerben*) to engrave.

2 *vr* **sich in etw** (*acc*) ~, (*Zähnen, Krallen*) to sink into sth; **das hat sich mir tief ins Gedächtnis gegraben** (*geh*) it has imprinted itself firmly on my memory; *siehe* **Grube**.

Graben m -s, ˵ ditch; (*trockener* ~, *Mil*) trench; (*Sport*) ditch; (*Sport: Wasser*~) water-jump; (*Burg*~) moat; (*Geol*) rift (valley), graben (*spec*). **im** ~ **liegen** (*Mil*) to be in the trenches.

Graben-: ~**kampf**, ~**krieg** m (*Mil*) trench warfare no *pl*, no indef *art*; ~**senke** f (rift) valley, graben (*spec*).

Gräber *pl of* **Grab**.

Gräber-: ~**feld** nt cemetery, burial ground; ~**fund** m grave find.

Grabes- (liter): ~dunkel nt sepulchral darkness; ~kälte f grave-like cold; ~luft f grave-like air; ~nacht f siehe ~dunkel; ~rand m: am ~rand on the very brink of the grave; ~ruhe, ~stille f deathly hush or silence; ~stimme f sepulchral voice.

Grab-: ~fund m siehe Gräberfund; ~geläute nt (a) (death) knell; (b) siehe ~gesang (b); ~geleit nt (geh) jdm das ~geleit geben to accompany or follow sb's coffin; ~gesang m (a) funeral hymn, dirge; (b) (fig) der ~gesang einer Sache (gen) sein to sound the death knell of sth; ~gewölbe nt vault; (von Kirche, Dom) crypt; ~hügel m mound (over a grave); (Archeol) barrow, tumulus (form); ~inschrift f epitaph, inscription (on gravestone etc); ~kammer f burial chamber; ~kapelle f chapel (attached to burial ground); ~kreuz nt (cross-shaped) gravestone, cross; ~legung f burial, interment.

Gräblein nt dim of Grab.

Grab-: ~licht nt candle (on a grave); ~mal nt -s, -mäler or (geh) -e monument; (~stein) gravestone; das ~(mal) des Unbekannten Soldaten the tomb of the Unknown Warrior or Soldier; ~nische f burial niche; ~pflege f care of the grave(s)/of graves; ~platte f memorial slab; ~rede f funeral oration; ~schänder(in f) m -s, - defiler of the grave(s)/of graves; ~schändung f defilement of graves; ~schaufel f shovel.

grabschen vti siehe grapschen.

Grab-: ~schmuck m flowers/wreaths pl etc (on a grave); ~schrift f siehe ~inschrift; ~spruch m epitaph, inscription (on a grave); ~stätte f grave; (Gruft) tomb, sepulchre; ~stein m gravestone, tombstone; ~stelle f (burial) plot; ~stichel m (Art) burin.

Grabung f (Archeol) excavation.

Grabungsfund m (Archeol) (archeological) find.

Grab-: ~urne f funeral urn; ~vase f grave vase; ~werkzeug nt (Zool) claw.

Gracchen ['graxn] pl die ~ (Hist) the Gracchi.

Gracht f -, -en canal.

Grad m -(e)s, -e (Sci, Univ, fig) degree; (Mil) rank; (Typ: Schrift~) size. ein Winkel von 45 ~ an angle of 45 degrees, a 45-degree angle; unterm 32. ~ nördlicher Breite latitude 32 degrees north; 4 ~ Kälte 4 degrees below zero or freezing point, 4 degrees below; 4 ~ Wärme 4 degrees above zero or freezing point; 20° (gesprochen: ~) Fahrenheit/Celsius 20 (degrees) Fahrenheit/Centigrade; um 5 ~ wärmer sein to be 5 degrees warmer; null ~ zero; Wasser auf 80 ~ erhitzen to heat water to 80 degrees; es kocht bei 100 ~ boiling occurs at 100 degrees; in ~e einteilen to calibrate, to graduate; Verwandte zweiten/dritten ~es a relative once/twice removed; Vetter zweiten ~es second cousin; Verbrennungen ersten ~es (Med) first-degree burns; in or bis zu einem gewissen ~e up to a certain point, to a certain degree; in hohem ~(e) to a great or large extent; im höchsten ~(e) extremely; siehe Gleichung.

grad- siehe gerade-.

Gradation f gradation.

grad(e) adj (inf) siehe gerade.

Grad-: ~bogen m (Surv, Mil) quadrant; ~einteilung f calibration, graduation.

Gradient [gra'diɛnt] m (Sci) gradient.

gradieren* vt (a) (in Grade einteilen) to calibrate, to graduate. (b) (abstufen) to grade.

Grad-: ~kreis m (Math) graduated circle; g~mäßig adj siehe graduell; ~messer m (fig) gauge (gen, für of); ~netz nt (Geog) latitude and longitude grid; ~skala f scale (of degrees).

graduell adj (allmählich) gradual; (gering) slight.

graduieren* 1 vt (a) (in Grade einteilen) to calibrate, to graduate. (b) (Univ) to confer a degree upon, to graduate. graduierter Ingenieur engineer with the diploma of a School of Engineering, engineering graduate. 2 vi (Univ) to graduate.

Graduierte(r) mf decl as adj graduate.

Graduierung f (Univ) graduation.

Grad-: ~unterschied m difference of degree; g~weise adj by degrees.

Graecum ['grɛːkʊm] nt -s, no pl (Univ, Sch) examination in Greek.

Graf m -en, -en count; (als Titel) Count; (britischer~) earl; (als Titel) Earl. wie ~ Koks von der Gasanstalt auftreten (inf) to turn up behaving like Lord Muck (hum inf); ~ Rotz (von der Backe) (sl) Lord Muck (hum inf).

Grafen-: ~familie f, ~geschlecht nt family of counts/earls; ~krone f (count's/earl's) coronet; ~stand m (Hist) (Rang) rank of count/earldom; (Gesamtheit der ~) counts/earls pl; jdn in den ~stand erheben to confer the rank of count/earl upon sb, to make sb a count/bestow an earldom upon sb.

Graffel nt -s, no pl (Aus inf) siehe Gerümpel.

Graffito m or nt -(s), **Graffiti** (Art) graffito.

Grafik siehe Graphik.

Gräfin f countess.

gräflich adj count's/earl's. das ~e Schloß the count's/earl's castle; ein ~er Diener one of the count's/earl's servants.

Grafo- siehe Grapho-.

Grafschaft f land of a count/earldom; (Admin) county.

Grahambrot nt (type of) wholemeal bread.

gräko- pref graeco-.

Gral m -s, no pl (Liter) der (Heilige) ~ the (Holy) Grail.

Grals- in cpds of the (Holy) Grail; ~hüter m (lit) keeper of the (Holy) Grail; (fig) guardian; ~suche f quest for the (Holy) Grail.

Gram m -(e)s, no pl (geh) grief, sorrow. vom or von ~ gebeugt bowed down with grief or sorrow.

gram adj pred (geh) jdm ~ sein to bear sb ill-will.

grämen 1 vr sich über jdn/etw ~ to grieve over sb/sth; sich zu Tode ~ to die of grief or sorrow. 2 vt to grieve.

gram|erfüllt adj (geh) grief-stricken, woebegone.

Gram-Färbung f (Med) Gram's method.

gramgebeugt adj (geh) bowed down with grief or sorrow.

grämlich adj morose, sullen; Gedanken morose.

Gramm nt -s, -e or (nach Zahlenangabe) - gram(me). 100 ~ Mehl 100 gram(me)s of flour.

Grammatik f grammar; (~buch) grammar (book).

grammatikalisch adj grammatical.

Grammatiker(in f) m -s, - grammarian.

Grammatikregel f grammatical rule.

grammatisch adj grammatical.

Gramm|atom nt gram(me) atom.

Grammel f -, -n (S Ger, Aus: Cook) siehe Griebe.

Grammo m or nt -s, -s (esp Sw inf) record player.

Grammolekül nt getrennt: Gramm-molekül gram(me) molecule.

Grammophon [gramo'foːn] nt -s, -e (dated) gramophone (dated), phonograph.

gram- (Med): ~negativ adj Gram-negative; ~positiv adj Gram-positive.

gramvoll adj grief-stricken, sorrowful.

Gran nt -(e)s, -e or (nach Zahlenangabe) - (old) (a) (Apothekergewicht) grain. (b) (auch Grän: Edelmetallgewicht) grain.

Granat m -(e)s, -e or (Aus) -en (a) (Miner) garnet. (b) (N Ger: Garnele) shrimp.

Granat-: ~apfel m pomegranate; ~(apfel)baum m pomegranate tree.

Granate f -, -n (Mil) (Geschoß) shell; (Hand~) grenade; (Ftbl sl: Schuß aufs Tor) cannonball (inf). voll wie eine ~ (sl) absolutely plastered (sl), smashed out of one's mind (sl).

Granat-: ~feuer nt shelling, shellfire; unter heftigem ~feuer liegen to be under heavy shellfire or shelling; ~splitter m shell/grenade splinter; ~trichter m shell crater; ~werfer m mortar.

Grand [grãː] m -s, -s (Cards) grand. ~ ouvert open grand; ~ Hand grand solo.

Grande m -n, -n grandee.

Grandeur [grã'døːr] f -, no pl (geh) grandeur.

Grandezza f -, no pl grandeur.

Grand Hotel, Grandhotel ['grãːhotɛl] nt luxury hotel.

grandios adj magnificent, superb; (hum) fantastic (inf), terrific (inf).

Grandiosität f magnificence.

Grandl nt -s, -n (S Ger, Aus) tub.

Grand Prix [grã'priː] m - -, - - Grand Prix.

Grandseigneur [grãsɛn'jøːr] m -s, -s or -e (geh) nobleman.

Grand-Tourisme-Wagen [grãtu'rism-], **GT-Wagen** [geːˈteː-] m (Aut) GT(-model).

Granit m -s, -e granite. auf ~ beißen (bei ...) to bang one's head against a brick wall (with ...); Geld von ihm leihen? damit wirst du bei ihm auf ~ beißen! borrow money from him? that'll be like trying to get blood out of a stone.

graniten adj attr granite, granitic (spec); (fig) rigid.

Granne f -, -n (a) (Ährenborste) awn, beard. (b) (bei Tieren) long coarse hair.

Grant m -s, no pl (inf: S Ger, Aus) einen ~ haben to be mad (inf) or cross (wegen about, auf jdn at sb).

grantig adj (S Ger, inf) grumpy.

Granulat nt granules pl.

granulieren* vti to granulate.

Grapefruit ['greːpfruːt] f -, -s grapefruit.

Graph[1] m -en, -en (Sci) graph.

Graph[2] nt -s, -e (Ling) graph.

Graphem nt -s, -e (Ling) grapheme.

Graphie f (Ling) written form.

Graphik f (a) no pl (Art) graphic arts pl; (Technik) graphics sing; (Entwurf) design. (b) (Art: Darstellung) graphic; (Druck) print; (Schaubild) illustration; (technisches Schaubild) diagram.

Graphiker(in f) m -s, - graphic artist; (Illustrator) illustrator; (Gestalter) (graphic) designer.

graphisch adj graphic; (schematisch) diagrammatic, schematic. ~e Farben printer's inks; ~es Gewerbe graphic trades pl.

Graphit m -s, -e graphite.

Graphit-: g~grau adj dark grey; ~stift m lead pencil.

Grapho-: ~loge m, ~login f graphologist; ~logie f graphology.

grapschen, grapsen (inf) 1 vt (sich dat) etw ~ to grab (inf); (S Ger, Aus hum: stehlen) to pinch (inf) or swipe (inf) sth. 2 vi unter etw (acc) nach etw ~ to make a grab under/at sth.

Gras nt -es, ¨er grass. ins ~ beißen (inf) to bite the dust (inf); das ~ wachsen hören to be highly perceptive, to have a sixth sense; (zuviel hineindeuten) to read too much into things; über etw (acc) ~ wachsen lassen (fig) to let the dust settle on sth; darüber ist ~ gewachsen (fig) that's dead and buried; da wächst kein ~ mehr! (fig inf) he/she really goes to town! (inf); wo er zuschlägt, wächst kein ~ mehr (inf) he really packs a punch; wo er hinlangt, da wächst kein ~ mehr once he gets his hands on something you'll never recognize it any more.

Gras- in cpds grass; ~affe m (dial pej) young pup(py) (dated), (young) whippersnapper (dated); g~bedeckt, g~bewachsen adj grassy, grass-covered; ~büschel nt tuft of grass.

Gräschen ['grɛːsçən] nt dim of Gras.

grasen vi to graze.

Gras-: ~fläche f grassland; (Rasen) piece or patch of grass; ~fleck m (a) grassy spot; (b) (auf Kleidern etc) grass stain; ~fresser m herbivore; ~frosch m grass frog; g~grün adj grass-green; ~halm m blade of grass; ~hüpfer m -s, - (inf) grasshopper.

grasig adj grassy.
Gras-: ~land nt, no pl grassland; ~mähmaschine f mower; ~mücke f (Orn) warbler; ~narbe f turf; ~nelke f (Bot) thrift; ~ pflanze f grass or graminaceous (form) plant.
Grass nt -, no pl (sl) grass (sl).
Gras-: ~samen m grass seed; ~schnitt m mowing.
grassieren* vi to be rife; (Krankheit auch) to be rampant, to rage.
gräßlich adj (a) hideous, horrible; Verbrechen auch heinous, abominable. (b) (intensiv, unangenehm) terrible, dreadful, awful; Mensch horrible, awful. ~ müde terribly or dreadfully or awfully tired.
Gräßlichkeit f (a) siehe adj (a) hideousness, horribleness; heinousness. (b) (gräßliche Tat etc) atrocity.
Gras-: ~stengel m siehe ~halm; ~steppe f savanna(h); ~streifen m strip of grass, grassy strip; ~teppich m (geh) sward no indef art, no pl (liter); ~wuchs m grass; g~überwachsen, g~überwuchert adj overgrown with grass.
Grat m -(e)s, -e (Berg~) ridge; (Tech) burr; (Archit) hip (of roof); (fig) (dividing) line, border.
Gräte f -, -n (fish-)bone. sich (dat) die ~n brechen (sl) to get (badly) smashed up (inf); ich brech' dir alle ~n einzeln! (sl) I'll break every bone in your body; nur noch in den ~n hängen (sl) to be dead on one's feet (inf).
Gratifikation f bonus.
gratinieren* vt (Cook) to brown (the top of). gratinierte Zwiebelsuppe onion soup au gratin.
gratis adv free; (Comm) free (of charge). ~ und franko (dated) free of charge.
Gratis- in cpds free; ~aktie f bonus share; ~anzeiger m (Sw) advertiser (contains only advertisements and is free of charge); ~mut m (iro) sham courage; ~probe f free sample.
Grätsche f -, -n (Sport) straddle.
grätschen 1 vi aux sein to do a straddle (vault). 2 vt Beine to straddle, to put apart.
Grätsch-: ~sitz m straddle position; ~sprung m straddle vault; ~stellung f straddle (position); in ~stellung gehen to take up a straddle position.
Gratulant(in f) m well-wisher. er war der erste ~ he was the first to offer his congratulations.
Gratulation f congratulations pl. zur ~ bei jdm erscheinen to call on sb to congratulate him/her.
Gratulations-: ~besuch m congratulatory visit; ~cour [-kuːɐ] f congratulatory reception; ~karte f congratulations card; ~schreiben nt letter of congratulation.
gratulieren* vi jdm (zu einer Sache) ~ to congratulate sb (on sth); jdm zum Geburtstag ~ to wish sb many happy returns (of the day); (ich) gratuliere! congratulations!; Sie können sich (dat) ~, daß alles gutgegangen ist you can count yourself lucky that everything went off all right.
Gratwanderung f (lit) ridge walk; (fig) tightrope walk.
grau adj grey, gray (esp US); Gesicht(sfarbe) auch ashen; (trostlos) gloomy, dark, bleak. ~e Haare bekommen, ~ werden (inf) to go grey; der Himmel or es sieht ~ in ~ aus the sky or it is looking very grey; er malte die Lage ~ in ~ (fig) he painted a gloomy or dark or bleak picture of the situation; ~e Eminenz éminence grise; der ~e Markt (Comm) the grey market; die (kleinen) ~en Zellen (hum) the little grey cells; die ~e Substanz (Anat) the grey matter; der ~e Alltag dull or drab reality, the daily round or grind; in ~er Vorzeit (fig) in the dim and distant or the misty past; das liegt in ~er Ferne (fig) it's in the dim and distant future; ~ ist alle Theorie (prov) theory is no use without practice; das ist bloß ~e Theorie that's all very well in theory.
Grau nt -s, -(s) grey; (fig) dullness, drabness.
Grau-: g~äugig adj grey-eyed; ~bär m grizzly bear; ~bart m (inf: Mensch) greybeard (inf); g~bärtig adj with a grey beard, grey-bearded; g~blau adj grey-blue; g~braun adj greyish brown; ~brot nt siehe Mischbrot.
Graubünden nt -s (Geog) the Grisons.
Graubündner(in f) m -s, - inhabitant of the Grisons.
grauen[1] vi (geh: Tag) to dawn. es begann zu ~ dawn began to break.
grauen[2] vi impers mir graut vor or es graut mir vor etw (dat)I dread sth; mir graut vor ihm I'm terrified of him.
Grauen nt -s, no pl (a) horror (vor d). mich überlief ein ~ I shuddered with horror. (b) (grauenhaftes Ereignis) horror.
grauen-: ~erregend, ~haft, ~voll adj terrible, atrocious; Schmerz auch gruesome.
Grau-: ~fuchs m grey fox; ~gans f grey(lag) goose; g~gestreift adj grey striped; g~grün adj grey-green; ~guß m (Tech) grey iron; g~haarig adj grey-haired; ~hörnchen nt (Zool) grey squirrel; ~kopf m (fig) grey-haired man/woman; g~köpfig adj grey-haired.
graulen (inf) 1 vi impers davor grault mir I dread it; mir grault vor ihm I'm scared or frightened of him. 2 vr sich vor jdm/etw ~ to be scared or frightened of sb/sth. 3 vt to drive out (aus of).
graulich, gräulich adj greyish.
graumeliert adj attr flecked with grey; Haar auch greying.
Graupe f -, -n grain of pearl barley. ~n pearl barley sing.
Graupel f -, -n (small) hailstone. ~n soft hail sing, graupel sing (spec).
graup(e)lig adj Schauer of soft hail. ~er Schnee snow mixed with fine hail; ~er Hagel soft hail; ~e Hagelschauer showers of soft hail.
graupeln vi impers es graupelt a soft hail is falling.
Graupel-: ~regen m, ~schauer m sleet; ~wetter nt soft hail.
Graupensuppe f barley broth or soup.
grauplig adj siehe graup(e)lig.
graus adj (old) afeared (old, liter); ganz ~ sore afraid (old,

liter), ein ~es Schicksal (obs) a terrible fate.
Graus m -es, no pl (old) horror. es war ein ~ zu sehen, wie ... it was terrible to see how ...; es ist ein ~ mit ihm he's impossible or the limit, will he never learn!; es ist ein ~ (mit ihm), wie dumm er ist it's exasperating how stupid he is; o ~! (old, hum) oh horror! (old, hum), (alack and) alas! (old, iro).
grausam adj (a) (gefühllos, roh) cruel (gegen, zu to). ~ ums Leben kommen to die a cruel death; sich ~ für etw rächen to take (a) cruel revenge for sth. (b) (inf) terrible, awful, dreadful.
Grausamkeit f (a) no pl cruelty. (b) (grausame Tat) (act of) cruelty; (stärker) atrocity.
Grau-: ~schimmel m (a) (Pferd) grey (horse); (b) (Pilz) grey mould; ~schleier m (von Wäsche) grey(ness); (fig) veil; g~schwarz adj greyish black.
grausen vi impers siehe grauen[2].
Grausen nt -s, no pl (a) siehe Grauen (a). (b) (inf) da kann man das große or kalte ~ kriegen it's enough to give you the creeps (inf) or willies (sl).
grausig adj siehe grauenhaft.
grauslich adj (dial) siehe gräßlich.
Grau-: ~specht m grey-headed woodpecker; ~tier nt (hum inf) (jack-)ass, donkey, mule; ~ton m grey colour; ~wal m grey whale; g~weiß adj greyish white; ~zone f (fig) grey area.
Graveur(in f) [graˈvøːɐ, -øːrɪn] m engraver.
Gravier- [graˈviːɐ-]: ~anstalt f engraving establishment; ~arbeit f engraving.
gravieren* [graˈviːrən] vt to engrave.
gravierend [graˈviːrənt] adj serious, grave.
Gravier- [graˈviːɐ-]: ~maschine f engraving machine; ~nadel f graver, burin.
Gravierung [graˈviːrʊŋ] f engraving.
Gravimetrie [gravimeˈtriː] f gravimetry.
gravimetrisch [gravi-] adj gravimetric.
Gravis [ˈɡraːvɪs] m -, - (Gram) grave accent.
Gravitation [gravitaˈtsioːn] f gravitation, gravitational pull.
Gravitations-: ~feld nt gravitational field; ~gesetz nt law of gravitation/gravity; ~kraft f gravitational force.
gravitätisch [graviˈtɛːtɪʃ] adj grave, solemn.
gravitieren* [graviˈtiːrən] vi (Phys, fig) to gravitate (zu towards).
Gravur [graˈvuːɐ], **Gravüre** [graˈvyːrə] f engraving.
Grazie [-iə] f (a) (Myth) Grace; (hum) beauty, belle. die ~n haben nicht an seiner Wiege gestanden (iro) God overlooked him when he gave out good looks (hum). (b) no pl (Liebreiz) grace(fulness).
grazil adj (delicately) slender, gracile (liter); (rare: geschmeidig) nimble. ~ gebaut sein to have a delicate figure.
Grazilität f siehe adj (delicate) slenderness; nimbleness.
graziös adj graceful; (lieblich) charming.
gräzisieren* vt to Graecize.
Gräzismus m (Ling) Graecism.
Gräzist(in f) m Greek scholar, Hellenist.
Gräzistik f Greek studies pl.
Greenhorn [ˈɡriːnhɔːn] nt -s, -s (inf) greenhorn (inf).
Greenwich-Zeit [ˈɡrɪnɪdʒ-, -ɪtʃ-], **Greenwicher Zeit** [ˈɡrɪnɪdʒɐ-] f (die) ~ GMT, Greenwich Mean Time.
Gregor m -s Gregory.
Gregorianik f Gregorian music.
gregorianisch adj Gregorian. G~er Gesang Gregorian chant, plainsong.
Greif m -(e)s, or -en, -e(n) (Myth) (Vogel) ~ griffin, griffon, gryphon.
Greif-: ~arm m claw arm; ~bagger m grab dredger; g~bar adj (konkret) tangible, concrete; (erreichbar) available; Ware available, in stock pred; g~bare Gestalt or g~bare Formen annehmen to take on (a) concrete or tangible form; g~bar nahe, in g~barer Nähe within reach; ~bewegung f grasping movement.
greifen pret griff, ptp gegriffen 1 vt (a) (nehmen, packen) to take hold of, to grasp; (grapschen) to seize, to grab; Saite to stop, to hold down; Akkord to strike. eine Oktave ~ to stretch or reach an octave; diese Zahl ist zu hoch/zu niedrig gegriffen (fig) this figure is too high/low; diese Argumentation ist zu kurz gegriffen this argument is oversimplified; zum G~ nahe sein (Sieg) to be within reach; (Folgerung) to be obvious (to anyone); die Gipfel waren zum G~ nahe you could almost touch the peaks; aus dem Leben gegriffen taken from life.
(b) (fangen) to catch. G~ spielen to play catch or tag; den werde ich mir mal ~ (inf) I'm going to tell him a thing or two (inf) or a few home truths.
2 vi (a) hinter sich (acc) ~ to reach behind one; um sich ~ (fig) to spread, to gain ground; unter etw (acc) ~ to reach under sth; in etw (acc) ~ to put one's hand into sth, to reach into sth; nach einer Sache ~ to reach for sth; (um zu halten) to clutch or (hastig) grab at sth; an etw (acc) ~ (fassen) to take hold of sth, to grasp sth; (berühren) to touch sth; zu etw ~ (zu Pistole) to reach for sth; (fig: zu Methoden, Mitteln) to turn or resort to sth; zur Flasche ~ to take or turn to the bottle; an den Hut ~ to tip or touch one's hat; sich (dat) an den Kopf or an die Stirn ~ (fig) to shake one's head in disbelief; er greift gern nach einem guten Buch he likes to settle down with a good book; tief in die Tasche ~ (fig) to dig deep in one's pocket(s); in die Saiten/Tasten ~ to sweep one's hand over the strings/keys; nach den Sternen ~ to reach for the stars; nach dem rettenden Strohhalm ~ to clutch at a straw; zu den Waffen ~ to take up arms; zum Äußersten ~ to resort to extremes; nach der Macht ~ to try to seize power; jdm an die Ehre ~ (geh) to tarnish sb's good name; die Geschichte greift ans Herz the story really tears or tugs at one's heartstrings.

(b) (*nicht rutschen, einrasten*) to grip; (*fig: wirksam werden*) to be effective.

Greifer *m* -s, - (a) (*Tech*) grab. (b) (*sl: Polizist*) cop (*sl*).

Greif-: ~fuß *m* prehensile foot; ~reflex *m* gripping reflex *or* response; ~vogel *m* bird of prey, raptor (*spec*); ~werkzeug *nt* prehensile organ; ~zirkel *m* (*outside*) callipers *pl*.

greinen *vi* (*pej*) to whine, to whimper.

Greis *m* -es, -e old man. **ein neunzigjähriger** ~ an old man of ninety, a ninety-year-old man.

greis *adj* aged; (*ehrwürdig*) venerable; (*altersgrau*) grey, hoary (*liter, hum*). **sein** ~**es Haupt schütteln** (*usu iro*) to shake one's wise old head.

Greisen-: ~**alter** *nt* extreme old age; **g**~**haft** *adj* very old, aged *attr*; (*von jüngerem Menschen*) like an old man/woman; ~**haftigkeit** *f* extreme old age; **seine frühzeitige** ~**haftigkeit** his being old before his time; ~**haupt** *nt* (*geh*) hoary head; (*iro*) wise old head.

Greisin *f* old lady. **eine neunzigjährige** ~ an old lady of ninety, a ninety-year-old lady.

Greißler, Greisler *m* -s, - (*Aus dated*) grocer.

grell *adj* Stimme, Schrei, Ton shrill, piercing; *Licht, Sonne* glaring, dazzling; *Farbe* garish, gaudy, loud; *Kleidung, Mode* loud, flashy; *Gegensatz* sharp; (*stärker*) glaring. ~ **gegen etw** (*acc*) **abstechen** to contrast very sharply with sth.

grell-: ~**beleuchtet, ~erleuchtet** *adj attr* dazzlingly bright; ~**bunt** *adj* gaudily coloured.

Grelle - (*rare*), *no pl*, **Grellheit** *f* siehe *adj* shrillness; glare, dazzling brightness; garishness, gaudiness; loudness, flashiness.

grellrot *adj* garish *or* gaudy red. ~ **geschminkt** painted a garish *or* gaudy red.

Gremium *nt* body; (*Ausschuß*) committee.

Grenadier *m* -s, -e (*Mil*) (a) (*Hist*) grenadier. (b) (*Infanterist*) infantryman.

Grenz- in *cpds* border, frontier; ~**abfertigung** *f* border *or* frontier clearance; ~**bach** *m* stream forming a/the boundary; (*bei Landesgrenze*) stream forming a/the border *or* frontier; ~**baum** *m* (*Schlagbaum*) frontier barrier; ~**begradigung** *f* straightening of the border/a border/borders; ~**bereich** *m* frontier *or* border zone *or* area; (*fig*) limits *pl*; **im** ~**bereich liegen** (*fig*) to lie at the limits; ~**bevölkerung** *f* inhabitants *pl* of the/a border zone; (*esp in unwegsamen Gebieten*) frontiersmen *pl*; ~**bewohner** *m* inhabitant of the/a border zone; (*esp in unwegsamen Gebieten*) frontiersman/-woman; ~**durchbruch** *m* breaking through the/a border *or* frontier; **gestern unternahm ein LKW-Fahrer einen gewaltsamen** ~**durchbruch** yesterday a lorry-driver attempted to crash his way through the border *or* frontier.

Grenze *f* -, -n border; (*Landes*~ *auch*) frontier; (*Stadt*~, *zwischen Grundstücken*) boundary; (*fig: zwischen Begriffen*) dividing line, boundary; (*fig: äußerstes Maß, Schranke*) limits *pl*, bounds *pl*. **die** ~ **zwischen Spanien und Frankreich** the Spanish-French border *or* frontier; **die** ~ **zu Österreich** the border with Austria, the Austrian border; **über die** ~ **gehen/fahren** to cross the border; (**bis**) **zur äußersten** ~ **gehen** (*fig*) to go as far as one can; **jdm** ~**n setzen** to lay down limits for sb; **einer Sache** (*dat*) ~**n setzen** *or* **stecken** to set a limit *or* limits to sth; **keine** ~**n kennen** (*fig*) to know no bounds; **seine** ~**n kennen** to know one's limitations; **seiner Großzügigkeit sind keine** ~**n gesetzt** there is no limit to his generosity; **seine Geduld war ohne** ~**n** his patience knew no bounds; **hart an der** ~ **des Erlaubten** bordering *or* verging on the limits of what is possible; **innerhalb seiner** ~**n bleiben** (*fig*) to stay within one's limits; (*finanziell*) to live within one's means; **jdn in seine** ~**n verweisen** (*fig*) to put sb in his place; **die** ~**n einhalten** to stay within the limits; **sich in** ~**n halten** (*fig*) to be limited; **die** ~**n des Möglichen** the bounds of possibility; **die oberste/unterste** ~ (*fig*) the upper/lower limit; **die** ~**n seines Amtes überschreiten** to exceed one's office; **über die** ~**n** (+ *gen*) ... **hinaus** (*fig*) beyond the bounds of ...; **an** ~**n stoßen** (*fig*) to come up against limiting factors; **alles hat seine** ~**n** there is a limit *or* there are limits to everything.

grenzen *vi* **an etw** (*acc*) ~ (*lit*) to border (on) sth; (*fig*) to border *or* verge on sth.

Grenzen-: **g**~**los** 1 *adj* (*lit, fig*) boundless; **sich ins** ~**lose verlieren** to disappear into the distance; (*fig*) to go too far; 2 *adv* boundlessly; (*fig*) immensely; ~**losigkeit** *f* boundlessness; (*fig*) immensity.

Grenzer *m* -s, - (*inf*) (*Zöllner*) customs man; (*Grenzsoldat*) border *or* frontier guard; *siehe auch* **Grenzbewohner**.

Grenz- in *cpds* border, frontier; ~**fall** *m* borderline case; ~**finanzer** *m* (*Aus*) customs officer; ~**fluß** *m* river forming a/the border *or* frontier; ~**gänger** *m* -s, - (*Arbeiter*) international commuter (*across a local border*); (*heimlicher* ~) illegal border *or* frontier crosser; (*Schmuggler*) smuggler; ~**gebiet** *nt* border *or* frontier area *or* zone; (*fig*) border(ing) area; ~**jäger** *m* (*old*) border *or* frontier guard; ~**konflikt** *m* border *or* frontier dispute; ~**land** *nt* border *or* frontier area *or* zone.

Grenzler(in *f*) *m* -s, - (*inf*) *siehe* **Grenzbewohner**.

Grenz-: ~**linie** *f* border; (*Sport*) line; ~**mark** *f* (*Hist*) border *or* frontier area *or* zone; **g**~**nah** *adj* close to the border *or* frontier; ~**nutzen** *m* (*Econ*) marginal utility; ~**pfahl** *m* boundary post; ~**posten** *m* border guard; ~**schutz** *m* (a) *no pl* protection of the border(s) *or* frontier(s); (b) (*Truppen*) border *or* frontier guard(s); ~**sicherungsanlagen** *pl* (*esp DDR*) border *or* frontier protection *sing*; ~**situation** *f* borderline situation; ~**soldat** *m* border *or* frontier guard; ~**sperre** *f* border *or* frontier barrier; (*fig: des Grenzverkehrs*) ban on border traffic; ~**stadt** *f* border town; ~**stein** *m* boundary stone; ~**streitigkeit** *f* boundary dispute; (*Pol*) border *or* frontier dispute; ~**übergang** *m* (a) border

or frontier crossing(-point); (b) *siehe* ~**übertritt**; **g**~**überschreitend** *adj attr* (*Comm, Jur*) across a/the border *or* frontier/(the) borders *or* frontiers; ~**übertritt** *m* crossing of the border; ~**verkehr** *m* border *or* frontier traffic; **kleiner** ~**verkehr** regular border traffic; ~**verlauf** *m* boundary line (*between countries*); ~**verletzer** *m* -s, - (*esp DDR*) border *or* frontier violator; ~**verletzung** *f* violation of the/a border *or* frontier; ~**wache** *f* siehe ~**posten**; ~**wacht** *f* (*Sw*) border *or* frontier guard; ~**wall** *m* border rampart; ~**wert** *m* (*Math*) limit; ~**zeichen** *nt* boundary marker; ~**ziehung** *f* drawing up of the/a border *or* frontier; ~**zwischenfall** *m* border incident *or* clash.

Gretchenfrage *f* (*fig*) crunch question (*inf*), sixty-four-thousand-dollar-question (*inf*).

Greuel *m* -s, - *no pl* (*Grauen, Abscheu*) horror. ~ **vor etw haben** to have a horror of sth.
(b) (~*tat*) atrocity.
(c) (*Gegenstand des Abscheus*) abomination. **sie/er/es ist mir ein** ~ I loathe *or* detest her/him/it; **die Prüfung ist mir ein** ~ I'm really dreading the exam; **es ist mir ein** ~, **das zu tun** I loathe *or* detest *or* cannot bear doing that.

Greuel-: ~**geschichte** *f* siehe ~**märchen**; ~**hetze** *f* siehe ~**propaganda**; ~**märchen** *nt* horror story; ~**meldung**, ~**nachricht** *f* report of an atrocity/atrocities; ~**propaganda** *f* atrocity propaganda, horror stories *pl*; ~**tat** *f* atrocity.

greulich *adj* siehe **gräßlich**.

Greyerzer ['graɪtsɐ] *m* -s, - ~ (*Käse*) Gruyère.

Griebe *f* -, -n = crackling *no indef art, no pl*, greaves *pl*.

Grieben-: ~**fett** *nt* bacon dripping; ~**schmalz** *nt* dripping with greaves *or* crackling.

Griebs(ch) *m* -es, -e (*dial*) (a) (*Apfel*~, *Birnen*~) core. (b) (*Gurgel*) throat, gullet.

Grieche *m* -n, -n Greek.

Griechenland *nt* -s Greece.

Griechentum *nt das* ~ (a) (*Volkstum*) Greekness, Hellenism. (b) (*Zivilisation*) Hellenism, (the) Greek civilization; (*Kultur*) Greek culture, things *pl* Greek. (c) (*Gesamtheit der Griechen*) the Greeks *pl*.

Griechin *f* Greek (woman/girl).

griechisch *adj* Greek; *Kleidung, Architektur, Vase, Stil, Profil auch* Grecian. **die** ~**e Tragödie** Greek tragedy; **das G**~**e** Greek; ~**es Kreuz** Greek cross; ~-**orthodox** Greek Orthodox; ~-**römisch** Graeco-Roman.

grienen *vi* (*N Ger inf*) to smirk (*inf*).

Griesgram *m* -(e)s, -e grouch (*inf*), misery.

griesgrämig *adj* grumpy, grouchy (*inf*).

Grieß *m* -es, -e (a) (*Cook*) semolina; (*Reis*~) ground rice. (b) (*Kies*) gravel (*auch Med*); (*Sand*) grit.

Grieß-: ~**brei** *m* semolina; ~**kloß** *m*, ~**klößchen** *nt* semolina dumpling; ~**pudding** *m* semolina pudding; ~**schmarren** *m* (*Aus*) (baked) semolina pudding.

Griff *m* -(e)s, -e (a) (*das Greifen*) **der** ~ **an etw** (*acc*) taking hold of sth, grasping sth; (*Berührung*) touching sth; **der** ~ **nach etw** reaching for sth; **einen** ~ **in die Kasse tun** to put one's hand in the till; **einen tiefen** ~ **in den Geldbeutel tun** (*fig*) to dig deep in one's pocket; **ihm blieb als einziger Ausweg der** ~ **zum Revolver** the only way out was to reach for his gun; **ihr blieb nichts anderes als der** ~ **nach der Flasche** she had no alternative but to turn *or* take to the bottle; **der** ~ **nach der Droge/der Flasche** turning *or* taking to drugs/the bottle; **der** ~ **nach der Macht/Vorherrschaft** the bid for power/dominance; **das ist ein** ~ **nach den Sternen** that's just reaching for the stars.
(b) (*Handgriff*) grip, grasp; (*beim Ringen, Judo, Bergsteigen*) hold; (*beim Turnen*) grip; (*Mus: Fingerstellung*) fingering; (*inf: Akkord*) chord; (*vom Tuch: Anfühlen*) feel, texture. **mit festem** ~ firmly; **einen** ~ **ansetzen** (*Ringen*) to put on *or* apply a hold; **jdn/etw im** ~ **haben** (*fig*) to have sb/sth under control, to have the upper hand of sb/sth; (*geistig*) to have a good grasp of sth; **ein falscher** ~ (*fig*) a false move; **jdn/etw in den** ~ **bekommen** (*fig*) to get the upper hand of sb/sth, to gain control of sb/sth; (*geistig*) to get a grasp of sth; (**mit jdm/etw) einen guten** *or* **glücklichen** ~ **tun** to make a wise choice (with sb/sth), to get on to a good thing (with sb/sth) (*inf*); **etw mit einem** ~ **tun** (*fig*) to do sth in the twinkling of an eye *or* in a flash.
(c) (*Stiel, Knauf*) handle; (*Pistolen*~) butt; (*Schwert*~) hilt; (*an Saiteninstrumenten*) neck.
(d) *usu pl* (*Hunt: Kralle*) talon.
(e) ~**e** *pl* (*Mil*) rifle positions *pl*; ~**e üben** *or* **kloppen** (*inf*) to do rifle drill.

griff *pret of* **greifen**.

Griff-: **g**~**bereit** *adj* ready to hand, handy; **etw g**~**bereit halten** to keep sth handy *or* ready to hand; ~**brett** *nt* (*Mus*) fingerboard.

Griffel *m* -s, - slate pencil; (*Bot*) style.

Griffelkasten *m* pencil case or box.

griffig *adj* Boden, Fahrbahn etc that has a good grip; Rad, Maschine auch that grips well; Gewebe firm; (*fig*) Ausdruck useful, handy; (*Aus*) Mehl coarse-grained. **etwas Glattes** ~ **machen** to make a slippery grip, to give a slippery thing some grip.

Griffloch *nt* finger hole.

Grill *m* -s, -s grill; (*Aut: Kühler*~) grille.

Grillade [grɪ'jaːdə] *f* (*Cook*) grill.

Grille *f* -, -n (a) (*Zool*) cricket. (b) (*dated inf: Laune*) silly notion *or* idea. ~**n im Kopf haben** to be full of big ideas; ~**n fangen** to be moody.

grillen 1 *vt* to grill. 2 *vr* **sich (in der Sonne)** ~ (**lassen**) (*inf*) to soak up the sun, to toast in the sun (*inf*).

grillenhaft *adj* (*dated*) (*trübsinnig*) moody; (*sonderbar*) strange, extraordinary.

Grillenhaftigkeit f (dated) siehe adj moodiness; strangeness.
Grill- (Cook): ~**gerät** nt grill; ~**gericht** nt grill; ~**restaurant** nt, ~**room** [-ruːm] m -s, -s, ~**stube** f grillroom, grill and griddle.
Grimasse f -, -n grimace. ~**n schneiden** or **ziehen** or **machen** to grimace, to make or pull faces; **sein Gesicht zu einer** ~ **verziehen** to twist one's face into a grimace.
Grimassenschneider(in f) m face-puller.
grimassieren* vi to grimace.
Grimm m -(e)s, no pl (old) fury, wrath (old, liter), ire (old, liter) (auf + acc against).
grimm adj (old) siehe **grimmig**.
Grimmdarm m colon.
Grimmen nt -s, no pl (S Ger) griping pains pl.
grimmig adj (a) (zornig) furious, wrathful (liter). ~ **lächeln** to smile grimly; ~**er Humor** grim or morbid humour. (b) (sehr groß, heftig) Kälte etc severe, harsh.
Grind m -(e)s, -e scab; (inf: Sw, S Ger: Kopf) bonce (inf).
grindig adj scabby, covered in scabs.
Grindwal m pilot whale.
grinsen vi to grin; (vor Schadenfreude, Dreistigkeit, höhnisch auch) to smirk.
Grinsen nt -s, no pl siehe vi grin; smirk.
grippal adj (Med) influenzal. ~**er Infekt** influenza infection.
Grippe f -, -n 'flu, influenza; (Erkältung) cold.
Grippe- in cpds 'flu, influenza; ~**welle** f wave of 'flu or influenza.
grippös adj attr influenzal.
Grips m -es, -e (inf) nous (Brit inf), sense. **nun strengt mal euren** ~ **an** use your nous (inf); ~ **zu etw haben** to have the nous to do sth (inf).
Grislybär, Grizzlybär ['grısli-] m grizzly (bear).
Griß nt -sses, no pl (Aus inf) siehe **G(e)riß**.
grob adj, comp ⁻**er**, superl ⁻**ste(r, s)** or adv am ⁻**sten** (a) (nicht fein) coarse; Arbeit dirty attr.
(b) (ungefähr) rough. ~ **geschätzt/gemessen** at a rough estimate; **in** ~**en Umrissen** roughly.
(c) (schlimm, groß) gross (auch Jur). **den** ⁻**sten Schmutz habe ich schon weggeputzt** I have already cleaned off the worst of the dirt; **ein** ~**er Fehler** a bad mistake, a gross error; **wir sind aus dem G**⁻**sten heraus** we're out of the woods (now), we can see the light at the end of the tunnel (now); ~ **fahrlässig handeln** to commit an act of culpable negligence.
(d) (brutal, derb) rough; (fig: derb) coarse; Antwort rude; (unhöflich) ill-mannered. ~ **gegen jdn werden** to become offensive (towards sb); **jdm** ~ **kommen** (inf) to get coarse with sb; **auf einen** ~**en Klotz gehört ein** ~**er Keil** (Prov) one must answer rudeness with rudeness; siehe **Geschütz**.
Grob- in cpds coarse; **g**~**fas(e)rig** adj coarse-fibred; **g**~**gemahlen** adj attr coarse-ground; ~**heit** f (a) no pl coarseness; (b) no pl (Brutalität) roughness; (fig: coarseness; (von Antwort) rudeness; (fig: Unhöflichkeit) ill-manneredness; (c) (Beschimpfung) nasty word or expression; **jdm** ~**heiten sagen** to be nasty to sb.
Grobian m -(e)s, -e boor, lout.
grob-: ~**knochig** adj big-boned; ~**körnig** adj coarse-grained.
gröblich adj (a) (form: schlimm) gross. (b) (geh: heftig, derb) gross. **jdn** ~ **beleidigen** to insult sb grossly; **jdn** ~ **beschimpfen** to call sb rude names.
Grob-: **g**~**maschig 1** adj large-meshed; (~ gestrickt) loose-knit attr; **2** adv coarsely; **g**~**schlächtig** adj coarse; Mensch big-built, heavily built; (fig auch) unrefined; ~**schlächtigkeit** f siehe adj coarseness; heavy or big build; lack of refinement; ~**schmied** m (old) (black)smith; ~**schnitt** m (Tabak) coarse cut.
Gröfaz m - (iro) der ~ the Big Chief (hum), the great General (iro).
Grog m -s, -s grog.
groggy ['grɔgi] adj pred (Boxen) groggy; (inf: erschöpft) all-in (inf).
grölen vti (pej) to bawl. ~**de Stimme/Menge** raucous voice/crowd; ~**d durch die Straßen ziehen** to roam rowdily through the streets.
Grölerei f (pej) bawling no pl.
Groll m -(e)s, no pl (Zorn) anger, wrath (liter); (Erbitterung) resentment. **einen** ~ **gegen jdn hegen** to harbour a grudge against sb.
grollen vi (geh) (a) to rumble; (Donner auch) to roll, to peal (liter). (b) (jdm) ~ (old) to be filled with wrath (against sb) (liter); (mit) **seinem Schicksal** ~ to bemoan one's fate.
Grönland nt -s Greenland.
Grönländer(in f) m -s, - Greenlander.
grönländisch adj Greenland attr.
Grönlandwal m bowhead.
Gros¹ [groː] nt -, - [groːs] major or greater part, majority, bulk; siehe **en gros**.
Gros² [grɔs] nt -ses, -se or (bei Zahlenangaben) - gross.
Groschen m -s, - (a) (Aus) groschen.
(b) (inf) 10-pfennig piece; (fig) penny, cent (US). **das kostet mich keinen** ~ it doesn't cost me a penny/cent; **seine paar** ~ **zusammenhalten** to scrape together a few pence or pennies/cents; **sich** (dat) **ein paar** ~ **verdienen** to earn (oneself) a few pence or pennies/cents, to earn (oneself) a bit of pocket money; **der** ~ **ist gefallen** (hum inf) the penny has dropped (inf); **bei ihm fällt der** ~ **pfennigweise** he's pretty slow on the uptake, it takes him a while to catch on; **nicht** (ganz or recht) **bei** ~ **sein** (inf) to have a screw loose (inf).
Groschen-: ~**blatt** nt (pej) (cheap) rag (inf), sensational (news)paper; **die** ~**blätter** the gutter press (pej); ~**grab** nt (hum) penny-eater (hum inf); (Spielautomat) one-armed

bandit; ~**heft** nt pulp magazine; (Krimi auch) penny dreadful (dated); ~**roman** m cheap or dime (US) novel; **g**~**weise** adj groschen by groschen, = penny by penny.
groß 1 adj, comp ⁻**er**, superl ⁻**te(r, s)** (a) big; Fläche, Raum, Haus, Hände auch large; Höhe, Breite great; Buchstabe big, capital; Größe, Tube, Dose, Packung etc large; (hoch, hochgewachsen) tall. **wie** ~ **bist du?** how tall are you?; **du bist** ~ **geworden** you've grown; **das ist gemein, du bist ja auch** ~**er als ich** that's not fair, you're bigger than me; **ein ganz** ~**es Haus/Buch** a great big house/book; **der** ~**e (Uhr)zeiger** the big or minute hand; **die Wiese ist 10.000 m²** ~ the field measures 10,000 square metres or is 100 metres square; **ein 2 Hektar** ~**es Grundstück** a 2 hectare piece of land; **er ist 1,80 m** ~ he is 1.80 metres (tall); **ein** ~**es Bier, ein G**~**es** (inf) = a pint (of beer); **die** ~**e Masse** (fig) the vast majority; ~**es Geld** notes pl (Brit), bills pl (US); **ich habe nur** ~**es Geld** I haven't any change on me; **im** ~**en und ganzen (gesehen)** (taken) by and large; **im G**~**en einkaufen** to buy in bulk or quantity.
(b) (zeitlich) Pause, Verzögerung, Rede big, long, lengthy. **die** ~**en Ferien** the long holidays, the long vacation (Univ).
(c) (älter) Bruder, Schwester big. **die G**~**en** (Erwachsene) the grown-ups; (ältere Kinder) the older children; **zu** ~ **für etw sein** to be too big for sth; **mit etw** ~ **geworden sein** to have grown up with sth; ~ **und klein** young and old (alike); **unsere G**~**e/unser G**~**er** our eldest or oldest (daughter/son); (von zwei) our elder daughter/son.
(d) (beträchtlich, heftig, wichtig) big; Erfolg, Interesse, Enttäuschung, Schreck, Hoffnung, Eile auch great; Summe auch large; Freude, Vergnügen, Schmerzen, Leid etc great; (bedeutend) Dichter, Werk, Erfindung, Schauspieler etc great; Lärm a lot of; Geschwindigkeit high. **die** ~**en Fragen unserer Zeit** the great or big questions of our time; ~**e Worte/Gefühle** big words/strong feelings; ~**e Worte machen** to use grand or big words; ~**en Hunger haben** to be very hungry; **eine** ⁻**e Summe** a biggish or largish or fair sum; **eine der** ⁻**eren Firmen** one of the major companies; **eine** ~**e Dummheit machen** to do something very stupid; **im** ~**ten Regen** in the midst of the downpour; **die** ~**e Nummer** (im Zirkus) the big number, the star turn; **ich habe** ~**e Lust zu etw/, etw zu tun** I would really like sth/to do sth; **ich habe keine** ~**e Lust** I don't particularly want to; ~**e Mode sein** to be all the fashion; **er ist ein** ~**es Kind** he's a big or a great big (inf) baby; **er ist kein** ~**er Esser/Trinker** (inf) he's not a big eater/drinker; **ich bin kein** ~**er Redner/Opernfreund** (inf) I'm no great speaker/opera-lover; **die** ~**e Welt** (die Fremde) the big wide world; (die oberen Zehntausend) high society; **die G**~**en** the great figures; **jds** ~**e Stunde** sb's big moment; **einen** ~**en Namen haben** to be a big name; **das** ~**e Ganze** the broader perspective, the wider view; **im Kleinen wie im G**~**en** in small matters as well as in big or larger ones, whether the scale be large or small; **er hat G**~**es geleistet** he has achieved great things.
(e) (~artig, bewundernswert) great. **das ist** or **finde ich ganz** ~ (inf) that's really great (inf).
(f) (in Eigennamen) Great; (vor Namen von Ballungsräumen) Greater. **Alfred/Friedrich der G**~**e** Alfred/Frederick the Great; **G**~**-Paris/-München** Greater Paris/Munich; **der G**~**e Ozean** the Pacific; **die G**~**en Seen** the Great Lakes.
(g) (Mus) ~**e Terz** major third.
2 adv, comp ⁻**er**, superl am ⁻**ten jdn** ~ **anblicken** to give sb a hard stare; **was ist das schon** ~? (inf) big deal! (inf), so what? (inf); **was soll man da schon** ~ **machen/sagen?** (inf) you can't really do/say anything or very much(, can you)? (inf), what are you supposed to do/say?; **keiner hat sich** ~ **gefreut** (inf) nobody was particularly delighted, nobody was exactly overjoyed; **ich kümmere mich nicht** ~ **darum** (inf) I don't take much notice; ~ **daherreden** (inf) to talk big (inf); ~ **und breit** (fig inf) at great or enormous length, at tedious length (pej); ~ **machen** (baby-talk) to do number two (baby-talk); **ein Wort** ~ **schreiben** to write a word with a capital or with a big A/B etc; ~ **in Mode sein** to be the fashion; **ganz** ~ **rauskommen** (sl) to make the big time (inf).
Groß- pref Great; (vor Namen von Ballungsräumen) Greater.
Groß-: ~**abnehmer** m (Comm) bulk purchaser or buyer; ~**admiral** m (Naut Hist) Grand Admiral, = Admiral of the Fleet; ~**agrarier** m (dated) big landowner; ~**aktionär** m major or principal shareholder; ~**alarm** m red alert; ~**alarm geben** to give a red alert; **g**~**angelegt** adj attr large-scale, on a large scale; ~**angriff** m large-scale or major attack; ~**anlaß** m (Sw) siehe ~**veranstaltung**; **g**~**artig** adj wonderful, superb, splendid; (prächtig) Bauwerk etc magnificent, splendid; **er hat** ~**artiges geleistet** he has achieved great things; **eine g**~**artige Frau** a wonderful or fine woman; **g**~**artig tun** (pej) to show off, to give oneself airs; ~**artigkeit** f (Pracht) magnificence, splendour; **die** ~**artigkeit des Festes/eines Kunstwerks** the magnificence of the festival/of a work of art; ... **und eine solchen** ~**artigkeit** such (a) wonderful ...; ~**aufnahme** f (Phot, Film) close-up; ~**bank** f major or big bank; ~**bauer** m big farmer; **g**~**bäuerlich** adj of a big farmer/big farmers; ~**baustelle** f construction site; ~**beben** nt (Geol) major earthquake; ~**behälter** m tank; (Container) container; ~**betrieb** m large concern; (Agr) big farm; ~**bezüger** m -s, - (Sw) siehe ~**abnehmer**; ~**bild** nt blow-up; ~**bildkamera** f plate camera; ~**bourgeoisie** f (Sociol, Pol pej) upper classes pl, upper bourgeoisie; ~**brand** m enormous blaze, major or big fire; ~**britannien** nt (Great) Britain; **g**~**britannisch** adj (Great) British, Britannic (rare); ~**buchstabe** m capital (letter), upper case letter (Typ); ~**bürger** m (Sociol) member of the upper classes; **g**~**bürgerlich** adj (Sociol) upper-class; ~**bürgertum** nt (Sociol) upper classes pl; **g**~**denkend** adj (geh) high-minded; **g**~**deutsch** adj (Hist) Pan-German; **das** ~**deutsche**

Reich (NS) the Reich; ~**deutschland** nt (NS) Greater Germany; ~**druckbuch** nt large-print book.

Größe f -, -n **(a)** (Format, Maßeinheit) size. **nach der ~** according to size; **er trägt** or **hat ~ 48** he takes or is size 48. **(b)** no pl (Höhe, Körper~) height; (Flächeninhalt) size, area, dimensions pl; (Dimension) size, dimensions pl; (Math, Phys) quantity; (Astron) magnitude. **nach der ~** according to height/size; **eine unbekannte ~** (lit, fig) an unknown quantity; **ein Stern erster ~** a star of the first magnitude. **(c)** no pl (Ausmaß) extent; (Bedeutsamkeit) significance. **(d)** no pl (Erhabenheit) greatness. **(e)** (bedeutender Mensch) leading light, important figure.

Groß-: ~**einkauf** m bulk purchase, bulk purchasing no indef art, no pl; ~**einsatz** m ~**einsatz der Feuerwehr/Polizei** etc large-scale operation by the fire brigade/police etc; **der ~einsatz von Truppen** the large-scale use or deployment of troops; **g~elterlich** adj attr of one's grandparents; **im g~elterlichen Haus wohnen** to live in one's grandparents' house; ~**eltern** pl grandparents pl; ~**enkel** m great-grandchild; (Junge) great-grandson; ~**enkelin** f great-granddaughter.

Größen-: ~**klasse** f (Astron) magnitude; (Comm) (size) class; ~**ordnung** f scale; (Größe) magnitude; (Math) order (of magnitude); **ich denke in anderen ~ordnungen** I think on a different scale.

großenteils adv mostly, for the most part. **er macht seine Arbeit ~ selbständig** he does his work mostly on his own, he does his work on his own for the most part.

Größen-: ~**unterschied** m (im Format) difference in size; (in der Höhe, im Wuchs) difference in height; (in der Bedeutung) difference in importance; ~**verhältnis** nt proportions pl (gen between); (Maßstab) scale; **im ~verhältnis 1:100** on the scale 1:100; **das ~verhältnis von etw/zwei Problemen richtig sehen, etw/zwei Probleme im richtigen ~verhältnis sehen** to see sth/two problems in perspective; ~**wahn(sinn)** m megalomania, delusions pl of grandeur; **g~wahnsinnig** adj megalomaniac(al); **g~wahnsinnig sein** to be a megalomaniac.

größer comp of **groß**.

größer(e)nteils adv siehe **großenteils.**

Groß-: ~**fahndung** f large-scale manhunt; ~**familie** f extended family; ~**feuer** nt major fire, enormous blaze; **g~flächig** adj extensive; Gesicht flat-featured; ~**flughafen** m major airport; ~**flugzeug** nt siehe ~**raumflugzeug;** ~**format** nt large size; (bei Büchern, Fotos auch) large format; **ein ... im ~format** a large-size .../large-format ...; **g~formatig** adj large-size; Bücher, Fotos auch large-format; ~**foto** nt giant photo(graph); ~**fresse** f (vulg) siehe ~**maul;** ~**fürst** m (Hist) grand prince; **(der) ~fürst Alexander** Grand Prince Alexander; ~**fürstentum** nt (Hist) grand principality; ~**fürstin** f (Hist) grand princess; **g~füttern** vt sep to raise, to rear; ~**garage** f large (underground) car park; ~**gemeinde** f municipality with several villages or districts; **g~gemustert** adj with a large pattern; **g~gewachsen** adj tall; ~**grundbesitz** m **(a)** large-scale land-holding; **(b)** (die ~grundbesitzer) big landowners pl; ~**grundbesitzer** m big landowner.

Großhandel m wholesale trade, wholesaling no art. **etw im ~ kaufen** to buy sth wholesale.

Großhandels- in cpds wholesale; ~**kaufmann** m wholesaler.

Groß-: ~**händler** m wholesaler; (inf: ~handlung) wholesaler's; ~**handlung** f wholesale business; **g~herzig** adj generous, magnanimous; **g~herzige Motive** the best of motives; ~**herzigkeit** f generosity, magnanimity; ~**herzog** m grand duke; **(der) ~herzog Roland** Grand Duke Roland; ~**herzogin** f grand duchess; **g~herzoglich** adj grand ducal; ~**herzogtum** nt grand duchy; **das ~herzogtum Luxemburg** the Grand Duchy of Luxembourg; ~**hirn** nt cerebrum; ~**hirnrinde** f cerebral cortex; ~**industrielle(r)** mf major or big industrialist; **die französischen ~industriellen** the major or big French industrialists; ~**inquisitor** m (Hist) Grand Inquisitor.

Grossist m siehe **Großhändler.**

Groß-: **g~jährig** adj (dated) of age, major (form); **g~jährig werden** to come of age, to reach the age of majority; ~**jährigkeit** f majority; **die ~jährigkeit erlangen** (form) to come of age, to attain one's majority (form); **g~kalib(e)rig** adj large-calibre.

Großkampf-: ~**schiff** nt capital ship; ~**tag** m (Mil) day of a/the great battle; **Montag ist bei uns im Büro meist ~tag** (hum) it's usually all systems go on Monday in the office (inf).

Groß-: ~**kapital** nt **das ~kapital** big business; ~**kapitalist** m big capitalist; **was, du willst 5 Mark? ich bin doch kein ~kapitalist!** what - you want 5 marks? I'm not made of money! (inf); **g~kariert** adj large-check(ed); ~**katze** f big cat; ~**kaufhaus** nt large (department) store; ~**kaufmann** m big merchant; ~**kind** nt (Sw) grandchild; ~**klima** nt macroclimate; ~**knecht** m (old) chief (farm)hand; ~**konzern** m big or large combine; ~**kopfe(r)te(r)** m decl as adj **(a)** (Aus, S Ger: pej) bigwig (inf), bigshot (inf); **(b)** (hum: Intellektueller) egghead (hum inf); ~**kotz** m (pej sl) swank (inf); **g~kotzig** adj (pej sl) swanky (inf); ~**kotzigkeit** f (pej sl) swank (inf); ~**kraftwerk** nt large power plant; ~**kreuz** nt Grand Cross; ~**küche** f canteen kitchen; ~**kundgebung** f mass rally; ~**lautsprecher** m giant loudspeaker; ~**loge** f grand lodge; **g~machen** vr sep (inf) to (try and) make oneself look important; **sich mit etw g~machen** to brag or boast about sth.

Großmacht f (Pol) big or great power.

Großmacht-: ~**politik** f (big-)power politics; ~**stellung** f great- or big-power status.

Groß-: ~**mama** f grandmama (dated), grandma; ~**mannssucht** f, no pl (pej) craving for status; ~**markt** m central market; ~**markthalle** f central market hall; **g~maschig** adj siehe **grobmaschig;** ~**mast** m mainmast; ~**maul** nt (pej inf) big-

mouth (inf), loudmouth (inf); **g~mäulig** adj (pej inf) big-mouthed attr (inf), loudmouthed (inf); **g~mäulig verkünden, daß ...** to brag that ...; ~**mäuligkeit** f, no pl (pej inf) big mouth (inf); ~**meister** m Grand Master; ~**mogul** m (Hist) Great Mogul; ~**mufti** m (Hist) grand mufti; ~**mut** f magnanimity; **g~mütig** adj magnanimous; ~**mütigkeit** f siehe ~**mut;** ~**mutter** f grandmother; **sie ist ~mutter geworden** she has become a grandmother; **das kannst du deiner ~mutter erzählen!** (inf) you can tell that one to the marines (inf), pull the other one (inf); **g~mütterlich** adj attr **(a)** (von der ~mutter) of one's grandmother; **im g~mütterlichen Haus wohnen** to live in one's grandmother's house; **das g~mütterliche Erbe** one's inheritance from one's grandmother; **(b)** (in der Art einer ~mutter) grandmotherly; **g~mütterlicherseits** adv on one's grandmother's side; ~**neffe** m great-nephew; ~**nichte** f great-niece; ~**offensive** f (Mil) major offensive.

Grossohandel m (old Comm) wholesalers pl; wholesaling.

Groß-: ~**oktav** nt large octavo; ~**onkel** m great-uncle; ~**papa** m grandpapa (dated), grandpa; ~**photo** nt siehe ~**foto;** ~**plastik** f large sculpture; **g~porig** adj large-pored; ~**produktion** f large-scale production; ~**produzent** m large-scale producer; ~**projekt** nt large-scale project; ~**putz** m siehe ~**reinemachen;** ~**quart** nt large quarto; ~**rat** m (Sw) member of a/the Cantonal parliament.

Großraum m **(a)** (einer Stadt) **der ~ München** the Munich area or conurbation, Greater Munich. **(b)** siehe **Großraumbüro.**

Großraum-: ~**büro** nt open-plan office; ~**flugzeug** nt large-capacity aircraft.

Groß-: **g~räumig** adj **(a)** (mit g~en Räumen) with large rooms; **g~räumig sein** to have large rooms; **(b)** (mit viel Platz, geräumig) roomy, spacious; **(c)** (über g~e Flächen) extensive; **(d)** (im g~en Umkreis) **g~räumiges Umfahren eines Gebietes** making a large detour around an area; ~**raumwagen** m (von Straßenbahn) articulated tram (Brit) or streetcar (US); (Rail) open-plan carriage (Brit) or car (US); ~**razzia** f large-scale raid; ~**reinemachen** nt thorough cleaning, ≈ spring-cleaning; ~**russe** m Great Russian; ~**schiffahrtsweg** m major waterway (for seagoing ships); ~**schnauze** f (pej sl) siehe ~**maul;** **g~schnäuzig** adj (pej sl) siehe **g~mäulig; g~schreiben** vt sep irreg **g~geschrieben werden** (fig inf) to be stressed, to be given pride of place, to be writ large; ~**schreibung** f capitalization; ~**segel** nt (Naut) mainsail; ~**sprecher** m (pej) boaster, bragger, braggart; ~**sprecherei** f (pej) **(a)** no pl (Angeberei) boasting, bragging; **(b)** (g~sprecherische Äußerung) boast; **g~sprecherisch** adj (pej) boastful, boasting attr, bragging attr; **g~spurig** adj (pej) flashy (inf), showy (inf); ~**spurigkeit** f (pej) flashiness (inf), showiness (inf).

Großstadt f city.

Großstadtbevölkerung f city population.

Großstädter m city-dweller.

großstädtisch adj big-city attr. **München wirkt ~er als Bonn** Munich has more of a big-city feel to it than Bonn; **~e Siedlungen** big or large conurbations.

Großstadt- in cpds city; ~**mensch** m city-dweller; **der ~mensch** urban man, city-dwellers pl; ~**pflanze** f (dated) city child.

Groß-: ~**tante** f great-aunt; ~**tat** f great feat; **eine medizinische ~tat** a great medical feat.

Großteil m large part. **zum ~** in the main, for the most part; **zu einem ~** for the most part.

großteils, größtenteils adv in the main, for the most part.

größte(r, s) superl of **groß.**

Größt-: ~**maß** nt (fig) siehe **Höchstmaß; g~möglich** adj attr greatest possible.

Groß-: ~**tuer** [-tu:ɐ] m -s, - (pej) boaster, bragger, show-off; ~**tuerei** [-tu:ə'rai] f (pej) **(a)** no pl boasting, bragging, showing off; **(b)** (g~tuerische Äußerung etc) boast; **g~tuerisch** [-tu:ərɪʃ] adj (pej) boastful, bragging; **g~tun** sep irreg (pej) **1** vi to boast, to brag, to show off; **2** vr sich mit etw **g~tun** to show off or boast or brag about sth; ~**unternehmen** nt siehe ~**betrieb;** ~**unternehmer** m big businessman or entrepreneur.

Großvater m grandfather.

großväterlich adj **(a)** (vom Großvater) of one's grandfather. **er hat den ~en Betrieb übernommen** he has taken over his grandfather's business; **das ~e Erbe** one's inheritance from one's grandfather. **(b)** (in der Art eines Großvaters) grandfatherly.

großväterlicherseits adv on one's grandfather's side.

Großvater-: ~**sessel,** ~**stuhl** m (inf) fireside armchair; ~**uhr** f (inf) grandfather clock.

Groß-: ~**veranstaltung** f big event; (~kundgebung) mass rally; **eine sportliche ~veranstaltung** a big sporting event; ~**verbraucher** m large consumer; ~**verdiener** m big earner; ~**versuch** m (esp Psych) large-scale experiment; ~**vieh** nt cattle and horses pl; ~**wesir** m (Hist) grand vizier; ~**wetterlage** f general weather situation; **die politische ~wetterlage** the general political climate.

Großwild nt big game.

Großwild-: ~**jagd** f big-game hunting; **eine ~jagd** a big-game hunt; **auf ~jagd gehen** to go big-game hunting; ~**jäger** m big-game hunter.

Groß-: ~**wörterbuch** nt large or comprehensive dictionary; **g~wüchsig** adj (form) siehe **g~gewachsen; g~ziehen** vt sep irreg to raise; Tier to rear; **g~zügig** adj generous, (weiträumig) spacious; Plan large-scale, ambitious; (inf: ungenau) generous, liberal; ~**zügigkeit** f siehe adj generosity; spaciousness; (large) scale, ambitiousness; generousness, liberality.

grotesk adj grotesque.

Grotesk f -, no pl (Typ) grotesque, sans serif.

Groteske f -, -n (Art) grotesque(rie); (Liter) grotesquerie.

groteskerweise adj ironically enough.

Grotte f -, -n grotto.

Grotten|olm m (Zool) olm (spec), salamander.

Groundhostess ['graunthɔstes] f ground hostess.

Groupie ['gru:pi] nt -s, -s groupie.

grub pret of **graben**.

Grubber m -s, - (Agr) grubber.

Grübchen nt dimple.

Grube f -, -n pit; (kleine) hole, hollow; (Min auch) mine; (dated: Gruft, Grab) grave. **wer andern eine ~ gräbt(, fällt selbst hinein)** (Prov) you can easily fall into your own trap; **in die ~ (ein)fahren** to go down the pit; **in die** or **zur ~ fahren** (old) to give up the ghost.

Grübelei f brooding no pl.

grübeln vi to brood (über +acc about, over).

Gruben- in cpds pit; **~arbeiter** m pitman; **~gas** nt firedamp; **~wagen** m mine car.

Grübler(in f) m -s, - brooder, brooding type.

grüblerisch adj pensive, brooding.

grüezi ['gry:ɛtsi] interj (Sw) hello, hi (inf), good morning/afternoon/evening.

Gruft f -, ⁻e tomb, vault; (in Kirchen) crypt; (offenes Grab) grave.

grummeln vi to rumble; (inf: brummeln) to mumble.

Grum(me)t nt -s, no pl (Agr) aftermath, rowen (dial, US).

grün adj (alle Bedeutungen) green; (Pol) ecologist. **~e Heringe** fresh herrings; **Aal ~** (Cook) (dish of) fresh eel (with parsley sauce); **~er Salat** lettuce; **die G~e Insel** the Emerald Isle; **ein ~er Junge** (inf) a greenhorn (inf); **~es Licht (für etw) geben/haben** (fig) to give/have got the green light (for sth); **komm an meine ~e Seite!** (inf) come and sit up close to me; **~en Tisch, vom ~en Tisch aus** from a bureaucratic ivory tower; **über die ~e Grenze fahren/kommen** (inf) to cross the border illegally (in a wood etc); **die ~e Hölle** (fig) the green hell of the jungle; **die ~en Lungen der Großstadt** (fig) the breathing spaces of the city; **~e Minna** (inf) Black Maria (Brit inf), paddy wagon (US inf); **der G~e Plan** (Pol) Agricultural Aid Plan; **sich ~ und blau** or **gelb ärgern** (inf) to be furious; **jdn ~ und blau** or **gelb schlagen** (inf) to beat sb black and blue; **wir haben ~e Weihnachten gehabt** we didn't have a white Christmas; **~e Welle** phased traffic lights; **~e Welle bei 60 km/h** traffic lights phased for 60 kmph; **~ im Gesicht werden** to go green (about the gills inf); **~e Witwe** (inf) lonely suburban housewife; **auf keinen ~en Zweig kommen** (fig inf) to get nowhere; **die beiden sind sich gar nicht ~** (inf) there's no love lost between them; **er ist dir nicht ~** (inf) you're not in his good books (inf).

Grün nt -s, - or (inf) -s green; (~flächen) green spaces pl; (Golf) green; (Cards: Pik) spades pl. **bei Mutter ~ schlafen** (dated inf) to sleep under the stars; **die Ampel steht auf ~** the light is at green; **das ist dasselbe in ~** (inf) it's (one and) the same (thing).

Grün- in cpds green; **~alge** f green alga; **~anlage** f green space or area; **g~äugig** adj green-eyed; **g~blau** adj greenish blue, greeny blue; **g~blind** adj suffering from red-green colourblindness.

Grund m -(e)s, ⁻e (a) no pl (Erdboden) ground; (old, dial: Erdreich auch) soil. **~ und Boden** land; **in ~ und Boden** sich blamieren, schämen utterly; verdammen outright; **jdn in ~ und Boden reden** not to leave sb a leg to stand on, to shoot sb's arguments to pieces; **bis auf den ~ zerstören/abtragen** to raze to the ground.
    (b) (Aus) (Bauplatz) (building) plot; (~stück) grounds pl, land no indef art, no pl.
    (c) no pl (esp Art) ground; (Her) field.
    (d) no pl (von Gefäßen, Becken etc) bottom; (Meeres~ auch) (sea)bed; (liter: Tal~) bottom of the/a valley. **~ suchen** (im Wasser) to look for a foothold, to try to find the bottom; **auf ~ stoßen** (Naut) (to run) to ground; **ein Schiff auf ~ setzen** to scuttle a ship; **das Glas/den Becher bis auf den ~ leeren** to drain the glass/tumbler.
    (e) no pl (lit, fig: Fundament) foundation(s pl); (das Innerste) depths pl. **von ~ auf** or **aus** entirely, completely; **etw von ~ auf ändern** to change sth fundamentally or from top to bottom; **von ~ auf neu gebaut/geplant** rebuilt/re-planned from scratch; **ein von ~ auf aufrechter Mensch** a thoroughly honest fellow; **den ~ zu etw legen** (lit, fig) to lay the foundations of or for sth; **einer Sache (dat) auf den ~ gehen** (fig) to get to the bottom of sth; **auf ~ von** or (+gen) on the basis of; **im ~e seines Herzens** in one's heart of hearts; **im ~e (genommen)** basically, fundamentally.
    (f) (Ursache, Veranlassung, Ausrede) reason; (Beweg~ auch) grounds pl. **aus gesundheitlichen etc ~en** for health etc reasons, on health etc grounds; **aus dem einfachen ~e, daß ...** for the simple reason that ...; **ohne ~** without reason; **auf ~ von Zeugenaussagen** on the basis or strength of the witnesses' testimonies; **auf ~ einer Verwechslung/seiner Eifersucht** owing to or because of a mistake/his jealousy; **die ~e für meinen Austritt** my reasons or grounds for leaving; **ich habe ~ zu der Annahme, daß ...** I have reason to believe or grounds for believing that ...; **~e und Gegengründe** pros and cons, arguments for and against; **einen ~ zum Feiern haben** to have good cause for (a) celebration; **es besteht kein** or **du hast keinen ~ zum Klagen** you have no cause to complain or for complaint; **die ~e für und wider** the cases for and against; **jdm ~ geben** to give sb good reason or cause (for sth); **ich habe ihm keinen ~ gegeben** I've given him no reason or cause for that/it; **jdm allen ~ geben, etw zu glauben** etc to give sb every reason to believe etc sth; **ich habe berechtigten ~ zu glauben, daß ...** I have good reason to believe or grounds for believing that ...; **aus diesem ~** for this reason; **aus guten ~en, mit gutem ~** with good reason; **aus welchem ~(e)?** for what reason?; **aus ~en** (+gen) for reasons (of).

Grund- in cpds basic; **~akkord** m (Mus) chord in root position; **~anschauung, ~ansicht** f fundamental philosophy; **g~anständig** adj thoroughly decent; **~anstrich** m first coat; (erstes Anstreichen) application of the first coat; **~bau** m (a) (Archit) foundation(s pl); **(b)** no pl (~arbeiten) laying of the foundations; **~besitz** m land, property; (das Besitzen) ownership of land or property; **~besitzer** m landowner; **~buch** nt land register; **~buchamt** nt land registry or office; **g~ehrlich** adj thoroughly honest; **~eigentum** nt siehe **~besitz**; **~eigentümer** m landowner; **~einstellung** f fundamental philosophy; **~eis** nt ground ice, anchor-ice; siehe **Arsch**.

gründen 1 vt to found; Argument etc to base (auf +acc on); Heim, Geschäft to set up. **eine Familie ~** to get married (and have a family). 2 vi to be based or founded (in +dat on). 3 vr **sich auf etw** (acc) **~** to be based or founded on sth.

Gründer(in f) m -s, - founder.

Gründerjahre pl (Hist) years of rapid industrial expansion in Germany (from 1871).

Grund-: **~erwerb** m acquisition of land; **~erwerbssteuer** f tax on land acquisition, land transfer tax.

Gründerzeit f (Hist) siehe **Gründerjahre**.

Grund-: **g~falsch** adj utterly wrong; **~farbe** f primary colour; (Grundierfarbe) ground colour; **~festen** pl (fig) foundations pl; etw bis in die or in seinen **~festen erschüttern** to shake sth to the or its very foundations; **an den ~festen von etw rütteln** to shake the (very) foundations of sth; **~fläche** f (Math) base; **~form** f basic form; (Gram) infinitive; **~gebühr** f basic or standing charge; **~gedanke** m basic idea; **g~gescheit** adj extremely bright.

Grundgesetz nt (a) (Grundprinzip) basic law. **(b)** (BRD) das **~** the Law.

Grundgesetz-: **~änderung** f alteration of the Basic Law; **g~widrig** adj contrary to the Basic Law.

Grund-: **g~gütig** adj (geh) extremely kind(-hearted); **~haltung** f basic position; **g~häßlich** adj extremely or dreadfully ugly; **~herr** m (Hist) lord of the manor; **~herrschaft** f (Hist) manorial system; **~idee** f siehe **~gedanke**.

grundieren* vt to undercoat; (Art) to ground.

Grundier-: **~farbe, ~schicht** f undercoat.

Grundierung f (a) no pl (das Grundieren) undercoating; (Art) grounding. **(b)** (Farbe, Fläche) undercoat; (Art) ground.

Grund-: **~irrtum** m fundamental error; **~kapital** nt share capital; (Anfangskapital) initial capital; **~kurs** m (Sch, Univ) basic or base course; **~lage** f basis; (Mus) root position; **als ~lage für etw dienen** to serve as a basis for sth; **auf der ~lage** +gen or **von on the basis of; 20.000 Mark sind wenigstens eine ~lage** 20,000 marks is at least a start; **die ~lagen einer Wissenschaft/eines Lehrfachs** the fundamental principles of a science/the rudiments of a subject; **etw auf eine neue ~lage stellen** Beziehungen to put sth on a different footing or basis; Organisation etc to change the basic structure(s) of sth; **jeder ~lage entbehren** to be completely unfounded or without foundation; **die beste ~lage für Alkohol** the best thing to line your stomach with before drinking alcohol; **~lagenforschung** f pure research; **g~legend** adj fundamental, basic (für to); Werk, Textbuch standard; **sich zu etw g~legend äußern** to make a statement of fundamental importance on sth; **~legung** f (lit, fig) laying of the foundations; (fig: ~riß) outline.

gründlich 1 adj thorough; Arbeit painstaking, careful; Vorbereitung auch careful. 2 adv thoroughly; (inf: sehr auch) really. **jdm ~ die Meinung sagen** to give sb a real piece of one's mind; **da haben Sie sich ~ getäuscht** you're completely mistaken there.

Gründlichkeit f, no pl siehe adj thoroughness; carefulness.

Gründling m (Zool) gudgeon.

Grund-: **~linie** f (Math, Sport) baseline; **~lohn** m basic pay or wage(s); **g~los** 1 adj (a) Tiefe etc bottomless; **(b)** (fig: unbegründet) groundless, unfounded; **g~loses Lachen** laughter for no reason (at all); 2 adv (fig) without reason, for no reason (at all); **~losigkeit** f (fig) groundlessness; **~mauer** f foundation wall; **bis auf die ~mauern niederbrennen** to be gutted; **~mittel** pl (esp DDR) siehe **Anlagevermögen**; **~moräne** f (Geol) ground moraine; **~nahrungsmittel** nt basic food(stuff).

Gründonnerstag [gry:n-] m Maundy Thursday.

Grund-: **~ordnung** f basic order; **~pfeiler** m (Archit) supporting pier; (fig) cornerstone, keystone; **~rechenart, ~rechnungsart** f basic arithmetical operation; **~ recht** nt basic or fundamental right; **~rente** f (Econ) ground rent; (Insur) basic pension; **~riß** m (von Gebäude) ground plan; (Math) base; (Abriß) outline, sketch; „~riß der chinesischen Grammatik" "Outline of Chinese Grammar".

Grundsatz m principle. **aus ~ on principle; ein Mann mit** or **von Grundsätzen** a man of principle; **an seinen Grundsätzen festhalten** or **bei seinen Grundsätzen bleiben** to stand by or keep to one's principles; **es sich** (dat) **zum ~ machen, etw zu tun** to make a principle of doing sth, to make it a matter of principle to do sth.

Grundsatz-: **~debatte, ~diskussion** f debate on (general) principles; **~entscheidung** f decision of general principle; **~erklärung** f declaration of principle.

grundsätzlich 1 adj fundamental; Frage of principle. 2 adv (allgemein, im Prinzip) in principle; (aus Prinzip) on principle; (immer) always; (völlig) absolutely. **sich zu etw ~ äußern** to make a statement of principle on sth; **er ist ~ anderer Meinung als sie** he always disagrees with her, he disagrees with her on principle; **ihre Meinungen sind ~ verschieden** their views are fundamentally different; **erlauben Sie so etwas? — ~ nicht** do you permit that sort of thing? — most definitely not, absolutely not; **das erlaube ich Ihnen ~ nicht** I will most definitely not permit that; **das ist ~ verboten** it is absolutely forbidden; **er hat ~ kein Interesse für so etwas** he has absolutely no interest in that sort of thing; **es ist ~ unmöglich, daß** ... it is absolutely impossible that ...

Grundsätzlichkeit f fundamental nature.

Grundsatz-: ~**referat** nt speech/paper setting out a basic principle; ~**urteil** nt judgement that establishes a principle.

Grund-: g~**schlecht** adj thoroughly bad; ~**schrift** f (Typ) base type; ~**schuld** f mortgage; ~**schule** f primary (Brit) or elementary school; ~**schüler** m primary/elementary(-school) pupil; ~**schullehrer** m primary/elementary(-school) teacher; g~**solide** adj very respectable; ~**sprache** f parent language; g~**ständig** adj (Bot) basal, basilar; ~**stein** m (lit, fig) foundation stone; **der ~stein zu etw sein** to form the foundation(s) of or for sth; **den ~stein zu etw legen** (lit) to lay the foundation stone of sth; (fig) to lay the foundations of or for sth; ~**steinlegung** f laying of the foundation stone; ~**stellung** f (Gymnastics) starting position; (Boxen) on-guard position; (Chess) initial or starting position; (Mus) root position; ~**steuer** f (local) property tax, = rates pl (Brit); ~**stimme** f bass; ~**stimmung** f prevailing mood; ~**stock** m basis, foundation; ~**stoff** m (Rohstoff) raw material; (Chem) element; ~**stoffindustrie** f primary industry.

Grundstück nt plot (of land); (Anwesen) estate; (Bau~ auch) site; (bebaut) property. **in ~en spekulieren** to speculate in property or in real estate.

Grundstücks-: ~**makler** m estate agent (Brit), realtor (US); ~**preis** m land price; ~**spekulant** m property speculator; ~**spekulation** f property speculation.

Grund-: ~**studium** nt (Univ) basic course; ~**stufe** f (a) first stage; (Sch) = junior (Brit) or grade (US) school; (b) (Gram) positive (degree); ~**tendenz** f, ~**tenor** m basic trend; (verborgen) underlying trend; ~**text** m original (text); ~**ton** m (Mus) (eines Akkords) root; (einer Tonleiter) tonic keynote; (~farbe) ground colour; ~**übel** nt basic or fundamental evil; (Nachteil) basic problem; ~**umsatz** m (Physiol) basal metabolism.

Gründung f founding, foundation; (Archit: Fundament) foundation(s pl); (das Anlegen des Fundaments) laying of the foundations; (von Heim, Geschäft) setting up. **die ~ einer Familie** getting married (and having a family).

Gründungs-: ~**jahr** nt year of the foundation; ~**kapital** nt initial capital; ~**rektor** m (Univ) first vice-chancellor; ~**versammlung** f inaugural meeting (of a new company).

Gründüngung f (Agr) green manuring.

Grund-: g~**verkehrt** adj completely wrong; ~**vermögen** nt landed property, real estate; g~**verschieden** adj totally or entirely different; ~**wasser** nt ground water; ~**wasserspiegel** m water table, ground-water level; ~**wehrdienst** m national (Brit) or selective (US) service; **den ~wehrdienst absolvieren** or **leisten** to do one's national/selective service; ~**wissenschaft** f fundamental discipline (für of); ~**wort** nt, pl ~**wörter** (Gram) root; ~**zahl** f (Math) base (number); (Kardinalzahl) cardinal number; ~**zins** m (Hist) feudal dues pl (Hist); ~**zug** m essential feature or trait; „**~züge der Geometrie**" "Basic Geometry", "(The) Rudiments of Geometry"; **etw in seinen ~zügen darstellen** to outline (the essentials of) sth; **dieses Werk entstand in seinen ~zügen schon** ... the essential features or the essentials of this work appeared as early as ...

grünen vi (geh) to turn green; (fig: Liebe, Hoffnung) to blossom (forth).

Grüne(r) m decl as adj (dated inf: Polizist) cop (inf), copper (Brit inf), bluebottle (dated Brit inf); (Pol) Ecologist.

Grüne(s) nt decl as adj (Farbe) green; (als Ausschmückung) greenery; (Gemüse) greens pl, green vegetables pl; (Grünfutter) green stuff. **ins ~ fahren** to go to the country; **wir essen viel ~s** (inf) we eat a lot of greens; ~**s in die Suppe tun** (inf) to put green vegetables in the soup.

Grün-: ~**fink** m greenfinch; ~**fläche** f green space or area; ~**futter** nt green fodder, greenstuff; g~**gelb** adj greenish yellow, greeny-yellow; ~**gürtel** m green belt; ~**kohl** m (curly) kale; ~**land** nt, no pl meadowland no indef art, grassland no indef art; g~**lich** adj greenish; ~**pflanze** f non-flowering or foliage plant; ~**rock** m (hum) gamekeeper; (Jäger) huntsman; ~**schnabel** m (inf) (little) whippersnapper (inf); (Neuling) greenhorn (inf); **sei still, du ~schnabel!** be quiet you little know-all! (inf); ~**span** m, no pl verdigris; ~**span ansetzen** or **bilden** to form verdigris; (fig) to grow hoary; ~**specht** m green woodpecker; ~**stich** m (Phot) green cast; g~**stichig** adj with a green cast; ~**stift** m (fig) blue pencil; ~**streifen** m central reservation (Brit), median (strip) (US, Austral); (am Straßenrand) grass verge.

grunzen vti to grunt.

Grünzeug nt greens pl, green vegetables pl; (Kräuter) herbs pl. **bei der Party war ein Haufen ~** a lot of the people at the party were still wet behind the ears (inf).

Grüppchen nt (usu pej) little group.

Gruppe f -, -n group (auch Math); (von Mitarbeitern auch) team; (Mil) = squad; (Aviat) = squadron (Brit), group (US); (von Pfadfindern) section; (Klasse, Kategorie auch) class. **eine ~ Zuschauer** or **von Zuschauern** a group of onlookers; **eine ~ von Beispielen** a list or series of examples; ~**n (zu je fünf/sechs) bilden** to form groups (into) or to make groups (of five/six).

Gruppen- in cpds group; ~**arbeit** f teamwork; ~**bild** nt group portrait; ~**bildung** f group formation, formation of groups; ~**dynamik** f (Psych) group dynamics; ~**egoismus** m self-interest of the/a group; ~**führer** m group leader; (Mil) squad leader; ~**leben** nt group living; ~**mitglied** nt member of the group, group member; ~**pädagogik** f group teaching; ~**psychologie** f group psychology; ~**reise** f group travel no pl; ~**sex** m group sex; ~**sieg** m (Sport) **den ~sieg erringen** to win

in one's group; ~**sieger** m (Sport) group winner, winner in or of a/the group; g~**spezifisch** adj group-specific; ~**therapie** f group therapy; ~**unterricht** m group learning; ~**vergewaltigung** f multiple rape, gang bang (sl); g~**weise** adv in groups; (Ind, Comm, Sport auch) in teams; (Mil) in squads; (Aviat) in squadrons.

gruppieren* 1 vt to group. 2 vr to form a group/groups, to group.

Gruppierung f (a) no pl grouping. (b) (Konstellation) grouping; (Gruppe) group; (Pol auch) faction.

Grus m -es, -e (Gesteinsschutt) rubble; (Kohlen~) slack.

Grusel-: ~**effekt** m horror effect; ~**film** m horror or gothic film; ~**geschichte** f tale of horror, horror or gothic story.

grus(e)lig adj horrifying, gruesome.

Gruselmärchen nt siehe **Gruselgeschichte**.

gruseln 1 vti impers **mich** or **mir gruselt auf Friedhöfen** cemeteries give me an eery feeling or give me the creeps; **ich kehre um, mir gruselt** I'm going back, I'm getting the creeps; **hier kann man das G~ lernen** this will teach you the meaning of fear.
2 vr **hier würde ich mich ~** a place like this would give me the creeps; **sie gruselt sich vor Schlangen** snakes give her the creeps.

Grusical ['gruːzikl] nt -s, -s (hum) comic horror or gothic film/play.

Grusinien [-iən] nt -s Georgia.

Grusinier(in f) [-iɐ, -iərin] m -s, - Georgian.

Gruskohle f slack.

gruslig adj siehe **grus(e)lig**.

Gruß m -es, ⁻e (a) greeting; (~geste, Mil) salute. **zum ~** in greeting; **der Deutsche ~** (NS) the Nazi salute; **er ging ohne ~ an mir vorbei** he walked past me without saying hello.
(b) (als Zeichen der Verbundenheit) **viele ~e** best wishes (an + acc to); **bestell Renate bitte viele ~e von mir** please give Renate my best wishes or my regards, remember me to Renate; **schick mir einen ~ aus Paris** drop me a line from Paris; **sag ihm einen schönen ~** say hello to him (from me); **einen (schönen) ~ an Ihre Gattin!** my regards to your wife.
(c) (als Briefformel) **mit bestem ~** or **besten ~en** yours; **mit brüderlichen/sozialistischem ~** (Pol) yours fraternally; **mit freundlichen ~en** or **freundlichem ~** (bei Anrede Mr/Mrs/Miss X) Yours sincerely, Yours truly (esp US); (bei Anrede Sir(s)/ Madam) Yours faithfully, Yours truly (esp US).

Gruß- (Pol): ~**adresse**, ~**ansprache**, ~**botschaft** f message of greeting.

grüßen 1 vt (a) to greet; (Mil) to salute. **grüßt er dich auch nicht?** doesn't he say hello to you either?; **sei gegrüßt** (old, geh, iro) greetings; **grüß dich!** (inf) hello there!, hi! (inf).
(b) (Grüße übermitteln) **Otto läßt dich (schön) ~** Otto sends his regards or best wishes or asked to be remembered to you; **ich soll Sie von ihm ~** he sends his regards etc; **grüß mir deine Mutter!, grüß deine Mutter von mir!** remember me to your mother, give my regards to your mother; **und grüß mir Wien/den Goldenen Löwen** and say hello to Vienna/the Golden Lion for me; **grüß Gott!** (S Ger, Aus) hello.
2 vi to say hello, to give a greeting (form); (Mil) to salute. **Otto läßt ~** Otto sends his regards; **die Berge grüßten aus der Ferne** (liter) the mountains greeted us in the distance.
3 vr **ich grüße mich nicht mehr mit ihm** I don't say hello to him any more.

Grußformel f form of greeting; (am Briefanfang) salutation; (am Briefende) complimentary close, ending.

Grüßfuß m (inf): **mit jdm auf (dem) ~ stehen** to have a nodding acquaintance with sb.

Gruß-: g~**los** adv without a word of greeting/farewell, without saying hello/goodbye; ~**ordnung** f (Mil) saluting hierarchy; ~**pflicht** f (Mil) obligation to salute; ~**schreiben** nt greeting; (Pol) letter of greeting; ~**telegramm** nt greetings telegram; (Pol) goodwill telegram; ~**wort** nt greeting.

Grütz-: ~**beutel** m (Med) wen; ~**brei** m gruel.

Grütze f -, -n (a) groats pl; (Brei) gruel. **rote ~** (type of) red fruit jelly. (b) no pl (inf: Verstand) brains (inf). **der hat ~ im Kopf** (inf) he's got brains (inf).

Grützkopf m (inf) (a) (Dummkopf) thickhead (inf), thickie (inf). (b) (Verstand) thick head.

Gschaftlhuber m -s, - (S Ger, Aus inf) busybody.

gschamig adj (Aus inf) bashful.

Gscherte(r) mf decl as adj (Aus inf) idiot.

Gschnas nt -, no pl (Aus inf) fancy-dress party.

gspaßig adj (Aus inf) funny.

Gspusi nt -s, -s (S Ger, Aus inf) (a) (Liebschaft) affair, carry-on (inf). (b) (Liebste(r)) darling, sweetheart.

Gstanz(e)l nt -s, -n (S Ger, Aus inf) ditty.

Gstätten f -, - (Aus inf) grassy patch of land on a hillside.

Guatemala nt -s Guatemala.

Guatemalteke m -n, -n, **Guatemaltekin** f Guatemalan.

guatemaltekisch adj Guatemalan.

Guayana [guaˈjaːna] nt -s Guiana; (ehem. Brit.-Guyana) Guyana.

Gu(a)yaner(in f) [guaˈjaːnɐ, -ərin] m -s, - Guianese; Guyanese.

guayanisch adj Guianese; Guyanese.

gucken ['gʊkn, (N Ger) 'kʊkn] 1 vi (sehen) to look (zu at); (heimlich auch) to peep, to peek; (hervorschauen) to peep (aus out of). **laß mal ~!** let's have a look, give us a look (inf); **jdm in die Karten ~** to look or have a look at sb's cards. 2 vt (inf) **Fernsehen ~** to watch television or telly (Brit inf).

Gucker m -s, - (inf) (a) (Fernglas) telescope; (Opernglas) opera glass(es). (b) pl (Augen) peepers (inf), eyes pl.

Guckfenster nt small window; (in Tür) judas window.

Gucki *m* -s, -s (*für Dias*) viewer.
Guck-: ~**indieluft** *m siehe* Hans; ~**kasten** *m* peepshow; (*inf: Fernseher*) telly (*Brit inf*), gogglebox (*Brit inf*), tube (*US inf*); ~**kastenbühne** *f* proscenium *or* fourth-wall stage; ~**loch** *nt* peephole.
Guerilla[1] [geˈrɪlja, geˈrɪla] *f* -, -s (a) (~*krieg*) guerilla war/warfare. (b) (~*einheit*) guerilla unit.
Guerilla[2] [geˈrɪlja] *m* -s, -s (~*kämpfer*) guerilla.
Guerilla- [geˈrɪlja-] *in cpds* guerilla.
Gugel-: ~**hupf** (*S Ger, Aus*), ~**hopf** (*Sw*) *m* -s, -e (*Cook*) gugelhupf.
Güggeli *nt* -s, - (*Sw Cook*) roast chicken.
Guillotine [gɪljoˈtiːnə, (*Aus*) gijoˈtiːna] *f* guillotine.
guillotinieren* [gɪljotiˈniːrən] *vt* to guillotine.
Guinea [gɪˈneːa] *nt* -s (*Geog*) Guinea.
Guineer(in *f*) [gɪˈneːɐ, -ərɪn] *m* -s, - Guinean.
guineisch [gɪˈneːɪʃ] *adj* Guinean.
Gulasch *nt or m* -(e)s, -e *or* -s goulash. **ich mache aus dir ~!** (*inf*) I'll beat the living daylights out of you (*inf*).
Gulasch-: ~**kanone** *f* (*Mil sl*) field kitchen; ~**kommunismus** *m* (*pej*) communism which is concerned only with material well-being; ~**suppe** *f* goulash soup.
Gulden *m* -s, - (*Hist*) florin; (*niederländischer* ~) gu(i)lder, gulden.
gülden *adj* (*poet*) golden.
Gülle *f* -, *no pl* (*S Ger, Sw*) *siehe* Jauche.
Gully [ˈguli] *m or nt* -s, -s drain.
gültig *adj* valid. **nach den** ~**en Bestimmungen** according to current regulations; **nach dem bis Mai noch** ~**en Gesetz** according to the law in force until May; **diese Münze ist nicht mehr** ~ this coin is no longer legal tender; **ab wann ist der Fahrplan** ~? when does the timetable come into effect *or* force?; ~ **für zehn Fahrten** valid *or* good for ten trips; ~ **werden** to become valid; (*Gesetz, Vertrag*) to come into force *or* effect; (*Münze*) to become legal tender.
Gültigkeit *f*, *no pl* validity; (*von Gesetz*) legal force. **das Fünfmarkstück verliert im Herbst seine** ~ the five-mark piece ceases to be legal tender in the autumn.
Gültigkeitsdauer *f* period of validity; (*eines Gesetzes*) period in force.
Gulyas [ˈguːlaʃ, ˈgulaʃ] *nt* -s, -e *siehe* Gulasch.
Gummi *nt or m* -s, -s (*Material*) rubber; (~*arabikum*) gum; (*Radier*~) rubber (*Brit*), eraser; (~*band*) rubber *or* elastic band; (*in Kleidung etc*) elastic; (*sl: Kondom*) rubber (*sl*), Durex ®.
Gummi- *in cpds* rubber; ~**anzug** *m* wetsuit; ~**arabikum** *nt* -s, *no pl* gum arabic; **g~artig** *adj* rubbery; **2** *adv* like rubber; ~**band** *nt* rubber *or* elastic band; (*in Kleidung*) elastic; ~**bär(chen** *nt*) *m* jelly bear; ~**baum** *m* rubber plant; ~**begriff** *m* (*inf*) elastic concept; ~**boot** *nt* inflatable boat, rubber dinghy; ~**elastikum** *nt* india rubber, caoutchouc.
gummieren* *vt* to gum.
Gummierung *f* (a) (*Verfahren*) gumming. (b) (*gummierte Fläche*) gum.
Gummi-: ~**gutt** *nt* -s, *no pl* gamboge; ~**harz** *nt* gum resin; ~**hose** *f*, ~**höschen** *nt* plastic pants *pl*; ~**kissen** *nt* inflatable rubber cushion; ~**knüppel** *m* rubber truncheon; ~**linse** *f* (*Phot*) zoom lens; ~**löwe** *m* (*hum*) paper tiger; ~**mantel** *m* plastic raincoat *or* mac (*Brit*); ~**paragraph** *m* (*inf*) ambiguous *or* meaningless paragraph; ~**rad** *nt* rubber tyre; ~**reifen** *m* rubber tyre; ~**sauger** *m* rubber teat (*Brit*) *or* nipple (*US*); ~**schlauch** *m* rubber hose; (*bei Fahrrad etc*) inner tube; ~**schutz** *m* (*dated*) sheath; ~**stiefel** *m* rubber boot, gumboot, wellington (boot) (*Brit*), wellie (*Brit inf*); (*bis zu den Oberschenkeln*) wader; ~**strumpf** *m* rubber *or* elastic stocking; ~**tier** *nt* rubber animal; (*aufblasbares* ~*tier*) inflatable animal; ~**unterlage** *f* rubber sheet; ~**waren** *pl* rubber goods *pl*; ~**zelle** *f* padded cell; ~**zug** *m* (piece of) elastic.
Gunst *f* -, *no pl* favour; (*Wohlwollen auch*) goodwill; (*Gönnerschaft auch*) patronage; (*des Schicksals etc*) benevolence. **zu meinen/deinen** ~**en** in my/your favour; **jdm eine** ~ **erweisen** (*geh*) to do sb a kindness; **jdm die** ~ **erweisen, etw zu tun** (*geh*) to be so gracious as to do sth for sb; **sich bei jdm in** ~ **setzen** to gain sb's favour; **jds** ~ **besitzen** *or* **genießen, in jds** ~ (*dat*) **stehen** to have *or* enjoy sb's favour, to be in favour with sb.
Gunst-: ~**beweis** *m*, ~**bezeigung** *f* mark of favour; ~**gewerbe** *nt* (*hum*) the oldest profession in the world (*hum*), prostitution; ~**gewerblerin** *f* (*hum*) lady of easy virtue, prostitute.
günstig *adj* favourable; (*zeitlich, bei Reisen etc*) convenient; *Angebot, Preis etc* reasonable, good. **jdm/einer Sache** ~ **gesinnt sein** (*geh*) to be favourably disposed towards sb/sth; **es trifft sich** ~**, daß ...** it's very lucky that ...; ~ **bei etw abschneiden** to do well in sth, to come out of sth very well; **bei** ~**er Witterung** weather permitting; **die Stadt liegt** ~ (**für**) **the** town is well situated (for); **wie komme ich am** ~**sten nach ...?** what's the best *or* easiest way to get to ...?; **die Fähre um 3 Uhr ist** ~**er** the 3 o'clock ferry is more convenient *or* better; **im** ~**sten Fall(e)** with luck; **im** ~**sten Licht** (*lit, fig*) in the most favourable light; **etw** ~ **kaufen/verkaufen** to buy/sell sth for a good price; **„Kinderwagen** ~ **abzugeben"** "pram for sale: bargain price"; **mit Geschäften und Erholungsmöglichkeiten in** ~**er Lage** convenient for shops and recreational facilities.
günstigstenfalls *adv* at the very best.
Günstling *m* (*pej*) favourite.
Günstlingswirtschaft *f* (*pej*) (system of) favouritism.
Gupf *m* -(e)s, -e (*Aus*) head.
Guppy [ˈgupi] *m* -s, -s (*Zool*) guppy.
Gurgel *f* -, -n throat; (*Schlund*) gullet. **jdm die** ~ **zudrücken** *or* **abdrücken** *or* **abschnüren** *or* **zuschnüren** (*lit, fig*) to strangle sb; **dann springt sie mir an die** ~! (*inf*) she'll kill me (*inf*); **sein Geld**

durch die ~ **jagen** (*inf*) to pour all one's money down one's throat *or* gullet (*inf*); **sich** (*dat*) **die** ~ **ausspülen** *or* **schmieren** (*hum*) to oil one's throat *or* gullet (*inf*).
gurgeln *vi* (a) (*den Rachen spülen*) to gargle. (b) (*Wasser, Laut*) to gurgle.
Gurgel-: ~**mittel**, ~**wasser** *nt* gargle.
Gürkchen *nt* midget gherkin.
Gurke *f* -, -n (a) cucumber; (*Essig*~) gherkin. **saure** ~**n** pickled gherkins. (b) (*hum inf: Nase*) hooter (*inf*), conk (*Brit inf*), nose; (*sl: Penis*) cock (*Brit inf*), prick (*vulg*).
gurken *vi aux sein* (*sl*) to drive.
Gurken-: ~**hobel** *m* slicer; ~**salat** *m* cucumber salad.
gurren *vi* (*lit, fig*) to coo.
Gurt *m* -(e)s, -e (*Gürtel, Patronen*~, *Ladestreifen*) belt; (*Riemen*) strap; (*Sattel*~) girth; (*Archit*) girder.
Gurtband *nt* waistband.
Gürtel *m* -s, - (*Gurt, Zone*) belt; (*Absperrkette*) cordon. **den** ~ **enger schnallen** (*lit, fig*) to tighten one's belt.
Gürtel-: ~**linie** *f* waist; **ein Schlag unter die** ~**linie** (*lit*) a punch/blow *etc* below the belt; **das war ein Schlag unter die** ~**linie** (*fig*) that really was (hitting) below the belt; ~**reifen** *m* radial (tyre); ~**rose** *f* (*Med*) shingles *sing or pl*; ~**schnalle** *f* belt buckle; ~**tier** *nt* armadillo.
gürten (*geh*) **1** *vt* to gird (*old*); *Pferd* to girth. **2** *vr* to gird oneself.
Guru *m* -s, -s guru.
Gusche *f* -, -n (*dial*) *siehe* Gosche.
Guß *m* **Gusses, Güsse** (a) (*Metal*) (*no pl: das Gießen*) casting, founding; (~*stück*) cast. (**wie**) **aus einem** ~ (*fig*) a unified whole. (b) (*Strahl*) stream, gush; (*inf: Regen*~) cloudburst, downpour. **kalte Güsse** (*Med*) cold affusions. (c) (*Zucker*~) icing, frosting (*esp US*); (*durchsichtig*) glaze. **einen Kuchen mit einem** ~ **überziehen** to ice a cake.
Guß-: ~**asphalt** *m* poured asphalt; ~**beton** *m* cast concrete; ~**eisen** *nt* cast iron; **g~eisern** *adj* cast-iron; ~**form** *f* mould; ~**naht** *f* seam; ~**stahl** *m* cast steel.
gustieren* *vt* (a) *siehe* goutieren (b) (*Aus*) to taste, to try.
gustiös *adj* (*Aus*) appetizing.
Gusto *m* -s, (*rare*) -s (*geh, Aus*) (a) (*Appetit*) ~ **auf etw** (*acc*) **haben** to feel like sth. (b) (*fig: Geschmack*) taste. **nach jds** ~ to sb's taste; **mit** ~ with gusto; **nach eignem** ~ ad lib, just as one/he *etc* likes.
Gustostückerl *nt* -s, -(n) (*Aus inf*) delicacy.
gut 1 *adj, comp* **besser**, *superl* **beste(r, s)** good. **probieren Sie unsere** ~**en Weine/Speisen!** try our fine wines/food; **er ist in der Schule/in Spanisch sehr** ~ he's very good at school/Spanish; ~**e Frau!** (*dated*) my dear lady; **er macht sich** (*dat*) **einen** ~**en Tag** (*faulenzt*) he's taking things easy for a day; (*amüsiert sich*) he's having a good day of it; **die** ~ **Stube** the best *or* good room; **das ist** ~ **gegen** *or* **für** (*inf*) **Husten** it's good for coughs; **wozu ist das** ~? (*inf*) what's that for?; **er ist immer für eine Überraschung** ~ (*inf*) he's always good for a surprise; **das war Pech, aber wer weiß, wozu es** ~ **ist** it was bad luck, but it's an ill wind ...; **sei so** ~ **(und) gib mir das** would you mind giving me that; **würden Sie so** ~ **sein und ...** would you be good enough to ...; **jdm** ~ **sein** (*old*) to love sb; **sie ist ihm von Herzen** ~ (*old*) her heart is his (*liter*); **bist du mir wieder** ~? (*dated*) are you friends with me again?; **dafür ist er sich zu** ~ he wouldn't stoop to that sort of thing; **sind die Bilder/die Plätzchen** ~ **geworden?** did the pictures/biscuits turn out all right?; **ist dein Magen wieder** ~? is your stomach better *or* all right again?; **es wird alles wieder** ~! everything will be all right, it is all ~, **daß ...** it's good that ...; **wie** ~**, daß ...** it's good that ..., how fortunate that ...; ~**, daß du das endlich einsiehst** it's a good thing *or* job (that) you realize it at last; **so was ist immer** ~ that's always useful; **ich will es damit** ~ **sein lassen** I'll leave it at that; **laß das** ~ **sein!** don't worry; **laß mal** ~ **sein!** that's enough, that'll do; **jetzt ist aber** ~! (*inf*) that's enough; **das ist ja alles** ~ **und schön, aber ...** that's all very well but ... *or* all well and good but ...; **ein** ~**es Stück Weg(s)** (*dated*) a good way; **ein** ~**es Pfund Reis** a good pound of rice; ~**e Besserung!** get well soon; **auf** ~**e Freundschaft!** here's to us!; **auf** ~**es Gelingen!** here's to success!; ~! good; (*in Ordnung*) (all) right, OK; **schon** ~! (it's) all right *or* OK; ~, ~! all right; **also** ~! all right *or* OK then; **nun** ~! fair enough, all right then; ~ **und schön** (*inf*) fair enough, that's all well and good; **du bist** ~! (*inf*) you're a fine one!

2 *adv, comp* **besser**, *superl* **am besten** well. ~ **schmecken/riechen** to taste/smell good; **sie spricht** ~ **Schwedisch** she speaks Swedish well, she speaks good Swedish; **es** ~ **haben** to have a good time of it; **unser Volk hat es noch nie so** ~ **gehabt** our people have never had it so good; **er hat es in seiner Jugend nicht** ~ **gehabt** he had a hard time (of it) when he was young; **er hatte es immer** ~ **bei seinen Eltern** his parents were always good to him; **du hast es** ~! you've got it made; **hier ist (es)** ~ **sein/leben** (*dated*) this is a good place to be/live; ~ **wohnen** to have a nice home; **das kann** ~ **sein** that may well be; **den Mantel lasse ich mir für** ~ (*inf*) I keep this coat for best; **so** ~ **wie nichts** next to nothing; **so** ~ **wie nicht hardly, scarcely**; **so** ~ **wie verloren** as good as lost; **so** ~ **ich kann** as best I can, as well as I can; **es dauert** ~**(e) drei Stunden** it lasts a good three hours; **nehmen Sie** ~ **ein Pfund Mehl** take a good pound of flour; **das ist aber** ~ **gewogen/eingeschenkt!** that's a generous measure; ~ **und gern** easily; **das läßt sich nicht** ~ **machen** that wouldn't be easy; (*das hast du*) ~ **gemacht!** well done!; **darauf kann man** ~ **verzichten** you can easily *or* well do without that; **mach's** ~! (*inf*) cheers, cheerio!, bye!; (*stärker*) look after yourself, take care; **paß** ~ **auf!** be very careful; **ich kann ihn jetzt nicht** ~ **im Stich lassen** I can't very well let him down now; **ich kann sie nicht** ~ (*danach*) **fragen** I can't very well ask her, can I?; *siehe* Gute(s).
Gut *nt* -(e)s, ¨-er (a) (*Eigentum*) property; (*lit, fig: Besitztum*)

possession. **irdische ~er** worldly goods; **geistige ~er** intellectual wealth; **nicht um alle ~er der Welt** (*geh*) not for all the world; **bewegliche/unbewegliche ~er** movables/immovables.

(b) *no pl* (*das Gute*) good, Good. **~ und Böse** good and evil, Good and Evil; **das höchste ~** (*Philos*) the greatest good; (*Gesundheit etc*) one's most valuable possession.

(c) (*Ware, Fracht~*) item. **~er** goods; (*Fracht~*) freight *sing*, goods (*esp Brit*).

(d) *no pl* (*dated: Material*) material (to be treated).

(e) (*Land~*) estate.

(f) *no pl* (*Naut*) rigging, gear. **laufendes/stehendes ~** running/standing rigging *or* gear.

-gut *nt suf in cpds* **(a)** *denotes material intended for or having undergone a process e.g.* **Saat~** seed; **Mahl~** substance(s) to be ground/ground substance(s).

(b) (*often not translated in English*) *denotes the totality of an abstract possession e.g.* **das deutsche Musik~/Gedanken~** (the body of) German music/thought.

Gut-: g~achten* *vi insep* (*usu infin, auch prp*) (*esp Jur*) to act as an expert witness; **~achten** *nt* -s, - report; **~achter(in** *f*) *m* -s, - expert; (*Schätzer auch*) valuator; (*Jur: Prozeß*) expert witness; **g~achtlich** *adj* (*form*) expert; **etw g~achtlich feststellen** to ascertain in an expert's report; **g~artig** *adj Kind, Hund etc* good-natured; *Geschwulst, Geschwür* benign; **~artigkeit** *f* (*von Kind etc*) good nature, good-naturedness; (*von Geschwulst*) benignity; **g~beleumdet** *adj attr* of high repute; **g~betucht** *adj attr* (*inf*) well-heeled (*inf*); **g~bezahlt** *adj attr* highly-paid; **g~bürgerlich** *adj* solid middle-class; *Küche* homely, good plain; **g~dotiert** *adj attr* well-paid; **~dünken** *nt* -s, *no pl* discretion; **nach (eigenem) ~dünken** at one's own discretion, as one sees fit, as one thinks fit *or* best.

Güte *f* -, *no pl* **(a)** (*Herzens~, Freundlichkeit*) goodness, kindness; (*Gottes auch*) loving-kindness. **würden Sie die ~ haben, zu ...** (*form*) would you have the goodness *or* kindness to ... (*form*); **ein Vorschlag zur ~** a suggestion; **in ~** amicably; **meine ~, ist der dumm!** (*inf*) my God, is he stupid! (*inf*); **ach du liebe** *or* **meine ~!** (*inf*) oh my goodness!, goodness me!

(b) (*einer Ware*) quality. **ein Reinfall erster ~** (*inf*) a first-class flop, a flop of the first order *or* water (*inf*).

Güte-: ~grad *m*, **~klasse** *f* (*Comm*) grade.

Gutenacht-: ~geschichte *f* bedtime story; **~kuß** *m* goodnight kiss.

Gute(r) *mf decl as adj* **mein ~r** (*old*) my dear friend/husband; **meine ~e** (*old*) my dear; **der/die ~** the dear kind soul; (*mitleidig*) the poor soul; **die ~n und die Bösen** the good and the bad; (*inf: in Westernfilmen etc*) the goodies and the baddies (*inf*).

Güter-: ~abfertigung *f* **(a)** *no pl* dispatch of freight *or* goods (*esp Brit*); **(b)** (*Abfertigungsstelle*) freight *or* goods (*esp Brit*) office; **~angebot** *nt siehe* **Warenangebot**; **~bahnhof** *m* freight *or* goods (*esp Brit*) depot; **~fernverkehr** *m* long-distance haulage; **~gemeinschaft** *f* (*Jur*) community of property; **in ~gemeinschaft leben** to have community of property; **~nahverkehr** *m* short-distance haulage (*up to 50 km*); **~schuppen** *m* freight depot, goods shed (*Brit*); **~trennung** *f* (*Jur*) separation of property; **in ~trennung leben** to have separation of property; **~verkehr** *m* freight *or* goods (*esp Brit*) traffic; **~wagen** *m* (*Rail*) freight car (*US*), goods truck (*Brit*); **~zug** *m* freight *or* goods (*esp Brit*) train.

Gute(s) *nt decl as adj* **~s tun** to do good; **es hat alles sein ~s** (*prov*) every cloud has a silver lining (*Prov*), it's an ill wind (that blows no good) (*Prov*); **alles ~e!** all the best!, good luck!; **man hört über sie nur ~s** you hear so many good things about her; **das führt zu nichts ~m** it'll lead to no good; **jdm (viel) ~s tun** to be (very) good to sb; **des ~n zuviel tun** to overdo things; **das ist des ~n zuviel** that is too much of a good thing; **das ~ daran** the good thing about it; **das ~e siegt** Good *or* good shall triumph; **das ~e im Menschen** the good in man; **im g~n wie im bösen** for better or for worse; **im g~n sich trennen** amicably; **ich sage es dir im g~n** I want to give you a friendly piece of advice.

Güte-: ~siegel *nt* (*Comm*) stamp of quality; **~termin** *m*, **~verhandlung** *f* (*Jur*) conciliation proceedings *pl*; **~zeichen** *nt* mark of quality; (*fig auch*) hallmark.

Gut-: g~gehen *sep irreg aux sein* 1 *vi impers* **es geht ihm g~** he is doing well *or* nicely; (*er ist gesund*) he is well; **sonst geht's dir g~!** (*iro*) are you feeling all right?, are you in your right mind?; 2 *vi* to go (off) well; **das ist noch einmal g~gegangen** it turned out all right; **wenn es g~geht** with luck; **das konnte ja nicht**

g~gehen it was bound to go wrong; **wenn das man g~geht!** (*N Ger*) that's asking for trouble; **hoffentlich geht es mit den beiden g~!** (*inf*) I hope things will work out for the two of them; **g~gehend** *adj attr* flourishing, thriving; **g~gelaunt** *adj* cheerful, in a good mood; **g~gelungen** *adj attr* very successful; *Überraschung* wonderful; **g~gemeint** *adj attr* well-meaning, well-meant; **g~gesinnt** *adj* well-disposed (+ *dat* towards); (*von edler Gesinnung*) right-thinking; **g~gläubig** *adj* trusting; (*vertrauensselig auch*) credulous; **~gläubigkeit** *f siehe adj* trusting nature, trustingness; credulity.

Guth. *abbr of* **Guthaben.**

Gut-: g~haben *vt sep irreg* **etw g~haben** to be owed with (*bei by*), to have sth coming (to one) (*bei from*) (*inf*); **~haben** *nt* -s, - (*Fin, Bank~*) credit; **auf meinem Konto ist** *or* **habe ich ein ~haben von DM 500** my account is DM 500 in credit; **g~heißen** *vt sep irreg* to approve of; (*genehmigen*) to approve; **~heißung** *f* approval; **g~herzig** *adj* kind-hearted, kindly; **~herzigkeit** *f* kind-heartedness, kind(li)ness.

gütig *adj* kind; (*edelmütig*) generous, gracious. **mit Ihrer ~en Erlaubnis** (*dated form*) with your kind permission; **würden Sie so ~ sein, zu ...** (*dated form*) would you be so kind as to ...

gütlich *adj* amicable. **sich an etw** (*dat*) **~ tun** to make free with sth.

Gut-: g~machen *vt sep* **(a)** (*in Ordnung bringen*) *Fehler* to put right, to correct; *Schaden* to make good; **das kann ich ja gar nicht wieder g~machen!** (*fig*) how on earth can I ever repay you!; **du hast viel an ihm g~zumachen** you've a lot to make up to him (for); **das mache ich dir wieder g~** (*inf*) I'll make it up to you; **(b)** (*gewinnen*) to make (*bei* out of, on); **g~mütig** *adj* good-natured; **~mütigkeit** *f* good-naturedness; **g~nachbarlich** 1 *adj* neighbourly; **2** *adv* in a neighbourly fashion, as good neighbours; **g~sagen** *vi sep* (*dated*) to vouch (*für* for).

Gutsbesitzer(in *f*) *m* lord of the manor; (*als Klasse*) landowner.

Gut-: ~schein *m* voucher, coupon; (*für Umtausch*) credit note; **g~schreiben** *vt sep irreg* to credit (*dat* to); **~schrift** *f* **(a)** *no pl* (*Vorgang*) crediting; **(b)** (*Bescheinigung*) credit note; (*Betrag*) credit (item).

Gutsel(e) *nt* -s, - (*S Ger*) (*Bonbon*) candy (*esp US*), sweet (*Brit*); (*Keks*) biscuit (*Brit*), cookie (*US*).

Guts-: ~haus *nt* manor (house); **~herr** *m* squire, lord of the manor; **~herrin** *f* lady of the manor; **~herrschaft** *f* squire and his family; **~hof** *m* estate.

gut-: ~situiert *adj attr* well-off; **~sitzend** *adj attr* well-fitting.

Gutsle *nt* -s, - (*S Ger*) *siehe* **Gutsel(e).**

Gutsverwalter(in *f*) *m* steward.

Guttapercha *f* - *or nt* -(s), *no pl* gutta-percha.

Gut-: ~templer(in *f*) *m* -s, - Good Templar; **g~tun** *vi sep irreg* **jdm g~tun** to do sb good; **das tut g~** that's good; **o, wie g~ das tut!** oh, that's good; **der Bub tut nicht g~** (*S Ger*) the boy is misbehaving.

Guttural -s, -e, **Gutturallaut** *m* (*Ling*) guttural (sound).

guttural *adj* guttural.

Gut-: g~unterrichtet *adj attr* well-informed; **g~verdienend** *adj attr* with a good salary, high-income; **g~willig** *adj* willing; (*entgegenkommend*) obliging; (*nicht böswillig*) well-meaning; **~willigkeit** *f siehe adj* willingness; obligingness; well-meaningness.

Gwirkst *nt* -s, *no pl* (*Aus inf*) hassle (*inf*).

gymnasial *adj attr* = at grammar schools (*Brit*), at high schools (*US*).

Gymnasial-: ~bildung *f* = grammar school education (*Brit*), high school education (*US*); **~lehrer, ~professor** *m* (*Aus*) = grammar school teacher (*Brit*), high school teacher (*US*).

Gymnasiast(in *f*) *m* -en, -en = grammar school pupil (*Brit*), high school student (*US*).

Gymnasium *nt* (**a**) (*Sch*) = grammar school (*Brit*), high school (*US*). **(b)** (*Hist*) gymnasium.

Gymnastik *f* keep-fit exercises *pl*; (*Turnen*) gymnastics *sing*. **~ machen** to do keep-fit (exercises)/gymnastics.

Gymnastiker(in *f*) *m* -s, - gymnast.

Gymnastik-: ~saal *m* gymnasium; **~unterricht** *m* gymnastics *sing*.

gymnastisch *adj* gymnastic.

Gynäkologe *m*, **Gynäkologin** *f* gynaecologist.

Gynäkologie *f* gynaecology.

gynäkologisch *adj* gynaecological.

Gyroskop [gyro'sko:p] *nt* -s, -e gyroscope.

H

H, h [haː] *nt* -, - H, h; (*Mus*) B.

h *abbr of* **hora(e)** (*Stunde*) hr. **Abfahrt 8ʰ/13ʰ** (*gesprochen acht/dreizehn Uhr*) departure 8 a.m./1 p.m. *or* 8⁰⁰/13⁰⁰ hours (spoken: eight/thirteen hundred hours); **120 km/h** (*gesprochen: Kilometer pro Stunde*) 120 km/h *or* kmph.

ha¹ *abbr of* **Hektar** hectare.

ha² *interj* ha; (*triumphierend*) aha; (*überrascht, erstaunt, verärgert*) oh; (*verächtlich*) huh. ~ **no** (*S Ger inf*) (*Selbstverständliches betonend*) why not; (*ungläubig*) well, well; (*aufmunternd*) come on; (*resignierend*) oh well.

hä *interj* what.

Haag *m* -s: **der ~, Den ~** The Hague; **in** *or* **im ~, in Den ~** in The Hague.

Haager *adj attr* Hague. **~ Konventionen** Hague Conventions; **~ Schiedshof** International Court of Justice in The Hague.

Haar *nt* -(e)s, -e (a) (*Menschen~*) hair. **sie hat schönes ~** *or* **schöne ~e** she has nice hair; **sich** (*dat*) **die ~e** *or* **das ~ schneiden lassen** to have *or* get one's hair cut, to have a haircut. (b) (*Bot, Zool, Material*) hair. (c) (*in Wendungen*) **~e auf den Zähnen haben** to be a tough customer; **~e lassen (müssen)** to suffer badly, to come off badly; **jdm kein ~ krümmen** not to harm a hair of sb's head; **darüber laß dir keine grauen ~e wachsen** don't worry your head about it, don't lose any sleep over it; **er findet immer ein ~ in der Suppe** he always finds something to quibble about; **jdm aufs ~ gleichen** to be the spitting image of sb; **sie gleichen sich aufs ~** they are the spitting image of each other, they're as alike as two peas in a pod; **das ist an den ~en herbeigezogen** that's rather far-fetched; **das hängt an einem ~** it's hanging by a thread; **sich** (*dat*) **die ~e raufen** to tear one's hair out; **sich** (*dat*) **durch die ~e fahren** to run one's fingers through one's hair; **an jdm/etw kein** *or* **nicht ein gutes ~ lassen** to pick *or* pull sb/sth to pieces; **sich** (*dat*) **in die ~e geraten** *or* **kriegen** (*inf*) to quarrel *or* squabble; **sich** (*dat*) **in den ~en liegen** to be at loggerheads; **jdm die ~e vom Kopf fressen** (*inf*) to eat sb out of house and home; **er hat mehr Schulden als ~e auf dem Kopf** he's up to his ears in debt; **um kein ~ besser** no better, not a bit *or* whit better; **um ein** *or* **ums ~ very** nearly, almost; **er hat mich um ein ~ getroffen** he just missed (hitting) me by a hair's breadth; *siehe* **Berg**.

Haar-: **~ansatz** *m* hairline; **~ausfall** *m* hair loss; **~balg** *m* (*Anat*) hair follicle; **~band** *nt* hairband; (*Schleife*) hair ribbon; **~boden** *m* scalp; **~breit** *nt*: **nicht ein** *or* **um kein ~breit** not an inch; **h~breit** *adv* almost; **entgehen** by a hair's breadth; **~bürste** *f* hairbrush; **~büschel** *nt* tuft of hair.

haaren 1 *vi* (*Tier*) to moult, to lose its coat *or* hair; (*Pelz etc*) to shed (hair); (*Teppich*) to shed. **2** *vr* (*Tier*) to moult.

Haar-: **~entferner** *m* -s, -, **~entfernungsmittel** *nt* hair remover, depilatory; **~ersatz** *m* (*form*) hairpiece; (*Perücke*) wig; (*Toupet*) toupet.

Haaresbreite *f inv* (**nur**) **um ~** almost, very nearly; *verfehlen* by a hair's breadth; **er wich nicht um ~ von seiner Meinung ab** he did not change his opinion one iota.

Haar-: **~farbe** *f* hair colour; **~festiger** *m* -s, - (hair) setting lotion; **~flechte** *f* (*old, geh*) plait, braid (*dated*); **~garn** *nt* yarn made from hair; **~gefäß** *nt* (*Anat*) capillary; **h~genau** *adj* exact; *Übereinstimmung* total; **die Beschreibung trifft h~genau auf ihn zu** the description fits him exactly *or* to a T (*inf*); **jdm etw h~genau erklären** to explain sth to sb in great detail; **das trifft h~genau zu** that is absolutely right.

haarig *adj* hairy (*inf*); (*heikel, gefährlich*) hairy (*inf*); (*schwierig*) nasty.

Haar-: **~klammer** *f* (*Klemme*) hairgrip; (*Spange*) hair slide, barrette (*US*); **~kleid** *nt* (*geh*) coat; **h~klein 1** *adj* (*inf*) *Beschreibung* detailed; **2** *adv* in great *or* minute detail; **er hat mir alles h~klein berechnet** he charged me for absolutely everything; **~klemme** *f* hairgrip; **~kranz** *m* (*von Männern*) fringe (of hair); (*Frauenfrisur*) plaits fixed around one's head; **~künstler** *m* (*usu hum*) hair artiste; **~lack** *m* hair lacquer; **h~los** *adj* hairless; (*glatzköpfig*) bald; **~losigkeit** *f siehe adj* hairlessness; baldness; **~mensch** *m* (*Med*) hirsute person; **~mode** *f* hairstyle; **~nadel** *f* hairpin; **~nadelkurve** *f* hairpin bend; **~netz** *nt* hairnet; **~öl** *nt* hair oil; **~pflege** *f* hair care; **zur ~pflege** (for caring) for one's hair; **~pinsel** *m* (a) (*zum Rasieren*) brush; (b) (*Art*) small animal-hair paintbrush; **~pracht** *f* superb head of hair; **~riß** *m* (*Tech*) (*in Metall, Pflaster etc*) hairline crack; **h~scharf** *adj Beschreibung, Wiedergabe* exact; *Gedächtnis* very sharp, very clear; *Unterschied* very fine; *Beobachtung* very close; **das hat ihn h~scharf verfehlt/getroffen** that only missed (hitting) him by a hair's breadth; **die Kugel ging h~scharf daneben** the bullet missed by a hair's breadth; **h~scharf an jdm vorbeizielen/vorbeischießen** to try to miss sb/to shoot just past sb; **der Glassplitter traf ihn h~scharf über dem Auge** the splinter of glass only just missed his eye; **~schleife** *f* hair ribbon; **~schmuck** *m* ornaments *pl* for one's hair; **~schneider** *m* -s, - (a) (*Gerät*) electric clippers *pl*; (b) (*inf: Friseur*) barber; **~schnitt** *m* (a) (*Frisur*) haircut, hairstyle; (b) (*das ~schneiden*) haircut; **~schopf** *m* mop *or* shock of hair; **ihr roter ~schopf** her mop *or* shock of red hair; **~schwund** *m siehe*

~ausfall; **~seite** *f* (*von Fell*) fleece side; (*von Pelz*) fur side; (*von Teppich*) pile side; **~sieb** *nt* fine sieve; **~spalter(in** *f*) *m* -s, - pedant, hairsplitter; **~spalterei** *f* splitting hairs *no indef art, no pl;* **eine solche ~spalterei** splitting hairs like that; **h~spalterisch** *adj* hairsplitting; *Unterschied* minute; **~spange** *f* hair slide, barrette (*US*); **~spitze** *f* end (of a hair); **gespaltene ~spitzen** split ends; **~spray** *nt or m* hairspray; **~strähne** *f* strand *or* (*dünner*) wisp of hair; **h~sträubend** *adj* hair-raising; (*empörend*) shocking, terrible; (*unglaublich*) *Frechheit* incredible; **~strich** *m* (*dünner Strich*) hairline, hairstroke; (*von Tierfell*) growth of the hair; **~teil** *nt* hairpiece; **~tolle** *f* quiff; (*Hahnenkamm*) cockscomb; **~töner** *m* -s, - hair-tinting lotion; **~tönung** *f* tinting; **~tracht** *f* (*dated, geh: Frisur*) hairstyle; **~transplantation** *f* hair transplant; (*Vorgang*) hair transplantation; **~trockner** *m* -s, - hair dryer; **~wäsche** *f* washing one's hair *no art;* **eine regelmäßige ~wäsche** washing one's hair regularly; **~waschmittel** *nt* shampoo; **~wasser** *nt* hair lotion; **~wechsel** *m* change of coat; **~wild** *nt* (*Hunt*) game animals *pl;* **~wirbel** *m* cowlick; (*am Hinterkopf*) crown; **~wuchs** *m* growth of hair; **einen kräftigen/spärlichen ~wuchs haben** to have a lot of hair *or* a thick head of hair/thin hair *or* a thin head of hair; **~wuchsmittel** *nt* hair restorer; **~wurzel** *f* root of a/the hair.

Hab *nt*: **~ und Gut** *sing vb* possessions, belongings, worldly goods *all pl*.

Habe *f* -, *no pl* (*geh*) possessions *pl*, belongings *pl*.

Habeaskorpus|akte *f* (*Jur*) Act of Habeas Corpus.

Habedank *nt* -s, *no pl* (*poet*) thanks *pl*. **ein herzliches ~** heartfelt thanks.

Habe die Ehre *interj* (*Aus*) (*Gruß*) hello; goodbye; (*Ausdruck des Erstaunens, der Entrüstung*) good heavens.

haben *pret* **hatte,** *ptp* **gehabt 1** *vt* (a) to have, to have got (*esp Brit*). **ein Meter hat 100 cm** there are 100 cm in a metre; **da hast du 10 Mark/das Buch** there's 10 Marks/the book; **was man hat, das hat man** (*inf*), **wer hat der hat** (*inf*) I/she *etc* might as well have it as not; (*in bezug auf Arbeit*) **once it's done it's done;** **die ~'s** (*ja*) (*inf*) **they can afford it;** **wie hätten Sie es gern?** how would you like it?; **man hat wieder lange Haare** long hair is in (fashion) again; **ich kann das nicht ~** (*inf*) I can't stand it; **sie hat heute Geburtstag** it's her birthday today; **Ferien ~** to be on holiday; **er wollte sie zur Frau ~** he wanted to make her his wife.

(b) (*über etw verfügen*) *Zeit, Geld, Beziehungen* to have; (*vorrätig ~, führen auch*) to have got (*esp Brit*). **damit hat es noch Zeit** *or* **eine gute Weile** (*geh*), **die Sache hat Zeit** it's not urgent, it can wait; **Zeit ~, etw zu tun** to have the time to do sth.

(c) (*Schülersprache*) *Lehrer, Unterricht, Schule* to have; *Note* to get; (*studieren*) *Fach* to do. **in der ersten Stunde ~ wir Mathe** we have maths first lesson; **was hast du diesmal in Englisch?** what did you get in English this time?

(d) (*von etw ergriffen, erfüllt, bedrückt sein*) *Zweifel, Hoffnung, Wunsch* to have. *Hunger/Durst/Angst/Sorgen* ~ to be hungry/thirsty/afraid/worried; **eine Krankheit ~** to have (got) an illness; *Fieber ~* to have (got) a temperature; **was hat er denn?** what's the matter with him?, what's wrong with him?; **hast du was?** are you all right?, is (there) something the matter with you?; **ich habe nichts** there's nothing wrong *or* the matter with me; **gute/schlechte Laune ~** to be in a good/bad mood.

(e) (*vorhanden sein, herrschen*) *gutes, schlechtes Wetter* to have. **morgen werden wir Nebel ~** we'll have fog tomorrow; **was ~ wir heute für ein Wetter?** what's the weather like today?; **wieviel Uhr ~ wir?** what's the time?; **heute ~ wir 10°** it's 10° today; **in Australien ~ sie jetzt Winter** it's winter in Australia now; **was für ein Datum ~ wir heute?, den wievielten ~ wir heute?** what's the date today?, what's today's date?

(f) (*mit adj*) **es gut/schön/bequem ~** to have it good/nice/easy; **sie hat es warm in ihrem Zimmer** it's warm in her room; **wir ~ es noch weit bis nach Hause** it's a long way home; **es schlecht ~** to have a bad time (of it); **er hat es nicht leicht mit ihr** he has a hard time (of it) with her.

(g) (*in Infinitivkonstruktion mit zu*) **ich habe nichts zu sagen/tun** I have nothing to say/do; **ich habe nichts mehr zu hoffen** I have nothing to hope for any more; **nichts vom Leben zu erwarten ~** to have no expectations in life; **du hast zu gehorchen** (*müssen*) you must *or* you have to obey; **ich habe nicht zu fragen** I'm not to ask questions; (*steht mir nicht zu*) it's not up to me to ask questions; **ich habe zu tun** I'm busy.

(h) (*in Infinitivkonstruktion mit Raumangabe*) **etw auf dem Boden liegen/an der Wand hängen ~** to have sth lying on the floor/hanging on the wall; **viele Bücher im Schrank stehen ~** to have a lot of books in the cupboard.

(i) (*in Infinitivkonstruktion mit sein*) **jd/etw ist zu ~** (*erhältlich*) sb/sth is to be had; (*nicht verheiratet*) sb is single; (*sexuell*) sb is available; **für etw zu ~ sein** to be keen on sth; **für ein gutes Essen ist er immer zu ~** he's always willing to have a good meal; **der ist doch für jeden Ulk zu ~** he's always one for a joke; **für gefährliche Sachen ist er immer zu ~** he's always game for anything dangerous; **er ist nicht dafür zu ~** (*nicht* *interessiert*) he's not keen on that; (*möchte nicht beteiligt sein*) he won't have anything to do with it.

(j) (*dial*) **es hat** (*es gibt*) there is/are.

(k) (*inf: leiden*) **es am Herzen/Magen/an der Leber ~** to have heart/stomach/liver trouble *or* trouble with one's heart/stomach/liver; **es in den Beinen ~** to have trouble with one's legs.

(l) (*Redewendungen*) **ich hab's** (*inf*) I've got it, I know; **dich hat's (wohl)!** (*inf*) you're daft (*inf*) *or* crazy (*inf*); **du kannst mich gern ~** (*inf*) I don't give a damn (*inf*); **da hast du's/~ wir's!** (*inf*) there you/we are; **woher hast du denn das?** where did you get that from?; **wie gehabt!** some things don't change.

(m) in *Verbindung mit Präpositionen siehe auch dort* **jd/etw hat eine nette Art/etwas Freundliches** *etc* **an sich** (*dat*) there is something nice/friendly *etc* about sb/sth; **sie werden schon merken, was hat er/sie/es so an sich** (*dat*) that's just the way he/she/it is; **das hat es in sich** (*inf*) (*schwierig*) that's tough, that's a tough one; (*alkoholreich*) that's strong; (*reichhaltig*) that's rich; **das hat etwas für sich** there's something to be said for that; **was hat es damit auf sich?** what is all this about, what is all this supposed to mean?; **was hat es mit ihm/ihr auf sich?** what is he/she up to?; **er hat es mit dem Malen/Bergsteigen** (*inf*) he has a thing about painting/mountaineering (*inf*); **man muß immer wissen, wen man vor sich hat** one must always know who one is talking to; **etwas mit jdm ~** (*euph*) to have a thing with sb (*inf*); **etwas von etw ~** (*inf*) to get something out of sth; **das hast du jetzt davon** now see what's happened *or* what's come of it; **das hat er von seinem Leichtsinn** that's what comes of his being frivolous; **nichts/mehr/weniger von etw ~** (*inf*) to get nothing/more/less out of *or* from sth; **da habe ich dann mehr davon** that way I get more out of it; **nichts davon/von etw ~** to get nothing out of it/sth *or* no benefit from it/sth; **viel/wenig von jdm ~** to take after/not to take after sb; **die blonden Haare hat sie von ihrem Vater** she gets her blonde hair from her father; **er hat etwas von einem Erpresser (an sich** *dat*) he's a bit of a blackmailer; **dieses Werk von Braque hat viel von Picasso** this work by Braque owes much to Picasso; **in seinem ganzen Gehabe hat er viel von einem Künstler** there's a good deal of the artist in *or* about his whole manner; **etw gegen jdn/etw ~** to have sth against sb/sth; **jd hat jdn/etw gegen sich** sb has sb/sth against him.

2 *vr* (*inf: sich anstellen*) to make a fuss. **was hast du dich denn so?** what are you making such a fuss about?; **hab dich nicht so** stop making such a fuss.

3 *vr impers* (*inf*) **und damit hat es sich** and that's that; **er gab ihr einen Kuß, und es hatte sich wieder** he gave her a kiss and everything was all right again; **die Sache hat sich** (*ist erledigt*) that's done; **es hat sich was mit der Liebe/Hoffnung** love/hope is a strange thing; **hat sich was!** (*inf*) some hopes!

4 *v aux* **ich habe/hatte gerufen** I have/had called, I've/I'd called; **du hättest den Brief früher schreiben können** you could have written the letter earlier; **er will ihn gesehen ~** he says (that) he saw him.

Haben *nt* **-s,** *no pl* credit. **im ~ stehen** to be on the credit side.

Habenichts *m* **-(es), -e** have-not.

Haben-: **~seite** *f* credit side; **~zinsen** *pl* interest on credit *sing*.

Haberer *m* **-s, -** (*Aus inf*) bloke (*inf*), chap (*inf*).

Habersack *m* (*old*) knapsack, haversack.

Hab-: **~gier** *f* greed, acquisitiveness; **h~gierig** *adj* greedy, acquisitive; **h~haft** *adj* **(a) jds/einer Sache h~haft werden** (*geh*) to get hold of sb/sth; **(b)** (*dial*) **Essen** substantial.

Habicht *m* **-s, -e** hawk; (*Hühner~*) goshawk.

Habichtsnase *f* hooked nose.

habil *adj* (*dated, geh*) skilful, clever.

habil. *abbr of* **habilitatus Dr. ~** doctor with postdoctoral university teaching qualification.

Habilitand(in *f*) *m* **-en, -en** person writing postdoctoral thesis to qualify as a university lecturer.

Habilitation *f* **(a)** (*Festakt*) ceremony at which sb receives his/her qualification as university lecturer. **(b)** (*Lehrberechtigung*) postdoctoral lecturing qualification.

Habilitationsschrift *f* postdoctoral thesis required for qualification as a university lecturer.

habilitieren* **1** *vr* to qualify as a university lecturer. **2** *vt* to confer qualification as a university lecturer on.

habilitiert *adj* qualified as a university lecturer.

Habit[1] [ha'bi:t, ha'bɪt] *nt or m* **-s, -e** (*Ordenskleid*) habit; (*geh: Aufzug*) attire.

Habit[2] ['hæbɪt] *nt or m* **-s, -s** (*Psych*) habit.

Habitat *nt* (*Zool*) habitat.

habituell *adj* (*geh*) habitual.

Habitus *m* **-,** *no pl* (*geh, Med*) disposition.

Habsburg *nt* **-s** Hapsburg, Habsburg.

Habsburger(in *f*) *m* **-s, -** Hapsburg, Habsburg.

Habsburger *adj attr*, **habsburgisch** *adj* Hapsburg *attr*, Habsburg *attr*, of the Hapsburgs *or* Habsburgs.

Hab-: **~schaft** *f*, **~seligkeiten** *pl* possessions, belongings, effects (*form*) *all pl*; **~sucht** *f siehe* **~gier; h~süchtig** *adj siehe* **h~gierig.**

Habtachtstellung *f* (*Mil*) attention. **in ~ stehen** *or* **sein** to stand *or* be at attention.

hach *interj* oh; (*verächtlich*) huh.

Haché [ha'ʃe:] *nt* **-s, -s** *siehe* **Haschee.**

Hachel *f* **-, -n** (*Aus*) slicer.

hacheln *vti* (*Aus*) to chop, to slice.

Hachse ['haksə] *f* **-, -n** (*dial*) *siehe* **Haxe.**

Hack-: **~bank** *f* butcher's chopping board; **~bau** *m* (*Agr*) hoe-farming; **~beil** *nt* chopper, cleaver; **~block** *m siehe* **~klotz;**

~braten *m* meat loaf; **~brett** *nt* **(a)** chopping board; **(b)** (*Mus*) dulcimer.

Hacke[1] *f* **-, -n (a)** (*dial: Ferse, am Strumpf*) heel. **(b)** (*dial, Mil: Absatz*) heel. **die ~n zusammenschlagen** *or* **-klappen** (*Mil*) to click one's heels; **die ~n zusammennehmen** (*Mil*) to put one's feet together; **die ~n voll haben, einen im ~n haben** (*N Ger inf*) to be pickled (*inf*); *siehe* **ablaufen.**

Hacke[2] *f* **-, -n (a)** (*Pickel*) pickaxe, pick; (*Garten~*) hoe. **(b)** (*Aus*) hatchet, axe.

Hackebeil *nt siehe* **Hackbeil.**

hacken **1** *vt* **(a)** (*zerkleinern*) to chop; (*im Fleischwolf*) to mince (*Brit*), to grind (*US*).

(b) *Garten, Erdreich* to hoe.

(c) (*mit spitzem Gegenstand*) *Loch* to hack, to chop; (*Vogel*) to peck.

2 *vi* **(a)** (*mit dem Schnabel*) to peck; (*mit spitzem Gegenstand*) to hack, to chop. **nach jdm/etw ~** to peck at sth/sb.

(b) (*im Garten etc*) to hoe.

3 *vr* (*sich verletzen*) to cut (oneself). **ich habe mich** *or* **mir in den Finger gehackt** I've cut my finger.

Hacken *m* **-s, -** *siehe* **Hacke**[1] **(a).**

Hackentrick *m* (*Sport*) backheel.

Hackepeter *m* **-s, -** **(a)** (*NGer*) mince (*Brit*), minced (*Brit*) *or* ground (*US*) meat. **(b)** (*S Ger*) seasoned raw meat loaf.

Hack-: **~fleisch** *nt* mince (*Brit*), minced (*Brit*) *or* ground (*US*) meat; **jdn zu** *or* **aus jdm ~fleisch machen** (*sl*) to make mincemeat of sb (*inf*); (*verprügeln*) to beat sb up; **~frucht** *f* root crop; **~klotz** *m* **(a)** chopping block; **(b)** (*fig: grober Kerl*) oaf (*inf*), clod (*inf*); **~ordnung** *f* (*lit, fig*) pecking order.

Häcksel *nt or m* **-s,** *no pl* chaff.

Häckselmaschine *f* chaffcutter.

Hack-: **~steak** *nt* hamburger; **~stock** *m* (*Aus*) *siehe* **~klotz (a).**

Hader *m* **-s,** *no pl* (*geh*) (*Zwist*) discord; (*Unzufriedenheit*) discontentment. **in ~ mit sich und der Welt leben** to be at odds with oneself and the world.

Haderer *m* **-s, -** (*geh: unzufriedener Mensch*) grumbler.

Haderlump *m* (*Aus, S Ger*) good-for-nothing.

Hadern *pl* rags *pl* (*for making paper*).

hadern *vi* (*dated, geh*) (*streiten*) to quarrel, to wrangle (*mit* with); (*unzufrieden sein*) to be at odds (*mit* with). **hadere nicht mit deinem Schicksal** you must accept your fate.

Hadernpapier *nt* rag paper.

Hades *m* **-,** *no pl* (*Myth*) Hades.

Hadrian [(*S Ger, Aus*) 'ha:drian] *m* **-s** Hadrian.

Hadschi *m* **-s, -s** hajji.

Hafen[1] *m* **-s, ¨ (a)** harbour; (*Handels~, für große Schiffe*) port; (*Jacht~*) marina; (*~anlagen*) docks *pl*. **in den ~ einlaufen** to put into harbour/port. **(b)** (*fig*) haven. **im ~ der Ehe landen** to get married; **in den ~ der Ehe einlaufen** to enter the state of matrimony.

Hafen[2] *m* **-s, ¨** *or* **-** (*dial*) **(a)** (*Kochtopf*) pot, pan; (*Schüssel*) dish, bowl; (*Krug*) jug. **(b)** (*Nachttopf*) chamber-pot.

Häfen *m* **-, -** (*Aus*) **(a)** (*sauce*)pan. **(b)** (*inf: Gefängnis*) jug (*inf*), clink (*inf*).

Hafen-: *in cpds* harbour; port; **~amt** *nt* harbour/port authority; **~anlagen** *pl* docks *pl*; **~arbeiter** *m* dockworker, docker; **~arzt** *m* port doctor; **~behörden** *pl* harbour/port authorities *pl*; **~blockade** *f* blockade of a harbour/port.

Häfenbruder *m* (*Aus inf*) jailbird (*inf*).

Hafen-: **~einfahrt** *f* harbour entrance; **die ~einfahrt von Dover** the entrance to Dover Harbour; **~gebühr** *f usu pl* harbour/port dues *pl*; **~kneipe** *f* (*inf*) dockland pub (*Brit*) *or* bar; **~meister** *m* harbourmaster; **~polizei** *f* port *or* dock police; **~rundfahrt** *f* (boat-)trip round the harbour; **~stadt** *f* port; (*am Meer auch*) seaport; **~viertel** *nt* dock area.

Hafer *m* **-s, -** oats *pl*. **ihn sticht der ~** (*inf*) he's feeling his oats (*inf*).

Hafer-: **~brei** *m* porridge; **~flocken** *pl* rolled oats *pl*; **~grütze** *f* porridge; **~korn** *nt* (oat) grain.

Haferlschuh *m* type of brogue.

Hafer-: **~mehl** *nt* oatmeal; **~sack** *m* fodder bag; **~schleim** *m* gruel.

Haff *nt* **-(e)s, -s** *or* **-e** lagoon.

Haflinger *m* **-s, -** Haflinger (horse).

Hafner, Häfner *m* **-s, -** (*dial*) (*Töpfer*) potter; (*Ofensetzer*) stove-fitter.

Hafnerei (*dial*) (*Töpferei*) pottery; (*Ofensetzerbetrieb*) stove-fitter's works *sing or pl*.

Haft *f* **-,** *no pl* (*vor dem Prozeß*) custody; (*~strafe*) imprisonment; (*~zeit*) prison sentence, term of imprisonment; (*politisch*) detention. **sich in ~ befinden** to be in custody/prison/detention; **eine schwere/leichte ~ verhängen** to impose a long/short term of imprisonment; **jdn aus der ~ entlassen** to release sb from custody/prison/detention; **eine ~ absitzen** (*inf*) to do time (*inf*); **in ~ sitzen** to be held in custody/prison/detention; **in ~ nehmen** to take into custody, to detain.

-haft *adj suf* **(a)** (*-artig*) -like; -ish; -ly. **kind~** childlike; **jungen~** boyish; **frauen~** womanly; **riesen~** gigantic. **(b)** (*auf Eigenschaft bezüglich*) -ly; -ive. **leb~** lively; **schwatz~** talkative. **(c)** (*in Verbableitungen*) -ing. **wohn~** residing, resident. **(d)** (*Möglichkeit bezeichnend*) -ible, -able. **glaub~** credible, believable.

Haft-: **~anstalt** *f* detention centre; **~ausschließungsgrund** *m* grounds *pl* for not imposing a prison sentence; **~aussetzung** *f* suspended prison sentence; (*Unterbrechung*) parole; **h~bar** *adj* (*für jdn*) legally responsible; (*für etw*) (legally) liable; **~barkeit** *f siehe adj* (legal) responsibility; (legal) liability; **~befehl** *m* warrant; **einen ~befehl gegen jdn ausstellen** to issue a warrant for sb's arrest; **~beschwerde** *f* appeal against a remand in custody; ~**dauer** f term of imprisonment.

Haftel nt -s, - (Aus) hook and eye sing.

Haftelmacher m (Aus) **aufpassen wie ein ~** to watch like a hawk.

haften[1] vi (Jur) **für jdn ~** to be (legally) responsible for sb; **für etw ~** to be (legally) liable for sth; **(jdm) für jdn/etw ~** (verantwortlich sein) to be responsible (to sb) for sb/sth; **die Versicherung hat für den Schaden nicht gehaftet** the insurance company did not accept liability (for the damage); **für Garderobe kann nicht gehaftet werden** the management can accept no responsibility for articles deposited, all articles are left at owner's risk.

haften[2] vi (a) (kleben) to stick (an +dat to); (Klebstoff auch, Reifen, Phys) to adhere; (sich festsetzen: Rauch, Schmutz, Geruch) to cling (an +dat to). **an jdm ~** (fig: Makel etc) to hang over sb, to stick to sb.
(b) (Eindruck, Erinnerung) to stick (in one's mind); (Blick) to become fixed. **an etw** (dat) **~** (hängen) to be fixed on sth; **der Taube haftete an den Lippen des Lehrers** the deaf man's attention was fixed on the teacher's lips; **bei den Schülern haftet nichts** nothing sinks in with these pupils; **~de Eindrücke** lasting impressions.

haftenbleiben vi sep irreg aux sein to stick (an or auf +dat to); (sich festsetzen: Rauch, Schmutz, Geruch) to cling; (Klebstoff auch, Phys) to adhere; (Eindruck, Gelerntes) to stick.

Haft-: ~**entlassung** f release from custody/prison/detention; ~**entschädigung** f compensation for wrongful imprisonment; h~**fähig** adj (a) Material adhesive; Reifen with good road-holding; **auf etw** (dat) **h~fähig sein** to stick to sth; (b) (Jur) fit to be kept in prison; ~**fähigkeit** f (a) (von Material) adhesiveness, adhesive strength; (von Reifen) road-holding; (b) (Jur) fitness to be kept in prison; ~**gläser** pl siehe ~**schalen;** ~**grund** m (a) (Jur) grounds pl for detaining sb (in custody); (b) (Tech) base.

Häftling m prisoner; (politisch auch) detainee.

Haft-: ~**organ** nt suction pad; ~**pflicht** f (a) (Schadenersatzpflicht) (legal) liability; (für Personen) (legal) responsibility; **die ~pflicht der Versicherung erstreckt sich nicht auf Glas und Silber** the insurance does not cover glass and silver; (b) (inf: ~**pflichtversicherung**) personal or public (US) liability insurance; (für Auto) = third party insurance; **ich bin in keiner ~pflicht** I don't have any personal or etc liability insurance; h~**pflichtig** adj liable; h~**pflichtversichert** adj h~**pflichtversichert sein** to have personal liability insurance; (Autofahrer) = to have third-party insurance; ~**pflichtversicherung** f personal or public (US) liability insurance no indef art; (von Autofahrer) = third-party insurance; ~**prüfung** f review of remand in custody; ~**psychose** f prison psychosis no indef art; ~**reibung** f (Phys) static friction; ~**richter** m magistrate; ~**schalen** pl contact lenses pl; ~**strafe** f prison sentence; h~**unfähig** adj (Jur) unfit to be kept in prison.

Haftung f (a) (Jur) (legal) liability; (für Personen) (legal) responsibility. **für Ihre Garderobe übernehmen wir keine ~** articles are left at owner's risk, the management accepts no responsibility for articles deposited. (b) (Tech, Phys, von Reifen) adhesion.

Haftungsklage f action to establish liability.

Haft-: ~**urlaub** m parole; ~**verschonung** f exemption from imprisonment; ~**zeit** f prison sentence.

Hag m -(e)s, -e (poet, old) (Hain) grove; (Hecke) hedge.

Hage-: ~**buche** f siehe Hainbuche; ~**butte** f -, -n rose hip; (inf: Heckenrose) dogrose; ~**buttentee** m rose-hip tea; ~**dorn** m hawthorn.

Hagel m -s, no pl (a) hail; (~schauer) hailstorm. (b) (große Menge) (von Steinen, Geschossen) hail; (von Vorwürfen, Drohungen, Anschuldigungen) stream; (von Schimpfworten) stream, torrent.

Hagelkorn nt (a) hailstone. (b) (Med) eye cyst.

hageln 1 vi impers **es hagelt** it's hailing. 2 vi etw **hagelt auf jdn/etw** (Schläge, Geschosse, Steine) sth rains down on sb/sth; (Vorwürfe, Schimpfworte) sb is showered with sth. 3 vt impers (lit) to hail (down). **es hagelte etw** (fig) sth rained down; Vorwürfe, Schimpfworte there was a shower of sth.

Hagel-: ~**schaden** m damage caused by hail; ~**schauer** m (short) hailstorm; ~**schlag** m (a) (Met) hail; (~schauer) hailstorm; (b) (Cook) sugar crystals pl; ~**schloße** f (dial) siehe ~**korn;** ~**sturm** m hailstorm; ~**wetter** nt (lit) hailstorm; (fig: von Schimpfworten, Vorwürfen etc) stream, torrent.

hager adj gaunt, thin; Mensch auch lean.

Hagerkeit f siehe adj gauntness, thinness; leanness.

Hagestolz m -es, -e (old, hum) confirmed bachelor.

Hagio-: ~**graph** m (form) hagiographer; ~**graphen** pl (Bibl) Hagiographa; ~**graphie** f (form) hagiography.

haha, hahaha interj haha, ha, ha, ha.

Häher m -s, - jay.

Hahn m -(e)s, -e (a) (männlicher Vogel) cock; (männliches Haushuhn auch) rooster; (jünger) cockerel; (Wetter~) weathercock. **der gallische ~** the French cockerel; **~ im Korb sein** (Mann unter Frauen) to be cock of the walk; (wichtige Person) to be a big shot (inf); **danach kräht kein ~ mehr** (inf) no one cares two hoots about that any more (inf); **jdm den (roten) ~ aufs Dach setzen** to set sb's house on fire.
(b) pl auch -en (Tech) tap, faucet (US); (Zapf~ auch) spigot; (Schwimmer~) ballcock.
(c) (Abzug) trigger.

Hähnchen nt chicken; (junger Hahn) cockerel.

Hahnen-: ~**balken** m (Build) ridge beam; ~**feder** f cock's plume; ~**fuß** m (Bot) buttercup; ~**fußgewächs** nt buttercup; ~**kamm** m (auch Frisur) cockscomb; ~**kampf** m (a) cockfight;

(Sport) cockfighting; (b) (Spiel) children's hopping game; ~**schrei** m cockcrow; **beim ersten ~schrei** (fig) at cockcrow; ~**sporn** m cock's spur; ~**tritt(muster** nt) m dogtooth check.

Hahnrei m -s, -e (dated) cuckold. **jdn zum ~ machen** to cuckold sb.

Hai m -(e)s, -e, **Haifisch** m (lit, fig) shark.

Haifischflossensuppe f shark-fin soup.

Hain m -(e)s, -e (poet, geh) grove.

Hainbuche f hornbeam.

Haiti [ha'i:ti] nt -s Haiti.

Haitianer(in f) [hai'tia:nɐ, -ərɪn], **Haitier(in** f) [ha'i:tiɐ, -iərɪn] m -s, - Haitian.

haitianisch [hai'ti-], **haitisch** adj Haitian.

Häkchen nt (a) (Sew) (small) hook. **was ein ~ werden will, krümmt sich beizeiten** (Prov) there's nothing like starting young. (b) (Zeichen) tick. (c) (Instrument) dental probe.

Häkelarbeit f crochet (work) no indef art; (das Häkeln auch) crocheting; (Gegenstand) piece of crochet (work).

Häkelei f crocheting, crochet work.

Häkelgarn nt crochet thread.

häkeln 1 vi (Fingerhakeln machen) to finger-wrestle. 2 vti (a) (Ftbl, Hockey etc) siehe **haken** 3. (b) (Rugby) to heel. (c) (beim Ringen) Gegner to get in a foot-lock.

häkeln vti to crochet.

Häkelnadel f crochet hook.

haken 1 vi (klemmen) to stick. **es hakt** (fig inf) there's some delay; **es hakt (bei jdm)** (inf: nicht verstehen) sb is stuck.
2 vt (a) (befestigen) to hook (an +acc to).
(b) (einhängen, um etw legen) to hook (in +acc in, um around). **einen Hund mit der Leine an etw** (acc) **~** to tie a dog up to sth by its lead.
3 vti (Sport) to trip up.

Haken m -s, - (a) hook; (aus Holz auch) peg. **~ und Öse** hook and eye; **mit ~ und Ösen spielen** (Ftbl inf) to foul.
(b) (inf: Schwierigkeit) snag, catch. **die Sache hat einen ~** there's a snag or a catch.
(c) (plötzlicher Richtungswechsel) **einen ~ schlagen** to dart sideways; **~ pl schlagen** to dart from side to side.
(d) (Boxen) hook.
(e) (Zeichen) tick, check (US); (auf Buchstaben) hachek (spec), wedge, diacritic in the form of an inverted circumflex.

Haken-: h~**förmig** adj hooked, hook-shaped; ~**kreuz** nt swastika; ~**nase** f hooked nose, hooknose.

hakig adj siehe hakenförmig.

Halali nt -s, -(s) (Hunt) mort.

halb 1 adj (a) (Bruchteil) half; Lehrauftrag etc part-time. **ein ~er Kuchen/Meter** etc half a cake/metre etc; **der ~e Kuchen/Tag** etc half the cake/day etc; **ein ~e Stunde** half an hour; **alle ~e Stunde** every half hour; **ein ~es Jahr** six months pl, half a year; **ein ~es Dutzend** half a dozen; **auf ~er Höhe** at half the normal height; (zum Gipfel) halfway up; **auf ~em Wege** or ~**er Strecke** (lit) halfway; (fig) halfway through; **jdm auf ~em Weg entgegen kommen** (fig) to meet sb halfway; **das ~e Hundert** fifty, half a hundred (old); **zum ~en Preis** (at) half price; **den Apfel nur ~ essen** to eat only half the apple; **Kleid mit ~em Arm** dress with half-length sleeves.
(b) (Mus) **eine ~e Note** a minim (Brit), a half-note (US); **ein ~er Ton** a semitone; ~**e Pause** minim/half-note rest.
(c) inv (Uhrzeit) **~ zehn** half past nine; **fünf Minuten vor/nach ~ zwei** twenty-five (minutes) past two/to three; **es schlägt ~** it's striking the half hour; **um drei/fünf Minuten nach ~** three minutes past the half hour/at twenty-five to.
(d) inv, no art (bei geographischen Namen) **~ Deutschland/London** half of Germany/London.
(e) (teilweise, stückhaft) Maßnahmen half; Reformen partial; (vermindert) Tempo half; Lächeln slight; Licht poor. ~**e Arbeit leisten** to do a bad job; **die ~e Freude** half the pleasure; **die ~e Wahrheit** half of or part of the truth; **mit ~er Stimme** in a low voice; **ein ~er Blick** a quick glance; **nichts H~es und nichts Ganzes** neither one thing nor the other; **mit ~em Ohr** with half an ear; **ein ~er Mensch/eine ~e Frau sein, sich nur wie ein ~er Mensch fühlen** not to feel a complete person/woman; (energielos) to feel half dead; **eine ~e Sache machen** not to do it properly; **keine ~en Sachen machen** not to do things by halves.
(f) (inf) (große Anzahl, großer Teil) **die ~e Stadt/Welt/Arbeit** half the town/world/work; **sie ist schon eine ~e Schottin** she is already half Scottish; **ein ~er Elektriker/Mechaniker** something of an electrician/mechanic; (noch) **ein ~es Kind sein** to be hardly or scarcely more than a child.
2 adv (a) (zur Hälfte) half. **~ rechts/links abzweigen** (Straße, Fahrer) to fork (off) to the right/left, to turn half right/left; **die Zeit ist ~ vorbei** half the time has already gone.
(b) (nicht ganz, teilweise) half. **~ so gut** half as good; **etw nur ~ verstehen** to only half understand something; **ich hörte nur ~ zu** I was only half listening; **das ist ~ so schlimm** it's not as bad as all that; (Zukünftiges) that won't be too bad; **er weiß alles nur ~** he only knows about things superficially **etw nur ~ machen** to only half-do sth (inf).
(c) (fast vollständig) almost, nearly; blind, roh half. **ich war schon ~ fertig** I was almost or nearly finished; **wir haben uns ~ totgelacht** we almost died laughing; **ich hätte mich ~ totärgern können** I could have kicked myself (inf).
(d) ~ **lachend, ~ weinend** half laughing, half crying; ~ **Mensch, ~ Pferd** half or part man, half or part horse.
(e) **mit jdm ~ und ~ or ~e-~e machen** (inf) to go halves with sb; ~ **und ~** (inf: beinahe) more or less; **gefällt es dir? — ~ und ~** do you like it? — sort of (inf) or so-so.

halb- pref (a) half. ~**voll/~leer** half-full/-empty. (b) (Tech) semi-.

Halb-: ~affe *m* prosimian; h~amtlich *adj* semi-official; ~bildung *f* smattering of knowledge *or* (*Ausbildung*) education; h~bitter *adj Schokolade* semi-sweet; ~blut *nt* -(e)s, *no pl* (a) (*Mensch*) half-caste; (b) (*Tier*) crossbreed; ~blüter *m* -s, - crossbreed; ~blütige(r) *mf decl as adj* half-caste; ~bruder *m* half-brother; h~bürtig *adj* half related by birth; h~dunkel *adj* half-dark, dim; ~dunkel *nt* semi-darkness, half-dark; (*Dämmerung*) dusk, twilight.

Halbe *f decl as adj* (*esp S Ger*) siehe **Halbe(r)**.

Halb|edelstein *m* semi-precious stone.

Halbe(r) *m decl as adj* half a litre (of beer). **trinken Sie noch einen ~n!** ≈ have another pint!

halber[1] *prep* +*gen* (*nachgestellt*) (*dated, geh*) (*wegen*) on account of; (*um ...willen*) for the sake of.

halber[2] *adj, adv* (*S Ger*) siehe **halb 1** (c), **2** (b, c).

-halber *adv suf* (*wegen*) on account of; (*um ...willen*) for the sake of. **gesundheits~** for reasons of health, for medical reasons; **vorsichts~** to be on the safe side, as a precaution; **sicherheits~** (*aus Sicherheitsgründen*) for safety reasons; (*um sicher zu sein*) to be on the safe side.

Halb-: h~erwachsen *adj attr* half grown (up); ~erzeugnis *nt* (*Comm*) semi-finished product.

Halbe(s) *nt decl as adj* siehe **Halbe(r)**.

Halb-: ~fabrikat *nt siehe* ~erzeugnis; h~fertig *adj attr* half-finished; (*fig*) immature; h~fest *adj attr Zustand, Materie* semi-solid; *Gelee* half-set; h~fett **1** *adj* (a) (*Typ*) secondary bold; (b) *Lebensmittel* medium-fat; **2** *adv* in secondary bold; ~finale *nt* semi-final; ~freie(r) *mf decl as adj person* halfway between serf and free person; h~gar *adj attr* half-cooked, half-done; h~gebildet *adj attr* half-educated; ~geschoß *nt* (*Archit*) mezzanine floor; ~geschwister *pl* half brothers and sisters *pl*; ~gott *m* (*Myth, fig*) demigod; ~götter in Weiß (*inf*) doctors.

Halbheit *f* (*pej*) half-measure. **er ist nicht für ~en** he is not one for half-measures, he doesn't do things by halves; **mach keine ~en** (*inf*) don't do things by halves.

Halb-: h~herzig *adj* half-hearted; ~herzigkeit *f* half-heartedness; h~hoch *adj Baum* half-grown; **den Ball h~hoch abspielen** to pass the ball at shoulder height; h~hoch fliegen to fly at half (its/one's *etc* normal) height.

halbieren* *vt* to halve, to divide in half *or* two; (*Geometrie*) to bisect; (*in zwei schneiden*) to cut in half. **eine Zahl ~** to divide a number by two.

Halbierung *f* halving, dividing in half *or* two; (*Geometrie*) bisection.

Halb-: ~insel *f* peninsula; ~invalide *m* semi-invalid.

Halbjahr *nt* half-year (*auch Comm*), six months. **im ersten/zweiten ~** in the first/last six months of the year.

Halbjahres-: ~bericht *m* half-yearly report; ~bilanz *f* half-yearly figures *pl*; ~kurs *m* six-month course; ~zeugnis *nt* (*Sch*) half-yearly report.

Halb-: h~jährig *adj Kind* six-month-old; *Lehrgang etc* six-month; *Kündigung* six months; h~jährlich **1** *adj* half-yearly (*auch Comm*), six-monthly; **in h~jährlichem Wechsel** changing every six months; **2** *adv* every six months, twice a year, twice yearly; ~jahrsausweis *m* (*Aus Sch*) half-yearly report; ~jahrskurs *m siehe* ~jahreskurs; ~jude *m* half Jew; ~jude sein to be half Jewish; ~kanton *m* sub-canton; ~konsonant *m* semi-consonant; ~kreis *m* semicircle; h~kreisförmig **1** *adj* semicircular; **2** *adv* in a semicircle; ~kugel *f* hemisphere; nördliche/südliche ~kugel northern/southern hemisphere; h~kugelförmig *adj* hemispherical; h~lang *adj Kleid, Rock* mid-calf length; *Haar* chin-length; (nun) mach (es) mal h~lang! (*inf*) now wait a minute!; h~laut **1** *adj* low; **2** *adv* in a low voice, in an undertone; ~leder *nt* (*Verfahren*) half-binding; in ~leder binden to bind in half-leather, to half-bind; ~lederband *m* (*Buch*) half-bound volume; (*Ausgabe*) half-bound edition; h~leinen *adj attr Stoff* made of a fifty per cent linen mixture; *Bucheinband* half-cloth; ~leinen *nt* (*Stoff*) fifty per cent linen material; (*Bucheinband*) half-cloth; ~leinenband *m* (*Buch*) volume bound in half-cloth; (*Ausgabe*) edition bound in half-cloth; ~leiter *m* (*Phys*) semiconductor; h~linke(r, s) *adj attr* (*Sport*) inside left; die h~linke Abzweigung/Straße the left fork; ~linke(r) *m decl as adj*, ~links *m* -, - (*Sport*) inside left; h~links *adv* (*Sport*) spielen (at) inside left; (*im Theater*) sitzen left of centre; h~links abbiegen to fork left; die Straße h~links the left fork; das Auto kam von h~links the car approached sharp left; h~mast *adv* (a) at half-mast; (eine Flagge) h~mast hissen to hoist a flag to half-mast; ~mast flaggen to fly a flag/flags at half-mast; auf h~mast stehen to fly *or* be at half-mast; (b) (hum: verrutschte Socken etc) at half-mast; h~matt *adj* (*Phot*) semimatt; ~messer *m siehe* Radius; ~metall *nt* semi-metal; ~monatsschrift *f* fortnightly periodical; ~mond *m* (*Astron*) half-moon; (*Symbol*) crescent; (an Fingernägeln) half-moon; bei ~mond when there is a half-moon; wir haben ~mond there's a half-moon; h~mondförmig *adj* crescent-shaped; h~nackt *adj attr* half-naked; *Arm* half-covered; h~offen *adj attr* half-open; *Gefängnis* open; h~part *adv* h~part machen (bei einer Unternehmung) to go halves; (bei Gewinn) to split it fifty-fifty; ~pension *f* half-board; in ~pension wohnen to have half-board; ~produkt *nt siehe* ~erzeugnis; h~rechte(r, s) *adj* (*Sport*) inside right; die h~rechte Abzweigung/Straße the right fork; ~rechte(r) *m decl as adj*, ~rechts *m* -, - (*Sport*) inside right; h~rechts *adv* (*Sport*) spielen (at) inside right; (*im Theater*) sitzen right of centre; h~rechts abbiegen to fork right; die Straße h~rechts the right fork; das Auto kam von h~rechts the car approached sharp right; h~reif *adj attr* half-ripe; ~relief *nt* half-relief, mezzo relievo; h~rund *adj attr* half round; *Tisch etc* semicircular; *Ecke* half-rounded; ~rund *nt* semicircle, half circle; im ~rund in a semicircle; ~schatten *m* half shadow;

(*Astron*) penumbra; ~schlaf *m* light sleep, doze; im ~schlaf sein to be half asleep; ~schuh *m* shoe; ~schwergewicht *nt* (a) *no pl* (*Klasse*) light-heavyweight division; ein Boxkampf im ~schwergewicht a light-heavyweight contest; (b) (*Boxer*) light-heavyweight; ~schwergewichtler *m* light-heavyweight; ~schwester *f* half-sister; ~seide *f* fifty per cent silk mixture; h~seiden *adj* (*lit*) fifty per cent silk; (*fig*) *Dame* fast; *Aussehen* flashy; (*schwul*) gay; h~seidenes Milieu/Kreise the demimonde; h~seitig *adj Anzeige etc* half-page; (*Med*) *Kopfschmerzen* in one side of one's head; h~seitige Lähmung hemiplegia; h~seitig gelähmt hemiplegic; h~staatlich *adj attr* partly state-run *or* state-controlled; h~stark *adj attr Sprache, Manieren, Jugendliche* rowdy; ~starke(r) *m decl as adj* young hooligan *or* rowdy, ≈ teddy boy (*Brit*); h~stündig *adj attr* half-hour *attr*, lasting half an hour; h~stündlich **1** *adj* half-hourly; **2** *adv* every half an hour, half-hourly; ~stürmer *m* (*Ftbl*) half-back; h~tags *adv* in the mornings/afternoons; (*in bezug auf Angestellte auch*) part-time.

Halbtags-: ~arbeit *f* (a) (*Arbeitsverhältnis*) half-day *or* morning/afternoon job; (*von Angestellten auch*) part-time job; (b) (*Arbeitszeit*) half-time/part-time working; ~beschäftigung *f* half-day *or* part-time *or* morning/afternoon job; ~kraft *f* worker employed for half-days *or* mornings/afternoons only; ~schule *f* half-day school.

Halb-: ~teil *m or nt siehe* Hälfte; ~ton *m* (*Mus*) semitone; (*Art, Phot*) half-tone; ~tonschritt *m* semitone; h~tot *adj* (*lit*) half dead; ~totale *f* (*Film*) medium shot; ~trauer *f* half-mourning; h~verdaut *adj attr* (*lit, fig*) half-digested; ~vers *m* half-line, hemistich; ~vokal *m* semivowel; h~voll *adj attr* half-filled; *Behälter auch* half-full; h~wach *adj attr* half awake; in h~wachem Zustand half awake; ~wahrheit *f* half-truth; ~waise *f child who has lost one parent*; er/sie ist ~waise he/she has lost one of his/her parents; h~wegs *adv* (a) partly; *gut, adäquat* reasonably; wenn es dir wieder h~wegs besser geht when you're feeling a bit better; wenn Sie h~wegs eine Vorstellung haben, ... if you have the least idea; (b) (*dated: auf halber Strecke*) halfway; ~welt *f* demimonde; ~weltdame *f* demimondaine; ~weltergewicht *nt* (*Klasse*) light-welterweight *no def art*; (*Sportler*) light-welterweight; ~wertszeit *f* (*Phys*) half-life; h~wild *adj attr* Mensch uncivilized; *Tier* half wild; wie die ~wilden (*inf*) like (a bunch of) savages; ~wissen *nt* (*pej*) superficial knowledge; h~wöchentlich **1** *adj* twice-weekly; **2** *adv* twice weekly; h~wüchsig *adj* adolescent; ~wüchsige(r) *mf decl as adj* adolescent; ~zeile *f* (*Poet*) half line; ~zeit *f* (*Sport*) (*Hälfte*) half; (*Pause*) half-time; ~zeitpfiff *m* half-time whistle; h~zivilisiert *adj attr* half-civilized.

Halde *f* -, -n (a) (*Abfall~*) mound, heap; (*Min*) (*Abbau~*) slagheap; (*von Vorräten*) pile. (b) (*geh: Abhang*) slope.

half *pret of* **helfen**.

Half-Back ['haːfbɛk] *m* -s, -s (*Sw*) half-back.

Hälfte *f* -, -n (a) half. die ~ der Kinder war abwesend half the children were absent; die ~ einer Sache (*gen*) *or* von etw half (of) sth; eine/die ~ des Apfels half of/half (of) the apple; wir haben schon die ~ (des Vorrats) verbraucht we have already used up half (the stocks); die ~ ist gelogen half of it is lies; Rentner zahlen die ~ pensioners pay half price; um die ~ mehr/zuviel half as much again/too much by half; um die ~ steigen to increase by half *or* fifty per cent; um die ~ kleiner/größer half as small *or* big/half as big again; es ist zur ~ fertig/voll it is half finished/full; die Beiträge werden je zur ~ vom Arbeitgeber und Arbeitnehmer bezahlt the employer and employee each pay half (of) the contribution; das werde ich zur ~ bezahlen I will pay half (of it); meine bessere ~ (hum inf) my better half (*hum inf*). (b) (*Mitte: einer Fläche*) middle. auf der ~ des Weges halfway.

hälften *vt* (*rare*) siehe **halbieren**.

Halfter[1] *m or nt* -s, - (für Tiere) halter.

Halfter[2] *f* -, -n *or nt* -s, - (*Pistolen*) holster.

halftern *vt* to halter, to put a halter on.

halkyonisch *adj* (*liter*) ~e Tage halcyon days.

Hall *m* -(e)s, -e (a) reverberation, echo. (b) (*Nachhall*) echo.

Halle *f* -, -n hall; (*Hotel~*) lobby, vestibule; (*Werks~, Fabrik~*) shed; (*Sport~*) (sports) hall, gym(nasium); (*Tennis~*) covered tennis court(s); (*Schwimm~*) indoor swimming pool; (*Flugzeug~*) hangar. in der ~ (*im Gegensatz zu draußen*) inside, indoors; Fußball in der ~ indoor football; in der ~ des Postamts (in the post office; in diesen heiligen ~n (iro) in these august surroundings (iro).

halleluja(h) *interj* halleluja(h).

Halleluja(h) *nt* -s, -s (*Rel, Mus*) halleluja(h). das ~ aus Händels „Messias" the Hallelujah Chorus from Handel's "Messiah".

hallen *vi* to reverberate, to echo (*auch fig*), to resound.

Hallen- *in cpds* (*Sport*) indoor; ~bad *nt* indoor swimming pool; ~fußball *m* indoor football; ~kirche *f* hall church; ~schwimmbad *nt* indoor swimming pool; ~sport *m* indoor sport(s); ~tennis *nt* indoor tennis.

Hallig *f* -, -en *a small island off Schleswig-Holstein*.

Hallimasch *m* -(e)s, -e (*Bot*) honey agaric.

hallo *interj* (a) ['halo] hello; (zur Begrüßung auch) hi (*inf*). (b) [ha'loː] (überrascht) hello.

Hallo *nt* -s, -s cheer *usu pl*; (*Gruß*) hello.

Hallodri *m* -s, -(s) (*Aus, S Ger inf*) rogue.

Hallstattzeit *f* (*Archeol*) Hallstatt period.

Halluzination *f* hallucination. an ~en leiden to suffer from hallucinations; ich leide wohl an ~en (*fig*) I must be seeing things.

halluzinatorisch *adj* hallucinatory.

halluzinieren* vi to hallucinate.

halluzinogen adj (Med) hallucinogenic.

Halluzinogen nt -s, -e (Med) hallucinogen.

Halm m -(e)s, -e stalk, stem; (Gras~) blade of grass; (Stroh~, zum Trinken) straw. **Getreide auf dem** ~ standing grain.

Halma nt -s, no pl halma.

Halmafigur f, **Halmastein** m halma piece.

Hälmchen nt dim of **Halm**.

Halo m -(s), -s or -nen [-'lo:nən] (Astron, Met) halo; (TV) shadow.

halogen adj halogenous.

Halogen nt -s, -e halogen.

Halogen-: ~(glüh)lampe f halogen lamp; ~licht nt halogen light; ~scheinwerfer m halogen headlamp.

Hals¹ m -es, ⁻e (a) (von außen gesehen) neck. **einen langen** ~ **machen, den** ~ **recken** to crane one's neck; **sich** (dat) **nach jdm/etw den** ~ **verrenken** (inf) to crane one's neck to see sb/sth; **jdm um den** ~ **fallen** to fling one's arms around sb's neck; **sich jdm an den** ~ **werfen** (fig inf) to throw oneself at sb; **sich** (dat) **den** ~ **brechen** (inf) to break one's neck; **etw kostet jdn** or **jdm** or **bricht jdm den** ~ (inf) sth will cost sb his/her neck; **sich um den** or **seinen** ~ **reden** (inf) to put one's head in the noose; ~ **über Kopf abreisen/den Koffer packen** to leave/pack one's case in a rush or hurry; **ihm steht das Wasser bis zum** ~ (fig) he is up to his neck in it (inf); **bis über den** ~ (fig inf) up to one's ears; **jdn auf dem** or **am** ~ **haben** (inf) to be lumbered or saddled with sb (inf); **jdm/sich etw auf den** ~ **laden** (inf) to lumber or saddle sb/oneself with sth (inf); **sich jdm auf den** ~ **schicken** or **hetzen** (inf) to put sb onto sb; **jdm mit etw vom** ~(e) **bleiben** (inf) to keep sth out of sb's hair (inf); **sich/jdm jdn/etw vom** ~e **schaffen** (inf) to get sb/sth off one's/sb's back (inf); **sich** (dat) **die Pest an den** ~ **ärgern (können)** to be mad or furious with oneself (mit over).

(b) (Kehle, Rachen) throat. **sie hat es am** or **im** ~ (inf) she has a sore throat; **aus vollem** ~(e) **lachen** to roar with laughter; **es hängt** or **wächst mir zum** ~ **heraus** (inf) I'm sick and tired of it, I've had it up to here (inf); **sie hat es in den falschen** or **verkehrten** ~ **bekommen** (inf) (sich verschlucken) it went down the wrong way; (falsch verstehen) she took it wrongly; **etw bleibt jdm im** ~ **stecken** (lit, fig) sth sticks in sb's throat; **er kann den** ~ **nicht voll (genug) kriegen** (fig inf) he is never satisfied.

(c) (Flaschen~, Geigen~, Säulen~) neck; (Noten~) stem; siehe **brechen**.

(d) (von Knochen) neck; (Gebärmutter~) cervix, neck of the womb.

Hals² m -es,-en (Naut) tack.

Hals-: ~abschneider m -s, - (pej inf) shark (inf); h~abschneiderisch adj (pej inf) Preise, Maßnahme extortionate, exorbitant; Mensch cutthroat (inf); ~ansatz m base of the neck; ~ausschnitt m neck(line); ~band nt (Hunde~) collar; (Schmuck) necklace; (eng anliegend) choker; h~brecherisch adj dangerous, risky; Tempo breakneck; Fahrt hair-raising; Weg treacherous; ~bund m, ~bündchen nt neckband.

Hälschen ['helsçən] nt dim of **Hals¹**.

halsen¹ vt (rare) to embrace.

halsen² vi (Naut) to wear.

Hals-: ~entzündung f sore throat; ~gericht nt (Hist) court dealing with capital offences.

-halsig adj suf -necked.

Hals-: ~kette f (Schmuck) necklace; (für Hund) chain; ~krause f (Fashion, Zool) ruff; ~länge f neck; (um) eine ~länge/zwei ~längen by a neck/half a length; h~los adj without a neck.

Hals-Nasen-Ohren-: ~-Arzt m ear, nose and throat specialist; ~-Heilkunde f ear, nose and throat medicine; ~-Krankheit f disease of the ear, nose and throat.

Hals-: ~partie f neck/throat area, area or region of the neck/throat; ~schlagader f carotid (artery); ~schmerzen pl sore throat sing; ~schmuck m necklace; (Sammelbegriff) necklaces pl; h~starrig adj obstinate, stubborn; ~starrigkeit f obstinacy, stubbornness; ~stück nt (Cook) neck; ~tuch nt scarf; ~- und Beinbruch interj good luck; ~weh nt siehe ~schmerzen; ~weite f neck size; ~wickel m (Med) hot compress (applied to the throat); ~wirbel m cervical vertebra.

Halt m -(e)s, -e (a) (für Füße, Hände, Festigkeit) hold; (lit, fig: Stütze) support; (fig: innerer ~) security no art. ~/einen besseren ~ **haben** (Ding) to hold/hold better; **keinen** ~ **haben** to have no hold/support; to be insecure; ~ **suchen/finden** to look for/find a hold/a support/security; **auf dem Eis den** ~ **verlieren** to lose one's footing on the ice; **ohne inneren** ~ insecure.

(b) (geh: Anhalten) stop. **ohne** ~ non-stop, without stopping.

halt¹ interj stop; (Mil) halt.

halt² adv (dial) (a) siehe **eben** 2 (d). (b) (Aus) **und so** ~ **and so on** or forth.

haltbar adj (a) (nicht leicht verderblich) ~ **sein** (Lebensmittel) to keep (well); ~e **Lebensmittel** food which keeps (well); **das ist sechs Monate** ~ that will keep for six months; **etw** ~ **machen** to preserve sth; ~ **bis 6.11.** use by 6 Nov; **nur begrenzt/schlecht** ~ perishable/highly perishable.

(b) (widerstandsfähig) durable; Stoff, Kleider hardwearing; Beziehung, Ehe long-lasting.

(c) Behauptung, Theorie, Annahme tenable.

(d) pred Festung defensible. **die Stadt ist nicht mehr** ~ the town can't be held any longer.

(e) Position, Rang, Platz tenable; Zustand, Lage tolerable. **diese Position ist nicht mehr** ~ this position can't be maintained any longer.

(f) (Sport) Ball, Wurf stoppable; Schuß auch savable.

haltbargemacht adj attr artificially preserved.

Haltbarkeit f siehe adj (a–c) (a) (von Lebensmitteln) **die** ~ **von Fisch beträgt nur ein paar Tage** fish will only keep for a few days; **eine längere** ~ **haben** to keep longer; **Lebensmittel von kurzer** ~ perishable food; **die begrenzte** ~ **von Fleisch** the perishability of meat.

(b) durability; hard-wearingness; long-lastingness.

(c) tenability.

Haltbarkeits-: ~datum nt eat-by date; ~dauer f length of time for which food may be kept; **eine kurze/lange** ~dauer **haben** to be/not to be perishable.

Halte-: ~bogen m (Mus) tie; ~griff m (a) grip, handle; (in Bus) strap; (an Badewanne) handrail; (b) (Sport) hold; ~gurt m seat or safety belt; (an Kinderwagen) safety harness.

halten pret **hielt**, ptp **gehalten** 1 vt (a) (festhalten, in Position ~) to hold; (fig: behalten) to keep; (aufhalten, zurückhalten) to stop. **jdm etw** ~ to hold sth for sb; **sich** (dat) **den Kopf/Bauch** ~ to hold one's head/stomach; **den Schnabel** or **Mund** ~ (inf) to keep one's mouth shut (inf), to hold one's tongue; **jdm den Mantel** ~ to hold sb's coat (for him/her); **ich konnte ihn/es gerade noch** ~ I just managed to grab hold of him/it; **sie läßt sich nicht** ~, **sie ist nicht zu** ~ (fig) there's no holding her; **es hält mich hier nichts mehr** there's nothing to keep me here any more; **es hält dich niemand** nobody's stopping you.

(b) (in Position bringen) **einen Fuß ins Wasser** ~ to put one's foot into the water; **etw gegen das Licht** ~ to hold sth up to the light; **den Arm in die Höhe** ~ to hold one's arm up.

(c) (tragen, stützen) Bild, Regal, Brücke to hold up.

(d) (zurückhalten, in sich ~, fassen) to hold; Tränen to hold or keep back. **die Wärme/Feuchtigkeit** ~ to retain heat/moisture; **dieses Material hält keinen Lack** this material will not take varnish; **er kann den Urin** or **das Wasser nicht** ~ he can't hold his water, he's incontinent.

(e) (Sport) to save.

(f) (unterhalten, besitzen) Haustier to keep; Chauffeur, Lehrer to employ; Auto to run. **sich** (dat) **jdn/etw** ~ to keep sb/sth; **jdm etw** ~ to keep sth for sb; **wir können uns kein Auto** ~ we can't afford to run a car.

(g) (abonniert haben) (sich dat) **eine Zeitung** etc ~ to take a paper etc.

(h) (behandeln) to treat. **er hält seine Kinder sehr streng** he's very strict with his children.

(i) (behalten) to keep; Besitz auch to hold on to; Festung to hold; Position to hold (on to); Rekord (innehaben) to hold; (beibehalten) to keep up.

(j) (beibehalten, aufrechterhalten) to keep up, to maintain; Disziplin, Temperatur to maintain; Kurs to keep to, to hold. **Ruhe** ~ to keep quiet; **die Balance** or **das Gleichgewicht** ~ to keep one's balance; **den Ton** ~ to stay in tune or in key; **die These läßt sich nicht länger/ist nicht länger zu** ~ this thesis is no longer tenable; **Kontakt** ~ to keep in touch, to maintain contact; (mit jdm) **Verbindung** ~ to keep in touch (with sb).

(k) (in einem Zustand, an einem Ort ~) to keep. **er hält sein Haus immer tadellos** he always keeps his house spotless; **den Abstand gleich** ~ to keep the distance the same; **ein Land besetzt** ~ to keep a country under occupation.

(l) (handhaben, verfahren mit) **es mit etw so/anders** ~ to deal with or handle sth like this/differently; **wie hältst du's mit der Religion?** what's your attitude towards religion?; **das kannst du** ~ **wie du willst** that's completely up to you.

(m) (Neigung haben für) **es (mehr or lieber) mit jdm/etw** ~ (Neigung haben für) to prefer sb/sth; (einverstanden sein) to agree with sb/sth; **er hält es mit der Bequemlichkeit/Sauberkeit** he likes things to be comfortable/clean; **er soll es ja angeblich mit seiner Sekretärin** ~ (hum) he's supposed to be having an affair with his secretary.

(n) (gestalten) to do; Aufsatz to write; Zimmer auch to decorate. **ein in Braun gehaltener Raum** a room decorated in brown; **das Kleid ist in dunklen Tönen gehalten** the dress is in dark colours; **das Mobiliar ist in einem hellen Holz gehalten** the furniture is made of a light wood; **etw einfach** ~ to keep sth simple.

(o) (veranstalten, abhalten) to give; Rede auch to make; Gottesdienst, Zwiesprache to hold; Wache to keep. **Mittagsschlaf** ~ to have an afternoon nap; **Winterschlaf** ~ to hibernate; **Unterricht** ~ to teach; **Selbstgespräche** ~ to talk to oneself.

(p) (einhalten, erfüllen) to keep. **man muß** ~, **was man verspricht** a promise is a promise; **der Film hält nicht, was er/der Titel verspricht** the film doesn't live up to expectations/its title.

(q) (einschätzen) jdn/etw für jdn/etw ~ to take sb/sth for or to be sb/sth; **ich habe ihn (irrtümlich) für seinen Bruder gehalten** I (mis)took him for his brother; **jdn für ehrlich** ~ to think or consider sb is honest; **es für Unsinn** ~ to think or consider sth is nonsense; **wofür** ~ **Sie mich?** what do you take me for?; **das halte ich nicht für möglich** I don't think that is possible.

(r) (denken über) etw von jdm/etw ~ to think sth of sb/sth; **ich halte nichts davon, das zu tun** I don't think much of doing that; **etwas/viel auf etw** (acc) ~ to place some/great emphasis on sth, to attach some/great importance or value to sth; **du solltest mehr auf dich** ~ (auf Äußeres achten) you should take more pride in yourself; (selbstbewußt sein) you should be more self-confident; **wenn man etwas auf sich** (acc) **hält ...** if you think you're somebody ...; **nicht viel von jdm/etw** ~ not to think much of sb/sth; **nicht viel vom Beten/Sparen** etc ~ not to be a great one for praying/saving etc (inf).

2 vi (a) (festhalten, zusammenhalten, standhalten) to hold; (haftenbleiben auch) to stick. **kannst du mal 'n Moment** ~? can you just hold that (for) a moment?

(b) (bestehen bleiben, haltbar sein, heil bleiben) to last;

(Konserven auch) to keep; *(Wetter auch, Frisur, Comm: Preise)* to hold; *(Stoff)* to wear well. **dieser Stoff hält lang** this material wears well.

(c) *(stehenbleiben, anhalten)* to stop. **ein ~der Wagen** a stationary car; **zum H~ bringen** to bring to a stop or standstill; **~ lassen** *(Mil)* to call a halt; **halt mal, ...** *(Moment mal)* hang *(inf)* or hold on, ...; **halt mal, stop** *(hum)* hang *(inf)* or hold on a minute!; *siehe* **halt[1]**.

(d) *(Sport)* to make a save. **unser Tormann hat heute wieder großartig gehalten** our goalkeeper made some good saves again today; **kann der denn (gut) ~?** is he a good goalkeeper?

(e) *(in einem Zustand erhalten)* **Sport hält jung** sport keeps you young; **die Plastikverpackung hält frisch** the plastic wrapping keeps things fresh.

(f) **auf etw** *(acc)* **~** *(zielen)* to aim at sth; *(steuern)* to head for sth; **etwas mehr nach links ~** to keep more to the left; *(zielen)* to aim more to the left; **nach Süden/auf Chikago ~** to head south/for Chicago.

(g) *(jdm beistehen, treu sein)* **zu jdm ~** to stand or stick by sb; *(favorisieren)* to support sb.

(h) *(Wert legen auf, praktizieren)* **(sehr) auf etw** *(acc)* **~** to attach (a lot of) importance to sth.

(i) *(stolz sein)* **auf sich** *(acc)* **~** *(auf Äußeres achten)* to take a pride in oneself; *(selbstbewußt sein)* to be self-confident.

(j) *(sich beherrschen)* **an sich** *(acc)* **~** to control oneself.

3 *vr* **(a)** *(sich festhalten)* to hold on *(an + dat* -to).

(b) *(sich nicht verändern, nicht verderben)* to keep; *(Blumen auch, Wetter)* to last; *(Preise)* to hold. **er hat sich gut gehalten** *(inf)* he's well-preserved.

(c) *(bleiben)* to stay. **der Autofahrer hielt sich ganz rechts** the driver kept to the right; **ich halte mich an meine alte Werkstatt/die alte Methode** I'll stick to or with or stay with my old workshop/the old method.

(d) *(nicht verschwinden)* to last; *(Schnee auch)* to stay; *(Geruch, Rauch)* to stay, to hang around.

(e) *(sich orientieren nach, sich richten nach)* to keep *(an +acc, nach* to). **sich an ein Versprechen ~** to keep a promise; **sich an die Tatsachen/den Text ~** to keep or stick to the facts/text; **sich (nach) links ~** to keep (to the) left; **sich nach Westen ~** to keep going westwards; *siehe* **Vorschrift**.

(f) *(seine Position behaupten)* to hold or hang on; *(haften)* to hold, to stick. **sich auf den Beinen ~** to stay on one's feet.

(g) *(sich behaupten)* to bear up; *(im Kampf)* to hold out. **sich gut ~** *(in Prüfung, Spiel etc)* to make a good showing, to do well.

(h) *(sich beherrschen)* to control oneself. **sich nicht ~ können** to be unable to control oneself.

(i) *(eine bestimmte Haltung haben)* to carry or hold oneself. **er hält sich sehr aufrecht/gerade** he holds or carries himself very erect/straight; **sich (im Gleichgewicht) ~** to keep one's balance; *siehe* **Bein**.

(j) **sich an jdn ~** *(sich wenden an)* to ask sb; *(sich richten nach)* to follow sb; *(sich gut stellen mit)* to keep in with sb; **ich halte mich lieber an den Wein** I'd rather keep or stick to wine.

(k) **er hält sich für einen Spezialisten/besonders klug** he thinks he's a specialist/very clever.

Halte-: **~platz** *m (Taxi~)* taxi rank or stand; **~punkt** *m (Rail)* stop.

Halter *m -s, -* **(a)** *(Halterung)* holder; *(Handtuch~)* (towel) rail/ring etc. **(b)** *(Feder~, Füll~)* pen. **(c)** *(Socken~)* garter; *(Strumpf~, Hüft~)* suspender *(Brit)* or garter *(US)* belt; *(Büsten~)* bra. *(Kerzen~)* candlestick, candle holder. **(e)** *(Jur) (Kraftfahrzeug~, Tier~)* owner. **(f)** *(rare: Griff)* handle.

Halteriemen *m* strap.

Halterung *f* mounting; *(für Regal etc)* support.

Halte-: **~schild** *nt* stop or halt sign; **~schlaufe** *f (in Bus etc)* strap; **~signal** *nt (Rail)* stop signal; **~stelle** *f* stop; **~verbot** *nt* (absolutes or uneingeschränktes) **~verbot** no stopping; *(Stelle)* no stopping zone; **eingeschränktes ~verbot** no waiting; *(Stelle)* no waiting zone; **hier ist ~verbot** there's no stopping here; **~verbot(s)schild** *nt* no stopping sign; **~vorrichtung** *f siehe* **Halterung**.

-haltig, -hältig *(Aus) adj suf* containing. **stark alkohol~** containing a lot of alcohol, with a high alcohol content.

Halt-: **h~los** *adj (schwach)* insecure; *(hemmungslos)* unrestrained; *(unbegründet)* groundless, unfounded; **~losigkeit** *f siehe adj* lack of security; uninhibitedness; groundlessness; **h~machen** *vi* say to stop; **vor nichts h~machen** *(fig)* to stop at nothing; **vor niemandem h~machen** *(fig)* to spare no-one; **~signal** *nt (Rail)* stop signal; **~taste** *f* pause button.

Haltung *f* **(a)** *(Körper~)* posture; *(Stellung)* position; *(esp Sport) (typische Stellung)* stance; *(bei der Ausführung)* style. **~ annehmen** *(esp Mil)* to stand to attention.

(b) *(fig) (Auftreten)* manner; *(Einstellung)* attitude. **in majestätischer/würdiger ~** with majestic/dignified bearing.

(c) *no pl (Beherrschtheit)* composure. **~ bewahren** to keep one's composure.

(d) *no pl (von Tieren, Fahrzeugen)* owning.

Haltungs-: **~fehler** *m* **(a)** *(Med)* bad posture *no indef art, no pl*; **(b)** *(Sport)* style fault; **~mängel** *pl* bad posture *sing*; **~schaden** *m* damaged posture *no pl*; **zu ~schaden führen** to damage one's posture.

Halt-: **~verbot** *nt (form) siehe* **Halteverbot**; **~zeichen** *nt siehe* **Haltesignal**.

Halunke *m -n, -n* **(a)** a scoundrel; **(b)** *(hum)* rascal, scamp.

Ham and eggs ['hæm ənd 'ɛgz] *pl* bacon or ham *(US)* and eggs *sing* or *pl*.

Hämatit *m -s, -e* haematite.

Hämatologe *m*, **Hämatologin** *f* haematologist.

Hämatologie *f* haematology.

hämatologisch *adj* haematological.

Hämatom *nt -s, -e* haematoma.

Hamburg *nt -s* Hamburg.

Hamburger[1] *m -s, - (Cook)* hamburger.

Hamburger[2] *adj attr* Hamburg.

Hamburger(in *f)* *m -s, -* native or *(Einwohner)* inhabitant of Hamburg.

hamburgern *vi* to speak with a Hamburg dialect.

hamburgisch *adj* Hamburg *attr*.

Häme *f -, no pl (rare)* malice.

hämisch *adj* malicious, spiteful. **er hat sich ~ gefreut** he gloated.

Hamit(in *f)* *m -en, -en* Hamite.

hamitisch *adj* Hamitic.

Hammel *m -s, -* or *(rare)* ⁈ **(a)** *(Zool)* wether, castrated ram. **(b)** *no pl (Cook)* mutton. **(c)** *(fig pej)* ass, donkey.

Hammel-: **~beine** *pl:* **jdm die ~beine langziehen** *(hum inf)* to give sb a dressing-down; **jdn bei den ~beinen nehmen/ kriegen** *(inf)* to take sb to task/get hold of sb; **~braten** *m* roast mutton; **~fleisch** *nt* mutton; **~herde** *f* herd or flock of wethers or rams; *(pej inf)* flock of sheep; **~keule** *f (Cook)* leg of mutton; **~sprung** *m (Parl)* division.

Hammer *m -s, -* ⁈ **(a)** *(Werkzeug, von Auktionator)* hammer; *(Holz~)* mallet. **~ und Sichel** hammer and sickle; **~ und Zirkel im Ährenkranz** hammer and pair of compasses in a garland of corn, symbol of the GDR; **unter den ~ kommen** to come under the hammer; **zwischen ~ und Amboß geraten** *(fig)* to come under attack from both sides; **das ist ein ~!** *(sl) (unerhört)* that's absurd!; *(prima)* that's fantastic! *(inf)*.

(b) *(Sportgerät)* hammer.

(c) *(Anat)* hammer, malleus.

(d) *(Klavier~, Glocken~)* hammer.

(e) *(sl: schwerer Fehler)* howler *(inf)*. **einen ~ haben** to be round the bend *(inf)* or twist *(inf)*.

(f) *(sl: Penis)* tool *(sl)*.

hämmerbar *adj* malleable.

Hämmerchen *nt dim of* **Hammer**.

Hammer-: **h~förmig** *adj* hammer-shaped; **~hai** *m* hammerhead (shark); **~kopf** *m* hammerhead; *(Sport: auch* **~kugel**) hammerhead.

hämmern 1 *vi* **(a)** to hammer; *(fig auch, mit den Fäusten etc)* to pound; *(inf: beim Klavierspielen etc)* to pound, to thump.

(b) *(~des Geräusch verursachen: Maschine, Motor)* to make a hammering sound.

(c) *(Puls, Herz, Blut)* to pound.

(d) *(Sport sl)* to hammer or slam the ball *(inf)*.

2 *vt* **(a)** to hammer; *Blech auch, Metallgefäße, Schmuck etc* to beat.

(b) *(inf) Melodie, Rhythmus etc* to hammer or pound out.

(c) *(Sport sl)* to hammer *(inf)*, to slam *(inf)*.

(d) *(fig inf: einprägen)* **jdm etw ins Bewußtsein etc ~** to hammer or knock sth into sb's head *(inf)*.

3 *vi impers* **es hämmert** there's a sound of hammering; **hörst du es nicht ~?** can't you hear the (sound of) hammering?

Hammer-: **~schlag** *m* **(a)** hammer blow; *(fig)* bolt from the blue; **(b)** *(Sport) (Boxen)* rabbit punch; *(Faustball)* smash; **(c)** *(Schmiederei)* hammer or mill scale; **~schmied** *m (old)* person working in a hammer mill; **~schmiede** *f (old)* hammer mill; **~stiel** *m* handle or shaft of a/the hammer; **~werfen** *nt -s, no pl (Sport)* hammer(-throwing); **~werfer** *m (Sport)* hammer thrower; **~werk** *nt (old)* hammer mill; **~wurf** *m (Sport)* **(a)** hammer throw; **(b)** *siehe* **~werfen**; **~zehe** *f (Med)* hammertoe.

Hammond|orgel ['hæmənd-] *f* electric organ.

Hämoglobin *nt -s, no pl* haemoglobin.

Hämophilie *f* haemophilia.

Hämorrhoiden [hɛmɔro'iːdən] *pl* piles *pl*, haemorrhoids *pl*.

Hämorrhoidenschaukel *f (hum)* boneshaker *(inf)*.

Hampelei *f (pej inf)* (continual) fidgeting *no pl*.

Hampelmann *m, pl -männer* **(a)** jumping jack. **(b)** *(inf) (zappeliger Mensch)* fidget. **er ist nur ein ~** he just lets people walk all over him; **jdn zu einem ~ machen** to walk all over sb. **(c)** *(Turnen)* exercise involving jumping and swinging the arms above the head.

hampeln *vi* to jump about; *(zappeln)* to fidget.

Hamster *m -s, -* hamster.

Hamsterbacken *pl (fig inf)* chubby cheeks *pl*.

Hamsterer(in *f)* *m -s, - (inf)* squirrel *(inf)*.

Hamster-: **~fahrt** *f* foraging trip; **auf ~fahrt gehen** to go foraging; **~kauf** *m* panic-buying *no pl*; **~käufe machen** to buy in order to hoard; *(bei Knappheit)* to panic-buy.

hamstern *vti (speichern)* to hoard; *(bei Hamsterfahrt)* to forage; *(Hamsterkäufe machen)* to panic-buy.

Hamster-: **~tasche** *f* large shopping bag; **~ware** *f siehe* **Hamster-** hoarded/foraged/panic-bought goods.

Hand *f -, ⁻e* **(a)** hand. **jdm die ~ geben** or **reichen** *(geh)* to give sb one's hand; **jdm die ~ drücken/schütteln/küssen** to press/shake/kiss sb's hand; **jdn an der ~ haben/an die** or **bei der ~ nehmen/der ~ fassen** to have/take/grab sb by the hand; **jdm etw aus der ~ nehmen** to take sth from or off sb *(auch fig)*, to take sth out of sb's hand; **etw in ~en halten** *(geh)* to hold or have sth in one's hands; **die Arbeit seiner ~ handiwork; in die ~e klatschen** to clap one's hands; **eine ~/zwei ~e breit** = six inches/a foot wide.

(b) *(old: ~schrift)* hand.

(c) *(Mus)* hand. **Stück für vier ~e** or **zu vier ~en** (piano) duet; **zu vier ~en spielen** to play a (piano) duet.

(d) *(Cards)* hand. **auf der ~** in one's hand.

(e) *no pl (Sport:* **~spiel**) hand-ball. **~ machen** to handle the ball.

(f) *(Boxen)* punch.

(g) *(Besitz, Obhut)* possession, hands. **aus** or **von**

privater ~ privately; etw aus der ~ geben to let sth out of one's sight; durch jds ~̈e or ~ gehen to pass or go through sb's hands; von ~ zu ~ gehen to pass from hand to hand; etw geht in jds ~̈e über sth passes to sb or into sb's hands; zu jds ~̈en, zu ~̈en von jdm for the attention of sb; siehe treu.

(h) (nicht mit Maschine, Hilfsmittel) mit der ~, von ~ by hand; von ~ geschrieben/genäht handwritten/handsewn; aus der ~ freehand; Vermittlung von ~ (Telec) operator-connected calls pl.

(i) (in Redewendungen) ~̈e hoch (put your) hands up; ~ aufs Herz cross your heart, word of honour; eine ~ wäscht die andere if you scratch my back I'll scratch yours; ich wasche meine ~ in Unschuld I wash my hands of it or the matter; er nimmt niemals ein Buch in die ~ he never picks up a book; bei etw die or seine ~ im Spiel haben to have a hand in sth; er hat überall seine ~ im Spiel he has a finger in every pie; etw hat ~ und Fuß sth is well done; etw hat weder ~ noch Fuß sth doesn't make sense; sich mit ~̈en und Füßen gegen etw wehren to fight sth tooth and nail; mit ~̈en und Füßen reden to talk or speak with one's hands; man konnte die ~ nicht vor den Augen sehen you couldn't see your hand in front of your face; die ~̈e überm Kopf zusammenschlagen to throw up one's hands in horror; die or seine ~̈e über jdn halten to protect or shield sb.

(j) (in Verbindung mit Adjektiv) rechter/linker ~, zur rechten/linken ~ on the right-/left-hand side; in guten/schlechten/sicheren ~̈en sein to be in good/bad/safe hands; eine ruhige/sichere ~ a steady hand; eine starke or feste ~ (fig) a firm hand; eine lockere or lose ~ haben (hum inf) to let fly (inf) at the slightest provocation; bei etw eine glückliche ~ haben to have a lucky touch with sth; ihm fehlt die leitende or lenkende ~ he lacks a guiding hand; in festen ~̈en sein to be spoken for; mit leeren/vollen ~̈en empty-handed/open-handedly; mit der flachen ~ with the flat or palm of one's hand; siehe rechte(r, s), linke(r, s) etc.

(k) (in Verbindung mit Verb) alle ~̈e voll zu tun haben to have one's hands full; jdm auf etw (acc) die ~ geben to give sb one's hand on sth; jdm etw in die ~ versprechen to promise sb sth or sth to sb; um jds ~ anhalten or bitten to ask for sb's hand (in marriage); jdm/sich or einander die ~ fürs Leben reichen to marry sb/to tie the knot; sich or einander (geh) die ~ reichen können to be tarred with the same brush; da können wir uns die ~ reichen snap! (inf); sich (dat) für jdn/etw die ~ abhacken lassen (inf) to stake one's life on sb/sth; seine or die ~ für jdn ins Feuer legen to vouch for sb; jdn auf ~̈en tragen to cherish sb; jdm aus der ~ fressen to eat out of sb's hand; die or seine ~ hinhalten or aufhalten (fig inf) to hold out one's hand (for money); (bei etw) mit ~ anlegen to lend a hand (with sth); letzte ~ an etw (acc) legen to put the finishing touches to sth; die ~̈e in den Schoß legen to sit back and do nothing; ~ an jdn legen (geh) to lay a hand on sb; ~ an sich legen (geh) to kill oneself; seine or die ~ auf etw (acc) legen (geh) to lay (one's) hands on sth; die ~ auf der Tasche halten (inf) to hold the purse-strings; die ~ auf etw (dat) haben or halten to keep a tight rein on sth; das liegt auf der ~ (inf) that's obvious.

(l) (in Verbindung mit Präpositionen) an ~ eines Beispiels/von Beispielen with an example/examples; an ~ dieses Berichts/dieser Unterlagen from this report/these documents; jdn an der ~ haben to know of sb; etw aus der ~ sagen können to be able to say sth offhand; etw aus erster/zweiter ~ wissen to know sth first/second hand; ein Auto aus erster/zweiter ~ a car which has had one previous owner/two previous owners; etw aus der ~ essen to eat sth out of one's hand; etw aus der ~ legen to put or lay sth aside; etw bei der or zur ~ haben to have sth to hand; Ausrede, Erklärung to have sth ready; mit etw schnell or gleich bei der ~ sein (inf) to be ready with sth; ~ in ~ hand in hand; jdm/einer Sache in die ~̈e arbeiten to play into sb's hands/the hands of sth; jdm in die ~ or ~̈e fallen or geraten or kommen to fall into sb's hands; jdn/etw in die ~ or ~̈e kriegen or bekommen to get one's hands on sb/sth; jdn (fest) in der ~ haben to have sb (well) in hand; von der ~ in den Mund leben to live from hand to mouth; etw in der ~ haben to have sth; ich habe die Entscheidung nicht in der ~ it's not in my hands; etw gegen jdn in der ~ haben to have something or some hold on sb; sich in der ~ haben to have oneself under control; etw in jds ~ or ~̈e legen to put sth in sb's hands; etw liegt or steht or ist in jds ~ sth is in sb's hands; in jds ~ sein to be in sb's hands; etw in die ~ nehmen to pick sth up; (fig) to take sth in hand; jdm etw in die ~ or ~̈e spielen to pass sth on to sb; hinter vorgehaltener ~ on the quiet; das ist mit ~̈en zu greifen that's as plain as a pikestaff or the nose on your face; etw zerrinnt or schmilzt jdm unter den ~̈en sb goes through sth like water or like nobody's business (inf); unter jds ~̈en/jdm unter der ~ or den ~̈en wegsterben to die while under sb's care; von jds ~ sterben to die at sb's hand; etw geht jdm flott or schnell/leicht von der ~ sb does sth quickly/finds sth easy; etw läßt sich nicht von der ~ weisen, etw ist nicht von der ~ zu weisen sth cannot be denied or gainsaid (form); zur ~ sein to be at hand; etw zur ~ nehmen to pick sth up; jdm zur or an die ~ gehen to lend sb a helping hand.

Hand-: ~abwehr f (Sport) save; durch ~abwehr klären to save, to clear; ~abzug m (Typ) proof pulled by hand; (Phot) print made by hand; ~antrieb m hand-driven mechanism; mit ~antrieb hand-driven; ~apparat m (a) reference books (on open shelves) pl; (b) (Telec) handset.

Hand|arbeit f (a) work done by hand; (Gegenstand) article made by hand, handmade article. etw in ~ herstellen to produce or make sth by hand; der Tisch ist ~ the table is handmade or made by hand.

(b) (körperliche Arbeit) manual work.

(c) (Nähen, Sticken etc, als Schulfach) needlework no pl;

(Stricken) knitting no pl; (Häkeln) crochet(ing) no pl. diese Tischdecke ist ~ this tablecloth is handmade; eine ~ aus dem 18. Jahrhundert a piece of needlework etc from the 18th century.

(d) (kunsthandwerklich) handicraft no pl. eine ~ a piece of handicraft work.

Hand|arbeiten nt -s, no pl (Sch) needlework.

hand|arbeiten vi insep to do needlework/knitting/crocheting.

Hand|arbeiter m manual worker.

Hand|arbeits-: ~geschäft nt needlework and wool shop; ~heft nt sewing, knitting and crocheting manual; ~korb m workbasket.

Hand-: ~aufheben nt -s, no pl (bei Wahl) show of hands; sich durch ~aufheben zu Wort melden to ask leave to speak by raising one's hand; ~auflegen nt -s, no pl, ~auflegung f laying on of hands; ~ausgabe f (Buch) concise edition; ~ball m (a) (Ball) handball; (b) no pl (inf auch nt) (Spiel) handball; ~ballen m (Anat) ball of the thumb; ~baller(in f) m -s, - (inf) siehe ~ballspieler; ~ballspiel nt (a) (Spiel) game of handball; (b) (Disziplin) handball no def art; ~ballspieler m handball player; h~bedient adj manually operated, hand-operated; ~bedienung f hand or manual operation or control; mit or für ~bedienung manually-operated; ~beil nt hatchet; ~besen m hand brush; ~betrieb m hand or manual operation; für or mit ~betrieb hand-operated; h~betrieben adj hand-operated; ~bewegung f sweep of the hand; (Geste, Zeichen) gesture; ~bibliothek f reference library or books pl (on open shelves); ~bohrer m gimlet, auger; ~bohrmaschine f (hand) drill; ~brause f siehe ~dusche; h~breit 1 adj = six-inch wide attr, six inches wide pred; 2 adv = six inches; ~breit f -, - = six inches; ~bremse f handbrake; ~buch nt handbook, reference book; (technisch) manual; ~bücherei f siehe ~bibliothek; ~bürste f nailbrush.

Händchen nt dim of Hand little hand. ~ halten (inf) to hold hands; für etw ein ~ haben (inf) to have a knack for sth; (gut können) to be good at sth; ~ geben to shake hands.

Händchen-: ~halten nt -s, no pl holding hands no def art; h~haltend adj holding hands.

Hand-: ~creme f hand cream; ~deutung f palmistry; ~druck m (Typ, Tex) block print; (Verfahren) block printing; ~dusche f shower attachment.

Hände-: ~druck m handshake; ~handtuch nt hand towel.

Hand|einstellung f (Tech) manual or hand-operated setting.

Händeklatschen nt applause no pl.

Handel[1] m -s, no pl (a) (das Handeln) trade; (esp mit illegaler Ware) traffic. ~ mit etw/einem Land trade in sth/with a country.

(b) (Warenverkehr) trade; (Warenmarkt) market. im ~ sein to be on the market; etw in den ~ bringen/aus dem ~ ziehen to put sth on/take sth off the market; (mit jdm) ~ (be)treiben to trade (with sb); ~ und Wandel (dated) doings and dealings pl.

(c) (Abmachung, Geschäft) deal, transaction; (inf) deal. mit jdm in den ~ kommen to do business with sb.

(d) (Wirtschaftszweig) commerce, trade; (die Handeltreibenden) trade.

(e) (dial: Handelsunternehmen) business. er betreibt/hat einen ~ in or mit Kohlen und Heizöl he runs/has a coal and fuel oil business.

Handel[2] m -s, ~̈ usu pl quarrel, argument.

Hand|elfmeter m penalty for a hand-ball.

handeln 1 vi (a) (Handel treiben) to trade. er handelt mit Gemüse he trades or deals in vegetables, he's in the vegetable trade; er handelt mit Drogen he traffics in drugs; er handelt in Gebrauchtwagen he's in the second-hand car trade; he sells second-hand cars; wir ~ nur en gros/en detail we're just wholesale/retail traders.

(b) (feilschen) to bargain, to haggle (um about, over); (fig: verhandeln) to negotiate (um about). ich lasse schon mit mir ~ I'm open to persuasion; (in bezug auf Preis) I'm open to offers.

(c) (tätig werden, agieren) to act. er ist ein schnell ~der Mensch he's a quick-acting person.

(d) (sich verhalten) to act, to behave. gegen jdn or an jdm gut/als Freund ~ (geh) to act or behave well/as or like a friend towards sb.

(e) (sprechen) von etw or über etw (acc) ~ to deal with sth; (Aufsatz etc auch) to be about sth.

2 vr impers (a) es handelt sich bei diesen sogenannten UFOs um optische Täuschungen these so-called UFO's are optical illusions; es handelt sich hier/dabei um ein Verbrechen it's a crime we are dealing with here/there; bei dem Festgenommenen handelt es sich um X the person arrested is X.

(b) (betreffen) sich um etw ~ to be about sth, to concern sth; worum handelt es sich, bitte? what's it about, please?; es handelt sich darum, daß ich einen Kredit beantragen möchte it is about or concerns a loan which I wish to apply for.

(c) (um etwas gehen, auf etw ankommen) sich um etw ~ to be a question or matter of sth; es handelt sich nur ums Überleben it's simply a question of survival.

3 vt (a) to sell (für at, for); (an der Börse) to quote (mit at); Drogen etc to traffic in.

(b) Preis etc (hinauf~) to push up, to raise; (herunter~) to bring down.

Handeln nt -s, no pl (a) (Feilschen) bargaining, haggling. (b) (das Handeltreiben) trading. das ~ mit Schmuck trading or dealing in jewellery. (c) (Verhalten) behaviour. (d) (das Tätigwerden) action.

handelnd adj die ~en Personen in einem Drama the characters in a drama, the dramatis personae pl; das ~e Subjekt the active subject.

Handels-: ~abkommen nt trade agreement; ~akademie f

(Aus) commercial college; ~akademiker *m (Aus)* graduate of a commercial college; ~artikel *m* commodity; ~attaché *m* commercial attaché; ~bank *f* merchant bank; ~beschränkung *f* trading restriction, restriction on trade; ~betrieb *m* trading or business concern; ~bezeichnung *f* trade name; ~beziehungen *pl* trade relations *pl*; ~bilanz *f* balance of trade; aktive/passive ~bilanz balance of trade surplus/deficit; ~brauch *m* trade or commercial practice; ~defizit *nt* trade deficit; h~einig, h~eins *adj pred* h~einig werden/sein to agree terms, to come to an agreement; h~fähig *adj Güter etc* marketable, merchantable; ~firma *f* (commercial or business) firm; ~flagge *f (Naut)* merchant flag; ~flotte *f* merchant fleet; ~freiheit *f* (a) *(Comm)* freedom of trade *no pl*; (b) *siehe* Handlungsfreiheit; h~gängig *adj* (a) *siehe* h~fähig; (b) *siehe* h~üblich; ~geist *m* commercialism; commercial spirit; ~gesellschaft *f* commercial company; ~gesetz *nt* commercial law; ~gesetzbuch *nt* code of commercial law; ~gewerbe *nt* commerce *no art*; ~gut *nt siehe* ~ware; ~hafen *m* trading port; ~haus *nt* business house, firm; ~kammer *f* chamber of commerce; ~kette *f* (a) chain of retail shops; (b) *(Weg der Ware)* sales route *(from manufacturer to buyer)*; ~klasse *f* grade; Heringe der ~klasse 1 grade 1 herring; ~krise *f* commercial crisis; ~lehrer(in *f*) *m* teacher of commercial subjects; ~macht *f* trading nation or power; ~makler *m* broker; ~mann *m, pl* -leute *(old) siehe* Hausierer(in); ~marine *f* merchant navy, mercantile marine *(form)*; ~marke *f* trade name; ~metropole *f* commercial metropolis; ~minister *m* = Trade Secretary *(Brit)*, Secretary of Commerce *(US)*; ~ministerium *nt* = Board of Trade *(Brit)*, Department of Commerce *(US)*; ~mission *f* trade mission; ~name *m siehe* ~bezeichnung; ~nation *f* trading nation; ~niederlassung *f* branch (of a trading organization); ~objekt *nt* commodity; ~organisation *f* (a) *(allgemein)* trading organization; (b) *(DDR)* state-owned commercial concern which runs stores, hotels etc; ~platz *m* trading centre; ~politik *f* trade or commercial policy; h~politisch 1 *adj* relating to trade or commercial policy; 2 *adv* as far as trade or commercial policy is concerned; ~privileg *nt, usu pl (Hist)* trade privilege; ~realschule *f (esp Sw) siehe* ~schule; ~recht *nt* commercial law *no def art, no pl*; h~rechtlich 1 *adj* of/about commercial law; 2 *adv* according to commercial law; ~register *nt* register of companies; ~reisende(r) *m decl as adj siehe* ~vertreter; ~schiff *nt* trading ship or vessel, merchantman *(old)*; ~schiffahrt *f* merchant shipping *no def art*; ~schranke *f usu pl* trade barrier; ~schule *f* commercial school or college; ~schüler *m* student at a commercial school or college; ~spanne *f* profit margin; ~sperre *f* trade embargo *(gegen* on*)*; ~sprache *f* commercial language; ~stadt *f* trading city or centre; ~stand *m (Sociol)* merchant class; ~straße *f (Hist)* trade route; h~üblich *adj* usual or customary (in the trade or in commerce); etw zu den h~üblichen Preisen kaufen to buy sth at normal retail prices.

Händelsucht *f* quarrelsomeness.
händelsüchtig *adj* quarrelsome.
Handels-: ~unternehmen *nt* commercial enterprise; ~verkehr *m* trade; ~vertrag *m* trade agreement; ~vertreter *m* commercial traveller or representative; ~vertretung *f* trade mission; ~volk *nt* trading nation; ~ware *f* commodity; ~waren *pl* commodities *pl*, merchandise *sing*; ~weg *m* (a) sales route; (b) *siehe* ~straße; ~wert *m* market value; ~wesen *nt* commerce, trade *no def art*; ~zentrum *nt* trading or commercial centre; ~zweig *m* branch.

handeltreibend *adj attr* trading.
Handeltreibende(r) *mf decl as adj* trader, tradesman/-woman.
Hände-: ~ringen *nt* -s, *no pl (fig)* wringing of one's hands; h~ringend *adv* wringing one's hands; *(fig)* imploringly; ~schütteln *nt* -s, *no pl* handshaking; ~trockner *m* hand drier; ~waschen *nt* -s, *no pl* washing one's hands; jdn zum ~waschen schicken to send sb to wash his/her hands; das ~waschen kostet ... it costs ... to wash your hands.
Hand-: ~feger *m* hand brush; wie ein wild gewordener ~feger *(inf)* like a wild thing; ~fertigkeit *f* dexterity; ~fessel *f* (a) manacle; etw als ~fessel benutzen to tie sb's hands together with sth; (b) *(Handschelle)* handcuff; h~fest *adj* (a) *(kräftig) Mensch* sturdy, robust; *Essen* solid, substantial; (b) *(fig) Schlägerei* violent; *Skandal* huge; *Vorschlag, Argument* well-founded, solid; *Beweis* solid, tangible; *Lüge, Betrug* flagrant, blatant; ~feuerlöscher *m* hand fire extinguisher; ~feuerwaffe *f* hand gun; ~fläche *f* palm or flat (of the/one's hand); ~furche *f siehe* ~linie; ~gas *nt (Aut)* (a) *(Vorrichtung)* hand throttle; ~gas haben/geben to have a/pull out the hand throttle; mit ~gas fahren to use the hand throttle; h~gearbeitet *adj* handmade; *Stickerei etc* handworked; h~gebunden *adj* hand-bound; h~gefertigt *adj siehe* h~gearbeitet; h~geknüpft *adj* handwoven; ~geld *nt (Sport)* transfer fee; *(Hist)* earnest money; *(Mil Hist)* bounty; ~gelenk *nt* wrist; aus dem ~gelenk *(fig inf) (ohne Mühe)* with the greatest of ease, effortlessly; *(improvisiert)* off the cuff; etw aus dem ~gelenk schütteln *(fig inf)* to do sth effortlessly or with no trouble at all; ein lockeres or loses ~gelenk haben *(inf)* to let fly at the slightest provocation; h~gemacht *adj* handmade; h~gemalt *adj* hand-painted; h~gemein *adj (mit jdm)* h~gemein werden to come to blows (with sb); ~gemenge *nt* scuffle, fight; h~genäht *adj* hand-sewn; ~gepäck *nt* hand luggage *no pl* or baggage *no pl*; ~gerät *nt (Sport)* hand apparatus; h~gerecht *adj, adv* handy; h~geschliffen *adj* hand-ground; h~geschmiedet *adj* hand-forged; h~geschöpft *adj Papier* handmade; h~geschrieben *adj* handwritten; h~gesetzt *adj (Typ)* handset, set by hand; h~gesponnen *adj* hand-spun;

h~gesteuert *adj (Tech)* hand-operated; h~gestrickt *adj* hand-knitted; h~gewebt *adj* handwoven; ~granate *f* hand grenade; h~greiflich *adj* (a) *Streit, Auseinandersetzung* violent; h~greiflich werden to become violent; (b) *(fig: offensichtlich)* clear; *Erfolg auch* visible; *Lüge* blatant, flagrant; etw h~greiflich vor Augen führen to demonstrate sth clearly; ~greiflichkeit *f siehe adj* (a) *usu pl* violence *no pl*; (b) clarity; blatancy, flagrance; ~griff *m* (a) *(Bewegung)* movement; *(im Haushalt)* chore; keinen ~griff tun not to lift a finger; mit einem ~griff öffnen with one flick of the wrist; *(schnell)* in no time; mit ein paar ~griffen in next to no time; (b) *(Gegenstand)* handle; h~groß *adj* hand-sized; h~habbar *adj* manageable; leicht/schwer h~habbar easy/difficult to manage; ~habe *f (fig)* ich habe gegen ihn keine ~habe I have no hold on him; etw als ~habe (gegen jdn) benutzen to use sth as a lever (against sb); h~haben* *vt insep* to handle; *Maschine auch* to operate, to work; *Gesetz* to implement, to administer; ~habung *f siehe vt* handling; operation, working; implementation, administration; ~harmonica *f* concertina; ~hebel *m* hand-operated or manually operated lever.
-händig *adj suf* -handed.
Handikap ['hɛndikɛp] *nt* -s, -s *(Sport, fig)* handicap.
handikapen ['hɛndikɛpn] *vt insep* to handicap.
Handikap-: ~rennen *nt* handicap (race); ~spiel *nt* handicap game.
Hand-in-Hand-Arbeiten *nt* -s, *no pl* cooperation.
händisch *adj (Aus)* manual.
Hand-: ~kamera *f* hand-held camera; ~kante *f* side of the/one's hand; ~kantenschlag *m* karate chop; ~karren *m* handcart; ~käse *m* strong-smelling round German cheese; ~katalog *m* ready-reference catalogue; ~koffer *m* (small) suitcase; h~koloriert *adj* hand-painted; ~korb *m* (small) basket; ~kurbel *f* hand crank; *(Aut)* starting handle; ~kuß *m* kiss on the hand; *(Eccl)* kiss *(on the ring of a bishop etc)*; die Damen wurden mit ~kuß begrüßt the ladies were greeted with a kiss on the hand; mit ~kuß *(fig inf)* with pleasure, gladly; zum ~kuß kommen *(Aus fig)* to come off worse; ~lampe *f siehe* ~leuchte; ~langer *m* -s, - odd-job man, handyman; *(fig: Untergeordneter)* dogsbody *(inf)*; *(fig pej: Gehilfe)* henchman; ~langerarbeit *f (pej)* donkey work *no pl*; ~langerdienst *m* dirty work *no pl*; ~lauf *m (an Treppen)* handrail.
Händler(in *f*) *m* -s, - trader, dealer; *(Auto~)* dealer; *(Laden-besitzer)* shopkeeper; *(Fisch~)* fishmonger; *(Fleisch~)* butcher; *(Gemüse~)* greengrocer. **ambulanter or fliegender ~** street trader.
Händler-: ~preis *m* trade price; ~rabatt *m* trade discount.
Hand-: ~lesekunst *f* (die) ~lesekunst palmistry, (the art of) reading palms; ~leser *m* palm reader, palmist; ~leuchte *f* inspection lamp.
handlich *adj* (a) *Gerät, Format, Form* handy; *Gepäckstück* manageable, easy to manage; *Auto* manoeuvrable.
(b) *(Sw: behende)* handy, dexterous.
(c) *(Sw: mit der Hand)* with one's hand(s).
Handlichkeit *f, no pl siehe adj* (a) handiness; manageability; manoeuvrability.
Hand-: ~linie *f* line (in the palm of the hand); ~liniendeutung *f* (die) ~liniendeutung palmistry.
Handlung *f* (a) *(Vorgehen, Handeln)* action, deed; *(Tat, Akt)* act.
(b) *(Geschehen)* action; *(~sablauf)* plot. der Ort der ~ the scene of the action.
(c) *(dated) (mit Waren)* business; *(Laden)* shop.
Handlungs-: ~ablauf *m* plot; h~arm *adj* thin or poor on plot; ~armut *f* lack of plot or action; ~art *f (Gram)* voice; ~bevollmächtigte(r) *mf* authorized agent, proxy; h~fähig *adj Regierung* capable of acting, able to act; *(Jur)* empowered or authorized to act; eine h~fähige Mehrheit a working majority; ~fähigkeit *f (von Regierung)* ability to act; *(Jur)* power to act; ~freiheit *f* freedom of action; ~gerüst *nt (Liter)* framework; h~reich *adj* action-packed, full of action; ~reichtum *m* abundance of action; ~reisende(r) *m (Comm)* commercial traveller, rep(resentative); ~spielraum *m* scope (of action); ~theorie *f (Sociol)* theory of action; h~unfähig *adj Regierung* incapable of acting, unable to act; *(Jur)* without power to act; ~unfähigkeit *f (von Regierung)* inability to act; *(Jur)* lack of power to act; ~verb *nt* transitive verb; ~verlauf *m siehe* ~ablauf; ~vollmacht *f* proxy; ~weise *f* way of behaving, behaviour *no pl*, conduct *no pl*; eine selbstlose/edelmütige ~weise unselfish behaviour or conduct/noble conduct.
Hand-: ~mehr *nt* -s, *no pl (Sw)* show of hands; es wurde durch ~mehr abgestimmt it was passed by a show of hands; ~mühle *f* hand-mill; ~pflege *f* care of one's hands; ~presse *f (Typ)* hand-press; ~pumpe *f* hand-pump; ~puppe *f* glove puppet; ~puppenspiel *nt (Technik)* glove puppetry; *(Stück)* glove puppet show; ~reichung *f* (a) helping hand *no pl*; (b) *(Instruktion, Empfehlung)* recommendation; ~rücken *m* back of the/one's hand; auf beiden ~rücken on the back of both hands; ~säge *f* hand-saw; ~satz *m (Typ)* hand-setting, hand-composition; ~schalter *m* manual switch; ~schaltung *f (Aut)* manual controls *pl*; ~schelle *f usu pl* handcuff; jdm ~schellen anlegen to handcuff sb, to put handcuffs on sb; in ~schellen in handcuffs, handcuffed; ~schlag *m* (a) *(Händedruck)* handshake; mit or durch or per ~schlag with a handshake; ein Geschäft durch ~schlag abschließen to shake on a deal; (b) keinen ~schlag tun not to do a stroke (of work); ~schreiben *nt* handwritten letter; ~schrift *f* (a) handwriting; *(fig)* (trade)mark; er hat eine gute/leserliche ~schrift he has a good/legible hand, he has good/legible handwriting; etw trägt/verrät jds ~schrift *(fig)* sth bears or has sb's (trade)mark; *(Kunstwerk auch)* sth shows the hand of sb; eine kräftige/gute ~schrift haben or

schreiben (*fig inf*) to be a hard/good hitter; **(b)** (*Text*) manuscript; ~**schriftendeutung** *f* **(die)** ~**schriftendeutung** the study of handwriting, graphology; **h**~**schriftlich 1** *adj* handwritten; **2** *adv* **korrigieren, einfügen** by hand; **sich bewerben** in writing; **einen Brief h**~**schriftlich beantworten/schreiben** to answer a letter in writing or by hand/to write a letter.

Handschuh *m* (*Finger*~) glove; (*Faust*~) mitten, mitt (*inf*).

Handschuh-: ~**fach** *nt*, ~**kasten** *m* (*Aut*) glove compartment; ~**macher** *m* glove maker.

Hand-: ~**schutz** *m* protection *no pl* for the hands; (*Handschuhe*) hand protection *no pl*; (*an Maschine*) hand guard; ~**setzer** *m* (*Typ*) hand compositor; **h**~**signiert** *adj* signed, autographed; ~**skizze** *f* rough sketch; ~**spiegel** *m* hand mirror or glass; ~**spiel** *nt, no pl* **(a)** (*Sport*) handball; **(b)** (*Cards*) (finishing a game by) playing all one's hand at once; ~**stand** *m* (*Sport*) handstand; ~**standüberschlag** *m* (*Sport*) handspring; ~**steuerung** *f* manual control; ~**streich** *m* in or durch einen ~**streich** in a surprise coup; (*Mil*) by surprise; **in einem** or **durch einen kühnen/detailliert geplanten** ~**streich** in a bold/minutely planned coup; ~**streichverfahren** *nt*: im ~**streichverfahren** in a surprise coup; ~**tasche** *f* handbag, purse (*US*); ~**teller** *m* palm (of the/one's hand); ~**trommel** *f* hand drum.

Handtuch *nt* **(a)** towel; (*Geschirr*~) tea towel, teacloth; (*Papier*~) paper towel. **das** ~ **werfen** or **schmeißen** (*inf*) (*lit*) to throw in the towel; (*fig*) to throw in the sponge or towel. **(b)** (*inf*) (*Raum*) long narrow place; (*Grundstück*) thin strip.

Handtuch-: in *cpds* towel; ~**halter** *m* towel-rail; ~**spender** *m* towel dispenser.

Hand-: ~**umdrehen** *nt* (*fig*): **im** ~**umdrehen** in the twinkling of an eye; **h**~**verlesen** *adj Obst etc* hand-graded; **h**~**vermittelt** *adj Telefongespräch* connected through or by the operator; ~**vermittlung** *f* connection by the operator; **eine durch** ~**vermittlung hergestellte Telefonverbindung** a call connected through or by the operator; ~**voll** *f* -, - (*lit, fig*) handful; ~**waffe** *f* hand weapon; ~**wagen** *m* handcart; **h**~**warm** *adj* hand-hot; **etw h**~**warm waschen** to wash sth in hand-hot water; ~**wäsche** *f* washing by hand; (*Wäschestücke*) hand wash; ~**webstuhl** *m* hand-loom.

Handwerk *nt* **(a)** (*Beruf*) trade; (*Kunst*~) craft; (*fig: Tätigkeit*) business. **das lederverarbeitende** ~ the leather worker's trade; **das** ~ **des Bäckers** the baking trade; **das** ~ **des Schneiders/Schreiners** the trade of tailor/joiner; **das** ~ **des Töpfers** the potter's craft; **der Krieg ist das einzige** ~, **das er versteht** or **beherrscht** war is the only business he knows anything about; **sein** ~ **verstehen** or **beherrschen** (*fig*) to know one's job; **jdm ins** ~ **pfuschen** (*fig*) to tread on sb's toes; **jdm das** ~ **legen** (*fig*) to put a stop to sb's game (*inf*) or to sb. **(b)** *no pl* (*Wirtschaftsbereich*) trade.

handwerkeln* *vi insep* (*hum*) to potter about (making things).

Handwerker *m* **-s,** - (skilled) manual worker; (*Kunst*~) craftsman. **wir haben seit Wochen die** ~ **im Haus** we've had workmen in the house for weeks; **dieser Schriftsteller ist ein guter** ~ (*fig*) this author is a real craftsman.

Handwerkerin *f* (skilled) manual worker; (*Kunst*~) craftswoman.

Handwerkerschaft *f* trade *sing* or *pl*.

handwerklich *adj Ausbildung* as a manual worker/craftsman; (*fig*) technical. ~**er Beruf** skilled trade; **die** ~**e Ausführung des Möbelstücks** the workmanship or craftsmanship of the piece of furniture; ~**es Können** craftsmanship; ~**e Fähigkeiten** manual skills; ~ **ist der Fotograf perfekt** technically the photographer is perfect.

Handwerks-: ~**beruf** *m* skilled trade; ~**betrieb** *m* workshop; ~**bursche** *m* (*old*) travelling journeyman; ~**kammer** *f* trade corporation; ~**mann** *m, pl* **-leute** (*obs*) *siehe* **Handwerker;** ~**zeug** *nt, no pl* tools *pl*; (*fig*) tools of the trade *pl*, equipment.

Hand-: ~**werkzeug** *nt* hand tools *pl*; ~**winde** *f* hand-winch; ~**wörterbuch** *nt* concise dictionary; ~**wurzel** *f* (*Anat*) carpus; ~**wurzelknochen** *m* (*Anat*) carpal bone; ~**zeichen** *nt* signal; (*Geste auch*) sign; (*bei Abstimmung*) show of hands; **durch** ~**zeichen** by a show of hands; **er gab mir durch ein** ~**zeichen zu verstehen, daß ich still sein sollte** he signalled to me to be quiet, he gave me a sign to be quiet; ~**zeichnung** *f* **(a)** (*Skizze*) sketch; **(b)** (*Art*) drawing; ~**zettel** *m* handout, leaflet, handbill.

hanebüchen *adj* outrageous, scandalous.

Hanf *m* **-(e)s,** *no pl* (*Pflanze, Faser*) hemp; (*Samen*) hempseed.

hanfen, hänfen *adj attr* (*rare*) hempen.

Hänfling *m* (*Orn*) linnet.

Hanf-: in *cpds* hemp-; ~**seil** *nt*, ~**strick** *m* hemp-rope.

Hang *m* **-(e)s,** ¨**e (a)** (*Abhang*) slope. **(b)** *no pl* (*Neigung*) tendency. **er hat einen (deutlichen)** ~ **zur Kriminalität** he has a (marked) tendency towards criminality.

Hangar ['haŋgaːɐ̯, haŋˈgaːɐ̯] *m* **-s,** -s hangar, shed.

Hänge-: ~**backen** *pl* flabby cheeks *pl*; ~**bauch** *m* drooping belly (*inf*); ~**brücke** *f* suspension bridge; ~**brust** *f*, ~**busen** *m* (*pej*) sagging or droopy (*inf*) breasts *pl* or bosom *no pl*; ~**dach** *nt* suspended roof; ~**gleiter** *m* (*Sport*) hang-glider; ~**kleid** *nt* loose dress, smock; ~**lampe** *f* drop-light.

Hängelleiter *f* (*Sport*) horizontal ladder.

hangeln *vir* **er hangelte (sich) an einem Tau über den Fluß** he moved hand over hand along a rope over the river; **er hangelte sich am Fels hinunter/über den Abgrund** he let himself down the cliff hand over hand/he crossed the chasm hand over hand.

Hänge-: ~**matte** *f* hammock; ~**mikrophon** *nt* hanging microphone.

hangen *vi* (*obs, dial*) (*dial: aux sein*) *siehe* **hängen 1.**

Hangen *nt*: **mit** ~ **und Bangen** with fear and trembling.

Hängen *nt* **-s,** *no pl* **(a) Tod durch** ~ death by hanging. **(b) mit** ~ **und Würgen** (*inf*) by the skin of one's teeth.

hängen 1 *vi pret* **hing**, *ptp* **gehangen (a)** to hang. **die Gardinen** ~ **schon** the curtains are already up; **die Tür hängt in den Angeln** the door hangs on its hinges.

(b) (*gehenkt werden*) to hang.

(c) (*herunter*~) to hang. **mit** ~**den Schultern** with drooping shoulders; **die Blumen ließen die Köpfe** ~ the flowers hung their heads; **den Kopf** ~ **lassen** (*fig*) to be downcast or crestfallen; **das Kleid hing ihr am Leib** the dress hung on her.

(d) (*sich neigen*) to lean. **der Wagen hängt (stark) nach rechts** the car leans (badly) to the right.

(e) (*inf: lässig sitzen*) to slouch. **in der Kurve** ~ (*Motorradfahrer*) to lean into the bend.

(f) (*befestigt sein*) to hang; (*Wohnwagen etc*) to be on (**an etw** (*dat*) sth); (*sich festhalten*) to hang on (**an** + *dat* to). **das Bild hängt an der Wand/am Nagel/an einem Aufhänger** the picture is hanging on the wall/on the nail/by a loop; **sie hing ihm am Hals/an der Schulter** she hung around his neck/clung to his shoulder; **das Kalb hängt am Euter der Mutter** the calf hangs on to its mother's udder; **der Knopf hängt nur noch an einem Faden** the button is only hanging (on) by a thread.

(g) (*angeschlossen, verbunden sein: Lautsprecher, Telefonapparat etc*) to be connected (up) (**an** + *dat* to). **der Patient hängt an der künstlichen Niere/am Tropf** the patient is on the kidney machine/connected (up) to the drip.

(h) (*inf: abhängen von*) **an jdm** ~ to depend on sb; **wo(ran) hängt es denn?** what's up (then)? (*inf*), what's the matter (then)?

(i) (*inf: dazugehören*) to be involved (**an** + *dat* in). **daran hängt viel Arbeit** there's a lot of work involved in that.

(j) (*behangen sein, vollgehängt sein*) to be full. **der Schrank hängt voll(er) Kleider** the cupboard is full of clothes; **der Baum hängt voller Früchte** the tree is laden with fruit.

(k) (*kleben*) to be stuck (**an** + *dat* on). **ihre Blicke** or **Augen hingen an dem Sänger** her eyes were fixed on the singer; **sie hing am Mund** or **an den Lippen des Redners** she hung on the speaker's every word.

(l) (*festhängen*) to be caught (*mit* by).

(m) (*schweben, im Raum stehen*) to hang. **eine Wolke hing im Tal** a cloud hung over the valley; **eine unerträgliche Spannung hing im Raum** there was an unbearable tension in the room; **eine Gefahr/ein Fluch hängt über uns** danger/a curse is hanging over us; *siehe* **Luft.**

(n) (*inf: sich aufhalten*) to hang about or around (*inf*). **er hängt den ganzen Tag vorm Fernseher/am Telefon** he spends all day in front of the telly/on the phone (*inf*); **wo hängt bloß der Jürgen schon wieder?** where on earth has Jürgen got to now?

(o) (*nicht vorankommen*) to hang fire; (*inf: vergeblich warten*) to hang about (*inf*); (*Sch inf, Sports sl*) to be behind. **die Partie hängt** (*Chess*) the game is held over or adjourned.

(p) (*sl: Geldschwierigkeiten, Schulden haben*) to be in debt or red (*inf*). **ich hänge bei meiner Schwester (mit 200 Mark)** I'm (200 marks) in debt to my sister, I owe my sister 200 marks.

(q) (*Chess: Figur*) to be vulnerable. **der Springer hängt** the knight is vulnerable.

(r) (*nicht verzichten mögen auf, lieben*) **an jdm/etw** ~ to be very attached to or fond of sb/sth; **er hängt am Leben** he clings to life.

2 *vt pret* **hängte**, *ptp* **gehängt**, (*dial auch*) *pret* **hing**, *ptp* **gehangen (a)** (*aufhängen, henken*) to hang. **wir müssen noch die Gardinen** ~ we still have to put up or hang the curtains; **er hängt sich all sein Geld** or **alles auf den Leib** (*inf*) he spends all his money on clothes; *siehe* **Nagel, Brotkorb, Glocke.**

(b) (*vollhängen, behängen mit*) to fill. **er hängte die Wand voll Bilder** he hung pictures all over the wall, he filled the wall with pictures.

(c) (*inf: aufwenden*) **etw in** or **an etw** (*acc*) ~ to put sth into sth; **in das alte Auto will ich nicht mehr viel Geld** ~ I don't want to spend much more money on the old car.

(d) (*einhängen*) **er hängte den Telefonhörer in die Gabel** he hung up or rang off, he put or placed the receiver back on the hook.

(e) (*hängenlassen, beugen*) to hang. **der Elefant hängte seinen Rüssel ins Wasser** the elephant dangled his trunk in the water; **seine Nase in etw** (*acc*) ~ (*inf: riechen*) to stick one's nose into sth (*inf*).

(f) (*an* + *acc* to) (*anschließen*) to connect; (*befestigen*) **Wohnwagen etc** to hitch up.

3 *vr pret* **hängte**, *ptp* **gehängt**, (*dial auch*) *pret* **hing**, *ptp* **gehangen (a) sich an etw** (*acc*) ~ to hang on to sth; **er hängte sich ihr an den Hals/Arm/Rockzipfel** he hung on to or clung to her neck/arm/apron-strings; **sich von etw/über etw** (*acc*) ~ to suspend oneself from/over sth; **sich unter etw** (*acc*) ~ to hang onto the underside of sth; **sich ins Seil/in die Seile** ~ (*Bergsteiger, Ringer*) to lean against the rope/ropes; **er hängte sich ans Telefon** or **an die Strippe** (*inf*) he got on the phone; **sich an die Flasche/an den Wasserhahn** ~ (*inf*) to have a good long drink.

(b) sich an etw (*acc*) ~ (*sich festsetzen*) to cling or stick to sth; **sich an jdn** ~ (*sich anschließen*) to latch on to sb (*inf*).

(c) sich an jdn/etw ~ (*gefühlsmäßig binden*) to become attached to sb/sth.

(d) (*verfolgen*) **sich an jdn/an ein Fahrzeug** ~ to set off in (hot) pursuit of sb/a vehicle.

(e) sich in etw (*acc*) ~ (*sl*) (*sich engagieren*) to get involved in sth; (*sich einmischen*) to meddle in sth.

(f) (*sl: sich setzen*) to park oneself (*inf*) or one's fanny (*sl*).

hängenbleiben *vi sep irreg aux sein* **(a)** to get caught (**an** + *dat* on).

(b) (*Sport*) (*zurückbleiben*) to get left behind; (*nicht durch-, weiterkommen*) not to get through. **der Aufschlag blieb im**

Netz hängen the ball didn't get past the net; **der Angriff blieb vor dem Strafraum hängen** the attack didn't get past the front of the penalty area; **die Mannschaft blieb schon in der ersten Runde hängen** the team didn't get past or through the first round.

(c) (*Sch inf: nicht versetzt werden*) to stay down.

(d) (*sich aufhalten*) to stay on. **bei einer Nebensächlichkeit ~** to get bogged down with a secondary issue, to get sidetracked.

(e) (*sich festsetzen, haftenbleiben*) to get stuck or caught (*in, an +dat* on); (*Blick, Augen*) to rest (*an +dat* on). **es bleibt ja doch alles an mir hängen** (*fig inf*) I'm stuck or landed with everything (*inf*); **der Verdacht ist an ihm hängengeblieben** suspicion rested on him; **vom Lateinunterricht ist bei ihm nicht viel hängengeblieben** (*fig inf*) not much of his Latin stuck (*inf*).

hängend 1 *prp of* **hängen. 2** *adj* hanging. **~e Gärten** hanging gardens; **mit ~er Zunge kam er angelaufen** (*fig*) he came running up panting; **mit ~em Kopf** (*fig*) in low spirits, crestfallen; **~ befestigt sein** to be hung up; **~e Ventile** (*Tech*) overhead valves.

hängenlassen *sep irreg, ptp.* **hängen(ge)lassen 1** *vt* **(a)** (*vergessen*) to leave behind. **(b)** (*inf: im Stich lassen*) to let down. **(c)** (*Sch: nicht versetzen*) to keep down. **2** *vr* to let oneself go. **laß dich nicht so hängen!** don't let yourself go like this!, pull yourself together!; **er läßt sich furchtbar hängen** he has really let himself go.

Hänge-: **~ohr** *nt* lop ear; **~partie** *f* (*Chess*) adjourned game; **~pflanze** *f* trailing plant.

Hänger *m* **-s, -** **(a)** *siehe* **Anhänger. (b)** *siehe* **Hängekleid. (c)** (*Mantel*) loose(-fitting) coat.

Hangerl *nt* **-s, -(n)** (*Aus*) **(a)** *siehe* **Lätzchen. (b)** *siehe* **Geschirrhandtuch.**

Hänge-: **~schloß** *nt siehe* **Vorhängeschloß; ~schrank** *m* wallcupboard; **~schultern** *pl* drooping shoulders *pl*.

hängig *adj* **(a)** (*Sw Jur*) *siehe* **anhängig. (b)** (*form*) sloping, inclined.

Hanglage *f* sloping site. **in ~** situated on a slope.

Hängolin *nt* **-s,** *no pl* (*hum*) anti-sex drug.

Hang-: **~segeln** *nt* (*Sport*) hang-gliding; **~täter** *m* (*Jur*) person with criminal tendencies.

Hannemann *m*: **~ geh du voran** (*inf*) you go first.

Hannibal *m* **-s** Hannibal.

Hannover [ha'no:fɐ] *nt* **-s** Hanover.

Hannoveraner [hanovə'ra:nɐ] *m* **-s, -** Hanoverian (horse).

Hannoveraner(in *f*) *m* **-s, -** Hanoverian.

hannoverisch [ha'no:fərɪʃ] (*rare*), **hannöversch** [ha'nø:fɐʃ] (*old*) *adj* Hanoverian.

Hans *m* **-' or -ens:** **~ Guckindieluft** Johnny Head-in-the-Air; **~ im Glück** (*fig*) lucky dog (*inf*) or devil (*inf*); **jeder ~ findet seine Grete** (*Prov*) every Jack has or shall have his Jill (*Prov*).

Hansa *f* **-,** *no pl* (*Hist*) *siehe* **Hanse.**

Hansaplast ® *nt* **-(e)s,** *no pl* Elastoplast ®.

Hänschen ['hɛnsçən] *nt* **-s** *dim of* **Hans; was ~ nicht lernt, lernt Hans nimmermehr** (*Prov*) = you can't teach an old dog new tricks (*Prov*).

Hansdampf *m* **-(e)s, -e** Jack-of-all-trades (and master of none). **er ist ein ~ in allen Gassen** he knows everybody and everything.

Hanse *f* **-,** *no pl* (*Hist*) Hanseatic League, Hansa, Hanse.

Hanseat(in *f*) *m* **-en, -en** citizen of a Hansa town; (*Hist*) Hanseatic merchant, merchant belonging to the Hanseatic League.

Hanseatengeist *m* Hanseatic spirit.

hanseatisch *adj* **(a)** (*Hist*) Hanseatic. **(b)** (*hansestädtisch*) Hanseatic. **(c)** (*fig*: *vornehm*) cool and reserved.

Hansebund *m* (*Hist*) Hanseatic League.

Hansel, Hänsel *m* **-s** *dim of* **Hans** (*dial*: *Trottel*) dolt, ninny (*inf*). **~ und Gretel** Hansel and Gretel; **ein paar ~** (*dial*: *wenige*) a few.

Hänselei *f* teasing *no pl.*

hänseln *vt* to tease.

Hanse-: **~stadt** *f* Hansa or Hanseatic or Hanse town; **h~städtisch** *adj* Hanseatic.

hansisch *adj* (*Hist*) Hanseatic.

Hans-: **~narr** *m* (*dated*) tomfool (*inf*); **~wurst** *m* **-(e)s, -e or -e** (*hum*) ̈e **(a)** buffoon, clown; **(b)** (*Theat*) fool, clown; **~wurstiade** *f* (a) (*auch* **~wursterei**) clowning, buffoonery; **(b)** (*Theat*) = harlequinade.

Hantel *f* **-, -n** (*Sport*) dumb-bell.

hanteln *vi* (*Sport*) to exercise with dumb-bells.

hantieren* *vi* **(a)** (*arbeiten*) to be busy. **(b)** (*umgehen mit*) **mit etw ~** to handle sth; **seine Geschicklichkeit im H~ mit Begriffen** (*fig*) his skill in handling ideas. **(c)** (*herum~*) to tinker or fiddle about (*an +dat* with, on).

hantig *adj* (*Aus, S Ger*) **(a)** (*bitter*) bitter. **(b)** (*barsch*) brusque, abrupt.

haperig *adj* (*N Ger*) *siehe* **stockend.**

hapern *vi impers* (*inf*) **es hapert an etw** (*dat*) (*fehlt*) there is a shortage or lack of sth; **es hapert bei jdm mit etw** sb is short of sth, sb is badly off for sth; **es hapert (bei jdm) mit etw** (*klappt nicht*) sb has a problem with sth; **mit der Grammatik hapert es bei ihm** he's weak in or poor at grammar.

Häppchen *nt* *dim of* **Happen** morsel, bit; (*Appetithappen*) titbit.

häppchenweise *adv* (*inf: lit, fig*) bit by bit.

Happen *m* **-s, -** (*inf*) mouthful, morsel; (*kleine Mahlzeit*) bite (*inf*), snack. **ein fetter ~** (*fig*) a good catch; **nach dem Theater aßen wir noch einen ~** after the theatre we had a bite to eat (*inf*) or a snack; **ich habe heute noch keinen ~ gegessen** I haven't had a bite to eat all day.

Happening ['hɛpənɪŋ] *nt* **-s, -s** (*Art*) action painting; (*Theat*) happening. **ein kleines ~ machen** (*fig inf*) to have a bit of fun.

happig *adj* (*inf*) steep (*inf*).

Happy-End, Happyend (*Aus*) ['hɛpɪ'|ɛnt] *nt* **-s, -s** happy ending. **ein Film/Buch/eine Geschichte mit ~** a film/book/story with a happy ending.

Harakiri *nt* **-(s), -s** harakiri.

Harald *m* **-s** Harold.

Härchen *nt* *dim of* **Haar** little or tiny hair.

Hard- ['ha:d-]: **~top** [-tɔp] *nt* **-s, -s** (*Aut*) (*Dach, Wagen*) hardtop; **ein Cabrio mit ~top** a cabriolet with a hardtop; **~ware** [-wɛə] *f* **-, -s** (*Computer*) hardware.

Harem *m* **-s, -s** (*auch hum*) harem.

Harems-: **~dame** *f* lady of the/a harem; **~wächter** *m* harem guard.

hären *adj* (*rare*) **~es Gewand** hairshirt.

Häresie *f* (*lit, fig*) heresy.

Häretiker(in *f*) *m* **-s, -** (*lit, fig*) heretic.

häretisch *adj* (*lit, fig*) heretical.

Harfe *f* **-, -n** harp.

Harfenist(in *f*) *m* harpist.

Harfen-: **~klang** *m* sound of the/a harp; **~spiel** *nt* *no pl* harp-playing; **~spieler** *m* harp-player, harpist.

Harfner(in *f*) *m* **-s, -** (*obs*) harp-player, harpist.

Harke *f* **-, -n** (*esp N Ger*) rake. **jdm zeigen, was eine ~ ist** (*fig inf*) to show sb what's what (*inf*).

harken *vti* (*esp N Ger*) to rake.

Harlekin ['harleki:n] *m* **-s, -e** Harlequin.

Harlekinade *f* *siehe* **Hanswurstiade.**

Harm *m* **-(e)s** *no pl* (*poet, obs*) sore affliction (*liter*), grief.

härmen *vtr* (*old*) *siehe* **grämen.**

harmlos *adj* **(a)** (*ungefährlich*) harmless; *Berg, Piste, Kurve* easy; *Schnupfen, Entzündung etc* slight, mild. **eine ~e Grippe** a mild bout of flu. **(b)** (*unschuldig, gutartig, naiv*) innocent; (*unbedenklich*) harmless, innocuous. **er ist ein ~er Mensch** he's harmless (enough), he's an innocuous type.

Harmlosigkeit *f*, *no pl* *siehe adj* **(a)** harmlessness; easiness; slightness, mildness. **(b)** innocence; harmlessness. **in aller ~** in all innocence.

Harmonie *f* (*Mus, fig*) harmony.

Harmonie-: **~gesetz** *nt* *usu pl* rule of harmony; **~lehre** *f* (*Gebiet*) harmony; (*Theorie*) harmonic theory; **~musik** *f* music for wind instruments.

harmonieren* *vi* (*Mus, fig*) to harmonize; (*farblich auch*) to go together, to match.

Harmonik *f*, *no pl* harmony.

Harmonika *f* **-, -s or Harmoniken** harmonica; (*Mund~ auch*) mouth organ; (*Zieh~*) accordion.

Harmonikatür *f* folding or accordion door.

harmonisch *adj* (*Mus, Math*) harmonic; (*wohlklingend, fig*) harmonious. **das klingt nicht sehr ~** that's not a very harmonious sound; **sie leben ~ zusammen** they live together in harmony.

harmonisieren* *vt* (*Mus*) to harmonize; (*fig*) to coordinate.

Harmonisierung *f* (*Mus*) harmonization; (*fig*) coordination.

Harmonium *nt* harmonium.

Harn *m* **-(e)s, -e** urine. **~ lassen** to pass water, to urinate.

Harn-: **~blase** *f* bladder; **~blasenentzündung** *f* *siehe* **Blasenentzündung; ~drang** *m* (*form*) urge or need to pass water or to urinate.

harnen *vi* (*form*) to urinate, to pass water, to micturate (*form*).

Harn-: **~entleerung** *f* urination, passing of water, micturition (*form*); **~flasche** *f* urinal.

Harnisch *m* **-(e)s, -e** armour. **in ~ sein** (*fig*) to be up in arms, to have one's hackles up; **jdn in ~ bringen** (*fig*) to get sb up in arms, to get sb's hackles up; **wenn sie das sieht, gerät or kommt sie in ~** it gets her hackles up when she sees that.

Harn-: **~lassen** *nt* **-s,** *no pl* (*form*) urination, passing of water, micturition (*form*); **~leiter** *m* ureter; **~organ** *nt* urinary organ; **~probe** *f* urine sample or specimen; **~röhre** *f* urethra; **~säure** *f* (*Chem*) uric acid; **~stein** *m* (*Med*) urinary calculus; **~stoff** *m* (*Chem*) urea, carbamide; **h~treibend** *adj* (*form*) diuretic; **~untersuchung** *f* urine analysis, urinalysis; **~vergiftung** *f* uraemia; **~wege** *pl* (*Anat*) urinary tract *sing*; **~zucker** *m* sugar in the urine.

Harpsichord [harpsi'kɔrt] *nt* **-(e)s, -e** (*old*) *siehe* **Cembalo.**

Harpune *f* **-, -n** harpoon.

Harpunengeschütz *nt*, **Harpunenkanone** *f*, **Harpunenwerfer** *m* harpoon-gun.

Harpunier *m* **-s, -e** harpooner.

harpunieren* *vti* to harpoon.

Harpyie [har'py:jə] *f* *usu pl* (*Myth*) Harpy.

Harrdigatti *interj* (*Aus*) Great Scott.

harren *vi* (*geh*) **jds/einer Sache ~, auf jdn/etw ~** to await sb/sth, to wait for sb/sth; *siehe* **Ding[1].**

Harsch *m* **-(e)s,** *no pl* frozen snow.

harsch *adj* **(a)** harsh. **(b)** (*verharscht*) *Schnee* frozen.

harschen *vi* to freeze over.

harschig *adj* *Schnee* frozen.

Harschschnee *m* frozen snow.

hart 1 *adj* **(a)** (*nicht weich, nicht sanft*) hard; *Matratze, Bett, Federung, Apfelschale auch* firm; *Aufprall, Ruck auch* violent; *Wind* strong; *Ei* hard-boiled. **~ werden** to get hard, to harden; **Eier ~ kochen** to hard-boil eggs; **der Boden ist ~ gefroren** the ground is frozen hard or solid; **er hat einen ~en Leib** (*Med old*) he is constipated; **er hat einen ~en Schädel or Kopf** (*fig*) he's pig-headed or obstinate; **ein ~es Herz haben** (*fig*) to have a hard heart, to be hard-hearted; **~ wie Stahl/Stein** as hard as steel/stone.

(b) (*scharf*) *Konturen, Kontrast, Formen*, (*Phot*) *Negativ* sharp; (*Gesichts*)*züge, Konsonant* hard; *Licht* harsh, hard; *Klang, Ton, Aussprache, Akzent* harsh.

(c) (rauh) Spiel, Gegner rough; (fig) Getränke, Droge, Pornographie hard; Kriminalfilm etc, Western tough.

(d) (widerstandsfähig, robust) tough. **kalte Duschen machen ~ cold** showers toughen you up or make you tough; **gelobt sei, was ~ macht** (prov, usu iro) anything for toughness!; treat 'em rough, make 'em tough! (inf); **er ist ~ im Nehmen** he's tough.

(e) (stabil, sicher) Währung, Devisen stable. **in ~en Dollars** in hard dollars.

(f) (streng, gnadenlos, kompromißlos) Mensch, Kampf hard; Wort auch strong, harsh; Winter, Frost, Vertragsbedingung auch severe; Strafe, Urteil, Kritik severe, harsh; Maßnahmen, Gesetze, Politik, Kurs tough; Auseinandersetzung violent. **er ist durch eine ~e Schule gegangen** (fig) he has been through a hard school; **~ bleiben** to stand or remain firm; **~ mit jdm sein** to be hard on sb, to be harsh with sb; **es fielen ~e Worte** hard or strong or harsh words were used; **es geht ~ auf ~** it's a tough fight or real battle.

(g) (schwer zu ertragen) Los, Schicksal, Tatsache hard, cruel; Verlust cruel; Wirklichkeit, Wahrheit harsh. **es war sehr ~ für ihn, daß er ...** it was very hard for him to ...; **oh, das war ~!** (inf: Witz etc) oh, that was painful!

(h) (mühevoll, anstrengend) Arbeit, Leben, Zeiten hard, tough.

(i) (Phys) Strahlen hard.

2 adv **(a)** hard. **er schläft gerne ~** he likes sleeping on a hard surface/bed.

(b) (scharf) kontrastiert sharply. **~ klingen** to sound harsh; **er spricht manche Laute zu ~ aus** he makes some sounds too hard.

(c) (heftig, rauh) roughly; fallen, aufprallen hard. **er läßt die Kupplung immer so ~ kommen** he always lets the clutch in so roughly or violently; **~ aneinandergeraten** (sich prügeln) to come to blows, to have a (real) set-to (inf); (sich streiten) to get into a fierce argument, to have a (real) set-to (inf); **~ einsteigen** (Sport) to go hard at it; **jdn ~ anfahren** to bite sb's head off (inf); **jdm ~ zusetzen** to press sb hard; **etw trifft jdn ~** (lit, fig) sth hits sb hard; **~ diskutieren** to have a vigorous discussion; **~spielen** (Sport) to play rough.

(d) (streng) severely, harshly. **~ durchgreifen** to take tough or rigorous action; **jdn ~ anfassen** to be hard on sb, to treat sb harshly.

(e) (mühevoll) hard. **~ arbeiten** to work hard; **es kommt mich ~ an** (geh) I find it hard.

(f) (nahe) close (an +dat to). **das ist ~ an der Grenze der Legalität/des Zumutbaren** that's pushing legality/reasonableness to its (very) limit(s), that's on the very limits of legality/of what's reasonable; **das ist ~ an der Grenze zum Kriminellen/zum Kitsch** that's very close to being criminal/kitsch; **wir fuhren ~ am Abgrund vorbei** (fig) we were (very) close to or on the (very) brink of disaster; **~ am Wind (segeln)** (Naut) (to sail) close to the wind; **~ auf ein Ziel zuhalten** (Naut) to head straight for a destination.

Hart-: ~bahn f (Sport) hard track; h~bedrängt adj attr hard-pressed; ~beton m (especially) hard concrete; h~blätt(e)rig adj (Bot) hard-leaved.

Härte f -, -n siehe adj **(a)** hardness; firmness; violence; (Härtegrad) degree or grade (of hardness). **die ~, mit der er bremste** the violence with which he braked.

(b) no pl (Schärfe) sharpness; hardness; harshness.

(c) (Rauheit) roughness no pl. **sie spielten mit größter ~** they played very rough.

(d) no pl (Robustheit) toughness.

(e) no pl (Stabilität) stability.

(f) no pl (Strenge) hardness; harshness; severity; toughness; violence. **eine Auseinandersetzung in großer ~ führen** to have a violent argument; **mit großer ~ diskutieren** to have a very heated discussion.

(g) (schwere Erträglichkeit) cruelty, harshness. **der Schicksalsschlag traf ihn in seiner ganzen ~** this blow of fate struck him with all its force or cruelty; **soziale ~n** social hardships; (Fälle) cases of social hardship.

(h) (Phys) degree of penetration.

Härte-: ~ausgleich m (Admin) compensation for (social) hardship; ~fall m case of hardship; (inf: Mensch) hardship case; ~fonds m hardship fund; ~grad m degree or grade of hardness; ~klausel f hardship clause; ~mittel nt (Metal) hardening agent.

härten 1 vt to harden; Stahl auch to temper. **2** vi to harden. **3** vr (Stoff) to harden; (rare: Mensch) to toughen oneself up.

Härte-: ~ofen m (Metal) tempering oven or furnace; ~paragraph m paragraph dealing with cases of hardship.

härter comp of hart.

Härter m -s, - (Tech) hardener, hardening agent.

Härteskala f scale of hardness, Mohs scale.

härteste(r, s) superl of hart.

Härtezustand m hard state. **im ~ läßt sich das Material wie Metall bearbeiten** in the hard state or when it is hard this material can be worked like metal.

Hart-: ~faserplatte f hardboard, fiberboard (US); h~gebrannt adj attr Ziegel, Keramik hard-baked; h~gefroren adj attr frozen, frozen stiff pred, frozen hard pred; h~gekocht adj attr Ei hard-boiled; (fig) Mensch auch hard-baked (inf); ~geld nt hard cash; h~gesotten adj **(a)** (fig) hard-baked (inf), hard-boiled; **(b)** (Aus) siehe h~gekocht; h~geworden adj attr hard; ~gummi nt hard rubber; h~herzig adj hard-hearted; ~herzigkeit f hard-heartedness; ~holz nt hardwood; h~hörig adj (old) siehe schwerhörig; ~käse m hard cheese; h~köpfig adj (dial) siehe dickköpfig; ~laubgewächs nt (Bot) sclerophyllous evergreen (spec); h~leibig adj (Med old) constipated; ~leibigkeit f (Med old) constipation;

h~löten vti sep to hard-solder; ~metall nt hard metal; h~näckig adj (stur) Mensch, Haltung obstinate, stubborn; (ausdauernd) Widerstand stubborn; Lügner persistent; Beharrlichkeit dogged, persistent; (langwierig) Krankheit, Fleck stubborn; ~näckigkeit f siehe adj obstinacy, stubbornness; persistence; doggedness; stubbornness; ~packung f hard pack; ~pappe f cardboard; ~platz m (Sport) hard sports area; (für Ballspiele) hard pitch; (Tennis) hard court; h~schalig adj Frucht hard-shelled, testaceous (spec); Apfel, Traube having a tough skin, tough-skinned; ~spiritus m methylated spirits in solid form.

Hartung m -s, -e (obs) January.

Härtung f (Tech) hardening; (von Stahl auch) tempering.

Hart-: ~ware f hardware no pl; ~weizengrieß m semolina; ~wurst f dry sausage.

Harz[1] nt -es, -e resin.

Harz[2] m -es (Geog) Harz Mountains pl.

harz|artig adj resin-like, resinous, resinoid.

harzen 1 vt Wein to treat with resin, to resinate. 2 vi (Baum, Holz) to secrete or exude resin.

Harzer[1] m -s, - (Cook) Harz cheese.

Harzer[2] adj (Geog) Harz. **~ Roller** (Zool) roller; (Cook) (roll-shaped) Harz cheese; **~ Käse** Harz cheese.

Harzer(in f) m -s, - native or (Einwohner) inhabitant of the Harz Mountains.

harzhaltig adj Holz resinous, containing resin.

harzig adj **(a)** Holz, Geruch, Geschmack, Wein resinous, resiny. **(b)** (Sw fig: zähflüssig) slow-moving.

Hasard [ha'zart] nt -s, no pl siehe Hasardspiel **(mit etw)** ~ **spielen** (fig geh) to gamble (with sth).

Hasardeur [hazar'dø:ɐ] m (geh) gambler.

hasardieren* vi (fig geh) to gamble, to take risks.

Hasardspiel [ha'zart-] nt game of chance; (fig geh) gamble. **glatte Fahrbahnen machen das Autofahren zum ~** slippy roads make driving a treacherous business.

Hasch nt -(s), no pl (inf) hash (inf).

Haschee nt -s, -s (Cook) hash.

Haschen nt -s, no pl catch, tag.

haschen[1] (dated, geh) 1 vt to catch. **hasch mich, ich bin der Frühling** (hum inf) come and get me boys! (hum). 2 vi nach etw **~** to make a grab at sth; **nach Beifall/Lob** etc **~** to fish or angle for applause/praise etc.

haschen[2] vi (inf) to smoke (hash) (inf).

Häschen ['hɛsçən] nt **(a)** dim of Hase young hare, leveret. **(b)** (inf: Kaninchen, Playboy~) bunny (inf). **(c)** (Kosename) sweetheart, sweetie(pie).

Hascher(in f) m -s, - (a) (inf) hash smoker. **(b)** (Aus inf) poor soul or thing (inf).

Häscher m -s, - (old, geh) henchman.

Hascherl m -s, -(n) (a) (Aus inf) poor soul or thing or creature. **(b)** (naiver Mensch) simple soul.

haschieren* vt (Cook) Fleisch to mince (Brit), to grind (US).

Haschisch nt or m -s, no pl hashish.

Haschischrausch m state of euphoria produced by hashish. **im ~** under the effects of hashish.

Haschmich m -s, no pl (inf) **einen ~ haben** to have a screw loose (inf), to be off one's rocker (inf).

Hase m -n, -n hare; (männlicher ~ auch) buck; (dial: Kaninchen, Oster~, in Märchen) rabbit. **falscher ~** (Cook) meat loaf; **wissen/sehen, wie der ~ läuft** (fig inf) to know/see which way the wind blows; **alter ~** (fig inf) old hand; **da liegt der ~ im Pfeffer** (inf) that's the crux of the matter; **mein Name ist ~ (, ich weiß von nichts)** I don't know anything about anything.

Hasel f -, -n (Bot) hazel.

Hasel-: ~busch m hazel-bush; ~gerte f hazel switch or rod; ~huhn nt hazel grouse; ~kätzchen nt (Bot) (hazel) catkin, lamb's tail (inf); ~maus f dormouse; ~nuß f hazelnut, cob-nut; ~rute f hazel rod or switch; ~strauch m hazel-bush.

Hasen-: ~braten m roast hare; ~brot nt (inf) left-over sandwich; ~fuß m **(a)** hare's foot; **(b)** (dated inf) milksop (dated); h~füßig adj (dated inf) chicken-hearted (dated inf), lily-livered (inf); ~herz nt (a) hare's heart; (b) (dated inf) siehe ~fuß (b); ~jagd f hare-hunt; **auf (die) ~jagd gehen** to go hunting hares or on a hare-hunt; **er ist auf ~jagd** he's hunting hares or on a hare-hunt; ~klein nt -s, no pl (Cook) jointed hare; ~panier nt **das ~panier ergreifen** (dated inf) to turn tail (and run); ~pfeffer m (Cook) ~ jugged hare; h~rein adj (Hunt) Hund trained to chase hares only on command; **jd/etw ist nicht (ganz) h~rein** (inf) sb/sth is not (quite) aboveboard, there's something fishy about sb/sth (inf); ~scharte f (Med) hare-lip.

Häsin f doe, female hare.

Haspel f -, -n (a) (Förderwinde) windlass. **(b)** (Garn~) reel.

haspeln vti (a) (inf: hastig sprechen) to splutter, to sputter; Gebete, Entschuldigung to sp(l)utter out. **(b)** (wickeln) to wind up, to reel up; (abwickeln) to unwind, to reel off.

Haß m Hasses, no pl (a) hatred, hate (auf +acc, gegen of). **Liebe und ~** love and hate or hatred; **sich (dat) jds ~ zuziehen, jds ~ auf sich** (acc) **ziehen** to incur sb's hatred.

(b) (inf: Wut, Ärger) **wenn ich so etwas sehe, könnt' ich einen ~ kriegen** (inf) when I see something like that I could get really angry; **einen ~ (auf jdn) schieben** (sl) or **haben** (inf) to be really sore (with sb) (inf).

Haß|ausbruch m burst of hatred.

hassen vti to hate, to detest, to loathe. **etw ~ wie die Pest** (inf) to hate sth like the plague (inf).

hassenswert adj hateful, odious, detestable.

Haß-: h~erfüllt adj full of hate or hatred; ~gefühl nt feeling of hatred.

häßlich adj **(a)** ugly. **~ wie die Nacht** or **die Sünde** (as) ugly as sin. **(b)** (gemein) nasty, mean. **das war ~ von ihm** that was nasty or mean of him; ~ **über jdn sprechen** to be nasty or mean about sb. **(c)** (*unerfreulich*) nasty; *Vorfall, Streit auch* ugly.

Häßlichkeit f *siehe adj* **(a)** ugliness *no pl.* **(b)** nastiness *no pl*, meanness *no pl*; (*Bemerkung*) nasty or mean remark. **(c)** nastiness; ugliness.

Haß-: ~**liebe** f love-hate relationship (*für* with); ~**liebe für jdn empfinden** to have a love-hate relationship with sb; ~**tirade** f tirade of hatred; **h~verzerrt** *adj Gesicht* twisted (up) with hatred.

hast 2. *pers sing present of* **haben.**

Hast f -, *no pl* haste. **voller** ~ in great haste, in a great hurry or rush; **ohne** ~ without haste, without hurrying or rushing; **mit fliegender/rasender** ~ in a tearing/frantic hurry; **mit einer solchen** ~ in such a hurry or rush, in such haste; **nur keine (jüdische)** ~! not so fast!, hold your horses! (*inf*).

haste (*inf*) *contr of* **hast du; (was)** ~ **was kannste** as quick or fast as possible; ~ **was, biste was** (*prov*) fortune brings status.

hasten vi *aux sein* (*geh*) to hasten (*form*), to hurry.

hastig *adj* hasty; *Essen auch, Worte* hurried, rushed. **nicht so** ~! not so fast!; **er schlang sein Essen** ~ **hinunter** he gobbled down his food; **sein** ~**es Rauchen** his hasty way of smoking.

Hastigkeit f hurriedness. **sie ißt/schwimmt** *etc* **mit einer solchen** ~ she eats/swims *etc* in such a hasty manner.

hat 3. *pers sing present of* **haben.**

Hätschelei f (*pej*) pampering, mollycoddling.

Hätschelkind nt (*Kind*) pampered child; (*fig: Liebling*) blue-eyed boy/girl (*inf*), darling.

hätscheln vt (*liebkosen*) to pet, to fondle; (*zu weich behandeln*) to pamper, to mollycoddle; (*bevorzugen*) to pamper, to indulge; (*hängen an*) *Plan, Idee* to cherish, to nurse; *Schmerz* to nurse, to indulge.

hatschen vi *aux sein* (*Aus, S Ger inf*) (*schlendern*) to amble along; (*mühsam gehen*) to trudge along; (*hinken*) to hobble. **durch die Berge** ~ to trudge through the mountains.

Hatscher m -s, - (*Aus inf*) **(a)** (*Marsch*) long haul, trudge. **(b)** *usu pl* (*Schuh*) worn-out shoe.

hatschert *adj* (*Aus inf*) hobbling. **er geht** ~ he hobbles (along).

hatschi *interj* atishoo. ~ **machen** (*baby-talk*) to sneeze.

hatte *pret of* **haben.**

Hat-Trick, Hattrick [ˈhættrɪk] m -s, -s (*Sport*) hat trick.

Hatz f -, -en **(a)** (*Hunt, fig*) hunt. **(b)** (*fig: esp S Ger, Aus*) rush.

hatzi *interj siehe* **hatschi.**

Hau m -s, -e (*inf*) bash (*inf*), clout (*inf*). **einen** ~ **haben** to be thick (*inf*).

Häubchen nt *dim of* **Haube.**

Haube f -, -n **(a)** bonnet; (*Aus, S Ger: Mütze*) (woollen) cap; (*von Krankenschwester etc*) cap. **jdn unter die** ~ **bringen** (*hum*) to marry sb off (*inf*); **unter der** ~ **sein/unter die** ~ **kommen** (*hum*) to be/get married. **(b)** (*bei Vögeln*) crest. **(c)** (*allgemein: Bedeckung*) cover; (*Trocken*~) (hair) dryer, drying hood (*US*); (*für Kaffee-, Teekanne*) cosy; (*Motor*~) bonnet, hood (*US*). **der hat einiges unter der** ~ (*inf*) it's got quite some engine (*inf*).

Hauben-: ~**lerche** f crested lark; ~**meise** f crested tit; ~**taucher** m (*Zool*) great crested grebe.

Haubitze f -, -n howitzer.

Hauch m -(e)s, -e (*geh, poet*) **(a)** (*Atem*) breath. **(b)** (*Luftzug*) breath of air, breeze. **(c)** (*Duft*) smell; (*von Parfüm auch*) waft. **ein** ~ **von Frühling/Harz lag in der Luft** (*liter*) a breath of spring/a delicate smell of resin was or hung in the air (*liter*). **(d)** (*Flair*) aura, air. **ihr Haus hat den** ~ **des Exotischen** their house has an exotic air (about it) or an aura of exoticism. **(e)** (*Andeutung, Anflug, Schicht*) hint, touch; (*von Lächeln*) hint, ghost. **Reif bedeckte den Rasen als zarter** ~ a touch of hoarfrost lay on the lawn.

hauchdünn *adj* extremely thin; *Scheiben, Schokoladentäfelchen* wafer-thin; (*fig*) *Mehrheit* extremely narrow; *Sieg* extremely close.

hauchen 1 vi to breathe. **gegen/auf etw** (*acc*) ~ to breathe on sth.

2 vt (*lit, fig, liter: flüstern*) to breathe. **jdn einen Kuß auf die Wange** ~ (*liter*) to brush sb's cheek with one's lips; **das Jawort** ~ (*liter*) to breathe "I will"; **jdm etw** (*acc*) **ins Ohr** ~ (*liter*) to whisper sth in sb's ear; **er hauchte mir den Zigarettenrauch ins Gesicht** he blew the cigarette smoke in(to) my face.

Hauch-: **h~fein** *adj* extremely fine; ~**laut** m (*Phon*) aspirate; **h~zart** *adj* very delicate; *Schokoladentäfelchen* wafer-thin.

Haudegen m (*fig*) old campaigner, (old) warhorse.

Haue f -, -n **(a)** (*S Ger, Sw, Aus*) *siehe* **Hacke²** **(a). (b)** *no pl* (*inf: Prügel*) (good) hiding (*inf*) or spanking. ~ **kriegen** to get a good hiding (*inf*) or spanking.

hauen *pret* **haute**, *ptp* **gehauen** or (*dial*) **gehaut** 1 vt **(a)** *pret auch* **hieb** (*inf: schlagen*) to hit, to clout (*inf*), to clobber (*inf*). **er haute den Stein in zwei Teile** he smashed the stone in two; **er haute ihr das Heft um die Ohren** he hit or clouted (*inf*) or clobbered (*inf*) her round the head with the exercise book. **(b)** (*inf: verprügeln*) to hit, to belt (*sl*), to thump (*inf*). **hau(t) ihn!** let him have it! (*inf*), belt or thump him (one) (*sl*). **(c)** (*meißeln*) *Statue, Figur* to carve; *Stufen* to cut, to hew (*form*); *Loch* to cut, to knock. **(d)** *pret* **hieb** (*geh: mit Waffe schlagen*) to make a thrust at sb. **jdn aus dem Sattel/vom Pferd** ~ to knock sb out of the saddle/from his horse. **(e)** (*inf: stoßen*) *jdn, Gegenstand* to shove (*inf*); *Körperteil* to bang, to knock (*an +acc* on, against). **das haut einen vom Stuhl or aus den Latschen or aus dem Anzug** or **den stärksten Mann aus dem Anzug** it really knocks you sideways (*inf*).

(f) (*inf*) (*werfen*) to chuck (*inf*), to fling; (*fig*) (*hinzufügen*) *Pfeffer, Kommas* to bung (*inf*) (*in +acc* in); (*nachlässig machen*) *Aufsatz, Skizze* to scribble, to scrawl (*auf +acc* on); *Farbe* to slap (*inf*) (*auf +acc* on). **er hat ihm eine 6 ins Zeugnis gehauen** he slammed a 6 on his report (*inf*). **(g)** (*dial*) (*fällen*) *Baum* to chop (down), to hew (down); (*mähen*) *Gras* to cut; (*zerhacken*) *Holz, Fleisch* to chop (up). **(h)** (*Min*) *Erz* to cut; *Kohle* to break.

2 vi **(a)** *pret auch* **hieb** (*inf: schlagen*) to hit. **jdm ins Gesicht** ~ to hit or clout (*inf*) or clobber (*inf*) sb in the face; **jdm auf die Schulter** ~ to clap or slap sb on the shoulder; **hau doch nicht so (auf die Tasten)** don't thump like that; **er haute und haute he** banged or thumped away. **(b)** (*inf: prügeln*) **nicht** ~, **Papi!** don't hit or thump (*inf*) me, daddy!; **er haut immer gleich** he's quick to hit out; **er hat ziemlich hart gehauen** he hit quite hard. **(c)** *pret* **hieb** (*geh: mit Waffe*) to lash out. **er hieb mit dem Degen (auf seinen Gegner)** he made a thrust (at his opponent) with his dagger; **es geht auf H~ und Stechen** (*fig*) there's a tough battle; **das H~ und Stechen war seine Leidenschaft nicht** (*geh*) he had no penchant for tough battles. **(d)** *aux sein* (*inf: stoßen*) to bang, to hit. **er ist mit dem Fuß gegen einen spitzen Stein gehauen** he banged or hit his foot against a sharp stone; **das Boot ist (mit dem Kiel) auf eine Sandbank gehauen** the boat's (keel) hit or struck a sandbank.

3 vr (*inf*) **(a)** (*sich prügeln*) to scrap, to fight. **sich mit jdm** ~ to scrap or fight with sb. **(b)** (*sich setzen, legen*) to fling oneself.

Hauer m -s, - **(a)** (*Min*) face-worker. **(b)** (*Aus*) *siehe* **Winzer(in). (c)** (*Zool*) tusk; (*hum: großer Zahn*) fang.

Häuer m -s, - (*Aus*) *siehe* **Hauer (a).**

Hauerei f (*inf*) scrap, fight.

Häufchen nt *dim of* **Haufen** small heap or pile. **ein** ~ **Unglück** a picture of misery; *siehe* **Elend.**

Haufe m -ns, -n (*rare*) *siehe* **Haufen.**

häufeln vt **(a)** *Kartoffeln, Spargel* to hill up. **(b)** (*Haufen machen aus*) to heap or pile up.

Haufen m -s, - **(a)** heap, pile. **jdn/ein Tier über den** ~ **rennen/fahren** *etc* (*inf*) to knock or run sb/an animal down, to run over sb/an animal; **jdn/ein Tier über den** ~ **schießen** (*inf*) or **knallen** (*inf*) to shoot sb/an animal down; **etw** (*acc*) **über den** ~ **werfen** (*inf*) or **schmeißen** (*inf*) (*verwerfen*) to throw or chuck (*inf*) sth out; (*durchkreuzen*) to mess sth up (*inf*); **der Hund hat da einen** ~ **gemacht** the dog has made a mess there (*inf*); **so viele Dummköpfe/soviel Idiotie/soviel Geld habe ich noch nie auf einem** ~ **gesehen** (*inf*) I've never seen so many fools/so much idiocy/money in one place before. **(b)** (*inf: große Menge*) load (*inf*), heap (*inf*). **ein** ~ **Arbeit/Geld/Bücher** a load or heap of work/money/books (*all inf*), piles or loads or heaps of work/money/books (*all inf*); **ein** ~ **Unsinn** a load of (old) rubbish (*inf*), a load of nonsense (*inf*); **ein** ~ **Zeit** loads or heaps of time (*inf*); **ich hab noch einen** ~ **zu tun** I still have loads or piles or heaps or a load to do (*all inf*); **in** ~ by the ton (*inf*); **er hat einen ganzen** ~ **Freunde** he has a whole load of friends (*inf*), he has loads or heaps of friends (*inf*). **(c)** (*Schar*) crowd; (*von Vögeln*) flock. **ein** ~ **Schaulustige(r)** a crowd of onlookers; **dichte** ~ **von Reisenden** dense crowds of travellers; **dem** ~ **folgen** (*pej*) to follow the crowd; **der große** ~ (*pej*) the common herd, the masses pl; **(einen)** ~ **bilden** to form a crowd; **die Leute kamen in hellen** ~ people flocked there *etc*, people came in their hundreds. **(d)** (*Gruppe, Gemeinschaft*) crowd (*inf*), bunch (*inf*); (*Mil*) troop.

häufen 1 vt to pile up, to heap up; (*sammeln*) to accumulate. **Bücher auf den Tisch** ~ to pile books onto the table; **ein gehäufter Teelöffel Salz** a heaped teaspoonful of salt; **Lob auf jdn** ~ (*fig*) to heap praise(s) on sb.

2 vr (*lit, fig: sich ansammeln*) to mount up; (*zahlreicher werden: Unfälle, Fehler, Zahlausdrücke etc*) to occur increasingly. **dieser Fehler tritt allerdings gehäuft auf** indeed this error occurs increasingly or occurs more and more frequently; **das kann schon mal vorkommen, es darf sich nur nicht** ~ these things happen, just as long as they don't happen too often.

Haufen-: ~**dorf** nt scattered village; **h~weise** *adv* **(a)** (*in Haufen*) in heaps or piles; **(b)** (*inf: in großer Zahl, Menge*) piles or heaps or loads of (*all inf*); **etw h~weise haben** to have piles or heaps or loads of sth (*all inf*); ~**wolke** f *siehe* **Kumuluswolke.**

häufig 1 *adj* frequent; (*weit verbreitet auch*) common, widespread. **seine Anfälle werden** ~**er** his attacks are becoming more frequent. 2 *adv* often, frequently.

Häufigkeit f frequency; (*räumliche Verbreitung*) commonness.

Häufigkeits- in *cpds* frequency-; ~**grad** m frequency rank; ~**zahl**, ~**ziffer** f frequency.

Häufung f **(a)** (*fig: das Anhäufen*) accumulation, amassment. **(b)** (*das Sich-Häufen*) increasing number. **in ähnlicher** *etc* ~ in similar *etc* numbers pl.

Haupt nt -(e)s, **Häupter** **(a)** (*geh: Kopf*) head. **entblößten** ~**es** bareheaded; **gesenkten/erhobenen** ~**es** with one's head bowed/raised; **zu jds Häupten** at sb's head; **jdn aufs** ~ **schlagen** (*fig: besiegen*) to vanquish; **eine Reform an** ~ **und Gliedern** a total or wide-reaching reform; **den Staat an** ~ **und Gliedern reformieren** to reform the state totally. **(b)** (*zentrale Figur*) head. **(c)** (*poet: von Berg*) peak.

Haupt- in *cpds* main, principal, chief; ~**achse** f main or principal axis; (*von Fahrzeug*) main axle; ~**akteur** m (*lit, fig*) leading light; (*pej*) kingpin; ~**aktion** f *siehe* **Haupt- und Staatsaktion**; ~**aktionär** m principal or main shareholder; ~**akzent** m **(a)** (*Ling*) main or primary accent or stress;

(b) (*fig*) main emphasis; **auf etw** (*acc*) **den ~akzent legen** to put *or* place the main emphasis on sth; **~altar** *m* high altar; **h~amtlich 1** *adj* full-time; **h~amtliche Tätigkeit** full-time office; **2** *adv* (on a) full-time (basis); **h~amtlich tätig sein** to work full-time; **~angeklagte(r)** *mf* main *or* principal defendant; **~anschluß** *m* (*Telec*) main extension; **nur einen ~anschluß haben** to have a phone without extensions; **~anteil** *m* main *or* principal part *or* share; **~arbeit** *f* main (part of the) work; **~ausgang** *m* main exit; **~bahnhof** *m* main *or* (*in Namen*) central station; **~belastungszeuge** *m* main *or* principal *or* chief witness for the prosecution; **~beruf** *m* chief *or* main occupation *or* profession; **er ist Lehrer im ~beruf** his main *or* chief occupation *or* profession is that of teacher; **h~beruflich 1** *adj Lehrer, Gärtner etc* full-time; **h~berufliche Tätigkeit** main *or* chief occupation; **2** *adv* full-time; **h~beruflich tätig sein** to be employed full-time, to be in full-time employment; **er ist h~beruflich bei dieser Firma tätig** (*voll angestellt*) he is employed full-time by this firm; (*im Gegensatz zu Nebenerwerb*) his main employment is at this firm; **~beschäftigung** *f* **(a)** main *or* chief occupation *or* pursuit; **(b)** (*Hauptberuf*) main *or* chief occupation *or* job; **~betrieb** *m* **(a)** (*Zentralbetrieb*) headquarters *sing or pl*; **(b)** (*geschäftigste Zeit*) peak period; (*Hauptverkehrszeit auch*) rush hour; **~buch** *nt* (*Comm*) ledger; **~büro** *nt* head office; **~darsteller(in** *f*) *m* principal actor/actress, leading man/lady; **~daten** *pl* main facts *pl*; **~deck** *nt* main deck; **~eingang** *m* main entrance; **~einnahmequelle** *f* main *or* chief source of income; **~einwand** *m* main *or* chief *or* principal objection (*gegen* to).

Häuptel *nt* **-s, -** (*Aus*) head (of lettuce *etc*).

Häuptelsalat *m* (*Aus*) lettuce.

Haupt-: **~entlastungszeuge** *m* main *or* principal witness for the defence; **~erbe¹** *m* principal heir; **~erbe²** *nt* principal inheritance; **~ereignis** *nt* main *or* principal event.

Haupteslänge *f* **jdn um ~ überragen** (*lit, fig*) to be head and shoulders above sb.

Haupt-: **~fach** *nt* (*Sch, Univ*) main *or* principal subject, major (*US*); **etw im ~fach studieren** to study sth as a main *or* principal subject, to major in sth (*US*); **~farbe** *f* main *or* principal colour; **~fehler** *m* main *or* chief *or* principal fault; **~feind** *m* main *or* chief enemy; **~feld** (*sl*), **~feldwebel** *m* (company) sergeant major; **~figur** *f* (*Liter*) central *or* main *or* principal character *or* figure; (*fig*) leading *or* central figure; **~film** *m* main film; **~forderung** *f* main *or* chief *or* principal demand; **~frage** *f* main *or* principal question *or* issue; **~gang** *m* **(a)** (*Archit etc*) main corridor; (*in Kirche, Theater, Kino*) central aisle; **(b)** (*Cook*) main course; **~gebäude** *nt* main building; **~gedanke** *m* main idea; **~gefreite(r)** *m* ≃ lance corporal (*Brit*), private first class (*US*); **~gegenstand** *m* **(a)** main *or* chief topic, main subject; **(b)** (*Aus Sch*) *siehe* **~fach**; **~gericht** *nt* main course.

Hauptgeschäft *nt* **(a)** (*Zentrale*) head office, headquarters *sing or pl*. **(b)** (*Hauptverdienst*) main business, major part of one's business.

Hauptgeschäfts-: **~stelle** *f* head office, headquarters *sing or pl*; **~straße** *f* main shopping street; **~zeit** *f* peak (shopping) period *or* hours *pl*.

Haupt-: **~gesichtspunkt** *m* main *or* major consideration; **~gewicht** *nt* (*lit*) major part of the weight, bulk of the weight; (*fig*) main emphasis; **~gewinn** *m* first prize; **~grund** *m* main *or* principal *or* chief reason; **~haar** *nt* (*geh*) hair (of the/one's head); **~hahn** *m* mains cock *or* tap (*Brit*); **~handlung** *f* (*Liter etc*) main plot; **~interesse** *nt* main *or* chief interest; **~kampflinie** *f* main front; **~katalog** *m* main catalogue; **~kennzeichen** *nt siehe* **~merkmal**; **~kläger** *m* principal plaintiff; **~last** *f* main load, major part of the load; (*fig*) main *or* major burden; **~lehrer** *m* (*dated*) head teacher; **~leitung** *f* mains *pl*; **~leute** *pl of* **~mann** (a); **~lieferant** *m* main *or* principal *or* chief supplier.

Häuptling *m* chief(tain); (*esp von Dorf*) headman.

häuptlings *adv* (*old, geh*) *siehe* **kopfüber**.

Haupt-: **~macht** *f* (*Mil*) bulk *or* main body of its/the forces; **~mahlzeit** *f* main meal; **~mangel** *m* main deficiency, main *or* principal defect; **~mann** *m*, *pl* **-leute** (a) (*Mil*) captain; (b) (*Hist: Führer*) leader; **~masse** *f* bulk, main body; **~merkmal** *nt* main feature, chief *or* principal characteristic; **~mieter** *m* main tenant; **~motiv** *nt* (a) (*Beweggrund*) primary *or* main motive; (b) (*Art, Liter, Mus*) main *or* principal motif; **~nahrungsmittel** *nt* staple *or* principal food; **~nenner** *m* (*Math, fig*) common denominator; **~niederlassung** *f* head office, headquarters *sing or pl*; **~person** *f* (*lit, fig*) central figure; **~portal** *nt* main portal *or* doorway; **~post** *f* (*inf*), **~postamt** *nt* main post office; **~probe** *f* final rehearsal; (*Kostümprobe*) dress rehearsal; **~problem** *nt* main *or* chief *or* principal problem; **~produkt** *nt* main product; (*esp im Gegensatz zu Nebenprodukt*) primary product; **~quartier** *nt* (*Mil, fig*) headquarters *sing or pl*; **~quelle** *f* (*lit, fig*) main *or* primary source; **~rechnungsart** *f* (*Math*) basic arithmetical operation; **~redner** *m* main *or* principal speaker; **~reisezeit** *f* peak travelling time(s *pl*)); **~revier** *nt siehe* **~wache**; **~rohr** *nt* main pipe; (*von Gas-/Wasserleitung*) main, mains pipe; **~rolle** *f* leading *or* main role *or* part, lead; **die ~rolle spielen** (*fig*) to be all-important; (*wichtigste Person sein*) to play the main role *or* part; **~runde** *f* (*Sport*) main round; **~sache** *f* main thing; (*in Brief, Rede etc*) main point; **in der ~sache** in the main, mainly; **~sache, es klappt/du bist glücklich** the main thing is that it comes off/you're happy; **h~sächlich 1** *adv* mainly, chiefly, principally; **2** *adj* main, chief, principal; **~saison** *f* peak *or* high season; **~saison haben** to have its/their peak season; **~satz** *m* (a) (*Gram*) (*übergeordnet*) main clause; (*alleinstehend*) sentence; (b) (*Mus*) first *or* main subject; (c) (*Philos*) main proposition; **~schalter** *m* (*Elec*) main *or* master switch;

~scheinwerfer *m* headlight, headlamp; **~schiff** *nt* (*Archit*) nave; **~schlagader** *f* aorta; **~schlüssel** *m* master key; **~schriftleiter** *m* (*dated*) *siehe* **Chefredakteur**; **~schriftleitung** *f* (*dated*) *siehe* **Chefredaktion**; **~schulabschluß** *m* den **~schulabschluß haben** ≃ to have completed secondary modern school (*Brit*) *or* junior high (school) (*US*); **~schuld** *f* main blame, principal fault (*esp Jur*); **~schuldige(r)** *mf* person mainly to blame *or* at fault, main offender (*esp Jur*); **er ist der ~schuldige** he is mainly to blame *or* at fault/he is the main offender; **~schule** *f* ≃ secondary modern (school) (*Brit*), junior high (school) (*US*); **~schüler** *m* ≃ secondary modern/junior high (school) pupil; **~schullehrer** *m* ≃ secondary modern/junior high (school) teacher; **~schwierigkeit** *f* main *or* chief *or* principal difficulty; **~segel** *nt* main sail; **~seminar** *nt* (*Univ*) seminar for advanced students; **~sicherung** *f* (*Elec*) main fuse; **~sitz** *m* head office, headquarters *sing or pl*; **~sorge** *f* main *or* chief worry; **~stadt** *f* capital (city); **~städter** *m* citizen of the capital, metropolitan; **h~städtisch** *adj* metropolitan, of the capital (city); **~stärke** *f* main *or* principal *or* chief strength; **~stoßrichtung** *f* (*Mil, fig*) main object of one's/the attack (*gegen* on); **~straße** *f* (*Durchgangsstraße*) main *or* major road; (*im Stadtzentrum etc*) main street; **~strecke** *f* (*Rail*) main line; (*Straße*) main *or* primary (*Admin*) route; **~strömung** *f* (*lit, fig*) main current; **~stütze** *f* (*fig*) mainstay, main support *or* prop; **~sünde** *f* (*Rel*) cardinal sin; **~täter** *m* main *or* chief *or* principal culprit; **~tätigkeit** *f* main *or* principal *or* chief activity; (*beruflich*) main occupation; **~teil** *m* main part; (*größter Teil auch*) major part; **~thema** *nt* main *or* principal topic; (*Mus, Liter*) main *or* principal theme; **~ton** *m* (*Ling*) main *or* primary stress; (*Mus*) principal note; **~treffer** *m* top prize, jackpot (*inf*); **den ~treffer machen** (*inf*) to win the top prize, to hit the jackpot (*inf*); **~treppe** *f* main staircase *or* stairs *pl*; **~tribüne** *f* main stand; (*Sport auch*) grandstand; **~typ(us)** *m* main *or* principal *or* major type; **~ und Staatsaktion** *f* aus etw eine **~-und Staatsaktion machen** to make a great issue of sth, to make a song and dance about sth (*inf*), to make a Federal case out of sth (*US inf*); **~unterschied** *m* main *or* principal difference; **~ursache** *f* main *or* chief *or* principal cause; **~verantwortliche(r)** *mf* person mainly *or* chiefly responsible; **~verantwortung** *f* main responsibility; **~verbandsplatz** *m* (*Mil*) main aid *or* dressing station; **~verdiener** *m* main *or* principal earner; **~verdienst¹** *m* main income; **~verdienst²** *nt* chief merit; **~verfahren** *nt* (*Jur*) main proceedings *pl*; **~verhandlung** *f* (*Jur*) main hearing.

Hauptverkehr *m* peak(-hour) traffic; (*Verkehrsteilnehmer*) main traffic, bulk of the traffic.

Hauptverkehrs-: **~ader** *f* main highway, arterial route; **~straße** *f* (*in Stadt*) main street; (*Durchgangsstraße*) main thoroughfare; (*zwischen Städten*) main highway, trunk road (*Brit*); **~zeit** *f* peak traffic times *pl*; (*in Stadt, bei Pendlern auch*) rush hour.

Haupt-: **~verlesen** *nt* (*Sw Mil*) roll call; **~versammlung** *f* general meeting; **~wache** *f* main police station; **~werk** *nt* (a) (*Art etc*) main *or* principal work; (b) (*Fabrik*) main factory *or* works *sing or pl*; **~wohnsitz** *m* main place of residence, main domicile (*form*); **~wort** *nt* (*Gram*) noun; **~wörterei** *f* (*pej*) over-fondness of nouns, over-nominalized style; **h~wörtlich** *adj* (*Gram*) nominal; **~zeit** *f* (*~saison*) peak times *pl*; (*in bezug auf Obst etc*) main season; **~zeuge** *m* principal *or* main *or* chief witness; **~ziel** *nt* main *or* principal aim *or* goal; **~zollamt** *nt* main customs office; **~zug** *m* (a) (*Rail*) scheduled train; (b) *usu pl* (*Charakteristikum*) main *or* principal feature, chief characteristic; **~zweck** *m* main *or* chief purpose *or* object.

hau ruck *interj* heave-ho.

Hauruck *nt* **-s, -s** heave.

Haus *nt* **-es, Häuser** (a) (*Gebäude*) (*esp Wohn~*) house; (*Firmengebäude*) building, premises *pl* (*form*). **er war nicht im ~, sondern im Garten** he wasn't in the house *or* indoors but in the garden; **laß uns ins ~ gehen** let's go in(doors) *or* inside *or* into the house; **Tomaten kann man im ~ ziehen** tomatoes can be grown indoors *or* inside *or* in the house; **der Klavierlehrer kommt ins ~** the piano teacher comes to the house; **er ist nicht im ~e** (*in der Firma*) he's not in the building *or* on the premises, he's not in; **aus dem ~ gehen** to leave the house; **mit jdm ~ an ~ wohnen** to live next door to sb; **wir wohnen ~ an ~** we live next door to each other, we are next-door neighbours; **von ~ zu ~ gehen** to go from door to door *or* from house to house; **das ~ Gottes** *or* **des Herrn** (*geh*) the House of God *or* of the Lord; **~ der Jugend** youth centre; **auf ihn kann man Häuser bauen** (*fig*) you can always count *or* rely on him, he's as safe as houses.

(b) (*Zuhause, Heim*) home. **~ und Hof** (*fig*) house and home; **~ und Herd verlassen** to leave house and home, to leave one's home (behind); **etw ins/frei ~ liefern** (*Comm*) to deliver sth to the door/to deliver sth free *or* carriage paid; **wir liefern frei ~** we offer free delivery; **ein großes ~ führen** (*fig*) to entertain lavishly *or* in style; **jdm das ~ führen** to keep house for sb; **jdm das ~ verbieten** not to allow sb in the house, to forbid sb (to enter) the house; **aus dem ~ sein** to be away from home; **außer ~ essen** to eat out; **im ~e meiner Schwester** at my sister's (house); **er hat nichts zu essen im ~** he has nothing in the house; **jdn ins ~ nehmen** to take sb in(to one's home); **ein Fernsehgerät kommt mir nicht ins ~!** I won't have a television set in the house!; **ins ~ stehen** (*fig*) to be coming up, to be forthcoming; (*Baby*) to be on the way; **jdm steht etw ins ~** (*fig*) sb is facing sth; **nach ~e** (*lit, fig*) home; **jdn nach ~e bringen** to take *or* see sb home; **komm mir bloß nicht damit nach ~e!** (*fig inf*) don't you (dare) come that one with me (*inf*)!; **jdn nach ~e schicken** (*fig inf*) to send sb packing (*inf*); **Grüße von ~ zu ~** (*form*) regards from ourselves to you all; **zu ~e** at home (*auch Sport*); **bei jdm zu ~e** at sb's (place), in sb's house *or* home;

bei uns zu ~e at home; wie geht's zu ~e? how are they (all) at home?, how are the folks? (*inf*); von zu ~e aus from home; für jdn/niemanden zu ~e sein to be at home to sb/nobody; irgendwo zu ~e sein (*Mensch, Tier*) to live somewhere; (*sich heimisch fühlen*) to be at home somewhere; (*Brauch*) to be customary *or* practised somewhere; in etw (*dat*) zu ~e sein (*fig*) to be at home in sth; sich wie zu ~e fühlen to feel at home; fühl dich wie zu ~e! make yourself at home!; damit kannst du zu ~e bleiben, bleib doch damit zu ~e (*fig inf*) you can keep it/them *etc* (*inf*).

(c) (*Bewohnerschaft eines ~es*) household. ein Freund des ~es a friend of the family; die Dame/Tochter *etc* des ~es (*form*) the lady/daughter *etc* of the house; der Herr des ~es (*form*) the master of the house.

(d) (*geh: Herkunft*) aus gutem/bürgerlichem ~(e) from a good/middle-class family; aus adligem ~(e) of noble birth, of *or* from a noble house (*form*); von ~e aus (*ursprünglich*) originally; (*von Natur aus*) naturally.

(e) (*Dynastie*) House. das ~ Habsburg the House of the Habsburgs, the Hapsburg dynasty; das ~ Windsor the House of Windsor; aus dem ~ Davids of the House of David.

(f) (*geh: Unternehmen*) House (*form*). das ~ Siemens the House of Siemens; „~ Talblick" (*Name*) "Talblick (House)"; das erste ~ am Platze (*Hotel*) the finest *or* best hotel in town; (*Kaufhaus*) the top *or* best store in town; ein gepflegtes *or* gut geführtes ~ (*Restaurant*) a well-run house.

(g) (*Theater*) theatre; (*Saal, Publikum*) house. vor vollem ~ spielen to play to a full house; das große/kleine ~ the large *or* main/small theatre.

(h) (*Parl*) House. Hohes ~! (*form*) = honourable members (of the House)!; dieses hohe ~ ... the *or* this House ...

(i) (*von Schnecke*) shell, house (*inf*).

(j) (*Astrol*) house.

(k) (*dated inf: Kerl*) chap (*Brit inf*), fellow. grüß dich Hans, (du) altes ~! (*inf*) hallo Hans, old chap (*inf*) *or* chum (*dated inf*).

Haus-: ~altar *m* family *or* house altar; ~andacht *f* family worship; ~angestellte(r) *mf* domestic servant; (*esp Frau*) domestic; ~anzug *m* hostess trouser (*Brit*) *or* pants suit; ~apotheke *f* medicine cupboard *or* chest; ~arbeit *f* (a) housework *no pl*; (b) (*Sch*) homework *no indef art, no pl*; ~arrest *m* (*im Internat*) detention; (*Jur*) house arrest; ~arrest haben to be in detention/under house arrest; Fritz kann nicht zum Spielen rauskommen, er hat ~arrest Fritz can't come out to play – he's being kept in; meine Eltern haben mich mit ~arrest bedroht my parents threatened to keep me in; ~arzt *m* family doctor, GP (*Brit*); (*von Heim, Anstalt*) resident doctor; ~aufgabe *f* (*Sch*) homework *no indef art, no pl*, piece of homework; ~aufgaben *pl* homework; ~aufgabenüberwachung *f* (*Sch*) homework supervision; ~aufsatz *m* (*Sch*) homework essay, essay for homework; h~backen *adj* (*fig*) homespun, drab, homely (*US*); *Kleidung* unadventurous; ~ball *m* (private) ball *or* dance; ~bank *f* bank; ~bar *f* home bar; (*Möbelstück*) cocktail *or* drinks cabinet; ~bau *m* house building *or* construction; (*das Bauen*) building of a/the house; ~berg *m* neighbouring *or* local mountain; ~besetzer *m* occupier of a/the house; (*esp um dort zu wohnen*) squatter; ~besetzung *f* siehe ~besetzer house occupation; squat(ting action); ~besitz *m* house ownership; ~besitz haben to own a house/houses; ~besitzer(in *f*) *m* house-owner; (*Hauswirt*) landlord/landlady; ~besorger *m* (*Aus*) siehe ~meister; ~besuch *m* home visit; (*von Handwerker*) house call; ~bewohner *m* (house) occupant *or* occupier; ~bibliothek *f* library; ~bock *m* (*Zool*) house longhorn; ~boot *nt* houseboat; ~brand *m* (a) house fire; (b) (*Brennstoff*) domestic *or* heating fuel; ~buch *nt* (a) (*häufig gelesenes Buch*) most frequent family reading *no indef art, no pl*; (*old: Haushaltsbuch*) housekeeping book; (c) (*DDR*) list of (house) occupants *or* of tenants; ~bursche *m* pageboy, bellboy (*US*), bellhop (*US*).

Häuschen ['hɔysçən] *nt* (a) *dim of* Haus.
(b) (*fig inf*) ganz aus dem ~ sein to be out of one's mind with joy/excitement/fear *etc* (*inf*); ganz aus dem ~ geraten to go berserk (*inf*); jdn (ganz) aus dem ~ bringen to make sb go berserk (*inf*).
(c) (*inf: Karo*) square, block.
(d) (*euph inf: Toilette*) loo (*Brit inf*), bathroom (*US*), smallest room (*hum inf*); (*außerhalb des Gebäudes*) privy, outside loo (*Brit inf*).

Haus-: ~dame *f* housekeeper; ~detektiv *m* house detective; (*von Kaufhaus*) store detective; ~diener *m* (a) (*in Privathaushalt*) manservant; (b) (*in Hotel*) hotel servant; (*Gepäckträger*) (hotel) porter; ~drachen *m* (*inf*) dragon (*inf*), battle-axe (*inf*); ~durchsuchung *f* (*Aus*) siehe ~suchung; h~eigen *adj* belonging to a/the hotel/firm *etc*; ~eigentümer *m* home owner; ~einfahrt *f* (*Aus*), ~eingang *m* (house) entrance.

Häusel *nt* -s, - (*Aus, dial*) siehe Häuschen (a, d).

Hausen *m* -s, - (*Zool*) sturgeon.

hausen *vi* (a) (*wohnen*) to live.
(b) (*wüten*) (*übel or schlimm*) ~ to wreak *or* create havoc; schrecklich ~ to wreak the most dreadful havoc; wie die Wandalen ~ to act like vandals.
(c) (*Sw, S Ger: sparsam sein*) to be economical.

Hauser *m* -s, - (*Aus, S Ger*) siehe Haushälter(in).

Häuser-: ~block *m* block (of houses); ~flucht *f* siehe ~reihe; ~front *f* front of a terrace *or* row of houses.

Häuserin *f* (*Aus, S Ger*) siehe Haushälterin.

Häuser-: ~kampf *m* (*Mil*) house-to-house fighting; (*Pol*) squatting actions *pl*; (*einzelner Fall*) squat(ting action); ~makler *m* estate agent, realtor (*US*); ~meer *nt* mass of houses; ~reihe, ~zeile *f* row of houses; (*aneinandergebaut*) terrace.

Haus-: ~flagge *f* (*Naut*) house flag; ~flur *m* (entrance) hall, hallway.

Hausfrau *f* (a) housewife; (*Gastgeberin*) hostess. (b) (*Aus, S Ger*) siehe Hauswirtin.

Hausfrauen-: ~art *f* Wurst *etc* nach ~art home-made-style sausage *etc*; ~brigade *f* (*DDR*) housewives' brigade; ~pflicht *f* housewifely duty.

Haus-: h~fraulich *adj* housewifely; ~freund *m* (a) (*Freund der Familie*) friend of the family; (b) (*euph inf*) man friend; ~friede(n) *m* domestic peace; ~friedensbruch *m* (*Jur*) trespass (*in sb's house*); ~gans *f* (domestic) goose; ~gast *m* (*von Pension etc*) resident, guest; ~gebrauch *m* für den ~gebrauch (*Gerät*) for domestic *or* household use; (*Obst-, Gemüsenbau*) for one's own consumption; sein Französisch reicht für den ~gebrauch (*inf*) his French is (good) enough to get by (on); ~gehilfin *f* home help; ~geist *m* (a) household spirit; (*Gespenst*) household ghost; (b) (*hum: ~angestellter*) faithful retainer (*old, hum*); h~gemacht *adj* home-made; ~gemeinschaft *f* household (community); mit jdm in ~gemeinschaft leben to live together with sb (in the same household); ~genosse *m* fellow tenant/lodger; ~götter *pl* (*Myth*) household gods *pl*; ~gottheit *f* (*Myth*) household deity *or* god.

Haushalt *m* -(e)s, -e (a) (*Hausgemeinschaft*) household; (*~sführung*) housekeeping. Geräte für den ~ household utensils; den ~ führen to run the household; jdm den ~ führen to keep house for sb. (b) (*fig: Biol etc*) balance. (c) (*Etat*) budget.

Haushalt- *in cpds* siehe **Haushalts-**.

haushalten *vi sep irreg* (a) (*sparsam wirtschaften*) to be economical. mit etw ~ mit Geld, Zeit to be economical with sth, to use sth economically; mit Kräften, Vorräten auch to conserve sth. (b) (*den Haushalt führen*) to keep house.

Haushälter(in *f*), **Haushalter(in** *f*) (*rare*) *m* -s, - housekeeper.

haushälterisch *adj* thrifty, economical. mit etw ~ umgehen siehe haushalten (a).

Haushalts- *in cpds* household; (*Pol*) budget; ~artikel *m* household item *or* article; ~buch *nt* housekeeping book; (ein) ~buch führen to keep a housekeeping book; ~debatte *f* (*Parl*) budget debate; ~fragen *pl* (*Pol*) budgetary questions *pl*; ~führung *f* housekeeping; ~geld *nt* housekeeping money; ~gerät *nt* household appliance; ~hilfe *f* domestic help; ~jahr *nt* (*Pol, Econ*) financial *or* fiscal year; ~kasse *f* household *or* family budget; ~mittel *pl* (*Pol*) budgetary funds *pl*; ~ordnung *f* budgetary regulations *pl*; ~packung *f* family pack; ~plan *m* (*Pol*) budget; ~planung *f* (*Pol*) budgetary planning, planning of a budget; ~politik *f* (*Pol*) budgetary policy; h~politisch *adj* concerning budgetary policy; die Regierung hat h~politisch versagt the government has failed in its budgetary policy; ~waage *f* kitchen scales *pl*; ~waren *pl* household goods *pl*.

Haushaltung *f* (a) (*das Haushaltführen*) housekeeping, household management; (*das Sparsamsein*) economizing (*mit* with). (b) (*form*) siehe Haushalt (a).

Haushaltungs-: ~buch *nt* housekeeping book; ~kosten *pl* household *or* housekeeping expenses; ~vorstand *m* (*form*) head of the household.

Haus-Haus-Verkehr *m* (*Rail*) siehe **Haus-zu-Haus-Verkehr**.

Haus-: ~herr *m* (a) head of the household; (*Gastgeber, Sport*) host; (b) (*Jur*) householder; (c) (*Aus, S Ger*) siehe ~besitzer(in); ~herrin *f* (a) lady of the house; (*Gastgeberin*) hostess; (b) (*Aus, S Ger*) siehe ~besitzer(in); h~hoch *adj* (as) high as a house/houses; (*fig*) Sieg crushing; der h~hohe Favorit the hot favourite (*inf*); 2 *adv* high (in the sky); jdn h~hoch schlagen to give sb a hammering (*inf*) *or* thrashing (*inf*); h~hoch gewinnen to win hands down *or* by miles (*inf*); jdm h~hoch überlegen sein to be head and shoulders above sb; ~hofmeister *m* (*old*) steward; h~hohe(r, s) *adj* siehe h~hoch 1; ~huhn *nt* domestic fowl.

hausieren *vi* to hawk, to peddle (*mit etw* sth). mit etw ~ gehen (*fig*) mit Plänen *etc* to hawk sth about; mit Gerüchten to peddle sth; „H~ verboten" "no hawkers *or* peddlers".

Hausierer(in *f*) *m* -s, - hawker, peddler, pedlar.

Haus-: h~intern *adj* siehe firmenintern; ~jacke *f* house jacket; ~jurist *m* company lawyer; ~kaninchen *nt* domestic rabbit; ~kapelle *f* (a) (*Rel*) private chapel; (b) (*Musikkapelle*) resident band; (*an Fürstenhof*) resident *or* private orchestra; ~katze *f* domestic cat; ~kauf *m* house-buying *no pl*, house purchase; ~kleid *nt* hostess gown; ~konzert *nt* family concert; ~korrektur *f* (*Typ*) proofreading (*carried out by the publishers*); ~lehrer(in *f*) *m* (private) tutor; ~leute *pl* (*dial, inf*) siehe Wirtsleute; (*Sw*) tenants *pl*.

häuslich *adj* Angelegenheiten, Pflichten, Friede *etc* domestic; (*der Familie gehörend*) family attr; (*an ~en Dingen interessiert*) domesticated; (*das Zuhause liebend*) home-loving. der ~e Herd the family home; sich irgendwo ~ niederlassen to make oneself at home somewhere; sich irgendwo ~ einrichten to settle in somewhere.

Häuslichkeit *f* domesticity.

Hausmacher-: ~art *f* Wurst *etc* nach ~art home-made-style sausage *etc*; ~kost *f* home cooking; ~wurst *f* home-made sausage.

Haus-: ~macht *f* (*Hist*) allodium; (*fig*) power base; ~mädchen *nt* (house)maid; ~mann *m*, *pl* ~männer (a) (*old: Hausmeister*) caretaker, janitor; (b) (*den Haushalt versorgender Mann*) man undertaking the role of housewife; ~mannskost *f* plain cooking *or* fare; ~mantel *m* housecoat; ~märchen *nt* folk tale; „~ und Kindermärchen" "Fairy Tales"; ~marke *f* (*eigene Marke*) own brand *or* label; (*bevorzugte Marke*) favourite brand; ~maus *f* house mouse; ~meier *m* (*Hist*) major-domo; ~meister *m* (a) caretaker, janitor; **(b)** (*Sw*) *siehe* ~**besitzer(in)**; ~**mitteilung** *f* memo; ~**mittel** *nt* household remedy; ~**musik** *f* music at home, family music; ~**mutter** *f* (*von Herberge etc*) housemother; ~**mütterchen** *nt* (*hum*) little mother; (*pej*) housewife, wife and mother; ~**nummer** *f* street *or* house number; ~**ordnung** *f* house rules *pl or* regulations *pl*; ~**partei** *f* (*Aus*) household; ~**perle** *f* maid; ~**pflege** *f* home care; ~**postille** *f* (*old*) collection of instructional reading for the family; (*fig*) manual; ~**putz** *m* house cleaning; ~**rat** *m* -**(e)s**, *no pl* household equipment *or* goods *pl*; ~**ratsversicherung** *f* (household) contents insurance; ~**recht** *nt* right(s *pl*) as a householder (*to forbid sb entrance*); **von seinem** ~**recht Gebrauch machen** to show sb the door, to tell sb to leave; ~**rind** *nt* domestic cattle *pl*; ~**sammlung** *f* house-to-house *or* door-to-door collection; ~**schlachten** *nt*, ~**schlachtung** *f* home slaughtering; ~**schlüssel** *m* front-door key, house key; ~**schuh** *m* slipper; ~**schwamm** *m* dry rot; ~**schwein** *nt* domestic pig.

Hausse ['ho:s(ə)] *f* -, -**n** (*Econ: Aufschwung*) boom (*an + dat* in); (*St Ex: Kurssteigerung*) bull market. ~ **haben** (*St Ex*) to rise on the Stock Exchange; **wenn man** ~ **hat, ...** (*St Ex*) when there's a bull market ...; **auf** ~ **spekulieren** (*St Ex*) to bull.

Haussegen *m* house blessing *or* benediction. **bei ihnen hängt der** ~ **schief** (*hum*) they're a bit short on domestic bliss (*inf*).

Haussespekulation ['ho:sə-] *f* (*St Ex*) bull speculation.

Haussier [(h)o'sie:] *m* -**s**, -**s** (*St Ex*) bull.

Haus-: ~**stand** *m* household, home; **einen** ~**stand gründen** to set up house *or* home; ~**suchung** *f* (*in einem Haus*) house search; (*in mehreren Häusern*) house-to-house search; ~**suchungsbefehl** *m* search-warrant; ~**taufe** *f* home baptism *or* christening (service); ~**telefon** *nt* internal telephone; ~**tier** *nt* domestic animal; (*aus Liebhaberei gehalten*) pet; ~**tochter** *f* lady's help; ~**trauung** *f* wedding at home; ~**tür** *f* front door; **gleich vor der** ~**tür** (*fig inf*) on one's doorstep; ~**tyrann** *m* (*inf*) domestic *or* household tyrant; ~**vater** *m* (*von Heim etc*) house-father; ~**verbot** *nt* ban on entering the house/a place; **jdm** ~**verbot erteilen** to bar *or* ban sb from the house, to forbid sb to enter the house; **in einem Lokal/bei jdm** ~**verbot haben** to be barred *or* banned from a pub (*Brit*) *or* bar/sb's house/a building; ~**versammlung** *f* (*esp DDR*) house meeting; ~**verwalter** *m* (house) supervisor; ~**verwaltung** *f* property *or* house management; ~**wappen** *nt* family coat of arms; ~**wart** *m* *siehe* ~**meister**; ~**wesen** *nt* (*dated*) household affairs *pl or* matters *pl*; ~**wirt** *m* landlord; ~**wirtin** *f* landlady.

Hauswirtschaft *f* **(a)** (*Haushaltsführung*) housekeeping; (*finanziell auch*) home economics *sing*. **(b)** (*Sch*) home economics *sing*, domestic science.

hauswirtschaftlich *adj* domestic. **ein** ~**er Kurs** a course on home economics *or* domestic science; ~ **interessiert** interested in domestic matters.

Hauswirtschafts-: ~**lehre** *f* (*Sch*) home economics *sing*, domestic science; ~**lehrer** *m* home economics *or* domestic science teacher; ~**leiterin** *f* housekeeper; ~**schule** *f* school of home economics *or* domestic science.

Haus-: ~**wurfsendung** *f* (house-to-house) circular; ~**zeitung**, ~**zeitschrift** *f* company newspaper; ~**zelt** *nt* frame tent; ~**zentrale** *f* (*Telec*) (internal) switchboard.

Haus-zu-Haus-: ~**-Transport** *m* (*Rail etc*) door-to-door service; ~**Verkehr** *m* (*Rail etc*) door-to-door service.

Haut *f* -, **Häute** skin; (*dick, esp von größerem Tier*) hide; (*geschälte Schale von Obst etc*) peel; (*inf: Mensch*) sort (*inf*). **naß bis auf die** ~ soaked to the skin; **nur** ~ **und Knochen sein** to be only *or* nothing but skin and bone; **viel** ~ **zeigen** (*hum*) to show all one's got (*hum*), to show a lot (of bare skin); **mit** ~ **und Haar(en)** (*inf*) completely, totally; **er ist ihr mit** ~ **und Haar(en) verfallen** (*inf*) he's head over heels in love with her, he's fallen for her hook, line and sinker (*inf*); **das geht** *or* **dringt unter die** ~ that gets under one's skin; **in seiner** ~ **möchte ich nicht stecken** I wouldn't like to be in his shoes; **er fühlt sich nicht wohl in seiner** ~ (*inf*), **ihm ist nicht wohl in seiner** ~ (*inf*) (*unglücklich, unzufrieden*) he's (feeling) rather unsettled; (*unbehaglich*) he feels uneasy *or* uncomfortable; **er kann nicht aus seiner** ~ **heraus** (*inf*) he can't change the way he is, a leopard can't change its spots (*prov*); **aus der** ~ **fahren** (*inf*) (*aus Ungeduld*) to work oneself up into a sweat (*inf*); (*aus Wut*) to go through the roof (*inf*), to hit the ceiling (*inf*); **das ist zum Aus-der-** ~**-Fahren!** it's enough to drive you up the wall (*inf*) *or* round the bend (*inf*); **auf der faulen** ~ **liegen** (*inf*), **sich auf die faule** ~ **legen** (*inf*) to sit back and do nothing, not to lift a finger (*inf*); **seine** ~ **zu Markte tragen** (*sich in Gefahr begeben*) to risk one's neck *or* hide (*inf*); (*euph: Frau*) to sell one's charms; **seine eigene** ~ **retten** to save one's (own) skin; (*esp vor Prügel*) to save one's (own) hide (*inf*); **seine** ~ **wagen** *or* **dransetzen** (*inf*) to risk one's neck (*inf*), to put one's life on the line (*inf*); **sich seiner** ~ **wehren** to defend oneself vigorously; **seine** ~ **so teuer wie möglich verkaufen** (*inf*) to sell oneself as dearly as possible; *siehe* **ehrlich**.

Haut- *in cpds* skin; ~**abschürfung** *f* graze; ~**arzt** *m* skin specialist, dermatologist; ~**atmung** *f* cutaneous respiration; **die** ~**atmung verhindern** to stop the skin from breathing; ~**ausschlag** *m* (skin) rash *or* eruption (*form*).

Häutchen *nt* -**s**, - *dim of* **Haut** (*auf Flüssigkeit*) skin; (*Anat, Bot*) membrane; (*an Fingernägeln*) cuticle.

haute *pret of* **hauen**.

Haute Couture [(h)o:tku'ty:ɐ] *f* - -, *no pl* haute couture.

häuten **1** *vt* *Tiere* to skin. **2** *vr* (*Tier*) to shed its skin; (*Schlange auch*) to slough (its skin); (*hum: Mensch*) to peel.

häut|eng *adj* skintight.

Hautevolee [(h)o:tvo'le:] *f* -, *no pl* upper crust.

Haut-: ~**falte** *f* skin fold; ~**farbe** *f* skin colour; **nur, weil er eine andere** ~**farbe hat** just because his skin is a different colour;

h~**farben** *adj* flesh-coloured; ~**flügler** *m* -**s**, - hymenopter(on); h~**freundlich** *adj* *Stoff* kind to one's *or* the skin; h~**freundliches Heftpflaster** micropore tape.

-**häutig** *adj suf* -skinned.

Haut-: ~**jucken** *nt* -**s**, *no pl* itching; **eine Creme gegen** ~**jucken** a cream for skin irritations; h~**nah** *adj* **(a)** (*Anat*) close to the skin; **(b)** (*sehr eng, Sport*) (very) close; h~**nah tanzen** to dance very close(ly); **(c)** (*fig inf: wirklichkeitsnah*) *Kontakt* (very) close; *Problem* that affects us/him *etc* directly; *Darstellung, Schilderung* deeply affective; h~**nah in Kontakt mit etw kommen** to come into (very) close contact with sth; ~**pflege** *f* skin care; ~**pilz** *m* (*Med*) fungal skin infection, dermatophyte (*spec*); h~**schonend** *adj* kind to the skin; *Spülmittel auch* kind to the hands; ~**spezialist** *m* skin specialist, dermatologist; ~**transplantation** *f* (*Operation*) skin graft; (*Verfahren*) skin grafting.

Häutung *f* skinning; (*von Schlange*) sloughing. **verschiedene** ~**en durchmachen** to slough several skins.

Hautwunde *f* superficial *or* skin wound.

Havanna(zigarre) [ha'vana-] *f* -, -**s** Havana (cigar).

Havarie [hava'ri:] *f* **(a)** (*Naut, Aviat*) (*Unfall*) accident; (*Schaden*) average (*spec*), damage *no indef art, no pl*. **(b)** (*Aus*) (*Kraftfahrzeugunfall*) accident; (*Kraftfahrzeugschaden*) damage *no indef art, no pl*.

havariert [hava'ri:ɐt] *adj* damaged.

Havarist [hava'rɪst] *m* (*Reeder*) owner of a/the damaged ship; (*Schiff*) damaged ship.

Hawaianer(in *f*) [havaɪ'a:nɐ, -ərɪn] *m* -**s**, - Hawaiian.

hawaianisch *adj* Hawaiian.

Hawaii [ha'vaii] *nt* -**s** Hawaii.

Hawaiigitarre *f* Hawaiian guitar.

hawaiisch [ha'vaiɪʃ] *adj* Hawaiian.

Haxe *f* -, -**n** (*Cook*) leg (joint); (*S Ger inf*) (*Fuß*) foot, plate of meat (*Brit sl*); (*Bein*) leg. „~**n abkratzen!"** "wipe your feet!".

Hbf *abbr of* **Hauptbahnhof**.

H-Bombe ['ha:-] *f* H-bomb.

h.c. [ha:'tse:] *abbr of* **honoris causa**.

HD [ha:'de:] *f* -, *no pl* (*Sw*) *abbr of* **Hilfsdienst**.

he *interj* hey; (*fragend*) hey.

Hearing ['hɪərɪŋ] *nt* -(**s**), -**s** hearing.

Hebamme *f* -, -**n** midwife.

Hebe-: ~**balken**, ~**baum** *m* lever; ~**bock** *m* (hydraulic) jack; ~**bühne** *f* hydraulic ramp.

Hebel *m* -**s**, - **(a)** (*Phys, Griff*) lever; (*an Maschinen auch*) handle. **den** ~ **ansetzen** to position the lever; (*fig*) to tackle it, to set about it; **den** ~ **an der richtigen Stelle ansetzen** (*fig*) to set about *or* tackle it in the right way; **alle** ~ **in Bewegung setzen** (*inf*) to move heaven and earth; **am längeren** ~ **sitzen** (*inf*) to have the whip hand.

(b) (*Sport*) *siehe* **Hebelgriff**.

Hebel-: ~**arm** *m* (lever) arm; ~**griff** *m* (*Sport*) lever hold; ~**kraft** *f* leverage; ~**wirkung** *f* leverage.

heben *pret* **hob**, *ptp* **gehoben 1** *vt* **(a)** (*nach oben bewegen*) to lift, to raise; *Augenbraue* to raise; *Kamera, Fernglas* to raise. **die Stimme** ~ (*lauter sprechen*) to raise one's voice, to speak up; (*höher sprechen*) to raise one's/the pitch; **die Hand/Faust gegen jdn** ~ (*geh*) to raise one's hand against sb/to shake one's fist at sb; **einen** ~ **gehen** (*inf*) to go for a drink; **er hebt gern einen** (*inf*) he likes *or* enjoys a drink; *siehe* **gehoben**.

(b) (*nach oben befördern, hochheben*) to lift; *Wrack* to raise, to bring up; *Schatz* to dig up; (*Sport*) *Gewicht* to lift. **er hob das Kind auf die Mauer/vom Baum** he lifted the child (up) onto the wall/(down) from the tree; **jdn auf die Schultern** ~ to hoist *or* lift sb onto one's shoulders *or* shoulder-high; **den Ball in den Strafraum/ins Tor** ~ to lob the ball into the penalty area/goal; **heb deine Füße!** pick your feet up!

(c) (*verbessern*) *Farbe* to bring out, to enhance; *Selbstbewußtsein, Effekt* to heighten; *Ertrag* to increase; *Geschäft* to increase, to boost; *Stimmung, Wohlstand* to improve; *Niveau* to raise, to increase; *jds Ansehen* to boost, to enhance. **jds Stimmung** ~ to cheer sb up; **das hebt den Mut** that boosts *or* raises one's morale.

(d) (*S Ger: halten*) to hold.

2 *vr* **(a)** (*sich nach oben bewegen*) to rise; (*Vorhang auch*) to go up; (*Nebel, Deckel*) to lift. **sich** ~ **und senken** (*Schiff*) to rise and fall; (*Busen*) to heave; **mein Magen hob sich bei dem Anblick** the sight turned my stomach *or* made me heave.

(b) (*geh: aufstehen*) to rise (*form*). **sich auf Zehenspitzen** ~ to rise onto tiptoe.

(c) (*geh: emporragen*) to tower up, to rise up.

(d) (*verbessern*) (*Stimmung, Konjunktur, Handel*) to improve. **da hob sich seine Stimmung** that cheered him up.

(e) (*S Ger: sich halten*) to hold on (*an + dat* to).

3 *vt impers* **es hebt jdm den Magen** *or* **jdn** (*inf*) sb feels sick; **es hebt mir den Magen** *or* **mich, wenn ich das sehe** (*inf*) seeing that makes me feel sick *or* turns my stomach (*inf*).

4 *vi* **(a)** (*Sport*) to do weight-lifting.

(b) (*S Ger: haltbar sein*) to hold; (*Nahrungsmittel*) to keep.

Heber *m* -**s**, - **(a)** (*Chem*) pipette. **(b)** (*Tech*) (hydraulic) jack. **(c)** (*Sport: Gewicht*~) weight-lifter.

-**hebig** *adj suf* (*Poet*) -footed.

Hebräer(in *f*) *m* -**s**, - Hebrew.

hebräisch *adj* Hebrew.

Hebräisch(e) *nt decl as adj* Hebrew; *siehe auch* **Deutsch(e)**.

Hebung *f* **(a)** (*von Schatz, Wrack etc*) recovery, raising.

(b) (*Geol*) elevation, rise (in the ground).

(c) (*fig: Verbesserung*) improvement; (*von Effekt, Selbstbewußtsein*) heightening; (*von Lebensstandard, Niveau*) rise. **seine Fröhlichkeit trug zur** ~ **der gedrückten Stimmung bei** his cheerfulness helped to relieve the subdued mood.

(d) (*Poet*) stressed *or* accented syllable.
Hechel *f* -, -n hatchel, heckle, card. **jdn/etw durch die ~ ziehen** (*fig dated*) to gossip about sb/sth, to pull sb/sth to pieces.
Hechelei *f* (*inf*) gossip *no pl*, bitching *no pl* (*sl*).
hecheln 1 *vt Flachs, Hanf* to hatchel, to heckle. 2 *vi* (a) (*inf: lästern*) to gossip. (b) (*keuchen*) to pant.
Hecht *m* -(e)s, -e (a) (*Zool*) pike; (*inf: Bursche*) chap (*inf*), bloke (*Brit inf*), guy (*inf*). **das ist ein ~** (*inf*) he's some guy (*inf*) *or* quite a guy (*inf*); **er ist (wie) ein ~ im Karpfenteich** (*fig*) (*sehr aktiv*) he certainly shakes people up; (*schockierend*) he's viewed as a dangerous crank.
(b) (*Sport*) *siehe* **Hechtsprung.**
(c) (*sl: Tabaksqualm*) fug (*inf*). **hier ist ein ~!** what a fug in here!
hechten *vi aux sein* (*inf*) to dive, to make a (headlong) dive; (*beim Schwimmen*) to do a racing dive; (*beim Geräteturnen*) to do a forward dive.
Hecht-: **~rolle** *f* (*Sport*) dive roll; **~sprung** *m* (*beim Schwimmen*) racing dive; (*beim Turnen*) forward dive; (*Ftbl inf*) (headlong *or* full-length) dive; **~suppe** *f*: **es zieht wie ~suppe** (*inf*) it's blowing a gale (in here) (*inf*), there's a terrible draught.
Heck *nt* -(e)s, -e (a) *pl auch* -s (*Naut*) stern; (*Aviat*) tail, rear; (*Aut*) rear, back. (b) (*N Ger: Gatter*) gate.
Heck|antrieb *m* (*Aut*) rear-wheel drive.
Hecke *f* -, -n hedge; (*am Wegrand*) hedgerow.
Hecken-: **~rose** *f* dogrose, wild rose; **~schere** *f* hedge-clippers *pl*; **~schütze** *m* sniper.
Heck-: **~fenster** *nt* (*Aut*) rear window *or* windscreen; **~flosse** *f* (*Aut*) tail fin; **~klappe** *f* (*Aut*) tailgate; **h~lastig** *adj* tail-heavy; **~licht** *nt* (*Aviat*) tail-light.
Heckmeck *m* -s, *no pl* (*inf*) (*dummes Gerede*) nonsense, rubbish; (*dumme Streiche*) stupid *or* daft (*inf*) things *pl*; (*Umstände*) fuss, palaver (*inf*); (*unnötiges Zeug*) rubbish. **mach doch keinen ~** don't be so stupid *or* daft (*inf*).
Heck-: **~motor** *m* (*Aut*) rear engine; **~scheibe** *f* (*Aut*) rear window *or* windscreen; **~schütze** *m* rear gunner; **~tür** *f* (*Aut*) tailgate; (*von Lieferwagen*) rear doors *pl*; **~türmodell** *nt* hatchback (car); **~welle** *f* (*Naut*) wash *no pl*.
heda *interj* hey there.
Hederich *m* -s, *no pl* (*Bot*) wild radish.
Hedonismus *m* hedonism.
hedonistisch *adj* hedonistic.
Heer *nt* -(e)s, -e (*lit, fig*) army. **beim ~** in the army; **in das ~ eintreten** to join the army, to enlist in the army; *siehe* **wild.**
Heerbann *m* (*Hist*) levy.
Heeres-: **~bericht** *m* military communiqué *or* despatch; **~bestände** *pl* army stores *pl or* supplies *pl*; **~dienst** *m, no pl* (*Hist*) military service; **~dienstvorschrift** *f* army regulations *pl*; **~gruppe** *f* army group; **~leitung** *f* command.
Heer(es)zug *m* (*Hist*) campaign.
Heer-: **~führer** *m* (*Hist*) army commander; **~lager** *nt* army camp; **der Flughafen glich einem ~lager** the airport was like a refugee camp; **~schar** *f* (*liter*) legion, troop; (*fig: große Menge*) host; **die himmlischen ~scharen** the heavenly hosts; **~schau** *f* (*old*) military parade; **~schau halten** to hold a military parade; **~straße** *f* military road; **~wesen** *nt* army.
Hefe *f* -, -n yeast. **die ~ des Volkes** (*geh: treibende Kraft*) the (driving) force behind the people; (*pej: Abschaum*) the scum of the earth.
Hefe(n)-: **~gebäck** *nt* yeast-risen pastry; **~kranz** *m* ≈ savarin; **~kuchen** *m* yeast cake; **~pilz** *m* yeast plant; **~stück(chen)** *nt* yeast pastry, ≈ Danish pastry; **~teig** *m* yeast dough; **wie ein ~teig auseinandergehen** (*fig inf*) to put on mounds of fat.
Heft[1] *nt* -(e)s, -e (*von Werkzeug, Messer*) handle; (*von Säge, Feile auch*) grip; (*von Dolch, Schwert*) hilt. **das ~ in der Hand haben** (*fig*) to hold the reins, to be at the helm; **das ~ in der Hand behalten** (*fig*) to remain in control *or* at the helm; **das ~ aus der Hand geben** (*fig*) to hand over control *or* the reins; **jdm das ~ aus der Hand nehmen** (*fig*) to seize control/power from sb; **ich lasse mir nicht das ~ aus der Hand nehmen** nobody's going to take over from me.
Heft[2] *nt* -(e)s, -e (a) (*Schreib~*) exercise book. (b) (*Zeitschrift*) magazine; (*Comic~*) comic; (*Nummer*) number, issue. „National Geographic 1979, ~ 3" "National Geographic 1979, No. 3". (c) (*geheftetes Büchlein*) booklet.
Heftchen *nt* (a) (*dim of* Heft[2]. (b) (*pej: billiger Roman*) rubbishy *or* cheap *or* pulp novel (*pej*); (*schlechte Zeitschrift, Comic~*) rag (*pej inf*). (c) (*Fahrkarten~*, *Eintrittskarten~*) book(let) of tickets; (*Briefmarken~*) book of stamps.
heften 1 *vt* (a) (*nähen*) Saum, Naht to tack (up), to baste; *Buch* to sew, to stitch; (*Klammern*) to clip (*an* +*acc* to); (*mit Heftmaschine auch*) to staple (*an* +*acc* to).
(b) (*befestigen*) to pin, to fix. **er heftete mit Reißzwecken eine Landkarte an die Wand** he pinned a map on the wall; **jdm ein Abzeichen an die Brust ~** to pin a decoration to sb's chest; **den Blick *or* die Augen auf jdn/etw ~** to gaze at *or* fix one's eyes on sb/sth, to stare fixedly at sb/sth.
2 *vr* (a) (*Blick, Augen*) **sich auf jdn/etw ~** to fix onto sb/sth.
(b) **sich an jdn ~** to latch on to sb; **sich an jds Spur *or* Fährte ~** to follow sb's trail; **sich an jds Fersen *or* Sohlen ~** (*fig*) (*jdn verfolgen*) to dog sb's heels; (*bei Rennen etc*) to stick to sb's heels.
(c) (*geh: verbunden werden*) **sich an jdn/etw ~** to be/become associated with sb/sth; **ein Makel hat sich an seinen Namen geheftet** he (now) has a blot on his name.
Hefter *m* -s, - (loose-leaf) file.
Heft-: **~faden** *m*, **~garn** *nt* tacking thread.
heftig *adj* (a) (*stark, gewaltig*) violent; *Kopfschmerzen auch* severe, acute; *Schmerz* intense, acute; *Erkältung* severe;

Fieber raging, severe; *Zorn, Ärger, Haß* violent, burning *no adv*, intense; *Leidenschaft, Liebe, Sehnsucht* ardent, burning *no adv*, intense; *Leidenschaft* violent, fierce; *Abneigung auch* intense; *Widerstand* vehement; *Weinen* bitter; *Lachen* uproarious; *Atmen* heavy; *Kontroverse, Kampf, Wind* fierce; *Regen* lashing *no adv*, driving *no adv*, heavy; *Frost* severe, heavy. **ein ~er Regenguß** a downpour; **der Regen schlug ~ gegen die Scheiben** the rain pounded *or* beat against the windows; **er hat sich ~ in sie verliebt** he has fallen violently *or* madly (*inf*) in love with her; **~ nicken/rühren** to nod/stir *or* beat vigorously; **sie knallte die Tür ~ ins Schloß** she slammed *or* banged the door (shut); **er hat ~ dagegen gewettert** he raged vehemently against it.
(b) (*jähzornig, ungehalten*) *Mensch, Art* violent(-tempered); *Ton* fierce, vehement; *Worte* violent. **~ werden** to fly into a passion.
Heftigkeit *f* -, *no pl siehe adj* (a) violence; severity, acuteness; intensity, acuteness; severity; fierceness; vehemence; intensity; bitterness; uproariousness; heaviness; ferocity, fierceness; heaviness; severity, heaviness. (b) violent temper, violence; fierceness, vehemence; violence.
Heft-: **~klammer** *f* staple; **~maschine** *f* stapler; **~naht** *f* (*Sew*) basted *or* tacked seam; (*Tech*) tack weld; **~pflaster** *nt* (sticking) plaster, adhesive tape (*US*); **~stich** *m* tacking-stitch; **~zwecke** *f* drawing-pin (*Brit*), thumb-tack (*US*).
Hegelianer *m* -s, - Hegelian.
hegelianisch, hegel(i)sch *adj* Hegelian.
Hegemonie *f* hegemony.
hegen *vt* (a) (*pflegen*) *Wild, Pflanzen* to care for, to tend; (*geh: umsorgen*) *jdn* to care for, to look after. **jdn ~ und pflegen** to lavish care and attention on sb.
(b) (*empfinden, haben*) *Haß, Groll, Verdacht* to harbour; *Mißtrauen, Achtung, Abneigung* to feel; *Zweifel* to entertain; *Hoffnung, Wunsch* to cherish; *Plan, Unternehmen* to foster. **ich hege den starken Verdacht, daß ...** I have a strong suspicion that ...; **ich hege schon lange den Plan auszuwandern** for a long time I've been contemplating emigrating.
Heger *m* -s, - gamekeeper.
Hehl *nt or m* **kein *or* keinen ~ aus etw machen** to make no secret of sth; **ohne ~** openly.
Hehler(in *f*) *m* -s, - receiver (of stolen goods), fence (*inf*). **der ~ ist schlimmer als der Stehler** (*Prov*) it is worse to condone a crime than to commit it.
Hehlerei *f* -, *no pl* receiving (of stolen goods).
hehr *adj* (*liter*) noble, sublime.
hei *interj* wow.
Heia *f* -, *no pl* (*baby-talk*) bye-byes (*baby-talk*), beddy-byes (*baby-talk*). **ab in die ~** off to bye-byes *etc*; **die ~ wartet auf dich** it's time for bye-byes *etc*; **in die ~ gehen** to go bye-byes *etc*; **h~ machen** to have a little nap *or* sleep.
Heiabett *nt* (*baby-talk*) beddy-byes (*baby-talk*).
Heide[1] *m* -n, -n, **Heidin** *f* heathen, pagan; (*Nichtjude*) Gentile.
Heide[2] *f* -, -n (a) moor, heath; (*~land*) moorland, heathland. (b) (*~kraut*) heather.
Heide-: **~kraut** *nt* heather; **~land** *nt* moorland, heathland.
Heidelbeere *f* bilberry, blueberry (*esp US, Scot*).
Heidelbeer-: **~kraut** *nt*, **~strauch** *m* bilberry *or* blueberry bush.
Heiden-: **~angst** *f* **eine ~angst vor etw** (*dat*) **haben** (*inf*) to be scared stiff of sth (*inf*); **~arbeit** *f* (*inf*) real slog (*inf*); **~geld** *nt* (*inf*) packet (*inf*); **~krach**, **~lärm** *m* (*inf*) unholy din (*inf*); **h~mäßig** (*inf*) 1 *adj* huge, massive; 2 *adv* incredibly; **h~mäßig Geld verdienen** to earn a (real) packet (*inf*); **sich h~mäßig freuen** to be as pleased as Punch; **~mission** *f* missionary work among the heathen; **~respekt** *m* (*inf*) healthy respect; **~spaß** *m* (*inf*) terrific fun; **einen ~spaß haben** to have a whale of a time (*inf*); **das macht ihm einen ~spaß** he finds it terrific fun; **~spektakel** *m* (*inf*) awful row; (*Schimpfen*) awful fuss.
Heidentum *nt, no pl* heathenism, heathendom, paganism. **das ~** (*Menschen*) the heathen *pl*, the pagans *pl*.
heidi *interj*: **~ ging es den Berg hinab** down the hill they/we *etc* went; **~(, dann geht's los)** here they/we *etc* go.
Heidin *f siehe* **Heide**[1].
heidnisch *adj* heathen; (*auf Götterkult bezüglich*) pagan. **~ leben** to live a heathen *or* pagan life.
Heidschnucke *f* -, -n German moorland sheep.
heikel *adj* (a) (*schwierig, gefährlich*) *Angelegenheit, Situation, Thema* tricky, delicate; *Frage* awkward, tricky.
(b) (*dial*) *Mensch* particular, pernickety (*inf*) (*in bezug auf* +*acc* about); (*wählerisch auch*) fussy; (*in bezug aufs Essen auch*) fussy, choosy.
(c) (*dial*) *Stoff, Farbe* difficult. **die Farbe/der Stoff ist mir zu ~** that colour/material is too much of a nuisance.
heil *adj* (a) (*unverletzt*) *Mensch* unhurt, uninjured; *Glieder* unbroken; *Haut* undamaged. **wieder ~ sein/werden** (*wieder gesund*) to be/get better again; (*Wunde*) to have healed/to heal up; (*Knochen*) to have mended/to mend; **~ nach Hause kommen** to get home safe and sound; **~ machen** (*inf*) (*heilen*) to make better; (*reparieren*) to fix, to mend; **etw ~ überstehen** *Unfall* to come through sth without a scratch; *Prüfung* to get through sth; **Gott sei Dank sind die Glieder noch ~** thank goodness there are no broken bones; **mit ~en Gliedern *or* am Ziel ankommen** to reach the finish without breaking any bones; **mit ~er Haut davonkommen** to escape unscathed *or* (*lit auch*) in one piece.
(b) (*inf: ganz*) intact; *Kleidungsstück* decent (*inf*). **die ~e Welt** an ideal world (*without problems, uncertainties etc*).
Heil 1 *nt* -s, *no pl* (a) (*Wohlergehen*) well-being, good. **sein ~ bei jdm versuchen** (*inf*) to try one's luck with sb; **jdm ~ und Segen wünschen** to wish sb every blessing.

(b) (*Eccl, fig*) salvation. **sein ~ in etw** (*dat*) **suchen** to seek one's salvation in sth; **sein ~ in der Flucht suchen** to flee for one's life; **zu jds ~(e) gereichen** (*geh*) to be sb's salvation; **im Jahr des ~s 1848** (*old*) in the year of grace 1848 (*old*).

2 *interj*: **~! hail!** (*old*); **~ dem König!** long live or God save the King!; **~ Hitler!** heil Hitler!; **Berg/Ski/Petri ~!** good climbing/skiing/fishing!

Heiland *m* **-(e)s, -e** (*Rel*) Saviour, Redeemer; (*fig geh: Retter*) saviour.

Heil-: **~anstalt** *f* nursing home; (*für Sucht- or Geisteskranke*) home; **~anstalt für Geisteskranke** mental home; **~bad** *nt* (*Bad*) medicinal bath; (*Ort*) spa, watering-place (*old*); **h~bar** *adj* curable; **~barkeit** *f* -, *no pl* curability; **h~bringend** *adj* (*Rel*) redeeming; **Wirkung, Kur** beneficial; **Kräuter** medicinal; **sie warteten auf den h~bringenden Regen** they were waiting for the vitally needed rain; **~butt** *m* halibut.

heilen 1 *vi aux sein* (*Wunde, Bruch*) to heal (up); (*Entzündung*) to clear up.

2 *vt Kranke, Krankheiten* to cure; *Wunde* to heal; (*Rel*) to heal. **als geheilt entlassen werden** to be discharged with a clean bill of health; **Jesus heilt uns von unseren Sünden** Jesus redeems us from our sins; **jdn von etw ~** (*lit, fig*) to cure sb of sth; **von jdm/etw geheilt sein** (*fig*) to have got over sb/sth; **die Zeit heilt (alle) Wunden** time heals all wounds.

heilend *adj* healing.

Heiler *m* **-s, -** (*geh*) healer.

Heil-: **~erde** *f* healing earth; **~erfolg** *m* success; **zum ~erfolg führen** to lead to a successful cure; **h~froh** *adj pred* (*inf*) jolly glad (*inf*); **~fürsorge** *f* (*dated*) medical service; **~gymnastik** *f* *etc siehe* **Krankengymnastik** *etc*; **~haut** *f* new skin; **ich habe eine gute ~haut** my skin heals easily.

heilig *adj* **(a)** holy; (*geweiht, geheiligt auch*) sacred; (*bei Namen von Heiligen*) Saint; (*old: fromm auch*) devout, saintly; (*pej*) holier-than-thou. **jdm ~ sein** (*lit, fig*) to be sacred to sb; **bei allem, was ~ ist** by all that is or I hold sacred; **die ~e Veronika/der ~e Augustinus** Saint Veronica/Augustine; **H~er Abend** Christmas Eve; **das ~e Abendmahl/die ~e Kommunion** Holy Communion; **die H~e Dreifaltigkeit/Familie/Stadt** the Holy Trinity/Family/City; **die H~e Jungfrau** the Blessed Virgin; **H~e Maria** Holy Mary; **der H~e Geist/Vater/Stuhl** the Holy Spirit/Father/See; **die H~en Drei Könige** the Three Kings or Wise Men, the Magi; **das H~e Land** the Holy Land; **die H~e Schrift** the Holy Scriptures *pl*; **das H~e Römische Reich** the Holy Roman Empire; **die H~e Allianz** the Holy Alliance; **das H~ste** (*lit, fig*) the holy of holies.

(b) (*fig: ernst*) *Eid, Pflicht* sacred, solemn; *Recht* sacred; *Eifer, Zorn* righteous; (*von Ehrfurcht erfüllt*) *Stille, Schauer* awed; (*unantastbar*) *Würde, Gefühl, Gewohnheit* sacred. **es ist mein ~er Ernst** I am deadly serious or in dead earnest.

(c) (*inf: groß*) incredible (*inf*); *Respekt auch* healthy. **mit jdm/etw seine ~e Not haben** to have a hard time with sb/sth; **von einer ~en Angst gepackt werden** to be scared out of one's wits.

(d) (*inf: in Ausrufen*) (*ach du*) **~er Bimbam** or **Strohsack, ~es Kanonenrohr!** holy smoke! (*inf*).

Heilig|abend *m* Christmas Eve.

heiligen *vt* (*weihen*) to hallow, to sanctify; (*heilighalten*) to hallow, to keep holy; *Sonntag etc* to keep holy, to observe. **der Zweck heiligt die Mittel** the end justifies the means; **durch die Zeit geheiligt** time-honoured; *siehe* **geheiligt**.

Heiligen-: **~bild** *nt* holy picture; **~legende** *f* life or story of the saints; **~schein** *m* halo; **jdn mit einem ~schein umgeben** (*fig*) to put sb on a pedestal; **sich mit einem ~schein umgeben** (*fig*) to be holier-than-thou; **~verehrung** *f* veneration of the saints.

Heilige(r) *mf decl as adj* (*lit, fig*) saint. **ein sonderbarer** or **wunderlicher ~r** (*inf*) a queer fish (*inf*).

Heilig-: **h~halten** *vt sep irreg* to keep holy or *Andenken auch* sacred; *Sonntag auch* to observe; **~keit** *f* holiness; (*Geweihtheit, Geheiligtheit auch, von Eigentum*) sacredness; (*von Zorn*) righteousness; **Eure/Seine ~keit** Your/his Holiness; **im Geruch der ~keit stehen** to be surrounded by an aura of sanctity; **h~mäßig** *adj Leben, Mensch* saintly; **h~sprechen** *vt sep irreg* to canonize; **~sprechung** *f* canonization; **~tum** *nt* (*Stätte*) shrine; (*Gegenstand*) (holy) relic; **Schändung eines ~tums** sacrilege; **jds ~tum sein** (*inf*) (*Zimmer*) to be sb's sanctum; (*Gegenstand etc*) to be sacrosanct (to sb).

Heiligung *f* **die ~ des Sonntags** Sunday or Lord's day observance; **die ~ des Sabbats** the observance of the Sabbath.

Heil-: **~klima** *nt* healthy climate; **~kraft** *f* healing power; **h~kräftig** *adj Pflanze, Tee* medicinal; **Wirkung** curative; **ein h~kräftiges Mittel** a curative; **~kraut** *nt usu pl* medicinal herb; **~kunde** *f* medicine; **h~kundig** *adj* skilled in medicine or the art of healing; **~kundige(r)** *mf decl as adj* person skilled in medicine or the art of healing, healer; **h~los** *adj* unholy (*inf*); *Durcheinander, Verwirrung auch* hopeless; *Schreck* terrible, frightful; **sich h~los verirren** to get hopelessly lost; **h~los verschuldet sein** to be up to one's ears in debt; **~methode** *f* cure; **~mittel** *nt* (*lit, fig*) remedy, cure; (*Medikament*) medicine; **~pädagogik** *f* remedial education; **~pflanze** *f* medicinal plant; **~praktiker** *m* non-medical practitioner; **~quelle** *f* medicinal spring; **~salbe** *f* (medicated) ointment; **h~sam** *adj* **(a)** (*dated: heilend*) *Wirkung* healing; *Arznei auch* curative; *Klima* salutary, beneficial; **(b)** (*fig: förderlich*) *Erfahrung, Strafe* salutary.

Heils-: **~armee** *f* Salvation Army; **~botschaft** *f* message of salvation, gospel.

Heil-: **~schlaf** *m* healing sleep (*induced for therapeutic ends*); **~serum** *nt* serum.

Heils-: **~geschichte** *f* heilsgeschichte, *interpretation of history stressing God's saving grace*; **~lehre** *f* (*Rel, fig*) doctrine of salvation; **~ordnung** *f* order of salvation; **~plan** *m* plan for the world's salvation.

Heilstätte *f* (*form*) sanatorium (*Brit*), sanitarium (*US*), clinic.

Heilung *f* (*das Heilen*) (*von Wunde*) healing; (*von Krankheit, Kranken*) curing; (*Rel*) healing; (*das Gesundwerden*) cure. **~ in etw** (*dat*) **finden** to find relief in sth.

Heilungsprozeß *m* healing process.

Heil-: **~verfahren** *nt* (course of) treatment; **~zweck** *m*: **zu ~zwecken** for medicinal purposes.

heim *adv* home. **~, bitte** let's go home; **~ ins Reich** (*NS*) back to the Reich (*referring to formerly German areas and their inhabitants*).

Heim *nt* **-(e)s, -e** (*Zuhause, Anstalt*) home; (*Obdachlosen ~, für Lehrlinge*) hostel; (*Studentenwohn ~*) hall of residence, hostel; (*von Sportverein*) clubhouse; (*Freizeit ~*) recreation centre. **~ und Herd** (*liter*) house and home.

Heim- *in cpds* home; **~abend** *m* social evening; **~arbeit** *f* (*Ind*) homework, outwork *both no indef art*; **etw in ~arbeit herstellen lassen** to have sth produced by homeworkers; **~arbeiter** *m* (*Ind*) homeworker.

Heimat *f* **-, -en** home; (*~ort auch*) home town; (*~land auch*) native country; (*Bot, Zool auch*) natural habitat. **die ~ verlassen** to leave one's home; **jdm zur ~ werden** to become sb's home.

Heimat- *in cpds* home; **~anschrift** *f* home address; **~dichter** *m* regional writer; **~dichtung** *f* regional literature; **~erde** *f* native soil; **~film** *m* sentimental film in idealized regional setting; **~forschung** *f* research into local history; **~front** *f* home front; **~hafen** *m* home port; **~kunde** *f* (*Sch*) local history; **h~kundlich** *adj* local history *attr*; **er hat h~kundliche Interessen** he is interested in local history; **~kunst** *f* regional art; **~land** *nt* native country or land; **h~lich** *adj* (*zur Heimat gehörend*) native; *Bräuche, Dialekt* local; (*an die Heimat erinnernd*) *Gefühle, Wehmut* nostalgic; *Klänge* of home; **die h~lichen Berge** the mountains of (one's) home; **das mutet mich h~lich an, das kommt mir h~lich vor** that reminds me of home; **h~licher Boden** native soil; **~liebe** *f* love of one's native country or land; **h~los** *adj* homeless; **~lose(r)** *mf decl as adj* homeless person; **die ~losen** the homeless; **~losigkeit** *f* homelessness; **~museum** *nt* museum of local history; **~ort** *m* **(a)** home town/village; **(b)** *siehe* **~hafen**; **~recht** *nt* right of domicile; **~schriftsteller** *m* regional writer; **~sprache** *f* native dialect; (*Baskisch etc*) native language; **h~vertrieben** *adj* displaced; **~vertriebene(r)** *mf decl as adj* displaced person, expellee (*esp from former Eastern German province*).

Heim-: **h~begeben*** *vr sep irreg* to make one's way home; **h~begleiten*** *vt sep* jdn h~begleiten to take or see sb home; **h~bringen** *vt sep irreg* (*nach Hause bringen*) to bring home; (*h~begleiten*) to take or see home; **~bügler** *m* rotary iron.

Heimchen *nt* (*Zool*) house cricket. **~ (am Herd)** (*pej: Frau*) housewife.

heim-: **~dürfen** *vi sep irreg* darf ich/sie **~?** may I/she go home?; **~eilen** *vi sep aux sein* to hurry home.

heimelig *adj* cosy, homely.

Heim-: **h~fahren** *vti sep irreg* (*vi: aux sein*) to drive home; **~fahrt** *f* journey home, return journey; (*Naut*) return voyage, voyage home; **h~finden** *vi sep irreg* to find one's way home; **h~führen** *vt sep* to take home; **ein Mädchen h~führen** (*dated*) to take a girl as one's wife (*dated*); **~gang** *m* (*euph geh: Tod*) passing away; **beim ~gang meiner Mutter** when my mother was called to her Lord or Maker (*euph*); **~gegangene(r)** *mf decl as adj* (*euph geh*) deceased; **unser lieber ~gegangener** our dear departed friend/father etc; **h~gehen** *sep irreg aux sein* 1 *vi* to go home; (*euph geh*) to pass away or on; 2 *vi impers* **es geht h~** we're going home; **h~geigen** *vi sep siehe* **h~leuchten**; **h~holen** *vt sep* to fetch home; **Gott hat ihn h~geholt** he has been called to his Maker; **~industrie** *f* cottage industry.

heimisch *adj* **(a)** (*einheimisch*) (*Zool, Bot*) indigenous, native (*in + dat* to); (*national*) home; (*ortsansässig*) local; (*regional*) regional; *Gewässer* home. **etw ~ machen** to introduce sth (*in + dat* to).

(b) (*vertraut*) familiar. **an einem Ort ~ sein** to feel at home in a place; **sich ~ fühlen** to feel at home; **vom ~en Herd weg sein** to be away from house and home; **in einer Sprache etc ~ sein** to be or feel at home in a language etc; **sich ~ machen** to make oneself at home; **~ werden** to become acclimatized (*an, in + dat* to), to settle in (*an, in + dat* to).

Heim-: **~kampf** *m* (*Sport*) home match or game or (*Boxen*) fight; **~kehr** *f* -, *no pl* homecoming, return; **h~kehren** *vi sep aux sein* to return home (*aus* from); **~kehrer** *m* -s, - homecomer; **~kind** *nt* institution child, child brought up in a home; **~kino** *nt* home movies *pl*; (*Ausrüstung*) home movie kit; (*inf: TV*) goggle-box (*Brit inf*); **heute abend machen wir ~kino** tonight we're going to watch some home movies; **h~kommen** *vi sep irreg aux sein* to come or return home; **h~können** *vi sep irreg* to be able to go home; **~kunft** *f* -, *no pl* (*geh*) *siehe* **~kehr**; **~leiter** *m* head or warden of a/the home/hostel; **~leitung** *f* person(s) in charge of a/the home/hostel; **ihr wurde die ~leitung übertragen** she was put in charge of the home etc; **h~leuchten** *vi sep* (*fig inf*) jdm h~leuchten to give sb a piece of one's mind.

heimlich 1 *adj* (*geheim, verborgen*) secret; *Treffen auch* clandestine; *Benehmen* secretive; *Bewegungen* furtive.

2 *adv* secretly; *treffen, tun auch* in secret; *lachen* inwardly. **er blickte sie ~ an** he stole a glance at her; **sich ~ entfernen** to steal or sneak away; **~, still und leise** (*inf*) quietly, on the quiet.

Heimlichkeit *f siehe adj* secrecy; clandestineness; secretiveness; furtiveness; (*Geheimnis*) secret. **in aller ~** secretly, in secret; **nur keine ~en!** (*inf*) stop being (so) secretive, no secrets now!

Heimlich-: **~tuer(in** *f*) *m* **-s, -** secretive person; **~tuerei** *f* secrecy, secretiveness; h~tun *vi sep irreg* to be secretive (*mit about*).

Heim-: h~**müssen** *vi sep irreg* to have to go home; ~**mutter** *f* mother of a/the home; (*von Jugendherberge*) warden; ~**ordnung** *f* rules and regulations of a/the home/hostel; ~**reise** *f* journey home, homeward journey; (*Naut*) voyage home, homeward voyage; h~**reisen** *vi sep aux sein* to travel home; ~**sauna** *f* home sauna; h~**schicken** *vt sep* to send home; ~**spiel** *nt* (*Sport*) home match or game; ~**statt** *f* (*liter*) home; **ohne** ~**statt** without a home; ~**stätte** *f* (a) (*Zuhause*) home; (b) (*Jur*) homestead.

heimsuchen *vt sep* to strike; (*für längere Zeit*) to plague; (*Feind auch*) to attack; (*Gespenst*) to haunt; (*Krankheit auch*) to afflict; (*Alpträume, Vorstellungen*) to afflict, to haunt; (*Schicksal*) to overtake, to afflict; (*inf: besuchen*) to descend on (*inf*). **von Dürre/Krieg/vom Streik heimgesucht** drought-stricken/war-torn or -ravaged/strike-torn; **Gott suchte die Ägypter mit schweren Plagen heim** God visited terrible plagues on the Egyptians.

Heimsuchung *f* (a) (*Schicksalsschlag*) affliction; (*Katastrophe*) disaster; (*Plage*) plague. (b) **Mariä** ~ the visitation of Mary.

heimtrauen *vr sep* to dare to go home.

Heimtücke *f, no pl siehe adj* insidiousness; maliciousness; insidiousness; treacherousness.

Heimtücker *m -s, -* (*inf*) devious character or bastard (*sl*).

heimtückisch *adj* (*hinterlistig*) insidious; (*boshaft*) malicious; *Krankheit* insidious; (*gefährlich*) *Glatteis, Maschine* treacherous.

Heim-: ~**vorteil** *m* (*Sport*) advantage of playing at home; h~**wärts** *adv* (*nach Hause zu*) home; (*auf dem* ~*weg*) on the way home; h~**wärts ziehen/gehen** to go homewards; ~**weg** *m* way home; **sich auf den** ~**weg machen** to set out or head for home; ~**weh** *nt* homesickness *no art*; ~**weh haben/bekommen** to be/become homesick (*nach* for); ~**weh nach Vergangenem/Verlorenem** nostalgia; **krank vor** ~**weh sein** to be pining for home, to be very homesick; h~**wehkrank** *adj* homesick; ~**werker** *m* handyman; h~**wollen** *vi sep* to want to go home; h~**zahlen** *vt sep* **jdm etw** h~**zahlen** to pay sb back for sth; h~**ziehen** *sep irreg* **1** *vi aux sein* to return home; **2** *vt impers* **es zog ihn** h~ he felt he wanted to go home; h~**zu** *adv* (*inf*) on the way home.

Hein *m:* **Freund** ~ (*old*) Death.

Heini *m -s, -s* (*inf*) bloke (*Brit inf*), guy (*inf*); (*Dummkopf*) idiot, fool.

Heinzelmännchen *nt* brownie.

Heirat *f -, -en* marriage; (*Feier*) wedding; (*Partie*) match.

Heiraten *nt -s, no pl* marriage, getting married *no def art*.

heiraten 1 *vt* to marry.

2 *vr* to get married.

3 *vi* to get married, to marry. **aufs Land/in die Stadt/nach Berlin** ~ to marry or get married and settle in the country/in town/in Berlin; **in eine reiche/alte Familie** ~ to marry into a rich/old family; ~ **müssen** (*euph*) to have to get married; „**wir** ~" "we are getting married"; „**geheiratet haben ...**" ≈ "marriages", "marriage announcements".

Heirats-: ~**absichten** *pl* marriage plans *pl*; ~**alter** *nt* marriageable or marrying age; (*Jur*) minimum legal age for marriage; ~**annonce** *f siehe* ~**anzeige** (b); ~**antrag** *m* proposal (of marriage); **jdm einen** ~**antrag machen** to propose to sb; ~**anzeige** *f* (a) (*Bekanntgabe*) announcement of a forthcoming marriage. (b) (*Annonce für Partnersuche*) advertisement for a marriage partner; ~**büro** *nt* marriage bureau; ~**erlaubnis** *f* consent (to a marriage); h~**fähig** *adj* marriageable; ~**kandidat** *m* (*Bräutigam*) husband-to-be; (*ehewilliger Junggeselle*) eligible bachelor, *person on the lookout for a wife*; ~**institut** *nt* marriage bureau; h~**lustig** *adj* eager to get married; ~**schwindel** *m* marriage proposal made under false pretences; ~**schwindler** *m* person who makes a marriage proposal under false pretences; ~**urkunde** *f* marriage certificate; ~**urlaub** *m* leave to get married; ~**vermittler** *m* marriage broker; ~**vermittlung** *f* matchmaking *no pl*; (*Büro*) marriage bureau; **diskrete** ~**vermittlung** marriages arranged discreetly; ~**versprechen** *nt* (*Jur*) promise of marriage; **Bruch des** ~**versprechens** breach of promise (of marriage).

heisa *interj* hey.

heischen *vt* (*geh*) (a) *Beifall, Hochachtung, Aufmerksamkeit etc* to demand. (b) (*dated: erbitten*) to beg or ask for.

heiser *adj* hoarse; (*dunkel klingend*) husky; *Laut* croaky. ~ **reden** to talk hoarsely or in a hoarse voice; **sich** ~ **schreien/reden** (*lit, fig*) to shout/talk oneself hoarse.

Heiserkeit *f siehe adj* hoarseness; huskiness.

heiß *adj* (a) hot; *Zone* torrid. **brennend/siedend/glühend** ~ burning/boiling/scorching hot; **drückend** ~ oppressively hot; **jdm ist/wird** ~ sb is/is getting hot; **sie hat einen** ~**en Kopf** (*wegen Fieber*) she has a burning forehead; (*vom Denken*) her head is spinning; **etw** ~ **machen** to heat sth up; **es überläuft mich** ~ **und kalt** I feel hot and cold all over; ~**e Tränen weinen** to cry one's heart out; **es wird nichts so** ~ **gegessen wie es gekocht wird** (*prov*) things are never as bad as they seem; **eine/ein Paar H**~**e** a hot sausage/a couple of hot sausages; ~**!** (*inf: fast gefunden*) you're hot; *siehe* **baden.**

(b) (*heftig*) *Diskussion, Kampf, Auseinandersetzung* heated, fierce; *Zorn* impassioned; *Begierde* passionate, burning; (*innig*) *Liebe, Wunsch* burning, fervent. **es ging** ~ **her** things got heated; **das Gebiet/die Stadt ist** ~ **umkämpft** the area/town is being hotly or fiercely fought over; **jdn/etw** ~ **und innig lieben** to love sb/sth madly; **sich die Köpfe** ~ **reden, sich** ~ **reden** or **diskutieren** to talk till one is blue in the face; ~**en Dank** very many thanks.

(c) (*aufreizend*) *Musik, Sachen, Bilder* hot; (*inf: sexuell erregt auch*) randy (*Brit inf*), horny (*inf*). ~**e Höschen** hot pants; **jdn** ~ **machen** (*inf*) to turn sb on (*inf*).

(d) (*gefährlich*) *Ware, Geld, (radioaktiv) Teilchen etc* hot; *Gegend, Thema* hotly-disputed. **das wird ein** ~**er Winter** things are going to be pretty hot this winter (*inf*); **ein** ~**es Eisen** a hot potato; **ein** ~**es Eisen anfassen** (*inf*) to grasp the nettle.

(e) *attr* (*inf*) *Favorit, Tip, Maschine* hot. **ein** ~**er Ofen** a motorbike; ~**er Draht** hot line; ~**e Spur** hot trail.

(f) *pred* (*inf: brünstig*) ~ **sein** to be on heat.

heißa *interj* hey.

heißblütig *adj* (*erregbar*) hot-tempered; (*leidenschaftlich*) hot-blooded.

heißen *pret* **hieß,** *ptp* **geheißen 1** *vt* (a) (*nennen*) to call; (*old: Namen geben*) **jdn, Ort** to name. **das heiße ich eine gute Geschichte/klug vorgehen!** that's what I call a good story/being clever; **jdn einen Lügner** *etc* ~ to call sb a liar *etc*; **oder wie heißt man das?** (*inf*) ... or what do you call it?; **... oder wie man das heißt** ... or whatever it's called.

(b) (*geh: auffordern*) to tell, to bid (*form*). **jdn etw tun** ~ to tell sb to do sth, to bid sb do sth; **jdn willkommen** ~ to bid sb welcome; **es hat dich niemand geheißen, das zu tun** no-one told you to do that; **etw mitgehen** ~ (*fig hum*) to appropriate sth.

2 *vi* (a) (*den Namen haben, bezeichnet werden*) to be called; (*als Titel haben auch*) to be titled. **wie** ~ **Sie/heißt die Straße?** what are you/is the street called?, what's your name/the name of the street?; **ich heiße Müller** I'm called or my name is Müller; **sie heißt jetzt anders** her name is different now, she has changed her name; **nach jdm** ~ to be called after (*Brit*) or for (*US*) sb; **wie kann man nur Gotthelf/so** ~? how can anyone have a name like Gotthelf/like that?; **wie heißt das?** what is that called?; **eigentlich heißt es richtig X** actually the correct word is X; **... und der Rest von them** ... **so wahr ich Franz-Josef heiße** (*als Bekräftigung*) ... as sure as I'm standing here; **... dann will ich Fridolin** ~ ... then I'm a Dutchman.

(b) (*bestimmte Bedeutung haben*) to mean. **was heißt „gut" auf englisch?** what is the English (word) for "gut"?; „**gut" heißt auf englisch „good"** the English (word) for "gut" is "good"; **ich weiß, was es heißt, allein zu sein** I know what it means to be alone.

(c) (*lauten*) to be; (*Spruch, Gedicht etc*) to go.

(d) **das heißt** that is; (*in anderen Worten*) that is to say.

3 *vi impers* (a) **es heißt, daß ...** (*es geht die Rede*) they say that ...; **es soll nicht** ~, **daß ...** never let it be said that ...

(b) (*zu lesen sein*) **in der Bibel/im Gesetz/in seinem Brief heißt es, daß ...** the Bible/the law/his letter says that ..., in the Bible *etc* it says that ...; **bei Hegel/Goethe etc heißt es ...** Hegel/Goethe says ...; **es heißt hier ...** it says here ...

(c) (*es ist nötig*) **es heißt, etw zu tun** you/we/he *etc* must do sth; **nun heißt es handeln** now it's time to act; **da heißt es aufgepaßt** or **aufpassen** you'd better watch out.

Heiß-: h~**ersehnt** *adj attr* much longed for; h~**geliebt** *adj* dearly beloved; ~**hunger** *m* ravenous or voracious appetite; **etw mit** ~**hunger essen** to eat sth ravenously or voraciously; **etw mit wahrem** ~**hunger verschlingen** (*fig*) to really devour sth; h~**hungrig** *adj* ravenous, voracious; h~**laufen** *vi sep irreg aux sein* (*Motor, Auto, Maschinenteil*) to overheat; (*Diskussionsteilnehmer etc*) to become heated; (*Telefonleitungen, -drähte*) to buzz.

Heißluft *f* hot air.

Heißluft-: ~**heizung** *f* hot-air heating; ~**motor** *m* hot-air or Stirling engine; ~**trockner** *m* hot-air dryer.

Heiß-: ~**mangel** *f* (*Gerät*) rotary iron; (*Ort*) laundry specializing in ironing sheets *etc*; ~**sporn** *m* hothead; h~**umkämpft** *adj attr* hotly disputed; h~**umstritten** *adj attr* hotly debated; ~**wasserbereiter** *m -s, -* geyser, water heater; ~**wasserspeicher** *m* hot (water) tank.

heiter *adj* (*fröhlich*) cheerful; *Mensch, Wesen auch* happy; (*ausgeglichen*) serene; (*amüsant*) *Geschichte* amusing, funny; (*leicht betrunken*) merry; (*hell, klar*) *Farbe, Raum* bright; *Himmel, Tag* bright, clear; *Wetter* clear, fine; (*Met*) fair. ~ **werden** to become cheerful; (*Gesicht*) to brighten; (*Wetter*) to brighten or clear up; ~**er werden** to cheer up; (*Wetter*) to brighten up, to become brighter; **das ist ja** ~**!** (*iro*) that's really wonderful (*iro*); **das kann ja** ~ **werden!** (*iro*) that sounds great (*iro*); **aus** ~**em Himmel** (*fig*) out of the blue.

Heiterkeit *f, no pl siehe adj* cheerfulness; happiness; serenity; amusingness, funniness; merriness; brightness; brightness, clearness; clearness, fineness; (*heitere Stimmung*) merriment; (*Belustigung*) amusement.

Heiterkeits-: ~**ausbruch** *m* fit of merriment; ~**erfolg** *m* einen ~**erfolg haben** to raise a laugh.

Heiz-: ~**anlage** *f* heating system; ~**apparat** *m siehe* ~**gerät**; h~**bar** *adj Heckscheibe etc* heated; *Zimmer auch* with heating; **der Saal ist schwer** h~**bar** the hall is difficult to heat; *siehe auch* **beheizbar**; ~**(bett)decke** *f* electric blanket; ~**element** *nt* heating element.

heizen 1 *vi* (*die Heizung anhaben*) to have the/one's heating on; (*Wärme abgeben*) to give off heat. **der Ofen heizt gut** the stove gives (off) a good heat; **mit Holz/Strom** *etc* ~ to use wood/electricity *etc* for heating; **ab November wird geheizt** the heating is put on in November.

2 *vt* (*warm machen*) to heat; (*verbrennen*) to burn; (*be*~) *Lokomotive* to stoke. **den Ofen heize ich nur mit Holz** I only burn wood in the stove.

3 *vr* **sich gut/schlecht** ~ to be easily heated or easy to heat/not easily heated or hard to heat.

Heizer *m -s, -* boilerman; (*von Lokomotive, Schiff*) stoker.

Heiz-: ~**fläche** *f* heating surface; ~**gas** *nt* fuel gas; ~**gerät** *nt* heater; ~**kessel** *m* boiler; ~**kissen** *nt* electric heat pad;

~**körper** m (Gerät) heater; (von Zentralheizung) radiator; (Element) heating element; ~**kosten** pl heating costs pl; ~**kraft** f calorific or heating power; ~**lüfter** m fan heater; ~**material** nt fuel (for heating); ~**ofen** m siehe ~**gerät**; ~**öl** nt heating or fuel oil; ~**platte** f hotplate; ~**sonne** f electric fire; ~**strahler** m electric (wall) heater.

Heizung f heating; (Heizkörper) heater; (von Zentralheizung) radiator.

Heizungs-: ~**anlage** f heating system; ~**monteur** m heating engineer; ~**rohr** nt heating pipe; ~**technik** f heating engineering.

Heizwert m calorific value.

Hektar nt or m -s, - hectare.

Hektik f -, no pl (Hast) hectic rush; (von Leben etc) hectic pace. sie ißt/arbeitet mit einer solchen ~ she eats/works at such a hectic pace; nur keine ~ take it easy.

hektisch adj (auch dated Med) hectic; Mensch auch frantic; Arbeiten frantic, furious. es geht ~ zu things are hectic; ich lebe zur Zeit ~ my life is very hectic just now; nur mal nicht so ~ take it easy.

Hekto-: ~**graph** m hectograph; ~**graphie** f (Verfahren) hectography; (Abzug) hectograph (copy); h~**graphieren*** vt insepto hectograph, to copy; ~**liter** m or nt hectolitre; ~**watt** nt hectowatt.

Helanca ® nt -, no pl stretch fabric.

helau interj greeting used at Carnival time.

Held m -en, -en hero. der ~ des Tages hero of the hour; kein ~ in etw (dat) sein not to be very brave about sth; (in Schulfach etc) to be no great shakes at sth (inf); du bist mir ein rechter or schöner ~! (iro) some hero you are!; den ~en spielen (inf) to come or play the (great) hero.

Helden-: ~**brust** f (hum) manly chest; ~**darsteller** m (Theat) heroic leading man; ~**dichtung** f epic or heroic poetry; ~**epos** nt heroic epic; ~**friedhof** m military cemetery; ~**gedenktag** m (old) ≈ Remembrance Day, Memorial Day (US); ~**gestalt** f hero; ~**grab** nt soldier's grave; h~**haft** adj heroic, valiant; ~**lied** nt (Liter) epic song or lay; ~**mut** m heroic courage; h~**mütig** adj siehe h~**haft**; ~**pose** f heroic pose; ~**rolle** f (Theat) hero's part or rôle; ~**sage** f heroic saga; ~**stück** nt: das war kein ~**stück** (inf) that didn't exactly cover you/him etc in glory; ~**tat** f heroic deed or feat; ~**tenor** m heroic tenor; ~**tod** m heroic death, hero's death; den ~**tod sterben** to die a hero's death; (Mil) to be killed in action; ~**tum** nt, no pl heroism.

Heldin f heroine.

helfen pret half, ptp geholfen vi (a) to help (jdm sb); (mit anfassen auch) to lend a hand. jdm bei etw ~ to help sb with sth, to lend sb a hand with sth; jdm etw tun ~ to help sb do sth; er half ihr aus dem Mantel/einer Verlegenheit he helped her out of her coat or off with her coat/out of a difficulty; ihm/dir ist nicht zu ~ (fig) he is/you are beyond help; dem Kranken ist nicht mehr zu ~ the patient is beyond help; ich kann mir nicht ~ I can't help it; ich kann mir nicht ~, ich muß es tun I can't help doing it; ich werd' dir/ihm (schon) ~! I'll give you/him what for (inf); ich werde dir ~, die Tapeten zu beschmieren I'll teach you to mess up the wallpaper (inf); er weiß sich (dat) zu ~ he is very resourceful; man muß sich (dat) nur zu ~ wissen (prov) you just have to use your head; er weiß sich (dat) nicht mehr zu ~ he is at his wits' end; hilf dir selbst, dann or so hilft dir Gott (Prov) God helps those who help themselves (Prov).
(b) auch wi impers (dienen, nützen) to help. es hilft nichts it's no use or no good; da ist nicht zu ~ there's no help for it; da hilft alles nichts ... there's nothing for it ...; da hilft kein Jammern und kein Klagen it's no use moaning; es hilft ihm nichts, daß ... it's no use to him that ...; das hilft mir wenig, damit ist mir nicht geholfen that's not much help to me; das hat mir schon viel geholfen that has been a great help to me; was hilft's? what's the use?; was hülfe es dem Menschen, wenn ... (Bibl) what does it profit a man if ... (Bibl).
(c) (heilsam sein) to help; (heilen auch: Arzt) to cure. diese Arznei hilft gegen or bei Kopfweh this medicine is good for headaches or helps to relieve headaches; jetzt kann nur noch eine Operation ~ only an operation will help now or do any good now.

Helfer m -s, - helper; (Mitarbeiter) assistant; (von Verbrecher) accomplice; (Gerät: Gerät) help. ~ in Steuersachen tax adviser; ein ~ in der Not a friend in need.

Helferin f siehe **Helfer**.

Helfershelfer m accomplice; (Jur: vor/nach begangener Tat) accessory before/after the fact.

Helikopter m -s, - helicopter.

Helium nt -s, no pl helium.

hell adj (a) (optisch) light; Licht, Beleuchtung, Himmel bright; Farbe auch pale; Kleidungsstück auch light-coloured; Haar, Teint fair; Hautfarbe (von Rasse) fair, pale; (fig) Zukunft bright. es wird ~ it's getting light; ~ bleiben to stay light; am ~en Tage in broad daylight; bis in den ~en Morgen schlafen to sleep late; in ~en Flammen in flames, ablaze; ~es Bier = lager.
(b) (akustisch) Laut, Ton, Stimme high(-pitched); Gelächter ringing.
(c) (inf: klug) Junge bright, intelligent; (geistig klar) Augenblicke lucid. er ist ein ~er Kopf, er hat einen ~en Kopf he has brains; siehe helle.
(d) attr (stark, groß) great; Verwunderung etc utter; Verzweiflung, Unsinn sheer, utter; Neid pure. von etw ~ begeistert/entzückt sein to be very enthusiastic/quite delighted about sth; in ~en Scharen or Haufen in great numbers; seine ~e Freude an etw (dat) haben to find great joy or pleasure in sth.

Hellas nt -' Hellas.

hell- in cpds (esp auf Farben bezüglich) light; ~**auf** adv completely, utterly; ~**auf lachen** to laugh out loud; ~**blau** adj light blue; ~**blond** adj very fair, blonde; ~**braun** adj light brown; H~**dunkel** nt (Art) chiaroscuro.

Helle f -, no pl siehe **Helligkeit**.

helle adj pred (inf) bright, clever. Mensch, sei ~! use your loaf, mate! (inf).

Hellebarde f -, -n (Hist) halberd.

Hellebardier m -s, -e, **Hellebardist** m halberdier.

Hellene m -n, -n (ancient) Greek, Hellene.

Hellenentum nt, no pl Hellenism, Hellenic culture.

hellenisch adj Hellenic.

hellenisieren* vt to hellenize.

Hellenismus m Hellenism.

Hellenist(in f) m Hellenist.

Hellenistik f classical Greek studies pl.

hellenistisch adj Hellenistic. die ~e Staatenwelt the Empire of Ancient Greece.

Heller m -s, - (Hist) heller. das ist keinen (roten or lumpigen) or nicht einen ~ wert that isn't worth a brass farthing; er besitzt keinen (roten or lumpigen) ~ he doesn't have a penny to his name, he doesn't have two pennies to rub together; darauf geb ich keinen (roten) ~ I wouldn't give you tuppence for it; auf ~ und Pfennig or bis auf den letzten ~ (down) to the last farthing or penny; stimmen down to the last detail.

Helle(s) nt decl as adj = lager.

hellleuchtend adj attr getrennt hell-leuchtend brightly shining; Farbe bright; Kleid brightly coloured.

hell-: ~**haarig** adj fair-haired; ~**häutig** adj fair-skinned; (von Rasse auch) pale-skinned; ~**hörig** adj keen of hearing; (Archit) poorly soundproofed; ~**hörig sein** (fig: Mensch) to have sharp ears; als er das sagte, wurde ich ~**hörig** when he said that I pricked up my ears; jdn ~**hörig machen** to make sb prick up their ears.

hellicht adj getrennt hell-licht: am ~en Tage in broad daylight; es ist ~er Tag it is broad daylight.

Helligkeit f, no pl siehe **hell** (a) lightness; brightness; paleness; fairness; paleness; brightness; (helles Licht) light; (Phys, Licht) light; (Phys, Astron) luminosity.

Helling f -, -en or **Helligen** or m -s, -e (Naut) slipway.

hellodernd adj attr getrennt hell-lodernd blazing.

hell-: ~**rot** adj bright red; ~**sehen** vi infin only ~**sehen können** to have second sight, to be clairvoyant; du kannst wohl ~**sehen!** you must have second sight or be clairvoyant; H~**seher(in** f) m (lit, fig) clairvoyant; ~**seherisch** adj attr clairvoyant; ~**sichtig** adj shrewd; H~**sichtigkeit** f, no pl shrewdness; ~**strahlend** adj attr brilliant, brightly shining; ~**wach** adj (lit) wide-awake; (fig) alert; H~**werden** nt -s, no pl daybreak.

Helm m -(e)s, -e helmet; (Archit) helm roof.

Helm-: ~**busch** m plume; ~**dach** nt helm roof; ~**schmuck** m crest; ~**sturz** m beaver.

Helot m -en, -en Helot.

Helotentum nt, no pl (Sklaverei) helotism, helotage; (alle Heloten) helotry.

hem [həm, hm] interj hem.

Hemd nt -(e)s, -en (Ober~) shirt; (Unter~) vest (Brit), undershirt (US). etw wie das or sein ~ wechseln (fig) to change sth with monotonous regularity; für dich gebe ich auch das letzte or mein letztes ~ her (inf) I'd give you the shirt off my back (inf); naß bis aufs ~ wet through, soaked to the skin; jdn bis aufs ~ ausziehen (fig inf) to have the shirt off sb's back (inf), to fleece sb (inf); das zieht einem ja das ~ aus (inf) it makes you cringe (inf), it's terrible; ein Schlag, und du stehst im ~ da (inf) I could floor you with one blow from my little finger; das ~ ist mir näher als der Rock (Prov) charity begins at home (Prov).

Hemd-: ~**ärmel** m siehe **Hemdsärmel**; ~**bluse** f shirt(-blouse), shirtwaist (US); ~**blusenkleid** nt shirtwaister (dress); ~**brust** f dickey.

Hemden-: ~**matz** m (inf) small child dressed only in a vest, ≈ Wee Willie Winkie; ~**stoff** m shirting.

Hemd-: ~**hose** f combinations pl, coms pl (inf); ~**knopf** m shirt button; ~**kragen** m shirt collar.

Hemds-: ~**ärmel** m shirt sleeve; in ~**ärmeln** in one's shirt sleeves; h~**ärmelig** adj shirt-sleeved; (fig inf: salopp) pally (inf); Ausdrucksweise, Empfang casual.

Hemisphäre f -, -n hemisphere.

hemisphärisch adj hemispheric(al).

hemmen vt Entwicklung, Fortschritt to hinder, to hamper; Lauf der Geschehnisse etc to check; (verlangsamen) to slow down; Maschine, Rad to check; Wasserlauf to stem; (Med) Blut to staunch; (Psych) to inhibit; Leidenschaften to restrain, to check. seinen Schritt ~ to slow down, to slow or check one's pace; jdn in seiner Entwicklung ~ to hinder or hamper sb's development; siehe gehemmt.

Hemmnis nt hindrance, impediment (für to).

Hemm-: ~**rad** nt (von Uhr) escapement; ~**schuh** m brake shoe; (fig) hindrance, impediment (für to); jdm einen ~**schuh in den Weg legen** (fig) to put a spanner in sb's works (inf); ~**stoff** m (Chem) inhibitor.

Hemmung f (a) (Psych) inhibition; (Bedenken) scruple. da habe ich ~en I've got scruples about that; an ~en leiden to suffer from inhibitions; keine ~en kennen to have no inhibitions, not to feel inhibited; nur keine ~en don't feel inhibited.
(b) siehe vt hindering, hampering; check (gen to); slowing down; checking; stemming; staunching.
(c) (von Gewehr) siehe **Ladehemmung**.
(d) (von Uhr) escapement.

Hemmungs-: h~**los** adj (rückhaltlos) unrestrained; (skrupellos) unscrupulous; ~**losigkeit** f siehe adj lack of restraint; unscrupulousness; ~**nerv** m inhibitor (nerve).

Hendl nt -s, -(n) (Aus) chicken.
Hengst m -(e)s, -e stallion; (Kamel~, Esel~) male; (sl: Mann) stud (sl); (sl: -heini) wallah (inf).
Hengst-: ~fohlen, ~füllen nt (male) foal, colt.
Henkel m -s, - handle.
Henkel-: ~glas nt glass with a handle; ~korb m basket with a handle; ~krug m jug (with a handle); ~mann m, pl -männer (inf) canteen; ~ohren pl (inf) big, sticking-out ears (inf); ~topf m pot or pan with a handle/handles.
henken vt (old) to hang.
Henker m -s, - hangman; (Scharfrichter) executioner. zum ~ (old inf) hang it all (inf), zounds (obs inf); was zum ~! (old inf) what the devil (inf); hol's der ~! (old inf) the devil take it! (old inf); hol mich der ~ (old inf) zounds (obs inf); scher dich or geh zum ~! (old inf) go to the devil! (inf); ich frage den ~ danach, ich schere mich den ~ drum (old inf) I don't care a hang or damn about it (inf).
Henker(s)beil nt executioner's axe.
Henkers-: ~hand f durch or von ~hand sterben to be executed; ~knecht m (Hist) hangman's or (von Scharfrichter) executioner's assistant; (fig) torturer; (Handlanger) henchman; ~mahl(zeit f) nt last meal before execution; (hum inf) last slap-up meal (before examination etc).
Henna f - or nt -(s), no pl henna. mit ~ färben to dye with henna.
Henne f -, -n hen.
Hepatitis f -, **Hepatitiden** hepatitis.
her adv siehe auch herkommen, hermüssen, hersein etc (a) (räumlich) von der Kirche/Frankreich/dem Meer ~ from the church/France/the sea; er winkte vom Nachbarhaus ~ he waved from the house next door; ~ zu mir! come here (to me); um mich ~ (all) around me; von weit ~ from a long way off or away, from afar (liter); ~ ist es ebensoweit wie hin it's the same distance both ways; siehe auch hin.
(b) (in Aufforderung) Bier/Essen ~! bring (me/us) some beer/food (here); ~ mit der Brieftasche! hand over the briefcase, give me the briefcase; (wieder) ~ mit den alten Bräuchen give me/us the old way of doing things, bring back the old customs I say; ~ damit! give me that, give that here (inf); immer ~ damit! let's have it/them (then).
(c) (von etwas aus gesehen) von der Idee/Form/Farbe ~ as for the idea/form/colour, as far as the idea/form/colour is concerned or goes; vom finanziellen Standpunkt ~ from the financial point of view; von den Eltern ~ gute Anlagen haben to have inherited good qualities from one's parents.
(d) (zeitlich) ich kenne ihn von früher ~ I know him from before or from earlier times, I used to know him (before); von der Schule/meiner Kindheit ~ since school/my childhood; von der letzten Saison ~ from last season; siehe hersein.
herab adv down. den Hügel/die Treppe ~ down the hill/stairs; von oben ~ (down) from above; siehe oben.
herab- pref down; siehe auch herunter-; ~blicken vi sep siehe ~sehen; ~flehen vt sep (liter) to call down; ~fließen vi sep irreg aux sein to flow down; ~hängen vi sep irreg to hang down; langes ~hängendes Haar long, flowing hair; ~kommen vi sep irreg aux sein (geh) to come down, to descend (liter, form); ~lassen sep irreg 1 vt to let down, to lower; 2 vr (a) (lit) to let oneself down, to lower oneself; (b) (fig) to lower oneself; sich zu etw ~ lassen to condescend or deign to do sth; sich auf jds Ebene (acc) ~lassen to descend to sb's level; wenn du dich ~lassen könntest, mir dabei zu helfen if you would condescend or deign to help me with it; ~lassend adj condescending; H~lassung f condescension; ~mindern vt sep (schlechtmachen) Leistung, Qualitäten to belittle, to disparage; (bagatellisieren) Gefahr, Problem to minimize, to make little of; (reduzieren) Geschwindigkeit, Länge, Niveau to reduce; ~rieseln vi sep aux sein to trickle down; (Schneeflocken, Staub, Musik) to float or waft down; ~sehen vi sep irreg (lit, fig) to look down (auf +acc on); ~senken vr sep (geh: Nebel, Dunkelheit, Abend) to fall; ~setzen vt sep Ware to reduce; Preise, Kosten auch to lower; Geschwindigkeit auch to slacken off; Niveau to lower, to debase; (schlechtmachen) Leistungen, Fähigkeiten, jdn to belittle, to disparage; zu stark ~gesetzten Preisen at greatly reduced prices; H~setzung f siehe vt reduction; lowering; slackening off; debasement, lowering; belittling, disparagement; (Kränkung) slight, snub; ~sinken vi sep irreg aux sein to sink (down); (liter: Nacht) to fall, to descend (liter); (Wasserstand) to drop, to fall; (fig: Mensch) to sink; bist du schon so weit ~gesunken? have you sunk so low?; ~steigen vi sep irreg aux sein to get down, to descend; (von Pferd) to dismount; (von Berg) to climb down, to descend; ~stoßen vi sep irreg aux sein to swoop (down); ~stürzen sep 1 vt to push off (von etw sth); 2 vi aux sein to fall off (von etw sth); (Felsbrocken) to fall down (von from); (geh: Wasserfall) to cascade or plunge down, to come rushing down; er stürzte vom Baugerüst ~ he fell off or from the scaffolding; 2 vr to jump off (von etw sth); er stürzte sich vom Turm ~ he threw himself or jumped off or from the tower; ~würdigen sep 1 vt to belittle, to disparage; 2 vr to degrade or lower oneself; H~würdigung f belittling, disparagement; ~ziehen vt sep irreg (lit) to pull down; (fig) jdn to drag down.
Heraldik f, no pl heraldry.
heraldisch adj heraldic.
heran adv rechts/links ~! over to the right/left; immer or nur ~! come on or along (then)!; bis an etw (acc) ~ close or near to sth, right by or beside sth; (mit Bewegungsverb) right up to sth.
heran-: ~arbeiten vr sep (sich nähern) to work one's way along; sich an jdn/etw ~arbeiten to work one's way (along or over) towards sb/sth; ~bilden vt sep to train (up); (in der Schule) to educate; ~bringen vt sep irreg (herbringen) to bring over; sein

Spurt brachte ihn näher an den führenden Läufer ~ his spurt brought him up towards or nearer to the leader; die Schüler bedächtig an diese schwierigen Probleme ~bringen to introduce the pupils slowly to these difficult problems; ~eilen vi sep aux sein to hurry or rush over; ~fahren vti sep irreg aux sein to drive or (mit Fahrrad) ride up (an +acc to); ~führen sep 1 vt jdn to lead up; Truppen to bring up; jdn an etw (acc) ~führen (lit) to lead/bring sb up to sth; (fig, Frage, Problem) to lead or bring sb to sth; (Lehrer etc) to introduce sb to sth; 2 vi an etw (acc) ~führen (lit, fig) to lead to sth; ~gehen vi sep irreg aux sein to go up (an +acc to); ich würde nicht näher ~gehen I wouldn't go any nearer or closer; an jdn/etw ~gehen (lit) to go up to sb/sth; (fig: angreifen) an Problem, Aufgabe to tackle or approach sth; an Gegner to set about sb; ~kommen vi sep irreg aux sein (a) (räumlich) to come or draw near (an +acc to), to approach (an etw (acc) sth); (zeitlich) to draw near (an +acc to), to approach (an etw (acc) sth); ich sah ihn langsam auf seinem Fahrrad ~kommen I saw him coming slowly along on his bicycle; das lasse ich mal an mich ~kommen (fig inf) I'll cross that bridge when I come to it (prov); die Verfolger kamen dicht an den führenden Läufer ~ those behind were almost catching up with the leader; die Verfolger kamen immer näher ~ our pursuers were gaining on us; unmittelbar an jdn ~kommen to come or get right near (close) to sb; auf 1:3 ~kommen to pull up or back to 1-3; er läßt alle Probleme an sich ~kommen he always adopts a wait-and-see attitude; (b) (erreichen, bekommen) an den Chef/Motor kommt man nicht ~ you can't get hold of the boss/get at or to the engine; wie komme ich nur an das Kapital ~? how do I get hold of or (wenn festgelegt) get at the capital? (c) (sich messen können mit) an jdn ~kommen to be up to the standard of sb; an etw (acc) ~kommen to be up to (the standard of) sth; an diesen Wissenschaftler kommt keiner ~ there's no-one who is a patch on this scientist; er kommt nicht an seinen Vater ~ he's not a patch on his father; (d) an etw (acc) ~kommen (grenzen an) to verge on sth; ~machen vr sep (inf) sich an etw (acc) ~machen to get down to sth, to get going on sth (inf); sich an jdn ~machen to approach sb, to have a go at sb (inf); an Mädchen to make up to sb, to chat sb up (inf); ~nahen vi sep aux sein (geh) to approach; (Katastrophe, Unwetter auch) to be imminent; ~reichen vi sep an jdn/etw ~reichen (lit) (Mensch) to reach sb/sth; (Weg, Gelände etc) to reach (up to) sth; (fig: sich messen können mit) to come up to (the standard of) sb/sth, to come near sb/sth; er reicht nicht an mich ~ (fig) he doesn't come up to my standard or come near me, he can't touch me (inf); ~reifen vi sep aux sein (geh) (Obst) to ripen; (fig) (Jugendliche) to mature; (Plan, Entschluß, Idee) to mature, to ripen; zur Frau/zum Mann/zum Erwachsenen ~reifen to mature into a woman/man/adult; ~rücken sep 1 vi aux sein (sich nähern) to approach (an etw (acc) sth); (Truppen auch) to advance (an +acc upon, towards); (dicht aufrücken) to come/go nearer or closer (an +acc to); er rückte mit seinem Stuhl ~ he brought or drew his chair up or nearer; 2 vt to pull/push over or up (an +acc to); rück deinen Stuhl ~ bring or draw up your chair; ~schaffen vt sep to bring (along); ~schleichen vi sep irreg (vi: aux sein) to creep up (an etw (acc) to sth, an jdn an sb); ~sprengen vi sep aux sein (liter) to gallop up; ~tasten vr sep (lit) to feel or grope one's way over (an +acc to); sich ~tasten to feel one's way; sich an eine Frage ~tasten to approach a matter cautiously; ~tragen vt sep irreg to bring (over), to carry over; etw an jdn ~tragen (fig) to take/bring sth to sb, to go to sb with sth; ~treten vi sep irreg aux sein (lit) to come/go up (an +acc to); näher ~treten to come/go nearer; bitte treten Sie näher ~! this way!, come along!; an jdn ~treten (fig) (konfrontieren: Probleme, Zweifel, Versuchung) to confront or face sb; mit etw an jdn ~treten (sich wenden an) to go to or approach sb with sth; ~wachsen vi sep irreg aux sein (geh) to grow; (Kind) to grow up; (fig: Probleme, Konkurrenz) to grow up (jdm around sb); zu einer schönen jungen Frau ~wachsen to grow (up) into or to be a lovely young woman; die ~wachsende Generation the rising generation, the up and coming generation; H~wachsende pl (Jur) adolescents pl; ~wagen vr sep to venture near, to dare to come/go near; sich an etw (acc) ~wagen (lit) to venture near sth, to dare to come/go near sth; (fig) to venture to tackle sth; er wagte sich nicht an sie ~ he did not dare to approach her; ~winken vt sep to beckon or wave over; Taxi to hail; einen Polizisten ~winken to call a policeman over; ~ziehen sep irreg 1 vt (a) (näher bringen) to pull over, to draw near (an +acc to); (b) (zu Hilfe holen) to call in; Literatur to consult; jdn zur Hilfe/Unterstützung ~ziehen to enlist sb's aid or help/support; (c) (einsetzen) Arbeitskräfte, Kapital to bring in; jdn zu einer Aufgabe ~ziehen to enlist sb to do a task; (d) (geltend machen) Recht, Paragraphen, Quelle, Zitat to call or bring into play; etw zum Vergleich ~ziehen to use sth by way of comparison; (e) (aufziehen) Tier, Kind to raise; Pflanze auch to cultivate; jdn zu etw ~ziehen to bring sb up to be sth; sich (dat) Revolutionäre/Jasager ~ziehen (pej) to make revolutionaries/yes-men for oneself; 2 vi aux sein to approach; (Mil) to advance.
herauf 1 adv up. vom Tal ~ up from the valley; von unten ~ up from below; vom Süden ~ (inf) up from the south. **2** prep +acc up. den Fluß/Berg/die Treppe ~ up the river/mountain/stairs.
herauf-: pref up; ~arbeiten vr sep (lit, fig) to work one's way up; ~bemühen* sep 1 vt to trouble to come up, to ask (to come) up; 2 vr to take the trouble to come up; ~beschwören* vt sep irreg (a) (wachrufen) Erinnerung, Vergangenheit to evoke; (b) (herbeiführen) Unglück, Streit, Krise to cause, to give rise to; ~bitten vt sep irreg to ask (to come) up; ~bringen vt sep irreg to bring up; ~dämmern vi sep aux sein (liter) to dawn; ~dringen vi sep irreg aux sein to rise (up) from below; (Geruch) to waft

up; **ein Geräusch drang zu ihm** ~ a noise from below reached him *or* his ears; **~dürfen** *vi sep irreg* (*inf*) to be allowed up; **~führen** *sep* 1 *vt Pferd etc* to lead up; *jdn* to show up; 2 *vi* (*Weg etc*) to lead up; **~kommen** *vi sep irreg aux* **sein** to come up; (*in oberes Stockwerk*) to come up(stairs); (*auf Boot, Kutsche*) to climb *or* come *or* get aboard; (*Mond, Geräusch, Nebel, Wolke auch*) to rise; (*Gewitter*) to approach; **~lassen** *vt sep irreg* to allow (to come) up; **er wollte mich nicht in den 2. Stock/auf die Leiter ~lassen** he wouldn't let me come up to the 2nd floor/ come up the ladder; **~reichen** *sep* 1 *vt* to hand *or* pass up; 2 *vi* to reach; **der Baum reicht bis zum Fenster** ~ the tree reaches (up to) *or* comes up to the window; **~setzen** *sep* 1 *vt Preise etc* to increase, to raise; 2 *vr* **komm setz dich zu mir** ~ come up here and sit with me, come and sit up here with me; **~steigen** *vi sep irreg aux* **sein** (a) to climb up; (*Dampf, Rauch*) to rise; (*Erinnerungen*) to well up (*in jdm in sb*); (b) (*liter: anbrechen*) (*Tag, neue Zeit*) to dawn; (*Dämmerung*) to break; **~ziehen** *sep irreg* 1 *vt* to pull up; **er zog ihn zu sich** ~ (*lit*) he pulled him up to him; (*fig*) he raised him to his own level; 2 *vi aux* **sein** (a) (*Gewitter, Unheil etc*) to approach; (*liter: Nacht, Tag, Zeitalter auch*) to draw nigh (*liter*) *or* near; (b) (*nach oben umziehen*) to move up.

heraus *adv siehe auch* **herauskommen, herausein** *etc* out. ~ **da!** (*inf*) get *or* come out of there!; **da** ~? out of there?; ~ **aus den Federn!** (*inf*) rise and shine! (*inf*); ~ **mit ihm** (*inf*) get him out!; ~ **damit!** (*inf*) (*gib her*) hand it over!; ~ **mit der Sprache** *or* **damit!** (*inf*) out with it! (*inf*); **zum Fenster** ~ out of the window; **nach vorn** ~ **wohnen** to live facing *or* at the front; **von innen** ~ to the core, through and through; **das rostet von innen** ~ **durch** it's rusting through from the inside; **mir ist von innen** ~ **kalt** I'm cold inside; **etw von innen** ~ **heilen** to cure sth from inside; **aus einem Gefühl der Verlassenheit/dem Wunsch** ~ out of a feeling of forlornness/the desire; *siehe* **freiheraus**.

heraus- *pref* out; **~arbeiten** *sep* 1 *vt* (*aus Stein, Holz*) to carve (*aus* of); (*fig*) to bring out; 2 *vr* to work one's way out (*aus* of); **~bekommen** *vt sep irreg* (a) *Fleck, Nagel etc* to get out (*aus* of); (b) (*ermitteln, ~finden*) *Täter, Ursache, Geheimnis* to find out (*aus jdm* from sb); *Lösung, Aufgabe* to work *or* figure out; (c) *Wechselgeld* to get back; **Sie bekommen noch 1 Mark** ~ you still have 1 mark change to come; **~bilden** *vr sep* to form, to develop (*aus* out of); **~boxen** *vt sep* (*inf*) (a) *Ball* to punch out; (*inf*) *jdn* to bail out (*inf*); **~bringen** *vt sep irreg* (a) (*lit*) to bring out (*aus* of); (b) (*inf: entfernen, ermitteln*) *siehe* **~bekommen** (a, b); (c) (*auf den Markt bringen*) to bring out; **neues Modell** *auch* to launch; **jdn/etw ganz groß ~bringen** to launch sb/sth in a big way, to give sb/sth a big build-up; **die Affäre wurde in allen Zeitungen groß ~gebracht** the affair made a big splash *or* they made a big splash of the affair in the papers; (d) (*hervorbringen*) *Worte* to utter, to say; **er brachte kein Wort/keinen Ton** ~ he couldn't utter a word/sound; **aus ihm war kein Wort ~zubringen** they couldn't get a (single) word out of him; **~drehen** *sep* 1 *vt Birne, Schraube* to unscrew (*aus* from); 2 *vr* (*inf*) to get oneself out of it (*inf*), to wriggle out of it (*inf*); **~dringen** *vi sep irreg aux* **sein** to come out (*aus* of); (*Wasser, Information auch*) to leak out (*aus* from); **aus dem Lokal drangen laute Geräusche** ~ loud noises came *or* issued from the bar; **~drücken** *vt sep* to squeeze out (*aus* of); **die Brust ~drücken** to stick one's chest out; **~fahren** *sep irreg* 1 *vi aux* **sein** (a) (*aus* of) to come out; (*Auto, Fahrer auch*) to drive out; (*Zug auch*) to pull *or* draw out; (*Radfahrer auch*) to ride out; **aufs Land/zu Besuch ~gefahren kommen** to drive *or* come out to the country/for a visit; (b) (*schnell herauskommen*) to leap out; (*entweichen*) to come out; (*Wort etc*) to slip out, to come out; **das Wort ist mir nur so ~gefahren** that word just came *or* slipped out somehow; 2 *vt* (a) (*aus* of) *Zug, Auto* to drive out; *Fahrrad* to ride out; (b) (*Sport*) **eine gute** *or* **schnelle Zeit/den Vorsprung ~fahren** to make good time/the lead; **einen Sieg ~fahren** to drive/ride to victory; **verlorene Minuten ~fahren** to make up for lost time; **~filtern** *vt sep* (*aus* of) to filter out; (*fig auch*) to sift out; **~finden** *sep irreg* 1 *vt Fehler, Fakten, Täter etc* to find out; (~**lesen**) *Gesuchtes* to pick out (*aus* from among, from), to find (*aus* (from) among); **er hat ~gefunden, daß** ... he has found out *or* discovered that ...; (*erkannt*) he has found *or* discovered that ...; 2 *vir* to find one's way out (*aus* of); **~fischen** *vt sep* (*inf*) to fish out (*inf*) (*aus* of); **sich** (*dat*) **etw ~fischen** to pick sth out (for oneself); **sich immer das Beste aus allem ~fischen** always to take the best of everything; **~fliegen** *sep irreg* 1 *vi aux* **sein** (*aus* of) (*lit*) to fly out; (*inf:* ~**fallen**) ~ to come flying out; 2 *vt* to fly out (*aus* of).

Herausforderer *m* -s, - challenger.

herausfordern *sep* 1 *vt* (*zu etw Sport*) to challenge (*zu* to); (*provozieren*) to provoke (*zu etw* to do sth); *Kritik, Protest* to invite; (*herausbeschwören*) *Gefahr* to court; *Unglück* to court, to invite. **das Schicksal** ~ to tempt fate *or* providence. 2 *vi* **zu etw** ~ (*provozieren*) to invite sth.

herausfordernd *adj* provocative; (*lockend auch*) inviting; *Blick auch* come-hither *attr*; (*Auseinandersetzung suchend*) *Reden, Haltung, Blick* challenging.

Herausforderung *f* challenge; (*Provokation*) provocation.

heraus-: ~**fühlen** *vt sep* (*fig*) to sense (*aus* from); ~**führen** *vti sep* (*lit, fig*) to lead out (*aus* of).

Herausgabe *f* (a) (*Rückgabe*) return, handing back; (*von Personen*) handing over, surrender, delivery. **Klage auf** ~ action for restitution *or* return (*für* of). (b) (*von Buch etc*) publication.

herausgeben *sep irreg* 1 *vt* (a) (*zurückgeben*) to return, to hand *or* give back; *Gefangene etc* to hand over, to surrender, to deliver.

(b) (*veröffentlichen, erlassen*) to issue; *Buch, Zeitung* to publish; (*bearbeiten*) to edit.

(c) (*Wechselgeld geben*) *Betrag* to give in *or* as change. **wieviel hat er dir herausgegeben?** how much change *or* what

change did he give you (back)?; 2 **DM/zu wenig** ~ to give 2 marks change/too little change.

(d) (*herausreichen*) to hand *or* pass out (*aus* of).

2 *vi* (*Wechselgeld geben*) to give change (*auf* + *acc* for). **er hat vergessen, mir herauszugeben** he's forgotten to give me my change; **können Sie (mir)** ~? can you give me change?, have you got the *or* enough change?; **falsch** ~ to give the wrong change.

Herausgeber(in *f*) *m* (*Verleger*) publisher; (*Redakteur*) editor.

heraus-: ~**gehen** *vi sep irreg aux* **sein** (*aus* of) to go out; (*Fleck, Korken etc*) to come out; **aus sich** ~**gehen** (*fig*) to come out of one's shell (*fig*); ~**greifen** *vt sep irreg* to pick *or* single out (*aus* of); *Beispiel* to take; **sich** (*dat*) **einzelne Demonstranten ~greifen** to pick on *or* single out individual demonstrators; ~**haben** *vt sep irreg* (*inf*) (a) (*entfernt haben*) to have got out (*aus* of); **ich will ihn aus der Firma ~haben** I want him out of the firm; (b) (*begriffen haben*) to have got (*inf*); (*gelöst haben*) *Problem, Rätsel, Aufgabe* to have solved; *Geheimnis* to have found out; **ich habe es jetzt** ~, **wie man das am besten macht** I've got it – I know the best way to do it now; **jetzt hat er die Handhabung der Maschine** ~ he's got the knack *or* hang of the machine now (*inf*); *siehe* **Dreh** etc; (c) (*zurückbekommen haben*) to have got back; **er will sein Geld wieder ~haben** he wants his money back; ~**halten** *sep irreg* 1 *vt* (a) (*lit*) *Hand, Gegenstand* to put *or* stick out (*aus* of); (b) (*fernhalten*) *Tiere, Eindringlinge* to keep out (*aus* of); (c) (*fig: nicht verwickeln*) to keep out (*aus* of); 2 *vr* to keep out of it; **sich aus etw ~halten** to keep out of sth; **halt du dich mal** ~! you keep *or* stay out of it this; ~**hängen** *sep* 1 *vt* to hang out (*aus* of); **den Intellektuellen ~hängen** (*inf*) to show off about being an intellectual (*inf*); 2 *vi irreg* to hang out (*aus* of); ~**hauen** *vt sep irreg* (a) *Bäume* to cut *or* chop down, to remove; (*aus Stein*) *Stufe, Figur, Relief* to carve, to cut (*aus* out of); (b) (*inf: erlangen*) *bessere Löhne, Bedingungen, Vorteile* to get; ~**heben** *sep irreg* 1 *vt* to lift out (*aus* of); (*fig: betonen*) to bring out; 2 *vr* to stand out; **er hebt sich durch seine Begabung** ~ he stands out on account of his talent; ~**helfen** *vi sep irreg jdm* ~**helfen** (*lit, fig*) to help sb out (*aus* of); **jdm aus dem Zug ~helfen** to help sb off the train; ~**holen** *vt sep* (a) (*lit*) (*aus* of) to get out; (~**bringen**) to bring *or* fetch out; (b) (*fig*) *Antwort, Geheimnis* to get out (*aus* of), to extract (*form*) (*aus* from); *Vorteil* to gain (*aus* from); *Zeit* to make up; *Ergebnis* to get, to achieve; *Sieg* to win, to gain; **er hat bei diesem Geschäft ganz schön viel (Geld)** ~**geholt** he has made *or* got a lot of money out of this deal; ~**hören** *vt sep* (*wahrnehmen*) to hear; (*fühlen*) to detect, to sense (*aus* in); ~**kehren** *vt sep* (*lit*) to sweep out (*aus* of); (*fig: betonen*) *Bildung, Überlegenheit* to parade; *Strenge* ~**kehren** to show one's sterner *or* stricter side; **den reichen Mann/Vorgesetzten** ~**kehren** to parade the fact that one is rich/the boss; ~**klingen** *vi sep irreg* to ring out (*aus* from); (*zum Ausdruck kommen*) to ring through (*aus etw* sth).

herauskommen *vi sep irreg aux* **sein** (a) to come out (*aus* of). **ich bin schon seit Tagen aus den Kleidern/dem Haus nicht herausgekommen** I haven't had these clothes off/I haven't been out of the house in days; **er ist nie aus seinem Land/Dorf herausgekommen** he has never been out of *or* has never left his country/village; **sie kommt zu wenig heraus** (*inf*) she doesn't go *or* get out enough; **aus sich** ~ to come out of one's shell; **er kam aus dem Staunen/der Verwunderung nicht heraus** he couldn't get over his astonishment/amazement; **er kam aus dem Lachen nicht heraus** he couldn't stop laughing; **wie kommen wir bloß hier heraus?** how do *or* shall we get out of here?

(b) (*inf: aus bestimmter Lage*) to get out (*aus* of). **aus seinen Schwierigkeiten/Sorgen** ~ to get over one's difficulties/worries; **aus den Schulden** ~ to get out of debt; **mit einem Gewinn** ~ to get *or* win a prize.

(c) (*auf den Markt kommen*) to come out; (*neues Modell auch*) to be launched. **mit einem neuen Modell** ~ to bring out a new model, to come out with a new model.

(d) (*bekanntgegeben werden*) to come out; (*Börsenkurse auch*) to be published; (*Gesetz*) to come into force; (*bekanntwerden: Schwindel, Betrug etc auch*) to come to light. **es wird bald** ~, **daß du das Auto gestohlen hast** they'll soon find out *or* it will soon come out that you stole the car.

(e) (*sichtbar werden*) to come out; (*Fleck*) to appear; (*zur Geltung kommen, hörbar werden*) to come over. **ganz groß** ~ (*inf*) to make a big splash (*inf*), to have a big impact.

(f) (*geäußert werden*) to come out. **mit etw** ~ to come out with sth; **mit der Sprache** ~ to come out with it (*inf*).

(g) (*Resultat haben*) **bei etw** ~ to come of sth, to emerge from sth; **und was soll dabei** ~? and what is that supposed to achieve?, and where is that supposed to get us?; **bei dieser Rechenaufgabe kommt 10 heraus** this sum comes to 10, the answer to this sum is 10; **es kommt nichts dabei heraus, da kommt nichts bei heraus** (*N Ger*) it doesn't lead anywhere *or* get us anywhere *or* achieve anything; **dabei wird nichts Gutes** ~ no good will come of it; **es kommt auf eins** *or* **auf dasselbe** *or* **aufs gleiche heraus** it comes (down) to *or* boils down to the same thing.

(h) (*Sw: ausgehen*) to turn out.

(i) (*inf: aus der Übung kommen*) to get out of practice.

(j) (*Cards*) to lead. **wer kommt heraus?** whose lead is it?, who leads?

heraus-: ~**kriegen** *vt sep* (*inf*) *siehe* ~**bekommen, rauskriegen;** ~**kristallisieren*** *sep* 1 *vt* (*Chem*) to crystallize (*aus* out of); (*fig*) *Fakten, Essenz, Punkte* to extract (*aus* from); 2 *vr* (*Chem*) to crystallize (out); (*fig*) to crystallize, to take shape; ~**lassen** *vt sep irreg* (a) (*lit, fig*) *Hemd, Neuigkeit* to let out (*aus* of); (b) (*inf: weglassen*) to leave out (*aus* of); ~**laufen** *sep irreg* 1 *vi aux* **sein**

to run out (*aus of*); **2** *vt* (*Sport*) *Vorsprung, Zeit, Sekunden* to gain; *Sieg, zweiten Platz auch* to win; **~lesen** *vt sep irreg* (**a**) (*erkennen*) to gather (*aus from*); **aus seinem Brief/seiner Miene las ich Kummer** ~ from his letter/expression I could tell or I gathered that he was worried; **was die Kritiker aus seinem Roman alles ~lesen wollen** the things the critics try to read into his novel; (**b**) (*aussondern*) to pick out (*aus from*); **~locken** *vt sep* (*aus of*) to entice out; *Gegner, Tier auch* to lure out; **etw aus jdm ~locken** (*ablisten*) to get or worm (*inf*) sth out of sb; **jdn aus seiner Reserve ~locken** to draw sb out of his shell; **~lügen** *vr sep irreg* to lie one's way out of it; **sich aus etw ~lügen** to lie one's way out of sth; **~machen** *sep* (*inf*) **1** *vt* (*aus of*) to take out; *Fleck* to get out; **2** *vr* (*sich gut entwickeln*) to come on (well); (*finanziell*) to do well; (*nach Krankheit*) to pick up; **sie hat sich prächtig ~gemacht** she has really blossomed or bloomed; **~müssen** *vi sep irreg* (**a**) (*entfernt werden müssen*) to have to come out; (**b**) (*aufstehen müssen*) to have to get up; (**c**) (*gesagt werden müssen*) to have to come out; **~nehmbar** *adj* removable; **~nehmen** *vt sep irreg* (**a**) to take out (*aus of*); (*inf*) *Zahn auch* to pull out; *Kind* (*aus der Schule etc*) to take away, to remove (*aus from*); **sich** (*dat*) **die Mandeln ~nehmen lassen** to have one's tonsils out; **den Gang ~nehmen** (*Aut*) to put the car into neutral; (**b**) (*inf: sich erlauben*) **es sich** (*dat*) **~nehmen, etw zu tun** to have the nerve to do sth (*inf*); **sich** (*dat*) **Freiheiten ~nehmen** to take liberties; **Sie nehmen sich zuviel** ~ you're going too far; **~pauken** *vt sep* (*inf*) **jdn** (**aus etw**) **~pauken** to get sb off the hook (*inf*), to bail sb out (of sth) (*inf*); **~picken** *vt sep* (*aus of*) (*Vögel*) to peck out; (*fig*) *das Beste* to pick out; **~platzen** *vi sep aux sein* (*inf*) (*spontan sagen*) to blurt it out; (*lachen*) to burst out laughing; **mit etw ~platzen** to blurt sth out; **~pressen** *vt sep* (*aus of*) to squeeze out; *Saft etc auch* to press out; *Geld, Geständnis auch* to wring out; **~putzen** *vt sep* **jdn** to dress up; (*schmücken*) *Stadt, Weihnachtsbaum, Wohnung etc* to deck out; **sich prächtig ~putzen** to get dressed up, to do oneself up (*inf*); *Zahn, Baum* to pull out; (**b**) **jdn aus etw ~reißen** (*aus Umgebung*) to tear sb away from sth; (*aus Arbeit, Spiel, Unterhaltung*) to drag sb away from sth; (*aus Schlaf, Träumerei*) to startle sb out of sth; (*aus Lethargie, Sorgen*) to shake sb out of sth; **jdn aus seinem Kummer ~reißen** to take sb out of himself; (**c**) (*inf: aus Schwierigkeiten*) **jdn ~reißen** to get sb out of it (*inf*); (**d**) (*inf: wiedergutmachen*) to save; **~rücken** *sep* **1** *vt* to push out (*aus of*); (*inf: hergeben*) *Geld* to cough up (*inf*); *Beute, Gegenstand* to hand over; **2** *vi aux sein* (**a**) (*lit*) to move out; (**b**) (*inf: hergeben*) **mit etw ~rücken** (*mit Geld*) to cough sth up (*inf*); (*mit Beute*) to hand sth over; (**c**) (*inf: aussprechen*) **mit etw ~rücken** to come out with sth; **rück schon mit deinem Problem ~!** come on (now), out with it, out with it now, what's the problem?; **mit der Sprache ~rücken** to come out with it; **~rufen** *sep irreg* **1** *vt* to call or shout out (*aus of*); **das Publikum rief den Schauspieler noch dreimal** ~ the audience called the actor back another three times; **2** *vi* to call or shout out (*aus of*); **~rutschen** *vi sep aux sein* (*lit*) to slip out (*aus of*); (*fig inf: Bemerkung*) to slip out; **das ist mir nur so ~gerutscht** it just slipped out somehow, I just let it slip (*out*) somehow; **~saugen** *vt sep* to suck out (*aus of*); **~schälen 1** *vt sep das Eßbare etc* (*aus of*) to get out, to dig out (*inf*); (*ausschneiden*) *schlechte Stelle auch* to scrape out; (*fig: absondern*) *Fakten, Elemente* to single out; **ein Kind aus seinen Kleidern ~schälen** to peel a child's clothes off; **sich aus seinen Sachen ~schälen** (*inf*) to peel off one's clothes; **2** *vr* (*fig: deutlich werden*) to become evident or apparent; **~schauen** *vi sep* (*dial*) (*Mensch*) to look out (*aus, zu of*); (**b**) (*zu sehen sein*) to show; (**c**) (*inf*) **dabei schauen Vorteile/schaut ein fetter Gewinn für ihn** ~ there's something/a handsome profit in it for him; **dabei schaut nichts** ~ there's nothing to be got out of it or to be gained by it; **was schaut bei dem Geschäft or dabei (für mich)** ~? what's in it for me? (*inf*), what do I get out of it?; **~schießen** *sep irreg* **1** *vi* (**a**) (*lit*) **aus einem Auto/Gebäude ~schießen** to shoot from a car/building; (**b**) *aux sein* (*auch* **~geschossen kommen**) (*aus of*) to shoot out; **2** *vt* to shoot out; **~schlagen** *sep irreg* **1** *vt* (**a**) (*lit*) to knock out (*aus of*); **aus einem Stein Funken ~schlagen** to strike sparks from or off a stone; (**b**) (*inf: erreichen*) *Geld* to make; *Erlaubnis, Verzögerung, Gewinn, Vorteil* to get; *Zeit* to gain; **seine Kosten ~schlagen** to cover one's costs; **2** *vi aux sein* (*Flammen*) to leap or shoot out; **die Flammen schlugen zum Dach** ~ the flames were leaping through the roof; **~schleudern** *vt sep* (*werfen*) to hurl out (*aus of*); (*fig*) *Fragen, Vorwürfe, wütende Worte* to burst out with; **~schlüpfen** *vi sep aux sein* (*lit, fig*) to slip out (*aus of*); **~schmecken** *sep* **1** *vt* to taste; **2** *vi* to be prominent (*over the other flavours*); **~schmeißen** *vt sep irreg* (*inf: lit, fig*) to throw or chuck (*inf*) or sling (*inf*) out (*aus of*); **~schneiden** *vt sep irreg* to cut out (*aus of*); **~schreiben** *vt sep irreg* *Stellen, Zitat etc* to copy out (*aus of*); **~schreien** *vt sep irreg* *Haß, Gefühle* to shout out.

heraussein *vi sep irreg aux sein* (*Zusammenschreibung nur bei infin und ptp*) (*inf*) (**a**) (*entfernt sein*) to be out; (*Blinddarm etc auch*) to have been taken out.
(**b**) (*hervorgekommen sein: Sterne, Blumen etc*) to be out.
(**c**) (*herausgekommen sein*) (*Buch, Programm etc*) to be out; (*Gesetz*) to be in force.
(**d**) (*bekannt sein*) to be known; (*entschieden sein*) to have been or to be settled or decided.
(**e**) (*hinter sich haben*) (*aus of*) to be out, to have got out. **aus der Schule** ~ to have left school; **aus dem Gröbsten or Ärgsten or Schlimmsten** ~ to have got past the worst (part); (*bei Krise, Krankheit*) to be over the worst; **wenn ich nur erst aus**

dieser Stadt heraus wäre if only I were out of this town; *siehe* **fein**.
(**f**) (*gesagt worden sein*) (*Wahrheit*) to be out; (*Worte*) to have come out.
heraußen *adv* (*S Ger, Aus*) out here.
heraus-: **~springen** *vi sep irreg aux sein* (*aus of*) (**a**) (*lit*) to jump or leap out; (**b**) (*sich lösen*) to come out; **aus dem Gleis ~springen** to jump the rails; (**c**) (*inf*) *siehe* **~schauen** (**c**); **~sprudeln** *sep* **1** *vi aux sein* to bubble out (*aus of*); **2** *vt Worte, Sätze* to come gushing out with; **~stehen** *vi sep irreg* (*S Ger: aux sein*) to stand or stick out, to protrude; **~stellen** *sep* **1** *vt* (**a**) (*lit*) to put outside; (*Sport*) to send off; (**b**) (*fig: hervorheben*) to emphasize, to underline; **jdn** to give prominence to; **2** *vr* (*Unschuld, Wahrheit*) to come to light; **sich als falsch/wahr/richtig/begründet ~stellen** to show itself to be or to prove (to be) wrong/true/correct/well-founded; **es stellte sich** ~, **daß** ... it turned out or emerged that ...; **es wird sich ~stellen, wer recht hat/was getan werden muß** we shall see who is right/what must be done; **das muß sich erst ~stellen** that remains to be seen; **~strecken** *vt sep* to stick out (*zu, aus of*); **~streichen** *vt sep irreg* (**a**) *Fehler etc* to cross out, to delete (*aus in*); (**b**) (*betonen*) *Verdienste etc* to stress, to lay great stress upon; **~strömen** *vi sep aux sein* (*aus of*) (*Flüssigkeit*) to stream or pour out; (*Gas*) to come out; (*Menschenmenge*) to pour out; **~stürzen** *vi sep aux sein* (**a**) (*auch* **~gestürzt kommen**) (*eilen*) to rush out (*aus of*); (**b**) (*fallen*) to fall out; **zum Fenster ~stürzen** to fall out of the window; **~suchen** *vt sep* to pick out; **~treten** *vi sep irreg aux sein* to step or come out (*aus of*), to emerge (*aus from*); (*Adern etc*) to stand out, to protrude; **~trommeln** *vt sep* (*inf*) to get out; **~wachsen** *vi sep irreg aux sein* to grow out (*aus of*); **~wagen** *vr sep* to dare to come out (*aus of*); to venture out (*aus of*) or forth (*liter*) (*aus from*); **~winden** *vr sep irreg* (*fig*) to wriggle out of it; **sich aus etw ~winden** to wriggle out of sth; **~wirtschaften** *vt sep* to make (*aus out of*); **~wollen** *vi sep* to want to get out (*aus of*); **nicht mit etw ~wollen** (*inf: sagen wollen*) not to want to come out with sth (*inf*); **er wollte nicht mit der Sprache** ~ (*inf*) he didn't want to come out with it (*inf*); **~ziehen** *sep irreg* **1** *vt* to pull out (*aus of*); (*~schleppen*) to drag out (*aus of*); (*Chem, Med*) to extract (*aus from*); *Truppen auch* to withdraw (*aus from*); **die Essenz aus einem Buch ~ziehen** to extract the main substance from a book; **muß ich dir die Antworten einzeln ~ziehen?** (*inf*) do I have to drag answers out of you bit by bit?; **2** *vr* to pull oneself out (*aus of*).
herb *adj* (**a**) *Geruch* sharp; *Geschmack auch, Parfüm* tangy; *Wein* dry. (**b**) *Enttäuschung, Verlust* bitter; *Erwachen* rude; *Erkenntnis, Wahrheit* cruel. (**c**) (*streng*) *Züge, Gesicht* severe, harsh; *Art, Wesen, Charakter, Mensch* dour; *Schönheit* severe, austere. (**d**) (*unfreundlich*) *Worte, Kritik* harsh.
Herbarium *nt* herbarium, herbary.
Herbe *f* -, *no pl* (*geh*) *siehe* **Herbheit**.
herbei *adv* (*geh*) come (here). (**alle Mann**) ~! come here (everybody)!
herbei-: **~bringen** *vt sep irreg jdn, Gegenstand* to bring over; *Indizien, Beweise* to provide; *Sachverständige* to bring in; **~eilen** *vi sep aux sein* to hurry or rush over; **~führen** *vt sep* (**a**) (*bewirken*) *Entscheidung, Konfrontation etc* to bring about; (*verursachen auch*) to cause; **den Tod etc ~führen** (*Med*) to cause death etc (*form*); (**b**) (*an einen Ort*) to bring; *Schaulustige* to draw; **~holen** *vt sep irreg* *Verstärkung* to bring in; *Arzt, Taxi, Polizisten* to fetch; **einen Arzt ~holen lassen** to send for a doctor; **~kommen** *vi sep irreg aux sein siehe* **herankommen**; **~lassen** *vr sep irreg* **sich zu etw ~lassen**, **sich ~lassen, etw zu tun** to condescend or deign to do sth; **~laufen** *vi sep irreg aux sein* to come running up; **~rufen** *vt sep irreg* *Taxi* to call over; *Verstärkung* to call in; *Arzt, Polizei, Taxi* to call; **~schaffen** *vt sep* to bring; *Geld* to get, to get hold of (*inf*); *Beweise* to produce; **~sehnen** *vt sep* to long for; **~strömen** *vi sep aux sein* to come flocking, to come in (their) crowds; **~winken** *vt sep irreg* to beckon over; **~ziehen** *sep irreg* **1** *vt siehe* **Haar**; **2** *vi aux sein siehe* **heranziehen 2**; **~zitieren*** *vt sep* (*inf*) to send for.
her-: **~bekommen*** *vt sep irreg* (*inf*) to get; **~bemühen*** *sep* (*geh*) **1** *vt jdn ~bemühen* to trouble sb to come here; **2** *vr* to take the trouble to come here; **~beordern*** *vt sep* to summon, to send for.
Herberge *f* -, **-n** (**a**) *no pl* (*Unterkunft*) lodging, accommodation *both no indef art*; (*fig*) refuge. (**b**) (*old, Gasthaus*) inn; (*Jugend~*) (youth) hostel.
Herbergs-: **~mutter** *f* (youth hostel) warden; **~vater** *m* (youth hostel) warden.
her-: **~bestellen*** *vt sep* to ask to come; **~beten** *vt sep* (*pej*) to rattle off.
Herbheit *f*, *no pl siehe adj* (**a**) sharpness; tanginess; dryness. (**b**) bitterness; rudeness; cruelness. (**c**) severity, harshness; dourness; severity, harshness, austerity. (**d**) harshness.
her-: **~bitten** *vt sep irreg* to ask to come; **~bringen** *vt sep irreg* to bring (here); **bring mir den Bleistift** ~ bring me the pencil (over); *siehe* **hergebracht**.
Herbst *m* -(**e**)**s**, **-e** autumn, fall (*US*). **im** ~ in autumn, in the fall (*US*); **der** ~ **des Lebens** (*liter*) the autumn of (one's) life (*liter*); **auch der** ~ **hat noch schöne Tage** (*Prov*) old age has its compensations.
Herbst- *in cpds* autumn, fall (*US*); **~anfang** *m* beginning of autumn; **~aster** *f* Michaelmas daisy.
herbsteln *vi impers* (*dial*) *siehe* **herbsten 1**.
herbsten 1 *vi impers* **es herbstet** (*liter*) autumn is nigh (*liter*). **2** *vt* (*dial*) *Wein* to harvest.
Herbstes- (*poet*) *in cpds siehe* **Herbst-**.
Herbst-: **~farben** *pl* autumn or autumnal colours *pl*; **~ferien** *pl*

autumn *or* fall (*US*) holiday(s); (*Sch*) half-term holiday(s) (*in the autumn term*); **h~lich** *adj* autumn *attr*; (*wie im Herbst auch*) autumnal; **das Wetter wird schon h~lich** autumn is in the air; **das Wetter ist schon h~lich** it's already autumn weather; **h~lich kühles Wetter** cool autumn weather; **das Wetter ist h~lich kühl** the cooler days of autumn *or* fall (*US*) are upon us; **~monat** *m* autumn month; **der ~monat** September; (*~mond* *m* (*obs*) September *no art*; **~-Tagundnachtgleiche** *f* autumnal equinox; **~zeitlose** *f* -n, -n meadow saffron.

Herd *m* -(e)s, -e (a) (*Küchen~*) cooker, stove; (*Kohle~*) range; (*fig: Heim*) home. **eigener ~ ist Goldes wert** (*Prov*) there's no place like home (*Prov*); **den ganzen Tag am ~ stehen** (*fig*) to slave over a hot stove all day.
(b) (*Med: Krankheits~*) focus; (*Geol: von Erdbeben*) epicentre; (*fig: von Rebellion etc*) seat.
(c) (*Tech*) hearth.

Herde *f* -, -n (*lit*) herd; (*von Schafen, fig geh: Gemeinde*) flock. **mit der ~ laufen, der ~ folgen** (*pej*) to follow the herd.

Herden-: **~instinkt** *m* (*lit, fig pej*) herd instinct; **~tier** *nt* gregarious animal; **~trieb** *m* (*lit, fig pej*) herd instinct; **h~weise** *adv* in herds; (*Schafe*) in flocks; (*fig auch*) in crowds.

Herdplatte *f* (*von Kohleherd*) (top) plate; (*von Elektroherd*) hotplate.

herein *adv* in. **~!** come in!, come! (*form*); **nur ~!** do come in!; **immer ~!** come along in!; **hier ~!** in here!; **von (dr)außen ~** from outside; **auf dem Wege von draußen ~** on the way in.

herein-: *pref* in; **~bekommen** *vt sep irreg* (*inf*) **Waren** to get in; **Radiosender** to get; **Unkosten etc** to recover; **~bemühen⁰** *sep* (*geh*) 1 *vt* to trouble to come in; 2 *vr* to take the trouble to come in; **~bitten** *vt sep irreg* to ask (to come) in; **~brechen** *vi sep irreg aux sein* (a) (*eindringen: Wasser, Flut, Wellen*) to gush in; **über jdn/etw ~brechen** (*lit, fig*) to descend upon sb/sth; (b) (*Gewitter*) to break; (*Krieg, Rest*) to break out; **das Unglück brach über ihn ~** misfortune overtook him; (c) (*liter: anbrechen*) (*Nacht, Abend*) to fall, to close in; (*Winter*) to set in; (d) (*lit: nach innen stürzen*) to fall in; **~bringen** *vt sep irreg* (a) to bring in; (b) (*inf: wettmachen*) **Geldverlust** to make good; **Zeit-, Produktionsverluste** to make up for; **Unkosten** to get back; (c) (*dial: unterbringen können*) to be able to get in (*in* *+acc* -to); **~drängen** *vir sep* to push one's way in; **~dringen** *vi sep irreg aux sein* (*Licht, Wasser*) to come in (*in* *+acc* -to); **ein Geräusch/Geruch drang or es drang ein Geräusch/Geruch ins Zimmer ~** a sound/smell reached the room; **~dürfen** *vi sep irreg* (*inf*) to be allowed in; **darf ich ~?** may *or* can I come in?; **~fahren** *vti sep irreg* (*vi: aux sein*) to drive in; (*mit Fahrrad*) to ride in; **~fallen** *vi sep irreg aux sein* (a) to fall in (*in* *+acc* -to); (b) (*inf*) to fall for it (*inf*); (*betrogen werden*) to be had (*inf*); **auf jdn/etw ~fallen** to be taken in by sb/sth, to be taken for a ride (by sb) (*inf*)/to fall for sth; **mit jdm/etw ~fallen** to have a bad deal with sb/sth; **~führen** *vt sep* to show in; **H~geschmeckte(r)** *mf decl as adj* (*S Ger*) newcomer (*in* *+dat* to); **er ist ein H~geschmeckter** he's not a local (man), he's not from these parts; **~holen** *vt sep* to bring in (*in* *+acc* -to); **~kommen** *vi sep irreg aux sein* to come in (*in* *+acc* -to); **wie ist er ~gekommen?** how did he get in?; **ins Haus ~kommen** to come in *or* inside; **~kriegen** *vt sep* (*inf*) *siehe* **~bekommen, reinkriegen**; **~lassen** *vt sep irreg* to let in (*in* *+acc* -to); **~legen** *vt sep* (a) to lay (down); **er legte das Kind zu mir ins Bett ~** he laid the child in bed beside me; (b) (*inf*) **jdn ~legen** (*betrügen*) to take sb for a ride (*inf*); (*anführen*) to take sb in; **~nehmen** *vt sep irreg* to bring in (*in* *+acc* -to); (*in Liste, Kollektion etc aufnehmen*) to put in, to include; (*Comm*) **Aufträge** to accept; **~nötigen** *vt sep* to urge to come in; **sie hat mich förmlich ~genötigt** she insisted that I come in; **~platzen** *vi sep aux sein* (*inf*) to burst *or* come bursting in (*in* *+acc* -to); **bei jdm ~platzen** to burst in on sb; **~regnen** *vi impers* **es regnet ~** the rain is coming in; **~reiten** *vi sep irreg* 1 *vti* (*vi: aux sein*) to ride in (*in* *+acc* -to); 2 *vr* (*inf*) to land oneself in it *or* in the soup (*inf*); **~rufen** *vt sep irreg* to call in; **~schauen** *vi sep* (*dial*) to look in (*in* *+acc* -to); (*bei jdm*) **~schauen** (*inf*) to look in on sb (*inf*), to look sb up (*inf*); **~schleichen** *vir sep irreg* (*vi: aux sein*) (*in* *+acc* to) to creep *or* slip in; (*heimlich*) to sneak in; **~schneien** *sep* 1 *vi impers* **es schneit ~** the snow's coming in; 2 *vi aux sein* (*inf*) to drop in (*inf*); **~sehen** *vi sep irreg* to see/look in (*in* *+acc* -to); **~spazieren⁰** *vi sep aux sein* to breeze in (*in* *+acc* -to); **~spaziert!** come right in!; **~stecken** *vt sep* (*in* *+acc* -to) to put in; **Kopf, Hand** *auch* to stick in; **~strömen** *vi sep aux sein* (*in* *+acc* -to) to stream *or* pour in; **~stürmen** *vi sep aux sein* to storm *or* come storming in (*in* *+acc* -to); **~stürzen** *vi sep aux sein* to rush in (*in* *+acc*-to); **~wagen** *vr sep* (*in* *+acc* -to) to dare to come in, to venture in; **~wollen** *vi sep* (*inf*) to want to come in.

Her-: **h~fahren** *sep irreg* 1 *vi aux sein* to come *or* get here; **hinter/vor jdm/etw h~fahren** to drive *or* (*mit Rad*) ride (along) behind/in front of *or* ahead of sb/sth; **der Detektiv fuhr hinter dem Auto h~** the detective followed *or* trailed the car; 2 *vt* to drive *or* bring here; **~fahrt** *f* journey here; **auf der ~fahrt** on the journey *or* way here; **h~fallen** *vi sep irreg aux sein* **über jdn h~fallen** to attack sb, to fall upon sb; (*mit Fragen*) to attack sb, to pitch into sb; (*kritisieren*) to pull sb to pieces; **über etw** (*acc*) **h~fallen** to descend upon sth; **über Geschenke, Eßbares etc** to pounce upon sth; **h~finden** *vi sep irreg* to find one's way here.

herfür *adv* (*obs*) *siehe* **hervor.**

herg. *abbr von* hergestellt manufactured, mfd.

Hergang *m* -(e)s, *no pl* (*von Schlacht*) course. **schildern Sie mir genau den ~ dieses Vorfalls** tell me exactly what happened; **der ~ des Unfalls** the way the accident happened, the details of the accident.

her-: **~geben** *sep irreg* 1 *vt* (*weggeben*) to give away; (*überreichen, aushändigen*) to hand over; (*zurückgeben*) to give back; **gib das ~!** give me that, let me have that; **viel/**

einiges/wenig ~geben (*inf: erbringen*) to be a lot of use/of some use/not to be much use; **das Buch gibt nicht viel ~** the book doesn't tell you/me (very) much; **das Thema gibt viel/nichts ~** there's a lot/nothing to this topic; **ein Essen, das was ~gibt** a fine spread; **was die Beine ~gaben** as fast as one's legs would carry one; **was die Lunge/Stimme ~gab** at the top of one's voice; **seinen Namen für etw ~geben** to lend one's name to sth; 2 *vr* **sich zu** *or* **für etw ~geben** to be (a) party to sth; **dazu gebe ich mich nicht ~** I won't have anything to do with it; **eine Schauspielerin, die sich für solche Filme ~gibt** an actress who allows herself to be involved in such films; **~gebracht** 1 *ptp of* **~bringen;** 2 *adj* (*traditionell*) **in ~gebrachter Weise** as is/was traditional; **~gehen** *sep irreg* (*aux sein*) 1 *vi* (a) **hinter/vor/neben jdm ~gehen** to walk (along) behind/in front of *or* ahead of/beside sb; (b) (*S Ger, Aus*) *siehe* **~kommen;** (c) **~gehen und etw tun** (*einfach tun*) just *or* simply to (go and) do sth; 2 *vi impers* (*inf*) (a) (*zugehen*) **so geht es ~** that's the way it goes *or* is; **es ging heiß ~** things got heated (*inf*), (the) sparks flew; **hier geht es hoch ~** there's plenty going on here; **es geht lustig ~** this is great fun; (b) **es geht über jdn/etw ~** (*wird kritisiert*) sb/sth is being got at (*inf*) *or* pulled to pieces; **es geht über etw** (*acc*) **~** (*wird verbraucht*) sth suffers (*hum*) *or* is depleted; **~gehören⁰** *vi sep* to belong here; (*fig auch*) to be relevant; **~gelaufen** 1 *ptp of* **~laufen;** 2 *adj attr* (*pej*) *siehe* **dahergelaufen;** **~haben** *vt sep irreg* (*inf*) **wo hat er das ~?** where did he get that from?; **~halten** 1 *vt* to hold out; 2 *vi* to suffer (for it), to pay for it; **für etw ~halten** to pay for sth; **er muß als Sündenbock ~halten** he is the scapegoat; **als Entschuldigung für etw ~halten** to serve *or* be used as an excuse for sth; **~holen** *vt sep* (*inf*) to fetch; **~holen lassen** to send for; **weit ~geholt sein** (*fig*) to be far-fetched; **~hören** *vi sep* (*inf*) to listen; **alle** *or* **alles mal ~hören!** listen (to me) *or* listen here (*inf*) *or* pay attention everybody, everybody listen to me).

Hering *m* -s, -e (a) herring. **ein gedörrter ~** a kipper; **wie die ~e zusammengedrängt** packed in like sardines (in a tin); **dünn wie ein ~** as thin as a rake.
(b) (*Zeltpflock*) (tent) peg.
(c) (*fig inf: schwächlicher Mensch*) shrimp (*inf*).

herinnen *adv* (*S Ger, Aus*) *siehe* **drinnen, innen.**

her-: **~jagen** *sep* 1 *vt* (*auf jdn zu*) to drive *or* chase over *or* across; **jdn vor sich** (*dat*) **~jagen** to drive sb along in front of one; 2 *vi aux sein* **hinter jdm ~jagen** to chase after sb; **hinter etw** (*dat*) **~jagen** to be after sth; **~kommen** *vi sep irreg aux sein* to come here; (*sich nähern*) to come, to approach; (*~stammen*) to come from; **komm ~!** come here!; **von jdm/etw ~kommen** (*stammen*) to come from sb/sth; **ich weiß nicht, wo das ~kommt** (*was der Grund ist*) I don't know why it is *or* what the reason is; **H~kommen** *nt* -s, *no pl* convention; **~kömmlich** *adj* conventional; **nach ~kömmlichem Brauch** according to convention; **~kriegen** *vt sep* (*inf*) to get; **ich kriege ihn einfach nicht ~** I simply can't get him to come (here).

Herkules *m* -, -se (*Myth, fig*) Hercules.

Herkules|arbeit *f* (*fig*) Herculean task.

herkulisch *adj* Herculean.

Herkunft *f* -, *no pl* origin; (*soziale*) background, origins *pl.* **er ist britischer** (*gen*) **~, er ist seiner ~ nach Brite** he is of British extraction *or* descent *or* origin; **er ist aristokratischer** (*gen*) **~** he comes from an aristocratic family, he is of aristocratic descent.

Herkunfts-: **~bezeichnung** *f* (*Comm*) designation of origin; **~land** *nt* (*Comm*) country of origin; **~ort** *m* place of origin.

her-: **~laufen** *vi sep irreg aux sein* to come running; **lauf doch mal ~ zu mir!** come over here to me; **hinter** (*lit, fig*)/**vor/neben jdm ~laufen** to run after/ahead of/beside sb; **~leiern** *vt sep* (*inf*) to spout (*inf*); **~leihen** *vt sep irreg* (*Aus, S Ger*) to lend (out); **~leiten** *sep* 1 *vt* (a) (*ableiten, folgern*) to derive (*aus* from); (b) (*an bestimmten Ort leiten*) to bring; 2 *vr* **sich von etw ~leiten** to come from sth, to be derived from sth; **~locken** *vt sep* to entice, to lure; **hinter sich** (*dat*) **~locken** to entice *or* lure along (behind one); **~machen** *sep* 1 *vr* **sich über etw** (*acc*) **~machen** (*in Angriff nehmen*) **Arbeit, Buch, Essen** to get stuck into sth (*inf*); (*Besitz ergreifen*) **Eigentum, Gegenstände** to pounce (up)on sth; **sich über jdn ~machen** to lay into sb (*inf*); 2 *vt* **~machen** to look impressive; **wenig ~machen** not to look very impressive; **nichts ~machen** not to be up to much (*inf*); **von jdm/etw viel ~machen** to crack sb/sth up to be quite fantastic (*inf*), to make a big thing of sb/sth (*inf*); **von jdm/etw wenig/nichts ~machen** not to make a big thing of sb/sth (*inf*); **viel von sich ~machen** to be full of oneself; **er macht wenig** *or* **nicht viel von sich ~** he's pretty modest.

Hermaphrodit *m* -en, -en hermaphrodite.

Hermelin¹ *nt* -s, -e (*Zool*) ermine.

Hermelin² *m* -s, -e (*Pelz*) ermine.

Hermeneutik *f, no pl* hermeneutics *sing.*

hermeneutisch *adj* hermeneutic(al).

hermetisch *adj* hermetic. **die Häftlinge sind ~ von der Außenwelt abgeschlossen** the prisoners are completely shut off from the outside world; **~ abgeriegelt** completely sealed off.

hermüssen *vi sep irreg* (*inf*) (a) **das muß her** I/we have to have it. (b) (*kommen müssen*) to have to come (here). **hinter jdm ~** to have to go after sb.

hernach *adv* (*dated, dial*) afterwards.

hernehmen *vt sep irreg* (a) (*beschaffen*) to get, to find. **wo soll ich das ~?** where am I supposed to get that from?
(b) (*dial inf*) **jdn ~** (*stark fordern, belasten*) to make sb sweat (*inf*); (*mitnehmen: Krankheit, Schock, Nachricht, Anstrengung*) to take it out of sb (*inf*).
(c) (*sich dat*) **jdn ~** (*dial: tadeln, verprügeln*) to give it to sb (*inf*), to let sb have it (*inf*).

   (d) *(dial: nehmen)* to take.
hernieder *adv (liter)* down.
heroben *adv (Aus, S Ger)* up here.
Heroe [he'ro:ə] *m* -n, -n *(geh) siehe* **Heros.**
Heroenkult(us) [he'ro:ən-] *m (geh)* hero-worship.
Heroin [hero'i:n] *nt* -s, *no pl* heroin.
Heroine [hero'i:nə] *f (dated Theat)* heroine.
heroisch [he'ro:ɪʃ] *adj (geh)* heroic.
heroisieren* [heroi'zi:rən] *vt jdn* to make a hero of; *Tat* to glorify.
Heroismus [hero'ɪsmʊs] *m, no pl (geh)* heroism.
Herold *m* -(e)s, -e *(Hist: Bote)* herald; *(fig: Vorbote auch)* harbinger.
Heros *m* -, **Heroen** hero.
herplappern *vt sep (inf)* to reel off. **was sie immer so herplappert** the things she's always talking about.
Herr *m* -(e)n, -en **(a)** *(Gebieter)* lord, master; *(Herrscher)* lord, ruler *(über + acc* of); *(von Hund)* master. **mein ~ und Gebieter** my lord and master; **der junge ~** *(form)* the young master; **die ~en der Schöpfung** *(hum: Männer)* the gentlemen; **sein eigener ~ sein** to be one's own master *or* boss; **~ im eigenen Haus sein** to be master in one's own house; **~ einer Sache** *(gen)* **sein/werden** *(in der Hand haben)* to have/get sth under control; **~ der Lage** *or* **Situation sein/bleiben** to be/remain master of the situation, to have/keep the situation under control; **nicht mehr ~ seiner Sinne sein** not to be in control of oneself any more; **~ über Leben und Tod sein** to have the power of life and death *(gen* over); **über jdn/etw ~ werden** to master sb/sth; **man kann nicht** *or* **niemand kann zwei ~en dienen** *(prov)* no man can serve two masters *(prov)*; **wie der ~, so's Gescherr!** *(prov)* like master, like man! *(prov)*; *siehe* **Land.**
   (b) *(Gott, Christus)* Lord. **Gott, der ~** the Lord God; **der ~ Jesus** the Lord Jesus; **der ~ der Heerscharen** the Lord of Hosts; **~, du meine Güte!** good(ness) gracious (me)!; **~ des Himmels!** good Lord!; **er ist ein großer Schwindler/Esser/Sportler** *etc* **vor dem ~n** *(hum inf)* what a great fibber/eater/sportsman *etc* he is.
   (c) *(feiner ~, Mann)* gentleman. **ein geistlicher/adliger ~** *or* **~ von Adel** a clergyman/nobleman; **„~en"** *(Toilette)* "gentlemen", "gents", "men"; **den (großen) ~n spielen** *or* **markieren** *(inf)* to give oneself airs; *siehe* **alt.**
   (d) *(vor Eigennamen)* Mr; *(vor Titeln) usu not translated; (in Anrede ohne Namen)* sir. **(mein) ~! sir!; bitte, der ~** *(beim Servieren)* there you are, sir; **der ~ wünscht?** what can I do for you, sir?; **Ihr ~ Vater** *(form)* your father; **~ Nachbar** *(form)* excuse me, sir; **~ Dr./Doktor/Professor Schmidt** Dr/Doctor/Professor Schmidt; **~ Doktor/Professor** doctor/professor; **~ Präsident/Vorsitzender** Mr President/Chairman; **der ~ Präsident/Vorsitzende** the President/Chairman; **lieber** *or* **werter** *(dated) or* **sehr verehrter** *(form)* **~ A** *(in Brief)* Dear Mr A; **an den ~n Abgeordneten C. Schmidt** C. Schmidt, MP; **werte** *or* **sehr geehrte ~en** *(in Brief)* Dear Sirs.
   (e) *(allgemein gesehen: Tanzpartner, Begleiter)* gentleman; *(auf eine bestimmte Dame bezogen)* partner; *(bei Cocktailparty, Theaterbesuch etc)* companion.
   (f) *(Sport)* **Vierhundert-Meter-Staffel der ~en** men's hundred metres relay.
Herrchen *nt (inf: von Hund)* master.
Her-: **h~reichen** *vt sep* to hand , to pass; **~reise** *f* journey here; **auf der ~reise von X** on the journey from X.
Herren- *in cpds* men's; *(auf Kleidung bezüglich auch)* gents' *(dated)*; *(auf einzelnes Exemplar bezüglich)* man's; gent's; **~abend** *m* stag night; **seinen ~abend haben** to have a night out with the boys *(inf)*; **~artikel** *pl* gentlemen's requisites *pl (dated)*; **~ausstatter** *m* -s, - gents' *or* men's outfitter; **~begleitung** *f* **~begleitung erwünscht** please bring a gentleman *or (bei Ball)* partner; **in ~begleitung** in the company of a gentleman; **~bekanntschaft** *f* gentleman acquaintance; **eine ~bekanntschaft machen** to make the acquaintance of a gentleman; **~bekleidung** *f* menswear; **~besuch** *m* (gentle)man visitor/visitors; **~doppel** *nt (Tennis etc)* men's doubles *sing*; **~einzel** *nt (Tennis etc)* men's singles *sing*; **~friseur** *m* men's hairdresser, barber; **~gesellschaft** *f* **(a)** *(gesellige Runde)* stag party; **(b)** *no pl (Begleitung von Herrn)* **in ~gesellschaft sein** to be in the company of gentlemen/a gentleman; **~haus** *nt* **(a)** manor house; **(b)** *(Hist)* upper chamber; **~jahre** *pl siehe* **Lehrjahr**; **~konfektion** *f* men's ready-to-wear clothes *pl*; **~leben** *nt* life of luxury and ease; **h~los** *adj* abandoned; *Hund etc* stray; **~mangel** *m* shortage of men; **~mensch** *m* member of the master race; **~mode** *f* men's fashion; **~partie** *f (Ausflug)* men-only outing; *(Gesellschaft)* stag party; **~rasse** *f* master race; **~reiten** *nt* amateur racing; **~reiter** *m* **(a)** *(Sport)* amateur jockey; **(b)** *(iro)* stuffed shirt *(inf)*; **~sattel** *m* (man's) saddle; **im ~sattel reiten** to ride astride; **~schneider** *m* gentlemen's tailor; **~schnitt** *m (Frisur)* haircut like a man's; **~sitz** *m* **(a)** *(Gutshof)* manor house; **(b)** **im ~sitz reiten** to ride astride; **~tiere** *pl siehe* **Primat²**; **~toilette** *f* men's toilet *or* restroom *(US)*, gents *sing*; **~volk** *nt* master race; **~welt** *f (dated hum)* gentlemen *pl*; **~winker** *m (hum)* kiss-curl; **~witz** *m* dirty joke; **~zimmer** *nt* study; *(Rauchzimmer)* smoking room.
Herrgott *m (dated inf) (Anrede)* God, Lord. **der ~ God,** the Lord (God); *(S Ger, Aus: Figur)* figure of the Lord; **~ (Sakrament)!** *(inf)* good God *or* Lord!; **~ noch mal!** *(inf)* damn it all! *(inf)*.
Herrgotts-: **~frühe** *f*: **in aller ~frühe** *(inf)* at the crack of dawn; **~schnitzer** *m (S Ger, Aus)* carver of crucifixes; **~winkel** *m (S Ger, Aus)* corner of a room with a crucifix.
herrichten *sep* 1 *vt* **(a)** *(vorbereiten)* to get ready *(dat, für* for); *Bett* to make; *Tisch* to set. **(b)** *(instand setzen, ausbessern)* to do up *(inf)*. 2 *vr (dial)* to get dressed up.

Herrin *f (Hist: Herrscherin)* female ruler; *(von Hund, old: Haus~)* mistress. **die ~** *(Anrede)* my lady.
herrisch *adj* overbearing, imperious; *Ton auch* peremptory.
herrje(h), herrjemine *interj* goodness gracious.
herrlich *adj* marvellous; *Anblick, Tag, Wetter auch* magnificent, glorious, lovely; *Kleid* gorgeous, lovely; *Essen, Witz, Geschichte auch* wonderful, lovely. **das ist ja ~** *(iro)* that's great; **du bist so ~ doof/naiv** *(iro)* you are so wonderfully stupid/naïve; **wir haben uns ~ amüsiert** we had marvellous fun.
Herrlichkeit *f* **(a)** *no pl (Schönheit, Pracht)* glory, magnificence, splendour. **die ~ Gottes** the glory of God; **Pracht und ~** pomp and circumstance; *(von Natur)* glory; **die ~ wird nicht lange dauern** *(iro inf)* this is too good to last; **ist das die ganze ~?** is that all there is to it?; **aus und vorbei mit der ~** here we go again. **(b)** *usu pl (prächtiger Gegenstand)* treasure. **(c)** *(obs: Anrede)* lordship.
Herrschaft *f* **(a)** *(Macht)* power; *(Staatsgewalt)* rule. **zur ~ gelangen** *or* **kommen** to come to power; **sich der ~ bemächtigen** to seize power; **unter der ~** under the rule *(gen, von* of); **unter jds ~** *(acc)* **fallen** to come under sb's rule.
   (b) *(Gewalt, Kontrolle)* control. **er verlor die ~ über sich** he lost his self-control; **er verlor die ~ über sein Auto** he lost control of his car, his car went out of control.
   (c) *(old: Dienst~)* master and mistress *pl*. **die ~en** *(Damen und Herren)* the ladies and gentlemen; **hohe ~en** *(dated)* persons of high rank *or* standing; **würden die ~en bitte …** would sir and madam please …/ladies and gentlemen, would you please …/ladies, would you please …/gentlemen, would you please …; **was wünschen die ~en?** what can I get you?; *(von Butler)* **you rang?; (meine) ~en!** ladies and gentlemen.
   (d) *(inf: Ausruf)* **~ (noch mal)** hang it (all) *(inf)*.
   (e) *(Hist: Landgut)* domain, estate, lands *pl*.
herrschaftlich *adj* of a person of high standing; *(vornehm)* grand. **die ~e Kutsche** his lordship's coach.
Herrschafts-: **~anspruch** *m* claim to power; *(von Thronfolger)* claim to the throne; **~bereich** *m* territory; **~form** *f* form *or* type of rule; **~gewalt** *f* authority, power; **h~los** *adj* without rule *or* government; **~losigkeit** *f* state of being without rule *or* government; **~system** *nt* system of rule.
herrschen 1 *vi* **(a)** *(Macht, Gewalt haben)* to rule; *(König)* to reign; *(fig) (Mensch)* to dominate; *(Geld)* to hold sway; *(Tod, Terror)* to rule, to hold sway.
   (b) *(vor~)* *(Angst, Ungewißheit, Zweifel)* to prevail; *(Verkehr, Ruhe, Betriebsamkeit)* to be prevalent; *(Nebel, Regen, Kälte)* to be predominant; *(Krankheit, Not)* to be rampant, to rage; *(Meinung, Ansicht)* to predominate. **überall herrschte Freude/Terror** there was joy/terror everywhere; **im Zimmer herrschte bedrückende Stille** it was oppressively quiet in the room; **bei uns herrscht schönes Wetter** we're having beautiful weather; **hier herrscht Ordnung** things are orderly round here; **hier herrscht ein anderer Ton** the atmosphere is different here; **hier ~ ja Zustände!** things are in a pretty state round here!; **bei uns herrscht die Grippe** we have a flu epidemic.
   (c) *(in herrischem Ton reden)* to snap, to bark.
2 *vi impers* **es herrscht schlechtes Wetter** the weather is bad, we're having bad weather; **es herrschte Schweigen** silence reigned; **es herrscht Ungewißheit darüber, ob …** there is uncertainty about whether …
herrschend *adj Partei, Klasse* ruling; *König* reigning; *Bedingungen, Verhältnisse, Meinungen* prevailing; *Mode* current. **die H~en** the rulers, those in power.
Herrscher(in *f) m* -s, - *(über + acc* of) ruler; *(König auch)* sovereign.
Herrscher-: **~blick** *m* imperious look; **mit ~blick** with an imperious look; **~familie** *f* ruling family; **~geschlecht** *nt* ruling dynasty; **~haus** *nt* ruling house *or* dynasty; **~miene** *f siehe* **~blick**; **~natur** *f* **(a)** *(Mensch)* domineering person; **(b)** *(Wesensart)* domineering character.
Herrschsucht *f* domineeringness.
herrschsüchtig *adj* domineering.
her-: **~rücken** *sep* 1 *vt* to move nearer *or* closer; 2 *vi aux sein* to move *or* come nearer *or* closer; **~rufen** *vt sep irreg* to call (over); *Tier* to call; **~rühren** *vi sep von etw* **~rühren** to be due to sth, to stem from sth; **~sagen** *vt sep* to recite; **~schaffen** *vt sep (inf) siehe* **herbeischaffen**; **~schauen** *vi sep (dial)* to look here *or* this way; **zu jdm ~schauen** to look in sb's direction; **da schau ~!** *(Aus inf)* well, I never! *(inf)*; **~schenken** *vt sep (inf) siehe* **verschenken**; **~schicken** *vt sep* to send; **jdn hinter jdm ~schicken** to send sb after sb; **~schleichen** *vir sep irreg (vi: aux sein)* **(a)** to creep up; **(b)** **(sich) hinter jdm ~schleichen** to creep along behind sb; **~schreiben** *vr sep irreg* **sich von etw ~schreiben** *(dated)* to originate from sth; **~sehen** *vi sep irreg* **(a)** to look here *or* this way; **zu jdm ~sehen** to look in sb's direction; **(b)** **hinter jdm/etw ~sehen** to follow sb with one's eyes; **~sein** *vi sep irreg aux sein* (Zusammenschreibung nur bei infin und ptp) **(a)** *(zeitlich)* **das ist schon 5 Jahre ~** that was 5 years ago; **es ist schon 5 Jahre ~, daß …** it was 5 years ago that …; **es ist kaum ein Jahr ~, daß …** it's hardly a year since …; **wie lange ist es ~?** how long ago was it?; **(b)** *(~stammen)* to come from; **mit jdm/etw ist es nicht weit ~** *(inf)* sb/sth is not up to much *(inf)*; **(c)** **hinter jdm/etw ~sein** to be after sb/sth; **dahinter ~sein, daß** **jd etw tut** to be on to sb to do sth; **~spionieren*** *vi sep* **hinter jdm ~spionieren** to spy on sb; **~stammen** *vi sep* **(a)** *(abstammen)* to come from; **wo stammst du ~?** where do you come from originally?; **(b)** *(~rühren)* **von etw ~stammen** to stem from sth; **(c)** *(~kommen)* **von jdm/etw ~stammen** to come from sb/sth.
herstellbar *adj* capable of being produced *or* manufactured. **schwer ~e Waren** goods which are difficult to produce *or* manufacture.

herstellen vt sep (a) (erzeugen) to produce; (industriell auch) to manufacture. **von Hand ~** to make or produce sth by hand; **in Deutschland hergestellt** made in Germany.

(b) (zustande bringen) to establish; Kontakt auch, (Telec) Verbindung to make; Stromkreis to complete.

(c) (gesundheitlich) jdn to restore to health; Gesundheit to restore. **er ist wieder ganz hergestellt** he has quite recovered.

(d) (an bestimmten Platz) to put or place here. **sich (zu jdm) ~** to come over (to sb); **etw zu jdm ~** to put sth by sb.

Hersteller m -s, - (Produzent) manufacturer; (im Verlag) production manager.

Hersteller-: ~betrieb m, ~firma f manufacturing firm, manufacturer.

Herstellung f, no pl (a) siehe vt (a) production; manufacture. **(b)** siehe vt (b) establishment; making; completion. **(c)** (von Gesundheit) restoration. **(d)** (Abteilung im Verlag) production department.

Herstellungs-: ~fehler m manufacturing defect or fault; ~kosten pl manufacturing or production costs pl; ~land nt country of manufacture; ~preis m cost of manufacture; ~verfahren nt manufacturing or production method.

her-: ~stürzen sep 1 vi aux sein (a) (auch ~gestürzt kommen) to come rushing up; **(b) hinter jdm/etw ~stürzen** to rush after sb/sth; **2** vr **sich hinter jdm ~stürzen** to throw oneself after sb; ~tragen vt sep irreg (a) (an bestimmten Ort) to carry here; **(b) etw vor/hinter jdm/etw ~tragen** to carry sth in front of/behind sb/sth; ~trauen vr sep to dare to come here; ~treiben sep irreg 1 vt (a) (an bestimmten Ort) to drive here; **(b) jdn/etw vor jdm/etw ~treiben** to drive (Strömung) to wash here; **etw zu uns ~treiben** to drive/blow/ wash sth over to us; **(b) jdn/etw vor jdm/etw ~treiben** to drive or (Wind) blow sb/sth in front of or before sb/sth; **jdn/etw hinter jdm/etw ~treiben** to drive or (Wind) blow sb/sth behind sb/sth; **was treibt dich ~?** what brings you here?; **2** vi aux sein to be driven (vor + dat in front of, before); (Wolken) to blow; (in der Strömung) to be washed; ~treten vi sep irreg aux sein to step up.

Hertz nt -, - (Phys, Rad) hertz.

herüben adv (S Ger, Aus) over here.

herüber adv over here; (über Fluß, Straße, Grenze etc) across. **~ und hinüber** to and fro, back and forth; **~ ist es nicht weiter als hinüber** (prov) coming or going, the distance is the same; **da ~** over/across there; siehe **herübersein**.

herüber- pref over; (über Straße, Fluß, Grenze etc) across; ~bitten vt sep irreg jdn to ask (to come) over; ~bringen vt sep irreg to bring over/across (über etw (acc) sth); ~dürfen vi sep irreg to be allowed to (come) over/across; ~fahren sep irreg 1 vi aux sein to come or (mit Auto etc) drive over/across (über etw (acc) sth); **2** vt (über etw (acc) sth) Auto etc to drive over/across; Fahrgast, Güter to take over/across; ~fliegen vti sep irreg (vi: aux sein) to fly over/across (über etw (acc) sth); ~geben vt sep irreg to pass (über + acc over); ~grüßen vi sep (zu jdm) ~grüßen to nod/call etc across to sb in greeting; ~holen vt sep to fetch; jdn to fetch over; ~kommen vi sep irreg aux sein to come over/across (über etw (acc) sth); (inf: zu Nachbarn) to pop round (inf); **wie sind die Leute (über die Mauer/den Fluß) ~gekommen?** how did the people get over (the wall)/across (the river)?; ~lassen vt sep irreg to allow (to come) over/across (über etw (acc) sth); (aus Land) to allow (to come) out; ~laufen vi sep irreg aux sein to run over/across (über etw (acc) sth); ~reichen sep 1 vt siehe ~geben; **2** vi to reach across (über etw (acc) sth); ~retten vt sep etw in die Gegenwart ~retten to preserve sth; ~schicken vt sep to send over/across; ~schwimmen vi sep irreg aux sein to swim across (über etw (acc) sth); ~sehen vi sep irreg to look over (über etw (acc) sth); **zu jdm ~sehen** to look over/across to sb; ~sein vi sep irreg aux sein (Zusammenschreibung nur bei infin und ptp) to be across; ~wechseln vi sep or auch haben (Tiere) to cross (über etw (acc) sth); **in unsere Partei/unseren Verein ~wechseln** to join our party/club, to swap parties/clubs (and join ours); ~wehen sep (über etw (acc) sth) 1 vi (a) (Wind) to blow over/across; **(b)** aux sein (Klang) to be blown over/across; (Duft) to waft over/across; **2** vt to blow over/across; ~werfen vt sep irreg to throw over/across (über etw (acc) sth); ~wollen vi sep to want to come over/across (über etw (acc) sth); ~ziehen sep irreg (über etw (acc) sth) 1 vt to pull over/across; (fig) to win over; **2** vi aux sein (Truppen, Wolken) to move over/across; (umziehen) to move.

herum adv (a) (örtlich richtungsangebend) **um ... ~** (a)round; **links/rechts ~** (a)round to the left/right; **hier/dort ~** (a)round here/there; **oben ~** (über Gegenstand, Berg) over the top; (in bezug auf Körper) round the top; **sie ist oben ~ ziemlich füllig** she's quite well endowed (hum); **unten ~** (unter Gegenstand) underneath; (um Berg, in bezug auf Körper) around the bottom; **oben/unten ~ fahren** to take the top/lower road; **wasch dich auch unten ~** (euph) don't forget to wash down below; **verkehrt ~** the wrong way round; (hinten nach vorn) back to front; (links nach außen) inside out; (oben nach unten) upside down; **immer um etw ~** round and round sth.

(b) (kreisförmig angeordnet, in der Nähe) **um ... ~** around; **hier ~** (a)round here; (in der Nähe auch) hereabouts; **alle um mich ~ wußten, daß ...** everyone around or round me knew that ...

(c) um ... ~ (ungefähre Mengenangabe) about, around; (Zeitangabe) (at) about or around' siehe auch **herumsein**.

herum- pref (a)round; siehe auch umher-; ~albern vi sep (inf) to fool or lark (inf) around; ~ärgern vr sep (inf) sich mit jdm/etw ~ärgern to keep struggling with sb/sth; ~balgen vr sep (inf) to romp about; ~basteln vi sep (inf) to tinker or mess (inf) about (an + dat with); ~bekommen vt sep irreg (inf) jdn to talk round; **etw ~bekommen** to (manage to) get sth round

(um etw sth); ~bessern vi sep an etw (dat) ~bessern to fiddle around correcting sth; ~blättern vi sep (in einem Buch) ~blättern to leaf or browse through a book; ~bohren vi sep (mit Stock, Finger etc) to poke around; (mit Bohrer) to drill; **sich (dat) in der Nase ~bohren** to pick one's nose; ~bringen vt sep irreg (inf) (a) siehe ~bekommen; **(b)** Zeit to get through; ~brüllen vi sep to yell; ~bummeln vi sep (inf) (a) (trödeln) to mess about (inf); **(b)** aux sein (spazieren) to stroll (a)round (in etw (dat) sth); ~doktern vi sep (inf) an jdm/einer Krankheit/einer Wunde ~doktern to try to cure sb/an illness/heal a wound (unsuccessfully, using many different remedies); **an etw (dat) ~doktern** (fig) to fiddle or tinker about with sth; ~drehen sep 1 vt Schlüssel to turn; (wenden) Decke, Tuch, Braten etc to turn (over); **jdm das Wort im Mund ~drehen** to twist sb's words; **2** vr to turn (a)round; (im Liegen) to turn over; **3** vi (inf) **an etw (dat) ~drehen** to fiddle or tinker about with sth; ~drücken sep 1 vr (inf) (a) (sich aufhalten) to hang (a)round (inf) (um etw sth); **(b)** (vermeiden) **sich um etw ~drücken** to dodge sth; **2** vi **an etw (dat) ~drücken** to squeeze sth; **3** vt Hebel to turn; ~drucksen vi sep (inf) to hum and haw (inf); ~erzählen vt sep etw bei jdm ~erzählen to tell sb about sth; **erzähl das nicht ~** don't spread that around; ~experimentieren* vi sep to experiment; ~fahren sep irreg 1 vi aux sein (a) (umherfahren) to go or travel or (mit Auto) drive around; **in der Stadt ~fahren** to go/drive (a)round the town; (um etw ~fahren) to go or (mit Auto) drive or (mit Schiff) sail (a)round; **(c)** (sich rasch umdrehen) to turn round quickly, to spin (a)round; **(d)** auch aux haben sich (dat) (mit den Händen) in den Haaren/im Gesicht ~fahren to run one's fingers through one's hair/to wipe one's face; **mit den Armen ~fahren** to wave one's arms about; **(e)** (inf: ~liegen) to be kicking around (inf); **2** vt to drive (a)round; ~fingern vi sep (inf) an etw (dat) ~fingern to fiddle about with sth; (an Körperteil) to finger sth; ~flattern vi sep aux sein (umherflattern) to flutter about; **um etw ~flattern** to flutter around sth; ~flegeln vi sep to loll about or around; ~fliegen sep irreg 1 vi aux sein to fly around (um jdn/etw sb/sth); (inf: ~liegen) to be kicking around (inf); **2** vt jdn to fly about or around; ~fragen vi sep (inf) to ask around (bei among); ~fuchteln vi sep (inf) (mit den Händen) ~fuchteln to wave one's hands about or around; **mit einer Pistole ~fuchteln** to wave a pistol around, to brandish a pistol; ~führen sep 1 vt (a) jdn, Tier to lead around (um etw sth); (bei Besichtigung) to take or show a(round); **jdn in einer Stadt/im Haus ~führen** to take or show sb (a)round a town/the house; **jdn an der Nase ~führen** to lead sb up the garden path; **(b)** (leiten, dirigieren) jdn/etw um etw ~führen to direct sb/sth around sth; **(c)** (bauen) etw um etw ~führen to build or take sth (a)round sth; **2** vi um etw ~führen to go (a)round sth; ~fuhrwerken vi sep (inf) to bustle about, to busy oneself; ~fummeln vi sep (inf) (an + dat with) to fiddle or fumble about; (an Auto) to mess about; (basteln) to tinker (about); ~geben vt sep irreg to hand or pass (a)round; ~gehen vi sep irreg aux sein (inf) (a) (um etw ~gehen) to walk or go (a)round (um etw sth); **(b)** (ziellos umhergehen) to go or wander (a)round (in etw (dat) sth); **es ging ihm im Kopf ~** it went round and round in his head; **(c)** (von einem zum andern gehen: Mensch) to go (a)round; (~gereicht werden) to be passed or handed (a)round; (weitererzählt werden) to go around (in etw (dat) sth); **etw ~gehen lassen** to circulate sth; **(d)** (zeitlich: vorbeigehen) to pass; ~geistern vi sep aux sein (inf) (Gespenster etc) to haunt (in etw (dat) sth); (Mensch) to wander (a)round; **in jds Kopf ~geistern** (Idee) to possess sb; ~gondeln vi sep aux sein (inf) to drive around; ~haben vt sep irreg (inf) (a) Zeit to have finished; **(b)** (überredet haben) to have talked round; ~hacken vi sep (fig inf) auf jdm ~hacken to pick on sb (inf); ~hängen vi sep irreg aux sein (inf) (a) (inf: unordentlich aufgehängt sein) to hang around; **(b)** (inf: sich lümmeln) to loll about; (sl: ständig zu finden sein) to hang out (inf); ~hantieren* vi sep (inf) to fiddle (about) (an + dat with); ~hetzen vi sep aux sein to rush around; ~horchen vi sep (inf) to keep one's ears open; ~huren vi sep (sl) to whore around (sl); ~irren vi sep aux sein to wander around; ~knobeln vi sep (inf) an etw (dat) ~knobeln to rack one's brains about sth; ~kommandieren* sep (inf) 1 vt to order about, to boss around or about (inf); **2** vi to give orders; ~kommen vi sep irreg aux sein (inf) (a) (um eine Ecke etc) to come round (um etw sth); **(b)** (~gehen, ~fahren etc können) to get round (um etw sth); **(c)** (vermeiden können) **um etw ~kommen** to get out of or avoid sth; **darum ~kommen, etw zu machen** to get out of or avoid doing sth; **mit den Armen um etw ~kommen** to be able to get one's arms (a)round sth; **wir kommen um die Tatsache nicht ~, daß ...** we cannot get away from or overlook the fact that ...; **(d)** (reisen) to get about or around (in etw (dat) sth); **er ist viel or weit ~gekommen** he has got around a great deal, he has seen a lot of the world; **(e)** (bewältigen können) **mit etw ~kommen** to manage sth; ~krabbeln vi sep aux sein (inf) to crawl around or about; ~kramen vi sep (inf) to rummage about or around; ~krebsen vi sep (inf) (a) (sich verzweifelt bemühen) to struggle; **(b)** (sich unwohl fühlen) to drag oneself around or about (inf); **(c)** aux sein (langsam or schwerfällig gehen) to trudge (a)round; ~kriechen vi sep irreg aux sein (inf) to crawl about or around (um etw sth); ~kriegen vt sep (inf) siehe ~bekommen; ~kritisieren*, ~kritteln vi sep to find fault (an + dat with), to pick holes (an + dat in); ~kurieren* vi sep siehe ~doktern; ~kutschieren* vti sep (vi: aux sein) to drive (a)round; ~laborieren* vi sep (inf) an etw (dat) ~laborieren to try to get rid of sth; ~laufen vi sep irreg aux sein (inf) (um etw ~laufen) to run round (um etw sth); (umherlaufen) to run or go about or around; **so kannst du doch nicht ~laufen** (fig inf) you can't run or go around (looking) like that; ~liegen vi sep irreg (inf) to lie around or about (um etw sth); ~lümmeln vir sep (inf) to loll around; ~**lungern** vi sep (inf) to hang about or around; ~**machen** sep (inf) **1** vi (a) (sich überlegen) to think about; **da braucht man doch nicht so lange ~zumachen** you don't need to think about it for so long; (b) (sich beschäftigen) **an jdm/etw ~machen** to fuss about sb/sth; **(c)** (~fingern) **an etw** (dat) ~**machen** to pick at sth; (an den Haaren) to fiddle with sth; **(d)** (~nörgeln) **an jdm/etw ~machen** to go on at sb/about sth (inf); **2** vt to put (a)round (um etw sth); ~**mäkeln** vi sep siehe ~**kritteln**; ~**nörgeln** vi sep an jdm/etw ~**nörgeln** to find fault with sb/sth; ~**pfuschen** vi sep (inf) to mess about (inf) (an +dat with); ~**pusseln** vi sep (inf) to fiddle about (an +dat with); ~**quälen** vr sep (inf) to struggle; (mit Problemen) to worry oneself sick (mit over) (inf); **sich mit Rheuma ~quälen** to be plagued by rheumatism; ~**raten** vi sep irreg (inf) to guess; ~**rätseln** vi sep (an etw dat) ~**rätseln** to (try to) figure sth out; ~**reden** vi sep (inf) (belangloses Zeug reden) to talk or chat away; **um etw** ~**reden** (ausweichend) to talk (a)round sth; ~**reichen** vt sep (a) (~geben) to pass round; (fig inf) Besucher to show off; (b) (lang genug sein) to reach (a)round (um etw sth); ~**reisen** vi sep aux sein to travel about; ~**reißen** vt sep irreg to pull or swing round (hard); **das Steuer ~reißen** (fig) to change or alter course; ~**reiten** vi sep irreg (a) aux sein (umherreiten) to ride around or about; (um etw ~reiten) to ride (a)round (um etw sth); (b) (fig inf) **auf jdm/etw ~reiten** to keep on at sb/about sth; ~**rennen** vi sep irreg aux sein (inf) (um etw ~rennen) to run round (um etw sth); (umherrennen) to run about or around; ~**rutschen** vi sep aux sein (inf) to fidget about; ~**scharwenzeln*** vi sep aux sein (inf) to dance attendance (um on); ~**schicken** vt sep (inf) jdn to send round (bei to); Brief etc to circulate; ~**schlagen** sep irreg **1** vt Papier, Tuch etc to wrap round (um etw sth); **2** vr (inf) **sich mit jdm ~schlagen** (lit) to fight or scuffle with sb; (fig) **sich mit jdm/etw ~schlagen** (fig) to keep struggling with sb/sth; ~**schleichen** vi sep irreg aux sein to creep (a)round (um etw sth); (umherschleichen) to drag around; ~**schlendern** vi sep aux sein to stroll or saunter about (in der Stadt (in) the town); ~**schleppen** vt sep (inf) Sachen to lug around (inf); jdn to drag around; **etw mit sich ~schleppen** Kummer, Sorge, Problem to be troubled or worried by sth; Krankheit, Infektion to be going around with sth; ~**schnüffeln** vi sep (inf) to sniff around (in etw dat) in); (fig) to snoop around (in +dat in); ~**schreien** vi sep irreg (inf) to shout out loud; ~**schwänzeln** vi sep aux sein (inf) siehe ~**scharwenzeln**; ~**sein** vi sep irreg aux sein (inf) (Zusammenschreibung nur bei infin und ptp) (a) (vorüber sein) to be past or over; (b) (verbreitet worden sein: Gerücht, Neuigkeit, Nachricht) to have got (a)round; (c) (in jds Nähe sein) **um jdn ~sein** to be (a)round sb; (d) (um etw gelaufen, gefahren sein) to be round (um etw sth); ~**sitzen** vi sep irreg aux sein to sit round (um jdm/etw sb/sth); ~**spielen** vi sep (inf) **mit etw ~spielen** to play about or around with sth; **an etw** (dat) ~**spielen** to fiddle about or around with sth; **auf etw** (dat) ~**spielen** to play around on sth; ~**sprechen** vr sep irreg to get about; **es dürfte sich ~gesprochen haben, daß …** it has probably got about that …; ~**spuken** vi sep to haunt; **die Idee spukt jdm im Kopf** or **in jds Kopf ~** sb has the idea; ~**stänkern** vi sep (inf) to moan, to gripe (inf), to bellyache (inf); ~**stehen** vi sep irreg aux sein (inf) (Sachen) to be lying around; **der Sessel steht blöd ~** the chair is in a stupid place; (b) (Menschen) to stand (a)round (um jdn/etw sb/sth); ~**stöbern** vi sep (inf) (a) (suchen) to rummage around or about; (b) (~schnüffeln) to snoop around; ~**stochern** vi sep (inf) to poke about; **im Essen ~stochern** to pick at one's food; **in den Zähnen ~stochern** to pick one's teeth; ~**stoßen** vt sep irreg (inf) jdn to shove around; ~**streichen** vi sep irreg aux sein (um jdn/etw sb/sth) to creep around; (Verbrecher, Katze) to prowl around; ~**streifen** vi sep aux sein to roam around; ~**streiten** vr sep irreg to squabble; ~**streunen**, ~**strolchen** vi sep aux sein (inf) to prowl around; ~**stromern** vi sep aux sein (inf) to wander or roam about or around; ~**tanzen** vi sep aux sein (inf) (umhertanzen) to dance around; **um jdn ~tanzen** to dance (a)round sb/sth; **sie tanzt ihm auf der Nase ~** she does as she pleases or likes with him; ~**tappen** vi sep aux sein (inf) to grope around or about; ~**tasten** vi sep (a) (tastend fühlen) to grope around or about; (b) aux sein (inf: tastend gehen) to grope around or about; ~**toben** vi sep (inf) (a) auch aux sein (umherlaufen) to romp around or about; (b) (schimpfen) to shout and scream; ~**tollen** vi sep aux sein (inf) to romp about or around; ~**tragen** vt sep irreg (inf) (a) to carry about or (a)round; **um etw ~tragen** to carry (a)round sth; **Sorgen mit sich ~tragen** to have worries; **eine Idee mit sich ~tragen** to be contemplating an idea, to be thinking about an idea; (b) (weitererzählen) to spread around; ~**trampeln** vi sep aux sein (inf) to trample (auf +dat on); **jdm auf den Nerven** or **auf jds Nerven ~trampeln** to get on sb's nerves; **auf jdm ~trampeln** (fig) to get at sb; ~**treiben** vr sep irreg (inf) (~ziehen in) to hang around or about (in +dat in) (inf); (liederlich leben) to hang around or about in bad places/company; **die treibt sich mal wieder irgendwo in Spanien ~** she's off gadding about in Spain again (inf); **sich mit jdm ~treiben** to hang or knock around with sb (inf).

Herumtreiber(in f) m -s, - (pej) (a) (Mensch ohne feste Arbeit, Wohnsitz) tramp. (b) (inf) (Streuner) vagabond; (liederlich) good-for-nothing; (Frau) tramp (inf).

herum-: ~**treten** vi sep irreg (inf) siehe ~**trampeln**; ~**trödeln** vi sep (inf) to dawdle (mit over); ~**turnen** vi sep aux sein (inf) to clamber or scramble about; ~**vagabundieren*** vi sep aux sein (pej) to roam about; ~**wälzen** sep **1** vt Stein to turn over; **2** vr to roll around; (sich schlaflos) **im Bett ~wälzen** to toss and turn in bed; ~**wandern** vi sep aux sein (inf) (umhergehen) to wander about; **um etw ~wandern** to wander (a)round sth; ~**werfen** sep irreg **1** vt (a) (achtlos werfen) to throw around (in etw (dat) sth); (b) (heftig bewegen) Kopf to turn (quickly); Steuer, Hebel to throw

around; **2** vr to roll over; **sich (im Bett) ~werfen** to toss and turn (in bed); **3** vi (inf) **mit Bemerkungen/Geld etc ~werfen** to fling or throw remarks/one's money etc around; ~**wickeln** vt sep (um etw sth) to wrap (a)round; ~**wirbeln** vti sep (vi: aux sein) jdn or mit jdm ~**wirbeln** to whirl or spin sb (a)round; (inf) ~**wühlen** vi sep (inf) to potter about; ~**wirtschaften** vi sep (inf) (Schwein) to root around; (~schnüffeln) to nose or snoop about or around; ~**wursteln** vi sep (inf) to fiddle or mess (inf) around or about (an +dat with); ~**zanken** vr sep to squabble; ~**zeigen** vt sep to show around; ~**ziehen** sep irreg **1** vi aux sein (a) (von Ort zu Ort ziehen) to move around; (inf: sich ~treiben in) to go around (in etw (dat) sth); **in der Welt ~ziehen** to roam the world; **mit jdm ~ziehen** (inf) to go or hang around with sb; (b) (um etw ~) to move around (um etw sth); **2** vt **etw mit sich ~ziehen** to take (around) with one; **3** vt etw ~**ziehen** (Hecke etc) to run (a)round sth; ~**ziehend** adj attr Händler itinerant; Musikant, Schauspieler wandering, strolling; ~**zigeunern*** vi sep aux sein (pej) to roam or wander (a)round (in etw dat sth).

herunten adv (S Ger, Aus) down here; siehe **herunterhaben**, **heruntersein**.

herunter 1 adv down. ~**!** get down!; ~ mit euch get/come down; ~ mit ihm get him down; ~ damit get or bring it down; (in bezug auf Kleider) get or take it off; da/hier ~ down there/here; den Hut ~, ~ mit dem Hut get or take your hat off; vom Berg ~ down the mountain; vom Himmel ~ down from heaven; bis ins Tal ~ down into the valley; der Franken ist bis auf eine Mark ~ (inf) the franc is down to one mark; siehe auch **herunterhaben**, **heruntersein** etc.

2 prep +acc (nachgestellt) down.

herunter- pref down; siehe auch **runter-**, **herab-**; ~**bekommen** vt sep irreg siehe ~**kriegen**; ~**bemühen*** sep **1** vt jdn ~**bemühen** to ask sb to come down; **2** vr to come down; ~**bitten** vt sep irreg (a) (Sonne) to burn or scorch down; (b) aux sein (Haus, Feuer etc) to burn down; ~**bringen** vt sep irreg (a) to bring down; (b) (zugrunde richten) to ruin; (c) (inf) siehe ~**kriegen**; ~**drücken** vt sep Hebel, Pedal to press down; Preise to force or bring down; Niveau to lower; ~**fahren** sep irreg **1** vi aux sein to go down; ~**gefahren kommen** to come down; **2** vt to bring down; ~**fallen** vi sep irreg aux sein to fall down; **von etw ~fallen** to fall off sth; **ihm fiel die Kinnlade ~** his jaw dropped; ~**fliegen** vi sep irreg aux sein to fly down; (inf) to fall down; ~**geben** vt sep irreg to hand down; ~**gehen** vi sep irreg aux sein to go down; (Fieber, Temperatur auch) to drop; (Preise auch) to come down, to drop; (Flugzeug) to descend; **von etw ~gehen** (inf) to get down from or get off sth; **auf etw** (acc) ~**gehen** (Preise) to go down to sth; (Geschwindigkeit) to slow down to sth; **mit den Preisen ~gehen** to lower or cut one's prices; ~**gekommen 1** ptp of ~**kommen**; **2** adj Haus dilapidated; Stadt run-down; Mensch, Mensch down-at-heel; ~**haben** vt sep irreg (inf) to have lost; (abgenommen haben) to have got down; ~**handeln** vt sep (inf) Preis to beat down; **etw um 20 Mark ~handeln** to get 20 marks knocked off sth; ~**hängen** vi sep irreg to hang down; (Haare) to hang; ~**hauen** vt sep irreg (inf) (a) **jdm eine ~hauen** to give sb a clip round the ear (inf); (b) (schnell machen) to dash or knock off (inf); ~**heben** vt sep irreg to lift down; ~**helfen** vi sep irreg jdm ~**helfen** to help sb down; ~**holen** vt sep to fetch down; (inf) Vogel to bring down, to bag; Flugzeug to bring down; ~**klappen** vt sep to turn down; Sitz to fold down; Deckel to close; ~**klettern** vi sep aux sein to climb down; ~**kommen** vi sep irreg aux sein (nach unten kommen) to come down; (inf: ~können) to get down; (b) (fig inf: verfallen) (Stadt, Firma) to go downhill; (gesundheitlich) to become run-down; **er ist soweit ~gekommen, daß …** (sittlich) he has sunk so low that …; siehe ~**gekommen**; (c) (fig inf: von etw wegkommen) (von schlechten Noten) to get over (von etw sth); **von Drogen/Alkohol ~kommen** to kick the habit (sl); ~**können** vi sep (inf) to be able to get down; ~**kriegen** vt sep (inf) (a) (~holen, schlucken können) to get down; (abmachen können) to get off; (b) (abnehmen) to lose; ~**kurbeln** vt sep Fensterscheibe to wind down; ~**lassen** sep irreg **1** vt (abseilen) Gegenstand to let down, to lower; Hose to take down; jdn to lower; **sie läßt mich nicht ~** (inf) she won't let me down; **2** vr (am Seil) to lower oneself; ~**leiern** vt sep (inf) to reel off; ~**lesen** vt sep irreg (pej) to read off; ~**machen** vt sep (inf) (a) (schlechtmachen) to run down, to knock (inf); (b) (zurechtweisen) to tell off; (c) (abmachen) to take down; Schminke, Farbe, Dreck to take off; ~**nehmen** vt sep to take down; (inf: von Schule) to take away; **etw vom Tisch etc ~nehmen** to take sth off the table etc; ~**putzen** vt sep (inf) jdn ~**putzen** to tear sb off a strip (inf); ~**rasseln** vt sep (inf) to rattle or reel off; ~**reichen** sep **1** vt to pass or hand down; **2** vi to reach down; ~**reißen** vt sep irreg (inf) (a) (von oben nach unten) to pull or tear down; (b) (abreißen) Pflaster, Tapete etc to pull off; (c) (sl) Zeit to get through; ~**rutschen** vi sep aux sein to slide down; siehe Buckel; ~**schalten** vi sep (Aut) to change or shift (US) down (in +acc into); ~**schießen** sep irreg **1** vti (mit Geschoß) to shoot down; **2** vi aux sein (sich schnell bewegen) to shoot down; ~**schlagen** vt sep (a) jdm den Hut etc ~**schlagen** to knock sb's hat etc off; etw vom Baum ~**schlagen** to knock sth off the tree; (b) Kragen, Hutkrempe to turn down; ~**schlucken** vt sep to swallow; ~**schrauben** vt sep (lit) Deckel etc to screw off; Petroleumlampe to turn down; (fig) Ansprüche, Niveau to lower; ~**sehen** vi sep irreg (a) (von oben) to look down; (b: fig: mustern) an jdm ~**sehen** to look sb up and down; (c) (fig: geringschätzig behandeln) auf jdn ~**sehen** to look down on sb; ~**sein** vi sep irreg aux sein (inf) (Zusammenschreibung nur bei infin und ptp) (a) (von oben) to be down; **(b)** (*~gelassen sein*) to be down; **(c)** (*abgeschnitten sein*) to be (cut) off; **(d)** (*Fieber, Preise*) to be lower or down; **wenn die 5 Kilo Übergewicht ~ sind** when I/you *etc* have lost those 5 kilos excess weight; **(e)** (*inf*) **mit den Nerven/der Gesundheit ~sein** to be at the end of one's tether/to be rundown; **für sein Alter ~sein** to be in poor health for one's age; **(f)** (*abgewirtschaftet haben*) to be in a bad way; **~setzen** *vt sep* (*inf*) *siehe* **herabsetzen; ~spielen** *vt sep* (*inf*) *Stück* to run through; (*verharmlosen*) *Problem, Vorfall* to play down; **~steigen** *vi sep irreg aux sein* to climb down; **~stürzen** *sep* 1 *vi aux sein* (*~fallen*) to fall or tumble down; (*inf: ~eilen*) to rush down; 2 *vt* **(a) jdn ~stürzen** to throw/push sb down; **(b)** (*inf: schnell trinken*) to gulp down; 3 *vr* to throw oneself down; **~werfen** *vt sep irreg* to throw down; (*unabsichtlich*) to drop; **~wirtschaften** *vt sep* (*inf*) to bring to the brink of ruin; **~wollen** *vi sep* (*inf*) to want to get down; **~ziehen** *sep irreg* 1 *vt* **(a)** to pull down; *Pullover etc* to pull off; **etw von etw ~ziehen** to pull sth off sth; **(b)** (*fig*) **jdn auf ein tieferes Niveau/seine Ebene/zu sich ~ziehen** to pull sb down to one's own level; 2 *vi aux sein* to go or move down; (*umziehen*) to move down; 3 *vr* to go down.

hervor *adv* **aus etw ~** out of sth; **hinter dem Tisch ~** out from behind the table; **~ mit euch** (*geh*) out you come.

hervor-: **~brechen** *vi sep irreg aux sein* (*geh*) to burst or break out; (*Sonne, fig: Gefühl*) to break through; (*Quelle, Flüssigkeit*) to gush out or forth (*liter*); **~bringen** *vt sep irreg* **(a)** to produce; *Blüten, Früchte, Pflanzen auch* to bring forth; *Worte* to utter; **(b)** (*verursachen*) *Unheil, Böses* to create; **~dringen** *vi sep irreg aux sein* (*a*) (*geh: entstammen*) to come (*aus from*); **aus der Ehe gingen zwei Kinder ~** the marriage produced two children; **(b)** (*sich ergeben, zu folgern sein*) to follow; **daraus geht ~, daß ...** from this it follows that ...; **(c)** (*etwas übersteigen*) to emerge; **als Sieger ~gehen** to emerge victorious; **aus etw ~gehen** to come out of sth; **~gucken** *vi sep* (*inf*) to peep out (*unter + dat* (from) under); **~heben** *vt sep irreg* to emphasize, to stress; **~holen** *vt sep* to bring out; **~kehren** *vt sep* (*geh*) to emphasize; **er kehrt immer den feinen Mann ~** he always emphasizes what a gentleman he is; **~kommen** *vi sep irreg aux sein* to come out (*hinter + dat* from behind); **~locken** *vt sep* to entice or lure out (*aus from, hinter + dat* from behind); **dein Gejammer lockt bei mir keine Träne ~** your moaning is not going to move me; **~quellen** *vi sep irreg aux sein* (*Wasser*) to gush forth (*aus from*) (*liter*); (*Tränen*) to well up (*aus in*); (*Blut*) to spurt out (*aus of*); (*Körperfülle*) to bulge or protrude (*aus from, unter + dat* from under); **~ragen** *vi sep* **(a)** (*Felsen, Stein etc*) to jut out, to project; (*Nase*) to protrude; **(b)** (*fig: sich auszeichnen*) to stand out; **er ragt unter den anderen/durch seine Intelligenz ~** he stands out from the others/because of his intelligence; **~ragend** *adj* **(a)** (*lit: vorstehend*) projecting; *esp Körperteil* protruding; **(b)** (*fig: ausgezeichnet*) excellent; *Mensch, Leistung etc auch* outstanding; **er hat H~ragendes geleistet** his achievement was outstanding; **~rufen** *vt sep irreg* **(a)** (*rufen*) **jdn ~rufen** to call (to) sb to come out; (*Theat etc*) to call for sb; **(b)** (*bewirken*) *Reaktion, Krankheit* to cause; *Eindruck* to create; **~sehen** *vi sep irreg* (*Unterrock*) to show; (*Mensch*) to look out; **hinter etw** (*dat*) **~sehen** (*Mensch*) to look out from behind sth; (*Mond, Sterne*) to shine out from behind sth; **~springen** *vi sep irreg aux sein* (*a*) to jump or leap out (*hinter + dat* from behind); **(b)** (*Felsen*) to project, to jut out; (*Nase*) to protrude, to stick out; **~sprudeln** *vi sep aux sein* to bubble or gush out; (*Worte*) to gush (out); **~stechen** *vi sep irreg aux sein* (*lit, fig*) to stand out; **~stechend** *adj* striking; **~stehen** *vi sep irreg aux sein* (*Spitze*) to project, to jut out; (*Nase, Ohren etc*) to stick out; **~stoßen** *vt sep irreg* (*fig*) *Worte* to gasp (out); **~stürzen** *vi sep aux sein* to rush or hurtle out (*hinter + dat* from behind); **~suchen** *vt sep* (*herausuchen*) to look out; **~trauen** *vr sep* (*inf*) *siehe* **~wagen; ~treten** *vi sep irreg aux sein* (*a*) (*heraustreten*) to step out, to emerge (*hinter + dat* from behind); (*Backenknochen*) to protrude; (*Adern*) to bulge; (*Sonne, Mond*) to emerge (*hinter + dat, aus* from behind); **(b)** (*sichtbar werden*) to stand out; (*fig auch*) to become evident; **(c)** (*an die Öffentlichkeit treten*) to come to the fore; **~tun** *vr sep irreg* to distinguish oneself; (*inf: sich wichtig tun*) to show off (*mit etw sth*); **~wagen** *vr sep* to dare to come out; **~zaubern** *vt sep* (*lit, fig*) to conjure up; **~ziehen** *vt sep irreg* to pull out (*unter + dat* from under); **etw aus/zwischen etw** (*dat*) **~ziehen** to pull sth out of/from among sth.

Her-: **h~wagen** *vr sep* to dare to come; **h~wärts** *adv* on the way here; **~weg** *m* way here; **auf dem ~weg** on the way here.

Herz *nt* **-ens, -en (a)** (*Organ, ~förmiges, Cook*) heart. **mir schlug das ~ bis zum Hals** my heart was thumping or pounding, my heart was in my mouth; **sein ~ schlug höher** his heart leapt; **die ~en höher schlagen lassen** to make people's hearts beat faster; **er drückte sie an sein ~** he clasped her to his breast; **komm an mein ~** come into my arms.

(b) (*Gemüt, Gefühl*) heart. **ein goldenes ~** a heart of gold; **ein gutes ~ haben** to be good-hearted, to have a good heart; **leichten/schweren/traurigen ~ens** light-heartedly or with a light heart/with a heavy/sad heart; **der Anblick rührte ihr das ~** the sight touched her heart; **es gab mir einen Stich ins ~** it hurt me; (*traurig stimmen*) it saddened me; **es ging mir bis ins ~** it cut me to the quick; (*traurig stimmen*) it saddened me very much; **es wird ihm das ~ abdrücken** it will almost kill him; **sich** (*dat*) **das ~ erleichtern** to unburden one's heart; **seinem ~en Luft machen** to give vent to one's feelings; **sich** (*dat*) **etw vom ~en finden** to get sth off one's chest; **den Weg in die or zu den ~en finden** to find one's way into people's hearts; **alle ~en im Sturm erobern** to capture people's hearts; **jdm ins ~ sehen** to see into sb's heart; **du sprichst mir aus dem ~en** you're voicing my innermost thoughts; **jdm das ~ schwer machen** to sadden

or grieve sb; **mir ist das ~ schwer** I have a heavy heart; **haben Sie doch ein ~!** have a heart!; **im Grund seines ~ens** in his heart of hearts; **aus tiefstem ~en** from the bottom of one's heart; **mit ganzem ~en** wholeheartedly; **er ist mit ganzem ~en bei der Arbeit** he is putting himself heart and soul into his work; **ein Mann nach meinem ~en** a man after my own heart; **ohne ~** heartless; **ich weiß, wie es dir ums ~ ist** I know how you feel; **es wurde ihr leichter ums ~** she felt easier or relieved; **es ging mir zu ~en** it touched me deeply.

(c) (*Liebe*) heart. **mein ~ gehört dir/der Musik** my heart belongs to you/to music; **jdm sein ~ schenken** to give sb one's heart; **dieser Hund ist mir ans ~ gewachsen** I have grown fond of or become attached to this dog; **ein ~ für etw haben** to feel sorry for sth; **sein ~ für etw entdecken** to start liking sth; **er hat sie in sein ~ geschlossen** he has grown fond of her; **sein ~ an jdn/etw hängen** to commit oneself heart and soul to sb/sth; **jds ~ hängt an jdm/etw** sb is committed heart and soul to sb/sth; (*an Geld*) sb is preoccupied with sth; **die Dame seines ~ens** the lady of his dreams.

(d) (*liter: Mut*) heart, courage. **sich** (*dat*) **ein ~ fassen** or **nehmen** to take heart; **sein ~ in beide Hände nehmen** to take one's courage in both hands; **jdm rutscht** or **fällt das ~ in die Hose(ntasche)** (*inf*) sb's heart sinks; **das ~ haben, etw zu tun** to have the heart to do sth.

(e) (*Inneres: von Salat, Stadt, Land*) heart.

(f) *pl* **- (Cards) ~** hearts *pl*; (*~karte*) heart.

(g) (*old: Kosewort*) dear (heart).

(h) (*Redewendungen*) **ein ~ und eine Seele sein** to be the best of friends; **alles, was das ~ begehrt** everything one's heart desires; **mir blutet das ~, mein ~ blutet** my heart bleeds (*auch iro*); **es zerreißt mir das ~** it breaks my heart; **jds ~ brechen/gewinnen/stehlen** to break/win/steal sb's heart; **gib deinem ~en einen Stoß!** go on!; **er hat das ~ auf dem or am rechten Fleck** his heart is in the right place; **mir lacht das ~ im Leibe** my heart leaps with joy; **das ~ auf der Zunge tragen** to speak one's mind; **jdm dreht sich das ~ im Leib um/jdm tut das ~ im Leibe weh** sb feels sick at heart; **wes das ~ voll ist, des geht or fließt der Mund über** (*Prov*) he/she *etc* is so excited that he/she can't stop talking about it; **es liegt mir am ~en** I am very concerned about it; **jdm etw ans ~ legen** to entrust sth to sb; **ich lege es dir ans ~, das zu tun** I (would) ask you particularly to do that; **es brennt mir auf dem ~en** it is of the utmost importance to me; **etw auf dem ~en haben** to have sth on one's mind; **jdn/etw auf ~ und Nieren prüfen** to examine sb/sth very thoroughly; **ein Kind unter dem ~en tragen** (*Bibl, old*) to be with child (*old*); **eine schwere Last or eine Zentnerlast fiel ihr vom ~en** a heavy load was lifted from her mind; **von ~en mit all one's heart; etw von ~en gern tun** to love doing sth; **jdn von ~en gern haben** to love sb dearly; **jdm von ganzem ~en danken** to thank sb with all one's heart; **von ~en kommend** heartfelt; **sich** (*dat*) **etw zu ~en nehmen** to take sth to heart.

herzählen *vt sep* to count.

Herz- *in cpds* (*Anat, Med*) cardiac; **h~allerliebst** *adj* (*old, hum*) most charming; **~allerliebste(r)** *mf decl as adj* (*old, hum*) darling, dearest; **~anfall** *m* heart attack; **~as** *nt* ace of hearts; **~attacke** *f* heart attack.

herzaubern *vt sep* to produce out of thin air.

Herz-: **~bad** *nt* spa specializing in treating heart disease; **h~beklemmend** *adj* oppressive; **~beklemmung** *f* **~beklemmungen bekommen** to feel as if one cannot breathe; **~beschwerden** *pl* heart trouble *sing*; **~beutel** *m* pericardium; **~beutelentzündung** *f* pericarditis; **h~bewegend** *adj* heart-rending; **~binkerl, ~bünkerl** *nt* **-s, -(n)** (*Aus*) darling; **~blatt** *nt* **(a)** (*Bot*) grass of Parnassus; **(b)** (*dated inf*) darling; **~blättchen** *nt* (*dated inf*) darling; **h~blättrig** *adj* heart-shaped; **~blut** *nt* (*poet*) lifeblood; **~bube** *m* jack or knave of hearts; **~bünkerl** *nt siehe* **~binkerl.**

Herzchen *nt* little heart; (*inf: Kosewort*) (little) darling.

Herz-: **~chirurg** *m* heart or cardiac surgeon; **~chirurgie** *f* heart or cardiac surgery; **~dame** *f* **(a)** (*Cards*) queen of hearts; **(b)** (*old, hum: Angebetete*) beloved; **~drücken** *nt*: **er stirbt nicht an ~drücken** (*inf*) he calls a spade a spade.

Herze *nt* **-ns, -n** (*old, poet*) heart.

herzeigen *vt sep* to show. **zeig (mal) her!** let me see, let's see; **das kann man ~** that's worth showing off.

Herzeleid *nt* (*old*) heartache.

herzen *vt* (*dated*) to hug.

Herzens-: **~angelegenheit** *f* (*dated*) affair of the heart, affaire de cœur; **~bedürfnis** *nt* (*dated*) **es ist mir ein ~bedürfnis** it is a matter dear to my heart; **~bildung** *f* (*geh*) nobleness of heart; **~brecher** *m* **-s, -** (*fig inf*) lady-killer; **~ergießung** *f*, **~erguß** *m* (*dated, hum*) emotional outpourings *pl*; **~freude** *f* (*dated*) **es ist mir eine ~freude** it warms my heart; **~freund** *m* (*old*) dear friend; **h~froh** *adj* (*old*) heartily glad; **~grund** *m* (*dated*) **aus tiefstem ~grund** from the very bottom of one's heart; **h~gut** *adj* good-hearted; **~güte** *f* good-heartedness; **~lust** *f* **nach ~lust** to one's heart's content; **~qual** *f* (*old*) *usu pl* great emotional torment *pl rare*; **~wunsch** *m* dearest wish.

Herz-: **h~erfreuend** *adj* heart-warming; **h~erfrischend** *adj* refreshing; **h~ergreifend** *adj* heart-rending; **h~erquickend** *adj* refreshing; **h~erwärmend** *adj* heart-warming; **h~erweichend** *adj* heart-rending; **~erweiterung** *f* cardiectasis (*spec*), dilation of the heart; **~fehler** *m* cardiac or heart defect; **~flattern** *nt* **-s, no pl** palpitations *pl* (of the heart); **~flimmern** *nt* **-s, no pl** heart flutter; (*Kammerflimmern*) (ventricular) fibrillation; **~flimmern haben** to have a heart flutter/to be in fibrillation; **h~förmig** *adj* heart-shaped; **~gegend** *f, no pl* cardiac region, area of the heart (*auch fig*); **~geräusche** *pl* heartbeats *pl*; **h~haft** *adj* **(a)** (*dated: mutig*) brave; **(b)** (*kräftig*) hearty; *Händedruck, Griff* firm; *Geschmack* strong;

h~**haft gähnen** to yawn widely; **alle packten h~haft zu** everyone got stuck in (inf); **das schmeckt h~haft** that's tasty; (c) (nahrhaft) Essen substantial.

herziehen sep irreg **1** vt to draw or pull closer or nearer. **jdn/etw hinter sich** (dat) ~ to pull or drag sb/sth (along) behind one.

2 vi **(a)** aux sein (herankommen) to approach. **hinter/neben/vor jdm** ~ to march along behind/beside/in front of sb. **(b)** aux sein (umziehen) to move here. **(c)** aux sein über jdn/etw ~ (inf) to knock sb/sth (inf), to pull sb/sth to pieces (inf).

herzig adj delightful, sweet.

Herz-: ~**infarkt** m heart attack, cardiac infarction (spec); h~**innig(lich)** adj (old) heartfelt; **sich h~innig(lich) umarmen** to embrace warmly; ~**insuffizienz** f cardiac degeneration; ~**Jesu-Bild** nt Sacred Heart painting; ~**kammer** f ventricle; ~**kirsche** f (bigarreau) cherry; ~**klappe** f cardiac or heart valve; ~**klappenentzündung** f endocarditis; ~**klappenfehler** m valvular heart defect; ~**klaps** m (inf) heart condition; ~**klopfen** nt -s, no pl **ich hatte/bekam ~klopfen** my heart was/started pounding; (durch Kaffee) I had/got palpitations; **mit ~klopfen** with a pounding heart, with one's heart in one's mouth; ~**knacks** m (inf) siehe ~**fehler**; ~**krampf** m heart spasm; h~**krank** adj suffering from a heart condition; h~**krank sein/werden** to have/get a heart condition; ~**krankheit** f heart condition; ~**kranzgefäß** nt usu pl coronary (blood) vessel; ~**land** nt, no pl heart; ~**leiden** nt siehe ~**krankheit**; h~**leidend** adj with a heart condition.

herzlich adj Empfang, Freundschaft warm; Wesen, Mensch warm(-hearted); Lachen hearty; Bitte sincere. **~e Grüße an Ihre Frau Gemahlin** kind(est) regards or remember me to your wife; **mit ~en Grüßen** kind regards; **~en Dank!** many thanks, thank you very much indeed; **~es Beileid!** you have my sincere or heartfelt sympathy or condolences pl; **zu jdm ~ sein** to be kind to sb; **eine ~e Bitte an jdn richten** to make a cordial request to sb; ~ **gern!** with the greatest of pleasure!; **ich würde ~ gern einmal wieder die Stätten meiner Kindheit besuchen** I should so much like to visit my childhood haunts again; ~ **schlecht** pretty awful; ~ **wenig** precious little; **ich habe es ~ satt** I am thoroughly or utterly sick of it, I'm sick and tired of it.

Herzlichkeit f siehe adj warmth; warm(-hearted)ness; heartiness; sincerity.

Herz-: ~**liebchen** nt (old) sweetheart, dearest; ~**liebste(r)** mf (old) siehe ~**allerliebste(r)**; ~**linie** f heart line; h~**los** adj heartless, unfeeling; ~**losigkeit** f heartlessness no pl; ~**Lungen-Maschine** f heart-lung machine; ~**massage** f heart massage; ~**mittel** nt cardiac drug; ~**muschel** f (Zool) cockle; ~**muskel** m heart or cardiac muscle.

Herzog ['hɛrtsoːk] m -s, ːe or (rare) -e duke. **Otto ~ von Stein** Otto Duke of Stein, Duke Otto of Stein.

Herzogin ['hɛrtsoːgɪn] f duchess.

herzoglich ['hɛrtsoːklɪç] adj attr ducal.

Herzogswürde f (Rang) dignity or rank of a duke; (Titel) dukedom. **der König verlieh ihm die ~** the king bestowed a dukedom or the rank of duke upon him.

Herzogtum nt dukedom, duchy.

Herz-: ~**patient** m heart or cardiac patient; ~**rhythmus** m heart or cardiac rhythm; ~**schlag** m (a) (einzelner) heartbeat; **einen ~schlag lang** (liter) for one fleeting second; **mit jedem ~schlag** (liter) with every beat of my/his etc heart; (b) (~tätigkeit) heart or pulse rate; (fig liter) throbbing or pulsating life; (c) (~stillstand) heart attack, heart failure no art, no pl; ~**schmerz** m stabbing pain in the chest; ~**schrittmacher** m pacemaker; ~**schwäche** f cardiac insufficiency no pl (spec); **wegen einer vorübergehenden ~schwäche** because my/his etc heart faltered for a moment; **an ~schwäche leiden** to have a weak heart; h~**stärkend** adj cardiotonic (spec); h~**stärkend wirken** to stimulate the heart; **ein h~stärkendes Mittel** a cardiac stimulant, a cardiotonic (spec); ~**stich** m usu pl stabbing pain in the chest; ~**stillstand** m cardiac arrest; ~**stolpern** nt irregular heartbeat; ~**stück** nt (fig geh) heart, core; ~**tätigkeit** f heart or cardiac activity; ~**tod** m death from heart disease.

herzu- siehe herbei-.

Herzug m (inf) **(a)** (Rail) downtrain. **(b)** (Umzug) **seit meinem ~** since I came here, since coming here.

Herz-: ~**verfettung** f fatty degeneration of the heart; h~**zerreißend** adj heartbreaking, heart-rending; h~**zerreißend weinen** to weep distressingly.

Hesekiel [he'zeːkieːl, -iɛl] m - Ezekiel.

Hesse m -n, -n, **Hessin** f Hessian.

Hessen nt -s Hesse.

hessisch adj Hessian.

Hetäre f -, -n (Hist) hetaira; (fig geh: Dirne) courtesan.

hetero adj pred (inf) hetero (inf), straight (sl).

Hetero-: h~**dox** adj heterodox; ~**doxie** f heterodoxy; h~**gen** adj (geh) heterogeneous; ~**genität** f (geh) heterogeneity; h~**nom** adj (geh) heteronomous; ~**nomie** f (geh) heteronomy; ~**sexualität** f heterosexuality; h~**sexuell** adj heterosexual.

Hethiter(in f) m -s, - Hittite.

hethitisch adj Hittite.

Hetz f -, (rare) -en (Aus inf) laugh (inf). **aus** or **zur ~** for a laugh.

Hetz- (pej) in cpds rabble-rousing (pej).

Hetze f -, -n (a) (Hunt) siehe **Hetzjagd. (b)** no pl (Hast) (mad) rush, hurry; (Getriebensein) hustle and bustle, (mad) rush. **(c)** no pl (pej) (Aufreizung) rabble-rousing propaganda.

hetzen 1 vt (a) (lit, fig: jagen) to hound. **die Hunde auf jdn/etw ~** to set the dogs on(to) sb/sth; siehe **Hund, gehetzt.** **(b)** (inf: antreiben) to rush, to hurry.

2 vr to hurry oneself, to rush oneself.

3 vi **(a)** (sich beeilen) to rush. **hetz nicht so** don't be in such a rush.

(b) aux sein (eilen) to tear, to race, to dash. **ich bin ganz schön gehetzt, um** ... I rushed like mad to ... (inf), I had an awful rush to ...; **hetz nicht so** don't go so fast.

(c) (pej: Haß schüren) to agitate, to stir up hatred; (inf: lästern) to say malicious things. **gegen jdn/etw ~** to agitate against or stir up hatred against sb/sth; **er hetzt immer gegen seinen Onkel** he's always running his uncle down or saying malicious things about his uncle; **sie hat so lange gehetzt, bis er** ... she kept on being nasty until he finally ...; **zum Krieg ~** to agitate for war; **gegen Minderheiten ~** to stir up hatred against minorities; **bei jdm gegen jdn ~** to try to turn or set sb against sb.

Hetzer(in f) m -s, - rabble-rouser, malicious agitator.

Hetzerei f **(a)** no pl (Hast) siehe **Hetze (b). (b)** (das Haß-schüren) rabble-rousing, malicious agitation, mischief-making. **politische ~** political agitation or mischief-making; ~ **zum Krieg** warmongering. **(c)** (hetzerische Äußerung) rabble-rousing attack (gegen on).

hetzerisch adj rabble-rousing attr, virulent.

Hetz-: h~**halber** adv (Aus inf) for a laugh (inf); ~**hund** m hound, hunting dog; ~**jagd** f (a) (lit, fig) hounding (auf + acc of); (b) (fig: Hast) rush, hurry; **es war die reinste ~jagd** it was one mad rush; **die ~jagd der Kinder durch den Garten** the children tearing or racing through the garden.

Hetzkampagne f malicious campaign.

Heu nt -(e)s, no pl (a) hay. **Geld wie ~ haben** (inf) to have pots or oodles of money (inf). **(b)** (sl: Marihuana) grass (sl).

Heu-: ~**boden** m, ~**bühne** (Sw) f hayloft; ~**bündel** nt bundle or bale of hay.

Heuchelei f hypocrisy. **spar dir deine ~en** cut out the hypocrisy or cant.

heucheln 1 vi to be a or play the hypocrite. **2** vt Zuneigung, Mitleid etc to feign, to simulate.

Heuchler(in f) m -s, - hypocrite.

heuchlerisch adj hypocritical. ~**es Gerede** hypocritical talk, cant.

heuen vi (dial) to make hay. **das H~** haymaking.

heuer adv (S Ger, Aus, Sw) this year.

Heuer f -, -n (Naut) pay.

Heuer-: ~**büro** nt (seamen's) employment office; ~**lohn** m siehe Heuer.

heuern vt to sign on, to engage, to hire.

Heu|ernte f hay harvest; (Ertrag) hay crop.

Heue(r)t m -s, -e, **Heuet** f -, -e (S Ger, Sw) siehe Heumonat.

Heuervertrag m contract of employment (of seaman).

Heu-: ~**fieber** nt siehe ~**schnupfen**; ~**forke** (N Ger), ~**gabel** f pitchfork, hayfork; ~**haufen** m haystack, hayrick.

Heulboje f (Naut) whistling buoy; (pej inf: Popsinger) groaner (inf); (Kind) wailing Willie (sl).

heulen vi **(a)** (inf: weinen) to howl, to bawl (inf), to wail; (vor Schmerz) to scream; (vor Wut) to howl. **ich hätte ~ können** I could have cried; **es ist einfach zum H~** it's enough to make you weep; siehe **Elend. (b)** (Meer, Flugzeug, Motor) to roar; (Wind auch, Tiere) to howl; (Sirene) to wail.

Heulen nt -s, no pl siehe vi **(a)** howling, bawling, wailing. ~ **und Zähneklappern** (Bibl) wailing and gnashing of teeth. **(b)** roaring; howling; wailing.

Heuler m -s, - **(a)** (von Motor) roar. **(b)** (Feuerwerkskörper) screamer. **(c)** (sl) **das ist ja der letzte ~** that's bloody incredible (sl).

Heulerei f (inf) constant bawling (inf) or blubbering (inf).

Heul-: (inf) ~**krampf** m fit of blubbering (inf); ~**peter** m, ~**suse** f cry-baby (inf); ~**ton** m (von Sirene) wail.

Heu-: ~**machen** nt -s, no pl, ~**mahd** f haymaking; ~**mond** (old liter), ~**monat** (old) m July; ~**ochs(e)** m (inf) oaf, dolt; ~**pferd** nt siehe ~**schrecke**; ~**reiter**, ~**reuter** m rickstand.

heurig adj attr (S Ger, Aus) this year's. **der ~e Wein** this year's wine.

Heurige pl decl as adj (esp Aus) early potatoes pl.

Heurige(r) m decl as adj (esp Aus) new wine.

Heuristik f (Philos) heuristics sing.

heuristisch adj (Philos) heuristic.

Heu-: ~**schnupfen** m hay fever; ~**schober** m barn; ~**schrecke** f -, -n grasshopper; (in heißen Ländern) locust; ~**speicher**, ~**stadel** m (S Ger, Aus, Sw) barn.

heute, heut (inf) adv **(a)** (an diesem Tag) today. ~ **morgen/abend** this morning/this evening or tonight; ~ **früh** this morning; ~ **nacht** tonight; „~ **geschlossen"** "closed today"; ~ **noch** (heutzutage) still ... today, even today; **ich muß ~ noch zur Bank** I must go to the bank today; **bis ~** (bisher, heute immer noch) to this day; **bis ~ nicht** (noch nicht) not ... to this day; **von ~ ab** or **an, ab ~** from today (on), from this day (forth) (liter); ~ **in einer Woche** a week today or from now, today week; ~ **vor acht Tagen** a week ago today; ~ **in einem Jahr** or **über ein Jahr** (dial) a year from today or now, a year hence (geh); **Milch/die Zeitung von ~** today's milk/paper; ~ **mir, morgen dir** (Prov) (it's my turn today,) your turn may come tomorrow; **lieber ~ als morgen** the sooner the better; **etw von ~ auf morgen verschieben** to put sth off until tomorrow; **von ~ auf morgen** (fig: rasch, plötzlich) overnight, from one day to the next.

(b) (in der gegenwärtigen Zeit) nowadays, these days, today. **das H~** the present, today; **das Italien/der Mensch von ~** present-day or contemporary or modern Italy/man; **der Bauer/die Frau/die Stadt von ~** the farmer/woman/town of today, today's farmers/women/towns; **die Jugend von ~** the young people of today, modern youth.

heutig adj attr today's; (von heute auch) the day's; (gegenwärtig) modern, contemporary. der ~e Tag today; am ~en Abend this evening; anläßlich Ihres ~en Geburtstags to mark your birthday today; unser ~es Schreiben (Comm) our letter of today('s date); die ~e Zeitung today's paper; bis zum ~en Tage to date, to this very day; aus ~er Sicht from today's standpoint, from a modern or contemporary point of view; wir H~en (geh) we people of today, we modern men and women.

heutigentags adv (dated) siehe **heute (b)**.

heutzutage adv nowadays, these days, today.

Heu-: ~wagen m haycart, haywagon; ~wender m -s, - tedder.

Hexa- [hɛksa-] in cpds hexa-; ~eder nt -s, - hexahedron; ~gon nt -s, -e hexagon; h~gonal adj hexagonal; ~gramm nt hexagram; ~meter [hɛ'ksa:metɐ] m hexameter.

Hexe f -, -n witch; (inf: altes Weib) old hag or crone. diese kleine ~! that little minx or hussy!

hexen 1 vi to practise witchcraft. er kann ~ he knows (how to work) black magic; ich kann doch nicht ~ (inf) I can't work miracles, I'm not a magician. 2 vt to conjure up. ~, daß ... to cast a (magic) spell so that ...

Hexen-: ~einmaleins nt magic square; ~glaube m belief in witches; ~haus nt enchanted house; ~häuschen nt gingerbread house; ~jagd f witch-hunt; ~kessel m (fig) pandemonium no art, bedlam no art; ein wahrer ~kessel absolute pandemonium or bedlam; ~kunst f witchcraft, sorcery, witchery; ~meister m sorcerer; ~probe f (Hist) witch's ordeal; ~prozeß m witch trial; ~ring m fairy ring; ~ritt m (fig) nightmare journey or trip; ~sabbat m witches' sabbath; (fig) bedlam no art, pandemonium no art; ~schuß m (Med) lumbago; ~verbrennung f burning of a witch/witches; ~verfolgung f witch-hunt; ~wahn m obsessive belief in witches; ~werk nt sorcery, witchcraft, witchery.

Hexer m -s, - sorcerer.

Hexerei f witchcraft no pl, sorcery, witchery no pl; (von Zaubertricks) magic no pl.

HG abbr of **Handelsgesellschaft**.

hg. abbr of **herausgegeben** ed.

Hiatus m -, - hiatus.

Hibiskus m -, **Hibisken** hibiscus.

hick interj hic.

Hickhack m or nt -s, -s squabbling no pl.

hie adv (old) here. ~ und da (manchmal) (every) now and then, every so often, (every) once in a while; (stellenweise) here and there; ~ ... ~ or da on the one side ... on the other (side).

hieb (geh) pret of **hauen**.

Hieb m -(e)s, -e (a) (Schlag) stroke, blow; (Faust~) blow; (Peitschen~) lash, crack; (Fechten) cut. auf den ersten ~ fällt kein Baum (prov) it takes more than one blow to fell a giant; auf einen ~ (inf) in one go; ein Glas auf einen ~ leer trinken (inf) to down a glass in one (inf).
(b) (~wunde) gash, slash. einen ~ haben (inf) to be daft (inf).
(c) ~e pl (dated: Prügel) hiding, thrashing, beating; ~e bekommen to get a hiding or thrashing or beating; gleich gibt es or setzt es ~e! you'll get a (good) hiding in a minute.
(d) (fig) dig, cutting remark. der ~ saß that (dig) went or struck home; ~e bekommen to be on the receiving end of some cutting remarks.

Hieb-: h~fest adj: ~- und stichfest adj (fig) watertight; ~waffe f cutting weapon; ~wunde f gash, slash.

hielt pret of **halten**.

hienieden adv (old liter) here below.

hier adv (a) (räumlich) here; (in diesem Land auch) (here) in this country; (~ am Ort auch) locally. das Haus ~ this house; dieser ~ this one (here); ~! (beim Appell) present!, here!; ~ und da here and there; Herr Direktor ~, Herr Direktor da (iro) yes sir, yes sir, three bags full sir; ~ draußen/drinnen out/in here; ~ entlang along here; ~ herum hereabouts, around here; ~ hinein in here; ~ oben/unten up/down here; ~ vorn/hinten in front at the back here, here in front/at the back; er ist von ~ he's a local (man), he comes from (a)round here; er ist nicht von ~ he's a stranger here, he's not a local; Tag Klaus, ~ (spricht) Hans (Telec) hello Klaus, Hans here; ~ spricht Dr. Müller (Telec) this is Dr Müller (speaking); von ~ ab from here (on or onwards); von ~ aus from here; ~ sehen Sie ... here you (can) see ...; ~ und heute (geh) here and now; das H~ und Heute (geh) the here and now; er ist ein bißchen ~ (sl) he's got a screw loose (inf).
(b) (zeitlich) now. ~ und da (every) now and then, every so often; von ~ ab or an from now on, henceforth (form).
(c) (fig) here. das steht mir bis ~ (sl) I'm fed up to here (inf) or to the back teeth (inf) (with it), I've had it up to here (inf); ~ versagte ihm die Stimme here or at this point or at this juncture his voice failed him.

hieran adv (a) (lit) here. (b) (fig) wenn ich ~ denke when I think of or about this; er erinnert sich ~ he remembers this; ~ erkenne ich es I recognize it by this; ~ kann es keinen Zweifel geben there can be no doubt about that.

Hierarchie f hierarchy.

hierarchisch adj hierarchic(al).

hier-: ~auf adv (a) (lit) on (here, on this; (b) (fig) on this; (daraufhin) hereupon; er setzte sich, und ~auf ... he sat down and then ...; ~aufhin adv hereupon; und ~aufhin ... and then ...; ~aus adv (a) (lit) out of/from this, from here; ~aus ist das Geld gestohlen worden the money was stolen from here; (b) (fig) from this; ~aus folgt/geht hervor, daß ... from this it follows that ..., hence (it follows that) ...; ~behalten vt sep irreg jdn/etw ~behalten to keep sb/sth here; ~bei adv (a) (lit) (währenddessen) doing this; (b) (fig) (bei dieser Gelegenheit) on this occasion; (in diesem Zusammenhang) in this connection; ~bleiben vi sep irreg aux sein to stay here; ~geblieben! stop!;

~durch adv (a) (lit) through here; (b) (fig) through this; ich lasse mich ~durch nicht ärgern I shan't let this annoy me; ~durch teilen wir Ihnen mit, daß ... we hereby inform you that ...; ~ein adv (a) (lit) in(to) this, in here; (b) (fig) in/to this; ~ein mußt du dich fügen you will just have to get used to the idea; ~für adv for this; ~gegen adv (lit, fig) against this; ~her adv here; (komm) ~her! come here or hither (liter, old); bis ~her (örtlich) up to here; (zeitlich) up to now, so far; mir steht's bis ~her (sl) I'm fed up to here or to the back teeth (inf); siehe bis[2]; ~herauf adv up here; bis ~herauf up to here.

hierher-: ~bemühen* sep 1 vt to ask or trouble to come (here); 2 vr to take the trouble to come (here); ~bitten vt sep irreg to ask to come (here); ~blicken vi sep to look this way or over here; ~bringen vt sep irreg to bring (over) here; ~fahren sep irreg 1 vi aux sein to come here; 2 vt etw to drive here; jdn to drive (here), to give a lift or ride (here); ~führen sep 1 vt to lead here; 2 vi (Weg etc) to lead here, to come this way; ~gehören* vi sep to belong here; (fig: relevant sein) to be relevant; ~gehörende Bemerkungen irrelevant remarks; ~holen vt sep to bring here; ~kommen vi sep irreg aux sein to come here; ~laufen vi sep irreg aux sein to run here; ~gelaufen kommen to come running up; ~legen sep 1 vt to lay (down) here; 2 vr to lie (down) here, to lay oneself (down) here; ~locken vt sep to entice or lure here; ~schaffen vt sep to bring here; ~schicken vt sep to send here; ~setzen sep 1 vt to put here; 2 vr to sit (down) here; ~stellen sep 1 vt to put here; 2 vr to stand here; ~tragen vt sep irreg to carry here.

hierherum adv around or round (esp Brit) here; (in diese Richtung) this way around; (inf: ungefähr hier) hereabouts, around here (somewhere).

hierher-: ~wagen vr sep to dare to come here; ~ziehen sep irreg 1 vt (fig) to bring here; 2 vi aux sein to come here.

hier-: ~hin adv here; ~hin und dorthin here and there, hither and thither (liter); bis ~hin up to here; ~hinab adv down here; ~hinauf adv up here; ~hinaus adv out here; ~hinein adv in here; ~hinter adv behind here; ~hinunter adv down here; ~in adv (lit, fig) in this; ~lassen vt sep irreg to leave here; ~mit adv with this, herewith (obs, form); ~mit ist der Fall erledigt this settles the matter; ~mit bin ich einverstanden I agree to this; ~mit erkläre ich ... (form) I hereby declare ... (form); ~mit bestätigen wir den Eingang Ihres Briefes we herewith or hereby acknowledge receipt of your letter; ~mit wird bescheinigt, daß ... this is to certify that ...; ~nach adv after this, afterwards; (daraus folgend) according to this; ~neben adv beside this, next to this.

Hieroglyphe [hiero'gly:fə] f -, -n hieroglyph(ic); (fig hum) hieroglyphic.

hier-: ~orts adv (geh) here; ~sein vi sep irreg aux sein (Zusammenschreibung nur bei infin und ptp) to be here; während meines H~seins during my stay; was ist der Zweck seines H~seins? what is the purpose of his being here or his presence?; ~selbst adv (old) in this very place, even here (old); ~über adv (a) (lit) over this or here; (oberhalb dieser Stelle) over it; (b) (fig) about this; (geh: währenddessen) in the midst of it (geh); ~über habe ich noch nicht nachgedacht I've never thought about it before; ~über ärgere ich mich this makes me angry; ~um adv (a) (lit) (a)round this or here; (b) (fig) about or concerning this; ~um handelt es sich nicht this isn't the issue; ~unter adv (a) (lit) under or beneath this or here; (b) (fig) by this or that; (in dieser Kategorie) among these; ~unter fallen auch die Sonntage this includes Sundays; ~von adv (a) (lit) (örtlich) from here or this; (von diesem etc) from this; (aus diesem Material) out of this; (b) ~von habe ich nichts gewußt I knew nothing of or about this; ~von abgesehen apart from this; ~von kannst du nichts haben you can't have any of this; ~vor adv (a) (lit) in front of this or here; (b) (fig) ~vor ekele/fürchte ich mich it revolts/frightens me; ~vor möge uns Gott bewahren may God preserve us from this; ~vor hat er großen Respekt he has a great respect for this; ~wider adv (old) siehe ~gegen; ~zu adv (a) (dafür) for this; (dazu) with this; (b) (außerdem) in addition to this, moreover; (c) (zu diesem Punkt) about this; ~zu gehören auch die Katzen this also includes the cat(s); ~zu habe ich etwas Wichtiges zu sagen I have something important to say on or about this; ~zu wünsche ich Ihnen viel Glück I wish you luck in this; vgl. ~zu S. 370 cf p 370; ~zulande adv in this country, in these parts, (over) here; ~zwischen adv between these.

hiesig adj attr local. die ~en Verhältnisse local conditions, conditions here; meine ~en Verwandten my relatives here; er ist kein H~er he is not a local (man), he's not from these parts.

hieß pret of **heißen**.

hieven ['hi:fn, 'hi:vn] vt (esp Naut) to heave.

Hi-Fi-Anlage ['haifi-] f hi-fi set or system.

Hifthorn nt (Hunt) hunting horn.

high [hai] adj pred (sl) high (sl).

highjacken ['haidʒɛkn] vt insep (inf) to hi(gh)jack.

Highjacker ['haidʒɛkɐ] m -s, - siehe **Hijacker**.

Highlife ['hailaif] nt -s, no pl high life. ~ machen (inf) to live it up (inf).

hihi interj hehe, teehee.

Hijacker ['haidʒɛkɐ] m -s, - hi(gh)jacker.

hilb adj (Sw) sheltered, protected from the wind.

hilf imper sing of **helfen**.

Hilfe f -, -n (a) no pl help; (finanzielle) aid, assistance, help; (für Notleidende) aid, relief. zu ~! help!; um ~ rufen/schreien to call/shout for help; jdm zu ~ kommen to come to sb's aid or assistance or rescue; jdn um ~ bitten to ask sb for help or assistance; jdm ~ leisten to help sb; bei jdm ~ suchen to seek sb's help or assistance; mit ~ with the help or aid (gen of); ohne ~ without help or assistance; (selbständig) unaided; etw zu ~

nehmen to use sth; **ohne fremde ~ gehen** to walk unaided; **jds Gedächtnis** (*dat*) **zu ~ kommen** to jog sb's memory; *siehe* **erste(r, s)**.

(b) (*Hilfsmittel, Hilfsstellung*) aid; (*Haushalts~*) (domestic) help. **~n geben** (*beim Turnen*) to give support; (*beim Reiten*) to give aids; **du bist mir eine schöne ~!** (*iro*) a fine help you are (to me)! (*iro*).

Hilfe-: **h~bringend** *adj attr* **endlich kam der h~bringende Regen/kamen die h~bringenden Nachschublieferungen** at last came aid *or* help *or* relief in the shape of the long-awaited rain/supplies; **~ersuchen** *nt* request for help; **h~flehend** *adj* imploring, beseeching; **~leistung** *f* aid, assistance; **unterlassene ~leistung** (*Jur*) denial of assistance; **~ruf** *m* call for help; **~schrei** *m* cry *or* shout for help, cry of "help"; **~stellung** *f* (*Sport, fig*) support; **jdm ~stellung geben** to give sb support; (*fig auch*) to back sb up; **h~suchend** *adj* **Mensch** seeking help; **Blick** imploring, beseeching; **täglich wenden sich Hunderte h~suchend an diese Organisation** hundreds turn every day to this charity seeking help; **die ~suchenden** those seeking help.

Hilf-: **h~los** *adj* helpless; (*schutzlos auch*) defenceless; (*ratlos auch*) clueless (*inf*); **~losigkeit** *f siehe adj* helplessness; defenceless; cluelessness (*inf*); **h~reich** *adj* helpful; (*nützlich auch*) useful; **eine ~reiche Hand** a helping hand; **er streckte ihr h~reich seine Hand** he held out a helping hand to her.

Hilfs-: **~aktion** *f* relief action; **~arbeiter** *m* labourer; (*in Fabrik*) unskilled worker; **~assistent** *m* (*Univ*) - tutorial assistant; **h~bedürftig** *adj* in need of help; (*notleidend*) needy, in need *pred*; **die ~bedürftigen** the needy, those in need; **~bedürftigkeit** *f* need(iness); **h~bereit** *adj* helpful, ready to help *pred*; **~bereitschaft** *f* helpfulness, readiness to help; **~bremser** *m* -s, - (*Univ hum*) - tutorial assistant; **~dienst** *m* emergency service; (*bei Katastrophenfall*) (emergency) relief service; (*Kfz~*) emergency *or* (emergency) breakdown service; **~feuerwehr** *f* auxiliary fire service; **~fonds** *m* relief fund; **~geistlicher** *m* curate; **~gelder** *pl* back-up funds *pl*; **~komitee** *nt* relief action committee; **~konstruktion** *f* (*Math*) rough diagram; (*fig*) temporary measure; **~kraft** *f* assistant helper; (*Aushilfe*) temporary worker; **wissenschaftliche/fachliche ~kraft** research/technical assistant; **~kreuzer** *m* (*Mil*) auxiliary cruiser; **~lehrer** *m* supply teacher; **~linie** *f* (*Math*) auxiliary line; **~maßnahme** *f* relief action *no pl*; (*zur Rettung*) rescue action *no pl*; **~mittel** *nt* aid; **~motor** *m* (*Aut*) auxiliary engine; **Fahrrad mit ~motor** moped, motor-assisted bicycle; **~organisation** *f* relief organization; **~personal** *nt* auxiliary staff; (*Aushilfspersonal*) temporary staff *or* help; **~polizei** *f* auxiliary police; **~polizist** *m* auxiliary policeman; **~prediger**, **~priester** *m* curate; **~programm** *nt* relief *or* aid programme; **~quelle** *f* (*a*) (*Geldquelle*) source of money, pecuniary *or* financial (re)sources *pl*; (*b*) (*für wissenschaftliche Arbeit*) source; **~ruder** *nt* (*Aviat*) auxiliary rudder; **~schiff** *nt* auxiliary vessel; **~schule** *f* (*dated*) school for backward children; **~schüler** *m* (*dated*) pupil at/from a school for backward children; **~schullehrer** *m* (*dated*) teacher at a school for backward children; **~schwester** *f* auxiliary (nurse); **~sheriff** *m* assistant *or* deputy sheriff; **~sprache** *f* auxiliary language; **~trupp** *m* group of helpers; **~truppe** *f* (*Mil*) auxiliary troops *pl*; (*Verstärkung*) reinforcements *pl*; (*Pol pej*) back-up army *or* boys *pl*; **~verb** *nt* auxiliary verb; **~werk** *nt* relief organization; **h~willig** *adj* willing to help *pred*; **~willige(r)** *mf decl as adj* voluntary helper; **~wissenschaft** *f* (*gen* to) complementary science; (*Geisteswissenschaft*) complementary subject; **~zeitwort** *nt siehe* **~verb**.

Himalaja *m* -(s) **der ~** the Himalayas *pl*.

Himbeere *f* raspberry.

Himbeer-: **~eis** *nt* raspberry ice(-cream); **~geist** *m, no pl* (white) raspberry brandy; **h~rot** *adj* raspberry-coloured; **~saft** *m* raspberry juice; **~strauch** *m* raspberry bush.

Himmel *m* -s, (*poet*) - (*a*) sky. **am ~** in the sky; **unter dem ~ Spaniens, unter spanischem ~** under *or* beneath a Spanish sky; **zwischen ~ und Erde** in midair; **~ und Menschen** (*dial*) all the world and his brother (*inf*); **in den ~ ragen** to tower (up) into the sky; **jdn/etw in den ~ (er)heben** *or* **loben** *or* **rühmen** to praise sb/sth to the skies; **jdm hängt der ~ voller Geigen** everything in the garden is lovely for sb; **gute Lehrer fallen nicht vom ~** good teachers don't grow on trees; **der Frieden fällt nicht einfach vom ~, sondern ...** peace doesn't just fall out of the blue, but ...; **eher stürzt der ~ ein, als daß ...** (*geh*) the skies will fall before ... (*liter*).

(b) (*Rel: ~reich*) heaven. **im ~** in heaven; **den Blick gen ~ richten** (*liter*) to look heavenward(s), to raise one's eyes towards heaven; **in den ~ kommen** to go to heaven; **zum ~ in den ~ auffahren, gen ~ fahren** to ascend into heaven; **der Sohn des ~s** (*Kaiser von China*) the Celestial Emperor; **der ~ auf Erden** heaven on earth; **dem ~ sei Dank** (*old*) thank God *or* Heaven(s); **der ~ ist** *or* **sei mein Zeuge** (*old*) as Heaven *or* God is my witness; **(das) weiß der ~!** (*inf*) God *or* Heaven (only) knows; **der ~ bewahre mich davor!** (*old*) may Heaven (*or* God) preserve me; **das schreit zum ~** it's a scandal; **es stinkt zum ~** (*inf*) it stinks to high heaven (*inf*); **der ~ verhüte** (*old*) Heaven *or* God forbid; **Gott im ~, gerechter ~!** (*old*) good Heaven!; **(ach) du lieber ~!** (*inf*) good Heavens!, good(ness) gracious!; **~ (noch mal)!** (*inf*) good God!, hang it all! (*inf*); **um(s) ~s willen** (*inf*) for Heaven's *or* goodness's sake (*inf*); **~, Herrgott, Sack!** (*inf*) damn and blast! (*inf*), hell's bells! (*inf*); **~, Arsch und Zwirn** (*sl*) *or* **Wolkenbruch** (*sl*) bloody hell! (*Brit sl*), Christ Almighty! (*sl*).

(c) (*Bett~ etc*) canopy; (*im Auto*) roof.

Himmel-: **h~an** *adv* (*poet*) heavenward(s); **h~angst** *adj pred* **mir wurde h~angst** I was scared to death; **~bett** *nt* four-poster

(bed); **h~blau** *adj* sky-blue, azure (*liter*); **~donnerwetter** *interj* (*sl*) damn it (*sl*); **~donnerwetter noch (ein)mal!** damn and blast it! (*sl*).

Himmelfahrt *f* (*a*) (*Rel*) **Christi ~** the Ascension of Christ; **Mariä ~** the Assumption of the Virgin Mary. (*b*) (*no art: Feiertag*) Ascension Day.

Himmelfahrts-: **~kommando** *nt* (*Mil inf*) suicide squad *or* (*Unternehmen*) mission; **~nase** *f* (*hum inf*) turned-up *or* snub nose; **~tag** *m der/am ~tag** Ascension Day/on Ascension Day.

Himmel-: **~herrgott** *interj* (*sl*) (*sl*), bloody hell (*Brit sl*); **~herrgott noch (ein)mal!** damn and blast! (*sl*); **~herrgottsakra** *interj* (*S Ger, Aus*) damn (it) (*sl*), bloody hell (*Brit sl*); **h~hoch** 1 *adj* sky-high; 2 *adv* **high into the sky**; **h~hoch jauchzend, zu Tode betrübt** up one minute and down the next; **~hund** *m* (*pej*) scoundrel, cur (*pej*); (*inf: Draufgänger*) clever bastard (*sl*); **~reich** *nt, no pl* (*Rel*) Kingdom of Heaven; **ins ~reich eingehen** *or* **kommen** to enter the Kingdom of Heaven; **ein ~reich für ...** I'd give anything *or* my right arm for ...

Himmels-: **~achse** *f* celestial axis; **~äquator** *m* celestial equator, equinoctial line *or* circle; **~bahn** *f* (*liter*) celestial path *or* orbit; **~braut** *f* (*liter*) bride of Christ (*liter*).

Himmel-: **~schlüssel** *m or nt siehe* **Himmelsschlüssel;** **h~schreiend** *adj* **Unrecht** outrageous, scandalous; **Unkenntnis, Verhältnisse** appalling; **Unsinn** utter *attr*; **Schande** crying *attr*.

Himmels-: **~erscheinung** *f* celestial phenomenon; **~feste** *f* (*liter*) firmament (*liter*); **~fürst** *m* (*Rel, liter*) King of Heaven; **~gabe** *f* (*geh*) gift from heaven; **~gegend** *f siehe* **~richtung;** **~gewölbe** *nt* (*liter*) vault of heaven (*liter*), firmament (*liter*); **~karte** *f* star map *or* chart; **~königin** *f* (*Rel*) Queen of Heaven; **~körper** *m* heavenly *or* celestial body; **~kugel** *f* (*liter*) celestial globe (*liter*) *or* sphere (*liter*); **~kunde** *f* astronomy; **~kuppel** *f* (*liter*) *siehe* **~gewölbe;** **~labor** *nt* (*Space*) space lab(oratory); **~leiter** *f* (*Bot*) Jacob's Ladder; **~macht** *f:* **die Liebe ist eine ~macht** love is a power of heaven; **~pforte** *f* (*liter*) gate of heaven; **~pol** *m* celestial pole; **~richtung** *f* direction; **die vier ~richtungen** the four points of the compass; **~schlüssel** *m or nt* (*Bot*) cowslip; **~schrift** *f* skywriting; **~spion** *m* (*inf*) spy satellite; **~strich** *m* (*liter*) area, region, clime (*liter*); **unter diesem ~strich** in these parts; **~stürmer** *m* (*liter*) (romantic) idealist; **~tor** *nt*, **~tür** *f* (*geh*) *siehe* **~pforte**.

himmelstürmend *adj attr* (*liter*) boundless.

Himmels-: **~wagen** *m* (*Astron*) Great Bear; **~zeichen** *nt siehe* **Tierkreiszeichen;** **~zelt** *nt* (*poet*) canopy of heaven (*poet*), firmament (*liter*); **~ziege** *f* (*inf*) church mouse (*inf*).

himmel-: **~wärts** *adv* (*liter*) heavenward(s); **~weit** *adj* (*fig inf*) tremendous, fantastic (*inf*); **zwischen uns besteht ein ~weiter Unterschied** there's a world of difference between us; **~weit voneinander entfernt, ~weit verschieden** (*fig*) poles apart; **wir sind noch ~weit davon entfernt** we're still nowhere near it.

himmlisch *adj* (*a*) *attr* (*göttlich*) heavenly, celestial (*liter*). **eine ~e Fügung** divine providence; **der ~e Vater** our Heavenly Father; **die H~en** (*old poet*) the gods; **das ~e Jerusalem** the new Jerusalem.

(b) (*fig*) (*wunderbar*) heavenly, divine; (*unerschöpflich*) **Geduld** infinite. **~ bequem** beautifully *or* wonderfully comfortable.

hin *adv* (*a*) (*räumlich*) **bis zum Haus ~** up to the house, as far as the house; **geh doch ~ zu ihr!** go to her; (*besuche sie auch*) go and see her; **nach Süden/Stuttgart ~** towards the south/Stuttgart; **über die ganze Welt ~** all over the world, throughout the world; **die Wüste erstreckt sich über 2000 km ~** the desert stretches for 2000 km; **nach außen ~** (*fig*) outwardly; **das Boot glitt über die Wellen ~** the boat glided along over the waves; **~ fahre ich mit dem Zug, zurück ...** on the way out I'll take the train, coming back ...; **die Fähre geht heute abend nur noch (zur Insel) ~** the ferry's only making the outward trip *or* is only going out (to the island) this evening; **das Boot bringt Sie zur Insel ~** the boat will take you across to the island; **zur anderen Seite ~ sind es 2 km** it's 2 kms to the other side; **bis zu diesem Punkt ~** up to this point; **die Straße verläuft nach rechts ~** the road goes off to the right; **dreht euch/seht mal alle zur Tafel ~** face the/look at the blackboard.

(b) (*als Teil eines Wortpaares*) **~ und her** (*räumlich*) to and fro, back and forth; (*~ und zurück*) there and back; **etw ~ und her überlegen/diskutieren** to think about sth a lot/to discuss sth over and over *or* a lot; **das H~ und Her** the comings and goings *or* to-ings and fro-ings *pl*; **nach langem H~ und Her** after a lot of to-ings and fro-ings; **das reicht nicht ~ und nicht her** (*inf*) that won't go very far at all, that's nothing like enough (*inf*); **Regen/Feiertag ~, Regen/Feiertag her** rain/holiday *or* no rain/holiday, whether it rains/whether it's a holiday or not; **Mörder/Sohn ~, Mörder/Sohn her** murderer/son or not, I don't care whether he *is* a murderer/his *etc* son; **~ und zurück** there and back; **eine Fahrkarte/einmal London ~ und zurück** a return (ticket), a round trip (*esp US*)/a return *or* round trip (*esp US*) to London; **~ und zurück? — nein, nur ~ bitte** return *or* round trip? — no, just a single please; **der Flug von X nach Y ~ und zurück kostet ...** the return flight *or* round trip from X to Y costs ...; **~ und wieder** (every) now and then, (every) now and again.

(c) (*zeitlich*) **es sind nur noch drei Tage ~** it's only three days (from) now; **bis zu den Ferien sind noch drei Wochen ~** it's (still) three weeks till *or* until the holidays; **noch weit ~** a long way off *or* away; **lange Zeit ~** for a long time, over a long period; **zum Sommer ~** towards summer, as summer draws nearer *or* approaches; **gegen Mittag ~** towards midday; **über die Jahre ~** over the years, as (the) years go by; **die Kälte zog sich bis in den Juni ~** the cold lasted up until (and during) June.

(d) (*fig*) **auf meine Bitte/meinen Vorschlag ~** at my

request/suggestion; **auf meinen Brief/Anruf** ~ on account of my letter/phone-call; **auf die Gefahr** ~, **... zu werden** at the risk of being ...; **auf sein Versprechen/seinen Rat** ~ on the basis of his promise/(up)on his advice; **etw auf etw** (*acc*) ~ **untersuchen/prüfen** to inspect/check sth for sth; **etw auf etw** (*acc*) ~ **planen/anlegen** to plan/design sth with sth in mind; **vor sich** ~ **sprechen** *etc* to talk *etc* to oneself; **vor sich** ~ **stieren** to stare straight ahead *or* into space; **vor sich** ~ **dösen** to doze.

(e) (*inf: als trennbarer Bestandteil von Adverbien*) **da will ich nicht** ~ I don't want to go (there); **wo geht ihr** ~? where are you going?

(f) (*elliptisch*) **nichts wie** ~ (*inf*) let's go (then)!, what are we waiting for? (*inf*); **wo ist es/sie** ~? where has it/she gone?; **ist es weit bis** ~? (*inf*) is it far?; *siehe* **hinein, nach, zu** *etc*.

hinab *adv, pref siehe* **hinunter.**

hinan *adv* (*liter*) upwards.

hinan- *pref siehe* **hinauf-.**

hin|arbeiten *vi sep:* **auf etw** (*acc*) ~ **auf ein Ziel** to work towards sth, to aim at sth; **auf eine Prüfung** to work for sth.

hinauf *adv* up. **den Berg/die Straße** ~ up the mountain/street; **den Fluß** ~ up the river; **die Treppe** ~ up the stairs, upstairs; **dort** ~ up there; **bis** ~ **zu** up to.

hinauf- *pref* up; ~**arbeiten** *vr sep* (*lit, fig*) to work one's way up; ~**begeben*** *vr sep irreg* to go up(stairs); ~**begleiten*** *vt sep* to take up(stairs); ~**bemühen*** *sep* 1 *vt* to trouble to go/come up(stairs); 2 *vr* to be so kind as to go/come up(stairs); ~**bitten** *vt sep irreg* to ask to go/come up(stairs); ~**blicken** *vi sep* to look up; ~**bringen** *vt sep irreg* to bring/take up; ~**fahren** *sep irreg* 1 *vi aux sein* to go up; (*in Auto auch*) to drive up; 2 *vt jdn* to take up; (*in Auto auch*) to drive up; *Aufzug* to take up; ~**fallen** *vi sep irreg aux sein:* **die Treppe** ~**fallen** (*hum*) to fall up the stairs; ~**führen** *vti sep* to lead up; ~**gehen** *vi sep irreg aux sein* to go up; (*Preise, Fieber auch*) to rise; **die Treppe** ~**gehen** to go or walk up the stairs; **einen Berg** ~**gehen** to climb *or* go up a mountain; **mit dem Preis** ~**gehen** to put up the price; ~**gelangen*** *vi sep aux sein* (*geh*) to (manage to) get up; ~**klettern** *vi sep aux sein* to climb up; **auf einen Baum** ~**klettern** to climb up a tree; ~**kommen** *vi sep irreg aux sein* to come up; (*schaffen*) to (manage to) get up; ~**laufen** *vi sep irreg aux sein* to run up; **die Treppe** ~**laufen** to run up the stairs; (*im Haus auch*) to run upstairs; ~**reichen** *sep* 1 *vi* to reach up; 2 *vt* to hand *or* pass up; ~**schauen** *vi sep* to look up; ~**schicken** *vt sep* to send up; ~**schieben** *vt sep irreg* to push up; ~**schrauben** *vt sep* to screw up; (*fig*) *Preise* to put up; *Produktion, Forderungen* to step up; ~**sehen** *vi sep irreg* to look up; ~**setzen** *vt sep* (*fig*) *Preis etc* to raise, to increase, to put up; ~**steigen** *vi sep irreg aux sein* to climb up; ~**tragen** *vt sep irreg* to carry *or* take up; ~**ziehen** *sep irreg* 1 *vt* to pull up; 2 *vi aux sein* to move up; 3 *vr* to pull oneself up; **sich an einem Seil** ~**ziehen** to pull oneself up with a rope.

hinaus *adv* (a) (*räumlich*) out. ~ (**mit dir**)! (get) out!, out you go!; **über** (+*acc*) ~ beyond, over; **aus dem** *or* **zum Fenster** ~ out of the window; **hier/dort** ~ this/that way out; **hinten/vorn** ~ at the back *or* rear/front; **nach hinten/vorn** ~ **wohnen** to live towards *or* facing the back/the front; **zur Straße** ~ facing the street; **durch die Tür** ~ out of *or* out through the door.

(b) (*zeitlich*) **auf Jahre/Monate** ~ for years/months to come; **über 65 Jahre** ~ **arbeiten** to work (on) after *or* beyond *or* past 65; **bis weit über die Siebzig** ~ until well over *or* after *or* past seventy; **wir werden damit über Mittwoch** ~ **beschäftigt sein** we'll be busy with that until after Wednesday.

(c) (*fig*) **über** (+*acc*) ~ over and above; (*über Gehalt, Summe auch*) on top of; **über das Grab** ~ beyond the grave; **darüber** ~ over and above this, on top of this, in addition to this; *siehe* **hinaussein, hinauswollen** *etc*.

hinaus-: ~**befördern*** *vt sep* (*inf*) *jdn* to kick out (*inf*), to chuck out (*inf*) (*aus of*); ~**begeben*** *vr sep irreg* (*geh*) to go out (*aus of*); ~**begleiten*** *vt sep* to see out (*aus of*); ~**beugen** *vr sep* to lean out (*aus of*); **sich zum Fenster** ~**beugen** to lean out of the window; ~**blicken** *vi sep* to look out (*aus of*); **zum Fenster** ~**blicken** to look out of the window; ~**bringen** *vt sep* (*aus of*) *etw* to take/bring out; *jdn* to take out; ~**bugsieren*** *vt sep* (*inf*) *jdn* to steer *or* hustle out (*aus of*); ~**drängen** *sep* 1 *vt* to force out (*aus of*); (*eilig*) to hustle out (*aus of*); (*fig*) to oust (*aus from*), to force out (*aus of*); 2 *vi aux sein* to push *or* force one's way out (*aus of*); ~**dürfen** *vi sep irreg* to be allowed to (go) out (*aus of*); **darf ich** ~? may I go out?; **über einen Punkt nicht** ~**dürfen** not to be allowed (to go) beyond a point; ~**eilen** *vi sep aux sein* (*geh*) to hurry out (*aus of*); **zum Zimmer** ~**eilen** to hurry out of the room; ~**ekeln** *vt sep* (*inf*) to drive out (*aus of*); ~**fahren** *sep irreg* 1 *vi aux sein* (a) **aus etw** ~**fahren** to go out of sth, to leave sth; (*in Fahrzeug auch*) to drive out of sth; (b) (*reisen*) to go out; **aufs Meer** ~**fahren** to sail out across the sea; (c) **über etw** (*acc*) ~**fahren** to go beyond sth; 2 *vt Wagen* to drive out (*aus of*); ~**fallen** *vi sep irreg aux sein* (a) to fall out; (*Licht*) to come out; ~**finden** *vi sep irreg* to find one's *or* the way out (*aus of*); **ich finde schon allein** ~ I can find my own way out, I can see myself out; ~**fliegen** *sep irreg* 1 *vi aux sein* (*aus of*) (a) to fly out; (*inf:* ~**fallen**) to go flying out (*inf*); **über ein Ziel** ~**fliegen** to fly past *or* go flying past a target/destination; (b) (*inf:* ~**geworfen werden**) to get kicked *or* chucked out (*inf*); 2 *vt* to fly out (*aus of*); ~**führen** *sep* 1 *vi* (a) (*nach draußen führen*) to lead out (*aus of*); (b) (*weiter führen als*) **über etw** (*acc*) ~**führen** (*lit, fig*) to go beyond sth; 2 *vt* to lead out (*aus of*); (*Weg, Reise*) to take (*über* +*acc* beyond); ~**gehen** *sep irreg aux sein* 1 *vi* (a) (*nach draußen gehen*) to go out(side); **aus dem Zimmer/auf die Straße** ~**gehen** to go *or* walk out of the room/out onto the street; (b) (*gesandt werden*) to go (out), to be sent out; (c) **auf etw** (*acc*) ~**gehen** (*Tür, Zimmer*) to open onto sth; (*Fenster*) to look (out) onto *or* open onto sth; **das Fenster geht**

nach Osten ~ the window looks *or* faces east; **zu** *or* **nach etw** ~**gehen** (*Straße, Weg*) to go out to; (d) (*fig: überschreiten*) **über etw** (*acc*) ~**gehen** to go beyond sth; **das geht über meine Kräfte** ~ it's too much for me to bear, I (just) can't take any more; **über seine Befugnisse** ~**gehen** to overstep one's authority, to exceed one's powers; **das geht über meine Geduld** ~ that's more than my patience can stand; 2 *vi impers* **wo geht es** ~? where's the way out?; ~**gelangen*** *vi sep aux sein* (*lit geh*) to get out; **über etw** (*acc*) ~**gelangen** (*fig*) to get beyond sth; ~**geleiten*** *vt sep* (*geh*) to show out (*aus of*); ~**graulen** *vt sep* (*inf*) to drive out (*aus of*); ~**greifen** *vi sep irreg* (*fig*) **über etw** (*acc*) ~**greifen** to reach beyond sth; ~**gucken** *vi sep* to look out (*aus of*); **zum Fenster** ~**gucken** to look out of the window; ~**halten** *vt sep irreg* to hold out; **den Kopf zum Fenster** ~**halten** to stick *or* put one's head out of the window; ~**hängen** *vti sep irreg* to hang out; **eine Fahne zum Fenster** ~**hängen** to hang a flag out of the window; ~**heben** *sep irreg* 1 *vt* **etw über etw** (*acc*) ~**heben** to raise *or* lift sth above sth, to put sth on a higher *or* different level to sth; 2 *vr* **sich über jdn/etw** ~**heben** to raise oneself above sb/sth; ~**jagen** *sep* (*aus of*) 1 *vt* (*lit: aus dem Zimmer, nach draußen*) to drive *or* chase out; (*fig: aus dem Haus*) to turn *or* drive out; 2 *vi aux sein* to bolt *or* dive out; ~**katapultieren*** *vt sep* (*Pol sl*) to throw out, to chuck out (*inf*) (*aus of*); ~**klettern** *vi sep aux sein* to climb out (*aus of*); ~**kommen** *vi sep irreg aux sein* (a) to come out(side); **ich bin den ganzen Tag noch nicht** ~**gekommen** I haven't been *or* got out(side) yet today; **er ist so dick, daß er kaum aus der Tür** ~**kommt** he's so fat that he can hardly get out of the door; **zu jdm aufs Land** ~**kommen** to come out to see sb in the country; (b) **über etw** (*acc*) ~**kommen** to go beyond sth; (*fig*) to get beyond sth; (c) (*fig:* ~**laufen**) **das kommt auf dasselbe** *or* **auf eins** *or* **aufs gleiche** ~ it boils *or* comes down to the same thing, it amounts *or* comes to the same thing; ~**komplimentieren*** *vt sep* (*hum*) to usher out (*aus of*); ~**lassen** *vt sep irreg* (*aus of*) to leave out; (~**begleiten**) to show out; ~**laufen** *vi sep irreg aux sein* (*aus of*) (a) (*lit*) to run out; (b) (*fig*) **auf etw** (*acc*) ~**laufen** to amount to sth; **es läuft auf dasselbe** *or* **auf eins** *or* **aufs gleiche** ~ it boils *or* comes down to the same thing, it amounts *or* comes to the same thing; **wo(rauf) soll das** ~**laufen?** how's it all going to end?, what are things coming to?; ~**lehnen** *vr sep* to lean out (*aus of*); **sich zum Fenster** ~**lehnen** to lean out of the window; ~**manövrieren*** *vt sep* **sich/jdn aus etw** ~**manövrieren** to manoeuvre oneself/sb out of sth; ~**müssen** *vi sep irreg* to have to go out (*aus of*); ~**nehmen** *vt sep irreg* to take out (*aus of*); ~**posaunen*** *vt sep* (*inf*) *siehe* **ausposaunen;** ~**ragen** *vi sep aux sein* (a) (*horizontal*) to project, to jut out (*über* +*acc* beyond); (*vertikal*) to tower up (*über* +*acc* above, over); (b) (*fig*) **über jdn/etw** ~**ragen** to tower above sb/sth; ~**reden** *vr sep* (*dial*) *siehe* **herausreden;** ~**reichen** *sep* 1 *vt* to hand *or* pass out (*aus of*); **jdm etw zum Fenster** ~**reichen** to hand *or* pass sb sth out of the window; 2 *vi* (*bis nach draußen reichen*) to reach, to stretch (*bis* as far as); (b) **über etw** (*acc*) ~**reichen** (*lit*) to stretch beyond sth; (*fig*) to go beyond sth; ~**rennen** *vi sep irreg aux sein* to run out (*aus of*); ~**rücken** *sep* 1 *vi aux sein* (*lit*) to move out (*aus of*); **die Soldaten rückten zur Stadt** ~ the soldiers marched *or* moved out of (the) town; 2 *vt* (*lit*) to shift *or* move out(side); (*fig*) to put off, to postpone; ~**schaffen** *vt sep* to take out (*aus of*); ~**schauen** *vi sep siehe* ~**blicken;** ~**scheren** *vr sep* to get out (*aus of*); ~**schicken** *vt sep* to send out (*aus of*); ~**schieben** *vt sep irreg* (a) *Gegenstand* to push out (*aus of*); (b) (*fig*) to put off, to postpone; ~**schießen** *vi sep irreg* (a) **er hat zum Fenster** ~**geschossen** he fired out of the window; (b) *aux sein* (~**rennen**) to shoot *or* dart out (*aus of*); **über das Ziel** ~**schießen** (*fig*) to go too far, to overshoot the mark; ~**schmeißen** *vt sep irreg* (*inf*) to kick *or* chuck out (*inf*) (*aus of*); **H**~**schmiß** *m* -sses, -sse (*inf*) man drohte ihm mit H~**schmiß** (aus der Kneipe) they threatened to kick *or* chuck him out (of the pub); **das war ein regelrechter H**~**schmiß** he was simply kicked *or* chucked out (*inf*); ~**schmuggeln** *vt sep* to smuggle out (*aus of*); ~**schreien** *sep irreg* 1 *vi* to shout out (*aus of*); **zum Fenster** ~**schreien** to shout out of the window; 2 *vt* (*geh*) *Schmerz, Haß* to proclaim (*geh*); ~**schwimmen** *vi sep irreg aux sein* (*aus of, über* +*acc* beyond, past) to swim out; (*Gegenstände*) to float out; ~**sehen** *vi sep irreg siehe* ~**blicken;** ~**sein** *vi sep irreg aux sein* (*Zusammenschreibung nur bei infin und ptp*) (a) (*lit inf:* ~**gegangen sein**) to be out, to have gone out; (b) (*fig: hinter sich haben*) **über etw** (*acc*) ~**sein über Kindereien, Dummheiten** to be past *or* beyond sth; **über Enttäuschungen** to be over sth, to have got over sth; **über ein Alter** to be past sth; ~**setzen** *sep* 1 *vt* to put out(side); **jdn** ~**setzen** (*inf*) to chuck *or* kick sb out (*inf*); 2 *vr* to (go and) sit outside; ~**stehlen** *vr sep irreg* (*geh*) to steal out (*geh*) (*aus of*); ~**steigen** *vi sep irreg aux sein* to climb out (*aus of*); **zum Fenster** ~**steigen** to climb out of the window; ~**stellen** *vt sep* to put *or* take out(side); *Sportler* to send off; **H**~**stellung** *f* (*Sport*) *et* **protestierte gegen seine H**~**stellung** he protested about being sent off; ~**strecken** *vt sep* to stick *or* put out (*aus of*); ~**strömen** *vi sep aux sein* to pour out, to come milling out (*aus of*); ~**stürmen** *vi sep aux sein* to storm out (*aus of*); ~**stürzen** *sep* (*aus of*) 1 *vi aux sein* (a) (~**fallen**) to fall out; (b) (~**eilen**) to rush *or* dash out; 2 *vr* to throw oneself *or* dive out; 3 *vt* to throw out; ~**tragen** *vt sep irreg* (a) to carry out (*aus of*); (b) (*geh*) **etw in alle Welt** ~**tragen** to carry sth into all the world (*liter*), to spread sth throughout the world; (c) (*weiter tragen als*) **über etw** (*acc*) ~**tragen** to carry sth over *or* beyond sth; ~**treiben** *vt sep irreg* to drive out (*aus of*); ~**treten** *vi sep irreg aux sein* to step out(side); **aus dem Haus** ~**treten** to step out of the house; **ins Leben** ~**treten** (*geh*) to go out into the world; ~**trompeten*** *vt sep* (*inf*) *siehe* **ausposaunen;** ~**wachsen** *vi sep irreg aux sein* **über etw** (*acc*) ~**wachsen** (*lit*) to grow taller than sth; (*fig: durch Reifer-*

werden, Fortschritte etc) to outgrow sth; **er wuchs über sich selbst ~** he surpassed himself; **~wagen** vr sep to venture out (aus of); **~weisen** sep irreg 1 vt **jdn ~weisen** to show sb the door, to ask sb to leave; **jdn aus einem Hotel ~weisen** to ask sb to leave a hotel; 2 vi to point out(wards); **über eine Frage/Sache ~weisen** (fig) to reach or point beyond a question/matter; **~werfen** vt sep irreg (aus of) (a) to throw or cast (liter) out; **einen Blick ~werfen** to glance or look out(side), to take a glance or look out(side); **das ist ~geworfenes Geld** it's money down the drain; **Geld zum Fenster ~werfen** to throw money out of the window or down the drain; **(b)** (inf) (entfernen) to chuck or kick out (inf); **~wollen** vi sep to want to go or get out (aus of); **worauf willst du ~?** (fig) what are you getting or driving at?; **hoch ~wollen** to aim high, to set one's sights high; **~ziehen** sep irreg 1 vt (a) (nach draußen ziehen) to pull out (aus of); **(b)** (fig) Verhandlungen etc to protract, to drag out; **Urlaub etc** to prolong; 2 vi aux sein to go out (aus of); **in die Welt ~ziehen** to go out into the world; **aufs Land/vor die Stadt ~ziehen** to move out into the country/out of town; **den Dampf/Rauch ~ziehen lassen** to let the steam/smoke out; 3 vr (Verhandlungen etc) to drag on; (Abfahrt etc) to be delayed, to be put off; 4 vt impers **es zog ihn ~ in die weite Welt** he felt the urge to be off into the big wide world; **mich zieht's wieder ~ in die Ferne** I've an urge to be off and away; **bei diesem schönen Wetter zieht's mich ~** I want to be out-of-doors with the weather like this; **~zögern** sep 1 vt to delay, to put off; 2 vr to be delayed, to be put off; **H~zögerung** f delaying, putting off.

hin-: **~begeben*** vr sep irreg sich zu jdm **~begeben** (form) to go to sb, to betake oneself to sb (old, form); **~bekommen*** vt sep irreg (inf) to manage; **das hast du gut ~bekommen** you've made a good job of it, you've managed it very well; **~bemühen*** sep 1 vt jdn **~bemühen** to trouble sb to go, to give sb the trouble of going; 2 vr to take the trouble to go; **~beordern*** vt sep to summon, to send for; **~bestellen*** vt sep to tell to go/come; **~biegen** vr sep irreg (fig inf) (a) etw to arrange, to sort out; **das or die Sache werden wir schon ~biegen** we'll sort it out or arrange matters somehow; **(b)** jdn to lick into shape (inf); **~blättern** vt sep (inf) to fork or shell out (inf), to cough up (inf); **H~blick** m: **im or in H~blick auf** (+acc) (angesichts) in view of; (mit Bezug auf) with regard to; **im H~blick darauf, daß ...** in view of the fact that ...; **~blicken** vi sep to look or glance (auf +acc, nach at, towards); **~brauchen** vi sep irreg (inf) to need to go; **~breiten** sep 1 vt to spread out; 2 vr to stretch out; **~bringen** vt sep irreg (a) etw to take there; (begleiten) jdn to take there; (in Auto auch) to drive there; **(b)** (fig) Zeit to spend, to pass; (in Muße) to idle or while away; **sein Leben kümmerlich ~bringen** to eke out an existence; **(c)** (fig inf: zustande bringen) to get done; **es ~bringen, etw zu tun** to manage to do ...

Hinde f -, -n (old, liter) siehe **Hindin**.

hin-: **~deichseln** vt sep (inf) etw to arrange, to sort out; **~denken** vi sep irreg **wo denkst du ~?** whatever are you thinking of!

hinderlich adj **~ sein** to be in the way, to be a nuisance; (Kleidungsstück auch) to be restricting; **ein ~er Gipsverband** a restricting plaster cast, a plaster cast that gets in the way or is a nuisance; **jds Fortkommen** (dat) **~ sein** (Gebrechen, Vorurteil etc) to be a hindrance or obstacle to sb's advancement, to get in the way of sb's advancement; **eher ~ als nützlich sein** to be more of a hindrance than a help; **sich ~ auswirken** to prove to be a hindrance; **jdm ~ sein** to get in sb's way.

hindern 1 vt (a) Fortschritte, Wachstum to impede, to hamper; jdn to hinder (bei in).

(b) (abhalten von) to prevent (an +dat from), to stop. **ja bitte, ich will Sie nicht ~** please do, I shan't stand in your way; **machen Sie, was Sie wollen, ich kann Sie nicht ~** do what you like, I can't stop or prevent you; **was hindert dich, hinzugehen?** what prevents or keeps you from going (there)?, what stops you going (there)?

2 vi (stören) to be a hindrance (bei to).

Hindernis nt (a) (lit, fig) obstacle; (Erschwernis, Behinderung) hindrance; (beim Sprechen) handicap, impediment. **sie empfand das Kind als ~/als ~ für ihre Karriere** she saw the child as a hindrance/as a hindrance to or an obstacle for her career; **gesetzliches ~** (form) legal impediment or obstacle; **jdm ~se in den Weg legen** (fig) to put obstacles in sb's path or way; **eine Reise mit ~sen** a journey full of hitches.

(b) (Sport) (beim ~lauf, auf Parcours) jump; (Hürde auch) hurdle; (beim Pferderennen auch) fence; (Golf) hazard.

Hindernis-: **~lauf** m steeplechase (in athletics); **~läufer** m steeplechaser (in athletics); **~rennen** nt steeplechase.

Hinderung f (a) siehe **Behinderung. ohne ~** without let or hindrance (Jur). **(b)** (Störung) obstruction.

Hinderungsgrund m obstacle. **etw als ~ angeben** to give sth as an excuse.

hindeuten vi sep to point (auf +acc, zu at). **es deutet alles darauf hin, daß ...** everything indicates that or points to the fact that ...

Hindi nt - Hindi.

Hindin f (old, liter) hind.

hin-: **~drängen** sep 1 vt jdn zum Ausgang etc **~drängen** to push sb towards the exit etc; 2 vr sich zu etw **~drängen** to push one's way towards sth; 3 vi zum Ausgang **~drängen** to push one's way towards the exit etc; **auf eine Änderung ~drängen** to agitate for a change; **alles in ihrem Innern drängte zum Künstlerberuf ~** everything within her urged her towards an artistic profession; **~drehen** vt sep (fig inf) siehe **~deichseln**.

Hindu m -(s), -(s) Hindu.

Hinduismus m Hinduism.

hinduistisch adj Hindu.

hindurch adv (a) (räumlich) through. **dort ~** through there; **mitten ~** straight through; **quer ~** straight across; **durch den Wald ~** through the wood.

(b) (zeitlich) through(out). **das ganze Jahr ~** throughout the year, all (the) year round; **die ganze Nacht ~** all (through the) night, throughout the night, all night long; **die ganze Zeit ~** all the time; **Jahre ~** for years (and years); **den ganzen Tag ~** all day (long); **durch etw ~** through sth.

hindurchgehen vi sep irreg aux sein (lit, fig) to go through (durch etw sth).

hindürfen vi sep irreg to be allowed to go (zu to). **da darfst du nicht mehr hin** you are not to or you mustn't go there any more.

Hindustan nt -s Hindustan.

Hindustani m -(s), -(s) Hindustani.

hineilen vi sep aux sein to rush or hurry (zu to). **ich eilte sofort hin** I rushed there at once.

hinein adv (a) (räumlich) in. **da ~** in there; **nur ~!** (inf) go right in!; **~ mit dir!** (inf) in you go!; **in etw** (acc) **~** into sth; **bis in etw** (acc) **~** right inside sth; **mitten ~ in etw** (acc) right into or right in the middle of sth; **leg es oben/unten ~** put it in the top/bottom; siehe **Blaue**[2].

(b) (zeitlich) into. **bis tief in die Nacht ~** well or far into the night.

hinein- pref in; siehe auch **ein-, herein-;** **~begeben*** vr sep irreg to enter (in etw (acc) sth); **~bekommen*** vt sep irreg (inf) to get in (in +acc -to); **~bemühen*** sep 1 vt to trouble to go in; 2 vr to be so kind as to go in (in +acc -to); **~blicken** vi sep to look in (in +acc -to); **ins Fenster ~blicken** to look in at the window; **~bohren** sep irreg (in +acc -to) 1 vt to dig in; 2 vr to bore one's way in; **~bringen** vt sep irreg (a) (~tragen) to bring/take in (in +acc -to); **(b)** siehe **~bekommen; ~bugsieren*** vt sep (inf) to manoeuvre in (in +acc -to); **~denken** vr sep irreg **sich in ein Problem ~denken** to think oneself into a problem; **sich in jdn ~denken** to put oneself in sb's position; **~deuten** vt sep to read sth into a sentence; **etw in die Natur ~deuten** to attribute nature with sth; **~drängen** sep (in +acc -to) 1 vt to push in; 2 vr (vi: aux sein) to push one's way in; **~fallen** vi sep irreg aux sein to fall in (in +acc -to); **~finden** vr sep irreg (fig) (sich vertraut machen) to find one's feet; (sich abfinden) to come to terms with it; **sich ~finden in etw** (acc) to get familiar with sth; to come to terms with sth; **~fressen** vt sep irreg (inf) etw in sich (acc) **~fressen** (lit) to wolf sth (down) (inf), to gobble sth down or up; (fig) Kummer etc to suppress sth; **~geheimnissen*** vt sep (inf) etw in etw (acc) **~geheimnissen** to read sth into sth; **~gehen** vi sep irreg aux sein (a) to go in (in etw (acc) **~gehen** to go into sth, to enter sth; **(b)** (~passen) to go in (in +acc -to); **in den Bus gehen 50 Leute ~** the bus holds 50 people, there is room for 50 people in the bus; **~gelangen*** vi sep aux sein (geh) to get in (in +acc -to); **~geraten*** vi sep irreg aux sein in etw (acc) **~geraten** to get involved in sth, to get into sth; **in ein Unwetter ~geraten** to get into a thunderstorm; **in eine Schlägerei ~geraten** to get into or get involved in a brawl; **~gießen** vt sep irreg to pour in (in +acc -to); **etw in sich ~gießen** (inf) to pour sth down one's throat (inf), to down sth; **~greifen** vi sep irreg to reach inside; **in etw** (acc) **~greifen** to reach into sth; **~gucken** vi sep (inf) (in Zimmer, Kiste) to look or take a look in (in +acc -to); (in Buch) to take a look in (in etw (acc) sth); **~halten** sep irreg 1 vt to put in (in etw (acc) sth); 2 vi (inf) (mit Gewehr etc) to aim (in +acc at); **mitten in die Menge ~halten** to aim into the crowd; **~heiraten** vi sep irreg **in eine Ehe einheiraten** to marry into; **~helfen** vi sep irreg jdm in den Mantel/ein Fahrzeug **~helfen** to help sb into his coat/into a vehicle; **~interpretieren*** vt sep siehe **~deuten; ~klettern** vi sep aux sein to climb in (in +acc -to); **~knien** vr sep (fig inf) **sich in etw** (acc) **~knien** to get into sth (inf); **~kommen** vi sep irreg aux sein (in +acc -to) (a) to come in; **(b)** (inf, fig: ~gelangen können) to get in; **nach 21 Uhr kommt man nicht (mehr) ~** you can't get in after 9 o'clock; **(c)** siehe **~geraten; ~komplimentieren*** vt sep to usher in (in +acc -to); **~kriechen** vi sep irreg aux sein to creep or slip in (in +acc -to); siehe **reinkriechen; ~kriegen** vt sep (inf) siehe **~bekommen; ~lachen** vi **sich in sich ~lachen** to laugh to oneself; **~lassen** vt sep irreg to let in (in +acc -to); **~laufen** vi sep irreg aux sein to run in (in +acc -to); **in sein eigenes Unglück ~laufen** to be heading for misfortune; **etw in sich ~laufen lassen** (inf) to knock sth back (inf); **~legen** vt sep (a) (lit, fig) Gefühl etc to put in (in +acc -to); **(b)** (~deuten) etw in jds Worte **~legen** to put sth in sb's mouth; **~lesen** sep irreg 1 vt etw in etw (acc) **~lesen** to read sth into sth; 2 vr **sich in ein Buch ~lesen** to get into or read one's way into a book; **~leuchten** vi sep to shine in (in +acc -to); **mit einer Lampe in eine Höhle ~leuchten** to shine a light into a cave; (in etw (acc)) **~leuchten** (fig) to throw light (up)on sth; **~manövrieren*** vt sep to manoeuvre in (in +acc -to); **~passen** sep 1 vi in etw (acc) **~passen** to fit into sth; (fig) to fit in with sth; 2 vt siehe **einpassen; ~pfuschen** vi sep (inf) jdm in seine Arbeit/Angelegenheiten **~pfuschen** to meddle or interfere in sb's work/affairs; **~platzen** vi sep aux sein (fig inf) to burst in (in +acc -to); **~pressen** vt sep (a) to press in (in +acc -to); **(b)** (fig) etw in ein Schema **~pressen** to force sth into a mould; **er läßt sich in kein Schema ~pressen** he won't be pigeon-holed (inf); **~projizieren*** vt sep to project (in +acc into); **sich in jdn ~projizieren** to project one's ideas/feelings etc into or onto sb; **~pumpen** vt sep to pump in (in +acc -to); **Geld auch** to pour in; **~ragen** vi sep aux sein (lit, fig) to project (in +acc into); **~reden** vi sep (a) (lit: unterbrechen) to interrupt (jdm sb); **jdm ~reden** (fig: sich einmischen) to interfere in sb's affairs; **jdm in seine Angelegenheiten/Entscheidungen/in alles ~reden** to meddle or interfere in sb's affairs/decision-making/in all sb's affairs; **(b)** ins Leere **~reden** to talk into a vacuum, to talk to oneself; **sich in (seine) Wut ~reden** to talk oneself into *or* work oneself up into a rage; ~**regnen** *vi impers sep* es regnet (ins Zimmer) ~ (the) rain is coming in(to) the room; ~**reichen** *sep* 1 *vt* to hand *or* pass in; (jdm) etw zum *or* durchs Fenster ~**reichen** to hand *or* pass sth in (to sb) through the window; 2 *vi* (*lang genug sein*) to reach in (*in + acc* -to); (*sich erstrecken*) to extend (*in + acc* as far as); in etw (*acc*) ~**reichen** (*zeitlich*) to go over into sth; Bräuche, die bis ins 20. Jahrhundert ~**reichen** customs that hang *or* come over into the 20th century; ~**reißen** *vt sep irreg* (*fig inf*) to drag in (*in + acc* -to); ~**reiten** *sep irreg* 1 *vi aux sein* to ride in (*in + acc* -to); 2 *vt* (*inf*) *siehe* reinreiten; ~**rennen** *vi sep irreg aux sein* to run in (*in + acc* -to); in sein Unglück/Verderben ~**rennen** to be heading for misfortune/disaster; ~**rufen** *vt sep irreg* to call *or* shout in (*in + acc* -to); ~**schaffen** *vt sep siehe* ~**bringen**; ~**schauen** *vi sep* to look in; ins Zimmer/Fenster ~**schauen** to look into the room/in at the window; eben mal ~**schauen** (*inf*) to look *or* pop in (*inf*); sich (*dat*) in etw nicht ~**schauen lassen** to keep sth to oneself; ~**schaufeln** *vt sep* to shovel in (*in + acc* -to); Essen in sich ~**schaufeln** (*inf*) to shovel food into oneself *or* down one's gullet (*inf*); ~**schießen** *vi sep irreg* (a) *aux sein* (*inf: Wasser etc*) to rush *or* gush in (*in + acc* -to); ~**geschossen kommen** (*Wasser*) to come gushing *or* rushing in; (*inf: Mensch*) to shoot in (*inf*), to come shooting in (*inf*); (b) **in eine Menschenmenge** ~**schießen** to shoot into a crowd; ~**schlagen** *vt sep irreg* (*in + acc* -to) Nagel to knock in; Eier to break in; Krallen to sink in; ein Loch ins Eis ~**schlagen** to knock a hole in the ice; ~**schleichen** *vi sep irreg* (*vi: aux sein*) (*inf*) to creep *or* sneak in (*in + acc* -to); ~**schlidern**, ~**schlittern** *vi sep aux sein* (*inf*) in etw (*acc*) ~**schlidern** *or* ~**schlittern** to get involved in *or* mixed up with sth; ~**schlingen** *vt sep irreg* etw (gierig) in sich ~**schlingen** to devour sth (greedily); ~**schlüpfen** *vi sep aux sein* to slip in (*in + acc* -to); ~**schmuggeln** *vt sep* to smuggle in (*in + acc* -to); ~**schneien** *sep* 1 *vi impers* es schneit (ins Zimmer) ~ the snow is coming in(to the room); 2 *vi aux sein siehe* hereinschneien; ~**schreiben** *vt sep irreg* to write in (*in etw* (*acc*) sth); ~**schütten** *vt sep* to pour in (*in + acc* -to); etw in sich ~**schütten** (*inf*) to knock sth back (*inf*); ~**sehen** *vi sep irreg siehe* ~**blicken**; ~**setzen** *sep* 1 *vt* to put in (*in + acc* -to); 2 *vr* (*in Fahrzeug*) to sit (oneself) inside (*in etw* (*acc*) sth); (*in Sessel*) to sit (oneself) down (*in + acc* in(to)); (*in Sessellift, Kettenkarussell etc*) to sit oneself in (*in etw* (*acc*) sth); sich in einen Haufen/die Brennnesseln ~**setzen** to sit (down) in a heap/the stinging nettles; sich in etw (*acc*) ~**setzen** (*Staub etc*) to settle into sth; sich wieder ~**setzen/ins Zimmer** ~**setzen** to go back and sit inside/in the room; ~**spazieren*** *vi sep aux sein* to walk in (*in + acc* -to); nur ~**spaziert!** please go in; ~**spielen** *sep* 1 *vi* (*beeinflussen*) to have a part to play (*in + acc* in); in etw (*acc*) ~**spielen** (*grenzen an*) to verge on sth; da spielen noch andere Gesichtspunkte ~ other factors have a part to play (in it) *or* enter into it; 2 *vt* (*Sport*) den Ball in den Strafraum etc ~**spielen** to play the ball into the penalty area *etc*; ~**sprechen** *vi sep irreg* ins Mikrophon ~**sprechen** to speak *or* talk into the microphone; ~**springen** *vi sep irreg aux sein* (*in + acc* -to) (a) to jump *or* leap *or* spring in; (b) (*inf:* ~**laufen**) to pop in (*inf*); ~**stecken** *vt sep* (*in + acc* -to) to put in; Nadel etc auch to stick in; den Kopf zum Fenster ~**stecken** to put *or* stick one's head in at *or* in through the window; Geld/Arbeit etc in etw (*acc*) ~**stecken** to put money/some work etc into sth; viel Mühe in etw (*acc*) ~**stecken** to put a lot of effort into sth; ~**steigern** *vt sep* to get into *or* work oneself up into a state, to get worked up; sich in seine Wut/Hysterie/seinen Ärger ~**steigern** to work oneself up into a rage/hysterics/a temper; sich in seinen Kummer/Schmerz ~**steigern** to let oneself be completely taken up with one's worries/to let the pain take one over completely; sich in seine Nervosität/Prüfungsangst/Reue ~**steigern** to work oneself up into a state (of nervousness)/a state (of worry) about the exams/an orgy of self-reproach; sie hat sich in die Vorstellung ~**gesteigert, daß** ... she has managed to convince herself that ..., she has talked herself into believing that ...; sich in eine Rolle ~**steigern** to become completely caught up in a role; ~**stopfen** *vt sep* to stuff *or* cram in (*in + acc* -to); Essen in sich (*acc*) ~**stopfen** to stuff *or* cram oneself with food; ~**stoßen** *sep irreg* 1 *vt* Schwert etc to thrust in (*in + acc* -to); jdn in etw ~**stoßen** (*lit*) to push sb into sth; (*fig*) to plunge sb into sth; 2 *vi aux sein* in eine Lücke ~**stoßen** to steer into a space; in ein Gebiet ~**stoßen** to enter a district; ~**strömen** *vi sep aux sein* to stream *or* flood in (*in + acc* -to); ~**stürzen** *sep* 1 *vi aux sein* to plunge in (*in + acc* -to); (~**eilen**) to rush in (*in + acc* -to); zur Tür ~**stürzen** to rush in through the door; 2 *vt* to throw *or* hurl in (*in + acc* -to); jdn ins Elend ~**stürzen** to plunge sb into misery; 3 *vr* (*in + acc* -to) to throw *or* hurl oneself in, to plunge in; sich in die Arbeit/in Schulden ~**stürzen** to throw oneself into one's work/to plunge oneself into debt; sich ins Vergnügen ~**stürzen** to plunge in and start enjoying oneself, to let it all hang out (*sl*); ~**tappen** *vi sep aux sein* (*fig inf*) to walk right into it (*inf*); in eine Falle ~**tappen** to walk into a trap; ~**tragen** *vt sep irreg* (*in + acc* -to) to carry in; (*fig*) to bring in; ~**treiben** *vt sep irreg* to drive in (*in + acc* -to); jdn in etw (*acc*) ~**treiben** (*fig*) to force sb into sth; ~**tun** *vt sep irreg* to put in (*in + acc* -to); einen Blick in etw (*acc*) ~**tun** to take a look in sth; ins Buch etc to take a look at sth; ~**versetzen*** *vr sep* sich in jdn *or* in jds Lage ~**versetzen** to put oneself in sb's position; sich in etw (*acc*) ~**versetzt fühlen** to imagine oneself in sth; sich in eine Rolle ~**versetzen** to empathize with a part; ~**wachsen** *vi sep irreg aux sein* in etw (*acc*) ~**wachsen** (*lit, fig*) to grow into sth; ~**wagen** *vr sep* to venture in (*in + acc* -to); ~**werfen** *vt sep irreg* (*in + acc* -to) to throw in; Truppen to send in; den Ball durchs Fenster ~**werfen** to throw the ball in at *or* through the window; ~**wollen** *vi sep* (*inf*) to want to go *or* get in (*in + acc* -to); das will mir nicht in den Kopf ~ I just can't understand it; ~**zerren** *vt sep* (*lit, fig*) to drag in

(*in + acc* -to); ~**ziehen** *sep irreg* 1 *vt* to pull *or* drag in (*in + acc* -to); jdn in eine Angelegenheit/einen Streit ~**ziehen** to drag sb into an affair/a quarrel; 2 *vi aux sein* (*in + acc* -to) to go in; (*in ein Haus*) to move in; ~**zwängen** *sep* (*in + acc* -to) 1 *vt* to force *or* squeeze in; 2 *vr* to squeeze (oneself) in; ~**zwingen** *vt sep irreg* to force in (*in + acc* -to).

hin-: ~**fahren** *sep irreg* 1 *vi aux sein* to go there; (*mit Fahrzeug auch*) to drive there; (*mit Schiff auch*) to sail there; mit der Hand über etw (*acc*) ~**fahren** (*fig*) to run one's hand over sth; fahre ~! (*old, poet*) farewell! (*old*), fare-thee-well! (*old, poet*); 2 *vt* to drive *or* take there; H~**fahrt** *f* journey there; (*Naut*) voyage out; (*Rail*) outward journey; auf der H~**fahrt** on the journey *or* way there etc; ~**fallen** *vi sep irreg aux sein* to fall (down).

hinfällig *adj* (a) frail. (b) (*fig: ungültig*) invalid; Argument auch untenable; etw ~ machen to render sth invalid, to invalidate sth.

Hinfälligkeit *f, no pl* frailness; (*von Argument*) invalidity.

hin-: ~**finden** *vir sep irreg* (*inf*) to find one's way there; ~**fläzen**, ~**flegeln** *vr sep* (*inf*) to loll about *or* around; ~**fliegen** *vi sep irreg aux sein* to fly there; (*inf:* ~**fallen*) to come a cropper (*inf*); der Ball flog über die Köpfe ~ the ball flew over their heads; H~**flug** *m* outward flight.

hinfort *adv* (*old*) henceforth (*old*).

hinführen *sep* 1 *vt* to lead there. jdn zu etw ~ (*fig*) to lead sb to sth. 2 *vi* to lead *or* go there. zu/zwischen etw (*dat*) ~ to lead to/between sth; wo soll das ~? (*fig*) where is this leading to?

hing *pret of* **hängen**.

Hingabe *f -, no pl* (*fig*) (*Begeisterung*) dedication; (*Selbstlosigkeit*) devotion; (*völliges Aufgehen*) (self-)abandon. mit ~ tanzen/singen *etc* to dance/sing etc with abandon; unter ~ seines Lebens (*geh*) by laying down one's life.

hingabefähig *adj siehe* n capable of dedication/devotion/(self-)abandon.

Hingang *m -s, no pl* (*old, form*) decease, demise (*form*).

hingeben *sep irreg* 1 *vt* to give up; Ruf, Zeit, Geld auch to sacrifice; Leben to lay down, to sacrifice.

2 *vr* (a) sich einer Sache (*dat*) ~ der Arbeit to devote *or* dedicate oneself to sth; dem Laster, Genuß, der Verzweiflung to abandon oneself to sth; sich Hoffnungen/einer Illusion ~ to cherish hopes/to labour under an illusion.

(b) sie gab sich ihm hin she gave herself *or* surrendered to him; sich Gott ~ to give oneself to God.

hingebend *adj* devoted.

Hingebung *f, no pl siehe* **Hingabe**.

hingebungsvoll 1 *adj* (*selbstlos*) devoted; (*begeistert*) abandoned. 2 *adv* devotedly; with abandon; lauschen raptly.

hingegen *conj* (*geh*) however; (*andererseits auch*) on the other hand.

hin-: ~**gegossen** *adj* (*fig inf*) sie lag/saß wie ~**gegossen auf dem** Bett she had draped herself artistically on the bed; ~**gehen** *vi sep irreg aux sein* (a) (*dorthin gehen*) to go (there); gehst du auch ~? are you going too?; wo gehst du ~? where are you going?; wo geht es hier ~? where does this go?; sein Blick ging über die Landschaft ~ he *or* his eyes scanned the scenery; (b) (*Zeit*) to pass, to go by; (c) (*fig: tragbar sein*) das geht gerade noch ~ that will just about do *or* pass; diesmal mag es noch ~**gehen** I'll let it go *or* pass this once; (jdm) etw ~**gehen lassen** to let sth pass, to let sb get away with sth; ~**gehören*** *vi sep* to belong; wo gehört das ~? where does this belong *or* go?; wo gehören die Gabeln ~? where do the forks live? (*inf*); ~**gelangen*** *vi sep aux sein* (*geh*) to get there; ~**geraten*** *vi sep irreg aux sein* irgendwo ~**geraten** to get somewhere; wo ist er ~**geraten?** (*inf*) where has he got to?; wo bin ich denn hier ~**geraten?** (*inf*) what kind of place is this then?; ~**gerissen** *ptp of* ~**reißen**; 2 *adj* enraptured, enchanted; ~**gerissen lauschen** to listen with rapt attention; ich bin ganz ~- und hergerissen (*iro*) absolutely great *or* fantastic! (*iro*); ~**gleiten** *vi sep irreg aux sein* to glide; (*geh: Zeit*) to slip away; ~**haben** *vt sep irreg* wo willst du dies ~**haben?** where do you want this (to go)?; ~**halten** *vt sep irreg* (a) (*entgegenstrecken*) to hold out (jdm to sb); (b) (*fig*) jdn to put off, to stall; (*Mil*) to stave off.

Hinhalte-: ~**politik** *f* stalling *or* delaying policy; ~**taktik** *f* stalling *or* delaying tactics.

hinhauen *sep irreg* (*inf*) 1 *vt* (a) (*nachlässig machen*) to knock off (*inf*).

(b) (*hinwerfen*) to slam *or* plonk (*inf*) *or* bang down.

(c) (*überraschen*) jdn ~ to knock sb out (*inf*).

2 *vi* (a) (*zuschlagen*) to hit hard. (mit der Faust) ~ to thump *or* clobber (*inf*) it/sth (with one's fist).

(b) *aux sein* (*fallen*) to fall flat.

(c) (*gutgehen*) es hat hingehauen I/we etc just managed it; das wird schon ~ it will be OK (*inf*) *or* all right.

(d) (*klappen, in Ordnung sein*) to work. ich habe das so lange geübt, bis es hinhaute I practised it till I could do it.

(e) (*ausreichen*) to do.

3 *vr* (*sl*) (sich hinflegeln, hinlegen) to flop down (*inf*); (*schlafen*) to have a kip (*Brit inf*).

4 *vt impers* es hat ihn hingehauen he fell over.

hin-: ~**hören** *vi sep* to listen; ~**kauern** *vr sep* to cower (down).

Hinkebein *nt*, **Hinkefuß** *m* (*inf*) (*verletztes Bein*) gammy leg (*inf*). das alte/du Hinkebein the old man with his/you with your gammy leg.

Hinkelstein *m* (*inf*) menhir.

hinken *vi* (a) (*gehbehindert sein*) to limp, to walk with a limp. mit *or* auf dem rechten Bein ~ to have a limp in one's right leg. (b) *aux sein* (*sich fortbewegen*) to limp. (c) (*fig*) (*Beispiel, Vergleich, Bild*) to be inappropriate; (*Formulierung auch*) to be inapt; (*Vers, Reim*) to be clumsy.

hin-: ~**knallen** sep (inf) **1** vt to slam or bang down; **2** vi aux sein to fall flat; ~**knien** vir sep (vi: aux sein) to kneel (down); ~**kommen** vi sep irreg aux sein **(a)** (an einen Ort ~) (da) ~**kommen** to get there; nach X ~**kommen** to get to X; kommst du mit ~? are you coming too?; wie komme ich zu dir ~? how do I get to your place?; könnt ihr alle zu ihm ~**kommen**? can you all go to his place?; **(b)** (an bestimmten Platz gehören) to go; wo ist das Buch ~**gekommen**? where has the book got to?; wo kämen wir denn ~, wenn ... (inf) where would we be if ...; wo kämen wir denn da ~? (inf) where would we be then?; **(c)** (inf: in Ordnung kommen) das kommt schon noch ~ that will turn out OK (inf); **(d)** (inf: auskommen) to manage; wir kommen (damit) ~ we will manage; **(e)** (inf: ausreichen, stimmen) to be right; ~**kriegen** vt sep (a) (fertigbringen) to do, to manage; wie er es nur immer ~**kriegt**, daß die anderen alles für ihn machen I don't know how he manages to get the others to do everything for him; **(b)** (in Ordnung bringen) to mend, to fix; (gesundheitlich) to cure; **H~kunft** f (Aus): in **H~kunft** in future; ~**künftig** (Aus) **1** adj future; **2** adv in future; ~**langen** vi sep (a) (zupacken) to grab him/her/it etc; (ziehen/schieben) to pull/push hard; (dial: anfassen) to touch; (zuschlagen) to take a (good) swipe (inf), (foulen) to play rough; siehe Gras; **(b)** (sich bedienen) to help oneself to a lot; (viel Geld verlangen) to overcharge; **(c)** (ausreichen) to do; (Geld) to stretch; mein Geld langt dafür nicht ~ my money won't stretch to that; **(d)** (auskommen) to manage; ~**länglich 1** adj (ausreichend) adequate; keine ~**längliche Anzahl** an insufficient number; **2** adv (ausreichend) adequately; (zu Genüge) sufficiently; ~**lassen** vt sep irreg jdn (da) ~**lassen** to let sb go (there); ~**laufen** vi sep irreg aux sein (a) (zu bestimmter Stelle laufen) to run there; (vorbei-, entlang-, dahinlaufen) to run; (inf: zu Veranstaltung, Amt, Rechtsanwalt etc) to rush; **(b)** (dial inf: nicht fahren) to walk; **(c)** (verlaufen: mit Ortsangabe, in bestimmte Richtung) to run; ~**legen** sep **1** vt (a) to put down; Zettel to leave (jdm for sb); (flach legen) Verletzten etc to lay down; (ins Bett, zum Schlafen) to put to bed; (inf: bezahlen müssen) to fork out (inf); **(b)** (inf: glänzend darbieten) to perform or Rede, Vortrag give effortlessly and brilliantly; er hat einen tollen Steptanz ~**gelegt** he did a neat bit of tap-dancing; **2** vr to lie down; ~**legen!** (Mil) down!; sich lang or der Länge nach ~**legen** (inf) to fall flat; da legst du dich ~! (inf) it's unbelievable; **3** vt impers (inf) es legt jdn ~ (lit: bringt zu Fall) sb falls over; ~**lenken** vt sep etw (auf etw acc) ~**lenken** Fahrzeug, Pferd to steer sth (towards sth); Fluß, Wasser, Blicke, jds Aufmerksamkeit to direct sth to sth; Schritte, Gespräch to turn sth to sth; etw (dort) ~**lenken** to steer etc sth there; ~**lümmeln** vr sep (inf) to loll or lounge about or around (auf +acc on).

hinmachen sep **1** vt (inf) (a) (anbringen) to put on; Bild to put up.
(b) (kaputtmachen) to wreck, to ruin; (sl: umbringen) to bump off (inf).
2 vi (a) (inf: Notdurft verrichten) to do one's/its etc business (euph).
(b) (dial: sich beeilen) to get a move on (inf).
(c) aux sein (dial inf: an bestimmten Ort gehen) to go there.
3 vr (inf: sich ruinieren) to wear oneself into the ground.

Hin-: ~**marsch** m way or (Mil) march there; **h~morden** vt sep (geh) to massacre; **h~murmeln** vti sep to murmur; **h~müssen** vi sep irreg to have to go; ~**nahme** f -, no pl acceptance; **h~nehmen** vt sep irreg (a) (ertragen) to take, to accept; Beleidigung to swallow; etw als selbstverständlich **h~nehmen** to take sth for granted; **(b)** (inf: mitnehmen) to take; **h~neigen** sep **1** vt Kopf, Körper to incline; **2** vr (zu towards) (Mensch) to lean; (fig) to incline or have leanings; (Zweige, Baum) to lean; (Landschaft) to incline; **3** vi (fig) zu etw **h~neigen** to incline towards sth; zu Vorbild to tend to follow.

hinnen adv (old, liter) von ~ hence; von ~ gehen or scheiden (fig) to depart this life, to pass on.

hin-: ~**passen** vi sep (Platz haben) to fit (in); (gut aussehen) to go (well); (Mensch: am Platz sein) to fit in; ~**pfeffern** vt sep (inf) Gegenstand to bang or slam down (inf); (fig) Antwort, Kritik (mündlich) to rap out; (schriftlich) to scribble down; ~**pfuschen** vt sep (inf) to dash off; ~**plappern** vt sep to say; Unsinn to talk; das hat sie nur so ~**geplappert** she said that without thinking; ~**plumpsen** vi sep aux sein (inf) to fall down (with a thud); etw ~**plumpsen lassen** to dump or plump (inf) sth down; sich ~**plumpsen lassen** to plump oneself down (inf), to flop down; ~**raffen** vt sep siehe **dahinraffen**; ~**reichen** sep **1** vt jdm etw ~**reichen** to hand or pass sb sth or sth to sb; Hand to hold out sth to sb; **2** vi (a) (ausreichen) to be enough, to suffice (form); **(b)** (sich erstrecken) bis zu etw ~**reichen** to stretch to sth; ~**reichend** adj (ausreichend) adequate; (genug) sufficient; (reichlich) ample; keine ~**reichenden Beweise** insufficient evidence; es ist noch ~**reichend Zeit** there is ample time; **H~reise** f journey there or out, outward journey; (mit Schiff) voyage out, outward voyage; **H~- und Rückreise** journey there and back; die **H~reise nach London** the journey to London; auf der **H~reise** on the way there; ~**reißen** vt sep irreg (fig) (a) (begeistern) to thrill, to enrapture; siehe ~**gerissen**, **(b)** (überwältigen) jdn zu etw ~**reißen** to force sb into sth; die Zuschauer zu Beifallsstürmen ~**reißen** to elicit thunderous applause from the audience; sich ~**reißen lassen** to let oneself be or get carried away; sich zu einer Entscheidung ~**reißen lassen** to let oneself be carried away into making a decision; ~**reißend** adj fantastic; Landschaft, Anblick enchanting; Schönheit, Mensch captivating; Redner auch thrilling; ~**reißend schön aussehen** to look quite enchanting; ~**reißend schön Klavier spielen** to play the piano quite enchantingly or delightfully; ~**rennen** vi sep irreg aux sein siehe ~**laufen** (a); ~**richten** vt sep (a) to execute; jdn durch den Strang/elektri-

schen Stuhl ~**richten** to hang sb/to send sb to the electric chair; **(b)** (inf) (herrichten) to prepare; (zurechtlegen) Kleider to lay out ready.

Hinrichtung f execution.
Hinrichtungs-: ~**kommando** nt execution or (bei Erschießen) firing squad; ~**stätte** f place of execution.

hin-: ~**rücken** sep **1** vt Gegenstand to push over; etw an die Wand ~**rücken** to push sth over to the wall; **2** vi aux sein to move up or over; ~**sagen** vt sep to say without thinking; ~**schaffen** vt sep to get there; ~**schauen** vi sep (dial) siehe ~**sehen**; ~**schaukeln** vt sep (sl) to fix (inf), to manage; ~**scheiden** vi sep irreg aux sein (liter) to pass away, to depart this life (form); der **H~geschiedene** the deceased, the (dear) departed; **H~scheiden** nt (liter) demise; ~**scheißen** vi sep irreg (vulg) to crap (vulg); ~**schicken** vt sep to send; ~**schieben** vt sep irreg to push over; **H~schied** m -(e)s, no pl (Sw) siehe **H~scheiden**; ~**schielen** vi sep to glance (zu at); ~**schlachten** vt sep to slaughter, to butcher; ~**schlagen** vi sep irreg (a) to strike or hit; **(b)** aux sein (~fallen) to fall over; der **Länge nach** or **längelang** or **lang** ~**schlagen** (inf) to fall flat (on one's face); ~**schleichen** vir sep irreg (vi: aux sein) to creep or steal or sneak up; ~**schleppen** sep **1** vt to carry, to lug (inf); (inf: mitnehmen) to drag along; **2** vr (Mensch) to drag oneself along; (fig) to drag on; ~**schludern** vt sep (inf) Arbeit to dash off; ~**schmeißen** vt sep irreg (inf) (hinwerfen) to fling or chuck down (inf); (fig: aufgeben) Arbeit etc to chuck or pack in (inf); ~**schmelzen** vi sep irreg aux sein (vam, inf) (Mensch) to swoon; (Wut) to melt away; ~**schmieren** vt sep (inf) Schmutz to spread, to smear; (pej) (malen) to daub; (flüchtig schreiben) to scribble; ~**schreiben** sep irreg **1** vt to write; (flüchtig niederschreiben) to bung down (inf), Aufsatz to dash off; **2** vi (inf) to write (there); ~**schwinden** vi sep irreg aux sein siehe **dahinschwinden**; ~**sehen** vi sep irreg to look; ich kann (gar) nicht ~**sehen** I can't bear to look; ohne ~**zusehen** without looking; bei genauerem **H~sehen** on looking more carefully; vor sich ~**sehen** to look or stare straight ahead.

hinsein vi sep irreg aux sein (Zusammenschreibung nur bei infin und ptp) (inf) (a) (kaputt sein) to have had it. **hin ist hin** what's done is done.
(b) (erschöpft sein) to be shattered (inf).
(c) (verloren sein) to be lost; (Ruhe) to have disappeared; (ruiniert sein) to be in ruins.
(d) (sl: tot sein) to have kicked the bucket (sl).
(e) (begeistert sein) (von etw) ~ to be mad about sth.
(f) bis dahin ist es noch lange hin it's a long time till then.

hinsetzen sep **1** vt to put or set down; jdn to seat, to put; Kind to sit down. **2** vr (a) (lit) to sit down. sich gerade ~ to sit up straight. **(b)** (inf: sich bemühen) to buckle down to it, to set to.

Hinsicht f -, no pl in dieser ~ in this respect or regard; in mancher or gewisser ~ in some or many respects or ways; in jeder ~ in every respect; in finanzieller/wirtschaftlicher ~ financially/economically; in beruflicher ~ with regard to my/his job; in ~ auf (+acc) siehe **hinsichtlich**.

hinsichtlich prep +gen (bezüglich) with regard to; (in Anbetracht) in view of.

hin-: ~**siechen** vi sep aux sein (geh) siehe **dahinsiechen**; ~**sinken** vi sep irreg aux sein (geh) to sink (down); (ohnmächtig werden) to faint, to swoon; (tot) to drop down dead; ~**sitzen** vi sep irreg aux sein (esp S Ger, Sw, Aus) to sit; sitz ~ sit down; ~**sollen** vi sep (inf) wo soll ich/das Buch ~? where do I/does the book go?; wo soll ich mit dem Paket ~? what should I do with this parcel?; eigentlich sollte ich ja zu der Party ~ I really ought to go to the party; **H~spiel** nt (Sport) first leg; ~**starren** vi sep to stare; ~**stellen** sep **1** vt (a) (niederstellen) to put down; (inf) Gebäude to put up; (abstellen) Fahrzeug to put, to park; er tut seine Pflicht, wo man ihn auch ~**stellt** he does his duty wherever he is; **(b)** (auslegen) Vorfall, Angelegenheit, Sachlage to describe; jdn/etw als jdn/etw ~**stellen** (bezeichnen) to make sb/sth out to be sb/sth; **2** vr to stand; (Fahrer) to park; sich gerade ~**stellen** to stand up straight; sich vor jdn or jdm ~**stellen** to stand in front of sb; sie hat sich vor mich/ihn ~**gestellt** she came and stood in front of me/went and stood in front of him; sich als etw ~**stellen** (fig) to make oneself out to be sth; ~**steuern** sep **1** vi (a) aux sein to steer; wo steuert sie ~? where is she going?; **(b)** (fig) in der Diskussion auf etw (acc) ~**steuern** to steer the discussion towards sth; auf ein Ziel ~**steuern** (fig) to aim at a goal; **2** vt to steer; ~**strecken** sep **1** vt (a) Hand, Gegenstand to hold out; **(b)** (liter) jdn to fell; **2** vr to stretch (oneself) out, to lie down; ~**strömen** vi sep aux sein (Fluß, Wasser) to flow; (Menschen) to flock there; sie strömten zur Ausstellung ~ they flocked to the exhibition; ~**stürzen** vi sep aux sein (a) (~fallen) to fall down heavily; **(b)** (~eilen) nach or zu jdm/etw ~**stürzen** to rush or dash towards sb/sth.

Hint|an-: **h~setzen** vt sep (zurückstellen) to put last; (vernachlässigen) to neglect; ~**setzung** f disregard; (Vernachlässigung) neglect; unter ~**setzung einer Sache** (gen) (form) regardless of or without regard for sth; **h~stellen** vt sep siehe **h~setzen**.

hinten adv (a) behind. von ~ from the back; (bei Menschen auch) from behind; nach ~ to the back; von weit ~ from the very back; ~ im Buch/in der Schlange/auf der Liste at the back of the book/queue/at the end of the list; sich ~ anstellen to join the end of the queue; ~ im Bild in the back of the picture; nach ~ abgehen (Theat) to exit at the back of the stage; nach ~ laufen to run to the back; jdn nach ~ transportieren (hinter der Front) to transport sb behind the lines; von ~ anfangen to begin from the end; das Alphabet von ~ aufsagen to say the alphabet backwards; etw ~ anfügen to add sth at the end; ~ bleiben (lit) to stay behind or at the back; (fig) to lag behind.

(b) (*am rückwärtigen Ende*) at the back; (*Naut*) aft; (*am Gesäß*) on one's behind. von ~ from behind; *jdn erkennen auch* from the back; ~ im Auto/Bus in the back of the car/bus; der Blinker ~ the rear indicator; ~ und vorn nichts haben (*inf*) to be as flat as a pancake (*inf*); nach ~ to the back; *fallen, ziehen* backwards; *jdn am liebsten von* ~ sehen (*inf*) to be glad to see the back of sb; nach ~ ausschlagen (*Pferd*) to kick out; *jdm* ~ hinein- *or* reinkriechen (*inf*) to lick sb's boots; *siehe* Auge.

(c) (*auf der Rückseite*) at the back; (*von Gebäude auch*) at the rear. das Buch ist ~ schmutzig the back (cover) of the book is dirty; ~ auf der Medaille on the back *or* the reverse side of the medal; ein nach ~ gelegenes Zimmer a room facing the back; ein Blick nach ~ a look behind; etw von ~ und vorn betrachten (*fig*) to consider sth from all angles.

(d) (*weit entfernt*) das Auto da ~ the car back there; sie waren ziemlich weit ~ they were quite far back; ~ im Walde deep in the forest; ~ in der Mongolei far away in Mongolia.

(e) (*fig*) ~ und vorn betrügen left, right and centre; *bedienen* hand and foot; *verwöhnen* rotten (*inf*); *egal sein* absolutely, utterly; das stimmt ~ und vorn nicht *or* weder ~ noch vorn that is absolutely untrue; das reicht *or* langt ~ und vorn nicht *or* weder ~ noch vorn that's nowhere near enough; dann heißt es Frau Schmidt ~ und Frau Schmidt vorn then it's Mrs Smith this and Mrs Smith that; ich weiß nicht mehr, wo ~ und vorn ist I don't know whether I'm coming or going.

hinten-: ~dran *adv* (*inf*) (*am hinteren Ende*) at the back; (*fig: im Hintertreffen*) behind; ~drauf *adv* (*inf*) on the back; (*von LKW*) in the back; (*auf Gesäß*) on one's behind; ~drein *adv siehe* hinterher; ~herum *adv* **(a)** (*von der hinteren Seite*) from the back; kommen Sie ~herum come round the back; **(b)** (*fig inf*) (*auf Umwegen*) in a roundabout way; (*illegal*) under the counter; er hat mir ~herum erzählt, daß sie ~ he told me behind her back that she ...; ~nach *adv* (*Aus, S Ger*) *siehe* hinterher; ~rum *adv* (*inf*) *siehe* ~herum; ~über *adv* backwards; er fiel/kippte ~über he fell over backwards.

hinter *prep* +*dat or* (*mit Bewegungsverben*) +*acc* **(a)** (*räumlich*) behind. ~ dem Haus behind *or* at the back *or* rear of the house; ~ jdm/etw her behind sb/sth; ~ etw (*acc*) kommen (*fig: herausfinden*) to get to the bottom of sth; ~ die Wahrheit kommen to get to the truth; sich ~ jdn stellen (*lit*) to stand behind sb; (*fig*) to support sb, to get behind sb; ~ jdm/etw stehen (*lit, fig*) to be behind sb/sth; jdn ~ sich (*dat*) haben (*lit, fig*) to have sb behind one; ~ dem Hügel/der Tür hervor (*out*) from behind the hill/door; jdn weit ~ sich (*dat*) lassen to leave sb far behind; (*im Rennen auch*) to outdistance sb; ~ etw (*dat*) stecken, sich ~ etw (*dat*) verbergen to be *or* lie behind sth; ~ seinen Reden steckt nicht viel there's not much in his speeches.

(b) +*dat* (*nach*) after. vier Kilometer ~ Glasgow/~ der Grenze four kilometres outside Glasgow/beyond the border; ~ diesem Satz steht ein Fragezeichen there is a question-mark at the end of this sentence; er ist ~ mir dran it's his turn after me.

(c) +*dat in Rangfolge*) after; (*in Bedeutung*) behind. an Talent nicht ~ jdm zurückstehen to be just as talented as sb; sie stand nicht ~ ihm zurück she did not lag behind him; ich stelle das Privatleben ~ der Arbeit zurück I put my work before my private life.

(d) etw ~ sich (*dat*) haben (*zurückgelegt haben*) to have got through sth; *Strecke* to have covered sth; *Land* to have left sth; (*überstanden haben*) to have got sth over (and done) with; *Krankheit, Zeit* to have been through sth; *anstrengende Tage* to have had sth; *Studium* to have completed *or* finished sth; sie hat viel ~ sich she has been through a lot; das Schlimmste haben wir ~ uns we're past *or* we've got over the worst; etw ~ sich (*acc*) bringen to get sth over (and done) with; *Strecke* to cover sth; *Arbeit* to get sth done; das liegt ~ ihr that is behind her; sich ~ etw (*acc*) machen to get down to sth; *siehe* hersein.

(e) (*inf*) *siehe* dahinter.

Hinter-: ~achse *f* rear *or* back axle; ~ansicht *f* rear *or* back view; ~ausgang *m* back *or* rear exit; ~backe *f usu pl* buttock; (*von Tier*) hindquarter; sich auf die ~backen setzen (*fig inf*) to get down to it; ~bänkler *m* -s, - (*Pol pej*) backbencher; ~bein *nt* hind leg; sich auf die ~beine stellen *or* setzen (*lit*) to rear up (on one's hind legs); (*fig inf*) (*sich widersetzen*) to kick up a fuss (*inf*); (*sich anstrengen*) to pull one's socks up (*inf*).

Hinterbliebenen-: ~fürsorge *f* welfare service for surviving dependents; ~rente *f* surviving dependents' pension.

Hinterbliebene(r) *mf decl as adj* surviving dependent. die ~n the bereaved family.

hinter-: ~bringen[1]* *vt insep irreg* jdm etw ~bringen to mention sth to sb; ~bringen[2] *vt sep irreg* (*dial inf*) to take back; (*hinunterschlucken können*) to be able to get down; H~deck *nt* (*Naut*) afterdeck; ~drein *adv siehe* ~her.

hintere *adj siehe* hintere(r, s).

hinter|einander *adv* (*räumlich*) one behind the other, behind each other; (*in einer Reihe nebeneinander*) next to one another; (*in Reihenfolge, nicht gleichzeitig, ohne Unterbrechung*) one after the other. ~ hereinkommen to come in one by one *or* one at a time; dicht ~ (*räumlich*) close behind one another; (*zeitlich*) close on one another; zwei Tage ~ two days running; dreimal ~ three times in a row; es hat monatelang ~ geregnet it has rained for months on end; etw ~ tun (*nicht gleichzeitig*) to do sth one after the other; (*der Reihe nach*) to do sth in turn; (*ohne Unterbrechung*) to do sth in one go *or* all at once.

hinter|einander-: ~fahren *vi sep irreg aux sein* (*mit Auto/Fahrrad*) to drive/ride behind one another *or* one behind the other; ~gehen *vi sep irreg aux sein* to walk behind one another *or* one behind the other; ~her *adv* behind one another; ~schalten *vt sep* (*Elec*) to connect in series; H~schaltung *f* (*Elec*) series connection; ~stehen *vi sep irreg aux haben or* (*S Ger*) *sein* to stand behind one another *or* one behind the other;

~weg *adv* (*zeitlich*) running, in a row; (*nacheinander*) one after the other.

Hinter|eingang *m* rear entrance.

Hintere(r) *m decl as adj* (*inf*) *siehe* Hintern.

hintere(r, s) *adj* back; (*von Tier, Gebäude, Zug auch*) rear. der/die/das H~ the one at the back; das ~ Ende des Saals the back *or* rear of the room; die H~n those at the back, those behind; am ~n Ende at the far end; *siehe* hinterste(r, s).

Hinter-: h~fotzig *adj* (*dial inf*) underhand(ed); ~fotzigkeit *f* (*dial inf*) underhandedness; (*Bemerkung*) underhand(ed) remark; h~fragen* *vt insep* to analyze; ~fuß *m* hind foot; ~gaumenlaut *m* velar (sound); ~gebäude *nt siehe* ~haus; ~gedanke *m* ulterior motive; ohne ~gedanken without any ulterior motive(s); h~gehen[1]* *vt insep irreg* (*betrügen*) to deceive; *Ehepartner etc auch* to be unfaithful to; (*umgehen*) *Verordnung, Gesetze, Prinzip* to circumvent; h~gehen[2] *vi sep irreg aux sein* (*dial inf*) to go to the back *or* rear (in +*acc of*); ~gestell *nt* (*hum inf*) (*Beine*) hind legs *pl* (*inf*), pins *pl* (*inf*); (*Po*) rump (*inf*), backside (*inf*); ~glasmalerei *f* (*Bild*) verre églomisé picture; (*Technik*) verre églomisé technique.

Hintergrund *m* (*von Bild, Raum*) background; (*von Bühne, Saal*) back; (*Theat: Kulisse*) backdrop, backcloth; (*fig: verborgene Zusammenhänge*) background *no pl* (*gen to*). im ~ in the background; im ~ der Bühne at the back of the stage; vor dem ~ (*lit, fig*) against the background; der musikalische/akustische ~ the background music/sounds *pl*; im ~ bleiben/stehen (*lit, fig*) to stay/be in the background; in den ~ treten *or* rücken (*fig*) to be pushed into the background.

Hinter-: h~gründig *adj* cryptic, enigmatic; ~gründigkeit *f* crypticness, enigmaticness; (*Bemerkung*) cryptic *or* enigmatic remark; h~haken *vi sep* (*inf*) to follow that/it *etc* up; ~halt *m* (*a*) ambush; jdn aus dem ~halt überfallen to ambush *or* waylay sb; jdn/etw aus dem ~halt angreifen (*esp Mil*) to ambush sb/sth; (*Sport, fig*) to make a surprise attack on sb/sth; im ~halt lauern *or* liegen to lie in wait *or* (*esp Mil*) ambush; (*inf*) etw im ~halt haben to have sth in reserve; ohne ~halt unreservedly; h~hältig *adj* underhand(ed); ~hältigkeit *f* underhandedness; (*Handlung*) underhand(ed) act; ~hand *f* (*von Pferd, Hund*) hindquarters *pl*; etw in der ~hand haben (*fig: in Reserve*) to have sth up one's sleeve; ~haupt *nt* back of one's/the head; ~haus *nt* part of a tenement house accessible only through a courtyard and thus considered inferior.

hinterher *adv* (*räumlich*) behind, after; (*zeitlich*) afterwards.

hinterher-: ~fahren *vi sep irreg aux sein* to drive behind (*jdm* sb); ~hinken *vi sep aux sein* to limp behind (*jdm* sb); (*fig*) to lag behind (*hinter etw dat*) sth, mit with, in); ~kommen *vi sep irreg aux sein* (*a*) (*danach kommen*) (*räumlich*) to follow (behind *or* after); (*zeitlich*) to come after; (*b*) (*als letzter kommen*) to bring up the rear; ~laufen *vi sep irreg aux sein* to run behind (*jdm* sb); jdm ~laufen (*fig inf: sich bemühen um*) to run (around) after sb; einem Mädchen ~laufen (*inf*) to run after a girl; ~schicken *vt sep* to send on (*jdm* to sb); jdn to send after (*jdm* sb); ~sein *vi sep irreg aux sein* (*Zusammenschreibung nur bei infin und ptp*) (*inf*) (*lit: verfolgen*) to be after (*jdm* sb); (*fig*) (*zurückgeblieben sein*) to lag behind; ~sein, daß ... to see to it that ...

Hinter-: ~hof *m* backyard; (*zwischen Vorder- und Hinterhaus*) courtyard; ~indien *nt* South-East Asia; ~kopf *m* back of one's head; etw im ~kopf haben/behalten (*inf*) to have/keep sth in the back of one's mind; ~lader *m* -s, - breech-loader; (*inf: Homosexueller*) fag (*pej*); ~lage *f* (*Sw*) security; ~land *nt* hinterland; (*Ind*) back-up area; h~lassen[1]* *vt insep irreg* to leave; (*testamentarisch auch*) to bequeath (*jdm etw* sb sth, sth to sb); h~lassene Werke/Schriften posthumous works; h~lassen[2] *vt sep irreg* (*dial inf*) (*inf*) jdn h~lassen to let sb go behind, to allow sb to go behind; ~lassenschaft *f* estate; (*literarisch, fig*) legacy; die ~lassenschaft seines Vorgängers aufarbeiten to finish (off) sb else's (unfinished) work; jds ~lassenschaft antreten (*beerben*) to inherit sb's estate; (*jdm nachfolgen*) to follow sb; ~lassung *f* (*form*) unter ~lassung von Schulden leaving (unsettled *or* unpaid) debts; h~lastig *adj* (*Aviat*) tail-heavy; (*Naut*) stern-heavy; ~lauf *m* (*Hunt*) hind leg; h~legen* *vt insep* (*a*) (*verwahren lassen*) to deposit; (*b*) (*als Pfand h~legen*) to leave.

Hinterlegung *f* deposit.

Hinterlegungs-: ~schein *m* deposit receipt; ~summe *f* sum deposited.

Hinterlist *f* -, *no pl* (*a*) *siehe adj* craftiness, cunning; treachery; deceitfulness. (*b*) (*Trick, List*) ruse, trick.

hinterlistig *adj* (*tückisch*) crafty, cunning; (*verräterisch*) treacherous; (*betrügerisch*) deceitful.

hinterm = hinter dem.

Hintermann *m, pl* ~er **(a)** person/car behind (one). mein ~ the person/car behind me. (*b*) (*inf*) (*Gewährsmann*) contact. die ~er des Skandals the men behind the scandal. (*c*) (*Fin: von Wechsel*) subsequent endorser.

Hintermannschaft *f* (*Sport*) defence.

hintern = hinter den.

Hintern *m* -s, - (*inf*) bottom (*inf*), backside (*inf*), behind. ein Tritt in den ~ a kick in the pants *or* up the backside (*inf*); jdm den ~ versohlen to tan sb's hide; ein paar auf den ~ *or* den ~ voll bekommen to get one's bottom smacked (*inf*); sich auf den ~ setzen (*hinfallen*) to fall on one's bottom *etc*; (*eifrig arbeiten*) to buckle down to work; jdm in den ~ kriechen to lick sb's boots, to suck up to sb; mit dem Zeugnis kann er sich (*dat*) den ~ wischen he might as well use that certificate for toilet paper.

Hinter-: ~pfote *f* hind paw; ~pfuiteufel *nt* -s, *no pl* (*pej inf*) *siehe* ~tupfing(en); ~rad *nt* rear *or* back wheel; ~radantrieb *m* rear wheel drive; h~rücks *adv* from behind; (*fig: heimtückisch*) behind sb's back.

hinters = hinter das.

Hinter-: ~**schiff** nt stern; ~**seite** f back; (von Münze) reverse side; (inf: Hintern) backside (inf); ~**sinn** m underlying or deeper meaning (gen behind); h~**sinnig** adj cryptic.

hinterste(r, s) adj superl of **hintere(r, s)** very back, backmost; (entlegenste) remotest. **die H~n** those at the very back; **das ~ Ende** the very end (or von Saal) back; **in der ~n Reihe** in the very back row; **das H~ zuvorderst kehren** (inf) to turn everything upside down.

Hinterste(r) m decl as adj (inf) siehe **Hintern.**

Hinter-: ~**steven** m (Naut) stern-post; (hum inf: Gesäß) backside (inf); ~**teil** nt (a) (inf) backside (inf); (von Tier) hindquarters pl; (b) auch m back or rear part; ~**treffen** nt im ~**treffen sein** to be at a disadvantage; **ins ~treffen geraten or kommen** to fall behind; h~**treiben*** vt insep irreg (fig) to foil, to thwart; **Gesetz** to block; **er hat es h~trieben, daß ich das machen durfte** he connived to stop me from being allowed to do it; ~**treibung** f siehe vt foiling, thwarting; blocking; ~**treppe** f back stairs pl; **etw von der ~treppe betrachten** to watch sth from the sidelines; ~**treppenroman** m (pej) cheap or trashy novel, penny dreadful (dated Brit), dime novel (US); ~**tupfing(en)** nt **-s, no pl** (inf) the back of beyond; ~**tür** f, (Aus) ~**türl** nt **-s, -(n)** back door; (fig inf: Ausweg, Umweg) loophole; **durch die ~tür** (fig) through the back door; **sich** (dat) **eine ~tür or ein ~türchen offenhalten** or **offenlassen** (fig) to leave oneself a loophole or a way out; ~**wäldler** m **-s, -** (inf) backwoodsman, hillbilly (esp US); h~**wäldlerisch** adj (inf) backwoods attr; **Ansichten, Benehmen, Methoden** auch hick attr; **ein h~wäldlerischer Mensch** a backwoodsman, a hillbilly (esp US); h~**ziehen*** vt insep irreg **Steuern** to evade; **Material** to appropriate; ~**ziehung** f siehe vt evasion; appropriation; ~**zimmer** nt back room.

hin-: ~**tragen** vt sep irreg to take or carry there; ~**treiben** sep irreg 1 vt (a) (Wind) to blow; (Strömung) to wash; (b) (fig) **jdn ~treiben** to drive sb there; 2 vt impers **es trieb ihn immer wieder ~** something always drove him back there; ~**treten** vi sep irreg (a) aux sein **vor jdn ~treten** to go up to sb; **vor Gott** to step before sb; **zu jdm/etw ~treten** to step over to sb/sth; (b) (mit Fuß stoßen) to kick (sth); ~**tun** vt sep irreg (inf) to put; **ich weiß nicht, wo ich ihn ~tun soll** (fig) I can't (quite) place him.

hinüber adv over; (über Grenze, Straße, Fluß auch) across. **da ~** over there; ~ **und herüber** back and forth; **quer** ~ right across; **bis zum anderen Ufer** ~ over or across to the other bank; siehe ~**sein.**

hinüber-: ~**befördern*** vt sep to transport across (über etw (acc) sth); ~**blicken** vi sep to look across (zu jdm to sb); ~**bringen** vt sep irreg to take across (über etw (acc) sth); ~**dämmern** vi sep aux sein (einschlafen) to doze off; (sterben) to pass away in one's sleep; ~**fahren** sep irreg 1 vt (über etw (acc) sth) **jdn** to take across; **Gepäck etc** auch to carry across; **Auto** to drive across; 2 vi aux sein to travel or go across; **nach Frankreich ~fahren** to cross or go across to France; **über den Fluß ~fahren** to cross the river; ~**führen** sep 1 vt (über die Straße/dort/in das andere Zimmer) ~**führen** to take sb across (the street)/over (there)/over (into the other room); 2 vi (verlaufen: Straße, Brücke) to go across (über etw (acc) sth); ~**gehen** vi sep irreg aux sein (a) to go or walk across; (über Brücke auch, zu anderem Haus, zu jdm) to go or walk over (über etw (acc) sth); (b) (euph: sterben) to pass away; ~**gelangen*** vi sep aux sein to get across (über etw (acc) sth); ~**helfen** vi sep irreg **jdm** ~**helfen** to help sb across (über etw (acc) sth); (fig: über Schwierigkeiten) to help sb out (über + acc of); **jdm** (ins Jenseits) ~**helfen** (leichten Tod verschaffen) to help sb to die; (töten) to bump sb off (inf); ~**kommen** vi sep irreg aux sein (über Brücke, Fluß auch, über Hindernis, zu Besuch) to come over; (~**können**) to get across/over; ~**lassen** vt sep irreg to let or allow across; (über Kreuzung, Brücke auch, zu Besuch) to let or allow over (über etw (acc) sth); ~**reichen** sep 1 vt to pass across; (über Zaun etc) to pass over (jdm to sb, über etw (acc) sth); 2 vi to reach across (über etw (acc) sth); (fig) to extend (in + acc into); ~**retten** sep 1 vt to bring to safety; (fig) **Humor, Tradition** to keep alive; **etw in die Gegenwart** ~**retten** to keep sth alive; 2 vr (über Grenze) to reach safety; (fig: Brauch) to be kept alive; ~**rufen** sep irreg 1 vt to call out; 2 vi to call over (über etw (acc) sth); ~**schaffen** vt sep to get across (über etw (acc) sth); ~**schicken** vt sep to send across or (zu Besuch) over (über etw (acc) sth); ~**schwimmen** vi sep aux sein (euph: sterben) to pass away; ~**schwimmen** vi sep irreg aux sein to swim across (über etw (acc) sth); ~**sein** vi sep irreg aux sein (Zusammenschreibung nur bei infin und ptp) (inf) (a) (verdorben sein) to be off or bad; (kaputt, unbrauchbar, tot sein) to have had it (inf); (ruiniert sein: Firma, Politiker) to be done for; (b) (eingeschlafen sein) to have dropped off; (betrunken sein) to be well away (inf); (betäubt sein) to be (knocked) out (inf); ~**spielen** sep 1 vi (geh) **dieses Rot spielt leicht ins Violett** ~ this red has a slight purple tinge or tinge of purple; 2 vt **Ball** to pass (jdm to sb); ~**steigen** vi sep irreg aux sein to climb over (über etw (acc) sth); ~**tragen** vt sep irreg to carry across (über etw (acc) sth); ~**wechseln** vi sep aux haben or sein to change over (zu, in + acc to); **zu einer anderen Partei** ~**wechseln** to go over to another party; ~**werfen** vt sep irreg to throw over (über etw (acc) sth); **einen Blick** ~**werfen** to glance over; ~**ziehen** sep irreg 1 vt to pull across (über etw (acc) sth); (fig: umstimmen) to win over (auf + acc to); 2 vi aux sein (a) (marschieren) to move or march across; (b) (sich bewegen: Rauch, Wolken) to move across (über etw (acc) sth); (c) (umziehen) to move; 3 vr (sich erstrecken) to stretch over (nach, zu to).

hin-und-her-: ~**bewegen*** vtr sep to move to and fro; ~**fahren** sep irreg 1 vi aux sein to travel to and fro or back and forth; 2 vt to drive to and fro or back and forth.

Hin|undhergerede, Hin-und-Her-Gerede nt (inf) **das ewige** ~ this continual argy-bargy (inf) or carrying-on (inf).

Hin-und-Rück-: ~**fahrt** f return journey, round trip (US); ~**flug** m return flight; ~**weg** m round trip.

hinunter 1 adv down. **bis** ~ **zu** down to; **ins Tal** ~ down into the valley; **am Hügel** ~ down the hill; **dort or da** ~ down there; ~ **mit ihm!** down with him; ~ **mit der Arznei** get this medicine down. 2 prep + acc (nachgestellt) down.

hinunter- pref down; ~**blicken** vi sep to look down; ~**bringen** vt sep irreg to take down; (inf: schlucken können) to be able to get down; ~**fahren** sep irreg 1 vi aux sein to go down; (Fahrstuhl, Bergbahn auch) to descend; **in etw** (acc)/**nach etw** ~**fahren** to go down into sth/to sth; 2 vt **Passagier** to take down; **Fahrzeug** to drive down; ~**fallen** vi sep irreg aux sein to fall down; ~**fließen** vi sep irreg aux sein to flow down; ~**gehen** vi sep irreg aux sein to go down; (zu Fuß auch) to walk down; (Flugzeug) to descend (auf + acc to); ~**gießen** vt sep irreg to pour down; **Getränke** to knock back (inf); ~**kippen** vt sep to tip down; (inf) **Getränke** to knock back (inf); ~**klettern** vi sep aux sein to climb down; ~**lassen** vt sep irreg to lower, to let down; **er läßt mich nicht** ~ (inf) he won't let me get down; ~**laufen** vi sep irreg aux sein to run down; **es lief ihm eiskalt den Rücken** ~ a shiver ran down his spine; ~**reichen** sep 1 vt to hand or pass down; 2 vi to reach down; (fig: in Rangfolge) to apply (bis zu down to); ~**reißen** vt sep irreg to pull or drag down; ~**schalten** vi sep (Aut) to change or shift (US) down; ~**schauen** vi sep (dial) to look down; ~**schlingen** vt sep irreg (inf) to gulp down; **Essen** to gobble down; ~**schlucken** vt sep to swallow (down); (fig) **Beleidigung** to swallow; **Kritik** to take; **Ärger, Tränen** to choke back; ~**schmeißen** vt sep irreg (inf) to throw or chuck (inf) down; ~**schütten** vt sep (inf) to throw or pour down; **Getränke** to knock back (inf); ~**schütten** vt sep to pour or tip down; **etw die Toilette/den Ausguß** ~**spülen** to flush sth down the toilet/drain; (b) **Essen, Tablette** to wash down; (fig) **Ärger** to soothe; ~**stürzen** sep 1 vi aux sein (a) (~fallen) to tumble or fall down; (b) (eilig ~laufen) to rush or dash down; 2 vt jdn to throw or hurl down; **Getränk** to gulp down; 3 vr to throw or fling oneself down; ~**werfen** vt sep irreg to throw down; (inf: fallen lassen) to drop; **einen Blick** ~**werfen** to glance down; ~**würgen** vt sep **Essen etc** to choke down; (fig) **Wut, Tränen** to choke back; ~**ziehen** sep irreg 1 vt to pull down; 2 vi aux sein to move down; 3 vr to run down.

Hin-: h~**wagen** vr sep to dare to go there; h~**wärts** adv on the way there; **die Strecke** h~**wärts** the way there; ~**weg** m way there; **auf dem** ~**weg** on the way there.

hinweg adv (a) (old: fort) away. ~ **mit euch** away with you; ~ **mit der Unterdrückung** down with oppression; **vom häuslichen Herd** ~ away from house and home.

(b) **über jdn/etw** ~ over sb or sb's head/sth; **über alle Hindernisse etc** ~ (fig) despite all the difficulties etc.

(c) (zeitlich) **über eine Zeit/zwei Jahre** ~ over a period of time/over (a period of) two years.

hinweg- pref away; ~**brausen** vi sep aux sein (geh) **über etw** ~**brausen** to rage over sth; ~**bringen** vt sep irreg (fig) **jdn über etw** (acc) ~**bringen** to help sb to get over sth; ~**gehen** vi sep irreg aux sein **über etw** (acc) ~**gehen** to pass over or across sth; (nicht beachten) to pass over or disregard sth; ~**helfen** vi sep irreg (fig) **jdm über etw** (acc) ~**helfen** to help sb get over sth; ~**kommen** vi sep irreg aux sein (fig) **über etw** (acc) ~**kommen** (überstehen, verwinden) to get over sth; (sich ~setzen können) to dismiss sth; **ich komme nicht darüber** ~, **daß ...** (inf) I can't get over the fact that ...; ~**raffen** vt sep (geh) to carry off; ~**sehen** vi sep irreg **über jdn/etw** ~**sehen** (lit) to see over sb or sb's head/sth; (fig) (ignorieren) to ignore sb/sth; (unbeachtet lassen) to overlook sb/sth; **darüber** ~**sehen, daß ...** to overlook the fact that ...; ~**setzen** sep 1 vi aux haben or sein **über etw** (acc) ~**setzen** to jump or leap over sth; 2 vr (fig) **sich über etw** (acc) ~**setzen** (nicht beachten) to disregard or dismiss sth; (überwinden) to overcome sth; ~**täuschen** vt sep **jdn über etw** (acc) ~**täuschen** to mislead or deceive sb about sth; **darüber** ~**täuschen, daß ...** to hide the fact that ...; **sich nicht darüber** ~**täuschen lassen, daß ...** not to blind oneself to the fact that ...; ~**trösten** vt sep **jdn über etw** (acc) ~**trösten** to console sb about sth; **deine Entschuldigung tröstet mich nicht darüber** ~, **daß ...** your apology does not make up for the fact that ...

Hinweis m **-es, -e** (a) (Rat) tip, piece of advice; (Bemerkung) comment; (amtlich) notice. **darf ich mir den** ~ **erlauben, daß ...** may I point out or draw your attention to the fact that ...; ~**e für den Benutzer** notes for the user.

(b) (Verweisung) reference. **unter** ~ **auf** (+ acc) with reference to.

(c) (Anhaltspunkt, Anzeichen) indication; (esp von Polizei) clue.

(d) (Anspielung) allusion (auf + acc to).

hinweisen sep irreg 1 vt **jdn auf etw** (acc) ~ to point sth out to sb. 2 vi **auf jdn/etw** ~ to point to sb/sth; (verweisen) to refer to sb/sth; **darauf** ~, **daß ...** to point out that ...; (nachdrücklich) to stress or emphasize that ...; (anzeigen) to indicate that ...

hinweisend adj (Gram) demonstrative.

Hinweis-: ~**schild** nt, ~**tafel** f sign.

hin-: ~**wenden** sep irreg 1 vt to turn (zu, nach towards); 2 vr (lit) to turn (zu, nach towards, to); (fig: Mensch) to turn (zu to); **die Entwicklung wandte sich zum Schlechten** ~ things took a turn for the worse; H~**wendung** f (fig) turning (zu to); **eine H~wendung zum Besseren** a turn for the better; ~**werfen** sep irreg 1 vt (a) (wegwerfen, zu Boden werfen) to throw down; (fallen lassen) to drop; **jdm etw** ~**werfen** to throw sth to sb; (b) (flüchtig machen) **Bemerkung** to drop casually; **Wort** to say casually; **Zeilen, Roman, Zeichnung** to dash off; **einen Blick** ~**werfen** to glance at it/them; **eine** ~**geworfene Bemerkung**

a casual remark; (c) (*inf: aufgeben*) *Arbeit, Stelle* to give up, to chuck (in) (*inf*); 2 *vr* to throw or fling oneself down; (*auf die Knie*) to go down or throw oneself down on one's knees.

hinwieder, hinwiederum (*old*) *adv* (*dagegen*) on the other hand; (*dann wieder*) in turn.

hin-: ~**wirken** *vi sep* auf etw (*acc*) ~**wirken** to work towards sth; **kannst du (nicht) (bei ihm) darauf** ~**wirken, daß er mich empfängt?** couldn't you use your influence to get him to or make him see me?; ~**wollen** *vi sep* (*inf*) to want to go.

Hinz *m*: ~ **und Kunz** (*inf*) every Tom, Dick and Harry; **von** ~ **zu Kunz** from pillar to post.

hin-: ~**zählen** *vt sep* to count out (*jdm* to sb); ~**zaubern** *vt sep* (*fig*) to rustle or whip up (*inf*); ~**ziehen** *sep irreg* 1 *vt* (a) (*zu sich ziehen*) to draw or pull (*zu* towards); (*fig: anziehen*) to attract (*zu* to); **das Heimweh/es zieht mich nach München** ~ homesickness is drawing me/I feel drawn to Munich; **es zieht sie zur Kunst** ~ she feels attracted to art; (b) (*fig: in die Länge ziehen*) to draw or drag out; 2 *vi aux sein* (a) (*sich in bestimmte Richtung bewegen*) to move (*über* +*acc* across, *zu* towards); (*weggehen, -marschieren*) to move or go away; (b) (*liter: Wolken, Rauch etc*) to drift, to move (*an* +*dat* across); (c) (*umziehen*) to move there; 3 *vr* (a) (*lange dauern, sich verzögern*) to drag on; (*sich verzögern*) to be delayed; (b) (*sich erstrecken*) to stretch, to extend; ~**zielen** *vi sep* auf etw (*acc*) ~**zielen** to aim at sth; (*Pläne etc*) to be aimed at sth; (*Bemerkung*) to refer to sth.

hinzu *adv* (*räumlich*) there, thither (*obs*); (*überdies, obendrein*) besides, in addition. ~ **kommt noch, daß ich ... moreover I ...**

hinzu-: ~**bekommen*** *vt sep irreg* to get or Kind have in addition; ~**denken** *vt sep irreg* to add in one's mind or imagination; ~**erfinden*** *vt sep irreg* etw ~**erfinden** to make up and add sth; ~**fügen** *vt sep* to add (*dat* to); (*beilegen*) to enclose; **H~fügung** *f* addition; **unter H~fügung von etw** (*form*) by adding sth; (*als Beilage*) enclosing sth; ~**gesellen*** *vr sep* to join (*jdm* sb); ~**gewinnen*** *vt sep irreg* to get in addition; **neue Mitglieder** **zu gain**; ~**kommen** *vi sep irreg aux sein* (a) (*hinkommen, eintreffen*) to arrive; **sie kam gerade** ~, **als ... she happened to come on the scene when ...; es werden später noch mehrere** ~**kommen** more people will join us or come along later; (*zu etw*) ~**kommen** (*sich anschließen*) to join sth; (b) (*zusätzlich eintreten*) to supervene, to ensue; (*beigefügt werden*) to be added; **zu etw** ~**kommen** to be added to sth; **es kommt noch** ~, **daß ... there is also the fact that ...; kommt sonst noch etwas** ~**?** will there be anything else?; ~**nehmen** *vt sep irreg* to include; **etw zu etw** ~**nehmen** to add sth to sth; ~**rechnen** *vt sep* to add on; ~**setzen** *vt sep* to add; ~**treten** *vi sep irreg aux sein* (a) (*herantreten*) to come up; **zu den anderen** ~**treten** to join the others; (b) (*zusätzlich*) siehe ~**kommen** (b); ~**tun** *vt sep irreg* (*inf*) to add; **H~tun** *nt* siehe **Dazutun**; ~**zählen** *vt sep* to add; ~**ziehen** *vt sep irreg* to consult; **H~ziehung** *f, no pl* consultation (*gen* with); **unter H~ziehung eines Lexikons** by consulting a dictionary; **unter H~ziehung Bayerns** including Bavaria.

Hiob *m* -s Job. **das Buch** ~ the Book of Job.

Hiobsbotschaft, Hiobspost (*old*) *f* bad news *no pl* or tidings *pl*.

Hippe *f* -, -n (*Messer*) pruning knife; (*Sense des Todes*) scythe.

hipp, hipp, hurra *interj* hip, hip, hurrah or hurray.

Hipphipphurra *nt* -s, -s cheer. **ein dreifaches** ~ three cheers.

Hippie ['hɪpi] *m* -s, -s hippie.

Hippodrom *nt* or *m* -s, -e hippodrome.

hippokratisch *adj* Hippocratic. ~**er Eid** Hippocratic oath.

Hirn *nt* -(e)s, -e (a) (*Anat*) brain.

  (b) (*inf*) (*Kopf*) head; (*Verstand*) brains *pl*, mind. **sich** (*dat*) **das** ~ **zermartern** to rack one's brain(s); **diese Idee ist doch nicht deinem** ~ **entsprungen?** that's not your own idea or brainwave, is it?

  (c) (*Cook*) brains *pl*.

Hirn- siehe auch **Gehirn-**; ~**anhang** *m*, ~**anhangsdrüse** *f* (*Anat*) pituitary gland; ~**gespinst** *nt* fantasy; ~**haut** *f* (*Anat*) meninges *pl*; ~**hautentzündung** *f* (*Med*) meningitis; **h~los** *adj* brainless; ~**rinde** *f* (*Anat*) cerebral cortex; **h~rissig** *adj* harebrained; ~**stamm** *m* brainstorm; ~**tumor** *m* brain tumour; **h~verbrannt** *adj* hare-brained; ~**windung** *f* (*Anat*) convolution of the brain; ~**zentrum** *nt* brain centre.

Hirsch *m* -es, -e (a) (*Paarhufer*) deer; (*Rot~*) red deer; (*männlicher Rot~*) stag; (*Cook*) venison. (b) (*dial sl: Könner*) smart or clever person. (c) (*inf: Schimpfwort*) clot (*inf*).

Hirsch-: ~**art** *f* kind or species *sing* of deer; ~**bock** *m* stag; ~**braten** *m* (*Cook*) roast of venison; (*Gericht*) roast venison; ~**brunft, ~brunst** *f* rut; **zur Zeit der** ~**brunft** during the rutting season; ~**fänger** *m* hunting knife; ~**geweih** *nt* antlers *pl*.

Hirschhorn *nt* horn.

Hirschhorn-: ~**knopf** *m* horn button; ~**salz** *nt* (*Chem*) ammonium carbonate.

Hirsch-: ~**jagd** *f* stag-hunt/-hunting; ~**käfer** *m* stag-beetle; ~**kalb** *nt* (male) fawn, (male) deer calf; ~**keule** *f* haunch of venison; ~**kuh** *f* hind; ~**leder** *nt* buckskin, deerskin; **h~ledern** *adj* buckskin, deerskin; ~**lederne** *f* decl as adj (*esp Aus*) buckskin breeches *pl*, buckskins *pl* (*US*).

Hirse *f* -, -n millet.

Hirse-: ~**brei** *m* millet gruel; ~**korn** *nt* millet seed.

Hirt *m* -en, -en herdsman; (*Schaf~*) shepherd. **wie der** ~, **so die Herde** (*Prov*) like master, like man (*prov*).

-hirt *m* in cpds -herd.

Hirte *m* -n, -n (a) (*liter*) siehe **Hirt**. (b) (*Eccl: Seelsorger*) shepherd. **der Gute** ~ the Good Shepherd.

hirten *vi* (*Sw*) to tend one's herd/sheep etc.

Hirten-: ~**amt** *nt* (*Eccl*) pastorate, pastorship; ~**brief** *m* (*Eccl*) pastoral; ~**dichtung** *f* siehe **Schäferdichtung**; ~**flöte** *f* shepherd's pipe; ~**gedicht** *nt* pastoral; ~**gott** *m* god of

shepherds; ~**hund** *m* sheepdog; ~**junge, ~knabe** (*liter*) *m* shepherd boy; ~**lied** *nt* shepherd's song; **h~los** *adj* (*lit, fig*) shepherdless; ~**mädchen** *nt* young shepherdess; ~**pfeife** *f* siehe ~**flöte**; ~**spiel** *nt* pastoral (play); ~**stab** *m* shepherd's crook; (*Eccl*) crosier; ~**täschel(kraut)** *nt* -s, - shepherd's-purse; ~**volk** *nt* pastoral people.

Hirtin *f* herdswoman; (*Schaf~*) shepherdess.

His, his *nt* -, - (*Mus*) B sharp.

Hispanien [-iən] *nt* -s, *no pl* (*obs*) Hispania (*old*).

hispanisch *adj* (*obs*) Hispanic.

hispanisieren* *vt* to Hispanicize.

Hispanismus *m* (*Ling*) Hispanicism.

Hispanist(in *f*) *m* Spanish specialist, Hispanist; (*Student*) Spanish student; (*Professor etc*) Spanish lecturer/professor.

Hispanistik *f* Spanish (language and literature).

hissen *vt* to hoist.

Histamin *nt* -s, *no pl* histamine.

Histologe *m*, **Histologin** *f* histologist.

Histologie *f* histology.

histologisch *adj* histological.

Histörchen *nt* anecdote; (*Klatschgeschichte*) little tale or story.

Historie [-iə] *f* (*old*) (a) (*Weltgeschichte*) history. (b) (*Erzählung*) story, tale.

Historien [-iən] *pl* **Shakespeares** ~ Shakespeare's history plays or histories.

Historien-: ~**maler** *m* painter of historical scenes; ~**malerei** *f* (art of) painting historical scenes.

Historik *f* history.

Historiker(in *f*) *m* -s, - historian.

Historiograph *m* historiographer.

Historiographie *f* historiography.

historisch *adj* historical; *Verständnis, Kenntnisse auch* of history; (*geschichtlich bedeutsam*) *Gestalt, Ereignis, Gebäude* historic. **das ist** ~ **belegt** there is historical evidence for this; ~ **denken** to think in historical terms; ~ **betrachtet** seen in the light of history.

historisch-kritisch *adj Ausgabe* historico-critical.

historisieren* *vi* to historicize.

Historismus *m, no pl* historicism.

historistisch *adj* historicist.

Histrione *m* -n, -n (*geh*) (play-)actor.

Hit *m* -s, -s (*Mus, fig inf*) hit.

Hitler *m* -s Hitler.

Hitler-: ~**gruß** *m* Hitler salute; ~**-Jugend** *f* Hitler Youth (organization); ~**junge** *m* member of the Hitler Youth; ~**reich** *nt* (Third) Reich; ~**zeit** *f* Hitler era.

Hit-: ~**liste** *f* top ten/twenty/thirty; ~**parade** *f* hit parade.

Hitze *f* -, -n (a) heat; (~**zeit**, ~**welle**) hot spell. **vor** ~ **umkommen** to be sweltering (in the heat); **eine** ~ **ist das!** the heat (is incredible)!; **die fliegende** ~ **bekommen** (*Med*) to get hot flushes; (*inf*) to get all hot and bothered; **bei starker/mittlerer/mäßiger** ~ **backen** (*Cook*) bake in a hot/medium/moderate oven.

  (b) (*fig*) passion. **in** ~**/leicht in** ~ **geraten** to get heated/to get worked up easily; **jdn in** ~ **bringen/sich in** ~ **reden** to get sb/oneself all worked up; **in der ersten** ~**/in der** ~ **des Gefecht(e)s** (*fig*) in the heat of the moment.

  (c) (*Zool*) heat.

Hitze-: **h~abweisend** *adj* heat-repellant; ~**ausschlag** *m* heat rash, prickly heat *no art*; **h~beständig** *adj* heat-resistant; ~**beständigkeit** *f* heat resistance; ~**bläschen** *nt* heat-spot; **h~empfindlich** *adj* sensitive to heat; ~**ferien** *pl* (*Sch*) time off from school on account of excessively hot weather; **h~frei** *adj* **h~frei haben** to have time off from school/work on account of excessively hot weather; ~**pickel** *m* (*inf*) siehe ~**bläschen**; ~**schild** *m* (*Space*) heat shield; ~**wallung** *f* usu *pl* (*Med*) hot flush; ~**welle** *f* heat wave.

hitzig *adj* (a) (*aufbrausend*) *Mensch* hot-headed; *Antwort, Reaktion, Debatte* heated; (*leidenschaftlich*) *Temperament, Typ, Diskussionsteilnehmer* passionate; *Blut* hot. ~ **werden** (*Mensch*) to flare up; (*Debatte*) to grow heated; **nicht so** ~**!** don't get so excited!, hold your horses!; **ein** ~**er Kopf** (*geh*) a hothead.

  (b) (*dated Med: fiebrig*) *Kopf, Gesichtsfarbe* fevered; *Fieber* high.

  (c) (*Zool*) on heat.

Hitzigkeit *f* siehe *adj* (a) hot-headedness; heatedness; passionateness.

Hitz-: ~**kopf** *m* hothead; **h~köpfig** *adj* hot-headed; ~**schlag** *m* (*Med*) heat-stroke.

Hiwi *m* -s, -s (a) *abbr of* **Hilfswillige(r)**. (b) (*Univ sl*) helper. (c) (*pej inf: Hilfskraft*) dogsbody (*inf*).

hj. *abbr of* **halbjährlich.**

Hj. *abbr of* **Halbjahr.**

hl. *abbr of* **heilig.**

Hl. *abbr of* **Heilige(r)** St.

hm *interj* hm.

H-Milch ['ha:-] *f* long-life milk.

h-Moll ['ha:-] *nt* -, *no pl* B-minor.

HNO-Arzt [ha:ɛn'ʔo:-] *m* ENT specialist.

hob *pret of* **heben.**

Hobby *nt* -s, -s hobby.

Hobbyraum *m* hobby-room, workroom.

Hobel *m* -s, - (*Tech*) plane; (*Cook*) slicer.

Hobel-: ~**bank** *f* carpenter's or joiner's bench; ~**eisen** *nt* plane-iron; ~ **maschine** *f* planer, planing machine; ~**messer** *nt* siehe

hobeln *vt* (a) auch *vi* (*Tech*) to plane (*an etw* (*dat*) sth); (*glätten*) *Brett* to plane down. **wo gehobelt wird, da fallen Späne** (*Prov*) you can't make an omelette without breaking eggs (*Prov*). (b) (*Cook*) to slice.

Hobelspan m, **Hobelscha(r)te** f (*Aus*) shaving.

Hobler m -s, - planer.

Hoboe [-'bo:ə] f -, -n (*old*) siehe **Oboe**.

Hoch nt -s, -s (a) (*Ruf*) ein (dreifaches) ~ für or auf jdn ausbringen to give three cheers for sb; ein ~ dem Brautpaar a toast to the bride and groom.
(b) (*Met, fig*) high.

hoch 1 adj, attr hohe(r, s) comp höher, superl ¨ste(r, s) (a) (*räumliche Ausdehnung*) high; Wuchs, Zimmer, Baum, Mast tall; Leiter tall, long; Schnee, Wasser deep. 10 cm ~ 10 cm high; auf dem hohen Roß sitzen (*fig*) to be on one's high horse.
(b) (*mengenmäßig, Ausmaß bezeichnend*) Preis, Verdienst, Temperatur, Druck etc high; Betrag, Summe large; Strafe, Gewicht heavy; Profit auch, Lotteriegewinn big; Verlust auch big, severe; Schaden extensive. mit hoher Wahrscheinlichkeit in all probability; in hohem Maße in or to a high degree.
(c) (*in bezug auf Rang, Ansehen, Bedeutung*) Stellung, Position, Amt, Adel, Meinung high; Geburt auch noble; Rang auch superior; Persönlichkeit distinguished; Ehre great; Fest auch, Besuch, Feiertag, Jubiläum important; Offizier high-ranking; Favorit hot; (*Jur, Pol*) high. ~ und niedrig rich and poor; das Hohe Haus (*Parl*) the House; hohe Frau! (*old*) noble lady!; ein hohes Tier (*inf*) a big fish (*inf*); hohe Herrschaften (*form*) ladies and gentlemen; die hohen Herrschaften, der Boß und seine Familie (*iro inf*) the boss and his family (*inf*); ein Mann von hohem Ansehen/hoher Bildung a man of high standing/of culture; siehe **Gewalt**.
(d) (*qualitativ, sehr groß*) Lebensstandard, Ansprüche high; Bedeutung, Genuß, Gut, Glück great.
(e) (*esp Mus*) high. das hohe C top C.
(f) Alter great, advanced. ein hohes Alter erreichen to live to a ripe old age; er ist ein hoher Siebziger he is well into his seventies; im hohen Mittelalter at the height of the Middle Ages.
(g) (*in Wendungen*) das ist mir zu ~ (*inf*) that's (well) above my head; in hoher Blüte stehen to be in full bloom; (*fig*) (*Mensch*) to be in one's prime; (*Kultur*) to be at its zenith; (*Wohlstand*) to flourish, to be flourishing; hohe Flut spring tide; die hohe Jagd deer hunt(ing); das Hohe Lied (*Bibl*) the Song of Songs; ein hohes Lied auf jdn/etw singen to sing sb's/sth's praises; die Hohe Schule (*beim Reiten*) haute école; (*old geh: Hochschule*) university, college; die Hohe Schule des Lebens/der Menschenkenntnis the school of life; es ist hohe Zeit (*geh*) it's high time; der hohe Norden the far North; siehe höchste(r, s), bestimmen.

2 adv, comp höher, superl am ¨sten (a) (*nach oben*) up. er sah zu uns ~ (*inf*) he looked up to us; ~ emporragend towering (up); ein ~ aufgeschossener Mann a very tall man; den Kopf ~ tragen to hold one's head high; die Nase ~ tragen (*inf*) to be stuck up or toffee-nosed, to go around with one's nose in the air (*all inf*); zwei Treppen ~ wohnen to live two floors up; nach Hamburg ~ up to Hamburg; er krempelte sich die Hosenbeine so ~, daß ... he rolled up his trouser-legs so far that ...
(b) (*in einiger Höhe*) high. ~ oben high up; ~ am Himmel high (up) in the sky; die Sonne steht ~ the sun is high in the sky; ~ zu Roß on horseback; ~ werfen/sitzen/wachsen to throw high/sit up high/grow tall; 4.000 m ~ fliegen to fly at a height of 4,000 metres.
(c) (*Bedeutung, Ansehen, Qualität bezeichnend*) verehren, schätzen, qualifiziert highly. das rechne ich ihm ~ an (I think) that is very much to his credit; ~ hinauswollen to aim high, to be ambitious; in der Rangordnung sehr ~ stehen to be very high up in the hierarchy.
(d) (*Ausmaß, Menge bezeichnend*) bezahlen, versichern, willkommen, begabt highly; besteuern, verlieren heavily; gewinnen handsomely; verschuldet deeply; zufrieden, beglückt, erfreut etc very. drei Mann ~ (*inf*) three of them; ~ (ein)schätzen/zu ~ (ein)schätzen to estimate generously/to overestimate; wie ~ kalkulieren Sie den Bedarf? how high would you put the requirements?; wenn es ~ kommt (*inf*) at (the) most, at the outside; ~ setzen or spielen (*im Spiel*) to play for high stakes; ~ favorisiert sein to be the hot favourite; wie ~ kommt das? how much is that?; ~ wetten to place high bets; ~ zu stehen kommen (*lit, fig*) to cost dearly; der Alkoholgehalt liegt sehr ~ the alcohol level is very high; er ist ~ an Jahren/betagt he has reached a ripe old age; er ist ~ in den Siebzigern well into his etc seventies; bis ~ ins 13. Jahrhundert until well into the 13th century; wie ~ steht das Thermometer? how high is the temperature?
(e) (*Math*) 7 ~ 3 7 to the power of 3, 7 to the 3rd.
(f) (*Mus*) high.
(g) (*in Wendungen*) es ging ~ her (*inf*) there were lively goings-on (*inf*); die See geht ~ the sea is running high; ~ lebe der König! long live the King!; ~ und heilig versprechen to promise faithfully; ~ und heilig schwören (*inf*) to swear blind (*inf*); ~! cheers!; die Menge rief ~! the crowd cheered; siehe **hochleben**.

hoch- pref (*in Verbindung mit Bewegungsverb*) up; (*in Verbindung mit adj*) bezahlt, qualifiziert, versichert, begabt etc highly; zufrieden, beglückt, erfreut, elegant etc very; besteuert heavily; verschuldet deeply.

Hoch-: h~achtbar adj attr (*dated*) highly respectable; h~achten vt sep to respect highly; ~achtung f deep respect; jdm seine ~achtung für seine Leistung zollen to be full of admiration for sb's achievement; bei aller ~achtung vor jdm/etw with (the greatest) respect for sb/sth; meine ~achtung! well done!; mit vorzüglicher ~achtung (*form: Briefschluß*) yours faithfully; h~achtungsvoll adv

(*Briefschluß*) yours faithfully; ~adel m high nobility; h~aktuell adj highly topical; h~alpin adj (high) alpine; ~altar m high altar; ~amt nt (*Eccl*) High Mass; h~angesehen adj attr highly regarded/esteemed; h~anständig adj very decent; ~antenne f roof aerial (*Brit*) or antenna (*US*); h~arbeiten vr sep to work one's way up; h~aufgeschossen adj attr Mensch lanky; Pflanze tall, that has shot up; ~aufgeständerte Straße or railroad (*US*), el (*US inf*); ~barock m or nt high baroque; ~bau m, no pl structural engineering; siehe ~und-Tiefbau; h~bäumen vr sep siehe aufbäumen; h~beansprucht adj attr (*Tech*) highly stressed; h~begabt adj attr highly gifted or talented; h~beglückt adj attr supremely or blissfully happy; h~beinig adj long-legged; Auto high on the road; h~bekommen* vt sep irreg Stein, Motorhaube etc to (manage to) lift or get up; Reißverschluß to (manage to) get or do up; h~beladen adj attr with a high load; h~berühmt adj very famous; h~betagt adj aged attr, advanced in years; ~betrieb m (*in Geschäft, Fabrik etc*) peak period; (*im Verkehr*) rush hour; (*Hochsaison*) high season; ~betrieb haben to be at one's/its busiest; h~biegen vtr sep irreg to bend up or upward(s); h~binden vt sep irreg Haare, Pflanze to tie up; h~blicken vi sep siehe h~sehen; ~blüte f (*fig*) (*von Geschichte, Literatur*) golden age; seine ~blüte haben to be at its zenith; h~bocken vt sep to jack up; h~bringen vt sep irreg (*inf*) (a) (*nach oben bringen*) to bring or take up; (b) (*inf: h~heben, h~drücken können*) to (manage to) get up; einen/keinen h~bringen (*sl*) to be able/not to be able to get it up (*sl*); (c) (*fig*) (*leistungsfähig machen*) to get going; Kranken to get back on his etc feet; Schüler to get up to scratch; (d) (*fig inf: ärgern*) jdn h~bringen to get sb's back up (*inf*); ~bunker m surface air-raid shelter; ~burg f (*fig*) stronghold; h~busig adj high-bosomed; ~decker m -s, - (*Aviat*) high-wing monoplane; h~deutsch adj standard or High German; die h~deutsche Lautverschiebung the High German sound shift; ~deutsch(e) nt standard or High German, the standard or High German language; h~dienen vr sep to work one's way up; h~dotiert adj attr Mensch highly remunerated; Arbeit highly remunerative; h~drehen vt sep Fenster to wind up; Motor to rev up.

Hochdruck m (a) (*Met*) high pressure.
(b) (*Typ*) (*no pl: Verfahren*) surface or relief printing; (*Gedrucktes*) relief print.
(c) (*Phys*) high pressure. (einen) ~ herstellen to create high pressure.
(d) (*Med: Blutdruck*) high blood pressure.
(e) (*fig*) mit ~ arbeiten to work at full stretch; im Betrieb herrscht ~ there's great pressure or work at work.

Hochdruck-: ~gebiet nt (*Met*) high-pressure area, anticyclone; ~verfahren nt (*Typ*) relief printing method.

Hoch-: ~ebene f plateau; h~empfindlich adj (*Tech*) Stoff, Material, Gerät, Instrumente highly sensitive; Film fast; Stoff very delicate; diese Farbe/dieser Teppich ist h~empfindlich this colour/carpet shows up everything; h~entwickelt adj attr Kultur, Volk, Land highly developed; (*verfeinert*) Geräte, Maschinen, Methoden sophisticated; h~erhoben adj attr raised high; h~erhobenen Hauptes (*fig*) with head held high; h~explosiv adj (*lit, fig*) highly explosive; h~fahren adj sep irreg 1 vi aux sein (a) (*nach oben fahren*) to go up; (*in Auto auch*) to drive up; (b) (*erschreckt*) to start (up); aus dem Schlaf h~fahren to wake up with a start; (c) (*aufbrausen*) to flare up; 2 vt to take up; (*in Auto auch*) to drive up; h~fahrend adj (a) (*überheblich*) arrogant; (b) siehe h~fliegend; h~fein adj (*von Qualität*) high quality; (*inf*) Mensch (terribly) posh (*inf*); ~finanz f high finance; ~fläche f siehe ~ebene; h~fliegen vi sep irreg aux sein to fly up; (*Vogel auch*) to soar; (*in die Luft geschleudert werden*) to be thrown up; h~fliegend adj ambitious; (*übertrieben*) high-flown; h~florig adj Samt, Teppich deep-pile attr; ~form f top form; ~format nt vertical format; h~frequent adj high frequency.

Hochfrequenz f (*Elec*) high frequency.

Hochfrequenz-: ~kamera f high-speed camera; ~strom m high-frequency current; ~technik f high-frequency engineering.

Hoch-: ~frisur f upswept hairstyle; sie hat eine ~frisur she wears her hair up; ~garage f multi-storey car park; h~gebenedeit adj (*old, Eccl*) most blessed; ~gebirge nt high mountains pl, high mountain region or area; ~gebirgspflanze f alpine plant; h~geboren adj (*dated*) high-born; (*Eure or Euer*) ~geboren (*Anrede*) your Honour; seine ~geboren his Honour; h~geehrt adj attr highly honoured; h~geehrter Herr (*old: im Brief*) esteemed Sir (*old*); h~gefühl nt elation; ein ~gefühl haben to have a feeling of elation, to feel elated; im ~gefühl des Sieges elated by the victory; h~gehen vi sep irreg aux sein (a) (*sich nach oben bewegen*) to rise; (*Preise auch*) to go up, to climb; (*Ballon auch*) to ascend; (*Wellen*) to surge; (b) (*inf: hinaufgehen*) to go up; (*inf: explodieren*) to blow up; (*Bombe*) to go off; etw h~gehen lassen to blow sth up; (d) (*inf: wütend werden*) to go through the roof; da geht einem der Hut h~ (*fig inf*) it's enough to make you blow your top (*inf*); (e) (*inf: gefaßt werden*) (*einzelner Verbrecher*) to get nabbed (*inf*); (*Bande auch*) to be blown sky-high (*inf*); jdn h~gehen lassen to blow the gaff on sb (*inf*); h~geistig adj highly intellectual; Lektüre, Mensch auch highbrow; h~gelegen adj attr high-altitude, high-lying; ein h~gelegener Ort in den Alpen a place situated high up in the Alps; h~gelehrt adj erudite, very learned; h~gemut adj (*geh*) cheerful, in good spirits; ~genuß m great or special treat; (*großes Vergnügen*) great pleasure; jdm ein ~genuß sein to be a real treat for sb; ~gericht nt (*Hist*) (*Gericht*) criminal court; (*Richtstätte*) scaffold; h~geschätzt adj attr Mensch highly esteemed; Sache greatly valued, much treasured; h~geschlossen adj Kleid etc high-necked;

h~gespannt adj (fig) Erwartungen extreme; h~gesteckt 1 ptp of h~stecken; 2 adj (fig) Ziele ambitious; h~gestellt adj attr (fig) Persönlichkeit high-ranking, important; h~gestochen adj (pej inf) highbrow; Reden high-faluting; Stil pompous; (eingebildet) stuck-up; h~gewachsen adj tall; h~gezüchtet adj (usu pej) Motor souped-up (sl); Geräte fancy (inf); Tiere, Pflanzen overbred.

Hochglanz m high polish or shine; (Phot) gloss. etw auf ~ polieren or bringen to polish sth until it gleams, to make sth shine like a new pin; (fig) to make sth spick and span.

Hochglanz|abzug m (Phot) glossy print.

hochglänzend adj Stoff, Oberfläche very shiny; Papier, Fotoabzug very glossy; Möbel highly polished.

Hochglanz-: ~papier nt high gloss paper; h~polieren* vt sep etw h~polieren to give sth a high or mirror polish; ~politur f (Oberfläche) mirror polish or finish; (Poliermittel) (furniture) polish.

Hoch-: ~gotik f high gothic period; h~gradig adj no pred extreme; (inf) Unsinn etc absolute, utter; h~gucken vi sep siehe h~sehen; h~hackig adj Schuhe high-heeled; h~halten vt sep irreg (a) (in die Höhe halten) to hold up; (b) (in Ehren halten) to uphold; ~haus nt high-rise or multi-storey building; (Wolkenkratzer) sky-scraper; h~heben vt sep irreg Hand, Arm to lift, to raise, to hold up; Kind, Last to lift up; durch ~heben der Hände abstimmen to vote by (a) show of hands; h~herrschaftlich adj very elegant or grand; Wohnung auch palatial; h~herzig adj generous, magnanimous; Mensch auch big-hearted; ~herzigkeit f generosity, magnanimity; (von Mensch auch) big-heartedness; h~industrialisiert adj attr highly industrialized; h~intelligent adj highly intelligent; h~interessant adj most interesting; h~jagen vt sep (inf) (a) (aufscheuchen) Vögel to scare up; Menschen to get up; (b) (sprengen) to blow up; (c) Motor to rev up; h~jubeln vt sep (inf) Künstler, Film, Politiker etc to build up (excessively); h~kämmen vt sep Haar to put up; h~kant adv (a) (lit) on end; h~kant stellen to up-end, to put on end; (b) (fig inf: auch h~kantig) h~kant hinauswerfen/hinausfliegen to chuck/be chucked out (inf); h~karätig adj Diamanten, Gold high-carat; (b) (fig) top-class; ~kirche f High Church; h~klappbar adj Tisch, Stuhl folding; Sitz tip-up; h~klappen sep 1 vt Tisch, Stuhl to fold up; Sitz to tip up; Kühlerhaube, Deckel to raise, to lift up; Mantelkragen to turn up; 2 vi aux sein (Tisch, Stuhl) to fold up; (Sitz) to tip up; h~klettern vi sep aux sein (lit, fig) to climb up; h~kommen vi sep irreg aux sein (a) (inf: hinauf-, heraufkommen) to come up; (b) (inf) das Essen ist ihm h~gekommen he threw up (his meal) (inf); es kommt mir h~ it makes me sick; (c) (aufstehen können) to (manage to) get up; (fig: sich aufraffen, gesund werden) to get back on one's feet; (d) (inf: beruflich, gesellschaftlich) to come up in the world; niemanden (neben sich dat) h~kommen lassen not to tolerate competition; ~konjunktur f boom; h~können vi sep irreg (inf) (aufstehen können) to be able to get up; (hinaufsteigen können) to be able to get up (auf etw (acc) onto sth, auf Berg the mountain); hinten nicht mehr h~können (inf) to be more dead than alive; h~konzentriert adj highly concentrated; h~krempeln vt sep Ärmel, Hosenbeine to roll up; h~kriegen vt sep (inf) siehe h~bekommen; er kann keinen h~kriegen (sl) he can't get it up (sl); h~kultiviert adj highly sophisticated; Lebensart highly civilized; ~kultur f (very) advanced civilization; h~kurbeln vt sep Fenster to wind up; ~land nt highland; das schottische ~land the Scottish Highlands pl; ~länder(in f) m -s, - highlander; ~lautung f (Ling) Standard German pronunciation; h~leben vi sep jdn h~leben lassen to give three cheers for sb; er lebe h~! three cheers (for him)!; h~ lebe der König! long live the King!; h~legen vt sep (a) Beine etc to put up; (b) (inf: nach oben legen) to put high up.

Hochleistung f first-class performance.

Hochleistungs-: ~motor m high-performance engine; ~öl nt heavy-duty oil; ~sport m competitive sport; ~sportler m top athlete; ~training nt intensive training.

höchlich(st) adv (dated) highly, greatly, most.

Hoch-: h~löblich adj (dated) very or highly praiseworthy; (iro) most appreciated; ~mittelalter nt high Middle Ages pl; h~modern adj very modern, ultra-modern; ~moor nt moor; ~mut m arrogance; ~mut kommt vor dem Fall (Prov) pride comes before a fall (Prov); h~mütig adj arrogant; ~mütigkeit f arrogance; h~näsig adj (inf) snooty (inf); ~näsigkeit f (inf) snootiness (inf); ~nebel m (low) stratus; h~nehmen vt sep irreg (a) (heben) to lift; Kind, Hund to pick or lift up; (b) (dial: in oberes Stockwerk) to take up; (c) (inf: necken) jdn h~nehmen to pull sb's leg; (d) (inf: schröpfen) jdn h~nehmen to fleece sb (inf); (e) (inf: verhaften) to pick up (inf); ~ofen m blast furnace; h~päppeln vt sep (inf) Tier, Kind, Kranken to feed up; (fig) to nurse back to health; ~parterre nt raised ground floor; ~plateau nt plateau; h~polymer adj (Chem) high-polymeric; h~prozentig adj alkoholische Getränke high-proof; Lösung highly concentrated; h~qualifiziert adj attr highly qualified; ~rad nt penny-farthing (bicycle); h~rädrig adj with high wheels; h~ragen vi sep aux sein or haben (Bäume) to rise (up); (Berge, Türme, Häuser) to tower (up), to rise up; h~ranken vir sep (vi: aux sein) to creep (up), to climb (up); h~rechnen sep 1 vt to project; 2 vi to make a projection; ~rechnung f projection; ~reck nt high or horizontal bar; h~recken sep 1 vt Arme, Hände to raise or stretch up; den Hals or Kopf h~recken to crane one's neck; 2 vr to draw oneself up; h~reißen vt sep irreg Arme to bring up; Kamera, Waffe to lift quickly; (Aviat) to put into a steep climb, to hoick (spec); ~relief nt high relief; ~renaissance f high renaissance; h~rot adj bright red; mit h~rotem Gesicht with one's face as red as a beetroot; ~ruf m cheer; h~rutschen vi sep aux sein (Kleidungsstück) to ride up;

(inf: aufrücken) to move up; ~saison f high season; h~schätzen vt sep siehe h~achten; h~schaukeln vr sep to work oneself up; h~scheuchen vt sep (inf) siehe aufscheuchen; h~schießen sep irreg 1 vi aux sein to shoot up; 2 vt Feuerwerksrakete, Leuchtkugel to send up; h~schlagen sep irreg 1 vt Kragen to turn up; 2 vi aux sein (Wellen) to surge up; (Flammen) to leap up; h~schnellen vi sep aux sein (Lachse) to leap up; (Feder, Mensch, Preise auch) to shoot up; h~schrauben vt sep (lit) to raise; (fig) Preise to force up; Erwartungen to raise; Forderungen, Ansprüche to increase; h~schrecken vti sep (vi: irreg aux sein) siehe aufschrecken.

Hochschul-: ~abschluß m degree; mit ~abschluß with a degree; ~absolvent m graduate; ~(aus)bildung f (Ausbildung) college/university training; (Bildung) university education.

Hochschule f college; (Universität) university. Technische ~ technical college, college of technology.

Hochschüler(in f) m student; (Universitäts~ auch) undergraduate.

Hochschul-: ~lehrer m college/university teacher, lecturer (Brit); ~politik f higher education policy; ~reform f university reform; ~reife f academic standard required for university entrance; er hat (die) ~reife = he's got his A-levels (Brit), he's graduated from high school (US); ~studium nt higher education, university education; ~wesen nt system of higher education, university system; ~zugang m university entrance or admission.

hochschwanger adj well advanced in pregnancy, very pregnant (inf).

Hochsee f high sea. auf ~ on the high seas or open sea.

Hochsee-: ~fischerei f deep-sea fishing; ~kutter m deep-sea cutter; ~schiffahrt f deep-sea shipping; h~tüchtig adj ocean-going.

Hoch-: h~sehen vi sep irreg to look up; ~seil nt high wire, tight-rope; ~seilakt m (von Artisten) high-wire or tightrope act; (fig) tightrope walk; ~sitz m (Hunt) (raised) hide; ~sommer m height of the summer; (Zeitabschnitt) midsummer no art; h~sommerlich adj very summery.

Hochspannung f (Elec) high voltage, high tension; (fig) high tension. „Vorsicht ~" "danger - high voltage".

Hochspannungs-: ~leitung f high tension line, power line; ~mast m pylon; ~technik f high-voltage engineering.

Hoch-: h~spielen vt sep (fig) to blow up, to play up; etw (künstlich) h~spielen to blow sth up out of all proportion; ~sprache f standard language; h~sprachlich adj standard; h~sprachlich heißt es ... in standard German/English etc that's ...; sich h~sprachlich ausdrücken to speak standard German/English etc; h~springen vi sep irreg aux sein (a) (inf: aufspringen) to jump up (an jdm on sb); auf etw (acc) h~springen to jump (up) on sth; (b) (inf: schnell hinauflaufen) to run up; (c) infin, ptp only (Sport) to do the high jump; ~springer m high jumper; ~sprung m (Disziplin) high jump; (Sprung) high jump.

höchst 1 adj siehe höchste(r, s). 2 adv (überaus) highly, extremely, most.

Höchst- in cpds (obere Grenze angebend) (mit n) maximum; (mit adj) siehe Hoch-; (mit adj: Intensität ausdrückend) extremely, most; ~alter nt maximum age.

Hoch-: h~stämmig adj Baum tall; Rosen long-stemmed; ~stand m (Hunt) siehe ~sitz; ~stapelei f (Jur) fraud; (einzelner Fall) swindle, con trick; (fig: Aufschneiderei) boasting no pl; h~stapeln vi sep (Jur) to be fraudulent, to practise fraud (form); (fig) to put one over (inf); ~stapler m -s, - confidence trickster, con man (inf); (fig) fraud; ~start m (Sport) standing start.

Höchst-: ~betrag m maximum amount; ~bietende(r) mf decl as adj highest bidder.

höchste adj siehe höchste(r, s).

Höchste siehe Höchste(r), Höchste(s).

hoch-: ~stecken vt sep to pin up; Haare auch to put up; ~stehend adj (a) (gesellschaftlich) of high standing; (kulturell) advanced; (geistig) highly intellectual; (b) (entwicklungsmäßig, qualitativ) superior; (c) Kragen turned-up; ~steigen vi sep irreg aux sein siehe hinauf-/heraufsteigen, aufsteigen.

höchst-: ~eigen adj, adv ~eigen, in ~eigener Person (dated, hum) in person; ~eigenhändig adv (dated, iro) personally; schreiben, malen, kochen etc with one's own (fair hum) hands.

hoch-: ~stellen vt sep (a) (an höhere Stelle) Stühle etc to put up; (außer Reichweite) to put or place high up; ~gestellte Zahlen superior numbers; (b) (inf: höher einstellen) Heizung, Ventilator etc to turn up; (c) Kragen to turn up; ~stemmen sep 1 vt to lift or raise up (with great effort); 2 vr to raise oneself up.

höchstenfalls adv at (the) most, at the outside.

höchstens adv (a) (nicht mehr, länger als) not more than; (bestenfalls) at the most, at best. (b) (außer) except.

Höchste(r) m decl as adj der ~ the Lord, the Supreme Being.

höchste(r, s) 1 adj, superl of hoch (a) (räumliche Ausdehnung) highest; Wuchs, Zimmer, Baum, Mast tallest; Leiter tallest, longest.

(b) Preis, Verdienst, Temperatur, Druck etc highest; Betrag, Summe largest; Strafe, Gewicht heaviest; Profit auch, Lotteriegewinn biggest; Verlust most severe; Schaden most expensive; (maximal) Verdienst, Temperatur, Geschwindigkeit etc maximum attr. im ~n Grade/Maße to the highest degree; im ~n Fall(e) at the most.

(c) (im Rang) highest; Ehre greatest; Fest most important; Offizier highest-ranking. das ~ Wesen the Supreme Being; die ~ Instanz the supreme court of appeal; sich an ~r Stelle beschweren to complain to the highest authority.

(d) attr (qualitativ, äußerst) Lebensstandard, Ansprüche highest; Bedeutung, Genuß, Glück greatest, supreme; Gu greatest; *Not, Gefahr, Wichtigkeit* utmost, greatest; *Freude* greatest; *Konzentration* extreme. **zu meiner ~n Zufriedenheit** to my great satisfaction.

(e) *Alter* greatest; (*Mus*) highest.

(f) (*in Wendungen*) ~ *Zeit or Eisenbahn* (*inf*) high time; **der ~ Norden** the extreme North; **das ist das ~ der Gefühle** that is the highest *or* most sublime feeling *or* of feelings; **aufs ~ erfreut** *etc* highly *or* greatly *or* tremendously (*inf*) pleased *etc*; **das ist das ~, was ich bezahlen/tun kann** that is the most I can do/pay.

2 *adv* **am ~n** (a) (*in größter Höhe*) highest. **mittags steht die Sonne am ~n** the sun is highest at noon.

(b) (*in größtem Ausmaß*) *verehren, schätzen* most (of all); *versichern, begabt* most; *besteuert, verlieren* (the) most heavily; *verschuldet* (the) most deeply. **in der Rangordnung am ~n stehen** to be the highest up in the hierarchy; **er ist am ~n qualifiziert** he is the.most (highly) qualified; **am ~n stehen** (*Kurse, Temperatur*) to be at its highest.

Höchste(s) *nt decl as adj* (*fig*) highest good. **nach dem ~n streben** to aspire to the ideal *or* to perfection.

Höchst-: **~fall** *m* im ~**fall** siehe **höchstens** (a); **~form** *f* (*Sport*) top form; **~frequenzwelle** *f* microwave; **~gebot** *nt* highest bid; **~geschwindigkeit** *f* top *or* maximum speed; **zulässige ~geschwindigkeit** speed limit; **~grenze** *f* upper limit.

Hoch-: **h~stielig** *adj* long-stemmed; **h~stilisieren*** *vt sep* to build up (*zu* into); **~stimmung** *f* high spirits *pl*.

Höchst-: **~leistung** *f* best performance; (*bei Produktion*) maximum output; **~maß** *nt* maximum amount (*an* + *dat* of); **h~persönlich** *adv* personally; **es ist der Prinz h~persönlich** it's the prince in person; **~preis** *m* top *or* maximum price.

Hoch-: **~straße** *f* fly-over; **h~streben** *vi sep aux sein* (a) siehe **aufstreben**; (b) (*fig: nach Höherem streben*) to aspire (*nach* to, after); **h~streifen** *vt sep Ärmel* to push up.

Höchst-: **h~richterlich** *adj* of the supreme court; **~satz** *m* (*beim Glücksspiel*) maximum stake; (*bei Versicherungen*) maximum rate; **~stand** *m* highest level; **~strafe** *f* maximum penalty; **h~wahrscheinlich** *adv* in all probability, most probably *or* likely; **~wert** *m* maximum value; **h~zulässig** *adj attr* maximum (permissible).

Hoch-: **~tal** *nt* high-lying valley; **h~tönend** *adj* high-sounding; **~tour** *f* auf **~touren laufen/arbeiten** (*Maschinen*) to run at full speed; (*fig: Mensch, Fabrik etc*) to run/work *etc* at full steam; **etw auf ~touren bringen** *Motor* to rev sth up to full speed; *Maschine, Produktion, Kampagne* to get sth into full swing; **jdn auf ~touren bringen** (*inf*) to get sb to work flat out (*inf*); **h~tourig** *adj Motor* high-revving; **h~tourig fahren** to drive at high revs; **h~trabend** *adj* (*pej*) pompous, turgid; **h~treiben** *vt sep irreg* (a) (*hinauftreiben*) to drive up; (b) (*fig*) *Preise, Löhne, Kosten* to force up; **~-und-Tiefbau** *m* structural and civil engineering; **h~verdient** *adj attr Mensch* of great merit; *Lob* much-deserved; (*in Brief*) esteemed (*old*); **h~verehrter Herr Vorsitzender ...** Mr Chairman ...; **h~verehrter Herr Präsident!** Mr President, Sir!; (*in Brief*) Dear Sir; **~verrat** *m* high treason; **~verräter** *m* person guilty of high treason, traitor; **h~verräterisch** *adj* treasonable; **h~verschuldet** *adj attr* deep in debt; **h~verzinslich** *adj* bearing *or* yielding a high rate/high rates of interest; **~wald** *m* timber forest.

Hochwasser *nt* (a) (*Höchststand von Flut*) high tide. (b) (*überhoher Wasserstand in Flüssen, Seen*) high water; (*Überschwemmung*) flood. **~ haben** (*Fluß*) to be in flood; **er hat ~** (*hum inf*) his trousers are at half-mast (*inf*).

Hochwasser-: **~gefahr** *f* danger of flooding; **~hosen** *pl* (*hum inf*) trousers at half-mast (*inf*); **~katastrophe** *f* flood disaster; **~schaden** *m* flood damage; **~stand** *m* high-water level.

Hoch-: **h~werfen** *vt sep irreg* to throw up; **h~wertig** *adj* high-quality *attr*, of high quality; *Nahrungsmittel* highly nutritious; *Stahl* high-grade; (*Chem*) high-valency *attr*, of high valency; **h~wichtig** *adj attr* highly *or* very important; **mit h~wichtiger Miene** looking self-important, full of one's own importance, looking extremely serious; **~wild** *nt* big game (including bigger game birds); **h~willkommen** *adj attr* most *or* very welcome; **h~wohlgeboren** *adj* (*obs*) honourable; (*Euer*) **~wohlgeboren** Your Honour; **h~wölben** *sep* **1** *vt* **etw h~wölben** to make sth bulge up; **2** *vr* to bulge up; **h~wollen** *vi sep* (*inf*) to want up (*inf*); (*aufstehen wollen auch*) to want to get up; (*in die Höhe wollen auch, nach Norden wollen*) to want to go up; **~würden** *m* **-s**, *no pl* (*dated: Anrede*) Reverend Father; **h~würdig** *adj* (*dated*) Reverend; **~zahl** *f* exponent.

Hochzeit¹ *f* **-**, **-en** (a) wedding; (*Eheschließung auch*) marriage. **~ machen/haben** to get married; **~ halten/feiern** to have a wedding; **etw zur ~ geschenkt bekommen/schenken** to get/ give sth as a wedding present; **grüne ~** wedding day; **silberne/goldene/diamantene ~** silver/golden/diamond wedding (anniversary); **man kann nicht auf zwei ~en tanzen** (*prov*) you can't have your cake and eat it (*prov*).

(b) (*Typ*) double.

Hochzeit² *f* **-**, **-en** (*liter: Blütezeit*) golden age.

hochzeiten *vi insep* (*dated, Aus, S Ger*) to marry.

Hochzeiter *m* **-s**, **-** (*dated, Aus, Sw, S Ger*) bridegroom. **die ~** the bride and groom.

hochzeitlich *adj* bridal *attr*, wedding *attr*. **die Braut/der Bräutigam war ~ gekleidet** the bride was in her wedding dress/ the groom was in his wedding attire; **~ geschmückt** decorated for the wedding.

Hochzeits- *in cpds* wedding; **~anzeige** *f* wedding announcement; **~bitter** *m* **-s**, **-** (*old*) *messenger who invites guests to a wedding*; **~feier** *f* wedding celebration; (*Empfang*) reception, wedding breakfast; **~fest** *nt* wedding celebration; **~flug** *m* (*Zool*) nuptial flight; **~gast** *m* wedding guest; **~kleid** *nt* wedding dress, bridal dress *or* gown; **~nacht** *f* wedding night;

~reise *f* honeymoon; **wohin geht die ~reise?** where are you going on (your) honeymoon?; **~reisende** *pl* honeymoon couple, honeymooners *pl*; **~tag** *m* wedding day; (*Jahrestag*) wedding anniversary; **~zug** *m* wedding procession.

hoch-: **~ziehen** *sep irreg* **1** *vt* (a) to pull up; *Hosen etc auch* to hitch up; *Fahne* to run up; *Augenbrauen* to raise, to lift; **die Maschine ~ziehen** (*Aviat*) to put the aircraft into a steep climb; (b) (*inf: bauen*) to throw up (*inf*); **2** *vr* to pull oneself up; **v sich an etw** (*dat*) **~ziehen** to climb up sth; (*fig inf*) to get a kick out of sth (*inf*); **H~ziel** *nt* (*geh*) ultimate goal.

Hock *m* **-s**, **:e** (*Sw, dial*) get-together.

Hocke¹ *f* **-**, **-n** squatting position; (*Übung*) squat; (*beim Turnen*) squat vault; (*beim Skilaufen*) crouch; (*beim Ringen*) mat position. **in die ~ gehen/in der ~ sitzen** to squat.

Hocke² *f* **-**, **-n** stook, shock.

hocken **1** *vi* (*S Ger: aux sein*) (a) (*in der Hocke sitzen*) to squat, to crouch. (b) (*inf: sitzen*) to sit; (*auf Hocker*) to perch. (c) (*pej inf*) to sit around. (d) (*Sport*) **übers Pferd ~** to squat-vault over the horse. **2** *vr* (a) (*in Hockstellung gehen*) to squat. (b) (*inf: sich setzen*) to sit down, to plonk oneself down (*inf*).

hockenbleiben *vi sep irreg aux sein* (*dial inf*) siehe **sitzenbleiben**.

Hocker *m* **-s**, **-** (a) (*Stuhl*) stool. (b) (*Archeol*) seated burial. (c) (*inf: Mensch*) stayer.

Höcker *m* **-s**, **-** (a) (*von Kamel, inf: Buckel*) hump; (*auf Schnabel*) knob. (b) (*Erhebung*) bump; (*in Gelände*) hump; (*kleiner Hügel*) hummock, hump.

Hockergrab *nt* seated burial.

höck(e)rig *adj* (*uneben*) bumpy; (*buckelig*) hunch-backed; *Nase* with a bump; *Schnabel* with a knob.

Hockey ['hɔki, 'hɔkɛ] *nt* **-s**, *no pl* hockey.

Hockey-: **~ball** *m* hockey ball; **~schläger** *m* hockey stick; **~spieler** *m* hockey player; **~stock** *m* siehe **~schläger**.

höckrig *adj* siehe **höck(e)rig**.

Hock-: **~sitz** *m* squat; **~sprung** *m* (*Sport*) (*über Gerät*) squat vault; (*beim Bodenturnen*) crouch jump; **~stellung** *f* crouched *or* squatting position; (*Archeol*) seated position.

Hode *m* **-n**, **-n**, *f* **-**, **-n**, **Hoden** *m* **-s**, **-** testicle.

Hoden-: **~bruch** *m* scrotal hernia; **~entzündung** *f* inflammation of the testicles, orchitis (*spec*); **~sack** *m* scrotum.

Hof *m* **-(e)s**, **:e** (a) (*Platz*) yard; (*Innen~*) courtyard; (*Schul~*) schoolyard, playground; (*Kasernen~*) square.

(b) (*Bauern~*) farm; (*Gebäudekomplex auch*) farmyard.

(c) (*Fürsten~*) court. **bei** *or* **am ~e** at court; **am ~e Ludwig XIV** at the court of Louis XIV.

(d) **einem Mädchen den ~ machen** (*dated, hum*) to court a girl (*dated*), to pay court to a girl (*form*).

(e) (*um Sonne, Mond*) halo.

(f) (*in Namen: Gasthof, Hotel*) hotel, inn.

Hof-: **~amt** *nt* court appointment; **~arzt** *m* court physician; **~ball** *m* court ball; **~dame** *f* lady-in-waiting; **~dichter** *m* court poet; (*in GB*) poet laureate.

höfeln *vi* (*Sw*) to flatter (*jdm* sb).

Hof-: **~erbe** *m* heir to a/the farm; **~etikette** *f* court etiquette; **h~fähig** *adj* acceptable at court; (*gesellschaftsfähig*) presentable; **~fähigkeit** *f* right/privilege to be present at court.

Hoffart *f* **-**, *no pl* (*dated*) pride, arrogance, haughtiness.

hoffärtig *adj* (*dated*) proud, arrogant, haughty.

hoffen **1** *vi* (a) (*von Hoffnung erfüllt sein*) to hope. **auf Gott ~** to trust in God; **auf jdn ~** to set one's hopes on sb; **auf etw ~** (*acc*) to hope for sth; **wer hier eintritt, hofft noch those who enter here still have hope; **da bleibt nur zu ~** one can only hope; **sie hofften auf ihre Verbündeten** (*auf Erscheinen*) they were waiting for their allies; (*auf Hilfe*) they set their hopes on their allies; **der Mensch hofft, solange er lebt** (*Prov*) hope springs eternal (*prov*); **H~ und Harren macht manchen zum Narren** (*Prov*) some people never give up hoping, pigs might fly (*inf*).

(b) (*wünschen und erwarten*) to hope. **~, daß ...** to hope that ...; **ich will nicht ~, daß das macht** I hope he doesn't do that; **ich will/wir wollen ~, daß ...** I/we can only hope that ..., it is to be hoped that ...

2 *vt* to hope for. **~ wir das Beste!** let's hope for the best!; **es ist zu ~ it is to be hoped; **ich hoffe es** I hope so; **das will ich (doch wohl) ~** I should (jolly well *Brit inf*) hope so; **das wollen wir ~** let's hope so; **ich will es nicht ~** I hope not; **sie hatten nichts mehr zu ~** they had nothing left to hope for.

hoffentlich *adv* hopefully. **~!** I hope so, let us hope so; **~ nicht** I/we hope not; **~ ist das bald vorbei** I/we hope that it will be over soon, hopefully it will be over soon; **du bist mir doch ~ nicht böse** I (do) hope (that) you're not angry with me.

-höffig *adj suf* (*Min*) promising a rich yield of.

höfflich *adj* (*Min*) promising a rich yield.

Hoffnung *f* hope; (*auf Gott*) trust (*auf* + *acc* in). **sich** (*dat*) **~en machen** to have hopes; **sich** (*dat*) **keine ~en machen** not to hold out any hopes; **er macht sich ~en bei ihr** (*inf*) he fancies his chances with her (*inf*); **mach dir keine ~(en)!** I wouldn't even think about it; **jdm ~en machen** to raise sb's hopes; **jdm ~en machen, daß ...** to lead sb to hope that ...; **jdm auf etw** (*acc*) **~en machen** to lead sb to expect sth; **jdm keine ~en machen** not to hold out any hopes for sb; **seine ~en auf jdn/etw setzen** to place one's hopes in *or* pin one's hopes on sb/sth; **die ~ aufgeben/verlieren** to abandon/lose hope; **eine ~ begraben** *or* **zu Grabe tragen** to abandon a hope; **eine ~ zerstören/enttäuschen** to dash/disappoint sb's hopes; **in der ~, bald von Ihnen zu hören** hoping to hear *or* in the hope of hearing from you soon; **sich einer ~/unbegründeten/falschen ~en hingeben** to cherish hopes/unfounded/false hopes; **zu schönen** *or* **zu den schönsten ~en berechtigen** to give rise to great hopes; **~ auf etw** (*acc*) **haben** to have hopes of getting sth; **guter ~ sein** (*euph: schwanger*) to be expecting.

Hoffnungs-: h~freudig, h~froh 1 *adj* hopeful; 2 *adv* in happy anticipation; ~funke(n) *m* glimmer of hope; ~lauf *m* (*Sport*) repechage; h~los *adj* hopeless; ~losigkeit *f*, *no pl* hopelessness; (*Verzweiflung*) despair; ~schimmer *m* glimmer of hope; ~strahl *m* ray of hope; h~voll 1 *adj* hopeful; (*vielversprechend*) promising; 2 *adv* full of hope.

Hof-: ~gang *m* yard exercise; ~geistliche(r) *m* court chaplain; ~gesellschaft *f* court society; ~gesinde *nt* (a) (*auf Bauernhof*) farm workers *pl*; (b) (*am Fürstenhof*) servants *pl* at the(a) court; h~halten *vi sep irreg* (*lit, fig*) to hold court; ~haltung *f* (holding of) court; ~herr *m* (*Gutsherr*) estate owner; (*in England*) squire; ~hund *m* watchdog.

hofieren* *vt* (*dated*) to court.

höfisch *adj* (a) (*eines Fürstenhofs*) Leben, Sitten, Vergnügen courtly *no adv*. (b) (*Liter*) Dichtung *etc* courtly *no adv*. (c) (*old: kultiviert*) Benehmen, Kleidung sophisticated.

Hof-: ~kapelle *f* (a) (*Kirche am Hof*) court chapel; (b) (*Mus*) court orchestra; ~knicks *m* court or formal curtsey; ~lager *nt* temporary residence; ~lager halten to hold court; ~leben *nt* court life.

höflich *adj* polite; (*zuvorkommend*) courteous. **ich bitte Sie ~** I (would) respectfully ask you; **wir teilen Ihnen ~(st) mit** we beg to inform you.

Höflichkeit *f* (a) *no pl siehe adj* politeness; courteousness. **jdm etw mit aller ~ sagen** to tell sb sth very politely *or* with the utmost politeness. (b) (*höfliche Bemerkung*) compliment. **jdm ~en sagen** to compliment sb.

Höflichkeits-: ~besuch *m* courtesy visit; ~bezeigung *f* act *or* mark of courtesy; ~floskel (*pej*), ~formel *f* polite phrase; h~halber *adv* out of courtesy.

Hoflieferant *m* purveyor to the court.

Höfling *m* courtier; (*pej: Schmeichler*) sycophant.

Hof-: ~marschall *m* (*Hist*) major-domo; (*in GB*) Lord Chamberlain; ~meister *m* (*Hist*) (a) (*Gutsverwalter*) steward, bailiff; (b) (*Erzieher*) (private) tutor; ~narr *m* (*Hist*) court jester; ~prediger *m* (*Hist*) court chaplain; ~rat *m* (a) (*Hist*) Court Counsellor; (*in GB*) Privy Counsellor; (b) (*Aus: Ehrentitel*) Hofrat, = Counsellor; ~sänger *m* (*Hist*) minstrel; ~schranze *f or* (*rare*) *m* (*Hist pej*) fawning courtier; ~seite *f* courtyard side (*of building*); ~staat *m* (*Hist*) (royal *etc*) household; ~statt *f*, -en *or* =en farmstead; ~theater *nt* (*Hist*) court *or* royal theatre; ~tor *nt* yard gate; ~trauer *f* court mourning; ~tür *f* yard gate.

HO-Geschäft [haː'loː-] *nt* (*DDR*) state retail shop.

hohe *adj siehe* hoch.

Höhe *f*, -n (a) (*Ausdehnung nach oben*) height; (*Flug~, Berg~, ~ über Meeresspiegel auch, Astron, Math*) altitude; (*von Schnee, Wasser*) depth. **in die/der ~** (up) into/in the air; **aus der ~** from above; **Ehre sei Gott in der ~** glory to God in the highest *or* on high; **an ~ gewinnen** (*Aviat*) to gain height, to climb; **in einer ~ von** at a height/an altitude of; **in die ~ gehen/treiben** (*fig: Preise etc*) to go up/force up; **einen Betrieb wieder in die ~ bringen** to put a business back on its feet again; **in die ~ gehen** (*fig inf*) to hit the roof (*inf*). (b) (*An~*) hill; (*Gipfel*) top, summit; (*fig: ~punkt, Blütezeit etc*) height. **auf der ~ sein** (*fig inf*) (*leistungsfähig*) to be at one's best; (*gesund*) to be fighting fit (*inf*); **die sanften ~n** the gentle slopes; **sich nicht auf der ~ fühlen, nicht auf der ~ sein** (*leistungsfähig*) to feel below par; (*gesundheitlich*) not to be up to scratch; **auf der ~ des Lebens** in the prime of (one's) life; **die ~n und Tiefen des Lebens** the ups and downs of life; **auf der ~ der Zeit** up-to-date; **das ist doch die ~!** (*fig inf*) that's the limit! (c) (*Ausmaß, Größe*) (*von Mieten, Preisen, Unkosten, Temperatur, Geschwindigkeit, Strafe, Phys: Stromspannung*) level; (*von Summe, Gewinn, Verlust, Gewicht, Geldstrafe*) size, amount; (*von Wert, Druck*) amount; (*von Einkommen*) size; (*von Schaden*) extent. **ein Zuwachs/Betrag in ~ von** an increase/amount of; **Zinsen in ~ von** interest at the rate of; **bis zu einer ~ von** up to a maximum of. (d) (*fig: Größe*) (*von Lebensstandard, Ansprüchen etc*) level. **trotz der ~ seines Alters ...** despite his great age ... (e) (*Mus: Ton~, von Stimme*) pitch; (*Rad: Ton~*) treble *no pl*. (f) (*Naut, Geog: Breitenlage*) latitude. **auf der ~ von** at the level of; **auf der ~ von Dover** (*Naut*) off Dover; **auf gleicher ~** level with each other.

Hoheit *f* (a) *no pl* (*Staats~*) sovereignty (*über +acc* over). (b) (*Mitglied einer fürstlichen Familie*) member of a/the royal family; (*als Anrede*) Highness. **Seine/Ihre Königliche ~** His/Her Royal Highness. (c) *siehe* **Erhabenheit.**

hoheitlich *adj* (*von Staatsgewalt ausgehend*) Befehl, Handlung sovereign; (*von einem Fürsten*) Gemächer royal; Auftreten, Geste majestic.

Hoheits-: ~abzeichen *nt* nationality marking; ~akt *m* act of sovereignty; ~bereich *m* (a) *siehe* ~gebiet; (b) (*Rechtsbereich*) jurisdiction; ~gebiet *nt* sovereign territory; ~gewalt *f* (national) jurisdiction; ~gewässer *pl* territorial waters *pl*; ~recht *nt usu pl* sovereign jurisdiction *or* rights *pl*; h~voll *adj* majestic; ~zeichen *nt* national emblem.

Hohelied *nt* Song of Songs; (*fig geh*) song.

Höhen-: ~angabe *f* altitude reading; (*auf Karte*) altitude mark; ~angst *f* fear of heights; ~flosse *f* (*Aviat*) tailplane; ~flug *m* high-altitude flight; (*geistiger/künstlerischer*) ~flug intellectual/artistic flight (of fancy); h~gleich 1 *adj* level; 2 *adv* on a level; ~grenze *f* altitude (on mountain) where vegetation ceases; ~klima *nt* mountain climate; ~krankheit *f* (*Med*) altitude sickness; (*im Gebirge auch*) mountain sickness; (*beim Fliegen auch*) aeroembolism (*spec*); ~kurort *m* mountain (health) resort; ~lage *f* altitude; ~leitwerk *nt* (*Aviat*) elevators *pl*; ~linie *f* contour (line); ~luft *f* mountain air; ~marke *f* bench mark; ~messer *m* -s, - (*Aviat*) altimeter, altitude

meter; ~messung *f* (a) (*Aviat*) measuring altitude; (b) (*Tech*) levelling; ~rekord *m* (*Aviat*) altitude record; ~rücken *m* (mountain) crest *or* ridge; ~ruder *nt* (*Aviat*) elevator; ~schicht *f* contour level; ~schreiber *m* (*Aviat*) altigraph; ~sonne *f* (*im Gebirge*) mountain sun; (*Lampe: auch künstliche* ~sonne) sunray lamp; (*Behandlung*) sunray treatment; ~steuer *nt siehe* ~ruder; ~strahlung *f* cosmic radiation; ~training *nt* (*Sport*) (high-)altitude training; ~unterschied *m* difference in altitude; ~verlust *m* loss of height *or* altitude; ~wind *m* high-altitude wind; ~zahl *f* (*auf Landkarten*) height above sea level; ~zug *m* range of hills, mountain range.

Hohepriester *m* high priest.

hohepriesterlich *adj* Gewänder, Amt high priest's *attr.*

Höhepunkt *m* highest point; (*des Abends, des Tages, des Lebens*) high point, high spot; (*einer Veranstaltung*) high spot, highlight; (*einer Karriere, des Ruhms, der Macht*) pinnacle, peak, height; (*des Glücks etc*) height, peak; (*einer Entwicklung*) peak, summit, apex; (*einer Kurve*) vertex; (*eines Stücks, Orgasmus*) climax. **auf den ~ bringen** to bring to a climax; **den ~ erreichen** to reach a or its/one's climax; (*Krankheit*) to reach *or* come to a crisis; **den ~ überschreiten** to pass the peak.

hohe(r, s) *adj siehe* hoch.

höher *adj comp of* hoch (*lit, fig*) higher; Macht superior; Klasse upper; Auflage bigger. ~e Berufsstände the professions; ~e Bildung higher education; ~es Lehramt = graduate teachership; ~e Schule secondary school, high school (*esp US*); ~e Töchterschule (*old, hum*) school for young ladies; ~e Tochter (*dated, hum*) young lady; ~e Gewalt an act of God; **in ~em Maße** to a greater extent; ~er Blödsinn (*iro*) utter nonsense; **in ~en Regionen or Sphären schweben** to have one's head in the clouds; **ihre Herzen schlugen ~** their hearts beat faster; **etw ~ bewerten** to rate sth higher *or* more highly; **sich ~ versichern** to increase one's insurance (premium); **sich zu H~em berufen fühlen** to feel (oneself) called to higher things *or* to greater things.

höher-: ~gestellt *adj attr* higher, more senior; ~liegend *adj attr* higher; ~schrauben *vt sep* (*fig*) Anforderungen to increase, to step up; Ansprüche to increase; Preise to force *or* push up; ~stehend *adj attr* higher; ~stufen *vt sep* Person to upgrade; ~wertig *adj* (*Chem*) of higher valency.

hohl *adj* (a) (*lit, fig: leer*) hollow; Geschwätz *etc* empty, shallow; Blick empty, vacant. (b) (*konkav*) hollow; Wangen *auch* sunken; Augen *auch* deep-set. **ein ~es Kreuz** a hollow back; **in der ~en Hand** in the hollow of one's hand; **aus der ~en Hand trinken** to drink with cupped hands; **eine ~e Hand machen** (*lit*) to cup one's hand; (*fig inf*) to hold one's hand out (for money, a tip etc); ~e Gasse narrow pass *or* defile. (c) Klang, Stimme, Husten hollow.

Hohl-: h~äugig *adj* hollow- *or* sunken-eyed; ~block(stein), ~blockziegel *m* cavity block.

Höhle *f* -, -n cave, cavern; (*in Baum*) hole, hollow bit; (*Tierbehausung*) cave, den; (*Augen~*) socket; (*fig: schlechte Wohnung*) hovel, hole (*inf*).

Höhlen- *in cpds* cave; ~bär *m* cave-bear; ~bewohner *m* cave dweller, caveman, troglodyte; ~forscher *m* cave explorer; (*unter der Erde auch*) potholer; ~forschung, ~kunde *f* speleology; ~gleichnis *nt* (*Philos*) Allegory of the Cave; ~malerei *f* cave painting; ~mensch *m* caveman; ~tier *m* cave-animal.

Hohl-: h~erhaben *adj* (*Phys*) concavo-convex; ~glas *nt* hollow glass(ware); ~heit *f no pl* (*fig*) *siehe adj* hollowness; emptiness; shallowness; ~kopf *m* (*pej*) blockhead (*inf*), numskull (*inf*), dunce; h~köpfig *adj* (*pej*) empty-headed, brainless, foolish; ~körper *m* hollow body; ~kreuz *nt* (*Med*) hollow back; ~kugel *f* hollow sphere; ~maß *nt* measure of capacity; (*für Getreide etc auch*) dry measure; ~nadel *f* (*Med*) cannula; ~raum *m* hollow space; (*Build auch*) cavity; ~saum *m* (*Sew*) hemstitch; ~saumarbeit *f* drawn-thread work; ~schliff *m* hollow grinding; **ein Messer mit ~schliff** a hollow-ground knife; ~spiegel *m* concave mirror; ~tiere *pl* coelenterata (*spec*).

Höhlung *f* hollow.

Hohl-: h~wangig *adj* hollow-cheeked; ~warze *f* inverted nipple; ~weg *m* narrow pass *or* defile; ~würmer *pl* aschelminthes *pl* (*spec*); ~ziegel *m* (a) (*Hohlstein*) cavity brick; (b) (*Dachziegel*) hollow tile.

Hohn *m* -(e)s, *no pl* scorn, derision, mockery. **jdn mit ~ und Spott überschütten** to heap *or* pour scorn on sb; **nur ~ und Spott ernten** to get nothing but scorn and derision; **das hat er mir zum ~ getan** he did it just to show his contempt for me; **ein ~ auf etw (acc)** a mockery of sth; **das ist der reine *or* reinste ~** it's a sheer *or* utter mockery; **der Tatsache (dat) zum ~** in defiance of the fact(s).

höhnen 1 *vt* (*geh*) jdn to mock. 2 *vi* to jeer, to scoff, to sneer (*über +acc* at).

Hohngelächter *nt* scornful *or* derisive *or* sneering laughter.

höhnisch *adj* scornful, mocking, sneering.

Hohn-: ~lächeln *nt* sneer, derisive *or* scornful smile; h~lächeln *vi insep or sep* to sneer, to smile derisively *or* scornfully; ~lachen *nt siehe* ~gelächter; h~lachen *vi sep* to laugh scornfully *or* derisively; **ich höre ihn schon h~lachen** I can hear his sneers already; h~sprechen *vi sep irreg* to make a mockery (*dat* of); **jdm h~sprechen** to mock at *or* deride sb; **das spricht jeder Vernunft h~** that flies right in the face of all reason.

hoho *interj* oho.

Höker(in *f*) *m* -s, - (*old*) street trader *or* pedlar.

Hökerfrau *f* (*old*), **Hökerweib** *nt* (*old, pej*) *siehe* Höker(in).

hökern *vi* (*old*) to peddle. **mit etw ~** to peddle sth.

Hokuspokus *m* -, *no pl* (*Zauberformel*) hey presto; (*Zauber-*

stück) (*conjuring*) trick(s); (*fig*) (*Täuschung*) hocus-pocus (*inf*), jiggery-pokery (*inf*); (*Drumherum*) palaver (*inf*), fuss. **die veranstalten immer einen ~, wenn Besuch kommt** they always make such a palaver (*inf*) or fuss when they have visitors.

hold *adj* (a) (*poet, dated*) fair, sweet; (*hum*) dear, beloved, fair. **~er Friede** sweet or blessed peace; **die ~e Weiblichkeit** (*hum*) the fair sex; **mein ~er Gatte** (*hum*) my dear or beloved husband (*hum*); **meine H~e** my sweet.
(b) *pred* (*geh: gewogen*) **jdm ~ sein** to be fond of or well-disposed to(wards) sb; **das Glück war ihm ~** fortune smiled upon him.

Holder *m* -s, - (*dial*) *siehe* **Holunder.**

Holdheit *f*, *no pl* (*liter*) fairness, sweetness.

Holdinggesellschaft *f* (*Comm*) holding company.

holdrio *interj* halloo.

Holdrio[1] *nt* -s, -s (shout of) halloo.

Holdrio[2] *m* -(s), -(s) (*dated*) devil-may-care fellow (*inf*).

holdselig *adj* (*liter*) sweet, lovely, fair.

holen *vt* (a) to fetch, to get; (*herunternehmen*) to get or take or fetch down; (*herausnehmen*) to get or take out. **Luft/Atem ~** to draw breath, to catch one's breath; **jdn aus dem Bett ~** to get or drag (*inf*) sb out of bed; **das Kind mußte geholt werden** the baby had to be pulled out; *siehe* **Teufel.**
(b) (*abholen*) to fetch, to pick up; **Verbrecher, Patienten** to take away.
(c) (*kaufen*) to get, to pick up (*inf*).
(d) (*herbeirufen, ~ lassen*) **Polizei, Hilfe** to fetch, to get. **jdn ~ lassen** to send for sb; **einen Moment, ich lasse ihn schnell ans Telefon ~** just a moment, I'll have someone fetch or get him to the phone; **der Professor hat seinen Assistenten an die neue Uni geholt** the professor took his assistant to the new university.
(e) (*erringen, gewinnen*) **Sieg, Preis** to win, to get.
(f) (*sich zuziehen*) **Krankheit** to catch, to get; **elektrischen Schlag** to get. **sich** (*dat*) **Schläge ~** to get a beating; **sonst wirst du dir etwas ~** or you'll catch something; **sich** (*dat*) **eine Erkältung/den Tod** (*inf*) **~** to catch a cold/one's death (*inf*).
(g) (*bekommen, erwerben*) to get. **sich** (*dat*) **etw ~** to get (oneself) sth; **dabei ist nichts zu ~** (*inf*) there's nothing in it; **bei ihm ist nichts zu ~** (*inf*) you *etc* won't get anything out of him.
(h) (*Naut*) **Anker** to raise, to hoist; **Segel, Taue** to take in.

holla *interj* hullo, hallo, hello, hey; (*überrascht*) hey; (*hoppla*) whoops.

Holland *nt* -s Holland, the Netherlands *pl*.

Holländer[1] *m* -s, - Dutchman. **die ~** the Dutch (people); **er ist ~** he is Dutch or a Dutchman; *siehe* **fliegend.**

Holländer[2] *m* -s, *no pl* Dutch cheese.

Holländer[3] *m* -s, - (*bei Papierherstellung*) hollander.

Holländerei *f* (*obs*) dairy farm.

Holländerin *f* Dutchwoman, Dutch girl.

holländern 1 *vt* (*Buchbinderei*) to sew, to stitch. **2** *vi* (*beim Eislauf*) to skate with arms crossed.

holländisch *adj* Dutch.

Holländisch(e) *nt decl as adj* Dutch, the Dutch language; *siehe* **Deutsch(e).**

Holle[1] *f* -, -n (*von Vogel*) crest, tuft.

Holle[2] *f*: **Frau ~** schüttelt die Betten aus it is snowing.

Hölle *f* -, (*rare*) -n hell. **in der ~** in hell; **die ~ auf Erden** hell on earth; **fahr zur ~!** (*liter*) go to the devil!; **in die ~ kommen** to go to hell; **ich werde ihm die ~ heiß machen** (*inf*) I'll give him hell (*inf*); **sie machte ihm das Leben zur ~** she made his life (a) hell (*inf*); **es war die (reinste) ~** (*inf*) it was (pure) hell (*inf*); **die ~ ist los** (*inf*) all hell has broken loose (*inf*).

Höllen- *in cpds* (*der Hölle*) of hell, infernal; (*inf: groß*) hellish (*inf*), infernal (*inf*); **~angst** *f* terrible fear; **eine ~angst haben** to be scared stiff (*inf*); **~brand** *m* (*liter*) hellfire; **~brut** *f* (*pej liter*) diabolical or fiendish mob or rabble; **~fahrt** *f* Descent into Hell; **~fürst** *m* (*liter*) Prince of Darkness; **~hund** *m* (*Myth*) hound of hell, hell-hound; **~lärm** *m* hellish (*inf*) or infernal (*inf*) noise; **~mächte** *pl* (*liter*) powers of darkness *pl*; **~maschine** *f* (*dated*) infernal machine (*dated*), time bomb; **~pein, ~qual** *f* (*liter*) torments *pl* of hell; (*fig inf*) agony; **eine ~qual/~qualen ausstehen** to suffer agony; **~rachen, ~schlund** *m* (*liter*) jaws *pl* of hell; **~spektakel** *m* (*inf*) *siehe* **~lärm; ~stein** *m* (*Chem*) silver nitrate, lunar caustic.

Holler *m* -s, - (*dial*) *siehe* **Holunder.**

Hollerithmaschine *f* Hollerith machine.

höllisch *adj* (a) *attr* (*die Hölle betreffend*) infernal, of hell.
(b) (*inf: außerordentlich*) dreadful, frightful, hellish (*inf*). **eine ~e Angst haben** to be scared stiff (*inf*); **~ fluchen** to swear like a trooper; **es tut ~ weh** it hurts like hell (*inf*), it's hellish(ly) painful (*inf*); **die Prüfung war ~ schwer** the exam was hellish(ly) difficult (*inf*).

Hollywoodschaukel *f* ['hɔlivud-] swing hammock.

Holm[1] *m* -(e)s, -e (a) (*von Barren*) bar; (*von Geländer*) rail; (*von Leiter*) side rail. (b) (*Aviat*) (*längs*) longeron; (*quer*) spar. (c) (*Stiel, Griff*) (*Axt~*) shaft, handle; (*Ruder~*) shaft.

Holm[2] *m* -(e)s, -e islet, small island.

Holographie *f* holography.

holp(e)rig *adj* (a) **Weg, Pflaster** bumpy. (b) (*schwerfällig*) **Rede, Verse** clumsy, jerky. **~ lesen** to read jerkily or haltingly.

holpern *vi* to bump, to jolt. **beim Lesen holpert er noch** he still stumbles (over his words) when reading, he still reads haltingly; **~de Verse** rough or stumbling or halting verse.

Holschuld *f* (*Comm*) debt to be collected from the debtor at his residence.

holterdiepolter *adv* helter-skelter. **der Wagen fuhr ~ den Berg hinunter** the cart went careering down the mountainside; **die Blechdose fiel ~ die Treppe hinunter** the tin went

crash bang wallop down the stairs (*inf*).

hol|über *interj* (*old*) **Fährmann ~!** ahoy there, ferryman or boatman!

Holunder *m* -s, - elder. **spanischer or blauer ~** lilac.

Holunder- *in cpds* elder; **~beere** *f* elderberry; **~busch, ~strauch** *m* elder bush; **~wein** *m* elderberry wine.

Holz *nt* -es, =er (a) wood; (*zum Bauen, Schreinern auch*) timber, lumber (*US*). **ein ~** a piece of wood or timber; (*~art*) a wood; **lange =er** long, untrimmed logs or timbers; **runde =er** short, untrimmed logs or timbers; **flüssiges ~** (*Tech*) plastic wood; **aus ~** made of wood, wooden; **~ fällen** to fell or cut down trees; **~ sägen** (*lit*) to saw wood; (*inf: schnarchen*) to snore, to saw wood (*US inf*); **aus einem anderen ~ (geschnitzt) sein** (*fig*) to be cast in a different mould; **aus grobem ~ geschnitzt sein** (*fig*) to be insensitive; **aus hartem or härterem ~ geschnitzt sein** (*fig*) to be made of stern or sterner stuff; **aus demselben ~ geschnitzt sein** (*fig*) to be cast in the same mould; **er saß da wie ein Stück ~** he sat there like a lump of wood or lead; **ich bin nicht aus ~!** I'm not made of stone, I am made of flesh and blood; **~ vor der Hütte or Tür haben** (*inf*) to be well-endowed or well-stacked (*inf*), to have big boobs (*inf*); **~!** (*Tennis etc*) wood!; **Dummheit und Stolz wachsen auf einem ~** (*Prov*) stupidity and pride grow on the same tree.
(b) (*Kegel*) skittle, ninepin. **~ schieben** to play skittles or ninepins; **gut ~!** have a good game!
(c) (*dated: Wald, Gehölz*) wood, woods *pl*. **zu ~e gehen** or **ziehen** to go to cover.

Holz- *in cpds* wood; (*aus ~ auch*) wooden; (*Build, Comm etc*) timber; **~apfel** *m* crab apple; **~arbeiter** *m* woodworker; (*im Wald*) woodcutter, woodman, lumberjack; **h~arm** *adj* **Gegend** sparsely wooded or timbered; **Papier** with (a) low wood content; **~art** *f* kind of wood or timber; **h~artig** *adj* woody, wood-like; **~asche** *f* wood-ashes *pl*; **~auge** *nt*: **~auge sei wachsam** (*inf*) be careful; **~bau** *m* -s (a) *no pl* wood- or timber-frame construction; (b) *pl* **-ten** wooden building; **~bearbeitung** *f* woodworking; (*im Sägewerk*) timber processing; **~bein** *nt* wooden leg; **~bestand** *m* stock of wood or timber, wood or timber stock; (*im Wald*) stand of timber; **~bildhauer** *m* wood carver; **~bläser** *m* woodwind player; **wo sitzen die ~bläser?** where do the woodwind sit or does the woodwind section sit?; **~blasinstrument** *nt* woodwind instrument; **~block** *m* block of wood; **~bock** *m* (a) (*Stützgestell*) wooden stand or trestle; (b) (*Insekt*) wood tick, dog tick; **~boden** *m* (a) (*Fußboden*) wooden floor; (b) (*für Holz*) wood- or timber-loft; (c) (*von Truhe etc*) wooden bottom; (d) (*Forstwesen*) wooded or timbered ground; **~bohrer** *m* (a) (*Tech*) wood drill; (b) (*Zool*) goat moth, leopard moth; **~brandmalerei** *f* (*Art*) poker-work, pyrography (*form*); **~brei** *m* wood pulp; **~bündel** *nt* bundle of wood, faggot.

Hölzchen *nt* small piece of wood; (*Streichholz*) match.

Holzdruck *m* (*Art*) wood engraving.

holzen 1 *vi* (a) (*Bäume fällen*) to cut down or fell timber, to lumber. (b) (*esp Ftbl*) to hack; (*Mus*) to play badly. **2** *vt* (*rare*) **Wald** to clear.

Holzer *m* -s, - (*pej inf*) hacker, rough player.

Holzerei *f* (*inf*) (*Rauferei*) roughhouse (*inf*); (*Ftbl auch*) rough game or match; (*Mus*) third- or fourth-rate playing.

hölzern *adj* (*lit, fig*) wooden. **so ein ~er Kerl** such a wooden sort of chap.

Holz-: **~fällen** *nt* -s, *no pl* tree-felling, lumbering; **~fäller** *m* -s, - woodcutter, woodsman, lumberjack; **~faser** *f* wood fibre; **~faserplatte** *f* (*wood*) fibreboard; **~fäule** *f* wood or dry/wet rot; **h~frei** *adj* **Papier** wood-free; **~frevel** *m* (*Jur*) offence against forest laws, infringement of forest regulations; **~hacken** *nt* -s, *no pl* cutting or chopping wood; **~hacker** *m* -s, - (*Aus, old*) (a) woodcutter; (b) *siehe* **~fäller; h~haltig** *adj* **Papier** woody; **~hammer** *m* mallet; **etwas mit dem ~hammer abgekriegt haben** (*inf*) to be not all there (*inf*); **jdm etw mit dem ~hammer beibringen** to hammer sth into sb (*inf*); **~hammermethode** *f* (*inf*) sledgehammer method (*inf*); **~handel** *m* timber trade; **~haufen** *m* woodpile, pile or stack of wood; **~haus** *nt* wooden or timber house.

holzig *adj* woody; **Spargel, Rettich** *auch* stringy, tough.

Holz-: **~kitt** *m* plastic wood; **~klotz** *m* wooden block, block of wood, log; (*Spielzeug*) wooden brick; **er saß da wie ein ~klotz** (*inf*) he sat there like a block or lump of wood; **~kohle** *f* charcoal; **~kopf** *m* (*fig inf*) blockhead (*inf*); **~lager** *nt* timberyard; **~nagel** *m* wooden nail or peg; **~ofen** *m* wood-burning oven; **~pantine** *f*, **~pantoffel** *m* clog; **~pflaster** *nt* wood-block paving; **~pflock** *m* (wooden) peg; **h~reich** *adj* well-timbered or -wooded; **ein h~reiches Land** a country rich in timber; **~schädling** *m* wood pest; **~scheit** *nt* piece of (fire)wood, log; **~schlag** *m* (*Vorgang*) tree-felling, lumbering; (*Ort*) felling or lumbering area; **~schliff** *m* mechanical wood pulp; **~schneider** *m* wood engraver; **~schnitt** *m* (*Art*) (a) *no pl* (*Kunst*) (art of) wood engraving; (b) (*Gegenstand*) wood engraving, woodcut; **~schnitzer** *m* wood carver; **~schnitzerei** *f* (art or craft of) wood carving; **~schuh** *m* wooden shoe, clog, sabot; **~schuhtanz** *m* clog dance; **~schwamm** *m* wood fungus, dry rot; **~span** *m* chip (of wood); (*beim Hobeln*) wood shaving; **~splitter** *m* splinter or sliver of wood; **~stich** *m* wood engraving; **~stift** *m* small wooden nail or pin; **~stock** *m* (engraved) wood block; **~stoß** *m* pile of wood; **~tafel** *f* wooden panel; (*Sch*) wooden blackboard; **~täfelung** *f* wood(en) panelling; **~taube** *f* woodpigeon; **h~verarbeitend** *adj attr* wood-processing; **~verarbeitung** *f* wood-processing; **~verkohlung** *f* carbonization, wood distillation; **~verschlag** *m* (a) (*Schuppen*) wooden shed; (b) (*Verpackung*) wooden crate; **~waren** *pl* wooden articles, articles made of wood; **~weg** *m* logging-path; **auf dem ~weg sein** (*fig inf*) to be on the wrong track (*inf*); **wenn du meinst, ich gebe dir das, dann bist du auf dem ~weg** if you think I'm going to give it to you, you've got another think coming (inf); ~**wirtschaft** f timber industry; ~**wolle** f woodwool; ~**wurm** m woodworm.

homerisch adj Homeric.

Homo m -s, -s (dated inf) homo (dated inf), queer (inf).

Homo- in cpds homo; h~**gen** adj homogeneous; h~**genisieren*** vt to homogenize; ~**genität** f homogeneity; ~**nym** nt -(e)s,-e homonym; h~**nym** adj homonymous; ~**nymie** f homonymy.

Homöopath m -en, -en homoeopath.

Homöopathie f, no pl homoeopathy.

homöopathisch adj homoeopathic.

Homo-: h~**phon** adj (Mus) homophonic; (Ling) homophonous; ~**sexualität** f homosexuality; h~**sexuell** adj homosexual; ~**sexuelle(r)** mf decl as adj homosexual.

Homunkulus m -, -sse or **Homunkuli** homunculus.

honen vt Sichel to hone.

honett adj (dated, geh) honest, upright, respectable.

Honig m -s, no pl honey. **türkischer** ~ nougat; **sie schmierte ihm** ~ **ums Maul** or **um den Bart** or **Mund** (inf) she buttered him up (inf).

Honig-: ~**ameise** f honey-ant; ~**biene** f honey-bee; ~**brot** nt (a) siehe ~**kuchen; (b)** bread and honey; h~**farben** adj honey-coloured; h~**gelb** adj honey-yellow; ~**klee** m (Bot) melilot; ~**kuchen** m honeycake; ~**kuchenpferd** nt (fig inf) simpleton; **grinsen wie ein** ~**kuchenpferd** to grin like a Cheshire cat; ~**lecken** nt (fig) **das ist kein** ~**lecken** it's no picnic; ~**mond** m (rare) honeymoon; ~**schlecken** nt siehe ~**lecken;** ~**schleuder** f honey extractor; h~**süß** adj as sweet as honey; (fig) Worte, Ton honeyed; **Lächeln** sickly sweet; **er lächelte** h~**süß** he smiled a sickly sweet smile; ~**tau** m (pflanzlich, tierisch) honeydew; ~**wabe** f honeycomb; ~**wein** m siehe Met; ~**zelle** f honeycomb cell.

Honneurs [(h)ɔ'nøːɛs] pl: **die** ~ **machen** (geh, iro) to do the honours, to welcome the guests.

honorabel adj (old) honourable.

Honorar nt -s, -e fee; (Autoren~) royalty.

Honorar-: ~**abrechnung** f statement of account; (von Schriftsteller) royalties account; h~**frei** adj free of charge; ~**professor** m honorary professor (with no say in faculty matters).

Honoratioren [honora'tsioːrən] pl dignitaries pl, notabilities pl.

honorieren* vt (Comm) Wechsel, Scheck to honour, to meet; (fig: anerkennen) to reward. **jdm etw** ~ to pay sb (a fee) for sth, to remunerate sb for sth; **meine Arbeit wird schlecht honoriert** my work is poorly remunerated.

Honorierung f (einer Rechnung) payment (of a fee); (Bezahlung) remuneration; (Comm: von Wechsel, Scheck) acceptance.

honorig adj (dated) (ehrenhaft) respectable, honourable; (anständig) decent.

honoris causa adv Dr. ~ ~ honorary doctor.

hopfen vt Bier to hop.

Hopfen m -s, - (Bot) hop; (beim Brauen) hops pl. **bei** or **an ihm ist** ~ **und Malz verloren** (inf) he's a hopeless case, he's a dead loss (inf).

Hopfen- in cpds hop; ~**(an)bau** m hop cultivation, hopgrowing; ~**darre** f hop drier or kiln; ~**stange** f hop-pole; (fig inf: Person) bean-pole (inf).

Hoplit m -en, -en (Hist) hoplite.

hopp interj quick. **bei ihr muß alles** ~ ~ **gehen** she insists on doing everything chop-chop or at the double or double-quick (all inf); **mach mal ein bißchen** ~! (inf) chop, chop! (inf); ~**e** ~**e Reiter machen** (baby-talk) to ride a cock-horse (on sb's knee).

hoppeln vi aux sein (Hase) to lollop.

Hoppelpoppel nt -s, - (dial) **(a)** breakfast made from scrambled egg with ham and fried potatoes. **(b)** (Getränk) eggnog.

hoppla interj (beim Stolpern, Zusammenstoßen, Fangen etc) whoops, oops; (beim Zuwerfen) catch. ~, **jetzt habe ich die richtige Idee!** aha or Eureka, now I've got it!; ~, **wer kommt denn da?** hullo, who's that coming there?; ~, **jetzt komm' ich!** look out, here I come!

Hops m -es, -e (inf) hop, jump. **einen** ~ **über etw** (acc) **machen** to hop or jump over sth.

hops¹ interj jump. ~ **waren sie über den Graben weg** with a jump they were over the ditch.

hops² adj pred ~ **sein** (inf: verloren) to be lost; (Geld) to be down the drain (inf); (inf: entzwei) to be broken or kaputt (inf); ~ **gehen** (inf: verlorengehen) to get lost; (inf: entzweigehen) to get broken; (sl: verhaftet werden) to get nabbed (inf); (sl: sterben) to kick the bucket (sl), to croak (sl); **etw** ~ **gehen lassen** (inf: stehlen) to pinch sth (inf); **jdn** ~ **nehmen** (sl: verhaften) to nab sb (inf).

hopsa interj siehe hoppla.

hopsala interj upsadaisy.

hopsasa interj up we go.

hopsen vi aux sein (inf) to hop, to skip, to jump.

Hopser m -s, - (a) (inf: kleiner Sprung) (little) jump or leap. **sein Herz tat vor Freude einen** ~ his heart gave a little leap for joy. **(b)** (Tanz) ecossaise.

Hopserei f (inf) (Hüpferei) jumping about or up and down; (pej: Tanzen) hopping about.

Hör-: ~**apparat** m hearing aid; h~**bar** adj audible; **sich** h~**bar machen** (inf) to speak up; ~**barkeit** f, no pl audibility; ~**bereich** m (des Ohrs) hearing range; (eines Senders) transmission area; ~**bild** nt (Rad) feature broadcast, radio feature; ~**brille** f hearing-aid glasses pl or spectacles pl.

horchen vi to listen (dat, auf +acc to); (heimlich) to eavesdrop. **horch!** (liter) hark! (old, liter).

Horcher m -s, - eavesdropper. **der** ~ **an der Wand hört seine eigne Schand'** (Prov) eavesdroppers never hear any good of themselves.

Horch-: ~**gerät** nt (Mil) sound detector or locator; (Naut) hydrophone; ~**posten** m (Mil) listening post; **auf** ~**posten sein** to be listening out for sth.

Horde¹ f -, -n (lit, fig) horde.

Horde² f -, -n rack.

hordenweise adv in hordes.

hören vti **(a)** to hear. **ich höre dich nicht** I can't hear you; **ich hörte ihn kommen** I heard him coming; **sei mal still, ich will das** ~ **be quiet,** I want to hear this or listen to this; **er hat an der Wand gehört** he was listening at the wall; **gut/schlecht** ~ to have good/bad hearing, to hear well; **schwer** ~ to be hard of hearing; **du hörst wohl schwer** or **schlecht!** (inf) you must be deaf, are you hard of hearing?; **hör, hört!** (Zustimmung) hear!; (Mißfallen) come, come!; **etw an etw** (dat) ~ to hear sth from sth; **das läßt sich** ~ (fig) that doesn't sound bad; **das läßt sich schon eher** ~ (inf) that sounds (a bit) more like it; **das werde ich noch lange** ~ **müssen** or **zu** ~ **bekommen** I shall never hear the end or last of it; **ich will gar nichts** ~! I don't want to hear it; **ich habe sagen** ~ I've heard said or tell; **ich habe es sagen** ~ I've heard it said; **er hört sich gern reden** he likes the sound of his own voice; **hör mal!,** ~ **Sie mal!** listen; **na hör mal!, na** ~ **Sie mal!** wait a minute!, look here!, listen here!

(b) (anhören) Hörspiel, Vortrag, Radio to listen to; Berichte, Sänger to hear; (zu Wort kommen lassen) to listen to, to hear; (Rad: empfangen) to get. **ich will auch gehört werden** I want to be heard too; **bei wem** ~ **Sie in diesem Semester?** whose lectures are you going to this term?; **dieses Semester höre ich nicht** I'm not going to lectures this term; **eine französische Vorlesung bei Professor X** ~ to go to a French lecture by Professor X.

(c) (sich nach etw richten) to listen, to pay attention; (dial: gehorchen) to obey, to listen. **auf jdn/etw** ~ to listen to or heed sb/sth; **wer nicht** ~ **will, muß fühlen** (Prov) what did I tell you?; **der Hund hört auf den Namen Tobias** the dog answers to the name of Tobias.

(d) (erfahren) to hear. **von etw** ~ to hear about or of sth; **von jdm gehört haben** to have heard of sb; **von jdm** ~ (Nachricht bekommen) to hear from sb; **Sie werden noch von mir** ~ or **zu** ~ **kriegen** (inf) (Drohung) you'll be hearing from me, you haven't heard the last of this; **man hörte nie mehr etwas von ihm** he was never heard of again; **nie gehört!** (inf) never heard of him/it; **etwas/nichts von sich** ~ **lassen** to get/not to get in touch; **lassen Sie von sich** ~ keep in touch; **ich lasse von mir** ~ I'll be in touch; **er ließ nichts von sich** ~ I etc haven't heard from him; **nach allem, was ich** (über ihn/darüber) **höre** from what I've heard or I hear (about him/it); **soviel man hört** from what I hear/one hears; **er kommt, wie ich höre** I hear he's coming; **man höre und staune!** would you believe it!; **das** or **so etwas habe ich ja noch nie gehört!** I've never heard anything like it (in all my life)!; **er wollte nichts** or **von nichts gehört haben** he pretended not to have heard anything about it; **ich will davon** or **von der Sache nichts gehört haben** I don't want to know anything about it; **ich will mal nichts gehört haben** (inf) I haven't heard a thing, right? (inf).

Hören nt -s, no pl hearing; (Radio~) listening. **das** ~ **von Musik** listening to music; **es verging ihm** ~ **und Sehen** he didn't know whether he was coming or going (inf); **er fuhr so schnell, daß mir** ~ **und Sehen verging** he drove so fast I almost passed out.

Hörensagen nt: **vom** ~ from or by hearsay.

hörenswert adj worth hearing or listening to.

Hörer m -s, - **(a)** (Rad) listener; (Univ) student/person (attending lectures). **sich als** ~ **einschreiben** to enrol for a lecture course.

(b) (Telec) receiver; (Kopf~) head- or earphone.

Hörerbrief m listener's letter.

Hörerin f siehe Hörer (a).

Hörerschaft f (Rad) listeners pl, audience; (Univ) number of students/people (attending a lecture).

Hör-: ~**fehler** m (Med) hearing defect; **diese falsche Information beruht auf einem** ~**fehler** the information was got wrong because something was misheard; **das war ein** ~**fehler** I/he etc misheard it; ~**folge** f (Rad) radio series; (Geschichte in Fortsetzung) radio serial; ~**funk** m sound radio; ~**gerät** nt, ~**hilfe** f hearing aid; ~**grenze** f auditory threshold, limit of hearing.

hörig adj enslaved; (Hist) in bondage. **jdm** (sexuell) ~ **sein** to be (sexually) dependent on sb, to be in sb's thrall (liter); **sich** (dat) **jdn** ~ **machen** to make sb sexually dependent on one; **er ist ihr** ~ she has sexual power over him, he's sexually enslaved to her.

Hörige(r) mf decl as adj (Hist) bondsman, bondswoman, serf; (fig: sexuell ~) person who is sexually dependent on sb.

Hörigkeit f (Hist) bondage, serfdom; (sexuell) sexual dependence.

Horizont m -(e)s, -e (lit, fig) horizon; (Geol auch) zone. **am** ~ on the horizon; **das geht über meinen** ~ (fig) that is beyond me or my comprehension; **er hat einen begrenzten** or **beschränkten** ~ he has limited horizons.

horizontal adj horizontal. **das** ~**e Gewerbe** (inf) the oldest profession in the world (inf).

Horizontale f -n, -(n) (Math) horizontal (line). **er befindet sich in der** ~**n** (inf) he is lying down (in bed); **sich in die** ~ **begeben** (inf) to adopt the horizontal (hum).

Hormon nt -s, -e hormone.

hormonal, hormonell adj hormone attr, hormonal. **jdn/etw** ~ **behandeln** to treat sb/sth with hormones, to give sb hormone treatment.

Hormon-: ~**behandlung** f hormone treatment; ~**drüse** f endocrine gland; ~**haushalt** *m* hormone *or* hormonal balance; ~**präparat** *nt* hormone preparation; ~**spiegel** *m* hormone level.

Hörmuschel *f* -, -n (*Telec*) earpiece.

Horn *nt* -(e)s, ⁓er (a) (*von Tieren, Trink*~) horn; (*fig inf: Beule*) bump, lump. **jdn mit den ⁓ern aufspießen** to gore sb; **sich** (*dat*) **die ⁓er ablaufen** *or* **abstoßen** (*inf*) to sow one's wild oats; **den Stier an** *or* **bei den ⁓ern packen** *or* **fassen** (*fig*) to take the bull by the horns; **jdm ⁓er aufsetzen** (*inf*) to cuckold sb, to give sb horns (*old*); **⁓er tragen** (*fig*) to be a cuckold.
(b) (*Mus*) horn; (*Mil*) bugle; (*von Auto etc*) horn, hooter. **die ⁓er** (*im Orchester*) the horns *pl*, the horn section; **ins ⁓ stoßen** to blow *or* sound the horn; **ins gleiche/in jds ⁓ blasen** *or* **stoßen** *or* **tuten** to chime in.
(c) (*bei Schnecke*) horn, feeler.

Horn-: **h~artig** *adj* horn-like; ~**berger Schießen** *nt:* **wie das ~berger Schießen ausgehen** *or* **enden** to come to nothing; ~**bläser** *m* (*Mus*) horn player; ~**blende** *f* (*Geol*) hornblende; ~**brille** *f* horn-rimmed glasses *pl or* spectacles *pl*.

Hörnchen *nt* -s, - (a) (*kleines Horn*) little horn. (b) (*Gebäck*) croissant. (c) (*Zool*) squirrel; (*Backen*~) chipmunk, ground squirrel; (*Flug*~) flying squirrel.

Hörnerklang *m* sound of horns *or* bugles.

hörnern *adj* (made of) horn.

Hörnerschlitten *m* *sledge with long horn-shaped runners.*

Hörnerv *m* auditory nerve.

Horn-: **h~förmig** *adj* horn-shaped; ~**haut** *f* (patch of) hard *or* horn skin, callous; (*des Auges*) cornea; ~**hautentzündung** *f* (*Med*) inflammation of the cornea, keratitis (*spec*); ~**hauttrübung** *f* (*Med*) corneal opacity.

hornig *adj* horny, like horn.

Hornisse *f* -, -n hornet.

Hornissennest *nt* hornet's nest.

Hornist *m* horn player; (*Mil*) bugler.

Horn-: ~**kamm** *m* horn comb; ~**ochs(e)** *m* (*fig inf*) blockhead (*inf*), idiot; ~**signal** *nt* (*Mil*) bugle call; (*Rail*) horn signal; (*Auto*) honk, hoot.

Hornung *m* -s, -e (*obs*) February.

Hornvieh *nt* horned cattle *pl*; (*fig*) *siehe* **Hornochs(e).**

Hör|organ *nt* organ of hearing.

Horoskop *nt* -s, -e horoscope. **jdm das ~ stellen** to cast sb's horoscope.

Hör-: ~**probe** *f* **jetzt eine ~probe aus seiner letzten Platte** now here's a sample from his latest record; **kann ich eine ~probe machen?** can I listen to it?, can I hear what it sounds like?; ~**prüfung** *f* hearing test.

horrend *adj* horrendous.

horribile dictu *adv* (*geh*) terrible to relate.

horrido *interj* (*Hunt*) halloo.

Horrido *nt* -s, -s halloo(ing). **ein ~ auf jdn ausbringen** to give three cheers for sb.

Hörrohr *nt* (a) ear trumpet. (b) (*Med*) stethoscope.

Horror *m* -s, *no pl* horror (*vor + dat* of). **ein unbeschreiblicher ~ überfiel mich** I was seized by an indescribable feeling of horror.

Horror- *in cpds* horror; ~**film** *m* horror film; ~**schocker** *m* (*Press sl*) horror film/novel/book.

Hör-: ~**saal** *m* (*Univ*) lecture room *or* hall *or* theatre; ~**schwelle** *f* auditory threshold.

Horsd'œvre [(h)ɔr'dø:vʀ, (h)o:ʀ'dø:vʀ] *nt* -s, -s hors d'œuvre.

Hörspiel *nt* (*Rad*) radio play.

Horst *m* -(e)s, -e (a) (*Nest*) nest; (*Adler*~) eyrie. (b) (*Gehölz*) thicket, shrubbery. (c) (*Geol*) horst. (d) *siehe* **Fliegerhorst.**

Hort *m* -(e)s, -e (a) (*old, poet: Schatz*) hoard, treasure. (b) (*geh: Zufluchtsstätte*) refuge, shelter. **ein ~ der Freiheit** a stronghold of liberty; **der Herr sei mein ~** (*Bibl*) the Lord be my refuge (*Bibl*). (c) (*Kinder*~) day-home for schoolchildren in the afternoon.

horten *vt* Geld, Vorräte *etc* to hoard; Rohstoffe *etc* to stockpile.

Hortensie [-iə] *f* hydrangea.

Hortnerin *f* attendant in a day-home (*for schoolchildren*).

Hörtrichter *m siehe* **Hörrohr** (a).

Hortung *f*, *no pl siehe* **horten** vt hoarding; stockpiling.

Hör-: ~**weite** *f* hearing range; **in/außer ~weite** within/out of hearing *or* earshot; ~**zentrum** *nt* (*Anat*) auditory *or* acoustic centre.

Hosanna *interj* hosanna.

Höschen ['hø:sçən] *nt* (a) (*Kinderhose*) (pair of) trousers *or* pants; (*Strampel*~) (pair of) rompers *pl*. **kurze(s) ~** (pair of) shorts *pl*. (b) (*Unterhose*) (pair of) panties *pl or* knickers *pl*; (*für Kinder*) (pair of) underpants *pl or* pants *pl* (*Brit*). (c) (*Zool: einer Biene*) pollen load *or* pellet.

Hose *f* -, -n trousers *pl*, pants *pl*; (*Damen- auch*) slacks *pl*; (*Bund*~) breeches *pl*; (*Reit*~) jodhpurs *pl*, (riding) breeches *pl*; (*Bade*~) swimming trunks *pl*; (*Unter*~) underpants *pl*, pants *pl* (*Brit*); (*von Vogel*) leg feathers *pl*. **ich brauche eine neue ~** I need a new pair of trousers *or* pants, I need some new trousers *or* pants; **zwei ~n** two pairs of trousers *or* pants; **die ~n anhaben** (*fig inf*) to wear the trousers *or* pants (*inf*); **das Herz fiel** *or* **rutschte ihm in die ~** (*inf*) his heart was in his mouth; **die ~n voll haben** (*lit*) to have dirtied oneself, to have made a mess in one's pants; (*fig inf*) to be scared shitless (*vulg*), to be wetting oneself (*inf*); **sich** (*dat*) **in die ~n machen** (*lit*) to dirty oneself, to make a mess in one's pants; (*fig inf*) to shit (*vulg*) *or* wet (*inf*) oneself; **in die ~ gehen** (*sl: Witz, Prüfung*) to be a complete wash-out (*inf*) *or* flop (*inf*); **sich auf die ~n setzen** (*fig inf*) to get stuck in (*inf*), to knuckle down.

Hosen-: ~**anzug** *m* trouser suit (*Brit*), pantsuit (*US*);

~**aufschlag** *m* turn-up (*Brit*), cuff (*US*); ~**band** *nt* knee-band; ~**bandorden** *m* Order of the Garter; ~**bein** *nt* trouser leg; ~**boden** *m* seat (of trousers); **den ~boden vollkriegen** (*inf*) to get a smacked bottom; **sich auf den ~boden setzen** (*inf*) (*arbeiten*) to get stuck in (*inf*), to knuckle down; (*stillsitzen*) to sit down and stay sitting down; ~**boje** *f* (*Naut*) breeches buoy; ~**bügel** *m* trouser hanger; ~**bund** *m* waistband; ~**klammer** *f* trouser clip, cycle clip; ~**klappe** *f* flap; ~**knopf** *m* trouser button; ~**laden** *m* (*inf*) **siehe ~stall**; ~**latz** *m* (*Verschluß*) flies *pl*, fly; (*von Latzhose*) bib; ~**matz** *m* (*inf*) (*kleines Kind*) **du** (*kleiner*) ~**matz** my little darling *or* chap *or* fellow; ~**naht** *f* trouser seam; **mit den Händen an der ~naht** (*Mil*) (stand to attention,) thumbs on (your) trouser seams; ~**rock** *m* divided skirt, culottes *pl*, pantskirt; ~**rolle** *f* (*Theat*) breeches part; ~**scheißer** *m* (a) (*inf: Kind*) mucky pup (*inf*); **du kleiner ~scheißer** you mucky little pup; (b) (*sl: Feigling*) chicken (*inf*); (*Junge*) scaredy-pants (*inf*); ~**schlitz** *m* flies *pl*, fly; ~**spanner** *m* trouser hanger; ~**stall** *m* (*inf*) (*Schlitz*) flies *pl*, fly; (*Latz, Klappe*) (front) flap; ~**tasche** *f* trouser pocket, pants *or* trousers pocket (*US*); ~**träger** *pl* (a pair of) braces *pl* (*Brit*) *or* suspenders *pl* (*US*); ~**türchen** *nt* (*inf*) (*Schlitz*) flies *pl*, fly; (*Latz*) flap.

hosianna *interj* hosanna.

Hosianna *nt* -s, -s hosanna.

Hospital *nt* -s, -e *or* **Hospitäler** (*dated*) (a) (*Krankenhaus*) hospital. (b) (*Pflegeheim*) (old people's) home.

Hospitalismus *m* (*Med*) hospitalism.

Hospitalit *m* -en, -en (*rare*) inmate *or* patient in a hospital.

Hospitalität *f* (*obs*) hospitality.

Hospitant *m* (*Univ*) someone sitting in on lectures/classes.

hospitieren* *vi* (*Univ*) to sit in on lectures/classes (*bei jdm* with sb).

Hospiz *nt* -es, -e hospice; (*christliches ~*) private hotel under religious management.

Hostess, Hosteß *f* -, **Hostessen** hostess.

Hostie ['hɔstiə] *f* (*Eccl*) host, consecrated wafer.

Hostien- [-iən]: ~**gefäß** *nt* pyx, ciborium; ~**kelch** *m* chalice; ~**schachtel** *f* box for communion wafers; ~**schrein** *m* tabernacle; ~**teller** *m* paten.

Hotel *nt* -s, -s hotel.

Hotel- *in cpds* hotel; ~**boy** [-bɔy] *m* page (boy), bellboy (*US*), bellhop (*US*); ~**fach** *nt* hotel management; ~**fachschule** *f* college of hotel management; ~**führer** *m* hotel guide.

Hotel garni *nt* bed and breakfast hotel.

Hotel-: ~**gewerbe** *nt* hotel business; ~**halle** *f* (hotel) lobby.

Hotellerie *f* (*Sw*) hotel business.

Hotelier [-'lie:] *m* -s, -s hotelier.

Hotel-: ~**page** *m siehe* ~**boy**; ~**portier** *m* hotel *or* hall porter; ~**silber** *nt* hotel cutlery; ~**- und Gaststättengewerbe** *nt* hotel and restaurant trade, catering industry.

hott *interj* (*vorwärts*) gee up; (*nach rechts*) gee.

Hottentotte *m* -n, -n Hottentot. **sie benehmen sich wie die ~n** (*inf*) they behave like savages.

Hottentottisch(e) *nt decl as adj* Hottentot, the Hottentot language.

hpts. *abbr of* **hauptsächlich.**

Hptst. *abbr of* **Hauptstadt.**

Hr. *abbr of* **Herr** Mr.

Hrn. *abbr of* **Herrn.**

hrsg. *abbr of* **herausgegeben** edited, ed.

Hrsg. *abbr of* **Herausgeber** ed.

hu *interj* (*Schaudern*) ugh; (*Schrecken, Kälte etc*) whew.

hü *interj* (*vorwärts*) gee up; (*nach links*) wo hi. **einmal sagt er ~, einmal hott** (*inf*) first he says one thing and then another, he's always chopping and changing.

Hub *m* -(e)s, ⁓e (*Tech*) (a) (*bei Maschinen: Kolben*~) (piston) stroke. (b) (*bei Kränen: Leistung*) lifting *or* hoisting capacity, lift.

Hub(b)el *m* -s, - (*inf*) bump.

hubb(e)lig *adj* (*inf*) bumpy.

Hubbrücke *f* lift bridge.

hüben *adv* over here, (on) this side. **~ und** *or* **wie drüben** on both sides.

Hubertusjagd *f* St Hubert's Day hunt.

Hub-: ~**insel** *f* drilling rig *or* platform; ~**karren** *m* lift(ing) truck; ~**kraft** *f* lifting *or* hoisting capacity; ~**raum** *m* (*Aut*) cubic capacity.

hübsch *adj* (a) (*gutaussehend*) pretty; (*reizvoll*) Ausflug, Geschenk lovely, delightful, nice; (*inf: nett*) lovely, nice. **sich ~ machen** to make oneself look pretty; **er macht das schon ganz ~** he's doing it very nicely; **das war ~/nicht ~ von dir** that was nice *or* lovely/not nice of you; **das wäre doch ~, wenn ...** it would be lovely if ...; **ihr** (*beiden*) **H~en** (*inf*) you two.
(b) (*iro inf: unangenehm*) fine, pretty, nice. **eine ~e Geschichte/Bescherung** a pretty kettle of fish, a fine how-d'ye-do; **das kann ja ~ werden** that'll be just great; **da hast du dir etwas H~es eingebrockt!** now you've got yourself into a fine *or* pretty mess!
(c) (*inf: beträchtlich*) tidy, pretty, nice. **ein ~es Vermögen/ein ~es Sümmchen** a pretty penny (*inf*), a tidy sum.
(d) *nur adv* (*ziemlich*) pretty. **es ist doch ganz ~ weit** it's pretty far, it's a fair old way; **da mußte ich aber ganz ~ arbeiten** I really had to work pretty hard; **ganz ~ viel bezahlen** to pay quite a bit.
(e) *nur adv* (*inf: wie es sein soll*) **das werde ich ~ bleiben lassen** I'm going to leave well alone; **das wirst du ~ lassen** you're going to do nothing of the kind; **sei ~ artig!** be a good boy/girl; **immer ~ langsam!** nice and easy does it, (take it) nice and slowly.

Hub-: ~**schrauber** *m* -s, - helicopter; ~**schrauberlandeplatz** *m* heliport; ~**stapler** *m* -s, - fork-lift truck; ~**volumen** *nt* (*Tech*) siehe ~**raum**.

huch *interj* ooh.

Hucke *f* -, -n (*obs*) (*Last*) load; (*Korb*) pannier. **jdm die ~ vollhauen** (*inf*) to give sb a good thrashing (*inf*) or hiding; **die ~ vollkriegen** (*inf*) to get a thrashing (*inf*) or hiding; **jdm die ~ vollügen** (*inf*) to tell sb a pack of lies; **sich** (*dat*) **die ~ vollsaufen** (*sl*) to have a skinful (*sl*).

huckepack *adv* piggy-back, pick-a-back. **ein Kind ~ nehmen/tragen** to give a child a piggy-back (ride), to carry a child piggy-back or pick-a-back.

Huckepackverkehr *m* (*Rail*) piggy-back transport (*US*), motorail service. **im ~** by motorail or rail.

Hudelei *f* (*esp S Ger, Aus inf*) slipshod or sloppy (*inf*) work.

hud(e)lig *adj* siehe **hudlig**.

hudeln *vi* (*esp S Ger, Aus inf*) to work sloppily, to do slipshod work.

Hudler *m* -s, - (*esp S Ger, Aus inf*) slipshod or sloppy worker, bungler (*inf*).

hudlig *adj* (*esp S Ger, Aus inf*) slipshod, sloppy (*inf*). **~ arbeiten** to work sloppily, to do sloppy or slipshod work.

Huf *m* -(e)s, -e hoof. **einem Pferd die ~e beschlagen** to shoe a horse.

Hufbeschlag *m* (horse)shoeing.

Hufeisen *nt* horseshoe.

Hufeisen-: **h~förmig** *adj* horseshoe-shaped, (in) the shape of a horseshoe; ~**magnet** *m* horseshoe magnet.

Hufendorf *nt* village arranged in a straight line with strips of farmland extending behind each house.

Huf-: ~**lattich** *m* (*Bot*) coltsfoot; ~**nagel** *m* horseshoe-nail; ~**schlag** *m* (*Getrappel*) hoofbeats *pl*; (*Stoß*) kick (from a horse); **dabei hat er einen ~schlag abbekommen** the horse kicked him; ~**schmied** *m* blacksmith, farrier; ~**schmiede** *f* smithy, blacksmith's or farrier's (workshop).

Hüft-: ~**bein** *nt* hip-bone; ~**bruch** *m* fractured hip, hip fracture.

Hüfte *f* -, -n hip; (*von Tieren*) haunch. **bis an die ~n reichen** to come up to the waist; **wir standen bis an die ~n in Brennesseln/im Wasser** we stood waist-high or up to the waist in stinging nettles/waist-deep or up to the waist in water; **aus der ~ schießen** to shoot from the hip; **die ~n wiegen** (*geh*), **mit den ~n wackeln** (*inf*) or swing one's hips; **die Arme in die ~n stützen** to put/have one's hands on one's hips; **er stand mit den Armen in die ~n gestützt da** he stood there hands on hips or with arms akimbo.

Hüft-: ~**gegend** *f* hip region; ~**gelenk** *nt* hip joint; ~**gürtel**, ~**halter** *m* girdle; ~**hoch** *adj* waist-high; *Wasser etc* waist-deep; **wir standen h~hoch im Farnkraut/Schlamm** we stood waist-high in ferns/waist-deep in mud; **h~hohe Gummistiefel** rubber waders.

Huftier *nt* hoofed animal, ungulate (*form*).

Hüft-: ~**knochen** *m* siehe ~**bein**; ~**leiden** *nt* hip trouble; ~**schmerz** *m* pain in the hip; ~**verrenkung** *f* dislocation of the hip.

Hügel *m* -s, - hill; (*Grab-, Erdhaufen*) mound. **ein kleiner ~** a hillock.

Hügel-: **h~ab** *adv* downhill; ~**abhang** *m* hillside, slope (of a hill); **h~an**, **h~auf** *adv* uphill; ~**grab** *nt* (*Archeol*) barrow, tumulus.

hüg(e)lig *adj* hilly, undulating, rolling *attr*.

Hügel-: ~**kette** *f* range or chain of hills; ~**land** *nt* hilly country.

Hugenotte *m* -n, -n, **Hugenottin** *f* Huguenot.

hüglig *adj* siehe **hüg(e)lig**.

hüh *interj* siehe **hu**.

huh *interj* siehe **hu**.

Huhn *nt* -(e)s, ~er (a) chicken (*auch Cook*); (*Henne auch*) hen; (*Gattung*) fowl, gallinaceous bird (*form*). **mit den ~ern aufstehen** (*inf*) to get up with the lark; **mit den ~ern zu Bett gehen** (*inf*) to go to bed early; **da lachen ja die ~er** (*inf*) what a joke, it's enough to make a cat laugh (*inf*); **ich sehe aus wie ein gerupftes ~** (*inf*) my hair looks like a haystack (*inf*).
(b) (*fig inf*) **du krankes ~** you poor old thing; **ein verrücktes** or **komisches** or **ulkiges ~** a queer bird (*inf*) or fish (*inf*); **ein dummes ~** a silly goose; **ein versoffenes ~** a tippler.

Hühnchen *nt* (young) chicken, pullet; (*Brat~*) (roast) chicken. **mit jdm ein ~ zu rupfen haben** (*inf*) to have a bone to pick with sb (*inf*).

Hühner-: ~**auge** *nt* (*Med*) corn; **jdm auf die ~augen treten** (*hum*) to tread on sb's corns (*inf*); ~**augenpflaster** *nt* corn plaster; ~**bouillon**, ~**brühe** *f* (clear) chicken broth; ~**brust** *f* (*Cook*) chicken breast; (*Med, fig*) pigeon-breast, chicken-breast (*US*); ~**dieb** *m* chicken thief; **er mußte sich wie ein ~dieb wegschleichen** he had to slink off with his tail between his legs; ~**draht** *m* chicken wire; ~**ei** *nt* hen's egg; ~**farm** *f* chicken farm; ~**frikassee** *nt* chicken fricassee; ~**futter** *nt* chicken feed; ~**habicht** *m* goshawk; ~**haus** *nt* henhouse, chicken-coop; ~**gott** *m* (*Miner*) holy-stone; ~**hof** *m* chicken run; ~**hund** *m* pointer; ~**klein** *nt* -s, no pl (*Cook*) chicken trimmings *pl*; ~**leiter** *f* chicken ladder; ~**mist** *m* chicken droppings *pl*; (*zum Düngen*) chicken manure; ~**pastete** *f* chicken pie; ~**pest** *f* (*Vet*) fowl pest; ~**stall** *m* henhouse, chicken-coop; ~**stange** *f* perch, (chicken) roost; ~**suppe** *f* chicken soup; ~**vögel** *pl* (*Orn*) gallinaceans *pl* (*form*), gallinaceous birds *pl* (*form*); ~**zucht** *f* chicken breeding or farming.

hui [huɪ] *interj* whoosh. **~, das war aber schnell!** wow, that was quick!; **im H~** in a flash (*inf*), in a jiffy (*inf*); **außen ~, innen pfui**, **oben ~, unten pfui** (*prov inf*) the outside's fine but underneath he/she *etc* is filthy.

Huld *f* -, no pl (*old liter*) (*Güte*) grace, graciousness; (*Gunst*) favour. **jdm seine ~ schenken** to bestow one's favour upon sb (*liter*); **sie stand in seiner ~** she was in his good graces.

huldigen *vi* +*dat* (*liter*) (a) **einem König, Papst etc** to render or do or pay homage to; **einem Künstler, Lehrmeister etc** to pay homage to; **einer Dame** to pay one's attentions or addresses to (*liter*). (b) **einer Ansicht** to subscribe to; **einer Sitte, einem Glauben etc** to embrace; **einem Laster** to indulge in.

Huldigung *f* (*old, liter*) (a) (*Hist: Treueeid*) homage, oath of allegiance. (b) (*Verehrung*) homage; (*einer Dame*) attentions *pl* (*liter*), addresses *pl* (*liter*); (*Beifall*) homage. **jdm seine ~ darbringen** to pay homage to sb.

huldreich, **huldvoll** *adj* (*old, liter*) gracious.

Hülfe *f* -, -n (*obs*) siehe **Hilfe**.

Hülle *f* -, -n (a) cover; (*Schallplatten~ auch*) sleeve; (*für Ausweiskarten etc auch*) holder, case; (*Cellophan~*) wrapping; (*liter, hum: Kleidung*) clothes *pl*, piece of clothing; (*liter: eines Menschen*) exterior; (*abgestreifte Schlangenhaut*) skin. **die ~ fallen lassen** to peel or strip off; **die letzten ~n fallen lassen** to shed the last layer; **der Körper als ~ der Seele** the body as the temple of the soul; **die sterbliche ~** the mortal remains *pl*.
(b) (*Anat*) integument.
(c) (*Bot*) involucre.
(d) (*Phys: Atom~*) shell.
(e) **in ~ und Fülle** in abundance; **Äpfel/Whisky/Frauen/Sorgen etc in ~ und Fülle** apples/whisky/women/worries galore; **es gab alles in ~ und Fülle** there was an abundance or plenty of everything.

hüllen *vt* (*geh*) to wrap. **in Dunkel gehüllt** shrouded in darkness; **in Flammen gehüllt** enveloped in flames; **in Wolken gehüllt** covered or enveloped or veiled (*liter*) in clouds; **sich fest in seinen Mantel ~** to wrap oneself up tight in one's coat; **sich (über etw acc) in Schweigen ~** to remain silent (on or about sth).

hüllenlos *adj* unclothed.

Hüllwort *nt* (*Ling*) euphemism.

Hülse *f* -, -n (a) (*Schale*) hull, husk; (*Schote*) pod; (*Bot: Frucht*) involucre (*form*). (b) (*Etui, Kapsel*) case; (*für Film*) cartridge; (*Phys: für gefährliche Stoffe*) capsule; (*von Geschoß*) case; (*von Patronen*) (cartridge) case. **er ist nur noch eine leere ~** he is now just an empty shell.

Hülsenfrucht *f usu pl* peas and beans *pl*, pulse (*form*).

human *adj* humane; (*verständnisvoll auch*) considerate.

Humangenetik *f* human genetics *sing*.

Humanisierung *f* humanization.

Humanismus *m* humanism; (*Hist*) Humanism.

Humanist(in *f*) *m* humanist; (*Hist: Humanist*); (*Altsprachler*) classicist.

humanistisch *adj* siehe *n* humanist(ic); Humanist; classical. **~ gebildet** educated in the classics or humanities; **~e Bildung** classical education, education in the classics or the humanities; **~es Gymnasium** secondary school with bias on Latin and Greek; ≈ grammar school (*Brit*).

humanitär *adj* humanitarian.

Humanität *f*, no pl humaneness, humanity; (*als Bildungsideal*) humanitarianism.

Humanitätsduselei *f* (*pej*) sentimental humanitarianism.

Human-: ~**medizin** *f* (human) medicine; ~**mediziner** *m* medic (*inf*); medical student; doctor of medicine.

Humbug *m* -s, no pl (*inf*) (*Schwindel*) humbug (*inf*); (*Unsinn auch*) stuff and nonsense (*inf*).

Hummel *f* -, -n bumble-bee. ~**n im** or **unterm Hintern haben** (*dated inf*) to have ants in one's pants (*inf*).

Hummer *m* -s, - lobster.

Hummer-: ~**krabben** *pl* king prawn; ~**mayonnaise** *f* lobster mayonnaise; ~**reuse** *f* lobster pot; ~**salat** *m* lobster salad; ~**schere** *f* lobster claw.

Humor *m* -s, (*rare*) -e humour; (*Sinn für ~*) sense of humour. **er hat keinen (Sinn für) ~** he has no sense of humour; **etw mit ~ nehmen/tragen** to take/bear sth with a sense of humour or cheerfully; **er nahm die Bemerkung mit ~ auf** he took the remark good-humouredly or in good humour; **er hat einen eigenartigen ~** he has a strange sense of humour; **er verliert nie den ~** he never loses his sense of humour; **langsam verliere ich den ~** it's getting beyond a joke; **da hat selbst er den ~ verloren** it was going too far even for him, even he didn't think it funny any more; **~ ist, wenn man trotzdem lacht** (*prov*) having a sense of humour means looking on the bright side.

Humoreske *f* -, -n (*liter*) humorous story/sketch; (*Mus*) humoresque.

humorig *adj* (*geh*) humorous, genial.

Humorist(in *f*) *m* humorist; (*Komiker*) comedian.

humoristisch *adj* humorous. **er ist/hat ein großes ~es Talent** he is a very funny or amusing person.

Humor-: **h~los** *adj* humourless; *Buch etc auch* lacking in or devoid of humour; *Mensch auch* lacking (a sense of) humour or in humour; **er hat recht h~los auf unsere Scherze reagiert** he didn't find our jokes funny at all; ~**losigkeit** *f* siehe *adj* humourlessness; lack of (a sense of) humour; **mit der für ihn typischen ~losigkeit** with his usual lack of humour; **h~voll** *adj* humorous, amusing; **er kann sehr h~voll erzählen** he is a very amusing or humorous talker.

Humpelei *f*, no pl (*inf*) hobbling.

humpeln *vi* (a) *aux sein* to hobble. (b) (*inf: ständig hinken*) to limp, to walk with or have a limp.

Humpen *m* -s, - tankard, mug; (*aus Ton*) stein.

Humus *m* -, no pl humus.

Humus-: ~**boden** *m*, ~**erde** *f* humus soil.

Hund *m* -(e)s, -e (a) dog; (*Jagd~ auch*) hound; (*sl: Schurke*) swine (*sl*), bastard (*sl*). **der Große/Kleine ~** (*Astron*) Great(er) Dog/Little or Lesser Dog; **junger ~** puppy, pup; **die Familie der ~e** the dog or canine family; ~**e, die** (*viel*

bellen, beißen nicht empty vessels make most noise (Prov); **getroffene ~e bellen** (inf) if the cap fits, wear it; **viele ~e sind des Hasen Tod** (Prov) there is not much one person can do against many; **wie ~ und Katze leben** to live like cat and dog, to lead a cat-and-dog life; **ich würde bei diesem Wetter keinen ~ auf die Straße jagen** I wouldn't send a dog out in this weather; **damit kann man keinen ~ hinterm Ofen hervorlocken** (inf) that's not going to tempt anybody; **müde wie ein ~ sein** (inf) to be dog-tired; **er ist bekannt wie ein bunter ~** (inf) everybody knows him; **kein ~ nimmt ein Stück Brot von ihm** everyone avoids him like the plague; **das ist (ja) zum Junge-~e-Kriegen** (inf) it's enough to give you kittens; **da wird der ~ in der Pfanne verrückt** (inf) it's enough to drive you round the twist (inf); **da liegt der ~ begraben** (inf) (so) that's what is/was behind it all; (Haken, Problem etc) that's the problem; **er ist mit allen ~en gehetzt** (inf) he knows all the tricks, there are no flies on him (inf); **er ist ein armer ~** he's a poor soul or devil (inf); **er ist völlig auf dem ~** (inf) he's really gone to the dogs (inf); **auf den ~ kommen** (inf) to go to the dogs (inf); **jdn auf den ~ bringen** (inf) to ruin sb; (gesundheitlich) to ruin sb's health; **die Weiber haben/der Suff hat ihn auf den ~ gebracht** (inf) women have/drink has been his ruin or downfall; **vor die ~e gehen** (sl) to go to the dogs (inf); (sterben) to die, to perish; (getötet werden) to cop it (inf), to be killed; **du blöder ~** (sl) you silly or stupid bastard (sl); **du gemeiner ~** (sl) you rotten bastard (sl); **du schlauer or gerissener ~** (sl) you sly or crafty devil or old fox; **kein ~** (inf) not a (damn inf) soul.
(b) (Min: Förderwagen) truck, tub.

Hündchen nt dim of **Hund** doggy (inf), little dog; (kleiner Hund) small or little dog; (junger Hund) puppy, pup, puppy-dog (baby-talk).

Hunde-: **~arbeit** f (fig inf): **eine ~arbeit an awful job, the devil's own job** (inf); **~art** f siehe **~rasse**; **~biß** m dog bite; **er hat einen ~biß abbekommen** he was/has been bitten by a dog; **~dreck** m dog's muck; **h~elend** adj (inf) **mir ist h~elend** I feel lousy (inf); **~fänger** m dog-catcher; **~floh** m dog flea; **~fraß** m (pej sl) (pig-)swill (pej inf); **~futter** nt dog food; **~gebell** nt barking (of dogs); **~gekläff** nt (pej) yapping (of dogs); **~gespann** nt team of dogs; **~halsband** nt dog collar; **~halter(in** f) m (form) dog owner; **~haltung** f owning dogs; **~hütte** f (lit, fig) (dog) kennel; **h~kalt** adj (inf) freezing cold; **~kälte** f (inf) freezing cold; **~kot** m dog dirt; **~kuchen** m dog-biscuit; **~leben** nt (inf) dog's life (inf); **~leine** f dog lead or leash; **~liebhaber** m dog-lover; **~lohn** m (pej inf) miserable or rotten (inf) wage(s); **~marke** f dog licence disc, dog tag (US); (hum inf: Erkennungsmarke) identity disc, dog-tag (US inf); **h~müde** adj pred, adv (inf) dog-tired; **~narr** m (inf) fanatical dog lover, dog-freak (inf); **~rasse** f breed (of dog); **~rennen** nt greyhound or dog racing no art, dogs (inf); (Wettkampf) greyhound race.

hundert num a or one hundred. **einige ~ Menschen** a few hundred people; **einer unter ~** one in a hundred; **in ~ Jahren** in a hundred years (from now); **ich wette ~ gegen eins** (inf) I'll bet or lay a hundred to one, I'll bet you anything (inf).

Hundert¹ f -, -en (Zahl) hundred.

Hundert² nt -s, -e hundred. **es geht in die ~e** it runs into the hundreds; **~e von Menschen** hundreds of people; **einer unter ~en** one out of hundreds; **zehn vom ~** ten per cent; **zu ~en by the hundred, in (their) hundreds; **einige ~ (Stecknadeln)** a few hundred (pins).

hundert|eins num a hundred and one.

Hunderter¹ m -s, - (a) (von Zahl) (the) hundred. (b) (Geldschein) hundred(-pound/-dollar etc note).

Hunderter² f -, - (inf) hundred-watt (electric) bulb.

hunderterlei adj inv a hundred and one.

Hundert-: **h~fach, h~fältig** (geh) 1 adj hundredfold; **die h~fache Menge** a hundred times the amount; 2 adv **a hundred times; **jdm etw h~fach zurückgeben/vergelten** (fig) to repay sb a hundredfold or a hundred times over for sth; **~fünfundsiebziger** m -s, - (dated sl) homo (dated inf), queer (inf); **h~fünfzigprozentig** adj (iro) fanatical; **er ist ein ~fünfzigprozentiger** he's a fanatic; **~jahrfeier** f centenary, centennial (US); (Festlichkeiten auch) centenary or centennial celebrations pl; **h~jährig** adj attr (one-)hundred-year-old; **der ~jährige Kalender** the Hundred Years' Calendar (for weather prediction); **der ~jährige Krieg** (Hist) the Hundred Years' War; **das Ergebnis einer h~jährigen Entwicklung/Arbeit** the result of a hundred years of development/work; **~jährige(r)** mf decl as adj centenarian; **h~jährlich** adj every hundred years; **h~mal** adv a hundred times; **ich hab' dir schon h~mal gesagt ...** if I've told you once I've told you a hundred times ...; **~meterlauf** m (Sport) der/ein **~meterlauf** the/a 100 metres sing; **h~prozentig** adj (a or one) hundred per cent; **Alkohol** pure; **ein h~prozentiger Konservativer** etc an out-and-out conservative etc; **er ist h~prozentig Amerikaner** etc he's one hundred per cent American etc; **Sie haben h~prozentig recht** you're absolutely right; **ich bin mir h~prozentig sicher** I'm a hundred per cent sure; **das weiß ich h~prozentig** that's a fact; **ich bin mit ihm h~prozentig einer Meinung** I agree with him one hundred per cent; **ich werde ihn h~prozentig im Krankenhaus besuchen** I'll definitely visit him in hospital; **h~prozentig?** (inf) are you absolutely sure?; **~satz** m (form) percentage; **~schaft** f (Mil) group of a or one hundred; (Hist) bei den Römern) century.

Hundertstel nt -s, - hundredth.

hundertste(r, s) adj hundredth. **vom H~n ins Tausendste kommen** (fig) to ramble on, to get carried away.

Hundert-: **h~tausend** num a or one hundred thousand; **~tausende von Menschen** hundreds of thousands of people; **~tausendstel** nt -s, - hundred thousandth; **h~undeins** num a

---

or one hundred and one.

hundertweise adv by the hundred, in hundreds.

Hunde-: **~salon** m dog parlour; **~scheiße** f (sl) dogshit (vulg), dog mess (inf); **~schlitten** m dog sled(ge) or sleigh; **~schnauze** f nose, snout; **kalt wie eine ~schnauze sein** (inf) to be ice-cold or as cold as ice; **~sohn** m (pej liter) cur; **~sperre** f ban on (bringing in) dogs; **~staffel** f dog branch; **~staupe** f (Vet) distemper; **~steuer** f dog licence fee; **~wache** f (Naut) dogwatch; **~wetter** nt (inf) foul or filthy weather; **~zucht** f dog breeding; **~zwinger** m (dog) compound; (städtisch) dog pound.

Hündin f bitch.

hündisch adj (fig) fawning attr, sycophantic. **~e Ergebenheit** dog-like devotion.

Hündlein nt dim of **Hund** doggy (inf), little dog; (kleiner Hund) little or small dog.

Hunds-: **~fott** m -s, ¨er (obs, dial) (miserable) cur; **h~föttisch** adj (obs, dial) dastardly (old); **h~gemein** adj (inf) shabby, mean; (schwierig) fiendishly difficult; **Schmerz** etc terrible; **es tut h~gemein weh** it hurts like hell (inf); **er kann h~gemein werden** he can get really nasty; **h~miserabel** adj (inf) abominable, abysmal (inf), lousy (inf); **mir geht es or ich fühle mich h~miserabel** I feel rotten (inf) or lousy (inf); **h~müde** adj (inf) siehe hundemüde; **~stern** m Dog Star; **~tage** pl dog days pl; **~veilchen** nt (heath) dog violet; **~wut** f (a) siehe Tollwut; (b) **eine ~wut auf jdn haben** (inf) to be livid with sb (inf).

Hüne m -n, -n: **ein ~ von Mensch** (geh) a giant of a man.

Hünen-: **~gestalt** f (geh) Titanic or colossal figure or frame; **ein Mann von ~gestalt** a man of Titanic or colossal stature; **~grab** nt megalithic grave; **h~haft** adj (geh) gigantic, colossal; **~weib** nt amazon.

Hunger m -s, no pl (lit, fig) hunger (nach for); (Hungersnot auch) famine; (nach Bildung auch) thirst; (nach fernen Ländern, Sonne etc) yearning; (nach Literatur) appetite. **~ bekommen/haben** to get/be hungry; **ich habe keinen richtigen ~** I'm not really hungry; **~ auf etw** (acc) **haben** to feel like (eating) sth; **den ~ bekämpfen** to combat hunger; **~ leiden** (geh) to go hungry, to starve; **ich habe ~ wie ein Wolf** or **Bär** (inf) I could eat a horse (inf); **~s** (liter) or **vor ~ sterben** to die of hunger or starvation, to starve to death; **ich sterbe vor ~** (inf) I'm starving (inf), I'm dying of hunger (inf); **~ ist der beste Koch** (Prov) hunger is the best sauce (Prov).

Hunger-: **~blockade** f hunger or starvation blockade; **~dasein** nt existence at starvation level; **~gefühl** nt hungry feeling; **~jahr** nt hungry year, year of hunger; **~künstler** m (professional) faster, person who, for pay, goes without nourishment for prolonged periods; **ich bin doch kein ~künstler** I'm not on a starvation diet; **~leben** nt siehe **~dasein**; **~leider** m -s, - (dated) starving wretch, starveling.

hungern 1 vi (a) (Hunger leiden) to go hungry, to starve. **jdn ~ lassen** to let sb go hungry; (zur Strafe auch) to make sb starve; **ich hungere schon seit fünf Tagen** I haven't eaten a thing for five days.
(b) (fasten) to go without food.
(c) (fig geh: verlangen) to hunger (nach for).
2 vt impers (geh) **es hungert mich, mich hungert** I am or feel hungry; **ihn hungert nach Macht** he hungers or is hungry for power.
3 vr **sich zu Tode ~** to starve oneself to death; **sich schlank ~** to go on a starvation diet; **er hat sich durch die Studentenzeit gehungert** he starved his way through university.

hungernd adj, no comp hungry, starving.

Hunger|ödem nt (Med) famine oedema (spec).

Hungersnot f famine.

Hunger-: **~streik** m hunger strike; **~tag** m (inf) fast day; **~tod** m death from starvation; **den ~tod erleiden** or **sterben** to die of hunger or starvation; **~tuch** nt (Eccl) Lenten veil; **am ~tuch nagen** (fig) to be starving, to be on the breadline (inf); **~turm** m (Hist) dungeon, oubliette.

hungrig adj (lit, fig) hungry (nach for). **Arbeit macht ~** work makes you hungry or gives you an appetite; **Gartenarbeit macht ~** gardening is hungry work; **~ nach** or **auf** (acc) **etw sein** to feel like (eating) sth; **~ nach Luft/Literatur** gasping for air/thirsting for good literature.

Hunne m -n -n, **Hunnin** f (Hist) Hun.

Hupe f -, -n horn. **auf die ~ drücken** to press/sound the horn.

hupen vi to sound or hoot or honk (Aut inf) the horn, to hoot. „~" "sound your horn".

hüpfen vi (esp S Ger) aux sein siehe hüpfen. **das ist gehupft wie gesprungen** (inf) it doesn't make any difference, it's six of one and half a dozen of the other (inf).

hüpfen vi aux sein to hop; (Lämmer, Zicklein etc) to frisk, to gambol; (Ball) to bounce. **vor Freude ~** to jump for joy; **die Kinder hüpften vor Freude im Zimmer herum** the children went skipping round the room in sheer delight; **sein Herz hüpfte vor Freude** his heart leapt for joy; **H~ spielen** to play (at) hopscotch.

Hüpfer, Hupfer (esp S Ger) m -s, - hop, skip, bounce. **mein Herz machte einen ~** my heart leapt.

Hüpfspiel nt hopscotch.

Hup-: **~konzert** nt (inf) chorus of hooting or horns; **~ring** m horn ring; **~signal** nt (Aut) hoot; siehe **~zeichen**; **~ton** m sound of a horn/hooter/whistle; **~zeichen** nt (Aut) hoot; „~zeichen geben" "sound your horn".

Hürde f -, -n (a) (Sport, fig) hurdle. **eine ~ nehmen** to take or clear a hurdle. (b) (Viehzaun) fold, pen.

Hürden-: **~lauf** m (Sportart) hurdling; (Wettkampf) hurdles pl or sing; **~läufer** m hurdler; **~rennen** nt (Horseracing) steeplechase.

Hure f -, -n whore.

huren vi (inf) to whore, to go whoring.

Huren-: ~**bock** *m* (*pej sl*) whoremonger; **h~haft** *adj* (*pej*) whorish; ~**haus** *nt* (*dated*) whorehouse (*sl*), brothel; ~**kind** *nt* (*old*) child of a whore; whoreson (*obs*); (*Typ*) widow; ~**sohn** *m* (*pej sl*) bastard (*sl*), son of a bitch (*esp US sl*).

Hurer *m* -s, - (*old pej*) whoremonger.

Hurerei *f* whoring.

hürnen *adj* (*obs*) *siehe* **hörnern. der** ~**e Siegfried** Siegfried the invulnerable.

hurra [hʊˈraː, ˈhʊra] *interj* hurray, hurrah.

Hurra *nt* -s, -s cheers *pl*. **ein dreifaches** ~ three cheers.

Hurra-: ~**geschrei** *nt* cheering; ~**patriot** *m* flag-waving patriot, jingoist, chauvinist; ~**patriotismus** *m* flag-waving, jingoism, chauvinism; ~**ruf** *m* cheer.

Hurrikan *m* -s, -e *or* (*bei engl Aussprache*) -s hurricane.

hurtig *adj* (*old*, *dial*) nimble; (*schnell*) quick.

Hurtigkeit *f*, *no pl* (*old*, *dial*) *siehe adj* nimbleness; quickness, speed.

Husar *m* -en, -en (*Hist*) hussar.

Husaren-: ~**streich** *m*, ~**stück** *nt* (*fig*) (daring) escapade *or* exploit.

husch *interj* (a) (*aufscheuchend*) shoo. (b) (*antreibend*) come on. (c) (*schnell*) quick, quickly now. **er macht seine Arbeit immer** ~ ~ (*inf*) he always whizzes through his work (*inf*); **und** ~, **weg war er and** whoosh! he was gone.

Husch *m* -(e)s, -e (*inf*) **im** ~ **in a** flash (*inf*) *or* jiffy (*inf*); **er kam auf einen** ~ **vorbei** he dropped in on me *or* by for a minute.

Husche *f* -, -n (*dial*) cloudburst. **schnell, sonst bekommen wir eine** ~ **ab!** hurry or we'll get a soaking!

huschen *vi aux sein* to dart, to flit; (*Mäuse etc auch*) to scurry; (*Lächeln*) to flash, to flit; (*Licht*) to flash.

hussa(sa) *interj* (*old*, *liter*) tally-ho; (*hü*) gee-up.

hüsteln *vi* to give a slight cough, to cough slightly. **er hüstelt noch** he still has a slight cough; **anstatt zu antworten, hüstelte er nur spöttisch** instead of answering he just cleared his throat sarcastically.

husten 1 *vi* to cough. **auf etw** (*acc*) ~ (*inf*) not to give a damn for sth (*inf*); **der Motor hustet** (*inf*) the engine is coughing (and spluttering). 2 *vt* to cough; *Blut* to cough (up). **denen werde ich was** ~ (*inf*) I'll tell them where they can get off (*inf*).

Husten *m* -s, *no pl* cough. ~ **haben** to have a cough.

Husten-: ~**anfall** *m* coughing fit; ~**bonbon** *m or nt* cough drop *or* sweet; ~**mittel** *nt* cough medicine/drop *or* sweet; ~**reiz** *m* tickle in *or* irritation of the throat; **seinen** ~**reiz unterdrücken** to suppress the need *or* urge to cough; ~**saft** *m* cough syrup *or* mixture; **h~stillend** *adj* cough-relieving; **das wirkt** ~**stillend** it relieves coughing *or* one's cough; ~**tee** *m* tea which is good for coughs; ~**tropfen** *pl* cough drops *pl*.

Hut[1] *m* -(e)s, ¨-e hat; (*von Pilz*) cap. **den** ~ **aufsetzen/abnehmen/ lüften** (*geh*) to put on/take off/raise one's hat; **den** *or* **mit dem** ~ **in der Hand** with his hat in his hand; **vor jdm den** ~ **abnehmen** *or* **ziehen** (*fig*) to take off one's hat to sb; **vor etw** (*dat*) **den** ~ **ziehen** (*fig*) to take off one's hat to sth; ~ **ab!** I take my hat off to him/you *etc*; ~ **ab vor solcher Leistung!** I take my hat off to you/that; **mit dem** ~**e in der Hand kommt man durch das ganze Land** (*Prov*) politeness will serve you well in life; **das kannst du dir an den** ~ **stecken!** (*inf*) you can stick (*sl*) *or* keep (*inf*) it; **unter einen** ~ **bringen** *or* **kriegen** (*inf*) to reconcile, to accommodate, to cater for; *Verpflichtungen, Termine* to fit in; **da geht einem der** ~ **hoch** (*inf*) it's enough to make you blow your top (*inf*); (*vor Spaß, Überraschung*) it is amazing, it beats everything; **da geht euch der** ~ **hoch** (*inf*) you'll have a whale of a time (*inf*); **den** *or* **seinen** ~ **nehmen (müssen)** (*inf*) to (have to) go, to (have to) pack one's bags (*inf*); **das ist doch ein alter** ~! (*inf*) that's old hat! (*inf*); **jdm eine auf den** ~ **geben** (*inf*) to give sb a rocket (*inf*) *or* wigging (*inf*); **eins auf den** ~ **kriegen** (*inf*) to get a rocket (*inf*) *or* wigging (*inf*).

Hut[2] *f* -, *no pl* (a) (*geh*) protection, keeping. **unter** *or* **in meiner** ~ in my keeping; (*Kinder*) in my care; **in guter** *or* **sicherer** ~ in safe keeping, in good *or* safe hands; **er befindet sich unter der besonderen** ~ **des Königs** he is under *or* enjoys the special protection of the king.

(b) **auf der** ~ **sein** to be on one's guard (*vor* +*dat* against).

Hut-: ~**ablage** *f* hat rack; ~**band** *nt* hatband; (*von Damenhut*) hat ribbon.

Hütchen *nt dim of* **Hut**[1] little hat.

Hütejunge *m* (*liter*) shepherd boy.

hüten 1 *vt* to look after, to mind; *Vieh etc auch* to tend, to keep watch over (*liter*); (*geh*) *Geheimnisse* to guard, to keep; (*geh*) *Briefe* to keep. **das Bett/Haus** ~ to stay in bed/indoors; **hüte deine Zunge!** (*liter*) guard your tongue! (*liter*).

2 *vr* to guard *or* to be on one's guard (*vor* +*dat* against), to beware (*vor* +*dat* of). **ich werde mich** ~! no fear!, not likely!, I'll do nothing of the kind!; **du wirst dich schwer** ~! you'll do nothing of the kind!; **ich werde mich** ~, **ihm das zu erzählen** there's no chance of me telling him that; **sich** ~, **etw zu tun** to take care not to do sth; **hüte dich, etwas zu verraten** take care not to give anything away, mind you don't give anything away; ~ **Sie sich vor ihm** be on your guard against him.

Hüter(in *f*) *m* -s, - guardian, keeper, custodian; (*Vieh~*) herdsman. **die** ~ **der Ordnung** (*hum*) the custodians of the law; **soll ich meines Bruders** ~ **sein?** (*Bibl*) am I my brother's keeper?

Hut-: ~**feder** *f* (hat) feather; (*größer, bei Tracht*) plume; ~**filz** *m* (hat) felt; ~**geschäft** *nt* hat shop, hatter's (shop); (*für Damen auch*) milliner's (shop); ~**größe** *f* hat size, size of hat; ~**krempe** *f* brim (of a hat); ~**laden** *m siehe* ~**geschäft**; ~**macher** *m* hatter, hat maker; (*für Damen auch*) milliner; ~**macherin** *f* milliner; ~**nadel** *f* hat pin; ~**schachtel** *f* hatbox.

Hutsche(n) *f* -, -n (*Aus*) *siehe* **Schaukel**.

hutschen (*Aus*) 1 *vi siehe* **schaukeln**. 2 *vr* (*inf*) to go away.

Hut-: ~**schleife** *f* hat bow; ~**schnur** *f* hat string *or* cord; **das geht mir über die** ~**schnur** (*inf*) that's going too far.

Hutschpferd *nt* (*Aus*) *siehe* **Schaukelpferd**.

Hutständer *m* hatstand.

Hütte *f* -, -n (a) hut; (*schäbiges Häuschen auch*) shack; (*hum: Haus*) humble abode; (*Jagd~*) (hunting) lodge; (*Holz~, Block~*) cabin; (*Wochenendhäuschen*) cottage; (*Schutz~*) hut, bothy (*Scot*); (*Hunde~*) kennel; (*Bibl*) Tabernacle; (*Naut*) poop. **hier laßt uns eine** ~ **bauen** let's stay here; *siehe* **Glanz**.

(b) (*Tech: Hüttenwerk*) iron and steel works *pl or sing*; (*Glas~*) glassworks *pl or sing*; (*Ziegel~*) brickworks *pl or sing*.

Hütten-: ~**arbeiter** *m* worker in an iron and steel works; ~**industrie** *f* iron and steel industry; ~**käse** *m* cottage cheese; ~**kombinat** *nt* (*DDR*) iron and steel combine; ~**kunde** *f* metallurgy; ~**rauch** *m* (*Chem*) flaky arsenic; (*Metal*) waste gases *pl*; ~**technik** *f* metallurgical engineering; ~**werk** *nt siehe* **Hütte** (b); ~**wesen** *nt siehe* ~**industrie**.

Hutzel *f* -, -n (*S Ger*) (a) dried pear. (b) (*inf*) wizened *or* wrinkled old woman.

Hutzelbrot *nt* (*S Ger*) fruit bread. **ein** ~ a fruit loaf.

hutz(e)lig *adj Obst* dried; *Mensch* wizened.

Hutzel-: ~**männchen**, ~**männlein** *nt* gnome; ~**weiblein** *nt siehe* **Hutzel** (b).

hutzlig *adj siehe* **hutz(e)lig**.

HwG-Mädchen [haːˈveːˈgeː-] *nt* (*Admin sl*) girl listed by police *or* medical authorities as being promiscuous.

Hyäne *f* -, -n hyena; (*fig*) wildcat.

Hyazinthe [hyaˈtsɪntə] *f* -, -n hyacinth.

hybrid *adj* (a) (*Biol, Ling*) hybrid. (b) (*liter: hochmütig*) arrogant, hubristic (*liter*).

Hybride *f* -, -n *or* *m* -n, -n (*Biol*) hybrid.

Hybris [ˈhyːbrɪs] *f*, *no pl* (*liter*) hubris (*liter*).

Hydra *f* - (*Zool, Myth, fig liter*) hydra.

Hydrant *m* hydrant.

Hydrat *nt* hydrate.

Hydraulik *f* hydraulics *sing*; (*Antrieb, Anlage*) hydraulic system, hydraulics *pl*.

hydraulisch *adj* hydraulic.

Hydrid *nt* -(e)s, -e hydride.

hydrieren* *vt* (*Chem*) to hydrogenate.

Hydro- [hydro-]: ~**biologie** *f* hydrobiology; ~**dynamik** *f* hydrodynamics *sing*; ~**graphie** *f* hydrography; **h~graphisch** *adj* hydrographic(al); ~**lyse** *f* -, -n (*Chem*) hydrolysis; ~**statik** *f* (*Phys*) hydrostatics *sing*; ~**therapie** *f* (*Med*) hydrotherapy.

Hygiene [hyˈgiːnə] *f* -, *no pl* hygiene.

hygienisch [hyˈgiːnɪʃ] *adj* hygienic.

Hygro-: ~**meter** *nt* (*Met*) hygrometer; ~**skop** *nt* -s, -e (*Met*) hygroscope.

Hymen [ˈhyːmən] *nt* -s, - (*Anat*) hymen, maidenhead.

Hymne [ˈhʏmnə] *f* -, -n hymn; (*National~*) (national) anthem.

hymnisch *adj* hymnal. ~**e Worte** (*liter*) paean (*liter*); **jdn/etw in** ~**en Worten loben** (*liter*) to sing paeans to sb/sth (*liter*).

Hymnus *m* -, **Hymnen** (*liter*) *siehe* **Hymne**.

Hyperbel *f* -, -n (*Math*) hyperbola; (*Rhetorik*) hyperbole.

hyperbolisch *adj* hyperbolic.

hyper-: ~**korrekt** *adj* hypercorrect; ~**kritisch** *adj* hypercritical; ~**modern** *adj* (*inf*) ultramodern; ~**sensibel** *adj* hypersensitive; ~**sensibilisieren*** *vt insep* (*esp Phot*) to hypersensitize.

Hyper-: ~**tonie** *f* (*Med*) hypertonia; **h~troph** *adj* (*Med*) hypertrophic; (*fig liter*) hypertrophied (*liter*); ~**trophie** *f* (*Med*) hypertrophy.

Hypnose *f* -, -n hypnosis. **unter** ~ **stehen** to be under hypnosis; **jdn in** ~ **versetzen** to put sb under hypnosis.

Hypnosebehandlung *f* hypnotherapy.

Hypnotikum *nt* -s, **Hypnotika** (*Pharm*) hypnotic.

hypnotisch *adj* hypnotic.

Hypnotiseur [hypnotiˈzøːɐ] *m* hypnotist.

hypnotisierbar *adj* hypnotizable.

hypnotisieren* *vt* to hypnotize.

Hypnotismus *m* hypnotism.

Hypochonder [hypoˈxɔndɐ] *m* -s, - hypochondriac.

Hypochondrie [hypoxɔnˈdriː] *f* hypochondria.

hypochondrisch *adj* hypochondriac(al).

Hypokrit [hypoˈkriːt] *m* -en, -en (*liter*) hypocrite.

hypokritisch *adj* (*liter*) hypocritical.

Hypophyse *f* -, -n (*Anat*) hypophysis (*spec*), pituitary gland.

Hypostase [hypoˈstaːzə] *f* -, -n (*liter, Philos*) hypostasis.

hypostasieren* *vti* (*liter, Philos*) to hypostatize.

Hypostasierung *f* (*liter, Philos*) hypostatization.

hypotaktisch *adj* (*Gram*) hypotactic.

Hypotaxe *f* -, -n (*Gram*) hypotaxis.

Hypotenuse *f* -, -n (*Math*) hypotenuse.

Hypothek *f* -, -en mortgage; (*fig*) (*Belastung*) burden of guilt; (*Handikap*) handicap. **eine** ~ **aufnehmen** to raise a mortgage; **etw mit einer** ~ **belasten** to mortgage sth.

hypothekarisch *adj* **das Haus ist** ~ **belastet** the house is mortgaged; ~**er Gläubiger** mortgagee; ~**er Kredit** mortgage credit; ~**e Sicherheit** mortgage security.

Hypotheken-: ~**bank** *f* bank specializing in mortgages; ~**brief** *m* mortgage deed *or* certificate; ~**darlehen** *nt* mortgage (loan); **h~frei** *adj* unmortgaged; ~**gläubiger** *m* mortgagee; ~**pfandbrief** *m* mortgage bond; ~**schuld** *f* mortgage debt; ~**schuldner** *m* mortgagor, mortgager; ~**urkunde** *f* siehe ~**brief**; ~**zinsen** *pl* mortgage interest.

Hypothese *f* -, -n hypothesis.

hypothetisch *adj* hypothetical.

Hysterie *f* hysteria.

Hysteriker(in *f*) *m* -s, - hysteric, hysterical person.

hysterisch *adj* hysterical. **einen** ~**en Anfall bekommen** (*fig*) to go into *or* have hysterics.

I

I, i [i:] *nt* I, i. **der Punkt** *or* **das Tüpfelchen auf dem** ~ (*lit*) the dot on the i; (*fig*) the final touch.
i [i:] *interj* (*inf*) ugh (*inf*). ~ **bewahre!** (*dated*) not on your life! (*inf*); ~ **wo!** not a bit of it! (*inf*), (good) heavens no!; ~ **gitt** (~ **gitt)! ugh!** (*inf*).
i.A. *abbr of* **im Auftrag** *pp.*
iah ['i:'a:, i'a:] *interj* hee-haw.
iahen* ['i:'a:ən, i'a:ən] *vi* to hee-haw (*inf*), to bray.
i. allg. *abbr of* **im allgemeinen.**
Iambus ['iambus] *m* -, **Iamben** *siehe* **Jambus.**
Iberer(in *f*) *m* -s, - Iberian.
iberisch *adj* Iberian. **die I~e Halbinsel** the Iberian Peninsula.
Ibero|amerika *nt* Latin America.
ibero|amerikanisch *adj* Latin-American.
ibid(em) *adv* ibid.
ich *pers pron gen* **meiner,** *dat* **mir,** *acc* **mich** I. **immer** ~! (it's) always me!; **immer** ~ **soll an allem schuld sein** it's always my fault; ~ **Idiot!** what an idiot I am!; **und** ~ **Idiot habe es gemacht** and I, like a fool, did it, and idiot that I am, I did it; ~ **nicht!** not me!, not I!; **ihr könnt ja hingehen, aber** ~ **nicht!** you're welcome to go, but I won't; **wer hat den Schlüssel?** — ~ **nicht!** who's got the key? — not me, I haven't!; ~ **selbst** I myself; **könnte** ~ **bitte den Chef sprechen? — das bin** ~ **(selbst)** could I speak to the boss? — I am the boss *or* that's me; ~ **(selbst) war es it was me** *or* I (*form*); **wer hat gerufen?** — ~! who called? — (it was) me, I did!; **wer steht denn draußen?** — ~ (bin's) who's out there? — (it's) me, I am!; **kennst du mich nicht mehr?** — ~ **bin's!** don't you remember me? it's me!; ~, **der immer so gutmütig ist** *or* **der** ~ **immer so gutmütig bin I,** who am always so good-natured.
Ich *nt* -(s), -(s) self; (*Pysch*) ego. **das eigene** ~ one's (own) self/ego; **das eigene** ~ **verleugnen** to deny the self; **mein anderes** *or* **zweites** ~ (*selbst*) my other self; (*andere Person*) my alter ego.
Ich-: ~**bewußtsein** *nt* awareness of the self; **i~bezogen** *adj* self-centred, egocentric; ~**erzähler** *m* first-person narrator; ~**erzählung** *f* story in the first person, first-person narrative; ~**form** *f* first person; ~**-Laut** *m* (*Phon*) *ch* sound as in *ich*, palatal fricative; ~**-Roman** *m* novel in the first person, first-person novel; ~**stärke** *f* (*Pysch*) ego strength; ~**sucht** *f* egoism; **i~süchtig** *adj* egoistic(al).
ideal *adj* ideal.
Ideal *nt* -s, -e ideal. **sie ist das** ~ **einer Lehrerin** she's the ideal *or* perfect teacher; **sie ist mein** ~ **einer Frau** she's my ideal (of a) woman.
Ideal- *in cpds* ideal; ~**bild** *nt* ideal; ~**fall** *m* ideal case; **im** ~**fall** ideally; ~**figur** *f* ideal figure; ~**gewicht** *nt* ideal *or* optimum weight.
idealisieren* *vt* to idealize.
Idealisierung *f* idealization.
Idealismus *m* idealism.
Idealist *m* idealist.
idealistisch *adj* idealistic.
Ideal-: ~**konkurrenz** *f* (*Jur*) commission of two or more crimes in one and the same act; ~**typus** *m* (*Sociol*) ideal type; ~**vorstellung** *f* ideal; ~**zustand** *m* ideal state of affairs.
Idee *f* -, -n [i'de:ən] **(a)** (*Einfall, Philos*) idea. **die** ~ **zu etw** the idea for sth; **überhaupt keine** ~**n haben** to have not a single idea in one's head, to have no ideas at all; **wie kommst du denn auf die** ~? whatever gave you that idea?; **ich kam auf die** ~, **sie zu fragen** I hit on the idea of asking her; **jdn auf die** ~ **bringen, etw zu tun** to give sb the idea of doing sth; **jdn auf andere** ~**n bringen** to make sb think about something else; **du machst dir keine** ~, **wie schwer das ist!** (*inf*) you've (got) no idea how difficult it is; ~**n müßte man haben!** what it is to have ideas!; **die künstlerische** ~ **ist rechtlich nicht geschützt** artistic ideas aren't protected by law.
(b) (*ein wenig*) shade, trifle. **eine** ~ **Salz** a touch *or* hint of salt; **keine** ~ **besser** not a whit better.
deell *adj* ideational (*form, Philos*); **Wert, Gesichtspunkt, Ziele** non-material; **Bedürfnisse, Unterstützung** spiritual.
Ideen- [i'de:ən-]: **i~arm** *adj* (*einfallsarm*) lacking in ideas; (*phantasiearm*) unimaginative, lacking in imagination; ~**armut** *f* lack of ideas; unimaginativeness, lack of imagination; ~**austausch** *m* exchange of ideas; ~**drama** *nt* drama of ideas; ~**fülle** *f* wealth of *or* richness in ideas; ~**gut** *nt* ideas *pl*, intellectual goods *pl*; **i~los** *adj* (*einfallslos*) devoid of ideas; (*phantasielos*) unimaginative, devoid of imagination; ~**losigkeit** *f* lack of ideas; unimaginativeness, lack of imagination; **i~reich** *adj* (*einfallsreich*) full of ideas; (*phantasiereich*) imaginative, full of imagination; ~**reichtum** *m* inventiveness; imaginativeness; ~**welt** *f* world of ideas *or* forms.
iden *pl* **die** ~ **des März** the Ides of March.
dentifikation *f* identification.
dentifizieren* **1** *vt* to identify. **2** *vr* **sich** ~ **mit** to identify (oneself) with.
dentifizierung *f* identification.
dentisch *adj* identical (*mit* with).

Identität *f* identity.
Identitäts-: ~**krise** *f* identity crisis; ~**nachweis** *m* proof of identity.
Ideologe *m*, **Ideologin** *f* ideologist.
Ideologie *f* ideology.
ideologisch *adj* ideological.
ideologisieren* *vt* to ideologize.
Ideologisierung *f* ideologization.
Idiom *nt* -s, -e idiom.
Idiomatik *f* idiomaticity; (*Redewendungen*) idioms *pl*.
idiomatisch *adj* idiomatic.
Idioplasma *nt* (*Biol*) germ plasm, idioplasm.
Idiot *m* -en, -en idiot; (*auch inf*) fool.
Idioten-: ~**hügel** *m* (*hum inf*) nursery *or* beginners' slope; **i~sicher** *adj* (*inf*) foolproof *no adv*; **etw i~sicher erklären** to explain sth so that even a fool *or* an idiot could understand it.
Idiotie *f* idiocy; (*inf*) lunacy, madness, craziness.
Idiotikon [i'dio:tikɔn] *nt* -s, **Idiotiken** *or* **Idiotika** (*old*) dictionary of idioms.
Idiotin *f* idiot; (*auch inf*) fool.
idiotisch *adj* idiotic.
Idiotismus *m* idiotism; (*inf*) lunacy, madness, craziness.
Idol *nt* -s, -e idol.
Idolatrie *f* idolatry.
Idyll *nt* -s, -e idyll; (*Gegend*) idyllic place *or* spot.
Idylle *f* -, -n idyll.
idyllisch *adj* idyllic.
IG [i:'ge:] *f* -, -s *abbr of* **Industriegewerkschaft.**
Igel *m* -s, - **(a)** (*Zool*) hedgehog; (*Blumen~*) pin-holder. **(b)** (*Mil*: ~**stellung**) position of all-round defence.
Iglu ['i:glu] *m* *or* *nt* -s, -s igloo.
Ignorant *m* ignoramus.
Ignoranz *f* ignorance.
ignorieren* *vt* to ignore.
ihm *pers pron dat of* **er, es**[1] (*bei Personen*) to him; (*bei Tieren und Dingen*) to it; (*nach Präpositionen*) him/it. **ich gab es** ~ I gave it (to) him/it; **ich gab** ~ **den Brief** I gave him the letter, I gave the letter to him; **ich sagte** ~, **daß ...** I told him that ..., I said to him that ...; **ich werde es** ~ **sagen** I'll tell him; **es war** ~, **als ob er träumte** he felt as though he were dreaming; **es ist** ~ **nicht gut** he doesn't feel well; **sie schnitt** ~ **die Haare/cremte** ~ **den Rücken ein** she cut his hair/creamed his back (for him); **ein Freund von** ~ a friend of his, one of his friends; **wir gingen zu** ~ (*haben ihn aufgesucht*) we went to see him; (*mit zu ihm nach Hause*) we went to his place; **ich habe** ~ **das gemacht** I did it for him; **sie hat** ~**einen Pulli gestrickt** she knitted him a sweater, she knitted a sweater for him.
ihn *pers pron acc of* **er** him; (*bei Tieren und Dingen*) it.
ihnen *pers pron dat of* **sie** *pl* to them; (*nach Präpositionen*) them; *siehe* **ihm.**
Ihnen *pers pron dat of* **Sie** to you; (*nach Präpositionen*) you; *siehe* **ihm.**
ihr **1** *pers pron* **(a)** *gen* **euer,** *dat* **euch,** *acc* **euch 2. pers pl nom** you. **I~** (*in Briefen*) you; (*obs, dial: als Anrede eines Erwachsenen*) thou (*obs, dial*).
(b) *dat of* **sie** *sing* (*bei Personen*) to her; (*bei Tieren und Dingen*) to it; (*nach Präpositionen*) her/it. **I~** (*obs: in der Anrede als eines weiblichen Wesens*) (to) thee (*obs, dial*); *siehe* **ihm.**
2 *poss pron* **(a)** (*einer Person*) her; (*eines Tiers, Dings, Abstraktum*) its.
(b) (*von mehreren*) their.
Ihr **1** *pers pron siehe* **ihr 1 (a, b). 2** *poss pron sing and pl* your. ~ **Franz Müller** (*Briefschluß*) yours, Franz Müller.
ihrer *pers pron* **(a)** *gen of* **sie** *sing* (*bei Personen*) of her. **wir werden** ~ **gedenken** we will remember her. **(b)** *gen of* **sie** *pl* of them. **es waren** ~ **zehn** there were ten of them, they were ten; **wir werden** ~ **gedenken** we will remember them.
Ihrer *pers pron gen of* **Sie** of you. **wir werden** ~ **gedenken** we will remember you.
ihre(r, s) *poss pron* (*substantivisch*) **(a)** (*einer Person*) hers; (*eines Tiers*) its. **der/die/das** ~ (*geh*) hers/its; **sie tat das** ~ (*geh*) she did her part; **I~ Majestät** Her Majesty; **sie und die I~n** (*geh: Familie*) she and hers; **das I~** (*geh: Besitz*) what is hers.
(b) (*von mehreren*) theirs. **der/die/das** ~ (*geh*) theirs; **sie taten das** ~ (*geh*) they did their bit.
Ihre(r, s) *poss pron sing and pl* (*substantivisch*) yours. **der/die/das** ~ (*geh*) yours; **stets** *or* **ganz der** ~ (*old*) yours ever; **schöne Grüße an Sie und die** ~**n** (*geh*) best wishes to you and your family; **tun Sie das** ~ (*geh*) you do your bit.
ihrerseits *adv* (*bei einer Person*) for her part; (*bei mehreren*) for their part; (*von ihrer Seite*) on her/their part.
Ihrerseits *adv* for your part; (*von Ihrer Seite*) on your part.
ihresgleichen *pron inv* (*von einer Person*) people like her; (*von mehreren*) people like them; (*von Dingen*) others like it, similar ones; (*pej auch*) her/their sort, the likes of her/them. **sie fühlt/fühlen sich am wohlsten unter** ~ she feels/they feel most at home among her/their own kind *or* among people like

her(self)/them(selves); **eine Frechheit, die ~ sucht! an** unparalleled cheek!; **nachdem ~** after he had lost his love, he sought in vain for somebody like her; **diese Bilder! ~ findet man nicht mehr** these paintings! you don't find any like them these days.

Ihresgleichen *pron inv* people like you; (*pej auch*) your sort, the likes of you. **Sie sollen Kontakt mit ~ pflegen** you should keep in contact with your own kind (of people) *or* with people like yourself *or* you; **jemand wie ~** somebody like you.

ihret-: ~**halben** (*dated*), ~**wegen,** ~**willen** *adv* (*bei Personen*) (*wegen ihr/ihnen*) (*sing*) because of her; (*pl*) because of them; (*ihr/ihnen zuliebe auch*) for her sake/their sake(s); (*um sie*) about her/them; (*für sie*) on her/their behalf; (*bei Dingen und Tieren*) (*sing*) because of it; (*pl*) because of them; **sie sagte, ~wegen könnten wir gehen** she said that, as far as she was concerned, we could go.

Ihret-: ~**halben** (*dated*), ~**wegen,** ~**willen** *adv* because of you; (*Ihnen zuliebe*) (*sing auch*) for your sake; (*pl auch*) for your sake(s); (*um Sie*) about you; (*für Sie*) on your behalf.

ihrige *poss pron* (*old, geh*) **der/die/das ~** (*von einer Person*) hers; (*von mehreren*) theirs; *siehe auch* **ihre(r, s).**

Ihrige *poss pron* (*obs*) **der/die/das ~** yours; *siehe auch* **Ihre(r, s).**

Ihro *poss pron* (*obs*) your.

i. J. *abbr of* **im Jahre.**

Ikone *f* -, -n icon.

Ilex *f or m* -, *no pl* holly.

Ilias *f* - Iliad.

ill. *abbr of* **illustriert.**

illegal *adj* illegal.

Illegalität *f* illegality.

illegitim *adj* illegitimate.

illiquid *adj* insolvent.

illoyal *adj* disloyal.

Illoyalität *f* disloyalty.

Illumination *f* illumination.

Illuminator *m* illuminator.

illuminieren* *vt* to illuminate.

Illuminierung *f siehe* **Illumination.**

Illusion *f* illusion. **jdm alle ~en nehmen** *or* **rauben** to rob sb of all his/her *etc* illusions; **sich** (*dat*) **~en machen** to delude oneself; **darüber macht er sich keine ~en** he doesn't have any illusions about it; **sich der ~ hingeben, daß ...** to be under the illusion that ..., to labour under the misapprehension that ...

illusionär *adj* illusionary.

Illusionismus *m* illusionism.

Illusionist *m* illusionist.

illusionistisch *adj* (*Art*) illusionistic.

illusionslos *adj* **ein ~er Mensch** a person with no illusions; **~ sein** to have no illusions; **~ werden** to lose one's illusions.

illusorisch *adj* illusory. **es ist völlig ~, zu glauben ...** it's a complete illusion to believe ...

illuster *adj* (*geh*) illustrious.

Illustration *f* illustration. **zur ~ von etw** to illustrate sth, as an illustration of sth.

illustrativ *adj* (**a**) (*mit Anschauungsmaterial*) illustrated. **etw ~ aufzeigen** to show sth with illustrations. (**b**) (*anschaulich*) illustrative. **er hat sehr ~ geschildert, wie ...** he described very vividly how ...

Illustrator *m* illustrator.

illustrieren* *vt* to illustrate (*jdm etw* sth for sb).

Illustrierte *f* -n, -n magazine, mag (*inf*).

Illustrierung *f* illustration.

Iltis *m* -ses, -se polecat.

im *prep contr of* **in dem** (**a**) (*räumlich*) in the. **~ zweiten Stock** on the second floor; **~ Kino/Theater** at the cinema/theatre; **die Beleuchtung ~ Kino/Theater** the lighting in the cinema/theatre; **Freiburg ~ Breisgau** Freiburg in Breisgau; **~ Bett** in bed; **~ „Faust"** in "Faust".

(**b**) (*zeitlich*) in the. **~ Mai** in May; **~ Jahre 1866** in (the year) 1866; **~ Alter von 91 Jahren** at the age of 91; **~ letzten/nächsten Jahr** last/next year; **~ letzten Jahr des Krieges** in the last year of the war; **~ nächsten Jahr ging er (in)** the next year he went.

(**c**) +*superl* **nicht ~ geringsten** not in the slightest.

(**d**) (*als Verlaufsform*) **~ Kommen/Gehen etc sein** to be coming/going *etc*; **etw ~ Liegen/Stehen etc tun** to do sth lying down/standing up *etc*.

(**e**) **~ Trab/Laufschritt** *etc* at a trot/run *etc*.

Image ['imitʃ] *nt* -(s), -s image.

Imagepflege *f* (*inf*) cultivation of one's image.

imaginär *adj* imaginary.

Imagination *f* (*geh*) imagination.

Imago *f* -, **Imagines** [i'ma:gine:s] (*Biol, Psych*) imago; (*Art*) image.

imbezil, imbezill *adj* (*old Med*) imbecile.

Imbiß *m* -sses, -sse snack.

Imbiß-: ~**halle** *f* snack bar; ~**stand** *m* ≃ hot-dog stall *or* stand; ~**stube** *f* cafe; (*in Kaufhaus etc*) cafeteria.

Imitation *f* imitation.

Imitator *m*, **Imitatorin** *f* imitator; (*von Schmuck, einem Bild*) copyist.

imitieren* *vt* to imitate. **imitierter Schmuck** imitation jewellery.

Imker *m* -s, - beekeeper, apiarist (*form*).

Imkerei *f* beekeeping, apiculture (*form*).

imkern *vi* to keep bees.

immanent *adj* inherent, intrinsic; *Kriterien* internal; (*Philos*) immanent. **einer Sache** (*dat*) **~ sein** to be inherent in sth; **~e Wiederholung** incorporative repetition.

Immanenz *f* (*Philos*) immanence.

immateriell *adj* incorporeal, immaterial.

Immatrikulation *f* matriculation (*form*), registration (*at university*).

immatrikulieren* **1** *vt* to register (*at university*) (*an* + *dat* at). **2** *vr* to matriculate (*form*), to register (*at university*).

Imme *f* -, -n (*poet*) bee.

immens *adj* immense, huge, enormous.

immer *adv* (**a**) (*häufig, ständig*) always. **schon ~** always; **auf** *or* **für ~** for ever, for always; **~ diese Aufregung/Nörgelei** this continual *or* there's always this excitement/niggling; **~ diese Probleme!** all these problems!; **~ diese Studenten/das Telefon** these wretched students/that wretched phone; **~, wenn ...** whenever ..., every time that ...; **~ mal** (*inf*) from time to time, now and again; **~ geradeaus gehen** to keep going straight on; **~ und ewig** (*liter*) for ever and ever; **~ langsam voran!** (*inf*), (*nur*) **~ schön langsam!** (*inf*) take your time (about it), take it slowly; **~ (schön) mit der Ruhe** (*inf*) take it easy; (*nur*) **~ her damit!** (*inf*) (just) hand it over!; **~ feste drauf!** (*inf*) keep hammering him/them *etc* (*inf*); **noch ~,** **~ noch still;** **~ noch nicht still not (yet); bist du denn ~ noch nicht fertig?** are you still not ready?, aren't you ready yet?; **nur ~ zu!** keep it up!, keep up the good work!; **~ wieder again and again, time after time, time and (time) again; etw ~ wieder tun** to keep on doing sth; **wie ~** as usual, as always; **du hast ja ~ keine Lust** you never want to.

(**b**) +*comp* **~ besser** better and better; **~ häufiger** more and more often; **~ mehr und mehr;** **es nimmt ~ mehr zu** it increases all the time *or* continually, it keeps on increasing; **~ größer werdende Schulden** constantly increasing debts; **sein Benehmen wird ~ schlechter** his behaviour gets worse and worse *or* goes from bad to worse.

(**c**) **wer/wie/wann/wo/was (auch) ~** whoever/however/whenever/wherever/whatever.

(**d**) (*inf: jeweils*) **gib mir ~ drei Bücher auf einmal** give me three books at a time; **stellt euch in einer Reihe auf, ~ zwei zusammen** line up in twos; **~ am dritten Tag** every third day.

immer-: ~**dar** *adv* (*liter*) forever, evermore; ~**fort** *adv* all the time, the whole time, constantly; ~**grün** *adj attr* (*lit, fig*) evergreen; **I~grün** *nt* evergreen; ~**hin** *adv* all the same, anyhow, at any rate; (*wenigstens*) at least; (*schließlich*) after all; ~**während** *adj attr* perpetual, eternal; *Kalender* perpetual; ~**zu** *adv siehe* ~**fort.**

Immigrant(in *f*) *m* immigrant.

Immigration *f* immigration.

immigrieren* *vi aux sein* to immigrate.

Immission *f* (*Jur*) effect on neighbouring property of gases, smoke, noise, smells etc.

immobil *adj* immobile, immoveable; *Vermögen, Besitz* real, immoveable.

Immobilien [-'bi:liən] *pl* real estate sing, real *or* immoveable property sing (*form*), immoveables pl (*form*); (*in Zeitungsannoncen*) property sing.

Immobilienhändler *m* (real) estate agent.

Immoralismus *m* immoralism.

Immoralität *f* immorality.

Immortalität *f* immortality.

Immortelle *f* (*Bot*) everlasting (flower), immortelle.

immun *adj* immune (*gegen* to).

immunisieren* *vt* to immunize (*gegen* against).

Immunisierung *f* (*form*) immunization (*gegen* against).

Immunität *f* immunity.

Imperativ *m* (*Gram*) imperative (form); (*Philos*) imperative.

imperativisch [-'ti:vɪʃ] *adj* (*Gram*) imperative.

Imperativsatz *m* (*Gram*) imperative sentence.

Imperator *m* (*Hist*) emperor; (*Mil*) general.

imperatorisch *adj* imperial; (*fig*) imperious.

Imperfekt *nt* -s, -e, **Imperfektum** *nt* -s, **Imperfekta** (*Gram*) imperfect (tense).

Imperialismus *m* imperialism.

Imperialist *m* imperialist.

imperialistisch *adj* imperialistic.

Imperium *nt* (*Gebiet*) empire; (*Herrschaft*) imperium.

impertinent *adj* (*geh*) impertinent, impudent.

Impertinenz *f* (*geh*) impertinence, impudence.

Impetus *m* -, *no pl* (*geh*) impetus, momentum; (*Tatkraft*) drive.

Impf-: ~**aktion** *f* vaccination *or* inoculation programme; ~**arzt** *m* vaccinator, inoculator.

impfen *vt* to vaccinate, to inoculate.

Impfling *m* person who has just been *or* is to be vaccinated.

Impf-: ~**paß** *m* vaccination card, record of the vaccinations one has been given; ~**pflicht** *f* compulsory vaccination *or* inoculation, requirement to be vaccinated *or* inoculated; ~**pistole** *f* vaccination gun; ~**schaden** *m* vaccine damage; ~**schein** *n* certificate of vaccination *or* inoculation; ~**schutz** *m* protection given by vaccination; ~**stoff** *m* vaccine, serum.

Impfung *f* vaccination, inoculation.

Impfzwang *m siehe* **Impfpflicht.**

Implantat *nt* implant.

Implantation *f* (*Med*) implantation.

implizieren* *vt* to imply.

implizit, implizite (*geh*) *adv* by implication, implicitly. **etw ~ sagen** to imply sth, to say sth by implication.

implodieren* *vi aux sein* to implode.

Implosion *f* implosion.

Imponderabilien [-'bi:liən] *pl* (*geh*) imponderables pl.

imponieren* *vi* to make an impression (*jdm* on sb), to impress (*jdm* sb). **dadurch hat er imponiert** he made an impression b... that; **es imponiert mir, wie sie das schafft** it impresses me ho... she manages it, I'm impressed by the way she manages it; **es imponiert immer von neuem, wie die primitiven Völker ... on...** never fails to be impressed by the way primitive people ...

imponierend adj impressive; *Gebäude auch* imposing.
Imponiergehabe nt (*Zool*) display pattern; (*fig pej*) exhibitionism.
Import m -(e)s, -e (a) (*Handel*) import. **der ~ sollte den Export nicht übersteigen** imports should not exceed exports; **der ~ von Obst und Gemüse ist gestiegen** the import *or* importation of fruit and vegetables has increased, fruit and vegetable imports have increased.
(b) (*~ware*) import. **der Salat ist holländischer ~** the lettuce was imported from Holland *or* is a Dutch import.
Importe f -, -n *usu pl* imported cigar.
Importeur [ɪmpɔrˈtøːɐ] m importer.
Import- *in cpds* import; **~geschäft** nt (*Handel*) import trade; (*Firma*) import business.
importieren* vt to import.
Importland nt importing country.
imposant adj *Gebäude, Kunstwerk, Figur* imposing; *Leistung* impressive; *Stimme* commanding.
impotent adj impotent.
Impotenz f impotence.
imprägnieren* vt to impregnate; (*wasserdicht machen*) to (water)proof.
Imprägnierung f impregnation; (*von Geweben*) (water)-proofing; (*nach der Reinigung*) reproofing.
impraktikabel adj impracticable.
Impresario m -s, -s *or* **Impresarii** impresario.
Impression f impression (*über* +acc of).
Impressionismus m impressionism.
Impressionist m impressionist.
impressionistisch adj impressionistic.
Impressum nt -s, **Impressen** imprint.
Improvisation [ɪmprovizaˈtsioːn] f improvization; (*von Rede, Gedicht, Musik auch*) extemporization.
Improvisationstalent nt talent for improvization; (*Mensch*) (great) improvizer.
improvisieren* [-viˈziːrən] vti to improvize; (*Mus auch*) to extemporize; *eine Rede auch* to ad-lib (*inf*), to extemporize.
Impuls m -es, -e impulse. **etw aus einem ~ heraus tun** to do sth on the spur of the moment *or* on impulse; **einer Sache** (*dat*) **neue ~e geben** to give sth new impetus *or* momentum; **äußere ~e veranlaßten ihn dazu** external factors made him do it.
impulsiv adj impulsive. **~e Äußerungen/Entschlüsse** spur of the moment *or* impulsive remarks/decisions; **~ handeln** to act impulsively *or* on impulse.
Impulsivität f impulsiveness.
imstande adj *pred* **~ sein, etw zu tun** (*fähig*) to be able to do sth, to be capable of doing sth; (*in der Lage*) to be in a position to do sth; **er ist zu allem ~** he's capable of anything; **er ist ~ und erzählt es meiner Mutter** he's (quite) capable of telling my mother.
in 1 *prep siehe auch* **im, ins** (a) (*räumlich*) (*wo?* +dat) in; (*innen auch*) inside; (*bei kleineren Orten auch*) at; (*wohin?* +acc) in, into. **sind Sie schon ~ Deutschland gewesen?** have you ever been to Germany?; **~ der Schweiz** in Switzerland; **~ die Schweiz** to Switzerland; **er ist Professor ~ London** he is a professor at London (University); **~ die Schule/Kirche gehen** to go to school/church; **er ist ~ der Schule/Kirche** he's at *or* in school/church; **die Heizung ~ der Schule/Kirche** the heating in the school/church; **er ging ~s Theater/Kino** he went to the theatre/cinema; **er verschwand ~s Theater** he disappeared into the theatre.
(b) (*zeitlich*) (*wann?* +dat) in; (*bis* +acc) into. **~ diesem Jahr** (*laufendes Jahr*) this year; (*jenes Jahr*) in that year; **heute/morgen ~ acht Tagen/zwei Wochen** a week/two weeks today/tomorrow; **bis ~s 18. Jahrhundert** into *or* up to the 18th century; **vom 16. bis ~s 18. Jahrhundert** from the 16th to the 18th century; **bis ~s 18. Jahrhundert zurück** back to the 18th century.
(c) **~ Englisch steht er sehr schwach** he's very weak in *or* at English; **das ist ~ Englisch** it's in English; **~s Englische übersetzen** to translate into English; **~ Mathe haben wir einen neuen Lehrer** we've a new teacher in *or* for maths; **~ die Hunderte gehen** to run into (the) hundreds; **sie hat es ~ sich** (*dat*) (*inf*) she's quite a girl; **der Text/die Rechenarbeit hat es ~ sich** (*dat*) (*inf*) the text/the arithmetic test is a tough one; **dieser Whisky hat es ~ sich** (*dat*) (*inf*) this whisky packs quite a punch *or* has quite a kick (*inf*); **er macht jetzt ~ Gebrauchtwagen** (*inf*) he's in the second-hand car business.
2 adj pred (*sl*) **~ sein** to be in (*inf*).
inadäquat adj inadequate.
inakkurat adj inaccurate.
inaktiv adj inactive; *Mitglied* non-active; (*Mil*) inactive, on the reserve list.
inaktivieren* vt *insep Sportler* to retire; (*Chem*) to inactivate; (*Mil*) to retire, to take off the active list.
inakzeptabel adj un- *or* inacceptable.
Inangriffnahme f -, *no pl* (*form*) starting, commencement (*form*).
Inanspruchnahme f -, *no pl* (*form*) (a) (*Beanspruchung*) demands pl, claims pl (*gen* on). **die ~ durch diese Nebenbeschäftigung** the demands *or* claims made on him by this second job; **im Falle einer ~ der Arbeitslosenunterstützung** where unemployment benefit has been sought (*form*); **bei ~ des Versicherungsschutzes entfällt der Rabatt** the discount is forfeited should an insurance claim be submitted.
(b) (*Auslastung: von Einrichtungen, Verkehrsystems etc*) utilization. **wegen zu geringer ~ des Freizeitzentrums** as a result of under-utilization of the leisure centre, because too few people have been availing themselves of the leisure centre.
inartikuliert adj inarticulate.

Inaugenscheinnahme f -, *no pl* (*form*) inspection.
Inauguration f inauguration.
inbegr. *abbr of* **inbegriffen.**
Inbegriff m -(e)s, *no pl* perfect example; (*der Schönheit, Güte, des Bösen etc*) epitome, embodiment. **sie war der ~ der Schönheit/Tugend** she was beauty/virtue personified *or* incarnate; **diese neue Kirche ist der ~ der modernen Architektur** this new church epitomizes modern architecture.
inbegriffen adj *pred* included. **die Mehrwertsteuer ist im Preis ~** the price includes VAT *or* is inclusive of VAT, VAT is included in the price.
Inbesitznahme f -, -n (*form*) taking possession.
Inbetriebnahme f -, -n (*form*) putting into operation; (*von Gebäude, U-Bahn etc*) inauguration. **die ~ des Geräts erfolgt in zwei Wochen** the appliance will be put into operation in two weeks.
Inbrunst f -, *no pl* fervour, fervency, ardour.
inbrünstig adj fervent, ardent.
Indanthren ® nt -s, -e *colour-fast dye.*
Indefinitpronomen nt indefinite pronoun.
indem 1 conj (a) (*während der ganzen Zeit*) while, whilst (*liter*); (*in dem Augenblick*) as. **~ er sich hinsetzte, sagte er ...** sitting down, he said ..., as he sat down he said ... (b) (*dadurch, daß*) **~ man etw macht** by doing sth. 2 adv (*old*) meanwhile, (in the) meantime.
Inder(in f) m -s, - Indian.
indes (*rare*), **indessen** 1 adv (a) (*zeitlich*) meanwhile, (in the) meantime. (b) (*adversativ*) however. 2 conj (a) (*geh*) (*zeitlich*) while. (b) (*adversativ*) **indes** (*liter*) however; (*andererseits*) whereas.
Index m -(es), -e *or* **Indizes** [ˈɪnditseːs] index; (*Eccl*) Index.
Indianer(in f) m -s, - (Red *or* American) Indian.
indianisch adj (Red *or* American) Indian.
Indianistik f American Indian studies pl.
Indien [ˈɪndiən] nt -s India.
indifferent adj (a) (*geh*) indifferent (*gegenüber* to). (b) (*Chem, Phys*) inert; *Gas auch* rare, inactive.
Indifferenz f (*geh*) indifference (*gegenüber* to, towards).
Indignation f (*geh*) indignation (*über* +acc at).
indigniert adj (*geh*) indignant.
Indignität f (*Jur*) incapability of inheriting.
Indigo nt *or* m -s, -s indigo.
indigoblau adj indigo blue.
Indikation f (*Med*) indication. **ethische/eugenische/medizinische/soziale ~** ethical/eugenic/medical/social grounds for the termination of pregnancy.
Indikationslösung f abortion on ethical, eugenic, medical *or* social grounds.
Indikativ m (*Gram*) indicative.
indikativisch [ˈɪndikatiːvɪʃ] adj (*Gram*) indicative.
Indikator m indicator.
Indio m -s, -s (Central/South American) Indian.
indirekt adj indirect. **~e Rede** indirect *or* reported speech.
indisch adj Indian.
indiskret adj indiscreet.
Indiskretion f indiscretion.
indiskutabel adj out of the question.
indisponiert adj (*geh*) indisposed.
Indisposition f (*geh*) indisposition.
indiszipliniert adj (*rare*) *siehe* **undiszipliniert.**
individualisieren* [ɪndividualiˈziːrən] vt to individualize.
Individualisierung [ɪndividualiˈziːrʊŋ] f individualization.
Individualismus [ɪndividuaˈlɪsmʊs] m individualism.
Individualist [ɪndividuaˈlɪst] m individualist.
individualistisch [ɪndividuaˈlɪstɪʃ] adj individualistic.
Individualität [ɪndividualiˈtɛːt] f (a) *no pl* individuality. (b) (*Charakterzüge*) individual characteristic.
individuell [ɪndiviˈdu̯ɛl] adj individual. **etw ~ gestalten** to give sth a personal note; **es ist ~ verschieden** it differs from person to person *or* case to case, it's different for each person.
Individuum [ɪndiˈviːdu̯ʊm] nt -s, **Individuen** [ɪndiˈviːdu̯ən] individual.
Indiz nt -es, -ien [-iən] (a) (*Jur*) clue; (*als Beweismittel*) piece of circumstantial evidence. **alles beruht nur auf ~ien** everything rests only on circumstantial evidence. (b) (*Anzeichen*) sign, indication (*für* of).
Indizes pl of **Index.**
Indizienbeweis m circumstantial evidence *no pl*; piece of circumstantial evidence.
indizieren* vt (*Med*) to indicate; (*Eccl*) to put on the Index.
Indochina nt Indochina.
indogermanisch adj Indo-Germanic, Indo-European.
Indoktrination f indoctrination.
indoktrinieren* vt to indoctrinate.
Indonesien [-iən] nt -s Indonesia.
Indonesier(in f) [-iɐ, -iərɪn] m -s, - Indonesian.
indonesisch adj Indonesian.
Indossament nt (*Comm*) endorsement.
Indossant m (*Comm*) endorser.
Indossat m -en, -en (*Comm*) endorsee.
indossieren* vt (*Comm*) to endorse.
Induktion f induction.
Induktionsstrom m induced current.
induktiv adj inductive.
industrialisieren* vt to industrialize.
Industrialisierung f industrialization.
Industrie f industry. **in der ~ arbeiten** to be *or* work in industry.
Industrie- *in cpds* industrial; **~anlage** f industrial plant *or* works pl; **~betrieb** m industrial firm *or* company; **~erzeugnis**

nt industrial product; ~**gebiet** *nt* industrial area; ~**gewerkschaft** *f* industrial (trade) union; ~**gewerkschaft Druck und Papier** printers' union; ~**kapitän** *m (inf)* captain of industry; ~**kaufladen** *m (DDR)* factory shop; ~**kaufmann** *m* industrial manager; ~**kombinat** *nt (DDR)* industrial combine; ~**landschaft** *f* industrial landscape.

industriell *adj* industrial.

Industrielle(r) *m decl as adj* industrialist.

Industrie-: ~**staat** *m* industrial nation *or* country; ~**stadt** *f* industrial town; ~**- und Handelskammer** *f* chamber of industry and commerce; ~**zweig** *m* branch of industry.

induzieren* *vt (Phys)* to induce.

in|effektiv *adj* ineffective, ineffectual; *(unproduktiv auch)* inefficient.

in|einander *adv* sein, liegen *etc* in(side) one another *or* each other; legen, hängen *etc* into one another *or* each other. ~ **übergehen** to merge (into one another *or* each other); **die Fäden haben sich alle ~ verwickelt** the threads have got all tangled up in each other *or* in one another; **sich ~ verlieben** to fall in love with each other.

in|einander-: ~**fließen** *vi sep irreg aux sein* to merge; *(Farben, Flüsse auch)* to flow into each other *or* one another; ~**fügen** *vt sep* to fit into each other *or* one another; ~**greifen** *vi sep irreg (lit)* to interlock; *(Zahnräder, Zinken auch)* to mesh *or* engage (with each other *or* one another); *(fig: Ereignisse, Ressorts etc)* to overlap; ~**passen** *vi sep* to fit into each other *or* one another, to fit together; ~**schieben** *vtr sep irreg* to telescope; **sich ~schieben lassen** to be telescopic.

infam *adj* infamous.

Infamie *f* infamy. **das ist eine ~** that's infamous *or* outrageous.

Infant *m* infante.

Infanterie *f* infantry.

Infanterieregiment *nt* infantry *or* foot regiment.

Infanterist *m* infantryman, foot soldier.

infantil *adj* infantile.

Infantilismus *m* infantilism.

Infantilität *f* childishness, puerility *(pej)*.

Infantin *f* infanta.

Infarkt *m* -(e)s, -e *(Med)* infarct *(spec)*; *(Herz~)* coronary (thrombosis).

Infekt *m* -(e)s, -e, **Infektion** *f* infection.

Infektions-: ~**gefahr** *f* danger of infection; ~**herd** *m* focus of infection; ~**krankheit** *f* infectious disease.

infektiös [ɪnfɛkˈtsi̯øːs] *adj* infectious.

infernalisch *adj (geh)* infernal.

Inferno *nt* -s, *no pl (lit, fig)* inferno.

Infiltration *f* infiltration.

infiltrieren* *vt* to infiltrate.

infinit *adj (Gram)* non-finite.

infinitesimal *adj (Math)* infinitesimal.

Infinitiv *m* infinitive.

Infinitiv-: ~**konstruktion** *f* infinitive construction; ~**satz** *m* infinitive clause.

infizieren* 1 *vt* to infect. 2 *vr* to be *or* get infected *(bei* by).

in flagranti *adv* in the act, red-handed, in flagrante delicto *(form)*.

Inflation *f* inflation.

inflationär [ɪnflatsi̯oˈnɛːɐ] *adj* inflationary. **sich ~ entwickeln** to develop in an inflationary way.

inflationistisch [ɪnflatsi̯oˈnɪstɪʃ] *adj* inflationary.

inflexibel *adj (lit, fig)* inflexible.

Inflexibilität *f (lit, fig)* inflexibility.

Influenz *f (Phys)* electrostatic induction.

Influenza *f* -, *no pl (obs)* influenza.

infolge *prep +gen or von* as a result of, owing to, because of.

infolgedessen *adv* consequently, as a result (of that), because of that.

Informatik *f* information studies *pl*.

Information *f* information *no pl (über +acc* about, on). **eine ~** (a piece of) information; ~**en weitergeben** to pass on information; **zu Ihrer ~** for your information.

informationell [ɪnfɔrmatsi̯oˈnɛl] *adj* informational.

Informations-: ~**austausch** *m* exchange of information; ~**büro** *nt* information bureau; ~**material** *nt* informative material; ~**quelle** *f* source of information; ~**theorie** *f* information theory.

informativ *adj* informative.

informatorisch *adj* informational.

informell *adj* informal.

informieren* 1 *vt* to inform *(über +acc, von* about, of). **da bist du falsch** *or* **nicht richtig informiert** you've been misinformed, you've been wrongly informed; **jdn nur unvollständig/einseitig ~** to give sb only part/one side of the information; **informierte Kreise** informed circles.

2 *vr* to find out, to inform oneself *(über +acc* about). **sich ständig über den neuesten Stand der Medizin ~** to keep oneself informed about the latest developments in medicine.

Informiertheit *f* knowledge. **wegen der zunehmenden ~ der Jugendlichen** since young people are becoming increasingly well-informed; **die mangelnde ~ der Bevölkerung** the population's lack of information *or* lack of knowledge of the facts.

Informierung *f* informing.

Infra-: **i~rot** *adj* infra-red; ~**rotstrahler** *m* -s, - infra-red lamp; ~**schall** *m* infrasonic *or* subsonic waves *pl*; ~**struktur** *f* infrastructure.

Infusion *f* infusion.

Ing. *abbr of* **Ingenieur.**

Ingenieur(in *f)* [ɪnʒeˈni̯øːɐ, -i̯øːrɪn] *m* engineer.

Ingenieur-: ~**büro** *nt* engineer's office; ~**schule** *f* school of engineering.

Ingrimm *m* -(e)s, *no pl (liter)* wrath, ire *(liter)*.

ingrimmig *adj (liter)* wrathful *(liter)*, ireful *(liter)*.

Ingwer *m* -s, *no pl* ginger.

Inh. *abbr of* **Inhaber** prop.; **Inhalt.**

Inhaber(in *f)* *m* -s, - *(von Geschäft, Firma)* owner; *(von Hotel, Restaurant auch)* proprietor/proprietress; *(von Konto, Aktie, Lizenz, Patent, Rekord, Orden)* holder; *(von Scheck, Paß)* bearer.

inhaftieren* *vt insep* to take into custody.

Inhaftierung *f (das Inhaftieren)* arrest; *(Haft)* imprisonment.

Inhalation *f (Med)* inhalation.

inhalieren* *vti insep (Med, inf)* to inhale.

Inhalt *m* -(e)s, -e **(a)** *(von Behälter, Paket)* contents *pl*.
(b) *(von Buch, Brief, Begriff)* content, contents *pl*; *(des Lebens)* meaning. **der Film ist obszönen/~s** the content of the film is obscene; **welchen ~ hatte der Film/das Gespräch?, was hatte der Film/das Gespräch zum ~?** what was the subject matter *or* content of the film/discussion?; **der Zensor befaßt sich nur mit dem ~ des Stückes, nicht mit der Form** the censor is only concerned with the content(s) of the play, not the form; **ein Brief des ~s, daß ...** *(form)* a letter to the effect that ...
(c) *(Math) (Flächen~)* area; *(Raum~)* volume. **der ~ der Flasche beträgt zwei Liter** the bottle has a volume of two litres, the bottle holds two litres.

inhaltlich *adj* as regards content.

Inhalts-: ~**angabe** *f* summary, précis *(esp Sch)*; **i~arm, i~leer** *adj (geh)* lacking (in) content; **Leben** meaningless; **i~los** *adj* empty; **Leben auch** meaningless; **Buch, Vortrag** lacking in content; **i~reich** *adj* full; **i~schwer** *adj (geh: bedeutungsvoll)* significant, of consequence; ~**übersicht** *f* summary of the contents; ~**verzeichnis** *nt* list *or* table of contents; „~verzeichnis" "contents".

inhärent *adj (geh)* inherent.

inhuman *adj (unmenschlich, brutal)* inhuman; *(unbarmherzig)* inhumane.

Inhumanität *f* inhumanity.

Initiale [iniˈtsi̯aːlə] *f* -, -n *(geh)* initial.

Initialzündung *f* booster detonation.

Initiation [initsi̯aˈtsi̯oːn] *f* initiation.

Initiationsritus *m* initiation rite.

initiativ [initsi̯aˈtiːf] *adj* ~ **werden** to take the initiative.

Initiative [initsi̯aˈtiːvə] *f* **(a)** *no pl* initiative. **aus eigener ~** on one's own initiative; **die ~ ergreifen** to take the initiative. **(b)** *(Anstoß)* initiative. **auf jds ~** *(acc)* **hin** on sb's initiative; *(Sw Pol)* **siehe Volksbegehren.**

Initiator(in *f)* [iniˈtsi̯aːtɔr, -ˈtoːrɪn] *m (geh)* initiator.

initiieren* [initsiˈiːrən] *vt (geh)* initiate.

Injektion *f* injection.

Injektionsspritze *f* hypodermic (syringe).

injizieren* [ɪnjiˈtsiːrən] *vt (form)* to inject *(jdm etw* sb with sth).

Inka *m* -(s), -s Inca.

Inkarnation *f* incarnation.

Inkasso *nt* -s, -s *or (Aus)* **Inkassi** *(Fin)* collection.

Inkaufnahme *f* -, *no pl (form)* acceptance. **unter ~ finanzieller Verluste** accepting the inevitable financial losses.

inkl. *abbr of* **inklusive.**

inklusive [-ˈziːvə] 1 *prep +gen* inclusive of. ~ **Heizung** heating included, inclusive of *or* including heating. 2 *adv* inclusive.

Inkognito *nt* -s, -s incognito.

inkognito *adv* incognito.

inkommodieren* *(old, hum)* 1 *vt* to incommode *(hum, form)*. 2 *vr* to incommode oneself *(hum, form)*.

inkompetent *adj* incompetent.

Inkompetenz *f* incompetence.

inkongruent *adj (Math)* non-congruent.

Inkongruenz *f (Math)* non-congruence.

inkonsequent *adj* inconsistent.

Inkonsequenz *f* inconsistency.

inkonstant *adj* inconstant.

Inkonstanz *f* inconstancy.

Inkorporation *f (geh)* incorporation.

inkorporieren* *vt* to incorporate *(in +acc* in, into).

inkorrekt *adj* incorrect.

Inkorrektheit *f* **(a)** *no pl (des Benehmens)* incorrectness, impropriety; *(der Arbeit etc)* incorrectness, inaccuracy. **(b)** *(Formfehler)* impropriety, breach of propriety; *(Ungenauigkeit)* inaccuracy.

Inkrafttreten *nt* -s, *no pl* coming into effect *or* force. **das ~ von etw verhindern** to prevent sth from coming into effect *or* force; **bei ~ von etw** when sth comes/came *etc* into effect *or* force.

inkriminieren* *vt* to incriminate.

Inkubation *f* incubation.

Inkubationszeit *f* incubation period.

Inkubator *m* incubator.

Inkubus [ˈɪnkubus] *m* -, **Inkuben** incubus.

inkulant *adj* disobliging.

Inkulanz *f* disobligingness.

Inkunabel *f* -, -n incunabulum.

Inland *nt* -(e)s, *no pl* **(a)** *(als Staatsgebiet)* home. **im ~ hergestellte Waren** home-produced goods, goods produced at home; **im In- und Ausland** at home and abroad; **die Gebühren für einen Brief im ~** inland *or* domestic letter rates. **(b)** *(Inneres eines Landes)* inland. **im ~** inland; **ins ~ ziehen** to move inland.

Inland- *in cpds (Comm)* home, domestic; *(Geog)* inland; ~**bedarf** *m* home *or* domestic requirements *pl*; ~**eis** *nt* ice sheet.

Inländer(in *f)* *m* -s, - *(rare)* native.

Inlandflug *m* domestic *or* internal flight.

inländisch adj home attr, domestic; (Geog) inland.
Inlands-: ~markt m home or domestic market; ~porto nt inland postage; ~verkehr m domestic traffic; (Handel) home trade; Briefe im ~verkehr letters within the country, inland or domestic letters; er ist Fernfahrer, aber nur im ~verkehr he's a long-distance driver, but only on inland or domestic routes.
Inlaut m im ~ vorkommen to occur (word) medially or in (word) medial position.
Inlett nt -(e)s, -e (Hülle) cambric case; (~stoff) cambric.
inliegend adj (form, Aus) enclosed. ~ senden wir Ihnen ... please find enclosed ...
inmitten 1 prep +gen in the middle or midst of. 2 adv ~ von amongst, surrounded by.
innehaben vt sep irreg (form) to hold.
innehalten sep irreg 1 vi to pause, to stop. er hielt im Satz/Sprechen inne he paused in mid-sentence/he stopped speaking; mit der Rede ~ to pause, to stop speaking; mit der Rede ~, um Luft zu holen to pause for breath. 2 vt (old) siehe einhalten.
innen adv (a) inside; (auf der Innenseite) on the inside; (im Haus) indoors, inside. ~ und außen inside and out(side); der Mantel hat ~ Pelz und außen Leder the coat has fur (on the) inside and leather (on the) outside; nach ~ inwards; tief ~ tut es doch weh deep down inside it really hurts; die Tür geht nach ~ auf the door opens inwards; die Truppen drangen nach ~ vor the troops pushed inland; das Einreibemittel wirkt tief nach ~ the rub penetrates deep; ein Schnitt der Erde, von außen nach ~ betrachtet a section of the earth viewed from (the) outside to (the) inside; das Band befördert die Kohle nach ~ the conveyor-belt carries the coal inside; die Haare nach ~ tragen to have one's hair curled under; nach ~ laufen to be pigeon-toed; von ~ from (the) inside; wie sieht das Haus von ~ aus? what does the house look like from the inside?, what does the inside of the house look like?; sich von ~ her aufwärmen to warm oneself from (the) inside, to get warm inside; ihr Lächeln kommt so von ~ heraus her smile really comes from the heart; Gefühle, die von ~ herauskommen feelings which come from deep down inside.
(b) (esp Aus) siehe drinnen.
Innen-: ~antenne f indoor aerial; ~arbeiten pl work on the interior; ~architekt m interior designer; ~architektur f interior design; ~aufnahme f indoor photo(graph); (Film) indoor shot or take; ~ausstattung f interior décor no pl; (das Ausstatten) interior decoration and furnishing; (von Auto) interior fittings pl; ~bahn f (Sport) inside lane; ~beleuchtung f interior lighting; ~dekoration f interior decoration; ~dienst m office duty; im ~dienst sein to work in the office; ~dienst machen or haben to work in the office, to be on office duty; i~drin adv (inf) inside; ~einrichtung f (interior) furnishings pl; (das Einrichten) interior furnishing no pl; ~fläche f (a) (innere Fläche) inside, inside or interior surface; (der Hand) palm; (b) (Flächeninhalt) internal surface area; ~hof m inner courtyard; (bei Universitäten, Klöstern) quadrangle, quad (inf); ~kurve f inside bend; ~leben nt, no pl (a) (inf: seelisch) inner or emotional life; sein ~leben offenbaren to reveal one's innermost thoughts or feelings; (b) (inf: körperlich) insides pl; ~minister m minister of the interior; (in GB) Home Secretary; (in den USA) Secretary of the Interior; ~ministerium nt ministry of the interior; (in GB) Home Office; (in den USA) Department of the Interior; ~politik f domestic policy/policies pl; (innere Angelegenheiten, Studienfach) home or domestic affairs pl; ~politiker m domestic politician; i~politisch adj domestic, internal, home attr; auf i~politischem Gebiet in the field of home affairs; i~politisch gesehen, aus i~politischer Sicht (seen) from the point of view of domestic policy; i~politisch hat die Regierung versagt the government has failed with its domestic policy/policies; ~raum m (a) ~räume inner rooms pl; die prächtigen ~räume des alten Schlosses the magnificent interior or rooms of the old castle; (b) no pl room inside; (von Wagen auch) interior; einen kleinen ~raum haben to be small inside, not to have much room inside; (von Wagen auch) to have a small interior; mit großem ~raum with a lot of room inside; (von Wagen auch) with a large interior; ~rolle f, no pl eine ~rolle tragen to have one's hair turned or curled under at the ends; sich (dat) eine ~rolle machen to turn or curl one's hair under at the ends; ~seite f inside; die ~seite von etw nach außen kehren to turn sth inside out; ~stadt f town centre, centre of the town; (einer Großstadt) city centre, centre of the city; ~tasche f inside pocket; ~temperatur f inside temperature; (in einem Gebäude) indoor temperature; wir haben 20° ~temperatur the temperature indoors is 20°; bei 20° ~temperatur when the temperature indoors or the indoor temperature is 20°, when it's 20° indoors; ~toilette f inside toilet; ~welt f inner world; er hat sich völlig in seine ~welt zurückgezogen he has withdrawn completely into his own private world; ~winkel m (Math) interior angle.
inner-: ~betrieblich adj internal company; das wird ~betrieblich geregelt werden that will be settled within the company or on an internal company basis; ~deutsch adj German domestic attr; ~deutscher Handel trade within Germany, domestic trade in Germany; diese Angelegenheiten sind rein ~deutsch these are purely (German) domestic matters.
Innereien pl innards pl; (von Geflügel auch) giblets pl.
innere(r, s) adj (a) (örtlich) inner; (im Körper befindlich, inländisch) internal. Facharzt für ~ Krankheiten internist; das ~ Ohr the inner ear; die ~n Angelegenheiten eines Landes the internal or home or domestic affairs of a country; der Whisky sorgte für die ~ Wärme (inf) the whisky warmed our/their etc insides (inf); I~Mission Home Mission; ~r Monolog (Liter) interior monologue; im innersten Herzen

deep in one's heart, in one's heart of hearts; eine ~ Uhr (inf) an internal or a biological clock; ~ Emigration inner emigration, withdrawal into private life of artists and intellectuals who remained in Germany through the Nazi period but did not support the Third Reich; any similar withdrawal; ~ Kämpfe in der Partei internal struggles within the party.
(b) (geistig, seelisch) inner. ~ Werte pl inner worth no pl; eine ~ Stimme an inner voice, a voice within; vor meinem ~n Auge in my mind's eye; ~ Führung (Mil) moral leadership.
Innere(s) nt decl as adj (a) inside; (von Kirche, Wagen, Schloß auch) interior; (Mitte) middle, centre. Minister des Inner(e)n minister of the interior; (in GB) Home Secretary; (in den USA) Secretary of the Interior; das ~ nach außen kehren to turn something inside out; ins ~ des Landes into the heart of the country; die Organe im ~n des Körpers the organs in(side) the body.
(b) (fig: Gemüt, Geist) heart. ich wußte, was in seinem ~n vorging I knew what was going on inside him; sein ~s rebellierte dagegen his inner self rebelled against it; im tiefsten ~n (deep) in one's heart, in one's heart of hearts.
innerhalb 1 prep +gen (a) (örtlich) inside, within. ~ dieser Regelung within this ruling. (b) (zeitlich) within. ~ von zehn Minuten within ten minutes, in ten minutes, inside (of) ten minutes. 2 adv inside; (eines Landes) inland. weiter ~ further in; weiter ~ im Lande further inland.
innerlich adj (a) (körperlich) internal. dieses Medikament ist ~ anzuwenden this medicament is to be taken internally.
(b) (geistig, seelisch) inward, inner no adv; Gedicht, Mensch inward; Hemmung inner. ein ~ gefestigter Mensch a person of inner strength; ~ schäumte er vor Wut inwardly or inside he was boiling with rage; ~ lachen to laugh inwardly or to oneself.
Innerlichkeit f (liter) inwardness.
inner-: ~parteilich adj within the party; ~parteiliche Schwierigkeiten internal difficulties in the party, difficulties within the party; eine ~parteiliche Diskussion a party discussion; ~parteiliche Demokratie democracy (with)in the party structure; ~politisch adj siehe innenpolitisch; ~staatlich adj domestic, internal.
innerste(r, s) adj superl of innere(r, s) innermost, inmost; (fig auch) deepest.
Innerste(s) nt decl as adj (lit) innermost part, heart; (fig) heart. tief im ~n liebte sie ihn in her heart of hearts or deep in her heart she loved him; bis ins ~ getroffen hurt to the quick, deeply or profoundly hurt.
innert prep +gen or dat (Aus, Sw) within, in, inside (of).
innesein vi sep irreg aux sein (Zusammenschreibung nur bei infin und ptp) (+gen) (geh) to be aware or cognizant (form) of.
innewerden vi sep irreg aux sein (sich dat) einer Sache (gen) ~ to become aware or cognizant (form) of sth.
innewohnen vi sep +dat to be inherent in.
innig adj Glückwünsche, Grüße heartfelt no adv, hearty; Beileid heartfelt, deep, profound; Vergnügen deep, profound; Freundschaft, Beziehung intimate (auch Chem). etw aufs ~ste erhoffen/wünschen to hope/wish for sth most fervently or ardently; mein ~ster Wunsch my dearest wish; jdn ~ lieben to love sb dearly or deeply or with all one's heart.
Innigkeit f (von Glückwünschen, Grüßen) warmth, sincerity; (von Empfindung) depth; (von Liebe) intensity; (von Freundschaft, Beziehung) intimacy. mit ~ beten/hoffen to pray/hope fervently or ardently.
inniglich adv (poet) (herzlich) sincerely, warmly; (tief) deeply, profoundly; lieben deeply, dearly; (eng) intimately, closely.
Innung f (trade) guild. du blamierst die ganze ~ (hum inf) you're letting the (whole) side down (inf).
inoffiziell adj unofficial. jdm etw ~ mitteilen to tell sb sth unofficially or off the record.
in|operabel adj (Med) inoperable.
in|opportun adj inopportune.
In|opportunität f inopportuneness, inopportunity.
in petto siehe petto.
in puncto siehe puncto.
Input ['mpʊt] m or nt -s, -s input.
Inquisition f Inquisition.
Inquisitions-: ~gericht nt Court of the Inquisition, inquisitional court; ~methode f inquisitional method.
Inquisitor m inquisitor.
inquisitorisch adj inquisitorial.
ins contr of in das. ~ Rollen/Rutschen geraten or kommen to start rolling/sliding.
Insasse m -n, -n, **Insassin** f (eines Fahrzeuges) passenger; (eines Autos auch) occupant; (einer Anstalt) inmate.
Insassenversicherung f passenger insurance.
insbesondere adv particularly, (e)specially, in particular.
Inschrift f inscription, legend (form).
Insekt nt -(e)s, -en insect.
Insekten-: ~bekämpfung f insect control, i~fressend adj attr insect-eating, insectivorous (form); ~fresser m insect-eater, insectivore (form); ~gift nt insecticide; ~kunde f entomology; ~plage f plague of insects; ~pulver nt insect powder, (powder) insecticide; ~schutzmittel nt insect-repellent; ~stich m (von Ameisen, Mücken, Flöhen) insect bite; (von Bienen, Wespen) (insect) sting; ~vertilgungsmittel nt insecticide.
Insektizid nt -s, -e (form) insecticide.
Insel f -, -n (lit, fig) island, isle (poet). die Britischen ~n the British Isles; die ~ Man the Isle of Man.
Inselbewohner m islander, inhabitant of an/the island.
Inselchen nt little island, islet (poet).
Insel-: ~gruppe f archipelago, group of islands; ~lage f island position; Großbritannien, infolge seiner ~lage ... Great Bri-

tain, because it is an island ...; i~**reich** adj with a lot of islands; ~**reich** nt island kingdom; ~**staat** m island state; ~**volk** nt island nation or race or people; ~**welt** f island world; **die ~welt** Mittelamerikas the world of the Central American islands.

Inserat nt advert (Brit inf), ad (inf), advertisement.

Inseratenteil m advertisement section, adverts pl (Brit inf), ads pl (inf).

Inserent m advertiser.

inserieren* vti to advertise. **etw in der Zeitung ~** to advertise sth in the paper, to insert or put an advertisement in the paper for sth.

insgeheim adv secretly, in secret.

insgemein adv (old) in general, on the whole, by and large.

insgesamt adv (alles zusammen) altogether; (im großen und ganzen) all in all, on the whole, by and large. **die Kosten belaufen sich auf ~ 1.000 DM** the costs amount to a total of DM 1,000; **ein Verdienst von ~ 2.000 DM** earnings totalling DM 2,000.

Insider ['ɪnsaɪdə] m -s, - insider. **der Witz war nur für ~ verständlich** that was an in-joke, that joke was just for the in-crowd; **~ der Jazz-Szene** those in on the jazz scene, those in the know about the jazz scene; **du arbeitest dort, du bist doch ~** you work there, you're the insider or you're on the inside.

Insignien [ɪn'zɪgniən] pl insignia pl.

insignifikant ['ɪnzɪgnifikant] adj (geh) insignificant, of no consequence.

insistieren* [ɪnzɪs'tiːrən] vi (geh) to insist (auf +dat on).

Inskription f inscription.

insofern 1 adv in this respect. **~ ... als** in so far as, inasmuch as, in that; **er hat ~ recht, als ...** he's right in so far as or inasmuch as or in that ... **2** [ɪnzo'fɛrn] conj (wenn) if.

insolvent ['ɪnzɔlvɛnt] adj (Comm) insolvent.

Insolvenz ['ɪnzɔlvɛnts] f (Comm) insolvency.

insoweit [ɪn'zoːvaɪt] adv, [ɪnzo'vaɪt] conj siehe **insofern**.

Insp. abbr of **Inspektor**.

in spe [ɪn'speː] adj (inf) to be, future. **unser Schwiegersohn ~ ~** our son-in-law to be, our future son-in-law.

Inspekteur [ɪnspɛk'tøːɐ] m (Mil) Chief of Staff.

Inspektion f (a) inspection; (Aut) service. **ich habe mein Auto zur ~ gebracht** I've taken my car in for a service or to be serviced. (b) (Behörde) inspectorate.

Inspektionsreise f tour of inspection.

Inspektor(in f) [ɪn'spɛktɔr, -'toːrɪn] m (Verwalter, Aufseher) superintendent.

Inspiration [ɪnspira'tsioːn] f inspiration.

inspirieren* [ɪnspi'riːrən] vt to inspire. **sich von etw ~ lassen** to get one's inspiration from sth.

Inspizient [ɪnspi'tsiɛnt] m (Theat) stage-manager; (Aufseher) inspector.

inspizieren* [ɪnspi'tsiːrən] vt to inspect.

Inspizierung f inspection.

instabil ['ɪnstabiːl] adj unstable.

Instabilität f instability.

Installateur [ɪnstala'tøːɐ] m plumber; (Elektro~) electrician, electrical fitter; (Gas~) gas-fitter.

Installation [ɪnstala'tsioːn] f (a) (no pl: das Installieren) installation; (Tech auch) fitting. (b) (Anlage) installation; (in Bauten) fittings pl, installations pl; (Wasser~) plumbing no pl. (c) (old, Sw: Amtseinsetzung) installation.

Installationsrohr nt services shaft.

installieren* [ɪnsta'liːrən] **1** vt to install (auch fig), to put in. **2** vr to install oneself.

instand adj in good condition or repair; (funktionsfähig) in working order, working. **etw ~ halten** to maintain sth, to keep sth in good condition or repair/in working order; **etw ~ setzen** to get sth into good condition or repair/into working order; (reparieren auch) to repair sth.

Instand-: ~**haltung** f (von Gerät) maintenance, servicing; (von Gebäude) maintenance, upkeep; ~**haltungskosten** pl maintenance costs pl; (von Gebäude auch) upkeep costs pl.

inständig adj urgent. **~ bitten** to beg, to implore, to beseech; **~ hoffen** to hope fervently.

Instand-: ~**setzung** f (von Gerät) overhaul; (von Gebäude) restoration; (Reparatur auch) repair; ~**setzungsarbeiten** pl repairs pl, repair work.

Instanz [ɪn'stants] f (a) (Behörde) authority. **er ging von einer ~ zur nächsten** he went from one office or department to the next.
(b) (Jur) court; (Verhandlungsstadium) (court-)case; (strafrechtlich auch) trial. **Verhandlung in erster/zweiter ~** first/second court-case, hearing at the court of second instance (form); **Berufung in erster/zweiter ~** first/second appeal; **ein Urteil letzter ~** (lit, fig) a final judgement; **er ging von einer ~ zu anderen** he went through all the courts; **vor der ~ des Über-Ichs** before the court (liter) or authority of the super-ego.

Instanzen-: ~**weg**, ~**zug** (Aus) m official or prescribed channels pl, channels pl (US); (Jur) stages pl of appeal; **auf dem** ~**weg** through (the official or prescribed) channels/the various stages of appeal.

Instinkt [ɪn'stɪŋkt] m -(e)s, -e (lit, fig) instinct. **aus ~** instinctively, by instinct.

instinkthaft adj instinctive.

Instinkthandlung f instinctive act. **das ist eine reine ~** it's purely instinctive (behaviour).

instinktiv [ɪnstɪŋk'tiːf] adj instinctive.

instinktmäßig 1 adj instinctive. **2** adv instinctively, by instinct; (Instinkte betreffend) as far as instinct is concerned.

Institut [ɪnsti'tuːt] nt -(e)s, -e institute; (Jur: Institution) institution.

Institution [ɪnstitu'tsioːn] f institution.

institutionalisieren* [ɪnstitutsio-] vt to institutionalize.

institutionell [ɪnstitutsioˈnɛl] adj institutional.

Institutsleiter m director of an/the institute.

instruieren* [ɪnstru'iːrən] vt to instruct; (über Unternehmen, Plan etc) to brief; **Anwalt** to brief.

Instrukteur [ɪnstrʊk'tøːɐ] m instructor.

Instruktion [ɪnstrʊk'tsioːn] f instruction. **laut ~** according to instructions.

instruktiv [ɪnstrʊk'tiːf] adj instructive.

Instrument [ɪnstru'mɛnt] nt instrument; (Hammer etc auch) tool, implement. **er ist ~ des ...** he is the instrument of ...

instrumental [ɪnstrumɛn'taːl] adj (Mus) instrumental.

Instrumental- in cpds instrumental; ~**begleitung** f instrumental accompaniment; **ohne ~begleitung singen** to sing unaccompanied; ~**flug** m (Aviat) siehe **Instrumentenflug**; ~**satz** m (Gram) instrumental clause; (Mus) (Bearbeitung) instrumental version; (Teilstück) instrumental section.

Instrumentarium [ɪnstrumɛn'taːriʊm] nt (lit) equipment, instruments pl; (Mus) instruments pl; (fig) apparatus.

instrumentell [ɪnstrumɛn'tɛl] adj with instruments.

Instrumenten-: ~**brett** nt instrument panel; ~**flug** m instrument flight; (das Fliegen auch) instrument flying, flying on instruments.

instrumentieren* [ɪnstrumɛn'tiːrən] vt (Mus) to arrange for instruments; (für Orchester) to orchestrate; (Tech) to fit out or equip with instruments.

Instrumentierung f instrumentation.

insuffizient ['ɪnzʊfitsiɛnt] adj (Med, geh) insufficient.

Insuffizienz ['ɪnzʊfitsiɛnts] f (Med, geh) insufficiency.

Insulaner(in f) m -s, - islander.

insular adj insular.

Insulin nt -s, no pl insulin.

Insulin- in cpds insulin; ~**schock** m insulin or hypoglycaemic (spec) shock; ~**stoß** m insulin boost.

Inszenator m (Theat) director; (fig) stage-manager.

inszenatorisch adj directing attr. **eine ~e Glanzleistung** a brilliant piece of directing or (fig) stage-management; **schwer zu lösen** hard to solve from a directing point of view.

inszenieren* vt (a) (Theat) to direct; (Rad, TV) to produce. (b) (fig) to stage-manage. **einen Streit ~** to start an argument; **ein Theater ~** to kick up a fuss (inf).

Inszenierung f production. **ein Stück in neuer ~ aufführen** to put on a new production of a play.

intakt adj intact. **ich bin nach meiner Grippe noch nicht ganz ~** (inf) I'm still feeling a bit fragile after my flu.

Intarsia f -, **Intarsien** [-iən], **Intarsie** [ɪn'tarziə] f usu pl marquetry no pl, inlay, inlaid work no pl.

integer adj (geh) **~ sein** to be full of integrity; **ein integrer Mensch** a person of integrity; **sich ~ verhalten** to behave with integrity.

integral adj attr integral.

Integral nt -s, -e integral.

Integralrechnung f integral calculus.

Integration f integration.

integrierbar adj capable of being integrated, assimilable; (Math) integrable.

integrieren* vt to integrate (auch Math). **integrierte Gesamtschule** comprehensive (school) (Brit).

Integrierung f integration no pl.

Integrität f integrity.

Intellekt m -(e)s, no pl intellect.

Intellektualismus m intellectualism.

intellektuell adj intellectual.

Intellektuelle(r) mf decl as adj intellectual.

Intellelle(r) mf decl as adj (hum inf) intellectual, egghead (inf).

intelligent adj intelligent (auch Psych), bright.

Intelligenz f intelligence; (Personengruppe) intelligentsia pl. **Elefanten haben eine hochentwickelte ~** elephants are highly intelligent or have a great deal of intelligence.

Intelligenzbestie f (pej inf) egghead (inf).

Intelligenzija [-'tsija] f -, no pl intelligentsia pl.

Intelligenzleistung f display of intelligence. **eine ~ von jdm** a display of sb's intelligence; **das war wieder eine ~ von dir!** (iro) that was intelligent or bright of you (iro).

Intelligenzler m -s, - (inf) egghead (inf).

Intelligenz-: ~**prüfung** f intelligence test; ~**quotient** m intelligence quotient, IQ; ~**test** m intelligence test; **einen ~test mit jdm machen** to give sb an intelligence test, to test sb's IQ.

intelligibel adj (Philos) knowable (only) to the mind, intelligible.

Intendant m director; theatre-manager.

Intendantur f (Amtszeit) period of directorship; (Amtssitz) director's office; theatre-manager's office. **während seiner ~** while he was director/theatre-manager, during his directorship or the period of his directorship.

Intendanz f (Amt) directorship; (Büro) director's/theatre-manager's office.

intendieren* vt (geh) to intend. **eine Beleidigung hatte ich damit nicht intendiert** I didn't intend that as an insult.

Intensität f intensity.

intensiv adj Arbeit, Forschung, Landwirtschaft intensive; Farbe, Gefühl intense; Geruch powerful, strong; Blick intent, intense. **jdn ~ beobachten** to watch sb intently.

intensivieren* [-'viːrən] vt to intensify.

Intensivierung f intensification.

Intensiv-: ~**pflege** f intensive care; ~**station** f intensive care unit.

Intention f (geh) intention, intent.

intentional [ɪntɛntsioˈnaːl] adj (Philos) intentional.

Inter- *in cpds* inter-; **~aktion** *f* interaction; **~city-Verkehr** *m* (*Rail*) inter-city traffic (*Brit*), express traffic; **~city-Zug** *m* inter-city train (*Brit*); **i~dependent** *adj* interdependent; **~dependenz** *f* interdependence.

Interdikt *nt* **-(e)s, -e** (*Eccl*) interdict.

interdisziplinär *adj* interdisciplinary.

interessant *adj* interesting. **zu diesem Preis ist das nicht ~ für uns** (*Comm*) we are not interested at that price; **das ist ja ~!** (that's) very interesting!; **sich ~ machen** to attract attention (to oneself); **sich bei jdm ~ machen** to attract sb's attention.

interessanterweise *adv* interestingly enough.

Interesse *nt* **-s, -n** interest. **~ an jdm/etw** *or* **für jdn/etw haben** to be interested in sb/sth; **aus ~** out of interest, for interest; **es liegt in Ihrem eigenen ~** it's in your own interest(s); **die ~n eines Staates wahrnehmen** to look after the interests of a state; **sein ~ gilt ...** his interest is *or* lies in ...; **he's interested in ...; das ist für uns nicht von ~** that's of no interest to us, we're not interested in that; **er tat es** *or* **handelte in meinem ~** he did it for my good *or* in my interest.

Interesse-: i~halber *adv* for *or* out of interest; **i~los** *adj* indifferent; **~losigkeit** *f* indifference.

Interessen-: ~bereich *m*, **~gebiet** *nt* field of interest; **das gehört nicht zu meinem ~bereich** that isn't one of my interests, that's outside my field of interests; **~gegensatz** *m* clash of interests; **~gemeinschaft** *f* (**a**) community of interests; (*Menschen*) group of people sharing interests; (**b**) (*Econ*) syndicate; **~gruppe** *f* interest group; **~sphäre** *f* (*Pol*) sphere of influence.

Interessent(in *f***)** *m* interested person *or* party (*form*); (*Bewerber auch*) applicant; (*Comm: Kauflustiger auch*) prospective customer. **~en werden gebeten ...** those interested are requested ...; **es haben sich mehrere ~en gemeldet** several people have shown interest.

Interessentenkreis *m* market.

Interessen-: ~verband *m* syndicate; **~vertretung** *f* representation of interests; (*Personen*) group representing one's interests; **eine ~vertretung wählen** to elect a group of people to represent one's interests.

interessieren* **1** *vt* to interest (*für, an* + *dat* in). **es würde mich doch sehr ~, was du damit machen willst** it would interest me very much to know *or* I'd be very interested to know what you want to do with it; **das interessiert mich (gar) nicht!** I'm not (the least *or* slightest bit) interested; **ich liege hier im Sterben, aber das interessiert dich gar nicht** here I am on my death-bed, but you don't care; **das hat dich nicht zu ~!** that's none of your business!, don't be so nosey! (*inf*).

2 *vr* to be interested (*für* in); (*mit Interesse verfolgen auch*) to take an interest (*für* in). **er begann schon mit acht Jahren, sich für Musik zu ~** he started to be interested *or* to take *or* show an interest in music when he was eight.

interessiert *adj* interested (*an* + *dat* in). **~ zuhören** *etc* to listen *etc* with interest; **vielseitig ~ sein** to have a wide range of interests; **politisch ~** interested in politics; **ein ~er Mensch** a person with a number of interests; **ein für alles ~er Mensch** a person interested in *or* with an interest in everything.

Interferenz *f* (*Phys, Ling*) interference *no pl*.

Interhotel *nt* (*DDR*) international hotel.

Interieur [ɛ̃te'riøːɐ] *nt* **-s, -s** *or* **-e** interior.

Interim *nt* **-s, -s** interim.

Interims- *in cpds* interim; **~regierung** *f* caretaker *or* provisional government; **~schein** *m* (*Fin*) scrip.

Interjektion *f* interjection.

Inter-: i~konfessionell *adj* interdenominational; **i~kontinental** *adj* intercontinental; **~kontinentalrakete** *f* intercontinental missile; **i~linear** *adj* interlinear.

Interludium *nt* (*rare*) interlude.

Intermezzo [-'mɛtso] *nt* **-s, -s** *or* **Intermezzi** (*Mus*) intermezzo; (*fig auch*) interlude; (*ärgerlich*) contretemps *sing*.

intermittierend *adj* intermittent.

intern *adj* internal. **~er Schüler** boarder; **diese Maßnahmen müssen vorläufig ~ bleiben** for the time being these measures must be kept private; **die ~en Schwierigkeiten des Landes** the country's internal *or* domestic difficulties.

-intern *adj suf* **schul-/ausschuß~e Angelegenheiten** internal school/committee matters; **etw schul~ regeln** to settle sth internally within the school(s).

internalisieren* *vt* (*spec*) to internalize.

Internat *nt* boarding school.

international [ɪntɐnatsio'naːl] *adj* international.

Internationale [ɪntɐnatsio'naːlə] *f* **-, -n** Internationale.

internationalisieren* [ɪntɐnatsio-] *vt* to make international.

Internationalismus *m* internationalism.

Internatsschüler *m* boarder, boarding (school) pupil.

internieren* *vt* to intern.

Internierte(r) *mf decl as adj* internee.

Internierung *f* internment.

Internierungslager *nt* internment camp.

Internist *m* internist.

interparlamentarisch *adj* interparliamentary.

Interpellant *m* questioner.

Interpellation *f* (parliamentary) question.

interpellieren* *vi* to ask a (parliamentary) question.

interplanetar(isch) *adj* interplanetary *no adv*.

Interpol *f* - Interpol.

Interpolation *f* interpolation.

interpolieren* *vt* to interpolate.

Interpret *m* **-en, -en** interpreter (*of music, art etc*).

Interpretation *f* interpretation; (*eines Liedes auch*) version.

interpretieren* *vt* to interpret. **etw falsch ~** to misinterpret sth.

Interpretin *f siehe* **Interpret.**

interpunktieren* *vt* to punctuate.

Interpunktion *f* punctuation.

Interpunktions-: ~regel *f* rule of punctuation, punctuation rule; **~zeichen** *nt* punctuation mark.

Interregnum *nt* **-s, Interregnen** *or* **Interregna** interregnum.

interrogativ *adj* interrogative.

Interrogativ-: ~pronomen *nt* interrogative pronoun; **~satz** *m* interrogative clause.

Interruptus *m* **-, *no pl*** (*inf*) coitus interruptus.

Intershop ['ɪntɐʃɔp] *m* **-s, -s** (*DDR*) international shop.

interstellar [-stɛ'laːɐ] *adj* interstellar.

Intervall [-'val] *nt* **-s, -e** interval (*auch Mus*). **sich in längeren ~en sehen** to see each other at infrequent intervals.

Intervalltraining *nt* interval training.

intervenieren* [-ve'niːrən] *vi* to intervene.

Intervention [-vɛn'tsioːn] *f* intervention.

Interview ['ɪntɐvjuː] *nt* **-s, -s** interview.

interviewen* [-'vjuːən] *vt* to interview (*jdn zu etw* sb on *or* about sth).

Interviewer(in *f***)** [-'vjuːɐ, -'vjuːərɪn] *m* **-s, -** interviewer.

Intervision [-vi'zioːn] *f* Intervision.

Interzonen- *in cpds* interzonal.

Inthronisation *f* enthronement.

inthronisieren* *vt* to enthrone.

intim *adj* intimate. **ein ~er Kenner von etw sein** to have an intimate knowledge of sth; **etw im ~en Kreis feiern** to celebrate sth with one's closest *or* most intimate friends; **meine ~en Angelegenheiten** my intimate personal affairs.

Intim-: ~bereich *m* (**a**) (*Anat*) genital area; (**b**) (*fig*) *siehe* **~sphäre**; **~feind** *m* favourite enemy; **~hygiene** *f* intimate hygiene.

Intimität *f* (**a**) *no pl* (*Gemütlichkeit, Vertraulichkeit*) intimacy. (**b**) (*private Angelegenheit*) intimacy. **jdm allerlei ~en erzählen** to tell sb all kinds of intimate details *or* intimacies; **bitte keine ~en!** please don't go into intimate details. (**c**) (*sexuell*) intimacy. **zwischen den beiden kam es zu ~en** they became intimate with each other; **~en austauschen** to kiss and pet; **bitte keine ~en in meinem Haus!** I'll have none of that sort of thing going on in my house!; **er hat sich einige ~en erlaubt** he became rather familiar.

Intim-: ~lotion *f* vaginal lotion; **~sphäre** *f* private life; **jds ~sphäre verletzen** to invade sb's privacy; **diese Frage greift in die ~sphäre ein** that question is an invasion of my/your *etc* privacy; **~spray** *nt* intimate deodorant spray.

Intimus *m* **-, Intimi** (*hum*) confidant.

Intimverkehr *m* intimacy. **~ mit jdm haben** to be intimate with sb.

intolerant *adj* intolerant (*einer Sache gegenüber* of sth, *jdm gegenüber* of *or* towards sb).

Intoleranz *f* intolerance.

Intonation *f* intonation.

intonieren* *vt* (**a**) **einen Satz falsch/anders ~** to give a sentence the wrong/a different intonation; **wie intoniert man diesen Fragesatz?** what's the intonation of this question?; **versuchen Sie, diesen Satz zu ~** try and say this sentence with the proper *or* correct intonation. (**b**) (*Mus*) *Melodie* to sing; (*Kapelle*) to play; *Ton* to give. **wer kann das Lied ~?** who can start the song off?, who can show us how the song goes?

intransigent *adj* (*liter*) intransigent.

Intransigenz *f* intransigence.

intransitiv *adj* intransitive.

intravenös [-ve'nøːs] *adj* intravenous.

intrigant *adj* (*geh*) scheming, designing.

Intrigant(in *f***)** *m* schemer, intriguer.

Intrige *f* **-, -n** intrigue, conspiracy, scheme.

Intrigen-: ~spiel *nt* intriguing, plotting; **~wirtschaft** *f* hive of intrigue.

intrigieren* *vi* to intrigue, to scheme *or* to plot.

Introduktion *f* introduction.

Introitus [ɪn'troːitus] *m* **-, -** (*Gesang*) introit; (*Anat*) introitus.

introvertiert [-vɛr'tiːɐt] *adj* introverted.

Introvertiertheit *f* introversion.

Intuition [ɪntui'tsioːn] *f* intuition.

intuitiv [ɪntui'tiːf] *adj* intuitive.

intus *adj* (*inf*) **etw ~ haben** (*wissen*) to have got sth into one's head (*inf*); *Essen, Alkohol* to have sth down (*inf*) *or* inside one (*inf*); **er hat schon etwas ~ einiges ~** he's had a few.

invalid(e) [ɪnva'liːt, -'liːdə] *adj* (*rare*) disabled, invalid *attr*.

Invalide [ɪnva'liːdə] *m* **-n, -n** disabled person, invalid. **er ist ~** he's disabled *or* an invalid; **der Krieg hat ihn zum ~n gemacht** he was disabled in the war; **ich mache dich zum ~n!** (*inf*) I'll cripple you! (*inf*).

Invaliden-: ~heim *nt* home for disabled persons *or* people, home for the disabled; **~rente** *f* disability pension; **~versicherung** *f* disability insurance.

invalidisieren* [ɪnvalidi'ziːrən] *vt* to retire due to ill health.

Invalidität [ɪnvalidi'tɛːt] *f* disability.

invariabel [ɪnva'riaːbl] *adj* invariable.

invariant [ɪnva'riant] *adj* invariant.

Invariante [-va-] *f* **-, -n** (*Math*) invariant, invariable.

Invasion [ɪnva'zioːn] *f* (*lit, fig*) invasion.

Invasor [ɪn'vaːzɔr] *m usu pl* invader.

Invektive [ɪnvɛk'tiːvə] *f* (*geh*) invective *no pl*.

Inventar [ɪnvɛn'taːɐ] *nt* **-s, -e** (**a**) (*Verzeichnis*) inventory; (*Comm*) assets and liabilities *pl*. **das ~ aufnehmen** to do the inventory; **etw ins ~ aufnehmen** to put sth on the inventory. (**b**) (*Einrichtung*) fittings *pl*; (*Maschinen*) equipment *no pl*,

plant *no pl*. lebendes ~ livestock; totes ~ fixtures and fittings *pl*; er gehört schon zum ~ (*fig*) he's part of the furniture.
Inventarisation [ɪnvɛnt-] *f* compilation of an inventory.
inventarisieren* [-ven-] *vt* to take *or* make an inventory of.
Inventarisierung *f siehe* **Inventarisation**.
Inventur [ɪnvɛn'tuːr] *f* stocktaking. ~ **machen** to stocktake.
Inversion [ɪnvɛr'zioːn] *f* (*Gram*) inversion.
invertiert [ɪnvɛr'tiːrt] *adj* inverted.
Invest- [ɪn'vɛst-] *in cpds* (*DDR*) investment.
investieren* [ɪnvɛs'tiːrən] *vti* (*Comm*) to invest; (*fig auch*) to put. **Geld in seine Freundin** ~ (*inf*) to invest money in one's girlfriend (*hum*); **Gefühle in jdn** ~ (*inf*) to become (emotionally) involved with sb.
Investierung, Investition [ɪnvɛst-] *f* investment.
Investitions- *in cpds* investment; ~**güter** *pl* capital goods *pl*; ~**hilfe** *f* investment aid.
Investitur [ɪnvɛsti'tuːr] *f* (*Eccl*) investiture.
Investment [ɪn'vɛstmənt] *nt* **-s, -s** investment.
Investment-: ~**fonds** *m* investment fund; ~**gesellschaft** *f* investment trust; ~**papier**, ~**zertifikat** *nt* investment fund certificate.
inwärts *adv siehe* **einwärts**.
inwendig *adj* (a) (*rare*) inside. (b) (*inf*) **jdn/etw in- und auswendig kennen** to know sb/sth inside out.
inwiefern, inwieweit *adv* (*im Satz*) to what extent, how far; (*alleinstehend*) in what way.
Inzahlungnahme *f* -, **-n** (*Comm*) **die** ~ **von etw** the acceptance of sth in part payment *or* as a trade-in; **bei** ~ **des alten Wagens** when the old car is traded in *or* is taken as a trade-in.
Inzest *m* **-(e)s, -e** incest *no pl*.
inzestuös *adj* incestuous.
Inzucht *f* inbreeding. **verfluchte** ~! (*sl*) bugger! (*sl*).
inzw. *abbr of* **inzwischen**.
inzwischen *adv* (in the) meantime, meanwhile. **ich gehe** ~ **auf die Post** I'll go to the post in the meantime; **sie hatte** ~ **davon erfahren** meanwhile *or* in the meantime she'd learnt of this; **er hat sich** ~ **verändert** he's changed since (then); **er ist** ~ **18 geworden** he's now 18.
Ion [ioːn, 'iːɔn] *nt* **-s, -en** ion.
IOK [iːloː'kaː] *nt* **-s** *abbr of* **Internationales Olympisches Komitee**.
Ionisation [ioniza'tsioːn] *f* ionization.
ionisch [io'nɪʃ] *adj* (*Archit, Poet*) ionic; (*Mus*) ionian.
ionisieren* [ioni'ziːrən] *vt* to ionize.
Ionosphäre [iono'sfɛːrə] *f* ionosphere.
I-Punkt [ˈiːpʊŋkt] *m* dot on the i. ~**e setzen** *or* **machen** to dot one's *or* the i's, to put the dots on the i's.
IQ *abbr of* **Intelligenzquotient** IQ.
i.R. [iːˈɛr] *abbr of* **im Ruhestand** retd.
Irak [iˈraːk, ˈiːrak] *m* **-s** (**der**) ~ Iraq.
Iraker(in *f*) *m* **-s, -** Iraqi.
irakisch *adj* Iraqi.
Iran *m* **-s** (**der**) ~ Iran.
Iraner(in *f*) *m* **-s, -** Iranian.
iranisch *adj* Iranian.
irden *adj* earthenware, earthen. ~**e Waren** earthenware.
irdisch *adj* earthly *no adv*. **den Weg alles I~en gehen** to go the way of all flesh.
Ire *m* **-n, -n** Irishman; Irish boy. **die** ~**n** the Irish; **er ist** ~ he is Irish.
irgend 1 *adv* at all. **wenn** ~ **möglich, wenn es** ~ **geht** if it's at all possible; **wann** ~ **du kannst, wann du** ~ **kannst** whenever you can; **was ich** ~ **kann ...** whatever I can ...; **wer (es)** ~ **kann, wer** ~ **es kann** whoever can; **so sanft wie** ~ **möglich** as gently as possible *or* as I/you *etc* possibly can; **so lange ich** ~ **kann** as long as I possibly can; **wo es** ~ **geht, wo** ~ **es geht** where it's at all possible, wherever (it's) possible.
2 *mit indef pron* ~ **jemand** somebody; (*fragend, verneinend, bedingend*) anybody; **ich bin nicht** ~ **jemand** I'm not just anybody; ~ **etwas** something; (*fragend, verneinend, bedingend*) anything; **was zieh' ich an?** — ~ **etwas** what shall I wear? — anything, any old thing (*inf*); ~ **so ein Tier** some animal; **ein Fuchs oder** ~ **so ein Tier** a fox or some such animal.
irgendein *indef pron* some; (*fragend, verneinend, bedingend*) any. **er hat so** ~ **Schimpfwort verwendet** he used some swearword *or* other; **ich will nicht** ~ **Buch** I don't want just any (old *inf*) book; **haben Sie noch** ~**en Wunsch?** is there anything else you would like?; **das kann** ~ **anderer machen** somebody *or* someone else can do it.
irgendeine(r, s) *indef pron* (*nominal*) (*bei Personen*) somebody, someone; (*bei Dingen*) something; (*fragend, verneinend, bedingend*) anybody, anyone/anything. **welchen wollen Sie?** — ~**n** which one do you want? — any one, any old one (*inf*).
irgendeinmal *adv* some time *or* other, sometime; (*fragend, bedingend*) ever.
irgendwann *adv* sometime. ~ **werde ich wohl kommen** I'll come some time *or* other *or* sometime; ~ **einmal** some time; (*fragend, bedingend*) ever.
irgendwas *indef pron* (*inf*) something; (*fragend, verneinend, bedingend*) anything. **er murmelte so** ~ **something or other; was soll ich sagen?** — ~ **what shall I say?** — anything *or* any old thing (*inf*).
irgendwelche(r, s) *indef pron* some; (*fragend, verneinend, bedingend, jede beliebige*) any. **sind noch** ~ **Reste da?** is there still anything left?, is there anything left?
irgendwer *indef pron* (*inf*) *siehe* **irgend 2**.
irgendwie *adv* somehow (or other). **ist es** ~ **möglich?** is it at all possible?; **kannst du dir das** ~ **vorstellen?** can you possibly imagine it?; **ich hab' das** ~ **schon mal gesehen** I've just got a feeling I've seen it before; **das macht man nicht** ~ **you**

shouldn't do that just anyhow *or* any old how (*inf*).
irgendwo *adv* somewhere (or other), someplace (*esp US inf*); (*fragend, verneinend, bedingend*) anywhere, any place (*esp US inf*).
irgendwoher *adv* from somewhere (or other), from someplace (*esp US inf*); (*fragend, verneinend, bedingend*) from anywhere *or* any place (*esp US inf*).
irgendwohin *adv* somewhere (or other), someplace (*esp US inf*); (*fragend, verneinend, bedingend*) anywhere, any place (*esp US inf*).
Iridium *nt* iridium.
Irin *f* Irishwoman; Irish girl. **sie ist** ~ she is Irish.
Iris *f* -, - *or* (*Opt auch*) **Iriden** iris.
irisch *adj* Irish. ~**-römisches Bad** Turkish bath.
irisieren* *vi* to iridesce. ~**d** iridescent.
Irland *nt* **-s** Ireland; (*Republik* ~) Eire.
Irländer(in *f*) *m* **-s, -** *siehe* **Ire, Irin**.
irländisch *adj* Irish. **I~es Moos** Irish moss.
Ironie *f* irony.
ironisch *adj* ironic, ironical.
ironisieren* *vt* to treat ironically.
irr *adj siehe* **irr(e)**.
irrational ['ɪratsionaːl] *adj* irrational (*auch Math*).
Irrationalismus *m* irrationalism.
irr(e) 1 *adj* (a) (*geistesgestört*) mad, crazy, insane; **Blick auch** crazed, demented, wild. **das macht mich ganz** ~ it's driving me mad *or* crazy *or* insane; **jdn für** ~ **halten** (*inf*)/**erklären** (*inf*) to think sb is mad/to tell sb he/she *etc* is mad; **wie** ~ (*fig inf*) like mad (*inf*) *or* crazy (*inf*); ~**es Zeug reden** (*fig*) to say crazy things, to babble away.
(b), *pred* (*verwirrt, unsicher*) muddled, confused. **an jdm/etw** ~ **werden** (*liter*) to lose (one's) faith in sb/sth.
(c) (*inf*) Party, Hut wild (*inf*), crazy (*inf*). **er war** ~ **angezogen** he was wearing way-out clothes (*sl*).
2 *adv* (a) (*verrückt*) insanely, in a mad *or* insane way. (b) (*sl: sehr*) incredibly (*inf*). ~ **gut/hübsch** (*sl*) way out (*sl*)/real pretty (*inf*).
Irre *f* -, *no pl*: **jdn in die** ~ **führen** (*lit, fig*) to lead sb astray; **sich in die** ~ **führen lassen** (*lit, fig*) to be led astray *or* to be misled; **in die** ~ **gehen** (*lit, fig*) to go astray.
irreal *adj* unreal.
Irre-: **i~führen** *vt sep* to mislead; (*lit auch*) to lead astray; **sich i~führen lassen** to be misled *or* led astray; **i~führend** *adj* misleading; ~**führung** *f* misleading; **durch bewußte** ~**führung der Öffentlichkeit** by deliberately misleading the public; **i~gehen** *vi sep irreg aux sein* (a) (*lit geh*) (*sich verirren*) to go astray, to lose one's way; (*umherirren*) to wander astray; (b) (*fig*) to be mistaken.
irregulär *adj* irregular.
Irregularität *f* irregularity.
irreleiten *vt sep* to mislead, to lead astray. **irregeleitete Jugendliche** misguided youth; ~**de Informationen** misleading information.
irrelevant ['ɪrelevant] *adj* irrelevant (*für* for, to).
Irrelevanz *f* irrelevance (*für* for, to).
irreligiös *adj* irreligious.
Irreligiosität *f* irreligion.
irremachen *vt sep* to confuse, to muddle.
irren 1 *vi* (a) *aux sein* (*ziellos umherschweifen*) to wander, to stray, to roam.
(b) (*sich täuschen*) to be mistaken *or* wrong. **I~ ist menschlich** (*Prov*) to err is human (*Prov*).
2 *vr* to be mistaken *or* wrong. **jeder kann sich mal** ~ anyone can make a mistake, everyone makes mistakes; **sich in jdm/etw** ~ to be mistaken in *or* about sb/about sth, to be wrong about sb/sth; **wenn ich mich nicht irre ...** if I'm not mistaken ..., unless I'm very much mistaken ...; **ich irre mich nie!** I'm never wrong *or* mistaken!, I never make mistakes!
Irren-: ~**anstalt** *f* (*dated*) lunatic asylum (*dated*), loony-bin (*inf*); ~**arzt** *m* (*old, pej*) psychiatrist; ~**haus** *nt* (*dated, pej*) lunatic asylum (*dated*), loony-bin (*inf*); **hier geht es zu wie im** ~**haus** (*inf*) this place is an absolute madhouse; **i~hausreif** *adj* (*inf*) **i~hausreif sein** to be cracking up (*inf*).
irreparabel *adj* irreparable.
Irre(r) *mf decl as adj* (*inf*) lunatic; (*fig auch*) madman. **ein armer** ~**r** (*hum inf*) a poor fool *or* idiot.
irrereden *vi sep* to rave, to rant, to talk dementedly.
Irr(e)sein *nt* insanity. **manisch-depressives** ~ manic depression, manic-depressive psychosis.
irreversibel ['ɪreverziːbl] *adj* (*Phys, Biol*) irreversible.
Irr-: ~**fahrt** *f* wandering, odyssey (*liter*); **nach langer** ~**fahrt** after a long period of wandering (*auch fig*); **das Leben ist eine lange** ~**fahrt** we are all wandering astray; ~**gang** *m* (*lit*) blind alley (*in maze, pyramid*); (*fig, usu pl*) maze, labyrinth; **die** ~**gänge des Gebäudes** the maze *or* labyrinth of corridors in the building; ~**garten** *m* maze, labyrinth; ~**glaube(n)** *m* (*Rel*) heretical belief, heresy (*auch fig*); (*irrige Ansicht*) mistaken belief; **i~gläubig** *adj* heretical; **die** ~**gläubigen** the heretics.
irrig *adj* incorrect, wrong, false.
irrigerweise *adv* wrongly, incorrectly. **etw** ~ **glauben to** believe sth mistakenly *or* wrongly.
irritieren* *vt* (*verwirren*) to confuse, to muddle; (*ärgern*) to irritate.
Irr-: ~**läufer** *m* (a) stray letter, document *etc* delivered to the wrong address; (b) (*Mil*) stray bullet/grenade *etc*; ~**lehre** *f* heresy, heretical *or* false doctrine; ~**licht** *nt* jack o'lantern, will-o'-the-wisp.
Irrnis *f* (*liter*), **Irrsal** *nt* **-(e)s, -e** (*liter*) erring *no pl*. **die Irrsale des Lebens** the pitfalls of life.
Irrsinn *m, no pl* madness, insanity. **das ist ja** ~! (*inf*) that's

(sheer or absolute) madness or lunacy!; **auf den ~ verfallen, etw zu tun** to have the mad or crazy idea of doing sth.
irrsinnig adj mad, crazy, insane; (inf: stark) terrific, tremendous. **wie ein I~er** like a madman; **das Kind schrie wie ~** the child yelled like mad (inf) or like crazy (inf); **ein ~er Verkehr** (inf) a terrific or a crazy (inf) amount of traffic; **~ viele Leute** (inf) a tremendous or terrific number of people.
Irrsinnigkeit f madness, craziness, insanity.
Irrsinns- in cpds (inf) terrific, tremendous; **~hitze** f (inf) **da ist eine ~hitze** the heat there is absolutely incredible; **~verkehr** m (inf) **da ist ein ~verkehr** there's a crazy (inf) or terrific amount of traffic there; **~tat** f insanity.
Irrtum m mistake, error. **ein ~ von ihm** a mistake on his part; **im ~ sein, sich im ~ befinden** to be wrong or mistaken, to be in error; **~!** wrong!, you're wrong there!; **~, ich war es gar nicht!** that's where you're wrong or you're wrong there, it wasn't me!; **~ vorbehalten!** (Comm) errors excepted; **einen ~ zugeben** to admit to (having made) a mistake or an error; **jdm einen ~ nachweisen** to show that sb has made a mistake.
irrtümlich 1 adj attr mistaken, erroneous. 2 adv mistakenly, erroneously; (aus Versehen) by mistake.
irrtümlicherweise adv mistakenly, erroneously; (aus Versehen) by mistake.
Irrung f (liter) **die ~en und Wirrungen meines Lebens** the aberrations of my life; siehe **Irrtum**.
Irr-: **~weg** m (a) wandering or tortuous path; (Irrfahrt) wandering; **die Hexe führte die Kinder über ~wege** or **auf ~wegen in den Wald** the witch led the children along wandering or tortuous paths that made them lose their way in the forest; (b) (fig) **auf dem ~weg sein** to be on the wrong track; **zu studieren erwies sich für ihn als ~weg** going to university turned out to be a mistake for him; **auf ~wege geraten** to go astray, to leave the straight and narrow; **~wisch** m -es, -e (a) siehe **Irrlicht**; (b) (lebhafter Mensch) imp.
-is adj suf (Mus) sharp.
Ischias m or nt -, no pl sciatica.
Ischiasnerv m sciatic nerve.
Isegrim m -s, -e (Liter) the big bad wolf.
Islam m -s, no pl Islam.
islamisch adj Islamic.
Island nt -s Iceland.
Isländer(in f) m -s, - Icelander.
isländisch adj Icelandic. **I~es Moos** Iceland moss.
Isobare f -, -n isobar.
isochron [izo'kro:n] adj isochronal, isochronous.
Isochronismus [izokro'nɪsmʊs] m isochronism.
Isolation f (a) (das Absondern, Isolieren) isolation (auch Med, Biol); (von Häftlingen auch) putting in solitary confinement; (das Isoliertsein) isolation (auch Med, Biol); (von Häftlingen) solitary confinement. **die Studenten protestierten gegen die ~**

politischer Häftlinge the students protested against political prisoners' being put in solitary confinement.
(b) (Elec, gegen Lärm, Kälte etc) insulation; (von Wasserleitung, Boiler, Speicher auch) lagging.
Isolationismus m isolationism.
Isolator m insulator.
Isolierband nt insulating tape.
isolierbar adj isolable; (Tech) insulable. **das Problem ist nicht ~** the problem cannot be looked at in isolation.
isolieren* 1 vt (a) (absondern) to isolate (auch Med, Biol); **Häftlinge auch** to put in(to) solitary confinement. **jdn isoliert halten** to keep sb in isolation or isolated/in solitary confinement; **völlig isoliert leben** to live in complete isolation, to live isolated from the world; **ein Problem isoliert betrachten** to look at a problem in isolation. (b) elektrische Leitungen, Häuser, Fenster to insulate; von Wasserleitungen, Speicher auch to lag. 2 vr to isolate oneself or cut oneself off (from the world).
Isolier-: **~haft** f solitary confinement; **~material** nt insulating material; (für Wasserleitungen, Speicher auch) lagging; **~schicht** f insulating layer; **~station** f isolation ward.
Isoliertheit f isolatedness.
Isolierung f siehe **Isolation**.
Isometrie f isometry.
isometrisch adj isometric.
isomorph adj isomorphic; Kristalle auch isomorphous.
Isotherme f -, -n isotherm.
Isotop nt -s, -e isotope.
Israel [ˈɪsraɛl] nt -s Israel. **das Volk ~** the people of Israel.
Israeli m -(s), -(s) Israeli.
israelisch adj Israeli.
Israelit m -en, -en Israelite.
israelitisch adj Israelite.
iß imper sing of **essen**.
ist 3. pers sing present of **sein**[1].
Ist-Bestand m (Geld) cash in hand; (Waren) actual stock.
Isthmus m -, **Isthmen** isthmus.
Ist-Stärke f (Mil) actual or effective strength.
Itaker m -s, - (pej) dago (pej), Eyetie (pej).
Italien [-iən] nt -s Italy.
Italiener(in f) [-ˈliɛːnɐ, -ərɪn] m -s, - Italian.
italienisch [-ˈliɛːnɪʃ] adj Italian. **die ~e Schweiz** Italian-speaking Switzerland.
iterativ adj (Gram) iterative.
I-Tüpfelchen nt dot (on the/an i). **bis aufs ~** (fig) (right) down to the last (little) detail.
Itzig m -(e)s, -e (dated pej) Yid (pej), Jewboy (pej).
i.V. [iːˈfau] abbr of **in Vertretung; im Vorjahre; in Vorbereitung**.
Iwan m -s, no pl (inf) **der ~** (Volk) the Russkies (inf) pl; (Mensch) the Russky (inf).

J

J, j [jɔt, (Aus) jeː] nt J, j.
ja adv (a) (zustimmend) yes, yeah (inf); aye (dial, Scot, Parl); yea (US Parl); (bei Trauung) I do. **kommst du morgen? — ~ are you coming tomorrow? — yes**(, I am); **haben Sie das gesehen? — ~** did you see it? — yes(, I did); **ich glaube ~** (yes) I think so; **sagen Sie doch ~** please say yes; **zu etw ~ sagen** to say yes to sth; **~ und amen zu etw sagen** (inf) to agree (slavishly) with sth; **wenn ~** if so; **~! ~!, riefen die Zuschauer** go on! go on!, shouted the crowd.
(b) (fragend) really? **er war gestern da — ~?** he was there yesterday — really?, was he?; **ich habe gekündigt — ~?** I've quit — have you?, really?; **~, bitte?** yes?, hello?
(c) (feststellend) **aber ~!** yes, of course, but of course; **ach ~!** oh yes; **nun ~** oh well; **~ doch** or **freilich** or **gewiß** yes, of course; **~ so!** I see.
(d) (zweifelnd, ungläubig) really? **ich esse gern rohen Fisch — ~?** I like raw fish — really?, do you?; **er braucht keinen Urlaub, er arbeitet lieber — ~?** he doesn't need any holiday, he'd rather work — really?, would he?
(e) (unbedingt) **komm ~ pünktlich!** be punctual; **sei ~ vorsichtig!** be careful; **vergessen Sie es ja nicht!** don't forget, whatever you do!; **tu das ja nicht, ich warne dich!** just don't do that, I'm warning you.
(f) (einräumend, schließlich) **es ist ~ noch früh** it's still early (after all); **sie ist ~ erst fünf** (after all) she's only five; **es ist ~ nicht so schlimm** it's not really as bad as all that, (after all) it's not that bad; **das ist ~ richtig, aber ...** that's (certainly) right, but ...; **der Hut ist ~ elegant, aber zu teuer** the hat is (certainly) elegant, but it's too dear; **ich kann es ~ mal versuchen, aber ... I could always try it, but ...**

(g) (als Steigerung) even, nay (liter). **das ist gut, ~ sogar sehr gut** it's good, in fact it's even very good.
(h) (feststellend) **da hat man's ~, da haben wir's ~** there you are (then); **da kommt er ~** there or here he is; **das ist es ~** that's just it; **hier ist ~ Herr Meier** here's Mr Meier himself; **~, was haben wir denn hier?** well, what have we here?; **das sag' ich ~!** that's just what I say; **das wissen wir ~ alle** we all know that (anyway); **Sie wissen ~, daß ... you** (already) know that ..., as you know ...; **Sie wissen ~, wie das so ist** you know how it is, (don't you?).
(i) (verstärkend, wirklich) just. **das ist ~ fürchterlich** that's (just) terrible, terrible, that's what it is!; **das weiß man ~ eben** nie vorher you just never know in advance.
(j) (aber) **~, sagen Sie mal** now look here; **~, was du nicht sagst!** you don't say!
(k) (vergewissernd) right?, OK? **du kommst doch morgen, ~?** you're coming tomorrow, right or aren't you?; **du rufst mich doch an, ~?** you'll give me a call, right or OK or won't you?; **das ist also abgemacht, ~?** that's agreed then, right or OK?
Ja nt -s, -(s) yes; aye (dial, Scot, Parl); yea (US Parl). **das ~ vor dem Traualtar sprechen** to say "I do" at the altar.
Jabo m -s, -s abbr of **Jagdbomber**.
Jacht f -, -en yacht.
Jacht-: **~klub** m yacht club; **~sport** m yachting, sailing.
jäck adj (dial) crazy.
Jäckchen nt (a) dim of **Jacke** little jacket. (b) (Baby~) matinée jacket.
Jacke f -, -n jacket, coat (esp US); (Woll~) cardigan; (Comm: Unterhemd) vest (Brit), undershirt (US). **das ist ~ wie Hose** (inf) it doesn't make any difference (either way), it's six of one

and half a dozen of the other (*inf*); **jdm die ~ vollhauen** (*inf*) to give sb a thrashing; **sich** (*dat*) **die/eine ~ anziehen** (*fig inf*) to take sth personally; **wem die ~ paßt ...** (*fig inf*) if the cap fits ...

Jacken-: ~kleid *nt* (*Kostüm*) costume, suit, two-piece; (*Kleid und Jacke*) two-piece; **~tasche** *f* jacket *or* coat (*esp US*) pocket.

Jacketkrone ['dʒɛkɪt-] *f* (*Zahnheilkunde*) jacket crown.

Jackett [ʒa'kɛt] *nt* **-s, -s** jacket, coat (*esp US*).

Jackettasche *f getrennt:* **Jackett-tasche** jacket *or* coat (*esp US*) pocket.

Jade *m or f* -, *no pl* jade.

jadegrün *adj* jade green.

Jagd *f* -, **-en** (a) hunt; (*Ausführung der ~*) hunting; (*mit dem Gewehr auch*) shoot, shooting; (*fig: Verfolgung*) hunt (*nach* for), chase (*nach* after); (*Wettlauf*) race. **die ~ auf Rotwild/Fasanen** deer-/pheasant-hunting; **hohe/niedere ~** big/small game-hunting; **auf der ~ sein/auf die ~ (nach etw) gehen** (*lit, fig*) to be/to go hunting (for sth), to be on the hunt (for sth); **auf jdn/etw ~ machen** (*lit, fig*) to hunt for sb/sth; **von der ~ leben** to live by hunting; **ein Buch über die ~** a book about hunting; **die Göttin der ~** the goddess of hunting *or* the hunt *or* the chase (*liter*); **die ~ nach Geld/Glück** the pursuit of *or* quest for money/fortune *etc*; **in wilder ~ sprengten sie über die Brücke** in their wild chase they charged over the bridge.
(b) (*~revier*) preserve, shoot.
(c) (*Wildbestand*) game.
(d) (*~gesellschaft*) hunt, hunting *or* shooting party.

Jagd-: ~aufseher *m* (*Angestellter*) gamekeeper; (*Beamter*) game warden; **j~bar** *adj* ... **sind j~bar** ... may be hunted, ... are fair game; **~beute** *f* bag; **~bomber** *m* (*Mil*) fighter-bomber; **~flieger** *m* (*Mil*) fighter pilot; **~flinte** *f* hunting rifle, sporting gun, shotgun; (*für Federwild auch*) fowling-piece; **~flugzeug** *nt* (*Mil*) fighter plane *or* aircraft; **~frevel** *m* (*form*) poaching; **~frevler** *m* (*form*) poacher; **~gebiet** *nt* hunting ground; **~geschwader** *nt* (*Mil*) fighter squadron; **~gesellschaft** *f* hunt, hunting *or* shooting party; **~gewehr** *nt* hunting rifle, sporting gun *or* rifle, shotgun; **~glück** *nt* good luck *or* fortune in hunting; **wir hatten kein ~glück** we didn't bag anything; **~göttin** *f* goddess of hunting *or* the hunt *or* the chase (*liter*); **~gründe** *pl*: **in die ewigen ~gründe eingehen** to go to the happy hunting-grounds; **~haus** *nt* hunting lodge; **~herr** *m* owner of a/the hunting ground; **~horn** *nt* hunting horn; **~hund** *m* hound; (*Vorstehhund*) pointer; (*Apportierhund*) retriever; **das ist ein guter ~hund** it's a good hunting dog; **~hütte** *f siehe* **~haus**; **~messer** *nt* hunting knife; **~pächter** *m* game tenant; **~recht** *nt* (a) hunting *or* shooting rights *pl*; (b) (*~bestimmungen*) game laws *pl*; **~rennen** *nt* steeplechase; **~revier** *nt* shoot; (*von Indianern etc*) preserve; **~schaden** *m* damage caused by hunting; **~schein** *m* hunting/shooting licence; **einen ~schein haben** (*hum sl*) to be certified (*inf*); **~schloß** *nt* hunting lodge; **~schutz** *m* (a) (*Hunt*) game protection; (b) (*Mil*) fighter cover; **~signal** *nt* hunting signal; **~staffel** *f* (*Mil*) fighter flight; **~tasche** *f* game bag; **~verbot** *nt* ban on hunting; (*als Strafe*) ban from hunting; **~wesen** *nt* hunting; **~wild** *nt* game; **~wurst** *f* smoked sausage; **~zeit** *f* hunting/shooting season.

jagen 1 *vt* (a) *Tier, Menschen* to hunt. **jagt ihn!** get *or* catch him!
(b) (*hetzen*) to chase, to drive; (*treiben*) *Wild* to drive. **jdn in die Flucht ~** to put sb to flight; **jdn zu Tode ~** to hound sb to death; **jdn aus dem Bett ~** (*inf*) to chase sb out of bed; **jdn aus dem Haus ~** to drive *or* chase sb out of the house; **jdm das Schwert in den Leib ~** to plunge *or* drive one's sword into sb; **jdm eine Spritze in den Arm ~** (*inf*) to stick a needle in sb's arm; **ein Unglück jagte das andere** one misfortune followed hard on (the heels of) the other; **am Freitag ~ viele Leute ihren ganzen Wochenlohn durch die Kehle** (*inf*) *or* **Gurgel** (*inf*) on Friday lots of people will pour all their week's earnings down their throats (*inf*); **mit diesem Essen kannst du mich ~** (*inf*) I wouldn't touch that food with a (ten-foot) barge pole (*Brit inf*) *or* a ten-foot pole (*US inf*).
(c) (*erlegen*) to bag.
2 *vi* (a) (*auf die Jagd gehen*) to hunt, to go hunting; (*mit dem Gewehr auch*) to shoot, to go shooting.
(b) *aux sein* (*rasen*) to race. **nach etw ~** to chase after sth; **in ~der Eile** in great haste.
3 *vr* (*Geschehnisse etc*) to follow one on the heels of the other.

Jäger *m* **-s, -** (a) hunter, huntsman. **~ und Sammler** hunters and gatherers. (b) (*Mil*) (*Gebirgs~*) rifleman; (*Jagdflieger*) fighter pilot; (*Sportflugzeug*) fighter (plane).

Jägerbataillon *nt* rifle battalion.

Jägerei *f, no pl* hunting; (*mit dem Gewehr auch*) shooting.

Jägerhut *m* Tyrolean hat.

Jägerin *f* huntress, huntswoman.

Jägerlatein *nt* (*inf*) hunters' yarns *pl*. **jdm ~ auftischen** to tell sb tall stories about one's hunting exploits.

Jägersmann *m, pl* **-leute** (*dated, liter*) hunter, huntsman.

Jägersprache *f* hunter's jargon.

Jaguar *m* **-s, -e** jaguar.

jäh(e) *adj* (*geh*) (a) (*plötzlich*) sudden; *Schmerz auch* sharp; (*unvermittelt*) *Wechsel, Ende, Bewegung auch* abrupt; *Flucht auch* headlong, precipitous. (b) (*steil*) sheer. **der Abhang steigt ~ an/fällt ~ herab** the slope rises/falls sharply *or* steeply *or* plunges *or* plummets down.

jählings *adv* (*liter*) (a) (*plötzlich*) suddenly; *aufhören, abbrechen auch* abruptly; (*fliehen*) headlong. (b) (*steil*) steeply, precipitously; (*hinabfallen*) headlong.

Jahr *nt* **-(e)s, -e** (a) year. **ein halbes ~** six months *sing or pl*; **ein dreiviertel ~** nine months *sing or pl*; **anderthalb ~e** one and a half years *sing*, eighteen months *sing or pl*; **zwei ~e Garantie** a two-year guarantee; **im ~(e) 1066** in (the year) 1066; **die sechziger ~e** the sixties *sing or pl*; **alle ~e** every year; **alle zehn ~e**

every ten years; **ein ~ ums andere** year after year; **auf ~e hinaus** for years ahead; **auf ~ und Tag** to the very day; **einmal im ~(e)** once a year; **das ganze ~ über** all year (round *or* through); **pro ~** a year, per annum; **das Buch/der Mann des ~es** the book/the man of the year; **noch nach ~en** years later; **nach ~ und Tag** after (many) years; **vor ~ und Tag** (many) years ago; **seit ~ und Tag** for years; **mit den ~en** as (the) years go by, over the years; **mit den ~en hat man sich ...** over the years one has ...; **zwischen den ~en** (*inf*) between Christmas and New Year.
(b) (*Alter, Lebens~*) **er ist zehn ~e** (*alt*) he is ten years old; **mit dreißig ~en, in seinem dreißigsten ~** (*liter*) at the age of thirty, in his thirtieth year (*liter*); **Personen über 18 ~e/unter 18 ~e** people over/under (the age of) 18; **die ~e zu etw haben** (*inf*) to be old enough for sth; **in die ~e kommen** (*inf*) to be getting on (in years); **man sieht ihm seine ~e nicht an** his age doesn't *or* his years don't show; **in den besten ~en sein** *or* **stehen** to be in the prime of one's life; **mit den ~en** as one gets older.

jahraus *adv*: **~, jahrein** year in, year out.

Jahrbuch *nt* yearbook; (*Ausgabe einer Sammlung etc*) annual; (*Kalender*) almanac.

Jährchen *nt* (*hum inf*) year.

jahrelang 1 *adj attr* lasting for years. **~es Warten/~e Planungen/Forschungen** years of waiting/planning/research. 2 *adv* for years. **und dann dauerte es noch ~, bevor ...** and then it took years until ...; **schon ~ verspricht man uns ... they've been promising us ...** for years.

jähren *vr* **heute jährt sich der Tag, daß ...** *or* **an dem ...** it's a year ago today that ...; **der Tag jährt sich zum dritten Mal, daß ...** *or* **an dem ...** it's three years ago that ...

Jahres- *in cpds* annual, yearly; **~abschluß** *m* (a) (*Comm*) annual closing of account; (b) (*~ende*) end of the year; **~anfang** *m siehe* **~beginn**; **~ausgleich** *m* (*Fin*) *siehe* Lohnsteuerjahresausgleich; **~ausklang** *m* (*geh*) zum **~ausklang** to see the old year out; **~beginn** *m* beginning of a/the new year; **~beitrag** *m* annual *or* yearly subscription; **~bericht** *m* annual *or* yearly report; **~bestzeit** *f* (*Sport*) best time of the year; **~bilanz** *f* (*Comm*) annual balance sheet; **~einkommen** *nt* annual income; **~ende** *nt* end of the year; **~feier** *f* anniversary; (*Feierlichkeiten*) anniversary celebrations *pl*; **~frist** *f*: **binnen/nach ~frist** within/after (a period of) one year; **~gehalt** *nt* annual salary; **~hauptversammlung** *f* (*Comm*) annual general meeting, AGM; **~karte** *f* annual season ticket; **~mitte** *f* middle of the year; **~mittel** *nt* (*Met*) average annual temperature; **~ring** *m* (*eines Baumes*) annual ring; **~tag** *m* anniversary; **~umsatz** *m* (*Comm*) annual *or* yearly turnover; **~urlaub** *m* annual holiday *or* leave; **~wechsel** *m*, **~wende** *f* new year; **jdm zum ~wechsel** Glück wünschen to wish sb a happy New Year; **~zahl** *f* date, year; **~zeit** *f* season; **für die ~zeit zu kalt** cold for the time of year.

Jahr-: ~fünft *nt* **-(e)s, -e** five years *pl*, quinquennium (*form*); **~gang** *m* (a) (*Sch, Univ*) year; **er ist ~gang 1950** he was born in 1950; **die ~gänge 1950-53** the 1950-53 age-group; **er ist mein/wir sind ein ~gang** we were born in the same year; (*alle Schulabgänger etc*) we were in the same year; (b) (*alle Zeitschriften etc von einem Jahr*) year's issues *pl*; (*einer Fachzeitschrift*) volume; **Nr. 20, ~gang 31 No. 20, 31st year; Spiegel, ~gang 1960** Spiegel of the year *or* for 1960; (c) (*von Wein*) vintage, year; **~hundert** *nt* **-s, -e** century; **das ~hundert der Aufklärung** the Age of Enlightenment; **~hunderte haben die Menschen ...** for centuries men have ...

jahrhunderte-: ~alt centuries-old; **~lang** 1 *adj* lasting for centuries; **eine ~lange Entwicklung** centuries of development; 2 *adv* for centuries.

Jahrhundert-: ~feier *f* centenary; (*Feierlichkeiten*) centenary celebrations *pl*; **~wende** *f* turn of the century.

-jährig *adj suf* (a) (*... Jahre alt*) -year-old. **ein Fünf~er** a five-year-old.
(b) (*Jahre dauernd*) years of. **nach elf~en Verhandlungen** after eleven years of negotiations; **nach drei~er Verspätung** after a three-year delay.
(c) (*Ordinalzahl*) anniversary of. **der 70.~e Gründungstag** the 70th anniversary (of the foundation).

jährlich 1 *adj* annual, yearly. 2 *adv* every year, annually, yearly; (*Comm*) per annum. **einmal/zweimal ~** once/twice a year *or* yearly.

Jährling *m* yearling.

Jahrmarkt *m* (fun-)fair. **ein ~ der Eitelkeiten** (*liter*) a vanity fair.

Jahrmarkts-: ~bude *f* booth *or* stall (at a fairground); (*Schaubude*) side-show; **~künstler** *m* fair-ground artiste.

Jahr-: ~millionen *pl* millions of years; **j~millionenlang** 1 *adj* millions of years of; 2 *adv* for millions of years; **~tausend** *nt* **-s, -e** millennium, a thousand years; **in unserem ~tausend** in our millennium; **~tausende** thousands of years; **j~tausendelang** *adj* thousands of years of; 2 *adv* for millennia *or* thousands of years; **~tausendfeier** *f* millennium; (*Feierlichkeiten*) millennium celebrations *pl*; **~zehnt** *nt* **-(e)s, -e** decade; **j~zehntelang** 1 *adj* decades of; 2 *adv* for decades.

Jahve, Jahwe ['ja:və] *m* **-s** Jehovah, Yahweh (*rare*).

Jähzorn *m* violent temper; (*plötzlicher Ausbruch*) violent outburst. **im ~** in a violent temper *or* rage; **zum ~ neigen** to be prone to violent outbursts (of temper).

jähzornig *adj* violent-tempered, irascible; (*~ erregt*) furious in a violent temper. **er ist manchmal so ~, daß ...** he sometimes becomes so furious *or* gets into such a violent temper that ..

Jakob *m* **-s** James; (*Bibl*) Jacob; *siehe* **wahr**.

Jakobiner(in *f*) *m* **-s, -** (*Hist*) Jacobin; (*Rel auch*) Dominican.

Jakobinermütze *f* liberty cap.

Jakobsleiter f (Bibl, Bot) Jacob's ladder; (Naut auch) rope ladder.
Jakobus m - James.
Jalousie [ʒalu'ziː] f venetian blind.
Jamaika nt -s Jamaica.
Jamaikaner(in f) m -s, - Jamaican.
jamaikanisch adj Jamaican.
Jamaika-: ~pfeffer m Jamaica pepper; ~rum m Jamaica rum.
Jambendichtung f iambic poetry.
Jambus m -, **Jamben** (Poet) iamb(us), iambic foot.
jambisch adj (Poet) iambic.
Jammer m -s, no pl (a) (Elend) misery, wretchedness. **ein Bild des ~s bieten** or **sein** to be the picture of misery; **der ~ überkam ihn** a feeling of misery came over him; **es ist ein ~, diesen Verfall mit ansehen zu müssen** it is a wretched thing or heart-breaking to have to watch this decay; **es ist ein ~, wie die Kosten steigen/wie wenig Zeit wir haben** it's deplorable the way costs are rising/it's terrible or awful how little time we have; **es wäre ein ~, wenn ...** (inf) it would be a crying shame if ... (inf).
(b) (Klage) wailing, lamentation.
Jammer-: ~bild nt (geh) picture of misery, piteous or wretched sight; ~geschrei nt (inf) siehe **Jammer** (b); ~gestalt f wretched figure; ~lappen m (sl) wet (sl), sissy (inf).
jämmerlich 1 adj wretched, pitiful; (beklagenswert auch) Zustand lamentable, deplorable; (inf) Erklärung, Bericht, Entschuldigung etc pitiful, pathetic (inf). **2** adv (inf: sehr) terribly (inf).
Jämmerlichkeit f wretchedness.
jammern 1 vi to wail (über + acc over); (sich beklagen auch) to moan, to yammer (inf). **nach jdm/etw ~** to whine or yammer (inf) for sb/sth; **der Gefangene jammerte um Wasser** the prisoner begged pitifully or moaned for water.
2 vt (old) to move to pity. **er jammert mich** I feel sorry for him, I pity him; **es kann einen ~, wenn man sieht, wie ...** you could really weep when you see how ...; **es kann einen Hund ~** (dated inf) it's a crying shame (inf).
Jammer-: j~schade adj **es ist j~schade** (inf) it's a terrible pity or a crying shame (inf); ~tal nt (Bibl, liter) vale of tears (inf); j~voll adj siehe **jämmerlich**.
Janker m -s, - (S Ger, Aus) Tyrolean jacket; (Strickjacke) cardigan.
Jänner m -s, - (Aus, Sw, S Ger) January.
Januar m -(s), -e January; siehe **März**.
Janus- (Myth, liter): ~gesicht nt, ~kopf m Janus face; j~gesichtig, j~köpfig adj Janus-faced.
Japan nt -s Japan.
Japaner(in f) m -s, - Japanese.
japanisch adj Japanese.
Japanisch(e) nt decl as adj Japanese; siehe **Deutsch(e)**.
Japanologe m, **Japanologin** f Japanese specialist; (Student) student of Japanese (studies).
Japanologie f Japanese studies.
Japanpapier nt Japanese paper.
jappen (N Ger), **japsen** vi (inf) to pant.
Jargon [ʒar'gõː] m -s, -s jargon, slang, lingo (inf).
Jasager m -s, - yes-man.
Jasmin m -s, -e jasmine.
Jaspis m -(ses), -se jasper.
Jastimme f vote in favour (of), vote for; (Parl auch) aye (Brit), yea (US).
jäten vti to weed.
Jauche f -, no pl liquid manure; (Med) sanies (form), ichor (form); (pej sl) (Getränk) (pig-)swill, piss (vulg); (Abwasser) sewage. **das stinkt wie ~** it stinks like nobody's business (inf), it stinks to high heaven.
Jauche(n)grube f cesspool, cesspit; (Agr) liquid manure pit.
jauchen vti to manure; (Med) to discharge (sanies or ichor).
Jauchewagen m liquid manure cart.
jauchzen vi (geh) to rejoice (liter), to exult (liter); (Publikum) to cheer; (Kinder) to shout and cheer; (Säugling) to chuckle, to laugh.
Jauchzer m -s, - jubilant cheer or shout. **sie stieß einen lauten, begeisterten ~ aus** she gave a loud yippee (inf), she cheered.
jaulen vi (lit, fig) to howl; (lit) to yowl.
Jause f -, -n (Aus) break (for a snack); (Proviant) snack. **eine ~ halten** or **machen** to stop for a snack.
jausen vi (Aus) to stop for a snack; (in der Arbeitspause) to have a tea break.
Jausenstation f (Aus) snack-bar.
Java ['jaːva] nt -s Java.
Javaner(in f) [ja'vaːnɐ, -ərɪn] m -s, - Javanese.
javanisch [ja'vaːnɪʃ] adj Javanese.
jawohl, jawoll (hum, inf) adv yes; (Mil) yes, sir; (Naut) aye, aye, sir. **stimmt das wirklich? — ~** is that really right? — yes, it is, yes, indeed; **haben Sie 50 DM gesagt? — ~** did you say 50 marks? — right, correct, I did, I did indeed; **~ habe ich dich gesehen** (inf) I most certainly did see you, you're damn right I saw you (inf).
jawollja adv (hum) yessir (hum).
Jawort nt **jdm das ~ geben** to consent to marry sb, to say yes to sb; (bei Trauung) to say "I do"; **sich** or **einander das ~ geben** to get married.
Jazz [dʒæz, dʒɛs, (dated, pej) jats] m -, no pl jazz.
Jazz- in cpds jazz.
Jazzer ['dʒɛsɐ] m -s, - (inf) jazz-man (inf).
Jazzkeller m (basement) jazz club.
je¹ 1 adv (a) (jemals) ever. **~ und ~** (dated) always; (bisweilen) now and again or then; siehe **eh**.
(b) (jeweils) every, each. **für ~ drei Stück zahlst du eine Mark** you pay one mark for (every) three; **~ zwei Schüler aus jeder Klasse** two children from each class; **ich gebe euch ~ zwei Äpfel** I'll give you two apples each or each of you two apples; **sie zahlten ~ eine Mark** they paid one mark each, each (of them) paid one mark.
2 prep + acc (pro) per. **~ Person zwei Stück** two per person; **~ zehn Exemplare ein Freiexemplar** one free copy for every ten copies.
3 conj (a) **~ eher, desto** or **um so besser** the sooner the better; **~ länger, ~ lieber** the longer the better.
(b) **~ nach** according to, depending on; **~ nach Wunsch** just as one wishes; **~ nachdem** it all depends; **~ nachdem, wie gut man arbeitet ...** depending on how well you work ...
je² interj **ach** or **o ~!** oh dear!; **o ~!** (old) alas! (old, Bibl, liter); **~ nun** (dated) oh, well.
Jeans [dʒiːnz] pl jeans.
Jeck m -en, -en (dial) siehe **Narr**.
jedenfalls adv anyhow, in any case; (zumindest) at least, at any rate. **~ ist es schon zu spät** it's too late now anyhow or in any case; **er ist nicht gekommen, aber er hat sich ~ entschuldigt** he didn't come but at least or at any rate he apologized or he did at least or at any rate apologize; **ob er krank ist, weiß ich nicht, ~ ist er nicht gekommen** I don't know whether he's ill or not, at any rate or in any case or anyhow he didn't come; **ob die Inflation zum Stillstand kommt, ist noch nicht abzusehen, ~ steigen die Preise nicht mehr so schnell** whether inflation will come to a stop is not yet predictable, but at any rate in any case or at least prices aren't going up so fast; **er ist nicht reif zum Studieren, ~ jetzt noch nicht** he's not mature enough to study, at least or at any rate not yet; **obwohl ich kein Theologe bin, bin ich ~ der Ansicht ...** I'm no theologian but in my opinion at any rate ...; **ich weiß nicht, ob das nötig ist, ~ ist es hier so üblich** I don't know if it's necessary, but it's what we do here (anyhow or at any rate).
jede(r, s) indef pron (a) (adjektivisch) (einzeln) each; (von zweien auch) either; (~ von allen) every; (~ beliebige) any. **das weiß doch ~s Kind** any or a child knows that, any or a child could tell you that; **ohne ~ Anstrengung/Vorstellung** etc without any effort/idea, with no effort/idea etc; **zu ~ Stunde** at all times; **es kann ~n Augenblick passieren** it can happen any minute or at any moment; **fern von ~r Kultur** far from all civilization.
(b) (substantivisch) (einzeln) each (one); (~ von allen) everyone, everybody; (~ beliebige) anyone, anybody. **~r von uns** each (one)/every one/any one of us; **ein ~r** (liter) each (one); **~r von uns beiden** each (one) of us; **er gab ~m von beiden ein Buch** he gave each or both of them a book; **~r von beiden kann sich verspäten** each or either of them could be late; **~r zweite** every other or second one; **~r für sich** everyone for himself; **~r/~/~s für sich ist ganz nett, aber beide zusammen** ... each one by himself/herself/itself or each one alone is quite nice, but together ...; **geht jetzt ~r in sein Bett!** go to bed now, both/all of you; **das kann ~r/nicht ~r** anyone or anybody can do that/not everyone or everybody can do that; **er spricht nicht mit ~m** he doesn't speak to just anybody or anyone.
jedermann indef pron everyone, everybody; (jeder, beliebige auch) anyone, anybody. **J~** (Theat) Everyman; **das ist nicht ~s Sache** it's not everyone's cup of tea (inf); **Herr/Frau J~** Mr/Mrs Average (Citizen).
Jedermannfunk m private walkie-talkies pl.
jederzeit adv at any time. **du kannst ~ kommen** you can come any time (you like); **ja, ~** sure, any time.
jedesmal adv every or each time. **~, wenn sie ...** each or every time she ..., whenever she ...; **~ ist es so(, daß ...)** it happens every or each time (that ...).
jedoch conj, adv however. **er verlor ~ die Nerven** he lost his nerve however or though.
jedwede(r, s) indef pron (old) siehe **jede(r, s)**.
Jeep [dʒiːp] m -s, -s jeep.
jegliche(r, s) indef pron (adjektivisch) any; (substantivisch) (old, liter: auch **ein ~r**) each (one).
jeher ['jeːheːɐ] adv: **von** or **seit ~** always; **das ist schon seit ~ so** it has always been like that.
Jehova [je'hoːva] m -s Jehovah. **die Zeugen ~s** Jehovah's witnesses.
jein adv (hum) yes and no.
Jelängerjelieber nt -s, - honeysuckle.
jemals adv ever.
jemand indef pron somebody, someone; (bei Fragen, bedingenden Sätzen auch, Negation) anybody, anyone. **ist da ~?** is anybody or somebody there?; **du lachst so, hat dir ~ ein Kompliment gemacht?** why are you smiling? has somebody or someone paid you a compliment?; **hat dir irgend or überhaupt ~ ein Kompliment gemacht?** did anyone or anybody pay you a compliment?; **ohne ~en zu fragen** without asking anybody or anyone; **ich brauche ~en, der mir den Fernseher repariert** I need somebody or someone to repair my television set; **~ Fremdes/Neues** a stranger/somebody or someone new.
jemine ['jeːmine] interj (old) siehe **ojemine, herrjemine**.
Jenaer Glas ® ['jeːnaɐ-] nt Pyrex ®, heatproof glass.
jene(r, s) dem pron (geh) (a) (adjektivisch) that; pl those; (der Vorherige, die Vorherigen) the former. **in ~m Leben** or **~r Welt** in the next life or world; **in ~n Tagen** in those days; (zukünftig) in those days ahead, in those days to come; **in ~r Zeit** at that time, in those times.
(b) (substantivisch) that one; pl those (ones); (der Vorherige, die Vorherigen) the former. **bald dieser, bald ~r** first one then the other; **von diesem und ~m sprechen** to talk about this and that.
jenseitig adj attr opposite, other. **die ~en Vororte** the suburbs

on the other side; **das~e Leben** the life hereafter, the life after death.
jenseits 1 *prep* +*gen* on the other side of. **2 km ~ der Grenze** 2 kms beyond the border *or* the other side of the border. **2** *adv* **~ von** on the other side of; **~ von Gut und Böse** beyond good and evil, over and above good and evil; (*hum inf*) past it (*inf*).
Jenseits *nt* -, *no pl* hereafter, next world. **jdn ins ~ befördern** (*inf*) to send sb to kingdom come (*inf*).
Jenseitsglaube *m* belief in a/the hereafter.
Jeremiade *f* (*old, liter*) jeremiad (*liter*).
Jeremias *m* - (*Bibl*) Jeremiah.
Jesaja *m* -s (*Bibl*) Isaiah.
Jesses *interj* (*inf*) Jesus (*inf*).
Jesuit *m* -en, -en Jesuit.
Jesuiten-: ~**orden** *m* Jesuit Order; ~**schule** *f* Jesuit school.
jesuitisch *adj* Jesuit.
Jesus *m gen* **Jesu**, *dat* - *or* **Jesu**, *acc* - *or* **Jesum** Jesus. **~ Christus** Jesus Christ; **~, Maria (und Josef)!** (*dial inf*) holy Mary mother of God! (*dial inf*).
Jesus-: ~**kind** *nt*: **das ~kind** the Infant Jesus, the Christ Child; ~**latschen** *pl* (*inf*) Jesus sandals *pl*.
Jet [dʒɛt] *m* -(s), -s (*inf*) jet.
Jeton [ʒə'tõ:] *m* -s, -s chip.
Jet-set ['dʒɛtzɛt] *m* -s, (*rare*) -s (*inf*) jet-set.
jetten ['dʒɛtn] *vi aux sein* (*inf*) to jet (*inf*).
Jet-Zeit|alter *nt* (*inf*) jet age.
jetzig *adj attr* present attr, current. **in der ~en Zeit** in our *or* present times; **im ~en Augenblick** at the present moment (in time).
jetzo *adv* (*obs*) *siehe* **jetzt.**
jetzt *adv* now; (*heutzutage auch*) nowadays. **sie ist ~ in der Schweiz** she's in Switzerland now, she's now in Switzerland; **bis ~ so far**; **ich bin ~ (schon) fünf Tage hier** I have been here five days now; **für ~** for now, for the present; **gleich ~, ~ gleich** right now, straight away; **schon ~ already**; **~ schon?** already?; **~ noch?** (what) now?; **das ist noch ~ der Fall** it's still the case today; **~ oder nie!** (it's) now or never!; **habe ich ~ den Brief eingeworfen?** now did I post that letter?, did I post that letter now?
Jetzt *nt* -, *no pl* (*geh*) present.
Jetztzeit *f*, *no pl* (*geh*) present (time), modern times *pl or* age.
Jeunesse dorée [ʒœnɛsdɔ're] *f* - -, *no pl* gilded youth, rich young people *pl*.
jew. *abbr of* **jeweils.**
jeweilig *adj attr* respective; (*vorherrschend*) *Verhältnisse, Bedingungen* prevailing. **die ~e Regierung** the government of the day.
jeweils *adv* at a *or* any one time; (*jedesmal*) each time; (*jeder einzelne*) each. **~ am Monatsletzten** on the last day of each month; **die ~ betroffenen Landesregierungen müssen ...** each of the governments concerned must ...; **die ~ durch Schiebetüren abgetrennten Räume** the rooms, each (of which are) separated (off) by sliding doors; **die ~ größten aus einer Gruppe** the biggest from each group.
Jg. *abbr of* **Jahrgang.**
Jh. *abbr of* **Jahrhundert.**
JH *abbr of* **Jugendherberge** YH.
jhrl. *abbr of* **jährlich.**
jiddeln *vi* (*inf*) *siehe* **jüdeln.**
jiddisch *adj* Yiddish.
Jiddisch(e) *nt decl as adj* Yiddish; *siehe* **Deutsch(e).**
Jiu-Jitsu ['dʒiːuː'dʒɪtsu] *nt* -s, *no pl* j(i)u-jitsu.
Job [dʒɔp] *m* -s, -s (*inf*) job.
jobben ['dʒɔbn] *vi* (*inf*) to work, to have a job.
Jobber ['dʒɔbɐ] *m* -s, - (*inf*) casual worker; (*Börsen~*) jobber.
Joch *nt* -(e)s, -e (a) (*lit, fig*) yoke. **Ochsen ins ~ spannen** to yoke *or* harness oxen; **ich habe mir dieses ~ selber auferlegt** I brought it (all) on myself; **sich einem ~ *or* unter ein ~ beugen** (*fig*) to submit to *or* bend under the yoke; **das ~ abwerfen *or* abschütteln** (*fig*) to shake *or* throw off the yoke. **(b)** (*dated: Gespann Ochsen*) yoke. **(c)** (*Archit*) truss; (*Kirchen~*) bay; (*Brücken~*) span. **(d)** (*Berg~*) ridge. **(e)** (*old: Feldmaß*) acre.
Joch-: ~**bein** *nt* cheek-bone, malar bone (*form*); ~**bogen** *m* (*a*) (*Anat*) zygomatic arch (*spec*), zygoma (*spec*); (b) (*Archit*) bay.
Jockei ['dʒɔke], **Jockey** ['dʒɔki] *m* -s, -s jockey.
Jockeymütze *f* jockey cap.
Jod *nt* -s, *no pl* iodine.
jodeln *vti* to yodel.
jodhaltig *adj* containing iodine, iodic (*form*).
Jodler *m* -s, - (*Ruf*) yodel.
Jodler *m* -s, - (*Mensch*) yodeller.
Jod-: ~**präparat** *nt* iodine preparation; ~**quelle** *f* iodine (-containing) spring; ~**salbe** *f* iodine ointment; ~**tinktur** *f* iodine tincture.
Joga *m* -(s), *no pl* yoga.
Joghurt *m or nt* -s, -(s) yoghurt, yoghourt.
Jogi *m* -s, -s yogi.
Johann *m* - *siehe* **Johannes.**
Johanna *f* - Joanna. **(die heilige) ~ von Orléans** (Saint) Joan of Arc.
Johannes *m* - *or* (*ohne Artikel*) **Johannis** (*Bibl*) John.
Johannes|evangelium *nt* St John's Gospel, Gospel according to St John.
Johanni(s) *nt siehe* **Johannistag.**
Johannis-: ~**beere** *f* **rote/schwarze ~beere** redcurrant/blackcurrant; ~**beerstrauch** *m* redcurrant/blackcurrant bush; ~**brot** *nt* (*Bot*) carob; ~**fest** *nt* Midsummer's Day; ~**feuer** *nt* Midsummer's Eve bonfire; ~**käfer** *m* (*Glüh-*

würmchen) glow-worm; (*Junikäfer*) summer chafer; ~**nacht** *f* Midsummer's Eve; ~**tag** *m* Midsummer's Day; ~**trieb** *m* (*Bot*) lammas shoot; (*fig*) late romantic stirrings *pl*; ~**würmchen** *nt siehe* ~**käfer.**
Johanniter *m* -s, - Knight of St John of Jerusalem. **~ Unfallhilfe** St John's Ambulance (Brigade).
Johanniter|orden *m* Order of St John of Jerusalem.
johlen *vi* to howl.
Joint [dʒɔɪnt] *m* -s, -s (*inf*) joint (*inf*).
Joker ['joːkɐ, 'dʒɔːkɐ] *m* -s, - (*Cards*) joker.
Jokus *m* -, -se (*dated, inf*) jape (*dated*), joke, prank. **da hat sich jemand einen ~ gemacht** someone's been playing a prank.
Jolle *f* -, -n (*Naut*) jolly-boat, dinghy.
Jollenkreuzer *m* cabin yacht.
Jona *m* -, **Jonas** *m* - (*Bibl*) Jonah.
Jongleur [ʒõ'gløːɐ] *m* juggler.
jonglieren* [ʒõ'gliːrən] *vi* (*lit, fig*) to juggle.
Joppe *f* -, -n (*dial*) jacket.
Jordan *m* -s Jordan. **über den ~ gehen** (*inf*) to cross the great divide (*inf*).
Jordanien [-ɪən] *nt* -s Jordan.
Jordanier(in *f*) [-ɪɐ, -ɪərɪn] *m* -s, - Jordanian.
jordanisch *adj* Jordanian.
Josef, Joseph *m* - s Joseph.
Jot *nt* -, - (the letter) J/j.
Jota *nt* -(s), -s iota. **kein *or* nicht ein ~ not a jot *or* one iota.**
Jour fixe [ʒuːr'fiks] *m* - -, *no pl* (*dated geh*) meeting day; (*in Privathaus*) at-home.
Journaille [ʒʊr'naljə] *f* -, *no pl* (*pej*) yellow press; (*Presse im allgemeinen*) press; (*Journalisten*) hacks *pl* (*pej*).
Journal [ʒʊr'naːl] *nt* -s, -e **(a)** (*dated: Tagebuch*) journal (*old*), diary; (*Comm*) daybook; (*Naut*) log(-book). **(b)** (*dated: Zeitschrift*) magazine, periodical; (*old: Zeitung*) journal (*old*); (*Fach~*) journal.
Journaldienst *m* (*Aus*) *siehe* **Bereitschaftsdienst.**
Journalismus [ʒʊrna'lɪsmʊs] *m*, *no pl* journalism.
Journalist(in *f*) [ʒʊrna'lɪst, -ɪstɪn] *m* journalist.
Journalistenjargon *m* journalese.
Journalistik [ʒʊrna'lɪstɪk] *f*, *no pl* journalism.
journalistisch [ʒʊrna'lɪstɪʃ] *adj* journalistic.
jovial [jo'viaːl] *adj* jovial.
Jovialität [joviali'tɛːt] *f*, *no pl* joviality.
jr. *abbr of* **junior** jnr., jr.
Jubel *m* -s, *no pl* (*von Volk, Menge etc*) jubilation; (~**rufe** *auch*) cheering. **~, Trubel, Heiterkeit** laughter and merriment.
Jubel-: ~**braut** *f* woman celebrating her wedding anniversary; ~**feier** *f*, ~**fest** *nt* jubilee; (*Feierlichkeiten*) jubilee celebration; ~**geschrei** *nt* (*pej*) shouting and cheering; ~**greis** *m* old person celebrating a jubilee *or* anniversary; (*fig inf*) gay old spark (*inf*); ~**hochzeit** *f* special wedding anniversary (*silver, golden etc anniversary*); ~**jahr** *nt* jubilee year; **nur alle ~jahre** (*einmal*) (*inf*) once in a blue moon (*inf*).
jubeln *vi* to cheer, to shout with joy, to rejoice (*liter*). **jubelt nicht zu früh** don't start celebrating too early.
Jubel-: ~**paar** *nt* happy couple (*celebrating a special, e.g. silver or golden, wedding anniversary*); ~**ruf** *m* (*triumphant*) cheer; ~**tag** *m* (*silver, golden etc*) wedding anniversary.
Jubilar(in *f*) *m* person celebrating an anniversary.
Jubilate *no art* (*Eccl*) Jubilate (Sunday).
Jubiläum *nt* -s, **Jubiläen** jubilee; (*Jahrstag*) anniversary.
Jubiläums- in *cpds* jubilee.
jubilieren* *vi* (*liter*) to rejoice (*liter*); (*Vögel*) to sing joyfully; *siehe* **jubeln.**
juchhe(i), juchheißa, juchhu (*inf*) *interj* hurrah, hooray.
Juchten *nt or m* -s, *no pl* **(a)** (~*leder*) Russia leather *or* calf, Russia. **(b)** (*Parfüm*) Russian leather.
Juchtenleder *nt* Russia leather *or* calf, Russia.
juchzen *vi* to shriek with delight.
juckeln *vi aux sein* (*inf*) **(a)** (*hin und her rutschen*) to fidget. **(b)** (*schaukelnd fahren: Auto, Zug*) to jog *or* chug along. **er ist durch die Stadt/über Land gejuckelt** he's been jogging around town/across country.
jucken 1 *vti* to itch. **es juckt mich am Rücken, der Rücken juckt mir *or* mich** my back itches; **der Stoff juckt mich** this material makes me itch; **es juckt mich, das zu tun** (*inf*) I'm itching to do it (*inf*); **ihn juckt das Geld dabei** (*inf*) he finds the money attractive; **das juckt mich doch nicht** (*inf*) I don't care; **ihn *or* ihm juckt das Fell** (*inf*) *or* **der Buckel** (*inf*) he's asking for a good hiding; **wen's juckt, der kratze sich** (*prov*) if you don't like it you know what you can do (*inf*). **2** *vt* (*kratzen*) to scratch.
Juck-: ~**pulver** *nt* itching powder; ~**reiz** *m* itching; **einen ~reiz in der Nase haben** to have an itch in one's nose.
Judäa *nt* -s Jud(a)ea.
Judaismus *m* Judaism.
Judas[1] *m* - (*Bibl*) Judas.
Judas[2] *m* -, -se (*fig liter*) Judas.
Judas-: ~**baum** *m* Judas tree; ~**kuß** *m* (*liter*) Judas kiss; **der ~kuß** (*Bibl*) the Betrayal; ~**lohn** *m* (*liter*) blood money, thirty pieces of silver *pl*.
Jude *m* -n, -n Jew. **er ist ~** he is a Jew; *siehe* **ewig.**
jüdeln *vi* (*inf*) to speak with a Jewish accent.
Juden-: ~**christ** *m* Judaist, Judaeo-Christian; ~**christentum** *nt* Judaeo-Christianity; ~**deutsch(e)** *nt* (*rare*) *siehe* **Jiddisch(e)**; ~**feind** *m*, ~**gegner** *m* anti-Semite; **j~feindlich** *adj* anti-Semitic; ~**haß** *m* anti-Semitism; ~**heit** *f* Jewry; ~**stern** *m* star of David; ~**tum** *nt* (a) (*Judaismus*) Judaism; (b) (*Gesamtheit der* ~) Jews *pl*, Jewry; (c) (*jüdisches Wesen*) Jewishness; ~**verfolgung** *f* persecution of (the) Jews; ~**viertel** *nt* Jewish quarter.

Judikative [-'ti:və], **Judikatur** *f* (old) siehe **Recht-sprechung.**
Jüdin *f* Jew(ess).
jüdisch *adj* Jewish.
judizieren* *vi* (old, Jur) siehe **urteilen.**
Judo¹ *m* -s, -s (BRD) Young Democrat.
Judo² *nt* -s, *no pl* judo.
Judoka *m* -s, -s judoka.
Jugend *f* -, *no pl* (a) (~zeit) youth; (Jungsein, Jugendlichkeit auch) youthfulness. **frühe** ~ early youth, adolescence; **in ihrer** ~ **waren sie** ... in their youth they were ...; **von** ~ **an** or **auf** from one's youth.
  (b) (junge Menschen) youth, young people *pl.* **die heutige** ~ young people or the youth of today, modern youth; **die weibliche/männliche** ~ young women/men; ~ **hat keine Tugend** (Prov) young people are all the same; **Haus der** ~ (BRD) youth centre; **er verkehrt nur mit** ~ he only mixes with young people.
  (c) (Sport) youth team.
Jugend-: ~**alter** *nt* adolescence; ~**amt** *nt* youth welfare department; ~**arbeit** *f*, *no pl* (a) (Arbeit Jugendlicher) youth employment; (b) (~fürsorge) youth work; ~**arrest** *m* (Jur) detention, borstal (Brit); ~**bekanntschaft** *f* friend of one's youth; **j~bewegt** *adj* (iro) **j~bewegte Typen** middle-aged or overgrown school-boys'-girls (hum); ~**bewegung** *f* (a) youth movement; (b) (Hist) German Youth Movement (of the early 1920's); ~**bild** *nt* picture or photo taken when one was young; **das ist ein** ~**bild von mir** that's a picture of me when I was young; ~**bilder Churchills** photographs of the young Churchill; ~**bildnis** *nt* (Art, fig) youth; ~**bildnis von X** portrait of X as a young man/woman; ~**brigade** *f* (DDR) youth brigade (work team consisting of young people); ~**buch** *nt* book for the younger reader or young people; ~**bücherei** *f* library for the younger reader; ~**buchverlag** *m* publishing house specializing in literature for young people; ~**elf** *f* youth team; ~**erinnerung** *f* youthful memory; **meine** ~**erinnerungen** memories of my youth; **j~frei** *adj* Film U-(certificate), G (US); ~**freund** *m* friend of one's youth; ~**funk** *m* (Rad) broadcasting or radio for young people; (Sendung) broadcast or programme for young people; ~**fürsorge** *f* youth welfare; (für Schulkinder) child guidance; ~**gedicht** *nt* youthful poem; **j~gefährdend** *adj* liable to corrupt the young; ~**gericht** *nt* juvenile court; ~**gespiele** *m*, ~**gespielin** *f* (hum) young playmate; ~**gruppe** *f* youth group; ~**heim** *nt* (a) youth club; (b) (Wohnheim) young people's home.
Jugendherberge *f* youth hostel.
Jugendherbergs-: ~**mutter** *f*, ~**vater** *m* youth hostel warden; ~**verband** *m* Youth Hostel Association.
Jugend-: ~**hof** *m* siehe ~**heim** (b); ~**irresein** *nt* (Med) dementia praecox; ~**jahre** *pl* days of one's youth *pl*; ~**kriminalität** *f* juvenile delinquency.
jugendlich *adj* (jung) young; (von Jugend, jung wirkend) youthful. **er kleidet sich immer sehr** ~ he always wears very youthful or young-looking clothes; **eine** ~**e Erscheinung** a young- or youthful-looking person; ~**e Banden** gangs of youths; **ein** ~**er Täter** a young offender, a juvenile delinquent; ~**er Leichtsinn** youthful frivolity; **das sagst du so in deinem** ~**en Leichtsinn** (hum) I admire your confidence.
Jugendliche(r) *mf decl as adj* young person; (männlicher ~ auch) youth.
Jugendlichkeit *f* youthfulness.
Jugend-: ~**liebe** *f* (a) young love; (b) (Geliebter) love or sweetheart of one's youth; ~**literatur** *f* literature for younger readers or young people; ~**mannschaft** *f* youth team; ~**organisation** *f* youth organization; ~**pflege** *f* youth welfare; ~**pfleger** *m* youth (welfare) worker; ~**psychologie** *f* adolescent psychology; ~**recht** *nt* law relating to young persons; ~**richter** *m* (Jur) magistrate in a juvenile court; ~**schriften** *pl* publications for young people; (eines Autors) youthful writings; ~**schriftsteller** *m* writer of books for young people; ~**schutz** *m* protection of children and young people; ~**sendung** *f* (Rad) programme for younger listeners or (TV) younger viewers; ~**spiele** *pl* youth games *pl*; ~**stil** *m* (Art) Art Nouveau; ~**strafanstalt** *f* (form) reform school, approved school (Brit), borstal (Brit); ~**strafe** *f* detention no art in a reform school etc; ~**streich** *m* youthful exploit or escapade; ~**sünde** *f* youthful misdeed; ~**theater** *nt* youth theatre; ~**torheit** *f* youthful folly, folly of one's youth; ~**traum** *m* youthful dream; ~**verband** *m* youth organization; ~**verbot** *nt* **für einen Film** ~**verbot aussprechen** to ban a film for young people; ~**vorstellung** *f* performance for young people; ~**weihe** *f* (Rel) initiation; (DDR) ceremony in which 12-year-olds are given adult social status; ~**werk** *nt* youthful work; ~**wohlfahrtspflege** *f* youth welfare; ~**wohnheim** *nt* home for young people; ~**zeit** *f* youth, younger days *pl*; ~**zentrum** *nt* youth centre.
Jugoslawe *m* -n, -n Yugoslav.
Jugoslawien [-ən] *nt* -s Yugoslavia.
Jugoslawin *f* Yugoslav.
jugoslawisch *adj* Yugoslav(ian).
Julei *m* -s, -s (esp Comm) siehe **Juli.**
Juli *m* -(s), -s July; siehe **März.**
julianisch *adj* **der J~e Kalender** the Julian Calendar.
Juliusturm *m* (inf) secret vault.
Jumbo(-Jet) ['jumbo(dʒet)] *m* -s, -s Jumbo (jet).
Jumper ['jumpɐ, 'dʒampɐ] *m* -s, - jumper (Brit), sweater.
jun. abbr of **junior** jun.
jung *adj, comp* ¨**er**, *superl* ¨**ste(r, s)** (lit, fig) young; Aktien new. ~ **und alt** (both) young and old; **von** ~ **auf** from one's youth; **der** ~**e Meyer** young Meyer; (Sohn) Meyer junior; **sie ist 18 Jahre** ~ (hum) she's 18 years young (hum); ~ **heiraten/sterben** to marry/die young; **sich** (dat) **ein** ~**es Herz bewahren** to stay

young at heart; ~ **gefreit, nie gereut** (Prov) if you marry young you won't regret it; **so** ~ **kommen wir nicht mehr zusammen** (hum) you're only young once; siehe **jünger, jüngste(r, s).**
Jung-: ~**akademiker** *m* graduate; ~**arbeiter** *m* juvenile employee or worker; ~**bauer** *m* young farmer; ~**brunnen** *m* fountain of youth; ~**bürger** *m* junior citizen.
Jungchen *nt* (inf) lad(die) (inf).
Jung-: ~**demokrat** *m* (BRD) Young Democrat; ~**dichter** *m* (iro) young poet.
Junge¹ *m* -n, -n or (dated inf) -ns or (inf) Jungs boy; (Lauf~) errand-boy; (Cards) jack, knave. ~, ~! (inf) boy oh boy (inf); **sie ist ein richtiger** ~ she's a real tomboy; **alter** ~ (inf) my old mate (inf) or pal (inf); **mein lieber** ~! my dear boy; (in Brief) my dear son; **ein schwerer** ~ (inf) a (big-time) crook; **unsere Jungs haben gewonnen** our boys or lads won.
Junge² *mf* -n, *no pl* (inf) **der/die** ~ Mr/Miss X junior, the young Mr/Miss X.
Jüngelchen *nt* (pej) young lad.
jungen *vi* to have young; (Hündin auch) to have pups; (Katze auch) to have kittens.
Jungen-: ~**gesicht** *nt* boy's or boyish face; **j~haft** *adj* boyish; **sie ist ein j~haftes Mädchen** she's a bit of a tomboy; ~**klasse** *f* (Sch) boys' class; ~**schule** *f* boys' school; ~**streich** *m* boyish prank or trick.
jünger *adj* (a) comp of **jung** younger. **sie sieht** ~ **aus, als sie ist** she looks younger than she is, she doesn't look her age; **Holbein der J~e** Holbein the Younger, the younger Holbein. (b) Geschichte, Entwicklung etc recent. **die** ~**e Steinzeit** the later or New Stone Age.
Jünger *m* -s, - (Bibl, fig) disciple.
jüngerhaft *adj* disciple-like, acolytic (liter). **sie scharten sich** ~ **um ihn** they gathered around him like disciples.
Jüngerin *f* disciple.
Jüngerschaft *f* disciples *pl*; (Jüngertum) discipleship.
Junge(s) *nt decl as adj* (Zool) young one; (von Hund) pup(py); (von Katze) kitten; (von Wolf, Löwe, Bär) cub; (von Vogel) young bird, nestling. **die** ~**n** the young.
Jungfer *f* -, -n (a) (old, hum) (ledige Frau) spinster. **eine alte** ~ an old maid. (b) (old: Jungfrau) virgin, maiden (old); (als Anrede) mistress (old). (c) (Kammer~) maid.
jüngferlich *adj* old-maidish.
Jungfern-: ~**fahrt** *f* maiden voyage; ~**flug** *m* maiden flight; ~**häutchen** *nt* (Anat) hymen (Anat), maidenhead; ~**inseln** *pl* Virgin Islands *pl*; ~**kranz** *m* (old) (bridal) bouquet; ~**rede** *f* (Parl) maiden speech; ~**reise** *f* siehe ~**fahrt**; ~**schaft** *f*, *no pl* siehe **Jungfräulichkeit**; ~**stand** *m* (old) spinsterhood; ~**zeugung** *f* (Biol) parthenogenesis.
Jungfilmer *m* young film maker. **die deutschen** ~ the young German film makers.
Jungfrau *f* virgin; (Astron, Astrol) Virgo no art. **ich bin** ~ I am a virgin; **I am (a) Virgo; die** ~ **Maria** the Virgin Mary; **die heilige** ~ the Blessed or Holy Virgin; **die** ~ **von Orléans** Joan of Arc, the Maid of Orleans; **dazu bin ich gekommen wie die** ~ **zum Kind(e)** it just fell into my hands; siehe **eisern.**
jungfräulich *adj* Mädchen, Schnee virgin; (liter) Seele pure, innocent.
Jungfräulichkeit *f* siehe *adj* virginity; purity, innocence.
Junggeselle *m* bachelor; (old: Handwerksgeselle) journeyman.
Junggesellen-: ~**bude** *f* (inf) bachelor pad (inf); ~**dasein** *nt*, ~**leben** *nt* bachelor's life; ~**tum** *nt* bachelorhood, bachelordom; ~**wirtschaft** *f* (inf) bachelor squalor; ~**wohnung** *f* bachelor flat; ~**zeit** *f* bachelor days *pl*.
Junggesellin *f* bachelor girl; (über 40) single woman.
Junglehrer *m* student teacher.
Jüngling *m* (liter, hum) youth.
Jünglings-: ~**alter** *nt* (liter) youth; **j~haft** *adj* (geh) youthful, boyish.
Jung-: ~**mädel** *nt* (dated) young girl; ~**mann** *m*, *pl* ~**männer** (dated) young man; ~**redakteur** *m* young journalist; ~**sozialist** *m* (BRD) Young Socialist.
jüngst *adv* (geh) recently, lately. **der** ~ **verstorbene** ... the late ...; **der** ~ **erlassene Befehl** the recent decree.
Jungsteinzeit *f* Neolithic age, New Stone Age.
jüngstens *adv* (old, liter) siehe **jüngst.**
jüngste(r, s) *adj* (a) superl of **jung** youngest. (b) Werk, Schöpfung, Ereignis latest, (most) recent; Zeit, Vergangenheit recent. **in der** ~**n Zeit** recently; **in ein Ausdruck aus der** ~**n Zeit** a recent expression; **das J~ Gericht** the Last Judgement; **der J~ Tag** Doomsday, the Day of Judgement; **man merkt, daß er/sie nicht mehr der J~** ist you can tell that he/she is not as young as he/she used to be; **sie ist auch nicht mehr die J~** she's no chicken (inf).
Jung-: ~**stier** *m* young steer; ~**tier** *nt* young animal; ~**türke** *m* (Pol sl) young Turk; ~**verheiratete(r)** *mf decl as adj* newly-wed; **j~vermählt** *adj* (geh) newly-wed, recently married; **die** ~**vermählten** the newly-weds; ~**vieh** *nt* young cattle *pl*; ~**wähler** *m* young voter; ~**wild** *nt* young game.
Juni *m* -(s), -s June; siehe **März.**
Junikäfer *m* chafer.
junior *adj* Franz Schulz ~ Franz Schulz, Junior.
Junior(in *f*) ['ju:niɔr, -'nio:rɪn] *m* (a) junior. **wie geht's dem** ~? how's junior? (b) (auch ~chef) son/nephew etc of the chairman/boss. **kann ich mal den** ~(chef) **sprechen?** can I speak to Mr X junior?
Juniorpartner *m* junior partner.
Junker *m* -s, - (Hist) squire; (preußisch) Junker.
Junkertum *nt*, *no pl* squirarchy; (in Preußen) Junkerdom.
Junktim *nt* -s, -s (Pol: Paket) package (deal). **zwischen X und Y besteht ein** ~ X is dependent on Y.

Juno m -s, -s (esp Comm) June.
Junta ['xʊnta, 'junta] f -, **Junten** (Pol) junta.
Jupe [ʒyp] m -s, -s (Sw) skirt.
Jupiter m -s Jupiter.
Jupiterlampe ® f klieg light.
jur. abbr of **juristisch**.
Jura[1] m -s, no pl (Geol, Geog) Jura (Mountains) pl.
Jura[2] no art (Univ) law.
Jurastudium nt study of law. **das ~ dauert acht Semester** the law degree (course) takes four years.
juridisch adj (old, Aus) siehe **juristisch**.
Jurisdiktion f (geh) administration of justice; (rare: Gerichtshoheit) jurisdiction.
Jurisprudenz f (geh) jurisprudence.
Jurist m jurist, legal eagle (hum inf); (Student) law student.
Juristen-: ~**deutsch** nt, ~**sprache** f, no pl legalese (pej), legal jargon or language.
Juristerei f, no pl (inf) law.
Juristin f jurist; law student.
juristisch adj legal; Problem etc auch juridical (form); Studium auch law attr. **die J~e Fakultät** the Faculty of Law; **eine ~e Person** a legal entity, a corporation, a corporate body.
Juror(in f) ['juːrɔr, -'roːrɪn] m juror, member of the jury; (bei Wettbewerb) member of the jury, judge, adjudicator.
Jurte f -, -n jurt.
Jury [ʒy'riː, 'ʒyːriː] f -, -s jury sing or pl; (bei Wettbewerb auch) judges pl, adjudicators pl.
Jus[1] nt -, no pl (Aus) siehe **Jura**[2].
Jus[2] [ʒy:] f or m or nt -, no pl (a) (Bratensaft) gravy; (geliert) dripping. (b) (Sw: Fruchtsaft) juice.
Juso m -s, -s (BRD) abbr of **Jungsozialist** Young Socialist.
just adv (old) precisely, exactly, just. **~ gekommen** just come.
justament adv (old) (a) (genau, richtig) precisely. (b) (erst recht) **wenn man ihn kritisierte, wollte er ~ nicht gehorchen** if you criticized him he would refuse to obey just out of spite.

justieren* vt to adjust; Gewehr, Zielfernrohr etc auch to collimate (form); Münzen auch to weight; (Typ) to justify.
Justierschraube f (Tech) adjusting screw.
Justierung f siehe vt adjustment; collimation (form); weighting; justification.
Justierwaage f adjusting balance.
Justitia [jus'tiːtsia] f -s Justice; (fig) the law.
justitiabel [justi'tsiaːbl] adj (geh) litigable.
Justitiar [justi'tsiaːr] m lawyer, legal adviser.
Justiz [jus'tiːts] f -, no pl (als Prinzip) justice; (als Institution) judiciary; (die Gerichte) courts pl.
Justiz-: ~**beamte(r)** m judicial officer; ~**behörde** f legal or judicial authority; ~**hoheit** f legal sovereignty; ~**irrtum** m miscarriage of justice; ~**minister** m minister of justice, justice minister, ≈ Attorney General (US), ≈ Lord (High) Chancellor (Brit); ~**ministerium** nt ministry of justice, ≈ Department of Justice (US); ~**mord** m judicial murder; ~**palast** m palace of justice; ~**verwaltung** f administration of justice; ~**vollzugsanstalt** f (form) place of detention; ~**wachtmeister** m court attendant.
Jute f -, no pl jute.
Jütland nt -s (Geog) Jutland.
juvenil [juve'niːl] adj (geh) juvenile.
Juwel[1] [ju'veːl] m or nt -s, -en jewel, gem. ~**en** (Schmuck) jewellery, jewelry.
Juwel[2] nt -s, -e (fig) jewel, gem.
Juwelier m -s, -e jeweller; (Geschäft) jeweller's (shop).
Juwelier-: ~**arbeit** f jewel(le)ry (work); ~**geschäft** nt jeweller's (shop); ~**waren** pl jewel(le)ry.
Jux m -es, -e (inf) **etw aus ~ tun/sagen** to do/say sth as a joke or in fun; **etw aus lauter ~ und Tollerei tun** to do sth out of sheer high spirits; **sich** (dat) **einen ~ aus etw machen** to make a joke (out) of sth.
juxen vi (inf) to joke.
jwd [jɔtve:'de:] adv (hum) in the back of beyond; (weit entfernt) miles out (inf).

K

K, k [kaː] nt -, - K, k.
Kaaba f -, no pl Kaaba, Caaba.
Kabale f -, -n (old) cabal (old).
Kabarett nt -s, -e or -s (a) cabaret; (Darbietung auch) cabaret show; (in Bar etc auch) floor show. **ein politisches ~** a satirical political revue, a political satire. (b) (Servierplatte) serving dish (divided into sections).
Kabarettist(in f) m cabaret artist.
kabarettistisch adj Darbietung cabaret; Stil revue attr; Eskapaden farcical.
Kabäuschen [ka'bɔysçən] nt (inf) (Zimmer) cubbyhole (inf); (Laube) hut, cabin.
Kabbala f - (Rel) cabbala.
Kabbalistik f cabbalism.
kabbalistisch adj cabbalistic.
Kabbelei f (inf) bickering, squabbling.
kabbelig adj Meer choppy.
kabbeln vir (inf) to bicker, to squabble.
Kabel nt -s, - (a) (Elec) wire; (von Elektrogeräten auch) flex; (Telefon~) flex, cord; (Strom- oder Telegraphenleitung) cable. (b) (old Naut: Tau) rope; (Drahtseil) cable. (c) (Telegramm) cable(gram).
Kabel-: ~**bericht** m cabled report; ~**dampfer** m cable ship; ~**fernsehen** nt cable television.
Kabeljau m -s, -e or -s cod.
Kabel-: ~**länge** f (Naut) cable, cable's length; ~**leger** m -s, - (Naut) cable layer; ~**mantel** m cable covering.
kabeln vti to cable.
Kabel-: ~**schiff** nt cable ship; ~**trommel** f cable drum or reel; ~**wort** nt **ein ~wort kostet 90 Pf** a cable costs 90 pfennigs per word.
Kabine f (Umkleide~, Anprobier~, Dusch~) cubicle; (Naut, Aviat, von Kran) cabin; (Telec, zum Plattenhören auch) booth; (Vorführ~) projection room; (Seilbahn~) car.
Kabinen-: ~**bahn** f cable railway; ~**koffer** m cabin trunk; ~**roller** m bubble-car.
Kabinett[1] nt -s, -e (a) (Pol) cabinet. (b) (für Kunstsammlungen) (Raum) gallery; (Schrank) cabinet. (c) (Zimmer) (Aus: kleines Zimmer) closet; (old: Arbeitszimmer) cabinet.
Kabinett[2] m -s, -e m siehe ~**wein**.
Kabinetts-: ~**beschluß** m cabinet decision; ~**frage** f (rare) siehe Vertrauensfrage; ~**justiz** f interference in the course of justice by a sovereign; ~**mitglied** nt cabinet member, member of the cabinet.

Kabinett-: ~**stück** nt (a) (old: einer Sammlung) showpiece, pièce de résistance; (b) (fig) masterstroke; ~**wein** m high quality German white wine.
Kabrio nt -(s), -s (inf) convertible.
Kabriolett [kabrio'let, (Aus, S Ger) kabrio'le:] nt -s, -s (a) (Aut) convertible. (b) (Hist) cabriolet.
Kabuff nt -s, -e or -s (inf) (poky) little corner.
Kachel f -, -n (glazed) tile. **etw mit ~n auslegen** to tile sth, to cover sth with or in tiles.
kacheln vt to tile.
Kachelofen m tiled stove.
Kacke f -, no pl (vulg) crap (vulg), shit (vulg).
kacken vi (vulg) to crap (vulg), to shit (vulg).
Kacker m -s, - (sl) stupid shit (sl).
kackig adj (sl) Farbe shitty (sl).
Kadaver [ka'daːvr] m -s, - carcass.
Kadavergehorsam m (pej) blind or slavish obedience.
Kadenz f cadence; (Improvisation) cadenza.
Kader m -s, - (Mil, Pol) cadre; (Sport) squad; (DDR, Sw) (Fachleute) group of specialists; (Fachmann) specialist; (Sw: Vorgesetzte) management.
Kaderleiter m (DDR) personnel officer.
Kadett m -en, -en (Mil) cadet. **ihr ~en!** (inf: ungezogene Jungen) you rascals.
Kadetten-: ~**anstalt** f cadet school; ~**schulschiff** nt naval (cadet) training ship.
Kadi m -s, -s (dated inf) beak (inf). **jdn vor den ~ schleppen** to take sb to court; **zum ~ laufen** to go to court.
Kadmium nt -s cadmium.
Käfer m -s, - (a) beetle (auch inf: VW). (b) (sl: Mädchen) bird (esp Brit inf), chick (esp US inf). **ein flotter ~** (dated inf) a nice bit of skirt (Brit inf).
Kaff nt -s, -s or -e (inf) dump (inf), hole (inf).
Kaffee[1] [or ka'fe:] m -s, -s (a) coffee. **zwei ~, bitte!** two coffees please; **~ mit Milch** white coffee (Brit), coffee with milk; ~ **verkehrt** (dated) white coffee (made with hot milk) (Brit), coffee with hot milk; **~ kochen** to make coffee; **das ist kalter ~** (inf) that's old hat (inf); **da kommt einem der ~ hoch** (sl) it makes you sick (inf); **dir haben sie wohl was in den ~ getan?** (inf) you must be joking or kidding (inf).
(b) no pl (Nachmittags~) ≈ (afternoon) tea. **~ und Kuchen** coffee and cakes; ≈ afternoon tea; **jdn zu ~ und Kuchen einladen** to invite sb for or to (afternoon) tea.
Kaffee[2] nt -s, -s (old) siehe **Café**.

Kaffee-: ~bohne f coffee bean; k~braun adj coffee-coloured; ~-Ersatz m coffee substitute; ~-Extrakt m coffee essence; ~filter m coffee filter; (inf: Filterpapier) filter (paper); ~geschirr nt coffee set; ~haube f siehe ~wärmer; ~haus nt café; ~hausmusik f (pej) palm court music; ~kanne f coffeepot; ~klatsch (inf) m -s, no pl, ~kränzchen nt coffee klatsch (US), hen party (inf), ≈ coffee morning; ich treffe mich mit meinen Freundinnen zu einem ~klatsch I'm meeting some friends for a chat over (a cup of) coffee or tea; ~löffel m coffee spoon; ~maschine f coffee machine; ~mischung f blended coffee; ~mühle f coffee grinder; ~mütze f siehe ~wärmer; ~pause f coffee break; ~satz m coffee grounds pl; aus dem ~satz wahrsagen or lesen to read (the) tea leaves; ~service nt coffee set; ~sieb nt coffee strainer; ~sorte f type or sort of coffee; ~strauch m coffee tree; ~stube f coffee shop; ~tante f (hum) coffee addict; (in Café) old biddy; ~tasse f coffee cup; ~tisch m (Frühstückstisch) breakfast table; (nachmittags) (afternoon) tea table; ~wärmer m -s, - cosy (for coffee pot); ~wasser nt water for coffee, coffee water; ich habe das ~wasser schon aufgesetzt I've just put the kettle on; ~zusatz m coffee additive.

Kaffer m (a) -n, -n kaffir; (pej inf) nigger. (b) -s, - (pej inf: dummer Kerl) thickhead (inf), duffer (inf).

Käfig m -s, -e cage. sie sitzt in einem goldenen ~ (fig) she is just a bird in a gilded cage.

Käfigvogel m cage bird.

Kafiller m -s, - (dial) knacker.

kafkaesk adj kafkaesque.

Kaftan m -s, -e caftan.

kahl adj Mensch, Kopf bald; (~geschoren) shaved, shorn; Vogel bald, featherless; Wand, Raum bare; Pflanze, Baum bare, leafless; Landschaft, Berge barren, bleak. eine ~e Stelle a bald patch; ~ werden (Mensch) to go bald; (Baum) to lose its leaves.

Kahl-: ~fraß m defoliation; k~fressen vt sep irreg to strip bare; Ernte to destroy completely; ~frost m black frost; k~geschoren 1 ptp of k~scheren; 2 adj Kopf shaven, shorn; ~heit f siehe adj baldness; featherlessness; bareness, leaflessness; barrenness, bareness; ~hieb m (Abholzung) clearing, clearance, deforestation; (abgeholzte Fläche) clearing; ~kopf m bald head; (Mensch) bald person; ein ~kopf sein to be bald; k~köpfig adj bald(-headed); ~köpfigkeit f baldness, baldheadedness; k~scheren vt sep irreg Schafe to shear; Hecken to cut right back; jdn k~scheren to shave sb's head; ~schlag m (a) (abgeholzte Fläche) clearing, (b) (Tätigkeit) deforestation; (c) (inf) (Aktion) ~schlag (Entlassungen) axing; (Abriß) demolition; k~schlagen vt sep irreg to deforest, to clear; ~wild nt (geweihlose, weibliche Tiere) does pl; (geweihlose Kälber) fawns pl.

Kahm m -(e)s, no pl mould.

kahmig adj mouldy.

Kahn m -(e)s, -̈e (a) (small) boat; (Stech~) punt. ~ fahren to go boating/punting. (b) (Lastschiff) barge. ein alter ~ (inf) an old tub (inf). (c) (inf) (Bett) bed, pit (inf); (Gefängnis) jug (dated inf); (Ftbl: Tor) net. ~e (inf) (große Schuhe) clodhoppers (inf).

Kahnfahrt f row; (in Stechkahn) punt.

Kai m -s, -e or -s quay; (Uferdamm auch) waterfront.

Kaianlage f quayside.

Kaiman m -s, -e (Zool) cayman.

Kaimauer f quay wall.

Kainsmal, Kainszeichen nt (Stigma) mark of Cain.

Kairo nt -s Cairo.

Kaiser m -s, - emperor. der deutsche ~ the German Emperor, the Kaiser; wo nichts ist, hat der ~ sein Recht verloren (Prov) you can't get blood from a stone; gebt dem ~, was des ~s ist! (Bibl) render unto Caesar the things which are Caesar's; (da,) wo selbst der ~ zu Fuß hingeht (dated hum) the smallest room (in the house) (hum); sich um des ~s Bart streiten (fig) to split hairs; das ist ein Streit um des ~s Bart that's just splitting hairs; er kommt sich vor wie der ~ von China (inf) he thinks he's the king of the castle or God.

Kaiser-: ~adler m imperial eagle; ~haus nt imperial family.

Kaiserin f empress.

Kaiserinmutter f dowager empress.

Kaiserkrone f (a) imperial crown. (b) (Bot) crown imperial.

kaiserlich adj imperial. diese Besitzungen waren früher ~ these possessions used to belong to the Emperor; Seine K~e Majestät His Imperial Majesty; ~ gesinnt monarchistic, imperialistic.

Kaiserliche(r) m decl as adj Imperialist.

kaiserlich-königlich adj imperial and royal (pertaining to the Dual Monarchy of Austro-Hungary).

Kaiser-: ~pfalz f imperial palace; ~reich nt empire; ~schmarr(e)n m -s, - (Aus) sugared, cut-up pancake with raisins; ~schnitt m Caesarean (section); ~stadt f imperial city.

Kaisertum nt (a) Empire. (b) siehe Kaiserwürde (b).

Kaiser-: ~wetter nt (dated) magnificent sunshine; ~würde f (a) (Ehre) honour or dignity of an emperor; (b) (Amt) emperorship.

Kajak m or nt -s, -s kayak.

Kaje f -, -n (N Ger) siehe Kai.

Kajütboot nt cabin boat.

Kajüte f -, -n cabin; (größer auch) stateroom.

Kakadu m -s, -s cockatoo.

Kakao [auch ka'kau] m -s, -s cocoa. jdn durch den ~ ziehen (inf) (veralbern) to make fun of sb, to take the mickey out of sb (inf); (boshaft reden) to run or do sb down.

Kakao-: ~bohne f cocoa bean; ~pulver nt cocoa powder; ~strauch m cacao palm.

kakeln vi (inf) to chat, to blether (inf).

Kakerlak m -s or -en, -en cockroach.

Kakophonie f (geh) cacophony.

Kaktee f -, -n [-eːən], **Kaktus** m -, Kakteen [-eːən] or (inf) -se cactus.

Kalabreser m -s, - slouch hat.

Kalabrien [-iən] nt -s Calabria.

Kalamität f (geh) calamity; (heikle Lage) predicament.

Kalander m -s, - (Tech) calender.

kalandern vt (Tech) to calender.

Kalauer m -s, - corny joke; (Wortspiel) corny pun; (alter Witz) old chestnut.

kalauern vi (inf) to joke; to pun.

Kalb nt -(e)s, -̈er (a) calf; (von Rehwild auch) fawn; siehe golden, stechen. (b) (inf: Mädchen) silly young girl or thing.

Kälbchen nt dim of Kalb.

Kalbe f -, -n heifer.

kalben vi (Kuh, Gletscher) to calve.

Kalberei f fooling or messing around or about (inf).

kälbern, kalbern vi (inf) to fool or mess about or around (inf).

Kälberne(s) nt decl as adj (S Ger, Aus) veal.

Kalb-: ~fell nt siehe Kalbsfell; ~fleisch nt veal; ~leder nt siehe ~sleder.

Kälblein nt dim of Kalb.

Kalbs-: ~braten m roast veal; ~fell nt (a) (Fell) calfskin; (b) (old: Trommel) drum; ~hachse, ~haxe f (Cook) knuckle of veal; ~keule f leg of veal; ~leber f calves' liver; ~leder nt calfskin; ~schnitzel nt veal cutlet.

Kaldaune f -, -n entrails pl.

Kalebasse f -, -n calabash.

Kaledonien [-iən] nt -s (liter) Caledonia.

Kaleidoskop nt -s, -e kaleidoscope.

kaleidoskopisch adj kaleidoscopic.

kalendarisch adj calendrical.

Kalendarium nt (geh, Eccl) calendar.

Kalender m -s, - calendar; (Taschen~) diary. etw im ~ rot anstreichen to make sth a red-letter day.

Kalender-: ~block m day-by-day calendar; ~jahr nt calendar year; ~monat m calendar month; ~spruch m calendar motto.

Kalesche f -, -n (Hist) barouche.

Kalfakter m -s, -, **Kalfaktor** m (a) (old: Heizer) boilerman, stoker. (b) (allgemeiner Gehilfe) odd-job man.

kalfatern* vti (Naut) to caulk.

Kali nt -s, -s potash.

Kaliber nt -s, - (lit, fig) calibre; (zum Messen) calibrator.

Kali-: ~bergwerk nt potash mine; ~dünger m potash fertilizer.

Kalif m -en, -en caliph.

Kalifat nt caliphate.

Kalifornien [-iən] nt -s California.

kalifornisch adj Californian.

kalihaltig adj containing potassium.

Kaliko m -s, -s calico; (für Buchbinderei) cloth.

Kali-: ~salpeter m saltpetre; ~salz nt potassium salt.

Kalium nt, no pl potassium.

Kalk m -(e)s, -e lime; (zum Tünchen) whitewash; (Anat) calcium. gebrannter/gelöschter ~ quicklime/slaked lime; Wände/Decken mit ~ bewerfen to whitewash walls/ceilings; bei ihm rieselt schon der ~ (inf) he's going a bit gaga (inf) or losing his marbles (inf).

Kalk-: k~artig adj chalky, calcareous (form); ~boden m chalky soil; ~brennerei f lime works sing or pl; ~bruch m siehe ~steinbruch.

kalken vt (a) (tünchen) to whitewash. (b) (Agr) to lime.

Kalk-: ~erde f chalky soil; ~grube f lime pit; k~haltig adj Boden chalky; Wasser hard; ~mangel m (Med) calcium deficiency; (von Boden) lime deficiency; ~ofen m lime kiln; ~stein m limestone; ~steinbruch m limestone quarry.

Kalkül m or nt -s, -e (a) calculation usu pl. (b) (Math) calculus.

Kalkulation f calculation; (Kostenberechnung) estimating.

Kalkulator m (old) siehe Buchhalter.

kalkulatorisch adj arithmetical. ~e Methoden methods of calculation; das ist ~ einwandfrei, aber ... the figures are perfect, but ...

kalkulieren* vt to calculate.

Kalligraphie f calligraphy.

kallös adj (Med) callous.

Kallus m -, -se (Biol, Med) callus.

Kalme f -, -n (Naut) calm.

Kalmen-: ~gürtel m, ~zone f calm belt or zones pl.

Kalmück(e) m -en, -en Kalmu(c)k (member of Mongol tribe).

Kalorie f calorie.

Kalorien- [-iən]: k~arm adj low-calorie; ~gehalt m calorie content; k~reich adj high-calorie.

kalt adj, comp -̈er, superl -̈este(r, s) or (adv) am -̈esten cold. mir ist/wird ~ I am/I'm getting cold; im K~en in the cold; ~ schlafen to sleep in an unheated room; ~e Platte cold meal; abends essen wir ~ we eat a cold meal in the evening; etw ~ stellen to put sth to chill; etw ~ bearbeiten (Tech) to work sth cold; die Wohnung kostet ~ 480 DM the flat costs 480 DM without heating; ~ rauchen (hum) to have an unlit cigarette in one's mouth; jdm die ~e Schulter zeigen to give sb the cold shoulder, to cold-shoulder sb; ~e Heimat (pej) former eastern areas of Germany, now Poland or Russia; da kann ich nur ~ lächeln (inf) that makes me laugh; ~er Angstschweiß trat ihm auf die Stirn he broke out in a cold sweat; ~es Grausen or Entsetzen überkam mich my blood ran cold; es überlief ihn ~ cold shivers ran through him; der ~e or K~e Krieg the Cold War; ~er Krieger cold warrior; auf ~em Wege unceremoniously; ein ~er Staatsstreich a bloodless coup.

Kalt-: k~bleiben vi sep irreg aux sein (fig) to remain unmoved *or* impassive; ~**blut** *nt, pl* ~**blüter** carthorse; ~**blüter** *m* -s, - (*Zool*) cold-blooded animal; **k~blütig** *adj* (a) (*fig*) *Mensch, Mord* cold-blooded; (*gelassen*) *Handlung* cool; *Mensch* cool, cool-headed, calm; **sie ist k~blütig hineingegangen** she just walked in as cool as you please; (b) (*Zool*) cold-blooded; ~**blütigkeit** *f siehe adj* cold-bloodedness; cool(ness); cool-headedness.

Kälte *f* -, *no pl* (a) (*von Wetter, Material etc*) cold; (~*periode*) cold spell. **die ~ des Stahls/Steins** *etc* the coldness *or* cold of the steel/stone *etc*; **fünf Grad ~** five degrees of frost *or* below freezing; **vor ~ zittern** to shiver with cold; **die ~ läßt nach** it is becoming milder; **bei dieser ~** in this cold; **hier ist eine solche ~, daß ...** it is so cold here that ...
(b) (*fig*) coldness, coolness. **geschlechtliche ~** sexual coldness, frigidity.

Kälte-: ~**anlage** *f* refrigeration plant; **k~beständig, k~fest** *adj* cold-resistant; ~**einbruch** *m* cold spell; **k~empfindlich** *adj* sensitive to cold; *Mensch auch* chilly; ~**erzeugung** *f* refrigeration; ~**gefühl** *nt* feeling of cold(ness); ~**grad** *m* degree of frost; ~**maschine** *f* refrigeration machine; ~**pol** *m* (*Geog*) cold pole, pole of cold; ~**resistenz** *f* cold-resistance, resistance to cold; ~**sturz** *m siehe* ~**einbruch**; ~**technik** *f* refrigeration technology; ~**tod** *m* **den** ~**tod sterben** to freeze to death, to die of exposure; (*Erde*) **to freeze over** completely; ~**welle** *f* cold spell.

Kalt-: ~**front** *f siehe* ~(**luft**)**front**; ~**haus** *nt* refrigerated glasshouse; **k~herzig** *adj* cold-hearted; **k~lächelnd** *adv* (*iro*) cool as you please; **k~lassen** *vt sep irreg* (*fig*) **jdn k~lassen** to leave sb cold; ~**leim** *m* wood glue; ~(**luft**)**front** *f* (*Met*) cold front; **k~machen** *vt sep* (*sl*) to do in (*inf*); ~**miete** *f* rent exclusive of heating; ~**schale** *f* (*Cook*) cold sweet soup; **k~schnäuzig** *adj* (*inf*) (*gefühllos*) cold, unfeeling, callous; (*unverschämt*) insolent; *Kritiker* sarky (*inf*), sarcastic; **k~schnäuzig sagte sie ...** as cool as you please she said ...; ~**schnäuzigkeit** *f* (*inf*) *siehe adj* coldness, unfeelingness, callousness; insolence; sarcasm; **k~stellen** *vt sep* (*inf*) **jdn** to demote, to put out of harm's way (*inf*); ~**wasserkur** *f siehe* **Kneippkur**; ~**welle** *f* (*Frisur*) cold perm *or* wave.

Kalvarienberg [kalˈvaːriən-] *m* Calvary.
kalvinisch [kalˈviːnɪʃ] *adj* calvinistic.
Kalvinismus [kalviˈnɪsmus] *m* Calvinism.
Kalvinist(in *f*) [kalviˈnɪst(ɪn)] *m* Calvinist.
kalvinistisch [kalviˈnɪstɪʃ] *adj* calvinist(ic).
Kalzium *nt, no pl* calcium.
kam *pret of* **kommen**.
Kamarilla [kamaˈrɪlja, kamaˈriːla] *f* -, **Kamarillen** (*geh*) political clique.
Kamee *f* -, -n [-eːən] cameo.
Kamel *nt* -(e)s, -e (a) camel. **eher geht ein ~ durchs Nadelöhr ...** it is easier for a camel to go through the eye of a needle ... (b) (*inf*) clot (*Brit inf*), clown (*inf*). **ich ~!** silly *or* stupid me!
Kamel-: ~**fohlen**, ~**füllen** *nt* camel foal; ~**haar** *nt* (*Tex*) camel hair.
Kamelie [-iə] *f* camellia.
Kamelle *f* *usu pl* (*inf*) **das sind doch alte** *or* **olle ~n** that's old hat (*inf*); **er hat nichts als alte** *or* **olle ~n erzählt** he just said the same old things.
Kameltreiber *m* camel driver, cameleer; (*pej: Orientale*) wog (*pej*).
Kamera *f* -, -s camera.
Kamerad *m* -en, -en (*Mil etc*) comrade; (*Gefährte, Lebens~*) companion, friend; (*dated: Arbeits~*) workmate; (*dated: Freund*) friend, buddy (*inf*), chum (*inf*).
Kameraderie *f* (*pej*) bonhomie.
Kameradschaft *f* comradeship, camaraderie.
kameradschaftlich *adj* comradely. **eine ~e Ehe** a companionate marriage.
Kameradschaftlichkeit *f* comradeship, comradeliness.
Kameradschafts-: ~**abend** *m* reunion; ~**ehe** *f* companionate marriage; ~**geist** *m* spirit of comradeship, esprit de corps.
Kameraführung *f* camera work.
Kameralistik *f* (*old*) finance.
Kamera-: ~**mann** *m, pl* ~**männer** cameraman; ~**schwenk** *m* pan.
Kamerun *nt* -s the Cameroons *pl*.
Kamille *f* -, -n camomile.
Kamillentee *m* camomile tea.
Kamin *m or* (*dial*) *nt* -s, -e (a) (*Schornstein*) chimney; (*Abzugsschacht*) flue. **etw in den ~ schreiben** to write sth off. (b) (*offene Feuerstelle*) fireplace. **eine Plauderei am ~** a fireside chat; **wir saßen am** *or* **vor dem ~** we sat by *or* in front of the fire *or* round the hearth. (c) (*Geol: Fels~*) chimney.
Kamin-: ~**feger**, ~**kehrer** *m* -s, - (*dial*) chimney sweep; ~**feuer** *nt* open fire, fire in the grate; ~**sims** *m or nt* mantelpiece; ~**vorsetzer** *m* -s, - fireguard.
Kamm *m* -(e)s, ~̈e (a) (*für Haar, Webe~*) comb. **sich** (*dat*) **mit dem ~ durch die Haare fahren** to run a comb through one's hair; **alle/alles über einen ~ scheren** (*fig*) to lump everyone/everything together; **bei denen liegt der ~ auf** *or* **neben der Butter** (*inf*) their place is a real pigsty (*inf*).
(b) (*von Vogel, Eidechse etc*) comb; *siehe* **schwellen**.
(c) (*von Pferd*) crest.
(d) (*Cook*) (*Hammelfleisch*) (middle) neck; (*Schweinefleisch*) spare rib; (*Rindfleisch*) neck.
(e) (*von Trauben*) stalk.
(f) (*Gebirgs~*) crest, ridge; (*Wellen~*) crest.
kämmen 1 *vt Haar, Baumwolle* to comb; *Wolle auch* to card, to tease. **sie kämmte ihm die Haare** she combed his hair. **2** *vr* to comb one's hair.
Kammer *f* -, -n (a) (*general*) chamber; (*Parl auch*) house;

(*Ärzte~, Anwalts~*) professional association; (*Herz~*) ventricle; (*Mil*) store *usu pl*. **Erste/Zweite ~** Upper/Lower House. (b) (*Zimmer*) (small) room, box room; (*dial: Schlafzimmer*) bedroom.
Kammer-: ~**bulle** *m* (*Mil sl*) quartermaster; ~**diener** *m* valet.
Kämmerei *f* (a) (*Hist: Finanzverwaltung*) treasury (*old*); finance department. (b) (*Tex*) combing works *sing or pl*.
Kämmerer *m* -s, - (a) (*Beamter*) finance officer. (b) (*Hist, Eccl*) chamberlain.
Kammer-: ~**frau** *f* (*Hist*) lady-in-waiting; ~**gericht** *nt* ≈ Supreme Court; ~**herr** *m* (*Hist*) chamberlain; ~**jäger** *m* (*Schädlingsbekämpfer*) pest controller; (*Leibjäger*) (head) gamekeeper; ~**jungfer** *f* lady-in-waiting; ~**konzert** *nt* chamber concert.
Kämmerlein *nt* chamber. **im stillen ~** in private.
Kammer-: ~**mädchen** *nt siehe* ~**jungfer**; ~**musik** *f* chamber music; ~**orchester** *nt* chamber orchestra; ~**sänger** *m*, ~**schauspieler** *m* (*Titel*) *title formerly given by Duke etc, now by authorities, to singer/actor for excellence*; ~**spiel** *nt* (a) (*Schauspiel*) play for a studio theatre; (b) (*Theater*) studio theatre; ~**ton** *m* concert pitch; ~**zofe** *f* chambermaid.
Kamm-: ~**garn** *nt* worsted; ~**muschel** *f siehe* **Kammuschel**; ~**rad** *nt* cogwheel; ~**stück** *nt* (*Cook*) shoulder.
Kammuschel *nt* getrennt Kamm-muschel scallop.
Kamp *m* -(e)s, ~̈e (*N Ger*) plot (of land), field.
Kampagne [kamˈpanjə] *f* -, -n (a) campaign. (b) (*bei Ausgrabungen*) stage.
Kämpe *m* -n, -n (*obs, iro*) (old) campaigner *or* soldier.
kampeln *vir* (*dial*) to quarrel.
Kampf *m* -(e)s, ~̈e fight, struggle (*um* for); (*Mil auch*) combat; (*Mil: Gefecht*) battle; (*Feindbegegnung*) engagement, encounter; (*Box~*) fight, bout, contest. **jdm/einer Sache den ~ ansagen** (*fig*) to declare war on sb/sth; **den ~/die ~e einstellen** to stop fighting; **für den ~ ungeeignet** unsuited for combat; **den ~ um etw verloren geben** to abandon the struggle for sth; **den ~ aufgeben** to give up the struggle; **den ~ abbrechen** (*Sport*) to stop the fight; **es kam zum ~** clashes occurred, fighting broke out; **auf in den ~!** (*hum*) once more unto the breach! (*hum*); **er ist im ~ gefallen** he fell in action *or* battle; **im ~ für die Freiheit/Frankreich** in the struggle for freedom/the battle for France; **der ~ ums Dasein** the struggle for existence; **der ~ der Geschlechter** *or* **zwischen den Geschlechtern** the battle of the sexes; **der~ um die Macht** the battle *or* struggle for power; **ein ~ auf Leben und Tod** a fight to the death; ~ **dem Atomtod!** fight the nuclear menace!; **St Georg im ~ mit dem Drachen** St George in combat with *or* fighting the dragon; **innere ~̈e** inner conflicts.
Kampf-: ~**abschnitt** *m* combat zone *or* sector; ~**abzeichen** *nt* campaign medal; ~**ansage** *f* declaration of war; (*Sport*) announcement; ~**bahn** *f* sports stadium, arena; ~**begier(de)** *f* (*liter*) bellicosity (*liter*); **k~bereit** *adj* ready for battle.
kämpfen 1 *vi* to fight, to struggle (*um, für* for); (*Sport: angreifen*) to attack. **gegen etw ~** to fight (against) sth; **die Rangers-Elf kämpft morgen gegen Celtic** Rangers are playing (against) Celtic tomorrow; **mit dem Tode ~** to fight for one's life; **mit den Tränen ~** to fight back one's tears; **gegen die Wellen ~** to battle against the waves; **ich hatte mit schweren Problemen zu ~** I had difficult problems to contend with; **ich habe lange mit mir ~ müssen, ehe ...** I had a long battle with myself before ...; **das ganze Publikum kämpfte mit dem Schlaf** the whole audience was struggling to keep awake.
2 *vt* (*usu fig*) *Kampf* to fight.
Kampfer *m* -s, *no pl* camphor.
Kämpfer *m* -s, - (*Archit*) impost.
Kämpfer(in *f*) *m* -s, - fighter; (*Krieger auch*) warrior.
kämpferisch *adj* aggressive; *Spiel auch* attacking.
kampferprobt *adj* battle-tried.
Kampfeslust *f* pugnacity.
Kampf-: **k~fähig** *adj* (*Mil*) fit for action; *Boxer* fit to fight; ~**flugzeug** *nt* fighter (plane); ~**geist** *m* fighting spirit; ~**gemeinschaft** *f* (*Pol*) action group; ~**gruppe** *f* task force; (*Mil auch*) combat group; ~**hahn** *m* (*lit, fig*) fighting cock; ~**handlung** *f usu pl* clash *usu pl*; ~**kraft** *f* fighting strength; **k~los** *adj* peaceful; **der Rückzug erfolgte k~los** they *etc* retreated without a fight; **sich k~los ergeben, k~los aufgeben** to surrender without a fight; **k~lustig** *adj* belligerent, pugnacious; ~**platz** *m* battlefield; (*Sport*) arena, stadium; ~**preis** *m* (a) (*in Wett~*) prize; (b) (*Comm*) competitive price; **die Konkurrenz mit ~preisen kaputtmachen** to undercut the competition; ~**richter** *m* (*Sport*) referee; (*Tennis*) umpire; (*Schwimmen, Skilaufen*) judge; ~**schrift** *f* broadsheet; ~**stärke** *f* (*Mil*) combat strength; ~**stoff** *m* weapon, warfare agent; **k~unfähig** *adj* (*Mil*) unfit for fighting *or* battle; (*Sport*) unfit; **einen Panzer/ein Schiff k~unfähig machen** to put a tank/ship out of action, to cripple a tank/ship; **k~unfähig schlagen** (*Boxen*) to put out of the fight; ~**wagen** *m* chariot; (*Panzer~*) armoured car.
kampieren* *vi* to camp (out). **im Wohnzimmer ~** (*inf*) to doss down in the sitting room (*inf*).
Kampl *m* -s, -(n) (*Aus inf*) mate (*inf*).
Kanaan [ˈkaːnaːn] *nt* -s (*Bibl*) Canaan.
Kanaaniter(in *f*) [kanaaˈniːtɐ, -ərɪn] *m* -s, - (*Bibl*) Canaanite.
Kanada *nt* -s Canada.
Kanadier [-iɐ] *m* -s, - Canadian; (*Sport*) Canadian canoe.
Kanadierin [-iərɪn] *f* Canadian (woman/girl).
kanadisch *adj* Canadian.
Kanaille [kaˈnaljə] *f* -, -n (*dated pej*) (*gemeiner Mensch*) scoundrel, rascal; (*Pöbel, Mob*) rabble, canaille.
Kanake *m* -n, -n (*Südseeinsulaner*) Kanaka; (*pej: Ausländer, Südländer*) wop (*pej*), dago (*pej*).

Kanal m -s, **Kanäle (a)** (*Schiffahrtsweg*) canal; (*Wasserlauf*) channel; (*zur Bewässerung auch*) ditch; (*zur Entwässerung*) drain; (*für Abwässer*) sewer. **der (Ärmel)k~** the (English) Channel; **sich** (*dat*) **den ~ vollaufen lassen** (*sl*) to get canned (*sl*); **den ~ voll haben** (*sl*) (*betrunken sein*) to be canned (*sl*); (*es satt haben*) to have had a bellyful (*sl*). **(b)** (*Radio, TV, fig: Weg*) channel. **etw durch die richtigen Kanäle weiterleiten** to pass sth on through the proper channels; **dunkle Kanäle** dubious channels.

Kanal-: **~arbeiter** m sewerage worker; **~bau** m canal building or construction.

Kanalisation f **(a)** (*für Abwässer*) sewerage system, sewers pl; (*das Kanalisieren*) sewerage installation. **(b)** (*Begradigung eines Flußlaufes*) canalization.

kanalisieren* 1 vt Fluß to canalize; (fig) Energie, Emotionen etc to channel. 2 vti to install or lay sewers (in).

Kanal-: **~tunnel** m channel tunnel; **~zone** f canal zone.

Kanapee nt -s, -s (*old, hum*) sofa, couch, settee.

Kanaren pl (*form*) Canary Islands pl.

Kanari m -s, - (*inf*), **Kanarienvogel** [-iən-] m canary.

Kanarische Inseln pl Canaries pl, Canary Islands pl.

Kandare f -, -n (curb) bit. **jdn an die ~ nehmen** (*fig*) to take sb in hand.

Kandel m -s, -n or f -, -n (*S Ger*) gutter.

Kandelaber m -s, - candelabra.

Kandidat m -en, -en candidate; (*bei Bewerbung auch*) applicant. **jdn als ~en aufstellen** to nominate sb, to put sb forward as a candidate; **~ der Philosophie** etc person about to take a philosophy etc exam.

Kandidatenliste f list of candidates.

Kandidatin f candidate; (*bei Bewerbung auch*) applicant.

Kandidatur f candidature, candidacy.

kandidieren* vi (*Pol*) to stand, to run (*für* for). **für das Amt des Präsidenten ~** to stand or run for president.

kandiert adj Frucht candied.

Kandis(zucker) m - rock candy.

Kaneel m -s, no pl cinnamon.

Känguruh ['kɛŋguru] nt -s, -s kangaroo.

Kanin nt -s, -e rabbit (fur).

Kaninchen nt rabbit. **sich wie ~ vermehren** (*inf*) to breed like rabbits.

Kaninchen-: **~bau** m rabbit warren; **~stall** m rabbit hutch.

Kanister m -s, - can.

Kann-Bestimmung, Kannbestimmung f (*Jur*) authorization.

Kännchen nt (*für Milch*) jug; (*für Kaffee*) pot. **ein ~ Kaffee** a pot of coffee.

Kanne f -, -n can; (*Tee~, Kaffee~*) pot; (*Milch~*) churn; (*Öl~*) can, tin; (*Wein~*) ≃ tankard; (*Gieß~*) watering can.

Kannegießer m (*old*) alehouse politician.

kanneliert adj (*Archit*) fluted.

Kannibale m -n, -n, **Kannibalin** f cannibal.

kannibalisch adj cannibalistic; (*brutal*) rough. **es geht mir ~ wohl** (*hum inf*) I'm feeling on top of the world; **ich habe ~en Hunger** (*hum inf*) I could eat a horse (*inf*).

Kannibalismus m cannibalism.

kannte pret of **kennen**.

Kanon m -s, -s (*alle Bedeutungen*) canon.

Kanonade f (*Mil*) barrage; (*fig auch*) tirade.

Kanone f -, -n (a) gun; (*Hist*) cannon; (*sl: Pistole*) rod (*US sl*), gat (*sl*), shooter (*sl*). **~n auffahren** (*lit, fig*) to bring up the big guns; **mit ~n auf Spatzen schießen** (*inf*) to take a sledgehammer to crack a nut. **(b)** (*fig inf: Könner*) ace (*inf*). **(c)** (*inf*) **das ist unter aller ~** that defies description.

Kanonen-: **~boot** nt gunboat; **~bootdiplomatie, ~bootpolitik** f gunboat diplomacy; **~donner** m rumbling of guns; **~futter** nt (*inf*) cannon fodder; **~kugel** f cannon ball; **~ofen** m cylindrical iron stove; **~rohr** nt gun barrel; **heiliges ~rohr!** (*inf*) good grief (*inf*).

Kanonier m -s, -e (*Mil*) gunner, artilleryman.

Kanoniker m -s, -, **Kanonikus** m -, **Kanonizi** (*Eccl*) canon.

Kanonisation f (*Eccl*) canonization.

kanonisch adj (*Eccl*) canonical. **~es Recht** canon law.

kanonisieren* vt (*Eccl*) to canonize.

Kanonisse f -, -n, **Kanonissin** f canoness.

Kanossa nt -s (*fig*) humiliation.

Kanossagang m: **einen ~ machen** or **antreten müssen** to eat humble pie.

Kantate[1] f -, -n (*Mus*) cantata.

Kantate[2] no art (*Eccl*) fourth Sunday after Easter.

Kante f -, -n (*eines Gegenstandes, einer Fläche*) edge; (*Rand, Borte*) border; (*Web~*) selvedge. **wir legten die Steine ~ an ~** we laid the stones end to end; **etw auf ~ kleben** to stick sth with the edges flush; **Geld auf die hohe ~ legen** (*inf*) to put money by (*inf*) or away; **Geld auf der hohen ~ haben** (*inf*) to have (some) money put by (*inf*) or away; **siehe abstoßen, fehlen.**

Kanten m -s, - (*N Ger*) crust, heel (*dial*).

kanten vt **(a)** to tilt. **nicht ~!** (*bei Kisten etc*) do not tilt!, this way up! **(b)** (*mit Kanten versehen*) to trim, to edge. **(c)** auch vi (*Ski*) to edge.

Kanter m -s, - canter.

Kant-: **~haken** m: **jdn beim ~haken nehmen** (*inf*) or **zu fassen kriegen** (*inf*) to haul sb over the coals (*inf*); **~holz** nt (*piece of*) squared timber.

kantig adj Holz edged, squared; Gesicht angular.

-kantig adj suf -edged.

Kantine f canteen.

Kantisch, kantisch adj Kantian.

Kanton m -s, -e canton.

Kantonist m: **ein unsicherer ~ sein** to be unreliable.

Kantor m choirmaster; (*in Synagoge*) cantor.

Kantorei f (church) choir.

Kantorin f choirmistress.

Kanu nt -s, -s canoe.

Kanüle f -, -n (*Med*) cannula.

Kanute m -n, -n canoeist.

Kanzel f -, -n **(a)** pulpit. **auf der ~** in the pulpit; **die ~ besteigen** to get into the pulpit; **von der ~ herab/aus** from the pulpit. **(b)** (*Aviat*) cockpit. **(c)** (*eines Berges*) promontory, spur. **(d)** (*Hunt*) (look-out) platform.

Kanzel-: **~deckel** m canopy; **~mißbrauch** m abuse of the pulpit (for political purposes); **~redner** m orator.

Kanzlei f **(a)** (*Dienststelle*) office; (*Büro eines Rechtsanwalts, Notars* etc) chambers pl. **(b)** (*Hist, Pol*) chancellery.

Kanzlei-: **~diener** m messenger; **~sprache** f official language; **~stil** m (*pej*) officialese.

Kanzler m -s, - **(a)** (*Regierungschef*) chancellor; siehe **Bundes~, Reichs~. (b)** (*diplomatischer Beamter*) chancellor, chief secretary. **(c)** (*Univ*) vice-chancellor.

Kanzlist m (*old*) clerk.

Kaolin m or nt -s, -e kaolin.

Kap nt -s, -s cape, headland. **~ der Guten Hoffnung** Cape of Good Hope; **~ Hoorn** Cape Horn.

kapabel adj (*obs*) capable.

Kapaun m -s, -e capon.

Kapazität f capacity; (*fig: Experte*) expert, authority.

Kapee nt: **schwer von ~ sein** (*inf*) to be slow on the uptake (*inf*).

Kapelle f **(a)** (*kleine Kirche* etc) chapel. **(b)** (*Mus*) band, orchestra.

Kapellmeister m (*Mus*) director of music; (*Mil, von Tanzkapelle* etc) bandmaster, bandleader.

Kaper[1] f -, -n (*Bot, Cook*) caper.

Kaper[2] m -s, - (*Naut*) privateer.

Kaperbrief m letter of marque.

Kaperei f privateering.

kapern vt (*Naut*) Schiff to seize, to capture; (*fig inf*) Ding to commandeer (*inf*), to grab; jdn to grab; (*mit Beschlag belegen*) to buttonhole, to collar (*inf*).

Kaperschiff nt privateer.

kapieren* vti (*inf*) to get (*inf*), to understand. **kapiert?** got it? (*inf*); **kapierst du (denn) jetzt?** do you get it now? (*inf*); **er hat schnell kapiert** he caught on quick (*inf*).

Kapillargefäß nt (*Anat*) capillary.

kapital adj **(a)** (*Hunt*) Hirsch royal. **einen ~en Bock schießen** (*fig*) to make a real bloomer (*inf*). **(b)** (*grundlegend*) Mißverständnis etc major.

Kapital nt -s, -e or -ien [-iən] **(a)** (*Fin*) capital no pl; (*pl: angelegtes ~*) capital investments pl. **flüssiges or verfügbares ~** ready or available capital; **er ist mit 35% am ~ dieser Firma beteiligt** he has a 35% stake in this firm.
(b) (*fig*) asset. **an seinem guten Aussehen besitzt er ein ~** his good looks are an asset to him, he has a very good asset in his good looks; **aus etw ~ schlagen** (*pej*) (*lit, fig*) to make capital out of sth; (*fig auch*) to capitalize on sth.

Kapital-: **~abwanderung** f exodus of capital; **~anlage** f capital investment, investment of capital; **~ertragssteuer** f capital gains tax; **~flucht** f flight of capital; **~gesellschaft** f (*Comm*) joint-stock company; **k~intensiv** adj capital-intensive.

kapitalisieren* vt to capitalize.

Kapitalismus m capitalism.

Kapitalist m capitalist.

kapitalistisch adj capitalist.

Kapital-: **~markt** m money market; **~verbrechen** nt serious crime; (*mit Todesstrafe*) capital crime or offence.

Kapitän m -s, -e **(a)** (*Naut, Mil*) captain; (*esp auf kleinerem Schiff auch*) skipper (*inf*); (*auf Handelsschiff auch*) master. **~ zur See** (*inf*) captain. **(b)** (*Sport*) captain. **(c)** (*Aviat*) captain.

Kapitänleutnant m lieutenant-commander.

Kapitänspatent nt master's certificate.

Kapitel nt -s, - **(a)** chapter; (*fig auch*) period; (*Angelegenheit*) chapter of events, story. **eines dunkles ~ in seinem Leben** a dark chapter in his life; **das ist ein anderes ~** that's another story; **das ist ein ~ für sich** that's a story all to itself; **für mich ist dieses ~ erledigt** as far as I'm concerned the matter is closed. **(b)** (*Eccl: Dom~*) chapter.

Kapitell nt -s, -e capital.

Kapitulation f (*von Armee, Land*) surrender, capitulation (*auch fig*) (*vor +dat* to, in the face of). **bedingungslose ~** unconditional surrender; **das ist eine ~ vor deinen Pflichten/Kindern** that's refusing to face up to your responsibilities/that's capitulating to your children.

kapitulieren* vi (*sich ergeben*) to surrender, to capitulate; (*fig: aufgeben*) to give up, to capitulate (*vor +dat* in the face of). **ich kapituliere, das ist zu schwierig** I give up, it's too difficult.

Kaplan m -s, **Kapläne** (*in Pfarrei*) curate; (*mit besonderen Aufgaben*) chaplain.

Kapo m -s, -s (*Aufseher*) overseer; (*S Ger inf: Vorarbeiter*) gaffer (*inf*). **(a)** (*Mil sl: Unteroffizier*) NCO; (*Feldwebel*) sarge (*sl*); (*Obergefreiter*) corp (*sl*); (*Küchen~*) cook-house wallah (*sl*).

Kapodaster m -s, - capo.

Kapok m -s, no pl (*Tex*) kapok.

kapores adj pred (*sl*) Auto etc kaput (*sl*); Firma bust (*inf*), broke (*inf*). **~ gehen** (*Auto*) to fall to pieces; (*Firma*) to go bust (*inf*).

Kapotthut m bonnet.

Kappe f -, -n cap; (*Flieger~, Motorradmütze*) helmet; (*Narrenmütze*) jester's cap; carnival or fancy-dress hat; (*von Jude*) skullcap; (*von Füllfederhalter, Saftflaschen auch*) top; (*Schuh~*) (*vorne*) toe(cap); (*hinten*) heelpiece; (*Archit*) coping.

eine ~ aus Schnee a snowcap; **das nehme ich auf meine ~** (*fig inf*) I'll take the responsibility for that, on my head be it; **das geht auf meine ~** (*inf: ich bezahle*) that's on me.

kappen *vt* (a) (*Naut*) *Tau, Leine* to cut; *Ast* to cut back, to trim; (*Med*) *Mandeln* to clip (off); (*fig inf*) *Finanzmittel* to cut (back). (b) (*kastrieren*) *Hähne* to caponize.

Kappen|abend *m* carnival fancy-dress party *where fancy-dress hats are worn*.

Kappes *m* -, - (*dial: Kohl*) cabbage. **~ reden** (*sl*) to talk (a load of) rubbish *or* baloney (*sl*).

Käppi *nt* -s, -s cap.

Kappnaht *f* French seam.

Kappus *m* -, - *siehe* **Kappes**.

Kaprice [ka'priːsə] *f* -, -n caprice.

Kapriole *f* -, -n capriole; (*fig*) caper. **~n machen** to cut capers.

Kaprize (*Aus*) *f* -, -n *siehe* **Kaprice**.

kaprizieren* *vr* (*geh*) to insist (*auf* +*acc* on).

kapriziös *adj* capricious.

Kapsel *f* -, -n (*Etui*) container; (*Anat, Bot, Pharm, Space etc*) capsule; (*an einer Flasche*) cap, top; (*Spreng~*) detonator.

kaptiös [kap'tsiøːs] *adj* (*obs*) *Frage* captious (*form*).

kaputt *adj* (*inf*) broken; *esp Maschine, Glühbirne etc* kaput (*sl*); (*erschöpft*) *Mensch* shattered (*inf*), done in (*inf*), knackered (*Brit sl*); *Ehe* broken; *Beziehungen, Gesundheit* ruined; *Nerven* shattered; *Firma* bust *pred* (*inf*). **das alte Auto/das Dach/ihre Ehe ist ~** (*irreparabel*) (*inf*) the old car/the roof/her marriage has had it (*inf*); **irgend etwas muß an deinem Auto ~ sein** something must be wrong with your car; **der Fernseher ist ~** (*vorläufig*) the TV is on the blink (*inf*); **mein ~es Bein** my gammy (*inf*) *or* bad leg; (*gebrochen*) my broken leg; **mein ~es Auge** my dud eye (*inf*); **meine Hose ist ~** (*nicht mehr tragbar*) my trousers have had it (*inf*); (*zerrissen*) my trousers are torn *or* ripped; (*am Saum*) my trousers are coming apart; **er ist ~** (*sl: tot*) he's kicked the bucket (*inf*); **das ~e Deutschland** the (war-)shattered Germany; **die ~e Welt** this mess of a world; **ein ~er Typ** (*sl*) a bum (*sl*).

kaputt-: **~fahren** *vt sep irreg* (*inf*) (*überfahren*) to run over; *Auto* to drive *or* run into the ground, to knacker (*Brit sl*); (*durch Unfall*) to smash (up), to write off; **~gehen** *vi sep irreg aux sein* (*inf*) to break; (*esp Maschine*) to go kaput (*sl*); (*esp Glühbirne, Elektronenröhre etc*) to go kaput (*sl*), to go phut (*inf*); (*Ehe*) to break up, to go on the rocks (*inf*) (*an* +*dat* because of); (*Beziehungen, Gesundheit, Nerven*) to be ruined, to go to pot (*inf*); (*Firma*) to go bust (*inf*), to fold up; (*Waschmaschine, Auto*) to break down, to pack up (*Brit inf*); (*Kleidung*) to come to pieces; (*zerrissen werden*) to tear; (*sl: sterben*) to kick the bucket (*inf*), to croak (*sl*); (*Blumen*) to die off; **der Fernseher ist schon wieder ~gegangen** (*vorläufig*) the TV has gone on the blink again (*inf*); **in dem Büro/an diesem Job gehe ich noch ~** this office/job will be the death of me (*inf*); **er ist am Alkohol ~gegangen** alcohol was his downfall, he was destroyed by drink; **~kriegen** *vt sep irreg* (*inf*) *Zerbrechliches* to break; *Auto* to ruin; *jdn* to wear out; **das Auto/der Hans ist nicht ~zukriegen** this car/Hans just goes on for ever; **wie hast du denn das ~gekriegt?** how did you (manage to) break it?; **~lachen** *vr sep* (*inf*) to die laughing (*inf*); **ich lach' mich ~!** what a laugh!; **ich hätte mich ~lachen können** I nearly killed myself (*sl*); **~machen** *sep* (*inf*) **1** *vt* to ruin; *Zerbrechliches* to break, to smash; *Brücke, Sandburg* to knock down; (*erschöpfen*) *jdn* to wear out, to knacker (*Brit sl*); **die ewigen Sorgen/die Kinder machen mich ~** these never-ending worries/the children will be the death of me (*inf*); **der Tod seiner Frau hat ihn völlig ~gemacht** after his wife's death he went completely to pieces (*inf*); **2** *vr* (*sich überanstrengen*) to wear oneself out, to slog oneself into the ground (*inf*), to knacker oneself (*Brit sl*); **~schlagen** *vt sep irreg* (*inf*) to break, to smash.

Kapuze *f* -, -n hood; (*Mönchs~*) cowl.

Kapuziner *m* -s, - (*Eccl*) Capucin (monk); (*Bot: auch* **~kresse** *f*) nasturtium.

Kar *nt* -(e)s, -e corrie, cwm, cirque.

Karabiner *m* -s, - (a) (*Gewehr*) carbine. (b) (*auch* **~haken** *m*) karabiner, snap link, crab (*inf*).

Karacho *nt* -s, *no pl*: **mit** *or* **im ~** (*inf*) at full tilt, hell for leather (*inf*); **er rannte/fuhr mit ~ gegen die Wand** he ran/drove smack into the wall.

Karaffe *f* -, -n carafe; (*mit Stöpsel*) decanter.

Karakulschaf *nt* karakul sheep.

Karambolage [karambo'laːʒə] *f* -, -n (*Aut*) collision, crash; (*Billard*) cannon.

Karambole *f* -, -n (*beim Billardspiel*) red (ball).

karambolieren* *vi aux sein* (*beim Billard*) to cannon; (*Autos*) to crash (*mit* into), to collide (*mit* with).

Karamel *m* -s, *no pl* caramel *no pl*.

Karamelle *f* caramel (toffee).

Karat *nt* -(e)s, -e *or* (*bei Zahlenangabe*) - (*Measure*) carat. **das Gold dieses Ringes hat 9 ~** this ring is made of 9-carat gold.

Karate *nt* -s, *no pl* karate. **~hieb** *m* karate chop.

-karäter *m* in *cpds* -s, - **Zehn~** ten-carat diamond/stone.

-karätig *adj suf* carat.

Karavelle [kara'vɛlə] *f* caravel.

Karawane *f* -, -n caravan.

Karawanenstraße *f* caravan route.

Karawanserei *f* caravanserai, caravansary.

Karbid *nt* -(e)s, -e carbide.

Karbidlampe *f* davy lamp.

Karbol *nt* -s, *no pl*, **Karbolsäure** *f* carbolic acid.

Karbol-: **~mäuschen** *nt* (*hum inf*) little nurse; **~seife** *f* carbolic soap.

Karbonat *nt* carbonate.

karbonisieren* *vt* to carbonize; *Getränke* to carbonate.

Karbunkel *m* -s, - (*Med*) carbuncle.

Kardamom *m* -s, *no pl* cardamom.

Kardan-: **~gelenk** *nt* universal joint; **~tunnel** *m* transmission tunnel; **~welle** *f* prop(eller) shaft.

Kardinal *m* -s, **Kardinäle** (a) (*Eccl*) cardinal. (b) (*Orn*) cardinal (bird).

Kardinalfehler *m* cardinal error.

Kardinalia *pl* cardinals *pl*.

Kardinal-: **~tugend** *f* (*Philos, Rel*) cardinal virtue; **~zahl** *f* cardinal (number).

Kardio-: **~gramm** *nt* cardiogram; **~logie** *f* cardiology.

Karenzzeit *f* waiting period.

Karfiol *m* -s, *no pl* (*Aus*) cauliflower. **zwei (Rosen) ~** two cauliflowers.

Karfreitag *m* Good Friday.

Karfunkel *m* -s, - (a) *siehe* **Karbunkel**. (b) *siehe* **Karfunkelstein**.

Karfunkelstein *m* red precious stone such as ruby or garnet, carbuncle (stone). **ihre Augen strahlten wie ~** (*liter*) her eyes sparkled like jewels.

karg *adj* (a) (*spärlich*) *Vorrat* meagre, sparse; (*unfruchtbar*) *Boden* barren; (*dürftig*) *Gehalt, Einkommen* meagre. **~ möbliert** sparsely furnished; **~ leben** to lead a meagre existence. (b) (*geizig*) mean, sparing. **er ist ~ mit seinem Lob** he is grudging with his praise; **ich erhielt ~en Dank** I received small *or* scant thanks; **etw ~ bemessen** to be mean *or* stingy (*inf*) with sth; **die Portionen sind sehr ~ bemessen** they are very mean *or* stingy (*inf*) with the helpings.

kargen *vi* (*sparsam sein*) to stint (*mit* on), to scrimp and save (*mit* with); (*knausern*) to be mean *or* stingy (*inf*) (*mit* with); (*mit Lob*) to be grudging. **er kargt nicht mit Lob** he is lavish with his praise.

Kargheit *f siehe adj* (a) meagreness, sparseness; barrenness; meagreness.

kärglich *adj Vorrat* meagre, sparse; *Mahl* frugal; (*dürftig*) *Gehalt, Einkommen* meagre. **unter ~en Bedingungen leben** to live in impoverished conditions; **sie leben ~** they lead a meagre existence.

Kärglichkeit *f siehe adj* meagreness, sparseness; frugality; meagreness.

Kargo *m* -s, -s cargo.

Karibe *m* -n, -n Carib.

Karibik *f* - **die ~** the Caribbean.

Karibin *f* Carib.

karibisch *adj* Caribbean. **das K~e Meer** the Caribbean Sea; **die K~en Inseln** the Caribbean Islands.

kariert *adj Stoff, Muster* checked, checkered (*esp US*); *Papier* squared. **red' nicht so ~!** (*inf*) don't talk such rubbish; **~ gucken** (*inf*) to look puzzled; **~ aussehen** (*inf*) to look soft in the head (*inf*).

Karies ['kaːriɛs] *f* -, *no pl* caries.

Karikatur *f* caricature. **eine ~ von jdm/etw zeichnen** (*lit*) to draw a caricature of sb/sth; (*lit, fig*) to caricature sb/sth.

Karikaturist(in *f***)** *m* cartoonist; (*Personenzeichner auch*) caricaturist.

karikaturistisch *adj* caricatural (*form*), caricature. **dieser Artikel ist ~** this article is a caricature.

karikieren* *vt* to caricature.

kariös *adj* Zahn carious, decayed.

Karitas *f* -, *no pl* (*Nächstenliebe*) charity; (*Verband auch*) charitable organization.

karitativ *adj* charitable.

Karkasse *f* -, -n (a) (*Cook*) carcass. (b) (*Aut: von Reifen*) casing.

Karl *m* -s Charles. **~ der Große** Charlemagne.

Karmeliter(in *f***)** *m* -s, - Carmelite.

Karmelitergeist *m* herbal medicine.

Karmesin *nt* -s, *no pl* crimson.

karmesin(rot) *adj* crimson.

karmin(rot) *adj* carmine (red).

Karneval ['karnəval] *m* -s, -e *or* -s carnival.

Karnevalszug *m* carnival procession.

Karnickel *nt* -s, - (*inf*) (a) bunny (rabbit) (*inf*), rabbit. (b) (*hum: Schuldiger*) culprit.

Karnickel-: **~bock** *m* buck rabbit; **~stall** *m* rabbit hutch.

karnivor [karni'voːr] *adj* (*Biol*) carnivorous.

Kärnten *nt* -s Carinthia.

Karo *nt* -s, -s (*Quadrat*) square; (*auf der Spitze stehend*) diamond, lozenge; (*Muster*) check; (*diagonal*) diamond; (*Cards*) diamonds *pl*. **ein ~ trocken** (*inf*) a slice of dry bread.

Karo- in *cpds* (*Cards*) of diamonds.

Karolinger *m* -s, - Carolingian.

karolingisch *adj* Carolingian. **K~e Minuskeln** Caroline minuscule.

Karomuster *nt* checked *or* chequered (*esp US*) pattern.

Karosse *f* -, -n (*Prachtkutsche*) (state) coach; (*fig: großes Auto*) limousine.

Karosserie *f* bodywork.

Karosserieschlosser *m* panelbeater.

Karotin *nt* -s, -e carotene, carotin.

Karotte *f* -, -n (*small*) carrot.

Karpaten *pl* Carpathian Mountains *pl*, Carpathians *pl*.

Karpell *nt* -s, -e *or* -a (*Bot*) carpel.

Karpfen *m* -s, - carp.

Karpfen-: **k~artig** *adj* (*lit*) carp-like; (*fig*) *Gesicht, Aussehen* fish-like; **~schwanz** *m* hummingbird; hawkmoth; **~teich** *m* carp pond; *siehe* **Hecht**.

Karre *f* -, -n (a) *siehe* **Karren**. (b) (*inf: klappriges Auto*) (old) crate (*inf*) *or* heap (*inf*).

Karree *nt* -s, -s (a) (*Viereck*) rectangle; (*Rhombus*) rhombus;

(*Quadrat*) square; (*Formation: esp Mil*) square. **(b)** (*Häuserblock*) block. **einmal ums ~ gehen** to walk round the block. **(c)** (*esp Aus: Cook*) loin.

Karren *m* **-s, -** **(a)** (*Wagen*) cart; (*esp für Garten, Baustelle*) (wheel)barrow; (*für Gepäck etc*) trolley. **ein ~ voll Obst** a cartload of fruit.

(b) (*fig inf*) **jdm an den ~ fahren** to take sb to task; **die beiden kann man nicht vor einen ~ spannen** the two of them go together like oil and water; (*bei der Arbeit*) those two couldn't work in harness; **den ~ einfach laufen lassen** to let things go or slide; **den ~ in den Dreck fahren** to ruin things, to get things in a mess; **der ~ ist hoffnungslos verfahren, der ~ steckt im Dreck** we/they *etc* are really in a mess; **den ~ aus dem Dreck ziehen** or **wieder flottmachen** to put things back on the rails, to get things sorted out.

karren **1** *vt* to cart. **jdn ~** (*inf: mit Auto*) to give sb a lift, to drive sb. **2** *vi aux sein* (*inf: mit dem Auto*) to drive (around).

Karrengaul *m* (*pej*) (old) nag.

Karrette *f* (*Sw*) (*Schubkarre*) (hand)cart, trolley.

Karriere [ka'riɛːrə, -iɛːrə] *f* **-, -n** **(a)** (*Laufbahn*) career. **~ machen** to make a career for oneself. **(b)** (*voller Galopp*) (full) gallop. **~ reiten** to gallop, to ride at a gallop.

Karrierefrau *f* career girl/woman.

Karrieremacher(in *f*)**, Karrierist(in** *f*) *m* careerist.

Karriol *nt* **-s, -e** or **-s** (*old*) cariole.

karriolen* *vi aux sein* (*dated inf*) to gallivant (around).

Kärrner *m* **-s, -** **(a)** (*Fuhrmann*) carter. **(b)** (*Kätner*) smallholder.

Kärrner|arbeit *f* hard labour or toil.

Karsamstag *m* Easter Saturday, Holy Saturday.

Karst[1] *m* **-(e)s, -e** (*Hacke*) two-pronged mattock or hoe.

Karst[2] *m* **-(e)s, -e** (*Geog, Geol*) karst.

karstig *adj* karstic.

Karstlandschaft *f* karst(ic) landscape.

Kartätsche *f* **-, -n** **(a)** (*Mil*) case shot. **(b)** (*Build*) plasterer's float, darby.

Kartause *f* **-, -n** chartreuse, Carthusian monastery.

Kartäuser *m* **-s, -** **(a)** (*Carthusian* (monk). **(b)** (*Likör*) chartreuse.

Karte *f* **-, -n** **(a)** (*Post~, Kartei~, Loch~ etc*) card.

(b) (*Fahr~, Eintritts~*) ticket; (*Einladungs~*) invitation (card); (*Bezugsschein*) coupon; (*Essens~*) luncheon voucher, meal ticket (*US*); (*Mitglieds~*) (membership) card. **die ~n, bitte!** tickets, please!

(c) (*Land~*) map; (*See~*) chart. **~n lesen** to map-read.

(d) (*Speise~*) menu; (*Wein~*) wine list. **nach der ~ à la carte.**

(e) (*Spiel~*) (playing) card. **jdm die ~n lesen** to tell sb's fortune from the cards; **mit offenen ~n spielen** (*lit*) to play with one's cards on the table; (*fig*) to put one's cards on the table; **er spielt mit verdeckten ~n** (*fig*) he's playing his cards or it very close to his chest; **du solltest deine ~n aufdecken** (*fig*) you ought to show your hand or put your cards on the table; **alle ~n in der Hand halten** (*fig*) to hold all the cards; **alle ~n in der Hand behalten** (*fig*) to keep hold of the reins; **er läßt sich nicht in die ~n sehen** or **gucken** (*fig*) he's playing it close to his chest; **jdm in die ~n sehen** (*lit*) to look or take a look at sb's cards; **es ist unmöglich, ihm in die ~n zu sehen** (*fig*) it's impossible to know what he's up to; **alles auf eine ~ setzen** (*lit*) to stake everything on one card; (*fig*) to stake everything on one chance; (*andere Möglichkeiten ausschließen*) to put all one's eggs in one basket (*prov*); **du hast auf die falsche ~ gesetzt** (*fig*) you backed the wrong horse.

Kartei *f* card file, card index.

Kartei-: **~karte** *f* file or record card; **~kasten** *m* file-card box; **~leiche** *f* (*hum*) sleeping or non-active member; **die meisten Mitglieder sind bloß ~leichen** most of the members are just names on the files; **~schrank** *m* filing cabinet.

Kartell *nt* **-s, -e** **(a)** (*Comm*) cartel. **(b)** (*Interessenvereinigung*) alliance; (*pej*) cartel.

Kartell-: **~amt** *nt*, **~behörde** *f* monopolies or anti-trust commission; **~gesetz** *nt* monopolies or anti-trust law.

Karten-: **~blatt** *nt* map, (map)sheet; **~brief** *m* letter-card; **~haus** *nt* (a) house of cards; **wie ein ~haus zusammenstürzen** or **in sich zusammenfallen** to collapse like a house of cards; **(b)** (*Naut*) chart room; **~kunststück** *nt* card trick; **~legen** *nt* **-s** (a) *siehe* **~lesen (b)**; **(b)** (*Patience*) patience; **~leger(in** *f*) *m* **-s, -** fortune-teller (*who reads cards*); **~lesen** *nt* (a) (*von Landkarten etc*) map-reading; **(b)** (*Wahrsagen*) fortune-telling (*using cards*), reading the cards, cartomancy (*form*); **~leser** *m* **(a)** (*von Landkarten*) map-reader; **(b)** (*auch ~schläger*) *siehe* **~leger(in)**; **~spiel** *nt* **(a)** (*das Spielen*) card-playing; (*ein Spiel*) card game; **beim ~spiel** when playing cards; **(b)** (*Karten*) pack or deck (*of cards*); **~stelle** *f* ticket office; **~vorverkauf** *m* advance sale of tickets; advance booking office; **~werk** *nt* map book, book of maps; **~zeichnen** *nt* (*map*) symbol; **~zeichner** *m* cartographer, mapmaker.

kartesianisch, kartesisch *adj* Cartesian.

Karthager(in *f*) *m* **-s, -** Carthaginian.

Karthago *nt* **-s** Carthage.

Kartoffel *f* **-, -n** (a) potato. **rin in die ~n, raus aus die ~n** (*sl*) first it's one thing, then (it's) another, you're/he's *etc* always chopping and changing; **jdn fallen lassen wie eine heiße ~** (*inf*) to drop sb like a hot potato; *siehe* **Bauer[1]**. **(b)** (*inf*) (*Nase*) hooter (*Brit inf*), conk (*inf*); (*Loch*) (spud) hole.

Kartoffel- *in cpds* potato; **~brei** *m* mashed potatoes *pl*; **~chips** *pl* potato crisps *pl*; **~ferien** *pl* autumn holiday(s); **~feuer** *nt* fire made from dried potato leaves *etc* with general celebration after potato harvest; **~käfer** *m* Colorado beetle; **~kraut** *nt* potato foliage or leaves; **~mehl** *nt* potato flour; **~miete** *f* (*Agr*) potato clamp; **~puffer** *m* potato fritter; **~püree** *nt* mashed

potatoes *pl*; **~salat** *m* potato salad; **~schalen** *pl* potato-skin; (*abgeschält*) potato peel(ings).

Kartograph(in *f*) *m* cartographer.

Kartographie *f* cartography.

kartographisch *adj* cartographical.

Karton [kar'tɔŋ, kar'tɔ̃ː, kar'toːn] *m* **-s, -s** **(a)** (*steifes Papier, Pappe*) card, cardboard. **ein ~ a** piece of card or cardboard. **(b)** (*Schachtel*) cardboard box. **(c)** (*Art*) cartoon. **(d)** (*Leerblatt*) blank page for one's own notes.

Kartonage [karto'naːʒə] *f* **-, -n** (*Verpackung*) cardboard packaging.

kartonieren* *vt Bücher* to bind in boards. **kartoniert** hardback, cased.

Kartothek *f* **-, -en** card file, card index.

Kartusche *f* **-, -n (a)** (*Archit, Her*) cartouche. **(b)** cartridge; (*Hist Mil: Patronentasche*) ammunition pouch.

Karussell *nt* **-s, -s** or **-e** merry-go-round, roundabout (*Brit*), carousel. **~ fahren** to have a ride on the merry-go-round *etc*; **das Ministerkarussell dreht sich wieder** (*Press sl*) the ministerial carousel goes round and round.

Karwoche *f* (*Eccl*) Holy Week.

Karyatide *f* **-, -n** (*Archit*) caryatid.

Karzer *m* **-s, -** (*Hist*) **(a)** (*Zelle*) detention cell (*in school or university*). **(b)** (*Strafe*) detention.

karzinogen *adj* (*Med*) carcinogenic.

Karzinologie *f* (*Med*) oncology.

Karzinom *nt* **-s, -e** (*Med*) carcinoma, malignant growth.

Kasack *m* **-s, -s** tunic.

Kaschemme *f* **-, -n** low dive.

kaschen *vt* (*inf*) to catch; (*verhaften*) to nab (*inf*).

kaschieren* *vt* **(a)** (*fig: überdecken*) to conceal. **(b)** *Bucheinband* to laminate.

Kaschmir[1] *nt* **-s** (*Geog*) Kashmir.

Kaschmir[2] *m* **-s, -e** (*Tex*) cashmere.

Kaschube *m* **-n, -n, Kaschubin** *f* Kashub(e).

Käse *m* **-s, -** **(a)** cheese. **weißer ~** curd cheese; **~ schließt den Magen** cheese rounds off a meal nicely. **(b)** (*inf: Unsinn*) rubbish, twaddle (*inf*).

Käse- *in cpds* cheese; **~blatt, ~blättchen** *nt* (*inf*) local rag (*inf*); **~brot** *nt* (open) cheese sandwich; **~gebäck** *nt* cheese savouries *pl*; **~glocke** *f* cheese cover; (*fig*) dome.

Kasein *nt* **-s, -e** casein.

Käsekuchen *m* cheesecake.

Kasel *f* **-, -n** (*Eccl*) chasuble.

Kasematte *f* **-, -n** casemate.

käsen *vi* (*rare*) to make cheese.

Käserei *f* **(a)** (*~betrieb*) cheese dairy. **(b)** (*Käseherstellung*) cheese-making.

Kaserne *f* **-, -n** barracks *pl*.

Kasernen-: **~arrest** *m* confinement to barracks; **~hof** *m* barrack square; **~hofton** *m*: **es herrscht ein richtiger ~hofton** it's like being on the parade ground; **im ~hofton** in his sergeant-major's voice.

kasernieren* *vt Truppen* to quarter in barracks; *Flüchtlinge, Obdachlose etc* to quarter, to billet. **wenn man die Leute so kaserniert ...** if you put people in these barrack-like places ...

Käse-: **~stange** *f* cheese straw; **~torte** *f* cheesecake; **k~weiß** *adj* (*inf*) white or pale (as a ghost).

käsig *adj* **(a)** (*fig inf*) *Gesicht, Haut* pasty, pale; (*vor Schreck*) white, pale. **(b)** (*lit*) cheesy.

Kasino *nt* **-s, -s (a)** (*Spielbank*) casino. **(b)** (*Offiziers~*) (officers') mess or club; (*Speiseraum*) dining room, cafeteria.

Kaskade *f* **(a)** (*Wasserfall*) waterfall, cascade (*poet*); (*in Feuerwerk*) cascade. **die Wasser stürzen in ~ hinab** the waters cascade down. **(b)** (*Zirkussprung*) acrobatic leap.

Kaskoversicherung *f* (*Aut*) (*Teil~*) ≈ third party, fire and theft insurance; (*Voll~*) fully comprehensive insurance; (*Naut*) hull insurance.

Kasper *m* **-s, -, Kasperl** *m* or *nt* **-s, -(n)** (*Aus, S Ger*), **Kasperle** *m* or *nt* **-s, -** (*S Ger*) (*im Puppenspiel*) Punch. **(b)** (*inf*) clown (*inf*), fool.

Kasperle-: **~figur** *f* glove puppet; **~theater** *nt* Punch and Judy (show); (*Gestell*) Punch and Judy theatre.

kaspern *vi* (*inf*) to clown (*inf*) or fool around.

Kaspisches Meer *nt* Caspian Sea.

Kassa *f* **-, Kassen** **(a)** (*esp Aus*) *siehe* **Kasse (a)**. **(b) gegen ~** (*Comm*) for cash.

Kassa-: **~buch** *nt* (*old*) cashbook, ledger; **~geschäft** *nt* (*Comm*) cash transaction; (*St Ex*) spot transaction; **~kurs** *m* spot rate; **~markt** *m* spot market.

Kassandraruf *m* prophecy of doom, gloomy prediction.

Kassation *f* **(a)** (*Jur*) quashing, reversal; (*von Urkunde*) annulment. **(b)** (*obs Mil*) cashiering. **(c)** (*Mus Hist*) cassation.

Kassationshof *m* (*Jur*) supreme court of appeal.

Kasse *f* **-, -n** **(a)** (*Zahlstelle*) cashdesk, till, cash point; (*Zahlraum*) cashier's office; (*Theat etc*) box office; (*in Bank*) cash point, cashdesk. **an der ~** (*in Geschäft*) at the desk.

(b) (*Geldkasten*) cashbox; (*in Läden*) cash register, till; (*Geldmittel*) coffers *pl*; (*bei Spielen*) kitty; (*in einer Spielbank*) bank. **in die ~ greifen** (*inf*) to dip into the till or cashbox; **der Film hat volle ~n gemacht** the film was a big box-office success; **die ~n klingeln** the tills are ringing, the money is really rolling in.

(c) (*Bargeld*) cash. **ein Verkauf per ~** (*form*) a cash sale; **bei ~ sein** (*inf*) to be flush (*inf*) or in the money (*inf*); **wie bist du bei ~?** (*inf*) how are you placed or off for cash?; **knapp/gut/schlecht bei ~ sein** (*inf*) to be short of cash or out of pocket/well-off/badly-off; **~ machen** to check one's finances; (*in Geschäft*) to cash up; (*sl: gut verdienen*) to be raking it in (*inf*), to make a bomb (*sl*); **die ~ führen** to be in charge of the money; **die ~**

stimmt! (*inf*) the money's OK (*inf*); **ein Loch in die** ~ **reißen** (*fig*) to make a dent *or* hole in one's finances; **zur** ~ **bitten** to ask for money; **jdn zur** ~ **bitten** to ask sb to pay up.
   (**d**) (*inf: Spar*~) (savings) bank.
   (**e**) *siehe* **Krankenkasse.**
Kasseler *nt* -s, - *lightly smoked pork loin.*
Kassen-: ~**abschluß** *m* cashing-up; ~**abschluß machen** to cash up; ~**arzt** *m doctor who treats members of sickness insurance schemes;* ≈ National Health general practitioner (*Brit*); ~**beamte(r)** *m* cashier; ~**bericht** *m* financial report; (*in Verein etc auch*) treasurer's report; ~**bestand** *m* cash balance, cash in hand; ~**bon** *m* sales slip; ~**buch** *nt* cashbook; ~**erfolg** *m* (*Theat etc*) box-office hit; ~**führer** *m* treasurer; ~**magnet** *m* (*Theat etc*) big draw; ~**patient** *m patient belonging to medical insurance scheme;* ≈ National Health patient (*Brit*); ~**preis** *m* cash price; ~**prüfung** *f* audit; ~**reißer** *m* (*inf*) (*Theat etc*) box-office hit; (*general*) big draw; ~**rekord** *m* record takings *pl*; ~**schalter** *m siehe* **Kasse** (**a**); ~**schlager** *m* (*inf*) (*Theat etc*) box-office hit; (*Ware*) big seller; ~**stunden** *pl* hours of business (of cashier's office *etc*); ~**sturz** *m* (*Comm*) cashing-up; ~**sturz machen** to check one's finances; (*Comm*) to cash up; ~**wart** *m* -s, -e treasurer; ~**zettel** *m* sales slip.
Kasserolle *f* -, -n saucepan; (*mit Henkeln*) casserole.
Kassette *f* (**a**) (*Kästchen*) case, box.
   (**b**) (*für Bücher*) slipcase; (*Bücher in* ~) set, pack (*Comm*); (*Geschenk*~) gift case/set; (*für Schallplatten*) box; set; (*Tonband*~, *Filmbehälter*) cassette; (*Aufbewahrungs*~) container; (*für Bücher*) library case; (*für Film*) can.
   (**c**) (*Archit*) coffer.
Kassetten-: ~**decke** *f* coffered ceiling; ~**recorder** *m* cassette recorder.
Kassiber *m* -s, - secret message, stiff (*US sl*).
Kassier *m* -s, -e (*S Ger, Aus, Sw*) *siehe* **Kassierer(in).**
kassieren* 1 *vt* (**a**) *Gelder etc* to collect (up), to take in; (*inf*) *Abfindung, Finderlohn* to pick up (*inf*). **nach seinem Tode kassierte sie 50.000 Mark** (*inf*) after his death she collected 50,000 marks; **bei jedem Verkauf kassiert er eine Menge Geld** (*inf*) he makes a packet on every sale (*inf*).
   (**b**) (*inf: wegnehmen*) to take away, to confiscate.
   (**c**) (*inf: verhaften*) to nab (*inf*).
   (**d**) (*Jur*) *Urteil* to quash.
   2 *vi* (**a**) (*abrechnen*) to take the money. **bei jdm** ~ to collect *or* get money from sb; **Sie haben bei mir schon kassiert** I've paid already; **darf ich** ~, **bitte?** would you like to pay now?
   (**b**) (*sl: Geld einnehmen*) to take the money; (*verdienen*) to make money. **seit Willi seine Würstchenbude hat, kassiert er ganz schön** since Willi has had his sausage stall, he's really been raking it in (*inf*) *or* making a bomb (*sl*); **warum soll ich eine Lebensversicherung abschließen, damit meine Erben** ~ **können?** why should I take out a life assurance policy just so my heirs can cash in (on it)?; **bei diesem Geschäft hat er ganz schön kassiert** he cleaned up very nicely on this deal (*inf*).
Kassierer(in *f*) *m* -s, - cashier; (*Bank*~) clerk, teller; (*Einnehmer*) collector; (*eines Klubs*) treasurer.
Kastagnette [kastan'jɛtə] *f* castanet.
Kastanie [-iə] *f* chestnut; (*Roß*~) (horse)chestnut; (*Edel*~) (sweet) chestnut. **glasierte** ~**n** marrons glacés; **für jdn die** ~**n aus dem Feuer holen** (*fig*) to pull sb's chestnuts out of the fire.
Kastanien-: [-iən]: ~**baum** *m* chestnut tree; **k**~**braun** *adj* maroon; *Pferd, Haar* chestnut; ~**holz** *nt* chestnut (wood).
Kästchen *nt* (*kleiner Kasten*) small box; (*für Schmuck*) case, casket. (**b**) (*auf kariertem Papier*) square.
Kaste *f* -, -n caste.
kasteien* *vr* (*als Bußübung*) to castigate *or* chastise oneself, to mortify the flesh (*liter*); (*sich Entbehrungen auferlegen*) to deny oneself.
Kasteiung *f* castigation, mortification of the flesh; self-denial.
Kastell *nt* -s, -e (small) fort; (*Naut, Hist*) castle.
Kastellan *m* -s, -e (*Aufsichtsbeamter, Hausmeister*) steward; (*old dial: in Schulen etc*) janitor, caretaker; (*Hist: Schloßvogt*) castellan.
Kasten *m* -s, - (**a**) box; (*Kiste*) crate, case; (*Truhe*) chest; (*Aus: Schrank*) cupboard; (*N Ger: Schublade*) drawer; (*Brief*~) postbox, letterbox; (*Schau*~) showcase, display case; (*Brot*~) breadbin; (*Sport: Gerät*) box.
   (**b**) (*inf*) (*altes Schiff*) tub (*inf*); (*alter Wagen, Flugzeug*) crate (*inf*); (*altes großes Haus*) barrack(s) *or* barn (of a place) (*inf*); (*Radio, Fernsehapparat etc*) box (*inf*).
   (**c**) (*inf: großer, breiter Mann*) heavyweight (*inf*), big bloke (*Brit inf*).
   (**d**) (*inf*) **er hat viel auf dem** ~ he's brainy (*inf*).
   (**e**) (*Mil sl*) cooler (*Mil sl*). **vier Tage** ~ four days in the cooler.
   (**f**) (*inf: Fußballtor*) goal. **sie müssen noch ein Tor in den** ~ **bringen** they need to put another one in the back of the net; **wie geht's in den** ~? who's going in goal?
Kasten-: ~**form** *f* (*Cook*) (square) baking tin; ~**geist** *m* (*Sociol, Rel*) caste spirit; (*von Cliquen*) clannishness, cliquishness; (*Klassenbewußtsein*) class spirit *or* outlook; ~**wagen** *m* (*Aut*) van, truck, panel truck (*US*); (*auf Bauernhof*) box cart; ~**wesen** *nt* caste system.
Kastilien [-iən] *nt* -s Castille.
Kastrat *m* -en, -en eunuch; (*Mus Hist*) castrato.
Kastration *f* castration.
Kastrations-: ~**angst** *f* fear of castration; ~**komplex** *m* castration complex.
kastrieren* *vt* (**a**) to castrate; *Tiere auch* to geld. (**b**) (*fig inf*) to castrate. **eine Kastrierte** (*sl*) a filter cigarette.
Kasuist *m* casuist.
Kasuistik *f* casuistry.

kasuistisch *adj* casuistic.
Kasus *m* -, - (*Gram*) case.
Kasus-: ~**bildung** *f* case formation, declension; ~**endung** *f* (case) ending.
Kata- *in cpds* cata-; ~**falk** *m* -s, -e catafalque; ~**klysmus** *m* (*liter*) cataclysm; ~**kombe** *f* -, -n catacomb.
Katalane *m* -n, -n, **Katalanin** *f* Catalan.
Katalanien [-iən] *nt* -s Catalonia.
Katalanisch(e) *nt decl as adj* Catalan.
Katalog *m* -(e)s, -e catalogue.
katalogisieren* *vt* to catalogue.
Katalogisierung *f* cataloguing.
katalogmäßig *adj Liste* catalogued. **er erfaßte seine Funde** ~ he made a catalogue of *or* catalogued his finds.
Katalonien [-iən] *nt* -s Catalonia.
Katalysator *m* (*lit, fig*) catalyst.
Katalyse *f* -, -n (*Chem*) catalysis.
katalytisch *adj* catalytic.
Katamaran *m* -s, -e catamaran.
Katapult *nt or m* -(e)s, -e catapult.
katapultieren* 1 *vt* to catapult. 2 *vr* to catapult oneself; (*Pilot*) to eject.
Katapultsitz *m* ejector *or* ejection seat.
Katarakt *m* -(e)s, -e cataract.
Katarrh *m* -s, -e catarrh.
katarrhalisch *adj* catarrhal.
Kataster *m or nt* -s, - land register.
Kataster|amt *nt* land registry.
katastrieren* *vt Grundstücke* to register, to enter in the land register.
katastrophal *adj* disastrous; *Auswirkungen etc auch* catastrophic; (*haarsträubend schlecht auch*) atrocious. **der Mangel an Brot ist** ~ **geworden** the bread shortage has become catastrophic; **das Zimmer sieht ja** ~ **aus** the room looks absolutely disastrous.
Katastrophe *f* -, -n disaster, catastrophe; (*Theat, Liter*) catastrophe, (*tragic*) dénouement. **der ist eine** ~ (*inf*) he's a real disaster (area) (*inf*) *or* catastrophe (*inf*).
Katastrophen-: ~**dienst** *m* emergency service; ~**einsatz** *m* duty *or* use in case of disaster; **für den** ~**einsatz** for use in case of disaster; ~**gebiet** *nt* disaster area; ~**schutz** *m* disaster control; (*im voraus*) disaster prevention.
Katatonie *f* (*Psych*) catatonia.
Kate *f* -, -n (*N Ger*) cottage, croft (*Scot*).
Katechese *f* -, -n catechesis.
Katechet(in *f*) *m* -en, -en catechist.
Katechismus *m* catechism.
Katechist(in *f*) *m* catechist.
kategorial *adj* categorical.
Kategorie *f* category. **er gehört auch zur** ~ **derer, die ...** he's one of those *or* of that sort who ...
kategorisch *adj* categorical, absolute; *Ablehnung auch* flat. **der K**~**e Imperativ** the categorical imperative; **ich weigerte mich** ~ I refused outright, I absolutely refused; **er lehnte** ~ **ab** he categorically refused; **... erklärte er** ~ **...** he declared emphatically.
kategorisieren* *vt* to categorize.
Kater *m* -s, - (**a**) *m* (tom(cat). **er ist verliebt wie ein** ~ (*dated*) he is smitten; **wie ein verliebter** ~ like an amorous tomcat; *siehe* **gestiefelt.** (**b**) (*Katzenjammer*) hangover.
Kater-: ~**frühstück** *nt breakfast (of pickled herring etc) to cure a hangover*; ~**idee** *f* (*inf*) hare-brained idea; ~**stimmung** *f* depression, the blues *pl* (*inf*); **nach der Party herrschte eine** ~**stimmung** after the party everyone was hung-over.
katexochen [katɛksɔ'xeːn] *adv* (*liter*) **Demokratie** ~ the epitome of democracy; **er ist der Übersetzer** ~ he is the epitome of a good translator.
Katgut *nt* -s, *no pl* catgut.
kath. *abbr of* **katholisch.**
Katharsis *f* -, *no pl* (*Liter, fig*) catharsis.
kathartisch *adj* (*Liter, fig*) cathartic.
Katheder *m or nt* -s, - (*in Schule*) teacher's desk; (*in Universität*) lectern. **ein Streit zwischen den** ~**n** (*fig*) an academic dispute, a dispute between two schools of thought; **etw vom** ~ **herab erklären** to declare sth ex cathedra (*hum, form*).
Kathedrale *f* -, -n cathedral.
Katheter *m* -s, - (*Med*) catheter.
Kathode *f* -, -n (*Phys*) cathode.
Kathoden-: ~**strahlen** *pl* (*Phys*) cathode rays *pl*; ~**strahlröhre** *f* (*TV etc*) cathode ray tube.
Kathole *m* -n, -n (*inf*) Catholic, Papist (*pej*).
Katholik(in *f*) *m* -en, -en (*Roman*) Catholic.
katholisch *adj* (*Roman*) Catholic. **sie ist streng** ~ she's a strict Catholic; **jdn** ~ **erziehen** to bring sb up (as) a Catholic.
Katholizismus *m* (*Roman*) Catholicism.
Katholizität *f* Catholicism.
katilinarisch *adj* Catilinian.
Kätner *m* -s, - (*N Ger*) smallholder, crofter (*Scot*).
katschen, kätschen *vi* (*S Ger, Sw*) to chomp (*inf*).
Katt|anker *m* (*Naut*) kedge.
Kattegatt *nt* -s Kattegat.
Kattun *m* -s, -e (*old*) cotton, calico.
Kattunkleid *nt* cotton *or* calico dress.
katzbalgen *vr* to romp around.
Katzbalgerei *f* romping.
katzbuckeln *vi* (*pej inf*) to bow and scrape, to grovel.
Kätzchen *nt* (**a**) (*junge Katze, inf: Mädchen*) kitten; (*Katze*) pussy (*inf*). (**b**) (*Bot*) catkin.
Katze *f* -, -n (**a**) cat. **sie ist eine falsche** ~ she's two-faced.
   (**b**) (*fig: in Wendungen*) **meine Arbeit war für die Katz** (*inf*)

my work was a waste of time; **das hat die ~ gefressen** the fairies took it (*hum inf*); **Katz und Maus mit jdm spielen** (*inf*) to play cat and mouse with sb; **wer hängt der ~ die Schelle um?** (*fig*) who will bell the cat?; **wie die ~ um den heißen Brei herumschleichen** to beat about the bush; **die ~ aus dem Sack lassen** (*inf*) to let the cat out of the bag; **laß die ~ endlich aus dem Sack** (*inf*) come on, spill the beans (*inf*); **die ~ im Sack kaufen** to buy a pig in a poke (*prov*); **die ~ läßt das Mausen nicht** (*Prov*) the leopard cannot change its spots (*Prov*); **bei Nacht sind alle ~n grau** all cats are grey at night; **wenn die ~ aus dem Haus ist, tanzen die Mäuse (auf dem Tisch)** (*Prov*) when the cat's away the mice will play (*Prov*).
(**c**) (*Raubtierart*) cat.
(**d**) (*Geld~*) (money) pouch.
Katzelmacher *m* (*S Ger, Aus: pej: Italiener*) Eyetie (*pej*).
Katzen-: ~**auge** *nt* (**a**) (*Straßenmarkierung*) cat's-eye; (*Rückstrahler*) reflector; (**b**) (*Min*) cat's-eye; ~**bär** *m* panda; ~**buckel** *m* arched back (of a cat); **einen ~buckel machen** to arch one's back; **k~freundlich** *adj* (*pej*) overfriendly; **k~haft** *adj* cat-like, feline; ~**hai** *m* dogfish; ~**jammer** *m* (*inf*) (**a**) (*Kater*) hangover; (**b**) (*jämmerliche Stimmung*) depression, the blues *pl* (*inf*); **ich habe ~jammer** I feel down (in the dumps) (*inf*), I've got the blues (*inf*); **k~jämmerlich** *adj* (*inf*) down (in the dumps) (*inf*), miserable; ~**kopf** *m* (*fig*) (**a**) (*Kopfstein*) cobble(stone); (**b**) (*Sch: Schlag*) cuff (on the head), box round the ears; ~**musik** *f* (*fig*) caterwauling, din, racket (*inf*); ~**sprung** *m* (*inf*) stone's throw; ~**tisch** *m* (*hum*) children's table; **die Kinder essen am ~tisch** the children are eating at their own table; ~**wäsche** *f* (*hum inf*) a lick and a promise (*inf*), a cat's lick (*inf*); ~**wäsche machen** to give oneself a lick and a promise; **ihr braucht heute nur ~wäsche zu machen** just a quick wash will do today; ~**zunge** *f* (*Schokolade*) langue de chat.
Kau-: ~**apparat** *m* masticatory apparatus; **setz mal deinen ~apparat in Bewegung** (*hum*) get stuck in (*inf*); ~**bewegung** *f* chewing movement.
Kauderwelsch *nt* -(s), *no pl* (*pej*) (*Fach- oder Geheimsprache*) lingo (*inf*), jargon; (*Gemisch aus mehreren Sprachen/Dialekten*) hotchpotch *or* mishmash (of different languages/dialects); (*unverständliche Sprache*) double dutch, gibberish.
kauderwelschen *vi siehe n* to talk jargon; to talk a hotchpotch *or* mishmash (of different languages/dialects); to talk double dutch *or* gibberish.
kauen **1** *vt* to chew; (*Med, form*) to masticate; **Nägel** to bite, to chew; **Wein** to taste.
2 *vi* to chew. **an etw** (*dat*) ~ to chew (on) sth; **an den Nägeln ~** to bite *or* chew one's nails; **daran hatte ich lange zu ~** (*fig*) it took me a long time to get over it; **daran wird er zu ~ haben** (*fig*) that will really give him food for thought *or* something to think about; **gut gekaut ist halb verdaut** (*Prov*) you should chew your food properly; **das K~** chewing; (*Med, form*) mastication.
kauern *vir* (*vi auch aux sein*) to crouch (down); (*ängstlich*) to cower; (*schutzsuchend*) to be huddled (up).
Kauf *m* -(e)s, **Käufe** (*das Kaufen*) buying *no pl*, purchase (*esp form*), purchasing *no pl* (*esp form*); (*das Gekaufte*) purchase (*esp form*), buy. **das war ein günstiger ~** that was a good buy; **diese Käufe haben sich gelohnt** it was worth buying these; **mit diesem Anzug machen Sie bestimmt einen guten ~** this suit is definitely a good buy; **ein ~ auf Kredit** a credit purchase; **etw zum ~ anbieten** to offer sth for sale; **einen ~ abschließen** *or* **tätigen** (*form*) to complete a purchase; **etw durch ~ erwerben** (*form*) to purchase sth; **leichten ~s davonkommen** (*fig*) to get off lightly; **etw in ~ nehmen** (*fig*) to accept sth.
Kauf-: ~**auftrag** *m* purchasing *or* buying order; ~**brief** *m* deed of purchase; (*esp für Grundstücke*) title deed.
kaufen **1** *vt* (**a**) (*auch sich* (*dat*)) ~ to buy, to purchase (*esp form*). **ich kauf' dir ein Geschenk** I'll buy you a present *or* a present for you; **ich habe (mir) einen neuen Anzug gekauft** I bought (myself) a new suit; **etw für teures Geld ~** (*inf*) to pay a lot (of money) for sth, to pay good money for sth; **diese Zigaretten werden viel/nicht gekauft** we sell a lot of these cigarettes/nobody buys these cigarettes; **jetzt wird nicht schon wieder eine neue Hose gekauft!** you're not going to buy another pair of trousers!; **dafür kann ich mir nichts ~** (*iro*), **was kann man sich (dat) dafür (schon)** ~ (*iro*) what use is that to me!, that's a fat lot of use! (*inf*).
(**b**) (*bestechen*) **jdn** to bribe, to buy off; **Spiel** to fix; **Stimmen** to buy. **der Sieg war gekauft** it was fixed.
(**c**) **sich** (*dat*) **jdn ~** (*inf*) to give sb a piece of one's mind (*inf*); (*tätlich*) to fix sb (*inf*).
(**d**) *auch vi* (*Cards*) to buy.
2 *vi* to buy; (*Einkäufe machen*) to shop. **auf dem Markt kauft man billiger** it is cheaper to shop *or* you can buy things cheaper at the market; **das K~** buying, purchasing (*esp form*).
Käufer(in *f*) *m* -s, - buyer, purchaser (*esp form*); (*Kunde*) customer, shopper.
Kauf-: ~**fahrer** *m*, ~**fahrteischiff** *nt* (*old*) merchant ship, merchantman; ~**halle** *f*, ~**haus** *nt* department store; ~**kraft** *f* (*von Geld*) buying *or* purchasing power; (*vom Käufer*) spending power; **dafür fehlt mir die ~kraft** I cannot afford that, I don't have enough money to buy that; **Kunden mit ~kraft** customers with money to spend; **k~kräftig** *adj* **eine k~kräftige Währung** a currency with good purchasing power; **k~kräftige Kunden** customers with money to spend; **der Dollar ist heutzutage in Japan nicht mehr besonders k~kräftig** these days the dollar has not retained its purchasing power in Japan.
Kaufkraft-: ~**lenkung** *f* control of (consumer) spending; ~**überhang** *m* excess *or* surplus (consumer) spending power;

Kauf-: ~**laden** *m* (**a**) (*rare: Ladengeschäft*) (small) shop; (**b**) (*Spielzeug*) toy shop; ~**leute** *pl of* ~**mann**.
käuflich *adj* (**a**) (*zu kaufen*) for sale, purchasable (*form*). **etwas, was nicht ~ ist** something which cannot be bought; **etw ~ erwerben** (*form*) to purchase sth.
(**b**) (*fig*) venal. ~**e Liebe** (*geh*) prostitution; **ein ~es Mädchen** (*geh*) a woman of easy virtue; **Freundschaft ist nicht ~** friendship cannot be bought.
(**c**) (*fig: bestechlich*) venal. ~ **sein** to be easily bought; **ich bin nicht ~** you cannot buy me!
Käuflichkeit *f* (**a**) purchasability (*form*). **Kennzeichen des Kapitalismus ist die ~ aller Dinge** it is a characteristic of capitalism that everything can be bought *or* is for sale. (**b**) (*fig*) (*Bestechlichkeit*) corruptibility, venality.
Kauf-: ~**lust** *f* desire to buy (things); (*St Ex*) buying; **die ~lust hat plötzlich zugenommen** people have suddenly gone on a spending spree; **k~lustig** *adj* inclined to buy, in a buying mood; **in den Straßen drängten sich die ~lustigen** the streets were thronged with shoppers.
Kaufmann *m*, *pl* -**leute** (**a**) (*Geschäftsmann*) businessman; (*Händler*) trader; (*Tabak~, Gewürz~, Woll~ etc*) merchant. **gelernter ~** person with qualifications in business *or* commerce; **jeder ~ lobt seine Ware** (*Prov*) a salesman will always praise his own wares.
(**b**) (*Einzelhandels~*) small shopkeeper, grocer. **zum ~ gehen** to go to the grocer's.
kaufmännisch *adj* commercial, business *attr*. ~**er Angestellter** clerk; **er wollte einen ~en Beruf ergreifen** he wanted to make a career in business *or* commerce; **er übt einen ~en Beruf aus** he is in business *or* commerce; **Fachschule für ~e Berufe** commercial college, business school; ~ **denken** to think in commercial *or* business terms; **alles K~e** everything commercial, everything to do with business; **alles K~e macht seine Frau für ihn** his wife looks after the business side of things for him; **er ist ~ tätig** he is in business *or* is a businessman; **sie ist ~ veranlagt** she is commercially minded, she has a good head for business.
Kaufmannschaft *f* (*geh*) merchants *pl*.
Kaufmanns-: ~**deutsch** *nt* business *or* commercial German; ~**gehilfe** *m* assistant, clerk; (*im Laden*) sales assistant, clerk (*US*); ~**laden** *m* (**a**) (*dated*) grocer's; (*Gemischtwarenhandlung*) general store; (**b**) (*Spielzeug*) toy grocer's shop; ~**lehrling** *m* management trainee; ~**stand** *m* merchant class.
Kauf-: ~**preis** *m* selling price; ~**summe** *f* money; ~**unlust** *f* consumer resistance; ~**vertrag** *m* bill of sale; ~**wert** *m* market value; ~**zwang** *m* obligation to buy; **kein/ohne ~zwang** no/without obligation.
Kaugummi *m* chewing gum.
Kaukasien [-iən] *nt* -s Caucasia.
Kaukasier(in *f*) [-iɐ, -iərɪn] *m* -s, - Caucasian.
kaukasisch *adj Rasse* Caucasian.
Kaukasus *m* -: **der ~** (the) Caucasus.
Kaulquappe *f* tadpole.
kaum **1** *adv* (**a**) (*noch nicht einmal*) hardly, scarcely, barely. **er verdient ~ 200 Mark/ich habe ~ noch 10 Liter** he earns hardly *etc* 200 marks/I've hardly *etc* 10 litres left; **das kostet ~ 200 Mark/man braucht ~ 10 Liter** it doesn't even cost 200 marks/you'll need less than 10 litres; **sie war ~ hereingekommen, als ... hardly** *or* scarcely *or* no sooner had she come in when ..., she had hardly *etc* come in when ...; ~ **jemand/jemals** hardly *or* scarcely anyone/ever; **es ist ~ möglich, daß ...** it is hardly *or* scarcely possible that ...; **es ist ~ zu glauben, wie ...** it's hardly *or* scarcely believable *or* to be believed how ...; **wir hatten ~ noch Benzin** we had hardly *or* scarcely any petrol left, we hardly *etc* had any petrol left; **ich hatte ~ noch Zeit, mich zu verabschieden** I hardly *etc* had time to say goodbye; **er kann ~ noch sprechen/laufen** he can hardly *etc* speak/walk any more; **ich hatte ~ noch damit gerechnet, daß ...** I hardly *or* scarcely thought ... any more.
(**b**) (*wahrscheinlich nicht*) hardly, scarcely. ~**!** hardly, scarcely; **wohl ~/ich glaube ~** I hardly *or* scarcely think so; **ich glaube ~, daß ...** I hardly *or* scarcely think that ...; **das wird wohl ~ stimmen** that can hardly *or* scarcely be right/true, surely that can't be right/true; **das wird ~ passieren** that's hardly *or* scarcely likely to happen; **das wird wohl ~ noch was werden** (*inf*) that's hardly *or* scarcely likely to come to anything.
2 *conj* hardly, scarcely. ~ **daß wir das Meer erreicht hatten ...** hardly *etc* had we reached the sea when ..., no sooner had we reached the sea than ...; ~ **gerufen, eilte der Diener herbei** no sooner summoned, the servant hurried in; **er verdient äußerst wenig,** ~ **daß er davon satt wird** he earns extremely little and can hardly even buy enough to eat.
Kaumuskel *m* jaw muscle, masseter (*spec*).
kausal *adj* causal.
Kausalgesetz *nt* law of causality.
Kausalität *f* causality.
Kausalitätsprinzip *nt* principle of causality.
Kausal-: ~**kette** *f* causal chain, chain of cause and effect; ~**nexus** *m* (*geh*) causal connection; ~**satz** *m* causal clause; ~**zusammenhang** *m* causal connection.
Kausativ *m* (*Gram*) causative.
kausativ *adj* (*Gram*) causative.
kaustisch *adj* (*Chem, fig*) caustic.
Kautabak *m* chewing tobacco.
Kautel *f* -, -en (*geh*) proviso.
Kaution *f* (**a**) (*Jur*) bail. ~ **stellen** to stand bail; **er stellte 1000 Mark ~** he put up 1000 marks (as) bail; **gegen ~** on bail; **jdn gegen ~ freibekommen** to bail sb out. (**b**) (*Comm*) security. (**c**) (*für Miete*) deposit.

Kautschuk m -s, -e (india)rubber.
Kautschuk-: ~**milch** f latex; ~**paragraph** m (inf) siehe Gummiparagraph.
Kauwerkzeuge pl masticatory organs pl.
Kauz m -es, **Käuze (a)** screech owl. **(b)** (Sonderling) odd or strange fellow, oddball (esp US inf). **ein komischer** ~ an odd bird; **ein wunderlicher alter** ~ a strange old bird.
Käuzchen nt dim of **Kauz (a).**
kauzig adj odd, cranky.
Kauzigkeit f crankiness.
Kavalier [kava'li:ɐ] m -s, -e (a) (galanter Mann) gentleman. **er ist immer** ~ he's always a gentleman or always chivalrous; **der** ~ **genießt und schweigt** one does not boast about one's conquests. **(b)** (dated: Begleiter einer Dame) beau (old), young man (dated).
Kavaliers-: ~**delikt** nt trivial offence, (mere) peccadillo; ~**schnupfen** m (hum) a dose of the clap (sl), a wound of honour (hum).
Kavalier(s)-: ~**start** m (Aut) racing start; ~**tuch** nt (dated) handkerchief in one's top pocket.
Kavalkade [kaval'ka:də] f cavalcade.
Kavallerie [kavalə'ri:] f (Mil) cavalry.
Kavalleriepferd nt cavalry horse.
Kavallerist [kavalə'rɪst] m (Mil Hist) cavalryman.
Kaventsmann [ka'vɛntsman] m, pl **-männer** (N Ger inf) whopper (inf).
Kaviar ['ka:viar] m -s, -e caviar.
Kaviarbrot nt French loaf.
Kcal abbr of **Kilokalorie.**
Kebab m -(s), -s kebab.
Kebse f -, -n, **Kebsweib** nt (old, Bibl) concubine.
keck adj (a) (dated: frech) cheeky, saucy. **(b)** (dated: flott) Mädchen pert; Hut auch cheeky, saucy. **sie trug den Hut** ~ **auf einem Ohr** she wore her hat at a jaunty or saucy angle over one ear. **(c)** (old: tapfer) bold.
keckern vi to snarl, to growl.
Keckheit f siehe adj **(a)** cheekiness, sauciness. **(b)** pertness; cheekiness, sauciness. **(c)** boldness.
Keeper ['ki:pɐ] m -s, - (Aus Sport) (goal)keeper.
Kefir m -s, no pl kefir (a milk product similar to yoghurt, of Turkish origin).
Kegel m -s, - (a) (Spielfigur) skittle, ninepin; (bei Bowling) pin. **wir schieben** ~ (inf) we play skittles or ninepins; we go bowling; ~ **aufsetzen** to set the skittles/pins up; siehe **Kind. (b)** (Geometrie) cone; (Berg~) peak. **(c)** (Licht~, Scheinwerfer~) beam (of light). **(d)** (Typ) body, shank.
Kegel-: ~**bahn** f (bowling) lane; (Anlage) skittle-alley; (automatisch) bowling alley; ~**bruder** m (inf) (eifriger Kegler) skittle-player; bowling fanatic; **die** ~**brüder** the skittle/bowling club; **ein** ~**bruder von dir** one of your skittle/bowling club pals; **k~förmig** adj conical; ~**kugel** f bowl; ~**mantel** m surface of a cone.
kegeln vi to play skittles or ninepins; (bei Bowling) to play bowls. ~ **gehen** to play skittles; to go bowling.
Kegel-: ~**rad** nt (Tech) bevelled or mitre wheel; **k~scheiben** (Aus), **k~schieben** vi sep irreg siehe **Kegel (a)**; ~**schnitt** m conic section; ~**sport** m bowling; ~**stumpf** m frustum.
Kegler(in f) m -s, - skittle-player; (bei Bowling) bowler.
Kehle f -, -n (a) (Gurgel) throat. **(sich dat) die** ~ **schmieren** (inf) or **anfeuchten** (inf) to wet one's whistle (inf); **das ist ihm in die falsche** ~ **gekommen**, **er hat das in die falsche** ~ **bekommen** (lit) it went down the wrong way or got stuck in his throat; (fig) he took it the wrong way; **eine rauhe** ~ **haben** to be hoarse; **er hat Gold in der** ~ (inf) his voice is/could be a real gold-mine; **aus voller** ~ at the top of one's voice or lungs.
(b) (ausgerundeter Winkel) moulding; (Rille) groove.
kehlig adj Aussprache guttural; Lachen, Alt throaty.
Kehlkopf m larynx.
Kehlkopf-: ~**entzündung** f, ~**katarrh** m laryngitis; ~**krebs** m cancer of the throat; ~**mikrophon** nt throat microphone; ~**spiegel** m laryngoscope.
Kehllaut m guttural (sound).
Kehlung f (Archit) groove, flute.
Kehlverschlußlaut m (Phon) glottal stop.
Kehr-: ~**aus** m -, no pl last dance; (fig: Abschiedsfeier) farewell celebration; **den** ~**aus machen** (fig) to have a farewell celebration; ~**besen** m broom; ~**blech** nt (S Ger) shovel.
Kehre f -, -n (a) (sharp) turn or bend; (Haarnadelkurve) hairpin bend. **(b)** (Turnübung) rear or back vault.
kehren¹ 1 vt (a) to turn. **die Augen** or **den Blick zum Himmel/zu Boden** ~ (liter) to turn one's eyes or gaze heavenwards/to cast one's eyes to the ground (liter); **in sich** (acc) **gekehrt** (versunken) pensive, wrapped in thought; (verschlossen) introspective, introverted; siehe **Rücken.**
(b) (kümmern) to bother. **was kehrt mich das?** what do I care about that?
2 vr (a) to turn. **diese Politik kehrt sich eindeutig gegen den Frieden** this policy is clearly aimed against peace; **eines Tages wird sich sein Hochmut gegen ihn** ~ one day his arrogance will rebound against him.
(b) **er kehrt sich nicht daran, was die Leute sagen** he doesn't mind or care what people say.
3 vi to turn (round); (Wind) to turn.
kehren² vti (esp S Ger: fegen) to sweep. **ich muß noch** ~ I've still got to do the sweeping; **jeder kehre vor seiner Tür!** (Prov) everyone should first put his own house in order; siehe **Besen.**
Kehricht m or nt -s, no pl (old, form) sweepings pl. **den** ~ **zusammenfegen** to sweep up the rubbish; siehe **feucht.**
Kehr-: ~**maschine** f (Straßen~) road-sweeper; road sweeping machine; (Teppich~) carpet-sweeper; ~**platz** m (Sw) turning

area; ~**reim** m chorus, refrain; ~**schaufel** f shovel; ~**seite** f **(a)** (von Münze) reverse; **(b)** (inf: Rücken) back; (hum: Gesäß) backside (inf), behind; (fig: Nachteil) drawback; **jdm seine** ~**seite zuwenden** to turn one's back on sb; **(c)** (fig: Schattenseite) other side; **die** ~**seite der Medaille** the other side of the coin; **jedes Ding hat seine** ~**seite** everything has its drawbacks.
kehrt interj (Mil) ganze Abteilung ~! company, about turn!
Kehrt-: **k~machen** vi sep to turn round, to do an about-turn; (zurückgehen) to turn back; (Mil) to about-turn; ~**wendung** f about-turn; **diese plötzliche** ~**wendung wurde scharf kritisiert** this sudden about-turn or volte-face was sharply criticized.
Kehr-: ~**um** m (dial): **im** ~**um** in a trice or flash; ~**wert** m reciprocal value; ~**wisch** m -s, -e (old, S Ger) (hand-)brush; ~**woche** f (S Ger) week when a resident has to take his/her turn to clean the communal areas of flats etc, cleaning week.
keifen vi to bicker.
Keiferei f (inf) bickering.
Keil m -(e)s, -e wedge (auch Mil); (als Hemmvorrichtung auch) chock; (Faust~) hand-axe; (Sew: Zwickel) gusset; (Kopf~) headrest. **einen** ~ **in etw** (acc) **treiben** to put a wedge in sth; (zum Befestigen auch) to wedge sth; **einen** ~ **zwischen zwei Freunde treiben** (fig) to drive a wedge between two friends; siehe **grob.**
Keil-: ~**absatz** m wedge heel, wedge; ~**bein** nt sphenoid (bone).
Keile pl (inf) thrashing, hiding. ~ **bekommen** or **kriegen** or **beziehen** to get or be given a thrashing or hiding; **dahinten gibt's gleich** ~ there's going to be a fight over there.
keilen 1 vt (a) (mit Keil) to wedge. **(b)** (sl: anwerben) Mitglieder to rope in (inf). 2 vr (inf: sich prügeln) to fight.
Keiler m -s, - wild boar.
Keilerei f (inf) punch-up (inf), brawl, fight.
Keil-: **k~förmig** adj wedge-shaped; ~**haue** f (Min) pick(axe); ~**hose** f, ~**hosen** pl ski pants pl; ~**kissen**, ~**polster** (Aus) nt wedge-shaped pillow (used as a headrest); ~**rahmen** m stretcher (for artist's canvas); ~**riemen** m drive-belt; (Aut) fan-belt; ~**schrift** f cuneiform script.
Keim m -(e)s, -e (a) (kleiner Trieb) shoot, sprout. **die ersten** ~**e ihrer jungen Liebe** (liter) the first blossomings or burgeoning of their young love (liter).
(b) (Embryo, fig) embryo, germ; (Krankheits~) germ. **im** ~**e** (fig) in embryo, in embryonic form; **etw im** ~ **ersticken** to nip sth in the bud; **der** ~ **eines werdenden Lebens** (geh) the beginnings of a new life.
(c) (fig: des Hasses, der Liebe etc) seed usu pl. **den** ~ **zu etw legen** to sow the seeds of sth; **den** ~ **des Hasses/des Bösen/der Hoffnung in jds Herz** (acc) **senken** (liter) to sow the seeds of hate/evil/hope in sb's breast.
Keim-: ~**blatt** nt (Bot) cotyledon; **(b)** (Zool) blastema; ~**drüse** f gonad; ~**drüsenhormon** nt sex hormone.
keimen vi (a) to germinate; (Pflanzen) to put out shoots, to shoot; (Knollen) to sprout. **(b)** (Verdacht) to be aroused; (Hoffnung auch) to stir (in one's breast liter). **das** ~**de Leben** (geh) the seeds of a new life.
Keim-: **k~frei** adj germ-free, free of germs pred; (Med auch, fig) sterile, **k~frei machen** to sterilize; **k~haft** adj (geh) embryonic, seminal; **k~haft vorhanden sein** to be present in embryo or in embryonic or seminal form; ~**ling** m (a) (Embryo) embryo; **(b)** (~pflanze) sprout, shoot; ~**plasma** nt germ plasm; **k~tötend** adj germicidal; **k~tötendes Mittel** germicide; ~**träger** m carrier.
Keimung f germination.
Keimzelle f germ cell.
kein, keine, keins, **kein** indef pron (a) (adjektivisch) no; (mit sing auch) not a; (mit pl n, bei Sammelbegriffen, bei Abstrakten auch) not any. ~ **Mann/**~**e Häuser/**~ **Whisky** ... no man/houses/whisky ...; **hast du** ~ **Herz?** have you no heart?; **hast du** ~ **Gefühl?** have you no or haven't you got any feeling?; **hast du** ~**en Bleistift?** haven't you got a or have you no pencil?; **hast du** ~**e Vorschläge/Geschwister?** haven't you got any or have you no suggestions/brothers and sisters?; **ich sehe da** ~**en Unterschied** I see no difference, I don't see any or a difference; **da sind** ~**e Häuser** there are no or there aren't any houses there; **er hatte** ~**e Chance** he had no or he didn't have a or any chance; ~ **echter Schotte würde** ... no true Scot would ...; **er ist** ~ **echter Schotte** he is no or not a true Scot; **er ist** ~ **Lehrer** he is not a teacher; (~ **guter auch**) he's no teacher; ~**e Widerrede/Ahnung!** no arguing/idea!; ~**e schlechte Idee** not a bad idea; ~**e Lust/Angst!** don't want to/don't worry; **das ist** ~**e Antwort auf unsere Frage** that's not an or the answer to our question; **ich habe noch** ~**en so sympathischen Lehrer gehabt** I've never had such a pleasant teacher; **er ist noch** ~ **erfahrener Lehrer** he is not yet an experienced teacher; ~ **bißchen** not a bit; **ich habe** ~ **bißchen Lust/Zeit** I've absolutely no desire to/time; **ich bin doch** ~ **Kind mehr!** I am not a child any longer or no longer a child; ~ **anderer als er** ... only he ..., no-one else but he ...; **das habe ich** ~**em anderen als dir gesagt** I have told nobody else or haven't told anybody else apart from you; ~**ein-ziger** (niemand) not a single one or person; ~**einziges Mal** not a single time; **in** ~**ster Weise** (incorrect) not in the least.
(b) (nicht einmal) less than. ~**e Stunde/drei Monate** less than an hour/three months; ~**e 5 Mark** under 5 marks.
keine(r, s) indef pron (substantivisch) (niemand) nobody (auch subj), no-one (auch subj), not anybody, not anyone; (von Gegenstand) not one, none; (bei Abstraktum) none; (obj) not any, none; (von Gegenständen, bei Abstrakta) none; (obj) not any, none. ~**r liebt mich** nobody or no-one loves me; **es war** ~**r** there was nobody etc there, there wasn't anybody etc there; (Gegenstand) there wasn't one there; **es waren** ~ **da** there wasn't anybody etc there; (Gegenstände) there weren't

any or there were none there; ich habe ~s I haven't got one; **von diesen Platten ist** ~ ... none or not one of these records is ...; **haben Sie Äpfel?** — nein, leider haben wir ~ have you any apples? — no, I'm afraid we haven't (any); **hast du schon ein Glas?** — nein, ich habe ~s have you a glass? — no, I haven't (got one) or no, I don't (US); ~r **von uns/von uns** (beiden) none/neither of us; (betont) not one of us; er hat ~n von beiden angetroffen he didn't meet either or he met neither of them; ~s **der** (beiden) **Kinder/Bücher** neither of the children/books; ~s **der sechs Kinder/Bücher** none of the six children/books; (betont) not one of the six children/books; **er kannte** ~s **der** (fünf) **Kinder** he didn't know any of or he knew none of the (five) children; **ist Bier da?** — nein, ich habe ~s **gekauft** is there any beer? — no, I didn't buy any; **Tee haben wir, aber Kaffee haben wir** ~n we've got tea but no coffee; **dumm/geschickt wie** ~r incredibly stupid/clever.

keinerlei adj attr inv no ... what(so)ever or at all.

keinerseits adv **sein Vorschlag fand** ~ **Zustimmung** his suggestion met with no support anywhere or from any side; **ich möchte mich** ~ **festlegen** I wouldn't like to commit myself in any direction.

keinesfalls adv under no circumstances, not ... under any circumstances. ~ **darfst du** ... under no circumstances or on no account must you ...; **aber er ist** ~ **dümmer als sein Bruder** he is at least as intelligent as his brother.

keineswegs adv not at all, by no means; (als Antwort) not in the least, not at all. **ich fühle mich** ~ **schuldig** I do not feel in the least or in any way guilty.

keinmal adv never once, not once. **er war noch** ~ **im Kino** he has never or not once been to the cinema, never or not once has he been to the cinema; siehe **einmal**.

keins = **keines** siehe **keine(r, s)**.

Keks m -es, -e or (Aus) nt -, - biscuit (Brit), cookie (US).

Kelch m -(e)s, -e (a) (Trinkglas) goblet; (Eccl) chalice, communion cup. **den** (bitteren) ~ (des Leidens) **bis zur Neige leeren** (fig) to drain the (bitter) cup of sorrow (to the last); **möge dieser** ~ **an mir vorübergehen** (Bibl) let this cup pass from me; **dieser** ~ **ist noch einmal an mir vorübergegangen** I have been spared again, the Good Lord has spared me again. (b) (Bot) calyx; (liter) cup, bell, chalice (poet).

Kelchblatt nt sepal.

Kelch-: k~förmig adj cup-shaped, bell-shaped; **die k~förmig geöffnete Blüte** the cup-shaped or bell-shaped blossom; ~glas nt goblet, goblet-shaped glass.

Kelim m -(s), -(s) kilim (Eastern carpet).

Kelle f -, -n (a) (Suppen~ etc) ladle; (Schaumlöffel) strainer, straining spoon. (b) (Maurer~) trowel. (c) (Signalstab) signalling disc. (d) (sl: Tischtennisschläger) bat, paddle; (Tennisschläger) racket.

Keller m -s, - cellar; (Geschoß) basement; (Gaststätte) (cellar) restaurant/bar. **im** ~ **sitzen** (inf: beim Kartenspiel) to have minus points.

Keller- in cpds cellar; basement; ~assel f wood-louse.

Kellerei f wine/champagne/fruit-juice producer's; (Lagerraum) cellar(s). **Wein direkt von der** ~ **kaufen** to buy wine direct from the producer's.

Keller-: ~geschoß nt basement; ~gewölbe nt vaulted cellar roof; (Keller) cellars pl; (Verlies) dungeon; ~kind nt unhealthy slum kid; ~kneipe f (inf), ~lokal nt cellar bar; ~meister m vintner; (in Kloster) cellarer; ~wechsel m (Fin) bill on fictitious drawee, dud bill; ~wohnung f basement flat.

Kellner m -s, - waiter.

Kellnerin f waitress.

kellnern vi (inf) to work as a waiter, to wait on tables (US).

Kelte m -n, -n, **Keltin** f Celt.

Kelter f -, -n winepress; (Obst~) press.

keltern vt Trauben, Wein to press.

Kemenate f -, -n lady's heated apartment(s) (in a castle); (fig) boudoir.

Kenia nt -s Kenya.

Kenianer(in f) m -s, - Kenyan.

kenianisch adj Kenyan.

kennen pret **kannte**, ptp **gekannt** vt to know; (~gelernt haben auch) to be acquainted with; (geh: er~) to recognize. **er kennt das Leben** he knows the ways of the world, he knows about life; **diese Vögel kennt man in Europa nicht** these birds are not known in Europe; **er kennt den Hunger nicht** he has never known hunger, he doesn't know what hunger is; **er kennt keine Müdigkeit** he never gets tired, he doesn't know what tiredness means; **kein Erbarmen/Mitleid** etc ~ to know no mercy/pity etc; **ich habe mich nicht mehr gekannt vor Wut** I was beside myself with anger; **so was** ~ **wir hier nicht!** we don't have that sort of thing here; **jdn als etw** ~ to know sb to be sth; ~ **Sie sich schon?** do you know each other (already)?; ~ **Sie den** (schon)? (Witz) have you heard this one?; **das** ~ **wir** (schon) (iro) we know all about that; **kennst du mich noch?** do you remember me?; **sie kennt uns nicht mehr/will uns nicht mehr** ~ she does not know/want to know us any more; **wie ich ihn kenne** ... if I know him (at all) ...; **ich trinke jetzt lieber kein Bier, ich kenne mich** I'd rather not have any beer now, I know me (inf) or I know what I'm like; **du kennst dich doch!** you know what you're like; **so kenne ich dich ja** (noch) **gar nicht!** I've never known you like this before; **da kennst du mich aber schlecht** you don't know me, that just shows how little you know me.

kennenlernen vt sep to get to know, to become acquainted with (form); (zum ersten Mal treffen) to meet. **sich** ~ to get to know each other; to meet each other; **jdn näher** ~ to get to know sb better, to become better acquainted with sb; **ich freue mich, Sie kennenzulernen** (form) (I am) pleased to meet you or to make your acquaintance (form); **der soll or wird mich noch** ~

(inf) he'll have me to reckon with (inf); **ich freue mich schon sehr auf unser K~** I look forward to meeting you/him etc; **bei näherem K~ erwies er sich als ... on closer acquaintance he proved to be ...

Kenner(in f) m -s, - (a) (Sachverständiger) expert (von or gen on/in), authority (von or gen on). ~ **der internen Vorgänge** those who know about the internal procedures; **da zeigt sich der** ~, **da merkt man den** ~ there you (can) see the (touch of the) expert. (b) (Wein~ etc) connoisseur, co(g)noscente (esp Art).

Kennerblick m expert's eye.

kennerhaft, **kennerisch** adj like a connoisseur. **mit** ~em **Blick/Griff** with the eye/touch of an expert.

Kenner-: ~miene f connoisseur's expression; **mit** ~miene **betrachtete er** ... he looked at ... like a connoisseur; **er versuchte, eine** ~miene **aufzusetzen** he tried to look like a connoisseur; (bei Erklärung etc) he tried to look knowledgeable; ~schaft f, ~tum nt connoisseurship (rare); (Fachkenntnis) expertise; **seine** ~schaft ... that he was a connoisseur ...

Kennkarte f (dated) identity card.

kenntlich adj (zu erkennen) recognizable, distinguishable (an + dat by); (deutlich) clear. **etw** ~ **machen** to identify or indicate sth (clearly); **etw für jdn** ~ **machen** to make sth clear to sb, to indicate sth to sb; **davon wird** ~, **daß** ... this indicates that ...; **etw gut** ~ **anbringen** to display sth clearly or prominently or visibly (an + dat on); **bei Dunkelheit gut** ~ **sein** to be easily visible or distinguishable in the dark.

Kenntlichkeit f siehe adj recognizability; clarity.

Kenntnis f (a) (Wissen) knowledge no pl. **über** ~se **von etw verfügen** to be knowledgeable about sth, to know about sth; **gute** ~se **in Mathematik haben** to have a good knowledge of mathematics; **dafür reicht seine** ~ **des Deutschen nicht aus** his knowledge of German is not sufficient for that, he does not know enough German for that; **ohne** ~ **des Englischen** without any or a knowledge of English, without knowing English. (b) no pl (form) **etw zur** ~ **nehmen** to note sth, to take note of sth; **ich nehme zur** ~, **daß** ... I note that ...; **jdn von etw in** ~ **setzen** to inform or advise (Comm, form) sb about sth; **von etw** ~ **erhalten** to learn or hear about sth; **das entzieht sich meiner** ~ I have no knowledge of it; **bei voller** ~ **der Sachlage** in full knowledge of the situation; **ohne** ~ **der Umstände** without any knowledge of the circumstances.

Kenntnis-: ~nahme f -, no pl (form) **zur** ~nahme **an** ... for the attention of ...; **nach** ~nahme **after perusal** (form); k~reich adj (geh) learned, knowledgeable.

-kenntnisse pl in cpds knowledge of ...

Kennung f (Telec) call sign; (von Leuchtfeuern) signal.

Kenn-: ~wort nt, pl ~wörter (Chiffre) code name; (Losungswort) password, code word; (Comm) reference; ~zahl f code or identification number; (Telec auch) code; ~zeichen nt (a) (Aut) number plate (Brit), license plate (US); (Aviat) markings pl; **amtliches/polizeiliches** ~zeichen **number plate** (Brit), license plate (US); (b) (Markierung) mark, sign; (bei Tier) marking(s); (in Personenbeschreibung) **unveränderliche** ~zeichen **distinguishing marks** or features; **besondere** ~zeichen **particular** characteristics; (c) (Eigenart, Charakteristikum) (typical) characteristic (für, gen of); (für Qualität) hallmark; (Erkennungszeichen) mark, sign; **ein typisches** ~zeichen **des Intellektuellen** a typical mark or sign of the intellectual; **als** ~zeichen **eine Nelke im Knopfloch vereinbaren** to agree on a carnation in one's buttonhole as a means of identification; **ein** ~zeichen **des Genies** a mark or sign or hallmark of genius; (d) (Anzeichen) symptom (für of); k~zeichnen insep 1 vt (a) to mark, to indicate; (durch Etikett auch) to label; **Weg** etc to mark, to signpost; (Logik) to denote; **etw als zerbrechlich** k~zeichnen to mark or label sth fragile; (b) (charakterisieren) to characterize; **jdn als etw** k~zeichnen to show sb to be sth, to mark sb out as sth; 2 vr to be characterized; k~zeichnend adj (charakteristisch) typical, characteristic (für of); ~ziffer f (code) number; (Math) characteristic; (Comm) reference number; (bei Zeitungsinserat) box number; (DDR) reference number (for production planning).

Kenotaph nt -s, -e cenotaph.

Kentaur m -en, -en centaur.

kentern vi aux sein (Schiff) to capsize.

Kentumsprache f centum language.

Kephalo- pref cephalo.

Keplersche Gesetze pl Kepler's laws pl.

keppeln vi (Aus inf) siehe **keifen**.

Keramik f (a) no pl (Art) ceramics pl; (als Gebrauchsgegenstände auch) pottery; (Arbeitszweig) ceramics sing. (b) (Kunstgegenstand) piece of ceramic work; (Gebrauchsgegenstand auch) piece of pottery. ~en ceramics/pottery.

keramisch adj ceramic; **Gebrauchsgegenstand** auch pottery.

Kerbe¹ f -, -n notch; (kleiner) nick. **in die gleiche** or **dieselbe** ~ **hauen** or **schlagen** (fig inf) to take the same line.

Kerbe² f -, -n (dial) siehe **Kirchweih**.

Kerbel m -s, no pl chervil.

Kerbelkraut nt chervil.

kerben vt Holz to cut or carve a notch/notches in, to notch; Inschrift, Namen to carve.

Kerbholz nt (fig inf) **etwas auf dem** ~ **haben** to have done something wrong or bad; **er hat so manches auf dem** ~ he has quite a record; **es gab fast keinen, der nichts auf dem** ~ **hatte** there was hardly anybody who had a completely clean record.

Kerbtier nt insect.

Kerbung f (das Kerben) notching; (die Kerben) notches pl; (kleiner) nicks pl.

Kerf m -(e)s, -e siehe **Insekt**.

Kerker m -s, - (a) (Hist, geh) dungeon (esp Hist), prison; (Strafe) imprisonment. (b) (Aus) siehe **Zuchthaus**.

Kerker-: ~**meister** m (Hist, geh) gaoler, jailer; ~**strafe** f (a) (Hist) imprisonment in the dungeons; (b) (Aus) siehe Zuchthausstrafe.

Kerl m -s, -e or -s (inf) chap, fellow, guy, bloke (Brit) (all inf); (pej) character; (Mädchen) girl, lass (inf). **du gemeiner** ~! you mean thing (inf) or swine (inf); **ein ganzer/richtiger** ~ a real man; **sie hat schon wieder einen neuen** ~ she's got another guy or bloke; **die langen** ~s (Hist) (soldiers of) the bodyguard of the King of Prussia.

Kern m -(e)s, -e (von Obst) pip, seed; (von Steinobst) stone; (Nuß~) kernel; (Phys, Biol) nucleus; (Holz~) heartwood; (fig) (von Problem, Sache) heart, crux, core; (von Stadt) centre; (von Gruppe) core. **jede Legende hat einen wahren** ~ at the heart of every legend there is a core of truth; **in ihr steckt ein guter** ~ there's some good in her somewhere; **bis zum** ~ **einer Sache vordringen** to get to the heart or the bottom of a matter.

Kern- in cpds (Nuklear-) nuclear; ~**beißer** m -s, - (Orn) hawfinch; ~**brennstoff** m nuclear fuel; ~**chemie** f nuclear chemistry; ~**energie** f nuclear energy; ~**explosion** f nuclear explosion; ~**fach** nt (Sch) core subject; ~**familie** f (Sociol) nuclear family; ~**forscher** m nuclear scientist or researcher; ~**forschung** f nuclear research; ~**frage** f central issue, central question; ~**frucht** f malaceous fruit (form), pome (form); ~**fusion** f nuclear fusion; ~**gebiet** nt heartland; ~**gedanke** m central idea; ~**gehäuse** nt core; **k~gesund** adj as fit as a fiddle, completely fit; ~**gruppe** f nucleus; ~**haus** nt siehe ~**gehäuse**; ~**holz** nt heartwood.

kernig adj full of pips; (fig) Ausspruch pithy; (urwüchsig) earthy; (kraftvoll) robust, powerful; (sl: gut) great (inf).

Kern-: ~**kräfte** pl forces in the nucleus pl, nuclear forces pl; ~**kraftwerk** nt nuclear power station, nuke (US sl); ~**ladungszahl** f atomic number; ~**land** nt heartland; **k~los** adj seedless, pipless; ~**mannschaft** f (Sport, fig) core or nucleus of a/the team; (von Partei) central caucus; (von Regierung) inner cabinet; ~**modell** nt model of the nucleus; ~**obst** nt malaceous fruit (form), pome (form); ~**pflichtfach** nt (Sch) (compulsory) core subject; ~**physik** f nuclear physics; ~**physiker** m nuclear physicist; ~**plasma** nt nucleoplasm; ~**problem** nt central problem; ~**punkt** m central point, crux; ~**reaktion** f nuclear reaction; ~**reaktor** m nuclear reactor; ~**satz** m (a) key sentence, key phrase; (b) (Ling) kernel sentence; (Satzform) simple sentence; ~**schatten** m complete shadow; (Astron) umbra; ~**seife** f washing soap; ~**spaltung** f nuclear fission; **die erste** ~**spaltung** the first splitting of the atom; ~**sprengstoff** m nuclear warhead; ~**spruch** m pithy saying; ~**stück** nt (fig) main item, centrepiece; (von Theorie etc) crucial or central element or part, core; (von Roman etc) crucial or key passage; ~**technik** f nuclear technology; ~**teilung** f (Biol) nuclear division; ~**truppe** f (Mil) core unit or division; (fig) core team; ~**unterricht** m (Sch) core curriculum; ~**verschmelzung** f (a) (Phys) siehe ~**fusion**; (b) (Biol) cell union.

Kernwaffe f nuclear weapon.

Kernwaffen-: **k~frei** adj nuclear demilitarized; ~**sperrvertrag** m Nuclear Nonproliferation Treaty; ~**versuch** m nuclear (weapons) test.

Kernzeit f core time.

Kerosin nt -s, -e kerosene.

Kerub m -s, -im or -e siehe **Cherub**.

Kerze f -, -n (a) (Wachs~) candle; (Blüte der Kastanie) candle, thyrus (form). (b) (Aut) plug. (c) (Turnen) shoulder-stand. (d) (Ftbl) skyer.

Kerzen-: ~**beleuchtung** f candlelight; ~**birne** f (Elec) candle bulb; ~**docht** m candle wick; ~**form** f (einer Glühbirne) candle-shape; **k~förmig** adj candle-shaped; **k~gerade** adj (as) straight as a die, erect; ~**gesicht** nt (Tech) appearance or look of a/the (spark) plug; ~**halter** m candlestick; (am Weihnachtsbaum, auf Kuchen etc) candle holder; ~**leuchter** m candlestick; ~**licht** nt, no pl candlelight; ~**schein** m candlelight; **im** ~**schein des Weihnachtsbaumes** in the light of the Christmas-tree candles, in the candle-lit glow of the Christmas-tree; ~**schlüssel** m (spark) plug spanner; ~**stummel**, ~**stumpf** m candle stump.

Kescher m -s, - fishing-net; (Hamen) landing-net.

keß adj (keck) saucy, pert; Kleid, Hut etc jaunty, saucy; (dial: frech) saucy, fresh (inf). **kesser Vater** (sl) (bull)dyke (sl).

Kessel m -s, - (a) (Tee~) kettle; (Wasch~) copper; (Koch~) pot; (für offenes Feuer) cauldron; (esp in Brauerei) vat; (Dampf~) boiler; (Behälter für Flüssigkeiten etc) tank.
(b) (Mulde) basin, basin-shaped valley; (Hunt) semi-circular ring of hunters; (Mil) encircled area. **als sie im** ~ **von Stalingrad lagen** when they were encircled at Stalingrad.

Kessel-: ~**flicker** m -s, - tinker; ~**haus** nt boiler house; ~**jagd** f siehe ~**treiben**; ~**pauke** f kettle drum; ~**raum** m boiler room; ~**schlacht** f (Mil) battle of encirclement; ~**stein** m scale, fur; ~**treiben** nt (Hunt) hunt using a circle of beaters; (fig: in Zeitung etc) witchhunt; ~**wagen** m (Rail) tank wagon or car.

Keßheit f siehe adj sauciness, pertness; jauntiness, sauciness; sauciness.

Ketchup ['ketʃap] m or nt -(s), -s ketchup.

Ketsch f -, -en (Naut) ketch.

ketschen vti siehe **catchen**.

Kette f -, -n (a) chain; (von Fahrzeug) (track) chain track. **einen Hund an die** ~ **legen** to put a dog on the chain, to chain up a dog; **in** ~n **liegen** (fig geh) to be in chains or bondage; **in** ~n **schlagen** (liter) to put in chains; **seine** ~n **zerreißen or sprengen** (fig geh) to throw off one's chains or shackles or fetters.
(b) (fig: ununterbrochene Reihe) chain; (von Menschen auch) line; (von Fahrzeugen) line, string; (von Unfällen, Erfahrungen

etc) series, string. **eine** ~ **von Ereignissen** a chain of events; **die** ~ **der Generationen, die ...** the succession of generations that ...
(c) (Berg~, Seen~) chain.
(d) (Hunt) (von Rebhühnern) covey; (von Wildenten) skein.
(e) (Aviat, Mil) flight.
(f) (Comm: von Läden) chain.
(g) (Tex) warp.

Kettel m -s, - or f -, -n (dial) siehe **Krampe**.

ketten vt to chain (an + acc to). **jdn an sich** ~ (fig) to bind sb to oneself; **sich an jdn/etw** ~ (fig) to tie or bind oneself to sb/sth.

Ketten-: ~**antrieb** m chain drive; **mit** ~**antrieb** chain-driven; ~**armband** nt chain bracelet; ~**brief** m chain letter; ~**brücke** f chain bridge; ~**fahrzeug** nt tracked vehicle, track-laying vehicle; ~**gebirge** nt mountain chain; ~**geschäft** nt chain store, multiple(-store); ~**glied** nt (chain-)link; ~**hemd** nt (Hist) coat of (chain-)mail; ~**hund** m guard-dog, watchdog; ~**karussell** nt merry-go-round (with gondolas suspended on chains); ~**laden** m siehe ~**geschäft**; ~**panzer** m siehe ~**hemd**; ~**rad** nt sprocket(-wheel); **k~rauchen** vi sep infin, ptp only to chainsmoke; ~**rauchen** nt chain-smoking; ~**raucher** m chain-smoker; ~**reaktion** f chain reaction; ~**reim** m (Poet) interlaced rhyme; ~**schaltung** f dérailleur gear; ~**schluß** m (Logik) sorites; ~**schutz** m chain guard; ~**spanner** m (bei Fahrrad etc) chain adjuster; ~**stich** m (Sew) chain stitch.

Ketzer m -s, - (Eccl, fig) heretic.

Ketzerei f heresy.

Ketzergericht nt (Hist) (court of) inquisition.

Ketzerin f siehe **Ketzer**.

ketzerisch adj (Eccl, fig) heretical.

Ketzertaufe f (Hist) heretical baptism.

keuchen vi (a) (schwer atmen) to pant, to puff, to gasp (for breath); (Asthmatiker etc) to wheeze. **mit** ~**dem Atem** panting, puffing; wheezing. (b) aux sein (sich schwer atmend fortbewegen) to pant, to puff; (Zug) to puff, to chug.

Keuchhusten m whooping cough.

Keule f -, -n (a) club, cudgel; (Sport) (Indian) club. (b) (Cook) leg; (von Wild auch) haunch. (c) (dial sl: als Anrede) mate (Brit inf), mac (US inf).

Keulen-: ~**hieb**, ~**schlag** m blow with a club or cudgel; **er bekam einen** ~**hieb auf den Kopf** he was hit on the head with a club or cudgel; **es traf ihn wie ein** ~**schlag** (fig) it hit him like a thunderbolt; ~**schwingen** nt -s, no pl (Sport) (Indian) club swinging.

keusch adj (lit, fig) chaste. ~ **und züchtig** pure and chaste.

Keusche f -, -n (Aus inf) cottage; (pej: baufälliges Haus) hovel.

Keuschheit f chasteness; (Unberührtheit auch) chastity.

Keuschheits-: ~**gelübde** nt vow of chastity; ~**gürtel** m chastity belt.

Keybordspieler ['ki:bɔrt-] m (Mus) keyboard player.

kfm abbr of **kaufmännisch**.

Kfz [kaˈʔɛfʦɛt] nt -(s), -(s) (form) abbr of **Kraftfahrzeug** motor vehicle.

Kfz- in cpds motor vehicle.

kg abbr of **Kilogramm** kg.

KG [kaˈgeː] f -, -s abbr of **Kommanditgesellschaft** limited partnership.

kgl abbr of **königlich** royal.

K-Gruppe ['ka:-] f (BRD Pol) Communist splinter group.

k.g.V., kgV abbr of **kleinstes gemeinsames Vielfaches** lowest common multiple, lcm.

Khaki[1] m -s, no pl (Stoff) khaki.

Khaki[2] nt -s, no pl (Farbe) khaki.

khaki adj pred khaki.

khakifarben adj khaki(-coloured).

Khartum nt -s Khartoum.

KHz, kHz abbr of **Kiloherz** kHz.

kibbeln vir (dial) siehe **kabbeln**.

Kibbuz m -, Kibbuzim or -e kibbutz.

Kicherei f giggling.

Kicher|erbse f chick-pea.

kichern vi to giggle.

Kick m -(s), -s (inf: Stoß) kick; (sl: Spiel) kick-about, kick-around.

Kickdown [kɪkˈdaun] nt -s, no pl (Aut) kickdown.

kicken (Ftbl inf) 1 vt to kick, to boot (inf). 2 vi to play football; (den Ball ~) to kick. **für eine Mannschaft** ~ to play for a team.

Kicker m -s, - (Ftbl inf) player.

Kick-off m -s, -s (Ftbl: esp Sw) kick-off.

Kickstarter m (bei Motorrad) kick-starter.

kidnappen ['kɪtnɛpn] vt insep to kidnap.

Kidnapper(in f) ['kɪtnɛpɐ, -ərɪn] m -s, - kidnapper.

Kidnapping ['kɪtnɛpɪŋ] nt -s, -s kidnapping.

kiebig adj (inf) cheeky, saucy, fresh (inf).

Kiebitz m -es, -e (Orn) lapwing, peewit, green plover; (Cards inf) kibitzer.

kiebitzen vi (inf) to spy; (Cards) to kibitz.

Kiefer[1] f -, -n pine (tree); (Holz) pine(wood).

Kiefer[2] m -s, - jaw; (~knochen) jawbone.

Kiefer-: ~**anomalie** f malformation of the jaw; ~**bruch** m broken or fractured jaw; ~**chirurg** m oral surgeon; ~**chirurgie** f oral surgery.

Kieferhöhle f (Anat) maxillary sinus.

Kieferhöhlen-: ~**entzündung** f sinusitis; ~**vereiterung** f sinus infection.

kiefern adj pine(wood).

Kiefern-: ~**holz** nt pine(wood); ~**nadel** f pine needle; ~**schonung** f pinery, pine plantation; ~**wald** m pine wood; (größer) pine forest; ~**zapfen** m pinecone.

Kiefer-: ~**orthopäde** m orthodontist; ~**orthopädie** f orthodontics; **k~orthopädisch** adj orthodontic.

kieken vi (dial) siehe **gucken**.

Kieker m -s, - (a) (N Ger inf) binoculars pl. (b) **jdn auf dem ~ haben** (inf) to have it in for sb (inf).

Kiel m -(e)s, -e (a) (Schiffs~) keel. **ein Schiff auf ~ legen** to lay down a ship. (b) (Feder~) quill.

Kiel-: ~**boot** nt keel boat; ~**feder** f quill pen; **k~holen** vt insep (Naut) (a) Schiff to careen; (b) Matrosen to keelhaul; ~**linie** f line ahead; **k~oben** adv bottom up; ~**raum** m bilge; ~**wasser** nt wake, wash; in jds ~**wasser segeln** or **schwimmen** (fig) to follow in sb's wake; **er bleibt immer im ~wasser der Geschäftsleitung** he always just follows on behind the management.

Kieme f -, -n gill. **voll bis an die ~n sein** (sl) to be full to the gills.

Kiemen- (Zool): ~**atmer** m -s, - gill-breather; ~**atmung** f gillbreathing; ~**füß(l)er** m -s, - branchiopod.

Kien¹ m -(e)s, no pl pine.

Kien² m: **auf dem ~ sein** (inf) to be on the alert, to keep one's wits about one.

Kien-: ~**apfel** m siehe **Kiefernzapfen**; ~**fackel** f pinewood torch; ~**holz** nt pine; ~**span** m pinewood spill; ~**topp** m or nt siehe **Kintopp**; ~**zapfen** m siehe **Kiefernzapfen**.

Kiepe f -, -n (dial) pannier, dosser.

Kiepenhut m poke-bonnet.

Kies m -es, -e (a) gravel; (am Strand) shingle. (b) no pl (inf: Geld) dough (inf), lolly (inf).

Kiesel m -s, - pebble.

Kieselerde f silica.

kieseln vt to gravel.

Kiesel-: ~**säure** f (Chem) (a) silicic acid; (b) (Siliziumdioxyd) silica; ~**stein** m pebble; ~**strand** m pebble beach, shingle beach.

kiesen pret **kor**, ptp **gekoren** vt (obs) to choose, to select.

Kiesgrube f gravel pit.

Kiesweg m gravel(led) path.

kiesig adj gravelly; Strand shingly.

Kie(t)z m -es, -e (dial) (a) (Stadtgegend) district, area. (b) (sl: Bordellgegend) red-light district.

Kif(f) m or nt -s, no pl (sl) pot (sl), grass (sl).

kiffen vi (sl) to smoke pot (sl) or grass (sl), to smoke (sl).

Kiffer(in f) m -s, - (sl) pot-smoker (sl).

kikeriki interj cock-a-doodle-doo.

Kikeriki¹ nt -s, -s (Hahnenschrei) cock-a-doodle-doo.

Kikeriki² m -s, -s (baby-talk) cock-a-doodle-doo (baby-talk).

Kilbi f -, **Kilbenen** (Sw) siehe **Kirchweih**.

killekille interj (baby-talk) tickle, tickle, kitchie, kitchie. (**bei jdm**) ~ **machen** to tickle sb.

killen¹ (sl) **1** vt to bump off (inf), to do in (inf), to kill; (esp mit Auftrag) to hit (sl). **2** vi to kill, to murder.

killen² vi (Naut) to shake, to shiver.

Killer(in f) m -s, - (sl) killer, murderer; (gedungener) hit-man.

Kilo nt -s, -(s) kilo.

Kilo- in cpds kilo-; ~**gramm** nt kilogram(me); ~**hertz** nt kilocycle; ~**kalorie** f kilocalorie.

Kilometer m kilometre; (inf: Stundenkilometer) k (inf). **bei ~ 547** (~**stein**) at kilometre 547; **wir konnten nur 80 ~ fahren** we could only do 80.

Kilometer-: ~**fresser** m (inf) long-haul driver; **er ist ein richtiger ~fresser** he really eats up the miles (inf); ~**geld** nt mileage (allowance); **k~lang 1** adj miles long; **k~lange Strände** miles and miles of beaches; **ein k~langer Stau** a tailback several miles/kilometres long; **2** adv for miles (and miles), for miles on end; ~**pauschale** f mileage allowance (against tax); ~**stand** m mileage; **der ~stand des Autos ist ...** the car has done ..., the car has ... on the clock (inf), the mileage on the car is ...; **bei ~stand x** when the car has done x miles/ kilometres; ~**stein** m milestone; **k~weit 1** adj miles long; **ein k~weiter Blick** a view for miles; **in k~weiter Entfernung** miles away in the distance; **ein k~weiter Marsch** a march of several miles/kilometres; **2** adv for miles (and miles); ~**zähler** m mileage indicator or counter, mileometer, odometer.

kilometrieren* vt (form) to divide up into kilometres.

Kilo-: ~**watt** nt kilowatt; ~**wattstunde** f kilowatt hour.

Kimbern pl (Hist) Cimbri pl.

Kimm f -, no pl (Naut) (a) (Horizont) apparent or visual horizon. (b) (am Schiffskörper) bilge.

Kimme f -, -n (a) (von Gewehr) back sight. (b) (inf: Gesäßfalte) cleft between the buttocks, great divide (hum). (c) (rare) siehe **Kerbe¹**.

Kimmung f (Naut) (a) (Horizont) visual horizon. (b) (Luftspiegelung) mirage.

Kimono m -s, -s kimono.

Kind nt -(e)s, -er child, kid (inf); (Kleinkind) baby; (esp Psych, Med) infant. **ein ~ erwarten/bekommen** or **kriegen** to be expecting a baby/to have a baby or child; **von ~ auf** or **an** since he/we etc was/were a child/children, from childhood; **einem Mädchen ein ~ machen** (sl) to knock a girl up (sl), to put a girl in the club (inf); **sie kriegt ein ~** she's going to have a baby or child; **aber ~!** child, child; **schönes ~!** (old: als Anrede) my pretty maid (old); **die ~er Gottes** (geh) the children of the Lord; **ein echtes Wiener ~** (dated) a true son/daughter of Vienna; **ein ~ seiner Zeit sein** to be a child of one's times; **sie ist kein ~ von Traurigkeit** (hum) she enjoys life; **er ist ein großes ~** he's a big baby; **sich freuen wie ein ~** to be as pleased as Punch; **er kann sich wie ein ~ freuen** he takes a childlike pleasure in (simple) things; **das weiß doch jedes ~!** any five-year-old would tell you that!; **du bist aber ein kluges ~!** (iro) clever kid!; **er ist red-licher/armer Leute ~** (dated) he was the child of upright/poor parents; **da kommt das ~ im Manne durch** all men are boys at heart; **es ist immer wieder lustig, das ~ im Manne zu beobachten** it's always amusing to see how men are boys at heart; **wie sag' ich's meinem ~e?** (hum) I don't know how to put it; (bei Aufklärung) what to tell your children; **das ist nichts für kleine ~er** (fig inf) that's not for your innocent or your young ears/eyes; **aus ~ern werden Leute** (Prov) children grow up quickly, don't they?; ~**er und Narren** or **Betrunkene sagen die Wahrheit** (fig) children and fools speak the truth; **ein ~ des Todes sein** (dated) to be a goner (inf); **jdm ein ~ in den Bauch reden können** (inf) to have the gift of the gab (inf), to have kissed the blarney (stone) (inf); **mit ~ und Kegel** (hum inf) with the whole family; **das ~ muß einen Namen haben** (fig) you/we etc have to call it something; **das ~ mit dem Bade ausschütten** to throw out the baby with the bathwater (prov); **wir werden das ~ schon schaukeln** (inf) we'll soon have that or everything sorted out; **los,** ~**er/hört mal alle her,** ~**er!** let's go, kids/listen, kids; ~**er,** ~**er!** dear, dear!, goodness me!, good heavens!.

Kind-: ~**bett** nt (old) childbed (old); **im ~bett** in confinement; ~**bettfieber** nt childbed fever.

Kindchen nt dim of **Kind** child; (zu Erwachsenen) kid(do) (inf).

Kindel nt -s, -(n) (dial) dim of **Kind** kiddy.

Kinder-: ~**arbeit** f child labour; **k~arm** adj with few children; Familie small; **ein k~armes Land** a country with a low birth rate; ~**art** f the way children are; ~**arzt** m paediatrician; ~**augen** pl children's eyes pl; **etw mit ~augen anschauen** to gaze wide-eyed at sth; **vor Erstaunen ~augen machen/ bekommen** to be wide-eyed with astonishment; ~**beihilfe** f (Aus) siehe ~**geld**; ~**beilage** f children's supplement, children's page; ~**bekleidung** f children's wear; ~**besteck** nt child's cutlery; ~**bett** nt cot; ~**bewahranstalt** f (old) day-nursery; (fig hum) kindergarten; ~**bild** nt childhood photograph; **das ist ein ~bild (von) meiner Mutter** that's a photograph of my mother as a child or when she was a child; ~**buch** nt children's book.

Kinderchen pl children pl.

Kinder-: ~**chor** m children's choir; ~**dorf** nt children's village; ~**ehe** f child marriage.

Kinderei f childishness no pl. ~**en** childishness, childish nonsense.

Kinder-: ~**erziehung** f bringing up of children; (durch Schule) education of children; **sie versteht nichts von ~erziehung** she knows nothing about bringing up/educating children; ~**fahrrad** nt child's or children's bicycle; ~**feind** m child-hater; **k~feindlich 1** adj hostile to children, anti-children; Architektur, Planung not catering for children; **k~feindliche Steuerpolitik** tax policies which penalize having children; **2** adv without regard to children; ~**feindlichkeit** f hostility to children, anti-children attitude; (von Architektur) failure to cater for children; ~**fernsehen** nt children's television; ~**fest** nt children's party or (von Stadt etc) fête; ~**film** m children's film; ~**frau** f, ~**fräulein** nt (dated) nanny, children's nurse; ~**freibetrag** m child allowance; ~**freund** m; ~**freund sein** to be fond of children; **k~freundlich 1** adj Mensch fond of children; Gesellschaft child-orientated; Möbel, Architektur etc catering for children; **eine k~freundliche Steuerpolitik** a tax policy which encourages one to have children; **2** adv with children in mind; ~**freundlichkeit** f siehe adj fondness for children; child-orientation; **die ~freundlichkeit dieser Möbel/Politik** the way this furniture caters for children/this policy which encourages one to have children; ~**freundschaft** f friendship between children; ~**funk** m children's radio or programmes pl; ~**garten** m nursery school, kindergarten; ~**gärtner(in** f) m nursery-school teacher; ~**geburtstag** m (Feier) children's birthday party; ~**geld** nt child allowance; ~**geschrei** nt screams pl of children; **er kann ~geschrei nicht vertragen** he can't stand children screaming; **dieses ~geschrei ...!** these children or kids (inf) screaming ...!; ~**gesicht** nt baby face; ~**glaube** m childlike faith; **im ~glauben an die liebe Gott ...** children believe that God has ..., in a child's belief God has ...; ~**gottesdienst** m children's service; ~**heilkunde** f paediatrics; **Facharzt für ~heilkunde** paediatrician; ~**heim** nt children's home; ~**hort** m day-nursery, crèche; ~**jahre** pl childhood years pl; ~**kleidung** f children's clothes pl; ~**klinik** f children's clinic, paediatric clinic; ~**korb** m baby-carrier; ~**kram** m (inf) kids' stuff (inf); ~**krankenhaus** nt children's hospital; ~**krankheit** f (allgemein) children's illness or disease; (eines bestimmten Menschen) childhood illness or disease; (fig) teething troubles pl; ~**kreuzzug** m (Eccl Hist) Children's Crusade; ~**kriegen** nt -s, no pl **sie hat keine Lust zum ~kriegen** she doesn't want to have children; **es ist zum ~kriegen** (inf) it's enough to drive you round the bend (inf); ~**krippe** f day-nursery, crèche; ~**laden** m (left-wing) play-group; ~**lähmung** f poliomyelitis, polio; ~**lähmungsimpfung** f polio vaccination or inoculation; **k~leicht** adj childishly simple, dead easy (inf); **es ist k~leicht** it's child's play or kid's stuff (inf).

Kinderlein pl children pl.

Kinder-: **k~lieb** adj fond of children; ~**liebe** f (Liebe zwischen ~n) children's love, children's affection; (Liebe zu ~n) love of or for children; ~**lied** nt = nursery rhyme; **k~los** adj childless; ~**losigkeit** f childlessness; ~**mädchen** f nanny; ~**märchen** nt (children's) fairy tale, fairy story; ~**moden** pl children's fashions pl; ~**mord** m child murder; (Jur) infanticide; **der beth-lehemitische ~mord, der ~mord zu Bethlehem** (Bibl) the massacre of the innocents; ~**mörder** m child-murderer; ~**mund** m (fig) children's talk, child's way of talking; **das wirkt spaßig, weil es aus ~mund kommt** that sounds funny coming from a child; ~**mund tut Wahrheit kund** (Prov) out of the mouths of babes and sucklings (prov); ~**narr** m great lover of children; **er ist ein ~narr** he adores children; ~**paradies** nt children's paradise; ~**pflegerin** f children's nurse; (~mädchen) nanny;

~**popo** m (inf) baby's bottom (inf); **glatt wie ein ~popo** smooth as a baby's bottom (inf); ~**psychologie** f child psychology; ~**raub** m baby-snatching; (Entführung) kidnapping (of a child/children); **k~reich** adj with many children; Familie large; ~**reichtum** m an abundance of children; **der ~reichtum Kenias** the abundance of children in Kenya; ~**reim** m nursery rhyme; ~**sachen** pl (Kleidung) children's clothes pl; (Gegenstände) children's things pl; (Spielsachen) toys pl; ~**schänder** m -s,- child molester; ~**schar** f swarm of children; ~**schreck** m bog(e)yman; ~**schuh** m child's shoe; ~**schuhe sind teuer** children's shoes are dear; **etw steckt noch in den ~schuhen** (fig) sth is still in its infancy; **den ~schuhen entwachsen sein** (fig) (Mensch) to have grown up; (Technik, Methode etc) to be no longer in its infancy; ~**schutz** m protection of children; ~**schwester** f siehe ~**pflegerin**; ~**segen** m (dated) children pl; **es war ihnen kein ~segen beschert** they were not blessed with children; **sein reicher ~segen war sein ganzer Stolz** his large family was his pride and joy; ~**sicherung** f (Aut) childproof safety catch; ~**sitz** m child's seat; (im Auto) child's safety seat; ~**spiel** nt children's game; (fig) child's play no art; ~**spielplatz** m children's playground; ~**spielzeug** nt (children's) toys pl; ~**sprache** f (von Kindern) children's language; (verniedlichend von Erwachsenen) baby talk no art; ~**station** f children's ward; ~**sterblichkeit** f infant mortality; ~**stimme** f child's voice; ~**streich** m childish prank; ~**stube** f (fig) upbringing; ~**stuhl** m child's chair; (Hochstuhl) high chair; ~**stunde** f children's hour; ~**tagesheim** nt, ~**tagesstätte** f day nursery, crèche; ~**taufe** f infant baptism; ~**theater** nt children's theatre; (Jugendtheater) youth theatre; ~**trommel** f toy drum; ~**vers** m nursery rhyme; ~**wagen** m pram (Brit), baby carriage (US), perambulator (form); (Sportwagen) pushchair (Brit), baby-stroller (US); ~**welt** f world of children; ~**zahl** f number of children; ~**zeichnung** f child's drawing; ~**zimmer** nt child's/children's room; (esp für Kleinkinder) nursery; ~**zulage** f, ~**zuschlag** m child benefit.

Kindes- ~**abtreibung** f abortion; ~**alter** nt childhood; **im ~alter** at an early age; **seit frühestem ~alter** from infancy; ~**annahme** f adoption; ~**aussetzung** f abandoning of children; ~**aussetzungen** cases of children being abandoned; ~**beine** pl: **von ~beinen an** from childhood, from an early age; ~**entführung** f kidnapping (of a child/children); ~**kind** nt grandchild; ~**liebe** f child's/children's love; ~**mißhandlung** f child abuse; ~**mord** m child-murder, murder of a child; ~**mörder** m child-murderer; ~**nöte** pl (old) travail (old); **in ~nöten sein** to be in travail (old); ~**raub** m siehe **Kinderraub**; ~**tötung** f (Jur: von eigenem Säugling) infanticide; ~**verwechs(e)lung** f confusion of children's identity.

Kind- **k~gemäß** adj suitable for a child/children; **k~haft** adj childlike; ~**heit** f childhood; (früheste ~heit) infancy; ~**heitserinnerung** f childhood memory.

kindisch adj (pej) childish. **sich ~ über etw** (acc) **freuen** to be as pleased as Punch about sth; **er kann sich ~ freuen** he takes a childlike pleasure in (simple) things.

Kindl nt -s, -(n) (dial) dim of **Kind**.

kindlich 1 adj childlike; (pej) childish. 2 adv like a child.

Kindlichkeit f childlikeness; (pej) childishness.

Kinds- in cpds siehe **Kindes-**; ~**bewegungen** pl (Med) foetal movements pl; ~**kopf** m (inf) big kid (inf); **sei kein ~kopf** don't be so childish; ~**lage** f (Med) presentation of the foetus.

Kindtaufe f (old) christening.

Kinemathek f -, -en film library or archive.

Kinematographie f cinematography.

Kinetik f kinetics sing.

kinetisch adj kinetic.

Kinigelhase m (Aus, dial) siehe **Kaninchen**.

Kinkerlitzchen pl (inf) knicknacks pl (inf); (dumme Streiche) tomfoolery sing (inf).

Kinn nt -(e)s, -e chin.

Kinn- ~**bart** m goatee (beard); ~**haken** m hook to the chin; ~**lade** f jaw(-bone); ~**riemen** m (am Helm) chinstrap; ~**schutz** m (Hockey) chin-guard.

Kino nt -s, -s cinema; (Gebäude auch) movie-theatre (US). **ins ~ gehen** to go to the cinema or pictures (Brit) or movies (esp US).

Kino- in cpds cinema, movie (esp US); ~**besuch** m visit to the cinema; (Besucherrate) cinema attendances pl; ~**besucher** m cinemagoer; ~**film** m cinema film; ~**gänger(in** f) m -s, - cinemagoer; ~**karte** f cinema ticket; ~**kasse** f cinema box office; ~**programm** nt film programme; (Übersicht) film guide; ~**reklame** f (a) cinema advertisement; (b) siehe ~**werbung**; ~**vorstellung** f performance, programme; ~**werbung** f cinema advertising.

Kintopp m or nt -s, -s or -e (dated) (a) pictures pl (Brit), movies pl (US). **im ~ sein** to be at the pictures/movies. (b) (als Kulturphänomen) cinema. **dieser alte Film ist noch richtiger ~** this old film is still good cinema.

Kiosk m -(e)s, -e kiosk.

Kipf m -(e)s, -e (S Ger) (stick) loaf.

Kipfe(r)l nt -s, -(n) (Aus) croissant.

Kipfler m (Aus) salad potatoes pl.

Kippe f -, -n (a) (Sport) spring.
(b) **auf der ~ stehen** (Gegenstand) to be balanced precariously; **sie steht auf der ~** (fig) it's touch and go with her; **es steht auf der ~, ob ...** (fig) it's touch and go whether ...
(c) (inf: Zigarettenstummel) cigarette stub, fag-end (Brit inf), dog-end (Brit inf); (sl: Zigarette) fag (Brit inf), butt (US sl).
(d) (Müll~, Min) tip.

kippelig adj (inf) (wackelig) wobbly; Möbel auch rickety; Angelegenheit shaky. **sie steht ~ in der Schule** she's a bit shaky at school.

kippeln vi (inf) to wobble, to be wobbly or rickety. **(mit dem Stuhl) ~** to tilt (on one's chair).

kippen 1 vt (a) Behälter, Fenster to tilt; Ladefläche, Tisch to tip or tilt (up). „**bitte nicht ~**" "please do not tilt"; **einen/ein paar ~** (inf: trinken) to have a drink/to down a few (inf).
(b) (mit Ortsangabe: schütten) to tip.
2 vi aux sein to tip over; (esp höhere Gegenstände) to topple (over); (Fahrzeug, Schiff) to overturn; (Mensch) to topple, to fall. **aus den Latschen or Pantinen ~** (fig inf) (überrascht sein) to fall through the floor (inf); (ohnmächtig werden) to pass out.

Kipper m -s, - (Aut) tipper, dump(er) truck; (Rail) (tipper) wagon.

Kippfenster nt pivot window.

kipplig adj siehe **kippelig**.

Kipp-: ~**lore** f tipper wagon; ~**schalter** m rocker switch; ~**wagen** m siehe **Kipper**.

Kirche f -, -n (Gebäude, Organisation) church; (bestimmte Glaubensgemeinschaft) Church; (Gottesdienst) church no art. **zur ~ gehen** to go to church; **die ~ im Dorf lassen** (fig) not to get carried away; **mit der ~ ums Dorf fahren** or **laufen** (prov) to go all round the houses (inf).

Kirchen- in cpds church; ~**älteste(r)** mf decl as adj church elder; ~**amt** nt (a) ecclesiastical office; (b) (Verwaltungsstelle) church offices pl; ~**austritt** m leaving the Church no art; ~**austritte** (cases of) people leaving the Church; ~**bank** f (church) pew; ~**bann** m excommunication; (Interdikt) interdict; **den ~bann über jdn verhängen** to excommunicate/interdict sb; ~**besuch** m church-going; ~**blatt** nt parish magazine; ~**buch** nt church register; ~**chor** m church choir; ~**diebstahl** m theft from a/the church; ~**diener** m sexton; **k~feindlich** adj anticlerical; ~**fenster** nt church window; ~**fest** nt religious or church festival; ~**fürst** m high dignitary of the Church; (katholisch) prince of the Church; ~**gemeinde** f parish; ~**geschichte** f church or ecclesiastical history; ~**glocke** f church bell; ~**gut** nt church property; ~**jahr** nt church or ecclesiastical year; ~**kampf** m struggle between Church and state; ~**lehrer** m Doctor of the Church; ~**leitung** f government of the Church; (Gremium) governing body of the Church; ~**licht** nt: **kein (großes) ~licht sein** (fig inf) to be not very bright; ~**lied** nt hymn; ~**mann** m, pl ~**männer** churchman; ~**maus** f: **arm wie eine ~maus** poor as a church mouse; ~**musik** f church or sacred music; ~**politik** f church policy; **k~politisch** 1 adj relating to church policy; 2 adv in relation to church policy; ~**rat** m (Person) member of the Church Council; (Gremium) Church Council; ~**raub** m theft from a/the church; (von geweihtem Gegenstand) sacrilege; ~**räuber** m church-robber; ~**recht** nt canon law; **k~rechtlich** adj canonical; ~**schänder** m -s, - desecrator, profaner; ~**schiff** nt (Längsschiff) nave; (Querschiff) transept; ~**spaltung** f schism; ~**sprengel** m siehe **Kirchspiel**; ~**staat** m (Hist) Papal States pl; (Vatikanstaat) Vatican City; ~**steuer** f church tax; ~**strafe** f ecclesiastical punishment; ~**tag** m Church congress; ~**tonart** f church or ecclesiastical mode; ~**vater** m Father of the Church, Church Father; ~**verfolgung** f persecution of the Church; ~**vorstand** m parish council.

Kirch-: ~**gang** m going to church no art; **der sonntägliche ~gang** going to church on Sunday; ~**gänger(in** f) m -s, - churchgoer; ~**hof** m churchyard; (Friedhof) graveyard.

kirchlich adj church attr; Zustimmung, Mißbilligung by the church; Amt auch, Gebot, Gericht ecclesiastical; Musik auch sacred, religious; Feiertag auch religious; Land, Mensch religious, devout; Recht canon. **sich ~ trauen lassen** to get married in church, to have a church wedding; ~ **bestattet werden** to have a religious funeral.

Kirchlichkeit f (von Mensch) religiosity, devoutness; (von Schule etc) attachment to the church.

Kirchner m -s, - (obs) siehe **Küster**.

Kirch-: ~**spiel** nt, ~**sprengel** m parish; ~**tag** m (Aus, S Ger) siehe ~**weih**.

Kirchturm m church steeple.

Kirchturm-: ~**politik** f (pej) parish pump politics pl; ~**politiker** m (pej) parochial politician; ~**spitze** f church spire.

Kirch-: ~**weih** f -, -en fair, kermis (US); ~**weihe** f consecration of a/the church.

Kirmes f -, -sen (dial) siehe **Kirchweih**.

kirre adj pred (inf) Tier tame; Mensch compliant. **jdn ~ machen** to soften sb up (inf).

Kirsch m -(e)s, - siehe **Kirschwasser**.

Kirsch- in cpds cherry; ~**baum** m cherry tree; (Holz) cherry (wood); ~**blüte** f cherry blossom; (Zeit) cherry blossom time.

Kirsche f -, -n cherry. **mit ihm ist nicht gut ~n essen** (fig) it's best not to tangle with him.

Kirschenmund m (poet) cherry(-red) lips pl.

Kirsch-: ~**entkerner**, ~**entsteiner** m -s, - cherry-stoner; ~**kern** m cherry stone; ~**likör** m cherry brandy; **k~rot** adj cherry(-red); ~**stein** m cherry stone; ~**torte** f cherry gateau; Schwarzwälder ~**torte** Black Forest gateau; ~**wasser** nt kirsch.

Kissen nt -s, - cushion; (Kopf~) pillow; (Stempel~, an Heftpflaster) pad; (Duft~, Haarshampoo~) sachet.

Kissen-: ~**bezug** m cushion cover; (Kopf~) pillow case; ~**schlacht** f pillow fight.

Kiste f -, -n (a) (Behälter) box; (für Obst auch, für Wein etc) case; (Latten~) crate; (Truhe) chest. **eine ~ Wein/Zigarren** a case of wine/box of cigars; **da füllen sich ~n und Kasten** (fig) the coffers get filled.
(b) (inf) (Auto, Flugzeug) crate (inf); (Schiff) tub (inf); (Fernsehen) box (inf).
(c) (inf: Angelegenheit) affair. **fertig ist die ~!** that's that (done)!; **das ist eine faule ~!** that's a fishy business! (inf).

kistenweise adv by the box/case etc.

Kitsch m -es, no pl kitsch.

kitschig adj kitschy.

Kitt m -(e)s, -e (Fenster~) putty; (für Porzellan, Stein etc) cement; (fig) bond. **der ganze ~** (inf) the whole caboodle (inf).

Kittchen nt (inf) clink (inf).

Kittel m -s, - **(a)** (Arbeits~) overall; (von Arzt, Laborant etc) (white) coat. **und damit ist der ~ geflickt** (fig inf) and we'll call it quits (inf). **(b)** (blusenartiges Kleidungsstück) smock. **(c)** (Aus: Damenrock) skirt.

Kittel-: ~**kleid** nt frock; ~**schürze** f overall.

kitten vt to cement, to stick together with cement; Fenster to putty; (füllen) to fill; (fig) to patch up.

Kitz nt -es, -e (Reh~) fawn; (Ziegen~, Gemsen~) kid.

Kitzel m -s, - tickle; (~gefühl) tickling feeling; (fig) thrill.

Kitzelgefühl nt tickling feeling.

kitz(e)lig adj (lit, fig) ticklish.

Kitzeligkeit f (lit, fig) ticklishness.

kitzeln 1 vt (lit, fig) to tickle. **jdn unter den Armen/am Bauch ~** to tickle sb under the arms/sb's stomach; **jdm das Zwerchfell ~** (fig) to make sb laugh. 2 vi to tickle. 3 vt impers **es kitzelt mich** I've got a tickle; **es kitzelt mich, das zu tun** I'm itching to do it.

Kitzeln nt -s, no pl tickling. **er findet das ~ angenehm** he likes being tickled; **ein angenehmes ~** a nice tickle.

Kitzler m -s, - (Anat) clitoris.

kitzlig adj siehe **kitz(e)lig**.

Kiwi m -s, - (Orn) kiwi.

klabastern* vi aux sein (N Ger) to plod, to clump, to stump.

Klabautermann m, pl -**männer** (Naut) ship's kobold.

klack interj click; (platschend) splosh.

klacken vi (inf) to click; (bei Aufprall) to crash; (klappern) to rattle.

klackern vti (dial) siehe **kleckern**.

klacks interj splosh.

Klacks m -es, -e (inf) **(a)** (Geräusch) splosh. **(b)** (von Kartoffelbrei, Sahne etc) dollop (inf); (von Senf, Farbe etc auch) blob (inf). **(c)** (fig) **das ist ein ~** (einfach) that's a piece of cake (inf); (wenig) that's nothing (inf); **die 500 Mark sind für ihn ein ~** the 500 marks are peanuts or chickenfeed to him (inf).

klacksen (inf) 1 vt Sahne, Kartoffelbrei etc to dollop (inf); Farbe to splash. **die Sahne/den Kartoffelbrei etc auf etw** (acc) ~ to put a dollop of cream/mashed potato on sth (inf). 2 vi (Brei, Sahne) to go smack; (Farbe) to splash.

Kladde f -, -n rough book; (Block) scribbling pad. **in ~** (inf) in rough.

kladderadatsch interj crash-bang-wallop.

Kladderadatsch m -(e)s, -e (inf) **(a)** (Geräusch) crash-bang-wallop (inf). **(b)** (fig) (Kram, Durcheinander) mess; (Streit) bust-up (inf); (Skandal) scandal. **da haben wir den ~!** what a mess!

klaffen vi to gape; (Spalte, Abgrund auch) to yawn. **da klafft eine Wunde/ein Loch** there is a gaping wound/a gaping hole; **zwischen uns beiden klafft ein Abgrund** (fig) we are poles apart; **zwischen den Aussagen klafft ein Widerspruch** there is a blatant contradiction between the statements.

kläffen vi (pej, fig) to yap.

klaffend adj gaping; Spalte, Abgrund auch yawning; (fig) irreconcilable; Widerspruch blatant.

Kläffer m -s, - (lit, fig: pej) yapper.

Klafter m or nt -s, - or (rare) f -, -n fathom.

klafter-: ~**lang** adj (fig) huge; ~**tief** (fig) 1 adj very deep; 2 adv deep down; ~**weise** adv (fig) by the ton.

klagbar adj (Jur) Sache actionable; Anspruch, Forderung enforceable.

Klage f -, -n **(a)** (Beschwerde) complaint. **(bei jdm) über jdn/etw ~ führen** to lodge a complaint (with sb) about sb/sth; **~n (über jdn/etw) vorbringen** to make complaints (about sb/sth); **Grund zu ~n/zur ~** reason for complaint or to complain; **daß mir keine ~n kommen!** (inf) don't let me hear any complaints.
(b) (Äußerung von Schmerz) complaint; (Äußerung von Trauer) lament(ation) (um, über + acc for); (~laut) plaintive cry.
(c) (Jur) (im Zivilrecht) action, suit; (im Strafrecht auch) charge; (Scheidungs~ auch) petition; (~schrift, Wortlaut) (im Strafrecht) charge; (im Zivilrecht) charge, plaint. **eine ~ gegen jdn einreichen/erheben** to institute proceedings against sb; **eine ~ auf etw** (acc) an action for sth; **öffentliche ~** criminal charge.

Klage-: ~**abweisung** f (Jur) dismissal of an action; ~**erhebung** f (Jur) institution of proceedings; ~**frau** f siehe ~**weib**; ~**frist** f (Jur) period for instituting proceedings; **k~führend** adj (Jur) suing; (in Scheidungssachen) petitioning; **die k~führende Partei** the plaintiff; **der k~führende Ehepartner** the petitioner; ~**gesang** m lament; ~**geschrei** nt wailing; ~**grund** m (Jur) cause of action; ~**laut** m plaintive cry; (schmerzerfüllt) cry of pain; ~**lied** nt lament; **ein ~lied über jdn/etw anstimmen** (fig) to start to moan about sth; ~**mauer** f **die ~mauer** The Wailing Wall; **sie müssen von der ~mauer weg** (fig) they must stop throwing up their hands in horror.

klagen 1 vi (a) (jammern) to moan, to wail; (Tiere) to cry.
(b) (trauern, Trauer äußern) to lament (um jdn/etw sb/sth), to wail.
(c) (sich beklagen) to complain. **über etw** (acc) ~ to complain about sth; **über Rückenschmerzen/Schlaflosigkeit ~** to complain of backache/insomnia; **über jdn nicht zu ~ haben** to have no complaints about sb; **ohne zu ~** without complaining; **ich kann nicht ~** (inf) mustn't grumble (inf).
(d) (Jur) to sue (auf + acc for). **auf Scheidung ~** to petition for divorce.

2 vt **(a)** jdm sein Leid/seine Not/seinen Kummer ~ to pour out one's sorrow/distress/grief to sb; **dem Himmel** or **Gott sei's geklagt** alas, alack.
(b) (Aus) siehe **verklagen**.

klagend adj (trauererfüllt) Mensch lamenting; Blick, Ton, Schrei plaintive; Gesicht sorrowful; (schmerzerfüllt) pained; (jammernd, sich beklagend) complaining. **der ~e Teil/die ~e Partei** the plaintiff.

Kläge-: ~**partei** f (Jur) plaintiff; ~**punkt** m usu pl particular of a charge/plaint/petition.

Kläger(in f) m -s, - (Jur) (im Zivilrecht) plaintiff; (in Scheidungssachen) petitioner; (im Strafrecht auch) prosecuting party. **wo kein ~ ist, ist auch kein Richter** (Prov) well, if no-one complains ...

Klage-: ~**ruf** m plaintive cry; (Schmerzensschrei) cry of pain; ~**schrift** f (Jur) charge; (bei Scheidung) petition; ~**ton** m plaintive sound; (pej) whine; ~**weg** m (Jur) **auf dem** or **im ~weg(e)** by (taking or bringing) legal action; **den ~weg beschreiten** to take legal action; ~**weib** nt wailer, mourner.

kläglich 1 adj pitiful; Ende auch wretched; Leistung auch pathetic; Rest miserable; Niederlage, Verhalten despicable; (pej: dürftig) pathetic. 2 adv (in beschämender Weise) miserably.

Kläglichkeit f siehe adj pitifulness; wretchedness; miserableness; despicableness. **die ~ des Angebots** the pathetic choice.

klaglos 1 adj (Jur) Schuld, Forderung non-actionable. 2 adv (ohne Klagen) uncomplainingly.

Klamauk m -s, no pl (inf) (Alberei) tomfoolery; (im Theater etc) slapstick; (Lärm) racket (inf); (Reklamewirbel) hullabaloo; (Aufheben) fuss, to-do; ~ **machen** (albern) to fool about; **laß den ~** stop fooling about/making this racket/making such a fuss; **wie kann man dem Publikum solch einen ~ anbieten?** how can they put on such utter slapstick?

klamm adj **(a)** (steif vor Kälte) numb. **(b)** (naß und kalt) clammy; Wäsche cold and damp. ~ **sein** (fig inf) to be hard up (inf).

Klamm f -, -en gorge.

Klammer f -, -n **(a)** (Wäsche~) peg; (Hosen~) clip; (Büro~) paperclip; (Heft~) staple. **seine Hände packten das Seil wie ~n** he held the rope in a vice-like grip.
(b) (Haar~) (hair)grip.
(c) (Med: Wund~) clip; (für Zähne) brace.
(d) (in Text, Math, ~ausdruck) bracket; (Mus) brace. ~ **auf/zu** open/close brackets; **in ~n** in brackets; **runde/eckige/spitze ~** round/square/pointed brackets; **geschweifte ~n** braces.
(e) (Bau~) clamp, cramp; (zur Verpackung) cramp.

Klammer-: ~**affe** m (Zool) spider monkey; **er ist ein richtiger ~affe** (fig inf) he's always clinging to you; **sie saß wie ein ~affe auf dem Motorrad** (inf) she sat on the motorcycle clinging on for dear life; ~**ausdruck** m bracket, bracketed expression; ~**beutel** m peg bag; **du bist wohl mit dem ~beutel gepudert worden** (sl) you must be off your rocker (sl); ~**hefter** m -s, - stapler.

klammern 1 vt (an + acc to) Wäsche to peg; Papier etc to staple; (Tech) to clamp; (Med) Wunde to clip; Zähne to brace. 2 vr **sich an jdn/etw ~** (lit, fig) to cling to sb/sth. 3 vi (Sport) to clinch.

klammheimlich (inf) 1 adj clandestine, on the quiet. 2 adv **on the quiet. ~ aus dem Haus gehen** to sneak out of the house.

Klamotte f -, -n **(a)** ~n pl (inf) (Kleider, Siebensachen) gear sing (inf); (Zeug) stuff no pl. **(b)** (sl) (großes Geschoß) great big thing; (Steinbrocken) great big rock. **(c)** (pej: Theaterstück, Film) rubbishy old play/film etc. **das ist doch eine alte ~, das sind doch alte ~n** (inf) that's old hat (inf).

Klamottenkiste f: **aus der ~ hervorholen** (pej inf) to dig up again.

Klampfe f -, -n (inf) guitar.

klamüsern* vt (N Ger inf) to puzzle over.

Klan m -s, -e siehe **Clan**.

klang pret of **klingen**.

Klang m -(e)s, -e sound; (Tonqualität) tone. **der ~ von Glocken/Glöckchen/Gläsern** the chiming of bells/tinkling of small bells/clinking of glasses; ~**e** (Mus) sounds, tones; **der Name hat einen guten ~** the name has a good ring to it; (guten Ruf) the name has a good reputation; siehe **Sang**.

Klang-: ~**bild** nt sound; (Phys) sound pattern; ~**boden** m siehe **Resonanzboden**; ~**effekt** m sound effect; ~**farbe** f tone colour; ~**folge** f tonal sequence; ~**fülle** f richness of tone; (von Stimme, Gedicht) sonority; **k~lich** 1 adj Qualität tonal; **k~liche Unterschiede** differences in sound; (von Tonqualität) tonal difference; 2 adv **k~lich gut sein** (Musik, Lied, Gedicht, Stimme) to sound good; (Instrument, Gerät) to have a good tone or sound; **k~los** adj toneless; siehe **sang-** und **klanglos**; ~**regler** m (Rad etc) tone control; **k~rein** adj pure; **k~rein sein** to have a pure tone or sound; ~**reinheit** f purity of tone or sound; **k~schön** adj beautiful sounding; **k~schön sein** to have a beautiful tone or sound; ~**schönheit** f beauty of tone or sound; **k~treu** adj Wiedergabe faithful; Empfänger high-fidelity; Ton true; **k~treu sein** to have high fidelity; ~**treue** f fidelity; **k~voll** adj Stimme, Sprache sonorous, euphonic (liter); Wiedergabe full; Melodie tuneful; (fig) Titel, Name finesounding; ~**wort** nt onomatopoeia.

klapp interj snap; (im Türschließen) click; siehe **klipp**.

Klapp-: ~**bett** nt folding bed; ~**brücke** f bascule bridge; ~**deckel** m hinged lid.

Klappe f -, -n **(a)** flap; (an Lastwagen) tailgate; (seitlich) sidegate; (an Kombiwagen) back; (von Tisch) leaf; (von Ofen) shutter, flap; (Klappdeckel) (hinged) lid; (Mus) key; (an Trompete) valve; (Falltür) trapdoor; (Film) clapperboard.

(b) (*Schulter~*) strap; (*Hosen~, an Tasche*) flap; (*Augen~*) patch; (*von Visier*) shutter.

(c) (*Fliegen~*) (fly) swat.

(d) (*Herz~*) valve.

(e) (*inf: Mund*) trap (*inf*). die ~ halten to shut one's trap (*inf*); die ~ aufreißen, eine große ~ haben, die große ~ schwingen to have a big mouth (*inf*).

(f) (*inf: Bett*) pit (*inf*). sich in die ~ hauen (*inf*) to hit the hay (*inf*) or sack (*inf*).

(g) (*Aus Telec*) extension.

(h) (*sl: von Homosexuellen*) pick-up spot, cottage (*sl*).

klappen 1 *vt* etw nach oben/unten ~ Sitz, Bett to fold sth up/down; Kragen to turn sth up/down; Deckel to lift sth up, to raise sth/to lower sth, to put sth down; etw nach vorn/hinten ~ Sitz to tip sth forward/back; Deckel to lift sth forward/back.

2 *vi* **(a)** to bang.

(b) (*fig inf*) to work; (*gutgehen auch*) to work out; (*reibungslos stattfinden: Aufführung, Abend*) to go smoothly. wenn das mal klappt if that works out; hat es mit den Karten/dem Job geklappt? did you get the tickets/job all right or OK (*inf*)?; mit dem Flug hat alles geklappt the flight went all right, there was no problem with the flight.

Klappen-: ~fehler *m* (*Med*) valvular defect; ~text *m* (*Typ*) blurb.

Klapper *f* -, -n rattle.

Klapper-: k~dürr *adj* (*inf*) thin as a rake; ~gestell *nt* (*hum inf*) (*Mensch*) bag of bones; (*Fahrzeug*) boneshaker (*inf*).

klapp(e)rig *adj* siehe **klapprig**.

Klapperkasten *m*, **Klapperkiste** *f* (*pej*) boneshaker (*inf*).

klappern *vi* **(a)** to clatter; (*Klapperschlange, Fenster, Baby*) to rattle; (*Lider*) to bat; (*Mühle*) to clack; (*auf der Schreibmaschine*) to clatter away; (*mit Stricknadeln*) to click. er klapperte vor Kälte/Angst mit den Zähnen his teeth were chattering with cold/fear; mit den Augen ~ (*hum inf*) to flutter one's eyelashes; K~ gehört zum Handwerk (*prov*) making a big noise is part of the business.

(b) *aux sein* (*sich ~d fortbewegen*) to clatter along; (*Auto etc auch*) to rattle along.

Klapper-: ~schlange *f* (*Zool*) rattlesnake; (*fig*) rattletrap; ~storch *m* (*baby-talk*) stork; er glaubt noch immer an den ~storch he still thinks babies are found under the gooseberry bush.

Klapp-: ~fahrrad *nt* folding bicycle; ~fenster *nt* top-hung window; ~hut *m* crush-hat; ~laden *m* folding shutter; ~messer *nt* flick knife; ~rad *nt siehe* ~fahrrad.

klapprig *adj* rickety, shaky; (*fig inf*) Mensch shaky, tottery.

Klapp-: ~sitz *m* folding seat; ~stuhl *m* folding chair; ~stulle *f* (*N Ger*) sandwich; ~tisch *m* folding table; ~tür *f* trapdoor; ~verdeck *nt* folding or collapsible hood; ~zylinder *m* opera hat.

Klaps *m* -es, -e **(a)** (*inf*) einen ~ haben to have a screw loose (*inf*), to be off one's rocker (*inf*); einen ~ bekommen to go crazy or bonkers (*Brit inf*). **(b)** (*Schlag*) smack, slap.

Klapsmühle *f* (*pej inf*) loony bin (*inf*), nut house (*inf*).

klar *adj* clear; (*fertig*) ready. ~ zum Gefecht/Einsatz (*Mil*) ready for action; ~ zum Start (*Sport*) ready (for the start); ~ Schiff (*lit, fig*)/Deck machen (*Naut*) to clear the decks; ein ~er Fall (*inf*) sure thing (*inf*); ein ~er Fall von ... (*inf*) a clear case of ...; das ist doch ~! (*inf*) of course!; na ~! (*inf*) of course!, sure! (*inf*); alles ~? everything all right or OK? (*inf*); jetzt ist or wird mir alles ~! now I understand; einen ~en Augenblick haben to have a lucid moment; bei ~em Verstand sein to be in full possession of one's faculties; (*inf*) to be in one's right mind; etw ~ und deutlich sagen to spell sth out; jdm etw ~ und deutlich sagen to tell sb sth straight (*inf*); etw ~ zum Ausdruck bringen to make sth clear; etw tritt ~ zutage sth becomes apparent or obvious or clear; ~ wie Kloßbrühe or dicke Tinte (*inf*) clear as mud (*inf*); sich (*dat*) über etw (*acc*) im ~en sein to be aware of sth; sich (*dat*) darüber im ~en sein, daß ... to realize that ...; ins ~e kommen to get things straight; mit jdm/seinem Privatleben ins ~e kommen to straighten things out with sb/to sort out one's private life; *siehe* **klipp**.

Klar *nt* -(e)s, -(e) (*Aus*) siehe **Eiweiß**.

Klär|anlage *f* sewage plant; (*von Fabrik*) purification plant.

Klär-: ~apfel *m* early dessert apple; ~blick *m* (*fig*) clear-sightedness; k~blickend *adj* clear-sighted; k~denkend *adj attr* clear-thinking.

klären 1 *vt* to clear; Wasser, Luft to purify; Abwasser to treat; Bier, Wein to fine; Fall, Sachlage to clarify, to clear up; Frage to settle.

2 *vi* (*Sport*) to clear (the ball).

3 *vr* (*Wasser, Himmel*) to clear; (*Wetter*) to clear up; (*Meinungen, Sachlage*) to become clear; (*Streitpunkte*) to be clarified; (*Frage*) to be settled.

Klare(r) *m decl as adj* (*inf*) schnapps.

Klar-: ~folie *f* transparent film; k~gehen *vi sep irreg aux sein* (*inf*) to be all right or OK (*inf*); ist es mit dem Examen k~gegangen? did the exam go all right or OK? (*inf*).

Klärgrube *f* cesspit.

Klarheit *f* **(a)** (*fig: Deutlichkeit*) clarity; (*geistige ~*) lucidity. sich (*dat*) ~ über etw (*acc*) verschaffen to find out about sth, to get clear about sth; über Sachlage to clarify sth; ~ über etw (*acc*) haben to be clear about sth; jdm etw in aller ~ sagen to tell sb sth in plain language. **(b)** (*Reinheit*) clearness.

klarieren* *vt* to clear (through customs).

Klarinette *f* clarinet.

Klarinettist(in *f*) *m* clarinettist.

Klarisse *f* -, -n, **Klarissin** *f* nun of the order of St Clare.

Klar-: k~kommen *vi sep irreg aux sein* (*inf*) to manage, to get by (*inf*); mit etw k~kommen to be able to cope with sth; mit jdm

k~kommen to be able to deal or cope with sb; k~kriegen *vt sep* (*inf*) to sort out; ein Problem k~kriegen to sort out or crack (*inf*) a problem; ~lack *m* clear varnish; k~legen *vt sep* to make clear, to explain; ~luftturbulenz *f* (*Aviat*) (pocket of) air turbulence; k~machen *sep* **1** *vt* to make clear, to explain; Schiff to make ready, to get ready; Flugzeug to clear; jdm etw k~machen to make sth clear to sb; sich (*dat*) etw/die Unterschiede etc k~machen to realize sth/get the differences etc clear in one's own mind; sich (*dat*) ein Thema k~machen to get a subject sorted out in one's mind; **2** *vr* (*sl: Toilette machen etc*) to get ready; **3** *vi* (*Naut*) to make ready, to get ready; zum Gefecht k~machen to clear the decks for action.

Klärschlamm *m* sludge.

Klar-: k~sehen *vi sep irreg* to see clearly; in etw (*dat*) k~sehen to have understood sth; ~sichtfolie *f* transparent film; k~sichtig *adj* (*fig*) clear-sighted; ~sichtpackung *f* transparent pack; ~sichtscheibe *f* (*Aut*) anti-mist panel; k~spülen *vti sep* to rinse; k~stellen *vt sep* (*klären*) to clear up, to clarify; (*k~machen*) to make clear; ich möchte k~stellen, daß ... I would like to make it clear that ...; ~stellung *f* clarification; ~text *m* uncoded text, text in clear; im ~text in clear; (*fig inf*) in plain English; mit jdm ~text reden (*fig inf*) to give sb a piece of one's mind.

Klärung *f* **(a)** purification. **(b)** (*fig*) clarification.

klarwerden *sep irreg aux sein* **1** *vr* sich (*dat*) (*über etw acc*) ~ to get (sth) clear in one's mind. **2** *vi* jdm wird etw klar sth becomes clear to sb; ist dir das noch immer nicht klargeworden? do you still not understand?

klaß *adj* (*Aus inf*) siehe **klasse**.

klasse *adj inv* (*inf*) great (*inf*); siehe **Klasse**.

Klasse *f* -, -n **(a)** class; (*Spiel~*) league; (*Steuer~ auch*) bracket; (*Wert~ auch*) rate; (*Güter~*) grade. ein Maler erster ~ a first-class or first-rate painter; ein Fahrschein zweiter ~ a second-class ticket; das ist (*große*) ~! (*inf*) that's great or tremendous or marvellous! (*all inf*). **(b)** (*Sch*) class, form; (*Raum*) classroom.

Klasse- in *cpds* (*sl*) top-class; ~frau *f* (*sl*) smasher (*inf*), stunner (*inf*); ~fußball *m* (*sl*) top-class football; ~mann *m* (*Sport sl*) (*Ftbl*) top-class player; (*bei Rennen etc*) top-class competitor.

Klassement [-'mã:] *nt* -s, -s (*Sport*) (list of) rankings *pl*.

Klassen-: ~älteste(r) *mf* oldest pupil in the class; ~arbeit *f* (written) class test; ~aufsatz *m* essay written in class; ~ausflug *m* class outing; ~beste(r) *mf* best pupil; wer ist ~beste(r)? who is top of the class?; ~bewußtsein *nt* class consciousness; ~bild *nt* class photograph; ~buch *nt* (class-) register; ~buchführer *m* pupil in charge of the class-register; ~clown *m* (*Sch sl*) class joker (*inf*); ~dünkel *m siehe* Standesdünkel; ~durchschnitt *m* class average; ~erste(r) *mf siehe* ~beste(r); ~feind *m* (*Pol*) class enemy; ~foto *nt* class photograph; ~frequenz *f* size of a/the class/the classes; ~gegensatz *m usu pl* (*Sociol*) class difference; ~geist *m* (*Sch dated, Sociol*) class spirit; ~gesellschaft *f* class society; ~haß *m* (*Sociol*) class hatred; ~herrschaft *f* class rule; ~interesse *nt* (*Sociol*) class interest; ~justiz *f* (*Pol*) legal system with class bias; ~kamerad *m* classmate; ~kampf *m* class struggle; k~kämpferisch **1** *adj* committed to the class struggle, supporting the class struggle; **2** *adv* in support of the class struggle; ~kasper *m* (*Sch sl*) class joker (*inf*); ~keile *f* (*Sch dated*) a thrashing from the rest of the class or from one's classmates; ~krieg *m* class warfare; ~lage *f* (*Sociol*) class position; die ~lage der Arbeiterschaft the position of the working classes; ~lehrer *m* class teacher, form teacher, form master/mistress; ~leiter *m* class teacher, form teacher, form master/mistress; ~lektüre *f* class reading; k~los *adj* Gesellschaft classless; Krankenhaus one-class; ~los *nt* draw ticket in a Klassenlotterie; ~lotterie *f* lottery in which draws are made on a number of different days and in which tickets can be bought for each individual draw; ~raum *m* classroom; ~schrank *m* classroom cupboard; ~schranke *f* class barrier; ~spiegel *m* (*Sch*) seating plan of the class; ~sprecher *m* (*Sch*) class spokesman, = form captain; ~staat *m* (*Pol*) state governed by one class; ~stärke *f* (*Sch*) size of a/the class/the classes; ~treffen *nt* (*Sch*) class reunion; ~unterschied *m* class difference; ~verband *m* im ~verband as a class; ~vorstand *m* (*esp Aus*) siehe ~lehrer; ~wahlrecht, ~wahlsystem *nt* electoral system based on class, class system of franchise; k~weise **1** *adj* by class; k~weiser Aufbau arrangement by class; **2** *adv* sitzen, sich aufstellen in classes; erscheinen as a class; ~ziel *nt* (*Sch*) required, standard; das ~ziel nicht erreichen not to reach the required standard; (*fig*) not to make the grade; ~zimmer *nt* classroom.

Klasse-: ~spieler *m* (*Sport sl*) star player, (top-)class player; ~weib *nt* (*sl*) smasher (*inf*), stunner (*inf*).

Klassifikation *f* classification.

klassifizierbar *adj* classifiable.

klassifizieren* *vt* to classify. ~d classificatory.

Klassifizierung *f* classification.

-klassig *adj suf* -class.

Klassik *f*, no *pl* classical period; (*inf: klassische Musik, Literatur*) classical music/literature. die antike ~ Classical Antiquity.

Klassiker(in *f*) *m* -s, - classic. ein ~ des Jazz/der modernen Musik a jazz classic/a classic of modern music; die antiken ~ the classics.

klassisch *adj* **(a)** (*die Klassik betreffend, antik, traditionell*) classical. **(b)** (*typisch, vorbildlich, zeitlos*) classic. **(c)** (*iro inf: prächtig*) classic. das hast du mal wieder ~ gesagt! another classic comment! (*iro*).

Klassizismus *m* classicism.

klassizistisch *adj* classical.

-kläßler(in f) m in cpds -s, - (Sch) -former.
klatsch interj splash, splosh; (bei Schlag, Aufprall) smack.
Klatsch m -(e)s, -e (a) splosh, splash; (bei Schlag, Aufprall) smack. (b) no pl (pej inf: Tratsch) gossip, scandal.
Klatschbase f (pej inf) (tratschend) scandalmonger, gossip; (redselig) chatterbox (inf).
Klatsche f -, -n (inf) (a) siehe **Klatschbase**. (b) (Sch) (Denunziant) sneak, telltale (inf); (Hilfsmittel) crib (inf). (c) (Fliegenklappe) fly swatter.
klatschen 1 vi (a) to clap. in die Hände ~ to clap one's hands. (b) (einen Klaps geben) to slap. jdm auf die Schenkel/sich (dat) gegen die Stirn ~ to slap sb's thighs/one's forehead; ruhig, sonst klatscht's (inf) be quiet or I'll smack you. (c) aux sein (aufschlagen) (harte Gegenstände) to go smack; (Flüssigkeiten) to splash. der Regen klatschte gegen die Fenster the rain beat against the windows. (d) (pej inf) (tratschen) to gossip; (dial: petzen) to sneak, to tell tales (bei to). über jdn/etw ~ to gossip or spread gossip about sb.
 2 vt (a) to clap; Takt to clap out. jdm Beifall ~ to applaud or clap sb. (b) (knallen) to smack, to slap; (werfen) to throw; Fliegen to swat. jdm eine (Ohrfeige) ~ (inf) to slap sb (across the face). (c) (pej dial: petzen) jdm etw ~ (Sch) to tell tales about sth to sb.
Klatschen nt -s, no pl (a) (Beifall~) applause. (b) (inf: Tratschen) gossiping.
klatschenaß adj (inf) siehe **klatschnaß**.
Klatscherei f (pej inf) (a) (Beifall~) clapping. (b) (Tratscherei) gossiping, gossipmongering.
Klatscher(in f) m -s, - (a) siehe **Klatschbase**. (b) (Beifall~) applauder.
Klatsch-: ~geschichte f (pej) gossip no pl; eine ~geschichte a piece of gossip; k~haft adj gossipy; ~haftigkeit f fondness for gossip; ~kolumnist m (inf) gossip columnist; ~maul nt (pej inf) (a) big mouth; (b) (Mensch) gossip, scandalmonger; ~mohn m (corn) poppy; k~naß adj (inf) sopping wet (inf); ~spalte f (Press inf) gossip column; ~sucht f passion for gossip; k~süchtig adj extremely gossipy; ein k~süchtiger Mensch a compulsive gossip; ~tante f, ~weib nt (pej inf) gossip(monger), scandalmonger.
klauben vt (a) (S Ger, Aus, Sw) (auflesen) to pick up; (auslesen) to pick out. etw in einen Korb ~ to pick sth up and put it in a basket; etw aus etw ~ to pick sth out from sth. (b) (Aus: sammeln) to collect; Holz, Pilze, Kräuter auch to gather; Beeren to pick. (c) (Sw: kneifen) to pinch. Worte ~ (dial) to split hairs.
Klaue f -, -n claw; (Huf) hoof; (pej inf: Hand) talons pl (pej inf); (pej inf: Schrift) scrawl (pej). in den ~n der Verbrecher etc in the clutches of the criminals etc; den ~n des Todes entkommen to escape from the jaws of death.
klauen (inf) **1** vt to nick (Brit inf), to pinch (inf) (jdm etw sth from sb); Ideen auch to crib (jdm etw sth from sb). **2** vi to steal, to nick (Brit inf) or pinch things (inf).
Klauenseuche f siehe **Maul- und Klauenseuche**.
Klause f -, -n (a) (von Mönch, Einsiedler) hermitage; (Klosterzelle) cell; (fig hum) den. (b) (mountain) defile.
Klausel f -, -n clause; (Vorbehalt) proviso; (Bedingung) condition, stipulation.
Klausner m -s, - siehe **Einsiedler**.
Klausnerzelle f hermit's cell.
Klaustrophobie f (Psych) claustrophobia.
klaustrophobisch adj (Psych) claustrophobic.
klausulieren* vt siehe **verklausulieren**.
Klausur f (a) (Univ auch ~arbeit) exam, paper. ~en korrigieren to mark scripts or exam papers. (b) no pl (Abgeschlossenheit) seclusion. eine Arbeit unter or in ~ schreiben to write an essay etc under examination conditions. (c) (Eccl: Räume) enclosure, cloister.
Klaviatur [klavia'tu:ɐ] f keyboard.
Klavichord [klavi'kɔrt] nt -(e)s, -e clavichord.
Klavier [-'vi:ɐ] nt -s, -e piano. ~ spielen to play the piano; er spielt ein hervorragendes ~ (sl) he's great on (the) piano (inf).
Klavier-: in cpds piano; ~auszug m piano score; ~bauer m piano-maker; ~bearbeitung f piano arrangement; ~begleitung f piano accompaniment; ~deckel m piano lid; ~hocker m piano stool; ~konzert nt (a) (Musik) piano concerto; (b) (Vorstellung) piano recital; ~schule f (Lehrbuch) piano tutor; ~sonate f piano sonata; ~spiel nt piano playing; ~spieler m pianist, piano player; ~stimmer m piano-tuner; ~stück nt piano piece, piece of piano-music.
Klebe-: ~band nt adhesive tape, sticky tape; ~binder m -s, - adhesive binder; ~bindung f (Typ) adhesive binding; ~ecke f siehe Fotoecke; ~falz m (gummed) stamp hinge or mount; ~folie f siehe Klebfolie; ~mittel nt adhesive.
kleben 1 vi to stick. an etw (dat) ~ (lit) to stick to sth; an den Traditionen ~ to cling or stick to tradition; an seinen Händen klebt Blut (fig) he has blood on his hands; klebt nicht so am Text don't stick so much or so close to the text. (b) (inf: für Sozialversicherung) to pay stamps. **2** vt to stick; (mit Klebstoff auch) to glue; (mit Leim auch) to paste; Film, Tonband to splice. Marken ~ (inf: Insur) to pay stamps; jdm eine ~ (inf) to belt sb one (inf).
klebenbleiben vi sep irreg aux sein to stick (an +dat to); (Sch inf) to stay down a year, to repeat a year; (fig inf: nicht wegkommen) to get stuck.
Klebe-: ~pflaster nt sticking plaster, adhesive plaster; ~presse f splicer.
Kleber m -s, - (a) (inf) siehe Klebstoff. (b) (im Mehl) gluten.
Klebe-: ~stelle f join; (an Film) splice; ~stoff m siehe Klebstoff; ~streifen m siehe Klebstreifen; ~zettel m gummed label.
Kleb-: ~festigkeit f adhesiveness; ~fläche f surface to be stuck; ~folie f adhesive film; (D-C-fix) fablon ®; (für Lebensmittel) cling film ®; ~kraft f adhesive strength; ~mittel nt siehe Klebemittel.
klebrig adj sticky; Farbe tacky; (klebfähig) adhesive.
Klebrigkeit f siehe adj stickiness; tackiness; adhesiveness.
Kleb-: ~stoff m adhesive; ~streifen m adhesive tape; (selbstklebend auch) sticky tape; (zum Befeuchten) gummed tape.
Klebung f bond.
Kleckerei f mess. ohne ~ geht's nicht you can't do it without making a mess.
kleckern 1 vt to spill; Farbe auch to splash. **2** vi (a) to make a mess. (b) (tropfen) to spill; (Farbe auch) to splash. (c) (inf: stückchenweise arbeiten) to fiddle about. gekleckert kommen to come in dribs and drabs.
kleckerweise adv in dribs and drabs.
Klecks m -es, -e (Tinten~) (ink)blot; (Farb~) blob; (Fleck) stain.
klecksen vi (mit Tinte) to make blots/a blot; (Kugelschreiber etc auch) to blot; (pej inf: malen) to daub.
Kleckserei f (pej inf) daubing; (von Schüler, Kugelschreiber) making blots.
Kledage [kle'da:ʒə], **Kledasche** f -, no pl (sl) clobber (sl), gear (inf).
Klee m -s, no pl clover. jdn/etw über den grünen ~ loben to praise sb/sth to the skies.
Kleeblatt nt cloverleaf; (Mot) cloverleaf (intersection); (fig: Menschen) threesome, trio. vierblättriges ~ four-leaf clover; das irische ~ the (Irish) shamrock.
Kleid nt -(e)s, -er (a) (Damen~) dress. ein zweiteiliges ~ a two-piece (suit). (b) ~er pl (Kleidung) clothes pl, clothing sing (esp Comm); garments pl (Comm); warme ~er mitbringen to bring warm clothes or clothing; ~er machen Leute (Prov) fine feathers make fine birds (Prov); in die ~er fahren to get into one's clothes, to get one's clothes on; ich bin zwei Tage nicht aus den ~ern gekommen I haven't been to bed for two days. (c) (old: Gewand) garment; (old, Sw, S Ger: Herrenanzug) suit; (liter: Uniform) uniform. (d) (liter) (Feder~) plumage; (Pelz) coat, fur; (fig: von Natur, Bäumen etc) mantle (liter), cloak (liter). der Winter hatte der Erde ein weißes ~ angezogen winter had clad the earth in white (liter).
-kleid nt in cpds Sommer-/Ordens-/Herbst~ summer dress/monastic robe/autumn cloak or mantle (liter).
Kleidchen nt dim of Kleid little dress; (leicht) flimsy dress.
kleiden 1 vr to dress; (Kleider anziehen auch) to dress oneself, to clothe oneself (liter, form). die Natur kleidet sich in Weiß (liter) nature dons a cloak or mantle of white (liter); siehe gekleidet.
 2 vt (a) (mit Kleidern versehen) to clothe, to dress; (fig) Gedanken, Ideen to clothe, to couch. die Armen ~ to clothe the poor; etw in schöne Worte ~ to dress sth up or to couch sth in fancy words. (b) jdn ~ (jdm stehen) to suit sb.
Kleider-: ~ablage f (Raum) cloakroom; (Garderobenablage) coat rack; (Ständer) hat- or coat-stand; ~bad nt, no pl etw ins ~bad geben to take sth to the (dry) cleaner's; die Flecken werden im ~bad rausgehen the spots will come out with dry cleaning; ~bügel m coathanger; ~bürste f clothes brush; ~haken m coat hook; ~kammer f (Mil etc) uniform store; ~kasten m (Aus, Sw) siehe ~schrank (a); ~macher(in f) m (Aus) siehe Schneider; ~ordnung f dress regulations pl; ~rechen m coat rack; ~schrank m (a) wardrobe; (b) (inf: Mensch) great hulk (of a man) (inf).
kleidsam adj flattering.
Kleidung f, no pl clothes pl, clothing (esp Comm). warme ~ warm clothing or clothes; für jds (Nahrung und) ~ sorgen to (feed and) clothe sb.
Kleidungsstück nt garment. ~e pl clothes pl; ein warmes ~ mitnehmen to bring something warm (to wear).
Kleie f, no pl bran.
klein adj (a) little, small; Finger little; Format, Gehalt, Rente, Zahl, (Hand)schrift, Buchstabe small; (Mus) Terz minor. die K~en Antillen etc the lesser Antilles etc; K~ Paris etc little or miniature Paris etc; der K~e Bär or Wagen the Little Bear, Ursa Minor; die K~e Strafkammer (Jur) the lower criminal court; haben Sie es nicht ~er? do you not have anything smaller?; ein ~ bißchen or wenig a little (bit); ein ~ bißchen or wenig Salat a little (bit of) salad; ein ~ Bier, ein K~es (inf) a small beer, = half a pint, a half; ~es Geld small change; das ~e Fräulein Braun (dated) little Miss Brown; K~ Roland little Roland; du ~er Teufel! you little devil!; ein süßes ~es Püppchen a sweet little thing; hallo, ~er Mann! hullo, little man; ein ~es Auto a nice little car; er fährt ein ~es Auto he drives a little or small car; mit seiner ~en Frau with his little wife; ich wußte nicht, daß seine Frau so ~ ist I didn't know his wife was so small or little; eine ~e, hübsche Wohnung a small, pretty flat; eine hübsche ~e Wohnung a nice little flat; mein ~er Bruder my little brother; er ist ~er als mein Bruder he's smaller than his brother; als ich (noch) ~ war when I was little; ~für sein Alter small or little for his age; er schreibt sehr ~ he writes very small, his writing is very small; sich ~ machen to bend down low; to curl up tight; um durch die enge Tür zu kommen, muß man sich ~ machen to get through this narrow door you have to squeeze yourself in; macht euch ein bißchen ~er! squeeze up closer; den mach' ich so ~ mit Hut!

(hum) I'll cut him down to size, I'll make him look *that* big; ~ **aber oho** (*inf*) good things come in small packages; **ein Wort** ~ **drucken/schreiben** to print/write a word with small initial letters, to use small initial letters; ~ **beigeben** (*inf*) to give in quietly *or* gracefully; **jdn** ~ **und häßlich machen** (*inf*) to make sb feel small; **ganz** ~ **(und häßlich) werden** (*inf*) to look humiliated *or* deflated; **im** ~**en** in miniature; **bis ins** ~**ste** in every possible *or* in minute detail, right down to the smallest detail; **von** ~ **an** *or* **auf** (*von Kindheit an*) from his childhood *or* early days; (*von Anfang an*) from the very beginning, from scratch; ~**e Kinder** ~**e Sorgen, große Kinder große Sorgen** (*prov*) bigger children just mean bigger problems; ~ **stellen** *or* **drehen** (*Cook*) to put sth on low *or* a low heat; **um ein** ~**es zu …** (*geh*) a little *or* a trifle too …

(b) (*kurz*) *Wuchs, Schritt* little, small, short; *Weile, Pause* little, short; *Vortrag* short. ~**en Augenblick, bitte!** just one moment, please; **ein Kopf** ~**er als jd sein** to be a head shorter than sb; **über ein** ~**es** (*obs*) in next to no time.

(c) (*geringfügig*) little, small, slight; *Betrag, Summe* little, small. **beim** ~**sten Schreck** at the slightest *or* smallest shock; **das** ~**ere Übel** the lesser evil; **ein paar** ~**ere Fehler** a few minor mistakes; **eine** ~**ere Unpäßlichkeit** a minor ailment; **es wäre ihm ein K**~**es, …** (*old*) it would be a mere nothing for him …

(d) (*unbedeutend*) petty (*pej*); *Leute* ordinary. **er ist ein** ~**er Geist** he is small-minded; **der** ~**e Mann** the ordinary citizen, the man in the street; **ein** ~**er Ganove** a small-time *or* petty crook; **die K**~**en** *or* ~**en Gauner fängt man, die Großen läßt man laufen** (*prov*) it's always the big fish that get away; **sein Vater war (ein)** ~**er Beamter** his father was a minor official; ~**e Leute übersieht man** (*hum*) I'm *etc* so small and insignificant.

(e) (*armselig*) *Verhältnisse* humble, lowly, modest. **aus** ~**en Anfängen aufgebaut** built up from small *or* humble *or* modest beginnings; ~ **anfangen** to start off in a small way.

(f) *Prüfung* intermediate.

-klein *nt* in *cpds* **-s,** *no pl siehe* **Gänse-, Hasen-** etc.

Klein-: ~**aktionär** *m* small shareholder; ~**anzeige** *f* small ad; ~**arbeit** *f* detailed work; **in zäher/mühseliger** ~**arbeit** with rigorous/painstaking attention to detail; ~**asien** *nt* Asia Minor; ~**auto** *nt siehe* ~**wagen**; ~**bahn** *f* narrow-gauge railway; ~**bauer** *m* small farmer, smallholder; **k**~**bekommen*** *vt sep irreg siehe* **k**~**kriegen**; ~**betrieb** *m* small business; **bäuerlicher/handwerklicher/industrieller** ~**betrieb** smallholding/(small) workshop/small factory; ~**bildkamera** *f* 35 mm camera; ~**buchstabe** *m* small letter; ~**bürger** *m* petty bourgeois; ~**bürgerlich** *adj* lower middle-class, petty bourgeois (*pej*); **er reagierte typisch k**~**bürgerlich** his reaction was typically lower middle-class *or* petty bourgeois; ~**bürgertum** *nt* (*Sociol*) lower middle class, petty bourgeoisie; ~**bus** *m* minibus.

Kleinchen *nt* (*dial*) little one; little boy/girl. **armes** ~ poor little thing *or* love (*inf*).

Kleinleutemilieu *nt* world of ordinary people.

Kleine(r) *mf decl as adj* (a) little one *or* child; little boy/girl; baby. **unser** ~**r** (*Jüngster*) our youngest (child); **die lieben** ~**n** (*iro*) the dear *or* sweet little things; **eine hübsche** ~ a pretty little girl *or* thing; **die Katze mit ihren** ~**n** the cat with its kittens *or* babies (*inf*).

(b) (*inf: auch* ~**s:** *Schatz, Liebling*) baby (*inf*). **na** ~**/**~**r!** (*zu einem Kind*) hullo little girl/sonny Jim!; **na** ~**r!** (*Prostituierte zu einem Passanten*) hullo, dear *or* love.

Kleine(s) *nt decl as adj*: **etwas** ~**s** (*inf*) a little baby *or* stranger (*hum*).

Klein-: ~**familie** *f* (*Sociol*) nuclear family; ~**format** *nt* small format; **ein Buch/Bild im** ~**format** a small-format book/picture; ~**garten** *m* allotment; ~**gärtner** *m* allotment holder; ~**gebäck** *nt* biscuits (*Brit*) *pl*, cookies (*US*) *pl*; **k**~**gedruckt** *adj attr* in small print; ~**gedruckte(s)** *nt* small print; ~**geist** *m* (*pej*) small-minded person; **k**~**geistig** *adj* (*pej*) small-minded, petty; ~**geld** *nt* (small) change; **das nötige** ~**geld haben** (*fig*) to have the necessary wherewithal (*inf*); **k**~**gemustert** *adj* small-patterned; **k**~**gewachsen** *adj* short, small; *Baum* small; **k**~**gläubig** *adj* (a) (*Rel*) doubting, sceptical; **der k**~**gläubige Thomas** doubting Thomas; **ihr** ~**gläubigen!** (*Bibl*) o ye of little faith; (b) (*zweifelnd*) timid; **k**~**gläubig sein** to lack conviction; **sei doch nicht so k**~**gläubig** don't be so timid; ~**gläubigkeit** *f* lack of faith, scepticism; timidity, lack of conviction; ~**gruppe** *f* (*Sociol*) small group; **k**~**hacken** *vt sep* to chop up small; ~**häusler** *m* **-s,** - (*Aus*) small farmer; ~**heit** *f* smallness, small size; **k**~**herzig** *adj* fainthearted; ~**hirn** *nt* (*Anat*) cerebellum; ~**holz** *nt, no pl* firewood, kindling; **aus etw** ~**holz machen, etw zu** ~**holz machen** to chop sth up; (*hum inf*) to smash sth to pieces; ~**holz aus jdm machen** (*inf*) to make mincemeat out of sb (*inf*).

Kleinigkeit *f* (a) little *or* small thing; (*Bagatelle*) small *or* trifling *or* trivial matter *or* thing, trifle; (*Einzelheit*) minor detail *or* point, small point. **ich habe noch ein paar** ~**en in der Stadt zu erledigen** I still have a few little things to attend to in town; **es war nur eine** ~ **zu reparieren** there was only something minor to be repaired; **die Reparatur/Prüfung war eine** ~ the repair job/exam was no trouble at all; **eine** ~ **essen** to have a bite to eat, to eat a little something; **jdm eine** ~ **schenken/bezahlen** to give/pay sb a little something; **die** ~ **von 1000 DM** (*iro*) the small matter of 1,000 marks; **das kostet eine** ~ (*iro*) that'll cost a pretty penny; **wegen** *or* **bei jeder** ~ for the slightest reason; **das war doch (nur) eine** ~**!** it was nothing; **das ist doch eine** ~**!** that isn't (asking) much; **das ist für mich keine** ~ that is no small matter for me; **wir haben noch ein paar** ~**en geändert** we've changed one or two details *or* made one or two small changes; **großen Wert auf** ~**en legen** to be a stickler for

detail(s); **bis auf die letzten** ~**en ist alles fertig** everything is ready apart from the last-minute odds and ends; **sich nicht mit** ~**en abgeben** *or* **befassen** not to bother over details.

(b) (*ein bißchen*) **eine** ~ a little (bit), a trifle, a shade; **eine** ~ **zu groß/nach rechts** a little (bit) *etc* too big/to the right; **das wird eine** ~ **dauern** it will take a little while.

Kleinigkeits-: ~**krämer** *m* (*pej*) stickler for detail, pedant; ~**krämerei** *f* (*pej*) pernicketiness, pedantry.

Klein-: ~**kaliber** *nt* small bore; ~**kalibergewehr** *nt* small-bore rifle; **k**~**kalibrig** *adj* small-bore *attr only*; **k**~**kariert** *adj* (*fig*) tuppenny-ha'penny *attr only* (*inf*), small-time (*inf*); (*lit rare*) finely checked *or* chequered; **k**~**kariert sein** (*fig*) to be small- *or* petty-minded; **k**~**kariert denken** to think small; ~**kind** *nt* small child, toddler (*inf*), infant (*Psych*); ~**klima** *nt* (*Met*) microclimate; ~**kram** *m* (*inf*) odds and ends *pl*; (*kleinere Arbeiten*) odd jobs *pl*; (*Trivialitäten*) trivialities *pl*, trivia *pl*; ~**kredit** *m* personal loan; ~**krieg** *m* (*fig*) battle; **einen** ~**krieg mit jdm führen** to be fighting a running battle with sb.

kleinkriegen *vt sep* (a) (*lit*) *Holz* to chop (up); *Nuß* to break. **er kann das Fleisch mit den Zähnen nicht** ~ he can't break up his meat with his teeth.

(b) (*inf: kaputtmachen*) to smash, to break.

(c) (*inf*) (*gefügig machen*) to bring into line (*inf*); (*unterkriegen, müde machen*) to get down; (*körperlich*) to tire out. **er/unser altes Auto ist einfach nicht kleinzukriegen** he just won't be beaten/our old car just goes on for ever; **er ließ sich auch trotz erpresserischer Drohungen nicht** ~ in spite of blackmail threats he was not to be intimidated.

(d) (*inf*) *Geld* to blow (*inf*), to get through.

Kleinkunst *f* cabaret.

Kleinkunstbühne *f* cabaret.

kleinlaut *adj* abashed, subdued, meek. **dann wurde er ganz** ~ it took the wind out of his sails, that made him shut up; **etw** ~ **zugeben** to admit sth shamefacedly; ~ **um Verzeihung bitten** to apologize rather sheepishly.

kleinlich *adj* petty; (*knauserig*) mean, stingy (*inf*); (*engstirnig*) narrow-minded.

Kleinlichkeit *f siehe adj* pettiness; meanness, stinginess (*inf*); narrow-mindedness.

kleinmachen *vt sep* (a) to chop *or* cut up. (b) (*inf*) *Geld* (*wechseln*) to change; (*ausgeben*) to blow (*inf*). (c) (*inf: erniedrigen*) **jdn** ~ to make sb look small.

Klein-: ~**möbel** *pl* smaller items of furniture; ~**mut** *m* faintheartedness, timidity; **k**~**mütig** *adj* fainthearted, timid.

Kleinod ['klaino:t] *nt* **-(e)s, -ien** [klai'no:diən] *or* **-e** (*lit, fig*) jewel, gem. **sie war sein** ~ (*liter*) she was his treasure *or* his pride and joy.

Klein-: ~**rentner** *m* person living on small pension; **k**~**schneiden** *vt sep irreg* to cut up small, to cut up into small pieces; **k**~**schreiben** *vt sep irreg* (*fig*) to set little store by; **k**~**geschrieben werden** to count for (very) little; ~**schreibung** *f* use of small initial letters; ~**staat** *m* small state; ~**stadt** *f* small town; ~**städter** *m* small-town dweller, provincial (*pej*); **k**~**städtisch** *adj* provincial, small-town *attr*.

Kleinstbetrag *m* small sum; (*bei Wetten*) minimum stake. ~**e unter DM 1 sind unzulässig** sums below the minimum of DM 1 are not acceptable.

kleinste(r, s) *superl of* **klein**.

Kleinst-: **k**~**möglich** *adj* smallest possible; ~**wohnung** *f* one-room apartment *or* flatlet (*Brit*).

Klein-: ~**tier** *nt* small animal; ~**vieh** *nt*: ~**vieh macht auch Mist** (*prov*) many a mickle makes a muckle, every little helps; ~**wagen** *m* small car; **k**~**weis** *adv* (*Aus*) gradually; **k**~**winzig** *adj* tiny little; ~**wohnung** *f* flatlet (*Brit*), small apartment; **k**~**wüchsig** *adj* (*geh*) small; *Volk auch* small in stature; ~**zeug** *nt* (*inf*) small odds and ends *pl*.

Kleister *m* **-s,** - (*Klebstoff*) paste; (*pej: dicke Speise*) goo (*inf*).

kleist(e)rig *adj* (*pej inf*) gooey (*inf*).

kleistern *vti* (a) (*zusammenkleben*) to paste. (b) (*dated inf*) **jdm eine** ~ to slap sb in the face *or* sb's face.

Klementine *f* clementine.

Klemmappe *f getrennt* **Klemm-mappe** spring folder *or* binder.

Klemme *f* **-, -n** (a) (*Haar*~, *für Papiere etc*) clip; (*Elec*) crocodile clamp *or* clip; (*Med*) clamp. (b) (*fig inf*) **in der** ~ **sitzen** *or* **sein** to be in a fix *or* tight spot *or* jam (*all inf*); **jdm aus der** ~ **helfen** to help sb out of a fix *or* tight spot *or* jam (*all inf*).

klemmen 1 *vt* (a) *Draht etc* to clamp, to clip; (*in Spalt*) to stick, to wedge, to jam. **sich** (*dat*) **den Finger in etw** (*acc*) ~ to catch *or* trap one's finger in sth; **sich** (*dat*) **etw unter den Arm** ~ to stick *or* tuck sth under one's arm; **sich** (*dat*) **eine Zigarette zwischen die Lippen** ~ (*inf*) to stick a cigarette in one's mouth.

(b) (*inf: stehlen*) to pinch (*inf*), to swipe (*inf*).

(c) (*sl: schwänzen*) *Arbeit* to skive (*Brit inf*), to skip, to cut. **2** *vr* to catch oneself (*in* +*dat* in). **sich hinter etw** (*acc*) ~ (*inf*) to get stuck into sth (*inf*); **sich hinter jdn** ~ (*inf*) to get on to sb.

3 *vi* *Tür, Schloß etc* to stick, to jam.

Klemmer *m* **-s,** - pince-nez.

Klemm-: ~**hefter** *m*, ~**mappe** *f siehe* **Klemmappe** ~**ring** *m* clamp(ing) ring; ~**tasche** *f* clutch bag.

Klempner *m* **-s,** - plumber.

Klempnerei *f* (a) *no pl* plumbing. (b) (*Werkstatt*) plumber's workshop.

Klempnerladen *m* plumber's (shop). **der General trägt** *or* **hat einen ganzen** ~ **auf der Brust** (*hum*) the general has a whole load of ironmongery on his breast (*inf*).

klempnern *vi* to do plumbing.

Kleopatra *f* - Cleopatra.

Klepper *m* **-s,** - nag, hack.

Klepper-®: ~**boot** *nt* faltboat, foldboat, folding boat; ~**mantel** *m* mackintosh, mac (*inf*).

Kleptomane m -n, -n kleptomaniac.
Kleptomanie f kleptomania.
Kleptomanin f kleptomaniac.
kleptomanisch adj kleptomaniac.
klerikal adj (pej) clerical.
Klerikalismus m (pej) clericalism.
Kleriker m -s, - cleric.
Klerisei f, no pl (old), **Klerus** m -, no pl clergy.
Klette f -, -n (Bot) burdock; (Blütenkopf) bur(r); (pej: lästiger Mensch) nuisance, bind (inf). sich wie eine ~ an jdn hängen to cling to sb like a limpet or barnacle; wie die ~n zusammenhalten to stick together.
Kletter-: ~affe m (inf) er ist ein richtiger ~affe he can climb like a monkey; ~baum m climbing tree.
Kletterer m -s, - climber.
Kletter-: ~gerüst nt climbing frame; ~max(e) m -es, -e (inf) steeplejack.
klettern vi aux sein to climb; (mühsam) to clamber. auf Bäume ~ to climb trees.
Kletter-: ~partie f climbing trip or outing; ~pflanze f climbing plant, climber; ~stange f climbing pole; ~tour f siehe ~partie.
Klętze f -, -n (S Ger, Aus) dried pear.
Kletzenbrot nt (S Ger, Aus) fruit bread.
klicken vi to click.
Klicker m -s, - marble; (Spiel) marbles sing.
klickern vi to play marbles.
klieben pret **kliebte** or **klob**, ptp **geklobt** or **gekloben** vt (Aus) Holz to chop.
Klient [kli'ɛnt] m -en, -en client.
Klientel [klien'tel] f -, -en clients pl, clientèle.
Klientin [kli'ɛntɪn] f client.
klieren vi (dial) to scrawl.
Kliff nt -(e)s, -e cliff.
Kliffküste f cliffs pl.
Klima nt -s, -s or -te [kli'ma:tə] (lit, fig) climate; (fig auch) atmosphere.
Klima-: ~änderung f climatic change; ~anlage f air-conditioning (system); mit ~anlage air-conditioned; ~kammer f climatic chamber.
Klimakterium nt climacteric, menopause.
Klima-: ~kunde f siehe Klimatologie; ~schwankung f climatic variation.
klimatisch adj no pred climatic.
klimatisieren* vt to air-condition.
Klimatologie f climatology.
Klimawechsel m (lit, fig) change in the climate.
Klimax f -, no pl (liter) climax.
Klimazone f (climatic) zone.
Klimbim m -s, no pl (inf) odds and ends pl; (Umstände) fuss (and bother).
klimmen pret **klomm** or **klimmte**, ptp **geklommen** or **geklimmt** vi aux sein (rare) to clamber, to scramble.
Klimmzug m (Sport) pull-up. geistige ~e machen (fig) to do intellectual or mental acrobatics.
Klimperei f (inf) tinkling; (stümperhaft) plonking (inf); (auf Banjo etc) twanging.
Klimperkasten m (inf) piano, joanna (inf).
klimpern vi to tinkle; (stümperhaft ~) to plonk away (inf); (auf Banjo) to twang. mit Geld etc ~ to jingle coins; mit den Wimpern ~ (inf) to flutter one's eyelashes.
kling interj clink, ting, ding. ~ machen (Metall, Glas etc) to clink; mit K~ und Klang (old) to the sound of music.
Klinge f -, -n blade; (liter: Schwert) sword, blade (liter). eine gute ~ schlagen (Fencing) to be a good swordsman; mit blanker ~ (liter) with drawn sword; er führt eine scharfe ~ (fig) he is a dangerous opponent; jdn über die ~ springen lassen (sl) (umbringen) to bump sb off (inf), to rub sb out (sl); (opfern) to leave sb to be killed.
Klingel f -, -n bell.
Klingel-: ~anlage f bell system; ~beutel m collection bag; ~draht m bell wire.
klingeling interj dingaling.
Klingelknopf m bell button or push.
klingeln vi to ring (nach for); (Motor) to pink, to knock. es hat schon zum ersten/zweiten/dritten Mal geklingelt (in Konzert, Theater) the three-/two-/one-minute bell has already gone; es hat schon geklingelt (in Schule) the bell has already gone; es hat geklingelt (Telefon) the phone just rang; (an Tür) somebody just rang the doorbell; immer wenn es an der Tür klingelt ... whenever the doorbell rings or goes ...; es klingelt an der Tür (als Bühnenanweisung) there is a ring at the door; hat es jetzt endlich geklingelt? (fig inf) has the penny finally dropped? (inf); K~ ringing.
Klingel-: ~partie f eine ~partie machen to ring doorbells and run away; ~schnur f bellpull; ~zeichen nt ring; auf ein ~zeichen hin at the ring of a bell; auf ein besonderes ~zeichen hin in response to a special ring; ~zug m bellpull.
klingen pret **klang**, ptp **geklungen** vi to sound; (Glocke, Ohr) to ring; (Glas) to clink; (Metall) to clang. nach etw ~ to sound like sth; mein linkes Ohr klingt I have a ringing (sound) in my left ear; das klingt mir wie Musik in den Ohren that is music to my ears; die Gläser ~ lassen to clink glasses; die Glocke klingt dumpf/hell the bell has a dull/clear ring.
klingend adj mit ~em Spiel (old Mil) with fife and drum; in or mit ~er Münze (old, liter) in coin of the realm; ~e Register (Mus) (sounding) stops pl; ~er Reim (Poet) feminine rhyme.
Klingklang m, no pl clinking, tinkle, tinkling (sound).
Klinik f -, -en clinic; (Universitäts~) (university) hospital.
Klinika, Kliniken pl of **Klinikum**.
Kliniker(in f) m -s, - (Med) clinician; (Univ) medical student

attached to a hospital.
Klinikum nt -s, **Klinika** or **Kliniken** (Univ) clinic.
klinisch adj clinical. ~ tot clinically dead.
Klinke f -, -n (Tür~) (door) handle; (Sperr~) catch, ratchet, pawl; (Telec) jack. ~n putzen (inf) to go or canvass/sell from door to door, to go or do door-to-door canvassing/selling.
Klinkenputzer m (inf) (Hausierer) hawker; (Vertreter) door-to-door salesman; (Wahlkandidat) door-to-door canvasser; (Bettler) beggar.
Klinker m -s, - (a) (Ziegelstein) clinker brick, (Dutch) clinker. (b) (Naut) clinker.
Klinker-: ~bau m clinker building; ~boot nt clinker(-built) boat; ~stein m siehe Klinker (a).
Klinomobil nt -s, -e mobile clinic.
klipp 1 interj ~, klapp click, clack; (Schuhe, Hufe) clip, clop. 2 adv: ~ und klar clearly, plainly; (offen) frankly, openly.
Klipp m -s, -e clip.
Klippe f -, -n (Fels~) cliff; (im Meer) rock; (fig) hurdle, obstacle. ~n umschiffen (lit, fig) to negotiate obstacles.
Klippen-: ~küste f rocky coast; k~reich adj rocky.
Klipp-: ~fisch m dried, salted cod; ~schule f (pej) second-rate school.
Klips m -es, -e siehe **Clip**.
klirren vi to clink; (Glas auch) to tinkle; (Fensterscheiben) to rattle; (Waffen) to clash; (Ketten, Sporen) to jangle; (Lautsprecher, Mikrophon) to crackle; (Eis) to crunch. ~de Kälte (liter) crisp cold; ~der Frost sharp frost; ~de Töne tinny sounds.
Klirrfaktor m distortion (factor).
Klischee nt -s, -s (Typ) plate, block; (fig: Ausdruck, Phrase) cliché.
Klischee-: ~anstalt f (Typ) plate-maker's; k~haft adj (fig) stereotyped, hackneyed; ~vorstellung f cliché, stereotype.
klischieren* vt (Typ) to make plates for, to stereotype.
Klistier nt -s, -e enema, clyster (spec).
Klistierspritze f enema (syringe).
Klitoris f -, - or **Klitorides** clitoris.
klitsch interj ~, klatsch slip, slop.
Klitsch m -(e)s, -e (dial) (a) (Schlag) slap, smack. (b) (Brei) doughy or soggy mass.
Klitsche f -, -n (pej inf) dilapidated building; (Theat) small-time theatre.
klitschig adj (dial) doughy, soggy.
klitschnaß adj (dial) drenched, soaking or sopping (inf) wet.
klittern vt Geschichte to concoct.
Klitterung f siehe **Geschichts~**.
klitzeklein adj (inf) tiny, teeny-weeny (inf).
Klivie ['kli:viə] f (Bot) clivia.
Klo nt -s, -s (inf) loo (Brit inf), john (US inf). aufs ~ gehen to go to the loo or john.
Kloake f -, -n sewer; (fig auch) cesspool; (Zool) cloaca.
Kloakentiere pl the monotremes pl (form), eg duck-billed platypus; porcupine; ant-eater.
klob pret of **klieben**.
Kloben m -s, - (a) (Holzklotz) log. (b) (Eisenhaken) hook.
klobig adj hefty (inf), bulky; Mensch hulking great (inf); Benehmen boorish; Hände massive, hefty (inf).
Klo-: ~bürste f (inf) toilet or loo (Brit inf) brush; ~frau f (inf) toilet or loo (Brit inf) attendant.
klomm pret of **klimmen**.
Klon m -s, -e clone.
klonen vti to clone.
klönen vi (N Ger inf) to (have a) natter (Brit inf).
Klönschnack m (N Ger inf) natter (Brit inf).
Klopapier nt (inf) toilet or loo (Brit inf) paper, bumf (dated Brit inf).
Klöpfel m -s, - (a) (Holzhammer) square mallet; (Steinmetzwerkzeug) stonemason's maul. (b) (old: Glocken~) tongue, clapper
klopfen 1 vt to knock; Fleisch, Teppich to beat; Steine to knock down. den Takt ~ to beat time; jdn aus dem Schlaf ~ to wake sb up.
2 vi to knock; (leicht auch) to tap; (Herz) to beat; (vor Aufregung, Anstrengung auch) to pound; (Puls, Schläfe) to throb; (Specht) to tap, to hammer; (Motor) to knock, to pink; (beim Kartenspiel) to pass. klopf doch noch mal! give another knock, knock again; sie klopften wiederholt heftig an die Tür they kept pounding away at the door; es klopft (Theat) there is a knock at the door; es hat geklopft there's someone knocking at the door; „bitte laut ~" "please knock loudly"; jdm auf die Schulter/den Rücken/den Hintern ~ to tap sb on the shoulder/to pat sb on the back/the bottom; jdm heftig auf die Schulter/den Rücken ~ to slap sb on the shoulder/back; jdm auf die Finger ~ (lit, fig) to give sb a rap or to rap sb on the knuckles; mit ~dem Herzen with beating or pounding heart; ~der Schmerz a throbbing pain; siehe Busch.
Klopfer m -s, - (Tür~) (door) knocker; (Fleisch~) (meat) mallet; (Teppich~) carpet beater.
Klopf-: ~fechter m (fig old) wrangler; k~fest adj antiknock; ~festigkeit f antiknock quality; ~zeichen nt knock.
Kloppe pl (dial inf) ~ kriegen to be given a hiding or thrashing.
Klöppel m -s, - (Glocken~) tongue, clapper; (Spitzen~) bobbin; (Trommel~) stick.
Klöppelarbeit f pillow lace.
Klöppelei f (pillow) lace making.
klöppeln vi to make (pillow) lace. eine Tischdecke ~ to make a lace tablecloth.
Klöppelspitze f pillow lace.
kloppen (N Ger inf) 1 vt to hit; siehe Griff, Skat. 2 vr to fight, to scrap (inf), to brawl.

Klopperei f (N Ger inf) fight, brawl.
Klöppler(in f) m -s, - (pillow) lace maker.
Klops m -es, -e (Cook) meatball.
Klosett nt -s, -e or -s lavatory, toilet.
Klosett-: ~becken nt lavatory or toilet bowl, lavatory pan; ~bürste f lavatory or toilet brush; ~deckel m lavatory or toilet seat lid; ~frau f lavatory attendant; ~papier nt lavatory or toilet paper.
Kloß m -es, ¨e dumpling; (Fleisch~) meatball; (Boulette) rissole. einen ~ im Hals haben (fig) to have a lump in one's throat.
Kloßbrühe f: klar wie ~ as clear as day; (iro) as clear as mud.
Kloster nt -s, ¨ cloister (old); (Mönchs~ auch) monastery; (Nonnen~ auch) convent, nunnery (old). ins ~ gehen to enter a monastery/convent, to become a monk/nun.
Kloster-: ~bruder m (old) monk; ~frau f (old) nun; ~gut nt land belonging to a monastery or convent; ~kirche f monastery/convent church; ~leben nt monastic/convent life.
klösterlich adj Leben monastic/convent; Stille, Abgeschiedenheit cloistered.
Klosterschule f monastic/convent school.
Klöten pl (sl) balls pl (sl).
Klotz m -es, ¨e (Holz~) block (of wood); (pej: Beton~) concrete block or monstrosity; (inf: Person) great lump (inf) or clod (inf). sich (dat) einen ~ ans Bein binden (inf) to tie a millstone around one's neck; schlafen wie ein ~ (inf) to sleep like a log.
Klötzchen nt dim of Klotz.
klotzen vi (sl) (hart arbeiten) to slog (away) (inf); (protzig auftreten) to show off.
klotzig adj (sl) huge, massive. ein ~es Geld, ~ viel Geld stacks of money (inf); ~ angeben to show off one's wealth.
Klub m -s, -s club.
Klub-: ~abend m club night; ~garnitur f club-style (three-piece) suite; ~haus nt clubhouse; ~jacke f blazer; ~leben nt club life; ~lokal nt club bar; ~sessel m club chair.
Klucker m -s, - siehe Klicker.
kluckern vi siehe gluckern.
Kluft f -, ¨e (a) (Erdspalte) cleft; (zwischen Felsenrändern auch) ravine; (in Bergen) crevasse; (Abgrund) chasm.
(b) (fig) gulf, gap. in der Partei tat sich eine tiefe ~ auf a deep rift opened up in the party.
(c) no pl (Uniform, Kleidung) uniform; (inf: Kleidung) gear (sl), garb (hum). sich in seine gute/beste ~ werfen to put on one's Sunday best or one's glad rags (hum).
klug adj, comp ¨er, superl ¨ste(r, s), adv superl am ¨sten clever, intelligent; Augen intelligent; Humor witty, sophisticated; (vernünftig) Entscheidung, Rat wise, sound; (Überlegung prudent; (geschickt) Antwort, Analyse, Geschäftsmann shrewd, clever. es wird am ~sten sein, wenn ... it would be most sensible if ..., it would be the best idea if ...; es wäre politisch/geschäftlich ~ ... it would make good political/business sense ...; ~ geschrieben/durchdacht cleverly or intelligently written/thought out; ein ~er Philosoph an astute philosopher; ein ~er Kopf a capable person; ein ~er Kopf, der Kleine he's a bright lad; in ~er Voraussicht with shrewd foresight; ich werde daraus nicht ~, da soll einer draus ~ werden I cannot make head or tail of it, I can't make it out; aus ihm werde ich nicht ~ I don't know what to make of him, I can't make him out; im nachhinein ist man immer ~er one learns by experience; du bist wohl nicht recht ~! (dated inf) you must be soft in the head; ~ reden or tun kann jeder ... anyone can talk ...; ~e Reden halten or führen (iro) to make fine-sounding speeches; ~e Bemerkungen/Ratschläge (iro) clever or helpful remarks/advice (iro); ein ganz K~er (iro) a right one (inf); wer war denn so ~ ... (iro) who was the bright or clever one ...; so ~ bin ich auch (iro) you don't say!; nun bin ich genau so ~ wie zuvor or vorher I am still none the wiser; der K~ere gibt nach (Prov) discretion is the better part of valour (Prov); der ~e Mann baut vor (Prov) the wise man takes precautions; wer ~ ist, fährt mit der Bahn it makes more sense to go by train; wenn du ~ bist, haust du sofort ab if you're smart you'll beat it (inf).
Klügelei f puzzling; (Rätsel) brain-teaser.
klügeln vi to puzzle (wie/was as to how/what). wieder etwas zum K~ für unsere Rätselfreunde another brain-teaser for our puzzle fans.
klugerweise adv (very) cleverly, (very) wisely.
Klugheit f siehe adj cleverness, intelligence; wisdom, soundness; prudence; shrewdness, cleverness. aus ~ (very) wisely; die ~ eines Sokrates the astuteness of a Socrates; menschliche ~ human understanding or insight; deine ~en kannst du dir sparen (iro) you can save your clever remarks.
Klügler m -s, - fiddle, fiddly person.
klüglich adv (old) wisely, cleverly.
Klug-: k~reden vi sep to talk big, to make fine-sounding speeches; ~redner m know-all; k~scheißen vi sep irreg (sl) to shoot one's mouth off (inf); ~scheißer m (sl) big mouth (inf), smart-aleck (inf), smart-ass (sl); k~schnacken vi (N Ger inf) siehe k~reden; ~schnacker m -s, - (N Ger inf) siehe ~redner.
Klump no art (inf) ein Auto zu ~ fahren to smash up a car; jdn zu ~ hauen to beat sb to a pulp (inf).
Klumpatsch m -s, no pl (inf): der ganze ~ the whole (kit and) caboodle (inf).
Klümpchen nt dim of Klumpen.
klumpen 1 vi (Sauce) to go lumpy. 2 vr to gather.
Klumpen m -s, - lump; (Erd~ auch) clod; (Gold~) nugget; (Blut~) clot. ~ bilden (Mehl etc) to go lumpy; (Blut) to clot; steht doch nicht alle auf einem ~! don't all stand in a huddle.
Klumpert nt -s, no pl (Aus) siehe Klumpatsch.
Klump-: ~fuß m club-foot; k~füßig adj club-footed.
klumpig adj lumpy.

Klüngel m s, - (inf: Clique) clique; (dial: Kram) mess.
Klüngelwirtschaft f (inf) nepotism no pl.
Klunker m -s, - (a) (sl: Edelstein) rock (sl). (b) siehe Troddel.
Kluppe f -, -n calipers pl; (Schneid~) die-stock.
Klüse f -, -n (Naut) hawsehole.
Klüver ['kly:vɐ] m -s, - (Naut) jib.
Klüverbaum m (Naut) jib boom.
km abbr of Kilometer km.
km/h abbr of Kilometer pro Stunde kph.
kn (Naut) abbr of Knoten kt.
knabbern vti to nibble. nichts zu ~ haben (inf) to have nothing to eat; daran wirst du noch zu ~ haben (fig inf) it will really give you something to think about or get your teeth into; an dieser Aufgabe habe ich lange zu ~ gehabt (fig inf) I spent ages puzzling over this exercise.
Knabe m -n, -n (liter) boy, lad. „~n" (old) boys; na alter ~! (inf) well old boy (inf) or chap (inf).
Knaben-: ~alter nt boyhood; im ~alter in his boyhood; ~chor m boys' choir; k~haft adj boyish; ~haftigkeit f boyishness; ~kraut nt (wild) orchid; ~liebe f (liter) paederasty, homosexual love; ~schänder m -s, - (liter) paederast; ~schule f (old) boys' school; ~stimme f boy's voice; (Mus auch) treble voice.
Knack m -(e)s, -e crack.
knack interj crack. ~ machen to crack, to go crack.
Knäckebrot nt crispbread.
knacken 1 vt (a) Nüsse, (fig inf) Rätsel, Kode, Geldschrank to crack; Läuse to squash, to crush.
(b) (inf) Auto to break into, to burgle; (Mil sl) Panzer to knock out.
2 vi (brechen) to crack, to snap; (Glas etc) to crack; (Dielen, Stuhl) to creak; (Holz) (knistern) to crackle. mit den Fingern ~ to crack one's fingers; es knackt im Radio the radio is crackling; es knackt im Gebälk the beams are creaking; an etw (dat) zu ~ haben (inf) to have sth to think about or chew on (inf); an dieser Aufgabe hatte ich ganz schön zu ~ (inf) I really had to sweat over this exercise.
Knacker m -s, - (a) siehe Knackwurst. (b) (pej inf) alter ~ old fog(e)y (inf).
Knacki m -s, -s (sl) jailbird (inf).
knackig adj crisp; Apfel auch crunchy; (inf) Mädchen juicy (inf).
Knacklaut m glottal stop.
Knackmandel f almond in the shell.
Knacks m -es, -e (a) (Sprung) crack.
(b) (inf: Schaden) das Radio/der Fernseher hat einen ~ there is something wrong with the radio/television; die Ehe der beiden hat schon lange einen ~ their marriage has been cracking up for a long time; er hat einen ~ (weg)bekommen he/his health/his nerves took a knock; er hat einen ~ weg he's a bit screwy (inf); his health isn't so good.
knacks interj crack, crash.
Knackwurst f type of frankfurter, the skin of which makes a cracking sound when bitten.
Knall m -(e)s, -e bang; (mit Peitsche) crack; (bei Tür) bang, slam; (von Korken) pop; (inf: Krach) trouble. der ~ eines Schusses a shot; ~ auf Fall (inf) all of a sudden; jdn ~ auf Fall entlassen (inf) to dismiss sb completely out of the blue (inf); einen ~ haben (inf) to be crazy (inf) or crackers (Brit inf).
Knall-: ~bonbon nt cracker; ~effekt m (inf) bombshell (inf); einen ~effekt haben/ein ~effekt sein to come as/be a real bombshell.
knallen 1 vi (a) to bang, to explode; (Schuß) to crack, to ring out; (Feuerwerk) to (go) bang; (Pfropfen) to (go) pop; (Peitsche) to crack; (Tür etc) to bang, to slam; (Auspuff) to misfire; (aux sein: auftreffen) to bang. mit der Peitsche ~ to crack the whip; mit der Tür ~ to bang or slam the door; mit den Absätzen ~ (Soldaten etc) to click one's heels; einen Pfropfen ~ lassen to pop a cork; draußen knallte es there was a shot/were shots outside; bleib stehen, sonst knallt's (inf) stand still or I'll shoot; sei nicht so frech, sonst knallt's (inf) don't be so cheeky, or there'll be trouble; der Fahrer ist gegen die Windschutzscheibe geknallt the driver hit the windscreen; er knallte gegen die Latte (inf) he banged or slammed the ball against the crossbar; der Ball knallte gegen den Pfosten (inf) the ball banged or slammed against the post.
(b) (inf: Sonne) to blaze or beat down.
2 vt (inf) to bang; Tür, Buch auch to slam; Ball auch to belt (inf); Schüsse to fire (off); Peitsche to crack. den Hörer auf die Gabel ~ (inf) to slam or bang down the receiver; jdm eine ~ (inf) to clout sb (inf), to belt sb (one) (inf); jdm ein paar vor den Kopf/ Latz ~ (sl) to clout sb one (sl), to stick one on sb (sl).
knallend adj Farbe bright, loud, gaudy.
Knall-: k~eng adj (inf) skintight; ihr Bikini war k~eng her bikini looked as though it was painted on; ~erbse f toy torpedo.
Knallerei f (inf) (Schießerei) shooting; (Feuerwerk) banging of fireworks.
Knall-: ~frosch m jumping jack; ~gas nt oxyhydrogen; k~gelb adj (inf) bright yellow; k~grün adj (inf) bright green; k~hart adj (inf) Film brutal; Porno hard-core; Job really tough; Truppen, Mensch really tough, as hard as nails; Schuß, Schlag really hard; ein k~harter Schuß/Schlag a real humdinger (of a shot/punch) (inf); der Film zeigt k~hart, wie ... the film shows brutally or without pulling any punches how ...; er sagte ihr k~hart ... he said to her quite brutally ...; k~heiß adj (inf) blazing or boiling hot; ~hitze f (inf) blazing heat, heatwave.
knallig adj (inf) Farben loud, gaudy.
Knall-: ~kopf (inf), ~kopp (inf) m fathead (inf), blockhead (inf); ~körper m fire-cracker; k~rot adj (inf) bright red,

scarlet; *Gesicht* as red as a beetroot (*inf*); ~**schleppe** *f* (*Aviat*) sonic boom.

knapp *adj* (**a**) (*nicht ausreichend vorhanden*) *Vorräte, Arbeitsstellen* scarce, in short supply; *Geld auch* tight; *Taschengeld* meagre; *Gehalt* low, meagre. **mein Geld ist** ~ my money is tight; **mein Geld wird** ~ I am running short of *or* out of money; **das Essen wird** ~ we/they *etc* are running short of *or* out of food; **mein Geld/meine Zeit ist** ~ **bemessen** I am short of money/time; **er hat ihr das Taschengeld** ~ **bemessen** he was mean with her pocket money; ~ **mit (dem) Geld sein** (*inf*) to be short of money.

(**b**) (*gerade noch ausreichend*) *Zeit, Geld, Miete* just *or* barely sufficient *or* enough; *Mehrheit* narrow, small, bare; *Sieg* narrow; *Kleidungsstück etc* (*eng*) tight; (*kurz*) short; *Bikini* scanty. **ich muß mit meinem** ~**en Geld auskommen** I have to get by on the small amount of money I have; **wir haben** ~ **verloren/gewonnen** we only just lost/won; **bei ihnen geht es** ~ **zu** they just get by *or* manage, they can just make ends meet; **ich verprügele dich, aber nicht zu** ~ (*dated*) I'll give you a thrashing, and how!

(**c**) (*nicht ganz*) almost. **ein** ~**es Pfund Mehl** just under a pound of flour; **seit einem** ~**en** *or* ~ **einem Jahr wohne ich hier** I have been living here for almost a year.

(**d**) (*kurz und präzis*) *Stil, Worte* concise; *Geste* terse; (*lakonisch*) *Antwort* pithy.

(**e**) (*gerade so eben*) just. **er ist** ~ **an mir vorbeigefahren** he just got *or* scraped past me; **mit** ~**er Not** only just, by the skin of one's teeth; **der Rock endete** ~ **über dem Knie** the skirt came to just above the knee.

Knappe *m* -**n**, -**n** (**a**) (*Hist: eines Ritters*) squire. (**b**) (*Min*) qualified miner.

knapphalten *vt sep irreg: jdn* ~ to keep sb short (*mit of*).

Knappheit *f* (*Lebensmittel*~) scarcity, shortage; (*von Zeit, Geld*) shortage; (*fig: des Ausdrucks*) conciseness, concision. **wegen der** ~ **der uns zur Verfügung stehenden Zeit** because of the shortness of the time at our disposal.

Knappschaft *f* (*Min*) miners' guild.

knapsen *vi* (*inf*) to scrimp (*mit, an* +*dat* on), to be stingy (*inf*) (*mit, an* +*dat* with).

Knarre *f* -, -**n** (**a**) (*sl: Gewehr*) shooter (*sl*). (**b**) (*Rassel*) rattle.

knarren *vi* to creak. **eine** ~**de Stimme** a rasping *or* grating voice.

Knast *m* -(**e**)**s**, *no pl* (*sl*) clink (*inf*), can (*US sl*). ~ **schieben** (*sl*) to do bird (*Brit sl*), to do time (*inf*).

Knastbruder *m* (*sl*) jailbird (*inf*).

Knaster *m* -**s**, - (*inf*) baccy (*inf*). **was rauchst du denn für einen** ~! what's that foul-smelling stuff you're smoking!

Knasterbart *m* (*dated inf*) old grumbler.

Knastologe *m* (*hum*) jailbird (*inf*).

Knatsch *m* -**es**, *no pl* (*inf*) trouble. **das gibt** ~ that means trouble.

knattern *vi* (*Motorrad*) to roar; (*Preßlufthammer*) to hammer; (*Maschinengewehr*) to rattle, to chatter; (*Schüsse*) to rattle out; (*Fahne im Wind*) to flap.

Knäuel *m or nt* -**s**, - ball; (*wirres*) tangle; (*fig: Durcheinander*) muddle; (*von Menschen*) group, knot; (*in Problemen*) knot, tangle; (*hum: Hund*) bundle of fluff (*inf*).

Knauf *m* -(**e**)**s**, **Knäufe** (*Tür*~) knob; (*von Schwert etc*) pommel.

Knauser *m* -**s**, - (*inf*) scrooge (*inf*).

Knauserei *f* (*inf*) meanness, stinginess (*inf*).

knauserig *adj* (*inf*) mean, stingy (*inf*).

knausern *vi* (*inf*) to be mean *or* stingy (*inf*) (*mit* with).

Knaus-Ogino-Methode *f* (*Med*) rhythm method.

knautschen *vti* (*inf*) to crumple (up); *Kleid etc auch* to crease.

knautschig *adj* (*inf*) *Anzug, Kleid* crumpled-up, crumply (*inf*).

Knautsch-: ~**lack** *m*, ~(**lack**)**leder** *nt* wet-look leather; ~**zone** *f* (*Aut*) crumple zone.

Knebel *m* -**s**, - (*Mund*~) gag; (*Paket*~) (wooden) handle; (*an Mänteln*) toggle; (*Fenster*~) (handle of) window catch.

Knebelbart *m* Van Dyke (beard).

knebeln *vt jdn, Presse* to gag.

Kneb(e)lung *f*, *no pl* (*lit, fig*) gagging.

Knecht *m* -(**e**)**s**, -**e** (**a**) servant; (*beim Bauern*) (farm-)labourer *or* worker; (*Stall*~) stableboy. (**b**) (*fig: Sklave*) slave (*gen* to). (**c**) ~ **Ruprecht** helper to St Nicholas (*Santa Claus*).

knechten *vt* (*geh*) to subjugate, to oppress. **die unterdrückten und geknechteten Völker** ... all oppressed and enslaved peoples ...; **sie wollten sich nicht mehr von ihm** ~ **lassen** they refused to be his slaves any longer.

knechtisch *adj* (*geh*) *Charakter* subservient, submissive; *Unterwürfigkeit, Verhalten auch* servile, slavish. **jdm/einer Sache** ~ **ergeben sein** to be a complete slave *or* totally enslaved to sb/sth.

Knechtschaft *f* slavery, servitude, bondage.

Knechtsgestalt *f* (*Bibl, liter*) form of a servant.

Knechtung *f*, *no pl* (*geh*) enslavement, subjugation.

kneifen *pret* **kniff**, *ptp* **gekniffen** 1 *vt* to pinch. **jdn/jdn** *or* **jdm in den Arm** ~ to pinch sb/sb's arm; **der Hund kniff den Schwanz zwischen die Beine** the dog put his tail between his legs.

2 *vi* (**a**) to pinch.

(**b**) (*Univ sl*) to fail to remain motionless during a student duel.

(**c**) (*inf*) (*ausweichen*) to chicken out (*sl*), to get *or* back out (*vor* +*dat* of); (*vor Arbeit auch*) to duck out (*vor* +*dat* of); (*vor Duell*) to back out, to show the white feather.

Kneifer *m* -**s**, - (**a**) (*Brille*) pince-nez. (**b**) (*inf*) (*Feigling*) yellowbelly (*inf*), chicken (*sl*); (*Drückeberger*) skiver (*Brit inf*), shirker.

Kneifzange *f* pliers *pl*; (*kleine*) pincers *pl*. **eine** ~ (a

pair of) pliers/(a pair of) pincers.

Kneip|abend *m siehe* **Kneipe** (**b**).

Kneipe *f* -, -**n** (*inf*) (**a**) (*Lokal*) pub (*Brit*), bar, saloon (*US*). (**b**) (*Gesellschaftsabend von Korpsstudenten*) club night, drinking evening.

Kneipenwirt *m* (*inf*), **Kneipier** [knaiˈpieː] *m* -**s**, -**s** (*hum inf*) publican (*Brit*), pub-owner (*Brit*), (pub) landlord (*Brit*), bar-keeper, saloon-keeper (*US*).

kneippen *vi* to undergo a Kneipp cure.

Kneippkur *f* Kneipp cure, *type of hydropathic treatment combined with diet, rest etc*.

kneisen *vt* (*Aus inf*) to notice.

Knet *m* -**s**, *no pl* modelling clay; (*Plastilin*) plasticine®.

knetbar *adj* workable; *Teig auch* kneadable.

Knete *f* -, *no pl* (*sl*) dough (*inf*).

kneten 1 *vt Teig* to knead; *Plastilin, Ton* to work; *Figuren* to model; *Muskeln, Rücken* to knead, to work; *siehe* **formen**. 2 *vi* (*mit Plastilin spielen*) to play with plasticine® *or* modelling clay.

Knet-: ~**gummi** *m or nt* plasticine®; ~**masse** *f* modelling clay.

Knick *m* -(**e**)**s**, -**e** *or* -**s** (**a**) (*leichter Sprung*) crack. (**b**) (*Kniff, Falte*) crease, crinkle; (*Eselsohr*) dog-ear; (*Biegung*) (sharp) bend; (*bei Draht, auf Oberfläche*) kink. **einen** ~ **machen** to bend sharply; *siehe* **Optik**. (**c**) *pl* -**s** (*N Ger: Hecke*) hedgerow.

Knickebein *m* -**s**, *no pl* advocaat.

knicken *vti* (*vi: aux sein*) to snap; *Papier* to fold, to crease. „**knick** ~!" "do not bend *or* fold"; *siehe* **geknickt**.

Knicker *m* -**s**, - (*inf*) scrooge (*inf*).

Knickerbocker [ˈknɪkrbɔkr] *pl* knickerbockers *pl* (*old*), plus-fours *pl*.

knick(e)rig *adj* (*inf*) stingy (*inf*), mean.

Knick(e)rigkeit *f* (*inf*) stinginess (*inf*), meanness.

knickern *vi* (*inf*) to be stingy (*inf*) (*mit* with).

Knickfuß *m* (*Med*) (type of) club-foot.

knickrig *adj* (*inf*) *siehe* **knick(e)rig**.

Knickrigkeit *f* (*inf*) *siehe* **Knick(e)rigkeit**.

Knicks *m* -**es**, -**e** bob; (*tiefer*) curts(e)y. **einen** ~ **machen** to drop a curts(e)y, to curts(e)y (*vor* +*dat* to). (**b**) (*heller Knacks*) crack, click.

knicksen *vi* to curts(e)y, to drop a curts(e)y (*vor* + *dat* to).

Knie *nt* -**s**, - (**a**) (*auch Hosen*~) knee. **auf** ~**n** on one's knees, on bended knee; **auf die** ~ **fallen, in die** ~ **sinken** (*geh*) to fall on *or* drop to one's knees; **sich vor jdm auf die** ~ **werfen** to throw oneself on one's knees in front of sb; **jdn auf** ~**n bitten** to go down on bended knees to sb (and beg); **jdm auf** ~**n danken** to go down on one's knees and thank sb; **in die** ~ **gehen** to kneel, to fall on one's knees; (*fig*) to be brought to one's knees; **jdn in** *or* **auf die** ~ **zwingen** to force sb to his knees; **jdn übers** ~ **legen** (*inf*) to put sb across one's knee; **etw übers** ~ **brechen** (*fig*) to rush (at) sth; **die** ~ **beugen** to bend one's knees; *siehe* **vor dem Altar** to bow, to genuflect (*form*); (*fig*) to give in, to bend the knee.

(**b**) (*Fluß*~) sharp bend; (*in Rohr*) elbow.

Knie-: ~**beuge** *f* (*Sport*) knee-bend; **in die** ~**beuge gehen** to bend one's knees; ~**fall** *m* genuflection (*form*); **einen** ~**fall vor jdm tun** (*geh*) *or* **machen** (*lit, fig*) to kneel before sb; (*fig auch*) to bow before sb; **k**~**fällig** 1 *adj Verehrung* humble, lowly; 2 *adv* on one's knees, on bended knee; **k**~**frei** *adj Rock* above the knee; ~**geige** *f* viola da gamba; ~**gelenk** *nt* knee joint; **k**~**hoch** *adj Schnee, Wasser* knee-deep; *Gras* knee-high; ~**hose** *f* knee breeches *pl*; ~**kehle** *f* back *or* hollow of the knee; ~**kissen** *nt* (*Eccl*) hassock; **k**~**lang** *adj* knee-length; **k**~**lings** *adv* (*rare*) on one's knees, kneeling.

knien [kniːn, ˈkniːən] 1 *vi* to kneel. **im K**~ on one's knees, kneeling. 2 *vr* to kneel (down). **sich in die Arbeit** ~ (*fig*) to get down to *or* stuck into (*inf*) one's work.

Knierohr *nt* elbow(-pipe).

Knies *m* -, *no pl* (*dial inf*) row, argument.

Knie-: ~**scheibe** *f* kneecap; ~**scheibenreflex**, ~**sehnenreflex** *m* knee *or* patellar (*spec*) reflex; ~**schnackler** *m* -**s**, - (*dial inf*) wobbly knees *pl*; ~**schützer** *m* -**s**, - kneepad, kneeguard; ~**strumpf** *m* knee-sock, knee-length sock; ~**stück** *nt* elbow joint; **k**~**tief** *adj* knee-deep; ~**welle** *f* knee circle.

kniff *pret of* **kneifen**.

Kniff *m* -(**e**)**s**, -**e** (**a**) (*inf*) trick. **den** ~ **bei etw heraushaben** to have the knack of sth (*inf*); **es ist ein** ~ **dabei** there is a (special) knack to it (*inf*). (**b**) (*Falte*) crease, fold. (**c**) (*Kneifen*) pinch.

Kniffelei *f* (*inf*) fiddly job.

kniff(e)lig *adj* (*inf*) fiddly; (*heikel*) tricky.

Knigge *m* -(**s**), - etiquette manual.

Knilch *m* -**s**, -**e** (*pej inf*) twit (*Brit inf*), clown (*inf*).

knille *adj* (*inf*) *siehe* **knülle**.

knips *interj* click.

knipsen 1 *vt* (**a**) *Fahrschein* to punch, to clip. (**b**) (*Phot inf*) to snap (*inf*). 2 *vi* (**a**) (*Phot inf*) to take pictures. (**b**) (*klicken*) to click. **mit den Fingern** ~ to snap one's fingers.

Knipser -**s**, - (*inf*), **Knipsschalter** *m* shutter.

Knirps *m* -**es**, -**e** (**a**) (*Junge*) whippersnapper; (*pej auch*) squirt. (**b**) ® folding *or* telescopic umbrella.

knirschen *vi* (*Sand, Schnee*) to crunch; (*Getriebe*) to grind. **mit den Zähnen** ~ to grind one's teeth; (*vor Wut auch*) to gnash one's teeth.

knistern *vi* (*Feuer*) to crackle; (*Papier, Seide*) to rustle. **mit Papier etc** ~ to rustle paper *etc*; **es knistert im Gebälk** (*fig*) there is trouble brewing *or* afoot (*gen* in).

Knittel *m* -**s**, - (*dial*) *siehe* **Knüppel**.

Knittelvers *m* rhyming couplets (using a four-stress line).

knitter-: ~**arm** *adj* crease-resistant; ~**frei** *adj Stoff, Kleid* non-crushable, crease-resistant.

knittern *vti* to crease, to crush.

Knobelbecher *m* (**a**) dice cup. (**b**) (*Mil sl*) army boot.

knobeln vi (a) (würfeln) to play dice; (um eine Entscheidung) to toss for it (inf). sie knobelten darum, wer bezahlen sollte they tossed (for it) to decide who should pay. (b) (nachdenken) to puzzle (an +dat over).

Knoblauch m -(e)s, no pl garlic.

Knoblauch-: ~geruch m smell of garlic; ~zehe f clove of garlic.

Knöchel m -s, - (a) (Fuß~) ankle. bis über die ~ up to the ankles, ankle-deep. (b) (Finger~) knuckle.

Knöchel-: ~bruch m broken ankle; k~lang adj ankle-length; k~tief adj ankle-deep.

Knochen m -s, - (a) bone; (pl sl) arms pl; legs pl; (Hände) paws pl (inf). Fleisch mit/ohne ~ meat on/off the bone; die Wunde geht bis auf den ~ the wound has penetrated to the bone; mir tun alle ~ weh (inf) every bone in my body is aching; er ist bis auf die ~ abgemagert he is just (a bag of) skin and bones; brich dir nicht die ~! (inf) don't break anything or your neck!; dem breche ich alle ~ einzeln (sl) I'll break every bone in his body; seine ~ zusammennehmen or zusammenreißen (Mil sl) to pull oneself together; das geht auf die ~ (sl) it knackers you (Brit sl) or breaks your back; ihm steckt or sitzt die Grippe/Angst in den ~ (inf) he's got flu/he's scared stiff (inf); naß bis auf die ~ (inf) soaked to the skin; kein Mark or keinen Mumm in den ~ haben (inf) to have no guts or spunk (inf); der Schreck fuhr ihm in die ~ he was paralyzed with shock; sich bis auf die ~ blamieren (inf) to make a proper fool of oneself (inf); er ist konservativ bis in or auf die ~ (inf) he is conservative through and through, he is a dyed-in-the-wool conservative. (b) (dated sl: Kerl) chap (inf), bloke (Brit inf). du fauler/ müder ~ you lazy/indolent so-and-so (inf). (c) (inf: großer Hausschlüssel) large door-key.

Knochen-: ~bau m bone structure; ~bruch m fracture; ~erweichung f (Med) softening of the bones, osteomalacia (spec); moralische ~erweichung (fig sl) softening or weakening of the moral fibre; ~gerüst nt skeleton; k~hart adj (inf) rock-hard; ~hauer m (old) butcher; ~haut f periosteum (spec); ~hautentzündung f periostitis (spec); ~leim m bone glue; ~mann m (liter) Death; ~mark nt bone marrow; ~markentzündung f osteomyelitis; ~mehl nt bone meal; ~naht f (Anat) bone suture; ~schinken m ham on the bone; ~schwund m bone atrophy, atrophy of the bone; k~trocken adj (inf) bone dry; (fig) Humor etc very dry; ~tuberkulose f bone tuberculosis, tuberculosis of the bone.

knöch(e)rig adj (a) (knochenartig) bony, bone-like, osseous (form). (b) siehe knöchern.

knöchern adj Gerät etc bone attr, of bone; Material auch bony, osseous (form); (inf: großknochig) Mensch, Körperbau bony; (pej inf: nicht anpassungsfähig) set in one's ways.

knochig adj bony.

Knöchlein nt dim of Knochen.

knöchrig adj siehe knöch(e)rig.

Knockdown [nɔk'daun] m -(s), -s knockdown.

Knockout [nɔk'laut] m -(s), -s knockout.

Knödel m -s, - dumpling. (einen) ~ im Hals (haben) (Aus, S Ger) to have a lump in one's throat.

knödeln vi to sing in a strangled voice.

Knofel m -s, no pl (inf) siehe Knoblauch.

Knöllchen nt (a) dim of Knolle. (b) (inf: Strafzettel) (parking) ticket.

Knöllchenbakterien pl rhizobia pl.

Knolle f -, -n (Bot) nodule, tubercule; (von Kartoffel, Dahlie) tuber; (Kartoffel) potato; (inf: Nase) conk (Brit inf).

Knollen m -s, - (a) siehe Knolle. (b) (Klumpen) lump.

Knollen-: ~blätterpilz, ~blätterschwamm m amanita; grüner ~blätterpilz deadly amanita, death cup, death angel; weißer ~blätterpilz destroying angel; ~nase f (Med) rhinophyma (spec), (nodular) swelling of the nose; (inf) conk (Brit inf).

knollig adj Wurzel tuberous; Auswuchs knobbly, knotty; Nase bulbous; (inf: klumpig) lumpy.

Knopf m -(e)s, -e (a) (an Kleidungsstück etc) button. etw an den ~en abzählen to decide sth by counting off one's buttons. (b) (an Gerät, elektrischer Anlage etc) (push-)button; (an Akkordeon) button. (c) (an Tür, Stock) knob; (Sattel~, Degen~) pommel. (d) (S Ger, Aus: Knoten) knob. (e) (inf: Kind) little chap or fellow/little lass(ie); (Kerl) chap, fellow. ein fieser ~ a nasty so-and-so. (f) (S Ger: Knospe) bud.

knöpfen, knöpfeln (Aus inf) vt to button (up). einen Kragen auf ein Kleid ~ to button a collar to a dress; ein Kleid zum K~ a dress that buttons up.

Knopf-: ~leiste f button tape; ~loch nt buttonhole; aus allen ~löchern platzen (inf) to be bursting at the seams; ihr schaut die Arroganz/Lebenslust aus allen ~löchern (inf) she oozes arrogance from every pore/she's bursting with the joy of living; aus allen ~löchern feuern (inf) to blaze away.

Knopp m -s, -e (dial) siehe Knopf.

knorke adj (dated sl) smashing (Brit inf), swell (esp US inf).

Knorpel m -s, - (Anat, Zool) cartilage; (Cook) gristle; (inf: Adamsapfel) Adam's apple.

knorpelig adj (Anat) cartilaginous; Fleisch gristly.

Knorren m -s, - (im Holz) knot; (an Weide) burl, burr; (Baumstumpf) (tree) stump; (Aststumpf) snag.

knorrig adj Baum gnarled; Holz, Klotz knotty; (fig) alter Mann rugged; (eigenwillig) Mensch, Charakter surly, gruff.

Knospe f -, -n bud. ~n ansetzen or treiben to bud; die zarte ~ ihrer Liebe (liter) the tender bud of their love; sie war wie eine ~ (liter) she was like a young blossom (liter).

knospen vi to bud. ~d (lit, fig liter) budding.

Knötchen nt dim of Knoten.

Knoten m -s, - (a) knot; (Med) (Geschwulst) lump; (Gicht~) tophus (spec); (Phys, Bot, Math, Astron) node; (fig: Verwicklung) plot. sich (dat) einen ~ ins Taschentuch machen (inf) to tie a knot in one's handkerchief; der ~ der Handlung schürzt sich the plot thickens. (b) (Naut) knot. (c) (Haar~) bun, knot. (d) siehe Knotenpunkt.

knoten vt Seil etc to (tie into a) knot, to tie a knot in.

Knoten-: ~bahnhof m junction; ~punkt m (Mot) (road) junction, (road) intersection; (Rail) junction; (fig) centre; (von Argumentation, Handlung etc) nodal point; ~schnur f quipu; ~stock m knobbly or gnarled (walking) stick.

Knöterich m knotgrass.

knotig adj knotty, knotted, full of knots; Äste, Finger gnarled; Geschwulst nodular.

Know-how ['nouhau] nt -s, no pl know-how.

Knubbel m -s, - (inf) lump.

Knuff m -(e)s, -e (inf) poke; (mit Ellbogen) nudge.

knuffen vti (inf) to poke (inf); (mit Ellbogen) to nudge.

Knülch m -s, -e (inf) siehe Knilch.

knülle adj pred (dial inf) tight (inf), stoned (sl).

knüllen vti to crumple, to crease (up).

Knüller m -s, - (inf) sensation; (Press) scoop.

knüpfen 1 vt Knoten to tie; Band to knot, to tie (up); Teppich to knot; Netz to mesh; Freundschaft to form, to strike up. jdn an den nächsten Baum/den Galgen ~ (inf) to hang sb from the nearest tree/the gallows, to string sb up (inf); etw an etw (acc) ~ (lit) to tie or knot sth to sth; (fig) Bedingungen to attach sth to sth; Hoffnungen to pin sth on sth; große Erwartungen an etw (acc) ~ to have great expectations of sth; Freundschaftsbande enger ~ to strengthen or tighten the bonds of friendship; Bande der Freundschaft ~ ihn an diese Schule he is attached or linked to the school by bonds or ties of friendship; siehe Band².

2 vr sich an etw (acc) ~ to be linked to or connected with sth; an diese Bemerkung knüpften sich einige Fragen this remark raised several questions; an diese Erfindung ~ sich viele technische Möglichkeiten this discovery has many technical possibilities.

Knüppel m -s, - (a) stick; (Waffe) cudgel, club; (Polizei~) truncheon; (Metal) billet. Politik des groben ~s big stick policy; man sollte mit dem ~ dreinschlagen (fig) someone ought to get tough or to wave the big stick; jdm (einen) ~ zwischen die Beine werfen (fig) to put a spoke in sb's wheel. (b) (Aviat) control stick, joystick; (Aut) gear stick. (c) (dial: Brötchen) ≃ crusty bridge roll.

Knüppel-: ~damm m log road; k~dick (inf) 1 adj Steak, Schicht very thick, good and thick pred; er schmiert sich die Butter k~dick aufs Brot he puts lashings of butter on his bread; 2 adv wenn's kommt, kommt's immer gleich k~dick it never rains but it pours (prov); bei dem kam es ja wirklich k~dick he had one problem after another; die Aufträge kamen k~dick we/they etc were inundated with orders, the orders came rolling in; so k~dick hättest du nicht auftragen dürfen you shouldn't have laid it on so thick (inf); ich hab's k~dick I'm fed-up to the back teeth (inf); k~dick(e) voll sein (Straßenbahn, Koffer etc) to be jam-packed, to be packed solid; (sl: betrunken) to be absolutely plastered (sl); k~hart adj (inf) rock-hard.

knüppeln 1 vi to use one's truncheon; (Sport sl) to hack, to kick wildly. 2 vt to club, to beat with a club or stick; (Polizei) to use one's truncheon on, to beat with one's truncheon.

Knüppel-: ~schaltung f (Aut) floor-mounted gear change; k~voll adj (inf) jam-packed, packed solid.

knurren 1 vi (Hund etc) to growl; (wütend) to snarl; (Magen) to rumble; (fig: sich beklagen) to moan, to groan (über +acc about). 2 vti (mürrisch sagen) to growl.

Knurren nt -s, no pl siehe vi growl(ing); snarl(ing); rumble, rumbling; moan(ing).

Knurrhahn m gurnard.

knurrig adj grumpy; Angestellte etc disgruntled.

Knusperhäuschen nt gingerbread house.

knusperig adj siehe knusprig.

knuspern vti to crunch. etwas zum K~ something to nibble; an etw (dat) ~ to crunch away at sth.

knusprig adj Braten crisp; Gebäck auch crunchy; Brötchen auch crusty; (fig) Mädchen scrumptious (inf).

Knust m -(e)s, -e or -e (N Ger) (end) crust, heel.

Knute f -, -n (old) knout (old), lash. jds ~ zu spüren bekommen to feel sb's lash; unter jds ~ (dat) stehen to be completely dominated by sb; jdn unter seine ~ bringen to get sb in one's clutches; unter jds ~ (dat) seufzen to live under sb's scourge or tyranny.

knutschen (inf) 1 vt to pet or smooch (inf) or neck (inf) with. 2 vir to pet, to smooch (inf), to neck (inf).

Knutscherei f petting, smooching (inf), necking (inf).

Knutschfleck m (inf) love bite (inf).

Knüttel m -s, - siehe Knüppel.

Knüttelvers m siehe Knittelvers.

k. o. [ka:'|o:] adj pred (Sport) knocked out; (fig inf) whacked (inf), all in (inf). jdn ~ schlagen to knock sb out.

K. o. [ka:'|o:] m -(s), -s knockout, K.O. Sieg durch ~ victory by a knockout.

ko|agulieren* vti (Med, Chem) to coagulate, to clot.

Koala m -s, -s, **Koalabär** m koala (bear).

ko|alieren* vi (esp Pol) to form a coalition (mit with).

Ko|alition f (esp Pol) coalition. kleine/große ~ little/grand coalition.

Ko|alitions- in cpds coalition; ~freiheit f freedom to form a coalition; ~krieg m (Hist) coalition war; ~recht nt right of

combination; ~**regierung** f coalition government.
ko|axial adj (Tech) co-axial.
Kobalt nt -s, no pl cobalt.
kobaltblau adj cobalt blue.
Kobel m -s, - (S Ger, Aus), **Koben** m -s, - (a) siehe **Schuppen**. (b) siehe **Stall**.
Kobold m -(e)s, -e goblin, imp.
Kobolz m: ~ **schießen** to turn or do somersaults.
Kobra f -, -s cobra.
Koch m -s, -̈e, **Köchin** f (a) cook; (von Restaurant etc auch) chef. viele ~̈e verderben den Brei (Prov) too many cooks spoil the broth (Prov). (b) (Aus: Brei) Apfel~ etc) purée; (Gries~ etc) pudding.
Koch-: ~**apfel** m cooking apple, cooker; k~**bar** adj suitable for boiling, that may be boiled; ~**buch** nt cookery book, cookbook; k~**echt** adj (Tex) Farbe fast at 100°, fast even in boiling water; Wäsche etc suitable for boiling, that may be boiled; ~**ecke** f kitchen or cooking area.
Köchelverzeichnis nt (Mus) Köchel index. ~ 25 Köchel or K. (number) 25.
kochen 1 vi (a) (Flüssigkeit, Speise) to boil. etw langsam or auf kleiner Flamme ~ lassen to let sth simmer or to simmer sth (over a low heat); etw zum K~ bringen to bring sth to the boil; jdn zum K~ bringen (fig inf) to make sb's blood boil; der Kühler/das Auto kocht (inf) the cooling system/car is overheating; er kochte vor Wut (inf) he was boiling or seething with rage; die See kocht (liter) the sea is raging; die ~de Volksseele (liter) the seething or turbulent mood of the people.
(b) (Speisen zubereiten) to cook; (als Koch fungieren) to do the cooking; (als Koch arbeiten) to work as a cook/chef. er kocht gut he's a good cook, he is good at cooking; er kocht scharf/pikant his cooking is (always) highly seasoned/spiced; die Franzosen sind dafür bekannt, daß sie gut ~ the French are noted for their good cooking or for their cuisine.
2 vt (a) Flüssigkeit, Nahrungsmittel, Wäsche to boil. etw langsam or auf kleiner Flamme ~ to simmer sth over a low heat.
(b) (zubereiten) Essen to cook; Kakao to make; (aufgießen) Kaffee, Tee to make, to brew. etw gar/weich ~ to cook sth through/until (it is) soft; Eier weich/hart ~ to soft-boil/hard-boil eggs.
3 vi impers (fig) to be boiling. es kocht in ihm he is boiling or seething with rage; im Stadion kochte es wie in einem Hexenkessel the atmosphere in the stadium was electric.
4 vr sich gut/schlecht ~ to cook/not to cook well.
kochend adj (lit, fig) boiling; (liter) See raging. ~ heiß sein to be boiling hot; (Suppe etc) to be piping hot.
kochendheiß adj attr boiling hot; Suppe etc piping hot.
Kocher m -s, - (Herd) cooker, stove; (Camping~) (primus) stove; (Kochplatte) hotplate; (Wasser~) ≈ (electric) kettle.
Köcher m -s, - (für Pfeile) quiver; (für Golfschläger) golf bag; (für Kameraobjektiv etc) case.
Kocherei f (inf) cooking.
Koch-: k~**fertig** adj ready-to-cook attr, ready to cook pred; k~**fest** adj (Tex) siehe kochecht; ~**fleisch** nt stewing or braising meat; ~**gelegenheit** f cooking facilities pl; ~**geschirr** nt (esp Mil) billy(can), mess tin (Mil); ~**herd** m siehe Herd.
Köchin f siehe Koch.
Koch-: ~**käse** m (type of) soft cheese; ~**kunst** f culinary art, art of cooking; seine ~**kunst** or ~**künste** his cooking (ability); ~**kurs(us)** m cookery course; ~**löffel** m cooking spoon; ~**nische** f kitchenette; ~**platte** f (a) (Herdplatte) hotplate; (b) (Kocher) cooker; ~**rezept** nt recipe; ~**salz** nt common salt; (Chem auch) sodium chloride; (Cook) cooking salt; ~**salzinfusion** f (Med) saline infusion; ~**schinken** m boiled ham; ~**topf** m (cooking) pot; (mit Stiel) saucepan; ~**wäsche** f washing that can be boiled; ~**wasser** nt cooking water, water in which (the) vegetables have been boiled; ~**zeit** f cooking time.
kodd(e)rig adj (N Ger inf) (a) (unwohl) sick, queasy. mir ist ganz ~ I feel sick or queasy. (b) (frech) insolent, impudent.
Kode [koːt, koːdə] m -s, -s code.
Kodein nt -s, no pl codeine.
Köder m -s, - bait; (fig auch) lure.
Köderfisch m bait fish.
ködern vt (lit) to lure; (fig) to tempt, to entice. er will dich mit diesen Versprechungen nur ~ these promises of his are only a bait (to lure you); jdn zu ~ versuchen to woo sb; jdn für etw ~ to rope sb into sth (inf); sich von jdm/etw nicht ~ lassen not to be tempted by sb/sth.
Kodex m - or -es, -e or **Kodices** or **Kodizes** (Gesetzbuch) codex, code; (Handschrift) codex, manuscript; (fig) (moral) code.
kodieren* vt to (en)code.
Kodifikation f codification.
kodifizieren* vt to codify; (fig geh) to write down. kodifiziertes Recht codified or statute law.
Ko|edukation f co-education.
Ko|effizient m coefficient.
Ko|existenz f coexistence.
Kofel m -s, - (Aus, S Ger) rounded or dome-shaped mountain top.
Koffein nt -s, no pl caffeine.
koffeinfrei adj decaffeinated.
Koffer m -s, - (a) (suit)case, bag; (Übersee~, Schrank~) trunk; (Arzt~) bag; (für Schreibmaschine, Kosmetika etc) (carrying) case. die ~ pl (Gepäck) the luggage or baggage or bags pl; die ~ packen (lit, fig) to pack one's bags; aus dem ~ leben to live out of a suitcase; einen ~ stehenlassen (fig sl) to fart (vulg).
(b) (Mil sl) heavy shell.

Koffer|anhänger m luggage label or tag.
Köfferchen nt dim of Koffer.
Koffer-: ~**gerät** nt portable (set); ~**kuli** m (luggage) trolley; ~**radio** nt portable radio; ~**raum** m (Aut) boot (Brit), trunk (US); (Volumen) luggage space; ~**schreibmaschine** f portable (typewriter); ~**träger** m porter.
Kogel m -s, - (Aus, S Ger) siehe Kofel.
Kogge f -, -n (Naut) cog.
Kognak [ˈkɔnjak] m -s, -s or -e brandy.
Kognakschwenker m -s, - brandy glass, balloon glass.
kognitiv adj (Philos, Psych) cognitive.
Kohabitation f (form) cohabitation.
Kohäsion f (Phys, geh) cohesion.
Kohl m -(e)s, -e (a) cabbage. das macht den ~ auch nicht fett (inf) that's not much help. (b) (inf: Unsinn) rubbish, nonsense. aufgewärmter ~ old stuff or story; alten ~ aufwärmen to rake up the past or an old story/old stories.
Kohldampf m, no pl (inf) ~ haben or schieben to be starving or famished.
Kohle f -, -n (a) (Brennstoff) coal; (Stück ~) (lump of) coal; (dial: Brikett) briquette. wir haben keine ~n mehr we have no coal left; zwei ~n two lumps of coal, two coals; weiße ~ white coal, water power, hydroelectric power; glühende ~n (lit) (glowing) embers; glühende or feurige ~n auf jds Haupt sammeln (geh) to heap coals of fire on sb's head; (wie auf (glühenden or heißen) ~n sitzen to be like a cat on hot bricks, to be on tenterhooks.
(b) (Verkohltes, Holz~) charcoal. (tierische or medizinische) ~ animal charcoal.
(c) (Art: ~stift) (stick of) charcoal. mit ~ zeichnen to draw with or in charcoal.
(d) (Tech) carbon.
(e) (inf: Geld) dough (inf), cash (inf). die ~n stimmen the money's right.
Kohle-: ~**filter** m charcoal filter; ~**hydrat** nt carbohydrate; ~**hydrierung** f (Tech) hydrogenation of coal.
kohlen[1] vi (a) (Naut, Rail) to take on coal. (b) (verkohlen) to char, to carbonize. (c) (Ruß erzeugen) to smoke.
kohlen[2] vti (inf) to talk a load of nonsense or rubbish (inf); (lügen) to lie, to tell lies. unglaublich, was der wieder kohlt it's incredible the nonsense he's been talking again/the lies he's been telling again.
Kohlen- in cpds coal; ~**bergbau** m coal-mining; ~**bergwerk** nt coalmine, pit, colliery; ~**bunker** m coalbunker; ~**dioxid** nt carbon dioxide; ~**gas** nt coal gas; ~**gebiet** nt coal-mining area; ~**grube** f coalmine, pit; ~**grus** m (coal) slack; ~**halde** f pile of coal; ~**halden** f coal stocks pl; ~**heizung** f coal heating; (Anlage) coal heating system; ~**herd** m range; ~**hydrat** nt siehe Kohlehydrat; ~**industrie** f coal industry; ~**kasten** m coal-box; ~**keller** m coal cellar; ~**lager** nt (a) (Vorrat) coal depot; (b) (im Stollen, Berg) coal seam or bed; ~**monoxyd** nt carbon monoxide; ~**ofen** m (coal-burning) stove; ~**pott** m (inf) (a) coal-mining area; (b) (Ruhrgebiet) siehe Ruhrpott; ~**revier** nt siehe ~gebiet; ~**sack** m coalsack; k~**sauer** adj k~**saurer Kalk/k~saures Natrium** calcium/sodium carbonate; ~**säure** f (a) (Chem) carbonic acid; (b) (inf: in Getränken) fizz (inf); ~**schaufel** f coal shovel; ~**staub** m coaldust; ~**staublunge** f anthracosis; ~**stoff** m carbon; ~**stoff-Datierung** f (radio)carbon dating; ~**trimmer** m -s, - (coal) trimmer; ~**wagen** m (a) (Rail: Tender) tender; (Waggon) coal truck; (b) (LKW) coal lorry (Brit) or truck; ~**wasserstoff** m hydrocarbon; ~**zange** f (pair of) fire or coal tongs; ~**zeche** f siehe ~bergwerk.
Kohlepapier nt carbon paper.
Köhler m -s, - charcoal burner.
Köhlerei f charcoal burning.
Kohle-: ~**stab** m (Tech) carbon rod; ~**stift** m (Art) piece or stick of charcoal; ~**tablette** f (Med) charcoal tablet; ~**zeichnung** f charcoal drawing.
Kohl-: ~**kopf** m cabbage; ~**meise** f great tit; k~**(pech)rabenschwarz** adj k~ Haar jet black, raven attr, raven-black; Nacht pitch-black; (b) (inf: sehr schmutzig) as black as coal; ~**rabi** m -(s), -(s) kohlrabi; ~**rübe** f (a) siehe Steckrübe; (b) (inf: Kopf) bonce (sl), nut (inf); ~**salat** m coleslaw; k~**schwarz** adj Haare, Augen jet black; Gesicht, Hände black as coal; ~**sprosse** f (Aus) (Brussels) sprout; ~**weißling** m cabbage white (butterfly).
Kohorte f -, -n (Hist) cohort.
koitieren* [koiˈtiːrən] vi (esp Med) to engage in coitus or sexual intercourse.
Koitus [ˈkoːitus] m -, - or -se (esp Med) coitus, coition.
Koje f -, -n (a) (esp Naut) bunk, berth; (inf: Bett) bed. sich in die ~ hauen (inf) to hit the sack (inf) or the hay (inf). (b) (Ausstellungs~) stand.
Kojote m -n, -n coyote.
Koka f -, - (Bot) coca.
Kokain nt -s, no pl cocaine.
kokainsüchtig adj addicted to cocaine. ein K~er a cocaine addict.
Kokarde f -, -n cockade.
kokeln vi (inf) to play with fire. mit Kerzen/Streichhölzern ~ to play with (lighted) candles/matches.
Kokerei f (Tätigkeit) coking; (Anlage) coking plant.
kokett adj coquettish, flirtatious.
Koketterie f (a) no pl (Eigenschaft) coquettishness, coquetry, flirtatiousness. (b) (Bemerkung) coquettish or flirtatious remark, coquetry.
kokettieren* vi to flirt. mit schönen Augen/einem rätselhaften Lächeln ~ to flirt with one's lovely eyes/an enigmatic smile; mit seinem Alter ~ to play up or upon one's age; mit einem

Gedanken/System etc ~ to toy with an idea/method etc.

Kokolores, Kokolorus m -, no pl (inf) **(a)** (Unsinn) rubbish, nonsense, twaddle (inf). **(b)** (Umstände) palaver (inf), fuss. mach doch nicht solchen ~ don't make such a palaver or fuss. **(c)** (Kram) den ganzen or all den ~ einpacken to pack in the whole caboodle (inf) or shebang (inf).

Kokon [ko'kõ:] m -s, -s (Zool) cocoon.

Kokos¹ f -, -n siehe **Kokospalme**.

Kokos² nt -, no pl coconut.

Kokos- in cpds coconut; ~fett nt coconut oil; ~flocken pl desiccated coconut; ~läufer m coconut matting; ~milch f coconut milk; ~nuß f coconut; ~palme f coconut palm or tree; ~raspeln pl desiccated coconut.

Kokotte f -, -n (old) cocotte.

Koks¹ m -es, -e coke; (inf: Unsinn) rubbish, nonsense; (Geld) dough (inf), cash (inf).

Koks² m or nt -es, no pl (sl: Kokain) coke (sl).

koksen vi **(a)** (inf: schlafen) to have a kip (inf). **(b)** (sl: Kokain nehmen) to take coke (sl).

Kokser(in f) m -s, - (sl) cocaine or coke (sl) addict.

Koksheizung f coke heating; (Anlage) coke-fired heating system.

Kola¹ f -, no pl siehe **Kolanuß**.

Kola² pl of **Kolon**.

Kola-: ~baum m cola or kola tree; ~nuß f cola or kola nut.

Kolben m -s, - **(a)** (dickes Ende, Gewehr~) butt; (Tech: Motor~, Pumpen~) piston; (Chem: Destillier~) retort; (von Glühlampe) bulb; (von Lötapparat) bit; (inf: Nase) conk (Brit inf), hooter (Brit inf), beak (inf); (sl: Penis) prick (vulg), cock (vulg), tool (sl). **(b)** (Bot) spadix; (Mais~) cob.

Kolben-: k~förmig adj club-shaped; etw verdickt sich k~förmig sth widens into a club shape; ~fresser m -s, - (inf) piston seizure; (den) ~fresser haben to have piston seizure; ~halter m plunger refill (fountain) pen; ~hub m (von Pumpe) plunger stroke; (den) ~fresser haben to have piston seizure; ~halter m plunger refill (fountain) pen; ~hub m (von Pumpe) plunger stroke; ~ring m piston ring.

kolbig adj siehe **kolbenförmig**.

Kolchos m or nt -, Kolchose, Kolchose f -, -n collective farm, kolkhos.

Kolchosbauer m worker on a collective farm.

Kolibakterien pl E. coli pl.

Kolibri m -s, -s humming bird, colibri (spec).

Kolik f -, -en colic.

kolikartig adj colicky.

Kolkrabe m raven.

kollabieren* vi aux sein (Med) to collapse.

Kollaborateur(in f) [-'tøːɐ, -'tøːrɪn] m (Pol) collaborator.

Kollaboration f collaboration.

kollaborieren* vi to collaborate.

Kollage [kɔ'laːʒə] f -, -n siehe **Collage**.

Kollaps m -es, -e (Med) collapse. einen ~ erleiden to collapse.

Kollation f (Liter) collation, comparison; (Typ) collation.

kollationieren* [kɔlatsio'niːrən] vt (Liter) to collate, to compare; (Typ) to collate.

Kolleg nt -s, -s or -ien [-iən] **(a)** (Univ: Vorlesung) lecture; (Vorlesungsreihe) (course of) lectures. **(b)** (Eccl) theological college.

Kollege m -n, -n, **Kollegin** f colleague; (Arbeiter auch) workmate. seine ~n vom Fach his professional colleagues, his fellow doctors/teachers etc; meine ~n the people I work with, my colleagues; seine ~n in der Ärzteschaft his fellow doctors; ~ kommt gleich! somebody will be with you right away; Herr ~! Mr X/Y; der (Herr) ~ (Müller) (Pol) the honourable member.

Kollegen-: ~rabatt m trade discount; ~schaft f colleagues pl.

Kolleg-: ~geld nt lecture fee; ~heft nt (student's) notebook.

kollegial adj cooperative. das war nicht sehr ~ von ihm that wasn't what you would expect from a colleague; mit ~en Grüßen ≈ yours sincerely; sich ~ verhalten to act like a good colleague.

Kollegialität f cooperativeness.

Kollegin siehe **Kollege**.

Kollegium nt **(a)** (Lehrer~ etc) staff; (Ausschuß) working party. **(b)** siehe **Kolleg**.

Kollegmappe f document case.

Kollekte f -, -n (Eccl) offering, collection, offertory.

Kollektion f collection; (Sortiment) range; (Fashion) collection. ~ (an Mustern) (set of) samples.

kollektiv adj collective.

Kollektiv nt collective.

Kollektiv-: ~arbeit f (Tätigkeit) collective work, collaboration; (Ergebnis) collective piece of work; ~begriff m (Ling) collective (term); ~geist m corporate or collective spirit.

kollektivieren* [-'viːrən] vt to collectivize.

Kollektivismus [-'vɪsmʊs] m, no pl collectivism.

Kollektivist(in f) [-'vɪst(ɪn)] m collectivist.

kollektivistisch [-'vɪstɪʃ] adj colletivist(ic).

Kollektiv-: ~schuld f collective guilt; ~strafe f collective punishment.

Kollektivum [-'tiːvʊm] nt -s, **Kollektiva** [-'tiːva] or **Kollektiven** [-'tiːvən] (Ling) collective (noun).

Kollektiv-: ~vertrag m collective agreement; (DDR Econ) house agreement; (Pol) multilateral treaty; ~wirtschaft f (Econ) collective economy.

Kollektor m (Elec) collector.

Koller m -s, - **(a)** (inf) (Anfall) silly or funny mood; (Wutanfall) rage; (Tropen~, Gefängnis~) tropical/prison madness. seinen ~ bekommen/haben to get into/to be in one of one's silly or funny moods; einen ~ haben/bekommen to be in/fly into a rage; wenn ihn der ~ packt when he gets into a silly or funny mood; when he gets angry.

(b) (Vet: bei Pferden) staggers sing.

kollern 1 vi **(a)** (Truthahn etc) to gobble; (Magen, Darm) to rumble. **(b)** aux sein (dial) siehe **kullern**. **2** vi impers es kollert in seinem Bauch his stomach is rumbling.

kollidieren* vi (geh) **(a)** aux sein (Fahrzeuge) to collide, to be in collision. **(b)** aux sein or haben (fig) to conflict, to be in conflict, to clash; (Termine) to clash. **miteinander** ~ to conflict, to clash, to be in conflict (with each other); er ist mit dem Gesetz kollidiert he has collided with the law.

Kollier [ko'lie:] nt -s, -s necklet, necklace.

Kollision f (geh) (Zusammenstoß) collision; (Streit) conflict, clash; (von Terminen) clash. **mit dem Gesetz in** ~ geraten or kommen to come into conflict with or to collide with the law.

Kollisionskurs m (Naut, Aviat) collision course. **auf** ~ gehen, einen ~ ansteuern (fig) to be heading for trouble.

Kolloid nt -s, -e (Chem) colloid.

Kolloquium nt colloquium; (Aus Univ: Prüfung) examination.

Köln nt -s Cologne.

Kölner adj attr Cologne. der ~ Dom Cologne Cathedral.

Kölner(in f) m -s, - inhabitant or (gebürtiger) native of Cologne. er ist ~ he lives in/comes from Cologne.

kölnisch adj Cologne. er spricht K~ he speaks (the) Cologne dialect.

Kölnischwasser, Kölnisch Wasser nt eau de Cologne, cologne.

Kolombine f (Theat) Columbine.

Kolon nt -s, -s or **Kola** (Typ, Anat) colon.

Koloniakübel m (Aus) dustbin (Brit), trash or garbage can (US).

kolonial adj (rare) colonial.

Kolonial- in cpds colonial; ~besitz m colonial possessions pl; das Land ist in ~besitz that country is a colony.

Kolonialismus m, no pl colonialism.

Kolonial-: ~macht f colonial power; ~stil m Colonial (style); ~waren pl groceries pl; (Erzeugnisse der Kolonien) colonial produce; ~warenhändler m (dated) grocer; ~warenhandlung f, ~warengeschäft nt (dated) grocer's (shop); ~zeit f colonial times pl; ein Relikt aus der ~zeit a relic of the colonial past or of colonial times.

Koloniawagen m (Aus) refuse lorry (Brit) or truck.

Kolonie f (alle Bedeutungen) colony; (Ansiedlung auch) settlement; (Ferien~) camp.

Kolonisation f siehe vt settlement; colonization.

kolonisieren* vt **(a)** (erschließen) Gebiet to settle in. **(b)** (zur Kolonie machen) Land to colonize.

Kolonist(in f) m colonist; (Siedler) settler.

Kolonnade f colonnade.

Kolonne f -, -n column; (Autoschlange, fig: Menge) queue (Brit), line; (zur Begleitung esp Mil) convoy; (Arbeits~) gang. „Achtung ~!" "convoy"; ~ fahren to drive in (a) convoy.

Kolonnen-: ~fahren nt -s, no pl driving in (a) convoy; ~springen nt jumping the (traffic) queue (Brit) or line; ~springer m queue-jumper (Brit); ~steller m -s, - (an Schreibmaschine) tabulator; ~verkehr m a queue/queues (Brit) or a line/lines of traffic, a tailback.

Kolophonium nt, no pl rosin, resin, colophony (spec).

Koloratur f coloratura.

kolorieren* vt to colour.

Kolorit nt -(e)s, -e (Art) colouring; (Mus) (tone) colour; (Liter, fig) atmosphere, colour.

Koloß m -sses, -sse colossus; (fig auch) giant. der ~ von Rhodos the Colossus of Rhodes.

kolossal 1 adj colossal, tremendous, enormous; (inf) Dummheit auch crass arrr. **2** adv (inf) tremendously, enormously. sich ~ verschätzen to make a colossal mistake.

Kolossal-: ~film m epic film, (film) epic; ~gemälde nt (inf) spectacular painting; ~schinken m (pej geh) spectacular.

Kolosser(in f) m -s, - **(a)** (Hist) Colossian. **(b)** (Bibl) siehe **Kolosserbrief**.

Kolosserbrief m Colossians sing, no def art.

Kolosseum nt -s, no pl das ~ the Colosseum.

Kolportage [kɔlpɔr'taːʒə] f -, -n **(a)** (Press) cheap sensationalism. **(b)** (minderwertige Literatur) trash, rubbish. **(c)** (old: Wandergewerbe) peddling.

Kolportage-: ~literatur f trashy literature; ~roman m trashy novel.

Kolporteur [-'tøːɐ] m (geh: Gerüchteverbreiter) rumour-monger.

kolportieren* vt **(a)** Nachricht to spread, to circulate; Gerüchte auch to peddle. die Zeitung kolportierte, daß ... the paper spread the story that ... **(b)** (old) Bücher etc to peddle.

kölsch adj siehe **kölnisch**.

Kölsch nt -, - (Bier) ≈ (strong) lager.

Kolumbianer(in f) m -s, - Colombian.

kolumbianisch adj Colombian.

Kolumbien [-iən] nt -s Colombia.

Kolumbier(in f) [-iɐ, -iərɪn] m -s, - Colombian.

Kolumbine f (Theat) Columbine.

kolumbisch adj Colombian.

Kolumbus m - siehe **Ei**.

Kolumne f -, -n (Typ, Press) column.

Kolumnist(in f) m columnist.

Koma nt -s, -s or ~ta (Med) coma.

Kombattant(in f) m (geh) combatant.

Kombi m -s, -s (Aut) estate (car) (Brit), station wagon (esp US).

Kombinat nt (Econ) combine.

Kombination f **(a)** (Verbindung, Zusammenstellung, Zahlen~) combination; (Sport: Zusammenspiel) concerted move, (piece of) teamwork. alpine/nordische ~ (Ski) Alpine/Nordic combination.

(b) (*Schlußfolgerung*) deduction, reasoning; (*Vermutung*) conjecture.

(c) (*Kleidung*) suit, ensemble; (*Hemdhose*) combinations *pl*, combs *pl* (*inf*); (*Arbeitsanzug*) overalls *pl*, boilersuit; (*Flieger~*) flying suit.

Kombinations-: ~**gabe** *f* powers of deduction *or* reasoning; ~**schloß** *nt* combination lock.

Kombinatorik *f* (*Math*) combination theory, theory of combinations.

kombinatorisch *adj* (a) *Fähigkeiten* deductive; *Problem, Logik* combinatory. (b) (*Ling*) ~**er Lautwandel** conditioned sound change.

kombinieren* **1** *vt* to combine; *Kleidungsstücke auch* to wear together. **Möbel zum K**~ unit furniture; **zum beliebigen K**~ to mix and match.

2 *vi* (a) (*folgern*) to deduce; (*vermuten*) to suppose. **gut** ~ **können** to be good at deducing *or* deduction; **ich kombiniere: ...** I conclude: ...; **du hast richtig kombiniert** your conclusion is/was right, you have come to the right conclusion.

(b) (*Sport*) to make a concerted move.

Kombi-: ~**wagen** *m* estate (car) (*Brit*), station wagon (*esp US*); ~**zange** *f* combination pliers *pl*.

Kombüse *f* -, -n (*Naut*) galley.

Komet *m* -en, -en comet; (*fig*) meteor.

kometen-: ~**artig** *adj* (a) (*Astron*) comet-like; (b) (*fig*) *siehe* ~**haft**; ~**haft** *adj* (*fig*) *Aufstieg, Karriere* meteoric; *Aufschwung* rapid.

Komfort [kɔm'foːɐ] *m* -s, *no pl* (*von Hotel etc*) luxury; (*von Möbel etc*) comfort; (*von Auto*) luxury features *pl*; (*von Gerät*) extras *pl*; (*von Wohnung*) amenities *pl*, mod cons *pl* (*inf*). **ein Auto mit allem** ~ a luxury car, a car with many luxury features.

-komfort *m in cpds* comfort. **Fahr~** (*motoring*) comfort; **ein Fernsehgerät mit großem Bedienungs~** a television set with easy-to-use controls.

komfortabel *adj* (*mit Komfort ausgestattet*) luxurious, luxury *attr*; *Haus, Wohnung* well-appointed; (*bequem*) *Sessel, Bett* comfortable; (*praktisch*) *Bedienung* convenient.

Komfortwohnung [kɔm'foːɐ-] *f* luxury flat.

Komik *f* -, *no pl* (*das Komische*) (*komische Wirkung*) comic effect; (*lustiges Element: von Situation*) comic element. **tragische** ~ tragi-comedy; **ein Sinn für** ~ a sense of the comic; **die** ~, **mit der er sich bewegt** the comical way he moves; **die peinliche Situation entbehrte andererseits nicht einer gewissen** ~ on the other hand, this awkward situation was not without an element of comedy *or* its comic side.

Komiker *m* -s, - comedian, comic; (*fig auch*) joker (*inf*). **Sie** ~ you must be joking.

Kominform *nt* -s, *no pl* (*Hist*) **das** ~ the Cominform.

Komintern *f* -, *no pl* (*Hist*) **die** ~ the Comintern.

komisch *adj* (a) (*spaßhaft, ulkig*) funny, comical; (*Theat*) *Rolle, Person, Oper* comic. **der** ~**e Alte** (*Theat*) the comic old man; **das K**~**e** (*Liter*) the comic; **das K**~**e daran** the funny thing about it.

(b) (*seltsam, verdächtig*) funny, strange, odd. **das K**~**e daran ist ...** the funny *or* strange *or* odd thing about it is ...; ~, **ich hab' schon wieder Hunger** funny, I'm hungry again already; ~, **daß ich das übersehen habe** it's funny *or* odd that I should have missed that; **mir ist/wird so** ~ (*inf*) I feel funny *or* strange *or* odd; **er war so** ~ **zu mir** he acted so strangely towards me.

komischerweise *adv* funnily enough.

Komitee *nt* -s, -s committee.

Komma *nt* -s, -s *or* -ta comma; (*Math*) decimal point. **fünf/null** ~ **drei** five/nought point three.

Kommandant *m* (*Mil*) commanding officer; (*Naut*) captain; (*von Festung auch*) commander; (*von Stadt*) commandant.

Kommandantur *f* (*Funktion*) command; (*Gebäude auch*) headquarters *sing*.

Kommandeur [kɔman'døːɐ] *m* commander.

kommandieren* **1** *vt* (a) (*befehligen*) to command, to be in command of.

(b) (*befehlen*) **jdm etw** ~ to order *or* command sb to do sth; **jdn an einen Ort/zu sich** ~ to order sb to a place/to appear.

2 *vi* (a) (*Befehlsgewalt haben*) to be in command. ~**der General** commanding general.

(b) (*Befehle geben*) to command, to give (the) orders. **er kommandiert gern** he likes to be the one to give (the) orders, he likes ordering people about.

Kommanditgesellschaft *f* (*Comm*) limited partnership.

Kommando *nt* -s, -s (a) (*Befehl*) command, order. **das** ~ **zum Schießen geben** to give the command *or* order to fire; **auf** ~ **schreit ihr alle ...** (up)on the command (you) all shout ...; **ich kann doch nicht auf** ~ **lustig sein** I can't be cheerful to order *or* on command; **ich mache nichts auf** ~ I don't do things to order *or* on command; **wie auf** ~ **stehenbleiben** to stand still as if by command; **der Hund gehorcht auf** ~ the dog obeys on command.

(b) (*Befehlsgewalt*) command. **wer hat das** ~? who is in command?; **das** ~ **haben** *or* **führen/übernehmen** to be in *or* have/take command (*über* +*acc* of).

(c) (*Mil*) (*Behörde*) command; (*Abteilung*) commando.

Kommando-: ~**brücke** *f* (*Naut*) bridge; ~**kapsel** *f* (*Space*) command module; ~**raum** *m* control room; ~**stab** *m* command (staff); ~**stand**, ~**turm** *m* (*Naut*) conning tower.

kommen *pret* **kam**, *ptp* **gekommen** *aux sein* **1** *vi* (a) to come; (*ankommen auch, geboren werden*) to arrive; (*herkommen*) to come over; (*in Gang* ~: *Motor, Feuer*) to start; (*sl: einen Orgasmus haben*) to come (*sl*); (*Telec: sich melden*) to come in. **ich komme (schon)** I'm (just) coming; **ich habe zwei Stunden gewartet, aber sie kam und kam nicht** I waited two hours but

she just didn't come; **er wird gleich** ~ he'll be here right away; **die Bedienung/der Nachtisch kommt gleich** we'll be served/the dessert is coming straight away; **da kommt er ja!** here he comes; **wann soll der Zug/das Baby** ~? when is the train/baby due?; **das Kind ist gestern nacht gekommen** the baby arrived last night; **bei Schmidts kommt ein Baby** the Schmidts are having *or* expecting a baby; **da kann** *or* **könnte ja jeder** ~ **und sagen ...** anybody *or* any Tom, Dick or Harry (*inf*) could come and say ...; **Torwart zu sein ist langweilig, wenn nie ein Ball kommt** it is boring to be a goalkeeper if the ball never comes your way; **mein Mann kommt alle drei Wochen** my husband comes home every three weeks; **nach Hause** ~ to come *or* get home; **von der Arbeit** ~ to come *or* get home from work; **zum Essen** ~ to come home for lunch/dinner *etc*; **der Wagen kommt in 16 sec. auf 100 km/h** the car reaches 100 km/h in 16 sec.

(b) (*auffordernd*) to come on *or* along. **komm, wir gehen/sag schon** come on *or* along, we're going/tell me; **komm, sei nicht so stur** come on *or* now, don't be so obstinate; **ach komm!** come on!; **komm, fang bloß nicht wieder damit an** come on, don't start that again; **komm, komm** (*beschwichtigend, zweifelnd*) come, come!; (*ermahnend*) come on; **komm, komm, wir müssen uns beeilen!** come on, we must hurry!; **komm, komm, werd nicht frech!** now now, don't be cheeky.

(c) (*Reihenfolge*) to come. **das Schlimmste kommt noch** the worst is yet to come; **warte, das kommt noch** wait, it's coming (later); **ich komme zuerst an die Reihe** I'm first, it's my turn first; **jetzt kommt's** here it comes, wait for it! (*inf*); **das Zitat/Lied kommt gleich/erst später** that line/song should be coming up soon/doesn't come till later; **das Lied kommt als nächstes** that song is next.

(d) (*erscheinen, auftauchen*) to come out; (*Zähne*) to come (through). **bohren, bis Öl/Grundwasser kommt** to bore until one strikes oil/finds water; **paß auf, ob hier eine Tankstelle kommt** watch out and see if there's a filling station; **jetzt muß bald die Grenze/Hannover** ~ we should soon be at the border/in Hanover; **die Kreuzung/das Zitat muß noch** ~ we haven't got *or* come to the crossing/that line yet; **wie sie (gerade)** ~ just as they come.

(e) (*stattfinden, eintreten*) (*Gewitter, Abend, Antwort, Reue*) to come; (*Zwischenfall*) to occur; (*Not*) to arise; (*TV, Rad, Theat etc: gegeben werden*) to be on. **der Mai ist gekommen** May is here *or* has come; **der Winter kommt mit großen Schritten** winter is rapidly *or* fast approaching; **ich glaube, es kommt ein Unwetter** I think there's some bad weather on the way; **sie stellten ihm die einfachsten Fragen, aber es kam nichts** they asked him the simplest questions but got nothing out of him; **was kommt diese Woche im Kino/Theater?** what's on at the cinema/theatre this week?

(f) (*geschehen, sich zutragen*) to happen. **egal, was kommt, ich bleibe fröhlich** whatever happens, I shall remain cheerful; **komme, was da wolle** come what may; **seine Hochzeit kam für alle überraschend** his wedding came as a surprise for everyone; **das mußte ja so** *or* **so mußte es ja** ~ it had to happen; **das hätte nicht** ~ **dürfen** that should never *or* shouldn't have happened; *siehe auch* **3**.

(g) (*Grund, Ursache angebend*) to come. **daher kommt es, daß ...** (and) that's (the reason) why ...; **das kommt davon, daß ...** that's because ...; **das kommt davon** *or* **daher, daß es soviel geregnet hat** that comes from *or* is because of all the rain we've had; **das kommt davon, wenn man nicht zuhört** that's what happens when you don't listen; **das kommt von** *or* that's what comes of not listening; **das kommt davon!** see what happens?

(h) (*in Verbindung mit Dativ*) *siehe auch* **n, adj wenn mir die Lust kommt** when I feel like it, when the fancy takes me; **ihm kamen Zweifel** he started to have doubts; **jdm kommen die Tränen** tears come to sb's eyes; **ihm kam das Grausen** terror seized him, he was terrified; **mir kommt ein Gedanke/eine Idee** I just thought of something *or* had a thought/idea, a thought/an idea occurs to me; **es kommt jdm** (*fällt ein*) it dawns on sb; (*wird klar*) it becomes clear to sb; **das Wort/sein Name kommt mir im Moment nicht** the word/his name escapes me for the moment; **das wird dir schon noch** ~ it'll come to you; **es kommt ihm** (*sl: er hat eine Ejakulation*) he's coming (*sl*); **du kommst mir gerade recht** (*iro*) you're just what I need; **das kommt mir gerade recht** that's just fine; **jdm frech/dumm** ~ to be cheeky to sb/to act stupid; **komm mir nur nicht so** don't you take that attitude with me!; **wie kommst du nur darauf?** what kind of attitude do you call that then?; **so darfst du mir nicht** ~ you'd better not take that attitude with me!

(i) (*in Verbindung mit vb siehe auch dort angelaufen/daher-marschiert* ~ to come running/marching along *or* (*auf einen zu*) up; **herbeigelaufen/heruntergeklettert** ~ to come running up/climbing down; **da kommt ein Vogel geflogen** there's a bird; **ich komme dann zu dir gefahren** I'll drive over to your place then; **kommt essen!** come and eat!; **jdn besuchen** ~ to come and visit sb; **auf dem Sessel/neben jdm zu sitzen** ~ to end up sitting in the armchair/next to sb; **jdn** ~ **sehen** to see sb coming; **ich habe es** ~ **sehen** I saw it coming; **die Zeit für gekommen halten** to think the time has come; **jdn** ~ **lassen** *Arzt, Polizei* to send for sb, to call sb in; (*zu sich rufen*) *Schüler, Sekretärin* to send for sb, to summon sb (*form*); **etw** ~ **lassen** *Mahlzeit, Taxi* to order; *Kupplung* to let in; **Sel** ~ to let come; *Motor* to start up.

(j) (*kosten, sich belaufen*) **wie hoch kommt das?** what does that come to *or* amount to *or* add up to?; **das kommt zusammen auf 20 DM** that comes to *or* adds up to *or* makes DM 20; **egal, wie oft ich zähle, ich komme nur auf 99** however many times I count it up, I only get 99 *or* make it 99; **ich komme auf 2 000 Mark im Monat** I get *or* make 2,000 marks a month.

(k) (*gelangen*) to get; (*mit Hand etc erreichen können*) to reach. **wie komme ich nach London?** how do I get to London?;

ich komme mit meiner Hand bis an die Decke I can reach up to the ceiling with my hand; **ich komme zur Zeit nicht an die frische Luft/aus dem Haus/ins Theater** at the moment I never get out into the fresh air/out of the house/to the theatre; **durch den Zoll/die Prüfung** ~ to get through customs/the exam; **zu einem Entschluß/einer Entscheidung/Einigung** ~ to come to a conclusion/decision/an agreement; **in das Alter** ~, **wo ...** to reach the age when ...; **die Entwicklung kam zu ihrem Höhepunkt** developments reached their climax.

(l) (geraten) to get. **ins Wackeln/in Bewegung/ins Erzählen** ~ to start shaking or to shake/moving or to move/talking or to talk; **zum Blühen/Wachsen** etc ~ to start flowering or to flower/growing or to grow; **zum Stehen/Stillstand** ~ to come to a halt or stop/standstill; **er schießt auf alles, was ihm vor die Flinte kommt** he shoots at everything he gets in his sights.

(m) (hingehören) to go, to belong. **das Buch kommt ins oberste Fach** the book belongs or goes on the top shelf; **in die Ecke kommt kein Schrank** another cupboard is to go in that corner; **das kommt unter „Sonstiges"** that comes or goes or belongs under miscellaneous; **da kommt ein Deckel drauf** it has to have a lid on it.

(n) (gebracht werden) to go. **ins Gefängnis** ~ to go or be sent to prison; **in die** or **zur Schule** ~ to go to or start school; **ins Altersheim/Krankenhaus** ~ to go into an old peoples' home/into hospital; **auf die Universität** ~ to go (up) to university.

(o) (sich entwickeln) (Samen, Pflanzen) to come on. **langsam kam ihm das Verständnis** understanding slowly came to him.

(p) (Redewendungen) **komm' ich heut nicht, komm' ich morgen** (prov) you'll see me when you see me; **kommt Zeit, kommt Rat** (Prov) things have a way of working themselves out; **wer zuerst kommt, mahlt zuerst** (Prov) first come first served.

2 vi mit Präpositionen siehe auch dort **an etw** (acc) ~ (berühren) to touch sth; (sich verschaffen) to get hold of sth; **auf etw** (acc) ~ (sich erinnern) to think of sth; (sprechen über) to come or get onto sth; **auf einen Gedanken/eine Idee** ~ to get an idea, to have a thought/an idea; **das kommt auf die Rechnung/auf mein Konto** that goes onto the bill/into my account; **auf ihn/darauf lasse ich nichts** ~ (inf) I won't hear or have a word against him/it; **auf jeden** ~ **fünf Mark** there are five marks (for) each; **auf jeden Haushalt** ~ 1½ m³ **Wasser pro Tag** each household consumes 1½ cu.m. of water per day; **wie kommst du darauf?** what makes you think that?; **darauf bin ich nicht gekommen** I didn't think of that; **ich komme im Moment nicht auf seinen Namen** his name escapes me or I can't think of his name for the moment; **hinter etw** (acc) ~ (herausfinden) to find sth out, to find out sth; **mit einer Frage/einem Anliegen** ~ to have a question (to ask)/a request (to make); **komm mir nicht wieder damit!** don't start that all over again!; **komm (mir) bloß nicht mit der Entschuldigung** don't come to me with that excuse; **damit kann ich ihm nicht** ~ (mit Entschuldigung) I can't give him that; (mit Bitte) I can't ask him that; **um etw** ~ (verlieren) um Geld, Besitz, Leben to lose sth; um Essen, Schlaf to (have to) go without sth, to miss (out on) sth; (vermeiden können) to get out of sth; **zu etw** ~ (Zeit finden für) to get round to sth; (erhalten) to come by sth, to get sth; **zu Ehre** to receive sth; (erben) to come into sth; (sich verschaffen) to get hold of sth, to get oneself sth; (inf: haben wollen) to want sth; **wie komme ich zu der Ehre?** to what do I owe this honour?; **hierzu kommt noch seine Kurzsichtigkeit** then there's his short-sightedness too or on top of that; **zu nichts/viel** ~ (zeitlich) not to get round to anything/to get round to doing a lot; (erreichen) to achieve nothing/a lot; **zu sich** ~ (Bewußtsein wiedererlangen) to come round, to come to one's senses; (aufwachen) to come to one's senses; (sich fassen) to recover, to get over it; (sich finden) to sort oneself out.

3 vi impers **es** ~ **jetzt die Nachrichten/die Clowns** and now (follows/follow) the news/clowns; **es werden viele Leute** ~ a lot of people will come; **es ist weit gekommen!** it has come to that!; **es kommen noch einmal so weit or dahin, daß ...** it will get to the point where ...; **so weit kommt es (noch)** that'll be the day (inf); **wie kommt es, daß du ...?** how is it that ...?, how come you ...? (inf); **ich wußte, daß es so** ~ **würde** I knew (that) that would happen; **dazu kam es gar nicht mehr** it didn't come to that; **wir wollten noch ...,** aber **es kam nicht mehr dazu** we still wanted to ..., but we didn't get (a)round to it; **es kam zum Streit** there was a quarrel; **es kam eins zum anderen** one thing led to another; **und dann kam es, daß ...** and then it happened that ...; **und so kam es, daß ...** and that is how it happened that ...; **es kam, wie es** ~ **mußte** the inevitable happened; **es kommt immer anders, als man denkt** (prov) things never turn out the way one expects; **es mag** ~, **wie es** ~ **will** whatever happens, come what may; **entweder gehe ich ins Kino oder trinken – wie es (gerade) kommt** (inf) either I'll go to the cinema or for a drink – or whatever (inf).

4 vt (inf: kosten) to cost.

Kommen nt -s, no pl coming. **ein einziges** ~ **und Gehen** a constant coming and going; **etw ist im** ~ sth is coming in, sth is on the way in; **jd ist im** ~ sb is on his/her way up.

kommend adj Jahr, Woche, Generation coming; Ereignisse, Mode future. **die nach uns K~en** (geh) the coming generations, generations to come; **der** ~**e Meister** the future champion; **(am)** ~**en Montag** next Monday; ~**e Weihnachten** next Christmas; **in den** ~**en Jahren** in the coming years, in the years to come.

kommensurabel adj (Mat., fig geh) commensurable.

Komment [kɔ'mãː] m -s, -s (Univ) code of conduct (of student fraternity).

Kommentar m (Bemerkung, Stellungnahme) comment; (Press, Jur, Liter) commentary. **jeden (weiteren)** ~ **ablehnen**

to decline to comment (further) or to make any (further) comment; **kein** ~! no comment; ~ **überflüssig!** no comment (necessary)!; **einen** ~ **(zu etw) (ab)geben** to (make a) comment on sth.

Kommentator m commentator.

kommentieren* vt (Press etc) to comment on; (Jur, Liter) to write a commentary on. **kommentierte Ausgabe** (Liter) annotated edition.

Kommers m -es, -e evening meeting of student fraternity with drinking ceremony.

Kommersbuch nt (students') book of drinking songs.

kommerzialisieren* vt (a) (vermarkten) to commercialize. **(b)** (Schulden umwandeln) **eine öffentliche Schuld** ~ to convert a public debt into a private loan.

Kommerzialisierung f siehe vt **(a)** commercialization. **(b)** conversion of a public debt into a private loan.

Kommerzialrat m (Aus) siehe **Kommerzienrat**.

kommerziell adj commercial. **rein** ~ **denken** to think purely in commercial terms or purely commercially.

Kommerzienrat [-ion-] m (Hist) title conferred on distinguished businessman.

Kommilitone m -n, -n, **Kommilitonin** f fellow student. **der** ~ **Müller** Mr Müller; **wir brauchen noch drei** ~**n, die Flugblätter verteilen** we need three more people or students to hand out leaflets; **Herr** ~! Sir, Mr X/Y.

Kommiß m -sses, no pl (dated inf) army. **beim** ~ **sein** to be in the army; **zum** ~ **müssen** to have to go into the army.

Kommissar, Kommissär (esp Aus) m (Admin) commissioner; (Polizei~) inspector; (ranghöher) (police) superintendent.

Kommissariat nt **(a)** (Admin) (Amt) commissionership; (Dienststelle, Amtsbereich) commissioner's department. **(b)** (Polizei) (Amt) office of inspector; office of superintendent; (Dienststelle, Amtsbereich) superintendent's department; (Aus: Polizeidienststelle) police station.

kommissarisch adj temporary.

Kommißbrot nt rye bread; army bread.

Kommission f **(a)** (Ausschuß) committee; (zur Untersuchung) commission. **(b)** (Comm) commission. **etw in** ~ **geben** to give goods (to a dealer) for sale on commission; **etw in** ~ **nehmen/haben** to take/have sth on commission. **(c)** (Sw) ~**en machen** to do the shopping.

Kommissionär m commission agent; (im Verlagswesen) wholesale bookseller, wholesaler.

kommissionieren* vt (Aus) to commission.

Kommissions-: ~**buchhandel** m wholesale book trade; ~**gebühr** f commission; ~**geschäft** nt commission or agency business.

Kommißstiefel m army boot; (fig pej) jackboot.

kommod adj (old, dial) comfortable.

Kommode f -, -n chest of drawers; (hohe) tallboy, highboy (US).

Kommodität f (old) comfort.

Kommodore m -s, -n or -s (Naut) commodore; (Aviat) wing commander (Brit), lieutenant colonel (US).

kommunal adj local; (von Stadt auch) municipal.

Kommunal|abgaben pl local rates and taxes pl.

kommunalisieren* vt to put under the control of the local authorities.

Kommunal-: ~**politik** f local government politics sing or pl; ~**verwaltung** f local government; ~**wahlen** pl local (government) or municipal elections pl.

Kommunarde m -n, -n (a) (Hist) Communard. **(b)** (Mitglied einer Wohngemeinschaft) member of a commune, commune-dweller, communard. **er ist ein** ~ he lives in a commune.

Kommune f -, -n **(a)** (Gemeinde) community. **(b)** (Wohngemeinschaft) commune. **(c)** (die Pariser~) the (Paris) Commune.

Kommunikant(in f) m (Eccl) communicant; (Erst~) first communicant.

Kommunikation f communication. **die** ~ **ist unmöglich geworden** communication has become impossible.

Kommunikations-: ~**mittel** nt means of communication; ~**schwierigkeiten** pl communication difficulties; ~**wissenschaften** pl communication studies.

kommunikativ adj communicative; Brief etc auch informative.

Kommunion f (Eccl) (Holy) Communion; (Erst~) first Communion.

Kommunion-: ~**bank** f Communion rail; ~**kind** nt first communicant.

Kommuniqué [kɔmyni'keː] nt -s, -s communiqué.

Kommunismus m communism.

Kommunist(in f) m Communist.

kommunistisch adj communist. **das K~e Manifest** the Communist Manifesto.

kommunizieren* vi **(a)** to communicate. ~**de Röhren** (Phys) communicating tubes. **(b)** (Eccl) to receive (Holy) Communion.

Komöde m -n, -n (geh) actor, Thespian (liter, hum).

Komödiant m (a) (old) actor, player (old). **(b)** (fig) play-actor.

Komödianten-: k~**haft** adj Gebaren theatrical, histrionic; ~**tum** nt histrionics pl; **in unserem Beruf ist ein gewisses** ~**tum unerläßlich** in our profession a certain histrionic ability is indispensable.

Komödiantin f (a) (old) actress. **(b)** (fig) play-actor.

komödiantisch adj (schauspielerisch) acting; (pej) theatrical, histrionic.

Komödie [-iə] f comedy; (fig) (heiteres Ereignis) farce; (Täu-

schung) play-acting. **die Stuttgarter ~** the Stuttgart Comedy Theatre; **~ spielen** (fig) to put on an act.
Komödin f (geh) actress, Thespian (liter, hum).
Kompagnon [kɔmpanˈjoː, ˈkɔmpanjõ] m -s, -s (Comm) partner, associate; (iro) pal (inf), chum (inf), buddy (inf).
kompakt adj compact; Gestein, Schicht, Brot, Masse auch solid.
Kompakt|auto nt compact (US), medium-sized family saloon.
Kompanie f (Mil) company; (old Comm) trading company; (Firma) firm. **damit kann man ja eine ganze ~ füttern** that's enough to feed a whole army.
Kompaniechef, Kompanieführer m (Mil) company commander.
Komparation f (Gram) comparison.
Komparatistik f comparative literature.
Komparativ m (Gram) comparative.
Komparse m -n, -n (Film) extra; (Theat) supernumerary. **er war nur ein ~** he only had a walk-on part.
Komparserie f extras pl; supernumeraries pl. **die ganze ~ ...** all those with walk-on parts ...
Kompaß m -sses, -sse compass. **nach dem ~** by the compass.
Kompaß-: ~häuschen nt (Naut) binnacle; **~nadel** f compass needle.
kompatibel adj (liter, Tech) compatible.
Kompatibilität f (liter, Tech) compatibility.
Kompendium nt (a) (Abriß) compendium. (b) (Phot) lenshood (with bellows extension).
Kompensation f compensation.
Kompensationsgeschäft nt barter (transaction).
Kompensator m (Tech) compensator.
kompensieren* vt to compensate for, to offset.
kompetent adj competent; (befugt auch) authorized. **für solche Fälle ist dieses Gericht nicht ~** this court has no jurisdiction in or is not competent to decide such cases; **der dafür ~e Kollege** the man responsible for that; **die dafür ~e Stelle** the office which deals with or is responsible for that; **dafür bin ich nicht ~** I'm not responsible for that; **er, als Sachverständiger, ist allein dafür ~** he alone, as an expert, is competent to do that.
Kompetenz f (area of) authority or competence; (eines Gerichts) jurisdiction, competence. **da hat er ganz eindeutig seine ~en überschritten** he has quite clearly exceeded his authority or powers here; **er hat die alleinige ~, hierüber zu entscheiden** he alone has the authority or competence or is competent to decide on this issue; **ich will dir nicht deine ~(en) streitig machen** I don't want to infringe on your field; **das fällt in die ~ dieses Amtes** that's the responsibility of this office; **seine mangelnde ~ in dieser Frage** his lack of competence in this issue.
Kompetenz-: ~bereich m area of competence; **~streitigkeiten** pl dispute over respective areas of responsibility or competence; (bei Gewerkschaften, fig) demarcation dispute; **~wirrwarr** m confusion or muddle about areas of responsibilities; demarcation confusion.
Kompilation f (geh) compilation.
kompilieren* vt (geh) to compile.
kompl. abbr of **komplett** complete.
Komplement nt (Math) complement.
komplementär adj Therapie, Beweise complementary.
Komplementär m fully liable partner in a limited partnership.
Komplementärfarbe f complementary colour.
Komplet¹ [kõˈpleː, kɔmˈpleː] nt -(s), -s (Fashion) matching dress/skirt and coat.
Komplet² [kɔmˈpleːt] f -, -e (Eccl) complin(e).
komplett 1 adj complete. **ein ~es Frühstück** a full or good breakfast; **ein ~es Menü** a (full) three course meal. 2 adv completely.
komplettieren* vt (geh) to complete.
Komplex m -es, -e complex. **er steckt voller ~e** he has so many complexes or hang-ups (inf).
komplex adj complex. **~ aufgebaut** complex in structure.
Komplexität f complexity.
Komplice [kɔmˈpliːtsə] m -n, -n siehe **Komplize**.
Komplikation f complication.
Kompliment nt compliment. **jdm ~e machen** to pay sb compliments, to compliment sb (wegen on); **mein ~!** my compliments!
Komplize m -n, -n, **Komplizin** f accomplice.
komplizieren* vt to complicate.
kompliziert adj complicated, involved; (Med) Bruch compound. **sei doch nicht so ~** don't be so complicated; **sich ~ ausdrücken** to express oneself in a complicated or an involved way.
Kompliziertheit f complexity.
Komplizin f siehe **Komplize**.
Komplizität f siehe **Komplexität**.
Komplott nt -(e)s, -e plot, conspiracy. **ein ~ schmieden** to hatch a plot; **ein ~ zur Ermordung ...** a plot or conspiracy to murder ...
Komponente f -, -n component.
komponieren* vti to compose; (Liter auch) to construct.
Komponist(in f) m composer.
Komposita pl of **Kompositum**.
Komposition f composition; (Liter auch) construction.
kompositorisch adj compositional.
Kompositum nt -s, **Komposita** (Gram, Pharm) compound.
Kompost m -(e)s, -e compost.
Kompost-: ~erde f compost; **~haufen** m compost heap.
kompostieren* 1 vt to compost. 2 vi to make compost.
Kompott nt -(e)s, -e stewed fruit, compote.
kompreß adv (Typ) solid.

Kompresse f compress.
Kompression f (Tech) compression.
Kompressions-: ~pumpe f pressure pump; **~verband** m compression or pressure bandage.
Kompressor m compressor.
komprimieren* vt to compress; (fig) to condense.
Kompromiß m -sses, -sse compromise. **einen ~ schließen** to (make a) compromise; **sie sind zu keinem ~ bereit** they are not prepared to compromise.
Kompromiß-: k~bereit adj prepared or willing to compromise; **~bereitschaft** f willingness to compromise; **k~los** adj uncompromising; **~lösung** f compromise solution.
kompromittieren* 1 vt to compromise. 2 vr to compromise oneself.
Komsomol m -, no pl Comsomol.
Komsomolze m -n, -n member of the Comsomol.
Komteß f - or -sse, -ssen countess.
Komtur m -s, -e commander (of a knightly order).
Kondensat nt condensate; (fig) distillation, condensation.
Kondensation f (Chem, Phys) condensation.
Kondensator m (Aut, Chem) condenser; (Elec auch) capacitor.
kondensieren* vti (lit, fig) to condense; (fig auch) to distil.
Kondens-: ~milch f condensed milk; **~streifen** m (Aviat) vapour trail; **~wasser** nt condensation.
Kondition f (a) condition, shape, form; (Durchhaltevermögen) stamina. **wie ist seine ~?** what sort of condition etc is he in?; **~ haben, in ~ sein** to be in good condition etc; (fig: beim Tanzen, Trinken etc) to have stamina; **er hat überhaupt keine ~** he is completely unfit; (fig) he has absolutely no stamina; **er zeigte heute eine ausgezeichnete ~** he was in top form today; **seine mangelnde ~** his lack of fitness. (b) (form: Bedingung) condition.
konditional [kɔnditsioˈnaːl] adj conditional.
Konditionalsatz m conditional clause.
konditionieren* [kɔnditsioˈniːrən] vt (Biol, Psych) to condition.
Konditions-: ~schwäche f lack of fitness no pl; **~training** nt fitness training.
Konditor m pastry-cook.
Konditorei f cake shop; (mit Café) café.
Konditorwaren pl cakes and pastries pl.
Kondolenz- in cpds of condolence; **~besuch** m visit of condolence; **~buch** nt condolences book.
kondolieren* vi (jdm) ~ to offer one's condolences (to sb), to condole with sb; **schriftlich ~** to write a letter of condolence.
Kondom m or nt -s, -e condom, contraceptive sheath.
Kondominium nt condominium.
Kondor m -s, -e condor.
Kondukteur [kɔndukˈtøːɐ] m (Aus, Sw) conductor.
Kondukteurin [kɔndukˈtøːrɪn] f (Aus, Sw) conductress.
Konen pl of **Konus**.
Konfekt nt -(e)s, -e confectionery.
Konfektion f (Herstellung) manufacture of off-the-peg or ready-made or ready-to-wear clothing; (Industrie) clothing industry, rag trade (inf); (Bekleidung) off-the-peg or ready-made or ready-to-wear clothes pl or clothing.
Konfektionär [kɔnfɛktsioˈnɛːɐ] m (dated) (Unternehmer) clothing manufacturer; (Angestellter) executive employee in the clothing industry.
Konfektions- in cpds off-the-peg, ready-made, ready-to-wear; **~anzug** m off-the-peg etc suit; **~geschäft** nt (off-the-peg) clothes shop or store; **~ware** f off-the-peg etc clothing.
Konferenz f conference; (Besprechung) meeting; (Ausschuß) committee.
Konferenz- in cpds conference; **~schaltung** f (Telec) conference circuit; (Rad, TV) (television/radio) link-up; **~teilnehmer** m person attending a conference/meeting.
konferieren* vi to confer, to have or hold a conference or discussion (über + acc on or about).
Konfession f (religious) denomination. **welche ~ haben Sie?** what denomination are you?; **die Augsburger ~** the Augsburg Confession.
Konfessionalismus m denominationalism, sectarianism.
konfessionell adj denominational.
Konfessions-: k~los adj non-denominational, undenominational; **~schule** f denominational school; **k~verschieden** adj (form) Ehe inter-denominational, mixed.
Konfetti nt -s, no pl confetti.
Konfetti-: ~regen m shower of confetti; (in US: bei Empfängen) shower of ticker-tape; **~schlacht** f confetti battle.
Konfident m (old) confidant; (Aus) police informer.
Konfiguration f configuration.
Konfirmand m -en, -en, **Konfirmandin** f (Eccl) candidate for confirmation, confirmand.
Konfirmanden|unterricht m confirmation classes pl.
Konfirmation f (Eccl) confirmation.
Konfirmations- in cpds confirmation; **~spruch** m confirmation text (chosen by confirmand as motto).
konfirmieren* vt (Eccl) to confirm.
Konfiserie f (Sw) (a) siehe **Konditorei**. (b) siehe **Konfekt**.
Konfiskation f confiscation.
konfiszieren* vt to confiscate.
Konfitüre f -, -n jam.
Konflikt m -s, -e conflict. **bewaffneter ~** armed conflict; **mit dem Gesetz in ~ geraten** to come into conflict with the law, to clash with the law; **kommst du da nicht mit deinem Gewissen in ~ ?** how can you reconcile that with your conscience?; **er befindet sich in einem ~** he is in a state of inner conflict.
Konflikt-: ~fall m conflict; **im ~fall** in case of conflict;

~forschung f conflict studies, research into the subject of conflict; ~herd m (esp Pol) centre of conflict; ~kommission f (DDR) grievance committee or tribunal; k~los adj without conflict; ~situation f conflict situation; ~stoff m cause for conflict.

Konföderation f confederacy.

konföderieren vr (liter) to confederate.

Konföderierte(r) m decl as adj confederate.

konform adj Ansichten etc concurring. mit jdm ~ gehen to agree or to be in agreement with sb (in + dat about); in etw (dat) ~ sein to agree in sth.

Konformismus m conformism.

Konformist(in f) m (pej) conformist.

konformistisch adj conformist, conforming.

Konformität f conformity.

Konfrater m (Eccl) fellow clergyman; fellow monk.

Konfrontation f confrontation.

konfrontieren vt to confront (mit with). zwei Parteien ~ to bring two parties face to face, to confront two parties with one another.

Konfrontierung f siehe Konfrontation.

konfus adj confused, muddled.

konfuzianisch adj Confucian.

Konfuzius m - Confucius.

kongenial adj (geh) sympathetic. ~e Geister kindred or congenial spirits.

Konglomerat nt (a) (Geol) conglomerate. (b) (Ansammlung) conglomeration.

Kongo m -(s) Congo.

Kongolese m -n, -n, **Kongolesin** f Congolese.

Kongreß m -sses, -sse (a) (Pol) congress; (fachlich) convention, conference. der Wiener ~ the Congress of Vienna. (b) (in USA) Congress.

Kongreß-: ~mitglied nt (a) person attending a congress/conference or convention; (b) (in USA) congressman/-woman; ~teilnehmer m person attending a congress/conference or convention.

kongruent adj (Math) congruent; (Gram) concordant, congruent; (geh) Ansichten concurring.

Kongruenz f (Math) congruence; (Gram) concord, agreement, congruence; (geh: von Ansichten) concurrence.

kongruieren vi to be congruent; (geh: Ansichten) to concur, to correspond.

K.-o.-Niederlage [ka:'|o:-] f KO defeat.

Konifere f -, -n conifer.

König m -s, -e king. des ~s Rock (old, liter) the king's uniform; die Heiligen Drei ~e The Three Kings or Magi; der ~ der Tiere/Lüfte the king of the beasts/lord of the skies.

Königin f (auch Zool) queen. ~ der Nacht (Bot) queen of the night, night-flowering cereus.

Königin-: ~mutter f queen mother; ~witwe f dowager queen.

königlich 1 adj royal; Auftreten, Stolz etc auch regal. das ~e Spiel chess, the royal game, the game of kings. **2** adv (inf) (köstlich, ungeheuer) sich ~ freuen to be as pleased as Punch (inf); sich ~ amüsieren to have the time of one's life (inf).

Königreich nt kingdom, realm (poet).

Königs-: k~blau adj royal blue; ~hof m royal or king's court; ~kerze f (Bot) mullein; ~kind nt (liter) king's son or daughter; ~krone f royal crown; ~macher m kingmaker; ~mord m regicide; ~paar nt royal couple; ~sohn m (liter) king's son, prince; ~tiger m Bengal tiger; ~tochter f (liter) king's daughter, princess; k~treu adj royalist; ~wasser nt (Chem) aqua regia; ~weg m (fig) ideal way; ~würde f royal dignity.

Königtum nt (a) no pl kingship. (b) (Reich) kingdom.

konisch adj conical.

Konjektur f (Vermutung) conjecture; (Liter: Lesart) conjectured version.

Konjugation f conjugation.

konjugieren vt to conjugate.

Konjunktion f (Astron, Gram) conjunction.

Konjunktionalsatz m (Gram) conjunctional clause.

Konjunktiv m (Gram) subjunctive.

konjunktivisch adj subjunctive.

Konjunktur f economic situation, economy; (Hoch~) boom. steigende/fallende or rückläufige ~ upward/downward economic trend, increasing/decreasing economic activity.

Konjunktur-: k~abhängig adj dependent on economic factors; ~aufschwung m economic upturn; k~bedingt adj influenced by or due to economic factors.

konjunkturell adj economic; Arbeitslosigkeit resulting from the economic situation, due to economic factors. ~ bedingt caused by economic factors.

Konjunktur-: ~forschung f economic research; ~politik f measures or policies aimed at preventing economic fluctuation; ~ritter m (inf) opportunist; ~zuschlag m refundable increase in taxation paid into the Bundesbank to help the national economy.

konkav adj concave.

Konkavspiegel m concave mirror.

Konklave [kɔn'kla:və, kɔŋ-] nt -s, -n (Eccl) conclave.

Konklusion f (geh, Philos) conclusion.

Konkordanz f concordance.

Konkordat nt concordat.

konkret adj concrete. ich kann es dir noch nicht ~ sagen I can't tell you definitely; ich kann dir nichts K~es sagen I can't tell you anything definite or concrete; drück dich etwas ~er aus would you put that in rather more concrete terms; ich kann mir ~ vorstellen, wie ... I can very clearly imagine how ...

konkretisieren vt to put in concrete form or terms.

Konkubinat nt concubinage.

Konkubine f concubine.

Konkurrent m rival; (Comm auch) competitor.

Konkurrenz f (Wettbewerb) competition, rivalry; (~betrieb) competitors pl; (Gesamtheit der Konkurrenten) competition, competitors pl. die ~ in diesem Sport/auf diesem Gebiet ist größer geworden the competition in this sport/field has increased; jdm ~ machen (Comm, fig) to compete with sb; (Comm) to be in/enter into competition with sb; zur ~ (über)gehen to go over to the competitor(s); außer ~ sein to have no competition.

Konkurrenz-: k~fähig adj competitive; ~kampf m competition; (zwischen zwei Menschen auch) rivalry; wir müssen mit einem sehr harten ~kampf rechnen we have to reckon with some very tough competition; ein ~kampf, bei dem wir uns durchgesetzt haben a competitive situation which we won; k~los adj without competition.

konkurrieren vi to compete; (Comm auch) to be in/go into competition.

Konkurs m -es, -e bankruptcy. in ~ gehen to go bankrupt; ~ machen (inf) to go bankrupt or bust (inf); siehe anmelden.

Konkurs-: ~masse f bankrupt's estate; ~verfahren nt bankruptcy proceedings pl; ~verwalter m receiver; (von Gläubigern bevollmächtigt) trustee.

können pret konnte, ptp gekonnt or (bei modal aux vb) ~ vti, modal aux vb **(a)** (vermögen) to be able to. ich kann es machen I can do it, I am able to do it; ich kann es nicht machen I cannot or can't do it, I am not able to do it; man konnte ihn retten they were able to or they managed to save him; man konnte ihn nicht retten they couldn't or were unable to save him; ich konnte es nicht verstehen I could not or couldn't or was unable to understand it; ich habe es sehen ~ I could see it, I was able to see it; es ist furchtbar, nicht schlafen zu ~ it's terrible not to be able to sleep; er hat es gekonnt he could do it, he was able to do it; weil er es nicht gekonnt hat because he couldn't or wasn't able to; morgen kann ich nicht I can't (manage) tomorrow; das hättest du gleich sagen ~ you could or might have said that straight away; das hätte ich dir gleich sagen ~ I could have told you that straight away; ich kann das nicht mehr sehen I can't stand the sight of it any more; ich kann das nicht mehr hören I don't want to hear that again; ich kann nicht mehr I can't go on; (ertragen) I can't take any more; (essen) I can't manage or eat any more; kannst du noch? can you go on?; (essen) can you manage some more?; mir kann keiner! (inf) I'm all right, Jack (inf); ich habe das alles schriftlich, mir kann keiner! I've got it all in writing, they can't touch me; so schnell er konnte as fast as he could or was able to; ~ vor Lachen! (inf) I wish I could, chance would be a fine thing (inf); man kann alles, wenn man (nur) will (Prov) where there's a will there's a way (Prov).

(b) (beherrschen) Sprache to know, to be able to speak; Gedicht, Lied to know; Schach to be able to play; Klavier spielen, lesen, schwimmen, Skilaufen etc to be able to, to know how to. sie kann keine Mathematik she can't do mathematics; er kann seine Schulaufgabe wieder nicht he can't do his homework again; (nicht gemacht) he hasn't done his homework again; was ~ Sie? what can you do?; was du alles kannst! the things you can do!; er kann was he's very capable or able; unser Chef kann viel/nichts our boss is a very capable or able man/our boss is incapable or useless; er kann gut Englisch he speaks English well.

(c) (dürfen) to be allowed or permitted to. kann ich jetzt gehen? can I go now?; könnte ich ...? could I ...?; er kann sich nicht beklagen he can't complain; man kann wohl sagen, daß ... one could well say that ...; du kannst mich (gern haben)! (inf) get lost! (inf); er kann mich (mal) (sl) he can get stuffed (sl), he can go to hell (sl); kann ich mit? (inf) can I come with you?

(d) (möglich sein) Sie könnten recht haben you could or might or may be right; er kann jeden Augenblick kommen he could or might or may come any minute; das kann nur er gewesen sein it can only have been him; wer kann/könnte das gewesen sein? who can/could or might it have been?; das kann nicht sein that can't be true; das kann fast nicht sein that can't be true, it's almost unbelievable; es kann sein/es kann nicht sein, daß er dabei war he could or might or may have been there/he couldn't or can't possibly have been there; kann sein maybe, could be.

(e) (mit Partikel) für etw ~ to be responsible or to blame for sth; ich kann nichts dafür it's not my fault; ich kann nichts dazu I can't do anything about it; ich könnte auf ein Bier (sl) I could just do with a beer (inf).

Können nt -s, no pl ability, skill.

Könner m -s, - expert.

Konnex m -es, -e (geh) connection; (Verbindung auch) contact.

Konnossement [kɔnɔsə'mɛnt] nt -s, -s (dated Comm) bill of lading.

konnte pret of können.

Konrektor m (an Schule) deputy headmaster (Brit) or principal; (an Universität) deputy vice-chancellor.

Konsanguinität [kɔnzaŋguini'tɛːt] f (geh) consanguinity.

Konsekration f (Eccl) consecration.

konsekrieren vt (Eccl) to consecrate.

konsekutiv adj consecutive.

Konsekutivsatz m consecutive clause.

Konsens m -es, -e agreement, assent, consent.

konsequent adj consistent; (Sport) Deckung close, tight. er hat ~ „nein" gesagt he stuck to his answer of "no"; ... werden gebeten, die Sicherheitsmaßnahmen ~ einzuhalten ... are required to observe the safety regulations strictly; wir werden ~ durchgreifen we will take rigorous action; eine ~e Anwendung der direkten Methode a consistent or strict or across-the-board application of the direct method; ~e Weiterentwicklung eines Stils logically consistent development of a style; **wenn du das ~ durchdenkst** if you follow it through to its logical conclusion; **eine Spur ~ verfolgen** to follow up a clue rigorously; **ein Ziel ~ verfolgen** to pursue an objective single-mindedly; **einen Fall ~ untersuchen** to investigate a case rigorously or thoroughly.

Konsequenz f **(a)** (Schlußfolgerung) consequence. **die ~en tragen** to take the consequences; **(aus etw) die ~en ziehen** to come to the obvious conclusion; to take the appropriate or logical step; **wenn es dir hier nicht gefällt, solltest du die entsprechenden ~en ziehen und gehen** if you don't like it here, you should do something about it and go; **ich werde meine ~en ziehen** there's only one thing for me to do. **(b)** siehe consistency; closeness, tightness; (bei Maßnahmen) rigorousness, rigour. **die ~, mit der er sein Ziel verfolgte** the single-mindedness with which he pursued his aim; **die ~, mit der er seinen Malstil weiterentwickelte** the logical consistency with which he developed his painting style.

Konservatismus [-va-] m siehe **Konservat(iv)ismus**.
konservativ [-va-] adj conservative; (Brit Pol) Conservative, Tory.
Konservative(r) [-va-] mf decl as adj conservative; (Brit Pol) Conservative, Tory.
Konservat(iv)ismus [-vat(iv)ismus] m conservatism.
Konservator [kɔnzɛr'vaːtɔr] m curator, keeper.
Konservatorium [kɔnzɛrva'toːrium] nt conservatory.
Konserve [kɔn'zɛrvə] f -, -n preserved food; (in Dosen) tinned (Brit) or canned food; (~ndose) tin (Brit), can; (Med: Blut~ etc) stored blood etc; blood bottle; (Rad, TV) pre-recorded or canned (inf) material; (Ton~) recorded/taped music. **sich aus or von ~n ernähren** to live out of cans.
Konserven-: ~büchse, ~dose f tin (Brit), can.
konservieren* [kɔnzɛr'viːrən] vt to preserve, to conserve; Leichen to preserve.
Konservierung f preservation, conservation; (der Umwelt) conservation; (von Leichen) preservation.
konsistent adj Masse solid.
Konsistenz f consistency; (von Gewebe) texture.
konskribieren* vt (old) to conscript.
Konsole f -, -n (Archit: Kragstein) console, corbel; (old: an Möbeln) bracket.
konsolidieren* vtr to consolidate; (Fin) Anleihen to fund, to consolidate.
Konsolidierung f consolidation.
konsonant adj consonant.
Konsonant m consonant.
konsonantisch adj consonant(al).
Konsonanz f (Mus) consonance.
Konsorten pl (pej inf) gang (inf), mob (inf), crowd (inf). **X und ~ X** and his gang etc.
Konsortium [kɔn'zɔrtsium] nt consortium, syndicate, group.
Konspiration [kɔnspira'tsioːn] f conspiracy, plot.
konspirativ [kɔnspira'tiːf] adj conspiratorial.
konspirieren* [kɔnspi'riːrən] vi to conspire, to plot.
konstant [kɔn'stant] adj constant.
Konstante [kɔn'stantə] f -(n), -n constant.
Konstantin ['kɔnstantiːn] m - Constantine.
Konstantinopel nt -s (old) Constantinople.
Konstanz¹ f (geh) constancy.
Konstanz² nt -' Constance.
konstatieren* [kɔnsta'tiːrən] vt to state, to notice. **ich bemerke, Sie haben schon wieder Ihre Hausaufgaben nicht gemacht** I see or notice you haven't done your homework once again; **in ihrer Rede konstatierte sie, daß ...** in her speech she made the point that ...; **wir müssen immer wieder ~, daß unsere Maßnahmen unwirksam sind** we are constantly forced to acknowledge that our measures are ineffective.
Konstellation [kɔnstela'tsioːn] f **(a)** constellation. **(b)** (fig) line-up; (von Umständen, Faktoren etc) combination. **diese wirtschaftliche ~** this economic situation; **die neue ~ in der Partei** the new line-up in the party; **die ~ in dem Gremium** the make-up of the committee.
konsternieren* [kɔnstɛr'niːrən] vt to scandalize.
konstituieren* [kɔnstitu'iːrən] **1** vt to constitute, to set up. **~de Versammlung** constituent assembly. **2** vr to be constituted or set up.
Konstitution [kɔnstitu'tsioːn] f (Pol, Med) constitution; (Phys auch) structure.
konstitutionell [kɔnstitutsio'nɛl] adj constitutional.
konstitutiv [kɔnstitu'tiːf] adj constitutive.
konstruieren* [kɔnstru'iːrən] vt to construct (auch Math); (Gram auch) to construe. **ein konstruierter Fall** a hypothetical case; **ein konstruiertes Wort** a made-up word; **der Satz klingt sehr konstruiert** the sentence sounds very artificial.
Konstrukteur [kɔnstruk'tøːr] m designer.
Konstruktion [kɔnstruk'tsioːn] f construction; (Entwurf, Bauart auch) design; (gedanklich, philosophisch auch) construct. **erlauben Sie mir die ~ des folgenden Falles** allow me to make up or construct the following case; **es bieten sich folgende ~en des Handlungsvorganges an** there are several possible reconstructions of the event.
Konstruktions-: ~büro nt drawing office; ~fehler m (im Entwurf) design fault; (im Aufbau) structural defect.
konstruktiv [kɔnstruk'tiːf] adj constructive.
Konstruktivismus [-'vismus] m (Art) constructivism.
Konsul m -s, -n consul.
konsularisch adj consular.
Konsulat nt consulate.
Konsultation f (form) consultation. **jdn zur ~ hinzuziehen** to consult sb.

konsultieren* vt (form) to consult.
Konsum m -s, -s **(a)** [kɔn'zuːm] no pl (Verbrauch) consumption. **(b)** ['kɔnzuːm, 'kɔnzum] (Genossenschaft) cooperative society; (Laden) cooperative store, co-op (inf).
Konsumartikel m consumer item. **~ pl** consumer goods pl.
Konsumation f (Aus, Sw) food and drink consumed in a restaurant.
Konsument m consumer.
Konsumentenhaltung f (pej) passive or non-participating attitude.
Konsum-: ~genossenschaft f siehe **Konsum (b)**; ~gesellschaft f consumer society; ~gut nt usu pl consumer item; ~güter consumer goods pl.
konsumieren* vt to consume.
Konsum-: ~terror m (pej) pressures pl of a materialistic society; ~zwang m (Sociol) compulsion to buy.
Kontakt m -(e)s, -e contact (auch Elec); (pl: Aut) contact breakers pl. **mit jdm in ~ kommen** to come into contact with sb; **mit jdm ~ bekommen, zu jdm ~ finden** to get to know sb; **ich bekomme mit ihm keinen ~** I don't feel I really know him; **mit jdm ~ aufnehmen** to get in contact or touch with sb, to contact sb; **mit jdm in ~ stehen** to be in contact or touch with sb; **~ herstellen** to make or establish contact; **den ~ unterbrechen** to break contact; **keinen ~ mehr haben, den ~ verloren haben** to have lost contact or touch, to be out of touch.
Kontakt-: ~abzug m (Phot) contact print; ~adresse f accommodation address; **er hinterließ eine ~adresse** he left behind an address where he could be contacted; ~anzeigen pl personal column; **k~arm** adj **er ist k~arm** he finds it difficult to make friends.
Kontakter m -s, - (im Werbeagentur) account executive.
Kontakt-: **k~freudig** adj sociable, outgoing; **sie ist k~freudig** she makes friends easily; ~linse f contact lens; **k~los** adj solitary; ~mangel m lack of contact; ~mann m, pl ~männer (Agent) contact; ~nahme f -, -n (form) contacting; **eine ~nahme mit ihm ist nötig** it is necessary to contact him; ~schale f siehe ~linse.
Kontamination f (Kerntechnik) contamination; (Gram) blend(ing).
kontaminieren* vi to contaminate, to pollute; (Gram) to blend.
Kontemplation f contemplation.
kontemplativ adj contemplative.
Konten pl of **Konto**.
Kontenance [kõta'nãːs] f -, no pl (geh) composure. **die ~ bewahren** to keep one's composure or countenance.
Konter- in cpds (Sport) counter-; ~admiral m rear-admiral; ~bande f -, no pl contraband.
Konterfei nt -s, -s or -e (old, hum) likeness, portrait.
konterfeien* vt to portray.
kontern vti Schlag, Angriff to counter.
Konter-: ~revolution f counter-revolution; ~schlag m (Sport, fig) counter-attack; (Boxen) counter(-blow or -punch).
Kontext m -(e)s, -e context.
Konti pl of **Konto**.
Kontinent m -(e)s, -e continent.
kontinental adj continental.
Kontinental-: ~europa nt the Continent; ~klima nt continental climate; ~sockel m continental shelf; ~sperre f (Hist) Continental System.
Kontingent [kɔntiŋ'gɛnt] nt -(e)s, -e (Mil: Truppen~) contingent; (Comm) quota, share; (Zuteilung) allotment, allocation.
kontingentieren* [kɔntiŋgɛn'tiːrən] vt (Comm) to allocate, to apportion. **den Import ~** to fix or impose import quotas.
Kontingenz f (Philos) contingency.
Kontinua pl of **Kontinuum**.
kontinuierlich adj continuous.
Kontinuität f continuity.
Kontinuum nt -s, **Kontinua** continuum.
Konto nt -s, **Konten** or **Konti** account. **auf meinem/mein ~** in my/into my account; **das geht auf mein ~** (inf) (ich bin schuldig) I am responsible or to blame for this; (ich zahle) this is on me (inf); **er hat ganz schön was or viel auf dem ~** (inf) he has a great deal to answer or account for.
Konto-: ~auszug m (bank) statement, statement (of account); ~bewegung f transaction.
Kontor nt -s, -e **(a)** (Büro) office; siehe **Schlag**. **(b)** (Handelsniederlassung) branch office.
Kontorist(in f) m clerk/clerkess.
Kontostand m balance, state of an account.
kontra prep +acc against; (Jur) versus.
Kontra nt -s, -s (Cards) double. **jdm ~ geben** (Cards) to double; (fig) to contradict sb.
Kontra-: ~baß m double-bass; **k~diktorisch** adj contradictory.
Kontrahent [kɔntra'hɛnt] m (Vertragsschließender) contracting party; (Gegner) opponent, adversary.
kontrahieren* [kɔntra'hiːrən] vt (Ling, Med) to contract.
Kontraindikation f (Med) contra-indication.
Kontrakt m -(e)s, -e contract.
Kontraktion f (Med) contraction.
Kontra-: ~post m -(e)s, -e (Art) contrapposto; ~punkt m (Mus) counterpoint; **k~punktisch** adj (Mus) contrapuntal.
konträr adj (geh) Meinungen contrary, opposite.
Kontrast m -(e)s, -e contrast.
Kontrast-: ~brei m (Med) barium meal; ~farbe f contrasting colour; ~filter m (Phot) yellow filter.
kontrastieren* vi to contrast.
Kontrast-: ~mittel nt (Med) contrast medium; ~programm nt alternative programme; ~regler m contrast (control); **k~reich** adj full of or rich in contrast, of many contrasts.

Kontratenor m counter-tenor.
Kontrazeption f (form) contraception.
kontribuieren* vt (old) to contribute.
Kontribution f (old) contribution.
Kontroll|abschnitt m (Comm) counterfoil, stub.
Kontrollampe f getrennt Kontroll-lampe pilot lamp; (Aut: für Ölstand) warning light.
Kontrollbeamte(r) m inspector; (an der Grenze) frontier guard; (zur Paßkontrolle) passport officer; (zur Zollkontrolle) customs officer; (zur Überwachung) security officer.
Kontrolle f -, -n (a) (Beherrschung, Regulierung) control. über jdn/etw die ~ verlieren to lose control of sb/sth; jdn/etw unter ~ haben/halten to have/keep sb/sth under control.
(b) (Nachprüfung) check (gen on); (Aufsicht) supervision; (Paß~) passport control; (Zoll~) customs examination. zur ~ haben wir noch einmal alles nachgerechnet we went over all the figures again to check; ~n durchführen to carry out or make checks; um die Qualität aufrechtzuerhalten, haben wir regelmäßige ~n eingebaut to maintain quality we have built in regular checks or controls; der Luftverkehr ist unter ständiger ~ air traffic is kept under constant surveillance, a constant check is kept on air traffic; nach einer sorgfältigen ~ der Waren after a careful inspection of or check on or of the goods; die ~ von Lebensmitteln the inspection of foodstuffs; Fernsehkameras zur ~ des Geschäfts television cameras to keep a check on the shop.
(c) (Person) inspector; (Paß~/Zoll~) passport/customs officer; (in Fabrik) security officer; (Polizist) (im Verkehr) traffic police; (an der Grenze) frontier guard; (in Bibliotheken etc) person at the check-out desk.
(d) (Stelle) (für Nach-/Überprüfung, Verkehr) checkpoint; (Paß~/Zoll~) passport control/customs; (vor Fabrik) gatehouse; (an der Grenze) border post; (in Bibliotheken etc) check-out desk.
Kontrolleur [kɔntrɔ'løːr] m inspector.
Kontroll-: ~funktion f controlling function; ~gang m (inspection) round.
kontrollierbar adj Behauptung checkable, verifiable.
kontrollieren* vt (a) (regulieren, beherrschen) to control.
(b) (nachprüfen, überwachen) to check; (Aufsicht haben über) to supervise; Paß, Fahrkarte etc to inspect, to check. um alle verschiedenen Operationen gleichzeitig ~ zu können in order to be able to keep a check on or to check up on all operations simultaneously; die Qualität der Waren muß streng kontrolliert werden a strict check must be kept on the quality of the goods; jdn/etw nach etw or auf etw (acc) ~ to check sb/sth for sth.
Kontrolliste f getrennt Kontroll-liste check-list.
Kontroll-: ~kommission f control commission; ~lampe f siehe Kontrollampe; ~liste f siehe Kontrolliste.
Kontrollor m (Aus) -s, -e siehe Kontrolleur.
Kontroll-: ~organ nt controlling organization; ~punkt m checkpoint; ~pflicht f control; seine ~pflicht vernachlässigen to neglect one's supervisory responsibilities; ~rat m: Alliierter ~rat Allied Control Council; ~stelle f checkpoint; ~stempel m inspection stamp; ~system nt control system; ~turm m control tower; ~uhr f time clock; ~zentrum nt (Space) control centre.
kontrovers [kɔntro'vɛrs] adj controversial.
Kontroverse [kɔntro'vɛrzə] f -, -n controversy.
Kontur f -, -en or (Art) m -s, -en outline, contour.
Konturenstift m liner.
konturieren* vt (lit, fig) to outline.
Konus m -, -se or (Tech) **Konen** (Math) cone; (Tech) taper; (Typ) body.
Konvektor [kɔn'vɛktor] m convector (heater).
Konvenienz [kɔnve'niɛnts] f (geh) propriety; (Bequemlichkeit) convenience.
Konvent [kɔn'vɛnt] m -(e)s, -e (Versammlung) convention; (Univ: in Verbindung) assembly; (Kloster) convent; (Mönchs~) monastery.
Konvention [kɔnvɛn'tsioːn] f (a) (Herkommen) convention. sich über die ~en hinwegsetzen to sweep aside or ignore (social) conventions. (b) (im Völkerrecht) convention.
Konventionalstrafe [kɔnvɛntsio'naːl-] f penalty or fine (for breach of contract).
konventionell [kɔnvɛntsio'nɛl] adj conventional.
konvergent [kɔnvɛr'gɛnt] adj convergent, converging.
Konvergenz [kɔnvɛr'gɛnts] f convergence.
Konvergenztheorie f theory of convergence.
konvergieren* [kɔnvɛr'giːrən] vi to converge.
Konversation [kɔnvɛrza'tsioːn] f conversation. ~ machen to make conversation or small talk (inf).
Konversationslexikon nt encyclopaedia.
Konversion [kɔnvɛr'zioːn] f conversion.
Konverter [kɔn'vɛrtɐ] m -s, - converter.
konvertibel [kɔnvɛr'tiːbl] adj (Fin) convertible.
Konvertibilität f (Fin) convertibility.
konvertierbar [kɔnvɛr'tiːrbaːr] adj (Fin) convertible.
Konvertierbarkeit f (Fin) convertibility.
konvertieren* [kɔnvɛr'tiːrən] 1 vt to convert (in +acc into). 2 vi aux haben or sein to be converted.
Konvertit(in f) [kɔnvɛr'tiːt(ɪn)] m -en- -en convert.
konvex [kɔn'vɛks] adj convex.
Konvex-: k~konkav adj convexo-concave; ~linse f convex lens; ~spiegel m convex mirror.
Konvikt [kɔn'vɪkt] nt -(e)s, -e seminary.
Konvoi ['kɔnvɔy, -'-] m -s, -s convoy. im ~ fahren to drive in convoy.
Konvolut [kɔnvo'luːt] nt -(e)s, -e (geh) bundle (of papers).

Konvulsion [kɔnvʊl'zioːn] f usu pl (Med) convulsion.
konvulsivisch [kɔnvʊl'ziːvɪʃ] adj (Med) convulsive.
konzedieren* vt (geh) to concede, to grant (jdm etw sb sth). man muß ihm ~, daß ... you have to concede or grant that ...
Konzentrat nt concentrate; (fig: eines Buches etc) condensed version.
Konzentration f concentration (auf +acc on).
Konzentrations-: ~fähigkeit f power of concentration usu pl; ~lager nt concentration camp; ~mangel m lack of concentration; ~schwäche f weak or poor concentration; ~vermögen nt siehe ~fähigkeit.
konzentrieren* 1 vt to concentrate (auf +acc on); Truppen auch to mass. 2 vr to concentrate (auf +acc on); (Untersuchung, Arbeit etc) to be concentrated (auf +acc on).
konzentriert adj (Chem) concentrated.
(b) mit ~er Aufmerksamkeit with all one's concentration; ~e Arbeit work requiring concentration; ~ arbeiten/zuhören to work/listen with concentration; ~ nachdenken to concentrate; der Pianist spielte nicht ~ genug the pianist didn't play with sufficient concentration.
konzentrisch adj (Math, Mil) concentric.
Konzept nt -(e)s, -e (Rohentwurf) draft, notes pl; (für Aufsatz etc auch) rough copy; (Plan, Programm) plan, programme; (Begriff, Vorstellung) concept. es ist jetzt wenigstens als or im ~ fertig at least the draft etc is ready now; jdn aus dem ~ bringen to put sb off, to break sb's train of thought; (inf: aus dem Gleichgewicht) to upset sb; aus dem ~ geraten to lose one's thread; (inf: aus dem Gleichgewicht) to get upset; das paßt mir nicht ins ~ that doesn't fit in with or suit my plans; (gefällt mir nicht) I don't like the idea; das paßt nicht ins ~ der Entspannung that doesn't fit in with the programme of détente; jdm das ~ verderben to spoil sb's plans.
Konzeption f (a) (Med) conception. (b) (geh) (Gedankengang) idea; (Entwurf) conception. seine ~ der Außenpolitik his idea or conception of foreign policy; ein schon in der ~ verfehltes Gedicht a poem which in its (very) conception was a failure.
konzeptionell [kɔntsɛptsio'nɛl] adj (geh) conceptional.
Konzeptions-: ~furcht f (Psych) conception phobia, fear of conceiving; k~los adj without a definite line; (Außenpolitik etc auch) amorphous; das Programm wirkt auf mich recht k~los the programme strikes me as lacking any definite line; ~losigkeit f lack of any definite line, amorphousness; ~verhütung f (Med) contraception.
Konzept-: ~kunst f conceptual art; ~papier nt rough paper.
Konzern m -s, -e combine, group (of companies). die ~e haben zuviel Macht the big companies have too much power.
Konzernbildung f formation of combines.
Konzert nt -(e)s, -e concert; (von klassischen Solisten auch) recital; (Komposition) concerto. das ~ der Großmächte the big powers; die Kinder heulten im ~ the children cried in unison.
Konzert-: ~abend m concert evening; ~agentur f concert artists' agency.
konzertant adj (Mus) in concerto form; Sinfonie concertante.
Konzert-: ~besucher m concert-goer; ~flügel m concert grand.
konzertieren* 1 vi to give a concert; (als Solist mitwirken) to play in a concert. 2 vt (geh: abstimmen) to concert.
konzertiert adj ~e Aktion (Fin, Pol) concerted action.
Konzertina f -, **Konzertinen** concertina.
Konzert-: ~meister m leader, concertmaster (US); ~pavillon m bandstand; ~pianist m concert pianist; ~saal m concert hall; ~sänger m concert singer.
Konzession f (a) (Gewerbeerlaubnis) concession, licence, franchise. (b) (Zugeständnis) concession (an +acc to).
Konzessionär(in f) m concessionaire, licensee.
Konzessions-: k~bereit adj ready or willing to make concessions; ~bereitschaft f readiness to make concessions.
konzessiv adj (Gram) concessive.
Konzessivsatz m (Gram) concessive clause.
Konzil nt -s, -e or -ien [-iən] (Eccl, Univ) council.
konziliant adj (versöhnlich) conciliatory; (entgegenkommend) generous.
Konzilianz f conciliatoriness; generosity.
Konzipient m (Aus) articled clerk.
konzipieren* 1 vt to conceive; (entwerfen auch) to design. 2 vi (Med) to conceive.
konzis adj (liter) concise.
Koofmich m -s, -s or -e (pej inf) businessman type.
Koog m -es, **Köge** (N Ger) siehe Polder.
Ko|operation f cooperation.
ko|operativ adj cooperative.
Ko|operative f (Econ) cooperative.
Ko|operator m (a) (Aus) curate. (b) (rare) cooperator.
ko|operieren* vi to cooperate.
Ko|optation f coopting, cooption.
ko|optieren* vt to coopt.
Ko|ordinate f -, -en (Math) coordinate.
Ko|ordinaten- (Math): ~achse f coordinate axis; ~kreuz, ~system nt coordinate system.
Ko|ordination f coordination.
Ko|ordinator m, **Ko|ordinatorin** f coordinator.
ko|ordinieren* vt to coordinate.
ko|ordinierend adj (Gram) coordinating.
Kopeke f -, -n copeck, kopeck.
Kopenhagen nt -s Copenhagen.
Köpenickiade f hoax involving impersonation.
Köper m -s, no pl (Tex) twill.
kopernikanisch adj Copernican.
Kopf m -(e)s, -e (a) (allgemein) head; (bei Plattenspieler) head, pick-up; (Pfeifen~) bowl; (Brief~) (letter-)head;

Kopf (*Zeitungs~*) head, heading. **mit bloßem** *or* **blankem ~** bareheaded; **~ an ~** shoulder to shoulder; (*Pferderennen, Sport*) neck and neck; **bis über den ~** (*im Wasser*) up to one's neck *or* (*in Schulden*) ears; **~ voraus** *or* **voran** headfirst; **~ weg!** (*inf*) mind your head!; **~ hoch!** chin up!; **~ runter** *or* **ab!** off with his/her/their head(s); **auf dem ~ stehen** to stand on one's head; **sich** (*dat*) **den ~ waschen** to wash one's hair; **jdm den ~ waschen** (*inf*) to give sb a piece of one's mind (*inf*); **den ~ in den Nacken werfen** to throw one's head back; **den ~ oben behalten** to keep one's chin up; **jdm den ~ abschlagen** to behead sb, to cut sb's head off; **jdn einen ~ kürzer machen** (*sl*) to cut *or* chop sb's head off; **jds ~ fordern** (*lit, fig*) to demand sb's head (*fig auch*) to cry for sb's blood; **von ~ bis Fuß** from top to toe, from head to foot; **sich** (*dat*) **an den ~ fassen** *or* **schlagen** (*fig*) to be (left) speechless; **das hältst du ja im ~ nicht aus!** (*sl*) it's absolutely incredible (*inf*); **ihm ist der ~ durch die Haare gewachsen** (*hum*) he's as bald as a coot; **die ~e zusammenstecken** to go into a huddle (*inf*); **einen schweren** *or* **dicken** (*inf*) **~ haben** to have a thick head *or* a hangover; **mit besoffenem ~** (*sl*) drunk out of one's mind (*inf*); **Geld etc auf den ~ hauen** (*inf*) to blow one's money etc (*inf*); **jdm auf den ~ spucken können** (*inf*) to tower above sb, to be head and shoulders above sb; **ich werde mir doch von denen nicht auf den ~ spucken lassen** (*fig inf*) I won't *or* I'm not going to stand any nonsense from them; **jdm über den ~ wachsen** (*lit*) to outgrow sb; (*fig*) (*Sorgen etc*) to be too much for sb, to be more than sb can cope with; (*Konkurrent etc*) to outstrip sb; **jdm auf dem ~ herumtrampeln** (*inf*) *or* **herumtanzen** (*inf*) to walk all over sb (*inf*); **den ~ für jdn/etw hinhalten** (*inf*) to take the blame *or* rap (*inf*) for sb/sth; **dafür halte ich meinen ~ nicht hin** (*inf*) I'm not putting my head on the chopping block for that; **etw auf den ~ stellen** (*lit, fig: durchsuchen*) to turn sth upside down; (*fig*) **Tatsachen** to stand facts on their heads; **und wenn du dich auf den ~ stellst, ...** (*inf*), du kannst dich auf den ~ stellen, ... (*inf*) no matter what you say/do ..., you can say/do what you like ...; **du kannst dich auf den ~ stellen, du wirst ihn nicht umstimmen** (*inf*) you can talk till you're blue in the face, you won't make him change his mind (*inf*); **jdn den ~ kosten** (*lit*) to cost sb his head; (*fig*) to cost sb his career *or* job; **das hat ihn den ~ gekostet** (*fig*) that was the end of the road for him; **~ und Kragen riskieren** *or* **wagen** (*inf*) to risk life and limb; (*beruflich etc*) to risk one's neck; **sich um seinen ~ reden** to sign one's own death warrant; **darauf steht der ~** (*inf*) it's a hanging matter; **auf jds ~** (*acc*) **eine Summe/Belohnung aussetzen** to put a sum of money/reward on sb's head; **es ist nicht auf den ~ gefallen** he's no fool; **jdm etw an den ~ werfen** *or* **schmeißen** (*inf*) to chuck (*inf*) *or* sling (*inf*) sth at sb; **jdm Beschimpfungen/Beleidigungen an den ~ werfen** (*inf*) to hurl insults at sb *or* in sb's face; **jdm etw auf den ~ zusagen** to say sth straight out to sb; **den ~ hängenlassen** (*lit*) to hang one's head; (*fig*) to be downcast *or* despondent; **jdn vor den ~ stoßen** to offend *or* antagonize sb; **jdm den ~ zurechtsetzen** *or* **-rücken** to bring sb to his/her senses; **mit dem ~ durch die Wand wollen** (*inf*) to be determined to get *or* bent on getting one's own way regardless; (**jdm**) **zu ~(e) steigen** to go to sb's head; **ich war wie vor den ~ geschlagen** I was dumbfounded *or* thunderstruck; **über jds** (*acc*) **hinweg** over sb's head; **du hast wohl was am ~!** (*sl*) you must be off your head! (*inf*); **ein ~ Salat/Kohl** a head of lettuce/cabbage; **~ oder Schrift?** heads or tails?

(b) (*Einzelperson*) person. **pro ~** per person *or* head *or* capita; **das Einkommen pro ~** the per capita income; **sie waren zehn ~e stark** there were ten of them; **eine zehn ~e starke Gruppe** a group of ten people; **eine Familie mit drei ~en** a family of three.

(c) (*fig*) (*Verstand*) head; (*Denker*) thinker; (*leitende Persönlichkeit*) leader; (*Bandenführer*) brains *sing*. **sich** (*dat*) **über etw** (*acc*) **den ~ zerbrechen** to rack one's brains over sth; **im ~ muß man's haben** (*inf*) you need brains, you have to have plenty up top (*inf*); **er ist nicht ganz richtig** *or* **klar im ~** (*inf*) he is not quite right in the head *or* up top (*inf*); **er hat einen hellen ~** he thinks clearly, he's got a good brain; **ein kluger/findiger ~** an intelligent/ingenious person; **er ist ein fähiger ~** he has a good head on his shoulders, he's a very capable person; **die besten ~e** the best brains *or* minds.

(d) (*Sinn*) head, mind; (*Erinnerung*) memory. **sich** (*dat*) **etw durch den ~ gehen lassen** to think about sth; **mir ist neulich in den ~ gekommen, daß ...** the other day *or* the idea crossed my mind that ...; **nichts als Tanzen/Fußball/Lesen etc im ~ haben** to think of nothing but dancing/football/reading etc; **andere Dinge im ~ haben** to have other things on one's mind; **ich habe den ~ voll genug** (*inf*) I've got enough on my mind; **ich weiß kaum, wo mir der ~ steht** I scarcely know whether I'm coming or going; **einen kühlen ~ bewahren** *or* **behalten** to keep a cool head, to stay cool-headed, to keep one's cool (*inf*); **den ~ verlieren** to lose one's head, not to keep one's head; **den ~ nicht verlieren** to keep one's head, not to lose one's head; **sich** (*dat*) **etw aus dem ~ schlagen** to put sth out of one's mind; **jdm den ~ verdrehen** to turn sb's head; **der Gedanke will mir nicht aus dem ~** *or* **geht mir im ~ herum** I can't get the thought out of my head *or* mind; **im ~** in one's head; **etw im ~ haben** to have sth in one's head; **etw im ~ rechnen** to work sth out in one's head *or* mentally; **ich habe die Melodie genau im ~** I know the tune exactly; **aus dem ~** from memory; **was man nicht im ~ hat, hat man in den Beinen** (*inf*) you'd/I'd forget your/my head if it wasn't screwed on (*inf*); **sie hat es sich** (*dat*) **in den ~ gesetzt, das zu tun** she has taken it into her head to do that, she has set her mind on doing that; **seinen ~ durchsetzen** to get one's own way; **seinen eigenen ~ haben** (*inf*) to have a mind of one's own; **es muß ja nicht immer alles nach deinem ~ gehen** you can't have things your own way all the time.

Kopf-: **~an-~-Rennen** *nt* neck-and-neck race; **~arbeit** *f* (a) brain-work; **~ an ~** shoulder to shoulder; (*Ftbl sl*) *siehe* **~spiel**; **~arbeiter** *m* brain-worker; **~bahnhof** *m* terminus (station); **~ball** *m* (*Ftbl*) header; **~bedeckung** *f* headgear; **als ~bedeckung trug er ...** on his head he wore ...; **ohne ~bedeckung** without a hat; **~betrag** *m* per capita sum, sum per head; **~bild** *nt* (portrait of sb's) head; **~blatt** *nt* (*Press*) local edition (*with different name*); **~brummen** *nt* -s, *no pl* (*inf*) headache; **~bruststück** *nt* (*Zool*) cephalothorax (*spec*).

Köpfchen *nt dim of* **Kopf** little head; (*fig hum*) brains. **~, ~!** clever stuff!; **~ haben** to have brains, to be brainy (*inf*); **du bist aber ein kluges ~** (*iro*) clever or smart cookie, eh! (*inf*).

köpfeln (*Aus*) **1** *vi* (*einen Kopfsprung machen*) to dive (head-first), to take a header. **2** *vti siehe* **köpfen (b)**.

köpfen *vti* (**a**) **jdn** to behead, to decapitate; (*hum*) *Flasche Wein* to crack (open). **in Frankreich wird immer noch geköpft** they still behead etc people in France. (**b**) (*verschneiden*) *Bäume* to poll; *Jungtriebe* to cut off the heads of. (**c**) (*Ftbl*) to head. **ins Tor ~** to head a goal, to head the ball in.

Kopf-: **~ende** *nt* head; **~form** *f* shape of (the) head; **~füßer** *m* -s, - (*Zool*) cephalopod (*spec*); **~geld** *nt* head money; **~griff** *m* (*Rettungsschwimmen*) chinhold; (*Ringen*) headlock; **~grippe** *f* flu (and headache), (epidemic) encephalitis (*spec*); **~haar** *nt* hair on one's head; (*einzelnes*) hair from the head; **~haltung** *f* **eine gerade ~haltung haben** to hold one's head straight; **~hängerei** *f* (*dated*) dejected *or* miserable attitude; **k~hängerisch** *adj* (*dated*) dejected, miserable, down in the mouth; **~haut** *f* scalp; **~hörer** *m* headphone.

-köpfig *adj suf* -headed. **eine fünf~e Familie** a family of five.

Kopf-: **~jäger** *m* head-hunter; **~jucken** *nt* itching of the scalp; **~keil** *m* (wedge-shaped) bolster; **~kissen** *nt* pillow; **~kissenbezug** *m* pillow case *or* slip; **~lage** *f* (*Med*) head presentation; **~länge** *f* **um eine ~länge by a head**; **k~lastig** *adj* (*lit, fig*) top-heavy; *Flugzeug* nose-heavy; **~lastigkeit** *f* top-heaviness; nose-heaviness; **~laus** *f* head louse; **~leiste** *f* (*Typ*) head rule; **k~los** *adj* (*fig*) in a panic, panicky, in a flap (*inf*); headless; **k~los werden** to lose one's head, to get into a flap (*inf*); **k~los handeln** to lose one's head; **~losigkeit** *f* (*fig*) panickiness; **~nicken** *nt* -s, *no pl* nod (of the head); **~nuß** *f* (*inf*) clip *or* clout (round the earhole) (*inf*); **~prämie** *f* reward; **~putz** *m* headdress; **k~rechnen** *vi infin only* to do mental arithmetic; **~rechnen** *nt* mental arithmetic; **~salat** *m* lettuce; **k~scheu** *adj* timid, nervous, shy; **jdn k~scheu machen** to intimidate sb; **lassen Sie sich nicht k~scheu machen** don't be intimidated; **~schmerz** *m usu pl* headache; **~schmerzen haben** to have a headache; **sich** (*dat*) **über** *or* **um etw** (*acc*) *or* **wegen etw ~schmerzen machen** (*fig*) to worry about sth; **~schmerztablette** *f* aspirin, headache tablet; **~schmuck** *m* headdress; **~schuppe** *f usu pl* dandruff *no pl*; **~schuß** *m* shot in the head; **~schütteln** *nt* -s, *no pl* shaking the head; **mit einem ~schütteln** with a shake of *or* the one's head; **sein ~schütteln zeigte mir, daß er ...** the way he shook his head told me that he ...; **k~schüttelnd 1** *adj* shaking one's head; **2** *adv* with a shake of one's head, shaking one's head; **~schutz** *m* protection for the head; **~schützer** *m* -s, - head-guard; **~seite** *f* (*von Münze*) head, face side; (*von Zeitung*) front page; **~spiel** *nt* (*Ftbl*) heading; **~sprung** *m* header, dive; **einen ~sprung machen** to take a header, to dive (headfirst); **~stand** *m* headstand; **einen ~stand machen** to stand on one's head; **k~stehen** *vi sep irreg aux sein* (a) (*lit*) to stand on one's head; (*vor Ausgelassenheit*) to go wild (with excitement); (*vor Aufregung*) to be in a state of excitement; (*vor Empörung*) to be in a (state of) turmoil; (*durcheinander sein*) to be in a jumble, to be all topsy-turvy (*inf*); **~stein** *m* cobble-stone; **~steinpflaster** *nt* cobble-stones *pl*; **eine Gasse mit ~steinpflaster** a cobbled street; **~steuer** *f* (*Hist*) poll tax; **~stimme** *f* (*Mus*) falsetto; (*Phon*) head voice; **~stoß** *m* (*Billiard*) massé; **~stück** *nt* (*Cook*) head end; **~stütze** *f* head-rest; **~tuch** *nt* (head)scarf; **k~über** *adv* (*lit, fig*) headfirst, headlong; **~verband** *m* (*Med*) head bandage; **~verletzung** *f* head injury; **~wäsche** *f* shampoo, hair-wash; **~weh** *nt siehe* **~schmerz**; **~wunde** *f* head wound; **~zahl** *f* number of persons; **~zerbrechen ist jdm ~zerbrechen machen** to be a worry to sb, to be a headache for sb (*inf*); **sich** (*dat*) **über etw** (*acc*) **~zerbrechen machen** to worry about sth.

Kopie [ko'pi:, (*Aus*) 'ko:piə] *f* copy; (*fig*) carbon copy; (*Durchschlag auch*) carbon (copy); (*Ablichtung*) photocopy; (*Phot*) print; (*Film*) print, copy; (*von Statue*) copy, replica. **das ist nicht das Original, sondern eine ~** it's not the original but a copy *or* imitation.

Kopier-: **~anstalt** *f* (*Film*) printing laboratory, print lab (*inf*); **~apparat** *m siehe* **~gerät**.

kopieren* *vti* (*lit, fig*) to copy; (*nachahmen*) to imitate; (*ablichten*) to photocopy; (*durchpausen*) to trace; (*Phot, Film*) to print. **etw mit Blaupapier ~** to make a carbon (copy) of sth; **oft kopiert, nie erreicht** often imitated but never equalled.

Kopier-: **~gerät** *nt* photocopying machine, photocopier; **~papier** *nt* photocopy paper; **~rad** *nt* (*Sew*) tracing wheel; **~rahmen** *m* printing frame; **~stift** *m* indelible pencil; **~verfahren** *nt* photocopying process.

Kopilot(in *f*) *m* copilot.

Kopist(in *f*) *m* (*Nachahmer*) imitator; (*Art*) copyist.

Koppe *f* -, -n *siehe* **Kuppe**.

Koppel¹ *nt* -s, - *or* (*Aus*) *f* -, -n (*Mil*) belt.

Koppel² *f* -, -n (a) (*Weide*) paddock, enclosure. **auf** *or* **in der ~** in the paddock etc. (b) (*Hunde~*) pack; (*Pferde~*) string. (c) (*Mus: Registerzug*) coupler.

koppeln *vt* (a) (*zusammenbinden*) *Hunde* to tie *or* leash together; *Pferde* to tie *or* string together. (b) (*verbinden*) to couple, to join (*etw an etw* (*acc*) sth to sth); **zwei Dinge** to couple *or* join together; *Raumschiffe auch* to link

up; (fig) to link, to couple; (als Bedingung) to tie; Ziele, Zwecke to conjoin, to combine. **eine Dienstreise mit einem Urlaub** ~ to combine a business trip with a holiday; **einen Vertrag mit einer Klausel** ~ to attach a clause to a contract; **seine Beförderung ist an (eine) Vertragsverlängerung gekoppelt** his promotion is tied to a contract extension.
   (c) (Elec) to couple.
   (d) (Typ) Wort to hyphenate.

Koppel-: ~**rick** nt -s, -e (Pferderennen) fence; ~**schloß** nt (Mil) belt buckle.
Kopp(e)lung f, no pl **(a)** (Elec) coupling. **(b)** (Verbindung) (lit) coupling, joining; (fig, von Raumschiffen) link-up. **(c)** (Mus) coupler.
Kopp(e)lungsmanöver nt (Space) docking manoeuvre. **ein** ~ **durchführen** to link up.
Köpper m -s, - (N Ger inf) header. **einen** ~ **machen** to take a header, to dive headfirst.
koppheister adv (N Ger) headfirst, headlong. ~ **schießen** to do a somersault.
Kopplung f siehe **Kopp(e)lung.**
Kopra f -, no pl copra.
Koproduktion f coproduction.
Koproduzent m coproducer.
Koprophagie [koprofaˈgiː] f, no pl (Psych) coprophagy.
Kopte m -n, -n, **Koptin** f Copt.
koptisch adj Coptic.
Kopula f -, -s or -e [leː] (Gram) copula.
Kopulation f (Biol) copulation, coupling; (Hort) splice grafting; (old Jur: Trauung) union.
kopulativ adj (Gram) copulative.
kopulieren* f (Hort) to splice-graft; (old Jur: trauen) to unite. **2** vi (koitieren) to copulate.
kor pret of **küren, kiesen.**
Koralle f -, -n coral.
Korallen-: ~**bank** f coral-reef; ~**fischer** m coral fisherman; ~**insel** f coral island; ~**kette** f coral necklace; ~**pilz** m goats-beard; ~**riff** nt coral-reef; **k**~**rot** adj coral(-red); ~**tiere** pl coral.
Koran m -s, no pl Koran.
Korb m -(e)s, ⁻e **(a)** basket; (Trag~ für Lasttiere auch) pannier; (Fisch~ auch) creel; (Bienen~) hive; (Förder~) cage; (Degen~, Säbel~) basket hilt. **ein** ~ **Äpfel** a basket of apples.
   (b) (~geflecht) wicker. **ein Sessel aus** ~ a wicker(work) or basket(work) chair.
   (c) (inf: Abweisung) refusal, rebuff. **einen** ~ **bekommen, sich** (dat) **einen** ~ **holen** to get a refusal, to be turned down; **jdm einen** ~ **geben** to turn sb down.
Korb-: ~**arbeit** f basketwork no pl, wickerwork no pl; ~**ball** m basket-ball; ~**blüt(l)er** m -s, - (Bot) composite (flower).
Körbchen nt **(a)** dim of **Korb. ins** ~**!** (baby-talk) off to or time for bye-byes (baby-talk) or beddy-byes (baby-talk). **(b)** (von Biene) (pollen) basket; (von Büstenhalter) cup.
Korb-: ~**flasche** f demijohn; ~**flechter(in f)** m -s, - siehe ~**macher(in);** ~**flechterei** f basket-making; ~**geflecht** nt basketwork, wickerwork; ~**macher(in f)** m basket-maker; ~**möbel** pl wicker(work) or basketwork furniture; ~**sessel** m wicker(work) or basket(work) chair; ~**wagen** m bassinet; ~**waren** pl basketwork or wickerwork (articles); ~**weide** f osier; **k**~**weise** adv by the basketful.
Kord m -(e)s, -e siehe **Cord.**
Kordel f -, -n cord.
Kordilleren pl (Geog) Cordilleras pl.
Kordon [kɔrˈdõː, kɔrˈdoːn] m -s, -s or (Aus) -e [kɔrˈdoːnə] (Mil, Bot) cordon; (Ordensband auch) ribbon.
Kore f -, -n (Archit) caryatid.
Korea nt -s Korea.
Koreaner(in f) m -s, - Korean.
koreanisch adj Korean.
Koreastraße f die ~ the Korea Strait.
Koreferat nt siehe **Korreferat.**
Koreferent(in f) m siehe **Korreferent.**
kören vt to select for breeding purposes.
Korfiot(in f) m -en, -en Corfuan, Corfiote.
Korfu nt -s Corfu.
Korhengst m stud.
Koriander m -s, no pl coriander.
Korinth nt -s Corinth.
Korinthe f -, -n currant.
Korinthenkacker m (sl) fusspot (inf).
Korinther m -s, - Corinthian.
Korintherbrief m (Epistle to the) Corinthians.
korinthisch adj Corinthian.
Kork m -(e)s, -e **(a)** (Bot) cork. **(b)** siehe **Korken.**
Korkeiche f cork oak or tree.
korken¹ vt to cork.
korken² adj attr (made of) cork.
Korken m -s, - cork; (aus Plastik) stopper.
Korken-: ~**geld** nt corkage; ~**zieher** m -s, - corkscrew; ~**zieherlocken** pl corkscrew curls pl.
Korkgeld nt siehe **Korkengeld.**
korkig adj corky.
Kork-: ~**mundstück** nt cork filter; ~**zieher** m siehe **Korkenzieher.**
Kormoran [kɔrmoˈraːn] m -s, -e cormorant.
Korn¹ nt -(e)s, ⁻er **(a)** (Samen~) seed, grain; (Pfeffer~) corn; (Salz~, Sand~, Tech, Phot, Typ) grain; (Hagel~) stone; (Staub~) speck. **(b)** no pl (Getreide) grain, corn (Brit). **das** ~ **steht gut** the corn etc looks promising.
Korn² m -(e)s, - or -s (Kornbranntwein) corn schnapps.
Korn³ nt -(e)s, -e (am Gewehr) front sight, bead. **jdn/etw aufs** ~

nehmen (lit) to draw a bead on sb/sth; (fig) to hit out at sth; **jdn aufs** ~ **nehmen** (fig) to start keeping tabs on sb.
Korn-: ~**ähre** f ear of corn (Brit) or grain; ~**blume** f cornflower; **k**~**blumenblau** adj cornflower blue; (hum: volltrunken) as drunk as a lord; ~**branntwein** m (form) corn schnapps.
Körnchen nt dim of **Korn¹** small grain, granule. **ein** ~ **Wahrheit** a grain of truth.
Körndlbauer m (Aus) corn-growing (Brit) or grain-growing farmer.
körnen vt to granulate, to grain; (aufrauhen) to roughen.
Korner m -s, - (Comm) corner.
Körner-: ~**fresser** m -s, - (Zool) grain-eating bird, granivore (form); ~**futter** nt grain or corn (Brit) (for animal feeding).
Kornett¹ nt -s, -e or -s (Mus) cornet.
Kornett² m -(e)s, -e or -s (old Mil) cornet (old).
Korn-: ~**feld** nt cornfield (Brit), grainfield; ~**futter** nt siehe **Körnerfutter;** ~**haus** nt (old) granary.
körnig adj granular, grainy.
-körnig adj suf -grained.
kornisch adj Cornish.
Korn-: ~**käfer** m corn weevil; ~**kammer** f (lit, fig) granary; ~**rade** f (Bot) corn-cockle; ~**speicher** m granary.
Körnung f (Tech) grain size; (Phot) granularity; (Hunt) decoy-place. **Schmirgelpapier mit feiner** ~ fine-grain sandpaper.
Korollar nt -s, -e (Logik) corollary.
Koromandelholz nt ebony.
Korona f -, **Koronen** corona; (inf) crowd (inf), gang (inf).
Koronar- (Med) in cpds coronary.
Körper m -s, - (alle Bedeutungen) body; (Schiffs~) hull. ~ **und Geist** mind and body; **das braucht der** ~ it's good for you; **am ganzen** ~ **beben** or **zittern/frieren** to tremble/to be cold all over; **ach, du armer** ~**!** (inf) good heavens! (inf).
Körper-: ~**bau** m physique, build; ~**bautyp** m physical type; ~**beherrschung** f physical control; **k**~**behindert** adj physically handicapped or disabled; ~**behinderte(r)** mf physically handicapped or disabled person; **die** ~**behinderten** the physically handicapped, the disabled; ~**ertüchtigung** f physical training, keep-fit exercises pl; **das dient der** ~**ertüchtigung** it helps keep you fit; ~**fülle** f (euph) corpulence; **trotz seiner** ~**fülle** in spite of being rather well-built; ~**geruch** m body odour, BO (inf); ~**gewicht** nt weight; ~**größe** f height; **k**~**haft** adj (geh) corporeal; ~**haltung** f posture, bearing; ~**kontakt** m physical or bodily contact; ~**kraft** f physical or bodily strength; ~**kultur** f **(a)** (DDR) physical education or training; **(b)** (~pflege) personal hygiene; ~**länge** f height; (von Schlange etc) (body) length.
körperlich adj physical; (stofflich) material, corporeal. ~**e Arbeit** manual work; ~**e Züchtigung** corporal punishment; **sich** ~ **ertüchtigen** to keep oneself physically fit; ~**e Vereinigung** (geh) physical union.
Körperlichkeit f corporeality.
Körper-: **k**~**los** adj bodiless, incorporeal; ~**maße** pl measurements pl; ~**öffnung** f (Anat) orifice of the body; ~**pflege** f personal hygiene; ~**puder** m or nt body powder; ~**säfte** pl (liter) blood sing; (~flüssigkeit) body or bodily fluids pl.
Körperschaft f corporation, (corporate) body. **gesetzgebende** ~ legislative body; ~ **des öffentlichen Rechts** public corporation or body.
Körperschaft(s)steuer f corporation tax.
Körper-: ~**schwäche** f physical weakness; ~**spray** m or nt body spray; ~**teil** m part of the body; ~**temperatur** f body temperature; ~**verletzung** f (Jur) bodily or physical injury; **fahrlässige** ~**verletzung** physical injury resulting from negligence; **schwere** ~**verletzung** grievous bodily harm; ~**verletzung im Amt** injury caused by a policeman/public official; ~**verletzung mit tödlichem Ausgang** manslaughter; ~**wärme** f body heat.
Korporal m -s, -e or **Korporäle** corporal.
Korporation f **(a)** (Studentenverbindung) student society, fraternity (US). **(b)** (Körperschaft) corporation.
korporativ adj Staat corporate.
korporiert adj pred ~ **sein** to be a member of a students' society which fights duels; **ein K**~**er** a member of a students' society which fights duels.
Korps [koːɐ] nt - [koːɐ(s)], - [koːɐs] (Mil) corps; (Univ) (duelling) corps.
Korps-: ~**bruder** m fellow member of a student (duelling) society; ~**geist** m esprit de corps; ~**student** m student belonging to a (duelling) society.
korpulent adj corpulent.
Korpulenz f, no pl corpulence.
Korpus¹ m -, -se (Art) body of Christ; (hum inf: Körper) body.
Korpus² nt -, **Korpora** **(a)** (Ling) corpus. **(b)** (Mus) resonance box.
Korpuskel nt -s, -n or f -, -n (Phys) particle, corpuscle.
Korreferat nt **(a)** (Vortrag) supplementary paper or report. **(b)** (Prüfung) second marking or assessment.
Korreferent(in f) m **(a)** (Redner) reader of a supplementary paper. **(b)** (Prüfer) second examiner.
korrekt adj correct; Frage civil.
korrekterweise adv to be correct, by rights.
Korrektheit f correctness.
Korrektiv nt corrective.
Korrektor m, **Korrektorin** f (Typ) proof-reader.
Korrektur f correction; (Typ) (Vorgang) proof-reading; (Verbesserung) proof correction; (~fahne) proof. ~ **lesen** to read or correct (the) proofs, to do (the) proof-reading (bei etw for sth), to proof-read (bei etw sth); **kann er** ~ **lesen?** can he proof-read?
Korrektur-: ~**abzug** m galley (proof); ~**bogen** m page proof;

~**fahne** f galley (proof); ~**zeichen** nt proofreader's mark.

Korrelat nt correlate.

korrelieren* vi to correlate.

Korrepetitor m (Mus) repetiteur, coach.

Korrespondent(in f) m correspondent.

Korrespondenz f correspondence. **mit jdm in ~ stehen** to be in correspondence with sb.

Korrespondenz-: ~**büro** nt news or press agency; ~**karte** f (Aus) postcard.

korrespondieren* vi (a) (in Briefwechsel stehen) to correspond. ~**des Mitglied** corresponding member. (b) (entsprechen) to correspond (mit to, with). ~**der Winkel** corresponding angle.

Korridor m -s, -e (auch Luft~ etc) corridor; (Flur) hall. **der (Polnische) ~** (Hist) the Polish Corridor.

korrigierbar adj able to be corrected, corrigible (form). **ein nicht so leicht ~er Sprachfehler** a speech defect which is not so easy to put right or correct.

korrigieren* vt (berichtigen) to correct; Aufsätze etc auch to mark; Meinung, Einstellung to alter, to change.

korrodieren* vti (vi: aux sein) to corrode.

Korrosion f corrosion.

Korrosions-: k~**beständig**, k~**fest** adj corrosion-resistant; k~**frei** adj non-corrosive, non-corroding; ~**schutz** m corrosion prevention.

korrosiv adj corrosive.

korrumpieren* vt to corrupt.

korrumpiert adj corrupt.

korrupt adj corrupt.

Korruption f, no pl corruption.

Korruptionsaffäre f corruption affair or business.

Korsage [kɔrˈzaːʒə] f -, -n corsage.

Korsar m -en, -en (Hist) corsair.

Korse m -n, -n Corsican.

Korselett [kɔrzəˈlet] nt -(e)s, -e or -s corselet.

Korsett nt -s, -s or -e corset(s pl).

Korsettstange f stay.

Korsika nt -s Corsica.

korsisch adj Corsican.

Korso m -s, -s (Pferderennen) horse-race; (Umzug) parade, procession; (breite Straße) avenue.

Kortex m -(es), **Kortizes** [ˈkɔrtiːtseːs] (Anat) cortex.

kortikal adj (Anat) cortical.

Kortison nt -s, -e (Med) cortisone.

Korund m -(e)s, -e (Geol) corundum.

Körung f selection for breeding purposes.

Korvette [kɔrˈvetə] f (Naut) corvette; (Sport) jump to handstand.

Korvettenkapitän m lieutenant commander.

Koryphäe [koryˈfɛːə] f -, -n genius; (auf einem Gebiet) eminent authority.

Kosak m -en, -en Cossack.

Kosakenmütze f cossack hat.

Koschenille [kɔʃəˈnɪljə] f -, no pl cochineal.

koscher adj (Rel, fig inf) kosher. **~ kochen/schlachten** to cook/slaughter according to kosher requirements.

K.-o.-Schlag [kaːˈʔoː-] m knockout blow. **durch ~ siegen** to win by a knockout.

Koseform f affectionate or familiar form (of proper name).

kosen vti (dated, geh) jdn/mit jdm ~ to fondle or caress sb; **~d strich ihre Hand über ...** her hand moved caressingly over ...; **miteinander ~** to bill and coo.

Kose-: ~**name** m pet name; ~**wort** nt term of endearment or affection.

K.-o.-Sieg [kaːˈʔoː-] m knock-out victory.

Kosinus m -, - or -se (Math) cosine.

Kosmetik f -, no pl beauty culture; (Kosmetika, fig) cosmetics pl. **eine Reform, die sich nicht nur auf ~ beschränkt** a reform which is not merely cosmetic.

Kosmetikberaterin f beauty counsellor or adviser.

Kosmetiker(in f) m -s, - beautician, cosmetician.

Kosmetikinstitut nt beauty parlour.

Kosmetikum nt -s, **Kosmetika** cosmetic.

kosmetisch adj cosmetic. **ein ~es Mittel** a cosmetic.

kosmisch adj cosmic. **~ beeinflußt werden** to be influenced by the stars or the cosmos.

Kosmo-: ~**biologie** f space or cosmic biology; ~**gonie** f cosmogony; ~**logie** f cosmology; ~**naut(in** f) m -en, -en cosmonaut; ~**polit(in** f) m -en, -en cosmopolitan; k~**politisch** adj cosmopolitan.

Kosmos m -, no pl cosmos.

Kost f -, no pl (a) (Nahrung, Essen) food, fare. **vegetarische/fleischlose ~** vegetarian/meatless diet; **geistige ~** (fig) intellectual fare; **leichte/schwere ~** (fig) easy/heavy going, heavy stuff (inf). (b) (dated: Beköstigung) board. **jdn in ~ nehmen** to take sb as a boarder; **bei jdm in ~ stehen** to board with sb; **(freie) ~ und Logis** or **Wohnung** (free) board and lodging.

kostbar adj (wertvoll) valuable, precious; (luxuriös) luxurious, sumptuous.

Kostbarkeit f (a) siehe adj value, preciousness; luxuriousness, sumptuousness. (b) (Gegenstand) treasure, precious object; (Leckerbissen) delicacy.

Kosten pl cost(s); (Jur) costs pl; (Un~) expenses pl; (Auslagen auch) outlay. **die ~ tragen** to bear the cost(s); **auf ~ von** or **+gen** at the expense of; **auf ~ des Steuerzahlers** at the expense of the tax-payer, at the tax-payer's expense; **auf meine ~** (lit, fig) at my expense; **auf seine ~ kommen** to cover one's expenses; (fig) to get one's money's worth, to have a very good time; **~ spielen keine Rolle** money's no object.

kosten¹ vti (a) (lit, fig) to cost. **was kostet das?** what or how much does it cost?, how much is it?; **was soll das ~?** what's it going to cost?; **das kostet/hat gekostet** (inf) it costs/it cost a bit or something; **koste es, was es wolle** whatever the cost; **das/die lasse ich mich etwas ~** I don't mind spending a bit of money on it/her; **jdn sein Leben/den Sieg ~** to cost sb his life/the victory; **was kostet die Welt?** (inf) the world's your/their etc oyster. (b) (in Anspruch nehmen) Zeit, Geduld etc to take.

kosten² 1 vt (probieren) to taste, to try, to sample; (fig) to taste; Freuden etc auch to taste of (liter). **2** vi to taste. **willst du mal ~?** would you like a taste?; **von etw ~** to taste etc sth.

Kosten-: ~**anschlag** m siehe ~**voranschlag**; ~**aufstellung** f statement of costs; ~**aufwand** m expense; **mit einem ~aufwand von 100.000 DM** at a cost of DM 100,000; ~**ersparnis** f cost saving; ~**erstattung** f reimbursement of costs or expenses; ~**explosion** f (inf) costs explosion; ~**frage** f question of cost(s); k~**frei** adj cost-free, free of cost; k~**intensiv** adj (Econ) cost-intensive; k~**los** adj, adv free (of charge); ~**miete** f rent which covers costs; k~**pflichtig** adj liable to pay costs, with costs; **eine Klage k~pflichtig abweisen** to dismiss a case with costs; **k~pflichtig verurteilt werden** to have costs awarded against one, to have to pay costs; **ein Kfz k~pflichtig abschleppen** to tow away a car at the owner's expense, to impound a car; ~**preis** m siehe **Selbstkostenpreis**; ~**punkt** m cost question; ~**punkt?** (inf) what'll it cost?, how much?; ~**punkt: 100 DM** (inf) cost, DM 100; ~**satz** m rate; k~**sparend** adj cost-saving; **etw k~sparend herstellen** to produce sth at low cost; ~**voranschlag** m (costs) estimate; ~**vorschuß** m advance.

Kost-: ~**gänger** m -s, - (dated) boarder; ~**geld** nt board.

köstlich adj (a) Wein, Speise exquisite; Luft magnificent. (b) (amüsant) priceless. **~, wie er darauf reagiert hat** (inf) it was priceless the way he reacted; **du bist ja ~** (inf) you're priceless; **sich ~ amüsieren** to have a great time.

Köstlichkeit f siehe adj (a) no pl exquisiteness; magnificence. (b) no pl pricelessness. (c) (Leckerbissen etc) (culinary) delicacy.

Kost-: ~**probe** f (von Wein, Käse) taste; (fig) sample; **das sind hier ~proben** these are free samples, these are for you to taste; **bei der ~probe** while tasting; **warst du auch bei der ~probe?** were you at the tasting too?; k~**spielig** adj costly, expensive.

Kostüm nt -s, -e (Theat: Tracht) costume. (b) (Schneider~) costume (dated), suit.

Kostüm-: ~**ball** m fancydress ball; ~**bildner(in** f) m costume designer; ~**fest** nt siehe ~**ball**; ~**film** m period film or picture.

kostümieren* vr to dress up.

Kostüm-: ~**probe** f (Theat) dress rehearsal; ~**verleih** m (theatrical) costume agency.

Kostverächter m: **kein ~ sein** (hum) (Feinschmecker sein) to be fond of or to enjoy one's food; (die Frauen lieben) to be one for the ladies, to be a bit of a lad (inf).

Kot m -(e)s, no pl (form) excrement, faeces (form) pl; (liter: Schmutz, Dreck) mire, filth.

Kotangens m (Math) cotangent.

Kotau m -s, -s (einen) ~ **machen** (pej) to kowtow (vor jdm to sb).

Kotblech nt siehe **Kotflügel**.

Kote¹ f -, -n (Surv) spot height.

Kote² f -, -n (Lappenzelt) tent.

Kotelett [kɔtəˈlet, kɔˈtlet] nt -(e)s, -s or (rare) -e chop, cutlet.

Kotelette [kɔtəˈlɛtə] f (usu pl) (side)whisker, sideboard, sideburn (US).

koten vi (form) to defecate (form).

Köter m -s, - (pej) cur.

Kotflügel m (Aut) wing.

Kothurn m -s, -e cothurn(us). **auf hohem ~ gehen** (fig liter) to speak/behave pompously.

kotig adj filthy.

Kotter m -s, - (dated Aus) detention cell.

Kotze¹ f -, no pl (vulg) vomit, puke (sl). **da kann man die ~ kriegen** it's enough to make you throw up or puke (sl).

Kotze² f -, -n (S Ger, Aus) coarse woollen blanket; (Umhang) poncho.

kotzen vi (vulg) to throw up (inf), to puke (sl). **das ist zum K~** (sl) it makes you sick; **du bist zum K~** (sl) you make me sick, you make me want to throw up or puke (sl); **da kann man das (kalte) K~ kriegen** (sl) it's enough to make you throw up or puke (sl).

kotz-: ~**langweilig** adj (sl) bloody (Brit inf) or dead (inf) boring; ~**übel** adj (sl) **mir ist ~übel** I feel like throwing up (inf).

KP [kaːˈpeː] f -, -en abbr of **Kommunistische Partei**.

KPD [kaːpeːˈdeː] f -, -en abbr of **Kommunistische Partei Deutschlands**.

KPdSU [kaːpeːdeːˈʔɛsˈʔuː] f - abbr of **Kommunistische Partei der Sowjetunion** Communist Party of the Soviet Union.

Krabbe f -, -n (a) (Zool) (klein) shrimp; (größer) prawn. (b) (dated inf: Kind) tot (inf), mite (inf). **eine süße kleine ~** a sweet little thing. (c) (Archit) crocket.

Krabbelalter nt crawling stage (of a baby).

krabbeln 1 vi aux sein to crawl. **2** vt (kitzeln) to tickle. **3** vti impers (kitzeln) to tickle; (jucken) to itch; siehe **kribbeln**.

Krach m -(e)s, -̈e (a) no pl (Lärm) noise, din, racket (inf); (Schlag) crash, bang. **~ machen** to make a noise etc. (b) (inf: Zank, Streit) row, quarrel, fight. **mit jdm ~ haben** to have a row etc with sb, to row or quarrel or fight with sb; **mit jdm ~ kriegen** to get into trouble with sb, to have a row with sb; **~ schlagen** to make a fuss. (c) (Börsen~) crash.

krach interj crash, bang.

krachen 1 vi (a) (Lärm machen) to crash, to bang; (Holz) to creak; (Schuß) to crack out; (Donner) to crash. **~d fallen** etc to fall with a crash or bang; **..., daß es nur so krachte** (lit) with a

bang or crash; (fig) with a vengeance; **sonst kracht's!** (inf) or there'll be trouble; **es hat gekracht** (inf) (Zusammenstoß) there's been a crash.
  (b) aux sein (inf) (aufplatzen) to rip (open), to split; (brechen) to break; (Eis) to crack; (Betrieb) to crash.
  (c) aux sein (inf: aufprallen) to crash.
  2 vr (inf) to have a row or fight or quarrel.
Kracher m -s, - banger (Brit), fire-cracker (US).
Kracherl nt -s, -(n) (Aus inf) pop (inf), fizzy pop (inf).
Krach-: k~ledern adj (fig hum) rustic; ~lederne f -n,-n leather shorts pl, lederhosen pl; ~macher(in f) m (inf) (lit) noisy person or character; (fig) trouble-maker; **hör auf, du ~macher!** must you make so much noise!; ~mandel f almond in its shell.
Krächzen nt -s, no pl croak(ing); (von Vogel) caw(ing).
krächzen vi to croak; (Vogel) to caw.
kracken ['krakn, 'krεkn] vt (Chem) to crack.
Kräcker m -s, - (Cook) cracker.
Krad nt -(e)s, ~er (Mil, dated) motor-cycle.
Krad-: ~fahrer m (dated) motor-cyclist; ~melder m (Mil) motor-cycle despatch rider.
Kraft f -, ~e (a) (körperlich, sittlich) strength no pl; (geistig, schöpferisch) powers pl; (von Prosa, Stimme) strength, power, force; (von Muskeln, Ringkämpfer) strength, power; (Energie) energy, energies pl. **er weiß nicht wohin mit seiner ~** (inf) he's just bubbling over with energy; **er kann vor ~ nicht mehr laufen** (hum) he's so muscle-bound he can hardly move; **die ~e (mit jdm) messen** to try or pit one's strength (against sb); (fig) to pit oneself against sb; **wenn man alle ~e anspannt** or **zusammennimmt** if you summon up all your strength; **seine ~e sammeln** to build up or recover one's strength; **mit frischer ~** with renewed strength; **mit letzter ~** with one's last ounce of strength; **die ~ aufbringen, etw zu tun** to find the strength to do sth; **mit vereinten ~en werden wir ...** if we combine our efforts or join forces we will ...; **mit seinen ~en haushalten** or **sparsam umgehen** to conserve one's strength or energy or energies; **die ~ der Verzweiflung** the strength born of desperation; **das geht über meine ~e** it's more than I can take; **ich bin am Ende meiner ~** I can't take any more; **mit aller** or **voller ~** with all one's might or strength; **er will mit aller ~ durchsetzen, daß ...** he will do his utmost to ensure that ...; **aus eigener ~** by oneself; (fig auch) by one's own efforts, single-handedly; **nach (besten) ~en** to the best of one's ability; **er tat, was in seinen ~en stand** he did everything (with)in his power; **nicht/wieder bei ~en sein** not to be in very good shape/to have (got) one's strength back; **wieder zu ~en kommen** to regain one's strength.
  (b) (Phys: einer Reaktion etc) force; (der Sonne etc) strength, power; (no pl: Wirksamkeit, liter, Bibl: Macht) power. **die treibende ~** (fig) the driving force; **das Gleichgewicht der ~e** (Pol) the balance of power; **das Parallelogramm der ~e** (Phys) the parallelogram of forces; **die ~ des Motors/der Flut** the power of the engine/the tide; **die heilende ~ der Sonne** the healing power of the sun; **die tröstende ~ der Musik** the comforting power of music.
  (c) (usu pl: in Wirtschaft, Politik etc) force.
  (d) no pl (Jur: Geltung) force. **in ~ sein/treten** to be in/come into force; **außer ~ sein/treten** to have ceased to be in force/to cease to be in force, to be no longer in force; **außer ~ setzen** to cancel, to annul.
  (e) no pl (Naut: Geschwindigkeit) **halbe/volle ~ voraus!** half/full speed ahead.
  (f) (Arbeits~) employee, worker; (Haushalts~) domestic help; (Lehr~) teacher. **~e staff**, personnel no pl.
kraft prep +gen (form) by virtue of; (mittels) by use of. **~ meines Amtes** by virtue of my office; **~ meiner Befugnisse** on the strength of or by virtue of my authority.
Kraft-: ~akt m strong-man act; (fig) show of strength; ~anstrengung f exertion; ~arm m (Phys) lever arm to which force is applied; ~aufwand m effort; unnützer ~aufwand wasted effort, waste of energy; ~ausdruck m swearword; ~ausdrücke strong language; ~brühe f beef tea; ~droschke f (form) Hackney carriage (form), taxicab; ~einheit f (Phys) unit of force.
Kräfteparallelogramm nt parallelogram of forces.
Kraft-: k~erfüllt adj (geh) vigorous; ~ersparnis f saving of energy or effort.
Kräfte-: ~verfall m loss of strength; ~verhältnis nt (Pol) balance of power; (von Mannschaften etc) relative strength; ~verlagerung f (Pol) power shift; ~verschleiß m waste of energy.
Kraftfahrer(in f) m (form) motorist, driver; (als Beruf) driver.
Kraftfahrergruß m (iro) tap on one's forehead etc (to indicate that a driver is mad), rude gesture.
Kraftfahr-: ~park m fleet of motor vehicles; k~technisch adj attr mechanical; k~technische Ausbildung training in motor mechanics; ~truppe f (Mil) motorized unit.
Kraftfahrwesen nt motoring no art.
Kraftfahrzeug nt motor vehicle.
Kraftfahrzeug-: ~brief m (vehicle) registration document, logbook (Brit); ~mechaniker m motor mechanic; ~schein m (vehicle) registration document; ~steuer f motor vehicle tax, road tax (Brit).
Kraft-: ~feld nt (Phys) force field; **im ~feld von jdm/etw stehen** (fig) to be exposed to the powerful influence of sb/sth; ~futter nt concentrated feed(stuff).
kräftig 1 adj strong; Mann, Geschmack, Muskel, Stimme auch powerful; Ausdrucksweise auch powerful, forceful; Haarwuchs, Pflanze auch healthy; Farbe auch rich; Schlag hard, powerful, hefty (inf); Händedruck firm, powerful; Fluch vio-

lent; Suppe, Essen nourishing; (groß) Portion big, massive; Preiserhöhung big, massive; Beifall loud. **~e Ausdrücke** strong language; **einen ~en Schluck nehmen** to take a good or big swig; **eine ~e Tracht Prügel** a good or sound or thorough beating.
  2 adv **(a)** gebaut strongly, powerfully; zuschlagen, treten, pressen, drücken, blasen hard; schütteln, lachen, mitsingen heartily; fluchen, niesen violently. **etw ~ schütteln/polieren/umrühren** to shake/polish/stir sth vigorously, to give sth a good shake/polish/stir; **jdn ~ verprügeln** to give sb a sound or good or thorough beating; **~ essen/trinken** to eat well/to drink a lot; **husten Sie mal ~** have a good cough; **er hat sich ~ dagegen gewehrt** he objected most strongly; (körperlich) he put up a strong resistance; **sich für etw ~ einsetzen** to support sth strongly or energetically.
  (b) (zur Verstärkung) really. **es hat ~ geregnet/geschneit** it really rained/snowed, it rained/snowed heavily; **es hat ~ geblitzt** there was tremendous lightning; **die Preise sind ~ gestiegen** prices have gone up a lot, prices have really gone up; **jdn ~ ausschimpfen** to give sb a good bawling out (inf), to really give sb a bawling out (inf); **sich ~ täuschen** (inf) to be really or very much or greatly mistaken; **jdn ~ belügen** (inf) to tell sb a pack of lies; **sich ~ ausweinen** to have a good cry; **sich ~ ärgern** to get really or mighty (inf) annoyed.
kräftigen vt (geh) jdn ~ to build up sb's strength; (Luft, Bad etc) to invigorate sb; (Essen, Mittel etc) to fortify sb; ~de Luft invigorating or bracing air; **ein ~des Mittel** a tonic.
Kräftigung f (geh) siehe vt strengthening; invigoration; fortification.
Kräftigungsmittel nt tonic.
Kraftlinien pl (Phys) lines of force pl.
kraftlos adj (schwach) feeble, weak; (schlaff) limp; (machtlos) powerless; (Jur) invalid. **~ sank er zurück** he fell feebly back.
Kraftlos|erklärung f (Jur) invalidation, annulment.
Kraftlosigkeit f siehe adj feebleness, weakness; limpness; powerlessness; invalidity.
Kraft-: ~meier m -s, - (inf) muscle man (inf); (fig) strong-man; ~mensch m strong-man, muscle man (inf); ~messer m -s, - dynamometer (form); (auf Jahrmarkt) test-your-strength machine; ~post f post(al) bus service; ~probe f test of strength; (zwischen zwei Gruppen, Menschen) trial of strength; ~protz m (inf) muscle man (inf); ~rad nt motorcycle, motorbike; ~sport m sport(s pl) involving strength; ~stoff m fuel; k~strotzend adj excluding vitality, vigorous; Pflanze healthy-looking, vigorous; (muskulös) with bulging muscles; **ein k~strotzendes Baby** a big strong bouncing baby; ~übertragung f power transmission; ~vergeudung f siehe ~verschwendung; ~verkehr m motor traffic; ~verschwendung f waste of energy or effort; k~voll adj (geh) Stimme powerful; ~wagen m motor vehicle; ~werk nt power station; ~wort nt siehe ~ausdruck.
Kragdach nt overhanging roof.
Krage f -, -n siehe **Kragstein**.
Kragen m -s, - or (S Ger, Sw auch) ~ collar. **jdn am** or **beim ~ packen** to grab sb by the collar; (fig inf) to collar sb; **mir platzte der ~** (inf) I blew my top (inf); **jetzt platzt mir aber der ~!** this is the last straw!; **jdn** or **jdm den ~ kosten** (fig) to be sb's downfall; (umbringen) to be the end of sb; **dem könnte ich den ~ umdrehen!** (inf) I could wring his neck! (inf); **es geht ihm jetzt an den ~** (inf) he's in for it now (inf); **siehe Kopf**.
Kragen-: ~knopf m collar stud; ~nummer f siehe ~weite; ~spiegel m (Mil) collar patch; ~weite f (lit) collar size; **eine ~weite zu groß für jdn sein** (fig inf) to be too much for sb (to handle); **das ist nicht meine ~weite** (fig inf) that's not my cup of tea (inf).
Kragstein m (Archit) console.
Krähe f -, -n **eine ~ hackt der anderen kein Auge aus** (Prov) birds of a feather stick together (Prov).
krähen vi to crow; siehe **Hahn**.
Krähen-: ~fuß m (Eisenkralle) crowbar; ~füße pl (an den Augen) crowsfeet pl; (Schriftkrakel) scrawl sing; ~nest nt (Naut) crow's nest.
Krähwinkel m (pej) cultural backwater.
Krakau nt -s Cracow.
Krakauer f -, - spicy smoked sausage with garlic.
Krakauer(in f) m -s, - Cracovian.
Krake m -n, -n octopus; (Myth) Kraken.
Krakeel m -s, no pl (inf) row. **~ machen** (inf) to kick up a row or racket (inf).
krakeelen* vi (inf) to make or kick up a row or racket (inf).
Krakeeler m -s, - (inf) rowdy (inf), rowdy type (inf).
Krakel m -s, - (inf) scrawl, scribble.
Krakelei f (inf) scrawl, scribble.
krakelig adj scrawly.
krakeln vti to scrawl, to scribble.
Kral m -s, -e kraal.
Kralle f -, -n claw; (von Raubvogel auch) talon; (pej: Fingernagel) claw, talon; (sl: Hand) paw (inf), mauler (sl). **jdn/etw in seinen ~n haben** (fig inf) to have sb/sth in one's clutches; (jdm) **die ~n zeigen** (fig) to show (sb) one's claws; **jdn aus den ~n des Todes retten** to rescue sb from the jaws of death; **auf die ~** (sl) (cash) on the nail (inf).
krallen 1 vr **sich an jdn/etw ~** (lit, fig) to cling to sb/sth; (Katze) **die ~n** to dig its claws into sb/sth; sich in etw (acc) ~ to sink its claws into sth; (mit Fingern) to dig one's fingers into sth.
  2 vt **(a) die Finger in etw** (acc)/**um etw ~** to dig one's fingers into sth/to clutch sth; **er krallte vor Schmerz die Finger in die Decke** he clawed (at) the blanket in pain.
  (b) (sl) to pinch (inf), to swipe (inf).
  3 vi to claw (an +dat at).

Kram m -(e)s, no pl (inf) (Gerümpel) junk; (Zeug) things pl, stuff (inf); (Angelegenheit) business. **den ~ satt haben/ hinschmeißen** to be fed up with/to chuck the whole thing or business (inf); **das paßt mir nicht in den ~** it's a confounded nuisance; **mach doch deinen ~ allein!** do it yourself!; **laß mich meinen ~ alleine machen** don't tell me what to do.
kramen 1 vi (a) to rummage about (in +dat in, nach for). (b) (Sw inf) to do a bit of shopping. 2 vt etw aus etw ~ to fish sth out of sth.
Krämer m -s, - small shopkeeper, grocer; (Laden) small general store, grocer's. **das ist kein Kaufhaus, das ist ein ~** it's not a department store, it's just a tatty old general store; **ein Volk von ~n** a nation of shopkeepers.
Krämer-: ~geist m, ~seele f small- or petty-minded person; **ein ~geist** or **eine ~seele sein** to be small- or petty-minded; **einen ~geist** or **eine ~seele haben** to have a small or petty mind.
Kramladen m (pej inf) tatty little shop (inf); (Trödelladen) junk shop.
Krampe f -, -n staple.
Krampen m -s, - staple; (Aus: Spitzhacke) pick(-axe).
Krampf m -(e)s, ⁻e (a) (Zustand) cramp; (Verkrampfung, Zuckung) spasm; (wiederholt) convulsion(s pl); (Anfall, Lach~) fit. **einen ~ haben/bekommen** to have/get (a) cramp; **er wand sich auf dem Boden in ⁻en** he curled up on the floor in convulsions.
(b) no pl (inf) (Getue) palaver (inf); (Unsinn) nonsense, rubbish.
Krampf-: ~ader f varicose vein; **k~artig** adj convulsive.
krampfen 1 vt Finger, Hand to clench (um etw around sth). **die Finger in etw** (acc) ~ to dig one's fingers into sth. 2 vr **sich um etw** ~ to clench sth. 3 vi (a) (Krämpfe haben) to have a convulsion/convulsions. (b) (Sw inf: hart arbeiten) to slave away (inf).
Krampf-: **k~haft** adj Zuckung convulsive; (inf: angestrengt, verzweifelt) frantic, desperate; Lachen forced no adv; **sich k~haft an etw** (dat) **festhalten** (lit, fig inf) to cling desperately to sth; ~husten m (Aus inf) whooping cough; **k~lindernd** adj antispasmodic (spec); **k~lösend** adj antispasmodic (spec).
Krampus m - (Aus) companion of St Nicholas.
Kran m -(e)s, ⁻e or -e (a) crane. (b) (dial: Hahn) tap, faucet (US).
Kranführer m crane driver or operator.
krängen vi (Naut) to heel (over).
Kranich m -s, -e (Orn) crane.
krank adj, comp ⁻er, superl ⁻ste(r, s) or adv am ⁻sten ill usu pred, sick (auch fig), not well; (leidend) invalid; Pflanze, Organ diseased; Zahn, Bein bad; Wirtschaft, Firma ailing; (Hunt) Wild wounded. **~ werden** to fall or be taken ill or sick; **schwer ~** seriously ill; **~ am Magen sein** (old) to have a stomach disorder; **~ am Herzen/an der Seele** (liter) sick at heart (liter); **vor Aufregung/Angst ~ sein** sick with excitement/fear; **vor Heimweh/Liebe ~** homesick/lovesick; **nach jdm ~ sein** to be sick with longing for sb, to be pining for sb; **sich ~ melden** to let sb/one's boss etc know that one is sick or ill; (telefonisch) to phone in sick; (esp Mil) to report sick; **sie hat sich ~ gemeldet** she is off sick; **jdn ~ schreiben** to give sb a medical certificate; (esp Mil) to put sb on the sick-list; **er ist schon seit einem halben Jahr ~ geschrieben** he's been off sick for six months; **sich ~ stellen** to pretend to be ill or sick, to malinger; **das macht/du machst mich ~!** (inf) it gets/you get on my nerves! (inf), it drives/you drive me round the bend! (inf); **du bist wohl ~!** (inf iro) there must be something wrong with you!; **der ~e Mann am Bosporus** the Sick Man of Europe.
kränkeln vi to be ailing (auch Wirtschaft, Firma), to be sickly, to be in bad or poor health. **sie ~ leicht** they're often poorly.
kranken vi to suffer (an +dat from). **das krankt daran, daß** (fig) it suffers from the fact that ...
kränken 1 vt **jdn ~** to hurt sb('s feelings), to wound sb; **sie war sehr gekränkt** she was very hurt; **es kränkt mich, daß ...** it hurts or grieves me that ...; **jdn in seiner Ehre ~** to offend sb's pride; **~d** hurtful. 2 vr **sich über etw** (acc) ~ (dated, dial) to feel upset about sth.
Kranken-: ~anstalten pl hospitals and/or clinics pl; ~auto nt siehe ~wagen; ~bericht m medical report; ~besuch m visit (to a sick person); (von Arzt) (sick) call; ~bett nt sick-bed; ~geld nt sickness benefit; (von Firma) sickpay; ~geschichte f medical history; ~gymnastik f physiotherapy; ~gymnastin f physiotherapist.
Krankenhaus nt hospital. **ins ~ gehen** (als Patient) to go into (the US) hospital; **im ~ liegen** to be in (the US) hospital; **jdn in einem ~ unterbringen** to put sb in a hospital; **an einem ~ sein** (Arzt, Schwester etc) to work in a hospital.
Krankenhaus- in cpds hospital; ~arzt m hospital doctor; ~aufenthalt m stay in hospital; ~kosten pl hospital charges pl or costs pl; ~rechnung f bill for hospital treatment.
Kranken-: ~kasse f (Versicherung) medical or health insurance; (Gesellschaft) medical or health insurance company; **ich bin in einer privaten ~kasse** I am in a private medical insurance scheme, I'm privately insured; **er ist in keiner ~kasse** he has no medical insurance; ~lager nt (Krankenbett) sick-bed; (Kranksein) illness; **das Fieber warf ihn aufs ~lager** (geh) the fever confined him to his sick-bed; ~pflege f nursing; **alle, die in der ~pflege tätig sind** all those who look after or care for the sick; ~pfleger m orderly; (mit Schwesternausbildung) male nurse; ~pflegerin f nurse; ~saal m ward; ~salbung f (Eccl) anointing of the sick; ~schein m medical insurance record card; ~schwester f nurse; ~stand m (dial, Aus) **im ~stand sein** to be sick or ill; **jdn in den ~stand schreiben** to give sb a medical certificate; ~stuhl m invalid chair; (Nachtstuhl) com-

mode; ~transport m transportation of sick people; (mittels Krankenwagen) ambulance service; (die Kranken selbst) shipload/busload etc of sick people; ~versicherung f medical or health insurance; soziale/private ~versicherung state or national/private health insurance; ~wagen m ambulance; ~wärter m orderly; ~zimmer nt sick-room; (im Krankenhaus) hospital room.
Kranke(r) mf decl as adj sick person, invalid; (Patient) patient. **die ~n** the sick.
krankfeiern vi sep (inf) to be off 'sick', to skive off work (Brit inf). **das K~ ist ein großes Problem** absenteeism is a great problem; **geh doch heute nicht ins Büro, feier doch krank** don't go in to the office today, say you're not feeling well; **ich glaube, ich muß morgen ~** I think I'll have to be off sick tomorrow.
krankhaft adj (a) Stelle, Zelle diseased; Vergrößerung, Zustand morbid; Aussehen sickly; Augen ill-looking. **die Untersuchungen haben keinen ~en Befund ergeben** the examinations revealed no sign(s) of disease; ~er Befund der Leber affected or diseased liver; ~e Veränderung affection; der ~e Zustand der britischen Wirtschaft the ailing condition of the British economy; **das K~e an unserer Gesellschaft** the sickness affecting our society.
(b) (seelisch) pathological; Mißtrauen, Eifersucht etc auch chronic, morbid. **sein Geiz/diese Vorstellung ist schon ~** his meanness/this idea is almost pathological or has reached almost pathological proportions.
Krankheit f (lit, fig) illness, sickness; (eine bestimmte ~ wie Krebs, Masern etc auch) disease; (von Pflanzen) disease. **wegen ~** due to illness; **eine ~ durchmachen** to have or suffer from a disease/an illness; (eine) ~ **vorschützen, eine ~ vortäuschen** to pretend to be ill, to fake an illness; **sich** (dat) **eine ~ zuziehen** to catch or contract (form) an illness or a disease; **von einer ~ befallen werden** to catch or contract (form) an illness or a disease; (Pflanze, Organ) to become diseased; **nach langer/schwerer ~** after a long/serious illness; **während/seit meiner ~** during/since my illness; **eine von ~ heimgesuchte Stadt** a city riddled with disease; **das soll ein Auto sein? das ist eine ~!** (fig inf) call that a car? that's just an apology or a miserable excuse for one or that's just a joke!
-krankheit f in cpds disease.
Krankheits-: ~bild nt symptoms pl, syndrome (spec); ~erreger m pathogene, disease-causing agent; **k~halber** adv due to illness; ~keim m germ (of a/the disease).
kränklich adj sickly, in poor or bad health.
Kränklichkeit f sickliness, poor or bad health.
Krank-: **k~machen** vi sep (inf) siehe **k~feiern**; ~meldung f notification of illness or sickness.
Kränkung f (a) insult. **etw als ~ empfinden** to take offence at sth, to be hurt by sth; **jdm eine ~ zufügen** to hurt sb. (b) (Kränken) offending, insulting. **das war eine ~ seiner Gefühle** that hurt his feelings.
Kranz m -es, ⁻e (a) wreath; (Sieger, Dichter~, Braut~ auch) garland; (fig: von Geschichten, Anekdoten etc) cycle. **da kannst du dir gleich einen ~ schicken lassen** (inf) you'll be signing your own death warrant; **das kommt nicht in die ⁻e** (Sw) it's out of the question.
(b) (kreisförmig Angeordnetes) ring, circle; (Haar~) plaits pl round one's head; (obs: von Mädchen) bevy.
(c) (Tech: Rad~) rim; (von Glocke auch) lip.
(d) (dial Cook) ring.
Kranz|arterie f coronary artery.
Kränzchen nt small wreath/garland; (fig: Kaffee~) (coffee) circle.
Kranz(e)ljungfer f (Aus) bridesmaid.
kränzen vt (liter) to garland, to adorn (with garlands).
Kranz-: ~gefäß nt (Anat) coronary artery; ~geld nt (Jur) money paid by a man to a woman as a fine on having sexual intercourse with her under the pretence of an offer of marriage; ~gesims nt (Archit) cornice.
Kranz|jungfer f siehe **Kranz(e)ljungfer**.
Kranzniederlegung f wreath-laying.
Krapfen m -s, -, **Kräppel** m -s, - (dial Cook) = doughnut.
Krapüle f -, -n (obs) rabble, riff-raff.
kraß adj (auffallend) Widerspruch, Gegensatz glaring, stark; Farben garish, glaring; Dissonanz harsh, jarring; Unterschied extreme; (unerhört) Ungerechtigkeit, Lüge blatant, gross; (extrem) Fall, Haltung extreme; Materialist, Unkenntnis crass; Egoist out-and-out, blatant; Außenseiter rank, complete; (unverblümt) Schilderung, Worte, Stil stark.
Krater m -s, - crater.
Krater-: ~landschaft f crater(ed) landscape; ~see m (Geol) crater lake.
Krätten m -s, - (S Ger, Sw) (small) basket.
Kratz-: ~beere f (dial) siehe **Brombeere**; ~bürste f wire brush; (inf) prickly character; **k~bürstig** adj (inf) prickly.
Krätzchen nt (Mil sl) forage cap.
Kratze f -, -n scraper; (Tex) carding machine.
Krätze[1] f -, no pl (a) (Med) scabies. (b) (Tech) scrapings pl, (metal) waste.
Krätze[2] f -, -n (S Ger) basket.
kratzen 1 vti (a) to scratch; (ab~ auch) to scrape (von off). **seinen Namen in die Wand ~** to scratch one's name on the wall; **der Pulli kratzt fürchterlich** the pullover scratches terribly or is terribly scratchy (inf); **der Rauch kratzt (mich) im Hals** the smoke irritates my throat; **es kratzt (mich) im Hals** my throat feels rough; **auf der Geige ~** (inf) to scrape away on the violin.
(b) (inf: stören) to bother. **das kratzt mich nicht** (inf), **das soll or kann mich nicht ~** (inf) I couldn't care less (about that), I don't give a damn (about that) (inf); **das braucht dich doch nicht

(zu) ~ it's nothing to do with you; **die Kritik hat ihn ganz schön gekratzt** the criticism really got to him *or* went home. (c) (*inf: stehlen*) to swipe (*inf*), to nick (*Brit sl*). (d) (*Tex*) to card, to tease. **2** *vr* to scratch oneself.

Kratzer *m* -s, - (*Schramme*) scratch.

Krätzer *m* -s, - (*inf*) rough *or* vinegary wine, plonk (*inf*) *no pl*; (*Aus*) sweet young Tirolean wine.

Kratzfuß *m* (*dated inf*) (low) bow (*with one foot drawn backwards*). **einen ~ machen** to bow low.

kratzig *adj* (*inf*) scratchy (*inf*).

krätzig *adj* scabious.

Kratz-: ~**putz** *m* sgraffito; ~**wunde** *f* scratch.

krauchen *vi aux sein* (*dial*) to crawl.

kraueln, krauen *vt siehe* **kraulen²**.

Kraul *nt* -(s), *no pl* (*Schwimmen*) crawl. **(im) ~ schwimmen** to do the crawl.

kraulen¹ (*Schwimmen*) *aux haben or sein* **1** *vi* to do *or* swim the crawl. **2** *vt* **er hat *or* ist die Strecke/100 m gekrault** he did the stretch using the crawl/he did a 100m's crawl.

kraulen² *vt* to fondle. **jdn am Kinn ~** to chuck sb under the chin; **jdn in den Haaren ~** to run one's fingers through sb's hair.

kraus *adj* crinkly; *Negerhaar auch, Haar, Kopf* frizzy; *Stirn* wrinkled, furrowed; (*zerknittert*) crumpled, wrinkled; (*fig: verworren*) muddled, confused. **die Stirn/Nase ~ ziehen** to wrinkle up *or* knit one's brow; (*mißbilligend*) to frown/to screw up one's nose.

Krause *f* -, -n (a) (*Hals~*) ruff; (*an Ärmeln etc*) ruffle, frill. **(b)** (*inf*) (*Krausheit*) crinkliness; (*von Negerhaar auch, von Haar, Kopf*) frizziness; (*Frisur*) frizzy hair/hairstyle. **im Regen bekomme ich eine ~** my hair goes frizzy in the rain; **Neger haben eine ~** negroes have crinkly *or* frizzy hair.

Kräuselkrepp *m* (*Tex*) crepe; (*Streifenkrepp*) seersucker.

kräuseln 1 *vt Haar* to make frizzy; (*mit Brennschere auch*) to crimp; (*mit Dauerwelle auch*) to frizz; (*Sew*) to gather (*in small folds*); (*Tex*) to crimp; *Stirn* to knit, to wrinkle; *Nase* to screw up; *Lippen* to pucker; *Wasseroberfläche* to ruffle.

2 *vr* (*Haare*) to go frizzy; (*Stoff*) to go crinkly; (*Stirn, Nase*) to wrinkle up; (*Lippen*) to pucker; (*Wasser*) to ripple; (*Rauch*) to curl (up).

krausen *vtr Haar, Stirn, Nase,* (*Sew*) *siehe* **kräuseln**.

Kraus-: **k~haarig** *adj* frizzy-haired; *Neger auch* crinkly-haired; ~**kopf** *m* frizzy head; (*Frisur*) frizzy hair/hairstyle; (*Mensch*) curly-head.

Kraut *nt* -(e)s, **Kräuter** (a) (*Pflanze: esp Heil~, Würz~*) herb. **dagegen ist kein ~ gewachsen** (*fig*) there is no remedy for that, there's nothing anyone can do about that. **(b)** *no pl* (*grüne Teile von Pflanzen*) foliage, stems and leaves *pl*, herbage; (*von Gemüse*) tops *pl*; (*Kartoffel~*) potato foliage; (*Spargel~*) asparagus leaves *pl*. **wie ~ und Rüben durcheinanderliegen** (*inf*) to lie (about) all over the place (*inf*); **ins ~ schießen** (*lit*) to run to seed; (*fig*) to get out of control, to run wild. **(c)** *no pl* (*Rot~, Weiß~*) cabbage; (*Sauer~*) sauerkraut. **(d)** (*pej: Tabak*) tobacco.

Kräuterbutter *f* herb butter.

Kräuter(er) *m* -s, - (*pej inf*) **ein alter ~** an old fogey (*inf*).

Kräuter-: ~**frau** *f* herb woman; ~**hexe** *f* (*pej*) herb woman; (*fig*) old hag (*pej*); ~**käse** *m* cheese flavoured with herbs; ~**kenner** *m* herbalist; ~**likör** *m* herbal liqueur; ~**sammler** *m* herbalist; ~**tee** *m* herb(al) tea; ~**weiblein** *nt* herb woman.

Kraut-: ~**junker** *m* (*pej*) country squire; ~**kopf** *m* (*S Ger, Aus*) (head of) cabbage; ~**salat** *m* ≈ coleslaw.

Krawall *m* -s, -e (*Aufruhr*) riot; (*inf*) (*Rauferei*) brawl; (*Lärm*) racket (*inf*), din (*inf*). ~ **machen** (*inf*) to kick up a row; (*randalieren*) to go on the rampage; (*auch* ~ **schlagen**: *sich beschweren*) to kick up a fuss.

Krawallbruder, Krawallmacher *m* (*inf*) hooligan; (*Krakeeler*) rowdy.

Krawatte *f* -, -n tie, necktie (*esp US*); (*kleiner Pelzkragen*) tippet; (*Ringkampf*) headlock.

Krawatten-: ~**halter** *m* tie clip; ~**knoten** *m* tie knot; ~**nadel** *f* tie-pin.

kraxeln *vi aux sein* (*S Ger*) to clamber (up).

Kreation *f* (*Fashion etc*) creation.

Kreativität [kreativi'tɛːt] *f* creativity.

Kreatur *f* (a) (*lit, fig, pej*) creature; (*abhängiger Mensch*) minion, creature (*liter*). **(b)** *no pl* (*alle Lebewesen*) creation. **die ~** all creation.

kreatürlich *adj* (*naturhaft*) natural; *Angst etc* animal *attr*.

Krebs *m* -es, -e (a) (*Taschen~, Einsiedler~*) crab; (*Fluß~*) crayfish, crawfish (*US*). **rot wie ein ~** red as a lobster. **(b)** (*Gattung*) crustacean; (*Hummer, Krabbe etc*) crayfish, crawfish (*US*). **(c)** (*Astron*) **der ~** Cancer, the Crab; (*Astrol*) Cancer. **(d)** (*Med*) cancer; (*Bot*) canker. **(e)** (*Typ inf*) return.

krebs-: ~**artig** *adj* (*Zool*) crablike; crayfish-like; crustaceous; (*Med*) cancerous; ~**auslösend** *adj* carcinogenic.

krebsen *vi* (a) (*Krebse fangen*) to go crabbing, to catch crabs. **(b)** (*inf: sich abmühen*) to struggle. **er hat es schwer zu ~** he really has to struggle, he finds it really hard going.

Krebs-: **k~erregend, k~erzeugend** *adj* carcinogenic; **k~erzeugend wirken** to cause cancer; ~**gang** *m* (*fig*) retrogression; **im ~gang gehen** to regress, to go backwards; ~**geschwulst** *f* (*Med*) cancer, cancerous tumour *or* growth; ~**geschwür** *nt* (*Med*) cancerous ulcer; (*fig*) cancer, cancerous growth; ~**kranke(r)** *mf* cancer victim; (*Patient*) cancer patient; **k~rot** *adj* red as a lobster; ~**schaden** *m* (*fig*) main trouble *or* problem; **das ist ein ~schaden** that's a big problem; ~**schere** *f* claws *pl or* pincers *pl* of the crab/crayfish; ~**tiere** *pl* crustaceans *pl*, crustacea *pl*; ~**zelle** *f* (*Med*) cancer cell.

Kredenz *f* (*dated, Aus*) sideboard.

kredenzen* *vt* (*liter*) **jdm etw ~** to proffer sb sth (*liter*).

Kredit¹ *m* -(e)s, -e credit; (*Darlehen auch*) loan; (*fig auch*) standing, (good) repute. **auf ~ on credit; einen ~ kündigen** to withdraw credit facilities *or* a credit; **er hat bei uns/der Bank ~** his credit is good with us/the bank; **in seiner Stammkneipe hat er ~** he gets credit at his local; **~ haben** (*fig*) to have standing *or* a good reputation; **jdm großen ~ verschaffen** (*fig*) to bring great credit to sb, to redound to sb's credit (*liter*); **das bringt ihn um allen ~** that completely discredits him.

Kredit² *nt* -s, -s (*Habenseite*) credit (side).

Kredit-: ~**anstalt** *f* credit institution, credit *or* loan bank; ~**aufnahme** *f* borrowing; **sich zu einer ~aufnahme entschließen** to decide to obtain a loan; ~**brief** *m* letter of credit; **k~fähig** *adj* credit-worthy; ~**geber** *m* creditor.

kreditieren* *vt* **jdm einen Betrag ~, jdm für einen Betrag ~** to advance sb an amount, to credit sb with an amount.

Kredit-: ~**institut** *nt* credit institution; ~**karte** *f* credit card; ~**nehmer** *m* borrower; **k~würdig** *adj* credit-worthy.

Kredo *nt* -s, -s (*lit, fig*) creed, credo.

kregel *adj* (*dial*) lively.

Kreide *f* -, -n chalk; (*Geol:* ~**zeit**) Cretaceous (period). **eine ~ a piece of chalk; bei jdm (tief) in der ~ sein** *or* **stehen** to be (deep) in debt to sb, to owe sb (a lot of) money.

Kreide-: **k~bleich** *adj* (as) white as chalk *or* a sheet; ~**felsen** *m* chalk cliff; ~**formation** *f* (*Geol*) Cretaceous (formation); **k~haltig** *adj* chalky, cretaceous (*spec*); ~**stift** *m* chalk; **k~weiß** *adj siehe* **k~bleich**; ~**zeichnung** *f* chalk drawing.

kreidig *adj* chalky.

kreieren* [kre'iːrən] *vt* (*Fashion, Theat etc, Eccl*) to create. **jdn zum Kardinal ~** (*form*) to create *or* appoint sb (a) cardinal.

Kreis *m* -es, -e (a) circle. **einen ~ beschreiben** *or* **schlagen** *or* **ziehen** to describe a circle; **einen ~ um jdn bilden** *or* **schließen** to form *or* make a circle around sb, to encircle sb; **im ~ (gehen/ sitzen)** (to go round/sit) in a circle; ~**e ziehen** (*lit*) to circle; (*weite*) ~**e ziehen** (*fig*) to have (wide) repercussions; **sich im ~ bewegen** *or* **drehen** (*lit*) to go *or* turn round in a circle; (*fig*) to go round in circles; **mir dreht sich alles im ~** everything's going round and round, my head is reeling *or* spinning; **der ~ schließt sich** (*fig*) we *etc* come full circle, the wheel turns full circle; **störe meine ~e nicht!** (*fig*) leave me in peace!

(b) (*Elec: Strom~*) circuit. **(c)** (*Bereich: von Interessen, Tätigkeit etc*) sphere; (*Ideer~*) body of ideas; (*Sagen~*) cycle. **im ~ des Scheinwerferlichtes** in the arc *or* pool of light thrown by the headlamps. **(d)** (*fig: von Menschen*) circle. **der ~ seiner Leser** his readership, his readers *pl*; **weite ~e der Bevölkerung** wide sections of the population; **im ~e von Freunden/seiner Familie** among *or* with friends/his family, in the family circle; **eine Feier im engen** *or* **kleinen ~e** a celebration for a few close friends and relatives; **ein Mann aus den besseren/besten ~en** a man belonging to high society *or* who moves in the best circles; **das kommt auch in den besten ~en vor** that happens even in the best society *or* the best of circles. **(e)** (*Stadt~, Land~*) district; (*Gemeindewahl~*) ward; (*Landeswahl~*) constituency. ~ **Leipzig** Leipzig District, the District of Leipzig.

Kreis-: ~**abschnitt** *m* segment; ~**ausschnitt** *m* sector; ~**bahn** *f* (*Astron, Space*) orbit; ~**bogen** *m* arc (of a circle).

kreischen *vi* (*old, hum: pret* **krisch**, *ptp* **gekrischen**) to screech; (*Vogel auch*) to squawk; (*Reifen, Bremsen auch*) to squeal; (*Mensch auch*) to shriek, to squeal.

Kreisel *m* -s, - (*Tech*) gyroscope; (*Spielzeug*) (spinning) top; (*inf: im Verkehr*) roundabout (*Brit*), traffic circle (*US*), rotary (*US*). **den ~ schlagen** to spin the top.

Kreisel-: ~**bewegung** *f* gyration; ~**kompaß** *m* gyroscopic compass, gyrocompass.

kreiseln *vi* (a) *aux sein or haben* (*sich drehen*) to spin around, to gyrate. **(b)** (*mit Kreisel spielen*) to play with a top, to spin a top.

kreisen *vi aux sein or haben* to circle (*um* round, *über + dat* over); (*um eine Achse*) to revolve (*um* around); (*Satellit, Planet auch*) to orbit (*um etw* sth); (*Blut, Öl etc*) to circulate (*in + dat* through); (*fig: Gedanken, Wünsche, Gespräch*) to revolve (*um* around). **die Arme ~ lassen** to swing one's arms around (in a circle); **den Becher ~ lassen** to hand the cup round.

Kreis-: ~**fläche** *f* circle; (~**inhalt**) area of a/the circle; **k~förmig** *adj* circular; **sich k~förmig bewegen** to move in a circle; **k~förmig angelegt** arranged in a circle; **k~frei** *adj* **k~freie Stadt** town which is an administrative district in its own right; ~**inhalt** *m* area of a/the circle; ~**kolbenmotor** *m* rotary piston engine.

Kreislauf *m* (*Blut~, Öl~, von Geld*) circulation; (*der Natur, des Wassers*) cycle.

Kreislauf-: ~**kollaps** *m* circulatory collapse; **nach der Anstrengung hatte ich einen kleinen ~kollaps** after the exercise I collapsed; ~**mittel** *nt* cardiac stimulant; ~**störungen** *pl* circulation *or* circulatory trouble *sing or* disorders *pl*.

Kreis-: ~**linie** *f* circle; **vom Mittelpunkt durch die ~linie** from the centre through the circumference (of a/the circle); **k~rund** *adj* (perfectly) circular; ~**säge** *f* circular saw; (*inf: Hut*) boater.

kreißen *vi* (*old*) to be in labour. **der Berg kreißt und gebiert eine Maus** (*prov*) the mountain laboured and brought forth a mouse.

Kreißsaal *m* delivery room.

Kreis-: ~**stadt** *f* chief town of a district, district town, ≈ county town (*Brit*); ~**tag** *m* district assembly, ≈ county council (*Brit*); ~**umfang** *m* circumference (of a/the circle); ~**verkehr** *m* roundabout (*Brit*) *or* rotary (*US*) traffic; (*Kreisel*) roundabout (*Brit*), traffic circle (*US*), rotary (*US*); **im ~verkehr muß man ... on a roundabout *etc* one must ...; dort gibt es viel ~verkehr**

there are a lot of roundabouts *etc* there; ~**wehrersatzamt** *nt* district recruiting office.

Krem *f* -, -s *or* *m* -s, -e (*inf*) *siehe* **Creme**.

Krematorium *nt* crematorium.

kremig *adj* creamy. **etw** ~ **schlagen** to cream sth.

Kreml *m* -s **der** ~ the Kremlin.

Krempe *f* -, -n (*Hut~*) brim. **ein Hut mit breiter** ~ a broad-brimmed hat.

Krempel[1] *m* -s, *no pl* (*inf*) (*Sachen*) stuff (*inf*), things *pl*; (*wertloses Zeug*) junk, rubbish. **ich werfe den ganzen** ~ **hin** I'm chucking the whole lot *or* business in (*inf*); **dann kannst du deinen** ~ **allein machen** then you can (damn well *inf*) do it yourself.

Krempel[2] *f* -, -n carding machine.

krempeln *vt* (a) (*Tex*) to card. (b) *siehe* **hoch~**, **um~** *etc*.

Kremser *m* -s, - charabanc.

Kren *m* -s, *no pl* (*Aus*) horse-radish.

Kreole *m* -n, -n, **Kreolin** *f* Creole.

kreolisch *adj* Creole.

krepieren* *vi aux sein* (a) (*platzen*) to explode, to go off. (b) (*sl: sterben*) to croak (it) (*sl*), to snuff it (*sl*), to kick the bucket (*inf*); (*inf: elend sterben*) to die a wretched death. **das Tier ist ihm krepiert** (*inf*) the animal died on him (*inf*).

Krepp *m* -s, -e *or* -s crepe.

Kreppapier *nt getrennt* **Krepp-papier** crepe paper.

Kreppsohle *f* crepe sole.

Kresse *f* -, *no pl* cress.

Kreta *nt* -s Crete.

Kreter(in *f*) *m* -s, - Cretan.

Krethi und Plethi *pl no art* (*inf*) every Tom, Dick and Harry.

Kretin [kre'tɛ̃:] *m* -s, -s (*Med, pej*) cretin.

Kretinismus *m* (*Med*) cretinism.

kretisch *adj* Cretan.

Kreton [kre'to:n] *m* -s, -e (*Aus*), **Kretonne** [kre'tɔn] *m or f* -, -s (*Tex*) cretonne.

kreucht (*obs, poet*) 3 *pers sing of* **kriechen**. **alles was da** ~ **und fleucht** all living creatures, all things that do creep and fly (*poet*).

Kreuz[1] *nt* -es, -e (a) cross; (*als Anhänger etc*) crucifix. **das** ~ **des Südens** (*Astron*) the Southern Cross; **jdn ans** ~ **schlagen** *or* **nageln** to nail sb to the cross; **ein** ~ **schlagen** *or* **machen** to make the sign of the cross; **sich bekreuzigen auch**) to cross oneself; **zwei Gegenstände über** ~ **legen** to put two objects crosswise one on top of the other; **mit jdm über** ~ **sein** *or* **stehen** (*fig*) to be on bad terms with sb; **sein** ~ **geduldig tragen** (*geh*) to bear one's cross with patience; **sein** ~ **auf sich nehmen** (*fig*) to take up one's cross; **es ist ein** ~ **ich habe mein** ~ **mit ihm/damit** he's/it's an awful problem; **ich mache drei** ~**e**, **wenn er geht** (*inf*) it'll be such a relief when he has gone; **er machte ein** ~ (**als Unterschrift/am Rand**) he put a cross (for his signature/in the margin); **zu** ~**e kriechen** (*fig*) to eat humble pie, to eat crow (*US*).

(b) (*Anat*) small of the back; (*von Tier*) back. **ich habe Schmerzen im** ~ I've got (a) backache; **ich hab's im** ~ (*inf*) I have back trouble; **aufs** ~ **fallen** to fall on one's back; (*fig inf*) to be staggered (*inf*), to fall through the floor (*inf*); **jdn aufs** ~ **legen** to throw sb on his back; (*fig inf*) to take sb for a ride (*inf*); (*vulg*) **Mädchen** to lay sb (*sl*); **jdm Geld aus dem** ~ **leiern** (*sl*) to wheedle some money out of sb.

(c) (*Archit: Fenster~*) mullion and transom.

(d) (*Typ*) dagger, obelisk.

(e) (*Mus*) sharp.

(f) (*Autobahn~*) intersection.

(g) (*Cards*) (*Farbe*) clubs *pl*; (*Karte*) club. **die** ~**-Dame** the Queen of Clubs.

Kreuz[2] *f*: **in die** ~ **und in die Quer** this way and that.

kreuz *adj*: ~ **und quer** all over; ~ **und quer durch die Gegend fahren** to drive/travel all over the place; **sie liefen/lagen** ~ **und quer durcheinander** they were running/lying all over the place.

Kreuz-: ~**abnahme** *f* Descent from the Cross; ~**band** *nt* (a) (*Anat*) crucial ligament; (b) (*Post: Streifband*) wrapper; ~**bein** *nt* (*Anat*) sacrum; (*von Tieren*) rump-bone; ~**blume** *f* (*Bot*) milkwort; (*Archit*) finial; ~**blütler** *pl* -s, - cruciferous plants *pl*; **k~brav** *adj* **Kind** terribly good *or* well-behaved, as good as gold; **k~dumm** *adj* (*inf*) awfully stupid, totally dense.

kreuzen 1 *vt* to cross (*auch Biol*). **die Degen** *or* **Klingen** *or* **Schwerter mit jdm** ~ (*lit, fig*) to cross swords with sb; **die Arme** ~ to fold *or* cross one's arms.

2 *vr* to cross; (*Meinungen, Interessen*) to clash; (*Biol*) to interbreed. **unsere Wege haben sich nie wieder gekreuzt** our paths have never crossed again.

3 *vi aux haben* or *sein* (*Naut*) to cruise; (*Zickzack fahren*) to tack.

Kreuzer *m* -s, - (a) (*Naut*) cruiser. (b) (*Hist: Münze*) kreutzer.

Kreuzes-: ~**tod** *m* (death by) crucifixion; **den** ~**tod erleiden** to die on the cross; ~**zeichen** *nt* sign of the cross.

Kreuz-: ~**fahrer** *m* (*Hist*) crusader; ~**fahrt** *f* (a) (*Naut*) cruise; **eine** ~**fahrt machen** to go on a cruise; (b) (*Hist*) crusade; ~**feuer** *nt* (*Mil, fig*) crossfire; **im** ~**feuer** (**der Kritik**) **stehen** (*fig*) to be under fire (from all sides); **ins** ~**feuer** (**der Kritik**) **geraten** (*fig*) to come under fire (from all sides); **k~fidel** *adj* (*inf*) happy as a sandboy (*inf*) *or* lark; **k~förmig** *adj* cross-shaped, cruciform (*form*); **etw k~förmig anordnen** to arrange sth crossways *or* crosswise; ~**gang** *m* cloister; ~**gelenk** *nt* (*Tech*) universal joint; ~**gewölbe** *nt* (*Archit*) cross *or* groin vault.

kreuzigen *vt* to crucify.

Kreuzigung *f* crucifixion.

Kreuz-: ~**knoten** *m* reef-knot; **k~lahm** *adj* **Pferd** broken-

backed; (*inf*) **Mensch** exhausted; **jetzt bin ich aber k~lahm** I'm exhausted and my back's killing me; ~**lähme** -, -n *f* (*Vet*) paralysis of the hindquarters; ~**mast** *m* (*Naut*) mizzen mast; ~**otter** *f* (*Zool*) adder, viper; ~**rippengewölbe** *nt* (*Archit*) ribbed vault; ~**ritter** *m* (*Hist*) crusader; (*vom deutschen Ritterorden*) knight of the Teutonic Order; ~**schmerzen** *pl* backache *sing*, pains *pl* in the small of the back; ~**schnabel** *m* (*Orn*) crossbill; ~**spinne** *f* (*Zool*) garden *or* cross spider; **k~ständig** *adj* (*Bot*) decussate; ~**stich** *m* (*Sew*) cross-stitch.

Kreuzung *f* (*Straßen*~) crossroads *sing or pl* (*esp Brit*), intersection (*esp US*). (b) (*das Kreuzen*) crossing; (*von Tieren auch*) cross-breeding, interbreeding. (c) (*Rasse*) hybrid; (*Tiere auch*) cross, cross-breed.

kreuzunglücklich *adj* absolutely miserable.

kreuzungsfrei *adj* without crossroads.

Kreuz-: ~**verband** *m* (*Med*) crossed bandage; (*Build*) cross bond; ~**verhör** *nt* cross-examination; **jdn ins** ~**verhör nehmen** to cross-examine sb; ~**weg** *m* (*Wegkreuzung, fig*) crossroads *sing*; (b) (*Rel: Christi Leidensweg*) way of the cross; (*Eccl: in Kirche auch*) stations of the cross *pl*; **den** ~**weg beten** to do the stations of the cross; **k~weise** *adv* crosswise, crossways; **du kannst mich k~weise**! (*sl!*) (you can) get stuffed! (*sl*); ~**worträtsel** *nt* crossword puzzle; ~**zeichen** *nt* sign of the cross; ~**zug** *m* (*lit, fig*) crusade.

Krevette [kre'vɛtə] *f* shrimp.

kribb(e)lig *adj* (*inf*) fidgety, edgy (*inf*); (*kribbelnd*) tingly (*inf*).

kribbeln 1 *vt* (*kitzeln*) to tickle; (*jucken*) to make itch; (*prickeln*) to make tingle.

2 *vi* (a) (*jucken*) to itch, to tickle; (*prickeln*) to prickle, to tingle. **auf der Haut** ~ to cause a prickling sensation; (*angenehm*) to make the skin tingle; **es kribbelt mir im Fuß** (*lit*) I have pins and needles in my foot; **es kribbelt mir** *or* **mich** (**in den Fingern**), **etw zu tun** (*inf*) I'm itching/I get an itch to do sth.

(b) *aux sein* (*Insekten*) ~ (**und krabbeln**) to scurry *or* swarm (around); **es kribbelt von Ameisen** the place is crawling *or* swarming *or* teeming with ants; **es kribbelt und krabbelt wie in einem Ameisenhaufen** it's like an ant-hill.

krickelig *adj* (*inf*) *siehe* **krakelig**.

Krickelkrakel *nt* -s, - *siehe* **Gekrakel**.

krickeln *vi* (*inf*) *siehe* **krakeln**.

Kricket *nt* -s, -s (*Sport*) cricket.

Krida *f* -, *no pl* faked bankruptcy.

kriechen *pret* **kroch**, *ptp* **gekrochen** *vi aux sein* to creep (*auch Pflanze, Tech*), to crawl (*auch Schlange*); (*langsam fahren*) to creep *or* crawl (along); (*fig: Zeit*) to creep by; (*fig: unterwürfig sein*) to grovel (*vor* +*dat* before), to crawl (*vor* +*dat* to). **aus dem Ei** ~ to hatch (out); **ins Bett** ~ (*inf*) to go to bed; (*sehr müde, erschöpft*) to crawl into bed; **unter die Bettdecke** ~ to slip under the covers *or* blankets; *siehe* **Kreuz**[1], **Leim**.

Kriecher *m* -s, - (*inf*) groveller, bootlicker (*inf*), crawler (*inf*).

kriecherisch *adj* (*inf*) grovelling, servile, bootlicking *attr* (*inf*).

Kriech-: ~**spur** *f* crawler lane; ~**strom** *m* (*Elec*) leakage current; ~**tier** *nt* (*Zool*) reptile.

Krieg *m* -(e)s, -e war; (*Art der Kriegsführung*) warfare. ~ **anfangen mit** to start a war with; **einer Partei** *etc* **den** ~ **ansagen** (*fig*) to declare war on a party *etc*; ~ **führen** (**mit** *or* **gegen**) to wage war (on); **in** ~ **und Frieden** in war and in peace; **im** ~**(e)** sein in war; (*als Soldat*) away in the war, away fighting; **im** ~ **sein** *or* **stehen** (**mit**), ~ **haben mit** to be at war (with); **im** ~**e fallen**, **im** ~ **bleiben** (*inf*) to be killed in the war *or* in action; **in den** ~ **ziehen** to go to war; **häuslicher** ~ (*fig*) domestic strife; **in einem ständigen** ~ **leben** (*fig*) to be constantly feuding.

kriegen *vt* (*inf*) to get; **Zug, Bus, Schnupfen, Weglaufenden auch** to catch; **Schlaganfall, eine Spritze, Besuch auch** to have; **Junge, ein Kind auch** to have; **sie kriegt ein Kind** she's going to have a baby; **graue Haare/eine Glatze** ~ to get grey hairs, to go grey/bald; **eine** ~ to catch one; **sie** *or* **es** ~ to get a hiding; **es mit der Angst/Wut** ~ to get scared/angry; **es mit jdm zu tun** ~ to be in trouble with sb; **wenn ich dich kriege!** just you wait till I catch you!; **sie** ~ **sich** (*in Kitschroman*) boy gets girl; **das werden wir schon** ~ we'll fix it, that's no problem; **dann kriege ich zuviel** then it gets too much for me; **was kriegt der Herr?** yes sir, what will you have?; **ich kriege ein Steak** I'll have a steak; ~ **Sie schon?** are you being *or* have you been served *or* done (*inf*)?; **jdn dazu** ~, **etw zu tun** to get sb to do sth; **etw gemacht** ~ to get sth done; **das kriege ich einfach nicht übersetzt** I just can't get it translated; **kann ich das bestätigt** ~? can I have *or* get that confirmed?

Kriegen *nt* -s, *no pl* (game of) tag.

Krieger *m* -s, - warrior; (*Indianer*~) brave. **alter** ~ veteran (soldier), old campaigner *or* warhorse; **ein müder** ~ **sein** (*fig inf*) to have no go left in one.

Kriegerdenkmal *nt* war memorial.

kriegerisch *adj* warlike *no adv*; **Haltung auch** belligerent. **eine** ~**e Auseinandersetzung** fighting *no pl*, military conflict.

Kriegerwitwe *f* war-widow.

Krieg-: **k~führend** *adj* belligerent, warring; **die** ~**führenden** the belligerents; ~**führung** *f* warfare *no art*; (*eines Feldherrn*) conduct of the war.

Kriegs-: ~**anleihe** *f* war loan; ~**ausbruch** *m* outbreak of war; **kurz nach** ~**ausbruch** shortly after the outbreak of war; **es kam zum** ~**ausbruch** war broke out; **k~bedingt** *adj* resulting from *or* caused by (the) war; ~**beginn** *m* start of the war; ~**beil** *nt* tomahawk; **das** ~**beil begraben/ausgraben** (*fig*) to bury the hatchet/to start a fight; ~**bemalung** *f* (*lit, hum*) warpaint; ~**berichterstatter** *m* war correspondent; **k~beschädigt** *adj* war-disabled; ~**beschädigte(r)** *mf decl as adj* war-disabled (ex-serviceman); ~**blinde(r)** *mf* war-blinded person; **die**

~**blinden** the war-blind; ~**dienst** m (old, form) military service; **den** ~**dienst verweigern** to be a conscientious objector.
Kriegsdienst-: ~**verweigerer** m -s, - conscientious objector; ~**verweigerung** f refusal to fight in a war; **wegen** ~**verweigerung wurde er ... because he was a conscientious** objector he was ...
Kriegs-: ~**einwirkung** f effects pl or aftermath no pl of war; ~**ende** nt end of the war; ~**entschädigungen** pl reparations pl; ~**erklärung** f declaration of war; ~**erlebnis** nt war-time experience; ~**fall** m (eventuality of) a war; **dann träte der** ~**fall ein** then war would break out; ~**film** m war film; ~**flagge** f naval ensign; ~**flotte** f navy, fleet; ~**flugzeug** nt military aeroplane or aircraft, warplane (US); ~**folge** f consequence of (a/the) war; ~**freiwillige(r)** mf (wartime) volunteer; ~**fuß** m (inf): **mit jdm auf** ~**fuß stehen** to be at loggerheads with sb; **mit der englischen Sprache auf** ~**fuß stehen** to find the English language heavy going (inf); ~**gebiet** nt war-zone; ~**gefahr** f danger of war; ~**gefahr zieht herauf** (geh) the war clouds are gathering; ~**gefangene(r)** mf prisoner of war, P.O.W.; ~**gefangenschaft** f captivity; **in** ~**gefangenschaft sein** to be a prisoner of war; **aus der** ~**gefangenschaft kommen** to return or be released from captivity; ~**gegner** m (a) opponent of a/the war; (Pazifist) pacifist, opponent of war; (b) (Gegner im Krieg) war-time enemy; ~**geheul** nt war-cry; ~**gericht** nt (war-time) court-martial; **jdn vor ein** ~**gericht stellen** to court-martial sb; ~**geschrei** nt war-cry; ~**gewinnler(in** f) m -s, - (pej) war-profiteer; ~**glück** nt (liter) fortunes of war pl; **dann verließ Hannibal sein** ~**glück** then the fortunes of war turned against or deserted Hannibal; ~**gott** m god of war; ~**göttin** f goddess of war; ~**gräberfürsorge** f War Graves Commission; ~**greuel** pl war atrocities pl; ~**grund** m reason for war; ~**hafen** m naval port or harbour; ~**handwerk** nt (old) soldiering; ~**held** m great warrior; (in moderner Zeit) military hero; ~**herr** m (Hist): **oberster** ~**herr** commander-in-chief; ~**hetze** f war-mongering; ~**hetzer** m -s, - (pej) war-monger; ~**hinterbliebene(r)** mf war-widow/orphan; **die** ~**hinterbliebenen** those who lost a husband or father in the war; ~**invalide(r)** mf siehe ~**beschädigte(r)**; ~**jahr** nt year of war; **die** ~**jahre** the war years; **im** ~**jahr 1945** (during the war) in 1945; **im dritten** ~**jahr** in the third year of the war; ~**kamerad** m fellow soldier, war(-time) comrade; ~**kasse** f war-chest; ~**kind** nt war-baby; ~**knecht** m (old) mercenary; ~**kosten** pl cost of the war sing; ~**kunst** f art of war(fare); ~**list** f (old, liter) ruse of war, stratagem; **k**~**lüstern** adj (pej) bellicose; ~**marine** f navy; **k**~**mäßig** adj for war; ~**minister** m (Hist, Pol pej) minister of war; ~**ministerium** nt (Hist) War Office (Brit), War Department (US); **k**~**müde** adj war-weary; ~**opfer** nt war victim; ~**pfad** m (liter): **auf dem** ~**pfad** on the war-path; ~**rat** m council of war; ~**rat halten** (fig) to have a pow-wow (inf); ~**recht** nt conventions of war pl; (Mil) martial law; ~**schäden** pl war damage; ~**schauplatz** m theatre of war; ~**schiff** nt war-ship, man-of-war; ~**schuld** f war guilt; ~**schulden** pl war debts pl; ~**spiel** nt war game; ~**stärke** f war establishment; **die Armee auf** ~**stärke bringen** to make the army ready for war; ~**teilnehmer** m combatant; (Staat) combatant nation, belligerent; (ehemaliger Soldat) ex-serviceman; ~**trauung** f war wedding; ~**treiber** m -s, - (pej) war-monger; **k**~**tüchtig** adj (old) fit for active service; **k**~**untauglich** adj unfit for active service; ~**verbrechen** nt war crime; ~**verbrecher** m war criminal; ~**verbrecherprozeß** m war crime trial; ~**verletzung** f war wound; **k**~**versehrt** adj siehe **k**~**beschädigt**; **k**~**verwendungsfähig** adj (form) fit for active service; ~**volk** nt (old, liter) soldiers pl, soldiery (old); ~**waise** f war orphan; ~**wesen** nt warfare; **k**~**wichtig** adj essential to the war effort; ~**wirren** pl (geh) chaos of war sing; ~**wirtschaft** f war economy; ~**zeit** f wartime; **in** ~**zeiten** in times of war; **sie erzählten von ihrer** ~**zeit** they told about their wartime experiences; **nach über zwanzigjähriger** ~**zeit** after over twenty years of war; **k**~**zerstört** adj destroyed by war; **Land** auch war-shattered; ~**zug** m (old) campaign, military expedition; ~**zustand** m state of war; **im** ~**zustand** at war.
Kriek|ente f (green-winged) teal.
Krill m -(s), no pl (Biol) krill.
Krim f - **die** the Crimea.
Krimi m -s, -s (inf) (crime) thriller; (mit Detektiv als Held) detective novel; (rätselhaft) murder mystery, whodunnit (inf); (moderner Film, Fernsehsendung) crime series sing; crime film.
Kriminalbeamte(r) m detective, CID officer (Brit).
Kriminale(r) m decl as adj (sl) plain-clothes man, detective, CID officer (Brit).
Kriminal-: ~**film** m crime thriller or film or movie (esp US); (rätselhaft) whodunnit (inf); ~**gericht** nt siehe **Strafgericht**; ~**groteske** f black comedy; ~**hörspiel** nt radio thriller; (rätselhaft) murder mystery, whodunnit (inf).
kriminalisieren* vt (a) (zum Kriminellen machen) **jdn** ~ **to make sb turn to crime; die** ~**den Wirkungen des Drogenmißbrauchs** the crime-inducing consequences of drug abuse.
(b) (als kriminell hinstellen) (durch Gesetz) to make a crime or a criminal offence; (in der öffentlichen Meinung) to represent as (being) criminal.
Kriminalist m criminologist.
Kriminalistik f criminology.
kriminalistisch adj criminological.
Kriminalität f crime; (Ziffer) crime rate.
Kriminal-: ~**kommissar** m detective superintendent; ~**komödie** f comedy thriller; ~**literatur** f crime literature; ~**museum** nt crime museum; ~**polizei** f criminal investigation department; ~**polizist** m detective, CID officer (Brit); ~**psychologie** f criminal psychology; ~**roman** m siehe **Krimi**

(crime) thriller; detective novel; murder mystery, whodunnit (inf); ~**stück** nt thriller; detective play; murder mystery, whodunnit (inf); **k**~**technisch** adj forensic.
kriminell adj (lit, fig inf) criminal. ~ **werden** to turn to crime, to become a criminal; (junger Mensch auch) to become delinquent.
Kriminelle(r) mf decl as adj criminal.
Kriminologie f criminology.
Krimkrieg m Crimean War.
Krimskrams m -es, no pl (inf) odds and ends pl, bits and pieces pl, rubbish.
Kringel m -s, - (der Schrift) squiggle; (Cook: Zucker~ etc) ring.
kringelig adj crinkly. **sich** ~ **lachen** (inf) to laugh oneself silly (inf), to kill oneself (laughing) (inf).
kringeln vr to go frizzy, to curl. **sich** ~ **vor Lachen** (inf) to kill oneself (laughing) (inf).
Krinoline f (Hist) crinoline.
Kripo f -, -s (inf) abbr of **Kriminalpolizei. die** ~ the cops (inf) pl, the CID (Brit).
Kripo- in cpds (inf) police.
Krippe f -, -n (a) (Futter~) (hay)rack, (hay)box. **sich an die** ~ **drängen** (fig) to start jockeying for position; **an der** ~ **sitzen** (fig) to live a life of ease, to live in comfort. (b) (Kinder~, Weihnachts~) crib; (Bibl auch) manger. (c) (Kinderhort) crèche. (d) (Astron) manger.
Krippenspiel nt nativity play.
krisch (old, hum) pret of **kreischen.**
Krise f -, -n crisis. **in eine** ~ **geraten** to enter a state of crisis; **er hatte eine schwere** ~ he was going through a difficult crisis.
kriseln vi impers (inf) **es kriselt** there is a crisis looming, there is trouble brewing.
Krisen-: **k**~**anfällig** adj crisis-prone; **k**~**fest** adj stable, crisis-proof; **er hat sein Geld k**~**fest in Grundbesitz angelegt** he put his money in property to secure it against or to hedge against economic crises; ~**gebiet** nt crisis area; ~**herd** m flash point, trouble spot; ~**management** nt crisis management; ~**stab** m (special) action or crisis committee.
Krisis f -, **Krisen** (liter) siehe **Krise.**
krisselig adj (dial) curdled.
Kristall[1] m -s, -e crystal. ~**e bilden** to crystallize, to form crystals.
Kristall[2] nt -s, no pl (~**glas**) crystal (glass); (~**waren**) crystalware, crystal goods pl.
Kristallbildung f crystallization.
kristallen adj (made of) crystal; **Stimme** crystal-clear.
Kristall-: ~**gitter** nt crystal lattice; ~**glas** nt crystal glass.
kristallin, kristallinisch adj crystalline.
Kristallisation f crystallization.
Kristallisationspunkt m (fig) focal point.
kristallisieren* vir (lit, fig) to crystallize.
Kristalleuchter m getrennt **Kristall-leuchter** crystal chandelier.
Kristall-: **k**~**klar** adj crystal-clear; ~**leuchter, ~lüster** (geh) m siehe **Kristalleuchter**; ~**nacht** f (Hist) Crystal night, night of 9th/10th November 1938, during which the Nazis organized a pogrom throughout Germany, burning synagogues and breaking windows of Jewish shops.
Kristallüster m getrennt **Kristall-lüster** siehe **Kristallleuchter.**
Kristall-: ~**waren** pl crystalware sing, crystal goods pl; ~**zucker** m refined sugar (in) crystals.
Kristiania m -s, -s (Ski) (stem) Christy, Christiania (turn).
Kriterium nt (a) criterion. (b) (Radfahren) circuit race.
Kritik f -, -en (a) no pl criticism (an + dat of). **an jdm/etw** ~ **üben** to criticize sb/sth; **Gesellschafts-/Literatur~** social/ literary criticism; **unter aller** ~ **sein** (inf) to be beneath contempt.
(b) (Rezensieren) criticism; (Rezension auch) review, notice, crit (inf). **eine gute** ~ **haben** to get good reviews etc.
(c) no pl (die Kritiker) critics pl.
(d) no pl (Urteilsfähigkeit) discrimination. **ohne jede** ~ uncritically.
(e) (Philos, kritische Analyse) critique.
Kritikaster m -s, - (dated pej) caviller, fault-finder, criticaster (rare).
Kritiker(in f) m -s, - critic.
Kritik-: ~**fähigkeit** f critical faculty; **k**~**los** adj uncritical.
kritisch adj (alle Bedeutungen) critical. **jdm/einer Sache** ~ **gegenüberstehen** to be critical of sb/sth, to regard or consider sb/sth critically; **dann wird es** ~ it could be critical.
kritisieren* vti to criticize. **er hat or findet an allem etw zu** ~ he always has or finds something to criticize.
Kritizismus m (Philos) critical philosophy.
Krittelei f fault-finding no pl, cavilling no pl.
kritteln vi to find fault (an + dat, über + acc with), to cavil (an + dat, über + acc at).
Kritzelei f scribble; (das Kritzeln) scribbling; (Männchenmalen etc) doodle; doodling; (an Wänden) graffiti.
kritzeln vti to scribble, to scrawl; (Männchen malen etc) to doodle.
Kroate m -n, -n, **Kroatin** f Croat, Croatian.
Kroatien [kro'a:tsiən] nt -s Croatia.
kroatisch adj Croat, Croatian.
Kroatzbeere f (esp S Ger) siehe **Brombeere.**
kroch pret of **kriechen.**
Krocket(spiel) ['krokət-, kro'ket-] nt -s, no pl croquet.
Krokant m -s, no pl (Cook) cracknel.
Krokette f (Cook) croquette.
Kroki nt -s, -s sketch map.
Kroko nt -s, no pl crocodile leather.

Krokodil *nt* -s, -e crocodile.
Krokodilleder *nt* crocodile leather *or* skin.
Krokodilstränen *pl* crocodile tears *pl*.
Krokus *m* -, *or* -se crocus.
Krönchen *nt dim of* **Krone.**
Krone *f* -, -n (a) crown; (*eines Grafen etc*) coronet. die ~ (*fig*) the Crown.
    (b) (*Mauer~*) coping; (*Schaum~*) cap, crest; (*Zahn~*) crown, cap; (*an Uhr*) winder; (*Geweih~*) surroyal (antler); (*Baum~*) top; (*Ernte~*) harvest wreath *or* crown. die ~ der Schöpfung the pride of creation, creation's crowning glory; die ~ des Lebens (*Bibl*) (a) crown of life; die ~ der Frechheit/Dummheit *etc* the height of impertinence/stupidity *etc*; die ~ des Ganzen war, daß … (*fig*) (just) what crowned *or* capped it all was that …; das setzt doch allem die ~ auf (*inf*) that beats everything; das setzt der Dummheit die ~ auf (*inf*) that beats everything for stupidity; meine Bemerkung ist ihr in die ~ gefahren she has taken offence *or* umbrage at *or* has gone into a huff at my remark; was ist ihm in die ~ gestiegen? (*inf*) what's up with him?, what's got into him? (*inf*); einen in der ~ haben (*inf*) to be tipsy, to have had a drop too much; dabei fällt dir keine Perle *or* kein Stein *or* Zacken aus der ~ (*inf*) it won't hurt you; wenn du mal mit der U-Bahn fährst, fällt dir auch kein Zacken aus der ~ (*inf*) surely it won't be too much of a blow to your dignity to travel by underground.
    (c) (*Währungseinheit*) (*Hist, in der CSSR*) crown; (*in Skandinavien*) krone; (*in Schweden*) krona.
krönen *vt* (*lit, fig*) to crown; *Bauwerk* to crown, to top, to cap. jdn zum König ~ to crown sb king; von Erfolg gekrönt sein/werden to be crowned with success; gekrönte Häupter crowned heads; damit wurde eine glänzende Laufbahn gekrönt this was the crowning achievement in *or* culmination of his career; der ~de Abschluß the culmination.
Kronen-: ~korken *m* crown cork; ~mutter *f* (*Tech*) castle nut.
Kron-: ~erbe *m* heir to the Crown *or* Throne; ~gut *nt* crown estate; ~kolonie *f* crown colony; ~land *nt* crown land.
Krönlein *nt dim of* **Krone.**
Kron-: ~leuchter *m* chandelier; ~prätendent *m* pretender (to the crown); ~prinz *m* crown prince; (*in Großbritannien auch*) Prince of Wales; (*fig*) heir apparent; ~prinzessin *f* crown princess; ~rat *m* crown council.
Kronsbeere *f* (*N Ger*) siehe **Preiselbeere.**
Krönung *f* coronation; (*fig*) culmination; (*von Veranstaltung*) high point, culmination; (*Archit*) coping stone.
Kronzeuge *m* (*Jur*) person who gives *or* turns King's/Queen's evidence *or* (*US*) State's evidence; (*fig*) main authority. ~ sein, als ~ auftreten to turn King's/Queen's/State's evidence.
Kropf *m* -(e)s, ¨e (a) (*von Vogel*) crop. (b) (*Med*) goitre.
Kröpfchen *nt dim of* **Kropf (a).**
kröpfen 1 *vt* (*füttern, nudeln*) to cram. 2 *vi* (*fressen: Raubvögel*) to gorge.
Kropftaube *f* pouter (pigeon).
Kroppzeug *nt* (*pej inf: Gesindel*) scum. dieses ganze ~ all this junk (*inf*).
kroß *adj* (*N Ger*) crisp; *Brötchen auch* crusty.
Krösus *m* -, -se Croesus. ich bin doch kein ~ (*inf*) I'm not made of money (*inf*).
Kröte *f* -, -n (*Zool*) toad. eine freche (kleine) ~ (*inf*) a cheeky (little) minx (*inf*); eine giftige ~ (*inf*) a spiteful creature. (b) ~n *pl* (*sl*) pennies (*inf*).
Krötentest *m* (*Med*) Hogben (pregnancy) test.
krötig *adj* (*inf*) stroppy (*inf*).
Krücke *f* -, -n (a) crutch; (*fig*) prop, stay. auf *or* an ~n (*dat*) gehen to walk on crutches. (b) (*Schirm~*) crook. (c) (*zum Harken etc*) rake. (d) (*sl: Stock*) stick. (e) (*sl: Nichtskönner*) dead loss (*inf*), washout (*inf*).
Krückstock *m* walking-stick; siehe **Blinde(r).**
krud(e) *adj* (*geh*) crude.
Krudität *f* (*geh*) crudity.
Krug *m* -(e)s, ¨e (a) (*Milch~ etc*) jug, pitcher (*old*); (*Wein~ auch*) flagon; (*Bier~*) (beer-)mug, stein, tankard; (*Maß~*) litre mug; (*Kruke*) jar. der ~ geht so lange zum Brunnen, bis er bricht (*Prov*) one day you/they *etc* will come unstuck *or* to grief. (b) (*N Ger: Wirtshaus*) inn, pub (*Brit*).
Krügel *nt* -s, - (*Aus*) half-litre mug.
Krüger *m* -s, - (*N Ger*) landlord (*Brit*), innkeeper.
Kruke *f* -, -n stone jar; (*Wärm~*) bed-warmer, earthenware *or* stone hot-water bottle. eine komische ~ (*dated inf*) a queer fish (*inf*).
Krümchen *nt dim of* **Krume** crumb.
Krume *f* -, -n (*geh*) (a) (*Brot~*) crumb. (b) (*liter: Acker~*) (top)soil.
Krümel *m* -s, - (a) (*Brot~ etc*) crumb. (b) (*inf: Kind*) little one, tiny tot (*inf*).
krümelig *adj* crumbly.
Krümelkacker *m* (*sl*) quibbler, nit-picker (*sl*).
krümeln *vti* to crumble; (*beim Essen*) to make crumbs.
krumm *adj* (a) (*lit*) crooked; (*verbogen auch*) bent; (*hakenförmig*) hooked; *Beine auch* bandy; *Rücken* hunched. ~e Nase hook(ed) nose; ~ gewachsen crooked; etw ~ biegen to bend sth; ~ und schief askew, skew-whiff (*inf*); sich ~ und schief lachen (*inf*) to fall about laughing (*inf*); sich ~ ärgern (*inf*) to be/get furious; ~ und lahm stiff (as a poker); jdn ~ und lahm schlagen to beat sb black and blue; keinen Finger ~ machen (*inf*) not to lift a finger; eine ~e Hand machen (*inf*) to hold one's hand out; einen ~en Rücken machen to stoop; (*fig*) to bow and scrape; mach nicht solchen ~en Rücken! straighten your shoulders, hold yourself straight; steh/sitz nicht so ~ da! stand/sit up straight, don't slouch; ~ gehen to walk with a stoop.

    (b) (*inf: unehrlich*) crooked (*inf*). ~er Hund (*pej*) crooked swine; ein ~es Ding drehen (*sl*) to do something crooked; er hat während seiner Zeit als Buchhalter viele ~e Dinger gedreht (*sl*) while he was a book-keeper he got up to all sorts of crooked tricks *or* he was up to all sorts of fiddles (*inf*); etw auf die ~e Tour versuchen to try to fiddle (*inf*) *or* wangle (*inf*) sth; er hat sie auf die ~e Tour herumgekriegt he conned her (*inf*); ~e Wege gehen to err from the straight and narrow.
krummbeinig *adj* bow-legged, bandy(-legged).
Krümme *f* -, -n (*old*) bend.
krümmen 1 *vt* to bend. die Katze krümmte den Buckel the cat arched its back; gekrümmte Oberfläche curved surface.
    2 *vr* to bend; (*Fluß*) to wind; (*Straße*) to bend, to curve; (*Wurm*) to writhe. sich ~ und winden (*fig*) to squirm; sich vor Lachen ~ to double up with laughter, to crease up (*inf*); sich vor Schmerzen (*dat*) ~ to double up *or* writhe with pain.
Krumm-: ~horn *nt* crumhorn, krummhorn; k~lachen *vr sep* (*inf*) to double up *or* fall about laughing *or* with laughter; k~legen *vr sep* (*inf*) to pinch and scrape (*inf*); k~liegen *vi sep irreg* (*inf*) to be on one's beam ends (*inf*); k~nasig *adj* (*pej*) hook-nosed; k~nehmen *vt sep irreg* (*inf*) (jdm) etw k~nehmen to take offence at sth, to take sth amiss; ~säbel *m* scimitar; ~schwert *nt* scimitar; ~stab *m* crook, crozier.
Krümmung *f* (a) (*das Krümmen*) bending. (b) (*Biegung*) (*von Weg, Fluß*) bend, turn; (*Math, Med, von Fläche*) curvature; (*Opt: von Linse*) curve, curvature, figure.
krump(e)lig *adj* (*dial*) creased, crumpled.
Kruppe *f* -, -n (*Zool*) croup, crupper.
Krüppel *m* -s, - cripple. ein seelischer/geistiger ~ sein to be an emotional/intellectual cripple, to be emotionally/intellectually stunted; zum ~ werden to be crippled; jdn zum ~ schlagen to (beat and) cripple sb.
krüpp(e)lig *adj Mensch* crippled, deformed; *Wuchs* stunted; siehe lachen.
Krustazeen [krusta'tse:ən] *pl* (*spec*) crustacea.
Kruste *f* -, -n crust; (*von Schweinebraten*) crackling; (*von Braten*) crisped outside.
krustig *adj* crusty; *Topf etc* encrusted.
Krux *f* -, *no pl* siehe **Crux.**
Kruzifix *nt* -es, -e crucifix. ~! (*inf*) Christ almighty!
Kruzifixus *m* -, *no pl* (the) crucified Christ.
Kruzitürken *interj* (*S Ger inf*) confound it, curse it.
Krypta ['krypta] *f* -, **Krypten** crypt.
Krypto-, krypto- [krypto-] *in cpds* crypto-.
Krypton ['krypton, kryp'to:n] *nt* -s, *no pl* krypton.
Kuba *nt* -s Cuba.
Kubaner(in *f*) *m* -s, - Cuban.
kubanisch *adj* Cuban.
Kübel *m* -s, - bucket, pail; (*für Jauche etc*) container; (*inf: im Gefängnis*) latrine *or* toilet bucket, crapper (*sl*); (*für Bäume*) tub. es regnet (wie) aus *or* in *or* mit ~n it's bucketing down; ~ von Schmutz *or* Unrat (*fig geh*) torrents of abuse; ~ von Hohn und Spott über jdn ausgießen (*fig geh*) to heap *or* pour scorn on sb.
kübeln *vi* (*inf: zechen*) to booze (*inf*).
Kuben *pl of* **Kubus.**
Kubik-: ~meter *m or nt* cubic metre; ~wurzel *f* cube root; ~zahl *f* cube number.
kubisch *adj* cubic(al); *Gleichung* cubic; *Lampen* cube-shaped.
Kubismus *m* (*Art*) cubism.
Kubist(in *f*) *m* (*Art*) cubist.
kubistisch *adj* (*Art*) cubist(ic).
Kubus *m* -, **Kuben** *or* - cube.
Küche *f* -, -n (a) kitchen; (*klein*) kitchenette. es wurde alles aufgetischt, was ~ und Keller zu bieten hatten he/they *etc* served up a meal fit for a king. (b) (*Kochkunst*) cooking, cuisine. gutbürgerliche ~ good home cooking; die ~ besorgen to do the cooking. (c) (*Speisen*) meals *pl*, dishes *pl*, food.
Kuchen *m* -s, - cake; (*Torte auch*) gateau; (*mit Obst gedeckt*) (fruit) flan, gateau.
Küchenabfälle *pl* kitchen scraps *pl*.
Küchenbenutzung *f* use of kitchen.
Küchenblech *nt* baking sheet *or* tin.
Küchen-: ~bulle *m* (*Mil sl*) cookhouse wallah (*Mil sl*); ~chef *m* chef; ~fee *f* (*hum inf*) (lady) cook.
Küchen-: ~form *f* cake tin; ~gabel *f* pastry fork.
Küchen-: ~gerät *nt* kitchen utensil; (*kollektiv*) kitchen utensils *pl*; (*elektrisch*) kitchen appliance; ~geschirr *nt* kitchenware *no pl*; ~gewürz *nt* herbs and spices *pl*; ~handtuch *nt* kitchen towel; ~herd *m* (electric/gas) cooker; ~hilfe *f* kitchen help; ~hobel *m* slicer, cutter; ~junge *m* (*dated*) apprentice cook *or* chef; ~kraut *nt siehe* ~gewürz; ~latein *nt* dog Latin; ~meister *m siehe* ~chef; ~messer *nt* kitchen knife; ~personal *nt* kitchen staff; ~schabe *f* (*Zool*) cockroach; ~schrank *m* (kitchen) cupboard.
Kuchenteig *m* cake mixture; (*Hefeteig*) dough.
Küchen-: ~tisch *m* kitchen table; ~uhr *f* kitchen clock; ~waage *f* kitchen scales *pl*; ~wagen *m* (*Mil*) mobile field-kitchen; ~zettel *m* menu.
Küchlein *nt* (a) small cake. (b) (*Küken*) chick.
Kücken *nt* -s, - (*Aus*) siehe **Küken.**
kucken *vi* (*inf, N Ger*) siehe **gucken.**
Kuckuck *m* -s, -e (a) cuckoo.
    (b) (*inf: Siegel des Gerichtsvollziehers*) bailiff's seal (for distraint of goods).
    (c) (*euph inf: Teufel*) devil. zum ~ (noch mal)! hell's bells! (*inf*); hol's der ~! botheration! (*inf*); geh *or* scher dich zum ~ go to blazes (*inf*); weiß der ~, wo das Buch ist heaven (only) knows where the book is (*inf*); das weiß der ~ heaven (only) knows (*inf*); das ganze Geld ist zum ~ all the money is gone.

kuckuck interj cuckoo.

Kuckucks-: ~ei nt cuckoo's egg; (inf: außerehelich gezeugtes Kind) illegitimate child; **jdm ein ~ei unterschieben** or **ins Nest legen** to father sb's child; ~**uhr** f cuckoo clock.

Kuddelmuddel m or nt -s, no pl (inf) muddle, mess, confusion; (Aufsatz etc auch) hotchpotch (inf).

Kufe f -, -n (a) (von Schlitten, Schlittschuh etc) runner; (von Flugzeug) skid. (b) (Holzbottich) tub.

Küfer m -s, - cellarman; (S Ger: Böttcher) cooper.

Kugel f -, -n (a) ball; (geometrische Figur) sphere; (Erd~) sphere, globe; (Sport sl: Ball) ball; (Kegel~) bowl; (Gewehr~) bullet; (für Luftgewehr) pellet; (Kanonen~) (cannon)ball; (Sport: Stoß~) shot; (Murmel) marble; (Papier~) ball; (kleine) pellet; (Christbaum~) glitter ball. **sich** (dat) **eine ~ durch den Kopf jagen** or **schießen** to blow one's brains out; **eine ruhige ~ schieben** (inf) to have a cushy number or job (inf); (aus Faulheit) to swing the lead (inf); **rund wie eine ~** (inf) like a barrel; **die ~ rollt** the roulette wheels are spinning; **er fuhr nach Las Vegas, wo die ~ rollt** he went to the gaming tables of Las Vegas.
    (b) (Gelenk~) head (of a bone).
    (c) (sl: Mark) mark; = quid (Brit inf), buck (US inf).

Kugel-: ~**abschnitt** m (Math) spherical segment; ~**ausschnitt** m (Math) spherical sector; ~**blitz** m (Met) ball-lightning.

Kügelchen nt dim of **Kugel**.

Kugel-: ~**fang** m butt; **die Leibwächter sollen als ~fang dienen** the bodyguards are meant to act as a bullet-screen; **k~fest** adj siehe **k~sicher**; ~**fläche** f (Math) spherical surface; **k~förmig** adj spherical; ~**gelenk** nt (Anat, Tech) ball-and-socket joint; ~**hagel** m hail of bullets.

kugelig adj (a) siehe **kugelförmig**. (b) (inf) **sich ~ lachen** to double up (laughing).

Kugel-: ~**kopf** m golf-ball; ~**kopfschreibmaschine** f golf-ball typewriter.

Kugellager nt ball-bearing.

kugeln 1 vi aux sein (rollen, fallen) to roll. **es ist zum K~** (inf) it's a scream (inf) or hoot (inf). **2** vr to roll (about). **sich** (vor Lachen) ~ (inf) to double up (laughing); **ich könnte mich ~** (inf) it's killingly funny (inf).

Kugel-: ~**regen** m siehe ~**hagel**; **k~rund** adj as round as a ball; (inf) Mensch tubby, barrel-shaped (inf); ~**schreiber** m ballpoint (pen), biro ®; ~**schreibermine** f refill (for a ballpoint pen); **k~sicher** adj bullet-proof; ~**stoßen** nt -s, no pl shot-putting, putting the shot; **Sieger im ~stoßen** winner in the shot(-put); ~**stoßer(in)** f m -s, - shot-putter; ~**ventil** nt (Tech) ball valve; ~**wechsel** m exchange of shots.

Kuh f -, -̈e cow; (pej sl: Mädchen, Frau) cow (sl). **wie die ~ vorm neuen Tor dastehen** (inf) to be completely bewildered; **heilige ~** (lit, fig) sacred cow.

Kuh-: ~**dorf** nt (pej inf) one-horse town (inf); ~**fladen** m cowpat; ~**fuß** m (Tech) crow-bar; ~**glocke** f cowbell; ~**handel** m (pej inf) horse-trading (inf) no pl; **ein ~handel** a bit of horse-trading; **k~handeln** vi insep (inf) to do horse-trading; ~**haut** f cow-hide; **das geht auf keine ~haut** (inf) that is absolutely staggering or incredible; ~**herde** f herd of cows; ~**hirt(e)** m cowhand, cowherd; cowboy.

kühl adj (lit, fig) cool; (abweisend) cold. **mir wird etwas ~** I'm getting rather chilly; **abends wurde es ~** in the evenings it got cool; **etw ~ lagern** to store sth in a cool place; **ein ~er Kopf** (fig) a cool-headed person; **einen ~en Kopf bewahren** to keep a cool head, to keep cool; **ein ~er Rechner** a cool, calculating person; **eine ~e Inszenierung** a low-key production; **die ~en, aber eleganten Bauten** the cold but elegant buildings; **aus diesem ~en Grunde** (hum) for this simple reason.

Kühl-: ~**anlage** f refrigeration plant, cold storage plant; ~**box** f cold box.

Kuhle f -, -n (N Ger) hollow; (Grube) pit.

Kühle f -, no pl (lit) cool(ness); (Abweisung) coldness. **mit einer solchen ~ inszeniert** produced in such a low-key fashion.

kühlen 1 vt to cool; (auf Eis) to chill; siehe **Mütchen. 2** vi to be cooling, to have a cooling effect. **bei großer Hitze kühlt Tee am besten** in very hot weather tea cools you down best.

Kühler m -s, - (Tech) cooler; (Aut) radiator; (inf: ~haube) bonnet (Brit), hood (US); (Sekt~) ice bucket. **jdn auf den ~ nehmen** (inf) to drive into or hit sb; **ich hätte die alte Frau beinahe auf den ~ genommen** (inf) the old lady almost finished up on my bonnet; **jdm vor den ~ rennen** (inf) to run (out) right in front of sb or right under sb's front wheels.

Kühler-: ~**figur** f (Aut) radiator mascot; ~**haube** f (Aut) siehe **Motorhaube**.

Kühl-: ~**fach** nt siehe **Gefrierfach**; ~**haus** nt cold-storage depot; ~**kette** f chain of cold storage units; ~**lagerung** f cold storage; ~**mittel** nt (Tech) coolant, cooling agent; ~**ofen** m (Tech) annealing oven; ~**raum** m cold store or storage room; ~**rippe** f (Aut) cooling fin; ~**schiff** nt refrigerator ship; ~**schrank** m refrigerator, fridge (Brit), icebox (US); ~**tasche** f cold bag; ~**truhe** f (chest) freezer, deep freeze (Brit); (in Lebensmittelgeschäft) freezer (cabinet); ~**turm** m (Tech) cooling tower.

Kühlung f (das Kühlen) cooling; (Kühle) coolness. **zur ~ des Motors** to cool the engine; **sich** (dat) ~ **verschaffen** to cool oneself (down); **er ging in den Schatten, um sich ~ zu verschaffen** he went into the shade to cool down or off; **auch bei ~ nur begrenzt haltbar** perishable even when kept in cold storage.

Kühl-: ~**vitrine** f refrigerated counter or cabinet; ~**wagen** m (a) (Rail) refrigerator or refrigerated or cold storage wagon; (b) (Lastwagen) refrigerator or refrigerated or cold storage truck; ~**wasser** nt radiator water; ~**wirkung** f cooling effect.

Kuh-: ~**magd** f (dated) milkmaid, dairymaid; ~**milch** f cow's milk; ~**mist** m cow dung.

kühn adj (lit, fig) bold. **eine ~ geschwungene Nase** an aquiline nose; **das übertrifft meine ~sten Erwartungen** it's beyond or it surpasses my wildest hopes or dreams.

Kühnheit f boldness.

Kuh-: ~**pocken** pl cowpox sing; ~**scheiße** f (sl) cow-shit (vulg); ~**stall** m cow-shed, byre; ~**stallwärme** f (fig) cosy camaraderie; **k~warm** adj Milch warm or fresh from the cow; ~**weide** f pasture.

Kujon [ku'joːn] m -s, -e (old) rapscallion, cullion (obs).

kujonieren* vt (old) to bully, to harass.

k.u.k. ['kaːʊnt'kaː] abbr of **kaiserlich und königlich** imperial and royal.

Küken nt -s, - (a) (Huhn) chick; (inf: junges Mädchen) young goose (inf); (inf: Nesthäken) youngest child, baby of the family (inf). (b) (Tech) plug.

Ku-Klux-Klan m -s Ku Klux Klan.

Kukuruz m -(es), no pl (Aus) maize, corn.

kulant adj obliging, accommodating; Bedingungen generous, fair.

Kulanz f, no pl siehe adj obligingness, accommodatingness; generousness, fairness.

Kule f -, -n siehe **Kuhle**.

Kuli m -s, -s (a) (Lastträger) coolie; (fig) slave. **wie ein ~ arbeiten** (inf) to work like a slave or black (inf). (b) (inf: Kugelschreiber) ballpoint, biro ®.

kulinarisch adj culinary; (fig) entertainment-orientated.

Kulisse f -, -n scenery no pl; (Teilstück) flat, piece of scenery; (hinten) backdrop; (an den Seiten auch) wing; (fig: Hintergrund) background, backdrop, back-cloth. **die ~n für das Stück** the scenery for the play; **das ist alles nur ~** (fig) that is only a façade; **hinter den ~n** behind the scenes; **hinter die ~n sehen, einen Blick hinter die ~n werfen** (fig) to have a look or glimpse behind the scenes.

Kulissen-: ~**fieber** nt siehe **Lampenfieber**; ~**maler** m scene-painter; ~**schieber(in)** f m -s, - scene-shifter.

Kuller m -s, - (a) (baby-talk) ring. (b) (dial: Murmel) marble.

Kuller-: ~**augen** pl (inf) big wide eyes pl; ~**ball** m (a) (baby-talk) baby's little ball; (b) (Sport inf) easy ball; (leicht zu haltender Schuß auch) dolly (inf).

kullern vti (vi: aux sein) (inf) to roll.

Kulmination f culmination; (fig auch) apex. **obere/untere ~** highest/lowest point.

Kulminationspunkt m (Astron) point of culmination; (fig) culmination, apex.

kulminieren* vi to culminate; (fig auch) to reach its peak.

Kulör f -, -en or -s siehe **Couleur**.

Kult m -(e)s, -e cult; (Verehrung) worship. **einen ~ mit jdm/etw treiben** to make a cult out of sb/sth, to idolize sb; **mit denen wird jetzt so ein ~ getrieben** they have become such cult figures.

Kult-: ~**bild** nt religious symbol; ~**gemeinschaft** f cult; ~**handlung** f ritual(istic) act.

kultisch adj ritual(istic), cultic (rare). **er wird geradezu ~ verehrt** they almost make a god out of him.

kultivierbar adj Land cultiv(at)able. **dieser Boden ist nur schwer ~** the soil is very hard to cultivate.

kultivieren* [kulti'viːrən] vt (lit, fig) to cultivate.

kultiviert adj cultivated, cultured, refined; Mensch, Geschmack, Unterhaltung auch sophisticated. **könnt ihr euch nicht etwas ~er unterhalten?** couldn't you make your language just a little more refined etc?; **in dieser Familie mußt du dich ein bißchen ~er benehmen als sonst** in this family you'll have to behave with a little more refinement or class (inf) than usual; **wenn Sie ~ reisen wollen** if you want to travel in style; **Kerzen beim Essen, das ist sehr ~** meals by candlelight, very civilized; **ja, danke, das ist noch mal 'ne ~e Zigarre** thank you, a very civilized cigar; **wenn man mal ~ essen will** if you want a civilized meal.

Kultivierung [kulti'viːruŋ] f (lit, fig) cultivation.

Kult-: ~**sprache** f language of worship; ~**stätte** f place of worship; ~**symbol** nt ritual symbol.

Kultur f (a) (no pl: Kunst und Wissenschaft) culture. **ein Volk von hoher ~** a highly cultured or civilized people; **er hat keine ~** he is uncultured.
    (b) (Lebensform) civilization. **dort leben verschiedene ~en harmonisch zusammen** different cultures live harmoniously together there.
    (c) (Bakterien~, Pilz~ etc) culture.
    (d) no pl (von Mikroben etc) culture; (des Bodens auch) cultivation.
    (e) (Bestand angebauter Pflanzen) plantation.

Kultur-: ~**abkommen** nt cultural agreement; ~**anthropologie** f cultural anthropology; ~**arbeit** f cultural activities pl; ~**attaché** m cultural attaché; ~**austausch** m cultural exchange; ~**autonomie** f independence in cultural (and educational) matters; ~**banause** m (inf) philistine; ~**beilage** f cultural or arts supplement or review; ~**betrieb** m (inf) culture industry; ~**beutel** m sponge or toilet bag (Brit), washbag; ~**boden** m cultivated or arable land; ~**denkmal** nt cultural monument.

kulturell adj cultural.

Kultur-: ~**erbe** nt cultural heritage; **k~fähig** adj siehe kultivierbar; ~**film** m documentary film; ~**föderalismus** m (Pol) cultural and educational devolution; ~**geographie** f human geography; ~**geschichte** f history of civilization; Sozial- und ~**geschichte der Etrusker** social and cultural history of the Etruscans; **k~geschichtlich** adj historico-cultural, concerning the history of civilization; ~**gut** nt cultural possessions pl or assets pl; ~**haus** nt (esp DDR) arts centre; **k~historisch** adj *siehe* k~geschichtlich; ~hoheit *f* independence in matters of education and culture; ~industrie *f* culture industry; ~kampf *m, no pl* cultural war; (*Hist*) Kulturkampf (*struggle between Church and State 1872–1887*); ~konsum *m* (*inf*) consumption of culture, cultural consumption; ~kreis *m* culture group *or* area; ~kritik *f* critique of (our) civilization *or* culture; ~kritiker *m* critic of (our) civilization *or* culture; ~land *nt* cultivated *or* arable land; ~landschaft *f* land developed and cultivated by man; ~leben *nt* cultural life; k~los *adj* lacking culture; *Mensch auch* uncultured; ~losigkeit *f* lack of culture; ~minister *m siehe* Kultusminister; ~ministerium *nt siehe* Kultusministerium; ~palast *m* (*esp DDR*) palace of culture or the arts; (*pej*) cultured extravagance; ~pessimismus *m* despair of civilization; ~pessimist *m* person who despairs of civilization; ~pflanze *f* cultivated plant; ~politik *f* cultural and educational policy; ~politiker *m* politician who concerns himself mainly with cultural and educational policies; k~politisch *adj* politico-cultural; k~politische Fragen matters with both a cultural and a political aspect; eine k~politische Dummheit an act of cultural and political folly; die k~politische Landschaft the cultural and political landscape; ~psychologie *f* psychology of culture; ~religion *f* culture-forming religion; ~revolution *f* cultural revolution; ~schaffende(r) *mf decl as adj* (*esp DDR*) creative artist; ~schande *f* crime against civilization, cultural outrage; (*fig inf*) insult to *or* offence against good taste; ~schock *m* cultural shock; ~soziologie *f* cultural sociology, sociology of culture; k~soziologisch *adj* socio-cultural; ~sprache *f* language of the civilized world; ~stätte *f* place of cultural interest; ~steppe *f* (*Geog*) cultivated steppe; ~stufe *f* stage *or* level of civilization; ~teil *m* (*von Zeitung*) arts section; ~träger *m* vehicle of culture *or* civilization; ~volk *nt* civilized people *sing or* nation; k~voll *adj* (*esp DDR*) cultured; ~wandel *m* cultural change; ~wissenschaft *f* study of civilization; ~wissenschaften cultural studies; ~zentrum *nt* (a) (*Stadt*) centre of cultural life, cultural centre; (b) (*Anlage*) arts centre.

Kultus-: ~beamte(r) *m* (*Rel*) synagogue official; ~freiheit *f* religious freedom, freedom of worship; ~gemeinde *f* religious community; ~minister *m* minister of education and the arts; ~ministerium *nt* ministry of education and the arts.

Kultwagen *m* ritual chariot.

Kumarin *nt -s, no pl* coumarin.

Kumme *f -, -n* (*N Ger*) bowl.

Kümmel *m -s, -* (a) *no pl* (*Gewürz*) caraway (seed). (b) (*inf: Schnaps*) kümmel.

Kümmelbranntwein *m* (*form*) kümmel.

kümmeln 1 *vt* to season with caraway (seeds). 2 *vti* (*inf*) to tipple. einen ~ to have a little drink.

Kümmel-: ~öl *nt* caraway oil; ~spalter(in *f*) *m -s, -* (*inf*) pedant, nit-picker (*inf*); ~türke *m* (*pej sl: Türke*) Turk, wog (*pej inf*); schuften wie ein ~türke (*inf*) to work like a black (*inf*) or slave.

Kummer *m -s, no pl* (*Gram, Betrübtheit*) grief, sorrow; (*Unannehmlichkeit, Ärger*) trouble, problems *pl*. hast du ~? is something wrong?, have you got problems?; aus *or* vor ~ sterben to die of sorrow *or* grief; vor ~ vergehen to be pining away with sorrow or grief; vor ~ nahm er sich (*dat*) das Leben in his grief *or* grief-stricken he took his life; er fand vor ~ keinen Schlaf mehr such was his grief *or* sorrow that he was unable to sleep; jdm ~ machen or bereiten to cause sb worry; wenn das dein einziger ~ ist if that's your only problem *or* worry; wir sind (an) ~ gewöhnt (*inf*) it happens all the time, nothing's ever perfect.

Kümmerer *m -s, -* (a) (*Hunt*) stag with stunted antlers. (b) (*inf: Freund*) companion. (c) (*inf: vergrämter Mensch*) woebegone person.

Kummerfalten *pl* wrinkles *pl*. das sind ~ that's the worry.

Kümmerform *f* (*Bot*) stunted form.

kümmerlich *adj* (a) (*karg, armselig*) wretched, miserable; *Reste, Ausbeute, Rente* miserable, meagre, paltry; *Lohn, Mahlzeit auch* measly (*inf*); *Aufsatz* scanty. sich ~ ernähren to live on a meagre diet. (b) (*schwächlich*) puny.

Kümmerling *m* (a) (*Zool*) stunted person/plant/animal. die Pflanze war von Anfang an ein ~ the plant always was a sickly thing. (b) (*inf: Schwächling*) weakling, weed (*pej inf*).

kümmern[1] *vi* (*Hunt, Zool*) to become *or* grow stunted.

kümmern[2] 1 *vt* to concern. was kümmert mich die Firma? why should I worry about the firm?, what do I care about the firm?; was kümmert Sie das? what business *or* concern is that of yours?; was kümmert mich das? what's that to me?
2 *vr* sich um jdn/etw ~ to look after sb/sth; sich um einen Kranken/jds Kinder ~ to look after *or* take care of a sick person/sb's children; sich um die Karten/das Essen ~ to look after *or* take care of *or* see to the tickets/the food; ich muß mich um ein Geschenk für ihn ~ I have to see about (getting) a present for him; sich darum ~, daß ... to see to it that ...; aber darum kümmert sich im Stadtrat ja keiner but nobody on the council does anything about it; kümmere dich nicht um Sachen, die dich nichts angehen don't worry about things that don't concern you; kümmere dich gefälligst um deine eigenen Angelegenheiten! mind your own business!; er kümmert sich nicht darum, was die Leute denken he doesn't mind *or* isn't worried about *or* doesn't care (about) what people think; *siehe* Dreck.

Kümmernis *f* (*liter*) troubles *pl*, worries *pl*.

Kummer-: ~speck *m* (*inf*) flab caused by overeating because of emotional problems; sie hat ganz schön ~speck angesetzt she's been putting on weight, it's the worry making her eat too much; k~voll *adj* sorrowful, sad, woebegone *no adv*.

Kümmerwuchs *m* stunted growth.

Kummet *nt -s, -e siehe* Kumt.

Kümo *nt -s, -s abbr of* Küstenmotorschiff coaster.

Kumpan(in *f*) *m -s, -e* (*dated inf*) pal (*inf*), chum (*inf*), mate (*Brit inf*), buddy (*esp US inf*).

Kumpanei *f* (*pej*) chumminess.

Kumpel *m -s, -* *or* (*inf*) **-s** *or* (*Aus*) **-n** (a) (*Min: Bergmann*) pitman, miner. (b) (*inf: Arbeitskollege, Kamerad*) pal (*inf*), chum (*inf*), mate (*Brit inf*), buddy (*esp US inf*).

Kumt *nt -(e)s, -e* horse collar.

Kumulation *f* (a) (*von Ämtern*) plurality. (b) (*von Wahlstimmen*) accumulation.

kumulativ *adj* cumulative.

kumulieren* *vt* to accumulate. ~de Bibliographie cumulative bibliography.

Kumulierung *f* cumulative voting; (*von Wahlstimmen*) accumulation.

Kumulus *m -, Kumuli*, **Kumuluswolke** *f* cumulus (cloud).

kund *adj inv* (*obs*): jdm etw ~ und zu wissen tun to make sth known to sb.

kündbar *adj Vertrag* terminable; *Anleihe* redeemable. Beamte sind nicht ohne weiteres ~ civil servants cannot be given (their) notice *or* dismissed just like that; die Mitgliedschaft ist sehr schwer ~ it is very difficult to terminate *or* cancel one's membership.

Kündbarkeit *f* (*von Vertrag*) terminability; (*von Anleihe*) redeemability. die ~ von Verträgen ist gesetzlich geregelt the termination of contracts is controlled by law; wegen der jährlichen ~ der Direktoren since the directors have to be given one year's notice.

Kunde[1] *f -, no pl* (*geh*) news *sing*, tidings *pl* (*old*). der Welt von etw ~ geben to proclaim sth to the world; von etw ~ geben *or* ablegen to bear witness to sth.

Kunde[2] *m -n, -* customer; (*pej inf*) customer (*inf*), character.

-kunde *f* in cpds science of.

künden 1 *vt* (*geh*) to announce, to herald. 2 *vi* (*geh*) von etw ~ to tell of sth, to bear witness to sth. 3 *vti* (*Sw*) *siehe* kündigen.

Kunden-: ~beratung *f* customer advisory service; ~dienst *m* after-sales service; (*Abteilung*) service department; ~fang *m* (*pej*) touting *or* looking for customers; das dient dem ~fang it helps to bring in the customers; auf ~fang sein to be touting *or* looking for customers; ein Vertreter auf ~fang a salesman chasing up some business; ~kreis *m* customers *pl*, clientèle; ~sprache *f* thieves' cant, argot; ~stock *m* (*Aus*) *siehe* ~kreis; ~werbung *f* publicity aimed at attracting custom *or* customers.

Künder(in *f*) *m -s, -* (*rare*) messenger, harbinger (*obs, liter*).

Kundgabe *f -, no pl* announcement, proclamation.

kundgeben *sep irreg* 1 *vt* (*dated*) to make known, to announce; *Meinung, Gefühle* to express, to declare. etw ~ to announce sth (*jdm* to sb), to make sth known (*jdm* to sb).
2 *vr* to be revealed.

Kundgebung *f* (a) (*Pol*) rally. (b) (*Bekanntgabe*) declaration, demonstration.

kundig *adj* (*geh*) well-informed, knowledgeable; (*sach~*) expert. einer Sache (*gen*) ~ sein to have a knowledge of sth.

-kundig *adj suf* with a good knowledge of.

kündigen 1 *vt Stellung* to hand in one's notice for; *Abonnement, Mitgliedschaft, Kredite* to cancel, to discontinue, to terminate; *Vertrag* to terminate; *Tarife* to discontinue; *Hypothek* (*Bank*) to foreclose (on); (*Hausbesitzer*) to terminate; (*strictly incorrect, Aus*) *Person* to sack (*inf*), to fire (*inf*), to dismiss. jdm die Wohnung ~, jdn aus einer Wohnung ~ (*Aus*) to give sb notice to quit his flat; ich habe meine Wohnung gekündigt I've given in notice that I'm leaving my flat, I've given in my notice for my flat; die Stellung ~ to hand *or* give in one's notice; jdm die Stellung ~ to give sb his/her notice; bei einer Firma die Stellung ~ to give *or* hand in one's notice to a firm; jdm Kredite ~ to cancel *or* discontinue *or* terminate sb's credit; Beträge über ... muß man ~ for sums in excess of ... notification must be given in advance; jdm die Freundschaft ~ to break off a friendship with sb; jdm den Gehorsam ~ to refuse to obey sb.
2 *vi* (*Arbeitnehmer*) to hand *or* give in one's notice; (*Mieter*) to give in one's notice, to give notice. jdm ~ (*Arbeitgeber*) to give sb his notice, to dismiss sb; (*Arbeitnehmer*) to hand *or* give in one's notice to sb; (*Vermieter*) to give sb notice to quit; (*Mieter*) to give in one's notice to sb; zum 1. April ~ to give *or* hand in one's notice for April 1st; (*Mieter*) to give notice for *or* give in one's notice for April 1st; (*bei Mitgliedschaft*) to cancel one's membership as of April 1st; ihm ist zum 1. Februar gekündigt worden he's been given his notice for *or* as from February 1st; (*bei Wohnung*) he's been given notice to quit for February 1st; ich kann nur zum Ersten eines Monats ~ I have to give a clear month's notice; bei jdm/einer Firma ~ to give *or* hand in one's notice to sb/a firm.

Kündigung *f* (a) (*Mitteilung*) (*von Vermieter*) notice to quit; (*von Mieter*) notice; (*von Stellung*) notice; (*von Vertrag*) termination; (*von Hypothek*) notice of foreclosure; (*von Anleihe*) notice of withdrawal; (*von Mitgliedschaft, Abonnement*) (letter of) cancellation.
(b) (*das Kündigen*) (*von Arbeitgeber*) dismissal; (*von Arbeitnehmer*) handing *or* giving in one's notice; (*von Vertrag*) termination; (*von Hypothek*) foreclosure; (*von Anleihe*) withdrawal; (*von Tarifen*) discontinuation; (*von Mitgliedschaft, Abonnement*) cancellation. die ~ meiner Wohnung wurde nötig I had to give in my notice for my flat; wegen schlechten Betragens des Mieters entschloß sich der Vermieter zur ~ the landlord decided to give the tenant his notice (to quit) because of his bad behaviour; ich drohte (dem Chef) mit der ~ I threatened to give *or* hand in my notice (to my boss), I threatened to quit; ich erwäge eine ~ meiner Stelle I'm considering handing *or* giving in my notice; Vertrag mit

vierteljährlicher ~ contract with three months' notice on either side; vierteljährliche ~ haben to have (to give) three months' notice.

Kündigungs-: ~frist f period of notice; ~grund m reason or grounds pl for giving notice; (von Arbeitgeber auch) grounds pl for dismissal; ~schutz m protection against wrongful dismissal.

Kundin f customer.

kundmachen vt sep (old, liter) siehe kundgeben 1.

Kundmachung f (Aus, Sw, S Ger) siehe Bekanntmachung.

Kundschaft f (a) customers pl. ~! shop!, service!; es ist ~ im Geschäft there are customers in the shop.
(b) (Erkundung) reconnaissance. jdn auf ~ ausschicken or senden (Mil) to send sb out to reconnoitre or on reconnaissance; auf ~ (aus)gehen (Mil) to go out on reconnaissance.
(c) siehe Kunde¹.

kundschaften* vi insep (Mil) to reconnoitre.

Kundschafter m -s, - spy; (Mil) scout.

kundtun ['kʊnttuːn] vt sep irreg (geh) to make known, to proclaim.

kundwerden vi sep irreg aux sein (liter) to become known.

künftig 1 adj future. ~en Jahres/Monats next year/month; das ~e Leben the next life, the life to come; meine ~e Frau/mein ~er Schwager my future wife/brother-in-law, my wife-to-be/brother-in-law to be. 2 adv in future.

künftighin adv (old, geh) in future.

Kungelei f (inf) fiddle (inf), fiddling no pl (inf).

kungeln vti (inf) to fiddle (inf). mit denen hat er viel gekungelt he did a lot of fiddles with them.

Kunst f -, ¨e (a) art. die schönen ¨e fine art sing, the fine arts; siehe bildend.
(b) (Können, Fertigkeit) art, skill. seine ~ an jdm versuchen to try or practise one's skills on sb; mit seiner ~ am or zu Ende sein to be at one's wits' end; die ~ besteht darin, ... the art or knack is in ...; ärztliche ~ medical skill; siehe Regel.
(c) (Kunststück) trick. er wandte alle ~e der Rhetorik an he used all the arts or tricks of rhetoric; sie versuchte all ihre ~e an ihm she used all her charms and wiles on him; das ist keine ~! it's like taking candy from a baby (inf); (ein Kinderspiel) it's a piece of cake (inf); so einfach ist das, das ist die ganze ~ it's that easy, that's all there is to it.
(d) (inf) das ist eine brotlose ~ there's no money in that; was macht die ~? (inf) how are things?, how's tricks? (inf).

Kunst- in cpds (Art) art; (künstlich) artificial; ~akademie f college of art, art college; ~auge nt artificial or glass eye; ~ausstellung f art exhibition; ~banause m (pej) philistine; ~blatt nt siehe ~druck; ~darm m artificial sausage skin; ~denkmal nt work of art (from an older culture); ~druck m art print; ~druckpapier nt art paper; ~dünger m chemical or artificial fertilizer.

Künstelei f affectation.

künsteln 1 vi (obs) to behave in an affected manner or way; siehe gekünstelt. 2 vt (rare: vortäuschen) to feign, to affect.

Kunst-: k~empfänglich adj artistic, appreciative of art; ~erzieher m art teacher; ~erziehung f (Sch) art; ~faser f man-made or synthetic fibre; ~fehler m professional error; (weniger ernst) slip; k~fertig adj (geh) skilful; ~fertigkeit f skill, skilfulness; ~flieger m stunt or aerobatic pilot, stunt flyer; ~flug m aerobatics sing, aerobatic or stunt flying; ein ~flug a piece of aerobatic or stunt flying; ~freund m art lover, patron or lover of the arts; ~gegenstand m objet d'art, art object; (Gemälde) work of art; k~gemäß, k~gerecht adj (fachmännisch) proficient, skilful; ~geschichte f history of art, art history; ~gewerbe nt arts and crafts pl; ein Fachgeschäft für ~gewerbe an arts and crafts shop, a craft shop; ~gewerbler(in f) m -s, - artisan, craftsman/-woman; k~gewerblich adj k~gewerbliche Gegenstände craft objects; k~gewerblicher Zweig arts and crafts department; sie hat k~gewerbliche Fähigkeiten she's skilled at arts and crafts; ~griff m trick, dodge (inf); ~handel m art trade; ~händler m art dealer; ~harz nt synthetic resin; k~historisch 1 adj art-historical, relating to art history; k~historisches Museum art history museum; k~historisches Interesse interest in art history; k~historische Forschungen/Studien research sing/ studies in art history; 2 adv from the point of view of art history; ~hochschule f siehe ~akademie; ~honig m artificial or synthetic honey; ~kenner m art connoisseur; ~kritik f, no pl art criticism; (die Kritiker) art critics pl; (Rezension) art review; ~kritiker m art critic; ~lauf m (Sport) figure skating; ~leder nt artificial or imitation leather.

Künstler(in f) m -s, - (a) artist; (Unterhaltungs~) artiste. bildender ~ visual artist. (b) (Könner) genius (in + dat at).

Künstler|eingang m stage door.

künstlerisch adj artistic.

Künstler-: ~kolonie f artists' colony, colony of artists; ~mähne f (inf) mane of hair; ~name m pseudonym; (von Schriftsteller auch) pen name, nom de plume; (von Schauspieler auch) stage name; ~pech nt (inf) hard luck; ~tum nt artistry, artistic genius.

künstlich adj artificial; Auge auch glass; Zähne, Wimpern, Fingernägel false; Faserstoffe synthetic, man-made; Diamanten imitation, fake (inf). jdn ~ ernähren (Med) to feed sb artificially; sich ~ aufregen (inf) to get all worked up (inf) or excited about nothing; sich ~ dumm stellen to pretend to be stupid; stell dich doch nicht ~ dumm, das weißt du doch don't be stupid, you know that; einen Schrank ~ auf alt trimmen to do a cupboard up to look old; siehe beatmen.

Künstlichkeit f artificiality.

Kunst-: ~licht nt (Phot) artificial light; ~lied nt composed or art song, kunstlied; k~los adj unsophisticated, simple; ~maler

---

m artist, painter; ~märchen nt literary fairytale; ~pause f (als Spannungsmoment) dramatic pause, pause for effect; (iro: beim Stocken) awkward pause, hesitation; eine ~pause machen to pause for effect; to pause awkwardly; k~reich adj (geh) siehe k~voll; ~reiter m trick or circus rider; ~richter m (dated) art critic; ~sammlung f art collection; ~schätze pl art treasures pl; ~schwimmen nt exhibition swimming; ~seide f artificial silk; ~sinn m artistic sense or taste, appreciation of or feeling for art; k~sinnig adj artistic, appreciative of art; ~sprache f artificial or invented language; ~springen nt diving; ~stoff m man-made or synthetic material or substance; k~stopfen sep infin and ptp only 1 vt to repair by invisible mending, to mend invisibly; 2 vi to do invisible mending; ~stück nt trick; ~stück! (iro) hardly surprising!, no wonder!; das ist kein ~stück (fig) there's nothing to it; (keine große Leistung) that's nothing to write home about; ~tischler m cabinet-maker; ~turnen nt gymnastics sing; ~verstand m feeling for or appreciation of art, artistic taste or sense; k~verständig adj appreciative of art, having artistic sense or taste; ~verständnis nt siehe ~verstand; k~voll adj artistic, elaborate; ~werk nt work of art; ~wissenschaft f aesthetics sing, art; ~wort nt artificial or made-up word.

kunterbunt adj Sammlung, Gruppe etc motley attr; (vielfarbig auch) multi- or many-coloured; Programm varied; Leben chequered. eine ~ zusammengewürfelte Gruppe a motley assortment; eine ~e Bibliothek a motley collection of books; ~ durcheinander all jumbled up, higgledy-piggledy (inf); hier sieht es ja ~ aus it looks a real muddle or jumble here; hier geht es ~ zu it's pretty chaotic here.

Kunterbunt nt -s, no pl motley mixture; (Vielfarbigkeit) colourfulness; (Durcheinander) jumble. das ~ des Jahrmarkts the gay profusion of the fair.

Kunz m siehe Hinz.

Kupee nt -s, -s siehe Coupé.

Kupfer nt -s, - (a) no pl (Chem) copper. etw in ~ stechen to do a copper engraving, to engrave or etch sth on copper. (b) no pl (Gegenstände aus ~, auch ~geld) copper. (c) siehe Kupferstich.

Kupfer- in cpds copper; ~blech nt sheet copper; ~draht m copper wire; ~druck m copperplate engraving or etching; ~geld nt coppers pl, copper coins pl; k~haltig adj containing copper, cupriferous (form).

kupf(e)rig adj coppery.

kupfern adj copper. ~e Hochzeit 7th wedding anniversary.

Kupfer-: k~rot adj copper-red, copper coloured; ~schmied m coppersmith; ~stecher m -s, - copper(plate) engraver; mein lieber Freund und ~stecher (inf) now then my dear old chap; ~stich m (a) copperplate (engraving or etching); (b) (Kunst) copper(plate) engraving or etching; ~vitriol nt blue vitriol; (dated Chem) copper sulphate.

kupieren* vt Schwanz, Ohren to crop, to dock; Karten to cut; (form) Wein to blend; (Med) Krankheit to check, to arrest.

Kupon [ku'põ:] m -s, -s coupon.

Kuppe f -, -n (Berg~) (rounded) hilltop; (von Straße) hump; (Finger~) tip.

Kuppel f -, -n dome, cupola.

Kuppeldach nt domed or dome-shaped roof.

Kuppelei f (Jur) procuring, procuration.

Kuppelmutter f procuress, bawd.

kuppeln 1 vt (a) siehe koppeln. (b) (Tech) to couple. 2 vi (Aut) to operate or use the clutch. (b) (inf: Paare zusammenführen) to match-make.

Kuppelpelz m: sich (dat) einen ~ verdienen (fig) to arrange or make a match.

Kuppelung f siehe Kupplung.

Kuppler(in f) m -s, - matchmaker (gen for); (Jur) procurer/ procuress.

Kupplung f (a) (Tech) coupling; (Aut etc) clutch. die ~ (durch)treten to disengage the clutch; die ~ kommen lassen (Aut) to let the clutch up or in. (b) (das Koppeln) coupling.

Kupplungs- in cpds (Aut) clutch; ~belag m clutch lining; ~pedal nt clutch pedal; ~scheibe f clutch plate; ~seil nt, ~zug m clutch cable.

Kur¹ f -, -en (in Badeort) (health) cure; (Haar~ etc) treatment no pl; (Schlankheits-, Diät~) diet. er ist zur ~ in Baden-Baden he's on a health cure or is taking a cure or the waters in Baden-Baden; in or zur ~ fahren to go to a health resort or spa; eine ~ machen to take or undergo a cure; (Schlankheits~) to diet; meine Haare sind so trocken, ich muß eine ~ machen my hair is so dry I'll have to condition it; ich mache zur Zeit eine ~ gegen meinen Ausschlag I'm taking a course of treatment for my rash; jdn zur ~ schicken to send sb on a cure or to a health resort or spa; jdn in die ~ nehmen (fig inf) to give sb what-for (inf); (Polizei etc) to give sb a grilling.

Kur² f -, no pl (obs: Wahl) election.

Kür f -, -en (a) (Sport) free section. eine ~ laufen to do the free skating; eine ~ tanzen/turnen to do the free section. (b) (old: Wahl) election.

Kurant nt -(e)s, -e (obs) coin possessing face value.

Kurant(in f) m (Sw) siehe Kurgast.

Küraß m -sses, -sse cuirass.

Kürassier m -s, -e (Mil Hist) cuirassier.

Kurat m -en, -en curate.

Kuratel f -, -en (obs) (Pflegschaft) trusteeship; (Vormundschaft) guardianship. unter (jds) ~ stehen (fig dated) to be under sb's thumb; jdn unter ~ stellen (old) to keep a watch on sb.

Kurator m (a) (Vormund) guardian. (b) (Verwalter einer Geldstiftung) trustee. (c) (Museum~) curator. (d) (Univ) ≈ registrar.

Kuratorium nt (a) (Vereinigung) committee. (b) (Amt) curatorship.

Kur-: ~aufenthalt m stay at a health resort or spa; ~bad nt siehe Heilbad.

Kurbel f -, -n crank; (an Fenstern, Rolläden etc) winder.

kurbeln vti to turn, to wind; (inf: filmen) to film, to shoot. wenn du daran kurbelst ... if you turn or wind it ...; die Markise vors Fenster ~ to wind up the awning in front of the window.

Kurbel-: ~stange f siehe Pleuelstange; ~welle f crankshaft.

Kürbis m -ses, -se pumpkin; (inf: Kopf) nut (inf).

Kürbisflasche f gourd.

Kurde m -n, -n, **Kurdin** f Kurd.

Kurdistan nt -s Kurdistan.

kuren vi (Sw, inf) to take a cure; (in Mineralbad) to take the waters.

küren pret kürte or kor (rare), ptp gekürt or gekoren vt (old, geh) to choose, to elect (zu as).

Kurfürst m Elector, electoral prince.

Kurfürstentum nt electorate.

kurfürstlich adj electoral.

Kur-: ~gast m visitor to/patient at a health resort or spa; ~haus nt assembly rooms pl (at a health resort or spa), spa rooms pl.

Kurie ['kuːriə] f (a) (Eccl) Curia. (b) (Hist) curia.

Kurienkardinal [-iən-] m cardinal of the Curia.

Kurier m -s, -e courier, messenger.

kurieren* vt (lit, fig) to cure (von of). von dieser Stadt/Idee/ihm bin ich kuriert I've gone right off this town/idea/him.

kurios adj (merkwürdig) curious, strange, odd.

Kuriosa pl of Kuriosum.

Kuriosität f (a) (Gegenstand) curio(sity). (b) (Eigenart) peculiarity, oddity.

Kuriositätenkabinett nt collection of curios; (fig) collection of odd people.

Kuriosum nt -s, **Kuriosa** (geh) curious or strange or odd thing.

Kurkonzert nt concert (at a health resort or spa), spa concert.

Kürlauf m free skating.

Kur-: ~ort m health resort, spa; ~park m spa gardens pl; ~pfalz f Palatinate, Palatine electorate; k~pfälzisch adj Palatine; k~pfuschen vi insep to play the quack; ~pfuscher m (pej inf) quack (doctor); ~pfuscherei f (pej inf) quackery; ~prinz m heir of an Elector; ~promenade f promenade (at a health resort or spa).

Kurre f -, -n (Naut) trawl (net).

kurrent adj (Aus) in gothic handwriting.

Kurrentschrift f (a) cursive writing or script. (b) (Aus) gothic handwriting.

Kurrikulum nt -s, **Kurrikula** (a) (Lehrplan) curriculum. (b) (obs: Lebenslauf) curriculum vitae.

Kurs m -es, -e (a) (Naut, Aviat, fig) course; (Pol, Richtung auch) line. harter/weicher ~ (Pol) hard/soft line; den ~ ändern/beibehalten (lit, fig) to change or alter/stick to or hold (one's) course; den ~ korrigieren (lit, fig) to adjust or correct one's course; den ~ halten to hold the (course); ~ nehmen auf (+acc) to set course for, to head for; auf (südwestlichen) ~ gehen/auf (südwestlichem) ~ sein to set a/be on a (southwesterly) course; ~ haben auf (+acc) to be heading for.
  (b) (Fin: Wechsel~) rate of exchange, exchange rate; (Börsen~, Aktien~) price, (going) rate; (Marktpreis) market value or price, going rate. zum ~ von at the rate of; die ~e fallen/steigen prices or rates are falling/rising; Geld außer ~ setzen to withdraw money from circulation; hoch im ~ stehen (Aktien) to be high; (fig) to be popular (bei with).
  (c) (Lehrgang) course (in +dat, für in). einen ~ besuchen or mitmachen to go to or attend a class.

Kurs-: ~änderung f (lit, fig) change of course; ~bericht m (Fin) siehe Börsenbericht; ~blatt nt siehe ~zettel; ~buch nt (Rail) (railway) timetable, Bradshaw (dated Brit).

Kurschatten m -s, - (hum inf) romance from/at the spa.

Kürschner(in f) m -s, - furrier.

Kürschnerei f (a) (Handwerk) furrier's trade. (b) (Werkstatt) furrier's workshop.

Kurse pl of Kursus.

Kurs-: ~einbuße f decrease or fall in value; das £ hat weitere ~einbußen hinnehmen müssen the £ suffered further losses (on the exchange market); ~gewinn m profit (on the stock exchange or (bei Wechsel) foreign exchange market); der jüngste ~gewinn des Pfundes the recent increase in the value of the pound; einen ~gewinn haben to make a profit.

kursieren* vi aux haben or sein to be in circulation, to circulate; (fig) to circulate, to go round.

kursiv adj italic. etw ~ drucken to print sth in italics, to italicize sth; Anmerkungen sind ~ notes are in italics.

Kursive [kur'ziːvə] f -, -n, **Kursivschrift** f italics pl. in ~ gesetzt printed in italics, italicized.

Kurs-: ~korrektur f (lit, fig) course correction or adjustment; (St Ex) corrective price or rate adjustment; ~notierung f (market) quotation, quotation (of stock exchange prices).

kursorisch adj: ~e Lektüre course reading.

Kursschwankung f fluctuation in rates of exchange or exchange rates; (St Ex) fluctuation in market rates or prices.

Kursus m -, **Kurse** (geh: Lehrgang) course.

Kurs-: ~verlust m (Fin) loss (on the stock exchange or foreign exchange market); das Pfund mußte ~verluste hinnehmen the pound suffered losses on the foreign exchange market; ~wagen m (Rail) through coach; ~wert m (Fin) market value or price; ~zettel m (Fin) stock exchange (price) list, list of quotations.

Kurtaxe f -, -n visitors' tax (at health resort or spa).

Kurtisane f -, -n courtesan.

Kür|übung f (Sport) free section.

Kurve ['kurvə, 'kurfə] f -, -n (Math, inf: Körperrundung) curve; (Biegung, Straßen~) bend; (an Kreuzung) corner; (von Geschoß) trajectory; (statistisch, Fieber~ etc) graph. die Straße macht eine ~ the road bends; eine ~ fliegen (Aviat) to bank, to do a banking turn; die ~ kratzen (inf) to scrape through (inf); (schnell weggehen) to make tracks (inf); die ~ nicht kriegen (inf) not to get round to it; die ~ raus- or weghaben (inf) to have the hang of it (inf).

kurven ['kurvn, 'kurfn] vi aux sein (inf) (Aviat) to circle. durch Italien ~ to drive around Italy.

Kurven-: ~lineal nt curve template or templet, French curve; k~reich adj Straße bendy, winding; (inf) Frau curvaceous, shapely; „k~reiche Strecke" "(series of) bends"; ~technik f (Sport) cornering technique.

kurvig ['kurviç] adj winding, twisting.

kurz 1 adj, comp ̈er, superl ̈este(r, s) short; Zeit, Aufenthalt, Besuch, Bericht, Antwort etc auch brief; Blick, Folge quick; Gedächtnis auch short-lived; (klein und stämmig) stocky, squat. etw ̈er machen to make sth shorter, to shorten sth; ich will es ~ machen I'll make it brief, I'll be brief; mach's ~! make it brief or quick, be brief, keep it short; ~e Hosen short trousers; (Shorts) shorts; ~e See (Naut) choppy sea; den ̈eren ziehen (fig inf) to come off worst, to get the worst of it; ~ verliert, lang gewinnt whoever draws the shortest (straw/match) loses; in or mit ein paar ~en Worten in a few brief words, briefly; eine ̈ere Lösung/ein ̈erer Weg a shorter or quicker solution/way; in ̈ester Frist before very long; zwei Minuten? o, das ist aber ~ two minutes? that's not very long or that's not much time; meine Zeit ist ~ I haven't much time; Pippin der K~e Pippin the Short.

2 adv, comp ̈er, superl am ̈esten (a) ~ atmen to breathe in or take short breaths; X hat ~ abgespielt (Sport) X's pass was short; (zu) ~ schießen/werfen etc to shoot/throw (too) short; die Hundeleine ~ halten to keep the dog on a short lead; eine Sache ~ abtun to dismiss sth out of hand; zu ~ kommen to come off badly, to get a raw deal (inf); ~ entschlossen without a moment's or the slightest hesitation; ~ gesagt in a nutshell, in a word; sich ~ fassen to be brief; ~ und bündig concisely, tersely (pej); ~ und gut in short, in a word; ~ und schmerzlos (inf) short and sweet; jdn/etw ~ und klein hauen or schlagen to beat sb up/to smash sth to pieces.
  (b) (für eine ~e Zeit) briefly. ich habe ihn nur ~ gesehen I only saw him briefly; ich bleibe nur ~ I'll only stay for a short while; darf ich mal ~ stören? could I just interrupt for a moment or second?; ich muß mal ~ weg I'll just have to go for a moment or second; darf ich mal ~ fragen ...? could I just quickly ask ...?; ich werde ~ mal gucken I'll have a quick look.
  (c) (zeitlich, räumlich: nicht lang, nicht weit) shortly, just. ~ bevor/nachdem shortly or just before/after; ~ vor Köln/Ostern shortly or just before Cologne/Easter; binnen ~em (form), in ~em (form) shortly, before long; er hat den Wagen erst seit ~em he's only had the car for a short or little while; seit ~em gibt es Bier in der Kantine recently there's been beer in the canteen; über ~ oder lang sooner or later; (bis) vor ~em (until) recently; ~ nacheinander shortly after each other.

Kurz-: ~arbeit f short time; k~arbeiten vi sep to be on or to work short time; ~arbeiter m short-time worker; k~ärm(e)lig adj short-sleeved; k~atmig adj (fig) feeble, lame; (Med) short-winded; ~atmigkeit f (Med) shortness of breath, dyspnoea (spec).

Kürze f -, -n (a) no pl shortness; (von Besuch, Bericht etc auch) brevity, briefness; (fig: Bündigkeit) brevity, conciseness; (fig: Barschheit) abruptness, curtness, bluntness. die ~ seines Atems his short-windedness; in ~ shortly, soon; in aller ~ briefly; der ~ halber for the sake of brevity; in der ~ liegt die Würze (Prov) brevity is the soul of wit.
  (b) (Poet: Silbe) short (syllable).

Kürzel nt -s, - (stenographisches Zeichen) shorthand symbol; (Kurzwort) contraction.

kürzen vt Kleid, Rede etc to shorten; Buch auch to abridge; (Math) Bruch to cancel (down); Gehalt, Etat, Produktion to cut (back). jdm das Gehalt etc ~ to cut back sb's salary etc.

Kurze(r) m decl as adj (inf) (a) (Schnaps) schnapps, short. (b) (Kurzschluß) short(-circuit).

kurzerhand adv without further ado; entlassen on the spot. etw ~ ablehnen to reject sth out of hand.

Kurz-: ~fassung f abridged version; ~film m short (film); ~form f shortened form (von, zu of, for); k~fristig 1 adj short-term; Wettervorhersage short-range; 2 adv (auf kurze Sicht) for the short term; (für kurze Zeit) for a short time; etw k~fristig erledigen to do sth without delay; k~fristig seine Pläne ändern to change one's plans at short notice; k~fristig gesehen looked at in the short term; k~gefaßt adj concise; ~geschichte f short story; k~geschnitten adj attr cropped; k~haarig adj short-haired; k~halsig adj short-necked; k~halten vt sep irreg jdn k~halten to keep sb short; k~hin adv (obs) tersely, curtly; k~lebig adj short-lived, ephemeral.

kürzlich adv recently, lately. erst or gerade ~ only or just recently, only a short time ago.

Kurz-: ~meldung f news flash; ~nachrichten pl the news headlines pl; (in Zeitung auch) the news in brief; ~parker m: „nur für ~parker" "short-stay or short-term parking only"; k~schließen vt sep irreg to short-circuit; ~schluß m (a) short-circuit; einen ~schluß haben/bekommen to be short-circuited/to short-circuit; (b) (fig: auch ~schlußhandlung) rash action; das war ein ~schluß or eine ~schlußhandlung something just went snap; ~schrift f shorthand; k~schriftlich 1 adj shorthand; 2 adv in shorthand; k~sichtig adj (lit, fig) short-sighted; ~sichtigkeit f (lit, fig) short-sightedness; ~streckenflugzeug nt short-haul or short-range aircraft;

~**streckenläufer** m (Sport) sprinter, short distance runner; k~**treten** vi sep irreg (Mil) to march with short steps; (fig inf) to go easy; k~**um** adv in short, in a word.
Kürzung f shortening; (eines Berichts, Buchs etc) abridgement; (von Gehältern, von Etat, der Produktion) cut (gen in).
Kurz-: ~**urlaub** m short holiday; (Mil) short leave; ~**waren** pl haberdashery (Brit), notions pl (US); k~**weg** adv siehe kurzerhand; ~**weil** f -, no pl (old) pastime, diversion; allerlei ~**weil treiben** to amuse oneself; zur ~**weil** as a pastime; k~**weilig** adj entertaining; ~**welle** f (Rad) short wave; ~**wellenempfänger** m short-wave receiver; ~**wellensender** m short-wave transmitter; ~**wort** nt abbreviation, abbreviated word.
kusch interj (an Hund) down.
kuschelig adj (inf) cosy, snug.
kuscheln vr sich an jdn ~ to snuggle up or cuddle up to sb; sich in etw (acc) ~ to snuggle up or cuddle up in sth.
kuschen vir (Hund etc) to get down; (fig) to knuckle under.
Kusine f (female) cousin.
Kuß m Kusses, Küsse kiss. Gruß und ~ Dein X (hum inf) love and kisses, yours X.
Küßchen nt little kiss, peck (inf). gib ~ give me a kiss.
küßdiehand, küß die Hand interj (Aus) your servant (old); (guten Tag auch) how do you do?; (auf Wiedersehen auch) good day.
kuß|echt adj Lippenstift kiss-proof.
küssen 1 vti to kiss. jdm die Hand ~ to kiss sb's hand; küß or küss die Hand (S Ger, Aus) siehe küßdiehand. 2 vr to kiss (each other).
Kuß-: k~**fest** adj siehe k~echt; ~**hand** f jdm eine ~hand zuwerfen to blow sb a kiss; mit ~**hand!** with (the greatest) pleasure!, gladly!; jdn/etw mit ~**hand nehmen** (inf) to be only too glad to take sb/sth; er wurde mit ~**hand genommen** they/we etc were only too glad to take him.
Küste f -, -n coast; (Ufer) shore. die zerklüftete ~ Schottlands the jagged coastline or coast of Scotland.
Küsten- in cpds coastal; ~**bewohner** m coast-dweller; die ~**bewohner Englands** people who live on the English coast; ~**fischerei** f inshore fishing or fishery (form); ~**gebiet** nt coastal area; ~**gewässer** pl, ~**meer** nt coastal waters pl;

~**schiffahrt** f coastal shipping; ~**strich** m stretch of coast; ~**wacht** f coastguard.
Küster m -s, - verger, sexton.
Küsterei f verger's or sexton's house.
Kustode m -n, -n, **Kustos** m -, **Kustoden** (in Museum) curator.
Kutikula f -, -s (spec) cuticle, cuticula (spec).
Kutschbock m coach-box.
Kutsche f -, -n coach, carriage; (inf: Auto) jalopy (inf).
kutschen vti (old) siehe kutschieren.
Kutscher m -s, - coachman, driver.
Kutschermanieren pl (pej) manners like a navvy pl.
kutschieren* 1 vi aux sein to drive, to ride. durch die Gegend ~ (inf) to drive or ride around. 2 vt to drive. jdn im Auto durch die Gegend ~ to drive sb around.
Kutschkasten m luggage compartment on a coach.
Kutte f -, -n habit.
Kuttel f -, -n usu pl siehe Kaldaune.
Kutter m -s, - (Naut) cutter.
Kuvert [ku'veːr, ku'veːr] nt -s, -s or [-'vert] -(e)s, -e (a) (Brief~) envelope. (b) (Gedeck) cover.
kuvertieren* [kuver'tiːrən] vt (form) to put into an envelope.
Kuvertüre [kuver'tyːrə] f -, -n (Cook) (chocolate) coating.
Kuwait nt -s Kuwait.
Kuwaiter(in f) m -s, - Kuwaiti.
kuwaitisch adj Kuwaiti.
kW abbr of Kilowatt.
kWh abbr of Kilowattstunde.
Kybernetik f cybernetics sing.
Kybernetiker(in f) m -s, - cybernetician.
kybernetisch adj cybernetic.
Kykladen pl Cyclades pl.
kymrisch adj Cymric, Welsh.
Kyniker m -s, - Cynic.
Kyrie(eleison) ['kyːrie(e'laizɔn)] nt -s, -s Kyrie (eleison).
kyrillisch adj Cyrillic.
KZ [kaː'tset] nt -s, -s concentration camp.
KZler(in f) [kaː'tsetln, -lərɪn] m -s, - (inf) concentration camp prisoner.

L

L, l [εl] nt -, - L, l.
l. abbr of Liter.
Lab nt -(e)s, -e rennin.
labb|rig adj (dial) Bier, Suppe watery; Kaffee, Tee auch weak; Essen mushy; Stoff etc floppy, limp; Hose flappy.
labbern vti (N Ger) to slurp; (Katze) to lap noisily; (Naut: Segel) to flap.
laben (liter) 1 vt (Mensch) to feast; (Quelle) to refresh. 2 vr to feast (oneself) (an + dat on); (an einer Quelle etc) to refresh oneself (mit, an + dat with). wir labten uns an dem Anblick we drank in or feasted our eyes on the view.
labern (inf) 1 vi to prattle or jabber (on or away) (inf). 2 vt to talk. was laberst du denn da? what are you prattling etc on about? (inf).
Labetrunk m (old liter) refreshing draught (liter).
labial adj (Ling) labial.
Labial(laut) m -s, -e labial.
labil adj (physisch) Gesundheit delicate; Kreislauf poor; Patient frail; (psychisch) Mensch, Charakter weak.
Labilität f siehe adj delicateness; poorness; frailness; weakness.
labiodental adj (Ling) labiodental.
Lab-: ~**kraut** nt (Bot) bedstraw; ~**magen** m (Zool) abomasum (spec), fourth stomach.
Labor nt -s, -s or -e laboratory, lab (inf).
Laborant(in f) m lab(oratory) technician.
Laboratorium nt laboratory.
laborieren* vi to labour (an + dat at); (leiden) to be plagued (an + dat by).
Labsal nt -(e)s, -e, (Aus auch) f -, -e (old, liter) refreshment.
Labskaus nt -, no pl (N Ger) stew made of meat, fish and mashed potato.
Labung f (liter) refreshment.
Labyrinth nt -(e)s, -e (lit, Med) labyrinth; (fig auch) maze.
labyrinthisch adj labyrinthine, maze-like.
Lach|anfall m laughing fit.
Lache¹ f -, -n puddle; (von Benzin, Blut etc auch) pool.
Lache² f -, -n (inf) laugh.
lächeln vi to smile. verlegen/freundlich ~ to give an embarrassed/a friendly smile.

Lächeln nt -s, no pl smile.
lachen 1 vi to laugh (über + acc at). jdn zum L~ bringen, jdn ~ machen to make sb laugh; zum L~ sein (lustig) to be hilarious; (lächerlich) to be laughable; mir ist nicht zum L~ (zumute) I'm in no laughing mood; daß ich nicht lache! (inf) don't make me laugh! (inf); da kann ich doch nur ~ I can't help laughing (at that); du hast gut ~! it's all right for you to laugh! (inf); lach du nur! you can laugh!; gezwungen/verlegen ~ to give a forced/an embarrassed laugh; wer zuletzt lacht, lacht am besten (Prov) he who laughs last, laughs longest (Prov); die ~**den Erben** (hum) the joyful heirs; die Sonne or der Himmel lacht the sun is shining brightly; ihm lachte das Glück/der Erfolg Fortune/success smiled on or favoured him; siehe Dritte(r).
  2 vt da gibt es gar nichts zu ~ that's nothing to laugh about; (es ist etwas Ernstes auch) that's no laughing matter, that's not funny; was gibt es denn da zu ~? what's so funny about that?; er hat bei seiner Frau nichts zu ~ (inf) he has a hard time of it with his wife; wenn dieses Versehen herauskommt, hast du nichts zu ~ (inf) you won't have anything to laugh about or it won't be funny if that mistake comes to light; das wäre doch gelacht if it would be ridiculous; sich schief or scheckig or krumm or bukkelig or krüpp(e)lig ~, sich (dat) einen Ast or Bruch ~ (inf) to split one's sides (laughing) (inf), to kill oneself (inf), to laugh oneself silly (inf); sich (dat) eins ~ (inf) to have a little snigger.
Lachen nt -s, no pl laughter, laughing; (Art des ~s) laugh. vor ~ schreien to shriek with laughter; dir wird das ~ schon noch vergehen! you'll soon be laughing on the other side of your face.
Lacher m -s, - (a) laugher. die ~ auf seiner Seite haben to have the last laugh; (einen Lacherfolg verbuchen) to get a laugh. (b) (inf: Lache) laugh. einen ~ ausstoßen to give a laugh.
Lach|erfolg m ein ~ sein, einen ~ haben or erzielen to make everybody laugh.
lächerlich adj (a) ridiculous, absurd, ludicrous; (komisch) comical, funny. jdn/etw ~ machen, to make sb/sth look silly or stupid (vor jdm in front of sb); jdn/sich ~ machen to make a fool of sb/oneself (vor jdm in front of sb); etw ins L~e ziehen to make fun of sth. (b) (geringfügig) Kleinigkeit, Anlaß trivial, petty; Preis ridiculously or absurdly low.
lächerlicherweise adv ridiculously enough.

Lächerlichkeit f (a) no pl ridiculousness; (von Argument etc auch) absurdity. **jdn der ~ preisgeben** to make a laughing stock of sb. (b) (Geringfügigkeit) triviality.
Lach-: ~**gas** nt laughing gas; l~**haft** adj ridiculous, ludicrous; Ansichten, Argument auch laughable; ~**krampf** m paroxysm (of laughter); **einen ~krampf bekommen** to go (off) into fits of laughter; **einen ~krampf haben** to be in fits (of laughter) (inf) or in stitches (inf), to fall about laughing (inf); ~**möwe** f black-headed gull; ~**muskel** m (Anat) risorius; **das ist was für Ihre ~muskeln** this will really make you laugh.
Lachs [laks] m -es, -e salmon.
Lachsalve f burst or roar of laughter.
Lachs-: l~**farben**, l~**farbig** adj salmon pink, salmon(-coloured); ~**forelle** f salmon or sea trout; ~**schinken** m smoked, rolled fillet of ham.
Lach-: ~**taube** f ringdove, Barbary dove; ~**zwang** m (hum) **es besteht kein ~zwang** you don't have to laugh.
Lack m -(e)s, -e (Holz~, Nagel~) varnish; (Auto~) paint; (für Lackarbeiten) lacquer; siehe **fertig**.
Lack-: ~**affe** m (pej inf) flash Harry (inf); ~**arbeit** f lacquer-work.
Lacke f -, -n (Aus) puddle.
Lackel m -s, - (S Ger, Aus) oaf.
lacken vti (Tech) to lacquer.
Lackfarbe f gloss paint.
Lackier|arbeiten pl (von Möbeln etc) varnishing; (von Autos) spraying.
lackieren* vti Holz to varnish; Fingernägel auch to paint; Auto to spray. **am Ende war ich der Lackierte** (inf) I ended up looking a fool.
Lackierer(in f) m -s, - varnisher; (von Autos) sprayer.
Lackiererei f (a) (Auto~) paint shop; (Möbel~) varnisher's. (b) (Handwerk) lacquerwork.
Lackierung f (a) (das Lackieren) (von Autos) spraying; (von Möbeln) varnishing. (b) (der Lack) (von Auto) paintwork; (Holz~) varnish; (für Lackarbeiten) lacquer.
Lackier-: ~**werkstatt**, ~**werkstätte** f siehe **Lackiererei (a).**
Lackleder nt patent leather.
lackmeiern vt siehe **gelackmeiert.**
Lackmus nt or m -, no pl litmus.
Lackmuspapier nt litmus paper.
Lack-: ~**schaden** m damage to the paintwork; ~**schuh** m patent-leather shoe.
Lade f -, -n chest; (inf: Schub~) drawer.
Lade-: ~**baum** m derrick; ~**brücke** f loading bridge; ~**bühne** f loading ramp; ~**fläche** f load area; ~**gewicht** nt load, capacity; ~**gut** nt (Ladung) load; (Fracht) freight no pl; **das Gewehr hat ~hemmung** the gun is jammed; **er hatte plötzlich ~hemmung** (inf) he had a sudden mental block; ~**höhe** f Lkw **mit einer ~höhe bis zu ... Meter** loads not exceeding ... metres (in height); ~**klappe** f tailboard; ~**kontrolle** f (Aut) (generator) charge indicator; ~**luke** f cargo or loading hatch.
laden¹ pret **lud**, ptp **geladen** 1 vt (a) (beladen) to load; (entladen) to unload. **einen Sack Mehl auf den Rücken ~** to load or hump a sack of flour on one's back; **das Schiff hat Autos geladen** the ship has a cargo of cars; **der Lkw hat zuviel geladen** the lorry is overloaded; **Verantwortung/Schulden auf sich** (acc) **~** to saddle or load oneself with responsibility/debts; **eine schwere Schuld auf sich** (acc) **~** to place oneself under a heavy burden of guilt; **da habe ich ja etwas auf mich geladen** I've taken on more than I'd bargained for; **jdn** (dat) **etw auf den Hals ~** (inf) to saddle oneself with sth (inf); **er hatte schon ganz schön geladen** (inf) he was already pretty tanked up (inf).
(b) Gewehr, Pistole to load; (Phys) to charge. **der Chef war mächtig geladen** (inf) the boss was absolutely hopping (mad) (inf); **mit Spannung geladen** charged with tension.
2 vi (a) to load (up).
(b) (Phys) to charge.
laden² pret **lud** ptp **geladen** vt (a) (liter: einladen) to invite. (b) (form: vor Gericht) to summon.
Laden¹ m -s, ˸ shop (esp Brit), store (US); (inf: Betrieb) outfit (inf). **der ~ läuft** (inf) business is good; **es wird eine Zeit dauern, bis der ~ läuft** (inf) it will be some time before the business gets going or off the ground; **dann kann er den ~ zumachen** or **dichtmachen** (inf) he might as well shut up shop (and go home) (inf); **den ~ schmeißen** (sl) to run the show; (zurechtkommen) to manage; **den (ganzen) ~ hinschmeißen** (inf) to chuck the whole lot in (inf).
Laden² m -s, ˸ or - shutter.
Laden-: ~**besitzer** m shopowner (esp Brit), storekeeper (US); ~**dieb** m shoplifter; ~**diebstahl** m shoplifting; ~**hüter** m non-seller; ~**kasse** f cashdesk, till; ~**kette** f chain of shops or stores; ~**mädchen** nt shopgirl (Brit), sales clerk (US); ~**preis** m shop price; ~**schild** nt shop (esp Brit) or store (US) sign.
Ladenschluß m **nach/vor ~** after/before the shops (esp Brit) or stores (US) shut; **kurz vor ~** (lit, fig) just before we/they shut up shop; **um fünf Uhr ist ~** the shops/stores shut at five o'clock.
Ladenschluß-: ~**gesetz** nt law governing the hours of trading; ~**zeit** f (shop) closing time.
Laden-: ~**schwengel** m (old, iro) shopboy, shoplad; ~**straße** f shopping street; ~**tisch** m shop counter; **über den/unter dem ~tisch** over/under the counter; ~**tochter** f (Sw) shop or sales assistant, salesgirl.
Lade-: ~**platz** m loading bay or area; ~**rampe** f loading ramp; ~**raum** m load room; (Aviat, Naut) hold; ~**stock** m ramrod.
lädieren* vt Kunstwerk, Briefmarke to damage. **lädiert sein** (hum)/**aussehen** (hum) to be/look the worse for wear.
Lädierung f damage no pl (gen to).

ladinisch adj Ladin.
Ladnerin f (old: S Ger, Aus) shop assistant.
Ladung f (a) load; (von Schnee, Steinen, Unflätigkeiten etc) whole load (inf); (von Sprengstoff) charge. **eine geballte ~ Schnee/Dreck** (inf) a handful of snow/mud; **eine geballte ~ von Schimpfwörtern** a whole torrent of abuse. (b) (Vorladung) summons sing.
Lady ['le:di] f -, -s or Ladies lady; (Adlige) Lady.
Lafette f (Mil) (gun)carriage.
Laffe m -n, -n (pej) flash Harry (inf).
lag pret of **liegen.**
Lage f -, -n (a) (geographische ~) situation, location. **in günstiger ~** well-situated; **eine gute/ruhige ~ haben** to be well/peacefully situated, to be in a good/peaceful location.
(b) (Art des Liegens) position. **eine bequeme ~ haben, sich in einer bequemen ~ befinden** to be lying comfortably, to be (lying) in a comfortable position.
(c) (Situation) situation. **dazu bin ich nicht in der ~** I'm not in a position to do that; **er wird wohl nie in die ~ kommen, das zu tun** he'll never be in a position to do it; **in der glücklichen/beneidenswerten ~ sein, etw zu tun** to be in the happy/enviable position of doing sth; **Herr der ~ sein/bleiben** to be/remain master of or in control of the situation; **die ~ der Dinge erfordert es, daß ...** the situation requires that ...; **in allen ~n** always, in all eventualities; siehe **peilen.**
(d) (Schicht) layer.
(e) (Mus) (Stimm~) register; (Ton~) pitch; (eines Instruments) position. **enge/weite ~** close/open harmony.
(f) (Runde) round. **eine ~ schmeißen** (sl) to buy or get or stand a round.
Lage-: ~**bericht** m report; (Mil) situation report; ~**besprechung** f discussion of the situation; **eine ~besprechung abhalten** to discuss the situation.
lagenweise adv in layers.
Lageplan m ground plan.
Lager nt -s, - (a) (Unterkunft) camp.
(b) (liter: Schlafstätte) bed. **die Krankheit fesselte ihn wochenlang ans ~** the illness kept him abed for weeks; **sie wachten am ~ des Königs** they kept watch at the King's bedside.
(c) (fig: Partei) camp; (von Staaten) bloc. **ins andere ~ überwechseln** to change camps or sides.
(d) pl auch ˸ (Vorratsraum) store(room); (von Laden) stockroom; (~halle) warehouse; (Vorrat) stock. **am ~ sein** to be in stock; **etw auf ~ haben** to have sth in stock; (fig) Witz etc to have sth on tap (inf) or (at the) ready.
(e) (Tech) bearing.
(f) (Geol) bed.
Lager-: ~**bestand** m stock; **den ~bestand aufnehmen** to do the stocktaking; l~**fähig** adj non-perishable; ~**feuer** nt campfire; ~**gebühr** f, ~**geld** nt storage charge; ~**halle** f warehouse; ~**haltung** f storekeeping; ~**haltung rentiert sich bei uns nicht** it doesn't pay us to keep a large stock; ~**haus** nt warehouse.
Lagerist(in f) m storeman/storewoman.
Lager-: ~**koller** m (inf) **er hat einen ~koller gekriegt** life in the camp turned his mind; ~**leben** nt camp life; ~**leiter** m camp commander; (in Ferien- etc) camp leader.
lagern 1 vt (a) (aufbewahren) to store. **kühl ~!** keep or store in a cool place.
(b) (hinlegen) jdn to lay down; Bein etc to rest. **den Kopf/einen Kranken weich ~** to rest one's head/lay an invalid on something soft; **das Bein hoch ~** to put one's leg up; **die Kranken müssen bequem gelagert werden** the invalids must be bedded down or must lie comfortably; siehe **gelagert.**
2 vi (a) (Lebensmittel etc) to be stored or kept.
(b) (liegen) to lie.
(c) (von Truppen) to camp, to be encamped.
3 vr (geh) to settle oneself (down).
Lager-: ~**raum** m storeroom; (in Geschäft) stockroom; ~**statt** f (old liter) bed, couch (liter); ~**stätte** f (a) (old liter) siehe ~**statt;** (b) (Geol) deposit.
Lagerung f storage; (das Lagern auch) storing.
Lagerverwalter m (a) stores supervisor. (b) siehe **Lagerleiter.**
Lageskizze f sketch-map.
Lagune f -, -n lagoon.
Lagunenstadt f town built on a lagoon; (Venedig) Venice.
lahm adj (a) (gelähmt) Bein, Mensch lame; (inf: steif) stiff. **er ist auf dem linken Bein ~** he is lame in his or the left leg; **er hat ein ~es Bein** he is lame in one leg, he has a gammy leg (inf).
(b) (inf: langsam, langweilig) dreary, dull; Ausrede, Entschuldigung, Geschäftsgang slow, sluggish. **eine ~e Ente sein** (inf) to have no zip (inf).
Lahm-: ~**arsch** m (sl) slowcoach (Brit inf), slowpoke (US inf); l~**arschig** adj (sl) bloody (Brit inf) or damn (inf) slow; **steh doch nicht so l~arschig herum!** get your finger out! (sl), get your arse in gear! (vulg).
lahmen vi to be lame (auf +dat in).
lähmen vt to paralyze; (fig) Industrie auch to cripple; Verhandlungen, Verkehr to hold up; Freude, Fest etc to spoil. **er ist durch einen Unfall/an beiden Beinen gelähmt** he was paralyzed in an accident, he is paralyzed in both legs; **vor Angst wie gelähmt sein** to be petrified, to be paralyzed with fear; ~**des Entsetzen befiel die Zuschauer** the onlookers were paralyzed with horror.
Lahme(r) mf decl as adj (old) cripple.
lahmlegen vt sep Verkehr, Produktion to bring to a standstill or halt; Industrie auch to paralyze.
Lahmlegung f bringing to a standstill no art, paralyzing no art. **zur ~ des Verkehrs führen** to bring the traffic to a standstill.
Lähmung f (lit) paralysis; (fig) immobilization. **der Unfall hatte**

die ~ des Verkehrs zur Folge the accident brought traffic to a standstill.

Lähmungs|erscheinungen *pl* signs *pl* of paralysis.

Lahn *f -, -en* (*Aus*) avalanche.

Laib *m -(e)s, -e* (*esp S Ger*) loaf.

Laich *m -(e)s, -e* spawn.

laichen *vi* to spawn.

Laich-: ~**platz** *m* spawning ground; ~**zeit** *f* spawning season.

Laie *m -n, -n* (*lit, fig*) layman. ~**n** the lay public; **die ~n** (*Eccl*) the laity; **da staunt der ~, der Fachmann wundert sich** (*hum inf*) that's a real turn-up for the book (*inf*).

Laien-: ~**apostolat** *nt* lay apostolate; ~**bruder** *m* lay brother; ~**bühne** *f* amateur dramatic society; (*Gebäude*) amateur theatre; **l~haft** *adj Arbeit* amateurish, unprofessional; *Urteil, Meinung* lay *attr only;* ~**prediger**, ~**priester** *m* lay preacher; ~**richter** *m* lay judge; ~**schwester** *f* lay sister; ~**spiel** *nt* amateur play; ~**stand** *m* laity; ~**theater** *nt* amateur theatre; (*Ensemble*) amateur theatre group; ~**tum** *nt* laity; **er mußte sich zwischen Priestertum und ~tum entscheiden** he had to decide whether to become a priest or remain a layman.

laisieren* [lai'zi:rən] *vt* to unfrock.

Laisierung *f* unfrocking.

Laisser-faire [lɛsɛ'fɛ:r] *nt -, no pl* (*Econ, fig*) laisser- or laissez-faire.

Laizismus [lai'tsısmus] *m* laicism.

laizistisch [lai'tsıstıʃ] *adj* laicistic.

Lakai *m -en, -en* (*lit, fig*) lackey.

Lake *f -, -n* brine.

Laken *nt -s, -* sheet.

lakonisch *adj* laconic.

Lakritz *m -es, -e* (*dial*), **Lakritze** *f -, -n* liquorice.

Laktose *f -, no pl* lactose.

lala *adv* (*inf*): **so ~** so-so (*inf*), not too bad (*inf*).

lallen *vti* to babble; (*Betrunkener*) to mumble.

Lama¹ *nt -s, -s* llama.

Lama² *m -(s), -s* (*Rel*) lama.

Lamaismus *m* Lamaism.

Lamakloster *nt* lamasery.

Lamäng *f:* **aus der (kalten) ~** (*sl*) just like that.

Lambrie *f* (*dated, S Ger*) skirting (board) (*Brit*), baseboard (*US*).

Lamé *m -s, -s* (*Tex*) lamé.

Lamelle *f* (a) (*Biol*) lamella. (b) (*Tech*) commutator bar or segment; (*von Jalousien*) slat.

lamellenförmig *adj* lamellate, lamellar.

lamentieren* *vi* to moan, to complain.

Lamento *nt -s, -s* (*Mus*) lament. **wegen etw ein ~ anstimmen** (*fig*) to bewail sth.

Lametta *nt -s, no pl* lametta; (*hum: Orden*) gongs *pl* (*inf*).

laminieren* *vt* (*Tex*) to draw; (*Typ*) to laminate.

Lamm *nt -(e)s, ˶er* lamb. **das ~ Gottes** the Lamb of God.

Lammbraten *m* roast lamb.

Lämmerwölkchen *pl* fleecy or cotton-wool clouds *pl* (*inf*).

Lamm(e)sgeduld *f* patience of a saint.

Lamm-: ~**fell** *nt* lambskin; ~**fleisch** *nt* lamb; **l~fromm** *adj Gesicht, Miene* innocent; **l~fromm sein** to be like a (little) lamb; **sie saßen l~fromm auf ihren Plätzen** they were sitting in their seats like little lambs or as good as gold.

Lammsgeduld *f siehe* **Lamm(e)sgeduld**.

Lammwolle *f* lambswool.

Lampe *f -, -n* light; (*Öl-, Steh~, Tisch~*) lamp; (*Glüh~*) bulb. **die ~n auf der Straße the street lights; einen auf die ~ gießen** (*inf*) to wet one's whistle; (*inf*), *siehe* **Meister**.

Lampen-: ~**fieber** *nt* stage fright; ~**licht** *nt* artificial light; ~**schirm** *m* lampshade.

Lamperie *f siehe* **Lambrie**.

Lampion [lam'piõ:, lam'piɔŋ] *m -s, -s* Chinese lantern.

lancieren* [lã'si:rən] *vt Produkt, Künstler* to launch; *Meldung, Nachricht* to put out. **jdn/etw in etw** (*acc*) ~ to get sb/sth into sth; **sein Onkel hat ihn in diese hohe Stellung lanciert** his uncle got him (into) that high position.

Lancierung *f* launching; putting out.

Land *nt -(e)s, ˶er* (a) (*Gelände, Festland*) land. **ein Stück ~ a** plot of land or ground; ~ **bestellen/bebauen** to till the soil or land/to cultivate the land; **an ~ gehen** to go ashore; **jdn an ~ setzen** to put sb ashore; **an ~ schwimmen** to swim to the shore; ~ **sehen** (*lit*) to see or sight land; **endlich können wir ~ sehen/ich sehe ich ~** (*fig*) at last we/I can see the light at the end of the tunnel; **kein ~ mehr sehen (können)** (*fig*) to be completely muddled *or* in a complete muddle; **etw/ein Boot/einen Fisch an ~ ziehen** to pull sth ashore/to beach a boat/to land a fish; **einen Millionär/einen Auftrag an ~ ziehen** (*inf*) to land a millionaire/an order; **er hat seinen Vermögensanteil sicher an ~ gezogen** (*inf*) he made sure of his share of the inheritance; ~ **in Sicht!** land ahoy!; ~ **unter!** land submerged!
(b) (*ländliches Gebiet*) country. **aufs ~** (in)to the country; **auf dem ~e** in the country; **über ~ fahren** (*old*) to travel.
(c) (*Staat*) country, land (*esp liter*); (*Bundes~*) (in *BRD*) Land, state; (in *Österreich*) province. **das ~ Hessen/Tirol** the state of Hesse/the province of Tyrol, Tyrol province; **außer ~es sein/gehen** to be out of/leave the country; **~ und Leute kennenlernen** to get to know the country and its inhabitants; **~e** *pl* (*poet*) lands *pl;* **in fernen ~en** (*liter*) in distant *or* far away lands; **durch die ~e ziehen** (*liter*) to roam abroad; **das ~ der tausend Seen** the land of the thousand lakes; **das ~ der aufgehenden Sonne** the land of the rising sun; **aus aller Herren ˶er(n)** from all over the world, from the four corners of the earth; **der Frühling war ins ~ gezogen** (*liter*) spring had arrived; **seitdem**

waren viele Jahre ins ~ gegangen *or* gezogen (*liter*) many years had passed since then.

Land-: **l~ab** *adv siehe* **l~auf;** ~**adel** *m* landed gentry; ~**ammann** *m* (*Sw*) highest official in a Swiss canton; ~**arbeit** *f* agricultural work; ~**arbeiter** *m* agricultural worker; ~**aristokratie** *f* landed aristocracy; **l~arm** *adj Bauer* with little land; ~**arzt** *m* country doctor.

Landauer *m -s, -* landau.

Land-: **l~auf** *adv:* **l~auf, l~ab** all over the country, the length and breadth of the country; **l~aus** *adv:* **l~aus, ~ein** all over the world; ~**bau** *m siehe* **Ackerbau;** ~**besitz** *m* landholding; ~**besitz haben** to be a landowner, to own land; ~**bewohner** *m* landowner; ~**bevölkerung** *f* rural population; ~**bewohner** *m* country dweller; ~**bewohner sind** ... people who live in the country are ...; ~**brot** *nt* brown bread usually made from rye flour; ~**brücke** *f* land bridge; ~**butter** *f* farm butter.

Lände *f -, -n* (*dial*) landing stage.

Lande-: ~**bahn** *f* landing strip; ~**brücke** *f siehe* **Landungsbrücke;** ~**erlaubnis** *f* landing permission, permission to land; ~**fähre** *f* (*Space*) landing module.

Land-: ~**eier** *pl* farm eggs *pl;* **l~ein** *adv siehe* **l~aus;** **l~einwärts** *adv* inland.

Lande-: ~**klappe** *f* landing flap; ~**kopf** *m* (*Mil*) bridgehead; ~**korridor** *m* (*Space*) re-entry corridor *or* window; ~**manöver** *nt* landing manoeuvre.

landen 1 *vi aux sein* to land; (*inf: enden*) to land up; (*inf: Eindruck machen*) to get somewhere. **weich ~** to make a soft landing; **alle anonymen Briefe ~ sofort im Papierkorb** all anonymous letters go straight into the wastepaper basket; **mit deinen Komplimenten kannst du bei mir nicht ~** your compliments won't get you anywhere *or* very far with me.

2 *vt* (*lit, fig*) to land; *siehe* **Coup**.

länden *vt* (*dial*) *Leiche* to recover (*aus* from).

Land|enge *f* isthmus.

Lande-: ~**piste** *f siehe* ~**bahn;** ~**platz** *m* (*für Flugzeuge*) place to land; (*ausgebaut*) landing strip; (*für Schiffe*) landing place.

Ländereien *pl* estates *pl.*

Länder-: ~**kampf** *m* (*Sport*) international contest; (~*spiel*) international (match); ~**kunde** *f* regional studies *pl;* ~**name** *m* name of a/the country; ~**spiel** *nt* international (match).

Landes-: ~**bank** *f* regional bank; ~**beamte(r)** *m* civil servant employed by a Land rather than the nation; ~**behörde** *f* regional authorities *pl;* ~**brauch** *m* national custom, custom of the country; **nach ~brauch ist es hier üblich** ... in this country it is customary ...; ~**ebene** *f: auf ~ebene* at the regional level; **l~eigen** *adj* owned by the Land/province; ~**farben** *pl* (*von Staat*) national colours *pl;* (*von Bundesland*) state colours *pl/*colours *pl* of the province; ~**gericht** *nt siehe* **Landgericht;** ~**grenze** *f* (*von Staat*) national boundary; (*von Bundesland*) state/provincial boundary; ~**hauptmann** *m* (*Aus*) head of the government of a province; ~**hauptstadt** *f* capital of a Land/province, provincial capital; ~**herr** *m* (*Hist*) sovereign, ruler; ~**innere(s)** *nt* interior; ~**kind** *nt* (*von Staat*) native of a/the country; (*von Bundesland*) native of a/the Land/province; **der König sprach zu seinen ~kindern** the king spoke to his subjects; ~**kirche** *f* national church; (*in Deutschland*) established Protestant church in some Länder; ~**kunde** *f* regional studies *pl;* **l~kundig** *adj* **l~kundiger Reiseleiter** courier who knows the country; **l~kundlich** *adj Themen, Aspekte* regional; ~**liste** *f* (*Parl*) regional list of parliamentary candidates for election to Federal parliament; ~**meister** *m* (*Sport*) regional champion; ~**mutter** *f* (*liter*) mother of the people (*liter*); **die britische ~mutter** the mother of the British nation (*liter*); ~**rat** *m* (*BRD*) highest official of an administrative district; (*Sw*) cantonal parliament; ~**recht** *nt* law of a Land/province; ~**regierung** *f* government of a Land/provincial government; ~**sprache** *f* national language; **der ~sprache unkundig sein** not to know the language; ~**teil** *m* region, area; ~**tracht** *f* national dress *or* costume; ~**trauer** *f* national mourning; **l~üblich** *adj* customary; **das ist dort l~üblich** that's the custom there; ~**vater** *m* (*liter*) father of the people (*liter*); **der bayrische ~vater** the father of the Bavarians (*liter*); ~**verrat** *m* treason; ~**verteidigung** *f* national defence; **l~verwiesen** *adj* (*rare*) expelled, banished (*old*); (*exiliert*) exiled.

Lande-: ~**übung** *f* landing exercise; ~**verbot** *nt* refusal of landing permission; ~**verbot erhalten** to be refused landing permission *or* permission to land.

Land-: ~**fahrer** *m* (*form*) vagrant; **l~fein** *adj* (*dated*) spruced up; **sich l~fein machen** to spruce oneself up; ~**flucht** *f* migration from the land, emigration to the cities; ~**frau** *f* countrywoman; ~**friede(n)** *m* (*Hist*) King's/Queen's Peace; ~**friedensbruch** *m* (*Jur*) breach of the peace; ~**funk** *m* farming (radio) programme; ~**gemeinde** *f* country community; ~**gericht** *nt* district court; ~**gewinnung** *f* land reclamation; ~**graf** *m* landgrave; ~**gut** *nt* estate; ~**haus** *nt* country house; ~**heer** *nt* army; ~**heim** *nt siehe* **Schullandheim;** ~**jäger** *m* (a) (*Hist*) country policeman; (b) (*Wurst*) pressed smoked sausage; ~**karte** *f* map; ~**klima** *nt* continental climate; ~**kreis** *m* administrative district; ~**krieg** *m* land warfare; **Luft- und ~krieg** war in the air and on the ground; **See- und ~krieg** war at sea and on land; ~**kriegsordnung** *f:* **Haager ~kriegsordnung** Hague Land Warfare Convention; **l~läufig** *adj* popular, common; **entgegen l~läufiger** *or* **der l~läufigen Meinung** contrary to popular opinion; ~**leben** *nt* country life.

Ländler *m -s, -* (*S Ger*) country dance.

Landleute *pl* country people *or* folk *pl.*

ländlich *adj* rural; *Tracht* country *attr; Tanz* country *attr,* folk *attr; Idylle* pastoral; *Stille, Frieden* of the countryside, rural.

Ländlichkeit *f* rural character *or* nature.

Land-: **l~liebend** *adj* country-loving *attr;* ~**luft** *f* country air;

~**macht** f land power; ~**mann** m, pl -**männer** (old, liter) husbandman (old, liter); ~**maschinen** pl agricultural machinery sing or machines pl; ~**messer** m siehe ~**vermesser**; ~**nahme** f -, -n (Hist) acquisition of land; ~**partie** f (old) country outing; ~**pfarrer** m country parson; ~**pfleger** m (Bibl) governor; ~**plage** f plague; (fig inf) pest; ~**pomeranze** f (dated pej) country cousin; ~**praxis** f (Med) country practice; ~**rat** m head of the administration of a Landkreis; ~**ratte** f (hum) landlubber; ~**regen** m steady rain; **ein anhaltender ~regen machte es unmöglich, ...** the steady rain made it impossible ...; ~**rücken** m ridge of land; ~**sasse** m -n, -n (Hist) freeholder.

Landschaft f scenery no pl; (Gemälde) landscape; (ländliche Gegend) countryside. **eine öde ~** a barren landscape or region; **die ~ um London** the countryside around London; **die ~en Italiens** the types of countryside in Italy; **wir sahen eine reizvolle ~** we saw some delightful scenery; **vor uns tat sich eine liebliche ~ auf** a lovely view appeared before us; **in der ~ herumstehen** (inf) to stand around; **da stand einsam ein Hochhaus in der ~** (herum) (inf) there was one solitary skyscraper to be seen; **die politische ~** the political scene or landscape.

landschaftlich adj Schönheiten etc scenic; Besonderheiten regional. **das Dorf liegt ~ einmalig** (inf) the village is surrounded by the most fantastic scenery; **diese Gegend ist ~ ausgesprochen reizvoll** the scenery in this area is particularly delightful; **das ist ~ unterschiedlich** it differs from one part of the country to another or in various parts of the country; **„Klempner" heißt ~ auch „Spengler"** in some areas the word "Spengler" is used for "Klempner".

Landschafts-: ~**bild** nt view; (Gemälde) landscape (painting); (Photographie) landscape (photograph); ~**form** f land form; ~**gärtner** m landscape gardener; ~**maler** m landscape painter; ~**schutzgebiet** nt nature reserve.

Land(schul)heim nt siehe **Schullandheim**.

Landser m -s, - (dated inf) private.

Landsitz m country seat.

Lands-: ~**mann** m, ~**männin** f, pl -**leute** compatriot, fellow countryman/-woman; ~**mannschaft** f (a) welfare and cultural association for Germans born in the eastern areas of the former Reich; (b) (Univ) association of students from the same region.

Land-: ~**stände** pl (Hist) body of representatives of various classes in medieval provincial politics; ~**störzer(in** f) m -s, - (obs) camp follower; ~**straße** f country road; (Straße zweiter Ordnung) secondary or B (Brit) road; (im Gegensatz zur Autobahn) ordinary road; ~**streicher(in** f) m -s, - (pej) tramp, hobo (US); ~**streicherei** f vagrancy; ~**streitkräfte** pl land forces pl; ~**strich** m area; **ein flacher ~strich** a flat belt of land; ~**sturm** m conscripted militia in times of war, = Home Guard (Brit); ~**tag** m Landtag (state parliament); ~**truppen** pl land forces pl.

Landung f (von Flugzeug, Truppen etc) landing. **zur ~ gezwungen werden** to be forced to land or forced down.

Landungs-: ~**boot** nt landing craft; ~**brücke** f jetty, landing stage; ~**steg** m landing stage; ~**truppen** pl land assault forces pl.

Land-: ~**urlaub** m shore leave; ~**(ver)messer** m land surveyor; ~**vermessung** f land surveying; ~**vogt** m (Hist) landvogt (governor of a royal province); ~**volk** nt country people pl or folk pl.

landw. abbr of **landwirtschaftlich**.

Land-: l~**wärts** adv landwards; ~**wehr** f territorial army; ~**wein** m vin ordinaire; ~**wind** m offshore wind; ~**wirt** m farmer.

Landwirtschaft f agriculture, farming; (Betrieb) farm; (Landwirte) farmers pl. ~ **betreiben** to farm; ~ **haben** (inf) to have a farm.

landwirtschaftlich adj agricultural. ~**e Geräte** agricultural or farm implements.

Landwirtschafts- in cpds agricultural; ~**ministerium** nt ministry of agriculture; ~**schule** f agricultural college.

Landzunge f spit (of land), promontory.

lang 1 adj, comp ~**er**, superl ~**ste(r, s)** (a) long; Film, Roman, Aufenthalt, Rede auch lengthy. **das ist/war seit ~em geplant** that has been planned (for) a long time/was planned a long time ago; **vor ~er Zeit** a long time ago; **in nicht allzu ~er Zeit** before too or very long, in the not too distant future; **ich habe ~e/~ere Zeit nichts von ihr gehört** I haven't heard from her for a long time/for (quite) some or a time; **das hat die ~ste Zeit gedauert!** that's gone on long enough!; **hier wird mir der Tag/die Zeit nicht ~** I won't get bored here; **etw ~er machen** to make sth longer, to lengthen sth; **es ist eine ~e Strecke bis Bristol, jedenfalls ~er, als ich gedacht hatte** it's a long way to Bristol, at least, further than I thought; **die Tage werden wieder ~er** the days are drawing out or getting longer; **er machte ein ~es Gesicht** his face fell; **man sah überall nur ~e Gesichter** you saw nothing but long faces; **etw von ~er Hand vorbereiten** to prepare sth carefully; **des ~en und breiten at great length**; **einen ~en Hals machen** (inf) to crane one's neck.

(b) (inf: groß gewachsen) Mensch tall. **eine ~e Latte, ein ~er Lulatsch, ein ~es Leiden** or **Laster** or **Elend** or **Ende sein** to be a (real) beanpole (inf); **er ist so ~ wie er dumm ist** he's as thick as two short planks (inf).

2 adv, comp ~**er**, superl am ~**sten**. **der ~ erwartete Regen** the long-awaited rain; **der ~ ersehnte Tag/Urlaub** the longed-for day/holiday; ~ **anhaltender Beifall** prolonged or long applause; **nur einen Augenblick ~** only for a moment or second; **zwei Stunden ~** for two hours; **mein ganzes Leben ~** all my life, my whole life; **mein ganzes Leben ~ werde ich das nicht vergessen** I'll never forget that as long as I live; ~ **und breit** at great length; siehe **entlang**.

lang-: ~**ärm(e)lig** adj long-sleeved; ~**armig** adj long-armed;

~**atmig** adj long-winded; L~**atmigkeit** f long-windedness; ~**beinig** adj long-legged.

lange, lang (S Ger, Aus) adv, comp ~**er**, superl am **längsten** (a) (zeitlich) a long time; (in Fragen, Negativsätzen) long. **die Sitzung hat heute ~/nicht ~ gedauert** the meeting went on (for) a long time/didn't go on (for) long today; **wie ~ lernst du schon Deutsch/bist du schon hier?** how long have you been learning German (for)/been here (for)?; **es ist noch gar nicht ~ her, daß wir diese Frage diskutiert haben** we discussed this question not long ago, it's not long since we discussed this question; **er wird es nicht mehr ~ machen** (inf) he won't last long, he's not got long to go; **bis Weihnachten ist es ja noch ~ hin** it's still a long time till Christmas, we're a long way from Christmas; **je ~er, je lieber** the more the better; (zeitlich) the longer the better; **Sauerkraut kann ich essen je ~er, je lieber** I could eat sauerkraut all day long.

(b) (inf: längst) noch ~ nicht not by any means, not by a long chalk (inf); ~ **nicht so ...** nowhere near as ..., not nearly as ...; **er verdient ~ nicht soviel** he doesn't earn nearly as much or anywhere near as much; **wenn er das schafft, kannst du das schon ~** if he can do it, you can do it easily.

Länge f -, -n (a) (zeitlich, räumlich) length; (inf: von Mensch) height. **eine ~ von 10 Metern haben** to be 10 metres long or in length; **ein Seil von 10 Meter ~** a rope 10 metres long; **ein Vortrag/eine Fahrt von einer Stunde ~** an hour-long lecture/an hour's journey; **Bauarbeiten auf 5 km ~** road works for 5 kms; **etw der ~ nach falten** to fold sth lengthways or lengthwise; **in die ~ gehen** (Kleidungsstücke) to stretch; **in die ~ schießen** or **wachsen** to shoot up; **etw in die ~ ziehen** to protract sth, to drag sth out (inf); **sich in die ~ ziehen** to go on and on; **der ~ nach hinfallen** to fall flat (on one's face); **einen Artikel in seiner vollen ~ abdrucken** to print an article in its entirety.

(b) (Sport) length. **mit einer ~ gewinnen** to win by a length; **die anderen Wagen kamen mit einigen ~n Abstand** the other cars came in several lengths behind.

(c) (in Buch, Film etc) long-drawn-out passage/scene.

(d) (Geog) longitude. **der Ort liegt auf** or **unter 20 Grad östlicher ~** the town has a longitude of 20 degrees east.

langelang adv (inf) ~ **hinfallen** to fall flat, to go sprawling.

langen (dial, inf) **1** vi (a) (sich erstrecken, greifen) to reach (nach for, in +acc into). **bis an/auf etw** (acc)/**zu etw ~** to reach sth.

(b) (fassen) to touch (an etw (acc) sth).

(c) (ausreichen) to be enough; (auskommen) to get by, to manage. **mir langt es** I've had/I have enough; **das Geld langt nicht** there isn't or we etc haven't enough money; **jetzt langt's mir aber!** I've had just about enough!; siehe **hinten**.

2 vt (reichen) **jdm etw ~** to give or pass or hand sb sth; **jdm eine ~** to give sb a clip on the ear (inf); **sich** (dat) **etw ~** to take sth; **ich werde ihn mir schon ~!** I'll teach him a thing or two!

längen vt Schuhe to stretch.

Längen-: ~**grad** m (a) degree of longitude; (b) (auch ~**kreis**) meridian; ~**maß** nt measure of length, linear measure (form).

länger comp of **lang, lange**.

längerfristig 1 adj longer-term. **2** adv in the longer term; **planen** for the longer term.

lang\|ersehnt adj attr longed-for.

Langeweile f (gen) - or **Langenweile**, (dat) - or **Langerweile**, no pl boredom. ~ **haben** to be bored.

Lang-: l~**fädig** adj (Sw) long-winded; ~**finger** m (hum) pickpocket; l~**fing(e)rig** adj long-fingered; (hum) light-fingered; ~**format** nt Briefumschläge/Zigaretten im ~**format** long envelopes/long-(length) cigarettes; l~**fristig 1** adj long-term. **2** adv in the long term; **planen** for the long term; l~**gehegt** adj attr Wunsch long-cherished; l~**gestreckt** adj long; Dorf auch strung-out; l~**gezogen** adj sustained; l~**glied(e)rig** adj long-limbed; l~**haarig** adj long-haired; ~**haarige(r)** mf decl as adj long-haired man/woman; **so ein ~haarige** some long-haired type; **diese dreckigen ~haarigen** (pej) these long-haired layabouts; ~**haarperücke** f long wig; ~**haus** nt nave; l~**hin** adv (rare) **ein l~hin schallender Ton** a sound which goes on and on resounding.

Lang-: ~**holz** nt uncut timber; ~**holzwagen** m timber lorry (Brit) or truck; l~**jährig 1** adj Freundschaft, Bekannter, Gewohnheit long-standing; Erfahrung, Verhandlungen, Recherchen many years of; Mitarbeiter of many years' standing; **2** adv for many years; ~**lauf** m (Ski) cross-country skiing; **Sieger im ~lauf** winner of the cross-country (event); ~**läufer** m (Ski) cross-country skier; l~**lebig** adj long-lasting; Stoff, Waren etc auch durable; Gerücht long-lived; Melodie enduring, long-lived; Mensch, Tier long-lived; l~**lebig sein** to last a long time or have a long life/be durable/long-lived/enduring/live to an old age or be long-lived; ~**lebigkeit** f siehe adj long-lastingness; durability; long life; longevity; l~**legen** vr sep to have a lie-down; (inf: hinfallen) to fall flat on one's face; (inf fig) to be struck all of a heap (inf).

länglich adj long, elongated.

Lang-: l~**liegen** vi sep irreg (inf) to be in bed; l~**mähnig** adj with a long mane, long-maned; (inf) Mensch long-haired; ~**mut** f -, no pl patience, forbearance; l~**mütig** adj patient, forbearing; ~**mütigkeit** f forbearance; l~**ohr** nt (hum) rabbit, bunny (inf); (Häschen) hare; **Meister ~ohr** Master Longears; ~**pferd** nt (Sport) (long) horse.

längs 1 adv lengthways, lengthwise. **2** prep +gen along. ~ **der Straße stehen Kastanien** chestnut trees line the road, there are chestnut trees along the road; **die Bäume ~ des Flusses** the trees along the (banks of) the river.

Längs\|achse f longitudinal axis.

langsam 1 adj slow.
2 adv (a) slowly. **geh/fahr/sprich ~er!** slow down!,

walk/drive/speak (a bit) more slowly or (a bit) slower! (inf); ~, ~!, immer schön ~! (inf) (take it) easy!, easy does it!; ~, aber sicher slowly but surely.

(b) (allmählich, endlich) es wird ~ Zeit, daß ... it's about time or it's high time that ...; ~ müßtest du das aber wissen it's about time or it's high time you knew that; ich muß jetzt ~ gehen I must be getting on my way, I'd better be thinking about going; kannst du dich ~ mal entscheiden? could you start making up your mind?; ~ (aber sicher) reicht es mir I've just about had enough; ist das ~ fertig? is it ready yet?

Langsamkeit f slowness.

langsamtreten vi sep irreg (inf) to go easy (inf); (gesundheitlich auch) to take things easy. Sie müssen langsamer treten! (inf) you'll have to take things a bit easier, you'll have to ease off a bit.

Lang-: ~schäfter m -s, - high boot; (aus Gummi) wader; l~schäftig adj Stiefel high; ~schiff nt nave; ~schläfer m late-riser; ~seite f siehe Längsseite.

Längs-: ~faden m warp; ~falte f lengthways fold; l~gestreift adj Stoff with lengthways stripes; Kleid, Vorhang etc auch with vertical stripes; ~linie f vertical line, line down.

Langspiel-: ~band nt long-playing tape; ~platte f long-playing record.

Längs-: ~richtung f longitudinal direction; in ~richtung zu etw verlaufen to run longitudinally along sth; l~schiffs adv broadside on; ~schnitt m longitudinal section; ~seite f long side; (Naut) broadside; l~seit(s) adv, prep +gen alongside; die beiden Boote lagen l~seit(s) the boats were lying alongside one another; ~streifen pl lengthways stripes pl; (von Kleid, Vorhängen auch) vertical stripes pl.

längst adv (a) (seit langem, schon lange) for a long time; (vor langer Zeit) a long time ago, long ago. er ist inzwischen ~ gestorben he has been dead (for) a long time now; das ist ~ nicht mehr so it hasn't been like that for a long time; als wir ankamen, war der Zug ~ weg when we arrived the train had long since gone.

(b) siehe **lange** (b).

Längstal ['lɛŋs-] nt longitudinal valley.

längstens adv siehe spätestens.

längste(r, s) superl of **lang**.

langstielig adj long-stemmed.

Langstrecken-: ~bomber m long-range bomber; ~flug m long-distance flight; ~flugzeug nt long-range or long-haul aircraft; ~lauf m (Disziplin) long-distance running; (Wettkampf) long-distance race; ~läufer, (auch) Langstreckler -s, - (inf) long-distance runner.

Längswand f long wall.

Languste [laŋ'gʊstə] f -, -n crayfish, crawfish (US).

langweilen insep 1 vt to bore. 2 vi to be boring. 3 vr to be/get bored. sich tödlich or zu Tode ~ to be/get bored to death or to tears; siehe **gelangweilt**.

Langweiler m -s, - bore; (langsamer Mensch) slowcoach (Brit inf), slowpoke (US inf).

langweilig adj (a) boring. (b) (inf: langsam) slow. er ist so ~ mit allem he's so slow or such a slowcoach (Brit inf) or slowpoke (US inf) at everything.

Langweiligkeit f siehe adj (a) boringness. (b) slowness.

Lang-: ~welle f long wave; l~wellig adj long-wave; l~wierig adj long, lengthy; Verhandlungen, Behandlung, Krankheit auch prolonged; l~wierig über etw (acc) beraten to have lengthy or prolonged discussions about sth; ~wierigkeit f lengthiness; ~zeitprogramm nt long-term programme; l~ziehen vt sep irreg to stretch; siehe **Ohr**, **Hammelbeine**.

Lanolin nt -s, no pl lanolin.

Lanze f -, -n lance; (zum Werfen) spear. für jdn eine ~ brechen (fig) to take up the cudgels for sb, to go to bat for sb (esp US).

Lanzen-: ~spitze f tip of a lance/spear; ~stich m lance/spear thrust; (Wunde) lance/spear wound; er wurde von einem ~stich getroffen he was hit by a lance/spear; ~stoß m lance/spear thrust.

Lanzette f (Med) lancet.

Lanzett-: ~fisch m, ~fischchen nt lancelet; l~förmig adj (Bot) lanceolate (spec).

Laos nt - Laos.

Laote m -n, -n, **Laotin** f Laotian.

laotisch adj Laotian.

Laotse m -s Lao-Tse.

lapidar adj succinct.

Lapislazuli m -, - lapis lazuli.

Lappalie [-iə] f trifle, petty little matter.

Läppchen nt (small) cloth.

Lappe m -n, -n, **Lappin** f Lapp, Lapplander.

Lappen m -s, - (a) (Stück Stoff) cloth; (Wasch~) face cloth, flannel. (b) (sl: Geldschein) note, bill (US). (c) (Hautstück) fold of skin. (d) (inf) jdm durch die ~ gehen to slip through sb's fingers; die Sendung ist mir durch die ~ gegangen I missed the programme.

läppern vr impers (inf) es läppert sich (all) mounts up.

lappig adj (inf) limp.

Lappin f siehe **Lappe**.

läppisch adj silly. wegen ~en zwei Mark macht er so ein Theater he makes such a fuss about a mere two marks.

Lappland nt -s Lapland.

Lappländer(in f) m -s, - siehe **Lappe**.

lappländisch adj Lapp.

Lapsus m -, - mistake, slip; (gesellschaftlich, diplomatisch) faux pas. ~ linguae [-'lɪŋguə] slip of the tongue; mir ist ein ~ unterlaufen or passiert, ich habe einen ~ begangen I've made a mistake/faux pas.

Lärche f -, -n larch.

large [larʒ] adj (Sw) generous.

Lärge f -, -n (dial, pej) Silesian.

Largo nt -s, -s or **Larghi** (Mus) largo.

larifari 1 interj nonsense, fiddlesticks, fiddle-de-dee. **2** adj inv airy-fairy.

Larifari nt -s, no pl (inf) nonsense.

Lärm m -(e)s, no pl noise; (Geräuschbelästigung auch) din, row, racket; (Aufsehen) fuss. ~ schlagen (lit) to raise the alarm; (fig) to kick up a fuss, to raise a commotion; „Viel ~ um nichts" "Much Ado about Nothing"; viel ~ um nichts machen to make a lot of fuss or ado about nothing; viel ~ um jdn/etw machen to make a big fuss about sb/sth.

Lärm-: ~bekämpfung f noise prevention; ~belästigung f noise nuisance; ~belästigung bekämpfen to fight noise pollution; sie beschwerten sich wegen der unzumutbaren ~belästigung they complained about the unacceptable noise level; l~empfindlich adj sensitive to noise.

lärmen vi to make a noise. ~d noisy.

lärm-: ~geplagt adj plagued with noise; ~geschädigt adj suffering physical damage as a result of exposure to noise.

larmoyant [larmoa'jant] adj (geh) lachrymose (liter).

Larmoyanz [larmoa'jants] f (geh) sentimentality.

Lärm-: ~quelle f source of noise/the noise; ~schäden, ~schädigungen pl injuries caused by excessive noise; ~schutz m noise prevention; l~unempfindlich adj insensitive to noise; ~wall m soundproof barrier.

Lärvchen nt (a) dim of **Larve**. (b) (dated inf: Gesicht) baby-doll face.

Larve ['larfə] f -, -n (a) (Tier~) larva. (b) siehe **Maske**.

las pret of **lesen**.

lasch adj (inf) (a) (schlaff) Bewegungen feeble; Händedruck limp. (b) Erziehung, Polizei, Eltern lax. (c) Speisen insipid, wishy-washy (inf).

Lasche f -, -n (Schlaufe) loop; (Schuh~) tongue; (als Schmuck, Verschluß) tab, flap; (Tech) splicing plate; (von Kette) side-plate; (Rail) fishplate.

Laschheit f siehe adj (a) feebleness; limpness. (b) laxity. (c) insipidity, wishy-washiness (inf).

Laser ['le:zɐ, 'la:zɐ] m -s, - laser.

Laserstrahl m laser beam.

lasieren* vt Bild, Holz to varnish; Glas to glaze.

laß adj (rare) siehe **lasch**.

laß imper sing of **lassen**.

lassen pret **ließ**, ptp **gelassen 1** vt (a) (unter~) to stop; (momentan aufhören) to leave. laß das (sein)! don't (do it)!; (hör auf) stop it!; laß das Jammern stop your moaning; laß diese Bemerkungen! that's enough of that kind of remark!; ~ wir das! let's leave it or that!; er kann das Rauchen/Trinken nicht ~ he can't stop smoking/drinking, he can't keep from smoking/drinking; sie kann Schokolade/Alkohol nicht ~ she can't keep away from chocolate/alcohol; er kann es nicht ~! he will keep on doing it!; er hat es versucht, aber er kann es nicht ~ he's tried, but he can't help it or himself; sich vor Freude nicht zu ~ wissen or ~ können to be delirious with joy; dann ~ wir es eben let's drop the whole idea; ich will aber nicht! — dann ~ wir es eben but I don't want to! — let's not bother then; wenn du nicht willst, dann laß es doch if you don't want to, then don't; ich habe es dann doch gelassen in the end I didn't; tu, was du nicht ~ kannst! if you must, you must!

(b) (zurück~) to leave. jdn allein ~ to leave sb alone; er dort viel Geld gelassen he left there with his pockets a lot lighter.

(c) (über~) jdm etw ~ to let sb have sth; (behalten ~) to let sb keep sth; das muß man ihr ~ (zugestehen) you've got to give or grant her that.

(d) (hinein~, hinaus~) to let (in +acc into, aus out of). Wasser in die Badewanne (laufen) ~ to run water into the bath; laß die Kinder nicht auf die Straße/auf das Sofa don't let the children (go) onto the street/(get) on(to) the sofa.

(e) (be~) to leave. etw ~, wie es ist to leave sth (just) as it is; etw ungesagt/ungetan ~ (geh) to leave sth unsaid/undone.

(f) (inf: los~) to let go; (in Ruhe ~) to leave alone, to let be; (gewähren ~) to let.

2 modal aux vb ptp ~ Übersetzung hängt oft vom Vollverb ab, siehe auch dort (a) (veranlassen) etw tun ~ to have or get sth done; sich (dat) etw schicken ~ to have or get sth sent to one; ich muß mich mal untersuchen ~ to run water into the bath; sich (dat) einen Zahn ziehen ~ to have a tooth out; jdm mitteilen/ausrichten ~, daß ... to let sb know or have sb informed (form)/leave a message for sb that ...; er läßt Ihnen mitteilen, daß ... he wants or wishes (form) you to know that ...; jdn rufen or kommen ~ to send for sb; mein Vater wollte mich studieren ~ my father wanted me to study; er hat gespart, nur um seine Kinder etwas lernen zu ~ he saved just so that his children could be educated; eine Versammlung einberufen ~ to have a meeting called; Goethe läßt Faust sagen: ... Goethe has or makes Faust say: ...

(b) (zu~) jdn etw wissen/sehen/hören ~ to let sb know/see/hear sth; etw kochen ~ to boil sth; sie hat mich nichts merken ~ she didn't show it/anything; ich muß es Sie wissen ~, daß ... I must tell you or let it be known that ...; einen Bart/sich (dat) die Haare wachsen ~ to grow a beard/one's hair, to let one's hair grow; den Tee ziehen ~ to let the tea draw; das Licht brennen ~ to leave the light on; jdn warten ~ to keep sb waiting; laß ihn nur kommen! just let him show his face or come!

(c) (erlauben) to let, to allow. er hat sich überreden/nicht überreden ~ he let himself be or allowed himself to be persuaded/he was not to be persuaded; ich lasse mich nicht belügen/zwingen I won't be lied to/coerced.

(d) (möglich sein) das Fenster läßt sich leicht öffnen the

window opens easily; **das Fenster läßt sich nicht öffnen** (*grundsätzlich nicht*) the window doesn't open; (*momentan nicht*) the window won't open; **das Wort läßt sich schwer/nicht übersetzen** the word is hard to translate/can't be translated *or* is untranslatable; **das läßt sich machen** that's possible, that can be done; **es läßt sich essen/trinken** it's edible *or* eatable/drinkable; **hier läßt es sich bequem sitzen** it's comfortable sitting here; **auf dieser Straße läßt es sich gut fahren** this road is good to drive on; **das läßt sich nicht mehr feststellen** that can no longer be established; **das läßt sich nicht mehr ändern** nothing can be done about that now, it's too late to do anything about it now; **daraus läßt sich schließen** *or* **folgern, daß ...** one can conclude from this that ...

(e) (*als Imperativ*) **laß uns gehen!** let's go!; **laß uns alles vergessen!** let's forget everything!; **laß es dir gutgehen!** take care of yourself!; **laß dir das gesagt sein!** let me tell you this!; **lasset die Kindlein zu mir kommen** (*Bibl*) suffer the little children to come unto me (*Bibl*); **lasset uns beten** let us pray.

3 *vi* (**a**) **laß mal, ich mache das schon** leave it, I'll do it; **laß mal, ich zahle das schon** no, that's all right, I'll pay; **ich lasse gern mit mir handeln** I'm quite willing to negotiate.

(b) (*ab~*) **von jdm/etw ~** to give sb/sth up.

lässig *adj* (*ungezwungen*) casual; (*nach~*) careless; (*sl: gekonnt*) cool (*sl*). **das hat er ganz ~ hingekriegt** (*sl*) pretty cool, the way he did that (*sl*).

Lässigkeit *f siehe adj* casualness; carelessness; coolness (*sl*).

läßlich *adj* (*Eccl*) **Sünde** venial, pardonable.

Läßlichkeit *f* (*Eccl*) veniality.

Lasso *m or nt* -s, -s lasso.

laßt *imper pl of* **lassen**.

Last *f* -, **-en** (**a**) load; (*Trag~ auch*) burden; (*lit, fig: Gewicht*) weight. **Aufzug nur für ~en** goods lift *or* hoist; **des Lebens und Mühe** (*liter*) the trials and tribulations of life.

(b) (*fig: Bürde*) burden. **eine ~ für jdn sein, jdm zur ~ fallen/werden** to be/become a burden on sb; **die ~ der Verantwortung/des Amtes** the burden of responsibility/the weight of office; **sich** (*dat*) **selbst eine ~ sein** to be a burden to oneself; **damit war uns eine schwere ~ vom Herzen** *or* **von der Seele genommen** that took a load off our minds; **jdm eine ~ abnehmen** to take a load off sb's shoulders; **jdm eine ~ legen** to lay sth to sb's charge; **man legte ihm zur ~, daß er betrunken gewesen war** he was charged with being drunk.

(c) **~en** (*Kosten*) costs; (*des Steuerzahlers*) charges; **soziale ~en** welfare costs *or* charges; **die steuerlichen ~en für die kleinen Unternehmen** the tax burden for small concerns; **auf dem Grundstück liegen erhebliche ~en** the land is heavily encumbered; **zu jds/eigenen ~en gehen** to be chargeable to sb/payable oneself.

Last-: **~arm** *m* (*Phys*) load arm; **~auto** *nt* van (*Brit*), panel truck (*US*).

lasten *vi* to weigh heavily (*auf + dat* on). **eine schwere Sorge hat auf ihr gelastet** a terrible worry weighed her down; **eine lähmende Schwüle lastete über der Stadt** (*geh*) an oppressive heat hung heavily over the town; **auf dem Haus lastet noch eine Hypothek** the house is still encumbered (with a mortgage) (*form*); **auf ihm lastet die ganze Verantwortung/Arbeit** all the work/responsibility rests on him/all the work falls on him.

Lasten-: **~aufzug** *m* hoist, goods lift *or* elevator (*US*); **~ausgleich** *m* system of financial compensation for losses suffered in the Second World War.

lastend *adj* (*geh*) **Stille, Schwüle** oppressive.

lastenfrei *adj* **Grundstück** unencumbered.

Laster[1] *m* -s, - (*inf*) lorry (*Brit*), truck.

Laster[2] *nt* -s, - vice; *siehe* **lang, Müßiggang**.

Lästerei *f* (*inf*) (**a**) *no pl* (*das Lästern*) running down (*über + acc* of), nasty comments *pl*. (**b**) (*Lästerwort*) nasty remark.

Lästerer *m* -s, - (**a**) **ein ~ sein** to have a vicious tongue (in one's head). (**b**) (*Gottes~*) blasphemer.

lasterhaft *adj* depraved.

Lasterhaftigkeit *f* depravity.

Lasterhöhle *f* den of vice *or* iniquity.

Lästerin *f siehe* **Lästerer**.

Lasterleben *nt* (*old, iro*) life of sin and depravity.

lästerlich *adj* malicious; (*gottes~*) blasphemous. **~e Bemerkung** gibe (*über + acc* at).

Lästermaul *nt* (*inf*) *siehe* **Lästerer (a)**.

lästern 1 *vi* **über jdn/etw ~** to make nasty remarks about sb/sth, to run sb/sth down; **wir haben gerade über dich gelästert** (*hum*) we were just talking about you, we were just taking your name in vain (*hum*). **2** *vt* (**a**) to be nasty about. (**b**) **Gott** to blaspheme against, to curse.

Läster-: **~wort** *nt, pl* **-worte** (**a**) gibe; (**b**) (*gegen Gott*) blasphemy; **~worte** blasphemous words; **~zunge** *f* vicious tongue.

Lastesel *m* pack mule.

Lastex ® *nt* -, *no pl* stretch fabric.

Lastex- ® *in cpds* stretch.

Last-: **~fahrzeug** *nt* goods vehicle; **~fuhre** *f* **der Fahrer hatte vorhin eine ~fuhre** the driver had previously been carrying goods; **mit dem Mietwagen dürfen keine ~fuhren unternommen werden** the hired car is not to be used for the carriage of goods.

lästig *adj* tiresome; (*ärgerlich auch*) annoying, irksome, aggravating; **Husten, Kopfschuppen etc** troublesome. **wie ~!** what a nuisance!; **jdm ~ sein** to bother sb; **der Regenschirm/dieser Verband ist mir ~** the umbrella is a nuisance/this bandage is bothering me; **jdm ~ fallen** to be a nuisance to sb; **jdm ~ werden** to become a nuisance (to sb); (*zum Ärgernis werden*) to get annoying to sb).

Lästigkeit *f siehe adj* tiresomeness; irksomeness; troublesomeness.

Last-: **~kahn** *m* barge; **~kraftwagen** *m* (*form*) heavy goods vehicle; **~schiff** *nt* freighter, cargo ship; **~schrift** *f* debit; (*Eintrag*) debit entry; **~tier** *nt* beast of burden, pack animal; **~träger** *m* carrier, porter; **~wagen** *m* lorry (*Brit*), truck; **~wagenfahrer** *m* lorry (*Brit*) *or* truck driver; **~zug** *m* truck-trailer (*US*), juggernaut (*Brit inf*).

Lasur *f* (*auf Holz, Bild*) varnish; (*auf Glas, Email*) glaze.

Lasurstein *m siehe* **Lapislazuli**.

lasziv *adj* (*geh*) lascivious.

Laszivität *f* (*geh*) lasciviousness.

Lätare *no art* (*Eccl*) Laetare Sunday, 3rd Sunday before Easter.

Latein *nt* -s Latin. **mit seinem ~ am Ende sein** to be stumped (*inf*).

Latein-: **~amerika** *nt* Latin America; **l~amerikanisch** *adj* Latin-American.

Lateiner *m* -s, - Latin scholar; (*Sch*) Latin pupil.

lateinisch *adj* Latin.

Lateinschule *f* (*Hist*) grammar school.

latent *adj* latent; **Selbstmörder** potential. **~ vorhanden sein** to be latent.

Latenz *f* latency.

Latenz-: **~periode** *f* latency period; **~zeit** *f* latent period.

lateral *adj* (*Sci*) lateral.

Laterna magica *f* magic lantern.

Laterne *f* -, **-n** (*Leuchte, Archit*) lantern; (*Straßen~*) streetlight, streetlamp. **so einen Ehemann kannst du mit der ~ suchen** husbands like that are few and far between.

Laternen-: **~licht** *nt* light of the streetlamp(s); **~pfahl** *m* lamppost.

Latex *m* -, **Latizes** latex.

Latifundium *nt usu pl* latifundium.

latinisieren* *vt* to latinize.

Latinismus *m* latinism.

Latinist(in *f*) *m* Latinist, Latin scholar.

Latinum *nt* -s, *no pl* **kleines/großes ~** ≃ Latin O-/A-level (exam) (*Brit*).

Latium *nt* -s Latium.

Latrine *f* latrine.

Latrinen-: **~parole** *f* (*inf*) rumour; **~reinigen** *nt* -s, *no pl* (*Mil*) latrine duty.

Latsche *f* -, **-n** (*Bot*) *siehe* **Latschenkiefer**.

Latschen *m* -s, - (*inf*) (*Hausschuh*) slipper; (*pej: Schuh*) worn-out shoe.

latschen *vi aux sein* (*inf*) to wander; (*durch die Stadt etc*) to traipse; (*schlurfend*) to slouch along; *siehe* **Bremse**[1].

Latschenkiefer *f* mountain pine.

latschig *adj* (*inf*) **Gang** sloppy (*inf*).

Latte *f* -, **-n** (**a**) (*schmales Brett*) slat. **nicht alle auf der ~ haben** (*sl*) to have a screw loose (*inf*). (**b**) (*Sport*) bar; (*Ftbl: cross*)bar. (**c**) (*fig: Liste*) **eine ganze ~ von Wünschen/Vorstrafen** a whole string of things that he *etc* wants/of previous convictions; *siehe* **lang**.

Latten-: **~holz** *nt* lath wood; **~kreuz** *nt* corner of the goalpost; **~verschlag** *m* crate; (*abgeteilte Fläche*) enclosure; (*für Hühner etc*) run; **~zaun** *m* wooden fence, paling.

Lattich *m* -s, **-e** (*Bot*) lettuce.

Latüchte *f* -, **-n** (*hum*) *siehe* **Laterne**.

Latz *m* **-es**, **-e** (*Aus*) -e (*Lätzchen, bei Kleidung*) bib; (*Hosen~*) (front) flap. **jdm eins vor den ~ knallen** (*sl*) *or* **ballern** (*sl*) to sock sb one (*sl*).

Lätzchen *nt* bib.

Latzhose *f* (*pair of*) dungarees *pl*.

lau *adj* (**a**) **Wind, Abend** mild. (**b**) (*~warm*) **Flüssigkeit** tepid, lukewarm; (*fig*) **Freundschaft, Begeisterung, Haltung** lukewarm, half-hearted.

Laub *nt* **-(e)s**, *no pl* leaves *pl*; (*an Bäumen etc auch*) foliage.

Laub-: **~baum** *m* deciduous tree; **~blatt** *nt* (*fallen*) leaf; **~dach** *nt* leafy canopy (*liter*).

Laube *f* -, **-n** (**a**) (*Gartenhäuschen*) summerhouse. (**b**) (*Gang*) arbour, pergola; (*Arkade*) arcade; *siehe* **fertig**.

Lauben-: **~gang** *m* arbour, pergola; **~kolonie** *f* area of allotments; **~pieper** *m* -s, - (*dial*) allotment gardener.

Laub-: **~fall** *m* **vor dem ~fall** before the leaves fall; **~färbung** *f* colouring of the leaves; **~frosch** *m* (*European*) tree-frog; **~hölzer** *pl* deciduous trees *pl*; **~hüttenfest** *nt* Feast of Tabernacles, Sukkoth; **~krone** *f* tree-top; **~säge** *f* fretsaw; **~sägearbeit** *f* fretwork; **l~tragend** *adj* deciduous; **~wald** *m* deciduous wood/forest; **~werk** *nt* foliage (*usu Art*).

Lauch *m* -(e)s, -e **allium** (*form*); (*esp S Ger: Porree*) leek.

Laudatio [lau'da:tsio] *f* -, **Laudationes** encomium, eulogy.

Laue(ne) *f* -, **-(ne)n** (*esp Sw*) avalanche.

Lauer *f* -, *no pl*: **auf der ~ sein** *or* **liegen** to lie in wait; **sich auf die ~ legen** to settle down to lie in wait.

lauern *vi* (*lit, fig*) to lurk, to lie in wait (*auf + acc* for); (*inf*) to wait (*auf + acc* for). **ein ~der Blick** a furtive glance.

Lauf *m* -(e)s, **Läufe** (**a**) (*schneller Schritt*) run; (*Sport: Wett~*) race. **sein ~ wurde immer schneller** he ran faster and faster; **einen ~ machen** to go for *or* have a run; **im ~ innehalten** to stop running for a moment.

(b) (*Verlauf*) course. **im ~e der Jahre** in the course of the years, over *or* through the years; **das Buch muß im ~e von drei Tagen zurückgegeben werden** the book must be returned within three days; **im ~e des Gesprächs** in the course of *or* during the conversation; **einer Entwicklung** (*dat*) **freien ~ lassen** to allow a development to take its (own) course; **sie ließ ihren Gefühlen freien ~** she gave way to her feelings; **den Dingen ihren ~ lassen** to let matters *or* things take their course; **das ist der ~ der Dinge** *or* **der Welt** that's the way of the world *or* the way things go; **die Dinge nahmen ihren ~** everything took its course.

(c) *(Gang, Arbeit)* running, operation.
(d) *(Fluß~, Astron)* course. **der obere/untere ~ der Donau** the upper/lower reaches of the Danube.
(e) *(Mus)* run.
(f) *(Gewehr~)* barrel. **ein Tier vor den ~ bekommen** to get an animal in one's sights.
(g) *(Hunt: Bein)* leg.

Laufbahn *f* career. **die ~ des Beamten einschlagen** to embark *or* enter on a career as a civil servant.

Laufbursche *m* errand-boy, messenger boy.

laufen *pret* **lief,** *ptp* **gelaufen 1** *vi aux sein* **(a)** *(rennen)* to run. **lauf doch!** get a move on! *(inf).*
(b) *(inf) (gehen)* to go; *(seine Notdurft verrichten)* to run (to the toilet) *(inf).* **er läuft dauernd ins Kino/auf die Polizei** he's always off to the cinema/running to the police.
(c) *(zu Fuß gehen)* to walk. **das Kind läuft schon** the child can already walk *or* is already walking; **das L~ lernen** to learn to walk; **er läuft sehr unsicher** he's very unsteady on his feet; **es sind noch/nur 10 Minuten zu ~** it's another/only 10 minutes' walk.
(d) *(fließen) (schmelzen: Käse, Butter)* to melt. **in Strömen ~** to stream *or* pour (in/out/down *etc);* **Wasser in einen Eimer/die Badewanne ~ lassen** to run water into a bucket/the bath; **das Bier muß ~** the beer must be kept flowing.
(e) *(undicht sein) (Gefäß, Wasserhahn)* to leak; *(Nase, Wunde)* to run. **seine Nase läuft, ihm läuft die Nase** his nose is running, he's got a runny nose.
(f) *(in Betrieb sein)* to run, to go; *(Uhr)* to go; *(Elektrogerät: eingeschaltet sein)* to be on; *(funktionieren)* to work. **wir haben jetzt drei neue Maschinen ~** *(inf)* we've got three new machines going *(inf);* **er hat vier Mädchen ~** *(sl)* he's got four girls out on the game *(sl) or* hustling for him *(sl).*
(g) *(fig: im Gange sein) (Prozeß, Verhandlung)* to go on, to be in progress; *(Bewerbung, Antrag)* to be under consideration; *(gezeigt werden) (Film)* to be on, to be showing; *(Stück)* to be on, to be playing. **der Film lief schon, als wir ankamen** the film had already started when we arrived; **der Film läuft über drei Stunden** the film goes on for three hours; **etw läuft gut/schlecht** sth is going well/badly; **die Sache/das Geschäft läuft jetzt** it/the shop is going well now; **sehen, wie die Sache läuft** see how things go; **alles/die Dinge ~ lassen** to let everything/things slide; **die Sache ist gelaufen** *(sl)* it's in the bag *(inf),* it's all wrapped up *(inf);* **es ist zu spät, die Sache ist schon gelaufen** *(sl)* it's too late now, it's all finished with; **jdm zeigen, wie es läuft** *(inf)* to show sb the ropes *(inf).*
(h) *(gültig sein: Vertrag, Abkommen)* to run.
(i) *(bezeichnet werden)* **das Auto läuft unter meinem Namen** *or* **auf meinen Namen** the car is in my name; **das Konto läuft unter der Nummer ...** the number of the account is ...; **der Agent läuft unter dem Decknamen „Spinne"** the agent goes by the cover-name of "Spider"; **das läuft unter „Sonderausgaben"** that comes under "special expenses".
(j) *(sich bewegen)* to run. **die Erde läuft um die Sonne** the earth moves round the sun; **es lief mir eiskalt über den Rücken** a chill ran *or* went up my spine; **auf eine Mine ~** to hit a mine; **in den Hafen ~** to come into port; *siehe* **Geld, Stapel.**
(k) *(verlaufen: Fluß etc)* to run; *(Weg auch)* to go.
2 *vt* **(a)** *aux haben or sein (Sport)* **Rekordzeit** to run; **Rekord** to set. **Rennen ~** to run (in races); **Ski/Schlittschuh/Rollschuh** *etc* **~** to ski/skate/rollerskate *etc; siehe* **Gefahr.**
(b) *aux sein (fahren: Auto etc)* **Geschwindigkeit, Strecke** to do.
(c) *aux sein (zu Fuß gehen)* to walk; *(schnell)* to run.
(d) **sich** *(dat)* **eine Blase ~** to give oneself a blister; **sich** *(dat)* **ein Loch in die Sohlen ~** to wear a hole in one's soles.
3 *vr* **sich warm ~** to warm up; **sich heiß ~** to overheat; **sich müde ~** to tire oneself out; **in den Schuhen läuft es sich gut/schlecht** these shoes are good/bad for walking/running in; **zu zweit läuft es sich besser** it's better walking/running in twos; **auf diesen Straßen läuft es sich nicht gut** these roads are not good for walking/running on.

laufend 1 *adj attr (ständig)* **Arbeiten, Ausgaben** regular; **Kredit** outstanding; *(regelmäßig)* **Wartung** routine; **Monat, Jahr, Konto** *(form)* current. **10 DM das ~e Meter** DM 10 per metre; **~e Nummer** serial number; *(von Konto)* number; **auf dem ~en bleiben/sein** to keep (oneself)/be in the picture *or* up-to-date *or* informed; **jdn auf dem ~en halten** to keep sb in the picture *or* up-to-date *or* informed; **mit etw auf dem ~en sein** to be up-to-date on sth; *siehe* **Band¹.**
2 *adv* continually, constantly.

laufenlassen *vt sep irreg (inf)* **jdn ~** to let sb go.

Läufer *m* **-s,** - **(a)** *(Sport)* runner; *(Hürden~)* hurdler; *(Ftbl)* halfback; *(dated: Laufbursche)* messenger-boy; *(Chess)* bishop. **rechter/linker ~** *(Ftbl)* right/left half.
(b) *(Teppich)* rug; *(Treppen~, Tisch~)* runner.
(c) *(Tech) (Laufkatze)* crab; *(Laufgewicht)* sliding weight.
(d) *(Build)* stretcher.
(e) *(junges Schwein)* young pig.

Lauferei *f (inf)* running about *no pl.*

Läuferin *f siehe* **Läufer (a).**

Läuferstange *f* stair-rod.

Lauf-: **~feuer** *nt*: **sich wie ein ~feuer verbreiten** to spread like wildfire; **~gewicht** *nt* sliding weight; **~gitter** *nt* playpen; **~graben** *m* approach trench.

läufig *adj* on heat.

Lauf-: **~junge** *m* errand-boy; **~katze** *f (Tech)* crab; **~kran** *m* (overhead) travelling crane; **~kunde** *m* occasional customer; **~kundschaft** *f* occasional customers *pl;* **~masche** *f* ladder *(Brit),* run; **~maschen aufnehmen** to mend ladders; **~paß** *m*: **jdm den ~paß geben** *(inf)* to give sb his marching orders *(inf);*

Freundin *etc auch* to pack sb in *(inf);* **~planke** *f (Naut)* gangplank; **~rad** *nt* traversing wheel; *(ohne Antrieb)* trailing wheel; *(in Turbine)* rotor; **~rinne** *f* foot-bath; **~rolle** *f* roller; *(unter Möbeln)* castor; **~rost** *m* duckboards *pl;* **~schritt** *m* trot; *(Mil)* double-quick, double-time; **im ~schritt** *(Mil)* at the double; **er näherte sich im ~schritt** he came trotting up; **~schuh** *m (inf)* walking shoe; **~stall** *m* **(a)** playpen; **(b)** *(für Tiere)* pen; **~ställchen** *nt (inf)* playpen; **~steg** *m* catwalk; **~werk** *nt* running gear; **~zeit** *f* **(a)** *(von Wechsel, Vertrag)* period of validity; **(b)** *(von Maschine) (Lebensdauer)* (operational) life; *(Betriebszeit)* running time; **(c)** *(Sport)* time; **(d)** *(Zool: Brunstzeit)* **während der ~zeit** while on heat; **die ~zeit dauert eine Woche** the animal is on heat for a week; **~zettel** *m (an Akten, Maschinen)* docket.

Lauge *f* **-,** **-n** *(Chem)* lye, leach; *(Seifen~)* soapy water; *(Salz~)* salt solution.

Lauheit, Lauigkeit *(rare) f* **(a)** *(von Wind, Abend)* mildness.
(b) *(von Flüssigkeit)* tepidness, tepidity, lukewarmness; *(fig: von Freundschaft etc)* lukewarmness, half-heartedness.

Laune *f* **-,** **-n** **(a)** *(Stimmung)* mood. **(je) nach (Lust und) ~** just as the mood *or* fancy takes one; **gute/schlechte ~ haben, (bei or in) guter/schlechter ~ sein** to be in a good/bad mood *or* temper; **jdn bei guter ~ *or* bei ~** *(inf)* **halten** to keep sb happy *or* in a good mood; **was hat er für ~?** what sort of (a) mood is he in?; **seine ~ an jdm auslassen** to take one's temper out on sb.
(b) *(Grille, Einfall)* whim, caprice. **die ~n des Glücks** the vagaries of fortune; **etw aus einer ~ heraus tun** to do sth on a whim.

launenhaft *adj* moody; *(unberechenbar)* capricious; **Wetter** changeable.

Launenhaftigkeit *f siehe adj* moodiness; capriciousness; changeableness.

launig *adj (dated)* witty.

launisch *adj siehe* **launenhaft.**

Laureat(in *f)* *m* **-en, -en** *(geh)* laureate.

Laus *f* **-,** **Läuse** louse; *(Blatt~)* greenfly; blackfly. **jdm/sich eine ~ in den Pelz setzen** *(inf)* to land sb/oneself in it *(inf),* to let sb/oneself in for it *(inf);* **ihm ist (wohl) eine ~ über die Leber gelaufen *or* gekrochen** *(inf)* something's biting him *(inf).*

Lausbub *m (dated)* rascal, scamp, scalliwag; *(jungenhaftes Mädchen)* tomboy.

Lausbubengesicht *nt (dated)* scampish *or* roguish face.

Lausbüberei *f (dated)* devilry, prank(s).

lausbübisch *adj (dated)* roguish, scampish, rascally; **Mädchen** tomboyish.

Lausch|angriff *m* bugging operation *(gegen* on).

lauschen *vi* **(a)** *(geh)* to listen *(dat, auf + acc* to). **(b)** *(heimlich zuhören)* to eavesdrop.

Läuschen ['lɔyʃən] *nt dim of* **Laus.**

Lauscher(in *f)* *m* **-s,** - **(a)** eavesdropper. **der ~ an der Wand hört seine eigene Schand** *(Prov)* people who listen at doors never hear any good of themselves. **(b)** *(Hunt: Ohr)* ear.

lauschig *adj* **Plätzchen** cosy, snug; *(im Freien)* secluded.

Lause-: **~bande** *f (inf) siehe* **~pack;** **~bengel, ~junge** *m (inf)* blighter *(Brit inf),* little devil *(inf); (wohlwollend)* scamp, rascal; **l~kalt** *adj (inf)* perishing *(inf),* freezing (cold); **~kälte** *f (inf)* freezing *or* perishing *(inf)* cold; **~lümmel** *m (inf) siehe* **~bengel.**

lausen *vt* to delouse. **jdn ~** *(inf: übervorteilen)* to fleece sb *(inf);* **ich denk', mich laust der Affe!** *(sl)* well blow me down! *(inf),* well I'll be blowed! *(inf).*

Lausepack *nt, no pl (sl)* riff-raff *pl,* trash *pl (inf).*

Lauser *m* **-s,** - *(S Ger) siehe* **Lausbub.**

lausig *(inf)* **1** *adj* lousy *(sl),* awful; **Kälte** freezing, perishing. **2** *adv* awfully; *(vor Adjektiv auch)* damn(ed) *(sl),* bloody *(Brit sl).*

laut¹ *adj* **(a)** loud. **~er sprechen** to speak louder *or* more loudly, to speak up; **~ auflachen** to burst out laughing, to laugh out loud; **etw ~(er) stellen** to turn sth up (loud).
(b) *(lärmend, voll Lärm)* noisy; *(auffällig, aufdringlich)* **Mensch** loudmouthed; **Farbe** *etc* loud. **er wird niemals/wird immer gleich ~** he never/always gets obstreperous.
(c) *(hörbar)* out loud *pred, adv,* aloud *pred, adv.* **etw ~ sagen** *(lit)* to say sth out loud; *(fig)* to shout sth from the rooftops, to tell sth to the whole world; **~ werden** *(bekannt)* to become known; **etw ~ werden lassen** to make sth known, to let sth be known.
(d) *(Hunt: windstill)* still.

laut² *prep* **+gen** *or* **dat** according to.

Laut *m* **-(e)s,** **-e** sound. **heimatliche ~e** sounds of home; **wir hörten bayerische ~e** we heard Bavarian accents; **keinen ~ von sich** *(dat)* **geben** not to make a sound; **~ geben** *(Hund)* to give tongue.

lautbar *adj:* **~ werden** to become known.

Lautbildung *f* articulation.

Laute *f* **-,** **-n** lute.

lauten *vi* to be; *(Rede, Argumentation)* to go; *(Schriftstück)* to read, to go. **dieser Erlaß lautet wörtlich: ...** the exact text of this decree is: ...; **auf den Namen ... ~** *(Paß)* to be in the name of ...; *(Scheck)* to be payable to *or* made out to ...; **die Anklage lautet auf Mord** the charge is (one of) murder.

läuten *vti* **(a)** to ring; *(Wecker)* to go (off). **es hat geläutet** the bell rang *or* went; **es läutet zur Stunde** *(Sch)* the bell is ringing *or* going for the next lesson; **jdn zu Grabe ~** *(liter)* to sound sb's funeral knell, to toll the bells for sb's funeral; **Feuer ~** *(liter)* to ring the fire-bell; **(nach) jdm ~** to ring for sb; *siehe* **Sturm.**
(b) **er hat davon (etwas) ~ hören** *(inf)* he has heard something about it.

Lautenist(in *f),* **Lautenspieler(in** *f)* *m* lute-player, lutenist.

lauter 1 *adj* **(a)** *(liter: rein)* **Gold, Wein** pure.

(b) (geh: aufrichtig) Mensch, Absichten honourable; **Wahrheit** honest.
   2 adv (nur) nothing/nobody but. ~ **Unsinn/Angst/Freude** etc pure or sheer nonsense/fear/joy etc; **das sind ~ Lügen** that's nothing but lies, that's all a pack of lies; **vor ~ Rauch/Autos kann man nichts sehen** you can't see anything for all the smoke/cars.

Lauterkeit f, no pl **(a)** (liter: Reinheit) purity. **(b)** (geh: Aufrichtigkeit) honourableness.

läutern vt (liter) to purify; (fig) to reform.

Läuterung f (liter) purification; (fig) reformation.

Läut(e)werk nt (Rail) signal bell.

laut-: ~(ge)treu adj phonetic; ~**hals** adv at the top of one's voice.

lautieren* vti (Phon) to read phonetically.

Laut-: ~**lehre** f phonetics sing; phonology; l~**lich** adj phonetic; l~**los** adj silent, soundless; noiseless; (wortlos) silent; **Stille** utter, complete; ~**losigkeit** f siehe adj silence, soundlessness; noiselessness; silence; completeness; l~**malend** adj onomatopoeic; ~**malerei** f onomatopoeia; (Ausdruck auch) onomatopoeic word; ~**schrift** f phonetics pl; (System auch) phonetic alphabet or script.

Lautsprecher m (loud)speaker. **über ~** over the loud-speaker(s).

Lautsprecher-: ~**anlage** f öffentliche ~**anlage** public address or PA system, tannoy ® (Brit); ~**wagen** m loudspeaker car/van.

Laut-: ~**stand** m (Ling) stage of development of the sound system; l~**stark** adj loud; (Rad, TV etc) high-volume; **Partei, Protest** vociferous; ~**stärke** f siehe adj loudness; volume; vociferousness; **ein Radio in voller ~stärke spielen lassen** to have a radio on full blast (inf) or (at) full volume; **das Radio auf volle ~stärke einstellen** to turn the radio right up or up as loud as it will go; ~**stärkeregler** m (Rad) volume control; l~**treu** adj siehe l~(ge)treu.

Lautung f (geh) articulation.

Laut-: ~**verschiebung** f sound shift; ~**wandel** m sound change.

Läutwerk nt (Rail) signal bell.

Lautzeichen nt phonetic symbol.

lauwarm adj slightly warm; **Flüssigkeit** lukewarm; (fig) lukewarm, half-hearted.

Lava ['la:va] f -, **Laven** ['la:vn] lava.

Lavabo nt -(s), -s (a) [la'va:bo] (Rel) lavabo. **(b)** ['la:vabo] (Sw) washbasin.

Lavendel [la'vɛndl] m -s, - lavender.

lavieren¹* [la'vi:rən] vi **(a)** (Naut) to tack. **(b)** (fig) to manoeuvre.

lavieren²* [la'vi:rən] vt (Art) to wash. **lavierte Zeichnung** wash drawing.

Lavoir [la'voa:ɐ̯] nt -s, -s (old, Aus) washbasin, washbowl.

Lawine f (lit, fig) avalanche.

Lawinen-: l~**artig** adj like an avalanche; l~**artig anwachsen** to snowball; ~**gefahr** f danger of avalanches.

lax adj lax.

Laxheit f laxity, laxness.

Layout ['le:jaut] nt -s, -s layout.

Layouter(in f) ['le:jautɐ, -ərɪn] m -s, - designer.

Lazarett nt -(e)s, -e (Mil) (in Kaserne etc) sick bay; (selbständiges Krankenhaus) hospital.

Lazarett-: ~**schiff** nt hospital ship; ~**zug** m hospital train.

Lazarus m -, -se (Bibl) Lazarus. **armer ~!** poor beggar or devil.

leasen ['li:zn] vt (Comm) to lease.

Leasing ['li:zɪŋ] nt -s, -s (Comm) leasing. **etw im ~ bekommen** to lease sth.

Lebedame f courtesan.

Lebehoch nt -(s), -(s) ≈ three cheers. **~ rufen** ≈ to give three cheers; **ein (dreifaches) ~ auf jdn ausbringen** ≈ to give sb three cheers.

Lebemann m, pl -**männer** roué, rake.

lebemännisch adj rakish.

Leben nt -s, - **(a)** life. **das ~** life; **das ~ des Menschen/der Tiere** etc the life of man/animals etc; **am ~ sein/bleiben** to be/stay alive; **das ~ als Briefträger** life as a postman, a postman's life; **das ~ Hemingways** Hemingway's life, the life of Hemingway; **das ~ vor/hinter sich** (dat) **haben** to have one's life ahead of or in front of or before/behind one; **solange ich am ~ bin** as long as I live; **sich des ~s freuen, das or sein ~ genießen** to enjoy life; **das or sein ~ verlieren** to lose one's life; **jdm das ~ retten** to save sb's life; **es geht um ~ und Tod, es ist eine Sache auf ~ und Tod** it's a matter of life and death; **wenn dir dein ~ lieb ist** if you value your life; **mit dem ~ davonkommen** to escape with one's life; **mit dem ~ spielen, sein ~ aufs Spiel setzen** to take one's life in one's hands, to dice with death; **mit dem ~ abschließen** to prepare for death; **einer Sache** (dat) **zu neuem ~ verhelfen** to breathe new life into sth, to revitalize sth; **etw ins ~ rufen** to bring sth into being; **jdn wieder ins ~ rufen** (liter) to bring sb back to life; **jdn vom ~ zum Tode bringen** (form) or **befördern** (inf) to kill sb, to take sb's life, to take care of sb (inf); (bei Hinrichtung auch) to put sb to death; **seines ~s nicht mehr sicher sein** to fear for one's life; **ums ~ kommen** to die, to lose one's life; **sein ~ lassen** (müssen) to lose one's life; **jdn am ~ lassen** to spare sb's life; **um sein ~ laufen or rennen** to run for one's life or for dear life; **sich** (dat) **das ~ nehmen** to take one's (own) life; **jdn wieder ins ~ zurückrufen** to bring sb back to life; **Bewußtlosen** to revive sb, to bring sb round; **was ist das für ein ~?** what kind of (a) life is that?; **der Mann/die Frau meines ~s** my ideal man/woman; **etw für sein ~ gern tun** to love doing sth, to be mad about doing sth (inf); **etw für sein ~ gern essen/trinken** to be mad about sth (inf), to love sth; **jdn künstlich am ~ erhalten** to keep sb alive artificially; **ein ~ in Frieden/in Armut** etc a life of peace/poverty etc; **er hat es nie leicht**

gehabt im ~ he has never had an easy life; **ein ~ lang** one's whole life (long); **zum erstenmal** or **das erstemal im ~** for the first time in one's life; **ich habe noch nie im or in meinem ~ geraucht** I have never smoked (in) all my life or in my whole life; **nie im ~!** never!; **sich durchs ~ schlagen** to struggle through (life); **ins ~ treten** to go out into the world; **im ~ stehen** to have some standing in the world; (nicht weltfremd sein) to know what life is all about; (draußen) **im ~ ist das ganz anders** in real life it's very different; **ein Roman, den das ~ schrieb** a novel of real life; **ein Film nach dem ~** a film from real life; **das ~ geht weiter** life goes on; **unser ~ währet siebzig Jahr ...** (Bibl) the days of our years are three score years and ten (Bibl); **so ist das ~ (eben)** that's life, such is life, that's the way the cookie crumbles (inf).
   (b) (Betriebsamkeit) life. **auf dem Markt herrscht reges ~** the market is a hive of activity; **in dieser Stadt ist wenigstens ~** at least there is some life in this town; **~ in etw** (acc) **bringen** (inf) to enliven or brighten sth up; **voller ~ stecken** to be full of life; **es war überhaupt kein ~ in seinem Vortrag** there wasn't a spark of life in his lecture; **das war eine Theateraufführung ohne ~** that was a lifeless performance, there was no life in the performance.

leben 1 vi (alle Bedeutungen) to live; (am Leben sein) to be alive; (weiter~) to live on. **er lebt noch/nicht mehr** he is still/is no longer alive; **er hat nicht lange gelebt** he didn't live (for) long; **ich möchte nicht mehr ~** I don't want to go on living; **er wird nicht mehr lange zu ~ haben** he won't live much longer; **von etw ~** to live on sth; **es/lang lebe der König!** long live the King!; **so wahr ich lebe!** (obs) 'pon my life! (obs); **wie geht es dir?** — **man lebt** (so) (inf) how are you? — surviving; **lebst du noch?** (hum inf) are you still in the land of the living? (hum); **genug zu ~ haben** to have enough to live on; **~ und ~ lassen** to live and let live; **so was lebt, und Schiller mußte sterben!** (hum inf) some mothers do have 'em (inf), it's a sad case (inf); **zum L~ zu wenig, zum Sterben zuviel, davon kann man nicht ~ und nicht sterben** it's barely enough to keep body and soul together; **das Bild** etc **lebt förmlich** that picture etc seems almost alive; **man lebt nur einmal!** you only live once; **einsam/christlich/gesund ~** to live a lonely/Christian/healthy life; **allein/glücklich ~** to live alone/happily; **ganz für sich ~** to live a secluded life; **für etw ~, einer Sache** (dat) **~** (geh) to live for sth; **lebe wohl!** (liter) farewell! (liter); **hier lebt es sich gut** or **läßt es sich** (gut) **~** it's a good life here; siehe **hoch, Ehe**.
   2 vt to live. **jeder muß sein eigenes Leben ~** we've all got our own lives to live or lead.

lebend adj live attr, alive pred; **Wesen, Seele, Beispiel, Sprache** living. **"Vorsicht, ~e Tiere"** "with care, live animals"; **ein noch ~er Zeuge** a witness who is still alive or living today; **ein Tier ~ fangen** to catch an animal alive; **~es Inventar** livestock; **die L~en** the living; ~**es Bild** tableau.

Lebend-: l~**gebärend** adj viviparous, live-bearing; ~**geburt** f live-birth; ~**gewicht** nt live weight; (von Rindern auch) weight on the hoof.

lebendig adj **(a)** (nicht tot) live attr, alive pred; **Wesen** living. ~**e Junge** young; ~**e Junge gebären** to bear one's young live; **die L~en und die Toten** (Bibl) the Quick and the Dead (Bibl); **er ist dort ~ begraben** (fig inf) it's a living death for him there; **jdn bei ~em Leibe** or **jdn ~en Leibes** (liter) verbrennen to burn sb alive; **wieder ~ werden** to come back to life; **er nimmt's von den L~en** (hum inf) he'll have the shirt off your back (inf), it's daylight robbery what he charges (inf).
   (b) (fig: lebhaft) lively no adv; **Darstellung, Szene, Bild, Erinnerung auch** vivid; **Glaube** deep, fervent.

Lebendigkeit f, no pl (fig) siehe adj **(b)** liveliness; vividness; depth, fervour.

Lebens-: ~**abend** m old age, autumn or twilight of one's life (liter); ~**abschnitt** m phase in or of one's life; ~**ader** f (fig) lifeline; ~**alter** nt age; **ein hohes ~alter erreichen** to have a long life; (Mensch auch) to reach a ripe old age (inf); ~**angst** f fear of life; ~**anschauung** f philosophy of life; ~**art** f, no pl **(a)** siehe ~**weise**. **(b)** (Manieren) manners pl; (Stil) style, savoir-vivre; **eine feine/kultivierte ~art haben** to have exquisite manners/style/to be cultivated; ~**auffassung** f attitude to life; ~**aufgabe** f life's work; ~**baum** m (Bot) arborvitae; (fig, Art) tree of life; ~**bedingungen** pl living conditions pl; l~**bejahend** adj positive; **eine l~bejahende Einstellung** a positive approach to life; ~**bejahung** f positive attitude to life; ~**berechtigung** f right to exist; (von Menschen, Tieren auch) right to live; ~**bereich** m area of life; ~**beschreibung** f biography; ~**bild** nt (fig) picture of sb's life; ~**dauer** f life(span); (von Maschine) life; l~**echt** adj true-to-life; ~**elixier** nt elixir of life; ~**ende** nt end of sb's/(one's) life, end; ~**erfahrung** f experience of life; ~**erinnerungen** pl memoirs pl; ~**erwartung** f life expectancy; ~**faden** m: **jdm den ~faden abschneiden** (liter) to cut the thread of sb's life (liter); l~**fähig** adj (Med) capable of life or of living, viable; (fig) capable of surviving, viable; ~**fähigkeit** f (Med) ability to live, viability; (fig) ability to survive, viability; ~**form** f (Biol) life-form; (Psych, Philos) form of life, type of man; (Form menschlichen Zusammenlebens) way of life; ~**frage** f vital matter; ~**fremd** adj remote from or out of touch with life; ~**freude** f joie de vivre, zest for life; l~**froh** adj merry, full of the joys of life; ~**führung** f life-style; ~**gefahr** f (mortal) danger; **„~gefahr!"** "danger"; **es besteht ~gefahr** there is danger (to life); **er ist** or **schwebt in ~gefahr** his life is in danger, he is in danger of his life; (Patient) he is in a critical condition; **außer ~gefahr sein** to be out of danger; **etw unter ~gefahr** (dat) **tun** to risk one's life doing sth; **der Film wurde unter ~gefahr gedreht** the film was made at great personal risk to the crew; l~**gefährlich** adj highly dangerous; **Krankheit, Verletzung** critical; ~**gefährte** m,

~**gefährtin** f companion through life (liter); ~**gefühl** nt, no pl feeling of being alive; **ein ganz neues** ~**gefühl haben** to feel (like) a different person; (neuen Auftrieb haben) to have a new lease of life; ~**geister** pl (hum inf) **jds/seine** ~**geister auffrischen** or **wecken** to pep sb/oneself up (inf), to put some life into sb/oneself; ~**gemeinschaft** f long-term relationship; (Biol, Zool) symbiosis; ~**genuß** m enjoyment of life; ~**geschichte** f life-story, life-history; ~**gewohnheit** f habit; l~**groß** adj lifesize; ~**größe** f lifesize; **eine Figur in** ~**größe** a lifesize figure; **etw in** ~**größe malen** to paint sth lifesize; **da stand er in voller** ~**größe** (hum) there he was (as) large as life (and twice as ugly) (inf); **er erhob sich zu seiner vollen** ~**größe** (hum) he drew himself up to his full height; ~**haltung** f (a) (Unterhaltskosten) cost of living; (b) (~führung) lifestyle; ~**haltungskosten** pl cost of living sing; ~**hilfe** f counselling; **er mißversteht Literatur als** ~**hilfe** he makes the mistake of thinking that literature can help him with the problems of life; ~**hunger** m thirst for life; l~**hungrig** adj eager or thirsty for life; ~**inhalt** m purpose in life, raison d'être; **etw zu seinem** ~**inhalt machen** to devote oneself to sth, to make sth one's mission in life; **das ist sein ganzer** ~**inhalt** his whole life revolves round it, it's the be-all and end-all of his existence; ~**jahr** nt year of (one's) life; **in seinem fünften** ~**jahr** in the fifth year of his life; **nach Vollendung des 18.** ~**jahres** on attaining the age of 18; ~**kamerad** m siehe ~**gefährte**; ~**kampf** m struggle for life or existence; ~**kraft** f vitality; ~**kreis** m (Lebensbereich) sphere of life; ~**künstler** m master or expert in the art of living; ~**lage** f situation; **in jeder** ~**lage** in any situation; l~**lang** adj Freundschaft, Siechtum lifelong; Haft, Gefangenschaft life attr, for life; l~**länglich** adj Rente, Strafe for life; Gefangenschaft auch life attr; **ein** ~**länglicher** (inf) **a lifer** (sl); **sie hat „l~länglich"** or ~**länglich bekommen** (inf) she got life (inf); l~**länglich im Zuchthaus** or **hinter Gittern sitzen** (inf) to be inside for life or behind bars for life (inf); ~**lauf** m life; (bei Bewerbungen) curriculum vitae, résumé (US); ~**licht** nt (a) (fig) flame of life (liter); **jdm das** ~**licht ausblasen** or **auslöschen** (liter) to snuff out sb's life; (b) (als Geburtstagskerze) candle; ~**linie** f lifeline; ~**lüge** f sham existence; **mit einer** ~**lüge leben** to live a lie; ~**lust** f zest for life, joie de vivre; l~**lustig** adj in love with life; ~**mitte** f middle years pl; **die Krise in der** ~**mitte** the mid-life crisis.

Lebensmittel pl food sing, food(stuff)s pl (form); (als Kaufware auch) groceries pl.

Lebensmittel-: ~**chemie** f food chemistry; ~**geschäft** nt grocer's (shop); ~**gesetz** nt food law; ~**karte** f food ration-card.

Lebens-: l~**müde** adj weary or tired of life; **ein** ~**müder** a potential suicide; ~**müdigkeit** f weariness or tiredness of life; ~**mut** m courage to face life; l~**nah** adj true-to-life; ~**nerv** m (fig) **eine Industrie/eine Stadt an ihrem** ~**nerv treffen** to cripple an industry/a town; **der Tourismus ist der** ~**nerv Mallorcas** tourism is Majorca's lifeblood; l~**notwendig** adj essential, vitally necessary; Organ, Sauerstoff etc vital (for life), essential for life; ~**notwendigkeit** f necessity of life, essential; ~**ordnung** f way of life; (Eccl) canons and ordinances pl (of the German Protestant Church); ~**pfad** m, no pl (liter) path of (one's/sb's) life; ~**philosophie** f philosophy of life; ~**qualität** f quality of life; ~**raum** m (Pol) lebensraum; (Biol) biosphere; ~**regel** f rule (of life); ~**reise** f, no pl (liter) journey through life; ~**retter** m rescuer; **du bist mein** ~**retter** you've saved my life; ~**rettungsmedaille** f lifesaving medal; ~**standard** m standard of living; ~**stellung** f job for life; ~**stil** m lifestyle, style of life; l~**tüchtig** adj able to cope with life; ~**überdruß** m weariness with life, world-weariness; ~**umstände** pl circumstances pl; **damals waren die** ~**umstände schwierig** conditions made life difficult in those days; ~**unterhalt** m (a) **seinen** ~**unterhalt verdienen** to earn one's living; **sie verdient den** ~**unterhalt für die Familie** she is the breadwinner of the family, she supports the family; **für jds** ~**unterhalt sorgen** to support sb; **etw zu seinem** ~**unterhalt tun** to do sth for a living or livelihood; **nur das Nötigste zum** ~**unterhalt haben** to have just enough to live on; (b) (Unterhaltskosten) cost of living; l~**untüchtig** adj unable to cope with life; l~**verneinend** adj negative; **eine** l~**verneinende Einstellung** a negative approach to life; ~**verneinung** f negative attitude to life; ~**versicherung** f life assurance or insurance; **eine** ~**versicherung abschließen** to take out a life assurance or insurance policy; ~**wandel** m way of life; **einen einwandfreien/zweifelhaften** etc ~**wandel führen** to lead an irreproachable/a dubious etc life; ~**weg** m journey through life; **den gemeinsamen** ~**weg antreten** to begin one's life together; **wir wollen unseren** ~**weg gemeinsam gehen** we want to go through life together; **alles Gute für den weiteren** or **ferneren** ~**weg** every good wish for the future; ~**weise** f way of life; ~**weisheit** f maxim; (~erfahrung) wisdom; ~**wende** f (geh) turning-point in (one's/sb's) life; ~**werk** nt life's work, lifework; l~**wert** adj worth living; l~**wichtig** adj essential, vital; Organ, Bedürfnisse vital; l~**wichtige Verbindungslinie** vital link, lifeline; ~**wille** m will to live; ~**zeichen** nt sign of life; **kein** ~**zeichen mehr von sich geben** to show no sign(s) of life; ~**zeit** f life(time); **auf** ~**zeit** for life; Beamter auf ~**zeit** permanent civil servant; Mitglied auf ~**zeit** life member; ~**ziel** nt goal or aim in life; ~**zweck** m purpose in life.

Leber f -, -n liver. **ich habe es mit der** ~ **zu tun** or **an der** ~ (inf) I've got liver trouble; **frei** or **frisch von der** ~ **weg reden** (inf) to speak out or frankly; **sich** (dat) **etw von der** ~ **reden** (inf) to get sth off one's chest; siehe **Laus**.

Leber-: ~**blümchen** nt liverwort; ~**entzündung** f hepatitis, inflammation of the liver; ~**fleck** m liver spot; ~**haken** m (Sport) hook to the liver; ~**käs(e)** m, no pl = meat loaf;

~**knödel** m liver dumpling; l~**krank** adj suffering from a liver disorder; ~**krebs** m cancer of the liver; ~**leiden** nt liver disorder; ~**pastete** f liver pâté; ~**tran** m cod-liver oil; ~**wurst** f liver sausage; siehe **beleidigt**.

Lebewesen nt living thing. **kleinste** ~ micro-organisms.

Lebewohl nt -s, no pl (liter) farewell (liter). **die Stunde des** ~**s** the hour of farewell; **jdm** ~ **sagen** to bid sb farewell or adieu.

lebhaft adj (a) (voll Leben, rege) lively no adv; alter Mensch auch sprightly; Temperament auch vivacious; Gespräch, Streit auch animated; (Comm) Geschäfte auch brisk; Verkehr brisk. **es geht** ~ **zu** it is or things are lively; **das Geschäft geht** ~ business is brisk or lively; **die Börse schloß** ~ business was brisk or lively on the Stock Exchange at the close of the day.

(b) (deutlich) Erinnerung, Vorstellungsvermögen vivid; (einfallsreich) Phantasie lively. **ich kann mir** ~ **vorstellen, daß ... I** can (very) well imagine that ...; **in** ~**er Erinnerung bleiben** to remain a vivid memory; **etw in** ~**er Erinnerung haben** to remember sth vividly.

(c) (kräftig) Muster, Interesse, Beifall lively; Farben auch bright. ~ **bedauern** to regret deeply, to be really sorry about.

Lebhaftigkeit f siehe adj (a) liveliness; sprightliness; vivaciousness; animation; briskness.

(b) vividness; liveliness.

(c) liveliness; brightness.

Leb-: ~**kuchen** m gingerbread; l~**los** adj Körper, Augen lifeless; Straße auch empty, deserted; l~**loser Gegenstand** inanimate object; ~**losigkeit** f siehe adj lifelessness; emptiness; ~**tag** m (inf) **mein/dein** etc ~**tag** all my/your etc life, all my/your etc born days; **das habe ich mein** ~**tag noch nicht gesehen** etc I've never seen the like (of it) in all my life or in all my born days; **das werde ich mein** ~**tag nicht vergessen** I'll never forget that as long as I live; ~**zeiten** pl **zu jds** ~**zeiten** (Leben) while sb is/was alive, in sb's lifetime; (Zeit) in sb's day; **schon zu** ~**zeiten eine Legende** a legend in his/her own lifetime.

lechzen vi (Hund) to pant, to have its tongue hanging out. **nach etw** ~ to thirst for or crave sth, to long for sth; **mit** ~**der Zunge** with one's tongue hanging out; siehe **Blut**.

Lecithin [letsi'tiːn] nt -s, no pl lecithin.

leck adj leaky. ~ **sein** to leak; ~ **schlagen** to hole.

Leck nt -(e)s, -s leak.

Leckage [lɛ'kaːʒə] f -, -n (a) (Gewichtsverlust) leakage. (b) (Leck) leak.

Lecke f -, -n (Hunt) saltlick.

lecken[1] vi (undicht sein) to leak.

lecken[2] vti to lick. **an jdm/etw** ~ to lick sb/sth; **sich** (dat) **die Wunden** ~ to lick one's wounds; siehe **Arsch, Finger, geleckt**.

lecker adj Speisen delicious, lovely, yummy (inf); (inf) Mädchen lovely, delectable.

Leckerbissen m (a) (Speise) delicacy, titbit. (b) (fig) gem.

Leckerei f (a) siehe **Leckerbissen** (a). (b) (Süßigkeit) dainty.

Lecker-: ~**maul**, ~**mäulchen** nt (inf) sweet-toothed child/person etc; **ein** ~**maul sein** to have a sweet tooth.

leckschlagen vti sep irreg siehe **leck**.

Leckstein m licking stone.

led. abbr of **ledig**.

Leder nt -s, - (a) leather; (Fenster~ auch) chamois, chammy; (Wild~) suede. **in** ~ **gebunden** leather-bound; **zäh wie** ~ as tough as old boots (inf); **vom** ~ **ziehen** to let rip (inf) or fly (inf).

(b) (dated inf: Haut) hide (inf). **jdm das** ~ **gerben** or **versohlen** to tan sb's hide; **jdm ans** ~ **wollen** to want to get one's hands on sb.

(c) (inf: Fußball) ball. **am** ~ **bleiben** to stick with the ball.

Leder- in cpds leather; l~**artig** adj Stoff leather-like; ~**band** m (Buch) leatherbound volume; ~**fett** nt dubbin; ~**garnitur** f leather-upholstered suite; ~**haut** f (Anat) dermis (spec), derma (spec); (um den Augapfel) sclera (spec); ~**hose** f lederhosen pl, leather/suede trousers pl or pants pl; (von Tracht) leather shorts pl; (Bundhose) leather breeches pl; ~**jacke** f leather/suede jacket.

ledern 1 adj (a) (aus Leder) leather. (b) (zäh) Fleisch, Haut leathery; (fig) Vortrag etc dry (as dust). 2 vt (gerben) to tan.

(b) (putzen) to leather.

Leder-: ~**nacken** m leathernecks pl; ~**rücken** m leather spine; ~**schurz** m leather apron; ~**waren** pl leather goods pl; ~**zeug** nt leather gear; (Mil) leathers pl.

ledig adj (a) (unverheiratet) single; (inf) Mutter unmarried; Kind illegitimate. ~ **gehen** to live separately for professional reasons.

(b) (geh: unabhängig) free. (los und) ~ **sein** to be footloose and fancy free; **aller Pflichten** (gen) (los und) ~ **sein** to be free of all commitments.

(c) Schiff unladen; Pferd riderless.

Ledigen(wohn)heim nt hostel for single people.

Ledige(r) mf decl as adj single person.

lediggehend adj living separately for professional reasons.

lediglich adv merely, simply.

Lee f -, no pl (Naut) lee. **in** ~ **liegen** to be on the lee side; **nach** ~ **drehen** to turn to leeward.

leer adj empty; Blätter, Seite auch blank; Gesichtsausdruck, Blick blank, vacant. **der** ~**e Raum** (geh) the cosmos; **eine** ~**e Stelle** an empty space; **vor einem** ~**en Haus** or **vor** ~**en Bänken spielen** (Theat) to play to an empty house; **ins L~e starren/treten** to stare/step into space; **ins L~e greifen** to clutch at thin air; **mit** ~**en Händen** (fig) empty-handed; **eine Zeile** ~ **lassen** to leave a line (blank or free); ~ **laufen** (Motor) to idle; (Maschine) to run idle; (Betrieb etc) to be idle; **du solltest bergab den Motor nicht** ~ **laufen lassen** you shouldn't coast down a hill (in neutral or with the car in neutral); **etw** ~ **machen** to empty sth; **den Teller** ~ **essen** to eat everything on the plate; ~ **stehen** to stand empty; **eine Wohnung** ~ **mieten** to rent an unfurnished flat, to rent a flat unfurnished; **einen Laden ~ kaufen** to buy a shop out; **an etw** (dat) **~ sein** (geh) to be devoid or empty of sth.

Leere f -, no pl (lit, fig) emptiness. **(eine) geistige ~** a mental vacuum; **(eine) gähnende ~** a yawning or gaping void.

leeren vt to empty; (völlig auch) to drain; **Briefkasten auch** to clear. **jdm die Taschen ~** (inf) to clean sb out (inf).

Leer-: l**~gefegt** adj (fig) (wie) l**~gefegt Straßen, Stadt etc** deserted; **~gewicht** nt unladen weight, tare; (von Behälter) empty weight of a container; **~gut** nt empties pl; **~lauf** m (a) (Aut) neutral; (von Fahrrad) freewheel; **im ~lauf fahren** to coast; **das Auto ist im ~lauf** the engine is in neutral; (stehend mit laufendem Motor) the engine is idling; **den Motor im ~lauf testen** to test the engine while it's idling; **l~laufen** vi sep irreg aux sein (Faß etc) to run dry; **l~laufen lassen** to empty, to drain; **~packung** f (empty) display package, dummy; **l~stehend** adj empty; **~taste** f (bei Schreibmaschine) space-bar.

Leerung f emptying. **die ~ der Mülltonnen erfolgt wöchentlich** the dustbins (Brit) or garbage cans (US) are emptied once a week; **nächste ~: 18 Uhr** (an Briefkasten) next collection: 6 p.m.

Lefze f -, -n usu pl chaps pl; (von Pferd) lip.

legal adj legal, lawful.

legalisieren* vt to legalize.

legalistisch adj legalistic.

Legalität f legality. **(etwas) außerhalb der ~** (euph) (slightly) outside the law.

Legasthenie f dyslexia.

Legastheniker(in f) m -s, - dyslexic.

legasthenisch adj dyslexic.

Legat¹ nt (Jur) legacy.

Legat² m -en, -en (Eccl, Hist) legate.

Legation f legation.

Legationsrat m counsellor to a legation.

Leg(e)henne f, **Leg(e)huhn** nt layer, laying hen.

Legel m -s, - (Naut) cringle, grummet.

legen 1 vt (a) (lagern) to lay down; (mit adv) to lay; **Flasche etc** to lay on its side; (zusammen~) **Wäsche** to fold; (dial) **Kartoffeln etc** to plant, to put in; (Sport) to bring down. **(b)** (mit Raumangabe) to put, to place. **wir müssen uns ein paar Flaschen Wein in den Keller ~** we must lay down a few bottles of wine; **etw beiseite ~** to put sth aside or (weglegen) away; **etw an die Luft ~** to put sth out to air; **etw in Essig etc ~** to preserve sth in vinegar etc; **ein Tier an die Kette ~** to chain an animal (up); **jdn in Ketten/Fesseln ~** to put sb in chains, to chain sb; (fig hum) to (en)snare sb; **sein Interesse auf etw** (acc) **~** (geh) to devote one's attention to sth. **(c)** (mit Angabe des Zustandes) **etw in Falten ~** to fold sth; **er legte die Stirn in Falten** he frowned, he creased his brow; **eine Stadt in Schutt und Asche ~** to reduce a town to rubble. **(d)** (verlegen) **Fliesen, Leitungen, Schienen, Minen etc** to lay, to put down; **Bomben** to plant. **Feuer** or **einen Brand ~** to start a fire; **sich** (dat) **die Haare ~ lassen** to have one's hair set; **sich** (dat) **Dauerwellen etc ~ lassen** to have a perm etc, to have one's hair permed etc. **(e)** auch vi (Hühner) to lay.

2 vr (a) (hin~) to lie down (auf + acc on). **sich ins or zu** (geh) **Bett ~** to go to bed, to retire (form); **sich in die Sonne ~** to lie in the sun; **sich ins Bett** (zum Hund) **lie!**; siehe **schlafen**. **(b)** (mit Ortsangabe) (nieder~) (Nebel, Rauch) to settle (auf + acc on). **sich auf die Seite ~** to lie on one's side; (Boot) to heel over, to go over onto its side; **sich in die Kurve ~** to lean into the corner; **sich auf ein Spezialgebiet ~** to concentrate on or specialize in a particular field. **(c)** (Lärm) to die down, to abate; (Sturm, Wind auch, Kälte) to let up; (Rauch, Nebel) to clear; (Zorn, Begeisterung auch, Arroganz, Nervosität) to wear off; (Anfangsschwierigkeiten) to sort themselves out. **das Fieber legt sich bald** his etc temperature will come down/the fever will lessen soon.

legendär adj legendary; (obskur) apocryphal. **er/das ist schon fast ~** he/it has already become almost legendary.

Legende f -, -n (alle Bedeutungen) legend.

legendenumwoben adj fabled, surrounded by legends.

leger [leˈʒeːr, leˈʒɛːr] adj casual, informal.

Legezeit f laying season or time.

Legföhre f siehe **Latschenkiefer**.

Leghenne f siehe **Leg(e)henne**.

legieren* vt (a) **Metall** to alloy. **(b)** (Cook) **Suppe etc** to thicken.

Legierung f alloy; (Verfahren) alloying.

Legion f legion. **die Zahl der Toten war ~** (geh) the number of the dead was legion (liter).

Legionär m legionary.

legislativ adj legislative.

Legislative f legislature, legislative assembly or body.

legislatorisch adj legislative.

Legislatur f (a) (rare: Gesetzgebung) legislation; (obs: gesetzgebende Gewalt) legislature. **(b)** (inf) siehe **Legislaturperiode**.

Legislaturperiode f parliamentary/congressional term.

legitim adj legitimate.

Legitimation f identification; (Berechtigung) authorization; (eines Kindes) legitimation.

legitimieren* 1 vt **jdn in Beziehung, Kind** to legitimize; (berechtigen) to entitle; (berechtigt erscheinen lassen) to justify, to warrant; (Erlaubnis geben) to authorize. **2** vr to show (proof of) authorization; (sich ausweisen) to identify oneself, to show proof of one's identity.

Legitimität f, no pl legitimacy.

Leguan m -s, -e iguana.

Lehen nt -s, - (Hist) fief, feoff, feu (Scot). **jdm ein Gut zu ~ geben** to enfeoff sb.

Lehens- in cpds siehe **Lehns-**.

Lehm m -(e)s, -e loam; (Ton) clay.

Lehm-: **~bau** m, **~bauweise** f clay building; **~boden** m clay soil; l**~farben**, l**~farbig** adj clay-coloured; **~hütte** f mud hut.

lehmig adj loamy; (tonartig) claylike, clayey.

Lehm-: **~packung** f mudpack; **~ziegel** m clay brick.

Lehn nt -s, - siehe **Lehen**.

Lehnbildung f (Ling) loan formation.

Lehne f -, -n (a) (Arm~) arm(-rest); (Rücken~) back(-rest). **(b)** (old, S Ger: Berghang) slope.

lehnen 1 vt to lean (an + acc against). **2** vi to be leaning (an + dat against). **3** vr to lean (an + acc against, auf + acc on). **„nicht aus dem Fenster ~!"** (Rail) "do not lean out of the window".

Lehnsdienst m (Hist) vassalage.

Lehnsessel m siehe **Lehnstuhl**.

Lehns-: **~herr** m (Hist) feudal lord; **~mann** m, pl **-männer** or **-leute** (Hist) vassal; **~pflicht** f (Hist) feudal duty.

Lehnstuhl m easy-chair.

Lehnswesen nt (Hist) feudal system, feudalism.

Lehn-: **~übersetzung** f (Ling) loan-translation; **~wort** nt (Ling) loan-word, borrowing.

Lehr-: **~amt** nt das **~amt** the teaching profession; **ein/sein ~amt ausüben** to hold a teaching post; **Prüfung für das höhere ~amt** examination for secondary school teachers; **sein ~amt ernst nehmen** (Univ) to take one's teaching responsibilities seriously; **~amtsanwärter**, **~amtskandidat** m prospective teacher; **~anstalt** f (form) educational establishment; **höhere ~anstalt** establishment of secondary education; **~auftrag** m (als Sonderlehrer) special teaching post; **einen ~auftrag für etw haben** (Univ) to give lectures on sth; l**~bar** adj teachable; **~barkeit** f teachability; **~beauftragte(r)** mf (Univ) **~beauftragter für etw sein** to give lectures on sth; **~befähigung** f teaching qualification; **~behalt** m (Aus) siehe **~mittel**; **~berechtigung** f jdm die **~berechtigung erteilen** to register sb as a teacher; **ihm wurde die ~berechtigung entzogen** he was struck off the register of teachers; **für Latein hat er keine ~berechtigung** he isn't qualified to teach Latin; **~beruf** m (a) (als Lehrer) teaching profession; **den ~beruf ergreifen** to go into teaching; **(b)** (Beruf mit ~zeit) trade requiring an apprenticeship, skilled trade; **~betrieb** m (Univ) teaching; **~brief** m (a) (Zeugnis) apprenticeship certificate; **(b)** (Lektion) correspondence lesson; **~bub**, **~bursche** m (dial) siehe **Lehrling**; **~buch** nt textbook; l**~buchgerecht** adj (a) **die l~buchgerechte Bearbeitung eines Textes** the revision of a text for a school edition; **(b)** (gutausgeführt) text-book attr, perfect; **~dichtung** f didactic poetry.

Lehre f -, -n (a) (das Lehren) teaching. **(b)** (von Christus, Buddha, Marx etc) teachings pl; (christlich, buddhistisch, marxistisch etc) (Lehrmeinung) doctrine; (das Lehren) teaching; (von Galileo, Kant, Freud etc) theory; (von Schall, Leben etc) science. **die christliche ~** Christian doctrine/teaching. **(c)** (negative Erfahrung) lesson; (Ratschlag) (piece of) advice; (einer Fabel) moral. **seine ~(n) aus etw ziehen** to learn a lesson from sth; (aus einer Fabel etc) to draw a moral from sth; **laß dir das eine ~ sein, laß es dir zur ~ dienen!** let that be a lesson to you! **(d)** (Berufs~) apprenticeship; (in nichtmanuellem Beruf) training. **bei jdm die ~ (durch)machen** or **in die ~ gehen** to serve one's apprenticeship with or under sb; **jdn in die ~ geben** to apprentice sb (bei, zu to); **du kannst bei ihm noch in die ~ gehen** (fig) he could teach you a thing or two. **(e)** (Tech) gauge; (Muster) template.

lehren vti to teach; (Univ auch) to lecture (ein Fach in a subject). **die Wissenschaft lehrt, daß ...** science tells us that ...; **jdn** or **jdm** (inf) **lesen etc ~** to teach sb to read etc; **die Zukunft wird es ~ time** (alone) will tell; **ich werde dich ~, so frech zu antworten!** I'll teach you to answer back! (inf).

Lehrer(in f) m -s, - teacher; (Privat~, Nachhilfe~ auch) tutor; (Flug~, Fahr~ etc) instructor/instructress. **er ist ~** he's a (school)teacher; **~ für Philosophie/Naturwissenschaften** teacher of philosophy/science; (in der Schule) philosophy/science teacher.

Lehrerausbildung f teacher training.

Lehrerin f siehe **Lehrer**.

Lehrer-: **~kollegium** nt (teaching)staff; **in diesem ~kollegium** amongst the teaching staff of this school; **~mangel** m teacher shortage; **~schaft** f (form) (teaching) staff; **~schwemme** f surplus of teachers; **~seminar** nt (für Referendare, inf: Pädagogische Hochschule) teacher training college; (Kurs) in-service course for teachers; **~zimmer** nt staff (esp Brit) or teachers' room.

Lehr-: **~fach** nt (a) subject; **(b) im ~fach tätig sein** (form) to be a member of the teaching profession; **~film** m educational film; **~freiheit** f freedom to teach what one sees fit; **~gang** m course (für in); **~gebäude** nt (fig) system of theories (Eccl) doctrinal system; **~gegenstand** m subject; **die Fortpflanzung des Menschen ist ~gegenstand für das 3. Schuljahr/die heutige Stunde** reproduction in humans is taught in the third year/is the subject of today's lesson; **~geld** nt (Hist) (apprenticeship) premium; (teures) **~geld für etw zahlen müssen** (fig) to pay dearly for sth; **laß dir dein ~geld zurückgeben!** (hum inf) go to the bottom of the class! (hum inf); **~gerüst** nt centring; l**~haft** adj didactic; **~herr** m master (of an apprentice); **~jahr** nt year as an apprentice; **~jahre sind keine Herrenjahre** (Prov) life's not easy at the bottom; **~junge** m siehe **Lehrling**; **~kanzel** f (Aus) siehe **~stuhl**; **~körper** m (form) teaching staff; (Univ auch) academic staff; **~kraft** f (form) teacher.

Lehrling m apprentice; (*in nicht manuellem Beruf*) trainee.
Lehrlings-: ~**ausbildung** f training of apprentices/trainees; ~**heim** nt apprentices' hostel; ~**vergütung** f apprentice's/trainee's pay.
Lehr-: ~**mädchen** nt siehe Lehrling; ~**meinung** f opinion; (*von einer bestimmten Gruppe vertreten*) school of thought; (*Eccl*) doctrine; **einer** ~**meinung angehören** to belong to a school of thought; ~**meister** m master; **seinen** ~**meister finden** to meet one's master; **du bist mir ein schöner** ~**meister** you're a fine example; ~**methode** f teaching method; ~**mittel** nt teaching aid; pl auch teaching materials; ~**plan** m (teaching) curriculum; (*für ein Schuljahr*) syllabus; ~**probe** f demonstration lesson, crit (*inf*); ~**programm** nt teaching programme; l~**reich** adj (*informativ*) instructive; *Erfahrung* educational; ~**satz** m (Math, Philos) theorem; (*Eccl*) dogma; ~**schwimmbecken** nt beginners' or teaching pool; ~**stand** m, no pl (*Hist*) teaching profession; (*Philos*) guardian-rulers pl; ~**stelle** f position for or (*aus Sicht des Lehrlings*) as an apprentice/a trainee; **wir haben zwei** ~**stellen zu vergeben** we have vacancies for two apprentices; ~**stoff** m subject; (*eines Jahres*) syllabus; **das ist** ~**stoff der dritten Klasse** that's on the syllabus for the third year; ~**stuhl** m (*Univ*) chair (*für* of); **jdn auf einen** ~**stuhl berufen** to offer sb a chair; ~**tochter** f (*Sw*) siehe Lehrling; ~**verhältnis** nt contractual relationship (*between apprentice and master/trainee and employer*); **in einem** ~**verhältnis stehen** (*form*) to be apprenticed (*bei* to); ~**vertrag** m indentures pl; contract as a trainee; ~**werk** nt (*form*) textbook; (*Buchreihe*) series of textbooks; ~**werkstatt** nt training workshop; ~**zeit** f apprenticeship.
Leib m -(e)s, -er (a) (*Körper*) body. **der ~ des Herrn** (*Eccl*) the Body of Christ; **Gefahr für ~ und Leben** (*geh*) danger to life and limb; ~ **und Leben wagen** (*geh*) to risk life and limb; **mit ~ und Seele heart and soul; wünschen with all one's heart; mit ~ und Seele singen/dabei sein** to sing one's heart out/put one's heart and soul or one's whole heart into it; **etw am eigenen** ~**(e) erfahren** or (*ver*)**spüren** to experience sth for oneself; **kein Hemd mehr am** ~ **haben** to be completely destitute; **keinen trocknen Faden am** ~ **haben** (*inf*) to be soaked to the skin (*inf*); **einen guten Schritt am** ~**(e) haben** (*inf*) to set a good pace; (*ständig*) to be a fast walker; **der hat vielleicht einen Ton am** ~**!** (*inf*) talk about rude!; **am ganzen** ~**(e) zittern/frieren/schwitzen** to shake/freeze/sweat all over; **sich** (*dat*) **alles an den** ~ **hängen** (*inf*) to spend everything on clothes; **die Rolle ist ihr wie auf den** ~ **geschrieben** the part is tailor-made for her; **der Beruf ist ihr wie auf den** ~ **geschnitten** that job is tailor-made for her or suits her to a T (*inf*); **kein Herz im** ~ **haben** to have no heart at all, to be completely heartless; **er hat kein Ehrgefühl/Taktgefühl im** ~ he hasn't an ounce of honour/tact (in him), he is completely devoid of honour/tact; **sich** (*dat*) **jdn/etw vom** ~**e halten** to keep or hold sb/sth at bay; **halt ihn mir vom** ~ keep him away from me; **jdm vom** ~ **bleiben** to keep away from sb; **geh mir vom** ~**!** get away (from) me!; (*laß mich in Ruhe*) get off my back! (*inf*); **bleib mir damit vom** ~**e!** (*inf*) stop pestering me with it (*inf*); siehe rücken.
(b) (*old, dial: Bauch*) stomach; (*Mutter~*) womb. **gut bei** ~**e sein** (*inf*) to be well-built (*euph*); **ich habe noch nichts im** ~**e** I haven't eaten yet.
Leib-: ~**arzt** m personal physician; ~**binde** f truss; (*nach Geburt*) abdominal binder.
Leibchen nt (a) (*old*) bodice. (b) (*Unterhemd*) vest (*Brit*), undershirt (*US*); (*Hemdchen*) top.
Leib-: l~**eigen** adj siehe Leibeigenschaft unfree, in bondage; serf attr; villein attr; l~**eigen sein** not to be a free man/woman; to be a serf/villein; ~**eigne(r)** mf decl as adj bond(s)man/bond(s)woman; serf; villein; **er behandelt seine Frau wie eine** ~**eigene** he treats his wife as though she were one of his possessions; ~**eigenschaft** f bondage; (*im Mittelalter*) serfdom; (*von Höhergestellten, mit Eigentum*) villeinage.
leiben vi: **wie er leibt und lebt** to the life, to a T (*inf*).
Leibes-: ~**erben** pl (*form*) issue sing (*form*); ~**erziehung** f physical education; ~**frucht** f (*geh*) unborn child, fruit of (one's/sb's) womb (*poet*); ~**kraft** f: **aus** ~**kräften schreien** etc to shout etc with all one's might (and main); ~**übung** f (*physical*) exercise; ~**übungen** (*Schulfach*) physical education no pl; ~**visitation** f body check; (*Mil*) physical inspection, medical.
Leib-: ~**garde** f (*Mil*) bodyguard; **die** ~**garde der englischen Königin** the Queen's Guards pl; ~**gardist** m soldier of a bodyguard; (*Brit*) lifeguard; ~**gericht** nt favourite meal.
leibhaft (*rare*), **leibhaftig 1** adj personified, incarnate. **die** ~**e Güte** etc goodness etc personified or incarnate; (*wie*) **der** ~**e Teufel** or **der L~e** (as) the devil himself. **2** adv in person, in the flesh.
Leibkoch m personal chef.
leiblich adj (a) (*körperlich*) physical, bodily. **die** ~**en Genüsse** the pleasures of the flesh; **die** ~**e Hülle** (*geh*) the mortal remains pl. (b) Mutter, Vater natural; Kind by birth; Bruder, Schwester full; Verwandte blood; (*emph: eigen*) (very) own.
Leib-: ~**pacht** f (*old*) life tenancy, lease for life; ~**rente** f life annuity; ~**riemen** m (*old*) belt; ~**schmerzen** pl (*old, dial*) stomach pains pl; ~**schneiden** nt (*old, dial*) colic pains pl; ~**speise** f favourite food; ~**wache** f bodyguard; ~**wächter** m bodyguard; ~**wäsche** f underwear, underclothes pl; ~**weh** nt (*old*) stomach-ache.
Leich m -(e)s, -e (*Liter*) lay.
Leiche f -, -n (a) body, corpse; (*menschlich auch*) stiff (sl); (*inf: Bier~, Schnaps~*) drunken body (*inf*). **die Insassen konnten nur noch als** ~**n geborgen werden** the passengers were dead when the rescuers arrived; **eine lebende** or **wandelnde** ~ (*inf*) a corpse; **wie eine lebende** or **wandelnde** ~ **aussehen** to look like death (warmed up *inf*); **er geht über** ~**n** (*inf*) he'd stick at

nothing, he'd sell his own grandmother (*inf*); **nur über meine** ~**!** (*inf*) over my dead body!
(b) (S Ger) (*Beerdigung*) funeral; (*Leichenschmaus*) funeral meal. **die** ~ **begießen** (*inf*) to drink the dead man's health.
(c) (*Typ*) omission.
Leichen-: ~**acker** m (*old*) graveyard; ~**begängnis** (*form*), ~**begräbnis** nt funeral; ~**beschauer** m -s, - doctor conducting a post-mortem; ~**bitter** m -s, - (*old*) person who invites people to a funeral; ~**bittermiene** f (*inf*) mournful or doleful expression; l~**blaß** adj deathly pale, as pale as death; ~**fledderei** f robbing of dead people; **diese** ~**fledderei nach dem Tod meiner Tante** the way the vultures descended after my aunt's death; **das ist die reinste** ~**fledderei** (*fig*) what vultures!; ~**fledderer** m -s, - person who robs dead people; (*fig*) vulture; ~**frau** f layer-out; ~**halle** f, ~**haus** nt mortuary; ~**hemd** nt shroud; ~**konservierung** f preservation of corpses; ~**öffnung** f autopsy; ~**rede** f funeral oration (*liter*) or address; ~**schändung** f desecration of corpses; (*sexuell*) necrophilia; (*fig hum: Ehe mit Greis*) grave-robbing (*hum*); **der zweite Schlag ist** ~**schändung** (*hum inf*) these fists are lethal weapons; ~**schau** f post-mortem (examination); ~**schauhaus** nt morgue; ~**schmaus** m funeral meal; ~**starre** f rigor mortis no art; ~**tuch** nt shroud; ~**verbrennung** f cremation; ~**wagen** m hearse; ~**zug** m funeral procession.
Leichnam m -s, -e (*form*) body.
leicht 1 adj (a) (*von geringem Gewicht, nicht schwerfällig, Mil*) light; (*aus* ~*em Material*) Koffer, Kleidung lightweight. **einen** ~**en Gang haben** to have an easy walk; **mit** ~**er Hand** lightly; (*fig*) effortlessly; **eine** ~**e Hand mit jdm/für etw haben** to have a way with sb/sth; ~**en Fußes** (*liter*) with a spring in one's step; ~ **zu tragen** light; **das wiegt** ~ that's light; (*Waren auch*) that weighs light; **gewogen und zu** ~ **befunden** (*fig*) tried and found wanting; **jdn um einiges** ~**er machen** to relieve sb of some of his money; **das Haus/Auto ist** ~ **gebaut** the house is built of light materials/the car is lightly built; **ein zu** ~ **gebautes Haus/Auto** a flimsily built house/car; ~ **bekleidet sein** to be scantily clad or dressed; ~ **gekleidet sein** to be (dressed) in light clothes; siehe Feder.
(b) (*schwach, geringfügig, nicht wichtig*) slight; Regen, Wind, Frost, Schläge, Schlaf, Berührung, Atmen light; (*Jur*) Diebstahl, Vergehen etc minor, petty. ~ **gewürzt/gesalzen** lightly seasoned/salted; **zu** ~ **gewürzt/gesalzen** not seasoned/salted enough; ~ **waschen** to wash gently.
(c) (*von geringem Gehalt*) Essen, Musik, Lektüre etc light.
(d) (*ohne Schwierigkeiten, einfach*) easy. **er hat eine** ~**e Auffassungsgabe** he's very quick to understand everything; ~**er Absatz** (*Comm*) quick turnover (*von* in); **mit dem werden wir (ein)** ~**es Spiel haben** he'll be a pushover (*inf*) or walkover (*inf*), he'll be no problem; **keinen** ~**en Stand haben** not to have an easy time (of it) (*bei, mit* with); **sie hat es immer** ~ **gehabt** (*im Leben*) she's always had it easy or had an easy time of it; **man hat's nicht** ~, **aber** ~ **hat's einen** (*inf*) it's a hard life; **das ist or geht ganz** ~ it's quite easy or simple; **das ist ihr ein** ~**es** (*geh*) that will present no problem to or for her; **nichts** ~**er als das!** nothing (could be) easier or simpler; **die Aufgabe ist** ~ **zu lösen** or **läßt sich** ~ **lösen** the exercise is easy to do; ~ **zu beantworten/verstehen** easily answered/understood, easy to answer/understand; **er ist** ~ **herumzukriegen/zu überzeugen** he's easy to win round/convince, he's easily won round/convinced; ~ **begreifen** to understand quickly or readily; **mach es dir nicht zu** ~ (*bequem*) don't make things too easy for yourself; (*sei gewissenhaft auch*) don't take the easy way out; (*vereinfache es nicht*) don't over-simplify things; **das ist** ~**er gesagt als getan** that's easier said than done; **du hast** ~ **reden/lachen** it's all very well or it's all right for you to talk/laugh.
(e) (*moralisch locker*) Lebenswandel loose. ~**es Mädchen** tart (*inf*).
(f) (*unbeschwert*) Herz, Gefühl light. **etw** ~**en Herzens or Sinnes tun** to do sth with a light heart; **sich** ~ **und beschwingt fühlen** to be walking on air, to be up in the clouds; **mir ist so** ~ **ums Herz** my heart is so light; **mir ist jetzt viel** ~**er** I feel a lot easier now; **nimm das nicht zu** ~ don't take it too lightly.
2 adv (*schnell, unversehens*) easily. **er wird** ~ **böse/ist** ~ **beleidigt** etc he is quick to get angry/take offence etc, he gets angry/takes offence etc easily; ~ **zerbrechlich** very fragile; **man kann einen Fehler** ~ **übersehen** it's easy to miss a mistake, mistakes are easily missed; **das ist** ~ **möglich** that's quite possible; **das kann ich mir** ~ **vorstellen** or **denken** I can easily or well imagine (it); ~ **entzündlich sein** (Gas, Brennstoff) to be highly inflammable; (*Haut*) to become easily inflamed; **man hat** ~ **etwas gesagt, was man nachher bereut** it's easy to say something (without thinking) that you regret later; **das passiert mir so** ~ **nicht wieder** I won't let that happen again in a hurry (*inf*); **das passiert mir so** ~ **nicht wieder, daß ich dir Geld borge** I won't lend you money again in a hurry (*inf*).
Leicht-: ~**athlet** m (track and field) athlete; ~**athletik** f (track and field) athletics; l~**athletisch 1** adj athletic attr; **2** adv as regards (track and field) athletics; ~**baustoff** m lightweight building material; l~**bau(weise** f) m lightweight construction; **in** ~**bauweise** using lightweight materials; ~**benzin** nt benzine; l~**beschwingt** adj attr Musik light; l~**beschwingte Melodien** melodies for easy listening; ~**beton** m lightweight concrete; l~**bewaffnet** adj attr lightly armed; l~**blütig** adj lighthearted; ~**entzündlich** adj attr Brennstoff etc highly inflammable; l~**entzündliche Haut** skin which easily becomes inflamed.
Leichter m -s, - (*Naut*) lighter.
leichtern vt (*Naut*) to lighten (*form*).
Leicht-: l~**fallen** vi sep irreg aux sein to be easy (*jdm* for sb);

Sprachen sind mir schon immer l~gefallen I've always found languages easy; **l~fertig** adj thoughtless; (moralisch) easygoing; **l~fertig handeln** to act without thinking; **etw l~fertig aufs Spiel setzen** to risk sth without giving it a thought; **~fertigkeit** f siehe adj thoughtlessness; easygoing nature; **l~flüssig** adj attr (easily) fusible; **~fuß** m (old): (Bruder) **~fuß** adventurer; **l~füßig** adj (liter) light-footed; **l~geschürzt** adj attr (hum) scantily clad or dressed; **~gewicht** nt (Sport, fig) lightweight; **Weltmeister im ~gewicht** world lightweight champion; **~gewichtler** m -s, - (Sport) lightweight; **~gewichtsklasse** f lightweight class; **l~gläubig** adj credulous; (leicht zu täuschen) gullible; **~gläubigkeit** f siehe adj credulity; gullibility.
Leichtheit f siehe adj (a) lightness. (b) slightness; lightness. (c) lightness. (d) easiness.
leichtherzig adj light-hearted.
leichthin adv lightly.
Leichtigkeit f ease. **mit** ~ easily, with no trouble (at all).
Leicht-: **~industrie** f light industry; **l~lebig** adj happy-go-lucky, easygoing; **~lebigkeit** f happy-go-lucky or easygoing nature; **~lohngruppe** f group of (usually female) workers paid less than workers in comparable jobs; **l~machen** vt sep **jdm etw l~machen** to make sth easy for sb; **sich** (dat) **etw l~machen, sich** (dat) **es mit etw l~machen** (es sich bequem machen) to make things easy for oneself with sth; (nicht gewissenhaft sein) to take it easy with sth; (vereinfachen) to oversimplify it; **er machte es sich** (dat) **leicht und vermied eine Entscheidung** he took the easy way out and avoided making a decision; **~matrose** m ordinary seaman; **~metall** nt light metal; **l~nehmen** vt sep irreg **etw l~nehmen** (nicht ernsthaft behandeln) to take sth lightly; (sich keine Sorgen machen) not to worry about sth; **~öl** nt light oil.
Leichtsinn m (unvorsichtige Haltung) foolishness; (Unbesorgtheit, Sorglosigkeit) thoughtlessness. **sträflicher** ~ criminal negligence; **unverzeihlicher** ~ unforgivable stupidity; **das ist (ein)** ~ that's foolish or silly; **so ein** ~! how silly/thoughtless (can you get)!
leichtsinnig adj foolish; (unüberlegt) thoughtless. ~ **mit etw umgehen** to be careless with sth.
Leichtsinnigkeit f siehe adj foolishness; thoughtlessness.
Leichtsinnsfehler m careless mistake, slip.
Leicht-: **l~verdaulich** adj attr easily digestible; **l~verderblich** adj attr perishable; **l~verletzt** adj attr slightly injured; (in Gefecht etc auch) slightly wounded; **~verletzte(r)** mf decl as adj slightly injured/wounded person; **l~verständlich** adj attr readily or easily understandable; **l~verwundet** adj attr slightly wounded; **~verwundete(r)** mf decl as adj slightly wounded soldier etc; **die ~verwundeten** the walking wounded.
leid adj pred (a) **etw tut jdm** ~ sb is sorry about or for sth; **es tut jdm** ~, **daß** ... sb is sorry that ...; **tut mir** ~! (I'm) sorry!; **es tut mir** ~, **daß ich so spät gekommen bin** I'm sorry for coming so late or (that) I came so late; **es tut mir nur** ~, **daß** ... I'm only sorry that ..., my only regret is that ..., I only regret that ...; **es tut uns** ~, **Ihnen mitteilen zu müssen** ... we regret to have to inform you ...; **es tut einem** ~, **zu sehen, wie** ... it makes you feel sorry when you see how ...; **er/sie tut mir** ~ I'm sorry for him/her, I pity him/her; **er/sie kann einem** ~ **tun** you can't help feeling sorry or you can't (help) but feel sorry for him/her; **du kannst einem** ~ **tun** you really are to be pitied; **es kann einem** ~ **tun, wenn** ... you can't help feeling sorry when ...; **es tut mir um ihn/darum** ~ I'm sorry about him/that; **das wird dir noch** ~ **tun** you'll regret it, you'll be sorry.
(b) (überdrüssig) **jdn/etw** ~ **sein** to be tired of sb/sth; **das lange Warten bin ich** ~ **geworden** I'm tired of all this waiting.
Leid nt -(e)s, no pl (a) (Kummer, Sorge) sorrow, grief no indef art; (Unglück) misfortune; (Böses, Schaden) harm. **jdm in seinem tiefen** ~ **beistehen** to stand by sb in his/her (hour of) affliction or sorrow; **um jdn** ~ **tragen** (geh) to mourn sb; **ihm ist großes** ~ **widerfahren** he has suffered great misfortune; **viel** ~ **erfahren/ertragen (müssen)** to suffer/have to suffer a great deal; **es soll dir kein** ~ **geschehen** or **zugefügt werden** you will come to no harm, no harm will come to you; **daraus soll niemandem ein** ~ **(es) werden** (liter) nobody should suffer because of that; **jdm ein** ~ **antun** (liter) to harm sb; (moralisch) to wrong sb, to do sb wrong; **jdm sein** ~ **klagen** to tell sb one's troubles, to cry on sb's shoulder; siehe antun.
(b) (Sw: Begräbnis) funeral.
(c) (Sw: Trauerkleidung) mourning. **(um jdn)** ~ **tragen, im** ~ **sein** to wear mourning (for sb), to be in mourning.
Leideform f (Gram) passive (voice).
leiden pret **litt,** ptp **gelitten** 1 vt (a) (ertragen müssen) Schaden, Hunger, Schmerz, Unrecht etc to suffer. **viel zu** ~ **haben** to have a great deal to bear or endure.
(b) (geh: zulassen, dulden) to allow, to permit, to suffer (old). **ich werde es nicht** ~, **daß dich irgend jemand beleidigt** I won't let you be insulted (by anyone); **er ist bei allen wohl gelitten** everybody holds him in high regard or great esteem.
(c) ich kann or mag ihn/es etc (gut) ~ I like him/it etc (very much); **ich kann or mag ihn/es etc nicht (gut)** ~ I don't like him/it etc very much, I'm not very fond of him/it etc.
2 vi to suffer (an + dat, unter + dat from). **die Farbe hat durch die grelle Sonne sehr gelitten** the harsh sun hasn't done the paint any good; siehe leidend.
Leiden nt -s, - (a) suffering; (Kummer auch) tribulation. **das sind (nun mal) die Freuden und** ~ **des Lebens!** ah, the ups and downs or the trials and tribulations of life!; **du siehst aus wie das** ~ **Christi** (inf) you look like death warmed up (inf).
(b) (Krankheit) illness; (Beschwerden) complaint. **das ist ja eben das** ~! (inf) that's just the trouble.
(c) (hum inf: Mensch) **ein langes** ~ a beanpole (inf).

-leiden nt in cpds complaint, condition.
leidend adj (kränklich) ailing; (inf) Miene long-suffering. ~ **aussehen** to look ill; **sich** ~ **fühlen** (form) to feel ill.
Leidenschaft f passion. **seine** ~ **für etw entdecken** to develop a passion for sth; **etw mit** ~ **tun** to do sth with passionate enthusiasm; **ich koche mit großer** ~ cooking is a great passion of mine; **er ist Lehrer aus** ~ he teaches for the love of it; **er hat seine ganze** ~ **in die Musik gelegt** music is his one great passion; **frei von (jeder)** ~ dispassionate.
leidenschaftlich adj passionate; Liebhaber auch ardent; Rede auch impassioned. **etw** ~ **gern tun** to be mad about (inf) or passionately fond of doing sth.
Leidenschaftlichkeit f passion; (im Beruf) dedication; (bei Hobby) burning enthusiasm.
leidenschaftslos adj dispassionate.
Leidens-: **~gefährte** m, **~gefährtin** f, **~genosse** m, **~genossin** f fellow-sufferer; **~geschichte** f tale of woe; **die ~geschichte (Christi)** (Bibl) Christ's Passion; **~miene** f (hum inf) (long-) suffering expression; **~weg** m life of suffering; **Christi ~weg** Christ's suffering; **seinen ~weg gehen** to bear one's cross.
leider adv unfortunately. ~ **Gottes ja!, ja** ~! (yes,) more's the pity (inf), I'm afraid so, yes, unfortunately; ~ **(Gottes) nein/nicht!** unfortunately not, I'm afraid not, no, worse luck (inf); **ich kann** ~ **(Gottes) nicht kommen** unfortunately or I'm afraid I can't come; **wir müssen Ihnen** ~ **mitteilen, daß** ... we regret to inform you that ...
leidgeprüft adj sorely afflicted.
leidig adj attr tiresome. **wenn bloß das ~e Geld nicht wäre** if only we didn't have to worry about money.
leidlich 1 adj reasonable, fair. **2** adv reasonably. **wie geht's?** — **danke,** ~! how are you? — not too bad or all right, thanks; **sie ist noch so** ~ **davongekommen** she didn't come out of it too badly.
Leidtragende(r) mf decl as adj (a) (Hinterbliebene(r) eines Verstorbenen) bereaved. **ein** ~**r** a bereaved person. **(b)** (Benachteiligte(r)) **der/die** ~ the sufferer, the one to suffer.
Leidwesen nt: **zu jds** ~ (much) to sb's disappointment or chagrin.
Leier f -, -n (a) (Mus) lyre; (Dreh~) hurdy-gurdy. **es ist immer dieselbe** or **die alte** or **die gleiche** ~ (inf) it's always the same old story. **(b)** (inf: Kurbel) crank. **(c)** (Astron) Lyra.
Leierkasten m barrel-organ, hurdy-gurdy.
Leierkastenmann m, pl **-männer** organ-grinder.
leiern 1 vt Drehorgel to grind, to play; (inf: kurbeln) to wind; (inf) Gedicht, Gebete to drone (out). **2** vi (Drehorgel spielen) to grind or play a barrel-organ; (inf: drehen) to crank (an etw (dat) sth); (inf: beim Beten, Gedichteaufsagen) to drone.
Leierschwanz m lyrebird.
Leih-: **~auto** nt hire(d) car; **~bibliothek, ~bücherei** f lending library.
Leihe f -, -n (das Verleihen) lending; (das Vermieten) hiring; (das Verpfänden) pawning; (inf: Leihhaus) pawnshop. **etw zur** ~ **haben** to have sth on loan/on hire; **etw in** ~ or **in die** ~ (inf) **geben** to pawn or pop (inf) sth; **etw in** ~ **nehmen** to take sth in pawn.
leihen pret **lieh,** ptp **geliehen** vt Geld to lend; Sachen auch to loan; (von jdm ent~) to borrow; (mieten, aus~) to hire. **ich habe es (mir) geliehen** I've borrowed/hired it, I've got it on loan/hire; **jdm seinen Beistand/sein Ohr/seine Aufmerksamkeit** ~ (geh) to lend sb one's support/one's ear/one's attention; **jdm sein Vertrauen** ~ (geh) to give sb one's trust.
Leih-: **~gabe** f loan; **~gebühr** f hire or rental charge; (für Buch) lending charge; **~haus** nt pawnshop; **~schein** m (in der Bibliothek) borrowing slip; (im ~haus) pawn ticket; **~verkehr** m ein Buch über den auswärtigen **~verkehr bestellen** to order a book on inter-library loan; **wir haben hier keinen ~verkehr** we don't lend books out here; **im ~verkehr erhältlich** available on loan; **~wagen** m hire(d) car; **l~weise** adv on loan.
Leim m -(e)s, -e glue; (zum Vogelfangen) (bird)lime. **jdn auf den** ~ **führen** or **locken** (inf) to take sb in; (inf) **aus dem** ~ **gehen** or **kriechen** (inf) to be taken in by sb; **aus dem** ~ **gehen** (inf) (Sache) to fall apart or to pieces; (Mensch) to lose one's figure.
leimen vt (zusammenkleben) to glue (together); (mit Leim bestreichen) to spread with glue; (zum Vogelfangen) to lime; (inf) Ehe to patch up (inf). **jdn** ~ (inf) to take sb for a ride (inf); **der Geleimte** the mug (inf).
Leimfarbe f distemper.
leimig adj sticky, gluey.
Leimrute f lime twig.
Lein m -(e)s, -e flax.
Leine f -, -n cord; (Tau, Zelt~) rope; (Schnur) string; (Angel~, Wäsche~, Naut) line; (Hunde~) lead, leash. **Hunde bitte an der** ~ **führen!** dogs should or must be kept on a leash; **den Hund an die** ~ **nehmen** to put the dog on the lead; **jdn an der** ~ **halten** or **haben** (inf) to keep sb on a tight rein; **jdn an die** ~ **legen** to hook sb (inf), to drag sb to the altar (inf); ~ **ziehen** (sl) to clear out (sl), to push off (inf).
leinen adj linen; canvas; cloth.
Leinen nt -s, - linen; (grob, segeltuchartig) canvas; (als Bucheinband) cloth.
Leinen- in cpds linen; canvas; cloth; **~band** m cloth(-bound) volume; **ein Buch als ~band haben** to have the cloth-bound edition of a book; **~tasche** f canvas bag; **~tuch** nt linen (cloth); (grob, segeltuchartig) canvas; **~zeug** nt linen.
Leineweber m linen weaver.
Leineweberei f (Fabrik) linen mill; (Herstellung) linen weaving.
Lein-: **~kraut** nt toadflax; **~kuchen** m linseed cake; **~öl** nt linseed oil; **~pfad** m towpath; **~samen** m linseed; **~tuch** nt (S Ger, Aus, Sw) sheet.
Leinwand f -, no pl canvas; (Film, für Dias) screen. **wenn der**

Film über die ~ läuft when the film is being shown or screened; jdn von der ~ kennen to know sb from (the) films; Dias auf die ~ werfen to show or project slides.

leise adj (a) quiet; Stimme, Schritt, Klopfen auch soft; Radio auch low; (aus der Ferne) faint. auf ~n Sohlen treading softly; das Radio (etwas) ~r stellen to turn the radio down (slightly); ... sagte er mit ~r Stimme ... he said in a low voice or quietly; sprich doch ~r! keep your voice down a bit.

(b) (gering, schwach) slight, faint; Schlaf, Regen, Berührung light; Wind, Wellenschlag light, gentle. nicht die ~ste Ahnung haben not to have the slightest or faintest or foggiest (inf) (idea); ich habe nicht die ~ste Veranlassung, ... there isn't the slightest or faintest reason why I ...; daran zweifle ich nicht im ~sten I don't doubt that in the slightest.

(c) (sanft, zart) soft, gentle; Musik soft.

Leisetreter m -s, - (pej, inf) pussyfoot(er) (pej, inf); (Duckmäuser) creep (pej inf).

Leiste f -, -n (a) (Holz~ etc) strip (of wood/metal etc); (Zier~) trim; (Umrandung) border; (zur Bilderaufhängung, zur Führung von Arbeitsstücken etc) rail; (Scheuer~) skirting (board), baseboard (US). (b) (Anat) groin.

leisten vt (a) (erringen, erreichen) to achieve; Arbeit, Überstunden to do; (Maschine, Motor) to manage. etwas/viel/nichts ~ (Mensch) (arbeiten) to do something/a lot/nothing; (schaffen auch) to get something/a lot/nothing done; (vollbringen) to achieve something/a great deal/nothing; (Maschine) to be quite good/very good/no good at all; (Auto, Motor etc) to be quite powerful/very powerful/have no power; Großartiges/Erstaunliches/Überragendes etc ~ to do or achieve something really great/amazing/excellent; gute/ganze Arbeit ~ to do a good/thorough job; die meisten Männer trauen den Frauen ja nicht zu, daß sie auch etwas ~ können most men don't think women are capable of anything much; in meiner Position muß ich schon etwas ~ in my position I have to do my work and do it well; er leistet genau soviel wie ich he's just as efficient as I am; was eine Mutter alles ~ muß the things that a mother has to cope with; er hat immer das Gefühl, nichts zu ~ he always has the feeling that he isn't doing a good job; seine Arbeit ~ to do one's work well; ich muß genauso meine Arbeit ~ wie jeder andere auch I've got my job to do like everybody else.

(b) in festen Verbindungen mit n siehe auch dort (jdm) Beistand/Hilfe ~ to lend (sb) one's support/give sb some help; jdm gute Dienste ~ (Gegenstand) to serve sb well; (Mensch) to be useful to sb; Folge ~ to comply (dat with); Zahlungen ~ to make payments; jdm eine Garantie/Gewähr ~ to give sb a guarantee (für/auf etw (acc) for/on sth, dafür, daß ... that ...).

(c) sich (dat) etw ~ to allow oneself sth; (sich gönnen) to treat oneself to sth; (kaufen) to buy sth; sich (dat) etw ~ können to be able to afford sth; sich (dat) etw ~ Frechheit/Frechheiten ~ to be cheeky or impudent; er leistete sich die Frechheit, ungebeten zu erscheinen he had the cheek or effrontery to turn up uninvited; diese Frechheit würde er sich bei mir nicht ~ he wouldn't try that sort of cheek with me; da hast du dir ja was (Schönes or Nettes) geleistet (iro) you've really done it now; er hat sich tolle Sachen/Streiche geleistet he got up to the craziest things/pranks.

Leisten m -s, - (Schuh~) last. alle/alles über einen ~ schlagen (fig) to measure everyone/everything by the same yardstick; siehe Schuster.

Leisten-: ~bruch m (Med) hernia, rupture; ~gegend f inguinal region (form), groin.

Leistung f (a) (Geleistetes) performance; (großartige, gute, Sociol) achievement; (Ergebnis) result(s); (geleistete Arbeit) work no pl. eine große ~ vollbringen to achieve a great success; das ist eine ~! that's quite or really something (inf) or quite an achievement or quite a feat; das ist keine besondere ~ that's nothing special; nach ~ bezahlt werden to be paid on results; hier wird man nur nach ~ befördert you get promotion here for performance; nicht das Geschlecht, nur die ~ zählt your sex isn't important, it's how you do the job that counts; das liegt weit unter der üblichen ~ that is well below the usual standard; die ~en sind besser geworden the levels of performance have improved; (in Fabrik, Schule auch) the standard of work has improved; seine schulischen/sportlichen ~en haben nachgelassen his school work/athletic ability has deteriorated; er ist auf seine sportlichen ~en stolz he's proud of his athletic achievement(s); eine ~ der Technik a feat of engineering; schwache ~! poor show! (dated inf), that's not very good.

(b) (~sfähigkeit) capacity; (eines Motors, einer Energiequelle) power; (einer Fabrik, Firma) potential output.

(c) (Jur) (Übernahme einer Verpflichtung) obligation; (Zahlung) payment. ~ eines Ersatzes obligation to provide a replacement.

(d) (Aufwendungen) (einer Versicherung, Krankenkasse, sozial) benefit; (Dienst~) service; (Zahlungs~) payment.

Leistungs-: ~abfall m (in bezug auf Qualität) drop in performance; (in bezug auf Quantität) drop in productivity; ~ausfall m loss of productivity; ~bilanz f (einer Firma) current balance including investments; (eines Landes) balance of payments including invisible trade; ~druck m pressure (to do well); l~fähig adj (konkurrenzfähig) competitive; (produktiv) efficient, productive; Motor powerful; Maschine productive; (Fin) able to pay, solvent; Mensch able, capable; Arbeiter efficient; Organe, Verdauungssystem etc functioning properly; ~fähigkeit f siehe adj competitiveness; efficiency, productivity; power(fulness); capacity; ability to pay, solvency; ability, capability; efficiency; capacity; das übersteigt meine ~fähigkeit that's more than I can manage; l~fördernd adj conducive to efficiency; (in Schule, Universität etc) conducive to learning; ~gesellschaft f meritocracy, achievement-

orientated society (pej); ~grenze f upper limit; ~klage f (Jur) suit for fulfilment of obligations; ~klasse f (Sport) class; ~kontrolle f (Sch, Univ) assessment; (in der Fabrik) productivity check; zur ~kontrolle (in order) to assess progress/check productivity; ~kraft f power; eine hohe ~kraft haben to be very powerful; ~kurs m (Sch) set; ~kurve f productivity curve; ~lohn m piece rates pl; ~messer m (Phys) power output meter; (Elec) wattmeter; ~messung f assessment of achievement; (in Fabrik) measuring or assessment of productivity; (Phys, Elec) measurement of power; ~motivation f achievement motivation; l~orientiert adj achievement-orientated; ~prämie f productivity bonus; ~prinzip nt achievement principle; ~prüfung f (Sch) achievement test; (Tech) performance test; ~schau f exhibition, show; ~sport m competitive sport; l~stark adj (konkurrenzfähig) highly competitive; (produktiv) highly efficient or productive; Motor very powerful; Maschine highly productive; ~steigerung f siehe Leistung (a, b) increase in performance/achievement etc; ~test m siehe ~prüfung; ~vermögen nt capabilities pl; ~wettkampf m competition; ~zulage f, ~zuschlag m productivity bonus; ~zwang m pressure to do well.

Leit-: ~artikel m leader; ~artikler(in f) m -s, - leader-writer; ~bild nt model; ~bündel nt (Bot) vascular bundle.

leiten vt (a) (in bestimmte Richtung lenken) to lead; (begleiten, führen auch) to conduct; (fig) Leser, Schüler etc to guide; Verkehr to route; Gas, Wasser to conduct; (um~) to divert. etw an die zuständige Stelle ~ to pass sth on to the proper authority; die Polizei auf die Spur ~ to put the police on the trail; jdn zu einem Entschluß ~ to bring or lead sb to a decision; sich von jdm/etw ~ lassen (lit, fig) to (let oneself) be guided by sb/sth; von Vorstellung, Idee, Emotion, Gesichtspunkt to be governed by sth; das Öl wird (durch Rohre) zum Hafen geleitet the oil is piped to the port.

(b) (verantwortlich sein für) to be in charge of; (administrativ auch) to run; Expedition, Partei, Regierung, Bewegung etc auch to lead, to head; Betrieb auch to manage; Orchester, Theatergruppe etc to direct, to run; Sitzung, Diskussion, Gespräch, Verhandlungen to lead; (als Vorsitzender) to chair; Geschick(e) to determine, to guide.

(c) (Phys) Wärme, Strom, Licht to conduct. (etw) gut/schlecht ~ to be a good/bad conductor (of sth).

leitend adj leading; Gedanke, Idee central, dominant; Stellung, Position managerial; Ingenieur, Beamter in charge; (Phys) conductive. nicht ~ (Phys) non-conductive; ~e(r) Angestellte(r) executive; ein ~er Beamter a senior official; die ~e Hand (fig) the guiding hand.

Leiter f -, -n (lit, fig) ladder; (Steh~) steps pl, stepladder; (Sport) wall-bars pl. an der ~ turnen to work on the wall-bars.

Leiter(in f) m -s, - (a) leader; (von Hotel, Restaurant, Geschäft) manager; (Abteilungs~ in Firma) head; (von Schule) head (esp Brit), principal (esp US); (von Orchester, Chor, Theatergruppe etc) director; (von Kirchenchor) choirmaster. kaufmännischer/künstlerischer ~ sales/artistic director.

(b) (Phys) conductor.

Leiter-: ~sprosse f rung; eine ~sprosse des Erfolgs höher kommen to climb one rung higher up the ladder of success; ~wagen m hand-cart.

Leit-: ~faden m (fig) main connecting thread or theme; (Fachbuch) introduction; l~fähig adj (Phys) conductive; ~fähigkeit f (Phys) conductivity; ~feuer nt beacon; ~fossil nt index fossil; ~gedanke m central idea; er machte diesen Spruch zum ~gedanken seines Lebens he made this saying his motto in life; ~gerade f (Math) directrix; ~gewebe nt (Biol) vascular tissue; ~hammel m bellwether; (fig inf) leader, bellwether (liter); ~hund m (Hunt) leader of the pack; ~idee f siehe ~gedanke; ~linie f (im Verkehr) broken (white) line; (fig) broad outline; (Bestimmung) guideline; (Math) directrix; ~motiv nt (Mus, Liter, fig) leitmotif; ~pfosten m reflector post; ~planke f crash-barrier; ~rad nt stator; ~satz m basic principle; ~schiene f guide rail; ~spindel f (Tech) lead screw; ~spruch m motto; ~stelle f regional headquarters pl; ~stern m (lit) lodestar; (fig auch) guiding star; ~strahl m (Aviat, Mil, Space) control beam; (Math) radius vector; ~tier nt leader (of a herd etc); ~ton m (Mus) leading note; ~trieb m leader.

Leitung f (a) no pl siehe vt (a) leading; conducting; guiding; routing; conducting; diversion, diverting.

(b) no pl (von Menschen, Organisationen etc) siehe vt (b) running; leadership; management; direction; leadership; chairmanship; (einer Schule) headship (esp Brit), principalship (esp US). die ~ einer Sache (gen) haben to be in charge of sth/to run/lead/manage/direct/lead/chair sth; (Sch) to be the head or principal of sth; unter der ~ von jdm (Mus) conducted by sb; die ~ des Gesprächs hat Horst Bauer Horst Bauer is leading the discussion.

(c) (die Leitenden) leaders pl; (eines Betriebes etc) management sing or pl; (einer Schule) head teachers pl.

(d) (für Gas, Wasser, Elektrizität etc bis zum Haus) main; (für Gas, Wasser, im Haus) pipe; (für Elektrizität im Haus) wire; (dicker) cable; (Überlandleitung für Elektrizität) line; (Telefon~) (Draht) wire; (dicker) cable; (Verbindung) line. die ~ ist ganz fürchterlich gestört (Telec) it's a terrible line, there's a lot of interference on the line; gehen Sie aus der ~ (inf) get off the line; da ist jemand in der ~ (inf) there's somebody else on the line; eine lange ~ haben (hum, inf) to be slow on the uptake, to be slow to catch on; bei dir steht wohl jemand or du stehst wohl auf der ~ (hum, inf) you're slow on the uptake, you're slow to catch on.

Leitungs-: ~anästhesie f (Med) nerve-block or conduction anaesthesia; ~draht m wire; ~mast m (Elec) (electricity) pylon; ~netz nt (Elec) (electricity) grid; (für Wasser, Gas) mains system; (Telec) (telephone) network; ~rohr nt main; (im Haus) (supply) pipe; ~wasser nt tapwater, mains water; ~widerstand m (Elec) resistance.

Leit-: ~vermögen nt (Phys) conductivity; ~währung f reserve currency; ~werk nt (Aviat) tail unit, empennage (spec); ~wert m conductance; ~wort nt motto; ~zinssatz m bank rate.

Lektion f lesson. jdm eine ~ erteilen (fig) to teach sb a lesson.

Lektor m, **Lektorin** f (Univ) foreign language assistant; (Verlags~) editor.

Lektorat nt (im Verlag) editorial office; (Gutachten) editorial report.

Lektüre f -, -n (no pl: das Lesen) reading; (Lesestoff) reading matter. das wird zur ~ empfohlen that is recommended reading; das ist eine gute/interessante etc ~ it makes good/interesting etc reading, it's a good/an interesting etc read; das ist eine schlechte ~ it doesn't make good reading, it's not a good read; ~ (be)treiben or machen (Sch inf) to do some reading; ich habe Ihnen einige ~n ausgesucht I've found some things for you to read; das ist keine (passende) ~ für dich/Kinder that's not suitable reading for you/children, that's not suitable for you/children to read; ich muß noch (etwas) leichte ~ besorgen I've still got to get something light to read.

Lemma nt -s, -ta lemma.

Lemming m lemming.

Lende f -, -n (Anat, Cook) loin.

Lenden-: ~braten m loin roast; ~gegend f lumbar region; l~lahm adj (dated) Pferd broken-backed; er ist l~lahm his back is crippling him; ~schurz m loincloth; ~stück nt piece of loin; ~wirbel m lumbar vertebra.

Leninismus m Leninism.

Leninist(in f) m Leninist.

leninistisch adj Leninist.

Lenk-: ~achse f pivoted axle; l~bar adj (Tech) steerable; Kind tractable; Rakete guided; leicht/schwer l~bar sein to be easy/difficult to steer, to have light/heavy steering; das Kind ist leicht/schwer l~bar the child can be easily guided/won't be guided.

lenken vt (a) (führen, leiten) to direct, to guide; (fig: beeinflussen) Sprache, Presse etc to influence; Kind to guide. gelenkte Wirtschaft planned economy.
(b) auch vi (steuern) Auto, Flugzeug, Schiff etc to steer; Pferde to drive. sich leicht ~ lassen to be easy to steer/drive.
(c) (fig) Schritte, Gedanken, seine Aufmerksamkeit, Blick to direct (auf +acc to); jds Aufmerksamkeit auch, Blicke (auf sich) to draw (auf +acc to); Verdacht to throw; (auf sich) to draw (auf +acc onto); Gespräch to lead, to steer; Schicksal to guide. seine Schritte heimwärts ~ (liter, hum) to wend one's way homewards, to turn one's steps to home (both liter, hum).

Lenker m -s, - (a) (Fahrrad~ etc) handlebars pl. (b) (Tech) guide; (Lenkung) steering gear. (c) (Mensch) driver; (fig) guide.

Lenk-: ~getriebe nt steering gear; ~rad nt (steering) wheel; jdm ins ~rad greifen to grab the (steering) wheel from sb.

Lenkrad-: ~schaltung f (Aut) column(-mounted) (gear) change or shift (US); ~schloß nt (Aut) steering(-wheel) lock.

lenksam adj malleable; (folgsam) docile, tractable.

Lenksamkeit f siehe adj malleability; docility, tractability.

Lenkstange f (Fahrrad~ etc) handlebars pl.

Lenkung f (a) siehe vt (das Lenken) direction, directing, guidance, guiding; influencing; (das Steuern) steering; driving; (fig) direction, directing; drawing; throwing; drawing; leading, steering. (b) (Tech: Lenkeinrichtung) steering.

Lenkverhalten nt (von Auto) steering no indef art.

Lenz m -es, -e (liter) (Frühling) spring(time), springtide (liter). der ~ des Lebens the springtime of one's life (liter); sie zählt 20 ~e she has seen 20 summers (liter, hum); einen ~ schieben or haben, sich (dat) einen (faulen or schönen) ~ machen (all inf) to laze about, to swing the lead (inf).

lenzen[1] vi impers (liter) es lenzt spring is in the air.

lenzen[2] (Naut) 1 vt (leerpumpen) to pump out. 2 vi (vor dem Wind segeln) to scud.

Lenzing m -s, -e (obs), **Lenzmonat**, **Lenzmond** m (obs) March.

Lenz-: ~pumpe f (Naut) bilge-pump; ~tag m (liter) spring day.

Leopard m -en, -en leopard.

Lepra f -, no pl leprosy.

Leprom nt -s, -e leprous lesion.

leprös, leprös adj leprous.

Leprosorium nt leprosarium.

leptosom adj (form) asthenic (form), leptosome (form).

Lerche f -, -n lark.

Lern-: l~bar adj learnable; ~begier(de) f eagerness to learn; l~begier adj eager to learn; l~behindert adj educationally handicapped; ~behinderte(r) mf educationally handicapped child/boy/girl; ~eifer m siehe ~begier(de); l~eifrig adj siehe l~begierig.

lernen 1 vt (a) to learn. lesen/schwimmen etc ~ to learn to read/swim etc; Stenographie/Schreibmaschine ~ to learn shorthand/typing or to type; ~, etw zu tun to learn to do sth; (sich Fähigkeit, Können aneignen auch) to learn how to do sth; etw von/bei jdm ~ to learn sth from sb; jdn lieben/schätzen ~ to come or learn to love/appreciate sb; er lernt's nie/wird's nie ~ he never learns/he'll never learn; siehe Hänschen.
(b) Beruf to learn; Bäcker, Schlosser etc to train as, to learn the trade of. das will gelernt sein it's a question of practice; gelernt ist gelernt (Prov) once you've learnt something ...; lerne was, so kannst/bist du was (prov) it never hurt anyone to learn anything; siehe gelernt.
2 vi (a) (Kenntnisse erwerben) to learn; (arbeiten) to study;

(Schulaufgaben machen) to do (one's) homework. die Mutter lernte drei Stunden mit ihm his mother spent three hours helping him with his homework; lerne fleißig in der Schule work hard at school; von ihm kannst du noch ~! he could teach you a thing or two; man lernt nicht für die Schule, sondern fürs Leben (Prov) learning is not just for school but for life.
(b) (sich in der Ausbildung befinden) to go to school; (in Universität) to study; (in Beruf) to train. er lernt bei der Firma Braun he's training at Braun's, Braun's are training him.
3 vr der Text/die Rolle lernt sich leicht/schwer/schnell the text/part is easy/hard to learn/doesn't take long to learn.

Lern-: ~hilfe f educational aid; ~kurve f (Psych) learning curve; ~maschine f teaching machine; ~mittel pl schoolbooks and equipment pl; ~mittelfreiheit f free provision of schoolbooks and equipment; ~psychologie f psychology of learning; ~schwester f student nurse.

Les-: ~art f (lit, fig) version; l~bar adj legible; Buch readable.

Lesbierin ['lɛsbiərɪn] f lesbian.

lesbisch adj lesbian.

Lese f -, -n (Ernte) harvest; (Weinart) vintage; (Beeren~) picking.

Lese-: ~abend m evening of readings; ~brille f reading glasses pl; ~buch nt reader; ~ecke f reading or readers' corner; ~kreis m reading circle; ~lampe f reading lamp.

lesen[1] pret las, ptp gelesen 1 vti (a) to read; (Eccl) Messe to say. hier/in der Zeitung steht or ist zu ~, daß ... it says here/in the paper that ...; die Schrift ist kaum zu ~ the writing is scarcely legible; siehe Leviten.
(b) (deuten) Gedanken to read. jdm (sein Schicksal) aus der Hand ~ to read sb's palm; in den Sternen ~ to read or see in the stars; aus ihren Zeilen habe ich einen Vorwurf/eine gewisse Unsicherheit gelesen I could tell from what she had written that she was reproaching me/felt a certain amount of uncertainty; etw in jds Augen/Miene (dat) ~ to see sth in sb's eyes/from sb's manner; es war in ihrem Gesicht zu ~ it was written all over her face, you could see it in her face.
2 vi (Univ) to lecture (über +acc on).
3 vr (Buch, Bericht etc) to read. bei diesem Licht liest es sich nicht gut this light isn't good for reading (in); sich satt ~ to have a good read; sich in den Schlaf ~ to read oneself to sleep.

lesen[2] pret las, ptp gelesen vt (a) (sammeln) Trauben, Beeren to pick; (nach der Ernte) Ähren to glean. (b) (ver~) Erbsen, Linsen etc to sort; Salat to clean.

lesenswert adj worth reading.

Lese-: ~probe f (a) (Theat) reading; (b) (Ausschnitt aus Buch) extract, excerpt; ~pult nt lectern.

Leser(in f)[1] m -s, - reader. seine Romane haben viele ~ gefunden his novels have gained a large readership.

Leser(in f)[2] m -s, - (Sammler) picker.

Leseratte f (inf) bookworm (inf).

Leserbrief m (reader's) letter. einen ~ an eine Zeitung schreiben to write a letter to a newspaper; „~e" "letters to the editor", "readers' letters".

Leserei f (inf) reading. kannst du jetzt nicht endlich mit der ~ aufhören? can't you take your nose out of your books? (inf).

Leser-: ~kreis m readership; l~lich adj legible; ~lichkeit f legibility; ~schaft f readership; ~wunsch m wish(es) of the readers; auf vielfachen ~wunsch at the request of many readers; ~zuschrift f siehe ~brief.

Lese-: ~saal m reading room; ~stoff m reading material; ich brauche noch ~stoff I need something to read; jdm etw als ~stoff geben to give sb sth to read; ~stück nt reading passage; ~wut f craze for reading; von (der) ~wut gepackt sein to have caught the reading bug (inf); ~zeichen nt bookmark(er); ~zimmer nt reading room; ~zirkel m magazine subscription club.

Lesung f (Dichter~, Parl) reading; (Eccl auch) lesson.

Lethargie f (Med, fig) lethargy.

lethargisch adj (Med, fig) lethargic.

Lethe f - (Myth) Lethe; (poet: Vergessenheit) waters pl of oblivion.

Lette m -n, -n, **Lettin** f Lett, Latvian.

Letten m -s, - (potter's) clay.

Letter f -, -n character.

lettisch adj Lettish, Latvian.

Lettland nt Latvia.

Lettner m -s, - (Archit) choir screen.

Letzt f: zu guter ~ finally, in the end.

letztendlich adv at (long) last.

letztens adv recently. erst ~, ~ erst just or only recently.

letzte(r, s) adj (a) (örtlich, zeitlich) last; (endgültig, aller~ auch) final; (restlich) last (remaining). ~(r) werden to be last; als ~(r) (an)kommen/(weg)gehen/fertig sein to arrive/leave/finish last, to be the last to arrive/leave/finish; als ~(r) gehen to be the last to go; (in Reihenfolge auch) to go last; (in Prozession etc) to bring up the rear; auf dem ~n Platz or an ~r Stelle liegen to be (lying) last; (in Tabelle, Liga auch) to be (lying) bottom; den ~n beißen die Hunde (Prov) (the) devil take the hindmost (prov); er wäre der ~, dem ich ... he would be the last person I'd ...; das ist das ~, was ich tun würde that's the last thing I'd do; das ~ Wort haben or behalten to have the last word; mein ~s Geld the last of my money; die ~n zwei Tage/ Jahre etc the last two days/years etc; (vor heute/diesem Jahr auch) the past two days/years etc; in ~r Zeit recently; zum ~n Mittel greifen to resort to drastic methods; jdm die ~ Ehre erweisen, jdm das ~ Geleit geben to pay one's last respects to sb; die ~n Dinge death and the life to come; die Lehre der ~n Dinge eschatology; das ~ und höchste Ziel meines Lebens/des Werkes the ultimate aim of my life/of the work; der L~ Wille last will and testament.

(b) zum dritten und zum ~n (*bei Auktion*) for the (third and) last time of asking; **bis aufs** ~ completely, totally; **bis ins** ~ (right) down to the last detail; **etw bis ins** ~ **kennen** to know sth like the back of one's hand; **bis zum** ~n to the utmost; **am** *or* **zum** ~n **last**; **fürs** ~ lastly.
(c) (*neueste*) *Mode, Nachricht, Neuigkeit etc* latest.
(d) (*schlechtester*) most terrible. **das ist der** ~e Schund/Dreck that's absolute trash; **er ist der** ~e Mensch (*inf*) he's a terrible person; **jdn wie den** ~n Dreck/Sklaven *etc* behandeln to treat sb like dirt *or* as though he/she *etc* were the scum of the earth/to treat sb like a slave *etc*.

Letzte(r) *mf decl as adj* last; (*dem Rang nach*) lowest. **der** ~ **seines Stammes** the last of his line; **der** ~ **des Monats** the last (day) of the month; **der/die** ~ **in der Klasse sein** to be bottom of the class; **die** ~n **werden die Ersten sein** (*Bibl*) the last shall be first (*Bibl*).

letztere(r, s) *adj* the latter; *siehe* **welch**.
Letzte(s) *nt decl as adj* last thing. **es geht ums** ~ everything is at stake; **sein** ~s **(her)geben** to give one's all, to do one's utmost; **bis zum** ~n **gehen** to do all that one possibly can; **das ist ja das** ~! (*inf*) that really is the limit.

letzt-: ~genannt *adj* the last-named; ~hin *adv siehe* letztens; ~jährig *adj attr* last year's *no art*; ~lich *adv* in the end; **das ist** ~lich **egal** it comes down to the same thing in the end; ~malig *adj attr* last; ~mals *adv* for the last time; ~möglich *adj attr* last possible; ~willig *adj* (*form*) ~willige Verfügung last will and testament; ~willig verfügen, daß ... to state in one's last will and testament that ...

Leu *m* -en, -en (*obs, poet*) lion.
Leucht-: ~boje *f* light-buoy; ~bombe *f* flare.
Leuchte *f* -, -n (*Leuchtkörper*) light; (*old: Laterne*) lamp, lantern; (*inf: Mensch*) genius. **auf einem Gebiet/in einem Fach eine** ~ **sein** to shine in a particular field/subject.
leuchten *vi* **(a)** to shine; (*Flammen, Feuer, Lava, Zifferblatt*) to glow; (*auf*~) to flash.
(b) (*Mensch*) mit einer Lampe in/auf etw (*acc*) *etc* ~ to shine a lamp into/onto *etc* sth; **mußt du mir direkt in die Augen** ~? do you have to shine that thing straight into my eyes?; **kannst du (mir) nicht mal** ~? can you point *or* shine the lamp/torch *etc* (for me)?; **leuchte mal hierher!** shine some light over here.
leuchtend *adj* (*lit, fig*) shining; *Farbe* bright, radiant. **etw in den** ~sten Farben schildern/preisen to paint sth/speak of sth in glowing colours.
Leuchter *m* -s, - (*Kerzen*~) candlestick; (*Arm*~) candelabra; (*Kron*~) chandelier; (*Wand*~) sconce.
Leucht-: ~farbe *f* fluorescent colour/paint/dye/ink; ~feuer *nt* navigational light; ~gas *nt* town gas; ~geschoß *nt* flare; ~käfer *m* glow-worm; ~kraft *f* brightness; (*von Birne etc auch*) luminous power (*form*); (*Stern auch*) luminosity (*form*); ~kugel *f* flare; ~patrone *f* flare; ~pistole *f* flare pistol; ~rakete *f* signal rocket; ~reklame *f* neon sign; ~röhre *f* fluorescent tube; ~schirm *m* fluorescent screen; ~schrift *f* neon writing; **eine** ~schrift a neon sign.
Leuchtspur *f* trail of light.
Leuchtspur-: ~geschoß *nt* (*Mil*) tracer bullet; ~munition *f* (*Mil*) tracer bullets *pl*.
Leucht-: ~tonne *f siehe* ~boje; ~turm *m* lighthouse; ~zeiger *m* luminous hand; ~zifferblatt *nt* luminous face *or* dial.
leugnen 1 *vt* to deny. ~, **etw getan zu haben** to deny having done sth; **es ist nicht zu** ~, **daß** ... it cannot be denied that ...; **der Angeklagte leugnete die Tat** the defendant denied the offence; (*vor Gericht*) the defendant pleaded not guilty. 2 *vi* to deny everything.
Leugnung *f* denial.
Leukämie *f* leukaemia.
leukämisch *adj* leukaemic.
Leukoplast ® *nt* -(e)s, -e sticking plaster, elastoplast ® (*Brit*).
Leukozyten *pl* leucocytes *pl* (*spec*), white corpuscles *pl*.
Leukozytenzählung *f* blood count (*of the white corpuscles*).
Leumund *m* -(e)s, *no pl* reputation, name.
Leumundszeugnis *nt* character reference.
Leutchen *pl* (*inf*) people *pl*, folk *pl* (*inf*). **kommt,** ~! come on everyone *or* folks (*inf*).
Leute *pl* **(a)** people *pl*; (*inf: Eltern auch*) folk(s) *pl* (*inf*). **arme/reiche/alte/junge** ~ poor/rich/old/young people *or* folk(s) (*inf*); **alle** ~ everybody; **die kleinen** ~ (*fig*) ordinary people *or* folk (*inf*); **die kleinen** ~ (*hum, inf: Kinder*) the little ones; **eine Sendung für die kleinen** ~ a programme for younger viewers/listeners; **die** ~ **waren von dem Stück begeistert** people were enthusiastic about the play; **was sollen denn die** ~ **davon denken?** what will people think?; **aber liebe** ~! (*inf*) come on now! (*inf*); ~, ~! (*inf*) dear me, (dear) oh dear!; **kommt,** ~! come on folks; **aber die Sache ist doch in aller** ~ **Mund!** but everybody's talking about it!; **sein Name war in aller** ~ **Mund** his name was on everybody's lips; **es ist nicht wie bei armen** ~n (*hum inf*) we're not on the breadline yet (*hum inf*); **ich kenne meine** ~! (*inf*) I know them/him *etc*; **etw unter die** ~ **bringen** (*inf*) *Gerücht, Geschichte* to spread sth around, to put sth about; *Geld* to spend sth; **unter die** ~ **kommen** (*inf*) (*Mensch*) to meet people; (*Gerüchte etc*) to go around, to go *or* do the rounds (*inf*); **das sind wohl nicht die richtigen** ~ they're not the right kind of people.
(b) (*Mannschaft, Arbeiter etc*) **der Offizier ließ seine** ~ **antreten** the officer ordered his men to fall in; **wir können nicht schneller arbeiten, wir haben ja keine** ~! we can't work any faster, we haven't the men/women/staff/workers; **dafür brauchen wir mehr** ~ we need more people/staff *etc* for that.
Leuteschinder *m* -s, - slavedriver.
Leutnant *m* -s, -s *or* -e (second) lieutenant; (*bei der Luftwaffe*) pilot officer (*Brit*), second lieutenant (*US*). ~ **zur See** sub-

lieutenant (*Brit*), lieutenant junior grade (*US*); **jawohl, Herr** ~! yes, sir; (*Naut*) aye aye, sir.
leutselig *adj* (*umgänglich*) affable; (*pej: freundlichherablassend*) genial.
Leutseligkeit *f siehe adj* affability; geniality.
Leuwagen *m* (*N Ger*) *siehe* **Schrubber**.
Levante [le'vantə] *f* -, *no pl* Levant.
Lever [lə've:] *nt* -s, -s (*liter*) levee.
Leviathan, Leviatan [le'via:tan, levia'ta:n] *m* -s (*Myth*) leviathan.
Levit [le'vi:t] *m* -en, -en (*Bibl*) Levite; (*Eccl*) deacon.
Leviten [le'vi:tən] *pl*: **jdm die** ~ **lesen** (*inf*) to haul sb over the coals (*inf*), to read sb the riot act (*inf*).
Levkoje [lɛf'koːjə] *f* -, -n (*Bot*) stock.
Lex *f* -, **Leges** (parliamentary) bill. ~ **Smythe/Braun** *etc* Smythe's/Braun's *etc* bill.
Lexem *nt* -s, -e (*Ling*) lexeme.
lexikalisch *adj* lexical.
Lexikographie *f* lexicography.
Lexikograph(in *f*) *m* lexicographer.
lexikographisch *adj* lexicographic(al).
Lexikologe *m*, **Lexikologin** *f* lexicologist.
Lexikologie *f* lexicology.
Lexikon *nt* -s, **Lexika** encyclopedia; (*Wörterbuch*) dictionary, lexicon.
lfd. *abbr of* laufend.
Liaison [lie'zõ:] *f* -, -s liaison.
Liane *f* -, -n liana.
Libanese *m* -n, -n, **Libanesin** *f* Lebanese.
libanesisch *adj* Lebanese.
Libanon *m* -(s) **der** ~ (*Land*) the Lebanon; (*Gebirge*) the Lebanon Mountains *pl*.
Libelle *f* (*Zool*) dragonfly; (*in Wasserwaage*) spirit level.
liberal *adj* liberal.
Liberale(r) *mf decl as adj* (*Pol*) Liberal.
liberalisieren* *vt* to liberalize.
Liberalisierung *f* liberalization.
Liberalismus *m* liberalism.
liberalistisch *adj* liberalist.
Liberalität *f* liberalness, liberality.
Libero *m* -s, -s (*Ftbl*) sweeper.
Libertin [liber'tɛ̃] *m* -s, -s (*old, geh*) libertine (*old*).
libidinös *adj* (*Psych*) libidinous, libidinal.
Libido *f* -, *no pl* (*Psych*) libido.
Librettist *m* librettist.
Libretto *nt* -s, -s *or* **Libretti** libretto.
Libyen *nt* -s Libya.
Libyer(in *f*) *m* -s, - Libyan.
libysch *adj* Libyan.
Licht *nt* -(e)s, -er *or* (*rare*) -e **(a)** *no pl* light. ~ **machen** (*anschalten*) to turn *or* switch *or* put on a light; (*anzünden*) to light a candle/lantern *etc*; **das** ~ **ist an** *or* **brennt** the light is on *or* is burning/the candle is burning; **das** ~ **des Tages/der Sonne** the light of day/the sun; **ich möchte es noch bei** ~ **fertigbekommen** I'd like to get it finished in daylight *or* while it's still light; ~ **ins Zimmer lassen** to let (the/some) light into the room; **in der ganzen Stadt fiel das** ~ **aus** all the lights in the town went out; **etw gegen das** ~ **halten** to hold sth up to the light; **gegen das** ~ **photographieren** to take a photograph into the light; **bei** ~e **besehen** *or* **betrachtet** (*lit*) in the daylight; (*fig*) in the cold light of day; **das ist nicht das richtige** ~ that's not the right sort of light; **das Bild hängt hier nicht im richtigen** ~ the light is wrong for the picture here; **du nimmst mir das ganze** ~ **weg** you're in the *or* my light; **jdm im** ~ **stehen** (*lit*) to stand in the *or* sb's light; (*fig*) to overshadow sb; **sich (***dat***) selbst im** ~ **stehen** (*fig*) to be one's own worst enemy; **(jdm) aus dem** ~ **gehen** to move *or* get out of the *or* sb's light; ~ **und Schatten** light and shade (*auch Art*); **wo** ~ **ist, ist auch Schatten** (*Prov*) there's no joy without sorrow (*prov*); **das** ~ **der Welt erblicken** (*geh*) to (first) see the light of day; **sein** ~ **leuchten lassen** (*inf*) to shine; **laß dein** ~ **leuchten!** don't hide your light under a bushel; **das** ~ **scheuen** (*lit*) to shun the light (of day); **Geschäfte, die das** ~ **scheuen** shady deals; **ein Treffpunkt für alle, die das** ~ **scheuen** a meeting place for all the more shady types; *siehe* **Scheffel**.
(b) (*fig*) light; (*Könner*) genius. **das** ~ **der Wahrheit/Erkenntnis** *etc* the light of truth/knowledge *etc*; ~ **in eine (dunkle) Sache bringen** to cast *or* shed some light on a matter; **im** ~(e) **unserer Erfahrungen** in the light of our experiences; **etw ans** ~ **bringen/zerren** to bring/drag sth out into the open; **ans** ~ **kommen** to come *or* get out, to come to light; **jdn hinters** ~ **führen** to pull the wool over sb's eyes, to lead sb up the garden path; **mir geht ein** ~ **auf(, warum ...)** now it's dawned on me (why ...), now I see (why ...); **etw in milderem** ~ **sehen** to see sth in a more favourable light; **ein schiefes/schlechtes** *or* **kein gutes** ~ **auf jdn/etw werfen** to show sb/sth in the wrong/a bad light; **das wirft ein bezeichnendes** ~ **auf ihn** that reveals a lot about him; **in ein schiefes** *or* **falsches** ~ **geraten** to be seen in the wrong light; **etw ins rechte/falsche** ~ **rücken** *or* **setzen** *or* **stellen** to show sth in a favourable/an unfavourable light; (*richtigstellen/falsch darstellen*) to show sth in its true light/put a wrong complexion on sth.
(c) (*Lichtquelle*) light; (*Kerze*) candle. ~er führen (*Naut*) to display *or* show lights; **jdm ein** ~ **aufstecken** *or* **aufsetzen** (*fig inf*) to put sb wise (*inf*).
(d) (*Hunt*) eye (*of deer etc*).
licht *adj* **(a)** (*hell*) light; (*liter*) *Morgen* bright. **am** ~en Tag in broad daylight; **es wird schon** ~ (*geh*) it is getting light, (the) day is dawning (*liter*); **einen** ~en Augenblick *or* Moment haben to have a lucid moment; (*fig inf*) to have a brainwave (*inf*),

auch ich habe ~e Augenblicke even I have my lucid moments. **(b)** *Wald* sparse; *Haar auch* thin. **eine ~e Stelle im Wald** a sparsely-wooded spot in the forest.

(c) *(Tech)* ~e **Höhe/Weite** headroom/(internal) width; ~er **Durchmesser** internal diameter.

Licht-: ~anlage *f* lights *pl*; **er hat sich** *(dat)* **eine ganze ~anlage gebastelt** he put together a whole lighting system; ~behandlung *f (Med)* phototherapy; l~beständig *adj* lightproof; *Farben, Stoff* non-fade; ~bild *nt (Dia)* transparency, slide; *(form: Photo)* photograph; ~bildervortrag *m* illustrated talk *or* lecture; ~blick *m (fig)* ray of hope; ~bogen *m* arc; l~brechend *adj (Opt)* refractive; ~brechung *f* refraction; ~bündel *nt* pencil (of rays); ~druck *m (Typ)* collotype; *(Phys)* light pressure; l~durchlässig *adj* pervious to light, light-transmissive *(form)*; *(durchsichtig)* transparent; *(durchscheinend)* translucent.

Lichte *f -, no pl* (internal) width.

Licht-: l~echt *adj* non-fade; ~echtheit *f* non-fade properties *pl*; ~effekt *m* lighting effect; ~einfall *m* incidence of light; ~einwirkung *f* action of light; l~elektrisch *adj* photoelectric; l~empfindlich *adj* sensitive to light, *(Tech auch)* photosensitive; ~empfindlichkeit *f* sensitivity to light; photosensitivity.

lichten[1] **1** *vt Wald* to thin (out). **2** *vr (Reihen, Wald, Dickicht, Haare)* to thin (out); *(Nebel)* to clear, to lift; *(Wolken, Dunkel)* to lift; *(Bestände)* to go down, to dwindle; *(fig: Angelegenheit)* to be cleared up.

lichten[2] *vt Anker* to weigh.

Lichter-: ~baum *m* Christmas tree; ~fest *nt* **(a)** *(liter: Weihnachten)* Yule *(old)*, Christmas; **(b)** *(jüdisches Fest)* Festival of Lights, Hanuk(k)ah; ~führung *f* showing of lights; ~glanz *m* blaze of lights; **in festlichem ~glanz erstrahlen** to be a blaze of festive lights; l~loh *adv* l~loh **brennen** *(lit)* to be ablaze; *(fig: Herz)* to be aflame; ~meer *nt (liter)* sea of light; **das ~meer von New York** the sea of light that is New York.

Licht-: ~filter *nt or m* (light) filter; ~geschwindigkeit *f* speed of light; ~hof *m* **(a)** *(Archit)* air well; **(b)** *(Phot)* halation *(spec)*; **(c)** *(des Mondes)* halo; ~hupe *f (Aut)* flash (of the headlights); **jdn durch ~hupe warnen** to warn sb by flashing one's lights; ~jahr *nt* light year; ~kegel *m (Phys)* cone of light; *(von Scheinwerfer)* beam (of light); **er stand im ~kegel** he stood in the spotlight/the beam of the headlights; ~kreis *m* circle *or* pool of light; ~lehre *f (old)* optics *sing*; ~leitung *f* lighting wire; l~los *adj* dark; **ein l~loser Raum** a room which doesn't get any light; ~mangel *m* lack of light; ~maschine *f (für Gleichstrom)* dynamo; *(für Drehstrom)* alternator; ~mast *m* lamppost; ~meß *no art Mariä* ~meß Candlemas; ~meßverfahren *nt (Mil)* flash ranging; ~nelke *f* catchfly, lychnis *(form)*; ~pause *f* photocopy; *(bei Blaupausverfahren)* blueprint; ~punkt *m* point of light; ~putzschere *f* wick-trimmer; ~quant *nt* photon; ~quelle *f* source of light; ~reklame *f* neon sign; ~satz *m (Typ)* film-setting, photocomposition; **in ~satz hergestellt** film-set; ~schacht *m* air shaft; ~schalter *m* light switch; ~schein *m* gleam of light; l~scheu *adj* averse to light; *(fig) Gesindel* shady; ~schimmer *m* gleam of light; ~schranke *f* light barrier, photoelectric beam; ~schutzfilter *m* light filter; ~setzmaschine *f (Typ)* photosetting machine; ~signal *nt* light signal; ~spielhaus *nt*, ~spieltheater *nt (dated)* cinema, picture palace *(old)*; l~stark *adj (Opt)* intense; *(Phot)* fast; ~stärke *f (Opt)* luminous intensity; *(Phot)* speed; ~stock *m siehe* Wachsstock; ~strahl *m* beam *or* ray of light; *(fig)* ray of sunshine; ~strom *m* **(a)** *(Opt)* luminous *or* light flux; **(b)** *(inf: Haushaltsstrom)* domestic current; **(c)** *(liter: Lichtbahn)* stream of light; l~undurchlässig *adj* opaque.

Lichtung *f* clearing, glade.

Licht-: ~verhältnisse *pl* lighting conditions *pl*; ~wechsel *m* change of light; *(Astron)* light variation; ~weg *m* light path; l~wendig *adj (Bot)* phototropic.

Lid *nt* -(e)s, -er eyelid.

Lidschatten *m* eye-shadow.

lieb *adj* **(a)** *(liebenswürdig, hilfsbereit)* kind; *(nett, reizend)* nice; *(niedlich) Kerl(chen), Ding* sweet, lovely, cute *(inf)*; *(artig) Kind, Schulklasse* good. **(es sendet Dir) ~e Grüße Deine Silvia** love Silvia; ~e **Grüße an Deine Eltern** give my best wishes to your parents; **sich ~ um jdn kümmern** to be very kind to sb; **er hat mir wirklich ~ geholfen** it was really sweet the way he helped me; **würdest du (bitte) so ~ sein und das Fenster aufmachen** *or*, **das Fenster aufzumachen?** would you do me a favour *or* (would you) be a love *(Brit inf)* *or* an angel (inf) and open the window; **willst du wohl (endlich) ~ sein?!** are you going to be good *or* to behave now?; **bei jdm ~ Kind sein** *(pej)* to be sb's (little) darling *or* pet; **beim Lehrer ~ Kind sein** *(pej)* to be teacher's pet; **sich bei jdm ~ Kind machen** *(pej)* to suck up to sb, to worm one's way into sb's good books.

(b) *Gast, Besuch (angenehm)* pleasant; *(willkommen)* welcome. **bei uns bist du jederzeit ein ~er Gast** you're always welcome, we're always pleased to see you.

(c) *(angenehm)* **etw ist jdm ~** sb likes sth; **es wäre mir ~, wenn ...** I'd be glad if ...; **I'd like it if ...; es ist mir ~, daß ...** I'm glad that ...; **es wäre ihm ~er** he would prefer it; **am ~sten hätte/würde ich ...** what I'd like most would be (to have) .../would be to..., most *or* best of all I'd like (to have) .../I'd like to ...; **am ~sten lese ich Kriminalromane/esse ich scharfe Speisen/gehe ich ins Kino** most *or* best of all I like detective novels/spicy food/going to the cinema; **am ~sten hätte ich ihm eine geklebt!** *(inf)* I could have stuck one on him *(sl)*; *siehe auch* lieb 2.

(d) *(geliebt, geschätzt)* dear, beloved *(iro, form)*; *(in Briefanrede)* dear; *(in Anrede von Publikum etc)* not translated. ~e **Monika, das geht doch nicht** (my) dear Monika, that's just not on; ~e **Brüder und Schwestern** *(Rel)* dearly beloved; **der ~e**

Gott the Good Lord; ~er **Gott** *(Anrede)* dear God *or* Lord; **unsere L~e Frau** *(Eccl)* Our Lady; **L~e Anna,** ~er **Klaus!** ... **Dear Anna and Klaus,** ...; *(mein)* **L~es** *(my)* love *or* pet, honey *(esp US)*; *(aber)* **meine L~e/mein L~er** *(iro)* (but) my dear *(woman/girl)*/man/boy; **jdn ~ behalten** to stay fond of sb; **er ist mir ~ und teuer** *or* **teuer** he's very dear to me; **den ~en langen Tag** *(inf)* the whole livelong day; **manch ~es Mal/manche ~e Stunde** *(dated, poet)* many a pleasant time/hour; **das ~e Geld!** the money, the money!; *(ach)* **du ~er Himmel!** *or* ~er **Güte!** *or* ~e **Zeit!**/~es **Lieschen** *or* **Lottchen**/~es **bißchen** *(inf)* good heavens *or* Lord!, goodness me!; *siehe* Not.

(e) ~ste(r, s) favourite; **sie ist mir die ~ste von allen** she is my favourite.

liebäugeln *vi insep* **mit etw ~** to have one's eye on sth; **mit einem neuen Auto ~** to be toying with the idea of getting a new car; **mit dem Gedanken ~, etw zu tun** to be toying *or* flirting with the idea of doing sth.

Liebchen *nt (old)* sweetheart.

Liebe *f -, -n* **(a)** love *(zu jdm, für jdn* for *or* of sb, *zu etw* of sth). **die große ~** the love of one's life, the real thing *(inf)*; **Heirat aus ~** love-match; **aus ~ zu jdm/einer Sache** for the love of sb/sth; **ein Kind der ~** *(liter)* a love child; **etw mit viel ~ tun** to do sth with loving care; **in ~ with love; in ~ Dein Theobald** with all my love, Theobald; ~ **macht blind** *(Prov)* love is blind *(Prov)*. **(b)** *(Sex)* sex. **eine Nacht der ~** a night of love; **von der ~ leben** *(Prostituierte etc)* to live off sex *or* off one's favours *(euph)*; **ein Meister der ~** an expert at love-making *or* in love; **sie/er ist gut in der ~** *(inf)* she/he is good at making love. **(c)** *(inf: Gefälligkeit)* favour. **tu mir doch bitte die ~ und ...** would you do me a favour and ... **(d)** *(Geliebte(r))* love. **sie ist eine alte ~ von mir** she is an old flame of mine.

Liebe-: l~bedürftig *adj* l~bedürftig **sein, ein** l~bedürftiges **Wesen haben** *or* **sein** to need a lot of love *or* affection; **ein** l~bedürftiges **Kind** a child who needs a lot of love *or* affection; ~dienerei *f (pej)* subservience, fawning *(gegenüber* to); l~dienern *vi insep (pej)* to fawn *(jdm* to sb); l~leer *adj* **Leben, Dasein** loveless.

Liebelei *f (inf)* flirtation; affair.

liebeln *vi (obs, liter)* **mit jdm ~** to flirt *or* dally *(old)* with sb.

lieben *vti* to love; *(als Liebesakt)* to make love *(jdn* to sb). **etw nicht ~** not to like sth; **ich liebe es nicht, wenn man mich unterbricht** I do not like being interrupted; **das liebe ich (gerade)!** *(iro)* marvellous, isn't it? *(iro)*; **etw ~d gern tun** to love to do sth; **sich** *or* **einander ~** to love one another *or* each other; *(euph)* to make love.

Liebende(r) *mf decl as adj* lover.

liebenlernen *vt sep* to come to love.

liebenswert *adj* lovable, endearing.

liebenswürdig *adj* kind. **würden Sie so ~ sein und die Tür schließen?** would you be so kind as to shut the door?

liebenswürdigerweise *adv* kindly.

Liebenswürdigkeit *f* **(a)** *(Höflichkeit)* politeness; *(Freundlichkeit)* kindness. **würden Sie die ~ haben, das zu tun** *or* **und das zu tun?** *(form)* would you be kind *or* good enough to do that?, would you have the goodness to do that?; **darf ich Sie um die ~ bitten, das zu tun?** *(form)* might I ask you to be so good enough to do that? **(b)** *(iro: giftige Bemerkung)* charming remark *(iro)*.

lieber 1 *adj comp of* lieb.
2 *adv comp of* gern **(a)** *(vorzugsweise)* rather, sooner. **das tue ich ~** *(im Augenblick)* I would *or* I'd rather *or* sooner do that; *(grundsätzlich auch)* I prefer doing that; **das würde ich ~ tun** I would *or* I'd rather *or* sooner do that, I would prefer to do that; **ich trinke ~ Wein als Bier** I prefer wine to beer; **(das möchte ich) ~ nicht!** I would *or* I'd sooner *or* rather not, I would *or* I'd prefer not to; **er sieht es ~, wenn du das nicht tust** he would *or* he'd prefer you not to do that, he would *or* he'd prefer it if you didn't do that, he would *or* he'd sooner *or* rather you didn't do that; *(grundsätzlich)* he prefers you not to do that, he prefers it if you don't do that.

(b) *(besser, vernünftigerweise)* better. **bleibe ~ im Bett** you had *or* you'd better stay in bed, I would *or* I'd stay in bed if I were you; **ich hätte ~ lernen/nachgeben etc sollen** I would have done better *or* I'd have done better to have studied/given in etc; **sollen wir gehen? — ~ nicht!** should we go? — better not; **nichts ~ als** there's nothing I'd rather do/have.

Liebes- in cpds love; ~abenteuer *nt* amorous adventure; ~affäre *f* (love-)affair; ~akt *m* love *or* sex act; ~apfel *m (obs)* tomato; ~bande *pl (liter)* bonds of love *pl*; ~beziehung *f* romantic attachment; (sexual) relationship; ~bote *m* messenger of love; ~brief *m* love letter; ~dienerin *f (inf)* lady of the night *(euph)*; ~dienst *m* labour of love; *(fig: Gefallen)* favour; **jdm einen ~dienst erweisen** to do sb a service of love/a favour; ~erklärung *f* declaration of love; **eine ~erklärung machen** to declare one's love to sb; ~film *m* love film; ~gabe *f (dated)* alms *pl*; ~gedicht *nt* love poem; ~geschichte *f* **(a)** *(Liter)* love story; **(b)** *(inf: Liebschaft)* love-affair; ~gott *m (geh)* god of love; ~göttin *f* goddess of love; ~handel, ~händel *m (obs)* love-affair; ~heirat *f* love-match; ~kummer *m* lovesickness; ~kummer **haben** to be lovesick; **vor ~kummer konnte sie nicht mehr essen** she was so lovesick that she couldn't eat; ~leben *nt* love-life; ~lied *nt* love song; ~müh(e) *f*: **das ist vergebliche** *or* **verlorene ~müh(e)** that is futile; ~nest *nt (inf)* love-nest; ~paar *nt* lovers *pl*; ~rausch *m* ecstasy of passion; ~roman *m* romantic novel; ~spiel *nt* loveplay; ~szene *f* love scene; l~toll *adj* love-stricken, lovelorn; ~trank *m (liter)* love potion; l~trunken *adj (geh)* in an ecstasy of love; ~verhältnis *nt* (sexual) relationship, liaison.

liebevoll *adj* loving.

lieb-: ~gewinnen* vt sep irreg to get or grow fond of; ~geworden adj attr well-loved; Brauch, Angewohnheit favourite; ein mir ~gewordenes Land a country of which I've grown very fond; ~haben vt sep irreg to love; (weniger stark) to be (very) fond of.

Liebhaber(in f) m -s, - (a) lover. (b) (Interessent, Freund) enthusiast; (Sammler) collector. ein ~ von etw a lover of sth; das ist nur etwas für ~ it's an acquired taste; das ist ein Wein/Auto für ~ that's a wine/car for connoisseurs.

Liebhaber-: ~aufführung f (für Kenner) performance for connoisseurs; (von Laien gespielt) amateur performance; ~bühne f siehe ~theater.

Liebhaberei f (fig: Steckenpferd, Hobby) hobby. etw aus ~ tun to do sth as a hobby.

Liebhaber-: ~preis m collector's price; ~theater nt (für Kenner) theatre for connoisseurs; (Laien~) amateur theatre; ~wert m collector's value.

liebkosen* vt insep (liter) to caress, to fondle.

Liebkosung f (liter) caress.

lieblich adj charming, lovely, delightful; Duft, Geschmack, Wein sweet. das ist ja ~! (iro) that's wonderful (iro).

Lieblichkeit f loveliness, delightfulness; sweetness. ihre ~, Prinzessin Sylvia (im Fasching) Her Sweetness Princess Sylvia (title of carnival princess).

Liebling m darling; (bevorzugter Mensch) favourite.

Lieblings- in cpds favourite.

Lieb-: l~los adj Ehemann, Eltern unloving; Bemerkung, Behandlung unkind; Benehmen inconsiderate; l~los gekocht/zubereitet etc cooked/prepared etc any old how (inf); ~losigkeit f (a) (no pl: liebloses Wesen) siehe adj unlovingness; unkindness; inconsiderateness; (b) (Äußerung) unkind remark; (Tat) unkind act; ~losigkeiten (Benehmen) unkind behaviour sing; ~reiz m (liter) charm; l~reizend adj (liter) charming; ~schaft f affair.

Liebste(r) mf decl as adj sweetheart.

Liebstöckel m or nt -s, - (Bot) lovage.

Lied nt -(e)s, -er song; (Kirchen~) hymn; (Weihnachts~) carol. das Ende vom ~ (fig inf) the upshot or outcome (of all this); das ist dann immer das Ende vom ~ it always ends like that; es ist immer dasselbe or das alte or gleiche ~ (inf) it's always the same old story (inf); davon kann ich ein ~ singen or weiß ich ein ~ zu singen I could tell you a thing or two about that (inf).

Lieder-: ~abend m evening of songs; (von Sänger) song recital; ~buch nt siehe Lied songbook; hymnbook; book of carols; ~dichter m lyrical poet; (des Mittelalters) minstrel; ~handschrift f collection of ballads.

Liederjan m -(e)s, -e (dated inf) wastrel.

liederlich adj (schlampig) slovenly attr, pred; (nachlässig auch) sloppy; (unmoralisch) Leben, Mann dissolute, dissipated; Frau, Mädchen loose. ein ~es Frauenzimmer (pej) a slut; Bruder L~ (old) wastrel.

Liederlichkeit f siehe adj slovenliness; sloppiness; dissoluteness; looseness.

Liederzyklus m song cycle.

Liedrian m -(e)s, -e siehe Liederjan.

lief pret of laufen.

Lieferant m supplier; (Auslieferer) deliveryman.

Lieferanten|eingang m tradesmen's entrance; (von Warenhaus etc) goods entrance.

Liefer-: ~auto nt siehe ~wagen; l~bar adj (vorrätig) available; (zustellbar) deliverable (rare); die Ware ist sofort l~bar the article can be supplied/delivered at once; diese Sachen sind auch kurzfristig l~bar these goods can be supplied/delivered at short notice; ~bedingungen pl conditions or terms of supply/delivery; ~firma f supplier; (Zusteller) delivery firm; ~frist f delivery period; die ~frist einhalten to meet the delivery date; das Auto hat eine lange ~frist there's a long waiting list for delivery of this car.

liefern vti (a) to supply; (zustellen) to deliver (in + acc to). jdm etw ~ to supply sb with sth/deliver sth to sb; wir können keine Rohstoffe mehr ins Ausland ~ we cannot supply any more raw materials abroad; wir ~ nicht ins Ausland/nach Frankreich we don't supply the foreign market/(to) France; eine Firma, die wegen Streiks nicht mehr ~ kann a firm which, because of a strike, cannot deliver any more.
(b) (zur Verfügung stellen) to supply; Beweise, Gesprächsstoff, Informationen, Sensationen auch to provide, to furnish; Ertrag to yield; (inf: stellen) to provide. jdm eine Schlacht/ein Wortgefecht ~ to do battle/verbal battle with sb; sie lieferten sich eine regelrechte Schlacht they had a real battle; (Sport) they put up a real fight; ein spannendes Spiel ~ (Sport) to put on an exciting game; jdm eine gute/schlechte Partie ~ to give/not to give sb a good game; siehe geliefert.

Liefer-: ~schein m delivery note; ~termin m delivery date.

Lieferung f (a) (Versand, Versandgut) delivery; (Versorgung) supply. bei ~ zu bezahlen payable on delivery; Zahlung bis 14 Tage nach ~ account payable within 14 days of delivery. (b) (von Buch) instalment.

Lieferungsbedingungen pl siehe Lieferbedingungen.

Liefer-: ~vertrag m contract of supply/delivery; ein ~vertrag über 5.000 Lastwagen a contract to supply/deliver 5,000 lorries; ~wagen m van, panel truck (US); (offen) pick-up; ~zeit f delivery period; ~zettel m delivery order.

Liege f -, -n couch; (Camping~) camp bed; (für Garten) lounger.

Liege-: ~deck nt (Naut) sundeck; ~geld nt (Naut) demurrage; ~kur f rest-cure.

liegen pret lag, ptp gelegen aux haben or (S Ger) sein vi (a) (flach ~, ausgebreitet sein) to lie; (Flasche etc) to lie on its side; (inf: krank sein) to be laid up (inf). das lange L~ lying

a long time; (von Mensch) lying in bed for a long time; hart/weich ~ to lie on hard/soft ground, to lie on a hard/soft surface, to lie on a hard/soft bed etc; in diesem Bett liegt es sich or liegt man hart/weich this bed is hard/soft; unbequem ~ to lie uncomfortably or in an uncomfortable position; auf den Knien ~ to be kneeling or on one's knees; im Bett/Krankenhaus ~ to be in bed/hospital; auf dem Boden ~ to lie on the floor; (zum Schlafen) to sleep on the floor; zu Bett ~ (form) to have retired (form); (krank sein) to have taken to one's bed (form); der Kranke muß unbedingt ~ the patient really must lie down; der Kopf muß hoch/tief ~ the head must be higher/lower than the rest of the body; flach ~ (lit) to lie flat; (inf: krank sein) to be laid up; er kam unter das Auto zu ~ he was run over or knocked down by the car; verstreut ~ to be scattered; der Ski-springer liegt ausgezeichnet in der Luft the ski-jumper is excellently positioned in the air; der Vogel/das Flugzeug liegt ganz ruhig in der Luft the bird/plane is flying quite smoothly; in der Kurve ~ (Auto) to hold the corner; (Rennfahrer) to corner; der Wagen liegt gut auf der Straße the car holds the road well; auf dem Boden haben sie teure Teppiche ~ they have expensive carpets on the floor; etw ~ lassen to leave sth (there); einen Ort links/rechts ~ lassen to pass by a place.
(b) (sich befinden, sein) to be. das Schiff liegt am Kai the ship is (tied up) alongside the quay; ich habe noch einen guten Wein im Keller ~ I have a good wine in the cellar; ein Lächeln lag auf ihrem Gesicht there was a smile on her face; die Preise ~ zwischen 60 und 80 Mark the prices are between 60 and 80 marks; der zweite Läufer liegt weit hinter dem ersten the second runner is or is lying a long way behind the first; die Betonung liegt auf der zweiten Silbe the stress is or lies on the second syllable; seine Fähigkeiten ~ auf einem anderen Gebiet his abilities lie in a different direction; in jds Absicht (dat) ~ to be sb's intention; es liegt in seiner Gewalt, das zu tun it is or lies within his power to do that.
(c) (einen bestimmten Rang haben) to be. an erster Stelle der Hitparade ~ to be number one (in the hit parade), to top the charts; auf den hintersten Plätzen/in Führung/an der Spitze ~ to be at the bottom/in the lead/right out in front.
(d) (lasten) auf dieser Familie scheint ein Fluch zu ~ there seems to be a curse on this family; die Verantwortung/Schuld dafür liegt bei ihm the responsibility/blame for that lies or rests with him; die Schuld liegt schwer auf mir my guilt weighs heavily on me; damit liegt die ganze Arbeit auf mir that means all the work falls on me; das liegt ganz bei dir that is completely up to you; die Entscheidung liegt beim Volk/bei Ihnen the decision rests with the people/you.
(e) (eine bestimmte Lage haben) to be; (Haus, Stadt etc auch) to be situated or located, to lie. nach Süden/der Straße ~ to face south/the road; ein idyllisch ~des Kirchlein an idyllically situated little church; das Haus liegt ganz ruhig the house is in a very quiet position or location; das liegt doch auf dem Weg/ganz in der Nähe it's on the way/quite nearby.
(f) (sich verhalten) to be. so, wie die Dinge jetzt ~ as things are or stand at the moment; damit liegst du (gold)richtig (inf) you're (dead (inf) or absolutely) right there; bei mir ~ Sie richtig (damit) (inf) you've come to the right person (for that).
(g) (begraben sein) to lie.
(h) (Schnee) to lie; (Hitze, Nebel auch) to hang. die Stadt lag in dichtem Nebel the town was enveloped in thick fog, thick fog hung or lay over the town; der Schnee liegt 50 cm hoch the snow is 50 cm deep; der Schnee bleibt nicht ~ the snow isn't lying.
(i) (wichtig sein) es liegt mir viel/wenig/nichts daran it matters a lot/doesn't matter much/at all to me, that is important/isn't very/at all important to me; es liegt mir viel an ihm/an meinem Beruf he/my job is very important or matters a lot to me; mir liegt an einer schnellen Fertigstellung des Hauses/an guten Beziehungen I am concerned that the house should be finished quickly/that there should be good relations; was liegt (dir) schon daran? what does it matter (to you)?
(j) (begründet sein) an jdm/etw ~ to be because of sb/sth; woran liegt es? why is that?, what is the reason (for that)?; das liegt daran, daß ... that is because..., the reason for that is that...; an mir soll es nicht ~! I'll go along with that; an mir soll es nicht ~, daß or wenn die Sache schiefgeht it won't be my fault if things go wrong.
(k) (geeignet sein, passen) jdm liegt etw nicht sth doesn't suit sb; (jds Art, Lebensart, Beruf) sth doesn't appeal to sb; (Mathematik etc) sb has no aptitude for sth; Krankenschwester liegt mir nicht (inf) nursing isn't my cup of tea (inf) or doesn't appeal to me; diese Rolle liegt ihr she suits or fits the part, the part suits her.
(l) (angeordnet sein) (Falten) to lie; (Haare) to stay in place. der Stoff liegt quer/90 cm breit the material is on the cross/is 90 cm wide.

liegenbleiben vi sep irreg aux sein (a) (nicht aufstehen) to remain lying (down). (im Bett) ~ to stay in bed; er blieb bewußtlos auf dem Boden liegen he lay unconscious on the floor; bleib liegen! don't get up!, stay down!
(b) (vergessen werden) to be or get left behind. mein Schirm muß irgendwo liegengeblieben sein I must have left my umbrella somewhere.
(c) (nicht verkauft werden) not to sell, to be left unsold. wenn uns diese Sachen ~ if we are left with these things (on our hands).
(d) (Auto) to conk out (inf).
(e) (nicht ausgeführt werden) to get or be left (undone), not to get done.

liegend adj (Art) reclining. ~ aufbewahren to store flat; Flasche etc to store on its side; ~e Güter immovable property sing (form), real estate.

Liegende f -n, -n (Art) reclining figure.
liegenlassen vt sep irreg, ptp - or (rare) **liegengelassen** (nicht erledigen) to leave; (vergessen) to leave (behind); (herum~) to leave lying about or around. sie hat alles liegengelassen, um dem Kind zu helfen she dropped everything (to go and) help the child; siehe links, stehenlassen.
Liegenschaft(en pl) f real estate sing, property sing.
Liege-: ~platz m place to lie; (auf Schiff, in Zug etc) berth; (Ankerplatz) moorings pl; (von großem Schiff) berth; ~sitz m reclining seat; (auf Boot) couchette; ~statt f (old, dial) bed; ~stuhl m (mit Holzgestell) deck chair; (mit Metallgestell) lounger; ~stütz m (Sport) press-up; ~stütze machen to do press-ups; in den ~stütz! press-ups!; ~wagen m (Rail) couchette coach or car (esp US); ~wagen buchen to book a couchette; ~wiese f lawn (for sunbathing); ~zeit f (a) (Naut) lay days pl (form); (b) rest period; eine Stunde ~zeit verschreiben to prescribe an hour's rest.
lieh pret of leihen.
Liek nt -(e)s, -en (Naut) boltrope.
lies imper sing of lesen.
Lieschen [liːsçən] nt Liz(zie). ~ Müller (inf) the average woman in the street; siehe fleißig, lieb.
ließ pret of lassen.
Lift m -(e)s, -e or -s (Personen~) lift (Brit), elevator (esp US); (Güter~) lift (Brit), hoist.
Liftboy ['lɪftbɔy] m -s, -s liftboy (Brit), elevator boy (US).
liften vt to lift. sich (dat) das Gesicht ~ lassen to have a facelift.
Liga f -, Ligen league.
Ligatur f ligature; (Mus: Verbindung zweier Noten) tie.
Liguster m -s, - privet.
liieren* 1 vt to bring or get together; Firmen etc to get to work together. liiert sein to have joined forces; (Firmen etc) to be working together; (Pol) to be allied; (ein Verhältnis haben) to have a relationship.
   2 vr to join forces; (Firmen etc) to work together; (Pol) to enter into an alliance; (ein Verhältnis eingehen) to get together, to form a liaison.
Likör m -s, -e liqueur.
lila adj inv purple.
Lila nt -s, (inf) -s purple.
Lilie [-iə] f lily. keusch wie eine ~ as pure as the driven snow.
Liliput- in cpds miniature.
Liliputaner(in f) m -s, - dwarf, midget; (Bewohner von Liliput) Liliputian.
Limburger (Käse) m -s, - Limburger, Limburg cheese.
Limerick m -(s), -s limerick.
Limes m -, - (a) no pl (Hist) limes. (b) (Math) limit.
Limit nt -s, -s or -e limit; (Fin) ceiling. jdm ein ~ setzen to set sb a limit.
limitieren* vt (form) to limit; (Fin) to put a ceiling on.
Limonade f lemonade; (in weiterem Sinn) soft drink.
Limone f -, -n lime.
Limousine [limuˈziːnə] f saloon (Brit), sedan (US).
lind adj (a) (liter) balmy; Regen gentle. (b) (Sw) ~ (gewürzt) lightly spiced.
Linde f -, -n linden or lime (tree); (~holz) limewood.
Lindenblütentee m lime blossom tea.
lindern vt to ease, to relieve, to alleviate; Hustenreiz, Sonnenbrand etc auch to soothe.
Linderung f easing, relief, alleviation; soothing.
Linderungsmittel nt pain reliever, analgesic.
Lind-: li~grün adj lime green; ~heit f siehe adj (a) balminess; gentleness; ~wurm m (Myth) lindworm (type of wingless dragon).
Lineal nt -s, -e ruler. einen Strich mit dem ~ ziehen to rule a line, to draw a line with a ruler; er geht, als ob er ein ~ verschluckt hätte (inf) he walks with his back as stiff as a ramrod or as straight as a die.
linear adj linear.
Lineatur f siehe Liniatur.
Liner ['laɪnɐ] m -s, - (Naut) liner.
lingual adj (form) lingual.
Linguist(in f) m linguist.
Linguistik f linguistics sing.
linguistisch adj linguistic.
Liniatur f ruling, lines pl.
Linie [-iə] f (a) (auch Sport, Pol, Naut, Abstammung, Straßenmarkierung) line; (Umriß auch) outline. ein Schreibblock mit ~n a ruled or lined notepad; die ~n (in) seiner Hand the lines of or on his hand; in einer ~ stehen to be in a line; sich in einer ~ aufstellen to line up; die Buchstaben halten nicht ~ (Typ) the letters are not in line; eine gemeinsame ~ als Grundlage für etw suchen to seek a common basis for sth; auf der gleichen ~ along the same lines; einer Sache (dat) fehlt die klare ~ there's no clear line to sth; eine klare ~ für sein Leben finden, seinem Leben eine klare ~ geben to give one's life a clear sense of direction; eine ~ ziehen zwischen ... (+dat) (fig) to draw a distinction between ...; auf der ganzen ~ (fig) all along the line; sie hat ein Gesicht mit klaren/verschwommenen ~n she has clear-cut/ill-defined features; auf die (schlanke) ~ achten to watch one's figure; die männliche/weibliche ~ eines Geschlechts the male/female line of a family; in erster/zweiter ~ kommen (fig) to come first/second, to take first/second place; in erster ~ muß die Arbeitslosigkeit bekämpft werden the fight against unemployment must come first or take priority; siehe erste(r, s).
   (b) (Mil) (Stellung) line; (Formation) rank. in ~ antreten! fall in!; in ~ zu drei Gliedern in ranks three deep; die feindliche/vorderste ~ the enemy lines pl/front line.
   (c) (Verkehrsverbindung, -strecke) route; (Bus~,Eisen-

bahn~ auch) line. fahren Sie mit der ~ 2 take a or the (number) 2; auf einer ~ verkehren to work a route; die ~ Köln-Bonn the Cologne-Bonn line.
Linien- [-iən]: ~blatt nt ruled sheet (placed under writing-paper), line guide; ~bus m public service bus, regular bus; ~dampfer m regular steamer; ~dienst m regular service; (Aviat) scheduled service; ~flug m scheduled flight; ~flugzeug nt scheduled (service) plane; ~führung f lines pl; ~netz nt network of routes; das ~netz der U-Bahn/der Straßenbahnen the underground (system)/the tram system; ~papier nt lined or ruled paper; ~richter m (Sport) linesman; ~schiff nt regular service ship; l~treu adj loyal to the party line; l~treu sein to follow or toe the party line; ~verkehr m regular traffic; (Aviat) scheduled traffic; im ~verkehr fliegen/fahren to fly on scheduled services/operate on regular services.
linieren*, liniieren* vt to rule, to draw or rule lines on. liniert lined, feint (spec).
Linierung, Liniierung f ruling.
Linke f -n, -n (a) (Hand) left hand; (Seite) left(-hand) side; (Boxen) left. zur ~n (des Königs) saß ... to the left (of the king) or on the (king's) left sat ... (b) (Pol) Left.
Linke(r) mf decl as adj (Pol) left-winger, leftist (pej), lefty (pej inf).
linke(r, s) adj attr (a) left; Rand, Spur etc auch left-hand. die ~ Seite the left(-hand) side; (von Stoff) the wrong side, the reverse (side); auf der ~n Seite on the left-hand side, on the left; ~r Hand, zur ~n Hand to or on the or one's left; ~ Masche (Stricken) purl (stitch); eine ~ Masche stricken to purl one; zwei ~ Hände haben (inf) to have two left hands (inf); das mache ich mit der ~n Hand (inf) I can do that with my eyes shut (inf); er ist heute mit dem ~n Bein or Fuß zuerst aufgestanden (inf) he got out of bed on the wrong side this morning (inf); ein ganz ~r Hund (pej inf) a nasty piece of work (pej inf); ein ganz ~s Ding drehen (inf) to get up to a bit of no good (inf).
   (b) (Pol) left-wing, leftist (pej), lefty (pej inf); Flügel left.
linkerseits adv to the left, on the left-hand side.
linkisch adj clumsy, awkward.
links 1 adv (a) on the left; schauen, abbiegen (to the) left. nach ~ (to the) left; von ~ from the left; ~ von etw (to or on the) left of sth; ~ von jdm to or on sb's left; sich ~ halten to keep to the left; weiter ~ further to the left; sich ~ einordnen to move into or take the left-hand lane; jdn ~ liegenlassen (fig inf) to ignore sb; weder ~ noch rechts schauen (lit) to look neither left nor right; (fig) not to let oneself be distracted.
   (b) (Pol) on the left. nach ~ to the left; ~ von jdm (to the) left of sb; ~ von der Mitte (to the) left of centre; ~ stehen or sein (inf) to be left-wing or on the left or a left-winger; ~ orientiert sein to lean or have leanings to(wards) the left.
   (c) (Mil) Augen ~! eyes left!; ~ um! left about turn; ~ schwenkt, marsch! left wheel!
   (d) (verkehrt) bügeln on the reverse or wrong side; tragen reverse or wrong side out; liegen reverse or wrong side up. ~ stricken to purl; eine (Masche) ~, drei (Maschen) rechts purl one, knit three; der Pullover ist nur ~ gestrickt the pullover is knitted all in purl.
   (e) (inf: mit der linken Hand) left-handed.
   2 prep +gen on or to the left of.
Links-: ~abbieger m motorist/cyclist/car etc turning left; ~abbiegerspur f left-hand turn-off lane; ~abweichler m -s, - (Pol inf) left-winger, leftist (pej), leftie (pej inf); ~außen m -s, - (Ftbl) outside left; (Pol) extreme left-winger; ~drall m (lit) (im Gewehrlauf) anticlockwise rifling; (von Geschoß, Billardball) swerve to the left; (von Auto, Pferd) pull to the left; (fig) leaning to the left; einen ~drall haben to swerve/pull/lean to the left; (fig) leaning to the left; l~drehend adj (Chem) laevorotatory (spec).
Linkser m -s, - (inf) left-hander.
Links-: ~extremist m left-wing extremist; l~gängig adj (Tech) left-handed; l~gerichtet adj (Pol) left-wing orientated no adv; ~gewinde nt left-handed thread; ~haken m left hook; ~händer(in f) m -s, - left-hander, left-handed person/player etc; ~händer sein to be left-handed; l~händig adj, adv left-handed; ~händigkeit f left-handedness; l~her adv (old) from the left; l~heran adv over to the left; l~herum adv (round) to the left; sich drehen etc anti-clockwise; l~hin adv (old) (to the) left; ~intellektuelle(r) mf left-wing intellectual; ~kurve f (von Straße) left-hand bend; (von Bahn auch) left-hand curve; l~lastig adj (lit) Boot listing to the left; Auto down at the left; (fig) leftist (pej), leaning to the left; l~lastig sein to list to the left/be down at the left/lean to the left; l~läufig adj Gewinde left-handed; Schrift right-to-left; ~partei f left-wing party; l~radikal adj (Pol) radically left-wing; die ~radikalen the left-wing radicals; ~radikalismus m (Pol) left-wing radicalism; l~rheinisch adj to or on the left of the Rhine; ~ruck, ~rutsch, ~schwenk m (Pol) shift to the left; l~herum; l~seitig adj on the left(-hand) side; l~seitig gelähmt paralysed in the left side; l~um adv (Mil) to the left; l~um machen (inf) to do a left turn; l~um kehrt! to the left about turn!; ~verkehr m, no pl driving on the left no def art; in Großbritannien ist ~verkehr they drive on the left in Britain; im ~verkehr muß man ... when driving on the left one must ...
Linnen nt -s, - (liter) siehe **Leinen**.
linnen adj (liter) siehe **leinen**.
Linoleum [liˈnoːleʊm] nt -s, no pl linoleum, lino.
Linolschnitt m (Art) linocut.
Linon [liˈnõ] m -(s), -s cotton/linen lawn.
Linse f -, -n (a) (Bot, Cook) lentil. (b) (Opt) lens.
linsen vi (inf) to peep, to peek (inf); (Sch) to copy (bei off, from).

Linsen-: ~gericht *nt* lentil dish; ~suppe *f* lentil soup.
Lippe *f* -, -n lip; (*Bot auch*) labium. eine (große *or* dicke) ~ riskieren (*sl*) to be brazen; das bringe ich nicht über die ~n I can't bring myself to say it; es wird *or* soll kein Wort über meine ~n kommen not a word shall cross *or* pass my lips; er brachte kein Wort über die ~n he couldn't say *or* utter a word; das Wort erstarb ihm auf den ~n (*liter*) the word froze on his lips; *siehe* .hängen.
Lippen-: ~bekenntnis *nt* lip-service; ein ~bekenntnis ablegen to pay lip-service (to one's ideals *etc*); ~blütler *m* -s, - (*Bot*) labiate; ~laut *m* (*Ling*) labial; ~stift *m* lipstick.
liquid *adj siehe* liquide.
Liquida *f* -, **Liquidä** *or* **Liquiden** (*Ling*) liquid.
Liquidation *f* (*form*) **(a)** (*Auflösung*) liquidation. in ~ treten to go into liquidation; sie haben die ~ beschlossen they decided to go into liquidation.
   (b) (*Rechnung*) account.
liquid(e) *adj* (*Econ*) Geld, Mittel liquid; Firma, Geschäftsmann solvent. ich bin nicht ~ (*inf*) I'm out of funds (*inf*), I'm short of the ready (*inf*).
liquidieren* *vt* **(a)** *Geschäft* to put into liquidation, to wind up; (*old*) *Betrag* to charge. **(b)** *jdn* to liquidate.
Liquidierung *f* (*von Geschäft, Menschen*) liquidation.
Liquidität *f* (*Econ*) liquidity.
lismen *vti* (*Sw*) to knit.
lispeln *vti* to lisp; (*flüstern*) to whisper.
List *f* -, -en (*Täuschung*) cunning, artfulness; (*trickreicher Plan*) trick, ruse. mit ~ und Tücke (*inf*) with a lot of coaxing; zu einer ~ greifen, (eine) ~ anwenden to use a bit of cunning, to resort to a ruse.
Liste *f* -, -n (*Aufstellung*) list; (*Wähler~*) register; (*von Parteien*) (party) list (*of candidates under the proportional representation system*). sich in eine ~ eintragen *or* (ein)schreiben to put oneself *or* one's name (down) on a list.
Listen-: ~führer *m* list keeper; ~platz *m* (*Pol*) place on the party list (*of candidates under the proportional representation system*); ~preis *m* list price; ~wahl *f* electoral system in which a vote is cast for a party rather than a specific candidate.
listig *adj* cunning, crafty, wily *no adv*.
listigerweise *adv* cunningly, craftily.
Litanei *f* (*Eccl, fig*) litany. eine ~ von Klagen/Beschwerden *etc* a long list *or* catalogue of complaints; immer dieselbe ~ beten to go on about the same old things all the time (*inf*).
Litauen *nt* -s Lithuania.
Litauer(in *f*) *m* -s, - Lithuanian.
litauisch *adj* Lithuanian.
Liter *m or nt* -s, - litre.
literarhistorisch *adj* literary historical *attr; Buch, Artikel auch* relating to literary history. ~ interessant of interest to literary history.
literarisch *adj* literary.
Literat *m* -en, -en man of letters; (*Schriftsteller*) literary figure. die ~en literati (*form*).
Literatur *f* literature.
Literatur-: ~angabe *f* bibliographical reference; (*Zusammenfassung*) bibliography; ~denkmal *nt* literary monument; ~gattung *f* literary genre; ~geschichte *f* history of literature; l~geschichtlich *adj* literarhistorisch; ~hinweis *m* literary reference (*auf* +*acc* to); ~kritik *f* literary criticism; (*Kritikerschaft*) literary critics *pl*; ~kritiker *m* literary critic; ~papst *m* literary pundit; ~preis *m* prize *or* award for literature, literary prize *or* award; ~verzeichnis *nt* bibliography; ~wissenschaft *f* literary studies *pl*; vergleichende ~wissenschaft comparative literature.
Liter-: ~leistung *f* power output per litre; ~maß *nt* litre measure; l~weise *adv* (*lit*) by the litre; (*fig*) by the gallon.
Litfaßsäule *f* advertising column.
Litho-: ~graph *m* lithographer; ~graphie *f* **(a)** (*Verfahren*) lithography; **(b)** (*Druck*) lithograph; l~graphieren* *vt* to lithograph; l~graphisch *adj* lithographic(al).
Litotes *f* -, *no pl* (*Liter*) litotes.
litt *ptp of* leiden.
Liturgie *f* liturgy.
liturgisch *adj* liturgical.
Litze *f* -, -n braid; (*Elec*) flex.
live [laif] *adj pred, adv* (*Rad, TV*) live.
Live-Sendung [laif-] *f* live programme *or* broadcast.
Livree [li'vre:] *f* -, -n [-'re:ən] livery.
livriert [li'vri:rt] *adj* liveried.
Lizentiat¹ [litsɛn'tsia:t] *nt* (*Univ*) licentiate (*form*).
Lizentiat² [litsɛn'tsia:t] *m* -en, -en (*Univ*) licentiate (*form*).
Lizenz *f* licence (*Brit*), license (*US*). eine ~ dafür haben, etw zu tun to have a licence to do sth, to be licensed to do sth; etw in ~ herstellen to manufacture sth under licence.
Lizenz-: ~abgabe *f* licence fee; (*im Verlagswesen*) royalty; ~ausgabe *f* licensed edition; ~geber *m* licenser; (*Behörde*) licensing authority; ~gebühr *f* licence fee; (*im Verlagswesen*) royalty.
lizenzieren* *vt* (*form*) to license.
Lizenz-: ~inhaber *m* licensee, licence holder; er ist ~inhaber he has a licence, he is licensed; ~nehmer *m* licensee; ~presse *f* (*Pol*) licensed press; ~spieler *m* (*Ftbl*) professional player; ~träger *m* licensee.
Lkw, LKW ['ɛlka:ve:, ɛlka:'ve:] *m* -(s), -(s) *abbr of* Lastkraftwagen.
Lob *nt* -(e)s, *no pl* praise. ~ verdienen to deserve praise *or* to be praised; (viel) ~ für etw bekommen to come in for (a lot of) praise for sth, to be (highly) praised for sth; ein ~ der Köchin (my/our) compliments to the chef!; Gott sei ~ und Dank praise be to God, God be praised; zum ~e Gottes in praise of

the Lord; über jedes ~ erhaben sein to be beyond praise; sein eigenes ~ singen (*inf*) to sing one's own praises, to blow one's own trumpet (*inf*); jdm ~ spenden *or* zollen to praise sb.
Lobby ['lɔbɪ] *f* -, -s *or* **Lobbies** lobby.
Lobbyismus [lɔbi'ɪsmʊs] *m* lobbyism.
Lobbyist [lɔbi'ɪst] *m* lobbyist.
loben *vt* to praise. sein neues Werk wurde allgemein sehr gelobt his new work was universally acclaimed; jdn/etw ~d erwähnen to commend sb/sth; das lob ich mir that's what I like (to see/hear *etc*); seinen Fleiß lob ich mir his diligence is most laudable; da lob ich mir doch ein gutes Glas Wein I always say you can't beat a good glass of wine; *siehe* Abend, Klee.
lobenswert, lobenswürdig *adj* praiseworthy, laudable.
lobesam *adj* (*obs*) virtuous.
Lobeshymne *f* (*fig*) hymn of praise, panegyric.
Lob-: ~gesang *m* song *or* hymn of praise; einen ~gesang auf jdn/etw anstimmen (*fig*) to sing sb's praises/the praises of sth; ~hudelei *f* (*pej*) gushing; l~hudeln *vi insep* jdm l~hudeln (*pej*) to gush over sb (*inf*).
löblich *adj* (*dated, iro*) commendable, laudable.
Lob-: ~lied *nt* song *or* hymn of praise; ein ~lied auf jdn/etw anstimmen *or* singen (*fig*) to sing sb's praises; ~preis *m* (*liter*) praise *no art*; l~preisen *vt insep ptp* l~(ge)priesen (*liter*) Gott to praise, to glorify; ~rede *f* eulogy, panegyric; eine ~rede auf jdn halten (*lit*) to make a speech in sb's honour; (*fig*) to eulogize *or* extol sb; sich in ~reden über jdn/etw ergehen to eulogize *or* extol sb/sth; ~redner *m* (*lit*) speaker; (*fig*) eulogist; l~singen *vi insep irreg ptp* l~gesungen +*dat* Gott to praise; (*fig*) to sing the praises of; ~spruch *m* eulogy (*über* +*acc* of), encomium (*form*); (*Gedicht*) panegyric.
Loch *nt* -(e)s, ̈-er (*Öffnung, Lücke*) hole; (*in Zahn auch*) cavity; (*in Reifen auch*) puncture; (*Luft~*) gap; (*Billard*) pocket; (*fig inf: elende Wohnung*) dump (*inf*), hole (*inf*); (*inf: Gefängnis*) jug (*sl*), clink (*sl*), can (*esp US sl*); (*vulg: Vagina*) cunt (*vulg*), hole (*sl*). sich (*dat*) ein ~ in den Kopf/ins Knie *etc* schlagen to gash one's head/knee *etc*, to cut one's head/knee *etc* open; jdm ein ~ *or* ̈-er in den Bauch fragen (*inf*) to pester the living daylights out of sb (with all one's questions) (*inf*); sich (*dat*) ein ~ *or* ̈-er in den Bauch reden (*inf*) to talk one's head off; sie redet einem ein ~ *or* ̈-er in den Bauch (*inf*) she could talk the hind legs off a donkey (*inf*); ein ~ *or* ̈-er in die Luft gucken *or* starren *or* in die Wand stieren (*inf*) to gaze into space *or* thin air; ein großes ~ in jds (Geld)beutel (*acc*) *or* Tasche (*acc*) reißen (*inf*) to make a big hole in sb's pocket; er machte ein ~ zu (*inf*) he robbed Peter to pay Paul (*prov*).
Loch|eisen *nt* punch.
lochen *vt* to punch holes/a hole in; to perforate; *Fahrkarte* to punch, to clip. gelochter Schreibblock tear-off file pad.
Locher *m* -s, - **(a)** punch. **(b)** (*Mensch*) punch-card operator.
löcherig *adj* full of holes, holey. ganz ~ sein to be full of holes.
löchern *vt* (*inf*) to pester (to death) with questions (*inf*). er löchert mich seit Wochen, wann ... he's been pestering me for weeks wanting to know when ...
Loch-: ~fraß *m* corrosion; ~kamera *f* pinhole camera; ~karte *f* punch card; ~kartenmaschine *f* punch card machine; ~säge *f* keyhole saw; ~stickerei *f* broderie anglaise; ~streifen *m* (punched) paper tape.
Lochung *f* punching; perforation.
Loch-: ~zange *f* punch; ~ziegel *m* airbrick.
Locke¹ *f* -, -n (*Haar*) curl. ~n haben to have curly hair.
Locke² *f* -, -n (*Pfeife*) (bird) call.
locken¹ *vtr* Haar to curl. gelocktes Haar curly hair.
locken² *vt* **(a)** *Tier* to lure. die Henne lockte ihre Küken the hen called to its chicks.
   (b) *jdn* to tempt; (*mit Ortsangabe*) to lure. es lockt mich in den Süden I can feel the call of the south; jdn in einen Hinterhalt ~ to lead *or* lure sb into a trap; das Angebot lockt mich sehr I'm very tempted by the offer; *siehe* Falle, Tasche.
löcken *vi*: wider den Stachel ~ (*geh*) to kick against the pricks.
lockend *adj* tempting, enticing, alluring.
Locken-: ~kopf *m* curly hairstyle; (*Mensch*) curlyhead; ~nadel *f* (*dated*) *siehe* Haarnadel; ~pracht *f* (*magnificent*) head of curls; ~schere *f* curling tongs *pl or* irons *pl* (*old*); ~stab *m* (electric) curling tongs *pl*; ~wickel, ~wickler *m* -s, - (*hair*-) curler; das Haar auf ~wickel drehen to put one's hair in curlers.
locker *adj* (*lit, fig*) loose; Schnee, Erdreich *auch* loose-packed; Kuchen, Schaum light; (*nicht gespannt*) slack; Haltung, Sitzweise relaxed; (*sl*) cool (*sl*). ~ werden (*lit, fig*) to get loose; (*Muskeln, Mensch*) to loosen up; (*Seil*) to get *or* go slack; (*Verhältnis*) to get more relaxed; (*Kuchen*) to be light; etw ~ machen to loosen sth/make sth light/slacken sth; jdn ~ machen to relax sb; etw ~ lassen to slacken sth off; *Bremse* to let sth off; ~ sitzen (*Ziegel, Schraube etc*) to be loose; (*Mensch*) to relax, to sit in a relaxed position; eine ~e Hand haben (*fig*) (*schnell züchtigen*) to be quick to hit out; (*beim Schreiben*) to have a flowing hand; bei ihr sitzt die Hand ziemlich ~ she's quick to lash out (*inf*); bei ihm sitzt der Revolver/das Messer ~ he's trigger-happy/he'd pull a knife at the slightest excuse; ein ~er Vogel (*inf*) *or* Zeisig (*dated inf*) a bit of a lad (*inf*) *or* rake (*dated*), a gay dog (*dated*); das mache ich ganz ~ (*sl*) I can do it just like that (*inf*); er hat ein ganz ~es Tor geschossen (*sl*) he scored a really slick goal (*inf*).
Lockerheit *f, no pl* looseness; (*von Kuchen etc*) lightness; (*von Seil etc*) slackness.
locker-: ~lassen *vi sep irreg* (*inf*) nicht ~lassen not to give *or* let up; ~machen *vt sep* (*inf*) Geld to shell out (*inf*), to part with; bei jdm 100 Mark ~machen to get sb to shell out (*inf*) *or* part with 100 marks.
lockern 1 *vt* **(a)** (*locker machen*) to loosen; *Griff auch* to relax;

Seil, (*lit, fig*) *Zügel* to slacken.
 (b) (*entspannen*) *Arme, Beine, Muskeln* to loosen up; (*fig*) *Vorschriften, Atmosphäre* to relax.
 2 *vr* to work itself loose; (*Sport*) to loosen up; (*zum Warmwerden*) to limber up; (*Verkrampfung, Spannung*) to ease off; (*Atmosphäre, Beziehungen, Mensch*) to get more relaxed.
Lockerung f *siehe vt* (a) loosening; relaxation; slackening. (b) loosening up; relaxation; (*von Beziehungen*) easing, relaxation.
Lockerungs-: ~**mittel** *nt* raising agent; ~**übung** f loosening up exercise; (*zum Warmwerden*) limbering-up exercise.
lockig *adj Haar* curly; *Mensch* curlyheaded.
Lock-: ~**mittel** *nt* lure; ~**pfeife** f (bird) call; (*für Hund*) whistle; ~**ruf** *m* call; ~**speise** f (*rare*) bait; ~**spitzel** *m* agent provocateur.
Lockung f lure; (*Versuchung*) temptation. **zur** ~ **der Käufer** to tempt customers.
Lockvogel *m* decoy (bird); (*fig*) lure, decoy.
Lode f -, -n sapling.
Loden *m* -s, - loden (cloth).
loden *adj* loden.
Lodenmantel *m* loden (coat).
lodern *vi* (*lit, fig*) to blaze; (*empor*~)to blaze up. **in seinen Augen loderte Haß/Gier** his eyes blazed with hatred/greed.
Löffel *m* -s, - (a) (*als Besteck*) spoon; (*als Maßangabe*) spoonful; (*von Bagger*) bucket. **den** ~ **abgeben** (*inf*) *or* **wegschmeißen** (*sl*) *or* **aus der Hand legen** (*inf*) to kick the bucket (*inf*); *siehe* **balbieren**.
 (b) (*Hunt*) ear; (*inf: von Mensch auch*) lug (*Brit sl*). **jdm ein paar hinter die** ~ **hauen** (*inf*), **jdm eins hinter die** ~ **geben** to give sb a clout round the ear(s); **sich** (*dat*) **etw hinter die** ~ **schreiben** (*inf*) to get sth into one's head (*inf*); **sperr doch deine** ~ **auf** (*inf*) pin back your lugholes (*Brit sl*), listen properly.
löffeln *vt* to spoon; (*mit der Kelle*) to ladle.
Löffel-: ~**stiel** *m* spoon-handle; l~**weise** *adv* by the spoonful.
Löffler *m* -s, - (*Zool*) spoonbill.
log *abbr of* **Logarithmus.**
log *pret of* **lügen.**
Log *nt* -s, -e (*Naut*) log.
Logarithmentafel f log table.
logarithmieren* **1** *vt* to find the log(arithm) of. **2** *vi* to find log(arithm)s/the log(arithm).
logarithmisch *adj* logarithmic.
Logarithmus *m* logarithm.
Logbuch *nt* log(book).
Loge ['lo:ʒə] f -, -n (a) (*Theat*) box. (b) (*Freimaurer*~) lodge. (c) (*Pförtner*~) lodge.
Logen- ['lo:ʒən-]: ~**bruder** *m* lodge brother; ~**meister** *m* master of a/the lodge; ~**platz** *m* (*Theat*) seat in a box; ~**schließer** *m* (*Theat*) box attendant.
Logger *m* -s, - (*Naut*) lugger.
Loggia ['lɔdʒa] f -, **Loggien** [-iən] (*Bogenhalle*) loggia; (*Balkon auch*) balcony.
Logglas *nt* log glass.
Logierbesuch [lo'ʒiːɐ̯-] *m* (*dated*) house-guest(s pl).
logieren* [lo'ʒiːrən] (*dated*) **1** *vi* to stay; (*als Zimmerherr*) to lodge. **2** *vt* **jdn** ~ to put sb up.
Logiergast [lo'ʒiːɐ̯-] *m* (*dated*) (*Besuch*) house-guest; (*Untermieter*) lodger.
Logik f logic. **in der** ~ in logic; **du hast vielleicht eine** ~! your logic is a bit quaint; **dieser Aussage fehlt die** ~ this statement is illogical *or* is lacking in logic.
Logiker(in f) *m* -s, - logician.
Logis [lo'ʒiː] *nt* -, - (*dated*) lodgings pl, rooms pl; (*Naut*) forecastle, crew's quarters pl. **Kost und** ~ board and lodging; **bei jdm in** *or* **zu** ~ **wohnen** to lodge with sb.
logisch *adj* logical; (*inf: selbstverständlich*) natural. **gehst du auch hin?** — ~ are you going too? — of course.
logischerweise *adv* logically.
Logistik f (a) (*Math*) logic. (b) (*Mil*) logistics sing.
Logleine f (*Naut*) logline.
logo *interj* (*sl*) you bet (*inf*).
Logopäde *m* -n, -n, **Logopädin** f speech therapist.
Logopädie f speech therapy.
Lohe¹ f -, -n (*liter*) raging flames pl.
Lohe² f -, -n (*Gerbrinde*) tan.
lohen¹ *vi* (*liter*) to blaze.
lohen² *vt Felle* to tan.
Loh-: ~**gerber** *m* tanner; ~**gerbung** f tanning.
Lohn *m* -(e)s, ⸚e (a) (*Arbeitsentgelt*) wage(s), pay **no pl, no indef art. wieviel** ~ **bekommst du?** how much do you get (paid)?, what are your wages?; **bei jdm in** ~ **und Brot stehen** (*old*) to be in sb's employ (*old*); **jdn in** ~ **und Brot nehmen** (*old*) to take sb into one's employ (*old*); **jdn um** ~ **und Brot bringen** (*old*) to deprive sb of a living *or* livelihood.
 (b) (*fig: Belohnung/Vergeltung*) reward; (*Strafe*) punishment. **als** *or* **zum** ~ **für ...** as a reward/punishment for ...; **sein verdienter** ~ one's just reward; **das ist nun der** ~ **für meine Mühe!** (*iro*), **das ist ein schlechter** ~ **für all die Mühe** that's what I get *or* that's all the thanks I get for my trouble.
Lohn-: ~**abbau** *m* reduction of earnings; l~**abhängig** *adj* on a payroll; ~**abhängige(r)** *mf* worker; ~**abkommen** *nt* wages *or* pay agreement; ~**abrechnung** f wages slip; *siehe* **Abrechnung**; ~**abzug** *m* deduction from one's wages; ~**arbeit** f labour; ~**ausfall** *m* loss of earnings; ~**ausgleich** *m* difference between sickness benefit and normal wages; ~**auszahlung** f payment of wages; ~**bewegung** f movement of wages; ~**buchhalter** *m* wages clerk; ~**buchhaltung** f wages accounting; wages office; ~**büro** *nt* wages office; ~**empfänger** *m* wage-earner.
lohnen 1 *vir* to be worthwhile, to be worth it. **es lohnt (sich), etw zu tun** it is worth *or* worthwhile doing sth; **die Mühe lohnt sich** it

---

is worth the effort, the effort is worthwhile: **der Film lohnt sich wirklich** the film is really worth seeing; **Fleiß lohnt sich immer** hard work always pays (off) *or* is always worthwhile; **das lohnt sich nicht für mich** it's not worth my while.
 2 *vt* (a) to be worth. **das Ergebnis lohnt die Mühe** the result makes all the effort worthwhile *or* amply repays all the effort; **das Museum lohnt einen Besuch** the museum is worth a visit *or* worth visiting.
 (b) **jdm etw** ~ to reward sb for sth; **er hat mir meine Hilfe mit Undank gelohnt** he repaid my help with ingratitude; **er hat mir meine Mühe schlecht gelohnt** he gave me poor thanks for my efforts.
löhnen **1** *vi* (*inf: viel bezahlen*) to pay up, to cough up (*inf*), to shell out (*inf*). **2** *vt* (*old: mit Lohn versehen*) to pay.
lohnend *adj* rewarding; (*nutzbringend*) worthwhile; (*einträglich*) profitable; (*sehens-/hörenswert*) worth seeing/hearing.
lohnenswert *adj* worthwhile. **es ist** ~, **etw zu tun** it is worth(-while) doing sth.
Lohn-: ~**erhöhung** f wage *or* pay rise, rise; ~**forderung** f wage demand *or* claim; ~**fortzahlung** f continued payment of wages; ~**gefälle** *nt* pay differential; ~**gruppe** f wage group; ~**herr** *m* (*old*) employer; ~**kürzung** f wage cut; ~**kutscher** *m* cabman, cabbie (*inf*); ~**liste** f payroll; ~**poker** *nt* (*fig*) wages haggling; ~**politik** f pay policy; ~-**Preis-Spirale** f (*Econ*) wage-price spiral; ~**satz** *m* rate of pay; ~**senkung** f cut in wages *or* pay; ~**skala** f pay *or* wages scale; ~**steuer** f income tax (*paid on earned income*).
Lohnsteuer-: ~**jahresausgleich** *m* annual adjustment of income tax; **beim letzten** ~**jahresausgleich habe ich 100 DM zurückbekommen** at the end of the last tax year I got back DM 100; ~**karte** f (income) tax card.
Lohn-: ~**stopp** *m* wages *or* pay freeze; ~**streifen** *m* pay slip; ~**tarif** *m* wage rate; ~**tüte** f pay packet.
Löhnung f (a) (*Auszahlung*) payment; (*auch* ~**stag** *m*) pay day. (b) (*Lohn*) pay.
Lohn-: ~**verhandlung** f pay *or* wage negotiations pl; ~**zahlung** f payment of wages; ~**zettel** *m* pay slip.
Loipe f -, -n cross-country ski run.
Lok f -, -s *abbr of* **Lokomotive** engine.
lokal *adj* (a) (*örtlich*) local. (b) (*Gram*) of place.
Lokal *nt* -s, -e (*Gaststätte*) pub (*esp Brit*), bar; (*auf dem Land auch*) inn (*Brit*); (*Restaurant*) restaurant. **das** ~ **verlassen** (*hum inf*) to leave.
Lokal- in cpds local; ~**anästhesie** f (*Med*) local anaesthesia; ~**augenschein** *m* (*Aus Jur*) *siehe* ~**termin**.
Lokale(s) *nt decl as adj* local news.
Lokalfernsehen *nt* local television.
Lokalisation f *siehe vt* (a) location. (b) localization; limiting.
lokalisieren* *vt* (a) (*Ort feststellen*) to locate. (b) (*Med*) to localize; (*auf einen Ort*) to limit (*auf +acc* to).
Lokalisierung f *siehe* **Lokalisation.**
Lokalität f (a) (*örtliche Beschaffenheit*) locality; (*Raum*) facilities pl. **sich mit den** ~**en auskennen** to know the district; **die** ~**en verlassen** to leave the premises.
 (b) (*hum inf: Lokal*) pub (*esp Brit*), bar.
 (c) (*hum inf: WC*) cloakroom (*euph*), washroom, bathroom (*US*). **ich muß hier mal die** ~ **aufsuchen** I must just inspect the plumbing (*hum inf*).
Lokal-: ~**kolorit** *nt* local colour; ~**nachrichten** pl local news sing; ~**patriotismus** *m* local patriotism; ~**reporter** *m* local reporter; ~**satz** *m* (*Gram*) (adverbial) clause of place; ~**stück** *nt* (*Theat*) play about a particular region; ~**teil** *m* local section; ~**termin** *m* (*Jur*) visit to the scene of the crime; ~**zeitung** f local newspaper.
Lokativ *m* (*Gram*) locative (case).
Lokführer *m* *abbr of* **Lokomotivführer.**
Lokomotive f locomotive, (railway) engine.
Lokomotiv-: ~**führer** *m* engine driver, engineer (*US*); ~**schuppen** *m* engine-shed.
Lokopreis *m* (*St Ex*) spot price.
Lokus *m* - *or* -ses, - *or* -se (*inf*) toilet, bathroom (*esp US*).
Lombard *m or nt* -(e)s, -e (*Fin*) loan on security.
Lombard-: ~**geschäft** *nt* loan on security; ~**satz** *m* rate for loans on security.
Longdrink ['lɔŋdrɪŋk] *m* long drink.
Longe ['lõːʒə] f -, -n (*für Pferde*) lunge; (*für Akrobaten*) harness.
longieren* [lõːˈʒiːrən] *vt Pferd* to lunge.
Look [lʊk] *m* -s, -s (*Mode*) look.
Looping ['luːpɪŋ] *m or nt* -s, -s (*Aviat*) looping the loop. **einen** ~ **machen** to loop the loop.
Lorbaß *m* -sses, -sse (*dial inf*) sly devil (*inf*), sharp one (*inf*).
Lorbeer *m* -s, -en (a) (*lit: Gewächs*) laurel; (*als Gewürz*) bayleaf; (~**kranz**) laurel wreath.
 (b) ~**en** pl (*fig: Erfolg*) laurels pl; **sich auf seinen** ~**en ausruhen** (*inf*) to rest on one's laurels; **seine ersten** ~**en ernten** to win one's first laurels; **damit kannst du keine** ~**en ernten** that's no great achievement.
Lorbeer-: ~**baum** *m* laurel (tree); ~**blatt** *nt* bayleaf; ~**kranz** *m* laurel wreath.
Lordose f -, -n (*Med*) lordosis (*spec*).
Lore f -, -n (a) (*Rail*) truck, wagon; (*Kipp*~) tipper, dumper. (b) (*Kohlenmaß: 200 Zentner*) 10,000 kilos (of coal).
Lorgnette [lɔrnˈjɛta] f lorgnette.
Lorgnon [lɔrnˈjõː] *nt* -s, -s lorgnon.
Los *nt* -es, -e (a) (*für Entscheidung*) lot; (*in der Lotterie, auf Jahrmarkt etc*) ticket. **das Große** ~ **gewinnen** *or* **ziehen** (*lit, fig*) to hit the jackpot; **etw durch das** ~ **entscheiden** *or* **bestimmen** *or* **ermitteln** to decide sth by drawing *or* casting lots; **jdn durch das** ~ **bestimmen** to pick sb by drawing lots; **etw durch das** ~ **gewinnen** to win sth in a lottery *or* (*bei Tombola*) raffle or (*auf*

los

Jahrmarkt) tombola; **das ~ hat mich getroffen** it fell to my lot.

(b) *no pl* (*Schicksal*) lot. **er hat ein hartes** *or* **schweres ~** his is a hard *or* not an easy lot; **das gleiche ~ erfahren** to share the same lot; **jds ~ teilen** to share sb's lot; **sein ~ ist nicht zu beneiden** his is an unenviable lot.

los 1 *adj pred* **(a)** (*nicht befestigt*) loose. **der Hund ist von der Leine ~** the dog is off the lead.

(b) (*frei*) **jdn/etw ~ sein** (*inf*) to be rid *or* shot (*inf*) of sb, to have got *or* gotten (*US*) rid of sb; **einer Sache** (*gen*) **~ und ledig sein** to be well and truly rid of sth; **ich bin mein ganzes Geld ~** (*inf*) I'm cleaned out (*inf*).

(c) (*inf*) **etwas ist ~/es ist nichts ~** (*geschieht*) there's something/nothing going on *or* happening; (*nicht in/in Ordnung*) there's something/nothing wrong *or* the matter; **mit jdm/etw ist etwas/nichts ~** there's something/nothing wrong *or* the matter with sb/sth; **mit jdm/etw ist nichts (mehr) ~** (*inf*) sb/sth isn't up to much (any more), sb/sth is a dead loss (now) (*inf*); **etwas ~ machen** (*sl*) to make sth happen; **was ist denn hier/da ~?** what's going on *or* what's up here/there (then)?; **was ist ~?** what's up?, what's wrong?, what's the matter?; **was ist da abends ~?** what is there going on there in the evenings?; **wo ist denn hier was ~?** where's the action here (*inf*)?; **als mein Vater das hörte, da war was ~!** when my father got to hear of it, you should have heard him.

2 *adv* **(a)** (*Aufforderung*) **~!** come on!; (*geh/lauf schon*) go on!, get going!; **nun aber ~!** let's get going; (*zu andern*) get going *or* moving (*inf*); **nichts wie ~!** let's get going; (**na**) **~, mach schon!** (come on,) get on with it; **~, nun frag doch endlich** (come on,) fire away!; **~, schreib/fahr etc doch endlich** come on, start writing/driving *etc*; **auf die Plätze** *or* **Achtung, fertig, ~** on your marks, get set, go!, ready, steady, go!

(b) (*weg*) **sie wollen ~ vom Reich/Kapitalismus** they want to break away from the Reich/capitalism; **wir wollen früh ~** we want to leave *or* to be off early.

los- *pref* +*vb* (*anfangen zu*) to start +*prp*; (*bei Verben der Bewegung auch*) *infin*+ (*befreien von, loslösen*) *infin*+ off.

-los *adj suf* -less.

lösbar *adj* soluble.

los-: ~bellen *vi sep* (*Hund*) to start barking; (*Mensch*) to start yelling; **~binden** *vt sep irreg* to untie (*von* from); **~brechen** *sep irreg* **1** *vt* to break off; **2** *vi aux sein* (*Gelächter etc*) to break out; (*Sturm, Gewitter*) to break; **~bröckeln** *vi sep aux sein* to crumble away.

Lösch-: ~arbeit *f usu pl* fire-fighting operations *pl*; **l~bar** *adj* **(a)** *Feuer, Flammen* extinguishable; *Kalk* slakable; *Durst* quenchable; *Schrift, Tonband* erasable; **die Hypothek/Schuld/Eintragung/das Konto ist l~bar** the mortgage/debt can be paid off/the entry can be deleted/the account can be closed; **(b)** (*Naut*) unloadable; **~blatt** *nt* sheet *or* piece of blotting paper; **~eimer** *m* fire-bucket.

löschen 1 *vt* **(a)** *Feuer, Brand, Flammen, Kerze* to put out, to extinguish; *Licht auch* to switch out *or* off, to turn out *or* off; *Kalk, Durst* to slake; *Durst* to quench; *Schrift (an Tafel), Tonband* to wipe *or* rub off, to erase; *Hypothek, Schuld* to pay off; *Eintragung* to delete; *Konto* to close; *Firma, Name* to strike off; (*aufsaugen*) *Tinte* to blot.

(b) (*Naut*) *Ladung* to unload.

2 *vi* **(a)** (*Feuerwehr etc*) to put out a/the fire.

(b) (*aufsaugen*) to blot.

(c) (*Naut*) to unload.

Löscher *m* -s, - (fire) extinguisher; **~kalk** *m* slaked lime; **Lösch-: ~fahrzeug** *nt* fire engine; **~mannschaft** *f* team of firemen/fire-fighters; **~mittel** *nt* (fire-)extinguishing agent; **~papier** *nt* (piece of) blotting paper.

Löschung *f* **(a)** (*von Schuld, Hypothek*) paying off; (*von Eintragung*) deletion; (*von Konto*) closing; (*von Firma, Namen*) striking off.

(b) (*von Ladung*) unloading.

Löschzug *m* set of fire-fighting appliances.

losdonnern *vi sep* (*lit, fig*) to start to thunder.

lose *adj* (*lit, fig*) loose; (*nicht gespannt*) *Seil* slack; (*schelmisch*) *Streich* mischievous. **etw ~ verkaufen** to sell sth loose; **du L~(r)** (*hum inf*), **du ~r Schelm** you devil (you); *siehe* **Maul, Zunge.**

Loseblatt|ausgabe *f* loose-leaf edition.

Lösegeld *nt* ransom (money).

los|eisen *sep* (*inf*) **1** *vt* to get *or* prise away (*von* from); **jdn von einer Verpflichtung/einer unangenehmen Stellung ~** to get sb out of an obligation/an awkward position. **2** *vr* to get away (*bei* from); (*von Verpflichtung etc*) to get out (*von* of).

losen[1] *vi* to draw lots (*um* for). **wir ~, wer ...** we'll draw lots to decide who ...

losen[2] *vi* (*S Ger, Aus, Sw*) to listen.

lösen 1 *vt* **(a)** (*losmachen, abtrennen, entfernen*) to remove (*von* from); *Boot* to cast off (*von* from); (*ab~*) *Fleisch, Briefmarken, Tapete etc auch* to get off (*von etw* sth); (*heraus~ auch*) to get out (*aus* of); (*aufbinden*) *Knoten, Fesseln, Gürtel, Haare* to undo; *Arme* to unfold; *Hände* to unclasp; *Handbremse* to take or let off; *Husten, Krampf* to ease; *Muskeln* to loosen up; (*lit, fig: lockern*) to loosen. **sie löste ihre Hand aus der seinen** she slipped her hand out of his; *siehe* **gelöst.**

(b) (*klären, Lösung finden für*) to solve; *Konflikt, Schwierigkeiten* to resolve.

(c) (*annullieren*) *Vertrag* to cancel; *Verlobung* to break off; *Verbindung, Verhältnis* to sever; *Ehe* to dissolve.

(d) (*zergehen lassen*) to dissolve.

(e) (*kaufen*) *Karte* to buy, to get.

2 *vr* **(a)** (*sich losmachen*) to detach oneself (*von* from); (*sich*

---

ab~ auch) to come off (*von etw* sth); (*Knoten, Haare*) to come undone; (*Schuß*) to go off; (*Husten, Krampf, Spannung*) to ease; (*Schleim, Schmutz*) to loosen; (*Atmosphäre*) to relax; (*Muskeln*) to loosen up; (*lit, fig: sich lockern*) to (be)come loose. **sich von etw ~** (*weggehen*) to break away from sb; **sich von etw ~** *von Verpflichtungen* to free oneself of sth; *von Vorstellung, Vorurteilen, Gedanken* to rid oneself of sth; *von Partnern, Vaterland, Vergangenheit* to break with sth *or* away from sth; **das Boot hat sich von der Verankerung gelöst** the boat has broken (away from) its moorings; **nur ungern löste sie sich aus seinen Armen** it was with reluctance that she freed herself from his arms; **eine Gestalt löste sich aus der Dunkelheit** (*liter*) a figure detached itself *or* emerged from the darkness.

(b) (*sich aufklären*) to be solved. **sich von selbst ~** (*Mordfall*) to solve itself; (*Problem auch*) to clear itself up, to resolve itself; **es hat sich alles zum Guten gelöst** it has all come out right in the end.

(c) (*zergehen*) to dissolve (*in* + *dat* in). **ihre Anspannung/ihr Schmerz löste sich in Tränen** her tension/pain found relief in tears.

los-: ~fahren *vi sep irreg aux sein* **(a)** (*abfahren*) to set off; (*Fahrzeug*) to move off; (*Auto*) to drive off; **(b)** (*inf: schimpfen, anfallen*) **auf jdn ~fahren** to lay into sb (*inf*), to attack sb; **~gehen** *vi sep irreg aux sein* **(a)** (*weggehen*) to set off; (*Schuß, Bombe etc*) to go off; (*mit dem Messer*) **auf jdn ~gehen** to go for sb (with a knife); (*Geschrei or Menge*) to go up; **gleich geht's ~** it's just about to start; (*bei Streit*) any minute now; **jetzt geht's ~!** here we go!; (*Vorstellung*) it's starting; (*Rennen*) they're off!; (*Reise, Bewegung*) we're/you're off!; **jetzt geht's wieder ~** (*mit ihren Klagen*) here we go again (with all her moans); **geht's bald ~?** will it start soon? (*Reise etc*) are we off soon?; **bei drei geht's ~** you/they *etc* start on the count of three; **jetzt geht's aber ~!** (*sl*) you're kidding! (*inf*); (*bei Frechheit*) do you mind!; **(c)** (*inf: abgehen*) to come off; **~haben** *vt sep irreg* (*inf*) **etwas/nichts ~haben** to be pretty clever (*inf*)/pretty stupid (*inf*); **~heulen** *vi sep* to burst out crying; **~kaufen** *vt sep* to buy out; *Entführten* to ransom; **~knüpfen** *vt sep* to untie, to undo; **~kommen** *vi sep irreg aux sein* (*Mensch*) to get away (*von* from); (*sich befreien*) to free oneself, to get free (*von* from); **das Flugzeug kam vom Boden ~/nicht ~** the plane left the ground/couldn't get off the ground; **das Boot kam von der Sandbank ~/nicht ~** the boat came off/wouldn't come off the sandbank; **von Schulden ~kommen** to get out of debt; **~kriegen** *vt sep* (*inf*) (*ablösen*) to get off; (*~werden*) *Mensch* to get rid *or* shot (*inf*) of; **~lachen** *vi sep* to burst out laughing; **laut ~lachen** to laugh out loud; **~lassen** *vt sep irreg* **(a)** (*nicht mehr festhalten*) to let go of; (*fig: nicht fesseln*) *Mensch* to let go; **der Gedanke/die Frage etc läßt mich nicht mehr ~** the thought/problem haunts me *or* won't go out of my mind; **das Buch läßt mich nicht mehr ~** I can't put the book down; **(b)** (*inf: abfeuern*) *Feuerwerk, Bombe* to let off; (*fig*) *Rede, Witze, Geschichte* to come out with; *Beschwerden, Schimpfkanonade* to launch into; *Schrift* to launch; *Brief* to send off; **(c)** **jdn (auf jdn) ~lassen** (*fig inf*) to let sb loose (on sb); **die Hunde auf jdn ~lassen** to put *or* set the dogs on(to) sb; **und so was läßt man nun auf die Menschheit ~!** (*hum inf*) what a thing to unleash on an unsuspecting world; **wehe, wenn sie ~gelassen ...** (*hum inf*) once let them off the leash ...; **~laufen** *vi sep irreg aux sein* (*zu laufen anfangen*) to start to run; (*weggehen*) to run out; **~legen** *vi sep* (*inf*) to get going *or* started; (*mit Schimpfen*) to let fly (*inf*) *or* rip (*inf*); **er legte gleich mit seinen Ideen ~** he started on about his ideas; **nun leg mal ~ und erzähle ...** now come on and tell me/us ...

löslich *adj* soluble. **leicht/schwer ~** readily/not readily soluble.

los-: ~lösen *sep* **1** *vt* to remove (*von* from); (*ablösen auch*) to take off (*von etw* sth); (*herauslösen auch*) to take out (*aus* of); (*lockern*) to loosen; **2** *vr* to detach oneself (*von* from); (*sich ablösen auch*) to come off (*von etw* sth); (*lockern*) to become loose; **sich von jdm ~lösen** to break away from sb; **Schottland will sich von Großbritannien ~lösen** Scotland wants to break away from Great Britain; **~machen** *sep* **1** *vt* to free; (*~binden*) to untie; *Handbremse* to let *or* take off; **jdn von einer Kette ~machen** to unchain sb; **2** *vi* **(a)** (*Naut*) to cast off; **(b)** (*inf: sich beeilen*) to step on it (*inf*), to get a move on (*inf*); **3** *vr* to get away (*von* from); **der Hund hat sich ~gemacht** the dog has got loose.

Losnummer *f* ticket number.

los-: ~platzen *vi sep aux sein* (*inf*) (*lachen*) to burst out laughing; (*spontan, vorzeitig äußern*) to start yapping (*inf*); **mit etw ~platzen** to burst out with sth; **platz nicht immer gleich ~** think before you speak; **mußt du immer gleich ~platzen!** can't you keep your mouth shut for two minutes?; **~prusten** *vi sep* (*inf*) to explode (with laughter); **~quatschen** *vi sep* (*inf*) to prattle away (*inf*); **~rasen** *vi sep aux sein* (*inf*) to race *or* tear off; **~reißen** *sep irreg* **1** *vt* to tear *or* rip off (*von etw* sth)/down (*von* from)/out (*aus* of)/up; **jdn ~reißen** to tear sb away; **2** *vr* **sich (von etw) ~reißen** (*Hund etc*) to break free *or* loose (*von* sth); (*fig*) to tear oneself away (*from* sth); **~rennen** *vi sep irreg aux sein* (*inf*) to run off; (*anfangen zu laufen*) to start to run.

Löß *m* -es *or* -sse, -e *or* -sse (*Geol*) loess.

lossagen *vr* **sich von etw ~** to renounce sth; **sich von jdm/seiner Vergangenheit ~** to dissociate oneself from *or* break with sb/the *or* one's past.

Lossagung *f siehe vr* renunciation (*von* of); dissociation (*von* from).

Lößboden *m* loess soil.

los-: ~schicken *vt sep* to send off; **~schießen** *vi sep irreg* **(a)** (*zu schießen anfangen*) to open fire; **schieß ~!** (*fig inf*) fire away! (*inf*); **(b)** *aux sein* (*schnell starten*) to shoot *or* race off; **auf jdn ~schießen** to race towards sb; **~schlagen** *sep irreg* **1** *vi* to hit out; (*Mil*) to (launch one's) attack; **auf jdn/aufeinander**

~schlagen to go for sb/one another or each other; 2 vt (a) (abschlagen) to knock off; (b) (inf: verkaufen) to get rid of; ~schnallen vt sep to unbuckle; ~schrauben vt sep to unscrew; (lockern auch) to loosen; ~springen vi sep irreg aux sein to jump; auf jdn/etw ~springen to leap for sb/sth; ~steuern vi sep aux sein auf jdn/etw ~steuern to head or make for sb/sth; ~stürzen vi sep aux sein to rush off; auf jdn/etw ~stürzen to pounce on sb/sth.

Lost m -(e)s, no pl (Chem) mustard gas.

los-: ~tigern vi sep aux sein (inf) to toddle off (inf); ~trennen vt sep siehe abtrennen.

Lostrommel f drum (containing lottery tickets).

Losung¹ f (a) (Devise, Parole) motto. (b) (Kennwort) password.

Losung² f (Hunt) droppings pl.

Lösung f (a) solution (gen to); (das Lösen) solution (gen of); (eines Konfliktes, von Schwierigkeiten) resolving. **zur ~ dieser Schwierigkeiten** to resolve these problems. (b) (Annullierung) (eines Vertrages) cancellation; (von Beziehungen, einer Verlobung) breaking off; (von Verbindung, eines Verhältnisses) severing, severance; (einer Ehe) dissolving. (c) (Chem) solution.

Lösungsmittel nt solvent.

Lösungswort nt password.

Losverkäufer m ticket seller (for lottery, raffle etc).

loswerden vt sep irreg aux sein to get rid of; Gedanken to get away from, to get out of one's mind; Angst etc auch to rid oneself of; Hemmungen auch, Geld (beim Spiel etc), Hab und Gut to lose; Geld (ausgeben) to spend. **er wird seine Erkältung einfach nicht los** he can't shake off or get rid of his cold.

losziehen vi sep irreg aux sein (a) (aufbrechen) to set out or off (in + acc, nach for). (b) **gegen jdn/etw ~** (inf) to lay into sb/sth (inf).

Lot¹ nt -(e)s, -e (a) (Senkblei) plumbline; (Naut auch) sounding line. **im ~ sein** to be in plumb.
(b) (old) old unit of weight varying between 16 and 50 gram.
(c) (Lötmetall) solder.
(d) (Math) perpendicular. **das ~ fällen** to drop a perpendicular; **seine Finanzen wieder ins ~ bringen** to put one's finances back on an even keel; **die Sache ist wieder im ~** things have been straightened out; **die Sache wieder ins (rechte) ~ bringen** to put things right, to put the record straight (inf); **mit ihm ist etwas nicht im ~** he is rather out of sorts.

Lot² m -s (Bibl) Lot.

Löt|apparat m soldering appliance.

lötbar adj solderable.

löten vt to plumb.

löten vti to solder.

Lothringen nt -s Lorraine.

Lothringer(in f) m -s, - Lorrainer. **~ Kreuz** Cross of Lorraine.

lothringisch adj of Lorraine, Lorrainese.

Lotion [lo'tsio:n] f -, -en lotion.

Löt-: ~kolben m soldering iron; ~lampe f blowlamp.

Lotleine f plumbline.

Lötmetall nt solder.

Lotophage [loto'fa:gə] m -n, -n (Myth) lotus-eater.

Lotos m -, - lotus.

Lotos-: ~blume f lotus (flower); ~sitz m lotus position.

lotrecht adj (Math) perpendicular.

Lotrechte f (Math) perpendicular.

Lotrohr nt blowpipe.

Lotse m -n, -n (Naut) pilot; (Flug~) air-traffic or flight controller; (Aut) navigator; (fig) guide.

lotsen vt to guide; Schiff auch to pilot. **jdn irgendwohin ~** (inf) to drag sb somewhere (inf); siehe Geld.

Lotsen-: ~boot nt pilot boat; ~dienst m pilot service; (Aut) driver-guide service; ~geld nt pilotage; ~zwang m compulsory pilotage; **auf dieser Strecke besteht ~zwang** all boats must carry a pilot on this stretch.

Löt-: ~stein m sal ammoniac block; ~stelle f soldered point.

Lotte f - abbr of Charlotte.

Lotter-: ~bett nt (old, hum) old bed; ~bube m (old, hum) wastrel.

Lotterie f lottery; (Tombola) raffle.

Lotterie-: ~gewinn m lottery/raffle prize or (Geld) winnings pl; ~los nt lottery/raffle ticket; ~spiel nt (lit) lottery; (fig) gamble.

lott(e)rig adj (inf) (a) slovenly no adv; Mensch, Arbeit auch sloppy (inf). ~ **herumlaufen** to go around looking a mess (inf). (b) (S Ger, Sw) ramshackle (inf); (lose) loose, wobbly.

Lotterleben nt (inf) dissolute life.

lottern vi (inf) (a) to lead a dissolute life. (b) (S Ger, Sw: lose sein) to wobble.

Lotterwirtschaft f (inf) muddle, slovenly mess.

Lotto nt -s, -s (a) national lottery. **(im) ~ spielen** to do the national lottery; **du hast wohl im ~ gewonnen** you must have won the pools (Brit). (b) (Gesellschaftsspiel) lotto.

Lotto-: ~geschäft nt, ~laden m (inf) Lotto agency; ~gewinn m Lotto win; (Geld) Lotto winnings pl; ~schein m Lotto coupon; ~- **und Totoannahmestelle** f Lotto and football pools agency; ~zahlen pl winning Lotto numbers pl.

lottrig adj (inf) siehe lott(e)rig.

Lotung f plumbing.

Lötung f (das Löten) soldering; (Lötstelle) soldered joint.

Lotus m -, - (Bot) (a) (Hornklee) birdsfoot trefoil. (b) siehe Lotos.

Lötzinn m solder.

Louis ['lu:i] m - ['lu:i(s)], - ['lu:is] (sl) ponce (inf), pimp.

Louisdor [lui'do:ɐ] m -s, -e or (bei Zahlenangaben) - (Hist) louis (d'or).

Löwe m -n, -n lion. **der ~** (Astron) Leo, the Lion; (Astrol) Leo;

---

im Zeichen des ~n geboren sein to have been born under (the sign of) Leo; **~ sein** to be (a) Leo; **sich in die Höhle des ~n begeben** (inf) to beard the lion in his den (prov).

Löwen-: ~anteil m (inf) lion's share; ~bändiger m lion-tamer; ~grube f (Bibl) lions' den; ~herz nt: Richard ~herz m Richard (the) Lionheart; ~jagd f lion hunt; ~mähne f (lit) lion's mane; (fig) flowing mane; ~maul nt, ~mäulchen nt snapdragon, antirrhinum; ~mut m (liter) leonine courage (liter); **mit ~mut** as brave as a lion; ~zahn m dandelion.

Löwin f lioness.

loyal [loa'ja:l] adj loyal (jdm gegenüber to sb). **einen Vertrag ~ auslegen** to interpret a contract faithfully.

Loyalität [loajali'tɛ:t] f loyalty (jdm gegenüber to sb).

LP [ɛl'pe:] f -, -s LP.

LP-Album [ɛl'pe:-] nt album, LP.

LPG [ɛlpe:'ge:] f -, -s (DDR) abbr of Landwirtschaftliche Produktionsgenossenschaft.

LSD [ɛlɛs'de:] nt -(s) LSD.

lt. abbr of laut².

lübisch adj (Hist) of Lübeck.

Luch f -, -e or nt -(e)s, -e (dial) marsh.

Luchs [luks] m -es, -e lynx. **Augen wie ein ~ haben** (inf) to have eyes like a lynx or hawk.

Luchs|augen pl (inf) eagle eyes pl.

luchsen ['luksn] vi (inf) to peep. **er luchste, um zu sehen ... he had a peep to see...**

Lücke f -, -n (lit, fig) gap; (zwischen Wörtern auch, auf Formularen etc) space; (Ungereimtheit, Unvollständigkeit etc) hole; (Gesetzes~) loophole; (in Versorgung) break. ~n (im Wissen) haben to have gaps in one's knowledge; **sein Tod hinterließ eine schmerzliche ~** (geh) his death has left a void in our lives.

Lücken-: ~büßer m (inf) stopgap; ~büßer spielen to be used as a stopgap; l~haft adj full of gaps; Bericht, Sammlung, Beweis etc auch incomplete; Kenntnisse auch sketchy; Versorgung deficient; Gesetz, Alibi full of holes; **sein Wissen ist sehr l~haft** there are great gaps in his knowledge; ~haftigkeit f siehe adj incompleteness; sketchiness; deficiency; wegen der ~haftigkeit des Berichts/des Gesetzes because of all the gaps in the report/loop-holes in the law; l~los adj complete; Kenntnisse, (Mil) Abwehr perfect; Versorgung, Überlieferung unbroken; ~losigkeit f siehe adj completeness; perfection; unbrokenness; ~test m (Sch) completion test.

Lucullus m - siehe Lukull.

lud pret of laden¹, laden².

Lude m -n, -n (sl) ponce (inf), pimp.

Luder nt -s, - (a) (Hunt: Aas) bait. (b) (inf) minx. **armes/dummes ~** poor/stupid creature; **so ein ordinäres ~!** what a common little hussy!

Luderjan m -(e)s, -e (inf) siehe Liederjan.

Ludwig m - Ludwig; (frz. Königsname) Louis.

Lues ['lu:ɛs] f -, no pl (Med) syphilis, lues (spec).

luetisch ['lue:tɪʃ] adj (Med) syphilitic, luetic (spec).

Luft f -, (liter) ⁻e (a) air no pl. **die ~e** pl (liter) the skies, the air sing; **frische ~ hereinlassen** to let some fresh air in; **im Zimmer ist schlechte ~** the room is stuffy, the air or it is stuffy in the room; **bei schlechter ~ kann ich nicht schlafen** I can't sleep when it's stuffy; **dicke ~** (inf) a bad atmosphere; ~ (acc) **kommen lassen** to let the air get to sth; **an or in die/der (frischen) ~** in the fresh air; **an die (frische) ~ gehen/kommen, (frische) ~ schnappen** (inf) or **schöpfen** (geh) to get out in the fresh air, to get some fresh air; **frische ~ in etw bringen** (fig) to breathe new life into sth; **die ~ ist rein** (inf) the coast is clear; **die ~ reinigen** (lit, fig) to clear the air; **jetzt ist das Flugzeug in der ~** the plane is now airborne or in the air; **aus der ~** from the air; **die ~ aus etw lassen** to let the air out of sth; **jdn an die (frische) ~ setzen** (inf) to show sb the door; (Sch) to send sb out; (entlassen) to give sb the push (inf); **in die ~ fliegen** (inf) to explode, to go up; **etw in die ~ jagen** (inf) or **sprengen** to blow sth up; **gleich** or **leicht** or **schnell in die ~ gehen** (fig) to be quick to blow one's top (inf), to be very explosive; **es liegt ein Gewitter/etwas in der ~** there's a storm brewing/something in the air; **in die ~ starren** or **gucken** to stare into space or thin air; **jdn/etw in der ~ zerreißen** (inf) to tear sb/sth to pieces; **das kann sich doch nicht in ~ auflöst haben** it can't have vanished into thin air; **in der ~ hängen** (Sache) to be (very much) up in the air; (Mensch) to be in (a state of) limbo, to be dangling; **die Behauptung ist aus der ~ gegriffen** this statement is (a) pure invention; **vor Freude in die ~ springen** to jump for or with joy; **von ~ und Liebe/von ~ leben** to live on love/air; **jdn wie ~ behandeln** to treat sb as though he/she just didn't exist; **er ist ~ für mich** I'm not speaking to him.
(b) (Atem) breath. **der Kragen schnürt mir die ~ ab** this collar is choking me, I can't breathe in this collar; **nach ~ schnappen** to gasp for breath or air; **die ~ anhalten** (lit) to hold one's breath; **nun halt mal die ~ an!** (inf) (rede nicht!) hold your tongue!, put a sock in it! (inf); (übertreibe nicht!) come off it! (inf), come on! (inf); **keine ~ mehr kriegen** not to be able to breathe; **tief ~ holen** (lit, fig) to take a deep breath; ... **da mußte ich erst mal tief ~ holen** (fig: war perplex) it really made me gasp; **mir blieb vor Schreck/Schmerz die ~ weg** I was breathless with shock/pain; **wieder ~ bekommen** or **kriegen/haben** (nach Sport etc) to get/have got one's breath back; (nach Schnupfen etc) to be able to breathe again; (fig) to get/have a chance to catch one's breath.
(c) (Wind) breeze. **linde/laue ⁻e** (liter) gentle/warm breezes; **sich** (dat) **~ machen** (fächeln) to fan oneself; **sich** (dat) **~ machen** (fig), **seinem Herzen ~ machen** to get everything off one's chest; **seinem Ärger/Zorn etc ~ machen** to give vent to one's annoyance/anger etc.

(d) (fig: Spielraum, Platz) space, room. **zwischen Wand und Regal etwas ~ lassen** to leave a space between the wall and the bookcase; **so langsam wird hier ~** we're beginning to get some space or room in here.

Luft-: **~abwehr** f (Mil) anti-aircraft defence; **~alarm** m air-raid alarm; **~angriff** m air-raid (auf + acc on); **einen ~angriff auf eine Stadt fliegen** to bomb a town, to carry out an air-raid on a town; **~aufklärung** f aerial reconnaissance; **~aufnahme** f aerial photo(graph); **~bad** nt (dated) **ein ~bad nehmen** to get some fresh air; **~ballon** m balloon; **~bewegung** f movement of the air; **~bild** nt aerial picture; **~bläschen** [-blɛːsçən] nt (Anat) air-sac; **~blase** f air bubble, bubble of air; **~bremse** f air-brake; **~brücke** f airlift; **über eine ~brücke** by airlift.

Lüftchen nt breeze.

Luft-: **l~dicht** adj airtight no adv; **die Ware ist l~dicht verpackt** the article is in airtight packaging; **ein l~dicht verschlossener Behälter** an airtight container, a container with an airtight seal; **~druck** m air pressure; **~druckwelle** f (Met) pressure wave; (Knallwelle) blast; **l~durchlässig** adj pervious to air; **~durchlässigkeit** f perviousness to air.

lüften 1 vt **(a)** to air; (ständig, systematisch) to ventilate. **(b)** (hochheben) Hut, Schleier to raise, to lift. **2** vi (Luft hereinlassen) to let some air in; (Betten, Kleider etc) to air.

Luftfahrt f aeronautics sing (mit Flugzeugen) aviation no art.

Luftfahrt-: **~karte** f aviation chart; **~medizin** f aeromedicine; **~schau** f air show.

Luft-: **~fahrzeug** nt aircraft; **~feuchtigkeit** f (atmospheric) humidity; **~filter** m or nt air filter; **~flotte** f air fleet; **~fracht** f air freight; **~geist** m (Myth) spirit of the air; **l~gekühlt** adj air-cooled; **l~getrocknet** adj air-dried; **~gewehr** nt air-rifle, airgun; **~hauch** m (geh) gentle breeze; **~heizung** f hot-air heating; **~herrschaft** f air supremacy; **~hoheit** f air sovereignty; **~hülle** f mantle of air; **l~hungrig** adj longing for fresh air; **ein l~hungriger Mensch** a fresh-air fanatic.

luftig adj Zimmer airy; Plätzchen breezy; Kleidung light. **in ~er Höhe** (liter) at a dizzy height.

Luftikus m -(es), -se (inf) happy-go-lucky sort of fellow.

Luft-: **~kampf** m air or aerial battle; **~kissen** nt air cushion; (von ~kissenboot) cushion of air; **~kissenboot**, **~kissenfahrzeug** nt hovercraft; **~klappe** f ventilation flap; **~koffer** m lightweight (suit)case; **~korridor** m air corridor; **~kreuz** nt, **~kreuzung** f centre of air routes; **~krieg** m aerial warfare; **~- und Seekrieg** warfare at sea and in the air; **~kühlung** f air-cooling; **~kurort** m (climatic) health resort; **~landetruppe** f airborne troops pl; **l~leer** adj (völlig) **l~leer sein** to be a vacuum; **l~leerer Raum** vacuum; **~linie** f **200 km etc ~linie** 200 km etc as the crow flies; **~loch** nt airhole; (Aviat) air pocket; **~masche** f (Sew) chain-stitch; **~massen** pl air masses pl; **~matratze** f airbed, lilo ®; **~pirat** m (aircraft) hijacker, skyjacker (esp US); **~piraterie** f (aircraft) hijacking, skyjacking (esp US).

Luftpost f airmail. **mit ~** by airmail.

Luftpost-: **~leichtbrief** m aerogramme, airletter (Brit); **~papier** nt airmail paper.

Luft-: **~pumpe** f air or pneumatic pump; (für Fahrrad) (bicycle) pump; **~raum** m airspace; **~recht** nt air traffic law; **~reifen** m pneumatic tyre; **~reiniger** m air purifier; **~röhre** f (Anat) windpipe, trachea; **~sack** m (Aut) air bag; (Orn) air sac; **~schacht** m ventilation shaft; **~schaukel** f swingboat; **~schicht** f (Met) layer of air; **~schiff** nt airship; **~schiffahrt** f aeronautics sing; **~schiffer** m (dated) airship pilot; **~schlacht** f air battle; **die ~schlacht um England** the Battle of Britain; **~schlange** f (paper) streamer; **~schlitz** m (Aut) ventilation slit; **~schloß** nt (fig) castle in the air, pipe dream; **~schlösser bauen** to build castles in the air; **~schneise** f air lane; **~schraube** f propeller, airscrew.

Luftschutz m anti-aircraft defence.

Luftschutz-: **~bunker**, **~keller**, **~raum** m air-raid shelter; **~übung** f air-raid drill; **~wart** m air-raid warden.

Luft-: **~sieg** m air victory; **~sperre** f (Mil) aerial barrage; **~spiegelung** f mirage; **~sprung** m jump in the air; **vor Freude einen ~sprung or ~sprünge machen** to jump for or with joy; **~straße** f air route; **~streitkräfte** pl air force sing; **~strom** m stream of air; **~strömung** f current of air; **~stützpunkt** m air base; **~tanken** nt in-flight refuelling; **~taxi** nt air taxi; **~temperatur** f air temperature; **~torpedo** m aerial torpedo; **l~trocken** adj air-dry; **~überwachung** f air surveillance; **~- und Raumfahrtindustrie** f aerospace industry; **~- und Raumfahrttechnik** f aerospace technology.

Lüftung f airing; (ständig, systematisch) ventilation.

Lüftungs-: **~klappe** f ventilation flap; **~schacht** m siehe **Luftschacht**.

Luft-: **~unterstützung** f (Mil) air support; **~veränderung** f change of air; **~verflüssigung** f liquefaction of air; **~verkehr** m air traffic; **~verkehrsgesellschaft** f airline; **~verkehrslinie** f air route; **~verpestung** f (pej); **~verschmutzung** f air pollution; **~versorgung** f air supplies pl; **~verteidigung** f air defence; **~waffe** f (Mil) air force; **die (deutsche) ~waffe** the Luftwaffe; **~weg** m (Flugweg) air route; (Atemweg) respiratory tract; **etw auf dem ~weg befördern** to transport by air; **~widerstand** m air resistance; **~zufuhr** f air supply; **~zug** m wind, (mild) breeze; (in Gebäude) draught.

Lug m: **~ und Trug** lies pl (and deception).

Lüge f -, -n lie, fib (euph inf), falsehood. **jdn einer ~ beschuldigen** to accuse sb of lying; **das ist alles ~** that's all lies; **jdn/etw ~n strafen** to give the lie to sb/sth; **~n haben kurze Beine** (prov) truth will out (prov).

lugen vi (dial) to peep, to peek.

lügen pret **log**, ptp **gelogen 1** vi to lie, to fib (euph inf). **ich müßte ~, wenn ...** I would be lying if ...; **wie gedruckt ~** (inf)

lie like mad (inf); **wer einmal lügt, dem glaubt man nicht, und wenn er auch die Wahrheit spricht** (Prov) remember the boy who cried 'wolf' (prov). **2** vt **das ist gelogen!, das lügst du doch!** (inf) that's a lie!, you're lying!; siehe **Blaue²**.

Lügen-: **~bericht** m fabrication; **~bold** m -(e)s, -e (dated inf) (inveterate) liar; **~detektor** m lie detector; **~dichtung** f, no pl tall story/stories; (Gattung) Munchausen-type stories pl; **~feldzug** m siehe **~kampagne**; **~gebäude** or **~gespinst** (geh) or **~gewebe** (liter) nt tissue or web of lies; **~geschichte** f pack of lies; **l~haft** adj Erzählung made-up, mendacious (form); Bericht auch false; **seine l~haften Geschichten** his tall stories; **~haftigkeit** f siehe adj mendacity (form), mendaciousness (form); falseness; **~kampagne** f campaign of lies; **~maul** nt (pej) liar; **~märchen** nt tall story, cock-and-bull story; **~propaganda** f propagandist lies pl, mendacious propaganda.

Lügerei f lying no pl, fibbing no pl.

Lügner(in f) m -s, - liar.

lügnerisch adj Mensch lying attr, untruthful, mendacious.

Lukas m - Luke.

Lukas|evangelium nt Gospel according to St. Luke, St. Luke's Gospel.

Luke f -, -n hatch; (Dach~) skylight.

lukrativ adj lucrative.

Lukull m -, **Lukullus** m - (lit) Lucullus; (fig: gen **Lukulls**) epicure, gourmet, gastronome.

lukullisch adj epicurean.

Lulatsch m -(es), -e (hum inf) **langer ~** beanpole (inf).

Lulle f -, -n (sl) fag (Brit inf), cig (inf), gasper (Brit sl).

lullen vt (dated) **ein Kind in den Schlaf ~** to lull a child to sleep.

Luller m -s, - (dial) comforter (esp US), dummy (Brit).

Lumbago f -, no pl lumbago.

lumbecken vt (Typ) to adhesive-bind.

Lumberjack ['lʌmbəʤæk] m -s, -s (dated) lumber jacket.

Lumme f -, -n guillemot.

Lümmel m -s, - (pej) **(a)** lout, oaf. **du ~, du** you rascal or rogue you. **(b)** (hum: Penis) willie (inf).

Lümmelei f (inf) sprawling about; (Flegelei) rudeness no pl.

lümmelhaft adj (pej) ill-mannered.

lümmeln vr (inf) to sprawl; (sich hin~) to flop down.

Lump m -en, -en (pej) rogue, blackguard (dated).

lumpen 1 vt (inf) **sich nicht ~ lassen** to splash out (inf). **2** vi (old, dial) to go/be out on the tiles (inf).

Lumpen m -s, - a) rag. **(b)** (S Ger: Lappen) cloth.

Lumpen-: **~gesindel** nt (pej) rabble pl (pej), riffraff pl (pej); **~händler(in** f) m rag-and-bone man/woman; **~hund**, **~kerl** m (sl) bastard (sl); **~pack** nt (pej) siehe **~gesindel**; **~proletariat** nt (Sociol) lumpenproletariat; **~sammler** m (a) siehe **~händler**; **(b)** (hum) last bus/tram/train, drunks' special (hum).

Lumperei f (inf) mean or dirty trick.

lumpig adj **(a)** Kleidung ragged, tattered. **~ herumlaufen** to go around in rags. **(b)** Gesinnung, Tat shabby, mean. **(c)** attr (inf: geringfügig) paltry, measly (inf). **~e 10 Mark** 10 paltry or measly (inf) marks.

Lunatiker(in f) m -s, - (Psych) sleepwalker, somnambulist (form).

lunatisch adj (Psych) sleepwalking attr, somnambulistic (form).

Lunatismus m (Psych) sleepwalking, somnambulism (form).

Lunch [lanʃ, lantʃ] m -(es) or -s, -e(s) or -s lunch, luncheon (form).

lunchen ['lanʃn, 'lantʃn] vi (geh) to lunch (form).

Lüneburger Heide f Lüneburg Heath.

Lunge f -, -n lungs pl; (~nflügel) lung. **(auf) ~ rauchen** to inhale; **sich (dat) die ~ aus dem Hals or Leib schreien** (inf) to yell till one is blue in the face (inf); **sich (dat) die ~ aus dem Leib husten** (inf) to cough one's lungs out (inf); **die (grünen) ~ einer Großstadt** the lungs of a city; siehe **eisern**.

Lungen-: **~bläschen** nt pulmonary alveolus (spec); **~braten** m (Aus) siehe **Lendenbraten**; **~embolie** f pulmonary embolism (spec); **~entzündung** f pneumonia; **~fisch** m lungfish; **~flügel** m lung; **~hasche** nt (Cook) hash made with calf's lights; **~heilstätte** f TB or tuberculosis sanatorium; **l~krank** adj tubercular; **l~krank sein** to have a lung disease; **~kranke(r)** mf decl as adj TB case; **~krankheit** f lung or pulmonary (form) disease; **~krebs** m lung cancer; **~schwindsucht** f (old) consumption (old); **~tuberkulose** f tuberculosis (of the lung), TB; **~tumor** m lung tumour; **~zug** m deep drag (inf); **einen ~zug machen** to inhale deeply, to take a deep drag (inf).

lungern vi (inf) to loaf or hang about (inf).

Lunte f -, -n **(a)** (Hist) fuse. **~ riechen** (Verdacht schöpfen) to smell a rat (inf); (Gefahr wittern) to smell (inf) or sense danger. **(b)** (Hunt: Fuchsschwanz) brush.

Lupe f -, -n magnifying glass. **so etwas/solche Leute kannst du mit der ~ suchen** things/people like that are few and far between; **jdn/etw unter die ~ nehmen** (inf) (beobachten) to keep a close eye on sb/sth; (prüfen) to examine sb/sth closely.

lupenrein adj (lit) Edelstein flawless; Diamant auch of the first water; (fig) Vergangenheit etc auch unimpeachable, unblemished; Gentleman, Intellektueller through and through pred. **das Geschäft war nicht ganz ~** the deal wouldn't stand close scrutiny or wasn't quite all above-board; **ein ~er KP-Mann** a communist with an unblemished party record.

lupfen, **lüpfen** vt (S Ger, Aus, Sw) to lift, to raise.

Lupine f lupin.

Lurch m -(e)s, -e amphibian.

Lure f -, -n lur.

Lurex ® nt -, no pl lurex ®.

Lusche¹ f -, -n (Cards) low card.

Lusche² f -, -n (dial: Pfütze) puddle.

Lusitanien [-iən] nt (Hist) Lusitania.

lusitanisch adj (Hist) Lusitanian.

Lust f -, -e (a) no pl (Freude) pleasure, joy. er hat die ~ daran verloren, die ~ daran ist ihm vergangen he has lost all interest in it; da kann einem die (ganze) or alle ~ vergehen, da vergeht einem die ganze ~ it puts you off; jdm die ~ an etw (dat) nehmen to take all the fun out of sth for sb; ich habe immer mit ~ und Liebe gekocht I've always enjoyed cooking; sie ging mit/ohne ~ (und Liebe) an die Arbeit she set to work enthusiastically/without enthusiasm.

(b) no pl (Neigung) inclination. zu etw ~ (und Liebe) haben to feel like sth; ich habe keine ~, das zu tun I don't really want to do that; (bin nicht dazu aufgelegt) I don't feel like doing that; ich habe keine ~ zu arbeiten I'm not in the mood to work or for working, I don't feel like work or working; ich habe ~, das zu tun I'd like to do that; (bin dazu aufgelegt) I feel like doing that; ich habe jetzt keine ~ I'm not in the mood just now; ich hätte ~ dazu I'd like to; das mache ich erst, wenn ich ~ dazu habe I'll do that when I feel like it or when I'm in the mood; hast du ~? how about it?; auf etw (acc) ~ haben to feel like or to fancy sth; mach, wie du ~ hast (inf) do as you like; er kann bleiben, so lange er ~ hat he can stay as long as he likes; ~ kriegen, etw zu tun to feel like doing sth; ich habe nicht übel ~, ... zu ... I've a good or half a mind to ...; ganz or je nach ~ und Laune (inf) just depending on how I/you etc feel or on my/your etc mood.

(c) (sinnliche Begierde) desire; (sexuell auch) lust (usu pej). ~ haben to feel desire; er/sie hat ~ (inf) he's/she's feeling like a bit (inf); seinen ~en leben or frönen to indulge one's desires/lusts (pej).

Lustbarkeit f (dated) festivity, junketing (old).

lustbetont adj pleasure-orientated, governed by the pleasure principle; Beziehung, Mensch sensual. ~ unterrichten to teach in such a way that learning is fun.

Luster m -s, - (Aus) siehe **Lüster (a)**.

Lüster m -s, - (a) (Leuchter) chandelier. (b) (Stoff, Glanzüberzug) lustre.

lüstern adj lecherous, lascivious. nach etw ~ sein to lust after or for sth.

Lüsternheit f lecherousness, lasciviousness.

Lust-: ~fahrt f (dated) outing; (auf Schiff) pleasure cruise; ~film m (dated) comedy film; ~garten m (old) pleasance; ~gefühl nt feeling of pleasure; (sexuell auch) desire; ~gewinn m pleasure; ~greis m (hum) dirty old man (inf), old lecher; ~haus, ~häuschen nt (old) summerhouse.

lustig adj (munter) merry, jolly; Mensch auch jovial; (humorvoll) funny, amusing; (emsig) happy, merry, cheerful. es wurde ~ things got quite merry; seid ~! liven up and have a bit of fun; L~e Person (Theat) clown, fool, buffoon; L~er Rat court jester or fool; Die L~e Witwe the Merry Widow; Bruder L~ (old) jolly or merry fellow (dated); das ist ja ~!, das finde ich aber ~! (iro) that's very or most amusing (iro); das kann ja ~ werden! (iro) that's going to be fun (iro); das kannst du tun, so lange du ~ bist (inf) you can do that as long as you like or please; sich über jdn/etw ~ machen to make fun of sb/sth.

Lustigkeit f siehe adj merriness, jolliness (dated); joviality; funniness.

Lustknabe m (old, hum) catamite.

Lüstling m debauchee, lecher. ein alter ~ an old lecher, a debauched old man.

Lust-: l~los adj unenthusiastic; (Fin) Börse slack, dull; ~molch m (hum inf) sex maniac (inf); (bewundernd) sexy beast (inf), sexpot (inf); ~mord m sex murder; ~mörder m sex killer or murderer; ~prinzip nt (Psych) pleasure principle; ~schloß nt summer residence; ~seuche f (old, hum) syphilis no pl, pox (old, hum); ~spiel nt comedy; ~spieldichter m comedy-writer, writer of comedies; l~voll 1 adj full of relish; 2 adv with relish; ~wäldchen nt (liter) spinney, copse; l~wandeln* vi insep aux sein or haben (liter) to (take a) stroll, to promenade (old); ~wiese f (hum) kingsize bed.

luth. abbr of lutherisch.

Lutheraner(in f) m -s, - Lutheran.

Lutherbibel f Lutheran translation (of the Bible).

Lutherisch, Lutherisch, lutherisch adj Lutheran.

Luther-: ~rock m clerical frock coat; ~tum nt Lutheranism.

lutschen vti to suck (an etw (dat)) sth.

Lutscher m -s, - lollipop.

lütt adj (N Ger) wee (esp Scot).

Lüttich nt -s Liège.

Luv [lu:f] f -, no pl (Naut) windward or weather side. nach/in ~ to windward.

luven ['lu:vn, 'lu:fn] vi (Naut) to luff (up).

Luvseite f windward side.

Luxation f (Med) dislocation.

Luxemburg nt -s Luxembourg.

Luxemburger(in f) m -s, - Luxembourger.

luxemburgisch adj Luxembourgian.

luxuriös adj luxurious. ein ~es Leben a life of luxury.

Luxus m -, no pl luxury; (pej: Verschwendung, Überfluß) extravagance. im ~ leben to live in (the lap of) luxury; den ~ lieben to love luxury; mit etw ~ treiben to be extravagant with sth, to lash out on sth (inf); ich leiste mir den ~ und ... I'll treat myself to the luxury of ...

Luxus- in cpds luxury; ~ausführung f de luxe model; ~ausgabe f de luxe edition; ~dampfer m luxury cruise ship; ~frau f (inf) piece of class (inf), classy woman; ~körper m (hum) beautiful body; ~limousine f limousine; ~restaurant nt first-class restaurant; ~schlitten m (inf) classy car (inf) or job (sl); ~weibchen nt (inf) classy piece (inf); ~zug m pullman (train).

Luzern nt -s Lucerne.

Luzerne f -, -n (Bot) lucerne.

luzid adj (liter) lucid; (durchsichtig) translucent.

Luzidität f (liter) siehe adj lucidity; translucency.

Luzifer ['lu:tsifɐ] m -s Lucifer.

luziferisch [lutsi'fe:rɪʃ] adj diabolical, satanic.

Lymphdrüse f siehe **Lymphknoten.**

Lymphe ['lʏmfə] f -, -n lymph.

Lymphknoten m lymph node, lymph(atic) gland.

lynchen ['lʏnçn, 'lɪnçn] vt (lit) to lynch; (fig) to kill.

Lynch- ['lʏnç-]: ~justiz f lynch-law; ~mord m lynching.

Lyoner f -, - (Wurst) pork/veal sausage.

Lyra f -, **Lyren** (Mus) lyre. die ~ (Astron) Lyra, the Lyre.

Lyrik f -, no pl lyric poetry or verse.

Lyriker(in f) m -s, - lyric poet, lyricist.

lyrisch adj (lit, fig) lyrical; Dichtung, Dichter lyric.

Lyzeum [ly'tse:ʊm] nt -s, **Lyzeen** [ly'tse:ən] girls' grammar school (Brit), girls' high school.

M

M, m [ɛm] nt -, - M, m.

m abbr of Meter.

MA. abbr of Mittelalter.

Mäander m -s, - (Geog, Art) meander.

mäandrisch adj meandering. sich ~ schlängeln to meander; ~ verziert (Art) decorated with meanders.

Maar nt -(e)s, -e (Geol) maar (spec), volcanic lake.

Maas f - Meuse, Maas.

Maat m -(e)s, -e or -en (Naut) (ship's) mate.

Mach nt -(s), - (Phys) Mach.

Machandel m -s, -, **Machandelbaum** m (N Ger) juniper (tree).

Machart f make; (Muster) design; (lit, fig: Stil) style.

machbar adj feasible, possible.

Mache f -, -n (inf) (a) (Technik) structure. die ~ des Stücks the way the play is put together, the structure of the play. (b) (Vortäuschung) sham. reine or pure ~ sein to be a) sham. (c) etw in der ~ haben (inf) to be working on sth, to have sth on the stocks; jdn in der ~ haben/in die ~ nehmen (sl) to be having/to have a go at sb (inf); (verprügeln auch) to be working or doing/to work or do sb over (inf).

machen 1 vt (a) (tun) to do. was macht dein Bruder (beruflich)? what does your brother do for a living?; was habe ich nur falsch gemacht? what have I done wrong?; gut, wird gemacht right, shall do (inf) or I'll get that done; das läßt sich ~/nicht ~, das ist zu/nicht zu ~ that can/can't be done; ich mache dir das schon I'll do that for you; (da ist) nichts zu ~ (geht nicht) (there's) nothing to be done; (kommt nicht in Frage) nothing doing; wie man's macht, ist's verkehrt whatever you do is wrong; ich mache das schon (bringe das in Ordnung) I'll see to that; (erledige das) I'll do that; was machst du da? what are you doing (there)?; was machst du denn hier? what (on earth) are you doing here?; was macht denn das Fahrrad hier im Hausflur? what's this bicycle doing here in the hall?; er macht, was er will he does what he wants; ich muß noch so viel ~ I still have so much to do; ich kann da auch nichts ~ I can't do anything about it either; was hast du denn nun wieder gemacht? what have you done now?; ich mache es wohl am besten so, daß ich etwas früher komme I'd do or be best to come a bit earlier; es ist schon gut gemacht, wie ... it's good the way ...; so etwas macht man nicht that sort of thing just isn't done; wie ~ Sie das nur? how do you do it?; damit/mit ihr kann man etwas ~

you could do something with it/her; *siehe* **gemacht.**

(b) *(herstellen, anfertigen, zu Erfolg verhelfen)* to make. **sich/jdm etw ~ lassen** to have sth made for oneself/sb; **Bilder** *or* **Fotos ~** to take photos; **mach mir mal einen (guten) Preis!** make me an offer, give me a price; **er ist für den Beruf wie gemacht** he's made for the job; **Bier wird aus Gerste gemacht** beer is made from barley; **aus Holz gemacht** made of wood.

(c) was macht die Arbeit? how's the work going?; **was macht dein Bruder?** how is your brother doing?, how are things with your brother?

(d) *(verursachen)* **Schwierigkeiten, Arbeit** to make *(jdm for* sb); **Mühe, Schmerzen, Aufregung** to cause *(jdm for* sb). **jdm Angst/Mut/Sorgen/Freude ~** to make sb afraid/brave/worried/happy; **jdm Hoffnung/Mut/Kopfschmerzen ~** to give sb hope/courage/a headache; **das macht Appetit/Hunger** that gives you an appetite/makes you hungry; *siehe* **schaffen.²**

(e) *(hervorbringen)* **Laut, Geräusch** to make; **miau, aua, brumm, mäh** to go; **Grimassen, böse Miene** to pull. **wie macht das Kindchen/feine Hündchen?** say please/sit up and beg.

(f) *(bilden, formen, darstellen)* **Kreuzzeichen, Kreis** to make; *(zeichnen)* **Kreis, Kurve** *auch* to draw. **die Straße macht einen Knick** the road bends.

(g) *(bewirken)* to do; *(+infin)* to make. **das macht die Kälte** it's the cold that does that; **jdn lachen/weinen/etw vergessen ~** to make sb laugh/cry/forget sth; **~, daß etw geschieht** to make sth happen; **mach, daß er gesund wird!** make him get better; **die Kälte macht, daß das Wasser gefriert** the cold makes the water freeze; **das ~ die vielen Zigaretten, daß du hustest** it's all those cigarettes you smoke that make you cough; **(viel) von sich reden ~** to be much talked about; **mach, daß du hier verschwindest!** (you just) get out of here!

(h) *(veranstalten)* **Fest, Party** to have, to give; **Seminar, Kurs** to do, to give; **Gruppenreise** to do.

(i) *(besuchen, teilnehmen an)* **Kurs, Seminar,** *(inf)* **Sehenswürdigkeiten, London** to do.

(j) *(zubereiten)* **Kaffee, Glühwein, Salat, Pfannkuchen** to make; **Frühstück, Abendessen** *auch* to get. **jdm einen Drink ~** to get sb a drink; *(Cocktail)* to make *or* mix sb a drink; **das Essen ~** to get the meal.

(k) *(mit unpersönlichem Objekt)* **mach's kurz!** make it *or* be brief; **mach's gut!** all the best; **er wird's nicht mehr lange ~** *(inf)* he won't last long; **es mit jdm ~** *(inf: Verkehr haben)* to make *or* do it with sb *(inf)*; **es jdm ~** *(sl: befriedigen)* to bring sb off *(sl)*; **mit mir kann man's ja ~!** *(inf)* the things I put up with! *(inf)*; **das läßt er nicht mit sich ~** he won't stand for that.

(l) *(ausmachen, schaden)* to matter. **macht nichts!** *(it)* doesn't matter; **macht das was?** does that matter?; **das macht sogar sehr viel** it matters a lot; **das macht durchaus etwas** it does indeed matter; **das macht mir doch nichts!** that doesn't matter to me; **der Regen/die Kälte** *etc* **macht mir nichts** I don't mind the rain/cold *etc*; **die Kälte macht dem Motor nichts** the cold doesn't hurt the engine; **es macht mir nichts, durch den Regen zu gehen** I don't mind walking in the rain.

(m) *(gewinnen, erzielen)* **Punkte, Freispiel, Preis** to get, to win; **Doktor, Diplom** *etc (studieren für)* to do; *(abschließen)* to get, to do; *(verdienen)* **Gewinne, Defizit** to make.

(n) **in Verbindung mit** *adj siehe auch dort* to make. **jdn nervös/unglücklich ~** to make sb nervous/unhappy; **etw größer/kleiner ~** to make sth bigger/smaller; **etw sauber/schmutzig ~** to get sth clean/dirty; **etw leer/kürzer ~** to vacate a chair; **jdn empty/shorten sth; einen Stuhl frei ~** to vacate a chair; **jdn alt/jung ~** *(aussehen lassen)* to make sb look old/young; **jdn wieder sehend ~** to make sb see again; **du hast dich am Ärmel schmutzig gemacht** you've got your sleeve dirty; **mach's dir doch bequem/gemütlich** make yourself comfortable/at home; **über's Wochenende habe ich es mir schön gemacht** I had a really nice weekend; **mach es ihm nicht noch schwerer** don't make it harder for him; **er macht es sich** *(dat)* **nicht leicht** he doesn't make it easy for himself.

(o) *(in Verbindung mit prep)* **etw aus jdm/etw ~** *(darstellen, interpretieren als)* to make sth of sb/sth; *(verwandeln in)* to make sth (out) of sb/out of sth, to turn *or* make sb/sth into sth; **was soll ich aus dieser Sache ~?** *(verstehen, interpretieren)* what am I meant to make of this?; **eine große Sache aus etw ~** to make a big thing of sth; **aus dem Haus könnte man schon etwas ~** you could really make something of that house; **sie weiß ~** you could really make something of herself; **jdn/etw zu etw ~** *(verwandeln in)* to turn sb/sth into sth; **etwas aus sich zu ~** she knows how to make the best of herself; **jdm etw zur Hölle/Qual** *etc* **~** to make sb/sth sth; **jdm etw zur Hölle/Qual** *etc* **~** to make sth hell/a misery *etc* for sb; **jdn zum Wortführer/Sklaven/zu seiner Frau ~** to make sb spokesman/slave/one's wife.

(p) *(Funktionsverb)* *siehe auch n auf jdn/etw* **Jagd ~** to hunt sb/sth; **Schicht/Nachtdienst ~** to work shifts/do night duty; **jdm die Rechnung ~** to make up sb's bill; **einen Spaziergang/Kopfsprung/Handstand ~** to go for a walk/to stand on one's head/do a handstand; **Pause/Halt ~** to have a break/call a halt; **ein Fragezeichen/einen Strich ~** to put a question mark/dash; **das Geschirr ~** to do the dishes; **eine Prüfung ~** to do *or* take an exam; **ein Spiel ~** to play a game.

(q) *(ordnen, reparieren, säubern)* to do. **die Küche muß mal wieder gemacht werden** *(gereinigt, gestrichen)* the kitchen needs doing again; **das Auto/den Kühlschrank ~ lassen** to have the car/refrigerator seen to or done; **er macht mir die Haare/Zähne** *(inf)* he does my hair/teeth; **das Bett ~** to make the bed; **mach den Fleck aus den Hosen** get that stain out of your trousers.

(r) *(inf: ergeben)* to make; *(Math)* to be. **drei und fünf macht** *or* **~ acht** three and five make(s) *or* is *or* are eight; **fünf mal vier macht** *or* **~ zwanzig** five fours are twenty, five times four

is twenty; **das macht (zusammen) 23** altogether that's 23; **was** *or* **wieviel macht sechs geteilt durch zwei?** what is six divided by two?; **100 cm ~ einen Meter** 100 cm make a metre; **was macht die Rechnung?** how much is the bill?, what does the bill come to?

(s) *(kosten)* to be. **was** *or* **wieviel macht das (alles zusammen)?** how much is that altogether?, what does that come to *or* make altogether?

(t) *(inf: eine bestimmte Rolle übernehmen)* **Dolmetscher, Schiedsrichter** *etc* to be; *(Theat)* to play. **jetzt macht er auf beleidigt** now he's playing the injured innocent; **den Ghostwriter für jdn ~** to act as sb's ghost writer, to ghost for sb.

(u) *(inf: Notdurft verrichten)* to do. **groß/klein ~** to do a big/little job *(baby-talk)*; **einen Haufen** *or* **sein Geschäft ~** to do one's business *(euph)*; *siehe* **Aa, Pipi** *etc.*

(v) *(inf: legen)* to put. **er machte sich** *(dat)* **Zucker in den Kaffee** he put some sugar in his coffee, he sugared his coffee.

2 *vi* **(a)** *(inf: sich beeilen)* to get a move on *(inf)*. **mach schon/mach (mal 'n bißchen) schneller/schnell!** get a move on! *(inf)*, hurry up; **ich mach ja schon!** I am hurrying; **sie machten, daß sie nach Hause kamen** they hurried home.

(b) *(inf)* **in etw** *(dat)* **~** *(beruflich)* to be in sth; *(pej: sich interessiert zeigen an)* to be into sth *(sl)*; **er macht in Politik/Malerei** he's in politics/doing some painting; **auf etw** *(acc)* **~** to play sth; **jetzt macht sie auf große Dame** she's playing the lady now; **sie macht auf verständnisvoll/gebildet** *etc* she's doing her understanding/cultured bit *(inf)*; **sie macht auf elegant/pazifistisch** she's playing the elegant lady/the pacifist; **er macht auf Schau** he's out for effect.

(c) laß ihn nur ~ *(hindre ihn nicht)* just let him do it; *(verlaß dich auf ihn)* just leave it to him; **laß mich mal ~** let me do it; **(ich bringe das in Ordnung)** let me see to that; **gut, mache ich right, will do** *(inf) or* I'll do that.

(d) *(inf: Notdurft verrichten)* to go to the toilet; *(Hund etc)* to do its business *(euph)*. **(sich** *dat)* **in die Hosen ~** *(lit, fig)* to wet oneself; **ins Bett ~** to wet the bed.

(e) *(dial: fahren, reisen)* to go. **nach Amerika ~** to go to America.

(f) das macht müde/gesund/schlank that makes you tired/healthy/slim; **das Kleid macht alt/schlank** that dress makes you look old/slim.

3 *vr* **(a)** *(sich entwickeln)* to come on *or* along. **wie macht sich der Garten?** how is the garden coming on *or* along?; **es wird sich schon ~** things will turn out all right.

(b) *(passen)* to look. **der Schal macht sich sehr hübsch zu dem Kleid** the scarf looks very pretty with that dress.

(c) sich an etw *(acc)* **~** to get down to sth/doing sth; **sich auf den Weg ~** to get going; **sich über das Essen ~** *(inf)* to get stuck in *(inf)*.

(d) sich verständlich/wichtig ~ to make oneself understood/important; **sich bei jdm beliebt/verhaßt ~** to make oneself popular with/hated by sb.

(e) sich *(dat)* **viel aus jdm/etw ~** to like sb/sth; **sich** *(dat)* **wenig aus jdm/etw ~** not to be very keen on sb/sth; **sich** *(dat)* **nichts aus etw ~** *(sich nicht ärgern)* not to let sth bother one; *(keinen Wert legen auf)* not to be very keen on sth; **sich** *(dat)* **einen schönen Abend/ein paar gemütliche Stunden ~** to have a nice evening/a few pleasant hours; **sich** *(dat)* **ein Vergnügen aus etw ~** to take delight in sth; **sich** *(dat)* **Umstände/Mühe ~** to go to a lot of bother/trouble; **sich** *(dat)* **Sorgen/Hoffnungen ~** to worry/get hopeful; **sich** *(dat)* **einen ~** *(sl)* to get one's knickers in a twist *(sl)*; **sich** *(dat)* **jdn zum Freund/Feind ~** to make sb one's friend/enemy; **sich** *(dat)* **etw zur Aufgabe/zum Grundsatz/Motto ~** to make sth one's job/a principle/a motto.

(f) sich zum Fürsprecher *etc* **~** to make oneself spokesman *etc*.

Machenschaften *pl* wheelings and dealings *pl*, machinations *pl*.

Macher *m* **-s, -** *(inf)* doer, man of action.

-macher(in *f) m in cpds* -maker.

Macherlohn *m* labour charge; *(bei Kleidung)* making-up charge.

Machete *f* **-, -n** machete.

machiavellistisch [makiavel-] *adj* Machiavellian.

Machinationen *pl (liter)* machinations *pl*.

Macht *f* **-, ¨e (a)** *no pl (Einfluß, Kraft)* power; *(Stärke auch)* might. **die ~ der Gewohnheit/Verhältnisse/des Schicksals** the force of habit/circumstance(s)/destiny; **alles, was in unserer ~ steht, alles in unserer ~ Stehende** everything (with)in our power; **es stand nicht in seiner ~, zu ...** it was not *or* did not lie within his power to ...; **mit aller ~** with might and main, with all one's might; **~ geht vor Recht** *(Prov)* might is right *(Prov)*.

(b) *no pl (Herrschaft, Befehlsgewalt)* power. **an die ~ ergreifen/erringen** to seize/gain power; **an die ~ gelangen** *(form) or* **kommen** to come to power; **an der ~ sein/bleiben** to be/remain in power; **seine ~ behaupten** to maintain control, to continue to hold sway; **die ~ übernehmen** to assume power, to take over.

(c) *(dated: Heeres~)* forces *pl.* **mit bewaffneter ~ angreifen** to make an armed attack.

(d) *(außerirdische Kraft, Groß~)* power. **die ¨e der Finsternis** *(old, liter)* the Powers of Darkness *(old, liter)*.

Macht-: **~anspruch** *m* claim to power; **~ausübung** *f* exercise of power; **jdn an der ~ausübung hindern** to prevent sb from exercising his power; **~befugnis** *f* power, authority *no pl*; **~bereich** *m* sphere of influence *or* control; **~block** *m* power bloc.

Mächtegruppierung *f* grouping of the powers.

Macht-: **~entfaltung** *f* display of power; **zur Zeit der größten ~entfaltung** at the height *or* peak of its power; **~ergreifung** *f* seizure of power; ~**fülle** f power no indef art; ~**gier** f lust for power; ~**haber** m -s, - (pej) dictator; **die ~haber in Ruritanien** the rulers of or powers-that-be in Ruritania; ~**hunger** m (liter) craving or hunger for power; **m~hungrig** adj (liter) power-hungry; **m~hungrig sein** to crave power.

mächtig 1 adj **(a)** (einflußreich) powerful. **die M~en (dieser Erde)** the powerful (of this world).

(b) (sehr groß) mighty; Baum, Felsen auch, Körper massive; Stimme, Wirkung, Schlag, Schultern auch powerful; Essen heavy; (inf: enorm) Hunger, Durst, Glück terrific (inf), tremendous. ~**e Angst** or **einen ~en Bammel haben** (inf) to be scared stiff.

(c) (liter) **seiner selbst** (gen) or **seiner Sinne** (gen) **nicht ~ sein** not to be in control of oneself; **einer Sprache** (gen) ~ **sein** to have a good command of a language.

2 adv (inf: sehr) terrifically (inf), tremendously; schneien, brüllen, sich beeilen like mad (inf). **sich ~ anstrengen** to make a terrific (inf) or tremendous effort; **da hast du dich ~ getäuscht** you've made a big mistake there.

Mächtigkeit f (Größe) mightiness; (von Baum, Felsen auch, von Körper) massiveness; (von Stimme, Wirkung, Schlag, Schultern auch) powerfulness; (von Essen) heaviness; (Geol, Min) thickness.

Macht-: ~**kampf** m power struggle, struggle for power; **m~los** adj powerless; (hilflos) helpless; **gegen diese Argumente war ich m~los** I was powerless against these arguments; ~**losigkeit** f, no pl powerlessness; helplessness; ~**mißbrauch** m abuse or misuse of power; ~**mittel** nt instrument of power; ~**politik** f power politics pl; ~**position** f position of power; ~**probe** f trial of strength; ~**spruch** m word (gen from); ~**stellung** f position of power; (einflußreiche Stellung auch) powerful position; ~**streben** nt striving for power; ~**übernahme** f takeover (durch by); ~**verhältnisse** pl balance of power sing; ~**voll** adj powerful; ~**vollkommenheit** f absolute power; **aus eigener ~vollkommenheit** (fig) high-handedly; ~**wort** nt word (gen from); **ein ~wort sprechen** to exercise one's authority.

Machwerk nt (pej) sorry effort. **das ist ein ~ des Teufels** that is the work of the devil.

Mach-Zahl f (Phys) Mach number.

Macke f -, -n (inf) **(a)** (Tick, Knall) quirk. **eine ~ haben** (sl) to be cracked (inf), to have a screw loose (inf). **(b)** (Fehler, Schadstelle) fault; (bei Maschinen auch) defect; (bei Kartoffeln etc) bad patch.

Macker m -s, - (sl) fellow (inf), bloke (Brit inf), guy (inf).

Madagaskar nt -s Madagascar; (Pol: heutzutage) Malagasy Republic.

Madagasse m -n, -n, **Madagassin** f Madagascan; Malagasy. **madagassisch** adj Madagascan; Malagasy.

Madam f -, -s or -en (hum dated) lady. **meine ~** my old woman or lady (inf).

Mädchen nt girl; (Tochter auch) daughter; (dated: Freundin) girl(friend); (Dienst~) maid. **ein unberührtes ~** a virgin; **ein ~ für alles** (inf) a dogsbody; (im Haushalt auch) a maid-of-all-work; siehe spät, leicht.

Mädchen-: **m~haft** adj girlish; **sich m~haft kleiden** to dress like a girl; **m~haft aussehen** to look like a (young) girl; ~**handel** m white slave trade; ~**händler** m white slaver, white slave trader; ~**klasse** f girls' class or form; ~**kleidung** f girls' clothing or clothes pl; ~**name** m **(a)** (Vorname) girl's name; ~**namen** girls' names; **(b)** (von verheirateter Frau) maiden name; ~**pensionat** nt girls' boarding school; **diese Kaserne ist kein ~pensionat!** (hum) these barracks aren't a finishing school; ~**schule** f girls' school; ~**zimmer** nt (dated) maid's room; (für Tochter) girl's room.

Made f -, -n maggot. **in dem Fleisch sind die ~n** the meat is maggoty, there are maggots in the meat; **wie die ~ im Speck leben** (inf) to live or be in clover, to live in (the lap of) luxury.

Madeira(wein) [ma'de:ra-, ma'daira-] m -s, -s Madeira.

Mädel nt -s, -(s) (dial), **Mäd(e)l** nt -s, -n (Aus) lass (dial), girl; siehe auch Mädchen.

Mäderl nt -s, -n (Aus) little lass (dial) or girl.

madig adj maggoty; Obst auch worm-eaten. **jdn/etw ~ machen** (inf) to run sb/sth down; **jdm etw ~ machen** (inf) to put sb off sth.

Madjar [ma'dja:r] m -en, -en Magyar.

Madl nt -s, -n (Aus), **Mädle** nt -s, - (S Ger) siehe Mädel.

Madonna f -, **Madonnen** Madonna.

Madonnen-: ~**bild** nt (picture of the) Madonna; **m~haft** adj madonna-like.

Madrigal nt -s, -e madrigal.

Maestro [ma'ɛstro] m -s, -s or **Maestri** maestro.

Ma(f)fia f -, no pl Mafia.

Magazin nt -s, -e **(a)** (Lager) storeroom; (esp für Sprengstoff, Waffen, old: Speicher auch) magazine; (Bibliotheks~) stockroom. **(b)** (am Gewehr) magazine. **(c)** (Zeitschrift) magazine, journal; (TV, Rad) magazine programme.

Magaziner m -s, - (Sw), **Magazineur** [-'nø:r] m (Aus) storeman.

magazinieren* vt to store, to put in store.

Magazinsendung f (Rad, TV) magazine programme.

Magd f -, ¨-e **(a)** (old) (Dienst~) maid; (Landarbeiterin) farm lass or girl; (Kuh~) milkmaid. **(b)** (liter: Mädchen, Jungfrau) maid(en) (old, liter). **Maria, die reine ~/die ~ des Herrn** Mary, the holy virgin/the handmaid of the Lord.

Mägd(e)lein nt (obs, poet) maid(en) (old, liter).

Magen m -s, ¨- or - stomach, tummy (inf). **mit leerem ~, auf nüchternen ~** on an empty stomach; **(die) Liebe geht durch den ~** (Prov) the way to a man's heart is through his stomach (prov).

etw liegt jdm (schwer or wie Blei or bleiern) **im ~** (inf) sth lies heavily on sb's stomach; (fig) sth preys on sb's mind; **der Kerl liegt mir im ~** (sl inf) I can't stomach or stand the fellow; **jdm auf den ~ schlagen** (inf) to upset sb's stomach, to give sb an upset stomach; (fig) to upset sb; **sich** (dat) **den ~ verderben** or **verkorksen** (inf) to get an upset stomach, to upset one's stomach; siehe umdrehen, knurren.

Magen-: ~**ausheilung** f (Med) ~**spülung**; ~**beschwerden** pl stomach or tummy (inf) trouble sing; ~**bitter** m bitters pl; ~**blutung** f stomach bleeding or haemorrhaging; ~**-Darm-Katarrh** m gastroenteritis; ~**-Darm-Trakt** m gastro-intestinal tract; ~**drücken** nt -s, - stomach-ache; ~**fahrplan** m (inf) (Diät) diet; (Speisekarte) menu; ~**gegend** f stomach region; ~**geschwür** nt stomach ulcer; ~**grube** f pit of the stomach; **ein Schlag in die ~grube** a blow in the solar plexus; ~**knurren** nt -s, no pl tummy (inf) or stomach rumbles pl; ~**krampf** m stomach cramp; **m~krank** adj with stomach trouble; **m~krank sein** to have stomach trouble; **jdn m~krank machen** to give sb stomach trouble; ~**krebs** m stomach cancer, cancer of the stomach; ~**leiden** nt stomach disorder or complaint; **m~leidend** adj siehe **m~krank**; ~**mittel** nt stomachic (spec); **jdm ein ~mittel verschreiben** to give sb something for his stomach; ~**saft** m gastric juice; ~**säure** f gastric acid; ~**schleimhaut** f stomach lining; ~**schleimhautentzündung** f gastritis; ~**schmerzen** pl stomach-ache sing, tummy-ache sing (inf); (Krämpfe auch) stomach pains pl; ~**spiegelung** f gastroscopy (spec); ~**spülung** f irrigation of the stomach; ~**verstimmung** f upset stomach, stomach upset; ~**weh** nt (S Ger) siehe ~**schmerzen**.

mager adj **(a)** (fettarm) Fleisch lean; Kost low-fat, low in fat. ~ **essen** to be on a low-fat diet.

(b) (dünn) thin, skinny (inf); (abgemagert) emaciated; (Typ) Druck roman.

(c) (unfruchtbar) Boden, Felder poor, infertile.

(d) (dürftig) meagre; Ernte, Ertrag auch lean; (Tech) Mischung weak; Ergebnis poor. **die sieben ~en Jahre** the seven lean years.

Magerkeit f, no pl siehe adj **(a)** leanness; low fat level (gen in). **(b)** thinness, skinniness (inf); emaciation. **(c)** poorness.

Mager-: ~**milch** f skimmed milk; ~**quark** m low-fat curd cheese; ~**sucht** f (Med) anorexia; (psychologisch bedingt) anorexia nervosa.

Maghreb ['magrɛp] m -, no pl Maghreb.

maghrebinisch adj Maghrebian.

Magie f, no pl magic.

Magier ['ma:giɐ] m -s, - magician. **die drei ~** the three Magi.

Maginot-Linie, Maginotlinie [maʒi'no-] f Maginot Line.

magisch adj magic(al); Quadrat, (Tech) Auge, (Econ) Dreieck, (Phys) Zahlen magic. **nach ~en Vorstellungen** according to various concepts of magic; **mit ~er Gewalt** with magical force; (fig) as if by magic; **von jdm/etw ~ angezogen werden** to be attracted to sb/sth as if by magic.

Magister m -s, - ~ **(Artium)** (Univ) M.A., Master of Arts; ~ **(pharmaciae)** (abbr Mag. pharm.) (Aus) M. Sc. or Master of Science in pharmacology.

Magistrat m -(e)s, -e municipal authorities pl.

Magma nt -s, **Magmen** (Geol) magma.

magna cum laude ['magna 'kʊm'laudə] adv (Univ) magna cum laude.

Magnat m -en, -en magnate (auch Hist).

Magnesia f -, no pl (Chem) magnesia; (Sport) chalk.

Magnesium nt, no pl magnesium.

Magnet m -s or -en, -(e)n (lit, fig) magnet.

Magnet- in cpds magnetic; ~**aufzeichnung** f magnetic recording; ~**band** nt magnetic tape; ~**berg** m (liter) mountain believed to draw ships to their doom by its magnetic properties; ~**bildverfahren** nt video recording; ~**eisenstein** m lodestone, magnetite; ~**feld** nt magnetic field.

magnetisch adj (lit, fig) magnetic. **eine ~e Anziehungskraft auf jdn ausüben** (fig) to have a magnetic attraction for sb.

Magnetiseur [-'zø:r] m healer who supposedly possesses magnetic powers which draw out illnesses.

magnetisieren* vt Metall to magnetize; **jdn** to use animal magnetism on.

Magnetismus m, no pl magnetism; (Mesmerismus) animal magnetism; (heutzutage) form of healing where the illness is supposedly drawn out by the magnetic power of the healer.

Magnet-: ~**kern** m (magnet) core; ~**kompaß** m magnetic compass; ~**nadel** f magnetic needle.

Magneton nt -s, -s magneton.

Magneto-: ~**phon** ® nt -(e)s, -e steel tape recorder, magnetophone ®; ~**phonband** ® nt steel recording tape; ~**sphäre** f magnetosphere.

Magnet-: ~**pol** m magnetic pole; ~**schalter** m (Aut) solenoid switch; ~**spule** f magnetic coil; ~**tonband** nt magnetic tape; ~**tongerät** nt magnetic (sound) recorder; ~**tonverfahren** nt magnetic (sound) recording; ~**zündung** f (Aut) magneto ignition.

Magnifikat nt -s, no pl magnificat.

Magnifizenz f (Univ) (Euer or Eure)/Seine ~ Your/His Magnificence (title given to German university rectors).

Magnolie [mag'no:liə] f magnolia.

Magyar [ma'dja:r] m -en, -en (Aus, liter) Magyar.

magyarisch [ma'dja:rɪʃ] adj (Aus, liter) Magyar.

mäh interj baa.

Mahagoni nt -s, no pl mahogany.

Maharadscha m -s, -s maharaja(h).

Maharani f -, -s maharani.

Mähbinder m reaper-binder, reaping-and-binding machine.

Mahd¹ f -, -en (dial) reaping; (das Abgemähte) cut grass.

Mahd² nt -(e)s, ⸚er (Sw, Aus) mountain pasture.
Mähder m -s, - (dial) siehe **Mäher**.
Mähdrescher m combine (harvester).
mähen¹ 1 vt Gras to cut; (für Heu) Getreide auch to reap; Rasen to mow. 2 vi to reap; (Rasen ~) to mow.
mähen² vi (Schaf) to bleat.
Mäher m -s, - mower; (von Getreide) reaper.
Mahl nt -(e)s, -e or ⸚er (liter) meal, repast (form); (Gast~) banquet. beim ~e sitzen (liter) to be at table.
mahlen pret mahlte, ptp gemahlen 1 vt to grind. 2 vi to grind; (Räder) to spin.
Mahl-: ~gang m (Tech) pair of millstones; ~gut nt material to be ground; (Getreide) grain (to be ground), grist.
mählich adj (poet) siehe allmählich.
Mahl-: ~statt, ~stätte f (Hist) meeting place of the Teutons; ~stein m millstone; (prähistorisch) quern; ~strom m siehe Malstrom; ~zahn m grinder.
Mahlzeit f meal. ~! (inf) greeting used around mealtimes; (guten Appetit) enjoy your meal; (prost) ~! (iro inf) that's just great (inf) or swell (esp US inf).
Mähmaschine f mower; (Rasen~ auch) mowing machine; (Getreide~) reaper.
Mahnbrief m reminder.
Mähne f -, -n (lit, fig) mane. du hast wieder eine ~! (inf) you're looking rather wild and woolly again (inf).
mahnen 1 vt (a) (erinnern) to remind (wegen, an +acc of); (warnend, mißbilligend) to admonish (wegen, an +acc on account of); Schuldner to send a reminder to. jdn schriftlich/brieflich ~ to remind sb in writing/by letter; gemahnt werden (Schuldner) to receive a reminder; eine ~de Stimme (liter) an admonishing or admonitory voice.
  (b) (auffordern) jdn zur Eile/Geduld/Ruhe etc ~ to urge or (warnend, mißbilligend) admonish sb to hurry/be patient/be quiet etc; jdn zur Mäßigkeit ~ to urge sb to be moderate, to urge moderation on sb.
  2 vi (a) (wegen Schulden etc) to send a reminder.
  (b) zur Eile/Geduld ~ to urge haste/patience; der Lehrer mahnte zur Ruhe the teacher called for quiet; die Uhr mahnte zur Eile the clock indicated that haste was called for.
Mahner m -s, - (liter) admonisher.
Mahn-: ~mal nt (liter) memorial; ~ruf m (liter) exhortation; ~schreiben nt reminder.
Mahnung f (a) (Ermahnung) exhortation; (warnend, mißbilligend) admonition. (b) (geh: warnende Erinnerung) reminder. zur ~ an (+acc) in memory of. (c) (Mahnbrief) reminder.
Mahn-: ~verfahren nt collection proceedings pl; ~wesen nt system for the collection of outstanding debts; ~zeichen nt (liter) warning.
Mähre f -, -n (old, pej) nag, jade.
Mähren nt -s Moravia.
mährisch adj Moravian.
Mai m -(e)s or - or (poet) -en, -e May. der Erste ~ May Day; des Lebens ~ (poet) the springtime of one's life (poet); wie einst im ~ (as if) in the first bloom or flush of youth, as if young again; siehe auch März.
Mai- in cpds May; (Pol) May Day; ~andacht f May devotions pl; ~baum m maypole; ~blume f, ~blümchen nt siehe ~glöckchen; große ~blume Solomon's seal; ~bowle f white wine punch (flavoured with woodruff); ~busch m (für Mädchen) sprig of birch left at one's sweetheart's window on May Day; (dial: als Schmuck) leafy twigs pl.
Maid f -, -en (old, liter) maid(en) (old, liter); (hum) wench (old, hum).
Maie f -, -n, **Maien** m -s, - (dial, obs) siehe **Maibusch**.
Mai-: ~feier f May Day celebrations pl; ~feiertag m (form) May Day no art; ~glöckchen nt lily of the valley; ~käfer m cockchafer; ~königin f Queen of (the) May; ~kundgebung f May Day rally.
Mailand nt -s Milan.
Mailänder adj attr Milan. die ~ Scala La Scala.
Mailänder(in f) m -s, - Milanese.
mailändisch adj Milanese.
Main m -s Main.
Mainlinie f line formed by the River Main roughly dividing North and South Germany.
Mais m -es, no pl maize, (Indian) corn (esp US).
Mais-: ~brei m thick maize porridge; ~brot nt corn bread.
Maischbottich m mash tub; (für Wein) fermenting vat.
Maische f -, -n (Bier~) mash; (Wein~) must; (Schnaps~) wort.
maischen vt to mash; Trauben to ferment.
Mais-: ~flocken pl cornflakes pl; m~gelb adj corn-coloured; ~kolben m corn cob; (Gericht) corn on the cob; ~korn nt grain of maize or corn (esp US); (als Sammelbegriff) maize or corn (esp US) grain; ~mehl nt maize or corn (esp US) meal; ~stärke f cornflour, cornstarch (US).
Maître de plaisir [mɛtrə(d)plɛ'ziːr] m - - -, -s - - (old, hum) Master of Ceremonies.
Maître d'hôtel [mɛtrədo'tɛl] m - -, -s - maître d'hôtel.
Majestät f (a) (Titel) Majesty. Seine/Ihre/Eure or Euer ~ His/Her/Your Majesty; die (kaiserlichen etc) ~en ... their (Imperial etc) Majesties ... (b) (liter) majesty, grandeur.
majestätisch adj majestic.
Majestäts-: ~beleidigung f lèse-majesté; ~verbrechen nt (Jur) crime against the crown.
Majolika f -, -s or **Majoliken** majolica.
Majonäse f -, -n siehe Mayonnaise.
Major m -s, -e (Mil) major; (in Luftwaffe) squadron leader (Brit), major (US).
Majoran m -s, -e marjoram.
Majorat nt (old) (a) (Jur) primogeniture. (b) (Erbgut) estate to which the eldest son is entitled.
Majordomus m -, - (Hist) major-domo.
majorenn adj (obs) of age. ~ werden to come of age, to attain one's majority.
Majorette f majorette.
majorisieren* vt to outvote.
Majorität f majority. die ~ haben to have a majority.
Majoritäts-: ~beschluß m majority decision; ~prinzip nt siehe Mehrheitsgrundsatz.
Majorsrang m (Mil) rank of major. im ~ sein to hold the rank of major.
Majorz m -es, no pl (Sw) first-past-the-post system; (Mehrheit) majority.
Majuskel f -, -n (geh) majuscule (spec), capital (letter).
makaber adj macabre; Witz, Geschichte sick.
Makedonien [-iən] nt -s Macedonia.
Makedonier(in f) [-iɐ, -iərin] m -s, - Macedonian.
makedonisch adj Macedonian.
Makel m -s, - (a) (Schandfleck) stigma. ohne ~ without a stain on one's reputation; (Rel) unblemished; ein ~ auf seiner blütenreinen Weste a blot on his escutcheon; mit einem ~ behaftet sein (liter) to be stigmatized.
  (b) (Fehler) blemish; (bei Waren) flaw, defect. ohne ~ without blemish, flawless.
Mäkelei f carping no pl, fault-finding no pl (an +dat, über +acc about, over).
mäk(e)lig adj (inf) finicky (inf).
makellos adj Reinheit, Frische spotless; Charakter, Lebenswandel, Gesinnung unimpeachable; Figur, Haut, Frisur perfect, flawless; Kleidung, Haare immaculate; Alibi watertight.
Makellosigkeit f (Reinheit) spotlessness; (moralisch) unimpeachability; (von Haut) flawlessness; (von Kleidung) immaculateness.
makeln 1 vi to act as a broker. 2 vt to be a broker for.
mäkeln vi (inf) (nörgeln) to carp, to cavil (an +dat at); (zu wählerisch sein) to be finicky (inf) (an +dat about, over).
Make-up [meːk'ap] nt -s, -s make-up; (flüssig) foundation, liquid make-up. sie braucht zwei Stunden fürs ~ she needs two hours for her or to put on her make-up.
Makkabäer pl Maccabees pl.
Makkaroni pl macaroni sing.
Makler m -s, - broker; (Grundstücks~) estate agent; (fig) middleman. der ehrliche ~ (fig) the honest broker.
Mäkler m -s, - (a) siehe Makler. (b) (inf) (nörglerisch) faultfinder, carper; (wählerisch) fusspot (inf).
Maklergebühr f broker's commission, brokerage.
Mako m or f or nt f -(s), -s (Tex) Egyptian cotton.
Makrele f -, -n mackerel.
Makro- in cpds macro-; ~kosmos m macrocosm.
Makrone f -, -n macaroon.
Makro-: ~ökonomie f macro-economics sing; m~zephal adj megacephalic.
Makulatur f (Typ) wastepaper; (fig pej) rubbish. ~ reden (inf) to talk rubbish (inf) or trash (inf).
Makulaturbogen m (Typ) waste or spoiled sheet.
makulieren* vt to pulp.
Mal¹ nt -(e)s, -e or (poet) ⸚er (a) (Fleck) mark; (fig liter: Kennzeichen auch) brand, sign. (b) (liter: Ehren~) memorial, monument. (c) (Sport) (Schlagball) base; (Rugby) posts pl; (~feld) touch.
Mal² nt -(e)s, -e time. das eine ~ once; erinnerst du dich an das eine ~ in Düsseldorf? do you remember that time in Düsseldorf? nur das eine ~ this once; (nur) dieses eine ~ (just) this once; das eine oder andere ~ now and then or again, from time to time; ein/kein einziges ~ once/not once; wenn du bloß ein einziges ~ auf mich hören würdest if you would only listen to me for once; manch liebes ~, manches liebe ~ (dated) many a time; ein für alle ~e once and for all; ein über das or ums andere ~, ein ~ über das or ums andere ~ time after time; voriges or das vorige ~ the time before; das soundsovielte or x-te ~ (inf) the umpteenth (inf) or nth time; ein erstes ~ (liter) for the first time ever; ein letztes ~ (liter) one last time; als ich letztes or das letzte ~ in London war (the) last time I was in London; beim ersten ~(e) the first time; beim zweiten/letzten etc ~ the second/last etc time; zum ersten/letzten etc ~ for the first/last etc time; zu verschiedenen ~en at various times; zu wiederholten ~en repeatedly, time and again; von ~ zu ~ each or every time; er wird von ~ zu ~ besser/dümmer he gets better and better/more and more stupid, he gets better/more stupid each or every time; für dieses ~ for the time being, for now; mit einem ~e all at once, all of a sudden, suddenly.
mal¹ adv (Math) times; (bei Maßangaben) by. zwei ~ zwei (Math) two times two, two twos, twice two.
mal² adv (inf) siehe einmal.
-mal adv suf times.
Malachit m -s, -e malachite.
malachitgrün adj malachite green.
malad(e) adj (inf) sick, ill.
Malagasy [mala'gaːsi] m, **Malagassi** nt - (Ling) Malagasy.
Malaga(wein) m -s, -s malaga.
Malaie [ma'laiə] m -n, -n, **Malaiin** [ma'laiɪn] f Malay.
malaiisch [ma'laiɪʃ] adj Malayan, Malay attr. M~er Bund (Hist) Federation of Malaya.
Malaise [ma'lɛːzə] f -, -n or (Sw) nt -s, - (geh) malaise.
Malaria f -, no pl malaria.
Malawi nt -s Malawi.
Malawier(in f) [-iɐ, -iərin] m -s, - Malawian.
malawisch adj Malawian, Malawi attr.
Malaysia [ma'laizia] nt -s Malaysia.
Malaysier(in f) [ma'laiziɐ, -iərin] m -s, - Malaysian.

malaysisch [ma'laizɪʃ] *adj* Malaysian.
Malbuch *nt* colouring book.
Malediven [male'di:vn] *pl* Maldives *pl*, Maldive Islands *pl*.
malen 1 *vti* to paint; (*inf: zeichnen*) to draw; (*inf: langsam schreiben*) to write with painstaking care. **sich** ~ **lassen** to have one's portrait painted; **etw rosig/schwarz** *etc* ~ (*fig*) to paint a rosy/black *etc* picture of sth; **er hat während des Vortrags (Männchen) gemalt** he was doodling during the talk; **er malt (als Beruf)** he's a painter or an artist; *siehe* **Teufel**.
  2 *vr* **(a)** to paint or do a self-portrait, to paint a picture of oneself.
  (b) (*fig liter*) to show itself, to be reflected.
Maler *m* -s, - painter; (*Kunst*~ *auch*) artist.
Malerei *f* (*no pl: Malkunst*) art; (*Bild*) painting; (*Zeichnung*) drawing.
Malerfarbe *f* paint.
Malerin *f* (woman) painter, artist.
malerisch *adj* **(a)** (*bildnerisch*) in painting; *Talent, Können* as a painter. **das** ~ **e Schaffen Leonardos** Leonardo's painting; **seine** ~**en Mittel** his technique as a painter.
  (b) (*pittoresk*) picturesque; *Altstadt, Fachwerkhaus auch* quaint; *Landschaft auch* scenic. ~ **auf das Sofa drapiert** draped artistically or decoratively over the sofa.
Maler-: ~**leinwand** *f* artist's canvas; ~**meister** *m* (master) painter; ~**schule** *f* school of painting.
Malesche *f* -, -**n** (*N Ger inf*) difficulty, trouble. **in** ~**n kommen** to land in trouble or the soup (*inf*).
Malheur [ma'løːɐ] *nt* -s, -s or -e mishap. **ihm ist ein kleines** ~ **passiert** (*inf*) he's had a little accident (*auch euph*) or a mishap; **das ist doch kein** ~! it's not serious.
Mali *nt* -s Mali.
Malier(in *f*) [-ɪɐ, -iɐrɪn] *m* -s, - Malian.
maligne *adj* (*Med*) malignant.
maliziös *adj* (*liter*) malicious.
Malkasten *m* paintbox.
mall *adj* (*Naut*) variable; (*N Ger inf*) barmy (*inf*), batty (*inf*).
Mallorca [ma'lɔrka, ma'jɔrka] *nt* -s Majorca, Mallorca.
mallorquinisch [malɔr'kiːnɪʃ] *adj* Majorcan.
malnehmen *vti sep irreg* to multiply (*mit* by).
Maloche *f* -, *no pl* (*sl*) graft (*sl*). **auf** ~ **sein** to be grafting (*sl*); **du mußt zur** ~ you've got to go to work.
malochen* *vi* (*sl*) to graft (*sl*), to sweat away (*inf*).
Malstift *m* crayon.
Malstrom *m* Maelstrom; (*fig liter*) maelstrom.
Malta *nt* -s Malta.
Maltechnik *f* painting technique.
Malteser *m* -s, - Maltese.
Malteser-: ~**kreuz** *nt* Maltese cross (*auch Tech*); ~**orden** *m* (Order of the) Knights *pl* of Malta or of St John; ~**ritter** *m* Knight of Malta, (Knight) Hospitaller.
maltesisch *adj* Maltese.
Maltose *f* -, *no pl* maltose.
malträtieren* *vt* to ill-treat, to maltreat.
Malus *m* -ses, - or -se (*Insur*) supplementary (high-risk) premium; (*Univ*) minus point.
Malve ['malvə] *f* -, -n (*Bot*) mallow; (*Stockrose*) hollyhock.
malvenfarbig, malvenfarben *adj* mauve.
Malz *nt* -es, *no pl* malt; *siehe* **Hopfen**.
Malz-: ~**bier** *nt* malt beer, ≈ stout; ~**bonbon** *nt* or *m* malt lozenge.
Malzeichen *nt* multiplication sign.
mälzen *vti* to malt.
Mälzer *m* -s, - maltster.
Mälzerei *f* malthouse, malting.
Malz-: ~**extrakt** *m* malt extract; ~**kaffee** *m* coffee substitute made from barley malt; ~**zucker** *m* maltose, malt sugar.
Mama¹ *f* -, -s (*inf*) mummy, mommy (*US*).
Mama² *f* -, -s (*dated*) mama (*dated*).
Mama-: ~**kind** *nt* (*pej*) mummy's boy/girl; ~**söhnchen** *nt* (*pej*) mummy's darling.
Mameluck *m* -en, -en (*Hist*) mameluke.
Mami *f* -, -s (*inf*) *siehe* **Mama¹**.
Mammon *m* -s, *no pl* Mammon. **der schnöde** ~ Mammon, filthy lucre; **dem** ~ **dienen** to serve Mammon; **ein Knecht des** ~**s sein** to be a servant of Mammon.
Mammonismus *m*, *no pl* (*liter*) mammonism (*liter*).
Mammonsdiener *m* (*pej*) servant of Mammon.
Mammut *nt* -s, -s or -e mammoth.
Mammut- *in cpds* (*lit, fig*) mammoth; (*lange dauernd*) marathon; ~**baum** *m* sequoia, giant redwood; ~**prozeß** *m* marathon trial.
mampfen *vti* (*inf*) to munch, to chomp (*inf*). **ich brauche was zu** ~ I want something to eat.
Mamsell *f* -, -en or -s (*dated hum*) lady; (*old: Wirtschafterin*) housekeeper.
man¹ *indef pron dat* **einem**, *acc* **einen** **(a)** you, one; (*ich*) one; (*wir*) we. ~ **kann nie wissen** you or one can never tell, there's no knowing; **das tut** ~ **nicht** that's not done; ~ **wird doch wohl noch fragen dürfen** there's no law against asking.
  (b) (*jemand*) somebody, someone. ~ **hat mir gesagt** ... I was told ..., somebody told me ...; ~ **hat mir erklärt, daß** ... it was explained or somebody explained to me that ...; ~ **hat festgestellt, daß** ... it has been established that ...
  (c) (*die Leute*) they *pl*, people *pl*. **früher glaubte** ~ **they or** people used to believe; ~ **will die alten Häuser niederreißen** they want to pull down the old houses; **diese Farbe trägt** ~ **nicht mehr** this colour isn't worn any more; ~ **hat öfters versucht** ... many attempts have been made ...
  (d) ~ **wende sich an** ... apply to ...; *siehe* **nehmen**.
man² *adv* (*N Ger inf*) just. **denn** ~ **los!** let's go then!; ~ **sachte!**

(just) take it easy!; **jetzt** ~ **schnell!** we'd/you'd *etc* better hurry.
Management ['mænɪdʒmənt] *nt* -s, -s management.
managen ['mɛnɪdʒn] *vt* (*inf*) to manage; (*hinkriegen auch*) to fix. **ich manage das schon!** I'll manage or fix it somehow!
Manager ['mɛnɪdʒɐ] *m* -s, - manager.
Managerkrankheit *f* (*inf*) executivitis (*hum*), stress disease.
manch *indef pron* **(a)** *inv* (*in Zusammensetzung mit ein, eine(r), s*), *substantiviertem Adjektiv und* (*liter*) *Substantiv*) many a. ~ **eine(r),** ~ **ein Mensch** many a person, (a good) many people, quite a few people; ~ **einem kann man nie Vernunft beibringen** you can never teach sense to some people; ~ **anderer** many another; ~ **Schönes** (*geh*) many a beautiful thing; ~ **Erlebnis/schöne Geschichte/Kind** (*all liter*) many an experience/a lovely story/a child.
  (b) (*adjektivisch*) ~**e(r, s)** a good many +*pl*, a fair number of +*pl*, quite a few +*pl*, many a +*sing*; (*pl: einige*) some +*pl*; ~**er,** **der** ... many a person who ..., many *pl* who ..., a good many people *pl* who ..., some (people) *pl* who ...; ~**e hundert Mark** some or several hundreds of marks; ~**es Schöne** a number of or quite a few or a good many beautiful things.
  (c) (*substantivisch*) ~**e(r)** a good many (people/men/women *etc*) *pl*, many a person/man/woman *etc*; (*pl: einige*) some (people/men/women *etc*); ~**es** (*vieles*) a good many things, a number of things, quite a few things *all pl*; (*einiges*) some things *pl*; **so or gar** (*old*) ~**es** a good many things *pl*, quite a few things *pl*; **in** ~**em hat er recht** he's right about a lot of/some things.
manchen|orts *adv siehe* **mancherorts**.
mancherlei *adj inv* (*adjektivisch mit pl n*) various, a number of; (*substantivisch*) various things *pl*, a number of things. ~ **Bier** various kinds of beer.
mancher|orts, mancher|orten *adv* in a number of places, in many a place.
Manchester [man'ʃɛstɐ] *m* -s, *no pl* (*Tex*) broad-ribbed cord(uroy).
Manchesterhose [man'ʃɛstɐ-] *f* corduroy trousers *pl*.
manchmal *adv* sometimes.
Mandant(in *f*) *m* (*Jur*) client.
Mandarin *m* -s, -e (*Hist*) mandarin.
Mandarine *f* mandarin (orange), tangerine.
Mandat *nt* **(a)** (*Auftrag, Vollmacht*) mandate (*auch Pol*), authorization (*gen from*); (*von Anwalt*) brief; (*Parl: Abgeordnetensitz*) seat. **sein** ~ **niederlegen** (*Parl*) to resign one's seat. **(b)** *siehe* **Mandatsgebiet**.
Mandatar *m* **(a)** (*rare: Beauftragter*) mandatary (*form*), agent. **(b)** (*Aus*) member of parliament, representative.
Mandatarstaat *m* mandatary.
Mandats-: ~**gebiet** *nt* mandated territory, mandate; ~**macht** *f* mandatory power; ~**verlust** *m* loss of a seat.
Mandel *f* -, -n **(a)** almond. **(b)** (*Anat*) tonsil. **(c)** (*obs Measure*) fifteen.
Mandel-: ~**augen** *pl* (*poet*) almond eyes *pl*; **m**~**äugig** *adj* (*poet*) almond-eyed; ~**baum** *m* almond tree; ~**entzündung** *f* tonsilitis; **m**~**förmig** *adj* almond-shaped; ~**kern** *m* almond (kernel); ~**kleie** *f* almond meal; ~**öl** *nt* almond oil.
Manderl (*Aus*), **Mandl** (*S Ger*) *nt* -s, -n (*inf*) **(a)** (*Männchen*) little man. **(b)** (*Vogelscheuche*) scarecrow.
Mandoline *f* mandolin.
Mandragora *f* -, **Mandragoren** (*Bot*) mandrake.
Mandrill *m* -s, -e (*Zool*) mandrill.
Mandschu¹ *m* -(s), - Manchu.
Mandschu² *nt* -(s), *no pl* (*Ling*) Manchu.
Mandschurei *f* - **die** ~ Manchuria.
mandschurisch *adj* Manchurian.
Manege [ma'ne:ʒə] *f* -, -n ring, arena.
mang *prep* +*dat or acc* (*N Ger inf*) among(st). **sie ist am liebsten** ~ **den or die Jungens** she likes being with the boys best.
Mangan [maŋ'ga:n] *nt* -s, *no pl* manganese.
Manganat [maŋga'na:t] *nt* (*Chem*) manganate.
Mangan- [maŋ'ga:n-]: ~**eisen** *nt* ferro-manganese; ~**erz** *nt* manganese ore; ~**stahl** *m* manganese steel.
Mangel¹ *f* -, -n mangle; (*Heiß*~) rotary iron. **durch die** ~ **drehen** to put through the mangle; (*fig inf*) to put through it (*inf*); **Prüfling** *etc* **auch** to put through the mill; **jdn in die** ~ **nehmen/in der** ~ **haben** (*fig inf*) to give sb a going-over (*inf*); (*ausfragen auch*) to give sb a grilling (*inf*).
Mangel² *m* -s, ⁻ **(a)** (*Fehler*) fault; (*bei Maschine auch*) defect; (*Unzulänglichkeit auch*) shortcoming; (*Charakter*~) flaw.
  (b) *no pl* (*das Fehlen*) lack (*an* + *dat* of); (*Knappheit auch*) shortage (*an* + *dat* of); (*Med auch*) deficiency (*an* + *dat* of). **aus** ~ **or wegen** ~**s an** (+ *dat*) for lack of, due to a lack of; **wegen** ~**s an Beweisen** for lack of evidence; ~ **an Vitamin C lack of vitamin C, vitamin C deficiency; es besteht or herrscht** ~ **an etw** (*dat*) there is a lack/shortage of sth; ~ **an etw** (*dat*) **haben or leiden** (*liter*) to be short of sth, to lack sth, to have a lack of sth.
  (c) *no pl* (*Entbehrung*) privation, need, want. ~ **leiden** (*liter*) to go short, to suffer hardship or privation; **keinen** ~ **leiden** to want for nothing.
-mangel *m in cpds* shortage of ...; (*Med*) ... deficiency.
Mängelbericht *m* list of faults.
Mangel-: ~**beruf** *m* undersubscribed or understaffed profession; ~**erscheinung** *f* (*Med*) deficiency symptom; **eine** ~**erscheinung sein** (*fig*) to be in short supply (*bei* with).
mangelfrei, mängelfrei *adj* free of faults or defects.
mangelhaft *adj* (*unzulänglich, schlecht*) poor; *Beleuchtung, Ausrüstung auch* inadequate; *Informationen, Interesse* insufficient; (*fehlerhaft*) *Sprachkenntnisse, Ware* faulty; (*Schulnote auch*) unsatisfactory.
Mangelhaftigkeit *f siehe adj* poorness; inadequacy; insufficiency; faultiness.

Mängelhaftung f (Jur) liability for faults or defects.
Mangelkrankheit f deficiency disease.
mangeln[1] 1 vt Wäsche to (put through the) mangle; (heiß ~) to iron, to press. 2 vi to use the mangle/rotary iron.
mangeln[2] 1 vi impers es mangelt an etw (dat) there is a lack of sth; (unzureichend vorhanden auch) there is a shortage of sth; er ließ es an nichts ~ he made sure that he/they etc lacked nothing or that nothing was lacking; es mangelt jdm an etw (dat) sb lacks sth; es mangelt ihm an Selbstvertrauen/Erfahrung he is lacking in or he lacks self-confidence/experience; ~des Selbstvertrauen/Verständnis etc a lack of self-confidence/understanding etc; wegen ~der Aufmerksamkeit through not paying attention; das Kino wurde wegen ~der Sicherheit geschlossen the cinema was closed because of inadequate safety precautions.
2 vi etw mangelt jdm/einer Sache sb/sth lacks sth; (Verständnis, Selbstvertrauen, Erfahrung auch) sb is lacking in sth.
mangels prep +gen (form) for lack of.
Mangel-: ~ware f scarce commodity, commodity in short supply; ~ware sein (fig) to be a rare thing; (Ärzte, gute Lehrer etc) not to grow on trees; ~wäsche f ironing (to be done in a rotary iron).
mangen vti siehe **mangeln**[1].
Mango[1] ['maŋgo] f -, -nen [maŋ'go:nən] or -s (auch ~pflaume) mango.
Mango[2] ['maŋgo] m -(s), -s (auch ~baum) mango (tree).
Mangold ['maŋgɔlt] m -(e)s, -e mangel(-wurzel).
Mangrove [maŋ'gro:və] f -, -n mangrove.
Mangroveküste f mangrove coastline.
Mangrovensumpf m mangrove swamp.
Manichäer m -s, - (Rel) Manichee, Manichaean.
Manie f (Med, fig) mania.
Manier f -, -en (a) no pl (Art und Weise) manner; (eines Künstlers etc) style. auf gute ~ as nicely as possible; in überzeugender ~ in a most convincing manner. (b) ~en pl (Umgangsformen) manners; ~en lernen to learn (some) manners, to learn (how) to behave; das ist doch keine ~ (inf) that's no way to behave. (c) (Angewohnheit) affectation.
maniert adj affected; Benehmen auch mannered.
Maniertheit f siehe adj affectation; manneredness.
Manierismus m (Liter, Art) mannerism.
manierlich 1 adj Kind well-mannered, well-behaved; Benehmen good; Aussehen, Frisur, Kleidung respectable. 2 adv essen politely; sich benehmen properly; sich kleiden respectably.
Manifest nt -(e)s, -e (a) manifesto. (b) (Naut) manifest.
manifest adj (liter) manifest.
Manifestant m (Sw) demonstrator.
Manifestation f manifestation; (offenkundiger Beweis) demonstration; (Sw: Kundgebung) demonstration.
manifestieren* (geh) 1 vt to demonstrate, to manifest. 2 vi (Sw) to demonstrate. 3 vr to manifest oneself.
Maniküre f -, -n (a) (Handpflege) manicure. (b) (Handpflegerin) manicurist.
maniküren* vt to manicure.
Manila nt -s Manil(l)a.
Manila-: ~hanf m Manil(l)a (hemp); ~zigarre f Manil(l)a (cigar).
Maniok m -s, -s (Bot) cassava.
Maniokwurzel f cassava root.
Manipulant m manipulator; (Aus: Amtshelfer) assistant.
Manipulation f manipulation; (Trick) manoeuvre.
Manipulator m (Tech) manipulator; (fig) conjurer, magician.
manipulierbar adj manipulable. leicht/schwer ~ easily manipulated/difficult to manipulate.
Manipulierbarkeit f manipulability.
manipulieren* vt to manipulate.
Manipulierung f manipulation.
manisch adj manic. ~-depressiv, ~-melancholisch manic-depressive; ~-melancholische Krankheit manic depression.
Manitu m -s Manitou.
Manko nt -s, -s (a) (Comm: Fehlbetrag) deficit. ~ haben (inf) or machen (inf) to be short (inf); ~ machen (inf: bei Verkauf) to make a loss. (b) (fig: Nachteil) shortcoming.
Mann m -(e)s, ¨-er (a) man. ein Überschuß an ~ern a surplus of males or men; der böse or schwarze ~ the bogeyman; ein feiner ~ a (perfect) gentleman; ein ~ aus dem Volk(e) a man of the people; der erste ~ or der ~ an der Spritze sein (fig sl) to be in charge; der ~ im Mond(e) the man in the moon; ein ~ der Feder/Wissenschaft a man of letters/science; ein ~ des Todes a dead man, a man marked for death; ein ~ von Format etc a man of stature etc; ein ~ von Wort a man of his word; wo ¨-er noch ¨-er sind where men are men; er ist unser ~ he's the man for us, he's our man; er ist nicht der ~ dafür or danach he's not the man for that; (nicht seine Art) he's not the sort; drei ~ hoch (inf) three of them together; wie ein ~ as a or one man; auf den ~ dressiert sein to be trained to go for people; etw an den ~ bringen (inf) to get rid of sth; seinen ~ gefunden haben (verkauft werden) to have found a buyer; seinen ~ stehen to hold one's own; (auf eigenen Füßen stehen) to stand on one's own two feet; einen kleinen ~ im Ohr haben (hum sl) to be crazy (inf); und ein ~, ein Wort, er hat's auch gemacht and, as good as his word, he did it; ~ an ~ close together, next to one another; ~ für ~ (einzeln hintereinander) one after the other; (allesamt) every single one; ~ gegen ~ man against man; pro ~ per head; ein Gespräch unter ¨-ern or von ~ zu ~ a man-to-man talk; siehe Mannen, Mann, tot et etc.
(b) (Ehe~) husband. jdn an den ~ bringen (inf) to marry sb off (inf), to find sb a husband; ~ und Frau werden to become man and wife.

(c) pl **Leute** (Besatzungsmitglied) hand, man. 20 ~ 20 hands or men; mit ~ und Maus untergehen to go down with all hands; (Passagierschiff) to go down with no survivors.
(d) pl **Leute** (Teilnehmer, Sport, Cards) player, man. auf den ~ spielen to play the ball at one's opponent; (beim Zuspielen) to pass accurately; den dritten ~ spielen (Cards) to play or take the third hand.
(e) (inf: als Interjektion) (my) God (inf); (auffordernd, bewundernd, erstaunt auch) hey, (hey) man (sl). ~, das kannst du doch nicht machen! hey, you can't do that!; mach schnell, ~! hurry up, man!; ~, oh ~! oh boy! (inf); (mein) lieber ~! my God! (inf); (erstaunt, bewundernd auch) wow! (inf); ~ Gottes! good God! (inf).
Männchen nt dim of Mann (a) little man; (Zwerg) man(n)ikin. ~ malen to draw (little) matchstick men, ≈ to doodle. (b) (Biol) male; (Vogel~ auch) cock. (c) ~ machen (Tier) to sit up on its hind legs; (Hund) to (sit up and) beg; (pej inf) (Mensch) to grovel; (hum: Soldat) to jump smartly to attention.
Männe m -, no pl (a) (dial) dim of Hermann. (b) (inf: Ehemann) hubby (inf).
Mannen pl (Hist: Gefolgsleute) men pl.
Mannequin [manə'kɛ̃:, 'manəkɛ̃] nt -s, -s (fashion) model.
Männer pl of Mann.
Männer-: ~bekanntschaft f usu pl man friend, boyfriend; von ~bekanntschaften leben to earn one's living from prostitution; ~bund m male organization; ~chor m male-voice choir; ~fang m auf ~fang ausgehen/sein to go/be looking for a man/men; (zwecks Heirat) to go be husband-hunting; ~freund m (Mann) man's man; (Frau) friend of the male sex; ~freundschaft f friendship between men; er hat immer ~freundschaften vorgezogen he has always preferred friendship(s) with other men; ~gesangverein m male choral society; ~haß m hatred of men; m~mordend adj man-eating; ~sache f (Angelegenheit) man's business; (Arbeit) job for a man, man's job; ~sachen men's affairs; Fußball war früher ~sache football used to be a male preserve; ~stimme f man's voice; (Mus) male voice; ~treu f -, - (Bot) speedwell; ~welt f (dated) men pl.
Mannes-: ~alter nt manhood no art; im besten ~alter sein to be in one's prime or in the prime of (one's) life; ~jahre pl years of manhood pl; in die ~jahre kommen to reach manhood; ~kraft f (dated, hum) virility.
Mannesmannrohr ® nt seamless metal tube, Mannesmann tube.
Mannes-: ~schwäche f (dated, euph) impotence, lack of virility; ~stamm m (old, liter) male line; ~stolz m masculine pride; ~treue f (old) loyalty between men; ~wort nt (old) word as a man; ~würde f (old) accoutrements of manhood pl; (hum) dignity as a man; ~zucht f (old) military discipline.
mannhaft adj manly no adv; (tapfer) manful, valiant; (entschlossen) resolute; Widerstand stout.
Mannhaftigkeit f, no pl siehe adj manliness; manfulness, valour; resolution; stoutness.
mannigfach adj attr manifold, multifarious.
mannigfaltig adj diverse, varied.
Mannigfaltigkeit f diversity, variety.
Männin f (Bibl) woman.
Männlein nt dim of Mann little man; (Zwerg) man(n)ikin. ~ und Weiblein (hum inf) boys and girls.
männlich adj (a) male; Reim, Wort masculine. (b) (fig: mannhaft) Stärke, Mut, Entschluß, Wesen manly; Auftreten, Stimme auch masculine; Frau masculine, mannish.
Männlichkeit f (fig) manliness; (von Auftreten, Stimme auch) masculinity; (von Frau) masculinity, mannishness.
Mannloch nt (Tech) manhole.
Mannsbild nt (dated pej) fellow, male.
Mannschaft f (Sport, fig) team; (Naut, Aviat) crew. ~(en) (Mil) men pl.
Mannschafts- in cpds (Sport) team; ~aufstellung f team line-up; (das Aufstellen) selection of the team; ~dienstgrad m (Mil) other rank usu pl; ~führer m (Sport) (team) captain; ~geist m team spirit; ~kampf m (Sport) team event; ~kost f (Sport) team fare; (Mil) troops' rations pl; (Naut, Aviat) crew's rations pl; ~raum m (Sport) team quarters pl; (Mil) men's quarters pl; (Naut) crew's quarters pl; (Umkleideraum) changing rooms pl; ~sieger m (Sport) winning team; ~spiel nt, ~sport m team sport; ~verpflegung f siehe ~kost; ~wagen m police van; (Mil) troop carrier.
Manns-: m~hoch adj as high as a man; der Schnee liegt m~hoch the snow is six feet deep; ~leute pl (dated inf) men pl; ~person f (dated pej) siehe ~bild; m~toll adj man-mad (inf); ~tollheit f nymphomania; ~volk nt (dated inf) men pl.
Mannweib nt (pej) masculine or mannish woman.
Manometer nt (Tech) pressure gauge. ~! (inf) wow! (inf), boy oh boy! (inf).
Manöver [ma'nø:vɐ] nt -s, - (lit, fig) manoeuvre. ins ~ gehen or ziehen to go on manoeuvres; nach größeren ~n ... (Mot, fig etc) after a lot of manoeuvring ...
Manöver-: ~gelände nt exercise area; (ständig) ranges pl; ~kritik f (fig) inquest, post-mortem; ~schaden m damage resulting from military manoeuvres.
manövrieren* [manø'vri:rən] vti (lit, fig) to manoeuvre.
Manövrier- [manø'vri:ɐ]: m~fähig adj manoeuvrable; ~fähigkeit f manoeuvrability; m~unfähig adj disabled.
Mansarde f -, -n garret; (Boden) attic.
Mansarden- in cpds attic.
Mansch m -es, no pl (inf) (Brei) mush; (Schlamm) mud; (Schneematsch) slush.
manschen vi (inf) to mess around (inf).
Manschette f (a) (Ärmelaufschlag) cuff. (b) (Umhüllung) frill.

(c) (Tech: Dichtung) sleeve.
(d) (Sport: Würgegriff) stranglehold. **~n haben** (inf) to be scared stupid (inf); **vor seinem Vater/der Prüfung hat er mächtige ~n** (inf) his father/the thought of the exam scares him stupid; **~n kriegen** (inf) to get cold feet.
Manschettenknopf m cufflink.
Mantel m -s, ¨ **(a)** coat; (loser ~) cloak; siehe Wind.
(b) (Tech) (Glocken~) cope; (Rohr~) jacket; (Geschoß~) jacket, casing; (Kabel~) casing; (Reifen~) outer tyre, casing.
(c) (Math) curved surface.
(d) (Fin) share certificate.
(e) (Comm: Firmen~) form.
(f) (Zool) mantle, pallium.
(g) (fig) cloak, mantle. **etw mit dem ~ der christlichen Nächstenliebe zudecken** to forgive and forget sth.
Mäntelchen nt dim of **Mantel**. **einer Sache** (dat) **ein ~ umhängen** to cover sth up.
Mantel- in cpds (Tex) coat; **~geschoß** nt jacketed bullet; **~gesetz** nt siehe **Rahmengesetz**; **~pavian** m sacred or hamadryas baboon; **~sack** m (old) portmanteau (old); **~stoff** m coating, coat fabric; **~tarif** m siehe **Rahmentarif**; **~tiere** pl tunicates pl (spec).
Mantik f (Rel) mantic art, divination.
Mantsch m -es, no pl (inf) siehe **Mansch**.
mantschen vi (inf) siehe **manschen**.
Manual nt -s, -e **(a)** (Mus) manual. **(b)** (old Comm) daily ledger.
manuell adj Arbeit manual. **etw ~ bedienen** to operate sth manually or by hand.
Manufaktur f (old, Sociol) **(a)** no pl manufacture. **(b)** (Fabrik) factory, manufactory (old).
Manufakturwaren pl manufactured goods pl; (Textilien) textiles pl.
Manus nt -, - (Typ: esp Aus) manuscript.
Manuskript nt -(e)s, -e manuscript; (Rad, Film, TV) script.
Maoismus m Maoism.
Maoist(in f) m Maoist.
maoistisch adj Maoist.
Maori m -(s), -(s) Maori.
Mappe f -, -n (Aktenhefter) folder, file; (Aktentasche) briefcase; (Schul~) (school) bag; (Feder~, Bleistift~) pencil case.
Mär f -, -en (old) siehe **Mär(e)**.
Marabu m -s, -s (Orn) marabou.
Marathon- in cpds marathon; **~lauf** m marathon; **~läufer** m marathon runner.
Marbel, Märbel f -, -n (dial) marble.
Märchen nt -s, - fairytale, fairy story; (inf) tall story.
Märchen- in cpds fairytale; **~buch** nt book of fairytales; **~dichtung** f writing of fairytales; **~erzähler** m teller of fairytales; (fig) storyteller; **~film** m film of a fairytale; **m~haft** adj fairytale attr, fabulous; (fig) fabulous, fantastic; **~land** nt fairyland; **~prinz** m Prince Charming; (fig auch) fairytale prince; **~stunde** f story time.
Marder m -s, - marten.
Marder-: **~fell** nt, **~pelz** m marten (fur).
Mär(e) f -(e), -en (old) (Nachricht) tidings pl, news; (Märchen) (fairy)tale; (hum inf) fairy story.
mären vi (dial) to mess around or about (inf).
Margarete f - Margaret.
Margarine [(Aus) -'ri:n] f margarine.
Marge ['marʒə] f -, -n (Comm) margin.
Margerite f -, -n daisy, marguerite.
marginal adj marginal.
Marginalie [-iə] f usu pl marginalia pl.
Maria f - Mary. **die Mutter ~** the Virgin Mary, Our (Blessed) Lady.
Mariä: **~ Empfängnis** f the Immaculate Conception; **~ Geburt** f (the) Nativity of Mary; **~ Himmelfahrt** f Assumption.
marianisch adj Marian.
Mariatheresientaler, Maria-Theresien-Taler [-te're:ziən-] m Maria Theresa thaler, Levant dollar.
Marie f - Mary; (sl: Geld) dough (sl), bread (sl). **dicke ~** (sl) bulging wallet.
Marien- [-iən]: **~altar** m Lady altar; **~bild** nt picture of the Virgin Mary; **~dichtung** f hymns and poems pl in praise of the Virgin Mary; **~fäden** pl gossamer sing; **~fest** nt Lady Day; **~käfer** m ladybird; **~kult** m Mariolatry (form), cult of the Virgin Mary; **~leben** nt (Art, Liter) Life of the Virgin Mary; **~verehrung** f adoration or veneration of the Virgin Mary.
Marihuana [mari'hua:na] nt -s, no pl marijuana.
Marille f -, -n (Aus) apricot.
Marinade f (Cook) marinade; (Soße) mayonnaise-based sauce. **~n** pl (Fischkonserven) canned or tinned (Brit) fish.
Marine f navy.
Marine- in cpds naval; **m~blau** adj navy blue; **~flieger** m naval pilot; **~flugzeug** nt naval aircraft or plane; **~infanterie** f marines pl; **~maler** m marine or seascape painter; **~minister** m minister of naval affairs; **~ministerium** nt ministry of naval affairs.
Mariner m -s, - (inf) sailor.
Marine-: **~soldat** m marine; **~truppen** pl marines pl; **~wesen** nt navy; **ein Begriff aus dem ~wesen** a nautical term.
marinieren* vt Fisch, Fleisch to marinate, to marinade. **marinierter Hering** pickled herring.
Marionette f marionette, puppet; (fig) puppet.
Marionetten- in cpds puppet; **~spieler** m puppeteer; **~theater** nt puppet theatre.
maritim adj maritime.
Mark¹ nt -(e)s, no pl (Knochen~) marrow; (Bot: Gewebe~) medulla, pith. **Brühe mit ~** (Cook) consommé with beef

marrow; **bis ins ~** (fig) to the core; **jdn bis ins ~ treffen** (fig) to cut sb to the quick; **es geht mir durch ~ und Bein** (inf) or **durch ~ und Pfennig** (hum inf) it goes right through me; **kein ~ in den Knochen haben** (fig) to have no guts or backbone; **jdm das ~ aus den Knochen saugen** (liter) to bleed sb dry.
Mark² f -, -en **(a)** (Grenzland) borderland, march (rare). **die ~ Brandenburg, die ~** (inf) the Mark Brandenburg, the Brandenburg Marches, die **~en** (Hist) the Marches.
(b) (Rugby) touch.
Mark³ f -, - or (hum) ¨er mark. **Deutsche ~** German mark, deutschmark; **~ der DDR** (East German) mark; **vier ~ zwanzig** four marks twenty (pfennigs); **mit jeder ~ rechnen, die or jede ~ umdrehen** to think twice before spending anything; **mit jeder ~ rechnen müssen** to have to count every penny.
markant adj (ausgeprägt) clear-cut; Schriftzüge clearly defined; (hervorstechend) Kinn etc prominent; (auffallend) Erscheinung, Persönlichkeit striking.
Mark Aurel m - - Marcus Aurelius.
markdurchdringend adj (geh) bloodcurdling.
Marke f -, -n **(a)** (bei Lebens- und Genußmitteln) brand; (bei Industriegütern) make. **du bist (vielleicht) eine ~!** (inf) you're a right or fine one (inf); **eine komische ~** (fig inf) a queer or rum customer or character.
(b) (Brief~) stamp. **zehn ~n à or zu fünfzig** ten fifty-pfennig stamps.
(c) (Essen~) voucher; (Rabatt~) (trading) stamp; (Lebensmittel~) coupon; (old: Renten~) stamp. **auf ~n** (inf) on coupons; **~n einführen** (inf) to introduce rationing or coupons; **~n kleben** (inf) to buy one's stamps.
(d) (Erkennungs~) disc, tag; (Garderoben~) cloakroom counter or (Zettel) ticket or check (US); (Polizei~) badge; (Spiel~) chip; (Pfand~ etc) token; siehe **Hundemarke**.
(e) (Rekord~) record; (Wasserstands~) watermark.
märken vt (Aus) Wäsche to mark.
Marken-: **~album** nt (inf) stamp album; **~artikel** m proprietary article; **~butter** f non-blended butter, best quality butter; **~erzeugnis, ~fabrikat** nt proprietary article; **m~frei** adj **(a)** (ohne Marken) unrationed, not on coupons; **(b)** (ohne Warenzeichen) non-branded; **~hersteller** m manufacturer of proprietary goods; **~name** m brand or proprietary name; **~schutz** m protection of trademarks; **~ware** f siehe **~artikel**.
Märker(in f) m -s, - inhabitant of the Mark Brandenburg.
markerschütternd adj siehe **markdurchdringend**.
Marketender(in f) m -s, - (Hist) sutler.
Marketenderware f (Mil) goods pl or (einzelner Artikel) article sold at army stores.
Marketing nt -s, no pl marketing.
Mark- (Hist): **~graf** m margrave; **~gräfin** f margravine; **m~gräflich** adj margravial; **~grafschaft** f margravate.
markieren* **1** vt (lit, fig, Sport) to mark; (inf: vortäuschen) to play. **den starken Mann ~** to come the strong man; **den Dummen** or **Dusseligen ~** (inf) to act daft (inf).
2 vi (inf: so tun, als ob) to put it on (inf). **markier doch nicht!** stop putting it on.
Markierung f marking; (Zeichen) mark.
Markierungs-: **~linie** f (marking) line; **~punkt** m marker.
markig adj (kraftvoll, kernig) vigorous, pithy; (iro: pathetisch) grandiloquent, bombastic.
Markigkeit f vigour, pithiness; (iro) grandiloquence, bombast.
märkisch adj of/from the Mark Brandenburg.
Markise f -, -n awning, (sun)blind.
Markknochen m (Cook) marrowbone.
Markscheide f (Min) boundary line.
Markscheide-: **~kunde, ~kunst** f mine surveying.
Markscheider m -s, - mine surveyor.
Mark-: **~schein** m mark note or bill (US); **10-~-Schein** or **Zehnmarkschein** ten-mark note or bill (US); **~stein** m (lit, fig) milestone; (an Feldern etc) boundary stone; **~stück** nt (one-) mark piece; **m~stückgroß** adj the size of a one-mark piece.
Markt m -(e)s, ¨e **(a)** market; (Jahr~) fair. **zum** or **auf den ~ gehen** to go to (the) market/to the fair; **~ abhalten** to hold or have a market; **dienstags/jede Woche einmal ist ~** or **wird ~ abgehalten** there is a market every Tuesday/week.
(b) (Comm) market; (Warenverkehr) trade. **auf dem** or **am ~** on the market; **auf den ~ bringen** to put on the market; **etw in großen Mengen auf den ~ werfen** to flood the market with sth; **auf den ~ gebracht werden** to come on the market.
(c) (~platz) marketplace, market square. **am ~** in the marketplace; **am ~ wohnen** to live on the marketplace.
(d) (geh: ~flecken) small market town.
Markt- in cpds market; **~absprache** f marketing agreement; **~anteil** m share of the market; **m~beherrschend** adj **m~beherrschende Stellung einnehmen** to control or dominate the market; **~bericht** m (Fin) stock market report; **~bude** f market stall.
markten vi (rare) siehe **feilschen**.
Markt-: **m~fähig** adj marketable; **~fahrer** m (Aus) (travelling) marketman; **~flecken** m small market town; **~forschung** f market research; **~frau** f market woman, (woman) stallholder; **m~gängig** adj marketable; Preis current; **m~gerecht** adj in line with or geared to market requirements; **~halle** f covered market; **~helfer** m market hand; **~lage** f state of the market; **~lücke** f gap in the market; **in eine ~lücke stoßen** to fill a gap in the market; **~ordnung** f market regulations pl; **~ort** m (small) market town; **~platz** m marketplace, market square; **am/auf dem ~platz** on/in the marketplace; **~psychologie** f marketing psychology; **~recht** nt (Hist) market rights pl; **~schreier** m barker, market crier; **m~schreierisch** adj loud and vociferous;

(fig) blatant; ~**stand** m market stall or stand; ~**weib** nt *(pej)* market woman; *(fig)* fish-wife; ~**wert** m market value; ~**wirtschaft** f market economy; siehe frei; m~**wirtschaftlich** adj attr free enterprise.

Markus m - Mark.

Markus|evangelium nt Gospel according to St Mark, St Mark's Gospel.

Marmarameer nt Sea of Marmara.

Marmel f -, -n marble.

Marmelade f jam; *(Orangen~)* marmalade.

Marmeláden-: ~**brot** nt jam sandwich; *(Scheibe)* slice of bread and jam; ~**glas** nt jam-jar.

marmeln vi to play marbles.

Marmor m -s, -e marble.

Marmor- in cpds marble; ~**bild** nt *(liter)* marble statue; ~**bruch** m marble quarry.

marmorieren* vt to marble. mit marmoriertem Schnitt with marbled edges, marbled.

Marmorkuchen m marble cake.

marmorn adj marble.

marode adj *(inf)* washed-out *(inf)*.

Marodeur [-'dø:ɐ] m marauder.

marodieren* vi to maraud.

Marokkaner(in f) m -s, - Moroccan.

marokkanisch adj Moroccan.

Marokko nt -s Morocco.

Marone[1] f -, -n, **Maroni** f -, - (sweet or Spanish) chestnut.

Marone[2] f -, -n **Maronenpilz** m chestnut boletus, boletus badius *(spec)*.

Maronibrater m -s, - *(Aus)* chestnut man *(inf)*, chestnut vendor.

Maronit m -en, -en Maronite.

Marotte f -, -n quirk. das ist ihre ~ that's one of her little quirks.

Marquis [mar'ki:] m -, - marquis.

Marquise [mar'ki:zə] f -, -n marquise.

Mars[1] m -, no pl *(Myth, Astron)* Mars.

Mars[2] m -, -e *(Naut)* top.

Marsbewohner m Martian.

marsch interj (a) *(Mil)* march. vorwärts ~! forward march!; **(im Laufschritt,)** ~! ~! (at the double,) quick march! (b) *(inf)* off with you. ~ ins Bett! off to bed with you at the double or chop, chop *(inf)*!; raus hier, ~! ~! get out of here at the double or chop, chop *(inf)*!

Marsch[1] m -(e)s, =e *(das Marschieren)* march; *(Wanderung)* hike. einen ~ **machen** to go on a march/hike; **sich in ~ setzen** to move off. (b) *(~musik)* march. **jdm den ~ blasen** *(inf)* to give sb a rocket *(inf)*.

Marsch[2] f -, -en marsh, fen.

Marschall m -s, **Marschälle** (field) marshal.

Marschallstab m (field) marshal's baton. **den ~ im Tornister haben** *(fig)* to be a potential leader of men.

Marsch-: ~**befehl** m *(Mil)* *(für Truppen)* marching orders pl; *(für einzelnen)* travel orders pl; m~**bereit** adj ready to move; ~**boden** m marshy soil.

Marschendorf nt fenland village.

Marsch-: m~**fertig** adj siehe m~**bereit**; ~**gepäck** nt pack.

marschieren* vi aux sein to march; *(fig)* to march off, to take oneself off. **getrennt ~, vereint schlagen** to unite for the attack.

Marsch-: ~**kolonne** f column; ~**kompaß** m compass; ~**land** nt marsh(land), fen; ~**lied** nt marching song; m~**mäßig** adj Ausrüstung etc marching attr; *(für Wanderung)* hiking attr; m~**mäßig angezogen** dressed for marching/hiking; ~**musik** f military marches pl; ~**ordnung** f marching order; ~**pause** f halt; ~**richtung** f march direction; ~**route** f *(lit)* route of march; *(fig)* line of approach; ~**tempo** nt marching time; *(Mus)* march time or tempo; ~**verpflegung** f rations pl; *(Mil)* field rations pl; ~**ziel** nt destination.

Marseille [mar'zɛ:j, mar'sɛ:j] nt -s Marseilles.

Marsfeld nt *(in Rom)* Campus Martius; *(in Paris)* Champs de Mars.

Marshallplan ['marʃal-] m *(Pol)* Marshall Plan.

Marsmensch m Martian.

Marssegel nt *(Naut)* topsail.

Marstall m -(e)s, **Marställe** *(Hist)* royal stables pl.

Marter f -, -n *(liter)* torment. **jdm ~n bereiten** or **zufügen** to cause sb anguish; **das kann zur ~ werden** it can be a painful ordeal.

Marter-: ~**gerät**, ~**instrument** nt instrument of torture.

Marterl nt -s, -n *(S Ger, Aus)* wayside shrine with a crucifix.

martern *(liter)* 1 vt to torture, to torment. **jdn zu Tode ~** to torture sb to death. 2 vr to torment or torture oneself.

Marter-: ~**pfahl** m stake; ~**tod** m *(liter)* siehe **Märtyrertod**.

Marterung f *(liter)* torment.

Marter-: m~**voll** adj *(liter)* anguished; **Stunden ~** of anguish; ~**werkzeug** nt siehe ~**gerät**.

martialisch [mar'tsia:lɪʃ] adj *(geh)* martial, warlike.

Martin-Horn ® nt siehe **Martinshorn**.

Martini nt -, no pl *(Eccl)* Martinmas.

Martins-: ~**fest** nt, ~**tag** m siehe **Martini**.

Martinshorn ® nt *(von Polizei und Feuerwehr)* siren. **mit ~** with its siren blaring or going.

Märtyrer, Martyrer *(Eccl)* m -s, - *(Eccl, fig)* martyr. **jdn zum ~ machen** to make a martyr of sb; **sich als ~ aufspielen** *(pej)* to make a martyr of oneself.

Märty(re)rin, Marty(re)rin *(Eccl)* f martyr.

Märtyrer-: ~**krone** f martyr's crown; ~**tod** m martyr's death; **den ~tod sterben** to die a martyr's death; ~**tum** nt martyrdom.

Martyrium nt (a) *(Opfertod)* martyrdom; *(fig)* ordeal. (b) *(Grabkirche)* martyry.

Marxismus m Marxism.

Marxismus-Leninismus m Marxism-Leninism.

Marxist(in f) m Marxist.

marxistisch adj Marxist.

Marxsch adj Marxian. **die ~e Dialektik** Marx's or Marxian dialectic.

März m -(es) or -en *(liter)*, -e March. **im ~** in March; **im Monat ~** in the month of March; **heute ist der zweite ~** today is the second of March or is March the second or March second *(US)*; **(geschrieben)** today is 2nd March or March 2nd; **am ersten ~ fahren wir nach ...** on the first of March we are going to ...; **in diesem ~** this March; **im Laufe des ~** during March; **der ~ war sehr warm** March was very warm; **Anfang/Ende/Mitte ~** at the beginning/end/in the middle of March; **den 4. ~ 1973** March 4th, 1973, **4th March 1973.**

Märzbecher, Märzenbecher m *(Bot)* snowflake; *(inf: Narzisse)* narcissus.

Märzen nt -(s), -, **März(en)bier** nt strong light beer.

März-: ~**flecken** pl *(Sw)* freckles pl; ~**fliege** f March fly; ~**gefallene** pl *(Hist)* revolutionaries pl killed during the 1848 revolution.

Marzipan nt [martsi'pa:n, *(Aus)* 'martsipa:n] -s, -e marzipan.

märzlich adj March-like.

März-: ~**revolution** f *(Hist)* Revolution of March 1848; ~**veilchen** nt sweet violet.

Masche f -, -n (a) *(Strick~, Häkel~)* stitch; *(von Netz)* hole; *(von Kettenhemd)* link; *(Lauf~)* ladder *(Brit)*, run. **die ~n eines Netzes** the mesh sing of a net; **dir läuft eine ~ am Bein/Strumpf (runter)** you've got a ladder or run (in your stocking); **(jdm) durch die ~n schlüpfen** to slip through sb's/the net; *(fig auch)* to slip through sb's fingers; **durch die ~n des Gesetzes schlüpfen** to slip through a loophole in the law.
  (b) *(S Ger, Aus: Schleife)* bow.
  (c) *(inf)* *(Trick)* trick, dodge *(inf)*; *(Eigenart)* fad, craze. **die ~ raushaben** to know how to do it; **er versucht es immer noch auf die alte ~** he's still trying the same old trick; **das ist die ~!** that's the thing!; **das ist seine neueste ~ or die neueste ~ von ihm** that's his latest (fad or craze).

Maschen-: ~**draht** m wire netting; ~**drahtzaun** m wire-netting fence; m~**fest** adj Strümpfe non-run; ~**netz** nt mesh, net; ~**werk** nt *(fig)* **sich im ~werk von etw verfangen** to become enmeshed in sth.

Maschin- *(Aus)* in cpds siehe **Maschine(n)-**.

Maschine f (a) machine; *(Motor)* engine; *(Flugzeug)* plane. **eine bloße ~ sein** *(fig)* to be no more than a machine; **zur ~ werden** *(fig)* to become a machine; **etw auf or mit der ~ schreiben** to type sth; **ich habe den Brief meiner Sekretärin in die ~ diktiert** my secretary typed the letter as I dictated it; **siehe maschine(n)schreiben.**
  (b) *(inf: dicke Frau)* fat old bag *(pej inf)*.

maschinell 1 adj Herstellung, Bearbeitung mechanical, machine attr. 2 adv mechanically, by machine.

Maschinen-: ~**antrieb** m machine drive; **mit ~antrieb** machine-driven, mechanically driven; ~**arbeit** f machine work; ~**bau** m mechanical engineering; ~**bauer** m mechanical engineer; ~**bauingenieur** m mechanical engineer; ~**defekt** m mechanical fault; ~**diktat** nt typing directly from dictation; ~**element** nt machine component; ~**fabrik** f engineering works sing or pl; ~**garn** nt machine thread; ~**genossenschaft** f agricultural machinery co-operative; m~**geschrieben** adj typewritten, typed; ~**geschütz** nt machine-gun; m~**gestrickt** adj machine-knitted; ~**gewehr** nt machine-gun; **mit ~gewehr(en) beschießen** to machine-gun; ~**gewehr-Schütze** m machine-gunner; ~**hammer** m mechanical hammer; ~**haus** nt machine room; ~**industrie** f engineering industry; ~**kanone** f siehe ~**geschütz**; ~**kraft** f mechanical power; m~**mäßig** adj in terms of machinery; m~**mäßige Ausstattung** machinery; ~**meister** m *(Aufseher)* machine minder; *(Theat)* stage technician; *(Typ)* pressman; ~**öl** nt lubricating oil; ~**park** m plant; ~**pistole** f submachine gun; ~**raum** m plant room; *(Naut)* engine-room; ~**revision** f *(Typ)* press proof; ~**saal** m machine room; *(Typ)* pressroom; *(in Setzerei)* caseroom; ~**satz** m (a) machine unit; (b) *(Typ)* machine setting or composition; ~**schaden** m mechanical fault; *(Aviat etc)* engine fault; ~**schlosser** m engine fitter.

Maschine(n)-: m~**schreiben** vi sep irreg *(Kleinschreibung nur bei infin und ptp)* to type; **sie schreibt Maschine** she types; ~**schreiben** nt typing, typewriting; ~**schreiber** m typist.

Maschinen-: ~**schrift** f typescript, typing; *(Schriftart)* typeface; **in ~schrift** typed, typewritten; m~**schriftlich** adj typewritten no adv; m~**schriftliches Manuskript** typescript, typewritten manuscript; ~**setzer** m machine compositor or typesetter; ~**stürmer** m -s, - machine wrecker; *(Hist)* Luddite; ~**stürmerei** f Luddism; ~**teil** nt machine part; ~**(-und)-Traktoren-Station** f *(DDR)* agricultural machinery centre; ~**waffe** f automatic weapon; ~**wärter** m machine minder; ~**zeitalter** nt machine age.

Maschinerie f (a) *(dated: Mechanismus)* piece of machinery. (b) *(Bühnen~)* stage machinery. (c) *(fig: Getriebe)* machinery.

Maschinist(in f) m *(Schiffs~)* engineer; *(Eisenbahn~)* engine-driver, engineer *(US)*.

Maser[1] f -, -n vein. **Holz mit feinen ~n** wood with a fine grain.

Maser[2] ['meɪzɐ, 'maːzɐ] m -s, - *(Phys)* maser.

Maserholz nt grained wood.

maserig adj grained.

masern 1 vt to grain. 2 vi to become grained.

Masern pl measles sing. **die ~ haben** to have (the) measles.

Maserung f grain.

Maske f -, -n (a) *(lit, fig, Sport, Med)* mask. **sein Gesicht wurde**

or erstarrte zur ~ his face froze (into a mask); die ~ abnehmen *or* ablegen to take off one's mask, to unmask; (*fig*) to drop all pretence, to let fall one's mask; die ~ fallen lassen *or* abwerfen (*fig*) to throw off one's mask; jdm die ~ herunterreißen *or* vom Gesicht reißen (*fig*) to unmask sb; ohne ~ (*fig*) undisguised; unter der ~ von etw (*fig*) under the guise of sth; das ist alles nur ~ that's all just pretence.
  (b) (*Theat: Aufmachung*) make-up. ~ machen to make up.
  (c) (*maskierte Person*) mask, domino (*old*); (*fig*) phony (*inf*).
Masken-: ~ball *m* masked ball; ~bildner *m* make-up artist; m~haft *adj* mask-like, like a mask; ~kleid, ~kostüm *nt* fancy-dress costume; ~spiele *pl* (*Liter*) masques *pl*; ~verleih *m* fancy-dress hire, theatrical costumier; ~zug *m* carnival procession.
Maskerade *f* (*Verkleidung*) costume; (*old*) masquerade.
maskieren* 1 *vt* **(a)** (*verkleiden*) to dress up; (*unkenntlich machen*) to disguise. **(b)** (*verbergen*) to mask, to disguise. 2 *vr* to dress up; (*sich unkenntlich machen*) to disguise oneself. sich als jd/etw ~ (*fig*) to masquerade as sb/sth.
maskiert *adj* masked.
Maskierung *f* **(a)** (*das Verkleiden*) dressing up; (*Sich-Unkenntlichmachen*) disguising oneself. **(b)** (*Verkleidung*) fancy-dress costume; (*von Spion etc*) disguise. **(c)** (*Verhüllung*) masking.
Maskottchen *nt* (lucky) mascot.
maskulin *adj* **(a)** (*Gram, Poet*) masculine. **(b)** [masku'li:n] (*betont männlich*) masculine.
Maskulinum *nt* -s, **Maskulina** masculine noun.
Maso *m* -s, *no pl* (*sl*) *abbr of* **Masochismus**.
Masochismus *m* -, *no pl* masochism.
Masochist(in *f)* *m* masochist.
masochistisch *adj* masochist.
maß *pret of* **messen**.
Maß[1] *nt* -es, -e **(a)** (*~einheit*) measure (*für* of); (*Zollstock*) rule; (*Bandmaß*) tape measure. ~e und Gewichte weights and measures; das ~ aller Dinge (*fig*) the measure of all things; das richtige *or* rechte ~ halten (*fig*) to strike the right balance; mit zweierlei *or* verschiedenem ~ messen (*fig*) to operate a double standard; das ~ ist voll (*fig*) that's enough (of that), enough's enough; und, um das ~ vollzumachen ... (*fig*) and to cap it all ...; in reichem ~(e) abundantly, in reichem ~(e) vorhanden sein to be abundant; (*Energie, Zeit etc*) to be plentiful; er hat sich in reichem ~e erkenntlich gezeigt he gave abundant proof of his gratitude; das (übliche) ~ überschreiten, über das übliche ~ hinausgehen to overstep the mark; die edlen ~e dieser Plastik (*geh*) the noble proportions of this statue.
  (b) (*Meßgröße*) measurement; (*von Zimmer, Möbelstück auch*) dimension. ihre ~e sind: ... her measurements *or* vital statistics are ...; sich (*dat*) etw nach ~ anfertigen lassen to have sth made to measure *or* order (*US*); ~ nehmen to measure up; bei jdm ~ nehmen to measure sb, to take sb's measurements; jdn ~ nehmen (*fig inf*) to give sb what for (*inf*); Schuhe/Hemden nach ~ shoes/shirts made to measure *or* order (*US*), custom (*US*) shoes/shirts.
  (c) (*Ausmaß*) extent, degree. ein solches/gewisses ~ an *or* von ... such a degree/a certain degree of ...; in hohem ~(e) to a high degree; in solchem ~(e) *or* in einem ~(e), daß ... to such an extent that ...; in nicht geringem ~(e) in no small measure; in großem ~e to a great extent; in vollem ~e fully; in demselben *or* gleichem ~e wie die Produktion steigt, steigt auch der Verbrauch when production increases, consumption increases accordingly; die Bäcker verlangen eine Lohnerhöhung in demselben *or* in gleichem ~e, wie die Fleischer the bakers are demanding a pay rise comparable to *or* with that of the butchers; in besonderem ~e especially; in gewissem/höherem *or* stärkerem/beschränktem ~ to a certain/greater/limited degree *or* extent; in höchstem ~e extremely; über alle ~en (*liter*) beyond (all) measure.
  (d) (*Mäßigung*) moderation. in *or* mit ~en in moderation; weder ~ noch Ziel kennen to know no bounds; ohne ~ und Ziel immoderately.
Maß[2] *f* -, - (*S Ger, Aus*) litre (tankard) of beer. zwei ~ Bier two litres of beer.
Massage [ma'sa:ʒə] *f* -, -n massage. ~n nehmen to have massage treatment.
Massage-: ~institut *nt siehe* ~salon; ~praxis *f* physiotherapy centre; ~salon *m* (*euph*) massage parlour; ~stab *m* vibrator.
Massaker *nt* -s, - massacre.
massakrieren* *vt* (*dated, inf*) to massacre.
Maß-: ~analyse *f* (*Chem*) volumetric analysis; ~angabe *f* measurement; (*bei Hohlmaßen*) volume *no pl*; Gläser in Restaurants müssen eine ~angabe haben glasses in restaurants must show how much they hold; ~anzug *m* made-to-measure *or* bespoke *or* made-to-order (*US*) *or* custom (*US*) suit; ~arbeit *f* (*inf*) das war ~arbeit that was a neat bit of work.
Masse *f* -, -n **(a)** (*Stoff*) mass; (*Cook*) mixture. die ~ für den Guß der Glocke the molten metal for casting the bell; die wogenden ~n ihres Körpers the heaving bulk of her body.
  (b) (*große Menge*) heaps *pl* (*inf*), stacks *pl* (*inf*); (*von Besuchern etc*) host. die (breite) ~ der Bevölkerung etc the bulk of the population *etc*; eine ganze ~ (*inf*) a lot *or* a great deal; sie kamen in wahren ~n they came in droves *or* in their thousands; das ist aber eine ~! (*inf*) that's heaps! (*inf*); die ~ muß es bringen (*Comm*) the profit only comes with quantity.
  (c) (*Menschenmenge*) crowd.
  (d) (*Bevölkerungs~*) masses *pl* (*auch pej*). die namenlose *or* graue *or* breite ~ the masses *pl*; der Geschmack der ~ the taste of the masses.
  (e) (*Konkurs~*) assets *pl*; (*Erb~*) estate.
  (f) (*Phys*) mass.

Massegläubiger *m* (*Jur*) preferential creditor.
Maß-: ~einheit *f* unit of measurement; ~einteilung *f* (measuring) scale.
Massel *m* -s, *no pl* (*sl*) ~ haben to be dead lucky (*inf*).
Massen- *in cpds* mass; ~absatz *m* bulk selling; das ist kein Artikel für den ~absatz that isn't intended for the mass market; ~andrang *m* crush; es herrschte ~andrang there was a terrible crush; ~angebot *nt* glut; sie waren im ~angebot auf dem Markt there was a glut of them on the market; ~anziehung *f* (*Phys*) gravitation; ~artikel *m* mass-produced article; ~aufgebot *nt* large body; in einem ~aufgebot erscheinen to turn up in force; ~bedarf *m* requirements of the masses *pl*; (*Comm*) requirements of the mass market *pl*; ~bedarfsgüter *pl* basic consumer goods *pl*; ~beeinflussung *f* mass propaganda; ~beförderungsmittel *nt* means of mass transportation *sing*; ~fabrikation, ~fertigung *f* mass production; ~gesellschaft *f* faceless society; ~grab *nt* mass grave; ~güter *pl* bulk goods *pl*; m~haft *adj* on a huge *or* massive scale; m~haft Fanbriefe/Sekt *etc* (*inf*) masses of fan letters/champagne *etc* (*inf*); ~herstellung *f siehe* ~produktion; ~karambolage *f* multiple (car) crash, pile-up (*inf*); ~kommunikationsmittel *nt* mass medium *usu pl*; ~medien *pl* mass media *pl*; ~mord *m* mass murder; ~mörder *m* mass murderer; ~partei *f* party of the masses; ~presse *f* popular press; ~produktion *f* mass production; ~psychologie *f* crowd psychology; ~psychose *f* mass hysteria; ~quartier *nt* camp; ~sterben *nt* mass of deaths; ~szene *f* crowd scene; ~terror *m* mass terror; ~verkehrsmittel *nt* means of mass transportation *sing*.
Massenvernichtung *f* mass extermination.
Massenvernichtungs-: ~lager *nt* extermination camp; ~mittel *nt* means of mass extermination *pl*.
Massen-: ~versammlung *f* mass meeting; ~wahn *m* mass hysteria; ~ware *f* mass-produced article; m~weise *adj siehe* m~haft; ~wirkung *f* mass effect.
Masseur [ma'søːɐ] *m* masseur.
Masseurin [-'søːrɪn] *f*, **Masseuse** [-'søːzə] *f* masseuse.
Maßgabe *f* (*form*) stipulation. mit der ~, daß ... with the proviso that ..., on (the) condition that ...; nach ~ (+*gen*) according to.
maßgebend, maßgeblich *adj* (*entscheidend, ausschlaggebend*) Einfluß, Bedingungen decisive; Meinung, Ansicht definitive; Text definitive, authoritative; Fachmann authoritative; (*wichtig*) Persönlichkeit leading; Beteiligung substantial; (*zuständig*) competent. ~e Kreise influential circles; von ~er Seite from the corridors of power; das/seine Meinung ist hier nicht ~ that/his opinion doesn't weigh *or* signify here; das war für mich nicht ~ that didn't weigh with me.
maßgeschneidert *adj* Anzug made-to-measure, made-to-order (*US*), custom *attr* (*US*). ein ~es Alibi a watertight alibi, the perfect alibi.
Maßhalte-: ~appell *m*, ~parole *f* appeal for moderation.
maßhalten *vi sep irreg* to be moderate, to practise moderation.
massieren[1]* 1 *vt* to massage. 2 *vi* to give (a) massage.
massieren[2]* 1 *vt* to mass. 2 *vr* to amass; (*Truppen*) to mass.
massig 1 *adj* massive, huge.
  2 *adv* (*inf: sehr viel*) ~ Arbeit/Geld *etc* masses *or* stacks of work/money *etc* (*inf*).
mäßig *adj* **(a)** moderate; Preise *auch* reasonable. in etw (*dat*) ~ sein to be moderate in sth; etw ~ tun to do sth in moderation; ~ essen to eat with moderation; ~ im Rauchen sein, ~ rauchen to be a moderate smoker, to smoke in moderation; ~, aber regelmäßig regularly but in moderation.
  (b) (*unterdurchschnittlich*) Leistung, Schulnote *etc* mediocre, indifferent; Begabung, Beifall moderate; Gesundheit middling, indifferent.
-mäßig *adj, adv suf* -wise.
mäßigen 1 *vt* (*mildern*) Anforderungen to moderate; Sprache *auch* to tone down; Zorn, Ungeduld to curb, to check. sein Tempo ~ to slacken one's pace, to slow down; *siehe* gemäßigt.
  2 *vr* (*im Essen, Trinken, Temperament*) to restrain *or* control oneself; (*Sturm*) to abate, to die down. ~ Sie sich! control yourself!; sich in seinem Temperament ~ to control *or* restrain oneself; ~ Sie sich in Ihren Wörten! tone down your language!
Massigkeit *f* massiveness, hugeness.
Mäßigkeit *f* **(a)** (*beim Essen, Trinken*) moderation, restraint; (*von Forderungen, Preisen etc*) moderateness. ~ üben *or* an den Tag legen to exercise *or* show moderation *or* restraint. **(b)** (*Mittelmäßigkeit*) mediocrity; (*von Begabung, Beifall*) moderateness.
Mäßigung *f* restraint; (*beim Essen etc auch*) moderation.
massiv *adj* **(a)** (*pur, nicht hohl, stabil*) solid. **(b)** (*heftig*) Beleidigung gross; Drohung, Kritik heavy; Anschuldigung severe. ~ werden (*inf*) to turn nasty.
Massiv *nt* -s, -e (*Geol*) massif.
Massivität *f* massiveness.
Maß-: ~kleidung *f* made-to-measure *or* made-to-order (*US*) *or* custom (*US*) clothing; ~krug *m* litre beer mug; (*Steinkrug*) stein; ~lieb *nt* -(e)s, -e, ~liebchen *nt* daisy, marguerite.
maßlos 1 *adj* extreme; (*übermäßig*) Forderungen *auch* excessive; (*grenzlos*) Trauer, Freude, Ehrgeiz *auch* boundless; Mensch (*in Forderungen etc auch, in Essen etc*) immoderate. er war ~ in seiner Wut/Freude *etc* his rage/joy knew no bounds; er ist im Rauchen/Trinken ~, er raucht/trinkt ~ he smokes/drinks to excess.
  2 *adv* (*äußerst*) extremely; (*übertreiben*) grossly, hugely. es ist alles ~ traurig (*inf*) it's all very *or* terribly (*inf*) sad.
Maßlosigkeit *f* .*siehe adj* extremeness; excessiveness; boundlessness; lack of moderation.
Maßnahme *f* -, -n measure. ~n treffen, um etw zu tun to take steps *or* measures to do sth; ~n gegen jdn/etw treffen *or*

ergreifen to take measures against sb/sth; **vor** ~**n zurück-schrecken** to shrink from taking action; **sich zu** ~**n gezwungen sehen** to be forced to take action.

maßnehmen vi sep irreg jdn ~ (inf) to give sb what for (inf).

Maßregel f rule.

maßregeln vt insep (zurechtweisen) to reprimand, to rebuke, to reprove; (bestrafen) to displicine; (Sport) to penalize.

Maßreg(e)lung f **(a)** no pl siehe vt reprimanding, rebuking, reproval; disciplining; penalizing. **(b)** (Rüge) reprimand, rebuke; (von Beamten) disciplinary action; (Sport) penalty.

Maßschneider m bespoke or custom (US) tailor.

Maßstab m **(a)** (Lineal) ruler; (Zollstock) rule.

(b) (Karten~) scale. **die Karte hat einen kleinen/großen** ~ it's a small-/large-scale map, the map is on a small/large scale; **beim/im** ~ **1:1000** on a scale of 1:1000; **im** ~ **1:25000 gezeichnet** drawn to a scale of 1:25000; **etw in verkleinertem** ~ **darstellen** to scale sth down.

(c) (fig: Richtlinie, Kriterium) standard. **einen hohen/strengen** ~ **anlegen** to apply a high/strict standard (an +acc to); **für jdn als** or **zum** ~ **dienen, für jdn einen** ~ **abgeben** to serve as a model for sb; **sich** (dat) **jdn/etw zum** ~ **nehmen** to take sb/sth as a yardstick; **das ist für mich kein** ~ I don't take that as my yardstick.

maßstäblich adj scale attr, to scale.

maßstab(s)-: ~**gerecht**, ~**getreu** adj (true) to scale; **eine** ~**gerechte Karte** an accurate scale map.

Maß-: ~**system** nt system of measures; **m**~**voll** adj moderate; ~**vorlage** f (Ftbl) spot-on (inf) or accurate pass; ~**werk** nt (Archit) tracery.

Mast[1] m **-(e)s, -en** or **-e** (Naut, Rad, TV) mast; (Stange) pole; (Elec) pylon.

Mast[2] f **-, -en** (das Mästen) fattening; (Futter) feed; (Schweine~) mast.

Mast-: ~**baum** m mast; ~**darm** m rectum.

mästen 1 vt to fatten. **2** vr (inf) to gorge or stuff (inf) oneself.

Mästerei f (Schweine~) pig fattening unit.

Mast- in cpds (zu mästen) feeder; (gemästet) fattened; ~**futter** nt (fattening) feed; (für Schweine) mast; ~**korb** m (Naut) top; ~**kur** f (hum inf) fattening diet; ~**schwein** nt (zu mästen) porker; (gemästet) fattened pig; **er sieht wie ein** ~**schwein aus** he looks like a little (fat) piggy.

Mästung, Mastung f fattening.

Masturbation f masturbation.

masturbieren* vtir to masturbate.

Masurka f **-, -s** siehe Mazurka.

Matador m **-s, -e** (Stierkämpfer) matador; (fig) kingpin.

Match [mɛtʃ] nt or m **-(e)s, -e(s)** match.

Match-: ~**ball** m (Tennis) match point; ~**beutel**, ~**sack** m duffel bag.

Mate [ˈmaːtə] m **-,** no pl maté, Paraguay tea.

Mater f **-, -n** (Typ) siehe Matrize.

material adj (Philos) material.

Material nt **-s, -ien** [-iən] material; (Bau~, Utensilien, Gerät) materials pl; (Beweis~, Belastungs~) evidence. **rollendes** ~ (Rail) rolling stock.

Material-: ~**ausgabe** f **(a)** (Raum) stores pl; **(b)** (Vorgang) issue of stores and equipment; ~**bedarf** m material requirements pl; ~**fehler** m material defect, defect in the material.

Materialisation f materialization.

materialisieren* vtr to materialize.

Materialismus m materialism.

Materialist(in f) m materialist.

materialistisch adj materialist(ic); (pej) materialistic.

Materialität f (Philos) materiality.

Material-: ~**kosten** pl cost of materials sing; ~**prüfung** f testing of materials; ~**sammlung** f collection of material; **ich habe jetzt die** ~**sammlung abgeschlossen** I have now finished collecting or gathering the material; ~**schaden** m material defect, defect in the material; ~**schlacht** f (Mil) matériel battle.

Materie [-iə] f **(a)** no pl (Phys, Philos) matter no art. **(b)** (Stoff, Thema) subject-matter no indef art. **die** ~ **beherrschen** to know one's stuff.

materiell adj **(a)** (Philos) material, physical; Recht substantive. **etw** ~ **erklären** to explain sth physically. **(b)** (wirtschaftlich) financial; Vorteile auch material; (gewinnsüchtig) materialistic. ~ **eingestellt sein** to be materialistic; **nur** ~**e Interessen haben** to be only interested in material things.

matern vt (Typ) to make a plate for.

Matetee [ˈmaːtə-] m siehe Mate.

Math. abbr of **Mathematik**.

Mathe f **-,** no pl (Sch sl) maths sing (Brit inf), math (US inf).

Mathematik f mathematics sing no art.

Mathematiker(in f) m **-s, -** mathematician.

mathematisch adj mathematical.

mathematisieren* vt **die Physik wird immer mehr mathematisiert** physics is becoming more and more mathematical.

Matinee f **-, -n** [-eːən] matinée.

Matjeshering, Matjes m **-, -** (inf) young herring.

Matratze f **-, -n** mattress. ~ **horchen** (sl) to have a kip (inf).

Mätresse f mistress.

Mätressenwirtschaft f petticoat government.

matriarchalisch adj matriarchal.

Matriarchat nt matriarchy, matriarchate.

Matrikel f **-, -n** (old, Aus) register; (Univ: Aufnahmeverzeichnis) matriculation register. **Student mit kleiner/großer** ~ occasional/full-time student.

Matrikelnummer f (Univ) registration or matriculation number.

Matrix f **-, Matrizen** or **Matrizes** [maˈtriːtseːs] (Math, Med, Biol) matrix.

Matrize f **-, -n** (Typ) matrix, mould; (für Schreibmaschine) stencil. **etw auf** ~ **schreiben** to stencil sth.

Matrone f **-, -n** matron.

matronenhaft adj matronly.

Matrose m **-n, -n** sailor; (als Rang) rating (Brit), ordinary seaman.

Matrosen- in cpds sailor; ~**mütze** f sailor's cap; ~**schenke** f sailors' pub; ~**uniform** f sailor's uniform.

matsch adj pred (dial) **(a)** Obst rotten, bad. **(b)** (Cards) beaten. ~ **werden** to be beaten; **er machte ihn** ~ he beat him hollow. **(c)** **sich** ~ **fühlen** to feel whacked (inf).

Matsch m **-(e)s,** no pl (inf: breiige Masse) mush; (Schlamm) mud, sludge; (Schnee~) slush.

Matschauge nt (sl) black eye, shiner (inf).

matschen vi (inf) to splash (about or around).

matschig adj (inf: breiig) gooey (inf), mushy; (schlammig) muddy, sludgy; Schnee slushy.

Matschwetter nt (inf) muddy/slushy weather or conditions pl.

matt adj **(a)** (schwach) Kranker weak; Stimme, Lächeln auch faint; Glieder weary. **sich** ~ **fühlen** to have no energy.

(b) (glanzlos) Augen, Metall, Farbe dull; (nicht glänzend) Farbe, Papier mat(t); (trübe) Licht dim, subdued; Glühbirne opal, pearl; Spiegel cloudy, dull.

(c) (undurchsichtig) Glas frosted, opaque.

(d) (fig) Ausdruck, Witz, Rede, Schluß lame, feeble; Echo faint; (St Ex: flau) slack.

(e) (Chess) (check)mate. **jdn** ~ **setzen** to checkmate sb (auch fig), to mate sb.

Matt nt **-s, -s** (Chess) (check)mate.

mattblau adj pale blue.

Matte[1] f **-, -n** mat. **jdn auf die** ~ **legen** to floor sb; (fig inf) to make mincemeat of sb (inf).

Matte[2] f **-, -n** (liter, Sw, Aus) alpine meadow.

Matt-: ~**glanz** m mat(t) finish; ~**glas** nt frosted or ground glass; ~**gold** nt dull gold; (Farbe) pale gold.

Matthäi [maˈtɛːi] gen of **Matthäus. bei ihm ist** ~ **am letzten** he's had it (inf).

Matthäus [maˈtɛːʊs] m **Matthäi** Matthew.

Matthäus|evangelium nt St Matthew's Gospel, Gospel according to St Matthew.

Mattheit f siehe adj **(a)** weakness; faintness; weariness; lack of energy. **(b)** dullness; mat(t) finish; dimness; opal or pearl finish; cloudiness, dullness. **(c)** opacity. **(d)** lameness, feebleness; faintness; slackness.

mattieren* vt to give a mat(t) finish to. **mattiert sein** to have a mat(t) finish; **mattierte Gläser** frosted glasses.

Mattigkeit f weariness; (von Kranken) weakness.

Matt-: ~**lack** m dull or mat(t) lacquer or varnish; ~**papier** nt mat(t) or unglazed paper.

Mattscheibe f **(a)** (Phot) focus(s)ing screen; (inf: Fernseher) telly (Brit inf), (goggle-)box (Brit inf), tube (US inf).

(b) (inf) **eine** ~ **haben/kriegen** (dumm sein) to be soft/go soft in the head (inf); (nicht klar denken können) to have/get a mental block; **als ich das gesagt habe, muß ich wohl eine** ~ **gehabt haben** I can't have been really with it when I said that (inf); **von dem Lärm kriegt man ja eine** ~ the noise makes it impossible to think straight.

Matur, Maturum nt **-s,** no pl (old) **Matura** f **-,** no pl (Aus, Sw) siehe Abitur.

Maturand(in f) m **-en, -en** (old, Sw), **Maturant(in** f) m (Aus) siehe Abiturient(in).

maturieren* vi **(a)** aux sein (old: reifen) to mature. **(b)** (Aus: Abitur machen) to take one's school-leaving exam, to graduate (from high school) (US).

Maturität f **(a)** (old: Reife) maturity. **(b)** (Sw: Hochschulreife) matriculation exam(ination).

Maturitäts- in cpds siehe Reife-.

Matz m **-es, -e** (dated inf) laddie (inf).

Mätzchen nt (inf) **(a)** antic. ~ **machen** to play or fool around (inf); **mach keine** ~, **schmeiß die Kanone weg!** don't try anything funny, just drop the gun! **(b)** dim of Matz.

Matze f **-, -n, Matzen** m **-s, -** (Cook) matzo.

mau adj pred (inf) poor, bad. **mir ist** ~ I feel poorly (inf); **die Geschäfte gehen** ~ business is slack.

Mauer f **-, -n (a)** wall. **etw mit einer** ~ **umgeben** to wall sth in; **in den** ~**n der Stadt** (fig) in the city. **(b)** (fig: des Schweigens etc) wall. **die** ~ **einreißen** to tear down the barriers.

Mauer-: ~**anschlag** m poster; ~**arbeit** f siehe Mau(r)erarbeit; ~**assel** f woodlouse; ~**blümchen** nt (fig inf) (beim Tanzen) wallflower; (schüchternes Mädchen) shy young thing; ~**brecher** m **-s, -** (Mil) battering ram; ~**haken** m (Bergsteigen) piton, peg; ~**kelle** f siehe Mau(r)erkelle; ~**krone** f wall coping.

mauern 1 vi to build, to lay bricks. **(b)** (Cards) to hold back; (Ftbl sl) to stonewall (sl), to play defensively; (fig) to stall, to stonewall (esp Parl). **2** vt to build; (mit Zement verfugen) to build with mortar. **der Beckenrand muß gemauert werden** the edge of the pool must be bedded in mortar.

Mauer-: ~**schwalbe** f, ~**segler** m swift; ~**speis** m **-es,** no pl, ~**speise** f (esp S Ger) siehe Mörtel; ~**stein** m building stone; ~**verband** m bond; ~**vorsprung** m projection on a/the wall; ~**werk** nt **(a)** (Steinmauer) stonework, masonry; (Ziegelmauer) brickwork; **ein mittelalterliches** ~**werk** a medieval stone structure; **(b)** (die Mauern) walls pl; ~**ziegel** m (building) brick.

Mauke f **-,** no pl (Vet) malanders pl.

Mauken pl (dial inf) hooves pl (hum).

Maul nt **-(e)s, Mäuler** mouth; (von Löwen etc) jaws pl; (sl: von

Menschen) gob (sl). ein böses or ungewaschenes or gottloses ~ (inf) an evil or a wicked or malicious tongue; ein loses or lockeres ~ haben (sl) (frech sein) to be an impudent so-and-so (inf); (indiskret sein) to be a blabbermouth (inf), to have a loose tongue; jdm übers ~ fahren (sl) to choke sb off (inf); das ~ zu weit aufreißen or zu voll nehmen (sl) to be too cocksure (inf); jdm ums ~ gehen (sl) to soft-soap sb (inf); ein großes ~ haben (sl) to have a big mouth, to be a big-mouth (inf); (hungrige) Mäuler stopfen (inf) to feed or fill (hungry) mouths; darüber werden sich die Leute das ~ zerreißen (inf) that will start people's tongues wagging; dem Volk or den Leuten aufs ~ schauen (inf) to listen to what people really say; (Meinung ermitteln) to sound out public opinion, to listen to the man in the street; halt's ~! (sl), ~ halten! (sl) shut your face or trap or gob (all sl); ein schiefes ~ machen or ziehen (inf) to pull a (long) face; das ~ hängen lassen (inf) to have a face as long as a fiddle (inf); jdm das ~ stopfen (sl) to shut sb up; sich (dat) das ~ verbrennen (inf) to talk one's way or oneself into trouble.

Maul-: ~**affen** pl (dated inf): ~**affen feilhalten** to stand gawping or gaping; ~**beerbaum** m mulberry (tree); ~**beere** f mulberry.

maulen vi (inf) to moan.

Maul-: ~**esel** m mule, hinny; **m**~**faul** adj (inf) uncommunicative; **sei doch nicht so m**~**faul** haven't you got a tongue in your head?; **sie ist nicht gerade m**~**faul** she's not exactly at a loss for words; ~**held** m (pej) loud-mouth (inf), show-off; ~**hurerei** f (geh) foul-mouthedness.

-mäulig adj suf -mouthed.

Maulkorb m (lit, fig) muzzle. **einem Hund/jdm einen** ~ **umhängen** to put a muzzle on a dog, to muzzle a dog/sb.

Maulkorb- (fig inf): ~**erlaß** m decree muzzling freedom of speech; ~**gesetz** nt law muzzling freedom of speech.

Maul-: ~**schelle** f (dated inf) slap in the face; ~**sperre** f: er kriegte die ~**sperre** (inf) his mouth dropped open; ~**taschen** pl (Cook) pasta squares pl; ~**tier** nt mule; ~**-und Klauenseuche** f (Vet) foot-and-mouth disease; ~**werk** nt (inf) siehe Mundwerk.

Maulwurf m -(e)s, **Maulwürfe** mole.

Maulwurfs-: ~**haufen**, ~**hügel** m mole-hill.

maunzen vi (S Ger) (winseln) to whine; (Katze) to mewl.

Maure m -n, -n (Hist) Moor.

Maurer m -s, - bricklayer, brickie (inf). ~ **lernen** to learn bricklaying or to be a bricklayer; **pünktlich wie die** ~ (hum) super-punctual; **pünktlich wie die** ~ **ließ er seinen Kugelschreiber fallen bang on the dot he put down his pen.**

Mau(r)er|arbeit f bricklaying (work) no pl.

Maurer-: ~**geselle** m journeyman bricklayer; ~**handwerk** nt bricklaying.

Mau(r)erkelle f (bricklayer's) trowel.

Maurer-: ~**kolonne** f bricklaying gang; ~**meister** m master builder; ~**polier** m foreman bricklayer.

Mauretanien [-iən] nt -s Mauritania, Mauretania.

Mauretanier(in f) [-iɐ, -iərin] m -s, - Mauritanian.

mauretanisch adj Mauritanian.

Maurin f (Hist) Moor.

maurisch adj Moorish.

Mauritier(in f) [mauˈriːtsiɐ, -iərin] m -s, - Mauritian.

Mauritius [mauˈriːtsiʊs] nt - Mauritius.

Maus f -, **Mäuse** (a) mouse. **weiße** ~ (fig inf) traffic cop (inf); **weiße Mäuse sehen** (fig inf) to see pink elephants (inf); **da beißt die** ~ **keinen Faden ab** (inf) there's nothing to be done about it. (b) (fig dated: Frau) **kleine** ~ little mouse; **eine graue** ~ (inf) a mouse (inf). (c) **Mäuse** pl (sl: Geld) bread (sl), dough (sl).

Mauschelei f (inf) (Korruption) fiddle (inf). **das war bestimmt** ~ it was definitely a fiddle.

mauscheln 1 vi (jiddisch sprechen) to talk Yiddish. **2** vti (manipulieren) to fiddle (inf).

Mauscheln nt -s (Cards) cheat.

Mäuschen [ˈmɔysçən] nt (a) little mouse. **da möchte ich mal** ~ **sein** or **spielen** (inf) I'd like to be a fly on the wall. (b) (fig) sweetheart (inf), love (Brit inf), honey (esp US). (c) siehe Musikantenknochen.

mäuschenstill [ˈmɔysçən-] adj dead quiet; Mensch auch (as) quiet as a mouse; (reglos) stock-still.

Mäusebussard m (common) buzzard.

Mausefalle, **Mäusefalle** (rare) f mouse-trap; (fig) police roadblock. **in eine** ~ **kommen** or **geraten** to get caught in a police roadblock.

Mäusegift nt mouse poison.

Mauseloch, **Mäuseloch** (rare) nt mouse-hole. **sich in ein** ~ **verkriechen** (inf) to crawl into a hole in the ground.

Mäusemelken nt: **das/es ist zum** ~ (dated inf) it's enough to drive you up the wall (inf).

mausen 1 vi to catch mice. **diese Katze maust gut** the cat is a good mouser. **2** vt (dated inf) to pinch (inf), to nick (Brit inf).

Mauser f -, no pl (Orn) moult. **in der** ~ **sein** to be moulting.

Mausergewehr nt Mauser (rifle).

Mäuserich m (hum) Mr Mouse (hum).

mausern vr (a) (Orn) to moult. (b) (inf) to blossom out (inf).

Mauser(pistole f) f -, -n Mauser.

mausetot adj (inf) stone-dead, as dead as a doornail.

maus-: ~**farben**, ~**farbig** adj mouse-coloured; ~**grau** adj (a) (~farben) mouse-grey; (b) (unauffällig) mousy.

mausig adj: **sich** ~ **machen** (inf) to get uppish or bolshie or stroppy (all inf).

Mausloch nt siehe Mäuseloch.

Mausoleum [-ˈleːʊm] nt -s, **Mausoleen** [-ˈleːən] mausoleum.

maustot adj (Aus) siehe mausetot.

Maut f -, -en (S Ger, Aus) toll.

Maut-: ~**gebühr** f toll(-charge); ~**straße** f toll-road, turnpike (US).

---

mauzen vi siehe maunzen.

max. abbr of **maximal**.

maxi adj pred maxi. ~ **tragen** to wear a maxi.

Maxi- in cpds maxi.

maximal 1 adj maximum. **2** adv (höchstens) at most. **bis zu** ~ $100 up to a maximum of $100.

Maximal- in cpds maximum.

Maxime f -, -n (Liter, Philos) maxim.

maximieren* vt (Econ) to maximize.

Maximierung f (Econ) maximization.

Maximum nt -s, **Maxima** maximum (an +dat of).

Maya [ˈmaːja] m -(s), -(s) Maya.

Mayonnaise [majoˈnɛːzə] f -, -n mayonnaise.

Mazedonien [-iən] nt -s siehe Makedonien.

Mäzen m -s, -e patron.

Mäzenatentum nt (a) (Kunstförderung) patronage. (b) (Wesen eines Mäzens) spirit of patronage.

Mazurka f -, -s mazurka.

MdB, M.d.B. [ɛmdeːˈbeː] m -s, -s abbr of **Mitglied des Bundestages** Member of the "Bundestag".

MdL, M.d.L. [ɛmdeːˈɛl] m -s, -s abbr of **Mitglied des Landtages** Member of the "Landtag".

m.E. abbr of **meines Erachtens** in my opinion.

mech. abbr of **mechanisch**.

Mechanik f (a) no pl (Phys) mechanics sing. (b) (rare) siehe **Mechanismus**.

Mechaniker(in f) m -s, - mechanic.

mechanisch adj (alle Bedeutungen) mechanical. ~**er Webstuhl** power loom; ~**e Werkstatt** (old) engineering workshop.

mechanisieren* vt to mechanize.

Mechanisierung f mechanization.

Mechanisierungsprozeß m process of mechanization.

Mechanismus m mechanism; (Methode, Arbeitsablauf) machinery.

mechanistisch adj (Philos, Psych) mechanistic.

meck interj (Ziege) ~, ~! meh, meh!

Meckerei f (inf) moaning, grumbling, grousing.

Meckerer m -s, - (inf) moaner, grumbler, grouser.

Mecker-: ~**fritze** (inf) m belly-acher (inf), wailing Willie (inf); ~**liese** f (inf) moaning Minny (inf).

meckern vi (Ziege) to bleat; (inf: Mensch) to moan, to bleat (inf), to grouse.

Meckerziege f (sl) sourpuss (inf), ratbag (inf).

med. abbr of **medizinisch**.

Medaille [meˈdaljə] f -, -n (Gedenkmünze) medallion; (bei Wettbewerben) medal.

Medaillengewinner [meˈdaljən-] m medallist, medal winner.

Medaillon [medalˈjõ] nt -s, -s (Bildchen) medallion; (Schmuckkapsel) locket.

medial adj (Gram) middle; (Med) medial, median; (Psych) mediumistic.

mediatisieren* vt (Hist) to mediatize.

Mediatisierung f (Hist) mediatization.

Mediävistik [mediɛˈvɪstɪk] f medieval studies sing or pl.

Mediävist(in f) [mediɛˈvɪst(ɪn)] m medievalist.

Medien [ˈmeːdiən] pl media pl.

Medien-: ~**forschung** f media research; **m**~**gerecht** adj suited to the media; ~**politik** f (mass) media policy; ~**verbund** m etw im ~**verbund lernen** to learn sth using the multi-media system.

Medikament nt medicine.

medikamentös adj medicinal.

Medikus m -, **Medizi** or -se (hum) quack (hum inf), doc (inf); (esp Student) medic (inf).

medioker adj (geh) mediocre.

Meditation f meditation.

meditativ adj (liter) meditative. **in** ~**er Versunkenheit** lost in meditation.

mediterran adj Mediterranean.

meditieren* vi to meditate.

Medium nt medium; (Gram) middle (voice).

Medizin f -, -en (a) no pl (Heilkunde) medicine. (b) (inf: Heilmittel) medicine. **das ist** ~ **für ihn** that's his medicine; (fig: Lektion, Denkzettel) that'll teach him a lesson.

Medizinal-: ~**assistent** m houseman (Brit), intern (US); ~**rat** m medical officer of health; ~**statistik** f medical statistics pl.

Medizinball m (Sport) medicine ball.

Mediziner(in f) m -s, - a doctor. (Univ) medic (inf).

medizinisch adj (a) (ärztlich) medical. **M**~**e Fakultät** school or faculty of medicine; **M**~**e Klinik** clinic for internal medicine; ~**-technische Assistentin** medical assistant. (b) (heilend) Kräuter, Bäder medicinal; Shampoo medicated.

Medizin-: ~**mann** m, pl -**männer** medicine man, witchdoctor; (hum: Arzt) quack (inf), medico (US inf); ~**schränkchen** nt medicine cabinet or cupboard; ~**student** m medical student.

Meduse f -, -n (a) (Myth) Medusa. (b) (Zool) medusa (spec), jellyfish.

Medusenhaupt nt (a) (Liter) head of Medusa. (b) (Med) caput medusae (spec).

Meer nt -(e)s, -e (a) sea; (Welt~) ocean. **am** ~(e) by the sea; **diesseits/jenseits des** ~**es** at home/across the sea; **übers** ~ **fahren** to travel (across) the seas; **ans** ~ **fahren** to go to the sea(side); **über dem** ~ above sea-level. (b) (liter: riesige Menge) sea.

Meer-: ~**busen** m gulf, bay; **Bottnischer** ~**busen** Gulf of Bothnia; ~**enge** f straits pl, strait.

Meeres-: ~**algen** pl seaweed, marine algae pl (spec); ~**arm** m arm of the sea, inlet; ~**boden** m siehe ~**grund**; ~**fauna** f marine fauna; ~**flora** f marine flora; ~**forschung** f oceanography; ~**freiheit** f (Jur) freedom of the seas; ~**grund** m seabed, sea-bottom, bottom of the sea; ~höhe f siehe ~spiegel; ~klima nt maritime climate; ~kunde f oceanography; m~kundlich adj oceanographic(al); ~leuchten nt marine phosphorescence; ~oberfläche f surface of the sea; ~spiegel m sea-level; über/ unter dem ~spiegel above/below sea-level; ~stille f calm (at sea); ~strand m (liter) seashore, strand (poet); ~straße f waterway; ~strömung f ocean current; ~tiefe f depth (of the sea or ocean); ~ufer nt seashore, coast.

Meer-: ~gott m (Myth) sea-god; ~göttin f sea-goddess; m~grün adj sea-green; ~jungfer, ~jungfrau f mermaid; ~katze f long-tailed monkey, guenon; ~rettich m horseradish; ~salz nt sea salt; ~schaum m (Miner) meerschaum; ~schaumpfeife f meerschaum (pipe); ~schweinchen nt guineapig, cavy (spec); ~spinne f spider crab; m~umschlungen adj (poet) seagirt (poet), sea-bound; ~ungeheuer nt sea-monster; m~wärts adv seawards.

Meerwasser nt sea water.

Meerwasser-: ~aufbereitung f treatment of sea water; ~entsalzung f desalination of sea water; ~entsalzungsanlage f desalination plant.

Meeting ['miːtɪŋ] nt -s, -s (esp DDR Pol, Sport) meeting.

mega-, Mega- in cpds mega-.

Megahertz nt megahertz.

Megalith m -en, -en (Archeol) megalith.

Megalith-: ~grab nt (Archeol) dolmen, megalithic tomb; ~kultur f (Hist) megalithic culture.

Megalo-: m~man adj (geh) megalomanic; ~manie f (geh) megalomania; ~polis [mega'loːpolis] f -, -polen [megalo'poːlən] megalopolis.

Megaphon [mega'foːn] nt megaphone.

Megäre f -, -n (a) (Myth) Megaera. (b) (fig liter) shrew, termagant (liter).

Mega-: ~tonne f megaton; ~tonnenbombe f megaton bomb; ~tote pl megadeaths pl; ~watt nt indecl megawatt.

Mehl nt -(e)s, -e flour; (grober) (Knochen~) bonemeal; (Pulver, Zement~) powder.

Mehl-: m~artig adj floury, mealy; ~beere f berry of the whitebeam; ~brei m pap, flummery.

mehlig adj Äpfel, Kartoffeln mealy.

Mehl-: ~kleister m flour paste; ~kloß m dumpling; ~papp m (inf) mush (inf); ~sack m flour bag; wie ein ~sack (inf) like a sack of potatoes; ~schwitze f (Cook) roux; ~speise f (a) (Gericht) flummery; (b) (Aus) (Nachspeise) sweet, dessert; (Kuchen) pastry; ~suppe f gruel; ~tau m (Bot) mildew.

mehr 1 indef pron inv comp of viel, sehr more. was wollen Sie ~? what more do you want?; zu ~ hat es nicht gelangt or gereicht that was all I/you etc could manage; ~ will er nicht bezahlen he doesn't want to pay (any) more; ist das alles, ~ kostet das nicht? is that all it costs?; je ~ er hat, je ~ er will (Prov) the more he has, the more he wants; sich für ~ halten (inf) to think one is something more; mit ~ oder weniger Erfolg with a greater or lesser degree of success.

2 adv (a) (in höherem Maße) more. immer ~ more and more; ~ oder weniger or minder (geh) more or less; ~ lang als breit more long than wide, longer than it is/they are wide; ~ Geschäftsmann als Arzt more (of) a businessman than a doctor; ~ ein juristisches Problem more (of) a legal problem; war er frech/sind Sie beleidigt/hat es Ihnen geschmeckt? — ~ als das was he cheeky/are you insulted/did you like it? — "cheeky/insulted/like" is not the word for it; würden Sie das gerne tun? — ja, nichts ~ als das would you like to? — there's nothing I'd rather do.

(b) (+ neg: sonst, länger) ich habe kein Geld ~ I have no more money, I haven't any more money; du bist doch kein Kind ~! you're not a child any longer or any more!, you're no longer a child!; es hat sich keiner ~ beworben nobody else has applied; es besteht keine Hoffnung ~ there's no hope left; kein Wort ~! not another word!; es war niemand ~ da there was no-one left, everyone had gone; daran erinnert sich niemand ~ nobody can remember that any more; er hat zu niemandem ~ Vertrauen he doesn't trust anyone any more or any longer, he no longer trusts anyone; wenn niemand ~ einsteigt, ... if nobody else gets in ...; das benutzt man nicht ~ that's not used any more or any longer, it's no longer used; er lebt nicht ~ he is dead; das darf nicht ~ vorkommen that must not or never happen again; nicht ~ not any longer, not any more, no more, no longer; nicht ~ lange not much longer; wenn unser Opa nicht ~ ist (euph) when Grandpa is no longer with us; nichts ~ nothing more; ich kann nichts ~ sagen I can say nothing more, I can't say anything more; nie ~ never again, nevermore (liter); ich will dich nie ~ wiedersehen I never want to see you again, I don't ever want to see you again; seit einer Woche kommt er kaum ~ ins Bett he's hardly been to bed at all for a week; mit nur ~ zwei Groschen (S Ger, Aus) with only two pence left.

Mehr nt -, no pl (a) (esp Sw: Mehrheit) majority. (b) (Zuwachs) increase. mit einem ~ an Mühe with more effort; auf das ~ oder Weniger an Erfahrung kommt es nicht an it's not a question of having more or less experience.

Mehr-: ~arbeit f overtime, extra time or work; ~aufwand m additional expenditure; ~ausgabe f extra or additional expense(s pl); m~bändig adj in several volumes, multivolume; ~bedarf m greater need (an + dat of, for); (Comm) increased demand, increase in or extra demand (an + dat for); ~belastung f excess load; (fig) extra or additional burden; ~betrag m (a) (zusätzliche Zahlung) extra or additional amount; (b) (Überschuß) surplus; m~deutig adj ambiguous, equivocal; ~deutigkeit f ambiguity, equivocalness; m~dimensional adj multi-dimensional; ~einnahme f additional revenue.

mehren 1 vt (liter) (vergrößern) to augment, to increase; (för-

dern) to further. 2 vr (geh: sich vermehren) to multiply. seid fruchtbar und mehret Euch! (Bibl) be fruitful and multiply!

Mehrer m -s, - (liter) augmenter (form).

mehrere indef pron several; (verschiedene auch) various.

mehreres indef pron several or various things pl.

mehrerlei indef pron inv (a) (substantivisch) several things pl. (b) (adjektivisch) several kinds of.

Mehr-: ~erlös m siehe ~einnahme; ~ertrag m additional yield, increase in yield.

mehrf. abbr of mehrfach.

mehrfach 1 adj multiple; (zahlreich) numerous; (wiederholt) repeated. ein ~er Millionär a multimillionaire; der ~e Meister im 100-m-Lauf the man who has several times been the 100 metres champion; die Unterlagen in ~er Ausfertigung einsenden to send in several copies of the documents.

2 adv (öfter) many or several times; (wiederholt) repeatedly.

Mehrfache(s) nt decl as adj das ~ or ein ~s des Kostenvoranschlags several times the estimated cost; verdient er wirklich mehr? — ja, ja, das ~ or ein ~s does he earn more? — oh yes, several times as much.

Mehrfachstecker m (Elec) multiple adaptor.

Mehr-: ~familienhaus nt multiple dwelling (form), house for several families; ~farbendruck m (a) no pl (Verfahren) colour or polychromatic (form) printing; (b) (Druck) colour or polychromatic (form) print; m~farbig adj multicoloured, polychromatic (form); ~gebot nt higher bid; ~gepäck nt excess baggage; ~gewicht nt additional or excess weight; (Übergewicht) excess weight.

Mehrheit f (a) no pl (größerer Teil) majority (with sing or pl vb). weitaus in der ~ in the vast majority.

(b) (Stimmenmehrheit) majority. die absolute/einfache or relative ~ an absolute/a simple majority; die ~ haben or besitzen/gewinnen or erringen to have/win or gain a majority; die ~ der Stimmen auf sich vereinigen to secure a majority of votes; die ~ verlieren to lose one's majority; mit zwei Stimmen ~ with a majority of two.

mehrheitlich adj wir sind ~ der Ansicht, daß ... the majority of us think(s) that ...; der Stadtrat hat ~ beschlossen ... the town council has reached a majority decision ...

Mehrheits-: ~beschluß m, ~entscheidung f majority decision; ~grundsatz m principle of majority rule; ~parteien pl majority parties pl; ~wahl f first-past-the-post election; ~wahlrecht nt first-past-the-post system, majority vote system.

Mehr-: m~jährig adj attr of several years; m~jährige Klinikerfahrung several years of clinical experience; ~kampf m (Sport) multi-discipline event; ~kämpfer m (Sport) allround athlete, all rounder; ~kosten pl additional costs pl; (in Hotel etc) additional expenses pl; ~ladegewehr nt, ~lader m -s, - repeater, repeater rifle; m~malig adj attr repeated; m~mals adv several times, repeatedly; m~motorig adj multiengined; ~parteiensystem nt multi-party system; ~phasenstrom m (Elec) multiphase or polyphase current; m~silbig adj polysyllabic, multisyllabic; m~sprachig adj multilingual, polyglot; m~sprachig aufwachsen to grow up multilingual or speaking several languages; ~sprachigkeit f multilingualism; m~stimmig adj (Mus) for several voices; m~stimmiges Lied part-song; m~stimmiger Gesang part-singing; m~stimmig singen to sing in harmony; ~stimmigkeit f (Mus) polyphony; m~stöckig adj multistorey; m~stöckig bauen to build or erect multistorey buildings; ~stufenrakete f multistage rocket; m~stufig adj multistage; m~ständig adj attr lasting several hours; m~ständiger Verspätung eintreffen to arrive several hours late; m~tägig adj attr Konferenz lasting several days; nach m~tägiger Abwesenheit after an absence of several days, after several days' absence; m~teilig adj in several parts.

Mehrung f (liter) increase.

Mehr-: ~verbrauch m additional consumption; ~wert m (Econ) surplus value; m~wertig adj (Chem) polyvalent, multivalent; ~wertsteuer f value added tax, VAT; m~wöchig adj attr lasting several weeks; Abwesenheit of several weeks.

Mehrw. St. abbr of Mehrwertsteuer.

Mehr-: ~zahl f, no pl (a) (Gram) plural; (b) (Mehrheit) majority; m~zeilig adj of several lines; m~zellig adj multicellular.

Mehrzweck- in cpds multipurpose.

meiden pret **mied**, ptp **gemieden** vt to avoid.

Meier m -s, - (old) steward, bailiff.

Meierei f (a) (dial: Molkerei) dairy (farm). (b) (old: Pachtgut) leasehold farm.

Meile f -, -n mile; (old: 4,8 km) league. das riecht man drei ~n gegen den Wind (inf) you can smell or tell that a mile off (inf).

Meilen-: m~lang 1 adj mile-long; 2 adv for miles; ~stein m (lit, fig) milestone; ~stiefel pl siehe Siebenmeilenstiefel; m~weit 1 adj of many miles; m~weite Sandstrände miles and miles of sandy beaches; 2 adv for miles; m~weit auseinander/entfernt (lit, fig) miles apart/away; ~zahl f mileage; ~zähler m mileometer, clock (inf).

Meiler m -s, - (Kohlen~) charcoal kiln or pile; (dated: Atom~) (atomic) pile.

mein 1 poss pron (a) (adjektivisch) my. ~ verdammtes Auto this damn (inf) car of mine; ich trinke so ~e fünf Flaschen Bier pro Tag I drink my five bottles of beer a day.

(b) (old: substantivisch) mine. ~ und dein verwechseln (euph) to take what doesn't belong to one; das M~ und Dein (old liter) mine and thine (old).

2 pers pron gen of ich (old, poet) of me.

Mein|eid m perjury no indef art. einen ~ leisten or ablegen to perjure oneself, to commit perjury.

mein|eidig *adj* perjured. ~ **werden** to commit perjury, to perjure oneself.

Mein|eidige(r) *mf decl as adj* perjurer.

meinen 1 *vi* (*denken, glauben*) to think. **ich würde/man möchte ~** I/one would think; **ich meine, ... I** think ..., I reckon ... (*inf*); **~ Sie?** (do) you think so?, do you reckon?; **ich meine nur so** (*inf*) it was just a thought; **wie Sie ~!** as you wish; (*drohend auch*) have it your own way; **wenn du meinst!** if you like, I don't mind; **man sollte ~** one would have thought.

2 *vt* (**a**) (*der Ansicht sein*) to think. **was ~ Sie dazu?** what do you think or say?; **~ Sie das im Ernst?** are you serious about that?; **das will ich ~!** I quite agree!; **das sollte man ~!** one would think so.

(**b**) (*sagen wollen*) to mean; (*inf: sagen*) to say. **was ~ Sie damit?, wie ~ Sie das?** what or how do you mean?; (*drohend*) (just) what do you mean by that?

(**c**) (*geh: bedeuten*) to mean.

(**d**) (*bezeichnen wollen*) to mean. **damit bin ich gemeint** that's meant for me, they mean/he means *etc* me.

(**e**) (*beabsichtigen*) to mean, to intend. **so war es nicht gemeint** it wasn't meant like that; **sie meint es gut** she means well; **er meint es ehrlich mit dem Mädchen** his intentions towards the girl are honourable; **sie meint es nicht böse** she means no harm, she doesn't mean any harm; **die Sonne hat es aber heute wieder gut gemeint** the sun's done its best for us again today.

meiner *pers pron gen of* **ich** of me.

meine(r, s) *poss pron* (*substantivisch*) mine. **der/die/das ~** (*geh*) mine; **ich tu das M~** (*geh*) I'll do my bit; **das M~** (*geh: Besitz*) what is mine; **die M~n** (*geh: Familie*) my people, my family.

meinerseits *adv* as far as I'm concerned, for my part. **ich ~ I** personally *or* myself, I for my part; **Vorschläge/Einwände ~** suggestions/objections from me; **ganz ~!** the pleasure's (all) mine; (*iro*) so do/are you.

meines-: **~gleichen** *pron inv* (*meiner Art*) people such as I or me, people like me or myself; (*gleichrangig*) my own kind, my equals; **Leute** *or* **Menschen ~gleichen** (*meiner Art*) people like me or myself; (*gleichrangig*) people of my own kind, my equals; **~teils** *adv* for my part.

meinet-: **~halben** (*dated*), **~wegen** *adv* (**a**) (*wegen mir*) because of me, on account of me, on my account; (*mir zuliebe auch*) for my sake; (*um mich*) about me; (*für mich*) on my behalf; (**b**) (*von mir aus*) as far as I'm concerned; **~wegen!** if you like; **wenn Ihr das tun wollt, ~wegen, aber ...** if you want to do that, fair enough (*inf*), but ...; **~willen** *adv:* **um ~willen** for my sake, on my account.

meinige *poss pron* **der/die/das ~** (*form, old*) mine; **die M~n** (*geh*) my family, my people.

meins *poss pron* mine.

Meinung *f* opinion; (*Anschauung auch*) view; (*Urteil*) judgement, estimation. **eine vorgefaßte ~** a preconceived idea; **nach meiner ~, meiner ~ nach** in my opinion or view; **ich bin der ~, daß ...** I'm of the opinion that ..., I take the view that ...; **seine ~ ändern** to change one's opinion or mind; **einer ~ sein** to share the same opinion, to think the same; **was ist Ihre ~ dazu?** what's your opinion or view (about or on that)?; **von seiner ~ eingenommen sein** to be opinionated; **das ist auch meine ~!** that's just what I think; **jdm (kräftig or vernünftig) die ~ sagen** (*inf*) to give sb a piece of one's mind (*inf*).

Meinungs-: **~äußerung** *f* (expression of) opinion; **~austausch** *m* exchange of views (*über* +*acc* on, about); **m~bildend** *adj* opinion-forming; **m~bildend wirken** to shape public opinion; **~bildung** *f* formation of opinion; **der Prozeß der ~bildung ist noch nicht abgeschlossen** we have not yet formed an opinion; **~forscher** *m* (opinion) pollster; **~forschung** *f* (public) opinion polling or research; **~forschungsinstitut** *nt* opinion research institute; **~freiheit** *f* freedom of speech; **m~los** *adj* without opinions, viewless; **m~los sein** to have no opinions; **~macher** *m* (*inf*) opinion-maker, opinion-leader; **~manipulation** *f* manipulation of (public) opinion; **~monopol** *nt* monopoly of opinion; **~terror** *m* repression of free thought; **~umfrage** *f* (public) opinion poll; **~umschwung** *m* swing of opinion; **~verschiedenheit** *f* difference of opinion, disagreement.

Meise *f* -, -n titmouse. **eine ~ haben** (*sl*) to be crackers (*inf*).

Meißel *m* -s, - chisel.

meißeln *vti* to chisel.

Meiß(e)ner *adj* ~ **Porzellan** Dresden *or* Meissen china.

meist *adv siehe* **meistens**.

Meist-: **m~begünstigt** *adj* (*Econ*) most-favoured; **~begünstigung** *f* (*Econ*) most-favoured-nation treatment; **~begünstigungsklausel** *f* (*Econ Pol*) most-favoured-nation clause; **m~bietend** *adj* highest bidding; **~bietender** highest bidder; **m~bietend versteigern** to sell or auction (off) to the highest bidder.

meisten: am ~ *adv* (**a**) *superl of* **viel** the most. (**b**) *superl of* **sehr** most of all. **am ~ bekannt** best known.

meistens *adv* mostly, more often than not; (*zum größten Teil*) for the most part.

meistenteils *adv siehe* **meistens**.

Meister *m* -s, - (**a**) (*Handwerks~*) master (craftsman); (*in Laden*) boss (*inf*); (*in Fabrik*) foreman, boss (*inf*); (*sl: als Anrede*) guv (*Brit sl*), chief (*Brit sl*), mac (*US sl*); (*Sport*) champion; (*Mannschaft*) champions *pl*. **seinen ~ machen** to take one's master craftsman's diploma; **jawohl, ~** yes, sir; (*Mus*) yes, maestro.

(**b**) (*Lehr~, Künstler*) master (*auch fig*). **alter ~** (*Art*) old master; **~ vom Stuhl** (*fig*) Master of the Lodge; **er hat seinen ~**

gefunden (*fig*) he's met his match; **~ einer Sache** (*gen*) *or* **in etw** (*dat*) past master at sth; **es ist noch kein ~ vom Himmel gefallen** (*Prov*) no-one is born a master.

(**c**) (*old liter*) master. **~ Zwirn** Snip, the tailor; **~ Knieriem** *or* **Pfriem/Lampe** Master Cobbler/Hare; **~ Urian** Old Nick.

meiste(r, s) *indef pron superl of* **viel** (**a**) (*adjektivisch*) **die ~n Leute** most people; **die ~n Leute, die ...** most people who ..., most of the people who ...; **meine ~ Zeit** most of my time; **du hast die ~ Zeit** you have (the) most time.

(**b**) (*substantivisch*) **die ~n** most people; **die ~n** (*von ihnen*) most (of them), the majority (of them); **das ~** most of it; **du hast das ~** you have (the) most.

Meister- *in cpds* master; **~brief** *m* master craftsman's diploma *or* certificate; **~gesang** *m* (*Liter*) poetry of the meistersingers; **m~haft 1** *adj* masterly; **2** *adv* in a masterly manner, **er versteht es m~haft, ...** he is brilliant at ...; **~hand** *f:* **von ~hand** by a master hand.

Meisterin *f* (*Handwerks~*) master craftswoman; (*Frau von Handwerksmeister*) master craftsman's wife; (*in Fabrik*) forewoman; (*Sport*) champion. **Frau ~!** madam!

Meister-: **~klasse** *f* master class; **~leistung** *f* masterly performance; (*iro*) brilliant achievement.

meisterlich *adj siehe* **meisterhaft**.

meistern *vt* to master; **Schwierigkeiten** to overcome. **sein Leben ~** to come to grips with one's life.

Meisterprüfung *f* examination for master craftsman's diploma *or* certificate.

Meisterschaft *f* (**a**) (*Sport*) championship; (*Veranstaltung*) championships *pl*.

(**b**) (*Können*) mastery. **es zu wahrer ~ bringen** (*als Künstler etc*) to become really proficient or expert, to achieve real mastery or proficiency; (*als Dieb etc*) to get it down to a fine art.

Meisterschaftsspiel *nt* (*Sport*) championship match.

Meister-: **~schüler** *m* (*Art, Mus*) pupil *in a master class*; **~schuß** *m* brilliant shot; **~schütze** *m* marksman; **~singer** *m* (*Hist*) meistersinger, mastersinger; **~stück** *nt* (*von Handwerker*) work done to qualify as master craftsman; (*fig*) masterpiece; (*geniale Tat*) master stroke; **~titel** *m* (*im Handwerk*) title of master craftsman; (*Sport*) championship title.

Meisterung *f, no pl* mastery.

Meister-: **~werk** *nt* masterpiece; **~würde** *f* (**a**) (*im Handwerk*) rank of master craftsman; (**b**) (*Sport sl*) championship, title.

Meist-: **~gebot** *nt* highest bid, best offer; **m~gebräuchlich** *adj attr* commonest; **m~gefragt** *adj attr* most popular, most in demand; **Wohngegend auch** most sought-after; **m~gekauft** *adj attr* best-selling; **m~gelesen** *adj attr* most widely read; **m~genannt** *adj attr* most frequently mentioned.

Mekka *nt* -s (*Geog, fig*) Mecca.

Melancholie [melaŋkoˈliː] *f* melancholy.

Melancholiker(in *f*) [melaŋˈkoːlikɐ, -ərɪn] *m* -s, - melancholic.

melancholisch [melaŋˈkoːlɪʃ] *adj* melancholy.

Melanesien [-iən] *nt* -s Melanesia.

Melanesier(in *f*) [-iɐ, -iərɪn] *m* -s, - Melanesian.

melanesisch *adj* Melanesian.

Melange [meˈlãːʒə] *f* -, -n (*rare: Mischung*) blend. (**b**) (*Aus: Milchkaffee*) white coffee (*Brit*), coffee with milk.

Melasse *f* -, -n molasses.

Melde-: **~amt** *nt*, **~büro** *nt* (*inf*) registration office; **~behörde** *f* registration authorities *pl*; **~fahrer** *m* (*Mil*) dispatch rider; **~frist** *f* registration period; **~gänger** *m* -s, - *siehe* **~fahrer**; **~hund** *m* (*Mil*) messenger dog.

melden 1 *vt* (**a**) (*anzeigen*) **Unfall, Verlust, ansteckende Erkrankungen** to report; (*berichten*) to report; (*registrieren*) to register; (*denunzieren*) to report. **eine Geburt/Änderungen (der Behörde) ~** to notify the authorities of a birth/changes; **wie soeben gemeldet wird** (*Rad, TV*) according to reports just coming in; **das wird gemeldet!** (*Sch*) I'll tell on you (*Sch inf*); **(bei jdm) nichts zu ~ haben** (*inf*) to have no say; **er hat hier nichts zu ~** (*inf*) he has no say in this; **melde gehorsamst** (*old Mil*) beg to report.

(**b**) (*ankündigen*) to announce. **ich ging zur Sekretärin und ließ mich beim Direktor ~** I went to the secretary and asked her to tell the director that I was there; **wen darf ich ~?** who(m) shall I say (is here)?, who(m) shall I announce?

2 *vi* (*Cards*) to meld.

3 *vr* (**a**) to report (*zu* for). **sich freiwillig ~** (*Mil*) to volunteer; **sich zu** *or* **für etw ~** (*esp Mil*) to sign up for or volunteer for sth; (*für Arbeitsplatz*) to apply for sth; (*für Lehrgang*) to enrol or sign on for sth; **sich krank/zum Dienst ~** to report sick/for work; **sich auf eine Anzeige ~** to answer an advertisement; **sich polizeilich** *or* **bei der Polizei ~** to register with the police; **sich stündlich ~** to report in every hour.

(**b**) (*fig: sich ankündigen*) to announce one's presence; (*Alter*) to make itself or its presence felt; (*Sport, zur Prüfung*) to enter (one's name) (*zu* for); (*Winter, Dunkelheit*) to draw or set in; (*durch Handaufheben*) to put one's hand up, to hold up one's hand; (*Rad, TV*) to come on the air.

(**c**) (*esp Telec: antworten*) to answer. **bitte ~!** (*Telec*) come in, please; **es meldet sich niemand** there's no answer.

(**d**) (*von sich hören lassen*) to get in touch (*bei* with). **melde dich wieder** keep in touch; **seitdem hat er sich nicht mehr gemeldet** he hasn't been heard of since; **wenn du was brauchst, melde dich** if you need anything give a shout (*inf*) or let me know.

Melde-: **~pflicht** *f* (**a**) compulsory registration, obligation to register; **polizeiliche ~pflicht** to apply for sth; **~pflicht des Arztes** the doctor's obligation to notify the authorities; **m~pflichtig** *adj* (**a**) obliged to register; (**b**) **Krankheit** notifiable.

Melder m -s, - siehe **Meldefahrer.**
Melde-: ~schein m registration form; ~schluß m closing date (for entries); ~stelle f place of registration; ~termin m closing date, deadline; ~vorschriften pl registration regulations pl; ~wesen nt system of registration; ~zettel m (Aus) certificate of registration.
Meldung f (a) (Mitteilung) announcement.
  (b) (Press, Rad, TV) report (über +acc on, about). ~en in Kürze news headlines pl; ~en vom Sport sports news sing.
  (c) (dienstlich) report. (eine) ~ machen to make a report.
  (d) (bei der Polizei) report.
  (e) (Sport, Examens~) entry. seine ~ zurückziehen to withdraw.
meliert adj Haar greying, streaked with grey; Wolle flecked. sein Haar war grau ~ his hair was streaked with grey.
Melioration f (Boden~) melioration.
meliorieren* vt to (a)meliorate.
Melisse f -, -n balm.
Melissengeist m balm spirit.
Melk- in cpds milking.
melken pret melkte or (old) molk, ptp gemolken or (rare) gemelkt vti (a) to milk. frisch gemolkene Milch milk fresh from the cow; eine ~de Kuh a milker, a milking or dairy cow; (fig) a milch-cow. (b) (fig inf) to milk (inf), to fleece (inf).
Melker m -s, - milker.
Melkerei f (Milchwirtschaft) dairy (farm).
Melkerin f milkmaid.
Melodie f melody; (Weise auch) tune. nach der ~ von ... to the tune of ...
Melodien- [-'di:ən-]: ~folge f, ~reigen m (Rad) medley of tunes.
Melodik f (a) (Theorie) melodics sing. (b) (musikalische Eigenart) musical idiom.
melodiös adj (geh) melodious.
melodisch adj melodic, tuneful.
Melodram(a) nt -s, Melodramen (liter) melodrama (auch fig).
melodramatisch adj melodramatic (auch fig).
Melone f -, -n (a) melon. (b) (Hut) bowler (Brit), derby (US).
Membran(e) f -, Membrane or Membranen (a) (Anat) membrane. (b) (Phys, Tech) diaphragm.
Memento nt -s, -s (liter) admonition, warning.
Memme f -, -n (inf) cissy (sl), yellow-belly (sl).
memmenhaft adj (inf) lily-livered (inf), yellow-bellied (sl).
Memoire [me'moa:r(ə)] nt -s, -s (Pol) siehe **Memorandum.**
Memoiren [me'moa:rən] pl memoirs pl.
Memorandum nt -s, Memoranden or Memoranda (Pol) memorandum.
Memorial nt -s, -s (esp Sport) memorial.
memorieren* vt (old) (a) to memorize, to commit to memory. (b) (aufsagen) to recite (from memory).
Menage [me'na:ʒə] f -, -n (a) (Gewürzständer) cruet (stand). (b) (Aus: Verpflegung) rations pl.
Menagerie [menaʒə'ri:] f menagerie.
menagieren* [mena'ʒi:rən] vi (Aus) to draw rations.
Menarche f -, no pl (Med) menarche (spec), first menstruation.
mendeln vi (Biol) to mendelize (spec), to conform to Mendel's laws.
Mendelsche Regeln pl (Biol) Mendel's laws pl.
Menetekel nt -s, - (liter) warning sign, portent. das ~ an der Wand the writing on the wall.
Menge f -, -n (a) (Quantum) amount, quantity. in ~n zu in quantities of.
  (b) (inf) (große Anzahl) lot, load (inf); (Haufen auch) pile (inf), heap (inf). eine ~ a lot, lots (inf); eine ~ Zeit/Häuser a lot or lots (inf) of time/houses; jede ~ masses pl (inf), loads pl (inf); jede ~ Zeit/Geld masses (inf) or loads (inf) of time/money; wir haben jede ~ getrunken we drank an enormous amount or a hell of a lot (inf); es gab Wein jede ~ there was masses or loads of wine (inf); eine ganze ~ quite a lot; sie bildet sich eine ~ auf ihre Schönheit ein she's incredibly conceited about her looks; Bücher in ~n any amount of books; siehe rauh.
  (c) (Menschen~) crowd; (geh: Masse) mass; (das Volk) people; (pej: Pöbel) mob.
  (d) (Math) set.
mengen 1 vt (geh) to mix (unter +acc with). **2** vr to mingle (unter +acc with); (fig: sich einmischen) to meddle, to interfere (in +acc with, in).
Mengen-: ~angabe f quantity, indication of quantity; ~begriff m uncountable noun; (Math) concept of the set; ~lehre f (Math) set theory; m~mäßig adj as far as quantity is concerned, quantitative; ~preis m bulk price; ~rabatt m bulk discount; ~verhältnis nt relative proportions pl (zwischen of), quantitative ratio (form) (zwischen between).
Menhir m -s, -e (Archeol) standing stone, menhir.
Meningitis [menɪŋ'gi:tɪs] f -, Meningitiden (Med) meningitis.
Meniskus m -, Menisken (Anat, Phys) meniscus (Phot auch) meniscal lens.
Meniskusriß m torn meniscus.
Menjoubärtchen ['menʒu-] nt pencil moustache.
Menkenke f -, -s or -n (dial) fuss.
Mennige f -, no pl minium, red lead.
Menopause f (Med) menopause.
Mensa f -, Mensen (Univ) canteen, refectory (Brit), commons (US).
Mensa|essen nt (Univ) (Mahlzeit) college meal, commons (US); (Kost) college food, commons (US).
Mensch¹ m -en, -en (a) (Person) person, man/woman. ein anderer ~ werden to become a different man/woman or person; ein neuer ~ werden to become a new person or man/

woman; von ~ zu ~ man-to-man/woman-to-woman; es war kein ~ da there was nobody or not a soul there; als ~ as a person; des ~en Wille ist sein Himmelreich (Prov) do what you want if it makes you happy (inf); das konnte kein ~ ahnen! no-one (on earth) could have foreseen that!; viel unter (die) ~en kommen to meet a lot of people, to get around (a lot); man muß die ~en nehmen, wie sie sind you have to take people as they are or come.
  (b) (als Gattung) der ~ man; die ~en man sing, human beings pl; die Ruritanier sind gutmütige ~en the Ruritanians are a good-natured race or are good-natured people; ein Tier, das keine ~en mag an animal that doesn't like people or humans; ~ bleiben (inf) to stay human; ich bin auch nur ein ~! I'm only human; wer so etwas macht, ist kein ~ mehr somebody who does something like that is not human; wie die ersten/letzten ~en (inf) like animals; ~ und Tier man and beast; alle ~en müssen sterben we are all mortal; alle ~en haben tierische Gelüste all human beings have animal cravings.
  (c) (die Menschheit) die ~ mankind, man; des ~en Sohn (Bibl) the Son of Man; Jesus ist gekommen, um die ~en zu retten Jesus came to save mankind; alle ~en everyone; so sind die ~en that's human nature.
  (d) (inf: als Interjektion) hey; (erstaunt auch) wow, blimey (Brit sl). ~, hat die Beine! hey or wow! has she got a pair of legs! (inf); ~, das habe ich ganz vergessen damn (inf), I completely forgot; ~, da habe ich mich aber getäuscht boy, was I wrong! (inf); ~, da habe ich mich beeilt/geärgert! boy, did I rush/was I angry! (inf); ~ Meier! golly! (inf), gosh! (inf).
Mensch² nt -(e)s, -er (sl) cow (sl); (liederlich) slut.
Mensch ärgere dich nicht nt - - - -, no pl (Spiel) ludo.
menscheln vi impers (a) es menschelt there's no escaping (from) one's humanity. (b) (in Märchen) es menschelt I smell or sense a human.
Menschen- in cpds human; ~affe m ape, anthropoid (ape); m~ähnlich adj man-like, like a human being/human beings; ~alter nt (a) (30 Jahre) generation; (b) (Lebensdauer) lifetime; ~ansammlung f gathering (of people); m~arm adj sparsely populated; ~art f (a) nach ~art like human beings/a human being; (b) (menschliche Schwäche) human nature; ~auflauf m crowd (of people); ~feind m misanthropist; m~feindlich adj Mensch misanthropic; Landschaft etc hostile to man, inhospitable; ~fleisch nt human flesh; ~fresser(in f) m -s, - (a) (inf: Kannibale) cannibal; (Raubtier) man-eater; ich bin doch kein ~fresser! I won't eat you!; (b) (Myth) ogre; ~fresserei f (inf) cannibalism; ~freund m philanthropist; m~freundlich adj Mensch philanthropic, benevolent; Gegend hospitable; diese Affenart ist nicht sehr m~freundlich this species of ape does not like humans; ~freundlichkeit f philanthropy, benevolence; aus reiner ~freundlichkeit from the sheer goodness of one's heart; ~führung f leadership; ~gedenken nt der kälteste Winter seit ~gedenken the coldest winter in living memory; hier hat sich seit ~gedenken nichts geändert nothing has changed here from time immemorial; ~gestalt f human form; ein Teufel or Satan or Scheusal in ~gestalt a devil in disguise; ~gewühl nt milling crowd; ~hai m man-eating shark, man-eater; ~hand f human hand; von ~hand geschaffen fashioned by the hand of man; das liegt nicht in ~hand that is beyond man's control; ~handel m slave trade; (Jur) trafficking (in human beings); (staatsfeindlicher) ~handel (DDR form) subversive smuggling of human beings; ~händler m slave trader; (Jur) trafficker (in human beings); (DDR pej) smuggler of human beings; ~haß m misanthropy, hatred of people; ~hasser m -s, - siehe ~feind; ~jagd f manhunts pl, man-hunting; eine ~jagd a manhunt; ~jäger m man-hunter; ~kenner m judge of character, connoisseur of human nature; ~kenntnis f, no pl knowledge of human nature; ~kenntnis haben to know human nature; ~kind nt creature, soul; ~kunde f anthropology; ~leben nt human life; ein ~leben lang a whole lifetime; ~leben beklagen to report fatalities; ~leben waren nicht zu beklagen there was no loss of life, no fatalities were reported; Verluste an ~leben loss of human life; das Unglück hat zwei ~leben gefordert the accident claimed two lives; m~leer adj deserted; ~liebe f (a) (Bibl) human love; (b) (Nächsten~) love of mankind, philanthropy; aus reiner ~liebe from the sheer goodness of one's heart; tätige ~liebe concrete humanitarianism, active philanthropy; ~masse f crowd or mass (of people); ~material nt (Mil sl) manpower; gutes ~material good (human) resources; ~menge f crowd (of people); m~möglich adj humanly possible; das ist doch nicht m~möglich! (inf) that's ridiculous (inf); das m~mögliche tun to do all that is humanly possible; ~opfer nt (a) human sacrifice; (b) (~leben) es waren ~opfer zu beklagen there were (some) fatalities; ~raub m (Jur) kidnapping; ~räuber m (Jur) kidnapper; ~recht nt human right; die Allgemeine Erklärung or Deklaration der ~rechte the Universal Declaration of Human Rights; ~rechtskonvention f Human Rights Convention; ~scheu f fear of people; krankhafte ~scheu anthropophobia (spec); m~scheu adj afraid of people; ~schinder m slavedriver; ~schlag m (inf) kind of people, breed (inf); ~seele f human soul; keine ~seele (fig) not a (living) soul.
Menschenskind interj good heavens, heavens above.
Menschen-: ~sohn m (Bibl) Son of Man; ~tum nt, no pl humanity; m~unmöglich adj absolutely impossible; das ~unmögliche versuchen/vollbringen to attempt/achieve the impossible; m~unwürdig adj beneath human dignity; Behandlung inhumane; Behausung unfit for human habitation; ~verächter m despiser of mankind; ~verachtung f contempt for mankind; ~verstand m human understanding no art; gesunder ~verstand common sense; ~werk nt (old, liter) work

of man; ~werk ist vergänglich all works of men are transient; ~würde f human dignity no art; m~würdig adj Behandlung humane; Unterkunft fit for human habitation; m~würdig leben to live in conditions fit for human beings; m~würdige Entlohnung decent living wage.

Menschewik m -en, -en or -i (Hist) Menshevik.

Menschewismus m (Hist) Menshevism.

Menschheit f die ~ mankind, humanity; zum Wohle der ~ for the benefit of mankind or the human race; Verdienste um die/im Namen der ~ services to/in the name of humanity.

Menschheits-: ~entwicklung f development of mankind; ~geschichte f history of the human race or of mankind.

menschlich adj (a) human. das ~e Leben human life; der ~e Körper/Geist the human body/mind; die ~e Gesellschaft/ Gemeinschaft the society of man/the human community; jede ~e Hilfe kam zu spät für sie she was beyond human help.
(b) (inf: zivilisiert) human. (einigermaßen) ~ aussehen (inf) to look more or less human; sich wieder ~ fühlen to feel more human (again).
(c) (human) Behandlung etc humane. eine ~e Seite haben to have a human side to one.

Menschlichkeit f, no pl humanity no art. aus reiner ~ on purely humanitarian grounds.

Menschlichkeitsverbrechen nt crime against humanity.

Menschwerdung f (a) (Bibl) incarnation. (b) (Biol) anthropogenesis.

Mensen pl of Mensa.

Menstruation [mɛnstrua'tsioːn] f menstruation.

menstruieren* vi to menstruate.

Mensur f (Univ) (students') fencing bout. eine ~ schlagen or fechten to fight a duel.

Mentalität f mentality.

Mentalreservation f (Jur, Philos) mental reservation.

Menthol nt -s, -e menthol.

Mentor m (a) (dated, geh) mentor. (b) (Sch) ≈ tutor.

Menü, Menu (geh) nt -s, -s (Tages~) set meal or menu, table d'hôte (form). ~ essen to have one of the set meals, to have the set menu; ~ des Tages (set) meal of the day.

Menuett nt -s, -e (Tanz, Kunstmusik) minuet.

Menükarte f (geh) bill of fare.

mephistophelisch adj (liter) Mephistophelian.

Mergel m -s, - (Geol) marl.

Mergelboden m (Geol) marly or marlaceous (spec) soil.

merg(e)lig adj marly, marlaceous (spec).

Meridian m -s, -e (Astron, Geog) meridian.

Meridiankreis m (Astron) meridian circle.

Merino m -s, -s, **Merinoschaf** nt merino (sheep).

Merinowolle f merino wool.

Meriten pl (geh) merits pl. sich (dat) ~ um etw erwerben to receive plaudits for sth; auf seinen alten ~ ruhen to rest on one's laurels or on one's past merits.

merkantil adj (Hist, geh) mercantile.

Merkantilismus m (Hist) mercantilism.

merkantilistisch adj (Hist) mercantilist(ic).

Merkantilsystem nt (Hist) mercantile system, mercantilism.

Merkatorprojektion f Mercator('s) projection.

Merk-: m~bar adj (a) (wahrnehmbar) noticeable; (b) (zu behalten) retainable; leicht/schwer m~bar easy/difficult to remember or retain; ~blatt nt leaflet; (mit Anweisungen auch) instructions pl; ~buch nt siehe Notizbuch.

merken 1 vt (a) (wahrnehmen, entdecken) to notice; (spüren) to feel; (erkennen) to realize. ich merke nichts! I can't feel anything!; davon habe ich nichts gemerkt I didn't notice anything; jdn etw ~ lassen to make sb feel sth; seine Gefühle ~ lassen to let one's feelings show; hat er dich etwas ~ lassen? did you notice anything in the way he behaved?; woran hast du das gemerkt? how could you tell that?; wie soll ich das ~? how am I supposed to tell (that)?; du merkst auch alles! (iro) nothing escapes you, does it?, you are observant, aren't you?; das merkt jeder/keiner! everyone/no-one will notice!; das ist kaum zu ~, davon merkt man kaum etwas it's hardly noticeable; das ist zu ~ you can tell; ich merke keinen Unterschied I can't tell the difference; (weil es keinen gibt) I can't see a difference.
(b) (im Gedächtnis behalten) to remember, to retain. das kann man leicht ~ that's easy to remember; merke: ... NB or note: ...

2 vr (a) (im Gedächtnis behalten) sich (dat) jdn/etw ~ to remember sb/sth; das werde ich mir ~!, ich werd's mir ~! (inf) I'll remember that, I won't forget that; das hat er sich gemerkt he's taken that/it to heart; merk dir das! mark my words!
(b) (im Auge behalten) to remember, to make a note of. sich (dat) eine Autonummer ~ to make a (mental) note of a licence number; ~ Sie sich (dat) den Mann! keep an eye on that man; diesen Schriftsteller wird man sich (dat) ~ müssen this author is someone to take note of.

Merk-: ~fähigkeit f memory; ~heft nt note book; ~hilfe f siehe Eselsbrücke.

merklich adj noticeable, marked, distinct. kein ~er Unterschied no noticeable difference.

Merkmal nt -s, -e characteristic, feature; (Biol, Zool) distinctive mark or marking. „besondere ~e: ..." "distinguishing marks: ...".

Merk-: (Sch) ~satz m mnemonic (sentence); ~spruch m mnemonic (form), memory aid.

Merkur m -s, no pl (Myth, Astron) Mercury; (obs: Quecksilber) quicksilver, mercury.

Merk-: ~vers m (Sch) jingle, mnemonic (rhyme) (form); m~würdig adj strange, odd, curious; er hat sich ganz m~würdig verändert he has undergone a curious change; m~würdigerweise adv strangely or oddly or curiously enough;

~würdigkeit f (a) no pl strangeness, oddness; (b) (rare) curiosity; ~zeichen nt mark(er).

Mesalliance [mezaˈliãːs] f -, -n (liter) misalliance, mésalliance (liter).

meschugge adj (sl) nuts (sl), barmy (Brit sl), meshuga (US sl).

Meskalin nt -s, no pl mescalin(e).

Mesmerismus m, no pl mesmerism.

Mesner m -s, - (dial) siehe Küster.

Mesokephale(r) mf decl as adj siehe Mesozephale(r).

Mesolithikum nt -s, no pl (Geol) Mesolithic period.

mesolithisch adj (Geol) Mesolithic.

Meson nt -s, -en [-'oːnən] (Phys) meson, mesotron.

Mesopotamien [-iən] nt -s Mesopotamia.

Mesopotamier(in f) [-iɐ, -iərin] m -s, - Mesopotamian.

mesopotamisch adj Mesopotamian.

Mesozephale(r) mf decl as adj mesocephalic.

Mesozoikum [-'tsoːikʊm] nt (Geol) Mesozoic.

Meß-: ~band nt siehe Bandmaß; m~bar adj measurable; ~becher m (Cook) measuring jug; ~buch nt (Eccl) missal, Mass book; ~diener m (Eccl) server, acolyte (form).

Messe¹ f -, -n (Eccl, Mus) mass. in die or zur ~ gehen to go to mass; die ~ lesen or halten to say mass; für jdn eine ~ lesen lassen to have a mass said for sb; die hohe ~ High Mass.

Messe² f -, -n (trade) fair. auf der ~ at the fair.

Messe³ f -, -n (Naut, Mil) mess.

Messe- in cpds fair; ~angebot nt exhibits pl (at a/the fair), fair exhibits pl; ~gast m visitor to a/the fair, fair visitor; ~gelände nt exhibition centre; ~gut nt exhibits pl (at a/the fair); ~halle f fair pavilion.

messen pret maß, ptp gemessen 1 vti to measure; (Tech: anzeigen auch) to gauge; Verlauf to time; (abschätzen) Entfernung etc to judge, to gauge. jds Blutdruck/Temperatur ~ (Arzt etc) to take sb's blood pressure/temperature; (Instrument) to measure sb's blood pressure/temperature; während ich lief, maß er die Zeit I ran and he timed me or took the time; seine Kräfte/Fähigkeiten mit jdm ~ to match one's strength/skills against sb's, to try or measure one's strength/skills with sb; seine Kräfte/Fähigkeiten an etw (dat) ~ to test one's strength/skills on sth; etw an etw (dat) ~ (ausprobieren) to try sth out on sth; (vergleichen) to compare sth with sth; jdn mit den Blicken ~ (geh) to look sb up and down.

2 vr (a) (mit against) (geh: im Wettkampf) to compete; (in geistigem Wettstreit, es jdm gleichtun wollen) to pit oneself.
(b) sich mit jdm/etw nicht ~ können to be no match for sb/sth.

Messer nt -s, - knife; (Tech auch) cutter, blade; (Rasier~) (cutthroat) razor. jdm ein ~ in den Leib stoßen, jdm ein ~ in den Bauch jagen (inf) to stick a knife into sb; unter dem ~ sein (Med inf) to be under the knife; jdm das ~ an die Kehle setzen (lit, fig) to hold a knife to sb's throat; die ~ wetzen (fig) to get ready or prepare for the kill; damit würden wir ihn ans ~ liefern (fig) that would be putting his head on the block; jdn der Mafia ans ~ liefern to shop sb (Brit sl) or inform on sb to the Mafia; ein Kampf/sich bekämpfen bis aufs ~ (fig) a fight/to fight to the finish; auf des ~s Schneide stehen (fig) to be or hang (very much) in the balance, to be on a razor-edge or razor's edge; es steht auf des ~s Schneide, ob ... it's touch and go or it's very much in the balance whether ...; es wird eine Nacht der langen ~ geben (fig) heads will roll; siehe locker.

Messer- in cpds knife; ~griff m, ~heft nt knife handle; ~held m (inf) knifer (inf); ~rücken m back of a/the knife; m~scharf adj (lit, fig) razor-sharp; m~scharf schließen (iro) to conclude with incredible logic (iro); ~schmied m cutler; ~schneide f knife edge; ~spitze f knife point; eine ~spitze (voll) (Cook) a pinch; ~stecher(in f) m -s, - knifer (inf); ~stecherei f knife fight; zur or in eine ~stecherei ausarten to end up in a knife fight; ~stich m knife thrust; (Wunde) stab wound; ~werfer m knife-thrower.

Messe-: ~stadt f (town with an) exhibition centre; ~stand m stand (at the/a fair).

Meß-: ~gerät nt (a) (für Öl, Druck etc) measuring instrument, gauge; (b) (Eccl) Mass requisites pl; ~gewand nt chasuble; ~glas nt graduated measure.

messianisch adj (Rel, Philos) Messianic.

Messianismus m, no pl Messianism.

Messias m -, -se (Rel, fig) Messiah.

Messing nt -s, no pl brass. mit ~ beschlagen brass-bound.

Messing- in cpds brass; ~blech nt sheet brass; ~schild nt brass plate.

Meß-: ~instrument nt gauge; ~opfer nt (Eccl) Sacrifice of the Mass; ~ordnung f (Eccl) ordinary (of the Mass); ~platte f (Surv) surveyor's staff or rod; ~stab m (a) (Surv) surveyor's staff, (b) (Aut: Ölmeßstab etc) dipstick; ~tisch m (Surv) surveyor's table; ~tischblatt nt ordnance survey map.

Messung f (a) (das Messen) measuring; (das Ablesen) reading; (von Blutdruck) taking; (Tech: das Anzeigen) gauging. (b) (Meßergebnis) measurement; (Ableseergebnis) reading.

Meß-: ~wein m (Eccl) Communion wine; ~wert m measurement; (Ableseergebnis) reading; ~zahl f measurement; ~zylinder m measuring cylinder, graduated measure.

Mestize m -n, -n mestizo.

Mestizin f mestiza.

Met m -(e)s, no pl mead.

Metall nt -s, -e (a) metal. (b) (geh: der Stimme) metallic ring or timbre.

Metall- in cpds metal; ~arbeiter m metalworker; m~artig adj metallic; ~bearbeitung f metal processing, metalworking.

metallen adj metal; (geh) Klang, Stimme metallic.

Metaller(in f) m -s, - (inf) metalworker.

Metall-: ~ermüdung f metal fatigue; ~geld nt specie, metallic

currency; m~haltig *adj* metalliferous, metalline.
metallisch *adj* metal; (*metallartig*), (*fig*) *Stimme, Klang* metallic. ~ **glänzen** to gleam like metal; ~ **schmecken** to have a metallic taste.
Metall-: ~**kunde** *f* metallurgy; ~**säge** *f* hacksaw.
Metallurg(e) *m* -(e)n, -(e)n, **Metallurgin** *f* metallurgist.
Metallurgie *f* metallurgy.
metallurgisch *adj* metallurgic(al).
Metall-: m~**verarbeitend** *adj* **die m~verarbeitende Industrie** the metal-processing industry; ~**verarbeitung** *f* metal processing; ~**waren** *pl* hardware *sing.*
Metamorphose [-'fo:zə] *f* -, -n metamorphosis.
Metapher [me'tafɐ] *f* -, -n (*Liter, Poet*) metaphor.
Metaphorik [-'fo:rɪk] *f* (*Liter, Poet*) imagery.
metaphorisch *adj* (*Liter, Poet*) metaphoric(al).
Metaphysik *f* metaphysics *sing.*
metaphysisch *adj* metaphysical.
Metapsychologie *f* metapsychology.
Metasprache *f* metalanguage.
Metastase [meta'sta:zə] *f* -, -n (*Med*) metastasis.
Metathese, Metathesis *f* -, **Metathesen** (*Ling*) metathesis.
Meteor *m or nt* -s, -e meteor.
Meteoreisen *nt* meteoric iron.
Meteorit *m* -en, -en meteorite.
Meteorologe *m* meteorologist; (*im Wetterdienst*) weather forecaster, weatherman (*inf*).
Meteorologie *f* meteorology.
Meteorologin *f* meteorologist; (*im Wetterdienst*) weather forecaster.
meteorologisch *adj* meteorological.
Meteorstein *m siehe* **Meteorit.**
Meter *m or nt* -s, - (a) metre (*Brit*), meter (*US*). **in einer Entfernung von 40** ~**(n)** at a distance of 40 metres; **in 500** ~ **Höhe** at a height of 500 metres; **nach** ~**n** by the metre. (b) (*Meterstab*) metric measure. (c) (*inf*) *siehe* **Metermaß.**
Meter-: m~**dick** *adj* metres thick; m~**hoch** *adj* metres high; m~**lang** *adj* metres long; ~**lange Lochstreifen** yards and yards of punch tape; ~**maß** *nt* (a) (*Bandmaß*) tape measure, measuring tape; (b) (*Stab*) (metre) rule; ~**stab** *m* metre rule(r); ~**ware** *f* (*Tex*) piece goods; m~**weise** *adv* by the metre; m~**weit** *adj* (*breit*) metres wide; (*lang*) metres long; **er schoß** m~**weit vorbei** his shot was yards or miles (*inf*) off target.
Methan *nt* -s, *no pl,* **Methangas** *nt* methane.
Methanol *nt* -s, *no pl siehe* **Methylalkohol.**
Methode *f* -, -n (a) method. **etw mit** ~ **machen** to do sth methodically *or* systematically; **das hat** ~ (*inf*) there's (a) method behind it; **er hat (so) seine** ~**n** (*inf*) he's got his methods. (b) ~**n** *pl* (*Sitten*) behaviour; **was sind denn das für** ~**n?** what sort of way is that to behave?
Methodenlehre *f siehe* **Methodologie.**
Methodik *f* methodology.
Methodiker(in *f*) *m* -s, - methodizer.
methodisch *adj* methodical.
Methodist(in *f*) *m* Methodist.
methodistisch *adj* Methodist.
Methodologie *f* methodology.
methodologisch *adj* methodological.
Methusalem *m* -s Methuselah. **alt wie** ~ old as Methuselah.
Methylalkohol *m* methyl *or* wood alcohol.
Metier [me'tie:] *nt* -s, -s (*hum*) job, profession. **sich auf sein** ~ **verstehen** to be good at one's job.
Metonymie *f* (*Liter*) metonymy.
metonymisch *adj* (*Liter*) metonymical.
Metrik *f* (*Poet, Mus*) metrics *sing.*
metrisch *adj* (*Sci*) metric; (*Poet, Mus auch*) metrical.
Metro *f* -, -s metro.
Metronom *nt* -s, -e (*Mus*) metronome.
Metropole *f* -, -n (a) (*größte Stadt*) metropolis. (b) (*Zentrum*) capital, centre. (c) (*Pol: Mutterland*) home country.
Metropolit *m* -en, -en metropolitan.
Metrum *nt* -s, **Metren** metre (*Brit*), meter (*US*).
Mett *nt* -(e)s, *no pl* (*Cook dial*) (lean) minced pork/beef.
Mettage [mɛ'ta:ʒə] *f* -, -n (*Typ*) make-up; (*Arbeitsort*) make-up room.
Mette *f* -, -n (*Eccl*) matins *sing*; (*Abend*~) vespers *sing.*
Metteur(in *f*) [-'tø:ɐ, -'tø:rɪn] *m* (*Typ*) make-up man/woman.
Metze¹ *f* -, -n, **Metzen** *m* -s, - (*obs*) measure for corn, ≈ peck.
Metze² *f* -, -n (*obs: Hure*) strumpet (*old*).
Metzelei *f* butchery, slaughter.
metzeln *vt* to slaughter, to butcher; (*S Ger: schlachten*) to slaughter.
Metzelsuppe *f* (*S Ger*) meat broth.
Metzger *m* -s, - (*dial*) butcher.
Metzger- *siehe* **Fleischer-.**
Metzgerei *f* butcher's (shop).
Meublement [møblə'mã:] *nt* -s, -s (*geh*) furniture, furnishings *pl.*
Meuchel-: ~**mord** *m* (treacherous) murder; ~**mörder** *m* (treacherous) assassin.
meucheln *vt* (*old*) to assassinate.
meuchlerisch *adj* (*old*) murderous; **Mörder** treacherous.
meuchlings *adv* treacherously.
Meute *f* -, -n pack (of hounds); (*fig pej*) mob. **die** ~ **loslassen** *or* **loskoppeln** to release the hounds.
Meuterei *f* mutiny; (*fig auch*) rebellion.
meutern *vi* to mutiny; (*inf auch*) to rebel; (*dial inf: meckern*) to moan, to grouch (*inf*). **die** ~**den Soldaten** the mutinous soldiers.
Mexikaner(in *f*) *m* -s, - Mexican.
mexikanisch *adj* Mexican.

Mexiko *nt* -s Mexico. ~ **City**, ~-**Stadt** Mexico City.
MEZ *abbr of* **mitteleuropäische Zeit.**
Mezzosopran *m* mezzo-soprano.
MG [ɛm'ge:] *nt* -(s), -(s) *abbr of* **Maschinengewehr.**
MHz *abbr of* **Megahertz.**
miau *interj* miaow.
miauen* *vi* to miaow.
mich 1 *pers pron acc of* **ich** me. 2 *reflexive pron* myself. **ich fühle** ~ **wohl** I feel fine.
Michael ['mɪçae:l, 'mɪçael] *m* -s Michael.
Michaeli(s) [mɪça'e:li, mɪça'e:lɪs] *nt* -, - Michaelmas.
Michaelis-: ~**fest** *nt*, ~**tag** *m* Michaelmas.
Michel *m* -s Mike, Mick. **der deutsche** ~ (*fig*) the plain honest German.
Michigansee ['mɪʃɪgən-] *m* Lake Michigan.
mick(e)rig *adj* (*inf*) pathetic; **Betrag** *auch* paltry; **altes Männchen** puny.
Mickymaus ['mɪki-] *f* Mickey Mouse.
midi *adj pred* (*Fashion*) midi.
mied *pret of* **meiden.**
Mieder *nt* -s, - (a) (*Leibchen*) bodice. (b) (*Korsage*) girdle.
Mieder-: ~**höschen** *nt* pantie-girdle; ~**waren** *pl* corsetry *sing.*
Mief *m* -s, *no pl* (*inf*) fug; (*muffig*) stale air; (*Gestank*) stink, pong (*Brit inf*). **im Büro ist so ein** ~ the air in the office is so stale; **der** ~ **der Provinz/des Kleinbürgertums** (*fig*) the oppressive claustrophobic atmosphere of the provinces/petty bourgeoisie.
miefen *vi* (*inf*) to stink, to pong (*Brit inf*); (*furzen*) to make a smell. **hier mieft es** there's a pong in here; (*muffig*) the air in here is so stale; **was mieft denn hier so?** what's this awful pong?
Miene *f* -, -n (*Gesichtsausdruck*) expression, face, mien (*liter*). **eine finstere** ~ **machen** to look grim; **gute** ~ **zum bösen Spiel machen** to grin and bear it; ~ **machen, etw zu tun** to make a move to do sth; **seine** ~ **verfinsterte** *or* **verdüsterte sich** his face darkened; **sich** (*dat*) **etw mit eisiger** ~ **anhören** to listen to sth in stony silence; *siehe* **verziehen¹.**
Mienenspiel *nt* facial expressions *pl.* **ein lebhaftes** ~ **haben** to express a lot with one's face.
mies *adj* (*inf*) rotten (*inf*), lousy (*inf*); **Lokal** *auch* crummy (*inf*); **Laune** *auch* foul. **jdn/etw** ~ **machen** to run sb/sth down; **mir ist** ~ I feel lousy *or* rotten (*inf*).
Miesepeter *m* -s, - (*inf*) misery-guts (*inf*).
miesepet(e)rig *adj* (*inf*) miserable, grouchy (*inf*).
Miesmacher *m* (*inf*) kill-joy.
Miesmacherei *f* (*inf*) belly-aching (*sl*).
Miesmuschel *f* mussel.
Miet-: ~**ausfall** *m* loss of rent; ~**auto** *nt* hire(d) car; ~**beihilfe** *f* rent allowance *or* subsidy/rebate.
Miete¹ *f* -, -n (*für Wohnung*) rent; (*für Gegenstände*) rental; (*für Dienstleistungen*) charge. **rückständige** ~ (rent) arrears; **zur** ~ **wohnen** to live in rented accommodation.
Miete² *f* -, -n (*Kartoffel*~) clamp (*Brit*), pit; (*Schober*) stack.
mieten *vt* to rent; **Boot, Auto** *auch* to hire.
Mieter(in *f*) *m* -s, - tenant; (*Untermieter*) lodger.
Miet|erhöhung *f* rent increase.
Mieterschaft *f* tenants *pl.*
Mieter-: ~**schutz** *m* rent control; ~**schutzgesetz** *nt* Rent Act.
Miet-: ~**ertrag** *m* rent(al) (income); m~**frei** *adj* rent-free; ~**ling** *m* (*obs*) hireling (*obs*), mercenary; ~**partei** *f* tenant (and family); ~**recht** *nt* rent law.
Miets-: ~**haus** *nt* block of (rented) flats (*Brit*), apartment house (*US*); ~**kaserne** *f* (*pej*) tenement house.
Miet-: ~**verhältnis** *nt* tenancy; ~**vertrag** *m* lease; ~**wagen** *m* hire car, hired car; m~**weise** *adv* on hire; ~**wert** *m* letting *or* rental value; ~**wohnung** *f* rented flat (*Brit*) *or* apartment (*US*); ~**wucher** *m* exorbitant rent; ~**wucher ist strafbar** charging exorbitant rent(s) is a punishable offence; ~**zahlung** *f* payment of the rent; ~**zins** *m* (*form, S Ger, Aus*) rent.
Mieze *f* -, -n (*inf*) (a) (*Katze*) pussy (*inf*). (b) (*Mädchen*) chick (*inf*), bird (*Brit inf*); (*als Anrede*) baby (*inf*), honey (*inf*).
Mieze-: ~**kätzchen** *nt* (*baby-talk*) (little) pussy(-cat); ~**katze** *f* (*baby-talk*) pussy(-cat).
Migräne *f* -, *no pl* migraine.
Migräne|anfall *m* attack of migraine.
Mikado¹ *nt* -s, -s (*Spiel*) pick-a-stick.
Mikado² *m* -s, -s (*old: Kaiser von Japan*) mikado.
Mikro- *in cpds* micro-.
Mikrobe *f* -, -n microbe.
Mikrofiche *m or nt* -s, -s microfiche.
Mikrofon *nt* -s, -e microphone.
Mikrokephale(r) *mf decl as adj siehe* **Mikrozephale(r).**
Mikrokosmos *m* microcosm.
Mikrometer *nt* micron; (*Gerät*) micrometer.
Mikron *nt* -s - micron.
Mikronesien [-iən] *nt* -s Micronesia.
Mikrophon *nt* -s, -e microphone.
Mikrophonstimme *f* microphone voice.
Mikroprozessor *m* microprocessor.
Mikroskop *nt* -s, -e microscope.
Mikroskopie *f* microscopy.
mikroskopieren* 1 *vt* (*rare*) to examine under *or* with the microscope. 2 *vi* to work with a/the microscope.
mikroskopisch *adj* microscopic. **etw** ~ **untersuchen** to examine sth under the microscope; ~ **klein** (*fig*) microscopically small.
Mikrozephale(r) *mf decl as adj* microcephalic.
Milan *m* -s, -e (*Orn*) kite.
Milbe *f* -, -n mite.
Milch *f* -, *no pl* (*alle Bedeutungen*) milk; (*Fischsamen*) milt, soft roe. **dicke** ~ curd(s); ~ **geben** (*Kuh*) to yield milk; **das Land,**

wo ~ und Honig fließt the land of or flowing with milk and honey; aussehen wie ~ und Blut to have a peaches-and-cream complexion.

Milch- in cpds milk; **m~artig** adj milky; **~bar** f milk bar; **~bart** m (inf) downy or fluffy beard, bum-fluff (inf); (fig pej: Jüngling) milksop; **~brei** m ≃ milk pudding; **~bruder** m (old) foster-brother; **~drüse** f mammary gland; **~eiweiß** nt lactoprotein; **~flasche** f milk bottle; **~frau** f (inf) dairywoman; **~gebiß** nt milk teeth pl; **~geschäft** nt dairy; **~gesicht** nt (inf) baby face; **~glas** nt frosted glass; **~handel** m dairy business; **~händler** m dairyman.

milchig adj milky.

Milch-: **~kaffee** m milky coffee; **~kanne** f milk can; (größer) (milk) churn; **~kuh** f milk or milch (spec) cow; (fig inf) milch cow, ever-open purse; **~kur** f milk diet; **~laden** m siehe **~geschäft**; **~mädchen** nt (~verkäuferin) dairy girl; (~kassiererin) milk girl; **~mädchenrechnung** f (inf) naïve fallacy; **~mann** m, pl **-männer** milkman; **~mixgetränk** nt milk shake.

Milchner m **-s**, **-** milter.

Milch-: **~pulver** nt dried or powdered milk; **~pumpe** f breast pump; **~reis** m rice pudding; **~saft** m (Bot) latex; **~säure** f lactic acid; **~schorf** m cradle cap; **~speise** f milky or milk-based food; **~straße** f Milky Way; **~straßensystem** nt Milky Way system or galaxy; **~suppe** f (a) ≃ warm blancmange; (b) (dated inf: Nebel) pea-souper (inf); **~tüte** f milk carton; **~wirtschaft** f dairy farming; **~zahn** m milk tooth; **~zucker** m lactose.

mild(e) adj (a) (sanft, lind) Wetter, Abend mild; Luft auch gentle.
(b) (nachsichtig, barmherzig) Behandlung, Beurteilung, Richter lenient; Worte mild. **jdn ~ stimmen** to put sb in a mild mood; **~ ausfallen** to be lenient; **eine ~e Gabe** alms pl; **~ gesagt/ausgedrückt** to put it mildly.
(c) Käse, Zigaretten mild; Seife auch gentle; Speisen light.

Milde f **-**, no pl siehe adj (a) mildness; gentleness. (b) leniency. **~ walten lassen** to be lenient.

mildern 1 vt (geh) Schmerz to ease, to soothe, to alleviate; Furcht to calm; Strafe, Urteil to moderate, to mitigate; Gegensätze to reduce, to make less crass or severe; Ausdrucksweise, Zorn to moderate. **~de Umstände** (Jur) mitigating or extenuating circumstances.
2 vr (Wetter) to become milder; (Gegensätze) to become less crass; (Zorn) to abate; (Schmerz) to ease.

Milderung f, no pl (von Schmerz) easing, soothing, alleviation; (von Ausdruck, des Klimas) moderation; (von Strafe) moderation, mitigation. **spüren Sie schon eine ~?** can you feel any easing (of the pain)?

Milderungsgrund m mitigating cause or circumstance.

Mild-: **m~herzig** adj (old) siehe **barmherzig**; **~herzigkeit** f, no pl (old) siehe **Barmherzigkeit**; **m~tätig** adj (geh) charitable; **er war sein ganzes Leben lang m~tätig** he performed charitable deeds throughout his life; **~tätigkeit** f (geh) charity.

Milieu [mi'ljøː] nt **-s**, **-s** (Umwelt) environment, milieu; (Lokalkolorit) atmosphere; (Verbrecher~) underworld; (von Prostitution) world of prostitutes.

Milieu-: **m~geschädigt**, **m~gestört** adj maladjusted (due to adverse social factors); **~schaden** m effects pl of adverse social factors; **~schilderung** f background description; **~studien** pl **~studien** treiben (usu hum) to study the locals (hum); **~theorie** f (Sociol) environmentalism no art; **~wechsel** m change of environment; (Abwechslung) change of scene.

militant adj militant.

Militanz f, no pl militancy.

Militär[1] nt **-s**, no pl military, armed forces pl. **beim ~ sein** (inf) to be in the forces; **zum ~ einberufen werden** to be called up; **zum ~ müssen** (inf) to have to join up; **zum ~ gehen** to join up; **(gegen jdn) ~ einsetzen** to use the military (against sb); **wir sind doch hier nicht beim ~!** we're not in the army, you know!; **da geht es zu wie beim ~** the place is run like an army camp.

Militär[2] m **-s**, **-s** (army) officer.

Militär- in cpds military; **~arzt** m army doctor; medical officer; **~bischof** m army bishop; **~dienst** m military service; **(seinen) ~dienst ableisten** to do national service; **~geistliche(r)** m (army) chaplain; **~gericht** nt military court, court martial; **Internationales ~gericht** International Military Tribunal; **vor ein ~gericht gestellt werden** to be tried by a court martial.

Militaria pl things military pl.

militärisch adj military. **~ grüßen** to give the military salute; **jdm ~ or die ~en Ehren erweisen** to give sb military honours; **mit allen ~en Ehren** with full military honours; **einen Konflikt ~ or mit ~en Mitteln lösen** to resolve a conflict with the use of troops; **es geht dort streng ~ zu** it's very regimented there; **~ abgehackt sprechen** to speak in a clipped military fashion; **sich ~ geben** to behave in a military fashion.

militarisieren* vt to militarize.

Militarismus m, no pl militarism.

Militarist(in f) m militarist.

militaristisch adj militaristic.

Militär-: **~pflicht** f siehe **Wehrpflicht**; **~pflichtige(r)** mf decl as adj siehe **Wehr(dienst)pflichtige(r)**; **~seelsorge** f spiritual welfare of the armed forces; **~wesen** nt military affairs pl; **~wissenschaft** f military science.

Military ['mɪlɪtərɪ] f **-**, **-s** (Sport) three-day event.

Militärzeit f army days pl, days pl as a soldier.

Miliz f **-**, **-en** militia.

Milizionär(in f) m militiaman/-woman.

Milizsoldat m (old) militiaman.

Mill. abbr of **Million(en)**.

mille: **pro ~** siehe **Promille**.

Mille f **-**, **-** (sl) grand (sl). **5 ~ 5** grand (sl).

Millennium nt (geh) millennium.

Milliardär(in f) m multi-millionaire, billionaire.

Milliarde f **-**, **-n** thousand millions (Brit), billion (US). **zwei ~n Mark** two thousand million marks (Brit), two billion marks (US); **~n (von) Menschen** thousands of millions of people, billions of people.

Milliardenbetrag m (amount of) thousands of millions (Brit), billions (US).

Milliardstel nt **-s**, **-** thousand millionth (Brit) or billionth (US) part.

milliardstel adj thousand millionth (Brit), billionth (US). **ein ~ Meter** a or one thousand millionth of a metre (Brit), a or one billionth of a meter (US), a or one bicron (US).

milliardste(r, s) adj thousand millionth (Brit), billionth (US).

Milli- in cpds milli-; **~bar** nt **-s**, **-** millibar; **~gramm** nt milligramme; **~meter** m or nt millimetre; **~meterpapier** nt graph paper.

Million f million. **eine ~ Londoner ist** or **sind unterwegs** a million Londoners are on their way; **zwei ~en** two millions; **zwei ~en Einwohner** two million inhabitants.

Millionär(in f) m millionaire(ss). **vom Tellerwäscher zum ~** from rags to riches; **es zum ~ bringen** to make a million.

Millionen-: **~auflage** f million copies pl; millions of copies; **~auftrag** m contract worth millions; **~dorf** nt (hum inf) urban or metropolitan village (hum), Munich; **~erbe** m, **~erbin** f inheritor of millions; **m~fach** 1 adj millionfold; 2 adv a million times; **~geschäft** nt multi-million-pound industry; **ein ~geschäft abschließen** to conclude a (business) deal worth millions; **~gewinn** m (a) (Ertrag) profit of millions; **manche Firmen haben ~gewinne gemacht** some firms have made profits running into millions; (b) (Lotterie~) prize of a million; **~heer** nt army of millions; **m~mal** adv a million times; **~schaden** m damage no pl amounting to or running into millions; **m~schwer** adj (inf) worth a few million; **~stadt** f town with over a million inhabitants.

Millionstel nt **-s**, **-** millionth part.

millionstel adj millionth.

millionste(r, s) adj millionth.

Milz f **-**, **-en** spleen.

Milzbrand m (Med, Vet) anthrax.

Mime m **-n**, **-n** (old, liter) mime (old), Thespian.

mimen (old) 1 vt to mime. **er mimt den Unschuldigen/den Kranken** (inf) he's acting the innocent/he's playing at being sick. 2 vi to play-act.

Mimesis f **-**, **Mimesen** (Liter, Philos) mimesis.

mimetisch adj (Liter, Philos) mimetic.

Mimik f, no pl facial expression. **etw durch ~ ausdrücken** to express sth facially.

Mimiker(in f) m **-s**, **-** mime(r).

Mimikry ['mɪmikri] f **-**, no pl (Zool, fig) mimicry.

mimisch adj mimic.

Mimose f **-**, **-n** mimosa. **empfindlich wie eine ~ sein** to be oversensitive.

mimosenhaft adj (fig) oversensitive.

Min., min. abbr of **Minute(n)**.

min. abbr of **minimal**.

Minarett nt **-s**, **-e** or **-s** minaret.

minder adv less. **mehr oder ~** more or less; **nicht mehr und nicht ~** neither more nor less, no more and no less; **nicht ~ wichtig** as no less important than; **und das nicht ~** and no less so.

Minder-: **m~begabt** adj less gifted; **~begabte** pl decl as adj less gifted people/ones pl; **m~begütert** adj less well-off; **~begüterte** pl decl as adj people pl in the lower income brackets; **~belastete(r)** m decl as adj (Jur) less incriminated person; **m~bemittelt** adj (dated) less well-off; **geistig m~bemittelt** (iro) mentally less gifted; **~bemittelte** pl decl as adj (dated) people pl with a limited income; (iro) not very bright people pl; **~einnahme** f decrease in receipts.

mindere(r, s) adj attr lesser; Güte, Qualität inferior.

Mindergewicht nt short weight.

Minderheit f minority.

Minderheiten- (Pol): **~frage** f minorities problem; **~schutz** m protection of minorities.

Minderheits- (Pol): **~rechte** pl rights of minorities pl; **~regierung** f minority government.

Minder-: **m~jährig** adj who is (still) a minor; **~jährige(r)** mf decl as adj minor; **~jährigkeit** f minority.

mindern 1 vt (herabsetzen) Würde, Verdienste to diminish; (verringern) Wert, Qualität to reduce, to diminish, to erode; Rechte to erode; Freude, Vergnügen to detract from, to lessen. 2 vr siehe vt to diminish; to be reduced, to diminish; to be eroded; to lessen.

Minderung f siehe vb diminishing no indef art; reduction (gen in); erosion; lessening.

Minderwert m (Jur) decrease in value.

minderwertig adj inferior; Waren, Material auch poor- or low-quality; Arbeit auch poor(-quality); Qualität auch low; Charakter low, base. **~es Subjekt** (pej) despicable character.

Minderwertigkeit f siehe adj inferiority; poor or low quality; poorness; lowness, baseness. **die ~ der Qualität** the low quality.

Minderwertigkeits-: **~gefühl** nt feeling of inferiority; **~gefühle haben** to feel inferior; **~komplex** m inferiority complex.

Minderzahl f minority. **in der ~ sein** to be in the minority.

Mindest- in cpds minimum; **~abstand** m minimum distance;

~alter *nt* minimum age; ~betrag *m* minimum amount; **Waren für einen** ~betrag **von DM 20** goods to a minimum value of DM 20.

mindestens *adv* at least.

mindeste *superl of* **wenig 1** *adj attr* least, slightest; *Ahnung auch* faintest, foggiest (*inf*). **nicht die** ~ **Angst** not the slightest or least trace of fear; **er hat nicht das** ~ **bißchen Arbeit geleistet** he didn't do a single stroke (of work); **das** ~ **the** (the very) least; **das macht mir den** ~n **Kummer** that's the least of my worries; **ich verstehe nicht das** ~ **von (der) Kunst** I don't know the slightest thing about art; **das wäre das** ~ **gewesen** that's the least he/she *etc* could have done.

2 *adv* **zum** ~n at least, at the very least; **(nicht) im** ~n (not) in the least; **das bezweifle ich nicht im** ~n I don't doubt that at all or in the slightest.

Mindest-: ~forderung *f* minimum demand; ~gebot *nt* (*bei Auktionen*) reserve or knockdown price; ~geschwindigkeit *f* minimum speed; ~größe *f* minimum size; (*von Menschen*) minimum height; ~lohn *m siehe* **Tariflohn**; ~maß *nt* minimum, minimum amount (*an + dat* of); **mit ihnen muß man mehr als ein** ~maß **an Geduld haben** you must have more than a little patience with them; **sich auf das** ~maß **beschränken** to limit oneself to the (absolute) minimum; ~preis *m* minimum price; ~reserve *f* (*Fin*) minimum reserves *pl*; ~strafe *f* minimum penalty; ~umtausch *m* minimum obligatory exchange; ~urlaub *m* minimum holiday entitlement; ~wert *m* minimum value; **im** ~wert **von** to a minimum value of; ~zahl *f* minimum number.

Mine *f* -, -n (a) (*Min*) mine. **in den** ~n **arbeiten** to work down or in the mines.

(b) (*Mil*) mine. **auf eine** ~ **laufen** to strike or hit a mine.

(c) (*Bleistift*~) lead; (*Kugelschreiber*~, *Filzstift*~) reservoir; (*Farb*~) cartridge; (*austauschbar*) refill. **die** ~ **ist leer/läuft aus** the biro/felt-tip has run out/is leaking; **eine neue** ~ **a refill**/new lead.

Minen-: ~feld *nt* (*Mil*) minefield; ~leger *m* -s, - (*Mil, Naut*) mine-layer; ~räumboot *nt* minesweeper; ~sperre *f* (*Mil*) mine barrage; ~suchboot *nt*, ~sucher *m* (*inf*) minesweeper; ~werfer *m* (*old Mil*) *siehe* **Mörser.**

Mineral *nt* -s, -e or -ien [-iən] mineral.

Mineral-: ~bad *nt* mineral bath; (*Ort*) spa; (*Schwimmbad*) swimming-pool fed from a mineral spring; ~brunnen *m* mineral spring; ~dünger *m* inorganic fertilizer.

Mineraliensammlung [-iən-] *f* collection of minerals.

mineralisch *adj* mineral.

Mineraloge *m*, **Mineralogin** *f* mineralogist.

Mineralogie *f* mineralogy.

mineralogisch *adj* mineralogical.

Mineral-: ~öl *nt* (mineral) oil; ~ölgesellschaft *f* oil company; ~ölsteuer *f* tax on oil; ~quelle *f* mineral spring; ~salz *nt* mineral salt; ~wasser *nt* mineral water.

mini *adj inv* (*Fashion*) mini. ~ **tragen/gehen** to wear a mini(-skirt/-dress *etc*).

Mini- *in cpds* mini-.

Miniatur *f* (*Art*) miniature; (*fig Liter*) thumb-nail sketch.

Miniatur- *in cpds* miniature; ~ausgabe *f* miniature version; (*Buch*) miniature edition; ~bild *nt* miniature; ~bildnis *nt* miniature portrait; ~format *nt* miniature format; **eine Bibel in** ~format a miniature Bible; ~gemälde *nt* miniature; ~maler *m* miniaturist; ~malerei *f* miniature painting; ~staat *m* tiny state or country.

Mini-: ~bikini *m* scanty bikini; ~car *m* minicab.

minieren* *vt* (*Min, Mil*) to mine.

Minigolf *nt* crazy golf.

minimal **1** *adj* Unterschied, Arbeitsaufwand minimal; *Verlust, Verbesserung, Steigerung* marginal; *Gewinn* very small; *Preise, Benzinverbrauch, Gehalt* very low. **mit** ~er **Anstrengung** with a minimum of effort. **2** *adv* (*wenigstens*) at least; (*geringfügig*) minimally, marginally.

Minimal- *in cpds* minimum; ~betrag *m* minimum amount; ~forderung *f* minimum demand; ~konsensus *m* basic area of agreement; ~programm *nt* basic programme; ~wert *m* minimum value.

Minimax ® *m* -es, -e fire-extinguisher.

minimieren* *vt* to minimize.

Minimierung *f* minimization.

Minimum *nt* -s, **Minima** minimum (*an + dat* of). **barometrisches** ~ (*Met*) barometric low.

Mini-: ~rock *m* mini-skirt; ~spion *m* miniaturized bugging device.

Minister(in *f*) *m* -s, - (*Pol*) minister (*Brit*) (*für* of), secretary (*für* for).

Ministeramt *nt* ministerial office.

Ministerial-: ~beamte(r) *m* ministry official; ~direktor *m* head of a government department, permanent secretary (*Brit*); ~dirigent *m* assistant head of government department, assistant secretary (*Brit*).

ministeriell *adj attr* ministerial.

Ministerium *nt* ministry (*Brit*), department.

Minister-: ~konferenz *f* conference of ministers, ministerial conference; ~präsident(in *f*) *m* prime minister; (*eines Bundeslandes*) chief minister of a Federal German state; ~rat *m* council of state; (*von EG*) Council of Ministers; ~sessel *m* ministerial post.

ministrabel *adj* (*geh*) eligible for ministerial office; (*aufgrund von Können auch*) of ministerial calibre.

Ministrant *m* (*Eccl*) server.

ministrieren* *vi* (*Eccl*) to serve, to act as server.

Minna *f* -, *no pl* (*dated: Hausangestellte*) maid; (*fig inf*) skivvy (*inf*). **jdn zur** ~ **machen** (*inf*) to give sb a piece of one's mind, to

tear a strip off sb (*inf*); *siehe* **grün.**

Minne *f* -, *no pl* (*Liter, Hist*) courtly love.

Minne-: ~dienst *m* homage rendered by a knight to his lady; **er hat** ~dienst (*dated hum*) he's out courting (*dated*); ~gesang *m siehe* ~sang; ~lied *nt* minnelied; ~sang *m* minnesong; ~sänger, ~singer *m* minnesinger.

minniglich *adj* (*obs, liter*) lovely, charming.

minoisch *adj* Minoan.

Minorität *f siehe* **Minderheit.**

Minuend *m* -en, -en (*Math*) minuend.

minus 1 *prep + gen* minus, less; (*Math*) minus. **2** *adv* minus; (*Elec*) negative. ~ **10 Grad, 10 Grad** ~ minus 10 degrees, 10 degrees below (zero); ~ **machen** (*inf*) to make a loss.

Minus *nt* -, - (a) (*Fehlbetrag*) deficit; (*auf Konto*) overdraft; (*fig: Nachteil*) bad point; (*in Beruf etc*) disadvantage. (b) (~zeichen) minus (sign).

Minus-: ~pol *m* negative pole; ~punkt *m* minus or penalty point; (*fig*) minus point; **ein** ~punkt **für jdn sein** to count against sb, to be a point against sb; ~temperatur *f* temperature below freezing or zero; ~zeichen *nt* minus sign.

Minute *f* -, -n minute; (*fig: Augenblick auch*) moment. **es ist 10 Uhr und 21** ~n (*form*) it is 21 minutes past 10 o'clock; **auf die** ~ (*genau/pünktlich*) (right) on the dot; **in letzter** ~ at the last moment or minute; ~ **auf or um** ~ verging or verstrich or verrann (*liter*) the minutes ticked by or went by; **auf die** ~ **kommt es nicht an** a few minutes one way or another don't matter; **es vergeht keine** ~, **ohne daß ...** not a moment goes by without ...

Minuten-: ~lang **1** *adj attr* several minutes of; **2** *adv* for several minutes; ~schnelle *f*: **in** ~schnelle in minutes, in a matter of minutes; ~zeiger *m* minute-hand.

minutiös [minu'tsiø:s], **minuziös** *adj* (*geh*) *Nachbildung, Mensch* meticulous; *Schilderung auch, Fragen* detailed.

Minze *f* -, -n (*Bot*) mint.

mir *pers pron dat of* **ich** to me; (*nach Präpositionen*) me. **ein Freund von** ~ a friend of mine; **von** ~ **aus!** (*inf*) I don't mind; ~ **nichts, dir nichts** (*inf*) (*unhöflich*) without so much as a by-your-leave; **es war** ~ **nichts, dir nichts weg** the next thing I knew it had gone; **wie du** ~, **so ich dir** (*prov*) tit for tat (*inf*); (*als Drohung*) I'll get my own back (on you); **und das** ~! why me (of all people)?; **daß ihr** ~ **nicht an die Bücher geht!** (*inf*) don't you touch those books!; **du bist** ~ **vielleicht einer!** (*inf*) you're a right one, you are! (*inf*); *siehe auch* **ihm.**

Mirabelle *f* mirabelle, small yellow plum.

Mirakel *nt* -s, - (*old liter*) miracle.

mirakulös *adj* (*old liter*) miraculous.

Misanthrop *m* -en, -en (*geh*) misanthropist.

Misanthropie *f* (*geh*) misanthropy.

Misch-: **m**~bar *adj* mixable, miscible (*form*); **m**~bar **sein** to mix; ~batterie *f* mixer tap; ~becher *m* (*Cook*) *siehe* **Mixbecher;** ~blut *nt* (*liter*) *siehe* **Mischling;** ~brot *nt* bread made from more than one kind of flour; ~ehe *f* mixed marriage.

mischen 1 *vt* to mix; *Tabak-, Tee-, Kaffeesorten auch* to blend; *Karten* to shuffle; *siehe* **gemischt.**

2 *vr* (*sich vermengen*) to mix. **sich unter jdn/etw** ~ to mix or mingle with sb/mix with sth; **sich in etw** (*acc*) ~ to meddle or interfere in sth; **sich in das Gespräch** ~ to butt or cut into the conversation.

3 *vi* (*Cards*) to shuffle. **wer mischt?** whose shuffle is it?

Mischer *m* -s, - (*inf*) (a) *siehe* **Mischpult.** (b) *siehe* **Mischtrommel.**

Misch-: ~farbe *f* mixed or blended colour; (*Phys*) secondary colour; ~form *f* mixture; (*von zwei Elementen auch*) hybrid (form); ~futter *nt* (*Agr*) *siehe* **Kraftfutter;** ~gas *nt* mixture of coal gas and water gas; ~kultur *f* (a) (*Agr*) mixed cultivation; ~kulturen **anbauen** to grow different crops side by side or in the same field; (b) (*Sociol*) mixed culture.

Mischling *m* (a) (*Mensch*) half-caste, half-breed. (b) (*Zool*) half-breed.

Mischlingskind *nt* half-caste child.

Misch-: ~masch *m* -(e)s, -e (*inf*) hotchpotch, mishmash (*aus* of); (*Essen auch*) concoction; **sie redet einen fürchterlichen** ~masch she speaks a horrible jumble or hotchpotch of different languages; ~maschine *f* cement-mixer; ~poke, ~poche *f* -, *no pl* (*sl*) clan (*inf*), mob (*inf*); ~pult *nt* (*Rad, TV*) mixing desk or panel; (*von Band*) sound mixer; ~rasse *f* (a) (*Tiere*) crossbreed; (b) (*Menschen*) mixed race; ~trommel *f* (drum in) cement-mixer.

Mischung *f* (a) (*das Mischen*) mixing; (*von Tee-, Kaffee-, Tabaksorten auch*) blending. (b) (*lit, fig: Gemischtes*) mixture; (*von Tee etc auch*) blend; (*von Süßigkeiten etc auch*) assortment; (*fig auch*) combination (*aus* of). (c) (*Chem*) *siehe* **Gemisch.**

Mischungsverhältnis *nt* ratio/proportions (of a mixture).

Misch-: ~volk *nt* mixed race; ~wald *m* mixed (deciduous and coniferous) woodland; ~wort *nt* hybrid word.

miserabel *adj* (*inf*) lousy (*inf*); *Gesundheit* miserable, wretched; *Gefühl* ghastly; *Benehmen* dreadful; *Leistungen auch* pathetic; (*gemein*) *Kerl etc* nasty.

Misere *f* -, -n (*von Leuten, Wirtschaft etc*) plight; (*von Hunger, Krieg etc*) misery, miseries *pl*. **in einer** ~ **stecken** to be in a terrible or dreadful state; (*Mensch*) to be in a mess, to have run into trouble; **jdn aus einer** ~ **herausholen** to get sb out of trouble or a mess; **die** ~ **der Inflation/des Skandals** the inflationary plight/the messy scandal; **das war eine einzige** ~ that was a real disaster; **es ist eine** ~, **wie/daß ...** it is dreadful how/that ...; **es gab einen Skandal und jetzt sitzt er in der** ~ there was a scandal and now he is suffering because of it; **es ist die** ~ **des Alltags, daß ...** it is one of life's hardships that ...

Miserere *nt* -(s), *no pl* (a) (*Eccl*) miserere. (b) (*Med*) faecal vomiting.

Misogyn m -s or -en, -en (liter) misogynist.
Mispel f -, -n medlar (tree).
Miß, Miss f -, **Misses** Miss.
miß imper sing of **messen**.
miß|achten* vt insep **(a)** (ignorieren) Warnung, Ratschlag to ignore, to disregard; Gesetz, Verbot to flout. **(b)** (geringschätzen) jdn to despise; Hilfe, Angebot to disdain.
Miß|achtung f **(a)** (Vernachlässigung) disregard; flouting. **(b)** (Geringschätzung) disrespect (gen for); disdain (gen of, for).
mißbehagen* infin auch **mißzubehagen** vi insep +dat das mißbehagte ihm that was not to his liking; es mißbehagt mir, schon wieder umziehen zu müssen it ill suits me to have to move again.
Mißbehagen nt (geh) (Unbehagen) uneasiness; (Mißfallen) discontent(ment). **jdm ~ bereiten** to cause sb uneasiness/discontent(ment).
mißbilden ptp **mißgebildet** vt insep to deform.
Mißbildung f deformity, malformation.
mißbilligen* vt insep to disapprove of, to object to.
mißbilligend adj disapproving.
Mißbilligung f disapproval.
Mißbrauch m abuse; (falsche Anwendung) misuse; (von Notbremse, Feuerlöscher etc) improper use; (geh: einer Person) sexual assault (gen on). **~ zur Unzucht** (Jur) sexual offence committed by person in position of authority over victim; **vor ~ wird gewarnt** use only as directed; (an Notbremse etc) do not misuse; **unter ~ seines Amtes** in abuse of his office.
mißbrauchen* vt insep to abuse; Güte auch to impose upon; (geh: vergewaltigen) to assault. **den Namen Gottes ~** (liter) to take the Lord's name in vain; **jdn für or zu etw ~** to use sb for sth or to do sth; **jdn zu allem möglichen ~** to impose on sb.
mißbräuchlich adj (form) Benutzung improper; Anwendung auch incorrect.
mißdeuten* vt insep to misinterpret.
Mißdeutung f misinterpretation.
missen vt (geh) to go or do without; Erfahrung to miss. **das möchte ich nicht ~** I wouldn't do without it/miss it (for the world); **ich möchte meine Kinder nicht ~** I could not do without my children; **wir können dich nur schwer ~** we can't really do without you.
Miß|erfolg m failure; (Theat, Buch etc auch) flop.
Miß|ernte f crop failure.
Missetat f (old, liter) misdeed, misdemeanour.
Missetäter(in f) m (old, liter) culprit; (Verbrecher auch) wrongdoer.
mißfallen* vi insep irreg +dat to displease. **es mißfällt mir, wie er ...** I dislike the way he ...
Mißfallen nt -s, no pl displeasure (über +acc at), disapproval (über +acc of). **jds ~ erregen** to incur sb's displeasure.
Mißfallens-: **~äußerung** f expression of disapproval or displeasure; **~bekundung**, **~kundgebung** f expression or demonstration of disapproval or displeasure.
mißfällig adj (rare) Bemerkung disparaging, deprecatory.
Mißgeburt f deformed person/animal; (fig inf) failure. **das Kind ist eine ~** the child was born deformed; **du widerliche ~!** you repulsive freak.
mißgelaunt adj (geh) bad-tempered, ill-humoured.
Mißgeschick nt mishap; (Pech, Unglück) misfortune. **ein kleines ~** a slight mishap; **vom ~ verfolgt werden** (geh) to be dogged by misfortune.
Mißgestalt f (liter) misshapen figure.
mißgestalt (liter), **mißgestaltet** (geh) adj misshapen.
mißgestimmt adj (geh) disgruntled. **~ sein** to be in an ill humour.
mißglücken* vi insep aux sein to fail, to be unsuccessful. **der Versuch ist (ihm) mißglückt** the/his attempt was a failure or failed; **er wollte mich überraschen, aber es ist ihm mißglückt** he wanted to surprise me but he failed.
mißgönnen* vt insep jdm etw ~ to (be)grudge sb sth; **sie mißgönnt es ihm, daß er erfolgreich ist** she (be)grudges him his success, she resents his success.
Mißgriff m mistake.
Mißgunst f resentment, enviousness (gegenüber of).
mißgünstig adj resentful (auf +acc towards).
mißhandeln* vt insep to ill-treat, to maltreat.
Mißhandlung f ill-treatment, maltreatment; (Kindes~) cruelty (to children).
Mißhelligkeit f (geh) disagreement, difference.
missingsch adv in a mixture of High and Low German.
Missingsch nt -, no pl mixture of High and Low German.
Mission f (Eccl, Pol, fig) mission; (diplomatische Vertretung) legation, mission (US); (Gruppe) delegation. **~ treiben** to do missionary work; **in der ~ tätig sein** to be a missionary.
Missionar(in f), **Missionär(in** f) (Aus) m missionary.
missionarisch adj missionary.
missionieren* **1** vi to do missionary work, to proselytize; (fig) to preach, to proselytize. **2** vt Land, Mensch to (work to) convert, to proselytize; (fig) to convert, to proselytize.
Missionierung f conversion, proselytization.
Missions-: **~chef** m head of a legation/leader of a delegation; **~gesellschaft** f missionary society; **~schule** f mission school; **~schwester** f nun working at a mission; **~wissenschaft** f mission studies.
Mißklang m discord (auch Mus), dissonance; (Mißton) discordant note. **ein ~** (fig) a note of discord, a discordant note.
Mißkredit m, no pl discredit. **jdn/etw in ~ bringen** to bring sb/sth into discredit, to discredit sb/sth; **in ~ geraten or kommen** to be discredited.
mißlang pret of **mißlingen**.

mißlaunig adj bad-tempered, ill-humoured.
mißlich adj (geh) awkward, difficult; Umstand auch, Verzögerung unfortunate, regrettable. **das ist ja eine ~e Sache** that is a bit awkward/unfortunate; **es steht ~ um jdn/etw** sb/sth is in a bad way; **es steht ~ um dieses Vorhaben** the outlook for this plan is not good.
Mißlichkeit f siehe adj awkwardness, difficulty; unfortunate nature.
mißliebig adj unpopular. **sich (bei jdm) ~ machen** to make oneself unpopular (with sb); **~e Ausländer** foreigners who have fallen out of favour.
mißlingen pret **mißlang**, ptp **mißlungen** vi aux sein to fail, to be unsuccessful. **der Versuch ist ihr mißlungen** her attempt failed or was unsuccessful; **das ist ihr mißlungen** she failed; **ihm mißlingt alles** everything he does goes wrong; **ein mißlungener Versuch** an unsuccessful attempt.
Mißlingen nt -s, no pl failure.
mißlungen ptp of **mißlingen**.
Mißmut m sullenness, moroseness; (Unzufriedenheit) displeasure, discontent. **seinen ~ über etw** (acc) **zeigen/äußern** to show/express one's displeasure or discontent at sth.
mißmutig adj sullen, morose; (unzufrieden) discontented; Äußerung, Aussehen disgruntled. **mach nicht so ein ~es Gesicht** don't look so morose; **sei nicht so ~** don't be so morose.
mißraten* **1** vi insep irreg aux sein to go wrong; (Kind) to become wayward. **der Kuchen ist mir ~** my cake went wrong or was a failure. **2** adj Kind wayward. **der ~e Kuchen** the cake which went wrong.
Mißstand m disgrace no pl, outrage; (allgemeiner Zustand) bad or deplorable state of affairs no pl; (Ungerechtigkeit) abuse; (Mangel) defect. **einen ~/~e beseitigen** to remedy something which is wrong/things which are wrong; **~e in der Regierung/im Management anprangern** to inveigh against misgovernment/mismanagement; **es ist ein ~, daß ...** it is a disgrace or disgraceful that ...
Mißstimmung f **(a)** (Uneinigkeit) friction, discord. **eine ~** a note of discord, a discordant note. **(b)** (Mißmut) ill feeling no indef art.
Mißton m (Mus, fig) discordant note; (fig auch) note of discord. **~e** (Klang) discordant sound; (fig) discord.
mißtönend, mißtönig (rare) adj discordant; Stimme, Instrument unpleasant(-sounding).
mißtrauen* vi insep +dat to mistrust, to be suspicious or wary of. **ich mißtraue mir selbst/meinem Gedächtnis** I don't trust myself/my memory.
Mißtrauen nt -s, no pl mistrust, distrust (gegenüber of); (esp einer Sache, Handlung gegenüber) suspiciousness (gegenüber of). **~ gegen jdn/etw haben** or **hegen** (liter), **jdm/etw ~ entgegenbringen** to mistrust sb/sth, to be suspicious of sb/sth.
Mißtrauens- (Parl): **~antrag** m motion of no confidence; **~votum** nt vote of no confidence.
mißtrauisch adj mistrustful, distrustful; (argwöhnisch) suspicious.
Mißvergnügen nt (geh) displeasure, disgruntlement.
mißvergnügt adj (geh) disgruntled, displeased.
Mißverhältnis nt discrepancy, disparity; (in Proportionen) imbalance. **seine Leistung steht im ~ zu seiner Bezahlung** there is a discrepancy or disparity between the work he does and his salary.
mißverständlich adj unclear. **~e Ausdrücke** expressions which could be misunderstood or misleading.
Mißverständnis nt **(a)** misunderstanding; (falsche Vorstellung) misconception. **(b)** usu pl (Meinungsverschiedenheit) misunderstanding, disagreement.
mißverstehen* infin auch **mißzuverstehen** vt insep irreg to misunderstand. **Sie dürfen mich nicht ~** please do not misunderstand me; **in nicht mißzuverstehender Weise** unequivocally.
Mißwahl, Misswahl f beauty contest.
Mißweisung f (form) (von Kompaß) magnetic declination or variation; (von Radar) indication error.
Mißwirtschaft f maladministration, mismanagement.
Mißwuchs m malformed growth, malformation.
Mist m -es, no pl **(a)** (Tierkot) droppings pl; (Pferde~, Kuh~ etc) dung; (Dünger) manure; (~haufen) manure or muck heap. **~ streuen or fahren** to spread manure or muck (inf); **das ist nicht auf seinem ~ gewachsen** (inf) he didn't think that up himself.
(b) (inf) (Unsinn) rubbish, nonsense; (Schund) rubbish, trash. **~!** blow!, blast! (inf); **so ein ~!** (inf) what a darned or blasted nuisance (inf); **er hat einen ~ geredet** he talked a load of rubbish; **da hat er ~ gemacht or gebaut** (sl) he really messed that up (inf); **allerlei ~ machen** to do all sorts of stupid things; **mach keinen ~!** (sl) don't be a fool!
Mistbeet nt (Hort) hotbed.
Mistel f -, -n mistletoe no pl.
Mistelzweig m sprig of mistletoe. **ein Kuß unterm ~** a kiss under the mistletoe.
misten¹ **1** vt (a) Stall to muck out; Acker to manure. **(b)** (inf) siehe ausmisten. **2** vi (im Stall) to do the mucking out; (düngen) to do the manuring.
misten² vi impers (Naut) **es mistet** it is misting over.
Mist-: **~fink** m (inf) dirty-minded character; (Journalist etc) muck-raker (inf); **~gabel** f pitchfork (used for shifting manure); **~grube** f siehe Jauche(n)grube; **~haufen** m manure heap; **~käfer** m dung beetle; **~stück**, **~vieh** nt (sl) (Mann) bastard (sl); (Frau auch) bitch (sl); **~wagen** m dung cart; **~wetter** nt (inf) lousy weather.
Miszellen pl (liter) short articles or items. **das fällt unter ~** that comes under miscellaneous.

mit 1 prep +dat (a) with; (versehen mit auch) and. Tee ~ Zitrone lemon tea, tea with lemon; ~ dem Hut in der Hand (with) his hat in his hand; ein Topf ~ Suppe a pot of soup; ein Kleid ~ Jacke a dress and jacket; wie wär's ~ einem Bier? (inf) how about a beer?

(b) (~ Hilfe von) with. ~ einer Zange with or using a pair of pliers; ~ der Bahn/dem Bus/dem Auto by train/bus/car; ich fahre ~ meinem eigenen Auto zur Arbeit I drive to work in my own car; ~ der Post by post; ~ Gewalt by force; ~ Bleistift/Tinte/dem Kugelschreiber schreiben to write in pencil/ink/ballpoint; ~ dem nächsten Flugzeug/Bus kommen to come on the next plane/bus; ~ etwas Liebe/Verständnis with a little love/understanding; ~ einem Wort in a word.

(c) (zeitlich) ~ dem Glockenschlage sechs at or on the stroke of six, at six on the dot; ~ achtzehn Jahren at (the age of) eighteen; ~ einem Mal all at once, suddenly, all of a sudden; ~ heutigem Tage (form) as from today; ~beginnendem Sommer at the start of summer; ~ der Zeit in time.

(d) (bei Maß-, Mengenangaben) ~ 1 sec Vorsprung gewinnen to win by 1 sec; etw ~ DM 50.000 versichern to insure sth for DM 50,000; ~ 80 km/h at 80 km/h; ~ 4:2 gewinnen to win 4–2.

(e) (einschließlich) with, including. ~ mir waren es 5 there were 5 with or including or counting me.

(f) (Begleitumstand, Art und Weise, Eigenschaft) with. er ~ seinem Herzfehler kann das nicht he can't do that with his heart condition; du ~ deinen dummen Ideen (inf) you and your stupid ideas; ~ Muße at (one's) leisure; ein junger Dichter, Rosenholz ~ Namen (old) a young poet, Rosenholz by name or called Rosenholz; ~ einem Schlage in a flash; ~ lauter Stimme in a loud voice; ~ Verlust at a loss.

(g) (betreffend) was ist ~ ihr los? what's the matter or what's up with her?; wie geht or steht es ~ deiner Arbeit? how is your work going?, how are you getting on with your work?; ~ meiner Reise wird's nichts my trip is off.

2 adv er wollte ~ (inf) he wanted to come too; er war ~ dabei he went or came too; er ist ~ der Beste der Gruppe/Mannschaft he is one of or among the best in the group/the team; das gehört ~ dazu that's part and parcel of it; etw ~ in Betracht ziehen to consider sth as well.

Mit|angeklagte(r) mf co-defendant.

Mit|arbeit f cooperation, collaboration; (Hilfe auch) assistance; (Teilnahme) participation (auch Sch). ~ bei/an etw work on sth; er ist an einer ~ bei diesem Projekt interessiert he is interested in working on this project; unter ~ von in collaboration with.

mit|arbeiten vi sep (mithelfen) to cooperate (bei on); (bei Projekt etc) to collaborate. an or bei etw ~ to work on sth; er hat beim Bau des Hauses mitgearbeitet he helped build the house; beim Unterricht ~ to take an active part in lessons; bei diesem Film hat die BBC mitgearbeitet the BBC collaborated on or in the making of this film; seine Frau arbeitet mit (inf) his wife works too.

Mit|arbeiter(in f) m (Betriebsangehöriger) employee; (Kollege) colleague; (an Projekt etc) collaborator. die ~ an diesem Projekt/bei dieser Firma those who work on this project/for this firm; freier ~ freelance.

Mit|arbeiterstab m staff.

Mitbegründer m co-founder.

mitbekommen* vt sep irreg (a) etw ~ to get or be given sth to take with one; Rat, Ausbildung to get or be given sth; (als Mitgift) to be given sth as a dowry. (b) (inf) (verstehen) to get (inf); (bemerken) to realize. hast du das noch nicht ~? (erfahren) you mean you didn't know that?

mitbenutzen*, **mitbenützen*** (S Ger) vt sep to share (the use of).

Mitbenutzung f joint use.

Mitbesitz m co-ownership, joint ownership/property. ~ an etw (dat) haben to have a share in the ownership of sth.

Mitbesitzer(in f) m joint owner, co-owner.

mitbestimmen* sep 1 vi to have a say (bei in); to participate (bei in). ~d sein or wirken to have an influence (bei, für on). 2 vt to have an influence on.

Mitbestimmung f participation (bei in). ~ der Arbeiter or am Arbeitsplatz worker participation.

Mitbestimmungs-: ~gesetz nt worker participation law; ~recht nt right of participation (in decision making etc).

Mitbewerber m (fellow) competitor; (für Stelle) (fellow) applicant.

Mitbewohner m (fellow) occupant. die ~ in unserem Haus the other occupants of the house.

mitbringen vt sep irreg (a) (beim Kommen bringen) to bring; Freund, Begleiter to bring along; (beim Zurückkommen) to bring back. jdm etw ~ to bring sth for sb or sb sth; jdm etw von der Stadt/vom Bäcker ~ to bring (sb) sth back from town/fetch (sb) sth from the baker's; was sollen wir der Gastgeberin ~? what should we take to our hostess?; die richtige Einstellung ~ to have the right attitude; bringt gute Laune mit come ready to enjoy yourselves; Sie haben schönes Wetter mitgebracht! lovely weather you've brought with you!

(b) Mitgift, Kinder to bring with one. etw in die Ehe ~ to have sth when one gets married; sie hat ein ansehnliches Vermögen in die Ehe mitgebracht she brought a considerable fortune with her when she got married; meine Frau hat den Hund in die Ehe mitgebracht my wife had the dog before our marriage; sie hat zwei Kinder aus der ersten Ehe mitgebracht she has two children from her first marriage.

(c) (fig) Befähigung, Voraussetzung etc to have, to possess.

Mitbringsel nt (Geschenk) small present; (Andenken) souvenir.

Mitbürger m fellow citizen. meine Stuttgarter ~ my fellow

citizens from Stuttgart; (in Anrede) fellow citizens of Stuttgart; die älteren ~ senior citizens.

mitdenken vi sep irreg (Gedankengänge/Beweisführung mitvollziehen) to follow sb's train of thought/line of argument. zum Glück hat er mitgedacht luckily he did not let me/us etc forget; du denkst ja mit! good thinking; denk mal mit help me/us etc think.

mitdürfen vi sep irreg to be allowed to go or come too or along.

Mit|eigentum nt siehe Mitbesitz.

Mit|eigentümer m siehe Mitbesitzer(in).

mit|einander adv with each other, with one another; (gemeinsam) together. alle ~! all together; wir haben lange ~ geredet we had a long talk; sie reden nicht mehr ~ they are not talking (to each other or one another) any more; guten Tag ~ (esp S Ger) hello everybody or all.

Mit|einander nt -s, no pl cooperation. ein ~ ist besser als ein Gegeneinander it is better to work with each other than against each other.

mit|empfinden* sep irreg 1 vt to feel too, to share. 2 vi jdm ~ to feel for sb, to sympathize with sb.

Mit|empfinden nt sympathy.

Mit|erbe m, **Mit|erbin** f joint heir. außer ihm sind es noch 4 ~ there are 4 other heirs apart from him.

mit|essen sep irreg 1 vt Schale etc to eat as well; Mahlzeit to share. 2 vi (bei jdm) ~ to eat or have a meal with sb; willst du nicht ~? why don't you have something to eat too?

Mit|esser m -s, - blackhead.

mitfahren vi sep irreg aux sein to go (with sb). sie fährt mit she is going too/with me/us etc; (mit jdm) ~ to go with sb; (auf Reise auch) to travel with sb; (mitgenommen werden) to get a lift with sb, to be given a lift by sb; jdn ~ lassen to allow sb to go; (jdn mitnehmen) to give sb a lift; kann ich (mit Ihnen) ~? can you give me a lift?; er fährt jeden Morgen mit mir im Auto mit I give him a lift in my car every morning; wieviel Leute können bei dir ~? how many people can you take (with you)?; ich fahre nicht gern mit ihm im Auto mit I don't like going in her car; obwohl der Bus eigentlich voll war, hat uns der Fahrer doch noch ~ lassen although the bus really was full the driver let us on.

Mitfahrer m fellow-passenger; (vom Fahrer aus gesehen) passenger.

Mitfahrerzentrale f agency for arranging lifts.

Mitfahrgelegenheit f lift. ~en nach Rom lifts offered to Rome.

mitfühlen vi sep siehe mitempfinden.

mitfühlend adj sympathetic, compassionate.

mitführen vt sep Papiere, Ware etc to carry (with one); (Fluß) to carry along.

mitgeben vt sep irreg jdn jdm ~ to send sb along with sb; jdm etw ~ to give sb sth to take with them; Rat, Erziehung to give sb sth; das gebe ich dir noch mit take that (with you) too.

Mitgefangene(r) mf fellow prisoner.

Mitgefühl nt sympathy.

mitgehen vi sep irreg aux sein (a) to go too or along. mit jdm ~ to go with sb; (begleiten auch) to accompany sb; gehen Sie mit? are you going (too)?; ich gehe bis zur Ecke mit I'll go to the corner with you/him etc; mit der Zeit ~ to move with the times.

(b) (fig: Publikum etc) to respond (favourably) (mit to). man merkt, wie die Zuhörer richtig (mit ihm) ~ you can see that the audience is really with him.

(c) (inf) etw ~ lassen to lift or pinch sth (inf).

Mitgift f -, -en dowry.

Mitgiftjäger m (inf) dowry-hunter.

Mitglied nt member (gen, bei, in +dat of). ~ eines Komitees sein to sit on or be a member of a committee.

Mitglieder-: ~liste f list of members; ~versammlung f general meeting.

Mitglieds-: ~ausweis m membership card; ~beitrag m membership subscription or fee or dues pl.

Mitgliedschaft f membership.

Mitgliedsstaat m member state or country.

mithaben vt sep irreg etw ~ to have sth (with one); jdn ~ to have brought sb with one; hast du alles mit? have you got everything?

mithalten vi sep irreg (sich beteiligen) to join in (mit with); (bei Leistung, Tempo etc nachkommen) (mit with) to keep up, to keep pace; (bei Versteigerung) to stay in the bidding. das ist lecker, willst du nicht ~? that's delicious, don't you want some too?; in der Kneipe hat er immer feste mitgehalten in the pub he would always drink as much as the rest; bei einer Diskussion ~ können to be able to hold one's own in a discussion; er kann so erstklassig Englisch, da kann keiner ~ he speaks such excellent English, no-one can touch him (inf); ich halte mit (mitmachen) count me in (on that).

mithelfen vi sep irreg to help. beim Bau des Hauses ~ to help build the house; hilf doch ein bißchen mit give us or lend us a hand.

Mitherausgeber m co-editor, joint editor; (Verlag) co-publisher.

Mithilfe f assistance, aid. unter ~ der Kollegen with the aid or assistance of colleagues.

mithin adv (dated) therefore, consequently.

mithören sep 1 vt to listen to (too); Gespräch to overhear; (heimlich) to listen in on; Vorlesung to attend, to go to. ich habe alles mitgehört I heard everything.

2 vi (zusammen mit jdm) to listen (too); (Radio hören, Gespräch belauschen) to listen in (bei on); (zufällig) to overhear. Feind hört mit (Mil prov) careless talk costs lives; (fig hum) someone may be listening.

3 vi impers es hört jd mit sb is listening.

Mit|inhaber *m* (*von Haus etc*) joint-owner, co-owner; (*von Firma auch*) joint-proprietor.

mitkämpfen *vi sep* to fight. **mit jdm** ~ to fight alongside sb.

Mitkämpfer *m* (*im Krieg*) comrade-in-arms; (*Sport*) team-mate; partner.

mitklingen *vi sep irreg* (*Ton, Saite*) to sound, to resonate. **bei dem ersten Lied klangen eigenartige Töne mit** there were some odd notes in the first song; **in ihrer Äußerung klang ein leichter Vorwurf mit** there was a slight note of reproach in her remark; **in diesem Wort klingt etwas Geheimnisvolles mit** there is something mysterious in the sound of this word; **Assoziationen, die bei diesem Wort** ~ associations contained in this word.

mitkommen *vi sep irreg aux sein* **(a)** to come along (*mit* with); (*Sendung, Brief etc*) to come, to arrive. **kommst du auch mit?** are you coming too?; **ich kann nicht** ~ I can't come; **komm doch mit!** (do) come with us/me etc!, why don't you come too?; **kommst du mit ins Kino?** are you coming to the cinema (with me/us)?; **bis zum Bahnhof** ~ to come as far as the station; **ich bin gerade noch mit dem Zug mitgekommen** I just caught the train.
(b) (*inf*) (*mithalten*) to keep up; (*verstehen*) to follow. **da komme ich nicht mit** that's beyond me; **sie kommt in der Schule/in Französisch gut mit** she is getting on well at school/with French.

mitkönnen *vi sep irreg (inf)* **(a)** to be able to come/go (*mit* with). **(b)** (*usu neg*) (*inf: verstehen*) to be able to follow. **da kann ich nicht mehr mit** I can't follow that.

mitkriegen *vt sep (inf)* *siehe* **mitbekommen**.

mitlaufen *vi sep irreg aux sein* to run (*mit* with); (*Rad, Zeiger etc*) to turn. **er läuft beim 100-m-Lauf mit** he's running in the 100 metres.

Mitläufer *m* (*Pol, pej*) fellow traveller.

Mitlaut *m* consonant.

Mitleid *nt, no pl* pity, compassion (*mit* for); (*Mitgefühl*) sympathy (*mit* with, for).

Mitleidenschaft *f*: **jdn/etw in** ~ **ziehen** to affect sb/sth (detrimentally).

mitleidig *adj* pitying; (*mitfühlend*) sympathetic; *Mensch auch* compassionate. ~ **lächeln** to smile pityingly.

Mitleid(s)-: **m~los** *adj* pitiless, heartless; **~losigkeit** *f* pitiless-ness, heartlessness; **m~voll** *adj* sympathetic, compassionate.

mitlernen *vti sep* to learn too; (*durch jdn lernen*) to learn (*mit* from).

mitlesen *vti sep irreg* to read too; *Text* to follow. **etw (mit jdm)** ~ to read sth at the same time as sb; **er liest mit** he is reading my paper/book *etc* at the same time as me.

mitmachen *vti sep* **(a)** (*teilnehmen*) *Spiel, Singen etc* to join in; *Reise, Expedition, Ausflug* to go on; *Kurs* to do; *Mode* to follow. **etw** *or* **bei etw** ~ to join in sth; **er will dabei** ~ he wants to join in; **er hat schon viele Partys mitgemacht** he has been to lots of parties; **er macht alles mit** he always joins in (all the fun); **jede Mode** ~ to follow every fashion; **bei der Mode** *or* **da mache ich nicht mit** that's not my scene (*inf*); **meine Augen/meine Beine machen nicht mehr mit** my eyes/legs are giving up; **wenn das Wetter mitmacht** if the weather cooperates.
(b) (*inf: einverstanden sein*) **da kann ich nicht** ~ I can't go along with that; **da macht mein Chef nicht mit** my boss won't go along with that; **das mache ich nicht mehr mit** I've had quite enough (of that); **ich mache das nicht mehr lange mit** I won't take that much longer.
(c) (*erleben*) to live through; (*erleiden*) to go through. **sie hat viel mitgemacht** she has been through a lot in her time.

Mitmensch *m* fellow man *or* creature, neighbour. **wir müssen in jedem den ~en sehen** we must see people as neighbours.

mitmenschlich *adj* *Kontakte, Probleme etc* human; *Verhalten* considerate.

mitmischen *vi sep (sl)* (*sich beteiligen*) to be involved (*in* +*dat*, *bei* in); (*sich einmischen*) to interfere (*in* +*dat*, *bei* in sth).

mitmüssen *vi sep irreg* to have to go/come too.

Mitnahme *f* -, *no pl* **die** ~ **von etw empfehlen** to recommend sb to take sth with them.

mitnehmen *vt sep irreg* **(a)** to take (with one); (*ausleihen*) to borrow; (*kaufen*) to take. **jdn (im Auto)** ~ to give sb a lift; **hast du aus der Predigt etwas mitgenommen?** did you get anything out of the sermon?; **der Bus konnte nicht alle** ~ the bus couldn't take everyone; **sie nimmt alles mit, was sich bietet** she makes the most of everything life has to offer; (*das ist*) **zum M~ please take one; **einmal Pommes frites zum M~** a bag of chips to take away.
(b) (*erschöpfen*) **jdn** to exhaust, to weaken; (*beschädigen*) to be bad for. **mitgenommen aussehen** to look the worse for wear.
(c) (*stehlen*) to walk off with.
(d) (*inf*) *Sehenswürdigkeit, Veranstaltung* to take in.

mitnichten *adv* (*old*) not at all, by no means, in no way.

Mitra *f* -, **Mitren** (*Eccl*) mitre.

mitrechnen *vt sep* to count; *Betrag* to count in.

mitreden *sep* **1** *vi* (*Meinung äußern*) to join in (*bei etw* sth); (*mitbestimmen*) to have a say (*bei* in). **da kann er nicht** ~ he wouldn't know anything about that; **da kann ich** ~ I should know; **da kann ich aus Erfahrung** ~ I know from my own experience; **sie will überall** ~ (*inf*) she always has to have her say.
2 *vt* **da möchte ich auch ein Wörtchen** ~ I'd like to have some say (in this) too; **Sie haben hier nichts mitzureden** this is none of your concern.

mitreisen *vi sep aux sein* to go/travel too (*mit* with).

Mitreisende(r) *mf* fellow passenger/traveller.

mitreißen *vt sep irreg* (*Fluß, Lawine*) to sweep *or* carry away; (*Fahrzeug*) to carry along. **der Schauspieler/seine Rede hat alle mitgerissen** everyone was carried away by the

actor's performance/his speech.

mitreißend *adj Rhythmus, Enthusiasmus* infectious; *Reden, Marschmusik* rousing.

mitsamt *prep* +*dat* together with.

mitschleifen *vt sep* to drag along.

mitschleppen *vt sep* **jdn/etw** ~ to drag *or* cart (*inf*) sb/sth with one *or* along.

mitschneiden *vt sep irreg* to record.

Mitschnitt *m* recording.

mitschreiben *sep irreg* **1** *vt* **etw** ~ to write *or* take sth down; (*Sekretärin*) to take sth down. **2** *vi* to take notes. **nicht so schnell, ich kann nicht mehr** ~ not so fast, I can't keep up.

Mitschrift *f* record; (*von Vorlesung etc*) notes *pl*. **zur** ~ for the record; **nicht zur** ~ **bestimmt** *or* **gedacht** off the record.

Mitschuld *f* share of the blame *or* responsibility (*an* +*dat* for); (*an einem Verbrechen*) complicity (*an* +*dat* in). **ihn trifft eine** ~ a share of the blame falls on *or* must be taken by him; (*an Verbrechen*) he is implicated (*an* +*dat* in).

mitschuldig *adj* (*an Verbrechen*) implicated (*an* +*dat* in); (*an Unfall*) partly responsible *or* to blame (*an* +*dat* for). **sich** ~ **machen** to incur (some) blame (*an* +*dat* for); (*an Verbrechen*) to become implicated (*an* +*dat* in).

Mitschuldige(r) *mf* accomplice; (*Helfershelfer*) accessory.

Mitschüler *m* school-friend; (*in derselben Klasse*) class-mate.

mitschwingen *vi sep irreg* (*lit*) to resonate too. **was bei** *or* **in diesem Wort mitschwingt** the overtones *or* associations con-tained in *or* conjured up by this word; **in seiner Stimme schwang ein Ton von Enttäuschung mit** there was a note of disappointment in his voice.

mitsingen *sep irreg* **1** *vt* to join in (singing). **2** *vi* to join in the singing, to sing along. **in einer Oper/einem Chor etc** ~ to sing in an opera/choir *etc*.

mitspielen *vi sep* **(a)** to play too; (*in Mannschaft etc*) to play (*bei* in). **in einem Film/bei einem Theaterstück** ~ to be in a film/play; **bei einem Orchester** ~ to play in an orchestra; **wer spielt mit?** who wants to play?; (*in Mannschaft*) who's playing?; (*Theat etc*) who's in it?
(b) (*fig inf: mitmachen*) to play along (*inf*).
(c) (*Gründe, Motive*) to play a part *or* role (*bei* in), to be involved (*bei* in).
(d) (*Schaden zufügen*) **er hat ihr übel/schlimm/arg/hart mitgespielt** he has treated her badly; **das Leben hat ihr übel** *etc* **mitgespielt** she has had a hard life, life has been hard to her.

Mitspieler *m* (*Sport*) player; (*Theat*) member of the cast. **seine** ~ his team-mates; the other members of the cast.

Mitsprache *f* a say.

Mitspracherecht *nt* right to a say in a matter. **jdm ein** ~ **ein-räumen** *or* **gewähren** to allow *or* grant sb a say (*bei* in); **bei dieser Entscheidung möchte ich ein** ~ I want to have a say in this matter.

mitsprechen *sep irreg* **1** *vt Gebet* to join in (saying). **etw (mit jdm)** ~ to say sth with *or* at the same time as sb. **2** *vi* to join in. **bei etw** ~ to join in sth; (*mitbestimmen*) to have a say in sth; **sie will überall** ~ she always wants to have her say.

Mitstreiter *m* (*geh*) comrade-in-arms.

mittag *adv* **gestern/heute/morgen** ~ at midday yester-day/today/tomorrow, yesterday/today/tomorrow lunchtime; **Dienstag** ~ midday Tuesday, Tuesday (at) midday, Tuesday lunchtime.

Mittag¹ *m* **-(e)s, -e** **(a)** midday. **gegen** ~ around *or* about midday *or* noon; **über** ~ at midday, at lunchtime(s); **jeden** ~ every day at midday, every lunchtime; **jeden** ~ **gegen halb eins** every day at half past twelve; **des ~s** (*geh*) around noon *or* midday; **eines ~s** (*geh*) one day around noon *or* midday; **zu** ~ **essen** to have lunch *or* dinner *or* one's midday meal; **etw Warmes zu** ~ **essen** to have a cooked lunch.
(b) (*old, liter: Süden*) south.
(c) (*inf: Pause*) lunch-hour, lunch-break. ~ **machen/haben** to take/have one's lunch-hour *or* lunch-break; **sie macht gerade** ~ she's (off) at lunch.

Mittag² *nt* **-s**, *no pl* (*inf*) lunch.

Mittag|essen *nt* lunch, midday meal. **er kam zum** ~ he came to lunch; **sie saßen beim** ~ they were having lunch *or* their midday meal.

mittägig *adj attr* midday.

mittäglich **1** *adj attr* midday, lunchtime; *Schläfchen* after-noon. **2** *adv* at lunchtime.

mittags *adv* at lunchtime. **die Deutschen essen** ~ **warm** the Germans have a hot meal at midday; ~ **(um) 12 Uhr, (um) 12 Uhr** ~ at 12 noon, at 12 o'clock midday; **sonnabends** ~ Saturday lunchtime.

Mittags-: ~**ausgabe** *f*, ~**blatt** *nt* midday *or* lunchtime edition; ~**brot** *nt* (*dial*) lunch; ~**glut** (*liter*), ~**hitze** *f* midday *or* noonday heat, heat of midday; ~**kreis** *m*, ~**linie** *f* (*Astron*) meridian; ~**mahl** *nt* (*liter*), ~**mahlzeit** *f* midday meal; ~**pause** *f* lunch-hour, lunch-break; ~**pause machen/haben** to take/have one's lunch-hour *or* lunch-break; ~**pause** (*Geschäft etc*) to close at lunch-time; ~**ruhe** *f* period of quiet (after lunch); (*in Geschäft*) midday-closing; ~**ruhe halten** to have a period of quiet after lunch; to close for lunch; ~**schlaf** *m* afternoon nap; ~**sonne** *f* midday sun; ~**stunde** *f* midday, noon; **um die** *or* **zur** (*geh*) ~**stunde** around midday *or* noon; ~**tisch** *m* (a) dinner-table; **den** ~**tisch decken** to lay the table for lunch; **den** ~**tisch abräumen** to clear away after lunch; **am** ~**tisch sitzen** to be sitting (at the table) having lunch; **(b)** (*im Restaurant*) businessman's lunch; ~**tisch für Studenten** student lunches, lunches for students; ~**zeit** *f* lunch-time; ~**zeit** (*geh*) at midday; **während** *or* **in der** ~**zeit** at lunch-time; **um die** ~**zeit** around midday *or* lunch-time; **zur** ~**zeit** (*geh*) at midday.

Mittäter(in *f*) *m* accomplice.

Mittäterschaft f complicity. die ~ leugnen or abstreiten to deny complicity.

Mittdreißiger(in f) m man/woman in his/her mid-thirties.

Mitte f -, -n **(a)** (Mittelpunkt, mittlerer Teil) middle; (fig auch, von Kreis, Kugel etc) centre; (der Stadt, Sport) centre. **das Reich der ~** (liter) the Middle Kingdom; **ein Buch bis zur ~ lesen** to read half of a book; **die ~ des Weges haben wir hinter uns** we have come more than halfway; **~ August** in the middle of August; **~ des Jahres/des Monats** halfway through the year/month; **er ist ~ Vierzig or der Vierziger** he's in his mid-forties; **die goldene ~** the golden mean; **die rechte ~** a happy medium; **du mußt in allem, was du tust, die rechte ~ finden** you must follow the path of moderation or be moderate in everything you do; **in der ~** in the middle; (zwischen zwei Menschen) in between (them/us etc); (zwischen Ortschaften) halfway, midway; **sie nahmen sie in die ~** they took her between them; siehe ab.

(b) (Pol) centre. **die linke/rechte ~** centre-left/-right; **in der ~ stehen** to be moderate; **in der ~ zwischen** midway between.

(c) (Gruppe, Gesellschaft) **einer aus unserer ~** one of us or our number; **ich möchte gern in eurer ~ sein** I would like to be with you; **in unserer ~** with us, in our midst, among(st) us; **wir haben ihn in unserer ~ willkommen geheißen** we welcomed him into our midst; **er wurde aus unserer ~ gerissen** he was taken from our midst or from amongst us.

mitteilbar adj communicable.

mitteilen sep **1** vt **jdm etw ~** to tell sb sth; (benachrichtigen) to inform sb of or about sth, to communicate sth to sb (form); (bekanntgeben) to announce sth to sb; (Comm, Admin) to inform or notify sb of sth; **wir erlauben uns, Ihnen mitzuteilen, daß ...** we beg to inform you that ...; **teile ihm die Nachricht schonend mit** break the news to him gently.

2 vr **(a)** to communicate (jdm with sb). **er kann sich gut/schlecht ~** he finds it easy/difficult to communicate.

(b) (geh: Stimmung) to communicate itself (jdm to sb).

mitteilsam adj communicative; (pej) talkative, garrulous.

Mitteilung f (Bekanntgabe) announcement; (Erklärung) statement; (Benachrichtigung) notification; (Comm, Admin) communication; (an Mitarbeiter etc) memo; (von Korrespondenten, Reporter etc) report. **jdm (eine) ~ (von etw) machen** (form) to inform sb (of sth), to report (sth) to sb; (bekanntgeben) to announce sth to sb; (Erklärung abgeben) to make a statement (about sth) to sb; (benachrichtigen) to inform or notify sb (of sth); **eine ~ bekommen, daß ...** to hear that ...; **wir bitten um ~ über die neuesten Publikationen** we request information on or about the latest publications.

Mitteilungsbedürfnis nt need to talk to other people.

mittel adj siehe **mittlere(r, s)**.

Mittel[1] nt -s, - **(a)** (Math: Durchschnitt) average. **im ~** on average; **arithmetisches/geometrisches ~** arithmetical/geometrical mean.

(b) (~ zum Zweck, Transport~ etc) means sing; (Maßnahme, Methode) way, method; (Werbe~, Propaganda~, zur Verkehrskontrolle) device; (Lehr~) aid. **~ und Wege finden** to find ways and means; **~ zum Zweck** a means to an end; **kein ~ unversucht lassen** to try everything; **~ gegen die Inflation** ways of beating inflation; **als letztes or äußerstes ~** as a last resort; **zu anderen ~n greifen, andere ~ anwenden** to use or employ other means or methods; **ihm ist jedes ~ recht** he will do anything (to achieve his ends); **ihm war jedes ~ recht, dazu war ihm jedes ~ recht** he did not care how he did it or what means he used to achieve his ends; **er ist in der Wahl seiner ~ nicht zimperlich** he is not fussy about what methods he chooses; **etw mit allen ~n verhindern/bekämpfen** to do one's utmost or everything one can to prevent/oppose sth; **etw mit allen ~n versuchen** to try one's utmost to do sth; **sie hat mit allen ~n gekämpft, um ...** she fought tooth and nail to ...

(c) pl (Geld~) funds pl, resources pl; (Privat~) means pl, resources pl.

(d) meist nicht übersetzt (Medikament, kosmetisch) preparation; (Med auch) drug; (Medizin) medicine; (Putz~) cleaning agent; (Flecken~) spot or stain remover; (Wasch~) detergent; (Haarwasch~) shampoo. **welches ~ nimmst du?** what do you use or (Med: einnehmen) take?; **ein ~ zum Einreiben** something or a lotion/an ointment/a cream to be rubbed in; **das ist ein ~ gegen (meinen) Durchfall/(meine) Schuppen** that is for (my) diarrhoea/dandruff; **~ zum Putzen** cleaning things pl or stuff; **sich (dat) ein ~ (gegen Kopfschmerzen/Husten etc) verschreiben lassen** to get the doctor to prescribe something (for headaches/a cough etc); **welches ~ hat der Arzt dir verschrieben?** what did the doctor give you?; **es gibt kein ~ gegen Schnupfen** there is no cure for the common cold; **das beste ~ für or gegen etw** the best cure or remedy for sth.

(e) (Phys, Chem) siehe **Medium**.

Mittel[2] f -, no pl (Typ) 14 point (type), English (type).

Mittel-: **~achse** f (von Fläche, Körper) central axis; (von Auto) central axle; **~alter** nt Middle Ages pl; **da herrschen Zustände wie im ~alter** (inf) it is positively medieval there; **m~alt(e)rig** adj (rare) middle-aged; **m~alterlich** adj medieval; **~amerika** nt Central America (and the Caribbean); **m~amerikanisch** adj Central American; **m~bar** adj indirect (auch Jur); Schaden consequential; **~bau** m (a) (Gebäude) central block; (b) (Univ) non-professorial teaching staff.

Mittelchen nt (a) siehe **Mittel** (d). (b) (Trick) dodge. **sie hat ihre ~** she has her ways.

Mittel-: **m~deutsch** adj (Geog, Ling) Central German; (BRD Pol) East German; (Mis deutsch nt Central German dialects pl; **~deutschland** nt Germany east of Harz Mountains excluding Pomerania etc; (BRD: als Land) East Germany; **~ding** nt (Mischung) cross; **ein/kein ~ding** (weder das eine noch das

andere) something/nothing in between; **entweder du willst oder du willst nicht, es gibt kein ~ding** either you want to or you don't, you can't have it both ways; **~europa** nt Central Europe; **~europäer** m Central European; **ich, als normaler ~europäer** (inf) any average person like myself; **m~europäisch** adj Central European; **m~europäische Zeit** Central European Time; **m~fein** adj Erbsen etc medium-sized; **Kaffee, Mehl etc** medium-ground; **~feld** nt (Sport) midfield; (die Spieler auch) midfield players pl; **~finger** m middle finger; **m~fristig** adj Finanzplanung, Kredite medium-term; Voraussage medium-range; **~gebirge** nt low mountain range; **~gewicht** nt middleweight; Meister im ~gewicht middleweight champion; **m~groß** adj medium-sized; **~hochdeutsch** nt Middle High German; **m~hochdeutsch** adj Middle High German; **~klasse** f (a) (Comm) middle of the market; **ein Wagen der ~klasse** a middle-market car; (b) (Sociol) middle classes pl; **~klassewagen** m middle-market car; **m~ländisch** adj Mediterranean; **das m~ländische Meer** (form) the Mediterranean Sea; **~latein** nt Medieval Latin; **m~lateinisch** adj Medieval Latin attr, in Medieval Latin pred; **~läufer** m (Sport) centre-half; **~linie** f centre line; **m~los** adj without means; (arm) impoverished; **~losigkeit** f lack of means; (Armut) impoverishment; **~maß** nt mediocrity no art; **das (gesunde) ~maß** the happy medium; **seine Leistungen bewegen sich im ~maß or gehen nicht über das ~maß hinaus** his performance is no more than mediocre; **m~mäßig 1** adj mediocre; Schriftsteller, Spieler etc auch indifferent; **als Redner gibt er eine recht m~mäßige Figur ab** he's a pretty mediocre or indifferent speaker; **2** adv indifferently; **wie gefällt es dir hier? — so m~mäßig** how do you like it here? — so-so; **~mäßigkeit** f mediocrity.

Mittelmeer nt Mediterranean (Sea), Med (inf).

Mittelmeer- in cpds Mediterranean.

mittelmeerisch adj Mediterranean.

Mittelmeerraum m Mediterranean (region), Med (inf).

Mittel|ohr-: **~entzündung, ~(ver)eiterung** f inflammation of the middle ear.

Mittel-: **m~prächtig** adj (hum inf) reasonable, not bad pred, so-so pred (inf); (ziemlich schlecht) pretty awful (inf); **~punkt** m (Math, räumlich) centre; (fig: visuell) focal point; **Marlene Dietrich war der ~punkt des Abends** Marlene Dietrich was the main attraction of the evening; **er muß immer ~punkt sein** he always has to be the centre of attention; **er steht im ~punkt des Interesses** he is the centre of attention; **~punktschule** f school at the centre of a rural catchment area.

mittels (geh), **mittelst** (old) prep +gen or dat by means of.

Mittel-: **~scheitel** m centre parting (Brit) or part (US); **~schicht** f (a) (Ind) middle shift; **~schicht haben** to be on the middle shift; (b) (Sociol) middle class; **~schiff** nt (Archit) nave; **~schule** f (a) (inf: Realschule) = secondary modern school (Brit), junior high (US); (b) (Sw, Aus, inf: Oberschule) secondary school, high school (US); **m~schwer** adj Text of medium difficulty pred; Verletzungen moderately severe.

Mittels-: **~mann** m, pl -männer or -leute, **~person** (form) f intermediary.

mittelst prep (old) siehe **mittels**.

Mittel-: **~stadt** f medium-sized town; **~stand** m middle classes pl; **m~ständig** adj (Bot) perigynous (spec); **m~ständisch** adj middle-class; **~ständler** m -s, - middle-class person; **~steinzeit** f Mesolithic period; **~stellung** f medium setting; (fig) intermediate position; **~stimme** f (Mus) middle part.

Mittelstrecke f (Sport) middle-distance event; (Aviat) medium haul; (von Rakete etc) medium range.

Mittelstrecken-: **~flugzeug** nt medium-haul aircraft; **~lauf** m middle-distance race; (Disziplin) middle-distance running; **~rakete** f medium-range missile.

Mittel-: **~streifen** m central reservation (Brit), median (strip) (US); **~stück** nt middle or centre part; (von Braten etc) middle; **~stufe** f (Sch) middle school (Brit), junior high (US); **~stürmer** m (Sport) centre-forward; **~teil** m or nt middle section; **~wasser** nt (Naut) normal (water) level; **~weg** m middle course; **der goldene ~weg** the happy medium, the golden mean; **einen ~weg einschlagen** to steer a middle course; **einen ~weg suchen** to try to find a happy medium; **~welle** f (Rad) medium wave(band); **auf ~welle senden** to broadcast on the medium waveband or on (the) medium wave; **~wert** m mean; **~wort** nt (Gram) participle; **~wort der Gegenwart/Vergangenheit** present/past participle.

mitten adv **~ an/in/auf/bei etw** (right) in the middle of sth; **~ aus etw** (right) from the middle of sth; (aus Gedränge etc auch) from the midst of sth; **~ durch etw** (right) through the middle of sth; **~ darin/darein** (right) in the middle of it; **~ darunter** (räumlich) right under it/them; (dabei) right amongst or in the middle of it/them; **~ (hin)durch** right through the middle; **~ im Urwald** in the middle or depths of the jungle; **~ in der Luft/im Atlantik** in mid-air/mid-Atlantic; **~ ins Gesicht** right in the face; **es ist noch ~ in der Nacht** it's still the middle of the night; **~ im Leben** in the middle of life; **er wurde ~ aus einem schaffensfrohen Leben gerissen** (geh) in the middle of his creative life he was called to his Maker; **~ in or bei der Arbeit** when I etc am/was etc in the middle of working; **~ beim Frühstück/Essen sein** to be in the middle of (one's) breakfast/of eating; **~ unter uns** (right) in our midst; **der Stock brach ~ entzwei** the stick broke clean in two.

mitten-: **~drin** adv (right) in the middle of it; **~drin in der Stadt/der Arbeit** (right) in the middle of the town/one's work; **~drin, etw zu tun** (right) in the middle of doing sth; **~drunter** adv (räumlich) right at the bottom; (dabei) (right) amongst it/them; **er ist immer ~drunter** (fig) he's always in the middle of things; **~durch** adv (right) through the middle; **~mang** (dial *inf*) **1** *prep* +*dat or* (*sl*) *acc* among; **sie spielte ~mang die Bengels** she was playing with the lads; **2** *adv* (right) in the middle of it/them.

Mitternacht *f* midnight *no art*.

mitternächtig, mitternächtlich *adj attr* midnight. **zu ~er Stunde** (*geh*) at the midnight hour.

Mitternachts-: ~**sonne** *f* midnight sun; ~**stunde** *f* witching hour; ~**vase** *f* (*hum*) chamberpot.

Mittfünfziger(in *f*) *m* man/woman in his/her mid-fifties.

Mittler *m* -s, - mediator; (*liter: Ideen, Sprache etc*) medium.

Mittler|amt *nt* mediatory position.

mittlere(r, s) *adj attr* (**a**) (*dazwischenliegend*) middle. **der/die/das ~** the middle one; **der M~ Osten** the Middle East; **der ~ Weg** (*fig*) the middle course.

(**b**) (*den Mittelwert bildend*) medium; (*mittelschwer*) *Kursus, Aufgabe* intermediate; (*durchschnittlich*) average; (*Math*) mean. **von ~m Wert** of medium value; ~**r Beamter** person in the section of the civil service for which the entry requirement is the Abitur, ≈ civil servant of the administrative class (*Brit*); ~**n Alters** middle-aged; *siehe* **Reife**.

Mittler-: ~**rolle** *f* role of mediator, mediatory role; **m~weile** *adv* in the meantime; **ich habe mich m~weile daran gewöhnt** I've got used to it in the meantime.

mit-: ~**tragen** *sep irreg* **1** *vt* to help (to) carry; **2** *vi* to help to carry it/them/everything; ~**trinken** *sep irreg* **1** *vt* to drink with us/them *etc*; **er wollte nichts ~trinken** he didn't want to join us/them *etc* in a drink; **2** *vi* to have a drink with us/them *etc*.

Mitt-: **m~schiffs** *adv* (*Naut*) (a)midships, ~**sechziger(in** *f*) *m* man/woman in his/her mid-sixties; ~**siebziger(in** *f*) *m* man/woman in his/her mid-seventies; ~**sommer** *m* midsummer; ~**sommernacht** *f* Midsummer's Night.

mittun *vi sep irreg* (*inf*) to join in.

Mitt-: ~**vierziger(in** *f*) *m* man/woman in his/her mid-forties; **m~wegs** *adv* (*old*) midway; ~**woch** *m* -s, -e Wednesday; *siehe auch* **Dienstag**; **m~wochs** *adv* on Wednesdays; *siehe auch* **dienstags**.

mit|unter *adv* from time to time, now and then *or* again, (every) once in a while.

mit|unterschreiben* *vti sep irreg* to sign too.

mitverantwortlich *adj* jointly responsible *pred*.

Mitverantwortlichkeit *f* joint responsibility.

Mitverantwortung *f* share of the responsibility. **~ haben** to have *or* bear a share of the responsibility; **die** *or* **jede ~ ablehnen** to abnegate (all) responsibility.

mitverdienen* *vi sep* to (go out to) work as well.

Mitverfasser *m* co-author.

Mitvergangenheit *f* (*Aus Gram*) imperfect (tense).

Mitverschulden *nt* **ihm wurde ein ~ nachgewiesen** he was shown to have been partially *or* partly to blame; **ihn trifft ein ~ an diesem Vorfall** he was partially *or* partly to blame for this incident.

Mitverschwor(e)ne(r) *mf decl as adj* fellow thinker/idealist *etc*, crony (*hum inf*); (*pej, bei Verbrechen*) conspirator.

Mitverschwörer *m* conspirator.

mitversichern* *vt sep* to include in the insurance.

Mitwelt *f* **die ~** the people *or* those about one; **es dauerte lange, bis die ~ seine Leistungen würdigte** it was a long time before his contemporaries learnt to appreciate his achievements.

mitwirken *vi sep* to play a part (*an* +*dat, bei* in); (*Fakten, Faktoren etc auch*) to contribute (*an* +*dat, bei* to); (*beteiligt sein*) to be involved (*an* +*dat, bei* in); (*Schriftsteller, Regisseur etc*) to collaborate (*an* +*dat, bei* on); (*mitspielen*) (*Schauspieler, Diskussionsteilnehmer*) to take part (*an* +*dat, bei* in); (*in Film*) to appear (*an* +*dat, bei* in); (*Tänzer, Orchester, Chor*) to perform (*an* +*dat, bei* in). **ohne das M~ des Ministers wäre das unmöglich gewesen** it would have been impossible without the minister's involvement.

Mitwirkende(r) *mf decl as adj* participant (*an* +*dat, bei* in); (*Mitspieler*) performer (*an* +*dat, bei* in); (*Schauspieler*) actor (*an* +*dat, bei* in). **die ~n** (*Theat*) the cast *pl*.

Mitwirkung *f* (*Beteiligung, Mitarbeit*) involvement (*an* +*dat, bei* in); (*Zusammenarbeit*) collaboration (*an* +*dat, bei* in); (*an Buch, Film*) collaboration (*an* +*dat, bei* on); (*Teilnahme*) (*an Diskussion, Projekt*) participation (*an* +*dat, bei* in); (*von Schauspieler*) appearance (*an* +*dat, bei* in); (*von Tänzer, Orchester, Chor*) performance (*an* +*dat, bei* in). **unter ~ von** with the assistance *or* aid *or* help of.

Mitwisser(in *f*) *m* -s, - (*Jur*) accessory (*gen* to). **~ sein** to know about it; **~ einer Sache** (*gen*) **sein** to know about sth; **jdn zum ~ machen** to tell sb (all) about it; (*Jur*) to make sb an accessory; **er wollte nicht so viele ~ haben** he didn't want so many people to know about it.

Mitwisserschaft *f* **er wurde wegen ~ angeklagt** he was charged with being an accessory (to the crime); **an seiner ~ kann kein Zweifel bestehen** there can be no doubt that he was an accessory to it; (*Jur*) *or* that he knew about it.

mitwollen *vi sep* to want to go/come along.

mitzählen *vi sep* *siehe* **mitrechnen**.

mitziehen *vi sep irreg aux sein* (*fig inf*) to go along with it.

Mixbecher *m* (cocktail) shaker.

mixen *vt Getränke,* (*Rad, TV*) to mix.

Mixer *m* -s, - (**a**) (*Bar~*) cocktail waiter. (**b**) (*Küchen~*) blender; (*Rührmaschine*) mixer. (**c**) (*Film, Rad, TV*) mixer.

Mixgetränk *nt* mixed drink; (*alkoholisch*) cocktail; (*Milch~*) milkshake.

Mixtur *f* (*Pharm, Mus, fig*) mixture.

ml *abbr of* **Milliliter** millilitre.

mm *abbr of* **Millimeter** millimetre.

Mnemo- [mnemo-]: ~**technik** *f* mnemonics *sing*; **m~technisch** *adj* mnemonic.

Mob *m* -s, *no pl* (*pej*) mob.

Möbel *nt* -s, - (~*stück*) piece of furniture. **~** *pl* furniture *sing*; **~ rücken** to shift the furniture.

Möbel- *in cpds* furniture; ~**lager** *nt* furniture showroom; ~**packer** *m* furniture packer, removal man; **wie ein ~packer** (*inf*) like a navvy; ~**schreiner** *m* cabinetmaker; ~**spedition** *f* removal firm; ~**stoff** *m* furnishing fabric; ~**stück** *nt* piece of furniture; ~**tischler** *m* cabinetmaker; ~**träger** *m* removal man; ~**wagen** *m* removal van (*Brit*) *or* truck, pantechnicon.

mobil *adj* (**a**) mobile; (*Comm, Jur*) *Vermögen, Kapital* movable. ~**es Vermögen** movables *pl*; **~ machen** (*Mil*) to mobilize. (**b**) (*inf: flink, munter*) lively. **jdn ~ machen** to liven sb up.

Mobile ['moːbilə] *nt* -s, -s mobile.

Mobiliar *nt* -s, *no pl* furnishings *pl*.

Mobilien [-iən] *pl* (*old*) furnishings *pl*; (*Jur*) chattels *pl*, movables *pl*.

mobilisieren* *vt* (*Mil, fig*) to mobilize; (*Comm*) *Kapital* to make liquid. **die Straße** *or* **den Mob ~** to rouse the mob.

Mobilität *f* mobility (*auch Sociol*); (*geistige* ~) agility.

Mobilmachung *f* (*Mil*) mobilization. **die ~ ausrufen/beschließen** to mobilize/decide to mobilize.

möbl. *abbr of* **möbliert** furnished.

möblieren* *vt* to furnish. **neu ~** to refurnish; **ein möbliertes Zimmer** a furnished room; **ein möblierter Herr** (*hum inf*) a lodger; **möbliert wohnen** to live in furnished accommodation.

Moçambique [mosamˈbɪk, -ˈbiːk] *nt* -s Mozambique.

Mocca *m* -s, -s *siehe* **Mokka**.

mochte *pret of* **mögen**.

Möchtegern- *in cpds* (*iro*) would-be.

mod. *abbr of* **modern.**

modal *adj* (*Gram*) modal.

Modalität *f* (**a**) *usu pl* (*von Plan, Vertrag etc*) arrangement; (*von Verfahren, Arbeit*) procedure. (**b**) (*Philos*) modality.

Modal- (*Gram*): ~**satz** *m* (adverbial) clause of manner; ~**verb** *nt* modal verb.

Modder *m* -s, *no pl* (*N Ger*) mud.

modd(e)rig *adj* (*N Ger*) muddy.

Mode *f* -, -n fashion; (*Sitte*) custom. ~**n** (*Kleider*) fashions, fashionwear *sing*, apparel *sing* (*esp US*); **~ sein** to be fashionable *or* the fashion *or* in vogue; (*Sitte*) to be the custom; **das ist jetzt ~** that's the latest fashion; **Radfahren/Alaska wird jetzt große ~** cycling/Alaska is becoming very fashionable nowadays; **in ~/aus der ~ kommen** to come into/go out of fashion; **die ~** *or* **alle ~n mitmachen, mit** *or* **nach der ~ gehen, sich nach der ~ richten** to keep up with the latest fashions; **sich nach der ~ kleiden** to dress in the height of fashion; **wir wollen keine neuen ~n einführen** (*inf*) we don't want any new-fangled ideas.

Mode-: ~**artikel** *m* (**a**) fashion accessory. (**b**) (*in Zeitung*) fashion article; ~**arzt** *m* fashionable doctor; ~**ausdruck** *m* in-phrase, trendy expression (*inf*); (*Wort*) in-word, vogue *or* trendy (*inf*) word; ~**bad** *nt* fashionable spa; **m~bewußt** *adj* fashion-conscious; ~**farbe** *f* fashionable colour, in-colour (*inf*); **m~gerecht** *adj* fashionable; ~**geschäft** *nt* fashion shop; ~**haus** *nt* fashion house; ~**heft** *nt*, ~**journal** *nt* fashion magazine; ~**krankheit** *f* fashionable complaint.

Modell *nt* -s, -e (**a**) model; (*naturgetreue Nachbildung auch*) mock-up. (**b**) (*Art, Foto~*) model. **zu etw ~ stehen** to be the model for sth; **jdm ~ stehen/sitzen** to sit for sb.

Modell-: ~**eisenbahn** *f* model railway; (*als Spielzeug*) train set; ~**flugzeug** *nt* model aeroplane *or* airplane (*US*).

modellieren* *vti* to model.

Modelliermasse *f* modelling clay.

Modell-: ~**kleid** *nt* model (dress); ~**versuch** *m* (*esp Sch*) experiment; ~**zeichnung** *f* drawing of a model; (*Art*) drawing from a model.

modeln 1 *vt* to model. **er läßt sich nicht ~** he's fixed in his habits. **2** *vi* **an jdm/etw ~** to change sb/sth.

Moden-: ~**schau** *f* fashion show; ~**zeitung** *f* fashion magazine.

Mode-: ~**puppe** *f*, ~**püppchen** *nt* model type (*inf*).

Moder *m* -s, *no pl* mustiness; (*geh: Verwesung*) decay; (*Schimmel*) mildew. **es riecht nach ~** it smells musty; **in ~ übergehen** (*Grabsteine etc*) to become mildewed.

Moderation *f* (*Rad, TV*) presentation. **die ~ heute abend hat:** ... tonight's presenter is ...

Moderator *m* presenter.

Modergeruch *m* musty odour.

moderieren* *vti* (*Rad, TV*) to present. **das M~** the presentation.

mod(e)rig *adj Geruch* musty.

modern[1] *vi aux sein or haben* to rot.

modern[2] *adj* modern *no adv*; (*zeitgemäß*) *Maschine, Vorrichtung auch* up-to-date *no adv*; (*modisch*) fashionable; *Politik, Ansichten, Eltern, Lehrer* progressive. **~ sein** (*Kleidung, Möbel*) to be fashionable; **~ werden** to come into fashion, to become fashionable; **ein ~ eingerichtetes Zimmer** a modern room; **der ~e Mensch** modern man.

Moderne *f* -, *no pl* (*geh*) modern age. **das Zeitalter der ~** the modern age.

modernisieren* **1** *vt Gebäude* to modernize; *Gesetz, Arbeitsmethoden, Betrieb auch* to bring up to date; *Kleidung* to revamp, to make more fashionable. **2** *vi* to get up to date.

Modernismus *m* modernism.

modernistisch *adj* modernistic.

Modernität *f* (*geh*) modernity.

Mode-: ~**sache** *f* **das ist reine ~sache** it's just the fashion; ~**salon** *m* **siehe ~haus**; ~**schau** *f* *siehe* **Modenschau**; ~**schmuck** *m* costume jewellery; ~**schöpfer(in** *f*) *m* fashion designer, couturier/couturière; ~**schrei** *m* **der letzte ~schrei** the latest fashion; ~**schriftsteller** *m* popular writer.

modest *adj* (*old*) modest.

Mode-: ~**tanz** m popular dance; ~**torheit** f fashion fad; ~**wort** nt in-word, vogue or trendy (inf) word; ~**zeichner** m fashion illustrator; ~**zeitschrift** f siehe **Modenzeitung**.
Modi pl of **Modus**.
Modifikation f modification.
modifizieren* vt to modify.
Modifizierung f modification.
modisch adj stylish, fashionable, modish.
Modistin f milliner.
Modul m -s, -n (Archit) module; (Math) modulus.
Modulation f modulation.
modulieren* vt to modulate.
Modus m -, **Modi** (a) way. ~ **vivendi** (geh) modus vivendi. **(b)** (Gram) mood.
Mofa nt -s, -s small moped, motor-assisted bicycle (form).
Mogelei f cheating no pl.
mogeln vi to cheat. **beim Kartenspiel/bei der Prüfung** ~ **to** cheat at cards/in an exam; **nicht** ~! no cheating!
Mogelzettel m (Sch) crib.
mögen pret **mochte**, ptp **gemocht** 1 vt to like. ~ **Sie ihn/Operettenmusik?** do you like him/operetta?; **ich mag ihn/Operettenmusik nicht** I don't like or care for him/operetta; **sie mag das (gern)** she (really) likes that; **sie mag kein Sauerkraut** she doesn't like sauerkraut; **was möchten Sie, bitte?** what would you like?; (Verkäufer) what can I do for you?; ~ **Sie eine Praline/etwas Wein?** (form) would you like or care for a chocolate/some wine?; **nein danke, ich möchte lieber Tee** no thank you, I would prefer tea or rather have tea.
2 vi **(a)** (wollen) (eine Praline/etwas Wein etc ~) to like one/ some; (etw tun ~) to like to. **ich mag nicht mehr** I've had enough; (bin am Ende) I can't take any more; **kommen Sie mit? — ich möchte gern, aber ...** are you coming too? — I'd like to, but ...
(b) (gehen/fahren wollen) to want to go. **ich möchte (gern) nach Hause** I want to go home; **ich möchte lieber in die Stadt** I would prefer to go or I would rather go into town.
3 ptp ~ modal aux vb **(a)** (im Konjunktiv: Wunsch) to like to +infin. **möchten Sie etwas essen?** would you like or care for something to eat?; **wir möchten (gern) etwas trinken** we would like something to drink; **ich möchte gern Herrn Schmidt sprechen** I would like to speak to Mr Schmidt; **hier möchte ich nicht wohnen** (würde nicht gern) I wouldn't like to live here; (will nicht) I don't want to live here; **ich möchte dazu nichts sagen** I don't want to say anything about that, no comment; **ich hätte gern/lieber dabeisein** ~ I would like or have liked/prefer or have preferred to have been there; **das möchte ich auch wissen** I'd like to know that too; **möge er/mögest du Erfolg haben** (old) may he/you be successful.
(b) (im Konjunktiv: einschränkend) **man möchte meinen, daß ...** you would think that ...; **ich möchte fast sagen ...** I would almost say ...
(c) (geh: Einräumung) **es mag wohl sein, daß er recht hat, aber ...** he may well be right, but ...; **wie dem auch sein mag** however that may be; **was sie auch sagen mag** whatever she says; **oder wie er auch heißen mag** or whatever he is or might be or may be called; **es mag für dieses Mal hingehen** it's all right this time; **mag kommen was da will** come what may; **mag es schneien, soviel es will** it can snow or let it snow as much as it likes; **von mir aus mag er warten** as far as I'm concerned he can wait; **man mag es tun, wie man will, aber ...** you can do it how you like, but ...; **mag er tun, was ihm gefällt** let him do what he wants; **nur Fachkräfte** ~ **sich melden** only qualified persons need or should apply.
(d) (Vermutung) **es mochten etwa fünf Stunden vergangen sein** about five hours must or would have passed; **sie mag/ mochte etwa zwanzig sein** she must or would be/have been about twenty; **wie alt mag sie sein?** how old might or would she be?, **how old is she, I wonder?**; **wo mag sie das gehört haben?** where could or might she have heard that?; **was mag das wohl heißen?** what might that mean?
(e) (wollen) to want. **sie mag nicht bleiben** she doesn't want to stay.
(f) (Aufforderung, indirekte Rede) (sagen Sie ihm,) **er möchte zu mir kommen** would you tell him to come and see me; **sie möchten zu Hause anrufen** you should call home; **du möchtest dich brieflich melden** you should write; **sie möchte Ihnen sagen lassen, daß ...** she asked me to tell you that ...
Mogler(in f) m -s, - cheat.
möglich 1 adj **(a)** possible; (ausführbar auch) feasible. **alles** ~**e** everything you or one can think of; **alles M~e tun** to do everything possible or everything one can; **aus allen** ~**en Richtungen** from all directions; **er hat allen** ~**en Blödsinn gemacht** he did all sorts of stupid things; **so viel/bald wie** ~ as much/soon as possible; **das ist schon** or **wohl** or **durchaus** ~ that's quite possible; **wenn es irgend** ~ **ist** if (it's) at all possible; **können Sie es** ~ **machen, daß Sie schon morgen kommen** or **schon morgen zu kommen?** could you manage to come tomorrow?; **es war mir nicht** ~ **mitzukommen** I couldn't manage to come, it wasn't possible for me to come; **das ist doch nicht** ~! that's impossible; **nicht** ~! never!, impossible!; **das wäre woanders nicht** ~ that couldn't happen anywhere else; **ist denn so was** ~? would you credit it? (inf); **er tat sein** ~**stes** he did his utmost or all he could.
(b) (attr: eventuell) **Kunden, Interessenten, Nachfolger** potential, possible. **alle** ~**en Fälle** every eventuality; **alles M~e bedenken** to consider everything.
2 adv siehe **möglichst**.
möglicherweise adv possibly. ~ **kommt er morgen** he may or might (possibly) come tomorrow; **ich habe meinen Regenschirm** ~ **im Bus vergessen** I may or might (possibly)

have left my umbrella on the bus; **da liegt** ~ **ein Mißverständnis vor** it's possible that there is a misunderstanding, there is possibly a misunderstanding.
Möglichkeit f **(a)** possibility; (no pl: Ausführbarkeit auch) feasibility. **es besteht die** ~**, daß ...** there is a possibility that ..., it is possible that ...; **es besteht die** ~ **zu kündigen** it would (always) be possible to hand in your notice; **alle** ~**en in Betracht ziehen** to take all the possibilities into account; **nach** ~ if possible; **ist denn das die** ~?, **ist es die** ~! (inf) it's impossible!, I don't believe it!
(b) (Aussicht) chance; (Gelegenheit auch) opportunity. **die** ~ **haben, etw zu tun** to have the or a chance/the or an opportunity to do sth or of doing sth; **wir bieten alle** ~**en, Sport zu treiben** we offer a wide range of sports facilities; **er hatte keine andere** ~ he had no other choice or alternative.
möglichst adv ~ **genau/schnell/oft** as accurately/quickly/often as possible; **in** ~ **kurzer Zeit** as quickly as possible.
Mogul m -s, -n or -e (Hist, fig) mogul.
Mohair, Mohär [mo'hɛːɐ] m -s, -e (Tex) mohair.
Mohammedaner(in f) [mohame'daːnɐ, -ərɪn] m -s, - Mohammedan.
mohammedanisch [mohame'daːnɪʃ] adj Mohammedan.
Mohär [mo'hɛːɐ] m -s, -e siehe **Mohair**.
Mohikaner [mohi'kaːnɐ] m -s, - Mohican. **der letzte** ~, **der Letzte der** ~ (lit) the last of the Mohicans; (fig) the very last one.
Mohn m -(e)s, -e (a) poppy. **(b)** (~samen) poppy seed.
Mohn- in cpds poppy; (Cook) (poppy)seed; ~**blume** f poppy.
Mohr m -en, -en (old) (blacka)moor (old). **Othello, der** ~ **von Venedig** Othello, the Moor of Venice; **schwarz** or **braungebrannt wie ein** ~ (dated inf) as brown as a berry; **der** ~ **hat seine Schuldigkeit getan, der** ~ **kann gehen** as soon as you've served your purpose they've no further interest in you.
Möhre f -, -n carrot.
Mohren-: ~**kopf** m small chocolate-covered cream cake; ~**wäsche** f (inf) attempt at whitewashing somebody.
Mohrrübe f carrot.
Moiré [moa'reː] m or nt -s, -s (Tex) moiré.
moiriert [moa'riːɐt] adj watered.
mokant adj (geh) sardonic, mocking.
Mokassin m -s, -s moccasin.
mokieren* vr to sneer (über +acc at).
Mokka m -s, -s mocha.
Mokka-: ~**löffel** m coffee spoon; ~**tasse** f, ~**täßchen** nt coffee cup.
Molar(zahn) m -s, -en molar (tooth).
Molch m -(e)s, -e salamander.
Mole[1] f -, -n (Naut) mole.
Mole[2] f -, -n (Med) mole.
Molekül nt -s, -e, **Molekel** (old) nt -s, - or f -, -n molecule.
molekular adj molecular.
Molesten pl (old) minor ailments pl.
molestieren* vt (old) to importune (old).
molk pret of **melken**.
Molke f -, no pl **Molken** (dial) m -s, no pl whey.
Molkerei f dairy.
Molkerei-: ~**butter** f blended butter; ~**genossenschaft** f dairy cooperative; ~**produkt** nt dairy product.
Moll nt -, - (Mus) minor. **in** ~ **übergehen** to go into the minor; **a-**~ A minor; **a-**~**-Tonleiter** scale of A minor; **Violinkonzert Nummer 4 a-**~ violin concerto Number 4 in A minor; **alles in** ~ **sehen** to see only the gloomy side of things.
Molle f -, -n beer. **eine** ~ **mit Korn** a beer and a (glass of) schnapps.
Mollenfriedhof m (hum) beer gut or belly (inf).
mollert adj (Aus inf) plump.
mollig adj (inf) **(a)** cosy; (warm, behaglich auch) snug. **(b)** (rundlich) plump.
Moll-: ~**tonart** f minor key; ~**tonleiter** f minor scale.
Molluske f -, -n (spec) mollusc.
Moloch m -s, -e Moloch.
Molotowcocktail ['moːlɔtɔfkɔkteːl] m Molotov cocktail.
Molukken pl (Geog) Moluccas pl, Spice Islands pl.
Molybdän nt -s, no pl (Chem) molybdenum.
Moment[1] m -(e)s, -e moment. **jeden** ~ any time or minute or moment; **einen** ~, **bitte one minute** or **moment please**; **kleinen** ~! just a second or tick (inf)!; ~ **mal!** just a minute!; **im** ~ at the moment; **im letzten/richtigen** etc ~ at the last/right etc moment; **im ersten** ~ for a moment.
Moment[2] nt -(e)s, -e (a) (Bestandteil) element. **(b)** (Umstand) fact; (Faktor) factor. **(c)** (Phys) moment; (Kraftwirkung) momentum.
momentan 1 adj **(a)** (vorübergehend) momentary. **(b)** (augenblicklich) present attr. 2 adv **(a)** (vorübergehend) for a moment, momentarily. **(b)** (augenblicklich) at the moment, at present.
Moment|aufnahme f (Phot) photo(graph).
Monaco ['moːnako, mo'nako] nt -s Monaco.
Monade f (Philos) monad.
Monadenlehre, Monadologie f (Philos) monadology.
Monarch(in f) m -en, -en monarch.
Monarchie f monarchy.
monarchisch adj monarchic(al).
Monarchist(in f) m monarchist.
monarchistisch adj monarchistic.
Monat m -(e)s, -e month. **der** ~ **Mai** the month of May; **sie ist im sechsten** ~ (schwanger) she's over five months pregnant or gone (inf), she's in the sixth month; **was verdient er im** ~? how much does he earn a month?; **am 12. dieses** or **des laufenden** ~**s** on the 12th (of this month); **auf** ~**e hinaus** months

ahead; **jdn zu drei ~en (Haft) verurteilen** to sentence sb to three months' imprisonment, to send sb down for three months (*inf*); **von ~ zu ~** month by month.

monatelang 1 *adj attr* **Verhandlungen**, *Kämpfe* which go/went *etc* on for months. **seine ~e Abwesenheit** his months of absence; **nach ~em Warten** after waiting for months *or* months of waiting; **mit ~er Verspätung** months late. **2** *adv* for months.

-monatig *adj suf* -month. **ein drei~er Urlaub** a three-month holiday.

monatlich *adj* monthly. **~ stattfinden** to take place every month.

-monatlich *adj suf* **zwei-/drei~** every two/three months; **all~** every month.

Monats-: **~anfang** *m* beginning of the month; **~binde** *f* sanitary towel; **~blutung** *f* menstrual period; **~einkommen** *nt* monthly income; **~ende** *nt* end of the month; **~erste(r)** *m decl as adj* first (day) of the month; **~frist** *f* innerhalb *or* binnen **~frist** within a month; **~gehalt** *nt* monthly salary; **ein ~gehalt** one month's salary; **~hälfte** *f* half of the month; **~karte** *f* monthly season ticket; **~lohn** *m* monthly wage; **~lohn bekommen** to be paid monthly; **~mitte** *f* middle of the month; **~name** *m* name of the/a month; **~rate** *f* monthly instalment; **~schrift** *f* monthly (journal *or* periodical); **~wechsel** *m* monthly allowance.

monat(s)weise 1 *adv* every month, monthly. **2** *adj* monthly.

Mönch *m* -(e)s, -e monk; (*Bettel~ auch*) friar. **wie ein ~ leben** to live like a monk.

mönchisch *adj* monastic. **ein ~es Leben führen** (*fig*) to live like a monk.

Mönchs-: **~kapuze** *f* cowl; **~kloster** *nt* monastery; (*von Bettelmönchen*) friary; **~kutte** *f* monk's/friar's habit; **~latein** *nt* dog Latin; **~leben** *nt* monastic life; **~orden** *m* monastic order.

Mönch(s)tum *nt* monasticism.

Mönchs-: **~wesen** *nt* monasticism; **~zelle** *f* monastic cell.

Mond *m* -(e)s, -e (**a**) moon. **den ~ anbellen** (*fig*) to bay at the moon; **auf *or* hinter dem ~ leben** (*inf*) to be *or* live behind the times; **du lebst wohl auf dem ~!** (*inf*) where have you been?; **drei Meilen hinter dem ~** (*inf*) in the Stone Age (*hum*); **in den ~ gucken** (*inf*) to go empty-handed; **deine Uhr geht nach dem ~** (*inf*) your watch/clock is way out (*inf*).
(**b**) (*old: Monat*) moon (*old*), month.

mondän *adj* chic.

Mond-: **~aufgang** *m* moonrise; **~auto** *nt* moon buggy *or* rover; **~bahn** *f* moon's orbit, orbit of the moon; (*Space*) lunar orbit; **m~beschienen** *adj* (*geh*) bathed in moonlight, moonlit.

Möndchen *nt* half-moon.

Mondesfinsternis *f* (*Aus*) eclipse of the moon, lunar eclipse.

Mondenschein, Mondesglanz *m* (*poet*) moonlight.

Mondesglanz *m* (*poet*) *siehe* **Mondenschein**.

Mond-: **~finsternis** *f* eclipse of the moon, lunar eclipse; **~gebirge** *nt* mountains of the moon *pl*; **~gesicht** *nt* moonface; (*gemalt*) simple representation of a face; **~gestein** *nt* moon rocks *pl*; **~göttin** *f* moon goddess; **m~hell** *adj* moonlit; **m~hell erleuchtet** lit by the moon, moonlit; **~jahr** *nt* lunar year; **~kalb** *nt* (**a**) (*Med*) mole; (**b**) (*dated inf: Dummkopf*) mooncalf; **~krater** *m* lunar crater; **~(lande)fähre** *f* (*Space*) lunar module; **~landschaft** *f* lunar landscape; **~landung** *f* lunar *or* moon landing; **~licht** *nt* moonlight; **m~los** *adj* (*geh*) moonless; **~nacht** *f* (*geh*) moonlit night; **~oberfläche** *f* surface of the moon; **~phasen** *pl* phases of the moon *pl*; **~schein** *m* moonlight; **der kann mir mal im ~schein begegnen!** (*inf*) he can get stuffed (*sl*); **~sichel** *f* (*liter*) crescent moon; **~sonde** *f* (*Space*) lunar probe; **~stein** *m* moonstone; **m~süchtig** *adj* **m~süchtig sein** to sleepwalk; **~süchtigkeit** *f* sleepwalking, somnambulism (*form*); **~umlaufbahn** *f* (*Space*) lunar orbit; **~untergang** *m* moonset; **~wechsel** *m* change from full to new moon.

Monegasse *m* -n, -n, **Monegassin** *f* Monegasque.

monegassisch *adj* Monegasque.

monetär *adj* monetary.

Monetarismus *m* (*Econ*) monetarism.

Moneten *pl* (*sl*) bread (*sl*), dough (*sl*). **~ machen** to make some bread (*sl*) *or* dough (*sl*).

Mongole *m* -n, -n, **Mongolin** *f* Mongolian, Mongol.

Mongolei *f* **die ~** Mongolia; **die Innere/Äußere ~** Inner/Outer Mongolia.

Mongolen-: **~falte** *f* epicanthus; **~fleck** *m* Mongolian spot.

mongolid *adj* Mongoloid.

Mongolide(r) *mf decl as adj* Mongoloid.

Mongolin *f siehe* **Mongole**.

mongolisch *adj* Mongolian.

Mongolismus *m* (*Med*) mongolism.

mongoloid *adj* (*Med*) mongoloid.

Mongoloide(r) *mf decl as adj* (*Med*) mongol.

monieren* 1 *vt* to complain about. **sie hat moniert, daß ... she** complained that ... **2** *vi* to complain.

Monismus *m* (*Philos*) monism.

Monitor *m* (*TV, Phys*) monitor.

Mono-, mono- *in cpds* mono-.

Mono-: **m~chrom** [mono'kroːm] *adj* monochrome; **m~color** *adj* (*Aus*) **eine m~colore Regierung** a single-party government; **m~gam** *adj* monogamous; **~gamie** *f* monogamy; **~gramm** *nt* monogram; **~graphie** *f* monograph.

Monokel *nt* -s, - monocle.

Monokultur *f* (*Agr*) monoculture.

Monolith *m* -en, -en monolith.

Monolog *m* -(e)s, -e (*Liter, fig*) monologue; (*Selbstgespräch*) soliloquy. **einen ~ sprechen** to hold a monologue/give a soliloquy; **einen ~ halten** (*fig*) to hold a monologue, to talk on and on.

monologisch *adj* monologic(al).

monologisieren* *vi siehe n* to hold a monologue; to soliloquize.

monoman *adj* (*liter*) monomaniacal.

Monomane *m* -n, -n, **Monomanin** *f* (*liter*) monomaniac.

Monomanie *f* (*liter*) monomania; (*fig*) obsession.

Monophthong [mono'ftɔŋ] *m* -s, -e (*Ling*) monophthong.

Monopol *nt* -s, -e monopoly (*auf +acc, für* on).

Monopol- *in cpds* monopoly; **~bildung** *f* monopolization *no pl*.

monopolisieren* *vt* (*lit, fig*) to monopolize.

Monopolisierung *f* monopolization.

Monopolist(in *f*) *m* monopolist.

Monopol-: **~kapital** *nt* (*Kapital*) monopoly capital; (*Kapitalisten*) monopoly capitalism; **~kapitalismus** *m* monopoly capitalism; **~kapitalist** *m* monopolist; **m~kapitalistisch** *adj* monopolistic; **~stellung** *f* monopoly.

Monotheismus [monote'ɪsmʊs] *m* monotheism.

monoton *adj* monotonous.

Monotonie *f* monotony.

Monoxid (*spec*), **Monoxyd** *nt* monoxide.

Monster *nt* -s, - (*inf*) *siehe* **Monstrum**.

Monster- *in cpds* (*usu pej*) mammoth, monster; **~film** *m* mammoth (film) production.

Monstra *pl of* **Monstrum**.

Monstranz *f* (*Eccl*) monstrance.

Monstren *pl of* **Monstrum**.

monströs *adj* monstrous; (*riesig groß*) monster.

Monstrosität *f* monstrosity; (*riesige Größe*) monstrous size; (*Ungeheuer*) monster.

Monstrum *nt* -s, **Monstren** *or* (*geh*) **Monstra** (*Ungeheuer*) monster; (*fig: Mißbildung*) monstrosity; (*inf: schweres Möbel*) hulking great piece of furniture (*inf*).

Monsun *m* -s, -e monsoon.

Monsunregen *m* monsoon rain.

Montag *m* Monday; *siehe* **Dienstag, blau**.

Montage [mɔn'taːʒə] *f* -, -n (**a**) (*Tech*) (*Aufstellung*) installation; (*von Gerüst*) erection; (*Zusammenbau*) assembly; (*Typ*) stripping. **auf ~** (*dat*) **sein** to be away on a job. (**b**) (*Art, Film, Liter*) montage.

Montage-: **~band** *nt* assembly line; **~halle** *f* assembly shop; **~werk** *nt* assembly plant.

montags *adv* on Mondays; *siehe* **dienstags**.

Montan-: **~industrie** *f* coal and steel industry; **~union** *f* European Coal and Steel Community.

Monteur(in *f*) [mɔn'tøːr, -'tøːrɪn] *m* (*Tech*) fitter; (*Aut*) mechanic; (*Heizungs~, Fernmelde~, Elektro~*) engineer; (*Elec*) electrician.

Monteur|anzug [-'tøːr-] *m* boiler suit.

montieren* *vt* (**a**) (*Tech*) to install; (*zusammenbauen*) to assemble; (*befestigen*) **Kotflügel, Autoantenne** to fit (*auf or an +acc* to); **Dachantenne** to put up; (*aufstellen*) **Gerüst** to erect. (**b**) (*Art, Film, Liter*) **Einzelteile** to create a montage from. **aus etw montiert sein** to be a montage of sth; **er hat die Erzählung aus verschiedenen Gesprächen montiert** he has written the story as a montage of various conversations.

Montur *f* (*inf*) (*hum: Arbeitskleidung*) gear (*inf*), rig-out (*inf*); (*Aus: Uniform*) uniform.

Monument *nt* monument.

monumental *adj* monumental.

Monumental- *in cpds* monumental.

Moor *nt* -(e)s, -e bog; (*Hoch~*) moor.

Moor-: **~bad** *nt* mud-bath; **~boden** *m* marshy soil; **~huhn** *nt* grouse.

moorig *adj* boggy.

Moor-: **~kolonie** *f* fen community; **~kultur** *f* cultivation of peat bogs; **~land** *nt* marshland; (*Hoch~*) moorland; **~packung** *f* mudpack; **~siedlung** *f siehe* **~kolonie**.

Moos¹ *nt* -es, -e moss. **von ~ überzogen** overgrown with moss, moss-grown; **~ ansetzen** to become covered with moss, to become moss-grown; (*fig*) to become hoary with age.

Moos² *nt* -es, *no pl* (*sl*) bread (*sl*), dough (*sl*).

moos-: **~bedeckt** *adj* moss-covered; **~grün** *adj* moss-green.

moosig *adj* mossy.

Moos-: **~rose** *f*, **~röschen** *nt* moss rose.

Mop *m* -s, -s mop.

Möp *m* -s, -s *or f* -, -s: **ein fieser** *or* **eine fiese ~** (*dial sl*) a nasty piece of work (*inf*).

Moped *nt* -s, -s moped.

Mopedfahrer *m* moped rider.

Moppel *m* -s, - (*inf*) tubby (*inf*).

moppen *vt* to mop.

Mops *m* -es, ̈-e (**a**) (*Hund*) pug (dog). (**b**) (*Dickwanst*) roly-poly (*inf*), dumpling (*inf*). (**c**) **~e** *pl* (*sl: Geld*) bread *sing* (*sl*), dough *sing* (*sl*).

mopsen 1 *vt* (*dated inf*) to nick (*Brit inf*), to pinch (*inf*). **2** *vr* (*inf*) (**a**) (*sich langweilen*) to be bored. (**b**) (*schmollen*) to sulk; (*sich ärgern*) to be peeved.

Mops-: **m~fidel** *adj* (*dated inf*) chirpy (*inf*); **~gesicht** *nt* (*inf*) pug-face, puggy face (*inf*).

mopsig *adj* (*inf*) (**a**) **Gesicht** puggy (*inf*). (**b**) (*frech*) **sich ~ machen, ~ werden** to get cheeky (*esp Brit*) or fresh (*esp US*).

Moral *f* -, *no pl* (**a**) (*Sittlichkeit*) morals *pl*; (*gesellschaftliche Norm auch*) morality. **eine hohe/keine ~ haben** to have high moral standards/no morals; **private ~** personal morals; **die ~ sinkt/steigt** moral standards are declining/rising; **die bürgerliche/sozialistische ~** bourgeois/socialist morality; **gegen die (geltende) ~ verstoßen** to violate the (accepted) moral code; **eine doppelte ~** double standards *pl*, a double standard; **~ predigen** to moralize (*jdm* to sb).
(**b**) (*Lehre, Nutzanwendung*) moral. **und die ~ von der Geschicht'** and the moral of this story.

(c) (*Ethik*) ethics *pl*, moral code. **nach christlicher ~** according to Christian ethics *or* the Christian (moral) code. (d) (*Disziplin: von Volk, Soldaten*) morale. **die ~ sinkt** morale is falling *or* getting lower.
Moral- *in cpds* moral; **~apostel** *m* (*pej*) upholder of moral standards; **~hüter** *m* guardian of public morals.
Moralin *nt* -s, *no pl* (*hum*) priggishness.
moralinsauer *adj* (*hum*) priggish.
moralisch *adj* moral. **ein ~ hochstehender Mensch** a person of high moral standing; **das war eine ~e Ohrfeige für die Regierung** that was one in the eye for the government (*inf*); **einen/seinen M~en haben** (*inf*) to have (a fit of) the blues (*inf*), to be down in the dumps (*inf*).
moralisieren* *vi* to moralize.
Moralismus *m* (*geh*) morality. **einem unbestechlichen ~ leben** to live a life of incorruptible morality.
Moralist(in *f*) *m* moralist.
moralistisch *adj* moralistic.
Moralität *f* morality; (*Theat*) morality play.
Moral-: **~kodex** *m* moral code; **~pauke** *f siehe* **~predigt**; **~philosophie** *f* moral philosophy; **~prediger** *m* moralizer; **~predigt** *f* homily, sermon; **~predigten halten** to moralize; **jdm eine ~predigt halten** to give sb a homily *or* sermon; **~theologie** *f* moral theology.
Moräne *f* -, -n (*Geol*) moraine.
Morast *m* -(e)s, -e *or* **Moräste** (*lit, fig*) mire; (*Sumpf auch*) morass.
morastig *adj* marshy; (*schlammig*) muddy.
Moratorium *nt* moratorium.
morbid *adj* (*Med*) morbid; (*fig geh*) degenerate.
Morbidität *f* morbidity, morbidness; (*fig geh*) degeneracy.
Morchel *f* -, -n (*Bot*) morel.
Mord *m* -(e)s, -e murder, homicide (*US*) (*an* +*dat* of); (*an Politiker etc*) assassination (*an* +*dat* of). **wegen ~es** for murder *or* homicide (*US*); **„~ an altem Mann"** "old man slain *or* murdered"; **politischer ~** political killing; **auf ~ sinnen** (*old liter*) to devise murderous schemes; **das ist ja ~!** (*inf*) it's (sheer) murder! (*inf*); **dann gibt es ~ und Totschlag** (*inf*) all hell will be let loose (*inf*), there'll be hell to pay (*inf*); **von ~ und Totschlag handeln** to be full of violence.
Mord-: **~anklage** *f* murder charge, charge of homicide (*US*); **~anklage erheben** to lay a murder charge *or* a charge of homicide (*US*); **unter ~anklage stehen** to be on a murder charge *or* charge of homicide (*US*); **~anschlag** *m* assassination (*auf* +*acc* of); (*erfolglos*) assassination attempt (*auf* +*acc* on), attempted assassination (*auf* +*acc* of); **einen ~anschlag verüben** to carry out an assassination attempt; **einen ~anschlag auf jdn verüben** to assassinate/try to assassinate sb; **~brenner** *m* (*old liter*) arsonist, incendiary; **~bube** *m* (*obs*) murderer; **~drohung** *f* threat on one's life, murder threat.
morden *vti* (*liter*) to murder, to kill, to slay (*liter*). **das sinnlose M~** senseless killing.
Mörder *m* -s, - murderer (*auch Jur*), killer; (*Attentäter*) assassin.
Mörder-: **~bande** *f* gang *or* bunch of murderers *or* killers; **~grube** *f*: **aus seinem Herzen keine ~grube machen** to speak frankly; **~hand** *f* (*old, liter*): **durch ~hand fallen/sterben** to die *or* perish (*old*) at the hands of a murderer.
Mörderin *f* murderer, murderess, killer; (*Attentäterin*) assassin.
mörderisch **1** *adj* (*fig*) (*schrecklich*) dreadful, terrible, murderous; *Tempo auch* breakneck *attr*; *Preise* iniquitous; *Konkurrenzkampf* cutthroat. **2** *adv* (*inf: entsetzlich*) dreadfully, terribly, murderously. **~ fluchen** to curse like blazes (*inf*); **~ schreien** to scream blue murder (*inf*).
Mord-: **~fall** *m* murder *or* homicide (*US*) (case); **der ~fall Dr Praun** the Dr Praun murder *or* homicide (*US*) (case); **~gier** *f* (*geh*) desire to kill; **m~gierig** *adj* (*geh*) bloodthirsty; **~instrument** *nt* murder weapon.
mordio *interj* (*old*) *siehe* zetermordio, Zeter.
Mord-: **~kommission** *f* murder squad, homicide squad *or* division (*US*); **~lust** *f* desire to kill; **~prozeß** *m* murder trial.
Mords- *in cpds* (*inf*) incredible, terrible, awful; (*toll, prima*) hell of a (*inf*); **~ding** *nt* (*inf*) whopper (*inf*); **~dusel** *m* (*inf*) tremendous stroke of luck; **einen ~dusel haben** to be dead lucky (*inf*); **~gaudi** *f* (*S Ger inf*) whale of a time (*inf*); **~geld** *nt* (*inf*) fantastic amount of money; **~glück** *nt* (*inf*) *siehe* **~dusel**; **~kerl** *m* (*inf*) (a) (*verwegener Mensch*) hell of a guy (*inf*); (b) (*starker Mann*) enormous fellow *or* guy (*inf*); **~krach** *m* (*inf*) hell of a *or* fearful *or* terrible din; **~lärm** *m* (*inf*) hell of a (*inf*) *or* fearful *or* terrible noise; **m~mäßig** (*inf*) **1** *adj* incredible; **2** *adv* (+*vb*) incredibly, terribly, awfully; (+*adj, ptp auch*) helluva (*sl*), bloody (*Brit sl*); **m~wenig** *adj* (*inf*) precious little; **~wut** *f* (*inf*) terrible temper *or* rage; **eine ~wut im Bauch haben** to be in a hell of a (*inf*) *or* terrible temper *or* rage.
Mord-: **~tat** *f* (*liter*) murderous deed; **~verdacht** *m* suspicion of murder; **unter ~verdacht** (*dat*) **stehen** to be suspected of murder; **~waffe** *f* murder weapon.
Mores ['moːreːs] *pl*: **jdn ~ lehren** (*dated inf*) to teach sb some manners.
Morgen *m* -s, - (a) (*Tagesanfang*) morning. **am ~, des ~s** (*geh*) in the morning; **gegen ~** towards (the) morning; **bis in den ~ (hinein)** into the wee small hours *or* the early hours; **~ für ~** (each and) every morning; **am nächsten** *or* **den nächsten ~** the next morning; **eines ~s** one morning; **den ganzen ~ (über)** the whole morning; **es wird ~** day is breaking; **der ~ dämmert** *or* **bricht an, der ~ graut** *or* **zieht herauf** (*all liter*) dawn is breaking; **guten ~!** good morning; **~!** (*inf*) morning, hello, hi (*inf*); **(jdm) guten ~ sagen** to say good morning (to sb); (*morgens kurz besuchen*) to say hello to sb; **schön** *or* **frisch wie**

der junge ~ (*liter*) fresh as a daisy. (b) *no pl* (*old, liter: Osten*) East. (c) (*liter: Zukunft*) dawn. **der ~ einer neuen Zeit bricht an** a new age is dawning. (d) (*Measure*) ≃ acre. **drei ~ Land** three acres of land.
morgen *adv* (a) tomorrow. **~ früh/mittag/abend** tomorrow morning/lunchtime/evening; **~ in acht Tagen** tomorrow week, a week (from) tomorrow; **~ um diese(lbe) Zeit** this time tomorrow; **bis ~/~ früh!** see you tomorrow/in the morning; **Kartoffeln gibt es erst wieder ~** we/they *etc* won't have any potatoes till tomorrow; **hast du ~ Zeit?** are you free tomorrow?; **~, ~, nur nicht heute, sagen alle faulen Leute** (*Prov*) tomorrow never comes (*Prov*); **~ ist auch (noch) ein Tag!** (*Prov*) there's always tomorrow; **die Technik von ~** the technology of tomorrow. (b) **gestern ~** yesterday morning.
Morgen- *in cpds* morning; **~ausgabe** *f* morning edition.
morgend *adj* (*old*) **der ~e Tag** the morrow (*old*), tomorrow.
Morgendämmerung *f siehe* **Morgengrauen**.
morgendlich *adj* morning *attr*; (*früh* ~) early morning *attr*. **die ~e Stille** the quiet of the early morning; **~ frisch aussehen** to look as fresh as a daisy.
Morgen-: **~dunst** *m* early morning mist; **~frühe** *f* early morning; **sie brachen in aller ~frühe auf** they left at break of dawn; **~gabe** *f* (*Hist*) gift given to a bride by her husband after the wedding night; **~grauen** *nt* -s, - dawn, daybreak; **im** *or* **beim ~grauen** in the first light of dawn; **~gymnastik** *f* morning exercises *pl*; **~gymnastik machen** to do one's morning exercises; **~land** *nt* (*old, liter*) Orient, East; **die Weisen aus dem ~land** the Three Wise Men from the East; **~länder(in** *f*) *m* -s, - (*old, iro*) Oriental; **m~ländisch** *adj* (*old, iro*) Oriental, Eastern; **~licht** *nt* early morning light; **~luft** *f* early morning air; **~luft wittern** (*fig inf*) to see one's chance; **~mantel** *m* dressing-gown; (*für Damen auch*) housecoat; **~muffel** *m* (*inf*) **er ist ein schrecklicher ~muffel** he's terribly grumpy in the mornings (*inf*); **~nebel** *m* early morning mist; **~post** *f* morning post (*Brit*) *or* mail; **~rock** *m* housecoat; **~rot** *nt* -s, *no pl*, **~röte** *f* -, -n sunrise; (*fig*) dawn(ing); **~rot deutet auf schlechtes Wetter hin** red sky in the morning, shepherd's warning (*prov*).
morgens *adv* in the morning. **(um) drei Uhr ~, ~ (um) drei Uhr** at three o'clock in the morning, at three a.m.; **~ und abends** morning and evening; (*fig: dauernd*) morning, noon and night; **von ~ bis mittags/abends** in the morning/from morning to night; **nur ~** mornings only; **Freitag ~** on Friday morning.
Morgen-: **~sonne** *f* morning sun; **~sonne haben** to get *or* catch the morning sun; **~stern** *m* morning star; (*Schlagwaffe auch*) flail; **~stunde** *f* morning hour; **zu früher ~stunde** early in the morning; **bis in die frühen ~stunden** into the early hours *or* wee small hours; **~stund(e) hat Gold im Mund(e)** (*Prov*) the early bird catches the worm (*Prov*); **~zug** *m* early (morning) train.
morgig *adj attr* tomorrow's. **die ~e Veranstaltung/Zeitung** tomorrow's event/paper; **der ~e Tag** tomorrow; **sein ~er Besuch** his visit tomorrow.
moribund *adj* (*Med, fig*) moribund.
Moritat ['moːritaːt] *f* -, -en (a) (*Vortrag*) street ballad. (b) (*Geschehen*) murderous deed.
Moritz *m* **der kleine ~** (*inf*) ≃ Simple Simon.
Mormone *m* -n, -n, **Mormonin** *f* Mormon.
mormonisch *adj* Mormon.
Morphem [morˈfeːm] *nt* -s, -e morpheme.
Morpheus ['morfoys] *m* -' Morpheus. **in ~' Armen ruhen** (*liter*) to be in the arms of Morpheus (*liter*).
Morphin [morˈfiːn] *nt* -s, *no pl* (*Chem*) *siehe* **Morphium**.
Morphinismus *m* morphine addiction.
Morphinist(in *f*) *m* morphine addict.
Morphium ['morfium] *nt* -s, *no pl* morphine, morphia.
Morphiumsucht *f siehe* **Morphinismus**.
morphiumsüchtig *adj* addicted to morphine.
Morphologie [morfoloˈgiː] *f* morphology.
morphologisch [morfoˈloːgʃ] *adj* morphological.
morsch *adj* (*lit, fig*) rotten; *Knochen* brittle; *Gebäude* ramshackle.
Morschheit *f* rottenness; brittleness; ramshackleness.
Morse-: **~alphabet** *nt* Morse (code); **im ~alphabet** in Morse (code); **~apparat** *m* Morse telegraph.
morsen **1** *vi* to send a message in Morse (code). **2** *vt* to send in Morse (code).
Mörser *m* -s, - mortar (*auch Mil*). **etw im ~ zerstoßen** to crush sth with a pestle and mortar.
Morsezeichen *nt* Morse signal.
Mortadella *f* -, *no pl* mortadella, baloney (*US*).
Mortalität *f*, *no pl* mortality rate.
Mörtel *m* -s, - (*zum Mauern*) mortar; (*Putz*) stucco.
Mosaik *nt* -s, -e(n) (*lit, fig*) mosaic.
Mosaik- *in cpds* mosaic; **~artig** *adj* like a mosaic, tessellated *no adv*; **~fußboden** *m* mosaic *or* tessellated floor; **~stein** *m* tessera.
mosaisch *adj* Mosaic.
Mosambik *nt* -s *siehe* **Moçambique**.
Moschee *f* -, -n [-ˈeːən] mosque.
Moschus *m* -, *no pl* musk.
Moschus|ochse *m* musk-ox.
Möse *f* -, -n (*vulg*) cunt (*vulg*).
Mosel[1] *f* - (*Geog*) Moselle.
Mosel[2] *m* -s, -, **Moselwein** *m* Moselle (wine).
mosern *vi* (*dial inf*) to gripe (*inf*), to belly-ache (*inf*). **er hat immer was zu ~** he always has something to gripe *or* belly-ache about (*inf*).
Moses[1] *m* - *or* (*liter*) **Mosis** Moses. **bin ich ~?** (*hum inf*) don't ask me; *siehe* **Buch**.

Moses[2] *m* -, - (*Naut inf*) ship's boy.
Moskau *nt* -s Moscow.
Moskauer *adj attr* Moscow *attr*.
Moskauer(in *f)* *m* -s, - Muscovite.
Moskito *m* -s, -s mosquito.
Moskitonetz *nt* mosquito net.
Moskowiter *adj attr* Muscovite.
Moskowiter(in *f)* *m* -s, - Muscovite.
Moslem *m* -s, -s Moslem.
moslemisch *adj attr* Moslem.
Most *m* -(e)s, no pl (a) (*unfermentet*) fruit juice; (*für Wein*) must. (b) (*S Ger, Sw: Obstwein*) fruit wine; (*Birnen~*) perry; (*Apfel~*) cider.
Most|apfel *m* cider apple.
Mostert *m* -s, no pl (*dial*) mustard.
Mostgewicht *nt* specific gravity of the must.
Mostrich *m* -s, no pl (*dial*) mustard.
Motel *nt* -s, -s motel.
Motette *f* (*Mus*) motet.
Motion *f* (a) (*Sw: Antrag*) motion. (b) (*Gram: Abwandlung*) inflexion (for gender).
Motiv *nt* -s, -e (a) (*Pysch, Jur, fig*) motive. **das ~ einer Tat** the motive for a deed; **aus welchem ~ heraus?** for what motive/reason?, what are your/his *etc* motives?; **ohne erkennbares ~** without any apparent motive. (b) (*Art, Liter*) subject; (*Leit~, Topos, Mus*) motif.
Motivation [-va'tsio:n] *f* motivation.
Motiv-: ~**forschung** *f* motivation research; **m~gleich** *adj* with the same theme *or* motif; **m~gleich sein** to have the same motif.
motivieren* [moti'vi:rən] *vt* (a) (*begründen*) etw (*jdm gegenüber*) ~ to give (sb) reasons for sth; (*rechtfertigend*) to justify sth (to sb); *Verhalten, Sinneswandel, Abwesenheit* to account for sth (to sb). (b) (*anregen*) to motivate.
Motivierung *f* motivation; (*erklärende Rechtfertigung*) explanation.
Moto *nt* -s, -s motorcycle.
Moto-Cross *nt* -, -e motocross.
Motor ['mo:tɔr, mo'to:r] *m* -s, -en [mo'to:rən] motor; (*von Fahrzeug*) engine; (*fig*) driving force (*gen* in).
Motor-: ~**antrieb** *m* motor drive; **mit ~antrieb** motor-driven; ~**block** *m* engine block; ~**boot** *nt* motorboat.
Motoren-: ~**geräusch** *nt* sound of the/an engine/engines; ~**lärm** *m* noise *or* roar of (the) engines; ~**öl** *nt* engine oil.
Motor-: ~**fahrrad** *nt* (*form*) motor-assisted bicycle (*form*); ~**fahrzeug** *nt* (*form*) motor vehicle; ~**haube** *f* bonnet, hood (*US*); (*Aviat*) engine cowling.
-motorig *adj suf* -engined.
Motorik *f* (*Physiol*) motor activity; (*Lehre*) study of motor activity.
Motoriker(in *f)* *m* -s, - (*Pysch*) motor type.
motorisch *adj* (*Physiol*) motor *attr*.
motorisieren* *vt* to motorize; *Landwirtschaft* to mechanize; (*mit Motor ausstatten*) to fit with an engine. **sich ~** to get motorized, to buy a car/motorcycle *etc*.
Motorisierung *f*, no pl siehe vt motorization; mechanization; fitting with an engine.
Motor-: ~**jacht** *f* motor yacht; ~**kühlung** *f* engine cooling system; ~**leistung** *f* engine performance.
Motorrad ['mo:tɔrra:t, mo'to:ʊra:t] *nt* motorbike, motorcycle (*esp Sport*). **fahren Sie (ein) ~?** do you ride a motorbike?
Motorrad-: ~**fahrer** *m* motorcyclist; ~**rennen** *nt* motorcycle race; (*Sportart*) motorcycle racing; ~**rennfahrer** *m* motorcycle racer; ~**sport** *m* motorcycle racing.
Motor-: ~**raum** *m* engine compartment; ~**roller** *m* (motor) scooter; ~**säge** *f* power saw; ~**schaden** *m* engine trouble no pl; ~**schiff** *nt* motor vessel *or* ship; ~**schlitten** *m* motorized sleigh; ~**sport** *m* motor sport.
Motte *f* -, -n (a) moth. **von ~n zerfressen** moth-eaten; **angezogen wie die ~n vom Licht** attracted like moths to a flame; **du kriegst die ~n!** (*sl*) blow me! (*inf*). (b) (*dated inf: Mädchen*) **eine kesse/flotte ~** a cheeky/bright young thing (*inf*). (c) (*sl: Lungentuberkulose*) **die ~n kriegen** to get TB.
Motten-: **m~fest** *adj* mothproof; **etw m~fest machen** to mothproof sth; ~**kiste** *f* (*fig*) **etw aus der ~kiste hervorholen** to dig sth out; **aus der ~kiste des 19. Jahrhunderts stammen** (*inf*) to be a relic of the 19th century; ~**kugel** *f* mothball; ~**pulver** *nt* moth powder; **m~zerfressen** *adj* moth-eaten.
Motto *nt* -s, -s (a) (*Wahlspruch*) motto. **unter dem ~ ... stehen** to have ... as a *or* one's motto. (b) (*in Buch*) epigraph. (c) (*Kennwort*) password.
motzen *vi* (*sl*) to beef (*inf*), to grouse (*inf*). **was hast du jetzt zu ~?** what are you beefing *or* grousing about now? (*inf*).
mouillieren* [mu'ji:rən] *vt* (*Ling*) to palatalize.
moussieren* [mu'si:rən] *vi* to effervesce.
Möwe *f* -, -n seagull, gull.
Mozambique [mozam'bik, -'bi:k] *nt* -s siehe Moçambique.
MP [ɛm'pɛ:] (a) *abbr of* **Militärpolizei** Military Police. (b) *abbr of* **Maschinenpistole**.
Mrd. *abbr of* **Milliarde**.
Ms., Mskr. *abbr of* **Manuskript** ms.
mtl. *abbr of* **monatlich**.
Mücke *f* -, -n (a) (*Insekt*) mosquito, midge, gnat. **aus einer ~ einen Elefanten machen** (*inf*) to make a mountain out of a molehill. (b) (*sl: Geld*) (**ein paar**) ~**n** (some) dough (*sl*).
Muckefuck *m* -s, no pl (*inf*) coffee substitute, ersatz coffee.
mucken 1 *vi* (*inf*) to mutter. **ohne zu ~** without a murmur. 2 *vr* to make a sound.
Mucken *pl* (*inf*) moods pl. (**seine**) ~ **haben** to be moody; (*Sache*)

to be temperamental; (*zu diesem Zeitpunkt*) (*Mensch*) to be in one of one's moods; (*Sache*) to play up; **jdm die ~ austreiben** to sort sb out (*inf*).
Mückenstich *m* mosquito *or* gnat bite.
Mucker *m* -s, - (*dated*) creep (*inf*).
muckerisch *adj* (*dated*) servile.
Muckertum *nt* (*dated*) servility.
muck(i)sch *adj* (*dial*) peeved.
Mucks *m* -es, -e (*inf*) sound. **einen/keinen ~ sagen** to make/not to make a sound; (*widersprechend*) to say/not to say a word; **ohne einen ~** (*widerspruchslos*) without a murmur.
mucksen *vr* (*inf*) **sich nicht ~** not to budge (*inf*), not to move (a muscle); (*sich nicht äußern*) not to make a sound; (*Mensch*) not to say a dickybird (*inf*), not to make a sound.
mucksmäuschenstill [-'mɔysçən-] *adj* (*inf*) (as) quiet as a mouse.
Mud, Mudd *m* -s, no pl (*Naut*) mud.
müde *adj* (a) tired; (*erschöpft auch*) weary; *Haupt* weary. **sich ~ laufen** to tire oneself out running about.
(b) (*überdrüssig*) tired, weary. **einer Sache (*gen*) ~ werden** to tire *or* weary of sth, to grow tired *or* weary of sth; **einer Sache (*gen*) ~ sein** to be tired *or* weary of sth; **des Wartens ~ sein** to be tired of waiting; **ich bin es ~, das zu tun** I'm tired *or* weary of doing that; **sie wird nicht ~, das zu tun** she never tires *or* wearies of doing that; **~ abwinken** to make a weary gesture (with one's hand).
-müde *adj suf* tired *or* weary of ...
Müdigkeit *f* (*Schlafbedürfnis*) tiredness; (*Schläfrigkeit*) sleepiness; (*Erschöpfung auch*) weariness, fatigue. **die ~ überwinden** to overcome one's tiredness; **sich (*dat*) die ~ vertreiben, gegen die ~ ankämpfen** to fight one's tiredness; **vor ~ (*dat*) umfallen** to drop from exhaustion; **nur keine ~ vorschützen!** (*inf*) don't (you) tell me you're tired.
Müesli ['my:ɛsli] *nt* -s, -s (*Sw*) muesli.
Muezzin [mu'ɛtsi:n] *m* -s, -s muezzin.
Muff[1] *m* -s, no pl (*N Ger*) (a) (*Schimmel, Moder*) mildew. (b) (*Modergeruch*) musty smell, mustiness; (*fig: Rückständigkeit*) fustiness.
Muff[2] *m* -(e)s, -e muff.
Muffe *f* -, -n (a) (*Tech*) sleeve. (b) (*sl*) ~ **kriegen/haben** to be scared stiff (*inf*), to get/have the shits (*sl*); **ihm geht die ~ (eins zu hunderttausend)** he's scared stiff (*inf*).
Muffel *m* -s, - (a) (*Hunt: Maul*) muzzle. (b) (*inf: Murrkopf*) grouch, grouser.
-muffel *m in cpds* (*inf*) stick-in-the-mud where ... is/are concerned (*inf*).
muff(e)lig *adj* (*inf*) grumpy.
muffeln[1] 1 *vi* (*inf*) (a) (*andauernd kauen*) to munch away (*an +dat* at). (b) (*mürrisch sein*) to be grumpy. 2 *vti* (*mürrisch reden*) to mutter.
muffeln[2], **müffeln** (*dial*) *vi* (*inf*) to smell musty. **es muffelt** there's a musty smell.
Muffensausen *nt* (*sl*) ~ **kriegen/haben** to be/get scared stiff (*inf*).
muffig, müffig (*dial*) *adj* (a) *Geruch* musty. (b) *Gesicht* grumpy.
Muffigkeit, Müffigkeit (*dial*) *f* (a) (*Modergeruch*) mustiness. (b) (*Verdrießlichkeit*) grumpiness.
mufflig *adj* (*inf*) grumpy.
Mufti *m* -s, -s mufti.
Mugel *m* -s, -n, **Mugl** *m* -s, -(n) (*Aus inf*) hillock, hummock.
muh *interj* moo.
Mühe *f* -, -n trouble; (*Anstrengung auch*) effort; (*Arbeitsaufwand auch*) bother. **ohne ~** without any trouble *or* bother; **nur mit ~** only just; **mit Müh und Not** (*inf*) with great difficulty; **er kann mit Müh und Not seinen Namen schreiben** (*inf*) he can just about write his name; **nur mit Müh und Not kriegt sie mal einen Blumenstrauß von ihm** (*inf*) she's lucky to get a bunch of flowers from him; **alle/viel ~ haben** to have a tremendous amount of/a great deal of trouble *or* bother (*etw zu tun* doing sth); **wenig/keine ~ haben** not to have much trouble *or* bother (*etw zu tun* doing sth); **mit jdm/etw seine ~ haben** to have a great deal of trouble *or* bother with sb/sth; **es ist der** (*gen*) *or* **die ~ wert, es lohnt die ~** it's worth the trouble *or* bother (*etw zu tun* of doing sth); **die kleine ~ hat sich gelohnt** it was worth the little bit of trouble; **sich (*dat*) etwas/mehr/keine ~ geben** to take some/more/no trouble; **er hat sich (*dat*) große ~ gegeben** he has taken great pains *or* a lot of trouble; **gib dir keine ~!** (*sei still*) save your breath; (*hör auf*) don't bother, save yourself the trouble; **sich (*dat*) die ~ machen/nicht machen, etw zu tun** to take the trouble to do sth, to go to the trouble *or* bother of doing sth/not to bother to do sth; **machen Sie sich (*dat*) keine ~!** (please) don't go to any trouble *or* bother; **sie hatte sich die ~ umsonst gemacht** her efforts were wasted; **jdm ~ machen** to give sb some trouble *or* bother; **wenn es Ihnen keine ~ macht** if it isn't any *or* too much trouble *or* bother; **viel ~ auf etw** (*acc*) **verwenden** to take a lot of trouble *or* bother with sth; **es hat viel ~ gekostet** it took a great deal of trouble *or* bother; **verlorene ~** a waste of effort.
mühelos *adj* effortless; *Sieg, Aufstieg auch* easy.
Mühelosigkeit *f siehe adj* effortlessness; ease.
muhen *vi* to moo, to low.
mühen *vr* to strive (*um* for). **sosehr er sich auch mühte ... strive** as he might ...; **sich mit etw ~** to labour with sth.
Mühe-: **m~voll** *adj* laborious, arduous; *Leben* arduous; ~**waltung** *f* (*form*) trouble.
Muhkuh *f* (*baby-talk*) moo-cow (*baby-talk*).
Mühlbach *m* mill-stream.
Mühle *f* -, -n (a) mill; (*Kaffee~*) grinder. (b) (*fig*) (*Routine*) treadmill; (*Bürokratie*) wheels of bureaucracy pl. (c) (~*spiel*)

nine men's morris. (d) (inf) (Flugzeug) crate (inf); (Auto auch) banger (inf), jalopy (inf); (Fahrrad) boneshaker (inf).

Mühl(en)- in cpds mill; ~**graben** m mill race; ~**rad** nt millwheel; ~**stein** m millstone.

Mühlespiel nt das ~ nine men's morris.

Muhme f -, -n (obs) aunt.

Mühsal ['myːzaːl] f -, -e (geh) tribulation; (Strapaze) toil. die ~e des Lebens the trials and tribulations of life.

mühsam ['myːzaːm] 1 adj Aufstieg, Weg, Leben arduous; Aufgabe, Amt auch laborious. 2 adv with difficulty. nur ~ vorwärtskommen to make painfully slow progress; ~ verdientes Geld hard-earned money.

mühselig ['myːzeːlɪç] adj arduous, toilsome (liter). Ihr M~en und Beladenen (Bibl) ye that labour and are heavy laden; sich ~ ernähren or durchschlagen to toil for one's living.

Mühseligkeit f laboriousness, toilsomeness (liter).

Mulatte m -n, -n, **Mulattin** f mulatto.

Mulde f -, -n (a) (Geländesenkung) hollow. (b) (Trog) trough. (c) (für Bauschutt) skip.

Muli nt or m -s, -(s) (a) (Maultier) mule. (b) (Ind inf: Gabelstapler) fork-lift (inf).

Mull m -(e)s, -e (a) (Torf~) garden peat. (b) (Gewebe) muslin; (Med) gauze.

Müll m -(e)s, no pl (Haushalts~) rubbish, garbage (esp US), trash (US), refuse (form); (Gerümpel) rubbish, junk, garbage (esp US); (Industrie~) waste; (inf: Unsinn) rubbish (inf), trash (inf). etw in den ~ werfen to throw sth out; „~ abladen verboten" "dumping prohibited", "no tipping" (Brit).

Müll-: ~**abfuhr** f (~abholung) refuse or garbage (US) or trash (US) collection; (Stadtreinigung) refuse etc collection department; ~**abladeplatz** m rubbish dump or tip (Brit), dump.

Müllbinde f gauze bandage.

Müll-: ~**deponie** f waste disposal site (form), sanitary (land)fill (US form); ~**eimer** m rubbish bin (Brit), garbage can (US).

Müller m -s, - miller.

Müllerbursch(e) m (obs) miller's lad.

Müllerin f (obs) miller's wife.

Müll-: ~**fahrer** m siehe ~**mann**; ~**grube** f rubbish (Brit) or refuse pit; ~**haufen** m rubbish or garbage (US) or trash (US) heap; ~**kasten** m (dial) siehe ~**tonne**; ~**kippe** f rubbish or garbage (US) dump; ~**kutscher** (N Ger), ~**mann** m, pl -**männer** or **Mülleute** (inf) dustman (Brit), trash collector (US); ~**schaufel**, ~**schippe** f dustpan; ~**schlucker** m -s, - refuse chute; ~**tonne** f dustbin (Brit), ashcan (US), trashcan (US).

Müllverbrennungs-: ~**anlage** f incinerating plant; ~**ofen** m incinerator.

Müll-: ~**verwertung** f refuse utilization; ~**wagen** m dust-cart (Brit), garbage truck (US).

Mullwindel f gauze nappy (Brit) or diaper (US).

Mulm m -s, no pl rotten wood.

mulmig adj (a) (morsch) Holz etc rotten. (b) (inf: bedenklich) uncomfortable. es wird ~ things are getting (a bit) uncomfortable; ich hatte ein ~es Gefühl im Magen, mir war ~ zumute (lit) I felt queasy; (fig) I had butterflies (in my tummy) (inf).

Multi m -s, -s (inf) multinational (organization).

Multi- in cpds multi-; m~**lateral** adj multilateral; ~**media** pl multimedia pl; m~**medial** adj multimedia attr; ~**millionär** m multimillionaire; m~**national** adj multinational.

multipel adj multiple. **multiple Sklerose** multiple sclerosis.

Multiplikand m -en, -en (Math) multiplicand.

Multiplikation f multiplication.

Multiplikationszeichen nt multiplication sign.

Multiplikator m multiplier.

multiplizierbar adj multipliable.

multiplizieren* 1 vt (lit, fig) to multiply (mit by). 2 vr (fig) to multiply.

Mumie ['muːmiə] f mummy. **wie eine wandelnde ~** (inf) like death warmed up (inf).

mumienhaft [-iən-] adj like a mummy.

mumifizieren* vt to mummify.

Mumifizierung f mummification.

Mumm m -s, no pl (inf) (a) (Kraft) strength. (b) (Mut) spunk (dated inf), guts pl (inf).

Mummelgreis m (inf) old dodderer (inf).

Mümmelmann m, pl -**männer** (hum) hare.

mummeln 1 vti (a) (undeutlich reden) to mumble. (b) (behaglich kauen) to chew slowly, to munch. 2 vtr (einhüllen) jdn/sich in etw (acc) ~ to wrap or muffle sb/oneself up in sth; sich ins Bett ~ to huddle up in bed.

mümmeln vi to nibble.

mummen vt (old) to swathe, to wrap (up).

Mummenschanz m -es, no pl masquerade.

Mumpitz m -es, no pl (inf) balderdash (dated inf).

Mumps m or (inf) f -, no pl (the) mumps sing.

München nt -s Munich.

Münch(e)ner adj attr Munich. **das ~ Abkommen** (Hist) the Munich Agreement.

Münch(e)ner(in f) m -s, - native of Munich; (Einwohner) inhabitant of Munich.

Münchhausen m -s, -(s) (fig) yarn-spinner.

Münchhaus(en)iade f cock-and-bull story, tall story.

Mund m -(e)s, ⁻er or (rare) -e or ⁻e mouth; (inf: Mundwerk) tongue. **ein Glas an den ~ setzen** to raise a glass to one's mouth or lips; **~ und Nase aufsperren** to gape (with astonishment or amazement); **etw in den ~ nehmen** to put sth in one's mouth; **dieses Wort nehme ich nicht in den ~** I never use that word; **den ~ aufmachen** or **auftun** (lit, fig) to open one's mouth; (fig: seine Meinung sagen) to speak up; **er hat wohl seinen ~ zu Hause gelassen** (inf) he seems to have lost his tongue; **einen großen ~ haben** (fig) (aufschneiden) to talk big (inf); (frech

sein) to be cheeky (esp Brit) or fresh (esp US); **jdm den ~ verbieten** to order sb to be quiet; **halt den ~!** shut up! (inf), hold your tongue!; **er kann den ~ einfach nicht halten** (inf) he can't keep his big mouth shut (inf); **jdm über den ~ fahren** to cut sb short; **jdm den ~ stopfen** (inf) to shut sb up (inf); **Sie haben mir das in den ~ gelegt** you're putting words into my mouth; **in aller ~ sein** to be on everyone's lips; **wie aus einem ~e** with one voice; **von ~ zu ~ gehen** to be passed on from person to person; **und das or so etwas aus deinem/seinem etc ~(e)!** and (that) coming from you/him etc too!; **an jds ~(e)** (dat) **hängen** (fig) to hang on sb's every word; **Sie nehmen mir das Wort aus dem ~(e)** you've taken the (very) words out of my mouth; **jdm nach dem ~(e) reden** (inf) to say what sb wants to hear; **sie ist nicht auf den ~ gefallen** (inf) she's never at a loss for words; **einen losen ~ haben** to have an unbridled tongue; **den ~ (zu/reichlich) voll nehmen** (inf) to talk (too/pretty) big (inf); **den ~ aufreißen** (inf) to talk big (inf).

Mund|art f dialect. **~ sprechen** to speak dialect.

Mund|art-: ~**dichter** m dialect poet; ~**dichtung** f dialect poetry/literature.

Mund|art(en)forschung f dialect research.

mund|artlich adj dialect(al). **das Wort wird ~ gebraucht** it's a dialect word, the word is used in dialect.

Mund|art-: ~**sprecher** m dialect speaker; ~**wörterbuch** nt dialect dictionary.

Mündel nt or (Jur) m -s, - ward.

Mündel-: ~**geld** nt trust money; m~**sicher** adj ≈ gilt-edged no adv.

munden vi (liter) **jdm trefflich/köstlich ~** to taste excellent/delicious to sb; **sich** (dat) **etw ~ lassen** to savour sth; **es mundete ihm nicht, es wollte ihm nicht ~** he found it unpalatable.

münden vi aux sein or haben (Bach, Fluß) to flow (in + acc into); (Straße, Gang) to lead (in + acc, auf + acc into); (fig: Fragen, Probleme) to lead (in + acc or dat to). **die B 3 mündet bei Celle in die B 1** the B3 joins the B1 at Celle.

Mund-: m~**faul** adj (inf) too lazy to say much; **sei doch nicht so m~faul!** make an effort and say something!; ~**fäule** f (Med) stomatitis; ~**flora** f (Med) (bacterial) flora of the oral cavity or mouth; m~**gerecht** adj bite-sized; **etw m~gerecht schneiden** to cut sth into bite-sized pieces; **jdm etw m~gerecht machen** (fig) to make sth attractive or palatable to sb; ~**geruch** m bad breath, halitosis; **etwas gegen ~geruch tun** to do something about one's (bad) breath; ~**harmonika** f mouth organ, harmonica; ~**höhle** f oral cavity.

mundig adj (geh) appetizing, savoury; Wein full-bodied.

mündig adj of age; (fig) mature, responsible. ~ **werden** to come of age, to reach or attain one's majority; **jdn (für) ~ erklären** to declare sb of age.

Mündigkeit f majority; (fig) maturity, responsibility.

Mündigkeits|erklärung f siehe **Volljährigkeitserklärung**.

Mündig-: m~**sprechen** vt sep irreg to declare of age; ~**sprechung** f declaration of (one's/sb's) majority.

mündlich adj verbal; Prüfung, Leistung oral. ~**e Verhandlung** (Jur) hearing; **einen Fall ~ verhandeln** (Jur) to hear a case; **etw durch ~e Überlieferung weitergeben** to pass sth on by word of mouth; **das M~e** (inf: Sch, Univ) (in Fremdsprache) the oral; (bei Dissertation etc) the viva (voce); **alles andere or weitere ~!** I'll tell you the rest when I see you.

Mündlichkeit f, no pl (Jur) **die ~ der Verhandlung ist vorgeschrieben** it is a legal requirement that every case be heard.

Mund-: ~**orgel** f cheng; ~**pflege** f oral hygiene no art; ~**propaganda** f verbal propaganda; ~**raub** m (Jur) theft of comestibles for personal consumption; ~**schenk** m (Hist) cupbearer; (fig) wine-waiter; ~**schleimhaut** f mucous membrane of the oral cavity or mouth; ~**schutz** m mask (over one's mouth); ~**spalte** f oral fissure.

M-und-S-Reifen ['ɛmʊnt'ɛs-] m winter tyre.

Mund-: ~**stellung** f position of the mouth, embouchure; **die falsche ~stellung haben** to have one's mouth in the wrong position; ~**stück** nt (von Pfeife, Blasinstrument) mouthpiece; (von Zigarette) tip; **ohne/mit ~stück** untipped/tipped; m~**tot** adj (inf) **jdn m~tot machen** to silence sb; ~**tuch** nt serviette, napkin.

Mündung f (von Fluß, Rohr etc) mouth; (Trichter~) estuary; (von Straße) end; (Gewehr~, Kanonen~) muzzle. **die ~ des Missouri in den Mississippi** the confluence of the Missouri and the Mississippi, the point where the Missouri flows into the Mississippi; **die ~ der Straße auf die B 11** the point where the road joins the B11.

Mündungsfeuer nt flash from the muzzle.

Mund-: ~**verkehr** m oral intercourse; ~**voll** m ein/ein paar ~**voll** a mouthful/a few mouthfuls; ~**vorrat** m provisions pl; ~**wasser** nt mouthwash; ~**werk** nt (inf) **ein gutes** or **flinkes ~werk haben** to be a fast talker (inf); **ein böses ~werk haben** to have a vicious tongue (in one's head); **ein freches/loses** or **lockeres/großes ~werk haben** to be cheeky (esp Brit) or fresh (esp US)/have a big mouth (inf)/talk big (inf); **der mit seinem großen ~werk!** him with all his big talk (inf); **ihr ~werk steht nie still** her tongue never stops wagging (inf); ~**winkel** m corner of one's mouth; ~**-zu-~-Beatmung** f mouth-to-mouth resuscitation.

Munition f ammunition; (Mil: als Sammelbegriff) munitions pl. ~ **fassen** (Mil) to be supplied with ammunition/munitions; **keine ~ mehr haben** (lit, fig) to have run out of ammunition; **seine ~ verschießen** (lit) to use up one's ammunition; (fig) to shoot one's bolt.

Munitions-: ~**depot** nt munitions or ammunition dump or store; ~**fabrik** f munitions or ordnance factory; ~**lager** nt

siehe ~depot; ~zug m (Rail) ammunition train.
Munkelei f rumour.
munkeln vti man munkelt or es wird gemunkelt, daß ... it's rumoured or there's a rumour that ...; ich habe ~ hören, daß ... I've heard it rumoured that ...; man munkelt allerlei, allerlei wird gemunkelt you hear all kinds of rumours; im Dunkeln ist gut ~ darkness is the friend of thieves/lovers.
Münster nt -s, - minster, cathedral.
munter adj **(a)** (lebhaft) lively no adv; (Farben) bright, gay; (fröhlich) cheerful, merry. ~ werden to liven up; ~ und vergnügt bright and cheery; ~ drauflos reden/gehen to prattle away merrily/to go at it with a will.
(b) (wach) awake; (aufgestanden) up and about. jdn ~/wieder ~ machen to wake sb up/to wake sb up (again).
Munterkeit f (Lebhaftigkeit) liveliness; (von Farben) brightness; (Fröhlichkeit) cheerfulness, merriness.
Münz-: ~anstalt f mint; ~automat m slot machine.
Münze f -, -n **(a)** (Geldstück) coin; (Münzsystem) coinage. jdm etw mit or in gleicher ~ heimzahlen (fig) to pay sb back in his own coin for sth; siehe bar. **(b)** (Münzanstalt) mint.
Münz-: ~einheit f unit of currency; ~einwurf m (coin) slot.
münzen vt to mint, to coin. das war auf ihn gemünzt (fig) that was aimed at or meant for him.
Münz(en)sammlung f coin or numismatic (form) collection.
Münz-: ~fälscher m (Jur) counterfeiter (of coins); ~fälschung f (Jur) counterfeiting of coins; ~fernsehen nt pay or coin-operated television; ~fernsprecher m (form) pay phone; (Telefonzelle auch) callbox (Brit); ~fund m find of coins; ~gaszähler m slot gas meter; ~geld nt coin; ~gewicht nt coin weight; ~hoheit f prerogative of coinage; ~kunde f numismatics sing; ~sammlung f siehe Münz(en)sammlung; ~schacht f coin slot; ~spielautomat m, ~spielgerät nt (form) coin-operated gaming machine (form), slot machine; ~stromzähler m slot electricity meter; ~system nt coinage; ~tank m coin-operated petrol (Brit) or gas(oline) (US) pump; ~wechsler m change machine; ~wesen nt coinage.
Mur f -, -en (Aus) mud.
Muräne f -, -n moray.
mürb(e) adj **(a)** crumbly; Gestein etc auch friable; (zerbrökkelnd) crumbling; Holz, Stoff auch rotten.
(b) Fleisch tender; (abgehangen) well-hung. ~ klopfen to tenderize, to hammer.
(c) Obst soft. etw ~ werden lassen to let sth ripen.
(d) (fig: zermürbt) jdn ~ machen to wear sb down; ~ werden/sein to be worn down; jdn ~ kriegen to break sb.
Mürbeteig m short(-crust) pastry.
Mure f -, -n (Geol) mudflow.
Murkel m -s, - (dial inf) squirt (inf), shrimp (inf).
murklig adj (dial inf) tiny, wee (esp Scot).
Murks m -es, no pl (inf) ~ machen to bungle things (inf), to botch things up (inf); das ist ~! that's a botch-up (inf); so ein ~! what a botch-up! (inf).
murksen vi (inf) to fiddle around; (vermurksen) to bungle things (inf), to botch things up (inf).
Murkserei f (inf) botching things up (inf). eine ~ a botch-up (inf).
Murmel f -, -n marble.
murmeln 1 vti to murmur; (undeutlich) to mumble; (brummeln) to mutter. etw vor sich (acc) hin ~ to mutter sth to oneself. 2 vi (mit Murmeln spielen) to play marbles.
Murmeltier nt marmot; siehe schlafen.
murren vi to grumble (über + acc about). etw ohne M~ or ohne zu ~ ertragen to put up with sth without grumbling.
mürrisch adj (abweisend) sullen, morose, surly; (schlechtgelaunt) grumpy.
Mus nt or m -es, -e mush; (Apfel~, Kartoffel~) puree; (Pflaumen~) jam. ~ aus Kartoffeln machen to cream or mash potatoes; sie wurden fast zu ~ zerdrückt or zerquetscht (inf) they were (nearly) squeezed to death.
Muschel f -, -n **(a)** mussel (auch Cook), bivalve; (Schale) shell. **(b)** (Ohr~) external ear, pinna. **(c)** (Telec) (Sprech~) mouthpiece; (Hör~) ear-piece.
Muschel-: ~bank f mussel bed; ~kalk m Muschelkalk (spec).
Muschi f -, -s (sl) pussy (sl).
Muschkote m -n, -n (Mil sl) private.
Muse f -, -n (Myth) Muse. die heitere or leichte ~ (fig) light entertainment; von der ~ geküßt werden (fig) to be inspired.
museal adj (geh) museum attr. das Haus sieht zu ~ aus the house looks too much like a museum.
Musel-: ~man(in f) m -en, -en, ~mann m, pl -männer (dated), ~männin f (dated) siehe Moslem.
Musen-: ~almanach m (old) poetry periodical published in the 17th and 18th centuries; ~sohn m (old, liter) poet; ~tempel m (old, liter) theatre.
Museum [mu'ze:ʊm] nt -s, Museen [mu'ze:ən] museum.
Museums-: ~diener m (dated) museum attendant; ~führer m museum guide; m~reif adj (hum) antique; m~reif sein to be almost a museum piece; ~stück nt museum piece.
Musical ['mju:zikl] nt -s, -s musical.
Musicbox ['mju:zik-] f -, -en siehe Musikbox.
Musik f -, -en **(a)** music. die ~ lieben to love music; etw in ~ setzen (geh) to set or put sth to music; ~ machen to play some music; das ist ~ in meinen Ohren (fig) that's music to my ears. **(b)** (~kapelle) band. hier ist die ~! (fig inf) this is where it's at (sl).
Musik|akademie f musical academy, academy of music.
Musikalien [-iən] pl music sing.
Musikalienhandlung [-iən-] f music shop (Brit) or store.
musikalisch adj musical. jdn ~ ausbilden to give sb a musical training or a training in music.

Musikalität f, no pl musicalness, musicality.
Musikant(in f) m musician, minstrel (old).
Musikantenknochen m funny bone, crazy bone (US).
Musik-: ~automat m musical box, music box (US); (~box) jukebox; m~begeistert adj fond of music, music-loving attr; ~begleitung f musical accompaniment; unter ~begleitung accompanied by music, to the accompaniment of music; ~berieselung f (inf) constant background music; ~box f jukebox; ~drama nt music drama.
Musiker(in f) m -s, - musician.
Musik-: ~erziehung f (form) musical education; ~freund m music-lover; ~geschichte f history of music; ~hochschule f college of music; ~instrument nt musical instrument; ~kapelle f band; ~konserve f (inf) canned music no pl; ~korps nt music corps sing; ~kritik f music criticism; (Rezension auch) music crit; (Kritikerschaft) music critics pl; ~kritiker m music critic; ~leben nt world of music; das ~leben Frankreichs the world of French music; ~lehrer m music teacher; ~lexikon nt encyclopaedia/dictionary of music; ~liebhaber m music-lover; ~programm nt music station; (Sendung) music programme; ~saal m music room; ~sendung f music programme; ~stück nt piece of music; ~stunde f music lesson; ~theater nt music theatre; ~truhe f radiogram, radio-phonograph (US); ~unterricht m music lessons pl; (Sch) music.
Musikus m -, Musizi (hum) musician.
Musik-: ~werk nt (geh) musical composition or work; ~wissenschaft f musicology; ~wissenschaftler m musicologist; ~zimmer nt music room.
musisch adj Fächer, Gymnasium (fine) arts attr; Begabung for the arts; Erziehung in the (fine) arts; Veranlagung, Mensch artistic.
Musizi pl of **Musikus**.
musizieren* vi to play a musical instrument. sie saßen auf dem Marktplatz und musizierten they sat in the market place playing their instruments; sonntags abends wird bei uns immer musiziert we always have a musical evening on Sundays.
Musizierstil m style of playing.
Muskat m -(e)s, -e siehe **Muskatnuß.**
Muskatblüte f mace.
Muskateller(wein) m -s, - muscatel.
Muskatnuß f nutmeg.
Muskel m -s, -n muscle. (viele) ~n haben to be muscular; seine ~n spielen lassen (lit, fig) to flex one's muscles.
Muskel-: ~dystrophie f muscular dystrophy; ~faser f muscle fibre; ~kater m aching muscles pl; ~kater haben to be stiff; er hatte (einen) ~kater in den Beinen his legs were stiff; ~kraft f physical strength; ~krampf m muscle cramp no indef art; ~mann m, ~paket nt, ~protz m (inf) muscleman (inf); ~riß m torn muscle; sich (dat) einen ~riß zuziehen to tear a muscle; ~schwund m muscular atrophy or wasting; ~starre f muscular rigidity; ~zerrung f pulled muscle.
Muskete f -, -n musket.
Musketier m -s, -e musketeer.
Muskulatur f muscular system, musculature (spec).
muskulös adj muscular. ~ gebaut sein to have a muscular build.
Muslem m -s, -s siehe **Moslem.**
Müsli nt -(s), -s muesli.
Muslim m -s, -s siehe **Moslem.**
Muß nt -, no pl das harte ~ grim necessity; es ist ein/kein ~ it's/it's not a must.
Muß-Bestimmung, Mußbestimmung f fixed regulation.
Muße f -, no pl leisure. (die) ~ für etw finden to find the time and leisure for sth; dafür fehlt mir die ~ I don't have the time or leisure; sich (dat) ~ gönnen to allow oneself some (time for) leisure; etw mit ~ tun to do sth in a leisurely way.
müssen 1 modal aux vb pret mußte, ptp ~ **(a)** (Zwang) to have to; (Notwendigkeit auch) to need to. ich muß (Zwang) I have to, I must only pres tense, I've got to (esp Brit); (Notwendigkeit auch) I need to; ich muß nicht (Zwang) I don't have to, I haven't got to (esp Brit); (Notwendigkeit auch) I don't need to, I needn't; muß er? have he?, does he have to?, has he got to? (esp Brit); mußtest du? did you have to?; das hat er tun/nicht tun ~ he had to/didn't have to do it; er hatte es tun ~ he had had to do it; es mußte ins Haus gebracht werden it had to be brought inside; das muß irgendwann mal gemacht werden it will have to be done some time; er sagte, er müsse bald gehen he said he would have to go soon; ich hätte es sonst allein tun ~ otherwise I would have had to do it alone; dafür ~/müßten Sie einen Polizisten fragen you'll/you'd have or need to ask a policeman about that; ich muß jeden Tag um sechs Uhr aufstehen I have to get up at six every day; ich muß jetzt gehen or weg (inf) I must be going or be off now, I must go now, I'll have to go now; man mußte lachen/weinen etc you couldn't help laughing/crying etc, you had to laugh/cry etc; wir ~ Ihnen leider mitteilen, daß ... we regret to (have to) inform you ...; muß das (denn) sein? is that (really) necessary?; must you/he?, do you/does he have to?; das muß sein it's necessary; I do/he does have to; wenn es (unbedingt) sein muß if it's absolutely necessary; if you/he must; das mußte (ja so) kommen that had to happen, that was bound to happen; sie muß immer zu spät kommen she always has to be late; das muß man sich (dat) mal vorstellen! (just) imagine that!, think of that!; jetzt muß ich dir mal was sagen now let me tell you something; was habe ich da hören ~? what's this I hear?
(b) (sollen) das müßte ich/müßtest du eigentlich wissen I/you ought to or should know that; ich hätte es gestern tun ~ I ought to or should have done it yesterday; das mußt du nicht tun! you

oughtn't to or shouldn't do that; „Zuspätkommende ~ sich beim Pförtner melden" "latecomers should report or are required to report (form) to the porter".

   (c) (Vermutung, Wahrscheinlichkeit) es muß geregnet haben it must have rained; es muß wahr sein it must be true, it has or it's got to be true; es muß nicht wahr sein it needn't be true; er muß es gewesen sein it must have been him, it has or it's got to have been him; es müßten zehntausend Zuschauer im Stadion gewesen sein there must have been ten thousand spectators in the stadium; er müßte schon da sein he should be there by now; es müßte schon viel falsch sein, bevor man es überhaupt merkt there would have to be a lot wrong before it would even be noticed; er müßte denn krank sein (old) unless he were ill; so muß es gewesen sein that's how it must have been; was ~ bloß die Leute (von uns) denken! what must people think (of us); was muß bloß in ihm vorgehen? what goes on in his mind?

   (d) (Wunsch) (viel) Geld müßte man haben! if only I were rich!; man müßte noch mal von vorn anfangen können! if only one could begin again!; man müßte nochmal zwanzig sein! oh, to be twenty again!

   2 vi pret **mußte**, ptp **gemußt (a)** to have to go. ich muß jetzt zur Schule I must or I've got to (esp Brit) or I have to go to school now; wann müßt ihr zur Schule? when do you have to go to school?; der Brief muß heute noch zur Post the letter must be or has to be mailed today.

   (b) (inf) ich muß mal I need to go to the loo (Brit inf) or bathroom (esp US).

   (c) (inf: an der Reihe sein) to be it.

   (d) (gezwungen sein) to have to. hast du gewollt? — nein, gemußt did you want to? — no, I had to; kein Mensch muß ~ there's no such thing as 'must'.

Mußestunde f hour of leisure. seine ~n one's leisure hours.

Mußheirat f (inf) shotgun wedding (inf). es war eine ~ they had to get married.

müßig adj (untätig) idle; Leben, Tage, Stunden of leisure; (überflüssig, unnütz) futile, pointless, otiose (form).

Müßig-: ~gang m (liter) siehe adj idleness; dem ~gang leben, sich dem ~gang hingeben to lead a life of idleness or an idle life; ~gang ist aller Laster Anfang (Prov) the devil finds work for idle hands (Prov); ~gänger(in f) m -s, - idler.

Müßigkeit f siehe adj futility, pointlessness, otiosity (form).

mußte pret of müssen.

Muß-Vorschrift f siehe **Muß-Bestimmung**.

Mustang m -s, -s mustang.

Muster nt -s, - (a) (Vorlage, Dessin) pattern; (für Brief, Bewerbung etc) specimen. nach einem ~ stricken etc to knit etc from a pattern.

   (b) (Probestück) sample, (Buch, Korrekturfahne etc) specimen. ~ ohne Wert sample of no commercial value.

   (c) (fig: Vorbild) model (an + dat of); (Verhaltens~) pattern. als ~ dienen to serve as a model; sich (dat) jdn zum ~ nehmen to take sb as one's model, to model oneself on sb; er ist ein ~ von einem Schüler/Ehemann/Staatsbürger he is a model student/husband/citizen; ein ~ an Tugend a paragon of virtue.

Muster- in cpds model; ~beispiel nt classic or prime example; ~betrieb m model factory/farm etc; ~bild nt (Vorbild) perfect specimen; (Prototyp) archetype; ein ~bild von einem Mann/Soldaten etc sein to be the perfect man/soldier etc; das ~bild eines Adligen/Komikers etc sein to be the archetypal aristocrat/comedian etc; ~buch nt pattern book; ~dorf nt model village; ~ehe f perfect marriage; ~exemplar nt fine specimen; ein ~exemplar von einer Frau/einem Idioten a model wife/a perfect idiot; ~gatte m model husband; m~gültig adj exemplary; ~gültigkeit f exemplariness; ~gut nt model farm; m~haft adj exemplary; er hat sich m~haft verhalten his conduct was exemplary; ~haftigkeit f exemplariness; ~knabe m (iro) paragon; ~koffer m sample case; ~kollektion f collection of samples; (Fashion) collection of models; ~messe f trade fair.

mustern vt **(a)** (betrachten) to scrutinize, to look over, to survey. jdn kühl/skeptisch ~ to survey or eye sb coolly/sceptically; jdn von oben bis unten ~ or von Kopf bis Fuß ~ to look sb up and down, to scrutinize sb from head to toe.

   (b) (Mil: inspizieren) to inspect, to review.

   (c) (Mil: für Wehrdienst) jdn ~ to give sb his/her medical.

   (d) Stoff siehe gemustert.

Muster-: ~packung f sample pack; (Attrappe) display pack; ~prozeß m test case; ~schüler m model pupil; (fig) star pupil; ~schutz m protection of patterns and designs; ~sendung f selection of samples; ~stadt f model town; ~stück nt (usu iro) siehe ~exemplar.

Musterung f **(a)** a pattern. **(b)** (Mil (von Truppen) inspection, review; (von Rekruten) medical examination for military service. **(c)** (durch Blicke) scrutiny.

Musterungs-: ~ausschuß m recruiting or draft (US) board; ~bescheid m notification of the recruiting or draft (US) board's decision; ~kommission f siehe ~ausschuß.

Mut m -(e)s, no pl **(a)** courage, pluck (inf); (Zuversicht) heart. ~ fassen to pluck up courage; ~/keinen ~ haben to have (a lot of/some)/not to have any courage; mit frischem ~ with new heart; nur ~! don't lose heart!, cheer up!, keep your pecker up! (Brit inf); jdm den ~ nehmen to discourage sb, to make sb lose heart; den ~ verlieren to lose heart; ~/wieder ~ bekommen to gain confidence/to take heart again; jdm ~ zusprechen or machen to encourage sb; das gab ihr wieder neuen ~ that gave her new heart; ihm sank der ~ his heart sank; mit dem ~ der Verzweiflung with the courage born of desperation or despair; der ~ zum Leben the will to live; der ~ zur Lücke (hum) the courage to admit when one doesn't know something.

   (b) (old: Laune, Stimmung) spirits pl. frohen/guten ~es sein

---

to be of good cheer (old), to be in good spirits; mit frohem ~ with good cheer (old).

Mutation f **(a)** mutation. **(b)** (Med) breaking of the voice. er hat die ~ gerade hinter sich his voice has just broken.

Mutbeweis m proof of his etc courage.

Mütchen nt sein ~ an jdm kühlen (inf) to take it out on sb (inf).

mutieren* vi **(a)** (sich erblich ändern) to mutate. **(b)** (Med, Aus) er hat schon mutiert his voice has already broken.

mutig adj (tapfer) courageous, brave, plucky (inf). dem M~en gehört die Welt (Prov) fortune favours the brave (Prov).

Mut-: m~los adj (niedergeschlagen) discouraged no adv, disheartened no adv; (bedrückt) despondent, dejected; jdn m~los machen to discourage sb, to make sb lose heart; ~losigkeit f siehe adj discouragement, disheartenment; despondency, dejection.

mutmaßen* vti insep to conjecture. es wurde viel über seine Abwesenheit gemutmaßt there was a lot of conjecture as to the reason for his absence.

mutmaßlich 1 adj attr Vater, Täter presumed. **2** adv die Fahrgäste sind ~ ums Leben gekommen it is presumed that all the passengers were killed; ~ soll er der Vater sein he is presumed to be the father.

Mutmaßung f conjecture. wir müssen uns auf ~en stützen we can only conjecture.

Mutprobe f test of courage.

Muttchen nt (inf) **(a)** (Mutter) mummy (inf), mommy (US inf). **(b)** (biedere Hausfrau) little housewife. **(c)** (alte Frau) grandma.

Mutter[1] f -, ¨ mother. sie ist jetzt ~ she's a mother now; ~ werden to have a baby; sie ist ~ von drei Kindern she's a mother of three; als Frau und ~ as a wife and a mother; ~ Natur/Erde (liter) Mother Nature/Earth; die ~ der Kompanie (Mil hum) the sergeant-major; wie bei ~n (dial) just like (at) home; (Essen) just like mother makes/used to make.

Mutter[2] f -, -n (Tech) nut.

Mütterberatungsstelle f child welfare clinic.

Mutter-: ~bindung f (Psych) mother fixation; ~boden m topsoil; ~brust f mother's breast; (Ernährung) mother's milk; an der ~brust at one's mother's breast; da war ich ja noch an der ~brust! I was just a babe-in-arms then.

Mütterchen nt **(a)** siehe Muttchen **(a).** **(b)** siehe Muttchen **(c).** **(c)** ~ Rußland Mother Russia.

Mutter-: ~erde f topsoil; (liter: Heimaterde) native soil; ~fahrzeug nt (Space) parent ship; ~freuden pl the joys of motherhood pl.

Müttergenesungsheim nt rest centre for mothers, especially of large families.

Mutter-: ~gesellschaft f (Comm) parent company; ~gewinde nt (Tech) female thread; ~glück nt das ~glück the joy of motherhood; ~gottes f -, no pl Mother of God; (Abbild) Madonna; ~gottesbild(nis) nt (image of the) Madonna; ~haus nt (Rel) training centre; (von Kloster) mother house; ~herz nt maternal heart; ~instinkt m maternal instinct; ~kirche f mother church; ~komplex m mother complex; ~korn nt (Bot) ergot; ~kuchen m (Anat) placenta; ~kult m mother cult; ~land nt mother country; ~leib m womb.

Mütterlein nt siehe Mütterchen **(a, b).**

mütterlich adj **(a)** maternal; Seite, Linie auch distaff. die ~en Pflichten one's duties as a mother; auf ~er Seite on his/her etc mother's side, on the distaff side. **(b)** (liebevoll besorgt) motherly no adv. jdn ~ umsorgen to mother sb.

mütterlicherseits adv on his/her etc mother's side, on the distaff side. sein Großvater ~ his maternal grandfather.

Mütterlichkeit f motherliness.

Mutter-: ~liebe f motherly love; m~los adj motherless; ~mal nt birthmark, mole; ~milch f mother's milk; etw mit der ~milch einsaugen (fig) to learn sth from the cradle; ~mord m matricide; ~mörder m matricide; ~mund m (Anat) cervix, neck of the uterus or womb.

Mutternschlüssel m (Tech) spanner.

Mutter-: ~paß m document held by expectant mothers in which the details of the pregnancy are entered; ~pferd nt dam; ~pflanze f parent (plant); ~recht nt (Sociol) matriliny; m~rechtlich adj (Sociol) matrilinear; ~schaf nt ewe.

Mutterschaft f motherhood.

Mutterschafts-: ~geld nt maternity grant; ~hilfe f maternity benefit; ~urlaub m maternity leave.

Mutter-: ~schiff nt (Space) parent ship; ~schutz m legal protection of expectant and nursing mothers; ~schutzgesetz nt law for the protection of expectant and nursing mothers; ~schwein nt sow; m~seelenallein adj, adv all alone, all on one's own; ~söhnchen nt (pej) mummy's boy; ~sprache f native language, mother tongue; Gälisch ist seine ~sprache Gaelic is his native language, he's a native speaker of Gaelic; ~stelle f: bei jdm ~stelle vertreten to be like a mother to sb; (Jur) to stand in loco parentis to sb.

Müttersterblichkeit f mortality in childbirth.

Mutter-: ~stute f dam; ~tag m Mother's Day; ~tier nt mother (animal); (Zuchttier) brood animal; ~witz m (Schläue) mother wit; (Humor) natural wit.

Mutti f -, -s (inf) mummy, mum, mommy (US).

Mutwille m -ns, no pl **(a)** (geh: Übermut) mischief. aus bloßem or reinem ~n out of pure mischief. **(b)** (böse Absicht) malice. etw mit or aus ~n tun to do sth out of malice; seinen ~n an jdm auslassen to vent one's spite on sb.

mutwillig 1 adj **(a)** (geh: übermütig) Streiche, Dummheiten mischievous. **(b)** (böswillig) malicious; Beschädigung, Zerstörung auch wilful. **2** adv (absichtlich) zerstören etc wilfully.

Mutwilligkeit f siehe Mutwille.

Mütze f -, -n cap. die ~ ziehen to doff one's cap; (fig) to take one's hat off (*vor jdm* to sb); **was auf die ~ kriegen** (*inf*) to get a ticking-off (*inf*); (*verprügelt etc werden*) to get thumped (*inf*); **eine ~ voll Schlaf** (*inf*) a good kip (*inf*).

Mützenschirm *m* peak.

Mykenä, Mykene *nt* **-s** Mycenae.

mykenisch *adj* Mycenean.

Myriade *f* (*lit, fig*) myriad.

Myrrhe ['myrə] *f* **-, -n** myrrh.

Myrrhen|öl *nt* oil of myrrh.

Myrte *f* **-, -n** myrtle.

Myrtenkranz *m* myrtle wreath.

Mysterien- [-iən-] (*Hist*): **~kult** *m* mystery cult; **~spiel** *nt* (*Theat*) mystery play.

mysteriös *adj* mysterious.

Mysterium *nt* (*alle Bedeutungen*) mystery.

Mystifikation *f* mystification.

mystifizieren* *vt* to mysticize.

Mystifizierung *f* mystification.

Mystik *f* mysticism *no art*.

Mystiker(in *f*) *m* **-s, -** mystic.

mystisch *adj* mystic(al); (*fig: geheimnisvoll*) mysterious.

Mystizismus *m* mysticism.

Mythe *f* **-, -n** *siehe* **Mythos**.

Mythen-: **~bildung** *f* zur **~bildung beitragen** to help to create a myth; **m~haft** *adj* mythical.

mythisch *adj* mythical.

Mythologie *f* mythology.

mythologisch *adj* mythologic(al).

Mythos, Mythus *m* **-, Mythen** (*lit, fig*) myth. **er war zeitlebens von einem ~ umgeben** he was a legend in his time.

N

N, n [ɛn] *nt* **-, - N, n. n-te** nth.

N *abbr of* **Norden**.

'n [n] *abbr of* **ein, einen**.

na¹ *interj* (*inf*) **(a)** (*Frage, Anrede*) well; (*Aufforderung*) then. **~, kommst du mit?** well, are you coming?, are you coming then?; **~, du?** well?

(b) (*zögernde Zustimmung, Resignation*) well. **~ ja** well; **~ ja, aber nur noch zehn Minuten** well yes *or* I suppose so, but only another ten minutes; **~ gut, ~ schön** all right, OK (*inf*).

(c) (*Bestätigung, Erleichterung*) well. **~ also!, ~ eben!** (well,) there you are (then)!; **~ und ob!** (*auf jeden Fall*) you bet! (*inf*), not half! (*inf*); (*und wie auch*) and how! (*inf*).

(d) (*Beschwichtigung*) come (on) (now).

(e) (*Ermahnung*) now; (*Zurückweisung*) well. **~ (~)!** now, now!, now then!; **~ warte!** just you wait!; **~ so was** *or* **so etwas!** well, I never!; **~ und?** so what?; **~ ich danke!** no thank you!

(f) (*Zweifel*) well. **~, wenn das mal klappt!** well, if it comes off.

na² *adv* (*S Ger, Aus inf*) *siehe* **nein**.

Nabe *f* **-, -n** hub.

Nabel *m* **-s, -** (*Anat*) navel, umbilicus (*spec*); (*Bot*) hilum. **der ~ der Welt** (*fig*) the hub of the universe, the centre of the world.

Nabel-: **~binde** *f* umbilical bandage; **~bruch** *m* umbilical hernia; **~schau** *f* **~schau betreiben** to be bound up in oneself; **~schnur** *f*, **~strang** *m* (*Anat*) umbilical cord; (*Space auch*) umbilical connector.

Nabob *m* **-s, -s** nabob.

nach 1 *prep* +*dat* **(a)** (*örtlich*) to. **ich nahm den Zug ~ Mailand** (*bis*) I took the train to Milan; (*in Richtung*) I took the Milan train *or* the train for Milan; **das Schiff/der Zug fährt ~ Kiel** the boat/train is going to Kiel; **er ist schon ~ London abgefahren** he has already left for London; **~ Osten/Westen** eastward(s)/westward(s), to the east/west; **von Osten ~ Westen** from (the east to (the) west; **~ links/rechts** (to the) left/right; **von links ~ rechts** from (the) left to (the) right; **~ jeder Richtung** *or* **allen Richtungen** (*lit*) in all directions; (*fig*) on all sides; **~ dem Bahnhof** (*dial*)/**meiner Tante** (*dial*) to the station/my aunt's; **~ hinten/vorn** to the back/front; (*in Wagen/Zug etc auch*) to the rear/front; **~ ... zu** towards ...; **~ Norden zu** *or* **hin** to(wards) the north.

(b) *in Verbindung mit vb siehe auch dort* **~ jdm/etw suchen** to look for sb/sth; **sich ~ etw sehnen** to long for sth; **~ etw schmecken/riechen** to taste/smell of sth.

(c) (*zeitlich*) after. **fünf (Minuten) ~ drei** five (minutes) past *or* after (*US*) three; **~ Christi Geburt** *or* **unserer Zeitrechnung** (*esp DDR*) AD, anno Domini (*form*); **sie kam ~ zehn Minuten** she came ten minutes later *or* after ten minutes; **~ zehn Minuten war sie wieder da** she was back in ten minutes (time) *or* ten minutes later; **~ zehn Minuten wurde ich schon unruhig** after ten minutes I was getting worried; **was wird man ~ zehn Jahren über ihn sagen?** what will people be saying about him in ten years (time)?; **~ Empfang** *or* **Erhalt** *or* **Eingang** on receipt; **drei Tage ~ Empfang** three days after receipt; **~ allem, was geschehen ist** after all that has happened.

(d) (*Reihenfolge*) after. **eine(r, s) ~ dem/der anderen** one after another *or* the other; **die dritte Straße ~ dem Rathaus** the third road after *or* past the town hall; **ich komme ~ Ihnen!** I'm *or* I come after you; (*bitte*) **~ Ihnen!** after you!; **der Leutnant kommt ~ dem Major** (*inf*) a lieutenant comes after a major; **"mit" steht den Dativ "mit"** is followed by *or* takes the dative.

(e) (*laut, entsprechend*) according to; (*im Einklang mit*) in accordance with. **~ dem Gesetz, dem Gesetz ~** according to the law; **~ römischem Gesetz** according to *or* under Roman law; **~ Artikel 142c** under article 142c; **manche Arbeiter werden ~ Zeit, andere ~ Leistung bezahlt** some workers are paid by the hour, others according to productivity; **etw ~ Gewicht kaufen** to buy sth by weight; **~ deutschem Geld** in German money; **~ Verfassern/Gedichtanfängen** in order of *or* according to authors/first lines; **die Uhr ~ dem Radio stellen** to put a clock right by the radio; **seinem Wesen** *or* **seiner Natur ~ ist er sehr sanft** he's very gentle by nature; **seiner Veranlagung ~ hätte er Musiker werden sollen** with his temperament he should have been a musician; **ihrer Sprache (zu urteilen)** from her language, judging by her language; **~ dem, was er gesagt hat** from *or* according to what he's said; **~ allem, was ich gehört habe** from what I've heard; **~ allem, was ich weiß** as far as I know; **Knödel ~ schwäbischer Art** Swabian dumplings.

(f) (*angelehnt an*) after. **~ dem Russischen** after the Russian; **~ einem Gedicht von Schiller** after a poem by Schiller.

(g) er wurde ~ seinem Großvater genannt he was called after *or* for (*US*) his grandfather.

2 *adv* **(a)** (*räumlich*) **mir ~!** (*old liter*) follow me!

(b) (*zeitlich*) **~ und ~** little by little, gradually; **~ wie vor** still; **wir treffen uns ~ wie vor im „Goldenen Handschuh"** we still meet in the "Golden Glove" as always.

nach|äffen *vt sep* (*pej*) *Moden, Ideen* to ape; *jdn* to take off, to mimic; (*imitieren*) to copy.

Nach|äfferei *f* (*pej*) *siehe vt* aping; mimicry; copying.

nach|ahmen *vt sep* to imitate; (*karikieren*) to take off, to mimic; (*nacheifern auch*) to emulate; (*kopieren*) to copy.

nach|ahmenswert *adj* exemplary.

Nach|ahmer(in *f*) *m* **-s, -** imitator; (*eines großen Vorbilds*) emulator; (*pej: Art, Liter*) copyist.

Nach|ahmung *f siehe vt* **(a)** (*das Imitieren*) imitation; taking off, mimicking; emulation; copying. **etw zur ~ anraten** *or* **empfehlen** to recommend sth as an example. **(b)** (*die Imitation*) imitation; take-off, impression; emulation; copy.

Nach|ahmungstrieb *m* imitative instinct.

nach|arbeiten *sep* **1** *vt* **(a)** (*aufholen*) to make up. **(b)** (*überarbeiten*) to work over; (*Art etc*) to touch up. **(c)** (*nachbilden*) to copy, to reproduce. **2** *vi* **wir müssen morgen ~** we'll have to make up the work tomorrow.

Nachbar ['naxbaːɐ] *m* **-n** *or* **-s, -n** neighbour; (*in ~wohnung, ~haus auch*) next-door neighbour. **Herr X war beim Konzert mein ~** Mr X sat next to me at the concert; **ich war eben bei ~s** (*inf*) I've just been round to the neighbours'; **~s Garten** the next-door garden; **die lieben ~n** (*iro*) the neighbours.

Nachbarhaus *nt* house next door, neighbouring house. **in unserem ~, bei uns im ~** in the house next door (to us).

Nachbarin *f* neighbour.

nachbarlich *adj* (*freundlich*) neighbourly *no adv*; (*benachbart*) neighbouring *no adv*.

Nachbarschaft *f* (*Gegend*) neighbourhood; (*Nachbarn*) neighbours *pl*; (*Nähe*) vicinity. **gute ~ halten** *or* **pflegen** to keep on good terms with the neighbours.

Nachbarschafts-: **~heim** *nt* community centre; **~hilfe** *f* neighbourly help; **man ist ja wohl zu ein bißchen ~hilfe verpflichtet** you have to help your neighbours a bit.

Nachbars-: **~familie** *f* next-door family, family next door; **~frau** *f* lady next door; **~kind** *nt* child next door; **~leute** *pl* neighbours *pl*; (*von nebenan auch*) people next door *pl*.

nachbehandeln* *vt sep* (*Med*) *jdn/etw* **~** to give sb after-care, to give sb/sth follow-up treatment.

Nachbehandlung *f* (*Med*) follow-up treatment *no indef art*.

nachbereiten* *vt sep* (*Sch*) to assess *or* evaluate afterwards.

nachbessern *sep* **1** *vt* to put the finishing touches to; (*beim Malen*) to touch up. **2** *vi* to add the finishing touches; to touch it up.

nachbestellen* *vt sep* to order some more; (*Comm*) to

reorder, to put in a repeat order for; (*nachträglich*) to put in or make a late order for. **ich habe gerade noch Sekt/noch zwei Flaschen Sekt nachbestellt** I've just ordered some more champagne/another two bottles of champagne.

Nachbestellung *f* (*gen* for) repeat order; (*nachträgliche Bestellung*) late order.

nachbeten *vt sep* (*inf*) to repeat parrot-fashion, to parrot.

Nachbeter *m* (*inf*) echoer, parrot (*inf*).

nachbezahlen* *sep* 1 *vt* to pay; (*später*) to pay later. **Steuern ~** to pay back-tax. 2 *vi* to pay the rest.

Nachbild *nt* (*Opt*) after-image.

nachbilden *vt sep* to copy; (*exakt*) to reproduce. **einer Sache** (*dat*) **nachgebildet sein** to be modelled on sth, to be a copy/reproduction of sth.

Nachbildung *f* copy; (*exakt*) reproduction.

nachblättern *vi sep* to have a quick look. **in etw** (*dat*) **~** to flick through sth again.

nachbleiben *vi sep irreg aux sein* (*dial*) to stay behind.

nachblicken *vi sep siehe* **nachsehen** 1 (a).

Nachblutung *f* (*Med*) secondary haemorrhage; (*nach Operation*) post-operative haemorrhage; (*nach Geburt*) post-partum haemorrhage.

nachbohren *sep* 1 *vt* Öffnung to drill out. 2 *vi* (*lit*) to drill out some more; (*fig inf*) to probe.

nachbringen *vt sep irreg* (*hinterherbringen*) to bring afterwards; (*zusätzlich servieren*) to bring some more. **er brachte mir den Schirm nach** he came after me with my umbrella.

nachbrummen *vi sep* (*inf*) **~** (**müssen**) to be kept in, to have detention.

nachchristlich *adj* **in den ersten ~en Jahrhunderten** in the first centuries AD.

nachdatieren* *vt sep* to postdate.

nachdem *conj* (a) (*zeitlich*) after. (b) (*modal*) *siehe* **je**[1] 3 (b). (c) (*S Ger: kausal*) since.

nachdenken *vi sep irreg* to think (*über* +*acc* about). **darüber darf man gar nicht ~** it doesn't bear thinking about; **denk doch mal nach!** think about it!; **denk mal gut** *or* **scharf nach!** think carefully!

Nachdenken *nt* thought, reflection. **nach langem ~** after (giving the matter) considerable thought; **gib mir ein bißchen Zeit zum ~** give me a bit of time to think (about it); **durch allzu langes ~ hat sie ihre Chance verpaßt** she spent so long thinking about it that she missed her chance.

nachdenklich *adj Mensch, Miene* thoughtful, pensive; *Geschichte, Worte* thought-provoking. **jdn ~ stimmen** *or* **machen** to set sb thinking; **~ gestimmt sein** to be in a thoughtful mood.

Nachdenklichkeit *f, no pl* thoughtfulness, pensiveness.

nachdichten *vt sep* (*Liter*) to give a free rendering of.

Nachdichtung *f* (*Liter*) free rendering.

nachdrängen *vi sep aux sein* to push from behind. **jdm ~** to throng after sb (*liter*).

Nachdruck *m* (a) *no pl* (*Betonung*) stress, emphasis; (*Tatkraft*) vigour, energy. **besonderen ~ darauf legen, daß ...** to put special emphasis on the fact that ...; **to stress** *or* **emphasize particularly that ...; etw mit ~ betreiben/sagen** to pursue sth with vigour/to say sth emphatically.
(b) (*das Nachdrucken*) reprinting; (*das Nachgedruckte*) reprint. **"~ verboten"** "no part of this publication may be reproduced without the prior permission of the publishers".

nachdrucken *vt sep* to reprint.

nachdrücklich *adj* emphatic; *Warnung auch* firm. **~ auf etw** (*dat*) **bestehen** to insist firmly (up)on sth; **jdm ~ raten** *or* **jdm den ~en Rat geben** to advise sb strongly *or* to urge sb to do sth; **jdn ~ warnen** to give sb a firm warning.

Nachdrücklichkeit *f* insistence.

nachdrucksvoll *adj* emphatic.

nachdunkeln *vi sep aux sein* to get *or* grow darker; (*Bild*) to darken.

nach|eifern *vi sep* **jdm/einer Sache ~** to emulate sb/sth.

nach|eifernswert *adj* worth emulating, worthy of emulation.

Nach|eiferung *f* emulation.

nach|eilen *vi sep aux sein* **jdm/einer Sache ~** to run *or* hurry after sb/sth.

nach|einander *adv* (*räumlich*) one after another *or* the other; (*zeitlich auch*) in succession. **zweimal ~** twice running *or* in a row; **kurz/unmittelbar ~** shortly/immediately after each other; **er schlief drei Tage ~** he slept for three whole days.

nach|empfinden *vt sep irreg* (a) *Stimmung* to feel; *Gedicht, Lied* to relate to. **niemand kann Werthers Schmerz ~** no-one can really feel Werther's grief; **ich kann** (*Ihnen*) **Ihre Entrüstung ~** I can understand how horrified you must be/have been; **das kann ich ihr ~** I can understand her feelings *or* how she feels/felt. (b) (*nachgestalten*) to adapt (*dat* from).

Nachen *m -s, -* (*liter*) barque (*poet*).

Nach|erbe *m* remainderman (*spec*).

Nach|ernte *f* second harvest; (*Ähren~*) gleaning; (*Ertrag*) gleanings *pl*. **~ halten** to glean the remains of the harvest.

nach|erzählen* *vt sep* to retell. **dem Türkischen nacherzählt** (*geh*) adapted from the Turkish.

Nach|erzählung *f* retelling; (*Sch*) (story) reproduction.

nach|exerzieren* *vi sep* (*Mil*) to do extra drill.

Nachf. *abbr of* **Nachfolger**.

Nachfahr *m -s, -en* (*liter*) descendant.

nachfahren *vi sep irreg aux sein* to follow (on). **jdm ~** to follow sb.

nachfassen *sep* 1 *vi* (a) (*nachgreifen*) to get a firmer grip; (*noch einmal zufassen*) to regain one's grip. (b) (*inf: nachforschen*) to probe a bit deeper. (c) (*inf: Essen ~*) to have a second helping. 2 *vt* (*inf: nachholen*) to have a second helping of. **Essen ~** to have a second helping.

Nachfeier *f* continuation of the party; (*später*) celebration *held some time after the event*.

nachfeiern *vi sep* (*weiterfeiern*) to carry on celebrating; (*auch vt: später feiern*) to celebrate later.

nachfeilen *vt sep* to file off.

Nachfolge *f, no pl* (a) succession. **jds/die ~ antreten** to succeed sb/succeed. (b) (*Nacheiferung*) emulation. **in der ~ seines Lehrmeisters** in emulation of his master; **die ~ Christi** the imitation of Christ.

nachfolgen *vi sep aux sein* (a) (*hinterherkommen*) to follow (on). **jdm ~** to follow sb; **jdm im Amt ~** to succeed sb in office; **sie ist ihrem Gatten nachgefolgt** (*euph*) she has gone to join her husband (*euph*). (b) **+dat** (*Anhänger sein*) to follow.

nachfolgend *adj* following. **wie im ~en ausgeführt** as detailed below; **~es, das N~e** the following; **können/konnten Sie aus den ~en Beispielen etwas entnehmen?** can/could you gather anything from the following/subsequent examples?

Nachfolge|organisation *f* successor organization.

Nachfolger(in *f*) *m -s, -* (a) (*im Amt etc*) successor. **Friedrich Reißnagel ~** successors to Friedrich Reissnagel. (b) (*Anhänger*) follower.

Nachfolgestaat *m* succession state.

nachfordern *vt sep* to put in another demand for. **der Erpresser forderte weitere 10.000 DM nach** the blackmailer demanded another 10,000 DM.

Nachforderung *f* subsequent demand.

nachforschen *vi sep* to try to find out; (*polizeilich etc*) to carry out an investigation (*dat* into); (*amtlich etc*) to make enquiries (*dat* into).

Nachforschung *f* enquiry; (*polizeilich etc*) investigation. **~en anstellen** to make enquiries.

Nachfrage *f* (a) (*Comm*) demand (*nach, in* +*dat* for). **danach besteht eine rege/keine ~** there is a great/no demand for it. (b) (*Erkundigung*) enquiry.

nachfragen *vi sep* to ask, to enquire.

Nachfrist *f* extension. **jdm eine ~ setzen** to extend sb's deadline, to give *or* grant sb an extension.

nachfühlen *vt sep siehe* **nachempfinden**.

nachfüllen *vt sep leeres Glas etc* to refill; *halbleeres Glas, Batterie etc* to top up. **darf ich (Ihr Glas) ~?** can I fill/top you up?, would you like a refill?

Nachgang *m* (*form*): **im ~** in addition.

nachgären *vi sep irreg aux haben* *or* *sein* to be lagered.

Nachgärung *f* lagering.

nachgeben *sep irreg* 1 *vi* (a) to give way (*dat* to); (*federn*) to give; (*fig*) (*Mensch*) to give in *or* way (*dat* to); (*aufgeben*) to give up *or* in.
(b) (*Comm: Preise, Kurse*) to drop, to fall.
2 *vt* (a) (*noch mehr geben*) **darf ich Ihnen noch etwas Gemüse ~?** may I give you a few more vegetables?; **er ließ sich** (*dat*) **Fleisch ~** he had another helping of meat.
(b) (*rare: schlechter sein*) **jdm nichts/nicht viel/wenig ~** to be sb's equal in everything/almost everything/most things.

nachgeboren *adj* (a) (*mit großem Altersunterschied*) late(r)-born. **die N~en** (*geh*) future generations. (b) (*nach Tod des Vaters geboren*) posthumous; (*nach Ehescheidung geboren*) born after a/the divorce.

Nachgebühr *f* excess (postage).

Nachgeburt *f* afterbirth; **expulsion of the afterbirth**.

Nachgefühl *nt* feeling. **das hinterließ ein unangenehmes ~ in mir** that left me with an unpleasant feeling.

nachgehen *vi sep irreg aux sein* (a) +*dat* (*hinterhergehen*) to follow; **jdm auch** to go after. (b) (*Uhr*) to be slow. **deine Uhr geht fünf Minuten nach** your clock is five minutes slow. (c) +*dat* (*ausüben*) *Beruf* to practise; *Studium, Vergnügungen etc* to pursue; *Geschäften* to go about. **welcher Tätigkeit gehen Sie nach?** what is your occupation? (d) +*dat* (*erforschen*) to investigate, to look into. (e) +*dat* (*zu denken geben*) to haunt.

nachgelassen 1 *ptp of* **nachlassen**. 2 *adj Werke, Briefe, Papiere* posthumously published. **seine ~en, bis heute noch veröffentlichten Fragmente** the fragments he left which remain unpublished to this day.

nachgemacht 1 *ptp of* **nachmachen**. 2 *adj Gold, Leder etc* imitation.

nachge|ordnet *adj* (*form*) *Behörde, Dienststelle* subordinate.

nachgerade *adv* (*geradezu*) practically, virtually; (*nach wie vor*) still.

nachgeraten* *vi sep irreg aux sein* **jdm ~** to take after sb; **sie ist ganz ihrer Mutter ~** she's just like her mother.

Nachgeschmack *m* (*lit, fig*) aftertaste. **einen üblen ~ hinterlassen** (*fig*) to leave a bad *or* nasty taste in one's *or* the mouth.

nachgewiesenermaßen *adv siehe* **erwiesenermaßen**.

nachgiebig *adj* (a) *Material* pliable; *Boden, Wand etc* yielding. **~ sein** to be pliable/to give. (b) (*fig*) *Mensch, Haltung* soft; (*konziliant*) accommodating, compliant. **sie behandelt die Kinder zu ~** she's too soft with the children; **jdn ~ machen** to soften sb up.

Nachgiebigkeit *f siehe adj* (a) pliability; softness. (b) softness; compliance.

nachgießen *vti sep irreg Wasser, Milch* to add. **er trinkt so schnell, daß man ständig ~ muß** he drinks so fast that you keep having to top up his glass; **darf ich Ihnen (noch etwas Wein) ~?** would you like some more (wine)?

nachglühen *vi sep* to go on glowing.

nachgreifen *vi sep irreg siehe* **nachfassen** 1.

nachgrübeln *vi sep* to think (*über* +*acc* about); (*sich Gedanken machen*) to ponder (*über* +*acc* on), to muse (*über* +*acc* about).

nachgucken *vti sep siehe* **nachsehen**.

nachhaken *vi sep (inf)* to dig deeper. **bei jdm ~** to pump sb *(inf)*.

Nachhall *m* reverberation; *(fig) (Anklang)* response *(auf + acc* to); *(Nachklang)* echo. **künstlicher ~** echo effect, artificial echo; **das Echo hatte einen langen ~** the echo went on reverberating a long while.

nachhallen *vi sep* to reverberate.

nachhaltig *adj* lasting *no adv; Widerstand* sustained *no adv.* **ihre Gesundheit hat sich ~ gebessert** there has been a lasting improvement in her health.

Nachhaltigkeit *f siehe adj* lastingness; sustainment.

nachhängen *vi sep irreg + dat* to give oneself up to, to abandon oneself to. **seinen Erinnerungen ~** to lose oneself in one's memories.

Nachhauseweg *m* way home.

nachhelfen *vi sep irreg* to help. **jdm ~** to help sb, to give sb a hand; **sie hat ihrer Schönheit etwas nachgeholfen** she has improved a little on Mother Nature *or* given nature a helping hand; **er hat dem Glück ein bißchen nachgeholfen** he engineered himself a little luck; **meine Güte, bist du braun! — na, ich hab' auch ein bißchen nachgeholfen** good heavens, you're brown! — well, I did help it *or* things along a bit.

nachher *adv* **(a)** *(danach)* afterwards; *(später auch)* later. **bis ~** see you later! **(b)** *(inf: möglicherweise)* **~ stimmt das gar nicht** that might not be true at all, (it) could be that's not true at all.

Nachhilfe *f* help, assistance; *(Sch)* private coaching *or* tuition. **Nachhilfe-: ~lehrer** *m* private tutor, crammer *(inf);* **~stunde** *f* private lesson; **~unterricht** *m* private coaching *or* tuition.

nachhinein *adv:* **im ~** afterwards; *(rückblickend)* in retrospect; *siehe* **klug**.

nachhinken *vi sep aux sein (fig inf)* to lag behind. **hinter jdm/etw ~** to lag behind.

Nachholbedarf *m* **einen ~ an etw** *(dat)* **haben** to have a lot to catch up on in the way of sth, to have a lot of sth to catch up on.

nachholen *vt sep* **(a)** *(nachkommen lassen)* to join sb to join one; *(von Übersee auch)* to fetch *or* get sb over. **(b)** *(aufholen) Versäumtes* to make up.

Nachhut ['na:xhu:t] *f* **-, -en** *(Mil)* rearguard. **bei der ~** in the rearguard.

Nach|impfung *f* *(Zweitimpfung)* reinoculation; *(Wiederholungsimpfung)* booster.

nach|industriell *adj (Sociol)* post-industrial.

nachjagen *vi sep aux sein + dat* to chase (after); *Vergnügungen, dem Glück auch* to pursue.

nachkauen *vt sep (inf)* to regurgitate.

nachkaufen *vt sep* to buy later. **kann man diese Knöpfe auch ~?** is it possible to buy replacements for these buttons?

Nachklang *m* **der ~ der Mandolinen** the sound of the mandolines dying away; **ein ferner ~ von Mallarmé** a distant echo of Mallarmé.

nachklassisch *adj* post-classical.

nachklingen *vi sep irreg aux sein (Ton, Echo)* to go on sounding; *(Worte, Erinnerung)* to linger on, to linger. **die Melodie klang noch lange in mir nach** the tune stayed in my head for some time.

Nachkomme *m* **-n, -n** descendant. **ohne ~n** without issue *(form)*.

nachkommen *vi sep irreg aux sein* **(a)** *(später kommen)* to follow *or* come (on) later. **jdm ~** to follow sb; **wir kommen gleich nach** we'll follow *or* come in just a couple of minutes; **Sie können Ihre Familie/Ihr Gepäck ~ lassen** you can let your family join you later/have your luggage sent on (after). **(b)** *(mitkommen, Schritt halten)* to keep up. **ich komme nicht nach!** I can't keep up (with you/them *etc*). **(c)** *+ dat (erfüllen) seiner Pflicht* to fulfil, to carry out; *einer Anordnung, Forderung, einem Wunsch* to comply with.

Nachkommenschaft *f* descendants *pl*, issue *(form)*. **seine zahlreiche ~** his numerous progeny *pl or* descendants.

Nachkömmling *m* **(a)** *(Nachzügler)* late arrival, latecomer; *(Kind)* afterthought *(hum)*. **(b)** *(old: Nachkomme)* descendant.

nachkontrollieren* *vt sep* to check (over).

Nachkriegs- *in cpds* post-war.

Nachkur ['na:xku:ɐ] *f* follow-up cure.

nachladen *vti sep irreg* to reload.

Nachlaß *m* **-lasses, -lasse** *or* **-lässe (a)** *(Preis~)* discount, reduction *(auf + acc* on). **(b)** *(Erbschaft)* estate. **den ~ eröffnen** to read the will; **literarischer ~** unpublished works *pl*; **Gedichte aus dem ~** unpublished poems.

nachlassen *vti sep irreg* **1** *vt* **(a)** *Preis, Summe* to reduce. **10% vom Preis ~** to give a 10% discount *or* reduction.
(b) *(locker lassen) Zügel, Seil* to slacken; *Schraube* to loosen.
(c) *(old: hinterlassen)* to bequeath; *siehe* **nachgelassen**.
2 *vi* to decrease, to diminish; *(Interesse auch)* to flag, to wane; *(Sehvermögen, Gehör auch)* to deteriorate; *(Regen, Sturm, Nasenbluten)* to ease off *or* up; *(Leistung, Geschäfte)* to fall *or* drop off; *(Preise)* to fall, to drop. **nicht ~!** keep it up!; **er hat in letzter Zeit sehr nachgelassen** he hasn't been nearly as good recently; **er hat in** *or* **mit seinem Eifer sehr nachgelassen** he's lost a lot of his enthusiasm; **das hat nachgelassen** it's got better; **sobald die Kälte nachläßt** as soon as it gets a bit warmer.

Nachlassenschaft *f siehe* **Hinterlassenschaft**.

Nachlaß-: ~gericht *nt* probate court; **~gläubiger** *m (Jur)* creditor of the estate.

nachlässig *adj* careless, negligent; *Arbeit auch* slipshod; *(unachtsam)* thoughtless. **~ gekleidet** carelessly dressed.

nachlässigerweise *adv* thoughtlessly.

Nachlässigkeit *f siehe adj* carelessness; thoughtlessness.

Nachlaß-: ~pfleger, ~verwalter *m* executor; **~verwaltung** *f* administration of the estate.

nachlaufen *vi sep irreg aux sein + dat* **jdm/einer Sache ~** to run after sb/sth; *(fig auch)* to chase sb/sth; **den Mädchen ~** to chase girls; **ich laufe doch nicht dem Finanzamt nach!** I'm not going to go running after *or* chasing the taxman!

nachleben *vi sep* **jdm ~** to model one's life on sb's; **einem Ideal ~** to live according to an ideal.

nachlegen *sep* **1** *vt* **noch Kohlen/Holz ~** to put some more coal/wood on (the fire). **2** *vi* to make up the fire.

Nachlese *f* second harvest; *(Ähren~)* gleaning; *(Ertrag)* gleanings *pl; (Liter)* further selection. **unter etw** *(dat)* **~ halten** to sift through sth.

nachlesen *sep irreg* **1** *vt* **(a)** *(Ähren)* to glean. **Beeren/Kartoffeln ~** to gather late berries/potatoes.
(b) *(in einem Buch)* to read; *(nachschlagen)* to look up; *(nachprüfen)* to check up. **man kann das in der Bibel ~** it says so in the Bible.
2 *vi* **(a)** to have a second harvest; *(Ähren ~)* to glean.
(b) *(nachschlagen)* to look it up; *(nachprüfen)* to check up.

nachliefern *sep* **1** *vt (später liefern)* to deliver at a later date; *(zuzüglich liefern)* to make a further delivery of; *(inf: später abgeben) Unterlagen* to hand in later. **könnten Sie mir noch einen Zentner ~?** could you deliver another hundredweight? **2** *vi* to make further deliveries.

Nachlieferung *f* delivery. **wir warten auf die ~** we're waiting for the rest to be delivered.

nachlösen *sep* **1** *vi* to pay on the train/when one gets off; *(zur Weiterfahrt)* to pay the extra. **2** *vt* **Fahrkarte** to buy on the train/when one gets off; *(zur Weiterfahrt)* to buy another.

Nachlöseschalter *m* excess fares (counter).

nachm. *abbr of* **nachmittags** p.m.

nachmachen *vt sep* **(a)** *(nachahmen)* to copy; *(nachäffen)* to take off, to mimic. **das Kind macht mir die Gesten nach** the child copies my gestures *or* the gestures I make; **sie macht mir alles nach** she copies everything I do; **das mach' mir mal einer nach!, das macht mir so schnell keiner nach!, das soll erst mal einer ~!** I'd like to see anyone else do that!
(b) *(fälschen) Unterschrift* to forge; *Geld auch* to counterfeit; *(imitieren)* to copy; *siehe* **nachgemacht**.
(c) *(inf: nachholen)* to make up.

nachmalen *vt sep* to copy; *(übermalen)* to touch up.

nachmalig *adj (old)* **der ~e Präsident** the future president; **der ~e Präsident X** President X, as he was to become.

nachmals *adv (old)* later, subsequently.

nachmessen *sep irreg* **1** *vt* to measure again; *Temperatur* to take again; *(prüfend messen)* to check. **2** *vi* to check.

Nachmieter *m* next tenant. **unser ~** the tenant after us.

Nachmittag *m* afternoon. **am ~** in the afternoon; **am heutigen ~** this afternoon; **am ~ des 14.** on the afternoon of October 14th; **im Laufe** *or* **während des ~s** during *or* in the course of the afternoon; *(heute)* sometime this afternoon; **vom ~ an** from about two o'clock; **bis zum ~** till the afternoon; **des ~s** *(geh)* in the afternoon.

nachmittag *adv* **gestern/morgen/Dienstag/heute ~** yesterday/tomorrow/Tuesday/this afternoon.

nachmittägig *adj attr* afternoon.

nachmittäglich *adj no pred* afternoon *attr.* **die ~ stattfindenden Kurse** the afternoon courses.

nachmittags *adv* in the afternoon; *(jeden Nachmittag)* in the afternoon(s). **von ~ an** from about two o'clock; **Dienstag** *or* **dienstags ~** every Tuesday afternoon, on Tuesday afternoons; **er ißt immer erst ~** he never eats till (the) afternoon.

Nachmittags-: ~schlaf *m* **~schlaf halten** to have a sleep after lunch; **~schläfchen** *nt (inf)* **sein ~schläfchen halten** to have one's afternoon nap *or* post-prandial snooze *(hum)*; **~sendung** *f (TV)* afternoon programme *or* show *(esp US)*; **~stunde** *f* hour of the afternoon; **zur frühen ~stunde** *(geh)* early in the afternoon; **~vorstellung** *f* matinée (performance).

Nachmusterung *f (Mil)* medical re-examination.

Nachnahme *f* **-, -n** cash *or* collect *(US)* on delivery, COD; *(inf: ~sendung)* COD parcel. **etw als** *or* **gegen** *or* **per ~ schicken** to send sth COD.

Nachnahme-: ~gebühr *f* COD charge; **~sendung** *f* COD parcel.

Nachname *m* surname, family *or* last name. **wie heißt du mit ~n?** what is your surname?

nachnehmen *vti sep irreg* to take (some) more.

nachplappern *vt sep* to repeat parrot-fashion. **jdm alles ~** to repeat everything sb says parrot-fashion.

nachpolieren* *vt sep* to polish up.

Nachporto *nt* excess postage (postage).

nachprägen *vt sep (nachträglich prägen)* to mint *or* strike some more; *(fälschen)* to forge. **es wurden 200 Stück nachgeprägt** a further 200 copies were struck.

Nachprägung *f (das Nachprägen)* further minting; *(Münze)* coin from a later minting.

nachprüfbar *adj* verifiable. **die Ergebnisse sind jederzeit ~** the results can be verified *or* checked at any time.

Nachprüfbarkeit *f* verifiability.

nachprüfen *sep* **1** *vt* **(a)** *(Aussagen, Tatsachen* to verify, to check. **(b)** *Kandidaten (nochmals prüfen)* to re-examine; *(später prüfen)* to examine at a later date. **2** *vi* to check.

Nachprüfung *f* **(a)** *(von Aussagen, Tatsachen)* check *(gen* on). **bei der ~ der Meldungen** when the reports were checked. **(b)** *(nochmalige Prüfung)* re-examination; *(Termin)* re-sit; *(spätere Prüfung)* later examination.

nachrasen *vi sep aux sein + dat* to race *or* chase after.

nachrechnen *vti sep* to check. **rechne noch einmal nach!** you'd better do your sums again, you'd better check your arithmetic.

Nachrede f (a) (*Verunglimpfung*) üble ~ (*Jur*) defamation of character; jdn in üble ~ bringen to damage sb's reputation, to bring sb into ill repute; üble ~ über jdn verbreiten or führen to cast aspersions on sb's character; in üble ~ geraten or kommen to get a bad reputation. (b) (*Epilog*) epilogue.

nachreden vt sep (a) (*wiederholen*) to repeat. er redet dir alles nach he repeats everything you say. (b) jdm (etwas) Übles/Schlechtes ~ to speak ill/badly of sb.

Nachredner m later or subsequent speaker. mein ~ the speaker after me.

nachreichen vt sep to hand in later.

Nachreife f afterripening.

nachreifen vi sep aux sein to afterripen.

nachreisen vi sep aux sein jdm ~ to follow sb.

nachreiten vi sep irreg aux sein +dat to ride after.

nachrennen vi sep irreg aux sein (inf) siehe nachlaufen.

Nachricht f -, -en (a) (*Mitteilung, Botschaft*) message; (*Meldung*) (piece of) news. eine ~ a message; some news, a piece of news; die ~en the news sing (auch Rad, TV); ~en hören to listen to the news; „Sie hören ~en" "this or here is the news"; das sind aber schlechte ~en that's bad news; wer teilt ihm diese unangenehme ~ mit? who's going to break this unpleasant (piece of) news to him?; die letzte ~ von ihm kam aus Indien the last news of him was from India; ~ erhalten, daß ... to receive (the) news that ...; wir geben Ihnen ~ we'll let you know.
(b) (*Bestätigung*) confirmation. wir sind bezüglich unserer Bestellung immer noch ohne ~ we are still awaiting confirmation of our order.

Nachrichten-: ~agentur f, ~büro nt news agency; ~dienst m (a) (Rad, TV) news service; (b) (Pol, Mil) intelligence (service); ~ magazin nt news magazine; ~satellit m (tele)communications satellite; ~sperre f news blackout or embargo; ~sprecher m newsreader, newscaster; ~technik f telecommunications sing; ~truppe f (old Mil) signals corps; ~übermittlung f communication; ~verbindung f line of communication (zu with, to); ~wesen nt communications pl.

Nachrichter m (old) siehe Scharfrichter.

nachrichtlich adv (form) ~ an +acc copy to.

nachrücken vi sep aux sein to move up; (Mil) to advance. dem Feind/nach Hanoi ~ to advance on the enemy/on Hanoi.

Nachruf m obituary.

nachrufen vti sep irreg +dat to shout after.

Nachruhm m fame after death.

nachrühmen vt sep jdm etw ~ to praise sb for sth; jdm ~, daß er etw getan hat to praise sb for doing or having done sth.

nachsagen vt sep (a) (*wiederholen*) to repeat. jdm alles ~ to repeat everything sb says; das ist kein Grund für dich, es nachzusagen that's no reason for you to say it too.
(b) jdm etw ~ to accuse sb of sth; jdm Schlechtes ~ to speak ill of sb; man kann ihr nichts ~ you can't say anything against her; ihm wird nachgesagt, daß ... it's said that he ...; ihm wird nachgesagt, daß er geizig ist he's said to be mean; das kannst du mir nicht ~ you can't accuse me of that; das lasse ich mir nicht ~! I'm not having that said of me!

Nachsaison f in der ~ after the season proper (has finished).

nachsalzen sep 1 vt to add more salt to. 2 vi to add more salt.

Nachsatz m (a) (*Nachschrift*) postscript; (*Nachtrag*) afterthought. in einem ~ sagte er, daß ... he added, as an afterthought, that ... (b) (*Gram*) clause in sentence final position.

nachschaffen vt sep irreg to reproduce.

nachschauen vti sep siehe nachsehen 1, 2 (a).

nachschenken vti sep jdm etw ~ to top sb up with sth; darf ich Ihnen noch (etwas) ~? may I top you up or top up your glass or give you a refill?; darf ich (dir) noch etwas Wein ~? can I give you a little or a drop more wine?; hat der Ober schon nachgeschenkt? has the waiter already topped up or refilled the glasses?

nachschicken vt sep to send on, to forward. bitte ~! please forward.

nachschießen sep irreg 1 vi (a) (Ftbl) to shoot again. (b) (Geld ~) to add something to it. 2 vt Geld to add to (it).

Nachschlag m (a) (Mus) nachschlag (spec), turn ending a trill. freier ~ any grace note following the main note. (b) (inf) second helping.

nachschlagen sep irreg 1 vt Stelle, Zitat to look up. 2 vi (a) aux sein (ähneln) jdm ~ to take after sb. (b) (Ftbl) (sich revanchieren) to retaliate; (von hinten foulen) to foul (one's opponent) from behind.

Nachschlagewerk nt reference book or work.

nachschleichen vi sep irreg aux sein +dat to creep after.

nachschleifen[1] vt sep (hinterherschleifen) to drag along.

nachschleifen[2] vt sep irreg eine Linse/ein Messer ~ to grind a lens a little more/to sharpen up a knife.

nachschleppen vt sep jdm etw ~ to lug sth after sb.

nachschleudern vt sep (fig) jdm etw ~ to fling or hurl sth after sb.

Nachschlüssel m duplicate key; (Dietrich) skeleton key.

nachschmeißen vt sep irreg (inf) jdm etw ~ to fling sth after sb; das ist ja nachgeschmissen! it's a real bargain.

nachschnüffeln vi sep (inf) to poke or sniff around (inf). jdm ~ to spy on sb.

nachschreiben vt sep irreg (nachträglich schreiben) to write later; (abschreiben) to write out.

Nachschrift f (Protokoll) transcript; (Zugefügtes) (abbr NS) postscript, PS. er hat eine ~ der Vorlesung angefertigt he wrote up the lecture afterwards.

Nachschub ['na:xʃu:p] m (Mil) supplies pl (an +dat of); (Truppe) reinforcements pl.

Nachschub- (Mil): ~basis f supply base; ~linie f supply line;

~weg m supply route.

Nachschuß m (a) (Comm) additional payment. (b) (Ftbl) second shot.

nachschütten vt sep Kies, Sand to tip in (some) more; Kohlen to put on (some) more; (inf: nachgießen) to pour (some) more.

nachschwatzen, nachschwätzen (S Ger, Aus) vt sep (inf) siehe nachplappern.

nachschwingen vi sep irreg siehe nachklingen.

nachsehen sep irreg 1 vi (a) jdm/einer Sache ~ to follow sb/sth with one's eyes, to watch sb/sth; (hinterherschauen) to gaze after sb/sth.
(b) (gucken) to have a look (and see), to look and see; (nachschlagen) to (have a) look.
2 vt (a) to (have a) look at; (prüfen) to check; Schulaufgaben etc to mark; (nachschlagen) to look up.
(b) (verzeihen) jdm etw ~ to forgive sb (for) sth.

Nachsehen nt: das ~ haben to be left standing; (keine Chance haben) not to get a look-in (inf), not to get anywhere; (nichts bekommen) to be left empty-handed.

Nachsende|antrag m application to have one's mail forwarded.

nachsenden vt sep irreg to forward. bitte ~! please forward.

nachsetzen sep 1 vi jdm ~ to pursue sb. 2 vt (a) Fuß to drag.
(b) siehe nachstellen 1 (a).

Nachsicht f -, no pl (Milde) leniency, clemency; (Geduld) forbearance. er wurde ohne ~ bestraft he was punished without mercy; er kennt keine ~ he knows no mercy; ~ üben or haben to be lenient/forbearing; jdn mit ~ behandeln to show leniency or clemency to sb, to be forbearing with sb; jdn um ~ bitten to ask sb to be lenient/forbearing.

nachsichtig, nachsichtsvoll adj (milde) lenient; (geduldig) forbearing (gegen, mit with).

Nachsichtigkeit f siehe Nachsicht.

Nachsilbe f suffix.

nachsingen vt sep irreg to sing.

nachsinnen vi sep irreg to ponder (über +acc over, about). jds Worten (dat) ~ (liter) to ponder sb's words.

nachsitzen vi sep irreg (Sch) ~ (müssen) to be kept in, to have detention; jdn ~ lassen to keep sb in, to give sb detention.

Nachsommer m Indian summer.

Nachsorge f (Med) after-care.

nachspähen vi sep jdm ~ to watch sb closely.

Nachspann m -s, -e credits pl.

Nachspeise f dessert, sweet (Brit). als ~ for dessert.

Nachspiel nt (Theat) epilogue; (Mus) closing section, postlude (form); (fig) sequel. das geht nicht ohne ~ ab that won't be without its consequences; das wird noch ein unangenehmes ~ haben that will have unpleasant consequences; ein gerichtliches ~ haben to have legal repercussions.

nachspielen sep 1 vt to play. 2 vi (Sport) to play extra time; (wegen Verletzungen) to play injury time. der Schiedsrichter ließ ~ the referee allowed extra time/injury time.

nachspionieren* vi sep (inf) jdm ~ to spy on sb.

nachsprechen sep irreg 1 vt to repeat. jdm etw ~ to repeat sth after sb. 2 vi wir mußten ihm ~ we had to repeat what he said.

nachspülen vti sep to rinse. ein Bier zum N~ (inf) a beer to wash it down.

nachspüren vi sep +dat to track or hunt down; einem Tier to track; einer Fährte to follow; einem Verbrechen, Fehler to go or look into.

nächst prep +dat (geh) (örtlich) next to, beside; (außer) apart or aside from.

nächstbeste adj attr der/die/das ~ ... the first ... I/you etc see; die ~ Frau/der ~ Zug/Job the first woman/train/job that comes along.

nachstehen vi sep irreg (a) (Gram) to come after. im Französischen steht das Adjektiv meist nach in French the adjective usually follows the noun.
(b) jdm ~ to take second place to sb; keinem ~ to be second to none (in +dat in); jdm in nichts (dat) ~ to be sb's equal in every way; jdm an Intelligenz (dat) nicht ~ to be every bit as intelligent as sb.

nachstehend adj attr Bemerkung, Ausführungen following; (Gram) postpositive (form). im ~en below, in the following; im ~en der Kläger genannt here(in)after referred to as the plaintiff; ~es müssen Sie beachten you must take note of the following; das ~e Adjektiv the adjective which follows the noun.

nachsteigen vi sep irreg aux sein jdm ~ (lit) to climb up after sb; (fig inf) to run after or chase sb.

nachstellen sep 1 vt (a) (Gram) im Französischen wird das Adjektiv (dem Substantiv) nachgestellt in French the adjective is put after the noun. (b) (Tech) (neu einstellen) to adjust; (zurückstellen) to put back. 2 vi jdm ~ to follow sb; (aufdringlich umwerben) to pester sb; einem Tier ~ to hunt an animal.

Nachstellung f (a) (Gram) postposition (form). (b) (Tech) adjustment; (Zurückstellung) putting back. (c) usu pl (old) (Verfolgung) pursuit no pl; (Aufdringlichkeit) pestering no pl; (Versuchung) temptation, snare.

Nächstenliebe f brotherly love; (Barmherzigkeit) compassion. ~ üben to love one's neighbour as oneself; siehe Mantel.

nächstens adv (a) (das nächste Mal) (the) next time; (bald einmal) some time soon, before long. (b) (am Ende) next.

nächste(r, s) adj superl of nah(e) (a) (nächstgelegen) nearest. der ~ Nachbar/das ~ Telefon the nearest neighbour/telephone; ist dies der ~ Weg zum Bahnhof? is this the shortest or quickest way to the station?; in ~r Nähe/Entfernung in the immediate vicinity/not far away; aus ~r Entfernung/Nähe from close by; sehen, betrachten at close quarters; schießen at close range; in ~r/aus der ~n Umgebung in/from the immediate vicinity or neighbourhood.

(b) (*unmittelbar folgend*) next. im ~n Haus in the next house, next door.

(c) (*zeitlich*) next. ~s Mal next time; bis zum ~n Mal! till the next time!, see you (some time)!; Dienstag ~r Woche Tuesday next week; Ende ~en Monats at the end of next month; am ~en Morgen/Tag(e) (the) next morning/day; ~r Tage, in den ~n Tagen in the next few days; bei ~er or bei der ~n Gelegenheit at the earliest opportunity; in ~r Zukunft in the near future; in den ~n Jahren in the next few years; in ~r Zeit some time soon.

(d) *Angehörige, Freunde etc* closest. die ~n Verwandten the immediate family; der ~ Angehörige the next of kin.

(e) (*in Adverbialkonstruktionen*) am ~n closest; (*räumlich auch*) nearest; fürs ~ for the time being.

Nächste(r) *mf decl as adj* (a) next one. der n~e, bitte next please, first please (*US, Scot*). (b) (*Mitmensch*) neighbour (*fig*). jeder ist sich selbst der ~ (*Prov*) it's every man for himself; du sollst deinen ~n lieben wie dich selbst (*Bibl*) (thou shalt) love thy neighbour as thyself.

Nächste(s) *nt decl as adj* das ~ the next thing; (*das erste*) the first thing; als ~s next/first; diese Vase war das ~ und Beste, was er auftreiben konnte this vase was the best he could dig up; das ~ wäre, ... the next/first thing or step would be ...

nächst-: ~folgend *adj attr* next; ~gelegen *adj attr* nearest; ~hin *adv* (*Sw*) *siehe* demnächst; ~höher *adj attr* one higher; ~jährig *adj attr* next year's; das ~jährige Jubiläum next year's anniversary; ~liegend *adj attr* (lit) nearest; (fig) most obvious; das N~liegende the most obvious thing (to do); ~möglich *adj attr* next possible.

nachstreben *vi sep* jdm/einer Sache ~ to emulate sb/to strive after sth.

nachstürzen *vi sep aux sein* (*Geröll*) to cave in. jdm ~ (*fig*) to dash or rush after sb.

nachsuchen *vi sep* (a) to look. such mal nach, ob ... (have a) look and see if ... (b) (*form: beantragen*) um etw ~ to request sth (*bei jdm* of sb), to apply for sth (*bei jdm* to sb).

Nachsuchung *f* (*form*) (*um for*) application, request.

Nacht *f* -, ⁻e (*lit, fig*) night. es wird/ist/war ~ it's getting/it is/was dark; als die ~ hereinbrach at nightfall, as night fell; in der or bei ~ at night; in der ~ vom 12. zum 13. April during the night of April 12th to 13th; in der ~ auf Dienstag during Monday night; diese ~ tonight; des ~s (*geh*) at night; spät in der ~ late in the or at night; in tiefster ~ at dead of night; bis tief in die ~ or bis in die späte ~ arbeiten to work late or far into the night; vor der ~ (*S Ger*) before evening; über ~ (*lit, fig*) overnight; über ~ bleiben to stay the night; zu(r) ~ essen (*S Ger, Aus*) to have supper; sich (*dat*) die ~ um die Ohren schlagen (*inf*) to make a night of it; die ~ zum Tage machen to turn night into day; eines ~s one night; letzte or vergangene ~ last night; ganze ⁻e for nights (on end); gute ~! good night!; na, dann gute ~! (*inf*) what a prospect!, what an outlook!; gute ~, schönes Leben! (*inf*) farewell, sweet life!; bei ~ und Nebel (*inf*) at dead of night; es wurde mir ~ vor den Augen everything went black; die ~ des Wahnsinns/der Barbarei/des Krieges (*liter*) the darkness of insanity/barbarism/war (*liter*); es wurde ~ über Deutschland (*liter*) the sun went down on Germany (*liter*).

nacht *adv* heute ~ tonight; (*letzte* ~) last night; Dienstag ~ (on) Tuesday night; 12 Uhr ~ (*Aus*) midnight.

nachtanken *sep* 1 *vi* to get some more (petrol *or* gas *US*). 2 *vt* fünf Liter ~ to put in another five litres.

Nacht- *in cpds* night; ~arbeit *f* night-work; ~asyl *nt* night shelter; ~ausgabe *f* late final (edition); ~blindheit *f* night blindness; ~dienst *m* night duty; ~dienst haben to be on night duty *or* nights.

Nachteil *m* -(e)s, -e disadvantage; (*Schaden auch*) detriment. ~e von *or* durch etw haben to lose by sth; jdm ~e bringen to bring sb disadvantages, to be disadvantageous to sb; im ~ sein, sich im ~ befinden to be at a disadvantage (*jdm gegenüber* with sb); daraus entstanden *or* erwuchsen ihm ~e this brought its disadvantages for him; der ~, allein zu leben the disadvantage of living alone; er hat sich zu seinem ~ verändert he has changed for the worse; das soll nicht Ihr ~ sein you won't lose by it; zu jds ~ to sb's disadvantage/detriment.

nachteilig *adj* (*ungünstig*) disadvantageous; (*schädlich*) detrimental. es ist nichts N~es über ihn bekannt nothing unfavourable is known about him; er hat sich sehr ~ über mich geäußert he spoke very unfavourably about me; die Pille wirkt bei manchen Frauen sehr ~ the pill has an adverse *or* a detrimental effect on some women; jdn ~ behandeln to treat sb unfavourably.

nächtelang *adv* night after night, for nights (on end).

nachten *vi impers* (*Sw, poet*) es nachtet it's growing dark, darkness *or* night is falling.

Nacht-: ~essen *nt* (*S Ger, Aus*) supper; ~eule *f* (*fig inf*) night owl; wie eine ~eule aussehen (*inf*) to look like an old hag; ~falter *m* moth; ~flug *m* night flight; ~frost *m* night frost; ~gebet *nt* evening prayer; sein/das ~gebet sprechen to say one's bedtime prayers; ~geschirr *nt* (*old, hum*) chamber pot; ~gespenst *nt* ghost (*that walks at night*); ~gewand *nt* (*geh*) nightrobe; ~gleiche *f* *siehe* Tagundnachtgleiche; ~hemd *nt* (*Damen*~) nightie, nightdress; (*Herren*~) nightshirt; ~himmel *m* night sky, sky at night.

Nachtigall *f* -, -en nightingale. ~, ick hör' dir trapsen (*hum dial*) I see it all now, now I see what you're/he's *etc* after.

nächtigen *vi* (*geh*) to spend the night.

Nachtisch *m* dessert, sweet (*Brit*); (*zu Hause auch*) pudding.

Nacht-: ~kästchen *nt* (*S Ger, Aus*) *siehe* ~tisch; ~klub *m* night club; ~lager *nt* (*Unterkunft*) place for the night; (*Mil auch*) bivouac; sein ~lager aufschlagen to settle *or* bed down for the night; (*Mil*) to bivouac; ~leben *nt* night life.

nächtlich *adj attr* (*jede Nacht*) nightly; (*in der Nacht*) night. die ~e Stadt the town at night; zu ~er Stunde at a late hour; ~e Ruhestörung (*Jur*) breach of the peace during the night.

nächtlicherweile *adv* (*rare*) by night.

Nacht-: ~lokal *nt* night club *or* spot; ~luft *f* night air; ~mahl *nt* (*Aus*) supper; n~mahlen *vi insep* (*Aus*) to have supper; ~mahr *m* -(e)s, -e (*old, liter*) nightmare; ~mensch *m* night person; ~mütze *f* nightcap (*lit*).

nachtönen *vi sep* to resound.

Nacht-: ~portier *m* night porter; ~programm *nt* late-night programme; ~quartier *nt* ein ~quartier somewhere for the night, a place to sleep; sein ~quartier aufschlagen to bed down (for the night).

Nachtrag *m* -(e)s, Nachträge postscript; (*zu einem Buch*) supplement.

nachtragen *vt sep irreg* (a) (*hinterhertragen*) jdm etw ~ (lit) to go after sb with sth, to take sth after sb; (fig) to hold sth against sb, to bear sb a grudge for sth. (b) (*hinzufügen*) to add; ~ Summe to enter up.

nachtragend, nachträgerisch (*rare*) *adj* unforgiving.

nachträglich *adj* (*zusätzlich*) additional; (*später*) later; (*verspätet*) belated; (*nach dem Tod*) posthumous.

Nachtrags- *in cpds* supplementary.

nachtrauern *vi sep* +dat to mourn.

Nachtruhe *f* night's rest *or* sleep; (*in Anstalten*) lights-out.

nachts *adv* at night. dienstags ~ (on) Tuesday nights.

Nacht-: ~schatten *m*, *no pl* (*Bot*) nightshade; ~schattengewächs *nt* (*Bot*) solanum (*spec*); (*fig inf*) night bird; ~schicht *f* night shift; ~schicht haben to be on night shift *or* nights; n~schlafend *adj*: bei *or* zu n~schlafender Zeit *or* Stunde in the middle of the night; ~schwärmer *m* (*Zool*) moth; (*fig hum*) night owl; ~schwester *f* night nurse; ~speicherofen *m* storage heater; ~strom *m* off-peak electricity; ~stuhl *m* (*old*) commode.

nachtsüber *adv* by night.

Nacht-: ~tarif *m* (*Verkehrsmittel*) night fares pl; (*Strom etc*) off-peak rate; ~tier *nt* nocturnal animal; ~tisch *m* bedside table; ~tischlampe, ~tischleuchte *f* bedside lamp; ~topf *m* chamber pot.

nachtun *vt sep irreg* es jdm ~ to copy or emulate sb.

Nacht-: ~vogel *m* nocturnal *or* night bird; ~vorstellung *f* late-night performance; ~wache *f* night-watch; (*im Krankenhaus*) night duty; bei einem Kranken ~wache halten to sit with a patient through the night; ~wache haben to be on night duty *or* on nights; ~wächter *m* (*Hist*) (night) watch; (*Betrieben etc*) night watchman; (*inf*) dope (*inf*); n~wandeln* *vi insep aux sein or haben* to sleepwalk, to walk in one's sleep; ~wanderung *f* night ramble *or* walk; ~wandler(in *f*) *m* -s, - sleepwalker; mit n~wandlerischer Sicherheit with instinctive assurance; ~zeit *f* night-time; ~zeug *nt* night things pl; ~zug *m* night train; ~zuschlag *m* night supplement.

Nachuntersuchung *f* (*weitere Untersuchung*) further examination; (*spätere Untersuchung*) check-up.

Nachurlaub *m* extra holiday.

Nachverbrennung *f* (*Tech*) after-burning *no pl*.

nachverlangen * *vt sep* 20 DM ~ to demand an additional DM 20.

nachversichern * *vt sep* Sie müssen neuerworbene Wertgegenstände ~ you must revise your insurance to cover newly-acquired valuables.

nachvollziehbar *adj* comprehensible.

nachvollziehen * *vt sep irreg* to understand, to comprehend.

nachwachsen *vi sep irreg aux sein* to grow again. die neue Generation, die jetzt nachwächst the young generation who are now taking their place in society.

Nachwahl *f* (*Pol*) ≈ by-election.

Nachwehen *pl* after-pains pl; (*fig*) painful aftermath *sing*.

nachweinen *vi sep* +dat to mourn. dieser Sache weine ich keine Träne nach *or* nicht nach I won't shed any tears over that.

Nachweis *m* -es, -e (*Beweis*) proof (*gen, für, über* +acc of); (*Zeugnis*) certificate; (*Zahlungs*~) proof of payment (*über* +acc of). als *or* zum ~ as proof; den ~ für etw erbringen *or* führen *or* liefern to furnish proof of sth; der ~ seiner Bedürftigkeit ist ihm geglückt he succeeded in proving his need.

-nachweis *m in cpds* (*Vermittlungsstelle*) agency; (*Aufstellung*) directory, list.

nachweisbar *adj* (*beweisbar*) provable; *Fehler, Irrtum* demonstrable; (*Tech*) detectable. dem Angeklagten ist keinerlei Schuld ~ it cannot be proved that the accused is in any way guilty.

nachweisen *vt sep irreg* (a) (*beweisen, aufzeigen*) to prove; *Staatsangehörigkeit, Identität auch* to establish proof of; (*Tech*) to detect. die Polizei konnte ihm nichts ~ the police could not prove anything against him; dem Angeklagten konnte seine Schuld nicht nachgewiesen werden the accused's guilt could not be proved. (b) (*vermitteln*) jdm etw ~ to arrange sth for sb, to fix sb up with sth.

nachweislich *adj* provable; *Fehler, Irrtum* demonstrable. er war ~ in London it can be proved that he was in London.

Nachwelt *f* die ~ posterity.

nachwerfen *vt sep irreg* jdm etw ~ (lit) to throw sth after *or* at sb; das ist nachgeworfen (*inf*) that's dirt cheap (*inf*) *or* a gift.

nachwiegen *sep irreg* 1 *vt* to weigh again. 2 *vi* to check the weight.

nachwinken *vi sep* jdm ~ to wave (goodbye) to sb.

Nachwinter *m* late winter.

nachwinterlich *adj* late-winter *attr*.

nachwirken *vi sep* to continue to have an effect.

Nachwirkung f after-effect; (fig) consequence.

Nachwort nt epilogue.

Nachwuchs m (a) (fig: junge Kräfte) young people pl (in the profession/sport etc). **es mangelt an** ~ there's a lack of young blood; **der wissenschaftliche** ~ the new generation of academics, the up-and-coming academics.
(b) (hum: Nachkommen) offspring pl.

Nachwuchs-: ~**autor** m up-and-coming young author; ~**kraft** f junior member of the staff; ~**sorgen** pl recruitment problems pl; ~**spieler** m (Sport) junior.

nachzahlen vti sep to pay extra; (später zahlen) to pay later. **20 Pfennig** ~ to pay 20 pfennigs extra.

nachzählen vti sep to check.

Nachzahlung f (nachträglich) back-payment; (zusätzlich) additional payment.

nachzeichnen vt sep siehe **nachziehen** 1 (b).

Nachzeitigkeit f (Gram) posteriority.

nachziehen sep irreg 1 vt (a) (hinterherziehen) etw ~ to pull or drag sth behind one; **das rechte Bein** ~ to drag one's right leg.
(b) Linie, Umriß to go over; Lippen to paint over or in; Augenbrauen to pencil over or in.
(c) Schraube, Seil to tighten (up).
2 vi (a) aux sein +dat (folgen) to follow.
(b) (Schach etc) to make the next move; (inf: gleichtun) to follow suit.

nachzotteln vi sep aux sein (inf) to lag behind.

Nachzug m (Rail) relief train.

Nachzügler ['na:xtsy:klɐ] m -s, - latecomer, late arrival (auch fig).

Nackedei m -(e)s, -e or -s (hum inf) naked body or person; (Kind) little bare monkey (hum inf).

Nacken m -s, - (nape of the) neck. **den** ~ **beugen** (fig) to submit; **jdm den** ~ **beugen** to bend sb to one's will; **jdm den** ~ **steifen** to encourage sb, to back sb up; **jdn im** ~ **haben** (inf) to have sb after one or on one's tail; **jdm im** ~ **sitzen** (inf) to breathe down sb's neck; **ihm sitzt die Furcht/der Geiz im** ~ he's frightened out of his wits (inf)/he's a miserly so-and-so (inf); **den** ~ **steif halten** (inf) to stand one's ground, to stand fast; **er hat einen starren/störrischen/unbeugsamen** ~ he's an obstinate/hardheaded/unbending character.

nackend adj (inf) Mensch naked.

Nacken-: ~**haar** nt hair at the nape of the neck; ~**hebel** m (Sport) nelson; ~**rolle** f bolster; ~**schlag** m rabbit-punch; (fig) hard knock; ~**schutz** m neck guard; ~**starre** f stiffness of the neck; ~**starre kriegen** to get a stiff neck; ~**stütze** f (Aut) headrest, head restraint.

nackig, nackert (Aus) adj (inf) bare; Mensch auch starkers pred (inf).

nackt adj (a) Mensch naked, nude (esp Art); Arm, Kinn, Haut etc bare; neugeborenes Tier naked. ~ **herumlaufen** to run around naked or in the nude; ~ **baden/schlafen** to bathe/sleep in the nude; **er stand ganz** ~ **da** he was standing there stark naked or absolutely starkers (inf).
(b) (unbewachsen, unbedeckt) Boden, Erde, Wand bare; Schwert naked.
(c) (fig) (unverblümt) naked; Wahrheit auch plain; Wirklichkeit stark; Tatsachen, Zahlen bare. **mit** ~**en Worten** without mincing one's words; **die** ~**e Armut** naked or sheer poverty; **das** ~**e Leben retten** to escape with one's bare life.

Nackt-: ~**baden** nt nude bathing, swimming in the nude; ~**badestrand** m nudist beach.

Nackte f decl as adj nude.

Nackt-: ~**frosch** m (hum) bare monkey (hum); ~**heit** f nakedness; (von Mensch auch) nudity; (Kahlheit) bareness; (von Landschaft auch) starkness; ~**kultur** f nudism, naturism; ~**modell** nt nude model; ~**schnecke** f slug; ~**tänzerin** f nude dancer.

Nadel f -, -n (a) needle; (Grammophon~, Gravier~, Radier~ auch) stylus; (Steck~) pin; (Häkel~) hook. **mit** ~ **und Faden umgehen können** to be able to wield a needle and thread; **er sitzt wie auf** ~**n** (inf) he's like a cat on hot bricks (inf).
(b) (Haar~, Hut~, Krawatten~) pin; (Brosche) brooch.
(c) (Blatt~, Eis~, Kristall~) needle.

Nadel-: ~**abweichung** f magnetic deviation or declination; ~**arbeit** f needlework no pl; **eine** ~**arbeit** a piece of needlework; ~**baum** m conifer; ~**brief** m packet of needles; ~**büchse** f pin tin; ~**einfädler** m -s, - needle-threader; n~**förmig** adj needlelike, needle-shaped; ~**geld** nt (old) dowry; ~**hölzer** pl conifers pl; ~**kissen** nt pin-cushion; ~**kopf** m pin-head.

nadeln vi (Baum) to shed (its needles).

Nadel-: ~**öhr** nt eye of a needle; siehe **Kamel**; ~**spitze** f point or tip (of a needle); (Handarbeit) needle-point (lace); ~**stärke** f size of needle; ~**stich** m prick; (beim Nähen, Med) stitch; **jdm** ~**stiche versetzen** (fig) to needle sb; **eine Politik der** ~**stiche** a policy of pinpricks; ~**streifen** pl pinstripes pl; ~**streifenanzug** m pinstripe(d) suit; ~**wald** m coniferous forest.

Nadir m -s, no pl nadir.

Nagel m -s, - nail (auch Anat); (Zwecke) tack; (aus Holz) peg; (an Schuhen) hobnail, stud; (Med) pin. **sich** (dat) **etw unter den** ~ **reißen** or **ritzen** (inf) to pinch sth (inf); **etw an den** ~ **hängen** (fig) to chuck sth in (inf); **den** ~ **auf den Kopf treffen** (fig) to hit the nail on the head; ~ **mit Köpfen machen** (inf) to do the job or thing properly; siehe **Sarg**, **brennen**.

Nagel-: ~**bett** nt (Anat) bed of the nail; (von Fakir) bed of nails; ~**bohrer** m gimlet; ~**bürste** f nailbrush; ~**feile** f nailfile; n~**fest** adj siehe **niet-** und **n~fest**; ~**haut** f cuticle; ~**hautentferner** m -s, - cuticle-remover; ~**kopf** m head (of a/the nail); ~**lack** m nail varnish or polish; ~**lackentferner** m nail varnish remover.

nageln vt to nail (an +acc, auf +acc (on)to; Teppich auch to tack; (Med) to pin; (mit Nägeln versehen) to hobnail or stud.

Nagel-: n~**neu** adj (inf) brand new; ~**pflege** f nail care; ~**pflege machen** to give oneself a manicure; ~**probe** f (fig) acid test; **morgen kommt es zur** ~**probe** tomorrow will be the acid test; ~**reiniger** m -s, - nail-cleaner; ~**schere** f (pair of) nail-scissors pl; ~**schuh** m hobnailed boot; (Bergstiefel) climbing boot; ~**zange** f nail clippers pl; (Tech) (pair of) pincers pl.

nagen 1 vi (lit, fig) to gnaw (an +dat at); (knabbern) to nibble (an +dat at); (Rost, Wasser) to eat (an +dat into). **an einem Knochen** ~ to gnaw (on or at) a bone; **eine schleichende Krankheit nagt an seiner Gesundheit** some insidious disease is eroding his health.
2 vt to gnaw. **wir haben nichts zu** ~ **noch zu beißen** (old) we've eaten our last crust.

nagend adj Hunger gnawing; Zweifel, Gewissen nagging.

Nager m -s, -, **Nagetier** nt rodent.

nah adj, adv siehe **nahe(e)** 1, 2.

Nah|aufnahme f (Phot) close-up.

Näharbeit f sewing no pl. **eine** ~ a piece of sewing.

nah(e) 1 adj, comp **näher**, superl **nächste(r, s)** (a) (örtlich) near pred, close pred, nearby. **der N~e Osten** the Middle East; **von** ~**em** from close to, at close quarters; **jdm** ~ **sein** to be near (to) sb; **in seinen letzten Stunden war sie ihm** ~ (liter) during his last hours she was at or by his side; **Gott ist uns** ~ (liter) God is nigh (liter); **Rettung/Hilfe ist nah** help is at hand.
(b) (zeitlich) near pred, approaching, nigh (liter) pred. **die** ~**e Zukunft** the near future.
(c) (eng) Freund, Beziehung etc close.
2 adv, comp **näher**, superl **am nächsten** (a) (örtlich) near, close. ~ **an** near or close to; ~**e bei** close to or by, near; ~ **beieinander** close together; ~ **liegend** nearby; ~ **vor** right in front of; **von** ~ **und fern** from near and far; **jdm zu** ~**(e) treten** (fig) to offend sb; **jdm/einer Sache zu** ~**(e) kommen** to get too close to sb/sth; siehe **daran**.
(b) (zeitlich) **mein Prüfungstermin rückt allmählich** ~ my examination is getting close; **Weihnachten steht** ~ **bevor** Christmas is just (a)round the corner or is almost upon us; ~ **bevorstehend** approaching; **sie ist** ~ **an (die) Achtzig** she's almost or nearing eighty.
(c) (eng) closely. **mit jdm** ~ **befreundet/verwandt sein** to be a close friend/near relative of sb's, to be closely related to sb.
3 prep +dat near (to), close to. **der Ohnmacht/dem Wahnsinn** etc ~**e sein** to be on the verge of fainting/madness.

Nähe f -, no pl (a) (örtlich) (Nahesein) nearness, closeness, proximity; (Umgebung, Nachbarschaft) vicinity, neighbourhood. **in meiner** ~/**der** ~ **des Gebäudes** near me/the building, in the vicinity of the building; **aus der** ~ from close to, at close quarters. (b) (zeitlich) closeness.

nahebei adv nearby, close to or by.

nahebringen vt sep irreg +dat (fig) **jdm etw** ~ to bring sth home to sb, to impress sth on sb; **jdn jdm** ~ to bring sb close to sb.

nahegehen vi sep irreg aux sein +dat (fig) to upset.

Nah|einstellung f (Film) close-up (shot).

nahekommen vi sep irreg aux sein +dat (fig) **jdm** ~ (vertraut werden) to get on close terms with sb, to get close to sb; **jdm/einer Sache** ~ (fast gleichen) to come close or near to sb/sth; **sich** or **einander** ~ to become close; **das kommt der Wahrheit schon näher** now that is getting nearer the truth.

nahelegen vt sep (fig) **jdm etw** ~ to suggest sth to sb; **jdm** ~, **etw zu tun** to advise sb to do sth; **er legte es mir nahe, von mir aus zu kündigen** he put it to me that I should resign.

naheliegen vi sep irreg (fig: Idee, Frage, Lösung) to suggest itself. **die Vermutung/die Annahme/der Verdacht liegt nahe, daß ...** it seems reasonable to suppose/assume/suspect that ...; **der Gedanke lag nahe, ihn zum Teilhaber zu machen** the idea of making him a partner seemed to suggest itself.

naheliegend adj Gedanke, Lösung which suggests itself; Verdacht, Vermutung natural. **das N~e wäre ...** the obvious thing to do would be ...; **aus** ~**en Gründen** for obvious reasons.

nahen vi aux sein (liter) to approach (jdm/einer Sache sb/sth), to draw near or nigh (liter) (jdm/einer Sache sb/sth).

nähen 1 vt to sew; (mit Stichen befestigen auch) to stitch; Kleid to make; Wunde, Verletzten to stitch (up), to suture (spec). **mit der Maschine/mit der** or **von Hand genäht** machine-/hand-sewn, sewn by machine/hand; **sich** (dat) **die Finger wund** ~ to sew one's fingers to the bone; siehe **doppelt**.
2 vi to sew.
3 vr dieser Stoff näht sich sehr gut/schlecht this material is very easy/difficult to sew.

näher comp of **nah(e)** 1 adj (a) (örtlich) closer, nearer. **jdm/einer Sache** ~ closer to or nearer (to) sb/sth; **dieser Weg ist** ~ this road is shorter or quicker; **die** ~**e Umgebung** the immediate vicinity.
(b) (zeitlich) closer, sooner pred. **der Tod ist ihm** ~, **als er glaubt** he is nearer to death than he thinks.
(c) (genauer) Auskünfte, Einzelheiten further attr, more detailed or precise.
(d) (enger) Verwandter, Bekannter, Beziehungen closer. **die** ~**e Verwandtschaft** the immediate family.
2 adv (a) (örtlich, zeitlich) closer, nearer. ~ **kommen** or **rücken** to come or draw nearer, to approach; **bitte treten Sie** ~ just step up!; (Beamter, Arzt) please come over here.
(b) (genauer) more closely; besprechen, erklären, ausführen in more detail. **ich habe mir das Bild** ~ **angesehen** I had a closer look at the picture; **sich mit etw** ~ **befassen** or **beschäftigen** to go into sth; **jdn/etw** ~ **kennenlernen** to get to know sb/sth better; **ich kenne ihn nicht** ~ I don't know him well; **der Sache** (dat) ~ **kommen** to be nearer the mark.

näherbringen vt sep irreg +dat jdm etw ~ to give sb an understanding of sth.

Näherei f (no pl: das Nähen) sewing; (Näharbeit) piece of sewing.

Nähere(s) nt decl as adj details pl; (über Stellenangebot etc) further details pl. ich kann mich des N~n nicht entsinnen (geh) I can't remember the (precise) details.

Näherin f seamstress.

näherkommen vi sep irreg aux sein (fig) jdm ~ to get closer to sb; sie sind sich or einander nähergekommen they've been closer.

näherliegen vi sep irreg (fig) to be more obvious; (Verdacht auch) to be more natural. ich denke, daß diese Entscheidung näherliegt I think this is the more obvious decision; das N~de the more obvious course.

nähern 1 vr sich (jdm/einer Sache) ~ to approach (sb/sth), to get closer or draw nearer (to sb/sth); die Politiker näherten sich und schüttelten sich die Hände the politicians went up to each other and shook hands; der Abend näherte sich seinem Ende the evening was drawing to a close.
2 vt to bring or draw closer.

näherstehen vi sep irreg +dat (fig) to be closer to.

nähertreten vi sep irreg aux sein +dat (fig) to get closer to. ich werde Ihrem Vorschlag ~ (form) I shall give full consideration to your proposal.

Näherung f (Math) approximation.

Näherungswert m (Math) approximate value.

nahestehen vi sep irreg +dat (fig) to be close to; (Pol) to sympathize with. sich ~ (Menschen, Ideen) to be close; wir stehen uns (geistig) sehr nahe our views are very close; dem Präsidenten ~de Quellen sources close to the president; eine den Konservativen ~de Zeitung a paper with Conservative sympathies or leanings.

nahezu adv nearly, almost, virtually. das ist ja ~ Wucher that's little short of profiteering.

Nähfaden m, **Nähgarn** nt (sewing) cotton or thread.

Nahkampf m (Mil) close combat, hand-to-hand fighting. beim ~ sein (fig sl) to be in a clinch (inf).

Nahkampfmittel, **Nahkampfwaffen** pl close- or short-range weapons pl.

Näh-: ~kästchen nt, ~kasten m work-box, sewing box; aus dem ~kästchen plaudern (inf) to give away private details; ~korb m work-basket, sewing basket.

nahm pret of nehmen.

Näh-: ~maschine f sewing machine; ~nadel f needle.

Nahost m in/aus ~ in/from the Middle East.

nah|östlich adj attr Middle East(ern).

Nähr-: ~bier nt high-extract beer, ≈ sweet stout; ~boden m (lit) fertile soil; (für Bakterien) culture medium; (fig) breeding-ground; ein guter ~boden (lit) fertile or good soil or land; diese Ideen fanden keinen guten ~boden these ideas didn't take root; ~brühe f siehe ~lösung; ~creme f skin food.

nähren 1 vt to feed; (fig) (steigern) to increase, to feed; Hoffnungen to build up; (haben) to nurse; Hoffnungen to nurture, to nurse. er sieht gut genährt aus he looks well-fed; das Handwerk nährt seinen Mann there's a good living to be made as a craftsman; er nährt den süßen Traum, berühmt zu werden he has fond hopes of becoming famous.
2 vr to feed oneself; (Tiere) to feed. sich von or mit etw ~ to live on sth; siehe bleiben.
3 vi to be nourishing.

nahrhaft adj Kost nourishing, nutritious; Boden fertile, rich; (fig) Beruf profitable, lucrative; Literatur edifying. ein ~es Essen a square meal.

Nähr-: ~kraft f nutritional value; ~lösung f nutrient solution; ~mittel pl cereal products pl; ~präparat nt nutrient preparation; ~stand m (Philos) farmers pl; ~stoff m nutrient, nutriment.

Nahrung f, no pl food. flüssige/feste ~ liquids/solids pl; geistige ~ intellectual stimulation; sie verweigerten jegliche ~ they refused all nourishment; einer Sache (dat) (neue) ~ geben to help to nourish or feed sth; dadurch fand or erhielt die ganze Sache neue ~ that just added fuel to the fire; dem Feuer ~ geben (liter) to build up the fire.

Nahrungs-: ~aufnahme f eating, ingestion (of food) (form); die ~aufnahme verweigern to refuse food or sustenance; ~mangel m food shortage.

Nahrungsmittel nt food(stuff).

Nahrungsmittel-: ~chemie f food chemistry; ~chemiker m food chemist; ~vergiftung f food poisoning.

Nahrungs-: ~sorgen pl worries about food pl; ~suche f search for food; ~verweigerung f refusal of food, refusal to eat; durch ~verweigerung by refusing food or to eat.

Nährwert m nutritional value. hat das einen praktischen ~? (inf) does that have any practical value?; das hat doch keinen (praktischen) ~ (inf) it's pretty pointless.

Nähseide f sewing-silk, silk thread.

Naht f -, ~e seam; (Tech auch) join; (Med) stitches pl, suture (spec); (Anat) suture. aus allen ~en platzen to be bursting at the seams.

nahtlos adj (lit) Teil, Anzug seamless; (fig) Übergang smooth, imperceptible. Vorlesung und Diskussion gingen ~ ineinander über there was a smooth transition from the lecture to the discussion.

Nahtstelle f (a) (lit) siehe Naht. (b) (fig) link.

Nahverkehr m local traffic. der öffentliche ~ local public transport; im ~ on local runs or journeys.

Nahverkehrs-: ~mittel pl means of local transport pl; ~zug m local train.

nahverwandt adj attr closely-related. N~e close relatives.

Nähzeug nt sewing kit, sewing things pl.

Nahziel nt immediate aim or objective.

naiv adj naive; (ungekünstelt auch) ingenuous. die N~e (Theat) the Ingénue.

Naivität [naivi'tɛːt] f naivety.

Naivling m (inf) simpleton. wie kann man bloß so ein ~ sein! how can anyone be so naive!

Najade f naiad.

Name m -ns, -n, **Namen** m -s, - (Benennung) name; (fig: Ruf) name, reputation. ein angenommener ~ an assumed name; (von Autoren etc) a pen name, a nom de plume, a pseudonym; der volle ~ his/her/their full name; mit ~n, des ~ns (geh) by the name of, called; dem ~n nach by name; ich kenne das Stück nur dem ~n nach I've heard of the play but that's all; dem ~n nach müßte sie Jugoslawin sein judging by her name she must be Yugoslavian; er ist nur dem ~n nach König he is king in name or title only; auf jds ~n (acc) in sb's name; unter dem ~n under the name of; er war unter dem ~n Schmidt bekannt he was known under or by the name of Schmidt, he was known as Schmidt; er nannte seinen ~n he gave his name; Ihr ~, bitte? your or the name, please?; wie war doch gleich Ihr (werter) ~? what was the name?; dazu gebe ich meinen ~n nicht her I won't lend my name to that; der ~ tut nichts zur Sache his/my etc name's irrelevant; einen ~n haben (fig) to have a name; sich (dat) einen ~n machen to make a name for oneself; die Dinge or das Kind (inf) beim (rechten) ~n nennen to call a spade a spade, to face facts; im ~n (+gen) on or in (US) behalf of; im ~n des Volkes in the name of the people; im ~n des Gesetzes in the name of the law; in Gottes ~n! (inf) for heaven's sake (inf); den Tag in Gottes ~n beginnen to start the day with a prayer.

Namen-: ~forschung f study of names; ~gebung f siehe Namen(s)gebung; ~gedächtnis nt memory for names; ~kunde f science of names; ~liste f siehe Namen(s)liste.

namenlos 1 adj (a) nameless (auch fig), unnamed; Helfer anonymous. er will ~ bleiben he wishes to remain anonymous; die Millionen der ~n the nameless millions. (b) (geh: unsäglich) nameless, unspeakable, unutterable. **2** adv (geh: äußerst) unspeakably, unutterably.

Namen-: ~nennung f siehe Namen(s)nennung; ~register nt siehe Namen(s)register.

namens adv (mit Namen) by the name of, called, named. **2** prep+gen (form: im Auftrag) in the name of.

Namen(s)- in cpds name; ~änderung f change of name; ~gebung f naming; eine unglückliche ~gebung für eine Ware an unfortunate choice of name for a product; ~liste f list of names, name list; ~nennung f naming names; auf ~nennung wollen wir doch verzichten we don't need to name names; ~register nt list of names, name list; ~schild nt nameplate; ~tag m name day, Saint's day; ~verzeichnis nt list of names, name list; ~vetter m namesake; ~zeichen nt initials pl; ~zug m signature; (Monogramm) monogram.

namentlich 1 adj by name. wir bitten, von einer ~en Aufführung der Spender abzusehen we would request you to refrain from naming the donors; ~e Abstimmung roll call vote; ~er Aufruf roll call. **2** adv (e)specially, in particular, particularly.

Namen-: ~verzeichnis nt siehe Namen(s)verzeichnis; ~wechsel m change of name.

namhaft adj (a) (bekannt) famous, renowned. ~ machen (form) to identify. (b) (beträchtlich) considerable, substantial.

Namibia nt -s Namibia.

nämlich 1 adv (a) namely, to wit (Jur, hum); (geschrieben) viz. (b) (denn) es ging nicht schneller, wir haben ~ einen Umweg machen müssen we couldn't be any quicker, we had to make a detour you see. **2** adj der/die/das ~e (old) the same.

nannte pret of nennen.

nanu interj well I never. ~, wer ist das denn? hello (hello), who's this?

Napalm nt -s, no pl napalm.

Napalmbombe f napalm bomb.

Napf m -(e)s, ~e bowl.

Napfkuchen m ≈ ring-shaped poundcake.

Naphtha ['nafta] nt -s or f -, no pl naphtha.

Naphthalin [nafta'liːn] nt -s, no pl naphthalene.

napoleonisch adj Napoleonic.

Nappa(leder) nt -s, ~s napa leather.

Narbe f -, -n (a) (lit, fig) scar; (Pocken~) pock(mark). eine ~ hinterlassen to leave a scar; die ~ bleibt, auch wenn die Wunde heilt (Prov) deep down, I/you etc still bear the scars. (b) (Bot) stigma. (c) (Gras~) turf. (d) (Leder~) grain.

Narben m -s, - grain.

Narben-: ~bildung f scarring; ~gesicht nt scarred face; (als Name) scarface.

narbig adj scarred.

Narkose f -, -n an(a)esthesia. jdm eine ~ geben to put sb under an(a)esthetic; in der ~ liegen to be under an(a)esthetic; ohne ~ without an(a)esthetic; aus der ~ aufwachen to come out of the an(a)esthetic.

Narkose-: ~apparat m an(a)esthetic apparatus no indef art; ~arzt m an(a)esthetist; ~maske f an(a)esthetic mask.

Narkotikum nt -s, **Narkotika** (Med) narcotic.

narkotisch adj narcotic; Düfte overpowering. der süße Geruch wirkte ~ auf uns the sweet smell had a druglike effect on us.

narkotisieren* vt (lit, fig) to drug.

Narr m -en, -en fool; (Hof~ auch) jester. den ~en spielen to act or play the fool; ich bin ein ~, daß ich immer wieder ... I am a fool always to ...; die ~en werden nicht alle (Prov) there's one born every minute (inf); jdn zum ~en haben or halten to make a fool of sb; ein verliebter ~ somebody blinded by love; er ist ein

narren

verliebter ~ he is love's dupe *or* fool; dieser verliebte ~ this love-lorn fool; *siehe* fressen.

narren *vt* (*geh*) jdn ~ (*zum besten haben*) to make a fool of *or* fool sb; (*täuschen*) to dupe *or* fool sb.

Narren-: ~freiheit *f* sie hat bei ihm ~freiheit he gives her (a) free rein; n~haft *adj* foolish; ~hände *pl:* ~hände beschmieren Tisch und Wände (*Prov*) only fools go round defacing things; ~haus *nt* madhouse; du gehörst ins ~haus you need locking up *or* putting away; ~kappe *f* fool's *or* jester's cap; ~possen *pl* (*obs*) (tom)foolery *no pl;* ~possen treiben to fool about *or* around; n~sicher *adj* foolproof; ~streich *m* (*old*) prank; (*dumme Tat*) act of stupidity; ~tum *nt* stupidity; ~zepter *nt* jester's *or* fool's sceptre, bauble; das ~zepter führen to carry the fool's sceptre.

Narretei *f* folly.

Narrheit *f* (a) *no pl* folly, stupidity. (b) (*Streich*) prank; (*dumme Tat*) act of stupidity, stupid thing to do.

Närrin *f* fool.

närrisch *adj* foolish, silly; (*verrückt*) mad; (*inf: sehr*) madly. die ~en Tage Fasching and the period leading up to it; das ~e Treiben Fasching celebrations; sich wie ~ gebärden to act like a madman, to act crazy; ganz ~ auf jdn/etw sein (*inf*) to be crazy about *or* mad (keen) on sb/sth (*inf*).

Narziß *m* -sses, -sse (*liter*) Narcissus.

Narzisse *f* -, -n narcissus.

Narzißmus *m* narcissism.

Narzißt *m* -en, -en (*Psych*) narcissist.

narzißtisch *adj* narcissistic.

Nasa, NASA ['na:za] *f* - NASA.

Nasal *m* -s, -e nasal.

nasal *adj* nasal. ~er Ton nasal twang.

nasalieren* *vti* to nasalize.

Nasallaut *m* nasal (sound).

naschen 1 *vi* to eat sweet things; (*heimlich kosten*) to pinch a bit (*inf*). darf ich mal ~? can I try a bit?; an etw (*dat*) ~ to pinch a bit of sth; (*anknabbern*) to (have a) nibble at sth; er hat von allem nur genascht (*lit*) he only had a taste of everything; (*fig*) he just dabbled in everything; die Kinder haben den ganzen Tag nur genascht the children have been nibbling all day; mein Mann nascht gerne (*hum*) my husband likes a little tipple.

2 *vt* to nibble. sie nascht gern Süßigkeiten she has a sweet tooth; hast du was zum N~? have you got something for my sweet tooth?

Näschen ['nɛ:sçən] *nt dim of* Nase.

Nascher(in *f*), **Näscher (in** *f*) (*old*) *m* -s, - nibbler; (*der Süßes mag*) sweet-eater.

Nascherei *f* (a) *no pl* nibbling; (*von Süßigkeiten*) sweet-eating. (b) ~en *pl* (*Süßigkeiten*) sweets and biscuits *pl* (*Brit*), candy and cookies *pl* (*US*).

Nasch-: n~haft *adj* fond of sweet things; die Kinder sind so n~haft the children are always nibbling at things; sei nicht so n~haft you and your sweet tooth; ~haftigkeit *f* fondness for sweet things; ~katze *f* (*inf*) guzzler; ich bin halt so eine alte ~katze I've got such a sweet tooth; ~sucht *f* craving for sweet things; ~werk *nt, no pl* (*old*) dainties *pl,* sweetmeats *pl* (*old*).

Nase *f* -, -n (a) (*Organ, Sinn, fig*) nose. durch die ~ reden to talk through one's nose; mir blutet die ~, meine ~ blutet I've got a nosebleed, my nose is bleeding; jdm/sich die ~ putzen to wipe sb's/one's nose; sich (*dat*) die ~ putzen (*sich schnäuzen*) to blow one's nose; pro ~ (*hum*) per head; es liegt vor deiner ~ (*inf*) it's right in front of *or* right under your nose (*inf*); wir haben die Weinberge genau vor der ~ (*inf*) the vine slopes are right on our doorstep; (*immer*) der ~ nachgehen (*inf*) to follow one's nose; eine gute ~ für etw haben (*inf*) to have a good nose for sth; die richtige ~ für etw haben (*inf*) to have the nose for sth; faß dich an deine eigene ~! (*inf*) you can (*iro*) *or* can't talk!; jdm etw/die Würmer aus der ~ ziehen (*inf*) to drag sth/it all out of sb; jdm etw unter die ~ reiben (*inf*) to rub sb's nose *or* face in sth (*inf*); jdm auf der ~ herumtanzen (*inf*) to play sb up (*inf*); seine ~ gefällt mir nicht (*inf*) I don't like his face; es muß nicht immer nach deiner ~ gehen (*inf*) you can't always have things your way; ihm wurde ein Neuer vor die ~ gesetzt (*inf*) they put a new man over him; ich sah es ihm an der ~ an (*inf*) I could see it on *or* written all over his face (*inf*); sich (*dat*) die ~ begießen (*hum*) to wet one's whistle (*inf*); mit langer ~ abziehen (*inf*) to be disappointed; auf der ~ liegen (*inf*) (*krank sein*) to be laid up; (*hingefallen sein*) to be flat on one's face (*inf*); steck deine ~ ins Buch! (*inf*) get on with your book; auf die ~ fallen (*lit, fig*) *or* fliegen (*inf*) to fall flat on one's face; jdm etw vor der ~ wegschnappen (*inf*) just to beat sb to sth; die Katze hat dem Hund das Futter vor der ~ weggeschnappt the cat took the dog's food away right from under its nose; der Zug fuhr ihm vor der ~ weg (*inf*) he missed the train by inches *or* seconds; jdm die Tür vor der ~ zuschlagen (*inf*) to slam the door in sb's face; jdm eine (lange) ~ drehen *or* machen (*inf*) to cock a snook at sb, to thumb one's nose at sb; jdm etw unter die ~ halten to shove sth right under sb's nose (*inf*); jdn mit der ~ draufstoßen (*inf*) to point it out to sb; (*überdeutlich werden*) to make it more than obvious to sb; jdm eins auf die ~ geben (*lit*) to punch sb on the nose; (*fig*) to tell sb what's what, to put sb in his place; die ~ voll haben (*inf*) to be fed up (*inf*), to have had enough; die ~ von jdm/etw voll haben (*inf*) to be sick (to death) of sb/sth (*inf*), to be fed up to the back teeth with sb/sth (*inf*); es sticht ihm in der ~, das zu tun he's dying *or* itching to do it; der Diamantring sticht mir in der ~ I'm itching to have that diamond ring; jdn an der ~ herumführen (*als Täuschung*) to lead sb by the nose; (*als Scherz*) to pull sb's leg; jdm etw auf die ~ binden (*inf*) to tell sb all about sth; jdm auf die ~ binden, daß ... (*inf*) to tell sb that ...; das werde ich ihm gerade auf die ~ binden (*iro*) you think I'd tell him that!; er steckt seine ~ in alles (hinein) (*inf*) he pokes

Nationalpreis

his nose into everything; er sieht nicht weiter als seine ~ (*inf*) he can't see further than the end of his nose; *siehe* Mund, Wind, hoch.

(b) (*Mech*) handle, horn.

(c) (*Farbtropfen*) run.

(d) (*Halbinsel*) promontory, headland, naze; (*Fels*~) overhang.

nas(e)lang *adv:* alle ~ all the time, again and again.

näseln *vi* to talk *or* speak through one's nose.

näselnd *adj* nasal.

Nasen-: ~bär *m* coati; (*fig inf*) silly-billy (*inf*); ~bein *nt* nose bone, nasal bone; ~bluten *nt* a nosebleed/nosebleed; ich habe ~bluten my nose is bleeding, I have a nosebleed; ~flügel *m* side of the nose; seine ~flügel fingen an zu zittern his nose *or* nostrils began to twitch; ~höhle *f* nasal cavity; ~länge *f* (*fig*) mit einer *or* um eine ~länge gewinnen to win by a nose; jdm eine ~länge voraus sein to be a hairsbreadth ahead of sb; ~loch *nt* nostril; verliebte ~löcher machen (*hum*) to make eyes; ~ring *m* (nose) ring; ~rücken *m* bridge *or* ridge of the nose; ~scheidewand *f* nasal septum (*spec*); ~schleim *m* nasal mucus; ~schleimhaut *f* mucous membrane (of the nose); ~schmuck *m* nose ornament(s); ~spitze *f* tip of the/sb's nose; ich seh es dir an der ~spitze an I can tell by your face, I can see it written all over your face; ~spray *m or nt* nasal *or* nose spray; ~stüber *m* -s, - bump on the nose; jdm einen ~stüber versetzen (*lit*) to bop sb on the nose; (*fig*) to tick *or* tell sb off; ~tropfen *pl* nose drops *pl;* ~wurzel *f* bridge of the nose.

Nase-: ~rümpfen *nt* wrinkling (up) *or* screwing up of one's nose; auf etw (*acc*) mit ~rümpfen reagieren to turn one's nose up at sth; n~rümpfend *adj* er sagte n~rümpfend screwing up *or* wrinkling (up) his nose, he said; die n~rümpfenden Eltern the disapproving parents; n~rümpfend gab er das Geschenk zurück he turned his nose up at the present; n~weis *adj* cheeky, saucy; (*vorlaut*) forward, precocious; (*neugierig*) nos(e)y (*inf*), inquisitive; ~weis *m* -es, -e (*Vorlauter*) cheeky (*esp Brit*) *or* precocious brat *or* monkey (*inf*); (*Neugieriger*) nos(e)y parker (*inf*); (*Überschlauer*) know-all, clever dick (*Brit inf*), wiseguy (*inf*).

nasführen* *vt insep* jdn ~ (*als Täuschung*) to lead sb by the nose; (*als Scherz*) to pull sb's leg (*inf*); ich war der/die Genasführte I was the dupe.

Nashorn *nt* rhinoceros, rhino.

-nasig *adj suf* -nosed.

Naß *nt* Nasses, *no pl* (*liter, hum*) water; (*Getränk*) liquid. hinein ins kühle ~ (*hum*) into the foaming brine; gierig trank er das erfrischende ~ (*liter*) eagerly he drank of the refreshing waters (*liter*).

naß *adj, comp* nasser *or* nässer, *superl* nasseste(r, s) *or* nässeste(r, s) am nassesten *or* nässesten wet. etw ~ machen to wet sth, to make sth wet; Bügelwäsche dampen sth; sich ~ machen (*inf*) to wet oneself; das Bett ~ machen to wet the bed; nun mach dich bloß nicht ~! (*sl*) keep your shirt (*inf*) *or* hair (*Brit inf*) on!, don't get your knickers in a twist! (*Brit sl*); durch und durch ~ wet through; mit nassen Augen with moist eyes, moist-eyed; wie ein nasser Sack (*sl*) like a wet rag (*inf*); ein nasses Grab (*fig*) a watery grave; der nasse Tod (*fig*) a watery death; für ~ (*dial*) for nothing, for free.

Nassauer *m* -s, - (*inf*) sponger (*inf*), scrounger.

nassauern *vi* (*inf*) to sponge (*inf*), to scrounge (*bei jdm on or off* sb).

Nässe *f* -, *no pl* wetness, damp(ness), moisture. in der ~ stehen to stand in the wet; „vor ~ bewahren *or* schützen" "keep dry"; vor ~ triefen to be dripping *or* wringing wet.

nässen 1 *vi* (*Wunde*) to weep, to discharge. **2** *vt* (*liter: feucht machen*) to dampen, to wet, to moisten; Bett to wet.

Naß-: n~forsch *adj* (*inf*) full of bravado; n~kalt *adj* cold *or* chilly and damp, raw; ~rasur *f* die ~rasur wet shaving; eine ~rasur a wet shave; ~wäsche *f* wet washing.

Nastuch ['na:stu:x] *nt* (*S Ger, Aus*) handkerchief.

Natalität *f* (*spec*) birth rate, natality (*US*).

Nation *f* nation. die Vereinten ~en the United Nations.

national *adj* national; (*patriotisch*) nationalist(ic). die Inflation muß ~ eingedämmt werden inflation must be checked nationally *or* at the national level.

National- *in cpds* national; n~bewußt *adj* nationally conscious; ~bewußtsein *nt* national consciousness; ~bibliothek *f* national library; ~charakter *m* national character; ~china *nt* Nationalist China; n~chinesisch *adj* Chinese Nationalist; ~einkommen *nt* national income; ~elf *f* international (football) team; die italienische ~elf the Italian (international) team, the Italian eleven; er hat dreimal in der ~elf gespielt he's played for his country three times, he's been capped three times; ~epos *nt* national epic; ~farben *pl* national colours *pl;* ~feiertag *m* national holiday; ~flagge *f* national flag; ~garde *f* National Guard; ~gefühl *nt* national feeling *or* sentiment; ~gericht *nt* national dish; ~getränk *nt* national drink; ~held *m* national hero; ~hymne *f* national anthem.

nationalisieren* [natsjonali'zi:rən] *vt* (a) (*einbürgern*) to naturalize. (b) (*verstaatlichen*) to nationalize.

Nationalisierung *f* (a) naturalization. (b) nationalization.

Nationalismus [natsjona'lɪsmʊs] *m* nationalism.

Nationalist(in *f*) [natsjona'lɪst(ɪn)] *m* nationalist.

nationalistisch [natsjona'lɪstɪʃ] *adj* nationalist(ic).

Nationalität [natsjonali'tɛːt] *f* nationality.

Nationalitäten-: ~frage *f* problem of different nationalities (within one state); ~staat *m* multinational state.

National- [natsjo'naːl-]: ~mannschaft *f* international team; er spielt in der schottischen ~mannschaft he plays for Scotland *or* in the Scotland team; ~ökonomie *f* economics *sing;* ~park *m* national park; ~preis *m* (*DDR*) annual award for achievement

in science, arts and technology; national prize *or* award;
~**preisträger** *m (DDR)* national prize *or* award holder; ~**rat** *m*
(a) *(Sw)* National Council; *(Aus)* National Assembly; **(b)** *(Sw)*
member of the National Council, ≈ MP; *(Aus)* deputy of *or* to
the National Assembly, ≈ MP; ~**sozialismus** *m* National
Socialism; ~**sozialist** *m* National Socialist; ~**spieler** *m* international (footballer *etc*); ~**staat** *m* nation-state; **n~staatlich** *adj*
of a nation-state/nation-states; *Ordnung* as a nation-state;
~**stolz** *m* national pride; ~**straße** *f* national highway; ~**theater**
nt national theatre; ~**tracht** *f* national dress *or* costume;
~**versammlung** *f* National Assembly.

NATO, Nato *f* -: die ~ NATO.
Natrium *nt* -s, *no pl* sodium.
Natron *nt* -s, *no pl* sodium compound, esp bicarbonate of soda.
kohlensaures ~ sodium carbonate; **doppeltkohlensaures** ~
bicarbonate of soda, sodium bicarbonate, bicarb (*inf*).
Natronlauge *f* caustic soda, sodium hydroxide.
Natter *f* -, -n adder, viper; *(fig)* snake, serpent. **eine** ~ **am
Busen nähren** (*liter*) to nurture a viper at one's breast *or* bosom.
Natternbrut *f*, **Natterngezücht** *nt* (*fig*) viper's brood.
Natur *f* **(a)** *no pl (Kosmos, Schöpfungsordnung)* nature. **sie ist
ein Meisterwerk der** ~ she is one of Nature's masterpieces; **die
drei Reiche der** ~ the three kingdoms of nature, the three
natural kingdoms; ~ **und Kultur** nature and civilization; **wider
die** ~ **sein** to be unnatural *or* against nature; **gegen die** ~
against nature.
  (b) *no pl (freies Land)* countryside. **die freie** ~, **Gottes freie**
~ (*liter*) the open country(side).
  (c) *no pl (~zustand)* nature. **ist ihr Haar gefärbt? — nein das
ist alles** ~ is her hair dyed? — no, it's natural; **sie sind von** ~ **so
gewachsen** they grew that way naturally; **ich bin von** ~ **aus
schüchtern** I am shy by nature; **sein Haar ist von** ~ **aus blond**
his hair is naturally blond; **zurück zur** ~! back to nature; **nach
der** ~ **zeichnen/malen** to draw/paint from nature.
  (d) *(Beschaffenheit, Wesensart)* nature; *(Mensch)* type. **es
liegt in der** ~ **der Sache or der Dinge** it is in the nature of
things; **das geht gegen meine** ~ it goes against the grain; **das
entspricht nicht meiner** ~, **das ist meiner** ~ **zuwider** it's not in
my nature; **eine Frage allgemeiner** ~ a question of a general
nature; **zurückhaltender** ~ **sein** to be of a retiring nature; **das
ist ihm zur zweiten** ~ **geworden** it's become second nature to
him; **eine eiserne** ~ **haben** to have a cast-iron constitution; **sie
hat eine glückliche** ~ she has a happy disposition *or* nature; **sie
ist eine gutmütige** ~ she's a good-natured type *or* soul; **seine** ~
erleichtern (*S Ger hum*) to answer the call of nature (*hum*).
Naturalien [-iən] *pl* **(a)** natural produce. **in** ~ **bezahlen** to pay
in kind; **Handel mit** ~ **barter(ing)** with goods. **(b)** *(Naturgeschichte)* natural history specimens *pl*.
Naturalien- [-iən-]: ~**kabinett** *nt (old)*; ~**sammlung** *f* natural
history collection.
naturalisieren* *vt* **(a)** *(Jur)* to naturalize. **(b)** *(Biol, Zool)*
naturalisiert werden, sich ~ to be naturalized, to naturalize.
Naturalisierung *f* naturalization.
Naturalismus *m* naturalism.
Naturalist (*in f*) *m* naturalist.
naturalistisch *adj* naturalistic; *Maler etc* naturalist(ic).
Natural-: ~**lohn** *m* payment in kind; ~**obligation** *f (old)* debt of
honour; ~**wert** *m* natural produce.
Natur-: ~**apostel** *m (hum)* health fiend (*inf*); ~**beobachtung** *f*
observation of nature; ~**beschreibung** *f* description of nature;
~**bursche** *m* nature-boy (*inf*); ~**denkmal** *nt* natural monument.
nature [na'ty:ɐ], **naturell** *adj (Cook)* Schnitzel/Fisch ~ cutlet/
fish not cooked in breadcrumbs; *Kaffee* ~ black coffee
without sugar; *Tee* ~ tea without milk or sugar.
Naturell *nt* -s, -e temperament, disposition.
Natur-: ~**ereignis** *nt* (impressive) natural phenomenon,
phenomenon of nature; ~**erscheinung** *f* natural phenomenon;
~**erzeugnis** *nt siehe* ~**produkt**; ~**farbe** *f* (a) natural colour; **(b)**
(auch ~**farbstoff**) natural dye; **n~farben** *adj* natural-
coloured; ~**forscher** *m* natural scientist; ~**forschung** *f* natural
science; ~**freund** *m* nature-lover; ~**gas** *nt* natural gas;
~**gefühl** *nt* feeling for nature; **n~gegeben** *adj (lit)* natural; *(fig
auch)* normal; **n~gemäß** *adj* natural; **n~gemäß ist es im
Mittelmeerraum wärmer als in Skandinavien** in the nature of
things it is warmer in the Mediterranean than in Scandinavia;
~**geschichte** *f* natural history; **n~geschichtlich** *adj* natural
history; **etw n~geschichtlich betrachten** to look at sth from a
natural history point of view; ~**gesetz** *nt* law of nature;
n~getreu *adj* lifelike, true to life; *(in Lebensgröße)* life-size,
full-scale; **etw n~getreu wiedergeben** to reproduce sth true to
life; **n~haft** *adj (geh)* natural; ~**heilkunde** *f* nature healing;
~**heilverfahren** *nt* natural cure *or* remedy; ~**katastrophe** *f*
natural disaster; ~**kind** *nt* child of nature; ~**kraft** *f* natural
energy *or* force; ~**kunde** *f* natural history; **n~kundlich** *adj*
Forschung, Zeitschrift natural history; ~**landschaft** *f* natural
or virgin landscape; ~**lehre** *f (Sch)* (physical) science.
natürlich 1 *adj (alle Bedeutungen)* natural. **in seiner** ~**en
Größe** life-size; **eines** ~**en Todes sterben** to die from *or* of
natural causes, to die a natural death; **es ist doch (nur zu)** ~, **daß
... it's (only) natural that ...;** ~**e Person** *(Jur)* natural person;
~**er Sohn** *(old: unehelich, nicht adoptiert)* natural son; ~**e Zahl**
natural number; **die** ~**ste Sache (von) der Welt** the most
natural thing in the world; **es geht nicht mit** ~**en Dingen zu or
nicht** ~ **zu** there's something odd *or* fishy (*inf*) going on, I smell
a rat (*inf*); ~**e Grenze** natural frontier *or* boundary; ~**e Auslese**
(Biol) natural selection.
  2 *adv* **(a)** naturally. **die Krankheit verlief ganz** ~ the illness
took its natural course.
  (b) *(selbstverständlich)* naturally, of course. ~! naturally!,
of course!, certainly!, sure! (*esp US*) surely!

natürlicherweise *adv* naturally, of course.
Natürlichkeit *f* naturalness.
Natur-: ~**mensch** *m* child of nature; ~**notwendigkeit** *f* physical
inevitability; ~**park** *m siehe* ~**(schutz)park**; ~**philosophie** *f*
philosophy of nature; ~**produkt** *nt* natural product; ~**produkte**
natural produce *sing*; ~**recht** *nt* natural right; **n~rein** *adj*
natural, pure, unadulterated; ~**schätze** *pl* natural resources *pl*;
~**schauspiel** *nt* natural spectacle, spectacle of nature; ~**schutz**
m conservation, nature conservancy; **unter** ~**schutz stehen** to
be listed, to be legally protected; ~**schutzgebiet** *nt* nature
reserve; ~**(schutz)park** *m* ≈ national park; ~**seide** *f* natural
silk; ~**stein** *m* natural stone; ~**talent** *nt* natural prodigy;
~**theater** *nt* open-air theatre; ~**treue** *f* trueness to life,
faithfulness, fidelity; ~**trieb** *m* (natural) instinct;
n~verbunden *adj* nature-loving, attached to nature;
~**verehrung** *f* nature worship; ~**volk** *nt* primitive people.
naturw. *abbr of* **naturwissenschaftlich**.
Natur-: ~**wein** *m* wine free of additives; **n~widrig** *adj*
unnatural, against nature; *(nicht normal)* abnormal;
~**wissenschaft** *f* natural sciences *pl*; *(Zweig)* natural science;
~**wissenschaftler** *m* (natural) scientist; **n~wissenschaftlich**
adj scientific; ~**wunder** *nt* miracle of nature, natural wonder;
~**zustand** *m* natural state.
'nauf *adv (dial) siehe* **hinauf**.
'naus *adv (dial) siehe* **hinaus**.
Nautik *f*, *no pl* nautical science, navigation.
nautisch *adj* navigational; *Instrumente auch*, *Ausbildung,
Ausdruck* nautical. ~**e Meile** nautical *or* sea mile.
Navigation [naviga'tsio:n] *f* navigation.
Navigations-: ~**fehler** *m* navigational error; ~**offizier** *m*
navigation officer; ~**raum** *m* charthouse, chartroom.
Navigator [navi'ga:tor] *m (Aviat)* navigator, navigation
officer.
navigieren* [navi'gi:rən] *vti* to navigate.
Nazarener *m* -s, - Nazarene.
Nazi *m* -s, -s Nazi.
Nazismus *m* **(a)** *(pej: Nationalsozialismus)* Nazi(i)sm. **(b)**
(Ling) Nazi term *or* expression.
nazistisch *adj (pej)* Nazi.
Nazizeit *f* Nazi period.
NB [ɛn'be:] *abbr of* **nota bene** NB.
n.Br. *abbr of* **nördlicher Breite**.
n.Chr. *abbr of* **nach Christus** AD.
NDR [ɛndeː'ʔɛr] *m* -s *abbr of* **Norddeutscher Rundfunk**.
ne *adv (inf)* no, nope (*inf*), nay (*old, dial*).
'ne *indef art (inf) abbr of* **eine**.
Neandertaler *m* -s, - Neanderthal man.
Neapel *nt* -s Naples.
Neapolitaner(in *f*) *m* -s, - Neapolitan; *(Aus: Waffel)* waffle.
nebbich *interj (sl) (schade)* shame; *(nun, wenn schon)* so what.
Nebel *m* -s, - mist; *(dichter)* fog; *(mit Abgasen)* smog; *(Mil:
künstlich)* smoke; *(Astron)* nebula; *(fig)* mist, haze. **über der
ganzen Sache lag ein** ~ *(fig)* the whole affair was shrouded in
mystery; **bei** ~ in mist/fog; **das fällt wegen** ~**(s) aus** *(sl)* it's all
off; *siehe* **Nacht**.
Nebel-: ~**bank** *f* fog bank; ~**bild** *nt (fig)* shade, shadow;
~**bildung** *f* fog; **stellenweise** ~**bildung** foggy patches; ~**fleck**
m (a) *(Astron)* nebula; **(b)** *(Zool)* leucoma (spec), clouding (of
the eye); ~**granate** *f* smoke grenade *or* canister.
nebelhaft *adj (fig)* nebulous. **es liegt in** ~**er Ferne** it's in the dim
distance; **es ist mir** ~, **wie ich das anpacken werde** I haven't the
foggiest idea (*inf*) *or* I've no idea (of) how to tackle it.
Nebelhorn *nt (Naut)* foghorn.
neb(e)lig *adv* misty; *(bei dichterem Nebel)* foggy.
Nebel-: ~**kammer** *f (Phys)* cloud chamber; ~**krähe** *f* hooded
crow; ~**meer** *nt* sea of mist; ~**monat** *m (liter)* November.
nebeln *vi impers* **es nebelt** it's misty/foggy.
Nebel-: ~**scheinwerfer** *m (Aut)* fog lamp; ~**schleier** *m (geh)*
veil of mist; ~**(schluß)leuchte** *f (Aut)* rear fog-light;
~**schwaden** *m usu pl* waft of mist.
Nebelung *m* -s, -e *(obs)* November.
Nebel-: ~**wand** *f* wall *or* bank of fog; *(Mil)* smokescreen;
~**werfer** *m (Mil)* multiple rocket launcher; ~**wetter** *nt*
misty/foggy weather.
neben *prep* **(a)** *(örtlich: +dat/acc)* beside, next to. **er fuhr** ~
dem Zug her he kept level with the train; **er ging** ~ **ihr** he
walked beside her; **ich stelle ihn** ~ **die größten Denker des 17.
Jahrhunderts** I rank him among *or* with the greatest thinkers of
the 17th century.
  (b) *(außer: +dat)* apart from, besides, aside from *(esp US)*.
du sollst keine anderen Götter haben ~ **mir** *(Bibl)* thou shalt
have no other gods before me *(Bibl)*; ~ **anderen Dingen** along
with *or* as well as *or* amongst other things.
  (c) *(verglichen mit: +dat)* compared with *or* to.
Neben-: ~**abrede** *f (Jur)* supplementary agreement, sub-
agreement; ~**absicht** *f* **eine** ~**absicht haben** *or* **verfolgen** to
have a secondary aim *or* objective; ~**altar** *m* side altar; ~**amt**
nt (a) *(Nebenberuf)* secondary *or* additional office; **(b)** *(Telec)*
branch *or* local exchange; **n~amtlich** *adj* *Tätigkeit* secondary,
additional; **das macht er nur n~amtlich** he does that just as a
secondary occupation.
neben|an *adv* next door. **die Tür** ~ the next door.
Neben-: ~**anschluß** *m (Telec)* extension; ~**arbeit** *f* (a)
(Zusatzarbeit) extra work *no indef art, no pl*, extra job; **(b)**
(Zweitberuf) second *or* extra job, sideline, side job; ~**arm** *m*
branch; ~**ausgabe** *f* incidental expense; ~**ausgaben** inciden-
tals, incidental expenses; ~**ausgang** *m* side exit; ~**bahn** *f (Rail)*
branch line; ~**bedeutung** *f* secondary meaning *or* connotation.
nebenbei *adv* **(a)** *(gleichzeitig)* at the same time. **etw** ~ **machen**
to do sth on the side.

(b) *(außerdem)* additionally, in addition. **die ~ entstandenen Kosten** the additional expenses.

(c) *(beiläufig)* incidentally. **~ bemerkt** *or* **gesagt** by the way, incidentally, by the by(e); **das mache ich so ~** *(inf)* that's just a sideline; *(kein Problem)* I'll do that with no bother *(inf)*.

Neben-: **~beruf** *m* second *or* extra job, sideline, side job; **er ist im ~beruf Nachtwächter** he has a second job as a night watchman, he moonlights as a night watchman *(inf)*; **n~beruflich 1** *adj* extra, supplementary; **n~berufliche Arbeit/Tätigkeit** extra work/job, sideline, side job; **2** *adv* as a second job, as a sideline *(inf)*, as a side job *(inf)*; **er verdient n~beruflich mehr als hauptberuflich** he earns more from his second job *or* from his moonlighting *(inf)* than he does from his main job; **~beschäftigung, ~betätigung** *f* **(a)** *(Zweitberuf)* second *or* extra job, sideline, side job; **(b)** *(Ablenkung)* **beim Fernsehen brauche ich immer eine kleine ~beschäftigung** I always need something else to do while I'm watching television; **~betrieb** *m* **(a)** branch industry; **(b)** *(Filiale)* *(Büro)* branch (office); *(Werk)* subsidiary factory; **~buhler(in** *f)* *m* rival; **~buhlerschaft** *f*, *no pl* rivalry; **~darsteller(in** *f)* *m* supporting actor/actress; **die ~darsteller** the supporting cast *sing*; **~dinge** *pl* secondary matters *pl*.

neben|einander *adv* **(a)** *(räumlich)* side by side; *(bei Rennen)* neck and neck. **sie gingen ~ durchs Ziel** they were neck and neck at the finish; **drei ~, zu dritt ~** three abreast. **(b)** *(zeitlich)* simultaneously, at the same time.

Neben|einander *nt* **-s**, *no pl* juxtaposition.

neben|einanderher *adv* side by side.

neben|einander-: **~legen** *vt sep* to lay side by side *or* next to each other; **~reihen** *vt sep* to place *or* put side by side *or* next to each other; **~schalten** *vt sep (Elec)* to put in parallel; **~setzen** *vt sep* to place *or* put side by side *or* next to each other; **~sitzen** *vi sep irreg (S Ger: aux sein)* to sit side by side *or* next to each other; **~stellen** *vt sep* to place *or* put side by side *or* next to each other; *(fig: vergleichen)* to compare.

Neben-: **~eingang** *m* side entrance; **~einkünfte, ~einnahmen** *pl* additional *or* supplementary income, extra money; **~erscheinung** *f* concomitant; *(von Krankheit)* secondary symptom; **das Medikament ruft unangenehme ~erscheinungen hervor** the drug has unpleasant side effects; **~erwerb** *m* second occupation; **~fach** *nt (Sch, Univ)* subsidiary (subject), minor *(US)*; **~flügel** *m* side wing; **~fluß** *m* tributary; **~form** *f (Biol)* variety; *(Ling)* variant; **~frage** *f* side issue; **~frau** *f* concubine; **~gasse** *f* side *or* back street; **~gebäude** *nt* **(a)** *(Zusatzgebäude)* annex(e), outbuilding; **(b)** *(Nachbargebäude)* neighbouring *or* adjacent building; **~gebühr** *f* supplementary fee *or* charge; **~gedanke** *m* ulterior motive; **~g(e)leis** *nt (Rail)* siding, sidetrack *(US)*; **jdn aufs ~g(e)leis schieben** *(inf)* to push sb into the background; **~geräusch** *nt (Rad, Telec)* interference, noise; *(bei Plattenspieler)* noise; **~geschäft** *nt* sideline; **~gestein** *nt (Min)* country rock; **~gewerbe** *nt siehe* **~erwerb**; **~handlung** *f (Liter)* subplot; **~haus** *nt* house next door, neighbouring house.

nebenher *adv* **(a)** *(zusätzlich)* in addition, on the side. **(b)** *(gleichzeitig)* at the same time, simultaneously.

nebenher- *pref* alongside, beside it/him *etc*.

nebenhin *adv* **(a)** *(inf: daneben)* next to it/them. **(b)** *(beiläufig)* in passing, by the way, casually.

Neben-: **~höhle** *f (Physiol)* sinus (of the nose); **~klage** *f (Jur)* incidental action; **~kläger** *m (Jur)* joint plaintiff; **~kosten** *pl* additional costs *pl*; **~kriegsschauplatz** *m* secondary theatre of war; **~linie** *f* **(a)** *(Familie)* collateral line; **(b)** *(Rail)* branch line; **~mann** *m*, *pl* **~männer Ihr ~mann** the person next to you, your neighbour; **~mensch** *m* fellow being; **~niere** *f* suprarenal gland *or* capsule, adrenal body.

neben|ordnen *vt sep infin and ptp only (Gram)* to coordinate.

Neben-: **~ordnung** *f (Gram)* coordination; **~person** *f* minor character; **~platz** *m* next seat; **auf meinem ~platz** in the seat next to me; **~produkt** *nt* by-product; **~raum** *m (benachbart)* adjoining *or* next room; *(weniger wichtig)* side room; **~rolle** *f* supporting rôle; *(fig)* minor rôle; **das spielt für mich nur eine ~rolle** that's only of minor concern to me; **~sache** *f* minor matter, trifle, triviality; **das ist ~sache** that's irrelevant *or* not the point; **n~sächlich** *adj* minor, peripheral; **etw als n~sächlich abtun** to dismiss sth as irrelevant *or* beside the point; **~sächliches** minor matters *pl*, trifles *pl*, trivia(lities) *pl*; **es ist doch völlig n~sächlich, wann er kommt** it doesn't matter a bit *or* it's quite irrelevant when he comes; **~sächlichkeit** *f* triviality; **~satz** *m (Gram)* subordinate clause.

nebenschalten *vt sep (Elec)* to wire *or* connect in parallel.

Neben-: **~schluß** *m (Tech)* parallel connection, side (of a parallel circuit); **~sonne** *f* mock sun, sundog, parhelion *(spec)*; **n~stehend** *adj* **n~stehende Erklärungen/Verbesserung** explanation/correction in the margin; **n~stehende Abbildung** illustration opposite; **im ~stehenden wird erklärt ...** the marginal note explains ...; **~stelle** *f (Telec)* extension; *(Comm)* branch; **~strafe** *f* additional penalty; **~straße** *f (in der Stadt)* side street; *(Landstraße)* minor road, by-road; **~strecke** *f (Rail)* branch *or* local line; **~thema** *nt (Mus)* minor theme; **~tisch** *m* adjacent table; **am ~tisch at** the next table; **sie saßen an einem ~tisch** they were sitting at a table near us; **~ton** *m (Ling)* secondary stress; **~ursache** *f* secondary cause; **~verdienst** *m* secondary *or* side *(inf)* income; **~weg** *m* byway; **auf ~wegen** *(lit, fig)* by a roundabout route; **~winkel** *m (Math)* adjacent angle; **~wirkung** *f* side effect; **~wohnung** *f* **(a)** next(-door) flat, flat next door; **in einer ~wohnung** in one of the flats next door; **(b)** *(Zweitwohnung)* second flat; **~zimmer** *nt* next *or* adjoining room; **in einem ~zimmer** in an adjoining room; **~zweck** *m* secondary aim.

neblig *adj siehe* **neb(e)lig**.

nebst *prep* **+dat** together with. **viele Grüße, Onkel Otto ~ Familie** greetings from Uncle Otto and family.

nebstdem *adv (Sw) siehe* **außerdem**.

nebulos, nebulös *adj* nebulous. **er redete so ~es Zeug** he was so vague *or* woolly *(inf)*.

Necessaire [nese'sɛːɐ] *nt* **-s**, **-s** *(Kulturbeutel)* vanity bag *or* case; *(zur Nagelpflege)* manicure case; *(Nähzeug)* sewing bag.

necken 1 *vt* to tease. **jdn mit jdm/etw ~** to tease sb about sb/sth. **2** *vr* **sich *or* einander ~, sich mit jdm ~** to tease each other, to have a tease *(inf)*; **was sich liebt, das neckt sich** *(Prov)* teasing is a sign of affection.

Neckerei *f* teasing *no pl*.

neckisch *adj (scherzhaft)* merry, teasing; *Einfall, Melodie* amusing; *Unterhaltung* bantering; *(inf: kokett, keß) Kleid, Frisur* coquettish, saucy; *Spielchen* mischievous, naughty. **~!** *(inf)* kinky! *(inf)*.

nee *adv (inf)* no, nope *(inf)*. **~, so was!** no, really!

Neer *f* **-**, **-en** *(N Ger)* eddy.

Neffe *m* **-n**, **-n** nephew.

Negation *f* negation.

Negativ *nt (Phot)* negative.

negativ *adj* negative. **jdm auf eine Frage ~ antworten** to answer sb's question in the negative; **sich ~ zu etw stellen** to adopt a negative attitude towards sth; **sich ~ zu etw äußern** to speak negatively about sth; **ich beurteile seine Arbeit sehr ~** I have a very negative view of his work; **die Untersuchung verlief ~** the examination proved negative; **etw ~ (auf)laden** to put a negative charge on sth.

Negativ-: **~bild** *nt* negative; **~druck** *m* reversing out; **~film** *m* negative (film).

Negativität *f* negativity, negativeness.

Neger *m* **-s**, **-** **(a)** negro. **angeben wie zehn nackte ~** *(inf)* to shoot one's big mouth off *(inf)*. **(b)** *(TV sl) (Gedächtnishilfe)* idiot card; *(Verdunklungstafel)* gobo.

neger *adj pred (Aus inf)* broke *(inf)*.

Negerin *f* negress.

Neger-: **~krause** *f (dated)* frizzy hair; **~kuß** *m* chocolate marshmallow.

Negerlein *nt dim of* **Neger** little negro.

Neger-: **~musik** *f* negro music; **~sklave** *m* negro slave.

negieren* *vt (verneinen)* Satz to negate; *(bestreiten) Tatsache, Behauptung* to deny.

Negligé, Négligé [negli'ʒeː] *(Sw) nt* **-s**, **-s** negligee, négligé.

negrid *adj* Rasse negro.

negroid *adj* negroid.

nehmen *pret* **nahm**, *ptp* **genommen** *vti* **(a)** *(ergreifen)* to take. **etw in die Hand ~** *(lit)* to pick sth up; *(fig)* to take sth in hand; **etw an sich** *(acc)* **~** *(aufbewahren)* to take care *or* charge of sth, to look after sth; *(sich aneignen)* to take (for oneself).

(b) *(wegnehmen)* to take; *Schmerz* to take away, to relieve; *(versperren) Blick, Sicht* to block. **jdm etw ~** to take sth (away) from sb; **jdm die Hoffnung/den Glauben/seine Illusionen/die Freude ~** to take away sb's hope/faith/illusions/joy, to rob *or* deprive sb of his hope/faith/illusions/joy; **um ihm die Angst zu ~** to stop him being afraid; **ihm sind seine Illusionen genommen worden** he was robbed *or* deprived of his illusions, his illusions were shattered; **er ließ es sich** *(dat)* **nicht ~, mich persönlich hinauszubegleiten** he insisted on showing me out himself; **diesen Erfolg lasse ich mir nicht ~** I won't be robbed of this success; **von deiner schlechten Laune lasse ich mir den Spaß nicht ~** I'm not having my fun spoiled by your bad temper; **woher ~ und nicht stehlen?** *(inf)* where on earth am I going to find any/one *etc*?; **sie ~ sich** *(dat)* **nichts** *(inf)* there's nothing to choose between them, one's as good as the other.

(c) *(benutzen)* Auto, Zug *etc* to take; *Bürste, Zutaten, Farbe* to use. **man nehme ...** *(Cook)* take ...; **sich** *(dat)* **etw ~** *Zimmer, Wohnung* to take sth; *(sich bedienen auch)* to help oneself to sth; **sich** *(dat)* **einen Anwalt/eine Hilfe ~** to get a lawyer/some help; **~ Sie sich doch bitte!** please help yourself.

(d) *(annehmen)* Geschenk to take; *(berechnen)* to charge. **was ~ Sie dafür?** how much will you charge for it?; **jdn zu sich ~** to take sb in; **Gott hat ihn zu sich genommen** *(euph)* he has been called home to his maker; **wie ~ wir es kommt** to take sth as it comes; **jdn ~, wie er ist** to take sb as he is; **etw auf sich** *(acc)* **~** to take sth upon oneself; **er ist immer der N~de** he does all the taking, with him it's just take take take *(inf)*; **die N~den und die Gebenden** the takers and the givers.

(e) *(einnehmen)* to take; *Essen auch* to have. **sie nimmt Rauschgift/die Pille** she's on *or* she takes drugs/the pill; **etw zu sich ~** to take sth, to partake of sth *(liter)*; **der Patient hat nichts zu sich ~ können** the patient has been unable to take nourishment.

(f) *(auffassen)* to take; *(behandeln)* to handle, to treat. **wenn Sie das so ~ wollen** if you care *or* choose to take it that way; **etw für ein *or* als Zeichen ~** to take sth as a sign *or* an omen; **wie man's nimmt** *(inf)* depending on your point of view; **wissen, wie man jdn ~ muß** *or* **soll** to know how to take sb; **sie weiß ihn zu ~** she knows how to take him.

(g) *(auswählen)* to take; *Essen, Menü auch* to have. **sich** *(dat)* **einen Mann/eine Frau ~** to take a husband/wife.

(h) *Hürde, Festung, Stadt, Frau* to take; *Schwierigkeiten* to overcome. **das Auto nahm den Berg im dritten Gang** the car took the hill in third gear.

(i) *in festen Verbindungen mit n siehe dort*.

Nehmer *m* **-s**, **-** **(a)** recipient. **(b)** *(Käufer)* taker.

Nehrung *f* spit (of land).

Neid *m* **-(e)s**, *no pl* envy, jealousy. **aus ~** out of envy *or* jealousy; **der ~ der Besitzlosen** *(inf)* sour grapes *(inf)*; **grün (und gelb) vor ~** *(inf)* green with envy; **das muß ihm der ~ lassen** *(inf)* you have to say that much for him, give the devil his due; **jds** *(acc)* *or* **bei jdm ~ erregen** to make sb jealous *or* envious, to arouse sb's jealousy; **vor ~ platzen** (*inf*) *or* **vergehen** to die of envy.

neiden *vt* **jdm etw ~** to envy sb (for) sth.

Neider *m* **-s,** - envious *or* jealous person. **reiche Leute haben viele ~** rich people are much envied.

Neid-: **n~erfüllt** *adj* filled with *or* full of envy *or* jealousy, envious, jealous; **~hammel** *m* (*inf*) jealous *or* envious person; **der alte/du alter ~hammel!** he's/you're just jealous.

neidisch, neidig (*S Ger, Aus*) *adj* jealous, envious. **auf jdn/etw ~ sein** to be jealous of sb/sth; **etw ~** *or* **mit ~en Blicken betrachten** to look enviously at sth, to cast covetous glances at sth.

neidlos *adj* ungrudging, without envy.

Neidlosigkeit *f* lack of envy *or* jealousy, ungrudgingness.

Neige *f* **-, -n** (**a**) (*Überrest*) remains *pl*. **das Glas bis zur ~ leeren** (*liter*) to drain the cup to the dregs; **den Kelch bis zur ~ leeren** *or* **trinken** (*fig liter*) to drain the bitter cup (*liter*); **etw bis zur ~ auskosten** (*genießen*) to savour sth to the full; **etw bis zur bitteren ~ auskosten** *or* **kennenlernen** to suffer sth to the full.

(**b**) *no pl* (*geh: Ende*) **zur ~ gehen** to draw to an end *or* a close; **die Sonne geht zur ~** the sun is sinking; **die Vorräte gehen zur ~** the provisions are fast becoming exhausted.

neigen 1 *vt* (*beugen*) *Kopf, Körper* to bend; (*zum Gruß*) to bow; (*kippen*) *Behälter, Glas* to tip, to tilt, to incline. **die Bäume ~ ihre Zweige bis zur Erde** (*geh*) the trees bow their branches to the ground; **geneigte Ebene** sloping surface, slope, incline.

2 *vr* (*Ebene*) to slope, to incline; (*Mensch*) to bend; (*liter: sich verneigen*) to bow; (*unter Last: Bäume etc*) to bow; (*Gebäude etc*) to lean; (*kippen*) to tip (up), to tilt (up); (*Schiff*) to list; (*liter: Tag, Leben*) to draw to a close *or* an end. **sich nach vorne/hinten ~** (*Mensch*) to lean *or* bend forward/backwards; (*Auto*) to tilt forward/backwards; (*Schiff, Wippe*) to dip/tilt up; **ein leicht zur Seite geneigtes Gebäude** a building which is leaning *or* tilting over slightly; **mit seitwärts geneigtem Kopf** with his/her head held on *or* to one side; **die Waagschale neigt sich zu seinen Gunsten** (*geh*) the scales are tipping in his favour, the tide is turning in his favour

3 *vi* **zu etw ~** to tend to sth, to have a tendency to sth; (*für etw anfällig sein*) to be susceptible *or* prone to sth; **er neigt zum Alkohol** he has a taste *or* predilection for alcohol, he has a tendency to drink; **er neigt zum Sozialismus** he tends *or* leans towards socialism, he has socialist leanings; **zu der Ansicht** *or* **Annahme ~, daß ...** to lean toward the view that ..., to be inclined to take the view that ...; **ich neige eher zur klassischen Musik** I tend rather towards classical music; *siehe* **geneigt.**

Neigung *f* (**a**) (*das Neigen*) inclination; (*Gefälle auch*) incline, slope, gradient (*esp Rail*); (*Schräglage auch*) tilt; (*von Schiff*) list; (*von Magnetnadel*) dip; (*Astron*) inclination.

(**b**) (*Tendenz*) tendency; (*Med auch*) proneness; (*Hingezogensein, Veranlagung*) leaning *usu pl*; (*Hang, Lust*) inclination. **er hat eine ~ zum Geiz/zum Trinken/zur Kritik** he has a tendency to be mean/to drink/to criticize, he inclines *or* tends to be mean/to drink/to criticize; **künstlerische/politische ~en** artistic/political leanings; **etw aus ~ tun** to do sth by inclination; **keine/geringe ~ verspüren, etw zu tun** to have *or* feel no/little inclination to do sth.

(**c**) (*Zuneigung*) affection, fondness. **zu jdm eine ~ fassen** to take a liking to sb; **jds ~ gewinnen** to win *or* gain (a place in) sb's affections; **jds ~ erwidern** to return sb's affection.

Neigungs-: **~ehe** *f* love match; **~messer** *m* **-s,** - inclinometer; **~winkel** *m* angle of inclination.

nein *adv* no; (*Überraschung*) no. **kommt er? — ~!** is he coming? — no, (he isn't); **ich sage nicht ~** I wouldn't say no; **~ und abermals ~** for the last time - no!; **~, ~, und nochmals ~** I won't say it again - no, spelt NO!; **Hunderte, ~ Tausende** hundreds, no *or* nay (*liter*) thousands; **~, so was!** well I never!, you don't say!; **~, doch! no!**; **o ~!, aber ~!** certainly not!, of course not!; **~, daß du dich auch mal wieder sehen läßt!** fancy seeing you again; **~ wie nett, mich mal zu besuchen!** well, how nice of you to visit me.

Nein *nt* **-s,** *no pl* no. **bei seinem ~ bleiben** to stick to one's refusal, to remain adamant; **mit Ja oder ~ stimmen** to vote yes *or* aye (*Pol*) *or* no *or* nay (*US Pol*).

Nein-: **~sager(in** *f*) *m* **-s,** - er ist ein ewiger **~sager** he always says no; **~stimme** *f* (*Pol*) no(-vote), nay (*US*).

Nekro-: **~log** *m* **-(e)s, -e** (*liter*) obituary (notice), necrology (*form*); **~philie** *f* necrophilia; **~pole** *f* **-, -n** necropolis.

Nektar *m* **-s,** *no pl* (*Myth, Bot*) nectar.

Nektarine *f* nectarine.

nektarisch, nektarn *adj* (*poet*) nectar-sweet.

Nelke *f* **-, -n** (**a**) pink; (*gefüllt*) carnation. (**b**) (*Gewürz*) clove.

Nelson *m* **-(s), -(s)** (*Sport*) nelson.

'nem *abbr of* **einem.**

Nemesis *f* **-,** *no pl* nemesis.

'nen *abbr of* **einen.**

nennbar *adj* specifiable; *Gefühl, Phänomen, Gedanke etc* nam(e)able. **nicht ~** unspecifiable; unnam(e)able.

Nennbetrag *m* (*Comm*) *siehe* **Nennwert.**

nennen *pret* **nannte,** *ptp* **genannt 1** *vt* (**a**) (*bezeichnen*) to call; (*einen bestimmten Namen geben auch*) to name. **jdn nach jdm ~** to name sb after *or* for (*US*) sb; **Friedrich II., genannt „der Große"** Frederick II, known as Frederick the Great; **das nenne ich Mut!** that's what I call courage!; **das nennst du schön?** you call that beautiful? *siehe* **eigen.**

(**b**) (*angeben, aufzählen*) to name. **die genannten Namen** the names mentioned; **können Sie mir einen guten Anwalt ~?** could you give me the name of a good lawyer?; *siehe* **Name.**

(**c**) (*erwähnen*) to mention. **das (weiter oben) Genannte** the above (mentioned); **das genannte Schloß** the above-mentioned castle, the castle referred to.

2 *vr* to call oneself; (*heißen*) to be called, to call oneself. **er**

nennt sich nur so that's just what he calls himself; **und so was nennt sich Liebe/modern** (*inf*) and they call that love/modern; **und so was nennt sich modern/Dichter** (*inf*) and he calls himself modern/a poet.

nennenswert *adj* considerable, not inconsiderable. **nicht ~** negligible, not worth mentioning; **keine ~en Schwierigkeiten** no great difficulties, no difficulties worth mentioning; **nichts N~es** nothing worth mentioning, nothing of any consequence.

Nenner *m* **-s,** - (*Math*) denominator. **etw auf einen (gemeinsamen) ~ bringen** (*lit, fig*) to reduce sth to a common denominator.

Nenn-: **~fall** *m* nominative; **~form** *f* infinitive; **~onkel** *m* er ist **kein richtiger Onkel, sondern nur ein ~onkel** he's not a proper uncle, I just call him uncle; **~tante** *f siehe* **~onkel.**

Nennung *f* (*das Nennen*) naming; (*Sport*) entry. **ich möchte mich mit der ~ weniger Beispiele begnügen** I should like to restrict myself to naming only a few examples.

Nenn-: **~wert** *m* (*Fin*) nominal *or* face *or* par value; **zum ~wert** at par; **über/unter dem ~wert** above/below par; **~wort** *nt siehe* **Substantiv.**

neo-, Neo-, *in cpds* neo-,

Neologismus *m* neologism.

Neon *nt* **-s,** *no pl* neon.

Neon-: **~licht** *nt* neon light; **~reklame** *f* neon sign; **~röhre** *f* neon tube *or* strip.

Nepal *nt* **-s** Nepal.

Nepalese *m* **-, -n, Nepalesin** *f* Nepalese.

nepalesisch *adj* Nepalese.

Nepotismus *m* nepotism.

Nepp *m* **-s,** *no pl* (*inf*) **so ein ~!, das ist ja ~!** that's daylight *or* highway robbery! (*inf*), it's a rip-off (*sl*).

neppen *vt* (*inf*) to fleece (*inf*), to rip off (*sl*). **da bist du aber geneppt worden!** they must have seen you coming (*inf*).

Nepplokal *nt* (*inf*) clipjoint (*inf*).

Neptun *m* **-s** Neptune.

'ner *abbr of* **einer.**

Nerv [nɛrf] *m* **-s** *or* **-en, -en** nerve; (*Bot auch*) vein; (*obs: Sehne*) sinew. **leicht die ~en verlieren** to scare easily, to get nervous easily; **er hat trotz allem die ~en behalten** *or* **nicht verloren** in spite of everything he kept calm *or* didn't lose his cool (*sl*); (*Selbstbeherrschung verlieren*) in spite of everything he didn't lose control; **die ~en sind mit ihm durchgegangen** he lost control *or* his cool (*sl*), he snapped (*inf*); **gute/schlechte** *or* **schwache ~en haben** to have strong *or* good/bad *or* weak nerves; **der hat (vielleicht) ~en!** (*inf*) he's got a cheek (*inf*) *or* nerve! (*inf*); **er hat ~en wie Drahtseile** *or* **Bindfäden** *or* **Stricke** he has nerves of steel; **es geht** *or* **fällt mir auf die ~en** (*inf*) it gets on my nerves; **jdm den (letzten) ~ töten** *or* **rauben** (*inf*) to break *or* shatter sb's nerve; **den ~ haben, etw zu tun** to have the nerve to do sth.

Nervatur [nɛrva'tuːɐ] *f* venation, nervation.

Nerven-: [ˈnɛrfn-]: **~anspannung** *f* nervous tension; **~arzt** *m* neurologist; **n~aufreibend** *adj* nerve-racking; **~bahn** *f* nerve; **~belastung** *f* strain on the nerves; **n~beruhigend** *adj* sedative; **~beruhigungsmittel** *nt* sedative, tranquillizer; **~bündel** *nt* fascicle; (*fig inf*) bag *or* bundle of nerves (*inf*); **~chirurgie** *f* neurosurgery; (*entzündung f* neuritis; **~faser** *f* nerve fibre; **~fieber** *nt* (*old*) *siehe* Typhus; **~gas** *nt* (*Mil*) nerve gas; **~gift** *nt* neurotoxin; **~heilanstalt** *f* psychiatric *or* mental hospital; **~heilkunde** *f* neurology; **~kitzel** *m* (*fig*) thrill; **etw als einen äußersten ~kitzel empfinden** to get a big thrill *or* kick (*inf*) out of sth, to find sth really thrilling; **~klinik** *f* psychiatric clinic; **~kostüm** *nt* (*hum*) **ein starkes/schwaches ~kostüm haben** to have strong/weak nerves; **~kraft** *f* strong nerves *pl*; **es erforderte einige ~kraft** it took strong nerves; **man verbraucht viel ~kraft** you use up a lot of nervous energy; **meine ~kraft ist erschöpft** my nerves can't take any more; **n~krank** *adj* (*geistig*) mentally ill *or* disturbed; (*körperlich*) suffering from a nervous disease; **~krankheit** *f* (*geistig*) mental illness *or* disorder; (*körperlich*) nervous disease *or* disorder; **~krieg** *m* (*fig*) war of nerves; **~lähmung** *f* neuroparalysis; **~leiden** *nt* nervous complaint *or* condition; **~mittel** *nt* sedative, tranquillizer; **~nahrung** *f* (*fig*) **das ist ~nahrung** it's good for my *etc* nerves; **~probe** *f* trial; **~sache** *f* (*inf*) question of nerves; **reine ~sache!** it's all a question of nerves; **~säge** *f* (*inf*) pain (in the neck) (*inf*); **n~schädigend** *adj* damaging to the nerves; **~schmerz** *m* neuralgia *no pl*; **~schock** *m* nervous shock; **n~schwach** *adj* with weak nerves, neurasthenic; **~schwäche** *f* weak nerves *pl*, neurasthenia; **n~stärkend** *adj* nerve-strengthening, tonic; **~strang** *m* nerve fibre; **~system** *nt* nervous system; **~zelle** *f* nerve cell; **~zerrüttung** *f* nervous exhaustion; **~zusammenbruch** *m* nervous breakdown, crack-up (*inf*).

nervig [ˈnɛrvɪç] *adj* *Faust, Hand, Gestalt* sinewy, wiry.

nervlich [ˈnɛrflɪç] *adj* **der ~e Zustand des Patienten** the state of the patient's nerves; **er ist ~ erschöpft** his nerves are at breaking point; **~ bedingt** nervous.

nervös [nɛrˈvøːs] *adj* nervous; (*aufgeregt auch*) jumpy (*inf*), jittery (*inf*), on edge. **die Krankheit ist rein ~ bedingt** the illness is purely nervous in origin; **jdn ~ machen** to make sb nervous; (*ärgern*) to get on sb's nerves.

Nervosität [nɛrvozɪˈtɛːt] *f* nervousness; (*Stimmung*) tension.

nervtötend [ˈnɛrf-] *adj* (*inf*) *Geräusch, Gerede* nerve-racking; *Arbeit* soul-destroying.

Nerz *m* **-es, -e** mink.

Nessel¹ *f* **-, -n** (*Bot*) nettle. **~n** (*Quaddeln*) nettle rash; **sich in die ~n setzen** (*inf*) to put oneself in a spot (*inf*).

Nessel² *m* **-s,** - (*auch ~tuch, ~stoff*) (untreated) cotton.

Nessel-: **~ausschlag** *m* nettle rash; **~fieber** *nt* nettle-rash fever; **~sucht** *f* nettle rash; **~tier** *nt* cnidarian (*spec*); jellyfish, sea anemone and corals.

Nest nt -(e)s, -er (a) (Brutstätte) nest.

(b) (fig: Schlupfwinkel) hideout, lair. ein ~ von Dieben a den of thieves; das ~ leer finden to find the bird/birds has/have flown.

(c) (fig: Heim) nest, home. sein eigenes ~ beschmutzen to foul one's own nest; sich ins warme ~ setzen (inf) to marry (into) money/to move straight into a good job; da hat er sich ins warme ~ gesetzt (inf) he's got it made (inf).

(d) (fig ing: Bett) bed. raus aus dem ~! rise and shine! (inf), show a leg! (inf).

(e) (pej inf: Ort) (schäbig) dump (inf), hole (inf), one-horse town (inf); (klein) little place.

Nest-: ~bau m nest-building; ~beschmutzer m (pej) runner-down (inf), knocker (inf) (of one's family or country); ~beschmutzung f (pej) running-down (inf), knocking (inf) (of one's family or country).

Nestel f -s, - (S Ger) lace (esp shoelace).

nesteln 1 vi an etw (dat) ~ to fumble or fiddle (around) with sth. 2 vt (rare) to fasten.

Nest-: ~flüchter m -s, - bird that leaves the nest early; (fig) person who leaves the family home at an early age; ~häkchen nt baby of the family; ~hocker m -s, - bird that stays a long time in its nest; (fig) person who stays with his parents for a long time.

Nestor m Nestor; (fig) doyen.

Nest-: n~warm adj warm from the nest; ~wärme f (fig) happy family life.

nett adj nice; (hübsch auch) pretty, cute. ein ganz ~es Sümmchen a nice little sum; eine ~e Stange Geld kosten (inf) to cost a pretty penny (inf) or tidy sum (inf); du bist mir ja ein N~er! (iro) well you're a nice or fine one!; das kann ja ~ werden! (iro) that'll be nice or great (inf) (I don't think!); sei so ~ und räum' auf! would you mind clearing up?, would you like to clear up?; Oma war so ~ und hat schon abgewaschen Grandma very nicely or kindly did the washing-up; ~, daß Sie gekommen sind! nice or good of you to come; das war (nicht) ~ von ihm that was(n't very) nice of him; was N~eres ist dir wohl nicht eingefallen? (iro) you do say/do some nice things.

netterweise adv kindly.

Nettigkeit f (a) no pl (nette Art) kindness, goodness. (b) (nette Worte) ~en nice or kind words or things.

netto adv (Comm) net. ich verdiene ~ £ 200 or £ 200 ~ im Monat I earn £200 net a month, I net £200 a month.

Netto- in cpds net.

Netz nt -es, -e (a) net; (Spinnen~) web; (Haar~) (hair)net; (Einkaufs~) string bag, net bag; (Gepäck~) (luggage) rack; (fig: von Lügen, Heuchelei) tissue, web; (Maschenwerk) netting. Fische mit dem ~ fangen to catch fish with nets, to net fish; ans ~ gehen (Sport) to go up to the net; ins ~ gehen (Ftbl) to go into the (back of the) net; (Tennis) to hit the net; ins ~ schlagen to play into the net; ~! (Tennis) let!; jdn in sein ~ locken or ziehen (fig) to lure sb into one's clutches; in jds ~ geraten (fig) to fall into sb's clutches; sich im eigenen ~ verstricken to be caught in one's own trap, to be hoist with one's own petard (prov); jdm ins ~ gehen (fig) to fall into sb's trap.

(b) (System) network; (Strom~) mains sing or pl; (Überland~) (national) grid.

(c) (Math) net; (Kartengitter) grid.

(d) (Anat) omentum (spec), caul (of the stomach).

Netz-: ~anschluß m (Elec) mains connection; ~arbeit f filet lace; n~artig adj netlike, reticular (form); ~auge nt compound eye; ~ball m (Tennis etc) netball.

netzen vti to moisten, to wet.

Netz-: ~flügler m -s, - neuropter (spec), ≈ lacewing; die ~Flügler the Neuroptera (spec); ~frequenz f mains frequency; ~gardine f net curtain; ~garn nt netting yarn; ~gerät nt mains receiver; ~gewebe nt gauze; ~gewölbe nt (Archit) fan vault.

Netzhaut f retina.

Netzhaut-: ~ablösung f detachment of the retina; ~entzündung f retinitis.

Netz-: ~hemd nt string vest (Brit) or undershirt (US); ~ka..e f (Rail) unlimited travel ticket, runabout ticket (Brit); ~magen m (Zool) second stomach; ~plan m critical path (diagram); ~plantechnik f critical path method; ~spannung f mains voltage; ~spiel nt net game; ~teil m mains adaptor; ~werk nt lace; (Elec, fig) network; (aus Draht) netting; ~wirkung f wetting effect; ~zwirn m netting twine.

neu adj new; Seite, Kräfte, Hoffnung, Truppen auch fresh; (kürzlich entstanden auch) recent; Wäsche, Socken clean; Wein young. das N~e Testament the New Testament; die N~e Welt the New World; jdm zum ~en Jahr Glück wünschen to wish sb (a) happy new year; ein ~er Anfang a fresh or new start; ~eren Datums of (more) recent date; ~e Hoffnung schöpfen to take new or fresh hope; eine ~e Mode/ein ~er Tanz a new fashion/dance; die ~(e)ste Mode/der ~(e)ste Tanz the latest fashion/dance; die ~esten Nachrichten the latest news; die ~eren Sprachen modern languages; ein ganz ~er Wagen a brand-new car; das ist mir ~! that's new(s) to me; mir ist die Sache ~ this is all new to me; schlechte Laune ist mir ~ an ihm it's something new for me to see him in a bad mood; sich wie ein ~er Mensch fühlen to feel like a new person; eine ~e Bearbeitung a revised edition; (von Oper etc) a new version; Geschichte der ~eren Zeit recent or modern history; in ~erer Zeit in modern times; erst in ~erer Zeit only recently; viele alte Leute finden sich in der ~en Zeit nicht mehr zurecht a lot of old people can't get on in the modern world; seit ~(e)stem recently; seit ~(e)stem gibt es ... since recently there has been ...; aufs ~e (geh) afresh, anew; auf ein ~es! (als Toast) (here's) to the New Year!; (Aufmunterung) let's try again; der/die N~e the newcomer, the new man/boy/woman/girl; the new president/pope

etc; the new guy (inf); die N~en the newcomers, the new people; was ist das N~e an dem Buch? what's new about the book?; das N~(e)ste in der Mode/auf dem Gebiet der Weltraumforschung the latest in fashion/in the field of space research; weißt du schon das N~(e)ste? have you heard the latest (news)?; was gibt's N~es? (inf) what's the latest?, what's new?; das N~(e)ste vom Tage the latest news, up-to-the-minute news; das N~(e)ste vom N~en the very latest (things); von ~em (von vorn) from the beginning, afresh, from scratch; (wieder) again; ~ beginnen to make a fresh start or start again from scratch; die Rollen ~ besetzen to recast the rôles; die Akten ~ ordnen to re-order the files; das Buch ist ~ erschienen the book is a recent publication or has recently or just come out or appeared; er ist ~ hinzugekommen he's joined (him/them) recently; ein Zimmer ~ einrichten to refurnish a room; sich/jdn ~ einkleiden to buy oneself/sb a new set of clothes.

Neu-: ~anfertigung f (das ~anfertigen) making (up), production (from scratch); (Produkt) newly-made article; ~anfertigung eines Anzugs dauert vier Wochen it takes four weeks to make up a suit; einer der Stühle ist eine ~anfertigung, die anderen sind antik one of the chairs is new, the others are antiques; ~ankömmling m newcomer; ~anschaffung f new purchase or acquisition; eine ~anschaffung würde sich rentieren it would be worth buying a new machine/part etc; n~apostolisch adj New Apostolic.

neuartig adj new. ein ~es Wörterbuch a new type of dictionary; es ist ganz ~ it is of a completely new type, it is a completely new departure.

Neuartigkeit f novelty.

Neu-: ~auflage f reprint; (mit Verbesserungen) new edition; ~ausgabe f new edition.

Neubau m new house/building.

Neubau-: ~siedlung f new housing estate; ~viertel nt new district; ~wohnung f newly-built flat.

Neu-: n~bearbeitet adj attr new; ~bearbeitung f revised edition; (von Oper etc) new version; (das ~bearbeiten) revision; reworking; ~beginn m new beginning; n~bekehrt adj attr newly or recently converted; ~bekehrte(r) mf decl as adj new or recent convert; ~belebung f revival; ~besetzung f replacement; (Theat) recasting; in der ~besetzung in the recast version; eine ~besetzung dieses Postens wurde nötig it was necessary to find a replacement for this position; ~bildung f (neues Gebilde) new entity; (Ling) neologism; (Med) renewal, repair; die ständige ~bildung von Staaten in Afrika the constant formation of new states in Africa; eine staatliche ~bildung a newly formed state; eine Kabinetts-~bildung wurde nötig it was necessary to form a new cabinet; bei der ~bildung von Begriffen in the formation of new concepts; ~bürger m new citizen; ~-Delhi nt ≈ New Delhi; n~deutsch adj (aus pej) new German, neo-German; ~druck m reprint; ~einrichtung f refurnishing; (Möbel) new furniture or furnishings pl; ~einstellung f new appointment; ~einstudierung f (stelle ~inszenierung; ~england nt New England; n~englisch adj modern English; n~entdeckt adj attr newly or recently discovered; ~entdeckung f rediscovery; (Mensch) new discovery; (Ort) newly discovered place; n~entwickelt adj attr newly developed; ~entwicklung f new development.

neuerdings adv recently; (rare: von neuem) again.

Neuerer m -s, - innovator.

neuerlich 1 adv lately, recently, of late; (rare: nochmals) again. 2 adj recent; (wiederholt) further.

Neu-: n~eröffnet adj attr newly-opened; (wiedereröffnet) reopened; ~eröffnung f (Wiedereröffnung) reopening; die ~eröffnung der Fluglinie the opening of the new airline; es gab zwanzig Geschäftsschließungen und nur zwei ~eröffnungen twenty shops were closed and only two new ones opened; ~erscheinung f new or recent publication; (Neuheit) new or recent phenomenon.

Neuerung f innovation; (Reform) reform.

neuerungssüchtig adj over-anxious to carry out reforms, reform-mad (inf).

Neuerwerbung f new acquisition. die ~ von Büchern the acquisition of new books.

neu(e)stens adv lately, recently.

Neu-: ~fassung f new or revised version; ~festsetzung f revision of a/the rate; new rate; ~fundland nt Newfoundland; ~fundländer m -s, - (Hund) Newfoundland (dog); n~gebacken adj attr fresh- or newly-baked; (fig) newly-fledged, brand-new; n~geboren adj newborn; sich wie n~geboren fühlen to feel (like) a new man/woman; ~geborene(s) nt decl as adj new-born child; ~geburt f (~geborenes) newborn child/animal; (~erscheinung) new phenomenon; (Wiedergeburt) rebirth; die ~geburten the newborn; n~geschaffen adj attr newly created; n~gestalten* vt sep to rearrange, to reorder; Platz, Stadion to redesign, to give a new layout; ~gestaltung f siehe vt rearrangement, reordering; redesigning, new layout; die ~gestaltung eines alten Themas the reworking of an old theme; n~gewählt adj attr newly elected.

Neugier(de) f -, no pl curiosity, inquisitiveness; (pej auch) nosiness (inf). aus ~ out of curiosity; seine ~ befriedigen to satisfy one's curiosity.

neugierig adj inquisitive, curious (auf +acc about); (pej) prying, nos(e)y (inf); (gespannt) longing or curious to know. ein N~er an inquisitive person; (pej auch) a nos(e)y parker (inf); jdn ~ machen to excite or arouse sb's curiosity; ich bin ~, ob I wonder if; da bin ich aber ~! this should be interesting, I can hardly wait (inf); sei nicht so ~! don't be so inquisitive or nos(e)y (inf) or such a nos(e)y parker (inf)!

Neu-: ~gliederung f reorganization, restructuring; ~gotik f

Gothic revival, neo-Gothic style; n~gotisch *adj* neo-Gothic; n~griechisch *adj* modern Greek; das ~griechische modern Greek; ~gründung *f* (*Wiederbegründung*) re-establishment, refoundation; die ~gründung von Universitäten the founding of new universities; der Verein/die Stadt ist eine ~gründung the club/town was only recently founded; ~gruppierung *f* regroupment, rearrangement; ~guinea *nt* New Guinea.

Neuheit *f* (a) *no pl* novelty. es wird bald den Reiz der ~ verlieren the novelty will soon wear off. (b) innovation, new thing/idea. dieses Gerät ist eine ~ auf dem Markt this apparatus has only recently come on(to) the market.

neuhochdeutsch *adj* New High German. das N~e New High German.

Neuigkeit *f* (piece of) news. die ~en the news *sing*; die ~ des Tages the big news of the day.

Neuinszenierung *f* new production.

Neujahr *nt* New Year. jdm zu(m) ~ gratulieren to wish sb a Happy New Year; ~ begehen *or* feiern to celebrate the New Year; Pros(i)t ~! (here's) to the New Year!

Neujahrs-: ~abend *m* New Year's Eve, Hogmanay (*Scot*); ~empfang *m* New Year reception; ~fest *nt* New Year's Day; (*Feier*) New Year celebrations *pl*; ~glückwunsch *m* New Year greeting; ~karte *f* New Year card; ~tag *m* New Year's day.

Neuland *nt*, *no pl* virgin land *or* territory, uncultivated land; (*fig*) new territory *or* ground. er betrat wissenschaftliches ~ he broke new ground in science.

neulateinisch *adj* neo-Latin, new Latin.

neulich 1 *adv* recently, the other day. ~ abend(s) the other evening. 2 *adj* (*strictly incorrect*) recent.

Neuling *m* newcomer, new man/woman/boy/girl; (*pej auch*) beginner, greenhorn (*inf*).

neumodisch *adj* (*pej*) new-fangled (*pej*). ~ unterrichten to teach in a new-fangled way/to teach new-fangled stuff.

Neumond *m* new moon. bei ~ at new moon; heute ist ~ there's a new moon today.

Neun *f* -, -en nine. die ~ ist eine heilige Zahl nine is a sacred number; er hat die ~ ausgespielt he played the nine; ach du grüne ~e! (*inf*) well I'm blowed! (*inf*); siehe auch Vier.

neun *num* nine. (*beim Kegeln*) alle ~(e)! strike!; er warf alle ~(e) he got a strike; *siehe auch* vier.

Neun|auge *nt* lamprey.

Neun-: ~eck *nt* nonagon; n~eckig *adj* nonagonal.

Neunerprobe *f* (*Math*) casting out nines.

Neun-: n~hundert *num* nine hundred; *siehe auch* vierhundert; n~mal *adv* nine times; das ist ~mal so viel! that's nine times as much; n~malklug *adj* (*iro*) smart-aleck *attr*; du bist ein ganz ~malkluger! you're a real smart-aleck; n~schwänzig *adj*: die n~schwänzige Katze the cat-o'-nine-tails; n~tausend *num* nine thousand; *siehe auch* viertausend.

Neuntel *nt* -s, - ninth; *siehe auch* Viertel[1].

neuntens *adv* ninth(ly), in the ninth place.

neunte(r, s) *adj* ninth; *siehe auch* vierte(r, s).

neunzehn *num* nineteen; *siehe auch* vierzehn.

neunzehnte(r, s) *adj* nineteenth; *siehe auch* vierte(r, s).

neunzig *num* ninety. auf ~ sein (*inf*) to be in a blind fury *or* a filthy temper (*inf*); *siehe auch* vierzig.

Neunziger(in *f*) *m* -s, - (*Mensch*) ninety-year-old, nonagenarian; *siehe auch* Vierziger(in).

neunzigste(r, s) *adj* ninetieth; *siehe* vierte(r, s).

Neu-: ~ordnung *f* reorganization, reordering; (*Reform*) reform; ~orientierung *f* reorientation; ~philologe *m* modern linguist; ~philologie *f* modern languages *sing or pl*; n~platonisch *adj* neo-Platonic; ~prägung *f* (*Münze*) new minting; (*Begriff*) new coinage; die ~prägung von Münzen/Begriffen the minting/coining of new coins/concepts.

Neuralgie *f* neuralgia.

neuralgisch *adj* neuralgic. ein ~er Punkt a trouble area; diese Kreuzung/Zypern ist ein ~er Punkt this crossroads/Cyprus is a trouble area *or* trouble spot.

Neurasthenie *f* neurasthenia.

Neurastheniker(in *f*) *m* -s, - neurasthenic.

neurasthenisch *adj* neurasthenic.

Neu-: ~reg(e)lung *f* adjustment, revision; eine ~regelung des Verkehrs a new traffic management scheme; n~reich *adj* nouveau riche; ~reiche(r) *mf* nouveau riche; die ~reichen the nouveaux riches.

Neuritis *f* -, **Neuritiden** neuritis.

Neuro- *in cpds* neuro; ~chirurgie *f* neurosurgery; ~loge *m* neurologist; ~logie *f* neurology; ~login *f* neurologist; n~logisch *adj* neurological.

Neuron *nt* -s, -e(n) [-'ro:na(n)] neuron.

Neuro-: ~pathie *f* neuropathy; ~pathologie *f* neuropathology.

Neurose *f* -, -n neurosis.

Neurotiker(in *f*) *m* -s, - neurotic.

neurotisch *adj* neurotic.

Neu-: ~satz *m* (*Typ*) new setting; ~schnee *m* fresh snow; über Nacht gab es ~schnee there was fresh snow *or* a fresh snowfall overnight; ~schöpfung *f* new creation; (*Ausdruck*) invention; die ~schöpfung von Begriffen the creation of new concepts; ~seeland *nt* New Zealand; n~seeländisch *adj* New Zealand; ~silber *nt* German silver; ~sprachler(in *f*) *m* -s, - modern linguist; n~sprachlich *adj* modern language; ~sprachliche Zweig (*Sch*) modern language side; n~sprachliches Gymnasium ≈ grammar school (*Brit*), high school (*esp US*, *Scot*) stressing modern languages; ~stadt *f* new town.

neustens *adv siehe* neu(e)stens.

neutral *adj* neutral; (*rare: Gram*) neuter. die N~en (*Pol*) the neutrals.

Neutralisation *f* neutralization. die ~ eines Rennens (*Sport*) the suspension of a race.

neutralisieren* *vt* to neutralize. das Rennen wurde neutralisiert (*Sport*) the race was suspended.

Neutralisierung *f* neutralization.

Neutralismus *m* (*Pol*) neutralism.

Neutralität *f* neutrality.

Neutralitäts-: ~abkommen *nt* treaty of neutrality; ~politik *f* policy of neutrality; ~zeichen *nt* sign of neutrality.

Neutron *nt* -s, -en [nɔy'tro:nən] neutron.

Neutrum *nt* -s, **Neutra** *or* **Neutren** (*Gram*, *fig*) neuter. ein ~ (*Gram*) a neuter noun; sie wirkt auf mich wie ein ~ I don't think of her as a woman.

Neu-: ~veranlagung *f* (*Fin*) reassessment; n~vermählt *adj* newly married *or* wed; die ~vermählten the newly-weds; ~wahl *f* (*Pol*) new election, re-election; die ~wahl des Präsidenten the election of a new president; n~weltlich *adj* (*geh*) new world; ~wert *m* value when new; ~wertig *adj* as new; ~wertversicherung *f* new-for-old insurance, replacement value insurance; ~zeit *f* modern age *or* era, modern times *pl*; Literatur/Gesellschaft der ~zeit modern literature/society; n~zeitlich *adj* modern; ~züchtung *f* new breed; (*Pflanze*) new variety; die ~züchtung von Tieren/Pflanzen the breeding/cultivation of new types of animal/plant; ~zugang *m* new entry; ~zulassung *f* (*Aut*) ≈ registration of a new vehicle; die meisten gestohlenen Autos waren ~zulassungen most of the stolen cars were *or* had new registrations.

Nibelungentreue *f* unshakeable loyalty.

nicht *adv* (a) (*Verneinung*) not. er raucht ~ (*augenblicklich*) he is not *or* isn't smoking; (*gewöhnlich*) he does not *or* doesn't smoke; alle lachten, nur er ~ everybody laughed except him, everybody laughed, only he didn't; kommst du? — nein, ich komme ~ are you coming? — no, I'm not (coming); ich weiß auch ~, warum I really don't know why; ich kann das ~ — ich auch ~ I can't do it — neither *or* nor can I; ~ mehr *or* länger not any longer; ~ mehr als no *or* not more than; ~ mehr und ~ weniger als no more and no less than; ~ heute und ~ morgen neither today nor tomorrow; ~ ihn meinte ich, sondern sie I didn't mean him, I meant her, it's not him I meant but her; er ~! not him, not he (*form*); ~ (ein)mal not even.

(b) (*Bitte, Gebot, Verbot*) ~ berühren! do not touch; (*gesprochen*) don't touch; ärgere dich ~! don't be angry, do not be angry (*often liter*); ~ rauchen! no smoking; ~! don't!, no!; tu's ~! don't do it!; ~ doch! stop it!, don't!; bitte ~! please don't; nur das ~! anything but that!; nun wein mal ~ gleich! now don't start crying.

(c) (*rhetorisch*) er kommt/sie kommen *etc*, ~ (wahr)? he's coming/they're coming *etc*, isn't he/aren't they? *or* is he not/are they not?; er kommt ~, ~ wahr? he isn't coming, is he?; ich darf kommen, ~ (wahr)? I can come, can't I *or* can I?; das ist schön, ~ (wahr)? it's nice, isn't it?; jetzt wollen wir Schluß machen, ~? let's leave it now, right *or* OK?

(d) (*doppelte Verneinung*) ~ uninteressant/unschön *etc* not uninteresting/unattractive *etc*; das hat mir keiner ~ gesagt (*incorrect*) I wasn't told that by nobody (*incorrect*); die Reichen brauchen keine Almosen ~ (*incorrect*) the rich don't need no alms (*incorrect*).

(e) (*Verwunderung, Resignation etc*) was die Kinder ~ alles wissen! the things children know about!; was ich ~ alles durchmachen muß! the things I have to go through!

Nicht-, nicht- *pref* non-.

Nicht-: ~achtung *f* (+*gen* for) disregard, lack of regard; jdn mit ~achtung strafen to send sb to Coventry; ~achtung des Gerichts contempt of court; n~amtlich *adj* unofficial; ~anerkennung *f* non-recognition; ~angriffspakt *m* non-aggression pact; ~arier *m* non-Aryan; ~beachtung, ~befolgung *f* non-observance; ~benutzung *f* (*form*) non-utilization (*form*); bei ~benutzung der Maschine when the machine is not in use *or* being used; n~berufstätig *adj attr* non-employed; ~bezahlung *f* non-payment; n~christlich *adj* non-Christian.

Nichte *f* -, -n niece.

Nicht-: n~ehelich *adj* (*Jur*) Kinder, Abstammung illegitimate; Mutter unmarried; Vater natural; n~eheliche Beziehungen zu jdm unterhalten to cohabit with sb; Kinder aus n~ehelichen Beziehungen children born outside wedlock (*form*); ~einhaltung *f* non-compliance (+*gen* with), non-observance (+*gen* of); ~einmischung *f* (*Pol*) non-intervention, non-interference; ~eisenmetall *nt* non-ferrous metal; ~erfüllung *f* (*Jur*) non-fulfilment (*of sth*), default; ~erscheinen *nt* non-appearance, failure to appear; ~fachmann *m* non-specialist, non-expert; ~gebrauch *m siehe* ~benutzung; ~gefallen *nt*: bei ~gefallen (zurück) if not satisfied (return); n~geschäftsfähig *adj attr siehe* geschäftsunfähig; ~-Ich *nt* non-self.

nichtig *adj* (a) (*Jur: ungültig*) invalid, void. etw für ~ erklären to declare sth invalid; Ehe *auch* to annul sth; dadurch *or* hierdurch ist der Vertrag ~ geworden the treaty has thereby become invalid; *siehe auch* null.

(b) (*unbedeutend*) trifling, trivial; Versuch vain; Drohung empty, vain. die ~en Dinge dieser Welt (*liter*) the vain things *or* the vanities (*liter*) of this life.

Nichtigkeit *f* (a) (*Jur: Ungültigkeit*) voidness, invalidity, nullity. (b) (*Bedeutungslosigkeit*) triviality, vainness, emptiness. (c) *usu pl* (*Kleinigkeit*) trifle, triviality, trivia *pl*.

Nichtigkeits-: ~erklärung *f* (*Jur*) annulment; ~klage *f* (*Jur*) nullity suit.

Nicht-: ~kombattant *m* (*form*) non-combatant; ~konvertierbarkeit *f* non-convertibility; n~leitend *adj* (*Elec*) non-conducting; ~leiter *m* -s, - (*Elec*) non-conductor; ~metall *nt* nonmetal; n~metallisch *adj* nonmetallic; ~mitglied *nt* non-member; n~öffentlich *adj attr* not open to the public, private; **n~öffentliche Sitzung/Konferenz** meeting/conference in camera (*Jur*) *or* behind closed doors; **n~organisiert** *adj attr Arbeiter* non-organized, non-union(ized); **~raucher** *m* (*auch Rail*) non-smoker; **ich bin ~raucher** I don't smoke, I'm a non-smoker; **„~raucher"** "no smoking" (*Brit*), "non-smoking car" (*US*); **~raucherabteil** *nt* no-smoking compartment; **n~rostend** *adj attr* rustproof, non-rust; *Stahl* stainless.

Nichts *nt* (a) **-**, *no pl* (*Philos*) nothingness; (*Leere*) emptiness, void; (*Kleinigkeit*) trifle, triviality, trivia *pl*. **etw aus dem ~ erschaffen/aufbauen** to create sth out of nothing(ness) *or* the void/to build sth up from nothing; **dieser Schriftsteller ist aus dem ~ aufgetaucht** this author sprang up from nowhere; **vor dem ~ stehen** to be left with nothing; **alle seine Hoffnungen endeten im ~** (*liter*) all his hopes came to nothing *or* nought. (b) **-es, -e** (*Mensch*) nobody, nonentity, (mere) cipher.

nichts *indef pron inv* nothing; (*fragend, bedingend auch*) not ... anything. **ich weiß ~** I know nothing, I don't know anything; **~ als** nothing but; **~ (anderes) als** nothing/not ... anything but *or* except; **~ von Bedeutung** nothing of (any) importance; **~ Besseres/Neues** *etc* nothing better/new *etc*; **~ da!** (*inf*) (*weg da*) no you don't!; (*ausgeschlossen*) nothing doing (*inf*), no chance (*inf*); **~ zu danken!** don't mention it, not at all; **für** *or* **um ~ for nothing, das ist ~ für mich** that's not (for) me, that's not my thing (*inf*) *or* not my cup of tea (*Brit inf*); **für ~ und wieder ~** (*inf*) for nothing at all, for damn all (*sl*); **~ zu machen** nothing doing (*inf*), you've had that (*inf*), nix (*sl*); **(es war) ~ mehr zu machen** there was nothing more that could be done; **~ mehr** nothing more, not ... anything more; **ich weiß ~ Näheres** *or* **Genaues** I don't know any details; **das war wohl ~** (*sl*) that's not much good, you can't win them all (*inf*); **es ging wie ~** (*inf*) it was over in a trice *or* flash (*inf*) *or* jiffy (*inf*); **~ wie raus/rein/hin** *etc* (*inf*) let's get out/in/over there *etc* (on the double); **aus ~ wird ~** (*Prov*) you can't make something out of nothing; **ich mag** *or* **will ~ mehr davon hören** I don't want to hear any more about it; **er ist zu ~ nutze** *or* **zu gebrauchen** he's useless *or* hopeless.

nichts-: **~ahnend** *adj* unsuspecting; **~bedeutend** *adj* trivial, trifling; *Funktionär* insignificant.

Nicht-: **~schwimmer** *m* non-swimmer; **sie ist ~schwimmer** she's a non-swimmer; **~schwimmerbecken** *nt* pool for non-swimmers.

nichts-: **~destominder** (*rare*), **~destotrotz** *adv* notwithstanding (*form*), nonetheless; **~destoweniger** *adv* nevertheless, nonetheless.

Nichtsein, Nicht-Sein *nt* non-existence, non-being.

Nichtser *m* **-s, -** (*S Ger inf*) nought, zero.

Nichtseßhafte(r) *mf decl as adj* (*form*) person of no fixed abode (*form*).

Nichts-: **~könner** *m* washout (*inf*), incompetent person; **er ist ein ~könner** he's (worse than) useless; **~nutz** *m* **-es, -e** good-for-nothing, useless bungler; **n~nutzig** *adj* useless, hopeless; (*unartig*) good-for-nothing; **~nutzigkeit** *f* uselessness, hopelessness; **die ~nutzigkeit dieser Kinder** these good-for-nothing children; **n~sagend** *adj Buch, Rede, Worte* empty, meaningless; *Vergnügen* trivial, trite, frivolous; *Mensch* insignificant; *Gesichtsausdruck* blank, vacant, expressionless; *Erklärung, Redensart* meaningless; **~tuer(in** *f*) *m* **-s, -** idler, loafer; **n~tuerisch** *adj* idle; **~tun** *nt* idleness, inactivity; (*Muße*) leisure; **das süße ~tun** dolce far niente, idle bliss; **viel Zeit mit ~tun verbringen** to spend a lot of time doing nothing; **n~würdig** *adj* base, despicable; *Mensch auch* worthless; (**du**) **~würdiger!** (*old, liter*) vile *or* base wretch! (*old, liter*); **~würdigkeit** *f siehe adj* baseness, worthlessness.

Nicht-: **~tänzer** *m* non-dancer; **ich bin ~tänzer** I don't dance; **~trinker** *m* non-drinker; **er ist ~trinker** he doesn't drink; **~übereinstimmung** *f* discrepancy (+*gen* in, of, between); (*Meinungsunterschied*) differences *pl*, disagreement; **~vorhandensein** *nt* absence; **~wählbarkeit** *f* ineligibility (for office); **~weitergabe** *f* (*von Atomwaffen*) non-proliferation; **~wissen** *nt* ignorance; **sich mit ~wissen entschuldigen** to plead ignorance; **~zahlung** *f* (*form*) non-payment; **im Falle der ~zahlung, bei ~zahlung** in default of payment; **n~zielend** *adj siehe* intransitiv; **~zustandekommen** *nt* (*form*) non-completion; **~zutreffende(s)** *nt decl as adj* (*etwas*) **~zutreffendes** something incorrect; **~zutreffendes** (*bitte*) **streichen!** (*please*) delete as applicable.

Nickel¹ *nt* **-s**, *no pl* nickel.

Nickel² *m* **-s, -** (*old*) 10-Pfennig piece, copper (*Brit*), nickel (*US*).

Nickel-: **~brille** *f* metal-rimmed glasses *pl*; **~legierung** *f* nickel alloy; **~stahl** *m* nickel steel.

nicken 1 *vi* (a) (*lit, fig*) to nod. **mit dem Kopf ~** to nod one's head; **ein leichtes N~** a slight nod.
(b) (*inf: schlummern*) to snooze, to doze, to nod.
2 *vt* (*jdm*) **Beifall/ein stummes Ja/einen Gruß ~** to nod (to sb) in approval *or* approvingly/in silent affirmation/in greeting.

Nickerchen *nt* (*inf*) nap, snooze, forty winks (*inf*). **ein ~ machen** to take *or* have forty winks *or* a nap *or* a snooze.

Nicki *m* **-s, -s** velour pullover; (**~hemd**) velour T-shirt.

nid *prep* +*dat* (*old*) beneath, under, 'neath (*poet*).

nie *adv* never. **~ im Leben** never ever; **machst du das? — ~ im Leben!** will you do it? — not on your life; **~ und nimmer** never ever; **~ wieder** *or* **mehr** never again; **ein ~ wiedergutzumachender Fehler** a mistake that can never be put right; **fast ~** hardly ever.

nieder 1 *adj attr* (a) (*esp S Ger: niedrig*) low. **die ~e Jagd** small game hunting.
(b) (*weniger bedeutend*) lower; *Beamte auch* minor; (*geringer*) *Geburt, Herkunft* lowly; *Volk* common; *Klasse,*

Stand lower. **der ~e Adel** the gentry, the lower *or* lesser aristocracy; **Hohe und N~e** (*liter*)/**hoch und ~** (*liter*) (both) the high and the low.
(c) *Triebe, Instinkt* low, base; *Arbeit* menial.
(d) (*primitiv*) *Kulturstufe* low, primitive; *Entwicklungsstufe* low, early.
2 *adv* down. **die Waffen ~!** lay down your arms; **auf und ~** up and down; **das Auf und N~** (*lit*) the bobbing up and down; (*fig*) the ups and (the) downs *pl*; **~ mit dem Kaiser!** down with the Kaiser!

Nieder-, nieder- *pref* (*Geog*) lower.

niederbeugen *sep* 1 *vt* (*lit, fig*) to bow down. 2 *vr* to bend down.

niederbrechen *vti sep irreg* (*vi: aux sein*) to break down.

niederbrennen *vti sep* (*irreg*) (*vi: aux sein*) to burn down.

niederbrüllen *vt sep Redner* to shout down.

niederdeutsch *adj* (a) (*Geog*) North German. (b) (*Ling*) Low German. **das N~e** Low German.

niederdonnern *sep* 1 *vi aux sein* (*Lawine*) to thunder down. 2 *vt* (*inf*) **jdn ~** to bawl sb out (*inf*).

Niederdruck *m* (*Tech*) low pressure.

niederdrücken *vt sep* (a) (*lit*) to press down; *Taste, Hebel auch* to press, to push, to depress (*form*). (b) (*bedrücken*) **jdn ~** to depress sb, to get sb down (*inf*); **~d** depressing; *siehe* **niedergedrückt.**

niederfahren *vi sep irreg aux sein* (*liter*) to descend.

niederfallen *vi sep irreg aux sein* (*liter*) to fall *or* drop down.

Niederfrequenz *f* low frequency; (*Akustik*) audio frequency.

Niedergang *m* (a) (*liter: der Sonne*) setting, going down (*poet*); (*fig: Verfall*) decline, fall. (b) (*Naut*) companionway.

niedergedrückt *adj* depressed, dejected.

niedergehen *vi sep irreg aux sein* to descend; (*Aviat*) to descend, to come down; (*Fallschirmspringer*) to drop; (*Vorhang*) to fall, to drop; (*Regen*) to fall; (*Gewitter*) to break (*auch fig*); (*Boxer*) to go down.

niedergeschlagen 1 *ptp of* niederschlagen. 2 *adj* dejected, despondent.

Niedergeschlagenheit *f* dejection, despondency.

niederhalten *vt sep irreg* to hold *or* keep down; *Volk* to oppress; (*Mil*) to pin *or* hold down.

niederhauen *vt sep irreg Baum* to cut *or* chop down, to fell; *Gegner* to floor, to knock down, to fell.

niederholen *vt sep Segel, Flagge* to haul down, to lower; *Ballon* to bring down.

Niederholz *nt, no pl* underwood, underbrush.

Niederjagd *f* small game hunting.

niederkämpfen *vt sep Feuer* to fight down *or* back; *Feind* to overcome; *Tränen* to fight back.

niederkauern *vir* (*vi: aux sein*) to crouch *or* cower down.

niederknallen *vt sep* to shoot down.

niederknien *vi sep aux sein* to kneel down.

niederknüppeln *vt sep* to club down.

niederkommen *vi sep irreg aux sein* (*old*) to be delivered (*old*) (*mit* of).

Niederkunft *f* **-, -̈e** (*old*) delivery.

Niederlage *f* (a) (*Mil, Sport, fig*) defeat; (*Mißerfolg*) failure, defeat. **eine ~ einstecken müssen** *or* **erleiden** to suffer a defeat; **jdm eine ~ zufügen** *or* **beibringen** to defeat sb, to inflict a defeat on sb; **ich kann dir jetzt schon eine ~ voraussagen** I can tell you now you're going to fail.
(b) (*Lager*) warehouse, store, depot.
(c) (*Filiale*) branch (office).

Niederlande *pl*: **die ~** the Netherlands *sing or pl*, the Low Countries *pl*.

Niederländer(in *f*) *m* **-s, -** Netherlander, Dutchman/Dutchwoman *etc*. **die ~** the Netherlanders, the Dutch.

niederländisch *adj* Dutch, Netherlands. **das N~e** Dutch.

niederlassen *vr sep irreg* (a) to sit down; (*sich niederlegen*) to lie down; (*Vögel*) to land, to alight.
(b) (*Wohnsitz nehmen*) to settle (down).
(c) (*Praxis, Geschäft eröffnen*) to set up in business, to establish oneself, to set up shop (*inf*). **sich als Arzt/Rechtsanwalt ~** to set up (a practice) as a doctor/lawyer; **die niedergelassenen Ärzte** general practitioners, GPs; **die niedergelassenen Rechtsanwälte** lawyers in private practice.

Niederlassung *f* (a) *no pl* (*das Niederlassen*) settling, settlement; (*eines Arztes etc*) establishment, setting-up. **die ~ eines Arztes in einer eigenen Praxis ist freigestellt** a doctor is free to set up his own practice. (b) (*Siedlung*) settlement. (c) (*Comm*) registered office; (*Zweigstelle*) branch.

Niederlassungsbewilligung *f* (*Sw*) residence permit.

niederlegen *sep* 1 *vt* (a) *Gegenstand, Menschen* to lay *or* put *or* set down; *Last auch* to cast off; (*liter, Bibl*) *Kranz, Blumen* to lay; *Waffen* to lay down.
(b) (*aufgeben*) *Dienst, Amt, Mandat* to resign (from), to give up; *Krone, Regierung, Führung* to renounce, to give up. **die Arbeit ~** (*aufhören*) to stop work(ing); (*bei manueller Arbeit auch*) to down tools; (*streiken*) to stop work, to strike.
(c) (*schriftlich festlegen*) to write *or* set down.
(d) (*rare: einreißen*) *Mauer, Gebäude* to pull down; *Baum* to fell, to cut down.
2 *vr* to lie down. **da legst' di' nieder!** (*S Ger inf*) well I'm blowed! (*inf*), by the 'eck! (*N Engl dial*).

Niederlegung *f* (a) (*von Kranz*) laying.
(b) (*von Amt, Dienst, Mandat*) resignation (from); (*von Kommando*) resignation (of); (*der Krone*) abdication. **~ der Arbeit** industrial action.
(c) (*schriftlich*) setting-out. **eine schriftliche ~ meiner Gedanken** setting out *or* putting down my thoughts in writing.

niedermachen, niedermetzeln *vt sep* to massacre, to butcher.

niedermähen vt sep (lit, fig) to mow down.
Nieder|österreich nt Lower Austria.
niederprasseln vi sep aux sein (Regen, Hagel etc) to beat down, to hammer down; (fig: Beschimpfungen, Vorwürfe) to rain or hail down.
niederreißen vt sep irreg jdn to pull or drag down; Gebäude to pull or knock down; (fig) Schranken to tear down.
Niederrhein m Lower Rhine.
niederrheinisch adj Lower Rhine.
niederringen vt sep irreg to fight down; (im Ringkampf auch) to floor; (fig auch) to fight back.
Niedersachsen nt Lower Saxony.
niedersausen vi sep aux sein to rain or hail down.
niederschießen sep irreg 1 vt to shoot down. 2 vi aux sein (Vogel etc) to shoot or plummet down.
Niederschlag m (a) (Met) precipitation (form); (Chem) precipitate; (Bodensatz) sediment, dregs pl. radioaktiver ~ (radioactive) fallout; für morgen sind heftige ~e gemeldet tomorrow there will be heavy rain/hail/snow; die statistischen Untersuchungen fanden ihren ~ in Gehaltserhöhungen the outcome of the statistical studies was a rise in wages, the statistical results resulted in a wage rise; in diesem Gedicht haben seine eigenen Erfahrungen ihren ~ gefunden his own experiences are reflected or find expression in this poem.
  (b) (Mus) downbeat.
  (c) (Boxen) knockdown blow; (über 10 Sekunden) knockout, KO. ~ bis 10 knockout, KO. Sieg durch ~ win by a knockout.
niederschlagen sep irreg 1 vt (a) jdn to knock down, to fell; (Regen, Hagel) Getreide to beat down, to flatten; Kragen, Hutkrempe to turn down; Aufstand, Revolte to quell, to put down, to suppress; Augen, Blick to lower, to cast down (liter); (Med) Fieber to bring down, to reduce, to lower. ~de Mittel antipyretics (spec); siehe auch niedergeschlagen.
  (b) (erlassen) Steuerschuld to waive. ein Verfahren ~ (Jur) to dismiss a case.
  (c) (Chem) to precipitate.
  2 vr (Flüssigkeit) to condense; (Bodensatz) to settle; (Chem) to precipitate; (Met) to fall. die Untersuchung schlug sich in einer Reform nieder the investigation resulted in a reform; sich in etw (dat) ~ (Erfahrungen etc) to find expression in sth.
Niederschlags-: n~arm adj with low precipitation (form); low-rainfall attr; with little snow; die Südinsel ist n~ärmer the south island has a lower rainfall/less snow or a lower level of precipitation (form); n~frei adj dry, without precipitation (form); nach drei n~freien Tagen after three rainless days/ three days without snow; ~menge f rainfall/snowfall, precipitation (form); n~reich adj with a lot of precipitation (form); high rainfall attr; with a lot of snow.
Niederschlagung f (von Strafverfahren) dismissal; (von Schulden, Abgaben, Steuern) waiving; (eines Aufstands) suppression.
niederschmettern vt sep to smash or batter down; (fig) to shatter.
niederschmetternd adj Nachricht, Ergebnis shattering.
niederschreiben vt sep irreg to write down.
niederschreien vt sep irreg to shout down.
Niederschrift f (das Niederschreiben) writing down; (Niedergeschriebenes) notes pl; (Schulaufsatz) composition, essay; (Protokoll) (einer Sitzung) minutes pl; (Jur) record. er brauchte viel Zeit für die ~ seiner Gedanken he needed a lot of time to write down his thoughts; die erste ~ eines Gedichts/Romans the first draft of a poem/novel.
niedersetzen sep 1 vt Kind, Glas to put or set down; Last auch to cast off (liter, Bibl). 2 vr to sit down; (Vogel) to perch, to settle, to alight.
niedersinken vi sep irreg aux sein (geh) to sink down.
Niederspannung f (Elec) low voltage or tension.
niederstechen vt sep irreg to stab or knife (down).
niedersteigen vti sep irreg aux sein (liter) to descend.
niederstimmen vt sep to vote down.
niederstoßen sep irreg 1 vt to knock down. 2 vi aux sein (Raubvogel) to shoot or plummet down.
niederstrecken sep (geh) 1 vt to lay low. 2 vr to lie down, to stretch out.
niederstürzen vi sep aux sein to crash down.
niedertourig [-tuːrɪç] adj Motor, Maschine low-revving. ~ fahren to drive with low revs.
Niedertracht f, no pl despicableness, vileness; (als Rache) malice, spite. so viel ~ hätte ich ihm nicht zugetraut I would not have suspected him of such a despicable or vile act; die ~, mit der er bei seinen Betrügereien vorgegangen ist the despicable way he went about his deceptions.
niederträchtig adj despicable, vile; (rachsüchtig) malicious, spiteful. jdn ~ verraten to betray sb in a despicable way.
Niederträchtigkeit f (a) no pl siehe Niedertracht. (b) (Tat) despicable/malicious behaviour no pl. das ist eine ~ that's despicable.
niedertrampeln vt sep to trample underfoot.
niedertreten vt sep irreg to tread or trample down; Erde to tread or stamp down; Teppich to wear (down).
Niederung f (Senke) depression; (Mündungsgebiet) flats pl; (sumpfig) marsh. die ~en des Lebens the dark or seamy side of life; in solche ~en begebe ich mich nicht (fig) I will not sink to such depths.
niederwalzen vt sep to flatten.
niederwärts adv (obs) down, downward(s).
niederwerfen sep irreg 1 vt to throw or hurl or cast (liter) down; Aufstand to suppress, to put down; Gegner (lit) to throw down, to floor; (fig) to defeat, to overcome. er wurde von einer Krankheit niedergeworfen he was laid low by or with an illness.
  2 vr to throw oneself down, to prostrate oneself.
Niederwerfung f (von Aufstand) suppression.
Niederwild nt small game.
niederzwingen vt sep irreg (lit) to force down; (fig) to defeat, to vanquish. er zwang seinen Gegner auf die Knie nieder (lit, fig) he brought his enemy to his knees.
niedlich adj sweet, cute, pretty little attr. das kann ja ~ werden! (iro) a fine prospect or look-out (inf)!, that's just fine!; das Kätzchen lag so ~ auf meinem Bett the kitten looked so sweet lying on my bed.
Niedlichkeit f sweetness, cuteness, prettiness.
Niednagel m agnail.
niedrig adj (a) (tief) low. ~ fliegen to fly low.
  (b) (gering) low; Stand, Herkunft, Geburt auch lowly, humble. hoch und ~, Hohe und N~e (liter) (both) the high and the low; ~ste Preise lowest or rock-bottom prices; ich schätze seine Chancen sehr ~ ein I don't think much of his chances, I think his chances are very slim or small; von jdm ~ denken, jdn ~ einschätzen to have a low or poor opinion of sb.
  (c) (gemein) low no adv, base.
Niedrigkeit f (a) lowness. die ~ des Wasserstandes the low water level; die ~ der Häuser the low-built style of the houses.
  (b) (von Gedanken, Beweggründen) lowness, baseness.
Niedrig-: n~stehend adj Volk, Kultur undeveloped, primitive; ~wasser nt (Naut) low tide, low water.
niemals adv never.
niemand indef pron nobody, no-one. es war ~ zu Hause there was nobody or no-one at home, there wasn't anybody or anyone at home; er ist ~es Freund he's nobody's friend; ~ anders or anderer (S Ger) kam nobody else came; ~ anders or anderer (S Ger) war da there wasn't anybody else there, nobody else was there; ich habe ~ anders or anderen (S Ger) gesehen I didn't see anybody else; herein kam ~ anders or anderer (S Ger) als der Kanzler selbst in came the Chancellor himself, no less, in came none other than the Chancellor himself; ~ Fremdes no strangers, not ... any strangers; er hat es ~(em) gesagt he hasn't told anyone, he has told no-one; sag das ~(em)! don't tell anybody.
Niemand m -s, no pl er ist ein ~ he's a nobody; wer hat es dir gesagt? — ein gewisser ~ or der große ~ or Herr ~ who told you? — a little bird(ie); der böse ~ (euph) Old Nick, the Evil One, the Tempter.
Niemandsland nt no man's land.
Niere f -, -n kidney. künstliche ~ kidney machine, artificial kidney; es geht mir an die ~n (inf) it gets me down.
Nieren- in cpds (Anat) renal; ~becken nt pelvis of the kidney; ~beckenentzündung f pyelitis (spec); ~entzündung f nephritis (spec); n~förmig adj kidney-shaped; ~kolik f renal colic; n~krank adj suffering from a kidney disease; ~krankheit f, ~leiden nt kidney disease; ~schale f kidney dish; ~stein m kidney stone, renal calculus (spec); ~tisch m kidney-shaped table; ~wärmer m -s, - kidney warmer.
nieseln vi impers to drizzle.
Nieselpriem m -s, -e (inf) misery-guts (inf), moaner.
Nieselregen m drizzle.
niesen vi to sneeze.
Niespulver nt sneezing powder.
Nieß-: ~brauch m (Jur) usufruct; ~braucher, ~nutzer m -s, - (Jur) usufructuary.
Nieswurz f -, no pl (Bot) hellebore.
Niet m -(e)s, -e (spec), **Niete** f -, -n rivet; (auf Kleidung) stud.
Niete f -, -n (Los) blank; (inf: Mensch) dead loss (inf), wash-out (inf). eine ~ ziehen (lit) to draw a blank; mit ihm haben wir eine ~ gezogen he is a dead loss.
nieten vt to rivet.
Nietenhose f (pair of) studded jeans pl.
niet- und nagelfest adj (inf) nailed or screwed down.
Niger¹ m -s (Fluß) Niger.
Niger² nt -s (Staat) Niger.
Nigeria nt -s Nigeria.
Nigerianer(in f) m -s, - Nigerian.
Nigger m -s, - (pej) nigger (pej), coon (pej).
Nigrer(in f) m -s, - Nigerian.
Nihilismus [nihi'lɪsmus] m nihilism.
Nihilist [nihi'lɪst] m nihilist.
nihilistisch [nihi'lɪstɪʃ] adj nihilistic.
Nikolaus m (a) (Name) Nicholas. (b) -, -e or (hum inf) Nikoläuse St Nicholas; (~tag) St Nicholas' Day.
Nikotin nt -s, no pl nicotine.
Nikotin-: n~arm adj low-nicotine; n~frei adj nicotine-free; ~gehalt m nicotine content; n~haltig adj containing nicotine; Zigarren sind n~haltiger als Zigaretten cigars contain more nicotine than cigarettes; ~vergiftung f nicotine poisoning.
Nil m -s Nile.
Nildelta nt Nile Delta.
Nille f -, -n (a) (vulg) prick (vulg). (b) (inf: Ball) ball.
Nilpferd nt hippopotamus, hippo.
Nilpferdpeitsche f bull whip.
Nimbus m -, -se (Heiligenschein) halo, aureole; (fig) aura. sich mit dem ~ der Anständigkeit umgeben to surround oneself with an aura of respectability; im ~ der Heiligkeit stehen to be thought of as a saint.
nimm imper sing of nehmen.
nimmer adv (a) (liter: niemals) never. (b) (S Ger, Aus) = nicht mehr.
Nimmerleinstag m siehe Sankt-Nimmerleins-Tag.
nimmermehr adv (liter) nevermore (liter), never again. nie und ~ never ever.
nimmermüde adj attr tireless, untiring.

Nimmersatt *m* -(e)s, -e glutton. **ein** ~ **sein** to be insatiable.

nimmersatt *adj* gluttonous, insatiable.

Nimmerwiedersehen *nt* (*inf*) **auf** ~! I don't *or* I never want to see you again; **ich habe meinen Koffer da stehen lassen — na dann, auf** ~ I left my case there — well, you've seen the last of that; **auf** ~ **verschwinden** to disappear never to be seen again; **ich habe es ihm geborgt, hoffentlich nicht auf** ~ I lent it to him, not permanently I hope *or* I hope not for ever.

Nimrod *m* -s, -e Nimrod.

Nippel *m* -s, - (*Tech*) nipple.

nippen *vti* to nip (*an* +*dat* at). **vom Wein** ~ to sip (at) the wine.

Nippes, Nippsachen *pl* ornaments *pl*, knick-knacks *pl*, bric-à-brac *sing*.

Nippflut, Nippzeit *f* neap tide.

nirgendhin *adv siehe* **nirgendwohin.**

nirgends *adv* nowhere, not ... anywhere. **ihm gefällt es** ~ he doesn't like it anywhere; **überall und** ~ here, there and everywhere; **er ist überall und** ~ **zu Hause** he has no real home; **er fühlt sich** ~ **so wohl wie** ... there's nowhere *or* there isn't anywhere he feels so happy as ...

nirgend(s)her *adv* from nowhere, not ... from anywhere.

nirgend(s)hin *adv siehe* **nirgendwohin.**

nirgendwo *adv siehe* **nirgends.**

nirgendwohin *adv* nowhere, not ... anywhere. **wohin gehst du?** — ~ where are you going? — nowhere; **wenn man** ~ **gehen kann, um zu übernachten** if you've got nowhere *or* if you haven't got anywhere to spend the night.

Nirosta ® *m* -, *no pl* stainless steel.

Nirwana, Nirvana *nt* -(s) nirvana.

Nische *f* -, -n niche; (*Koch~ etc*) corner.

Niß *f* -, **Nisse** (*rare*), **Nisse** *f* -, -n nit.

Nissenhütte *f* Nissen hut.

nisten 1 *vi* to nest; (*fig*) to take possession (*in* +*dat* of). **dieses Vorurteil nistete in seinem Hirn** this prejudice lodged in his mind. 2 *vr* **Haß nistete sich in ihr Herz** (*liter*) hatred gripped *or* filled her heart.

Nist-: ~**kasten** *m* nest(ing) box; ~**platz** *m* nesting place; ~**zeit** *f* nesting time, (the) nesting season.

Nitrat *nt* nitrate.

nitrieren* *vt* to nitrate.

Nitro- ['nitro] *in cpds* nitro; ~**benzol** *nt* nitrobenzene; ~**glyzerin** *nt* nitroglycerine; ~**lack** *m* nitrocellulose paint; ~**vergiftung** *f* lead poisoning.

Niveau [ni'vo:] *nt* -s, -s (*lit, fig*) level. **auf gleichem** ~ **liegen** to be on the same level; **intelligenzmäßig steht er auf dem** ~ **eines Dreijährigen** he has the mental age of a three-year-old; **diese Schule hat ein hohes** ~ this school has high standards; **seine Arbeit hat ein sehr schlechtes** ~ the level *or* standard of his work is very poor; **unter** ~ below par; **unter meinem** ~ beneath me; ~**/kein/wenig** ~ **haben** to be of a high/low/fairly low standard; (*Mensch*) to be cultured/not at all/not very cultured; **ein Hotel mit** ~ a hotel with class.

Niveau- [ni'vo:] ~**linie** *f* contour line; **n~los** *adj* mediocre; ~**unterschied** *m* (*lit, fig*) difference of level; **n~voll** *adj* high-class.

nivellieren* [nive'li:rən] 1 *vt* (*lit, fig*) to level off *or* out. 2 *vi* (*Surv*) to level.

Nivellier|instrument *nt* (dumpy) level.

Nivellierung [nive'li:rʊŋ] *f* (*Surv*) levelling; (*Ausgleichung*) levelling out.

Nivellierwaage *f* (dumpy) level.

nix *indef pron* (*inf*) *siehe* **nichts.**

Nix *m* -es, -e water-sprite; (*mit Fischschwanz*) merman.

Nixe *f* -, -n water-sprite, water-nymph, nix(ie); (*mit Fischschwanz*) mermaid; (*hum: Bade~*) bathing belle.

Nizza *nt* -s Nice.

NN *abbr of* **Normalnull.**

NNO *abbr of* **Nordnordost** NNE.

NNW *abbr of* **Nordnordwest** NNW.

NO *abbr of* **Nordosten.**

nobel *adj* (*edelmütig*) noble; (*inf*) (*großzügig*) generous, lavish; (*kostspielig*) extravagant; (*elegant*) posh (*inf*). ~ **geht die Welt zugrunde** (*iro*) there's nothing like bowing out in style; **sich** ~ **zeigen** (*inf*) to be generous; **er zeigte sich sehr** ~ **und verzieh ihm** he nobly forgave him; **ein nobler Kunde** (*iro inf*) a pleasant customer, a nice type of person.

Nobelherberge *f* (*inf*) posh *or* classy hotel (*inf*).

Nobelpreis *m* Nobel prize.

Nobelpreisträger *m* Nobel prize winner.

Noblesse [no'blɛsə] *f* -, *no pl* (*geh*) noblesse. **dafür hat er zu viel** ~ he's much too high-minded for that.

noch 1 *adv* (a) (*weiterhin, bis jetzt, wie zuvor*) still. ~ **nicht** still not, not yet; **bist du fertig?** — ~ **nicht** are you ready? — not yet; **er ist** ~ **nicht da** he still isn't here, he isn't here yet; **immer** ~, ~ **immer** still; **sie ist immer** ~ **nicht fertig** she still isn't ready (yet), she isn't ready yet; **du bist** ~ **zu klein** you're still too young; **er schläft** ~ he's still asleep, he is sleeping yet (*liter*); ~ **nie** never; **das habe ich** ~ **nie gehört** I've never known that (before); **ich gehe kaum** ~ **aus** I hardly go out any more; **ich möchte gerne** ~ **bleiben** I'd like to stay on longer; **ich habe** ~ **keinen Biber gesehen** I've never seen a beaver; **ich warte schon zwei Stunden und habe** ~ **keinen Biber gesehen** I've been waiting two hours and still haven't seen a beaver *or* haven't seen a beaver yet.

(b) (*irgendwann*) some time, one day. **er wird sich (schon)** ~ **daran gewöhnen** he'll get used to it (some time *or* one day); **das kann** ~ **passieren** that just might happen, that might still happen; **er wird** ~ **kommen** he'll come (yet).

(c) (*eben, nicht später als*) **das muß** ~ **vor Dienstag fertig sein** it has to be ready by Tuesday; **ich habe ihn** ~ **vor zwei**

Tagen gesehen I saw him only two days ago; **er ist** ~ **am selben Tag gestorben** he died the very same day; **ich tue das** ~ **heute** *or* **heute** ~ I'll do it today *or* this very day; ~ **im 18. Jahrhundert** as late as the 18th century; **gerade** ~ (only) just; ~ **gestern war er frisch und munter** (only) yesterday he was still bright and cheerful; ~ **keine drei Tage** not three days.

(d) (*einschränkend*) (only) just. (**gerade**) ~ **gut genug** (only) just good enough.

(e) (*außerdem, zusätzlich*) **wer war** ~ **da?** who else was there?; (**gibt es**) ~ **etwas?** (is there) anything else?; **ich will** ~ **etwas sagen** there's something else *or* another thing I want to say; ~ **etwas Fleisch** some more meat, a bit more meat; ~ **einer** another (one); ~ **ein Bier** another beer; ~ **zwei Bier** two more beers, another two beers; **und** ~ **eins!** and another thing!; ~ **einmal** *or* **mal** (once) again, once more; **das ist zu teuer,** ~ **dazu, wenn man an die schlechte Qualität denkt** it's too expensive, especially when you consider the poor quality; **und es regnete auch** ~ *or* **dazu and on top of that it was raining; **dumm und** ~ **dazu frech** stupid and cheeky with it (*inf*); **ich gebe Ihnen** ~ **zwei dazu** I'll give you two extra; ~ **ein Wort!** (not) another word!

(f) (*bei Vergleichen*) even, still, yet. ~ **größer** even *or* still *or* yet bigger; **er will** ~ **mehr haben** he wants even *or* still more; **das ist** ~ **besser** that's even better, that's better still *or* still better; **das ist** ~ **viel wichtiger als** ... that is far more important yet *or* still than ...; **seien sie auch** ~ **so klein** however small they may *or* might be; **und wenn du auch** ~ **so bittest** ... however much you ask ...

(g) (*inf*) ~ **und** ~ **Geld, Geld** ~ **und** ~**er** (*hum inf*) heaps and heaps of money (*inf*); **er kann** ~ **und** ~ **erzählen** he can go on telling stories for ever; **ich kann Ihnen Beispiele** ~ **und** ~ **geben** I can give you any number of examples; **sie hat** ~ **und** ~ **versucht,** ... she tried again and again to ...

2 *conj* (*weder* ... ~ ...) nor. **nicht X,** ~ **Y,** ~ **Z** not X nor Y nor Z.

nochmalig *adj attr* renewed. **eine** ~**e Überprüfung** another check.

nochmals *adv* again.

Nockenwelle *f* camshaft.

Nocturne [nɔk'tyrn] *nt* -s, -s *or* f -, -s, **Nokturne** *f* -, -n (*Mus*) *siehe* **Notturno.**

NOK [ɛn|o:'ka] *nt* -s *abbr of* **Nationales Olympisches Komitee.**

nölen *vi* (*N Ger inf*) to be slow, to dawdle.

nolens volens ['no:lɛns 'vo:lɛns] *adv* (*geh*) like it or not *or* no, willy-nilly.

Nolimetangere ['no:lime'taŋgerə] *nt* -, - (*Bot*) touch-me-not.

Nomade *m* -n, -n (*lit, fig*) nomad.

Nomaden- *in cpds* nomadic; **n~haft** *adj* (*lit, fig*) nomadic; ~**tum** *nt* nomadism.

Nomadin *f* (*lit, fig*) nomad.

nomadisch *adj* nomadic.

nomadisieren* *vi* to lead a nomadic existence. ~**de Stämme** nomadic tribes.

Nomen *nt* -s, **Nomina** (*Gram*) noun. **n~ est omen** (*geh*) true to your/his *etc* name.

Nomenklatur *f* nomenclature.

Nomina *pl of* **Nomen.**

nominal *adj* nominal.

Nominal- *in cpds* (*Gram, Fin*) nominal; ~**stil** *m* nominal style; ~**wert** *m* (*Fin*) nominal *or* face *or* par value.

Nomination *f* (*Eccl*) nomination.

Nominativ *m* nominative.

nominell *adj* nominal.

nominieren* *vt* to nominate.

Nonchalance [nõʃa'lã:s] *f* -, *no pl* (*geh*) nonchalance.

nonchalant [nõʃa'lã:] *adj* (*geh*) nonchalant.

Nonius *m* -, **Nonien** (-iən) *or* -se vernier (scale).

Nonkonformist(in *f*) *m* nonconformist.

nonkonformistisch *adj* nonconformist.

Nonne *f* -, -n (a) nun. (b) (*Schmetterling*) nun moth. (c) (*Dachziegel*) concave tile.

Nonnen-: **n~haft** *adj* nunnish; **sie lebte n~haft** she lived like a nun; **sie tut so n~haft** she pretends to be so chaste; ~**kloster** *nt* convent, nunnery (*old, hum*).

Nonplus|ultra *nt* -s, *no pl* (*geh*) ultimate, non plus ultra.

Nonsens *m* -(es), *no pl* nonsense.

nonstop [nɔn'ʃtɔp, nɔn'stɔp] *adv* non-stop.

Nonstop- *in cpds* non-stop; ~**betrieb** *m*: **im** ~**betrieb** non-stop; ~**flug** *m* non-stop flight; ~**kino** *nt* cinema with a continuous programme.

Noppe *f* -, -n (*Knoten*) burl; (*Schlinge*) loop. **Garn mit** ~**n** bouclé; **ein Teppich mit** ~**n** a loop pile carpet.

noppen *vt* (*entfernen*) Rohgewebe to burl; *siehe* **genoppt.**

Nord *m* -(e)s, (*rare*) -e (a) (*Naut, Met, liter*) north. **aus** *or* **von/nach** ~ from the/to the north. (b) (*liter: Wind*) north wind.

Nord- *in cpds* (*in Ländernamen*) (*politisch*) North; (*geographisch auch*) the North of ..., Northern; ~**afrika** *nt* North Africa; ~**amerika** *nt* North America; ~**atlantikpakt** *m* North Atlantic Treaty; **n~deutsch** *adj* North German; *Dialekt, Spezialität, Mentalität auch* Northern German; **die n~deutsche Tiefebene** the North German lowlands *pl*; **n~deutscher Bund** (*Hist*) North German Confederation; **die** ~**deutschen** the North Germans; ~**deutschland** *nt* North(ern) Germany, the North of Germany.

Norden *m* -s, *no pl* north; (*von Land*) North. **aus dem** ~, **von** ~ **her** from the north; **gegen** *or* **gen** (*liter*) *or* **nach** ~ north(wards), to the north; **der Balkon liegt nach** ~ the balcony faces north(wards); **nach** ~ **hin** to the north; **im** ~ **der Stadt/des Landes** in the north of the town/country; **im hohen** ~ in the far north; **weiter** *or* **höher im** ~ further north.

norden vt Karte to orient(ate).

Nord-: ~england nt the North of England; n~friesisch adj North Fri(e)sian; ~irland nt Northern Ireland, Ulster.

nordisch adj Wälder northern; Völker, Sprache nordic. ~e Kombination (Ski) nordic combined.

Nordist(in f) m expert on/student of nordic languages.

Nordistik f nordic studies sing.

Nord-: ~kap nt North Cape; ~küste f north(ern) coast; ~länder(in f) m -s, - northern.

nördlich 1 adj northern; Kurs, Wind, Richtung northerly. der ~e Polarkreis the Arctic Circle; der ~e Wendekreis the Tropic of Cancer; N~es Eismeer Arctic Ocean; 52 Grad ~er Breite 52 degrees north.
   2 adv (to the) north. ~ von Köln (gelegen) north of Cologne; es liegt ~er or weiter ~ it is further (to the) north.
   3 prep +gen (to the) north of.

Nordlicht nt northern lights pl, aurora borealis.

Nordnord-: ~ost m (a) (Naut, Met, liter) north-north-east, nor'-nor'-east (Naut); (b) (liter: Wind) nor'-nor'-easterly; ~osten m north-north-east, nor'-nor'-east (Naut); n~östlich adj north-north-east(erly), nor'-nor'-east(erly) (Naut); ~west m (a) (Naut, Met, liter) north-north-west, nor'-nor'-west (Naut); (b) (liter: Wind) nor'-nor'-westerly; ~westen m north-north-west, nor'-nor'-west (Naut); n~westlich adj north-north-west(erly), nor'-nor'-west(erly) (Naut).

Nordost m (a) (Met, Naut, liter) north-east, nor'-east (Naut). aus ~ from the north-east. (b) (liter: Wind) north-east(erly) wind, north-easter, nor'-easter (Naut).

Nordost- in cpds north-east; (bei Namen) North-East.

Nordosten m north-east; (von Land) North East. aus or von ~ from the north-east; nach ~ to the north-east, north-east(wards).

nordöstlich 1 adj Gegend north-eastern; Wind north-east(erly). 2 adv (to the) north-east. 3 prep +gen (to the) north-east of.

Nord-Ostsee-Kanal m Kiel Canal.

Nordpol m North Pole.

Nordpolar-: ~gebiet nt Arctic (Zone); ~meer nt Arctic Ocean.

Nordpol|expedition f North Pole or Arctic expedition.

Nordrhein-Westfalen nt North Rhine–Westphalia.

nordrhein-westfälisch adj North Rhine–Westphalian.

Nordsee f North Sea.

Nord-: ~seite f north(ern) side; (von Berg) north(ern) face; ~stern m North Star, Polar Star; ~wand f (von Berg) north face.

nordwärts adv north(wards). der Wind dreht ~ the wind is moving round to the north.

Nordwest m (a) (Met, Naut, liter) north-west. aus ~ from the north-west. (b) (liter: Wind) north-west(erly) wind, north-wester, nor'-wester (Naut).

Nordwest- in cpds north-west; (bei Namen) North-West.

Nordwesten m north-west; (von Land) North-West. aus or von ~ from the north-west; nach ~ to the north-west, north-west(wards).

nordwestlich 1 adj Gegend north-western; Wind north-west(erly). 2 adv (to the) north-west. ~ von (to the) north-west of. 3 prep +gen (to the) north-west of.

Nordwind m north wind.

Nörgelei f moaning, grumbling; (Krittelei) carping.

nörg(e)lig adj grumbly (inf), moaning; (krittelig) carping.

nörgeln vi to moan, to grumble; (kritteln) to carp (an +dat about). er hat immer an allem zu ~ he always finds something to moan about.

Nörgler(in f) m -s, - grumbler, moaner; (Krittler) carper.

Norm f -, -en (a) norm; (Größenvorschrift) standard (specification). als ~ gelten, die ~ sein to be (considered) normal, to be the usual thing; dieses Muster gilt als ~ this is the standard pattern.
   (b) (Leistungssoll) quota, norm. die ~ erreichen to achieve one's quota, to meet one's target.
   (c) (Typ) signature (at foot of page).

normal adj normal; Format, Maß, Gewicht standard. benimm dich doch mal ~! act like a normal human being, can't you?

Normal- in cpds (a) (üblich) normal; (b) (genormt) standard; ~benzin nt regular (petrol Brit or gas US).

Normale f -(n), -n (Math) normal.

normalerweise adv normally, usually.

Normal-: ~fall m normal case; im ~fall normally, usually; ~film m standard film; ~gewicht nt normal weight; (genormt) standard weight.

normalisieren* 1 vt to normalize. 2 vr to return or get back to normal.

Normalisierung f normalization.

Normalität f normality, normalcy.

Normal-: ~maß nt standard (measure); ~null nt -s, no pl (abbr NN) ≈ sea level; ~spur f (Rail) standard gauge; ~uhr f (old) (synchronized) clock; ~verbraucher m average consumer; (geistiger) ~verbraucher (inf) middlebrow; Otto ~verbraucher (inf) the average person or punter (sl), John Doe (US); ~zeit f standard time; ~zustand m normal state; (normale Verhältnisse) normal conditions pl; (Chem, Phys) natural state.

Normandie f - Normandy.

Normanne m -n, -n, **Normannin** f Norman.

normannisch adj Norman.

normativ adj normative.

Normativbestimmungen pl (Jur) basic stipulations pl.

Normblatt nt standard specifications sheet.

normen, normieren* vt to standardize. normierter Vertrag (Jur) standard contract.

Normierung f standardization.

Norm-: ~schrift f standard print/handwriting; ~teil nt (Tech) standard part.

Normung f (Tech) standardization.

normwidrig adj deviant; (Tech) non-standard.

Norwegen nt -s Norway.

Norweger(in f) m -s, - Norwegian.

norwegisch adj Norwegian. das N~e Norwegian.

Nostalgie f nostalgia.

nostalgisch adj nostalgic.

Not f -, ¨-e (a) no pl (Mangel, Elend) need(iness), want, poverty. hier herrscht große ~ there is great poverty here; eine Zeit der ~ a time of need, a lean time; aus ~ out of poverty; ~ leiden to suffer deprivation; jds ~ (acc) erleichtern or lindern to improve sb's lot; in ~ leben to live in poverty; wenn ~ am Mann ist if you/they etc are short (inf); (im Notfall) in an emergency; ~ macht erfinderisch (Prov) necessity is the mother of invention (Prov); ~ bricht Eisen (Prov) where there's a will there's a way (Prov); in der ~ frißt der Teufel Fliegen or schmeckt jedes Brot (Prov) beggars can't be choosers (prov); ~ kennt kein Gebot (Prov) necessity knows no law (Prov); siehe Geldnot, Zeitnot.
   (b) (Bedrängnis) distress no pl, affliction; (Problem) problem. die ~e des Alltags the problems of everyday living; in seiner ~ in his hour of need; in unserer ~ blieb uns nichts anderes übrig in this emergency we had no choice; jdm seine ~ klagen to tell sb one's troubles, to cry on sb's shoulder (inf); in ~ sein to be in distress; in ~ geraten to get into serious difficulties; Freunde in der ~ (gehen tausend auf ein Lot) (Prov) a friend in need (is a friend indeed) (Prov); in ~ und Tod (liter) come what may, through thick and thin; der/als Retter in der ~ sb's knight/like a knight in shining armour; Hilfe in höchster ~ help in the nick of time; in Ängsten und ~en schweben to be in fear and trembling; jdm in der ~ beistehen to help sb in or through times of trouble or in his need; jdn aus der ~ retten to come to sb in his need.
   (c) no pl (Sorge, Mühe) difficulty, trouble. er hat seine liebe ~ mit ihr/damit he really has problems with her/it, he really has his work cut out with her/it (inf); die Eltern hatten ~, ihre fünf Kinder zu ernähren the parents had difficulty in feeding their five children; es hat or damit hat's keine ~ (old) there's no rush; siehe knapp, Mühe.
   (d) (Zwang, Notwendigkeit) necessity. der ~ gehorchend bowing to necessity; etw nicht ohne ~ tun not to do sth without having to; zur ~ if necessary, if need(s) be; (gerade noch) at a pinch, just about; aus der ~ eine Tugend machen to make a virtue (out) of necessity.

not adj (geh) ~ tun or sein to be necessary; ihm tat Hilfe ~ he needed help; uns allen täte ein bißchen mehr Bescheidenheit ~ we could all benefit from a little more modesty.

Notabeln pl (geh) notabilities pl.

nota bene adv (geh) please note, let it be noted.

Not|anker m sheet anchor.

Notar m notary.

Notariat nt notary's office.

notariell adj notarial. ~ beglaubigt attested by a notary.

Not-: ~arzt m doctor on emergency call; ~aufnahmelager nt reception centre, transit camp; ~ausgang m emergency exit; ~behelf m stopgap (measure), makeshift; ~beleuchtung f emergency lighting; ~bremse f emergency brake; die ~bremse ziehen to pull the communication cord (Brit); ~bremsung f emergency stop; ~brücke f temporary bridge.

Notdurft f -, no pl (a) (euph geh) call of nature (euph). seine ~ verrichten to relieve oneself, to answer the or a call of nature (euph). (b) (old) need. des Lebens ~ the bare necessities of life; des Leibes ~ enough to keep body and soul together.

notdürftig adj (kaum ausreichend) meagre, poor; (behelfsmäßig) makeshift no adv, rough and ready no adv. wir konnten uns mit den Einheimischen ~ verständigen we could just about communicate with the natives; damit Sie sich wenigstens ~ verständigen können so that you can at least communicate to some extent; nachdem wir den Reifen ~ geflickt hatten when we had patched up the tyre in a makeshift or rough-and-ready way.

Note f -, -n (a) (Mus) note. ganze ~ semibreve (Brit), whole note (US); halbe ~ minim (Brit), half note (US); ~n pl music; ~n lesen to read music; nach ~n spielen/singen to play/sing from music; nach ~n (fig inf) thoroughly; das ging ja (wie) nach ~n (fig inf) it went like clockwork.
   (b) (Sch) mark.
   (c) (Pol) note.
   (d) (Bank~) (bank)note.
   (e) no pl (Eigenart) (in bezug auf Gespräch, Brief etc) note; (in bezug auf Beziehungen, Atmosphäre) tone, character; (in bezug auf Einrichtung, Kleidung) touch. das ist meine persönliche ~ that's my trademark; einer Sache (dat) eine persönliche ~ verleihen to give sth a personal touch; ein Parfüm mit einer herben ~ a perfume with something tangy about it or with a tangy quality.
   (f) ~n pl (Liter) notes pl.

Noten-: ~austausch m (Pol) exchange of notes; ~bank f issuing bank, bank of issue; ~blatt nt sheet of music; ~deckung f (Fin) (bank)note cover; ~heft nt (mit Noten) book of music; (ohne Noten) manuscript book; ~linie f lines pl (of a stave); Papier mit ~linien manuscript paper; ~papier nt manuscript paper; ~presse f money press; ~pult nt music stand; ~schlüssel m clef; ~schrift f musical notation; ~ständer m music stand; ~umlauf m (Fin) circulation (of banknotes); ~wechsel m (Pol) exchange of notes.

Notfall m emergency. für den ~, daß ein Feuer ausbricht in case of fire, in case a fire breaks out; für den ~ nehme ich einen

Schirm mit I'll take an umbrella (just) in case; **im** ~ if necessary, if need(s) be; **bei einem** ~ in case of emergency.

notfalls *adv* if necessary, if need(s) be.

Notflagge *f* distress flag.

notgedrungen 1 *adj* essential, imperative. **2** *adv* of necessity, perforce. **ich muß mich** ~ **dazu bereit erklären** I'm forced to agree, I've no choice but to agree, I must perforce agree.

Not-: ~**geld** *nt* emergency money; ~**gemeinschaft** *f* emergency organization; **im Luftschutzbunker waren wir alle eine** ~**gemeinschaft** in the air raid shelter we were all brothers in misfortune; ~**groschen** *m* nest egg; **sich** (*dat*) **eine Summe als** ~**groschen zurücklegen** to put some money away for a rainy day; ~**hafen** *m* harbour of refuge; **wegen der Epidemie mußte das Schiff einen** ~**hafen anlaufen** because of the epidemic the ship had to make an emergency stop; ~**helfer** *m* (*Rel*) auxiliary saint; ~**hilfe** *f* assistance in an emergency.

notieren* 1 *vti* (**a**) (*Notizen machen*) to note down, to make a note of; (*schnell*) to jot down. **ich notiere** (**mir**) **den Namen** I'll make a note of the name; **Fräulein, bitte** ~ **Sie!** please take a note/a letter/a memo, Miss X; **was möchten Sie bestellen? ich notiere** what would you like to order? I'll make a note of it *or* I'll take it down; **haben Sie mich verstanden?** — **ja, ich notiere** did you understand me? — yes, I've got that (down).

(**b**) (*vormerken*) (*Comm*) *Auftrag* to note, to book. **zu welchem Termin waren Sie notiert?** what time was your appointment?; **jdn** ~ to put sb's name *or* sb down.

(**c**) (*St Ex: festlegen*) to quote (*mit* at).

2 *vi* (*St Ex: wert sein*) to be quoted (*auf +acc* at).

Notierung *f* (**a**) (*Comm*) note. (**b**) (*St Ex*) quotation. (**c**) (*Mus*) notation.

nötig 1 *adj* necessary. **das für die Reise** ~**e Geld** the necessary money for the journey, the money needed *or* necessary for the journey; **ist das unbedingt** ~? is that really *or* absolutely necessary?; **es ist nicht** ~, **zu sagen, wie ...** it's not necessary *or* there's no need to say how ...; **es ist nicht** ~, **daß er kommt it's** not necessary *or* there's no need for him to come, he doesn't need to come; **das war wirklich nicht** ~ that really wasn't necessary, there was no need for that; (*nach spitzer Bemerkung auch*) that was uncalled for; **die** ~**en Unkosten** the unavoidable costs; **wenn** ~ if necessary, if need(s) be; **etw** ~ **haben** to need sth; **etw bitter** ~ **haben** to need sth badly; **er hat das natürlich nicht** ~ (*iro*) but, of course, he's different; **ich habe es nicht** ~, **mich von dir anschreien zu lassen** I don't need *or* have to let you shout at me; **die haben's gerade** ~ (*inf*) that's the last thing they need; **du hast es gerade** ~, **so zu reden** (*inf*) you can *or* can't talk (*inf*), you're a fine one to talk (*inf*); **das habe ich nicht** ~! I can do without that, I don't need that; **etw** ~ **machen** to necessitate sth, to make sth necessary; **das N**~**e** the necessary; **das Nötigste** the (bare) necessities *or* essentials; **alles zum Bergsteigen unbedingt N**~**e** everything necessary *or* needed for mountaineering.

2 *adv* (*dringend*) **etw** ~ **brauchen** to need something urgently; **ich muß mal** ~ (*inf*) I'm dying to go (*inf*).

nötigen *vt* (*geh: zwingen*) to force, to compel; (*Jur*) to coerce; (*auffordern*) to urge, to press. **jdn ins Zimmer** ~ to force sb to go into a room; **sich** ~ **lassen** to need prompting *or* urging; **lassen Sie sich nicht (erst)** ~! don't wait to be asked; *siehe* **genötigt.**

nötigenfalls *adv* (*form*) *siehe* **notfalls.**

Nötigung *f* (*Zwang*) compulsion; (*Jur*) coercion. ~ **zum Diebstahl** coercion to commit theft.

Notiz *f* -, -en (**a**) (*Vermerk*) note; (*Zeitungs*~) item. **sich** (*dat*) ~**en machen** to make *or* take notes; **sich** (*dat*) **eine** ~ **von etw machen** to make a note of sth. (**b**) ~ **nehmen von** to pay attention to, to take notice of; **keine** ~ **nehmen von** to ignore; **nimm keine** ~! take no notice, don't take any notice.

Notiz-: ~**block** *m* notepad, jotter; ~**buch** *nt* notebook; ~**zettel** *m* piece of paper; **er hinterließ mir einen** ~**zettel mit seiner Adresse** he left me a note of his address on a piece of paper.

Notjahr *nt* year of need, difficult year.

Notlage *f* crisis; (*Elend*) plight. **in** ~**n** in an emergency; **die wirtschaftliche** ~ **Großbritanniens** Great Britain's economic plight; **jds** ~ (*acc*) **ausnützen** to exploit sb's situation; **in eine** ~ **geraten** to get into serious difficulties; **sich in einer** ~ **befinden** to find oneself in serious difficulties.

notlanden *pret* **notlandete** *ptp* **notgelandet,** *infin auch* **notzulanden** *vi aux* **sein** to make a forced landing *or* an emergency landing.

Notlandung *f* forced *or* emergency landing.

notleidend *adj* needy; (*Comm*) *Wechsel, Wertpapier* dishonoured. **die N**~**en** the needy.

Not-: ~**leine** *f* emergency cord; ~**leiter** *f* fire escape; ~**lösung** *f* less-than-ideal solution; (*provisorisch*) temporary solution; ~**lüge** *f* white lie; ~**maßnahme** *f* emergency measure; ~**nagel** *m* (*fig inf*) last resort; ~**opfer** *nt* emergency contribution.

notorisch *adj* notorious.

Not-: ~**pfennig** *m siehe* ~**groschen**; ~**ruf** *m* (*Telec*) (*Gespräch*) emergency call; (*Nummer*) emergency number; ~**rufanlage** *f* emergency telephone; ~**rufsäule** *f* emergency telephone.

notschlachten *pret* **notschlachtete,** *ptp* **notgeschlachtet,** *infin auch* **notzuschlachten** *vt* to destroy, to put down.

Not-: ~**schlachtung** *f* putting down; ~**schrei** *m* (*liter*) cry of distress, cry for help; ~**signal** *nt* distress signal; ~**situation** *f* emergency; ~**sitz** *m* foldaway seat, tip-up seat.

Notstand *m* crisis; (*Pol*) state of emergency; (*Jur*) emergency. **innerer** ~ domestic *or* internal state of emergency; **äußerer** ~ threat of invasion *or* attack; **ziviler** ~ disaster; **übergesetzlicher** ~ emergency situation in which a law no longer holds; **den** ~ **ausrufen** to declare a state of emergency; **einen** ~ **beheben** to end *or* put an end to a crisis.

Notstands-: ~**gebiet** *nt* (*wirtschaftlich*) depressed *or* deprived area; (*bei Katastrophen*) disaster area; ~**gesetze** *pl*, ~**verfassung** *f* (*Pol*) emergency laws *pl*.

Not-: ~**taufe** *f* emergency baptism; **n**~**taufen** *pret* **n**~**taufte,** *ptp* **n**~**getauft,** *infin auch* **n**~**zutaufen** *vt* **jdn n**~**taufen** to administer an emergency baptism to sb.

Notturno *nt* -s, -s *or* **Notturni** nocturne.

Not-: ~**unterkunft** *f* emergency accommodation; ~**verband** *m* emergency *or* first-aid dressing; ~**verordnung** *f* emergency decree.

notwassern *pret* **notwasserte,** *ptp* **notgewassert,** *infin auch* **notzuwassern** *vi* to ditch (*Aviat sl*), to make a crash-landing in the sea.

Notwehr *f, no pl* self-defence. **aus/in** ~ in self-defence.

notwendig *adj* necessary; (*unvermeidlich auch*) inevitable. ~ **brauchen** to need urgently; **es folgt** ~ it necessarily follows; **es mußte** ~ **zum Zusammenstoß kommen** the collision was inevitable; **es ist** ~, **daß sie selbst kommt** it is necessary that she come(s) herself; **das N**~**e** the necessary, what is necessary; **ich habe alles N**~**e erledigt** I've done everything (that's) necessary; **das N**~**ste** the (bare) necessities *or* essentials; **sich auf das N**~**ste beschränken** to stick to essentials.

notwendigerweise *adv* of necessity, necessarily, inevitably.

Notwendigkeit *f* (**a**) *no pl* necessity. **mit** ~ of necessity; **die** ~, **etw zu tun** the necessity of doing sth. (**b**) (*notwendige Sache*) necessity, essential.

Notzeichen *nt* distress signal.

Notzucht *f* (*Jur*) rape. ~ **begehen** *or* **verüben** to commit rape (*an +dat* on).

notzüchtigen, *pret* **notzüchtigte,** *ptp* **genotzüchtigt,** *infin auch* **notzuzüchtigen** *vt* (*Jur*) to rape, to ravish, to violate.

Notzuchtverbrechen *nt* crime of rape.

Nougat, Nugat ['nu:gat] *m or nt* -s, -s nougat.

Nova *pl of* **Novum.**

Novelle [no'vɛlə] *f* (**a**) novella. (**b**) (*Pol*) amendment.

novellieren* [nove'li:rən] *vt* (*Pol*) to amend.

Novellierung [nove'li:rʊŋ] *f* (*Pol*) amendment.

Novellist(in *f)* [nove'lɪst(ɪn)] *m* novella writer.

novellistisch [nove'lɪstɪʃ] *adj* novella-like. **den Stoff** ~ **behandeln** to use the material for *or* in a novella.

November [no'vɛmbə] *m* -s, - November; *siehe* **September.**

novemberlich [no'vɛmbəlɪç] *adj* November-like.

Novene [no've:nə] *f* -, -n novena.

Novität [novi'tɛːt] *f* (*geh*) innovation, novelty; (*Buch*) new publication; (*Theat*) new play. **dieser Hut ist eine** ~ this hat is the latest *or* newest thing.

Novize [no'vi:tsə] *m* -n, -n, *f* -, -n novice.

Noviziat [novi'tsia:t] *nt* novitiate.

Novizin *f* novice.

Novum ['no:vʊm] *nt* -s, **Nova** ['no:va] novelty.

NPD [ɛnpeː'deː] *f* - *abbr of* **National-Demokratische Partei Deutschlands.**

Nr. *abbr of* **Numero, Nummer** No.

NS *abbr of* **Nachschrift** PS; **nationalsozialistisch.**

NT *abbr of* **Neues Testament** NT.

Nu *m*: **im** ~ in no time, in a flash *or* trice.

nu *adv* (*dial inf*) *siehe* **nun.**

Nuance ['nyãːsə] *f* -, -n (*kleiner Unterschied*) nuance; (*Kleinigkeit*) shade. **um eine** ~ **zu laut** a shade too loud.

nuancenreich *adj* full of nuances.

nuancieren* [nyã'si:rən] *vt* to nuance.

'nüber *adv* (*dial*) *siehe* **hinüber.**

nüchtern *adj* (**a**) (*ohne Essen*) **der Patient muß** ~ **sein** the patient must have an empty stomach; **eine Medizin** ~ **einnehmen** to take a medicine on an empty stomach; **mit** ~**em/auf** ~**en Magen** with/on an empty stomach; **das war ein Schreck auf** ~**en Magen** my heart skipped a beat.

(**b**) (*nicht betrunken*) sober. **wieder** ~ **werden** to sober up.

(**c**) (*sachlich, vernünftig*) down-to-earth *no adv*, rational; *Mensch auch* no-nonsense *attr*; *Zahlen, Tatsachen* bare, plain.

(**d**) (*schmucklos*) sober; *Essen* (*fade*) dull, insipid; (*nicht gewürzt*) plain.

Nüchternheit *f* (**a**) **überzeugen Sie sich von der** ~ **des Patienten** make sure that the patient's stomach is empty.

(**b**) (*Unbetrunkenheit*) soberness, sobriety.

(**c**) (*Sachlichkeit, Vernünftigkeit*) rationality.

(**d**) (*Schmucklosigkeit*) soberness; (*von Essen*) (*Fadheit*) dul(l)ness, insipidness, insipidity; (*Ungewürztheit*) plainness.

Nuckel *m* -s, - (*inf*) (*auf Fläschchen*) teat (*Brit*), nipple (*US*); (*Schnuller*) dummy (*Brit*), pacifier (*US*).

nuckeln *vi* (*inf*) (*Mensch*) to suck (*an +dat* at); (*Tier*) to suckle (*an +dat* from). **am Daumen** ~ to suck one's thumb.

Nuckelpinne *f* (*inf*) old banger (*Brit inf*) *or* crate (*inf*).

Nucki *m* -s, - (*Sw*) dummy (*Brit*), pacifier (*US*).

Nudel *f* -, -n *usu pl* (**a**) (*als Beilage*) pasta *no pl*; (*als Suppeneinlage, chinesische*) noodle; (*Faden*~) vermicelli *pl*. (**b**) (*inf: Mensch*) (*dick*) dumpling (*inf*); (*komisch*) character.

Nudel-: ~**brett** *nt* pastryboard; **n**~**dick** *adj* (*inf*) podgy (*inf*); ~**holz** *nt* rolling pin.

nudeln *vt* (**a**) *Gans* to force-feed; (*inf*) *Kind* to stuff (*inf*), to overfeed. **ich bin genudelt** (*inf*) I'm full to bursting (*inf*). (**b**) (*dial: umarmen*) to cuddle.

Nudel-: ~**suppe** *f* noodle soup; ~**teig** *m* pasta/noodle dough.

Nudismus *m* nudism.

Nudist(in *f)* *m* nudist.

Nudität *f usu pl* (*geh*) nude (picture).

Nugat *m or nt siehe* **Nougat.**

nuklear *adj attr* nuclear.

Nuklearmacht *f* nuclear power.

Nukleus ['nu:kleʊs] *m* -, **Nuklei** ['nu:klei] nucleus.

Null[1] f -, -en (a) (Zahl) nought, naught (US), zero; (Gefrierpunkt) zero. **die ~ the figure nought, zero; das Thermometer steht auf ~** the thermometer is at or on zero; **gleich ~ sein** to be absolutely nil or zero; **in ~ Komma nichts** (inf) in less than no time; **~ Komma ~** (sl) damn-all (sl), sweet Fanny Adams (Brit sl); **jdn auf ~ bringen** (inf) to fix sb for good (inf); **die Augen auf ~ stellen** (sl) to croak (sl); **seine Stimmung sank auf or unter ~** (inf) he sank into the depths of gloom; **im Jahre ~** in the year nought; **die Stunde ~** the new starting point.
(b) (inf: Mensch) wash-out (inf), dead loss (inf).

Null[2] m or nt -(s), -s (Cards) nullo.

null num zero; (inf: kein) zero (sl); (Telec) O [əʊ] (Brit), zero (US); (Sport) nil, nothing; (Tennis) love. **~ Komma eins** (nought) point one; **es ist ~ Uhr zehn** it's ten past twelve or midnight; **zwei Minuten ~ Sekunden** (bei Zeitansagen) two minutes precisely; (bei Rennen) two minutes dead or flat; **~ Grad zero degrees; ~Fehler** no or zero (sl) mistakes; **es steht ~ zu ~** there's no score; **das Spiel wurde ~ zu ~ beendet** the game was a goalless draw; **~ zu eins** one-nil, one-nothing; **~ und nichtig** (Jur) null and void; **für ~ und nichtig erklären** (Jur) to declare null and void, to annul.

null|achtfünfzehn, null|achtfuffzehn (inf) 1 adj inv run-of-the-mill (inf). 2 adv in a run-of-the-mill way.

Null|achtfünfzehn-, Null|achtfuffzehn- in cpds (inf) run-of-the-mill.

Nulleiter m getrennt: **Null-leiter** (Elec) earth (wire) (Brit), ground (wire) (US).

Nullinie f getrennt: **Null-linie** zero, nought, naught (US).

Nullmeridian m Greenwich or prime Meridian.

Null-Null nt or m -, no pl (inf) loo (Brit inf), restroom (US).

Null ouvert [u'vɛːʀ] m or (rare) nt - -, - -s (Cards) null ouvert.

Nullpunkt m zero. **die Stimmung sank unter den ~** the atmosphere froze; **seine Karriere hatte den ~ erreicht** his career had reached rock-bottom; **auf dem ~ angekommen sein** (fig) to have sunk to or reached rock-bottom.

Null-: **~spiel** nt (Cards) nullo; **~stellung** f zero position; **in der ~stellung sein** to be on zero; **~tarif** m (für Verkehrsmittel) free travel; (freier Eintritt) free admission; **~wachstum** nt (Pol) nil or zero growth.

Nulpe f -, -n (sl) clot (inf), dope (sl), jerk (sl).

Numerale nt -s, **Numeralia** or **Numeralien** [-liən] (Gram) numeral.

Numeri pl of **Numerus**.

numerieren* vt to number.

Numerierung f numbering.

numerisch adj numeric(al).

Numero nt -s, -s (old, hum) **~ eins/zwei** number one/two.

Numerus m -, **Numeri** (Gram) number. **~ clausus** (Univ) restricted entry.

Numismatik f numismatics sing.

Nummer f -, -n (Math, von Zeitschrift, Varieté~) number; (Größe) size; (inf: Mensch) character; (sl: Koitus) screw (sl); (mit Prostituierter) trick (sl). **unser Haus hat die ~ 25** our house is number 25; **Bahnhofstraße 15** number 15 Bahnhofstraße; **nur eine ~ unter vielen sein** (fig) to be a cog in the machine); **er hat eine ruhige ~** (inf) he's onto a cushy number (inf); **~ Null** (inf) the loo (Brit inf) or restroom (US); **auf ~ Sicher gehen** (inf) to play (it) safe; **auf or in ~ Sicher sein** (sl) to be in the jug (sl) or can (US sl); **bei jdm eine (gute) ~ haben** (inf) to be in sb's good books (inf); **Gesprächsthema ~ eins** the number one talking point; **sie ist die ~ eins in Hollywood** she's number one or the number one star in Hollywood; **eine ~ abziehen** (sl) to put on an act; **eine ~ machen or schieben** (sl) to have it off or away (sl).

Nummern-: **~scheibe** f (Telec) dial; **~schild** nt (Aut) number plate, registration plate (Brit), license plate (US).

nun 1 adv (a) (jetzt) now. **von ~ an** from now on, as from or of now, from here on in (US); **~ und nimmer(mehr)** (liter) nevermore (liter); **~, da er da ist, können wir anfangen** now that he's here we can get started; **~ erst, erst ~** only now; **~ist aber genug!** now that's enough; **~ endlich** (now) at last; **was ~?** what now?; **was ~ (schon wieder)?** what (is it) now?
(b) (danach) then. **~ erst ging er** only then did he go.
(c) **ich bin ~ eben dumm** I'm just stupid, that's all; **er will ~ mal nicht** he simply doesn't want to; **wir hatten uns ~ eben entschlossen, zu gehen** ... after all, we had decided to go ...; **dann muß ich das ~ wohl tun!** then I'll just have to do it; **~, wenn's unbedingt sein muß** well, if I/you etc really must; **~, du hast ja recht, wenn du das sagst, aber** ... well or OK (inf) or fair enough (inf), what you say is true but ...; **das ist ~ (ein)mal so** that's just the way things are; **~ ja or gut, aber** ... all right or OK (inf), but ...; **~ ja** well yes; **~ gut** (well) all right, (well) OK (inf); **~, meinetwegen** well, as far as I'm concerned; **er mag ~ wollen oder nicht** (liter) whether he wants to or not or no; **~ gerade erst or erst recht!** just for that (I'll do it)!; **~ taten wir's gerade erst nicht or erst recht nicht** just because they/he/she etc said/did that, we didn't do it.
(d) (Folge) now. **das hast du ~ davon!** (it) serves you right.
(e) (Aufforderung) come on, go on. **~ denn** (geh) well then; **~, wird's bald?** (inf) come on then, hurry up then.
(f) (bei Fragen) well. **~?** well?
(g) (beschwichtigend) come on. **~, ~!** (warnend) come on now, come, come, now, now; (tröstend) there, there.
2 conj (obs) since (that obs), now that.

nunmehr adv (geh) (jetzt) now, at this point; (von jetzt an) henceforth (form), from now on, as from or of now. **die ~ herrschende Partei** the currently ruling party.

nunmehrig adj attr (form) present, current.

'nunter adv (dial) abbr of **hinunter**.

Nuntius ['nʊntsiʊs] m -, **Nuntien** ['nʊntsiən] nuncio.

nur adv (a) (einschränkend) only, just. **er ist ein sehr schneller Arbeiter, ~ müßte er etwas gründlicher sein** he is a very fast worker but or only he should be rather more thorough; **ich habe ~ ein Stück Brot gegessen** I've only eaten a piece of bread, I've eaten only or just a piece of bread; **alle, ~ ich nicht** everyone except or but me; **~ ich weiß** I'm the only one who knows, only I know; **~ schade, daß** ... it's just a pity that ...; **~ daß** it's just that, only; **~ noch zwei Minuten** only or just two minutes left or to go; **der Kranke ißt fast ~ noch Obst** the sick man eats virtually nothing but fruit these days; **nicht ~ ..., sondern auch** not only or just ... but also; **alles, ~ das nicht!** anything but that!; **dieses eine Bild ~ wollte er haben** he wanted only this one picture; **warum möchtest du das denn wissen? — ach, ~ so!** why do you want to know? — oh I just do or oh just because or oh no special reason; **ich hab' das ~ so gesagt** I was just talking; **warum hast du das gemacht? — so why did you do that? — I just did; ~ kann man nie wissen, ob** ... only or but you never can or can never tell if ...
(b) (verstärkend) just. **wie schnell er ~ redet** doesn't he speak fast!; **daß es ~ so krachte** making a terrible din; **er fuhr, so schnell er ~ (fahren) konnte** he drove just as fast as he possibly could, he drove for all he was worth.
(c) (mit Fragepronomen) -ever, on earth (inf). **was/wer/wie etc ~?** but what/who/how etc?; **warum sie ~ dahin geht?** whyever or why on earth (inf) does she go there?; **was hat er ~?** whatever or what on earth is the matter with him?; **wie kannst du ~ (so etwas sagen)?** how could you (say such a thing)?; **wie bekommt alles, was sie ~ will** she gets whatever she wants.
(d) (Wunsch, Bedingung) wenn **er ~ (erst) käme** if only he would come, if he would only come; **wüßte ich ~, wie** if only I knew how, if I only knew how; **es wird klappen, wenn er ~ nicht die Nerven verliert** it will be all right as long as or so long as (inf) or provided (that) he doesn't lose his nerve; **es hätte geklappt, wenn er ~ nicht die Nerven verloren hätte** it would have been all right if only he hadn't lost his nerve.
(e) (mit Negationen) just, ... whatever you do. **laß das ~ niemand wissen!** just don't let anyone find out, (but) don't let anyone find out whatever you do; **sagen Sie das ~ nicht Ihrer Frau!** just don't tell your wife (whatever you do).
(f) (Aufforderung) just. **geh ~!** just go, go on; **~ zu!** go on; **sieh ~ just look; ~ her damit!** (inf) let's have it; **sagen Sie es ~, Sie brauchen es ~ zu sagen** just say (the word), you only have to say (the word); **er soll ~ lachen!** let him laugh; **~ fort!** (old, liter) away! (old, liter).
(g) **~ mehr** (dial, esp Aus) only ... left; **ich habe ~ mehr eine Mark** I've only one mark left.

Nurhausfrau f full-time housewife.

Nürnberg nt -s Nuremberg. **jdm etw mit dem ~er Trichter beibringen** (inf) to drum sth into sb.

nuscheln vti (inf) to mutter, to mumble.

Nuß f -, **Nüsse** (a) nut. **eine harte ~ zu knacken haben** (fig) to have a tough nut to crack. (b) (inf: Mensch) drip (sl), jerk (sl). **eine taube ~** a dead loss (inf), a wash-out (inf). (c) (inf: Kopf~) punch (in the head).

Nuß-: **~baum** m (Baum) walnut tree; (Holz) walnut; **~baumholz** nt walnut; **n~braun** adj nutbrown, hazel; **~kern** m (nut) kernel; **~knacker** m nutcracker, (pair of) nutcrackers pl; **~kohle** f nut coal; **~schale** f nutshell; (fig: Boot) cockleshell, frail little boat.

Nüster f -, -n nostril.

Nut f -, -en (spec), **Nute** f -, -n groove, flute, chase; (zur Einfügung) rabbet, slot; (Keil~) keyway, key seat. **~ und Feder** tongue and groove; **~ und Zapfen** mortise and tenon.

nuten vt siehe **Nut** to groove, to flute; to rabbet, to slot; to cut a keyway in, to key seat.

Nutria f -, -s (Tier, Pelz) coypu, nutria (rare).

Nutte f -, -n (inf) tart (inf), pro (Brit sl), hooker (esp US sl).

nutz adj (S Ger, Aus) siehe **nütze**.

Nutz m: **zu ~ und Frommen** + gen (old liter) for the greater good of (form).

Nutz|anwendung f practical application; (einer Geschichte) moral.

nutzbar adj us(e)able, utilizable; Bodenschätze exploitable; Boden fertile, productive. **~ machen** to make us(e)able or utilizable; Sonnenenergie to utilize, to harness, to turn to good use; Sümpfe to reclaim; Bodenschätze to exploit.

Nutzbarkeit f siehe adj us(e)ability, utilizability; exploitability; fertility, productivity.

Nutzbarmachung f utilization; (von Sümpfen) reclamation; (von Bodenschätzen) exploitation.

Nutzbau m -(e)s, -ten functional building.

nutzbringend adj profitable. **etw ~ anwenden** to use sth profitably or to good effect, to put sth to good use, to turn sth to good account.

nütze, nutz (S Ger, Aus) adj pred **zu etw/nichts ~ sein** to be useful for sth/to be no use for anything.

Nutz|effekt m effectiveness, efficiency.

Nutzen m -s, - (a) use; (Nützlichkeit) usefulness. **es hat keinen ~, das zu tun** there's no use or point (in) doing that; **zum ~ der Öffentlichkeit** for the benefit of the public; **jdm von ~ sein** to be useful or of use to sb; (einer anderen Person auch) to be of service to sb.
(b) (Vorteil) advantage, benefit; (Gewinn) profit. **jdm ~ bringen** (Vorteil) to be of advantage to sb; (Gewinn) to bring sb profit, to prove profitable to sb; **sich (dat) großen ~ von etw versprechen** to expect to benefit or profit greatly from sth; **von etw ~ haben** to gain or profit by sth; **aus etw ~ ziehen** to reap the benefits of sth; **er sucht immer nur seinen eigenen ~** he's always seeking his own advantage; **etw mit ~ verkaufen** to sell sth at a profit.

nutzen, nützen 1 vi to be of use, to be useful (jdm zu etw to sb for sth). **die Ermahnungen haben genützt/nichts genützt** the warnings had the desired effect/didn't do any good; **es nützt nichts** it's no use *or* good, it's useless; **alle Anstrengungen haben nichts genützt** all our efforts were useless *or* in vain; **da nützt alles nichts** there's nothing to be done; **das nützt (mir/dir) nichts** that won't help (me/you); **das nützt niemandem** that's of no use to anybody; **es nützt wenig** it isn't much use *or* good; **wozu soll das alles ~?** what's the use *or* point of that?

2 *vt* to make use of, to use; *Gelegenheit* to take advantage of. **nütze den Tag!** gather ye rosebuds while ye may (*liter*).

Nutz-: ~**fahrzeug** *nt* farm vehicle; military vehicle *etc*; (*Comm*) commercial vehicle, goods vehicle; (*Straßenbahn etc*) public vehicle; ~**fläche** *f* utilizable *or* us(e)able floor space; (*Agr*) (agriculturally) productive land; ~**garten** *m* vegetable *or* kitchen garden; ~**gegenstand** *m* article of purely practical value; **für mich ist ein Auto ein reiner ~gegenstand** for me a car is just a means of getting from A to B; ~**holz** *nt* (utilizable) timber; ~**last** *f* maximum load; ~**leistung** *f* efficiency, effective capacity *or* output; (*Aut*) performance.

nützlich *adj* useful; *Hinweis, Wissen, Kenntnisse, Buch auch* helpful. **~ für die Gesundheit** beneficial for the health; **er könnte dir eines Tages sehr ~ werden** he might be very useful to you one day; **~ für das Wohl des Volkes** in the interest(s) of the people; **sich ~ machen** to make oneself useful; **kann ich Ihnen ~ sein?** may I be of service to you?

Nützlichkeit *f* usefulness, utility (*form*); (*Vorteil*) advantage; (*Dienlichkeit*) usefulness, helpfulness. **die ~ eines Onkels bei der Polizei** the advantage of having an uncle in the police.

Nützlichkeits-: ~**denken** *nt* utilitarian thinking; ~**prinzip** *nt* utility principle.

Nützling *m* beneficial insect.

nutzlos *adj* (a) useless; (*unergiebig, vergeblich*) futile, vain *attr*, in vain *pred*. **es ist völlig ~, das zu tun** it's absolutely useless *or* pointless *or* futile doing that; **er hat seine Zeit ~ mit Spielen zugebracht** he frittered away *or* wasted his time playing.
  (b) (*unnötig*) needless. **sein Leben ~ aufs Spiel setzen** to risk one's life needlessly *or* unnecessarily.

Nutzlosigkeit *f* uselessness; (*Uneinträglichkeit, Vergeblichkeit*) futility, vainness.

Nutznießer(in *f*) *m* **-s, -** beneficiary; (*Jur*) usufructuary.

Nutznießung *f* (*Jur*) usufruct.

Nutz-: ~**pflanze** *f* useful plant; ~**tier** *nt* working animal.

Nutzung *f* (*Gebrauch*) use; (*das Ausnutzen*) exploitation; (*Jur: Ertrag*) benefit; (*Einkommen*) revenue (+*gen* from), return(s) (+*gen* on). **ich habe ihm meinen Garten zur ~ überlassen** I gave him the use of my garden; **die ~en aus etw ziehen** (*Jur*) to enjoy the benefit of sth.

Nutzungsdauer *f* (useful) life.

Nutzungsrecht *nt* (*Jur*) usufruct.

n.u.Z. *abbr of* **nach unserer Zeitrechnung** AD.

NW *abbr of* **Nordwesten** NW.

Nylon ['nailɔn] ⑭ *nt* **-(s)**, *no pl* nylon.

Nylons ['nailɔns] *pl* nylons *pl*, nylon stockings *pl*.

Nylonstrumpf ['nailɔn-] *m* nylon (stocking).

Nymphe ['nʏmfə] *f* **-, -n** (*Myth*) nymph; (*fig*) sylph; (*Zool*) nymph(a). **die ~n** (*Anat*) the nymphae *pl*.

Nymphomanie [nʏmfo-] *f* nymphomania.

Nymphomanin [nʏmfo-] *f* nymphomaniac.

nymphomanisch [nʏmfo-] *adj* nymphomaniac.

O, o [oː] *nt* **-, -** O, o.

O *abbr of* **Osten**.

o *interj* oh. **~ Sünder!** (*liter*) O sinner.

Oase *f* **-, -n** oasis; (*fig*) haven, oasis.

ob 1 *conj* (a) (*indirekte Frage*) if, whether. **wir gehen spazieren, ~ es regnet oder nicht** we're going for a walk whether it rains or not; **Sie müssen kommen, ~ Sie (nun) wollen oder nicht** like it or not, you have to come; **~ reich, ~ arm** whether rich or poor; **~ er (wohl) morgen kommt?** I wonder if he'll come tomorrow?; **~ wir jetzt Pause machen?** shall we have a break now?; **~ ich nicht lieber gehe?** maybe I'd better go, hadn't I better go?; **~ ich keine Angst gehabt hätte, fragte er** hadn't I been afraid, he asked; **er hat gefragt, ~ du's geklaut hast — ~ ich was?** (*inf*) he asked if you pinched it — if I what?; **hast du's geklaut? — ~ ich was?** (*inf*) did you pinch it? — did I what?; **kommst du mit? — was? — ~ du mitkommen willst?** are you coming? — what? — are you coming?; **~ Sie mir wohl mal helfen können?** could you possibly help me?, I wonder if you could help me?
  (b) (*verstärkend*) **und ~** (*inf*) you bet (*inf*), of course; **und ~ ich das gesehen habe!** you bet (*inf*) *or* of course I saw it!
  (c) (*vergleichend*) **als ~** as if; (*so*) **tun als ~** (*inf*) to pretend; **tu nicht so als ~!** stop pretending!
  (d) **~ ... auch, ~ ... gleich** (*liter*) even though.
  2 *prep* + *gen* (a) (*old, liter*) on account of.
  (b) (*in Ortsnamen*) (up)on.

OB [oːˈbeː] *m* **-s, -s** *abbr of* **Oberbürgermeister**.

o.B. *abbr of* **ohne Befund**.

Obacht *f* **-**, *no pl* (*esp S Ger*) **~!** watch out!, look out!, careful!; **~ geben auf** (+*acc*) (*aufmerken*) to pay attention to; (*bewachen*) to keep an eye on; **du mußt ~ geben, daß du keine Fehler machst** you must be careful not to make any mistakes; **gib or hab doch ~!** (*inf*) be careful!, watch it! (*inf*).

ÖBB *abbr of* **Österreichische Bundesbahnen**.

Obdach *nt*, *no pl* (*geh*) shelter. **jdm (ein) ~ gewähren** *or* **geben** to give *or* offer sb shelter; **kein ~ haben** to be homeless; (*vorübergehend*) to have no shelter.

Obdach-: o~**los** *adj* homeless; o~**los werden** to be made homeless; **die Flüchtlinge zogen o~los umher** the refugees wandered about with no home to go to; ~**lose(r)** *mf decl as adj* homeless person; **die ~losen** the homeless.

Obdachlosen-: ~**asyl**, ~**heim** *nt* hostel/shelter for the homeless; ~**siedlung** *f* settlement for the homeless.

Obdachlosigkeit *f* homelessness.

Obduktion *f* post-mortem (examination), autopsy.

obduzieren* *vt* to carry out *or* do a post-mortem *or* autopsy on.

O-Beine *pl* (*inf*) bow *or* bandy legs *pl*.

o-beinig *adj* bow- *or* bandy-legged.

Obelisk *m* **-en, -en** obelisk.

oben *adv* (a) (*am oberen Ende*) at the top; (*an der Oberfläche*) on the surface; (*im Hause*) upstairs; (*in der Höhe*) up. **(hier) ~!** (*auf Kisten etc*) this way *or* this side up!; **so ist das Leben, mal bist du ~, mal bist du unten** that's life, sometimes you're up, sometimes you're down; **~ und unten (von etw) verwechseln** to get sth upside down; **wo ist ~ (bei dem Bild)?** which is the top (of the picture)?, which is the right way up (for the picture)?; **die Leute, die ~ wohnen** the people on the floor above us/you *etc or* (who live) upstairs; **wir möchten lieber ~ wohnen** we'd rather live high(er) up; **möchten Sie lieber ~ schlafen?** (*im oberen Bett*) would you like the top bunk *or* to sleep on top?; **wir wohnen rechts ~ or ~ rechts** we live on the top floor to the right; **~ rechts** *or* **rechts ~ (in der Ecke)** in the top right-hand corner; **die Abbildung ~ links** *or* **links ~ auf der Schautafel** the illustration on the top left *or* in the top left-hand corner of the diagram; **der ist ~ nicht ganz richtig** (*inf*) he's not quite right up top (*inf*); **Kleid/Kellnerin mit ~ ohne** (*inf*) topless dress/waitress; **~ ohne gehen** *or* **tragen** (*inf*) to be topless; **ganz ~** right at the top; **ganz ~ auf dem Stapel/in der Rangordnung** right at the top of the pile/of the hierarchy; **hier/dort ~** up here/there; **die ganze Sache steht mir bis hier ~** (*inf*) I'm sick to death of *or* fed up to the back teeth with the whole thing (*inf*); **bis ~ (hin)** to the top; **hoch ~** high (up) above; **~ an der Tafel** at the top of the table; **beim Festessen saß er weiter ~ an der Tafel** at the banquet he sat nearer the top of the table; **~ auf dem Berg/der Leiter/dem Dach** on top of the mountain/ladder/roof; **~ an der Erde** above ground; **~ am Himmel** up in the sky; **~ im Himmel** up in heaven, in heaven above (*liter*); **~ in Schottland** up in Scotland; **~ im Norden** up in the north; **~ herum** round the top; (*von Frau*) up top; (*von Jacke*) round the chest; **nach ~** up, upwards; (*im Hause*) upstairs; **der Fahrstuhl fährt nach ~** the lift is going up; **wir sind mit dem Fahrstuhl nach ~ gefahren** we went up in the lift; **die Bergsteiger sind auf dem Weg nach ~** the climbers are on their way up; **der Weg nach ~** (*fig*) the road to the top; **endlich hat sie den Weg nach ~ geschafft** (*fig*) she finally got to the top *or* made it (to the top); **nach ~ zu** *or* **hin** towards the top; **von ~ (her)** down; (*im Hause*) down(stairs); **ich komme gerade von ~ (am Berg)** I've just come from the top; (*im Hause*) I've just been upstairs; **von ~ (aus)** **hat man eine schöne Aussicht** there's a nice view from the top; **von ~ bis unten** from top to bottom; (*von Mensch*) from top to toe; **jdn von ~ bis unten mustern** to look sb up and down; **jdn von ~ herab behandeln** to be condescending to sb, to treat sb condescendingly; **jdn von ~ herab ansehen** to look down on sb; **weiter ~ further up; das Gehöft liegt weiter ~ (am Berg/im Tal)** the farm is further *or* higher up (the mountain/valley).
  (b) (*inf: die Vorgesetzten*) **die da ~** the powers that be (*inf*), the top brass (*inf*); **das wird ~ entschieden** that's decided higher up; **er will sich nur ~ beliebt machen** he's just sucking up to the management (*inf*); **etw nach ~ (weiter)melden/weitergeben** to report sth/to pass sth on to a superior; **der**

Befehl kommt von ~ it's orders from above.
  (c) (*vorher*) above. **siehe** ~ see above; **wie** ~ **erwähnt** as mentioned above; **der** ~ **schon erwähnte Herr** the abovementioned *or* aforementioned gentleman; **der weiter** ~ **erwähnte Fall** the case referred to before *or* above.

oben-: ~**an** *adv* at the top *or* on (the) top; **sein Name steht** ~**an (auf der Liste)** his name is (at the) top (of the list); **an der Tafel saß er** ~**an** he sat at the top of the table; **er will immer** ~**an** (*fig*) he always wants to be on top; ~**auf** *adv* on (the) top; (*an der Oberfläche*) on the top *or* surface; **gestern war er krank, aber heute ist er wieder** ~**auf** (*inf*) he wasn't well yesterday, but he's back on form today; **sie ist immer** ~**auf** (*inf*) she is always bright and cheery (*inf*); ~**drauf** *adv* (*inf*) on top; ~**drein** *adv* (*inf*) on top of everything (*inf*); ~**erwähnt** *adj attr* abovementioned; ~(**he**)**raus** *adv* (*inf*) **er ist immer gleich** ~(**he**)**raus** he blows his top at the slightest little thing (*inf*); ~**hin** *adv* superficially; **etw nur so** ~**hin sagen** to say sth lightly *or* casually *or* in an offhand way; **es schien mir (so)** ~**hin gesagt** he seemed so offhand *or* casual about it; ~**hinaus** *adv* ~**hinaus wollen** (*inf*) to have big ideas; ~**ohne** *adj attr* topless; ~**raus** *adv* **siehe** ~(**he**)**raus.**

Ober *m* -s, - **(a)** (*Kellner*) waiter. **Herr** ~! waiter! **(b)** (*Cards*) = Queen.

Ober- *in cpds* (*Geog*) Upper; (*im Rang*) senior, chief; (*fig*) first class; ~**arm** *m* upper arm; (*im Rang*) senior, chief; (*fig*) first class; ~**arm** *m* upper arm; ~**arzt** *m* senior physician; ~**aufseher** *m* (head) supervisor, superintendent; (*im Gefängnis*) head warden *or* guard; ~**aufsicht** *f* supervision, superintendence; **die** ~**aufsicht haben** to be in *or* have overall control (*über* +*acc* of); ~**bau** *m* (*a*) (*von Brücke*) superstructure; **(b)** (*Rail*) permanent way; ~**befehl** *m* (*Mil*) supreme command; **den** ~**befehl haben** to be commander-in-chief *or* supreme commander, to be in supreme command (*über* +*acc* of); ~**befehlshaber** *m* (*Mil*) commander-in-chief, supreme commander; ~**begriff** *m* generic term; ~**bekleidung** *f* outer clothing, top clothes; ~**bett** *nt* quilt; ~**bürgermeister** *m* mayor; (*von englischer Großstadt*) Lord Mayor; (*Scot*) provost; ~**deck** *nt* upper *or* top deck; **o**~**deutsch** *adj* (*Ling*) Upper German; **im O**~**deutschen** in Upper German *or* the Upper German dialects.

obere(r, s) *adj attr* Ende, Stockwerke, (*Schul*)*klassen* upper, top; *Flußlauf* upper. **die O**~**n** (*inf*) the top brass (*inf*), the bosses; (*Eccl*) the superiors; **die** ~**en Zehntausend** (*inf*) high society; **siehe oberste(r, s).**

Ober-: **o**~**faul** *adj* (*inf*) very peculiar *or* odd *or* funny (*inf*); ~**feld** *m* (*sl*) sarge (*sl*); ~**feldwebel** *m* (**a**) (*Heer*) staff sergeant (*Brit*), first sergeant (*US*); **(b)** (*Luftwaffe*) flight sergeant (*Brit*), master sergeant (*US*).

Oberfläche *f* surface; (*Tech, Math*) surface area. **an die** ~ **kommen** (*lit*) to come to the surface, to surface; (*fig*) to emerge; **an der** ~ **schwimmen** to float; **an der** ~ **bleiben** (*lit*) to remain on the surface; **sein Referat blieb völlig an der** ~ his paper was completely superficial *or* only scratched the surface; **die Unterhaltung plätscherte an der** ~ **dahin** the conversation never got beyond small talk.

oberflächlich *adj* (*an der Oberfläche*) superficial. ~**e Verletzung** surface wound; **er ist nur** ~ **verletzt** he's only got superficial injuries.
  (b) (*flüchtig*) superficial; *Kenntnisse auch* shallow. **bei** ~**er Betrachtung** at a quick glance; **seine Kenntnisse sind nur** ~ his knowledge doesn't go very deep *or* far *or* doesn't go beyond the surface; ~ **arbeiten** to work superficially; **eine Arbeit** ~ **machen** to do a job superficially, to skip through a piece of work; **etw** ~ **lesen** to skim through sth; **er ist sehr** ~ **in seiner Arbeit** his work is very superficial; **jdn (nur)** ~ **kennen** to know sb (only) slightly, to have a nodding acquaintance with sb; **etw (nur)** ~ **kennen** to have (only) a shallow *or* superficial knowledge of sth; **nach** ~**er Schätzung** at a rough estimate *or* guess.
  (c) (*seicht*) *Mensch, Unterhaltung* superficial, shallow.

Oberflächlichkeit *f* superficiality.

Ober-: ~**förster** *m* head forester; **o**~**gärig** *adj* Bier top fermented; ~**gefreite(r)** *m* (**a**) (*Heer*) lance-corporal (*Brit*), private first class (*US*); **(b)** (*Luftwaffe*) senior aircraftsman (*Brit*), airman first class (*US*); **(c)** (*Marine*) seaman first class (*Brit*), seaman (*US*); ~**geschoß** *nt* upper *or* top floor; **im zweiten** ~**geschoß** on the second (*Brit*) *or* (*US*) third floor; ~**grenze** *f* upper limit; **o**~**halb 1** *prep* +*gen* above; **2** *adv* above; **o**~**halb von Basel** above Basel; **weiter o**~**halb** further *or* higher up; ~**hand** *f* (*fig*) upper hand; **die** ~**hand gewinnen** *or* **bekommen** to get *or* gain the upper hand (*über* +*acc* over); **to get the better (of sb/sth); die** ~**hand haben** to have the upper hand; ~**haupt** *nt* (*Repräsentant*) head; (*Anführer*) leader; ~**haus** *nt* (*Pol*) upper house; (*in GB*) House of Lords; ~**hemd** *nt* shirt; ~**herr** *m* (*old*) sovereign; ~**herrschaft** *f* sovereignty, supremacy (*über* +*acc* over); **unter der** ~**herrschaft Englands** under English rule; ~**hirte** *m* spiritual head *or* leader; ~**hoheit** *f* supremacy, sovereignty, overlordship; **die** ~**hoheit über jdn gewinnen** to gain *or* win supremacy over sb.

Oberin *f* (**a**) (*im Krankenhaus*) matron. **(b)** (*Eccl*) Mother Superior.

Ober-: ~**ingenieur** *m* chief engineer; ~**inspektor** *m* senior inspector; **o**~**irdisch** *adj* above ground; ~**kellner** *m* head waiter; ~**kiefer** *m* upper jaw; ~**kirchenrat** *m* (church assembly); **(b)** member of the church assembly; ~**klasse** *f* (**a**) (*Sch*) ~**klassen** top classes *or* forms; **(b)** (*Sociol*) upper class; ~**kleid** *nt* (*liter*) outer garment(s); ~**kleidung** *f* outer clothing; ~**kommandierende(r)** *m decl as adj* Commander-in-Chief, Supreme Commander; ~**kommando** *nt* (~*befehl*) Supreme Command; (*Befehlsstab*) headquarters *pl*; ~**körper** *m* trunk, upper part of the body; **mit bloßem** *or* **freiem** *or* **nacktem** ~**körper** stripped to the waist; **den** ~**körper frei machen** to strip to the waist; ~**land** *nt* (*Geog*) uplands; **das Berner**

~**land** the Bernese Oberland; ~**landesgericht** *nt* provincial high court and court of appeal; ~**länge** *f* upstroke; (*Typ*) ascender; **o**~**lastig** *adj* (*Naut*) top-heavy; ~**lauf** *m* upper reaches *pl*; **am** ~**lauf des Rheins** in the upper reaches of the Rhine; ~**leder** *nt* (leather) uppers *pl*; ~**lehrer** *m* (*old*) senior primary school teacher; ~**leitung** *f* (a) (*Führung*) direction; **die** ~**leitung eines Projekts haben** to be in overall charge of a project; **(b)** (*Elec*) overhead cable; ~**leutnant** *m* (a) (*Heer*) lieutenant (*Brit*), first lieutenant (*US*); **(b)** (*Luftwaffe*) flying officer (*Brit*), first lieutenant (*US*); **(c)** (*Marine*) ~**leutnant zur See** lieutenant; ~**licht** *nt* (*hochgelegenes Fenster*) small, high window; (*Lüftungsklappe, über einer Tür*) fanlight, transom (window); (*Sport*) top *or* first league; ~**lippe** *f* upper lip; ~**maat** *m* (*Naut*) = leading seaman; ~**meister** *m* (a) head of craft guild; **(b)** (*bei Polizei*) = sergeant; ~**postdirektion** *f* (*Behörde*) regional post office (administration); (*Bezirk*) postal area *or* district; ~**postdirektion Köln** Cologne postal district; ~**priester** *m* high priest; ~**prima** *f* top form of German grammar school = upper sixth, ≈ senior grade (*US*); ~**primaner(in** *f*) *m* = sixth former, ≈ senior (*US*); **o**~**rheinisch** *adj* upper Rhine; **die** ~**rheinische Tiefebene** the upper Rhine valley; **im** ~**rheinischen** along *or* around the upper Rhine; ~**richter** *m* (*Sw*) = high court judge.

Obers *nt* -, *no pl* (*Aus*) cream.

Ober-: ~**schenkel** *m* thigh; ~**schenkelbruch** *m* broken thighbone *or* femur, fracture of the thighbone *or* femur; ~**schenkelhals** *m* head of the thighbone *or* femur; ~**schenkelknochen** *m* thighbone, femur; ~**schicht** *f* top layer; (*Sociol*) upper strata (of society) *pl*; ~**schule** *f* (old: *Gymnasium*) grammar school (*Brit*), high school (*US*); (*DDR: weiterführende Schule*) secondary school; ~**schulrat** *m* school inspector, HMI (*Brit inf*); ~**schurke** *m* (*inf*) chief villain, baddy (*inf*); ~**schwester** *f* senior nursing officer; ~**seite** *f* top (side); ~**sekunda** *f* seventh year of German secondary school; ~**sekundaner(in** *f*) *m* pupil in seventh year of German secondary school.

Oberst *m* -en, -e(n) **(a)** (*Heer*) colonel. **b)** (*Luftwaffe*) group captain (*Brit*), colonel (*US*).

Ober-: ~**staatsanwalt** *m* public prosecutor, procurator fiscal (*Scot*), district attorney (*US*); ~**stadt** *f* upper town, upper part of a town; ~**stadtdirektor** *m* town clerk; ~**steiger** *m* head foreman (in a mine).

oberste(r, s) *adj* (*ganz oben*) *Stockwerk, Schicht* topmost, uppermost, very top. **das O**~**zu unterst kehren** to turn everything *or* things upside down.
  (b) *Gebot, Gesetz, Prinzip* supreme; *Dienstgrad* highest, most senior, top. **die** ~**n Kreise der Gesellschaft** the upper circles *or* echelons of society; **O**~**es Gericht, O**~**er Gerichtshof** supreme court; (*in GB*) High Court (of Justice); (*in USA*) Supreme Court.

Oberstimme *f* soprano; (*Knaben*~) treble; (*Diskant*) descant.

Oberstleutnant *m* **(a)** (*Heer*) lieutenant colonel. **(b)** (*Luftwaffe*) wing commander (*Brit*), lieutenant colonel (*US*).

Ober-: ~**stübchen** *nt* (*inf*): **er ist nicht ganz richtig im** ~**stübchen** he's not quite right up top (*inf*); ~**studiendirektor** *m* headmaster (*Brit*), principal (*US*); ~**studienrat** *m* senior teacher; ~**stufe** *f* upper school; (*Univ*) advanced level; ~**tasse** *f* (*form*) cup; ~**teil** *nt or m* upper part, top; ~**tertia** *f* fifth year of German secondary school; ~**tertianer(in** *f*) *m* pupil in fifth year of German secondary school; ~**töne** *pl* (*Mus, fig*) overtone(s); ~**trottel** *m* (*inf*) prize *or* first-class idiot; ~**volta** *nt* -s Upper Volta; ~**wasser** *nt* (a) (*von Wehr*) backwater; **(b)** (*fig inf*) **sobald sein älterer Bruder dabei ist, hat er (wieder)** ~**wasser** as soon as his elder brother is there he opens up *or* out (again); **seitdem wir unser Geschäft haben, bekommen wir** ~**wasser** since we did up the shop we've been going great guns (*inf*); ~**weite** *f* bust measurement; **sie hat** ~**weite 94** she has a 38-inch bust; **die hat eine ganz schöne** ~**weite!** she's very well endowed; ~**welt** *f* (*liter*) world (of the living).

obgleich *conj* although, (even) though.

Obhut *f* -, *no pl* (*geh*) (*Aufsicht*) care; (*Verwahrung*) keeping, care. **jdn/etw jds** ~ (*dat*) **anvertrauen** to place *or* put sb/sth in sb's care; **jdn in** ~ **nehmen** to take care of sb, to look after sb; **jdn bei jdm in** ~ **geben** to put *or* place sb in sb's care.

obige(r, s) *adj attr* above. **vergleiche** ~ **Abbildung** compare the illustration above *or* the above illustration; **der O**~ (*form*) the above (*form*).

Objekt *nt* -(e)s, -e (*auch Gram*) object. **das** ~ **der Untersuchung** the object under examination.

objektiv *adj* objective. ~ **über etw** (*acc*) **urteilen** to make an objective judgement about sth, to judge sth objectively; **etw** ~ **betrachten** to view sth objectively.

Objektiv *nt* (*object*) lens, objective.

objektivieren* [ɔpjɛkti'viːrən] **1** *vi* to objectify. **du mußt mal** ~ you must try to see things objectively *or* in perspective. **2** *vt* *Problem* to treat objectively, to objectivize.

Objektivität *f* objectivity. **sich um größte** ~ **bemühen** to try to be as objective as possible.

Objektsatz *m* object clause.

Objektträger *m* slide.

Oblate *f* -, -n wafer; (*Eccl*) host.

obliegen *sep or* (*esp S Ger, Aus*)* *insep irreg aux haben or sein* (+*dat*) **1** *vi* (*old*) *einer Aufgabe, seinen Studien* to apply oneself to (*form*). **2** *vi impers* (*form*) **es obliegt ihm** it's incumbent upon him (*form*); **ihm oblag die Betreuung der Flüchtlinge** he was responsible for looking after the refugees.

Obliegenheit *f* (*form*) duty, obligation, incumbency (*form*).

obligat *adj* obligatory. **der** ~**e Dudelsackpfeifer** the obligatory bagpiper; **mit** ~**em Cembalo** (*Mus*) with (a) cembalo obligato.

Obligation *f* (*auch Fin*) obligation. **die Firma übernimmt keine**

~ the firm is under or accepts no obligation.
obligatorisch adj obligatory; Fächer, Vorlesung compulsory; Qualifikationen necessary, requisite.

Obligo nt -s, -s (Fin) guarantee. frei von or ohne ~ without recourse.

Obmann m, pl -männer or -leute, **Obmännin** f representative.

Oboe [o'bo:ə] f -, -n oboe.

Oboist [obo'ɪst] m oboist, oboe player.

Obolus m -, -se contribution.

Obrigkeit f (a) (als Begriff) authority. (b) (Behörden) die ~ the authorities pl; die geistliche/weltliche ~ the spiritual/secular authorities.

obrigkeitlich adj authoritarian. das Leben der Beamten war ~ geprägt the lives of the civil servants bore the stamp of authoritarian attitudes.

Obrigkeitsstaat m authoritarian state.

Obrist m colonel.

obschon conj (liter) although, albeit (nur in verbloser Konstruktion).

Observanz [ɔpzɛr'vants] f observance. ein Orden (von) der strengen ~ a strict or closed order; er ist einer von der strengen ~ (fig) he's a stickler for the rules.

Observatorium [ɔpzɛrva'to:rɪum] nt observatory.

observieren* [ɔpzɛr'vi:rən] vt (form) to observe. er ist schon einige Monate observiert worden he has been under surveillance for several months.

obsiegen vi sep or insep* (obs) to prevail (dat over).

obskur adj (a) (unbekannt) obscure. (b) (verdächtig) Gestalten, Kneipe, Gassen suspect, dubious. diese ~en Gestalten der Unterwelt these twilight figures of the underworld.

Obskurantismus m obscurantism.

obsolet adj (liter) obsolete.

Obst nt -(e)s, no pl fruit; siehe danken.

Obst-: ~**bau** m fruit-growing; ~**baum** m fruit-tree; ~**garten** m orchard.

obstinat adj (geh) obstinate.

Obst-: ~**jahr** nt ein gutes ~**jahr** a good year for fruit; ~**kuchen** m fruit flan/tart.

Obstler m -s, - (dial) fruit schnapps.

Obstmesser nt fruit-knife.

Obstruktion f (a) (Med) obstruction, blockage. (b) (Pol) obstruction, filibuster. das Regierungsprogramm scheiterte an der ~ der Opposition the Government's programme failed because of the Opposition's obstructive or filibustering tactics or obstructionism; ~ betreiben to obstruct, to block, to filibuster.

Obstruktionspolitik f obstructionist or filibustering policies, obstructionism.

Obst-: ~**saft** m fruit juice; ~**tag** m legen Sie jede Woche einen ~**tag** ein eat only fruit one day a week; meine Frau hat heute ihren ~**tag** my wife's on her fruit diet today; ~**torte** f fruit flan/tart; ~**wein** m fruit wine.

obszön adj obscene.

Obszönität f obscenity.

Obus m -ses, -se (inf) trolley (inf), trolley bus.

obwalten vi sep or insep* (form: herrschen) to prevail.

obwohl conj although, (even) though.

obzwar conj (rare) siehe obwohl.

Ochs(e) ['ɔks(ə)] m -n, -n (a) ox, bullock. ~ am Spieß roast ox; er stand da wie der ~ vorm Scheunentor or am Berg (inf) he stood there like a cow at a five-barred gate (inf). (b) (inf: Dummkopf) twit (Brit inf), ass (inf), dope (inf).

ochsen ['ɔksn] (Sch sl) 1 vt to swot up (inf), to mug up (inf). 2 vi to swot (up) (inf), to mug (up) (inf), to cram (inf).

Ochsen-: ['ɔksn-]: ~**gespann** nt yoke of oxen; ~**schwanzsuppe** f oxtail soup; ~**tour** f (inf) (a) (Schinderei) slog (inf), sweat (inf); (b) er brauchte sich nicht über die ~**tour** heraufzudienen he did not have to work his way up the hard way; ~**ziemer** m bull's pizzle, bullwhip.

ochsig ['ɔksɪç] adv (S Ger inf) really hard. ~ viel an awful lot.

Ochsle ['œkslə] nt -s, - measure of alcohol content of drink according to its specific gravity.

Ocker m or nt -s, - ochre.

ockerbraun, ockergelb adj ochre.

od. abbr of oder.

Ode f -, -n ode.

öd(e) adj (a) (verlassen) Stadt, Strand deserted, empty, abandoned; (unbewohnt) desolate, empty, bleak; (unbebaut) waste, barren. öd und leer dreary and desolate. (b) (fig: fade) dull, dreary, tedious; Dasein, Stunden auch barren.

Öde f -, -n (liter) (einsame Gegend) desert, waste (land). (b) (Langeweile) barrenness, dreariness, monotony.

Odem m -s, no pl (poet, Bibl) breath.

Ödem nt -s, -e oedema, edema.

oder conj (a) or. ~ aber or else; ~ auch or even or maybe or perhaps; eins ~ das andere one or the other, it's either or; entweder ... ~ either ... or.
(b) (in Fragen) so war's doch, ~ (etwa) nicht? that was what happened, wasn't it?, wasn't that how it happened?, it happened like that, didn't it?; du kommst doch, ~? you're coming, aren't you?; die Zeit des Nationalismus ist endgültig vorüber, ~? the days of nationalism are gone for ever, don't you think or don't you agree or (bezweifelnd) ... or are they?; der Mörder hat sein Opfer nie vorher gesehen, ~ doch? the murderer had never seen his victim before, or had he?; ~ soll ich lieber mitkommen? maybe I should come along?; lassen wir es so, ~? let's leave it at that, right or OK?

Ödipuskomplex m Oedipus complex.

Ödium nt -s, no pl (liter) odium.

Ödland nt barren land.

Odyssee f -, -n [-e:ən] (Liter) Odyssey; (fig) odyssey.

Oeuvre ['ø:vrə, œ:vrə] nt, -s (Liter) work, works pl.

OEZ abbr of **Osteuropäische Zeit**.

Öfchen nt dim of **Ofen**.

Ofen m -s, ⁻ (a) (Heiz~) heater; (Elektro~, Gas~ auch) fire; (Öl~, Petroleum~ auch) stove; (Kohle~) stove; (Heizungs~) boiler. hinter dem ~ hocken to be a stay-at-home; jetzt ist der ~ aus (sl) that's it (inf), that does it (inf).
(b) (Herd) oven, stove; (Kohle~) stove, range; (Back~) oven.
(c) (Tech) furnace, oven; (Brenn~) kiln; (Trocken~) drying oven or kiln; (Hoch~) blast furnace; (Schmelz~) smelting furnace.

Ofen-: ~**bank** f fireside (bench), hearth; auf der ~**bank** by the hearth or fire or fireside; ~**blech** nt tray for catching falling coals; ~**ecke** f inglenook; o~**fertig** adj Gericht oven ready; o~**frisch** adj Brot oven fresh; ~**heizung** f stove heating; Zimmer mit ~**heizung** room with stove (heater); ~**klappe** f (a) siehe ~**tür**; (b) (Lüftungsklappe) damper; ~**loch** nt stove door; ein paar Kohlen fielen aus dem ~**loch** some coal fell out of the front of the stove; ~**rohr** nt stovepipe; (old inf: Zylinder) stovepipe (hat); ~**röhre** f (slow) oven; ~**schirm** m firescreen; ~**setzer** m stove fitter; ~**tür** f stove door.

offen adj (a) open; Bein ulcerated; Flamme, Licht naked; Feuer open; Haare loose. ein ~er Brief an open letter; er geht mit ~em Hemd he wears an open neck; die Haare ~ tragen to wear one's hair loose; der Laden hat bis 7 Uhr ~ the shop is or stays open until 7 o'clock; das Turnier ist für alle ~ the tournament is open to everybody; die Teilnahme ist für alle ~ anyone can take part; ~er Wein wine by the carafe/glass; Wein ~ verkaufen to sell wine on draught; auf ~er Strecke (Straße) on the open road; (Rail) between stations; wir hielten auf ~er Strecke we stopped in the middle of nowhere; auf ~er Straße in the middle of the street; (Landstraße) on the open road; auf ~er See on the open sea; auf ~er Szene or Bühne on the open stage; Beifall auf ~er Szene spontaneous applause, an outburst of applause; bei ~er Szene or Bühne verwandelt sich das Bild the scene changed without a curtain; ~e Flanke (Mil) open or exposed flank; ~e Stadt (Mil) open or undefended town; wir sahen die Stadt ~ daliegen we saw the town spread out before us; endlich lag das Ziel ~ vor ihnen (da) at last their goal lay before them; mit ~em Munde dastehen (fig) to stand gaping; mit ~em Munde atmen to breathe with one's mouth open; ~e Türen einrennen (fig) to kick at an open door; Tag der ~en Tür open day; ein ~es Haus haben or führen to keep open house; überall ~e Türen finden (fig) to find a warm welcome everywhere; Haus der ~en Tür open house; Politik der ~en Tür open-door policy; jdn mit ~en Armen empfangen to greet or welcome sb with open arms; mit ~en Augen or Sinnen durchs Leben gehen to go through life with one's eyes open; eine ~e Hand haben (fig) to be openhanded; sich (dat) einen ~en Blick für etw bewahren to keep an open mind about or for sth, to be open-minded about sth; allem Neuen gegenüber ~ sein to be open or receptive to (all) new ideas; etw ~ in sich (dat) aufnehmen to absorb or soak up or take in sth; ~e Handlungsgesellschaft general partnership; siehe Buch, Karte.
(b) (frei) Stelle vacant. ~e Stellen vacancies; (Press auch) "situations vacant".
(c) (unerledigt, unentschieden) Frage, Ausgang, Partie open; Rechnung outstanding.
(d) (aufrichtig, freimütig) Mensch, Bekenntnis, Aussprache open. er hat einen ~en Blick he's got an open or honest face; er hat keinen ~en Blick he's got a shifty look in his eyes; ~ standen or gesagt to tell you the truth, quite honestly, to be frank; etw ~ eingestehen or zugeben to confess or admit (to) sth openly or frankly; seine Meinung ~ sagen to speak one's mind, to say what one thinks; ~ mit jdm reden to speak openly to sb, to be frank with sb; ein ~es Wort mit jdm reden to have a frank talk with sb.

offenbar 1 adj obvious. sein Zögern machte ~, daß ... it showed or was obvious from the way he hesitated that ...; ~ werden to become obvious or clear, to emerge.
2 adv (vermutlich) apparently. er hat ~ den Zug verpaßt he must have missed the train; da haben Sie sich ~ geirrt you seem to have made a mistake.

offenbaren* insep ptp auch (old) geoffenbart 1 vt to reveal. 2 vr (a) (erweisen) to show or reveal itself/oneself. sich als etw ~ to show oneself to be sth; nun wird sich ~, wer recht hat now we'll find out or see who's right.
(b) (kundtun) sich jdm ~ to reveal oneself to sb; (Liebe erklären) to reveal one's feelings to sb.

Offenbarung f revelation.

Offenbarungsleid m (Jur) oath of disclosure or manifestation. den ~ leisten (lit) to swear an oath of disclosure or manifestation; mit diesem Programm hat die Partei ihren ~ geleistet with this programme the party has revealed its political bankruptcy.

offen-: ~**bleiben** vi sep irreg aux sein to remain open; alle ~**gebliebenen** Probleme all unsolved or remaining problems; ~**halten** vt sep irreg to keep open; die Ohren ~**halten** to keep one's ear to the ground or open; jdm eine Stelle or eine Stelle für jdn ~**halten** to keep a job open for sb.

Offenheit f openness, frankness, candour. schonungslose ~ brutal frankness.

offen-: ~**herzig** adj (a) open, frank, candid; Mensch auch open-hearted, outspoken; (b) (hum inf) Kleid revealing; sie ist ja heute wieder sehr ~**herzig** she's being very revealing again today (hum inf); O~**herzigkeit** f openness, frankness, candour; ~**kundig** adj obvious, clear; Beweise clear; Lüge, Interesse obvious, manifest; es ist ~**kundig, daß** ... it is obvious or clear *or* evident that ...; **~lassen** *vt sep irreg* to leave open; **~sichtlich** *adj* obvious; *Irrtum, Lüge auch* blatant; *Unterschied auch* clear; **es war ~sichtlich, daß er uns mied** it was plain *or* evident *or* obvious he was avoiding us, he was obviously avoiding us; **er hat sich da ganz ~sichtlich vertan** he's obviously *or* clearly *or* evidently made a mistake there.

offensiv *adj* offensive.

Offensive *f* offensive. **in die ~ gehen** to take the offensive.

Offensivkrieg *m* offensive war.

offenstehen *vi sep irreg* (*S Ger auch: aux sein*) **(a)** (*Tür, Fenster*) to be open; (*Knopf*) to be undone.
(b) (*Comm: Rechnung, Betrag*) to be *or* remain unpaid *or* unsettled, to be outstanding.
(c) jdm ~ (*fig: zugänglich sein*) to be open to sb; **die (ganze) Welt steht ihm offen** he has the (whole) world at his feet, the world's his oyster; **es steht ihr offen, sich uns anzuschließen** she's free to join us; **die Teilnahme an der Veranstaltung steht auch Nichtmitgliedern offen** the function is also open to non-members.

öffentlich *adj* **(a)** (*allgemein zugänglich, sichtbar*) *attr* public; *pred* open to the public, public; *adv* in public, publicly. **etw ~ bekanntmachen** to make sth public, to publicize sth; **~ versteigern** to sell by public auction, to auction publicly; **eine Persönlichkeit des ~en Lebens** a person in public life *or* in the public eye; **im ~en Leben stehen** to be in public life; **jdn ~ anschuldigen/hinrichten** to accuse/execute sb publicly; **ein ~es Haus** (*euph*) a house of ill repute (*euph*).
(b) *attr* (*die Allgemeinheit betreffend*) *Wohl, Interesse* public. **die ~e Meinung/Moral** public opinion/morality; **die ~e Ordnung** law and order; **~es Recht** (*Jur*) public law; **Anstalt des ~en Rechts** public institution.
(c) (*staatlich*) public. **~e Schule** state school, public school (*US*); **die ~e Hand** (central/local) government; **Ausgaben der ~en Hand** public spending; **etw in die ~e Hand überführen** to take sth into public ownership, to take sth under public control.

Öffentlichkeit *f* **(a)** **der Verteidiger bestand auf der ~ der Verhandlung** the defence counsel insisted that the trial take place in public; **~ der Rechtsprechung** administration of justice in open court; **~ der Prüfungen war eine Hauptforderung der Studenten** one of the students' main demands was that exams should be open to the public; **die ~ einer Versammlung herstellen** to make a meeting public.
(b) (*Allgemeinheit*) the (general) public. **die ~ scheuen** to shun publicity; **in** *or* **vor aller ~** in public; **unter Ausschluß der ~** in secret *or* private; (*Jur*) in camera; **als er das erstemal vor die ~ trat** when he made his first public appearance; **mit etw an** *or* **vor die ~ treten, etw vor die ~ bringen** to bring sth to the public eye *or* before the public; **etw der ~ übergeben** (*form*) (*eröffnen*) to declare sth officially open; (*veröffentlichen*) to publish sth.

Öffentlichkeits|arbeit *f* public relations work.

öffentlich-rechtlich *adj attr* (under) public law.

offerieren* *vt* (*Comm, form*) to offer.

Offerte *f* **-, -n** (*Comm*) offer.

Offizial-: **~delikt** *nt* (*Jur*) offence for which proceedings are brought directly by the public prosecutor's department; **~verteidiger** *m* (*Jur*) lawyer appointed by the court; (*US*) public defender.

offiziell *adj* *Meinung, Erklärung, Besuch* official; *Einladung, Besuch auch* formal. **etw ~ bekanntgeben** to announce sth officially; **wie von ~er Seite verlautet** according to official sources; **auf dem Empfang ging es schrecklich ~ zu** the reception was terribly formal.

Offizier *m* **-s, -e** officer. **~ werden** to become an officer, to get *or* be given *or* gain a commission; (*als Beruf*) to become *or* be an army officer; **erster/zweiter ~** first/second officer.

Offiziers-: **~anwärter** *m* officer cadet; **~kasino** *nt* officers' mess; **~korps** *nt* officer corps, the officers *pl*; **~messe** *f* officers' mess; **~patent** *nt* (*old*) commission.

Offizin *f* **-, -en** **(a)** (*Druckerei*) print shop. **(b)** (*old: von Apotheke*) dispensary.

offizinell *adj* (*old: Pharm*) officinal.

offiziös *adj* semiofficial.

öffnen 1 *vt* to open. **jdm den Blick für etw ~** to open sb's eyes to sth, to make sb aware *or* conscious of sth; **eine Leiche ~** to open (up) a corpse; **das Museum wird um 10 geöffnet** the museum is open *or* opens at 10; **„bitte ~"** "open this end *or* here".
2 *vi* to open. **es hat geklingelt, könnten Sie mal ~?** that was the doorbell, would you answer it *or* would you get it?; **der Nachtportier öffnete mir** the night porter opened the door for me.
3 *vr* (*Tür, Blume, Augen*) to open; (*weiter werden*) to open out. **die Erde öffnete sich** the ground opened (up); **nach Norden hin öffnete sich die Schlucht** the gully widens *or* opens out further north; **das Tal öffnet sich nach Süden** the valley opens *or* is open to the south.

Öffner *m* **-s, -** opener.

Öffnung *f* **(a)** *no pl* (*das Öffnen*) opening. **~ der Leiche** post-mortem, autopsy; **die ~ nach links** (*Pol*) the move *or* swing to the left. **(b)** (*offene Stelle*) opening.

Öffnungszeiten *pl* hours of business *pl*.

Offsetdruck [ˈɔfsɛt-] *m* offset (printing).

oft *adv, comp* **~er,** (*rare*) *superl* **am ~esten** (*häufig*) often, frequently; (*in kurzen Abständen*) frequently. **der Bus fährt nicht ~, die Bahn verkehrt ~er** the bus doesn't go very often, the train goes more often; **schon so ~, ~ genug** often enough; **wie ~ fährt der Bus?** how often *or* frequently does the bus go?; **wie ~ warst du schon in Deutschland?** how often *or* how many times have you been to Germany?; **wie ~ wir das schon gehört haben!** how often we've heard that!, how many times have we

heard that before!; **des ~eren** quite often *or* frequently; **je ~er ... the more often ...**

öfter(s) *adv* on occasion, (every) once in a while; (*wiederholt*) from time to time, (every) now and then. **~ mal was Neues** (*inf*) variety is the spice of life (*prov*).

oftmals *adv* (*geh*) often, oft (*poet*), oftimes (*poet*).

oh *interj siehe* **o.**

Oheim, Ohm *m* **-s, -e** (*old*) uncle.

OHG *abbr of* **Offene Handelsgesellschaft.**

Ohm *nt* **-(s), -** ohm. **~sches Gesetz** Ohm's Law.

ohne 1 *prep* +*acc* **(a)** without. **~ (die) Vororte hat die Stadt 100.000 Einwohner** the city has 100,000 inhabitants excluding *or* not including *or* not counting the suburbs; **~ mich!** count me out!; **er ist nicht ~** (*inf*) he's not bad (*inf*), he's got what it takes (*inf*); **die Sache ist (gar) nicht (so) ~** (*inf*) (*interessant*) it's not bad; (*schwierig*) it's not that easy (*inf*); **~ ihn wären wir immer noch dort** without him *or* but for him *or* if it weren't for him we'd still be there; **~ etw sein** to be without *or* minus (*inf*) sth; **~ Auto** without a *or* one's car; **er ist ~ jede Begabung (für Musik)** he lacks *or* is without any (musical) talent; **~ einen** *or* **jeden Pfennig Geld** penniless, without a penny *or* dime (*US*), without two halfpennies to rub together; **ich rauche immer ~** (*inf*) I always smoke untipped cigarettes.
(b) ich hätte das ~ weiteres getan I'd have done it without a second thought *or* without thinking twice about it; **so etwas kann man ~ weiteres sagen** it's quite all right to say that; **so etwas kann man in feiner Gesellschaft nicht ~ weiteres sagen** you can't say that sort of thing in polite society; **ja, das kann man ~ weiteres sagen** yes, that's true enough; **ich würde ~ weiteres sagen, daß ...** I would not hesitate to say that ...; **er hat den Brief ~ weiteres unterschrieben** he signed the letter just like that *or* straight away; **das Darlehen ist ~ weiteres bewilligt worden** the loan was granted without any bother *or* problem *or* straight away; **ihm können Sie ~ weiteres vertrauen** you can trust him implicitly; **das läßt sich ~ weiteres arrangieren** that can easily be arranged; **hast du das Geld gekriegt? — ja, ~ weiteres** did you get the money? — yes, no bother (*inf*); **das sagst du so ~ weiteres, aber ...** that's easily said *or* it's easy enough to say that but ...; **dem Kerl kann man nicht ~ weiteres glauben** you can't just believe anything *or* whatever that guy says; **das kann man nicht ~ weiteres voraussetzen** you can't just assume that automatically; **diesem Vorschlag kann ich nicht ~ weiteres zustimmen** I can't accept the suggestion without some qualification; **er lief so ~ weiteres hinaus** he simply *or* just ran out; **du kannst doch nicht so ~ weiteres aus der Schule weglaufen** you can't just run away from school like that.
2 *conj* **~ zu zögern** without hesitating; **~ daß ich ihn darum gebeten hätte, kam er mich besuchen** he came to see me without my *or* me inviting him; **wer redet, ~ gefragt zu sein ...** anybody who talks without being asked ...

ohne-: **~dem** (*old*), **~dies** *adv siehe* **~hin;** **~einander** *adv* without one another, without each other; **~gleichen** *adj inv* unparalleled; **ein Erfolg ~gleichen** an unparalleled success; **diese Frechheit ist ~gleichen!** I've never known such a cheek *or* nerve!; **seine Frechheit ist ~gleichen** I've never known anybody have such a nerve; **er singt ~gleichen** as a singer he is without compare *or* he's in a class by himself; **~hin** *adv* anyway; **wir sind ~hin zu viel Leute** there are too many of us already *or* as it is; **es ist ~hin schon spät** it's already late, it's late enough already, it's late enough as it is; **das hat ~hin keinen Zweck** there is no point in (doing) that anyway.

Ohnmacht *f* **-, -en (a)** (*Med*) faint, swoon (*old*). **in ~ fallen** to faint, to swoon (*old*); **aus der ~ erwachen** to come round *or* to, to recover consciousness. **(b)** (*geh: Machtlosigkeit*) powerlessness, helplessness, impotence.

ohnmächtig *adj* **(a)** (*bewußtlos*) unconscious. **~ werden** to faint, to pass out; **Hilfe, sie ist ~!** help, she's fainted!; **~ sank sie in seine Arme** she fainted *or* collapsed unconscious into his arms; **die O~en wurden auf Tragen hinausgebracht** those who had fainted *or* had lost consciousness *or* passed out were brought out on stretchers.
(b) (*geh: machtlos*) powerless, impotent, helpless. **~e Wut, ~er Zorn** impotent *or* helpless rage; **einer Sache** (*dat*) **~ gegenüberstehen** to stand *or* be helpless in the face of sth; **~ zusehen** to look on helplessly; **der Kaiser war nur noch eine ~e Figur** the Emperor was nothing but a powerless *or* an impotent figure.

Ohnmachts|anfall *m* (*lit, fig*) fainting fit. **als ich das hörte, habe ich fast einen ~ bekommen** (*inf*) when I heard that I nearly fainted *or* nearly passed out.

oho *interj* oho, hello; *siehe* **klein.**

Ohr *nt* **-(e)s, -en** ear. **seine ~en sind nicht mehr so gut** his hearing isn't too good any more; **auf einem ~(e) taub sein** to be deaf in one ear; **auf dem ~ bin ich taub** (*fig*) nothing doing (*inf*), I won't hear of it; **bei jdm ein aufmerksames/geneigtes/offenes ~ finden** to find sb a ready/willing/sympathetic listener; **jdm ein geneigtes ~ leihen** *or* **schenken** to lend sb one's ear *or* a willing ear; **lange ~en machen** (*inf*) to prick up one's ears; **ein musikalisches ~ haben** to have a musical ear *or* an ear for music; **ein scharfes** *or* **feines ~ haben** to have a good ear; **die ~en hängenlassen** (*inf*) to look down in the mouth (*inf*) *or* downhearted *or* down in the dumps (*inf*); **die ~en anlegen** to put its ears back; **mach** *or* **sperr die ~en auf!** (*inf*) wash *or* clean out your ears (*inf*); **mir klingen die ~en** my ears are burning; **jdm die ~en volljammern** (*inf*) to keep (going) on *or* moaning at sb; **die Wände haben ~en** walls have ears; **ganz ~ sein** (*hum*) to be all ears; **sich aufs ~ legen** *or* **hauen** (*inf*) to turn in (*inf*), to hit the hay (*inf*), to kip down (*inf*); **sich** (*dat*) **die Mütze schief aufs ~ setzen** to wear one's cap at a jaunty angle *or* tipped over one ear; **sitzt er auf seinen ~en?** (*inf*) is he deaf or something?; **jdn bei den ~en nehmen, jdm die ~en langziehen** (*inf*) to tweak sb's ear(s); **für deutsche/englische ~en klingt das komisch** that sounds odd to German/English ears; **diese Nachricht war nicht für fremde ~en bestimmt** this piece of news was not meant for other ears; **jdm eins hinter die ~en geben** (*inf*) to give sb a clip round the ear; **jdm etw um die ~en hauen** (*inf*) or **schlagen** (*inf*) to hit sb over the head with sth; **schreib es dir hinter die ~en** (*inf*) will you (finally) get that into your (thick) head (*inf*), has that sunk in? (*inf*); **noch naß** or **feucht** or **nicht trocken hinter den ~en sein** to be still wet behind the ears; **jdm etw ins ~ sagen** to whisper sth in sb's ear; **die Melodie geht (leicht) ins ~** the tune is very catchy; **du hast wohl Dreck/Watte in den ~en!** (*inf*) are you deaf or something?, is there something wrong with your ears?; **ich habe seine Worte noch deutlich im ~** I can still hear his words clearly, his words are still ringing in my ears; **jdm in den ~en liegen** to badger sb, to keep on at sb (*inf*); **mit halbem ~(e) hin-** or **zuhören** to half listen or listen with half an ear; **jdn übers ~ hauen** to take sb for a ride (*inf*), to pull a fast one on sb (*inf*); **bis über die** or **beide ~en verliebt sein** to be head over heels in love; **viel um die ~en haben** (*inf*) to have a lot on (one's plate) (*inf*), to be rushed off one's feet (*inf*); **es ist mir zu ~en gekommen** it has come to my ears (*form*); **zum einen ~ hinein und zum anderen wieder hinaus gehen** (*inf*) to go in one ear and out the other (*inf*).

Öhr *nt* -(e)s, -e eye.

Ohren-: **~arzt** *m* ear specialist; *siehe* **Hals-Nasen-Ohren-**; **~beichte** *f* (auricular) confession; **o~betäubend** *adj* (*fig*) earsplitting, deafening; **~bläser** *m* (*old inf*) schemer, plotter; **~klappe** *f* earflap; **~kriecher** *m siehe* **Ohrwurm**; **~sausen** *nt* (*Med*) buzzing in one's ears; **~schmalz** *nt* earwax; **~schmaus** *m* **das Konzert war ein richtiger ~schmaus** the concert was a real delight to hear or a feast or treat for the ears; **moderne Musik ist oft kein ~schmaus** modern music is often far from easy to the ear; **~schmerzen** *pl* earache; **~schützer** *pl* earmuffs *pl*; **~sessel** *m* wing chair; **~zeuge** *m* earwitness.

Ohrfeige *f* -, -n slap (on or round the face); (*als Strafe*) box on or clip round the ears. **jdm eine ~ geben** or **verabreichen** to slap sb's face; **eine ~ bekommen** to get a slap round the face; **wenn du nicht gleich ruhig bist, bekommst du eine ~** if you don't shut up I'll box your ears.

ohrfeigen *vt* **jdn ~** to slap or hit sb, to box sb's ears; **ich könnte mich selbst ~, daß ich das gemacht habe** I could hit or kick myself for doing it.

Ohrfeigengesicht *nt* (*inf*) fish face (*inf*). **er hat so ein richtiges ~** he's got the sort of face you'd like to put your fist into.

Ohr-: **~gehänge** *nt* (*form*) drop earrings; (*hum*) dangly earrings; **~läppchen** *nt* (ear)lobe; **~muschel** *f* (outer) ear, auricle (*form*); **~ring** *m* earring; **~wurm** *m* earwig; **der Schlager ist ein richtiger ~wurm** (*inf*) that's a really catchy record (*inf*).

oje, ojemine, ojerum (*old*) *interj* oh dear.

okay [o'keː] *interj* okay, OK.

Okay [o'keː] *nt* -s, -s okay, OK.

okkult *adj* occult. **das O~e** the occult.

Okkultismus *m* occultism.

Okkupant *m* occupier. **die ~en** the occupying forces or powers.

Okkupation *f* occupation.

okkupieren* *vt* to occupy.

Ökologe *m*, **Ökologin** *f* ecologist.

Ökologie *f* ecology.

ökologisch *adj* ecological, environmental.

Ökonom *m* (a) economist. (b) (*obs*) bailiff.

Ökonomie *f* (a) (*Wirtschaftlichkeit*) economy. **die ~ des Unternehmens könnte gesteigert werden** the concern could be made to run more economically; **durch kluge ~ hat er das Unternehmen wieder auf die Beine gestellt** by clever economies he put the concern back on its feet again. (b) (*Wirtschaft*) economy. (c) (*Wirtschaftswissenschaft*) economics *sing*. **politische ~ studieren** to study political economy.

ökonomisch *adj* (a) economic. (b) (*sparsam*) economic(al).

Oktaeder [ɔkta'eːdɐ] *nt* -s, - octohedron.

Oktanzahl *f* octane number or rating. **Benzin mit einer hohen ~** high octane petrol.

Oktav *nt* -s, -e octavo.

Oktavband *m* octavo volume.

Oktave [ɔk'taːvə] *f* -, -n octave.

Oktett *nt* -s, -e octet.

Oktober *m* -s, - October; *siehe* **März**.

Oktoberfest *nt* Munich beer festival.

Oktoberrevolution *f* October Revolution.

oktroyieren* [ɔktroa'jiːrən] *vt* (*geh*) to force, to impose (*jdm etw* sth on sb).

Okular *nt* -s, -e eyepiece, ocular.

okulieren* *vt* **Obstbäume, Rosen** to graft, to bud.

Okumene *f* -, *no pl* ecumenical movement.

ökumenisch *adj* ecumenical. **~es Konzil** Ecumenical Council.

Okzident *m* -s, *no pl* (*liter*) occident.

Öl *nt* -(e)s, -e oil. **auf ~ stoßen** to strike oil; **~ fördern** to extract oil; **ätherische ~e** (*Chem*) essential oils; **in ~ malen** to paint in oils; **~ auf die Wogen gießen** (*prov*) to pour oil on troubled waters; **~ ins Feuer gießen** (*prov*) to add fuel to the fire (*prov*).

Öl-: **~baum** *m* olive tree; **~berg** *m* (a) Mount of Olives; (b) (*Art*) sculpture or painting showing Christ with 12 sleeping Apostles on the Mount of Olives; **~bild** *nt* oil painting, oil; **~bohrung** *f* oil drilling, drilling for oil; **~druck** *m* (a) (*Bild*) oleograph; (b) (*Tech*) oil pressure; **~druckbremse** *f* hydraulic brake.

Oldtimer ['oʊldtaɪmə] *m* -s, - (a) (*Auto*) veteran car; (*Rail*) historic train; (*Aviat*) veteran plane, old bus or crate (*pej inf*). (b) (*Sport*) veteran, old timer. (c) (*Pferd*) old or retired racehorse.

Ole|ander *m* -s, - oleander.

ölen *vt* to oil. **wie geölt** (*inf*) like clockwork (*inf*); **wie ein geölter Blitz** (*inf*) like (a streak of) greased lightning (*inf*).

Öl-: **~farbe** *f* oil-based paint; (*Art*) oil (paint or colour); **mit ~farben malen** to paint in oils or oil colours; **~feld** *nt* oil field; **~film** *m* film of oil; **~gemälde** *nt* oil painting; **~gesellschaft** *f* oil company; **~götze** *m* (*inf*) wie **ein ~götze** like a stuffed or tailor's dummy (*inf*); **~heizung** *f* oil-fired central heating.

ölig *adj* oily; (*fig auch*) greasy.

Oligarchie *f* oligarchy.

Olim (*dated inf*): **seit ~s Zeiten** since the year dot (*inf*); **zu** or **in ~s Zeiten** in the year dot (*inf*).

oliv *adj pred* olive(-green). **ein Kleid in O~** an olive-green dress.

Olive [o'liːvə] *f* -, -n olive.

Oliven-: **~baum** *m* olive tree; **o~farben, o~farbig** *adj attr* olive green; **~hain** *m* olive grove; **~öl** *nt* olive oil.

olivgrün *adj* olive-green.

Öl-: **~kanne** *f*, **~kännchen** *nt* oil can; **~kuchen** *m* oil cake.

oll *adj* (*N Ger*) old. **der ~e Hans** old Hans; **das sind ~e Kamellen** (*inf*) that's nothing new, that's old hat (*inf*); **je ~er, je doller** (*prov inf*) there's no fox like an old fox (*prov inf*).

Olle(r) *mf decl as adj* (*N Ger*) **der ~** the old man; **mein ~r** (*inf*) my or the old man (*inf*); **meine ~** (*inf*) my old woman (*inf*), the old lady (*inf*).

Öl-: **~malerei** *f* oil painting; **~meßstab** *m* (*Aut*) dip stick; **~mühle** *f* oil mill; **~ofen** *m* oil stove or heater; **~papier** *nt* oil paper; **~pest** *f* oil pollution; **~plattform** *f* oil-rig; **ö~reich** *adj* oil-rich; **~sardine** *f* sardine; **6 Leute im Wagen, da sitzt ihr ja wie die ~sardinen** (*inf*) with 6 people in the car, you must be crammed in like sardines (*inf*); **~schalter** *m* (*Elec*) oil switch; **~scheich** *m* (*pej*) oil sheik; **~schinken** *m* (*pej*) daub (*pej*); **~sockel** *m* dado; **~stand** *m* oil level; **~standsanzeiger** *m* oil pressure gauge; **~teppich** *m* oil slick.

Ölung *f* oiling. **die Letzte ~** (*Eccl*) extreme unction, the last rites.

Öl-: **~vorkommen** *nt* oil deposit; **~wanne** *f* (*Aut*) sump (*Brit*), oil pan (*US*); **~wechsel** *m* oil change; **ich muß mit dem Wagen zum ~wechsel** I must take my car in for an oil change; **den ~wechsel machen** to change the oil, to do an oil change.

Olymp *m* -s (a) (*Berg*) Mount Olympus. **die Götter des ~** the gods of or on Mount Olympus. (b) (*Theat*) **der ~** the gods.

Olympia *nt* -(s), *no pl* (*liter*) *siehe* **Olympiade**.

Olympiade *f* (a) (*Olympische Spiele*) Olympic Games *pl*, Olympics *pl*. (b) (*liter: Zeitraum*) Olympiad.

Olympia-: **~medaille** *f* Olympic medal; **~sieger** *m* Olympic champion or gold-medallist; **~stadion** *nt* Olympic stadium.

Olympier [o'lʏmpiɐ] *m* -s, - (*liter*) Olympian (*liter*). **Goethe, der ~** Goethe, that Olympian figure.

Olympionike *m* -n, -n (*liter*) Olympic athlete.

olympisch *adj* (a) (*den Olymp betreffend*) Olympian (*auch fig*). **die ~en Götter, die O~en** (*liter*) the gods of or on Mount Olympus, the Olympian deities (*liter*). (b) (*die Olympiade betreffend*) Olympic. **die O~en Spiele** the Olympic Games.

Öl-: **~zeug** *nt* oilskins *pl*; **~zweig** *m* (*lit, fig*) olive-branch.

Oma *f* -, -s (*inf*) granny (*inf*), grandma (*inf*). **die alte ~ da drüben** the old dear (*inf*) or old granny (*inf*) over there.

Ombudsmann *m*, *pl* **-männer** ombudsman.

Omelett [ɔm(ə)'lɛt] *nt* -(e)s, -e or -s, **Omelette** *f* -, -n omelette.

Omen *nt* -s, - or **Omina** omen.

ominös *adj* (*geh*) ominous, sinister.

Omnibus *m* bus; (*im Überlandverkehr*) bus, coach (*Brit*).

Omnibus-: **~linie** *f* bus route; **~verkehr** *m* (*Stadtverkehr*) bus service; (*Überlandverkehr*) bus or coach (*Brit*) service.

omnipotent *adj* (*liter*) omnipotent.

Omnipotenz *f*, *no pl* (*liter*) omnipotence.

Onanie *f* masturbation, onanism.

onanieren* *vi* to masturbate.

Onanist *m* masturbator.

Ondit [õ'diː] *nt* -, -s (*geh*) **einem ~ zufolge** as the rumour has it, as is being noised abroad (*liter*).

ondulieren* *vt* to crimp.

Onkel *m* -s, - (a) uncle. (b) (*Kindersprache: erwachsener Mann*) uncle. **sag dem ~ guten Tag!** say hallo to the nice man!; **sieh mal den komischen ~ da!** look at the funny (old) man or guy (*inf*) over there!; **der ~ Doktor** the nice doctor. (c) (*inf*) **der große** or **dicke ~** your/his *etc* big toe; **über den ~ gehen** to walk pigeon-toed.

Onkel-: **~ehe** *f cohabitation of widow with a man so that she keeps pension rights etc*; **o~haft** *adj* avuncular.

ONO *abbr of* **Ostnordost** ENE.

Onomasiologie *f* onomasiology.

onomatopoetisch [onomatopo'eːtɪʃ] *adj* (*form*) onomatopoetic.

ontisch *adj* ontic.

Ontogenese *f* -, *no pl* ontogenesis, ontogeny.

ontogenetisch *adj* ontogenetic, ontogenic.

Ontologie *f* ontology.

ontologisch *adj* ontological. **der ~e Gottesbeweis** the ontological proof or argument.

Onyx *m* -(es), -e onyx.

OP [oː'peː] *m* -s, -s *abbr of* **Operationssaal**.

o.P. *abbr of* **ordentlicher Professor**.

Opa *m* -s, -s (*inf*) grandpa (*inf*), grandad (*inf*); (*fig*) old grandpa or grandad. **na ~, nun mach mal schneller!** come on grandpa, hurry up!

opak *adj* opaque.

Opal *m* -s, -e opal.

opalisieren* *vi* to opalesce.

Op-art *f* -, *no pl* op art.

Opec-Länder [ˈoːpɛk-] pl Opec countries pl.

Oper f -, -n opera; (Ensemble) Opera; (Opernhaus) Opera, Opera House. **in die ~ gehen** to go to the opera; **an die** or **zur ~ gehen** to take up opera-singing, to become an opera singer.

Operateur [-ˈtøːɐ] m (a) (Med) surgeon. (b) (old: im Kino) projectionist.

Operation f operation.

Operations-: ~**saal** m operating theatre (Brit) or room (US); ~**schwester** f theatre sister (Brit), operating room nurse (US).

operativ adj (a) (Med) operative, surgical. **das ist nur durch einen ~en Eingriff zu beseitigen** that can only be removed by (means of) surgery; **eine Geschwulst ~ entfernen** to remove a growth surgically or by surgery. (b) (Mil) Pläne, Planung, Stab operational, strategic. ~ **denken** to think strategically.

Operator m, **Operatorin** f (computer) operator.

Operette f operetta.

Operettenkaiser m (hum) stage emperor.

operieren* 1 vt Patienten, Krebs, Magen to operate on. **jdn am Magen ~** to operate or perform an operation on sb's stomach; **der Blinddarm muß sofort operiert werden** that appendix must be operated on at once or needs immediate surgery.
2 vi (a) (Med) to operate. **die Ärzte haben drei Stunden an ihm operiert** the doctors operated on him for three hours; **sich ~ lassen** to have an operation. (b) (Mil) to operate. (c) (fig: arbeiten) to operate. **Arbeiter, die mit großen Maschinen ~** workers who operate large machines; **wir müssen in den Verhandlungen sehr vorsichtig ~** we must go or tread very carefully in the negotiations.

Opern-: ~**arie** f (operatic) aria; ~**ball** m opera ball; ~**glas** nt opera glasses pl; ~**haus** nt opera house; ~**sänger** m opera singer; ~**text** m libretto.

Opfer nt -s, - (~gabe) sacrifice (auch fig). **zum** or **als ~ as a sacrifice; die Gottheit verlangte zehn Jungfrauen zum** or **als ~** the god demanded the sacrifice of ten virgins; **sie brachten ein ~ aus Wein und Wasser dar** they made an offering of water and wine; **jdm etw zum ~ bringen** or **als ~ darbringen** to offer sth as a sacrifice to sb, to make a sacrificial offering of sth to sb; **für ihre Kinder scheut sie keine ~** she sacrifices everything for her children, for her children she considers no sacrifice too great; **wir müssen alle ~ bringen** we must all make sacrifices; **ein ~ für jdn bringen** to make a sacrifice for sb. (b) (geschädigte Person) victim. **jdm/einer Sache zum ~ fallen** to be (the) victim of sb/sth; **sie fiel seinem Charme zum ~** she fell victim to his charm; **ein ~ einer Sache** (gen) **werden** to be a victim of sth, to fall victim to sth; **täglich werden 28 Kinder ~ des Straßenverkehrs** every day 28 children are the victims of road accidents; **das Erdbeben forderte große ~ an Leben und Gut** the earthquake took a heavy toll of life and property; **das Erdbeben forderte viele ~** the earthquake took a heavy toll or claimed many victims.

Opfer-: o~**bereit** adj ready or willing to make sacrifices; ~**bereitschaft** f readiness or willingness to make sacrifices; o~**freudig** adj willing to make sacrifices; ~**gabe** f (liter) (sacrificial) offering; (Eccl) offering; ~**gang** m (liter) sacrifice of one's honour/life; **Veronika begleitete Christus auf seinem ~gang** Veronica accompanied Christ on his way to the cross; **sie erklärte sich zu dem ~gang bereit, um ihren Geliebten zu retten** she said she was ready to sacrifice her honour/life to save her beloved; ~**lamm** nt sacrificial lamb; **der Bräutigam schritt wie ein ~lamm zum Altar** the groom walked to the altar like a lamb to the slaughter; ~**mut** m self-sacrifice; **mit bewundernswürdigem ~mut stürzte er sich in das brennende Haus** with an admirable disregard for his own safety he plunged into the burning house.

opfern 1 vt (a) (als Opfer darbringen) to sacrifice, to immolate (form); Tiere auch to make a sacrifice of; Feldfrüchte etc to offer (up). **sein Leben ~** to give up or sacrifice one's life. (b) (fig: aufgeben) to give up, to sacrifice.
2 vi to make a sacrifice, to sacrifice. **einem Gotte ~** (liter) to pay homage to (liter) or worship a god.
3 vr (a) (sein Leben hingeben) to sacrifice oneself or one's life. (b) (inf: sich bereit erklären) to be a martyr (inf). **wer opfert sich, die Reste aufzuessen?** who's going to be a martyr and eat up the remains?, who's going to volunteer to eat up the remains?

Opfer-: ~**pfennig** m small contribution; ~**stätte** f sacrificial altar; ~**stock** m offertory box; ~**tier** nt sacrificial animal; ~**tod** m self-sacrifice, death; **er rettete durch seinen ~tod den anderen das Leben** by sacrificing his own life, he saved the lives of the others; **der ~tod Christi am Kreuz** Christ's sacrifice or death on the cross; **Christus starb den ~tod (für unsere Sünden)** Christ gave up his life (for our sins).

Opferung f (das Opfern) sacrifice; (Eccl) offertory.

Opfer-: ~**wille** m spirit of sacrifice; o~**willig** adj self-sacrificing, willing to make sacrifices.

Opiat nt opiate.

Opium nt -s, no pl opium. **Religion ist ~ des Volkes** religion is the opium of the masses.

Opium-: ~**höhle** f opium den; ~**raucher** m opium smoker.

Opponent(in f) m opponent.

opponieren* vi to oppose (gegen jdn/etw sb/sth), to offer opposition (gegen to). **ihr müßt auch immer ~** do you always have to oppose or be against everything?

opportun adj (geh) opportune.

Opportunismus m opportunism.

Opportunist(in f) m opportunist.

opportunistisch adj opportunistic, opportunist. **~ handeln** to

act in an opportunist fashion; **da hat er sehr ~ gehandelt** that was very opportunist(ic) of him.

Opportunität f (geh) opportuneness, appropriateness.

Opposition f opposition. **etw aus (lauter) ~ tun** to do sth out of or from (sheer) contrariness; **diese Gruppe macht ständig ~ (gegen den Klassenlehrer)** (inf) this group is always making trouble (for the teacher).

oppositionell adj Gruppen, Kräfte opposition.

Optativ m optative.

optieren* vi (Pol form) ~ **für** to opt for.

Optik f (a) (Phys) optics. (b) (Linsensystem) lens system. **du hast wohl einen Knick in der ~!** (sl) can't you see straight? (inf), are you blind?; **das ist eine Frage der ~** (fig) it depends on your point of view. (c) (fig) **das ist nur hier wegen der ~** it's just here because it looks good or for visual or optical effect; **die Partei muß sehen, daß sie die ~ ihrer Politik ein bißchen verbessert** the party must try to present their policies in a better light; **etw in die rechte ~ bringen** to put sth into the right perspective.

Optiker(in f) m -s, - optician.

optimal adj optimal, optimum attr.

optimieren* vt to optimize.

Optimismus m optimism.

Optimist m optimist.

optimistisch adj optimistic.

Optimum nt -s, Optima optimum.

Option [ɔpˈtsioːn] f (a) (Wahl) option (für in favour of). (b) (Anrecht) option (auf + acc on).

optisch adj visual; Gesetze, Instrumente optical. ~**er Eindruck** visual or optical effect; ~**e Täuschung** optical illusion.

opulent adj Mahl lavish, sumptuous.

Opus nt -, (rare) pl **Opera** work; (Mus, hum) opus; (Gesamtwerk) (complete) works pl, opus.

Orakel nt -s, - oracle. **das ~ befragen** to consult the oracle; **er spricht in ~n** (fig) he speaks like an oracle, he has an oracular way of putting things.

orakelhaft adj (liter) oracular, delphic (liter).

orakeln* vi (a) (rätseln) **wir haben lange orakelt, was der Satz bedeuten sollte** we spent a long time trying to figure out what the sentence meant or trying to decipher the sentence. (b) (über die Zukunft) to prognosticate (hum).

oral adj oral.

Oral|erotik f oral eroticism.

Orange¹ [oˈrãːʒə] f -, -n (Frucht) orange.

Orange² [oˈrãːʒə] nt -, - or (inf) -s orange.

orange [oˈrãːʒə] adj inv orange. **ein ~** or **~ner** (inf) **Rock** an orange skirt.

Orangeade [orãˈʒaːdə] f orangeade.

Orangeat [orãˈʒaːt] nt candied (orange) peel.

orange(n)- [oˈrãːʒə(n)-]: ~**farben**, ~**farbig** adj orange(-coloured).

Orangenmarmelade [oˈrãːʒən-] f orange marmalade.

Orangerie [orãʒəˈriː] f orangery.

Orang-Utan m -s, -s orang-utan, orang-outang.

Oranien [-iən] nt -s Orange. **Wilhelm von ~** William of Orange.

Oranjefreistaat [oˈranjə-] m Orange Free State.

Oratorium nt (a) (Mus) oratorio. (b) (Betraum) oratory.

Orchester [ɔrˈkɛstɐ, (old) ɔrˈçɛstɐ] nt -s, - (a) orchestra. (b) (~raum) orchestra (pit).

orchestral [ɔrkɛsˈtraːl, (old) ɔrçɛsˈtraːl] adj orchestral.

orchestrieren* [ɔrkɛsˈtriːrən, (old) ɔrçɛsˈtriːrən] vt to orchestrate.

Orchestrierung f orchestration.

Orchidee f -, -n [-ˈdeːən] orchid.

Orden m -s, - (a) (Gemeinschaft) (holy) order. **in einen ~ (ein)-treten, einem ~ beitreten** to become a monk/nun. (b) (Ehrenzeichen) decoration; (Mil auch) medal. ~ **tragen** to wear one's decorations; **jdm einen ~ (für etw) verleihen** to decorate sb (for sth); **einen ~ bekommen** to be decorated, to receive a decoration.

ordengeschmückt adj decorated, covered in decorations or (Mil auch) medals.

Ordens-: ~**band** nt ribbon; (Mil) medal ribbon; ~**bruder** m (a) (Eccl) monk; **meine ~brüder** my brother monks; (b) (von Ritterorden etc) brother member (of an order); ~**burg** f medieval castle built by a religious order; ~**frau** f (old) nun; ~**geistliche(r)** m priest in a religious order; ~**kleid** nt (liter) habit; ~**meister** m master of an order; ~**regel** f rule (of the order); ~**schnalle** f medal clasp; ~**schwester** f nursing sister or nun; ~**tracht** f habit.

ordentlich adj (a) Mensch, Zimmer tidy, neat, orderly. **in ihrem Haushalt geht es sehr ~ zu** she runs a very orderly household; **kannst du die Wörter nicht ~ untereinander schreiben?** can't you write the words neatly or tidily under one another?; **bei ihr sieht es immer ~ aus** her house always looks neat and tidy; **stell den Stuhl wieder ~ hin** put the chair back neatly; ~ **arbeiten** to be a thorough and precise worker. (b) (ordnungsgemäß) ~**es Gericht** court of law, law court; ~**es Mitglied** full member; ~**er Professor** (full) professor. (c) (anständig) respectable. **sich ~ benehmen** to behave properly. (d) (inf: tüchtig) ~ **essen/trinken** to eat/drink (really) well or heartily; **ihr habt sicher Hunger, greift ~ zu** you're sure to be hungry, tuck in; **ein ~es Frühstück** a proper or good breakfast; **wir haben ~ gearbeitet** we really got down to it; **eine ~e Tracht Prügel** a real beating, a proper hiding; **jetzt bin ich ~ erschrocken** that's given me a real or proper (inf) shock. (e) (inf: richtig) real, proper. (f) (annehmbar, ganz gut) Preis, Leistung reasonable.

Order f -, -s or -n (a) (Comm: Auftrag) order. **einen Scheck/**

Wechsel an (die) ~ **der Firma M ausstellen** to make a cheque/bill payable or make out a cheque/bill to the firm of M; **an** ~ **lautend** made out to order.
 (b) (dated: Anweisung) jdm ~ **erteilen** to order or direct or instruct sb; **sich an eine** ~ **halten** to keep to one's orders; **ich habe meine** ~, **und daran halte ich mich** orders are orders, I have my orders and I'm sticking to them.
Ordinalia pl ordinals pl.
Ordinalzahl f ordinal number.
ordinär adj **(a)** (gemein, unfein) vulgar, common. **(b)** (alltäglich) ordinary. **was, Sie wollen so viel für eine ganz** ~**e Kiste?** what, you're wanting that much for a perfectly ordinary box or for that old box? **(c)** (old Comm: regulär) **Preis** regular, normal.
Ordinariat nt **(a)** (Univ) chair. **(b) Bischöfliches** ~ bishop's palace.
Ordinarius m -, **Ordinarien** [-iən] **(a)** (Univ) professor (für of). **(b)** (Eccl) bishop, ordinary. **(c)** (old Sch) form or class teacher.
Ordinate f -, -n ordinate.
Ordinaten|achse f axis of ordinate.
Ordination f **(a)** (Eccl) ordination, ordaining. **(b)** (old Med) (Verordnung) prescription; (Sprechstunde) surgery.
ordinieren* **1** vt **(a)** (Eccl) to ordain. **sich** ~ **lassen** to be ordained. **(b)** (old Med) to prescribe. **2** vi (old Med) to hold or have surgery (hours).
ordnen 1 vt **(a)** Gedanken, Einfälle, Material to order, to organize; Demonstrationszug, Verkehrswesen to organize; Akten, Finanzen, Hinterlassenschaft, Privatleben to put in order, to straighten out; siehe **geordnet.**
 (b) (sortieren) to order, to arrange.
 2 vr to get into order. **allmählich ordnete sich das Bild** (fig) the picture gradually became clear, things gradually fell into place; **die Menge ordnete sich zu einem Festzug** the crowd formed itself into a procession.
Ordner m -s, - **(a)** steward; (bei Demonstration auch) marshal. **(b)** (Akten~) file.
Ordnung f **(a)** (das Ordnen) ordering. **bei der** ~ **der Papiere** when putting the papers in order.
 (b) (geordneter Zustand) order. ~ **halten** to keep things tidy; **du mußt mal ein bißchen** ~ **in deinen Sachen halten** you must keep your affairs a bit more in order, you must order your affairs a bit more; **in dem Aufsatz sehe ich keine** ~ I can see no order or coherence in the essay; ~ **schaffen, für** ~ **sorgen** to sort things out, to put things in order, to tidy things up; **seid ruhig, sonst schaff ich gleich mal** ~ (inf) be quiet or I'll come and sort you out (inf); **Sie müssen mehr für** ~ **in Ihrer Klasse sorgen** you'll have to keep more discipline in your class, you'll have to keep your class in better order; **auf** ~ **halten** or **sehen** to be tidy; **etw in** ~ **halten** to keep sth in order; Garten, Haus etc auch to keep sth tidy; **etw in** ~ **bringen** (reparieren) to fix sth; (herrichten) to put sth in order; (bereinigen) to clear sth up, to sort sth out; **ich finde es (ganz) in** ~, **daß** ... I think or find it quite right that ...; **ich finde es nicht in** ~, **daß** ... I don't think it's right that ...; **(das ist) in** ~! (inf) (that's) OK (inf) or all right!; **geht in** ~ (inf) sure (inf), that's all right or fine or OK (inf); **Ihre Bestellung geht in** ~ we'll see to your order, we'll get your order through; **der ist in** ~ (inf) he's OK (inf) or all right (inf); **da ist etwas nicht in** ~ there's something wrong there; **mit ihm/der Maschine ist etwas nicht in** ~ there's something wrong or the matter with him/the machine; **die Maschine ist (wieder) in** ~ the machine's fixed or in order or all right (again); **es ist alles in bester** or **schönster** ~ everything's fine, things couldn't be better; **der Fahrstuhl ist nicht in** ~ the lift is not working properly; **jdn zur** ~ **rufen** to call sb to order; **ein Kind zur** ~ **anhalten** or **erziehen** to teach a child tidy habits; ~ **muß sein!** we must have order!; ~ **ist das halbe Leben** (Prov) tidiness or a tidy mind is half the battle; **hier** or **bei uns herrscht** ~ we like to have a little order around here; **hier herrscht ja eine schöne** ~ (iro) this is a nice mess; siehe **Ruhe.**
 (c) (Gesetzmäßigkeit) routine. **alles muß (bei ihm) seine** ~ **haben** (räumlich) he has to have everything in its right or proper place; (zeitlich) he does everything according to a fixed schedule; **das Kind braucht seine** ~ the child needs a routine.
 (d) (Vorschrift) rules pl. **sich an eine** ~ **halten** to stick or keep to the rules; **ich frage nur der** ~ **halber** it's only a routine or formal question, I'm only asking as a matter of form; **der** ~ **gemäß** according to the rules or the rule book.
 (e) (Rang, Biol) order. **Straße erster** ~ first-class road; **das war ein Fauxpas erster** ~ (inf) that was a faux pas of the first order or first water (inf); **ein Stern fünfter** ~ a star of the fifth magnitude.
Ordnungs-: ~**amt** nt = town clerk's office; ~**fanatiker** m fanatic for order; **nicht alle Deutschen sind** ~**fanatiker** not all Germans have a mania or passion for order; **o~gemäß** adj according to or in accordance with the rules, proper; **ich werde mich selber um die o~gemäße Abfertigung ihrer Bestellung kümmern** I will see to it myself that your order is properly or correctly dealt with; **der Prozeß ist o~gemäß abgelaufen** the trial took its proper course; **o~halber** adv as a matter of form, for the sake of form; ~**hüter** m (hum) custodian of the law (hum); ~**liebe** f love of order; **o~liebend** adj tidy, tidy-minded; ~**ruf** m call to order; **in der Debatte mußte der Präsident mehrere** ~**rufe erteilen** during the debate the chairman had to call the meeting to order several times; **einen** ~**ruf bekommen** to be called to order; ~**sinn** m idea or conception of tidiness or order; ~**strafe** f fine; **jdn mit einer** ~**strafe belegen** to fine sb; **o~widrig** adj irregular; Parken, Verhalten (im Straßenverkehr) illegal; **o~widrig handeln** to go against or infringe rules or regulations; ~**widrigkeit** f infringement (of law or rule); ~**zahl** f **(a)** ordinal number; **(b)** (Phys) atomic number.

Ordonnanz f orderly.
Ordonnanz|offizier m aide-de-camp, ADC.
Organ nt -s, -e **(a)** (Med, Biol) organ. **kein** ~ **für etw haben** (inf) not to have any feel for sth.
 (b) (inf: Stimme) voice.
 (c) (fig: Zeitschrift) organ, mouthpiece.
 (d) (Behörde) organ, instrument; (Beauftragter) agent; (der Polizei) branch, division. **die ausführenden** ~**e** the executors; **wir sind nur ausführendes** ~ we are only following orders; **beratendes** ~ advisory body.
Organbank f transplant bank.
Organisation f organization.
Organisationstalent nt talent or flair for organization. **er ist ein** ~ he has a talent or flair for organization.
Organisator m organizer.
organisatorisch adj organizational. **eine** ~**e Höchstleistung** a masterpiece of organization; **er ist ein** ~**es Talent** he has a gift for organizing or organization; **das hat** ~ **gar nicht geklappt** organizationally, it was a failure.
organisch adj Chemie, Verbindung, Salze organic; Erkrankung, Leiden physical. **ein** ~**es Ganzes** an organic whole; **sich** ~ **einfügen** to merge, to blend (in +acc with, into).
organisieren* **1** vt **(a)** to organize. **er kann ausgezeichnet** ~ he's excellent at organizing. **(b)** (sl: stehlen) (Beauftragter) to lift (sl), to get hold of. **2** vr to organize.
organisiert adj organized.
Organismus m organism.
Organist(in f) m organist.
Organ-: ~**spender** m donor (of an organ); ~**verpflanzung** f transplant(ation) (of organs).
Organza m -s, no pl organza.
Orgasmus m orgasm.
orgastisch adj orgasmic.
Orgel f -, -n organ.
orgeln vi **(a)** (inf: Orgel spielen) to play the organ. **(b)** (Hunt: Hirsch) to bell; (fig) to thunder.
Orgelpfeife f organ pipe. **die Kinder standen da wie die** ~**n** (hum) the children were standing in order of height or were standing like a row of Russian dolls.
orgiastisch adj orgiastic.
Orgie [-iə] f orgy. ~**n feiern** (lit) to have orgies/an orgy; (fig) to go wild; (Phantasie etc) to run riot.
Orient ['o:rient, o'rient] m -s, no pl **(a)** (liter) Orient. **das Denken des** ~**s** Eastern thought; **der Vordere** ~ the Near East; **vom** ~ **zum Okzident** from east to west. **(b)** (inf) = Middle East.
Orientale [orien'ta:lə] m -n, -n, **Orientalin** f a person from the Middle East.
orientalisch [orien'ta:lɪʃ] adj Middle Eastern.
Orientalist [orienta'lɪst] m = specialist in Middle Eastern and oriental studies.
Orientalistik [orienta'lɪstɪk] f = Middle Eastern studies. ~**studieren** ≃ to do Middle Eastern studies.
orientieren* [orien'ti:rən] **1** vti **(a)** (unterrichten) to put sb in the picture (über +acc about). **unser Katalog orientiert (Sie) über unsere Sonderangebote** our catalogue gives (you) information on or about our special offers; **darüber ist er gut/falsch/nicht orientiert** he is well/wrongly/not informed on or about that.
 (b) (ausrichten) (lit, fig) to orientate (nach, auf to, towards). **ein positivistisch orientierter Denker** a positivistically orientated thinker; **ein Brechtisch orientierter Dramatiker** a Brecht-orientated dramatist; **links orientiert sein** to tend to the left; **links orientierte Gruppen** left-wing groups.
 (c) (hinweisen) (auf +acc to) to orientate, to orient. **einige Betriebe** ~ **ihre Mitarbeiter darauf, ihren Urlaub im Sommer zu nehmen** some firms encourage their employees to take their holidays in the summer.
 2 vr **(a)** (sich unterrichten) to inform oneself (über +acc about or on).
 (b) (sich zurechtfinden) to orientate oneself (an +dat, nach by), to find or get one's bearings. **in einer fremden Stadt kann ich mich gar nicht** ~ I just can't find my way around in a strange city; **von da an kann ich mich alleine** ~ I can find my own way from there; **ich muß ungefähr wissen, wieviel Gehalt ich bekomme, damit ich mich** ~ **kann** I have to know roughly how much salary I'll earn so that I can work things out.
 (c) (sich einstellen) to orient or orientate (oneself) (an +dat, auf +acc to).
Orientierung [orien'ti:rʊŋ] f **(a)** (Unterrichtung) information. **man müßte doch darüber eine bessere** ~ **erwarten** one would expect more information or to be better informed about it; **zu Ihrer** ~ for your information.
 (b) (das Zurechtfinden) orientation. **hier fällt einem die** ~ **schwer** it's difficult to find or get one's bearings here; **die** ~ **verlieren** to lose one's bearings.
 (c) (das Ausrichten) orientation.
Orientierungs-: ~**punkt** m point of reference; ~**sinn** m sense of direction.
Orig. abbr of Original.
Original nt -s, -e **(a)** original. **(b)** (Mensch) character.
original adj original. ~ **Meißener Porzellan** real or genuine Meissen porcelain; ~ **aus USA** guaranteed from USA.
Original-: ~**ausgabe** f first edition; ~**fassung** f original (version); **in der englischen** ~**fassung** in the original English version; **o~getreu** adj true to the original; **etw o~getreu nachmalen** to paint a very faithful copy of sth; **die Kopie sieht sehr o~getreu aus** the copy looks very like the original.
Originalität f, no pl **(a)** (Echtheit) authenticity, genuineness. **(b)** (Urtümlichkeit) originality.
originär adj Idee original.

originell adj (selbständig) Idee, Argumentation, Interpretation original; (neu) novel; (geistreich) witty. **das hat er sich** (dat) **sehr ~ ausgedacht** that's a very original idea of his; **er ist ein ~er Kopf** he's got an original mind; **das finde ich ~** (von ihm) that's pretty original/witty.

Orkan m -(e)s, -e (a) hurricane. **der Sturm schwoll zum ~ an** the storm increased to hurricane force. **(b)** (fig) storm. **ein ~ des Beifalls brach los** thunderous applause broke out.

Orkan-: o**~artig** adj hurricane(like); **bei unserer letzten Überfahrt hatten wir o~artige Winde** on our last crossing it was really blowing a gale; **~stärke** f hurricane force.

Ornament nt decoration, ornament. **der Fries ist reines ~** the frieze is purely ornamental or decorative; **eine Vase mit figürlichen ~en** a vase decorated with figures.

ornamental adj ornamental.

ornamentieren* vt to embellish, to ornament.

Ornat m -(e)s, -e regalia pl; (Eccl) vestments pl; (Jur) official robes pl. **in vollem ~** (inf) dressed up to the nines (inf).

Ornithologe m, **Ornithologin** f (form) ornithologist.

Orpheus m - Orpheus.

Orphik f Orphism.

orphisch adj Orphic.

Ort¹ m -(e)s, -e (a) (Platz, Stelle) place. **der ~ des Treffens** meeting place, venue; **hier bin ich wohl nicht am rechten ~** I've obviously not come to the right place; **ein ~ der Stille/des Friedens** a place of quiet/of peace; **ein ~ der Einkehr** a place for thinking quietly; **~ der Handlung** (Theat) scene of the action; **an den ~ der Tat** or **des Verbrechens zurückkehren** to return to the scene of the crime; **der Stuhl steht wieder an seinem ~** the chair is back in (its) place again; **hier ist nicht der ~, darüber zu sprechen** this is not the (time or) place to talk about that; **am angegebenen ~** in the place quoted, loc cit abbr; **ohne ~ und Jahr** without indication of place and date of publication; **an ~ und Stelle** on the spot, there and then; **an ~ und Stelle ankommen** to arrive (at one's destination); **das ist höheren ~s entschieden worden** (hum, form) the decision came from higher places or from above; **höheren ~s ist das bemerkt worden** (hum. form) it's been noticed in high places.

(b) (~schaft) place. **in einem kleinen ~ in Cornwall** in a little spot in Cornwall; **jeder größere ~ hat ein Postamt** a place of any size has a post office; **~e über 100.000 Einwohner** places with more than or with over 100,000 inhabitants; **er ist im ganzen ~ bekannt** everyone knows him, the whole village/town etc knows him; **wir sind mit dem halben ~ verwandt** we're related to half the people in the place; **am ~ in the place; das beste Hotel am ~** the best hotel in town; **wir haben keinen Arzt am ~** we have no resident doctor; **am ~ wohnen** to live in the same village/town; **die Waren sind alle am ~ erzeugt** the goods are all produced locally; **sich an einem dritten ~ treffen** to meet in a neutral place or on neutral ground; **mitten im ~** in the centre (of the place/town); **der nächste ~** the next village/town etc; **von ~ zu ~** from place to place.

Ort² m -(e)s, ⁻er (a) position; (Geometry) locus. **(b)** (Min) coal face, (working) face. **vor ~** at the (coal) face; (fig) on the spot.

Örtchen nt das (stille) ~ (inf) the smallest room (inf).

orten vt U-Boot, Flugzeug to locate, to fix the position of, to get a fix on; Heringsschwarm to locate.

orthodox adj (lit, fig) orthodox.

Orthodoxie f orthodoxy.

Orthographie f orthography.

orthographisch adj orthographic(al). **er schreibt nicht immer ~ richtig** his spelling is not always correct.

Orthopäde m -n, -n, **Orthopädin** f orthopaedist, orthopaedic specialist.

orthopädisch adj orthopaedic.

örtlich adj local. **das ist ~ verschieden** it varies from place to place; **der Konflikt war ~ begrenzt** it was limited to a local encounter; **jdn/etw ~ betäuben** to give sb/sth a local anaesthetic; **er war nur ~ betäubt** he was only under or had only had a local anaesthetic.

Örtlichkeit f locality. **sich mit der ~/den ~en vertraut machen** to get to know the place; **er ist mit den ~en gut vertraut** he knows his way about; **die ~en** (euph) the cloakroom (euph).

Orts-: **~angabe** f place of publication; (bei Anschriften) (name of the) town; **ohne ~angabe** no place of publication indicated; o**~ansässig** adj local; **eine schon lange o~ansässige Familie** a long established local family; **sind Sie schon lange o~ansässig?** have you been living here or locally for a long time?; **die ~ansässigen** the local residents; **~bestimmung** f Fehler bei der ~bestimmung navigational error; **zur ~bestimmung braucht man Kompaß und Sextant** for fixing or to fix one's bearings one needs a compass and a sextant; **~bestimmung der heutigen Philosophie** perspectives in modern philosophy.

Ortschaft f -, -en village; town. **geschlossene ~** built-up or restricted area.

Orts-: o**~fremd** adj non-local; **ich bin hier o~fremd** I'm a stranger here; **ein ~fremder** a stranger; **~gespräch** nt (Telec) local call; **~gewaltige(r)** m decl as adj (hum) local bigwig (hum); **~gruppe** f local branch or group; **~kenntnis** f local knowledge; (gute) **~kenntnisse haben** to know one's way around (well); **~klasse** f classification of area according to cost of living for entitlement to salary weighting allowances; **~krankenkasse** f Allgemeine ~krankenkasse compulsory medical insurance scheme for workers, old people etc; o**~kundig** adj nehmen Sie sich einen o~kundigen Führer get a guide who knows his way around; **ich bin nicht sehr o~kundig** I don't know my way around very well; **ein ~kundiger** somebody who knows his way around or who knows the place; **~name** m place name; **~netz** nt (Telec) local (telephone) exchange area; (Elec) local grid; **~netzkennzahl** f (Telec) dialling code;

~schild nt place name sign; **~sinn** m sense of direction; **~tarif** m (bei Briefen) local postal charge; (Telec) charge for local phone-call; o**~üblich** adj local; **das ist hier o~üblich** it is usual or customary here, it is (a) local custom here; **~verkehr** m local traffic; **selbst im ~verkehr hat der Brief noch drei Tage gebraucht** even a local letter took three days; **Gebühren im ~verkehr** (Telec) charges for local (phone) calls; (von Briefen) local postage rates; **handvermittelter ~verkehr** (Telec) local calls connected by the operator; **~zeit** f local time; **~zulage** f, **~zuschlag** m (local) weighting allowance.

Ortung f locating. **bei (der) ~ eines feindlichen U-Boots ...** when locating an or fixing the position of or getting a fix on an enemy submarine ...

Öse f -, -n loop; (an Kleidung) eye; siehe Haken.

Osmane m -n, -n Ottoman.

osmanisch adj Ottoman.

OSO abbr of Ostsüdost.

Ost m -(e)s, no pl (liter) (a) East. **aus ~ und West** from East and West; **von ~ nach West** from East to West; **der Wind kommt aus ~** the wind is coming from the East; **wo ~ und West zusammentreffen** where East and West meet, where East meets West; **10 Mark ~** (inf) 10 East German marks. **(b)** (~wind) East or easterly wind.

Ost- in cpds (bei Ländern, Erdteilen) (als politische Einheit) East; (geographisch auch) Eastern, the East of ...; (bei Städten, Inseln) East; **~afrika** nt East Africa; **~asien** nt Eastern Asia; **~Berlin** nt East Berlin; **~berliner** m East Berliner; **~besuch** m (inf) visit from East Germany; **zu Weihnachten haben wir ~besuch** over Christmas we have visitors from East Germany; **~block** m Eastern bloc; **~blockland** nt, **~blockstaat** m country belonging to the Eastern bloc, Iron Curtain country; o**~deutsch** adj East German; **~deutschland** nt (Pol) East Germany; (Geog) Eastern Germany.

Osten m -s, no pl (a) East. **der Ferne ~** the Far East; **der Nahe ~** the Middle East, the Near East; **der Mittlere ~** area stretching from Iran and Iraq to India, Middle East; **im Nahen and Mittleren ~** in the Middle East; **im ~** in the East; **in den ~** to the East; **von ~** from the East; **gen ~** (liter) eastwards. **(b)** (Pol) der ~ (Ostdeutschland) East Germany; (Ostblock) the East; East Berlin.

ostentativ adj pointed. **ihre Trauer war etwas zu ~** her mourning was somehow too put on or studied; **der Botschafter drehte sich ~ um und verließ den Raum** the ambassador pointedly turned round and left the room.

Oster-: **~ei** nt Easter egg; **~feiertag** m Easter holiday; **am 2. ~feiertag** on Easter Monday; **über die ~feiertage fahren wir weg** we're going away over the Easter weekend; **~fest** nt Easter; **das jüdische ~fest** the Jewish Feast of the Passover; **~feuer** nt bonfire lit on Easter Saturday; **~glocke** f daffodil; **~hase** m Easter bunny; **~insel** f Easter Island; **~lamm** nt paschal lamb.

österlich adj Easter.

Oster-: **~montag** m Easter Monday; **~morgen** m Easter morning.

Ostern nt -, - Easter. **frohe** or **fröhliche ~!** Happy Easter!; **ein verregnetes ~, verregnete ~** a rainy Easter; **an ~** on Easter day; **zu ~** at Easter; (zu or über) **~ fahren wir weg** we're going away at or over Easter; **wenn ~ und Pfingsten auf einen Tag fällt** (hum) if pigs could fly (hum).

Österreich nt -s Austria. **~-Ungarn** (Hist) Austria-Hungary.

Österreicher(in f) m -s, - Austrian. **er ist ~** he's (an) Austrian.

österreichisch adj Austrian. **~-ungarisch** (Hist) Austro-Hungarian; **das Ö~e** (Ling) Austrian.

Oster-: **~sonntag** m Easter Sunday; **~spiel** nt Easter (passion) play; **~woche** f Easter week.

Ost-: **~europa** nt East(ern) Europe; o**~europäisch** adj East European; **~geld** nt (inf) East German money; o**~germanisch** adj (Ling) East Germanic; **~gote** m (Hist) Ostrogoth.

ostinat adj (Mus) **~er Baß** ground bass, bass ostinato.

Ost-: o**~indisch** adj East Indian; **~indische Kompanie** East India Company; **~jude** m East European Jew; **~kirche** f Orthodox or Eastern Church; **~kolonisation** f (Hist) German medieval colonization of Eastern Europe; **~küste** f East coast.

Ostler(in f) m -s, - (inf) East German.

östlich 1 adj Richtung, Winde easterly; Gebiete eastern. **30° ~er Länge** 30° (longitude) east.

2 adv **~ von Hamburg/des Rheins** (to the) east of Hamburg/of the Rhine.

3 prep +gen (to the) east of.

Ost-: **~mark** f (a) (Hist) Austria; (b) (inf) East German Mark; o**~mitteldeutsch** adj (Ling) East Middle German; **~nordost(en)** m east-north-east; **~paket** nt parcel to East Germany/East Berlin; **~politik** f Ostpolitik, West German foreign policy regarding the Eastern block especially East Germany and East Berlin; **~preuße** m East Prussian; **~preußen** nt East Prussia; o**~preußisch** adj East Prussian; **~rom** nt (Hist) Eastern (Roman) Empire, Byzantine Empire.

Ostsee f: die ~ the Baltic (Sea).

Ostsee- in cpds Baltic.

Ost-: **~staaten** pl (in USA) the Eastern or East coast states; **~südost(en)** m east-south-east; o**~wärts** adv eastwards; **~West-Achse** f East-West link; **~-West-Verhandlungen** pl East-West negotiations; **~wind** m east or easterly wind.

oszillieren* vi to oscillate.

Oszillograph m oscillograph.

Otter¹ m -s, - otter.

Otter² f -, -n viper, adder.

Otterngezücht nt (Bibl) brood of vipers.

Ottomane f -, -n ottoman.

Ottomotor *m* internal combustion engine, otto engine.
ottonisch *adj* (*Hist*) Ottonian.
Ouvertüre [uver'ty:rə] *f* -, -n overture.
oval [o'va:l] *adj* oval.
Oval [o'va:l] *nt* -s, -e oval.
Ovation [ova'tsio:n] *f* ovation. **jdm eine ~ or ~en darbringen** to give sb an ovation *or* a standing ovation.
Overall ['ouvərɔ:l] *m* -s, -s overalls *pl*.
ÖVP [øfau'pe:] *f* - *abbr of* Österreichische Volkspartei.
Ovulation [ovula'tsio:n] *f* ovulation.
Ovulationshemmer *m* -s, - ovulation inhibitor.

Oxid, Oxyd *nt* -(e)s, -e oxide.
Oxidation, Oxydation *f* oxidation.
oxidieren*, oxydieren* *vti aux sein or haben* to oxidise.
Ozean *m* -s, -e ocean. **ein ~ von Tränen** an ocean of tears.
Ozeandampfer *m* ocean steamer.
Ozeanien [-iən] *nt* -s Oceania.
ozeanisch *adj Flora* oceanic; *Sprachen* Oceanic.
Ozeanographie *f* oceanography.
Ozelot *m* -s, -e ocelot.
Ozon *nt or* (*inf*) *m* -s, *no pl* ozone.

P

P, p [pe:] *nt* -, - P, p.
Pa *m* -s, *no pl* (*inf*) daddy (*inf*).
Paar *nt* -s, -e pair; (*Mann und Frau auch*) couple. **ein ~ Schuhe** a pair of shoes; **zwei ~ Socken** two pairs of socks; **ein ~ Ochsen** a yoke of oxen; **ein ~ Würstchen** a couple of *or* two sausages; **ein ~ bilden** to make *or* form a pair; **ein ~ mit jdm bilden** to pair off with sb; **ein ~ werden** (*liter*) to become man and wife (*form*), to be made one (*liter*); **zu ~en treiben** (*old*) to put to flight, to rout; **ein ungleiches ~** an odd pair; (*Menschen auch*) an odd *or* unlikely couple.
paar *adj inv* **ein ~ a few**; (*zwei oder drei auch*) a couple of; **ein ~ Male** a few times, a couple of times, once or twice; **schreiben Sie mir ein ~ Zeilen** drop me a line; **die ~ Pfennige, die es kostet** ... the few pence that it costs ...; **der Bus fährt alle ~ Minuten** there's a bus every few minutes; **wenn er alle ~ Minuten mit einer Frage kommt** ... if he comes along with a question every other minute ...; **du kriegst ein ~!** (*inf*) I'll land you one! (*inf*).
paaren 1 *vt Tiere* to mate, to pair; (*Sport*) to match. **in seinen Bemerkungen sind Witz und Geist gepaart** his remarks show a combination of wit and intellect, in his remarks wit is coupled with intellect. **2** *vr* (*Tiere*) to mate, to copulate; (*fig*) to be coupled *or* combined.
Paarhufer *pl* (*Zool*) cloven-hoofed animals *pl*, even-toed ungulates *pl* (*spec*).
paarig *adj* in pairs. **~e Blätter** paired leaves.
Paar-: **~lauf** *m*, **~laufen** *nt* pair-skating, pairs *pl*; **p~laufen** *vi sep irreg aux sein infin, ptp only* to pair-skate.
paarmal *adv* **ein ~** a few times; (*zwei- oder dreimal auch*) a couple of times.
Paarreim *m* (*Poet*) rhyming couplet.
Paarung *f* (a) (*Sport, fig liter*) combination; (*Sport: Gegnerschaft*) draw, match. (b) (*Kopulation*) mating, copulation; (*Kreuzung*) crossing, mating.
Paarungszeit *f* mating season.
Paar-: **p~weise** *adv* in pairs, in twos; **~zeher** *m siehe* **~hufer**.
Pacht *f* -, -en lease; (*Entgelt*) rent. **etw in ~ geben** to lease sth (out), to let out sth on lease; **etw zur ~ freigeben** to release sth for leasing, to allow sth to be leased; **etw in ~ nehmen** to take sth on lease, to lease sth; **etw in or zur ~ haben** to have sth on lease *or* (on) leasehold.
Pachtbrief *m* lease.
pachten *vt* to take a lease on, to lease. **du hast das Sofa doch nicht für dich gepachtet** (*inf*) don't hog the sofa (*inf*), you haven't got a monopoly on the sofa (*inf*); **er tat so, als hätte er die Weisheit für sich (allein) gepachtet** (*inf*) he behaved as though he was the only clever person around.
Pächter(in *f*) *m* -s, - tenant, leaseholder, lessee (*form*). **der Herzog und seine ~** the duke and his tenants *or* tenantry; **er ist ~ auf einem Bauernhof or eines Bauernhofs** he's a tenant farmer.
Pacht-: **~ertrag** *m* net rent; **~geld** *nt* rent; **~grundstück** *nt* leasehold property; **~gut** *nt*, **~hof** *m* smallholding.
Pachtung *f* leasing.
Pacht-: **~vertrag** *m* lease; **p~weise** *adv* leasehold, on lease; **~zins** *m* rent.
Pack¹ *m* -(e)s, -e *or* ⸚e (*von Zeitungen, Büchern, Wäsche*) stack, pile; (*zusammengeschnürt*) bundle, pack. **zwei ~(e) Spielkarten** two packs of (playing) cards.
Pack² *nt* -s, *no pl* (*pej*) rabble *pl* (*pej*), riffraff *pl* (*pej*). **~ schlägt sich, ~ verträgt sich** (*Prov*) rabble like that are at each other's throats one minute and friends again the next.
Päckchen *nt* package, (small) parcel; (*Post*) small parcel; (*Packung*) packet, pack. **ein ~ Zigaretten** a packet *or* pack (*esp US*) of cigarettes; **ein ~ Spielkarten** a pack of (playing) cards; **ein ~ aufgeben** to post *or* mail a small parcel; **jeder hat sein ~ zu tragen** (*fig inf*) we all have our cross to bear.
Pack|eis *nt* pack ice.
packeln *vi* (*Aus inf*) *siehe* **paktieren (b)**.

packen 1 *vti* (a) *Koffer* to pack; *Paket* to make up; (*verstauen*) to stow *or* pack (away). **Sachen in ein Paket ~** to make things up into a parcel; **etw ins Paket ~** to put *or* pack sth into the parcel; **etw in Holzwolle/Watte ~** to pack sth (up) in wood shavings/to pack *or* wrap sth (up) in cotton wool; **jdn ins Bett ~** (*inf*) to tuck sb up (in bed); *siehe* **Watte**.
(b) (*fassen*) to grab (hold of), to seize, to grasp; (*Gefühle*) to grip, to seize. **jdn am or beim Kragen ~** (*inf*) to grab *or* seize sb by the collar; **von der Leidenschaft gepackt** in the grip of passion; **jdn bei der Ehre ~** to appeal to sb's sense of honour; **den hat es aber ganz schön gepackt** (*inf*) he's got it bad(ly) (*inf*).
(c) (*fig: mitreißen*) to grip, to thrill, to enthrall. **das Theaterstück hat mich gepackt** I was really gripped by the play.
(d) (*sl: schaffen*) to manage. **hast du die Prüfung gepackt?** did you (manage to) get through the exam?
(e) (*sl: aufhören*) **ich pack's jetzt!** I'm going to pack it in (*inf*).
(f) (*inf: gehen*) **~ wir's!** let's go.
(g) (*inf: kapieren*) **er packt es nie** he'll never get it (*inf*).
2 *vr* (*inf*) to clear off. **pack euch (fort)!** clear off! (*inf*), beat it! (*inf*); **pack dich nach Hause!** clear off home! (*inf*).
Packen *m* -s, - heap, pile, stack; (*zusammengeschnürt*) package, bundle. **ein ~ Arbeit** (*inf*) a pile of work.
Packer(in *f*) *m* -s, - packer; (*Hunt*) boarhound.
Packerei *f* (a) packing department. (b) *no pl* (*inf*) packing.
Pack-: **~esel** *m* pack-ass, pack-mule; (*fig*) packhorse; **~leinen** *nt*, **~leinwand** *f* burlap, gunny, bagging; **~material** *nt* packing material; **~papier** *nt* wrapping *or* brown paper; **~pferd** *nt* packhorse; **~raum** *m siehe* **Packerei (a)**; **~sattel** *m* packsaddle; **~tier** *nt* pack animal, beast of burden.
Packung *f* (a) (*Schachtel*) packet, pack; (*von Pralinen*) box. **eine ~ Zigaretten** a packet *or* pack (*esp US*) of cigarettes. (b) (*Med*) compress, pack; (*Kosmetik*) beauty pack. (c) (*Tech*) gasket; (*Straßenbau*) pitching *no pl*, ballast *no pl*. (d) (*inf: Niederlage*) thrashing, hammering (*inf*).
Pack-: **~wagen** *m* luggage van (*Brit*), baggage car (*US*); **~zettel** *m* packing slip, docket.
Pädagoge *m*, **Pädagogin** *f* educationalist, pedagogue (*form*).
Pädagogik *f* education, educational theory, pedagogy (*rare*).
pädagogisch *adj* educational, pedagogical (*form*). **P~e Hochschule** college of education, teacher-training college (*for primary teachers*); **eine ~e Ausbildung** a training in education, a pedagogical training; **seine ~en Fähigkeiten** his ability to teach, his teaching ability; **das ist nicht sehr ~** that's not a very educationally sound thing to do; **sein Unterricht ist nicht sehr ~** he has no teaching ability; **~ falsch** wrong from an educational point of view; **~ unbedarfte Eltern** parents who have no idea how to bring up their children.
pädagogisieren* 1 *vt* (*pädagogisch ausrichten*) to bring into line with educational *or* pedagogical theory. **2** *vi* (*inf*) (*über Pädagogik reden*) to talk education.
Paddel *nt* -s, - paddle.
Paddel-: **~boot** *nt* canoe; **~bootfahrer** *m* canoeist.
paddeln *vi aux sein or haben* to paddle; (*als Sport*) to canoe; (*schwimmen*) to dog-paddle.
Paddler(in *f*) *m* -s, - canoeist.
Päderast *m* -en, -en pederast.
Päderastie *f* pederasty.
Pädiatrie *f* p(a)ediatrics *sing*.
pädiatrisch *adj* p(a)ediatric.
paff *interj* bang.
paffen 1 *vi* (*inf*) (a) (*heftig rauchen*) to puff away. (b) (*nicht inhalieren*) to puff. **du paffst ja bloß!** you're just puffing at it! **2** *vt* to puff (away) at.
Page ['pa:ʒə] *m* -n, -n (*Hist*) page; (*Hotel~*) page (boy), bellboy, bellhop (*US*).
Pagen-: **~frisur** *f*, **~kopf** *m* page-boy (hair style *or* cut).
paginieren* *vt* to paginate.
Pagode *f* -, -n pagoda.
pah *interj* bah, pooh, poof.

Paillette [pai'jɛtə] f sequin.
Pair [pɛːʀ] m -s, -s (Hist) peer.
Pak f -, -s abbr of **Panzerabwehrkanone** anti-tank gun.
Paket nt -s, -e (Bündel) pile, stack; (zusammengeschnürt) bundle, package; (Packung) packet; (Post) parcel; (fig: von Angeboten, Gesetzesvorschlägen) package.
Paket-: ~adresse f stick-on address label; ~annahme f parcels office; ~ausgabe f parcels office; ~boot nt packet (boat), mailboat; ~karte f dispatch form; ~post f parcel post; ~schalter m parcels counter.
Pakistan nt -s Pakistan.
Pakistaner(in f) m -s, -, Pakistani m -(s), -(s) Pakistani.
pakistanisch adj Pakistani.
Pakt m -(e)s, -e pact, agreement. einen ~ (ab)schließen (mit) to make a pact or agreement or deal (inf) (with); einem ~ beitreten to enter into an agreement.
paktieren* vi (a) (old: Bündnis schließen) to make a pact or an agreement. (b) (pej) to make a deal (inf).
Paladin m -s, -e (Hist) paladin; (pej) (Gefolgsmann) henchman, hireling; (Land) satellite.
Palais [pa'lɛː] nt -, - palace.
paläo- pref palaeo-.
Palast m -(e)s, Paläste (lit, fig) palace.
palast|artig adj palatial.
Palästina nt -s Palestine.
Palästinenser(in f) m -s, - Palestinian.
palästinensisch, palästinisch adj Palestinian.
Palast-: ~revolution f (lit, fig) palace revolution; ~wache f palace guard.
palatal adj palatal.
Palatallaut m palatal (sound).
Palatschinke f -, -n (Aus) stuffed pancake.
Palaver [pa'laːvɐ] nt -s, - (lit, fig inf) palaver.
palavern* [pa'laːvɐn] vi (lit, fig inf) to palaver.
Paletot ['palɐto] m -s, -s (obs) greatcoat, overcoat.
Palette f (a) (Malerei) palette; (fig) range. ihr Gesicht sah aus wie eine ~ she was made up to the eyeballs (inf). (b) (Stapelplatte) pallet.
paletti adv (sl) OK (inf).
Palimpsest m or nt -es, -e palimpsest.
Palisade f palisade.
Palisaden-: ~wand f, ~zaun m palisade, stockade.
Palisander(holz nt) m -s, - jacaranda.
Palliativ(um) nt (Med) palliative.
Palme f -, -n palm. die ~ des Sieges erringen (liter) to bear off or carry off the palm (liter); jdn auf die ~ bringen (inf) to make sb see red (inf), to make sb's blood boil (inf).
Palmfett nt (Palmbutter) palm butter; (Palmöl) palm oil.
Palmin ® nt -s, no pl cooking fat (made from coconut oil).
Palm-: ~kätzchen nt pussy willow, catkin; ~öl nt palm oil; ~sonntag m Palm Sunday; ~wedel m siehe ~zweig; ~wein m palm wine; ~zweig m palm leaf.
Pamp m -s, no pl (inf) slop (inf), mush (inf).
Pampa f -, -s pampas pl.
Pampe f -, no pl (inf) paste; (pej) slop (inf), mush (inf).
Pampelmuse f -, -n grapefruit.
Pampf m -s, no pl (inf) slop (inf), mush (inf).
Pamphlet nt -(e)s, -e lampoon.
Pamphletist m lampoonist.
pampig adj (inf) (a) (breiig) gooey (inf); Kartoffeln soggy. (b) (frech) stroppy (inf).
Pan m -s (Myth) Pan.
pan- pref pan-. ~amerikanisch pan-American; ~arabisch pan-Arab; P~slawismus pan-Slavism.
Panama nt -s (a) Panama. (b) (auch ~hut) Panama (hat).
Panamakanal m Panama Canal.
panaschieren* vi (Pol) to split one's ticket. 2 vt panaschierte Blätter variegated leaves.
Panda m -s, - panda.
Pandämonium nt (Myth, fig) pandemonium.
Pandekten pl (Jur) Pandects pl, Digest.
Paneel nt -s, -e (form) (einzeln) panel; (Täfelung) panelling, wainscoting.
paneelieren* vt (form) to panel.
Panflöte f panpipes pl, Pan's pipes pl.
päng interj bang.
Panier nt -s, -e (obs) banner, standard. Freiheit sei euer ~! (liter) let freedom be your watchword or motto! (liter); unter dem ~ der Freiheit kämpfen (liter) to fight under the banner of freedom; sich (dat) etw aufs ~ schreiben (fig) to take or adopt sth as one's motto.
panieren* vt to bread, to coat with breadcrumbs.
Paniermehl nt breadcrumbs pl.
Panik f -, -en panic. (eine) ~ brach aus or breitete sich aus panic, to get into a panic; von ~ ergriffen panic-stricken; nur keine ~! don't panic!; die ~, die ihn zu überwältigen drohte the feeling of panic that threatened to overwhelm him.
Panik-: ~mache f (inf) panicmongering; ~stimmung f state of panic.
panisch adj no pred panic-stricken. ~e Angst panic-stricken fear, terror; sie hat ~e Angst vor Schlangen she's terrified of snakes, snakes scare her out of her wits; er hatte eine ~e Angst zu ertrinken he was terrified of drowning; ~er Schrecken panic; sich ~ fürchten (vor) to be terrified or petrified (by); sie rannten ~ durcheinander they ran about in panic.
Pankreas nt -, Pankreaten (Anat) pancreas.
Panne f -, -n (a) (Störung) hitch (inf), breakdown, trouble no

indef art; (Reifen~) puncture, flat (tyre), blow-out (inf). ich hatte eine ~ mit dem Fahrrad, mein Fahrrad hatte eine ~ I had some trouble with my bike/I had a puncture etc; ich hatte eine ~ mit dem Auto, mein Auto hatte eine ~ my car broke down/I had a puncture etc; mit der neuen Maschine passieren dauernd ~n things keep going wrong with the new machine, the new machine keeps breaking down.
(b) (fig inf) slip, boob (Brit inf), goof (US inf). mit jdm/etw eine ~ erleben to have (a bit of) trouble with sb/sth; mit unserem Urlaub haben wir vielleicht eine ~ erlebt just about everything went wrong with our holiday; uns ist eine ~ passiert we've made a slip etc or we've slipped up or boobed (Brit inf) or goofed (US inf); da ist eine ~ passiert mit dem Brief something has gone wrong with the letter.
Pannen-: ~dienst m, ~hilfe f breakdown service; ~koffer m emergency toolkit; ~kurs m car maintenance course.
Pan|optikum nt -s, Pan|optiken (von Kuriositäten) collection of curios; (von Wachsfiguren) waxworks pl.
Panorama nt -s, Panoramen panorama.
Panorama-: ~aufnahme f panorama, panoramic view; ~bus m coach with panoramic windows, panorama coach; ~gemälde nt panoramic painting; ~spiegel m (Aut) panoramic mirror.
panschen 1 vt to adulterate; (verdünnen) to water down, to dilute. 2 vi (inf) to splash (about).
Panscher m -s, - (inf) (a) (pej) adulterator. (b) du bist vielleicht ein ~! you're a messy thing!
Panscherei f siehe vb (a) adulteration; watering down, dilution. (b) splashing (about). was für eine ~ du gemacht hast! what a flood or mess you've made!
Pansen m -s, - (Zool) rumen; (N Ger inf) belly (inf).
Pantheismus m pantheism.
Pantheist m pantheist.
pantheistisch adj pantheistic.
Panther m -s, - panther.
Pantine f (N Ger) clog; siehe kippen.
Pantoffel m -s, -n slipper. unterm ~ stehen (inf) to be henpecked; unter den ~ kommen or geraten (inf) to become a henpecked husband; bei Müllers schwingt sie den ~ (inf) Mrs Müller rules the roost or has her husband under her thumb.
Pantoffelblume f slipper flower, calceolaria.
Pantöffelchen nt slipper.
Pantoffel-: ~held m (inf) henpecked husband; ~kino nt (inf) telly (Brit inf), (goggle-)box (Brit inf), tube (US inf); ~tierchen nt (Biol) slipper animalcule, paramecium (spec).
Pantolette f slip-on (shoe).
Pantomime¹ f -, -n mime.
Pantomime² m -n, -n mime.
pantomimisch adj Darstellung in mime. sich ~ verständlich machen to communicate with gestures or in sign language.
pantschen vti siehe panschen.
Panzer m -s, - (a) (Mil) tank. die deutschen ~ the German tanks pl or armour sing.
(b) (Hist: Rüstung) armour no indef art, suit of armour.
(c) (Panzerung) armour plating, armour plate.
(d) (von Schildkröte, Insekt) shell; (dicke Haut) armour.
(e) (fig) shield. sich mit einem ~ (gegen etw) umgeben to harden oneself (against sth); sich mit einem ~ aus etw umgeben to put up or erect a defensive barrier of sth; ein ~ der Gleichgültigkeit a wall of indifference.
Panzer-: ~abwehr f anti-tank defence; (Truppe) anti-tank unit; ~abwehrkanone f anti-tank gun; ~besatzung f tank crew; p~brechend adj armour-piercing; ~deckungsloch nt slit trench; ~division f armoured division; ~falle f tank trap; ~faust f bazooka; ~glas nt bulletproof glass; ~graben m anti-tank ditch; ~granate f armour-piercing shell; ~grenadier m armoured infantryman; ~hemd nt coat of mail; ~kampfwagen m armoured vehicle; ~kette f tank-track; ~kreuzer m (Naut) (armoured) cruiser.
panzern 1 vt to armour-plate. gepanzerte Fahrzeuge armoured vehicles. 2 vr (lit) to put on one's armour; (fig) to arm oneself.
Panzer-: ~platte f armour plating no pl, armour plate; ~schrank m safe; ~spähwagen m armoured scout car; ~sperre f anti-tank obstacle, tank trap; ~truppe f tanks pl, tank division; ~turm m tank turret.
Panzerung f armour plating; (fig) shield.
Panzer-: ~wagen m armoured car; ~weste f bulletproof vest.
Papa¹ m -s, -s (inf) daddy (inf), pa (US inf), pop(s) (US inf).
Papa² m -s, -s papa.
Papagallo m -s, Papagalli (pej) (Latin) wolf or romeo.
Papagei m -s, -en parrot. er plappert alles wie ein ~ nach he repeats everything parrot fashion, he parrots everything he/she etc says.
Papageienkrankheit f (Med) parrot fever, psittacosis.
Papier ['peɪpə] nt -s, - paper.
Paperback ['peɪpəbæk] nt paperback.
Papeterie [papetə'riː] f (Sw) stationer's.
Papi m -s, no pl (inf) daddy (inf).
Papier nt -s, -e (a) no pl (Material) paper. ein Blatt ~ a sheet or piece of paper; das existiert nur auf dem ~ it only exists on paper; das steht nur auf dem ~ that's only on paper, that's only in theory; seine Gedanken zu ~ bringen to set or put one's thoughts down on paper or in writing, to commit one's thoughts to paper; ~ ist geduldig (Prov) you can say what you like on paper, you can write what you like.
(b) (politisches Dokument, Schriftstück) paper.
(c) ~e pl (identity) papers pl; (Urkunden) documents pl; er hatte keine ~e bei sich he had no or he was carrying no means of identification on him; seine ~e bekommen (entlassen werden) to get one's cards.
(d) (Fin, Wert~) security.

Papierdeutsch nt officialese, gobbledygook (inf).
papier(e)n adj (a) (lit form) paper. (b) (fig) Stil, Sprache prosy, bookish.
Papier-: ~fabrik f paper mill; ~fetzen m scrap or (little) bit of paper; ~format nt paper size; ~geld nt paper money; ~korb m (waste)paper basket or bin; ~kram m (inf) bumf (inf); ~krieg m (inf) vor lauter ~krieg kommen wir nicht zur Forschung there's so much paperwork we can't get on with our research; erst nach einem langen ~krieg after going through a lot of red tape; einen ~krieg (mit jdm) führen to go through a lot of red tape (with sb); ~maché [papiema'ʃe:] nt -s, -s siehe Pappmaché; ~manschette f paper frill; (am Ärmel) false cuff; ~mühle f paper mill; ~schere f paper scissors pl; ~schlange f streamer; ~schnitzel m or nt scrap of paper; Konfetti confetti; ~serviette f paper serviette or napkin; ~taschentuch nt paper hanky or handkerchief, tissue; ~tiger m (fig) paper tiger; p~verarbeitend adj attr paper-processing; ~verschwendung f waste of paper; ~währung f paper currency; ~waren pl stationery no pl; ~warengeschäft nt, ~warenhandlung f stationer's (shop).
Papist m (pej) papist (pej).
papistisch adj (Hist) papal; (pej) popish.
Papp m -s, no pl (S Ger) siehe **Pappe** (b).
papp adj (inf) ich kann nicht mehr ~ sagen I'm full to bursting (inf), I'm about to go pop (inf).
Papp-: ~band m (Einband) pasteboard; (Buch) hardback; ~deckel m (thin) cardboard; einen ~deckel unterlegen to put a piece of cardboard underneath.
Pappe f -, -n (a) (Pappdeckel) cardboard; (Dach~) roofing felt. dieser linke Haken war nicht von ~ (inf) that left hook really had some weight or force behind it, that was no mean left hook; X ist ein guter Sprinter, aber Y ist auch nicht von ~ (inf) X is good but Y is no mean sprinter either.
(b) (S Ger inf) (Leim) glue; (Brei) paste; (pej) slop (pej inf), mush (pej inf). ich kann diese ~ von Porridge nicht essen I can't eat this porridge muck (pej inf).
Papp|einband m pasteboard.
Pappel f -, -n poplar.
Pappel|allee f avenue of poplars.
päppeln vt (inf) to nourish.
pappen (inf) 1 vt to stick, to glue (an or auf + acc on). jdm eine ~ to stick one on sb (inf). 2 vi (inf) (klebrig sein) to be sticky; (Schnee) to pack. der Leim pappt gut the glue sticks or holds well; das Hemd pappt an mir my shirt is sticking to me.
Pappen-: ~deckel m (S Ger) siehe Pappdeckel; ~heimer pl: ich kenne meine ~heimer (inf) I know you lot/that lot (inside out) (inf); ~stiel m (fig inf): das ist doch ein ~stiel (billig) that's chicken feed (inf); (leicht) that's child's play (inf); das ist keinen ~stiel wert that's not worth a thing or a penny or a straw; das hab ich für einen ~stiel gekauft I bought it for a song or for next to nothing.
papperlapapp interj (inf) rubbish, (stuff and) nonsense.
pappig adj (inf) sticky.
Papp-: ~kamerad m (Mil sl) silhouette target; ~karton m (Schachtel) cardboard box; (Material) cardboard; ~maché nt -s, -s papier-mâché; ~schachtel f cardboard box; ~schnee m wet or sticky snow.
Paprika m -s, -(s) (no pl: Gewürz) paprika; (~schote) pepper.
Paprikaschote f pepper. gefüllte ~n stuffed peppers.
Paps m -, no pl (inf) dad (inf), daddy (inf), pops (US inf).
Papst m -(e)s, -e pope; (fig) high priest.
päpstlich adj papal; (fig pej) pontifical. ~er als der Papst sein to be more Catholic than the Pope, to be more royal than the king.
Papst-: ~tum nt, no pl papacy; ~wahl f papal elections pl; ~würde f papal office.
Papua m -(s), -(s) Papuan.
papuanisch adj Papuan.
Papyrus m -, Papyri papyrus.
Papyrusrolle f papyrus (scroll).
Parabel f -, -n (a) (Liter) parable. (b) (Math) parabola, parabolic curve.
parabolisch adj (Liter) parabolic. eine ~e Erzählung a parable. (b) (Math) parabolic.
Parabolspiegel m parabolic reflector or mirror.
Parade f (a) (Mil) parade, review. die ~ abnehmen to take the salute.
(b) (Sport: Fechten, Boxen) parry; (Ballspiele) save; (Reiten) check. jdm in die ~ fahren (fig) to cut sb off short.
Parade-: ~anzug m (Mil) dress uniform; (inf: gute Kleidung) best bib and tucker (inf), Sunday best (inf); ~beispiel nt prime example; ~bett nt fourposter (bed).
Paradeiser m -s, - (Aus) tomato.
Parade-: ~kissen nt scatter cushion; ~marsch m (a) parade step; (Stechschritt) goose-step; im ~marsch marschieren to march in parade step/to goose-step; (b) (Marschmusik) (military) march; ~pferd nt show horse; (fig) showpiece; ~platz m parade ground; ~schritt m siehe ~marsch (a); ~stück nt (fig) showpiece; (Gegenstand auch) pièce de résistance; ~uniform f dress uniform.
paradieren vi to parade. mit etw ~ (fig) to show off or flaunt sth.
Paradies nt -es, -e (a) (lit, fig) paradise. die Vertreibung aus dem ~ the expulsion from Paradise; hier ist es so schön wie im ~ it's like paradise here, this is paradise; da haben sie wie im ~ gelebt they were living in paradise; ein ~ für Kinder a children's paradise, a paradise for children; das ~ auf Erden heaven on earth.
(b) (Archit) galilee.
paradiesisch adj (fig) heavenly, paradisiac(al) (liter). hier ist

es ~ schön it's (like) paradise here, this is paradise; sich ~ wohl fühlen to be blissfully happy, to be in paradise; ~ leere Strände blissfully empty beaches.
Paradiesvogel m bird of paradise.
Paradigma nt -s, Paradigmen paradigm.
paradigmatisch adj paradigmatic.
paradox adj paradoxical.
Paradox nt -es, -e, **Paradoxon** nt -s, **Paradoxa** paradox.
paradoxerweise adv paradoxically.
Paradoxie f paradox, paradoxicalness.
Paraffin nt -s, -e (Chem) (~öl) (liquid) paraffin; (~wachs) paraffin wax.
Paragraph m (Jur) section; (Abschnitt) paragraph.
Paragraphen-: ~reiter m (inf) pedant, stickler for the rules; p~weise adv in paragraphs; ~zeichen nt paragraph (marker).
Parallaxe f -, -n (Math) parallax.
parallel adj parallel. ~ laufen to run parallel; der Weg (ver)läuft ~ zum Fluß the path runs or is parallel to the river; die Entwicklung dort verläuft ~ zu der in der BRD the development there is parallel to or parallels that of West Germany; ~ schalten (Elec) to connect in parallel.
Parallele f -, -n (lit) parallel (line); (fig) parallel. eine ~ zu etw ziehen (lit) to draw a line parallel to sth; (fig) to draw a parallel to sth.
Parallel-: ~erscheinung f parallel; ~fall m parallel (case).
Parallelismus m parallelism.
Parallelität f parallelism.
Parallel-: ~klasse f parallel class; ~kreis m parallel (of latitude).
Parallelogramm nt -s, -e parallelogram.
Parallelschaltung f parallel connection.
Paralyse f -, -n (Med, fig) paralysis.
paralysieren* vt (Med, fig) to paralyse.
Paralytiker(in f) m -s, - (Med) paralytic.
paralytisch adj paralytic.
paramilitärisch adj paramilitary.
Paranoia [para'nɔya] f -, no pl paranoia.
paranoid [parano'i:t] adj paranoid, paranoiac.
Paranoiker [para'no:ikɐ] m -s, - paranoiac.
paranoisch [para'no:ɪʃ] adj paranoid, paranoiac.
Paranuß f (Bot) Brazil nut.
Paraphe f -, -n (form) (Namenszug) signature; (Namenszeichen) initials pl; (Stempel) signature stamp.
paraphieren* vt (Pol) to initial.
Paraphierung f (Pol) initialling.
Paraphrase f paraphrase; (Mus) variation.
paraphrasieren* vt to paraphrase; (Mus) to write variations on.
Parapsychologie f parapsychology.
Parasit m -en, -en (Biol, fig) parasite.
parasitär, parasitisch adj (Biol, fig) parasitic(al). ~ leben to live parasitically.
Parasol m or nt -s, -s or -e (old) parasol, sunshade.
parat adj Antwort, Beispiel etc ready, prepared; Werkzeug etc handy, ready. halte dich ~ be ready; halte den Korkenzieher ~ keep the corkscrew ready or handy or out; er hatte immer eine Ausrede ~ he always had an excuse ready or on tap (inf), was always ready with an excuse; seine stets ~e Ausrede his ever-ready excuse.
parataktisch adj (Ling) coordinated; (ohne Konjunktion) paratactic(al).
Parataxe f -, -n (Ling) coordination; (ohne Konjunktion) parataxis.
Pärchen nt (courting) couple. ihr seid mir so ein ~! (iro) you're a fine pair!
pärchenweise adv in pairs.
Parcours [par'ku:r] m -, - show-jumping course; (Sportart) show-jumping. einen ~ reiten to jump a course; sie reitet nicht gern ~ she doesn't like show-jumping.
pardauz interj (old) whoops.
Pardon [par'dõ:] m or nt -s, no pl (a) pardon. jdn um ~ bitten to ask sb's pardon; jdm kein(en) ~ geben (old) to show sb no mercy, to give sb no quarter.
(b) (inf) kein ~ kennen to be ruthless; wenn die Firma erst mal anfängt zu sparen, dann gibt's kein ~ if the firm starts saving there'll be no mercy shown; wenn er sich (dat) was in den Kopf gesetzt hat, gibt's kein ~ or kennt er kein ~ once he's set on something he's merciless or ruthless; das Zeug räumst du auf, da gibt's kein ~ you'll clear that stuff up and that's that! (inf).
pardon [par'dõ:] interj (Verzeihung) sorry; (nicht verstanden) sorry, beg pardon, pardon me (US). o ~! sorry!, I'm so sorry!; (empört) excuse me!
Parenthese f -, -n parenthesis. in ~ in parenthesis or parentheses; etw in ~ setzen to put sth in parentheses.
parenthetisch adj parenthetic(al).
par excellence [parɛksɛ'lã:s] adv par excellence.
Parforce- [par'fɔrs]: ~jagd f hunt, course; (Jagdart) coursing; wir machen eine ~jagd we're going hunting or going on a hunt; ~ritt m forced ride.
Parfum [par'fœ:] nt -s, -s, **Parfüm** nt -s, -e or -s perfume, scent.
Parfümerie f perfumery.
Parfümfläschchen nt scent or perfume bottle.
parfümieren* 1 vt to scent, to perfume. 2 vr to put perfume or scent on. du parfümierst dich zu stark you put too much scent or perfume on.
Parfümzerstäuber m scent spray, perfume or scent atomizer.
pari adv (Fin) par. al ~ at par (value), at nominal value; über ~

above par, at a premium; **unter** ~ below par, at a discount; **die Chancen stehen** ~ (~) the odds are even *or* fifty-fifty.
Paria *m* -s, -s (*lit, fig*) pariah.
parieren* 1 *vt* (a) (*Fechten, fig*) to parry; (*Ftbl*) to deflect. (b) (*Reiten*) to rein in. 2 *vi* to obey, to do what one is told. **aufs Wort** ~ to jump to it.
Parikurs *m* (*Fin*) par of exchange.
Pariser[1] *m* -s, - (a) Parisian. (b) (*inf: Kondom*) rubber (*inf*).
Pariser[2] *adj attr* Parisian, Paris.
Pariserin *f* Parisienne.
Parität *f* (*Gleichstellung*) parity, equality; (*von Währung*) parity, par of exchange.
paritätisch *adj* equal. ~e **Mitbestimmung** equal representation.
Park *m* -s, -s (a) park; (*von Schloß*) grounds *pl*. (b) (*rare*) *siehe* **Fuhrpark.**
Parka *m* -(s), -s *or f* -, -s parka.
Park-: ~anlage *f* park; p~artig *adj* park-like; ~bahn *f* (*Space*) parking orbit.
parken *vti* to park. **ein** ~des **Auto** a parked car; „**P**~ **verboten!**“ "No Parking"; **sein Auto parkte ...** his car was parked ...
Parkett *nt* -s, -e (a) (*Fußboden*) parquet (flooring). **ein Zimmer mit** ~ **auslegen** to lay parquet (flooring) in a room; **sich auf jedem** ~ **bewegen können** (*fig*) to be able to move in any society; **auf dem internationalen** ~ in international circles. (b) (*Tanzfläche*) (dance) floor. **eine tolle Nummer aufs** ~ **legen** (*inf*) to put on a great show; *siehe* **Sohle.** (c) (*Theat*) stalls *pl*, parquet (*US*). **das** ~ **klatschte Beifall** there was applause from the stalls; **wir sitzen** ~ (*inf*) we sit in the stalls.
Parkett(fuß)boden *m* parquet floor.
parkettieren* *vt* to lay with parquet, to lay *or* put down parquet in, to parquet.
Parkett-: ~platz, ~sitz *m* (*Theat*) seat in the stalls *or* parquet (*US*).
Park-: ~gebühr *f* parking fee; ~haus *nt* multi-storey car park.
parkieren* *vti* (*Sw*) *siehe* **parken.**
Parkinsonsche Krankheit *f*, **Parkinsonismus** *m* Parkinson's disease.
Park-: ~landschaft *f* parkland; ~licht *nt* parking light; ~lücke *f* parking space.
Parkometer *nt siehe* **Parkuhr.**
Park-: ~platz *m* car park, parking lot (*esp US*); (*für Einzelwagen*) (parking) space, place to park; **bewachter/unbewachter** ~platz car park with/without an attendant; ~raum *m* parking space; ~raumnot *f* shortage of parking space; ~scheibe *f* parking disc; ~uhr *f* parking meter; ~verbot *nt* parking ban; **hier ist** ~verbot there's no parking *or* you're not allowed to park here; ~verbotsschild *nt* no-parking sign; ~wächter *m* (*Aut*) car-park attendant; (*von Anlagen*) park keeper *or* attendant; ~zeit *f* parking time.
Parlament *nt* parliament. **das** ~ **auflösen** to dissolve parliament; **jdn ins** ~ **wählen** to elect sb to parliament.
Parlamentär *m* peace envoy, negotiator.
Parlamentärflagge *f* flag of truce.
Parlamentarier(in *f*) [-iɐ, -iərɪn] *m* -s, - parliamentarian.
parlamentarisch *adj* parliamentary. ~ **regieren** to govern by a parliament; ~er **Staatssekretär im Verteidigungsministerium** non-Cabinet minister with special responsibility for defence; **der P**~e **Rat** the Parliamentary Council; **ein** ~**demokratisches System** a democratic parliamentary system; ~e **Demokratie** parliamentary democracy.
Parlamentarismus *m* parliamentarianism.
parlamentieren* *vi* (a) (*obs Mil*) to parley. (b) (*inf*) to haggle (*über + acc* about).
Parlaments-: ~ausschuß *m* parliamentary committee; ~beschluß *m* vote *or* decision of parliament; ~ferien *pl* recess; **in die** ~ferien **gehen** to go into recess; ~gebäude *nt* parliamentary building(s); (*in London*) Houses of Parliament *pl*; (*in Washington*) Capitol; ~mitglied *nt* member of parliament; (*in GB*) Member of Parliament, MP; (*in USA*) Congressman; ~sitzung *f* sitting (of parliament); ~wahl *f usu pl* parliamentary election(s).
parlieren* *vi* to talk away. **er ist so schüchtern, ich hätte nie geglaubt, daß er so** ~ **könnte** he's so shy I'd never have believed that he could talk so fluently.
Parmesan(käse) *m* -s, *no pl* Parmesan (cheese).
Parnaß *m* -sses (*liter*) (Mount) Parnassus.
Parodie *f* parody, take-off (*auf + acc* on, *zu* of). **er ist nur noch eine** ~ **seiner selbst** he is now only a parody of his former self; **eine** ~ **von jdm geben** to do a parody *or* take-off of sb, to take sb off.
parodieren* *vt* (a) (*Parodie schreiben auf*) to parody. (b) (*karikieren*) to take off, to parody.
Parodist *m* parodist; (*von Persönlichkeiten*) impersonator.
parodistisch *adj* parodistic (*liter*). ~e **Sendung** parody, take-off; **er hat** ~e **Fähigkeiten** he's good at taking people off, he's a good impersonator; ~e **Literatur** literary parodies.
Parodontose *f* -, -n periodontosis (*spec*), shrinking gums.
Parole *f* -, -n (a) (*Mil*) password. (b) (*fig: Wahlspruch*) motto, watchword; (*Pol*) slogan.
Paroli *nt*: **jdm** ~ **bieten** (*old*) to defy sb.
Paroxysmus *m* paroxysm.
Part *m* -s, -e (a) (*Anteil*) share. (b) (*Theat, Mus*) part.
Partei *f* (a) (*Pol*) party. **bei** *or* **in der** ~ **in the party**; **die** ~ **wechseln** to change parties; **als Bundespräsident steht er über den** ~en **as Federal President he takes no part in party politics**. (b) (*Jur*) party. **die streitenden** ~en **the disputing parties**; **die vertragsschließenden** ~en **the contracting parties**; **meine** ~ **my client.**

(c) (*fig*) ~ **sein** to be bias(s)ed; **jds** ~ (*acc*) *or* **für jdn** ~ **ergreifen** *or* **nehmen** to take sb's side *or* part, to side with sb; **gegen jdn** ~ **ergreifen** *or* **nehmen** to side *or* to take sides against sb; **es mit keiner** ~ **halten, es mit keiner von beiden** ~en **halten** to be on neither side, to be neutral; **es mit beiden** ~en **halten** to run with the hare and hunt with the hounds (*prov*); **ein Richter sollte über den** ~en **stehen** a judge should be impartial.
(d) (*im Mietshaus*) tenant, party (*form*).
Partei-: ~abzeichen *nt* party badge; ~anhänger *m* party supporter; ~apparat *m* party machinery *or* apparatus; ~bonze *m* (*pej*) party bigwig *or* boss; ~buch *nt* party membership book; **das richtige** ~buch **haben** to belong to the right party; ~chef *m* party leader *or* boss; ~chinesisch *nt* (*pej*) party jargon; ~freund *m* fellow party member; ~führer *m* party leader; ~führung *f* leadership of a party; (*Vorstand*) party leaders *pl or* executive; ~gänger *m* -s, - party supporter *or* follower; ~genosse *m* party member; p~intern *adj* internal party; **etw** p~intern **lösen** to solve sth within the party.
parteiisch *adj* bias(s)ed, partial.
Partei-: ~kongreß *m* convention, party congress; ~leitung *f siehe* ~führung.
parteilich *adj* (a) (*rare: parteiisch*) bias(s)ed. (b) (*eine Partei betreffend*) party. **Maßnahmen, die nicht** ~ **gebunden sind** measures which are independent of party politics. (c) (*DDR: linientreu*) in accordance with party thought.
Parteilichkeit *f* bias, partiality.
Parteilinie *f* party line. **auf die** ~ **einschwenken** to toe the party line.
parteilos *adj Abgeordneter, Kandidat* independent, non-party. **der Journalist war** ~ the journalist wasn't attached to *or* aligned with any party.
Parteilose(r) *mf decl as adj* independent.
Parteilosigkeit *f* independence. ~ **ist oft ein Vorteil** it's often an advantage not to belong to any party.
Partei-: ~mitglied *nt* party member; ~nahme *f* -, -n partisanship; ~organ *nt* party organ; ~politik *f* party politics *pl*; p~politisch *adj* party political; ~präsidium *nt* party executive committee; ~programm *nt* (party) manifesto *or* programme; ~tag *m* party conference *or* convention.
Parteiungen *pl* (*old*) factions *pl*.
Partei-: ~versammlung *f* party meeting; ~vorsitzende(r) *m* party leader; ~vorstand *m* party executive; ~wesen *nt* party system; ~zugehörigkeit *f* party membership; **was hat er für eine** ~zugehörigkeit? what party does he belong to?
parterre [par'tɛr] *adv* on the ground (*Brit*) *or* first (*US*) floor.
Parterre [par'tɛr] *nt* -s, -s (a) (*von Gebäude*) ground floor (*Brit*), first floor (*US*). **im** ~ **wohnen** to live on the ground floor. (b) (*old Theat*) rear stalls, pit (*Brit*), parterre (*US*).
Parterrewohnung *f* ground-floor flat (*Brit*), first-floor apartment (*US*).
partial- [par'tsiaːl] *in cpds* partial.
Partie *f* (a) (*Teil, Ausschnitt*) part; (*eines Buchs auch*) section.
(b) (*Theat*) part, role; (*Mus*) part.
(c) (*Sport*) game; (*Fechten*) round. **eine** ~ **Schach spielen** to play *or* have a game of chess; **die** ~ **verloren geben** (*lit, fig*) to give the game up as lost.
(d) (*old: Land*~) outing, trip. **eine** ~ **machen** to go on *or* for an outing *or* a trip.
(e) (*Comm*) lot, batch.
(f) (*inf*) catch. **eine gute** ~ (**für jdn**) **sein** to be a good catch (for sb); **eine gute** ~ (**mit jdm**) **machen** to marry (into) money.
(g) **mit von der** ~ **sein** to join in, to be in on it; **da bin ich mit von der** ~ count me in, I'm with you.
(h) (*Aus: Arbeitergruppe*) gang.
Partie-: ~exemplar, ~stück *nt* free copy.
partiell [par'tsiɛl] *adj* partial. **diese Lösung ist** ~ **richtig** this solution is partly *or* partially right.
partienweise [par'tiːən-] *adv* (*Comm*) in lots.
Partikel *f* -, -n (*Gram, Phys*) particle.
Partikularismus *m* particularism.
Partikularist *m* particularist.
partikularistisch *adj* particularistic.
Partisan(in *f*) *m* -s *or* -en, -en partisan.
Partisanen-: ~kampf *m* guerrilla warfare; (*Kampfhandlung*) guerrilla battle; ~krieg *m* partisan war; (*Art des Krieges*) guerrilla warfare.
Partita *f* -, **Partiten** (*Mus*) partita.
partitiv *adj* (*Gram*) partitive.
Partitur *f* (*Mus*) score.
Partizip *nt* -s, -ien [-iən] (*Gram*) participle. ~ **Präsens/Perfekt** present/past participle.
Partizipation *f* participation (*an + dat* in).
Partizipationsgeschäft *nt* (*Comm*) transaction conducted by several parties.
Partizipial-: ~konstruktion *f* participial construction; ~satz *m* participial clause.
partizipieren* *vi* to participate (*an + dat* in).
Partizipium *nt* -s, **Partizipien** (*old*) *siehe* **Partizip.**
Partner(in *f*) *m* -s, - partner; (*Film*) co-star. **als jds** ~ **spielen** (*in Film*) to play opposite sb; (*Sport*) to be partnered by sb, to be sb's partner; *siehe* **Gesprächspartner.**
Partnerschaft *f* partnership.
partnerschaftlich *adj* ~es **Verhältnis** (relationship based on) partnership; **in unserer Ehe haben wir ein** ~es **Verhältnis** our marriage is a partnership; ~e **Zusammenarbeit** working together as partners; **sein** ~er **Führungsstil** his style of leadership which involves treating people as equal partners; **in gutem** ~em **Einvernehmen** in a spirit of partnership; **sie haben ihre Kinder** ~ **erzogen** they brought their children up as their

equals; das haben wir ~ gelöst we solved it together or jointly.

Partner-: ~staat m partner (country); ~tausch m (a) (Tanz, Tennis) change of partners; (b) (sexuell) partner-swopping; ~wahl f choice of partner; jetzt ist ~wahl (beim Tanz) take or choose your partners, please!; ~wechsel m siehe ~tausch (a).

partout [par'tuː] adv (dated) er will ~ ins Kino gehen he insists on going to the cinema; er muß ~ wieder zu spät kommen he had to be late again of course; sie will ~ nicht nach Hause gehen she just doesn't want to go home.

Party ['paːɐti] f -, -s or **Parties** party. eine ~ geben or veranstalten to give or have a party; bei or auf einer ~ at a party; auf eine or zu einer ~ gehen to go to a party.

Partylöwe m (iro) socialite.

Parvenü [parve'nyː, -vɔ'nyː] m -s, -s (dated) parvenu, upstart.

Parze f -, -n (Myth) Parca. die ~n the Fates.

Parzelle f plot, lot, parcel of land.

parzellieren* vt to parcel out.

Pasch m -(e)s, -e or ⸚e (beim Würfelspiel) doublets pl; siehe Viererpasch.

Pascha m -s, -s pasha. wie ein ~ like Lord Muck (inf).

Paspel f -, -n piping no pl.

paspelieren*, paspeln vt to pipe.

Paß m **Passes, Pässe (a)** passport. (b) (im Gebirge etc) pass. (c) (Ballspiele) pass. (d) (Reitsport) siehe **Paßgang**.

passabel adj passable, reasonable; Aussehen auch presentable. mir geht's ganz ~ I'm OK (inf), I'm all right.

Passage [pa'saːʒə] f -, -n (alle Bedeutungen) passage; (Ladenstraße) arcade.

Passagier [pasa'ʒiːɐ] m passenger. ein blinder ~ a stowaway.

Passagier-: ~dampfer m passenger steamer; ~flugzeug nt passenger aircraft, air-liner; ~gut nt passenger luggage; ~liste f passenger list.

Passah ['pasa] -s, no pl, **Passahfest** nt (Feast of the) Passover.

Paßamt nt passport office.

Passant(in f) m passer-by.

Passat(wind) m -s, -e, **Passatströmung** f trade wind.

Paßbild nt passport photo(graph).

passé [pa'seː] adj pred passé. diese Mode ist längst ~ this fashion went out long ago; die Sache ist längst ~ that's all ancient history (inf), that's all in the past.

Passe f -, -n yoke.

passen¹ 1 vi (a) (die richtige Größe, Form haben) to fit. die Schuhe ~ (mir) gut the shoes fit (me) well or are a good fit (for me); dieser Schlüssel paßt nicht (ins Schloß) this key doesn't or won't fit (the lock); der Deckel paßt nicht the lid doesn't or won't fit (on); wie angegossen ~ to fit like a glove.

(b) (harmonieren) zu etw ~ to go with sth; zu etw im Ton ~ to match sth; zu jdm ~ (Mensch) to be suited to sb, to suit sb; zueinander ~ to go together; (Menschen auch) to be suited (to each other), to suit each other, to be well matched; sie paßt gut zu ihm she suits him well, she's well suited to him, she's just right for him; das paßt zu ihm, so etwas zu sagen that's just like him to say that; es paßt nicht zu dir, Bier zu trinken it doesn't look right for you to drink beer, you don't look right drinking beer; diese Einstellung paßt gut zu ihm that attitude is typical of him or is just like him; so ein formeller Ausdruck paßt nicht in diesen Satz such a formal expression is out of place or is all wrong in this sentence; das Rot paßt da nicht the red is all wrong there; das Bild paßt besser in das andere Zimmer the picture would look or go better in the other room; er paßt nicht zum Lehrer (dated) he isn't suited to teaching or to being a teacher; er paßt nicht in diese Welt/in dieses Team he doesn't fit or is out of place in this world/in this team.

(c) (genehm sein) to suit, to be suitable or convenient. er paßt mir einfach nicht I just don't like him; Sonntag paßt uns nicht Sunday is no good for us; das paßt mir gar nicht (kommt ungelegen) that isn't at all convenient, that doesn't suit me at all; (gefällt mir nicht) I don't like that at all, I don't think much of that; das paßt mir gar nicht, daß du schon gehst I don't want you to go now; es paßt ihr gar nicht, daß sie jetzt schlafen gehen soll she doesn't like the idea of having to go to bed now; wenn's dem Chef paßt ... if it suits the boss ..., if the boss gets the idea into his head ...; du kannst doch nicht einfach kommen, wann es dir paßt you can't just come when it suits you or when you like; das könnte dir so ~! (inf) you'd like or love that, wouldn't you?; ihre Raucherei paßt mir schon lange nicht this smoking of hers has been annoying me for a long time.

2 vr (inf) to be proper. so solches Benehmen paßt sich nicht hier you can't behave like that here; das paßt sich nicht für eine Dame ladies shouldn't do that kind of thing.

3 vt to fix.

passen² vi (Cards) to pass. (ich) passe! (I) pass!; bei dieser Frage muß ich ~ (fig) I'll have to pass on this question.

passen³ vti (Ftbl) to pass.

passend adj (a) (in Größe, Form) gut/schlecht ~ well-/ill-fitting; er trägt kaum mal einen ~en Anzug he hardly ever wears a suit that fits; ein ~er Schlüssel (zu diesem Schloß) a key that fits or to fit (this lock).

(b) (in Farbe, Stil) matching. etwas dazu P~es something that goes with it or to go with it or to match; ich muß jetzt dazu ~e Schuhe kaufen now I must buy some matching shoes or some shoes to go with it or that go with it; die zu diesem Parfüm ~e Seife the soap that goes with or matches this perfume; eine im Ton genau dazu ~e Tasche a bag which matches it exactly.

(c) (genehm) Zeit, Termin convenient, suitable. er kam zu jeder ~en und unpassenden Zeit he came at any time, no matter how inconvenient.

(d) (angemessen) Bemerkung, Benehmen, Kleidung suitable, appropriate, fitting; Wort right, proper. sie trägt zu jeder Gelegenheit einen ~en Hut she always wears a hat to suit or

match the occasion; er findet immer das ~e Wort he always knows the right thing to say.

(e) Geld exact. haben Sie es ~? have you got it exactly?, have you got the right money?

Passepartout [paspar'tuː] m or nt -s, -s (alle Bedeutungen) passe-partout.

Paß-: ~form f fit; eine gute ~form haben to be a good fit; ~foto nt passport photo(graph); ~gang m amble; im ~gang gehen to amble; ~gänger m -s, - ambler; ~höhe f top of the pass.

passierbar adj passable; Fluß, Kanal negotiable.

passieren* 1 vt (a) auch vi to pass. der Zug passierte die Brücke/zwei Stationen the train crossed or went or passed over the bridge/went through or passed (through) two stations; die Grenze ~ to cross (over) or pass (over or through) the border; die Zensur ~ to get through the censor, to be passed by the censor; jdn ungehindert ~ lassen to let sb pass.

(b) (Cook) to strain.

2 vi aux sein (sich ereignen) to happen (mit to). ihm ist etwas Schreckliches passiert something terrible has happened to him; ihm ist beim Bergsteigen etwas passiert he had an accident while mountaineering; ist ihm etwas passiert? has anything happened to him?; beim Sturz ist ihm erstaunlicherweise nichts passiert miraculously he wasn't hurt or injured in the fall; was ist denn passiert? what's the matter?; es wird dir schon nichts ~ nobody's going to hurt you, nothing is going to happen to you; es ist ein Unfall passiert there has been an accident; das kann auch nur mir ~! that could only happen to me!, just my luck!; daß mir das ja nicht mehr or nicht noch mal passiert! see that it doesn't happen again!; so etwas passiert schließlich nicht alle Tage! after all, it doesn't happen every day; jetzt ist es passiert! ich hatte dich gewarnt now it's happened! I warned you; jetzt ist es passiert! jetzt kriegen wir Ärger that's done it or torn it (inf), now we'll be in trouble; so was ist mir noch nie passiert! that's never happened to me before!; (empört) I've never known anything like it!

Passier-: ~schein m pass, permit; ~schlag m (Tennis) passing shot; ~sieb nt strainer; ~stelle f crossing point.

Passion f passion; (religiös) Passion. er ist Jäger aus ~ he has a passion for hunting.

passioniert adj enthusiastic, passionate.

Passions-: ~blume f passionflower; ~spiel nt Passion play; ~weg m Via Dolorosa, Way of the Cross, road to Calvary; ~woche f Holy Week, Passion Week; ~zeit f (Karwoche) Holy or Passion Week; (Fastenzeit) Lent.

passiv adj passive. sich ~ verhalten to be passive; ~e Bestechung corruption no pl, corrupt practices pl; ~es Mitglied non-active member; ~er Widerstand passive resistance; ~er Wortschatz passive vocabulary; ~e Handelsbilanz (Comm) adverse trade balance; siehe Wahlrecht.

Passiv nt -s, -e, **Passivum** [pa'siːvum] nt (Gram) passive (voice). das Verb steht im ~ the verb is in the passive (voice).

Passiva [pa'siːva], **Passiven** [pa'siːvn] pl (Comm) liabilities pl.

Passivbildung f (Gram) formation of the passive.

passivieren* [pasi'viːrən] vt (Comm) to enter on the debit side.

passivisch [pa'siːvɪʃ] adj (Gram) passive. dieses Verb kann nur ~ gebraucht werden this verb can only be used in the passive (voice) or passively.

Passivität [pasivi'tɛːt] f passiveness, passivity; (Chem) passivity.

Passiv- (Comm): ~posten m debit entry; ~saldo m debit account; ~seite f debit side.

Passivum nt (Gram) siehe Passiv.

Paß-: ~kontrolle f passport control; ~kontrolle! (your) passports please!; durch die ~kontrolle gehen to go through passport control; ~photo nt passport photo(graph); ~stelle f passport office; ~straße f (mountain) pass.

Passung f (Tech) fit.

Passus m -, - passage.

Paßzwang m requirement to carry a passport. es besteht kein ~ you don't have to carry a passport.

Paste f -, -n, **Pasta** f -, **Pasten** paste.

Pastell nt -s, -e pastel. in ~ arbeiten to work in pastels; ein schönes ~ a beautiful pastel (drawing).

Pastell-: ~farbe f pastel (crayon); (Farbton) pastel (shade or colour); p~farben adj pastel(-coloured); etw p~farben streichen to paint sth in pastel colours or in pastels; ~maler m pastellist; ~malerei f drawing in pastels, pastel drawing; ~stift m pastel (crayon); ~ton m pastel shade or tone.

Pastetchen nt vol-au-vent.

Pastete f -, -n (a) (Schüssel~) pie; (Pastetchen) vol-au-vent; (ungefüllt) vol-au-vent case. (b) (Leber~ etc) pâté.

Pasteurisation [pastøriza'tsioːn] f siehe Pasteurisierung.

pasteurisieren* [pastøri'ziːrən] vt to pasteurize.

Pasteurisierung [pastøri'ziːrʊŋ] f pasteurization.

Pastille f -, -n pastille.

Pastor m siehe Pfarrer(in).

pastoral adj pastoral.

Pastorale nt -s or f -, -n (Mus) pastorale; (Art) pastoral. Beethovens ~ Beethoven's Pastoral Symphony.

Pastorin f siehe Pfarrer(in).

Pate m -n, -n (a) (Taufzeuge) godfather, godparent; (Firmzeuge) sponsor. bei einem Kind ~ stehen to be a child's godparent/sponsor; bei etw ~ gestanden haben (fig) to be the force behind sth.

(b) (obs: Täufling) godchild.

Patene f -, -n (Eccl) paten.

Paten-: ~kind nt godchild; godson; goddaughter; ~onkel m godfather; ~schaft f godparenthood; sponsorship; er übernimmt die ~schaft für das Kind he's going to be the godfather; er nahm seine ~schaft nicht ernst he didn't take his responsibilities as godfather *or* godparent very seriously; ~**sohn** *m* godson; ~**stadt** *f* twin(ned) town.

patent *adj* ingenious, clever; *Lösung auch* neat; *(praktisch) Mensch, Messer auch* handy *(inf)*; *Werkzeug auch* nifty *(inf)*. **ein** ~**er Kerl** a great guy/girl *(inf)*; **sie ist eine** ~**e Frau** she's a tremendous woman; **er hat sich** ~ **angestellt** he managed it very well; **das war** ~ **(von dir!)** *(iro)* that was clever of you.

Patent *nt* -(e)s, -e (a) *(Erfindung, Urkunde)* patent; *(inf: Mechanismus)* apparatus. **der Reißverschluß, so ein blödes** ~ this zip, the stupid thing; **etw als** *or* **zum** ~ **anmelden, ein** ~ **auf** *or* **für etw anmelden** to apply for a patent on *or* for sth; **ein** ~ **auf eine Erfindung haben** to have a patent on an invention; **,,zum** ~**angemeldet"** patent pending. (b) *(Ernennungsurkunde)* commission. (c) *(Sw)* permit, licence.

Patent-: ~**amt** *nt* Patent Office; ~**anmeldung** *f* application for a patent.

Patentante *f* godmother.

Patent-: ~**anwalt** *m* patent agent *or* attorney *(US)*; **p**~**fähig** *adj* patentable; ~**geber** *m* patentor; ~**gebühr** *f* *(bei Anmeldung)* (patent) filing fee; *(jährlich)* patent annuity; ~**gesetz** *nt* Patents Act.

patentierbar *adj* patentable.

patentieren* *vt* to patent. **sich** *(dat)* **etw** ~ **lassen** to take out a patent on sth, to have sth patented.

Patent-: ~**inhaber** *m* patentee, patent-holder; ~**lösung** *f (fig)* easy answer, patent remedy; **bei der Kindererziehung gibt es keine** ~**lösung** there's no instant recipe for success in bringing up children.

Patentochter *f* goddaughter.

Patent-: ~ **recht** *nt* patent law; ~**register** *nt* Patent Rolls *pl*; ~**rezept** *nt (fig) siehe* ~**lösung**; ~**schrift** *f* patent specification; ~**schutz** *m* patent right, protection by (letters) patent; ~**streit** *m* dispute over a patent; ~**urkunde** *f* letters patent *pl*; ~**verschluß** *m* swing stopper.

Pater *m* -s, - *or* **Patres** *(Eccl)* Father.

Paterfamilias *m* -, - paterfamilias.

Paternoster[1] *nt* -s, - *(Gebet)* Lord's Prayer, paternoster. **das** ~ **aufsagen** *or* **beten** to say the Lord's Prayer *or* paternoster.

Paternoster[2] *m* -s, - *(Aufzug)* paternoster.

pathetisch *adj* emotional; *Beschreibung auch* dramatic; *Rede, Stil auch* emotive; *Gehabe auch* histrionic. **das war zu** ~ **gespielt** it was overacted.

Pathologe *m*, **Pathologin** *f* pathologist.

Pathologie *f* pathology.

pathologisch *adj* pathological.

Pathos *nt* -, *no pl* emotiveness, emotionalism. **ein Gedicht mit** ~ **vortragen** to read a poem with feeling; **die Rede enthielt zu viel falsches** ~ the speech contained too much false emotionalism; **mit viel** ~ **in der Stimme** in a voice charged with emotion; **mit viel** ~ **versuchte sie, ihn zu überzeugen** she made a highly emotional attempt to persuade him.

Patience [pa'siã:s] *f* -, -n patience *no pl*. ~**n legen** to play patience; **eine** ~ **legen** to play (a game of) patience.

Patient(in *f)* [pa'tsient(in)] *m* -en, -en patient. **ich bin** ~ **von** *or* **bei Dr. X** I'm Dr X's patient, I'm being treated by Dr X.

Patin *f* godmother, godparent; *(Firm*~*)* sponsor.

Patina *f* -, *no pl (lit, fig)* patina. ~ **ansetzen** *(lit)* to patinate, to become coated with a patina; *(fig)* to take on a hallowed air of tradition.

patinieren* *vt* to patinate, to coat with a patina.

Patres *pl of* **Pater**.

Patriarch *m* -en, -en *(lit, fig)* patriarch.

patriarchalisch *adj (lit, fig)* patriarchal. **er regiert** ~ he rules patriarchally; **in seiner Familie herrscht er** ~ he rules his family like a patriarch.

Patriarchat *nt* patriarchy.

Patriot(in *f)* *m* -en, -en patriot.

patriotisch *adj* patriotic. ~ **gesinnt** patriotically-minded, patriotic.

Patriotismus *m* patriotism.

Patrize *f* -, -n punch.

Patriziat *nt* patriciate.

Patrizier [-iɐ] *m* patrician.

Patriziergeschlecht *nt* patrician family.

patrizisch *adj* patrician.

Patron *m* -s, -e (a) *(Eccl)* patron saint. (b) *(old: Schirmherr)* patron. (c) *(inf)* frecher ~ cheeky beggar *(inf)*.

Patronage [patro'na:ʒə] *f* -, -n patronage.

Patronat *nt* patronage *(über +acc* of). **unter jds** ~ *(dat)* **stehen** to be under sb's patronage.

Patrone *f* -, -n *(Film, Mil, von Füller)* cartridge; *(Tex)* point paper design.

Patronen-: ~**gurt** *m* ammunition belt; ~**gürtel** *m* cartridge belt, bandolier; ~**hülse** *f* cartridge case; ~**rahmen** *m* (cartridge) clip; ~**tasche** *f* ammunition pouch.

Patronin *f* (a) *(Eccl)* patron saint. (b) *(old: Schirmherrin)* patron, patroness.

Patronym *nt* -s, -e, **Patronymikon** *nt* -s, **Patronymika** patronymic.

Patrouille [pa'truljə] *f* -, -n patrol. ~ **gehen** to patrol.

Patrouillen- [pa'truljən-]: ~**boot** *nt* patrol boat; ~**gang** *m* patrol.

patrouillieren* [patrul'ji:rən] *vi* to patrol.

patsch *interj* splash, splat; *(bei Ohrfeige)* smack. **er trat** ~**! in die Pfütze** he went splash *or* splat into the puddle; ~**! das spritzt!** that's splashing!; **wenn du so frech bist, macht's gleich** ~**!** if you go on being so cheeky you'll get a good smack.

Patsch *m* -es, -e *(inf)* smack, slap. **einen** ~ **auf den Hintern kriegen** to get a smack *or* slap on the bottom, to get a smacked bottom.

Patsche *f* -, -n *(inf)* (a) *(Hand)* paw *(inf)*, mitt *(inf)*. (b) *(Matsch)* mud; *(Schneematsch)* slush; *(fig)* jam *(inf)*, fix *(inf)*, (tight) spot *(inf)*. **in der** ~ **sitzen** *or* **stecken** to be in a jam *etc*; **jdm aus der** ~ **helfen, jdn aus der** ~ **ziehen** to get sb out of a jam *etc*; **jdn in der** ~ **(sitzen) lassen** to leave sb in the lurch. (c) *(Feuer*~*)* beater; *(Fliegen*~*)* swat.

patschen *vi* (a) to splash. **das Baby patschte mit der Hand in die Suppe** the baby went splat *or* splash with his hand in the soup; **er ist durch die Pfützen gepatscht** he splashed *or* went splashing through the puddles. (b) *(inf)* **das Baby patschte auf den Tisch/an die Möbel** the baby smacked *or* slapped the table/the furniture (with its hands); **die Kinder** ~ **mit den Händen** the children clap their hands (together); **der Hund patschte über den Flur** the dog padded across the hall; **er patschte der Sekretärin auf den Hintern** he gave his secretary a pat on the bottom, he patted his secretary on the bottom; **jetzt patscht es aber gleich!** you'll get a smack *or* get smacked in a minute; **ich patsche dir gleich eine!** I'll give you a smack *or* a slap *or* I'll smack you in a minute.

Patsch-: ~**hand** *f (inf)*, ~**händchen** *nt (inf)* paw *(inf)*, mitt *(inf)*; *(von Kindern)* (little) hand; **p**~**naß** *adj (inf)* soaking *or* dripping wet; **p**~**naß ist es draußen!** it's soaking wet outside.

patt *adj pred, adv (Chess, fig)* in stalemate. **das Spiel endete** ~ the game ended in (a) stalemate; **jetzt sind wir beide** ~ **now** we've both reached a stalemate.

Patt *nt* -s, -s *(lit, fig)* stalemate. **ein** ~ **erreichen** to reach *or* come to (a) stalemate.

patzen *vi (inf)* to slip up, to boob *(Brit inf)*, to goof *(US inf)*. **die Straßenarbeiter haben gepatzt** the road-workers botched the job (up) *or* boobed; **der Pianist/Schauspieler hat gepatzt** the pianist/actor fluffed a passage/his lines *or* boobed *etc*.

Patzen *m* -s, - *(Aus)* blotch, splodge; *(Tinte auch)* blot.

Patzer *m* -s, - *(inf)* (a) *(Fehler)* slip, boob *(Brit inf)*, goof *(US inf)*. **mir ist ein** ~ **unterlaufen** I made a slip *or* boob. (b) *(S Ger: Klecks)* botch, splodge; *(Tinte auch)* blot. (c) *(Mensch)* bungler; *(Aus: Kleckser)* messy thing *(inf)*.

patzig *adj (inf)* snotty *(inf)*, insolent.

Paukant *m (Univ sl)* duellist.

Paukboden *m (Univ sl)* duelling floor.

Pauke *f* -, -n (a) *(Mus)* kettledrum, timpani *pl*. **jdn mit** ~**n und Trompeten empfangen** to roll out the red carpet for sb, to give sb the red-carpet treatment; **mit** ~**n und Trompeten durchfallen** *(inf)* to fail miserably *or* dismally; **auf die** ~ **hauen** *(inf) (angeben)* to blow one's own trumpet, to brag; *(feiern)* to paint the town red. (b) *(dated Sch: Schule)* swot-shop *(dated sl)*.

pauken 1 *vi* (a) *(inf: Pauke spielen)* to drum. (b) *(von Korpsstudenten)* to fence. (c) *(inf: lernen)* to swot *(inf)*, to cram *(inf)*. **meine Mutter hat immer mit mir gepaukt** my mother always helped me with my swotting. 2 *vt* to swot up *(inf)*. **mit jdm Geschichtszahlen** ~ to help sb swot up their dates.

Pauken-: ~**schlag** *m* drum beat; **wie ein** ~**schlag** *(fig)* like a thunderbolt; **die Sinfonie mit dem** ~**schlag** the Surprise Symphony; ~**schläger** *m* drummer; ~**schlegel** *m* drumstick; ~**spieler** *m* drummer; ~**wirbel** *m* drum roll, roll on the drums.

Pauker *m* -s, - (a) *(inf: Paukenspieler)* drummer. (b) *(Sch inf: Lehrer)* teacher. **da geht unser** ~ there's sir *(inf)*.

Paukerei *f* (a) *(inf: das Paukespielen)* drumming. (b) *(Sch inf)* swotting *(inf)*. **ich hab diese** ~ **satt** I'm fed up with school.

Paukist(in *f)* *m* timpanist.

Pausbacken *pl* chubby cheeks *pl*.

pausbäckig *adj* chubby-cheeked.

pauschal *adj* (a) *(vorläufig geschätzt)* estimated; *(einheitlich)* flat-rate *attr only*; *(inklusiv)* inclusive. **ich schätze die Baukosten** ~ **auf etwa eine Million DM** I'd estimate the overall building costs to be DM1 million; **die Werkstatt rechnet** ~ **pro Inspektion 25 DM** the garage has a flat rate of DM25 per service; **die Einkommensteuer kann** ~ **festgesetzt werden** income tax can be set at a flat rate; **die Gebühren werden** ~ **bezahlt** the charges are paid in a lump sum; **Strom berechnen wir Ihnen** ~ we'll charge you a flat rate for electricity; **die Reisekosten verstehen sich** ~ the travelling costs are inclusive; **alle bekommen** ~ **£ 6 pro Woche mehr** there will be an across-the-board increase of £6 a week, they'll get £6 a week more across the board. (b) *(fig)* **so** ~ **kann man das nicht sagen** that's much too sweeping a statement; **ein Volk** ~ **verurteilen** to condemn a people wholesale *or* lock, stock and barrel; **diese Probleme hat er ganz** ~ **in einem kurzen Kapitel behandelt** he treated these problems all lumped together in a single short chapter.

Pauschale *f* -, -n *or nt* -s, **Pauschalien** [-iən] *(Einheitspreis)* flat rate; *(vorläufig geschätzter Betrag)* estimated amount.

Pauschalgebühr *f (Einheitsgebühr)* flat rate (charge); *(vorläufig geschätzter Betrag)* estimated charge.

pauschalieren* *vt* to estimate at a flat rate *or* in a lump sum.

Pauschal-: ~**preis** *m (Einheitspreis)* flat rate; *(vorläufig geschätzter Betrag)* estimated price; *(Inklusivpreis)* inclusive *or* all-in price; ~**reise** *f* package holiday/tour; ~**steuer** *f (vorläufige Steuer)* estimated tax; *(einheitliche Steuer)* tax at a flat rate; ~**summe** *f* lump sum; ~**urteil** *nt* sweeping statement; **er neigt sehr zu** ~**urteilen** he tends to make sweeping statements; ~**versicherung** *f* comprehensive insurance *no pl*.

Pauschbetrag *m* flat rate.

Pause *f* -, -n (a) *(Unterbrechung)* break; *(Rast)* rest; *(das Innehalten)* pause; *(Theat)* interval, intermission; *(Sch)* break, recess *(US)*; *(Pol)* recess. **(eine)** ~ **machen** to take *or* have *or* make a break; *(rasten)* to rest, to have *or* take a rest; *(innehalten)* to pause, to make a pause; **nach einer langen** ~ **sagte er ...** after a long silence he said ...; immer wieder entstanden ~n in der Unterhaltung the conversation was full of gaps or silences; ohne ~ arbeiten to work non-stop or without stopping or continuously; die große ~ break, recess (US); (in einer Grundschule) playtime.

(b) (Mus) rest. die ~n einhalten to make the rests; eine halbe/ganze ~ a minim (Brit) or half-note (US)/semi-breve (Brit) or whole-note (US) rest.

(c) (Durchzeichnung) tracing; (Photokopie) (photo)copy.

pausen vt to trace.

Pausen-: ~brot nt something to eat at break; ~halle f break or recess (US) hall; ~hof m playground, schoolyard; p~los adj no pred non-stop, continuous, incessant; er arbeitet p~los he works non-stop; ~stand m half-time score; score at the interval; ~zeichen nt (Mus) rest; (Rad) call sign.

pausieren* vi to (take or have a) break. der Torwart mußte wegen einer Verletzung ~ the goalkeeper had to rest up because of injury.

Pauspapier nt tracing paper; (Kohlepapier) carbon paper.

Pavian ['pa:via:n] m -s, -e baboon.

Pavillon ['pavil'jõ:] m -s, -s pavilion.

Pazifik m -s Pacific.

pazifisch adj Pacific. der P~e Ozean the Pacific (Ocean).

Pazifismus m pacifism.

Pazifist(in f) m pacifist.

pazifistisch adj pacifist.

Pech nt -(e)s, -e **(a)** (Stoff) pitch. schwarz wie ~ (as) black as pitch; ihr Haar ist schwarz wie ~ her hair is jet black; die beiden halten zusammen wie ~ und Schwefel (inf) the two are as thick as thieves or are inseparable.

(b) no pl (inf: Mißgeschick) bad or hard or tough (inf) luck. bei etw ~ haben to be unlucky in or with sth, to have bad or tough (inf) or lousy (inf) luck in or with sth; ~ gehabt! tough! (inf); sie ist vom ~ verfolgt bad luck follows her around; das ist sein ~! that's his hard or bad or tough (inf) luck!; so ein ~! just my/our etc luck!

Pech-: ~blende f (Min) pitchblende; ~draht m waxed thread; ~fackel f (pitch) torch, link; ~kohle f bituminous coal; p~(raben)schwarz adj (inf) pitch-black; Haar jet-black; ~strähne f (inf) run or streak of bad luck, unlucky patch; eine ~strähne haben to have a run or streak of bad luck, to go through an unlucky patch; ~vogel m (inf) unlucky person, walking disaster area (hum inf); (Frau auch) Calamity Jane.

Pedal nt -s, -e pedal. (fest) in die ~e treten to pedal (hard).

Pedant m pedant.

Pedanterie f pedantry.

pedantisch adj pedantic.

Peddigrohr nt cane.

Pedell m -s, -e (old) (Sch) caretaker, janitor; (Univ) porter.

Pediküre f -, -n **(a)** no pl (Fußpflege) pedicure. **(b)** (Fußpflegerin) chiropodist.

pediküren* vt to give a pedicure to.

Pegasus m - Pegasus.

Pegel m -s, - (in Flüssen, Kanälen, Meer) water depth gauge; (Elec) level recorder.

Pegelstand m water level.

Peil-: ~anlage f direction finding equipment, direction-finder; (Naut) sounding equipment; ~antenne f directional antenna.

peilen vt Wassertiefe to sound, to plumb; U-Boot, Sender, Standort to get a fix on, to get or take the bearings of; Richtung to plot; (entdecken) to detect. die Umgebung ~ (inf) to find one's bearings; die Lage ~ (inf) to see how the land lies, to see which way the wind's blowing; über den Daumen ~ (inf) to guess roughly; über den Daumen gepeilt (inf) roughly speaking, at a rough estimate.

Peiler m -s, - detector.

Peil-: ~funk m radio direction finder; ~gerät nt direction finder; ~lot nt plumb-line; ~station f direction finding station.

Peilung f (von Wassertiefe) sounding, plumbing; (von U-Boot, Sender) locating; (von Richtung) plotting. was für eine ~ haben wir für das U-Boot? what's our bearing on the submarine?

Pein f -, no pl agony, suffering. seine Leben war nur eine einzige ~ his life was one long torment; es ist eine ~, ihm zuzuhören it's agony or painful to hear him; jdm das Leben zur ~ machen to make sb's life a misery.

peinigen vt to torture; (fig) to torment. jdn bis aufs Blut ~ to torture sb till he bleeds; (fig) to torment sb mercilessly; von Schmerzen/Zweifeln gepeinigt tormented by pain/doubt, racked with pain/doubt.

Peiniger(in f) m -s, - (liter) torturer; (fig) tormentor.

Peinigung f (liter) torture; (fig) torment.

peinlich adj **(a)** (unangenehm) (painfully) embarrassing; Lage, Fragen auch awkward; Überraschung nasty. ein ~es Gefühl an uncomfortable feeling; ich habe das ~e Gefühl, daß ... I have a terrible feeling that ...; es war ihm ~(, daß ...) he was or felt embarrassed (because ...); es ist mir sehr ~, aber ich muß es Ihnen einmal sagen I don't know how to put it, but you really ought to know; es ist mir sehr ~, aber die Arbeit ist immer noch nicht fertig I'm really sorry but the work still isn't finished; das ist mir ja so ~ I feel awful about it; ~ berührt sein (hum) to be profoundly shocked (iro); ~ wirken to be embarrassing, to cause embarrassment; es war so schlecht, daß es schon ~ war (inf) it was so bad it was really painful (inf).

(b) (gewissenhaft) painstaking, meticulous; Sparsamkeit careful. in seinem Zimmer/auf seinem Schreibtisch herrschte ~e or ~ste Ordnung his room/his desk was meticulously or scrupulously tidy; jdn einem ~en Verhör unterziehen to question sb very closely; ~ sauber scrupulously or meticulously clean; der Koffer wurde ~ genau untersucht the case was gone through very thoroughly or was given a very thorough going-over (inf); er vermied es ~st, davon zu sprechen he was at

pains not to talk about it; etw ~st geheimhalten to keep sth strictly secret or top secret.

Peinlichkeit f **(a)** (Unangenehmheit) awkwardness, embarrassment. die ~ der Situation/seines Benehmens the awkwardness of the situation, the embarrassing or awkward situation/his embarrassing behaviour; diese ~en auf der Bühne these embarrassing or painful (inf) scenes on stage.

(b) (Gewissenhaftigkeit) thoroughness, meticulousness, painstakingness.

peinsam adj (hum) painful, embarrassing.

peinvoll adj (old) painful.

Peitsche f -, -n whip. er gab seinem Pferd die ~ he whipped his horse on; siehe Zuckerbrot.

peitschen vti to whip; (fig) to lash.

Peitschen-: ~hieb m stroke, lash; ~knall m crack of a whip; ~leuchte f street lamp; ~schlag m lash of a whip; ~schlageffekt m (Med) whiplash; ~schnur f (whip)lash, thong; ~stiel m whip handle, whipstock.

pejorativ adj pejorative.

Pekinese m -n, -n pekinese, peke (inf).

Pektin nt -s, -e pectin.

pekuniär adj pecuniary, financial.

Pelerine f (old) pelerine (old), cape.

Pelikan m -s, -e pelican.

Pelle f -, -n (inf) skin. der Chef sitzt mir auf der ~ (inf) I've got the boss on my back (inf); er geht mir nicht von der ~ (inf) he won't stop pestering me; siehe rücken.

pellen (inf) 1 vt Kartoffeln, Wurst to skin, to peel; siehe Ei. 2 vr (Mensch, Körperhaut) to peel. meine Haut pellt sich my skin's peeling, I'm peeling.

Pellkartoffeln pl potatoes pl boiled in their jackets.

Peloponnes m -(es) or f - Peloponnese.

Pelz m -es, -e fur; (nicht gegerbt auch) pelt, hide, skin; (Kleidung) fur; (fig: Haarwuchs) fur no pl. ~ ist wieder in Mode fur is or furs are in fashion again; jdm eins auf den ~ brennen (inf) to singe sb's hide; sich (dat) die Sonnen auf den ~ brennen lassen (inf) to toast oneself (inf); siehe rücken.

Pelz-: ~besatz m fur trimming; p~besetzt adj trimmed with fur, fur-trimmed; ~futter nt fur lining; p~gefüttert adj fur-lined, lined with fur; ~händler m furrier; (Fellhändler) fur trader; ~handschuh m fur glove.

pelzig adj furry; Zunge furred(-over), furry.

Pelz-: ~imitation f imitation fur; ~jäger m skin-hunter; (Fallensteller) (fur-)trapper; ~kragen m fur collar; ~mantel m fur coat; ~mütze f fur hat; ~stiefel m fur or furry (inf) boot; (p~gefüttert) fur-lined boot; ~stoff m fur fabric; ~tier nt animal with a valuable fur, animal prized for its fur; ~tiere jagen to hunt animals for their fur; (mit Fallen) to go trapping; ~tierfarm f fur farm; ~tierjäger m siehe ~jäger; ~tierzucht f fur-farming; p~verbrämt adj (liter) siehe p~besetzt; ~waren pl furs; ~werk nt fur.

Pendant [pã'dã:] nt -s, -s counterpart, opposite number.

Pendel nt -s, - pendulum. keiner kann das ~ der Zeit aufhalten time and tide wait for no man (prov); das ~ schlug nach der entgegengesetzten Seite aus (fig) the pendulum swung in the other direction.

Pendelausschlag m swing of a pendulum.

pendeln vi **(a)** (schwingen) to swing (to and fro), to oscillate (form). er ließ die Beine ~ he let his legs dangle, he dangled his legs. **(b)** aux sein (hin- und herfahren) (Zug, Fähre etc) to run or operate a shuttle-service, to shuttle; (Mensch) to commute; (fig) to vacillate, to fluctuate.

Pendel-: ~schlag m swing of the pendulum; er spielte zum ~schlag des Metronoms he played in time to the metronome; der ~schlag der Zeit the march of time; ~schwingung f swing of the pendulum; (Phys auch) oscillation (of a pendulum); ~tür f swing door; ~uhr f pendulum clock; ~verkehr m shuttle service; (Berufsverkehr) commuter traffic.

Pendler(in f) m -s, - commuter.

Penes pl of **Penis.**

penetrant adj **(a)** Gestank, Geschmack penetrating, pungent; Gestank, Parfüm auch overpowering. das schmeckt ~ nach Knoblauch you can't taste anything for garlic, it has a very strong taste of garlic.

(b) (fig: aufdringlich) pushing, insistent. der Typ war mir zu ~ he was too pushing or pushy (inf) for my liking; seine Selbstsicherheit ist schon ~ his self-confidence is overpowering; ein ~er Kerl a pest, a nuisance.

Penetranz f, no pl (von Geruch, Geschmack) pungency; (fig: Aufdringlichkeit) insistence, aggressiveness. er ist von einer unausstehlichen ~ he's unbearably overpowering.

Penetration f penetration.

penetrieren* vt to penetrate.

peng interj bang.

penibel adj **(a)** pernickety (inf), precise, exact. **(b)** (dial: peinlich) Lage, Angelegenheit painful, embarrassing.

Penicillin [penitsi'li:n] nt -s, -e siehe **Penizillin.**

Penis m -, -se or **Penes** penis.

Penizillin nt -s, -e penicillin.

Pennal nt -s, -e **(a)** (old inf: Schule) high (inf), high school, grammar (Brit inf), grammar school (Brit). **(b)** (S Ger, Aus: Federmäppchen) pencil case.

Pennäler(in f) m -s, - (dated) high-school boy/girl, grammar-school boy/girl (Brit).

Pennbruder m (inf) tramp, bum (inf), hobo (US).

Penne f -, -n **(a)** (Sch sl) school. **(b)** (inf: Herberge) doss house (inf), flophouse (inf).

pennen vi (inf) to kip (inf). ich habe gerade ein bißchen gepennt I've just been having a kip (inf) or sleep, I've just been kipping (inf); der Meier pennt schon wieder im Unterricht Meier's having a little sleep again during the lesson; **du bist daran, penn nicht!** it's your turn, wake up!

Penner(in f) m -s, - (inf) **(a)** tramp, bum (inf), hobo (US). **(b)** (verschlafener Mensch) sleepyhead (inf).

Pensa, Pensen pl of **Pensum**.

Pension [pãˈzioːn, pãˈsioːn, penˈzioːn] f -, -en **(a)** (Fremdenheim) guest-house, pension.

(b) no pl (Verpflegung, Kostgeld) board. **halbe/volle ~** half/full board; **die ~ pro Tag macht 30 DM** half/full board is DM30 a day.

(c) (Ruhegehalt) pension, superannuation.

(d) no pl (Ruhestand) retirement. **in ~ gehen** to retire, to go into retirement; **in ~ sein** to be retired, to be in retirement.

Pensionär(in f) [pãzioˈnɛːr, -ɛːərin, pãsioˈnɛːr, -ɛːərin, penziˈoːr, -ɛːərin] m **(a)** (Pension beziehend) pensioner; (im Ruhestand befindlich) retired person. **(b)** (Pensionsgast) paying guest; (ständiger Pensionsgast) boarder.

Pensionat [pãzioˈnaːt, pãsioˈnaːt, penzioˈnaːt] nt (dated) boarding school.

pensionieren* [pãzioˈniːrən, pãsioˈniːrən, pensioˈniːrən] vt to pension off, to retire. **sich ~ lassen** to retire.

pensioniert adj retired, in retirement.

Pensionierung f (Zustand) retirement; (Vorgang) pensioning-off. **die Firma entschloß sich zur ~ der älteren Mitarbeiter** the firm decided to pension off the older workers.

Pensionist [pãzioˈnist, pãsioˈnist, pensioˈnist] m (S Ger, Aus) siehe **Pensionär(in) (a)**.

Pensions-: **~alter** nt retiring or retirement age; **~anspruch** m right to a pension; **p~berechtigt** adj entitled to a pension; **~fonds** m pension fund; **~gast** m paying guest; **~kasse** f siehe **~fonds**; **~preis** m price for full board; **~preis DM 21** full board DM21; **p~reif** adj (inf) ready for retirement; **~rückstellungen** pl pension reserve(s).

Pensum nt -s, **Pensa** or **Pensen** workload; (Sch) curriculum. **tägliches ~** daily quota; **er hat sein ~ nicht geschafft** he didn't achieve his target; **ein hohes** or **großes ~ an Arbeit** a heavy workload.

Pentagon nt -s, -e pentagon.

Pentagramm nt pentagram.

Pentameter m (Poet) pentameter.

Pentateuch m -s Pentateuch.

Penthouse [ˈpenthaus] nt -s, -s penthouse (flat).

Pep m -(s), no pl (inf) pep (inf), life. **etw mit ~ machen** to put a bit of pep (inf) or life or zip (inf) into doing sth; **das Kleid hat ~** that dress has style or flair.

Peperoni pl chillies pl.

Pepita m or nt -s, -s shepherd('s) check or plaid.

Pepmittel nt (inf) pep pill (inf).

Pepsin nt -s, -e pepsin.

per prep **(a)** (mittels, durch) by. **~ Adresse** (Comm) care of, c/o; **mit jdm ~ du sein** (inf) to be on Christian-name terms or first-name terms with sb; **~ procura** (Comm) per procura, pp abbr, for; **~ pedes** (hum) on shanks's pony (hum), on foot; **~ se** per se. **(b)** (Comm: gegen) against. **~ cassa**, **~ Kasse** (old) against cash.

(c) (Comm: bis, am) by.

(d) (Comm: pro) per.

perennierend adj perennial.

perfekt adj **(a)** (vollkommen) perfect. **~ Englisch sprechen** to speak perfect English, to speak English perfectly.

(b) pred (abgemacht) settled. **etw ~ machen** to settle or conclude sth; **die Sache ~ machen** to clinch the deal, to settle the matter; **der Vertrag ist ~** the contract is signed, sealed and delivered (inf), the contract is all settled; **damit war die Niederlage ~ total** defeat was then inevitable.

Perfekt nt -s, -e, **Perfektum** nt -s, **Perfekta** perfect (tense).

Perfektion f perfection. **das war Artistik in höchster ~** that was the epitome of artistry, that was perfect artistry.

perfektionieren* [perfektsioˈniːrən] vt to perfect.

Perfektionismus [perfektsioˈnismus] m perfectionism.

Perfektionist(in f) [perfektsioˈnist(m)] m perfectionist.

perfektionistisch [perfektsioˈnistiʃ] adj perfectionist.

Perfektum nt siehe **Perfekt**.

perfid(e) adj (liter) perfidious.

Perfidie f (liter) perfidy.

Perforation f perforation.

perforieren* vt to perforate.

Pergament nt **(a)** (präparierte Tierhaut) parchment; (Kalbs~ auch) vellum. **dieses Buch ist in ~ gebunden** this book is vellum-bound or bound in vellum. **(b)** (Handschrift) parchment. **(c)** (~papier) greaseproof paper.

Pergamentband m vellum(-bound) book.

pergamenten adj (liter) parchment; (aus Kalbshaut) vellum.

Pergament-: **~papier** nt greaseproof paper; **~rolle** f (parchment) scroll; **~rücken** m vellum spine.

Pergola f, **Pergolen** arbour, bower.

Periode f -, -n period (auch Physiol); (von Wetter auch) spell; (Math) repetend; (Elec) cycle. **0,33 ~ 0.33** recurring; **ihre ~ ist ausgeblieben** she didn't get or have her period; **~n pro Sekunde** cycles per second.

Periodensystem nt periodic system; (Tafel) periodic table.

Periodikum nt -s, **Periodika** usu pl periodical.

periodisch adj periodic(al); (regelmäßig) regular; (Phys) periodic. **~er Dezimalbruch** recurring fraction; **diese Zeitschrift erscheint ~ alle 4 Monate** this publication comes out at 4-monthly intervals or every 4 months.

periodisieren* vt to divide up into periods.

Periodizität f periodicity; (Math: von Bruch) recurrence.

Peripetie f peripeteia.

peripher adj (liter) peripheral.

Peripherie f periphery; (von Kreis) circumference; (von Stadt) outskirts pl. **an der ~ Bonns** in or on the outskirts of Bonn.

Periskop nt -s, -e periscope.

periskopisch adj periscopic.

Peristaltik f peristalsis.

Perle f -, -n **(a)** (Muschel~) pearl. **~n vor die Säue werfen** (prov) to cast pearls before swine (prov); siehe **Krone**. **(b)** (aus Glas, Holz etc) bead; (Luftbläschen) bubble; (von Wasser, Schweiß) bead, drop, droplet. **(c)** (fig) pearl, gem; (dated inf: Hausmädchen) maid.

perlen vi (sprudeln) to sparkle, to bubble, to effervesce; (fallen, rollen) to trickle, to roll. **~des Lachen** (liter) rippling or bubbling laughter; **der Tau perlt auf den Blättern** drops or beads of dew glisten on the leaves; **der Schweiß perlte ihm von/auf der Stirn** beads of sweat were running down/stood out on his forehead; **Wasser perlt auf einer Fettschicht** water forms into droplets on a greasy surface.

Perlen-: **~auster** f pearl oyster; **p~besetzt** adj set with pearls; **p~bestickt** adj embroidered or decorated with pearls; **~fischer** m pearl fisher, pearler; **~fischerei** f pearl fishing; **~kette** f, **~kollier** nt string of pearls, pearl necklace, pearls pl; **~schnur** f string of beads, beads pl; **~stickerei** f beadwork; **~taucher** m pearl diver.

Perl-: **~garn** nt mercerized yarn; **p~grau** adj pearl grey; **~huhn** nt guinea fowl; **~muschel** f pearl oyster; **~mutt** nt -s, no pl, **~mutter** f -, no pl or nt -s, no pl mother-of-pearl; **~mutterknopf**, **~muttknopf** m (mother-of-)pearl button; **p~muttern** adj mother-of-pearl; (fig) pearly; **ihre Zähne schimmerten p~muttern** her teeth gleamed like pearls.

Perlon ® nt -s, no pl = nylon.

Perlon-: **~strümpfe** pl nylons pl, nylon stockings pl; **p~verstärkt** adj nylon-reinforced.

Perl-: **~schrift** f (Typ) pearl; **~wein** m sparkling wine; **~zwiebel** f cocktail or pearl onion.

permanent adj permanent.

Permanenz f permanence. **in ~** continually, constantly.

permeabel adj (Bot, Phys, Tech) permeable.

perniziös adj malignant.

Perpendikel m or nt -s, - (von Uhr) pendulum.

Perpetuum mobile nt - -, - -(s) perpetual motion machine.

perplex adj dumbfounded, thunderstruck.

Perron [peˈrõː] m -s, -s (old, Sw, Aus) platform.

Persenning f -, -e(n) tarpaulin, tarp (US inf).

Perser(in f) m -s, - **(a)** (Mensch) Persian. **(b)** (inf) siehe **Perserteppich**.

Perserteppich m Persian carpet; (Brücke) Persian rug.

Persianer m -s, - **(a)** (Pelz) Persian lamb. **(b)** (auch ~mantel) Persian lamb (coat).

Persien [-iən] nt -s Persia.

Persiflage [perziˈflaːʒə] f -, -n pastiche, satire (gen, auf +acc on, of).

persiflieren* vt to satirize, to write a pastiche of.

Persilschein m (hum inf) clean bill of health (inf); denazification certificate.

persisch adj Persian.

Person f -, -en (Einzel~) person, individual. **jede ~ bezahlt ... each person** or everybody pays ...; **~en** people, persons (form); **eine aus 6 ~en bestehende Familie** a family of 6; **pro ~** per person; **die eigene ~** oneself; **was seine eigene ~ betrifft** as for himself; **ich für meine ~...** I myself ..., as for myself I ..., I for my part ...; **ich wußte nicht, daß ich den Chef in ~ vor mir hatte** I didn't know that I was actually talking to the boss himself; **in (eigener) ~ erscheinen** to appear in person or personally; **er ist Finanz- und Außenminister in einer ~** he's the Chancellor of the Exchequer and Foreign Secretary rolled into one; **jdn zur ~ vernehmen** (Jur) to question sb concerning his identity; **von ~ bekannt** (Jur) of known identity; **natürliche/juristische ~** (Jur) natural/juristic or artificial person; **die drei göttlichen ~en** the Holy Trinity, God in three persons; **eine hochgestellte ~** a high-ranking personage or person.

(b) (Mensch) person; (pej: Frau) female. **sie ist die Geduld in ~** she's patience personified; **Tiere treten in Fabeln als ~en auf** animals figure in fables as human beings or as people; **die Zeit als ~ dargestellt** time represented as a person or human being; **die ~ des Königs ist unantastbar** (the person of) the king is inviolable; **es geht um die ~ des Kanzlers, nicht um das Amt** it concerns the chancellor as a person, not the office; **lassen wir seine ~ aus dem Spiel** let's leave personalities out of it; **wir müssen die ~ von der Sache trennen** we must keep the personal and the factual aspects separate; **er ist klein von ~** he's small in stature, he's a small person.

(c) (Liter, Theat) character. **die ~en der Handlung** the characters (in the action); (Theat auch) the dramatis personae; **eine stumme ~** a non-speaking part.

(d) (Gram) person.

Personal nt -s, no pl personnel, staff; (Dienerschaft auch) servants pl; (Liter: Romanfiguren) characters pl. **fliegendes ~** aircrew; **ständiges ~** permanent staff; **ausreichend/ungenügend mit ~ versehen sein** to be adequately staffed/understaffed.

Personal-: **~abbau** m reductions pl in staff or personnel, personnel or staff cuts pl; **~abteilung** f personnel (department); **~akte** f personal file; **~angaben** pl particulars pl; **~ausweis** m identity card; **~bestand** m number of staff or employees or personnel; **~büro** nt siehe **~abteilung**; **~chef** m personnel manager, head of the personnel department; **~direktor** m personnel director; **~einsparung** f personnel reduction or cutdown; **~gesellschaft** f unlimited company.

Personalien [-iən] *pl* particulars *pl*.
personalisieren* *vti* to personalize. **er personalisiert immer** he always personalizes everything *or* reduces everything to a personal level.
Personalisierung *f* personalization.
Personalität *f* personality.
Personal-: ~**kartei** *f* personnel index; ~**kosten** *pl* personnel costs *pl*; ~**leiter** *m siehe* ~**chef**; ~**politik** *f* staff *or* personnel policy; ~**pronomen** *nt* personal pronoun; ~**rabatt** *m* staff discount; ~**rat** *m* (*Ausschuß*) *staff council for civil servants*; (*einzelner*) *representative on a staff council for civil servants*; ~**union** *f* personal union; **er ist Kanzler und Parteivorsitzender in** ~**union** he is at the same time Prime Minister and party chairman.
Persönchen *nt* (*inf*) little lady (*inf*).
personell *adj* staff *attr*, personnel *attr*. **die Verzögerungen unserer Produktion sind** ~ **bedingt** the delays in production are caused by staff *or* personnel problems; **unsere Schwierigkeiten sind rein** ~ our difficulties are simply to do with staffing *or* personnel.
Personen-: ~**aufzug** *m* (passenger) lift (*Brit*), elevator (*US*); ~**auto** *nt siehe* ~**kraftwagen**; ~**beförderung** *f* carriage *or* conveyance of passengers; **die Bahn hat ein finanzielles Defizit bei der** ~**beförderung** the railways' passenger(-carrying) services show a deficit; ~**beschreibung** *f* (personal) description; ~**dampfer** *m* passenger boat *or* steamer; ~**gedächtnis** *nt* memory for faces; ~**kraftwagen** *m* (*form*) (private) car, motorcar (*form*), automobile (*US*); ~**kreis** *m* group of people; ~**kult** *m* personality cult; **mit Che Guevara wird viel** ~**kult getrieben** a great personality cult has been built up around Che Guevara; ~**schaden** *m* injury to persons; ~**schaden ist bei dem Unfall nicht entstanden** no-one was injured *or* received any injuries in the accident; ~**stand** *m* marital status; ~**standsregister** *nt* register of births, marriages and deaths; ~**verkehr** *m* passenger services *pl*; ~**versicherung** *f* personal injury insurance; ~**verzeichnis** *nt* register (of persons); (*Liter*) list of characters; ~**waage** *f* scales *pl*, pair of scales; ~**wagen** *m* (*Rail*) carriage; (*Aut*) (private) car, automobile (*US*); ~**zahl** *f* number of persons (*form*) *or* people; ~**zug** *m* (*Gegensatz: Schnellzug*) slow *or* stopping train; (*Gegensatz: Güterzug*) passenger train.
Personifikation *f* personification.
personifizieren* *vt* to personify. **er läuft herum wie das personifizierte schlechte Gewissen** he's going around with guilt written all over his face.
Personifizierung *f* personification.
persönlich 1 *adj* personal; *Atmosphäre, Umgangsformen* friendly. ~**e Auslagen** out-of-pocket *or* personal expenses; ~**e Meinung** personal *or* one's own opinion; ~ **werden** to get personal; ~**es Fürwort** personal pronoun.
2 *adv* personally; (*auf Briefen*) private (and confidential). **der Chef** ~ the boss himself *or* in person *or* personally; **etw** ~ **meinen/nehmen** *or* **auffassen** to mean/take sth personally; **er interessiert sich** ~ **für seine Leute** he takes a personal interest in his people; **Sie müssen** ~ **erscheinen** you are required to appear in person *or* personally; ~ **haften** (*Comm*) to be personally liable.
Persönlichkeit *f* (a) *no pl* (*Charakter*) personality. **er besitzt wenig** ~ he hasn't got much personality. (b) (*bedeutender Mensch*) personality. **er ist eine** ~ he's quite a personality; ~**en des öffentlichen Lebens** public figures.
Persönlichkeits-: ~**entfaltung** *f* personality development, development of the personality; ~**wahl** *f* electoral system in which a vote is cast for a candidate rather than a party; **diese Wahl war eine reine** ~**wahl** (*inf*) this election boiled down to a question of the candidates' personalities.
Perspektiv *nt* small telescope, perspective (*obs*).
Perspektive [-'tiːvə] *f* (*Art, Opt*) perspective; (*Blickpunkt*) angle; (*Gesichtspunkt*) point of view, angle; (*fig: Zukunftsausblick*) prospects *pl*. **aus dieser** ~ **wirkt das Haus viel größer** the house looks much bigger from this angle; **wenn du das Problem aus meiner** ~ **betrachtest** if you look at the problem from my angle *or* point of view; **das eröffnet ganz neue** ~**n für uns** that opens new horizons for us.
perspektivisch [-'tiːvɪʃ] *adj* perspective *attr*; in perspective. **die Zeichnung ist nicht** ~ the drawing is not in perspective; **manche Tiere können nicht** ~ **sehen** some animals can't see in perspective; ~**e Verkürzung** foreshortening.
Peru *nt* -s Peru.
Peruaner(in *f*) *m* -s, - Peruvian.
peruanisch *adj* Peruvian.
Perücke *f* -, -n wig.
pervers [per'vɛrs] *adj* perverted, warped (*inf*). **ein** ~**er Mensch** a pervert.
Perversion [perver'zioːn] *f* perversion.
Perversität [perverzi'tɛːt] *f* perversion.
pervertieren* [perver'tiːrən] 1 *vt* to pervert, to warp. 2 *vi aux sein* to become *or* get perverted.
Pervertiertheit *f* pervertedness, perversion.
pesen *vi aux sein* (*inf*) to belt (*inf*), to charge (*inf*).
Pessar *nt* -s, -e pessary; (*zur Empfängnisverhütung*) cap, diaphragm.
Pessimismus *m* pessimism. **immer dieser** ~! you're/he's *etc* always so pessimistic!, this eternal pessimism!
Pessimist(in *f*) *m* pessimist.
pessimistisch *adj* pessimistic. **etw** ~ **beurteilen** to take a pessimistic view of sth, to view sth pessimistically.
Pest *f* -, *no pl* (*Hist, Med*) plague, pestilence, pest. **sich wie die** ~ **ausbreiten** to spread like the plague *or* like wildfire; **jdn/etw wie die** ~ **hassen** (*inf*) to loathe (and detest) sb/sth, to hate sb's

guts (*inf*); **jdn wie die** ~ **meiden** (*inf*) to avoid sb like the plague; **wie die** ~ **stinken** (*inf*) to stink to high heaven (*inf*); **jdm die** ~ **an den Hals wünschen** (*inf*) to wish sb would drop dead (*inf*).
Pest-: **p**~**artig** *adj* (*Med*) pestilential; (*fig*) *Gestank* fetid, miasmic (*liter*); **sich p**~**artig verbreiten** to spread like the plague; ~**beule** *f* plague spot; ~**geruch**, ~**gestank** *m* (foul) stench, stink; ~**hauch** *m* (*poet*) miasma (*liter*), fetor (*liter*).
Pestilenz *f* (*old*) pestilence.
Pest-: **p**~**krank** *adj* sick of the plague (*old*), plague-stricken; ~**kranke(r)** *mf* person with *or* who has the plague; **die** ~**kranken** those who had (been stricken by) the plague.
Petersilie [-iə] *f* parsley. **du siehst aus, als ob es dir die** ~ **verhagelt hätte** (*inf*) you look as though you've lost a pound and found a sixpence (*inf*).
Peterskirche *f* St Peter's.
Peterwagen *m* (*inf*) police *or* patrol car, panda car (*Brit*).
Petition *f* petition.
Petitionsrecht *nt* right to petition.
Petro(l)chemie *f* petrochemistry.
Petroleum [pe'troːleum] *nt* -s, *no pl* paraffin (oil), kerosene (*esp US*).
Petroleum-: ~**kocher** *m* paraffin stove, primus (stove); ~**lampe** *f*, ~**licht** *nt* paraffin *or* oil *or* kerosene (*esp US*) lamp.
Petschaft *nt* -s, -e (*old*) seal.
Petticoat ['pɛtikoːt] *m* -s, -s stiff(ened) petticoat.
Petting *nt* -s, -s petting.
petto *adv*: **etw in** ~ **haben** (*inf*) to have sth up one's sleeve (*inf*).
Petunie [-iə] *f* petunia.
Petz *m* -es, -e (*liter*) **Meister** ~ (*Master*) Bruin.
Petze *f* -, -n (*inf*) sneak (*Sch sl*), telltale (*tit*) (*Sch sl*).
petzen (*inf*) 1 *vt* **der petzt alles** he always tells; **er hat gepetzt, daß ... he** (went and) told that ...; **er hat's dem Lehrer gepetzt** he told sir (*Sch sl*). 2 *vi* to tell (tales).
Petzer *m* -s, - (*inf*) *siehe* **Petze**.
Petzliese *f siehe* **Petze**.
peu à peu [pøa'pø] *adv* (*inf*) gradually, little by little.
Pf *abbr of* Pfennig.
Pfad *m* -(e)s, -e path, track. **den** ~ **der Tugend wandeln** (*liter*) to follow the path of virtue; **neue** ~**e in der Medizin** new directions in medicine.
Pfadfinder *m* -s, - (boy) scout. **er ist bei den** ~**n** he's in the (Boy) Scouts.
Pfadfinderbewegung *f* (Boy) Scout movement, (Boy) Scouts *pl*.
Pfadfinderin *f* girl guide (*Brit*), girl scout (*US*).
Pfaffe *m* -n, -n (*pej*) cleric (*pej*), parson.
pfäffisch *adj* (*pej*) sanctimonious (*pej*).
Pfahl *m* -s, -̈e post; (*Zaun- auch*) stake; (*Stütze auch*) support; (*Palisade*) palisade, pale, stake; (*Brücken*~) pile, pier; (*Marter*~) stake. **jdm ein** ~ **im Fleisch sein** (*liter*) to be a thorn in sb's flesh.
Pfahl-: ~**bau** *m* -s, -ten (a) *no pl* (*Bauweise*) building on stilts; **im** ~**bau** on stilts; (b) (*Haus*) pile dwelling, house built on stilts; ~**brücke** *f* pile bridge; ~**dorf** *nt* pile village.
pfählen *vt* (a) (*Hort*) to stake. (b) (*hinrichten*) to impale.
Pfahl-: ~**werk** *nt* (*Stützwand*) pilework; (*Palisade*) palisade, paling; ~**wurzel** *f* taproot.
Pfalz *f* -, -en (a) *no pl* (*Rhein*~)Rhineland *or* Lower Palatinate, Rheinpfalz. (b) *no pl* (*Ober*~) Upper Palatinate. (c) (*Hist*) (*Burg*) palace; (*Gebiet eines Pfalzgrafen*) palatinate.
Pfälzer(in *f*) *m* -s, - (a) person from the Rhineland/Upper Palatinate. **er ist (ein)** ~ he comes from the (Rhineland/Upper) Palatinate. (b) (*Wein*) wine from the Rhineland Palatinate.
Pfalz-: ~**graf** *m* (*Hist*) count palatine; **p**~**gräflich** *adj* of a/the count palatine.
pfälzisch *adj* Palatine, of the (Rhineland) Palatinate.
Pfand *nt* -(e)s, -̈er security, pledge; (*beim Pfänderspiel*) forfeit; (*Flaschen*~) deposit; (*fig*) pledge. **etw als** ~ **geben, etw zum** ~ **setzen** (*liter*) to pledge sth, to give sth as (a) security; (*fig*) to pledge sth; (*beim Pfänderspiel*) to pay sth as a forfeit; **ich gebe mein Wort als** ~ I pledge my word; **etw gegen** ~ **leihen** to lend sth against a security *or* pledge; **auf der Flasche ist** ~ there's something (back) on the bottle (*inf*), there's a deposit on the bottle; **auf die Flasche ist 10 Pf** ~ there's 10Pf (back) on the bottle (*inf*); **ein** ~ **einlösen** to redeem a pledge; **etw als** ~ **behalten** to keep sth as (a) security, to hold sth in pledge.
pfändbar *adj* (*Jur*) distrainable (*form*), attachable (*form*). **der Fernseher ist nicht** ~ the bailiffs can't take the television.
Pfandbrief *m* (*von Bank, Regierung*) bond, debenture.
pfänden *vt* (*Jur*) to impound, to seize, to distrain upon (*form*). **man hat ihm die Möbel gepfändet** the bailiffs *or* they took away his furniture; **jdn** ~ to impound *or* seize some of sb's possessions; **jdn** ~ **lassen** to get the bailiffs onto sb.
Pfänderspiel *nt* (game of) forfeits.
Pfand-: ~**haus** *nt* pawnshop, pawnbroker's; ~**leihe** *f* (a) (*das Leihen*) pawnbroking; (b) (~*haus*) pawnshop, pawnbroker's; ~**leiher** *m* -s, - pawnbroker; ~**recht** *nt* right of distraint (*an* +*dat* upon) (*form*), lien (*an* +*dat* on) (*form*); **wenn du deine Miete nicht bezahlst, hat der Vermieter ein** ~**recht an deinen Möbeln** if you don't pay your rent the landlord is entitled to seize *or* impound your furniture; ~**schein** *m* pawn ticket.
Pfändung *f* seizure, distraint (*form*), attachment (*form*). **der Gerichtsvollzieher kam zur** ~ the bailiff came to seize *or* impound their possessions.
Pfändungs-: ~**befehl** *m*, ~**verfügung** *f* distress warrant.
Pfand-: ~**verkauf** *m* sale of pawned articles; ~**zettel** *m siehe* ~**schein**.
Pfanne *f* -, -n (*Cook*) pan; (*Anat*) socket; (*Dach*~) pantile; (*Zünd*~) pan. **ein paar Eier in die** ~ **schlagen** *or* **hauen** (*inf*) to bung a couple of eggs in the pan (*inf*), to fry up a couple of eggs;

jdn in die ~ **hauen** (sl) to do the dirty on sb (inf); (vernichtend schlagen) to wipe the floor with sb (inf), to give sb a thrashing (inf) or hammering (Brit sl); (ausschimpfen) to bawl sb out (inf), to give sb a bawling-out (inf).

Pfann(en)kuchen m pancake. Berliner ~ (jam) doughnut; wie ein ~ **aufgehen** (inf) to turn into or to get to be a real dumpling (inf) or roly-poly (inf).

Pfarr|amt nt priest's office.

Pfarrbezirk m, **Pfarre** f -, -n (old) parish.

Pfarrei f (Gemeinde) parish; (Amtsräume) priest's office.

Pfarrer(in f) m -s, - (katholisch, evangelisch) parish priest; (anglikanisch auch) vicar; (von Freikirchen) minister; (Gefängnis~, Militär~ etc) chaplain, padre. **guten Morgen, Herr ~!** good morning, (katholisch) Father or (evangelisch, anglikanisch) Vicar or (von Freikirchen) Mr ... or (Gefängnis etc) Padre; **als nächster wird Herr ~ Schmidt sprechen** the Reverend Michael Schmidt is going to speak next.

Pfarr-: ~**gemeinde** f siehe Pfarrei; ~**haus** nt (anglikanisch) vicarage; (methodistisch, Scot) manse; (katholisch) presbytery; ~**helfer(in** f) m curate; ~**kind** nt parishioner; ~**kirche** f parish church; ~**stelle** f parish, (church) living, benefice.

Pfau m -(e)s or -en, -en peacock. **er stolziert daher wie wie ein ~** he struts around like a peacock; **aufgedonnert wie ein ~** (inf) dressed or done up to the nines (inf).

Pfauen-: ~**auge** nt (Tag~) peacock butterfly; (Nacht~) peacock moth; ~**feder** f peacock feather; ~**henne** f peahen.

Pfeffer m -s, - pepper. ~ **und Salz** (lit) salt and pepper; (Stoffmuster) pepper-and-salt; **das brennt wie ~** that's red-hot; (Schmerz) that really stings; **er kann hingehen or bleiben, wo der ~ wächst!** (inf) he can go to hell (sl), I have a running jump (inf); **sie hat ~ im Hintern** (inf) or **Arsch** (vulg) she's got lots of get-up-and-go (inf).

Pfeffergurke f pickled gherkin.

pfeff(e)rig adj peppery.

Pfeffer-: ~**korn** nt peppercorn; ~**kuchen** m gingerbread; ~**kuchenhäuschen** nt gingerbread house.

Pfefferminz(bonbon) nt -es, -(e) peppermint.

Pfefferminze f -, no pl peppermint.

Pfefferminz(likör) m -es, -e crème de menthe.

Pfefferminz-: ~**plätzchen** nt peppermint; ~**tee** m peppermint tea.

Pfeffermühle f pepper-mill.

pfeffern vt (a) (Cook) to season with pepper, to pepper; siehe gepfeffert. (b) (inf: heftig werfen) to fling, to hurl; (hinauswerfen) to chuck out (inf), to sling out (inf). **jdm eine ~, jdm eine gepfefferte Ohrfeige geben** to give sb a clout (inf), to clout sb one (inf).

Pfeffer-: ~**nuß** f gingerbread ball; ~**strauch** m pepper (plant); ~**-und-Salz-Muster** nt pepper-and-salt (pattern).

Pfeifchen nt dim of Pfeife (b).

Pfeife f -, -n (a) whistle; (Quer~) fife (esp Mil), piccolo; (Bootsmanns~, Orgel~) pipe. **nach jds ~ tanzen** to dance to sb's tune. (b) (zum Rauchen) pipe. **eine ~ rauchen** to smoke or have a pipe; ~ **rauchen** to smoke a pipe. (c) (inf: Versager) wash-out (inf).

pfeifen pret **pfiff**, ptp **gepfiffen** vti to whistle (dat for); (auf einer Trillerpfeife) to blow one's whistle; (Mus: auf einer Pfeife spielen) to pipe; (inf) **Spiel** to ref (inf). **mit P~ und Trommeln zogen sie durch die Stadt** they made their way through the town amid piping and drumming or with pipes piping and drums beating; **auf dem letzten Loch ~** (inf) (erschöpft sein) to be on one's last legs (inf); (finanziell) to be on one's beam ends (inf); **der Wind pfeift aus einem anderen Loch** (inf) things are very different; **ich pfeife darauf!** (inf) I couldn't care less, I don't give a damn (inf); **ich pfeife auf seine Meinung** (inf) I couldn't care less about what he thinks; **das ~ ja schon die Spatzen von den Dächern** that's common knowledge, it's all over town; **ich werde dir was ~!** (inf) you've got another think coming! (inf); ~**der Atem** wheezing; **sein Atem ging ~d** his breath was coming in wheezes or wheezily.

Pfeifen-: ~**deckel** m pipe lid; ~**deckel!** (inf) not likely! (inf); ~**kopf** m bowl (of a pipe); ~**reiniger** m pipe-cleaner; ~**ständer** m pipe stand or rack; ~**stiel** m pipe stem; ~**stopfer** m tamper; ~**tabak** m pipe tobacco; ~**werk** nt pipes pl, pipework.

Pfeifer m -s, - piper, fifer (esp Mil).

Pfeiferei f (inf) whistling.

Pfeif-: ~**kessel** m whistling kettle; ~**konzert** nt barrage or hail of catcalls or whistles; ~**ton** m whistle, whistling sound or tone; ~**topf** m siehe ~kessel.

Pfeil m -s, -e arrow; (bei Armbrust auch) bolt; (Wurf~) dart. ~ **und Bogen** bow and arrow; **die ~e seine Spotts** (liter) the barbs of his mockery; **alle seine ~e verschossen haben** (fig) to have run out of arguments, to have shot one's bolt; **Amors ~ Cupid's arrow** or dart; **er schoß wie ein ~ davon** he was off like a shot.

Pfeiler m -s, - (lit, fig) pillar; (Brücken~ auch) pier; (von Hängebrücke) pylon; (Stütz~) buttress.

Pfeil-: ~**flügel** m sweptback wing; **p~förmig** adj arrow-shaped, V-shaped; **p~förmig angeordnet** arranged in the shape of an arrow or in a V; **p~förmige Tragflügel** sweptback or V-shaped wings; **p~gerade** adj as straight as a die; **eine ~gerade Linie** a dead-straight line; **sie kam p~gerade auf uns zu** she made a beeline for us, she headed straight for us; **der Vogel flog p~gerade von einem Baum zum nächsten** the bird flew straight as an arrow from one tree to the next; **p~geschwind** adj siehe p~schnell; ~**gift** nt arrow poison; ~**köcher** m quiver; **p~schnell** adj as quick as lightning, as swift as an arrow (liter); **er startete p~schnell** he was off like a shot; ~**schuß** m arrowshot; **durch einen ~schuß getötet** killed by an arrow; **einen ~schuß abgeben** to shoot an arrow, to let loose an arrow; ~**schütze** m bowman, archer; ~**spitze** f

arrowhead, tip of an arrow; ~**wurfspiel** nt darts pl; ~**wurz** f arrowroot no pl.

Pfennig m -s, -e or (nach Zahlenangabe) - pfennig (one hundredth of a mark). **30 ~ 30 pfennigs; er hat keinen ~ Geld** he hasn't got a penny to his name or two pennies to rub together or a dime (US); **es ist keinen ~ wert** (fig) it's not worth a thing or a red cent (US); **dem/dafür gebe ich keinen ~** (lit) I won't give him/it a penny; **für ihn gibt der Arzt keinen ~ mehr** (fig inf) the doctor doesn't give much for his chances (inf); **für seine Chancen/Gesundheit etc gebe ich keinen ~** I don't give much for his chances (inf), I wouldn't put much money on his chances (inf); **nicht für fünf ~** (inf) not the slightest (bit of); **er hat nicht für fünf ~ Anstand/Verstand** (inf) he hasn't an ounce of respectability/intelligence; **das interessiert mich nicht für fünf ~** (inf) that doesn't interest me in the slightest; **auf den ~ sehen** (fig) to watch or count every penny; **mit dem or jedem ~ rechnen müssen** (fig) to have to watch or count every penny; **jeden ~ (dreimal) umdrehen** (fig inf) to think twice about every penny one spends; **wer den ~ nicht ehrt, ist des Talers nicht wert** (Prov) take care of the pennies, and the pounds will look after themselves (Prov); siehe Heller.

Pfennig-: ~**absatz** m stiletto heel; ~**betrag** m (amount in) pence or pennies; **es war nur ein ~betrag** it was only a matter of pence or pennies; ~**fuchser** m -s, - (inf) skinflint (inf), miser (inf); **p~groß** adj **ein p~großes Geschwür** a boil the size of a sixpence; ~**stück** nt pfennig (piece); **p~weise** adv penny by penny, one penny at a time; siehe Groschen.

Pferch m -es, -e fold, pen.

pferchen vt to cram, to pack.

Pferd nt -(e)s, -e (Tier, Turngerät) horse; (Reit~ auch) mount; (beim Schachspiel) knight, horse (US inf). **zu ~e** on horseback; **aufs falsche/richtige ~ setzen** (lit, fig) to back the wrong/right horse; **die ~e gehen ihm leicht durch** (fig) he flies off the handle easily (inf); **immer langsam or sachte mit den jungen ~en** (inf) hold your horses (inf); **wie ein ~ arbeiten** (inf) to work like a Trojan; **das hält ja kein ~ aus** (inf) it's more than flesh and blood can stand; **keine zehn ~e brächten mich dahin** (inf) wild horses wouldn't drag me there; **mit ihm kann man ~e stehlen** (inf), **er ist ein Kerl zum ~e stehlen** (inf) he's a great sport (inf); **er ist unser bestes ~ im Stall** he's our best man.

Pferde-: ~**apfel** m piece of horse-dung; ~**äpfel** horse-droppings pl or dung no pl; ~**bahn** f horse-drawn tram, horsecar (US); **p~bespannt** adj horse-drawn; ~**bremse** f horsefly; ~**decke** f horse blanket; ~**dieb** m horse thief; ~**droschke** f hackney-cab; ~**fleisch** nt horsemeat or -flesh; ~**fliege** f siehe ~bremse; ~**fuhrwerk** nt horse and cart; ~**fuß** m (fig: des Teufels) cloven hoof; **die Sache hat aber einen ~fuß** there's just one snag; ~**gebiß** nt horsey mouth or teeth; ~**geschirr** nt harness no pl; ~**gesicht** nt horsey face, face like a horse; ~**haar** nt horsehair; ~**händler** m horse dealer; ~**huf** m horse's hoof; ~**knecht** m groom; ~**koppel** f paddock; ~**kur** f (fig) siehe Roßkur; ~**länge** f length; ~**rennbahn** f race course or track; ~**rennen** nt (Sportart) (horse-)racing; (einzelnes Rennen) (horse-)race; ~**schlachter** m knacker; ~**schlachterei** f knacker's; ~**schlitten** m horse-drawn sleigh; ~**schwanz** m horse's tail; (Frisur) pony-tail; ~**sport** m equestrian sport; ~**stall** m stable; ~**stärke** f horse power no pl, hp abbr; ~**wagen** m (für Personen) horse and carriage, trap, horse-buggy (US); (für Lasten) horse and cart; ~**zucht** f horse breeding; (Gestüt) stud-farm; ~**züchter** m horse breeder.

pfiff pret of pfeifen.

Pfiff m -s, -e (a) whistle; (Theat auch) catcall. (b) (Reiz) flair, style. **der Soße fehlt noch der letzte ~** the sauce still needs that extra something; **einem Kleid den richtigen ~ geben** to add flair to a dress, to give a dress real style. (c) (inf: Trick) **jetzt hast du den ~ heraus** you've got the knack or hang of it now (inf); **das ist ein Ding mit 'nem ~** there's a special knack to it.

Pfifferling m chanterelle. **er kümmert sich keinen ~ um seine Kinder** (inf) he doesn't give or care a fig or give a damn about his children (inf); **keinen ~ wert** (inf) not worth a thing.

pfiffig adj smart, sharp, cute.

Pfiffigkeit f sharpness, cuteness.

Pfiffikus m - or -ses, -se (dated) crafty thing (inf).

Pfingsten nt -, - Whitsun, Pentecost (Eccl). **zu or an ~** at Whitsun.

Pfingst-: ~**ferien** pl Whit(sun) holiday(s); ~**fest** nt siehe Pfingsten.

pfingstlich adj no pred Whit(sun) attr. **die Wiesen sehen schon ~ aus** the fields have taken on a spring-time look; **die Kirche ~ schmücken** to decorate the church for Whitsun.

Pfingst-: ~**montag** m Whit Monday; ~**ochse** m: **herausgeputzt wie ein ~ochse** (inf) dressed or done up to the nines (inf); ~**rose** f peony; ~**sonntag** m Whit Sunday, Pentecost (Eccl); ~**woche** f Whit week; ~**zeit** f Whitsun(tide).

Pfirsich m -s, -e peach.

Pfirsich-: ~**baum** m peach tree; ~**blüte** f peach blossom; **p~farben** adj peach(-coloured); ~**haut** f (lit) peach skin; (fig) peaches-and-cream complexion.

Pflanze f -, -n (a) (Gewächs) plant. (b) (inf: Mensch) **du bist vielleicht eine ~!** you're a fine or right one! (inf); **er/sie ist eine komische or seltsame ~** he/she is an odd bird (inf); **eine Berliner ~** (dated) a typical Berlin lass.

pflanzen 1 vt to plant. **einem Kind etw ins Herz ~** (liter) to implant sth in the heart of a child (liter). 2 vr (inf) to plant (inf) or plonk (inf) oneself.

Pflanzen-: ~**butter** f vegetable butter; ~**farbstoff** m vegetable dye; ~**faser** f plant fibre; ~**fett** nt vegetable fat; **p~fressend** adj attr herbivorous; ~**fresser** m herbivore; ~**kost** f vegetable

foodstuffs pl; ~kunde, ~lehre f botany; ~margarine f vegetable margarine; ~öl nt vegetable oil; ~reich nt vegetable
kingdom; ~schädling m pest; garden pest; ~schutz m protection of plants; (gegen Ungeziefer) pest control; ~schutzmittel
nt pesticide; ~welt f plant world; die ~welt des Mittelmeers
the plant life or the flora of the Mediterranean.

Pflanzer(in f) m -s, - planter.

Pflanzkartoffel f seed potato.

pflanzlich adj attr vegetable.

Pflänzling m seedling.

Pflanzung f (das Pflanzen) planting; (Plantage) plantation.

Pflaster nt -s, - **(a)** (Heft~) (sticking-)plaster; (fig:
Entschädigung) sop (auf + acc to). das ~ erneuern to put on a
fresh or new (piece of) (sticking-)plaster.
(b) (Straßen~) (road) surface; (Kopfstein~) cobbles pl. ~
treten (inf) to trudge the streets, to trudge or traipse around;
ein gefährliches or heißes ~ (inf) a dangerous place; ein teures
~ (inf) a pricey place (inf).

Pflasterer m -s, - road worker.

pflastermüde adj (inf) dead on one's feet (inf).

pflastern vt (a) Straße, Hof to surface; (mit Kopfsteinpflaster)
to cobble; (mit Steinplatten) to pave. eine Straße neu ~ to
resurface a road; siehe Vorsatz. **(b)** (inf: ohrfeigen) jdm eine ~
to sock sb (one) (inf); du kriegst gleich eine gepflastert I'll sock
you one in a minute (inf).

Pflasterstein m (Kopfstein) cobble(stone); (Steinplatte)
paving stone, flagstone; (inf: Pfefferkuchen) gingerbread.

Pflasterung f surfacing; (mit Kopfsteinpflaster) cobbling;
(mit Steinplatten) paving; (Pflaster) surface; (Kopfsteinpflaster) cobbles pl; (Steinplatten) paving no pl.

Pflaume f -, -n **(a)** plum. getrocknete ~ prune. **(b)** (inf:
Mensch) dope (inf), twit (Brit inf). **(c)** (vulg) cunt (vulg).

pflaumen vi (inf) to tease, to kid (inf).

Pflaumen-: ~baum m plum(tree); ~kern m plum stone;
~kompott nt stewed plums pl; ~kuchen m plum tart; ~mus nt
plum jam; p~weich adj (inf) soft; (pej) Haltung spineless; die
Knie wurden ihm p~weich his knees turned to jelly.

Pflege f -, no pl care; (von Kranken auch) nursing; (von Garten
auch) attention; (von Beziehungen, Künsten) fostering,
cultivation; (von Maschinen, Gebäuden) maintenance, upkeep.
jdn/etw in ~ nehmen to look after sb/sth; jdn/etw in ~ geben to
have sb/sth looked after; sie gaben den Hund bei den Nachbarn
in ~ they gave their dog to the neighbours to look after; ein
Kind in ~ nehmen (dauernd) to foster a child; ein Kind in ~
geben to have a child fostered; (von Behörden) to foster a child
out (zu jdm with sb); die ~ von jdm/etw übernehmen to look
after sb/sth; Katzen brauchen kaum/viel ~ cats hardly need
any looking after/need a lot of looking after; der Garten/der
Kranke braucht viel ~ the garden/sick man needs a lot of care
and attention; das Kind/der Hund hat bei uns gute ~ the
child/dog is well looked after or cared for by us; jdm gute ~
angedeihen lassen to take good care of sb, to look after sb well.

Pflege-: p~bedürftig adj in need of care (and attention); wenn
alte Leute p~bedürftig werden when old people start to need
looking after; ~eltern pl foster parents pl; ~fall m case for
nursing; ~geld nt (für ~kinder) boarding-out allowance; (für
Kranke) attendance allowance; ~heim nt nursing home;
~kind nt foster child; p~leicht adj easy-care; ~mutter f foster
mother.

pflegen 1 vt to look after, to care for; Kranke auch to nurse;
Garten, Blumen, Rasen auch to tend; Haar, Bart auch to
groom; Beziehungen, Kunst, Freundschaft to foster, to cultivate; Maschinen, Gebäude, Denkmäler to maintain, to keep up.
etw regelmäßig ~ to attend to sth regularly, to pay regular
attention to sth; siehe gepflegt, Umgang.
2 vi (a) (gewöhnlich tun) to be in the habit (zu of), to be accustomed (zu to). sie pflegte zu sagen she used to say, she was in
the habit of saying; zum Mittagessen pflegt er Bier zu trinken
he's in the habit of drinking beer with his lunch, he usually
drinks beer with his lunch; wie es so zu gehen pflegt as usually
happens; wie man zu sagen pflegt as they say.
(b) der Ruhe (gen) ~ (old) to take a rest; mit jdm Rat(s) ~
(obs) to take counsel with sb (old).
3 vr (a) to care about one's appearance.
(b) (sich schonen) to take it or things easy (inf).

Pfleger m -s, - (im Krankenhaus) orderly; (voll qualifiziert)
(male) nurse; (Vormund) guardian; (Nachlaß~) trustee.

Pflegerin f nurse.

pflegerisch adj nursing. der Fall kann nur ~ behandelt
werden it's a case for terminal care.

Pflege-: ~satz m hospital and nursing charges pl; ~sohn m
foster son; ~station f nursing ward; ~tochter f foster
daughter; ~vater m foster father.

pfleglich adj careful. etw ~ behandeln to treat sth carefully or
with care.

Pflegling m foster child; (Mündel) ward.

Pflegschaft f (Vormundschaft) guardianship, tutelage (form);
(Vermögens~) trusteeship.

Pflicht f -, -en **(a)** (Verpflichtung) duty. ich habe die traurige ~
... it is my sad duty ...; als Abteilungsleiter hat er die ~, ... it's his
duty or responsibility as head of department ...; Rechte und
~en rights and responsibilities; seine ~ erfüllen to do one's
duty; der ~ gehorchen (geh) to obey the call of duty; jdn in die
~ nehmen to remind sb of his duty; eheliche ~en conjugal or
marital duties; die bürgerlichen ~en one's civic duties or
responsibilities; die ~ ruft duty calls; ich habe es mir zur ~
gemacht I've taken it upon myself, I've made it my duty; ich tue
nur meine ~ I'm only doing my duty; etw nur aus ~ tun to do
sth merely because one has to; das/Schulbesuch ist ~ you have
to do that/to go to school, it's/going to school is compulsory; es

ist seine (verdammte inf) ~ und Schuldigkeit(, das zu tun)
he damn well or jolly well ought to (do it) (inf).
(b) (Sport) compulsory section or exercises pl. bei der ~ in
the compulsory section or exercises.

Pflicht-: ~begriff m concept of duty; ~besuch m duty visit;
p~bewußt adj conscientious, conscious of one's duties; er ist
sehr p~bewußt he takes his duties very seriously, he has a
great sense of duty; ~bewußtsein nt sense of duty; ~eifer m
zeal; p~eifrig adj zealous.

Pflichtenkreis m duties pl.

Pflicht-: ~erfüllung f fulfilment of one's duty; sein ganzes
Leben war Arbeit und ~erfüllung he spent his whole life
working and in the fulfilment of his duties; ~exemplar nt
deposit copy; ~fach nt compulsory subject; Deutsch ist ~fach
German is compulsory or is a compulsory subject; ~gefühl nt
siehe ~bewußtsein; p~gemäß adj dutiful; ich teile Ihnen
p~gemäß mit it is my duty to inform you; p~getreu adj dutiful;
~jahr nt a year's compulsory community service for girls
during Nazi period; ~kür f compulsory exercise; ~lauf m
(Eiskunstlauf) compulsory figures pl; ~lektüre f compulsory
reading; (Sch auch) set book(s); ~mitglied nt statutory
member; p~schuldig adj dutiful; ~teil m or nt legal portion;
p~treu adj dutiful; ~treue f devotion to duty; ~übung f
compulsory exercise; p~vergessen adj irresponsible;
~vergessenheit f neglect of duty, irresponsibility;
~verletzung f breach of duty; ~versäumnis f neglect or
dereliction of duty no pl; er machte sich häufiger
~versäumnisse schuldig he was frequently guilty of neglecting his duties; p~versichert adj compulsorily insured;
~versicherte(r) mf compulsorily insured person;
~versicherung f compulsory insurance; ~verteidiger m
counsel for the defence appointed by the court and paid from
the legal aid fund; ~vorlesung f compulsory lecture; p~widrig
adj contrary to duty; er hat sich p~widrig verhalten he
behaved in a manner contrary to (his) duty.

Pflock m -(e)s, -e peg; (für Tiere) stake. einen ~ or ein paar ~e
zurückstecken (fig) to back-pedal a bit.

pflücken vt to pick, to pluck; (sammeln) to pick.

Pflücker(in f) m -s, - picker.

Pflug m -es, -e plough, plow (US). unter dem ~ under the
plough.

pflügen vti (lit, fig) to plough, to plow (US); (lit auch) to till
(liter). das Schiff pflügte die Wellen (liter) the ship ploughed
(through) the waves.

Pflüger m -s, - ploughman, plowman (US).

Pflug-: ~schar f -, -en ploughshare, plowshare (US); ~stellung
f (Ski) snowplough or snowplow (US) position; ~sterz m
plough-handle, plow-handle (US).

Pfortader f portal vein.

Pforte f -, -n (Tor) gate; (Geog) gap. das Theater hat seine ~n
für immer geschlossen the theatre has closed its doors for
good; Nepal, die ~ zum Himalaya Nepal, the gateway to the
Himalayas; die ~n des Himmels (liter) the gates or portals
(liter) of Heaven.

Pförtner m -s, - (Anat) pylorus.

Pförtner(in f) m -s, - porter; (von Fabrik) gateman; (von
Wohnhaus, Behörde) doorman; (von Schloß) gatekeeper.

Pförtnerloge [-lo:ʒə] f porter's office; (in Fabrik) gatehouse;
(in Wohnhaus, Büro) doorman's office.

Pfosten m -s, - post; (senkrechter Balken) upright; (Fenster~)
jamb; (Tür~) jamb, doorpost; (Stütze) support, prop; (Ftbl)
(goal)post, upright.

Pfostenschuß m (Ftbl) das war nur ein ~ it hit the (goal)post
upright.

Pfötchen nt dim of **Pfote** little paw. (gib) ~! shake hands!

Pfote f -, -n **(a)** paw.
(b) (inf: Hand) mitt (inf), paw (inf). sich (dat) die ~n verbrennen (inf) to burn one's fingers; seine ~n überall drin haben
(fig inf) to have a finger in every pie (inf).
(c) (inf: schlechte Handschrift) scribble, scrawl. er hat vielleicht eine ~ he's got a terrible scribble or scrawl.

Pfriem m -(e)s, -e awl.

Pfropf m -(e)s, -e or ~e, **Pfropfen** m -s, - (Stöpsel) stopper;
(Kork, Sekt~) cork; (Watte~ etc) plug; (von Faß, Korbflasche)
bung; (Med: Blut~) (blood) clot; (verstopfend) blockage. er hat
einen ~ im Ohr his ears are bunged up (inf) or blocked up.

pfropfen vt (a) Pflanzen to graft. **(b)** (verschließen) Flasche to
bung. **(c)** (inf: hineinzwängen) to cram. er pfropfte den Korken
in die Flasche he shoved the cork in the bottle (inf); gepfropft
voll jam-packed (inf), crammed full.

Pfröpfling m graft, scion.

Pfropf-: ~messer nt grafting knife; ~reis nt graft, scion.

Pfründe f -, -n (Kirchenamt) (church) living, benefice; (Einkünfte auch) prebend; (fig) sinecure.

Pfuhl m -s, -e (liter) mudhole; (fig) (quag)mire, slough (liter).

Pfühl m or nt -(e)s, -e (poet, dial) (Kissen) pillow; (weiches
Bett) downy or feather bed.

pfui interj (Ekel) ugh, yuck; (Mißbilligung) tut tut; (zu Hunden)
oy, hey; (Buhruf) boo. faß das nicht an, das ist ~ (inf) don't
touch it, it's dirty or nasty; ~ Teufel or Deibel or Spinne (all inf)
ugh, yuck; ~ schäme dich shame on you!; ~ über sein
Benehmen/ihn his behaviour/he is an absolute disgrace; da
kann ich nur ~ sagen it's simply disgraceful.

Pfuiruf m boo.

Pfund nt -(e)s, -e or (nach Zahlenangabe) - **(a)** (Gewicht) (in
Deutschland) 500 grams, half a kilo(gram); (in England) pound.
drei ~ Äpfel three pounds of apples; er bewegte seine
~e mit Mühe he moved his great bulk with effort.
(b) (Währungseinheit) pound. in ~ in pounds; zwanzig ~
Sterling twenty pounds sterling; das ~ sinkt sterling/the pound

is falling; **mit seinem ~e wuchern** (*liter*) to make the most of one's opportunities *or* chances.

Pfund- in *cpds* pound; **~betrag** *m* amount in pounds, sterling sum.

-pfünder *m* **-s, -** in *cpds* -pounder; (*Brot*) -pound loaf.

pfundig *adj* (*dated inf*) great *no adv*, fantastic, swell *no adv* (*US*). **das hast du ~ gemacht** you've made a great job of that.

-pfündig *adj suf* -pound.

Pfunds- in *cpds* (*inf*) great (*inf*), swell (*US inf*), super (*inf*); **~kerl** *m* (*inf*) great guy (*inf*).

pfundweise *adv* by the pound.

Pfusch *m* **-(e)s,** *no pl* (*inf*) *siehe* **Pfuscherei.**

Pfusch|arbeit *f* (*inf*) slapdash work. **sie haben richtige ~ geleistet** they did a really sloppy job (*inf*).

pfuschen *vi* (a) to bungle; (*einen Fehler machen*) to slip up, to come unstuck (*inf*). **jdm ins Handwerk ~** to poke one's nose into *or* meddle in sb's affairs. (b) (*Sch*) to cheat.

Pfuscher(in *f*) *m* **-s, -** (*inf*) bungler, botcher (*inf*).

Pfuscherei *f* (*das Pfuschen*) bungling *no pl*; (*gepfuschte Arbeit*) botch-up (*inf*), botched-up job.

Pfütze *f* **-, -n** puddle.

PH [peː'haː] *f* **-, -s** *abbr of* **Pädagogische Hochschule.**

Phalanx *f* **-, Phalangen** (*Hist*) phalanx; (*fig*) battery.

Phallen, Phalli *pl of* **Phallus.**

phallisch *adj* phallic.

Phallus *m* **-, -se** *or* **Phalli** *or* **Phallen** phallus.

Phallus-: **~kult** *m* phallus worship; **~symbol** *nt* phallic symbol.

Phänomen *nt* **-s, -e** phenomenon. **dieser Mensch ist ein ~** this person is phenomenal *or* is an absolute phenomenon.

phänomenal *adj* phenomenal.

Phänomenologie *f* phenomenology.

Phänotyp *m* **-s, -en** phenotype.

Phantasie *f* (a) *no pl* (*Einbildung*) imagination. **er hat ~** he's got imagination; **eine schmutzige ~ haben** to have a dirty mind; **in seiner ~** in his mind *or* imagination; **er spielt ohne ~** he plays unimaginatively *or* without any imagination. (b) *usu pl* (*Trugbild*) fantasy.

Phantasie-: **p~arm** *adj* unimaginative, lacking in imagination; **p~begabt** *adj* imaginative; **~bild** *nt* fantasy (picture); **~blume** *f* imaginary flower; **~gebilde** *nt* (a) (*phantastische Form*) fantastic form; (b) (*Einbildung*) figment of the *or* one's imagination; **p~los** *adj* unimaginative, lacking in imagination; **~losigkeit** *f* lack of imagination, unimaginativeness; **p~reich** *adj siehe* **p~voll.**

phantasieren* 1 *vi* to fantasize (*von* about); (*von Schlimmem*) to have visions (*von* of); (*Med*) to be delirious; (*Mus*) to improvise. **sie phantasiert von einer neuen Puppe** she's dreaming about a new doll; **er phantasiert von einem großen Haus auf dem Lande** he has fantasies about a big house in the country.
2 *vt* **Geschichte** to dream up; (*Mus*) to improvise. **was phantasierst du denn da?** (*inf*) what are you (going) on about? (*inf*); **er hat das alles phantasiert** that's all just (in) his imagination; **er phantasiert, daß die Welt untergeht** he has visions of the world coming to an end; **sie phantasiert, daß sie auswandern will** she indulges in fantasies of *or* fantasizes about wanting to emigrate.

Phantasie-: **p~voll** *adj* highly imaginative; **~vorstellung** *f* figment of the imagination.

Phantast *m* **-en, -en** dreamer, visionary.

Phantasterei *f* fantasy.

phantastisch *adj* fantastic; (*unglaublich auch*) incredible.

Phantom *nt* **-s, -e** (a) (*Trugbild*) phantom. **einem ~ nachjagen** (*fig*) to tilt at windmills. (b) (*Modell*) (*für Unterricht*) anatomical model, manikin; (*beim Fechten*) dummy.

Phantomschmerz *m* phantom limb pain.

Pharao *m* **-s, Pharaonen** Pharaoh.

Pharaonen- in *cpds* of the Pharaohs.

Pharisäer *m* **-s, -** (*Hist*) pharisee; (*fig auch*) hypocrite.

pharisäerhaft, pharisäisch *adj* pharisaic(al); (*fig auch*) holier-than-thou, self-righteous.

Pharisäertum *nt* (*fig*) self-righteousness.

pharm. *abbr of* **pharmazeutisch.**

Pharmakologe *m*, **Pharmakologin** *f* pharmacologist.

Pharmakologie *f* pharmacology.

pharmakologisch *adj* pharmacological.

Pharmazeut(in *f*) *m* **-en, -en** pharmacist, druggist (*US*).

Pharmazeutik *f siehe* **Pharmazie.**

pharmazeutisch *adj* pharmaceutical.

Pharmazie *f* pharmacy, pharmaceutics *sing*.

Phase *f* **-, -n** phase.

Phasen-: **p~gleich** *adj* in phase; **~gleichheit** *f* phase coincidence; **~spannung** *f* voltage to neutral, phase voltage; **~verschiebung** *f* phase difference *or* displacement.

-phasig *adj suf* -phase.

Philanthrop *m* **-en, -en** philanthropist.

Philanthropie *f* philanthropy.

philanthropisch *adj* philanthropic(al).

Philatelie *f* philately.

Philatelist(in *f*) *m* philatelist.

philatelistisch *adj* philatelic.

Philharmonie *f* (*Orchester*) philharmonia, philharmonic (orchestra); (*Konzertsaal*) philharmonic hall.

Philharmoniker *m* **-s, -** (*Musiker*) member of a philharmonic orchestra. **die ~** the philharmonic (orchestra).

philharmonisch *adj* philharmonic.

Philippika *f* **-, Philippiken** (*Hist*) Philippic; (*fig*) philippic.

Philippine *m* **-n, -n, Philippino** *f* Filipino.

Philippinen *pl* Philippines *pl*, Philippine Islands *pl*.

philippinisch *adj* Philippine.

Philister *m* **-s, -** (*lit*) Philistine; (*fig*) philistine.

philisterhaft *adj* (*fig*) philistine. **sich ~ verhalten** to behave like a philistine.

Philologe *m*, **Philologin** *f* philologist.

Philologie *f* philology.

philologisch *adj* philological.

Philosoph *m* **-en, -en** philosopher.

Philosophie *f* philosophy.

philosophieren* *vi* to philosophize (*über* +*acc* about).

philosophisch *adj* philosophical.

Phimose *f* **-, -n** phimosis.

Phiole *f* **-, -n** phial, vial.

Phlegma *nt* **-s,** *no pl* apathy, torpor, torpidity.

Phlegmatiker(in *f*) *m* **-s, -** apathetic person.

Phlegmatikus *m* **-, -se** (*inf*) apathetic so-and-so (*inf*).

phlegmatisch *adj* apathetic.

Phlox [floks] *m* **-es, -e** *or f* **-, -e** phlox.

Phobie [foˈbiː] *f* phobia (*vor* about).

Phon [foːn] *nt* **-s, -s** phon.

Phonem *nt* **-s, -e** phoneme.

Phonetik *f* phonetics *sing*.

Phonetiker(in *f*) *m* **-s, -** phonetician.

phonetisch *adj* phonetic. **~e Schrift** phonetic transcription *or* script; **etw ~ schreiben** to write *or* transcribe sth phonetically *or* in phonetics.

Phönix *m* **-(es), -e** phoenix. **wie ein ~ aus der Asche steigen** to rise like a phoenix from the ashes.

Phönizier(in *f*) [-iɐ, -iərɪn] *m* **-s, -** Phoenician.

phönizisch *adj* Phoenician.

Phonograph *m* phonograph.

Phonologie *f* phonology.

phonologisch *adj* phonological.

Phonotypistin *f* audio-typist.

Phon-: **p~stark** *adj Lautsprecher* powerful; *Lärm* loud; **~zahl** *f* decibel level.

Phosphat [fɔsˈfaːt] *nt* phosphate.

Phosphor [ˈfɔsfɔr] *m* **-s,** *no pl* phosphorus.

Phosphoreszenz *f* phosphorescence.

phosphoreszieren* *vi* to phosphoresce.

phosphorhaltig *adj* phosphorous.

phosphorig *adj* **~e Säure** phosphorous acid.

Phosphor-: **~säure** *f* phosphoric acid; **~vergiftung** *f* phosphorus poisoning.

phot. *abbr of* **photographisch.**

Photo¹ *nt* **-s, -s** photo(graph), snap(shot) (*inf*). **ein ~ machen** to take a photo(graph); *siehe auch* **Foto¹.**

Photo² *m* **-s, -s** (*inf*) camera.

Photo- in *cpds* photo; *siehe auch* Foto-; **~album** *nt* photograph album; **~amateur** *m* amateur photographer; **~apparat** *m* camera; **~arbeiten** *pl* photographic work; **~archiv** *nt* photo archives *pl*; **~artikel** *pl* photographic equipment; **~atelier** *nt* (photographic) studio; **~chemie** *f* photochemistry; **p~elektrisch** *adj* photoelectric.

photogen *adj* photogenic.

Photogeschäft *nt* photographic shop.

Photograph *m* photographer.

Photographie *f* (a) photography. (b) (*Bild*) photo(graph), snap(shot) (*inf*).

photographieren* 1 *vt* to photograph, to take a photo(graph) of. **sich ~ lassen** to have one's photo(graph) *or* picture taken; **sie läßt sich gut ~** she photographs well, she comes out well in photos. 2 *vi* to take photos *or* photographs.

Photographin *f* photographer.

photographisch 1 *adj* photographic. 2 *adv* photographically.

Photo-: **~industrie** *f* photographic industry; **~kopie** *f* photocopy; **~kopierautomat** *m*, **~kopierer** (*inf*) *m* **-s, -** photocopying machine, photocopier; **p~kopieren*** *vt insep* to photocopy, to make a photocopy of; **~laborant(in** *f*) *m* photographic lab(oratory) assistant; **p~mechanisch** *adj* photomechanical; **~montage** *f* photomontage.

Photon *nt* **-s, -en** photon.

Photo-: **~reporter** *m* press photographer; **~synthese** *f* photosynthesis; **p~trop** *adj* phototropic; **~zeitschrift** *f* photographic magazine; **~zelle** *f* photoelectric cell.

Phrase *f* **-, -n** phrase; (*pej*) empty *or* hollow phrase. **abgedroschene ~** cliché, hackneyed phrase; **das sind alles nur ~n** that's just (so many) words, that's just talk; **leere** *or* **hohle ~n** empty *or* hollow words *or* phrases; **~n dreschen** (*inf*) to churn out one cliché after another.

Phrasen-: **~drescher** *m* (*pej*) windbag; **~drescherei** *f* (*pej*) phrase-mongering; (*Geschwafel*) hot air, **p~haft** *adj* empty, hollow; **er drückt sich p~haft aus** he speaks in empty phrases; **p~reich** *adj* cliché-ridden.

Phraseologie *f* phraseology; (*Buch*) dictionary of idioms.

phraseologisch *adj* phraseological. **~es Wörterbuch** dictionary of idioms.

phrasieren* *vt* to phrase.

Phrasierung *f* phrasing.

Physik *f* **-,** *no pl* physics *sing*.

physikalisch *adj* physical. **~e Experimente durchführen** to carry out physics experiments *or* experiments in physics; **das ist ~ nicht erklärbar** that can't be explained by physics; **~e Therapie** physiotherapy, physical therapy.

Physiker(in *f*) *m* **-s, -** physicist; (*Student auch*) physics student.

Physiksaal *m* physics lab *or* laboratory.

Physikum *nt* **-s,** *no pl* (*Univ*) preliminary examination in medicine.

Physiognomie [fyziɔgnoˈmiː] *f* (*liter*) physiognomy.

physiognomisch [fyziɔˈgnoːmɪʃ] *adj* physiognomical.

Physiologe *m*, **Physiologin** *f* physiologist.

Physiologie f physiology.
physiologisch adj physiological.
Physiotherapeut m physiotherapist.
Physiotherapie f physiotherapy, physical therapy.
physisch adj physical.
Pi nt -(s), -s pi.
Pianino nt -s, -s pianino, cottage or piccolo piano.
Pianist(in f) m pianist.
Piano nt -s, -s (geh: Klavier) piano.
Pianoforte nt -s, -s pianoforte.
picheln vi (inf) to booze (inf), to knock it back (inf).
Picke f -, -n pick(axe).
Pickel m -s, - (a) spot, pimple. (b) (Spitzhacke) pick(axe); (Eis~) ice axe.
Pickelhaube f spiked (leather) helmet.
pick(e)lig adj spotty, pimply.
picken vti to peck (nach at).
Picknick nt -s, -s or -e picnic. zum ~ fahren to go for a picnic; ~ machen to have a picnic.
picknicken vi to (have a) picnic.
picobello, pikobello adj (inf) immaculate, impeccable. ein Zimmer ~ aufräumen to make a room look immaculate.
Piefke m -s, -s (a) (Aus inf: Deutscher) Kraut (inf), Jerry (inf). (b) ein kleiner ~ a (little) pipsqueak.
pieken, piken, pieksen, piksen vti (inf) to prick. es hat nur ein bißchen gepiekt it was just a bit of a prick, I/he etc just felt a bit of a prick.
piekfein, pikfein adj (inf) posh (inf), swish (inf).
pieksauber adj (inf) spotless, clean as a whistle or a new penny.
pieksen vti siehe pieken.
piep interj tweet(-tweet), chirp(-chirp), cheep(-cheep). er traute sich nicht mal ~ zu sagen or machen (inf) he wouldn't have dared (to) say boo to a goose (inf).
Piep m -s, -e (inf) er sagt keinen ~ he doesn't say a (single) word; keinen ~ mehr machen to have had it (inf); du hast ja einen ~! you're off your head (inf).
piepe, piep|egal adj pred (inf) all one (inf). das ist mir ~! (inf) I couldn't care less (inf), it's all one to me (inf).
piepen, piepsen vi (Vogel) to cheep, to chirrup; (Kinderstimme) to pipe, to squeak; (Maus) to squeak; (Funkgerät etc) to bleep. bei dir piept's wohl! (inf) are you off your head?; es war zum P~! (inf) it was a scream (inf); mit ~der Stimme in a piping voice.
Piepen pl (dated sl) lolly (inf), dough (sl).
Piepmatz m (baby-talk: Vogel) dickybird (baby-talk); (Kind) tiny tot. du kleiner ~ you little rascal.
piepsen vi siehe piepen.
piepsig adj (inf) squeaky.
Piepvogel m (baby-talk) dickybird (baby-talk).
Pier m -s, -e or -s or f -, -s jetty, pier.
Pierrot [pie'ro:] m -s, -s Pierrot.
piesacken vt (inf) (quälen) to torment; (belästigen) to pester. er piesackt mich schon den ganzen Tag, daß ich ihn mitnehme he's been pestering me all day to take him with me.
Piesepampel m -s, - (inf) square (inf).
Pietà [pie'ta] f -, -s pietà.
Pietät [pie'tɛ:t] f (Ehrfurcht vor den Toten) reverence no pl; (Achtung) respect (gegenüber jdm/etw, vor etw (dat) for sb/sth); (Frömmelei) piety. das verstößt gegen jede ~ that goes against every feeling of respect or sense of reverence.
pietätlos [pie'tɛ:t-] adj irreverent, lacking in respect, impious.
Pietätlosigkeit [pie'tɛ:t-] f irreverence, impiety; (Tat) impious act. bei einer Beerdigung eine Zigarette zu rauchen, ist eine grobe ~ to smoke a cigarette at a funeral shows a complete lack of reverence.
pietätvoll [pie'tɛ:t-] adj pious, reverent.
Pietismus [pie'tɪsmʊs] m Pietism; (pej) pietism, piety, piousness.
Pietist(in f) [pie'tɪst(ɪn)] m Pietist; (pej auch) holy Joe (inf).
pietistisch [pie'tɪstɪʃ] adj pietistic; (pej auch) pious.
piff paff interj bang bang, pow pow (inf).
Pigment nt pigment.
Pigmentation f pigmentation.
Pigmentfleck m pigmentation mark.
pigmentieren* (form) **1** vi to become pigmented, to pigment. **2** vt to pigment.
Pik[1] m (inf) einen ~ auf jdn haben to have something or a grudge against sb.
Pik[2] nt -s, -s (Cards) spade. ~-As ace of spades; dastehen wie ~-Sieben (inf) to look completely bewildered or at a loss.
pikant adj piquant; Witz, Geschichte auch racy.
Pikanterie f (a) siehe adj piquancy; raciness. (b) (Bemerkung) piquant or racy remark.
Pike f -, -n pike. von der ~ auf dienen (fig) to rise from the ranks, to work one's way up; etw von der ~ auf lernen (fig) to learn sth starting from the bottom.
Pikee m or nt -s, -s piqué.
piken vti siehe pieken.
pikfein adj siehe piekfein.
pikieren* vt Blumen to prick out, to transplant; Bäume to transplant.
pikiert adj (inf) put out, peeved, piqued. sie machte ein ~es Gesicht she looked put out or peeved; ~ reagieren to get put out or peeved.
Pikkolo m -s, -s (a) (Kellnerlehrling) apprentice or trainee waiter. (b) (fig: kleine Ausgabe) mini-version, baby; (auch ~flasche) quarter bottle of champagne. (c) (Mus: auch ~flöte) piccolo.
pikobello adj siehe picobello.
piksen vti siehe pieken.

Pilger(in f) m -s, - pilgrim.
Pilger-: ~chor m pilgrims' chorus; ~fahrt f pilgrimage; auf ~fahrt gehen to go on a pilgrimage.
Pilgerin f siehe **Pilger(in).**
pilgern vi aux sein to make a pilgrimage; (inf: gehen) to make or wend one's way.
Pilgerschaft f pilgrimage.
Pilger-: ~stab m pilgrim's staff; ~zug m procession of pilgrims.
Pilgrim m -s, -e (poet) pilgrim.
Pille f -, -n pill, tablet; (Antibaby~) pill. eine ~ (ein)nehmen or schlucken to take a pill; sie nimmt die ~ she's on the pill, she takes the pill; das war eine bittere ~ für ihn (fig) that was a bitter pill for him (to swallow); jdm eine bittere ~ versüßen or verzuckern (fig) to sugar or sweeten the pill for sb.
Pillen-: ~dreher m (a) (Zool) scarab; (b) (inf: Apotheker) chemist, druggist (US); ~knick m birth-rate slump caused by the pill.
Pilot(in f) m -en, -en pilot.
Pilot-: ~ballon m pilot balloon; ~studie f pilot study.
Pils -, -, **Pils(e)ner** nt -s, - Pilsner (lager).
Pilz m -es, -e (a) fungus; (giftig) toadstool; (eßbar) mushroom; (Mikro~) mould; (Atom~) mushroom cloud. in die ~e gehen (inf) to go mushrooming or mushroom-picking; wie ~e aus der Erde or aus dem Boden schießen or sprießen to spring up like mushrooms, to mushroom.
  (b) (Haut~) ringworm; (Fuß~ auch) athlete's foot.
pilzförmig adj mushroom-shaped. der Rauch stieg ~ auf the smoke climbed up in a mushroom-shaped cloud.
Pilz-: ~kopf m (inf) Beatle; (Frisur) Beatle haircut; ~krankheit f fungal disease; ~kunde f mycology; p~tötend adj fungicidal; ~vergiftung f fungus poisoning.
Pimmel m -s, - (inf: Penis) willie (inf).
pimp(e)lig adj (inf) (wehleidig) soppy (inf); (verweichlicht auch) namby-pamby (inf), cissyish.
Pimpelliese f (inf) cissy, softy (inf).
Pimperlinge pl (dated inf) die paar ~ the odd penny.
pimpern (sl) **1** vt to have it off with (sl). **2** vi to have it off (sl).
Pimpf m -(e)s, -e (a) (inf) squirt (pej). so ein süßer kleiner ~ such a nice little chap or man. (b) (Hist) member of Hitlerian organization for 10–14-year-olds.
pimplig adj siehe **pimp(e)lig.**
pingelig adj (inf) finicky (inf), fussy.
Pingpong nt -s, -s (inf) ping-pong.
Pinguin ['pɪŋguiːn] m -s, -e penguin.
Pinie ['piːniə] f pine (tree).
Pinkel m -s, - (inf) ein feiner or vornehmer ~ a swell, Lord Muck (inf).
pinkeln vi (inf) to pee (inf), to piddle (inf). ich muß mal ~ I need a pee (inf).
Pinkelpause f (inf) break. der Bus hielt zu einer ~ the bus made a toilet stop or a convenience stop.
Pinke(pinke) f -, no pl (dated sl) dough (sl), lolly (inf). heute gibt's ~ pay-day today!
Pinne f -, -n (a) (inf: Stift) pin. (b) (für Kompaßnadel) pivot. (c) (Ruder~) tiller.
Pinscher m -s, - pinscher; (inf: Mensch) self-important little pipsqueak (inf).
Pinsel m -s, - (a) brush; (Hunt) tuft of hair. (b) (inf) ein eingebildeter ~ a self-opinionated twit (inf), a jumped-up so-and-so (inf). (c) (sl: Penis) willie (inf).
Pinselei f (pej) daubing (pej); (Gemälde auch) daub (pej).
Pinselführung f brushwork.
pinseln vti (inf: streichen) to paint (auch Med); (pej: malen) to daub; (inf: schreiben) to pen.
Pinselstrich m stroke (of a brush), brushstroke.
Pint m -s, -e (vulg) prick (vulg), tool (vulg).
Pinte f -, -n (a) (inf: Lokal) boozer (Brit inf). (b) (Measure) pint.
Pin-up-girl [pɪn'apɡœrl] nt -s, -s pin-up (girl).
Pinzette f (pair of) tweezers pl.
Pionier m -s, -e (a) (Mil) sapper, engineer. (b) (fig) pioneer. (c) (DDR) member of a political organization similar to the Boy Scouts.
Pionier|arbeit f pioneering work.
Pipeline ['paiplain] f -, -s pipeline.
Pipette f pipette.
Pipi nt or m -s, -s (baby-talk) wee(-wee) (baby-talk). ~ machen to do or have a wee(-wee).
Piranha [pi'ranja] m -(s), -s piranha.
Pirat m -en, -en pirate.
Piraten-: ~schiff nt pirate ship; ~sender m pirate radio station.
Piraterie f (lit, fig) piracy.
Pirol m -s, -e oriole.
Pirouette [pi'ruɛtə] f pirouette.
Pirsch f -, no pl stalk. auf (die) ~ gehen to go stalking.
pirschen vi to stalk, to go stalking.
Pirschgang m stalk. auf ~ gehen to go stalking.
pispern vi (dial) to whisper.
Piß m Pisses, no pl (vulg) piss (vulg), slash (Brit sl).
Pisse f -, no pl (vulg) piss (vulg).
pissen vi (vulg) to (have a) piss (vulg); (regnen) to piss down (vulg).
Pissoir [pɪ'soaːr] nt -s, -s or -e (dated) urinal.
Pißpott m (sl) potty (inf).
Pistazie [pɪs'taːtsiə] f pistachio.
Piste f -, -n (Ski) piste, (ski-)run; (Rennbahn) track, circuit; (Aviat) runway, tarmac; (behelfsmäßig) landing-strip, air-strip; (im Zirkus) barrier.
Pistole f -, -n (a) pistol. jdn mit vorgehaltener ~ zwingen to

force sb at gunpoint; **jdn auf ~n fordern** to challenge sb to a duel (with pistols); **jdm die ~ auf die Brust setzen** (fig) to hold a pistol to sb's head; **wie aus der ~ geschossen** (fig) like a shot. **(b)** (Hist: Goldmünze) pistole.

Pistolen-: ~**griff** m pistol butt; ~**kugel** f (pistol) bullet; ~**schuß** m pistol shot; ~**tasche** f holster.

pitsch(e)naß, pitsch(e)patsch(e)naß (inf) adj soaking (wet); Kleidung, Mensch auch dripping (wet).

pitsch, patsch interj pitter-patter.

pittoresk adj picturesque.

Pizza f -, -s pizza.

Pizzeria f -, -s pizzeria.

Pkw ['peːkaːveː] m -s, -s siehe **Personenkraftwagen**.

pl., Pl. abbr of **Plural** pl.

placieren* [plaˈtsiːrən] vt, **Placierung** f siehe **plazieren**, **Plazierung**.

placken vr (inf) to slave (away) (inf).

Placken m -s, - (dial) patch.

Plackerei f (inf) grind (inf).

pladdern (N Ger) **1** vi aux sein (Regen) to pelt (down). **2** vi impers to pelt down.

plädieren* vi (Jur, fig) to plead (für, auf +acc for).

Plädoyer [plɛdoaˈjeː] nt -s, -s (Jur) address to the jury, summation (US), summing up; (fig) plea.

Plafond [plaˈfõː] m -s, -s (lit, fig) ceiling.

Plage f -, -n **(a)** plague. **(b)** (fig: Mühe) nuisance. **sie hat ihre ~ mit ihm** he's a trial for her; **man hat schon seine ~ mit dir** you do make life difficult, you are a nuisance; **ein jeder hat seine ~** we all have our cross to bear; **zu einer ~ werden** to become a nuisance.

Plagegeist m nuisance, pest.

plagen 1 vt to plague, to torment; (mit Bitten und Fragen auch) to pester, to harass. **dich plagt doch etwas, heraus mit der Sprache** something's worrying or bothering you, out with it; **ein geplagter Mann** a harassed man; **jdn (damit) ~, etw zu tun** to pester sb to do sth.

2 vr **(a)** (leiden) to be troubled or bothered (mit by). **schon die ganze Woche plage ich mich mit meinem Heuschnupfen** I've been bothered or troubled all week by my hay fever, my hay fever's been bothering or troubling me all week.

(b) (arbeiten) to slave or slog away (inf); (sich Mühe geben) to go to or take a lot of trouble or great pains (mit over or with).

Plagiat nt plagiarism. **da hat er ein ~ begangen** that's a plagiarism, he plagiarized that.

Plagiator m plagiarist.

plagiieren* vti to plagiarize.

Plaid [pleːt] nt or m -s, -s tartan travelling rug.

Plakafarbe ® f poster paint.

Plakat nt -(e)s, -e (an Litfaßsäulen etc) poster, bill; (aus Pappe) placard.

Plakat-: ~**ankleber** m -s, - billposter, billsticker; ~**farbe** f poster paint.

plakatieren* vt to placard; (fig) to broadcast.

plakativ adj Wirkung striking, bold; Sprache pithy.

Plakat-: ~**maler** m poster painter or artist; ~**säule** f advertisement pillar; ~**schrift** f block lettering; ~**träger** m sandwichman; ~**werbung** f poster advertising.

Plakette f (Abzeichen) badge; (Münze) commemorative coin; (an Wänden) plaque.

plan adj flat, level; Ebene, Fläche plane attr.

Plan¹ m -(e)s, ⸚e **(a)** plan. **die ⸚e zur Renovierung der Stadt** the plans for the renovation of the city; **den ~ fassen, etw zu tun** to form the intention of doing sth, to plan to do sth; **wir haben den ~, ...** we're planning to ...; **⸚e machen or schmieden** to make plans, to plan; **nach ~ verlaufen** to run or go according to plan.

(b) (Stadt~) (street-)map, town plan; (Grundriß, Bau~) plan, blueprint; (Zeittafel) schedule, timetable.

Plan² m -(e)s, ⸚e (obs: ebene Fläche) plain. **auf dem ~ erscheinen, auf den ~ treten** (fig) to arrive or come on the scene; **jdn auf den ~ rufen** (fig) to bring sb into the arena.

Plane f -, -n tarpaulin, tarp (US inf); (von LKW) hood; (Schutzdach) canopy, awning.

Plänemacher m planner. **er ist ein großer ~** he's a great one for making plans.

planen vti to plan; Attentat, Verbrechen auch to plot.

Planer(in f) m -s, - planner.

Planerfüllung f realization of a/the plan. **uns trennen nur noch 5% von der ~** we're only 5% short of our planned target.

planerisch adj planning. **~e Ausarbeitung** working out of the plans; **~ vorgehen** to proceed methodically; **ein Projekt ~ betreuen** to be in charge of the planning of a project; **~ hat das Team versagt** the team's planning was a failure.

Planet m -en, -en planet.

planetarisch adj planetary.

Planetarium nt planetarium.

Planeten-: ~**bahn** f planetary orbit; ~**system** nt planetary system.

Planetoid m -en, -en planetoid, asteroid.

plangemäß adj siehe **planmäßig**.

planieren* vt Boden to level (off); Werkstück to planish.

Planierraupe f bulldozer.

Planke f -, -n plank, board; (Leit~) crash barrier. **~n** (Umzäunung) fencing, boarding (gen round).

Plänkelei f (old Mil) skirmish; (fig auch) squabble.

plänkeln vi (old Mil) to skirmish, to engage in skirmishes; (fig) to squabble, to have a squabble.

Plankton nt -s, no pl plankton.

planlos adj unmethodical, unsystematic; (ziellos) random.

Planlosigkeit f lack of planning.

planmäßig adj (wie geplant) as planned, according to plan; (pünktlich) on schedule, as scheduled; (methodisch) methodical. **~e Ankunft/Abfahrt** scheduled time of arrival/departure; **wir sind ~ um 7 angekommen** we arrived on schedule or as scheduled or on time at 7; **~ kommt der Zug um 7 Uhr an** the train is scheduled to arrive or is due in at 7 o'clock.

Planmäßigkeit f (Methodik) methodicalness, method; (Pünktlichkeit) punctuality; (Regelmäßigkeit) regularity.

Planquadrat nt grid square.

Planschbecken nt paddling pool.

planschen vi to splash around.

Planscherei f splashing around.

Plan-: ~**soll** nt output target; ~**stelle** f post.

Plantage [planˈtaːʒə] f -, -n plantation.

Planung f planning. **diese Straße ist noch in ~** this road is still being planned; **schon in der ~ sein** to be in or at the planning stage.

Planungs-: ~**abteilung** f planning department; ~**kommission** f planning commission.

Plan-: ~**wagen** m covered wagon; ~**wirtschaft** f planned economy.

Plapperei f (inf) chatter(ing), prattling.

Plappermaul nt (inf) (Mund) big mouth (inf); (Kind) chatterbox (inf); (Schwätzer) tittle-tattler (inf), blabber (inf).

plappern 1 vi to prattle, to chatter; (Geheimnis verraten) to talk, to blab (inf).

2 vt **was plapperst du denn da für Blödsinn?** don't talk rubbish.

Plappertasche f (inf) tittle-tattler (inf).

plärren vti (inf: weinen) to howl, to bawl; (Radio) to blare (out); (schreien) to yell, to shriek; (unschön singen) to screech.

Pläsier nt -s, -e (dated) pleasure, delight. **nun laß ihm doch sein ~** let him have his bit of fun.

Pläsierchen nt: **jedem Tierchen sein ~** (hum) each to his own.

pläsierlich adj (old) pleasurable, pleasing.

Plasma nt -s, **Plasmen** plasma.

Plastik¹ nt -s, -s (Kunststoff) plastic.

Plastik² f **(a)** (Bildhauerkunst) sculpture, plastic art (form). **(b)** (Skulptur) sculpture. **(c)** (Med) plastic surgery. **jdm eine ~ machen** to give sb plastic surgery. **(d)** (fig: Anschaulichkeit) vividness.

Plastik-: ~**bombe** f plastic bomb; ~**folie** f plastic film; ~**material** nt plastic; ~**tüte** f plastic bag.

Plastilin nt -s, -e plasticine ®.

plastisch adj **(a)** (knetbar) malleable, plastic, workable. **(b)** (dreidimensional) three-dimensional, 3-D; (fig: anschaulich) vivid. **~es Vorstellungsvermögen** ability to imagine things in three dimensions; **~ hervortreten** to stand out; **~e Sprache** vivid or graphic language; **sich** (dat) **einen Gegenstand ~ vorstellen** to form a concrete mental image of an object; **das kann ich mir ~ vorstellen** I can just imagine or picture it. **(c)** (Art) plastic. **die ~e Kunst** plastic art; **~e Arbeiten** sculptures, plastic works. **(d)** (Med) plastic.

Plastizität f, no pl **(a)** (Formbarkeit) malleability, plasticity, workability. **(b)** (fig: Anschaulichkeit) vividness, graphicness.

Platane f -, -n plane tree.

Plateau [plaˈtoː] nt -s, -s **(a)** plateau; (Tafelland auch) tableland. **(b)** (von Schuh) platform.

Plateausohle [plaˈtoː-] f platform sole.

Platin nt -s, no pl platinum.

platinblond adj platinum blonde.

Platitüde f -, -n platitude.

Plato(n) m - Plato.

Platoniker m -s, - Platonist.

platonisch adj Platonic, Platonist; (nicht sexuell) platonic; (geh: unverbindlich) non-committal.

Platonismus m Platonism.

platsch interj splash, splosh.

platschen vi (inf) to splash; (regnen) to pelt, to pour.

plätschern vi (Bach) to babble, to splash; (Brunnen) to splash; (Regen) to patter; (planschen) to splash (about or around). **eine ~de Unterhaltung** light conversation.

platschnaß adj (inf) soaking (wet); Kleidung, Mensch auch dripping (wet), drenched.

platt adj **(a)** (flach) flat. **etw ~ drücken** to press sth flat, to flatten sth; **einen Reifen ~ fahren** (inf) or **einen ~en Reifen haben** to have a flat (inf) or a flat tyre; **das ~e Land** the flat country; (nicht Stadt) the country.

(b) (fig: geistlos) Bemerkung, Witz flat, boring, dull; Mensch dull, uninspired.

(c) (inf: verblüfft) **~ sein** to be flabbergasted (inf); **da bist du ~, nicht?** that's surprised you.

Platt nt -(s), no pl (inf) Low German, Plattdeutsch.

Plättbrett nt (dial) ironing-board; (sl) skinny Lizzy (inf).

Plättchen nt little tile; (Computers) microchip.

plattdeutsch adj Low German. **das P~e** Low German, Plattdeutsch.

Platte f -, -n **(a)** (Holz~) piece of wood, wood no pl, board; (zur Wandverkleidung) panel; (Tischtennis~) ping-pong table; (Glas~/Metall~/Plastik~) piece or sheet of glass/metal/plastic; (Beton~, Stein~) slab; (zum Pflastern) paving stone, flagstone; (Kachel, Fliese) tile; (Grab~) gravestone, slab; (Herd~) hotplate; (Tisch~) (table-)top; (ausziehbare) leaf; (Felsen~) shelf, ledge; (Geog: ebenes Land) flat or low land; (Druckstock) plate; (Phot) plate; (Gebiß) (dental) plate; (Gedenktafel) plaque. **ein Ereignis auf die ~ bannen** to capture an event on film; **die ~ putzen** (inf) to hop it (inf).

(b) (Fleisch-, Gemüseteller) serving-dish, plate; (Torten~) cake plate; (mit Fuß) cake-stand. **eine ~ Aufschnitt** a plate of selected cold meats; **kalte ~** cold dish; **das kommt nicht auf die ~!** (fig inf) that's just not on! (inf).

   (c) (Schall~) record, disc. **etw auf ~ sprechen/aufnehmen** to make a record of sth, to record sth; **eine ~ mit Marschmusik** a record of march music.

   (d) (fig inf) **die ~ kenne ich schon** I've heard all that before, I know that line; **er legte die alte ~ auf** he started on his old theme; **leg doch mal eine neue ~ auf!** change the record, can't you!; **die ~ hat einen Sprung** the record's stuck.

   (e) (inf: Glatze) bald head; (kahle Stelle) bald spot or patch.

Plätte f -, -n (N Ger inf), **Plätt|eisen** nt (dial, Hist) iron, smoothing iron (Hist).

plätten vt (dial) to iron, to press; siehe **geplättet**.

Platten-: ~kondensator m plate condenser; ~leger m -s, - paver; ~sammlung f record collection; ~see m der ~see Lake Balaton; ~spieler m record-player; ~teller m turntable; ~wechsler m -s, - autochanger, record changer; ~weg m paved path.

platterdings adv: ~ **unmöglich** absolutely impossible.

Plätterei f (dial) **(a)** (Betrieb) business which does ironing. **(b)** (inf: das Plätten) ironing.

Plätterin f ironer, presser.

Platt-: ~fisch m flatfish; ~form f -, -en platform; (fig: Grundlage) basis; ~fuß m flat foot; (inf: Reifenpanne) flat (inf); **p~füßig** adj, adv flat-footed; ~heit f **(a)** no pl (Flachheit) flatness; (Geistlosigkeit auch) dullness; **(b)** usu pl (Redensart etc) commonplace, platitude, cliché.

plattieren* vt Metall to plate.

Platt-: **p~nasig** adj flat-nosed; ~stich m satin stitch; ~stickerei f satin stitch embroidery.

Plättwäsche f (dial) ironing.

Platz m -es, -e **(a)** (freier Raum) room, space. **~ für jdn/etw schaffen** to make room for sb/sth; **~ für etw finden** to find room or space for sth; **es wird ~ finden** there'll be room or space for it; **seine Fähigkeiten finden hier keinen ~** there's no scope for his abilities here; **~ greifen** to spread, to gain ground; **~ einnehmen** or **brauchen** to take up or occupy room or space; **~ für etw (frei) lassen** to leave room or space for sth; **das Buch hat keinen ~ mehr im Regal** there's no more room or space on the bookshelf for that book; **mehr als 10 Leute haben hier nicht ~** there's not room or space for more than 10 people here; **jdm den (ganzen) ~ wegnehmen** to take up all the room; **jdm ~ machen** to make room for sb; (vorbeigehen lassen) to make way for sb (auch fig); **~ machen** to get out of the way (inf); **mach mal ein bißchen ~** make a bit of room; **~ dem König** make way for the king!; **der ~ ist beengt** space is restricted, there's only a limited amount of room or space; **~ für jdn/etw bieten** to hold sb/sth, to have room for sb/sth; **~ da!** (inf) (get) out of the way there! (inf), gangway! (inf).

   (b) (Sitzplatz) seat. **~ nehmen** to take a seat; **bitte ~ nehmen zum Mittagessen** please take your seats for lunch; **behalten Sie doch bitte ~!** (form) please remain seated (form); **ist hier noch ein ~ frei?** is there a free seat here?; **dieser ~ ist belegt** or **besetzt** this seat's taken, this is somebody's seat; **sich von seinem ~ erheben** (geh) to rise (form); **der Saal hat 2.000 ~e** the hall seats 2,000 or has seating for 2,000 or has 2,000 seats; **mit jdm den ~ tauschen** or **wechseln** to change places with sb; **erster/zweiter ~** front/rear stalls; **~!** (zum Hund) sit!

   (c) (Stelle, Standort, Rang, Sport) place. **das Buch steht nicht an seinem ~** the book isn't in (its) place; **etw (wieder) an seinen ~ stellen** to put sth (back) in (its) place; **fehl** or **nicht am ~e sein** to be out of place; **auf die ~e, fertig, los!** (beim Sport) on your marks, get set, go!; **er wich nicht vom ~(e)** he wouldn't yield (an inch); **seinen ~ behaupten** to stand one's ground, to hold one's own; **alles hat seinen festen ~** everything has its proper place; **das Buch hat einen festen ~ auf der Bestsellerliste** the book is firmly established on the bestseller list; **die Literatur hat einen festen ~ in ihrem Leben** literature is very much a part of her life; **ihr ~ ist an der Seite ihres Mannes** her (proper) place is at her husband's side; **den ersten ~ einnehmen** (fig) to take first place, to come first; **auf ~ zwei** in second place; **jdn auf ~ drei/den zweiten ~ verweisen** to beat sb into third/second place; **jdn auf die ~e verweisen** (fig) to beat sb; **auf ~ wetten** to make a place bet; **ein ~ an der Sonne** (lit, fig) a place in the sun.

   (d) (Arbeits~, Studien~ etc) place. **im Kindergarten sind noch ein paar ~e frei** there are still a few vacancies or places left in the kindergarten; **wir haben noch einen freien ~ im Büro** we've still got one vacancy in the office.

   (e) (umbaute Fläche) square. **auf dem ~** in or on the square; **ein freier ~ vor der Kirche** an open space in front of the church.

   (f) (Sport~) playing field; (Ftbl, Hockey) pitch, field; (Handball~, Tennis~) court; (Golf~) (golf) course, (golf) links pl. **einen Spieler vom ~ stellen** or **verweisen** to send a player off; **auf gegnerischem/eigenem ~** away/at home.

   (g) (Ort) town, place; (Handels~) centre. **das erste Hotel or Haus am ~** the best hotel in town or in the place.

   (h) (Lager~) (store or storage) yard.

   (i) (Bau~) site.

Platz-: ~angst f (Psych) agoraphobia; (inf: Beklemmung) claustrophobia; ~angst **bekommen** to get claustrophobic or claustrophobia; ~anweiser(in f) m -s, - usher(ette).

Plätzchen nt **(a)** dim of **Platz** spot, little place. **(b)** (Gebäck) biscuit (Brit), cookie (US).

Platze f (inf): **da kann man ja die ~ kriegen** it's enough to drive you up the wall (inf) or round the bend (Brit inf).

platzen vi aux sein **(a)** (aufreißen) to burst; (Naht, Hose, Augenbraue, Haut) to split; (explodieren: Granate, Bombe) to explode; (einen Riß bekommen) to crack. **mir ist unterwegs ein Reifen geplatzt** I had a blow-out on the way, a tyre burst on the way; **ihm ist eine Ader geplatzt** he burst a blood-vessel; **wenn du so weiterißt, platzt du!** if you go on eating like that you'll burst; **wir sind vor Lachen fast geplatzt** we split our sides laughing, we laughed till our sides ached or split; **ins Zimmer ~** (inf) to burst into the room; **jdm ins Haus ~** (inf) to descend on sb; **(vor Wut/Neid/Ungeduld) ~** (inf) to be bursting (with rage/envy/impatience); siehe **Kragen, Naht**.

   (b) (inf: scheitern) (Plan, Geschäft) to fall through; (Freundschaft) to break up; (Theorie) to fall down, to collapse; (Spionagering, Verschwörung) to collapse; (Wechsel) to bounce (inf). **die Verlobung ist geplatzt** the engagement is (all) off; **etw ~ lassen** Plan to make sth fall through; Freundschaft, Verlobung to break sth up; Theorie to explode sth; Spionagering to break sth up, to smash sth; Wechsel to make sth bounce (inf).

Platz-: ~herren pl (Sport) home team; ~karte f (Rail) seat reservation (ticket); **ich bestelle mir eine ~karte** I'll reserve (myself) a seat, I'll get a seat reservation; ~konzert nt open-air concert; ~mangel m shortage or lack of space or room; **wir leiden sehr unter ~mangel** we're terribly short of space or room, we've a space problem; ~miete f (Theat) season ticket; (Sport) ground rent; ~patrone f blank (cartridge); **p~raubend** adj space-consuming; ~regen m cloudburst; **das ist nur ein ~regen** it's only a (passing) shower; **p~sparend** adj space-saving attr; **etw p~sparend stapeln** to stack sth away compactly or with a minimum use of space; **das ist p~sparender** that saves more space; ~verweis m sending-off; **es gab drei ~verweise** three players were sent off; ~wahl f toss-up; **die ~wahl haben/verlieren** to win/lose the toss; **die ~wahl vornehmen** to toss up; ~wart m (Sport) groundsman; ~wechsel m change of place; (Sport) change of position; ~wette f place bet; ~wunde f cut, laceration.

Plauderei f chat, conversation; (Press) feature; (TV, Rad) chat show.

Plauderer m -s, -, **Plauderin** f conversationalist.

plauderhaft adj Ton conversational, chatty.

plaudern vi to chat, to talk (über + acc, von about); (verraten) to talk. **mit ihm läßt sich gut ~** he's easy to talk to; siehe **Schule**.

Plauder-: ~stündchen nt chat; **ein angenehmes ~stündchen zubringen** to have a pleasant chat or a cosy little chat; ~tasche f (inf) chatterbox (inf); ~ton m conversational or chatty tone.

Plausch m -(e)s, -e (inf) chat.

plauschen vi (inf) to chat, to have a chat or a natter (inf).

plausibel adj plausible. **jdm etw ~ machen** to make sth clear to sb, to explain sth to sb.

plauz interj (old) crash, bang.

Plauz m -es, -e (inf) (Geräusch) bang, crash; (Fall) fall. **einen ~ tun** or **machen** to have a fall, to fall down.

Plauze f -, -n (dial inf) chest. **es auf der ~ haben** (inf) to have a chesty cough, to be chesty (inf).

Play-back ['pleɪbæk] nt -s, -s (Band) (bei der Schallplatte) backing track; (TV) recording; (~ verfahren) (bei der Schallplatte) double-tracking no pl; (TV) miming no pl. **ein ~ von einem Lied machen** to double-track a song; (TV) to prerecord a song, to make a recording of a song; **etw im ~ machen** to double-track sth; (TV) to mime to (a recording of) sth.

Play-: ~boy ['pleɪbɔɪ] m -s, -s playboy; ~girl ['pleɪɡœrl] nt -s, -s playgirl.

Plazenta f -, -s or **Plazenten** placenta.

Plazet nt -s, -s approval, OK (inf). **sein ~ zu etw geben** to approve or OK sth, to give sth one's approval or OK.

plazieren*¹ vt **(a)** (Platz anweisen) to put; Soldaten, Wächter to put, to place, to position; (Tennis) to seed. **der Kellner plazierte uns in die or der Nähe der Band** the waiter directed or showed us to a place or put us near the band.

   (b) (zielen) Ball to place, to position; Schlag, Faust to land. **gut plazierte Aufschläge** well-placed or well-positioned services; **ein (gut) plazierter Schlag** a well-placed or well-aimed blow; **plaziert schießen** to position one's shots well; **er hat plaziert in die rechte Torecke geschossen** he tucked the ball away neatly in the right corner of the goal.

   (c) (anlegen) Geld to put, to place.

2 vr **(a)** (inf: sich setzen, stellen etc) to plant oneself (inf).

   (b) (Sport) to be placed, to get a place; (Tennis) to be seeded. **der Läufer konnte sich gut/nicht ~** the runner was well-placed/wasn't even placed.

Plazierung f (Einlauf) order; (Tennis) seeding; (Platz) place. **welche ~ hatte er?** where did he come in?, what position did he come in?

Plebejer(in f) m -s, - (lit, fig) plebeian, pleb (inf).

plebejisch adj (lit) plebeian no adv; (fig auch) plebby (inf), common. **sich ~ benehmen** to behave like a pleb (inf).

Plebiszit nt -(e)s, -e plebiscite.

Plebs¹ f -, no pl (Hist) plebs pl.

Plebs² m -es, no pl (pej) plebs pl.

pleite adj pred, adv (inf) Mensch broke (inf); Firma auch bust (inf). **~ gehen** to go bust.

Pleite f -, -n (inf) bankruptcy, collapse; (fig) flop (inf), washout (inf). **~ machen** to go bankrupt or bust (inf); **damit/mit ihm haben wir eine ~ erlebt** it/he was a disaster.

Pleitegeier m (inf) **(a)** (drohende Pleite) vulture. **in meinem Geldbeutel sitzt der ~** I'm almost broke (inf); **über der Firma schwebt der ~** the vultures are or the threat of bankruptcy is hovering over the firm. **(b)** (Bankrotteur) bankrupt.

Plektron, Plektrum nt -s, **Plektren** or **Plektra** plectrum.

Plempe f -, -n (dial) dishwater (inf).

plempern vi (inf) **(a)** (trödeln) to dawdle. **(b)** (verschütten) to splash.

plemplem adj pred (sl) nuts (sl), round the bend (Brit inf). **jd**

~ **machen** to drive sb round the bend (inf) or up the wall (inf).

Plena pl of **Plenum**.

Plenar-: ~**saal** m assembly room; ~**sitzung**, ~**versammlung** f plenary session.

Plenum nt -s, **Plena** plenum.

Pleonasmus m pleonasm.

pleonastisch adj pleonastic.

Pleuelstange f connecting rod.

Plexiglas ® nt acrylic glass.

plieren, plinkern vi (N Ger) to screw up one's eyes.

Plissee nt -s, -s pleats pl, pleating no pl.

Plissee-: ~**falte** f pleat; ~**rock** m pleated skirt.

plissieren* vt to pleat.

Plombe f -, -n (a) (Siegel) lead seal. (b) (Zahn~) filling.

Plombenzieher m -s, - (hum inf) dentist's delight (hum inf).

plombieren* vt (a) (versiegeln) to seal, to put a seal on. (b) Zahn to fill. er hat mir zwei Zähne plombiert he did two fillings.

Plombierung f (a) (das Versiegeln) sealing; (Vorrichtung) seal. (b) (beim Zahn) filling.

Plörre f -, -n (dial) dishwater.

Plot m or nt -s, -s (Liter) plot.

plötzlich 1 adj sudden. 2 adv suddenly, all of a sudden. **aber etwas ~!** (inf) make it snappy! (inf), look sharp! (inf); **das kommt alles so ~** (inf) it all happens so suddenly.

Plötzlichkeit f suddenness.

Pluderhose f Turkish trousers pl; (knielang) knickerbockers pl, baggy breeches pl.

Plumeau [ply'moː] nt -s, -s eiderdown, quilt.

plump adj Figur, Hände, Form ungainly no adv; Bewegung, Gang auch awkward; Ausdruck clumsy; Bemerkung crass; Mittel, Schmeichelei, Lüge, Betrug obvious, crude. **der Film ist sehr ~ (gemacht)** the film is very crudely made; **etw ~ ausdrücken** to express sth clumsily; **sich ~ verhalten** to behave crassly; ~**e Annäherungsversuche** very obvious advances.

Plumpheit f siehe adj ungainliness; awkwardness; clumsiness; crassness; obviousness, crudeness.

plumps interj bang; (lauter) crash. ~, **da lag er** crash, he'd fallen over.

Plumps m -es, -e (inf) (Fall) fall, tumble; (Geräusch) bump, thud. **einen ~ machen** (baby-talk) to fall; **mit einem ~ ins Wasser fallen** to fall into the water with a splash.

plumpsen vi aux sein (inf) to tumble, to fall. **ich habe es ~ gehört** I heard a bang; **ich ließ mich einfach aufs Bett ~** I just flopped (down) onto the bed; **er plumpste ins Wasser** he went splash into the water, he fell into the water with a splash.

Plumpsklo(sett) nt (inf) earth closet.

plump-vertraulich 1 adj hail-fellow-well-met. 2 adv in a hail-fellow-well-met sort of way.

Plunder m -s, no pl junk, rubbish.

Plünd(e)rer m -s, - looter, plunderer.

Plundergebäck nt flaky pastry.

plündern vti (a) to loot, to plunder, to pillage; (ausrauben) to raid; Obstbaum to strip. **jemand hat unsere** or **auf unserer Obstplantage geplündert** somebody's raided our orchard.

Plünderung f looting, pillage, plunder.

Plural m -s, -e plural. **im ~ stehen** to be (in the) plural; **den ~ zu etw bilden** to form the plural of sth.

Pluraletantum nt -s, -s or **Pluraliatantum** plural noun.

pluralisch adj plural. **nur ~ gebraucht** only used in the plural.

Pluralismus m pluralism.

pluralistisch adj pluralistic.

Pluralität f plurality; (Mehrheit) majority, plurality (US).

plus 1 prep +gen plus. 2 adv plus. **bei ~ 5 Grad** or **5 Grad ~** at 5 degrees (above freezing or zero).

Plus nt -, - (a) (~zeichen) plus (sign). **ein ~ machen** to put a plus (sign). (b) (Phys inf: ~pol) positive (pole). (c) (Comm) (Zuwachs) increase; (Gewinn) profit; (Überschuß) surplus. (d) (fig: Vorteil) advantage. **das ist ein ~ für dich** that's a point in your favour; **das können Sie als ~ für sich buchen** that's one up to or for you (inf), you've scored a point there (inf).

Plüsch m -(e)s, -e plush. **Stofftiere aus ~** soft toys made of fur fabric.

Plüsch- in cpds plush; ~**bär** m furry teddy bear; ~**tier** nt ~ soft toy.

Plus-: ~**pol** m (Elec) positive pole; ~**punkt** m (Sport) point; (Sch) extra mark; (fig) advantage; **einen ~punkt machen** to win a point; **deine Erfahrung ist ein ~punkt für dich** your experience counts in your favour or is a point in your favour; ~**quamperfekt** nt pluperfect, past perfect.

plustern 1 vt Federn to fluff up. 2 vr to fluff oneself up.

Pluszeichen nt plus sign.

Plutokrat m -en, -en plutocrat.

Plutokratie f plutocracy.

Plutonium nt -s, no pl plutonium.

Pneu [pnøː] m -s, -s (esp Sw) tyre.

pneumatisch [pnɔy'maːtɪʃ] adj pneumatic. ~**e Kammer** pressure chamber.

Po m -s, -s (inf) siehe **Popo**.

Pöbel m -s, no pl rabble, mob.

Pöbelei f vulgarity, bad language no pl.

Pöbel-: p~**haft** adj uncouth, vulgar; ~**herrschaft** f mob rule.

pöbeln vi to swear, to use bad language.

pochen vi to knock; (leise auch) to tap; (heftig) to thump, to bang; (Herz) to pound, to thump; (Blut) to throb, to pound. **auf etw** (acc) ~ (fig) to insist on sth; **auf sein (gutes) Recht ~** to insist on or stand up for one's rights.

pochieren* [pɔ'ʃiːrən] vt Ei to poach.

Pocke f -, -n pock. ~**n** pl smallpox.

Pocken-: ~**narbe** f pockmark; p~**narbig** adj pockmarked; ~(**schutz)impfung** f smallpox vaccination.

Podest nt or m -(e)s, -e (Sockel) pedestal (auch fig); (Podium) platform; (Treppenabsatz) landing.

Podex m -es, -e (hum inf) posterior (hum inf), behind (inf).

Podium nt (lit, fig) platform; (des Dirigenten) podium; (bei Diskussion) panel.

Podiums-: ~**diskussion** f, ~**gespräch** nt panel discussion, brains trust.

Poem nt -s, -e (usu pej) poem, doggerel (pej) no indef art.

Poesie [poe'ziː] f (lit, fig) poetry.

Poesiealbum nt autograph book.

Poet m -en, -en (old: Dichter) poet, bard (liter); (pej) poetaster, versifier.

Poetaster [poe'tastr] m -s, - (old pej) poetaster.

Poetik f poetics sing.

poetisch adj poetic. **eine ~e Ader haben** to have a poetic streak.

pofen vi (sl) to kip (inf).

Pogrom nt or m -s, -e pogrom.

Pogromstimmung f bloodthirsty mood.

Pointe ['poɛ̃tə] f -, -n (eines Witzes) punch-line; (einer Geschichte) point. **die ~ einer Geschichte begreifen** to get the (main) point of a story.

pointieren* [poɛ̃'tiːrən] vt to emphasize, to stress.

pointiert [poɛ̃'tiːrt] adj trenchant, pithy.

Pointillismus [poɛ̃tɪ'jɪsmʊs] m pointillism.

Pokal m -s, -e (zum Trinken) goblet; (Sport) cup. **das Endspiel um den ~** the cup final.

Pokal-: ~**sieger** m cup-winners pl; ~**spiel** nt cup-tie.

Pökel m -s, - brine, pickle.

Pökel-: ~**fleisch** nt salt meat; ~**hering** m salt or pickled herring.

pökeln vt Fleisch, Fisch to salt, to pickle.

Poker nt -s, no pl poker.

Pokergesicht nt, **Pokermiene** f poker face. **ein Pokergesicht machen, eine Pokermiene aufsetzen** to put on a poker-faced or deadpan expression.

pokern vi to play poker. **um etw ~** (fig) to haggle for sth.

pokulieren* vi (old, hum) to quaff (old, hum).

pol. abbr. of **politisch, polizeilich**.

Pol m -s, -e pole. **der ruhende ~** (fig) the calming influence.

polar adj polar. ~**e Kälte** arctic coldness; ~ **entgegengesetzt** diametrically opposed, poles apart pred.

Polar- in cpds polar; ~**fuchs** m arctic fox.

polarisieren* 1 vt to polarize. 2 vr to polarize, to become polarized.

Polarisierung f polarization.

Polarität f polarity.

Polar-: ~**kreis** m polar circle; nördlicher/südlicher ~**kreis** Arctic/Antarctic circle; ~**licht** nt polar lights pl; ~**stern** m Pole Star, North Star, Polaris; ~**zone** f Frigid Zone, polar region.

Polder m -s, - polder.

Pole m -n, -n Pole. **er ist ~** he's Polish, he's a Pole.

Polemik f polemics sing; (Streitschrift) polemic. **die ~ dieses Artikels** the polemic nature of this article; **seine ~ ist kaum mehr erträglich** his polemics are becoming unbearable.

Polemiker(in f) m -s, - controversialist, polemicist.

polemisch adj polemic(al).

polemisieren* vi to polemicize. ~ **gegen** to inveigh against.

polen vt to polarize.

Polen nt -s Poland. **noch ist ~ nicht verloren** (prov) the day is or all is not yet lost.

Polente f -, no pl (inf) cops pl (inf), fuzz pl (inf).

Police [po'liːsə] f -, -n (insurance) policy.

Polier m -s, -e site foreman.

polieren* vt to polish; Schuhe auch to shine; (fig) to polish or brush up. **jdm die Fresse** or **Schnauze** or **Visage ~** (sl) to smash sb's face in (sl).

Polier-: ~**mittel** nt polish; ~**scheibe** f polishing wheel or disc; ~**tuch** nt polishing cloth; ~**wachs** nt wax polish.

Poliklinik f (Krankenhaus) clinic (for outpatients only); (Abteilung) outpatients' department, outpatients sing.

Polin f Pole, Polish woman.

Polio f -, no pl polio, poliomyelitis.

Politesse f (woman) traffic warden.

Politbüro nt Politburo.

Politik f (a) no pl politics sing; (politischer Standpunkt) politics pl. **welche ~ vertritt er?** what are his politics?; **in die ~ gehen** to go into politics; **über ~ sprechen** to talk (about) politics; ~ **verdirbt den Charakter** (Prov) power corrupts and absolute power corrupts absolutely (Prov). (b) (bestimmte ~) policy. **eine ~ der starken Hand treiben** to take a tough line; **eine ~ verfolgen** or **betreiben** to pursue a policy; **ihre gesamte ~** all their policies.

Politika pl of **Politikum**.

Politiker(in f) m -s, - politician. **führender ~** leading politician, statesman.

Politikum nt -s, **Politika** political issue.

Politikwissenschaft f siehe **Politologie**.

politisch adj political; (klug) politic, judicious. **jdn ~ schulen** to educate sb politically; **er ist ein P~er** he's a political prisoner.

politisieren* 1 vi to talk politics, to politicize. 2 vt to politicize; **jdn** to make politically aware.

Politisierung f politicization. **sind Sie für die ~ des Unterrichts?** are you in favour of politicizing school lessons?; **er kümmerte sich um die ~ seiner Schüler** he saw to it that his pupils were made politically aware.

Politökonomie f political economy.

Politologe m, **Politologin** f political scientist.

Politologie f political science, politics sing.

Politur f (Poliermittel) polish; (Glanz) shine, polish; (das Polieren) polishing. die ~ ist runter (inf) (lit) the polish has worn off; (fig) the glamour's gone.

Polizei f police pl; (Gebäude) police station. auf die or zur ~ gehen to go to the police; er ist bei der ~ he's in the police (force); siehe dumm.

Polizei- in cpds police; ~aktion f police operation; ~apparat m police force; ~aufsicht f police supervision; unter ~aufsicht stehen to have to report regularly to the police; ~beamte(r) m police official; (Polizist) police officer; ~behörde f police authorities pl; sich bei der ~behörde anmelden to register with the police; ~chef m chief constable, chief of police (US); ~dienststelle f (form) police station; ~direktion f police headquarters pl; ~funk m police radio; ~griff m wrist-hold, police hold; er wurde im ~griff abgeführt they put a wrist-hold on him and led him away, he was frogmarched away; ~haft f detention; ~hund m police dog; ~knüppel m truncheon; ~kommissar m (police) inspector.

polizeilich adj no pred police attr. diese Regelung ist ~ angeordnet this is a police regulation, this regulation is by order of the police; ~es Führungszeugnis certificate issued by the police, stating that the holder has no criminal record; ~e Meldepflicht legal requirement to register with the police; er wird ~ überwacht he's being watched by the police; sich ~ melden to register with the police; ~ verboten against the law; „Parken ~ verboten" "police notice – no parking".

Polizei-: ~präsident m chief constable, chief of police (US); ~präsidium nt police headquarters pl; ~revier nt (a) (~wache) police station; ins or aufs ~revier gehen to go (down) to the (police) station; (b) (Bezirk) (police) district, precinct (US), patch (inf); ~schutz m police protection; ~sirene f (police) siren, hee-haw (inf); ~spitzel m police informer, nark (Brit sl); ~staat m police state; ~streife f police patrol; ~stunde f closing time; ~verordnung f police regulation; ~wache f siehe ~revier (a); ~wesen nt police force; p~widrig adj illegal; sich p~widrig verhalten to break the law.

Polizist m policeman.

Polizistin f policewoman.

Polka f -, -s polka.

Pollen m -s, - pollen.

Poller m -s, - capstan, bollard.

Pollution f (Med) (seminal) emission.

polnisch adj Polish. ~e Wirtschaft (inf) shambles sing.

Polnisch(e) nt decl as adj Polish; siehe auch Deutsch(e).

Polo nt -s, -s polo.

Polohemd nt sports shirt; (für Frau) casual blouse.

Polonaise [polo'nɛːzə], **Polonäse** f -, -n polonaise.

Polster nt or (Aus) m -s, - (a) cushion; (Polsterung) upholstery no pl; (bei Kleidung) pad, padding no pl. das ~ vom Sessel muß erneuert werden the chair needs re-upholstering; seine Jacke als ~ für seinen Kopf benutzen to use one's jacket as a pillow. (b) (fig) (Fett~) flab no pl (inf), layer of fat; (Bauch) spare tyre; (Geldreserve) reserves pl. sie hat ein ganz schönes ~ am Hintern she's pretty well-upholstered or well-padded behind.

Pölsterchen nt (inf) (a) (Rücklage) nest-egg. (b) (Fettpolster) (layer of) fat; (an Hüften) spare tyre. sie hat einige ~ she's well-upholstered or well-padded.

Polsterer m -s, - upholsterer.

Polster-: ~garnitur f three-piece suite; ~möbel pl upholstered furniture.

polstern vt to upholster; Kleidung, Tür to pad. etw neu ~ to re-upholster sth; sie ist gut gepolstert she's well-upholstered or well-padded; sie ist finanziell gut gepolstert she's not short of the odd penny.

Polster-: ~sessel m armchair, easy chair; ~sitz m upholstered or padded seat; ~stoff m upholstery or upholstering fabric; ~stuhl m upholstered or padded chair; ~tür f padded door.

Polsterung f (Polster) upholstery; (das Polstern) upholstering.

Polterabend m party on the eve of a wedding, at which old crockery is smashed to bring good luck, ≈ shower (US).

Polterer m -s, - noisy person; (beim Sprechen) ranter, blusterer.

Poltergeist m poltergeist.

poltern vi (a) (krachen) to crash about. (~d umfallen) to go crash. die Kinder ~ oben the children are crashing about or banging about upstairs or are making a din or racket (inf) upstairs; was hat da oben so gepoltert? what was that crash or bang?; es fiel ~d zu Boden it crashed to the floor, it fell with a crash to the floor; es polterte fürchterlich, als er ... there was a terrific crash or bang when he ...; es poltert (an der Tür/vor dem Haus) there's a real racket (inf) or din going on (at the door/in front of the house); ein ~der Lärm a din or racket (inf); an die Tür ~ to thump or bang on the door. (b) aux sein (sich laut bewegen) to crash, to bang. über das Pflaster ~ to clatter over the cobbles. (c) (inf: schimpfen) to rant (and rave), to carry on (inf). (d) (inf: Polterabend feiern) to celebrate on the eve of a wedding.

Poly-: ~ester m -s, - polyester; p~gam adj polygamous; ~gamie f polygamy; p~glott adj polyglot no adv.

Polynesien [-iən] nt -s Polynesia.

Polynesier(in f) [-iə, -iərin] m -s, - Polynesian.

polynesisch adj Polynesian.

Polyp m -en, -en (a) (Zool) polyp. (b) (Med) ~en adenoids. (c) (hum inf: Polizist) cop (inf).

Poly-: ~technikum nt polytechnic, poly (inf); p~technisch adj polytechnic.

Pomade f hair-cream; (Hist, für krause Haare) pomade.

pomadig adj (inf) (a) Haare smarmed down (inf), Brylcreemed

®. (b) (schleimig) smarmy (inf). (c) (langsam) sluggish.

Pomeranze f -, -n Seville or bitter orange.

Pommer(in f) m -n, -n Pomeranian.

Pommern nt -s Pomerania.

Pommes frites [pɔm'frits] pl chips pl (Brit), French fries pl (US), French fried potatoes pl (form).

Pomp m -(e)s, no pl pomp.

pompös adj grandiose.

Poncho m -s, -s poncho.

Pond nt -s, - (Phys) weight of 1 gramme mass under standard gravity.

Pontifikalamt nt Pontifical Mass.

Pontifikat nt or m -(e)s, -e pontificate.

Pontius ['pɔntsius] m: von ~ zu Pilatus from pillar to post.

Ponton [pɔ'tõː, pɔn'tõː, 'pɔntõ] m -s, -s pontoon.

Pontonbrücke f pontoon bridge.

Pony¹ ['pɔni] nt -s, -s pony.

Pony² ['pɔni] m -s, -s (Frisur) fringe, bangs pl (US).

Ponyfrisur f hairstyle with a fringe or with bangs (US). sie hat eine ~ she has a fringe/bangs.

Pool [puːl] m -s, -s pool.

Pool(billard ['puːl(biljart]) nt pool, pocket billiards no pl.

Pop m -s, no pl (Mus) pop; (Art) pop-art; (Mode) pop fashion.

Popanz m -es, -e (a) (Schreckgespenst) bogey, bugbear. etw als ~ hinstellen to make a bogey or bugbear of sth. (b) (willenloser Mensch) puppet.

Pope m -n, -n priest; (pej) cleric.

Popel m -s, - (inf) (Nasen~) bogey (baby-talk), (piece of) snot (sl); (Mensch) pleb (inf), prole (inf).

pop(e)lig adj (a) (knauserig) stingy (inf). ~e zwei Mark a lousy two marks (inf). (b) (dürftig) crummy (inf). ihre Wohnung war recht ~ eingerichtet her flat had really crummy furniture. (c) (spießig) small-minded, narrow-minded.

Popelin m -s, -e, **Popeline** f -, - poplin.

popeln vi (inf) (in der Nase) ~ to pick one's nose.

Popo m -s, -s (inf) bottom, behind (inf), botty (baby-talk).

Poposcheitel m (inf) middle or centre parting.

poppig adj (inf) (Art, Mus) pop no adv; Kleidung trendy.

populär adj popular (bei with). etw ~ darstellen to present sth in a popular way.

popularisieren* vt to popularize.

Popularität f popularity.

populärwissenschaftlich adj popular science. seine Bücher sind mehr ~ his books are rather more popular science; etw ~ darstellen to present sth in a popular scientific way.

Population f (Biol, Sociol) population.

Pore f -, -n pore.

porig adj Gestein porous. die Haut ist ~ the skin has pores.

-porig adj suf with ... pores.

Porno m -s, -s (inf) porn (inf).

Porno- in cpds (inf) porn (inf); ~film m porn or blue film.

Pornographie f pornography.

pornographisch adj pornographic.

porös adj (durchlässig) porous; (brüchig: Gummi, Leder) perished. ~ werden to perish.

Porosität f porosity.

Porree ['pɔre] m -s, -s leek.

Port m -(e)s, -e (a) (poet) haven (poet). (b) (~wein) port.

Portable ['pɔrtəbl] nt -s, -s portable TV or television (set).

Portal nt -s, -e portal.

Portefeuille [pɔrt(ə)'føːj] nt -s, -s (Pol, obs) portfolio; (obs: Brieftasche) wallet.

Portemonnaie [pɔrtmo'neː, pɔrtmo'nɛː] nt -s, -s purse.

Porti pl of Porto.

Portier [pɔr'tieː] m -s, -s porter; siehe Pförtner(in).

portieren* vt (Sw, Pol) to put up.

Portierloge [pɔr'tieːloːʒə] f porter's lodge; siehe Pförtnerloge.

Portion f (a) (beim Essen) portion, helping. eine halbe ~ a half portion; (fig inf) a half-pint (inf); eine zweite ~ a second helping; eine ~ Kaffee a pot of coffee; eine ~ Butter a portion of butter. (b) (fig inf: Anteil) amount. er besitzt eine ganze ~ Frechheit he's got a fair amount of cheek (inf); sie brachte eine gute ~ Geduld auf she showed a fair amount of patience (inf).

portionenweise, portionsweise adv in helpings or portions.

Porto nt -s, -s or **Porti** postage no pl (für in, for); (für Kisten etc) carriage. ~ zahlt Empfänger postage paid; das ~ für den Brief macht 70 Pfennig the postage on or for the letter is 70 Pfennig.

Porto-: ~auslagen pl postal or postage expenses pl; p~frei adj post free, postage paid; ~kasse f ≈ petty cash (for postal expenses); p~pflichtig adj liable or subject to postage.

Porträt, Portrait [pɔr'trɛː] nt -s, -s (lit, fig) portrait.

Porträtaufnahme f portrait photo(graph).

porträtieren*, portraitieren* vt (fig) to portray. jdn ~ to paint a portrait of sb, to paint sb's portrait.

Porträtist, Portraitist, Porträtmaler m portrait painter, portraitist.

Porträt-, Portrait-: ~malerei f portraiture; ~photographie f portrait photo(graph); ~studie f sketch for a portrait.

Portugal nt -s Portugal.

Portugiese m, -n, -n, **Portugiesin** f Portuguese.

portugiesisch adj Portuguese.

Portwein m port.

Porzellan nt -s, -e (Material) china, porcelain; (Geschirr) china. unnötig ~ zerbrechen or zerschlagen (fig) to cause a lot of unnecessary bother or trouble.

Porzellan- in cpds china, porcelain; ~erde f china clay, kaolin;

~geschirr nt china, crockery; ~laden m china shop; siehe Elefant; ~manufaktur f porcelain or china factory; (Herstellung) porcelain or china production.

Posaune f -, -n trombone; (fig) trumpet. die ~n des Jüngsten Gerichts the last trump.

posaunen* (inf) 1 vi (Posaune spielen) to play the trombone. 2 vti (fig: laut sprechen) to bellow, to bawl, to yell. etw in alle Welt or in die Gegend ~ to shout sth from the rooftops or hilltops, to tell or proclaim sth to the whole world.

Posaunen-: ~bläser m trombonist, trombone player; ~chor m trombone band (usually connected with a church); ~engel m (lit) cherub with a trumpet; (fig) (little) chubby-cheeks (inf).

Posaunist(in f) m siehe **Posaunenbläser.**

Pose f -, -n pose.

posieren* vi to pose. er posiert in der Rolle des Wohltäters he's playing the benefactor.

Position f position; (Comm: Posten einer Liste) item. in gesicherter ~ sein to have a secure position.

Positions-: ~lampe f, ~licht nt navigation light.

positiv adj positive. eine ~e Antwort an answer in the affirmative, an affirmative (answer); das ist sehr ~ (inf) that's really great (inf); etw ~ wissen to know sth for certain or for a fact, to be positive; ich weiß nichts P~es I don't know anything definite; ~ zu etw stehen to be in favour of sth; sich ~ zu einer Sache äußern to respond or react positively to sth.

Positiv¹ m (Gram) positive.

Positiv² nt (Phot) positive.

Positivismus m positivism.

positivistisch adj positivist.

Positur f posture; (stehend auch) stance. sich in ~ setzen/ stellen to take up or adopt a posture; sie setzte sich vor ihrem Chef in ~ she sat neatly posed for her boss; sich in ~ werfen to strike a pose.

Posse f -, -n farce.

Possen m -s, - (dated) prank, tomfoolery no pl. ~ reißen to lark or fool or clown around; jdm einen ~ spielen to play a prank on sb; mit jdm ~ treiben (old) to play pranks on sb; er tat es mir zum ~ he did it just to annoy me.

Possen-: p~haft adj farcical; ~reißer m -s, - clown, buffoon; ~spiel nt (liter) pranks pl.

possessiv adj possessive.

Possessiv(pronomen) nt -s, -e, **Possessivum** nt possessive pronoun.

possierlich adj comical, funny.

Post f -, -en (a) post, mail; (~amt, ~wesen) post office. war die ~ schon da? has the post or mail come yet?; ist ~ für mich da? is there any post or mail for me?, are there any letters for me?; er las seine ~ he read his mail; etw mit der ~ schicken to send sth by post or mail; etw auf die ~ geben to post or mail sth; auf die or zur ~ gehen to go to the post office; mit gleicher ~ by the same post; mit getrennter ~ under separate cover; mit der ersten ~ kommen to come with or in the first post, to come first post; etw durch die ~ beziehen to order sth by post.
(b) (~kutsche) mail coach; (~bus) mail bus.
(c) (obs: Nachricht) news no pl.

Post|abholer m -s, - someone who collects his mail from a PO box.

postalisch adj postal.

Postament nt pedestal, base.

Post-: ~amt nt post office; ~anschrift f postal address; ~anweisung f remittance paid in at a Post Office and delivered by post ≈ postal (Brit) or money order; ~auto nt post-office van; (Lieferwagen) mail van (Brit) or truck (US); (Bus) mail bus; ~beamte(r) m, ~beamtin f post office official; ~bedienstete(r) mf (form) post office worker; ~bezirk m postal district or area or zone (US); ~boot nt mail boat, packet (boat); ~bote m postman, mailman (US); ~bus m mail bus.

Pöstchen nt dim of **Posten** little position or job.

Postdienst m postal service, the mails pl (US).

Posten m -s, - (a) (Anstellung) post, position, job.
(b) (Mil: Wachmann) guard; (am Eingang auch) sentry; (Stelle) post. ~ stehen to stand guard; (am Eingang auch) to stand sentry; ~ beziehen to take up one's post; ~ aufstellen to post guards, to mount a guard.
(c) auf dem ~ sein (aufpassen) to be awake; (gesund sein) to be fit; nicht ganz auf dem ~ sein to be (a bit) under the weather, to be off-colour; siehe verloren, ausharren.
(d) (Streik~) picket. ~ aufstellen to set up pickets or a picket-line.
(e) (Comm: Warenmenge) quantity, lot.
(f) (Comm: im Etat) item, entry.

Posten-: ~dienst m guard duty; ~dienst haben to be on guard duty; ~jäger m (inf) go-getter (inf), pusher (inf); ~kette f cordon.

Poster ['poːstɐ] nt -s, -(s) poster.

Postf. abbr of **Postfach.**

Post-: ~fach nt post-office or PO box; ~fachnummer f (PO or post-office) box number; p~fertig adj ready for posting or for the post; ~flugzeug nt mail plane; p~frisch adj mint; ~gebühr f postal (and telephone) charge or rate; ~geheimnis nt secrecy of the post; ~halterei f coaching house or inn; ~horn nt posthorn.

posthum adj posthumous.

postieren* 1 vt to post, to station, to position. 2 vr to station or position oneself.

Postillion [pɔstɪl'joːn, pɔstɪljoːn] m -s, -e mail coach driver.

Postillon d'amour [pɔstijõdaˈmuːr] m - -, - -s - go-between.

Postkarte f postcard, postal card (US), postal (US inf).

Postkarten-: ~format nt, ~größe f postcard size; in ~größe postcard sized.

Post-: ~kasten m pillar box (Brit), postbox, mailbox (US); ~kutsche f mail coach, stagecoach; p~lagernd 1 adj to be called for; 2 adv poste restante; ~leitzahl f post(al) code, Zip code (US).

Postler(in f) m -s, - (inf) post office official/worker.

Post-: ~meister m postmaster; ~minister m postmaster general; ~paket nt parcel (sent by post); per ~paket (by) parcel-post; ~sache f post office mail no pl; ~sack m mailbag; ~schalter m post office counter; ~scheck m (Post Office or National) Giro cheque (Brit); ~scheckamt nt National Giro office (Brit); ~scheckkonto nt National or Post Office Giro account (Brit); ~schließfach nt siehe ~fach; ~skript nt -(e)s, -e, ~skriptum nt -s, -e or ~skripta postscript, PS abbr; ~sparbuch nt Post Office savings book; ~sparkasse f Post Office savings bank; ~stelle f sub post office; ~stempel m postmark.

Postulat nt (Annahme) postulate; (Eccl: Probezeit) postulancy.

postulieren* vt to postulate.

postum adj siehe **posthum.**

Post-: ~wagen m (Rail) mail car or van (Brit); p~wendend adv by return (of post), by return mail; ~wertzeichen nt (form) postage stamp (form); ~wesen nt Post Office; ~wurfsendung f postal door-to-door delivery; ~zug m mail train; ~zustellung f postal or mail delivery.

Pot nt -s, no pl (sl: Haschisch) pot (sl).

Potemkinsche Dörfer pl façade, sham.

potent adj potent; (fig) Phantasie powerful; Mensch high-powered.

Potentat m -en, -en potentate.

Potential [potɛn'tsiaːl] nt -s, -e potential.

Potentialität [potɛntsialiˈtɛːt] f (geh) potentiality.

potentiell [potɛn'tsiɛl] adj potential. er ist ~ mein Gegner he's a potential opponent, he's potentially my opponent.

Potenz f (a) (Med) potency; (fig) ability. schöpferische ~ creative power.
(b) (Math) power. zweite/dritte ~ square/cube; eine Zahl in die sechste ~ erheben to raise a number to the power of six or to the sixth power; die zweite/dritte ~ zu zwei ist vier/acht the square/cube of two is four/eight, two to the power of two/three is four/eight; die sechste ~ zu zwei two to the sixth (power); in höchster ~ (fig) to the highest degree; er spinnt in höchster ~ (inf) he must be absolutely crazy (inf).
(c) (Philos) potentiality.

potenzieren* vt (Math) to raise to the power of; (fig: steigern) to multiply, to increase. 2 potenziert mit 4 2 to the power of 4, 2 to the fourth.

Potpourri ['pɔtpuri] nt -s, -s (Mus) potpourri, medley (aus +dat of); (fig) potpourri, assortment.

Pott m -(e)s, ¨e (inf) pot; (Schiff) ship, tub (hum inf).

Pott-: ~asche f potash; p~egal adj pred (inf) es ist p~egal it doesn't matter a bit (inf); das ist mir p~egal I couldn't care less; ~fisch, ~wal m sperm whale; p~häßlich adj (inf) ugly as sin, plug-ugly (inf).

potz Blitz, potztausend interj (old) upon my soul (old).

poussieren [pu'siːrən] 1 vi (dated inf: flirten) to flirt. 2 vt (old: schmeicheln) jdn ~ to curry favour with sb.

power ['poːvɐ] adj (inf) poor; Essen, Geschenke meagre. der Ring sieht ~ aus the ring looks cheap; er hat mir zwei Mark gegeben, das war recht ~ he gave me two marks, that was really mean (of him).

Prä nt: das ~ haben to come first.

prä-, prae- pref pre-.

Präambel f preamble (gen to).

Pracht f -, no pl splendour, magnificence; (fig: Herrlichkeit) splendour. in seiner vollen or ganzen ~ in all its splendour or magnificence; große ~ entfalten to put on a show or display of great splendour; es ist eine wahre ~ it's (really) marvellous or fantastic; er kann singen, daß es eine ~ ist he can sing marvellously or fantastically.

Pracht-: ~ausgabe f de luxe edition; ~bau m splendid or magnificent building; ~entfaltung f display of splendour, magnificent display; zur vollen ~entfaltung kommen to display its/their full splendour; ~exemplar nt splendid or prime specimen, beauty (inf); (von Buch: ~ausgabe) de luxe copy; (fig: Mensch) fine specimen; mein ~exemplar von Sohn (iro) my brilliant son (iro).

prächtig adj (prunkvoll) splendid, magnificent; (großartig) splendid, marvellous.

Pracht-: ~kerl m (inf) great guy (inf), good bloke (Brit inf); (~exemplar) beauty (inf); ~straße f boulevard, magnificent avenue; ~stück nt siehe ~exemplar; p~voll adj siehe prächtig; ~weib nt (inf) fine specimen of a woman or of womanhood.

Prädestination f predestination.

prädestinieren* vt to predestine, to predetermine. sein diplomatisches Geschick prädestinierte ihn zum Politiker with his diplomatic skill he was predestined to be a politician; er ist für diese Aufgabe wie prädestiniert he seems to have been made for the job.

Prädikat nt (Gram) predicate; (Bewertung) rating; (Sch: Zensur) grade; (Rangbezeichnung) title. Wein mit ~ special quality wine.

prädikativ adj predicative.

Prädikativ(um) nt predicative noun/adjective/pronoun.

Prädikatsnomen nt predicative noun/pronoun.

prädisponieren* vt to predispose (für to).

Präfekt m -en, -en prefect.

Präferenz f (geh) preference.

Präferenzstellung f special or privileged status.

Präfix nt -es, -e prefix.

Prag nt -s Prague. ~er Frühling (Pol) Spring of Prague.
Präge f -, -n, **Präge|anstalt** f mint.
prägen vt (a) to stamp; Münzen to mint, to strike; Leder, Papier, Metall to emboss; (erfinden) Begriffe, Wörter to coin. seine Worte prägten sich ihr ins Herz (liter) his words engraved themselves in her heart (liter).
(b) (fig: formen) Charakter to shape, to mould; (Erlebnis, Kummer, Erfahrungen) jdn to leave its/their mark on. ein vom Leid geprägtes Gesicht a face marked by suffering; das moderne Drama ist durch Brecht geprägt worden Brecht had a forming or formative influence on modern drama.
(c) (kennzeichnen) Stadtbild, Landschaft etc to characterize.
Präge-: ~ort m mint; ~stempel m die, stamp; ~stock m punch.
Pragmatiker(in f) m -s, - pragmatist.
pragmatisch adj pragmatic.
Pragmatismus m pragmatism.
prägnant adj succinct, concise, terse.
Prägnanz f succinctness, conciseness, terseness.
Prägung f (a) siehe vt (a, b) stamping; minting, striking; embossing; coining; shaping, moulding. (b) (auf Münzen) strike; (auf Leder, Metall, Papier) embossing. (c) (Eigenart) character; (von Charakter) mould.
prähistorisch adj prehistoric.
prahlen vi (mit about) to boast, to brag, to swank (inf).
Prahler(in f) m -s, - boaster, bragger, braggard.
Prahlerei f (Großsprecherei) boasting no pl, bragging no pl; (das Zurschaustellen) showing-off, swank (inf). ~en boasts, showing-off, swanking (inf).
prahlerisch adj (großsprecherisch) boastful, bragging attr; (großtuerisch) swanky (inf).
Prahl-: ~hans m -es, -hänse (inf) show-off; ~sucht f boastfulness.
Prahm m -(e)s, -e or ¨e barge, lighter.
präjudizieren* vt insep (Jur) to prejudge.
Praktik f (Methode) procedure, method; (usu pl: Kniff) practice, trick. undurchsichtige ~en shady or dark practices.
Praktika pl of **Praktikum**.
praktikabel adj practicable, practical.
Praktikant(in f) m student doing a period of practical training, trainee.
Praktiker(in f) m -s, - practical man/woman; (auf wissenschaftlichem Gebiet auch) practician; (inf: praktischer Arzt) GP. was halten Sie als ~ von der Pädagogik? what do you, as a practising teacher, think of educational theory?
Praktikum nt -s, **Praktika** practical, (period of) practical training.
Praktikus m -, -se (inf) handyman (inf).
praktisch 1 adj practical; (nützlich auch) handy. sie hat einen ~en Verstand she's practically minded; ~er Arzt general practitioner; ~es Jahr practical year; ~e Ausbildung practical or in-job training; ~es Beispiel concrete example.
2 adv (in der Praxis) in practice; (geschickt) practically; (so gut wie) practically, virtually.
praktizieren* 1 vi to practise. ein ~der Katholik a practising Catholic. 2 vt (a) (pej: ausführen) to put into practice, to practise. (b) (inf: geschickt an eine Stelle bringen) to conjure.
Prälat m -en, -en prelate.
Präliminarien [-iən] pl preliminary talks or discussions pl.
Praline f, **Praliné, Pralinee** (Aus) nt -s, -s chocolate, chocolate candy (US).
prall adj Sack, Beutel, Brieftasche bulging; Segel billowing, full; Tomaten firm; Euter swollen, full; Luftballon hard; Wange full, chubby; Brüste full, well-rounded; Hintern wellrounded; Arme, Schenkel big strong attr; Sonne blazing. ~gefüllt filled to bursting; das Segel war ~ vom Wind gefüllt the sail billowed out in the wind; ihre Brüste wölbten sich ~ unter dem Pullover her breasts curved firmly under her sweater; die Hose spannte sich ~ über ihrem Hintern her trousers stretched tightly over her bottom; die Sonne brannte ~ auf den Strand the sun blazed or beat down onto the beach.
Prall m -(e)s, -e collision (gegen with).
prallen vi aux sein gegen etw ~ to collide with sth, to crash into sth; (Ball) to bounce against or off sth; er prallte mit dem Kopf gegen die Windschutzscheibe he hit or crashed his head on or against the windscreen; die Sonne prallte gegen or auf die Fenster the sun beat or blazed down on the windows.
Prallheit f (von Ballon) hardness; (von Brüsten, Hintern) fullness, well-roundedness; (von Euter) fullness, swollenness. die ~ der Segel the fullness of the sails, the billowing sails; die ~ ihrer Schenkel her big strong thighs; der ~ seiner Brieftasche nach zu urteilen judging by his bulging wallet or the bulge in his wallet.
prallvoll adj full to bursting; Brieftasche bulging.
Präludium nt prelude; (sexuell) foreplay.
Prämie [-iə] f premium; (Belohnung) bonus; (Preis) prize.
prämien- [-iən] -:~begünstigt adj concession- or premiumcarrying, with benefit of premiums; P~los nt winning premium bond; ~sparen vi sep infin, ptp only to save on a system benefiting from government premiums in addition to interest.
prämieren*, prämiieren* vt (auszeichnen) to give an award; (belohnen) to give a bonus. etw mit dem ersten Preis/mit 1000 Mark ~ to award sth first prize/a prize of 1000 marks or a 1000 mark prize; jedes Tor ~ to give a bonus for every goal.
Prämierung, Prämiierung f (a) (das Prämieren) für diesen Film kommt eine ~ nicht in Frage we can't possibly give this film an award; wir sind gegen die ~ von Toren we don't think there should be bonuses for goals.
(b) (Veranstaltung) presentation. die ~ der Preisträger the presentation to the prizewinners.

Prämisse f -, -n premise.
pränatal adj attr prenatal; Vorsorge antenatal.
prangen vi (liter) to be resplendent. an der Tür prangte ein Schild/sein Name in großen Lettern a notice hung resplendent on the door/his name was emblazoned in big letters on the door.
Pranger m -s, - stocks pl, pillory. jdn/etw an den ~ stellen (fig) to pillory sb/sth; am ~ stehen (lit) to be in the stocks or pillory; (fig) to be being pilloried.
Pranke f -, -n (Tier~) paw; (inf: Hand) paw (inf), mauler (inf).
Prankenhieb m swipe or blow from a paw. ein ~ des Löwen streckte die Antilope nieder one blow or swipe from the lion's paw laid the antelope low.
Präparat nt preparation; (für Mikroskop) slide preparation.
präparieren* 1 vt (a) (konservieren) to preserve. (b) (Med: zerlegen) to dissect. (c) (geh: vorbereiten) to prepare. 2 vr (dated) to prepare (oneself), to do one's preparation (für, auf +acc for).
Präposition f preposition.
präpositional adj prepositional.
Prärie f prairie.
Präriewolf m prairie wolf, coyote.
Präsens nt -, **Präsenzien** [-iən] present (tense).
präsent adj (anwesend) present; (geistig rege) alert. etw ~ haben to have sth at hand; sein Name ist mir nicht ~ his name escapes me; ~e Konzentration/Geistesgegenwart ready concentration/presence of mind.
Präsent nt -s, -e present, gift.
präsentabel adj presentable.
präsentieren* 1 vt to present. jdm etw ~ to present sb with sth; präsentiert das Gewehr! present arms! 2 vr (sich zeigen) to present oneself; (sich vorstellen auch) to introduce oneself. 3 vi (Mil) to present arms.
Präsentierteller m (old) salver.
Präsenz f -, no pl (geh) presence. die ständig abnehmende ~ im Büro the constantly decreasing numbers in the office.
Präsenz-: ~bibliothek f reference library; ~liste f (attendance) register.
Präservativ nt contraceptive, condom, sheath.
Präsidentenwahl f presidential election.
Präsident(in f) m president. Herr/Frau ~ Mister/Madam President.
Präsidentschaft f presidency.
Präsidentschaftskandidat m presidential candidate.
präsidieren* vi to preside. einem Ausschuß ~ to preside over or be president of a committee.
Präsidium nt (Vorsitz) presidency; (Führungsgruppe) committee; (Polizei~) (police) headquarters pl. ins ~ gewählt werden to be elected to the committee; das ~ übernehmen to take the chair.
prasseln vi (a) aux sein to clatter; (Regen, Hagel) to drum; (fig: Vorwürfe, Fragen) to rain or hail down. ~der Beifall a hail of applause, thunderous applause.
(b) (Feuer) to crackle.
prassen vi (schlemmen) to feast; (in Luxus leben) to live the high life.
Prasser m -s, - glutton; (Verschwender) spendthrift.
Prasserei f (Schlemmerei) feasting; (Luxusleben) high life.
Prätendent m pretender.
prätentiös [prɛtɛn'tsiø:s] adj pretentious.
Präteritum nt -s, **Präterita** preterite.
Pratze f -, -n (S Ger inf) paw; (fig: Hand) paw (inf), mauler (sl).
präventiv [prɛvɛn'ti:f] adj prevent(at)ive.
Präventiv-: ~behandlung f (Med) preventive treatment; ~krieg m preventive or pre-emptive war; ~maßnahme f preventive measure.
Praxis f -, **Praxen** (a) (no pl) practice; (Erfahrung) experience; (Brauch) practice, custom. in der ~ in practice; das stimmt nicht mit der ~ überein that doesn't correspond with the facts or reality; die ~ sieht anders aus the facts are different; eine Idee in die ~ umsetzen to put an idea into practice; ein Mann der ~ a man with practical experience; ein Beispiel aus der ~ an example from real life; das lernt man erst durch die ~ you only learn that by doing it, that's only learnt through practical experience; seine langjährige ~ his long years of experience.
(b) (eines Arztes, Rechtsanwalts) practice.
(c) (Behandlungsräume, Sprechstunde) surgery (Brit); tor's office (US); (Anwaltsbüro) office.
Präzedenzfall m precedent. einen ~ schaffen to set or create or establish a precedent.
präzis(e) adj precise.
präzisieren* vt to state more precisely; (zusammenfassen) to summarize. nach seiner ~den Erklärung ... after the explanation he gave stating things more precisely ...
Präzision f precision.
Präzisions- in cpds precision; ~arbeit f precision work; ~arbeit leisten to work with precision.
predigen 1 vt (a) to preach. solche Leute ~ immer Moral people like that are always preaching (about) or sermonizing about morality.
(b) (fig) jdm etw ~ to lecture sb on sth; sie predigt ihm andauernd, daß er sich die Zähne putzen soll she keeps lecturing him on the importance of cleaning his teeth.
2 vi to give a sermon, to preach; (fig: mahnen) to preach, to sermonize. tauben Ohren ~ to preach to deaf ears.
Prediger(in f) m -s, - preacher/woman preacher.
Predigt f -, -en (lit, fig) sermon. jdm eine lange ~ über etw (acc) halten (fig) to give sb a long sermon on or about sth.
Predigttext m text for a sermon.
Preis m -es, -e (a) price (für of); (Fahrgeld) fare (für for);

(Gebühr, Honorar) fee (für of). der ~ für die Hose beträgt 10 Mark the price of the trousers is 10 marks; hoch or gut im ~ stehen to be in demand; (weit) unter(m) ~ cut-price; zum halben ~ half-price; um jeden ~ (fig) at all costs; ich gehe um keinen ~ hier weg (fig) I'm not leaving here at any price; auch um den ~ seines eignen Glücks even at the expense of his own happiness.

(b) (bei Wettbewerben) prize; (Auszeichnung) award. in diesem Rennen ist kein ~ ausgesetzt there's no prize in or for this race; den ersten ~ gewinnen to win (the) first prize; jdm einen ~ zusprechen or zuerkennen or verleihen to award or give sb a prize/to give sb an award.

(c) (Belohnung) reward. einen ~ auf jds Kopf aussetzen to put a price on sb's head.

(d) no pl (liter: Lob) praise (auf + acc of). ein Gedicht zum ~ von ... a poem in praise of ...

Preis-: ~abbau m price reduction; ~angabe f price quotation; alle Kleider sind mit ~angabe all dresses are priced, the prices of all dresses are given; ~anstieg m rise in prices; ~aufgabe f prize competition; die erste ~aufgabe besteht darin, ... the first part of the competition is ...; ~aufschlag m supplementary charge, supplement; ~auftrieb m price increase; ~ausschreiben nt competition; ~bewegung f movement of prices; p~bewußt adj price-conscious; ~bildung f price fixing; ~bindung f price fixing; ~bindung der zweiten Hand retail price maintenance; ~brecher m (Produkt) (all-time) bargain, snip (inf); (Firma) undercutter; diese Firma wirkt als ~brecher auf dem Markt this firm undercuts the market; ~disziplin f price restraint.

Preiselbeere f cranberry.

preisen pret **pries**, ptp **gepriesen** vt (geh) to extol, to praise, to laud (liter). Gott sei gepriesen praise be to God; sich glücklich ~ to consider or count or think oneself lucky.

Preis-: ~entwicklung f price trend; ~erhöhung f price increase; ~ermäßigung f price reduction; ~explosion f price explosion; ~frage f (a) question of price; (b) (beim ~ausschreiben) prize question (in a competition); (inf: schwierige Frage) sixty-four-thousand dollar question (inf), big question; ~gabe f (geh) (Aufgabe) surrender, relinquishment, abandoning; (von Geheimnis) betrayal, divulgence; sie wurden zur ~gabe ihrer Position gezwungen they were forced to surrender or abandon or relinquish their position.

preisgeben vt sep irreg (geh) (a) (ausliefern) to expose, to leave to the mercy of. jdm/einer Sache preisgegeben sein to be exposed to or at the mercy of sb/sth; das Haus war dem Verfall preisgegeben the building was left to decay.

(b) (aufgeben) to abandon, to relinquish; Gebiete auch to surrender.

(c) (verraten) to betray; Geheimnis auch to divulge.

Preis-: ~gefälle nt price gap; ~gefüge nt price structure; p~gekrönt adj award-winning; p~gekrönt werden to be given an award; ~gericht nt jury, team of judges; gestaltung f price structuring; ~grenze f price limit; p~günstig adj inexpensive; etw p~günstig bekommen to get sth at a low or good price; ~index m price index; ~kontrolle f price control; ~lage f price range; in jeder ~lage at all prices, at prices to suit every pocket; ~lawine f (inf) snowballing prices pl.

preislich adj no pred price attr, in price. dieses Angebot ist ~ sehr günstig this offer is a bargain; die Waren sind nur ~ verschieden the goods only differ in price.

Preis-: ~liste f price list; ~nachlaß m price reduction; 10% ~nachlaß bei Barbezahlung 10% off cash sales; ~niveau nt price level; ~politik f prices policy; ~rätsel nt prize competition; ~richter m judge (in a competition), jury-member; ~schießen nt shooting competition or contest, shoot; ~schild nt price-tag; ~schlager m (all-time) bargain; ~schwankung f price fluctuation; ~senkung f price cut; ~spanne f price margin; p~stabil adj stable in price; ~stabilität f stability of prices; ~steigerung f price increase; ~stopp m price freeze; ~sturz m sudden fall or drop in prices; „~stürze!" drastic reductions; ~träger(in f) m prizewinner; (Kultur-)winner; siehe Nobelpreis; ~treiber m person who forces prices up; ~treiberei f forcing up of prices; (Wucher) profiteering; das ist nur ein Vorwand für die ~treiberei der Industrie that's only an excuse for industry to force up prices; ~überwachung f siehe ~kontrolle; ~vergleich m price comparison; einen ~vergleich machen to shop around; ~verleihung f presentation (of prizes/awards); ~verzeichnis nt siehe ~liste; p~wert adj good value pred; ein (sehr) p~wertes Angebot a (real) bargain; ein p~wertes Kleid a dress which is good value (for money); hier kann man p~wert einkaufen you get good value (for money) here.

prekär adj (peinlich) awkward, embarrassing; (schwierig) precarious.

Prell-: ~ball m game similar to volleyball in which the ball is bounced over the net; ~bock m (Rail) buffers pl, buffer-stop; der ~bock sein (fig) to be the scapegoat or fallguy (esp US inf).

prellen 1 vt (a) to bruise; (anschlagen) to hit. (b) (fig inf: betrügen) to swindle, to cheat. jdm um etw ~ to swindle or cheat sb out of sth; die Zeche ~ to avoid paying the bill. (c) (Sport) to bounce. 2 vr to bruise oneself. ich habe mich am Arm geprellt I've bruised my arm.

Prellerei f swindle, fraud. das ist doch ~ that's fraud.

Prellschuß m ricochet, ricocheting bullet.

Prellung f bruise, contusion.

Premier [prə'mie:, pre-] m -s, -s premier.

Premiere [prə'mie:rə, pre-, -'miɛːrə] f -, -n premiere.

Premieren-: ~besucher pl, ~publikum nt premiere audience no pl; ~kino nt first-run cinema.

Premierminister [prə'mie:-, pre-] m prime minister.

Presbyterianer(in f) m Presbyterian.

presbyterianisch adj Presbyterian.

preschen vi aux sein (inf) to tear, to dash.

pressant adj (dated, dial) urgent.

Presse f -, -n (a) (mechanische ~) press; (Sch sl: Privatschule) crammer (sl). in die ~ gehen to go to press; frisch or eben aus der ~ hot from the press. (b) (Zeitungen) press. eine gute ~ haben to have or get a good press.

Presse-: ~agentur f press or news agency; ~amt nt press office; ~ausweis m press card; ~bank f press bench; ~baron m (inf) press baron (inf); ~bericht m press report; ~büro nt siehe ~agentur; ~dienst m news service; ~empfang m press reception; ~erklärung f statement to the press, press release; ~fotograf m press photographer; ~freiheit f freedom of the press; ~gesetz nt press law; ~kampagne f press campaign; ~karte f press or review ticket; ~kommentar m press commentary; ~konferenz f press conference; ~meldung f press report.

pressen 1 vt (a) to press; Obst auch to squeeze; hohe Töne to squeeze out; (fig: zwingen) to force (in + acc into); (fig dated: unterdrücken) to oppress. (b) (Naut) Segel ~ to make too much sail. 2 vi (Sänger) to squeeze the/one's notes out.

Presse-: ~notiz f paragraph in the press; ~organ nt organ; ~recht nt press laws pl; ~referent m press officer; ~stelle f press office; ~stimme f press commentary; (kulturell) press review; ~tribüne f press box; (Parl) press gallery; ~verband m association of newspaper owners; ~vertreter m representative of the press; ~wesen nt press; ~zar m (inf) press king.

Preßglas nt pressed glass.

pressieren* (S Ger, Aus, Sw) 1 vi to be in a hurry. 2 vi impers es pressiert it's urgent; (bei) ihm pressiert es immer he's always in a hurry; ich konnte es nicht fertigmachen, weil es wieder mal pressierte I couldn't finish it since time was pressing again.

Pression f pressure. ~en anwenden to put on the pressure.

Preß-: ~kohle f siehe Brikett; ~luft f compressed air; ~luftbohrer m pneumatic drill; ~lufthammer m pneumatic or air hammer.

Prestige [prɛs'tiːʒə] nt -s, no pl prestige. ~ verlieren to lose (one's) prestige.

Prestige-: ~frage f question or matter of prestige; ~gewinn m gain in prestige; ~sache f siehe ~frage; ~verlust m loss of prestige.

Pretiosen [pre'tsioːzn] pl (geh) valuables pl.

Preuße m -n, -n, **Preußin** f Prussian. so schnell schießen die ~n nicht (inf) things don't happen that fast.

Preußen nt -s Prussia.

preußisch adj Prussian.

preußischblau adj Prussian blue.

preziös adj (geh) precious.

Pricke f -, -n (Naut) shallows marker.

prickeln vi (kribbeln) to tingle; (kitzeln) to tickle; (Bläschen bilden) to sparkle, to bubble. die Limonade prickelt in der Nase the lemonade's tickling my nose; ein angenehmes P~ auf der Haut a pleasant tingling of the skin; ich spürte ein P~ in meinem Bein I had pins and needles in my leg.

prickelnd adj siehe vi tingling; tickling; sparkling, bubbling; (fig: würzig) piquant; (fig: erregend) Gefühl tingling. Horrorfilme üben einen ~en Reiz auf mich aus horror films give me a thrill or kick (inf); der ~e Reiz der Neuheit the thrill of novelty; etwas P~es für den Gaumen something to titillate the tastebuds (hum), something tasty for the palate.

Priel m -(e)s, -e narrow channel (in North Sea mud flats), tideway.

Priem m -(e)s, -e quid of tobacco.

priemen vi to chew tobacco.

pries pret of preisen.

Priester m -s, - priest.

Priester|amt nt priesthood.

Priesterin f priestess.

priesterlich adj priestly no adv; Kleidung auch clerical.

Priester-: ~rock m cassock; ~schaft f priesthood; ~seminar nt seminary; ~tum nt priesthood; ~weihe f ordination (to the priesthood); die ~weihe empfangen to be ordained (to the priesthood or to a priest).

prima adj inv (a) (inf) fantastic (inf), great no adv (inf). das hast du ~ gemacht you did that fantastically (well) or beautifully or just great. (b) (Comm) first-class, top-quality.

Prima f -, Primen (Sch) eighth and ninth year of German secondary school; (Aus) first year of secondary school.

Prima-: ~ballerina f prima ballerina; ~donna f -, -donnen prima donna.

Primaner(in f) m -s, - (Sch) ≈ sixth-former; (Aus) first-former.

primär adj primary.

Primärliteratur f primary literature or sources pl.

Primarschule f (Sw) primary or junior school.

Primas m -, -se or Primaten (Eccl) primate; (in Zigeunerkapelle) first violin.

Primat[1] m or nt -(e)s, -e priority, primacy (vor over); (des Papstes) primacy; (Erstgeburtsrecht) primogeniture.

Primat[2] m -en, -en (Zool) primate.

Primaten pl of Primas and Primat[2].

Primel f -, -n (Wald~) (wild) primrose; (Schlüsselblume) cowslip; (farbige Garten~) primula; (mit verzweigtem Stiel) polyanthus. wie eine ~ eingehen (fig) to fade or wither away.

Primen pl of Prima.

Primi pl of Primus.

primitiv adj primitive; Maschine auch crude.

Primitive(r) mf decl as adj primitive person; (Art) primitive.

Primitivität f siehe adj primitiveness; crudeness.

Primitivling m (pej inf) peasant (pej inf), primitive (pej inf).

Primus m -, -se or **Primi** top of the class or form, top or star pupil.

Primzahl f prime (number).

Prinz m -en, -en prince. wie ein ~ leben (inf) to live like a lord or a king; unser kleiner ~ (inf) our son and heir (inf).

Prinzessin f princess. eine ~ auf der Erbse (fig) a hot-house plant.

Prinzgemahl m prince consort.

Prinzip nt -s, -ien [-iən] or (rare) -e principle. aus ~ on principle; das hat er aus ~ getan he did it on principle or as a matter of principle; im ~ in principle; das funktioniert nach einem einfachen ~ it works on a simple principle; nach einem ~ handeln to act according to a principle; er ist ein Mann von or mit ~ien he is a man of principle.

Prinzipal m -s, -e (old) (Geschäftsinhaber) proprietor; (Lehrherr) master.

prinzipiell adj (im Prinzip) in principle; (aus Prinzip) on principle. ~ bin ich einverstanden I agree in principle; das tue ich ~ nicht I won't do that on principle.

Prinzipien- [-iən-]: p~fest adj firm-principled; er ist ein p~fester Mann he's a man of very firm principles; ~frage f matter or question of principle; p~los adj unprincipled; ~losigkeit f lack of principle(s); ~reiter m (pej) stickler for one's principles; ~reiterei f (pej) going-on about principles (pej); ~streit m dispute about principles.

Prinzregent m prince regent.

Prior m prior.

Priorin f prioress.

Priorität f priority. ~en pl (Comm) preference shares pl, preferred stock (US); ~ vor etw (dat) haben to have or take priority or precedence over sth; ~en setzen to establish one's priorities; die richtigen ~en setzen to get one's priorities right.

Prise f -, -n (a) (kleine Menge) pinch. eine ~ Humor a touch of humour. (b) (Naut) prize.

Prisma nt -s, **Prismen** prism.

prismatisch adj prismatic.

Prismen pl of **Prisma**.

Prismenglas nt prismatic telescope.

Pritsche f -, -n (a) (Narren~) fool's wand. (b) (von LKW) platform. (c) (Liegestatt) plank bed.

Pritschenwagen m platform truck.

privat [pri'vaːt] adj private; Telefonnummer auch home attr. ~ ist der Chef sehr freundlich the boss is very friendly out(side) of work; ~ ist er ganz anders he's quite different socially; jdn ~ sprechen to speak to sb in private or privately; jdn ~ unterbringen to put sb up privately; dazu hat er sich ~ ganz anders geäußert what he said about it in private was quite different; ich sagte es ihm ganz ~ I told him quite confidentially or in absolute confidence; etw an P~ verkaufen (Comm) to sell sth to the public or to private individuals.

Privat- in cpds private; ~adresse f private or home address; ~angelegenheit f private matter; das ist meine ~angelegenheit that's my own business, that's a private matter; ~besitz m private property; viele Gemälde sind in ~besitz many paintings are privately owned or in private ownership; ~detektiv m private detective or investigator or eye (inf); ~dozent m outside lecturer; ~druck m privately published edition; als ~druck erschienen published privately; ~eigentum nt private property; ~gelehrte(r) m scholar; ~gespräch nt private conversation or talk; (am Telefon) private call.

Privatier [priva'tieː] m -s, -s (dated) man of independent or private means.

Privat-: ~initiative f private initiative; ~interesse nt private interest.

privatisieren* [privati'ziːrən] 1 vt to take into private ownership. 2 vi to live on a private income or on independent means.

Privat-: ~klage f private action or suit; ~kläger m private litigant; ~klinik f private clinic or hospital, nursing-home; ~leben nt private life; ~lehrer m private tutor; ~leute pl private individuals pl or people pl; ~mann m, pl ~leute private person or individual; ~mittel pl private means pl; ~person f private individual or person; ~quartier nt private quarters pl; ~recht nt private or civil law; p~rechtlich adj Klage, Verfahren private or civil law attr; sich p~rechtlich auseinandersetzen to settle a dispute in private or civil law; p~rechtlich ist die Frage ganz eindeutig the matter is quite clear in private or civil law; ~sache f private matter; das ist meine ~sache that's my own business, that's a private matter; ~schule f private school; (Eliteschule auch) public school (Brit); ~sekretär m private secretary; ~sektor m private sector; ~unternehmen nt private enterprise; ~unterricht m private tuition; ~vergnügen nt (inf) private pleasure; ~vermögen nt private fortune; ~versicherung f private insurance; ~weg m private way; ~wirtschaft f private industry; ~wohnung f private flat (Brit) or apartment (US)/house.

Privileg [privi'leːk] nt -(e)s, -ien [-iən] or -e privilege.

privilegieren* [privile'giːrən] vt to favour, to privilege. die privilegierten Schichten the privileged classes.

pro prep per. ~ Jahr per annum (form), a or per year; ~ Person per person; ~ Kopf per person, per capita (form); P~-Kopf-Einkommen nt per capita income; ~ Stück each, apiece.

Pro nt (das) ~ und (das) Kontra the pros and cons pl.

Proband m -en, -en guinea-pig, experimentee.

probat adj no adv (dated) tried, proved, tested.

Probe f -, -n (a) (Prüfung) test. eine ~ auf etw (acc) machen to test sth, to do a test on sth; die ~ (auf eine Rechnung) machen to check a calculation; wenn du die ~ gemacht hättest if you'd

checked it or given it a check; ein Beamter auf ~ a probationary civil servant; er ist auf ~ angestellt he's employed for a probationary period; jdn/etw auf ~ nehmen to take sb/sth on trial; jdn/etw auf die ~ stellen to put sb/sth to the test, to try sb/sth; meine Geduld wurde auf eine harte ~ gestellt my patience was sorely tried; jdn/etw einer ~ unterziehen to subject sb/sth to a test; zur ~ for a trial, to try out.

  (b) (Theat) rehearsal. ~n abhalten to rehearse, to hold rehearsals.

  (c) (Teststück, Beispiel) sample. er gab eine ~ seines Könnens he showed what he could do.

Probe-: ~abzug m proof; ~alarm m practice alarm; heute ist ~alarm the alarms will be tested today; ~angebot nt trial offer; ~arbeit f test or specimen piece, trial work no pl; ~belastung f stress test; ~bohrung f test drill, probe; ~druck m trial print; ~exemplar nt specimen (copy); p~fahren sep irreg infin, ptp only 1 vt to test-drive; 2 vi aux sein to go for a test drive or run; ~fahrt f test drive or run/trial sail; eine ~fahrt machen to go for a test drive etc; ~flug m test flight; p~halber adv for a test; ich möchte dieses Auto p~halber eine Woche lang fahren I'd like to try out this car for a week; ~jahr nt probationary year; ~lauf m test or trial run; (Sport) practice run; ~lehrer m (Aus) probationary teacher.

proben vti to rehearse.

Proben-: ~arbeit f rehearsals pl; ~entnahme f sampling.

Probe-: ~nummer f trial copy; ~seite f specimen or sample page; ~sendung f sample pack; ~stück nt sample, specimen; ~stunde f test lesson (given by a probationary teacher); ~vorlesung f test lecture (given by a probationary lecturer); p~weise adv on a trial basis; ich habe mir p~weise einen anderen Kaffee gekauft I've bought another kind of coffee to try (out); ~zeit f probationary or trial period.

probieren* 1 vt (versuchen) to try, to have a go or try at; (kosten) Speisen, Getränke to try, to taste, to sample; (prüfen) to try (out), to test. ~ Sie es noch mal! try (it) again!, have another go or try!; laß es mich mal ~! let me try!, let me have a try or a go!

  2 vi (a) (versuchen) to try, to have a try or go. Kinder lernen durch P~ children learn by trial and error; P~ geht über Studieren (Prov) the proof of the pudding is in the eating (Prov).

  (b) (kosten) to have a taste, to try. probier mal try some, have a taste.

Probierer m -s, - taster.

Probier-: ~glas nt (a) taster, tasting glass; trinken Sie ein ~glas try a sample, have a taste; (b) siehe Reagenzglas; ~stube f sampling room.

Problem nt -s, -e problem. vor einem ~ stehen to be faced or confronted with a problem; das wird zum ~ it's becoming (something of) a problem.

Problematik f (Schwierigkeit) problem, difficulty (gen with); (Fragwürdigkeit) questionability, problematic nature. die ~ der modernen Soziologie the problems of modern sociology.

problematisch adj problematic; (fragwürdig) questionable.

Problem-: ~bewußtsein nt appreciation of the difficulties or problem; ~kind nt problem child; ~kreis m problem area; p~los adj problem-free; ~stellung f way of looking at a problem; dieses Buch ist von der ~stellung her interessant this book looks at or approaches the problem in an interesting way; ~stück nt problem play.

Produkt nt -(e)s, -e (lit, fig) product. landwirtschaftliche ~e agricultural produce no pl or products; das ~ aus 2 mal 2 the product of 2 × 2; ein ~ seiner Phantasie a figment of his imagination.

Produkten-: ~handel m produce business or trade; ~markt m produce market.

Produktion f production.

Produktions- in cpds production; ~anlagen pl production plant; ~ ausfall m loss of production; ~beschränkung f limitation of production; ~genossenschaft f (DDR) collective, cooperative; landwirtschaftliche ~genossenschaft (DDR) collective farm; ~kosten pl production costs pl; ~kraft f production capacity; ~leistung f (potential) output, production capacity; ~leiter m production manager; p~mäßig 1 adj production attr; 2 adv in terms of production; ~menge f output; ~mittel pl means of production pl; ~rückgang m falling off or drop in production; ~stand m production level; ~stätte f production centre; ~zweig m line of production.

produktiv adj productive.

Produktivität f productivity.

Produktivkräfte pl (Sociol) productive forces pl, forces of production pl.

Produzent(in f) m producer.

produzieren* 1 vt (a) auch vi to produce. (b) (inf: hervorbringen) Lärm to make; Entschuldigung to come up with (inf); Romane to churn out (inf). wer hat denn das produziert? who's responsible for that? 2 vr (pej) to show off.

Prof. abbr of **Professor**.

profan adj (weltlich) secular, profane; (gewöhnlich) mundane.

Profanbau m secular building.

profanieren* vt (form) to profane.

Profession f (old form) profession. eine ~ ausüben to ply a trade (old), to follow a profession (form).

Professional [pro'fɛʃənəl] m -s, -s professional.

professionell adj professional. eine P~e (inf) a pro (inf), a tart (inf).

professioniert adj (rare) professional.

Professor m (a) (Hochschul~) professor. (b) (Aus, S Ger: Gymnasial~) master/mistress. Herr ~! Sir!; Frau ~! Miss!

Professorenschaft f professors pl.

Professorin f (lady) professor.

Professur f chair (für in, of).

Profi m -s, -s (inf) pro (inf).

Profil nt -s, -e (a) (von Gesicht) profile; (Archit) elevation; (fig: Ansehen) image. im ~ in profile; ~ haben or besitzen (fig) to have a (distinctive or personal) image; **die Partei hat in den letzten Jahren mehr ~ bekommen** over the last few years the party has sharpened its image; **dadurch hat er an ~ gewonnen/verloren** that improved/damaged his image.
(b) (von Reifen, Schuhsohle) tread.
(c) (Querschnitt) cross-section; (Längsschnitt) vertical section; (Geog) (vertical) section; (Aviat) wing section; (fig: Skizze) profile. im ~ in section.

profilieren* 1 vt (mit Profil versehen) Schuhsohlen, Reifen to put a tread on; (fig: scharf umreißen) to define. 2 vr (sich ein Image geben) to create a distinctive personal image for oneself; (Besonderes leisten) to distinguish oneself. **er will sich akademisch/politisch** etc ~ he wants to make a mark for himself academically/in politics etc, he wants to make his mark academically/in politics etc.

profiliert adj Schuhe, Reifen with a tread, treaded; (fig: scharf umrissen) clear-cut no adv; (fig: hervorstechend) distinctive. **ein ~er Politiker/Wissenschaftler** a politician/scientist who has made his mark.

Profilierung f (a) (das Profilieren: von Schuhen, Reifen) treading; (fig) (personal) image. **die PR-Arbeit hatte eine günstigere ~ des Parteichefs zum Ziel** the PR work was aimed at giving the party leader a sharper or more clearly defined (personal) image.
(b) (das Sich-Profilieren) making one's mark no art.
(c) (Profil: von Schuhen, Reifen) tread.

profillos adj Politiker, Firma lacking any distinct (personal) image; Sohle, Reifen treadless.

Profil-: ~neurose f (hum) neurosis about one's image, image neurosis; ~sohle f sole with a tread, treaded sole; ~stahl m sectional steel.

Profit m -(e)s, -e profit. ~ aus etw schlagen or ziehen (lit) to make a profit from or out of sth; (fig) to reap the benefits or to profit from sth; **den/keinen ~ von etw haben** to profit/not to profit from sth; **ohne/mit ~ arbeiten** to work unprofitably/profitably.

profitabel adj profitable.

Profit-: p~bringend adj profitable; ~gier f greed for profit, profit lust; p~gierig adj greedy for profit, profit-greedy.

profitieren* vti to profit; (fig auch) to gain. **viel/etwas ~** (lit) to make a large profit/to make something of a profit; (fig) to profit greatly/somewhat; **davon hat er wenig profitiert** (lit) he didn't make much of a profit from it; (fig) he didn't profit much or didn't gain a great deal from it; **dabei kann ich nur ~** I only stand to gain from it, I can't lose; **und was profitierst du dabei or davon?** what do you stand to gain from or by it?

Profit-: ~jäger, ~macher m (inf) profiteer; ~macherei f (inf) profiteering; ~maximierung f maximisation of profit(s pl); ~streben nt profit seeking.

pro forma adv as a matter of form, for appearance's sake.

Pro-forma-Rechnung f pro forma invoice.

profund adj (geh) profound, deep. **er ist ein ~er Kenner +gen** he has a profound or deep knowledge of ...

Prognose f -, -n prediction, prognosis; (Wetter~) forecast. **eine ~ stellen/wagen** to give or make/venture a prediction or prognosis.

prognostisch adj prognostic.

prognostizieren* vt to predict, to prognosticate (form).

Programm nt -s, -e programme, program (US, Computers); (Tagesordnung) agenda; (Theat: Vorstellungsablauf auch) bill; (TV: Sender) channel; (Sendefolge) programmes pl; (gedrucktes Radio~, TV~) programme guide; (Verlags~) list; (beim Pferderennen) card; (Kollektion) range. **nach ~** as planned; **auf dem ~ stehen** to be on the programme/agenda; **ein ~ für den Urlaub machen** to work out a programme for one's holidays; **für heute habe ich schon ein ~** I've already got something planned for today; **unser ~ für den heutigen Abend** our programmes for this evening.

programmatisch adj programmatic.

Programm-: ~folge f order of programmes or (Theat) acts; ~füller m (inf) (programme) filler; p~gemäß adj according to plan or programme; ~gestaltung f programme planning; ~heft nt programme; ~hinweis m (Rad, TV) programme announcement; **wir bringen noch einige ~hinweise für morgen** and now a look at some of tomorrow's programmes.

programmieren* vt (a) (auch vi) to programme; (fig auch) to condition. **auf etw (acc) programmiert sein** (fig) to be geared or conditioned to sth; **programmiertes Lernen** programmed learning. (b) (entwerfen) to draw up a programme for; (planen) to schedule, to plan.

Programmierer(in f) m -s, - programmer.

Programmiersprache f programming language.

Programmierung f programming; (fig auch) conditioning.

Programmpunkt m item on the agenda; (TV) programme; (bei Show) act.

Programmusik f getrennt: Programm-musik programme music.

Programm-: ~vorschau f preview (für of); (Film) trailer; ~zeitschrift f programme guide; ~zettel m programme.

Progreß m -sses, -sse progress.

Progression f progression.

progressiv adj progressive.

Progymnasium nt secondary school (for pupils up to 16).

Prohibition f Prohibition.

Projekt nt -(e)s, -e project.

Projektgruppe f project team.

projektieren* vt (entwerfen) to plan, to project, to lay plans for; (planen) to project.

Projektil nt -s, -e (form) projectile.

Projektion f projection.

Projektions-: ~apparat m siehe Projektor; ~ebene f plane of projection; ~fläche f projection surface; ~lampe f projection lamp; ~schirm m projection screen.

Projektleiter m project leader.

Projektor m projector.

projizieren* vt to project.

Proklamation f proclamation.

proklamieren* vt to proclaim.

Prokrustesbett nt Procrustean bed.

Prokura f -, Prokuren (form) procuration (form), power or letter of attorney. **jdm ~ erteilen** to grant sb procuration (form) or power or letter of attorney.

Prokurist(in f) m attorney, procurator (old).

Prolet m -en, -en (pej) prole (pej), pleb (pej).

Proletariat nt proletariat.

Proletarier [-iɐ] m -s, - proletarian. **~ aller Länder, vereinigt euch!** workers of the world, unite!

proletarisch adj proletarian.

proletarisieren* vt to proletarianize.

proletenhaft adj (pej) plebeian (pej), plebby (pej inf).

Prolog m -(e)s, -e prologue.

prolongieren* [prolɔŋ'giːrən] vt to prolong, to extend.

Promenade f (old: Spaziergang) promenade, constitutional (old, hum); (Spazierweg) promenade.

Promenaden-: ~deck nt promenade deck; ~konzert nt promenade concert; ~mischung f (hum) mongrel, cross-breed.

promenieren* vi aux sein (geh) to promenade.

prometheisch [prome'teːɪʃ] adj (liter) Promethean (liter).

Prometheus m - Prometheus.

Promille nt -(s), - thousandth (part); (inf: Alkoholspiegel) alcohol level. **er hat zuviel ~ (im Blut)** he has too much alcohol in his blood, his alcohol level is too high; **0,8 ~ 80 millilitres** alcohol level.

Promillegrenze f legal (alcohol) limit.

prominent adj prominent.

Prominente(r) mf decl as adj prominent figure, VIP.

Prominenten- in cpds posh; ~herberge f (inf) posh hotel (inf); ~suite f VIP suite.

Prominenz f VIP's pl, prominent figures pl.

Promiskuität [promɪskui'tɛːt] f promiscuity.

Promotion¹ f (Univ) doctorate, PhD. **während seiner ~** while he was doing his doctorate or PhD; **nach seiner ~** after he got his PhD; **jds ~ befürworten** to recommend sb for a doctorate.

Promotion² [prɔ'moʊʃən] f (Comm) promotion.

promovieren* [promo'viːrən] 1 vi to do a doctorate or a doctor's degree or a PhD (über + acc in); (Doktorwürde erhalten) to receive a doctorate etc. 2 vt to confer a doctorate or the degree of doctor on.

prompt 1 adj prompt. 2 adv promptly; (natürlich) naturally, of course.

Promptheit f promptness, promptitude (form).

promulgieren* vt to promulgate.

Pronomen nt -s, - or Pronomina pronoun.

pronominal adj pronominal.

Pronominal-: ~adjektiv nt pronominal adjective; ~adverb nt pronominal adverb.

prononciert [pronõ'siːɐt] adj (geh) (deutlich) distinct, clear; (nachdrücklich) definite.

Propädeutik f preparatory course.

propädeutisch adj preparatory.

Propaganda f -, no pl propaganda; (dated: Werbung) publicity. **~ für etw machen** or **treiben** to make propaganda for sth; **~ mit etw machen** to make propaganda out of sth; **das ist (doch) alles nur ~** that's just (so much) propaganda.

Propaganda-: ~apparat m propaganda machine; ~feldzug m propaganda campaign; (Werbefeldzug) publicity campaign; ~rummel m (inf) deluge or torrent or flood of propaganda; p~wirksam adj effective or good propaganda pred; **etw p~wirksam ausnützen** to make effective propaganda out of sth.

Propagandist(in f) m (a) propagandist. (b) (Comm) demonstrator.

propagandistisch adj propagandist(ic). **etw ~ ausnutzen** to use sth as propaganda.

propagieren* vt to propagate.

Propan nt -s, no pl propane.

Propangas nt propane gas.

Propeller m -s, - (Luftschraube) propeller, prop (inf), airscrew; (Schiffsschraube) propeller, screw.

Propeller-: ~antrieb m propeller-drive; **ein Flugzeug mit ~antrieb** a propeller-driven plane; ~flugzeug nt, ~maschine f propeller-driven plane; ~turbine f turboprop.

proper adj (inf) trim, neat, (clean and) tidy.

Prophet(in f) m -en, -en prophet. **der ~ gilt nichts in seinem Vaterland** (Prov) a prophet is without honour in his own country (Prov); siehe Berg.

Prophetie [profe'tiː] f prophecy.

Prophetin f prophetess.

prophetisch adj prophetic.

prophezeien* vt to prophesy; (vorhersagen auch) to predict, to foretell. **Kassandra hat den Trojanern ihren Untergang prophezeit** Cassandra prophesied that the Trojans would meet their downfall; **das kann ich dir ~!** I can promise you that!

Prophezeiung f prophecy.

Prophylaktikum nt -s, Prophylaktika (Med) prophylactic; (Präservativ) contraceptive.

prophylaktisch adj prophylactic (form), preventive.
Prophylaxe f -, -n prophylaxis.
Proportion f proportion. **das Bild ist in den** ~**en falsch** the proportions are wrong in the picture.
proportional [proportsio'naːl] adj proportional, proportionate. **die Steuern steigen** ~ **(zu** or **mit) dem Einkommen** taxes increase in proportion to or proportionally to income; **umgekehrt** ~ (Math) in inverse proportion.
proportioniert [proportsio'niːɐt] adj proportioned.
Proporz m -es, -e proportional representation no art.
Proppen m -s, - (N Ger) (a) siehe **Pfropfen**. (b) (inf: Mensch) dumpling (inf).
proppe(n)voll adj (inf) jam-packed (inf).
Propst m -(e)s, ¨-e provost.
Prorektor m (old Sch) deputy rector; (Univ) deputy vice-chancellor.
Prosa f -, no pl prose; (fig) prosaicness.
Prosadichtung f prose writing.
Prosaiker [pro'zaːikɐ] m -s, - (a) (old) siehe **Prosaist(in)**. (b) (fig: nüchterner Mensch) prosaic person.
prosaisch [pro'zaːɪʃ] adj (a) (nüchtern) prosaic. (b) (Liter) prose attr, prosaic (form). **ein Thema** ~ **bearbeiten** to treat a subject in prose.
Prosaist(in f) [proza'ɪst(ɪn)] m, **Prosaschriftsteller(in** f) m prosewriter.
Proselyt m -en, -en (liter) proselyte. ~**en machen** to pro-selytize.
Proseminar nt an introductory seminar course for students in their first and second year.
prosit interj your health. ~ **Neujahr!** (here's to) the New Year!
Prosit m -s, -s toast. **ein** ~ **der Köchin!** here's to the cook!; **auf jdn ein** ~ **ausbringen** to toast sb, to drink to sb, to drink sb's health; **sie rief mir ein** ~ **zu** she called out 'cheers' to me.
Prosodie f prosody.
prosodisch adj prosodic.
Prospekt [pro'spɛkt] m -(e)s, -e (a) (Reklameschrift) brochure, pamphlet (gen about); (Werbezettel) leaflet; (von Internaten etc) prospectus; (Verzeichnis) catalogue. (b) (Ansicht) view, prospect (old). (c) (Theat) back-drop, back-cloth.
prospektieren* [prospɛk'tiːrən] vt to prospect (in).
prospektiv [prospɛk'tiːf] adj prospective.
Prospektmaterial [pro'spɛkt-] nt brochures pl, pamphlets pl, literature.
prosperieren* [prospe'riːrən] vi (geh) to prosper.
Prosperität [prosperi'tɛːt] f (geh) prosperity.
prost interj cheers, cheerio; (hum: beim Niesen) bless you. **na denn** ~! cheers then!, bottoms up! (hum); siehe **Mahlzeit**.
Prostata f -, no pl prostate gland; (inf: Prostataleiden) prostate.
prosten vi to say cheers.
prösterchen interj (hum) cheers, bottoms up (hum).
prostituieren* [prostitu'iːrən] **1** vr (lit, fig) to prostitute one-self. **2** vt (old) to prostitute.
Prostituierte [prostitu'iːɐtə] f -n, -n prostitute.
Prostitution [prostitu'tsioːn] f prostitution.
Proszenium nt proscenium.
Proszeniumsloge f proscenium or stage box.
Protagonist m (lit, fig) protagonist.
Protegé [prote'ʒeː] m -s, -s protégé.
protegieren* [prote'ʒiːrən] vt von Schriftsteller, Projekt to sponsor; Land, Regime to support. **er wird vom Chef protegiert** he's the boss's protégé.
Protein nt -s, -e protein.
Protektion f (Schutz) protection; (Begünstigung) patronage. **unter jds** ~ (dat) **stehen** (Schutz) to be under sb's protection; (Begünstigung) to be under sb's patronage.
Protektionismus [protɛktsio'nɪsmʊs] m (a) (Econ) protec-tionism. (b) (Günstlingswirtschaft) nepotism.
Protektor m (old: Beschützer) protector; (Schirmherr) patron.
Protektorat nt (Schirmherrschaft) patronage; (Schutzgebiet) protectorate.
Protest m -(e)s, -e (a) protest. (scharfen) ~ **gegen jdn/etw erheben** to make a (strong) protest against sb/sth; **etw aus** ~ **tun** to do sth in protest or as a protest; **unter** ~ **protesting**; (gezwungen) under protest.
(b) (Fin) ~ **mangels Annahme/Zahlung** protest for non-acceptance/non-payment; **einen Wechsel zu** ~ **gehen lassen** to protest a bill.
Protest|aktion f protest.
Protestant(in f) m Protestant.
protestantisch adj Protestant.
Protestantismus m Protestantism.
Protest-: ~**bewegung** f protest movement; ~**demonstration** f (protest) demonstration, demo (inf).
protestieren* 1 vi to protest (gegen against, about). **2** vt (Fin) to protest.
Protestkundgebung f (protest) rally.
Protestler(in f) m -s, - (inf) protester.
Protest-: ~**marsch** m protest march; ~**note** f (Pol) letter of pro-test; ~**ruf** m call of protest; ~**sänger** m protest singer; ~**schreiben** nt letter of protest; ~**song** m protest song; ~**streik** m protest strike; ~**sturm** m storm of protest; ~**versammlung** f protest meeting; ~**welle** f wave of protest.
Prothese f -, -n (a) artificial limb/joint, prosthesis (Med, form); (Gebiß) set of dentures. (b) (Ling) prothesis.
Prothesenträger(in f) m (a) person with an artificial limb. **er ist** ~ he has an artificial limb. (b) (Gebiß) denture-wearer.
Protokoll nt -s, -e (a) (Niederschrift) record; (Bericht) report; (von Sitzung) minutes pl; (bei Polizei) statement; (bei Gericht) transcript. **das** ~ **aufnehmen** to take sth down; (bei Sitzung) to

take (down) the minutes; (bei Polizei) to take (down) sb's state-ment; (bei Gericht) to keep a record of the proceedings, to make a transcript of the proceedings; (das) ~ **führen** (bei Sit-zung) to take or keep the minutes; (bei Gericht) to keep a record of or make a transcript of the proceedings; (beim Unterricht) to write a report; **etw zu** ~ **geben** to have sth put on record; (bei Polizei) to say sth in one's statement; **etw zu** ~ **nehmen** to take sth down, to record sth; **wenn man auf Dienstreise ist, muß man über alle Ausgaben** ~ **führen** on a business trip one must keep a record or (check)list of all expenses.
(b) (diplomatisch) protocol.
(c) (Strafzettel) ticket.
Protokollant(in f) m secretary; (Jur) clerk (of the court).
protokollarisch adj (a) (protokolliert) on record; (in Sitzung) minuted. **folgende Maßnahmen wurden** ~ **festgelegt** the fol-lowing measures were agreed on.
(b) (zeremoniell) ~**e Vorschriften** rules of protocol; ~ **ist das so geregelt, daß ...** protocol requires that ...; ~ **ist alles in Ord-nung** as regards protocol, everything is in order; **diese Vor-schriften sind rein** ~ these are merely rules of protocol.
Protokoll-: ~**chef** m head of protocol; ~**führer** m siehe **Protokollant(in)**.
protokollieren* 1 vi (bei Sitzung) to take the minutes (down); (bei Polizei) to take a/the statement down; (in der Schule) to write notes. **2** vt to take down; Sitzung to minute; Bemerkung auch to put or enter in the minutes; Stunde to write up.
Proton nt -s, **Protonen** proton.
Proto- in cpds proto-; ~**plasma** nt protoplasm; ~**typ** m (Erstanfertigung) prototype; (Inbegriff auch) archetype.
Protz m -es or -en, -e(n) (inf) swank (inf).
protzen vi (inf) to show off. **mit etw** ~ to show sth off.
Protzerei f (inf) showing off, swanking (inf).
protzig adj (inf) swanky (inf), showy (inf).
Protzigkeit f (inf) swankiness (inf), showiness (inf).
Provenienz [prove'niɛnts] f (geh) provenance.
Provenzale [proven'tsaːlə, proven'saːlə, prova'saːlə] m -n, -n, **Provenzalin** f Provençal.
provenzalisch [proven'tsaːlɪʃ, proven'saːlɪʃ] adj Provençal.
Proviant [pro'viant] m -s, (rare) -e provisions pl, supplies pl (esp Mil); (Reise~) food for the journey. **sich mit** ~ **versehen** to lay in provisions/to buy food for the journey.
Proviantlager nt supply camp.
Provinz [pro'vɪnts] f -, -en province; (im Gegensatz zur Stadt) provinces pl (auch pej), country. **das ist finsterste** or **hinterste** ~ (pej) it's so provincial, it's a cultural backwater.
Provinz- in cpds provincial; ~**bewohner** m provincial.
provinziell [provɪn'tsiɛl] adj provincial (auch pej).
Provinzler(in f) [pro'vɪntslɐ, -ərɪn] m -s, - (pej) provincial.
provinzlerisch [pro'vɪntslərɪʃ] adj (pej) provincial.
Provinzluft f (pej) provincial or small-town atmosphere.
Provision [provi'zioːn] f commission. **auf** ~ on commission.
Provisionsbasis f commission basis. **auf** ~ **arbeiten** to work on a commission basis.
Provisor [pro'viːzɔr] m (old) manager of a chemist's shop.
provisorisch [provi'zoːrɪʃ] adj provisional, temporary. ~**e Regierung** caretaker or provisional government; **das ist alles noch sehr** ~ in unserem Haus things are still very makeshift in our house; **Straßen mit** ~**em Belag** roads with a temporary sur-face; **wir wollen es** ~ **so lassen** let's leave it like that for the time being; **ich habe den Stuhl** ~ **repariert** I've fixed the chair up for the time being.
Provisorium [provi'zoːriʊm] nt stop-gap, temporary or provi-sional arrangement.
provokant [provo'kant] adj provocative, provoking.
Provokateur [provoka'tøːr] m troublemaker; (Pol auch) agitator, agent provocateur.
Provokation [provoka'tsioːn] f provocation.
provokativ, provokatorisch [provoka-] adj provocative, provoking.
provozieren* [provo'tsiːrən] vti to provoke.
Prozedur f (a) (Vorgang) procedure. **ein Auto zu bauen ist eine lange** ~ making a car is a lengthy procedure or business.
(b) (pej) carry-on (inf), palaver (inf). **die ganze** ~, **bis man endlich zur Universität zugelassen wird** all the rigmarole (inf) before you are finally admitted to university; **die** ~ **beim Zahnarzt** the ordeal at the dentist's.
Prozent nt -(e)s, -e or (nach Zahlenangaben) - per cent no pl. ~**e percentage; fünf** ~ five per cent; **wieviel** ~? what percen-tage?; **zu zehn** ~ at ten per cent; **zu hohen** ~**en** at a high percen-tage; **etw in** ~**en ausdrücken** to express sth as a percentage or in per cent; **dieser Whisky hat 35** ~ **(Alkoholgehalt)** this whisky contains 35 per cent alcohol; ~**e (in einem Geschäft) bekommen** to get a discount (in a shop).
Prozentbasis f percentage or (von Vertreter auch) commission basis. **auf** ~ **arbeiten** to work on a commission basis.
-prozentig adj suf per cent. **hoch~** high percentage.
Prozent-: ~**punkt** m point; ~**rechnung** f percentage calcula-tion; ~**satz** m percentage; (Zins) rate of interest, interest rate.
prozentual adj percentage attr. ~**er Anteil** percentage; **diese Zahlen sind** ~ **(gesehen)** these figures are (expressed as) percentages; **etw** ~ **ausdrücken/rechnen** to express/calculate sth as a percentage or in percentages; **sich an einem Geschäft** ~ **beteiligen** to have a percentage (share) in a business; ~ **gut abschneiden** to get a good percentage; **die Beteiligung war** ~ **sehr hoch** that's a very high percentage.
prozentuell adj (esp Aus) siehe **prozentual**.
Prozeß m -sses, -sse (a) (Straf~) trial; (Rechtsfall) (court) case. **einen** ~ **gewinnen/verlieren** to win/lose a case; **gegen jdn einen** ~ **anstrengen** to take or institute legal proceedings against sb, to bring an action against sb; **er führt zur Zeit gegen**

fünf Firmen einen ~ at the moment he's taking five companies to court *or* is involved in legal action against five companies; **es ist sehr teuer, einen** ~ **zu führen** going to court *or* taking legal action is very expensive; **es zum** ~ **kommen lassen** to go to court; **es kann zum** ~ **kommen** it might come to a court case; **mit jdm im** ~ **liegen** to be involved in a court case *or* in a lawsuit *or* in litigation (*form*) with sb; **jdm den** ~ **machen** (*inf*) to take sb to court; **mit jdm/etw kurzen** ~ **machen** (*fig inf*) to make short work of sb/sth (*inf*).
  (b) (*Vorgang*) process.
Prozeß-: ~**akten** *pl* case files *pl*; **p**~**fähig** *adj* able *or* entitled to take legal action; ~**fähigkeit** *f* ability *or* entitlement to take legal action; **p**~**führend** *adj* **p**~**führende Partei** litigant; ~**führung** *f* handling of a case; ~**hansel** *m* (*inf*) someone who is always going to law.
prozessieren* *vi* to go to court. **er prozessiert mit fünf Firmen** he's got cases going on against five firms; **sie haben jahrelang gegen mich prozessiert** they've been bringing an action against me for years, they've had a case going on against me for years.
Prozession *f* procession.
Prozeß-: ~**kosten** *pl* legal costs *pl*; **er mußte die** ~**kosten tragen** he had to pay costs; ~**ordnung** *f* code *or* rules of procedure, legal procedure; ~**recht** *nt* procedural law; **p**~**süchtig** *adj* litigious; **p**~**unfähig** *adj* not entitled to take legal action; ~**unfähigkeit** *f* inability to take legal action; ~**verschleppung** *f* protraction of a case; ~**vollmacht** *f*, *no pl* power of attorney (*for a lawsuit*); (*Formular*) letter of attorney.
prüde *adj* prudish.
Prüderie *f* prudishness, prudery.
prüfen 1 *vt* **(a)** (*auch vi*) (*Sch, Univ*) jdn to examine; *Kenntnisse auch* to test. **jdn in etw** (*dat*) ~ to examine sb in sth; **wer hat bei dir geprüft?** who examined you?; **morgen wird in Englisch geprüft** the English exams are tomorrow; **schriftlich geprüft werden** to have a written examination; **ein staatlich geprüfter Dolmetscher** a qualified interpreter.
  (b) (*überprüfen*) to check (*auf* +*acc* for); (*untersuchen*) to examine, to check; (*durch Ausprobieren*) to test; (*auf die Probe stellen*) to test; *Alibi* to check (out), to check up on; *Geschäftsbücher* to audit, to check, to examine; *Lebensmittel, Wein* to inspect, to test. **es wird geprüft, ob alle anwesend sind** they check *or* there's a check to see if everyone is present; **den Wein auf sein Aroma** ~ to sniff *or* test the bouquet of the wine; **Metall auf den Anteil an Fremdstoffen** ~ to check the level of impurities in metal; **Babynahrung wird chemisch geprüft** baby foods are chemically tested; **jdn auf seine Ehrlichkeit** ~ to test *or* try sb's honesty; **wir werden die Beschwerde/Sache** ~ we'll look into *or* investigate the complaint/matter; **sie wollte ihn nur** ~ she only wanted to test him; **drum prüfe, wer sich ewig bindet** (*prov*) marry in haste, repent at leisure (*Prov*).
  (c) (*erwägen*) to consider. **etw nochmals** ~ to reconsider *or* review sth.
  (d) (*mustern*) to scrutinize. **ein** ~**der Blick** a searching look.
  (e) (*heimsuchen*) to try, to afflict. **er ist im Leben schwer geprüft worden** he's been sorely tried *or* much afflicted in his life; **ein schwer geprüfter Vater** a sorely tried *or* much afflicted father.
2 *vr* (*geh*) to search one's heart. **du mußt dich selber** ~**, ob ...** you must decide for yourself *or* you must enquire of yourself (*liter*) whether ...
Prüfer(in *f*) *m* **-s,** - examiner; (*Wirtschafts*~) inspector.
Prüf-: ~**gerät** *nt* testing apparatus *or* equipment; ~**lampe** *f* control light tester.
Prüfling *m* examinee, (examination) candidate.
Prüf-: ~**stand** *m* test bed; (*Space*) test stand; ~**stein** *m* (*fig*) touchstone (*für* of *or* for), measure (*für* of).
Prüfung *f* **(a)** (*Sch, Univ*) exam, examination. **eine** ~ **machen** to take *or* do an exam.
  (b) (*Überprüfung*) check, checking *no indef art*; (*Untersuchung*) examination, checking *no indef art*; (*durch Ausprobieren*) test, testing *no indef art*; (*von Geschäftsbüchern*) audit, examination, checking *no indef art*; (*von Lebensmitteln, Wein*) inspection, testing *no indef art*. **eine gründliche** ~ **einer Maschine vornehmen** to check *or* examine *or* test a machine thoroughly, to give a machine a thorough check *or* examination *or* test; **nach der** ~ **wird das Auto ...** after being checked *or* tested the car is ...; **bei nochmaliger** ~ **der Rechnung** on re-checking the account; **er führt (Wirtschafts)**~**en bei Firmen durch** he audits firms' books; **nach/bei** ~ **Ihrer Beschwerde/dieser Sache ...** after/on looking into *or* investigating your complaint/the matter.
  (c) (*Erwägung*) consideration. **die** ~ **seiner Entscheidung** the reconsideration of one's decision.
  (d) (*Heimsuchung*) test, trial.
Prüfungs-: ~**angst** *f* exam nerves *pl*; ~**arbeit** *f* dissertation; ~**aufgabe** *f* exam(ination) question; ~**ausschuß** *m* board of examiners, examining board; (*bei Sachen*) board of inspectors; ~**gebühr** *f* examination fee; ~**kandidat** *m* siehe **Prüfling**; ~**kommission** *f* siehe ~**ausschuß**; ~**ordnung** *f* exam(ination) regulations *pl*; ~**termin** *m* (*Sch, Univ*) date of examination *or* test; (*Jur*) meeting of creditors; ~**unterlagen** *pl* exam(ination) papers *pl*; ~**zeugnis** *nt* exam(ination) certificate.
Prüfverfahren *nt* test procedure.
Prügel *m* **-s,** - **(a)** (*inf*) club, cudgel. **(b)** *pl* beating, thrashing. ~ **bekommen** *or* **beziehen** (*lit, fig*) to get a beating *or* thrashing; siehe **Tracht**.
Prügelei *f* (*inf*) fight, punch-up (*Brit inf*).
Prügelknabe *m* (*fig*) whipping boy.
prügeln 1 *vti* to beat. **unser Lehrer prügelt grundsätzlich nicht** our teacher doesn't use corporal punishment on principle.
2 *vr* to fight. **sich mit jdm** ~ to fight sb; **Eheleute, die**

sich ~ married people who come to blows; **sich um etw** (*acc*) ~ to fight over *or* for sth.
Prügel-: ~**strafe** *f* corporal punishment; ~**szene** *f* fight; (*Theat*) fight scene.
Prunk *m* **-s,** *no pl* (*Pracht*) splendour, magnificence, resplendence; (*von Saal, Rokoko auch*) sumptuousness; (*von Stadt, Gebäude auch*) grandeur; (*von höfischer Zeremonie auch*) pomp and circumstance, pageantry. **Ludwig XIV liebte** ~ Louis XIV had a passion for grandeur; **der** ~ **im Saal** the splendour *or* magnificence *or* resplendence of the hall; **die Schlösser sind voller** ~ the castles are sumptuously appointed; **großen** ~ **entfalten** to put on a show of great splendour.
Prunk- in *cpds* magnificent, resplendent; ~**bett** *nt* four-poster bed; magnificent bed.
prunken *vi* to be resplendent. **mit etw** ~ to flaunt sth, to make a great show of sth.
Prunk-: ~**gemach** *nt* state apartment; **p**~**haft** *adj* siehe **p**~**voll**; **p**~**los** *adj* unostentatious, modest; ~**saal** *m* sumptuous *or* palatial room; ~**stück** *nt* showpiece; ~**sucht** *f* great love of splendour, passion for the grand scale; **p**~**süchtig** *adj* **ein p**~**süchtiger König** a king with a craving for splendour; **meine p**~**süchtige Frau** my wife with her passion for finery and grandeur; **p**~**süchtig sein** to have a craving for splendour *etc*; **p**~**voll** *adj* splendid, magnificent.
prusten *vi* (*inf*) to snort. **vor Lachen** ~ to snort with laughter; **sie prustete laut vor Lachen** she gave a loud snort (of laughter).
PS [peː'|ɛs] *nt* ~ *abbr of* **Pferdestärke** hp.
P.S., PS [peː'|ɛs] *nt* -, - *abbr of* **Postskript(um)** PS.
Psalm *m* **-s, -en** psalm.
Psalmist *m* psalmist.
Psalter *m* **-s,** - **(a)** (*Eccl*) psalter. **(b)** (*Mus*) psaltery.
pseudo- in *cpds* pseudo.
Pseudonym *nt* **-s, -e** pseudonym; (*eines Schriftstellers auch*) nom de plume, pen-name.
psst *interj* pst; (*ruhig*) sh, hush.
Psyche *f* -, **-n** psyche; (*Myth*) Psyche.
psychedelisch *adj* psychedelic.
Psychiater *m* **-s,** - psychiatrist.
Psychiatrie *f* psychiatry.
psychiatrisch *adj* psychiatric. ~ **betrachtet** from a psychiatric point of view, (considered) psychiatrically.
psychisch *adj Belastung, Auswirkungen, Defekt* emotional, psychological; *Phänomen, Erscheinung* psychic; *Vorgänge* psychological. ~**e Erkrankung** mental illness; **eine** ~ **bedingte Krankheit** a psychologically determined illness; ~ **gestört** emotionally *or* psychologically disturbed; **jdn** ~ **beanspruchen** to make emotional *or* psychological demands on sb; **er ist** ~ **völlig am Ende** his nerves can't take any more; ~ **unter großem Druck stehen, unter großem** ~**en Druck stehen** to be under a great deal of emotional *or* psychological pressure, to have a great deal of emotional *or* psychological pressure on one.
Psycho- in *cpds* psycho-; ~**analyse** *f* psychoanalysis; ~**analytiker** *m* psychoanalyst; **p**~**analytisch** *adj* psychoanalytic(al); **jdn p**~**analytisch behandeln** to psychoanalyze sb; **ein Gedicht p**~**analytisch interpretieren** to interpret a poem psychoanalytically; ~**diagnostik** *f* psychodiagnostics *sing*; **p**~**gen** *adj* psychogenic; ~**gramm** *nt* **-s, -e** profile (*auch fig*), psychograph; ~**loge** *m*, ~**login** *f* psychologist; ~**logie** *f* psychology; **p**~**logisch** *adj* psychological; **p**~**logische Kampf-** *or* **Kriegsführung** psychological warfare; **p**~**logisieren*** *vt* to psychologize; ~**neurose** *f* psychoneurosis; ~**path(in** *f*) *m* **-en, -en** psychopath; ~**pathie** *f* psychopathy; **p**~**pathisch** *adj* psychopathic; **p**~**pathisch reagieren** to react psychopathically; ~**pharmakon** *nt* **-s, -pharmaka** *usu pl* psychiatric drug.
Psychose *f* -, **-n** psychosis.
Psycho-: ~**somatik** *f* psychosomatics *sing*; **p**~**somatisch** *adj* psychosomatic; ~**therapeut** *m* psychotherapist; **p**~**therapeutisch** *adj* psychotherapeutic; ~**therapie** *f* psychotherapy.
Psychotiker(in *f*) *m* **-s,** - psychotic.
psychotisch *adj* psychotic.
Ptolemäer [ptoleˈmɛːɐ] *m* **-s,** - Ptolemy.
ptolemäisch [ptoleˈmɛːɪʃ] *adj* Ptolemaic.
Ptolemäus [ptoleˈmɛːʊs] *m* - Ptolemy.
pubertär *adj* of puberty, adolescent. **ein Junge im** ~**en Alter** a boy at the age of puberty *or* in puberty; ~ **bedingte Störungen** disorders caused by puberty, adolescent disorders.
Pubertät *f* puberty. **er steckt mitten in der** ~ he's going through his adolescence.
Pubertäts-: ~**alter** *nt* age of puberty; **im** ~**alter** at the age of puberty; ~**erscheinung** *f* symptom of puberty *or* adolescence; **das ist bloß eine** ~**erscheinung** that's just a thing adolescents go through; ~**störungen** *pl* adolescent disturbances *pl*, growing-up problems *pl* (*inf*); ~**zeit** *f* puberty (period).
pubertieren* *vi* to reach puberty. ~**d** pubescent.
Publicity [pʌˈblɪsɪti] *f* -, *no pl* publicity.
publicityscheu *adj* **er ist** ~ he shuns publicity.
Public Relations [pʌblɪkrɪˈleɪʃənz] *pl* public relations *pl*.
publik *adj pred* public. ~ **werden** to become public knowledge; **die Sache ist längst** ~ that's long been common knowledge.
Publikation *f* publication.
Publikum *nt* **-s,** *no pl* public; (*Zuschauer, Zuhörer*) audience; (*Sport*) crowd. **er muß ja immer ein** ~ **haben** (*fig*) he always has to have an audience; **das** ~ **im Kaufhaus/in dem Lokal ist sehr gemischt** you get a very mixed group of people using this store/pub, the customers in this store/pub are very mixed; **in diesem Lokal verkehrt ein sehr schlechtes** ~ this pub attracts a very bad type of customer *or* a very bad clientele; **sein** ~ **finden** to find a public.

Publikums-: ~**erfolg** m success with the public, popular success; ~**geschmack** m public or popular taste; ~**interesse** nt interest of the public; ~**liebling** m darling of the public; ~**renner** m -s, - (inf) hit with the public (inf); ~**verkehr** m ~**verkehr im Rathaus ist von 8 bis 12 Uhr** the town hall is open to the public from 8 till 12 o'clock; „**heute kein ~verkehr**" "closed today for public business"; **wir haben heute viel** ~**verkehr** we've a lot of people coming in today; **p~wirksam** adj **p~wirksam sein** to have public appeal; **ein Stück p~wirksam inszenieren** to produce a play in a popular way or with a view to public appeal; **sehr p~wirksame Tricks** tricks with great public appeal or appeal to the public.

publizieren* vti to publish. **er hat in verschiedenen Fachzeitschriften publiziert** he's had things or work published or he has been published in various journals.

Publizist(in f) m publicist; (Journalist) journalist.

Publizistik f journalism.

publizistisch adj journalistic. **sich** ~ **betätigen** to write for newspapers.

Publizität f publicity.

Puck m -s, -s puck.

puckern vi (inf) to throb. **es puckert im Zahn** my tooth's throbbing.

Pudding m -s, -s thick custard-based dessert often flavoured with vanilla, chocolate etc = blancmange. **kaltgerührter** ~ instant whip.

Puddingpulver nt custard powder.

Pudel m -s, - (a) (Hund) poodle. **das ist des** ~**s Kern** (fig) that's what it's really all about; **siehe begossen. (b)** (inf: Fehlwurf beim Kegeln) miss.

Pudel-: ~**mütze** f bobble cap or hat, pom-pom hat (inf); **p~nackt** adj (inf) stark-naked, starkers pred (inf); **p~naß** adj dripping or soaking wet, drenched; **p~wohl** adj (inf) **sich p~wohl fühlen** to feel completely contented; **nach der Sauna fühle ich mich p~wohl** after the sauna I feel like a million dollars (inf) or on top of the world (inf).

Puder m or (inf) nt -s, - powder.

Puderdose f powder tin; (für Gesichtspuder) (powder) compact.

puderig adj powdery.

pudern 1 vt to powder. **sich** (dat) **das Gesicht** ~ to powder one's face. 2 vr (Puder auftragen) to powder oneself; (Puder benutzen) to use powder. **ich muß mich noch** ~ I still have to powder my nose or face; **ich stark** ~ to use a lot of powder.

Puder-: ~**quaste** f powder puff; ~**zucker** m icing sugar.

pueril [pue'ri:l] adj (geh) puerile; (knabenhaft) boyish.

Puertoricaner(in f) [puertori'ka:nɐ, -ərɪn] m -s, - Puerto Rican.

puertoricanisch [puertori'ka:nɪʃ] adj Puerto Rican.

Puerto Rico [pu'ɛrto'ri:ko] nt - -s Puerto Rico.

puff interj bang.

Puff¹ m -(e)s, ¨e (a) (Stoß) thump, blow; (in die Seite) prod, dig; (vertraulich) nudge. **einen** ~ **or einige** ~**e aushalten können** (fig) to be thick-skinned. **(b)** (Geräusch) bang.

Puff² m -(e)s, -e (a) (Wäsche~) linen basket. **(b)** (Bausch) puff. **(c)** (Sitz~) pouf(fe).

Puff³ m or nt -s, -s (inf) brothel, whorehouse (sl), cathouse (esp US inf).

Puff|ärmel m puff(ed) sleeve.

puffen 1 vt (a) (schlagen) to thump, to hit; (in die Seite) to prod, to dig; (vertraulich stoßen) to nudge. **(b)** Rauch to puff. **(c)** Ärmel to puff. 2 vi (inf: puff machen) to go bang; (leise) to go phut (inf); (Rauch, Abgase) to puff.

Puffer m -s, - (a) (Rail) buffer. **(b)** (Cook) siehe **Kartoffelpuffer.**

Puffer-: ~**staat** m buffer state; ~**zone** f buffer zone.

Puff-: ~**gegend** f (inf) red-light district; ~**mais** m popcorn; ~**mutter** f (inf) madam(e), bawd; ~**reis** m puffed rice; ~**straße** f (inf) brothel street.

puh interj (Abscheu) ugh; (Erleichterung) phew.

pulen 1 vi (inf) to pick. **in der Nase** ~ to pick one's nose; **an einem Loch** ~ to pick (at) a hole. 2 vt (N Ger) Krabben to shell; Erbsen auch to pod.

Pulk m -s, -s or (rare) -e (a) (Mil) group. **(b)** (Menge) (von Menschen) group, bunch; (von Dingen) pile.

Pulle f -, -n (inf) bottle. **eine** ~ **Schnaps** a bottle of schnapps; **volle** ~ **fahren** (sl) to drive flat out (inf) or full pelt (inf).

pullen vi (Naut) to row.

pulle(r)n vi (inf) to pee (inf).

Pulli m -s, -s (inf), **Pullover** [pʊ'lo:vɐ] m -s, - jumper (Brit), pullover, sweater, jersey.

Pullunder m -s, - tank top, slipover.

Puls m -es, -e (lit, fig) pulse. **sein** ~ **geht** or **schlägt regelmäßig** his pulse is regular; **jdm den** ~ **fühlen** to feel or take sb's pulse; **sein Ohr am** ~ **der Zeit haben** to have one's finger on the pulse of the time(s).

Puls|ader f artery. **sich** (dat) **die** ~**(n) aufschneiden** to slash one's wrists.

pulsen vi (liter) to pulse, to pulsate, to throb.

pulsieren* vi (lit, fig) to pulsate, to throb. ~**der Gleichstrom** intermittent direct current.

Puls-: ~**schlag** m pulse-beat; (fig) pulse; (das Pulsieren) throbbing, pulsing, pulsation; **an der Börse fühlt man den** ~**schlag der Wirtschaft** at the stock exchange you have your finger on the pulse of the economy; **in Schwabing spürte sie den** ~**schlag der Großstadt** in Schwabing she felt the throbbing or puls(at)ing of the city; **den** ~**schlag der Zeit spüren** to feel life pulsing around one; **hier oben in den Highlands merkt man nichts vom** ~**schlag der Zeit** up here in the Highlands time and the world seem far away; **in der Einsamkeit der Berge, fern**

vom ~**schlag der Zeit** in the loneliness of the mountains, far from the throb of civilization; ~**wärmer** m -s, - wristlet; ~**zahl** f pulse count.

Pult nt -(e)s, -e desk.

Pulver ['pʊlfɐ, -lvɐ] nt -s, - powder; (Schieß~) gunpowder, powder; (sl: Geld) dough (sl). **er hat das** ~ **nicht erfunden** (fig) he'll never set the Thames on fire (prov); **sein** ~ **verschossen haben** (fig) to have shot one's bolt.

Pulver-: ~**dampf** m gunsmoke, gunpowder smoke; ~**fabrik** f gunpowder factory; ~**faß** nt barrel of gunpowder, powder barrel or keg; (fig) powder keg, volcano; **(wie) auf einem** ~**faß sitzen** (fig) to be sitting on (top of) a volcano; **den Funken ins** ~**faß schleudern, die Lunte ans** ~**faß legen** (fig) to trigger or spark the whole thing off; **Nordirland gleicht einem** ~**faß** Northern Ireland is like a powder keg; **p~fein** adj finely ground.

pulv(e)rig ['pʊlf(ə)rɪç, -lv(ə)rɪç] adj powdery no adv. **den Kaffee** ~ **mahlen** to grind the coffee to a powder.

Pulverisator [pʊlveri'za:tɔr] m pulverizer.

pulverisieren* [pʊlveri'zi:rən] vt to pulverize, to powder.

Pulver-: ~**kaffee** m (inf) instant coffee; ~**kammer** f (Hist), ~**magazin** nt magazine; ~**mühle** f siehe ~**fabrik.**

pulvern ['pʊlfɐn] 1 vt to pulverize, to powder. **zu Silvester werden Millionenbeträge in die Luft gepulvert** on New Year's Eve vast sums of money go up in smoke. 2 vi (inf) to shoot.

Pulver-: ~**schnee** m powder snow; ~**turm** m (Hist) magazine; ~**verschwörung** f (Hist) Gunpowder Plot.

Puma m -s, -s puma.

Pummel m -s, - (inf), **Pummelchen** nt (inf) dumpling (inf), pudding (inf), roly-poly (inf).

pumm(e)lig adj (inf) chubby, plump.

Pump m -(e)s, no pl (inf) credit, tick (inf). **etw auf** ~ **kaufen** to buy sth on credit or on tick; **etw auf** ~ **kaufen** (auf Raten) to buy sth on the never-never (Brit inf) or on the cuff (US inf); **auf** ~ **leben** to live on credit or tick.

Pumpe f -, -n (a) pump. **(b)** (inf: Herz) ticker (inf).

pumpen vti (a) to pump. **(b)** (inf: entleihen) to borrow; (verleihen) to lend, to loan. (sich dat) **Geld bei jdm** ~ to borrow money from or off (inf) sb; **er pumpt in den Geschäften** he gets things from the shops on credit or tick (inf).

Pumpenschwengel m pump handle.

pumpern vi (S Ger, Aus inf) to thump, to hammer. **sein Herz pumperte vor Aufregung** his heart was thumping (away) or hammering away with excitement.

Pumpernickel m -s, - pumpernickel.

Pumphose f baggy breeches pl, knickerbockers pl; (Unterhose) knickerbockers pl.

Pumps¹ [pœmps] m -, - (dated) pump.

Pumps² m -es, -e (dial: Furz) rude noise/smell.

pumpsen vi (dial) to make a rude noise/smell.

Pumpstation f pumping station.

puncto prep + gen: **in** ~ X where X or in so far as X is concerned.

Punier(in f) [pu'ni:ɐ, -iərɪn] m -s, - Phoenician.

punisch adj Punic.

Punkt m -(e)s, -e (a) (Tupfen) spot, dot. **grüne** ~**e in den Augen** green flecks in one's eyes; **das Schiff war nur noch ein kleiner** ~ **in der Ferne** the ship was only a small speck or dot or spot in the distance.

(b) (Satzzeichen) full stop, period (esp US); (Typ) point; (auf dem i, Mus, Auslassungszeichen, von ~linie) dot. **einen** ~ **setzen** or **machen** to put a full stop; **der Satz endet mit drei** ~**en** the sentence ends with a row of dots or with suspension points; **nun mach aber mal einen** ~! (inf) come off it! (inf); **einen** ~ **hinter eine Angelegenheit setzen** to make an end to a matter; **ohne** ~ **und Komma reden** (inf) to talk nineteen to the dozen (inf), to rattle on and on (inf); **den** ~ **aufs i setzen** (fig) to dot the i's and cross the t's; **und sagte,** ~**,** ~**,** ~ and said dot, dot, dot.

(c) (Stelle) point. **zwischen den** ~**en A und B** between (the) points A and B; ~ **12 Uhr** at 12 o'clock on the dot; **wir sind auf** or **an dem** ~ **angelangt, wo ...** we have reached the stage or point where ...; **ein dunkler** ~ (fig) a dark chapter; **bis zu einem gewissen** ~ up to a certain point; **siehe tot.**

(d) (Bewertungseinheit) point, mark; (bei Prüfung) mark. **nach** ~**en siegen/führen** to win/lead on points.

(e) (bei Diskussion, von Vertrag etc) point. **in diesem** ~ on this point; **etw** ~ **für** ~ **widerlegen** to disprove sth point by point; **etw in allen** ~**en widerlegen** to refute sth in every respect; **der strittige** ~ the disputed point, the area of dispute; **sein Aufsatz ist in vielen** ~**en anfechtbar** many points in his essay are disputable.

Punktball m punchball, punchbag.

Pünktchen nt little dot or spot. **drei** ~ **three dots; dann kam der** ~**,** ~**,** ~ (statt nicht salonfähigem Ausdruck) then that dot, dot, dot came; **da fehlt aber auch nicht das** ~ **auf dem i!** (fig) it's got every i dotted and every t crossed.

Punkt-: ~**feuer** nt (Mil) precision fire; **p~gleich** adj (Sport) level; **die beiden Mannschaften liegen p~gleich** the two teams are lying level (on points) or are level pegging; **der Boxkampf ging p~gleich aus** the fight ended in or was a draw; ~**gleichheit** f (Sport) level score; **bei** ~**gleichheit** if the scores are level; **wegen** ~**gleichheit** because the score was level.

punktieren* vt (a) (Med) to aspirate. **(b)** (mit Punkten versehen) to dot; Fläche auch to stipple. **einen Umriß** ~ to dot an outline; **punktierte Linie** dotted line.

Punktion f (Med) aspiration.

pünktlich 1 adj (a) punctual. **(b)** (genau) exact, precise, meticulous.

2 adv (a) on time. **er kam** ~ **um 3 Uhr** he came punctually at 3 o'clock or at 3 o'clock sharp; **der Zug kommt immer sehr** ~ the train is always dead on time or very punctual; ~ **da sein** to be

there on time; **es wird ~ erledigt** it will be promptly dealt with; (*rechtzeitig*) it will be dealt with on time. **(b)** (*genau*) precisely, meticulously.

Pünktlichkeit *f siehe adj* **(a)** punctuality. **~ ist die Höflichkeit der Könige** (*Prov*) punctuality is the politeness of princes. **(b)** exactness, precision, meticulousness.

Punkt-: **~linie** *f* dotted line; **~niederlage** *f* defeat on points, points defeat.

punkto *prep* +*gen* **~ X** where X *or* as far as X is concerned; **~ meiner Anfrage** concerning *or* reference (*Comm*) *or* re (*Comm*) my enquiry.

Punkt-: **~richter** *m* judge; **~schrift** *f* Braille; **p~schweißen** *vti sep infin, ptp only* (*Tech*) to spot-weld; **~sieg** *m* win on points, points win; **~sieger** *m* winner on points; **~spiel** *nt* points game, game decided on points.

punktuell *adj* selective, dealing with certain points. **wir haben uns nur ~ mit diesem Thema befaßt** we only dealt with certain *or* selected points of this topic; **einige ~e Ergänzungen anbringen** to expand a few points; **~e Verkehrskontrollen** spot checks on traffic; **die Kontrollen erfolgten nur ~** they only did spot checks.

Punktum *interj* and that's flat, and that's that. **Schluß, aus, ~!** and that's/that was the end of that!

Punkt-: **~wertung** *f* points system; **in der ~wertung liegt er vorne** he's leading on points; **~zahl** *f* score.

Punsch *m* **-es, -e** (hot) punch.

Punschglas *nt* punch cup.

Punze *f* **-, -n (a)** (*Tech*) punch. **(b)** (*Aus: Gütezeichen*) hallmark.

punzen *vt* **(a)** (*Tech*) to punch. **(b)** (*Aus*) Gold to hallmark.

Pup *m* **-(e)s, -e** *siehe* **Pups.**

pupen *vi siehe* **pupsen.**

Pupille *f* **-, -n** pupil.

Pupillen-: **~erweiterung** *f* dilation of the pupil; **~verengung** *f* contraction of the pupil, miosis (*spec*).

Püppchen *nt* **(a)** (*kleine Puppe*) little doll *or* dolly (*inf*). **(b)** (*hübsches Mädchen*) little sweetie; (*Teenager*) dolly bird (*inf*). **ein süßes kleines ~** a sweet little thing.

Puppe *f* **-, -n (a)** (*Kinderspielzeug*) doll, dolly (*inf*); (*Marionette*) puppet, marionette; (*Schaufenster~, Mil: Übungs~*) dummy; (*inf: Mädchen*) doll (*inf*), bird (*esp Brit inf*); (*als Anrede*) baby (*inf*), doll (*esp US inf*). **die ~n tanzen lassen** (*inf*) to paint the town red (*inf*), to live it up (*inf*); **bis in die ~n schlafen** (*inf*) to sleep to all hours. **(b)** (*Zool*) pupa. **(c)** (*Getreide~*) stook, shock.

Puppen- *in cpds* doll's; **~doktor** *m* dolls' doctor; **~gesicht** *nt* baby-doll face; **p~haft** *adj* doll-like; **~haus** *nt* doll's house, dollhouse (*US*); **~spiel** *nt* puppet show; **~spieler** *m* puppeteer; **~stube** *f* doll's house, dollhouse (*US*); **~theater** *nt* puppet theatre; **~wagen** *nt* doll's pram.

puppern *vi* (*inf*) (*zittern*) to tremble, to shake, to quake; (*klopfen*) to thump, to thud.

puppig *adj* cute.

Pups *m* **-es, -e, Pupser** *m* **-s, -** (*inf: Furz*) rude noise/smell.

pupsen *vi* (*inf*) to make a rude noise/smell.

Pupser *m siehe* **Pups.**

pur *adj* (*rein*) pure; (*unverdünnt*) neat, straight; (*bloß, völlig*) sheer, pure. **~er Unsinn** absolute nonsense; **~er Wahnsinn** sheer *or* pure *or* absolute madness; **~er Zufall** sheer *or* mere coincidence; **Whisky ~** straight *or* neat whisky.

Püree *nt* **-s, -s** puree; (*Kartoffel~*) mashed *or* creamed potatoes *pl*.

Purgatorium *nt* purgatory.

purgieren* *vt* to purge.

purifizieren* *vt* (*liter*) to purify.

Purismus *m* purism.

Purist(in *f*) *m* purist.

puristisch *adj* puristic.

Puritaner(in *f*) *m* **-s, -** Puritan.

puritanisch *adj* (*Hist*) Puritan; (*pej*) puritanical.

Puritanismus *m* Puritanism.

Purpur *m* **-s, no pl** crimson. **den ~ tragen** (*fig*) to wear the purple.

Purpur-: **p~farben, p~farbig** *adj* crimson; **der Morgenhimmel strahlte p~farben** the morning sky shone a deep crimson; **~mantel** *m* crimson *or* purple robe.

purpurn *adj* (*liter*) crimson.

purpurrot *adj* crimson (red).

Purzelbaum *m* somersault. **einen ~ machen** *or* **schlagen** *or* **schießen** to turn *or* do a somersault.

purzeln *vi aux sein* to tumble. **über etw** (*acc*) **~** to trip *or* fall over sth.

pusselig *adj* (*inf*) Mensch pernickety (*inf*), finicky (*inf*), fussy; Arbeit, Aufgabe fiddly (*inf*).

pusseln *vi* (*inf*) **(a)** to fuss. **sie pusselt den ganzen Tag im Haus** she fusses about the house all day. **(b)** (*herumbasteln*) to fiddle about.

Pußta *f* **-, Pußten** puszta (*plain in Hungary*).

Puste *f* **-, no pl** (*inf*) puff (*inf*), breath. **außer ~ sein** to be puffed out (*inf*), to be out of puff (*inf*); **(ja) ~(kuchen)!** (*inf*) no chance! (*inf*); *siehe* **ausgehen.**

Pusteblume *f* (*inf*) dandelion.

Pustel *f* **-, -n** (*Pickel*) spot, pimple; (*Med*) pustule.

pusten (*inf*) **1** *vi* (*blasen*) to puff, to blow; (*keuchen*) to puff (and pant).
2 *vt* **(a)** (*blasen*) to puff, to blow.
(b) (*inf*) **komm bloß nicht so spät nach Hause, sonst werd' ich dir was ~!** don't be late home or there'll be trouble; **er hat gesagt, ich soll das alles alleine machen, dem werd' ich was ~!** he said I was to do it all by myself, I'll tell him where he can get off! (*inf*); **ich soll dir 1.000 Mark leihen, ich werd' dir was ~!** I should lend you 1,000 marks, you must be *or* you've got to be joking! (*inf*).

Pusterohr *nt* (*inf*) pea-shooter.

putativ *adj* (*geh*) putative.

Pute *f* **-, -n** turkey (hen). **dumme ~** (*inf*) silly goose (*inf*); **eingebildete ~** (*inf*) conceited *or* stuck-up little madam (*inf*).

Puter *m* **-s, -** turkey (cock).

puterrot *adj* scarlet, bright red. **~ werden** to go as red as a beetroot (*inf*), to go scarlet *or* bright red.

Putsch *m* **-(e)s, -e** coup (d'état), revolt, putsch.

putschen *vi* to rebel, to revolt. **in Südamerika wird permanent geputscht** they're always having coups *or* revolts in South America.

Putschist(in *f*) *m* rebel.

Putschversuch *m* attempted coup (d'état).

Pütt *m* **-s, -s** (*dial*) pit, mine.

Putte *f* **-, -n** (*Art*) cherub.

putten *vt* to putt.

put(t) put(t) *interj* chick, chick, chick.

Putz *m* **-es, no pl** (*dated: Kleidung*) finery; (*Besatz*) frills and furbelows *pl*. **in vollem ~ erscheinen** to arrive all dressed up in one's Sunday best; **seinen festtäglichen ~ ablegen** to take off one's glad rags (*dated inf*) *or* Sunday best.
(b) (*Build*) plaster; (*Rauh~*) roughcast. **eine Mauer mit ~ verkleiden** *or* **bewerfen** to plaster *or* roughcast a wall; **unter ~** under the plaster.
(c) **auf den ~ hauen** (*inf*) (*angeben*) to show off; (*ausgelassen feiern*) to have a rave-up (*inf*); (*meckern*) to kick up a fuss (*inf*).

putzen 1 *vt* **(a)** to clean; (*scheuern auch*) to scrub; (*polieren auch*) to polish; (*wischen auch*) to wipe; Gemüse to clean; Pferd to brush down, to groom; Docht to trim. **die Schuhe ~** to clean *or* polish one's shoes; **Fenster ~** to clean the windows; **sich** (*dat*) **die Nase ~** to wipe one's nose; (*sich schneuzen*) to blow one's nose; **sich** (*dat*) **die Zähne ~** to clean *or* brush one's teeth; **einem Baby den Hintern/die Nase ~** to wipe a baby's bottom/nose.
(b) (*dated: schmücken*) to decorate.
(c) Mauer to roughcast, to plaster.
2 *vr* **(a)** (*sich säubern*) to wash *or* clean oneself.
(b) (*dated: sich schmücken*) to dress *or* do oneself up.

Putzer *m* **-s, -** (*Offiziers~*) batman.

Putzerei *f* **(a)** *no pl* (*inf*) cleaning. **hör doch endlich mal auf mit der ~!** will you stop all this damn cleaning! (*inf*). **(b)** (*Aus: Reinigung*) dry cleaner's.

Putzfrau *f* cleaner, cleaning lady, char(woman) (*Brit*).

putzig *adj* (*inf*) (*komisch*) funny, comical, amusing; (*niedlich*) cute; (*merkwürdig*) funny, strange, odd.

Putz-: **~lappen** *m* cloth; (*Staubtuch*) duster; **~leder** *nt* chamois *or* chammy (leather), wash-leather; **~macherin** *f* (*dated*) milliner; **~mittel** *nt* (*zum Scheuern*) cleanser, cleansing agent; (*zum Polieren*) polish; **~mittel** *pl* cleaning things *pl*; **p~munter** *adj* (*inf*) full of beans (*inf*); **~schere** *f* wick trimmer; **~sucht** *f* (*dated*) obsession with dressing up; **p~süchtig** *adj* (*dated*) excessively fond of dressing up; **~tag** *m* cleaning day; **~teufel** *m* (*inf: Frau*) maniac for keeping things clean; **sie ist ein richtiger ~teufel** she's excessively house-proud; **vom ~teufel besessen sein, den ~teufel haben** to have a mania for keeping things clean, to have the cleaning bug (*inf*); **~tuch** *nt* (*Staubtuch*) duster; (*Wischlappen*) cloth; **~wolle** *f* wire *or* steel wool; **~zeug** *nt* cleaning things *pl*.

puzzeln ['pazəln] *vi* to do a jigsaw (puzzle).

Puzzle(spiel) ['pazl-, 'pasl-] *nt* **-s, -s** jigsaw (puzzle).

Pygmäe [py'gmɛːə] *m* **-n, -n** Pygmy.

pygmäenhaft *adj* pygmy-like, pygmy *attr*.

Pyjama [py'dʒaːma, py'ʒaːma, pi'dʒaːma, pi'ʒaːma] *m* **-s, -s** pair of pyjamas (*Brit*) *or* pajamas (*US*) *sing*, pyjamas *pl* (*Brit*), pajamas *pl* (*US*). **wo ist mein ~?** where are my pyjamas?; **im ~** in his pyjamas; **ich wollte einen ~ kaufen** I wanted to buy some pyjamas *or* a pair of pyjamas.

Pyjamahose *f* pyjama (*Brit*) *or* pajama (*US*) trousers *pl*.

Pykniker(in *f*) *m* **-s, -** stocky person.

pyknisch *adj* stockily built.

Pylon *m* **-en, -en, Pylone** *f* **-, -n** (*Archit, von Brücken*) pylon; (*Absperrmarkierung*) traffic cone.

Pyramide *f* **-, -n** pyramid.

pyramidenförmig *adj* pyramid-shaped *no adv*, pyramidal (*form*). **~ konstruiert** built in the shape of a pyramid.

Pyrenäen [pyre'nɛːən] *pl* **die ~** the Pyrenees *pl*.

Pyrenäenhalb|insel *f* Iberian Peninsula.

Pyro-: **~mane** *mf* **-n, -n** pyromaniac; **~manie** *f* pyromania; **~technik** *f* pyrotechnics *sing*; **~techniker** *m* pyrotechnist; **p~technisch** *adj* pyrotechnic.

Pyrrhussieg ['pyrus-] *m* Pyrrhic victory.

pythagoreisch [pytago'reːɪʃ] *adj* Pythagorean. **~er Lehrsatz** Pythagoras's theorem, law of Pythagoras.

Python(schlange *f*) ['pyːtɔn-] *m* **-s, -s** python.

Q

Q, q [ku:] *nt* -, - Q, q.
qkm *abbr of* Quadradkilometer.
qm *abbr of* Quadratmeter.
Qu-, qu- [kv-].
qua *adv* (*geh*) qua.
quabbelig *adj Frosch, Qualle* slimy; *Pudding* wobbly.
quabbeln *vi* to wobble.
Quackelei *f* (*inf*) nattering (*inf*), chattering, blethering (*inf*).
Quacksalber *m* -s, - (*pej*) quack (doctor).
Quacksalberei *f* quackery, quack medicine.
quacksalbern* *vi insep* to quack (*rare*). **sowas nenne ich ~** I'd call that quack medicine *or* quackery.
Quaddel *f* -, -n hives *pl*, rash; (*durch Insekten*) bite; (*von Sonne*) heat spot.
Quader *m* -s, - *or f* -, -n (*Math*) cuboid, rectangular solid; (*Archit: auch* ~stein) ashlar, square stone block.
Quadrant *m* quadrant.
Quadrat[1] *nt* -(e)s, -e (*Fläche, Potenz*) square. **eine Zahl ins ~ erheben** to square a number; **vier zum ~** four squared; **drei Meter im ~** three metres square.
Quadrat[2] *nt* -(e)s, -e(n) (*Typ*) quad, quadrat.
Quadrat- *in cpds* square; ~arsch *m* (*inf*) great big bum (*Brit inf*) *or* backside (*inf*).
quadratisch *adj Form* square; (*Math*) *Gleichung* quadratic.
Quadrat-: ~latschen *pl* (*inf*) (*Schuhe*) clodhoppers (*inf*), beetle-crushers (*inf*); (*Füße*) plates of meat (*Brit sl*); ~meter *m or nt* square metre; ~schädel *m* (*inf: Kopf*) big head, great bonce (*Brit inf*); **das will einfach nicht in seinen ~schädel hinein!** that just won't sink into his thick skull! (*inf*).
Quadratur *f* quadrature. **die ~ des Kreises** *or* Zirkels the squaring of the circle; **das käme der ~ des Kreises** *or* Zirkels gleich that's like trying to square the circle.
Quadrat-: ~wurzel *f* square root; ~zahl *f* square number.
quadrieren* *vt Zahl* to square.
Quadriga *f* -, Quadrigen four-horsed chariot.
Quadrille [kva'drɪlja, ka-] *f* -, -n quadrille.
Quadrophonie *f* quadrophonic sound, quadrophony. **in ~** in quadrophonic, in quad (*inf*).
quadrophonisch *adj* quadrophonic.
Quai [kɛ:, ke:] *m or nt* -s, -s *siehe* **Kai.**
quak *interj* (*von Frosch*) croak; (*von Ente*) quack.
quaken *vi* (*Frosch*) to croak; (*Ente*) to quack; (*inf: Mensch*) to squawk (*inf*), to screech (*inf*).
quäken* *vti* (*inf*) to screech, to squawk.
Quäker(in *f*) *m* -s, - Quaker.
Qual *f* -, -en (*Schmerz*) (*körperlich*) pain, agony; (*seelisch*) agony, anguish. **tapfer ertrug er alle ~en** he bore all his suffering *or* pain bravely; **jds ~(en) lindern** *or* **mildern** (*liter*) to lessen sb's suffering; **unter großen ~en** to die in agony *or* great pain; **Gott/der Tod hat ihn von seinen ~en erlöst** *or* **befreit** (*form*) God/death released *or* freed him from his suffering *or* pain *or* agony; **sein Leben war eine einzige ~** his life was a living death; **es ist eine ~, das mit ansehen zu müssen** it is agonizing to watch; **die letzten Monate waren für mich eine ~** the last few months have been sheer agony for me; **jeder Schritt/das Bücken wurde ihm zur ~** every step/bending down was agony for him; **er machte ihr den Aufenthalt/das Leben/die Tage zur ~** he made her stay/her life/her days a misery; **es bereitete ihm ~en, sie so leiden zu sehen** it tormented him to see her suffering so; **die ~en des Gewissens** (*geh*)/des Zweifels agonies of conscience/of doubt *or* indecision; **die ~en, die sie um ihn** *or* **seinetwegen ausgestanden hat** the suffering she has gone through because of him.
quälen 1 *vt* to torment; *Tiere auch* to tease; (*inf*) *Motor* to punish; (*mit Bitten etc*) to pester, to plague. **jdn zu Tode ~** to torture sb to death; ~de Ungewißheit/Zweifel agonizing uncertainty/doubts, agonies of uncertainty/doubt; ~der Schmerz agonizing *or* excruciating pain; ~der Durst/Husten-reiz excruciating thirst/cough; *siehe* gequält.
2 *vr* (a) (*seelisch*) to torture *or* torment oneself; (*leiden*) to suffer, to be in agony.
(b) (*sich abmühen*) to struggle. **sie quälte sich in die enge Hose** she struggled into *or* squeezed herself into her tight slacks; **er mußte sich ~, damit er das schaffte** it took him a lot of effort *or* it was a struggle for him to do it; **sich durch ein Buch ~** to struggle *or* plough *or* wade through a book; **ich quäle mich jeden Morgen aus dem Bett** it's a struggle for me to get out of bed every morning; **er quälte sich aus dem Sessel** he heaved himself out of the chair; **das Auto quälte sich über den Berg** the car laboured *or* struggled over the hill.
Quälerei *f* (a) (*Grausamkeit*) atrocity, torture; (*seelische, nervliche Belastung*) agony, torment. **diese Tierversuche sind in meinen Augen ~** in my view these experiments on animals are cruel; **es ist doch eine ~ für das Tier** that is cruel to the animal; **die letzten Monate waren eine einzige ~** the last few months were sheer agony *or* were one long agony.
(b) (*mühsame Arbeit*) struggle. **das war vielleicht eine ~!** that was really a struggle *or* hard going.

quälerisch *adj attr* tormenting, agonizing.
Quälgeist *m* (*inf*) pest (*inf*).
Qualifikation *f* qualification. **für diese Arbeit fehlt ihm die nötige ~** he lacks the necessary qualifications for this work; **er hat die ~ zu diesem Amt** he has the qualifications *or* is qualified for this office; **mit diesem Sieg gelang der Mannschaft die ~** the team qualified with this win; **zur ~ fehlten ihr nur wenige Zentimeter/Sekunden** she only needed a few more centimetres/seconds to qualify.
Qualifikations-: ~runde *f* qualifying round; ~spiel *nt* qualifying match *or* game.
qualifizieren* **1** *vt* **(a)** (*befähigen*) to qualify (*für, zu* for).
(b) (*geh: differenzieren*) to qualify.
(c) (*geh: einstufen*) to designate, to label, to qualify. **man hat den Artikel als minderwertig qualifiziert** the article has been designated *or* labelled poor quality.
2 *vr* **(a)** (*allgemein, Sport*) to qualify. **er hat sich zum Facharbeiter qualifiziert** he qualifed as a specialist.
(b) (*sich erweisen*) to show *or* reveal oneself (*als* to be).
qualifiziert *adj* **(a)** *Arbeiter, Nachwuchs* qualified; *Arbeit* expert, professional. **(b)** (*Pol*) *Mehrheit* requisite.
Qualität *f* quality. **dieses Leder ist in der ~ besser als das andere** this leather is better quality than that; **von der ~ her** as far as quality is concerned, for quality; **die Ware ist von ausgezeichneter ~** the product is (of) top quality.
qualitativ *adj* qualitative.
Qualitäts- *in cpds* quality; ~arbeit *f* quality work; **unsere Firma hat sich durch (ihre) ~arbeit einen Namen gemacht** our firm made its name by the quality of its work *or* has got itself a reputation for quality; ~erzeugnis *nt* quality product; ~kontrolle *f* quality control; ~ware *f* quality goods *pl*; ~wein *m* wine of certified origin and quality.
Qualle *f* -, -n jellyfish.
Qualm *m* -(e)s, *no pl* (thick *or* dense) smoke; (*Tabaks*~) fug.
qualmen 1 *vi* **(a)** to give off smoke, to smoke. **es qualmt aus dem Schornstein/hinten aus dem Auto** clouds of smoke are coming *or* billowing from the chimney/from the back of the car.
(b) (*inf: Mensch*) to smoke. **wenn sie nervös ist, fängt sie an zu ~** when she's nervous she starts to smoke a lot *or* starts puffing away (at cigarettes); **sie qualmt einem die ganze Bude voll** she fills the whole place with smoke.
2 *vt* (*inf*) *Zigarette, Pfeife* to puff away at (*inf*).
Qualmerei *f* (*inf*) smoking; (*von Ofen*) smoke. **der einzige Nachteil ist die ~** the only drawback is the smoke *or* fug.
qualmig *adj* smoke-filled, smoky.
qualvoll *adj* painful; *Schmerzen* agonizing, excruciating; *Vorstellung, Gedanke* agonizing; *Anblick* harrowing.
Quant *nt* -s, -en quantum.
quanteln *vt* to quantize.
Quanten *pl* **(a)** *pl of* **Quant, Quantum. (b)** (*sl: Füße*) feet, plates of meat (*Brit sl*).
Quanten-: ~mechanik *f* quantum mechanics *sing*; ~theorie *f* quantum theory.
Quantität *f* quantity. **diese Artikel haben wir in großer ~** we have large quantities *or* a large quantity of these items.
quantitativ *adj* quantitative.
Quantum *nt* -s, Quanten (*Menge, Anzahl*) quantum, quantity; (*Anteil*) quota, quantum (*an* +*dat* of).
Quappe *f* -, -n **(a)** (*Kaul*~) tadpole. **(b)** (*Aal*~) burbot.
Quarantäne *f* -, -n quarantine. **in ~ liegen** *or* **sein** to be in quarantine; **unter ~ stellen** *Personen* to put in quarantine; *Gebiet, Stadt auch* to put under quarantine, to quarantine (off); **über das Gebiet wurde sofort ~ verhängt** the area was immediately placed in *or* under quarantine *or* was quarantined off.
Quarantänestation *f* quarantine *or* isolation ward.
Quark *m* -s, *no pl* **(a)** (soft) curd cheese.
(b) (*inf: Unsinn*) rubbish; (*unbedeutende Sache*) (little) trifle. **so ein ~!** stuff and nonsense!; ~ **reden** to talk rubbish; **sie kümmern sich einen ~ darum, was ...** they don't care in the slightest *or* don't give a hoot (*inf*) what ...; **das geht ihn einen ~ an!** it's none of his business!
Quark-: ~kuchen *m siehe* Käsekuchen; ~speise *f* pudding made with curd cheese, sugar, milk, fruit etc; ~tasche *f*, ~teilchen *nt* curd cheese turnover.
Quart[1] *f* -, -en **(a)** (*Mus: auch* ~e) fourth. **ein Sprung über eine ~ nach oben/unten** a jump up/down a fourth. **(b)** (*Fechten*) quarte.
Quart[2] *nt* -s, -e **(a)** (*old: Maß*) ≈ quart. **(b)** (*Typ*) *no pl siehe* **Quartformat.**
Quarta *f* -, Quarten (*Sch*) third year of German secondary school.
Quartal *nt* -s, -e quarter (year). **Kündigung zum ~** quarterly notice date; **es muß jedes ~ bezahlt werden** it has to be paid quarterly *or* every quarter.
Quartal(s)-: ~abschluß *m* end of the quarter; ~säufer *m* periodic heavy drinker; **sein Vater ist ein ~säufer** every so often his father goes on a binge (*inf*); **q~weise** *adj* quarterly.

Quartaner(in f) m -s, - (Sch) pupil in third year of German secondary school.

Quartär nt -s, no pl quaternary.

Quartband m quarto volume.

Quarte f -, -n siehe Quart¹ (a).

Quarten pl of Quart¹, Quarta, Quarte.

Quartett nt -(e)s, -e (a) (Mus) quartet. (b) (Cards) (Spiel) ≃ happy families; (Karten) set of four cards.

Quartformat nt quarto (format).

Quartier nt -s, -e (a) (Unterkunft) accommodation. wir sollten uns ein ~ suchen we should look for accommodation or a place to stay; **die Jugendlichen sind in verschiedenen ~en untergebracht/auf mehrere ~e verteilt worden** the youngsters have been accommodated or given accommodation or put up in various different places; **wir hatten unser ~ in einem alten Bauernhof** we stayed in an old farmhouse.
(b) (Mil) quarters pl, billet. **bei jdm in ~ liegen** to be quartered or billeted with or on sb; **~ machen** to arrange quarters or billets.
(c) (Stadtviertel) district, quarter.

Quartier-: ~macher m (Mil) billeting officer; ~meister m (old Mil) quartermaster.

Quarz m -es, -e quartz.

Quarz-: ~glas nt quartz glass; **q~haltig** adj quartziferous (form), which contains quartz; ~lampe f quartz lamp; ~uhr f quartz clock.

Quasar m -s, -e quasar.

quasi 1 adv virtually. 2 pref quasi. **~-wissenschaftlich** quasi-scientific.

Quasselei f (inf) gabbling (inf), gabbing (inf), blethering (inf).

quasseln vti to gabble (inf), to blether (inf). **was quasselst du denn da für ein dummes Zeug?** what are you blethering about now? (inf).

Quasselstrippe f (inf) chatterbox (inf); (beleidigend) windbag (inf), blabbermouth (inf).

Quast m -(e)s, -e (dial) wide paint brush.

Quaste f -, -n (Troddel) tassle; (von Pinsel) brush, bristles pl; (Schwanz~) tuft; siehe Puderquaste.

Quästur f (Univ) bursary.

Quatember m -s, - (a) (Eccl) Ember day. (b) (obs) quarter day.

quatsch interj squelch.

Quatsch m -es, no pl (a) (inf: Unsinn) rubbish. **das ist der größte ~, den ich je gehört habe** that is the biggest load of rubbish I have ever heard; **red keinen ~!** don't talk rubbish!; **ach ~! rubbish!; ach ~, das hast du ganz falsch verstanden** don't be silly, you've understood it all wrong; **so ein ~!** what (a load of) rubbish; **~ mit Soße!** stuff and nonsense!
(b) (inf: Dummheiten) nonsense. **hört doch endlich mit dem ~ auf!** stop being so stupid or silly!; **was soll denn der ~!** what's all this nonsense in aid of then!; **laß den ~ cut it out! (inf); ~ machen** to mess about or around (inf); **mach damit keinen ~** don't mess about or around with it (inf), don't do anything stupid with it; **mach keinen ~, sonst knallt's** don't try anything silly or funny or I'll shoot; **mach keinen ~, du kannst doch jetzt nicht krank werden** don't be silly, you can't get ill now!
(c) (esp S Ger: Matsch) mud, sludge.

quatschen¹ (inf) 1 vti (dummes Zeug reden) to gab (away) (inf), to blather (inf), to gabble (inf). **sie quatscht mal wieder einen Blödsinn** she's talking a load of nonsense or rubbish again.
2 vi (a) (plaudern) to blather (inf), to chatter, to natter (Brit inf). **er hat stundenlang gequatscht** he blathered or gabbled on for hours; **ich hab' mit ihm am Telefon gequatscht** I had a good natter with him on the phone.
(b) (etw ausplaudern) to squeal (inf), to talk.

quatschen² vi (Schlamm) to squelch.

Quatscherei f (inf) blathering (inf), yacking (inf); (in der Schule) chattering.

Quatsch-: ~kopf m (pej inf) (Schwätzer) windbag (inf); (Dummkopf) fool, twit (Brit inf); **q~naß** adj (inf) soaking or dripping wet.

Quecke f -, -n couch grass.

Quecksilber nt (a) (Chem) mercury, quicksilver. **~ im Leib haben** (fig) to have ants in one's pants (inf). (b) (dated: Mensch) fidget.

Quecksilber- in cpds mercury; **q~haltig** adj mercurial.

quecksilb(e)rig adj (fig) fidgety, restless.

Quell m -(e)s, -e (poet) spring, source.

Quelle f -, -n (a) spring; (von Fluß auch) source; (Erdöl~, Gas~) well. **heiße ~n** hot springs; **eine ~ erschließen** to develop or exploit a source; **eine neue ~ der Energie** a new source of energy.
(b) (fig) (Ursprung) source; (für Waren) source (of supply), supplier. **die ~ allen Übels** the root of all evil; **eine ~ der Freude** a source of pleasure; **~n der Weisheit** fountain of knowledge; **aus zuverlässiger/sicherer ~** from a reliable/trustworthy source; **aus welcher ~ haben Sie das?** what source did you get that from?, what's your source for that?; **an der ~ sitzen** (fig) to be well-placed; to be able to get inside information; **kannst du mir einige Bücher besorgen, du sitzt doch an der ~?** can you get me some books, after all you can get them from source.

quellen 1 vi pret **quoll**, ptp **gequollen** aux sein (a) (herausfließen) to pour, to stream, to well. **der Bauch quillt ihm aus der Hose** his stomach hangs out or bulges out over his trousers; **die Augen quollen ihm aus dem Kopf** his eyes were popping out of his head.
(b) (Holz, Reis, Erbsen) to swell. **lassen Sie die Bohnen über Nacht ~** leave the beans to soak overnight.
2 vt pret **quellte**, ptp **gequellt** (rare) Erbsen to soak.

Quellen-: ~angabe f reference; **achten Sie bei der ~angabe darauf, daß ... make** sure when doing or giving the references that ...; ~forschung f source research; ~sammlung f (collection of) source material; (~werk) source book; ~studium nt study of sources; **ich bin immer noch mit dem ~studium beschäftigt** I am still studying the sources; ~werk nt source book.

Quell-: ~fluß m source (river); ~gebiet nt headwaters pl; ~wasser nt spring water.

Quengelei f (inf) whining.

queng(e)lig adj whining. **die Kinder wurden ~** the children started to whine; **er ist sonst nicht so ~** he doesn't usually whine so much.

quengeln vi (inf) to whine.

Quengler m -s, - (inf) whiner.

Quentchen nt (old) tiny bit, spot. **ein ~ Salz** a speck or dash of salt; **ein ~ Glück** a modicum of luck; **ein ~ Mut** a scrap of courage; **kein ~** not a jot, not an iota.

quer adv (schräg) crossways, crosswise, diagonally; (rechtwinklig) at right angles. **sollen wir den Teppich lieber ~ legen?** why don't we lay the carpet crosswise or crossways or diagonally?; **der Baumstamm trieb ~ den Fluß hinunter** the log floated crossways or crosswise down the river; **er legte sich ~ aufs Bett** he lay down across the bed; **die Spur verläuft ~ zum Hang** the path runs across the slope; **die Straße/Linie verläuft ~ the road/the line** runs at right angles; **der Wagen stand ~ zur Fahrbahn** the car was at right angles to the road; **der Lastzug lag ~ über der Straße** the truck was lying (diagonally/at right angles) across the road; **wenn Sie sich ~ stellen, habe ich mit meinem Wagen auch noch Platz** if you park diagonally/at right angles I'll have room to park my car too; **~ durch etw gehen/laufen** etc to cross sth, to go through sth; **~ über etw (acc) gehen/laufen** to cross sth, to go across sth; **der Hund ist ~ über die Wäsche gelaufen** the dog ran straight or right over or across the washing; **die Kamera ~ nehmen** to hold the camera lengthways or crossways; **den Stoff ~ nehmen** to use the cross-grain of the material; siehe kreuz.

Quer-: ~balken m crossbeam; (von Türrahmen) transom, lintel; (Her) bar; (Mus) line joining quavers etc; **q~beet** adv (inf) (wahllos) at random; (durcheinander) all over the place (inf); (~feldein) across country; **q~durch** adv straight through.

Quere f -, no pl der ~ nach widthways, breadthways; **jdm in die ~ kommen** to cross sb's path; **es muß ihm etwas in die ~ gekommen sein, sonst hätte er sich nicht verspätet** something must have cropped up otherwise he would not be late; **der Lastwagen kam mir in die ~** the lorry got in my way; siehe Kreuz².

Querele f -, -n (geh) dispute, quarrel.

queren 1 vt to cross. 2 vi to cross.

querfeldein adv across country.

Querfeldein-: ~lauf m cross-country (run); (Wettbewerb) cross-country (race); ~rennen nt cross-country; (Auto~) autocross; (Motorrad~) motocross; (Fahrrad~) cyclecross; (Pferde~) point-to-point.

Quer-: ~flöte f (transverse) flute; ~format nt oblong format; **wenn du das Photo im ~format machst** if you take the photo lengthways; **q~gehen** vi sep irreg aux sein (inf) to go wrong; **heute geht mir alles q~** I can't do a thing right today; **q~gestreift** adj attr horizontally striped, cross-striped; **tragen Sie lieber q~gestreift** you'd be better to wear horizontal or cross stripes; ~holz nt siehe ~balken; ~kopf m (inf) awkward so-and-so (inf) or customer (inf); **q~köpfig** adj awkward, perverse; ~lage f (Med) transverse presentation, crossbirth; ~latte f crossbar; **q~legen** vr (fig inf) to be awkward; ~paß m cross; ~pfeife f fife; ~ruder nt aileron; **q~schießen** vi sep irreg (inf) to be awkward, to spoil things; ~schiff nt transept; ~schläger m ricochet (shot).

Querschnitt m (lit, fig) cross-section.

Querschnitt(s)-: **q~gelähmt** adj paraplegic; **seit dem Autounfall ist er q~gelähmt** since the car accident he has been paralyzed from the waist down; ~gelähmte(r) mf paraplegic; ~lähmung f paraplegia; ~zeichnung f sectional drawing.

Quer-: **q~schreiben** vt sep irreg (Fin) Wechsel to accept, to underwrite; ~schuß m (fig) objection; **q~stellen** vr sep (fig inf) to be awkward; ~straße f das ist eine ~straße zur Hauptstraße it runs at right angles to the high street; **in dieser ~straße muß das Geschäft sein** the shop must be down this turning; **bei or an der zweiten ~straße fahren Sie links ab** turn (off to the) left at the second junction, go left at the second turning; **die ~straßen zur Königstraße sehen alle gleich aus** the streets (going) off Königstraße all look the same; **die Kaiserallee hat viele ~straßen** there are lots of streets (going) off the Kaiserallee; ~streifen m horizontal stripe; ~strich m (horizontal) stroke or line; (Typ inf: Gedankenstrich) dash; (Bruchstrich) line; **einen ~strich durch etw machen** to put a line through sth; (streichen auch) to cross sth out; **er macht beim T nie die ~striche** he always forgets to cross his T's; ~summe f (Math) sum of digits of a number; **die ~summe bilden** to add the digits in a number; ~treiber m (inf) troublemaker, awkward customer (inf); ~treiberei f (inf) awkwardness, troublemaking; **er versucht jetzt, die Sache durch ~treiberei zu verhindern** now he's trying to obstruct things by being awkward.

Querulant(in f) m grouser (inf), grumbler.

querulieren* vi to grouse (inf), to grumble.

Quer-: ~verbindung f connection, link; (von Eisenbahn) connecting line; (von Straße) link road; **hier läßt sich doch eine ~verbindung zur deutschen Geschichte herstellen** you can surely make a connection here with German history, you can surely link this up with German history; ~verweis m cross-reference.

quetschen 1 *vt* (*drücken*) to squash, to crush; (*aus einer Tube*) to squeeze; *Kartoffeln* to mash; (*Med: usu pass*) to crush. **etw in etw** (*acc*) ~ to squeeze *or* squash sth into sth; **jdn halbtot** ~ to crush sb (nearly) to death; **jdm/sich den Finger** ~ to squash sb's/one's finger; **du hast mir den Finger in der Tür gequetscht** you caught my finger in the door.

2 *vr* (*sich klemmen*) to be caught *or* squashed *or* crushed; (*sich zwängen*) to squeeze (oneself). **du kannst dich noch ins Auto** ~ you can still squeeze into the car.

Quetsch-: ~**kartoffeln** *pl* (*dial*) mashed potatoes *pl*; ~**kommode** *f* (*hum inf*) squeeze box (*inf*).

Quetschung, Quetschwunde *f* (*Med*) bruise, contusion (*form*). **der Fahrer kam mit** ~**en davon** the driver escaped with bruises *or* bruising; ~ **innerer Organe** internal bruising.

Queue [kø:] *nt or m* -s, -s (*Billard*) cue.

quick *adj* (*dial*) quick-witted, alert. **er ist immer** ~ **bei der Sache** he is always on the ball (*inf*).

quicklebendig *adj* (*inf*) *Kind* lively, active; *ältere Person auch* spry.

quiek *interj* squeak.

quiek(s)en *vi* to squeal, to squeak.

quietschen *vi* (*Tür, Schloß*) to squeak; (*Reifen, Mensch*) to squeal. **das Kind quietschte vergnügt** *or* **vor Vergnügen** (*inf*) the child squealed with delight; **das** *or* **es war zum Q~!** (*inf*) it was a (real) scream! (*inf*).

quietschfidel, quietschvergnügt *adj* (*inf*) full of beans (*inf*).

quill *imper sing* of **quellen**.

Quinta *f* -, **Quinten** (*Sch*) second year of German secondary school.

Quintaner(in *f*) *m* -s, - (*Sch*) pupil in second year of German secondary school.

Quint(e) *f* -, -n (a) (*Mus*) fifth. (b) (*Fechten*) quinte.

Quinten *pl* of **Quinta, Quinte**.

Quint|essenz *f* quintessence.

Quintett *nt* -(e)s, -e quintet.

Quintole *f* -, -n quintuplet.

Quirl *m* -s, -e (a) (*Cook*) whisk, beater. (b) (*Bot*) whorl, verticil. (c) (*dated inf: Mensch*) live wire (*inf*).

quirlen *vt* to whisk, to beat.

quirlig *adj* lively, effervescent.

Quisling *m* (*Pol pej*) quisling.

quitt *adj* ~ **sein** (**mit jdm**) to be quits *or* even (with sb); **jdn/etw** ~ **sein** (*dial*) to be rid of sb/sth.

Quitte *f* -, -n quince.

quitte(n)gelb *adj* (sickly) yellow.

quittieren* **1** *vt* (a) (*bestätigen*) *Betrag, Rechnung, Empfang* to give a receipt for. **lassen Sie sich** (*dat*) **die Rechnung** ~ **get a** receipt for the bill.

(b) (*beantworten*) to meet, to answer, to counter.

(c) (*verlassen*) *Dienst* to quit, to resign.

2 *vi* (a) (*bestätigen*) to sign.

(b) (*old: zurücktreten*) to quit, to resign.

Quittung *f* (a) receipt. **gegen** ~ on production of a receipt; **eine** ~ **über 500 Mark** a receipt for 500 marks; **eine** ~ **ausstellen** (**über** *or* **für etw**) to make out *or* give a receipt (for sth).

(b) (*fig*) **das ist die** ~ **für Ihre Unverschämtheit** that is what you get for being so insolent, that's what comes of being so insolent; **das ist die** ~ **dafür, daß** ... that's the price you have to pay for ...; **jetzt haben Sie die** ~! now you have paid the penalty!; **du wirst die** ~ **für deine Faulheit bekommen** you'll pay the penalty for being lazy; **er hat seine** ~ **bekommen** he's paid the penalty *or* price.

Quittungsblock *m* receipt book.

Quiz [kvɪs] *nt* -, - quiz.

Quizmaster [ˈkvɪsmaːstɐ] *m* -s, - quizmaster.

quoll *pret* of **quellen**.

Quorum *nt* -s, *no pl* quorum.

Quote *f* -, -n (a) (*Statistik*) (*Anteilsziffer*) proportion; (*Rate*) rate.

(b) (*Econ, Quantum*) quota.

Quotient [kvoˈtsiɛnt] *m* quotient.

quotieren* *vt* (*Comm*) *Preis, Kurs* to quote.

Quotierung *f* (*Comm*) quotation.

R

R, r [ɛr] *nt* -, - R, r. **das R rollen** to roll one's r's.

Rabatt *m* -(e)s, -e discount. **mit 10%** ~ at *or* with (a) 10% discount.

Rabatte *f* (a) (*Beet*) border. (b) (*am Kragen*) revere, revers (*US*); (*Ärmelaufschlag*) cuff.

rabattieren* *vt* (*Comm*) to give a discount on.

Rabattmarke *f* (*Comm*) (trading) stamp.

Rabatz *m* -es, *no pl* (*inf*) row, din, shindy (*sl*).

Rabauke *m* -n, -n (*inf*) hooligan, lout (*inf*), rowdy (*inf*).

Rabaukentum *nt* hooliganism, rowdyism.

Rabbi *m* -(s), -s, *or* **Rabbinen, Rabbiner** *m* -s, - rabbi.

rabbinisch *adj* rabbinical.

Rabe *m* -n, -n raven. **wie ein** ~ **stehlen** (*inf*) to thieve like a magpie.

Raben-: ~**aas** *nt* (*dated inf*) bad lot (*inf*); ~**eltern** *pl* (*inf*) bad parents *pl*; ~**mutter** *f* (*inf*) bad mother; **r~schwarz** *adj Nacht* pitch-black, black as pitch; *Augen, Seele auch* coal-black, black as coal; *Haare* jet-black, raven(-black); ~**vater** *m* (*inf*) bad father; ~**vieh,** ~**viech** *nt* (*Aus inf*) siehe ~**aas**.

rabiat *adj Kerl* violent, rough; *Autofahrer* breakneck, wild; *Geschäftsleute* ruthless; *Umgangston* aggressive; *Methoden, Konkurrenz* ruthless, cut-throat. ~ **werden** (*wütend*) to go wild; (*aggressiv*) to get violent *or* physical (*inf*); ~ **arbeiten/ fahren** to work/drive furiously.

Rabulist *m* sophist, quibbler.

Rabulisterei, Rabulistik *f* sophistry, quibbling.

rabulistisch *adj* sophistic, quibbling.

Rache *f* -, *no pl* revenge, vengeance. **die** ~ **des kleinen Mannes** (*inf*) sweet revenge; **Tag der** ~ (*liter*) day of reckoning; **das ist die** ~ **für eine Untat** this is the retribution for my misdeed; ~ **brüten, auf** ~ **sinnen** to contemplate *or* plot revenge; ~ **schwören** to swear vengeance; (**an jdm**) ~ **nehmen** *or* **üben** to take revenge *or* have one's revenge (on *or* upon sb); **etw aus** ~ **tun** to do sth in revenge; ~ **ist Blutwurst** (*inf*) you'll/he'll *etc* be sorry (*inf*); ~ **ist süß** (*prov*) revenge is sweet (*prov*).

Rache-: ~**akt** *m* act of revenge *or* vengeance; ~**durst** *m* thirst *or* longing for revenge *or* vengeance; **r~durstig** *adj* thirsting *or* longing for revenge *or* vengeance; ~**engel** *m* avenging angel; ~**gefühl** *nt* feeling of bitter resentment; ~**gefühle haben** to harbour bitter resentment; ~**göttin** *f* avenging goddess, goddess of vengeance; **wie eine** ~**göttin** like a Fury.

Rachen *m* -s, - throat, pharynx (*spec*); (*von großen Tieren*) jaws *pl*; (*fig*) jaws *pl*, abyss, maw. **der** ~ **des Todes** the jaws of death;

jdm etw in den ~ **werfen** *or* **schmeißen** (*inf*) to shove sth down sb's throat (*inf*); **jdm den** ~ **stopfen** (*inf*) to give sb what he/she wants; **er kann den** ~ **nicht voll (genug) kriegen** (*inf*) he can't get enough; **halt den** ~ (*sl*) shut your face (*sl*), belt up (*sl*).

rächen 1 *vt jdn, Untat* to avenge (*etw an jdm* sth on sb). **er schwor, diese Schmach zu** ~ he swore to take vengeance for *or* to avenge this dishonour; **dieses Unrecht werde ich noch an ihm** ~ I intend to avenge myself on him for this injustice.

2 *vr* (*Mensch*) to get one's revenge, to take revenge *or* vengeance (*an jdm für etw* on sb for sth); (*Schuld, Sünde, Untat*) to be avenged. **deine Faulheit/Unehrlichkeit wird sich** ~ you'll pay for being so lazy/dishonest.

Rachen-: ~**blütler** *m* -s, - (*Bot*) figwort; ~**höhle** *f* pharynx, pharyngeal cavity; ~**katarrh** *m* pharyngitis; ~**mandel** *f* pharyngeal tonsil; ~**putzer** *m* (*hum inf*) gutrot (*inf*).

Racheplan *m* plan of revenge. **Rachepläne schmieden** to plot revenge.

Rächer(in *f*) *m* -s, - avenger.

Rache-: **r~schnaubend** *adj* swearing vengeance; ~**schwur** *m* oath of revenge *or* vengeance.

Rach-: ~**gier** *f* siehe ~**sucht**; **r~gierig** *adj* siehe **r~süchtig**.

Rachitis *f* -, *no pl* rickets, rachitis (*spec*).

rachitisch *adj* rickety, rachitic (*spec*); *Symptom* of rickets.

Rach-: ~**sucht** *f* vindictiveness; **r~süchtig** *adj* vindictive.

Racker *m* -s, - (*inf: Kind*) rascal, scamp, monkey (*all inf*).

Rackerei *f* siehe **Plackerei**.

rackern *vir* (*inf*) to slave (away) (*inf*).

Racket [ˈrɛkət, raˈkɛt] *nt* -s, -s (*Aus*) siehe **Rakett**.

Rad *nt* -(e)s, ̈-er (a) wheel; (*Rolle*) castor; (*Sport*) cartwheel. **ein** ~ **schlagen** (*Sport*) to do *or* turn a cartwheel; **der Pfau schlägt ein** ~ the peacock is fanning out its tail *or* spreading its tail *or* opening its fan; **jdn aufs** ~ **flechten** (*Hist*) to break sb on the wheel; **alle** ̈~**er greifen ineinander, ein** ~ **greift ins andere** (*fig*) it all knits together, all the parts knit together; **nur ein** ~ *or* **Rädchen im Getriebe sein** (*fig*) to be only a cog in the works; **das** ~ **der Geschichte** the wheels of history; **das** ~ **der Geschichte** *or* **Zeit läßt sich nicht zurückdrehen** you can't turn *or* put the clock back; **unter die** ̈~**er kommen** *or* **geraten** (*inf*) to get *or* fall into bad ways; **das fünfte** ~ **am Wagen sein** (*inf*) to feel *or* be out of place *or* de trop; (*bei Paaren*) to play gooseberry (*inf*).

(b) (*Fahr~*) bicycle, bike (*inf*), cycle. **mit dem** ~ **fahren/ kommen** to go/come by bicycle; *siehe* **radfahren**.

Rad|achse f axle(tree).
Radar m or nt -s, no pl radar.
Radar- in cpds radar; ~**abwehrnetz** nt (Mil) radar defence network; ~**anlage** f radar (equipment) no indef art; ~**falle** f speed trap; ~**gerät** nt radar unit; **r~gesteuert** adj radar-controlled; ~**kontrolle** f radar speed check; ~**schirm** m radar screen, radarscope.
Radau m -s, no pl (inf) row, din, racket (inf). ~ **machen** to kick up a row; (Unruhe stiften) to cause or make trouble.
Radaubruder m (inf) rowdy (inf), hooligan, yobbo (Brit inf).
Rad|aufhängung f (Aut) (wheel) suspension.
Radaumacher m (inf) siehe **Radaubruder**.
Radball m, no pl bicycle polo.
Rädchen nt dim of Rad small wheel; (für Schnittmuster) tracing wheel; (Cook) pastry wheel; siehe **Rad**.
Raddampfer m paddle-steamer.
Rade f -, -n corncockle.
radebrechen vti insep to speak broken English/German etc. er radebrechte auf Italienisch, er wolle ... he said in broken Italian that he wanted ...; **da haben wir einfach ~ müssen** so we just had to get by in a mixture of languages.
radeln[1] vi aux sein (inf) to cycle.
radeln[2], **rädeln** vt Schnittmuster to trace; (Cook) to cut out.
Rädelsführer m ringleader.
-räd(e)rig adj suf -wheeled.
rädern vt (Hist) to break on the wheel; siehe **gerädert**.
Räderwerk nt (Mech) mechanism, works pl; (fig) machinery, cogs pl.
radfahren vi sep irreg aux sein (Kleinschreibung nur bei infin und ptp) (a) to cycle. **ich fahre Rad** I ride a bicycle; **kannst du ~?** can you ride a bike?; **R~ verboten** no cycling. (b) (pej inf: kriechen) to crawl (inf), to suck up (inf).
Radfahrer(in f) m (a) cyclist. (b) (pej inf) crawler (inf).
Radfahr-: ~**sport** m siehe Radsport; ~**weg** m siehe Radweg.
Radgabel f fork.
Radi m -s, - (S Ger, Aus) radish. **einen ~ kriegen** (inf) to get a rocket (inf), to catch it (inf).
radial adj radial.
Radialgeschwindigkeit f (Astron) radial velocity.
Radiator m radiator.
radieren* vti (a) to rub out, to erase. **auf dieser Seite hat er dreimal radiert** he's rubbed three things out on this page, there are three erasures on this page. (b) (Art) to etch.
Radierer m -s, - (a) (inf) siehe **Radiergummi**. (b) (Art) etcher.
Radier-: ~**gummi** m rubber (Brit), eraser (esp US, form); ~**kunst** f (Art) etching; ~**messer** nt (steel) eraser, erasing knife; ~**nadel** f (Art) etching needle.
Radierung f (Art) etching.
Radieschen [ra'di:sçən] nt radish. **sich** (dat) **die ~ von unten an- or besehen** (hum sl) to be pushing up the daisies (hum).
radikal adj radical; Vereinfachung, Methode auch drastic; Vertilgung, Entfernen total; Verneinung categorical; Ablehnung flat, categorical. **mit diesen Mißbräuchen muß ~ Schluß gemacht werden** a definitive stop must be put to these abuses; **etw ~ verneinen/ablehnen** to deny sth categorically/to refuse sth flatly; ~ **vorgehen** to be drastic; ~ **gegen etw vorgehen** to take radical steps against sth.
Radikal nt -s, -e (Math) root; (Chem) radical.
Radikalen|erlaß m (pej) ban on the employment of radical teachers and civil servants.
Radikale(r) mf decl as adj radical.
Radikalinski m -s, -s (Pol pej) lefty (inf), commie (pej), bolshie (pej), radical.
radikalisieren* vt to radicalize.
Radikalisierung f radicalization.
Radikalismus m (Pol) radicalism.
Radikalkur f (inf) drastic remedy, kill-or-cure remedy.
Radio nt or (Sw, S Ger auch) m -s, -s radio, wireless (esp Brit). ~ **hören** to listen to the radio; **im ~** on the radio.
Radio- in cpds radio; **r~aktiv** adj radioactive; **r~aktiv machen** to activate, to make radioactive; **r~aktiver Niederschlag** (radioactive) fall-out; ~**aktivität** f radioactivity; ~**amateur** m radio ham (inf) or amateur; ~**apparat** m radio ~**gerät**; ~**astronomie** f radio astronomy; ~**bastler** m (inf) radio buff (inf) or enthusiast; ~**biologie** f radiobiology; ~**chemie** f radiochemistry; ~**durchsage** f radio announcement; ~**empfänger** m radio (set); (von Funkamateur) radio receiver; ~**gehäuse** nt radio cabinet; (von Kofferradio) casing; ~**gerät** nt radio (set); ~**geschäft** nt electrical shop; ~**gramm** m (Med) X-ray (photograph), radiograph (esp US); ~**graphie** f radiography; ~**isotop** nt radioisotope; ~**karbonmethode** f radiocarbon (dating) technique or method; ~**kompaß** m (Aviat, Naut) radio compass, automatic direction finder; ~**loge** m, ~**login** f (Med) radiologist; ~**logie** f (Med) radiology; ~**mechaniker** m radio technician or engineer; ~**metrie** f radiometry; ~**quelle** f (Astron) radio source; ~**röhre** f radio valve (esp Brit) or tube (esp US); ~**sender** m (Rundfunkanstalt) radio station; (Sendeeinrichtung) radio transmitter; ~**sendung** f radio programme; ~**skopie** f radioscopy; ~**sonde** f (radio-equipped) weather balloon, radiosonde; ~**station** f radio or broadcasting station; ~**strahlung** f radio signal; ~**technik** f radio technology; ~**techniker** m siehe ~**mechaniker**; ~**telegrafie** f radiotelegraphy; ~**teleskop** nt radio telescope; ~**therapeut** m radiotherapist; ~**therapie** f radiotherapy; ~**übertragung** f (radio) broadcast or transmission.
Radium nt radium.
Radium-: ~**behandlung**, ~**bestrahlung** f (Med) siehe ~**therapie**; **r~haltig** adj containing radium; **r~haltig sein** to contain radium; ~**strahlen** pl (Phys, Med) radium rays pl;

~**therapie** f radium therapy or treatment.
Radius m -, **Radien** [-ən] radius.
Rad-: ~**kappe** f hub cap; ~**kasten** m wheel casing; (Naut) paddle-box; ~**kranz** m rim (of a/the wheel); ~**lager** nt wheel bearing.
Radler(in f) m -s, - (inf) cyclist.
Radlermaß f (S Ger inf) shandy.
Rad-: ~**macher** m siehe Stellmacher; ~**mantel** m (a) (Bereifung) bicycle tyre; (b) (Kleidung) cycle or cycling cape; ~**nabe** f (wheel) hub; ~**rennbahn** f cycle (racing) track; ~**rennen** nt (Sportart) cycle racing; (einzelnes Rennen) cycle race; ~**rennfahrer** m racing cyclist; ~**rennsport** m cycle racing; ~**schaufel** f blade (of a wheel); **r~schlagen** vi sep irreg (Kleinschreibung nur bei infin und ptp) to do or turn cartwheels; **ich schlage ~** I do cartwheels; ~**schuh** m brake; ~**sport** m cycling; ~**sportler** m cyclist; ~**stand** m (Aut, Rail) wheelbase; ~**sturz** m (Aut) camber; ~**tour** f cycling or cycle tour; ~**wechsel** m wheel change; (einen) ~**wechsel machen** to change a wheel, to do a wheel change; ~**weg** m cycle track.
Raffel f -, -n (dial) (a) (Reibeisen) grater. (b) (Tex) hackle, flax comb. (c) (inf: Schwätzerin) blatherer (inf). **eine ~ haben** to be a blatherer (inf).
raffeln (dial) 1 vti (a) to grate. (b) (Tex) to comb, to hackle. 2 vi (schwatzen) to rattle on.
raffen vt (a) (anhäufen) to pile, to heap. **er will immer nur Geld ~** he's always after money; **sein ganzes Leben hat er nur Geld gerafft** he spent his whole life making money; **etw an sich** (acc) ~ to grab or snatch sth. (b) Stoff, Gardine to gather; langes Kleid, Rock to gather up.
Raff-: ~**gier** f greed, avarice; **r~gierig** adj greedy, grasping.
raffig adj (dial) siehe **raffgierig**.
Raffinade f (Zucker) refined sugar.
Raffination f (von Öl, Zucker) refining.
Raffinement [rafinə'mã:] nt -s, -s (geh) siehe **Raffinesse** (b).
Raffinerie f refinery.
Raffinesse f (a) (Feinheit) refinement, finesse no pl. **ein Auto mit allen ~n** a car with all the refinements. (b) (Schlauheit, Durchtriebenheit) cunning no pl, craftiness no pl, wiliness no pl. **mit allen ~n** with all one's cunning.
raffinieren* vt Zucker, Öl to refine.
raffiniert adj (a) Zucker, Öl refined.
(b) (inf) Kleid, Frisur, Apparat, Kleidung fancy (inf), stylish; Apparat fancy (inf). **sie kleidet sich sehr ~** she certainly knows how to dress.
(c) (schlau) clever, cunning; (durchtrieben auch) crafty. **sie ist eine ~e Frau** she knows all the tricks in the book; **ein ~es Luder** or **Weib** (pej) a cunning bitch (inf).
Raffiniertheit f siehe adj (b, c) fanciness (inf), stylishness; fanciness (inf); cleverness, cunning; craftiness.
Raffke m -s, -s (inf) money-grubber (inf). **Herr/Frau ~** a typical member of the nouveau riche.
Rage ['ra:ʒə] f -, no pl (a) (Wut) rage, fury. **jdn in ~ bringen** to infuriate sb; **in ~ kommen** or **geraten** to get or become furious, to fly into a rage or fury. (b) (inf: Aufregung, Eile) hurry, rush.
ragen vi to rise, to tower, to loom; (heraus~) to jut.
Ragionenbuch [ra'dʒo:nən-] nt (Sw) business register.
Raglan- in cpds raglan; ~**ärmel** m raglan sleeve; ~**schnitt** m raglan style.
Ragmusik ['ræg-] f siehe **Ragtime**.
Ragout [ra'gu:] nt -s, -s ragout.
Ragtime ['ræg-] m -s, no pl ragtime.
Rah(e) f -(e), -(e)n (Naut) yard.
Rahm m -(e)s, no pl (dial) cream; siehe **abschöpfen**.
Rähmchen nt dim of Rahmen (Dia~) mount.
rahmen vt to frame; Dias to mount.
Rahmen m -s, - (a) frame; (vom Schuh) welt.
(b) (fig) (Bereich, Liter: ~handlung) framework; (Atmosphäre) setting; (Größe) scale. **im ~** within the framework (gen of); **seine Verdienste wurden im ~ einer kleinen Feier gewürdigt** his services were honoured in a small ceremony; **im ~ des Möglichen** within the bounds of possibility; **wir werden Ihnen im ~ des Möglichen helfen** we will help you if it is at all within the bounds of possibility; **im ~ bleiben** not to go too far; **aus dem ~ fallen** to go too far; **mußt du denn immer aus dem ~ fallen!** do you always have to show yourself up?; **ein Geschenk/Getränk, das aus dem ~ des Üblichen fällt** a present/drink with a difference; **dieses Buch fällt aus dem ~ unserer normalen Produktion** this book is outside our usual line (of business); **in den ~ von etw passen, sich in den ~ von etw einfügen** to fit (in) or blend in with sth, to go with sth; **den ~ von etw sprengen, über den ~ von etw hinausgehen** to go beyond the scope of sth; **das würde den ~ sprengen** it would be beyond our scope; **einer Feier einen würdigen/der richtigen ~ geben** to provide the appropriate setting for a celebration; **in größerem/kleinerem ~** on a large/small scale; **die Feier fand nur in engem** or **in engstem ~ statt** the celebration was just a small-scale affair.
Rahmen-: ~**antenne** f frame aerial (esp Brit) or antenna; ~**erzählung** f (Liter) framework story; ~**gesetz** nt general outline of a law providing guidelines for specific elaboration; ~**handlung** f (Liter) background story, story which forms the framework; ~**plan** m framework, outline plan; ~**programm** nt (a) framework; (b) siehe ~**plan**; ~**richtlinien** pl guidelines pl; ~**sucher** m (Phot) viewfinder; ~**tarif** m (Ind) general agreement concerning minimum pay scales; ~**vertrag** m (Ind) general agreement concerning conditions of employment.
rahmig adj (dial) creamy.
Rahmkäse m cream cheese.
Rahsegel nt (Naut) square sail.

Rain m -(e)s, -e (liter) margin, marge (poet).
räkeln vr siehe rekeln.
Rakete f -, -n rocket (auch Space); (Mil auch) missile. **fern-gelenkte** or **ferngesteuerte** ~ guided missile.
Raketen- in cpds rocket; (Mil auch) missile; ~**abschuß** m (rocket) launch(ing); ~**(abschuß)basis** f (Mil) missile or rocket base; (Space) launch(ing) site; ~**abwehr** f antimissile defence; ~**abwehrrakete** f antimissile missile; ~**antrieb** m rocket propulsion; **mit** ~**antrieb** rocket-propelled; ~**apparat** m rocket(-line) apparatus; ~**basis** f siehe ~**(abschuß)basis**; **r~bestückt** adj missile-carrying or -equipped; ~**flugzeug** nt rocket-propelled aircraft; ~**geschoß** nt missile; ~**satz** m set of rockets/missiles; ~**start** m (rocket) launch(ing); (Start mittels Raketen) rocket-assisted take-off; ~**stufe** f stage (of a rocket/missile); ~**stützpunkt** m missile base; ~**ver-suchsgelände** nt rocket range; (Space) launch(ing) site; ~**wer-fer** m rocket launcher; ~**wesen** nt rocketry; ~**zeitalter** nt space age.
Rakett nt -s, -s or -e (old Sport) racket, racquet.
Rallye ['rali,'rɛli] f -, -s rally. **eine** ~ **fahren** to drive in a rally; ~ **fahren** to go rallying.
Rallyefahrer m rally-driver.
Ramm-: ~**bock**, ~**bock** m siehe **Ramme**; **r~dösig** adj (inf) giddy, dizzy.
Ramme f -, -n ram(mer); (für Pfähle) pile-driver.
Rammelei f (a) (inf: Gedränge) crush, scrum (inf). (b) (sl) banging away (sl).
rammeln 1 vt siehe **gerammelt**. 2 vir (dial: herumtoben) to charge about or around. 3 vi (Hunt) to mate; (sl) to have it off or away (sl).
rammen vt to ram.
Rammler m -s, - buck.
Rampe f -, -n (a) ramp. (b) (Theat) apron, forestage.
Rampenlicht nt (Theat) footlights pl. **sie möchte im** ~ **stehen** (Theat) she'd like to go on the stage; (fig) she wants to be in the limelight; **im** ~ **der Öffentlichkeit stehen** (fig) to be in the limelight.
ramponieren* vt (inf) to ruin; Möbel to bash about (inf). **er sah ziemlich ramponiert aus** he looked the worse for wear (inf).
Ramsch m -(e)s, no pl (a) (inf) junk, rubbish, trash. **im** ~ **kaufen** (Comm) to buy a job lot. (b) (Skat) (einen) ~ **spielen** to play (a) ramsch.
ramschen 1 vi (a) (inf) to buy cheap junk. (b) (beim Skat) to play (a) ramsch. 2 vt (Comm) to buy up.
Ramsch-: ~**händler** m (pej) junk dealer; ~**laden** m (pej) junk shop; ~**verkauf** m oddments sale; ~**ware** f (pej) trashy goods pl, rubbish.
ran interj (inf) come on, go it (inf). ~ **an den Feind!** let's go get 'em! (inf); ~ **an die Bouletten** (sl) get stuck in (inf); siehe **heran**.
Ranch [rɛntʃ, ra:ntʃ] f -, -(e)s ranch.
Rancher ['rɛntʃr, 'ra:ntʃr] m -s, -(s) rancher.
Rand¹ m -es, -̈er (a) edge; (von Weg, Straße, Schwimmbecken etc auch) side; (von Brunnen, Tasse) top, rim, brim; (von Abgrund) brink. **voll bis zum** ~ full to the brim, brimful; **am** ~**e erwähnen, zur Sprache kommen** by the way, in passing; **interessieren** marginally; **beteiligt sein** marginally, on the fringe; **miterleben** on the sidelines; **etw am** ~**e bemerken** or **vermerken** to mention sth in passing or in parentheses; **am** ~**e des Waldes** at the edge of the forest; **am** ~**e der Stadt** on the outskirts of the town; **am** ~ **der Verzweiflung/des Wahnsinns** on the verge of despair/madness; **am** ~**e des Grabes/Todes** at death's door; **am** ~**e des Untergangs** or **Ruins** on the brink or verge of ruin; **am** ~**e eines Krieges** on the brink of war; **die Schweizer haben den Krieg nur am** ~**e miterlebt** the Swiss were only marginally involved in the war or only experienced the war from the sidelines; **er hat die Russische Revolution noch am** ~**e miterlebt** he was around at the beginning/end of the Russian Revolution; **eine kleine Szene am** ~**e des Krieges** a small incident on the fringe of the war; **am** ~**e der Gesellschaft/der politischen Landschaft** on the fringes of society/the political scene.
(b) (Umrandung) border; (Teller~) edge, side; (Brillen~) rim; (von Hut) brim; (Seiten~, Buch~, Heft~) margin. **wenn er so über die** ~**er seiner Brille schielt** when he peers over the top of his glasses like that; **mit schwarzem** ~ black-edged, with a black border; **etw an den** ~ **schreiben** to write sth in the margin.
(c) (Schmutz~) ring; (um Augen auch) circle; (in der Badewanne auch) tide-mark. **rote** ~**er um die Augen haben** to have red rims around one's eyes.
(d) (fig) **das versteht sich am** ~**e** that goes without saying; **sie waren außer** ~ **und Band** there was no holding them, they were going wild; **allein komme ich damit nicht zu** ~**e** I can't manage (it) by myself; **halt den** ~! (sl) shut your face (sl).
Rand² m -s, -(s) (Währung) rand.
randalieren* vi to rampage (about). ~**de Jugendliche** (young) hooligans; ~**de Studenten** rioting students; **die Jugendlichen zogen** ~**d durch die Straßen** the youths rampaged or went on the rampage or ran wild through the streets; **die Gefangenen fingen an zu** ~ the prisoners started to get violent.
Randalierer m -s, - hooligan, trouble-maker.
Rand-: ~**auslöser** m margin release; ~**bemerkung** f note in the margin, marginal note; (fig) (passing) comment; **etw in einer** ~**bemerkung erwähnen** (fig) to mention sth in passing.
Rande f -, - (Sw) beetroot.
Rand|einstellung f margin setting.
rändeln vt Münze to mill.
-ränd(e)rig adj suf -edged.
rändern vt to edge, to border.
Rand-: ~**erscheinung** f phenomenon of peripheral importance;

(Nebenwirkung) side effect; **das Problem des ... ist nur eine** ~**erscheinung** the problem of ... is only of peripheral importance; ~**figur** f minor figure; ~**gebiet** nt (Geog) edge, fringe; (Pol) border territory; (fig) subsidiary; **r~genäht** adj Schuhe welted; ~**glosse** f marginal note; ~**gruppe** f fringe group.
-randig adj suf -edged.
Rand-: **r~los** adj Brille rimless; Hut brimless; ~**persönlichkeit** f (Sociol) marginal man; ~**staat** m border state; **die** ~**staaten des Mittelmeers** the countries around or bordering on the Mediterranean; **die** ~**staaten der Nordsee** the North Sea countries; ~**stein** m siehe **Bordstein**; ~**steller** m -s, - margin stop; ~**zone** f peripheral zone or area; **in der** ~**zone** on the periphery; **diese Staaten sind vorerst noch** ~**zonen der Weltpolitik** these states are still on the periphery or perimeter of world politics.
Ranft m -(e)s, -̈e (dial) crust, heel (US, Scot, dial).
rang pret of **ringen**.
Rang m -(e)s, -̈e (a) (Mil) rank; (in Firma) position; (gesellschaftliche Stellung auch) position, station (dated). **im** ~**(e) eines Hauptmanns stehen** to have the rank of captain; **im** ~ **höher/tiefer stehen** to have a higher/lower rank/position, to rank higher/lower; **ein Offizier in hohem** ~ a high-ranking officer; **einen hohen** ~ **bekleiden** to hold a high office; (Mil) to have a high rank; **ein Mann von** ~ **und Würden** a man of considerable or high standing, a man of status; **ein Mann ohne** ~ **und Namen** a man without any standing or reputation; **jdm den** ~ **streitig machen** (fig) to challenge sb's position; **jdm den** ~ **ablaufen** (fig) to outstrip sb.
(b) (Qualität) quality, class. **ein Künstler/Wissenschaftler von** ~ an artist/scientist of standing, a top artist/scientist; **von hohem** ~ high-class; **ein Essen ersten** ~**es** a first-class or first-rate meal; **minderen** ~**es** low-class, second-rate; **Qualität minderen** ~**es** low quality.
(c) (Theat) circle. **erster/zweiter** ~ dress/upper circle, first/second circle; **wir sitzen (erster/zweiter)** ~ **Mitte** (inf) we're sitting in the middle of the (dress/upper) circle; **vor leeren/überfüllten** ~**en spielen** to play to an empty/a packed house.
(d) ~**e** pl (Sport) stands pl.
(e) (Gewinnklasse) prize category.
Rang-: ~**abzeichen** nt (Mil) badge of rank, insignia; ~**älteste(r)** m (Mil) senior officer.
Range f -, - urchin.
rangehen vi sep irreg aux sein (inf) to get stuck in (inf). **geh ran!** go on!; **der geht aber ran wie Blücher!** he's a fast worker (inf); siehe **herangehen**.
Rangelei f (inf) siehe **Gerangel**.
rangeln (inf) 1 vi to scrap; (um Sonderangebote auch) to tussle (um for); (um Posten) to wrangle (um for). 2 vr to sprawl about.
Rang-: ~**folge** f order of rank (esp Mil) or standing; **nach der** ~**folge, der** ~**folge nach** in order of rank (esp Mil) or standing; ~**höchste(r)** mf senior person/member etc; (Mil) highest-ranking officer.
Rangierbahnhof [rã'ʒiːn-] m marshalling yard.
rangieren* [rã'ʒiːrən] 1 vt (a) (Rail) to shunt, to switch (US). (b) (inf: abschieben) to shove (inf), to shunt (inf).
2 vi (Rang einnehmen) to rank. **er rangiert gleich hinter** or **unter dem Abteilungsleiter** he comes directly beneath the head of department; **seine Familie rangiert nur am Rande in seinem Leben** his family take second place; **die Mathilde rangiert bei mir unter „ferner liefen"** (inf) as far as I'm concerned Mathilde is an "also-ran"; **der Intelligenz nach rangiert er ganz vorne** he's quite high up the list as far as intelligence goes; **an erster/letzter Stelle** ~ to come first/last, to take first/last place.
Rangierer [rã'ʒiːrn] m -s, - (Rail) shunter.
Rangier- [rã'ʒiːn-]: ~**gleis** nt siding, sidetrack (US); ~**lok(omotive)**, ~**maschine** f shunter, switcher (US).
Rang-: ~**klasse** f rank category; ~**liste** f (a) (Mil) active list; (b) (Sport) (results) table; ~**loge** f (Theat) box (in the circle); **r~mäßig** adj according to rank; **r~mäßig stehe ich unter ihm** I'm lower than him in rank; ~**ordnung** f hierarchy; (Mil) (order of) ranks; ~**platz** m (Theat) seat in the circle; ~**stufe** f rank; **auf der gleichen** ~**stufe stehen** to be of or to have the same rank; ~**unterschied** m social distinction; (Mil) difference of rank; **der Chef macht keine** ~**unterschiede** the boss doesn't make any distinctions on the basis of seniority; **wir machen hier keine** ~**unterschiede** we're not status-conscious here.
ranhalten vr sep irreg (inf) (a) (sich beeilen, sich umtun) to get a move on (inf). (b) (schnell zugreifen) to dig in (inf), to get stuck in (inf).
ranhauen vi sep irreg (sl) to get stuck in (inf).
rank adj (liter) ~ **und schlank** slender and supple; Mädchen auch slim and sylphlike.
Ranke f -, -n tendril; (von Brom-, Himbeeren) branch; (von Erd-beeren) stalk; (von Weinrebe) shoot.
Ränke pl (liter) intrigue, cabal (liter). ~ **schmieden** to hatch a plot, to intrigue, to cabal (liter).
ranken 1 vr sich um etw ~ to entwine itself around sth; (fig: Geschichten etc) to have grown up around sth. 2 vi aux haben or sein an etw (dat) ~ to entwine itself around sth.
Ranken-: ~**gewächs** nt climbing plant, climber; (Efeu etc) creeper; ~**werk** nt (Art) arabesques pl; (fig) embellishment.
Ränke-: ~**schmied** m (liter) intriguer; ~**spiel** nt (liter) intrigue, cabal (liter); **r~süchtig**, **r~voll** adj (liter) scheming, caballing (liter).
rankig adj (Bot) climbing. **die Pflanzen wachsen** ~ **am Gemäuer hoch** the plants twine their way up the walls.
ranklotzen vi sep (sl) to get stuck in (inf).
rankommen vi sep irreg aux sein (inf) **an etw** (acc) ~ to get at sth; **an die Helga ist nicht ranzukommen** you won't get anywhere with Helga (inf); **an unseren Chef ist schwer ran-**

zukommen our boss isn't very easy to get at (*inf*); **niemanden an sich ~ lassen** to be standoffish (*inf*), to keep oneself to one-self; *siehe* **herankommen.**

ranlassen *vt sep irreg* (*inf*) **jdn ~** to let sb have a go; **sie läßt jeden ran** (*sl*) she's anybody's (*inf*), she's an easy lay (*sl*); **sie läßt keinen mehr (an sich** *acc*) **ran** (*sl*) she won't let anybody near her.

ranmachen *vr sep* (*inf*) *siehe* **heranmachen.**

rann *pret of* **rinnen.**

rannte *pret of* **rennen.**

ranschmeißen *vr sep irreg* (*inf*) **sich an jdn ~** to fling oneself at sb (*inf*).

Ranschmeißer *m* -s, - (*sl*) fast worker (*inf*), goer (*sl*).

Ränzel *nt or m* -s, - (*old, dial*) knapsack, pack. **sein** *or* **den ~ schnüren** (*liter*) to pack up one's belongings.

Ranzen *m* -s, - (**a**) (*Schul~*) satchel. (**b**) (*inf: Bauch*) belly (*inf*), gut (*sl*). **sich** (*dat*) **den ~ vollschlagen** to stuff oneself (*inf*) *or* one's face (*sl*). (**c**) (*inf: Buckel*) hunchback, hump(back). **jdm** (*ordentlich*) **den ~ vollhauen** to give sb a (good) thrashing.

ranzig *adj* rancid.

rapid(e) *adj* rapid.

Rapier *nt* -s, -e rapier.

Rappe *m* -n, -n black horse; *siehe* **Schuster.**

Rappel *m* -s, - (*inf*) (**a**) (*Fimmel*) craze; (*Klaps*) crazy mood. **seinen ~ kriegen** to get one of one's crazes/crazy moods; **du hast wohl einen ~!** you must be crazy!
(**b**) (*Wutanfall*) **einen ~ haben/kriegen** to be in a foul *or* filthy mood *or* temper/to throw a fit; **dabei kann man ja einen ~ kriegen** it's enough to drive you mad *or* up the wall (*inf*).

rapp(e)lig *adj* (*inf*) (**a**) (*verrückt*) crazy, cracked (*inf*). **bei dem Lärm kann man ja ~ werden** the noise is enough to drive you crazy *or* round the twist (*inf*). (**b**) (*nervös, unruhig*) jumpy (*inf*).

Rappel-: **~kopf** *m* (*inf*) (*jähzornig*) hothead (*inf*); (*Dickkopf*) awkward devil (*inf*); **r~köpfig** *adj* (*inf*) (*jähzornig*) hotheaded; (*eigensinnig*) awkward.

rappeln *vi* (**a**) (*lärmen*) to rattle; (*Aus: verrückt sein*) to be crazy. **es rappelt an der Tür** somebody is shaking *or* rattling the door; **bei dir rappelt's wohl!** (*inf*) are you crazy?; **bei dem rappelt's manchmal** he just flips sometimes (*sl*).

Rappen *m* -s, - (*Sw*) centime.

Rapport *m* -(e)s, -e (**a**) (*old*) report. **sich zum ~ melden** to report; **er ist beim Kommandeur zum ~** he's making a report to the commander. (**b**) (*Psych*) rapport.

Raps *m* -es, -e (*Bot*) rape.

Raps|öl *nt* rape(seed) oil.

Raptus *m* -, -se (*Med*) fit, raptus (*spec*).

Rapunzel *f* -, -n (**a**) (*Bot*) corn salad, lamb's lettuce. (**b**) (*Märchen*) Rapunzel.

Rapunzelsalat *m* corn salad.

rar *adj* rare. **sich ~ machen** (*inf*) to keep *or* stay away; (*sich zurückziehen*) to make oneself scarce.

Rarität *f* rarity.

Raritäten-: **~händler** *m* dealer in rare objects; **~kabinett** *nt* collection of rare objects *or* curios.

rasant *adj* (**a**) *Schuß-, Flugbahn* level, flat.
(**b**) (*inf*) *Tempo, Spurt* terrific, lightning *attr* (*inf*); *Auto, Fahrer* fast; *Aufstieg, Karriere* meteoric; *Entwicklung, Zerfall* rapid. **das ist vielleicht ein ~es Auto** this car really can shift (*inf*); **sie fuhr ~ die Straße hinunter** she tore *or* raced down the street; **sie haben das Presto in ~em Tempo gespielt** they really raced *or* rattled (*inf*) through the presto.
(**c**) (*inf: imponierend*) *Frau* vivacious; *Leistung* terrific.

Rasanz *f*, *no pl* (**a**) (*Mil*) levelness, flatness.
(**b**) (*inf: Geschwindigkeit*) speed. **er jagte mit unheimlicher ~ davon** he tore off at a terrific speed *or* lick (*inf*); **er nahm die Kurve mit gekonnter ~** he took the bend fast and well *or* with daredevil skill; **etw mit ~ tun** to do sth in great style.

rasch 1 *adj* (**a**) (*schnell*) quick, rapid, swift; *Tempo* great.
(**b**) (*übereilt*) rash, (over-)hasty.
2 *adv* (**a**) quickly, rapidly, swiftly. **nicht so ~!** not so fast *or* quick; **~ machen** to hurry (up), to get a move on (*inf*); **ich habe so ~ wie möglich gemacht** I was as quick *or* fast as I could be; **ein bißchen ~, bitte!** make it quick, be quick.
(**b**) **mit etw ~ bei der Hand sein** to be rash *or* (over-)hasty about sth, to be too quick off the mark with sth (*inf*).

rascheln *vi* to rustle. **es raschelt (im Stroh/Laub)** there's something rustling (in the straw/leaves); **mit etw ~** to rustle sth.

Raschheit *f* (**a**) quickness, rapidity, swiftness. (**b**) (*Übereiltheit*) rashness, (over-)hastiness.

rasen *vi* (**a**) (*wüten, toben*) to rave; (*Sturm*) to rage. **er raste vor Schmerz/Wut** he was going wild with pain/he was mad with rage; **er raste vor Eifersucht** he was half-crazed with jealousy; **die Zuschauer rasten vor Begeisterung** the spectators were/went wild with excitement.
(**b**) *aux sein* (*sich schnell bewegen*) to race, to tear; (*Puls*) to race. **der Rennwagen raste in die Menge/gegen einen Baum** the racing car crashed *or* smashed into the crowd/a tree; **das Auto raste in den Fluß** the car crashed into the river; **wenn wir den Zug noch erreichen wollen, müssen wir ~** (*inf*) if we're going to catch that train we'll have to shift (*inf*); **ras doch nicht so!** (*inf*) don't go so fast!; **die Zeit rast** time flies.
(**c**) *aux sein* (*inf: herumhetzen*) to race *or* run around.

Rasen *m* -s, - lawn, grass *no indef art, no pl*; (*von Sportplatz*) turf, grass; (*Sportplatz*) field, pitch; (*Tennis*) court. **einen ~ anlegen** to lay a lawn; „**bitte den ~ nicht betreten**" "please keep off the grass"; **jetzt deckt ihn der kühle** *or* **grüne ~ zu** (*liter*), **ihn deckt jetzt der grüne ~** (*liter*) now he lies beneath the green sward (*liter*); **unter dem grünen ~ ruhen** (*liter*) to be at rest in God's green acre (*liter*).

Rasen-: **~bank** *f* grassy bank; **r~bedeckt, r~bewachsen** *adj*

---

grassy, grass-covered, covered with grass.

rasend 1 *adj* (**a**) (*enorm*) terrific; *Eile auch* tearing; *Hunger, Durst auch* raging; *Beifall auch* wild, rapturous; *Eifersucht* burning; *Schmerz auch* excruciating. **~e Kopfschmerzen** a splitting headache.
(**b**) (*wütend*) furious, livid, raging. **jdn ~ machen** to make sb furious *or* livid *or* wild (*inf*); **er macht mich noch ~** he'll drive me crazy; **ich könnte ~ werden** I could scream; **es ist zum R~werden** it's absolutely infuriating *or* maddening.
2 *adv* (**a**) terrifically, enormously; **weh tun, sich beeilen, applaudieren** like mad (*inf*) *or* crazy (*inf*); **lieben, verliebt, eifersüchtig sein** madly (*inf*). **~ viel Geld** heaps *or* pots of money (*inf*); **~ gern!** I'd simply love to!

Rasende(r) *mf decl as adj* madman/madwoman, maniac.

Rasen-: **~fläche** *f* lawn; **~mäher** *m*, **~mähmaschine** *f* lawn-mower; **~platz** *m* (*Ftbl etc*) field, pitch; (*Tennis*) grass court; **~spiel** *nt* (*Sport*) game played on grass, outdoor game; **~sport** *m* sport played on grass, outdoor sport; **~sprenger** *m* (*lawn*) sprinkler; **~stück** *nt* patch of grass; **~walze** *f* (*lawn*) roller.

Raser *m* -s, - (*inf*) speed maniac (*inf*) *or* merchant (*inf*).

Raserei *f* (**a**) (*Wut*) fury, rage, frenzy. (**b**) (*inf: schnelles Fahren, Gehen*) mad rush.

Rasier- *in cpds* shaving; **~apparat** *m* razor; (*elektrisch auch*) shaver; **~creme** *f* shaving cream.

rasieren* 1 *vt* (**a**) to shave. **sich ~ lassen** to have a shave; **sie rasiert sich** (*dat*) **die Beine** she shaves her legs. (**b**) (*inf: streifen*) to scrape. 2 *vr* to (have a) shave. **sich naß/trocken ~** to have a wet shave/to use an electric shaver.

Rasier-: **~klinge** *f* razor blade; **~messer** *nt* (open) razor, cut-throat razor; **~napf** *m siehe* **~schale**; **~pinsel** *m* shaving brush; **~schale** *f* shaving mug; **~seife** *f* shaving soap; **~wasser** *nt* aftershave/pre-shave (lotion); **~zeug** *nt* shaving things *pl or* tackle (*inf*) *or* equipment.

Räson [rɛˈzõ:] *f* -, *no pl* **er will keine ~ annehmen** he refuses to *or* won't listen to reason; **jdn zur ~ bringen** to make sb listen to reason, to make sb see sense.

räsonieren* *vi* (*old*) to grumble.

Raspel *f* -, -n (**a**) (*Holzfeile*) rasp. (**b**) (*Cook*) grater.

raspeln *vt* to grate; *Holz* to rasp; *siehe* **Süßholz.**

raß, räß *adj* (*S Ger, Sw*) *Most, Speise* sharp; *Witz* earthy; *Pferd* fiery; *Kellnerin* buxom; (*Sw*) *Mensch* wild.

Rasse *f* -, -n (*Menschen~*) race; (*Tier~*) breed; (*fig*) spirit, hot-bloodedness. **das Mädchen hat ~** she's a hot-blooded girl; **das Pferd/der Hund hat ~** that horse/dog has spirit.

Rassehund *m* pedigree *or* thoroughbred dog.

Rassel *f* -, -n rattle.

Rasselbande *f* (*dated inf*) mischievous bunch (*inf*).

rasseln *vi* (**a**) to rattle. **mit** *or* **an etw** (*dat*) **~** to rattle sth. (**b**) *aux sein* (*inf*) **durch eine Prüfung ~** to flunk an exam (*inf*).

Rassen- *in cpds* racial; **~bewußtsein** *nt* racial consciousness; **~diskriminierung** *f* racial discrimination; **~doktrin** *f* racial doctrine; **~forschung** *f* ethnogeny (*form*), racial research; **~frage** *f* race *or* racial problem; (*Farbige betreffend*) colour problem; **~haß** *m* race *or* racial hatred; **~hygiene** *f* (*NS*) eugenics *sing*; **r~hygienisch** *adj* (*NS*) eugenical; **~kampf** *m* racial struggle; **~krawall** *m* race *or* racial riot; **~kreuzung** *f* (*von Tieren*) cross-breeding; (*Tier*) crossbreed, crossbred; **~kunde** *f* ethnogeny (*form*), study of race; **~merkmal** *nt* racial characteristic; **~mischung** *f* mixture of races; (*bei Tieren*) cross-breeding; (*Tier*) crossbreed, crossbred; **~problem** *nt* *siehe* **~frage**; **~schande** *f* Nazi term for sexual relations with a non-Aryan; **~schranke** *f* racial barrier, barrier of race; (*Farbige betreffend*) colour bar; **~theorie** *f* racial theory, theory of race; **~trennung** *f* racial segregation; **~vermischung** *f siehe* **~mischung.**

Rasse-: **~pferd** *nt* thoroughbred (horse); **r~rein** *adj siehe* **reinrassig**; **~reinheit** *f* racial purity; **~vieh** *nt* thoroughbred *or* pure-bred animal(s).

rassig *adj* *Pferd, Auto* sleek; *Frau* vivacious and hot-blooded; *Erscheinung, Gesichtszüge* sharp, striking; *Wein* spirited, lively; *Zigeuner, Spanier* fiery, hot-blooded. **ihre Kleidung hat eine sehr ~e Note** her clothes have great flair.

rassisch *adj* racial. **jdn ~ verfolgen** to persecute sb because of his/her race.

Rassismus *m* racialism, racism.

rassistisch *adj* racialist, racist.

Rast *f* -, *no pl* rest, repose (*liter*). **~ machen** to stop (to eat); (*Mil*) to make a halt; **die schöne Aussicht lädt zur ~** (*liter*) the beautiful view invites repose (*liter*); **er gönnt sich keine ~** he won't rest, he allows himself no respite; **ohne ~ und Ruh** (*liter*) without pause for rest, without respite.

Raste *f* -, -n notch.

rasten *vi* to rest; (*Mil*) to make a halt. **er hat nicht gerastet und geruht, bis ...** (*liter*) he did not rest until ...; **wer rastet, der rostet** (*Prov*) you have to keep active; you have to keep in practice.

Raster *m* -s, - (*Archit*) grid; (*Typ*) halftone *or* raster screen; (*Phot: Gitter*) screen; (*TV*) raster; (*fig*) framework.

Raster-: **~ätzung** *f* halftone (engraving); **~bild** *nt* (*Typ*) half-tone picture; (*TV*) frame; **~druck** *m* (*Typ*) halftone printing.

Rasterpunkt *m* (*Typ*) (halftone) dot; (*TV*) picture element; (*Typ*) halftone screening.

Rasterung *f* (*TV*) scanning.

Rast-: **~haus** *nt* (*travellers'*) inn; (*an Autobahn: auch* **~hof**) service area (including motel); **r~los** *adj* (*unruhig*) restless; (*unermüdlich*) tireless, untiring; **r~los tätig sein** to work tirelessly *or* ceaselessly; **~losigkeit** *f* restlessness; **~platz** *m* resting place, place to rest; (*an Autostraßen*) picnic area;

~stätte f service area, services pl; **~tag** m rest day; **das Gasthaus hat ~tag** the pub is closed all day.

Rasur f (a) (Bart~) shave. (b) (radierte Stelle) erasure.

Rat m -(e)s (a) pl **Ratschläge** (Empfehlung) advice no pl, counsel no pl (liter). **ein ~** a piece of advice; **jdm einen ~ geben** to give sb a piece of advice; **jdm den ~ geben, etw zu tun** to advise sb to do sth; **jdn um ~ fragen, sich** (dat) **bei jdm ~ holen** to ask sb's advice or sb for advice; **gegen jds ~ handeln** to go against or act against or ignore sb's advice; **auf jds ~** (acc) **(hin)** on or following sb's advice; **jdm mit ~ und Tat beistehen** or **zur Seite stehen** to support sb or back sb up in (both) word and deed; **da ist guter ~ teuer** it's hard to know what to do.

(b) no pl (Beratung) **mit jdm zu ~e gehen** (liter) to seek sb's advice, to consult sb; **ich muß erst mit mir zu ~e gehen** I'll have to consider it first; **jdn/etw zu ~e ziehen** to consult sb/sth; **einen Anwalt/Arzt zu ~e ziehen** to take legal/medical advice, to consult a lawyer/doctor; **einen Kollegen zu ~e ziehen** to get a second opinion, to consult a colleague; **mit jdm ~ halten** (liter) or **pflegen** (liter) to take counsel with sb (liter).

(c) no pl (Abhilfe) **~ (für etw) wissen** to know what to do (about sth); **~ schaffen** (liter) to show what is to be done; **sie wußte sich** (dat) **keinen ~ mehr** she was at her wits' end; **sich** (dat) **keinen ~ mehr wissen** not to know what to do about sth.

(d) pl **¨e** (Körperschaft) council; (Sowjet) soviet. **der ~ der Gemeinde/Stadt** = the district council; **der Große ~** (Sw) the cantonal parliament; **der Hohe ~** (Bibl) the Sanhedrin; **den ~ einberufen** to call a council meeting; **im ~ sitzen** to be on the council.

(e) pl **¨e** (Person) senior official; siehe **wissenschaftlich, geheim.**

Rate f -, -n instalment (Brit), installment (US). **auf ~n kaufen** to buy in instalments or on hire purchase (Brit) or on the installment plan (US); **in ~n zahlen** to pay in instalments.

raten pret **riet**, ptp **geraten** vti (a) (Ratschläge geben) to advise. **jdm gut/richtig/schlecht ~** to give sb good/correct/bad advice; **jdm zu etw ~** to recommend sth to sb, to advise sb to do/take/buy etc sth; **jdm ~, etw nicht zu tun** to advise sb not to do sth, to advise sb against doing sth; **zu dieser langen Reise kann ich dir nicht ~** I must advise you against making this long journey; **das würde ich dir nicht ~** I wouldn't advise or recommend it; **das möchte ich dir nicht ~ or geraten haben** I wouldn't advise or recommend it, I wouldn't if I were you; **das möchte ich dir auch geraten haben!** you better had (inf), see that you do/are (inf); **was or wozu ~ Sie mir?** what do you advise or recommend?; **er läßt sich nicht ~** he won't listen to or take advice; **laß dir ~!** take some advice, be advised; **ich weiß mir nicht zu ~** (old) I'm at a loss; **wem nicht zu ~ ist, dem ist auch nicht zu helfen** (prov) a bit of advice never hurt anybody; **ich halte es für geraten** I think it would be advisable; **ich hielte es für geraten, wenn du dich sofort verabschiedest** I think you would be well-advised or it would be advisable for you to leave at once.

(b) (erraten, herausfinden) to guess; Kreuzworträtsel etc to solve, to do. **hin und her ~** to make all sorts of guesses; **rate mal!** (have a) guess; **dreimal darfst du ~** I'll give you three guesses (auch iro); **das rätst du nie!** you'll never guess!; **(gut) geraten!** good guess!; **falsch geraten!** wrong!; **das kann ich nur ~** I can only make a guess, I can only guess at it; **das hab' ich nur so geraten** I was only guessing, it was only a guess.

Raten-: **~kauf** m (Kaufart) hire purchase (Brit), HP (Brit inf), the installment plan (US); **durch viele ~käufe** by buying a lot of items on hire purchase etc; **~sparen** vi sep infin only siehe **prämiensparen; r~weise** adv in instalments; **~zahlung** f (Zahlung einer Rate) payment of an instalment; (Zahlung in Raten) payment by instalments.

Rater m -s, - (inf) guesser; (von Rätsel) solver of riddles.

Räteregierung f soviet government.

Raterei f (a) (das Schätzen) guessing. **laß mal die ~** must we have these guessing games? (b) (Rätselraten) puzzle-solving.

Räterepublik f soviet republic (esp in Bavaria 1919).

Ratespiel nt guessing game; (TV) quiz; (Beruferaten etc auch) panel game.

Rat-: **~geber** m adviser, counsellor (form); **~haus** nt town hall; (einer Großstadt) city hall; **~haussaal** m council chamber; **Konzert im ~haussaal** concert in the town hall.

Ratifikation f ratification.

ratifizieren* vt to ratify.

Ratifizierung f ratification.

Rätin f siehe **Rat (e).**

Ratio ['ra:tsio] f -, no pl reason. **es ist ein Gebot der ~, zu ...** reason demands that ..., it's only rational to ...

Ration [ra'tsio:n] f ration. **jeder bekommt eine bestimmte ~** everyone gets fixed rations; **eiserne ~** iron rations pl.

rational [ratsio'na:l] adj rational.

rationalisieren* [ratsionali'zi:rən] vti to rationalize.

Rationalisierung [ratsionali'zi:ruŋ] f rationalization.

Rationalisierungs-: **~fachmann** m efficiency expert, time and motion (study) expert or man; **~maßnahme** f rationalization or efficiency measure.

Rationalismus [ratsiona'lɪsmʊs] m rationalism.

Rationalist [ratsiona'lɪst] m rationalist.

rationalistisch [ratsiona'lɪstɪʃ] adj rationalist(ic).

Rationalität [ratsionali'tɛ:t] f rationality; (Leistungsfähigkeit) efficiency.

rationell [ratsio'nɛl] adj efficient.

rationenweise [ratsio:nən-] adv in rations.

rationieren* [ratsio'ni:rən] vt to ration.

Rationierung [ratsio'ni:ruŋ] f rationing.

Rationierungssystem nt rationing system.

rationsweise [ratsi'o:nz-] adv siehe **rationenweise.**

ratlos adj helpless. **ich bin völlig ~(, was ich tun soll)** I'm at a complete loss (as to what to do), I just don't know what to do; **~e Eltern** parents who are at a loss to know what to do with their children; **sie machte ein ~es Gesicht** she looked helpless or at a loss; **einer Sache** (dat) **~ gegenüberstehen** to be at a loss when faced with sth; **sie sahen sich ~ an** they looked at each other helplessly.

Ratlosigkeit f helplessness. **in meiner ~ ...** not knowing what to do ..., being at a loss ...

Rätoromane m Rhaetian.

rätoromanisch adj Rhaetian; Sprache Rhaeto-Romanic.

ratsam adj advisable. **ich halte es für ~, das zu tun** I think it (would be) advisable to do that.

Ratsbeschluß m decision of the local council.

ratsch interj rip.

Ratsche, Rätsche f -, -n (S Ger, Aus) rattle.

ratschen, rätschen vi (S Ger, Sw) (a) (mit der Ratsche) to rattle. (b) (inf: schwatzen) to blather (inf).

Ratschlag m piece or bit of advice. **ein guter ~** a good piece of advice, good advice; **Ratschläge** advice; **drei Ratschläge** three pieces of advice; **deine klugen Ratschläge kannst du dir sparen** keep your advice for yourself; **jdm einen ~ geben or erteilen** to give sb a piece of advice or some advice.

ratschlagen vi insep to deliberate, to consult (together). **sie ratschlagten, wie man es am besten machen sollte** they deliberated as to or on how best to do it.

Ratschluß m (liter) decision. Gottes **~** the will of God; **Gottes unerforschlichem ~ hat es gefallen ...** it has pleased the Lord in his mysterious wisdom ...

Ratsdiener m (old) (town hall) porter.

Rätsel nt -s, - (a) riddle; (Kreuzwort~) crossword (puzzle); (Silben~, Bilder~ etc) puzzle. **jdm ein ~ aufgeben** to give or ask sb a riddle; **das plötzliche Verschwinden des Zeugen gab der Polizei ~ auf** the sudden disappearance of the witness baffled the police.

(b) (fig: Geheimnis) riddle, mystery, enigma (um of). **die Polizei konnte das ~ lösen** the police have solved the riddle or mystery; **vor einem ~ stehen** to be faced with a riddle or mystery, to be baffled; **es ist mir ein ~, wie ...** it's a mystery to me how ..., it baffles or beats (inf) me how ...; **er ist mir ein ~** he's a mystery or an enigma to me; **in ~n sprechen** to talk in riddles; **das ist des ~s Lösung!** that's the answer.

Rätsel-: **~ecke** f puzzle corner; **~frage** f (Quizfrage) question; **r~haft** adj mysterious; Gesichtsausdruck, Lächeln auch enigmatic; **auf r~hafte Weise** mysteriously; **es ist mir r~haft** it's a mystery to me, it baffles me; **~haftigkeit** f mysteriousness; **~heft** nt puzzle book; **~löser** m -s, - puzzle-solver.

rätseln vi to puzzle (over sth), to rack one's brains.

Rätsel-: **~raten** nt guessing game; **~raten ist nicht meine starke Seite** guessing isn't/guessing games aren't my forte; **r~voll** adj (geh) mysterious; **~zeitung** f siehe **~heft.**

Rats-: **~herr** m councillor (esp Brit), councilman (US); **~keller** m rathskeller (US) (cellar bar/restaurant under the town hall); **~schreiber** m (old) clerk to the council; **~sitzung** f council meeting; **~stube** f bar/restaurant near the town hall.

ratsuchend adj seeking advice. **sich ~ an jdn wenden** to turn to sb for advice; **R~e** people/those wanting or seeking advice.

Ratsversammlung f (a) siehe **Ratssitzung.** (b) (Rat) council.

Ratte f -, -n rat. **eine widerliche ~** (sl) a dirty rat (sl); **die ~n verlassen das sinkende Schiff** (prov) the rats are leaving the sinking ship; siehe **schlafen.**

Ratten-: **~bekämpfung** f rat control; **~fänger** m rat-catcher; (Hund) ratter; (fig) rabble-rouser; **der ~fänger von Hameln** the Pied Piper of Hamelin; **~gift** nt rat poison; **~schwanz** m (a) (lit) rat's tail; (b) usu pl (inf: Zopf) bunch; (c) (fig inf: Serie, Folge) string.

rattern vi to rattle, to clatter; (Maschinengewehr) to chatter.

Ratz m -es, -e (dial) rat. **wie ein ~ schlafen** (inf) to sleep like a log (inf).

ratzekahl adv (inf) completely, totally. **alles ~ aufessen** (Vorräte) to eat the cupboard bare (inf); (Portion) to polish off the lot (inf).

ratzen vi (dial inf) to kip (inf). **ich hab' vielleicht geratzt** I had a really good kip (inf).

Raub m -(e)s, no pl (a) (das Rauben) robbery. **auf ~ ausgehen** (Tiere) to go out hunting or on the prowl; (Räuber) to go out pillaging.

(b) (Entführung) abduction. **der ~ der Sabinerinnen** the rape of the Sabine women.

(c) (Beute) booty, loot, spoils pl. **ein ~ der Flammen werden** (liter) to fall victim to the flames.

Raub-: **~bau** m, no pl overexploitation (of natural resources); (am Wald) overfelling; (an Ackern) overcropping; (an Weideland) overgrazing; **~bau an etw** (dat) **treiben** to overexploit etc sth; **am Fischbestand eines Flusses ~bau treiben** to overfish a river; **mit seiner Gesundheit ~bau treiben** to ruin one's health; **~druck** m pirate(d) edition; (das Drucken) pirating.

rauben 1 vt (a) (wegnehmen) to steal. **jdm etw ~** to rob sb of sth.

(b) (entführen) to abduct, to carry off.

(c) (fig) **jdm etw ~** to rob sb of sth; **das hat uns viel Zeit geraubt** it cost us a lot of time; **jdm einen Kuß ~** to steal a kiss from sb; **jdm die Unschuld ~** (obs, iro) to take sb's virginity; **du raubst mir noch die letzten Nerven!** you'll drive me mad or crazy (inf).

2 vi to rob, to plunder, to pillage.

Räuber m -s, - robber, brigand (old); (bei Banküberfall etc auch) raider; (Wegelagerer) highwayman. **Ali Baba und die vierzig ~** Ali Baba and the forty thieves; **unter die ~ fallen** or

geraten to fall among thieves; **der Fuchs ist ein** ~ the fox is a beast of prey *or* a predator; ~ **und Gendarm** cops and robbers.
Räuberbande *f* robber band, band of robbers; (*pej*) bunch of thieves.
Räuberei *f* (*inf*) robbery.
Räuber-: ~**geschichte** *f* (a) story about robbers; (b) (*fig*) cock-and-bull story (*inf*); ~**gesindel** *nt* (*pej*) thieving riffraff; ~**hauptmann** *m* robber-chief; ~**höhle** *f* (a) (*lit*) robbers' cave; (b) (*fig*) (*inf*) (*Spelunke*) low dive (*inf*); (*Durcheinander*) pigsty.
räuberisch *adj* rapacious, predatory. ~**er Diebstahl** (*Jur*) theft *in which force or the threat of violence is used to remain in possession of the stolen goods;* ~**e Erpressung** (*Jur*) armed robbery, *robbery using the threat of violence*; **in** ~**er Absicht** with intent to rob.
räubern *vi* (*inf*) to thieve. **in der Speisekammer** ~ to raid the larder.
Räuber-: ~**pistole** *f siehe* ~**geschichte**; ~**roman** *m* novel *about robbers who are on the side of justice*; ~**zivil** *nt* (*hum inf*) scruffy old clothes *pl* (*inf*); **komm einfach in** ~**zivil!** come just as you are, don't bother to dress up.
Raub-: ~**fisch** *m* predatory fish, predator; ~**gier** *f* (*liter*) rapacity; **r**~**gierig** *adj* (*liter*) rapacious; ~**katze** *f* (predatory) big cat; ~**krieg** *m* war of conquest; **der** ~**krieg gegen unser Land** the rape of our country; ~**mord** *m* robbery with murder; ~**mörder** *m* robber and murderer; ~**ritter** *m* robber baron.
Raubtier *nt* predator, beast of prey.
Raubtier-: ~**haus** *nt* lion house; ~**käfig** *m* lion's/tiger's *etc* cage.
Raub-: ~**überfall** *m* robbery; (*auf Bank etc auch*) raid; **einen** ~**überfall auf jdn begehen** to hold sb up; „~**überfall auf Taxifahrer**" "taxi-driver attacked and robbed"; ~**vogel** *m* bird of prey, predator; ~**wild** *nt* (*Hunt*) predatory game; ~**zeug** *nt* (*Hunt*) vermin *pl*; ~**zug** *m* series *sing* of robberies; (*pej*: *Angriffskrieg*) rape (*nach, gegen* of); (*von Tieren*) hunting excursion; **auf** ~**zug gehen** (*Einbrecher*) to commit a series of robberies; (*Tier*) to go hunting *or* on the prowl.
Rauch *m* -(e)s, *no pl* smoke; (*giftig auch*) fumes *pl*. **in** ~ **und Flammen aufgehen** to go up in smoke *or* flames; **in** ~ **aufgehen** (*lit, fig*), **sich in** ~ **auflösen** (*fig*) to go up in smoke; **Würste in den** ~ **hängen** to hang sausages up to smoke; **kein** ~ **ohne Feuer** (*Prov*) there's no smoke without fire (*prov*).
Rauch-: ~**abzug** *m* smoke outlet; **r**~**arm** *adj* smokeless; **r**~**bar** *adj* smok(e)able; **hast du was** ~**bares?** have you got anything to smoke?; ~**bildung** *f siehe* ~**entwicklung**; ~**bombe** *f* smoke bomb.
rauchen 1 *vi* (*Rauch abgeben*) to smoke, to give off smoke. **sie sah, daß es in unserer Küche rauchte** she saw smoke in/coming from our kitchen; **sonst raucht's** (*inf*) or there'll be trouble, or else (*inf*); **mir raucht der Kopf** my head's spinning.
2 *vti* to smoke. **möchten Sie** ~? do you want to smoke?; (*Zigarette anbietend*) would you like a smoke *or* a cigarette?; **nach dem Essen rauche ich gern** I like a *or* to smoke after a meal; **eine** ~ to have a smoke; **hast du was zu** ~? have you got a smoke?; „**R**~ **verboten**" "no smoking"; **sich** (*dat*) **das R**~ **an-/abgewöhnen** to take up/give up smoking; **viel** *or* **stark** ~ to be a heavy smoker, to smoke a lot; ~ **Sie?** do you smoke?
Rauch|entwicklung *f* production *or* formation of smoke. **mit großer/geringer** ~ with high/low smoke levels.
Raucher *m* -s, - (a) smoker. (b) (*Rail*: ~*abteil*) smoker, smoking compartment.
Raucher|aal *m* smoked eel.
Raucher|abteil *nt* smoking compartment, smoker.
Räucher-: ~**faß** *nt* (*Eccl*) censer; ~**gefäß** *nt* incense burner; ~**hering** *m* kipper, smoked herring.
Raucherhusten *m* smoker's cough.
räucherig *adj* (*inf*) smoky.
Raucherin *f* smoker.
Räucher-: ~**kammer** *f* smoking chamber, smokehouse; ~**kerze** *f* scented candle.
räuchern 1 *vt* to smoke. **2** *vi* (*inf:* mit Weihrauch) to burn incense. **hier räuchert's** there's a burning smell in here.
Räucher-: ~**schinken** *m* smoked ham; ~**speck** *m* = smoked bacon; ~**stäbchen** *nt* joss stick; ~**waren** *pl* smoked foods *pl*.
Rauch-: ~**fahne** *f* smoke trail, trail of smoke; ~**fang** *m* (~*abzug*) chimney hood; (b) (*Aus*) chimney; ~**fangkehrer** *m* (*Aus*) (chimney) sweep; **r**~**farben**, **r**~**farbig** *adj* smoke-coloured; ~**faß** *nt* (*Eccl*) censer; ~**fleisch** *nt* smoked meat; **r**~**frei** *adj* smokeless; ~**garnitur** *f* smoker's set; ~**gase** *pl* fumes *pl*; **r**~**geschwängert** *adj* smoke-filled, heavy with smoke; **r**~**geschwärzt** *adj* blackened by smoke, smoke-blackened; ~**glas** *nt* smoked glass; ~**glocke** *f* pall of smoke.
rauchig *adj* smoky.
Rauch-: ~**kammer** *f* (*Rail*) smokebox; **r**~**los** *adj* smokeless; ~**maske** *f* smoke mask; ~**opfer** *nt* burnt offering; ~**pilz** *m* mushroom cloud; ~**quarz** *m* smoky quartz, cairngorm; ~**salon** *m* smoking *or* smoke room; ~**säule** *f* column *or* pillar of smoke; ~**schleier** *m* veil of smoke; ~**schwaden** *pl* drifts of smoke *pl*; ~**schwalbe** *f* swallow; ~**service** *nt* smoker's set; ~**signal** *nt* smoke signal; ~**tabak** *m* (*form*) tobacco; ~**tisch**(**chen**) *nt m* smoker's table; ~**topas** *nt siehe* ~**quarz**; ~**utensilien** *pl* smoker's requisites *pl*; ~**verbot** *nt* smoking ban, ban on smoking; **hier herrscht** ~**verbot** smoking is not allowed here, there's no smoking here; ~**vergiftung** *f* fume poisoning; **eine** ~**vergiftung erleiden** to be overcome by fumes; ~**verzehrer** *m* -s, - smoke dispeller, *small, often ornamental device for neutralizing tobacco smoke*; ~**vorhang** *m*, ~**wand** *f* smokescreen; ~**waren**[1] *pl* tobacco (products *pl*); ~**waren**[2] *pl* (*Pelze*) furs *pl*; ~**warenhändler** *m* furrier; ~**wolke** *f* cloud of smoke; ~**zimmer** *nt* smoking *or* smoke room.
Räude *f* -, -n (*Vet*) mange.

räudig *adj* mangy. **du** ~**er Hund!** (*old inf*) you dirty dog!
rauf *adv* (*inf*) ~! (get) up!; *siehe* **herauf, hinauf**.
Raufbold *m* -(e)s, -e (*dated*) ruffian, roughneck.
Raufe *f* -, -n hay rack.
raufen 1 *vt Unkraut* to pull up; *Flachs* to pull. **sich** (*dat*) **die Haare** ~ to tear (at) one's hair. **2** *vir* to scrap, to fight.
Rauferei *f* scrap, rough-house (*inf*). **nur eine harmlose** ~ just a harmless little scrap.
Rauf-: ~**handel** *m* (*old, form*) affray (*form*); ~**lust** *f* pugnacity; **r**~**lustig** *adj* ready for a fight *or* scrap, pugnacious.
rauh *adj* (a) rough. **eine** ~**e Schale haben** (*fig*) to be a rough diamond.
(b) *Hals, Kehle* sore; *Stimme* husky; (*heiser*) hoarse; (*unfreundlich*) rough.
(c) (*nicht mild, streng*) *Wetter* rough, raw; *Wind, Luft* raw; *See* rough; *Klima, Winter* harsh, raw; (*unwirtlich*) *Gebiet* bleak, stark; *Stadt* tough. **im** ~**en Norden** in the rugged north; (**die**) ~**e Wirklichkeit** harsh reality, the hard facts *pl*; **hier herrschen ja** ~**e Methoden** their/his *etc* methods are brutal.
(d) (*barsch, grob*) *Benehmen, Wesen* rough; (*hart*) *Mann* tough, rugged; *Sitten auch* rough-and-ready; *Ton, Worte, Behandlung auch* harsh. ~, **aber herzlich** bluff; *Begrüßung, Ton* rough but jovial; **er ist** ~, **aber herzlich** he's a rough diamond; **in unserer Familie geht es** ~, **aber herzlich zu** we're a pretty hale and hearty lot in our family.
(e) (*inf*) **in** ~**en Mengen** by the ton (*inf*), galore (*inf*); **Zucker in** ~**en Mengen** sugar by the ton, sugar galore.
Rauh-: ~**bauz** *m* -es, -e (*dated inf*) *siehe* ~**bein**; **r**~**bauzig** *adj* (*dated inf*) *siehe* **r**~**beinig**; ~**bein** *nt* (*inf*) rough diamond; **r**~**beinig** *adj* (*inf*) rough-and-ready.
Rauheit *f, no pl siehe rauh* (a) roughness. (b) soreness; huskiness; hoarseness; roughness. (c) roughness, rawness; rawness; roughness; harshness; bleakness; toughness. (d) roughness; toughness; rough-and-readiness; harshness.
rauhen *vt siehe* **aufrauhen**.
Rauh-: ~**fasertapete** *f* woodchip paper; ~**frost** *m siehe* ~**reif**; ~**futter** *nt* roughage; ~**haardackel** *m* wire-haired dachshund; **r**~**haarig** *adj* coarse-haired; *Hund auch* wire-haired; *Fell, Wolle* coarse.
Rauhigkeit *f siehe* **Rauheit**.
Rauh-: ~**putz** *m* roughcast; ~**reif** *m* hoarfrost, white frost; (*gefrorener Nebel*) rime.
raum *adj* (*spec*) *Wald* open, clear; (*Naut*) *Wind* following *attr*.
Raum *m* -(e)s, **Räume** (a) *no pl* (*Platz*) room, space; (*Weite*) expanse. ~ **schaffen** to make some space *or* room; **auf engstem** ~ **leben** to live in a very confined space; **einer Sache** (*dat*) ~ **geben** (*geh*) to yield to sth; **eine Frage/ein Problem steht im** ~ there's one question/one problem; **eine Frage in den** ~ **stellen** to pose a question; **eine Frage im** ~ **stehen lassen** to leave a question unresolved *or* hanging.
(b) (*Spielraum*) room, scope.
(c) (*Zimmer*) room.
(d) (*Gebiet, Bereich*) area; (*fig*) sphere. **der** ~ **Frankfurt** the Frankfurt area; **im geistigen** ~ in the intellectual sphere; ~ **gewinnen** (*Mil, fig*) to gain ground.
(e) *no pl* (*Phys, Space*) space *no art.* **der offene** *or* **leere** ~ the void; *siehe* **luftleer**.
Raum-: ~**anordnung** *f* floor plan; ~**anzug** *m* spacesuit; ~**aufteilung** *f siehe* ~**anordnung**; ~**ausstatter**(**in** *f*) *m* -s, - interior decorator; ~**bild** *nt* stereoscopic *or* 3-D picture; ~**bildverfahren** *nt* stereoscopy.
Räumboot *nt* minesweeper.
Raum|einheit *f* unit of volume.
räumen 1 *vt* (a) (*verlassen*) *Gebäude, Gebiet* to clear, to evacuate; (*Mil: Truppen*) to move out of, to withdraw from; *Wohnung* to vacate, to move out of; *Hotelzimmer* to vacate, to check out of; *Sitzplatz* to vacate, to give up. **wir müssen die Wohnung bis Mittwoch** ~ we have to be out of the flat by Wednesday; *siehe* **Feld**.
(b) (*leeren*) *Gebäude, Straße, Warenlager* to clear (*von* of). „**wir** ~" "clearance sale"; **wegen Einsturzgefahr mußte das Gebäude geräumt werden** the building had to be evacuated *or* cleared because of the danger of it collapsing.
(c) (*woanders hinbringen*) to shift, to move; (*entfernen*) *Schnee, Schutt auch* to clear (away); *Minen* to clear; (*auf See*) to sweep, to clear. **räum deine Sachen in den Schrank** put your things away in the cupboard; **er hat seine Sachen aus dem Schrank geräumt** he cleared his things out of the cupboard; **kannst du deine Bücher vom Tisch** ~? can you clear your books off the table?; *siehe* **Weg**.
2 *vi* (*auf*~) to clear up; (*um*~) to rearrange things. **in etw** (*dat*) ~ to rummage around in sth; **wir waren so tief eingeschneit, daß wir erst stundenlang** ~ **mußten** we were so badly snowed in that it took us hours to clear (away) the snow.
Raum-: ~**entweser** *m* -s, - (*form*) pest exterminator; ~**ersparnis** *f* space-saving; **aus Gründen der** ~**ersparnis** to save space, for reasons of space; ~**fähre** *f* space shuttle; ~**fahrer** *m* spaceman, astronaut; (*sowjetisch*) cosmonaut.
Raumfahrt *f* space travel *no art or* flight *no art*. **die Ausgaben für die** ~ **erhöhen** to increase the space budget; **mit der Entwicklung der** ~ with the development of space technology; **das Zeitalter der** ~ the space age.
Raumfahrt- *in cpds space*; ~**behörde** *f* space authority; ~**medizin** *f* space medicine; ~**programm** *nt* space programme; ~**technik** *f* space technology; ~**zeitalter** *nt* space age.
Raumfahrzeug *nt* spacecraft.
Räumfahrzeug *nt* bulldozer; (*für Schnee*) snow-clearer.
Raum-: ~**flug** *m* space flight; (*Forschungsflug auch*) space mission; ~**forschung** *f* space research; ~**gestaltung** *f* interior

design; ~gewinn m extra space gained; der ~gewinn war nicht sehr groß we didn't gain much space; ~gitter nt (Min) (crystal or space) lattice; ~inhalt m volume, (cubic) capacity; ~kapsel f space capsule; ~klang m stereoscopic sound; ~lehre f geometry.

räumlich adj (a) (den Raum betreffend) spatial. ~e Verhältnisse physical conditions; ~e Nähe physical closeness, spatial proximity; wir wohnen ~ sehr beengt we live in very cramped conditions; rein ~ ist das unmöglich (just) from the point of view of space it's impossible; hier hat sich ~ viel verändert the layout of this place has changed a lot.
(b) (dreidimensional) three-dimensional. ~es Anschauungsvermögen capacity to think in three dimensions; ~ sehen to see in three dimensions or three-dimensionally; ich kann mir das nicht ~ vorstellen I can't really picture it.

Räumlichkeit f (a) no pl three-dimensionality. (b) ~en pl premises pl; dazu fehlen uns die ~en our premises aren't big enough.

Raum-: ~mangel m lack of space or room; ~maß nt unit of capacity; ~meter m or nt cubic metre (of stacked wood); ~not f shortage of space; ~ordnung f environmental planning; ~ordnungsplan m development plan; ~pflegerin f cleaner, cleaning lady.

Räumpflug m snowplough, snowplow (US).

Raum-: ~planung f (das Planen) development planning; (Plan) development plan; ~schiff nt spaceship; ~schiffahrt f siehe ~fahrt; ~sonde f space probe; r~sparend adj siehe platzsparend; ~station f space station; ~transporter m space shuttle.

Raumtrupp m clearance gang or workers pl.

Räumung f clearing; (von Wohnung, Gebäude) vacation; (wegen Gefahr etc) evacuation; (unter Zwang) eviction; (von Lager, Vorräten, Geschäft) clearance. „wegen ~ alle Preise radikal herabgesetzt!" "all prices reduced to clear".

Räumungs-: ~arbeiten pl clearance operations pl; ~befehl m eviction order; ~frist f (period of) notice; ~klage f action for eviction; ~verkauf m clearance sale.

Raumverschwendung f waste of space.

raunen vti (liter) to whisper. man raunt sich ins Ohr, daß ... it's (being) whispered that ...; es ging ein R~ durch die Menge a murmur went through the crowd.

raunzen vi (inf: S Ger, Aus) to grouse (inf), to grouch (inf).

Raunzer m -s, - (inf: S Ger, Aus) grouse(r) (inf), grouch(er) (inf).

Raupe f -, -n (a) caterpillar. (b) (Planier~) caterpillar; (Kette) caterpillar track or tread.

Raupen-: ~fahrzeug nt caterpillar (vehicle); ~kette f caterpillar track; ~schlepper m caterpillar (tractor).

raus adv (inf) ~! (get) out!; siehe heraus, hinaus.

Rausch m -(e)s, **Räusche** (a) (Trunkenheit) intoxication, inebriation; (Drogen~) state of euphoria, high (sl). sich (dat) einen ~ antrinken to get drunk; einen ~ haben to be drunk; etw im ~ tun/sagen to do/say sth under the influence or while one is drunk; seinen ~ ausschlafen to sleep it off.
(b) (liter: Ekstase) ecstasy, transport (liter), rapture; (Blut~, Mord~ etc) frenzy. im ~ der Leidenschaft inflamed with passion; im ~ der Gefühle in an ecstasy of emotion; der ~ der Geschwindigkeit the thrill of speed.

rausch|arm adj (Rad) low-noise.

Rauschebart m (inf) big bushy beard; (Mann) man with a big bushy beard, beardy (hum inf).

rauschen vi (a) (Wasser, Meer, Wasserfall) to roar; (sanft) to murmur; (Brandung) to boom, to roar; (Baum, Wald) to rustle; (Wind) to murmur; (Seide) to rustle, to swish; (Korn) to swish; (Regen) to pour or swoosh down; (Radio, Lautsprecher etc) to hiss; (Muschel) to sing; (Applaus) to resound. im ~den Walde in the gently murmuring forest; mit ~den Flügeln with a swish or swoosh of its wings; ~de Feste glittering parties; eine ~e Ballnacht a glittering ball.
(b) aux sein (sich bewegen) (Bach) to rush; (Bumerang, Geschoß) to whoosh.
(c) aux sein (inf: Mensch) to sweep. sie rauschte in das/aus dem Zimmer she swept into/out of the room.

Rauscher m -s, - (dial) sweet cider (half fermented).

Rauschgift nt drug, narcotic; (Drogen) drugs pl, narcotics pl. ~ nehmen to take drugs; (regelmäßig auch) to be on drugs.

Rauschgift-: ~dezernat nt narcotics or drug squad; ~handel m drug trafficking; ~händler m drug trafficker; ~sucht f drug addiction; r~süchtig adj drug-addicted; er ist r~süchtig he's addicted to drugs, he's a drug addict; ~süchtige(r) mf drug addict.

Rausch-: ~gold nt gold foil; ~goldengel m ≃ Christmas tree fairy; r~haft adj (fig) ecstatic; ~mittel nt (form) intoxicant (form).

rausfeuern vt sep (inf) to chuck or sling out.

rausfliegen vi sep irreg aux sein (inf) to be chucked or slung out (inf); (entlassen werden auch) to be given the boot (inf) or the push (inf).

rauskriegen vt sep (inf) to get out; (herausfinden) to find out; (lösen können) to be able to do.

rauspauken vt sep (inf) jdn ~ to get sb out of trouble or off the hook (inf); mein Anwalt hat mich rausgepaukt my lawyer got me off.

räuspern vr to clear one's throat.

rausreißen vt sep irreg (inf) jdn ~ to save sb, to save sb's bacon (inf), to get sb out of trouble; der Mittelstürmer/das hat noch alles rausgerissen the centre-forward/that saved the day.

rausschmeißen vt sep irreg (inf) to chuck or sling or kick out (all inf); (entlassen auch) to give the boot (inf); (wegwerfen) to chuck out or away (inf); Geld to chuck away (inf), to chuck

down the drain (inf). das ist rausgeschmissenes Geld that's money down the drain (inf).

Rausschmeißer(in f) m -s, - (inf) bouncer; (letzter Tanz) last number or dance.

Rausschmiß m -sses, -sse (inf) booting out (inf). man drohte uns mit dem ~ they threatened us with the boot (inf) or push (inf).

Raute f -, -n (a) (Bot) rue. (b) (Math) rhombus; (Her) lozenge.

rautenförmig adj rhomboid, diamond-shaped, lozenge-shaped.

Rayon [rɛ'jõ:] m -s, -s (Aus) department; (old) region.

Razzia ['ratsia] f -, **Razzien** ['ratsiən] raid, swoop (inf). die Polizei machte in ein paar Lokalen ~ the police swooped on (inf) or raided or made a raid on three or four bars.

Re nt -s, -s (Cards) redouble. ~ ansagen to redouble.

Reader ['riːdɐ] m -s, - (Lehrbuch) reader.

Reagens nt -, **Reagenzien** [-iən], **Reagenz** nt -es, -ien [-iən] (Chem) reagent.

Reagenz-: ~glas, ~röhrchen nt (Chem) test-tube.

reagieren* vi to react (auf + acc to). auf etw (acc) verärgert ~ to react angrily to sth; miteinander ~ (Chem) to react (together).

Reaktion f (a) reaction (auf + acc to). (b) (Pol pej) reaction. ein Vertreter der ~ a representative of reactionary thinking.

reaktionär adj (Pol pej) reactionary.

Reationär(in f) [reaktsio'nɛːɐ, -ərɪn] m (pej) reactionary.

Reaktions-: ~fähigkeit f reactions pl; Alkohol vermindert die ~fähigkeit alcohol slows down the or one's reactions; ~geschwindigkeit f speed of reaction; r~schnell adj with fast reactions; er bremste r~schnell he reacted quickly and braked; r~schnell sein to have fast reactions; ~verlauf m (Chem) course of the reaction; ~wärme f (Chem) heat of reaction; ~zeit f reaction time.

reaktiv adj (geh) reactive. wir werden nur ~ tätig we will only act if prompted; er verhält sich nur ~ he doesn't act – he only reacts.

reaktivieren* [reakti'viːrən] vt (Sci) to reactivate; (Agr, Biol, fig) to revive; Kenntnisse, Können to brush up, to polish up; Glieder to rehabilitate; (Mil) to call up again.

Reaktivierung f siehe vt reactivation; revival; brushing or polishing up; rehabilitation; new call-up.

Reaktor m reactor.

real adj real; (wirklichkeitsbezogen) realistic.

Real-: ~büro nt (Aus) estate agency; ~einkommen nt real income; ~enzyklopädie f specialist dictionary/encyclopaedia; ~gymnasium nt ≃ grammar school (Brit), high school (esp US) (stressing modern languages, maths and science).

Realien [re'aːliən] pl realities pl, real facts pl; (old Sch) science and modern languages pl.

Real-: ~index m (dated) subject index; ~injurie [-iə] f (Jur) ≃ assault.

Realisation f (Verwirklichung, Fin) realization; (TV, Rad, Theat) production.

realisierbar adj (a) practicable, feasible, realizable. (b) (Fin) realizable.

Realisierbarkeit f practicability, feasibility, realizability.

realisieren* vt (a) Pläne, Ideen, Programm to carry out; (TV, Rad, Theat) to produce. (b) (Fin) to realize; Verkauf to make, to conclude. (c) (verstehen) to realize.

Realisierung f siehe Realisation.

Realismus m realism.

Realist(in f) m realist.

Realistik f (rare) realism.

realistisch adj realistic.

Realität f (a) reality. die ~ anerkennen to face facts; ~en pl (Gegebenheiten) realities pl, facts pl. (b) ~en pl (Aus: Grundstücke) real estate.

Realitäten-: ~händler, ~vermittler m (Aus) (real) estate agent, realtor (US).

Realitäts-: r~feindlich adj (pej) r~feindlich sein to refuse to accept the realities of the situation; r~fremd adj out of touch with reality; ~sinn m sense of realism; er hat einen gesunden ~sinn he has a firm hold on reality.

realiter [re'aːlitɐ] adv (geh) in reality, in (point of) fact.

Real-: ~kanzlei f (Aus) siehe ~büro; ~kapital nt physical assets pl, non-monetary capital; ~katalog m subject catalogue; ~konkurrenz f (Jur) in ~konkurrenz mit in conjunction with; ~lexikon nt specialist dictionary/encyclopaedia; ~lohn m real wages pl; ~politik f political realism, Realpolitik; ~politiker m political realist, practitioner of Realpolitik; ~schule f ≃ secondary school, secondary modern school (Brit); (Aus) ≃ grammar school (Brit), high school (US); ~schüler m ≃ secondary modern pupil (Brit), student at secondary school (US); (Aus) ≃ grammar school pupil (Brit), high school student (US); ~wert m (Fin) real value.

Re|animation f (Med) resuscitation.

re|animieren* vt (Med) to resuscitate.

Rebbach m -s, no pl (sl) siehe Reibach.

Rebbe m -n, -n siehe Rabbiner.

Rebe f -, -n (Ranke) shoot; (Weinstock) vine.

Rebell(in f) m -en, -en rebel.

rebellieren* vi to rebel, to revolt.

Rebellion f rebellion, revolt.

rebellisch adj rebellious.

Reben-: ~blut nt (liter), ~saft m (liter) wine, juice of the vine (liter), grape (liter).

Rebhuhn nt (common) partridge.

Reb-: ~laus f phylloxera (spec), vine pest; ~ling m young vine; ~schnur f (Aus) rope; ~sorte f type of vine; ~stock m vine.

Rebus m or nt -, -se rebus, picture puzzle.

Rechaud [re'ʃoː] *m or nt* **-s, -s** spirit burner; tea/coffee *etc* warmer; (*für Fondue*) spirit burner.

Rechen *m* **-s, -** (*S Ger*) (*Harke*) rake; (*Gitter an Bächen, Flüssen*) grill.

rechen *vt* (*S Ger*) to rake.

Rechen-: ~**anlage** *f* computer; ~**art** *f* type of calculation; **die vier** ~**arten** the four arithmetical operations; ~**aufgabe** *f* sum, (arithmetical) problem; ~**automat** *m* (automatic) adding machine, comptometer; ~**brett** *nt* abacus; ~**buch** *nt* arithmetic book; ~**exempel** *nt* sum; **das ist doch ein ganz einfaches** ~**exempel** it's a matter of simple arithmetic; ~**fehler** *m* miscalculation, (arithmetical) error or mistake; ~**heft** *nt* arithmetic book; ~**künstler** *m* mathematical genius or wizard (*inf*); ~**lehrer** *m* arithmetic teacher; ~**maschine** *f* adding machine; ~**operation** *f* calculation.

Rechenschaft *f* account. **jdm über etw** (*acc*) ~ **geben** or **ablegen** to account to sb for sth, to give or render account to sb for sth (*liter*); **sich** (*dat*) **über etw** (*acc*) ~ **ablegen** to account to oneself for sth; **jdm** ~ **schuldig sein** or **schulden** to be accountable to sb, to have to account to sb; **dafür bist du mir** ~ **schuldig** you owe me an explanation for that; **jdn** (*für etw*) **zur** ~ **ziehen** to call sb to account (for or over sth); (**von jdm**) ~ **verlangen** or **fordern** to demand an explanation or account (from sb).

Rechenschafts-: ~**bericht** *m* report; ~**legung** *f* report; **jdm gegenüber zur** ~**legung verpflichtet sein** to be accountable to sb.

Rechen-: ~**schieber**, ~**stab** *m* slide-rule; ~**stunde** *f* arithmetic lesson; ~**tabelle** *f* ready-reckoner; ~**tafel** *f* arithmetic slate; (*an der Wand*) (squared) blackboard; ~**zentrum** *nt* computer centre.

Recherche [re'ʃɛrʃə, rə-] *f* **-, -n** investigation, enquiry. ~**n anstellen** to make investigations or enquiries (*über etw* (*acc*)) about or into sth).

recherchieren* [reʃɛr'ʃiːrən, rə-] *vti* to investigate.

rechnen 1 *vt* (a) (*addieren etc*) to work out, to calculate; **Aufgabe** to work out. **wir** ~ **gerade Additionsbeispiele** we're doing addition sums at the moment; **rund gerechnet** in round figures; **was für einen Unsinn hast du da gerechnet!** how did you get that absurd result?, how did you work that out?
    (b) (*einstufen*) to count. **jdn/etw zu etw** ~, **jdn/etw unter etw** (*acc*) ~ to count sb among sth, to class sb/sth as sth; **er wird zu den größten Physikern** or **unter die größten Physiker gerechnet** he is rated as or is reckoned to be one of the greatest physicists, he is counted among the greatest physicists.
    (c) (*veranschlagen*) to estimate, to reckon. **wir hatten nur drei Tage gerechnet** we were only reckoning on three days; **für vier Personen rechnet man ca. zwei Pfund Fleisch** for four people you should reckon on about two pounds of meat; **das ist zu hoch/niedrig gerechnet** that's too high/low (an estimate).
    (d) (*einberechnen*) to include, to count, to take into account. **alles in allem gerechnet** all in all, taking everything into account; **den Ärger/die Unkosten mit dazu gerechnet** what with all the trouble/expense too or on top of that.
    2 *vi* (a) (*addieren etc*) to do or make a calculation/calculations; (*esp Sch*) to do sums. **falsch/richtig** ~ to go wrong or make a mistake (in one's calculations)/to calculate correctly; (**da hast du**) **falsch gerechnet!** you got that wrong; **gut/schlecht** ~ **können** to be good/bad at sums (*esp Sch*) or arithmetic or with figures; **rechne doch selbst!** work it out for yourself; ~ **lernen** to learn arithmetic; **ein Kaufmann muß schnell** ~ **können** a businessman has to be quick at working out figures.
    (b) (*eingestuft werden*) to count. **er rechnet noch als Kind** he still counts as a child.
    (c) (*sich verlassen*) **auf jdn/etw** ~ to reckon or count on sb/sth.
    (d) **mit jdm/etw** ~ (*erwarten, einkalkulieren*) to reckon on or with sb/sth; (*berücksichtigen*) to reckon with sb/sth; **du mußt damit** ~, **daß es regnet** you must reckon on or with it raining; **mit ihm/dieser Partei wird man** ~ **müssen** he/this party will have to be reckoned with; **damit hatte ich nicht gerechnet** I wasn't expecting that, I hadn't reckoned on or with that; **mit so etwas muß man** ~ you have to reckon on or with that sort of thing happening; **er rechnet mit einem Sieg** he reckons he'll win; **mit allem/dem Schlimmsten** ~ to be prepared for anything/the worst; **wir hatten nicht mehr mit ihm/seinem Kommen gerechnet** we hadn't reckoned on him coming any more; **damit** ~ **müssen, daß ...** to have to be prepared for the fact that ...; **ich rechne morgen fest mit dir** I'll be expecting you tomorrow.
    (e) (*inf: haushalten*) to be thrifty, to economize. **seine Frau kann gut** ~ his wife knows how to economize, his wife is thrifty.

Rechnen *nt* **-s, no pl** arithmetic; (*esp Sch*) sums *pl*.

Rechner *m* **-s, -** (a) arithmetician. **ein guter** ~ sein to be good at arithmetic or figures. **(b)** (*Elektronen~*) computer; (*Taschen~*) calculator.

Rechnerei *f* (*inf*) calculation. **das ist eine furchtbare** ~ it's incredibly difficult to work out; **die ganze** ~ **überlasse ich ihm** I leave all the calculations or figurework to him.

rechnerisch *adj* arithmetical. **ein** ~**es Beispiel** an example with some figures; **ich bin rein** ~ **überzeugt, aber ...** I'm convinced as far as the figures go but ...

Rechnung *f* (a) (*Berechnung*) calculation; (*als Aufgabe*) sum. **die** ~ **geht nicht auf** (*lit*) the sum doesn't work out; (*fig*) it won't work (out); *siehe* **Strich.**
    (b) (*schriftliche Kostenforderung*) bill (*Brit*), check (*US*); (*von Firma auch*) invoice; (*für Kundenkonto*) statement of account. **das geht auf meine** ~ I'm paying, this one's on me; **auf** ~ **kaufen/bestellen** to buy/order on account; **laut** ~ as per invoice; **laut** ~ **vom 5. Juli** as per our invoice of July 5th; **auf** or **für eigene** ~ on one's own account; (**jdm**) **etw in** ~ **stellen**

to charge (sb) for sth; **einer Sache** (*dat*) ~ **tragen, etw in** ~ **ziehen** to take sth into account, to bear sth in mind; **auf seine** ~ **kommen** to have one's money's worth; **wenn du das glaubst, dann hast du die** ~ **ohne den Wirt gemacht** (*inf*) if you think that, you've got another think coming; **aber er hatte die** ~ **ohne den Wirt gemacht** (*inf*) but there was one thing he hadn't reckoned with.

Rechnungs-: ~**abschluß** *m* making-up of (the) accounts; **den** ~**abschluß machen** to do the books; ~**amt** *nt* audit office; ~**art** *f* *siehe* **Rechenart;** ~**betrag** *m* (total) amount of a bill or check (*US*)/invoice/account; ~**buch** *nt* account(s) book or ledger; ~**einheit** *f* unit of account; ~**führer** *m* chief accountant; ~**führung** *f* *siehe* **Buchführung;** ~**hof** *m* ≈ Auditor-General's office (*Brit*), audit division (*US*); ~**jahr** *nt* financial or fiscal year; ~**legung** *f* tendering of account; ~**prüfer** *m* auditor; ~**prüfung** *f* audit; ~**wesen** *nt* (*Führung*) accountancy, bookkeeping; (*Prüfung*) auditing.

Recht *nt* **-(e)s, -e** (a) (*Rechtsordnung, sittliche Norm*) law; (*Gerechtigkeit auch*) justice. ~ **sprechen** to administer or dispense justice; **nach geltendem/englischem** ~ in law/in or under or according to English law; **muß** ~ **bleiben** (*Naturrecht*) fair's fair; (*Gesetz*) the law's the law; **für das** ~ **kämpfen** to fight for justice; **das Schwurgericht hat für** ~ **erkannt ...** the court has reached the following verdict or has decided ...; **von** ~**s wegen** legally, as of right; (*inf: eigentlich*) by rights (*inf*).
    (b) ~**e** *pl* (*form: Rechtswissenschaft*) jurisprudence; **Doktor der** or **beider** ~**e** Doctor of Laws.
    (c) (*Anspruch, Berechtigung*) right (*auf* + *acc* to). **sein** ~ **fordern** to demand one's rights; **seine** ~**e geltend machen** to insist on one's rights; **ich nehme mir das** ~, **das zu tun** I shall make so bold as to do that; **sein** ~ **bekommen** or **erhalten** or **kriegen** (*inf*) to get one's rights, to get what is one's by right; **zu seinem** ~ **kommen** (*lit*) to gain one's rights; (*fig*) to come into one's own; **auch das Vergnügen muß zu seinem** ~ **kommen** there has to be a place for pleasure too; **der Körper verlangt sein** ~ (*auf Schlaf*) the body demands its due or its rightful sleep; **gleiches** ~ **für alle!** equal rights for all!; **gleiche** ~**e, gleiche Pflichten** equal rights, equal duties; **das** ~ **des Stärkeren** the law of the jungle; **in jds** ~**e** (*acc*) **treten** (*form*) to assume sb's rights; **mit** or **zu** ~ rightly, with justification; **und** (**das**) **mit** ~ and rightly so; **Sie stellen diese Frage ganz zu** ~ you are quite right to ask this question; **im** ~ **sein** to be in the right; **das ist mein gutes** ~ it's my right; **es ist unser gutes** ~, **zu erfahren ...** we have every right to know ...; **woher nimmt er das** ~, **das zu sagen?** what gives him the right to say that?; **mit welchem** ~? by what right?; *siehe* **vorbehalten.**

recht 1 *adj* (a) (*richtig*) right. **mir ist es** ~, **es soll mir** ~ **sein** it's all right or OK (*inf*) by me; **ganz** ~! quite right; **ist schon** ~! (*inf*) that's all right, that's OK (*inf*); **alles, was** ~ **ist** (*empört*) there is a limit, fair's fair; (*anerkennend*) you can't deny it; **ich will zum Bahnhof, bin ich hier** ~? (*esp S Ger*) I want to get to the station, am I going the right way?; **bin ich hier** ~ **bei Schmidts?** (*esp S Ger*) is this the Smiths' place (all right *inf*)?; **bin ich hier** ~ **bei Herrn Meyer?** (*esp S Ger*) is this Mr. Meyer's office?; **hier geht es nicht mit** ~**en Dingen zu** there's something odd or not right here; **ich habe keine** ~**e Lust** I don't particularly feel like it; **ein** ~**er Narr** (*old*) a real or right fool; **nichts R**~**es** no good; **aus dem Jungen kann nichts R**~**es werden** that boy will come to no good; **aus ihm ist nichts R**~**es geworden** (*beruflich etc*) he never really made it; **er hat nichts R**~**es gelernt** he didn't learn any real trade; **nach dem R**~**en sehen** to see that everything's OK (*inf*); **Tag, ich wollte nur mal nach dem R**~**en sehen** hello, I just thought I'd come and see how you're doing or how things are; **es ist nicht mehr als** ~ **und billig** it's only right and proper; **was dem einen** ~ **ist, ist dem andern billig** (*Prov*) what's sauce for the goose is sauce for the gander (*Prov*).
    (b) ~ **haben** to be right; **er hat** ~ **bekommen** he was right; ~ **behalten** to be right; **er will immer** ~ **behalten** he always has to be right; **ich hatte** ~, **und ich habe** ~ **behalten** I was right and I'm still right; **jdm** ~ **geben** to agree with sb, to admit that sb is right; ~ **daran tun, zu ...** to be or do right to ...
    2 *adv* (a) (*richtig*) properly; (*wirklich*) really. **verstehen Sie mich** ~ don't get me wrong (*inf*), don't misunderstand me; **ich verstehe ihn nicht so** ~, **wie kann er nur ...?** I just don't understand him, how can he ...?; **wenn ich Sie** ~ **verstehe** if I understand you rightly or aright (*form*); **sehe/höre ich** ~? am I seeing/hearing things?; **ich werde daraus nicht** ~ **klug** I don't really or rightly know what to make of it; **das geschieht ihm** ~ it serves him right; **du kommst gerade** ~, **um ...** you're just in time to ...; **das ist** or **kommt mir gerade** ~ (*inf*) that suits me fine; **du kommst mir gerade** ~ (*iro*) you're all I needed; **gehe ich** ~ **in der Annahme, daß ...?** am I right or correct in assuming that ...?; **es hat mir nicht mehr** ~ **gefallen** I didn't really like it any more; **hat es dir gefallen? – nicht so** ~ did you like it? - not really; **ich weiß nicht** ~ I don't really or rightly know; **man kann ihm nichts** ~ **machen** you can't do anything right for him; **man kann es nicht allen** ~ **machen** you can't please all of the people all of the time; **ich mache es Ihnen** (**auch**) ~ (*inf*) I'll make it worth your while; **sie versuchte, es ihm immer** ~ **zu machen** she always tried to do everything right for him.
    (b) (*ziemlich, ganz*) quite, fairly, pretty (*inf*). ~ **viel** quite a lot.
    (c) (*sehr*) very, right (*dial*). ~ **herzlichen Dank!** thank you very much indeed.

Rechte *f* **-n, -n** (a) (*Hand*) right hand; (*Boxen*) right. **(b)** (*Pol*) right, Right.

Recht-: ~**eck** *nt* rectangle; **r**~**eckig** *adj* rectangular.

Rechtehandregel *f* (*Phys*) right-hand rule.

rechten *vi* (*geh*) to argue, to dispute.

Rechtens *gen of* **Recht** (*form*) **es ist** ~/**nicht** ~, **daß er das**

gemacht hat he was/was not within his rights to do that; **die Sache war nicht ~** the matter was not right *or (Jur)* legal.

rechte(r, s) *adj attr* **(a)** right, right-hand. **~r Hand** on *or* to the right; **jds ~ Hand sein** to be sb's right-hand man. **(b) ein ~r Winkel** a right angle. **(c)** *(konservativ)* right-wing, rightist. **der ~ Flügel** the right wing.

rechterseits *adv* on the right-hand side.

rechtfertigen *insep* 1 *vt* to justify; *(berechtigt erscheinen lassen auch)* to warrant. **das ist durch nichts zu ~** that can in no way be justified, that is completely unjustifiable. 2 *vr* to justify oneself.

Rechtfertigung *f siehe vt* justification; warranting. **zu meiner ~** in my defence, in justification of what I did/said *etc*.

Rechtfertigungs-: **~grund** *m (Jur)* justification; **~schrift** *f* apologia; **~versuch** *m* attempt at self-justification.

Recht-: **r~gläubig** *adj* orthodox; **~gläubigkeit** *f* orthodoxy; **~haber** *m -s, -* *(pej)* know-all *(inf)*, self-opinionated person; **~haberei** *f (pej)* know-all attitude *(inf)*, self-opinionatedness; **r~haberisch** *adj* know-all *attr (inf)*, self-opinionated; **er ist so r~haberisch** he's such a know-all *(inf)*, he's so self-opinionated; **r~haberisch bestand er darauf** he insisted on it in his self-opinionated way.

rechtlich *adj* **(a)** *(gesetzlich)* legal. **~ verpflichtet** bound by law, legally obliged; **~ zulässig** permissible in law, legal; **~ nicht zulässig** not permissible in law, illegal; **~ unmöglich** impossible for legal reasons; **jdn ~ belangen** to take sb to court, to take legal action against sb. **(b)** *(old: redlich)* honest, upright, upstanding *(old)*. **~ denken/handeln** to think/act in an honest *etc* way.

Recht-: **r~los** *adj* **(a)** without rights; **(b)** *Zustand* lawless; **~lose(r)** *mf decl as adj* person with no rights; *(Vogelfreier)* outlaw; **~losigkeit** *f* **(a)** *(von Mensch)* lack of rights; **in völliger ~losigkeit leben** to have no rights whatever; **(b)** *(in Land)* lawlessness; **r~mäßig** *adj (legitim)* lawful, legitimate; *Erben, Thronfolger, Besitzer auch* rightful; *(dem Gesetz entsprechend)* legal, in accordance with the law; **für r~mäßig erklären** to legitimize; to declare legal; **jdm etw r~mäßig zuerkennen** to recognize sb's legal right *or* entitlement to sth; **~mäßigkeit** *f (Legitimität)* legitimacy; *(Legalität)* legality.

rechts 1 *adv* on the right. **nach ~** (to the) right; **von ~** from the right; **~ von etw** (on *or* to the) right of sth; **~ von jdm** to *or* on sb's right; *(Pol)* to the right of sb; **das Haus liegt weiter ~** the house is further to the right; **sich ~ einordnen** to move into *or* take the right-hand lane; **~ vor links** right before left *(rule of the priority system for driving)*; **sich ~ halten** to keep (to the) right; **Augen ~!** *(Mil)* eyes right!; **~ schwenkt, marsch!** *(Mil)* right wheel!; **~ stehen** *or* **sein** *(Pol)* to be right-wing *or* on the right *or* a right-winger; **~ stricken** to knit (plain); **ein ganz ~ gestrickter Pullover** a pullover knitted in garter stitch; **zwei ~, zwei links** *(beim Stricken)* knit two, purl two, two plain, two purl; **ich weiß nicht mehr, wo ~ und links ist** *(inf)* I don't know whether I'm coming or going *(inf)*.

2 *prep +gen* **~ des Rheins** to *or* on the right of the Rhine.

Rechts- in *cpds (Jur)* legal; **~abbieger** *m -s, -* motorist/cyclist/car *etc* turning right; **die Spur für ~abbieger** the right-hand turn-off lane; **~abweichler** *m -s, - (Pol inf)* right-winger, rightist *(pej)*; **~angelegenheit** *f* legal matter; **~anspruch** *m* legal right *or* entitlement; **einen ~anspruch auf etw** *(acc)* **haben** to be legally entitled to sth, to have a legal right *etc* to sth; **aus etw einen ~anspruch ableiten** to use sth to create a legal precedent; **~anwalt** *m* lawyer, attorney *(US)*; *(als Berater auch)* solicitor *(Brit)*; *(vor Gericht auch)* barrister *(Brit)*; *(vor Gericht auch)* advocate *(Scot)*; **sein ~anwalt behauptete vor Gericht, ...** his counsel maintained in court ...; **sich (dat) einen ~anwalt nehmen** to get a lawyer *or* an attorney *(US) etc*; **~auffassung** *f* **(a)** conception of legality; **(b)** *(Auslegung)* interpretation of the law; **~auskunft** *f* legal advice; **~ausleger** *m (Boxen)* southpaw; *(Pol hum)* extreme right-winger (of a party); **~außen** *m -, - (Ftbl)* outside-right; *(Pol inf)* extreme right-winger; **~beistand** *m* legal advice; *(Mensch)* legal adviser; **~belehrung** *f siehe* **~mittelbelehrung**; **~berater** *m* legal adviser; **~beratung(sstelle)** *f ≈* citizens' advice bureau *(Brit)*; **~beugung** *f* perversion of the course of justice; **~brecher** *m -s, -* law-breaker, criminal; **~bruch** *m* breach *or* infringement of the law.

rechtschaffen 1 *adj* **(a)** *(ehrlich, redlich)* honest, upright. **(b)** *(inf: stark, groß)* **~en Durst/Hunger haben** to be really thirsty/hungry; **to be parched** *(inf)*/**to be starving** *(inf)*. 2 *adv* really, tremendously. **sich ~ bemühen** to try really *etc* hard.

Rechtschaffenheit *f* honesty, uprightness.

Rechtschreib(e)buch *nt* spelling dictionary.

rechtschreiben *vi infin only* to spell.

Rechtschreiben *nt* spelling.

Rechtschreibfehler *m* spelling mistake.

rechtschreiblich *adj (form) siehe* **orthographisch**.

Rechtschreibung *f* spelling.

Rechts-: **~drall** *m (in Gewehrlauf)* clockwise rifling; *(von Geschoß, Billardball)* swerve to the right; *(von Auto, Pferd)* pull to the right; *(Pol inf)* leaning to the right; **einen ~drall haben** to swerve/pull/lean to the right; **~drehung** *f* turn to the right.

rechtsseitig *adj siehe* **rechtsseitig**.

Rechts|empfinden *nt* sense of justice.

Rechtser(in) *f) m -s, - (dial) siehe* **Rechtshänder(in)**.

Rechts-: **~extremist** *m* right-wing extremist; **r~fähig** *adj (Jur)* legally responsible, having legal capacity *(form)*; **~fähigkeit** *f (Jur)* legal responsibility *or* capacity *(form)*; **~fall** *m* court case; *(in der ~geschichte auch)* legal case; **~frage** *f* legal question *or* issue; **~frieden** *m (Jur)* peace under the law; **~gang**[1] *m (Jur)* legal procedure; **im ersten ~gang** at the first court-case; **~gang**[2] *m (Tech)* right-handed thread; **r~gängig**

adj (Tech) right-handed; **~gefühl** *nt siehe* **~empfinden)**; **~gelehrsamkeit** *f (old) siehe* **~wissenschaft**; **~gelehrte(r)** *mf* jurist, legal scholar; **r~gerichtet** *adj (Pol)* orientated towards the right; **~geschäft** *nt* legal transaction; **einseitiges/mehrseitiges ~geschäft** unilateral/multilateral legal transaction; **~geschichte** *f* legal history; *(Geschichte der ~wissenschaft auch)* history of law; **~gewinde** *nt* right-handed thread; **~grund** *m* legal justification; **~grundsatz** *m* legal maxim; **r~gültig** *adj* legally valid, legal; *Vertrag auch* legally binding; **~gültigkeit** *f* legal validity, legality; **~gut** *nt* something enjoying legal protection, legally protected right; **~gutachten** *nt* legal report; **~haken** *m (Boxen)* right hook; **~handel** *m (liter)* lawsuit; **~händer(in)** *f) m -s, -* right-handed person, right-hander *(esp Sport)*; **~händer sein** to be right-handed; **r~händig** *adj* right-handed; **~händigkeit** *f* right-handedness; **~handlung** *f* legal act; **r~hängig** *adj (Jur)* sub judice *pred*; **~hängigkeit** *f* state of being sub judice; **im Falle der ~hängigkeit** where a case is sub judice; **r~her** *adv* from the right; **r~heran** *adv* over to the right; **r~herum** *adv* (round) to the right; *sich drehen etc auch* clockwise; **~hilfe** *f* (mutual) assistance in law enforcement; **~hilfeabkommen** *nt* law enforcement treaty; **r~hin** *adv* (to the) right; **~kraft** *f, no pl* force of law; *(Gültigkeit: von Vertrag etc)* legal validity; **~kraft erlangen** to become law, to come into force; **die ~kraft eines Urteils** the finality *or* legal force of a verdict; **r~kräftig** *adj* having the force of law; *Urteil* final; *Vertrag* legally valid; **r~kräftig sein/werden** *(Verordnung)* to have the force of law/to become law; *(Urteil)* to be/become final; *(Gesetz)* to be in/come into force; **r~kundig** *adj* familiar with *or* versed in the law; **~kurve** *f (von Straße)* right-hand bend; *(von Bahn auch)* right-hand curve; **~lage** *f* legal position; **r~lastig** *adj* listing to the right; *Auto auch* down at the right; *(fig)* leaning to the right; **r~lastig sein** to list to/be down at/lean to the right; **r~läufig** *adj* *Gewinde* right-handed; *Schrift* left-to-right; **~lehre** *f siehe* **~wissenschaft**; **~lehrer** *m (form)* professor of jurisprudence *(form)*; **~mißbrauch** *m* abuse of the law; **~mittel** *nt* means of legal redress; **~mittel einlegen** to lodge an appeal; **~mittelbelehrung** *f* statement of rights of redress *or* appeal; **~nachfolge** *f* legal succession; **~nachfolger** *m* legal successor; **~norm** *f* legal norm; **~ordnung** *f* eine **~ordnung** a system of laws; **die ~ordnung** the law; **~partei** *f* right-wing party; **~pflege** *f* administration of justice; **~pfleger** *m* official with certain judicial powers; **~philosophie** *f* philosophy of law.

Rechtsprechung *f* **(a)** *(Rechtspflege)* administration of justice; *(Gerichtsbarkeit)* jurisdiction. **(b)** *(richterliche Tätigkeit)* administering *or* dispensation of justice. **(c)** *(bisherige Urteile)* precedents *pl*.

Rechts-: **r~radikal** *adj* radical right-wing; **die ~radikalen** the right-wing radicals; **~radikalismus** *m* right-wing radicalism; **~referendar** *m* articled clerk; **~referendar sein** to be under articles; **r~rheinisch** *adj* to *or* on the right of the Rhine; **~ruck, ~rutsch** *m (Pol)* swing to the right; **r~rum** *adv (inf)* to the right; **~sache** *f* legal matter; *(Fall)* case; **~schutz** *m* legal protection; **~schutzversicherung** *f* legal costs insurance; **r~seitig** *adj* on the right(-hand) side; **r~seitig gelähmt** paralysed in the right side; **~sprache** *f* legal terminology *or* language; **~spruch** *m* verdict; **~staat** *m* state under the rule of law; **r~staatlich** *adj* of a state under the rule of law; **r~staatliche Ordnung** law and order; **seine r~staatliche Gesinnung** his predisposition for law and order; **~staatlichkeit** *f* rule of law; *(einer Maßnahme)* legality; **die r~staatlichkeit dieses Landes ist umstritten** how far this country is under the rule of law is a matter of controversy; **r~stehend** *adj attr* right-hand, on the right; *(Pol)* right-wing, on the right; **~stellung** *f* legal position; **~steuerung** *f* right-hand drive; **~streit** *m* lawsuit; **~titel** *m* legal title.

rechtsuchend *adj attr* seeking justice.

rechts|um *adv (Mil)* to the right. **~ machen** to do a right turn; **~ (kehrt)!** *(Mil)* right about turn!

Rechts-: **~unsicherheit** *f* uncertainty (about one's legal position); **r~verbindlich** *adj* legally binding; *Auskunft* legally valid; **~verbindlichkeit** *f siehe adj* legal bindingness; legal validity; **~verdreher** *m -s, - (pej)* shyster *(inf)*, Philadelphia lawyer *(US)*; *(hum inf)* legal eagle *(inf)*; **~vergleichung** *f* comparative law; **~verhältnis** *nt* facts of the case *pl*; **~verkehr** *m* driving on the right *no def art*; **in Deutschland ist ~verkehr** in Germany they drive on the right; **im ~verkehr muß man ...** when driving on the right one must ...; **~verletzung** *f* infringement *or* breach of the law; **~verordnung** *f ≈* statutory order; **~vertreter** *m* legal representative; **~weg** *m* legal action; **den ~weg beschreiten** *or* **einschlagen** to have recourse to *or* take legal action, to go to law; **unter Ausschluß des ~weges** without possibility of recourse to legal action; **der ~weg ist ausgeschlossen** ≈ the judges' decision is final; **r~widrig** *adj* illegal; **~widrigkeit** *f* illegality; **~wissenschaft** *f* jurisprudence.

Recht-: **r~wink(e)lig** *adj* right-angled; **r~zeitig** 1 *adj (früh genug)* timely; *(pünktlich)* punctual; **um eine r~zeitige Erkennung von Krebs zu ermöglichen** in order that the presence of cancer may be determined in (good) time; **um r~zeitige Anmeldung wird gebeten** you are requested to apply in good time; 2 *adv (früh genug)* in (good) time; *(pünktlich)* on time; **gerade noch r~zeitig ankommen** to arrive *or* be just in time; **komm r~zeitiger als letztes Mal** try to arrive in better time than last time; **r~zeitigkeit** *f siehe adj* timeliness; punctuality.

Reck *nt -(e)s, -e (Sport)* horizontal bar.

Recke *m -n, -n (obs)* warrior.

recken 1 *vt* **(a)** *(aus-, emporstrecken)* to stretch. **den Kopf/Hals ~** to crane one's neck; **die Glieder ~** to stretch (oneself), to have a stretch. **(b)** *(dial: glattziehen)* etw **~** to pull the creases out of sth. **2** *vr* to stretch (oneself). **sich ~ und strecken** to have a good stretch.

Recken-: **~art** *f* (*obs*) heroic manner; **nach alter ~art** as in the heroic days of yore (*old liter*); **r~haft** *adj* (*obs*) doughty (*old*); **~tum** *nt* (*obs*) warriorship (*rare*); (*die Recken*) warriors *pl*.

Reck-: **~stange** *f* horizontal bar; **~turnen** *nt* bar exercises *pl*.

Recorder [re'kɔdɐ] *m* -s, - (cassette) recorder.

Red. *abbr of* **Redakteur** ed; **Redaktion**.

Redakteur(in *f*) [-'tøːɐ, -'tøːrɪn] *m* editor.

Redaktion *f* **(a)** (*das Redigieren*) editing. **die ~ dieses Buches hatte XY** this book was edited by XY. **(b)** (*Personal*) editorial staff. **(c)** (*~sbüro*) editorial office(s). **als ich in die ~ zurück-fuhr** as I drove back to the office; **der Reporter rief seine ~ an** the reporter phoned his office *or* paper.

redaktionell [redaktsio'nɛl] *adj* editorial. **die ~e Leitung im Ressort Wirtschaft hat Herr Müller** Herr Müller is the editor responsible for business and finance; **etw ~ überarbeiten** to edit sth.

Redaktions-: **~geheimnis** *nt* press secret; **~konferenz** *f* editorial conference; **~schluß** *m* time of going to press; (*Einsende-schluß*) copy deadline; **diese Nachricht ist vor/nach ~schluß eingegangen** this news item arrived before/after the paper went to press *or* bed (*sl*); „**nach ~schluß eingegangen**" "stop-press (news)".

Redaktor *m* (*Sw*) editor.

Redaktrice [-'triːsə] *f* -, -n (*Aus*) editor.

Redder *m* -s, - (*N Ger*) lane.

Rede *f* -, -n **(a)** speech; (*Ansprache*) address. **die Kunst der ~** (*form*) the art of rhetoric; **eine ~ halten** *or* **schwingen** (*sl*) to make *or* give a speech; **die ~ des Bundeskanzlers** the Chancellor's speech, the speech given by the Chancellor; **der langen ~ kurzer Sinn** (*prov*) the long and the short of it.
(b) (*Äußerungen, Worte*) words *pl*, language *no pl*. **seine frechen ~n** his cheek; **große ~n führen** *or* **schwingen** (*sl*) to talk big (*inf*); **jdn zur ~ kommen lassen** to let sb speak, to let sb get a word in (*inf*); (*mitreden lassen*) to let sb have a say; **das ist meine ~!** that's what I've always said; **das ist nicht der ~ wert** it's not worth mentioning; (**es ist) nicht der ~ wert!** don't mention it, it was nothing.
(c) (*das Reden, Gespräch*) conversation, talk. **jdm in die ~ fallen** to interrupt sb; **die ~ fiel** *or* **kam auf** (*+acc*) the conversation *or* talk turned to; **die in ~ stehende Person** (*form*) the person in question *or* under discussion; **es war von einer Gehaltserhöhung die ~** there was talk *or* mention of a salary increase; **von Ihnen war eben die ~** we were just talking about you; **von Liebe war doch gar nicht die ~!** who was talking about love!; **aber davon war doch nie die ~!** but no-one was ever talking about that; **wovon ist die ~?** what are you/we *etc* talking about?; **von einer Gehaltserhöhung kann keine ~ sein** there can be no question of a salary increase; **von Großzügigkeit kann keine ~ sein, das war nur ...** there's no question of it being generosity, it was just ...; **davon kann keine ~ sein** it's out of the question.
(d) (*Ling, Liter*) speech. **direkte/indirekte ~** direct/indirect speech *or* discourse (*US*); **gebundene/ungebundene ~** verse/prose; **in freier ~** without (consulting) notes.
(e) (*Gerücht, Nachrede*) rumour. **kümmere dich doch nicht um die ~n der Leute!** don't worry (about) what people say; **es geht die ~, daß** there's a rumour that, rumour has it that.
(f) (*Rechenschaft*) **(jdm) ~ (und Antwort) stehen** to justify oneself to sb; **(jdm) für etw ~ und Antwort stehen** to account (to sb) for sth; **jdn zur ~ stellen** to take sb to task.

Rede-: **~duell** *nt* verbal exchange *or* duel; **~figur** *f* (*Liter*) figure of speech; **~fluß** *m* volubility; **sie hat einen unwahrscheinlichen ~fluß** she is incredibly voluble; **er stockte plötzlich in seinem ~fluß** his flow of words suddenly stopped; **ich will Ihren ~fluß nicht unterbrechen, aber ...** I don't wish to interrupt your flow but ...; **~freiheit** *f* freedom of speech; **~gabe** *f* eloquence; **r~gewandt** *adj* eloquent; **~gewandtheit** *f* eloquence; **~kunst** *f* **die ~kunst** rhetoric.

reden 1 *vi* **(a)** (*sprechen*) to talk, to speak. **R~ während des Unterrichts** talking in class; **mit sich selbst/jdm ~** to talk *or* speak to oneself/sb; **wie redst du denn mit deiner Mutter!** that's no way to talk *or* speak to your mother; **so lasse ich nicht mit mir ~!** I won't be spoken to like that!; **sie hat geredet und geredet** she talked and talked; **mit jdm über jdn/etw ~** to talk *or* speak to *or* with sb about sb/sth; **~ wir nicht mehr davon** *or* **darüber** let's not talk *or* speak about it any more, let's drop it (*inf*); **~ Sie doch nicht!** (*inf*) come off it! (*inf*); **(viel) von sich ~ machen** to become (very much) a talking point; **das Buch/er macht viel von sich ~** everyone is talking about the book/him; **viel R~s von einer Sache machen** to make a great to-do about sth; **du hast gut** *or* **leicht ~!** it's all very well for you (to talk); **ich habe mit Ihnen zu ~!** I would like to speak *or* talk to you, I would like a word with you; **ich rede gegen eine Wand** *or* **Mauer** it's like talking to a brick wall (*inf*); **darüber läßt** *or* **ließe sich ~** that's a possibility; (*über Preis, Bedingungen*) I think we could discuss that; **darüber läßt** *or* **ließe sich eher ~** that's more like it, now you're talking; **er läßt mit sich ~** he could be persuaded; (*in bezug auf Preis*) he's open to offers; (*gesprächsbereit*) he's open to discussion; **sie läßt nicht mit sich ~** she is adamant; (*bei eigenen Forderungen auch*) she won't take no for an answer; **R~ ist Silber, Schweigen ist Gold** (*Prov*) (speech is silver but) silence is golden (*Prov*); **das ist ja mein R~ (seit 33)** (*inf*) I've been saying that for (donkey's *inf*) years; *siehe* **Wasserfall**.
(b) (*klatschen*) to talk (*über +acc* about). **schlecht von jdm ~** to talk *or* speak ill of sb; **in so einem Dorf wird natürlich viel geredet** in a village like that naturally people talk a lot.
(c) (*eine Rede halten*) to speak. **er redet nicht gerne öffentlich** he doesn't like public speaking; **er kann nicht/gut ~** he is

no/a good talker *or* (*als Redner*) speaker.
(d) (*euph: gestehen, aussagen*) to talk. **jdn zum R~ bringen** to get sb to talk, to make sb talk; **er will nicht ~** he won't talk.
2 *vt* **(a)** to talk; **Worte** to say. **einige Worte ~** to say a few words; **kein Wort ~** not to say *or* speak a word; **sich** (*dat*) **etw von der Seele** *or* **vom Herzen ~** to get sth off one's chest; **jdm/einer Sache das Wort ~** to speak (out) in favour of sb/sth.
(b) (*klatschen*) to say. **es kann dir doch nicht egal sein, was über dich geredet wird** it must matter to you what people say about you; **Schlechtes von jdm** *or* **über jdn ~** to say bad things about sb; **damit die Leute wieder was zu ~ haben** so that people have something to talk about again.
3 *vr* **sich heiser ~** to talk oneself hoarse; **sich in Zorn** *or* **Wut ~** to talk oneself into a fury;

Redens|art *f* (*Phrase*) hackneyed expression, cliché; (*Redewendung*) expression, idiom; (*Sprichwort*) saying; (*leere Versprechung*) empty promise. **das ist nur so eine ~** it's just a way of speaking; **bloße ~en** empty talk; **jdn mit ~en besoffen machen** (*sl*) to overwhelm sb with fine-sounding phrases.

Rederei *f* **(a)** (*Geschwätz*) chattering *no pl*, talking *no pl*. **du mit deiner ~, du bist doch zu feige dazu** you're all talk, you're too scared to do it. **(b)** (*Klatsch*) gossip *no pl*, talk *no pl*. **zu ~en Anlaß geben** to make people talk, to give rise to gossip.

Rede-: **~schwall** *m* torrent *or* flood of words; **~schwulst** *m* bombastic verbiage; **ein ~schwulst** a stream of bombastic verbiage; **~strom** *m* flow of words; **~verbot** *nt* ban on speaking; **jdm ~verbot erteilen** to ban sb from speaking; (*allgemeines*) **~verbot** no talking!; **~weise** *f* style *or* manner (of speaking); **~wendung** *f* idiom, idiomatic expression.

redigieren* *vt* to edit.

redlich *adj* honest. **~ denken** to be honest; **~ handeln** to be honest, to act honestly; **er meint es ~** he is being honest; **sich** (*dat*) **etw ~ verdienen haben** to have really *or* genuinely earned sth; **Geld, Gut** to have acquired sth by honest means; **~ (mit jdm) teilen** to share (things) equally (with sb); **sich ~ durchs Leben schlagen** to make an honest living.

Redlichkeit *f* honesty.

Redner(in *f*) *m* -s, - speaker; (*Rhetoriker*) orator. **ich bin kein (großer) ~ aber ...** unaccustomed as I am to public speaking ...

Redner-: **~bühne** *f* platform, rostrum; **~gabe** *f* gift of oratory.

rednerisch *adj* rhetorical, oratorical. **~e Begabung** talent for public speaking; **~ begabt sein** to be a gifted speaker.

Rednerpult *nt* lectern.

Redoute [re'duːtə, rə-] *f* -, -n **(a)** (*old Mil*) redoubt. **(b)** (*old: Festball*) grand ball.

redselig *adj* talkative.

Redseligkeit *f* talkativeness.

Reduktion *f* **(a)** (*Einschränkung*) diminution; (*von Preisen, Ausgaben, Verbrauch*) reduction (*gen* in). **(b)** (*Zurückführung*) reduction (*auf +acc* to). **(c)** (*Chem*) reduction.

Reduktions-: **~mittel** *nt* (*Chem*) reducing agent; **~ofen** *m* (*Metal*) reducing furnace.

redundant *adj* redundant. **er drückt sich ~ aus** a lot of what he says is redundant.

Redundanz *f* redundancy, redundance *no pl*.

Reduplikation *f* reduplication.

reduplizieren* *vt* to reduplicate.

reduzierbar, reduzibel *adj* reducible (*auf +acc* to).

reduzieren* 1 *vt* **(a)** (*einschränken*) to reduce. **(b)** (*zurück-führen*) to reduce (*auf +acc* to). **(c)** (*Chem*) to reduce. **2** *vr* to decrease, to diminish.

Reduzierung *f siehe* **Reduktion**.

Reede *f* -, -n (*Naut*) roads *pl*, roadstead. **auf der ~ liegen** to be (lying) in the roads.

Reeder *m* -s, - ship owner.

Reederei *f* shipping company.

Reedereiflagge *f* house flag.

reell *adj* **(a)** (*ehrlich*) honest, straight, on the level (*inf*); (*Comm*) **Geschäft, Firma** solid, sound; **Preis** realistic, fair; **Bedienung** good. **das ist etwas R~es!** it's the real thing. **(b)** (*wirklich, echt*) real. **(c)** (*Math*) **Zahlen** real.

Reep *nt* -(e)s, -e (*N Ger*) rope.

Reet *nt* -s, *no pl* (*N Ger*) reed.

Reet-: **~dach** *nt* thatched roof; **r~gedeckt** *adj* thatched.

REFA-Fachmann, REFA-Mann ['reːfa-] (*inf*) *m* time and motion expert *or* man (*inf*), work-study man (*inf*).

Refaschisierung *f* fascist revival (*gen* in).

Refektorium *nt* (*Eccl*) refectory.

Referat *nt* **(a)** (*Univ*) seminar paper; (*Sch*) project. **ein ~ vortragen** *or* **halten** to give *or* read *or* present a seminar paper/to present a project. **(b)** (*Admin: Ressort*) department.

Referendar(in *f*) *m* trainee (in civil service); (*Studien~*) student teacher; (*Gerichts~*) articled clerk.

Referendarzeit *f* traineeship; (*Studien~*) teacher training; (*Gerichts~*) time under articles.

Referendum *nt* -s, **Referenden** *or* **Referenda** referendum.

Referent(in *f*) *m* (*Sachbearbeiter*) consultant, expert; (*Redner, Berichterstatter*) speaker; (*Univ: Gutachter*) examiner.

Referenz *f* reference. **jdn als ~ angeben** to give sb as a referee.

referieren* *vi* to (give a) report, to give a review (*über +acc* on).

Reff[1] *nt* -(e)s, -e (*Naut*) reef.

Reff[2] *nt* -(e)s, -e (*dial*) pannier, dosser (*rare*).

Reff[3] *nt* -(e)s, -e (*pej*) old hag *or* crow.

reffen *vt* (*Naut*) to reef.

Refinanzierung *f* financing of financing, rediscounting.

Reflektant *m* (*form*) (*Kauflustiger*) prospective purchaser; (*Stellungsbewerber*) applicant.

reflektieren* 1 *vt* to reflect. **2** *vi* **(a)** (*nachdenken*) to reflect, to ponder (*über* + *acc* (up)on). **(b)** (*streben nach*) **auf etw** (*acc*) ~ to be interested in sth. **(c)** (*Phys*) to reflect. **entblendete Rückspiegel** ~ **nicht tinted rear-view mirrors eliminate dazzle.**

Reflektor *m* reflector.

reflektorisch 1 *adj* **(a)** (*motorisch*) reflex. **(b)** (*geistig*) reflective. **2** *adv* by reflex action.

Reflex *m* **-es, -e (a)** (*Phys*) reflection. **(b)** (*Physiol*) reflex. **(c)** (*Sociol*) reflection.

Reflexbewegung *f* reflex action.

Reflexion *f* **(a)** (*Phys*) reflection. **(b)** (*Überlegung*) reflection. **über etw** (*acc*) ~**en anstellen** to reflect on sth.

Reflexionswinkel *m* (*Phys*) angle of reflection.

reflexiv *adj* (*Gram*) reflexive.

Reflexiv *nt* **-s, -e, Reflexivum** *nt* reflexive (pronoun/verb).

Reflexivpronomen *nt* reflexive pronoun.

Reform *f* **-, -en** reform.

Reformation *f* Reformation.

Reformations-: ~**fest** *nt* Reformation Day (*Oct 31st*); ~**zeitalter** *nt* age of the Reformation.

Reformator *m* Reformer.

reformatorisch *adj* reforming.

Reform-: **r**~**bedürftig** *adj* in need of reform; ~**bestrebungen** *pl* striving for *or* after reform; ~**bewegung** *f* reform movement; ~**eifer** *m* reforming zeal.

Reformer *m* **-s, -** reformer.

reformerisch *adj* reforming.

Reform-: **r**~**freudig** *adj* avid for reform; ~**gesetz** *nt* reform bill *or* law; ~**haus** *nt* health food shop.

reformieren* *vt* to reform.

reformiert *adj* (*Eccl*) Reformed.

Reformierte(r) *mf decl as adj* member of the Reformed Church.

Reformismus *m* (*Pol*) reformism.

Reformist *m* (*Pol*) reformist.

reformistisch *adj* (*Pol*) reformist.

Reform-: ~**kost** *f* health food; ~**kurs** *m* policy of reform; **einen** ~**kurs steuern** to follow a policy of reform; **auf** ~**kurs gehen** to embark on a policy of reform; ~**plan** *m* plan for reform.

Refrain [rə'frɛ̃ː, re-] *m* **-s, -s** (*Mus*) chorus, refrain.

refraktär *adj* (*Med, liter*) refractory.

Refraktion *f* (*Phys*) refraction.

Refraktor *m* (*Phys, Opt*) refractor.

Refrigerator *m* (*form*) refrigeration plant.

Refugium *nt* (*geh*) refuge.

Regal[1] *nt* **-s, -e (a)** (*Bord*) shelves *pl*; (*Typ*) stand. **(b)** (*Mus*) (*tragbare Orgel*) regal; (*Orgelteil*) vox humana.

Regal[2] *nt* **-s, -ien** [-iən] (*Jur*) regale (*spec*).

Regatta *f* **-, Regatten** regatta.

Regattastrecke *f* regatta course.

Reg. Bez. *abbr of* **Regierungsbezirk.**

rege *adj* **(a)** (*betriebsam*) active, busy; *Verkehr* busy; *Handel* flourishing; *Briefwechsel* lively. **ein** ~**s Treiben** a busy to-and-fro, a hustle and bustle; **auf dem Marktplatz herrschte ein** ~**s Treiben** the market place was bustling with activity *or* life; **Tendenz** ~ (*St Ex*) brisk activity; ~ **werden** to become active. **(b)** (*lebhaft*) lively; *Unterhaltung auch* animated; *Phantasie auch* vivid; *Interesse auch* avid. **ein** ~**r Geist** a lively soul; (*Verstand*) an active mind; **körperlich und geistig** ~ **sein** to be mentally and physically active, to be active in mind and body; **noch sehr** ~ **sein** to be very active still; **in ihm wurde die Hoffnung** ~ his hopes rose; **in ihm wurde der Gedanke** ~ **the** thought stirred within him; ~ **Beteiligung** lively participation; (*zahlreich*) good attendance *or* turnout. **(c)** (*zahlreich*) numerous; (*häufig*) frequent. ~**r Besuch** high attendance; **das Museum wurde nach der Eröffnung** ~ **besucht** when it opened the museum was very well visited.

Regel *f* **-, -n (a)** (*Vorschrift, Norm*) rule; (*Verordnung*) regulation. **die** ~**n der ärztlichen Kunst** the rules of the medical profession; **nach allen** ~**n der Kunst** (*fig*) thoroughly; **sie überredete ihn nach allen** ~**n der Kunst, ...** she used every trick in the book to persuade him ... **(b)** (*Gewohnheit*) habit, rule. **sich** (*dat*) **etw zur** ~ **machen** to make a habit *or* rule of sth; **in der** ~ as a rule; **zur** ~ **werden** to become a habit. **(c)** (*Monatsblutung*) period; (*Menstruation*) menstruation *no art.* **die** ~ **haben/bekommen** to have/get one's period, to menstruate; **sie hat mit zehn ihre** ~ **bekommen** her periods started when she was ten.

Regel-: **r**~**bar** *adj* (*steuerbar*) adjustable; (*klärbar*) easily arranged; ~**detri** *f* **-, *no pl* (*Math*) rule of three; ~**fall** *m* rule; **im** ~**fall as a rule;** **r**~**los** *adj* (*ungeregelt*) irregular; (*unordentlich*) disorderly, haphazard; *Leben* disorderly; **in r**~**loser Folge** at irregular intervals; **ein r**~**loses Durcheinander** a disorderly confusion; ~**losigkeit** *f* siehe **adj** irregularity; disorderliness, haphazardness; disorderliness; **r**~**mäßig** *adj* regular; *Lebensweise auch* well-ordered, orderly; **r**~**mäßig spazierengehen** to take regular walks; **r**~**mäßige Beschwerden** regularly recurring complaints; **er kommt r**~**mäßig zu spät** he's always late; ~**mäßigkeit** *f* regularity; **er kommt mit sturer** ~**mäßigkeit zu spät** he is persistently late.

regeln 1 *vt* **(a)** (*regulieren*) *Verkehr* to control; *Temperatur etc auch* to regulate; *siehe* **geregelt.** **(b)** (*erledigen*) to see to; (*endgültig*) to settle; *Problem etc* to sort out; (*in Ordnung bringen*) *Unstimmigkeiten* to settle, to resolve; *Finanzen* to put in order. **das läßt sich** ~ that can be arranged; **das werde ich schon** ~ I'll see to it. **(c)** (*festsetzen, einrichten*) to settle. **wir haben die Sache so geregelt ...** we have arranged things like this ...; **gesetzlich geregelt sein** to be laid down by law.

2 *vr* to sort itself out, to resolve itself.

Regel-: **r**~**recht** 1 *adj* real, proper; *Betrug, Erpressung, Beleidigung etc* downright; **er wollte einen r**~**rechten Prozeß** he wanted a full-blown trial; **das Spiel artete in eine r**~**rechte Schlägerei** the match degenerated into a regular brawl; **2** *adv* really; *unverschämt, beleidigend* downright; ~**studienzeit** *f* period of time within which a student must complete his studies; ~**technik** *f* control engineering; ~**techniker** *m* control engineer.

Regelung *f* **(a)** (*Regulierung*) regulation, control(ling). **(b)** (*Erledigung*) settling, settlement; (*von Unstimmigkeiten*) resolution. **ich habe die** ~ **meiner finanziellen Angelegenheiten meinem Bruder übertragen** I have entrusted my brother with the management of my financial affairs; **die** ~ **der Unterhaltszahlung liegt beim Gericht** the court settles *or* determines maintenance payments; **ich werde für die** ~ **dieser Angelegenheit sorgen** I shall see to this matter. **(c)** (*Abmachung*) arrangement; (*Bestimmung*) ruling. **wir haben eine** ~ **gefunden** we have come to an arrangement.

Regelungstechnik *f* control engineering.

Regel-: **r**~**widrig** *adj* against the rules; (*gegen Verordnungen verstoßend*) against the regulations; **r**~**widriges Verhalten im** Verkehr breaking the traffic regulations; **r**~**widrige Transaktion** irregular transaction; **ein r**~**widriger Einwurf/Elfmeter** a foul throw-in/an improperly taken penalty; ~**widrigkeit** *f* irregularity; (*Verstoß auch*) breach of the rules; (*Verstoß gegen Verordnungen auch*) breach of regulations.

regen 1 *vt* (*bewegen*) to move. **keinen Finger (mehr)** ~ (*fig*) not to lift a finger (any more).

2 *vr* (*Mensch, Glied, Baum etc*) to move, to stir; (*Gefühl, Gewissen, Zweifel, Wind etc*) to stir. **unter den Zuhörern regte sich Widerspruch** there were mutterings of disapproval from the audience; **kein Lüftchen regt sich** (*poet*) not a breeze stirs the air; **reg dich!** look lively!; **sich nicht/kaum** ~ **können** not/hardly to be able to move; (*fig*) not to have enough/to have just enough to keep body and soul together; **sich** ~ **bringt Segen** (*Prov*) hard work brings its own reward.

Regen *m* **-s, -** rain; (*fig: von Schimpfwörtern, Blumen etc*) shower. **in den** ~ **kommen** to be caught in the rain; **es gibt bald** ~ it's going to rain soon; **so ein** ~! what *or* some rain!; **in/bei strömendem** ~ in the pouring rain; **ein warmer** ~ (*fig*) a windfall; **jdn im** ~ **stehenlassen** (*fig*) to leave sb out in the cold; **vom** ~ **in die Traufe kommen** (*prov*) to fall out of the frying-pan into the fire (*prov*).

Regen-: **r**~**arm** *adj* dry, rainless; ~**bö** *f* rainy squall.

Regenbogen *m* rainbow.

Regenbogen-: ~**farben** *pl* colours *pl* of the rainbow; **in allen** ~**farben schillern** to shine like shot silk, to iridesce (*liter*); **r**~**farbig, r**~**farben** *adj* rainbow-coloured; ~**haut** *f* (*Anat*) iris; ~**hautentzündung** *f* iritis (*spec*), inflammation of the iris; ~**presse** *f* trashy *or* pulp magazines *pl*; ~**trikot** *nt* (*Sport*) multi-coloured jersey.

Regen-: ~**dach** *nt* canopy; (*hum:* ~**schirm**) brolly (*Brit inf*), bumbershoot (*US inf*); **r**~**dicht** *adj* rainproof.

Regeneration *f* regeneration; (*fig auch*) revitalization.

regenerationsfähig *adj* capable of regeneration; (*fig auch*) capable of regenerating itself *or* of revitalization.

Regenerator *m* (*Tech*) regenerator.

regenerieren* 1 *vr* (*Biol*) to regenerate; (*fig*) to revitalize *or* regenerate oneself/itself; (*nach Anstrengung, Schock etc*) to recover. **2** *vt* (*Biol*) to regenerate; (*fig auch*) to revitalize.

Regenerierung *f* siehe **Regeneration.**

Regen-: ~**fall** *m usu pl* (fall of) rain; **ein** ~**fall** rain, a shower; **tropische** ~**fälle** tropical rains; ~**faß** *nt* water-butt, rain barrel; ~**flut** *f usu pl* torrential rain *usu sing*, torrent of rain; **r**~**frei** *adj* rainless; ~**guß** *m* downpour; ~**haut** ® *f* plastic mac (*Brit inf*) *or* raincoat; ~**hut** *m* waterproof hat, rainhat; ~**jahr** *nt* rainy year; ~**kleidung** *f* rainwear; ~**mantel** *m* raincoat, mac (*Brit inf*), mac(k)intosh (*esp Brit*); ~**pfeifer** *m* plover; **r**~**reich** *adj* rainy, wet; ~**rinne** *f siehe* **Dachrinne;** ~**schatten** *m* (*Geog*) rain shadow; ~**schauer** *m* shower (of rain); ~**schirm** *m* umbrella; *siehe gespannt*; **r**~**schwer** *adj* ~**schwere Wolken** black *or* rain clouds, clouds heavy with rain.

Regent(in *f***)** *m* sovereign, reigning monarch; (*Stellvertreter*) regent.

Regen-: ~**tag** *m* rainy day; ~**tonne** *f* water-butt, rain barrel; ~**tropfen** *m* raindrop.

Regentschaft *f* reign; (*Stellvertretung*) regency. **die** ~ **antreten** to ascend the throne; (*als Stellvertreter*) to become regent; **die** ~ **übernehmen** to take over as regent.

Regen-: ~**wald** *m* (*Geog*) rain forest; ~**wand** *f* wall *or* curtain of rain; ~**wasser** *nt* rainwater; ~**wetter** *nt* rainy weather, rain; **er macht ein Gesicht wie drei** *or* **sieben Tage** ~**wetter** (*inf*) he's got a face as long as a month of Sundays (*inf*); ~**wolke** *f* rain cloud; ~**wurm** *m* earthworm; ~**zeit** *f* rainy season, rains *pl*.

Regie [re'ʒiː] *f* **(a)** (*künstlerische Leitung*) direction; (*Theat, Rad, TV auch*) production (*Brit*). **die** ~ **bei etw haben** *or* **führen** to direct/produce sth; **die** ~ **bei diesem Film/dieser Sendung führte** *or* **hatte Heinz Krüger** this film/programme was directed/produced by Heinz Krüger; **unter der** ~ **von** directed/produced by; „ ~: **A.G. Meier"** "Producer/Director A.G. Meier". **(b)** (*Leitung, Verwaltung*) management. **etw in eigener** ~ **führen** to control sth directly *or* personally; **etw in eigene** ~ **nehmen** to take *or* assume direct *or* personal control of sth; **etw in eigener** ~ **tun** to do sth oneself. **(c)** (*Aus: staatliches Monopol*) state monopoly. **Tabak**~ state tobacco monopoly.

Regie- [re'ʒiː-]: ~**anweisung** *f* (stage) direction; ~**assistent** *m* assistant producer/director; ~**betrieb** *m* (*Admin*) state-owned factory; ~**fehler** m (fig) slip-up; ~**film** m sein erster ~film the first film he directed; ~**kosten** pl (Aus) administrative costs pl; ~**pult** nt (Rad) control desk or console.

regieren* 1 vi (herrschen) to rule; (Monarch auch, fig) to reign. der R~de Bürgermeister von Berlin the Mayor of West Berlin. 2 vt (beherrschen, lenken) Staat to rule (over), to govern; (Monarch auch) to reign over; Markt, Fahrzeug to control; (Gram) to govern.

Regierung f (a) (Kabinett) government. die ~ Wilson the Wilson government.
(b) (Herrschaft) government; (Zeitabschnitt) period of government; (nichtdemokratisch) rule; (von Monarch) reign; (Führung) leadership. an die ~ kommen to come to power; (durch Wahl auch) to come into or take office; jdn an die ~ bringen to put sb into power; (durch Wahl auch) to put sb into office; die ~ antreten to take power; (nach Wahl auch) ~ take office.

Regierungs-: ~**anhänger** m government supporter; ~**antritt** m taking of power; (nach Wahl auch) taking of office; bei ~**antritt** when the government took power/office; ~**bank** f government bench; ~**beamte(r)** m government official; ~**bezirk** m primary administrative division of a "Land", ≈ region (Brit), ≈ county (US); ~**bildung** f formation of a government; ~**blatt** nt (pej) pro-government newspaper; ~**chef** m head of a/the government; der belgische ~chef the head of the Belgian government; ~**direktor** m senior government official; ~**erklärung** f inaugural speech; (in GB) King's/Queen's Speech; r~**feindlich** adj anti-government no adv; sich r~**feindlich verhalten/äußern** to act/speak against the government; ~**form** f form or type of government; r~**freundlich** adj pro-government no adv; r~**fromm** adj (pej) toadying to the government (pej); ~**hauptstadt** f administrative capital; ~**kreise** pl government circles pl; ~**krise** f government(al) crisis; ~**partei** f ruling or governing party, party in power; ~**präsident** m chief administrator of a ~bezirk, ≈ chairman of the regional council (Brit), ≈ county manager (US); ~**präsidium** nt highest authority in a ~bezirk, ≈ regional council (Brit) or board (US); ~**rat** m senior civil servant; (Sw: Organ) legislature; ~**sitz** m seat of government; ~**sprecher** m government spokesman; ~**system** nt system of government, governmental system; ~**treu** adj loyal to the government; ~**umbildung** f cabinet reshuffle; ~**vorlage** f government bill; ~**wechsel** m change of government; ~**zeit** f reign; (von Monarch auch) reign; (von gewählter Regierung, Präsident) period or term of office.

Regime [re'ʒi:m] nt -s, -s (pej) regime.

Regime-: ~**anhänger** m supporter of the regime; ~**gegner** m opponent of the regime; ~**kritiker** m critic of the regime, dissident.

Regiment nt -(e)s, -e or (Einheit) -er (a) (old: Herrschaft) rule. das ~ führen (inf) to be the boss (inf), to give the orders; ein strenges or straffes ~ führen (inf) to be strict; (Vorgesetzter etc auch) to run a tight ship (inf); der Winter führt ein strenges ~ the winter is harsh and stern. (b) (Mil) regiment.

regimenterweise adj (in Regimentern) in regiments; (nach Regimentern) by regiment(s). die Soldaten wurden ~ in den Tod geschickt whole regiments were sent to their deaths.

Regiments- in cpds regimental; ~**kommandeur** m regimental commander.

Region f region; siehe schweben.

regional adj regional. ~ verschieden or unterschiedlich sein to vary from one region to another.

Regionalismus m regionalism.

Regional-: ~**liga** f regional league (lower leagues of professional clubs); ~**programm** nt (TV, Rad) regional station or (TV auch) channel; (Sendung) regional programme.

Regisseur(in f) [reʒɪ'søːɐ, -'søːrɪn] m director; (Theat, Rad, TV auch) producer (Brit).

Register nt -s, - (a) (amtliche Liste) register. ein ~ (über etw acc) führen to keep a register (of sth); etw ins ~ (eines Amtes etc) eintragen to register sth (with an office etc).
(b) (Stichwortverzeichnis) index.
(c) (Daumen~) thumb index.
(d) (Mus) register; (von Orgel auch) stop. alle ~ spielen lassen or ziehen (fig) to pull out all the stops; andere ~ ziehen (fig) to get tough.
(e) (fig inf) ein langes/altes ~ a tall/an old type (inf).

Register-: ~**tonne** f (Naut) register ton; ~**zug** m (Mus: bei Orgel) stop.

Registrator m (old) registrar.

Registratur f (a) (das Registrieren) registration. (b) (Büro) records office. (c) (Aktenschrank) filing cabinet. (d) (Mus: bei Orgel) stops pl.

Registrierballon m (Met) sounding balloon.

registrieren* vt (a) (eintragen, verzeichnen) to register; (zusammenzählen) to calculate. sie ist registriert she is a registered prostitute. (b) (inf: zur Kenntnis nehmen) to note. sie hat überhaupt nicht registriert, daß ich da war the fact that I wasn't there didn't register with her at all.

Registrier-: ~**kasse** f cash register; ~**stelle** f registration office.

Registrierung f registration.

Reglement [reglə'mãː] nt -s, -s (old) rules pl, conventions pl.

reglementarisch 1 adj regulation. 2 adv according to (the) regulations. etw ~ festlegen to make a regulation about sth.

reglementieren* vt to regulate; jdn to regiment.

Reglementierung f siehe vt regulation; regimentation.

reglement-: [reglə'mãː-]: ~**mäßig** adj (old) according to regulation(s); ~**widrig** adj (old) contrary to regulations.

Regler m -s, - regulator, control; (Elektromotor, Fern-

---

steuerung) control(ler); (von Benzinmotor) governor.

Reglette f (Typ) lead.

reglos adj motionless.

Reglung f siehe Regelung.

regnen vti impers to rain. es regnet in Strömen it's pouring (with rain); es regnet Glückwünsche/Proteste congratulations/protests are pouring in; es regnete Vorwürfe reproaches hailed down; es regnete Schimpfwörter the air was blue.

regnerisch adj rainy.

Regreß m -sses, -sse (a) (Philos) regress. (b) (Jur) recourse, redress. einen ~ auf jdn or an jdm nehmen to have recourse against sb.

Regreßanspruch m (Jur) claim for compensation.

Regression f regression, retrogression.

regressiv adj (Biol) regressive, retrogressive; (fig) retrograde, retrogressive. die Ausweitung verlief ~ the expansion dropped off.

Regreß-: ~**pflicht** f liability for compensation; r~**pflichtig** adj liable for compensation.

regsam adj active, alert, lively.

Regsamkeit f alertness, liveliness.

regulär adj (üblich) normal; (vorschriftsmäßig) proper, regular; Arbeitszeit normal, basic, regular. ~e Truppen regular troops, regulars; ~e Bankgeschäfte normal banking transactions; etw ~ kaufen/verkaufen (zum normalen Preis) to buy/sell sth at the normal price; (auf normale Weise) to buy/sell sth in the normal way.

Regulation f (Biol) regulation.

Regulations-: ~**störung** f (Biol) malfunction of a regulatory system; ~**system** nt (Biol) regulatory system.

regulativ adj regulatory, regulative. in etw (acc) ~ eingreifen to regulate sth.

Regulativ nt counterbalance (Med). als ~ wirken to have a regulating effect.

Regulator m wall clock.

regulierbar adj regul(at)able, adjustable.

regulieren* 1 vt (a) to regulate; (nachstellen auch) to adjust. (b) Rechnung, Forderung to settle. 2 vr to become more regular. sich von selbst ~ to be self-regulating.

Regulierhebel m (Tech) regulating lever.

Regulierung f regulation; (Nachstellung auch) adjustment.

Regung f (Bewegung) movement; (des Gefühls, des Gewissens, von Mitleid) stirring. ohne jede ~ without a flicker (of emotion); einer ~ des Herzens folgen (liter) to follow the dictates of one's heart (liter); zu keiner ~ fähig sein (fig) to be paralyzed; eine menschliche ~ verspüren (hum) to have to answer a call of nature (hum).

regungslos adj motionless.

Regungslosigkeit f motionlessness.

Reh nt -s, -e deer; (im Gegensatz zu Hirsch etc) roedeer. scheu wie ein ~ (as) timid as a fawn.

Rehabilitand m -en, -en person undergoing rehabilitation.

Rehabilitation f rehabilitation; (von Ruf, Ehre) vindication.

rehabilitieren* 1 vt to rehabilitate; Ruf, Ehre to vindicate. 2 vr to rehabilitate (form) or vindicate oneself.

Rehabilitierung f siehe **Rehabilitation**.

Reh-: ~**bock** m roebuck; ~**braten** m roast venison; r~**braun** adj russet; Augen hazel; ~**geiß** f doe (of the roedeer); ~**kalb**, ~**kitz** nt fawn or kid (of the roedeer); ~**keule** f (Cook) haunch of venison; ~**leder** nt deerskin; r~**ledern** adj deerskin.

Rehling m (Bot dial) chanterelle.

Reh-: ~**posten** m (Hunt: grober Schrot) buckshot; ~**rücken** m (Cook) saddle of venison; ~**wild** nt (Hunt) roedeer.

Reibach m -s, no pl (inf) killing (inf). einen ~ machen (inf) to make a killing (inf).

Reibe f -, -n (Cook) grater.

Reibeisen nt rasp; (Cook) grater; (fig: zänkisches Weib) shrew. rauh wie ein ~ (inf) like sandpaper.

Reibe-: ~**kuchen** m (Cook dial) ≈ potato waffle; ~**laut** m (Ling) fricative.

reiben pret **rieb**, ptp **gerieben** 1 vti (a) to rub. etw blank ~ to rub sth till it shines; etw or an etw (dat) ~ to rub sth; sich (dat) die Augen (vor Müdigkeit) ~ to rub one's eyes (because one is tired); sie rieb dem Kranken die Salbe in die Haut she rubbed the ointment into the patient's skin; jdm den Rücken ~ to rub sb's back; sich (dat) die Hände ~ to rub one's hands.
(b) (zerkleinern) to grate.
2 vr to rub oneself (an +dat on, against); (sich verletzen) to scrape oneself (an +dat on). die beiden haben sich ständig aneinander gerieben those two were constantly rubbing each other up the wrong way; ich würde mich ständig an ihm ~ there would always be friction between him and me; sich an etw (dat) wund ~ to scrape oneself raw on sth; ich habe mich beim Radfahren wund gerieben I got chafed cycling.

Reiberei f usu pl (inf) friction no pl. (kleinere) ~en (short) periods of friction; ihre ständigen ~en the constant friction between them.

Reibfläche f (für Streichholz) striking surface; (von Reibe) scraping surface.

Reibung f (a) (das Reiben) rubbing; (Phys) friction. (b) (fig) friction no pl. es kommt zu ~en friction occurs.

Reibungs-: ~**elektrizität** f frictional electricity; ~**fläche** f (fig) source of friction; (viele) ~**flächen bieten** to be a potential cause of friction; r~**los** adj frictionless; (fig inf) trouble-free; r~**los verlaufen** to go off smoothly or without a hitch; ~**verlust** m friction(al) loss; ~**wärme** f (Phys) frictional heat; ~**widerstand** m (Phys) frictional resistance.

Reich nt -(e)s, -e (a) (Herrschaft(sgebiet), Imperium) empire; (König~) realm, kingdom. das ~ der aufgehenden Sonne (liter) the land of the rising sun; das Deutsche ~ the German Reich; (bis 1919 auch) the German Empire; das Dritte ~ the Third Reich; das himmlische ~ (liter) the Kingdom of Heaven, the Heavenly Kingdom; das ~ Gottes the Kingdom of God.

(b) (Bereich, Gebiet) realm. das ~ der Tiere/Pflanzen the animal/vegetable kingdom; das ~ der Natur the world or realm of nature; das ist mein ~ (fig) that is my domain; da bin ich in meinem ~ that's where I'm in my element.

reich adj **(a)** (vermögend, wohlhabend) rich, wealthy; Erbschaft substantial; Partie, Heirat good. ~ heiraten (inf) to marry (into) money.

(b) (kostbar) costly no adv, rich; Schmuck costly no adv, expensive. ~ geschmückt richly decorated; Mensch richly adorned; ein ~ ausgestattetes Haus a richly or lavishly furnished house; eine ~ ausgestattete Bibliothek a well stocked library; ~ mit Vorräten ausgestattet well or amply stocked up with supplies.

(c) (ergiebig, üppig) rich, copious; Ernte auch bountiful, abundant; Mahl sumptuous, lavish. jdn ~ belohnen to reward sb well, to give sb a rich reward; damit bin ich ~ belohnt (fig) I am richly or amply rewarded; jdn ~ beschenken to shower sb with presents; eine mit Kindern ~ beschenkte Familie a family blessed with many children; ~ an etw (dat) sein to be rich in sth; ~ an Fischen/Wild/Steinen abounding with or full of fish/game/stones; er ist ~ an Erfahrungen/guten Einfällen he has had a wealth of experiences/he is full of good ideas.

(d) (groß, vielfältig) large, copious; Auswahl wide, large; Erfahrungen, Kenntnisse wide; Blattwerk, Vegetation rich, luxuriant. die ~en Eindrücke the wealth of impressions; eine ~e Fülle a rich abundance; in ~em Maße vorhanden sein to abound, to be found in large quantities; ~ illustriert richly or copiously illustrated.

reichbegütert adj wealthy, affluent.

reichen 1 vi **(a)** (sich erstrecken) to stretch, to extend (bis zu to), to reach (bis zu etw sth); (Stimme) to carry (bis zu to), to reach (bis zu jdm/etw sb/sth); (Kleidungsstück) to reach (bis zu etw sth). sein Swimmingpool reicht bis an mein Grundstück his swimming pool comes right up to my land; der Garten reicht bis ans Ufer the garden stretches or extends or goes right down to the riverbank; das Wasser reicht mir bis zum Hals the water comes up to my neck; wenn das Wasser bis zur 5 m Marke reicht if the water comes up to or reaches the 5m mark; jdm bis zur Schulter ~ to come up to sb's shoulder; er reicht mit dem Kopf bis zur Decke his head reaches or touches the ceiling; so weit der Himmel reicht in the whole sky; so weit ~ meine Beziehungen/Fähigkeiten nicht my connections are not that extensive/my skills are not that wide-ranging; ... aber sein Arm reichte nicht so weit ... but his arm wouldn't reach that far; so weit das Auge reicht as far as the eye can see.

(b) (langen) to be enough, to suffice (form); (zeitlich auch) to last. der Saal reicht nicht für so viele Leute the room isn't big enough or won't suffice (form) for so many people; der Zucker reicht nicht there won't be enough sugar; reicht mein Geld noch bis zum Monatsende? will my money last until the end of the month?; reicht das Licht zum Lesen? is there enough light to read by?; reicht die Butter für einen Kuchen? is there enough butter for a cake?; dazu reicht meine Geduld/~ meine Fähigkeiten nicht I haven't got enough patience/I'm not skilled enough for that; das muß für vier Leute ~ that will have to be enough or suffice (form) or do (inf) for four people; das sollte eigentlich ~ that should be enough, that should do (inf); mir reicht's (inf) (habe die Nase voll) I've had enough (inf); (habe genug gehabt) that's enough for me; als das dann noch passierte, reichte es ihm when that happened it was just too much for him; jetzt reicht's (mir aber)! that's the last straw!; (Schluß) that's enough!; das reicht ja, um den Geduldigsten aus der Fassung zu bringen! it's enough to try the patience of a saint!; es reichte ja schon, daß er frech war it was bad enough that he was cheeky, his being cheeky was bad enough.

(c) (inf) mit dem Essen/der Zeit etc ~ to have enough food/time etc.

2 vt (entgegenhalten) to hand; (geben auch) to give; (herüber-, hinüber- auch) to pass (over); (anbieten) to serve; (Eccl) Abendmahl to give, to administer. jdm etw ~ to hand/give/pass sth to sb, to hand/give/pass sth to sb; sie reichte mir die Wange zum Kuß she proffered her cheek for a kiss; jdm die Hand ~ to hold out one's hand (to sb); sich die Hände ~ to join hands; (zur Begrüßung) to shake hands; es wurden Erfrischungen gereicht refreshments were served; siehe Hand.

Reiche(r) mf decl as adj rich or wealthy man/woman etc. die ~n the rich or wealthy.

Reich-: r~geschmückt adj attr richly adorned; Gegenstand auch richly decorated; r~haltig adj extensive; Auswahl auch wide, large; Essen rich; Informationen comprehensive; Programm varied; ~haltigkeit f siehe adj extensiveness; wideness; richness; comprehensiveness; variety; die ~haltigkeit der Auswahl the range of choice.

reichlich 1 adj **(a)** (sehr viel, groß) ample, large, substantial; Vorrat auch plentiful; Portion, Trinkgeld auch generous; Geschenke numerous.

(b) (mehr als genügend) Zeit, Geld, Platz ample, plenty of; Belohnung ample.

(c) (inf: mindestens) good. eine ~e Stunde a good hour.

2 adv **(a)** (sehr viel) belohnen, sich eindecken amply; verdienen richly. jdn ~ beschenken to give sb lots of or numerous presents; ~ Trinkgeld geben to tip generously.

(b) (mehr als genügend) ~ Zeit/Geld haben to have plenty of or ample time/money; ~ vorhanden sein to abound, to exist in plenty; mehr als ~ belohnt/bezahlt more than amply rewarded/paid more than enough; der Mantel ist ~ ausgefallen the coat is

on the big side; das war ~ gewogen/abgemessen that was very generously weighed out/measured out; das ist ~ gerechnet that's a generous estimate.

(c) (inf: mindestens) ~ 1.000 Mark a good 1,000 marks.

(d) (inf: ziemlich) pretty.

Reichs-: ~abt m (Hist) abbot of an abbey under imperial protection; ~acht f (Hist) outlawry in the Emperor's name; ~adler m (Her, Hist) imperial eagle; ~apfel m (Her, Hist) imperial orb; ~bahn f state railway; (DDR) East German State Railways; ~bann m (Hist) siehe ~acht; ~gebiet nt prewar Germany; im ~gebiet inside Germany's prewar boundaries; ~gericht nt (Hist) German supreme court (until 1945); ~grenze f border of the empire; prewar German border; ~gründung f foundation of the Reich or Prussian Empire; ~hauptstadt f (1933-45) capital of the Reich; (vor 1933) imperial capital; ~insignien pl (Hist) imperial regalia pl; ~kanzler m (bis 1918) Imperial Chancellor; (1918-34) German Chancellor; ~kleinodien pl (Hist) imperial regalia pl; ~konkordat nt Reich Concordat; ~mark f reichsmark, (old) German mark; ~präsident m German president (until 1934); ~regierung f German government (until 1945); ~stadt f (Hist) free city (of the Holy Roman Empire); freie ~stadt free city; ~stände pl (Hist) estates of the Empire pl; ~tag m Parliament; (in Deutschland 1871-1945) Reichstag; (in Deutschland vor 1871, in Japan) Imperial Diet; ~tagsbrand m burning of the Reichstag; r~unmittelbar adj (Hist) self-governing under the Kaiser; ~vogt m (Hist) protector; ~wehr f German army (1921-35).

Reichtum m **(a)** wealth no pl, richness no pl; (Besitz) riches pl. zu ~ kommen to become rich, to make one's fortune; ~er erwerben to gain riches; die ~er der Erde/des Meeres the riches of the earth/sea; der innere or seelische ~ richness of spirit; damit kann man keine ~er gewinnen you won't get rich that way.

(b) (fig: Fülle, Reichhaltigkeit) wealth, abundance (an + dat of). der ~ an Fischen the abundance of fish.

reichverziert adj attr richly ornamented.

Reichweite f (von Geschoß, Sender) range; (greifbare Nähe) reach; (fig: Einflußbereich) scope. in ~ within range/the reach (gen of); jd ist in ~ sb is nearby or around; außer ~ out of range/reach (gen of); innerhalb der ~ + gen within range/the scope of; außerhalb der ~ + gen outside the range of/beyond the scope of.

Reif[1] m -(e)s, no pl siehe **Rauhreif**.

Reif[2] m -(e)s, -e (old, liter) (Stirn~, Diadem) circlet; (Arm~) bangle; (Fingerring) ring; (im Rock) hoop.

reif adj **(a)** (voll entwickelt) Früchte, Getreide ripe; Mensch, Ei mature. der Pickel/das Geschwür ist ~ (inf) the spot/abscess has come to a head; er brauchte nur noch die ~e Frucht zu pflücken (fig liter) it was all his for the taking.

(b) (erfahren, älter) mature. in ~(er)em Alter, in den ~eren Jahren in one's mature(r) years; die ~ere Jugend those of mellower years; im ~eren Alter von ... at the ripe old age of ...

(c) (vorbereitet) ready, ripe; (durchdacht) Urteil, Arbeit, Gedanken mature. ~ zur Veröffentlichung ready or ripe for publication; die Zeit ist ~/noch nicht ~ the time is ripe/not yet ripe; eine ~e Leistung (inf) a brilliant achievement.

(d) für etw ~ sein (inf) to be ready for sth; ~ sein (sl) to be in for it (inf) or for the high jump (inf).

Reife f -, no pl **(a)** (das Reifen) ripening.

(b) (das Reifsein) ripeness; (Geschlechts~, von Ei) maturity. zur ~ kommen to ripen; (geh: Mädchen) to come to or reach maturity; zur ~ bringen to ripen.

(c) (fig: von Menschen, Gedanken etc) maturity. ihm fehlt die (sittliche) ~ he lacks maturity, he's too immature.

(d) mittlere ~ (Sch) first public examination in secondary school, ≈ O-Levels pl (Brit); Zeugnis der ~ (form) siehe **Reifezeugnis**.

Reifegrad m degree of ripeness.

reifen[1] vi impers es reift there has been/will be a frost.

reifen[2] 1 vt Obst to ripen; jdn to mature. das hat ihn zum Manne gereift (liter) that made a man out of him; siehe gereift.

2 vi aux sein **(a)** (Obst) to ripen; (Mensch, Ei) to mature. er reifte zum Manne he became a man.

(b) (fig: Plan, Entscheidung) to mature. zur Wirklichkeit ~ to come to fruition, to become reality; zur Gewißheit ~ to harden into certainty.

Reifen m -s, - tyre; (Spiel~, von Faß, von Rock) hoop; (Arm~) bangle. (den) ~ treiben/spielen to bowl a hoop.

Reifen-: ~defekt m, ~panne f puncture, flat; (geplatzt auch) blowout; ~profil nt tyre tread; ~schaden m **(a)** faulty tyre; **(b)** siehe ~panne; ~spiel nt bowling a hoop; ~wechsel m tyre-change.

Reife-: ~prüfung f (Sch) siehe Abitur; ~zeit f ripening time; (von Ei) period of incubation; (Pubertät) puberty no def art; ~zeugnis nt (Sch) "Abitur" certificate, ≈ A-Level certificate (Brit), high-school graduation certificate (US).

reiflich adj thorough, careful. nach ~er Überlegung after careful consideration, upon mature reflection (liter); sich (dat) etw ~ überlegen to consider sth carefully.

Reif-: ~rock m (Hist) farthingale, hoop skirt; ~spiel nt bowling a hoop.

Reifung f ripening; (von Ei) maturing, maturation.

Reifungsprozeß m process of ripening; (von Ei) maturation process.

Reigen m -s, - round dance, roundel(ay) (old); (fig geh) round. den ~ eröffnen or anführen (fig geh) to lead off; den ~ beschließen (fig geh) to bring up the rear.

Reihe f -, -n **(a)** (geregelte Anordnung) row, line; (Sitz~, beim Stricken) row; (fig: von Beispielen, Reden) series sing. in ~n antreten to line up; (Mil) to fall in; in ~n zu (je) drei antreten/

marschieren to line up/march in rows of three *or* in threes; **sich in einer ~ aufstellen** to line up, to form a row *or* line; **sich in die/eine ~ stellen** to join the row *or* line/to line up; (*Mil*) to fall in; **in einer ~ stehen** to stand in a row *or* line; **in Reih und Glied antreten** to line up in formation; **sie standen in Reih und Glied vor dem Lehrer** they stood lined up in front of their teacher; **aus der ~ tanzen** (*fig inf*) to be different; (*gegen Konventionen verstoßen*) to step out of line; **die ~ herumgehen** (*Gegenstand*) to be passed around, to go the rounds; **die ~n schließen** (*Mil*) to close ranks; **die ~n lichten sich** (*fig*) the ranks are thinning; **in den eigenen ~n** within our/their *etc* own ranks; **die ~ eröffnen** (*fig*) to start off; **in einer ~ mit jdm stehen** (*fig*) to be on a par with sb; **sich in eine ~ mit jdm stellen** (*fig*) to put oneself on a par *or* on an equal footing with sb.

(b) (*Reihenfolge*) **er ist an der ~** it's his turn, he's next; (*beim Spiel etc auch*) it's his go; **die ~ ist an jdm** it's sb's turn; **er kommt an die ~** he's next, it's his turn *or* him (*inf*) next; **warte, bis du an die ~ kommst** wait till it's your turn/go; **er kommt immer außer der ~** he always comes just when he pleases; **der ~ nach, nach der ~** in order, in turn; **sie sollen der ~ nach hereinkommen** they are to come in one by one *or* one at a time; **erzähl mal der ~ nach, wie alles war** tell us how it was in the order it all happened; **außer der ~** out of order; (*bei Spielen auch*) out of turn; (*zusätzlich, nicht wie gewöhnlich*) out of the usual way of things; **ich genehmige mir auch mal außer der ~ eine Havanna** I sometimes smoke a Havana at times when I wouldn't normally; **wenn ich das Auto mal außer der ~ brauche** if I should happen to need the car at a time when I don't normally have it; **es kommt ganz selten vor, daß ich mal außer der ~ da bin** it's very rare for me to be there out of my routine.

(c) (*Serie, Math, Mus*) series *sing*; (*Biol: Ordnung*) order.
(d) (*unbestimmte Anzahl*) number. **in die ~ der Mitgliedsstaaten eintreten** to join the ranks of the member states; **in der ~ der Stars** amongst the ranks of the stars; **eine ganze ~ (von)** a whole lot (of); **eine ganze ~ von Beispielen** a whole string of examples.

(e) (*inf: Ordnung*) **aus der ~ kommen** (*in Unordnung geraten*) to get out of order; (*verwirrt werden*) to lose one's equilibrium; (*gesundheitlich*) to fall ill; **wieder in die ~ kommen** to get one's equilibrium back; (*gesundheitlich*) to get back on form; **nicht in der ~ sein** not to be well *or* one hundred per cent (*inf*); **in die ~ bringen** to put in order, to put straight.
reihen 1 *vt* **(a)** **Perlen auf eine Schnur ~** to string beads (on a thread); **sie reihte die Pilzstücke auf einen Faden** she strung the pieces of mushroom up (on a thread).
(b) (*Sew*) to tack.
2 *vr* **etw reiht sich an etw** (*acc*) sth follows (after) sth; **eine Enttäuschung reihte sich an die andere** let-down followed letdown.
Reihen *m* -s, - (*S Ger*) instep.
Reihen-: ~dorf *nt* village built along a road, ribbon development (*spec*); **~fabrikation, ~fertigung** *f* serial production.
Reihenfolge *f* order; (*notwendige Aufeinanderfolge*) sequence. **der ~ nach** in order; **in zwangloser ~** in no particular *or* special order; **alphabetische/zeitliche ~** alphabetical/chronological order.
Reihen-: ~haus *nt* terraced house; **~(haus)siedlung** *f* estate of terraced houses; **~schaltung** *f* (*Elec*) series connection; **in ~schaltung** in series; **~untersuchung** *f* mass screening; **r~weise** *adv* **(a)** (*in Reihen*) in rows; **(b)** (*fig: in großer Anzahl*) by the dozen; **sie sind r~weise ohnmächtig geworden** they fainted by the dozen, dozens of them fainted; **~zahl** *f* (*Math*) member of a series.
Reiher *m* -s, - heron. **kotzen wie ein ~** (*sl*) to spew *or* puke one's guts up (*sl*).
Reiher-: ~beize *f* heron hawking; **~busch** *m* (*old*) aigrette, egret; **~feder** *f* heron's feather; (*als Hutschmuck*) aigrette; **~horst** *m* heron's nest.
reihern *vi* (*sl*) to puke (up) (*sl*), to spew up (*sl*).
Reiherschnabel *m* (*Bot*) common stork's-bill.
Reihgarn *nt* tacking thread.
-reihig *adj suf* -rowed. **zwei~e Jacke** double-breasted jacket.
reihum *adv* round. **es geht ~** everybody takes their turn; **etw ~ gehen lassen** to pass sth round.
Reim *m* -(e)s, -e rhyme. **im ~ mit etw stehen** to rhyme with sth; **ein ~ auf „Hut" ein** a rhyme for "hat"; **~e bilden** *or* **machen** *or* **drechseln** (*hum*) *or* **schmieden** (*hum*) to make *or* write rhymes, to versify (*hum*); **etw in ~e bringen** to make sth rhyme; **sich** (*dat*) **einen ~ auf etw** (*acc*) **machen** (*inf*) to make sense of sth; **ich mache mir so meinen ~ darauf** (*inf*) I can put two and two together (*inf*), I think I can see what's going on; **ich kann mir keinen ~ darauf machen** (*inf*) I can't make head (n)or tail of it, I can see no rhyme (n)or reason in it.
Reimart *f* type of rhyme.
reimen 1 *vt* to rhyme (*auf* + *acc*, *mit* with). **ich kann das Wort nicht ~** I can't find a rhyme for this word *or* anything to rhyme with this word. **2** *vi* to make up rhymes, to rhyme (*liter*), to versify (*hum*). **3** *vr* to rhyme (*auf* + *acc*, *mit* with). **das reimt sich nicht** (*fig*) it doesn't hang together *or* make sense.
Reimer *m* -s, - (*pej*) rhymester, versifier.
Reimerei *f* **(a)** (*das Reimen*) versifying. **(b)** (*Gedicht*) doggerel *no pl*. **eine ~** a piece of doggerel.
Reim-: ~lexikon *nt* rhyming dictionary; **r~los** *adj* unrhymed, non-rhyming; **~paar** *nt* rhyming couplet.
Reimport *m* (*Fin, Comm*) reimportation.
Reim-: ~schema *nt* rhyming pattern, rhyme scheme; **~schmied** *m* (*hum*) rhymester, versifier; **~sucht** *f* rhyming mania; **~wort** *nt*, *pl* **~worte** rhyme; **ein ~wort zu etw sein** to rhyme with sth; **ein ~wort zu etw finden** to find a rhyme for sth *or* a word to rhyme with sth.

rein¹ *adv* (*inf*) = **herein, hinein**.
rein² **1** *adj* **(a)** pure; (*absolut, völlig auch*) sheer; **Wahrheit** plain, straight, unvarnished; **Gewinn** clear. **das ist die ~ste Freude/der ~ste Hohn** *etc* it's pure *or* sheer joy/mockery *etc*; **er ist der ~ste Künstler/Akrobat** he's a real artist/acrobat; **das Kind ist der ~ste Vater** (*dial*) the child is just like his father; **er ist die ~ste Bestie** he's an absolute *or* downright brute; **mit ihren Kindern hat sie nicht immer die ~ste Freude** she doesn't find her children exactly an unmixed blessing; **die ~e Arbeit kostet ...** the work alone costs ...; **er ist ein Demokrat ~sten Wassers** *or* **von ~stem Wasser** he is the archetypal *or* a pure democrat; **jdm ~en Wein einschenken** (*fig*) to give it to sb straight (from the shoulder); **eine ~e Jungenklasse** an all boys' class; **eine ~e Industriestadt** a purely industrial town.
(b) (*sauber*) clean; **Haut, Teint** clear, pure. **etw ~ machen** to clean sth; **~ Schiff!** (*Naut*) = swab the decks!; **~ klingen** to make a pure sound; **~ singen** to have a pure voice; **~en Tisch machen** (*fig*) to get things straight, to sort things out; **ich habe ~e Hände** (*fig*) my hands are clean; **die Hände ~ behalten** (*fig*) to keep one's nose clean (*inf*); **siehe Weste**.
(c) (*klar, übersichtlich*) **etw ins ~e schreiben** to write out a fair copy of sth, to write sth out neatly; **etw ins ~e bringen** to clear sth up; **die Sache ist ins ~e gekommen** things are cleared up, things have cleared themselves up; **mit sich selbst ins ~e kommen** to get things straight with oneself, to straighten *or* sort things out with oneself; **mit etw ins ~e kommen** to get straight about sth; **mit jdm/sich selbst im ~en sein** to have got things straightened *or* sorted out with sb/oneself; **mit etw im ~en sein** to have got sth straightened *or* sorted out; **mit seinem Gewissen im ~en sein** to have a clear conscience; **er ist mit sich selbst nicht im ~en** he is at odds with himself.
(d) (*unschuldig*) pure; **Gewissen** clear. **er ist ~ von Schuld** (*old*) he is free of guilt; **dem R~en ist alles ~** (*prov*) to the pure all things are pure.
2 *adv* **(a)** (*ausschließlich*) purely. **~ hypothetisch gesprochen** speaking purely hypothetically.
(b) (*inf: ganz, völlig*) absolutely. **~ alles/unmöglich** absolutely everything/impossible; **~ gar nichts** absolutely nothing, sweet Fanny Adams (*sl*); **das ist ~ erfunden** it's all pure invention; **~ weg sein** (*dated sl*) to be sent (*inf*).
Rein(e) *f* -, -en (*S Ger, Aus: Cook*) = casserole.
Reineclaude [rɛnəˈkloːdə] *f* -, - *siehe* **Reneklode**.
Reineinnahme *f siehe* **Reinertrag**.
Reineke Fuchs *m* (*Liter*) Reynard the Fox.
Rein(e)machefrau *f* cleaner, cleaning lady.
Reinemachen *nt* -s, *no pl* (*inf*) cleaning.
Rein-: r~erbig *adj* (*Biol*) homozygous (*spec*); **~erlös, ~ertrag** *m* net profit(s) *or* proceeds *pl*.
Reinette [rɛˈnɛtə] *f siehe* **Renette**.
rein(e)weg *adv* (*inf*) completely, absolutely. **das ist ~ eine Frechheit/erlogen** it's a downright cheek/lie; **das ist ~ zum Verrücktwerden** it's enough to drive you absolutely mad.
Reinfall *m* (*inf*) disaster (*inf*); (*Pleite auch*) flop (*inf*). **mit der Waschmaschine/dem Kollegen haben wir einen ~ erlebt** the washing machine/this colleague was a real disaster.
reinfallen *vi sep irreg aux sein* (*inf*) *siehe* **hereinfallen, hineinfallen**.
Reinfektion *f* reinfection.
Reingeschmeckte(r) *mf decl as adj* (*S Ger*) outsider.
Rein-: ~gewicht *nt* net(t) weight; **~gewinn** *m* net(t) profit; **~haltung** *f* keeping clean; (*von Wasser auch, von Rasse*) keeping pure; **die ~haltung des Spielplatzes** keeping the playground clean.
Reinheit *f* purity; (*Sauberkeit*) cleanness; (*von Haut*) clearness.
Reinheits-: ~gebot *nt* beer/wine purity regulations *pl*; **~grad** *m* (*Chem*) (degree of) purity.
reinigen 1 *vt* **(a)** (*saubermachen, putzen*) to clean; (*chemisch auch*) to dry-clean. **etw chemisch ~** to dry-clean sth; **sich** (*dat*) **die Hände ~** to clean one's hands.
(b) (*säubern*) to purify; **Metall** to refine; **Blut** *auch* to cleanse. **ein ~des Gewitter** (*fig inf*) a row which clears/cleared the air.
(c) (*zensieren*) **Text** to clean up, to bowdlerize; **Sprache** to purify. **eine Sprache/einen Text von etw ~** to purify *or* purge a language/text of sth.
2 *vr* to clean itself; (*Mensch*) to cleanse oneself. **normalerweise kann ein Fluß sich von selbst ~** normally a river can cleanse itself *or* keep itself clean; **sich von einer Schuld/einem Verdacht ~** (*liter*) to cleanse oneself of a sin (*liter*)/to clear oneself of suspicion.
Reinigung *f* **(a)** (*das Saubermachen*) cleaning. **(b)** (*chemische ~*) (*Vorgang*) dry cleaning; (*Anstalt*) (dry) cleaner's. **(c)** (*das Säubern*) purification; (*von Metall*) refining; (*von Blut auch*) cleansing. **(d)** (*von Text*) cleaning up, bowdlerization; (*von Sprache*) purification. **(e)** (*Rel*) purification.
Reinigungs-: ~creme *f* cleansing cream; **~milch** *f* cleansing milk; **~mittel** *nt* cleansing agent.
Reinkarnation *f* reincarnation.
reinkriechen *vi sep irreg aux sein* (*fig sl*) **jdm hinten ~** to suck up to sb (*inf*).
reinkriegen *vt sep* (*inf*) to get in.
Reinkultur *f* (*Biol*) cultivation of pure cultures. **Kitsch/Faschismus** *etc* **in ~** (*inf*) pure unadulterated rubbish/fascism.
reinlegen *vt sep* (*inf*) *siehe* **hereinlegen, hineinlegen**.
reinleinen *adj* pure linen.
reinlich *adj* **(a)** (*sauberkeitsliebend*) cleanly. **(b)** (*ordentlich*) neat, tidy. **(c)** (*gründlich, klar*) clear.
Reinlichkeit *f siehe adj* **(a)** cleanliness. **(b)** neatness, tidiness. **(c)** clearness.

Rein-: ~**machefrau** f siehe **Rein(e)machefrau; r**~**rassig** adj of pure race, pure-blooded; Tier purebred, thoroughbred; ~**rassigkeit** f racial purity; (von Tier) pure breeding; **r**~**reiten** vt sep irreg **jdn** (ganz schön) **r**~**reiten** (inf) to get sb into a (right) mess (inf); ~**schiff** nt (Naut): ~**schiff machen** ≈ to swab the decks; ~**schrift** f writing out a fair copy no art; (Geschriebenes) fair copy; **etw/Notizen in** ~**schrift schreiben** to write out a fair copy of sth/to write up notes; **r**~**schriftlich** adj **r**~**schriftliches Exemplar** fair copy; **es wird nur das benotet, was r**~**schriftlich vorhanden ist** only that which has been written out properly or as a fair copy will be marked; **r**~**seiden** adj pure silk; ~**vermögen** nt net assets pl; **r**~**waschen** sep irreg **1** vt (von of) to clear; (von Sünden) to cleanse; **2** vr (fig) to clear oneself; (von Sünden) to cleanse oneself; ~**weg** adv siehe **rein(e)weg; r**~**wollen** adj pure wool; ~**zucht** f (von Tieren) inbreeding; (von Bakterien) cultivation of pure cultures.

Reis¹ nt -es, -er (old, liter) (Zweig) twig, sprig; (Pfropf~) scion.
Reis² m -es, -e rice. **Huhn auf** ~ chicken with rice.
Reis-: ~**auflauf** m rice pudding; ~**bau** m rice-growing no art, cultivation of rice; ~**besen** m siehe **Reisigbesen;** ~**branntwein** m siehe ~**schnaps;** ~**brei** m ≈ creamed rice; ~**bündel** nt siehe **Reisigbündel.**

Reise f -, -n journey, trip; (Schiffs~) voyage; (Space) voyage, journey; (Geschäfts~) trip. **seine** ~**n durch Europa** his travels through Europe; **eine** ~ **mit der Eisenbahn/dem Auto** a train/car journey, a journey by rail/car; **eine** ~ **zu Schiff** a sea voyage; (Kreuzfahrt) a cruise; **er plant eine** ~ **durch Afrika** he's planning to travel through Africa; **eine** ~ **machen** to go on a journey; **weite** ~**n mache ich lieber mit dem Auto** I prefer doing long journeys by car; **wir konnten die geplante** ~ **nicht machen** we couldn't go away as planned; **er hat in seinem Leben viele interessante** ~**n gemacht** he has travelled to a lot of interesting places in his lifetime; **wann machst du die nächste** ~? when are you off (on your travels) again?, when's the next trip?; **ich muß mal wieder eine** ~ **machen** I must go away again; **die** ~ **nach Afrika habe ich allein gemacht** I travelled to Africa by myself; **auf** ~**n sein** to be away (travelling); **er ist viel auf** ~**n** he does a lot of travelling; **jeden Sommer gehen wir auf** ~**n** we go away every summer; **wann gehen Sie auf die** ~? when do you go (away) on your trip?; **er geht viel auf** ~**n** he travels a lot; **jdn auf die** ~ **schicken** to see sb off on his/her journey; **wohin geht die** ~? where are you off to?; **die letzte** ~ **antreten** (euph liter) to enter upon one's last journey (liter); **glückliche** or **gute** ~! bon voyage!, have a good journey!; **wenn einer eine** ~ **tut, so kann er was erzählen** (prov) strange things happen when you're abroad.

Reise-: ~**andenken** nt souvenir; ~**apotheke** f first aid kit; ~**bedarf** m travel requisites pl; ~**begleiter** m travelling companion; (~leiter) courier; (für Kinder) chaperon; ~**bekanntschaft** f acquaintance made while travelling; ~**bericht** m report or account of one's journey; (Buch) travel story; (Film) travel film, travelogue; (in Tagebuch) holiday diary; ~**beschränkungen** pl travel restrictions pl; ~**beschreibung** f description of a journey/one's travels etc; traveller's tale, travel book or story/film; (Film) travelogue; ~**büro** nt travel agency; ~**bürokaufmann** m travel agent; ~**erleichterungen** pl easing of travel restrictions; ~**fabrik** f (pej) tour operator; **r**~**fertig** adj ready (to go or leave); **r**~**fertige Gäste warten bitte in der Hotelhalle** would guests who are ready to leave please wait in the hotel foyer; ~**fieber** nt (fig) travel nerves pl; ~**führer** m (Buch) guidebook; (Person) siehe ~**leiter;** ~**gefährte** m travelling companion; ~**geld** nt fare; ~**genehmigung** f travel permit; ~**gepäck** nt luggage, baggage (esp US, Aviat); ~**geschwindigkeit** f cruising speed; ~**gesellschaft** f (tourist) party; (im Bus auch) coach party; (inf: Veranstalter) tour operator; **eine japanische** ~**gesellschaft** a party of Japanese tourists; ~**gewerbe** nt **Leute im** ~**gewerbe** travelling salesmen; ~**koffer** m suitcase; ~**kosten** pl travelling expenses pl; ~**kostenvergütung** f payment or reimbursement of travelling expenses; **die Firma übernimmt volle** ~**kostenvergütung** the firm will pay all (your) travelling expenses; **100 Mark** ~**kostenvergütung** 100 marks (in respect of) travelling expenses; ~**krankheit** f travel sickness; ~**leiter** m courier; ~**leitung** f (das Leiten) organization of a/the tourist party; (~leiter) courier(s); **möchten Sie die** ~**leitung für eine Englandtour übernehmen?** would you like to take a party for a tour of England?; **wegen schlechter** ~**leitung** because of the poor way in which the party was run; ~**lektüre** f reading-matter (for a journey); **etw als** ~**lektüre mitnehmen** to take sth to read on the journey; ~**lust** f travel urge, wanderlust; **mich packt die** ~**lust** I've got itchy feet (inf) or the travel bug (inf); **r**~**lustig** adj fond of or keen on travel(ling), travel-mad (inf); ~**mitbringsel** nt souvenir.

reisen vi aux sein to travel. **in den Urlaub** ~ to go away on holiday; **in etw** (dat) ~ (Comm) to travel in sth; **viel gereist sein** to have travelled a lot, to be well-travelled.
Reisende(r) mf decl as adj (a) traveller; (Fahrgast) passenger; (Comm) (commercial) traveller, travelling salesman.
Reise-: ~**necessaire** nt (für Nagelpflege) travelling manicure set; (Nähzeug) travelling sewing kit; ~**onkel** m (hum inf) globetrotter (hum); ~**paß** m passport; ~**pläne** pl plans pl (for a/the journey); **meine Mutter schmiedet dauernd irgendwelche** ~**pläne** my mother is always planning some journey or trip or other; ~**prospekt** m travel brochure; ~**proviant** m food for the journey, provisions pl (usu hum).
Reiserbesen m siehe **Reisigbesen.**
Reiserei f (endless) travelling around.
Reise-: ~**route** f route, itinerary; ~**scheck** m traveller's cheque (Brit), traveler's check (US); ~**schilderung** f description of a journey/one's travels; (Buch) travel story; ~**schreibmaschine**

f portable typewriter; ~**spesen** pl travelling expenses pl; ~**stipendium** nt travelling scholarship; ~**tablette** f travel sickness pill; ~**tante** f (hum inf) globetrotter (hum); ~**tasche** f grip, travelling bag; ~**verkehr** m holiday traffic; ~**vorbereitungen** pl travel preparations pl, preparations for a/the journey; ~**wetter** nt travelling weather; ~**wetterbericht** m holiday weather forecast; ~**zeit** f time for travelling; **die beste** ~**zeit für Ägypten** the best time to go to Egypt; ~**ziel** nt destination.
Reis-: ~**feld** nt paddy-field; ~**holz** nt (old) siehe **Reisig.**
Reisig nt -s, no pl brushwood, twigs pl.
Reisig-: ~**besen** m besom; ~**bündel** nt bundle of twigs, faggot.
Reis-: ~**korn** nt grain of rice; ~**mehl** nt ground rice; ~**papier** nt (Art, Cook) rice paper.
Reißahle f scriber, scratch-awl.
Reißaus m: ~ **nehmen** (inf) to clear off (inf), to make oneself scarce (inf), to take to one's heels.
Reiß-: ~**blei** nt graphite; ~**brett** nt drawing-board; ~**brettstift** m siehe ~**zwecke.**
Reis-: ~**schleim** m rice water; ~**schnaps** m rice spirit.
reißen pret **riß,** ptp **gerissen 1** vt **(a)** (zer~) to tear, to rip. **ein Loch ins Kleid** ~ to tear or rip a hole in one's dress.
  (b) (ab~, ent~, herunter~, weg~) to tear, to pull, to rip (etw von etw sth off sth); (mit~, zerren) to pull, to drag. **jdn zu Boden** ~ to pull or drag sb to the ground; **jdn/etw in die Tiefe** ~ to pull or drag sb/sth down into the depths; **der Fluß hat die Brücke mit sich gerissen** the river swept the bridge away; **jdn aus der Gefahr** ~ to snatch sb from danger; **aus diesem Leben gerissen** snatched from this life; **jdn aus seinen Gedanken** ~ to interrupt sb's thoughts; (aufmuntern) to make sb snap out of it; **jdn aus dem Schlaf/seinen Träumen** ~ to wake sb from his sleep dreams; **etw aus dem Zusammenhang** ~ to take sth out of context; **in etw** (dat) **Lücken** ~ to make gaps in sth; **jdn ins Verderben** ~ to ruin sb; **hin und her gerissen werden/sein** (fig) to be torn.
  (c) **etw an sich** (acc) ~ to seize sth; Macht auch to usurp sth; Unterhaltung to monopolize sth; siehe **Nagel.**
  (d) (Sport) (Gewichtheben) to snatch; (Hochsprung, Pferderennen) to knock off or down.
  (e) (töten) to take, to kill.
  (f) (inf: machen) Witze to crack (inf); Possen to play.
  (g) (Aus sl) **jdm eine** ~ to clout sb (one) (inf); **einen Stern** ~ to fall; **damit kannst du nichts** ~ that's not going to impress anybody.
  (h) (Wunde beibringen) **sich** (dat) **eine Wunde an etw** (dat) ~ to cut oneself on sth; **sich** (dat) **etw blutig** ~ to tear sth open.
2 vi **(a)** aux sein (zer~) to tear, to rip; (Muskel) to tear; (Seil) to tear, to break, to snap; (Risse bekommen) to crack. **mir ist die Kette/der Faden gerissen** my chain/thread has broken or snapped; **da riß mir die Geduld** or **der Geduldsfaden** then my patience gave out or snapped; **es reißt mir in allen Gliedern** (inf) I'm aching all over; **wenn alle Stricke** or **Stränge** ~ (fig inf) if the worst comes to the worst, if all else fails.
  (b) (zerren) (an + dat at) to pull, to tug; (wütend) to tear.
  (c) (Sport) (Gewichtheben) to snatch; (Hochsprung, Pferderennen) to knock the bar off or down.
3 vr **(a)** (sich verletzen) to cut oneself (an + dat on).
  (b) (sich los~) to tear oneself/itself.
  (c) (inf) **um jdn/etw** ~ to scramble to get sb/sth.
Reißen nt -s, no pl (inf: Glieder~) ache.
reißend adj Fluß torrential, raging; Tier rapacious; Schmerzen searing; Verkauf, Absatz massive. ~**en Absatz finden** to sell like hot cakes (inf).
Reißer m -s, - (Theat, Film, Buch: inf) thriller; (inf: Ware) hot item (inf) or line (inf), big seller.
reißerisch adj sensational.
Reiß-: ~**feder** f (Art) (drawing) pen; **r**~**fest** adj tearproof; ~**festigkeit** f (tensile) strength; ~**kohle** f (Art) charcoal; ~**leine** f ripcord; ~**nagel** m siehe ~**zwecke;** ~**schiene** f T-square; ~**stift** m siehe ~**zwecke;** ~**verschluß** m zip(-fastener) (Brit), zipper; **den** ~**verschluß an etw** (dat) **auf-/zumachen** to zip sth up/to unzip sth; ~**wolf** m shredder, shredding machine; ~**wolle** f shoddy; ~**zahn** m carnassial (tooth) (spec); ~**zeug** nt drawing instruments pl; ~**zirkel** m drawing compass(es); ~**zwecke** f drawing pin (Brit), thumb tack (US).
Reiswein m rice wine.
Reit-: ~**anzug** m riding-habit; ~**bahn** f arena.
reiten pret **ritt,** ptp **geritten 1** vi aux sein **(a)** to ride. **auf etw** (dat) ~ to ride (on) sth; **im Schritt/Trab/Galopp** ~ to ride at a walk/trot/gallop; **gerritten kommen** to ride up, to come riding up; **das Schiff reitet vor Anker** (Naut) the ship is riding at anchor; **auf diesem Messer kann man** ~! (inf) you couldn't cut butter with this knife!
  (b) (sl: koitieren) to ride (sl).
2 vt to ride. **Schritt/Trab/Galopp** ~ to ride at a walk/trot/gallop; **ein schnelles Tempo** ~ to ride at a fast pace; **sich** (dat) **Schwielen** ~ to get saddle-sore; **jdn zu Boden** or **über den Haufen** (inf) ~ to trample sb down; **ein Steckenpferd** ~ (inf) to have a hobby; **Prinzipien** ~ (inf) to insist on one's principles; **krumme Touren** ~ (sl) to be up to some crooked tricks (inf).
reitend adj mounted. ~**e Artillerie** horse artillery.
Reiter m -s, - **(a)** rider, horseman; (Mil) cavalryman. **ein Trupp preußischer** ~ a troop of Prussian horse. **(b)** (an Waage) rider; (Kartei~) index-tab. **(c)** (Mil: Absperrblock) barrier. **spanische** ~ pl barbed-wire barricade.
Reiter-: ~**angriff** m cavalry charge; ~**aufzug** m cavalcade.
Reiterei f **(a)** (Mil) cavalry. **(b)** (inf: das Reiten) riding.
Reiterin f rider, horsewoman.
Reiterregiment nt cavalry regiment.
Reitersmann m, pl **-männer** (liter) horseman.
Reiterstandbild nt equestrian statue.

Reit-: ~**gerte** f riding crop; ~**hose** f riding-breeches pl; (Hunt, Sport) jodhpurs pl; ~**kleid** nt riding-habit; ~**knecht** m (old) groom; ~**kunst** f horsemanship, riding skill; ~**peitsche** f riding whip; ~**pferd** nt saddle-horse, mount; ~**sattel** m (riding) saddle; ~**schule** f riding school; ~**sitz** m riding position; (rittlings) straddling position; **im** ~**sitz sitzen** to sit astride (auf etw (dat) sth); ~**sport** m (horse-)riding, equestrian sport (form); ~**stall** m riding-stable; ~**stiefel** m riding-boot; ~**stunde** f riding lesson; ~**tier** nt mount, animal used for riding; ~**turnier** nt horse show; (Geländereiten) point-to-point; ~-**und Fahrturnier** nt horse show; ~**unterricht** m riding lessons pl; ~**weg** m bridle-path; ~**zeug** nt riding equipment or things pl.

Reiz m -es, -e **(a)** (Physiol) stimulus. **einen** ~ **auf etw** (acc) **ausüben** to act as a stimulus on sth.
   (b) (Verlockung) attraction, appeal; (des Unbekannten, Fremdartigen, der Großstadt auch) lure; (Zauber) charm. **der** ~ **der Neuheit/des Verbotenen** the lure or appeal of novelty/forbidden fruits; **(auf jdn) einen** ~ **ausüben** to have or hold great attraction(s) (for sb); **das erhöht den** ~ it adds to the thrill or pleasure; **einen/keinen** ~ **für jdn haben** to appeal/not to appeal to sb; **seinen** or **den** ~ **verlieren** to lose all one's/its charm; **an** ~ **verlieren** to be losing one's/its charm or attraction or appeal, to begin to pall; **seine** ~**e spielen lassen** to display one's charms; **weibliche** ~**e** feminine charms; **seine** ~**e zeigen** (euph, iro) to reveal one's charms.

Reiz-: ~**auslöser** m stimulant; (von krankhaftem Zustand) irritant; **r~bar** adj (empfindlich) sensitive, touchy (inf); (erregbar) irritable; (Med) irritable, sensitive; **leicht r~bar sein** to be very sensitive/irritable; (ständig erregbar auch) to be quick-tempered or hot-tempered; **r~bare Schwäche** (Med) irritability; (fig) sensitive spot or point; ~**barkeit** f siehe adj sensitiveness, sensitivity, touchiness (inf); irritability; irritability, sensitivity; ~**behandlung** f (Med) stimulation therapy; ~**blase** f irritable bladder; **r~empfänglich** adj responsive; (Physiol) receptive to stimuli; ~**empfänglichkeit** f responsiveness; (Physiol) receptiveness to stimuli.

reizen 1 vt **(a)** (Physiol) to irritate; (stimulieren) to stimulate. **(b)** (verlocken) to appeal to. **jds/den Gaumen** ~ to make sb's/one's mouth water; **jds Verlangen** ~ to waken or rouse sb's desire; **es würde mich ja sehr** ~, **...** I'd love to ...; **es reizt mich, nach Skye zu fahren** I've got an itch to go to Skye; **es hat mich ja immer sehr gereizt, ...** I've always had an itch to ...; **Ihr Angebot reizt mich sehr** I find your offer very tempting; **sie versteht es, Männer zu** ~ she knows how to appeal to men.
   (c) (ärgern) to annoy; Tier auch to tease; (herausfordern) to provoke. **ein gereiztes Nashorn** a rhinoceros when provoked; **jds Zorn** ~ to arouse sb's anger; **die Kinder reizten sie bis zur Weißglut** the children really made her see red; siehe **gereizt.**
   (d) (Skat) to bid.
2 vi **(a)** (Med) to irritate; (stimulieren) to stimulate. **auf der Haut** ~ to irritate the skin etc; **der Rauch reizt zum Husten** the smoke makes you cough; **zum Widerspruch** ~ to invite contradiction.
   (b) (Skat) to bid. **hoch** ~ (lit, fig) to make a high bid.

reizend adj charming. **es ist** ~ (von dir) it is charming or lovely (of you); **das ist ja** ~ (iro) (that's) charming.

Reizhusten m chesty cough; (nervös) nervous cough.

Reizker m -s, - (Bot) saffron milk-cap.

Reiz-: ~**klima** nt bracing climate; **r~los** adj dull, uninspiring; **das ist ja r~los** that's no fun; ~**losigkeit** f dullness, uninspiring nature; ~**mittel** nt (Med) stimulant; ~**schwelle** f (Physiol) stimulus or absolute threshold; (Comm) sales resistance; ~**stoff** m irritant; ~**therapie** f (Med) stimulation therapy; ~**überflutung** f overstimulation.

Reizung f **(a)** (Med) stimulation; (krankhaft) irritation. **(b)** (Herausforderung) provocation.

Reiz-: **r~voll** adj charming, delightful; Aufgabe, Beruf attractive; **die Aussicht ist nicht gerade r~voll** the prospect is not particularly enticing or appealing; **es wäre r~voll, mal dahin zu fahren/das ganz anders zu machen** it would be lovely to go there some time/it would be interesting to do it quite differently; ~**wäsche** f (inf) sexy underwear; ~**wort** nt emotive word.

Rekapitulation f recapitulation.

rekapitulieren* vt to recapitulate.

Rekelei f (inf) lolling about (inf).

rekeln vr (inf) (sich herumlümmeln) to loll about (inf); (sich strecken) to stretch. **sich noch ein paar Minuten im Bett** ~ to stretch out in bed for a few more minutes; **er rekelte sich im behaglichen Sessel vor dem Feuer** he snuggled down in the comfy chair in front of the fire; **die Katze rekelte sich behaglich in der Sonne** the cat lay lazily sunning itself.

Reklamation f query; (Beschwerde) complaint. „**spätere** ~**en können nicht anerkannt werden**" "we regret that money cannot be refunded after purchase".

Reklame f -, -**n (a)** (Werbewesen, Werbung) advertising. ~ **für jdn/etw machen** to advertize sb/sth; (fig) to do a bit of advertizing for sb/sth; **mit jdm/etw** ~ **machen** (pej) to show sb off/to show off about sth; **das ist keine gute** ~ **für die Firma** it's not a very good advertisement for the company.
   (b) (Einzelwerbung) advertisement, advert (Brit inf), ad (inf); (TV, Rad auch) commercial.

Reklame-: ~**artikel** m free gift, sales gimmick (often pej); (Probe) (free) sample; ~**broschüre** f (advertising) brochure, handout; ~**broschüren** advertizing literature; ~**fachmann** m, pl -**leute** advertizing executive, adman (inf); **die** ~**fachleute** the publicity boys; ~**feldzug** m advertizing campaign; ~**film** m advertizing film, commercial; ~**plakat** nt (advertizing) poster, advertisement; ~**rummel** m (pej) (advertizing) ballyhoo (inf); ~**schild** nt advertizing sign; ~**sendung** f commercial break,

commercials pl; **eine verkappte** ~**sendung** a disguised commercial; ~**spot** m (advertizing) spot, commercial; ~**tafel** f hoarding; ~**trick** m sales trick; ~**trommel** f: **die** ~**trommel für jdn/etw rühren** (inf) to beat the (big) drum for sb/sth; ~**zettel** m (advertizing) leaflet, handout.

reklamieren* **1** vi (Einspruch erheben) to complain, to make a complaint. **bei jdm wegen etw** ~ to complain to sb about sth; **die Rechnung kann nicht stimmen, da würde ich** ~ the bill can't be right, I would query it.
   2 vt **(a)** (bemängeln) to complain about (etw bei jdm sth to sb); (in Frage stellen) Rechnung, Rechnungsposten to query (etw bei jdm sth with sb).
   (b) (in Anspruch nehmen) jdn/etw für sich ~ to lay claim to sb/sth, to claim sb/sth as one's own.

rekommandieren* **1** vt (Aus) Brief, Sendung to register. **einen Brief rekommandiert aufgeben** to register a letter, to send a letter by registered mail. **2** vr (obs, Aus) **sich jdm** ~ to present one's compliments to sb.

Rekompenz f (Aus, Admin) compensation.

rekonstruieren* vt to reconstruct.

Rekonstruktion f reconstruction.

Rekonvaleszent(in f) [rekɔnvaleˈtsɛnt(ɪn)] m convalescent.

Rekonvaleszenz [rekɔnvaleˈtsɛnts] f convalescence.

Rekord m -s, -e record. **das Zeitalter der** ~**e** the age of superlatives; (des Fortschritts) the age of achievement.

Rekord- in cpds record; ~**brecher** m recordbreaker; ~**halter**, ~**inhaber** m record-holder; ~**lauf** m record(-breaking) run.

Rekordler m -s, - (inf) record-holder.

Rekord-: ~**marke** f (Sport, fig) record; **die bisherige** ~**marke im Weitsprung war ...** till now the long-jump record stood at or was ...; **auf der** ~**marke (von)** at the record or (fig) record level (of); ~**versuch** m attempt on the/a record; ~**zeit** f record time.

Rekrut m -en, -en (Mil) recruit.

Rekruten-: ~**ausbildung** f (Mil) basic training; ~**aushebung** f (old Mil) levy (old).

rekrutieren* **1** vt (Mil, fig) to recruit. **2** vr (fig) **sich** ~ **aus** to be recruited or drawn from.

Rekrutierung f recruitment, recruiting.

Rekrutierungsstelle f (Mil) recruiting centre.

Rekta pl of Rektum.

rektal adj (Med) rectal. ~ **einführen** to insert through the rectum; **Temperatur** ~ **messen** to take the temperature rectally.

Rektifikation f **(a)** (old) correction; (Berichtigung auch) rectification. **(b)** (Chem, Math) rectification.

rektifizieren* vt **(a)** (old) to correct; (berichtigen auch) to rectify. **(b)** (Chem, Math) to rectify.

Rektion f (Gram) government. **die** ~ **eines Verbs** the case governed by a verb.

Rektor m, **Rektorin** f (Sch) headmaster/-mistress, principal (esp US); (Univ) vice-chancellor, rector (US); (von Fachhochschule) principal.

Rektorat nt (Sch) (Amt, Amtszeit) headship, principalship (esp US); (Zimmer) headmaster's/-mistress's study, principal's room (esp US); (Univ) vice-chancellorship, rectorship (US); vice-chancellor's or rector's (US) office; (in Fachhochschule) principalship; principal's office.

Rektoratsrede f (Univ) (vice-chancellor's or rector's US) inaugural address.

Rektorin f siehe Rektor.

Rektum nt -s, **Rekta** (form) rectum.

rekurrieren* vi **(a)** (old Jur) to appeal. **(b)** (liter: auf etw zurückkommen) to return (auf +acc to).

Rekurs m -es, -e (old Jur) appeal.

Rel. abbr of Religion.

Relais [rəˈlɛː] nt -, - (Elec) relay.

Relaisstation f (Elec) relay station.

Relation f relation. **in einer/keiner** ~ **zu etw stehen** to bear some/no relation to sth.

relativ **1** adj relative. ~**e Mehrheit** (Parl) simple majority; **alles ist** ~ everything is relative. **2** adv relatively.

Relativ nt relative pronoun.

Relativ|adverb nt relative adverb.

relativieren* [relatiˈviːrən] (geh) **1** vt Begriff, Behauptung etc to qualify. **2** vi to see things or to think in relative terms.

Relativismus [-ˈvɪsmʊs] m relativism.

relativistisch [-ˈvɪstɪʃ] adj relativistic.

Relativität [relativiˈtɛːt] f relativity.

Relativitätstheorie f theory of relativity, relativity theory no art.

Relativ-: ~**pronomen** nt relative pronoun; ~**satz** m relative clause.

Relativum [-ˈtiːvʊm] nt (form) relative pronoun.

Relegation f (form) expulsion.

relegieren* vt (form) to expel.

relevant [releˈvant] adj relevant.

Relevanz [releˈvants] f relevance.

Relief [reˈliɛf] nt -s, -s or -e relief.

Relief-: ~**druck** m relief printing; ~**karte** f relief map.

Religion f religion; (Schulfach) religious instruction or education, RI (inf), RE (inf). ~ **sehr gut, Kopfrechnen schwach** (inf) virtuous but stupid.

Religions-: ~**bekenntnis** nt denomination; ~**buch** nt religion or religious textbook; ~**ersatz** m substitute for religion; ~**freiheit** f religious freedom, freedom of worship; ~**friede(n)** m religious peace; ~**gemeinschaft** f religious community; ~**geschichte** f history of religion; ~**krieg** m religious war, war of religion; ~**lehre** f religious education or instruction; ~**lehrer** m teacher of religious education, RI or RE teacher (inf); **r~los** adj not religious; (bekenntnislos) non-denominational; ~**losigkeit** f siehe adj lack of religion; non-denominationalism; ~**stifter** m founder of a religion; ~**streit** m religious controversy; ~**stunde** f religious education or instruction lesson, RI or RE lesson (inf); ~**unterricht** m (a) siehe ~**lehre**; (b) siehe ~**stunde**; ~**wissenschaft** f religious studies pl; vergleichende ~**wissenschaft** comparative religion; ~**zwang** m religious compulsion.

religiös adj religious. ~ **erzogen werden** to have or receive a religious upbringing.

Religiosität f religiousness. **ein Mensch von tiefer** ~ a deeply religious person.

Relikt nt -(e)s, -e relic.

Reling f -, -s or -e (Naut) (deck) rail.

Reliquiar nt reliquary.

Reliquie [-iə] f relic.

Reliquienschrein [-iən-] m reliquary.

Remanenz f (Phys) remanence, residual magnetism.

Rembours [rãˈbuːɐ] m -, - (Fin) reimbursement, payment.

Remboursgeschäft [rãˈbuːɐ-] nt (Fin) documentary credit trading/transaction.

Remedur f (obs) remedy, corrective. ~ **schaffen** to remedy the situation.

Remigrant(in f) m returning/returned emigrant.

remilitarisieren* vti to remilitarize.

Remilitarisierung f remilitarization.

Reminiszenz f (geh) (Erinnerung) memory (an +acc of); (Ähnlichkeit) similarity, resemblance (an +acc to). **ich habe aus seinem Vortrag ~en an Spengler herausgehört** I found his lecture in some ways reminiscent of Spengler.

remis [rəˈmiː] adj inv drawn. ~ **spielen** to draw; **die Partie ist** ~ the game has ended in a draw or has been drawn; **die Vereine trennten sich** ~ the clubs held each other to a draw.

Remis [rəˈmiː] nt -, - or -en [rəˈmiːzn] (a) (, Schach, Sport) draw. **gegen jdn ein** ~ **erzielen** to hold sb to a draw. (b) (fig) stalemate, deadlock. **mit einem** ~ in stalemate or deadlock.

Remise f -, -n (old) shed, outbuilding.

Remission f (Med, old: Erlaß) remission; (Comm) remittance.

Remittende f -, -n (Comm) return.

Remittent m (Fin) drawee, payee.

remittieren* 1 vt (Comm) Waren to return; Geld to remit. 2 vi (Med: nachlassen) to remit (form).

Remmidemmi nt -s, no pl (sl) (Krach) row, rumpus (inf); (Trubel) rave-up (sl). ~ **machen** to make a row etc/to have a rave-up (sl).

Remoulade [remuˈlaːdə], **Remouladensoße** f (Cook) remoulade.

Rempelei f (inf) barging (inf), jostling, pushing and shoving; (im Sport) pushing.

rempeln vti (inf) to barge (jdn into sb) (inf), to jostle, to elbow; (im Sport) to barge (jdn into sb); (foulen) to push.

Rem(p)ter m -s, - (in Klöstern) refectory; (in Burgen) banquet(ing) hall.

Remuneration f (Aus) (Gratifikation) bonus; (Vergütung) remuneration.

Ren nt -s, -e reindeer.

Renaissance [rənɛˈsãːs] f -, -en (a) (Hist) renaissance. (b) (fig) revival, rebirth; (von Kunstformen auch) renaissance.

Renaissance- [rənɛˈsãːs-] in cpds renaissance; ~**mensch** m renaissance man no art.

Rendezvous [rãdeˈvuː, ˈrãːdevu] nt -, - rendezvous (liter, hum), date (inf); (Space) rendezvous.

Rendezvousmanöver nt (Space) rendezvous manoeuvre.

Rendite f -, -n (Fin) yield, return on capital.

Renegat m -en, -en (Eccl, Pol) renegade.

Reneklode f -, -n greengage.

Renette f rennet.

renitent adj awkward, refractory.

Renitenz f awkwardness, refractoriness.

Renke f -, -n whitefish.

Renn- in cpds race; ~**bahn** f (race)track; ~**boot** nt powerboat.

rennen pret **rannte**, ptp **gerannt** 1 vi aux sein (a) (schnell laufen) to run; (Sport) (Mensch, Tier) to run, to race; (Auto etc) to race. **um die Wette** ~ to have a race; **ins Verderben or Unglück** ~ to rush headlong into disaster; **(aufs Klo)** ~ (inf) to run (to the loo Brit inf or bathroom US).

(b) (inf: hingehen) to run (off). **sie rennt wegen jeder Kleinigkeit zum Chef** she goes running (off) to the boss at the slightest little thing; **er rennt zu jedem Fußballspiel** he goes to every football match; **sie rennt jeden Tag in die Kirche** she goes running off to church every day.

(c) (stoßen) an or gegen jdn/etw ~ to run or bump or bang into sb/sth; **er rannte mit dem Kopf gegen ... he bumped or banged his head against...; mit dem Kopf durch/gegen die Wand** ~ (fig) to bang one's head against a brick wall.

2 vt (a) aux haben or sein (Sport) to run.

(b) jdn zu Boden or über den Haufen ~ to knock sb down or over; sich (dat) (an etw) ein Loch in den Kopf ~ to crack one's head (against sth); sich an etw (dat) ~ (dial) to knock or bang into sth, to knock or bang oneself on sth.

(c) (stoßen) Messer etc to run.

Rennen nt -s, - running; (Sport) (Vorgang) racing; (Veranstaltung) race. **totes** ~ dead heat; **gehst du zum** ~? (bei Pferde~, Hunde~ etc) are you going to the races?, are you going racing?; (bei Auto~ etc) are you going to the racing?; **gut im** ~ **liegen** (lit, fig) to be well placed; **das** ~ **ist gelaufen** (lit) the race is over; (fig) it's all over; **das** ~ **machen** (lit, fig) to win (the race); **aus dem** ~ **ausscheiden** (lit, fig) to drop out; **das** ~ **aufgeben** (lit) to drop out (of the race); (fig auch) to throw in the towel.

Renner m -s, - (inf: Verkaufsschlager) winner, worldbeater; (Pferd auch) flier.

Rennerei f (inf) (lit, fig: das Herumrennen) running around; (Hetze) mad chase (inf). **die** ~, **bis ich endlich meinen Paß kriegte** all that running around until I finally got my passport; **nach meinem Umzug hatte ich tagelange** ~**en** after moving I was running around for days; **diese** ~ **zum Klo** this running to the loo (Brit inf) or bathroom (US).

Renn-: ~**fahrer** m (Rad~) racing cyclist; (Motorrad~) racing motorcyclist; (Auto~) racing driver; ~**jacht** f racing yacht; ~**leiter** m race organizer; ~**leitung** f organization of a race meeting; (die ~**leiter**) race organizers pl; ~**maschine** f racer; ~**pferd** nt racehorse; **aus einem Ackergaul kann man kein** ~**pferd machen** (prov) you can't make a silk purse out of a sow's ear (Prov); ~**piste** f (race)track; ~**platz** m racecourse; ~**rad** nt racing bicycle or bike (inf); ~**rodeln** nt bob(sleigh) racing; ~**saison** f racing season; ~**schlitten** m bob(sleigh), bobsled; ~**schuhe** pl (Sport) spikes pl; ~**sport** m racing; ~**stall** m (Tiere, Zucht) stable; ~**strecke** f (~**bahn**) (race)track; (zu laufende Strecke) course, distance; **eine** ~**strecke von 100 km** a 100 km course, a distance of 100km; ~**tag** m day of the race; **das Rennen erstreckt sich über drei** ~**tage** the race is a three-day event; ~**tier** nt siehe Ren; ~**veranstaltung** f races pl, race meeting; ~**wagen** m racing car; ~**wette** f bet (on a race); **Ergebnisse der** ~**wetten** betting results.

Renommee nt -s, -s reputation, name.

renommieren* vi to show off, to swank (inf); (aufschneiden auch) to brag.

Renommier-: ~**onkel** m (inf) rich uncle; ~**schule** f (inf) posh or classy school (inf); ~**stück** nt pride and joy; (inf: Aufführung) showpiece.

renommiert adj renowned, famed, famous (wegen for).

Renommist m (geh) show-off; (Aufschneider auch) braggart.

Renommisterei f (geh) showing off; bragging.

renovieren* [renoˈviːrən] vt to renovate, to do up (inf).

Renovierung [renoˈviːrʊŋ] f renovation.

rentabel adj profitable; Firma auch viable. **es ist nicht** ~, **das reparieren zu lassen** it is not worth(while) having it repaired; ~ **wirtschaften** (gut einteilen) to spend one's money sensibly; (mit Gewinn arbeiten) to make or show a profit; ~ **kalkulieren** (gut einteilen) to budget sensibly; (Gewinn einplanen) to think in terms of profit(s), to go for profit(s); **das ist eine rentable Sache or Angelegenheit** it will pay (off).

Rentabilität f profitability; (von Firma auch) viability.

Rentabilitäts-: ~**gesichtspunkte** pl profitability point of view; ~**grenze** f limit of profitability; ~**prüfung** f investigation into profitability; ~**rechnung** f profitability calculation; ~**schwelle** f break-even point.

Rent|amt nt (old, Admin) bursary.

Rente f -, -n (Alters~, Invaliden~) pension; (aus Versicherung, Lebens~) annuity; (aus Vermögen) income, (St Ex: ~npapier) fixed-interest security. **auf** ~ **gehen** (inf)/**sein** (inf) to start drawing one's pension/to be on a pension; **jdn auf** ~ **setzen** (inf) to pension sb off (inf).

Renten-: ~**anpassung** f tying of pensions to the national average wage; ~**anpassungsgesetz** nt law tying pensions to the national average wage; ~**anspruch** m right to a pension; ~**basis** f annuity basis; ~**bemessungsgrundlage** f basis of calculation of a/the pension/pensions; ~**berechnung** f calculation of a/the pension/pensions; r~**berechtigt** adj entitled to a pension; Alter pensionable; ~**bescheid** m notice of the amount of one's pension; ~**empfänger** m pensioner; ~**erhöhung** f pension increase; ~**mark** f (Hist) rentenmark; ~**markt** m market in fixed-interest securities; r~**pflichtig** adj responsible for paying a pension; ~**reform** f reform of pensions; ~**versicherung** f pension scheme; ~**zahltag** m pension day.

Rentier¹ nt siehe Ren.

Rentier² [rɛnˈtieː] m -s, -s (old) man of private means, gentleman of leisure; (mit staatlicher Rente) pensioner.

rentieren* vir to be worthwhile; (Geschäft, Unternehmen etc auch, Maschine) to pay. **es hat sich doch rentiert, daß ich noch ein bißchen dageblieben bin** it was worth(while) staying on a bit; **das rentiert (sich) nicht** it's not worth it; **ein Auto rentiert sich für mich nicht** it's not worth my having a car; **der Film rentiert sich doch nicht** (sl) the film's not worth seeing.

Rentner(in f) m -s, - pensioner; (Alters~ auch) senior citizen, old age pensioner (Brit).

Re|okkupation f (Mil) reoccupation.

re|okkupieren* vt (Mil) to reoccupy.

Re|organisation, Re|organisierung f reorganization.

re|organisieren* vt to reorganize.

reparabel adj repairable.

Reparation f reparations pl. ~**en leisten** or **zahlen** to pay or make reparations.

Reparations-: ~**ausschuß** m reparations committee; ~**zahlungen** pl reparations pl.

Reparatur f repair. ~**en am Auto** car repairs; ~**en am Haus vornehmen** to do some repairs on or to the house; **in** ~ being repaired; **er übernimmt** ~**en von Schuhen** he does shoe repairs, he mends shoes; **etw in** ~ **geben** to have sth repaired or mended; Auto to have sth repaired.

Reparatur-: r~**anfällig** adj prone to break down; r~**bedürftig** adj in need of repair; ~**kosten** pl repair costs pl; ~**werkstatt** f workshop; (Auto~) garage.

reparieren* vt to repair, to mend; Auto to repair.

repatriieren* vt (wieder einbürgern) to renaturalize. (b) (heimschicken) to repatriate.

Repatriierung f siehe vt renaturalization; repatriation.

Repertoire [reperˈtoaːɐ] nt -s, -s repertory, repertoire (auch fig).

Repertoire- [reperˈtoaːɐ-]: ~**stück** nt repertory or stock play; ~**theater** nt repertory theatre, rep (inf).

Repetent m (form, Aus) pupil who has to repeat a year.
repetieren* 1 vt (a) (old) Stoff, Vokabeln to revise. (b) (wiederholen) to repeat; (form, Aus) Klasse to repeat, to take again; Jahr to repeat, to stay down for. 2 vi (a) (old) to do revision, to revise. (b) (form, Aus) to stay down, to repeat a class.
Repetier-: ~gewehr nt (old) repeating rifle; ~uhr f (old) repeater.
Repetition f (a) (old: von Stoff etc) revision. (b) (Wiederholung) repetition. **im Falle einer ~ muß der Schüler ...** (form, Aus) if it is necessary to repeat a class or to stay down for a year the pupil must ...
Repetitor m (Univ) coach, crammer (inf).
Repetitorium nt (Buch) revision book; (Unterricht) revision or cramming (inf) course.
Replik f -, -en (a) (Jur) replication; (fig geh) riposte, reply. (b) (Art) replica.
replizieren* vti (a) (Jur) to reply; (fig geh auch) to ripost. (b) (Art) to make a replica of.
Report m -(e)s, -e (a) report; (Enthüllungsbericht auch) exposé. **Schulmädchen-/Fensterputzer~** Confessions of a Schoolgirl/Window-Cleaner. (b) (St Ex) contango.
Reportage [repor'taːʒə] f -, -n report.
Reporter m -s, - reporter. **Sport-/Wirtschafts~** sports/economics correspondent.
reportieren* 1 vt (geh) to report (on). 2 vi to report.
Reposition f (Med) resetting.
repräsentabel adj impressive, prestigious; Frau (highly) presentable.
Repräsentant(in f) m representative.
Repräsentantenhaus nt (US Pol) House of Representatives.
Repräsentanz f (a) (Pol) representation. (b) (Aus: Geschäftsvertretung) branch.
Repräsentation f (a) (Stellvertretung) representation.
  (b) **der ~ dienen** to create a good image, to have good prestige value, to make the right impression; **die Diplomatenfrau fand die Pflichten der ~ sehr anstrengend** the diplomat's wife found her life of official and social functions very tiring; **die einzige Funktion des Monarchen ist heute die ~** the sole function of the monarch today is that of an official figurehead.
repräsentativ adj (a) (stellvertretend, typisch) representative (für of).
  (b) Haus, Auto, Ausstattung prestigious; Erscheinung auch presentable, personable. **zu ~en Zwecken** for purposes of prestige.
  (c) **die ~en Pflichten eines Botschafters** the social duties of an ambassador; **seine Stellung schließt ~e Pflichten ein in** his job includes being a public/social representative of his company; **der ~e Aufwand des Königshauses/der Firma** the expenditure for maintaining the royal household's/company's image; **ein großes Konferenzzimmer für ~e Zwecke** a large conference room to provide a suitable setting for functions.
Representativ|umfrage f representative survey.
repräsentieren* 1 vt to represent. 2 vi to perform official duties. **eine Diplomatenfrau muß ~ können** a diplomat's wife must be able to perform social duties.
Repressalie [-iə] f reprisal. **~n anwenden or ergreifen** to take reprisals.
Repression f repression.
repressionsfrei adj free of repression.
repressiv adj repressive.
Reprise f -, -n (a) (Mus) recapitulation; (TV, Rad) repeat; (Film, Theat) rerun; (nach längerer Zeit) revival. (b) (Mil) recapture.
Reprivatisierung [reprivati'ziːruŋ] f denationalization.
Reproduktion f reproduction; (Typ auch) repro (sl).
Reproduktions-: ~faktor m (Econ) production factor; ~prozeß m reproductive process.
reproduktiv adj reproductive. **er arbeitet rein ~** he merely reproduces what others have done.
reproduzierbar adj reproducible.
Reproduzierbarkeit f reproducibility.
reproduzieren* vt to reproduce.
Reprographie f (Typ) reprography.
Reptil nt -s, -ien [-iən] reptile.
Reptilienfonds [-iən-] m (Pol) secret fund.
Republik f -, -en republic.
Republikaner(in f) m -s, - republican.
republikanisch adj republican.
Republik-: ~flucht f (DDR) illegal crossing of the border; r~flüchtig adj (DDR) illegally emigrated; **r~flüchtig werden** to cross the border illegally; ~flüchtling m (DDR) illegal emigrant.
repulsiv adj (geh) repulsive.
Repunze f -, -en hallmark, plate-mark.
Reputation f (old) (good) reputation.
reputierlich adj (old) reputable, of good or high renown (old, liter).
Requiem ['reːkviem] nt -s, -s or (Aus) **Requien** ['reːkviən] requiem.
requirieren* vt (Mil) to requisition, to comandeer.
Requisit nt -s, -en equipment no pl, requisite (form). **ein unerläßliches ~** an indispensable piece of equipment; ~en (Theat) props, properties (form).
Requisiteur [-'tøːr] m (Theat) props or property manager.
Requisition f requisition(ing), commandeering.
Requisitionsschein m (Mil) requisition order.
resch adj (Aus) (knusprig) Brötchen etc crisp, crunchy, crispy; (fig: lebhaft) Frau dynamic.
Reseda -, **Reseden**, **Resede** f -, -n (Gattung) reseda; (Garten~) mignonette.

reservat [rezer'vaːt] adj (Aus) classified.
Reservat [rezer'vaːt] nt (a) (old: Sonderrecht) right, discretionary power. **sich** (dat) **das ~ vorbehalten, etw zu machen** to reserve the right to do sth. (b) (Wildpark) reserve. (c) (für Volksstämme) reservation.
Reservation [rezerva'tsioːn] f (a) (old: Sonderrecht) siehe **Reservat** (a). (b) (für Volksstämme) reservation.
Reservatrecht [rezer'vaːt-] nt discretionary power. **sich** (dat) **das ~ vorbehalten, etw zu machen** to reserve the right to do sth.
Reserve [re'zervə] f -, -n (a) (Vorrat) reserve(s) (an + dat of); (Geld) savings pl; (Mil, Sport) reserves pl. **(noch) etw in ~ haben** to have sth (still) in reserve; **in ~ liegen** (Mil) to stay back in reserve.
  (b) (Zurückhaltung) reserve; (Bedenken) reservation. **jdn aus der ~ locken** to break down sb's reserve, to bring sb out of his shell (inf); **aus der ~ heraustreten** to lose one's reserve, to come out of one's shell (inf); **sich** (dat) **~ auferlegen** to be reserved.
Reserve-: ~fonds m reserve fund; ~kanister m spare can; ~mann m, pl -männer or -leute (Sport) reserve; ~offizier m reserve officer; ~rad nt spare (wheel); ~reifen m spare (tyre); ~tank m reserve tank; ~truppen pl reserves pl; ~übung f (army) reserve training no pl.
reservieren* [rezer'viːrən] vt to reserve.
reserviert adj Platz, Mensch reserved.
Reserviertheit f reserve, reservedness.
Reservierung f reservation.
Reservist [rezer'vist] m reservist.
Reservoir [rezer'voaːr] nt -s, -e reservoir; (fig auch) pool.
Resident m envoy, resident (rare).
Residenz f (a) (Wohnung) residence, residency. (b) (Hauptstadt) royal seat or capital.
Residenzstadt f royal seat or capital.
residieren* vi to reside.
residual adj (geh) residual.
Residuum nt -s, **Residuen** [re'ziːduən] (geh) residue, residuum (form).
Resignation f (geh) resignation. **(über etw** acc**) in ~ verfallen, sich der ~ überlassen** to become resigned (to sth).
resignieren* vi to give up. **resigniert resigned; ... sagte er ~d or resigniert ...** he said with resignation or in a resigned way.
resistent adj (Med) resistant (gegen to).
Resistenz f (Med) resistance (gegen to).
resistieren* vi (Med) to resist.
resolut adj purposeful, decisive. **etw ~ tun** to do sth purposefully.
Resolution f (Pol) (Beschluß) resolution; (Bittschrift) petition.
Resonanz f (a) (Mus, Phys) resonance. (b) (fig) response (auf + acc to). **keine/wenig/große ~ finden** to meet with or get no/little/a good response.
Resonanz-: ~boden m sounding-board; ~kasten m soundbox.
Resopal ® nt -s, no pl Formica ®.
resorbieren* vt to absorb.
Resorption f absorption.
resozialisieren* vt to rehabilitate.
Resozialisierung f rehabilitation.
resp. abbr of **respektive**.
Respekt m -s, no pl (Achtung) respect; (Angst) fear. **jdm ~ einflößen** (Achtung) to command or inspire respect from sb; (Angst) to put the fear of God into sb; **vor jdm den ~ verlieren** to lose one's respect for sb; **bei allem ~ (vor jdm/etw)** with all due respect (to sb/for sth); **vor jdm/etw ~ haben** (Achtung) to respect sb/sth, to have respect for sb/sth; (Angst) to be afraid of sb/sth; **sich** (dat) **~ verschaffen** to make oneself respected; **allen ~!** well done!
respektabel adj respectable.
respekt-: ~einflößend adj authoritative; **ein wenig ~einflößender Mensch** a person who commands or inspires little respect; ~heischend adj demanding respect.
respektieren* vt to respect; Wechsel to honour.
respektive [respɛk'tiːvə] adv (geh, Comm) (a) (jeweils) and ... respectively. **Fritz und Franz verdienen 40 ~ 50 Mark pro Tag** Fritz and Franz earn 40 and 50 marks per day respectively.
  (b) (anders ausgedrückt) or rather; (genauer gesagt) (or) more precisely.
  (c) (oder) or.
  (d) (und) and. **Herr Meyer ~ seine Frau danken ...** Mr and Mrs Meyer thank ...
Respekt-: r~los adj disrespectful, irreverent; **eine r~lose Person** an irreverent person; ~losigkeit f (a) (no pl: Verhalten) disrespect(fulness), lack of respect, irreverence; (b) (Bemerkung) disrespectful, remark or comment.
Respektsperson f person to be respected; (Beamter etc) person in authority.
Respekt-: ~tage pl (Comm) days of grace; r~voll adj respectful; r~widrig adj disrespectful, irreverent.
Respiration f (form) respiration.
Respirations|apparat, Respirator m respirator.
respirieren* vi (form) to respire.
Ressentiment [rɛsãti'mãː, rə-] nt -s, -s resentment no pl, feeling of resentment (gegen against).
Ressort [re'soːr] nt -s, -s department. **in das ~ von jdm/etw fallen** to be sb's/sth's department.
Ressort-: r~mäßig adj departmental, on a departmental basis, **ich weiß nicht, wo der Antrag r~mäßig hingehört** I don't know which department the application comes under; ~minister m department minister; **der ~minister für die Polizei** the minister responsible for the police.
Rest m -(e)s, -e (a) rest. **die ~e einer Kirche/Stadt/Kultur** the remains or remnants of a church/city/civilization; **90% sind**

schon fertig, den ~ mache ich 90% is done, I'll do the rest or remainder; **am Anfang hatte ich 25 Schüler, die 3 hier sind noch der ~ (davon)** at the beginning I had 25 pupils, these 3 are what's left or all that is left; **der letzte ~** the last bit; **der letzte ~ vom Schützenfest** (hum) the last little bit; **bis auf einen ~** except for a little bit or a small amount; **dieser kleine ~** this little bit that's left (over); **der kümmerliche ~** (vom meinem Geld) all that's left, the miserable remains; (vom Essen) the sad remnants; **jdm/einer Sache den ~ geben** (inf) to finish sb/sth off; **sich** (dat) **den ~ holen** (inf) to make oneself really ill.
   (b) ~e pl (Essens~) left-overs pl.
   (c) (Stoff~) remnant.
   (d) (Math) remainder. 2 ~ 3 2 and 3 over, 2 remainder 3.
Rest- in cpds remaining; ~**abschnitt** m remaining part.
Restant m (Comm) **(a)** (Schuldner) defaulter. **(b)** (Ladenhüter) slow or slow-moving line.
Rest|auflage f remainder(ed) stock, remainders pl.
Restaurant [rɛsto'rã:] nt -s, -s restaurant.
Restaurateur [rɛstora'tø:r] m (old) restaurateur.
Restauration¹ f restoration. **die ~** (Hist) the Restoration.
Restauration² [rɛstora'tsio:n] f (old, Aus) inn, tavern (old); (im Bahnhof) refreshment rooms pl.
Restaurations-: ~**betrieb** m catering business; ~**zeit** f period of ultraconservatism; **die ~zeit** (Hist) the Restoration.
Restaurator m restorer.
restaurieren* 1 vt to restore. 2 vr (old) to partake of some refreshment (old, form).
Restaurierung f restoration.
Rest-: ~**bestand** m remaining stock; **wir haben noch einen kleinen ~bestand an Bikinis** we still have a few bikinis left; ~**betrag** m remaining or outstanding sum.
Reste-: ~**essen** nt left-overs pl; ~**verkauf** m remnants sale.
restituieren* vt (form) to make restitution of (form).
Restitution f (form) restitution (form).
Restitutions-: ~**edikt** nt Edict of Restitution; ~**klage** f action for a retrial.
restlich adj remaining, rest of the ... **die ~en** the rest.
restlos 1 adj complete, total. 2 adv completely, totally; begeistert wildly.
Restposten m (Comm) remaining stock. **ein ~** remaining stock; **ein großer ~ Bücher/Zucker** a lot of books/sugar left in stock; „~" "reduced to clear".
Restriktion f (form) restriction.
Restriktionsmaßnahme f restriction, restrictive measure.
restriktiv adj (geh) restrictive.
Rest-: ~**summe** f balance, amount remaining; ~**zahlung** f final payment, payment of the balance.
Resultante f -, -n (Math) resultant.
Resultat nt result; (von Prüfung auch) results pl. **zu einem ~ kommen** to come to or arrive at a conclusion.
resultatlos adj fruitless, without result. **das Spiel verlief ~** the game was resultatlos or in a draw.
resultieren* vi (geh) to result (in + dat in). **aus etw ~** to be the result of sth, to result from sth; **aus dem Gesagten resultiert, daß ...** from what was said one must conclude that ...; **die daraus ~den ... the resulting ...
Resultierende f -n, -n (Math) resultant.
Resümee, Resümé (Aus, Sw) [rezy'me:] nt -s, -s (geh) summary, résumé; (am Ende einer Rede auch) recapitulation.
resümieren* vti (geh) to summarize, to sum up; (am Ende einer Rede auch) to recapitulate.
Retardation f retardation.
retardieren* vt to retard. **ein ~des Moment** a delaying factor or element.
retirieren* vi aux sein (old Mil, hum) to beat a retreat.
Retorte f -, -n (Chem) retort. **aus der ~** (inf) synthetic; **Baby aus der ~** test-tube baby.
Retortenbaby nt test-tube baby.
retour [re'tu:r] adv (Aus, dial) back.
Retourbillett [re'tu:rbil'jet] nt (Sw) return (ticket), round-trip ticket (US).
Retoure [re'tu:r] f -, -n usu pl (Aus) return.
Retour- [re'tu:r-]: ~**gang** m (Aus) reverse (gear); ~**karte** f (Aus) return (ticket), round-trip ticket (US); ~**kutsche** f (inf) tit-for-tat answer; **deins hat mir auch gut geschmeckt — ach, bitte keine ~kutschen** yours was lovely too — oh please, you don't have to return the compliment.
retournieren* [retur'ni:rən] vt (old, Aus) to return.
Retourspiel [re'tu:r-] nt (Aus) return (match).
retrograd adj (liter) retrograde.
retrospektiv (liter) 1 adj retrospective. 2 adv in retrospect.
Retrospektive f (liter) retrospective.
retten 1 vt to save; (aus Gefahr auch, befreien) to rescue. **jdm das Leben ~** to save sb's life; **jdn vor jdm/etw ~** to save sb from sb/sth; **ein ~der Gedanke** a bright idea that saved the situation or his/our etc bacon (inf); **der Patient/die alte Kirche ist noch/nicht mehr zu ~** the patient/the old church can still be saved or is not yet past saving/is past saving; **er hat wieder geheiratet? er ist nicht mehr zu ~** he got married again? he's beyond redemption or past saving or helping; **bist du noch zu ~?** (inf) are you out of your mind, have you gone completely round the bend? (inf).
   2 vr to escape. **sich auf/unter etw** (acc) **/aus etw ~** to escape onto/under/from sth; **sich vor jdm/etw ~** to escape (from) sb/sth; **sich durch die Flucht ~** to escape; **sich vor etw nicht mehr ~ können** or **zu ~ wissen** (fig) to be swamped with sth; **rette sich, wer kann!** it's every man for himself!
Retter(in f) m -s, - rescuer, saviour (liter), deliverer (liter); (Rel) Saviour. **ach mein ~!** oh my hero!; siehe Not.
Rettich m -s, -e radish.

Rettung f rescue, deliverance (liter); (von Waren) recovery; (Rel) salvation, deliverance. **die ~ und Erhaltung historischer Denkmäler** the saving and preservation of historical monuments; **Gesellschaft zur ~ Schiffbrüchiger** Lifeboat Service; **die ~ kam in letzter Minute** the situation was saved in the last minute; (für Schiffbrüchige etc) help came in the nick of time; **auf ~ hoffen** to hope to be saved, to hope for deliverance (liter); **an seine (eigene) ~ denken** to worry about one's own safety; **Trinker, für die jegliche ~ ...** alcoholics for whom any salvation ...; **für den Patienten/unsere Wirtschaft gibt es keine ~ mehr** the patient/our economy is beyond saving, our economy is beyond salvation; **das war meine ~** that saved me, that was my salvation; **das war meine ~, daß ...** I was saved by the fact that ...; **das war meine letzte ~** that was my last hope; (hat mich gerettet) that was my salvation, that saved me.
Rettungs-: ~**aktion** f rescue operation; ~**anker** m sheet anchor; (fig) anchor; ~**arzt** m siehe Notarzt; ~**boje** f lifebelt; (Hosenboje) breeches buoy; ~**boot** nt lifeboat; ~**dienst** m rescue service; ~**floß** nt life-raft; ~**flugzeug** nt rescue aircraft; ~**gerät** nt rescue equipment no pl or apparatus no pl; ~**gürtel** m lifebelt; ~**insel** f inflatable life-raft; ~**kommando** nt rescue squad; ~**leine** f lifeline; ~**leiter** f rescue ladder; **r~los** 1 adj beyond saving; **Lage** hopeless, irredeemable; **Verlust** irrecoverable; 2 adv verloren hopelessly, irretrievably; ~**mannschaft** f rescue team or party; ~**medaille** f lifesaving medal; ~**ring** m lifebuoy, lifebelt; (hum: Bauch) spare tyre (hum); ~**schwimmen** nt lifesaving; ~**schwimmer** m lifesaver; (am Strand) lifeguard; ~**station**, ~**stelle** f rescue centre; (für Erste Hilfe) first-aid post; (mit ~**booten**) lifeboat or coast-guard station; ~**trupp** m siehe ~**kommando**; ~**versuch** m rescue attempt or bid; (von Arzt etc) attempt to save sb; ~**wagen** m (Aus) ambulance; ~**wesen** nt rescue services pl.
Retusche f -, -n (Phot) retouching.
Retuscheur(in f) [retu'ʃø:r, -'ʃø:rɪn)] m retoucher.
retuschieren* vt (Phot) to retouch, to touch up (inf, auch fig).
Reue f -, no pl remorse (über + acc at, about), repentance (auch Rel) (über + acc of), rue (old, liter) (über + acc at, of); (Bedauern) regret (über + acc at, about).
reuelos adj unrepentant.
reuen vt (liter) **etw reut jdn** sb regrets or rues (liter, old) sth; **es reut mich, daß ich das getan habe** I regret or rue (liter, old) having done that.
reuevoll adj siehe reumütig.
Reugeld nt (old) indemnity (for a cancelled contract).
reuig adj (liter) siehe reumütig.
reumütig adj (voller Reue) remorseful, repentant; Sünder, Missetäter contrite, penitent; (betreten, zerknirscht) rueful. **gestand er ... full of remorse he confessed ...; **du wirst bald ~ zu mir zurückkommen, sagte der Ehemann** you'll soon come back feeling sorry, said the husband.
Reuse f -, -n fish trap.
Reuße m -n, -n (obs) Russian, Muscovite. **Zar aller ~n** Czar of all the Russias.
re|üssieren* vi (old) to succeed, to be successful (bei, mit with).
Revanche [re'vã:ʃ(ə)] f -, -n **(a)** (Sport) revenge; (~partie) return match. **du mußt ihm ~ geben!** you'll have to let him have his revenge, you'll have to give him a return match. **(b)** no pl (Pol) revenge, vengeance.
Revanche- [re'vã:ʃə-]: ~**krieg** m war of revenge; **r~lüstern** adj revanchist; ~**partie** f (Sport) return match; ~**politik** f (pej) revanchist policy/politics pl; ~**spiel** nt (Sport) return match.
revanchieren* [revã'ʃi:rən] vr **(a)** (sich rächen) to get one's revenge, to get one's own back (bei jdm für etw on sb for sth).
   (b) (sich erkenntlich zeigen) to reciprocate. **ich werde mich bei Gelegenheit mal ~** I'll return the compliment some time; (für Hilfe) I'll do the same for you one day, I'll return the favour one day; **das Problem bei Geschenken/Einladungen ist, daß man meint, sich ~ zu müssen** the problem with getting presents/invitations is that one always feels one has to give something (back) in return/to invite somebody back (in return); **sich bei jdm für eine Einladung/seine Gastfreundschaft ~** to return sb's invitation/hospitality.
Revanchismus [revã'ʃɪsmʊs] m revanchism.
Revanchist [revã'ʃɪst] m revanchist.
revanchistisch [revã'ʃɪstɪʃ] adj revanchist.
Reverenz f (old) (Hochachtung) reverence; (Verbeugung) obeisance, reverence (old). **jdm seine ~ erweisen** to show one's reverence or respect for sb; **seine ~en machen** (old), to bow.
Revers¹ [re've:r, re've:r, rə-] nt or m -, - (an Kleidung) lapel, revere, revers (esp US).
Revers² [re'vɛrs] m -es, -e or [re've:r, rə've:r] m -, - (old: Rückseite) reverse.
Revers³ [re'vɛrs] m -es, -e (Erklärung) declaration.
reversibel [rever'zi:bl] adj reversible.
Reversion [rever'zio:n] f (Biol, Psych) reversion.
revidieren* [revi'di:rən] vt to revise; Korrekturen to check; (Comm) to audit, to check.
Revier [re'vi:r] nt -s, -e **(a)** (Polizei~) (Dienststelle) (police) station, station house (US); (Dienstbereich) beat, district, precinct (US), patch (inf); (von Prostituierter) beat, patch (inf).
   (b) (Zool: Gebiet) territory. **die Küche ist mein ~** the kitchen is my territory or preserve.
   (c) (Hunt: Jagd~) hunting ground, shoot.
   (d) (old: Gebiet, Gegend) district, area.
   (e) (Mil: Kranken~) sick-bay. **auf dem or im ~ liegen** to be in the sick-bay.
   (f) (Min: Kohlen~) (coal)mine. **im ~ an der Ruhr** in the mines of the Ruhr; **das ~ Ruhr; the Saar.**

Revier-: ~**förster** m forester, forest ranger (US); ~**försterei** f forester's lodge; **r~krank** adj (Mil) hospitalized, in the sickbay; ~**kranke(r)** m (Mil) soldier in the sick-bay; ~**stube** f sickbay; ~**wache** f duty room; ~**wachtmeister** m station sergeant.
Revirement [revirə'mã:, revir'mã:] nt -s, -s (Pol) reshuffle.
Revision [revi'zio:n] f (a) (von Meinung, Politik etc) revision.
  (b) (Comm: Prüfung) audit.
  (c) (Typ: letzte Überprüfung) final (proof-)read. ~ **lesen** to do the final (proof-)read.
  (d) (Jur: Urteilsanfechtung) appeal (an +acc to).
Revisionismus [revizio'nɪsmʊs] m (Pol) revisionism.
Revisionist [revizio'nɪst] m (Pol) revisionist.
revisionistisch [revizio'nɪstɪʃ] adj (Pol) revisionist.
Revisions-: ~**bogen** m page-proof; ~**frist** f time for appeal; ~**gericht** nt court of appeal, appeal court; ~**verhandlung** f appeal hearing.
Revisor [re'vi:zɔr] m (Comm) auditor; (Typ) proof-reader.
Revolte [re'vɔltə] f -, -n revolt.
revoltieren* [revɔl'ti:rən] vi to revolt, to rebel; (fig: Magen) to rebel.
Revolution [revolu'tsio:n] f (lit, fig) revolution. **eine** ~ **der Moral** a moral revolution, a revolution in morals.
revolutionär [revolutsio'nɛ:r] adj (lit, fig) revolutionary.
Revolutionär(in f) [revolutsio'nɛ:r, -'nɛ:ər(ɪn)] m revolutionary.
revolutionieren* [revolutsio'ni:rən] vt to revolutionize.
Revolutions- in cpds revolutionary.
Revoluzzer [revo'lutsr] m -s, - (pej) would-be revolutionary.
Revolver [re'vɔlvr] m -s, - revolver, gun.
Revolver-: ~**blatt** nt (pej) scandal sheet; ~**griff** m butt (of a/the revolver); ~**held** m (pej) gunslinger; ~**lauf** m barrel (of a/the revolver); ~**mündung** f mouth (of a/the revolver); **plötzlich starrte er in eine** ~**mündung** he suddenly found himself staring down the barrel of a revolver; ~**presse** f (pej) gutter press; ~**schnauze** f (sl) (Mundwerk) loud mouth (inf); (Mensch) loud-mouth (inf).
Revue [rə'vy:] f -, -n [-'vy:ən] (a) (Theat) revue.
  (b) (rare: Zeitschrift) review.
  (c) (old, Mil) review. **etw** ~ **passieren lassen** (fig) to let sth parade before one, to pass sth in review.
Revuetänzerin [rə'vy:-] f chorus-girl.
Rezensent m reviewer.
rezensieren* vt to review.
Rezension f review, write-up (inf).
Rezensions|exemplar nt review copy.
rezent adj (a) (Biol) living; (Ethnologie) Kulturen surviving.
  (b) (dial: säuerlich, pikant) tart, sour.
Rezept nt -(e)s, -e (a) (Med) prescription; (fig) cure, remedy (für, gegen for). **auf** ~ on prescription. **(b)** (Cook, fig) recipe.
Rezept-: ~**block** m prescription pad; **r~frei** 1 adj available without prescription; **2** adv over the counter, without a prescription.
rezeptieren* vt (form) to prescribe.
Rezeption f (a) (liter: Übernahme) adoption. (b) (von Hotel: Empfang) reception.
rezeptiv adj receptive. **der Kritiker als** ~**er Mensch** the critic as one who assimilates or receives ideas.
Rezept-: ~**pflicht** f prescription requirement; **der** ~**pflicht unterliegen** to be available only on prescription; **dafür besteht jetzt keine** ~**pflicht mehr** you don't need a prescription for it now; **r~pflichtig** adj available only on prescription; **etw r~pflichtig machen** to put sth on prescription.
Rezeptur f (form) dispensing.
Rezeß m -sses, -sse (Jur) written settlement or agreement.
Rezession f (Econ) recession.
rezessiv adj (Biol) recessive.
reziprok adj (Math, Gram) reciprocal. **sich** ~ **zueinander verhalten** to be in a reciprocal relationship.
Rezitation f recitation.
Rezitations|abend m poetry evening.
Rezitativ nt (Mus) recitative.
Rezitator m reciter.
rezitieren* vti to recite.
R-Gespräch ['ɛr-] nt transfer or reverse charge call (Brit), collect call (US). **ein** ~ **führen** to make a transfer charge call etc, to transfer or reverse the charges (Brit), to call collect (US).
Rh [ɛr'ha:] abbr of **Rhesusfaktor positiv.**
rh [ɛr'ha:] abbr of **Rhesusfaktor negativ.**
Rhabarber m -s, no pl (auch Gemurmel) rhubarb.
Rhapsode m -n, -n rhapsodist.
Rhapsodie f (Mus, Liter) rhapsody.
rhapsodisch adj (Mus, Liter) rhapsodic(al).
Rhein m -s Rhine.
Rhein-: **r~ab(wärts)** adv down the Rhine; **r~auf(wärts)** adv up the Rhine; **r~bund** m (Hist) Confederation of the Rhine; ~**fall** m Rhine Falls pl, Falls of the Rhine pl.
rheinisch adj attr Rhenish, Rhineland.
Rhein-: ~**länder** m -s, - (a) Rhinelander; (b) (Tanz) ≈ schottische; **r~ländisch** adj Rhenish, Rhineland; ~**land-Pfalz** no art Rhineland-Palatinate; ~**wein** m Rhine wine, Rhenish (wine); (weißer auch) hock.
rhenanisch adj (old) siehe rheinisch.
Rhesus-: ~**affe** m rhesus monkey; ~**faktor** m (Med) rhesus or Rh factor; ~**(faktor) positiv/negativ** rhesus positive/negative.
Rhetor m (liter) orator, rhetor (rare).
Rhetorik f rhetoric.
Rhetoriker m -s, - rhetorician (form), master of rhetoric; (Redner) orator.
rhetorisch adj rhetorical. ~**e Frage** rhetorical question.
Rheuma nt -s, no pl rheumatism.

Rheumamittel nt (inf) cure for rheumatism or the rheumatics (inf).
Rheumatiker(in f) m -s, - rheumatic, rheumatism sufferer.
rheumatisch adj rheumatic.
Rheumatismus m rheumatism.
Rheumatologe m, **Rheumatologin** f rheumatologist.
Rhinozeros nt -(ses), -se rhinoceros, rhino (inf); (inf: Dummkopf) fool, twit (Brit inf), sap (inf).
Rhodesien [-iən] nt -s Rhodesia.
Rhodesier(in f) [-iɐ, -iərɪn] m -s, - Rhodesian.
rhodesisch adj Rhodesian.
Rhododendron [rodo'dendrɔn] m or nt -s, **Rhododendren** rhododendron.
Rhodos ['ro:dɔs, 'rɔdɔs] nt - Rhodes.
Rhomben pl of **Rhombus.**
rhombisch adj rhomboid(al).
Rhomboid nt -(e)s, -e rhomboid.
Rhombus m -, **Rhomben** rhombus, rhomb.
Rhythmik f rhythmics sing; (inf: Rhythmus) rhythm.
Rhythmiker(in f) m -s, - rhythmist.
rhythmisch adj rhythmic(al). ~**e Prosa** rhythmic prose; ~**e Gymnastik** rhythmics sing, music and movement.
rhythmisieren* vt to make rhythmic, to put rhythm into. **rhythmisiert** rhythmic.
Rhythmus m (Mus, Poet, fig) rhythm.
RIAS abbr of **Rundfunk im amerikanischen Sektor.**
ribbeln vt (dial) to rub.
Ribis(e)l f -, -n (Aus) siehe Johannisbeere.
Richt-: ~**antenne** f directional aerial (esp Brit) or antenna; ~**baum** m tree used in the topping-out ceremony; ~**beil** nt executioner's axe; ~**blei** nt plumbline, plummet; ~**block** m (execution) block.
Richte f -, no pl etw in die ~ **bringen** (fig) to straighten sth out; (dial) to straighten sth up; **in die** ~ **kommen** (fig) to straighten itself out.
richten 1 vt (a) (lenken) to direct (auf +acc towards), to point (auf +acc at, towards); Gewehr auch to train (auf +acc on); Scheinwerfer auch to turn (auf +acc on); Augen, Blicke, Aufmerksamkeit to direct, to turn (auf +acc towards), to focus (auf +acc on); Pläne, Wünsche, Tun to direct (auf +acc towards). **den Kurs nach Norden/Osten** etc ~ to set or steer a northerly/easterly etc course; **die Augen gen Himmel** ~ (liter) to raise or lift one's eyes heavenwards (liter) or to heaven (liter); **richt euch!** (Mil) right dress!; (Sch) get in a straight line!; **einen Verdacht gegen jdn** ~ to suspect sb.
  (b) (aus~) etw nach jdm/etw ~ to suit or fit sth to sb/sth; Lebensstil, Verhalten to orientate sth to sb/sth.
  (c) (adressieren) Briefe, Anfragen to address, to send (an +acc to); Bitten, Forderungen, Gesuch to address, to make (an +acc to); Kritik, Vorwurf to level, to direct, to aim (gegen at, against).
  (d) (S Ger) (zurechtmachen) to prepare, to get ready; (in Ordnung bringen) to do, to fix; (reparieren) to fix; Essen auch to get, to fix; Haare to do; Tisch to lay (Brit), to set; Betten to make, to do. **jdm ein Bad** ~ (form, S Ger) to draw (form) or run a bath for sb.
  (e) (einstellen) to set; (S Ger: geradebiegen) to straighten (out), to bend straight.
  (f) (Aus pej) sich's (dat) ~ to get oneself off (inf).
  (g) (old: hinrichten) to execute, to put to death. **sich selbst** ~ (liter) to find death by one's own hand (liter); **sich von selbst** ~ (fig) to condemn oneself; siehe zugrunde.
2 vr (a) (sich hinwenden) to focus, to be focussed (auf +acc on), to be directed (auf +acc towards); (Gedanken, Augen auch) to turn, to be turned (auf +acc towards).
  (b) (sich wenden) to consult (an jdn sb); (Maßnahme, Vorwurf etc) to be directed or aimed (gegen at).
  (c) (sich anpassen) to follow (nach jdm/etw sb/sth). **sich nach den Vorschriften** ~ to go by the rules; **sich nach jds Wünschen** ~ to comply with or go along with sb's wishes; **mir ist es egal, ob wir früher oder später gehen, ich richte mich nach dir** I don't mind if we go earlier or later, I'll fit in with you or I'll do what you do; **wir** ~ **uns ganz nach unseren Kunden** we are guided entirely by our customers' wishes; **warum sollte die Frau sich immer nach dem Mann** ~? why should the woman always do what the man wants?; **sich nach den Sternen/der Wettervorhersage/dem, was er behauptet,** ~ to go by the stars/the weather forecast/what he maintains; **und richte dich (gefälligst) danach!** (inf) (kindly) do as you're told.
  (d) (abhängen von) to depend (nach on).
  (e) (S Ger: sich zurechtmachen) to get ready. **für die Party brauchst du dich nicht extra zu** ~ you don't have to get specially done up for the party (inf).
3 vi (liter: urteilen) to judge (über jdn sb), to pass judgement (über +acc on). **milde/streng** ~ to be mild/harsh in one's judgement; **richtet nicht, auf daß ihr nicht gerichtet werdet!** (Bibl) judge not, that ye be not judged (Bibl).
Richter(in f) m -s, - judge. **jdn/etw vor den** ~ **bringen** to take sb/sth to court; **der gesetzliche** ~ the right to a fair trial; **die** ~ the Bench, the judiciary, the judges pl; **das Buch der** ~ (Bibl) (the Book of) Judges; **sich zum** ~ **aufwerfen** or **machen** (fig) to set (oneself) up in judgement; **der höchste** ~ (liter: Gott) the Supreme Judge; **vor dem höchsten** ~ **stehen** (liter: vor Gott) to stand before the Judgement Seat or the Throne of Judgement.
Richter-: ~**amt** nt judicial office; **das** ~**amt ausüben** to sit on the Bench; ~**gesetz** nt law defining the functions and powers of judges.
Richterin f siehe Richter.
Richter-: **r~lich** adj attr judicial; ~**schaft** f judiciary, Bench; ~**-Skala** f (Geol) Richter scale; ~**spruch** m (a) (Jur) ≈ judge-

ment; **(b)** (*Sport*) judges' decision; (*Pferderennen*) stewards' decision; ~**stuhl** *m* Bench; **der** ~**stuhl (Gottes)** the Judgement Seat, the Throne of Judgement.

Richt-: ~**fest** *nt* topping-out ceremony; ~**feuer** *nt* (*Naut*) leading lights *pl*; (*Aviat*) approach lights *pl*; ~**funk** *m* directional radio; ~**funkbake** *f* (*Naut*) directional radio beacon; ~**geschwindigkeit** *f* recommended speed.

richtig 1 *adj* **(a)** right *no comp*; (*zutreffend auch*) correct. **eine** ~**e Erkenntnis/Voraussetzung** *etc* a correct realization/presupposition *etc*; **der** ~**e Mann am** ~**en Ort** the right man for the job; **ich halte es für** ~**/das** ~**ste, ...** I think it would be right/best ...; **nicht ganz** ~ **(im Kopf) sein** (*inf*) to be not quite right (in the head) (*inf*); **bin ich hier** ~ **bei Müller?** (*inf*) is this right for the Müllers?; **der Junge ist** ~ (*inf*) that boy's all right (*inf*) *or* OK (*inf*).

(b) (*wirklich, echt*) real, proper. **der** ~**e Vater/die** ~**e Mutter** the real father/mother; **ein** ~**er Drache/Idiot** *etc* a real *or* proper *or* right (*inf*) dragon/idiot *etc*.

2 *adv* **(a)** (*korrekt*) correctly, right; *passen, funktionieren, liegen etc auch* properly. **die Uhr geht** ~ the clock is right *or* correct; **habe ich** ~ **gehört?** (*iro*) do my ears deceive me?, am I hearing things?; (*Gerücht betreffend*) is it right what I've heard?; **wenn man es** ~ **nimmt** (*inf*) really, actually, properly speaking; **du kommst gerade** ~**!** you're just in time; (*iro*) you're just what I need.

(b) (*inf: ganz und gar*) really, proper (*dial*), real (*esp US inf*); *sich schämen, verlegen, schlagen auch* thoroughly.

(c) (*wahrhaftig*) right, correct. **du bist doch Konrads Schwester** — ~**!** you're Konrad's sister — (that's) right; **das ist doch Paul!** — **ach ja,** ~ that's Paul — oh yes, so it is; **wir dachten, es würde gleich regnen und** ~**, kaum ...** we thought it would soon start raining and, sure enough, scarcely ...

Richtige(r) *mf decl as adj* right person/man/woman *etc*; (*zum Heiraten auch*) Mr/Miss Right. **du bist mir der** ~**!** (*iro*) you're a fine *or* right one (*inf*), some mothers do have them! (*inf*); **sechs** ~ **im Lotto** six right in the lottery.

Richtige(s) *nt decl as adj* right thing. **das ist das** ~ that's right; **das ist genau das** ~ that's just right *or* the thing *or* the job (*inf*); **das ist auch nicht das** ~ that's not right either; **ich habe nichts** ~**s gegessen/gelernt** I haven't had a proper meal/I didn't really learn anything; **ich habe noch nicht das** ~**/endlich was** ~**s gefunden** I haven't found anything right *or* suitable/at last I've found something suitable.

richtiggehend 1 *adj attr Uhr, Waage* accurate; (*inf: regelrecht*) real, regular (*inf*), proper. **2** *adv* (*inf*) ~ **intelligent** really intelligent; **das ist ja** ~ **Betrug** that's downright deceit.

Richtigkeit *f* correctness, accuracy; (*von Verhalten, Vorgehen, einer Entscheidung*) rightness, correctness. **an der** ~ **von etw zweifeln, bei etw an der** ~ **zweifeln** (*inf*) to doubt whether sth is correct *or* right; **die** ~ **einer Abschrift bescheinigen** to certify a copy as being accurate; **das hat schon seine** ~ it's right enough; **es wird schon seine** ~ **haben** it's bound to be right *or* OK (*inf*); **damit hat es seine** ~ it's right.

Richtig-: **r~liegen** *vi sep irreg* (*inf*) to fit in; **bei jdm r~liegen** to get on well with sb; *siehe* **liegen (f); r~stellen** *vt sep* to correct; **ich muß Ihre Behauptung r~stellen** I must put you right there; ~**stellung** *f* correction.

Richt-: ~**kanonier** *m* (*Mil*) gun-layer; ~**kranz**, ~**krone** *f* (*Build*) wreath used in the topping-out ceremony; ~**linien** *pl* guidelines *pl*; ~**maß** *nt siehe* **Eichmaß**; ~**mikrophon** *nt* directional microphone *or* mike (*inf*); ~**platz** *m* place of execution; ~**preis** *m* recommended price; **unverbindlicher** ~**preis** recommended price; ~**scheit** *nt* (*Build*) (spirit) level; ~**schnur** *f* **(a)** (*Build*) guide line; (*senkrecht*) plumb-line; **(b)** (*fig: Grundsatz*) guiding principle; ~**schütze** *m* (*Mil*) gun-layer; ~**schwert** *nt* (*old*) executioner's sword; ~**spruch** *m* (*old*) judgement; ~**stätte** *f* (*old*) place of execution; ~**strahlantenne** *f*, ~**strahler** *m* beam *or* directional antenna.

Richtung *f* **(a)** direction. **in** ~ **Hamburg/Süden** towards Hamburg/the south, in the direction of Hamburg/in a southerly direction; (*auf Autobahn*) towards Hamburg/on the southbound carriageway (*Brit*) *or* lane; **in nördliche** ~ northwards, towards the north, in a northerly direction; **die Autobahn/der Zug** ~ **Hamburg** the Hamburg autobahn/train; **nach allen** ~**en/in alle** ~**en** in all directions; **die** ~ **ändern** *or* **wechseln** to change direction(s); **die** ~ **anzeigen** to indicate the direction, to point the way; (*mit Fahrzeug*) to indicate which way one is going to turn; **eine** ~ **nehmen** *or* **einschlagen** to head *or* drive/walk *etc* in a direction; **seine Gedanken/Argumente nahmen eine neue** ~ his thoughts/arguments took a new turn, (*die Vertreter einer* ~) movement; (*Denk~, Lehrmeinung*) school of thought. **die herrschende** ~ the prevailing trend; **Picasso begann eine völlig neue** ~ **in der Malerei** Picasso started a completely new direction in painting; **die beiden** ~**en in der katholischen Kirche** the two lines of thought in the Catholic church; **sie gehören den verschiedensten politischen** ~**en an** they have the most varied political sympathies; **die ganze** ~ **paßt uns nicht!** that's not the sort of thing we want.

richtunggebend *adj* pointing the way; (*in der Mode*) trend-setting. **für jdn/etw** ~ **sein** to set the pattern for sb/sth.

Richtungs-: ~**änderung** *f* change of *or* in direction; ~**fahrbahn** *f* carriageway (*Brit*), roadway (*US*); **r~los** *adj* lacking a sense

of direction; ~**losigkeit** *f* lack of a sense of direction; ~**wechsel** *m* (*lit, fig*) change of direction.

richtungweisend *adj* pointing the way. ~ **sein** to point the way (ahead).

Richt-: ~**waage** *f siehe* **Wasserwaage**; ~**zahl** *f* approximate figure.

Ricke *f* **-, -n** doe.

rieb *pret of* **reiben**.

riechen *pret* **roch**, *ptp* **gerochen 1** *vt* **i** to smell. **gut/schlecht** ~ to smell good/bad; **nach etw** ~ to smell of sth; **an jdm/etw** ~ to smell sb/sth, to sniff (at) sb/sth; **ich rieche Gas** I (can) smell gas; **ich rieche das Gewürz gern** I like the smell of this spice; **aus dem Mund** ~ to have bad breath; **riech mal** have a sniff *or* smell; **das riecht nach Betrug/Verrat** (*fig inf*) that smacks of deceit/treachery; **Lunte** *or* **den Braten** ~ (*fig sl*) to smell a rat (*inf*); **er kann kein Pulver** ~ (*fig inf*) he's yellow (*inf*) *or* chicken (*inf*); **ich kann das nicht** ~ (*inf*) I can't stand the smell of it; (*fig: nicht leiden*) I can't stand it; **jdn nicht** ~ **können** (*inf*) not to be able to stand sb, to hate sb's guts (*inf*); **das konnte ich doch nicht** ~**!** (*inf*) how was I (supposed) to know?, I'm not psychic (*inf*).

2 *vi* (*Geruchssinn haben*) to have a sense of smell, to be able to smell. **nicht mehr** ~ **können** to have lost one's sense of smell.

3 *vi impers* to smell. **es riecht angebrannt** there's a smell of burning, there's a burning smell; **es riecht nach Gas** there's a smell of gas; **es riecht nach armen Leuten** (*inf*) there's poverty in the air.

Riecher *m* **-s, -** (*inf*) **einen guten** *or* **den richtigen** ~ **(für etw) haben** (*inf*) to have a nose (for sth) (*inf*); **da habe ich doch den richtigen** ~ **gehabt!** I knew it all along!

Riech-: ~**fläschchen** *nt* (bottle of) smelling salts *pl*; ~**kolben** *m* (*sl*) hooter (*sl*), conk (*sl*), s(c)hnozzle (*sl*); ~**nerv** *m* olfactory nerve; ~**organ** *nt* organ of smell, olfactory organ; ~**salz** *nt* smelling salts *pl*; ~**stoff** *m* aromatic substance.

Ried *nt* **-s, -e (a)** (*Schilf*) reeds *pl*. **(b)** (*S Ger: Moor*) marsh.

Riedgras *nt* sedge.

rief *pret of* **rufen**.

Riefe *f* **-, -n** groove, channel; (*in Säulen*) flute.

riefelig, riefig *adj* grooved, channelled; *Säule* fluted.

riefeln, riefen *vt* to groove, to channel; *Säule* to flute.

Riege *f* **-, -n** (*Sport*) team, squad.

Riegel *m* **-s, - (a)** (*Verschluß*) bolt. **den** ~ **an etw** (*dat*) **vorlegen** to bolt sth; **vergiß nicht, den** ~ **vorzulegen!** don't forget to bolt the door *etc*; **den** ~ **an etw** (*dat*) **zurückschieben** to unbolt sth; **einer Sache** (*dat*) **einen** ~ **vorschieben** (*fig*) to put a stop to sth, to clamp down on sth; **ein** ~ **gegen aggressive Politik** a restraint on *or* against aggressive policies; *siehe* **Schloß**.

(b) (*Schokolade*) bar; (*Seife auch*) cake.

(c) (*Sew*) (*Lasche*) tab; (*von Jackett*) strap; (*für Haken*) eye; (*am Knopfloch*) bar tack.

Riegel-: ~**bau** *m* (*Sw*) half-timbering; (*Gebäude*) half-timbered building; ~**stellung** *f* (*Mil*) switch line *or* position; ~**werk** *nt* (*dial*) half-timbering.

Riegen-: ~**führer** *m* team *or* squad leader *or* captain; **r~weise** *adv* in teams *or* squads.

Riemchenschuh *m* strap shoe.

Riemen[1] *m* **-s, -** (*Treib~, Gürtel*) belt; (*an Schuhen, Kleidung, Koffer~, Gepäck~*) strap; (*Schnürsenkel*) leather shoelace; (*Peitschen~*) thong; (*vulg: Penis*) prick (*vulg*), cock (*vulg*). **jdn mit einem** ~ **verdreschen** to strap sb, to give sb the strap *or* belt; **den** ~ **enger schnallen** (*fig*) to tighten one's belt; **sich am** ~ **reißen** (*fig inf*) to get a grip on oneself.

Riemen[2] *m* **-s, -** (*Sport*) oar. **die** ~ **einlegen** to ship oars; **sich in die** ~ **legen** (*lit, fig*) to put one's back into it.

Riemen-: ~**antrieb** *m* belt-drive; ~**werk** *nt* strapping.

Ries *nt* **-es, -e** (*Measure*) German ream, ~ 2 reams.

Riese[1]: **das machst nach Adam** ~ **DM 3.50** (*hum inf*) the way I learned it at school that makes DM 3.50.

Riese[2] *m* **-n, -n** (*lit, fig*) giant; (*sl: Tausendmarkschein*) 1000 mark note, big one (*esp US sl*). **ein böser** ~ **an ogre**; **ein** ~ **von Mensch** *or* **von einem Menschen** a giant of a man/woman.

Rieselfelder *pl* sewage farm.

rieseln *vi aux sein* (*Wasser, Sand*) to trickle; (*Regen*) to drizzle; (*Schnee*) to float *or* flutter down. **der Kalk rieselt von der Wand** lime is crumbling off the wall; **Schuppen** ~ **ihm vom Kopf** dandruff is flaking off his head; **ein angenehmes Lustgefühl rieselte durch seinen Körper** a pleasurable sensation ran *or* thrilled through his body; **ein Schauder rieselte mir über den Rücken/durch alle Glieder** a shiver went down my spine/through me.

Riesen- *pref* gigantic, enormous, colossal; (*Zool, Bot etc auch*) giant; ~**ameise** *f* carpenter ant; ~**arbeit** *f* (*Pensum*) gigantic *etc* job; (*Anstrengung*) gigantic *etc* effort; ~**bau** *m* gigantic *etc* building; ~**chance** *f* tremendous chance; ~**erfolg** *m* gigantic *etc* success; (*Theat, Film*) smash hit; ~**fräulein** *nt* giantess; ~**gebirge** *nt* (*Geog*) Sudeten Mountains *pl*; ~**gestalt** *f* **(a)** (*Größe*) gigantic *etc* frame; **(b)** (*Riese*) giant; **r~groß, r~haft** *adj siehe* **riesig**; ~**haftigkeit** *f* gigantic *etc* size; ~**hai** *m* basking shark; ~**hunger** *m* (*inf*) enormous appetite; **ich habe einen** ~**hunger** (*inf*) I could eat a horse (*inf*); ~**kraft** *f* gigantic *etc* strength; **mit** ~**kräften with a gigantic** *or* **an enormous effort**; ~**rad** *nt* big *or* Ferris wheel; ~**salamander** *m* giant salamander; ~**schildkröte** *f* giant tortoise; ~**schlange** *f* boa; ~**schritt** *m* giant step *or* stride; **sich mit** ~**schritten nähern** (*fig*) to be drawing on apace; ~**slalom** *m* giant slalom; **r~stark** *adj* enormously strong; ~**trara** *nt* (*inf*) ballyhoo, great fuss *or* to-do (*inf*); ~**werk** *nt* colossal work; (*Gesamtwerk*) colossal works *pl*; ~**wuchs** *m* giantism; (*Med auch*) gigantism.

riesig 1 *adj* gigantic, colossal, enormous. **2** *adv* (*inf: sehr*) enormously, tremendously, immensely.

Riesin *f* giantess.

Riesling m Riesling.
Riester m -s, - leather patch.
riet pret of **raten**.
Riff nt -(e)s, -e **(a)** (Felsklippe) reef. **(b)** (Mus) riff.
Riffel f -, -n (Tex) (flax) hackle, flax comb.
riffeln vt **(a)** Flachs to comb. **(b)** (Tech) siehe **riefeln**.
Rigg nt -s, no pl (Naut) rigging.
Riggung f (Naut) rigging.
rigide adj (geh) rigid.
Rigidität f (Med, Psych) rigidity.
Rigole f -, -n (Agr) (drainage) trench.
Rigorismus m (geh) rigour.
rigoristisch adj (geh) rigorous.
rigoros adj rigorous. **ich bleibe dabei, da bin ich ganz ~** I'm sticking to that, I'm adamant.
Rigorosität f rigorousness.
Rigorosum nt -s, **Rigorosa** or (Aus) **Rigorosen** (Univ) (doctoral or PhD) viva.
Rikscha f -, -s rickshaw.
Rille f -, -n groove; (in Säule) flute.
Rillen-: r~förmig adj groove-like; ~**profil** nt tread.
rillig adj (rare) fluted.
Rimesse f (Fin) remittance.
rin- pref (dial) siehe **herein-, hinein-**.
Rind nt -(e)s, -er **(a)** (Tier) cow. ~**er cattle** pl; **10 ~er** 10 head of cattle. **(b)** (inf: Rindfleisch) beef. **vom ~** of beef; **Hackfleisch vom ~** minced (Brit) or ground (US) beef, mince.
Rinde f -, -n (Baum~) bark; (Brot~) crust; (Käse~) rind; (Anat) cortex.
rindenlos adj Baum barkless; Käse rindless.
Rinder-: ~**bouillon** f beef stock or bouillon (form); ~**braten** m (roh) joint of beef; (gebraten) roast beef no indef art; ~**bremse** f horsefly; ~**brühe** f beef broth; ~**brust** f brisket (of beef); ~**filet** nt fillet of beef; ~**herde** f herd of cattle; ~**hirt** m cowherd; (in Nordamerika) cowboy; (in Südamerika) gaucho; (in Australien) drover.
rindern vi (Kuh) to be on or in heat.
Rinder-: ~**pest** f (Vet) rinderpest; ~**talg** m beef dripping; ~**zucht** f cattle farming or raising; ~**zunge** f ox tongue.
Rind-: ~**fleisch** nt beef; ~**fleischbrühe** f beef broth.
Rinds- in cpds (Aus, S Ger) siehe **Rinder-**; ~**leder** nt leather; r~**ledern** adj attr leather; ~**stück** nt (Cook) joint of beef.
Rindvieh nt **(a)** no pl cattle. **10 Stück ~** 10 head of cattle. **(b)** pl **Rindviecher** (sl) ass (inf).
Ring m -(e)s, -e **(a)** ring; (Ketten~) link; (Wurf~) quoit; (Einweck~) seal, rubber; (Rettungs~) lifebuoy, lifebelt. **die ~e tauschen** or **wechseln** to exchange rings.
(b) (Kreis) (Jahres~, Rauch~) ring; (auf dem Wasser, von Menschen auch) circle; (~straße) ring road.
(c) (Sport) (Box~) ring; (von Schießständen) ring, circle. ~**e** (Turnen) rings; **acht ~e schießen** to score an eight; **~ frei!** seconds out or away!; (fig) clear the decks!
(d) (Astron, Met, Chem) ring.
(e) (Vereinigung) circle, group; (von Großhändlern, Erzeugern) group; (Bande) ring.
(f) (liter: Kreislauf) circle, cycle. **der ~ schließt sich** the circle is completed or closed, the wheel comes or turns full circle; **und hiermit schließt sich der ~ des Jahres** and thus the year's cycle is complete or the year has come full circle.
Ring-: r~**artig** adj ring-like; ~**bahn** f circle line.
Ringel m -s, - ring; (Locke) ringlet.
Ringelblume f marigold.
Ringelchen nt (inf) little ring.
Ringelgedicht nt siehe **Rondeau**.
ring(e)lig adj ringleted.
Ringellocke f ringlet. ~**n tragen** to wear one's hair in ringlets, to have ringlets.
ringeln 1 vt (Pflanze) to (en)twine; Schwanz etc auch to curl; siehe **geringelt**.
2 vr to go curly, to curl; (Rauch) to curl up(wards). **die Schlange ringelte sich durch das Unterholz** the snake wriggled through the undergrowth; **der Schwanz des Schweins ringelt sich** the pig has a curly tail; **die Schlange ringelte sich um den Baum** the snake coiled or curled itself around the tree.
Ringel-: ~**natter** f grass snake; ~**pie(t)z** m -es, -e (hum inf) hop (inf); ~**pie(t)z mit Anfassen** hop (inf); ~**reigen, ~reihen** ring-a-ring-o' roses; **einen ~reigen tanzen** to play ring-a-ring-o' roses; ~**schwanz** m, ~**schwänzchen** nt (inf) curly tail; ~**spiel** nt (Aus) merry-go-round, roundabout (Brit); ~**taube** f woodpigeon, ringdove; ~**wurm** m ringed worm, annelid (spec).
ringen pret **rang**, ptp **gerungen 1** vt **die Hände ~** to wring one's hands; **er rang ihr das Messer aus der Hand** he wrenched or wrested the knife from her hand; **ein Schluchzen rang sich aus ihrer Brust** (liter) a sob was wrung from her breast (liter).
2 vi **(a)** (lit, fig: kämpfen) to wrestle. **mit sich/dem Tode ~** to wrestle with oneself/death; **mit den Tränen ~** to struggle or fight to keep back one's tears.
(b) (streben) **nach** or **um etw ~** to struggle for sth; **er rang um Fassung** he struggled to maintain his composure; **ums Überleben ~** (liter) to struggle to survive.
Ringen nt -s, no pl (Sport) wrestling; (fig) struggle.
Ringer m -s, - wrestler.
Ringergriff m wrestling hold.
ringerisch adj wrestling attr.
Ring-: ~**finger** m ring finger; r~**förmig** adj ring-like; **der Wallgraben umschließt die Stadt** r~**förmig** the rampart rings or encircles the town; r~**förmige Verbindungen** (Chem) cyclic or ring compounds; ~**kampf** m fight; (Sport) wrestling match; ~**kämpfer** m wrestler; ~**lein** nt ring; ~**leitung** f (Elec etc) ring main; ~**lotte** f -, -n (Aus) siehe **Reneklode**; ~**mauer** f circular

wall; **die ~mauer rund um die Burg** the wall encircling or surrounding the castle; ~**muskel** m sphincter; ~**panzer** m articulated or jointed armour; ~**richter** m (Sport) referee.
rings adv (all) around. **die Stadt ist ~ von Bergen umgeben** the town is completely surrounded or encircled by mountains, there are mountains all around the town; **das Blumenbeet ist ~ mit Tulpen bepflanzt** tulips are planted around the edge of the flowerbed; **ich bin ~ um die Kirche gegangen** I went all the way round (the outside of) the church; **wir mußten uns alle ~ im Kreis aufstellen** we all had to get into or make a circle.
Ring-: ~**scheibe** f (Sport) target (marked with concentric rings); ~**sendung** f (Rad, TV) link up (transmission).
ringsherum adv (all the way) around.
Ringstraße f ring road.
rings-: ~**um** adv (all) around; ~**um konnte ich nichts sehen** I could see nothing around me; **ein breiter Graben lief ~um a** wide ditch went all round; ~**umher** adv around.
Ring-: ~**tausch** m exchange of rings; (von Wohnungen) three-way house exchange; ~**tennis** nt (Sport) quoits sing, deck tennis; ~**vorlesung** f series of lectures by different speakers; ~**wall** m siehe ~**mauer**.
Rinne f -, -n (Rille) groove; (Furche, Abfluß~, Fahr~) channel; (Bach~, inf: Rinnstein) gutter; (Geog) gap.
rinnen pret **rann**, ptp **geronnen** vi **(a)** aux sein (fließen) to run. **das Blut rann ihm in Strömen aus der Wunde** blood streamed from his wound; **die Zeit rinnt (dahin)** (liter) time is slipping away (liter); **das Geld rinnt ihm durch die Finger** (fig) money slips through his fingers.
(b) (naß sein) to run (vor with).
(c) (undicht sein) to leak.
Rinn-: ~**sal** nt -(e)s, -e rivulet; ~**stein** m (Gosse) gutter; (old: Ausguß) drain; **jdn aus dem ~stein holen** or **auflesen** (fig) to pick sb out of the gutter; **im ~stein enden** to come to a sorry end.
Rippchen nt (Cook) slightly cured pork rib.
Rippe f -, -n **(a)** (Anat, Cook) rib. **bei ihm kann man die ~n zählen** (inf) you could play a tune on his ribs (inf); **er hat nichts auf den ~n** (inf) he's just skin and bones; ... **damit du was auf die ~n kriegst** (inf) ... to put a bit of flesh on you; **ich kann es mir nicht aus den ~n schneiden** (inf), **ich kann es doch nicht durch die ~n schwitzen** (inf) I can't just produce it from nowhere.
(b) (Blatt~, Gewölbe~, Boots~) rib.
(c) (von Heizkörper, Kühlaggregat) fin.
(d) (von Apfelsine) segment; (von Schokolade) row (of squares).
rippen vt to rib.
Rippen-: ~**bogen** m (Anat) costal arch; ~**bruch** m broken or fractured rib; ~**fell** nt pleura; ~**fellentzündung** f pleurisy; ~**gewölbe** nt (Archit) ribbed vaulting; ~**quallen** pl ctenophorans pl (spec); ~**speer** m or nt (Cook) spare rib; **Kaßler** or **Kasseler ~speer** slightly cured pork spare rib; ~**stoß** m nudge, dig in the ribs; (schmerzhaft) thump (inf) or dig in the ribs; **ein freundschaftlicher ~stoß** (fig) a quiet or friendly word; ~**stück** nt (Cook) joint of meat including ribs.
Rippli pl (Sw) ribs pl.
Rippspeer m siehe **Rippenspeer**.
rips interj ~, raps! rip!
Rips m -es, -e (Tex) rep.
Risiko nt -s, -s or **Risiken** or (Aus) **Risken** risk. **auf eigenes ~** at one's own risk; **bitte, Sie können das machen, aber auf eigenes ~** do it by all means, but on your own head be it; **ohne ~** without risk; **etw ohne ~ tun** to do sth without taking a risk; **es ist nicht ohne ~**, **das zu tun** there is a risk involved in doing that, doing that is not without a risk; **die Sache ist ohne ~** there's no risk involved.
risikofreudig adj venturesome, prepared to take risks.
riskant adj risky, chancy (inf). **das ist mir zu ~** that's too risky or chancy for me.
riskieren* vt **(a)** (aufs Spiel setzen) to risk. **etwas/nichts ~ to** take risks or chances/no risks or chances; **seine Stellung/sein Geld ~** to risk losing one's job/money, to put one's job/money at risk; **sein Geld bei etw ~** to risk one's money on sth.
(b) (wagen) to venture. **traust du dich, hier runterzuspringen? — ja, ich riskier's!** do you think you dare jump down? — yes, I'll risk or chance it!; **in Gegenwart seiner Frau riskiert er kein Wort** when his wife is present he dare not say a word.
Rispe f -, -n (Bot) panicle.
rispenförmig, rispig adj (Bot) panicled, paniculate.
riß pret of **reißen**.
Riß m Risses, Risse **(a)** (in Stoff, Papier etc) tear, rip; (in Erde, Gestein) crevice, fissure; (Sprung in Wand, Behälter etc) crack; (Haut~) chap; (Tiefe: Kluft) rift, split. **die Freundschaft hat einen (tiefen) ~ bekommen** a rift has developed in their friendship; **durch das Volk geht ein tiefer ~** there is a deep split in the people, the people are deeply divided.
(b) (Archit: Zeichnung) sketch, sketch plan.
(c) (Hunt: Raubwildbeute) kill.
rissig adj Boden, Wand, Leder cracked; Haut, Hände chapped.
Rißwunde f laceration, lacerated wound.
Rist m -(e)s, -e **(a)** (am Fuß) instep; (an der Hand) back (of the hand). **(b)** (beim Pferd) withers pl.
ristornieren* vt (Comm) to cancel.
Ristorno m or nt -s, -s (Comm) cancellation.
rite adv (Univ) lowest pass grade in doctoral examinations.
Riten pl of **Ritus**.
ritsch interj ~, ratsch! rip!
ritt pret of **reiten**.
Ritt m -(e)s, -e ride. **einen ~ machen** to go for a ride; **in scharfem ~ jagte er über die Felder** riding furiously he chased across the fields; **in einem** or **auf einen ~** (inf) at one go (inf).

Ritter m -s, - (a) (im Mittelalter, im alten Rom) knight; (Kavalier) cavalier. **fahrender ~** knight errant; **jdn zum ~ schlagen** to knight sb, to dub sb knight; **der ~ von der traurigen Gestalt** the Knight of the Sorrowful Countenance; **ein ~ ohne Furcht und Tadel** (lit) a doughty knight; (fig) a knight in shining armour.
  (b) (Adelstitel) ≃ Sir. **X ~ von Y** ≃ Sir X of Y.
  (c) (Ordensträger) knight.
  (d) (Schmetterling) swallowtail.
  (e) (Cook) **arme ~** pl sweet French toast soaked in milk.

Ritter-: **~burg** f knight's castle; **~drama** nt late eighteenth century and Romantic drama featuring Medieval (German) knight as hero, romance of chivalry; **~gut** nt ≃ manor; **~gutsbesitzer** m ≃ lord of the manor; **r~haft** adj siehe **r~lich**; **~kreuz** nt (Mil) Knight's Cross; **~kreuz mit Eichenlaub** ≃ Knight's Cross with bar; **~kreuzträger** m holder of the Knight's Cross; **r~lich** adj (lit) knightly; (fig) chivalrous; **~lichkeit** f chivalry, chivalrousness; **~orden** m order of knights; **der Deutsche ~orden** the Teutonic Order; **~roman** m (Liter) romance of chivalry; **~schaft** f (a) (die Ritter) knights pl, knighthood; (b) (Ritterfahrt) **auf ~schaft ziehen** to go out as a knight errant; (c) (Ritterehre) knighthood; **~schlag** m (Hist) dubbing; **den ~schlag empfangen** to be knighted, to be dubbed knight; (jdm) **den ~schlag erteilen** to confer a knighthood (on sb).

Rittersmann m, pl -leute (poet) knight.

Ritter-: **~sporn** m (Bot) larkspur, delphinium; **~stand** m knighthood; **in den ~stand erhoben werden** to be raised to the knighthood, to be knighted; **~tum** nt knighthood; **~-und-Räuber-Roman** m (Liter) late eighteenth century sentimental novel about knights and robbers, romance of chivalry; **~wesen** nt knighthood; **~zeit** f Age of Chivalry.

rittig adj Pferd broken in, rideable.

rittlings adv astride (auf etw (dat) sth).

Rittmeister m (old Mil) cavalry captain, captain (of horse).

Ritual nt -s, -e or -ien [-iən] (lit, fig) ritual.

Rituale nt -, no pl (Eccl) ritual. **~ Romanum** missal.

Ritualhandlung f ritual act.

Ritualien [-iən] pl (Eccl) ritual objects pl.

Ritualismus m (Rel) Ritualism.

Ritualmord m ritual murder.

rituell adj ritual.

Ritus m -, **Riten** rite; (fig) ritual.

Ritz m -es, -e (a) (Kratzer) scratch. (b) (Spalte) chink, crack.

Ritze f -, -n (Spalte, Po~) crack; (Fuge) join, gap. **auf der ~ schlafen** (hum inf) to sleep in the middle.

Ritzel nt -s, - (Tech) pinion.

ritzen 1 vt to scratch; (einritzen) Initialen, Namen etc auch to carve. **die Sache ist geritzt** (inf) it's all fixed up. 2 vr to scratch oneself.

Ritzer m -s, - (inf) scratch.

Rivale [ri'va:lə] m -n, -n, **Rivalin** [ri'va:lɪn] f rival.

rivalisieren* [rivali'zi:rən] vi mit jdm ~ to compete with sb; **34 ~de Parteien** 34 rival parties.

Rivalität [rivali'tɛ:t] f rivalry.

Rizinus m -, - or -se (a) (Bot) castor-oil plant. (b) (auch ~öl) castor oil.

Roastbeef ['ro:stbi:f] nt -s, -s (roh) beef; (gebraten) roast beef.

Robbe f -, -n seal.

robben vi aux sein (Mil) to crawl.

Robben-: **~fang** m sealing, seal hunting; **~fänger** m sealer, seal hunter; **~jagd** f siehe **~fang**.

Robe f -, -n (a) (Abendkleid) evening gown. **in großer ~** in evening dress. (b) (Amtstracht) (official) robe or robes pl.

Robinie [-iə] f robinia.

Robinsonade f Robinsonade; (Sport) flying save (towards attacker).

roboten vi (sl) to slave (inf).

Roboter ['robotɐ, ro'bo:tɐ] m -s, - (a) robot. (b) (sl: Schwerstarbeiter) slave (inf). (c) (Sport) ball-feeder.

robust adj (a) (derb) rough. (b) (widerstandsfähig) robust.

Robustheit f siehe adj (a) roughness. (b) robustness.

roch pret of **riechen**.

Rochade [rɔ'xa:də, rɔ'ʃa:də] f (Chess) castling; (Ftbl) switchover, change of position. **die kleine** or **kurze/große** or **lange ~** castling king's side/queen's side.

Röcheln nt -s, no pl groan; (Todes~) death rattle. **das ~ der Verletzten** the groans or groaning of the wounded.

röcheln vi to groan; (Sterbender) to give the death rattle.

Rochen m -s, - ray.

rochieren* [rɔ'xi:rən, rɔ'ʃi:rən] vi to castle; (Ftbl) to change or switch positions.

Rock m -(e)s, ⁼e (a) (Damen~) skirt; (Schotten~) kilt; (Sw: Kleid) dress. (b) (geh: Herren~) jacket. **den bunten ~ anziehen** (old) to take the King's shilling (old); **der grüne ~ (des Försters)** (old) the green coat of a forester; **der schwarze ~ (des Geistlichen)** (old) the black gown or cassock of a priest.

Rock|aufschlag m lapel.

Röckchen nt dim of **Rock**.

Rocken m -s, - (Tex) distaff.

Rocker m -s, - rocker.

Rock-: **~falte** f (von Damenrock) inverted pleat; (von Jackett) vent; **~futter** nt skirt lining.

Rockhacke f mattock.

Rock-: **~saum** m hem of a/the skirt; **~schoß** m coat-tail; **an jds ~schößen hängen**, **sich jdm an die ~schöße hängen** (inf) to cling to sb's coat-tails (inf); **~zipfel** m: **der Mutter am ~zipfel** or **an Mutters ~zipfel hängen** (inf) to cling to (one's) mother's apron-strings (inf).

Rodel m -s, -, (S Ger, Aus) f -, -n sledge, toboggan, sleigh.

Rodelbahn f toboggan-run.

rodeln vi aux sein or haben to toboggan (auch Sport), to sledge.

Rodel-: **~schlitten** m toboggan, sledge; **~sport** m tobogganning.

roden vt Wald, Land to clear; Kartoffeln to lift.

Rodeo m or nt -s, -s rodeo.

Rodler(in f) m -s, - tobogganer; (Sport auch) tobogganist.

Rodung f (das Roden, Siedlung) clearing.

Rogate f -, -n (Eccl) Rogation Sunday.

Rogen m -s, - roe.

Rog(e)ner m -s, - spawner.

Rogenstein m (Geol) oolite, oolitic limestone.

Roggen m -s, no pl rye.

Rogner m -s, - siehe **Rog(e)ner**.

roh adj (a) (ungebraten, ungekocht) raw; Milch ordinary.
  (b) (unbearbeitet) Bretter etc rough; Stein auch undressed, unhewn; Diamant auch uncut; Eisen, Metall crude; Felle untreated. **etw aus dem ~en arbeiten** (Art) to work sth from the rough; **die Statue/das Bild/das Manuskript ist im ~en fertig** the rough shape of the statue/the rough sketch of the picture/the rough draft of the manuscript is finished; siehe Ei.
  (c) (unkultiviert, brutal) rough. **~e Gewalt** brute force; **wo ~e Kräfte sinnlos walten ...** (prov) brute force does it.

Roh-: **~bau** m (a) (Bauabschnitt) shell of a/the house); **das Haus ist im ~bau fertig(gestellt)** the house is structurally complete; **die ~bauten** the shells of the unfinished houses; (b) siehe Klinkerbau; **~baumwolle** f raw cotton; **~benzin** m naphtha; **~bilanz** f trial balance sheet; **~bogen** m unbound sheet; **~diamant** m rough or uncut or unpolished diamond; **~einnahme** f siehe **~ertrag**; **~eisen** nt pig iron.

Roheit f (a) no pl (Eigenschaft) roughness; (Brutalität auch) brutality. (b) (Tat) brutality. (c) (ungekochter Zustand) rawness.

Roh|ertrag m gross proceeds pl.

roherweise adv roughly.

Roh-: **~faser** f raw fibre; **~gewicht** nt gross weight; **~gummi** m or nt raw rubber; **~kost** f raw fruit and vegetables pl; **~köstler(in** f) m -s, - person who prefers fruit and vegetables uncooked; **~leder** nt rawhide, untanned leather; **~ling** m (a) (Grobian) brute, ruffian. (b) (Tech) blank; **~material** nt raw material; **~öl** nt crude oil; **~produkt** nt raw material; **~produktenhändler** m siehe Schrotthändler.

Rohr nt -(e)s, -e (a) (Schilf~) reed; (Röhricht, Schilf) reeds pl; (Zucker~) cane; (für Stühle etc) cane, wicker no pl. **aus ~ geflochtene Stühle** wicker(work) or basketwork or cane chairs; **wie eine schwankendes ~ im Wind** (liter) like a reed in the wind (liter); **spanisches ~** (old) cane.
  (b) (Tech, Mech) pipe; (Geschütz~) (gun) barrel; (Blas~) blowpipe. **aus allen ~en feuern** to fire with all its guns.
  (c) (dial, Aus: Backröhre) oven.

Rohr-: **~ammer** f (Orn) reed bunting; **~blatt** nt (Mus) reed; **~bruch** m burst pipe.

Röhrchen nt tube; (Chem) test tube; (inf: zur Alkoholkontrolle) breathalyzer. **ins ~ blasen** (inf) to be breathalyzed, to have or take a breathalyzer test.

Rohrdommel f -, -n (Orn) bittern.

Röhre f -, -n (a) (Ofen~) warming oven; (Back~) oven; (Drainage~) drainage pipe. **in die ~ gucken** (inf) to be left out.
  (b) (Neon~) (neon) tube or strip; (Elektronen~) valve (Brit), tube (US); (fig: Fernsehgerät) telly (Brit inf), box (Brit inf), tube (US inf). **in die ~ gucken** or **glotzen** (inf) to watch telly (Brit inf) or the tube (US inf), to sit in front of the box (Brit inf).
  (c) (Höhlung, Hohlkörper) tube; (in Knochen) cavity.
  (d) (Hunt: Gang im Tierbau) gallery.

rö(h)ren vi (Hunt) to bell.

Röhren-: **~blüter** m (Bot) tubiflorae pl (spec); **~brunnen** m fountain; **r~förmig** adj tubular; Hosenbein drainpipe attr; **~hose** f (inf) drainpipe trousers pl; **~knochen** m long bone; **~pilz** m siehe Röhrling.

Rohr-: **r~farben** adj beige, fawn; **~flöte** f (Mus) reed pipe; (Orgel~) rohrflöte, rohr flute; (Pan~) pan pipes pl; **~geflecht** nt wickerwork, basketwork.

Röhricht nt -s, -e (old) reeds pl, reed bed.

Rohr-: **~kolben** m (Bot) reed mace, cat's tail; **~krepierer** m -s, - (Mil sl) barrel burst; **zum ~krepierer werden, ein ~krepierer sein** (fig) to backfire; **~leger** m -s, - pipe fitter; **~leitung** f pipe, conduit; **~leitungssystem** nt network or system of pipes.

Röhrling m (Bot) boletus.

Rohr-: **~matte** f rush or reed mat; **~möbel** pl cane furniture sing; **~muffe** f (Tech) socket; **~netz** nt network of pipes; **~palme** f calamus; **~post** f pneumatic dispatch system; **~postkarte** f (dated) postcard sent by pneumatic dispatch; **~sänger** m (Orn) warbler; **~spatz** m: **schimpfen wie ein ~spatz** (inf) to make a fuss; (Schimpfwörter gebrauchen) to curse and swear; **~stock** m cane; **~stuhl** m basketwork or wickerwork chair; **~zange** f pipe wrench; **~zucker** m cane sugar.

Roh-: **~seide** f wild silk; **r~seiden** adj wild silk.

Rohstoff m raw material; (St Ex) commodity.

Rohstoff-: **~mangel** m shortage of raw material; **~reserven** pl reserves of raw materials pl.

Roh-: **~tabak** m tobacco; (ungetrocknet) uncured tobacco; (ungeschnitten) leaf tobacco; **~übersetzung** f rough translation; **~zucker** m crude or unrefined sugar; **~zustand** m natural or unprocessed state or condition; **das Denkmal/Manuskript ist noch im ~zustand** the memorial/manuscript is still in a fairly rough state.

rojen vti (Naut) to row.

Rokoko nt -(s), no pl Rococo period; (Stil) Rococo, rococo.

Rolladen m -s, **Rolläden** or - getrennt **Roll-laden** (an Fenster, Tür etc) shutters pl; (von Schreibtisch) roll top.

Rollbahn f (Aviat) taxiway; (Start-, Landebahn) runway.

Röllchen nt little roll; (von Garn) reel.

Rolle f -, -n (a) (Zusammengerolltes) roll; (Garn~, Zwirn~) reel, bobbin (spec); (Urkunde) scroll. eine ~ Garn/Zwirn a reel of thread; eine ~ Bindfaden a ball of string; eine ~ Film a roll of film; (im Kino) a reel of film.
   (b) (walzenförmig) roller; (an Möbeln, Kisten) caster, castor; (an Flaschenzug) pulley; (Gardinen~) runner.
   (c) (dial: Wäschemangel) roller iron.
   (d) (Sport) forward roll; (Aviat) roll. eine ~ machen to do a forward roll/roll; die ~ rückwärts the backward roll.
   (e) (Theat, Film, fig) role, part; (Sociol) role. es war ein Spiel mit vertauschten ~n (fig) it was a situation where the roles were reversed; ein Stück mit verteilten ~n lesen to read a play with the parts cast or (in Schule) given out; der literarische Kreis liest jeden Dienstag ein Stück mit verteilten ~n the literary circle has a play-reading every Tuesday; eine Ehe mit streng verteilten ~n a marriage with strict allocation of roles; jds ~ bei etw (fig) sb's role or part in sth; in der ~ von jdm/etw auftreten to appear in the role of sb/sth; er gefällt sich (dat) in der ~ des ... (fig) he likes to think of or see himself in the role of the ...; sich in die ~ eines anderen versetzen (fig) to put oneself in sb else's place; bei or in etw (dat) eine ~ spielen to play a part in sth; (Mensch auch) to play a role in sth; als Verteidiger hat er eine klägliche ~ gespielt as a defence counsel he was not up to much or he left much to be desired; etw spielt eine große ~ (bei jdm) sth is very important (to sb); es spielt keine ~, (ob) ... it doesn't matter (whether) ..., it doesn't make any difference (whether) ...; das spielt hier keine ~ that does not concern us now, that is irrelevant; bei ihm spielt Geld keine ~ with him money is no object; bei wem Geld eine ~ spielt, der sollte lieber nicht mitfahren if you've got to think about money, you'd be better not to come along; bei ihm/dieser Entscheidung spielt persönliche Zuneigung überhaupt keine ~ he is not influenced by personal inclination/personal inclination plays no part in or doesn't come into this decision; aus der ~ fallen (fig) to forget oneself; seine ~ ausgespielt haben (fig) to have played one's part.

rollen 1 vi (a) aux sein to roll; (Flugzeug) to taxi. der Stein kommt ins R~ (fig) the ball has started rolling; etw/den Stein ins R~ bringen (fig) to set or start sth/the ball rolling; es werden einige Köpfe ~ heads will roll.
   (b) mit den Augen ~ to roll one's eyes.
   2 vt to roll; Teig to roll out; Teppich, Papier to roll up; (dial: mangeln) Wäsche, Bettücher to mangle.
   3 vr to curl up; (Schlange auch) to curl itself up.

Rollen-: ~besetzung f (Theat, Film) casting; ~erwartung f (Sociol) role expectation; ~fach nt (Theat) character or type part; der jugendliche Liebhaber ist sein ~fach he's a character actor specializing in the young lover; r~förmig adj cylindrical; ~gedicht nt (Liter) dramatic monologue; r~gelagert adj mounted on roller bearings; ~konflikt m role conflict; ~lager nt roller bearings pl; r~spezifisch adj role-specific; ~tausch m exchange of roles; (Sociol auch) role reversal; ~zug m siehe Flaschenzug.

Roller m -s, - (a) scooter. (b) (Naut: Welle) roller. (c) (Aus: Rollo) (roller) blind. (d) (Orn) Harzer ~ canary, roller. (e) (Walze) roller.

Rollerfahren nt riding a scooter.

rollern vi aux sein to ride one's scooter.

Roll-: ~feld nt runway; ~film m roll film; ~fuhrdienst m road-rail haulage; ~geld nt carriage, freight charge; ~gerste f (Agr) pot-barley, hulled barley; ~gut nt (Rail) freight; ~hockey nt roller-skate hockey; ~kommando nt raiding party; ~kragen m roll or polo neck; ~kunstlauf m roller-skating; ~kur f (Med) treatment for stomach disorders where the patient takes medicine, lies for 5 minutes on his back, 5 minutes on his side, then on his front etc; ~kutscher m (old) drayman; ~mops m rollmops.

Rollo nt -s, -s (roller) blind.

Roll-: ~schinken m smoked ham; ~schnellauf m speed (roller-) skating; ~schrank m roll-fronted cupboard.

Rollschuh m roller-skate. ~ laufen to roller-skate.

Rollschuh-: ~bahn f roller-skating rink; ~laufen nt roller-skating; ~läufer m roller-skater; ~sport m roller-skating.

Roll-: ~sitz m (im Rennboot) sliding seat; ~splitt m loose chippings pl; ~sport m siehe ~schuhsport; ~steg m travolator, moving pavement (Brit), mobile walkway (US); (Naut) gangplank, gangway; ~stuhl m wheel-chair; ~tabak m tobacco plug; ~treppe f escalator; ~werk nt (Archit) cartouche, scroll-work.

Rom nt -s Rome. ~ ist auch nicht an einem Tag erbaut worden (prov) Rome wasn't built in a day (Prov); viele Wege führen nach ~ (Prov) all roads lead to Rome (Prov); das sind Zustände wie im alten ~ (inf) (unmoralisch) it's disgraceful; (primitiv) it's medieval (inf).

Roman m -s, -e novel; (höfisch, ritterlich etc auch) romance. ich könnte einen ~ schreiben! (inf) I could write a book about it!; (jdm) einen ganzen ~ erzählen (inf) to give sb a long rigmarole (inf); erzähl keine ~e! (inf) don't tell stories! (inf).

romanartig adj novelistic.

Romanautor m, **Romancier** [romã'sie:] m -s, -s novelist.

Romane m -n, -n person speaking a Romance language.

Romanentum nt Latin nature.

Roman-: r~haft adj like a novel; ~heft nt cheap pulp novel, penny dreadful (dated); ~held m hero of a/the novel.

Romania f - die ~ (Liter) all Romance languages and culture.

Romanik f (Archit, Art) Romanesque period; (Stil) Romanesque (style).

Romanin f siehe Romane.

romanisch adj Volk, Sprache Romance; (Art) Romanesque.

Romanist(in f) m (Univ) teacher/student/scholar of Romance languages and literature.

Romanistik f (Univ) Romance languages and literature.

romanistisch adj Romance.

Roman-: ~leser m novel reader; ~literatur f fiction, novels pl; ~schreiber m (inf) novelist; (pej) scribbler; ~schriftsteller m novelist.

Romantik f (a) (Liter, Art, Mus) Romanticism; (Epoche) Age of Romanticism, Romantic period. die blaue Blume der ~ (Liter) the Blue Flower of the Romantics. (b) (fig) romance, romanticism; (Gefühl, Einstellung) romanticism. keinen Sinn für ~ haben to have no sense of romance.

Romantiker(in f) m -s, - (Liter, Art, Mus) Romantic; (fig) romantic.

romantisch adj romantic; (Liter etc) Romantic.

romantisieren* vt to romanticize.

romantsch, romaun(t)sch, romontsch, rumantsch adj siehe rätoromanisch.

Romanze f -, -n (Liter, Mus, fig) romance.

Römer[1] m -s, - (Weinglas) wineglass in various sizes with clear glass bowl and green or brown coiled stem.

Römer[2] m -s der ~ town hall of Frankfurt am Main.

Römer(in f) m -s, - Roman. die alten ~ the (ancient) Romans.

Römer-: ~brief m Letter or Epistle of Paul to the Romans, Romans sing, no art; ~reich nt Roman Empire; ~straße f Roman road; ~topf m (Cook) ~ (chicken) brick; ~tum nt Roman culture etc; die Haupttugenden des ~tums the main virtues of Rome; das ~tum hat zahlreiche griechische Elemente absorbiert Rome absorbed many elements from Greece.

Romfahrer m pilgrim to Rome.

römisch adj Roman.

römisch-katholisch adj Roman Catholic.

Rommé [rɔ'me:, 'rome] nt -s, no pl rummy.

Rondeau nt -s, -s (a) [rõ'do:] (Liter, Mus) rondeau, rondel. (b) [rɔn'do:] (Aus: Rondell) circular flowerbed.

Rondell nt -s, -e (a) (Archit) round tower. (b) circular flowerbed.

Rondo nt -s, -s (Mus) rondo.

röntgen vt to X-ray; Körperteil auch to take an X-ray of.

Röntgen nt -s, no pl X-raying. er ist zur Zeit beim ~ he's being X-rayed at the moment.

Röntgen-: ~apparat m X-ray equipment no indef art, no pl; ~aufnahme f X-ray (plate); ~augen pl (hum) X-ray eyes pl (hum); ~behandlung f, ~bestrahlung f radiotherapy, X-ray treatment or therapy; ~diagnostik f X-ray diagnosis; ~film m X-ray film.

röntgenisieren* vt (Aus) siehe röntgen.

Röntgenogramm nt -s, -e X-ray (plate), radiograph (esp US).

Röntgenographie f radiography.

Röntgenologe m, **Röntgenologin** f radiologist, roentgenologist (form).

Röntgenologie f radiology, roentgenology (form).

Röntgenoskopie f radioscopy.

Röntgen-: ~röhre f X-ray tube; ~strahlen pl X-rays pl; jdn mit ~strahlen behandeln to treat sb with X-rays, to give sb X-ray treatment; ~therapie f siehe ~behandlung; ~untersuchung f X-ray examination.

Roof m or nt -(e)s, -e (Naut) deckhouse.

rören vi siehe rö(h)ren.

rosa adj inv pink. ein ~ or ~nes (inf) Kleid a pink dress; die Welt durch eine ~(rote) Brille sehen to see the world through rose-coloured or rose-tinted glasses; in ~(rotem) Licht in a rosy light; er malt die Zukunft ~rot he paints a rosy picture of the future.

Rosa nt -s, -s pink.

rosa-: ~farben, ~farbig, ~rot siehe rosa.

rösch adj (S Ger: knusprig) Brot crusty; Fleisch crisp; Mädchen bonnie (esp N Engl, Scot).

Röschen ['rø:sçən] nt (little) rose; (von Rosenkohl) Brussel(s) sprout.

Rose f -, -n (a) (Blume) rose; (Kompaßblatt auch) compass card; (Archit) rose window. er ist nicht auf ~n gebettet (fig) life isn't a bed of roses for him; keine ~ ohne Dornen (prov) no rose without a thorn (prov). (b) (Med) erysipelas (spec), rose. (c) (Hunt: am Hirschgeweih) burr.

rosé adj inv pink. Schuhe in ~ pink shoes.

Rosé m -s, -s rosé (wine).

Rosen-: r~artig adj rose-like, rosaceous (spec); ~blatt nt rose petal; ~duft m scent or perfume of roses; r~farben, r~farbig adj rose-coloured, pink, rosy; r~fing(e)rig adj (poet) roseate (poet); ~garten m rose garden; ~gewächse pl rosaceae pl (spec); ~holz nt rosewood; ~käfer m rose chafer, rose beetle; ~knospe f rosebud; ~kohl m Brussel(s) sprouts pl; ~kranz m (Eccl) rosary; einen ~kranz beten to say a rosary; ~kreu(t)zer pl (Rel) the Rosicrucians pl; ~kriege pl (Hist) the Wars of the Roses pl; ~montag m Monday preceding Ash Wednesday; ~montagszug m Carnival parade which takes place on the Monday preceding Ash Wednesday; ~öl nt attar of roses; ~quarz m rose quartz; r~rot adj Wangen, Lippen rosy (red); Schneeweißchen und ~rot (Liter) Snow White and Rose Red; ~stock m rose (tree); ~strauch m rosebush; ~zucht f rose-growing; ~züchter m rose-grower.

Rosette f rosette.

Roséwein m rosé wine.

rosig adj (lit, fig) rosy. etw in ~em Licht sehen (inf) to see sth in a rosy light; etw in ~en Farben schildern (inf) to paint a glowing or rosy picture of sth, to show sth in a rosy light.

Rosine f raisin. (große) ~n im Kopf haben (inf) to have big ideas; sich (dat) die (besten or größten) ~n (aus dem Kuchen)

herauspicken (inf) to take the pick of the bunch.
Rosinenbomber m (hum) plane which flew food etc into Berlin during the 1948 airlift.
Röslein nt (little) rose.
Rosmarin m -s, no pl rosemary.
Roß nt Rosses, Rosse or (S Ger, Aus) **Rösser** (liter) steed; (S Ger, Aus) horse; (inf: Dummkopf) dolt (inf). ~ und Reiter nennen (fig geh) to name names; der Ritter hoch zu ~ (liter) the knight astride his steed (liter); siehe hoch.
Roß-: ~apfel m (hum inf) horse droppings pl; ~breiten pl (Naut) horse latitudes pl.
Rössel, Rößl nt -s, - (Chess) knight; (S Ger: Pferd) horse.
Rosselenker m (poet) reinsman (liter).
Rösselsprung m (a) (Chess) knight's move. (b) (Rätselart) type of crossword puzzle in which certain individual letters make up a phrase or saying.
Roß-: ~haar nt horsehair; ~haarmatratze f horsehair mattress; ~käfer m siehe Mistkäfer; ~kastanie f horse chestnut; ~kastanienextrakt m extract of horse chestnut used as a medicament for varicose veins; ~kur f (hum) drastic cure, kill-or-cure remedy; eine ~kur (durch)machen to follow a drastic cure.
Rößli(spiel), Rössliritti nt -s, - (Sw) merry-go-round, roundabout (Brit).
Roß-: ~schlächter m horse butcher; ~schlächterei f horse butchery; ~täuscher m (old, fig) horse-trader; ~täuscherei f (fig) horse-trading no pl.
Rost¹ m -(e)s, no pl (auch Bot) rust. ~ ansetzen to start to rust.
Rost² m -(e)s, -e (Ofen~) grill; (Gitter~) grating, grille; (dial: Bett~) base, frame. auf dem ~ braten (Cook) to barbecue, to grill on charcoal.
Rost-: ~ansatz m signs of rust pl; r~beständig adj rust-resistant; ~bildung f rust formation; ~braten m (Cook) = roast; ~bratwurst f grilled or barbecued sausage; r~braun adj russet; Haar auburn.
Röstbrot nt siehe Toast.
Röste f -, -n (Metal) roasting.
rosten vi aux sein or haben to rust, to get rusty (auch fig). alte Liebe rostet nicht (Prov) old love never dies; siehe rasten.
rösten vt (a) Kaffee to roast; Brot to toast. sich in der Sonne ~ lassen to lie in the sun and bake. (b) Erz to roast, to calcine.
Rösterei f roast(ing) house. frisch aus der ~ fresh from the roast, freshly roasted.
Rost-: r~farben, r~farbig adj siehe r~braun; ~fleck m spot or patch of rust, rust spot or patch; r~frei adj (Stahl) stainless.
rostig adj (lit, fig) rusty.
Röstkartoffeln pl siehe Bratkartoffeln.
Rost-: ~krankheiten pl (Bot) rust diseases pl; ~laube f (hum) rust-heap (hum); r~rot adj rust-coloured, russet.
Rostschutz m anti-rust protection.
Rostschutz-: ~farbe f anti-rust paint; ~mittel nt rust-proofer.
Rost|umwandler m (Aut) rust converter.
rot adj red (auch Pol). ~e Bete or Rüben beetroot; ~e Johannisbeeren pl redcurrants pl; das R~e Kreuz the Red Cross; der R~e Halbmond the Red Crescent; der R~e Löwe the Red Cross in Iran; der R~e Platz Red Square; das R~e Meer the Red Sea; die R~e Armee the Red Army; die R~en (pej) the reds; die ~e Flut (pej) the red peril; in den ~en Zahlen stecken to be in the red; Gewalt zieht sich wie ein ~er Faden durch die Geschichte violence runs like a thread through history; ~ werden to blush, to go red (inf); bis über beide Ohren ~ werden to blush furiously, to turn crimson; ~ wie ein Krebs red as a lobster; ~ Ohren bekommen (hum), einen ~en Kopf bekommen or kriegen (inf) to blush, to go red (inf); ~ (angehaucht) sein (Pol inf) to have left-wing leanings; sich (dat) etw ~ (im Kalender) anstreichen (inf) to make sth a red-letter day; den Tag werde ich mir ~ im Kalender anstreichen that will be a red-letter day; siehe Grütze, rotsehen, Tuch, Hahn.
Rot nt -s, -s or - red; (Wangen~) rouge. bei or auf ~ at red; bei ~ anhalten! stop (when the lights are) at red, stop when the lights are (at) red; die Ampel stand auf ~ the lights were (at) red; bei ~ über die Ampel fahren to jump or shoot (inf) the lights.
Röt nt -(e)s, no pl (Geol) upper layer of bunter sandstone.
Rotarier [ro'ta:riɐ] m -s, - rotarian.
Rot|armist m soldier in or of the Red Army. die ~en zogen durch die Stadt the Red Army moved through the town.
Rota (Romana) f - (-), no pl (Eccl) rota.
Rotation f (Phys) rotation; (Math auch) curl.
Rotations-: ~achse f (Math, Phys) axis of rotation; ~druck m (Typ) rotary (press) printing; ~fläche f (Math, Phys) surface of revolution; ~maschine, ~presse f (Typ) rotary press.
Rot-: ~auge nt (Zool) roach; r~bäckig, r~backig adj rosy-cheeked; ~barsch m rosefish; ~bart m red-beard; Kaiser ~bart Emperor Frederick Barbarossa; r~bärtig adj red-bearded; r~blond adj Haar sandy; Mann sandy-haired; Frau, Tönung, (Frauen)haar strawberry blonde; r~braun adj reddish brown; ~buche f (common) beech; ~dorn m hawthorn.
Röte f -, no pl redness, red; (Erröten) blush. die ~ des Abendhimmels the red glow of the evening sky; die ~ stieg ihr ins Gesicht her face reddened.
Rote-Kreuz-Lotterie f etc siehe Rotkreuzlotterie etc.
Rötel m -s, - red chalk.
Röteln pl German measles sing.
Rötelzeichnung f (Art) red chalk drawing.
röten 1 vt to turn red, to make red; Himmel to turn red. die frische Luft rötete ihre Wangen the fresh air gave her rosy cheeks or made her cheeks (go) red; ein gerötetes Gesicht a flushed face. 2 vr to turn or become red, to flush.
Rot-: ~filter nt or m (Phot) red filter; ~front f (Pol) red front; ~fuchs m red fox; (Pferd) sorrel or bay (horse); (fig inf) carrot-

---

top (inf); ~gardist m Red Guard; r~gesichtig adj florid, red-faced; r~glühend adj Metall red-hot; der r~glühende Abendhimmel the red glow of the evening sky; ~glut f (Metal) red heat; ~grünblindheit f red-green colour-blindness; ~guß m (Metal) red brass; r~haarig adj red-haired; ~haut f (dated hum) redskin; ~hirsch m red deer.
rotieren * vi to rotate. anfangen zu ~ (sl) to get into a flap (inf); am R~ sein (sl) to be rushing around like a mad thing (inf).
Rot-: ~kabis m (Sw) red cabbage; ~käppchen nt (Liter) Little Red Ridinghood; ~kehlchen nt robin; ~kohl m red cabbage; ~kopf m (inf) redhead; ~kraut nt (S Ger, Aus) red cabbage.
Rotkreuz-: ~lotterie f Red Cross lottery; ~sammlung f Red Cross appeal or collection; ~schwester f Red Cross nurse.
Rotlauf m -s, no pl (Vet) swine erysipelas (spec).
rötlich adj reddish.
Rot-: ~licht nt red light; ~liegende(s) nt decl as adj (Geol) rot(h)liegendes (spec), red bed of sandstone.
Rotor m rotor.
Rotorflügel m (Aviat) rotor blade.
Rot-: ~schwanz m, ~schwänzchen m redstart; r~sehen vi sep irreg (inf) to see red (inf); ~sehen nt -s, no pl (Med) erythropsia (spec); ~stift m red pencil; den ~stift ansetzen (fig) to cut sth back drastically; dem ~stift zum Opfer fallen (fig) to be scrapped or rejected or cancelled; ~tanne f Norway spruce.
Rotte f -, -n gang; (bei Jugendorganisation) troop; (Mil) rank; (Mil Aviat, Mil Naut) pair (of planes/ships operating together); (von Hunden etc) pack; (Hunt: von Sauen) herd, sounder (spec).
Rotten-: ~führer m (von Arbeitern) foreman; (bei Jugendorganisation) troop-leader; r~weise adv in groups; die Hunde fielen r~weise über das Reh her packs of dogs attacked the deer.
Rottweiler m -s, - Rottweiler.
Rotunde f -, -n (Archit) rotunda.
Rötung f reddening.
Rot-: r~wangig adj rosy-cheeked; ~wein m red wine; r~welsch adj argot, thieves' cant; ~welsch(e) nt decl as adj argot, thieves' cant; ~wild nt red deer; ~wurst f = black pudding.
Rotz m -es, no pl (a) (sl) snot (inf). jdm ~ auf die Backe schmieren (sl) to suck up to sb (inf); ~ und Wasser heulen (inf) to blubber; Baron or Graf ~ (inf) Lord Muck (inf); der ganze ~ (sl) the whole bloody (Brit) or goddam (US) show (sl). (b) (Vet) glanders sing, farcy. den ~ haben to have glanders. (c) (Bot) soft rot.
Rotzbengel, Rotzbub (S Ger, Aus) m (inf) snotty-nosed brat (inf).
rotzen vi (sl) to blow one's nose.
Rotz-: ~fahne f (sl) snot-rag (sl); r~frech adj (inf) cocky (inf).
rotzig adj (a) (sl: lit, fig) snotty (sl). (b) (Vet) glanderous.
Rotz-: ~junge m (sl) snotty-nosed kid (inf); ~lappen m (sl) snot-rag (sl); ~löffel (Aus), ~lümmel (sl) m cheeky brat (inf); ~nase f (a) (sl) snotty nose (inf); (b) (inf: Kind) snotty-nosed brat (inf); r~näsig adj (sl) (a) snotty-nosed (inf); (b) (frech) snotty (sl); ~nigel m (Aus) snotty-nosed brat (inf).
Rotzunge f (Zool) witch flounder.
Rouge [ru:ʒ] nt -s, -s rouge.
Roulade [ru'la:də] f (Cook) = beef olive.
Rouleau [ru'lo:] nt -s, -s siehe Rollo.
Roulett(e) [ru'let(ə)] nt -s, - or -s roulette.
roulieren * [ru'li:rən] vt (Sew) to roll.
Route ['ru:tə] f -, -n route. wir sind die ~ über Bremen gefahren we took the Bremen route.
Routine [ru'ti:nə] f (Erfahrung) experience; (Gewohnheit, Trott) routine. das ist bei mir zur ~ geworden that has become routine for me.
Routine-: ~angelegenheit f routine matter; r~mäßig 1 adj routine; 2 adv ich gehe r~mäßig zum Zahnarzt I make a routine visit to the dentist's; das wird r~mäßig überprüft it's checked as a matter of routine; Sie sollten sich r~mäßig untersuchen lassen you should have a routine check-up; ich werde das r~mäßig abwickeln I'll deal with it in the usual way; ~sache f routine matter; ~untersuchung f routine examination.
Routinier [ruti'nie:] m -s, -s old hand.
routiniert [ruti'ni:rt] adj experienced.
Rowdy ['raudi] m -s, -s or Rowdies hooligan; (zerstörerisch) vandal; (lärmend) rowdy (type); (Verkehrs~) roadhog (inf).
Rowdytum ['rauditu:m] nt, no pl hooliganism; vandalism. das ~ im Verkehr bekämpfen to combat roadhogs.
Royalismus [roaja'lısmʊs] m royalism.
Royalist [roaja'lıst] m royalist.
royalistisch [roaja'lıstıʃ] adj royalist.
rubbeln vti to rub.
Rübchen nt dim of Rübe small turnip. Teltower ~ (Cook) glazed turnip with bacon.
Rübe f -, -n (a) turnip. gelbe ~ (S Ger: Mohr~) carrot; rote ~ beetroot; weiße ~ white turnip; jdn über die ~n jagen (sl) to send sb packing (inf); siehe Kraut. (b) (sl: Kopf) nut (inf). eins auf die ~ bekommen or kriegen to get a bash on the nut (inf); jdm eins über die ~ ziehen to give sb a bash or crack on the nut (inf); die ~ (für etw) hinhalten to take the rap (for sth) (inf); jdm die ~ abhacken (fig) to have sb's guts for garters (sl); ~ ab! off with his/her head!
Rübel m -s, - rouble. der ~ rollt (inf) the money's rolling in (inf).
Rüben-: r~artig adj turnip-like; ~saft m, ~kraut nt sugar beet syrup; ~zucker m beet sugar.
rüber- in cpds (inf) siehe herüber-, hinüber-.
Rübezahl m -s spirit of the Sudeten Mountains.
Rubikon m -s Rubicon. den ~ überschreiten (fig geh) to cross the Rubicon.

Rubin m -s, -e ruby.
rubinrot adj ruby-red, ruby.
Rüb-: ~kohl m siehe Kohlrabi; ~öl nt rapeseed oil, rape oil.
Rubra, Rubren (geh) pl of Rubrum.
Rubrik f (a) (Kategorie) category. das gehört in die ~ „Militaria" this belongs under the category or heading "military". (b) (Zeitungs~) section, column.
rubrizieren* vt to categorize, to put under a heading/headings. Politiker unter Rabauken ~ to categorize or put politicians under the heading of hooligans.
Rubrizierung f categorization.
Rubrum nt -s, Rubra or Rubren (geh) rubric.
Ruch-: r~bar adj r~bar werden (old, liter) to become known; r~los adj (old, liter) dastardly (liter); ~losigkeit f (old, liter) dastardliness (liter).
ruck interj (beim Ziehen) heave; (beim Schieben) push. ~, zuck in a flash; (Imperativ) jump to it!; das geht ~, zuck it won't take a second; wenn er nicht gehorcht, fliegt er raus, das geht ~, zuck if he doesn't obey he'll be out, just like that; siehe hau ruck.
Ruck m -(e)s, -e jerk, tug; (von Fahrzeug) jolt, jerk; (Pol) swing, shift. auf einen or mit einem ~ in one go, with one heave; er stand mit einem ~ auf he sprang to his feet, he stood up suddenly; sich (dat) einen ~ geben (inf) to make an effort, to give oneself a kick up the backside (hum inf); etw in einem ~ erledigen to do sth at one fell swoop.
Rück-: ~ansicht f back or rear view; ~antwort f reply, answer; um ~antwort wird gebeten please reply; Telegramm mit ~antwort reply-paid telegram.
ruck|artig 1 adj jerky. das Auto machte einige ~e Bewegungen the car jerked a few times. 2 adv jerkily. er stand ~ auf he shot to his feet.
Rück-: ~äußerung f reply, answer; ~berufung f recall; ~besinnung f recollection; die ~besinnung auf die Werte der Vergangenheit thinking back to past values, the recollection of past values; ~bezüglich adj (Gram) reflexive; ~bildung f (Ling) back-formation; (Biol) degeneration; ~blende f flashback; ~blick m look back (auf +acc at); im ~blick auf etw (acc) looking back on sth; einen ~blick auf etw (acc) werfen to look back on or at sth; wenn ich mir einen ~blick auf jene Zeit gestatte when I look back on or at that time; r~blickend adj retrospective; r~blickend läßt sich sagen, daß ... in retrospect or retrospectively or looking back we can say that ...; ein auf das vergangene Jahr r~blickender Bericht a report that looks back at or over the last year; r~datieren* vt sep infin, ptp only to backdate; ~deckungsversicherung f (Econ) firm's private pension plan for employees; r~drehend adj (Met) Wind backing.
rucken vi (Fahrzeug) to jerk, to jolt; (Taube) to coo.
Rücken m -s, - (Anat, Stuhl~, Hand~, Sew) back; (Nasen~) ridge; (Fuß~) instep; (Messer~) blunt edge, back; (Hügel~, Berg~) crest; (Buch~) spine. auf dem/den ~ on one's back; ich bin ja auf den ~ gefallen! (fig) you could have knocked me down with a feather (inf); den Feind im ~ haben to have the enemy in one's rear; die Sonne im ~ haben to have the sun behind one or in one's back; den Wind im ~ haben to have a tail or following wind; er hat doch die Firma des Vaters im ~ but he's got his father's firm behind him; ich habe nicht gern jemanden im ~ I don't like having somebody sitting/standing right behind my back; jdm die Hände auf den ~ binden to tie sb's hands behind his back; mit dem ~ zur Tür/Wand with one's back to the door/wall; mit dem ~ zur Wand stehen (fig) (aus Feigheit) to cover oneself; (aus Unterlegenheit) to have one's back to the wall; der verlängerte ~ (hum inf) one's posterior (hum inf); ~ an ~ back to back; ein schöner ~ kann auch entzücken (hum inf) you've got a lovely back; hinter jds ~ (dat) (fig) behind sb's back; jdm/einer Sache den ~ kehren (lit, fig) or zuwenden (lit) or wenden (fig) or zudrehen (lit) to turn one's back on sb/sth; den ~ wenden to turn one's back; jdm in den ~ fallen (fig) to stab sb in the back; (Mil) to attack sb from the rear; sich (dat) den ~ freihalten (inf) or decken to cover oneself; jdm den ~ decken (fig inf) to back sb up (inf); schon viele Jahre/viel Erfahrung auf dem ~ haben (inf) to be getting on in years/to have a lot of experience under one's belt (inf); auf seinen ~ geht viel (inf) he can take it; jdm den ~ beugen or brechen (fig) to break sb; jdm den ~ stärken or steifen (fig inf) to give sb encouragement; siehe breit.
rücken 1 vi aux sein to move; (Platz machen) to move up or (zur Seite auch) over; (weiter~: Zeiger) to move on (auf +acc to). näher ~ to move or come closer; (Zeit) to come or get closer; ins Feld (old)/ins Manöver/an die Front ~ to take the field/to go off on manoeuvres/to go up to the front; mit etw ~ to move sth; sie rückten ungeduldig mit den Stühlen they shuffled their chairs about impatiently; an etw (dat) ~ an Uhrzeiger to move sth; an Krawatte to pull sth (straight); (schieben) to push at sth; (ziehen) to pull at sth; an jds Seite ~ to move up close beside sb; an jds Stelle (acc) ~ to take sb's place; nicht von der Stelle ~ not to budge an inch (inf); in weite Ferne ~ to recede into the distance; jdm auf den Leib or Pelz (inf) or Balg (inf) or die Pelle (sl) ~ (zu nahe kommen) to crowd sb; (sich jdn vorknöpfen) to get on at sb; (hum: besuchen) to move in on sb; einer Sache (dat) zu Leibe ~ to have a go at sth, to tackle sth; siehe Bude.
2 vt to move; siehe Licht.
Rücken-: ~deckung f (fig) backing; jdm ~deckung geben to back sb; ~flosse f dorsal fin; ~flug m (Aviat) inverted flight; ~kraulen nt (Sport) back crawl, backstroke; r~kraulen vi sep infin only to do or swim back crawl or backstroke; ~lage f supine position; er mußte 3 Monate in ~lage verbringen he had to spend 3 months lying (flat) on his back or in a supine

---

position (form); er schläft in ~lage he sleeps on his back; ~lehne f back, back-rest; ~mark nt spinal cord; ~mark(s)entzündung f myelitis; ~muskel m back muscle; ~muskulatur f back muscles pl, muscles of the/one's back pl; ~schmerz(en) pl m backache; ich habe ~schmerzen I've got backache, my back aches; ~schwimmen nt backstroke, swimming on one's back; r~schwimmen vi sep infin only to swim on one's back, to do the or swim backstroke; ~stärkung f (fig) moral support; ~stück nt (Cook) (vom Rind) chine; (vom Reh, Hammel) saddle; ein schönes ~stück a nice piece of back; ~trage f carrying-frame.
Rück|entwicklung f (allgemein) fall-off (gen in); (Biol) degeneration.
Rücken-: ~wind m tail or following wind; ~wirbel m siehe Brustwirbel.
Rück-: ~erinnerung f memory (an +acc of); r~erstatten* vt sep infin, ptp only to refund; Ausgaben to reimburse; ~erstattung f refund; reimbursement; ~fahrkarte f, ~fahrschein m return ticket, round-trip ticket (US); ~fahrscheinwerfer m (Aut) reversing light; ~fahrt f return journey; ~fall m (Med, fig) relapse; (Jur) subsequent offence, repetition of an/the offence; ein ~fall in alte Gewohnheiten a relapse into one's old habits; Diebstahl im ~fall a repeated case of theft; r~fällig adj (Med, fig) relapsed; (Jur) recidivist (form); ein r~fälliger Dieb a thief who repeats his offence; r~fällig werden (Med) to have a relapse; (fig) to relapse; (Jur) to lapse back into crime; ~fällige(r) mf decl as adj (Med, fig) person who relapses/has relapsed; (Jur) subsequent offender, recidivist (form); ~falltäter m recidivist (form), recidivistic offender (form); ~flug m return flight; ~fluß m reflux, flowing back; ~forderung f ~forderung des Geldes/des Buches demand for the return of the money/the book; ~fracht f return load; ~frage f question; nach ~frage bei der Zentrale ... after querying or checking this with the exchange ...; mit ~fragen können Sie sich auch an meine Kollegin wenden you can take your queries or questions to my colleague as well; bei jdm ~frage halten to query it/sth with sb; r~fragen vi sep infin, ptp only to inquire, to check; ich habe im Fundbüro r~gefragt I inquired or checked at the lost-property office; ich muß beim Chef r~fragen I'll have to check with the boss or query it with the boss; ~front f back, rear façade; ~führung f (a) (Deduktion) tracing back; die ~führung der Probleme auf (+acc) tracing the problems back to; (b) (von Menschen) repatriation, return; ~gabe f return; ~gaberecht nt right of return; ~gang m fall, drop (gen in); einen ~gang or ~gänge zu verzeichnen haben to report a drop or fall; r~gängig adj (a) (Comm: zurückgehend) declining, falling, dropping; (b) r~gängig machen (widerrufen) to undo; Bestellung, Geschäft, Vertrag, Termin to cancel; Verlobung, Hochzeit to call off; chemischen Prozeß to reverse; ~gängigmachung f (form) cancellation; (Chem) reversal; r~gebildet adj (Biol) degenerate; ~gewinnung f recovery; (von Land, Gebiet) reclaiming, reclamation; (aus verbrauchten Stoffen) recycling; ~glie-derung f (Pol) reintegration.
Rückgrat nt -(e)s, -e spine, backbone. er ist ein Mensch ohne ~ (fig) he's a spineless creature, he's got no backbone; das ~ der Wirtschaft the backbone or mainstay of the economy; jdm das ~ stärken (inf) to give sb encouragement or a boost; jdm das ~ brechen to break or ruin sb.
Rückgratverkrümmung f curvature of the spine.
Rück-: ~griff m (a) wenn ein ~griff auf vorhandene Reserven nicht möglich ist if it is not possible to fall back on available resources; erlauben Sie mir einen ~griff auf bereits Gesagtes allow me to revert to something that has already been said; (b) (Jur) siehe Regreß; ~halt m (a) (Unterstützung) support, backing; an jdm einen ~halt haben to find a support in sb; (b) (Einschränkung) ohne ~halt without reservation; ~haltlos adj complete; Unterstützung auch unqualified; Vertrauen auch implicit; sich r~haltlos zu etw bekennen to proclaim one's total allegiance to sth; ~hand f (Sport) backhand; ~hand spielen to play backhand; er kann erstklassig ~hand spielen he has a first-rate backhand; den Ball (mit der) ~hand schlagen to hit the ball (on one's) backhand; ~handschlag m (Sport) backhand (stroke); ~kampf m (Sport) return match.
Rückkauf m repurchase.
Rückkaufs-: ~recht nt right of repurchase; ~wert m repurchase value.
Rück-: ~kehr f -, no pl return; bei seiner ~kehr on his return; jdn zur ~kehr (nach X/zu jdm) bewegen to persuade sb to return (to X/to sb); ~koppeln vti sep infin, ptp only (alle Bedeutungen) to feed back; ~kopp(e)lung f feedback; ~kreuzung f back-cross; (Vorgang) back crossing; ~kunft f -, no pl (liter) return; ~lage f (Fin: Reserve) reserve, reserves pl; (Ersparnisse auch) savings pl; ~lauf m, no pl reverse running; (von Maschinenteil) return travel; (Gegenströmung) countercurrent; (TV) flyback; (Naut) slip; (beim Tonband) fast rewind; (von Schußwaffe) recoil; r~läufig adj declining, falling, dropping; Tendenz downward; eine r~läufige Entwicklung a decline, a falling off; r~läufiges Wörterbuch reverse index; ~licht nt tail or rear light; (bei Fahrrad auch) back light; r~lings adv (r~wärts) backwards; (von hinten) from behind; (von der Rücken) on one's back; ~marsch m (Mil) march back; (~zug) retreat.
Rückmelde-: ~frist f (Univ) re-registration period; ~gebühren pl (Univ) re-registration fee.
Rück-: ~meldung f (Univ) re-registration; ~nahme f -, -n taking back; die ~nahme des Gerätes ist unmöglich it is impossible for us to take this set back; ich bestehe auf der ~nahme des Gerätes I must insist that you take this set back ~paß m (Sport) return pass; ~porto nt return postage; ~prall

m rebound; (*von Kugel, Stein etc*) ricochet; ~**reise** *f* return journey; ~**reisevisum** *nt* return visa; ~**ruf** *m* (a) (*am Telefon*) **Herr X hat angerufen und bittet um ~ruf** Mr X called and asked you to call (him) back; (b) (*Jur*) rescission of permission to manufacture under licence.

Rucksack *m* rucksack.

Rück-: ~**schalttaste** *f siehe* ~**(stell)taste;** ~**schau** *f* reflection (*auf + acc* on); (*in Medien*) review (*auf + acc* of); ~**schau halten** to reminisce, to reflect; **auf etw** (*acc*) ~**schau halten** to look back on sth; **in** ~**schau auf das vergangene Jahr** ... looking back on the past year ...; ~**schein** ≈ recorded delivery slip; ~**schlag** *m* (a) (*von Ball*) rebound; (*von Gewehr*) recoil; (*fig*) set-back; (*bei Patient*) relapse; (b) (*Biol*) atavism; ~**schläger** *m* (*Sport*) receiver; ~**schlagventil** *nt* check valve; ~**schluß** *m* conclusion; **den** ~**schluß gestatten, daß** ... to admit of the conclusion that ...; **den** ~**schluß ziehen, daß** ... to draw the conclusion *or* to conclude that ...; ~**schlüsse ziehen** (*euph*) to draw one's own conclusions (*aus* from); ~**schritt** *m* (*fig*) retrograde step, step backwards; **ein gesellschaftlicher** ~**schritt** a retrograde social step, a social step backwards; **r**~**schrittlich** *adj* reactionary; **Entwicklung** retrograde.

Rückseite *f* back; (*von Blatt Papier, Geldschein auch*) reverse; (*von Buchseite, Münze*) reverse, verso; (*von Zeitung*) back page; (*von Mond auch*) far side; (*von Gebäude auch*) rear. **siehe** ~ see over(leaf).

rückseitig *adj* on the back *or* reverse. **die** ~**en Bemerkungen** the remarks overleaf; **der Garten liegt** ~ the garden is at the back; **das Papier soll auch** ~ **beschrieben werden** you should write on both sides of the paper.

rucksen *vi* (*Taube*) to coo.

Rücksendung *f* return.

Rücksicht *f* -, -en (*Schonung, Nachsicht*) consideration. ~**en** *pl* (*Gründe, Interessen*) considerations *pl*; **aus** *or* **mit** ~ **auf jdn/etw** out of consideration for sb/sth; **ohne** ~ **auf jdn/etw** with no consideration for sb/sth; **ohne** ~ **auf Verluste** (*inf*) regardless; **auf jdn/etw** ~ **nehmen** to consider sb/sth, to show consideration for sb/sth; **er hat keine** ~ **auf seine Gesundheit genommen** he did not consider his health; **er kennt keine** ~ he's ruthless; **da kenne ich keine** ~! I can be ruthless.

rücksichtlich *prep + gen* (*old*) in view of.

Rücksichtnahme *f* -, *no pl* consideration.

Rücksichts-: **r**~**los** *adj* (a) inconsiderate, thoughtless; (*im Verkehr*) reckless; **er verfolgt r**~**los seine Interessen** he follows his own interests without consideration for others; (b) (*unbarmherzig*) ruthless; ~**losigkeit** *f* (a) inconsiderateness *no pl*, thoughtlessness *no pl*; **das ist doch eine** ~**losigkeit!** how inconsiderate *or* thoughtless; (b) ruthlessness; **r**~**voll** *adj* considerate, thoughtful (*gegenüber, gegen* towards).

Rück-: ~**sitz** *m* (*von Fahrrad, Motorrad*) pillion; (*von Auto*) back seat; ~**spiegel** *m* (*Aut*) rear(-view) *or* driving mirror; (*außen*) outside mirror; ~**spiel** *nt* (*Sport*) return match; ~**sprache** *f* consultation; **laut** ~**sprache mit Herrn Müller** ... I have consulted Herr Müller and he informs me that ...; ~**sprache mit jdm nehmen** *or* **halten** to confer with *or* consult (with) sb; **r**~**spulen** *vt sep infin, ptp only* **Tonband, Film** to rewind; ~**spulknopf** *m* (*von Kamera*) rewind knob; ~**spultaste** *f* (*von Tonbandgerät*) rewind key.

Rückstand *m* (a) (*Überrest*) remains *pl*; (*bei Verbrennung, Bodensatz*) residue.
(b) (*Verzug*) delay; (*bei Aufträgen*) backlog. **im** ~ **sein/in** ~ **kommen** to be/fall behind; (*bei Zahlungen auch*) to be/get in arrears *pl*; **seinen** ~ **aufholen** to make up for one's delay/to catch up on a backlog; (*bei Zahlungen*) to catch up on one's payments; (*in Leistungen*) to catch up.
(c) (*Außenstände*) arrears *pl*. **wie hoch ist mein** ~? how much are my arrears?; ~**e eintreiben/bezahlen** to collect/pay arrears.
(d) (*Sport*) amount by which one is behind. **mit 0:2 im** ~ **sein** to be 2 goals/points *etc* down; **ihr** ~ **gegenüber dem Tabellenführer beträgt 4 Punkte** they are 4 points behind the leader.

rückständig *adj* (a) (*überfällig*) **Betrag** overdue; **Mensch** in arrears. ~**er Betrag** amount overdue. (b) (*zurückgeblieben*) **Land, Mensch** backward; **Methoden, Ansichten auch** antiquated. ~ **denken** to have antiquated ideas.

Rückständigkeit *f, no pl* backwardness.

rückstand(s)frei *adj* without residue; **Verbrennung auch** clean. **ein Diamant verbrennt** ~ a diamond burns without leaving any residue; **dieses Öl verbrennt nahezu** ~ this oil burns cleanly.

Rück-: ~**stau** *m* (*von Wasser*) backwater; (*von Autos*) tailback; ~**(stell)taste** *f* (*an Schreibmaschine*) backspacer; (*an Tonband*) rewind key; ~**stellung** *f* (*Fin*) reserve; ~**stoß** *m* repulsion; (*bei Gewehr*) recoil; (*von Rakete*) thrust; ~**stoßantrieb** *m* (*Aviat*) reaction propulsion; **r**~**stoßfrei** *adj* **Geschütze** recoilless; ~**strahler** *m* -s, - reflector; ~**strom** *m* (*Elec*) reverse current; (*von Menschen, Fahrzeugen*) return; **der** ~**strom der Urlauber aus Italien** the stream of holiday makers returning from Italy; ~**taste** *f siehe* ~**(stell)taste;** ~**transport** *m* return transport; (*bei Schreibmaschine*) return.

Rücktritt *m* (a) (*Amtsniederlegung*) resignation; (*von König*) abdication. **seinen** ~ **einreichen** *or* **erklären** to hand in *or* tender (*form*) one's resignation. (b) (*Jur*) (*von Vertrag*) withdrawal (*von* from), rescission (*form*) (*von* of). ~ **vom Versuch** abandonment of intent. (c) (*inf*) *siehe* **Rücktrittbremse.**

Rücktrittbremse *f* backpedal *or* coaster brake.

Rücktritts-: ~**drohung** *f* threat to resign/abdicate; ~**frist** *f* period for withdrawal; ~**gesuch** *nt* resignation; **das** ~**gesuch einreichen** to tender one's resignation (*form*); ~**klausel** *f* withdrawal clause; ~**recht** *nt* right of withdrawal; ~**vorbehalt** *m* option of withdrawal.

Rück-: **r**~**übersetzen*** *vt sep infin, ptp only* to translate back into the original language; ~**übersetzung** *f* retranslation into the original language; **r**~**vergüten*** *vt sep infin, ptp only* to refund (*jdm etw* sb sth); ~**vergütung** *f* refund; ~**versicherer** *m* reinsurer; (*fig*) hedger; ~**versichern*** *sep* 1 *vti* to reinsure; 2 *vr* to check (up *or* back); ~**versicherung** *f* reinsurance; ~**versicherungsvertrag** *m* (*Hist*) Reinsurance Treaty; ~**verweis** *m* reference back; ~**verweisen*** *vti sep irreg infin, ptp only* to refer back; ~**wand** *f* (*von Zimmer, Gebäude etc*) back wall; (*von Möbelstück etc*) back; ~**wanderer** *m* returning emigrant, remigrant; ~**wanderung** *f* remigration; **r**~**wärtig** *adj* back; **Tür, Eingang, Ausgang auch,** (*Mil*) rear; **r**~**wärtige Verbindungen** (*Mil*) lines of communication.

rückwärts *adv* (a) (*zurück, rücklings*) backwards. **Rolle/Salto** ~ backward roll/back somersault; ~ **einparken** to back *or* reverse into a parking space. (b) (*Aus: hinten*) behind, at the back. **von** ~ from behind.

Rückwärts-: ~**drehung** *f* reverse turn; ~**fahren** *nt* reversing; ~**gang** *m* reverse gear; **den** ~**gang einlegen** to change into reverse, to put the car *etc* into reverse; **im** ~**gang fahren** to reverse; **r**~**gehen** *sep irreg aux sein* (*fig*) 1 *vi* to go downhill; 2 *vi impers* **von da an ging es r**~ things went downhill from then on; **mit etw ist es r**~**gegangen** sth has gone downhill; **r**~**gewandt** *adj* (*fig*) backward-looking, retrogressive.

Rückweg *m* way back. **auf dem** ~ **vorbeikommen** to call in on one's way back; **den** ~ **antreten, sich auf den** ~ **begeben** to set off back; **sich auf den** ~ **machen** to head back; **jdm den** ~ **abschneiden** to cut off sb's line of retreat.

ruckweise *adv* jerkily. **sich** ~ **bewegen** to jerk, to move jerkily.

Rück-: ~**wendung** *f* return (*zu, auf + acc* to); **r**~**wirkend** *adj* (*Jur*) retrospective; **Lohn-, Gehaltserhöhung** backdated; **es wird r**~**wirkend vom 1. Mai bezahlt** it will be backdated to the 1st May; **das Gesetz tritt r**~**wirkend vom 1. Januar in Kraft** the law is made retrospective to the 1st January; ~**wirkung** *f* repercussion; **eine Zahlung/Gesetzesänderung mit** ~**wirkung von** ... a payment backdated to/an amendment made retrospective to ...; **r**~**zahlbar** *adj* repayable; ~**zahlung** *f* repayment; ~**zieher** *m* -s, - (a) (*inf*) **einen** ~**zieher machen** to back out (*inf*); (*sl: beim Verkehr*) to pull (it) out (*sl*), to be careful (*euph*); (b) (*Ftbl*) overhead *or* bicycle kick; **r**~**zielend** *adj* (*Gram rare*) reflexive.

ruck, zuck *interj siehe* **ruck.**

Ruckzuck *nt* -s, *no pl* (*inf*) **etw mit** ~ **machen** to do sth at the double (*inf*); **dein ewiges** ~ your continual "get on with it" (*inf*).

Rückzug *m* (*Mil*) retreat. **auf dem** ~ in the retreat; **den** ~ **antreten** (*lit, fig*) to retreat, to beat a retreat; *siehe* **blasen.**

Rückzugs-: ~**gebiet** *nt* retreat; ~**gefecht** *nt* (*Mil, fig*) rearguard action.

rüd *adj* (*Aus*) *siehe* **rüde.**

Rüde *m* -n, -n (*Männchen*) dog, male; (*Hetzhund*) hound.

rüde, rüd (*Aus*) *adj* impolite; **Antwort** curt, brusque. **das war sehr** ~ **von dir** that was a very rude thing to do.

Rudel *nt* -s, - (*von Hunden, Wölfen*) pack; (*von Wildschweinen, Hirschen*) herd; (*fig dated*) swarm, horde. **in** ~**n auftreten** to go round in packs/herds/swarms *or* hordes.

rudelweise *adv* in packs/herds/swarms *or* hordes.

Ruder *nt* -s, - (*von* ~**boot, Galeere etc*) oar; (*Naut, Aviat: Steuer*~) rudder; (*fig: Führung*) helm. **das** ~ **fest in der Hand haben** (*fig*) to be in control of the situation; **die** ~ **auslegen/einziehen** to put out/ship oars; **am** ~ **sein** (*lit, fig*)/**ans** ~ **kommen** (*fig*) to be at/to take over (at) the helm; **sich in die** ~ **legen** (*lit, fig*), **sich für etw in die** ~ **legen** (*fig*) to put one's back into it/sth; **das** ~ **herumwerfen** (*fig*) to change course *or* tack.

Ruder-: ~**bank** *f* rowing seat; (*in Galeere*) rowing bench; ~**blatt** *nt* (oar) blade; ~**boot** *nt* rowing boat, rowboat (*esp US*); ~**dolle** *f* rowlock.

Ruderer *m* -s, - oarsman, rower.

Rudergänger *m* -s, - (*Naut*) helmsman.

Ruderhaus *nt* (*Naut*) wheelhouse, pilot house.

-rud(e)rig *adj suf* -oared.

Ruderin *f* oarswoman, rower.

rudern 1 *vi* (a) *aux* **haben** *or* **sein** to row. (b) (*Schwimmvögel*) to paddle. **mit den Armen** ~ (*fig*) to flail *or* wave one's arms about. 2 *vt* to row.

Ruder-: ~**pinne** *f* tiller; ~**regatta** *f* rowing regatta; ~**schlag** *m* stroke; ~**sport** *m* rowing *no def art*; ~**stange** *f* tiller.

Rudiment *nt* rudiment.

rudimentär *adj* rudimentary; (*Biol*) **Organ auch** vestigial. ~ **ausgebildet** rudimentary.

Rudrer(in *f*) *m* -s, - *siehe* **Ruderer, Ruderin.**

Ruf *m* -(e)s, -e (a) (*Aus*~, **Vogel**~, *fig: Auf*~) call; (*lauter*) shout; (*Schrei, gellend*) cry. **ein** ~ **ertönte** a cry rang out; **in den** ~ „...." **ausbrechen** to burst into cries *or* shouts of "...."; **der** ~ **des Muezzins** the call of the muezzin; **der** ~ **der Wildnis** the call of the wild; **dem** ~ **des Herzens/Gewissens folgen** (*fig*) to obey the voice of one's heart/conscience; **der** ~ **nach Freiheit/Gerechtigkeit** (*fig*) the call for freedom/justice; **der** ~ **nach dem Henker** (*fig*) the call to bring back hanging/the chair *etc*; **der** ~ **zu den Waffen** the call to arms; **der** ~ **zur Ordnung** (*fig*) the call to order.

(b) (*Ansehen, Leumund*) reputation. **einen guten** ~ **haben** *or* **genießen, sich eines guten** ~ **erfreuen** (*geh*) to have *or* enjoy a good reputation; **dem** ~ **nach** by reputation; **eine Firma von** ~ a firm with a good reputation *or* of high repute, a firm with a good name; **sich** (*dat*) **einen** ~ **als etw erwerben** to build up a reputation *or* make a name for oneself as sth; **ein Mann von schlechtem** ~ a man with a bad reputation *or* of low repute, a man with a bad name; **von üblem** *or* **zweifelhaftem** ~ with a bad reputation; **von üblem** *or* **zweifelhaftem** ~ **sein** to have a bad reputation; **jdn/etw in schlechten** ~ **bringen** to give sb/sth a bad name; **jdn bei jdm in schlechten ~ bringen** to bring sb into disrepute with sb; **sie/das ist besser als ihr/sein ~** she/it is better than she/it is made out to be, she/it is not as black as she/it is painted; **ist der ~ erst ruiniert, lebt man völlig ungeniert** (prov) you live freely if you haven't a reputation to lose.

(c) (Univ: Berufung) offer of a chair or professorship. **er hat einen ~ nach Mainz erhalten** he has been offered a chair or professorship at Mainz; **einem ~ auf einen Lehrstuhl folgen** to accept a chair, to take up a professorship.

(d) (Fernruf) telephone number. „**,~: 2785**" "Tel: 2785".

Rufe, Rüfe f -, -n (Sw) **(a)** (Steinlawine) rockfall; (Erdrutsch) landslide. **(b)** (auf Wunde) scab.

rufen pret **rief**, ptp **gerufen 1** vi to call; (Mensch: laut ~) to shout; (Gong, Glocke, Horn etc) to sound (zu for). **um Hilfe ~** to call or cry for help; **die Pflicht ruft** duty calls; **die Arbeit ruft** my/your etc work is waiting; **nach jdm/etw ~** to call for sb/sth; **nach dem Henker ~** (fig) to call for the return of hanging/the chair etc; **der Muezzin ruft zum Gebet** the muezzin calls the faithful to prayer.

2 vi impers **es ruft eine Stimme** a voice is calling; **es hat gerufen** somebody called.

3 vt **(a)** to call; (aus~) to cry; (Mensch: laut ~) to shout. **jdm/sich etw in Erinnerung** or **ins Gedächtnis ~** to bring back (memories of) sth to sb/to recall sth; **jdn zur Ordnung ~** to call sb to order; **jdn zur Sache ~** to bring sb back to the point; **jdn zu den Waffen ~** to call sb to arms; **bravo/da capo ~** to shout hooray/encore; **sich heiser ~** to shout oneself hoarse.

(b) (kommen lassen) to send for; Arzt, Polizei auch, Taxi to call. **jdn zu sich ~** to send for sb; **Gott hat sie zu sich gerufen** God has called her to Him; **Sie haben mich ~ lassen?** you called, sir/madam?; **~ Sie ihn bitte!** please send him to me; **jdn vor Gericht ~** to summon sb to appear in court; **jdn zu Hilfe ~** to call on sb to help; **du kommst wie gerufen** you're just the man/woman I wanted; **das kommt mir wie gerufen** that's just what I needed; (kommt mir gelegen) that suits me fine.

Rufen nt -s, no pl calling no indef art; (von Mensch: laut) shouting no indef art. **haben Sie das ~ nicht gehört?** didn't you hear him/her etc calling/shouting?

Rufer m -s, - der ~ im Streit (liter) the leader in battle; **der ~ in der Wüste** the voice (crying) in the wilderness.

Ruferei f (inf) siehe **Rufen**.

Rüffel m -s, - (inf) telling- or ticking-off (inf).

rüffeln vt (inf) to tell or tick off (inf).

Ruf-: **~mord** m character assassination; **~mordkampagne** f smear campaign; **~name** m forename (by which one is generally known); **~nummer** f telephone number; **~säule** f (für Taxi) telephone; (Mot: Not~) emergency telephone; **~weite** f: **in ~weite** within earshot, within calling distance; **außer ~weite** out of earshot; **~zeichen** nt (a) (Telec) call sign; (von Telefon) ringing tone; **(b)** (Aus) exclamation mark.

Rugby [ˈrakbi] nt -, no pl rugby, rugger (inf).

Rugbyspiel nt (Veranstaltung) rugby match. **das ~** (Sportart) rugby.

Rüge f -, -n (Verweis) reprimand, rebuke; (Kritik) criticism no indef art; (scharfe Kritik) censure no indef art. **jdm eine ~ erteilen** to reprimand or rebuke/criticize/censure sb (für, wegen for).

rügen vt (form) jdn to reprimand (wegen, für for); etw to reprehend. **ich muß dein Verhalten ~** I must reprimand you for your behaviour.

rügenswert adj reprehensible.

Ruhe f -, no pl **(a)** (Schweigen, Stille) quiet, silence. **~!** quiet!, silence!; **~, bitte!** quiet, please; **gebt ~!** be quiet!; **ihr sollt ~ geben!** once and for all – (will you) be quiet!; **jdn zur ~ ermahnen** to tell sb to be quiet; **sich** (dat) **~ verschaffen** to get quiet or silence; **es herrscht ~** all is silent, silence reigns (liter); (fig: Disziplin, Frieden) all is quiet; **~ halten** (lit, fig) to keep quiet or silent; **die ~ der Natur** the stillness of nature; **himmlische ~** heavenly peace; **~ und Frieden** peace and quiet; **in ~ und Abgeschiedenheit** in peaceful seclusion; **es herrschte die ~ des Grabes** or **des Friedhofs** it was as still or silent as the grave; **die ~ vor dem Sturm** (fig) the calm before the storm.

(b) (Ungestörtheit, Frieden) peace, quiet; (~stätte) resting place. **~ ausstrahlen** to radiate a sense of calm; **in ~ und Frieden leben** to live a quiet life; **~ und Ordnung** law and order; **~ ist die erste Bürgerpflicht** (prov) the main thing is to keep calm/quiet; **die ~ wiederherstellen** to restore order; **ich brauche meine ~** I need a bit of peace; **laß mich in ~!** leave me in peace, stop bothering me; **ich will meine ~ haben!, mei Ruh will i ham!** (S Ger) leave or let me alone or be; **dann hat die liebe Seele Ruh** then perhaps we'll get a bit of peace; **vor jdm ~ haben wollen** to want a rest from sb; (endgültig) to want to get or be rid of sb; **jdm keine ~ lassen** or **gönnen** (Mensch) not to give sb any peace; **das läßt ihm keine ~** he can't stop thinking about it; **zur ~ kommen** to get some peace; (solide werden) to settle down; **jdn zur ~ kommen lassen** to give sb a chance to rest; **keine ~ finden (können)** to know no peace, not to be able to find any peace of mind; **jdn zur letzten ~ betten** (liter) to lay sb to rest (liter); **die letzte ~ finden** (liter) to be laid to rest (liter).

(c) (Erholung) rest, repose (liter); (~stand) retirement; (Stillstand) rest. **der Patient braucht viel ~** the patient needs a great deal of rest; **das Pendel befindet sich in ~** the pendulum is stationary; **jdm keine ~ gönnen** not to give sb a minute's rest; **sich zur ~ begeben** (form), **zur ~ gehen** to retire (to bed) (form); **angenehme ~!** sleep well!; **sich zur ~ setzen** to retire.

(d) (Gelassenheit) calm(ness); (Disziplin) quiet, order. **die ~ weghaben** (inf) to be unflappable (inf); **~ bewahren** to keep calm; **die ~ selbst sein** to be calmness itself; **jdn aus der ~ bringen** to throw sb (inf); **sich nicht aus der ~ bringen lassen, nicht aus der ~ zu bringen sein** not to (let oneself) get worked

up; **er trank noch in aller ~ seinen Kaffee** he drank his coffee as if he had all the time in the world; **überlege es dir in aller ~** think about it calmly; **sich** (dat) **etw in ~ ansehen** to look at sth in one's own time; **immer mit der ~** (inf) don't panic.

Ruhe-: **~bank** f bench, seat; **~bedürfnis** nt need for quiet/peace/rest; **r~bedürftig** adj in need of quiet/peace/rest; **~bett** nt bed; **~gehalt** nt (form) superannuation; **r~gehaltsfähig** adj (form) superannuable; **~geld** nt (form), **~genuß** m (Aus) pension; **~kissen** nt bolster; siehe **Gewissen**; **~lage** f (von Mensch) reclining position; (Med: bei Bruch) immobile position; (Tech) (von Maschine) resting position; (von Zeiger) neutral position; (Unbeweglichkeit) immobility; **sich in ~lage befinden** (Mensch, Maschine) to be at rest; (Wein) to be kept still; (unbeweglich sein) to be immobile; **r~liebend** adj fond of peace and quiet; **r~los** adj restless; **eine r~lose Zeit** a time of unrest; **~losigkeit** f restlessness; **~masse** f (Phys) rest mass.

ruhen 1 vi **(a)** (aus~) to rest. **nach dem Essen soll man ruhn oder tausend Schritte tun** (Prov) after a meal one should either rest or take some exercise; **ich möchte etwas ~** I want to take a short rest, I want to rest a little; **nicht (eher) ~ or nicht ~ und rasten, bis ...** (fig) not to rest until ...; **ich wünsche wohl zu ~!** (form) I wish you a good night (form); **(ich) wünsche, wohl geruht zu haben!** (form) I trust that you slept well (form).

(b) (geh: liegen) to rest (an or auf +dat on); (Gebäude auch) to be supported (auf +dat by); (Fluch) to lie (auf +dat on). **möge Gottes Segen auf dir ~** may God's blessing be with you; **auf ihm ruht ein Verdacht** suspicion hangs over him (liter).

(c) (stillstehen) to stop; (Maschinen) to stand idle; (Arbeit auch, Verkehr) to cease; (Waffen) to be laid down; (unterbrochen sein: Verfahren, Verhandlung, Vertrag) to be suspended. **laß die Arbeit jetzt ~** (geh) leave your work now.

(d) (tot und begraben sein) to lie, to be buried. „**hier ruht (in Gott) ...**" "here lies ..."; „**ruhe in Frieden!**" "Rest in Peace"; „**ruhe sanft!**" "rest eternal".

2 vi impers **hier ruht es sich gut** this is good to rest on; **nach der Anstrengung ruht es sich gut** it is good to rest after all that exertion.

ruhend adj resting; Kapital dormant; Maschinen idle; Verkehr stationary. **~e Venus** Venus reclining.

ruhenlassen vt sep irreg Vergangenheit, Angelegenheit to let rest; Verhandlungen, Prozeß to adjourn; Teig to allow to rest.

Ruhe-: **~pause** f break; (wenig Betrieb, Arbeit) slack or quiet period; **eine ~pause einlegen** to take or have a break; **~platz** m resting place; **~posten** m sinecure; **~punkt** m place of rest; **~raum** m rest room; **~sitz** m (Haus) retirement home; **er hat seinen ~sitz in Ehlscheid aufgeschlagen** he has retired to Ehlscheid; **~stand** m retirement; **im ~stand sein/leben** to be retired; **er ist Bankdirektor im ~stand** he is a retired bank director; **in den ~stand treten** or **gehen** to retire, to go into retirement; **jdn in den ~stand versetzen** to retire sb; **~ständler** m -s, - retired person; **~standsbeamte(r)** m retired civil servant; **~statt, ~stätte** f resting-place; **letzte ~stätte** last or final resting-place; **~stellung** f (von Körper) resting position; (von beweglichem Gegenstand) resting point; (von Maschinen) off position; **der Arm muß in ~stellung bleiben** the arm must not be moved; **r~störend** adj **r~störender Lärm** (Jur) disturbance of the peace; **~störer** m disturber of the peace; **~störung** f (Jur) disturbance of the peace; **~tag** m rest-day, day off; (von Geschäft etc) closing day; **einen ~tag einlegen** to have a day's rest, to take a day off; „**Mittwoch ~tag**" "closed (on) Wednesdays"; **~zeit** f rest period; (Saison) off-season.

ruhig 1 adj **(a)** (still) quiet; Wetter, Meer calm. **seid ~!** be quiet!; **ihr sollt ~ sein!** (will you) be quiet!; **sitz doch ~!** sit still!

(b) (geruhsam) quiet; Urlaub, Feiertage, Leben auch peaceful; Farbe restful; (ohne Störung) Überfahrt, Verlauf smooth; (Tech auch) smooth. **gegen 6 Uhr wird es ~er** it quietens down around 6 o'clock; **das Flugzeug liegt ~ in der Luft** the plane is flying smoothly; **alles geht seinen ~en Gang** everything is going smoothly.

(c) (gelassen) calm; Gewissen easy. **nur ~ (Blut)!** keep calm, take it easy (inf); **bei ~er Überlegung** on (mature) consideration; **du wirst auch noch ~er!** you'll calm down one day; **du kannst/Sie können ganz ~ sein** I can assure you.

(d) (sicher) Hand, Blick steady.

(e) (teilnahmslos) calm. **etw ~ mitansehen** to stand by and watch sth; **~ dabeistehen** just to stand by.

2 adv **du kannst ~ hierbleiben** feel free to stay here, you're welcome to stay here if you want; **ihr könnt ~ gehen, ich passe schon auf** you just go and I'll look after things; **hier kann jeder ~ seine Meinung sagen** here everyone is free to speak his mind; **man kann ~ behaupten/sagen/annehmen, daß ...** (mit Recht) one may well assert/say/assume that ..., one need have no hesitation in or about asserting/saying/assuming that ...; **die können ~ etwas mehr zahlen** (leicht) they could easily pay a little more; **wir können ~ darüber sprechen** we can talk about it if you want; **du könntest ~ mal etwas für mich tun!** it's about time you did something for me!

Ruhm m -es, no pl glory; (Berühmtheit) fame; (Lob) praise. **des ~es voll sein** to be full of praise (über +acc for); **mit etw keinen ~ ernten** (inf) not to win any medals with or for sth; **sich in seinem ~ sonnen** to rest on one's laurels; **siehe beklecksen**.

Ruhm-: **r~bedeckt** adj covered with glory; **~begier(de)** f thirst for glory; **r~begierig** adj thirsting for glory.

rühmen 1 vt (preisen, empfehlen) to sing the praises of; Tugenden, Schönheit auch to extol. **jdn ~d erwähnen** to give sb an honourable mention; **etw ~d hervorheben** to single sth out for or give sth special praise.

2 vr **sich einer Sache** (gen) **~** (prahlen) to boast about sth; (stolz sein) to pride oneself on sth; **sich einer Sache** (gen) **~**

können to be able to boast of sth; **die Stadt rühmt sich eines eigenen Schwimmbads** (iro) the town boasts its own swimming pool; **ohne mich zu** ~ without wishing to boast.

rühmenswert adj praiseworthy, laudable.

Ruhmes-: ~**blatt** nt (fig) glorious chapter; ~**halle** f hall of fame; ~**tag** m glorious day; ~**tat** f glorious deed.

rühmlich adj praiseworthy, laudable; Ausnahme notable. **kein** ~**es Ende finden** or **nehmen** to meet a bad end; **sich** ~ **hervortun** to distinguish oneself.

Ruhm-: r~**los** adj inglorious; ~**losigkeit** f, no pl ingloriousness; r~**redig** adj (obs) vainglorious (old, liter); r~**reich** adj (liter) glorious; ~**sucht** f siehe ~**begier(de)**; r~**süchtig** adj siehe r~**begierig**; r~**voll** adj glorious; r~**würdig** adj laudable.

Ruhr¹ f - (Geog) Ruhr.

Ruhr² f -, no pl (Krankheit) dysentery.

Ruhr|ei nt scrambled egg; (als Gericht) scrambled eggs pl.

rühren 1 vi (a) (um~) to stir.

  (b) **an etw** (acc) ~ (anfassen) to touch sth; (fig: erwähnen) to touch on sth; **daran wollen wir nicht** ~ let's not go into it; (in bezug auf Vergangenes) let sleeping dogs lie; **rühret nicht daran!** (liter) let us not dwell on that.

  (c) **von etw** ~ to stem from sth; **das rührt daher, daß** ... that is because ...; **daher rührt sein Mißtrauen!** so that is the reason for his distrust!

  2 vt (a) (um~) Teig, Farbe to stir; (schlagen) Eier to beat.

  (b) (bewegen) to move. **er rührte ein Glied** he didn't stir at all; **er rührte keinen Finger** or **keine Hand, um mir zu helfen** (inf) he didn't lift a finger to help me (inf).

  (c) (Gemüt bewegen) to move; Herz to stir. **das kann mich nicht** ~! that leaves me cold; (stört mich nicht) that doesn't bother me; **jdn zu Tränen** ~ to move sb to tears; **sie war äußerst gerührt** she was extremely moved or touched.

  (d) (Mus) Trommel to strike, to beat; Saiten to touch; Harfe to sound.

  (e) **ihn hat der Schlag gerührt** (inf) he was thunderstruck; **ich glaubte, mich rührt der Schlag** (inf) you could have knocked me down with a feather (inf); siehe Donner.

  3 vr (a) (sich bewegen) Blatt, Mensch to stir; (Körperteil) to move; (sich von der Stelle bewegen) to move; (aktiv sein) to buck up (inf); (sich beeilen) to bestir oneself, to get a move on (inf). **rührt Euch!** (Mil) at ease!; ~ **lassen** (Mil) to give the order to stand at ease; **kein Lüftchen rührte sich** the air was still, there was not the slightest breeze; **er rührt sich nicht mehr** (inf) he won't get up again; **hier kann man sich nicht** ~ you can't move in here; **nichts hat sich gerührt** nothing happened.

  (b) (Gewissen, Mitleid, Reue) to stir, to be awakened; (inf: sich melden) to say something. **sie hat sich schon 2 Jahre nicht gerührt** (inf) I haven't heard from her for 2 years.

Rühren nt -s, no pl stirring. **ein menschliches** ~ (verspüren) (to feel) a stirring of human pity; (hum) (to have to answer) a or the call of nature (hum).

rührend adj touching. **das ist** ~ **von Ihnen** that is sweet of you.

Ruhrgebiet nt Ruhr (area).

rührig adj active.

Rührigkeit f, no pl activeness.

ruhrkrank adj suffering from dysentery.

Rühr-: ~**löffel** m mixing spoon; ~**maschine** f mixer; (in Bäckerei) mixing machine; ~**michnichtan** nt -, - (Bot) touch-me-not.

Ruhrpott m (inf) Ruhr (Basin or Valley).

Rühr-: r~**selig** adj (pej) touching, tear-jerking (pej inf); ~**seligkeit** f, no pl sentimentality; ~**stück** nt (Theat) melodrama; ~**teig** m sponge mixture.

Rührung f, no pl emotion. **vor** ~ **nicht sprechen können** to be choked with emotion.

Ruin m -s, no pl ruin. **vor dem** ~ **stehen** to be on the brink or verge of ruin; **seinem/dem** ~ **entgegengehen** to be on the way to ruin; **das ist mein** ~! that will be my ruin or the ruin of me; **du bist noch mein** ~! (hum inf) you'll be the ruin of me.

Ruine f -, -n (lit, fig) ruin.

Ruinen-: ~**feld** nt sea of debris; r~**haft** adj ruined; ~**stadt** f ruined city.

ruinieren* vt to ruin. **sich** ~ to ruin oneself.

ruinös adj ruinous.

Rülps m -es, -e (dial) siehe **Rülpser**.

rülpsen vi to belch. **das R~** belching.

Rülpser m -s, - (inf) belch.

Rülpswasser nt (sl) gassy stuff (inf).

rum adv (inf) siehe **herum**.

Rum m [(S Ger, Aus auch) ru:m] m -s, -s rum.

Rumäne m -n, -n, **Rumänin** f Romanian.

Rumänien [-iən] nt -s Romania.

rumänisch adj Romanian.

Rumba f -, -s or (inf) m -s, -s rumba. ~ **tanzen** to (dance the) rumba.

Rumbakugel, Rumbarassel f maraca.

rumkriegen vt sep (inf) jdn ~ to talk sb round.

Rummel m -s, no pl (a) (inf) (Betrieb) (hustle and) bustle; (Getöse) racket (inf); (Aufheben) fuss (inf). **der ganze** ~ **the whole business** or **carry-on** (inf); **den** ~ **kennen** to know all about it; **großen** ~ **um jdn/etw machen** to make a great fuss or to-do about sb/sth (inf).

  (b) (~platz) fair. **auf den** ~ **gehen** to go to the fair.

Rummelplatz m (inf) fairground.

Rummy ['rœmi] nt -s, -s (Aus) rummy.

Rumor m -s, no pl (inf) racket (inf), row, din.

rumoren* 1 vi to make a noise; (Mensch) to rumble about; (Bauch) to rumble; (Gewissen) to play up; (Gedanke) to float about. **etw rumort in den Köpfen** sth is going through people's minds.

---

  2 vi impers **es rumort in meinem Magen** or **Bauch** or **mir im Leib** my stomach's rumbling; **es rumort im Volk** (fig) there is growing unrest among the people.

rump(e)lig adj (inf) siehe **holp(e)rig**.

Rumpelkammer f (inf) junk room (inf).

rumpeln vi (a) (Geräusch machen) to rumble. **er fiel** ~**d die Treppe hinunter** he fell down the stairs with a clatter. (b) aux sein (sich polternd bewegen) to rumble; (Mensch) to clatter.

Rumpelstilzchen nt -s Rumpelstiltskin.

Rumpf m -(e)s, ⁻e trunk; (Sport) body; (von geschlachtetem Tier) carcass; (Statue) torso; (von Schiff) hull; (von Flugzeug) fuselage. ~ **beugt/streckt!** (Sport) bend/stretch.

Rumpfbeuge f forward bend.

rümpfen vt **die Nase** ~ to turn up one's nose (über +acc at).

Rumpfparlament nt (Hist) Rump (Parliament).

Rumpsteak ['rʊmp-ste:k] nt rump steak.

rums interj bang.

Rum-: ~**topf** m rumpot (soft fruit in rum); ~**verschnitt** m blended rum.

rund 1 adj round; Figur, Arme plump; Ton, Klang full; Wein mellow. **du wirst mit jedem Jahr** ~**er** you're getting bigger or plumper every year; ~**e 50 Jahre/2000 Mark** a good 50 years/2,000 marks; **ein** ~**es Dutzend Leute** a dozen or more people; **das Kind machte** ~**e Augen** the child's eyes grew round; **Konferenz am** ~**en Tisch** round-table talks pl.

  2 adv (a) (herum) (a)round. ~ **um** right (a)round; ~ **um die Uhr** right (a)round the clock.

  (b) (ungefähr) (round) about, roughly. ~ **gerechnet 200** call it 200.

  (c) (fig: glattweg) abschlagen, ablehnen flatly. **jetzt geht's** ~ (inf) this is where the fun starts (inf); **wenn er das erfährt, geht's** ~ (inf) there'll be a to-do when he finds out (inf); **es geht** ~, **wenn sie zu Besuch kommen** (inf) there'll be great goings-on when they come to stay (inf); **es geht** ~ **im Büro** (inf) there's a lot on at the office.

Rund-: ~**bank** f circular bench; ~**bau** m rotunda; ~**blick** m panorama; ~**bogen** m (Archit) round arch; ~**brief** m circular.

Runde f -, -n (a) (Gesellschaft) company. **sich zu einer gemütlichen** ~ **treffen** to meet informally; **in der** ~ **herumgehen** to be passed around, to do or go the rounds.

  (b) (Rundgang) walk, turn; (von Wachmann) rounds pl; (von Briefträger etc) round. **die/seine** ~ **machen** to do the/one's rounds; (Gastgeberin) to circulate; (herumgegeben werden) to be passed round; **eine** ~ **durch die Lokale machen** to go on a pub crawl; **eine** ~ **machen** to go for a walk; (mit Fahrzeug) to go for a ride; **eine** ~ **um etw machen** to go for a walk or take a turn round sth; (mit Fahrzeug) to ride round sth; **zwei** ~**n um etw machen** to do two circuits of sth.

  (c) (Sport) (bei Rennen) lap; (von Turnier, Wettkampf) round; (Gesprächs~, Verhandlungs~) round. **seine** ~**n drehen** or **ziehen** to do one's laps; **über die** ~**n kommen** (Sport, fig) to pull through; **etw über die** ~**n bringen** (fig) to manage sth, to get through sth; **eine** ~ **schlafen** (sl) to have a kip.

  (d) (von Getränken) round. **(für jdn) eine** ~ **spendieren** or **ausgeben** or **schmeißen** (sl) to buy or stand sb a round.

  (e) (liter: Umkreis) surroundings pl. **in die/der** ~ **round about.**

runden 1 vt Lippen to round. 2 vr (lit: rund werden) (Bauch) to become round; (Gesicht auch) to become full; (Lippen) to grow round; (fig: konkrete Formen annehmen) to take shape. **sich zu etw** ~ (fig) to develop into sth.

Rund-: ~**erlaß** m circular (directive); r~**erneuern*** vt sep in fin, ptp ~ to remould; r~**erneuerte Reifen** remoulds; ~**erneuerung** f remoulding; ~**fahrt** f tour; **eine** ~**fahrt machen/an einer** ~**fahrt teilnehmen** to go on a tour; ~**flug** m (Besichtigungsflug) sightseeing flight; (Reiseroute) round trip; ~**frage** f survey (an +acc, unter +dat of).

Rundfunk m broadcasting; (besonders Hörfunk) radio, wireless (esp Brit dated); (Organisation) broadcasting company or corporation. **der** ~ **überträgt etw sth is broadcast; im/über** ~ on the radio; ~ **hören** to listen to the radio; **beim** ~ **arbeiten** or **(tätig) sein** to work or be in broadcasting.

Rundfunk- in cpds radio; ~**ansager** m (radio) announcer; ~**anstalt** f broadcasting corporation; ~**durchsage** f special announcement (on the radio); ~**empfang** m radio reception; ~**empfänger** m radio receiver; ~**gebühr** f radio licence fee; ~**gerät** nt radio set; ~**gesellschaft** f broadcasting company; ~**hörer** m (radio) listener; ~**programm** nt (Kanal, inf: Sendung) radio programme; (Sendefolge) radio programmes; (gedrucktes ~programm) radio programme guide; ~**sender** m (a) (Sendeanlage) radio transmitter; (b) (Sendeanstalt) radio station; ~**sendung** f radio programme; ~**sprecher** m radio announcer; ~**station** f radio station; ~**technik** f radiotechnology; ~**techniker** m radio engineer; ~**teilnehmer** m owner of a radio set; ~**übertragung** f radio broadcast; ~**zeitschrift** f radio programme guide.

Rund-: ~**gang** m (Spaziergang) walk; (zur Besichtigung) tour (durch of); (von Wachmann) rounds pl; (von Briefträger etc) round; **einen** ~**gang machen** to go for a walk; to go on a tour; **seinen** ~**gang machen** to do one's rounds/round; ~**gesang** m (Mus) chorus song (in which a different person sings each verse); (Kanon) round; ~**heit** f roundness; r~**heraus** adv flatly, bluntly, straight out; r~**heraus gesagt** frankly; r~**herum** adv all round; (fig inf: völlig) totally; ~**kurs** m circuit; r~**lich** adj plump; ~**lichkeit** f plumpness; ~**ling** m circular village grouped round a green, nuclear village; ~**reise** f tour (durch of); ~**schädel** m shorthead; ~**schau** f (Rad, TV) magazine programme ~**schild** m (Hist) round shield; ~**schnitt** m round haircut; ~**schreiben** nt circular; ~**sicht** f panorama; ~**spruch** m (Sw) siehe ~**funk**; ~**spruchemission** f (Sw) radio programme; ~**stricknadel** f circular needle; ~**stück** nt (N Ger) roll; **r~um** adv all around; (fig) completely, totally; **r~umher** adv schauen, blicken around.

Rundung f curve.

Rund-: ~**verkehr** m siehe Kreisverkehr; **r~weg** adv siehe **r~heraus**; ~**zange** f round-nosed pliers pl.

Rune f -, -n rune.

Runen- in cpds runic; ~**reihe** f runic alphabet; ~**schrift** f runic writing; ~**stein** m rune-stone; ~**zeichen** nt runic character.

Runge f -, -n stake.

Runkelrübe f, **Runkel** f -, -n (Aus) mangel-wurzel.

runter adv (inf) siehe herunter, hinunter. ~! down!

runter- pref (inf) down; ~**holen** vt sep to get down; **jdm/sich einen** ~**holen** (sl) to jerk sb/(oneself) off (sl); ~**kommen** vi sep irreg aux sein (sl: von Drogen) to come off drugs/heroin etc; ~**lassen** vt sep irreg siehe herunterlassen; **die Hosen** ~**lassen** (sl) to come clean (inf); ~**sein** vi sep irreg aux sein (Zusammenschreibung nur bei infin und ptp) (inf) (erschöpft sein) to be run down; (sl: vom Rauschgift etc) to be off drugs/heroin etc; **gesundheitlich** ~**sein** to be under the weather (inf), to feel off (inf); **mit den Nerven** ~**sein** to be at the end of one's tether (inf).

Runzel f -, -n wrinkle; (auf Stirn auch) line. ~n **bekommen** (Mensch) to get wrinkles; (Haut) to get or become wrinkled.

runz(e)lig adj wrinkled; Stirn auch lined.

runzeln 1 vt Stirn to wrinkle, to crease; Brauen to knit. 2 vr to become wrinkled.

runzlig adj siehe runz(e)lig.

Rüpel m -s, - lout, yob(bo) (Brit sl).

Rüpelei f (rüpelhafte Art) loutishness; (rüpelhafte Handlung/ Bemerkung) loutish act/remark etc.

rüpelhaft adj loutish.

Rüpelhaftigkeit f siehe Rüpelei.

rupfen vt Gänse, Hühner, Enten to pluck; Gras, Unkraut to pull up. **jdn** ~ (fig inf) to fleece sb (inf), to take sb to the cleaners (inf); **wie ein gerupftes Huhn aussehen** to look like a shorn sheep; siehe Hühnchen.

Rupfen m -s, - (Tex) gunny; (für Wandbehänge) hessian.

Rupie ['ru:pjə] f rupee.

ruppig adj (grob) rough; Benehmen, Antwort gruff; Autofahren wild. ~ **spielen** to play rough.

Ruppsack m (dated inf) blackguard (old).

Ruprecht m Rupert; siehe Knecht.

Rüsche f -, -n ruche, frill.

Rush-hour ['rʌʃ-aʊə] f -, no pl rush hour.

Ruß m -es, no pl soot; (von Kerze) smoke; (von Petroleumlampe) lampblack.

rußbedeckt adj covered in or with soot.

Russe m -n, -n Russian, Russian man/boy.

Rüssel m -s, - snout (auch sl: Nase); (Elefanten~) trunk; (von Insekt) proboscis.

rüsselförmig adj snoutlike; trunklike; proboscidean (spec).

rußen 1 vi (Öllampe, Kerze) to smoke; (Ofen) to produce soot. **es rußt** there's a lot of soot; **eine stark** ~**de Lampe** a very smoky lamp.

2 vt (Sw, S Ger) **den Ofen/den Kamin** ~ to clean the soot out of the stove/to sweep the chimney.

Russen-: **r~freundlich** adj pro-Russian; **ein r~freundlicher Mensch** a Russophile; ~**kittel** m smock; ~**stiefel** m Cossack boot.

Ruß-: **r~farben**, **r~farbig** adj soot-black; ~**fleck** m sooty mark; ~**flocke** f soot particle; **r~geschwärzt** adj soot-blackened.

rußig adj sooty.

Russin f Russian, Russian woman/girl.

russisch adj Russian. ~**es Roulett** Russian roulette; ~**e Eier** (Cook) egg(s) mayonnaise; ~**er Salat** (Cook) Russian salad; **R~es Brot** (Cook) alphabet biscuits.

Russisch(e) nt decl as adj Russian; siehe Deutsch(e).

Rußland nt -s Russia.

Rüste f: **zur** ~ **gehen** (poet: Sonne) to sink (below the horizon), to set.

rüsten 1 vi (Mil) to arm. **zum Krieg/Kampf** ~ to arm for war/battle; **gut/schlecht gerüstet sein** to be well/badly armed; **um die Wette** ~ to be involved in an arms race.

2 vr to prepare (zu for); (lit, fig: sich wappnen) to arm oneself (gegen for). **sich zur Abreise/zum Fest** ~ to get ready to leave/to prepare for the festival.

3 vt (a) (old: vorbereiten) to prepare; Nachtlager auch to make ready.

(b) (Build) Haus to scaffold.

Rüster f -, -n elm.

rüstern adj attr elm.

Rüster(n)holz nt elm(wood).

rüstig adj sprightly.

Rüstigkeit f sprightliness.

rustikal adj rustic. **sich** ~ **einrichten** to furnish one's home in a rustic or farmhouse style.

Rüst-: ~**kammer** f (Mil, fig) armoury; ~**tag** m (Rel) day of preparation.

Rüstung f (a) (das Rüsten) armament; (Waffen) arms pl, weapons pl. (b) (Ritter~) armour.

Rüstungs- in cpds arms; ~**beschränkung** f arms limitation; ~**betrieb** m, ~**fabrik** f armaments or ordnance factory; ~**industrie** f armaments industry; ~**kontrolle** f arms control; ~**produktion** f arms production; ~**wettlauf** m arms race.

Rüst-: ~**zeiten** pl (Rel) siehe ~**tag**; ~**zeug** nt, no pl (a) (old) siehe Handwerkszeug; (b) (fig) qualifications pl.

Rute f -, -n (a) (Gerte) switch; (esp Stock zum Züchtigen) cane, rod; (Birken~) birch (rod); (von Gertenbündel) birch. **jdn mit einer** ~ **schlagen** to cane/birch sb, to beat sb with a cane/birch; **mit eiserner** ~ **regieren** (fig) to rule with a rod of iron. (b) (Wünschel~) (divining or dowsing) rod; (Angel~) (fishing) rod. **mit der** ~ **gehen** to go divining. (c) (Hunt: Schwanz) tail. (d) (Tierpenis) penis; (sl: von Mann) cock (vulg), prick (vulg). (e) (Aus: Schneebesen) whisk. (f) (old: Measure) rod.

Ruten-: ~**bündel** nt (Hist) fasces pl; ~**gänger(in** f) m -s, - diviner, dowser; ~**hieb** m stroke (of the birch).

Ruthenium nt, no pl (Chem) ruthenium.

Rütlischwur m (Hist) oath taken on the Rütli Mountain by the founders of Switzerland.

rutsch interj whee, whoomph.

Rutsch m -es, -e slip, slide, fall; (Erd~) landslide; (von Steinen) rockfall; (fig Pol) shift, swing; (inf: Ausflug) trip, outing. **wir machten einen kleinen** ~ **nach Wien** (inf) we went on a little trip or outing to Vienna; **guten** ~! (inf) Happy New Year!; **in einem** ~ in one go.

Rutschbahn f, **Rutsche** f -, -n (Mech) chute; (Kinder~) slide.

rutschen vi aux sein (a) (gleiten) to slide; (aus~, entgleiten) to slip; (Aut) to skid; (fig: Preise, Kurse) to slip; (Regime, Hierarchie) to crumble. **auf dem Stuhl hin und her** ~ to fidget or shift around on one's chair.

(b) (inf: rücken) to move or shove (inf) up. **zur Seite** ~ to move or shove (inf) up or over; **ein Stück(chen)** ~ to move or shove (inf) up a bit.

(c) (herunter~) to slip down; (Essen, Tablette) to go down; siehe Herz.

(d) (auf Rutschbahn) to slide. **darf ich mal** ~? can I have a go on the slide?

(e) (~d kriechen) to crawl. **auf den Knien gerutscht kommen** (fig inf) to go down on one's bended knees; **auf den Knien** ~ (lit) to move along on one's knees.

Rutscher m -s, - (Aus) (Abstecher) small detour; (kleine Strecke) stone's throw.

Rutsch-: **r~fest** adj non-slip; ~**gefahr** f danger of skidding; „~**gefahr**" "slippery road";

rutschig adj slippery, slippy (inf).

Rutsch-: ~**partie** f (hum inf) (auf Eis, auf ~bahn) slide; (das Ausrutschen) slip; (von Auto) skid; **eine** ~**partie machen** to go sliding; (ausrutschen) to slip; (mit Auto) to go into a skid; **r~sicher** adj non-slip.

Rüttelei f shaking; (von Fahrzeug, Zug) jolting; (von Fenstern, Türen) rattling. **die Fahrt war eine einzige** ~ we were jolted about the whole way.

rütteln 1 vt to shake (about); Getreide etc to riddle, to sieve. **jdn am Arm/an der Schulter** ~ to shake sb's arm/shoulder, to shake sb by the arm/shoulder.

2 vi to shake; (Fahrzeug) to jolt; (Fenster, Tür: im Wind) to rattle. **an etw** (dat) ~ an Tür, Fenster etc to rattle (at) sth; (fig) **an Grundsätzen, Glauben** to shake sth; **daran ist nicht or daran gibt es nichts zu** ~ (inf) there's no doubt about that.

Rüttelsieb nt sieve, riddle.

S

S, s [ɛs] nt -, - S, s.
S abbr of **Süden** S.
S. abbr of **Seite** p.
s. abbr of **siehe** v.
SA [ɛs'|a] f -, no pl abbr of **Sturmabteilung** (NS).
s.a. abbr of **siehe auch**.
Saal m -(e)s, **Säle** hall; (für Sitzungen etc) room; (Lese~) reading room; (Tanz~, Ball~) ballroom; (für Hochzeiten, Empfänge) function suite; (Theater~) auditorium.
Saal-: ~ordner m usher; ~schlacht f (Brit inf) brawl, punch-up (inf); ~tochter f (Sw) waitress.
Saar f - Saar.
Saar-: ~gebiet, ~land nt Saarland; ~länder(in f) m -s, - Saarlander; s~ländisch adj (of the) Saarland.
Saat f -, -en (a) (das Säen) sowing.
  (b) (Samen, ~gut) seed(s) (auch fig). wenn die ~ aufgeht (lit) when the seed begins to grow; (fig) when the seed bears fruit; die ~ für etw legen (fig) to sow the seed(s) of sth; wie die ~, so die Ernte (prov)/ohne ~ keine Ernte (prov) as you sow, so shall you reap (Prov).
  (c) (junges Getreide) young crop(s), seedlings pl.
Saatenstand m state of the crop(s).
Saat-: ~feld nt cornfield (Brit), grainfield; ~gut nt, no pl seed(s); ~kartoffel f seed potato; ~korn nt seed corn; ~krähe f rook; ~zeit f seedtime, sowing time.
Saba nt -s (Hist) Sheba. die Königin von ~ the Queen of Sheba.
Sabbat m -s, -e Sabbath.
Sabbat-: ~jahr nt (Rel) sabbatical year; ~schänder m -s, - desecrator of the Sabbath.
Sabbel m -s, no pl (dial) siehe **Sabber**.
sabbeln vti (dial) siehe **sabbern**.
Sabber m -s, no pl (dial) slobber, saliva, slaver.
Sabberei f (inf) (dial) slobbering; (fig: Geschwätz) drivel (inf).
Sabberlätzchen nt (dial) bib.
sabbern (inf) 1 vi to slobber, to slaver. vor sich hin ~ (fig) to mutter away to oneself. 2 vt to blather (inf). dummes Zeug ~ to talk drivel (inf).
Säbel m -s, - sabre; (Krumm~) scimitar. jdn auf ~ fordern to challenge sb to a (sabre) duel; mit dem ~ rasseln (fig) to rattle the sabre.
Säbel-: ~beine pl (inf) bow or bandy legs pl; s~beinig adj (inf) bow-legged, bandy-legged; ~fechten nt sabre fencing; ~gerassel nt siehe ~rasseln; ~hieb m stroke of one's sabre.
säbeln (inf) 1 vt to saw away at. 2 vi to saw away (an + dat at).
Säbel-: ~rasseln nt -s, no pl sabre-rattling; s~rasselnd adj sabre-rattling; ~raßler(in f) m -s, - sabre-rattler.
Sabinerinnen pl der Raub der ~ the rape of the Sabines or the Sabine women.
Sabotage [zabo'ta:ʒə] f -, -n sabotage. ~ treiben to perform acts of sabotage.
Sabotageakt m act of sabotage.
Saboteur (in f) [-'tø:r, -'tø:rɪn] m saboteur.
sabotieren* vt to sabotage.
Sa(c)charin nt -s, no pl saccharin.
Sach-: ~anlagevermögen nt (Econ) tangible fixed assets pl; ~bearbeiter m specialist; (Beamter) official in charge (für of); der ~bearbeiter für Anträge ist nicht da the person who deals with applications isn't here; ~bereich m (specialist) area; ~beschädigung f damage to property; s~bezogen adj Wissen, Fragen, Angaben relevant, pertinent; ~buch nt non-fiction book; im Bereich ~bücher in the non-fiction area; s~dienlich adj useful; es ist nicht s~dienlich, wenn ... it won't help the matter if ...
Sache f -, -n (a) thing; (Gegenstand auch) object; (Jur: Eigentum) article of property. ~n pl (inf: Zeug) things pl; (Jur) property; der Mensch wird zur ~ man is reduced to or becomes an object; das liegt in der Natur der ~ that's in the nature of things; ~n gibt's(, die gibt's gar nicht)! (inf) would you credit it! (inf).
  (b) (Angelegenheit) matter; (Rechtsstreit, ~fall) case; (Aufgabe) job. eine ~ der Polizei/der Behörden a matter for the police/authorities; es ist ~ der Polizei/der Behörden, das zu tun it's up to the police/authorities or it's for the police/authorities to do that; das mit dem Präsidenten war eine unangenehme ~ that was an unpleasant business with the president; das ist eine ganz tolle/unangenehme ~ it's really fantastic/unpleasant; die ~ macht sich (inf) things are coming along; ich habe mir die ~ anders vorgestellt I had imagined things differently; das ist eine andere ~ that's a different matter, that's a different kettle of fish (inf); das ist meine/seine ~ that's my/his affair or business; in ~n or in der ~ A gegen B (Jur) in the case (of) A versus B; zu einer ~ vernommen werden (Jur) to be questioned in a case; das ist nicht jedermanns ~ it's not everyone's cup of tea (inf); er versteht seine ~ he knows what he's doing or what he's about (inf); er macht seine ~ gut he's doing very well; (beruflich) he's doing a good job; das Innenministerium, das ist eine ~ für sich the Home Office is a thing apart or is a world unto itself; diese Frage können wir nicht hier mitbesprechen,

das ist eine ~ für sich we can't discuss this question now, it's a separate issue all to itself; und was hat deine Frau gesagt?/was meinen Sie zu diesen Streiks? — das ist eine ~ für sich and what did your wife say?/what do you think about these strikes? — that's another story; das ist so eine ~ (inf) it's a bit tricky, it's a bit of a problem; das ist 'ne ~ (inf: prima) great (inf); der ~ zuliebe for the love of it; die ~ mit der Bank ist also geplatzt so the bank job fell through; er ist für illegale ~n nicht zu haben you won't get him to do anything illegal; solche ~n liegen mir nicht I don't like things like that.
  (c) (Vorfall) business, affair. ~n pl (Vorkommnisse) things pl; die ~ mit dem verschwundenen Schlüssel the business or affair with the disappearing key; machst du bei der ~ mit? are you with us?; bei der ~ mache ich nicht mit I'll have nothing to do with it; wann ist die ~ passiert? when did it (all) happen?; was hat die Polizei zu der ~ gesagt? what did the police say about it or about all this business?; das ist (eine) beschlossene ~ it's (all) settled; die ~ hat geklappt/ist schiefgegangen everything or it worked/went wrong; mach keine ~n! (inf) don't be silly or daft! (inf); was machst du bloß für ~n! (inf) the things you do!; was sind denn das für ~n? what's all this?
  (d) (Frage, Problem) matter, question; (Thema) subject; (Ideal, Anliegen) cause. eine ~ der Erziehung/des Geschmacks a matter or question of education/taste; mehr kann ich zu der ~ nicht sagen that's all I can say on the subject; um die ~ herumreden to talk (all) round the subject; zur ~! let's get on with it; (Parl, Jur etc) come to the point!; das tut nichts zur ~ that doesn't matter; sich (dat) seiner ~ sicher or gewiß sein to be sure of one's ground; bei der ~ sein to be with it (inf), to be on the ball (inf); sie war nicht bei der ~ her mind was elsewhere; bei der ~ bleiben to keep one's mind on the job; (bei Diskussion) to keep to the point.
  (e) (Sachlage) things pl, no art. so steht die ~ also so that's the way things are; die ~ ist die, daß ... the thing is that ...
  (f) (Tempo) mit 60/100 ~n (inf) at 60/100.
-sache f in cpds a matter of ...
Sach|einlage f (Econ) contribution in kind.
Sächelchen nt (inf) little thing; (Angelegenheit) small or little matter. mit 150 ~ (inf) at 150.
Sachenrecht nt (Jur) law of property.
Sachertorte f a rich chocolate cake, sachertorte.
Sach-: ~frage f factual question; ~- und Personalfragen questions relating to work and to personnel matters; s~fremd adj irrelevant; ein paar s~fremde Exemplare in der Kollektion a couple of extraneous copies in the collection; ~gebiet nt area; s~gemäß, s~gerecht adj proper; bei s~gemäßer Anwendung if used properly; etw s~gemäß machen to do sth properly; ~katalog m subject index; ~kenner m expert (in + dat on); ~kenner auf einem or für ein Gebiet sein to be an expert in a field; ~kenntnis f (in bezug auf Wissensgebiet) knowledge of the/his subject; (in bezug auf ~lage) knowledge of the facts; ~kunde f, no pl (a) siehe ~kenntnis; (b) (Schulfach) general knowledge; s~kundig adj (well-)informed no adv; sich s~kundig machen to inform oneself; s~kundig antworten to give an informed answer; ~kundige(r) mf deci as adj siehe ~kenner; ~lage f situation, state of affairs; ~leistung f payment in kind; (der Krankenkasse etc) benefit in kind.
sachlich adj (a) (faktisch) Irrtum, Angaben factual; Unterschied auch material; Grund, Einwand practical; (sachbezogen) Frage, Wissen relevant. rein ~ hast du recht from a purely factual point of view you are right.
  (b) (objektiv) Kritik, Bemerkung objective; (nüchtern, unemotional) matter-of-fact. bleiben Sie mal ~ don't get carried away; (nicht persönlich werden) don't get personal, stay objective.
  (c) (schmucklos) functional, businesslike.
sächlich adj (Gram) neuter.
Sachlichkeit f (a) siehe adj (b) objectivity; matter-of-factness. mit ~ kommt man weiter you get on better if you stay objective. (b) (Schmucklosigkeit) functionality. die Neue ~ (Art, Archit) the new functionalism.
Sach-: ~mängel pl material defects pl; ~mängelhaftung f liability for material defects; ~mittel pl (form) materials pl; (Zubehör) equipment no pl; ~register nt subject index; ~schaden m damage (to property); bei dem Unfall hatte ich nur ~schaden only my car was damaged in the accident.
Sachse ['zaksə] m -n, -n, **Sächsin** ['zeksɪn] f Saxon.
sächseln ['zeksln] vi (inf) to speak with a Saxon accent or in the Saxon dialect.
Sachsen ['zaksn] nt -s, Saxony.
sächsisch ['zeksɪʃ] adj Saxon. ~er Genitiv Saxon genitive.
Sächsisch(e) ['zeksɪʃ(ə)] nt decl as adj Saxon (dialect).
Sachspende f gift. wir bitten um Geld- und ~n we are asking for donations of money, food and clothes.
sacht(e) adj (leise) soft; (sanft) gentle; (vorsichtig) cautious, careful; (allmählich) gentle, gradual. mit ~n Schritten softly; ~, ~! (inf) take it easy!
Sach-: ~verhalt m -(e)s, -e facts pl (of the case);

~verständigenausschuß *m* committee of experts; **~verständigengutachten** *nt* specialist report; **~verständige(r)** *mf decl as adj* expert, specialist; (*Jur*) expert witness; **~verzeichnis** *nt siehe* **~register**; **~walter(in** *f*) *m* -s, - (*geh*) (*Verwalter*) agent; (*Treuhänder*) trustee; (*fig*: *Fürsprecher*) champion; **~wert** *m* real *or* intrinsic value; **~werte** *pl* material assets *pl*; **~wörterbuch** *nt* specialist dictionary; **~wörterbuch der Kunst/Botanik** dictionary of art/botany, art/botanical dictionary.

Sack *m* -(e)s, ̈e **(a)** sack; (*aus Papier, Plastik*) bag. **drei ~ Kartoffeln/Kohlen** three sacks of potatoes/sacks *or* bags of coal; **in ~ und Asche** in sackcloth and ashes; **mit ~ und Pack** (*inf*) with bag and baggage; **den ~ schlägt man, und den Esel meint man** (*Prov*) to kick the dog and mean the master (*prov*); **ihr habt wohl (zu Hause) ̈e vor der Tür** (*sl*) were you born in a field?; **ich habe in den ~ gehauen** (*sl*) I chucked it (in) (*sl*), I packed it in (*inf*); **ein ganzer ~ voll Neuigkeiten** (*inf*) heaps of news (*inf*); **jdn in den ~ stecken** (*fig inf*) to put sb in the shade. **(b)** (*Anat, Zool*) sac. **(c)** (*S Ger, Aus: Hosentasche*) (trouser *Brit or* pants *US*) pocket. **etw im ~ haben** (*sl*) to have sth in the bag (*inf*); **Geld im ~ haben** to have money in one's pocket. **(d)** (*vulg: Hoden*) balls *pl* (*sl*). **(e)** (*sl: Kerl, Bursche*) sod (*Brit sl*), bastard (*sl*), cunt (*vulg*). **fauler ~** lazy bugger (*Brit sl*) *or* bastard (*sl*).

Sackbahnhof *m* terminus.

Säckel *m* -s, - (*S Ger*) (*Beutel*) bag; (*Hosentasche*) pocket; (*Geld~*) moneybag. **tief in den ~ greifen müssen** to have to dig deep (into one's pockets); **sich** (*dat*) **den ~ füllen** to line one's (own) pockets; *siehe* **Staatssäckel**.

sacken¹, säckeln (*dial*) *vt* to put into sacks, to sack.

sacken² *vi aux* **sein** (*lit, fig*) to sink; (*Flugzeug*) to lose height; (*durchhängen*) to sag. **in die Knie ~** to sag at the knees.

sackerlot, sackerment *interj* (*old*) *siehe* **sapperlot**.

säckeweise *adj* by the sack/bag.

Sack-: ~förmig *adj* like a sack, sack-like; **~gasse** *f* dead end, blind alley, cul-de-sac (*esp Brit*); (*fig*) dead end; **in eine ~gasse geraten** (*fig*) to finish up a blind alley; (*Verhandlungen*) to reach an impasse; **in einer ~gasse stecken** (*fig*) to be (stuck) up a blind alley; (*mit Bemühungen etc*) to have come to a dead end; **~hüpfen** *nt* -s, *no pl* sack-race; **~karre** *f* barrow, hand-cart; **~kleid** *nt* sack dress; **~leinen** *nt*, **~leinwand** *f* sacking, burlap (*US*); **~pfeife** *f siehe* **Dudelsack**; **~träger** *m* carrier; **~tuch** *nt* **(a)** *siehe* **~leinen**; **(b)** (*S Ger, Aus, Sw: Taschentuch*) handkerchief.

Sadismus *m* **(a)** *no pl* sadism. **(b)** (*Handlung*) sadistic act.

Sadist(in *f*) *m* sadist.

sadistisch *adj* sadistic.

Sadomasochismus *m* sado-masochism.

säen *vti* to sow; (*fig*) to sow (the seeds of). **dünn** *or* **spärlich** *or* **nicht dick gesät** (*fig*) thin on the ground, few and far between.

Safari *f* -, -s safari. **eine ~ machen** to go on safari.

Safarianzug *m* safari suit.

Safe [ze:f] *m or nt* -s, -s safe.

Saffian *m* -s, *no pl*, **Saffianleder** *nt* morocco (leather).

Safran *m* -s, -e (*Krokus, Gewürz*) saffron.

safrangelb *adj* saffron (yellow).

Saft *m* -(e)s, ̈e (*Obst~*) (fruit) juice; (*Pflanzen~*) sap; (*Braten~, Fleisch~*) juice; (*Flüssigkeit*) liquid; (*Husten~ etc*) syrup; (*Magen~*) juices *pl*; (*old: Körper~*) humour (*old*); (*inf: Strom, Benzin*) juice (*inf*). **roter ~** lifeblood; **Blut ist ein ganz besonderer ~** blood is a very special stuff; **der ~ der Reben** the juice of the grape; **im ~ stehen** (*liter*) to be full of sap; **die ̈e der Natur** (*liter*) the vital forces of nature; **von ~ und Kraft** (*fig*) dynamic, vital, vibrant; **ohne ~ und Kraft** (*fig*) wishywashy (*inf*), effete; *siehe* **schmoren**.

Saftbraten *m* (*Cook*) roast.

Säftchen *nt dim of* **Saft** (*Frucht~*) juice; (*pej: Arznei*) mixture, medicine.

Saft-: s~grün *adj* luscious green; **~heini** *m* (*sl*) sap (*sl*), berk (*Brit sl*).

saftig *adj* **(a)** (*voll Saft*) *Obst, Fleisch* juicy; *Wiese, Grün* lush. **(b)** (*inf: kräftig*) *Witz* juicy (*inf*); *Rechnung, Ohrfeige* hefty (*inf*); *Brief, Antwort, Ausdrucksweise* potent. **da habe ich ihm einen ~en Brief geschrieben** so I wrote him a pretty potent letter *or* one hell of a letter (*inf*).

Saftigkeit *f* (*von Obst, Witz*) juiciness; (*von Wiese etc*) lushness.

Saft-: ~kur *f* fruit-juice diet; **~laden** *m* (*pej inf*) dump (*pej inf*); **s~los** *adj* not juicy, juiceless; **~presse** *f* fruit-press; **~sack** *m* (*sl*) stupid bastard (*sl*) *or* bugger (*Brit sl*); **~tag** *m* juice day; **einen ~tag haben/einlegen** to have a day on juices (*inf*).

saft- und kraftlos *adj* wishy-washy (*inf*), effete.

Saga *f* -, -s saga.

sagbar *adj* sayable.

Sage *f* -, -n legend; (*altnordische*) saga. **es geht die ~, daß ...** legend has it that ...; (*Gerücht*) rumour has it that ...

Säge *f* -, -n **(a)** (*Werkzeug*) saw. **(b)** (*Aus: ~werk*) sawmill.

Säge-: s~artig *adj* like a saw, saw-like; **~blatt** *nt* saw blade; **~bock** *m* sawhorse; **~fisch** *m* sawfish; **~maschine** *f* mechanical saw; **~mehl** *nt* sawdust; **~messer** *nt* serrated knife; **~mühle** *f* sawmill.

sagen *vt* **(a)** (*äußern*) to say. **jdm etw ~** to say sth to sb; (*mitteilen, ausrichten*) to tell sb sth; **sich** (*dat*) **etw ~** to say sth to oneself; **das hättest du dir selbst ~ können** *or* **müssen!** you might have known *or* realised that!; **im Vertrauen gesagt** in confidence; **unter uns gesagt** between you and me (and the gatepost *hum inf*); **genauer/deutlicher gesagt** to put it more precisely/clearly; **könnten Sie mir ~ ...?** could you tell me ...?; **ich sag's ihm** I'll tell him; **sag mir, was du liest, und ich sage dir,**

wer du bist (*prov*) tell me what you read and I'll tell you what kind of person you are; **jdm etw ~ lassen** to ask somebody to tell sb sth; **ich habe mir ~ lassen, ...** I've been told ...; **was ich mir von ihm nicht alles ~ lassen muß!** the things I have to take from him!; **das kann ich Ihnen nicht ~** I couldn't say, I don't know; **das kann ich noch nicht ~** (that) I can't say yet; **so was sagt man doch nicht!** you mustn't say things like that; (*bei Schimpfen, Fluchen*) (watch *or* mind your) language!; **sag nicht so etwas** *or* **so was!** (*inf*) don't say things like that!, don't talk like that!; **wie kannst du so etwas ~?** how can you say such things?; **das sage ich nicht!** I'm not saying *or* telling; **er hat auf alles etwas zu ~** he's got an answer for everything; **was ich noch ~ wollte, ...** (*inf*) there's something else I wanted to say ...; **oh, was ich noch ~ wollte, vergiß nicht ...** (*inf*) by the way, don't forget ...; **dann will ich nichts gesagt haben** in that case forget I said anything; **wie ich schon sagte** as I said before; **ich sage, wie es ist** I'm just telling you the way it is; **es ist nicht zu ~** it doesn't bear thinking about!; (*entrüstet*) there just aren't any words to describe it!; **um nicht zu ~** not to say; **sag an, ...** (*old, liter*) pray tell (*old*).

(b) (*befehlen*) **jdm ~, er solle etw tun** to tell sb to do sth; **hat er im Betrieb etwas zu ~?** does he have a say in the firm?; **du hast hier (gar) nichts zu ~** that isn't for you to say; **das S~ haben** to have the say; **hier habe ich das S~** what I say goes!; **laß dir von mir ~ or gesagt sein, ...** let me tell you, take it from me; **er läßt sich** (*dat*) **nichts ~** he won't be told, you can't tell him anything; **das laß ich mir von dem nicht ~** I won't take that from him; **sie ließen es sich** (*dat*) **nicht zweimal ~** they didn't need to be told a second time *or* to be told twice.

(c) (*Meinung äußern*) to say. **was ~ Sie dazu?** what do you think about it?; **was soll man dazu ~?** what can you say?; **haben Sie dazu etwas zu ~?** do you have anything to say (about *or* on that)?; **das möchte** *or* **will ich nicht ~** I wouldn't say that; **das würde ich (wieder) nicht ~** I wouldn't say that; **ich sag's ja immer ...** I always say ...; **I've always said ...; ich möchte fast ~, ...** I'd almost say ..., one could almost say ...; **wenn ich so ~ darf** if I may say so; **sag, was du willst, ...** (*inf*) say what you like ...; **da soll noch einer ~, ...** never let it be said ...

(d) (*bedeuten, meinen*) to mean. **was will er damit ~?** what does he mean (by that)?; **willst du vielleicht ~, daß ...** are you trying to tell me *or* to say that ...?, do you mean to tell me *or* to say that ...?; **ich will damit nicht ~, daß ...** I don't mean to imply *or* to say that ...; **damit ist nichts gesagt** that doesn't mean anything; **damit ist viel/wenig gesagt** that's saying a lot/not saying much; **damit ist alles gesagt** that says everything, that says it all; **sein Gesicht sagte alles** it was written all over his face; **damit ist nicht gesagt, daß ...** that doesn't mean (to say) that ...; **das hat nichts zu ~** that doesn't mean anything; **sagt dir der Name etwas?** does the name mean anything to you?

(e) (*Redewendungen*) **Sie mal/sag mal, ...** tell me, ..., say, ...; **du, Veronika, sag mal, wollen wir ...** hey, Veronika, listen, shall we ...; **sag mal, Peter, kannst du mir fünf Mark leihen?** (say,) Peter, can you lend me five marks?; **sag mal, willst du nicht endlich Schluß machen?** come on *or* hey, isn't it time to stop?; **nun ~ Sie/sag mal selber, ist das nicht unpraktisch?** you must admit that's impractical; **wem ~ Sie das!** you don't need to tell me that!; **sag bloß!** you don't say, get away (*Brit inf*); **was Sie nicht ~!** you don't say!; **ich sage gar nichts mehr!** I'm not saying another word; (*verblüfft*) good heavens!, did you ever! (*inf*); **das kann man wohl ~** you can say that again!; **ich muß schon ~** I must say; **das muß man ~** you have to *or* you must admit that; **wie man so sagt** as they say, as the saying goes; **das ist nicht gesagt** that's by no means certain; **das ist schnell gesagt** I can tell you in two words; (*leicht gesagt*) that's easily said; **leichter gesagt als getan** easier said than done; **gesagt, getan** no sooner said than done; **wie (schon) gesagt** as I/you *etc* said; **ich bin, ~ in einer Stunde da** I'll be there in, let's say, an hour; **sage und schreibe 100 Mark** 100 marks, would you believe it; *siehe* **offen, Dank, Meinung**.

sägen 1 *vti* to saw. **2** *vi* (*inf*) to snore, to saw wood (*US inf*).

Sagen-: ~buch *nt* book of legends; **~dichtung** *f* sagas *pl*; **s~haft** *adj* **(a)** (*nach Art einer Sage*) legendary; **(b)** (*enorm*) fabulous; **(c)** (*inf: hervorragend*) fantastic (*inf*), terrific (*inf*); **~kreis** *m* group of sagas; **s~umwoben** *adj* legendary; **~welt** *f* mythology, legend.

Sägerei *f* **(a)** *siehe* **Sägewerk**. **(b)** *no pl* (*inf*) sawing.

Säge-: ~späne *pl* wood shavings *pl*; **~werk** *nt* sawmill; **~zahn** *m* saw tooth.

Sago *m or nt* -s, *no pl* sago.

Sagopalme *f* sago palm.

sah *pret of* **sehen**.

Sahara [za'ha:ra, 'za:hara] *f* - Sahara (Desert).

Sahne *f* -, *no pl* cream.

Sahne-: ~baiser *nt* cream meringue; **~bonbon** *m or nt* toffee; **~eis** *nt* icecream; **~käse** *m* cream cheese; **~torte** *f* cream gateau.

sahnig *adj* creamy. **etw ~ schlagen** to whip *or* beat sth until creamy.

Saibling *m* char(r).

Saison [zɛ'zɔ̃:, zɛ'zɔŋ] *f* -, -s *or* (*Aus*) -en season. **außerhalb der ~, in der stillen** *or* **toten ~** in the off-season.

saisonal [zɛzo'na:l] *adj* seasonal.

Saison- [zɛ'zõ:] *in cpds* seasonal; **~arbeit** *f* seasonal work; **~arbeiter** *m* seasonal worker; **~ausverkauf** *m* end-of-season sale; **s~bedingt** *adj* seasonal; **~beginn** *m* start of the season; **~beschäftigung** *f* seasonal job; **~betrieb** *m* (*Hochsaison*) high season; (*~geschäft*) seasonal business; **~eröffnung** *f* opening of the season; **~geschäft** *nt* seasonal business; **~gewerbe** *nt* seasonal trade; **~industrie** *f* seasonal industry; **~schluß** *m* end of the season; **~schwankung** *f* seasonal fluctuation;

~stellung f seasonal job; in ~stellung gehen to take a seasonal job; ~wanderung f (Econ) seasonal movement of labour; ~zuschlag m in-season supplement.

Saite f -, -n (a) (Mus, Sport) string. (b) (fig liter) eine ~ in jdm berühren or anschlagen, eine ~ in jdm zum Klingen bringen to strike a chord in sb; eine empfindliche ~ berühren to touch a tender or sore spot; andere ~n aufziehen (inf) to get tough.

Saiten-: ~instrument nt string(ed) instrument; ~klang m (liter) sound of strings; ~spiel nt, no pl playing of a stringed instrument.

-saitig adj suf -stringed.

Sakko m or nt -s, -s sports jacket (Brit), sport coat (US); (aus Samt etc) jacket.

sakra interj (S Ger, Aus) good God, my God.

sakral adj sacred, sacral.

Sakral-: ~bau m sacred building; ~kunst f religious art, sacral art.

Sakrament nt sacrament. das ~ der Taufe the sacrament of baptism; ~ (noch mal)! (sl) Jesus Christ! (sl).

sakramental adj sacramental.

Sakramentalien [-iən] pl (Eccl) sacraments pl.

Sakrament(s)häuschen nt tabernacle.

Sakrileg nt -s, -e, **Sakrilegium** nt (geh) sacrilege.

sakrisch adv (dial inf) damned (inf); schreien like hell (inf).

Sakristan m -s, -e sacristan.

Sakristei f sacristy.

sakrosankt adj sacrosanct.

säkular adj (a) (weltlich) secular. (b) (zeitüberdauernd) timeless.

Säkularisation f secularization.

säkularisieren* vt to secularize.

Säkulum nt -s, **Säkula** (geh) century.

Salamander m -s, - salamander.

Salami f -, -s salami.

Salamitaktik f (inf) policy of small steps.

Salär nt -s, -e (old, Sw) salary.

Salat m -(e)s, -e (a) (Pflanze, Kopf~) lettuce. (b) (Gericht) salad. da haben wir den ~! (inf) now we're in a fine mess or a pretty pickle (inf).

Salat-: ~besteck nt salad servers pl; ~gurke f cucumber; ~kartoffel f potato used for potato salad; ~kopf m (head of) lettuce; ~öl nt salad oil; ~pflanze f (a) (Setzling) lettuce (plant); (b) (Sorte) salad; ~platte f salad; ~schüssel f salad bowl; ~soße f salad dressing.

Salbader m -s, - (old pej) sanctimonious old windbag.

Salbaderei f (pej geh) sanctimonious prating.

salbadern* vi to prate.

Salbe f -, -n ointment.

Salbei m -s, no pl or f -, no pl sage.

salben vt (liter) to anoint. jdn zum König ~ to anoint sb king.

Salböl nt consecrated oil.

Salbung f anointing, unction.

salbungsvoll adj (pej) unctuous (pej).

saldieren* vt (Comm) to balance; (Aus) to confirm payment.

Saldo m -s, -s or **Saldi** or **Salden** (Fin) balance. per ~ (lit, fig) on balance; per ~ bezahlen/remittieren to pay off the balance in full; in ~ bleiben/sein to stay/be in debt.

Saldoübertrag, Saldovortrag m (Fin) balance brought forward or carried forward.

Säle pl of **Saal**.

Saline f salt-works sing or pl.

salisch adj (Hist) Salian, Salic.

Salizylsäure f salicylic acid.

Salm m -(e)s, -e (a) (Lachs) salmon. (b) (inf: Gerede) rigmarole (inf).

Salmiak m or nt -s, no pl sal ammoniac, ammonium chloride.

Salmiakgeist m (liquid) ammonia.

Salmonellen pl salmonellae.

Salmonellose f -, -n salmonellosis.

Salomo(n) m -s or (geh) **Salomonis** Solomon.

salomonisch adj of Solomon; Urteil worthy of a Solomon. ein wahrhaft ~es Urteil! a real Solomon!

Salon [za'lõ:, za'lɔŋ] m -s, -s (a) (Gesellschaftszimmer) drawing room; (Naut) saloon. (b) (Friseur~, Mode~, Kosmetik~ etc) salon. (c) (Hist: literarischer etc Zirkel) salon. (d) (auf Messe) stand, exhibition stand. (e) (Kunst~) exhibition room.

Salon- [za'lõ:-]: ~anarchist m (pej) drawing-room revolutionary; s~fähig adj (iro) socially acceptable; Leute, Aussehen presentable; ein nicht s~fähiger Witz an objectionable joke; (unanständig auch) a rude or naughty joke; nicht s~fähige Ausdrucksweise uncouth language, not the sort of language to be used in polite society; ~löwe m socialite, society man, social lion; ~musik f palm court music; ~wagen m (Rail) Pullman (carriage), special coach.

salopp adj (a) (nachlässig) sloppy, slovenly; Manieren slovenly; Ausdruck, Sprache slangy. (b) (ungezwungen) casual.

Salpeter m -s, no pl saltpetre, nitre.

salpet(e)rig adj nitrous.

Salpetersäure f nitric acid.

Salto m -s, -s or **Salti** somersault; (Turmspringen auch) turn. ein anderthalbfacher ~ a one-and-a-half somersault or turn; einen ~ mortale machen (Zirkus) to perform a death-defying leap; (Aviat) to loop the loop; ein logischer/gedanklicher ~ mortale a logical/an intellectual leap.

Salut m -(e)s, -e (Mil) salute. ~ schießen to fire a salute; 21 Schuß ~ 21-gun salute.

salutieren* vti (Mil) to salute.

Salutschuß m man gab or feuerte fünf Salutschüsse ab a five-gun salute was fired.

Salve ['zalvə] f -, -n salvo, volley; (Ehren~) salute; (fig) (Lach~) burst of laughter; (von Applaus) volley, burst. eine ~ auf jdn abschießen (lit, fig) to fire a salvo or volley at sb.

Salz nt -es, -e salt. in ~ legen to salt down or away; das ~ der Erde (liter) the salt of the earth; das ist das ~ in der Suppe (fig) that's what gives it that extra something; wie eine Suppe ohne ~ (fig) like ham without eggs (hum); er gönnt einem nicht das ~ in der Suppe he even begrudges you the air you breathe.

Salz-: s~arm adj (Cook) low-salt, with a low salt content; s~arm essen/leben to eat low-salt food/to live on a low-salt diet; ~bergwerk nt salt mine; ~brezel f pretzel.

salzen vt to salt; siehe gesalzen.

Salz-: ~faß, ~fäßchen nt saltcellar; ~fleisch nt (Cook) salt meat; s~frei adj salt-free; Diät auch no-salt attr; ~gebäck nt savoury biscuits pl; ~gurke f pickled gherkin; s~haltig adj salty, saline; ~hering m salted herring.

salzig adj salty, salt.

Salzigkeit f saltiness.

Salz-: ~kartoffeln pl boiled potatoes pl; ~korn nt grain of salt; ~lake f brine; s~los adj salt-free; s~los essen not to eat salt; ~lösung f saline solution; ~mandel f salted almond; ~napf m siehe ~faß; ~säule f: zur ~säule erstarren (Bibl) to turn into a pillar of salt; (fig) to stand as though rooted to the spot; ~säure f hydrochloric acid; ~see m salt lake; ~sieder m -s, - (Hist) salt-maker; ~siederei f (Hist) saltworks sing or pl; ~sole f brine; ~stange f pretzel stick; ~streuer m -s, - salt shaker, salt cellar; ~wasser nt salt water; ~wüste f salt desert, salt flat.

SA-Mann m, pl **SA-Leute** [ɛs'|aː-] storm-trooper, SA-man.

Sämann m, pl **Sämänner** (old liter) sower.

Samariter m -s, - (a) (Bibl, fig) Samaritan. der Barmherzige ~ the good Samaritan. (b) (Angehöriger des Arbeiter-Samariterbunds) first-aid volunteer, ≈ St John's Ambulance man (Brit).

Samariterdienst m act of mercy. jdm einen ~ erweisen to be a good Samaritan to sb.

Samba m -s, -s or f -, -s samba.

Sambesi m -(s) Zambesi.

Sambia nt -s Zambia.

Sambier(in f) [-iə, -iərɪn] m -s, - Zambian.

sambisch adj Zambian.

Same m -ns, -n (liter) siehe **Samen**.

Samen m -s, - (a) (Bot, fig) seed; (fig auch) seeds pl. (b) (Menschen~, Tier~) sperm. (c) (liter, Bibl: Nachkommen) seed (liter, Bibl).

Samen-: ~anlage f (Bot) ovule; ~bank f sperm bank; ~blase f seminal vesicle; ~erguß m ejaculation, emission of semen, seminal discharge or emission; ~faden m spermatozoon; ~flüssigkeit f semen, seminal fluid; ~händler m seedsman, seed merchant; ~handlung f seed shop; ~kapsel f seed capsule; ~korn nt seed; ~leiter m vas deferens; ~strang m spermatic cord; s~tragend adj seed-bearing; ~zelle f sperm cell; ~zwiebel f seed onion.

Sämereien pl seeds pl.

sämig adj thick, creamy.

Sämischleder nt chamois (leather).

Sämling m seedling.

Sammel-: ~album nt (collector's) album; ~anschluß m (Telec) private (branch) exchange; (von Privathäusern) party line; ~band m anthology; ~becken nt collecting tank; (Geol) catchment area; (fig) melting pot (von for); ~begriff m (Gram) collective name or term; ~bestellung f joint or collective order; ~bezeichnung f siehe ~begriff; ~büchse f collecting tin or box; ~karte f (für mehrere Fahrten) multi-journey ticket; (für mehrere Personen) group ticket; ~mappe f file.

sammeln 1 vt to collect; Holz, Ähren, Fakten, Material, Erfahrungen auch to gather; Blumen, Pilze etc to pick, to gather; Truppen, Anhänger to gather, to assemble. neue Kräfte ~ to build up one's energy again; seine Gedanken ~ to collect one's thoughts.

2 vr (a) (zusammenkommen) to gather, to collect; (sich anhäufen: Wasser, Geld etc) to collect, to accumulate; (Lichtstrahlen) to converge, to meet.

(b) (sich konzentrieren) to collect or compose oneself or one's thoughts; siehe gesammelt.

3 vi to collect (für for).

Sammel-: ~name m siehe ~begriff; ~nummer f (Telec) private exchange number, switchboard number; ~paß m group passport; ~platz m (a) (Treffpunkt) assembly point; (Lagerplatz) collecting point; (Deponie) dump; ~punkt m (a) (Treffpunkt) assembly point; (b) (Opt) focus; ~sendung f joint consignment; Güter als ~sendung schicken to send goods part-load.

Sammelsurium nt conglomeration.

Sammel-: ~tasse f ornamental cup, saucer and plate; ~transport m (von Gütern) general shipment; (von Personen) group transport; ~visum nt collective visa; ~werk nt compilation; (über ein Thema) symposium; ~wut f collecting mania.

Sammet m -s, -e (obs, Sw) velvet.

Sammler(in f) m -s, - collector; (von Beeren) picker; (von Holz) gatherer.

Sammlerfleiß m collector's enthusiasm. diese Kollektion ist mit großem ~ zusammengetragen it has taken a lot of hard work to put this collection together; dank dem ~ des Museumsdirektors thanks to the efforts of the museum director in building the collection.

Sammlung f (a) collection. (b) (fig: Konzentration) composure. ihm fehlt die innere ~ he lacks composure; zur ~ (meiner Gedanken) to collect myself or my thoughts.

Samos(wein) m -, - Samian wine, wine from Samos.

Samowar *m* -s, -e samovar.
Samstag *m* -(e)s, -e Saturday; *siehe* **Dienstag**.
samstägig *adj* Saturday.
samstags *adj* on Saturdays.
samt 1 *prep + dat* along *or* together with. **sie kam ~ Katze** (*hum*) she came complete with cat. **2** *adv* **~ und sonders** the whole lot (of them/us/you), the whole bunch (*inf*); **die Teilnehmer wurden ~ und sonders verhaftet** all the participants were arrested, the whole lot of them.
Samt *m* -(e)s, -e velvet. **in ~ und Seide** (*liter*) in silks and satins; **zart wie ~ und Seide** (*liter*) as soft as silk.
Samt- *in cpds* velvet; **s~artig** *adj* velvety, like velvet; **~band** *nt* velvet ribbon; **~blume** *f* (*Bot*) marigold.
samten *adj* (*liter*) velvet.
Samthandschuh *m* velvet glove. **jdn mit ~en anfassen** (*inf*) to handle sb with kid gloves (*inf*).
samtig *adj* velvety.
sämtlich *adj* (*alle*) all; (*vollständig*) complete. **~e Unterlagen waren verschwunden, die Unterlagen waren ~ verschwunden** all the *or* every one of the documents had disappeared, the documents had all disappeared; **Schillers ~e Werke** the complete works of Schiller; **~e Anwesenden** all those present; **sie mußten ~en Besitz zurücklassen** they had to leave all their possessions behind.
Samt-: **~pfötchen** *nt* (*inf*) velvet paw; **~pfötchen machen** (*Katze*) to draw in/have drawn in its claws; (*fig*) to go all soft; **s~weich** *adj* (as) soft as velvet, velvet-soft, velvety.
Sanatorium *nt* sanatorium.
Sand *m* -(e)s, -e sand; (*Scheuer~*) scouring powder. **mit ~ bestreuen** to sand; **das/die gibt's wie ~ am Meer** (*inf*) there are heaps of them (*inf*); **auf ~ laufen** *or* **geraten** to run aground; **auf ~ bauen** (*fig*) to build upon sandy ground; **jdm ~ in die Augen streuen** (*fig*) to throw dust in sb's eyes; **~ ins Getriebe streuen** to throw a spanner in the works; **im ~ verlaufen** (*inf*) to peter out, to come to naught *or* nothing; **den Kopf in den ~ stecken** to stick *or* bury *or* hide one's head in the sand.
Sandale *f* -, -n sandal.
Sandalette *f* high-heeled sandal.
Sand- *in cpds* sand; **~bank** *f* sandbank, sandbar; **~blatt** *nt* wrapper, leaf; **~boden** *m* sandy soil; **~dorn** *m* (*Bot*) sea buckthorn.
Sandelholz *nt* sandalwood.
sandeln *vi* (*S Ger, Aus, Sw*) to play in the sand.
Sandelöl *nt* sandalwood oil.
Sand-: **s~farben, s~farbig** *adj* sand-coloured; **~grube** *f* sandpit (*esp Brit*), sandbox (*US*); (*Golf*) bunker, sand trap; **~haufen** *m* pile *or* heap of sand; (*~kasten*) sandpit (*esp Brit*), sandbox (*US*); **~hose** *f* sand column *or* spout, dust devil.
sandig *adj* sandy.
Sand-: **~kasten** *m* sandpit (*esp Brit*), sandbox (*US*); (*Mil*) sand table; **~kastenspiele** *pl* (*Mil*) sand-table exercises *pl*; (*fig*) tactical manoeuvrings *pl*; **~korn** *nt* grain of sand; **~kuchen** *m* (*Cook*) sand-cake (*a Madeira-type cake*); (*von Kindern*) mud pie.
Sandler(in *f*) *m* -s, - (*Aus*) ne'er-do-well.
Sandlerin *f* (*inf*) steerer (*a person employed to entice patrons*).
Sand-: **~mann** *m*, **~männchen** *nt* (*in Geschichten*) sandman; **~meer** *nt* (*geh*) sea of sand; **~papier** *nt* sandpaper; **~sack** *m* sandbag; (*Boxen*) punchbag.
Sandstein *m* sandstone. **ein Haus aus rotem ~** a red sandstone house, a brownstone (house) (*US*).
Sandstein- *in cpds* sandstone; **~fels(en)** *m* sandstone cliff.
Sand-: **~strahl** *m* jet of sand; **etw mit ~strahl abblasen** *or* **reinigen** to sandblast sth; **s~strahlen** *vti insep* to sandblast; **~strahlgebläse** *nt* sandblasting equipment *no indef art, no pl*; **~strand** *m* sandy beach; **~sturm** *m* sandstorm.
sandte *pret of* **senden**¹.
Sand-: **~uhr** *f* hour-glass; (*Eieruhr*) egg-timer; **~weg** *m* dirt road, track.
Sandwich ['zɛntvɪtʃ] *nt or m* -(s), -(e)s sandwich.
Sandwich-: **~bauweise** *f* sandwich construction; **~mann** *m, pl* -**männer** (*hum*) sandwichman; **~wecken** *m* (*Aus*) long thin white loaf, French loaf.
Sandwüste *f* sandy waste; (*Geog*) (sandy) desert.
sanft *adj* gentle; *Berührung, Stimme, Farbe, Licht, Wind, Regen auch* soft; *Unterlage, Haut* soft; *Schlaf, Tod* peaceful. **sich ~ anfühlen** to feel soft; **mit ~er Gewalt** gently but firmly; **mit ~er Hand** with a gentle hand; **von ~er Hand** by a woman's fair hand; **sie lächelte ~** she smiled softly; **sie schaute das Kind mit ~en Augen an** she looked tenderly at the child; **~ schlafen** to be sleeping peacefully; **er ist ~ entschlafen** he passed away peacefully, he fell gently asleep (*auch iro*); **~ wie ein Lamm** (as) gentle as a lamb; *siehe* **ruhen**.
Sänfte *f* -, -n litter; (*esp im 17., 18. Jh. Europas*) sedan-chair; (*in Indien*) palanquin; (*auf Elefant*) howdah.
Sänftenträger *m* litter-bearer; sedan bearer; palanquin bearer.
Sanftheit *f siehe adj* gentleness; softness.
sänftigen *vt* (*obs*) *siehe* **besänftigen**.
Sanftmut *f, no pl* (*liter*) gentleness.
sanftmütig *adj* (*liter*) gentle; (*Bibl*) meek.
sang *pret of* **singen**.
Sang *m* -(e)s, ̈e (*old liter*) (*Gesang*) song; (*das Singen*) singing. **mit ~ und Klang** (*lit*) with drums drumming and pipes piping; (*fig iro*) **durchfallen** disastrously, catastrophically; *entlassen werden* with a lot of hullaballoo; **ohne ~ und Klang** (*inf*) without any ado, quietly; **ohne ~ und Klang verschwinden** to just simply disappear.
Sänger *m* -s, - (a) singer; (*esp Jazz~, Pop~ auch*) vocalist. (b) (*old liter: Dichter*) bard (*old*), poet. **da(rüber) schweigt des ~s**

Höflichkeit modesty forbids me to say. (c) (*Singvogel*) songbird, songster.
Sänger-: **~bund** *m* choral union; **~fest** *nt* choral festival.
Sängerin *f* singer; (*esp Jazz~, Pop~*) vocalist.
Sanges-: **~bruder** *m* (*inf*) chorister; **~freude, ~lust** *f* (*dated*) love of song *or* singing; **s~freudig, s~lustig** *adj* (*dated*) fond of singing, song-loving.
Sanguiniker(in *f*) [zaŋ'guiːnikn, -ərɪn] *m* -s, - (*Psych*) sanguine person.
sanguinisch [zaŋ'guiːnɪʃ] *adj* (*Psych*) sanguine.
sang- und klanglos *adv* (*inf*) without any ado, quietly. **sie ist ~ verschwunden** she just simply disappeared.
Sani *m* -s, -s (*Mil inf*) medical orderly.
sanieren* 1 *vt* (a) (*gesunde Lebensverhältnisse schaffen*) to renovate; *Stadtteil* to redevelop.
  (b) (*Econ*) *Unternehmen, Wirtschaft* to put (back) on it's feet, to put on an even keel, to rehabilitate.
  2 *vr* (a) (*inf: Mensch*) to line one's own pocket (*inf*). **bei dem Geschäft hat er sich saniert** he made a killing on the deal (*inf*).
  (b) (*Unternehmen, Wirtschaft, Industrie*) to put itself on an even keel, to put itself (back) in good shape.
Sanierung *f* (a) *siehe vt* (a) renovation; redevelopment.
  (b) (*Econ*) rehabilitation. **Maßnahmen zur ~ des Dollars** measures to put the dollar back on an even keel *or* on its feet again.
  (c) (*inf: Bereicherung*) self-enrichment. **er ist nur auf die eigene ~ bedacht** he is only interested in lining his own pocket (*inf*).
Sanierungs-: **~gebiet** *nt* redevelopment area; **~gewinn** *m* profit from property speculation in a redevelopment area; **~maßnahme** *f* (*für Gebiete etc*) redevelopment measure; (*Econ*) rehabilitation measure; **für den Dollar kamen alle ~maßnahmen zu spät** all attempts to put the dollar back on its feet were too late; **~plan** *m* redevelopment plan *or* scheme; (*Econ*) rehabilitation plan.
sanitär *adj no pred* sanitary. **~e Anlagen** sanitation (facilities), sanitary facilities; **ein Haus ~ ausstatten** to install sanitation in a house.
Sanität *f* (*Aus, Sw*) (a) medical service; (*Krankenpflege*) nursing. (b) (*inf: Krankenwagen*) ambulance.
Sanitäter *m* -s, - first-aid attendant; (*Mil*) (medical) orderly; (*in Krankenwagen*) ambulance man.
Sanitäts-: **~auto** *nt* ambulance; **~behörde** *f* health authorities *pl*; **~dienst** *m* (*Mil*) medical duty; (*Heeresabteilung*) medical corps; **~flugzeug** *nt* ambulance plane, air ambulance; **~gefreite(r)** *m* (medical) orderly; **~kasten** *m* first-aid box *or* kit; **~kompanie** *f* medical company; **~korps** *nt* medical corps; **~offizier** *m* (*Mil*) Medical Officer, MO; **~wache** *f* first-aid post; **~wagen** *m* ambulance; **~wesen** *nt* (*Mil*) medical service.
sank *pret of* **sinken**.
Sanka [zaŋka] *m* -s, -s (*Mil inf*) ambulance.
Sankt *adj inv* saint. **~ Nikolaus** Santa (Claus), Father Christmas; (*Rel*) St *or* Saint Nicholas.
Sanktion *f* sanction.
sanktionieren* *vt* to sanction.
Sanktionierung *f* sanctioning.
Sankt-Lorenz-Strom *m* St Lawrence river.
Sankt-Nimmerleins-Tag *m* (*hum*) never-never day. **ja, am ~** yes yes, and pigs might fly (*hum*).
sann *pret of* **sinnen**.
Sansibar *nt* -s Zanzibar.
Sanskrit *nt* -s, *no pl* Sanskrit.
Saphir *m* -s, -e sapphire.
sapperlot, sapperment *interj* (*old*) stap me (*old*), upon my soul (*old*).
sapphisch ['zapfɪʃ, 'zafɪʃ] *adj* Sapphic.
Sarabande *f* -, -n (*Mus*) saraband.
Sarazene *m* -n, -n **Sarazenin** *f* Saracen.
sarazenisch *adj* Saracen.
Sarde *m* -n, -n, **Sardin** *f* Sardinian.
Sardelle *f* anchovy.
Sardellen-: **~butter** *f* anchovy butter; **~paste** *f* anchovy paste.
Sardin *f siehe* **Sarde**.
Sardine *f* sardine.
Sardinenbüchse *f* sardine-tin. **wie in einer ~** (*fig inf*) like sardines (*inf*).
Sardinien [-iən] *nt* -s Sardinia.
Sardinier(in *f*) [-ɪn, -iərɪn] *m* -s, - Sardinian.
sardinisch, sardisch *adj* Sardinian.
sardonisch *adj* (*liter*) sardonic.
Sarg *m* -(e)s, ̈e coffin, casket (*US*). **ein Nagel zu jds ~ sein** (*hum inf*) to be a nail in sb's coffin; **du kannst dir schon deinen ~ machen lassen** (*hum inf*) you'd better start arranging your funeral.
Sarg-: **~deckel** *m* coffin lid, casket lid (*US*); **~nagel** *m* coffin nail; (*fig inf auch: Zigarette*) cancer-stick (*hum inf*); **~tischler** *m* coffin-maker, casket-maker (*US*); **~träger** *m* pall-bearer.
Sari *m* -(s), -s sari.
Sarkasmus *m* sarcasm.
sarkastisch *adj* sarcastic.
Sarkophag *m* -(e)s, -e sarcophagus.
saß *pret of* **sitzen**.
Satan *m* -s, -e (*Bibl, fig*) Satan. **dieses Weib ist ein ~** this woman is a (she-)devil.
satanisch *adj* satanic.
Satanismus *m* Satanism.
Satans-: **~braten** *m* (*hum inf*) young devil; **~kult** *m* satan-cult; **~pilz** *m* boletus satanas (*spec*).
Satellit *m* -en, -en (*alle Bedeutungen*) satellite.

Satelliten- in *cpds* satellite; **~bahn** *f* satellite orbit; **~staat** *m* satellite state; **~stadt** *f* satellite town; **~station** *f* space station; **~übertragung** *f* (*Rad, TV*) satellite transmission.

Satin [za'tɛ̃] *m* **-s, -s** satin; (*Baumwoll~*) sateen.

satinieren* *vt Papier* to glaze.

Satinpapier [za'tɛ̃] *nt* glazed paper.

Satire *f* **-, -n** satire (*auf +acc* on).

Satiriker(in *f*) *m* **-s, -** satirist.

satirisch *adj* satirical.

Satisfaktion *f* (*old*) satisfaction. **ich verlange** *or* **fordere ~!** I demand satisfaction.

satisfaktionsfähig *adj* (*old*) capable of giving satisfaction.

Satrap *m* **-en, -en** (*Hist*) satrap.

satt *adj* (a) (*gesättigt*) *Mensch* replete (*hum, form*), full (up) (*inf*); *Magen, Gefühl* full; (*sl: betrunken*) smashed (*sl*), bloated (*sl*). **~ sein** to have had enough (to eat), to be full (up) (*inf*); (*sl: betrunken*) to have had a skinful (*sl*); **~ werden** to have enough to eat; **von so was kann man doch nicht ~ werden** it's not enough to satisfy you *or* fill you up; **das macht ~** it's filling; **sich (an etw** *dat*) **~ essen** to eat one's fill (of sth); (*überdrüssig werden auch*) to have had one's fill (of sth); **sie haben nicht ~ zu essen** (*inf*) they don't have enough to eat; **wie soll sie ihre Kinder ~ kriegen?** (*inf*) how is she supposed to feed her children?; **er ist kaum ~ zu kriegen** (*inf: lit, fig*) he's insatiable; **er konnte sich an ihr nicht ~ sehen/hören** he could not see/hear enough of her; **~ sanken er in den Sessel zurück** having eaten his fill he sank back into his chair; **wie ein ~er Säugling** (*inf*) with a look of contentment, like a contented cow (*inf*).

(b) **jdn/etw ~ haben** *or* **sein** to be fed up with sb/sth (*inf*); **jdn/etw ~ bekommen** *or* **kriegen** (*inf*) to get fed up with sb/sth (*inf*).

(c) (*blasiert, übersättigt*) well-fed; (*selbstgefällig*) smug.

(d) (*kräftig, voll*) *Farben* rich, full; (*sl: stramm*) *Brust* full; *Hintern* well-padded. **~e 100 Mark** (*inf*) a cool 100 marks (*inf*).

(e) (*großartig*) great *no adv* (*inf*), tremendous.

Sattel *m* **-s, ̈** (a) saddle. **ohne/mit ~ reiten** to ride bareback *or* without a saddle/with a saddle; **sich in den ~ schwingen** to swing (oneself) into the saddle; (*auf Fahrrad*) to jump onto one's bicycle; **sich im ~ halten** (*lit, fig*) to stay in the saddle; **jdn aus dem ~ heben** (*herunterhelfen*) to help sb (to) dismount; (*lit, fig: zu Fall bringen*) to unseat sb; **er ist in allen ~n gerecht** *or* **sicher** (*fig*) he can turn his hand to anything; **fest im ~ sitzen** (*fig*) to be firmly in the saddle.

(b) (*Berg~*) saddle; (*Geigen~*) nut; (*Nasen~*) bridge.

Sattel-: **~dach** *nt* saddle roof; **~decke** *f* saddlecloth; **s~fest** *adj* **s~fest sein** (*Reiter*) to have a good seat; **in etw** (*dat*) **s~fest sein** (*fig*) to have a firm grasp of sth; **~gurt** *m* girth; **~knopf** *m* pommel.

satteln *vt Pferd* to saddle (up). **für etw gesattelt sein** (*fig*) to be ready for sth.

Sattel-: **~nase** *f* saddlenose; **~pferd** *nt* saddle horse; **~platz** *m* paddock; **~schlepper** *m* articulated lorry (*Brit*), artic (*Brit inf*), semitrailer (*US*), semi (*US inf*); **~tasche** *f* saddlebag; (*Gepäcktasche am Fahrrad, aus Stroh*) pannier; **~zeug** *nt* saddlery.

Sattheit *f* (a) (*rare: Gesättigtsein*) repletion; (*Gefühl*) feeling of repletion *or* of being full. (b) (*Selbstgefälligkeit*) smugness, self-satisfaction. (c) (*von Farben*) richness, fullness.

sättigen 1 *vt* (a) *Hunger, Neugier* to satisfy, to satiate; *jdn* to make replete; (*ernähren*) to feed, to provide with food. **ich bin gesättigt** I am *or* feel replete. (b) (*Comm, Chem*) to saturate. **2** *vi* to be filling. **3** *vr* **sich an etw** (*dat*) *or* **mit etw ~** to eat one's fill of sth.

sättigend *adj Essen* filling.

Sättigung *f* (a) (*geh*) (*Sattsein*) repletion. **die ~ der Hungrigen** the feeding of the hungry; **er aß bis zu seiner ~** he ate until he was replete; **das Essen dient nicht nur der ~** eating does not only serve to satisfy hunger. (b) (*Chem, Comm, von Farbe*) saturation.

Sättigungs-: **~grad** *m* degree of saturation; **~punkt** *m* saturation point.

Sattler *m* **-s, -** saddler; (*Polsterer*) upholsterer.

Sattlerei *f siehe* **Sattler** saddlery; upholstery; (*Werkstatt*) saddler's; upholsterer's.

Sattler-: **~geselle** *m* journeyman saddler/upholsterer; **~meister** *m* master saddler/upholsterer.

sattsam *adv* amply; *bekannt* sufficiently.

saturieren* 1 *vt* (*liter*) to satisfy, to content. **2** *vr* (*geh*) to do well for oneself.

saturiert *adj* (*geh*) *Markt* saturated; *Klasse* prosperous. **~ leben** to prosper, to live prosperously.

Saturn *m* **-s** (*Myth, Astron*) Saturn. **die Ringe des ~s** the rings of Saturn.

Saturnalien [-iən] *pl* (*Hist*) Saturnalia *pl*.

Satyr *m* **-s** *or* **-n, -n** *or* **-e** satyr.

Satz *m* **-es, ̈e** (a) *sentence*; (*Teilsatz*) clause; (*Jur: Gesetzabschnitt*) clause. **ich kann nur ein paar ~e Italienisch** I only know a few phrases of Italian; **mitten im ~** in mid-sentence; **abhängiger/selbständiger ~** subordinate/principal clause; **eingeschobener ~** appositional phrase.

(b) (*Lehr~, Philos*) proposition; (*Math*) theorem. **der ~ des Pythagoras** Pythagoras' theorem.

(c) (*Typ*) (*das Setzen*) setting; (*das Gesetzte*) type *no pl*. **etw in ~ geben** to send sth for setting; **in ~ gehen** to go for setting; **das Buch ist im ~** the book is set.

(d) (*Mus*) movement.

(e) (*Boden~*) dregs *pl*; (*Kaffee~*) grounds *pl*; (*Tee~ auch*) leaves *pl*.

(f) (*Zusammengehörige*) set; (*Hunt: Wurf*) litter.

(g) (*Sport*) set; (*Tischtennis*) game.

(h) (*Tarif~*) charge; (*Spesen~*) allowance.

(i) (*Sprung*) leap, jump. **einen ~ machen** *or* **tun** to leap, to jump; **mit einem ~** in one leap *or* bound.

Satz-: **~aussage** *f* (*Gram*) predicate; **~ball** *m* (*Sport*) set point; (*Tischtennis*) game point; **~bau** *m* sentence construction; **~ergänzung** *f* (*Gram*) object; **~fehler** *m* (*Typ*) printer's error; **~gefüge** *nt* (*Gram*) complex sentence; **~gegenstand** *m* (*Gram*) subject; **~glied** *nt* part of a/the sentence.

-sätzig *adj* (*Mus*) in ... movements.

Satz-: **~lehre** *f* (*Gram*) syntax; **~melodie** *f* (*Phon*) intonation; **~reihe** *f* sequence of clauses; **~spiegel** *m* (*Typ*) type area, area of type; **~teil** *m* part *or* constituent of a/the sentence.

Satzung *f* constitution, statutes *pl*; (*Vereins~*) rules *pl*.

satzungsgemäß *adj* according to the statutes/rules.

Satz-: **~verbindung** *f* clause construction; **s~weise** *adj* a (*Ling*) sentence by sentence; **eine Sprache lernt man besser s~weise** you are better to learn a language in phrases; (b) (*Tech*) in sets; **~zeichen** *nt* punctuation mark; **~zusammenhang** *m* context of the sentence.

Sau *f* **-, Säue** *or* (*Hunt*) **-en** (a) sow; (*inf: Schwein*) pig; (*Hunt*) wild boar. **die ~ rauslassen** *or* **loszmachen** (*fig sl*) to let it all hang out (*sl*); **wie eine gestochene ~ bluten** (*sl*) to bleed like a (stuck) pig; **wie eine gesengte ~** (*sl*) like a maniac (*inf*).

(b) (*pej inf: Schmutzfink*) dirty swine (*inf*); (*Frau auch*) bitch (*sl*). **du alte ~!** (*vulg*) you dirty bastard (*sl*), you son-of-a-bitch (*esp US sl*); **unter aller ~** bloody (*Brit sl*) *or* goddamn (*sl*) dirty bitch (*sl*).

(c) (*fig sl*) **da war keine ~ zu sehen** there wasn't a bloody (*Brit sl*) *or* goddamn (*sl*) soul to be seen; **jdn zur ~ machen** to bawl sb out (*inf*); **unter aller ~** bloody (*Brit sl*) *or* goddamn (*sl*) awful *or* lousy.

Sau-: **~arbeit** *f* (*sl*) bloody (*Brit sl*) *or* damn (*inf*) awful job; (*schlampige Arbeit*) lousy piece of work (*inf*); **~bande** *f* (*inf*) gang of hoodlums (*inf*).

sauber 1 *adj* (a) (*rein, reinlich*) clean. **~ sein** (*Hund etc*) to be house-trained; (*Kind*) to be (potty-)trained; **etw ~ putzen** to clean sth; **~ singen/spielen** to sing/play on key.

(b) (*ordentlich*) neat, tidy; (*Aus, S Ger: hübsch*) *Mädel* pretty; (*exakt*) accurate.

(c) (*anständig*) honest, upstanding. **~ bleiben** to keep one's hands clean; **bleib ~!** (*sl*) keep your nose clean (*inf*).

(d) (*inf: großartig*) fantastic, great. **~! ~!** that's the stuff! (*inf*); **du bist mir ja ein ~er Freund!** (*iro*) a fine friend you are! (*iro*); **eine ~e Gesellschaft!** (*iro*) a bunch of crooks; **das ist ja ~!** (*iro*) that's great (*iro*).

2 *adv* (*Aus, S Ger: verstärkend*) really and truly.

sauberhalten *vt sep irreg* to keep clean.

Sauberkeit *f* (a) (*Hygiene, Ordentlichkeit*) cleanliness; (*Reinheit*) (*von Wasser, Luft etc*) cleanness; (*von Tönen*) accuracy. (b) (*Anständigkeit*) honesty, upstandingness.

Sauberkeitsfimmel *m* (*pej*) mania for cleanliness, thing about cleanliness (*inf*).

säuberlich *adj* neat and tidy. **fein ~** neatly and tidily.

saubermachen *vt sep* to clean.

säubern *vt* (a) to clean. **er säuberte seinen Anzug von den Blutflecken** he cleaned the bloodstains off his jacket; **das Wasser (von Verschmutzung) ~** to cleanse the water.

(b) (*fig euph*) *Partei, Buch* to purge (*von* of); *Saal, (Mil) Gegend* to clear (*von* of).

Säuberung *f siehe vt* (a) cleaning; cleansing. (b) purging; clearing; expurgation; (*Pol: Aktion*) purge.

Säuberungs|aktion *f* cleaning-up operation; (*Pol*) purge.

Sau-: **s~blöd, s~blöde** *adj* (*sl*) bloody (*Brit sl*) *or* damn (*inf*) stupid (*inf*); **sich s~blöd anstellen** to behave like a bloody (*Brit sl*) *or* damn (*inf*) idiot; **~bohne** *f* broad bean.

Sauce ['zoːsə] *f* **-, -n siehe Soße.**

Sauciere [zo'sieːrə, -'sieːrə] *f* **-, -n** sauce boat.

Saudi-: **~araber** *m* Saudi; **~-Arabien** *nt* Saudi Arabia; **s~arabisch** *adj* Saudi *attr*, Saudi-Arabian.

saudumm *adj* (*inf*) damn stupid (*inf*). **sich ~ benehmen** to behave like a stupid idiot (*inf*).

sauen *vi* (a) to litter. (b) (*inf: Dreck machen*) to make a mess. (c) *aux sein* (*S Ger inf: rennen*) to run.

sauer *adj* (a) (*nicht süß*) sour; *Wein, Bonbons* acid(ic), sharp; *Obst auch* sharp, tart. **saure Drops** acid drops; *siehe* **aufstoßen.**

(b) (*verdorben*) off *pred*; *Milch auch* sour; *Geruch* sour, sickly. **es roch so ~** there was a sickly smell; **~ werden** (*Milch, Sahne*) to go sour *or* off, to turn (sour).

(c) (*mit Säure zubereitet*) *Gurke, Hering* pickled; *Sahne* soured. **~ einlegen** to pickle.

(d) (*sumpfig*) *Wiese, Boden* acidic.

(e) (*Chem*) acid(ic). **~ reagieren** to react acidically.

(f) (*inf: schlecht gelaunt*) (*auf +acc* with) mad (*inf*), cross. **eine ~e Miene machen** to look sour *or* annoyed; **~ reagieren** to get annoyed.

(g) (*unerfreulich, unter Schwierigkeiten*) **sich** (*dat*) **etw ~ werden lassen** (*old*) to find sth very difficult *or* trying; **das habe ich mir ~ erworben** I got that the hard way; **~ erworbenes Geld** hard-earned money; **es kommt mich ~ an** I find it difficult; **jdm das Leben ~ machen** to make sb's life a misery, to make life miserable for sb; **gib ihm Saures!** (*sl*) let him have it! (*inf*).

Sauer-: **~ampfer** *m* sorrel; **~braten** *m* braised beef (marinaded in vinegar), sauerbraten (*US*); **~brunnen** *m* (*Heilquelle*) acidic spring; (b) (*Wasser*) acidic mineral water.

Sauerei *f* (*sl*) (a) (*Unflätigkeit*) **~en erzählen** to tell filthy stories; **eine einzige ~** (*inf*) a load of filth. (b) **das ist eine ~!**, **so eine ~!** it's a bloody (*Brit sl*) *or* downright disgrace *or* scandal. (c) (*Dreck*) mess. **(eine) ~ machen** to make a mess.

Sauer-: **~kirsche** *f* sour cherry; **~klee** *m* wood sorrel, oxalis; **~kohl** *m* (*dial*), **~kraut** *nt* sauerkraut, pickled cabbage.

säuerlich *adj* (*lit, fig*) sour; *Wein auch* sharp; *Obst auch* sharp, tart.

Säuerlichkeit f siehe adj sourness; sharpness; sharpness, tartness.
Säuerling m **(a)** siehe **Sauerbrunnen. (b)** (Bot) siehe **Sauerampfer.**
Sauermilch f sour milk.
säuern 1 vt Brot, Teig to leaven. **2** vi to go or turn sour, to sour.
Sauerstoff m, no pl oxygen.
Sauerstoff- in cpds oxygen; ~**apparat** m breathing apparatus; s~**arm** adj low in oxygen; (zu wenig) oxygen-deficient; ~**entzug** m (Med) oxygen deficiency; (Chem) deoxygenation; ~**flasche** f siehe **Sauerstoffflasche**; ~**gerät** nt breathing apparatus; (Med) (für künstliche Beatmung) respirator; (für Erste Hilfe) resuscitator; s~**haltig** adj containing oxygen.
Sauerstoffflasche f getrennt: **Sauerstoff-flasche** oxygen cylinder or (kleiner) bottle.
Sauerstoff-: ~**mangel** m lack of oxygen; (akut) oxygen deficiency; ~**maske** f oxygen mask; ~**patrone** f oxygen cartridge; ~**zelt** nt oxygen tent; ~**zufuhr** f oxygen supply; **mittels** ~**zufuhr** by supplying oxygen.
Sauer-: ~**teig** m sour dough; ~**topf** m (old, hum) sourpuss (inf); s~**töpfisch** adj (old, hum) sour; Mensch auch sour-faced.
Säuerung f leavening.
Sauf-: ~**aus** m -, -, ~**bold** m -(e)s, -e (old pej) sot (old), drunkard; ~**bruder** m (pej inf) (Kumpan) drinking companion; (Säufer) soak (inf), boozer (inf).
saufen pret **soff**, ptp **gesoffen** vti **(a)** (Tiere) to drink. **(b)** (sl: Mensch) to booze (inf), to drink. **das S~** boozing; **sich dumm/zu Tode** ~ to drink oneself silly/to death; **wie ein Loch** or **Bürstenbinder** (dated) ~ to drink like a fish.
Säufer(in f) m -s, - (inf) boozer (inf), drunkard.
Sauferei f (inf) **(a)** (Trinkgelage) booze-up (inf). **(b)** no pl (Trunksucht) boozing (inf).
Säufer-: ~**leber** f (inf) gin-drinker's liver (inf); ~**nase** f boozer's nose; ~**wahn(sinn)** m the DT's pl (inf).
Sauf-: ~**gelage** nt (pej inf) drinking bout, booze-up (inf); ~**kumpan**, ~**kumpel** m (pej inf) drinking pal.
Saufraß m (sl) muck (inf).
Säug|amme f (old) wet nurse.
Saugbagger m suction dredger.
saugen pret **sog** or **saugte**, ptp **gesogen** or **gesaugt** vti to suck; (Pflanze, Schwamm) to draw up, to absorb; (inf: mit Staubsauger) to vacuum. **an etw** (dat) ~**to** suck sth; **an Pfeife** to draw on sth; siehe **Finger.**
säugen vt to suckle.
Sauger m -s, - **(a)** (auf Flasche) teat (Brit), nipple (US); (Schnuller) dummy (Brit), pacifier (US). **(b)** (inf: Staub~) vacuum (cleaner).
Säuger m -s, -, **Säugetier** nt mammal.
Saug-: s~**fähig** adj absorbent; ~**fähigkeit** f absorbency; ~**flasche** f (form) feeding bottle.
Säugling m baby, infant (form).
Säuglings- in cpds baby, infant (form); ~**alter** nt babyhood; **das Kind ist noch im** ~**alter** the child is still a baby; ~**fürsorge** f infant welfare; ~**gymnastik** f exercises for babies; ~**heim** nt home for babies; ~**pflege** f babycare; ~**schwester** f infant nurse; ~**sterblichkeit** f infant mortality.
Saug-: ~**massage** f suction or vacuum massage; ~**napf** m sucker; ~**organ** nt suctorial organ (form); ~**pumpe** f suction pump; (für Brust) breast pump; ~**reflex** m sucking reflex.
saugrob adj (sl) (gewalttätig) very rough; (unanständig) very crude.
Saug-: ~**rohr**, ~**röhrchen** nt pipette; ~**rüssel** m (Zool) proboscis; ~**würmer** pl trematodes pl (spec).
Sau-: ~**hatz** f (Hunt) wild boar hunt; ~**haufen** m (sl) bunch of layabouts (inf); ~**hirt** m (old) swineherd (old); ~**hund** m (dated sl) bastard (sl); ~**igel** m (inf) siehe **Schweinigel**; s~**igeln** vi insep (inf) siehe **schweinigeln.**
säuisch adj (sl) Benehmen, Witze filthy, swinish (sl).
Sau-: ~**jagd** f siehe ~**hatz**; s~**kalt** adj (sl) bloody (Brit sl) or damn (inf) cold; ~**kälte** f (sl) bloody (Brit sl) or damn (inf) freezing weather; **ist das eine** ~**kälte** it's bloody (Brit sl) or frigging (esp US sl) freezing; ~**kerl** m (sl) bastard (sl); ~**klaue** f (sl) scrawl (inf).
Säule f -, ~**n** column; (Rauch~, Wasser~ auch, inf: Pfeiler, fig: Stütze) pillar. **die** ~**n des Herkules** the Pillars of Hercules.
Säulen-: ~**abschluß** m capital; ~**bau** m building with columns; s~**förmig** adj like a column/columns, columnar (form); ~**fuß** m base; ~**gang** m colonnade; (um einen Hof) peristyle; ~**halle** f columned hall; ~**heilige(r)** mf stylite; ~**ordnung** f order of columns; **die dorische** ~**ordnung** the Doric Order; ~**portal** nt colonnaded doorway; ~**reihe** f row of columns; ~**schaft** m shaft of a column; ~**tempel** m colonnaded temple.
Saulus m - (Bibl) Saul. **vom** ~ **zum Paulus werden** (fig liter) to have seen the light.
Saum m -(e)s, **Säume** (Stoffumschlag) hem; (Naht) seam; (fig: Wald~) edge. **ein schmaler** ~ **am Horizont** a thin band of cloud on the horizon.
saumäßig (sl) **1** adj lousy (inf); (zur Verstärkung) hell of a (inf). **2** adv lousily (inf); (zur Verstärkung) like hell (inf). **das hat er** ~ **gemacht** he made a real mess of it.
säumen[1] vt (Sew) to hem; (fig geh) to line.
säumen[2] vi (liter) to tarry (liter).
säumig adj (geh) Schuldner defaulting; Zahlung outstanding, overdue; Schüler dilatory. ~ **sein/bleiben/werden** to be/remain/get behind.
Säumigkeit f dilatoriness.
Säumnis f (obs) delay.
Saum-: ~**pfad** m mule track; s~**selig** adj (old liter) dilatory; ~**seligkeit** f (old liter) dilatoriness; ~**stich** m hemstitch; ~**tier** nt pack animal.

Sauna f -, -s or **Saunen** sauna.
Saupreuße m (S Ger sl) Prussian swine.
Säure f -, -n **(a)** (Chem, Magen~) acid. **(b)** siehe **sauer (a)** sourness; acidity, sharpness; sharpness, tartness. **dieser Wein hat zuviel** ~ this wine is too sharp.
Säure-: s~**arm** adj low in acid; ~**bad** nt acid bath; s~**beständig**, s~**fest** adj acid-resistant; s~**frei** adj acid-free; ~**gehalt** m acid content.
Sauregurkenzeit f bad time or period; (in den Medien) silly season.
Säure-: s~**haltig** adj acidic; s~**löslich** adj acid-soluble.
Säure(s) nt decl as adj siehe **sauer (g).**
Säurevergiftung f acid poisoning.
Saurier [-iɐ] m -s, - dinosaur, saurian (spec).
Saus m: **in** ~ **und Braus leben** to live like a lord.
Sause f -, -n (inf) pub crawl. **eine** ~ **machen** to go on a pub crawl.
säuseln 1 vi (Wind) to murmur, to sigh; (Blätter) to rustle; (Mensch) to purr. **mit** ~**der Stimme** in a purring voice. **2** vt to murmur, to purr.
sausen vi **(a)** (Ohren, Kopf) to buzz; (Wind) to whistle; (Sturm) to roar. **ihr sauste das Blut in den Ohren** (geh) the blood pounded in her ears; **mir** ~ **die Ohren, es saust mir in den Ohren** my ears are buzzing.
(b) aux sein (Geschoß, Peitsche) to whistle.
(c) aux sein (inf: Mensch) to tear (inf), to charge (inf); (Fahrzeug) to roar. **saus mal schnell zum Bäcker** nip round (Brit) or run round to the baker's; **in den Graben** ~ to fly into the ditch; **durch eine Prüfung** ~ to fail or flunk (inf) an exam.
(d) (inf) **jdn/etw** ~ **lassen** to drop sb/sth; **das Kino heute abend laß ich** ~ I'll not bother going to the cinema tonight.
(e) einen ~ **lassen** (sl) to let off (sl) a fart vulg).
Sauser m -s, - (S Ger) fermented apple/grape juice.
Sausewind m **(a)** (dated inf) (lebhaft) live wire (inf); (unstet) restless person. **(b)** (baby-talk: Wind) wind.
Sau-: ~**stall** m (sl) (unordentlich) pigsty (inf); (chaotisch) mess; ~**wetter** nt (sl) bloody (Brit sl) or damn (inf) awful weather; s~**wohl** adj pred (sl) bloody (Brit sl) or really good; **mir ist** or **ich fühle mich** s~**wohl** I feel bloody (Brit sl) or really good; ~**wut** f (sl) flaming rage (inf); **eine** ~**wut** (im Bauch) **haben** to be flaming mad; **eine** ~**wut auf jdn/etw haben** to be flaming mad at sb/sth.
Savanne [za'vanə] f -, -n savanna(h).
Savoyen [za'vɔyən] nt -s Savoy.
Saxophon nt -(e)s, -e saxophone, sax (inf).
Saxophonist(in f) m saxophone player, saxophonist.
S-Bahn [ˈɛs-] f abbr of **Schnell-, Stadtbahn.**
S-Bahnhof [ˈɛs-] m suburban line station.
S-Bahn-Netz [ˈɛs-] nt suburban rail network.
SBB abbr of **Schweizerische Bundesbahn.**
s. Br. abbr of **südlicher Breite.**
sch interj shh; (zum Fortscheuchen) shoo.
Schabau m -s, no pl (dial) spirits pl.
Schabe f -, -n cockroach.
Schabefleisch nt (Cook dial) minced steak (Brit), ground beef (US) (often eaten raw).
Schab(e)messer nt scraping knife, scraper.
schaben vt to scrape; Fleisch to chop finely; Leder, Fell to shave. **sich** (dat) **den Bart** ~ (hum) to scrape one's face (hum).
Schaber m -s, - scraper.
Schabernack m -(e)s, -e **(a)** prank, practical joke. **jdm einen** ~ **spielen/mit jdm einen** ~ **treiben** to play a prank on sb; **allerlei** ~ **treiben** to get up to all sorts of pranks; **ich bin zu jedem** ~ **bereit** I'm always ready for a laugh. **(b)** (Kind) monkey (inf).
schäbig adj **(a)** (abgetragen) shabby. **(b)** (niederträchtig) mean, shabby; (geizig) mean, stingy; Bezahlung poor, shabby.
Schäbigkeit f siehe adj **(a)** shabbiness. **(b)** meanness, shabbiness; meanness, stinginess; poorness, shabbiness; (Verhalten) mean or shabby behaviour no pl.
Schablone f -, -n **(a)** stencil; (Muster) template.
(b) (fig pej) (bei Arbeit, Arbeitsweise) routine, pattern; (beim Reden) cliché. **nach (der)** ~ **arbeiten** to work according to a/one's (set) routine; **in** ~**n denken** to think in a stereotyped way; **in** ~**n reden** to speak in clichés; **etw geht nach** ~ sth follows the same routine; **etw nach der gleichen** ~ **behandeln** to treat sth in the same stereotyped way; **alles was er sagt, ist nur** ~ everything he says is clichéd, he always talks in clichés; **der Präsident lächelte, aber das war reine** ~ the President smiled but it was just a matter of convention; **das ist alles nur** ~ that's all just for show.
schablonenhaft 1 adj (pej) Denken, Vorstellungen, Argumente stereotyped; Ausdrucksweise clichéd. **2** adv in stereotypes/clichés.
Schabmesser nt siehe **Schab(e)messer.**
Schabracke f -, -n **(a)** (Satteldecke) saddlecloth. **(b)** (altes Pferd) nag; (sl: alte Frau) hag. **(c)** (Querbehang) pelmet.
Schabsel pl shavings pl.
Schach nt -s, no pl chess; (Stellung im Spiel) check. **kannst du** ~ **(spielen)?** can you play chess?; ~ **(dem König)!** check; ~ **und matt** checkmate; **im** ~ **stehen** or **sein to be in check; jdm** ~ **bieten** (lit) to put sb in check, to check sb; (fig) to thwart sb; **jdn in** ~ **halten** (fig) to stall sb; (mit Pistole etc) to cover sb, to keep sb covered.
Schach-: ~**aufgabe** f chess problem; ~**brett** nt chessboard; s~**brettartig** adj chequered; Platten s~**brettartig anlegen** to lay tiles in a chequered pattern or like a chessboard; **die Straßen sind** s~**brettartig angeordnet** the roads are laid out like a grid; ~**brettmuster** nt chequered pattern.
Schacher m -s, no pl (pej) (das Feilschen) haggling (um over); (Wucher) sharp practice; (fig Pol auch) horse-trading (um

Schächer about). ~ **treiben** to indulge in haggling *etc.*

Schächer *m* -s, - (*Bibl*) thief.

Schacherei *f* (*pej*) *siehe* **Schacher.**

Schacherer *m* -s, - (*pej*) haggler; (*Wucherer*) sharper; (*Pol*) horse-trader.

schachern *vi* (*pej*) **um etw** ~ to haggle over sth.

Schach-: ~**feld** *nt* square (on a chessboard); ~**figur** *f* chess piece, chessman; (*fig*) pawn; **s~matt** *adj* (*lit*) (check)mated; (*fig: erschöpft*) exhausted, shattered (*inf*); **s~matt!** (check-) mate; **jdn s~matt setzen** (*lit*) to (check)mate sb; (*fig*) to snooker sb (*inf*); ~**partie** *f* game of chess; ~**spiel** *nt* (*Spiel*) game of chess; (*Spielart*) chess *no art*; (*Brett und Figuren*) chess set; ~**spieler** *m* chess player.

Schacht *m* -(e)s, ⁔e shaft; (*Brunnen~*) well; (*Straßen~*) man-hole; (*Kanalisations~*) drain.

Schachtel *f* -, -n (a) box; (*Zigaretten~*) packet. **eine ~ Streichhölzer/Pralinen** a box of matches/chocolates. (b) (*sl: Frau*) bag (*sl*).

Schachtel-: ~**halm** *m* (*Bot*) horsetail; ~**satz** *m* complicated or multi-clause sentence.

schächten *vti* to slaughter (*according to Jewish rites*).

Schach-: ~**turnier** *nt* chess tournament; ~**zug** *m* (*fig*) move.

Schade *m* (*old*): **es soll dein ~ nicht sein** it will not be to your disadvantage.

schade *adj pred* (*das ist aber*) ~**!** what a pity or shame; **es ist** (zu) ~, **daß** ... it's a (real) pity or shame that ...; **es ist ~ um jdn/etw** it's a pity or shame about sb/sth; **um sie ist es nicht ~** she's no great loss; **für etw zu ~ sein** to be too good for sth; **sich** (*dat*) **für etw zu ~ sein** to consider oneself too good for sth; **sich** (*dat*) **für nichts zu ~ sein** to consider nothing (to be) beneath one.

Schädel *m* -s, - skull. **ein kahler ~** a bald head; **jdm den ~ einschlagen** to beat sb's skull or head in; **jdm den ~ spalten/zertrümmern** to split or cleave/crush sb's skull; **sich** (*dat*) **den ~ einrennen** (*inf*) to crack one's skull; **mir brummt der ~** (*inf*) my head is going round and round; (*vor Kopfschmerzen*) my head is throbbing; **einen dicken ~ haben** (*fig inf*) to be stubborn.

Schädel-: ~**basisbruch** *m* fracture at the base of the skull; ~**bruch** *m* fractured skull; ~**decke** *f* top of the skull; ~**lage** *f* vertex presentation; ~**naht** *f* suture; ~**stätte** *f* (*Bibl*) place of a skull.

schaden *vi* +*dat* to damage, to harm; **einem Menschen** to harm, to hurt; **jds Ruf** to damage. **sich** (*dat*) **selbst ~** to harm or hurt oneself, to do oneself harm; **das/Rauchen schadet Ihrer Gesundheit/Ihnen** that/smoking is bad for your health/you; **das schadet nichts** it does no harm; (*macht nichts*) that doesn't matter; **es kann nichts ~, wenn** ... it would do no harm if ...; **das kann nicht(s) ~** that won't do any harm, it wouldn't hurt; **das schadet dir gar nichts** it serves you right; **was schadet es, wenn ...?** what harm can it do if ...?

Schaden *m* -s, ⁔ (a) (*Beschädigung, Zerstörung*) damage *no pl, no indef art* (*durch* caused by); (*Personen~*) injury; (*Verlust*) loss; (*Unheil, Leid*) harm. **einen ~ verursachen** to cause damage; **ich habe einen ~ am Auto my car has been damaged; **zu jds ~ gereichen** (*geh*) to be to sb's detriment; **es soll sein ~ nicht sein** it will not be to his disadvantage; **es ist nicht zu deinem ~** it won't do you any harm; **den ~ von etw haben** to suffer for sth; **in etw** (*acc*) **zum ~ der Firma investieren** to invest in sth to the detriment of the firm; **zu ~ kommen** to suffer; (*physisch*) to be hurt or injured; **nicht zu ~ kommen** not to come to any harm; **an etw** (*dat*) **~ nehmen** to damage or harm sth; **jdm/einer Sache ~ zufügen** to harm sb/to harm or damage sth; **geringe/einige ~ aufweisen** to have suffered little/some damage; **~ von etw abwenden** (*fig*) to preserve sth from harm; **aus or durch ~ wird man klug** (*Prov*) you learn by or from your mistakes; **wer den ~ hat, braucht für den Spott nicht zu sorgen** (*Prov*) don't mock the afflicted.

(b) (*Defekt*) fault; (*körperlicher Mangel*) defect. ~ **an der Lunge** lung damage; ~ **aufweisen** to be defective; (*Organ*) to be damaged; **ein ~ an der Leber** a damaged liver.

Schaden-: ~**ersatz** *m siehe* **Schadensersatz**; ~**feststellung** *f* assessment of damage; ~**freude** *f* malicious joy, gloating; ... **sagt er mit ~freude** ... he gloated; **s~froh** *adj* gloating.

Schadens|ersatz *m* compensation. **jdn auf ~ verklagen** to claim compensation from sb; **~ leisten** to pay compensation.

Schadens|ersatz-: ~**anspruch** *m* claim for compensation; ~**klage** *f* action for damages; **s~pflichtig** *adj* liable for compensation.

schadhaft *adj no adv* faulty, defective; (*beschädigt*) damaged; (*abgenutzt*) **Kleidung** worn; **Zähne** decayed; **Gebäude** dilapidated.

Schadhaftigkeit *f siehe adj* faultiness, defectiveness; damaged/worn/decayed/dilapidated state.

schädigen *vt* to damage; **jdn** to hurt, to harm; **Firma** *auch* to hurt. **man muß die Firma ~, wo man nur kann** (*iro*) you've got to get what you can out of the firm.

Schädigung *f siehe vt* (*gen* done to) damage; hurt, harm.

schädlich *adj* harmful; **Wirkung, Einflüsse** detrimental, damaging; ~ **für etw sein** to be damaging to sth; ~**es Tier** pest.

Schädlichkeit *f* harmfulness.

Schädling *m* pest.

Schädlings-: ~**bekämpfung** *f* pest control *no art*; ~**bekämpfungsmittel** *nt* pesticide.

schadlos *adj*: **sich an jdm/etw ~ halten** to take advantage of sb/sth; **wir halten uns dafür am Bier ~** (*hum*) ... but we'll make up for it in the beer.

Schadstoff *m* harmful substance.

Schaf *nt* -(e)s, -e sheep; (*inf: Dummkopf*) twit (*Brit inf*), dope (*inf*). **das schwarze ~** to be the black sheep (*in* +*dat, gen* of); ~**e zählen** (*fig*) to count sheep; *siehe* **Bock¹** (a).

Schafbock *m* ram.

Schäfchen *nt* lamb, little sheep; (*inf: Dummerchen*) silly billy (*inf*). ~ *pl* (*Gemeinde, Anvertraute*) flock *sing*; **sein ~ ins trockene bringen** (*prov*) to see oneself all right (*inf*); **sein ~ im trockenen haben** to have feathered one's own nest.

Schäfchenwolken *pl* cotton-wool clouds *pl*, fleecy clouds *pl*.

Schäfer *m* -s, - shepherd.

Schäferdichtung *f* (*Liter*) pastoral poetry.

Schäferei *f* (a) (*Schafhaltung*) sheep-rearing or -farming. (b) (*Betrieb*) sheep farm.

Schäferhund *m* alsatian (dog) (*Brit*), German shepherd (dog) (*US*).

Schäferin *f* shepherdess.

Schäfer-: ~**roman** *m* (*Liter*) pastoral novel; ~**stündchen** *nt* (*euph hum*) bit of hanky-panky (*hum inf*).

Schaffell *nt* sheepskin.

Schaffen *nt* -s, *no pl* **die Freude am ~** the joy of creation; **sein musikalisches/künstlerisches ~** his musical/artistic works *pl* or creations *pl*; **der Künstler bei seinem ~** the artist at work; **auf dem Höhepunkt seines ~s** at the peak of his creative powers or prowess.

schaffen¹ *pret* **schuf**, *ptp* **geschaffen** *vt* (a) to create. **die ~de Natur** the creative power of nature; **der ~de Mensch** the creative human being; **dafür ist er wie geschaffen** he's just made for it; **wie ihn Gott geschaffen hatte** as God made him.

(b) *pret auch* **schaffte** (*herstellen*) to make; **Bedingungen, Möglichkeiten, System, Methode** to create. **Raum or Platz ~** to make room; **Ruhe ~** to establish order; **Linderung ~** to bring relief (*für* to).

schaffen² 1 *vt* (a) (*bewältigen, zustande bringen*) **Aufgabe, Hürde, Portion** *etc* to manage; **Prüfung** to pass. ~ **wir das zeitlich?** are we going to make it?; **schaffst du's noch?** (*inf*) can you manage?; **wir haben's geschafft** we've managed it; (*Arbeit erledigt*) we've done it; (*gut angekommen*) we've made it; **so, das hätten wir** *or* **das wäre geschafft!** there, that's done; **das ist nicht zu ~** that can't be done; **das hast du wieder mal geschafft** you've done it again; **er schafft es immer, sie zu verärgern** he always manages to annoy her; **wir haben nicht viel geschafft** *or* **geschafft gekriegt** (*inf*) we haven't managed to do much or haven't got much done; **er schafft es noch, daß ich ihn rauswerfe/er rausgeworfen wird** he'll end up with me throwing him out/(by) being thrown out.

(b) (*inf: überwältigen*) **jdn** to see off (*inf*). **das hat mich geschafft** it took it out of me; (*nervlich*) it got on top of me; **geschafft sein** to be shattered (*inf*); **die schafft keiner** (*sl*) she can't get enough (from anyone).

(c) (*bringen*) **etw in etw** (*acc*) ~ to put sth in sth; **wie sollen wir das in den Keller/auf den Berg ~?** how will we manage to get that into the cellar/up the mountain?; **etw aus etw ~** to get sth out of sth; **einen Koffer zum Bahnhof ~** to take a case to the station; **alte Zeitungen auf den Boden ~** to put old newspapers in the attic; **etw aus der Welt ~** to settle sth (for good); **sich** (*dat*) **jdn/etw vom Hals(e)** *or* **Leib(e) ~** to get sb/sth off one's back; *siehe* **beiseite.**

(d) (*verursachen*) **Ärger, Unruhe, Verdruß** to cause, to create.

2 *vi* (a) (*tun*) to do. **ich habe damit nichts zu ~** that has nothing to do with me; **was haben Sie dort zu ~?** what do you think you're doing (there)?; **sich** (*dat*) **an etw** (*dat*) **zu ~ machen** to fiddle about with sth; **sich mit etw zu ~ machen** to busy oneself with sth.

(b) (*zusetzen*) **jdm** (*sehr or schwer*) **zu ~ machen** to cause sb (a lot of) trouble; (*bekümmern*) to worry sb (a lot); **das macht ihr heute noch zu ~** she still worries about it today.

(c) (*S Ger: arbeiten*) to work.

Schaffens-: ~**drang** *m* energy; (*von Künstler*) creative urge; ~**freude** *f* (creative) zest or enthusiasm; **s~freudig** *adj* (creatively) enthusiastic; *Künstler* creative; ~**kraft** *f* creativity.

Schaffer *m* -s, - (*inf*) hard worker.

Schaffleisch *nt* mutton.

Schaffner(in *f*) *m* -s, - (a) (*im Bus*) conductor; (*Rail*) ticket collector; (*im Zug*) guard (*Brit*), conductor (*US*), ticket inspector; (*im Schlafwagen*) attendant. (b) (*old*) (*Verwalter*) major-domo; (*Wirtschafterin*) housekeeper.

schaffnerlos *adj* without a conductor *etc.* ~**e Busse** one-man buses.

Schaffung *f* creation.

Schaf- *siehe auch* **Schafs-;** ~**garbe** *f* yarrow; ~**herde** *f* flock of sheep; ~**hirt** *m* shepherd; ~**hürde** *f* sheep pen, (sheep)fold.

Schäflein *nt* (*lit, fig*) lamb; (*pl fig*) flock *sing or pl*.

Schafott *nt* -(e)s, -e scaffold.

Schaf-: ~**pelz** *m siehe* **Schafspelz;** ~**scherer(in** *f*) *m* -s, - sheep-shearer; ~**schur** *f* sheepshearing.

Schafs-: ~**käse** *m* sheep's milk cheese; ~**kopf** *m* (a) sheep's head; (*pej: Dummkopf*) blockhead, dolt, numskull; (b) (*Cards*) German card game, a simplified version of skat; ~**milch** *f* sheep's milk; ~**pelz** *m* sheepskin; *siehe* **Wolf.**

Schafstall *m* sheepfold.

Schaft *m* -(e)s, ⁔e shaft (*auch Archit*); (*von Gewehr*) stock; (*von Stiefel*) leg; (*von Schraube, Schlüssel*) shank; (*Bot*) stalk.

Schaftstiefel *pl* high boots *pl*; (*Mil*) jackboots *pl*.

Schaf-: ~**weide** *f* sheep pasture; ~**wolle** *f* sheep's wool; ~**zucht** *f* sheep breeding *no art*.

Schah *m* -s, -s Shah.

Schakal *m* -s, -e jackal.

Schäker *m* -s, - (*inf*) flirt; (*Witzbold*) joker.

Schäkerei *f* (*inf*) flirting; (*Witzelei*) fooling around.

Schäkerin *f* (*inf*) flirt, coquette; (*Witzbold*) joker.

schäkern *vi* to flirt; (*necken*) to play about.

Schal *m* -s, -s *or* -e scarf; (*Umschlagtuch*) shawl.

schal *adj* **Getränk** flat; **Wasser, Geschmack** stale; (*fig: geistlos*)

Witz stale, weak; *Leben* empty; *Gerede* vapid, empty.

Schälchen *nt* dim of **Schale**[1] (small) bowl.

Schale[1] *f* -, -n bowl; *(flach, zum Servieren etc)* dish; *(von Waage)* pan; *(Sekt~)* champagne glass; *(esp S Ger, Aus: Tasse)* cup.

Schale[2] *f* -, -n *(von Obst, Gemüse)* skin; *(abgeschält)* peel *no pl*; *(Rinde)* rind; *(von Käse)* rind; *(von Nüssen, Eiern, Muscheln)* shell; *(von Getreide)* husk, hull; *(Hunt)* hoof; *(fig: äußeres Auftreten)* appearance. **sich in ~ werfen** *or* **schmeißen** *(inf)* to get dressed up; *(Frau auch)* to get dolled up *(inf)*; **Kartoffeln in der ~** jacket potatoes; **in seiner rauhen ~ steckt ein guter Kern** beneath that rough exterior (there) beats a heart of gold *(prov)*; *siehe* **rauh.**

schälen 1 *vti* to peel; *Tomate, Mandel* to skin; *Nüsse* to shell; *Getreide* to husk. **2** *vr* to peel; *(Schlange)* to slough its skin. **sich aus den Kleidern ~** to peel off (one's clothes); **ich schäle mich auf der Nase** my nose is peeling.

Schal(en)|obst *nt* nuts *pl*.

Schalen-: **~sessel** *m* shell chair; **~sitz** *m* bucket seat; **~wild** *nt siehe* **Schalwild.**

Schalheit *f* flatness; *(von Wasser, Geschmack)* staleness; *(fig: Geistlosigkeit, von Witz)* staleness, weakness.

Schalhengst *m siehe* **Zuchthengst.**

Schalholz *nt* shuttering wood.

Schalk *m* -(e)s, -e *or* ¨e joker. **ihm sitzt der ~ im Nacken** he's in a devilish mood; **ihr schaut der ~ aus den Augen** she (always) has a roguish *or* mischievous look on her face.

schalkhaft *adj* roguish, mischievous.

Schalkhaftigkeit *f* roguishness, mischievousness.

Schalkragen *m* shawl collar; *(mit losen Enden)* scarf collar.

Schalks-: **~knecht** *m (obs pej)* ne'er-do-well; **~narr** *m (obs)* **(a)** *(Hofnarr)* jester, fool; **(b)** *(Schalk)* wag, prankster, rogue.

Schall *m* -s, -e *or* ¨e sound. **Ruhm vergeht wie ~ und Rauch** *(geh)* fame is but a transient shadow; **Name ist ~ und Rauch** what's in a name?; **das ist alles ~ und Rauch** it's all hollow words.

Schall-: **~becher** *m (Mus)* bell; **~boden** *m* sound(ing)-board; **s~dämmend** *adj* sound-deadening; **~dämmung** *f* sound absorption; *(Abdichtung gegen Schall)* soundproofing; **s~dämpfend** *adj* Wirkung sound-muffling *or* -deadening; *Material* soundproofing; **~dämpfer** *m* sound absorber; *(von Auto)* silencer *(Brit)*, muffler *(US)*; *(von Gewehr etc)* silencer; *(Mus)* mute; **~dämpfung** *f* sound absorption; *(Abdichtung gegen Schall)* soundproofing; *(von Auto etc)* silencing; **s~dicht** *adj* soundproof; **s~dicht abgeschlossen sein** to be fully sound-proofed.

Schalleiter *m getrennt:* **Schall-leiter** conductor of sound.

schallen *vi* to sound; *(Stimme, Glocke, Beifall)* to ring (out); *(widerhallen)* to resound, to echo. **das Schlagen der Turmuhr schallte zu uns herüber** we could hear the church clock ring out; **er schlug die Tür zu, daß es (im Zimmer) schallte** he slammed the door so that the room reverberated.

schallend *adj Beifall, Ohrfeige* resounding; *Gelächter* ringing; **~ lachen** to roar with laughter.

Schall-: **~geschwindigkeit** *f* speed of sound; **~grenze, ~mauer** *f* sound barrier; **~leiter** *m siehe* **Schalleiter; ~messung** *f* sound ranging.

Schallplatte *f* record.

Schallplatten-: **~album** *nt* record case; **~archiv** *nt* (gramophone) record archive; **~aufnahme** *f* (gramophone) recording.

Schall-: **~schirm** *m siehe* **~wand; s~schluckend** *adj* sound-absorbent; *Material* soundproofing; **s~sicher** *adj* soundproof; **s~tot** *adj Raum* completely soundproof; **~trichter** *m* horn; *(von Trompeten etc)* bell; **~wand** *f* baffle *(of loudspeaker etc)*; **~welle** *f* soundwave; **~wort** *nt* onomatopoeic word.

Schalmei *f* shawm.

Schal|obst *nt siehe* **Schal(en)obst.**

schalt *pret of* **schelten.**

Schalt-: **~anlage** *f* switchgear; **~bild** *nt* circuit diagram, wiring diagram; **~brett** *nt* switchboard, control panel.

schalten 1 *vt* to switch, to turn; *(in Gang bringen)* to switch *or* turn on. **etw auf „2" ~** to turn *or* switch sth to "2"; **etw auf die höchste Stufe ~** to turn sth on full, to turn sth full on *or* up; **in Reihe/parallel ~** *(Elec)* to connect in series/in parallel; **das Gerät läßt sich schwer ~** *or* **schaltet sich schwer** this device has a difficult switch (to operate); **das Auto läßt sich spielend ~** *or* **schaltet sich leicht** it's easy to change gear in this car. **2** *vi* **(a)** *(Gerät)* to switch *(auf +acc* to); *(Aut)* to change gear. **in den 2. Gang ~** to change *or* shift *(US)* (up/down) into 2nd gear.

(b) *(fig: verfahren, handeln)* **~ und walten** to bustle around; **frei ~ (und walten) können** to have a free hand (to do as one pleases); **jdn frei ~ und walten lassen** to give sb a free hand, to let sb manage things as he sees fit.

(c) *(inf: begreifen)* to latch on *(inf)*, to get it *(inf)*, to get the message *(inf)*; *(reagieren)* to react.

Schalter *m* -s, - **(a)** *(Elec etc)* switch. **(b)** *(in Post, Bank, Amt)* counter; *(mit Fenster auch)* window; *(im Bahnhof)* ticket window.

Schalter-: **~beamte(r)** *m* counter clerk; *(in Bahnhof)* ticket clerk; **~dienst** *m* counter duty; **~halle** *f*, **~raum** *m (in Post)* hall; *(in Bank)* (banking) hall; *(im Bahnhof)* booking *or* ticket hall; **~stunden** *pl* hours of business *pl*, business hours *pl*.

schaltfaul *adj (inf)* reluctant to change gear.

Schalthebel *m* switch lever; *(Aut)* gear lever, gearshift (lever). **an dem ~ der Macht sitzen** to hold the reins of power.

Schaltier *nt* crustacean.

Schalt-: **~jahr** *nt* leap year; **alle ~jahre** *(inf)* once in a blue moon; **~kasten** *m* switchbox; **~knüppel** *m (Aut)* gear lever;

(Aviat) joystick; **~pause** *f (TV, Rad)* pause *(before going over to another region or station)*; **~plan** *m siehe* **~bild; ~pult** *nt* control desk; **~satz** *m (Ling)* parenthetic clause; **~skizze** *f siehe* **~bild; ~stelle** *f (fig)* coordinating point; **~tafel** *f siehe* **~brett; ~tag** *m* leap day.

Schaltung *f* switching; *(Elec)* wiring; *(Aut)* gear change, gearshift.

Schalung *f* formwork, shuttering.

Schaluppe *f* -, -n sloop.

Schalwild *nt* hoofed game.

Scham *f* -, *no pl* **(a)** shame. **er wurde rot vor ~** he went red with shame; **die ~ stieg ihm ins Gesicht** *(old)* a blush of shame mounted to his cheeks; **ich hätte vor ~ (in den Boden) versinken können** I wanted the floor to swallow me up *or* to open up under me; **er versteckte sich vor ~** he hid himself in shame; **aus falscher ~** from a false sense of shame; **nur keine falsche ~!** *(inf)* no need to feel *or* be embarrassed!; **no need for embarrassment!; sie hat kein bißchen ~ (im Leibe)** she doesn't have an ounce of shame (in her); **ohne ~** unashamedly.

(b) *(geh: Genitalien)* private parts *pl*; *(von Frau)* pudenda *pl*.

Schamane *m* -n, -n shaman.

Scham-: **~bein** *nt* pubic bone; **~berg** *m (geh) siehe* **~hügel; ~bogen** *m* pubic arch.

schämen *vr* to be ashamed. **du solltest dich ~!, du sollst dich was ~** *(inf)* you ought to be ashamed of yourself!; **sich einer Sache** *(gen)* **or für** *or* **wegen etw ~** to be ashamed of sth; **sich jds/einer Sache** *or* **wegen jdm/etw** *(inf)* **~** to be ashamed of sb/sth; **sich für jdn ~** to be ashamed for sb; **sich vor jdm ~** to be *or* feel ashamed in front of sb; **ich schäme mich so vor ihm** he makes me feel so ashamed; **schäme dich!** shame on you!

Scham-: **~fuge** *f* pubic symphysis *(spec)*; **~gefühl** *nt* sense of shame; **ganz ohne ~gefühl sein** to have no (sense of) shame; **~gegend** *f* pubic region; **~haar** *nt* pubic hair; **s~haft** *adj* modest; *(verschämt)* bashful, coy; **die heutige Jugend ist nicht sehr s~haft** today's young people have very little modesty; **~haftigkeit** *f* modesty; **~hügel** *m* mount of Venus, mons veneris *(form)*; **~lippen** *pl* labia *pl*, lips *pl* of the vulva; **s~los** *adj* shameless; *(unanständig auch)* indecent; *(unverschämt auch)* brazen; *Frechheit, Lüge* brazen, barefaced; **sich s~los zeigen** to flaunt oneself brazenly *or* shamelessly; **sich s~los kleiden** to dress indecently; **~lose Reden führen** to make indecent remarks; **~losigkeit** *f siehe adj* shamelessness; indecency; brazenness.

Schamott *m* -s, *no pl* **(a)** *(inf)* junk *(inf)*, trash *(inf)*, rubbish. **(b)** *(Aus, S Ger) siehe* **Schamotte.**

Schamotte *f* -, *no pl* fireclay.

Schamotte-: **~stein** *m* firestone; **~ziegel** *m* firebrick.

schamottieren* *vt* to line with firebricks.

Schampun *nt* -s, -s *(rare) siehe* **Shampoo(n).**

Schampus *m* -, *no pl (dated inf)* champers *sing (dated inf)*.

Scham-: **s~rot** *adj* red (with shame); **s~rot werden** *or* **anlaufen** to turn red *or* to blush *or* flush with shame; **~röte** *f* flush *or* blush of shame; **die ~röte stieg ihr ins Gesicht** her face flushed with shame; **~teile** *pl* private parts *pl*, genitals *pl*.

schandbar *adj* shameful, disgraceful.

Schande *f* -, *no pl* disgrace; *(Unehre auch)* shame, ignominy. **er ist eine ~ für seine Familie** he is a disgrace to his family; **das ist eine (wahre) ~!** this is a(n absolute) disgrace!; **~!** *(euph inf)* sugar! *(euph inf)*, hell! *(inf)*; **es ist doch keine ~, Gefühle zu zeigen** *or* **wenn man Gefühle zeigt** there is no shame *or* disgrace in showing one's feelings; **~ über jdn bringen** to bring disgrace *or* shame upon sb, to disgrace sb; **~ über dich!** *(dated)* shame on you!; **er hat das arme Mädchen in ~ gebracht** he brought shame *or* dishonour upon the poor girl, he dishonoured the poor girl; **jdm/einer Sache ~ machen** to be a disgrace to sb/sth; **mach mir keine ~** don't show me up *(inf)*, don't be a disgrace to me; **zu meiner (großen) ~ muß ich gestehen, . . .** to my great *or* eternal shame I have to admit that . . .; *siehe* **Schimpf.**

schänden *vt Leichnam, Grab, Denkmal* to violate, to defile; *Heiligtum auch* to desecrate; *Sabbat, Sonntag etc* to violate, to desecrate; *Frauen, Kinder* to violate; *Ansehen, Namen* to dishonour, to discredit, to sully.

Schand-: **~fleck** *m* blot *(in +dat on)*; **er war der ~fleck der Familie** he was the disgrace of his family; **~geld** *nt (inf)* ridiculous *or* extortionate price.

schändlich *adj* disgraceful, shameful. **jdn ~ im Stich lassen/betrügen** shamefully to leave sb in the lurch/to deceive sb shamefully.

Schändlichkeit *f* disgracefulness, shamefulness.

Schand-: **~mal** *nt* brand, stigma; **~maul** *nt (pej)* malicious *or* evil tongue; **er ist ein ~maul** he has a malicious *or* evil tongue; **~pfahl** *m* pillory; **~tat** *f* scandalous *or* disgraceful deed; *(hum)* prank, escapade; **zu jeder ~tat bereit sein** *(inf)* to be always ready for mischief *or* a lark *(inf)*.

Schändung *f siehe vt* violation, defilement; desecration; violation; dishonouring, discrediting, sullying.

schanghaien *vt (Naut)* to shanghai.

Schani *m* -s, - *(Aus)* **(a)** *(Freund)* mate *(inf)*, buddy *(US inf)*. **(b)** *(Diener)* servant.

Schank *m* -s, ¨e *(obs)* selling *or* retail of alcohol; *(Aus)* bar.

Schank-: **~betrieb** *m* bar service; **nach 24°° kein ~betrieb mehr** the bar closes at 12 midnight; **~bier** *nt* draught beer.

Schanker *m* -s, - chancre.

Schank-: **~erlaubnis** *f* licence *(of publican)* *(Brit)*, excise license *(US)*; **~fräulein** *nt (Aus)* barmaid; **~konzession** *f siehe* **~erlaubnis; ~stube** *f* (public) bar *(Brit)*, saloon *(US)*; **~tisch** *m* bar; **~wirt** *m (old)* taverner *(old)*, publican *(Brit)*, saloon keeper *(US)*, barkeeper *(US)*; **~wirtschaft** *f (old, Aus)* tavern *(old)*, public house *(Brit)*, saloon *(US)*.

Schanz-: **~arbeit** *f* trench digging, trenchwork; **~arbeiten**

entrenchments, trenchwork; ~**bau** m *siehe* **Schanzenbau.**

Schanze f -, -n (*Mil*) fieldwork, entrenchment; (*Naut*) quarterdeck; (*Sport*) (ski-)jump. **sein Leben in die ~ schlagen** (*geh*) to risk one's life, to put one's life at risk *or* in jeopardy.

schanzen vi (a) (*Mil*) to dig (trenches). (b) (*Sch inf*) to work like mad (*inf*). **auf die Mathearbeit habe ich unheimlich geschanzt** I really slogged myself to death (*inf*) over my maths.

Schanzen-: ~**bau** m construction of fieldwork *or* entrenchments; ~**rekord** m (*Sport*) ski-jump record.

Schanzwerk nt entrenchment.

Schar[1] f -, -en crowd, throng (*liter*); (*von Vögeln*) flock; (*von Insekten, Heuschrecken etc*) swarm; (*Reiter~, Soldaten~ etc*) band, company; (*von Jägern*) party; (*Pfadfinder*) company, troop; (*von Engeln*) host, band, throng (*liter*). ~**en von Hausfrauen** stürzten sich auf die Sonderangebote hordes *or* crowds of housewives descended on the special offers; **die Schlachtenbummler verließen das Stadion in (hellen) ~en** the away supporters left the stadium in droves *or* swarmed away from the stadium; **die Menschen kamen in (hellen) ~en nach Lourdes** people flocked to Lourdes.

Schar[2] f -, -en (*Pflug~*) (plough)share (*Brit*), (plow)share (*US*).

Scharade f charade. ~ **spielen** to play charades.

Scharbockskraut nt (lesser) celandine.

Schäre f -, -n skerry.

scharen 1 vt **Menschen/Anhänger um sich ~** to gather people/to rally supporters around one. 2 vr **sich um jdn ~** to gather around sb; (*Anhänger auch*) to rally around sb.

scharenweise adv (*in bezug auf Menschen*) in droves. **die Heuschrecken/Vögel fielen ~ über die Saat her** swarms of locusts/whole flocks of birds descended on the seedcrop; ~ **drängten sich die Leute vor dem Schaufenster** people crowded *or* thronged in front of the shop window.

scharf adj, comp ⁼**er**, superl ⁼**ste(r, s)** *or* adv am ⁼**sten** (a) *Kante, Kurve* sharp; *Messer, Klinge auch* keen attr (*liter*); (*durchdringend auch*) *Wind* keen, biting, cutting; *Kälte* biting; *Luft* raw, keen; *Frost* sharp, keen; *Ton* piercing, shrill. **das „s"** wird oft ~ ausgesprochen "s" is often voiceless *or* pronounced as an "s" and not a "z"; **das ~e s** (*inf, Aus*) the "scharfes s" (*German symbol ß*); **ein Messer ~ machen** to sharpen a knife.

(b) (*stark gewürzt*) hot; (*mit Salz, Pfeffer*) highly seasoned; *Geruch, Geschmack* pungent, acrid; *Käse* strong, sharp; *Alkohol* (*stark*) strong; (*brennend*) fiery; (*ätzend*) *Waschmittel, Lösung* caustic. ~ **nach etw riechen** to smell strongly of sth; ~ **würzen** to season highly, to make hot (*inf*); *Fleisch* ~ **anbraten** to sear meat; ~ **gebackenes Brot** crisp-baked bread; *Kaffee* ~ **brennen** to give coffee a burnt taste; **der Kaffee ist mir zu ~ gebrannt** the coffee has too much of a burnt taste for my liking; ~**e Sachen** (*inf*) hard stuff (*inf*).

(c) (*hart, streng*) *Mittel, Maßnahmen* tough, severe, drastic; (*inf*) *Prüfung, Untersuchung* strict, tough; *Lehrer, Polizist* tough; *Bewachung* close, tight; *Hund* fierce. **jdn ~ bewachen** to guard sb closely.

(d) (*schonungslos, stark*) *Worte, Kritik* sharp, biting, harsh; *Widerstand, Konkurrenz* fierce, tough; *Gegner, Protest* strong, fierce; *Auseinandersetzung* bitter, fierce. **eine ~e Zunge haben** to have a sharp tongue, to be sharp-tongued; **jdn/etw in ~er Form kritisieren** to criticize sb/sth in strong terms; **etw in ~ster Form** *or* **aufs ~ste verurteilen** to condemn sth in the strongest possible terms; **das ist ja das ~ste!** (*sl*) this is too much! (*inf*).

(e) (*deutlich, klar, genau*) sharp; *Unterschied auch* marked; *Brille, Linse* sharply focusing; *Augen auch* keen; *Töne* clear, precise; *Verstand, Intelligenz, Gehör auch* keen, acute; *Beobachter* keen. **etw ~ einstellen** *Bild, Diaprojektor etc* to bring sth into focus; *Sender* to tune sth in (properly); ~ **eingestellt in** (sharp) focus; (properly) tuned in; ~ **sehen/hören** to have sharp eyes/ears; ~ **aufpassen/zuhören** to pay close attention/to listen closely; **jdn ~ ansehen** to give sb a scrutinizing look; (*mißbilligend*) to look sharply at sb; **etw ~ umreißen** (*fig*) to outline sth precisely *or* clearly; ~ **nachdenken** to have a good *or* long think, to think long and hard; ~ **kalkulieren** to calculate exactly; **ein ~es Auge für etw haben** (*fig*) to have a keen *or* sharp eye for sth; **mit ~em Blick** (*fig*) with penetrating insight; **etw ~er ins Auge fassen** (*fig*) to take a closer look at sth, to look more closely at sth.

(f) (*heftig, schnell*) *Ritt, Trab* hard. ~ **reiten** to ride hard; **ein ~es Tempo fahren** (*inf*) to drive hell for leather (*inf*), to drive at quite a lick (*inf*); **einen ~en Stil fahren** (*inf*) to drive hard; ~ **bremsen** to brake sharply *or* hard.

(g) (*echt*) *Munition etc, Schuß* live. **~ machen** to arm sth; **~e Schüsse abgeben** to shoot *or* fire live bullets; **das Gewehr war ~ geladen** the rifle was loaded with live ammunition; ~ **schießen** (*lit*) (*mit ~er Munition*) to shoot with live ammunition; (*auf den Mann*) to aim to hit; (*fig*) to let fly; **in der Diskussion wurde ziemlich ~ geschossen** (*fig*) the discussion became rather heated, sparks flew in the discussion.

(h) (*sl*) (*geil*) randy (*Brit inf*), horny (*inf*); (*aufreizend*) *Frau, Kleidung, Bilder* sexy (*inf*); *Film* sexy (*inf*), blue attr; (*aufregend*) *Auto, Film* cool (*inf*), great (*inf*). ~ **werden** to get turned on (*inf*), to get randy (*Brit inf*) *or* horny (*inf*); **jdn ~ machen** to turn sb on (*inf*); **auf jdn/etw ~ sein** to be keen on (*inf*) *or* hot for (*sl*) sb/sth, to fancy sb/sth (*inf*); **der Kleine/Alte ist ~ wie Nachbars Lumpi** *or* **tausend Russen** *or* **sieben Sensen** he's a randy little/old beggar (*sl*); *siehe* **scharfmachen.**

Scharfblick m (*fig*) perspicacity, keen insight, penetration.

Schärfe f -, -n *siehe adj (a-e)* (a) sharpness; keenness; keenness; shrillness.

(b) hotness; pungency; causticity.

(c) toughness; severity; toughness; closeness, tightness. **mit ~ vorgehen** to take tough *or* severe *or* drastic measures.

(d) sharpness, harshness; ferocity, toughness; ferocity; bitterness, ferocity. **ich möchte in aller ~ sagen, daß ... I'm** going to be quite harsh (about this) and say that ...

(e) sharpness; sharp focus; keenness; clarity; keenness; (*an Kamera, Fernsehen*) focus; (*an Radio*) tuning. **dem Bild fehlt die ~** the picture lacks sharpness (of focus) *or* definition.

Scharf|einstellung f focusing.

schärfen vt (*lit, fig*) to sharpen.

Schärfen|einstellung f focusing control.

Scharf-: s~**kantig** adj with sharp edges, sharp-edged; s~**machen** vt sep (*inf*) to stir up, to get up in arms; ~**macher** m (*inf*) rabble-rouser, agitator; ~**macherei** f (*inf*) rabble-rousing, agitation; ~**richter** m executioner; ~**schütze** m marksman; s~**sichtig** adj keen- *or* sharp-sighted; (*fig*) perspicacious, clear-sighted; ~**sinn** m astuteness, acumen, keen perception; s~**sinnig** adj *Bemerkung* astute, penetrating; *Detektiv etc* astute, sharp-witted; **wie er s~sinnig bemerkte** as he so astutely remarked.

Schärfung f (*lit, fig*) sharpening.

Scharlach m -s, no pl (a) scarlet. (b) (*~fieber*) scarlet fever.

Scharlach-: s~**farben** adj scarlet; ~**fieber** nt scarlet fever; s~**rot** adj scarlet (red).

Scharlatan m -s, -e charlatan; (*Arzt auch*) quack.

Scharlatanerie f charlatanism.

Scharm m -s, no pl *siehe* **Charme.**

scharmant adj *siehe* **charmant.**

Scharmützel nt -s, - (*old*) skirmish, brush with the enemy.

Scharnier -s, -e, **Scharniergelenk** nt hinge.

Schärpe f -, -n sash.

scharren vti to scrape; (*Pferd, Hund*) to paw; (*Huhn*) to scratch; (*verscharren*) to bury (hurriedly). **mit dem Huf ~** to paw the ground.

Scharte f -, -n nick; (*in Bergkamm*) wind-gap; (*Schieß~*) embrasure; (*in Kampfwagen*) gunport. **eine ~ auswetzen** (*fig*) to make amends, to patch things up.

Scharteke f -, -n (*pej*) (old) hag; (*Buch*) tattered old volume.

schartig adj jagged, notched.

scharwenzeln* vi aux sein *or* haben (*inf*) to dance attendance (*um* (up)on).

Schaschlik nt -s, -s (shish-)kebab.

schassen vt (*inf*) to chuck out (*inf*), to boot out (*inf*).

Schatten m -s, - (*lit, fig*) shadow; (*schattige Stelle*) shade; (*Geist*) shade. **im ~ sitzen** to sit in the shade; **40 Grad im ~** 40 degrees in the shade; ~ **geben** *or* **spenden** to give *or* provide shade; **einen ~ auf etw** (*acc*) **werfen** (*lit*) to cast a shadow on sth; (*fig*) to cast a shadow *or* cloud (up)on sth; **aus dem ~ ans Licht treten** (*lit, fig*) to come out of the shadows; **große Ereignisse werfen ihre ~ voraus** great events are often foreshadowed; **in jds ~** (*dat*) **stehen** (*fig*) to stand *or* be in sb's shadow; **im ~ bleiben** (*fig*) to remain in the background *or* shadows; **jdn/etw in den ~ stellen** (*fig*) to put sb/sth in the shade, to overshadow *or* eclipse sb/sth; **man kann nicht über seinen eigenen ~ springen** (*fig*) the leopard cannot change his spots (*prov*); **sich vor seinem eigenen ~ fürchten** (*fig*) to be afraid of one's own shadow; **nur noch ein ~ (seiner selbst) sein** to be (only) a shadow of one's former self; **die ~ des Todes/der Nacht** (*liter*) the shades of death/night (*liter*); **Reich der ~** (*liter*) realm of shades (*liter*); **es fiel nicht der leiseste ~ des Verdachts auf ihn** not a shadow of suspicion fell on him; **nicht der ~ eines Beweises** not the slightest proof; ~ **unter den Augen** shadows under the eyes; **du hast ja einen ~** (*sl*) you must be nuts (*sl*); *siehe* **Licht.**

Schatten-: ~**bild** nt silhouette; (*in ~spiel*) shadow picture, shadow(graph); ~**boxen** nt shadow-boxing; ~**dasein** nt shadowy existence; s~**haft** adj shadowy, shadow-like; (*fig: vage*) shadowy, fuzzy, vague; **etw s~haft zeichnen** to draw sth with shadowy outlines; ~**kabinett** nt (*Pol*) shadow cabinet; s~**los** adj shadowless; ~**morelle** f morello cherry; s~**reich** adj shady; ~**reich** nt (*liter*) realm of shadows (*liter*) *or* shades (*liter*); ~**riß** m silhouette; ~**seite** f shady side; (*von Planeten*) dark side; (*fig: Nachteil*) drawback, disadvantage; **die ~seite(n) des Lebens** the dark side of life, life's dark side; (*in Milieu, Slums etc*) the seamy side of life; s~**spendend** adj attr shady; ~**spiel** nt shadow play *or* show; (*Art*) contrast, shadow play.

schattieren* vt to shade.

Schattierung f (*lit, fig*) shade; (*das Schattieren*) shading. **aller politischen ~en** of every political shade.

schattig adj shady.

Schattseite f (*Aus*) *siehe* **Schattenseite.**

schattseitig adj (*Aus*) shady.

Schatulle f -, -n casket; (*Geld~*) coffer; (*pej*) bag (*inf*).

Schatz m -es, ⁼e (a) (*lit, fig*) treasure. ⁼**e** pl (*Boden~*) natural resources pl; (*Reichtum*) riches pl, wealth sing; **nach ~en graben** to dig for (buried) treasure; **du bist ein ~!** (*inf*) you're a (real) treasure *or* gem!; **für alle ~e der Welt** (*fig*) for all the money in the world, for all the tea in China.

(b) (*Liebling*) sweetheart; (*als Anrede*) love, darling.

Schatz-: ~**amt** nt Treasury; ~**anweisung** f treasury bond.

schätzbar adj assessable. **gut/schlecht/schwer ~** easy/hard/difficult to assess *or* estimate.

Schätzchen nt darling.

schätzen 1 vt (a) (*veranschlagen*) to estimate, to assess (*auf +acc* at); *Wertgegenstand, Gemälde etc* to value, to appraise; (*annehmen*) to reckon, to think. **die Besucherzahl wurde auf 500.000 geschätzt** the number of visitors was estimated at *or* to be 500,000; **wie alt ~ Sie mich denn?** how old do you reckon I am *or* would you say I am, then?; **was schätzt du, wie lange/wie viele/wie alt ...?** how long/how many/how old ... do you reckon *or* would you say ...?; **was/wieviel schätzt du denn?**

what/how much do you reckon it is or would you say it was?; **ich hätte sie älter geschätzt** I'd have said she was older, I'd have thought her older; *siehe* **hoch.**

(b) (*würdigen*) to regard highly, to value. **jdn ~** to think highly of sb, to hold sb in high regard or esteem; **mein geschätzter Kollege** (*form*) my esteemed colleague (*form*); **etw zu ~ wissen** to appreciate sth; **das schätzt er (überhaupt) nicht** he doesn't care for or appreciate that (at all); **sich glücklich ~** to consider or deem (*form*) oneself lucky.

2 *vi* (*veranschlagen, raten*) to guess. **schätz mal** have a guess.

schätzenlernen *vt sep* to come to appreciate or value.

schätzenswert *adj* estimable.

Schätzer *m* -s, - valuer; (*Insur*) assessor.

Schatz-: **~fund** *m* find (*of treasure*), treasure-trove (*Jur*); **~gräber** *m* -s, - treasure-hunter; **~kammer** *f* treasure chamber or vault; **~kanzler** *m* (*Pol*) minister of finance, Chancellor of the Exchequer (*Brit*), secretary to the Treasury (*US*); **~kästchen, ~kästlein** *nt* casket, (small) treasure chest; (*fig: als Buchtitel etc*) treasury; **~meister** *m* treasurer.

Schätzpreis *m* valuation price.

Schätzung *f* estimate; (*das Schätzen*) estimation; (*von Wertgegenstand*) valuation, appraisal. **nach meiner ~ ...** I reckon that ...; (*ungefähr*) approximately, roughly.

schätzungsweise *adv* (*so vermutet man*) it is estimated or thought; (*ungefähr*) approximately, roughly; (*so schätze ich*) I think, I reckon. **die Inflationsrate wird sich ~ verdoppeln** it is thought or estimated (that) the rate of inflation will double; **es werden ~ 3.000 Zuschauer kommen** an estimated 3,000 spectators will come; **das wird ~ länger dauern** I think or reckon (that) that'll take longer; **wann wirst du ~ kommen?** when do you think or reckon you'll come?

Schätzwert *m* estimated value.

schau *adj pred* (*dated sl*) smashing (*dated inf*), wizard (*dated sl*).

Schau *f* -, -en **(a)** (*Vorführung*) show; (*Ausstellung auch*) display, exhibition. **etw zur ~ stellen** (*ausstellen*) to put sth on show, to display or exhibit or show sth; (*fig*) to make a show of sth, to parade sth; (*protzen mit*) to show off sth; **sich zur ~ stellen** to make a spectacle or exhibition of oneself; **etw zur ~ tragen** to display sth.

(b) (*inf*) **eine ~ abziehen** to put on a display or show; (*Theater machen*) to make a big show (*inf*); **das war eine ~!** that was really great or fantastic (*inf*); **das ist nur ~** it's only show; **er macht nur (eine) ~** he's (only) putting it on; **jdm die ~ stehlen** or **klauen** to steal the show from sb.

(c) (*liter: mystische Vision*) vision.

(d) (*geh: Blickwinkel*) (point of) view.

Schau-: **~bild** *nt* diagram; (*Kurve*) graph; **~bude** *f* (show) booth; **~bühne** *f* (*old*) theatre; (*fig*) stage, scene.

Schauder *m* -s, - shudder; (*vor Angst, Kälte auch*) shiver. **ein ~ lief mir über den Rücken** a shiver/shudder ran down my spine.

schauder-: **~bar** *adj* (*hum*) terrible, dreadful, awful; **~erregend** *adj* terrifying, fearsome, horrifying; (*Vorstellung, Vision, Geschichte auch*) horrific; **~haft** *adj* (*lit*) horrible, ghastly, terrible; (*fig inf*) terrible, dreadful, awful.

schaudern *vi* (*vor Grauen, Abscheu*) to shudder; (*vor Kälte, Angst auch*) to shiver; (*vor Ehrfurcht*) to tremble, to quiver. **mich schauderte bei dem Anblick/Gedanken** I shuddered/shivered/trembled or quivered at the sight/thought (of it); **ihr schauderte vor ihm** he makes her shudder/shiver.

schauen **1** *vi* (*esp dial*) to look. **verärgert/traurig etc ~** to look angry/sad etc; **auf etw** (*acc*) **~** to look at sth; **um sich ~** to look around (one); **die Sonne schaut durch die Wolken** the sun is peeping or shining through the clouds or from behind the clouds; **jdm** (*fest*) **in die Augen ~** to look sb (straight) in the eye; **jdm (verliebt) in die Augen ~** to gaze (adoringly) into sb's eyes; **ihm schaut der Ärger/Zorn/Schrecken aus den Augen** annoyance/anger/fright is written all over his face; **nach jdm/etw ~** (*suchen*) to look for sb/sth; (*sich kümmern um*) to look after sb/sth; **da schaust du aber!** there, see!, there you are!; **schau, schau!** (*inf*), **da schau her!** (*S Ger*) well, well!, what do you know! (*inf*), how about that! (*inf*); **schau, daß du ...** see or mind (that) you ...

2 *vt* (*geh*) to see, to behold (*old, liter*); (*erkennen*) to see. **Gott ~** to see God.

Schauer *m* -s, - **(a)** (*Regen~*) shower. **(b)** (*Schauder*) shudder.

Schauergeschichte *f* horror story; (*Liter*) gothic tale or story; (*inf: Lügengeschichte*) horror story.

schauerlich *adj* **(a)** (*inf*) horrific, horrible; (*Anblick, Schrei, Erzählung auch*) spine-chilling, bloodcurdling; (*gruselig*) eerie, creepy (*inf*). **(b)** (*inf: fürchterlich*) terrible, dreadful, awful.

Schauerlichkeit *f siehe adj* **(a)** horribleness; eeriness, creepiness (*inf*).

Schauer-: **~mann** *m, pl* -leute docker, longshoreman (*US*); **~märchen** *nt* (*inf*) horror story.

schauern **1** *vi* to shudder. **2** *vt impers* **mich schauert** I shudder; **mich schauert bei dem bloßen Gedanken** the very thought (of it) makes me shudder.

Schauerroman *m* (*lit, fig inf*) horror story; (*Liter auch*) Gothic novel.

Schaufel *f* -, -n shovel; (*kleiner: für Mehl, Zucker*) scoop; (*Kehricht~*) dustpan; (*von Bagger*) scoop; (*von Wasserrad, Turbine*) vane; (*Geweih~*) palm; (*Hunt: von Auerhahn*) fan. **zwei ~n (voll) Sand/Kies** two shovel(ful)s of sand/gravel.

schaufelförmig *adj* shaped like a shovel, shovel-shaped.

schaufeln *vti* to shovel; *Grab, Grube* to dig; *siehe* **Grab.**

Schaufel-: **~rad** *nt* (*von Dampfer*) paddlewheel; (*von Turbine*)

---

vane wheel, impeller; **~raddampfer** *m* paddle-steamer; **s~weise** *adv* in shovelfuls.

Schaufenster *nt* display window; (*von Geschäft auch*) shop window.

Schaufenster-: **~auslage** *f* window display; **~bummel** *m* window-shopping expedition; **einen ~bummel machen** to go window-shopping; **~dekorateur** *m* window-dresser; **~gestaltung** *f* window-dressing; **~puppe** *f* display dummy.

Schau-: **~fliegen** *nt* stunt flying; (*Veranstaltung*) air display; **~flug** *m* stunt flight; **~geschäft** *nt* show business; **~kampf** *m* exhibition bout or fight; **~kasten** *m* showcase.

Schaukel *f* -, -n swing.

schauk(e)lig *adj* Brücke swaying *attr*; Überfahrt rough; Auto, Fahrt bouncy. **ein ~es Boot** a boat which rocks.

schaukeln **1** *vi* **(a)** (*mit Schaukel*) to swing; (*im Schaukelstuhl*) to rock. **auf or mit dem Stuhl ~** to swing or rock back and forth in one's chair, to tip one's chair back and forth.

(b) (*sich hin und her bewegen*) to swing or sway (to and fro or back and forth); (*sich auf und ab bewegen*) to rock up and down; (*Fahrzeug*) to bounce (up and down); (*Schiff*) to rock, to pitch and toss.

(c) *aux sein* (*sich ~d bewegen*) (*Schiff*) to pitch and toss; (*gemütlich fahren*) to jog along.

2 *vt* to rock. **jdn durch die Gegend ~** (*inf*) to take sb for a spin round the place (*inf*); **wir werden das Kind** or **das** or **die Sache schon ~** (*inf*) we'll manage it.

3 *vi impers* **bei der Überfahrt/im Auto hat es geschaukelt** the boat pitched and tossed on the way over/it was a bouncy ride.

Schaukel-: **~pferd** *nt* rocking horse; **~politik** *f* seesaw(ing) politics *pl*/policy; **~stuhl** *m* rocking chair.

Schau-: **~laufen** *nt* exhibition skating; (*Veranstaltung*) skating display; **s~lustig** *adj* curious; **~lustige** *pl decl as adj* (curious) onlookers *pl*.

Schaum *m* -s, **Schäume** foam, froth; (*Seifen~, Shampoo~*) lather; (*von Waschmittel*) lather, suds *pl*; (*Cook: auf Speisen, Getränken*) froth; (*auf Marmelade, Flüssen, Sümpfen*) scum; (*von Bier*) head, froth. **~ vor dem Mund haben** (*lit, fig*) to froth or foam at the mouth; **etw zu ~ schlagen** (*Cook*) to beat or whip sth until frothy; **zu ~ schlagen** (*fig inf*) to be all hot air.

Schaum-: **~bad** *nt* bubble or foam bath; **~blase** *f* bubble.

schäumen *vi* to foam, to froth; (*Seife, Shampoo, Waschmittel*) to lather (up); (*Limonade, Wein*) to bubble; (*inf: wütend sein*) to foam at the mouth. **das Waschmittel schäumt stark/schwach** it's a high-/low-lather detergent; **vor Wut ~** to be foaming with rage.

Schaum-: **~feuerlöscher** *m* foam fire extinguisher; **~geborene** *f* (*liter*) goddess born of the foam of the sea (*liter*); **~gummi** *nt or m* foam rubber.

schaumig *adj siehe* **Schaum** foamy, frothy; lathery, lathery, sudsy; frothy; scummy; frothy.

Schaum-: **~kelle** *f* skimmer; **~krone** *f* whitecap, white crest or horse; **~löffel** *m* skimmer; **~löscher** *m*, **~löschgerät** *nt* foam extinguisher; **~schläger** *m* (*fig inf*) hot-air merchant (*inf*); **~schlägerei** *f* (*fig inf*) hot air (*inf*); **~stoff** *m* foam material.

Schaummünze *f* medal, medallion; (*Gedenkmünze*) commemorative coin.

Schaumwein *m* sparkling wine.

Schau-: **~packung** *f* dummy (package); **~platz** *m* scene; **vom ~platz berichten** to give an on-the-spot report; **am ~platz sein** to be on or at the scene or on the spot; **auf dem ~platz erscheinen** to appear on the scene; **vom ~platz (der Politik) abtreten** to leave the (political) scene or arena; **~prozeß** *m* show trial.

schaurig *adj* gruesome; *Schrei* spine-chilling, bloodcurdling; (*inf: sehr schlecht*) dreadful, abysmal (*inf*), awful.

Schaurigkeit *f siehe adj* gruesomeness; spine-chillingness; dreadfulness.

schaurig-schön *adj* gruesomely beautiful; (*unheimlich*) eerily beautiful.

Schauspiel *nt* **(a)** (*Theat*) drama, play. **(b)** (*fig*) spectacle. **wir wollen doch den Leuten kein ~ bieten** let's not make a spectacle of ourselves.

Schauspieler *m* actor, player; (*fig*) (play-)actor.

Schauspielerei *f* acting; (*fig: Verstellung*) play-acting.

Schauspielerin *f* (*lit*) actress; (*fig*) (play-)actress.

schauspielerisch **1** *adj* acting. **2** *adv* as regards acting, as far as (the) acting is/was concerned.

schauspielern *vi insep* to act; (*fig*) to (play-)act.

Schauspiel-: **~haus** *nt* playhouse, theatre; **~kunst** *f* dramatic art, drama; (*in bezug auf Schauspieler*) acting; **~schule** *f* drama school; **~schüler** *m* drama student; **~unterricht** *m* acting or drama lessons *pl* or classes *pl*.

Schau-: **~steller** *m* -s, - showman; **~stück** *nt* showpiece; **~tafel** *f* (*zur Information*) (notice) board; (*~bild*) diagram; **~tanz** *m* exhibition dance; **~turnen** *nt* gymnastic display.

Scheck *m* -s, -s or (*rare*) -e cheque (*Brit*), check (*US*). **mit (einem)** or **per ~ bezahlen** to pay by cheque; **ein ~ auf** or **über DM 200** a cheque for DM 200.

Scheck-: **~betrug** *m* cheque/check fraud; **~betrüger** *m* cheque/check fraud; **~buch** *nt* chequebook (*Brit*), checkbook (*US*).

Schecke *m* -n, -n or *f* -, -n (*Pferd*) dappled horse/pony; (*Rind*) spotted ox/bull/cow.

Scheck-: **~fälschung** *f* cheque/check forgery; **~heft** *nt siehe* **~buch.**

scheckig *adj* spotted; *Pferd* dappled; (*inf: kunterbunt*) gaudy; (*verfärbt*) blotchy, patchy.

Scheck-: **~karte** *f* cheque card (*Brit*), check card (*US*), banker's card; **~verkehr** *m* cheque/check transactions *pl*.

scheel *adj* **(a)** (*old: schielend*) cross-eyed. **auf einem Auge war**

sie ~ she had a squint (in one eye). **(b)** (*mißgünstig*) envious, jealous; (*abschätzig*) disparaging. ein ~er Blick a dirty look; jdn ~ ansehen to give sb a dirty look; (*abschätzig*) to look askance at sb.

scheel|äugig adj (old) siehe scheel.

Scheffel m -s, - (*Gefäß, Hohlmaß*) ≈ bushel (*contains anything from 30 to 300 litres*); (*Flächenmaß*) area between 12 and 42 ares. sein Licht unter den ~ stellen (inf) to hide one's light under a bushel.

scheffeln 1 vt Gold, Orden to pile up, to accumulate; Geld to rake in (inf). 2 vi er scheffelt seit Jahren he's been raking it in for years (inf).

scheffelweise adv in large quantities, by the sackful. ~ Geld verdienen to be raking it in (inf).

scheibchenweise adv (fig) bit by bit, little by little, a bit or little at a time.

Scheibe f -, -n **(a)** disc; (*Schieß~*) target; (*Eishockey*) puck; (*Wähl~*) dial; (*Tech*) (*Unterleg~, Dichtungs~*) washer; (*Kupplungs~, Brems~*) disc; (*Töpfer~*) wheel; (inf: *Schallplatte*) disc (inf).
  (b) (*abgeschnittene* ~) slice; (*Längs~: von Orange etc*) segment. etw in ~n schneiden to slice sth (up), to cut sth (up) into slices; von ihm könntest du dir eine ~ abschneiden (fig inf) you could take a leaf out of his book (inf).
  (c) (*Glas~*) (window)pane; (*Fenster, von Auto*) window; (inf: *Windschutz~*) windscreen (Brit), windshield (US); (*Spiegel~*) glass.
  (d) (euph inf) ~! sugar! (euph inf).

Scheiben-: ~bremse f disc brake; ~gardine f net curtain; ~honig m comb honey; ~honig! (euph inf) sugar! (euph inf); ~kleister interj sugar! (euph inf); ~kupplung f disc or plate clutch; ~schießen nt target shooting; ~waschanlage f windscreen (Brit) or windshield (US) washers pl; s~weise adv in slices; ~wischer m windscreen (Brit) or windshield (US) wiper.

Scheibtruhe f (Aus) siehe Schubkarre.

Scheich m -s, -e sheik(h); (inf) bloke (Brit inf), guy (inf).

Scheichtum nt sheik(h)dom.

Scheide f -, -n **(a)** a sheath; (*von Schwert auch*) scabbard; (*Vagina*) vagina. das Schwert aus der ~ ziehen to unsheathe or draw one's sword; das Schwert in die ~ stecken to put up or sheathe one's sword. **(b)** (obs, fig: *Grenze*) border.

Scheide-: ~linie f (lit) border(line); (fig) dividing line; ~mittel nt (Chem) separating agent.

scheiden pret **schied**, ptp **geschieden** 1 vt **(a)** (geh: *trennen*) to separate; (*voneinander* ~ auch) to divide; (Chem) to separate (out); siehe Geist, Spreu.
  (b) (auflösen) Ehe to dissolve; Eheleute to divorce. eine geschiedene Frau a divorced woman, a divorcee; sich ~ lassen to get divorced, to get a divorce; er will sich von ihr ~ lassen he wants to divorce her or get a divorce (from her); er läßt sich nicht von ihr ~ he won't give her a divorce; von dem Moment an waren wir (zwei) geschiedene Leute (inf) after that it was the parting of the ways for us (inf).
  2 vi aux sein (liter) (sich trennen) to part; (weggehen) to depart. aus dem Dienst/Amt ~ to retire from service/one's office; aus dem Leben ~ to depart this life; S~ tut weh (prov) parting is such sweet sorrow (Prov).
  3 vr (Wege) to divide, to part, to separate; (Meinungen) to diverge, to part company.

Scheiden-: ~abstrich m vaginal smear; ~krampf m vaginal cramp, vaginismus (form); ~vorfall m prolapse of the vagina.

Scheide-: ~wasser nt (Chem) nitric acid, aqua fortis; ~weg m (fig) crossroads sing; am ~weg stehen to be at a crossroads.

Scheidung f **(a)** (das Scheiden) separation.
  (b) (Ehe~) divorce. die ~ dieser Ehe the dissolution of this marriage; die ~ aussprechen to grant the divorce; in ~ leben or liegen to be in the middle of divorce proceedings, to be getting a divorce; die ~ einreichen to file a petition for divorce.

Scheidungs-: ~grund m grounds pl for divorce; (hum: *Mensch*) reason for his/her etc divorce; ~klage f petition for divorce; ~prozeß m divorce proceedings pl; ~recht nt divorce law(s pl); ~urkunde f divorce certificate; ~urteil nt decree of divorce.

Schein[1] m -s, no pl **(a)** (Licht) light; (matt) glow; (von Gold, Schwert etc) gleam, glint. einen (hellen) ~ auf etw (acc) werfen to shine (brightly) on sth, to cast a (bright) light on sth.
  (b) (An~) appearances pl; (Vortäuschung) pretence, sham. ~ und Sein appearance and reality; das ist mehr ~ als Sein it's all (on) the surface; der ~ trügt or täuscht appearances are deceptive; dem ~ nach on the face of it, to all appearances; den ~ wahren to keep up appearances; seine Freundschaft ist nur ~ his friendship is only (a) pretence or sham; etw nur zum ~ tun only to pretend to do sth, to make only a pretence or a show of doing sth.

Schein[2] m -s, -e (Geld~) note, bill (US); (Bescheinigung) certificate; (Univ) (end of semester) certificate; (Fahr~) ticket. ~e machen (Univ) to get certificates.

Schein-: ~angriff m feint (attack); s~bar adj apparent, seeming attr; (vorgegeben) feigned, ostensible; er hörte s~bar interessiert zu he listened with apparent or seeming/ feigned interest; ~blüte f illusory flowering; (Econ) illusory boom; ~dasein nt phantom existence; ~ehe f fictitious or sham marriage.

scheinen pret **schien**, ptp **geschienen** vi **(a)** (leuchten) to shine.
  (b) auch vi impers (den Anschein geben) to seem, to appear. es scheint, daß .../als (ob) ... it seems or appears that .../as if ...; mir scheint, (daß) ... it seems or appears to me that ...; wie es scheint as it seems or would appear, apparently; es scheint nur ...

so it only seems or appears to be like that; er kommt scheint's nicht mehr (dial inf) it would seem that he won't come now, seemingly he's not coming now; du hast scheint's vergessen, daß ... (dial inf) you seem to have forgotten that ...

Schein-: ~firma f phoney or fictitious firm; ~friede m phoney peace, peace in name only, semblance no pl of peace; ~gefecht nt mock or sham fight; ~grund m spurious reason; (Vorwand) pretext; s~heilig adj hypocritical; (Arglosigkeit vortäuschend) innocent; s~heilig tun to be hypocritical; (Arglosigkeit vortäuschen) to act innocent, to play it innocent; ~heilige(r) mf siehe adj hypocrite; sham; ~heiligkeit f siehe adj hypocrisy; feigned innocence; ~schwangerschaft f false pregnancy; ~tod m apparent death, suspended animation; s~tot adj in a state of apparent death or of suspended animation; ~werfer m (zum Beleuchten) floodlight; (im Theater) spotlight; (Such~) searchlight; (Aut) (head)light, headlamp; ~werferlicht nt siehe ~werfer floodlight(ing); spotlight; searchlight (beam); light or beam of the headlights or headlamps; (fig) limelight; im ~werferlicht (der Öffentlichkeit) stehen (fig) to be in the glare of publicity; ein Problem in das ~werferlicht rücken to spotlight or highlight a problem; ~widerstand m sham resistance; (Elec) impedance, apparent resistance.

Scheiß m -, no pl (sl) shit (vulg), crap (vulg). ein ~ a load of shit (vulg) or crap (vulg); ~ machen (herumalbern) to bugger (sl) or mess (inf) about; (Fehler machen) to make a balls-up (vulg); mach keinen ~! don't do anything so bloody (Brit sl) or daft (inf) silly; red' doch keinen ~! don't talk crap! (vulg), cut (out) the crap! (vulg).

Scheiß- in cpds (sl) bloody (Brit sl), bleeding (Brit sl), damn(ed) (inf), fucking (vulg).

Scheißdreck m (vulg: Kot) shit (vulg), crap (vulg); (sl) (blödes Gerede, schlechtes Buch, schlechte Ware etc) load of shit (vulg); (unangenehme Sache, Arbeit) effing thing (sl), bloody thing (Brit sl); (Angelegenheiten) effing business (sl), bloody business (Brit sl). ~! shit! (vulg); wegen jedem ~ about every effing (sl) or bloody (Brit sl) little thing; das geht dich einen ~ an it's none of your effing (sl) or bloody (Brit sl) business, it's got bugger-all to do with you (sl); einen ~ werd' ich tun! like (bloody Brit sl) hell I will!; sich einen ~ um jdn/etw kümmern not to give a shit (vulg) or a bloody damn (Brit sl) about sb/sth.

Scheiße f -, no pl (vulg: Kot) shit (vulg), crap (vulg); (sl) (unangenehme Lage) shit (vulg); (Unsinn) shit (vulg), crap (vulg). ~ sein to be bloody awful (Brit sl) or goddamn (sl) awful; (ärgerlich) to be a bloody (Brit sl) or goddamn (sl) nuisance; das ist doch alles ~ it's all a bloody (Brit sl) mess, it's all shit (vulg); (Unsinn) it's all a load of shit (vulg); das ist doch alles ~, ich geb's auf it's no bloody (Brit sl) or shitting (vulg) good, I'm giving up; ~! bloody hell! (Brit sl), shit! (vulg), bugger (sl); in der ~ sitzen to be in the shit (vulg), to be up shit creek (vulg); siehe auch Scheiß.

scheiß|egal adj (sl) das ist mir doch ~! I don't give a shit (vulg) or a bloody damn (Brit sl).

scheißen pret **schiß**, ptp **geschissen** vi (vulg) to shit (vulg), to crap (vulg). sich (dat) vor Angst in die Hosen ~ to have or get the shits (vulg), to shit oneself (vulg); auf etw (acc) ~ (fig) not to give a shit about sth (vulg); ich scheiß' auf deine guten Ratschläge/auf ein tolles Auto to hell with your good advice/fancy cars (sl), you can stick your good advice/fancy car (sl); scheiß der Hund drauf to hell with that! (sl), bugger that! (sl).

Scheißer m -s, - (sl: Arschloch) bugger (sl); (inf: Kosename) chubby cheeks sing (hum inf).

Scheißerei (sl), **Scheißeritis** (hum inf) f die ~ the runs (inf), the shits (vulg).

Scheiß-: s~freundlich adj (sl) as nice as pie (iro inf); ~haus nt (vulg) shithouse (vulg); ~kerl m (sl) bastard (sl), sod (sl), son-of-a-bitch (US sl), mother(fucker) (US vulg); s~vornehm adj (sl) bloody posh (Brit sl).

Scheit m -(e)s, -e or (Aus, Sw) -er log, piece of wood.

Scheitel m -s, - **(a)** (Haar~) parting (Brit), part (US); (liter: Haupthaar) locks pl. vom ~ bis zur Sohle from top to toe. **(b)** (höchster Punkt) vertex.

scheiteln vt to part.

Scheitel-: ~punkt m vertex; ~wert m peak (value); ~winkel m vertical angle.

scheiten vt (Sw) Holz to chop.

Scheiterhaufen m (funeral) pyre; (Hist: zur Hinrichtung) stake. die Hexe wurde auf dem ~ verbrannt the witch was burned at the stake.

scheitern vi aux sein **(a)** (an +dat because of) (Mensch, Unternehmen) to fail; (Verhandlungen, Ehe) to break down; (Plan, Vorhaben auch) to fall through; (Regierung) to founder (an +dat on); (Mannschaft) to be defeated (an +dat by); siehe Existenz. **(b)** (Schiff) to be wrecked.

Scheitern nt -s, no pl siehe vi **(a)** failure; breakdown; falling through; foundering; defeat. das war zum ~ verurteilt or verdammt that was doomed to failure; etw zum ~ bringen to make sth fail/break down/fall through. **(b)** wrecking.

Scheitholz nt firewood.

Schelf m or nt -s, -e (Geog) (continental) shelf.

Schelfmeer nt shelf sea.

Schellack m -(e)s, -e shellac.

Schelle f -, -n **(a)** bell; (dial: Klingel) bell. **(b)** (Tech) clamp. **(c)** (Hand~) handcuff. **(d)** (dial) siehe Ohrfeige. **(e)** (Cards) ~n pl ≈ diamonds sing or pl (shaped like bells on traditional German cards).

schellen vi to ring (nach jdm for sb). es hat geschellt the bell has gone; bei jdm or an jds Tür (dat) ~ to ring at sb's door.

Schellen-: ~baum m (Mus) Turkish crescent, pavillon chinois; ~bube m ≈ jack or knave of diamonds; ~geläut(e) nt jingling (of bells); mit ~geläute fuhr der Pferdeschlitten vorbei the sleigh passed by with its bells jingling; ~kappe f cap and bells, fool's cap; ~könig m = king of diamonds; jdn über den ~könig loben (fig dial) to praise sb to the skies; ~ober m = queen of diamonds (a man on traditional German cards); ~unter m = jack or knave of diamonds.

Schellfisch m fish of the cod group.

Schelm m -(e)s, -e (dated: Spaßvogel) rogue, wag (dated); (obs: Gauner) knave (obs); (Liter) picaro. den ~ im Nacken haben to be up to mischief; ein ~, der Böses denkt honi soit qui mal y pense (prov), evil to him who evil thinks (prov).

Schelmen-: ~gesicht nt mischievous face; ~roman m picaresque novel; ~streich m (dated) roguish prank; ~stück nt (dated) knavery (old); (obs: Missetat) villainous deed (old).

Schelmerei f (old: Missetat) villainous deed (old); (dated: Streich) prank.

schelmisch adj mischievous.

Schelte f -, -n scolding. er hat ~ bekommen he got a scolding.

schelten pret schalt, ptp gescholten 1 vt to scold, to chide. jdn einen Dummkopf ~ to call sb a blockhead. 2 vi (schimpfen) to curse. über or auf jdn/etw ~ to curse sb/sth, to rail at sb/sth (old); mit jdm ~ to scold sb.

Scheltwort nt word of abuse. ~e words of abuse, invective sing.

Schema nt -s, Schemen or -ta scheme; (Darstellung) diagram; (Ordnung, Vorlage auch) plan; (Muster) pattern; (Philos, Psych) schema. nach ~ F in the same (old) way; etw nach einem ~ machen to do sth according to a pattern.

schematisch adj schematic; (mechanisch) mechanical.

schematisieren* vti to schematize.

Schematismus m schematism.

Schemel m -s, - stool.

Schemen m -s, - silhouette; (Gespenst) spectre.

schemenhaft 1 adj shadowy. 2 adv etw ~ sehen/zeichnen to see the outlines of sth/to sketch sth in; die Bäume hoben sich ~ gegen den Himmel ab the trees were silhouetted against the sky.

Schenke f -, -n tavern, inn.

Schenkel m -s, - (a) (Anat) (Ober~) thigh. sich (dat) auf die ~ schlagen to slap one's thighs; dem Pferd die ~ geben to press a horse on; siehe Unterschenkel. (b) (von Zirkel) leg; (von Zange, Schere) shank; (Math: von Winkel) side.

Schenkel-: ~bruch m fracture of the thigh(bone) or femur; ~hals m neck of the femur; ~halsbruch m fracture of the neck of the femur.

schenken 1 vt (a) (Geschenk geben) jdm etw ~ to give sb sth or give sth to sb (as a present or gift); sich (dat) (gegenseitig) etw ~ to give each other sth (as a present or gift); etw geschenkt bekommen/sich (dat) etw ~ lassen to get sth as a present or gift; etw zum Geburtstag/zu Weihnachten geschenkt bekommen to get sth for one's birthday/for Christmas; zu Weihnachten hat er nichts geschenkt bekommen he didn't get anything or any presents for Christmas; so was kaufe ich nicht, das lasse ich mir immer ~ I don't buy anything like that, I always like to get these things as presents; ich möchte nichts geschenkt haben! (lit) I don't want any presents!; (fig: bevorzugt werden) I don't want any special treatment!; ich nehme nichts geschenkt! I'm not accepting any presents!; das ist geschenkt! (inf) (ist ein Geschenk) it's a present; (nicht der Rede wert) that's no great shakes (inf); (sl: nichts wert) forget it! (inf); das ist (fast) geschenkt! (inf: billig) that's dirt cheap (inf) or a give-away (inf); das möchte ich nicht mal geschenkt haben! I wouldn't want it if it was given to me; einem geschenkten Gaul sieht man nicht ins Maul (Prov) don't look a gift horse in the mouth (Prov).
(b) (erlassen) jdm etw ~ to let sb off sth; ihm ist nie etwas geschenkt worden (fig) he never had it easy.
(c) in Verbindung mit n siehe auch dort jdm die Freiheit/das Leben ~ (begnadigen) to set sb free/to spare sb's life; einem Kind das Leben ~ (geh) to give birth to a child; jdm seine Liebe/seine Aufmerksamkeit etc ~ to give sb one's love/one's attention etc; jdm/einer Sache (keinen) Glauben ~ to give (no) credence to sb/sth; jdm Vertrauen ~ to put one's trust in sb.
(d) (eingießen) to pour.
2 vi to give presents.
3 vr (a) sich (dat) etw ~ to skip sth (inf); deine Komplimente kannst du dir ~! you can keep your compliments (inf); sich (dat) die Mühe ~ to save oneself the trouble; er hat sich (dat) nichts geschenkt he spared no pains; die beiden haben sich nichts geschenkt neither was giving anything away.
(b) sich jdm ~ (liter: Frau) to give oneself to sb.

Schenkung f (Jur) gift.

Schenkungs-: ~steuer f gift tax; ~urkunde f deed of gift.

Schenkwirt m siehe Schankwirt.

scheppern vi (dial) to clatter. es hat gescheppert there was a clatter; (loser, Gegenstand) there was a rattle; (Autounfall) there was a bang; (Ohrfeige) he/she got a clip round the ear.

Scher m -(e)s, -e (S Ger, Aus, Sw) mole.

Scherbe f -, -n fragment, (broken) piece; (Glas~, Porzellan~, Keramik~) broken piece of glass/china/pottery; (Archeol) shard, potsherd. etw in ~n schlagen to shatter sth; in ~n gehen to break, to shatter; (fig) to fall or go to pieces; ~n machen to break something; (fig) to put one's foot in it; die ~n zusammenkehren to sweep up the (broken) pieces; (fig) to pick up the pieces; es hat ~n gegeben (fig) there was lots of trouble; (bei Streit) sparks flew; die ~n unseres Glücks the shattered remains of our happiness; ~n bringen Glück (Prov) broken crockery brings you luck.

scherbeln vi (dated inf) to dance, to swing a leg (inf).

Scherben m -s, - (S Ger, Aus) siehe Scherbe.

Scherbengericht nt ostracism. über jdn ein ~ abhalten (geh) to ostracize sb.

Schere f -, -n (a) (Werkzeug) (klein) scissors pl; (groß) shears pl; (Draht~) wire-cutters pl. eine ~ a pair of scissors/shears/wire-cutters. (b) (Zool) pincer; (von Hummer, Krebs etc auch) claw. (c) (Turnen, Ringen) scissors sing.

scheren[1] pret schor, ptp geschoren vt to clip; Schaf, (Tech) to shear; Haare to crop; Bart (rasieren) to shave; (stutzen) to trim. er war/seine Haare waren kurz geschoren his hair was cropped short; siehe kahlscheren, Kamm.

scheren[2] vtr (a) sich nicht um jdn/etw ~ not to care or bother about sb/sth; was schert mich das? what do I care (about that)?, what's that to me?; er scherte sich nicht im geringsten darum he couldn't have cared less about it; siehe Teufel.
(b) (inf) scher dich (weg)! scram! (inf), beat it! (inf); scher dich heim! go home!; scher dich ins Bett! get to bed!; es ist Zeit, daß du dich nach Hause scherst it's time you were off home.

Scheren-: ~fernrohr nt binocular periscope; ~gitter nt concertina barrier; ~schlag m scissors kick; ~schleifer m scissor(s) grinder, knife grinder; ~schnitt m silhouette.

Schererei f usu pl (inf) trouble no pl.

Scherflein nt (Bibl) mite. sein ~ (zu etw) beitragen or dazu geben or beisteuern (Geld) to contribute one's mite (towards sth); (fig) to do one's bit (for sth) (inf).

Scherge m -n, -n (a) (geh: Büttel) thug. (b) (obs) siehe Häscher.

Schergendienst m dirty work. zu ~en bereit willing to do (the) dirty work.

Scher-: ~kopf m shaving head; ~maus f (Aus, S Ger) vole; (Sw) mole; ~messer nt shearing knife; ~wolle f fleece.

Scherz[1] m -es, -e joke, jest; (Unfug) tomfoolery no pl. aus or zum/im ~ as a joke/in jest; einen ~ machen to make a joke; (Streich) to play a joke; mach keine ~e! (inf) you're joking!, you must be kidding! (inf); mit so etwas macht man keine ~e you don't joke or make jokes about things like that; seine ~e über jdn/etw machen to make or crack jokes about sb/sth; seine ~e (mit jdm) treiben to play jokes; ... und solche ~e (inf) ... and what have you (inf); (ganz) ohne ~! (inf) no kidding! (inf).

Scherz[2] m -es, -e, Scherzel nt -s, - (Aus) hunk of bread; (Endstück) heel.

Scherzartikel m usu pl joke (article).

scherzen vi (a) (old, geh) to joke, to jest; (albern) to banter; (nicht ernst nehmen) to trifle (mit with). mir scheint, du scherzt you can't be serious; ich scherze nicht (old, geh) I'm not joking; Sie belieben wohl zu ~! (old, geh) surely you are in jest (old, liter); mit jdm/etw ist nicht zu ~ one can't trifle with sb/sth.
(b) (old, flirten) to dally.

Scherz-: ~frage f riddle; ~gedicht nt humorous poem; s~haft adj jocular, jovial; Angelegenheit joking; (spaßig) Einfall playful; etw s~haft sagen/meinen/aufnehmen to say sth jokingly or as a joke or in jest/to mean sth as a joke/to take sth as a joke.

Scherzo ['skɛrtso] nt -s, -s or Scherzi scherzo.

Scherzwort nt witticism, jocular or joking remark.

schesen vi aux sein (dial) to rush.

scheu adj (schüchtern) shy; (ängstlich) Reh, Tier auch timid; (zaghaft) Versuche, Worte cautious. jdn ~ machen to make sb shy; (ängstigen) to frighten or scare sb; mach doch die Pferde or Gäule nicht ~ (fig inf) keep your hair on (inf); ~ werden (Pferd) to be frightened.

Scheu f -, no pl fear (vor + dat of); (Schüchternheit) shyness; (von Reh, Tier) shyness, timidity; (Hemmung) inhibition; (Ehrfurcht) awe. seine ~ verlieren to lose one's inhibitions; ohne jede ~ without any inhibition; sprechen quite freely.

Scheuche f -, -n siehe Vogelscheuche.

scheuchen vt to shoo (away); (verscheuchen) to frighten or scare away or off.

scheuen 1 vt Kosten, Arbeit to shy away from; Menschen, Licht to shun. weder Mühe noch Kosten ~ to spare neither trouble nor expense; keine Mühe ~ to go to endless trouble.
2 vr sich vor etw (dat) ~ (Angst haben) to be afraid of sth; (zurückschrecken) to shy away from sth; sich (davor) ~, etw zu tun (Angst haben) to be afraid of doing sth; (zurückschrecken) to shrink back from doing sth; und ich scheue mich nicht, das zu sagen and I'm not afraid of saying it.
3 vi (Pferd etc) to shy (vor + dat at).

Scheuer f -, -n barn.

Scheuer-: ~besen m scrubbing broom; ~bürste f scrubbing brush; ~frau f char (Brit), cleaning woman; ~lappen m floorcloth; ~leiste f skirting board (Brit), baseboard (US).

scheuern 1 vti (a) (putzen) to scour; (mit Bürste) to scrub.
(b) (reiben) to chafe. der Rucksack scheuert mich am Rücken the rucksack is chafing my back; der Kragen scheuert am Hals the collar chafes at the neck.
(c) jdm eine ~ (inf) to clout sb one (inf).
2 vr sich (an etw dat) ~ to rub (against sth); sich (acc) (wund) ~ to chafe oneself.

Scheuer-: ~sand m scouring powder; ~tuch nt floorcloth.

Scheuklappe f blinker. ~n haben or tragen (lit, fig) to be blinkered, to wear blinkers; mit ~n herumlaufen or durchs Leben laufen to be wearing blinkers.

Scheune f -, -n barn.

Scheunen-: ~drescher m: wie ein ~drescher fressen (inf) to eat like a horse (inf); ~tor nt barn door; siehe Ochse.

Scheusal nt -s, -e or (inf) Scheusäler monster.

scheußlich adj dreadful; (abstoßend häßlich) hideous. es hat ~ weh getan (inf) it hurt dreadfully (inf), it was horribly or terribly painful.

Scheußlichkeit f siehe adj dreadfulness; hideousness.

Schi m -s, -er or - siehe **Ski**.
Schicht f -, -en (a) (Lage) layer; (dünne ~) film; (Geol, Sci auch) stratum; (Farb~) coat; (der Gesellschaft) level, stratum. breite ~en der Bevölkerung large sections of the population; aus allen ~en (der Bevölkerung) from all walks of life.
(b) (Arbeitsabschnitt, -gruppe etc) shift. er hat jetzt ~, er ist auf ~ (inf) he's on shift; zur ~ gehen to go on shift; er muß ~ arbeiten he has to work shifts.
Schicht-: ~arbeit f shift-work; ~arbeiter m shift-worker.
Schichte f -, -n (Aus) siehe **Schicht (a)**.
schichten 1 vt to layer; Holz, Heu, Bücher etc to stack. 2 vr (Geol) to form layers; (Gestein) to stratify.
schichtenspezifisch adj (Sociol) specific to a particular social stratum.
Schichtlohn m shift(-work) rates pl.
Schichtung f layering; (von Holz, Heu, Büchern etc) stacking; (Sociol, Geol, Met) stratification.
Schicht-: ~unterricht m teaching in shifts; ~unterricht haben to be taught in shifts; ~wechsel m change of shifts; um 6 Uhr ist ~wechsel bei uns we change shifts at six o'clock; s~weise adv in layers; (Farbe, Lack) in coats.
schick adj elegant, smart; Frauenmode chic; Haus, Wohnung auch, Möbel stylish; Auto smart; (inf: prima) great (inf).
Schick m -s, no pl style; (von Frauenmode, Frau auch) chic.
schicken 1 vt to send. (jdm) etw ~ to send sth (to sb), to send (sb) sth; jdn einkaufen/Bier holen ~ to send sb to do the shopping/to fetch or for some beer; (jdn) nach jdm/etw ~ to send (sb) for sb/sth.
2 vr, vr impers (sich ziemen) to be fitting or proper. das schickt sich nicht für ein Mädchen it does not befit or become a girl.
3 vr (a) (old: sich abfinden) sich in etw (acc) ~ to resign or reconcile oneself to sth; schließlich schickte er sich drein eventually he became reconciled to this.
(b) (old, dial: sich beeilen) to hurry up.
Schickeria f -, no pl (iro) in-people pl.
schicklich adj Kleidung or proper, fitting; Verhalten seemly, becoming. es ist nicht ~ zu pfeifen it is unseemly or unbecoming to whistle.
Schicklichkeit f propriety, decorum.
Schicksal nt -s, -e fate, destiny; (Pech) fate. das ~ wollte es, (daß) ... as fate would have it, ...; ~ spielen to play at fate; die ~e der Flüchtlinge the fate of the refugees; manche schweren ~e many a difficult fate; das sind (schwere) ~e those are tragic cases; er hat ein schweres ~ gehabt or durchgemacht fate has been unkind to him; (das ist) ~ (inf) that's life; jdn seinem ~ überlassen to leave or abandon sb to his fate; sein ~ herausfordern to tempt fate or providence; sein ~ war besiegelt his fate was sealed; dem ~ haben wir es zu verdanken, daß ... we have to thank our good fortune that ...; das ~ hat es gut mit uns gemeint fortune has smiled on us.
schicksalhaft adj fateful.
Schicksals-: ~frage f fateful question; ~gefährte m companion in misfortune; ~gemeinschaft f wir waren eine ~gemeinschaft we shared a common destiny; ~glaube m fatalism; ~göttin f goddess of destiny; die ~göttinnen the Fates; (Nornen) the Norns; ~schlag m great misfortune, stroke of fate; ~tragödie f tragedy of fate or destiny; ~wende f change in fortune.
Schickse f -, -n (pej inf) floozy (pej inf).
Schickung f (liter) act of providence.
Schiebe-: ~bühne f traverser; (Theat) sliding stage; ~dach nt sunroof; ~fenster nt sliding window.
schieben pret schob, ptp geschoben 1 vt (a) to push, to shove; Fahrrad, Rollstuhl etc auch to wheel. etw von sich (dat) ~ (fig) to put sth aside; Schuld, Verantwortung to reject sth; etw vor sich (dat) her ~ (fig) to put off sth; etw von einem Tag auf den andern ~ to put sth off from one day to the next; etw auf jdn/etw ~ to blame sb/sth for sth, to put the blame onto sb/sth; die Schuld/Verantwortung auf jdn ~ to put the blame on sb/the responsibility at sb's door.
(b) (stecken) to put; Hände auch to slip. jdm/sich etw in den Mund ~ to put sth into sb's/one's mouth.
(c) (inf: handeln mit) to traffic in; Drogen to push (inf).
(d) (inf) Wache/Dienst ~ to do guard duty/duty; siehe Kohldampf etc.
(e) (Rail) to shunt.
2 vi (a) to push, to shove.
(b) (inf) mit etw/Drogen ~ to traffic in sth/push (inf) drugs.
(c) (inf: begünstigen) to wangle (inf). da wurde viel geschoben there was a lot of wangling (inf) going on.
3 vr (a) (mit Anstrengung) to push, to shove. sich an die Spitze ~ to push one's way to the front. (b) (sich bewegen) to move.
Schieber m -s, - (a) slide; (am Ofen etc) damper; (inf: Bettpfanne) bedpan; (Eßbesteck für Kinder) pusher. (b) (inf: Tanz) shuffle. (c) (Schwarzhändler) black marketeer; (Waffen~) gun-runner; (Drogen~) pusher (inf).
Schieberei f (inf) (a) (Drängelei) pushing, shoving. (b) (Begünstigung) wangling (inf).
Schiebergeschäft nt shady deal; (Schwarzhandel) siehe **Schieber** (c) black marketeering; trafficking; pushing (inf).
Schiebe-: ~sitz m sliding seat; ~tür f sliding door; ~wand f sliding partition (wall).
Schiebelehre f calliper rule.
Schiebung f (Begünstigung) string-pulling; (Sport) rigging; (Schiebergeschäfte) shady deals pl. der ~ beschuldigt werden to be accused of rigging; das war doch ~ that was rigged or a fix; die Zuschauer riefen „~!" the spectators shouted "fix!"
schiech [ʃiːç] adj (Aus) (a) (häßlich) ugly. (b) (bang) jdm wird ~ sb gets scared.

schied pret of **scheiden**.
schiedlich adv: ~ und friedlich amicably.
Schieds-: ~gericht nt, ~gerichtshof m court of arbitration; s~gerichtlich 1 adj arbitral; 2 adv by arbitration; ~mann m, pl ~leute arbitrator, arbiter; ~richter m arbitrator, arbiter, umpire; (Fußball, Eishockey, Boxen) referee; (Hockey, Tennis, Federball, Kricket, Mil) umpire; (Preisrichter) judge; ~richterentscheidung f (Sport) referee's/umpire's decision; s~richterlich adj siehe ~richter arbitrational, arbitral, umpiring; refereeing; umpiring; judging; das muß s~richterlich entschieden werden the arbitrator/arbiter etc decides; s~richtern* vi insep (inf) siehe ~richter to arbitrate, to umpire; to referee; to umpire; to judge; ~spruch m (arbitral) award; ~verfahren nt arbitration proceedings pl.
schief adj crooked, not straight pred; (nach einer Seite geneigt) lopsided, tilted; Winkel oblique; Blick, Lächeln wry; Absätze worn(-down); (fig: unzutreffend) inappropriate; Deutung wide of the mark, inappropriate; Bild distorted. ~ laufen to walk lopsidedly; das Bild hängt ~ the picture is crooked or isn't straight; ~e Ebene (Phys) inclined plane; auf die ~e Bahn geraten or kommen (fig) to leave the straight and narrow; du siehst die Sache ganz ~! (fig) you're looking at it all wrong!; jdn ~ ansehen (fig) to look askance at sb; einen ~en Mund or ein ~es Gesicht ziehen (fig inf) to pull a (wry) face; der S~e Turm von Pisa the Leaning Tower of Pisa; siehe **Licht**.
Schiefe f -, no pl crookedness; (Neigung) lopsidedness, tilt; (von Ebene) inclination; (von Winkel) obliqueness.
Schiefer m -s, - (Gesteinsart) slate; (esp Aus: Holzsplitter) splinter.
Schiefer-: ~bruch m slate quarry; ~dach nt slate roof; s~grau adj slate-grey; ~kasten m pencil box; ~platte f slate; ~stift m slate pencil; ~tafel f slate.
schief-: ~gehen vi sep irreg aux sein to go wrong; es wird schon ~gehen! (hum) it'll be OK (inf); ~gewickelt adj pred (inf) on the wrong track; da bist du ~gewickelt you've got a surprise coming to you there (inf).
Schiefheit f siehe adj crookedness; lopsidedness, tilt; obliqueness; wryness; inappropriateness; distortion.
schief-: ~lachen vr sep (inf) to kill oneself (laughing) (inf); ~laufen sep irreg 1 vt siehe ~treten; 2 vi aux sein (inf) to go wrong; ~liegen vi sep irreg (inf) to be wrong; mit einer Meinung ~liegen to be on the wrong track; ~mäulig adj (lit) with a crooked mouth; (fig) envious; ~treten vt sep irreg Absätze to wear down; die Schuhe ~treten to wear down the heels of one's shoes; ~wink(e)lig adj oblique-angled.
schieläugig adj cross-eyed, squint-eyed, boss-eyed.
schielen vi to squint, to be cross-eyed or boss-eyed. auf or mit einem Auge ~ to have a squint in one eye; auf etw (acc) ~ (inf) to steal a glance at sth; er schielte auf ihre Beine (inf) he was ogling her legs; nach jdm/etw ~ (inf) to look at sb/sth out of the corner of one's eye; (begehrlich) to eye sb/sth up; (heimlich) to sneak a look at sb/sth.
schien pret of **scheinen**.
Schienbein nt shin; (~knochen) shinbone. jdm gegen or vor das ~ treten to kick sb in the shin(s).
Schienbein-: ~schoner, ~schutz, ~schützer m shin-pad, shin-guard.
Schiene f -, -n rail; (Med) splint; (von Lineal) edge, guide; (von Winkelmesser) blade. ~n (Rail) track sing, rails pl; aus den ~n springen to leave or jump the rails.
schienen vt Arm, Bein auch to put in a splint/splints, to splint.
Schienen-: ~bahn f (a) track transport; (b) siehe ~fahrzeug; ~bremse f slipper brake; ~bus m rail bus; ~fahrzeug nt track vehicle; ~netz nt (Rail) rail network; ~räumer m -s, - track clearer; ~strang m (section of) track; ~weg m railway (Brit) or railroad (US) line; etw auf dem ~weg versenden to send sth by rail.
schier[1] adj pure; (fig) sheer.
schier[2] adv (beinahe) nearly, almost.
Schierling m hemlock.
Schierlingsbecher m (cup of) hemlock.
Schieß-: ~befehl m order to fire or shoot; ~bude f shooting gallery; ~budenfigur f target figure or doll; (fig inf) clown; du siehst ja aus wie eine ~budenfigur you look like something out of a pantomime; ~eisen nt (sl) shooting iron (sl).
schießen pret schoß, ptp geschossen 1 vt to shoot; Kugel, Rakete to fire; (Ftbl etc) to kick; Tor auch to score; (mit Stock, Schläger) to hit. jdn in den Kopf/Bauch ~ to shoot sb in the head/stomach; etw an der Schießbude ~ to win sth at the shooting gallery; ein paar Bilder ~ (Phot inf) to take a few shots; Blicke auf jdn ~ to shoot glances at sb; sie hat ihn zum Krüppel geschossen she shot and crippled him.
2 vi (a) to shoot. auf jdn/etw ~ to shoot at sb/sth; nach etw ~ to shoot at sth; aufs Tor/ins Netz ~ to shoot or kick at goal/into the net; das ist zum S~ (inf) that's a scream (inf).
(b) aux sein (in die Höhe ~) to shoot up; (Samenstand entwickeln) to run to seed. die Pflanzen/Kinder sind in die Höhe geschossen the plants/children have shot up; aus dem Boden ~ (lit, fig) to spring or sprout up; siehe **Kraut**.
(c) aux sein (inf: sich schnell bewegen) to shoot. er ist or kam um die Ecke geschossen he shot round the corner; jdm durch den Kopf ~ (fig) to flash through sb's mind; etw ~ lassen (inf) to drop or forget sth (inf).
(d) aux sein (Flüssigkeit) to shoot; (spritzen) to spurt. das Blut schoß ihm ins Gesicht blood rushed or shot to his face; die Tränen schossen ihr in die Augen tears flooded her eyes.
(e) aux sein (S Ger, Aus: verbleichen) to fade.
3 vr to have a shoot-out.
Schießerei f gun battle, shoot-out; (das Schießen) shooting.
Schieß-: ~gewehr nt (hum) gun; ~hund m: wie ein ~hund

aufpassen (inf) to keep a close watch, to watch like a hawk; ~kunst f marksmanship no pl; ~platz m (shooting or firing) range; ~prügel m (sl) iron (sl); ~pulver nt gunpowder; ~scharte f embrasure; ~scheibe f target; ~sport m shooting; ~stand shooting range; (~bude) shooting gallery; ~übung f shooting or target practice no pl.

Schiet m -s, no pl (N Ger inf) siehe **Scheiße**.

Schiff nt -(e)s, -e (a) ship. das ~ der Wüste (geh) the ship of the desert; das ~ des Staates (geh) the ship of state; siehe klar. (b) (Archit) (Mittel~) nave; (Seiten~) aisle; (Quer~) transept. (c) (in Kohleherd) boiler. (d) (Typ: Setz~) galley.

Schiffahrt f getrennt: Schiff-fahrt shipping; (~skunde) navigation.

Schiffahrts-: ~gesellschaft f shipping company; ~kunde f navigation; ~linie f (a) (Schiffsweg) shipping route; (b) (Unternehmen) shipping line; ~recht nt maritime law; ~straße f, ~weg m (Kanal) waterway; (~linie) shipping lane or lane.

Schiff-: s~bar adj navigable; ~barkeit f navigability; ~barmachung f (von Fluß) canalization; ~bau m shipbuilding; ~bauer m shipwright; ~bruch m shipwreck; ~bruch erleiden (lit) to be shipwrecked; (fig) to fail; (Unternehmen) to founder; s~brüchig adj shipwrecked; s~brüchig werden to be shipwrecked; ~brüchige(r) mf decl as adj shipwrecked person.

Schiffchen nt (a) (zum Spielen) little boat. (b) (Mil, Fashion) forage cap. (c) (Tex, Sew) shuttle. (d) (Bot) keel, carina (spec). (e) (für Weihrauch) boat.

Schiffchen|arbeit f tatting.

schiffen 1 (a) aux sein (old) (Schiff fahren) to ship (old), to go by ship; (Schiff steuern) to steer. (b) (sl: urinieren) to piss (sl). **2** vi impers (sl: regnen) to piss down (sl).

Schiffer(in f) m -s, - boatman, sailor; (von Lastkahn) bargee; (Kapitän) skipper.

Schiffer-: ~klavier nt accordion; ~knoten m sailor's knot; ~mütze f yachting cap; ~scheiße f (vulg) frech/geil/dumm wie ~scheiße cheeky as hell (inf)/randy (Brit) or horny as hell (sl)/thick as pigshit (vulg).

Schiffs- in cpds ship's; ~arzt m ship's doctor; ~bauch m bilge; ~besatzung f ship's company.

Schiffschaukel f swing boat.

Schiffs-: ~eigner m (form) shipowner; ~junge m ship's boy; ~kapitän m ship's captain; ~koch m ship's cook; ~körper m (form) hull; ~ladung f shipload; ~makler m ship-broker; ~mannschaft f ship's crew; ~modell nt model ship; ~papiere pl ship's papers pl; ~raum m hold; ~register nt register of shipping; ~rumpf m hull; ~schnabel m bow; ~schraube f ship's propeller; ~tagebuch nt ship's log; ~tau nt (ship's) rope; ~taufe f christening or naming of the ship; ~verkehr m shipping; ~werft f shipyard; ~zwieback m ship's biscuit.

Schikane f -, -n (a) harassment; (von Mitschülern) bullying no pl. diese neuerlichen ~n an der Grenze this recent harassment at the border; das hat er aus reiner ~ gemacht he did it out of sheer bloody-mindedness; die Schüler brauchen sich nicht alle ~n gefallenzulassen the pupils don't have to put up with being messed around (inf). (b) mit allen ~n (inf) with all the trimmings. (c) (Sport) chicane.

schikanieren* vt to harass; Ehepartner, Freundin etc to mess around; Mitschüler to bully. ich lasse mich nicht weiter von diesem Weibsstück ~ I won't let this female mess me around any more (inf); er hat mich einmal so schikaniert, daß ... he once gave me such a rough time that ...

schikanös adj Mensch bloody-minded; Maßnahme etc harassing; Mitschüler, Ehemann, Vorgesetzter bullying. jdn ~ behandeln to mess sb around, to give sb a rough time; die Behinderungen des Verkehrs waren rein ~ holding up the traffic was pure harassment.

Schild[1] m -(e)s, -e shield; (Wappen~) escutcheon; (von ~kröte) shell, carapace (spec). jdn auf den ~ erheben (fig) to choose sb as leader; ein Einhorn im ~(e) führen (Her) to bear a unicorn in one's coat of arms; etwas/nichts Gutes im ~e führen (fig) to be up to something/to be up to no good.

Schild[2] nt -(e)s, -er (Aushang, Waren~, Verkehrs~) sign; (Wegweiser) signpost; (Namens~, Tür~) nameplate; (Kennzeichen) number plate (Brit), license plate (US); (Preis~) ticket; (Etikett, an Käfig, Gepäck etc) label; (Plakette) badge; (Plakat) placard; (von Plakatträger) board; (an Monument, Haus, Grab) plaque; (von Mütze) peak. im Fenster stand ein ~ there was a sign or notice in the window.

Schildbürger m (Liter) = Gothamite; (hum) fool.

Schildbürgerstreich m foolish act. das war ein ~ that was a stupid thing to do, that was a bit Irish (hum inf).

Schildchen nt siehe Schild[2] small sign; small plate etc.

Schilddrüse f thyroid gland. an der ~ leiden to have a thyroid complaint.

Schilddrüsenhormon nt thyroid hormone.

Schilderer m -s, - portrayer.

Schilder-: ~haus, ~häuschen nt sentry-box; ~maler m sign-writer.

schildern vt Ereignisse, Erlebnisse, Vorgänge to describe; (skizzieren) to outline; Menschen, Landschaften to portray. es ist kaum zu ~ it's almost impossible to describe; es ist kaum zu ~, wie frech er war he was indescribably cheeky; ~ Sie den Verlauf des Unfalls give an account of how the accident happened.

Schilderung f (Beschreibung) description; (Bericht, von Zeuge) account; (literarische ~) portrayal.

Schilderwald m (hum) forest or jungle of traffic signs.

Schild-: ~knappe m (Hist) squire, shield-bearer; (Land~) tortoise; (Wasser~) turtle; ~krötensuppe f turtle soup; ~laus f scale insect; ~patt nt -s, no pl tortoiseshell.

~wache f (old) sentry; ~wache stehen to stand sentry.

Schilf nt -(e)s, -e reed; (mit ~ bewachsene Fläche) reeds pl.

Schilfdach nt thatched roof.

schilfern vir (dial) siehe abschilfern.

Schilfgras nt, **Schilfrohr** nt siehe Schilf.

Schiller m -s, no pl (a) (Schimmer, Glanz) shimmer. (b) (Wein) rosé (wine).

Schiller-: ~kragen m Byron collar; ~locke f (a) (Gebäck) cream horn; (b) (Räucherfisch) strip of smoked rock-salmon.

schillern vi to shimmer.

schillernd adj Farben, Stoffe shimmering; (in Regenbogenfarben) iridescent; (fig) Charakter enigmatic. ~e Seide shot silk.

Schillerwein m rosé (wine).

Schilling m -s, - or (bei Geldstücken) -e shilling; (Aus) schilling.

schilpen vi to twitter, to chirp.

schilt imper sing of schelten.

Schimäre f -, -n chimera.

schimärisch adj chimerical.

Schimmel[1] m -s, - (Pferd) white horse, grey. ein weißer ~ (hum) a pleonasm.

Schimmel[2] m -s no pl (auf Nahrungsmitteln) mould; (auf Leder, Papier etc) mildew.

schimm(e)lig adj siehe Schimmel[2] mouldy; mildewy. ~ riechen to smell mouldy; ~ werden to go mouldy; to become covered with mildew.

schimmeln vi aux sein or haben (Nahrungsmittel) to go mouldy; (Leder, Papier etc) to go mildewy.

Schimmel-: ~pilz m mould; ~reiter m (Myth) ghost rider.

Schimmer m -s no pl glimmer, gleam; (von Licht auf Masse, Perlen, Seide) shimmer; (von Metall) gleam; (im Haar) sheen. beim ~ der Lampe/Kerzen by or in the soft glow of the lamp/glimmer of the candles; beim blassen ~ des Mondes in the pale moonlight; keinen (blassen) ~ von etw haben (inf) not to have the slightest idea or the faintest (inf) about sth.

schimmern vi to glimmer, to gleam; (Licht auf Wasser auch, Perlen, Seide) to shimmer; (Metall) to gleam. der Stoff/ihr Haar schimmert rötlich the material/her hair has a tinge of red.

schimmlig adj siehe schimm(e)lig.

Schimpanse m -n, -n chimpanzee, chimp (inf).

Schimpf m -(e)s, no pl (liter) insult, affront. mit ~ und Schande in disgrace; jdm einen ~ antun to affront or insult sb.

schimpfen 1 vi to get angry; (sich beklagen) to moan, to grumble, to bitch (inf); (fluchen) to swear, to curse; (Vögel, Affen etc) to bitch (inf). mit jdm ~ to scold sb, to tell sb off; heute hat der Lehrer (fürchterlich) geschimpft, weil ich ... the teacher told me off today because I ... (inf); auf or über jdn/etw ~ to bitch (inf) about sb/sth, to curse (about or at) sb/sth; vor sich hin ~ to grumble to oneself. **2** vt (aus~) to tell off, to scold. jdn einen Idioten ~ to call sb an idiot. **3** vr sich etw ~ (inf) to call oneself sth.

Schimpferei f cursing and swearing; (Geschimpfe) scolding; (Beschimpfung) row, set-to (inf), slanging match (inf); (das Murren) moaning, grumbling, bitching (inf); (von Vögeln, Affen etc) bitching (inf).

schimpfieren* vt (inf) to spoil.

Schimpfkanonade f barrage of abuse.

schimpflich adj (geh) (beleidigend) insulting; (schmachvoll) humiliating. jdn ~ verjagen to drive sb away in disgrace.

Schimpf-: ~name m nickname; Tricky Dicky war sein ~name they dubbed him Tricky Dicky; ~wort nt swearword; mit ~wörtern um sich werfen to curse and swear.

Schinakel nt -s, -(n) (Aus inf) (Ruderboot) rowing boat; (klappriges Fahrzeug) rattletrap (inf).

Schind|anger m (old) knacker's yard.

Schindel f -, -n shingle.

Schindeldach nt shingle roof.

schinden pret schindete or (rare) schund, ptp geschunden **1** vt (a) (quälen) Gefangene, Tiere to maltreat; (ausbeuten) to overwork, to drive hard; Maschine, Motor, Auto to flog. der geschundene Leib Christi the broken body of Christ. (b) (old: abdecken) to skin, to flay. (c) (inf: herausschlagen) Zeilen to pad (out); Arbeitsstunden to pile up. Zeit ~ to play for time; (bei jdm) Eindruck ~ to make a good impression (on sb), to impress (sb); Mitleid ~ to get some sympathy. **2** vr (hart arbeiten) to struggle; (sich quälen) to strain. sich mit etw ~ to slave away at sth.

Schinder m -s, - (a) (old: Abdecker) knacker. (b) (fig: Quäler) slavedriver.

Schinderei f (a) (old: Abdeckerei) knacker's yard. (b) (Plakkerei) struggle; (Arbeit) slavery no end art.

Schinderkarren m (old) knacker's cart.

Schindluder nt (inf) mit jdm ~ treiben to make sb suffer; mit etw ~ treiben to misuse sth; mit dem Essen ~ treiben to throw one's food about; mit seiner Gesundheit/seinen Kräften ~ treiben to abuse one's health/strength.

Schindmähre f (old) nag.

Schinken m -s, - (a) ham; (gekocht und geräuchert auch) gammon. (b) (pej inf) hackneyed and clichéed play/book/film; (großes Buch) tome; (großes Bild) great daub (pej inf).

Schinken-: ~brötchen nt ham roll; ~röllchen nt roll of ham; ~speck m bacon; ~wurst f ham sausage.

Schinn m no pl, **Schinnen** pl (N Ger) dandruff no pl.

Schippe f -, -n (a) (esp N Ger: Schaufel) shovel, spade. jdn auf die ~ nehmen (fig inf) to pull sb's leg (inf); dem Tod von der ~ springen (inf) to be snatched from the jaws of death. (b)

(*Cards*) spades. **(c)** (*inf: Schmollmund*) pout. **eine ~ machen** *or* **ziehen** to pout.

schippen *vt* to shovel. **Schnee ~** to clear the snow.

Schiri *m* -s, -s (*Ftbl inf*) ref (*inf*).

Schirm *m* -(e)s, -e **(a)** (*Regen~*) umbrella; (*Sonnen~*) sunshade, parasol; (*von Pilz*) cap.

    (b) (*Mützen~*) peak. **eine Mütze mit ~** a peaked cap.

    (c) (*Röntgen~, Wand~, Ofen~*) screen; (*Lampen~*) shade.

    (d) (*liter: Schutz*) **unter seinem Schutz und ~** under his protection; **jdm** *or* **jds ~ und Schild sein** to be sb's protector.

Schirm-: **~akazie** *f* umbrella thorn; **~bild** *nt* x-ray (picture); **~bildaufnahme** *f* (*form*) x-ray; **ich muß zur ~bildaufnahme** I've got to go for an x-ray; **~bildstelle** *f* x-ray unit.

schirmen *vt* (*geh*) to shield, to protect (*vor* +dat from, *gegen* against).

Schirm-: **~futteral** *nt* umbrella cover *or* case; **~herr(in** *f*) *m* patron; (*Frau auch*) patroness; **~herrschaft** *f* patronage; **unter der ~herrschaft von** under the patronage of; (*von Organisation*) under the auspices of; **die ~herrschaft übernehmen** to become patron; **~hülle** *f* umbrella cover; **~mütze** *f* peaked cap; **~pilz** *m* parasol mushroom; **~ständer** *m* umbrella stand.

Schirokko *m* -s, -s sirocco.

Schisma ['ʃɪsma, 'sçɪ-] *nt* -s, **Schismen** *or* (*geh*) -ta (*Eccl, Pol*) schism.

Schismatiker(in *f*) [ʃɪs'maːtikɐ, -ərɪn, sçɪ-] *m* -s, - (*liter*) schismatic.

schismatisch [ʃɪs'maːtɪʃ, sçɪ-] *adj* (*geh*) schismatic.

schiß *pret of* **scheißen**.

Schiß *m* -sses, *no pl* (*sl*) shit (*vulg*), crap (*vulg*). **(fürchterlichen) ~ haben** to be shit scared (*vor* +dat of) (*vulg*); **~ kriegen** to get the shits (*vulg*).

schizophren *adj* **(a)** (*Med*) schizophrenic. **(b)** (*pej: widersinnig*) contradictory, topsy-turvy.

Schizophrenie *f* **(a)** (*Med*) schizophrenia. **(b)** (*pej: Widersinn*) contradictoriness. **das ist die reinste ~** that's a flat contradiction.

Schlabberei *f* (*inf*) slurping, slobbering.

schlabberig *adj* (*inf*) slithery, slimy; *Maul* slobbery; *Brei, Suppe* watery.

Schlabbermaul *nt* (*inf*) **(a)** (*von Hund*) slobbery mouth. **(b)** (*Schwätzer*) bletherer (*inf*), gab(ber) (*inf*).

schlabbern (*inf*) **1** *vi* to slobber, to slurp; (*inf: quatschen*) to blether (*inf*), to gab (*inf*). **er schlabberte beim Essen** he slobbered *or* slurped his food. **2** *vt* to slurp.

Schlacht *f* -, -en battle. **die ~ bei** *or* **um X** the battle of X; **in die ~ gehen** *or* **ziehen** to go into battle; **jdm eine ~ liefern** to fight sb, to battle with sb; **die Kelten lieferten den Römern eine ~, die …** the Celts gave the Romans a battle that …

Schlachtbank *f:* **jdn (wie ein Lamm) zur ~ führen** to lead sb (like a lamb) to the slaughter.

Schlachtefest *nt siehe* **Schlachtfest**.

schlachten 1 *vt Schwein, Kuh* to slaughter, to butcher; *Huhn, Kaninchen, Opfertier etc* to slaughter, to kill; (*hum*) *Sparschwein* to break into.

    2 *vi* to do one's slaughtering. **unser Fleischer schlachtet selbst** our butcher does his own slaughtering; **heute wird geschlachtet** we're/they're *etc* slaughtering today.

Schlachten-: **~bummler** *m* (*inf: Sport*) visiting *or* away supporter *or* fan; **~maler** *m* painter of battle scenes.

Schlachter(in *f*) *m* -s, - (*esp N Ger*) butcher.

Schlächter *m* -s, - (*dial, fig*) butcher.

Schlachterei *f* (*esp N Ger*) butcher's (shop).

Schlächterei *f* **(a)** (*dial*) butcher's (shop). **(b)** (*fig: Blutbad*) slaughter, butchery *no pl*, massacre.

Schlachterladen, Schlächterladen *m* (*dial*) *siehe* **Schlachterei**.

Schlacht-: **~feld** *nt* battle-field; **auf dem ~feld bleiben** (*lit*) to fall in battle; (*fig*) (*nach Schlägerei etc*) to be left lying; (*esp Pol*) to be finished; **das ~feld räumen** (*aufräumen*) to clear the (battle-)field; (*verlassen*) to leave the (battle-)field; (*fig*) to drop out of contention; **das Zimmer sieht aus wie ein ~feld** the room looks like a battle-field *or* looks as if a bomb has hit it (*inf*); **~fest** *nt* a country feast to eat up meat from freshly slaughtered pigs; **~gesang** *m* battle song; **~getümmel** *nt* thick of the battle, fray; **~gewicht** *nt* dressed weight; **~gewühl** *nt siehe* **~getümmel**; **~haus** *nt*, **~hof** *m* slaughter-house, abattoir; **~kreuzer** *m* battle cruiser; **~linie** *f* battle line; **~messer** *nt* butcher's knife; **~opfer** *nt* sacrifice; (*Mensch*) human sacrifice; **~ordnung** *f* battle formation; **~plan** *m* battle plan; (*für Feldzug*) campaign plan; (*fig auch*) plan of action; **~platte** *f* (*Cook*) ham, German sausage, made with meat from freshly slaughtered pigs and served with sauerkraut; **s~reif** *adj* (*lit, fig*) ready for the slaughter; **~roß** *nt* (*liter*) warhorse, charger; (*fig inf*) heavyweight; **~ruf** *m* battle cry; **~schiff** *nt* battleship; (*inf: Auto*) tank (*inf*); **~tag** *m* slaughtering day.

Schlachtung *f siehe vt* slaughter(ing), butchering; slaughter(ing), killing.

Schlachtvieh *nt, no pl* animals *pl* for slaughter; (*Rinder auch*) beef cattle *pl*.

Schlacke *f* -, -n (*Verbrennungsrückstand*) clinker *no pl*; (*Aschenteile auch*) cinders *pl*; (*Metall*) slag *no pl*; (*Geol*) scoria *pl* (*spec*), slag *no pl*; (*Physiol*) waste products *pl*.

Schlacken-: **~bahn** *f* (*Sport*) cinder track; **s~frei, s~los** *adj* (*ohne Verbrennungsrückstand*) non-clinker, clinker-free; (*ohne Stoffwechselrückstand*) free of waste products; **Anthrazit brennt s~frei** anthracite burns without clinkering.

schlackern *vi* (*inf*) to tremble, to shake; (*vor Angst auch*) to quake; (*Kleidung*) to hang loosely, to be baggy. **mit den Knien ~** to tremble at the knees; **mit den Ohren ~** (*fig*) to be (left) speechless.

Schlaf *m* -(e)s, *no pl* sleep; (*Schläfrigkeit auch*) sleepiness. **einen leichten/festen/tiefen ~ haben** to be a light/sound/deep sleeper; **keinen ~ finden** to be unable to sleep; **um seinen ~ kommen/gebracht werden** to lose sleep; (*überhaupt nicht schlafen*) to not get any sleep; **jdn um seinen ~ bringen** to keep sb awake; **halb im ~e** half asleep; **im ~ reden** to talk in one's sleep; **ein Kind in den ~ singen** to sing a child to sleep; **~ haben** to be sleepy; **jdm sieht der ~ aus den Augen** sb looks sleepy; **sich** (*dat*) **den ~ aus den Augen reiben** to rub the sleep out of one's eyes; **in tiefstem ~ liegen** to be sound *or* fast asleep; **aus dem ~ erwachen** (*geh*) to awake, to waken (from sleep); **den ewigen** *or* **letzten ~ schlafen** (*euph*) to sleep one's last sleep; **den Seinen gibt's der Herr im ~** the devil looks after his own; **es fällt mir nicht im ~(e) ein, das zu tun** I wouldn't dream of doing that; **das macht** *or* **tut** *or* **kann er im ~** (*fig inf*) he can do that in his sleep.

Schlaf-: **~anzug** *m* pyjamas *pl* (*Brit*), pajamas *pl* (*US*); **s~bedürftig** *adj* (*besonders*) **s~bedürftig sein** to need a lot of sleep; **Kinder sind s~bedürftiger als Erwachsene** children need more sleep than adults; **~bursche** *m* (*dated*) lodger (*who only has a bed*).

Schläfchen *nt* nap, snooze. **ein ~ machen** to have a nap *or* snooze.

Schlafcouch *f* studio couch, sofa bed.

Schläfe *f* -, -n temple. **graue ~n** greying temples.

schlafen *pret* **schlief**, *ptp* **geschlafen** **1** *vi* to sleep; (*nicht wach sein auch*) to be asleep; (*euph: tot sein*) to be asleep (*euph*); (*geh: Stadt, Land auch*) to be quiet, to slumber (*liter*); (*inf: nicht aufpassen*) (*bei bestimmter Gelegenheit*) to be asleep; (*immer*) not to pay attention. **er schläft immer noch** he's still asleep, he's still sleeping; **tief** *or* **fest ~** (*zu diesem Zeitpunkt*) to be fast *or* sound asleep; (*immer*) to be a deep *or* sound sleeper; **~ gehen** to go to bed; **sich ~ legen** to lie down to sleep; **jdn ~ legen** to put sb to bed; **schläfst du schon?** are you asleep?; **jetzt wird (aber) geschlafen!** go to sleep this minute; **lange ~** to sleep for a long time; (*spät aufstehen*) to sleep late, to have a long lie (in); **schlaf gut** *or* (*geh*) **wohl** sleep well; **hast du gut geschlafen?** did you sleep well?, did you have a good sleep?; **mittags** *or* **über Mittag ~** to have an afternoon nap; **wie ein Murmeltier** *or* **Bär** *or* **Sack** *or* **Stein** *or* **eine Ratte** (*all inf*) **schlafen** to sleep like a log; **bei jdm ~** to stay overnight with sb; **er kann nachts nicht mehr ~** (*fig*) he can't sleep nights; **das läßt ihn nicht ~** (*fig*) it preys on his mind, it gives him no peace; **darüber muß ich erst mal ~** (*fig: überdenken*) I'll have to sleep on it; **mit jdm ~** (*euph*) to sleep with sb; **sie schläft mit jedem** she sleeps around; **schlaf nicht!** wake up!

    2 *vr impers* **auf dieser Matratze schläft es sich schlecht** this mattress is terrible to sleep on.

Schlafenbein *nt* temporal bone.

schlafend 1 *adj* sleeping. **im ~en Zustand** asleep. **2** *adv* asleep. **sich ~ stellen** to pretend to be asleep.

Schlafengehen *nt* going to bed. **vor dem ~** before going to bed.

Schlafenszeit *f* bedtime.

Schlaf|entzug *m* sleep deprivation.

Schläfer(in *f*) *m* -s, - sleeper; (*fig*) dozy person (*inf*).

schläfern *vt impers* (*geh*) **mich/ihn schläfert** I'm/he's sleepy, I feel/he feels sleepy *or* drowsy.

schlaff *adj* limp; (*locker*) *Seil, Segel* loose, slack; *Moral* lax, loose; *Disziplin* lax; *Haut* flabby, loose; *Muskeln* flabby, floppy; (*erschöpft*) worn-out, shattered (*inf*), exhausted; (*energielos*) listless, floppy.

Schlaffheit *f siehe adj* limpness; looseness, slackness; laxity, looseness; laxity; flabbiness, looseness; flabbiness, floppiness; exhaustion; listlessness, floppiness.

Schlaf-: **~gelegenheit** *f* place to sleep; **wir haben ~gelegenheit für mehrere Leute** we can put up several people; **~gemach** *nt* (*liter*) bedchamber (*liter*).

Schlafittchen *nt:* **jdn am** *or* **beim ~ nehmen** *or* **kriegen** (*inf*) to take sb by the scruff of the neck; (*zurechtweisen*) to give sb a dressing down (*inf*).

Schlaf-: **~kammer** *f* (*dial*) bedroom; **~krankheit** *f* sleeping sickness; **~lied** *nt* lullaby; **s~los** *adj* (*lit, fig*) sleepless; **s~los liegen** to lie awake; **s~losigkeit** *f* sleeplessness, insomnia (*Med*); **sie verbrachte die folgenden Nächte in ~losigkeit** she spent the following nights unable to sleep; **~maus** *f* dormouse; **~mittel** *nt* sleeping drug *or* pill; (*fig iro*) soporific; **diese Zeitung ist das reinste ~mittel** this newspaper just sends you to sleep; **~mittelvergiftung** *f* (poisoning from an) overdose of sleeping pills, = barbiturate poisoning; **~mütze** *f* **(a)** nightcap; **(b)** (*fig*) dope (*inf*); **diese ~mützen im Parlament** that dozy lot in Parliament (*inf*); **s~mützig** *adj* (*inf*) dozy (*inf*), dopey (*inf*); **~mützigkeit** *f* doziness (*inf*), dopeyness (*inf*); **~pille** *f* (*inf*) sleeping pill; **~pulver** *nt* sleeping powder; **~raum** *m* dormitory, dorm (*inf*).

schläfrig *adj* sleepy; *Mensch auch* drowsy; (*fig auch: träge*) lethargic.

Schläfrigkeit *f siehe adj* sleepiness; drowsiness; lethargy.

Schlaf-: **~rock** *m* dressing-gown; **Äpfel im ~rock** baked apples in puff pastry; **Würstchen im ~rock** = sausage roll; **~saal** *m* dormitory; **~sack** *m* sleeping-bag; **~stadt** *f* dormitory town; **~stelle** *f* place to sleep; **~stube** *f* (*dial*) bedroom; **~sucht** *f* hypersomnia; **~tablette** *f* sleeping pill; **~trank** *m* (*old*) sleeping draught (*old*); (*hum inf: Alkohol*) nightcap; **s~trunken 1** *adj* (*geh*) drowsy, half asleep; **2** *adv* drowsily, half-asleep; **~wagen** *m* sleeping-car, sleeper; **~wagenschaffner** *m* sleeping-car attendant; **s~wandeln** *vi insep aux sein or haben* to sleepwalk, to walk in one's sleep, to somnambulate (*form*); **~wandler(in** *f*) *m* -s, - sleepwalker, somnambulist (*form*); **s~wandlerisch** *adj* (*geh*) sleepwalking *attr*, somnambulatory (*form*); **mit s~wandlerischer Sicherheit wählen, Fragen beantworten** intuitively, instinctively; **das Kind lief mit s~wandlerischer Sicherheit durch den dichten Verkehr** the child ran through the heavy traffic with instinctive assurance; **~zimmer** *nt* bedroom; **~zimmerblick** *m* (*hum inf*) come-to-bed eyes *pl* (*inf*); **~zimmergeschichte** *f* (*inf*) sexual adventure, bedroom antic (*inf*).

Schlag *m* -(e)s, ¨e (a) (*lit, fig*) blow; (*Faust~ auch*) punch; (*mit der Handfläche*) smack, slap; (*leichter*) pat; (*Handkanten~, Judo etc*) chop (*inf*); (*Ohrfeige*) cuff, clout; (*mit dem Fuß, Huf*) kick; (*Ftbl sl: Schuß*) shot; (*mit Rohrstock etc*) stroke; (*Peitschen~*) stroke, lash; (*einmaliges Klopfen*) knock; (*dumpf*) thump, thud; (*leichtes Pochen*) tap; (*Glocken~*) chime; (*Standuhr~*) stroke; (*von Metronom*) tick, beat; (*Gehirn~, ~anfall, Kolben~, Ruder~, Schwimmen, Tennis*) stroke; (*Herz~, Puls~, Trommel~, Wellen~*) beat; (*Blitz~*) bolt, stroke; (*Donner~*) clap; (*Strom~*) shock. **man hörte die ¨e des Hammers/der Trommeln** you could hear the clanging of the hammer/beating of the drums; **¨e kriegen** to get a hiding or thrashing or beating; **zum entscheidenden ~ ausholen** (*fig*) to strike the decisive blow; **~ auf ~** (*fig*) in quick succession, one after the other; **~ or s~** (*Aus*) **acht Uhr** (*inf*) at eight on the dot (*inf*), on the stroke of eight; **ein ~ ins Gesicht** (*lit, fig*) a slap in the face; **ein ~ ins Kontor** (*inf*) a nasty shock or surprise; **ein ~ ins Wasser** (*inf*) a washout (*inf*), a let-down (*inf*); **ein ~ aus heiterem Himmel** a bolt from the blue; **mit einem or auf einen ~** (*inf*) all at once; (*auf einmal, zugleich auch*) in one go; **mit einem ~ berühmt werden** to become famous overnight; **einen ~ arbeiten** (*inf*) to do a (little) spot of work; **die haben keinen ~ getan** (*inf*) they haven't done a stroke (of work); **einen ~ weghaben** (*sl*) (*blöd sein*) to have a screw loose (*inf*); (*betrunken sein*) to be tiddly (*inf*); **ihn hat der ~ getroffen** (*Med*) he had a stroke; **ich dachte, mich rührt or trifft der ~** (*inf*) I was flabbergasted (*inf*) or thunderstruck; **ich glaube, mich trifft der ~** I don't believe it; **wie vom ~ gerührt or getroffen sein** to be flabbergasted (*inf*) or thunderstruck (*inf*), to be knocked all of a heap (*inf*).

(b) (*inf: Wesensart*) type (of person *etc*). **vom ~ der Südländer sein** to be a Southern type; **vom gleichen ~ sein** to be cast in the same mould; (*pej*) to be tarred with the same brush; **vom alten ~** of the old school.

(c) (*Vogel~*) song.

(d) (*Wagen~*) door.

(e) (*Tauben~*) cote.

(f) (*Aus: ~sahne*) cream.

(g) (*inf: Portion*) helping.

(h) (*sl*) **er hat ~ bei Frauen** he has a way with the ladies.

Schlag-: **~abtausch** *m* (*Boxen*) exchange of blows; (*fig*) (*verbaler*) exchange; **~ader** *f* artery; **~anfall** *m* stroke; **s~artig** 1 *adj* sudden, abrupt; 2 *adv* suddenly; **~ball** *m* rounders *sing*; (*Ball*) rounders ball; **s~bar** *adj* beatable; **diese Mannschaft ist durchaus s~bar** this team is by no means invincible or unbeatable; **~baum** *m* barrier; **~bohrer** *m* percussion drill; **~bolzen** *m* firing pin.

Schläge *pl* of **Schlag**.

Schlägel *m* -s, - (*Min*) (miner's) hammer. **~ und Eisen** crossed hammers, miner's symbol.

schlagen *pret* **schlug**, *ptp* **geschlagen** 1 *vti* (a) to hit; (*hauen*) to beat; (*einmal zu~, treffen auch*) to strike; (*mit der flachen Hand*) to slap, to smack; (*leichter*) to pat; (*mit der Faust*) to punch; (*mit Schläger*) to hit; (*treten*) to kick; (*mit Hammer, Pickel etc*) **Nagel, Loch** to knock. **jdn bewußtlos ~** to knock sb out or unconscious; (*mit vielen Schlägen*) to beat sb unconscious; **etw in Stücke or kurz und klein ~** to smash sth up or to pieces; **nach jdm/etw ~** to hit out or lash out at sb; **um sich ~** to lash out; **mit dem Hammer an die Nagel ~** to hit the nail with the hammer; **mit der Faust an die Tür/auf den Tisch ~** to beat or thump on the door/table with one's fist; **gegen die Tür ~** to hammer on the door; **jdm or (rare) jdn auf die Schulter ~** to slap sb on the back; (*leichter*) to pat sb on the back; **jdm or (rare) jdn auf den Kopf ~** to hit sb on the head; **jdm ein Buch auf den Kopf ~** to hit sb on the head with a book; **jdm etw aus der Hand ~** to knock sth out of sb's hand; **jdm or (rare) jdn ins Gesicht ~** to hit/slap/punch sb in the face; **ihm schlug das Gewissen** his conscience pricked him; **einer Sache** (*dat*) **ins Gesicht ~** (*fig*) to be a slap in the face for sth; **das schlägt dem guten Geschmack ins Gesicht** that goes against all canons or standards of good taste; **siehe grün, Boden, Wahrheit etc.**

(b) **Teig, Eier** to beat; (*mit Schneebesen*) to whisk; **Sahne** to whip. **ein Ei in die Pfanne/die Suppe ~** to crack an egg into the pan/beat an egg into the soup; **etw durch ein Sieb ~** to rub sth through a sieve.

(c) (*läuten*) to chime. **Stunde** to strike. **die Uhr hat 12 geschlagen** the clock has struck 12; **eine geschlagene Stunde** a full hour; **wissen, was es or die Uhr or Glocke geschlagen hat** (*fig inf*) to know what's what (*inf*); **siehe dreizehn.**

(d) (*heftig flattern*) **mit den Flügeln ~, die Flügel ~** (*liter*) to beat or flap its wings.

(e) (*Chess*) to take, to capture.

2 *vt* (a) (*besiegen, übertreffen*) **Gegner, Rekord** to beat. **jdn in etw** (*dat*) **~** to beat sb at sth; **unsere Mannschaft schlug den Gegner** (*mit*) **2:1** our team beat their opponents (by) 2-1; **das schlägt alles bisher Dagewesene!** this or that beats everything!; **na ja, ehe ich mich ~ lasse!** (*hum inf*) yes, I don't mind if I do, I suppose you could twist my arm (*hum inf*); **sich geschlagen geben** to admit that one is beaten, to admit defeat.

(b) (*liter: treffen*) **das Schicksal schlug sie hart** fate dealt her a hard blow; **ein vom Schicksal geschlagener Mann** a man dogged by fate.

(c) (*Bibl: bestrafen*) to strike (down), to smite (*Bibl*). **mit Blindheit** (*lit, fig*)**/Dummheit geschlagen sein** to be blind/dumb.

(d) (*fällen*) to fell.

(e) (*fechten*) **Mensuren** to fight.

(f) (*liter: krallen, beißen*) **seine Fänge/Zähne in etw** (*acc*) **~** to sink one's talons/teeth into sth.

(g) (*Hunt: töten*) to kill.

(h) (*spielen*) **Trommel** to beat; (*liter*) **Harfe, Laute** to pluck, to play. **das S~ der Trommeln** the beat(ing) of the drums.

(i) (*prägen*) **Münzen** to mint, to coin; **Medaillen** *auch* to strike.

(j) (*hinzufügen*) to add (*auf +acc, zu to*); **Gebiet** to annexe.

(k) **in Verbindung mit n** *siehe auch dort.* **Kreis, Bogen** to describe; **Purzelbaum, Rad** to do; **Alarm, Funken** to raise; **Krach** to make. **Profit aus etw ~** to make profit from sth; **eine Schlacht ~** to fight a battle.

(l) **den Kragen nach oben ~** to turn up one's collar; **die Hände vors Gesicht ~** to cover one's face with one's hands.

(m) (*wickeln*) to wrap.

3 *vi* (a) (*Herz, Puls*) to beat; (*heftig*) to pound, to throb. **sein Puls schlug unregelmäßig** his pulse was irregular.

(b) *aux sein* (*auftreffen*) **mit dem Kopf auf/gegen etw** (*acc*) **~** to hit one's head on/against sth.

(c) *aux sein* (*gelangen*) **ein leises Wimmern schlug an sein Ohr** he could hear a faint whimpering.

(d) (*Regen*) to beat; (*Wellen auch*) to pound.

(e) *aux sein or haben* (*Flammen*) to shoot out (*aus of*); (*Rauch*) to pour out (*aus of*).

(f) (*Blitz*) to strike (*in etw* (*acc*) sth).

(g) (*singen: Nachtigall, Fink*) to sing.

(h) *aux sein* (*fig: ähneln*) **er schlägt sehr nach seinem Vater** he takes after his father a lot; *siehe* **Art.**

(i) (*betreffen*) **in jds Fach/Gebiet** (*acc*) **~** to be in sb's field/line.

(j) *aux sein* (*esp Med: in Mitleidenschaft ziehen*) **auf die Augen/Nieren etc ~** to affect the eyes/kidneys; **jdm auf die Augen etc ~** to affect sb's eyes etc.

4 *vr* (a) (*sich prügeln*) to fight; (*sich duellieren*) to duel (*auf +dat* with). **als Schuljunge habe ich mich oft geschlagen** I often had fights when I was a schoolboy; **sich mit jdm ~** to fight (with) sb, to have a fight with sb; (*duellieren*) to duel with sb; **sich um etw ~** (*lit, fig*) to fight over sth; **er schlägt sich nicht um die Arbeit** he's not too keen on work.

(b) (*sich selbst ~*) to hit or beat oneself.

(c) (*sich bewähren*) to do, to fare. **sich tapfer** or **gut ~** to make a good showing.

(d) (*sich begeben*) **sich nach rechts/links/Norden ~** to strike out to the left/right/for the North; **sich auf jds Seite ~** to side with sb; (*die Fronten wechseln*) to go over to sb; **sich zu einer Partei ~** to throw in one's lot with a party; *siehe* **Leben, Busch.**

(e) (*Mech*) **sich auf etw** (*acc*) **~** to affect sth.

schlagend *adj* (*treffend*) **Bemerkung, Vergleich** apt, appropriate; (*überzeugend*) **Beweis** striking, convincing. **etw ~ beweisen/widerlegen** to prove/refute sth convincingly; *siehe* **Verbindung, Wetter²**.

Schlager *m* -s, - (a) (*Mus*) pop-song; (*erfolgreich*) hit-song, hit.

(b) (*inf*) (*Erfolg*) hit; (*Waren*) bargain; (*Verkaufs~, Buch*) bestseller.

Schläger *m* -s, - (a) (*Tennis~, Federball~*) racquet (*Brit*), racket (*US*); (*Hockey~, Eishockey~*) stick; (*Golf~*) club; (*Kricket~, Baseball~*) bat; (*Tischtennis*) bat, paddle; (*Polo~*) mallet.

(b) (*Spieler*) (*Kricket*) batsman; (*Baseball*) batter.

(c) (*Raufbold*) thug, ruffian.

(d) (*Waffe*) straight-bladed sabre used by students in duelling bouts.

Schlägerbande *f* gang of thugs.

Schlägerei *f* fight, brawl.

Schlägerkartei *f* (*inf*) criminal records *pl*, police files *pl*.

Schlägermusik *f* pop music.

Schlägermütze *f* cap.

schlägern *vti* (*Aus*) **Bäume** to fell.

Schlager-: **~parade** *f* hit-parade; **~sänger** *m* pop singer; **~sendung** *f* pop music programme; **~text** *m* (pop music) lyrics *pl*; **~texter** *m* writer of pop music lyrics, lyricist.

Schlägertyp *m* (*inf*) thug.

Schlagetot *m* -s, -s (*old*) cutthroat.

Schlag-: **s~fertig** *adj* quick-witted; **~fertigkeit** *f* quick-wittedness; **~fluß** *m* (*obs*) *siehe* **~anfall**; **~instrument** *nt* percussion instrument; **~kraft** *f* (*lit, fig*) power; (*Boxen*) punch(ing power); (*Mil*) strike power; **s~kräftig** *adj* **Boxer, Armee, Argumente** powerful; **Beweise** clear-cut; **~licht** *nt* (*Art, Phot*) highlight; **ein bezeichnendes ~licht auf etw** (*acc*) **werfen** (*fig*) to highlight or spotlight sth; **s~lichtartig** *adj* etw **s~lichtartig beleuchten** to give a sudden insight into sth; **~loch** *nt* pothole; **~mann** *m, pl* **-männer** (*Rudern*) stroke; (*Baseball*) batsman; (*Baseball*) batter; **~obers** *nt* (*Aus*), **~rahm** *m* (*S Ger*) *siehe* **~sahne**; **~ring** *m* (a) knuckleduster; (b) (*Mus*) plectrum; **~sahne** *f* (whipping) cream; (*geschlagen*) whipped cream; **~schatten** *m* (*Art, Phot*) shadow (of person or object); **~seite** *f* (*Naut*) list; **~seite haben** (*Naut*) to be listing, to have a list; (*hum inf*) to be half-seas over (*inf*); **~stock** *m* (*form*) truncheon, baton, nightstick (*US*); **~stöcke einsetzen** to charge with batons; **~stockeinsatz** *m* (*form*) baton charge; **~werk** *nt* striking mechanism (of a clock); **~wetter** *nt* (*Min*) firedamp; **~wort** *nt* (a) (*Stichwort*) headword; (b) (*Parole*) catchword, slogan; **~wortkatalog** *m* subject catalogue; **~zeile** *f* headline; **~zeilen machen** (*inf*) to hit the headlines; **~zeug** *nt* drums *pl*; (*in Orchester*) percussion no *pl*; **~zeuger(in** *f*) *m* -s, - drummer; (*inf: im Orchester*) percussionist; **~zeugspieler** *m* percussionist.

Schlaks m -es, -e (N Ger inf) gangling or gawky youngster.
schlaksig (esp N Ger inf) **1** adj gangling, gawky. **2** adv in a gangling way, gawkily.
Schlamassel m or nt -s, - (inf) (Durcheinander) mix-up; (mißliche Lage) mess. **der** or **das (ganze)** ~ (Zeug) the whole lot or whole caboodle (inf); **da haben wir den** ~ now we're in a right mess (inf).
Schlamm m -(e)s, -e or ~e mud; (Schlick auch) sludge.
Schlammbad nt mudbath.
schlämmen vt (a) (reinigen) Hafenbecken to dredge; Kreide to wash. (b) (weißen) Wand to whitewash.
schlammig adj muddy; (schlickig auch) sludgy.
Schlämmkreide f whiting.
Schlammschlacht f (inf) mudbath.
schlampampen* vi (inf) siehe **schlemmen**.
Schlampe f -, -n (pej inf) slut (inf).
schlampen vi (inf) to be sloppy (in one's work). **bei einer Arbeit** ~ to do a piece of work sloppily; **die Behörden haben wieder einmal geschlampt** (once again) the authorities have done a sloppy job.
Schlamper(in f) m -s, - (S Ger inf) sloppy person; (unordentlich) untidy person.
Schlamperei f (inf) sloppiness; (schlechte Arbeit) sloppy work; (Unordentlichkeit) untidiness. **das ist eine** ~! that's a disgrace.
schlampig, schlampert (Aus, S Ger) adj (inf) sloppy, careless; Arbeit auch slipshod; (unordentlich) untidy; (liederlich) slovenly.
schlang pret of **schlingen**[1], **schlingen**[2].
Schlange f -, -n (a) snake, serpent (liter); (fig: Frau) Jezebel. **die** ~ (Astron) Serpens, the Serpent; **eine falsche** ~ a snake in the grass; **sich winden wie eine** ~ (fig) to go through all sorts of contortions.
(b) (Menschen~, Auto~) queue (Brit), line (US). ~ **stehen** to queue (up) (Brit), to stand in line (US).
(c) (Tech) coil.
schlängelig adj Weg winding.
Schlängellinie f wavy line.
schlängeln vr (Weg) to wind (its way), to snake; (Fluß auch) to meander; (Schlange) to wriggle. **sich um etw** ~ to wind around sth; **sich durch etw** ~ (fig) to worm one's way or wriggle through sth; **sich aus der Affäre** ~ (fig) to wriggle out of the situation; **eine geschlängelte Linie** a wavy line.
Schlangen-: s~artig adj snakelike; ~beschwörer m -s, - snake-charmer; ~biß m snakebite; ~brut f (old liter) brood of vipers (liter); ~fraß m (pej inf) muck no indef art; ~gezücht nt brood of vipers; ~gift nt snake venom or poison; s~haft adj snake-like; ~haut f snake's skin; (Leder) snakeskin; ~leder nt snakeskin; ~linie f (in) ~linien fahren to swerve about; ~mensch m contortionist.
Schlangestehen nt queuing (Brit), standing in line (US).
schlank adj slim; Hals, Bäume auch slender. ~ **werden** to slim; **ihr Kleid macht sie** ~ her dress makes her look slim; **Joghurt macht** ~ yoghurt is slimming or is good for the figure; **sich** ~ **machen** (fig) to breathe in, slim; **schlanke Linie**.
Schlankel m -s, -(n) (Aus inf) rogue, rascal.
Schlankheit f siehe adj slimness; slenderness.
Schlankheitskur f (Med) course of slimming treatment. **eine** ~ **machen/anfangen** to be/go on a diet.
schlankweg adv (inf) ablehnen, sagen point-blank, flatly.
Schlapfen m -s, - (Aus, S Ger: Pantoffel) slipper.
schlapp adj (inf) (erschöpft, kraftlos) worn-out, shattered (inf); (energielos) listless, floppy; (nach Krankheit etc) run-down; (feige) Haltung, Gesinnung, Mensch lily-livered (inf), yellow (inf). **sich** ~ **lachen** (inf) to laugh oneself silly.
Schlappe f -, -n (inf) set-back; (esp Sport) defeat. **eine** ~ **erleiden** or **einstecken (müssen)** to suffer a set-back/defeat; **jdm eine** ~ **beibringen** or **erteilen** to defeat sb.
schlappen 1 vi aux sein or haben (inf) (lose sitzen) to be baggy; (Schuhe) to flap. **2** vt (Tier) to lap.
Schlappen m -s, - (inf) slipper.
Schlappheit f (Erschöpfung) exhaustion, fatigue; (Energielosigkeit) listlessness, floppiness; (Feigheit) cowardice, yellowness (inf).
Schlapp-: ~hut m floppy hat; s~machen vi sep (inf) to wilt; (zusammenbrechen, ohnmächtig werden) to collapse; **die meisten Manager machen mit 40 s~** most managers are finished by the time they're 40; **Leute, die bei jeder Gelegenheit s~machen, können wir nicht gebrauchen** we can't use people who can't take it or who can't stand the pace (inf); ~ohr nt (hum: Kaninchen) bunny (rabbit) (inf); ~ohren pl floppy ears pl; ~schuh m (inf) slipper; ~schwanz m (pej inf) weakling, softy (inf).
Schlaraffenland nt Cockaigne, land of milk and honey.
schlau adj clever, smart; Mensch, Idee auch shrewd; (gerissen) cunning, crafty, wily; (nicht anstrengend) Leben, Posten easy, cushy (inf); Sprüche clever. **er ist ein** ~er Kopf he has a good head on his shoulders; **ein** ~er Bursche a crafty or cunning devil (inf); **sie tut immer so** ~ she always thinks she's so clever or smart; **ein** ~es Buch (inf) a clever book; **etw** ~ **anfangen** or **anstellen** to manage sth cleverly; **ich werde nicht** ~ **aus ihm/dieser Sache** I can't make him/it out; siehe **Fuchs**.
Schlaube f -, -n (dial) skin.
Schlauberger m -s, - (inf) clever-dick (inf), smart alec (inf).
Schlaubergerei f, no pl (iro inf) know-all attitude.
Schlauch m -(e)s, **Schläuche** (a) hose; (Garten~ auch) hosepipe; (Fahrrad~, Auto ~) (inner) tube; (Wein~ etc) skin. **das Zimmer ist ein richtiger** ~ the room is really narrow. (b) (inf: Strapaze) slog (inf), grind. (c) (sl: Übersetzungshilfe) crib (inf).

Schlauch-: s~artig adj tube-like, tubular; ~boot nt rubber dinghy.
schlauchen 1 vt (inf) (Reise, Arbeit etc) jdn to wear out; (Chef, Feldwebel etc) to drive hard. **2** vi (a) (inf: Kraft kosten) to wear you/one etc out; **das schlaucht** to take it out of you/one etc (inf). (b) (sl: schmarotzen) to scrounge (inf).
schlauchlos adj Reifen tubeless.
Schläue f -, no pl cunning, craftiness, slyness.
schlauerweise adv cleverly, shrewdly; (gerissen) craftily, cunningly, slyly. **wenn du das wußtest, hättest du mich** ~ **benachrichtigen können** if you'd had any sense, you could have informed me.
Schlaufe f -, -n (an Kleidungsstück, Schuh etc) loop; (Aufhänger) hanger.
Schlauheit, Schlauigkeit (rare) f siehe **schlau** cleverness, smartness; shrewdness; cunning, craftiness, guile; easiness; cushiness (inf); (Bemerkung) clever remark.
Schlaukopf m, **Schlaule** nt -s, - (S Ger inf), **Schlaumeier** m siehe **Schlauberger**.
Schlawiner m -s, - (hum inf) villain, rogue.
schlecht 1 adj (a) bad; Zustand, Aussprache, Geschmack, Zensur, Leistung auch poor; Qualität auch poor, inferior; Luft auch stale; Zeiten auch hard. **das S~e in der Welt/im Menschen** the evil in the world/in man; **das ist ein** ~er Scherz that is a dirty trick; **er ist in Latein** ~er als ich he is worse at Latin than I am; **sich zum S~en wenden** to take a turn for the worse; **nur S~es von jdm** or **über jdn sagen** not to have a good word to say for sb.
(b) pred (ungenießbar) off. **die Milch/das Fleisch ist** ~ **werden** milk/meat has gone off or is off; ~ **werden** to go off.
(c) (gesundheitlich etc) Zustand poor; Nieren, Herz bad; Durchblutung bad, poor. **jdm ist (es)** ~ sb feels sick or ill; **es ist zum S~werden** (fig inf) it makes or is enough to make you sick (inf); **in** ~er Verfassung sein to be in a bad way; ~ **aussehen** (Mensch) to look bad or sick or ill; (Lage) to look bad; **mit jdm/etw sieht es** ~ **aus** sb/sth looks in a bad way; **damit sieht es** ~ **aus** things look bad; siehe **schlechtgehen**.
2 adv (a) badly. **sich** ~ **vertragen** (Menschen) to get along badly; (Dinge, Farben etc) not to go well together; **die beiden können sich** ~ **leiden** the two of them don't get along (with each other); **an jdm** ~ **handeln** to do sb wrong, to wrong sb; ~ **über jdn sprechen/von jdm denken** to speak/think ill of sb.
(b) (mit Schwierigkeiten) hören, sehen badly; lernen, begreifen with difficulty. **er kann** ~ **nein sagen** he finds it hard to say no, he can't say no; **da kann man** ~ **nein sagen** you can hardly say no or it's hard to say no to that; **heute geht es** ~ today is not very convenient; **das läßt sich** ~ **machen, das geht** ~ that's not really possible or on (inf); **das läßt sich** ~ **vermeiden** that can't really be avoided; **er ist** ~ **zu verstehen** he is hard to understand; **sie kann sich** ~ **anpassen** she finds it difficult or hard to adjust; **sie kann ich** ~ **sagen** it's hard to say, I can't really say; **sie kann es sich** ~ **leisten, zu ...** she can ill afford to really say; **...; ich kann sie** ~ **sehen** I can't see her very well.
(c) in festen Redewendungen **auf jdn/etw** ~ **zu sprechen sein** not to have a good word to say for sb/sth; ~ **gerechnet** at the very least; ~ **und recht, mehr** ~ **als recht** (hum) after a fashion.
(d) (inf) **er hat nicht** ~ **gestaunt** he wasn't half surprised (inf).
schlecht-: ~beraten adj attr ill-advised; ~bezahlt adj attr low-paid, badly paid.
schlechterdings adv (völlig) absolutely; (nahezu) virtually.
schlecht-: ~gehen vi impers sep irreg aux sein **es geht jdm** ~ sb is in a bad way; (finanziell) sb is doing badly; **wenn er das erfährt, geht's dir** ~ if he hears about that you'll be for it (inf); **in der Prüfung ist es ihm** ~gegangen he did badly in the exam; ~gelaunt adj attr bad-tempered; ~hin adv (vollkommen) quite, absolutely; (als solches, in seiner Gesamtheit) as such, per se; **er gilt als** or **ist der romantische Komponist** ~hin he is the epitome of the Romantic composer; **Studenten/die deutsche Sprache** ~hin students/the German language as such or per se.
Schlechtigkeit f (a) no pl badness; (qualitativ auch) inferiority. (b) (schlechte Tat) misdeed.
Schlecht-: s~machen vt sep to denigrate, to run down; s~weg adv siehe s~hin; ~wetter nt bad weather; ~wettergeld nt bad-weather money or pay; ~wetterperiode f spell of bad weather.
Schleck m -s, -e (S Ger, Sw) sweets pl (Brit), candies pl (US). **das ist kein** ~ (Vergnügen) that's no fun.
schlecken (Aus, S Ger) **1** vti siehe **lecken**[2]. **2** vi (Süßigkeiten essen) to eat sweets (Brit) or candies (US). **Lust auf was zum S~ haben** to feel like eating something sweet.
Schleckerei f (Aus, S Ger) (a) no pl (das Lecken) licking. (b) no pl (das Naschen) eating sweet things. **die** ~ **der Kinder** the children eating sweet things. (c) (Leckerbissen) delicacy; (Süßigkeit) sweet (Brit), sweetie (Brit inf), candy (US).
Schleckermaul nt (hum inf) **sie ist ein richtiges** ~ she really has a sweet tooth.
schleckig adj (S Ger inf) fussy, finicky (about one's food).
Schlegel m -s, - (a) stick; (Trommel~ auch) drumstick. (b) (Min) miner's hammer. (c) (S Ger, Aus: Cook) leg; (von Geflügel auch) drumstick.
Schlehdorn m blackthorn, sloe.
Schlehe f -, -n sloe.
Schlei m -(e)s, -s siehe **Schleie**.
schleichen pret **schlich**, ptp **geschlichen 1** vi aux sein to creep; (heimlich auch) to sneak, to steal; (Fahrzeug) to crawl; (fig: Zeit) to crawl (by). **um das Haus** ~ to prowl around the house.
2 vr (a) to creep, to sneak, to steal; (fig: Mißtrauen) to enter. **sich in jds Vertrauen** ~ to worm one's way into sb's confidence; **sich in jds Herz** ~ (Zweifel etc) to enter sb's heart.

(b) (*Aus: weggehen*) to go away. **schleich dich** get lost (*inf*).

schleichend *adj attr* creeping; *Krankheit, Gift* insidious; *Fieber* lingering.

Schleicher *m* -s, - hypocrite.

Schleicherei *f* hypocrisy, insincerity.

Schleich-: ~**handel** *m* illicit trading (*mit* in); **der ~handel mit Waffen/Alkohol** gun-running/bootlegging; ~**händler** *m siehe* ~**handel** illicit trader; gun-runner/bootlegger; ~**pfad**, ~**weg** *m* secret *or* hidden path; **auf ~wegen** (*fig*) on the quiet, surreptitiously; ~**werbung** *f* a plug; ~**werbung vermeiden** to avoid giving plugs.

Schleie *f* -, -n (*Zool*) tench.

Schleier *m* -s, - (*lit, fig*) veil; (*von Wolken, Nebel auch*) haze. **das Photo hat einen ~** the photo is foggy *or* fogged; **die Berggipfel waren in ~ von Nebel gehüllt** the mountain tops were veiled in mist; **einen ~ vor den Augen haben** *or* **wie durch einen ~ sehen** to have a mist in front of one's eyes; **den ~ (des Geheimnisses) lüften** to lift the veil of secrecy; **einen ~ über etw** (*acc*) **ziehen** *or* **breiten** (*fig*) to draw a veil over sth; **der ~ des Vergessens** the veil of oblivion; **den ~ nehmen** (*liter*) to take the veil.

Schleier-: ~**eule** *f* barn owl; **s~haft** *adj* (*inf*) baffling, mysterious; **es ist mir völlig s~haft** it's a complete mystery to me; ~**schwanz** *m* goldfish; ~**tanz** *m* veil-dance.

Schleifbank *f* grinding machine.

Schleife *f* -, -n (a) loop (*auch Aviat, beim Schlittschuhlaufen*); (*Fluß~*) bow, horse-shoe bend; (*Straßen~*) twisty bend. **(b)** (*von Band*) bow; (*Schuh~*) bow(-knot); (*Fliege*) bow tie; (*Kranz~*) ribbon.

schleifen[1] **1** *vt* **(a)** (*lit, fig*) to drag; (*ziehen auch*) to haul; (*Mus*) *Töne, Noten* to slur. **jdn vor Gericht ~** (*fig*) to drag *or* haul sb into court; **jdn ins Konzert ~** (*hum inf*) to drag sb along to a concert.
(b) (*niederreißen*) to raze (to the ground).
2 *vi aux sein or haben* to trail, to drag.
(b) (*reiben*) to rub. **die Kupplung ~ lassen** (*Aut*) to slip the clutch; **die Zügel ~ lassen** (*lit, fig*) to slacken the reins.

schleifen[2] *pret* **schliff**, *ptp* **geschliffen** *vt* **(a)** *Rasiermesser, Messer, Schere* to sharpen, to whet; *Beil, Sense auch* to grind; *Werkstück, Linse* to grind; *Parkett* to sand; *Edelstein, Glas* to cut; *siehe* **geschliffen. (b)** (*inf: drillen*) **jdn ~** to drill sb hard.

Schleifer *m* -s, - **(a)** grinder; (*Edelstein~*) cutter. **(b)** (*Mus*) slurred note. **(c)** (*Mil sl*) slave-driver.

Schleiferei *f* **(a)** *no pl siehe* **schleifen**[2] **(a)** grinding, whetting; grinding; sanding; cutting. **(b)** (*Werkstatt*) grinding shop. **(c)** (*Mil sl: Drill*) square-bashing (*inf*).

Schleif-: ~**lack** *m* (coloured) lacquer *or* varnish; ~**lackmöbel** *pl* lacquered furniture *sing*; ~**maschine** *f* grinding machine; ~**papier** *nt* abrasive paper; ~**rad** *nt*, ~**scheibe** *f* grinding wheel; ~**stein** *m* grinding stone, grindstone; **er sitzt da wie ein Affe auf dem ~stein** (*sl*) he looks a proper idiot *or* a proper Charlie (*inf*) sitting there.

Schleifung *f* razing.

Schleim *m* -(e)s, -e **(a)** slime; (*Med*) mucus; (*in Atemorganen auch*) phlegm; (*Bot*) mucilage. **(b)** (*Cook*) gruel.

Schleim-: ~**absonderung** *f* mucous secretion; ~**beutel** *m* (*Physiol*) bursa (*spec*); ~**drüse** *f* mucous gland; (*von Schnecken etc*) slime gland.

schleimen *vi* to leave a coating or film; (*fig inf: schmeicheln*) to fawn, to crawl (*inf*).

Schleimhaut *f* mucous membrane.

schleimig *adj* **(a)** slimy; (*Med*) mucous; (*Bot*) mucilaginous. **(b)** (*pej: unterwürfig*) slimy (*inf*).

Schleimigkeit *f* (*pej*) sliminess (*inf*).

Schleim-: **s~lösend** *adj* expectorant; ~**pilz** *m* slime mould *or* fungus; ~**scheißer** *m* (*sl*) bootlicker (*inf*), arse-licker (*vulg*); ~**suppe** *f* gruel.

schleißen *pret* **schleißte** *or* **schliß**, *ptp* **geschleißt** *or* **geschlissen 1** *vt* (*rare*) *Späne* to split off; *Federn* to strip. **2** *vi aux sein* (*obs*) to fall apart, to wear out.

schleißig (*Aus*) **1** *adj* (*lit, fig*) shabby; *Essen* poor. **2** *adv* badly; (*moralisch auch*) shabbily. **mir geht's ~** I feel rotten.

schlemmen 1 *vi* (*üppig essen*) to feast; to have a feast; (*üppig leben*) to live it up. **2** *vt* to feast on.

Schlemmer(in *f*) *m* -s, - gourmet, bon vivant.

Schlemmerei *f* feasting; (*Mahl*) feast.

schlemmerhaft, schlemmerisch *adj* gourmandizing, gluttonous (*pej*).

Schlemmermahl *nt* feast, banquet.

Schlemmertum *nt* feasting.

schlendern *vi aux sein* to stroll, to amble.

Schlendrian *m* -(e)s, *no pl* (*inf*) casualness, inefficiency; (*Trott*) rut.

Schlenker *m* -s, - swerve. **einen ~ machen** to swerve.

schlenk(e)rig *adj* swinging, flapping. **er geht ~** he flaps along.

schlenkern 1 *vti* to swing, to dangle. **mit den Beinen ~, die Beine ~** to swing *or* dangle one's legs. **2** *vi* (*Auto*) to swerve, to sway.

schlenzen *vi* (*Sport*) to scoop.

Schlepp *m* (*Naut, fig*): **jdn/etw in ~ nehmen** to take sb/sth in tow; **in** *or* **im ~ haben** to have in tow.

Schleppdampfer *m* tug(boat).

Schleppe *f* -, -n (a) (*von Kleid*) train. (b) (·*Hunt*) drag.

schleppen 1 *vt* (*tragen*) *Lasten* to lug, to schlepp (*US sl*); (*zerren*) to drag, to haul, to schlepp (*US sl*); *Auto, Schiff* to tow; (*fig*) to drag; (*inf*) *Kleidung* to wear continually. **jdn vor den Richter ~** to haul sb (up) before the judge.
2 *vi* (*inf: nachschleifen*) to drag, to trail.
3 *vr* to drag *or* haul oneself; (*Verhandlungen etc*) to drag on.

schleppend *adj Gang* dragging, shuffling; *Bedienung, Abfertigung* sluggish, slow; *Absatz, Nachfrage* slack, sluggish;

Gesang dragging, slow. **wehmütig ~e Klänge** melancholy languorous sounds; **die Unterhaltung kam nur ~ in Gang** conversation was very slow to start *or* started sluggishly; **nach ein paar Stunden wurde die Unterhaltung immer ~er** after a few hours the conversation began to drag more and more.

Schlepp(en)kleid *nt* dress with a train.

Schleppenträger *m* trainbearer.

Schlepper *m* -s, - **(a)** (*Aut*) tractor. **(b)** (*Naut*) tug. **(c)** (*sl: Zuhälter, für Lokal*) tout. **(d)** (*Univ sl*) somebody who writes an exam paper for somebody else.

Schlepperei *f* (*inf*) lugging around *or* about.

Schlepp-: ~**kahn** *m* lighter, (canal) barge; ~**lift** *m* ski tow; ~**lohn** *m* (*Naut*) towage; ~**netz** *nt* trawl (net); ~**schiff** *nt* tug(boat); ~**tau** *nt* (*Naut*) tow rope; (*Aviat*) dragrope, trail rope; **ein Schiff/jdn ins ~tau nehmen** to take a ship/sb in tow; ~**zug** *m* string of barges pulled by a tug.

Schlesien [-iən] *nt* -s Silesia.

Schlesier(in *f*) [-iɐ, -iərɪn] *m* -s, - Silesian.

schlesisch *adj* Silesian.

Schleuder *f* -, -n **(a)** (*Waffe*) sling; (*Wurfmaschine*) catapult, onager; (*Zwille*) catapult, slingshot (*US*). **(b)** (*Zentrifuge*) centrifuge; (*für Honig*) extractor; (*Wäsche~*) spin-drier.

Schleuder-: ~**ball** *m* (*Sport*) **(a)** heavy leather ball with a strap attached, swung round the head and then thrown; **(b)** *no pl* a game using such a ball; ~**honig** *m* extracted honey; ~**maschine** *f* (*Wurfmaschine*) catapult, onager; (*für Milch etc*) centrifuge; (*für Honig*) extractor.

schleudern 1 *vti* **(a)** (*werfen*) to hurl, to sling, to fling. **jdm etw ins Gesicht** *or* **an den Kopf ~** to hurl *or* fling sth in sb's face.
(b) (*Tech*) to centrifuge, to spin; *Honig* to extract; *Wäsche* to spin-dry. **die Maschine schleudert nicht mehr** the machine isn't spinning *or* extracting.
2 *vi aux sein or haben* (*Aut*) to skid. **ins S~ kommen** *or* **geraten** to go into a skid; (*fig inf*) to run into trouble.

Schleuder-: ~**preis** *m* giveaway price, throwaway price; **immer noch die alten ~preise** we're still practically giving it/them away; ~**sitz** *m* (*Aviat*) ejection *or* ejector seat; (*fig*) hot seat; ~**spur** *f* skidmark; ~**start** *m* (*Aviat*) catapult start; ~**ware** *f* cut-price goods *pl*, cheap goods *pl*.

schleunig *adj attr usu superl* prompt, speedy; *Schritte* quick, rapid. **nur ~stes Eingreifen kann jetzt helfen** only immediate measures can help now.

schleunigst *adv* at once, straight away, immediately. **verschwinde, aber ~!** beat it, on the double!; **ein Bier, aber ~!** a beer, and make it snappy!

Schleuse *f* -, -n (*für Schiffe*) lock; (*zur Regulierung des Wasserlaufs*) sluice, floodgate; (*für Abwasser*) sluice. **der Himmel öffnete seine ~n** (*liter*) the floodgates of heaven opened, the rain sluiced down.

schleusen *vt Schiffe* to pass through a lock, to lock; *Wasser* to channel; (*langsam*) *Menschen* to filter; *Antrag* to channel; (*fig: heimlich*) to smuggle. **er wurde in den Saal geschleust** he was smuggled into the hall.

Schleusen-: ~**geld** *nt* lock dues *pl*, lockage; ~**kammer** *f* (lock) basin; ~**meister** *m* lockmaster; ~**tor** *nt* (*für Schiffe*) lock gate; (*zur Regulierung des Wasserlaufs*) sluice gate, floodgate; ~**wärter** *m* lock keeper.

Schleusung *f* lockage, locking. **bei der ~ größerer Schiffe** when putting bigger ships through the locks.

Schlich *m* -(e)s, -e *usu pl* ruse, trick, wile *usu pl*. **alle ~e kennen** to know all the tricks; **jdm auf** *or* **hinter die ~e kommen** to catch on to sb, to get on to sb, to get wise to sb.

schlich *pret* of **schleichen**.

schlicht *adj* simple. **die ~e Wahrheit/Tatsache** the plain *or* simple truth/fact; ~ **und einfach** plain and simple; **das ist ~ und einfach nicht wahr** that's just simply not true; **der ~e Menschenverstand** basic common sense; **das geht über den ~en Menschenverstand** this is beyond the normal human mind *or* beyond human comprehension; **er sagte ~ und ergreifend nein** he said quite simply no; **diese Gedichte sind ~ und ergreifend** (*iro*) these poems are not exactly brilliant; **unser Abschied war ~ und ergreifend** our parting was short and sweet; **der Roman endet ~ und ergreifend mit der Hochzeit der beiden** the novel ends typically enough with the two getting married.

schlichten *vti* **(a)** *Streit* (*vermitteln*) to mediate, to arbitrate (*esp Ind*); (*beilegen*) to settle. **Ruritanien soll zwischen den beiden Ländern ~** Ruritania is to mediate between the two countries; **er wollte ~d in den Streit eingreifen** he wanted to intervene in the quarrel (to settle it).
(b) (*glätten*) *Werkzeug, Leder, Gewebe* to dress; *Holz* to smooth (off).

Schlichter(in *f*) *m* -s, - mediator; (*Ind*) arbitrator.

Schlichtfeile *f* smooth-cut file.

Schlichtheit *f* simplicity.

Schlichthobel *m* smoothing plane.

Schlichtung *f siehe vti* **(a)** mediation, arbitration; settlement.

Schlichtungs-: ~**ausschuß** *m* arbitration *or* conciliation commission; ~**stelle** *f* arbitration *or* conciliation board; ~**verhandlungen** *pl* arbitration (negotiations); ~**versuch** *m* attempt at mediation *or* arbitration.

Schlick *m* -(e)s, -e silt, ooze, mud; (*Öl~*) slick.

schlickig *adj* muddy, slimy.

schliddern *vi aux haben or sein* (*N Ger*) *siehe* **schlittern**.

schlief *pret* of **schlafen**.

Schliere *f* -, -n streak, schlieren *pl* (*Tech*).

schließbar *adj* (*rare*) closable; (*zuschließbar*) lockable.

Schließe *f* -, -n fastening, fastener.

schließen *pret* **schloß**, *ptp* **geschlossen 1** *vt* **(a)** (*zumachen*) to close, to shut; (*verriegeln*) to bolt; (*Betrieb einstellen*) to close *or* shut down; *Stromkreis* to close. eine Lücke ~ (*lit*) to close a gap; (*fig auch*) to fill a gap; die Reihen ~ (*Mil*) to close ranks.

(b) (*beenden*) *Versammlung* to close, to conclude, to wind up; *Brief* to conclude, to close.

(c) (*eingehen*) *Vertrag, Bündnis* to conclude; *Frieden auch* to make; *Bündnis auch* to enter into; *Freundschaft* to form. wo wurde Ihre Ehe geschlossen? where did your marriage take place?; wer hat Ihre Ehe geschlossen? who married you?

(d) (*geh: umfassen*) etw in sich (*dat*) ~ (*lit, fig*) to contain sth, to include sth; (*indirekt*) to imply; jdn in die Arme ~ to embrace sb; laß dich in die Arme ~ let me embrace you; jdn/etw in sein Herz ~ to take sb/sth to one's heart.

(e) (*befestigen*) etw an etw (*acc*) ~ to fasten sth to sth; daran schloß er eine Bemerkung he added a remark (to this).

2 *vr* to close, to shut; (*Wunde*) to close; (*fig geh: Wunde*) to heal. daran schließt sich eine Diskussion this is followed by a discussion; sich um etw ~ to close around sth.

3 *vi* (a) to close, to shut; (*Betrieb einstellen*) to close *or* shut down; (*Schlüssel*) to fit. die Tür schließt nicht the door doesn't *or* won't close *or* shut; „geschlossen" "closed".

(b) (*enden*) to close, to conclude; (*St Ex*) to close. leider muß ich jetzt ~ (*in Brief*) I'm afraid I must conclude *or* close now; die Börse schloß munter the market closed on a lively note.

(c) (*schlußfolgern*) to infer. aus etw auf etw (*acc*) ~ to infer sth from sth; auf etw (*acc*) ~ lassen to indicate sth, to suggest sth; von sich auf andere ~ to judge others by one's own standards; *siehe* geschlossen.

Schließer *m* -s, - (*inf*) (a) jailer, warder. (b) (*Schnappschloß*) springlock.

Schließ-: ~fach *nt* left-luggage locker; (*Post~*) post-office box, PO box; (*Bank~*) safe-deposit box; ~korb *m* hamper.

schließlich *adv* (*endlich*) in the end, finally, eventually; (*immerhin*) after all. er kam ~ doch he came after all; ~ und endlich at long last; ~ und endlich bist du doch kein Kind mehr after all you're not a child any more.

Schließmuskel *m* (*Anat*) sphincter.

Schließung *f* (a) (*das Schließen*) closing, shutting; (*Betriebseinstellung*) closure.

(b) (*Beendigung*) (*einer Versammlung*) closing, breaking-up; (*von Debatte etc*) conclusion, closing; (*Geschäftsschluß*) closing(-time); (*Parl*) closure.

(c) (*Vereinbarung*) (*von Frieden, Vertrag, Ehe*) conclusion; (*von Bündnis auch*) forming.

Schliff *m* -(e)s, -e (*von Glas, von Edelstein*) (*Prozeß*) cutting; (*Ergebnis*) cut; (*fig: Umgangsformen*) refinement, polish. jdm ~ beibringen *or* geben to give sb some polish *or* refinement; einer Sache/jdm den letzten ~ geben (*fig*) to put the finishing touch(es) to sth/to perfect sb.

schliff *pret of* schleifen².

schlimm *adj* (a) (*moralisch*) bad, wicked; (*unartig auch*) naughty. es gibt S~ere als ihn there are worse than him; ein ~er Bösewicht (*old*) an out-and-out villain; Sie sind ja ein ganz S~er! you are naughty *or* wicked.

(b) (*inf: krank, entzündet*) bad.

(c) (*übel*) bad; *Krankheit auch* nasty, *Wunde auch* nasty, ugly; *Nachricht auch* awful, terrible. sich ~ verletzen to hurt oneself badly; ~, ~! terrible, terrible!; das war ~ that was awful *or* terrible; es ist ~, wie schlecht sie aussieht it's awful how bad she looks; mit der neuen Frisur siehst du ~ aus you look awful with that new hairdo; ~ genug, daß ... it is/was bad enough that ...; das finde ich nicht ~ I don't find that so bad; eine ~e Geschichte (*inf*) a nasty state of affairs; eine ~e Zeit bad times (*inf*); das ist halb so/nicht so ~! that's not so bad!, it doesn't matter!; er ist ~ dran (*inf*) he's in a bad way; zu Anfang (um ihn) things aren't looking too good (for him); zu Anfang war es ~ für ihn in the beginning he had a hard time of it; ist es ~ or etwas S~es? is it bad?; wenn's weiter nichts ~ kommt if things are really bad; wenn es nichts S~eres ist! if that's all it is!; es gibt S~eres it or things could be worse; es hätte ~er kommen können it or things could have been worse; ~er kann es nicht mehr werden things can hardly get any worse; um so or desto ~er all the worse; im ~sten Fall if the worst comes to the worst; das S~ste the worst; was aber das S~ste ist, ... but the worst of it is that ...; das S~ste liegt hinter uns the worst (of it) is behind us.

schlimmstenfalls *adv* at (the) worst. ~ wird er nur sein Geld verlieren at worst, he will only lose his money; ~ kann ich dir £100 leihen if the worst comes to the worst I can lend you £100.

Schlinge *f* -, -n loop; (*an Galgen*) noose; (*Med: Armbinde*) sling; (*Falle*) snare. jdm in die ~ gehen (*lit, fig*) to fall into sb's trap; ~n legen to set snares; den Kopf or sich aus der ~ ziehen (*fig*) to get out of a tight spot; (bei jdm) die ~ zuziehen (*fig*) to tighten the noose (on sb).

Schlingel *m* -s, - rascal.

schlingen¹ *pret* schlang, *ptp* geschlungen (*geh*) 1 *vt* (*binden*) *Knoten* to tie; (*umbinden*) *Schal* to wrap; (*flechten auch*) to plait. die Arme um jdn ~ to wrap one's arms around sb, to hug sb. 2 *vr* sich um etw ~ to coil (itself) around sth; (*Pflanze auch*) to twine (itself) around sth.

schlingen² *pret* schlang, *ptp* geschlungen *vi* to gobble, to gulp, to bolt one's food.

Schlingerbewegung *f* rolling (motion).

schlingern *vi* (*Schiff*) to roll; (*fig*) to lurch from side to side.

Schlinggewächs *nt*, **Schlingpflanze** *f* creeper.

Schlips *m* -es, -e tie, necktie (*US*). mit ~ und Kragen (*inf*) wearing a collar and tie; jdm auf den ~ treten (*inf*) to tread on sb's toes; sich auf den ~ getreten fühlen (*inf*) to feel offended, to be put out (*inf*).

Schlips-: ~knoten *m* knot (in a tie); ~nadel *f* tiepin.

---

schliß *pret of* schleißen.

Schlitten *m* -s, - (a) sledge, sled; (*Pferde~*) sleigh; (*Rodel~*) toboggan. ~ fahren to go tobogganing; mit jdm ~ fahren (*inf*) to have sb on the carpet (*inf*), to give sb a bawling out (*inf*).

(b) (*Tech*) (*Schreibmaschinen~*) carriage; (*zum Stapellauf*) cradle.

(c) (*sl: Auto*) car, motor (*inf*).

Schlitten-: ~bahn *f siehe* Rodelbahn; ~fahren *nt* sledging; (*Rodeln*) tobogganing; (*mit Pferde~ etc*) sleighing; ~fahrt *f* sledge ride; (*mit Rodel*) toboggan ride; (*mit Pferde~ etc*) sleigh ride; ~partie *f* sleigh ride.

Schlitterbahn *f* slide.

schlittern *vi* (a) *aux sein or haben* (*absichtlich*) to slide. (b) *aux sein* (*ausrutschen*) to slide, to slip; (*Wagen*) to skid; (*fig*) to slide, to stumble. in den Konkurs/Krieg ~ to slide into bankruptcy/war.

Schlittschuh *m* (ice-)skate. ~ laufen or fahren (*inf*) to (ice-)skate.

Schlittschuh-: ~bahn *f siehe* Eisbahn; ~laufen *nt* (ice-)skating; ~läufer(in *f*) *m* (ice-)skater.

Schlitz *m* -es, -e slit; (*Einwurf~*) slot; (*Hosen~*) fly, flies *pl*; (*Kleider~*) slit; (*Jackett~*) vent.

Schlitz-: ~auge *nt* slit or slant eye; (*pej: Chinese*) Chink (*pej*); s~äugig *adj* slit- or slant-eyed; er grinste s~äugig he grinned a slant- or slit-eyed grin.

schlitzen *vt* to slit.

Schlitz-: ~ohr *nt* (*fig*) sly fox; s~ohrig *adj* (*fig*) shifty, crafty; ~verschluß *m* (*Phot*) focal-plane shutter.

schlohweiß *adj Haare* snow-white.

schloß *pret of* schließen.

Schloß *nt* -sses, ̈sser (a) castle; (*Palast*) palace; (*großes Herrschaftshaus*) mansion, stately home; (*in Frankreich*) château. ~sser und Burgen castles and stately homes; ̈sser im Mond (*fig*) castles in the air, castles in Spain.

(b) (*Tür~, Gewehr~ etc*) lock; (*Vorhänge~*) padlock; (*an Handtasche etc*) fastener, clasp. ins ~ fallen to lock (itself); die Tür ins ~ werfen to slam the door shut; hinter ~ und Riegel sitzen/bringen to be/put behind bars.

Schloß-: s~artig *adj* palatial; ~bau *m* (*Vorgang*) building of a castle/of castles etc; (b) (*Architektur von Schlössern*) castle etc building; (c) (*Anlage*) castle etc; ~berg *m* castle etc hill; ~besitzer *m* owner of a castle etc.

Schlößchen *nt dim of* Schloß small castle etc.

Schlosser *m* -s, - fitter, metalworker; (*für Schlösser*) locksmith.

Schlosserei *f* (a) (~handwerk) metalworking. (b) (~werkstatt) metalworking shop.

Schlosser-: ~handwerk *nt* metalworking; ~meister *m* master fitter; ~werkstatt *f* metalworking shop.

Schloß-: ~garten *m* castle etc gardens *pl*; ~herr *m* owner of a castle etc; (*Adliger*) lord of the castle; ~hof *m* courtyard; ~hund *m* (*obs: Kettenhund*) watchdog; heulen wie ein ~hund (*inf*) to howl one's head off; ~kapelle *f* castle etc chapel; ~park *m* castle etc grounds *pl*, estate; ~platz *m* castle etc square; ~vogt *m* (*Hist*) castellan; ~wache *f* castle etc guard.

Schlot *m* -(e)s, -e or (*rare*) ̈e (a) (*Schornstein*) chimney (stack), smokestack; (*Naut, Rail auch*) funnel; (*von Vulkan*) chimney. rauchen or qualmen wie ein ~ (*inf*) to smoke like a chimney (*inf*). (b) (*inf: Flegel*) slob (*inf*), peasant (*inf*).

Schlotbaron *m* (*dated pej*) industrial magnate or baron.

schlott(e)rig *adj* (*inf*) (a) (*zitternd*) shivering *attr*; (*vor Angst, Erschöpfung*) trembling *attr*. (b) *Kleider* baggy.

schlottern *vi* (a) (*zittern*) to shiver; (*vor Angst, Erschöpfung*) to tremble. an allen Gliedern ~ to shake all over; er schlotterte mit den Knien he was shaking at the knees, his knees were knocking. (b) (*Kleider*) to hang loose, to be baggy.

Schlucht *f* -, -en gorge, ravine.

schluchzen *vti* (*lit, fig*) to sob.

Schluchzer *m* -s, - sob.

Schluck *m* -(e)s, -e or (*rare*) ̈e drink; (*ein bißchen*) drop; (*das Schlucken*) swallow; (*großer*) gulp; (*kleiner*) sip. der erste ~ war mir ungewohnt the first mouthful tasted strange; er stürzte das Bier in einem ~ herunter he downed the beer in one gulp or in one go; etw ~ für ~ austrinken to drink every drop; einen (*kräftigen*) ~ nehmen to take a (long) drink or swig (*inf*).

Schluck|auf *m* -s, *no pl* hiccups *pl*. einen/den ~ haben to have (the) hiccups.

Schluckbeschwerden *pl* difficulties *pl* in swallowing.

Schlückchen *nt dim of* Schluck drop; (*von Alkohol auch*) nip.

schlückchenweise *adv* in short sips. ~ trinken to sip.

schlucken 1 *vt* (a) to swallow; (*hastig*) to gulp down; (*sl*) *Alkohol* to booze (*inf*).

(b) (*inf: absorbieren, kosten*) to swallow up; *Benzin, Öl* to guzzle.

(c) (*inf: hinnehmen*) *Beleidigung* to swallow, to take.

(d) (*inf: glauben*) to swallow (*inf*).

2 *vi* to swallow; (*hastig*) to gulp; (*sl*) to booze (*inf*). da mußte ich erst mal trocken or dreimal ~ (*inf*) I had to take a deep breath or to count to ten.

Schlucken *m* -s, *no pl siehe* Schluckauf.

Schlucker *m* -s, - (*inf*): armer ~ poor devil.

Schluck-: ~impfung *f* oral vaccination; ~specht *m* (*inf*) boozer (*inf*); s~weise *adv* in sips.

Schluder|arbeit *f* (*inf*) botched-up or sloppy job (*inf*).

Schluderei *f* (*inf*) sloppiness, bungling. das ist eine ~! how sloppy can you get!

schlud(e)rig *adj* (*inf*) *Arbeit* sloppy, slipshod *no adv*. ~ arbeiten to work sloppily or in a slipshod way.

Schlud(e)rigkeit *f* (*inf*) sloppiness.

schludern (*inf*) 1 *vt* to skimp. das ist geschludert! this is a sloppy piece of work! **2** *vi* to do sloppy work, to work sloppily.

schludrig *adj* (*inf*) *siehe* **schlud(e)rig**.

schlug *pret of* **schlagen**.

Schlummer *m* -s, *no pl* (*liter*) (light) slumber (*liter*).

Schlummerlied *nt* (*geh*) cradlesong, lullaby.

schlummern *vi* (*geh*) to slumber (*liter*); (*fig auch*) to lie dormant.

Schlummerrolle *f* bolster.

Schlund *m* -(e)s, -̈e (*Anat*) pharynx, gullet; (*fig liter*) maw (*liter*).

Schlunze *f* -, -n (*dial*) *siehe* **Schlampe**.

schlunzen *vi* (*dial*) *siehe* **schludern**.

Schlupf *m* -(e)s, *no pl* (*Elec, Naut*) slip; (*Tech*) slip, slippage.

schlüpfen *vi aux sein* to slip; (*Küken*) to hatch (out).

Schlüpfer *m* -s, - panties *pl*, knickers *pl*.

Schlupfloch *nt* hole, gap; (*Versteck*) hideout, lair; (*fig*) loophole.

schlüpfrig *adj* (**a**) slippery. (**b**) (*fig*) *Bemerkung* lewd, risqué.

Schlüpfrigkeit *f siehe adj* slipperiness; lewdness.

Schlupf-: ~**wespe** *f* ichneumon (fly) (*form*); ~**winkel** *m* hiding place; (*fig*) quiet corner.

schlürfen 1 *vt* to slurp; (*mit Genuß*) to savour. **er schlürfte die letzten Tropfen** he slurped up the last drops. **2** *vi* to slurp.

Schluß *m* -sses, -̈sse *no pl* (*Ende*) end; (*eines Romans, Gedichts, Theaterstücks auch*) ending, conclusion; (*hinterer Teil*) back, end, rear. ~! that'll do!, stop!; ~ **für heute!** that's it or all for today, that'll do for today; ~ **damit!** stop it!, that'll do!; **... und damit** ~! ... and that's that!, ... and that's the end of it!; **nun ist aber** ~!, ~ **jetzt!** that's enough now!; **dann ist** ~ that'll be it; ~ **folgt** to be concluded; ~ **haben** (*inf*) to be closed *or* shut; **am/zum** ~ **des Jahres** at the end of the year; **zum** ~ **sangen wir ...** at the end we sang ...; **zum** ~ **hat sie's dann doch erlaubt** finally *or* in the end she allowed it after all; **bis zum** ~ **bleiben** to stay to the end; **zum** ~ **kommen** to conclude; **zum** ~ **möchte ich noch darauf hinweisen, daß ...** to conclude *or* in conclusion I would like to point out that ...; ~ **machen** (*inf*) (*aufhören*) to finish, to call it a day (*inf*); (*zumachen*) to close, to shut; (*Selbstmord begehen*) to put an end to oneself, to end it all; (*Freundschaft beenden*) to break *or* call it off; **ich muß** ~ **machen** (*in Brief*) I'll have to finish off now; (*am Telefon*) I'll have to go now; **mit etw** ~ **machen** to stop *or* end sth, to finish with sth (*inf*); **mit der Arbeit** ~ **machen** to stop *or* leave off work; **mit jdm** ~ **machen** to finish with sb, to break with sb. (**b**) *no pl* (*das Schließen*) closing. (**c**) (*Folgerung*) conclusion. **aus etw den** ~ **ziehen, daß ...** to draw the conclusion *or* to conclude from sth that ...; **ich ziehe meine** ~̈**sse daraus!** I can draw my own conclusions! (**d**) (*Tech*) **die Tür hat einen guten/schlechten** ~ the door is a good/bad fit. (**e**) (*Mus*) cadence. (**f**) (*St Ex*) minimum amount allowed for dealing.

Schluß-: ~**abrechnung** *f* final statement *or* account; ~**akkord** *m* final chord; ~**akt** *m* (*lit, fig*) final act; ~**ansprache** *f* closing address *or* speech; ~**bemerkung** *f* final observation, concluding remark; ~**bestimmung** *f* final clause; ~**bilanz** *f* (*lit*) final balance (sheet); (*fig*) final position.

Schlüssel *m* -s, - (*lit, fig*) key; (*Chiffren*~ *auch*) cipher; (*Sch: Lösungsheft*) key; (*Tech*) spanner, wrench; (*Verteilungs*~) ratio (of distribution); (*Mus*) clef.

Schlüssel-: ~**bein** *nt* collarbone, clavicle (*form*); ~**blume** *f* cowslip; ~**brett** *nt* keyboard; ~**bund** *m* key ring; bunch of keys; ~**erlebnis** *nt* (*Psych*) crucial experience; **s**~**fertig** *adj* *Neubau* ready for moving in to, ready for occupancy; ~**figur** *f* key figure; ~**gewalt** *f* (*Jur*) a wife's power to represent her husband in matters concerning the household; (*Eccl*) power of the keys; ~**industrie** *f* key industry; ~**kind** *nt* (*inf*) latchkey child (*inf*); ~**loch** *nt* keyhole; ~**position** *f* key position; ~**ring** *m* key ring; ~**roman** *m* roman à clef; ~**stellung** *f* key position; ~**tasche** *f* key wallet; ~**wort** *nt* keyword; (*für Schloß*) combination, code.

Schluß-: **s**~**endlich** *adv* (*geh*) to conclude, in conclusion *or* closing; ~**ergebnis** *nt* final result.

schlußfolgern* *vi insep* to conclude, to infer.

Schluß-: ~**folgerung** *f* conclusion, inference; ~**formel** *f* (*in Brief*) complimentary close; (*bei Vertrag*) final clause.

schlüssig *adj* conclusive. **sich** (*dat*) (**über etw** *acc*) ~ **sein** to have made up one's mind (about sth).

Schlüssigkeit *f* conclusiveness.

Schluß-: ~**kapitel** *nt* concluding *or* final chapter; ~**kommuniqué** *nt* final communiqué; ~**kurs** *m* (*St Ex*) closing prices *pl*; ~**läufer** *m* last runner; (*in Staffel*) anchor (man); ~**licht** *nt* taillight, tail lamp; (*inf: bei Rennen etc*) tailender, back marker; ~**licht der Tabelle/in der Klasse sein** to be bottom of the table/class; **das** ~**licht bilden** (*fig*) (*beim Laufen etc*) to bring up the rear; (*in einer Tabelle*) to be bottom of the league; ~**mann** *m*, *pl* -**männer** (*Sport sl*) goalie (*inf*), keeper (*inf*); ~**note** *f siehe* ~**schein**; ~**notierung** *f* (*St Ex*) closing quotation; ~**pfiff** *m* final whistle; ~**phase** *f* final stages *pl*; ~**punkt** *m*: **einen** ~**punkt unter etw** (*acc*) **setzen** to round off sth; (*bei etwas Unangenehmem*) to write sth off; ~**rechnung** *f* (**a**) (*Comm*) final account *or* settlement; (**b**) (*Math: Dreisatz*) computation using the rule of three; ~**runde** *f* (*Boxen etc, fig*) final round; (*in Rennsport, Leichtathletik*) final lap; (*bei Ausscheidungskämpfen*) final heat; (*Endausscheidung*) final(s); ~**rundenteilnehmer** *m* finalist; ~**satz** *m* closing *or* concluding sentence; (*Logik*) conclusion; (*Mus*) last *or* final movement; ~**schein** *m* (*Comm*) contract note; ~**sprung** *m* standing jump; (*beim Turnen*) finishing jump; ~**stand** *m* final result; (*von Spiel auch*) final score; ~**stein** *m* (*Archit, fig*) keystone; ~**strich** *m* (*fig*) final stroke; **einen** ~**strich**

unter etw (*acc*) **ziehen** to consider sth finished; ~**verkauf** *m* (end-of-season) sale; ~**wort** *nt* closing words *or* remarks *pl*; (~**rede**) closing *or* concluding speech; (*Nachwort*) postscript.

Schmach *f* -, *no pl* (*geh*) disgrace, ignominy, shame *no indef art*; (*Demütigung auch*) humiliation. **etw als** ~ **empfinden** to see sth as a disgrace; **to feel humiliated by sth**; **jdm eine** ~ **antun** to bring shame upon sb.

schmachbedeckt *adj* (*liter*) covered in shame; humiliated.

schmachten *vi* (*geh*) (**a**) (*leiden*) to languish. **vor Durst** ~ to be parched; **vor Hunger** ~ to starve. (**b**) (*sich sehnen*) **nach jdm/etw** ~ to pine *or* yearn for sb/sth; **jdn** ~ **lassen** to torment sb.

schmachtend *adj* yearning, soulful; *Liebhaber* languishing.

Schmachtfetzen *m* (*dated hum*) tear-jerker (*inf*).

schmächtig *adj* slight, frail, weedy (*pej*).

Schmächtigkeit *f* slightness, frailty, weediness (*pej*).

Schmacht-: ~**lappen** *m* (*dated hum*) Romeo (*inf*); ~**locke** *f* (*dated hum*) kiss-curl.

schmachvoll *adj* (*geh*) *Niederlage* ignominious; (*demütigend auch*) *Frieden* humiliating.

schmackhaft *adj* (*wohlschmeckend*) palatable, tasty; (*appetitanregend*) appetizing. **jdm etw** ~ **machen** (*fig*) to make sth palatable to sb.

Schmackhaftigkeit *f* palatability.

Schmäh *m* -s, -(s) (*Aus inf*) (*Trick*) con (*inf*), dodge (*inf*). **einen** ~ **führen** (*Witze machen*) to clown around; **jdn am** ~ **halten** to make a fool out of sb.

Schmähbrief *m* defamatory *or* abusive letter.

schmähen *vti* (*geh*) to abuse, to revile (*liter*), to vituperate against (*liter*).

schmählich *adj* (*geh*) ignominious, shameful; (*demütigend*) humiliating.

Schmäh-: ~**rede** *f* (*geh*) invective, diatribe; ~**reden** (**gegen jdn**) **führen** to launch diatribes (against sb); ~**schrift** *f* defamatory piece of writing; (*Satire*) lampoon; ~**sucht** *f* (*liter*) love of slander; **s**~**süchtig** *adj* (*liter*) vituperative (*liter*).

Schmähung *f* (*geh*) abuse, vituperation (*liter*). (**gegen jdn**) ~**en und Verwünschungen ausstoßen** to hurl abuse (at sb).

Schmähwort *nt*, *pl* -e (*liter*) abusive word, term of abuse. ~**e** abuse *sing*, invective *sing*.

schmal *adj*, *comp* -er *or* -̈er, *superl* -ste(r, s) *or* -̈ste(r, s), *adv superl* **am** -sten *or* -̈sten (**a**) narrow; *Hüfte, Taille auch, Mensch* slim, slender; *Band, Buch* slim; *Gelenke, Lippen* thin. **er ist sehr** ~ **geworden** he has got very thin. (**b**) (*fig: karg*) meagre, slender. ~**e Kost** slender fare.

schmalbrüstig *adj* narrow-chested; (*fig*) limited.

schmälen *vt* (*obs, dial*) to abuse.

schmälern *vt* to diminish, to reduce, to lessen; (*heruntermachen*) to detract from, to belittle, to diminish.

Schmälerung *f siehe vt* diminishing, reduction, lessening; detraction, belittlement. **eine** ~ **seines Ruhms** a detraction from *or* diminishing of his fame.

Schmal-: ~**film** *m* cine-film; ~**filmfreund** *m* home-movie enthusiast *or* buff (*inf*); (*euph*) blue-movie freak (*inf*); ~**filmkamera** *f* cine-camera; ~**hans** *m* (*inf*): **bei ihnen/uns ist** ~**hans Küchenmeister** their/our cupboard is nearly always bare; **s**~**lippig** *adj* thin-lipped; **s**~**schult(e)rig** *adj* narrow-shouldered; ~**seite** *f* narrow side; ~**spur** *f* (*Rail*) narrow gauge; ~**spur-** *in cpds* (*pej*) small-time; ~**spurbahn** *f* narrow-gauge railway; **s**~**spurig** *adj* (*Rail*) *Strecke* narrow-gauge; **s**~**spurig fahren** to run on narrow gauge.

Schmalz¹ *nt* -es, -e (**a**) fat; (*Schweine*~) lard; (*Braten*~) dripping. (**b**) *siehe* **Ohrenschmalz**.

Schmalz² *m* -es, *no pl* (*pej inf*) schmaltz (*inf*).

schmalzig *adj* (*pej inf*) schmaltzy (*inf*), slushy (*inf*).

Schmalzler *m* -s, - (*S Ger*) snuff.

Schmankerl *nt* -s, -n (*S Ger, Aus*) *siehe* **Leckerbissen**.

Schmant *m* -(e)s, *no pl* (*dial*) (**a**) (*Sahne*) cream. (**b**) (*Matsch*) muck.

schmarotzen* *vi* to sponge, to scrounge, to freeload (*esp US*) (**bei** on, off); (*Biol*) to be parasitic (**bei** on).

Schmarotzer(in *f*) *m* -s, - (*Biol*) parasite; (*fig auch*) sponger, scrounger, freeloader (*esp US*).

schmarotzerhaft, schmarotzerisch *adj* (*Biol, fig*) parasitic.

Schmarotzer-: ~**pflanze** *f* parasitic plant; ~**tier** *nt* (*animal*) parasite; ~**tum** *nt*, *no pl* (*Biol, fig*) parasitism.

Schmarre *f* -, -n (*dial*) cut, gash; (*Narbe*) scar.

Schmarr(e)n *m* -s, - (*S Ger, Aus*) (*Cook*) pancake cut up into small pieces. (**b**) (*inf: Quatsch*) rubbish, tripe (*inf*). **das geht dich einen** ~ **an!** that's none of your business!

Schmatz *m* -es, -e (*inf: Kuß*) smacker.

schmatzen *vi* to eat noisily. **er aß** ~**d seine Suppe** he slurped his soup; **schmatz nicht so!** don't make so much noise when you eat!; **mit den Lippen** ~ to smack one's lips; **Oma küßte das Kind** ~**d** grandma gave the child a real smacker of a kiss.

schmauchen 1 *vt* to puff away at. **2** *vi* to puff away.

Schmaus *m* -es, **Schmäuse** (*dated*) feast.

schmausen (*geh*) **1** *vi* to feast. **2** *vt* to feast on.

schmecken 1 *vi* (**a**) (*Geschmack haben*) to taste (**nach** of); (*gut* ~) to be good, to taste good *or* lovely; (*probieren auch*) to have a taste. **ihm schmeckt es** (*gut finden*) he likes it; (*gut haben*) he likes his food; **ihm schmeckt es nicht** (*keinen Appetit*) he's lost his appetite, he's off his food; **das schmeckt ihm nicht** (*lit, fig*) he doesn't like it; **die Arbeit schmeckt ihm nicht** this work doesn't agree with him, he has no taste for this work; **wie schmeckt die Ehe?** how does marriage agree with you?; **nach etw** ~ (*fig*) to smack of sth; **das schmeckt nach nichts** it's tasteless; (*ist fad*) **das schmeckt nach mehr!** (*inf*) it tastes more-ish (*hum inf*); **schmeckt es (Ihnen)?** do you like it?, is it good?; **are you enjoying your food** *or* **meal?** (*esp form*); **das hat ge-**

schmeckt that was good; **und das schmeckt!** and it tastes so good, and it's so good; **das schmeckt nicht (gut)** it doesn't taste good or nice; **es schmeckt mir ausgezeichnet** it is or tastes really excellent; **Hauptsache, es schmeckt** (inf) the main thing is it tastes nice; **es sich ~ lassen** to tuck in.
(b) (S Ger, Aus, Sw: riechen) to smell.
2 vt **(a)** (probieren auch) to have a taste of. **etw zu ~ bekommen** (fig inf) to have a taste of sth.
(b) (S Ger, Aus, Sw: riechen) to smell; (fig: ahnen) to sense.

Schmeichelei f flattery; (Komplimente auch) flattering remark or compliment. **so eine ~!** such flattery!

schmeichelhaft adj flattering; Bemerkung auch complimentary.

schmeicheln vi **(a)** to flatter (jdm sb); (um etw zu erreichen auch) to butter up (inf) (jdm sb). **es schmeichelt mir, daß ...** it flatters me that ..., I find it flattering that ...; **... sagte sie ~d ...** she wheedled; **sich** (dat)**~ ...** (geh) to flatter oneself (that) ...
(b) (verschönen) to flatter. **das Bild ist aber geschmeichelt!** the picture is very flattering.
(c) mit jdm ~ to caress or fondle sb.

Schmeichelwort nt, pl -e (geh) flattery, honeyed word.

Schmeichler(in f) m -s, - flatterer; (Kriecher) sycophant, fawner.

schmeichlerisch adj flattering; (lobhudelnd auch) unctuous, fawning, sycophantic.

schmeißen pret **schmiß,** ptp **geschmissen** (inf) **1** vt **(a)** (werfen) to sling, to chuck (inf), to fling; Tür to slam. **sich auf etw** (acc)**~** to throw oneself into sth; **die Frauen schmissen sich auf die Sonderangebote** the women made a rush at the special offers; **sich jdm an den Hals ~** (fig) to throw oneself at sb; **er schmiß sich mutig zwischen die beiden** he courageously flung or threw or hurled himself between the two.
(b) (spendieren) **eine Runde** or **Lage ~** to stand a round; **eine Party ~** (sl) to throw a party.
(c) (managen) **den Laden ~** to run the (whole) show; **die Sache ~** to handle it.
2 vi (werfen) to throw, to chuck (inf). **mit Steinen ~** to throw or chuck (inf) stones; **mit etw um sich ~** to throw sth about, to chuck sth around (inf); **mit Fremdwörtern um sich ~** to bandy loanwords or foreign words about.

Schmeißfliege f bluebottle.

Schmelz m -(e)s, -e (Glasur) glaze; (Zahn~) enamel; (geh) (einer Farbe) lustre, glow; (Wohllaut) melodiousness, mellifluousness.

Schmelz-: **s~bar** adj fusible, meltable; **Eisen ist leicht s~bar** iron is easily melted or melts easily; **~barkeit** f fusibility.

Schmelze f -, -n **(a)** (Metal) melt. **(b)** (Schmelzen) melting; (Metal: von Erz) smelting. **(c)** (Schmelzhütte) smelting plant or works sing or pl.

schmelzen pret **schmolz,** ptp **geschmolzen 1** vi auch sein (lit, fig: erweichen) to melt; (fig: schwinden auch) to melt away. **es ist ihr gelungen, sein hartes Herz zum S~ zu bringen** she succeeded in melting his heart of stone. **2** vt Metall, Fett to melt; Erz to smelt.

schmelzend 1 prp of **schmelzen. 2** adj (geh) Gesang, Ton, Stimme mellifluous.

Schmelzerei f siehe **Schmelzhütte.**

Schmelz-: **~farbe** f (Tech) vitrifiable pigment or colour; **~glas** nt enamel; **~hütte** f smelting plant or works sing or pl; **~käse** m cheese spread; **~ofen** m melting furnace; (für Erze) smelting furnace; **~punkt** m melting point; **~tiegel** m (lit, fig) melting pot; **~wärme** f (Metal) heat of fusion; **~wasser** nt melted snow and ice; (Geog, Phys) meltwater.

Schmer m or nt -s, no pl (old, dial) pork fat.

Schmer-: **~bauch** m (inf) paunch, potbelly; **s~bäuchig** adj (inf) paunchy, potbellied.

Schmerle f -, -n loach.

Schmerz m -es, -en pain pl rare; (Kummer auch) grief no pl. **ihre ~en** her pain; **dumpfer ~** ache; **stechender ~** stabbing pain; **sie schrie vor ~en** she cried out in pain; **~en haben** to be in pain; **~en in der Nierengegend/in den Ohren/im Hals haben** to have a pain in the kidneys/to have ear-ache/to have a sore throat; **wo haben Sie ~en?** where does it hurt?, where's the pain?; **wenn der Patient wieder ~en bekommt** ... if the patient starts feeling pain again ...; **von dem Essen habe ich ~en im Leib bekommen** the meal gave me a stomach ache; **jdm ~en bereiten** to cause sb pain; (seelisch auch) to pain sb; **mit ~en** (fig) regretfully; **jdn/etw mit ~en erwarten** to wait impatiently for sb/sth; **unter ~en** painfully; (fig) regretfully; **jdn mit ~(en) erfüllen** (fig) to grieve or hurt sb.

Schmerz-: **s~betäubend** adj pain-killing; **s~empfindlich** adj Mensch sensitive to pain; Wunde, Körperteil tender; **~empfindlichkeit** f siehe adj sensitivity to pain; tenderness.
-schmerzen pl in cpds pain in the ...; (Bauch~, Ohren~, Kopf~) -ache; (Hals~, Gelenk~) sore ...

schmerzen (geh) **1** vt to hurt, to pain; (körperlich) to hurt.
2 vi to hurt; (Wunde etc) to be sore; (Kopf, Bauch auch) to ache. **mir schmerzt der Kopf** my head aches; **es schmerzt** (lit, fig) it hurts; **eine ~de Stelle** a painful spot or area; **eine ~de Stille** a painful silence.

Schmerzens-: **~geld** nt (Jur) damages pl; **~laut** m (geh) cry of pain; **~schrei** m scream of pain.

Schmerz-: **s~erfüllt** adj (geh) racked with pain; (seelisch) grief-stricken; **s~frei** adj free of pain; Operation painless; **s~haft** adj (lit, fig) painful; **s~lich** adj (geh) painful; Lächeln sad; **es ist mir sehr s~lich, Ihnen mitteilen zu müssen, daß ... it** is my painful duty to inform you that ...; **s~lindernd** adj pain-relieving, analgesic; **~linderung** f relief or alleviation of pain; **s~los** adj (lit, fig) painless; siehe kurz; **s~loser** less painful; **~losigkeit** f (lit, fig) painlessness; **~mittel** nt pain-killing

drug, pain-killer; **~schwelle** f pain threshold; **s~stillend** adj pain-killing, pain relieving, analgesic (Med); **s~stillendes Mittel** pain-killing drug, pain-killer, analgesic (Med); **~tablette** f pain-killer, ≈ aspirin (inf); **s~unempfindlich** adj insensitive to pain; Körperteil auch numb; **s~verzerrt** adj pain-racked, agonized; **s~voll** adj (fig) painful.

Schmetterball m smash.

Schmetterling m (Zool, inf: Schwimmart) butterfly. **kannst du ~ schwimmen?** can you do the butterfly?

Schmetterlings-: **~blütler** m -s, - **die ~blütler** the papilionaceae (spec); **ein ~blütler** a member of the papilionaceae family (spec); **~netz** nt butterfly net; **~stil** m butterfly stroke.

schmettern 1 vt **(a)** (schleudern) to smash; Tür to slam; (Sport) Ball to smash. **etw in Stücke ~** to smash sth to pieces.
(b) Lied to bellow out; (Vogel) to sing, to warble.
2 vi **(a)** (Sport) to smash, to hit a smash.
(b) (Trompete etc) to blare (out); (Sänger) to bellow; (Vogel) to sing, to warble.

Schmetterschlag m (Sport) smash.

Schmied m -(e)s, -e (black)smith; siehe **Glück.**

schmiedbar adj malleable.

Schmiede f -, -n smithy, forge.

Schmiede-: **~arbeit** f (das Schmieden) forging; (Gegenstand) piece of wrought-iron work; **~eisen** nt wrought iron; **s~eisern** adj wrought-iron; **~hammer** m blacksmith's hammer; **~kunst** f skill in wrought-iron work.

schmieden vt to forge (zu into); (fig: zusammenfügen auch) to mould; (ersinnen) Plan to hatch, to concoct; (hum) Verse to concoct. **geschmiedet sein** (Gartentür etc) to be made of wrought-iron; **jdn in Ketten ~** (liter) to bind sb in chains.

schmiegen 1 vr sich an jdn ~ to cuddle or snuggle up to sb; **sich an/in etw** (acc)**~** to nestle or snuggle into sth; **die Weinberge/Häuser ~ sich an die sanften Hänge** the vineyards/houses nestle into the gentle slopes; **sich um etw ~** to hang gracefully on sth; (Haare) to fall gracefully round sth.
2 vt **etw an/in etw** (acc)**~** to nestle sth into sth; **etw um etw ~** to wrap sth around sth; **die an den Felsen geschmiegte Kapelle** the chapel nestled or nestling in the cliffs.

schmiegsam adj supple; Stoff soft; (fig: anpassungsfähig) adaptable, flexible.

Schmiegsamkeit f siehe adj suppleness; softness; adaptability, flexibility.

Schmiere f -, -n **(a)** (inf) grease; (Salbe) ointment; (feuchter Schmutz auch) mud; (pej: Schminke) paint; (Aufstrich) spread.
(b) (pej) (Wanderbühne) (troop of) barnstormers; (schlechtes Theater) flea-pit.
(c) (sl) **~ stehen** to be the look-out, to keep cave (dated Brit Sch sl).

schmieren 1 vt **(a)** (streichen) to smear; Butter, Aufstrich to spread; Brot to butter; Salbe, Make-up to rub in (in +acc -to); (einfetten, ölen) to grease; (Tech) Achsen, Gelenke etc to grease, to lubricate. **es geht** or **läuft wie geschmiert** it's going like clockwork; **jdm eine ~** (inf) to clout sb one (inf).
(b) (pej: schreiben) to scrawl.
(c) (inf: bestechen) **jdn ~** to grease sb's palm (inf).
2 vi **(a)** (pej) (schreiben) to scrawl; (malen) to daub.
(b) (Stift, Radiergummi, Scheibenwischer) to smear.
(c) (inf: bestechen) to give a bribe/bribes.

Schmieren-: **~komödiant** m (pej) ham (actor); **~komödie** f (pej) slapstick farce, pantomime; (fig) pantomime, farce; **~schauspieler** m barnstormer; (pej) ham (actor); **~theater** nt (pej) (troop of) barnstormers; (schlechtes Theater) flea-pit.

Schmierer(in f) m -s, - **(a)** (pej inf) scrawler, scribbler; (von Parolen) slogan dauber; (in Toiletten, an Gebäuden) graffiti writer; (Maler) dauber; (Autor, Journalist) hack, scribbler. **(b)** (Aus Sch) crib.

Schmiererei f (pej inf) (Geschriebenes) scrawl, scribble; (Parolen etc) graffiti pl; (Malerei) daubing; (Schriftstellerei) scribbling; (das Schmieren von Parolen etc) scrawling, scribbling; (von Stift, Scheibenwischer etc) smearing.

Schmierestehen nt (sl) keeping look-out.

Schmier-: **~fett** nt (lubricating) grease; **~fink** m (pej) **(a)** (Autor, Journalist) hack, scribbler; (Skandaljournalist) muckraker (inf); **(b)** (Schüler) messy writer, scrawler; **~geld** nt (inf) bribe, bribe-money; **~heft** nt jotter, rough-book.

schmierig adj greasy; Restaurant auch grimy; (fig) (unanständig) dirty, filthy; (schleimig) greasy, smarmy (inf).

Schmier-: **~käse** m (dated) cheese spread; **~mittel** nt lubricant; **~öl** nt lubricating oil; **~papier** nt rough or jotting paper; **~seife** f soft soap.

Schmierung f lubrication.

Schmierzettel m piece of rough or jotting paper.

schmilz imper sing of **schmelzen.**

Schminke f -, -n make-up.

schminken 1 vt to make up. **sich** (dat) **die Lippen/Augen ~** to put on lipstick/eye make-up. **2** vr to make oneself up, to put on make-up. **sich selten/zu stark ~** to wear make-up rarely/to wear too much make-up.

Schmink-: **~koffer** m vanity case; **~täschchen** nt make-up bag; **~tisch** m dressing table.

Schmirgel m -s, no pl emery.

schmirgeln 1 vt to sand, to rub down. **2** vi to sand.

Schmirgel-: **~papier** nt sandpaper; **~scheibe** f sanding disc.

Schmiß m -sses, -sse **(a)** (Fechtwunde) gash, wound; (Narbe) duelling scar. **(b)** (dated: Schwung) dash, élan. **~ haben** (Musik etc) to go with a swing; (Mensch) to have go (inf).

schmiß pret of **schmeißen.**

schmissig adj (dated) dashing; Musik auch spirited.

Schmock m -(e)s, -e or -s (pej) hack (inf).

Schmok m -s, no pl (N Ger) smoke.
schmöken vti (N Ger) to smoke.
Schmöker m -s, - book (usu of light literature); (dick) tome.
schmökern (inf) **1** vi to bury oneself in a book; (in Büchern blättern) to browse. **2** vt to bury oneself in.
schmollen vi to pout; (gekränkt sein) to sulk. **mit jdm ~** to be annoyed with sb.
Schmoll-: ~**mund** m pout; **einen** ~**mund machen** to pout; ~**winkel** m (inf) **im** ~**winkel sitzen** to have the sulks (inf); **sich in den** ~**winkel zurückziehen** to go off into a corner to sulk.
schmolz pret of schmelzen.
Schmonzes m -, (dated) balderdash (dated), tripe (inf).
Schmorbraten m pot-roast.
schmoren **1** vt to braise; Braten auch to pot-roast. **2** vi **(a)** (Cook) to braise; (inf: schwitzen) to roast, to swelter. **jdn (im eigenen Saft or Fett) ~ lassen** to leave sb to stew (in his/her own juice). **(b)** (unbearbeitet liegen) to lie there.
Schmorfleisch nt (Cook) braising steak; (Braten) pot roast.
Schmu m -s, no pl (inf) cheating; (esp mit Geld auch) fiddling (inf). **das ist ~!** that's a cheat or a fiddle! (inf); ~ **machen** to cheat; to fiddle (inf); **bei der Abrechnung/Prüfung ~ machen** to fiddle the expenses/cheat in the exam.
schmuck adj (dated) Haus etc neat, tidy; Schiff neat, trim; Bursche, Mädel smart, spruce; Paar smart. **sich ~ machen** to spruce oneself up.
Schmuck m -(e)s, (rare) -e **(a)** (~stücke) jewellery (Brit) no pl, jewelry no pl.
(b) (Verzierung) decoration; (fig) embellishment. **der ~ am Christbaum** the decorations on the Christmas tree; **im** ~ **der Blumen/Fahnen** (liter) decked with flowers/flags; **der Baum stand im** ~ **seiner Blüten** (liter) the tree was bedecked with blossom; **Natürlichkeit ist der schönste** ~ **eines Mädchens** naturalness is the greatest adornment a girl can have.
schmücken **1** vt to decorate, to adorn; Rede to embellish. **die mit Blumenkränzen geschmückten Tänzerinnen** the dancers adorned with garlands of flowers; **mit Juwelen geschmückt** bejewelled; ~**des Beiwerk/Beiwort** embellishment.
2 vr (zum Fest etc) (Mensch) to adorn oneself; (Stadt) to be decorated. **sich mit Blumenkränzen** ~ to garland oneself with flowers; siehe fremd.
Schmuck-: ~**gegenstand** m ornament; (Ring etc) piece of jewellery; ~**kassette** f, ~**kästchen** nt, ~**kasten** m jewellery box; **ihr Haus war ein** ~**kästchen** her house was a picture; **s~los** adj plain; Fassade unadorned; Einrichtung, Stil auch simple; (fig) Stil, Prosa etc simple, unadorned; ~**losigkeit** f siehe adj plainness; unadornedness; simplicity; simplicity, unadornedness; ~**sachen** pl jewellery (Brit) sing, jewelry sing; ~**stein** m (Edelstein) precious stone, gem; (Halbedelstein) semi-precious stone; ~**stück** nt (Ring etc) piece of jewellery; (~gegenstand) ornament; (fig: Prachtstück) gem; (fig inf) (Frau) better half (inf); (Freundin, als Anrede) sweetheart (inf); ~**waren** pl jewellery (Brit) sing, jewelry sing.
Schmuddel m -s, no pl (N Ger inf) (Schmutz) mess; (auf Straße) dirt, mud.
Schmuddelei f (inf) mess no pl; (schlechtes Arbeiten) messy work; (schlechte Arbeit) messy piece of work.
schmudd(e)lig adj messy; (schmutzig auch) dirty; (schmierig, unsauber) filthy; (schlampig) Bedienung sloppy; Frau, Schüler sloppy, slovenly.
Schmuggel m -s, no pl smuggling. ~ **treiben** to smuggle; **der** ~ **von Heroin** heroin smuggling.
Schmuggelei f smuggling no pl. **seine kleinen** ~**en** his small-scale smuggling.
schmuggeln vti (lit, fig) to smuggle. **mit etw** ~ to smuggle sth.
Schmuggelgut nt -s, no pl smuggling.
Schmuggelware f smuggled goods pl, contraband no pl.
Schmuggler(in f) m -s, - smuggler. ~ **von Rauschgift/Waffen** drug-smuggler/arms smuggler, gun-runner.
Schmuggler-: ~**bande** f smuggling ring, ring of smugglers; ~**pfad** m smugglers' path.
schmunzeln vi to smile.
Schmunzeln nt -s, no pl smile.
Schmus m -es, no pl (inf) (Unsinn) nonsense; (Schmeicheleien) soft soap (inf). ~ **erzählen** to talk nonsense; to soft soap sb (inf).
schmusen vi (inf) **(a)** (zärtlich sein) to cuddle; (mit Freund, Freundin auch) to canoodle (inf). **mit jdm** ~ to cuddle up to, to canoodle with sb (inf). **(b)** (schmeicheln) to soft-soap sb (inf).
Schmuser m -s, - **(a)** (zärtlicher Mensch) affectionate person. **er ist ein kleiner** ~ he likes a cuddle. **(b)** (Schmeichler) soft-soaper (inf), flatterer.
Schmutz m -es, no pl **(a)** dirt; (Schlamm auch) mud. **die Handwerker haben viel** ~ **gemacht** the workmen have made a lot of mess; **sie leben in** ~ they live in real squalor; **der Stoff nimmt leicht** ~ **an** the material dirties easily.
(b) (fig) filth, dirt, smut. ~ **und Schund** obscene or offensive material; **jdn/etw in den** ~ **ziehen or zerren** to drag sb/sth through the mud; siehe bewerfen.
Schmutz-: ~**blatt** nt (Typ) half-title (page); ~**bürste** f stiff brush.
schmutzen vi (inf) to dirty.
Schmutz-: ~**fänger** m dust trap; ~**farbe** f (dated) dirty colour; ~**fink** m (inf) (unsauberer Mensch) dirty slob (inf); (Kind) mucky pup (inf); (fig) (Mann) dirty old man; (Journalist) muck-raker (inf); ~**fleck** m dirty mark.
schmutzig adj (unsauber, unanständig) dirty, filthy; Geschäft dirty, sordid; Witze, Geschichten auch smutty. **sich** ~ **machen** to get oneself dirty; **Geld ist doch nicht** ~ money is money no matter where it comes from; ~**e Wäsche (vor anderen Leuten) waschen** to wash one's dirty linen in public; ~**e Reden führen** to use bad or foul language.

Schmutzigkeit f siehe adj dirtiness, filthiness; dirtiness, sordidness; smuttiness; (Witz, Bemerkung) dirty etc joke/remark.
Schmutz-: ~**literatur** f dirty or smutty literature; ~**titel** m (Typ) half-title; ~**wäsche** f dirty washing; ~**wasser** nt dirty water.
Schnabel m -s, ¨ **(a)** (Vogel~) beak, bill.
(b) (von Kanne) spout; (von Krug) lip; (von Schiff) prow.
(c) (Mus: Mundstück) mouthpiece.
(d) (inf: Mund) mouth. **halt den** ~! shut your mouth (inf) or trap (sl); **den** ~ **aufreißen** (vor Erstaunen) to gape; (reden) to open one's big mouth (inf); **mach doch den** ~ **auf** say something; **reden, wie einem der** ~ **gewachsen ist** to say exactly what comes into one's head; (unaffektiert) to talk naturally.
Schnäbelei f (lit, fig) billing and cooing.
Schnabelhieb m peck.
schnäbeln vi (lit, fig) to bill and coo.
Schnabel-: ~**schuh** m pointed shoe (with turned-up toe); ~**tasse** f feeding cup; ~**tier** nt duckbilled platypus.
schnabulieren* vi (inf: essen) to nibble.
Schnack m -(e)s, -e (N Ger inf) (Unterhaltung) chat; (Ausspruch) silly or amusing phrase. **das ist ein dummer** ~ that's a silly phrase.
schnackeln vi (S Ger) (Mensch) to shake. **mit den Fingern** ~ to snap or click one's fingers; **jdm** ~ **die Knie** sb's knees are trembling or shaking; **es hat (bei jdm) geschnackelt** it's clicked.
schnacken vi to chat.
Schnackerl m or nt -s, no pl (Aus) hiccup. **den** ~ **haben** to have (the) hiccups.
Schnake f -, -n **(a)** (inf: Stechmücke) gnat, midge. **(b)** (Weberknecht) daddy-long-legs.
Schnakenstich m (inf) gnat bite.
Schnalle f -, -n **(a)** (Schuh~, Gürtel~) buckle. **(b)** (an Handtasche, Buch) clasp. **(c)** (Aus, S Ger: Tür~) handle. **(d)** (sl: Flittchen) tarty type (inf).
schnallen vt to strap; Gürtel to buckle, to fasten; siehe Gürtel.
Schnallenschuh m buckled shoe.
schnalzen vi (mit den Fingern) ~ to snap or click one's fingers; **mit der Peitsche** ~ to crack one's whip, to give a crack of one's whip; **mit der Zunge** ~ to click one's tongue.
Schnalzer m -s, - (inf) (mit Zunge) click; (mit Fingern auch) snap; (von Peitsche) crack. ~ **von sich geben** to make clicks.
Schnalzlaut m (Ling) click.
schnapp interj snap; siehe schnipp.
schnappen **1** vi **(a) nach jdm/etw** ~ to snap or take a snap at sb/sth; (greifen) to snatch or grab at sb/sth; siehe Luft.
(b) aux sein (sich bewegen) to spring up. **die Tür schnappt ins Schloß** the door snaps or clicks shut.
2 vt **(a)** (ergreifen) to snatch, to grab. **jdn am Arm** ~ to grab sb's arm or sb by the arm; **schnapp dir einen Zettel** grab a piece of paper (inf).
(b) (fangen) to catch, to nab (inf).
Schnapper m -s, - (inf) **(a)** (von Hund etc) snap. **(b)** siehe Schnäpper.
Schnäpper m -s, - **(a)** (Med) lancet. **(b)** (inf: Schloß) latch.
Schnapp-: ~**feder** f spring catch; ~**hahn** m (Hist) highwayman; ~**messer** nt clasp-knife; ~**sack** m (obs) knapsack (dated); ~**schloß** nt (an Tür) springlock; (an Schmuck) spring clasp; ~**schuß** m (Foto) snap(shot).
Schnaps m -es, ¨e (klarer) ~ schnapps; (inf: Branntwein) spirits pl; (inf: Alkohol) drink, booze (inf), liquor (esp US inf). **ich möchte lieber einen** ~ **trinken** I'd rather have a short (inf).
Schnaps-: ~**brenner** m distiller; ~**brennerei** f **(a)** (Gebäude) distillery; **(b)** (das Brennen) distilling of spirits or liquor; ~**bruder** m (inf) boozer (inf).
Schnäpschen ['ʃnɛpsçən] nt (inf) little drink, wee dram (esp Scot).
schnapseln (Aus), **schnapsen** vi (inf) to booze (inf).
Schnaps-: ~**fahne** f (inf) boozy breath (inf); ~**flasche** f bottle of booze (inf) or spirits or liquor; ~**glas** nt small glass for spirits; ~**idee** f (inf) crazy or crackpot idea; ~**laden** m off-licence (Brit), liquor store (US); ~**leiche** f (inf) drunk; ~**nase** f (inf) boozer's nose (inf); ~**zahl** f (inf) multi-digit number with all digits identical.
schnarchen vi to snore.
Schnarcher(in f) m -s, - snorer.
Schnarre f -, -n rattle.
schnarren vi (Wecker, Radio, Saite etc) to buzz; (Maschine, Spinnrad etc) to clatter; (Uhrwerk) to creak; (Vogel) to croak. **mit** ~**der Stimme** in a rasping or grating voice.
Schnatter-: ~**gans**, ~**liese** f, ~**maul** nt (all inf) chatterbox.
schnattern vi (Gans) to gabble; (Ente) to quack; (inf: schwatzen) to natter (inf). **sie schnatterten vor Kälte** her teeth are chattering with (the) cold.
schnauben pret schnaubte or schnob (old), ptp geschnaubt or geschnoben (old) **1** vi **(a)** (Tier) to snort. **(b)** vor Wut/Entrüstung ~ to snort with rage/indignation. **2** vt **(b)** Unverschämtheit, schnaubte er disgraceful, he snorted. **(b)** (liter: Pferd etc) to breathe. **3** vr **sich (dat) die Nase** ~, **sich** ~ to blow one's nose.
schnaufen vi **(a)** (schwer atmen) to wheeze; (keuchen) to puff, to pant; (fig) (Lokomotive) to puff; (inf: Auto) to struggle. **(b)** (esp S Ger: atmen) to breathe. **(c)** aux sein (sich keuchend bewegen) Auto to struggle. **ich bin in den fünften Stock geschnauft** (inf) I went/came puffing and panting up to the fifth floor.
Schnaufer m -s, - (inf) breath. **ein** ~ **frische Luft** a breath of fresh air; **den letzten** ~ **tun** to breathe one's last, to kick the bucket (inf).

Schnauferl nt -s, - or (Aus) -n (hum: Oldtimer) veteran car.

Schnaufpause f (Aus, S Ger) short breather (inf).

Schnauzbart m walrus moustache.

Schnäuzchen nt dim of **Schnauze** nose.

Schnauze f -, -n (a) (von Tier) muzzle. eine feuchte ~ haben to have a wet nose; mit einer Maus in der ~ with a mouse in its mouth.
(b) (Ausguß an Kaffeekanne etc) spout; (an Krug etc) lip.
(c) (inf) (von Fahrzeugen) front; (von Flugzeug, Schiff) nose.
(d) (sl: Mund) gob (sl), trap (sl). ~! shut your gob (sl) or trap (sl); auf die ~ fallen to fall flat on one's face; (fig) to come a cropper (inf); jdm die ~ einschlagen or polieren or lackieren to smash sb's face in (sl); die ~ (gestrichen) voll haben to be fed up to the back teeth (inf); eine große ~ haben to have a big mouth, to be a big-mouth (inf); die ~ halten to hold one's tongue; etw frei nach ~ machen to do sth any old how (inf); frei nach ~ gehen/fahren etc to follow one's nose.

schnauzen vi (inf) to shout; (jdn anfahren) to snap, to bark.

Schnauzer m -s, - (a) (Hundeart) schnauzer. (b) (inf) siehe **Schnauzbart**.

Schneck m -s, -en (Aus, S Ger) siehe **Schnecke** (a, b).

Schnecke f -, -n (a) (Zool, fig) snail; (Nacktschnecke) slug; (Cook auch) escargot. wie eine ~ kriechen to crawl at a snail's pace; jdn zur ~ machen (inf) to give sb a real bawling-out (inf).
(b) (inf: Kosename) pet (inf).
(c) (Anat) cochlea (spec).
(d) (Archit, an Säule) volute; (Treppe) spiral staircase.
(e) (Tech) (Schraube) worm, endless screw; (Förderschnecke) worm or screw conveyor.
(f) usu pl (Frisur) earphone.
(g) (Cook: Gebäck) = Chelsea bun.

Schnecken-: s~förmig adj spiral; (Archit) ornament scroll-shaped; ~gehäuse, ~haus nt snail-shell; sich in sein ~haus zurückziehen (fig inf) to retreat into one's shell; ~linie f spiral; ~nudel f (dial) = Chelsea bun; ~post f (hum inf) du bist wohl mit der ~post gefahren? you must have crawled your way here; ~tempo nt (inf) im ~tempo at a snail's pace; dein ~tempo kenn' ich schon I know how slowly you do things.

schnedderengteng interj tarantara.

Schnee m -s, no pl (a) (auch TV) snow. vom ~ eingeschlossen sein to be snowbound; unser Geld schmilzt wie ~ (an der Sonne) our money is dwindling fast; ein Auto aus dem Jahre ~ (Aus) an ancient car; im Jahre ~ (Aus) ages ago.
(b) (Ei~) whisked egg-white. Eiweiß zu ~ schlagen to whisk the egg-white(s) till stiff.
(c) (sl: Heroin, Kokain) snow (sl).

Schnee-: ~ball m snowball; (Bot) snowball, guelder rose; ~ballschlacht f snowball fight; eine ~ballschlacht machen to have a snowball fight; ~ballsystem nt accumulative process; (Comm) pyramid selling; das vermehrt sich nach dem ~ballsystem it snowballs; s~bedeckt adj snow-covered; Berg auch snow-capped; ~besen m (Cook) whisk; s~blind adj snow-blind; ~blindheit f snow blindness; ~brille f snow-goggles pl; ~decke f blanket or (Met) covering of snow; ~-Eule f snowy owl; ~fall m snowfall, fall of snow; dichter ~fall behindert die Sicht heavy falling snow is impairing visibility; ~flocke f snowflake; ~fräse f snow blower; s~frei adj free of snow; ~gans f snow goose; ~gestöber nt (leicht) snow flurry; (stark) snowstorm; ~glätte f hard-packed snow no pl; ~glöckchen nt snowdrop; ~grenze f snow-line; ~hang m snow slope; ~hase m blue hare; ~hemd nt (Mil) white anorak for camouflage in snow; ~hütte f hut made of snow.

schneeig ['ʃneːɪç] adj snowy.

Schnee-: ~kette f (Aut) snow chain; ~könig m: sich freuen wie ein ~könig to be as pleased as Punch; ~kristall m snow crystal; ~landschaft f snowy landscape; ~mann m, pl -männer snowman; ~matsch m slush; ~pflug m (Tech, Ski) snowplough (Brit), snowplow (US); ~raupe f snow cat; ~regen m sleet; ~schaufel, ~schippe f snow-shovel, snowpusher (US); ~schläger m whisk; ~schmelze f thaw; ~schuh m snow-shoe; (dated: Ski) ski; ~sturm m snowstorm; (stärker) blizzard; ~treiben nt driving snow; ~verhältnisse pl snow conditions pl; ~verwehung f snowdrift; ~wächte f snow cornice; ~wasser nt water from melting snow, snowmelt (US); ~wehe f snowdrift; s~weiß adj snow-white, as white as snow; Haare snowy-white; Hände lily-white; Gewissen clear; ~weißchen, ~wittchen nt Snow White; ~zaun m snow fence.

Schneid m -(e)s, no pl, (Aus) f -, no pl (inf) nerve, courage. ~/keinen ~ haben to have/not to have guts (inf); den ~ verlieren to lose one's nerve.

Schneidbrenner m (Tech) oxyacetylene cutter, cutting torch.

Schneide f -, -n (sharp or cutting) edge; (von Messer, Schwert) blade; siehe **Messer**.

schneiden pret **schnitt**, ptp **geschnitten** 1 vi to cut; (Med) to operate; (bei Geburt) to do an episiotomy. Ärzte, die gern ~ (inf) knife-happy doctors (inf); jdm ins Gesicht/in die Hand etc ~ to cut sb on the face/on the hand; der Wind/die Kälte schneidet the wind is biting/it is bitingly cold; jdm ins Herz or in die Seele ~ to cut sb to the quick.
2 vt (a) Papier etc, Haare, (fig: meiden) to cut; Getreide auch to mow; (klein~) Schnittlauch, Gemüse etc to chop; (Sport) Ball to slice, to cut; (schnitzen) Namen, Figuren to carve; (Math auch) to intersect with; (Weg) to cross. eine Kurve ~ to cut a corner; sein schön/scharf geschnittenes Gesicht his clean-cut/sharp features or face; Gesichter or Grimassen ~ to make or pull faces; die Luft ist zum S~ (fig inf) the air is very bad; die Atmosphäre ist zum S~ (fig inf) you could cut the atmosphere with a knife; jdn ~ (beim Überholen) to cut in on sb; weit/eng geschnitten sein (Sew) to be cut wide/narrow.
(b) Film, Tonband to edit.

(c) (inf: operieren) to operate on; Furunkel to lance. jdn ~ to cut sb open (inf); (bei Geburt) to give sb an episiotomy; geschnitten werden (bei Geburt) to have an episiotomy.
3 vr (a) (Mensch) to cut oneself. sich in den Finger etc ~ to cut one's finger etc; siehe **Fleisch**.
(b) (inf: sich täuschen) da hat er sich aber geschnitten! he's made a big mistake, he's very mistaken.
(c) (Linien, Straßen etc) to intersect.

schneidend adj biting, Hohn, Bemerkung auch cutting; Wind, Kälte auch piercing, bitter; Schmerz sharp, searing; Stimme, Ton piercing.

Schneider m -s, - (a) (Beruf) tailor; (Damen~) dressmaker; siehe **frieren**.
(b) (Cards) einen ~ machen to score half (the full) points; im ~ sein to have less than half points; aus dem ~ sein to have slightly more than half points; (fig) to be out of the woods.
(c) (Gerät) cutter; (inf: für Brot etc) slicer.

Schneiderei f (a) no pl (Handwerk) tailoring; (für Damen) dressmaking. (b) (Werkstatt) tailor's/dressmaker's.

Schneider-: ~geselle m journeyman tailor/dressmaker; ~handwerk nt tailoring no art; dressmaking no art.

Schneiderin f siehe **Schneider** (a).

Schneider-: ~kostüm nt tailored suit; ~kreide f tailor's chalk; ~lehrling m tailor's/dressmaker's apprentice; ~meister m master tailor/dressmaker.

schneidern 1 vi (beruflich) to be a tailor/dressmaker; (als Hobby) to do dressmaking. 2 vt to make, to sew; Herrenanzug to tailor, to make.

Schneider-: ~puppe f tailor's/dressmaker's dummy; ~sitz m im ~sitz sitzen to sit cross-legged; ~werkstatt f tailor's/dressmaker's workshop.

Schneide-: ~tisch m (Film) editing or cutting table; ~werkzeug nt cutting tool; ~zahn m incisor.

schneidig adj dashing, sharp; Musik rousing; Tempo fast.

Schneidigkeit f (von Mensch) dashing character; (von Musik) rousing character or tempo; (von Tempo) speed.

schneien 1 vi impers to snow.
2 vt impers es schneit dicke Flocken big flakes (of snow) are falling; es schneite Konfetti confetti rained down.
3 vi aux sein (fig) to rain down. jdm ins Haus ~ (inf) (Besuch) to drop in on sb; (Rechnung, Brief) to arrive through one's letterbox or in the post.

Schneise f -, -n break; (Wald~) aisle, lane; (Feuer~) fire-break; (Flug~) path.

schnell adj quick; Bedienung, Fahrt, Tempo, Läufer auch fast; Auto, Zug, Verkehr, Fahrer, Strecke fast; Schritte, Puls, Verbesserung auch fast, rapid; Abreise, Bote, Hilfe speedy; Antwort auch speedy, prompt; Genesung, Besserung quick, rapid, speedy. ~ gehen/fahren to walk/drive quickly/fast; etw in ~em Tempo singen to sing sth quickly or fast; er kam in ~em Lauf dahergerannt he came running up quickly; sie wird ~ böse/ist ~ verärgert she loses her temper quickly, she is quick to get angry; er ist sehr ~ mit seinem Urteil/seiner Kritik he's very quick to judge/to criticize; nicht so ~! not so fast!; kannst du das vorher noch ~ machen? (inf) can you do that quickly first?; ich muß mir nur noch ~ die Haare kämmen I must just give my hair a quick comb; sein Puls ging ~ his pulse was very fast; das geht ~ (grundsätzlich) it doesn't take long; das mache ich gleich, das geht ~ I'll do that now, it won't take long; das ging ~ that was quick; es ist mit dem Patienten ~ gegangen it was all over quickly; mit dicker Wolle geht es ~, einen Pullover zu stricken knitting a pullover with thick wool is very quick; an der Grenze ist es ~ gegangen things went very quickly at the border; das ging alles viel zu ~ it all happened much too quickly or fast; in unserem Büro muß alles ~ gehen in our office things must be done quickly; das werden wir ~ erledigt haben we'll soon have that finished; ~ machen! hurry (up)!; das werde ich so ~ nicht vergessen/wieder tun etc I won't forget that/do that etc again in a hurry; das werden wir ~ sehen (bald) we'll soon see about that; ich kann nicht so ~ machen I can't go so fast; siehe **Schnelle**.

Schnelläufer m getrennt: Schnell-läufer (Sport) sprinter; (Astron) high-velocity star; (Tech) high-speed machine.

Schnell-: ~bahn f high-speed railway; ~bauweise f high-speed building methods pl; ~boot nt speedboat; ~dienst m express service.

Schnelle f -, -n (a) no pl (Schnelligkeit) quickness, speed. (b) (Strom~) rapids pl. (c) etw auf die ~ machen to do sth quickly or in a rush; das läßt sich nicht auf die ~ machen we can't rush that, that will take time; Sex/ein Bier auf die ~ (inf) a quickie (inf).

schnellebig adj getrennt: schnell-lebig Zeit fast-moving.

schnellen 1 vi aux sein (lit, fig) to shoot. in die Höhe ~ to shoot up; ein Gummiband ~ lassen to flick a rubber band. 2 vt (rare) to shoot; (mit Gummiring) to flick, to shoot. sich in die Höhe ~ (auf Sprungbrett etc) to bounce up.

Schnell-: ~feuer nt (Mil) rapid fire; ~feuergeschütz nt automatic rifle; ~feuergewehr nt automatic pistol; s~füßig adj (geh) fleet-footed (liter), fleet of foot (liter); ~gaststätte f cafeteria, fast-food store (US); ~gericht nt (a) (Jur) summary court; (b) (Cook) convenience food; ~hefter m spring folder.

Schnelligkeit f (von Auto, Verkehr, Abreise) speed; (von Bewegung, Tempo auch) quickness; (von Schritten, Besserung, Verbesserung auch, von Puls) rapidity; (von Bote, Hilfe) speediness; (von Antwort) speediness, promptness.

Schnell-: ~imbiß m (a) (Essen) (quick) snack; (b) (Raum) snack-bar; ~kochplatte f high-speed ring; ~kochtopf m (Dampfkochtopf) pressure cooker; (Wasserkochtopf) = electric kettle; ~kraft f (von Feder, Sprungbrett) springiness, resilience; (von Sportler, Fischen) ability to jump; ~kurs m crash course; ~**läufer** m siehe **Schnelläufer**; **s~lebig** adj siehe **schnellebig**; ~**paket** nt express parcel; ~**presse** f high-speed printing machine or press; ~**reinigung** f express cleaning service.

schnellstens adv as quickly as possible.

Schnell-: ~**straße** f expressway; ~**verfahren** nt (Jur) summary trial; (Mil) summary court-martial; **im ~verfahren abgeurteilt** to be sentenced by a summary trial/court-martial; ~**verkehr** m fast traffic; (im Transportwesen) express service; etw **im ~verkehr schicken** to send sth express delivery; ~**zug** m fast train; (Fern~) express (train); ~**zugzuschlag** m supplementary charge for travel on a fast/an express train; (inf: Karte) supplementary ticket.

Schnepfe f -, -n snipe; (pej inf) silly cow (sl).

Schnepper m -s, - siehe **Schnäpper**.

schnetzeln vt (S Ger, Sw) Frucht, Gemüse to slice; Fleisch to shred.

schneuzen 1 vr to blow one's nose. 2 vt **einem Kind/sich die Nase ~** to blow a child's/one's nose.

Schnickschnack m -s, no pl (inf) (Unsinn) twaddle (inf) no indef art, poppycock (inf) no indef art; (Kinkerlitzchen) paraphernalia (inf) no indef art. **ach ~!** (dated) (dated) balderdash!, fiddlesticks! (dated).

schniefen vi (dial) (bei Schnupfen) to sniff(le); (beim Weinen) to sniffle, to snivel. **schnief, schnief** (hum inf) boo-hoo (hum inf), sob, sob (hum inf).

schniegeln (inf) 1 vt Kleidung, Kinder, Auto to spruce up. 2 vr to get spruced up, to spruce oneself up; siehe **geschniegelt**.

schnieke adj (N Ger sl: schick) swish (inf).

Schnipfel m -s, - (dial) siehe **Schnipsel**.

schnipp interj snip. ~, **schnapp** snip, snip.

Schnippchen nt (inf) **jdm ein ~ schlagen** to play a trick on sb, to trick sb; **dem Tod ein ~ schlagen** to cheat death.

Schnippel m or nt -s, - (inf) siehe **Schnipsel**.

schnippeln vti (inf) to snip (an +dat at); (mit Messer) to hack (an +dat at). **an ihr haben die Ärzte schon was geschnippelt!** she has already been hacked about a bit by the doctors (inf).

schnippen 1 vi **mit den Fingern ~** to snap one's fingers. 2 vt **etw von etw ~** to flick sth off or from sth.

schnippisch adj saucy, pert.

Schnipsel m or nt -s, - (inf) scrap; (Papier~) scrap or bit of paper.

schnipseln vti (inf) siehe **schnippeln**.

schnipsen vti (inf) siehe **schnippen**.

schnitt pret of **schneiden**.

Schnitt m -(e)s, -e (a) cut; (Kerbe auch) notch, nick; (Med auch) incision; (von Heu, Getreide) crop. **Blumen für den ~** flowers (suitable) for cutting. **(b)** (Haar~) (hair)cut. **einen kurzen ~ bitte** cut it short please. **(c)** (Sew) cut; (~muster) pattern. **(d)** (Form) (von Edelstein) cut; (von Gesicht, Augen) shape; (von Profil) line. **(e)** (Film) editing no pl. **der Film ist jetzt beim ~** the film is now being edited or cut; **~: L. Schwarz** editor – L. Schwarz. **(f)** (Math) (~punkt) (point of) intersection; (~fläche) section; (inf: Durch~) average. **im ~** on average; **im ~ liegen bei** to average. **(g)** (Längs~, Quer~) section. **im ~ gezeichnet** drawn in section. **(h)** (inf: Gewinn) profit. **(i)** (Typ) (das Beschneiden) cut; (Buchrand) (trimmed) edge. **dann kommt das gebundene Buch zum ~** then the bound book is cut or trimmed. **(j)** (Hort: von Bäumen etc) cutting no indef art.

Schnitt-: ~**blumen** pl cut flowers pl; (im Garten) flowers (suitable) for cutting; ~**bohnen** pl French or green beans pl.

Schnitte f -, -n slice; (belegt) open sandwich; (zusammengeklappt) sandwich. **womit soll ich dir die ~ belegen?** what shall I put on your (slice of) bread?

Schnittebene f (Math) sectional plane.

Schnitter(in f) m -s, - reaper.

Schnitt-: **s~fest** adj Tomaten firm; ~**fläche** f section.

schnittig adj smart; Mann, Auto, Formen auch stylish; Tempo auch snappy (inf). **er ist ganz schön ~ gefahren** he nipped or zipped along (inf).

Schnitt-: ~**lauch** m, no pl chives pl; ~**lauchlocken** pl (hum inf) straight hair; ~**linie** f (Math) line of intersection; (Sew) cutting line; ~**muster** nt (Sew) (paper) pattern; ~**musterbogen** m (Sew) pattern chart; ~**punkt** m (von Straßen) intersection; (Math auch) point of intersection; ~**wunde** f cut; (tief) gash; ~**winkel** m angle of intersection.

Schnitz m -es, -e (S Ger, Aus) piece; (von Orange auch) segment; (von Apfel auch) slice.

Schnitzarbeit f siehe **Schnitzerei**.

Schnitzel¹ nt or m -s, - (Papier~) bit or scrap of paper; (Holz~) shaving; (Fetzen, Karotten~, Kartoffel~) shred, sliver. **~ pl** (Abfälle) scraps pl.

Schnitzel² nt -s, - (Cook) veal/pork cutlet, schnitzel.

Schnitzeljagd f paper-chase.

schnitzeln vt Gemüse to shred; Holz to chop (up) (into sticks).

schnitzen vti to carve. **wir haben in der Schule S~ gelernt** we learnt wood carving at school; siehe **Holz**.

Schnitzer m -s, - (a) wood carver. **(b)** (inf: Benehmen) blunder, boob (Brit inf), goof (US inf); (Fehler) howler (inf).

Schnitzerei f (wood-)carving.

Schnitz-: ~**kunst** f (art of) wood carving; ~**messer** nt wood-carving knife; ~**werk** nt (wood) carving.

schnob (old) pret of **schnauben**.

schnodd(e)rig adj (inf) rude and offhand, brash.

Schnodd(e)rigkeit f (inf) brashness.

schnöd(e) adj (niederträchtig) despicable, contemptible, base; Geiz, Verrat base; Gewinn vile; Behandlung, Ton, Antwort contemptuous, disdainful. **~r Mammon/~s Geld** filthy lucre; **jdn ~ verlassen** to leave sb in a most despicable fashion.

Schnödigkeit f **(a)** (Gemeinheit) despicableness, contemptibleness, baseness; (Geringschätzung) contempt no pl, disdain no pl. **(b)** (gemeine Handlung, Bemerkung) despicable or contemptible thing (to do/say).

Schnorchel m -s, - (von U-Boot, Taucher) snorkel; (~maske) snorkel mask.

Schnörkel m -s, - flourish; (an Möbeln, Säulen) scroll; (fig: Unterschrift) squiggle (hum), signature.

schnörkelig adj ornate; Schrift auch full of flourishes; Rede auch flowery.

schnorren vti (inf) to cadge (inf), to scrounge (inf) (bei from).

Schnorrer m -s, - (inf) cadger (inf), scrounger (inf).

Schnösel m -s, - (inf) snotty(-nosed) little upstart (inf).

schnöselig adj (inf) Benehmen, Jugendlicher snotty (inf), snotty-nosed (inf).

Schnuckelchen nt (inf) sweetheart, pet, baby (esp US).

schnuckelig adj (inf) (gemütlich) snug, cosy; Wärme cosy; (niedlich) cute.

Schnüffelei f (inf) **(a)** (von Hund, Mensch) snuffling no pl, sniffing no pl; (von Mensch auch) sniffling no pl. **(b)** (fig: das Spionieren) snooping no pl (inf).

schnüffeln vi **(a)** (schnuppern, riechen) to sniff; (Hund auch) to snuffle. **an etw** (dat) **~** to sniff (at) sth. **(b)** (bei Erkältung etc) to sniffle, to snuffle. **(c)** (fig inf: spionieren) to snoop around (inf), to nose around or about (inf).

Schnüffler(in f) m -s, - (inf) (fig) snooper (inf), Nosey Parker (inf); (Detektiv) sleuth (inf), private eye (inf).

Schnuller m -s, - (inf) dummy (Brit), pacifier (US); (auf Flasche) teat (Brit), nipple (US).

Schnulze f -, -n (inf) schmaltzy film/book/song (inf). **das sind alles ~n** it's all schmaltz (inf).

schnulzig adj (inf) slushy, soppy, schmaltzy (all inf).

schnupfen vti (Tabak) **~** to take snuff; **willst du auch ~?** would you like some snuff too?

Schnupfen m -s, - cold. **(einen) ~ bekommen, sich** (dat) **einen ~ holen** (inf) to catch (a) cold; **(einen) ~ haben** to have a cold.

Schnupfer(in f) m -s, - snuff-taker.

Schnupf-: ~**tabak** m snuff; ~**tabak(s)dose** f snuffbox; ~**tuch** nt (S Ger) handkerchief, hanky (inf).

schnuppe adj pred (inf) **jdm ~ sein** to be all the same to sb; **das Wohl seiner Angestellten ist ihm völlig ~** he couldn't care less (inf) about the welfare of his employees.

schnuppern 1 vi (Hund, Mensch) to sniff; (Hund auch) to snuffle. **an etw** (dat) **~** to sniff (at) sth. 2 vt to sniff.

Schnur f -, ¨e (Bindfaden) string; (Kordel, an Vorhang) cord; (Litze) braid no indef art, no pl, piping no indef art, no pl; (Zelt~) guy (rope); (Angel~) (fishing) line; (Kabel) flex, lead. **über die ~ hauen** (dated) to overstep or overshoot the mark.

Schnür-: ~**band** nt lace; ~**boden** m (Theat) flies pl.

Schnürchen nt dim of **Schnur** bit of string. **es läuft or geht or klappt alles wie am ~** everything's going like clockwork; **etw wie am ~ hersagen** to say or recite sth off pat.

schnüren 1 vt Paket, Strohbündel to tie up; Schuhe auch, Mieder to lace (up); Körper to lace in. **Schuhe zum S~** lace-up shoes, lace-ups. 2 vi **(a)** (inf: eng sein) to be too tight. **(b)** aux sein (Hunt) to run in a straight line. 3 vr (Frauen) to lace oneself up or in.

Schnur-: **s~gerade** adj (dead) straight; **s~gerade auf jdn/etw zugehen** to make a bee-line for sb/sth (inf), to go straight up to sb/sth; ~**keramik** f (Archeol) string ceramics sing.

Schnürleibchen nt siehe **Schnürmieder**.

Schnürl- (Aus): ~**regen** m pouring or streaming rain; ~**samt** m corduroy.

Schnürmieder nt lace-up corset.

Schnurrbart m moustache (Brit), mustache (US).

schnurrbärtig adj with a moustache, mustachioed.

Schnurre f -, -n **(a)** (Erzählung) funny story. **(b)** (Posse) farce.

schnurren vi (Katze) to purr; (Spinnrad etc) to hum, to whirr.

Schnurrhaare pl whiskers pl.

Schnurriemen m siehe **Schnürsenkel**.

schnurrig adj amusing, droll; alter Mann quaint, funny.

Schnür-: ~**schuh** m lace-up or laced shoe; ~**senkel** m shoelace; (für Stiefel) bootlace; ~**stiefel** m lace-up or laced boot.

schnurstracks adv straight, directly. **du gehst jetzt ~ nach Hause!** you are to go straight home (now), you are to go home directly; **~ auf jdn/etw zugehen** to make a bee-line for sb/sth (inf), to go straight up to sb/sth.

schnurz adj (inf) **das ist ihm ~** he couldn't care less (about it) (inf), he couldn't give a darn (about it) (inf).

Schnute f -, -n (inf) (Mund) mouth; (Schmollmund) pout; (pej: Mundwerk) big mouth (inf). **eine ~ ziehen** or **machen** to pout, to pull a face.

schob pret of **schieben**.

Schober m -s, - (S Ger, Aus) **(a)** (Scheune) barn. **(b)** (Heuhaufen) hay stack or rick.

Schock¹ m -(e)s, -e (obs) three score (old).

Schock² m -(e)s, -s or (rare) -e (Schreck, elektrisch) shock. **unter ~ stehen** to be in (a state of) shock.

schockant adj shocking.

Schock-: ~**behandlung** f shock therapy; (elektrisch auch) electro-convulsive therapy; (elektrisch auch) **unter ~einwirkung** f state of shock; **unter ~einwirkung stehen** to be in (a state of) shock.

schocken vt (inf) to shock. **jdn elektrisch ~** (Med) to give sb an electric shock, to administer an electric shock to sb (form).

Schocker m -s, - (inf) shock film/novel, film/novel aimed to shock.

schockieren* vti to shock; (stärker) to scandalize. **sich leicht ~ lassen** to be easily shocked; **schockiert sein** to be shocked (über +acc at).

Schock-: **~therapie** f shock therapy; (elektrisch auch) electro-convulsive therapy; **s~weise** adv (obs) by the score (old).

schofel, schof(e)lig adj (inf) Behandlung, Ausrede mean, rotten no adv (inf); Spende, Geschenk, Mahlzeit miserable.

Schöffe m -n, -n = juror.

Schöffen-: **~amt** nt = jury service; **~bank** f = jury bench; **~gericht** nt court (with jury); **einen Fall vor einem ~gericht verhandeln** ≈ to try a case by jury.

Schöffin f = juror.

schöflig adj (inf) siehe schofel.

Schokolade f chocolate.

schokoladen adj attr chocolate.

Schokoladen- in cpds chocolate; **s~braun** adj chocolate-coloured; **~guß** m chocolate icing; **~raspel** f chocolate flake.

Scholar m -en, -en (Hist) itinerant scholar.

Scholastik f scholasticism.

Scholastiker(in f) m -s, - scholastic.

scholastisch adj scholastic.

scholl pret of schallen.

Scholle[1] f -, -n (Fisch) plaice.

Scholle[2] f -, -n (Eis~) (ice) floe; (Erd~) clod (of earth). **mit der ~ verbunden sein** (fig) to be a son of the soil.

Scholli m: **mein lieber ~!** (inf) (drohend) now look here!; (erstaunt) my goodness me!, my oh my!

schon adv (a) (bereits) already; (in Fragen: überhaupt ~) ever. **er ist ~ da** is there already, he's already there; **ist er ~ da?** is he there yet?; **warst du ~ dort?** have you been there yet?; (je) **have you ever been there?**; **danke, ich habe ~** (inf) no thank you, I have some (already); **ich habe den Film ~ gesehen** I've already seen that film, I've seen that film before; **ich werde ~ bedient** I'm (already) being served; **mußt du ~ gehen?** must you go already or so soon?; **ich bin ~ drei Jahre alt** I'm three (years old); **er wollte ~ die Hoffnung aufgeben, als ...** he was just about to give up hope when ...

(b) (mit Zeitangaben) **ich warte nun ~ seit drei Wochen** I've already been waiting (for) three weeks; **~ vor drei Wochen** three weeks ago; **~ damals** even then; **~ damals, als ...** even when ...; **~ früher wußte man ~** in years gone by they knew ...; **~ vor 100 Jahren/im 13. Jahrhundert** as far back as 100 years ago/as early or as far back as the 13th century; **das haben wir ~ gestern or gestern ~ gemacht** we did that yesterday; **~ am nächsten Tag** the very next day; **es ist ~ 11 Uhr** it's 11 o'clock already; **der Briefträger kommt ~ um 6 Uhr** the postman comes as early as 6 o'clock; **kommt er ~ heute?** will he come today (already)?

(c) ~ (ein)mal before; (in Fragen: je) ever; **ich habe das ~ mal gehört** I've heard that before; **warst du ~ (ein)mal dort?** have you ever been there?; **ich habe Sie ~ (ein)mal gesehen** I've met or seen you before somewhere; **ich habe dir ~ (ein)mal gesagt, daß ...** I've already told you once that ...; **das habe ich dir doch ~ hundertmal gesagt** I've told you that a hundred times (before); **ich habe das Buch ~ zweimal gelesen** I've read that book twice already; **das habe ich ~ oft gehört** I've heard that often; **das ist ~ längst vorbei/vergessen** that's long past/forgotten; **das ist ~ längst erledigt** that was done a long time ago or was done ages ago; **ich bin ~ lange fertig** I've been ready for ages; **wie lange wartest du ~?** how long have you been waiting?; **wartest du ~ lange?** have you been waiting (for) long?; **wie ~ so oft** as so often (before); **wie ~ erwähnt** as has (already) been mentioned; **~ immer** always; **ich habe ~ immer dunkle Haare** I've always had dark hair; **~ wieder zurück** back again, she's back again; (~ zurück) she's back already; **was, ~ wieder?** what – again?; **was denn nun ~ wieder?** what is it now?, now what is it? (inf).

(d) (allein, bloß) just; (ohnehin) anyway. **allein ~ das Gefühl ...** just the very feeling ...; **~ die Tatsache, daß ...** just the fact that ...; **die Preise sind jetzt ~ hoch genug** the prices are high enough anyway or as it is; **wenn ich das ~ sehe/höre/lese!** if I even see/hear/read that!; **~ deswegen** if only because of that; **~ weil** if only because.

(e) (bestimmt) all right. **du wirst ~ sehen** you'll see (all right); **das wirst du ~ noch lernen** you'll learn that one day; **sie wird es ~ machen** (don't worry,) she'll do it (all right); (schaffen) she'll manage it all right.

(f) (ungeduldig) **hör ~ auf damit!** will you stop that!; so ant-worte ~! come on, answer; **geh ~** go on; **nun sag ~!** come on, tell me (inf); **mach ~!** get a move on! (inf), get on with it!; **wenn doch ~ ...!** if only ...; **ich komme ja ~!** I'm just coming!, I'm on my way! (inf).

(g) (tatsächlich, allerdings) really. **das ist ~ eine Frechheit!** what a cheek!, that's a real cheek!; **das ist ~ etwas, (wenn ...)** it's really something (if ...); **da gehört ~ Mut/Geschick etc dazu** that takes real courage/skill etc; **da müßten wir ~ großes Glück haben** we'd be very lucky; **da müßte ~ etwas ganz Schlimmes passieren, um ihn zu erschüttern** it would take something really terrible to shake him; **das ist ~ gut!** it's pretty good; **du müßtest ~ etwas mehr arbeiten** you really ought to work a bit harder; **das ist ~ möglich** that's quite possible, that's not impossible; **das müßt du ~ machen!** you really ought to do that.

(h) (bedingt) siehe wenn, wennschon.

(i) (einschränkend) ~ or ja ~, aber ... (inf) yes (well), but ...; **da haben Sie ~ recht, aber ...** yes, you're right (there), but ...

(j) (in rhetorischen Fragen) **was macht das ~, wenn ...** what-(ever) does it matter if ...; (was hilft das ~) what(ever) use is it (ever) does it matter if ...; **wer fragt ~ danach, ob ...** who wants to know if ...; **aber wer fragt ~ danach** (resignierend) but, no-one wants to know;

500 km, was ist das ~ bei den heutigen Flugverbindungen? 500 km is nothing with today's air travel; **10 Mark, was ist das ~, was sind heute ~ 10 Mark?** 10 marks goes nowhere these days, what's 10 marks these days?; **die paar Tropfen, was ist das ~, das ist doch kein Regen** a few drops, what are you talking about, that's not rain; **3 Seiten schreiben, was ist das ~?** write 3 pages? that's nothing.

(k) (inf: Füllwort) **und wenn ~!, na wenn ~!** so what? (inf); ~ **gut!** all right, okay (inf); **ich verstehe ~** I understand, that's all right (inf); ~ **I know**; **danke, es geht ~** thank you, I/we etc will manage; **so ~ I know** that's even more impossible, you certainly can't do that; **für Krimis gebe ich kein Geld aus, und für Pornoheftchen ~ gar nicht** I won't spend money on thrillers and certainly not on pornography.

schön 1 adj (a) (hübsch anzusehen) beautiful, lovely; Mann handsome. **das S~e** beauty; **das S~e dieser Landschaft** the beauty of this countryside; **ein ~es Fräulein** (old, hum) my pretty one or maid (old); **na, ~es Kind** (inf) well then, beautiful (inf).

(b) (nett, angenehm) good; Erlebnis, Stimme, Musik, Wetter auch lovely; Gelegenheit great, splendid. **die ~en Künste** the fine arts; **die ~e Literatur** belles-lettres; **das ist ein ~er Tod** that's a good way to die; **die ~e Hand** (baby-talk) the right hand; **eines ~en Tages** one fine day; **(wieder) in ~ster Ordnung** (nach Krach etc) back to normal (again); **in ~ster Eintracht/Harmonie** in perfect harmony; **das S~e beim Skilaufen ist ...** the nice thing about skiing is ...; **das S~ste daran ist ...** the best thing about it is ...; **das ist ... das S~e, der nicest or best thing about it is ...; **~e Ferien/~en Urlaub!** have a good or nice holiday; **~es Wochenende** have a good or nice weekend; **~en guten Tag a** very good morning/evening etc to you; **war es ~ im Urlaub/bei Tante Veronika?** did you have a nice or good holiday/did you have a nice or good time at Aunty Veronika's?; ~, **daß du gekommen bist** (how) nice of you to come; **~er, heißer Kaffee** nice hot coffee; **ein ~er frischer Wind** a nice fresh wind.

(c) (iro) Unordnung fine, nice, lovely; Überraschung, Wetter lovely; Unsinn, Frechheit absolute. **da hast du etwas S~es angerichtet** you've made a fine or nice or lovely mess/muddle; **du bist mir ein ~er Freund/Vater/Held etc** a fine friend/father/hero etc you are, you're some friend/father/hero etc; **du machst or das sind mir ja ~e Sachen or Geschichten** here's or this is a pretty state of things, here's a pretty kettle of fish (inf); **von dir hört man ~e Sachen or Geschichten** I've been hearing some nice or fine things about you; **das wäre ja noch ~er** (inf) that's (just) too much!; **es wird immer ~er** (inf) things are going from bad to worse; siehe Bescherung.

(d) (inf: gut) nice. **das war nicht ~ von dir** (inf) that wasn't very nice of you; **zu ~, um wahr zu sein** (inf) too good to be true; ~, ~, (also) ~, **sehr** ~, **na** ~ fine, okay, all right; ~ **und gut, aber ...** (that's) all well and good but ..., that's all very well but ...

(e) (beträchtlich, groß) Erfolg great; Strecke, Stück Arbeit, Alter good. **ein ~es Stück weiterkommen** to make good progress; **eine ganz ~e Leistung/Arbeit/Menge** quite an achievement/quite a lot of work/quite a lot; **das hat eine ~e Stange Geld gekostet** (inf) that cost a pretty penny.

2 adv (a) (bei Verben) (gut) well; sich waschen, verarbeiten lassen easily; scheinen brightly; schreiben beautifully; (richtig, genau) ansehen, durchlesen etc carefully. **sich ~ anziehen** to get dressed up; **es ~ haben** to be well off; (im Urlaub etc) to have a good time (of it); **du hast's ~** you're all right!, it's all right for you!; **etw am ~sten machen** to do sth best; siehe danke, bitte.

(b) (angenehm) ~ **weich/warm/stark etc** nice and soft/warm/strong etc.

(c) (bei Wünschen) **schlaf ~** sleep well; **amüsiere dich ~** have a nice or good time; **erhole dich ~** have a good rest; siehe grüßen.

(d) (inf: brav, lieb) nicely. **iß mal ~ deinen Teller leer** eat it all up nicely (now), be a good girl/boy and eat it all up; **sag ~ „Guten Tag"** say "hallo" nicely; **sei ~ still/ordentlich etc** (als Aufforderung) be nice and quiet/tidy etc; **sei ~ brav** be a good boy/girl; **fahr ~ langsam** drive nice and slowly; siehe bleiben-lassen.

(e) (inf: sehr, ziemlich) (vor Verb, Partizip) really; (vor Adjektiv auch) pretty. **sich ~ dat** ~ **weh tun** to hurt oneself a lot; **sich ~ täuschen** to make a big mistake; **sich ~ ärgern** to be very angry; **jdn ~ erschrecken** to give sb quite a or a real fright; **ganz ~ teuer/kalt** pretty expensive/cold; ~ **weit weg a** long or good way off, quite a distance away; **ganz ~ lange** quite a while; ~ **viel Geld kosten** to cost a pretty penny.

Schonbezug m (für Matratzen) mattress cover; (für Möbel) loose cover; (für Autositz) seat cover.

Schöndruck m (Typ) first printing.

Schöne f -n, -n (liter, hum: Mädchen) beauty, belle (liter, hum). **nun, ihr beiden ~ ~!** (inf) now, my beauties (inf).

schonen 1 vt Gesundheit, Herz, Körperteil, Buch, Kleider to look after, to take care of; eigene Nerven to go easy on; jds Nerven, Gefühle, Kraft to spare; Gegner, Kind to be easy on; (nicht stark beanspruchen) Teppich, Schuhsohlen to save; (Mensch) Bremsen, Auto to go easy on; Füße, (iro) Gehirn to save; (schützen) to protect. **ein Waschmittel, das die Hände/Wäsche schont** a detergent that is kind to your hands/washing; **vernünftiges Schalten schont das Getriebe** careful gear-changing makes the gears last longer or saves the gears; **ein Licht, das die Augen schont** lighting that is easy on or kind to the eyes; **sie trägt eine Schürze, um ihre Kleider zu ~** she wears an apron to save her clothes; **er muß den Arm noch ~** he still has to be careful with or look after his arm; **um seine Nerven/die Nerven seiner Mutter zu ~** for the sake of his/his mother's nerves; **ein Beruf, der die Nerven nicht gerade schont** a job that isn't exactly easy on the nerves;

du brauchst mich nicht zu ~, sag ruhig die Wahrheit you don't need to spare me or my feelings – just tell me the truth. **2** vr to look after or take care of oneself; (Patient auch) to take things easy.

schönen vt (a) Farbe to brighten. (b) Wein to clarify.

schonend adj gentle; (rücksichtsvoll) considerate; Waschmittel auch, Politur mild. **jdm etw ~ beibringen** to break sth to sb gently; **jdn ~ behandeln** to be or go easy on sb; Kranken to treat gently; **etw ~ behandeln** to treat sth with care, to look after sth.

Schoner[1] m -s, - (Naut) schooner.

Schoner[2] m -s, - cover; (für Rückenlehnen) antimacassar, chairback; (Ärmel~) sleeve-protector.

Schön-: **s~färben** sep 1 vt (fig) to gloss over; **2** vi to gloss things over; **~färber** m (fig) someone who tends to gloss things over; **~färberei** f (fig) glossing things over.

Schonfrist f period of grace. **eine ~ von 12 Tagen** 12 days' grace.

Schöngeist m aesthete.

schöngeistig adj aesthetic. **~e Literatur** belletristic literature.

Schönheit f beauty.

Schönheits-: **~chirurgie** f cosmetic surgery; **~fehler** m blemish; (von Gegenstand) flaw; (~fleck m beauty spot; **~ideal** nt ideal of beauty; **~königin** f beauty queen; **~konkurrenz** f beauty contest; **~korrektur** f correction of an imperfection/imperfections; (fig) cosmetic alteration; **~operation** f cosmetic operation; **~pflästerchen** nt (artificial) beauty spot; **~pflege** f beauty care; **~salon** m beauty parlour or salon; **~sinn** m sense of beauty; **~wettbewerb** m beauty contest.

Schonkost f light diet.

Schönling m (pej) pansy (inf), pretty boy (inf).

Schön-: **s~machen** sep 1 vt Kind to dress up; Wohnung, Straßen to decorate; **2** vr to get dressed up, to dress (oneself) up; (sich schminken) to make (oneself) up; **3** vi (Hund) to sit up (and beg); **s~reden** vi sep to use flattery; **das ~reden** smooth talking, flattery; **~redner** m flatterer, smooth-talker; **~schreiben** nt writing; **~schreibheft** nt writing book; (mit vorgedruckten Buchstaben) copy-book; **~schrift** f in **~schrift** in one's best (copy-book) (hand)writing.

schönstens adv most beautifully; bitten, fragen respectfully. **jdn ~ grüßen** to give sb one's kindest regards; **ich danke ~** thank you so much.

Schön-: **~tuerei** f flattery, blandishments pl, soft-soap (inf); **s~tun** vi sep irreg **jdm s~tun** (schmeicheln) to flatter or soft-soap (inf) sb; (sich lieb Kind machen) to pay court to sb, to play or suck (inf) up to sb.

Schonung f (a) (Waldbestand) (protected) forest plantation area.

(b) (das Schonen) (von Gefühlen, Kraft) sparing; (von Teppich, Schuhsohlen, Kleider) saving; (das Schützen) protection. **der Patient/Arm braucht noch ein paar Wochen ~** the patient/arm still needs looking after for a few weeks; **zur ~ meiner Gefühle/der Gefühle anderer** to spare my feelings/the feelings of others; **auf ~ seiner Gesundheit/Nerven Wert legen** to value one's health/to attach importance to the state of one's nerves; **Gummihandschuhe/ein mildes Waschmittel zur ~ der Hände** rubber gloves that protect your hands/mild detergent that is kind to your hands; **zur ~ Ihrer Augen/Waschmaschine** to look after your eyes/washing machine; **zur ~ des Getriebes** to give your gears a longer life.

(c) (Nachsicht, Milde) mercy.

Schonungs-: **s~bedürftig** adj in need of care; (in bezug auf Gefühle, Nerven) in need of careful handling; **s~los** adj ruthless, merciless; Wahrheit blunt; Kritik savage; **~losigkeit** f ruthlessness, mercilessness; (von Kritik) savageness; **mit einer solchen ~losigkeit** so ruthlessly, so mercilessly; so savagely; **s~voll** adj gentle.

Schönwetter nt (lit) fine weather. **~ machen** (fig inf) to smooth things over; **bei jdm um ~ bitten** (fig inf) to be as nice as pie to sb (inf).

Schönwetter-: **~front** f warm front; **~periode** f period of fine weather; **~wolke** f (inf) cloud that means good weather.

Schonzeit f close season; (fig) honeymoon period.

Schopf m -(e)s, -e (shock of) hair; (von Vogel) tuft, crest. **jdn beim ~ packen** to grab sb by the hair; **eine Gelegenheit beim ~ ergreifen or packen or fassen** to seize or grasp an opportunity with both hands.

Schöpf-: **~brunnen** m draw well; **~eimer** m pail, bucket.

schöpfen vt (a) auch vi (aus from) Wasser to scoop; Suppe to ladle; Papier to dip. **Wasser aus einem Boot ~** to bale out a boat.

(b) Atem to draw, to take; Mut, Kraft to summon up; Vertrauen, Hoffnung to find. **Vertrauen/Hoffnung/Mut etc aus etw ~** to draw confidence/hope/courage etc from sth.

(c) auch vi (old: schaffen) Kunstwerk to create; neuen Ausdruck, Wörter auch to coin, to invent.

Schöpfer(in f) m -s, - (a) creator; (Gott) Creator. **seinem ~ danken** to thank one's Maker or Creator. (b) (inf: Schöpflöffel) ladle. (c) (Papier~) paper maker.

Schöpfer-: **~geist** m creative spirit; (Rel) Holy Spirit; **~hand** f (Rel) Hand of the Creator.

schöpferisch adj creative. **~er Augenblick** moment of inspiration, creative moment; **~e Pause** (hum) pause for inspiration; **~ tätig sein** to be creative.

Schöpferkraft f creative power, creativity.

Schöpf-: **~kelle** f, **~löffel** m ladle.

Schöpfung f creation; (Wort, Ausdruck) coinage, invention. **die ~** (Rel) the Creation; (die Welt) Creation; siehe Herr, Krone.

Schöpfungs-: **~bericht** m, **~geschichte** f story of the Creation; **~tag** m (Rel) day of the Creation.

Schöppchen nt (dial) glass of wine.

schöppeln vti (dial) (einen) ~ to have a drink.

schoppen vt (Aus, S Ger: inf) to stick (inf).

Schoppen m -s, - (a) (old: Flüssigkeitsmaß) half-litre (measure); (S Ger: Glas Wein) glass of wine; (S Ger: Glas Bier) ≈ half-pint of beer, glass of beer.

(b) (dial: Beisammensein) zum ~ gehen to go for a drink; **sich beim ~ treffen** to meet for or over a drink.

(c) (S Ger, Sw: Babyfläschchen) bottle.

(d) (dial) siehe Schuppen.

schoppenweise adv (dial) by the glass(ful).

Schöps m -es, -e (Aus) siehe Hammel.

Schöpserne(s) nt decl as adj (Aus) lamb; mutton.

schor pret of scheren[1].

Schorf m -(e)s, -e (a) crust, scaly skin; (Wund~) scab. (b) (Pflanzenkrankheit) scab.

schorfig adj Wunde that has formed a scab; Haut scaly. (b) Pflanzen scabby.

Schorle f -, -n or nt -s, -s (dial) wine and soda water mix.

Schornstein m chimney; (von Schiff, Lokomotive) funnel, (smoke)stack; (von Fabrik auch) stack. **etw in den ~ schreiben** (inf) to write sth off as a dead loss (inf); **damit der ~ raucht** (inf) to keep body and soul together.

Schornstein-: **~brand** m chimney fire; **~feger(in** f), **~kehrer(in** f) m -s, - chimney-sweep.

Schose f -, -n (dated inf) siehe Chose.

schoß pret of schießen.

Schoß[1] m -sses, -sse (Bot) shoot.

Schoß[2] -es, -e (a) lap. **die Hände in den ~ legen** (lit) to put one's hands in one's lap; (fig) to sit back (and take it easy); **das ist ihm nicht in den ~ gefallen** (fig) it wasn't handed (to) him on a plate, it didn't just fall into his lap; siehe Abraham.

(b) (liter) (Mutterleib) womb; (Scheide) vagina. **Soldaten haben ihren ~ geschändet** she was ravished by soldiers; **im ~e der Familie/Kirche** in the bosom of one's family/of the church; **im ~ der Erde** in the bowels of the earth; **im ~ der Vergessenheit liegen** to have sunk into oblivion; **im ~ der Zukunft** in the lap of the gods.

(c) (an Kleidungsstück) tail.

Schoß[3] f -, -en or -e (Aus) skirt.

Schoß-: **~hund** m lap-dog; **~kind** nt spoilt child; Mamas **~kind** mummy's little boy/girl; **ein ~kind des Glücks** (geh) a child of Fortune.

Schößling m (Bot) shoot.

Schot f -, -en, **Schote** f -, -n (Naut) sheet.

Schote f -, -n (Bot) pod. **~n** (inf: Erbsen) peas (in the pod).

Schott m -(e)s, -e, **Schotte** f -, -n (Naut) bulkhead.

Schotte m -n, -n Scot, Scotsman. **er ist ~** he's a Scot, he's Scottish; **die ~n** the Scots, the Scottish.

Schotten-: **~karo**, **~muster** nt tartan; Rock mit or im **~muster** tartan skirt; **~rock** m tartan skirt; kilt.

Schotter m -s, - gravel; (im Straßenbau) (road-)metal; (Rail) ballast.

Schotterdecke f gravel surface.

schottern vt siehe **in** to gravel (over); to metal; to ballast.

Schotterstraße f gravel road.

Schottin f Scot, Scotswoman. **sie ist ~** she's a Scot, she's Scottish; **die ~nen** Scottish women, Scotswomen.

schottisch adj Scottish, Scots.

Schottland nt -s Scotland.

schraffieren* vt to hatch.

Schraffierung, Schraffur f hatching.

schräg 1 adj (a) (schief, geneigt) sloping; Schrift auch slanting; Augen slanted, slanting; Kante bevelled.

(b) (nicht gerade, nicht parallel) oblique; Linie auch diagonal.

(c) (inf: verdächtig) suspicious, fishy (inf). **ein ~er Vogel** a queer fish (inf).

(d) Musik, Klavier hot.

2 adv (a) (geneigt) at an angle; halten on the slant, slanting; (krumm auch) skew, off the straight, skew-whiff (inf). **den Hut ~ aufsetzen** to put one's hat on at an angle; **~ stehende Augen** slanting or slanted eyes.

(b) (nicht gerade, nicht parallel) obliquely; überqueren, gestreift diagonally; (Sew) on the bias; schneiden on the cross or bias. **~ gegenüber/hinter** diagonally opposite/behind; **~ rechts/links** diagonally to the right; **~ rechts/links abbiegen** (Auto, Fähre) to bear or fork right/left; **die Straße biegt ~ ab** the road forks off; **~ gedruckt** in italics; **den Kopf ~ halten** to hold one's head at an angle or cocked to one side; **~ parken** to park at an angle; **die Sonne schien ~ ins Fenster** the sun slanted in through the window; **jdn ~ ansehen** or **angucken** (lit) to look at sb out of the corner of one's eye; (fig) to look askance at sb; **~ zum Hang queren/fahren** to traverse; **~ zum Fadenlauf** on the bias.

Schrägband nt siehe **Schrägstreifen** (b).

Schräge f -, -n (a) (schräge Fläche) slope, sloping surface; (schräge Kante) bevel(led edge). (b) (Schrägheit) slant, angle; (von Dach auch) pitch, slope; (im Zimmer) sloping ceiling. **eine ~ haben** to be on the slant, to slope, to slant; (Zimmer) to have a sloping ceiling.

Schragen m -s, - (dial) trestle; (Sägebock) sawhorse; (Bett) pallet.

schrägen vt to chamfer; Kanten to bevel.

Schrägheit f slant, angle; (von Wand auch) slope; (von Dach auch) pitch, slope; (von Schrift, Augen) slant.

Schräg-: **~kante** f bevelled edge; **~lage** f angle, slant; (von Flugzeug) bank(ing); (im Mutterleib) oblique position; **etw in ~lage bringen/aufbewahren** to put/keep sth at an angle or on the slant; **das Baby ist in ~lage** the baby is in an oblique position; s~laufend adj diagonal, oblique; ~linie f diagonal line, oblique (line); ~schrift f (Handschrift) slanting hand(writing) or writing; (Typ) italics pl; ~streifen m (a) (Muster) diagonal stripe; (b) (Sew) bias binding; ~strich m oblique.

schrak (old) pret of **schrecken**.

Schramme f -, -n scratch.

Schrammelmusik f popular Viennese music for violins, guitar and accordion.

Schrammeln pl (Aus) quartet playing Schrammelmusik.

schrammen vt to scratch. **sich** (dat) **den Arm/sich ~** to scratch one's arm/oneself.

Schrank m -(e)s, -e cupboard, closet (US); (Kleider~) wardrobe; (für Bücher) bookcase; (im Wohnzimmer, Vitrinen~, Medizin~ auch) cabinet; (Platten~) record cabinet; (Umkleide~, Mil: Spind) locker; (inf: Mann) giant; siehe **Tasse**.

Schrankbett nt fold-away bed.

Schränkchen nt dim of **Schrank** small cupboard; (Arznei~, im Badezimmer) cabinet; (neben dem Bett) bedside cupboard or cabinet.

Schranke f -, -n (a) barrier; (Barrikade) barricade; (Rail: Gatter) gate; (fig) (Grenze) limit; (Hindernis) barrier. **meine Geduld hat ~n** there are limits to my patience; **vor den ~n des Gerichts** before the court; **keine ~n kennen** to know no bounds; (Mensch) not to know when to stop; **er kennt keine ~n mehr** there's no restraining him; **sich in ~n halten** to keep or to remain within reasonable limits; **meine Begeisterung hält sich in ~n** I'm not exactly overwhelmed by it; **etw in ~n halten** to keep sth within reasonable limits or bounds; **einer Sache** (dat) **(enge) ~n setzen** to put a limit on sth; **seiner Geduld sind keine ~n gesetzt** his patience knows no bounds.
    (b) ~n pl (Hist) lists pl; **jdn in die ~n fordern** (fig) to challenge sb; **jdn in seine ~n (ver)weisen** (fig) to put sb in his place; **für jdn/etw in die ~n treten** (old) to enter the lists for sb/sth.

Schranken m -s, - (Aus) (level-crossing) barrier.

Schranken-: s~los adj (fig) Weiten boundless, unbounded, unlimited; Verhalten, Forderungen, Ansprüche unrestrained, unbridled; ~losigkeit f siehe adj boundlessness; unrestraint (gen in), unrestrainedness; ~wärter m gatekeeper (at level crossing).

Schrank-: ~fach nt shelf; **im obersten ~fach** on the top shelf; **s~fertig** adj Wäsche washed and ironed; ~koffer m wardrobe trunk; ~spiegel m wardrobe mirror; ~wand f wall unit.

Schranze f -, -n or m, -n (obs pej) lickspittle (obs), sycophant.

Schrapnell nt -s, -e or -s shrapnel.

Schrapper m -s, - scraper.

Schrat, Schratt m -(e)s, -e forest demon.

Schraubdeckel m screw(-on) lid.

Schraube f -, -n (a) screw; (ohne Spitze) bolt. **bei ihr ist eine ~ locker** (inf) she's got a screw loose (inf). (b) (Naut, Aviat) propeller, prop (inf). (c) (Sport) twist. (d) **alte ~** (pej inf) old bag (inf).

schrauben vti to screw. **etw höher/niedriger ~** to screw sth up/down; **etw fester ~** to screw sth tighter; **etw in die Höhe ~** (fig) Preise, Rekorde to push sth up; Ansprüche, Erwartungen to raise; **etw niedriger ~** (fig) to lower sth; **das Flugzeug schraubte sich in die Höhe** the plane spiralled upwards; siehe **geschraubt**.

Schrauben-: ~bolzen m bolt; ~dampfer m propeller-driven steamer; ~flügel m propeller blade; ~gewinde nt screw thread; ~kopf m screw head; ~schlüssel m spanner; ~windung f screw thread; (Umdrehung) turn; ~zieher m -s, - screwdriver.

Schraub-: ~fassung f screw fixture (on light bulb); ~stock m vice; **etw wie ein ~stock umklammern** (fig) to clasp sth in a vice-like grip; ~verschluß m screw top or cap.

Schrebergarten m allotment.

Schreck m -s, (rare) -e fright, scare. **vor ~** in fright; **zittern with fright**; **zu meinem großen ~(en)** to my great horror or dismay; **einen ~(en) bekommen** to get a fright or scare; **jdm einen ~(en) einjagen** to give sb a fright or scare; **der ~ fuhr mir in die Glieder or Knochen** my knees turned to jelly (inf); **mir sitzt** or **steckt der ~ noch in allen Gliedern or Knochen** my knees are still like jelly (inf); **auf den ~ (hin)** to get over the fright; **sich vom ersten ~ erholen** to recover from the initial shock; **mit dem ~(en) davonkommen** to get off or escape with no more than a fright; **freudiger ~** thrill of joy; **ach du ~!** (im Dustern) (inf) (oh) crumbs! (inf), blast! (inf); **o ~ laß nach** (hum inf) for goodness sake! (inf), for heaven's sake! (inf).

Schreckbild nt terrible or awful vision, nightmare.

schrecken pret **schreckte**, ptp **geschreckt** 1 vt (a) (ängstigen) to frighten, to scare; (stärker) to terrify. **jdn aus dem Schlaf/aus seinen Träumen ~** to startle sb out of his sleep/dreams.
    (b) (Cook) to dip quickly in cold water.
    2 pret auch (old) **schrak**, ptp auch (old) **geschrocken** vi (a) aus sein au dem Schlaf/aus den Gedanken ~ to be startled out of one's sleep/to startle sb, to give sb a start.
    (b) (Hunt) to start up.

Schrecken m -s, - (a) (plötzliches Erschrecken) siehe **Schreck**.
    (b) (Furcht, Entsetzen) terror, horror. **einer Sache** (dat) **den ~ nehmen** to make a thing less frightening or terrifying; **seinen ~ vor etw** (dat) **verlieren** to lose one's fear of sth; **er war der ~ der ganzen Lehrerschaft** he was the terror of all the teachers; siehe **Ende**.

schrecken|erregend adj terrifying, horrifying.

Schreckens-: s~blaß, s~bleich adj as white as a sheet or ghost; ~botschaft f terrible or alarming piece of news; ~herrschaft f (reign of) terror; ~kammer f chamber of hor-

---

rors; ~nachricht f terrible news no pl or piece of news; ~tat f atrocity; ~vision f terrifying or terrible vision, nightmare; ~zeit f time of terror.

Schreck-: ~gespenst nt nightmare; **das ~gespenst des Krieges/der Inflation** the bogey of war/inflation; s~haft adj easily startled; Mensch auch jumpy (inf); ~haftigkeit f nervousness; jumpiness (inf).

schrecklich adj terrible, dreadful; (inf: sehr, groß auch) awful, frightful; Freude great. **er war ~ in seinem Zorn** (geh) his wrath was terrible (to behold) (liter); **es ist mir ~** I feel terrible or dreadful or awful; **sich ~ freuen** (inf) to be terribly or awfully or frightfully pleased; ~ gerne! (inf) I'd absolutely love to; ~ **schimpfen** to swear dreadfully or terribly.

Schrecklichkeit f terribleness, dreadfulness.

Schrecknis nt (old) horror(s pl), terror(s pl).

Schreck-: ~schraube f (pej inf) (old) battle-axe (inf); (in bezug auf Äußeres) dolled-up old bag (sl); ~schuß m (lit) warning shot; **einen ~schuß abgeben** (lit, fig) to give or fire a warning shot; ~schußpistole f blank gun; ~sekunde f moment of shock.

Schrei m -(e)s, -e cry, shout; (brüllender) yell; (gellender) scream; (kreischender) shriek; (von Vogel, von Wild) cry, call; (von Esel) bray; (von Eule etc) screech; (von Hahn) crow. **einen ~ ausstoßen** to give a cry or shout/yell/scream or shriek; **einen ~ unterdrücken** to suppress a cry; **ein spitzer ~** a sharp cry; **der ~ nach Freiheit/Rache** the call for freedom/revenge; **ein ~ der Entrüstung** an (indignant) outcry; **der letzte ~** (inf) the latest thing, all the rage (inf); **nach dem letzten ~ gekleidet** (inf) dressed in the latest style or in the height of fashion.

Schreib-: ~art f style; ~bedarf m writing materials pl, stationery; **alles, was Sie für Ihren ~bedarf brauchen** everything you need in the way of writing materials or stationery; ~block m (writing) pad.

schreiben pret **schrieb**, ptp **geschrieben** 1 vt (a) to write; (ausstellen) Scheck auch, Rechnung to make out, to write out; (mit Schreibmaschine) to type (out); Klassenarbeit, Übersetzung, Examen to do; (berichten: Zeitung etc) to say; (nieder~) to write (down). **sie schreibt eine gute Handschrift** her handwriting is good. she has nice handwriting; **sie schreibt einen guten Stil** she has or writes a good style; **jdm or an jdn einen Brief ~** to write a letter to sb, to write sb a letter; **jdm ein paar Zeilen ~** to write or drop sb a few lines, to write a few lines to sb; **seinen Namen unter etw** (acc) ~ to put one's signature to sth, to sign sth; **sich** (dat) **etw von der Seele or dem Herzen ~** to get sth off one's chest; **wo steht das geschrieben?** where does it say that?; **es steht geschrieben** (Rel) it is written; **es steht Ihnen auf der Stirn or im Gesicht geschrieben** it's written all over your face; siehe **Handschrift, Stern[1], krank, gesund**.
    (b) (orthographisch) to spell. **ein Wort falsch ~** to misspell a word, to spell a word wrong(ly); **etw groß/klein ~** to write or spell sth with a capital/small letter.
    (c) (Datum) **wir ~ heute den 10. Mai** today is the 10th May; **den wievielten ~ wir heute?** what is the date today?; **man schrieb das Jahr 1939** the year was 1939, it was (in) 1939.
    (d) (verbuchen) **jdm etw auf sein** (Bank)konto/die Rechnung ~ to credit sth to sb's (bank) account/to put sth on sb's bill.
    2 vi to write; (Schriftsteller sein auch) to be a writer; (tippen) to type; (berichten) to say. **jdm ~** to write to sb, to write sb (US); **ich schrieb ihm, daß ...** I wrote and told him that ...; **er schreibt orthographisch richtig** his spelling is correct; **an einem Roman etc ~** to be working on or writing a novel etc; **über etw** (acc) **~** (abhandeln) to write about sth; (Univ auch) to work on sth; **ich kann nicht mit der Maschine ~** I can't type; **wieviel Silben schreibt sie pro Minute?** what is her (typing) speed?, how many words a minute can or does she do?; **mit Bleistift ~** to write in pencil, to write with a pencil; **hast du was zum S~?** have you something or anything to write with?
    3 vr impers to write. **mit diesem Kuli schreibt es sich gut/schlecht** this biro writes well/doesn't write properly; **auf diesem Papier schreibt es sich gut/schlecht** this paper is easy or good/difficult to write on.
    4 vr (a) (korrespondieren) to write (to one another or to each other), to correspond. **ich schreibe mich schon lange mit ihm** (inf) I've been writing to him for a long time.
    (b) (geschrieben werden) to be spelt. **wie schreibt er sich?** how does he spell his name?, how is his name spelt?; **wie schreibt sich das?** how is that spelt?, how do you spell that?
    (c) (dated: heißen) to call oneself. **seit wann schreibst du dich wieder mit deinem Mädchennamen?** how long have you been calling yourself by your maiden name again?

Schreiben nt -s, - (a) no pl writing. (b) (Mitteilung) communication (form); (Brief auch) letter.

Schreiber(in f) m -s, - (a) (Verfasser) writer, author; (Brief~) (letter-)writer; (Hist) scribe; (Angestellter, Gerichts~) clerk; (Sw: Schriftführer) secretary; (pej: Schriftsteller) scribbler.
    (b) (inf: Schreibgerät) writing implement. **einen/keinen ~ haben** to have something/nothing to write with.
    (c) (Tech) (Fahrten~) tachograph; (an Meßgerät) recording instrument, recorder; (Fern~) teleprinter, telex.

Schreiberei f (inf) (das Schreiben, Geschriebenes) writing no indef art; (Schriftverkehr) paperwork no indef art, no pl; (pej: von Schriftsteller) scribbling.

Schreiberling m (pej) (Schriftsteller) scribbler; (kleiner Angestellter) pen-pusher.

Schreib-: s~faul adj lazy (about letter-writing); **ich bin s~faul** I'm no great letter-writer, I'm a poor correspondent; ~faulheit f laziness (about letter-writing); ~feder f (pen) nib; (Federhalter) ink pen; (Gänse~) quill (pen); ~fehler m (spelling) mistake; (aus Flüchtigkeit) slip of the pen; (Tippfehler) (typing) mistake or error; ~gerät nt writing implement; (Tech) recording instrument, recorder; ~heft nt exercise book;

(*Schönschreibheft*) copy-book; ~**kraft** *f* typist; ~**krampf** *m* writer's cramp; **einen** ~**krampf (in der Hand) bekommen** to get writer's cramp; ~**maschine** *f* typewriter; **auf** *or* **mit der** ~**maschine schreiben** to type; **mit der** ~**maschine geschrieben** typewritten, typed; ~**maschinenpapier** *nt* typing paper; ~**material** *nt* writing materials *pl*, stationery *no pl*; ~**papier** *nt* (*typing*) paper; (*Briefpapier*) writing paper, letter paper, notepaper; ~**pult** *nt* (writing) desk; ~**schrank** *m* writing desk; ~**schrift** *f* cursive (hand)writing, script; (*Typ*) script; ~**stube** *f* (*Hist*) writing room; (*Büro*) (typists') office, typing room; (*Mil*) orderly room; ~**tafel** *f* (*Hist*) tablet; (*für Schüler*) slate; (*Wandtafel*) blackboard; ~**tisch** *m* desk; ~**tischmörder**, ~**tischtäter** *m* mastermind *or* brains *sing* behind the scenes (of a/the crime); ~**übung** *f* writing exercise.

Schreibung *f* spelling. **falsche** ~ **eines Namens** misspelling of a name.

Schreib-: **s**~**unkundig** *adj* unable to write; ~**unterlage** *f* pad; (*auf* ~*tisch*) desk pad; **ein Buch als** ~**unterlage benutzen** to use a book to rest (one's paper) on; ~**waren** *pl* stationery *sing*, writing materials *pl*; ~**warenhändler** *m* stationer; ~**warenhandlung** *f* stationer's (shop), stationery shop; ~**weise** *f* (*Stil*) style; (*Rechtschreibung*) spelling. ~**zeug** *nt* writing things *pl*; ~**zimmer** *nt* (*Büro*) (typists') office, typing room; (*von Schriftsteller*) study.

schreien *pret* **schrie**, *ptp* **geschrie(e)n 1** *vi* to shout, to cry out; (*gellend*) to scream; (*vor Angst, vor Schmerzen*) to cry out/to scream; (*kreischend*) to shriek; (*brüllen*) to yell; (*inf: laut reden*) to shout; (*inf: schlecht und laut singen*) to screech; (*heulen, weinen: Kind*) to howl; (*jammern*) to moan; (*Esel*) to bray; (*Vogel, Wild*) to call; (*Eule, Käuzchen etc*) to screech; (*Hahn*) to crow. **vor Lachen** ~ to roar *or* hoot with laughter; (*schrill*) to scream with laughter; **es war zum S**~ (*inf*) it was a scream (*inf*) *or* a hoot (*inf*); **nach jdm** ~ to shout for sb; **nach etw** ~ (*fig*) to cry out for sth; *siehe* **Hilfe**.

2 *vt* **Befehle etc** to shout (out). **jdm etw ins Gesicht** ~ to shout sth in sb's face.

3 *vr* **sich heiser** ~ to shout oneself hoarse; (*Baby*) to cry itself hoarse; **sich** (*dat*) **die Kehle heiser** *or* **aus dem Hals** ~ (*inf*) to shout oneself hoarse, to shout one's head off (*inf*).

schreiend *adj* **Farben** loud, garish, gaudy; **Unrecht** glaring, flagrant.

Schreier(in *f*) *m* -**s**, - (*inf*) (*Baby*) bawler (*inf*); (*Unruhestifter*) rowdy, noisy troublemaker; (*fig: Nörgler*) moaner, grouser (*inf*).

Schreierei *f* (*inf*) bawling (*inf*) *no pl*, yelling *no pl*.

Schrei-: ~**hals** *m* (*inf*) (*Baby*) bawler (*inf*); (*Unruhestifter*) rowdy, noisy troublemaker; ~**krampf** *m* screaming fit; **wenn meine Mutter das sieht, bekommt sie einen** ~**krampf** when my mother sees that she'll have a fit.

Schrein *m* -**(e)s**, -**e** (*geh*) shrine; (*Reliquien*~ *auch*) reliquary; (*old: Sarg*) coffin. **im** ~ **seines Herzens** *or* **seiner Seele** (*liter*) in the innermost recesses of his heart (*liter*).

Schreiner *m* -**s**, - (*esp S Ger*) carpenter.

schreinern (*esp S Ger*) **1** *vi* to do carpentry. **mein Mann kann gut** ~ my husband is good at carpentry *or* woodwork *or* is a good carpenter. **2** *vt* to make.

schreiten *pret* **schritt**, *ptp* **geschritten** *vi aux sein* (*geh*) (*schnell gehen*) to stride; (*liter: Zeit*) to march on; (*feierlich gehen*) to walk; (*vorwärts*) to proceed; (*stolzieren*) to strut, to stalk. **im Zimmer auf und ab** ~ to stride *or* pace up and down the room; **zu etw** ~ (*fig*) to get down to sth, to proceed with sth; **es wird Zeit, daß wir zur Tat** ~ it's time we got down to work *or* action; **zum Äußersten** ~ to take extreme measures; **zur Abstimmung/Wahl** ~ to proceed *or* go to a vote.

schrie *pret of* **schreien**.

schrieb *pret of* **schreiben**.

Schrieb *m* -**s**, -**e** (*inf*) missive (*hum*).

Schrift *f* -, -**en** **(a)** (*Hand*~ *auch*) handwriting; (~*system*) script; (*Typ*) type, typeface. **gotische** *or* **deutsche** ~ Gothic script; **in lateinischer/kyrillischer** ~ **schreiben** to write in the Roman/Cyrillic alphabet *or* in (the) Cyrillic script; **er hat eine schlechte** ~ he has bad handwriting, he writes *or* has a poor hand.

(b) (~*stück*) document; (*Bericht*) report; (*Eingabe*) petition.

(c) (*Broschüre*) leaflet; (*Buch*) work; (*kürzere Abhandlung*) paper. **seine früheren** ~**en** his early writings *or* works; **Schopenhauers sämtliche** ~**en** the complete works of Schopenhauer; **die (Heilige)** ~ the (Holy) Scriptures *pl*.

Schrift-: ~**art** *f* (*Hand*~) script; (*Typ*) type, typeface; ~**auslegung** *f* (*Bibl*) interpretation (of the Bible); ~**bild** *nt* script; ~**deutsch** *nt* (*nicht Umgangssprache*) written German; (*nicht Dialekt*) (good) standard German; ~**deutung** *f* graphology.

Schriften-: ~**nachweis** *m*, ~**verzeichnis** *nt* bibliography.

Schrift-: ~**form** *f* (*Jur*) **dieser Vertrag erfordert die** ~**form** this contract must be drawn up in writing; ~**führer** *m* secretary; (*Protokollführer auch*) clerk; ~**gelehrte(r)** *m* (*Bibl*) scribe; ~**gießer** *m* typefounder; ~**grad** *m* type size; ~**guß** *m* typefounding; ~**höhe** *f* x-height (*spec*), height of the type; ~**kunst** *f* calligraphy; ~**leiter** *m* editor; ~**leitung** *f* (*Redaktionsstab*) editorial staff *pl*; (*Redaktionsleitung*) editorship; ~**lesung** *f* (*Eccl*) lesson.

schriftlich 1 *adj* written. **in** ~**er Form/auf** ~**em Wege** in writing; **die** ~**e Prüfung, das S**~**e** (*inf*) the written exam; **ich habe nichts S**~**es darüber** I haven't got anything in writing.

2 *adv* in writing. **ich bin** ~ **eingeladen worden** I have had a written invitation; **ich muß mich bei ihm** ~ **für das Geschenk bedanken** I must write and thank him for the present; **etw** ~ **festhalten/niederlegen/machen** (*inf*) to put sth down in writing; **das kann ich Ihnen** ~ **geben** (*fig inf*) I can tell you that for free (*inf*).

Schrift-: ~**linie** *f* (*Typ*) type line; ~**probe** *f* (*Hand*~) specimen of one's handwriting; (*Typ*) specimen (proof); ~**rolle** *f* scroll; ~**sachverständige(r)** *mf* handwriting expert; ~**satz** *m* (*a*) (*Jur*) legal document; (*b*) (*Typ*) form(e); ~**setzer** *m* typesetter, compositor, comp (*Typ sl*); ~**sprache** *f* (*nicht Umgangssprache*) written language; (*nicht Dialekt*) standard language; **die französische** ~**sprache** written/(good) standard French; **s**~**sprachlich** *adj* **Ausdruck, Konstruktion** used in the written language; **s**~**sprachlich würde man ... sagen** in the written language one would say ...

Schriftsteller *m* -**s**, - author, writer.

Schriftstellerei *f* writing.

Schriftstellerin *f* author(ess), writer.

schriftstellerisch *adj* literary. ~ **tätig sein** to write; **er ist** ~ **begabt** he has literary talent *or* talent as a writer.

schriftstellern* *vi insep* (*inf*) to try one's hand at writing *or* as an author. **der General Patschke** General Patschke, who also writes in his free time.

Schriftstellername *m* pen name, nom de plume.

Schrift-: ~**stück** *nt* paper; (*Jur*) document; ~**tum** *nt*, *no pl* literature; ~**verkehr** *m* correspondence; **im** ~**verkehr stehen** to be in correspondence; ~**wart** *m siehe* ~**führer**; ~**wechsel** *m siehe* ~**verkehr**; ~**zeichen** *nt* character; ~**zug** *m usu pl* stroke; (*Duktus*) hand.

schrill *adj* **Ton, Stimme** shrill; (*fig*) **Mißton, Mißklang** jarring. **sie lachte** ~ **auf** she gave a shriek *or* screech of laughter.

schrillen *vi* to shrill; (*Stimme auch*) to sound shrilly.

Schrippe *f* -, -**n** (*dial*) (bread) roll.

schritt *pret of* **schreiten**.

Schritt *m* -**(e)s**, -**e (a)** (*lit, fig*) step; (*weit ausholend*) stride; (*hörbar*) footstep. **mit schnellen/langsamen** ~**en** quickly/slowly, with quick/slow steps; **mit schleppenden** ~**en** dragging one's feet, with dragging feet; **sie näherte sich ihm mit trippelnden** ~**en** she tripped towards him; **einen** ~ **zurücktreten/zur Seite gehen** to step back/aside *or* to one side; ~ **vor** ~ **setzen** to put one foot in front of the other; **ein paar** ~**e spazierengehen** to go for *or* take a short walk *or* stroll; **einen** ~ **machen** *or* **tun** to take a step; **kleine** *or* **kurze/große** *or* **lange** ~**e machen** to take small steps/long strides; **ich habe seit Wochen keinen/kaum einen** ~ **aus dem Haus getan** I haven't/have hardly set foot outside the house for weeks; **die ersten** ~**e machen** *or* **tun** to take one's first steps; (*fig*) to take the first step; **den ersten** ~ **tun** (*fig*) to make the first move; (*etw beginnen*) to take the first step; **den** ~ **tun** (*fig*) to take the plunge; ~**e gegen jdn/etw unternehmen** to take steps against sb/sth; **den zweiten** ~ **vor dem ersten tun** (*fig*) to try to run before one can walk; **im gleichen** ~ **und Tritt** (*lit, fig*) in step; **auf** ~ **und Tritt** (*lit, fig*) wherever *or* everywhere one goes; ~ **um** *or* **für** ~ step by step; (*fig auch*) little by little, gradually; **Politik der kleinen** ~**e** step-by-step *or* gradualistic policy.

(b) (*Gang*) walk, gait; (*Tempo*) pace. ~ **halten** (*lit, fig*) to keep pace, to keep up; **mit der Zeit** ~ **halten** to keep abreast of the times; **einen schnellen/unwahrscheinlichen** ~ **am Leib** (*inf*) *or* **an sich** (*dat*) **haben** to walk quickly/incredibly quickly; **gemessenen/leichten/langsamen** ~**es** (*geh*) with measured/light/slow step(s) *or* tread; **seinen** ~ *or* **seine** ~**e beschleunigen/verlangsamen** (*geh*) to increase/slow one's pace, to speed up/slow down; **den** ~ **anhalten** to stop; **sein** ~ **stockte** (*geh*) he stopped.

(c) (~*geschwindigkeit*) walking pace. **(im)** ~ **fahren** to go at a crawl, to drive at walking speed; „„~**fahren**" "dead slow"; **im** ~ **reiten/gehen** to walk.

(d) (*Maßangabe*) = yard. **mit zehn** ~ *or* ~**en Abstand** at a distance of ten paces; **sich** (*dat*) **jdn drei** ~**(e) vom Leib halten** (*inf*) to keep sb at arm's length.

(e) (*Hosen*~) crotch; (~*weite*) crotch measurement.

Schrittempo *nt* **getrennt Schritt-tempo** walking speed. **im** ~ **fahren** to crawl along; „„~" "dead slow".

Schritt-: ~**länge** *f* length of one's stride; **s**~**lings** *adv* (*old*) *siehe* **s**~**weise**.

Schrittmacher *m* (*Sport, Med*) pacemaker; (*fig auch*) pacesetter. **die Universitäten waren** ~ **der Revolution** the universities were in the van(guard) of *or* led the way in the revolution.

Schrittmacher-: ~**dienste** *pl* (*fig*) **jdm** ~**dienste leisten** to smooth the path *or* way for sb; ~**maschine** *f* (*Sport*) pacemaker.

Schritt-: ~**messer** *m* -**s**, - *siehe* ~**zähler**; ~**tempo** *nt siehe* **Schrittempo**; **s**~**weise 1** *adv* gradually, little by little; **2** *adj* gradual; ~**weite** *f* (*Sew: von Hose*) (waist-to-)crotch measurement; (*von Kleid, Rock*) hemline; ~**zähler** *m* pedometer.

Schrofen, Schroffen *m* -**s**, - (*Aus, S Ger*) crag.

schroff *adj* (*rauh, barsch*) curt, brusque; (*kraß, abrupt*) **Übergang, Bruch** abrupt; (*steil, jäh*) **Fels, Klippe** precipitous, steep. **das** ~**e Nebeneinander von Arm und Reich** the stark juxtaposition of rich and poor; ~**e Gegensätze** stark *or* sharp contrasts.

Schroffheit *f siehe adj* curtness, brusqueness; abruptness; precipitousness, steepness; (*schroffes Wort*) curt remark.

schröpfen *vt* (*Blut absaugen*) to bleed, to cup (*old*). **jdn** ~ (*fig*) to fleece sb (*inf*), to rip sb off (*sl*).

Schröpfkopf *m* (*Med*) cupping glass.

Schrot *m or nt* -**(e)s**, -**e (a)** whole-corn/-rye *etc* meal; (*Weizen*) wholemeal (*Brit*), wholewheat (*US*). **ein Schotte von echtem** ~ **und Korn** a true Scot; **er ist ein Bauer von echtem** ~ **und Korn** he is a farmer through and through; **vom alten** ~ **und Korn** (*fig*) of the old school; **vom selben** ~ **und Korn** (*fig*) of the same ilk.

(b) (*Hunt*) shot. **einem Hasen eine Ladung** ~ **aufbrennen** (*inf*) to pepper a hare with shot.

Schrot-: ~**brot** *nt* whole-corn/-rye *etc* bread; wholemeal (*Brit*) *or* wholewheat (*US*) bread; ~**büchse** *f* (*Hunt*) shotgun; ~**effekt** *m* (*Elec*) shot effect.

schroten vt Getreide to grind coarsely; Alteisen to break up.

Schrot-: ~flinte f shotgun; ~korn nt (a) grain; (b) (Hunt) pellet; ~kugel f pellet; ~ladung f round of shot; ~mehl nt wholecorn-/rye etc flour; (Weizen) wholemeal (Brit) or wholewheat (US) flour; ~meißel m blacksmith's chisel; ~säge f crosscut saw; ~schuß m round of shot or pellets.

Schrott m -(e)s, no pl scrap metal; (aus Eisen auch) old iron; siehe fahren.

schrotten vt siehe verschrotten.

Schrott-: ~halde f scrap heap; ~handel m scrap trade; ~händler m scrap dealer or merchant; ~haufen m (lit) scrap heap; (fig: Auto) pile or heap of scrap; ~platz m scrap yard; s~reif adj ready for the scrap heap, only fit for scrap; siehe fahren; ~wert m scrap value.

Schrotwaage f (Tech) spirit level.

schrubben 1 vti to scrub. das Deck ~ to swab or scrub the deck/decks. 2 vr to scrub oneself.

Schrubber m -s, - (long-handled) scrubbing brush.

Schrulle f -, -n (a) quirk. sich (dat) die ~ in den Kopf setzen, etw zu tun (inf) to take it into one's head to do sth; was hast du dir denn da für eine ~ in den Kopf gesetzt? (inf) what strange idea have you got into your head now? (b) (pej: alte Frau) old crone.

schrullenhaft, schrullig adj odd, cranky.

Schrullenhaftigkeit, Schrulligkeit f crankiness.

Schrumpel f -, -n (dial) wrinkle.

schrump(e)lig adj (inf) wrinkled.

schrumpeln vi aux sein (inf) to go wrinkled.

schrumpfen vi aux sein (a) (lit) to shrink; (Leber, Niere) to atrophy; (Muskeln) to waste, to atrophy; (Metall, Gestein etc) to contract; (runzlig werden) to get wrinkled.
(b) (fig) to shrink; (Kapital auch, Exporte, Mitgliederschaft, Interesse) to dwindle; (Währung) to depreciate; (Industriezweig) to decline.

schrumplig adj siehe schrump(e)lig.

Schrumpf-: ~kopf m shrunken head; ~leber f cirrhosis of the liver; ~niere f cirrhosis of the kidney.

Schrumpfung f shrinking; (Raumverlust) shrinkage; (von Fundamenten, Metall) contraction; (Med) atrophy(ing); (von Kapital, Arbeitskräften, Exporten) dwindling, diminution; (von Währung) depreciation; (von Industriezweig etc) decline.

Schrund m -(e)s, -̈e (Berg~) crevasse.

Schrunde f -, -n (in der Haut) crack; (durch Kälte) chap; (Fels~, Gletscherspalte) crevasse.

schrundig adj cracked; (durch Kälte) chapped.

schruppen vt (a) (Tech) (mit Feile) to rough-file; (mit Hobel) to rough-plane; (mit Maschine) to rough-machine. (b) siehe **schrubben.**

Schrupp-: ~feile f rough file; ~hobel m jack plane.

Schub m -(e)s, -̈e (a) (Stoß) push, shove. (b) (Phys) (Vortriebskraft) thrust; (Scherung) shear. (c) (Med) phase. (d) (Gruppe, Anzahl) batch. (e) (Kegel~) throw. alle neune auf einen ~ a strike; auf zwei ~e in two throws. (f) (inf: ~fach) drawer.

schubben vt (N Ger) to scratch.

Schuber m -s, - slipcase.

Schub-: ~fach nt drawer; ~haft f (Jur) siehe **Abschiebehaft.**

Schubiack m -s, -s (N Ger) beggar; (Schurke) rogue.

Schub-: ~karre f, ~karren m wheelbarrow; ~kasten m drawer; ~kraft f (Phys) thrust; (Scherung) shearing stress.

Schublade f -, -n drawer.

Schubladengesetz nt (Pol pej) law kept in reserve to deal with a special situation.

Schubladkasten m (Aus) chest of drawers.

Schublehre f vernier calliper.

Schubs m -es, -e (inf) shove (inf), push; (Aufmerksamkeit erregend) nudge. jdm einen ~ geben to give sb a shove (inf) or push/nudge; (fig) to give sb a prod.

Schubschiff nt tug (boat) (which pushes).

schubsen vti (inf) to shove (inf), to push; (Aufmerksamkeit erregend) to nudge.

Schub-: ~stange f siehe **Pleuelstange;** s~weise adv in batches; (Med) in phases.

schüchtern adj shy; (scheu auch) bashful. einen ~en Versuch unternehmen (iro) to make a half-hearted attempt.

Schüchternheit f shyness; (Scheu auch) bashfulness.

schuckeln vi (inf, dial) siehe **wackeln.**

schuf pret of **schaffen[1].**

Schuft m (e)s, -e heel (inf), cad, blackguard (old).

schuften vi (inf) to graft (away) (sl), to slave away. wie ein Pferd ~ (inf) to work like a horse or a Trojan.

Schufterei f (inf) graft (sl), hard work.

schuftig adj mean, shabby.

Schuftigkeit f meanness, shabbiness. das war eine ~ von ihm that was a mean thing he did, that was mean of him.

Schuh m -(e)s, -e (a) shoe. jdm etw in die ~e schieben (inf) to lay the blame for sth at sb's door, to put the blame for sth on sb; wissen, wo jdn der ~ drückt to know what is bothering or troubling sb; wo drückt der ~? what's the trouble?, what's bothering you?; umgekehrt wird ein ~ draus! (inf) quite the reverse is true.
(b) (Brems~) shoe.
(c) (obs: Längenmaß) = foot.

Schuh- in cpds shoe; ~absatz m heel (of a/one's shoe); ~anzieher m shoehorn; ~band nt shoelace.

Schühchen nt dim of **Schuh.**

Schuh-: ~creme f shoe polish or cream; ~haus nt shoe shop; ~löffel m shoehorn; ~macher m shoemaker; (Flickschuster) cobbler; ~nummer f (inf) shoe size; jds ~nummer sein (fig) to be sb's cup of tea (inf); ein paar/mindestens zwei ~nummern zu

groß für jdn (fig) out of sb's league; die Stelle war ein paar ~nummern zu klein für ihn the job wasn't big enough for him (inf); ~plattler m -s, - Bavarian folk dance; ~putzer m bootblack, shoe-shine boy (US); jdn wie einen ~putzer behandeln to treat sb like dirt; ich bin doch nicht dein ~putzer! I'm not your slave!; ~riemen m strap (of a/one's shoe); (Schnürsenkel) shoelace; ~sohle f sole (of a/one's shoe); ~sohlen sparen to save shoe-leather; ~spanner m shoetree; ~waren pl footwear sing; ~werk nt, no pl footwear; ~wichse f (inf) shoe polish; ~zeug nt, no pl footwear.

Schuko-®: ~steckdose f safety socket; ~stecker m safety plug.

Schul-: ~abgänger(in f) m -s, - school-leaver; ~alter nt school age; im ~alter of school age; ins ~alter kommen to reach school age; ~amt nt education authority; ~anfang m beginning of term; (~eintritt) first day at school; morgen ist ~anfang school starts tomorrow; ~anfänger m child just starting school; ~arbeit f (a) usu pl homework no pl, prep no pl (Brit inf); (b) (Aus) test; ~arzt m school doctor; ~aufgaben pl homework sing; ~aufsatz m class essay; ~aufsicht f supervision of schools; die ~aufsicht obliegt dem Kultusministerium the Department of Education is responsible for schools; ~aufsichtsbehörde f education authority; ~ausflug m school outing or trip; ~ausgabe f school edition; ~bank f school desk; die ~bank drücken (inf) to go to school; ~bau m building of a/the school; (im allgemeinen) building of schools; (Gebäude) school building; ~beginn m (~jahrsbeginn) beginning of school building; ~beginn m (~jahrsbeginn) beginning of the school year; (nach Ferien) beginning of term; (der) ~beginn ist um neun school starts at nine; ~behörde f education authority; ~beispiel nt (fig) classic example (für of); ~besuch m school attendance; ~bildung f (school) education; ~bub m (S Ger, Aus) schoolboy; ~buch nt schoolbook, textbook; ~buchverlag m educational publishing company; ~bus m school bus.

schuld adj pred ~ sein or haben to be to blame (an +dat for); war or hatte ~ an dem Streit the argument was his fault, he was to blame for the argument; das Wetter/ich war ~ daran, daß wir zu spät kamen the weather/I was to blame for us being late, it was my fault that we were late; bin ich denn ~, wenn ...? is it my fault if ...?; du hast or bist selbst ~ that's your own fault, that's nobody's fault but your own; jdm/etw ~ geben to blame sb/sth; er gab ihr ~, daß es nicht klappte he blamed her for it not working or for the fact that it didn't work.

Schuld f -, -en (a) no pl (Ursache, Verantwortlichkeit) die ~ an etw (dat) haben or tragen (geh) to be to blame for sth; die ~ auf sich (acc) nehmen to take the blame; jdm die ~ geben or zuschreiben or zuschieben to blame sb; die ~ auf jdn abwälzen or schieben to put the blame on sb; die ~ bei anderen suchen to try to blame somebody else; die ~ liegt bei mir I am to blame (for that); das ist meine/deine ~ that is my/your fault, I am/you are to blame (for that); das ist meine eigene ~ it's my own fault, I've nobody but or only myself to blame; durch meine/deine ~ because of me/you; das ist die ~ der Umstände/Gesellschaft circumstances are/society is to blame.
(b) no pl (~haftigkeit, ~gefühl) guilt; (Unrecht) wrong; (Rel: Sünde) sin; (im Vaterunser) trespasses pl. die Strafe sollte in einem angemessenen Verhältnis zur ~ stehen the punishment should be appropriate to the degree of culpability; sich frei von ~ fühlen to consider oneself completely blameless; ich bin mir keiner ~ bewußt I'm not aware of having done anything wrong; ich bin mir meiner ~ bewußt I know that I have done wrong; ihm konnte seine ~ nicht nachgewiesen werden his guilt could not be proved; ihm konnte keine ~ nachgewiesen werden it couldn't be proved that he had done anything wrong; ~ auf sich (acc) laden to burden oneself with a deep sense of guilt; seine ~ sühnen to atone for one's sins; für seine ~ büßen to pay for one's sin/sins; ~ und Sühne crime and punishment.
(c) (Zahlungsverpflichtung) debt. ich stehe tief in seiner ~ (lit) I'm deeply in debt to him; (fig) I'm deeply indebted to him; ~en machen to run up debts; ~en haben to be in debt; DM 10.000 ~en haben to have debts totalling or of DM10,000, to be in debt to the tune of DM10,000; in ~en geraten to get into debt; mehr ~en als Haare auf dem Kopf haben (inf) to be up to one's ears in debt (inf); das Haus ist frei von ~en the house is unmortgaged.

Schuld-: ~anerkenntnis nt admission of one's guilt; (~schein) promissory note, IOU; ~bekenntnis nt confession; s~beladen adj burdened with guilt; ~beweis m proof or evidence of one's guilt; s~bewußt adj Mensch feeling guilty; Gesicht, Miene guilty; ~bewußtsein nt feelings of guilt.

schulden vt to owe. das schulde ich ihm I owe him that, I owe it to him; jdm Dank ~ to owe sb a debt of gratitude.

Schulden-: s~frei adj free of debt(s); Besitz unmortgaged; ~last f debts pl; ~macher m (inf) habitual debtor; er ist ein notorischer/ewiger ~macher he is notorious for/is forever running up debts; ~masse f (Jur) aggregate liabilities pl; ~tilgung f discharge of one's debt(s).

Schuld-: ~forderung f claim; ~frage f question of guilt; s~frei adj blameless; ~gefängnis nt (Hist) debtors' prison; ~gefühl nt sense no pl or feeling of guilt; ~haft f (Hist) imprisonment for debt; s~haft adj (Jur) culpable.

Schul-: ~diener m (old) school janitor or caretaker; ~dienst m (school-)teaching no art; in den ~dienst treten or gehen to go into teaching; im ~dienst (tätig) sein to be a teacher, to be in the teaching profession.

schuldig adj (a) (schuldhaft, straffällig, schuldbeladen) guilty; (verantwortlich) to blame pred (an +dat for); (Rel) sinful. einer Sache (gen) ~ sein to be guilty of sth; jdn einer Tat (gen) (für) ~ erklären or befinden (Jur) to find sb guilty of or to convict sb of an offence; sich einer Sache (gen) ~ machen to be

guilty of sth; **jdn ~ sprechen** to find *or* pronounce sb guilty, to convict sb; **sich ~ bekennen** to admit one's guilt; (*Jur*) to plead guilty; **~ geschieden sein** to be the guilty party in a/the divorce; **an jdm ~ werden** (*geh*) to wrong sb.
(b) (*geh: gebührend*) due. **jdm die ~e Achtung/den ~en Respekt zollen** to give sb the attention/respect due to him/her.
(c) (*verpflichtet*) **jdm etw** (*acc*) **~ sein** (*lit, fig*) to owe sb sth; **ich muß Ihnen 2 Mark ~ bleiben** I'll have to owe you 2 marks; **was bin ich Ihnen ~?** how much *or* what do I owe you?; **jdm Dank ~ sein** to owe sb a debt of gratitude; **sie blieb mir die Antwort ~/nicht ~** she didn't answer me *or* didn't have an answer/she hit back at me; **er blieb ihr nichts ~** (*fig*) he gave (her) as good as he got.

Schuldige(r) *mf decl as adj* guilty person; (*zivilrechtlich*) guilty party.
Schuldiger *m* -s, - (*Bibl*) trespasser. **wie auch wir vergeben unseren ~n** as we forgive those who trespass against us.
Schuldigkeit *f, no pl* duty. **seine ~ tun** to do one's duty.
Schuldigsprechung *f* conviction.
Schul-: **~direktor** *m* headmaster (*esp Brit*), principal; **~direktorin** *f* headmistress (*esp Brit*), principal.
Schuld-: **~komplex** *m* guilt complex; **s~los** *adj* (*an Verbrechen*) innocent (*an* +dat of); (*an Fehler, Unglück etc*) blameless, free from blame; **er war vollständig s~los an dem Unglück** he was in no way to blame for the accident; **s~los geschieden sein** to be the innocent party in a/the divorce; **~losigkeit** *f siehe adj* innocence; blamelessness.
Schuldner(in *f*) *m* -s, - debtor.
Schuld-: **~prinzip** *nt* (*Jur*) principle of the guilty party; **~recht** *nt* (*Jur*) law of contract; **~schein** *m* IOU, promissory note; **~spruch** *m* verdict of guilty; **~turm** *m* (*Hist*) debtors' prison; **~verhältnis** *nt* (*Jur*) relationship of debenture; **~verschreibung** *f* (*Fin*) debenture bond.
Schule *f* -, -n **(a)** (*Lehranstalt, Lehrmeinung, künstlerische Richtung*) school. **in die** *or* **zur ~ kommen/gehen** to start school/go to school; **er hat nie eine ~ besucht** he has never been to school; **auf** *or* **in der ~ sein** at school; **die ~ wechseln** to change schools; **von der ~ abgehen** to leave school; **sie ist an der ~** she is a (school)teacher; **die ~ ist aus** school is over, the schools are out; **er ist bei Brecht in die ~ gegangen** (*fig*) he was greatly influenced by Brecht; **darin hat er bei seinen Eltern eine gute ~ gehabt** his parents have given him a good schooling in that; **durch eine harte ~ gegangen sein** (*fig*) to have learned in a hard school; **~ machen** to become the accepted thing; **aus der ~ plaudern** to tell tales out of school (*inf*).
(b) (*Reiten*) school of riding; *siehe* **hoch.**
(c) (*Lehrbuch*) tutor. **~ der Geläufigkeit** book of études.
schulen *vt* to train; *Auge, Gedächtnis, Pferd auch* to school; (*Pol*) to give political instruction to.
Schul-: **~englisch** *nt* schoolboy/schoolgirl English; **zwei Jahre ~englisch** two years' English at school; **mein ~englisch** the English I learnt at school; **s~entlassen** *adj* **kaum s~entlassen, begann er ...** hardly had he left school when he began ...; **die s~entlassene Jugend** the young people who have recently left school; **~entlassung** *pl* school-leavers *pl*; **~entlassung** *f* **der Tag der ~entlassung** the day one leaves school; **nach seiner/der ~entlassung** after leaving school; **~entlassungsfeier** *f* school-leavers' day; **~entlassungszeugnis** *nt* school-leaving certificate.
Schüler(in *f*) *m* -s, - schoolboy/schoolgirl; (*einer bestimmten Schule*) pupil; (*einer Oberschule auch*) student; (*Jünger*) follower, disciple. **als ~ habe ich ...** when I was at school I ...; **alle ~ und ~innen dieser Stadt** all the schoolchildren of this town; **ein ehemaliger ~** (*der Schule*) an old boy *or* pupil (of the school).
Schüler-: **~austausch** *m* school *or* student exchange; **~ausweis** *m* (school) student card; **s~haft** *adj* schoolboyish/schoolgirlish; (*pej*) childish, puerile; **~heim** *nt* (school) boarding house.
Schülerin *f siehe* **Schüler(in).**
Schüler-: **~karte** *f* school season-ticket; **~lotse** *m* pupil acting as road-crossing warden; **~mitverwaltung** *f* school *or* student council; **~mütze** *f* school cap; **~parlament** *nt* inter-school student council; **~schaft** *f* pupils *pl*; **~sprache** *f* school slang; **~vertretung** *f* pupil *or* student representation; **~zeitung** *f* school magazine.
Schul-: **~erziehung** *f* schooling; **~fach** *nt* school subject; **~feier** *f* school function; **~ferien** *pl* school holidays *pl* (*Brit*) *or* vacation; **~fernsehen** *nt* schools' *or* educational television; **~fest** *nt* school function; **~film** *m* educational film; **s~frei** *adj* **ein s~freier Nachmittag** an afternoon when one doesn't have to go to school; **nächsten Samstag ist s~frei** there's no school next Saturday; **die Kinder haben morgen s~frei** the children don't have to go to school tomorrow; **~freund** *m* schoolfriend; **~funk** *m* schools' radio; **~gebäude** *nt* school building; **~gebrauch** *m:* **zum** *or* **für den ~gebrauch** for use in schools; **~gegenstand** *m* (*Aus*) school subject; **~gelände** *nt* school grounds *pl*; **~geld** *nt* school fees *pl*; **laß dir dein ~geld wiedergeben!** (*inf*) school didn't do you much good!; **~gelehrsamkeit** *f* (*old, pej*) booklearning; **~gesetz** *nt* education act; **~grammatik** *f* (school) grammar book *or* grammar (*inf*); **~haus** *nt* schoolhouse; **~heft** *nt* exercise book; **~hof** *m* school playground (*Brit*), schoolyard.
schulisch *adj Leistungen, Probleme, Verbesserung* at school; (*rein akademisch*) scholastic; *Angelegenheiten* school *attr.* **seine ~en Leistungen/Probleme** his progress/problems at school; **er hat ~ große Fortschritte gemacht** he has improved greatly at school; **~e Angelegenheiten** school matters; **aus ~er Sicht** from the school angle.
Schul-: **~jahr** *nt* school year; (*Klasse*) year; **ihre ~jahre** her schooldays; **~jugend** *f* schoolchildren *pl*; **die heutige ~jugend** schoolchildren today; **~junge** *m* schoolboy; **~kamerad** *m*

schoolmate, schoolfriend; **~kenntnisse** *pl* knowledge *sing* acquired at school; **~kind** *nt* schoolchild; **~klasse** *f* (school) class; **~landheim** *nt* country house used by school classes for short visits; **~lehrer** *m* schoolteacher; **~leiter** *m* headmaster (*esp Brit*), principal; **~leiterin** *f* headmistress (*esp Brit*), principal; **~lektüre** *f* book/books read in schools; **~lektüre sein** to be read in schools; **~mädchen** *nt* schoolgirl; **~mappe** *f* schoolbag; **s~mäßig** *adj Unterricht, Kurs, Lehrbuch* didactic; **s~mäßig ist die Stadt ganz gut versorgt** the town is well provided with schools; **s~mäßig gekleidet** dressed for school; **es war alles s~mäßig reglementiert** everything was regimented just like in school; **~medizin** *f* orthodox medicine; **~mediziner** *m* orthodox medical practitioner; **~meinung** *f* received opinion; **~meister** *m* (*old, hum, pej*) schoolmaster; **s~meisterlich** *adj* (*pej*) schoolmasterish; **sich s~meisterlich aufspielen** to play the schoolmaster; **s~meistern*** *insep* 1 *vt* to lecture (at or to); 2 *vi* to lecture; **~ordnung** *f* school rules *pl*; **~pflicht** *f* compulsory school attendance *no art*; **allgemeine ~pflicht** compulsory school attendance for all children; **es besteht ~pflicht** school attendance is compulsory; **s~pflichtig** *adj Kind* required to attend school; **~politik** *f* education policy; **~psychologe** *m* educational psychologist; **~ranzen** *m* (school) satchel; **~rat** *m* schools inspector; **~reform** *f* educational reform; **~regel** *f* school adage; **~reife** *f* school readiness (*spec*); **die ~reife haben** to be ready to go to school; **~reifetest** *m* school readiness test; **~schiff** *nt* training ship; **~schluß** *m* end of school; (*vor den Ferien*) end of term; **~schluß ist um 13[10]** school finishes at 13.10; **kurz nach ~schluß** just after school finishes/finished; **~schwänzen** *nt* truancy; **~schwänzer** *m* -s, - truant; **~speisung** *f* free school meals *pl*; **~sport** *m* school sport; **~sprecher(in** *f*) *m* head boy/girl (*Brit*); **~sprengel** *m* (*Aus*) (school) catchment area; **~streß** *m* stress at school; **im ~streß sein** to be under stress at school; **~stunde** *f* (school) period *or* lesson; **~system** *nt* school system; **~tag** *m* schoolday; **der erste ~tag** the/one's first day at school; **~tasche** *f* schoolbag.
Schulter *f* -, -n shoulder. **mit gebeugten/hängenden ~n gehen** to be round-shouldered, to have round/sloping shoulders; (*fig: niedergeschlagen*) to look careworn/down in the mouth *or* downcast; **breite ~n haben** (*lit*) to be broad-shouldered, to have broad shoulders; (*fig*) to have a broad back; **er ließ die ~n hängen** he was slouching; (*niedergeschlagen*) he hung his head; **sich** (*dat*) **eine Jacke über die ~n hängen** to put a jacket round one's shoulders; **sich** (*dat*) **den Fotoapparat über die ~ hängen** to sling one's camera over one's shoulder; **jdm die Hand auf die ~ legen** to put one's hand on sb's shoulder; **jdm auf die Schulter klopfen** *or* **schlagen** to give sb a slap on the back, to clap sb on the back; (*lobend*) to pat sb on the back; **sich** (*dat*) **selbst auf die ~ klopfen** (*fig*) to blow one's own trumpet; **jdm** *or* **jdn um die ~ fassen** to put one's arm round sb's shoulders; **~ an ~** (*dichtgedrängt*) shoulder to shoulder; (*gemeinsam, solidarisch*) side by side; **die** *or* **mit den ~n zucken** to shrug one's shoulders; **jdn auf die ~ legen** *or* **werfen** to get sb in a shoulder-press; **die Verantwortung ruht auf seinen ~n** the responsibility rests on his shoulders *or* lies at his door; **etw auf die leichte ~ nehmen** to take sth lightly; **jdn über die ~ ansehen** (*fig*) to look down one's nose at sb; *siehe* **kalt.**
Schulter-: **~blatt** *nt* shoulder blade; **s~frei** *adj Kleid* off-the-shoulder; (*ohne Träger*) strapless; (*mit Nackenträger*) halterneck; **sie war/kam s~frei** her shoulders were bare, she was wearing a dress which left her shoulders bare; **~gelenk** *nt* shoulder joint; **~höhe** *f* shoulder height; **in ~höhe** at shoulder level *or* height; **das Wasser stand (mir) in ~höhe** the water came up to my shoulders.
-schult(e)rig *adj suf* -shouldered.
Schulter-: **~klappe** *f* (*Mil*) epaulette; **s~lang** *adj* shoulder-length.
schultern *vt* to shoulder. **das Gewehr ~** to shoulder arms.
Schulter-: **~polster** *nt* shoulder pad; **~riemen** *m* shoulder strap; **~sieg** *m* (*Sport*) fall; **~stand** *m* (*Sport*) shoulder stand; **~stück** *nt* (**a**) (*Mil*) epaulette; (**b**) (*Cook*) piece of shoulder; **~wurf** *m* (*Sport*) shoulder-throw.
Schultheiß *m* -en, -en (*Hist*) mayor.
Schulträger *m* (*form*) **der ~** (*dieser Schule*) **ist der Staat** the school is supported *or* maintained by the State.
-schultrig *adj suf siehe* **-schult(e)rig.**
Schul-: **~tüte** *f* large conical bag of sweets given to children on their first day at school; **~typ** *m* type of school.
Schulung *f* (*Ausbildung, Übung*) training; (*von Auge, Gedächtnis, Pferd auch*) schooling; (*Pol*) political instruction.
Schulungs-: **~kurs** *m* training course; **~lager** *nt* training camp.
Schul-: **~uniform** *f* school uniform; **~unterricht** *m* school lessons *pl*; **~wanderung** *f* school hike; **~weg** *m* way to/from school; (*Entfernung*) distance to/from school; (*Route*) route to/from school; **ich habe einen ~weg von 20 Minuten** it takes me 20 minutes to get to/from school; **~weisheit** *f* (*pej*) booklearning; **~wesen** *nt* school system; **~wissen** *nt* knowledge acquired at school; **~wörterbuch** *nt* school dictionary.
Schulze *m* -n, -n (*Hist*) *siehe* **Schultheiß.**
Schul-: **~zeit** *f* (**~jahre**) schooldays *pl*; **nach 13jähriger ~zeit** after 13 years at school; **seit der ~zeit** since we/they were at school, since our/their schooldays; **~zentrum** *nt* school complex; **~zeugnis** *nt* school report; **~zwang** *m siehe* **~pflicht**; **~zwecke** *pl:* **für ~zwecke, zu ~zwecken** for school; (*als geeignetes Lehrmittel*) for use in schools.
schummeln *vi* (*inf*) to cheat. **in Latein/beim Kartenspiel ~** to cheat in Latin/at cards.
Schummelzettel *m* (*Sch sl*) crib.
schumm(e)rig *adj Beleuchtung* dim; *Raum* dimly-lit. **bei ~em**

schummern

Licht in the half-light; **es war schon ~** it was already getting dark.

schummern 1 *vi impers* (*N Ger*) **es schummert** dusk is falling. **2** *vt* (*Geog*) to shade (in).

Schummerstunde *f* (*N Ger*) twilight hour.

Schummerung *f* (*Geog*) shading.

schummrig *adj siehe* **schumm(e)rig**.

schund (*rare*) *pret of* **schinden**.

Schund *m* **-(e)s**, *no pl* (*pej*) trash, rubbish. **was für ~/einen ~ hast du denn da?** what's that trash/trashy book you're reading?; *siehe* **Schmutz**.

Schund-: **~literatur** *f* trash, trashy literature; **~roman** *m* trashy novel.

Schunkellied *nt* German drinking song.

schunkeln *vi* to link arms and sway from side to side.

Schupfen *m* **-s**, - (*esp S Ger*) *siehe* **Schuppen**.

Schupfer *m* **-s**, - (*Aus*) *siehe* **Schubs**.

Schupo¹ *f* **-**, *no pl abbr of* **Schutzpolizei**.

Schupo² *m* **-s**, **-s** (*dated inf*) *abbr of* **Schutzpolizist** cop (*inf*), copper (*Brit inf*).

Schuppe *f* **-**, **-n** (**a**) (*Bot, Zool*) scale; (*von Ritterrüstung, Tierpanzer*) plate. **es fiel mir wie ~n von den Augen** the scales fell from my eyes. (**b**) (*Kopf~*) **~n** *pl* dandruff *sing*.

Schuppen *m* **-s**, - (**a**) shed; (*Flugzeug~*) hangar. (**b**) (*inf*) (*Haus, Wohnung etc*) joint (*sl*), hole (*pej inf*), hovel (*pej*); (*übles Lokal*) dive (*inf*).

schuppen 1 *vt* (**a**) *Fische* to scale. (**b**) (*N Ger inf*) *siehe* **schubsen**. **2** *vr* to flake.

Schuppen-: **s~artig** *adj* scale-like; **die Ziegel sind s~artig angeordnet** the tiles are arranged so that they overlap; **~bildung** *f*, *no pl* dandruff; **~flechte** *f* (*Med*) psoriasis (*spec*); **s~förmig** *adj siehe* **s~artig**; **~panzer** *m* scale armour; **~tier** *nt* scaly ant-eater.

schuppig *adj* scaly; (*abblätternd auch*) flaking. **die Haut löst sich ~ ab** his *etc* skin is flaking (off).

Schup(p)s *m* **-es**, **-e** *siehe* **Schubs**.

schup(p)sen *vti siehe* **schubsen**.

Schur *f* **-**, **-en** (*das Scheren*) shearing; (*geschorene Wolle*) clip.

Schüreisen *nt siehe* **Schürhaken**.

schüren *vt* (**a**) *Feuer, Glut* to rake, to poke. (**b**) (*fig*) to stir up; *Zorn, Eifersucht, Leidenschaft, Haß* to fan the flames of.

schürfen 1 *vi* (*Min*) to prospect (*nach* for). **tief ~** (*fig*) to dig deep. **2** *vt* *Bodenschätze* to mine. **3** *vtr* to graze oneself. **sich** (*dat*) **die Haut ~, sich ~** to graze oneself *or* one's skin; **sich am Knie ~** to graze one's knee.

Schürf-: **~grube** *f*, **~loch** *nt* (*Min*) test pit; **~recht** *nt* mining rights *pl*; **~wunde** *f* graze, abrasion.

Schürhaken *m* poker.

schurigeln *vt* (*inf*) (*hart anfahren*) to lay into (*inf*); (*schikanieren*) to bully.

Schurke *m* **-n**, **-n** (*dated*) villain, scoundrel, rogue.

Schurkenstreich *m*, **Schurkentat**, **Schurkerei** *f* (*old*) (piece of) villainy.

schurkisch *adj* (*dated*) base, despicable.

schurren *vi* (*dial*) (*Schlitten*) to grate. **mit den Füßen ~** to shuffle one's feet; (*beim Gehen*) to drag one's feet.

Schurrmurr *m* **-s**, *no pl* (*dial*) junk, rubbish.

Schurwolle *f* virgin wool. **„reine ~"** "pure new wool".

Schurz *m* **-es**, **-e** loincloth; (*von Schmied, Arbeiter etc, dial*) apron.

Schürze *f* **-**, **-n** apron; (*Frauen~, Kinder~ mit Latz auch*) pinafore, pinny (*inf*). **sich** (*dat*) **eine ~ umbinden** to put an apron on; **er hängt der Mutter noch an der ~** he's still tied to his mother's apron strings; **er ist hinter jeder ~ her** (*dated inf*), **er läuft jeder ~ nach** (*dated inf*) he runs after anything in a skirt (*inf*).

schürzen *vt* (**a**) (*dated*) *Rock* to gather (up). (**b**) (*geh: schlingen*) *Knoten* to tie; *Faden* to knot, to tie a knot in. (**c**) (*geh: aufwerfen*) **die Lippen/den Mund ~** (*zum Pfeifen*) to purse one's lips; (*verführerisch*) to pout; **ihr geschürzter Mund** her pursed lips/her pout.

Schürzen-: **~band** *nt* apron-string; **er hängt der Mutter noch am ~band** he's still tied to his mother's apron strings; **~jäger** *m* (*inf*) philanderer, one for the girls (*inf*).

Schurzfell *nt* leather apron.

Schuß *m* **-sses**, **-̈sse** (**a**) shot; (*~ Munition*) round. **sechs ~ or ~̈sse** six shots/rounds; **zum ~ kommen** to have a chance to shoot; **ein ~ ins Schwarze** (*lit, fig*) a bull's-eye; **weit vom ~ sein** (*fig inf*) to be miles from where the action is (*inf*); **er ist keinen ~ Pulver wert** (*fig*) he is not worth tuppence (*inf*); **das war ein ~ (schöner) ~ vor den Bug** (*fig*) that was a warning not to be ignored; **ein ~ in den Ofen** (*sl*) a complete waste of time.

(**b**) (*Min: Sprengung*) blast, charge.

(**c**) (*Ftbl*) kick; (*zum Tor auch*) shot. **zum ~ kommen** to get the ball; (*zum Tor*) to get a chance to shoot.

(**d**) (*Ski*) schuss. **im ~ fahren** to schuss.

(**e**) (*Spritzer*) (*von Wein, Essig etc*) dash; (*von Whisky*) shot; (*von Humor, Leichtsinn etc auch*) touch.

(**f**) (*Tex: Querfäden*) weft, woof.

(**g**) (*inf*) **in ~ sein/kommen** to be in/get into (good) shape; (*Mensch, Sportler auch*) to be on form/get into good form; (*Schüler, Klasse*) to be/get up to the mark; (*Party*) to be going well/get going; **etw in ~ bringen/halten** to knock sth into shape/keep sth in good shape; *Schulklasse* to bring/keep sth up to the mark; *Party* to get/keep sth going; **ich werde dafür sorgen, daß der Garten wieder in ~ kommt** I will see that the garden is put into good shape *or* is set to rights again.

Schuß-: **~bereich** *m* (firing) range; **im ~bereich** within range; **s~bereit** *adj* ready to fire; *Gewehr auch* cocked.

Schussel *m* **-s**, - (*inf*) *or* *f* **-**, **-n** (*inf*) dolt (*inf*); (*zerstreut*) scatterbrain (*inf*); (*ungeschickt*) clumsy clot (*inf*).

Schüssel *f* **-**, **-n** bowl; (*Servier~ auch*) dish; (*Wasch~*) basin. **vor leeren ~n sitzen** (*nach dem Essen*) to sit staring at the dirty dishes; (*in Notzeit*) to go hungry.

schusselig *adj* (*inf*) daft; (*zerstreut*) scatterbrained (*inf*), muddle-headed (*inf*); (*ungeschickt*) clumsy, all thumbs *pred*.

Schusseligkeit *f* (*inf*) daftness; (*Zerstreutheit*) muddle-headedness (*inf*); (*Ungeschick*) clumsiness.

schusseln *vi* (*inf*) (*zerstreut sein*) to be scatterbrained (*inf*) *or* muddle-headed (*inf*); (*ungeschickt vorgehen*) to be clumsy; (*sich ungeschickt bewegen*) to bumble (*inf*).

Schusser *m* **-s**, - (*dial*) marble.

schussern *vi* (*dial*) to play marbles.

Schuß-: **~faden** *m* (*Tex*) weft thread; **~fahrt** *f* (*Ski*) schuss; (*das ~fahren*) schussing; **~feld** *nt* field of fire; (*Übungsplatz*) firing range; **s~fest** *adj* bulletproof; **s~frei** *adj* clear for firing; **s~freie Bahn haben** to have a clear line of fire; **~geschwindigkeit** *f* velocity (*of bullet etc*); **~kanal** *m* (*Med*) path of a/the bullet through the body.

schußlig *adj* (*inf*) *siehe* **schusselig**.

Schußligkeit *f* (*inf*) *siehe* **Schusseligkeit**.

Schuß-: **~linie** *f* line of fire; (*fig auch*) firing line; **~richtung** *f* direction of fire; **s~sicher** *adj* bulletproof; **~verletzung** *f* bullet wound; **~waffe** *f* firearm; **~waffengebrauch** *m* (*form*) use of firearms; **~wechsel** *m* exchange of shots *or* fire; **~weite** *f* range (of fire); **in/außer ~weite** within/out of range; **~winkel** *m* angle of fire; **~wunde** *f* bullet wound; **~zahl** *f* (*Tex*) number of weft threads; **~zeit** *f* (*Hunt*) shooting season.

Schuster *m* **-s**, - shoemaker; (*Flick~*) cobbler. **auf ~s Rappen** (*hum*) by Shanks's pony; **~, bleib bei deinem Leisten!** (*Prov*) cobbler, stick to your last (*Prov*).

Schuster-: **~ahle** *f* shoemaker's awl; **~draht** *m* waxed thread.

Schusterei *f* (**a**) (*Werkstatt*) shoemaker's; (*von Flickschuster*) cobbler's. (**b**) (*pej inf: Pfuscherei*) botching (*inf*).

Schuster-: **~handwerk** *nt* shoemaking; cobbling; **~junge** *m* (**a**) (*old: ~lehrling*) shoemaker's/cobbler's apprentice. (**b**) (*Typ*) widow.

schustern *vi* (**a**) to cobble *or* repair *or* mend shoes. (**b**) (*pej inf*) to do a botch job (*inf*).

Schuster-: **~pech** *nt* shoemaker's *or* cobbler's wax; **~pfriem(en)** *m siehe* **~ahle**; **~werkstatt** *f* shoemaker's/cobbler's workshop.

Schute *f* **-**, **-n** (**a**) (*Naut*) lighter. (**b**) (*Damenhut*) poke (bonnet).

Schutt *m* **-(e)s**, *no pl* (*Trümmer, Bau~*) rubble; (*Geol*) debris, detritus (*spec*). **„~ abladen verboten"** "no tipping"; **eine Stadt in ~ und Asche legen** to reduce a town to rubble; **in ~ und Asche liegen** to be in ruins.

Schuttabladeplatz *m* tip, dump.

Schütt-: **~beton** *m* cast concrete; **~boden** *m* strawloft; (*für Getreide*) granary.

Schütte *f* **-**, **-n** (**a**) (*Bund*) stock. (**b**) (*Behälter*) wall-mounted drawer-like canister for sugar, flour etc.

Schüttel-: **~becher** *m* (cocktail) shaker; **~frost** *m* (*Med*) shivering fit, fit of the shivers (*inf*); **~lähmung** *f* (*Med*) Parkinson's disease.

schütteln 1 *vt* to shake; (*rütteln*) to shake about, to jolt (about). **den** *or* **mit dem Kopf ~** to shake one's head; **von Angst/Entsetzen geschüttelt werden** to be gripped with fear/horror; **von Fieber geschüttelt werden** to be racked with fever; *siehe* **Hand, Staub**.

2 *vr* to shake oneself; (*vor Kälte*) to shiver (*vor* with); (*vor Ekel*) to shudder (*vor* with, in). **sich vor Lachen ~** to shake with laughter.

Schüttel-: **~reim** *m* goat rhyme, rhyme in which the consonants of the rhyming syllables are transposed in the next line; **~rutsche** *f* (*Tech*) vibrating chute; **~sieb** *nt* riddle.

schütten 1 *vt* to tip; *Flüssigkeiten* to pour; (*ver~*) to spill. **„keine heiße Asche in die Mülltonnen ~"** "do not put hot ashes in the dustbins". **2** *vi impers* (*inf*) **es schüttet** it's pouring (with rain), it's bucketing (down) (*inf*).

schütter *adj* *Haar* thin.

Schüttgut *nt* bulk goods *pl*.

Schutt-: **~halde** *f* (*~haufen*) rubble tip; (*Geol*) scree slope; **~haufen** *m* pile *or* heap of rubble; **etw in einen ~haufen verwandeln** to reduce sth to a pile of rubble; **~kegel** *m* (*Geol*) cone of scree *or* debris; **~platz** *m* tip.

Schütt-: **~stein** *m* (*S Ger, Sw*) sink; **~stroh** *nt* bedding straw.

Schutz *m* **-es**, *no pl* protection (*vor +dat, gegen* against, from); (*Zuflucht auch*) shelter, refuge (*vor +dat, gegen* from); (*esp Mil: Deckung*) cover. (*Natur, Umwelt etc*) conservation; **jdn um ~ bitten** to ask sb for protection; **bei jdm ~ suchen** to look to sb for protection; to seek shelter *or* refuge with sb; **unter einem Baum ~ suchen** to shelter under a tree, to take *or* seek refuge under a tree; **im ~(e) der Nacht** *or* **Dunkelheit/des Artilleriefeuers** under cover of night *or* darkness/artillery fire; **zum ~ von Leib und Leben** for the protection of life and limb; **jdn/etw als ~ mitnehmen** to take sb/sth with one for protection; **zum ~ der Augen** to protect the eyes; **jdn in ~ nehmen** (*fig*) to take sb's part, to stand up for sb; **zu ~ und Trutz zusammenstehen** (*old, liter*) to stand together.

Schutz-: **~anstrich** *m* protective coat; **~anzug** *m* protective clothing *no indef art, no pl*; **~ärmel** *m* sleeve-protector; **~aufsicht** *f* (*Jur*) supervision by a social worker; **s~bedürftig** *adj* in need of protection; **~befohlene(r)** *mf decl as adj siehe* **Schützling**; **~behauptung** *f* lie to cover oneself; **~blech** *nt* mudguard; **~brief** *m* (**a**) (letter of) safe-conduct; (**b**) *siehe* **Auslandsschutzbrief**; **~brille** *f* protective goggles *pl*; **~bündnis** *nt* defensive alliance; **~dach** *nt* porch; (*an Haltestelle*) shelter; **~deck** *nt* shelter deck.

Schütze *m* **-n**, **-n** (**a**) marksman; (*Schießsportler*) rifleman;

(*Hunt*) hunter; (*Bogen*~) archer; (*Hist*) bowman, archer; (*Ftbl: Tor*~) scorer. **er ist der beste** ~ he is the best shot. **(b)** (*Mil: Dienstgrad*) private; (*Maschinengewehr*~) gunner. **(c)** (*Astrol*) Sagittarius *or* art; (*Astron auch*) Archer. **sie ist** ~ she's Sagittarius *or* a Sagittarius. **(d)** (*Weberschiffchen*) shuttle.

Schützen *m* -s, - (*Tex*) shuttle.

schützen **1** *vt* to protect (*vor* +*dat*, *gegen* from, against); (*Zuflucht bieten auch*) to shelter (*vor* +*dat*, *gegen* from); (*absichern: Versicherung etc auch*) to safeguard; (*esp Mil: Deckung geben*) to cover. **urheberrechtlich/gesetzlich/patentrechtlich geschützt** protected by copyright/registered/patented; **ein geschützter Platz** a sheltered spot *or* place; **vor Hitze/Sonnenlicht** ~**!** keep away from heat/sunlight; **vor Nässe** ~**!** keep dry; **Gott schütze dich!** (*old*) (may) the Lord protect *or* keep you.

2 *vi* to give *or* offer protection (*vor* +*dat*, *gegen* against, from); (*Zuflucht bieten auch*) to give *or* offer shelter (*vor* +*dat*, *gegen* from); (*esp Mil: Deckung geben*) to give cover.

3 *vr* to protect oneself (*vor* +*dat*, *gegen* from, against); (*sich absichern auch*) to safeguard oneself (*vor* +*dat*, *gegen* against). **er weiß sich zu** ~ he knows how to look after himself.

Schützen-: ~**anger** *m siehe* ~**wiese**; ~**bruder** *m* member of a rifle club.

schützend *adj* protective. **ein** ~**es Dach** (*gegen Wetter*) a shelter; **ein** ~**es Dach über sich** (*dat*) **haben** to be under cover; **der** ~**e Hafen** (*lit*) the protection of the harbour; (*fig*) a/the safe haven; **seine** ~**e Hand über jdn halten** *or* **breiten** to take sb under one's wing.

Schützenfest *nt fair featuring shooting matches.*

Schutz|engel *m* guardian angel.

Schützen-: ~**gesellschaft**, ~**gilde** *f siehe* ~**verein**; ~**graben** *m* trench; ~**haus** *nt* clubhouse (*of a rifle club*); ~**hilfe** *f* (*fig*) support; **jdm** ~**hilfe geben** to back sb up, to support sb; ~**kette** *f* (*Mil*) firing line; ~**könig** *m* champion rifleman at a Schützenfest; ~**linie** *f* (*Mil*) firing line; ~**loch** *nt* (*Mil*) foxhole; ~**panzer(wagen)** *m* armoured personnel carrier; ~**platz** *m siehe* ~**wiese**; ~**verein** *m* rifle *or* shooting club; ~**wiese** *f* fairground at which a rifle club holds its competitions; ~**zug** *m* procession of riflemen.

Schutz-: ~**farbe**, ~**färbung** *f* (*Biol*) protective *or* adaptive colouring; ~**frist** *f* term of copyright; ~**gebiet** *nt* (*Pol*) protectorate; ~**gebühr** *f* (*token*) fee; ~**gebühren** *pl* (*euph sl*) protection money *sing*; ~**geist** *m* (*Myth*) protecting *or* tutelary (*liter*) spirit; ~**geländer** *nt* guard-rail; ~**geleit** *nt siehe* Geleitschutz; ~**gitter** *nt* (*um Denkmal etc*) protective barrier; (*vor Maschine, Fenster, Tür*) protective grille; (*um Leute zu schützen*) safety barrier/grille; (*vor Kamin*) (fire)guard; (*Elec*) screen grid; ~**gott** *m* tutelary god (*liter*); ~**göttin** *f* (*Myth*) tutelary goddess (*liter*); ~**hafen** *m* port of refuge; (*Winterhafen*) winter harbour; ~**haft** *f* (*Jur*) protective custody; (*Pol*) preventive detention; ~**haube** *f* protective hood; (*für Schreibmaschine*) cover; ~**haut** *f* protective covering; ~**heilige(r)** *mf* patron saint; ~**helm** *m* safety helmet; (*von Bauarbeiter auch*) hard hat (*inf*); ~**herr(in** *f*) *m* patron; ~**herrschaft** *f* (*Pol*) protection, protectorate; (*Patronat*) patronage; ~**hülle** *f* protective cover; (*Buchumschlag*) dust cover *or* jacket; **s~impfen** *pret* **s~impfte**, *ptp* **s~geimpft**, *infin auch* **s~zuimpfen** *vt* to vaccinate, to inoculate; ~**impfung** *f* vaccination, inoculation; ~**kappe** *f* (protective) cap; ~**karton** *m* cardboard box; (*für Buch*) slipcase; ~**klausel** *f* protective *or* let-out clause; ~**kleidung** *f* protective clothing; ~**kontakt** *m* (*Elec*) safety contact; ~**kontakt(steck)dose** *f* (*Elec*) *siehe* Schukosteckdose; ~**kontaktstecker** *m* (*Elec*) *siehe* Schukostecker; ~**leiste** *f* protective strip; (~**planke**) guard-rail.

Schützling *m* protégé; (*esp Kind*) charge.

schutzlos *adj* (*wehrlos*) defenceless; (*gegen Kälte etc*) without protection, unprotected. **jdm/einer Sache** ~ **ausgeliefert** *or* **preisgegeben sein** to be at the mercy of sb/sth, to be defenceless/without protection against sb/sth.

Schutzlosigkeit *f* defencelessness; unprotectedness.

Schutz-: ~**macht** *f* (*Pol*) protecting power, protector; ~**mann** *m*, *pl* -**leute** (*dated*) policeman, constable (*Brit*); ~**mantel** *m* (*Tech*) protective casing; (*gegen Strahlen*) radiation shield; ~**marke** *f* trademark; ~**maske** *f* (protective) mask; ~**maßnahme** *f* precaution, precautionary measure; (*vorbeugend*) preventive measure; ~**mauer** *f* protecting wall; (*von Festung*) defensive wall; ~**mechanismus** *m* (*esp Psych*) protective mechanism; ~**mittel** *nt* means of protection *sing*; (*Substanz*) protective substance; (*Med auch*) prophylactic (*gegen* for); ~**netz** *nt* (*im Zirkus*) safety net; (*an Damenfahrrad*) skirt guard; (*gegen Stechmücken etc*) mosquito net; ~**patron** *m* saint; ~**pflanzung** *f* protective planting; ~**polizei** *f* (*form*) police force, constabulary (*Brit form*); ~**polizist** *m* (*form*) police officer, (police) constable (*Brit*), policeman; ~**raum** *m* shelter; ~**schicht** *f* protective layer; (*Überzug*) protective coating; ~**schild** *m* shield; (*an Geschützen*) gun shield; ~**schirm** *m* (*Tech*) protective screen; ~**staffel** *f* (*Hist*) SS; **s~suchend** *adj* seeking protection; (*nach Obdach*) seeking refuge *or* shelter; ~**tracht** *f* (*Biol*) mimicry; (~**färbung auch**) adaptive coloration; ~**truppe** *f* (*Hist*) colonial army *or* force; ~**umschlag** *m* dust cover *or* jacket; ~**und-Trutz-Bündnis** *nt* (*old*) defensive and offensive alliance; ~**verband** *m* (**a**) protective association; **der** ~**verband der ...** (*in Namen*) the Association for the Protection of ...; (**b**) (*Med*) protective bandage *or* dressing; ~**vorrichtung** *f* safety device; ~**wall** *m* protective wall (*gegen* to keep out), barrier; ~**weg** *m* (*Aus*) pedestrian crossing; **s~würdig** *adj* worthy of protection; **Gebäude, Sitten** worth preserving, worthy of preservation; ~**zoll** *m* protective duty *or* tariff.

Schwa *nt* -s, *no pl* (*Ling*) schwa.

schwabbelig *adj* (*inf*) *Körperteil* flabby; *Gelee* wobbly.

schwabbeln *vi* (*inf*) to wobble (about).

Schwabe¹ *f* -, -**n** (*Zool*) *siehe* Schabe.

Schwabe² *m* -**n**, -**n** Swabian.

schwäbeln *vi* (*inf*) to speak Swabian *or* the Swabian dialect; (*mit Akzent*) to speak with a Swabian accent.

Schwaben *nt* -s Swabia.

Schwabenstreich *m* piece of folly.

Schwäbin *f* Swabian (woman/girl).

schwäbisch *adj* Swabian. **S~e Alb** Swabian mountains *pl*; **das S~e Meer** (*hum*) Lake Constance.

schwach *adj*, *comp* ¨**er**, *superl* ¨**ste(r, s)** *or adv* **am** ¨**sten** weak (*auch Gram*); *Mensch, Greis, Begründung, Versuch, Aufführung, Alibi, Widerstand auch* feeble; *Konstitution auch* frail; *Gesundheit, Beteiligung, Gedächtnis* poor; *Ton, Anzeichen, Hoffnung, Bewegung* faint, slight; *Gehör* poor, dull; *Stimme auch* feeble; faint; *Licht* poor, dim; *Wind* light; (*Comm*) *Nachfrage, Geschäft* slack, poor. ~**es Augen** weak *or* poor (eye)sight; **das ist ein** ~**es Bild** (*inf*) *or* **eine** ~**e Leistung** (*inf*) that's a poor show (*inf*); **ein** ~**es Lob** faint praise; **trotz des** ~**en Erfolgs des Buchs** in spite of the book's lack of success *or* of the book's poor reception; **jds** ~**e Seite/Stelle** sb's weak point/spot; **ein** ~**er Trost** cold *or* small comfort; **in einem** ~**en Augenblick, in einer** ~**en Stunde** in a moment of weakness, in a weak moment; **jdn** ~ **machen** (*inf*) to soften sb up, to talk sb round; **mach mich nicht** ~**!** (*inf*) don't say that! (*inf*); **in etw** (*dat*) ~ **sein** to be weak in sth; **auf** ~**en Beinen** *or* **Füßen stehen, auf** ~**em Boden stehen** (*fig*) to be on shaky ground; (*Theorie*) to be shaky; **alles, was in meinen** ~**en Kräften steht** everything within my power; **jdn an seiner** ~**en** *or* ~**sten Stelle treffen** to strike at *or* hit sb's weak spot; **mir wird** ~ (*lit*) I feel faint; (*fig inf*) it makes me sick (*inf*); **nur nicht** ~ **werden!** don't weaken!; ~**er werden** to grow weaker, to weaken; (*Augen*) to fail, to grow worse; (*Stimme*) to grow fainter; (*Licht*) to (grow) dim; (*Ton*) to fade; (*Nachfrage*) to fall off, to slacken; ~ **besiedelt** *or* **bevölkert** sparsely populated; ~ **besucht** poorly attended; ~ **gesalzen/gesüßt** slightly salted/sweetened; **sich** ~ **verteidigen** to put up a weak *or* feeble defence; **die S~en** the weak; **der S~ere** the weaker (person); (*gegenüber Gegner*) the underdog.

schwach-: ~**besiedelt**, ~**bevölkert** *adj attr* sparsely populated; ~**betont** *adj attr* weakly stressed; ~**bewegt** *adj attr Meer* gently rolling; **schon bei** ~**bewegtem Meer werde ich seekrank** as soon as there's the slightest swell I get sea-sick; ~**brüstig** *adj* (*hum*) feeble.

Schwäche *f* -, -**n** (**a**) *no pl siehe adj* weakness; feebleness; frailty; poorness; faintness, slightness; dullness; feebleness; faintness; dimness; lightness; slackness. **eine** ~ **überkam sie** a feeling of weakness came over her; **sie brach vor** ~ **zusammen** she was so weak she collapsed. (**b**) (*Nachteil, Fehler*) weakness. (**c**) (*Vorliebe*) weakness (*für* for). (**d**) (*Charaktermangel*) weakness, failing. **menschliche** ~**n** human failings *or* frailties; **jeder Mensch hat seine** ~**n** we all have our little weaknesses *or* failings.

Schwäche-: ~**anfall** *m* sudden feeling of weakness; ~**gefühl** *nt* feeling of weakness.

schwächen **1** *vt* (*lit, fig*) to weaken. **2** *vr* to weaken oneself. **3** *vi* **etw schwächt** sth has a weakening effect.

Schwäche-: ~**punkt** *m* low point; **einen** ~**punkt erreichen** to reach a low point *or* low ebb (in the day); ~**zustand** *m* condition of weakness *or* debility (*spec*), weak condition.

Schwachheit *f* (**a**) *no pl* (*fig*) weakness, frailty. ~**, dein Name ist Weib** (*prov*) frailty, thy name is woman! (*prov*). (**b**) *no pl* (*rare: Kraftlosigkeit*) *siehe* Schwäche (**a**). (**c**) (*inf*) **bilde dir die** ~ **nicht!** (*inf*) don't you believe it!

Schwach-: ~**kopf** *m* (*inf*) dimwit (*inf*), idiot, thickie (*inf*); **s~köpfig** *adj* (*inf*) daft, idiotic.

schwächlich *adj* weakly; (*zart auch*) puny.

Schwächlichkeit *f siehe adj* weakness; puniness.

Schwächling *m* (*lit, fig*) weakling.

Schwachmatikus *m* -, -**se** *or* **Schwachmatiker** *m* (*hum inf*) weakling.

Schwach-: **s~sichtig** *adj* (*Med*) poor- *or* weak-sighted; ~**sichtigkeit** *f* (*Med*) dimness of vision, amblyopia (*spec*); ~**sinn** *m* (*Med*) mental deficiency, feeble-mindedness (*dated*); (*fig inf*) (*unsinnige Tat*) idiocy *no indef art*; (*Quatsch*) rubbish (*inf*); **leichter/mittelschwerer/schwerer** ~**sinn** mild/severe to moderate/profound mental deficiency, moronism/imbecility/idiocy; **s~sinnig** *adj* (*Med*) mentally deficient, feeble-minded (*dated*); (*fig inf*) daft, idiotic; ~**sinnige(r)** *mf decl as adj* mental defective, feeble-minded person (*dated*); (*fig inf*) idiot, moron (*inf*), imbecile (*inf*); ~**stelle** *f* weak point.

Schwachstrom *m* (*Elec*) low-voltage *or* weak current.

Schwachstrom-: ~**leitung** *f* low-voltage (current) line; ~**technik** *f* (*dated*) communications engineering *or* technology.

Schwächung *f* weakening.

Schwade *f* -, -**n**, **Schwaden** *m* -s, - swath(e), windrow (*spec*).

Schwaden *m* -s, - *usu pl* cloud.

Schwadron *f* -, -**en** (*Mil Hist*) squadron.

Schwadroneur [ʃvadroˈnøːɐ̯] *m* blusterer.

schwadronieren* *vi* to bluster.

Schwafelei *f* (*pej inf*) drivel *no pl* (*inf*), twaddle *no pl* (*inf*); (*das Schwafeln*) drivelling *or* blethering on (*inf*).

schwafeln (*pej inf*) **1** *vi* to drivel (on), to blether (on), to talk drivel (*all inf*); (*in einer Prüfung*) to waffle (*inf*). **2** *vt* **dummes Zeug** ~ to talk drivel (*inf*); **was schwafelst du da?** what are you drivelling *or* blethering on about? (*inf*).

Schwafler(in f) m -s, - (pej inf) wind-bag, gas-bag, bletherer (all inf).

Schwager m -s, ⸚ (a) brother-in-law. (b) (obs: Postillion) coachman.

Schwägerin f sister-in-law.

Schwägerschaft f (Jur) relationship by marriage, affinity (spec).

Schwäher m -s, - (obs) brother-in-law.

Schwaige f -, -n (S Ger, Aus) siehe **Sennhütte**.

Schwaiger m -s, - (S Ger, Aus) siehe **Senner**.

Schwälbchen nt dim of **Schwalbe**.

Schwalbe f -, -n swallow. eine ~ macht noch keinen Sommer (Prov) one swallow doesn't make a summer (Prov).

Schwalben-: ~nest nt (a) swallow's nest; (b) (Mil) (bandsman's) epaulette; (c) (Naut) sponson; (d) (Cook) bird's nest soup; ~nestersuppe f bird's nest soup; ~schwanz m (a) (Zool) swallowtail (butterfly); (b) (inf) (Frack) swallow-tailed coat, swallow-tails pl, cutaway; (Frackschoß) (swallow-)tails pl; (c) (Tech) dovetail; mit einem ~schwanz verbinden to dovetail; ~wurz f -, -e (Bot) swallowwort.

Schwall m -(e)s, -e flood, torrent; (von Worten auch) effusion.

schwamm pret of **schwimmen**.

Schwamm m -(e)s, ⸚e (a) sponge. etw mit dem ~ abwischen to sponge sth (down), to wipe sth with a sponge; ~ drüber! (inf) (let's) forget it! (b) (dial: Pilz) fungus; (eßbar) mushroom; (giftig) toadstool. (c) (Haus~) dry rot. den ~ haben to have dry rot. (d) (Feuer~) touchwood, tinder, punk all no pl.

Schwämmchen nt (a) dim of **Schwamm**. (b) (Med) thrush.

Schwammerl nt -s, -(n) (S Ger, Aus inf) siehe **Schwamm**.

schwammig adj (a) (lit) spongy. (b) (fig) Gesicht, Hände puffy, bloated; (vage) Begriff woolly.

Schwammigkeit f siehe adj sponginess; puffiness, bloated appearance; woolliness.

Schwan m -(e)s, ⸚e swan. mein lieber ~! (inf) (überrascht) my goodness!; (drohend) my lad/girl.

schwand pret of **schwinden**.

schwanen vi impers ihm schwante etwas he had forebodings, he sensed something might happen; mir schwant nichts Gutes I don't like it, I've a feeling something nasty is going to happen.

Schwanen-: ~gesang m (fig) swansong; ~hals m swan's neck; (fig) swanlike neck; (Tech) goose-neck, swan-neck; ~haus, ~häuschen nt swan house; ~jungfrau f (Myth) swan maiden; ~see m Swan Lake; ~teich m swan pond; s~weiß adj (geh) lily-white.

schwang pret of **schwingen**.

Schwang m: im ~(e) sein to be in vogue, to be "in" (inf); in ~ kommen to come into vogue.

schwanger adj pregnant. ~ sein or gehen to be pregnant; mit etw ~ gehen (fig) to be big with sth; mit großen Ideen ~ gehen (fig) to be full of great ideas.

Schwangere f decl as adj pregnant woman.

schwängern vt to make pregnant, to impregnate (form). mit etw geschwängert sein (fig) to be impregnated with sth; die Luft war mit Rauch/Weihrauch geschwängert the air was thick with smoke/heavy or impregnated with incense.

Schwangerschaft f pregnancy.

Schwangerschafts-: ~abbruch m termination of pregnancy, abortion; ~nachweis m pregnancy test; ~narbe f, ~streifen m stretch mark; ~unterbrechung f siehe ~abbruch; ~verhütung f contraception.

Schwängerung f die ~ einer Frau making a woman pregnant; das wird eine ~ nicht immer verhindern that won't always prevent a pregnancy.

schwank adj (poet): ~en Schrittes with faltering steps, shakily, falteringly.

Schwank m -(e)s, ⸚e (Liter) merry or comical tale; (Theat) farce. ein ~ aus der Jugendzeit (hum) a tale of one's youthful exploits.

schwanken vi (a) (wanken, sich wiegen) to sway; (Schiff) (auf und ab) to pitch; (seitwärts) to roll; (beben) to shake, to rock. der Boden schwankte unter meinen Füßen (lit, fig) the ground rocked beneath my feet.
   (b) aux sein (gehen) to stagger, to totter.
   (c) (Preise, Temperatur, Stimmung etc) to fluctuate, to vary; (Gesundheit, Gebrauch) to vary; (Phys, Math) to fluctuate; (Kompaßnadel etc) to swing, to oscillate.
   (d) (hin und hergerissen werden) to vacillate; (wechseln) to alternate. sie schwankte zwischen Stolz und Mitleid she alternated between pride and pity.
   (e) (zögern) to hesitate; (sich nicht schlüssig sein) to waver, to vacillate. ~, ob to hesitate as to whether, to be undecided (as to) whether.
   (f) ins S~ kommen or geraten (Baum, Gebäude etc) to start to sway; (Erde) to start to shake or rock; (Preise, Kurs, Temperatur etc) to start to fluctuate or vary; (Autorität, Überzeugung etc) to begin to waver; (Institution) to begin to totter.

schwankend adj (a) siehe vi (a) swaying; pitching; rolling; shaking, rocking. auf ~en Füßen/~em Boden stehen (fig) to be shaky/to be on shaky ground.
   (b) Mensch staggering; Gang rolling; Schritt unsteady.
   (c) siehe vi (c) fluctuating esp attr; varying; oscillating; Kurs, Gesundheit auch unstable.
   (d) (unschlüssig) uncertain, wavering attr; (zögernd) hesitant; (unbeständig) vacillating, unsteady. jdn ~ machen/~ sb waver; ~ werden to waver; sie ist sehr ~ in ihren Entschlüssen she vacillates a lot.

Schwankung f (hin und her) swaying no pl; (auf und ab) shaking no pl, rocking no pl. um die ~en des Turms zu messen to measure the extent to which the tower sways.
   (b) (von Preisen, Temperatur, Stimmung etc) fluctuation,

variation (gen in); (von Kompaßnadel etc) oscillation. seelische ~en fluctuations in one's mental state, mental ups and downs (inf).

Schwankungsbereich m range.

Schwanz m -es, ⸚e (a) (lit, fig) tail; (inf: von Zug) (tail-)end. den ~ zwischen die Beine klemmen und abhauen (inf, fig sl) to put one's tail between one's legs and run; den ~ hängen lassen (lit) to let its tail droop; (fig inf) to be down in the dumps (inf); das Pferd or den Gaul beim or am ~ aufzäumen (fig) to do things back to front; kein ~ (inf) not a (blessed) soul (inf); siehe **treten**.
   (b) (Univ inf) einen ~ machen to fail part of an exam; seinen ~ einziehen to resit part of an exam.
   (c) (sl: Penis) prick (vulg), cock (vulg). sich (dat) den ~ verbrennen (sl) to get VD or a dose (sl) or the clap (sl).

Schwänzchen nt dim of **Schwanz**.

Schwänzelei f siehe vi (a) tail-wagging. (b) crawling (inf). (c) sashaying (esp US inf).

schwänzeln vi (a) (Hund: mit dem Schwanz wedeln) to wag its tail. (b) (fig pej: Mensch) to crawl (inf). (c) aux sein (geziert gehen) to sashay (esp US inf).

Schwänzeltanz m (Zool) dance used by bees as a form of communication.

schwänzen (inf) 1 vt Stunde, Vorlesung to skip (inf), to cut (inf); Schule to play truant or hooky (esp US inf) from, to skive off (Brit sl). 2 vi to play truant, to play hooky (esp US inf), to skive (Brit sl).

Schwanz-: ~ende nt end or tip of the tail; (fig) tail-end; (von Flugzeug) tail; ~feder f tail feather; ~flosse f tail or caudal fin; (Aviat) tail fin; s~lastig adj (Aviat) tail-heavy; s~los adj tailless (auch Aviat); ~lurch m (Zool) caudate (spec), urodele (spec); ~meise f (Orn) long-tailed tit; ~spitze f tip of the tail; ~stachel m (Zool) sting (in the tail); ~stern m (old) comet; tail; ~wirbel m (Anat) caudal vertebra.

schwapp interj slosh, splash; (schwups) slap, smack.

Schwapp m -(e)s, -e slosh, splash.

schwappen vi (a) to slosh around. (b) aux sein (über~) to splash, to slosh.

schwaps interj siehe **schwapp**.

Schwaps m -(e)s, -e siehe **Schwapp**.

Schwär m -(e)s, -e (old liter), **Schwäre** f -, -n (liter) ulcer, festering sore.

schwären vi (liter) to fester. eine ~de Wunde (lit, fig) a festering sore.

Schwarm m -(e)s, ⸚e (a) swarm; (Flugzeugformation) flight.
   (b) (inf) (Angebeteter) idol; (Schauspieler, Popsänger auch) heart-throb (inf); (Vorliebe) passion, big thing (inf). der neue Englischlehrer ist ihr ~ she's got a crush on the new English teacher (inf).

schwärmen vi (a) aux sein to swarm.
   (b) (begeistert reden) to enthuse (von about), to go into raptures (von about). für jdn/etw ~ (außerordentlich angetan sein) to be mad or wild or crazy about sb/sth (inf); (verliebt sein, verehren auch) to worship sb/sth, to be smitten with sb/sth (liter, hum); ins S~ kommen or geraten to go or fall into raptures; ich schwärme nicht gerade für ihn (iro) I'm not exactly crazy about him (inf); sie schwärmt für die Bühne she is stagestruck.

Schwärmer m -s, - (a) (Begeisterter) enthusiast, zealot; (Phantast) dreamer, visionary; (sentimentaler ~) sentimentalist. (b) (Zool) hawkmoth, sphinx moth. (c) (Feuerwerkskörper) jumping jack.

Schwärmerei f (Begeisterung) enthusiasm; (in Worten ausgedrückt) effusion no pl; (Leidenschaft) passion; (Verzückung) rapture. sich in ~en über jdn/etw ergehen to go into raptures over sb/sth; sich in ~en verlieren to get or become carried away.

Schwärmerin f siehe **Schwärmer (a)**.

schwärmerisch adj (begeistert) enthusiastic; Worte, Übertreibung effusive; (verliebt) infatuated, gooey (inf); (verzückt) enraptured; Illusion, Glaube, Gemüt fanciful. die Romantiker hatten alle etwas ~es the Romantics were all filled with a great emotional passion.

Schwärm-: ~geist m (Phantast) visionary; (Eiferer) zealot; s~weise adv in swarms.

Schwärmzeit f swarming time.

Schwarte f -, -n (a) (Speck~) rind; (Hunt: Haut) skin, hide; (Abfallholz) slab. arbeiten, daß or bis die ~ kracht (inf) or knackt (inf) to work oneself into the ground (inf). (b) (inf) (Buch) old book, tome (hum); (Gemälde) daub(ing) (pej); (Sch sl) crib (inf).

Schwartenmagen m (Cook) brawn.

schwartig adj (rare) rindy.

schwarz adj, comp ⸚er, superl ⸚este(r, s) or adv am ⸚esten (a) (lit, fig) black; (schmutzig auch) dirty; (stark sonnengebräunt) deeply tanned, brown. ~e Blattern or Pocken smallpox; das S~e Brett the notice-board; ~e Diamanten black diamonds; der S~e Erdteil the Dark Continent; der S~e Freitag Black Friday; ~e Gold (fig) black gold; ~er Humor black humour; ~er Kaffee/Tee black coffee/tea; die S~e Kunst (Buchdruckerkunst) (the art of) printing; (Magie) Black Art; ~e Liste blacklist; jdn auf die ~e Liste setzen to blacklist sb, to put sb on the blacklist; ~e Magie Black Magic; der ~e Mann (Schornsteinfeger) the (chimney-)sweep; (Kinderschreck) the bogeyman; (dated: die ~e Rasse) the Black Man, the Negro; das S~e Meer the Black Sea; eine ~e Messe a Black Mass; S~er Peter (Cards) children's card-game; jdm den S~en Peter zuschieben or zuspielen (fig) (die Verantwortung abschieben) to pass the buck to sb (inf), to leave sb holding the baby; (etw Unangenehmes abschieben) to give sb the worst of the deal; das ~e Schaf (in der Familie) the black sheep

(of the family); **eine ~e Seele** a black or evil soul; **~er Star** (Med) amaurosis (spec); **ein ~er Tag** a black day; **~e Tat** a black deed; **der ~e Tod** the Black Death; **die S~e Witwe** the Black Widow (spider); **etw ~ auf weiß haben** to have sth in black and white; **~ von Menschen** crowded or black with people; **~ wie die Nacht/wie Ebenholz** jet-black; **in den ~en Zahlen** in the black; **sich ~ ärgern** to get extremely annoyed, to get hopping mad (inf); **er wurde ~ vor Ärger** his face went black; **mir wurde ~ vor den Augen** everything went black, I blacked out; **er kam ~ wie ein Neger aus dem Urlaub zurück** he came back from his holidays as brown as a berry; **~ werden** (Cards) to lose every trick, to be whitewashed (inf); **da kannst du warten/schreien, bis du ~ wirst** (inf) you can wait till the cows come home (inf)/shout until you're blue in the face (inf).
(b) (inf: ungesetzlich) illicit. **der ~e Markt** the black market; **~e Geschäfte machen** to do shady deals; **sich** (dat) **etw ~ besorgen** to get sth illicitly/on the black market; **über die Grenze gehen** to cross the border illegally; **etw ~ verdienen** to earn sth on the side (inf).
(c) (inf: katholisch) Catholic, Papist (pej). **dort wählen alle ~** they all vote conservative there.
Schwarz nt -, no pl inv black. **in ~ gehen** to wear black.
Schwarz-: **~afrika** nt Black Africa; **~arbeit** f illicit work, work on the side (inf); (nach Feierabend) moonlighting (inf); **s~arbeiten** vi sep to do illicit work, to work on the side (inf); to moonlight (inf); **~arbeiter** m person doing illicit work or work on the side (inf); moonlighter (inf); **s~äugig** adj dark-eyed; **Schönheit** auch sloe-eyed (liter); **~beere** f (S Ger, Aus) siehe **Heidelbeere**; **s~blau** adj bluish black, inky blue; Tinte blueblack; **~blech** nt black plate; **s~braun** adj dark brown; **~brenner** m illicit distiller, moonshine distiller (inf); **~brennerei** f illicit still, moonshine still (inf); **~brot** nt (braun) brown rye bread; (schwarz, wie Pumpernickel) black bread, pumpernickel; **~bunte** f -n, -n Friesian; **~dorn** m (Bot) blackthorn; **~drossel** f blackbird.
Schwarze f -n, -n (Negerin) black woman; (Schwarzhaarige) brunette.
Schwärze f -, -n (a) (no pl: Dunkelheit) blackness. **(b)** (Farbe) black dye; (Drucker~) printer's ink.
schwärzen vtr to blacken.
Schwarze(r) m decl as adj (Neger) black; (Schwarzhaariger) dark man/boy; (pej sl: Katholik) Catholic, Papist (pej); (Aus: schwarzer Mokka) black (mocha) coffee. **die ~n** (pej sl) the Conservatives.
Schwarz|erde f (Geol) black earth.
Schwarze(s) nt decl as adj black. **das kleine ~** (inf) one's or a little black dress; **ins ~ treffen** (lit, fig) to score a bull's-eye; **jdm nicht das ~ unter den Nägeln gönnen** (dated) to begrudge sb the very air he/she breathes.
Schwarz-: **s~fahren** vi sep irreg aux sein (ohne zu zahlen) to travel without paying, to dodge paying the fare (inf); (ohne Führerschein) to drive without a licence; **~fahrer** m fare dodger (inf); driver without a licence; **~fahrt** f ride without paying; drive without a licence; **sie wurde bei einer ~fahrt geschnappt** she was caught travelling without a ticket or taking a free ride (inf)/driving without a licence; **~fäule** f (Bot) black rot; **~fernseher** m siehe **~seher (b)**; **~filter** m (Phot) black filter; **s~gestreift** adj attr with black stripes; **s~grau** adj greyblack, greyish-black; **s~haarig** adj black-haired; **eine ~haarige** a brunette; **~handel** m, no pl black market; (Tätigkeit) black-marketeering; **im ~handel** on the black market; **~händler** m black marketeer; **~hemden** pl (Hist) Blackshirts pl; **s~hören** vi sep (Rad) to use a radio without having a licence; (dated Univ inf) to go to lectures without paying the fees; **~hörer** m (Rad) radio-owner without a licence; (dated Univ inf) student (attending a lecture) who hasn't paid the lecture fees; **~kittel** m (inf) wild boar; (pej: Geistlicher) priest.
schwärzlich adj blackish; Haut dusky.
Schwarz-: **s~malen** sep 1 vi to be pessimistic; 2 vt to be pessimistic about; **~maler** m pessimist; **~malerei** f pessimism; **~markt** m black market; **~markthändler** m black marketeer; **~marktpreis** m black-market price; **~meerflotte** f Black Sea fleet; **~pappel** f black poplar; **~pulver** nt black (gun)powder; **~rock** m (pej) priest; **~-Rot-Gold** nt: die Fahne/Farben **~-Rot-Gold** the black-red-and-gold flag/colours (of West Germany); **s~rotgolden** adj Fahne black-red-and-gold; **s~schlachten** sep 1 vi to slaughter pigs etc illegally or illicitly; 2 vt to slaughter illegally or illicitly; **s~sehen** sep irreg 1 vt to be pessimistic about; 2 vi (a) to be pessimistic; für jdn/etw **s~sehen** to be pessimistic about sb/sth; **(b)** (TV) to watch TV without a licence; **~seher** m (a) pessimist; **(b)** (TV) (TV) licence-dodger (inf); **~seherei** f pessimism; **s~seherisch** adj pessimistic, gloomy; **~sender** m pirate (radio) station; **~specht** m black woodpecker; **~storch** m black stork.
Schwärzung f blackening.
Schwarz-: **~wal** m black whale; **~wald** m Black Forest; **~wälder** adj attr Black Forest; **~wälder(in** f) m -s, - inhabitant of/person from the Black Forest; **~wälder Kirsch** m, **~wälder Kirschwasser** m kirsch; **~wälder Kirschtorte** f Black Forest gateau.
schwarzweiß adj black-and-white attr, black and white.
Schwarzweiß-: **~aufnahme** f black-and-white (shot); **~empfänger** m black-and-white or monochrome set; **~fernsehen** nt black-and-white or monochrome television; **~fernseher** m black-and-white or monochrome television (set); **~film** m black-and-white film; **~foto** nt black-and-white (photo); **~gerät** nt black-and-white or monochrome set; **s~malen** vti sep (fig) to depict in black and white (terms); **in den Berichten über die Unruhen wurde deutlich s~gemalt** the reports about the unrest made everything black and white;

das kann man doch nicht so **s~malen** it's not as black and white as that; **~malerei** f (fig) black-and-white portrayal; **die ~malerei älterer Geschichtsbücher** the way older history books make everything seem black and white or reduce everything to black and white (terms); **~malerei ist ein primitives Mittel der Propaganda** reducing everything to black and white (terms) is a primitive means of propaganda.
Schwarzweiß-: **s~rot** adj black-white-and-red (the colours of the German imperial flag); **~rot** nt: die Farben/Fahne **~rot** the black-white-and-red colours/flag.
Schwarzweißzeichnung f black-and-white (drawing).
Schwarz-: **~wild** nt wild boars pl; **~wurzel** f viper's grass; (Cook) salsify.
Schwatz m -es, -e (inf) chat, chinwag (inf). **auf einen ~ kommen** to come (round) for a chat.
Schwatz-, Schwätz- (S Ger) **~base** f gossip; **~bude** f (inf) talking shop.
schwatzen vti (N Ger) to talk; (pej) (unaufhörlich) to chatter; (über belanglose, oberflächliche Dinge, kindisch) to prattle; (Unsinn reden) to blether (inf); (klatschen) to gossip. **über Politik ~** to prate on about politics (pej); **dummes Zeug ~** to talk a lot of rubbish (inf) or drivel (inf).
schwätzen vti (S Ger, Aus) siehe **schwatzen**.
Schwätzer m -s, - (pej) chatterer; (Kind, Schüler) chatterbox; (Schwafler) wind-bag, gas-bag, bletherer (all inf); (Klatschmaul) gossip.
Schwätzerei f (pej) (Gerede, im Unterricht) talk, chatter; (über Belanglosigkeiten, kindisch) prattle; (Unsinn) drivel (inf); (Klatsch) gossip.
Schwätzerin f (pej) chatterer, chatterbox; (Schwaflerin) bletherer (inf), wind-bag (inf); (Klatschbase) gossip.
schwätzerisch adj windy (inf), gassy (inf).
schwatzhaft adj (geschwätzig) talkative, garrulous; (klatschsüchtig) gossipy.
Schwatzhaftigkeit f siehe adj talkativeness, garrulousness; gossipy nature.
Schwatz-: **~liese** f siehe **~base**; **~maul** nt (inf) big mouth (inf).
Schwebe f -, no pl sich in der **~ halten** (Ballon) to hover, to float in the air; (Waage) to balance; (fig) to hang in the balance; **in der ~ sein/bleiben** (fig) to be/remain in the balance, to be/remain undecided; (Jur, Comm) to be/remain pending.
Schwebe-: **~bahn** f suspension railway; (Seilbahn) cable railway; **~balken** m balance beam; **~baum** m (Sport) beam; **~fähre** f aerial ferry.
schweben vi (a) to hang; (in der Luft, in Flüssigkeit auch) to float; (an Seil etc auch) to be suspended, to dangle; (sich unbeweglich in der Luft halten: Geier etc) to hover; (nachklingen, zurückbleiben: Klänge, Parfüm) to linger (on). **ein Lächeln schwebte auf seinen Lippen** a smile hovered about his lips; **und der Geist Gottes schwebte über den Wassern** (Bibl) and the Spirit of the Lord moved over the waters (Bibl); **ihr war, als ob sie schwebte** she felt she was walking or floating on air; **etw schwebt jdm vor Augen** (fig) sb envisages sth, sb has sth in mind; (Bild) sb sees sth in his mind's eye; **in großer Gefahr ~** to be in great danger; **in höheren Regionen or Sphären or über den Wolken ~** to have one's head in the clouds.
(b) aux sein (durch die Luft gleiten) to float, to sail; (hoch~) to soar; (nieder~) to float down; (an Seil etc) to swing; (mit Fahrstuhl) to soar, to zoom; (sich leichtfüßig bewegen) to glide, to float.
(c) (schwanken) to hover, to waver; (Angelegenheit) to hang or be in the balance, to be undecided; (Jur) to be pending.
schwebend adj (Tech, Chem) suspended; (fig) Fragen etc unresolved, undecided; Verfahren, (Comm) Geschäft pending; (Comm) Schulden floating; (Poet) Betonung hovering.
Schwebe-: **~reck** nt trapeze; **~zug** m hovertrain; **~zustand** m (fig) state of suspense; (zwischen zwei Stadien) in-between state.
Schwebfliege f hover-fly.
Schwede m -n, -n Swede. **alter ~** (inf) (my) old fruit (Brit inf) or chap.
Schweden nt -s Sweden.
Schweden-: **~platte** f (Cook) smorgasbord; **~punsch** m arrack punch, Swedish punch; **~stahl** m Swedish steel.
Schwedin f Swede, Swedish girl/woman.
schwedisch adj Swedish. **hinter ~en Gardinen** (inf) behind bars; **hinter ~e Gardinen kommen** (inf) to be put behind bars.
Schwedisch(e) nt decl as adj Swedish; siehe auch **Deutsch(e)**.
Schwefel m -s, no pl sulphur, brimstone (old, Bibl).
Schwefel- in cpds sulphur; **~artig** adj sulphur(e)ous; **~blume, ~blüte** f flowers of sulphur; **s~gelb** adj sulphurous yellow; **s~haltig** adj containing sulphur, sulphur(e)ous; **~hölzchen** nt (old) match, lucifer (old).
schwefelig adj siehe **schweflig**.
Schwefel-: **~kies** m iron pyrites sing or pl; **~kohlenstoff** m carbon disulphide.
schwefeln vt to sulphurize.
Schwefelsäure f sulphuric acid.
Schwefelung f sulphurization.
Schwefel-: **~verbindung** f sulphur compound; **~wasserstoff** m hydrogen sulphide, sulphuretted hydrogen.
schweflig adj sulphurous. **es roch ~** there was a smell of sulphur.
Schweif m -(e)s, -e (auch Astron) tail.
schweifen 1 vi aux sein (lit geh, fig) to roam, to wander, to rove. **warum in die Ferne ~ ...?** why roam so far afield ...?; **sein Blick schweifte von einem zum anderen** his gaze roamed from one to the other; **seine Gedanken in die Vergangenheit ~ lassen** to let one's thoughts roam or wander over the past.
2 vt Bretter, Blechgefäß to curve.

Schweif-: ~haar nt tail hair(s); ~säge f fretsaw; ~stern m comet.

Schweifung f curving; (geschweifte Form) curve.

schweifwedeln* vi insep (Hund) to wag its tail; (fig old: liebedienern) to fawn.

Schweige-: ~geld nt hush-money; ~marsch m silent march (of protest); ~minute f one minute('s) silence.

schweigen pret **schwieg**, ptp **geschwiegen** vi to be silent; (still sein auch) to keep quiet; (sich nicht äußern auch) to remain silent, to say nothing; (aufhören: Musik, Geräusch, Wind) to cease, to stop. ~ Sie! be silent or quiet!; kannst du ~? can you keep a secret?; seit gestern ~ die Waffen yesterday the guns fell silent; plötzlich schwieg er suddenly he fell or went silent; er kann ~ wie ein Grab he knows how to keep quiet; auf etw (acc)/zu etw ~ to make no reply to sth; schweig mir davon! (obs) do not speak to me of that!; ganz zu ~ von ..., von ... ganz zu ~ to say nothing of ...

Schweigen nt -s, no pl silence. jdn zum ~ bringen to silence sb (auch euph); siehe reden.

schweigend adj silent. die ~e Mehrheit the silent majority; ~ über etw (acc) hinweggehen to pass over sth in silence; ~ zuhören to listen in silence or silently.

Schweigepflicht f pledge of secrecy; (von Anwalt) requirement of confidentiality. die ärztliche ~ medical confidentiality or secrecy; die priesterliche ~ a priest's duty to remain silent; unter ~ stehen to be bound to observe confidentiality.

Schweiger m -s, - man of few words. der große ~ the strong silent type; (als Beiname) the silent.

schweigsam adj silent, quiet; (als Charaktereigenschaft) taciturn, reticent; (verschwiegen) discreet.

Schweigsamkeit f siehe adj silence, quietness; taciturnity, reticence; discretion, discreetness.

Schwein nt -s, -e (a) pig, hog (US); (Fleisch) pork. ~e pl pigs pl, hogs pl (US), swine pl; sich wie die ~e benehmen (inf) to behave like pigs (inf); bluten wie ein ~ (sl) to bleed like a stuck pig; mit jdm (zusammen) ~e gehütet haben (hum) to be on familiar terms (with sb); das falsche ~ schlachten (fig) to get the wrong one.
(b) (inf: Mensch) pig (inf), swine; (gemein, Schweinehund) swine (inf), bastard (sl). ein armes/faules ~ a poor/lazy sod or bastard (sl); kein ~ nobody, not one single person.
(c) no pl (inf: Glück) ~ haben to be lucky; ~ gehabt! that's a bit of luck.

Schweinchen nt dim of **Schwein** little pig; (baby-talk) piggy(-wiggy) (baby-talk); (fig inf: kleiner Schmutzfink) mucky pup (inf).

Schweine-: ~bande f (fig inf) pack; ~bauch m (Cook) belly of pork; ~braten m joint of pork; (gekocht) roast pork; ~bucht f (Geog) die ~bucht the Bay of Pigs; ~fett nt pig fat; ~filet nt fillet of pork; ~fleisch nt pork; ~fraß m (fig sl) muck (inf); ~futter nt pig feed; (flüssig) pig swill; ~geld nt (sl) ein ~geld a packet (inf); ~haltung f pig-keeping; ~hirt(e) m (esp liter) swineherd (esp old, liter); ~hund m (sl) bastard (sl), swine (inf); den inneren ~hund überwinden (inf) to conquer one's weaker self; ~kerl m (sl) swine (inf), bastard (sl); ~koben, ~kofen m pigsty; ~kotelett nt pork chop; ~mast f pig-fattening; (Futter) pig food; ~mästerei f piggery; ~mett nt (N Ger Cook) minced (Brit) or ground (US) pork; ~pack nt (pej sl) vermin; ~pest f (Vet) swine fever.

Schweinerei f (inf) (a) no pl mess. es ist eine ~, wenn ... it's disgusting if ...; so eine ~! how disgusting!; Fische zu schuppen, ist eine ~ scaling fish is a messy business; diese ~ muß eine andere werden (hum inf) (this won't do,) things will have to change.
(b) (Skandal) scandal; (Gemeinheit) dirty or mean trick (inf). ich finde es eine ~, wie er sie behandelt I think it's disgusting the way he treats her; (so eine) ~! what a dirty trick! (inf).
(c) (Zote) smutty or dirty joke; (unzüchtige Handlung) indecent act. ~en machen to do dirty or filthy things; das Buch besteht nur aus ~en the book is just a lot of dirt or filth.
(d) (iro: Leckerbissen) delicacy.

Schweinerippchen nt (Cook) cured pork chop.

schweinern adj pork. S~es pork.

Schweine-: ~rüssel m pig's snout; ~schmalz nt dripping; (als Kochfett) lard; ~schnitzel nt pork cutlet, escalope of pork; ~stall m (lit, fig) pigsty, pig pen (esp US); (korruptes System) corrupt shambles sing; ~zucht f pig-breeding; (Hof) pig farm; ~züchter m pig-breeder.

Schweinigel m (inf) dirty pig (inf) or so-and-so (inf).

Schweinigelei f (inf) (Witz) dirty or smutty joke; (Bemerkung) dirty or smutty remark; (das Schweinigeln) dirty or smutty jokes pl/remarks pl.

schweinigeln vi insep (inf) (Witze erzählen) to tell dirty jokes; (Bemerkungen machen) to make dirty or smutty remarks; (Schmutz machen) to make a mess.

schweinisch adj (inf) Benehmen piggish (inf), swinish (inf); Witz dirty. benimm dich nicht so ~! stop behaving like a pig!

Schweinkram m (inf) dirt, filth. dann mach doch deinen ~ allein! then do the stupid job yourself!

Schweins-: ~augen, ~äuglein pl (inf) piggy eyes pl (inf); ~blase f pig's bladder; ~borste f pig's bristle; ~füße pl (Cook dial) (pig's) trotters pl; ~galopp m: im ~galopp davonlaufen (hum inf) to go galumphing off (inf); ~haxe f (S Ger Cook) knuckle of pork; ~kopf m (Cook) pig's head; ~leder nt pigskin; s~ledern adj pigskin; ~ohr nt (a) pig's ear; (Gebäck) (kidney-shaped) pastry; (b) (Bot) (Kalla) calla (lily); (Pilz) cantharellus clavatus (spec); ~stelze f (Aus) siehe ~füße.

Schweiß m -es, no pl sweat; (von Mensch auch) perspiration; (Hunt) blood. in ~ geraten or kommen to break into a sweat, to start sweating/perspiring; der ~ brach ihm aus allen Poren he was absolutely dripping with sweat; der ~ brach ihm aus broke out in a sweat; naß ~ soaked with perspiration or sweat; kalter ~ cold sweat; das hat viel ~ gekostet it was a sweat (inf); im Schweiße seines Angesichts (Bibl, liter) in the sweat of his brow (Bibl, liter); die Früchte seines ~es (liter) the fruits of his toil or labour(s).

Schweiß-: ~absonderung f perspiration; ~apparat m welding equipment no indef art, no pl; ~ausbruch m sweating no indef art, no pl; ~band nt sweatband; s~bar adj (Tech) weldable; s~bedeckt adj covered in sweat; ~bläschen pl (Med) prickly heat sing, miliaria sing (spec); ~brenner m (Tech) welding torch; ~brille f (Tech) welding goggles pl; ~draht m (Tech) welding rod or wire; ~drüse f (Anat) sweat or perspiratory (form) gland.

schweißen 1 vt (Tech) to weld. **2** vi (a) (Tech) to weld. (b) (Hunt) to bleed.

Schweißer(in f) m -s, - (Tech) welder.

Schweiß-: ~fährte f (Hunt) trail of blood, blood track; ~flamme f welding flame; ~fleck m sweat stain, perspiration mark; ~fuß m sweaty foot; s~gebadet adj bathed in sweat; Mensch auch bathed in perspiration; ~geruch m smell of sweat or perspiration; ~hund m (Hunt) bloodhound.

schweißig adj sweaty; (Hunt) Tier bleeding; Fährte bloody.

Schweiß-: ~naht f (Tech) weld, welded joint; s~naß adj sweaty; ~perle f bead of perspiration or sweat; ~stahl m welding steel; ~stelle f weld; ~technik f welding (engineering); s~treibend adj causing perspiration, sudorific (spec); s~treibendes Mittel sudorific (spec); s~triefend adj dripping with perspiration or sweat; ~tropfen m drop of sweat or perspiration; ~tuch nt (a) (obs: Taschentuch) handkerchief; (b) das ~tuch der Veronika the sudarium, Veronica's veil.

Schweißung f welding; (Naht, Stelle) weld.

Schweiz f - die ~ Switzerland.

Schweizer m -s, - (a). (b) (Melker) dairyman. (c) (Eccl: Pförtner) beadle. (d) (päpstlicher Leibgardist) Swiss Guard. **2** adj attr Swiss.

Schweizer-: ~degen m (Typ) compositor-printer; ~deutsch nt Swiss German; s~deutsch adj Swiss-German; ~franken m Swiss franc.

Schweizergarde f Swiss Guard.

Schweizerin f Swiss (woman/girl).

schweizerisch adj Swiss.

Schweizer-: ~käse m Swiss cheese; ~land nt (geh, Sw) Switzerland no art; ~volk nt (geh, Sw) Swiss people pl.

Schwelbrand m smouldering fire.

schwelen 1 vi (lit, fig) to smoulder. **2** vt Rasen to burn off (slowly); Koks to carbonize at a low temperature.

schwelgen vi to indulge oneself (in + dat in). von S~ und Prassen hat er nichts gehalten he had no time for self-indulgence and feasting; wir schwelgten in Kaviar und Sekt we feasted on caviar and champagne; in Farben/Worten ~ to revel in colour/in the sound of words; im Überfluß ~ to live in the lap of luxury; in Gefühlen etc ~ to revel in one's emotions; in Erinnerungen ~ to indulge in reminiscences.

Schwelgerei f high living no pl, indulgence no pl; (Schlemmerei) feasting no pl.

Schwelger(in f) m -s, - high liver; (Schlemmer) gourmand.

schwelgerisch adj (üppig) Mahl, Farbe sumptuous; Akkorde auch voluptuous; (genießerisch) self-indulgent.

Schwel-: ~kohle f high-bituminous brown coal; ~koks m low-temperature coke.

Schwelle f -, -n (a) (Tür-, fig, Psych) threshold; (Stein etc) sill. einen/keinen Fuß über die ~ setzen to set foot/not to set foot in sb's house; er darf mir nicht mehr über die ~ kommen, er darf meine ~ nie wieder betreten he shall or may not darken my door again (liter), he may not cross my threshold again (liter); an der ~ einer neuen Zeit on the threshold of a new era; an der ~ des Grabes or Todes at death's door.
(b) (Rail) sleeper (Brit), tie (US).
(c) (Geog) rise.

schwellen 1 vi pret **schwoll**, ptp **geschwollen** aux sein to swell; (lit: Körperteile auch) to swell up. der Wind schwoll zum Sturm the wind grew into a storm; ihm schwoll der Kamm (inf) (vor Eitelkeit, Übermut) he got swollen-headed (esp Brit) or swell-headed (esp US) or above himself; (vor Wut) he saw red; siehe geschwollen.
2 vt (geh) Segel to swell or belly (out); (fig) Brust to swell.

Schwellenangst f (Psych) fear of entering a place.

schwellend adj (geh) swelling; Lippen full.

Schwellenwert m (Phys, Psych) threshold value.

Schweller m -s, - (Mus) swell.

Schwellkörper m (Anat) erectile tissue.

Schwellung f swelling; (von Penis) tumescence (spec).

Schwelung f (Tech) low-temperature carbonization.

Schwemmboden m siehe **Schwemmland**.

Schwemme f -, -n (a) (für Tiere) watering place. (b) (Überfluß) glut (an + dat of). (c) (Kneipe) bar, public bar (Brit). (d) (Aus: im Warenhaus) bargain basement; (einzelner Tisch) bargain counter.

-schwemme f in cpds glut of.

schwemmen vt (treiben) Sand etc to wash; Vieh to water; (wässern) Felle to soak; (Aus: spülen) Wäsche to rinse.

Schwemm-: ~land nt alluvial land; ~sand m alluvial sand.

Schwengel m -s, - (Glocken~) clapper; (Pumpen~) handle; (sl: Penis) dong (US sl), tool (sl).

Schwenk m -e(s), -s (Film) pan, panning shot.

Schwenk-: ~arm m swivel arm; s~bar adj swivelling; auch swivel attr; Geschütz traversable; ~bereich m jib range.

schwenken 1 vt (a) (schwingen) to wave; (herumfuchteln mit auch) to brandish;

(b) *Lampe etc* to swivel; *Kran* to swing, to slew; *Geschütz auch* to traverse, to swing; *Kamera* to pan.
(c) *(Cook) Kartoffeln, Nudeln* to toss.
(d) *Tanzpartnerin* to swing round, to spin (round).
(e) *(dial: spülen) Wäsche, Geschirr* to rinse.
2 *vi* to swing; *(Kolonne von Soldaten, Autos etc)* to wheel; *(Geschütz auch)* to traverse; *(Kamera)* to pan; *(fig)* to swing over, to switch. **links schwenkt!** *(Mil)* left wheel!

Schwenker *m* -s, - balloon glass.
Schwenkkran *m* swing crane.
Schwenkung *f* swing; *(Mil)* wheel; *(von Kran auch)* slewing; *(von Geschütz)* traverse; *(von Kamera)* pan(ning). **eine ~ vollziehen** *(Mil)* to wheel; *(fig)* to swing around.

schwer 1 *adj* **(a)** *(lit, fig)* heavy; *(massiv) Gold* solid. **ein 10 kg ~er Sack** a sack weighing 10 kgs or 10 kgs in weight; **~ beladen/bewaffnet sein** to be heavily laden/armed; **~ auf jdm/etw liegen/lasten** to lie/weigh heavily on sb/sth; **die Beine wurden mir ~** my legs grew heavy; **er ist fünf Millionen ~** *(inf)* he is worth five million.
(b) *(stark) Fahrzeug, Maschine* powerful; *Artillerie, Kavallerie, Wein, Parfüm* heavy; *Zigarre* strong; *(nährstoffreich) Boden* rich. **~es Wasser** *(Phys)* heavy water; *siehe* **Geschütz.**
(c) *(heftig) Sturm, See, Angriff, Artilleriefeuer* heavy; *Winter* hard, severe.
(d) *(ernst) Sorge, Bedenken, Unrecht, Unfall, Verlust, Krankheit* serious, grave; *Fehler, Enttäuschung, Beleidigung auch* big; *Zeit, Leben, Schicksal* hard; *Leiden, Belastungsprobe, Strafe, Buße* severe; *Musik* heavy. **~ erkältet sein** to have a heavy cold; **~er Verluste** heavy losses; **ein ~er Traum** a nightmare; **~ geprüft sein** to be sorely tried; **S~es erlebt or durchgemacht haben** to have been through (some) hard times, to have had a hard time (of it); **~ verletzt/krank sein** to be seriously wounded/ill; **~ stürzen/verunglücken** to have a heavy fall/serious accident; **~ bestraft werden** to be punished severely; **~ betroffen sein** to be hard hit; **das war ein ~er Schlag für ihn** it was a hard blow for him; *siehe* **Stunde.**
(e) *(hart, anstrengend) Amt, Aufgabe, Dienst, Arbeit, Tag* hard; *Geburt, Tod* difficult. **es ~ haben** to have a hard time (of it); **~ schuften müssen** to have to work hard; **er lernt ~** he's a slow learner; **~ hören** to be hard of hearing.
(f) *(schwierig) Frage, Entscheidung, Übung* hard, difficult, tough. **~ zu sehen/sagen** hard or difficult to see/say; **sich ~ entschließen können** to find it hard or difficult to decide.
(g) *(inf: enorm)* **~es Geld machen** to make a packet *(inf)*.
2 *adv (inf: sehr)* really; *gekränkt, verletzt* deeply. **da mußte ich ~ aufpassen** I really had to watch out; **~ reich** stinking rich *(inf)*; **~betrunken** rolling drunk *(inf)*; **~ verdienen** to earn a packet *(inf)*; **sich ~ blamieren** to make a proper fool of oneself; **ich werde mich ~ hüten** there's no way (I will) *(inf)*; **~ im Irrtum sein** to be badly or seriously mistaken; **er ist ~ in Ordnung** he's OK *(inf)*, he's a good bloke *(Brit inf)* or guy *(inf)*.

Schwer-: **~arbeit** *f* heavy labour; **~arbeiter** *m* labourer; **~athlet** *m* weight-lifter; boxer; wrestler; **~athletik** *f* weightlifting sports, boxing, wrestling etc; **s~beladen** *adj attr* heavily-laden; **~benzin** *nt* heavy benzene, naphtha; **s~bepackt** *adj attr* heavily-loaded or -laden; **s~beschädigt** *adj attr (seriously)* disabled; **~beschädigte(r)** *mf* disabled person; **s~bewaffnet** *adj attr* heavily armed; **s~blütig** *adj* serious, ponderous; **ein s~blütiger Mensch** a ponderous (sort of) person; **~blütigkeit** *f* seriousness, ponderousness.

Schwere *f* -, *no pl siehe adj* **(a)** heaviness. **(b)** power; heaviness; strength; richness. **(c)** heaviness; hardness, severity. **(d)** seriousness, gravity; hardness; severity. **die ganze ~ des Gesetzes** the full severity of the law. **(e)** hardness; difficulty. **(f)** *(Phys: Schwerkraft)* gravitation.

Schwere-: **~feld** *nt* field of gravity, gravitational field; **s~los** *adj* weightless; **~losigkeit** *f* weightlessness.
Schwerenöter *m* -s, - *(dated)* philanderer.
schwer|erziehbar *adj attr* maladjusted.
schwerfallen *vi sep irreg aux sein* to be difficult or hard *(jdm* for sb). **das dürfte dir doch nicht ~** you shouldn't find that too difficult or hard.
schwerfällig *adj (unbeholfen) Gang, Bewegungen* clumsy, heavy, awkward; *(langsam) Verstand* slow, dull, ponderous; *Humor* ponderous, heavy-handed; *Stil, Übersetzung* awkward, ponderous, cumbersome. **~ gehen/sprechen** to walk/speak clumsily or awkwardly.
Schwerfälligkeit *f siehe adj* clumsiness, heaviness, awkwardness; slowness, dullness, ponderousness; ponderousness, heavy-handedness; awkwardness, ponderousness, cumbersomeness.

Schwer-: **s~geprüft** *adj attr* sorely afflicted; **~gewicht** *nt* **(a)** *(Sport, fig)* heavyweight; **(b)** *(Nachdruck)* stress, emphasis; **das ~gewicht verlagern** to shift the emphasis; **das ~gewicht auf etw** *(acc)* **legen** to put the stress or emphasis on sth; **s~gewichtig** *adj* heavyweight; **~gewichtler(in** *f) m* -s, - *(Sport)* heavyweight; **s~halten** *vi impers sep irreg* **es wird or dürfte s~halten** it will be difficult; **s~hörig** *adj* hard of hearing; **~hörigkeit** *f* hardness of hearing; **~industrie** *f* heavy industry; **~industrielle(r)** *mf* industrialist (in heavy industry); **~kraft** *f* gravity; **s~krank** *adj attr* seriously or critically or dangerously ill; **~kranke(r)** *mf* seriously or critically or dangerously ill patient; **s~kriegsbeschädigt** *adj attr* seriously disabled (in war); **~kriegsbeschädigte(r)** *mf* seriously disabled ex-serviceman/woman or war veteran (US).
schwerlich *adv* hardly, scarcely.
Schwer-: **s~löslich** *adj attr* not easily dissoluble; **s~machen** *vt sep* **(a) jdm das Herz s~machen** to make sb's heart sad or heavy; **jdm das Leben s~machen** to make life difficult or hard for sb; **(b) es jdm/sich s~machen** to make it or things difficult

or hard for sb/oneself; **~metall** *nt* heavy metal.
Schwermut *f* -, *no pl* melancholy.
schwermütig *adj* melancholy.
schwernehmen *vt sep irreg* **etw ~** to take sth hard.
Schwer|öl *nt* heavy oil.
Schwerpunkt *m* *(Phys)* centre of gravity; *(fig) (Zentrum)* centre, main focus; *(Hauptgewicht)* main emphasis or stress. **er hat Französisch mit ~ Linguistik studiert** he studied French with the main emphasis or main stress on linguistics; **den ~ einer Sache** *(gen)* **bilden** to occupy the central position in sth; **den ~ auf etw** *(acc)* **legen** to put the main emphasis or stress on sth.
-schwerpunkt *m in cpds* main emphasis on sth.
Schwerpunkt-: **~bildung** *f* concentration; **~industrie** *f* main industry; **~programm** *nt* programme or plan of main points of emphasis; **~streik** *m* pinpoint strike; **~verlagerung** *f* shift of emphasis.
Schwer-: **s~reich** *adj attr (inf)* stinking rich *(inf)*; **~spat** *m* heavy spar, barite, barytes *sing*.
Schwerst-: **~arbeiter** *m* heavy labourer; **~beschädigte(r)** *mf* totally disabled person.
Schwert *nt* -(e)s, -er **(a)** sword. **das ~ ziehen** or **zücken** to draw one's sword; **sich mit dem ~ gürten** *(liter)* to gird (on) one's sword. **(b)** *(von Segelboot)* centreboard.
Schwert|adel *m* *(Hist, fig)* military nobility.
Schwerter-: **~geklirr** *nt (liter)* ring(ing) or clash(ing) of swords; **~tanz** *m* sword dance.
Schwert-: **~feger** *m* -s, - *(obs)* armourer; **~fisch** *m* swordfish; **s~förmig** *adj* sword-shaped; *Blatt auch* gladiate *(spec)*; **~griff** *m* (sword) hilt; **~hieb** *m* sword stroke, stroke or blow of the sword; **~klinge** *f* sword blade; **~knauf** *m* (sword) pommel; **~leite** *f* -, -n *(Hist)* accolade; **~lilie** *f (Bot)* iris; **~schlucker** *m* -s, - sword-swallower; **~streich** *m siehe* **~hieb**; **~tanz** *m siehe* **Schwertertanz**; **~träger** *m (Zool)* swordtail.
schwertun *vr irreg (inf)* **sich** *(dat)* **mit** or **bei etw ~** to make heavy weather of sth *(inf)*.
Schwertwal *m* killer whale.
Schwer-: **~verbrecher** *m* criminal, felon *(esp Jur)*; **s~verdaulich** *adj attr Speisen* indigestible; *(fig auch)* difficult; **~verdaulichkeit** *f* indigestibility; *(fig auch)* difficulty; **s~verdient** *adj attr Geld* hard-earned; **s~verletzt** *adj attr* seriously injured; **~verletzte(r)** *mf* serious casualty; *(bei Unfall etc auch)* seriously injured person; **s~verständlich** *adj attr* difficult or hard to understand, incomprehensible; **s~verträglich** *adj attr Speisen* indigestible; *Medikament* not easily assimilable or assimilated; **s~verwundet** *adj attr* seriously wounded; **~verwundete(r)** *mf* major casualty; **s~wiegend** *adj (fig)* serious.
Schwester *f* -, -n sister; *(Kranken~)* nurse; *(Stations~)* sister; *(Ordens~)* nun, sister; *(Gemeinde~)* district nurse; *(inf: ~firma)* sister or associate(d) company.
Schwesterbank *f* affiliated or associated bank.
Schwesterchen *nt* little sister, baby sister
Schwester-: **~firma** *f* sister or associate(d) company; **~herz** *nt (inf)* (dear) sister, sis *(inf)*; **~kind** *nt (dial)* sister's child.
Schwesterlein *nt siehe* **Schwesterchen.**
schwesterlich *adj* sisterly.
Schwesterlichkeit *f* sisterliness.
Schwesterliebe *f* sisterly love.
Schwestern-: **~heim** *nt* nurses' home; **~helferin** *f* nursing auxiliary *(Brit)* or assistant *(US)*; **~liebe** *f* sisterly love; **~orden** *m* sisterhood; **~paar** *nt* two sisters *pl*; **~schaft** *f* nursing staff; *(von Orden)* sisterhood; **~schule** *f* nurses' training college; **~tracht** *f* nurse's uniform; **~wohnheim** *nt* nurses' home.
Schwester-: **~partei** *f* sister party; **~schiff** *nt* sister ship; **~sohn** *m (dial)* nephew; **~tochter** *f (dial)* niece.
Schwibbogen *m (Archit)* flying buttress.
schwieg *pret of* **schweigen.**
Schwieger-: **~eltern** *pl* parents-in-law *pl*; **~leute** *pl (inf)* in-laws *pl (inf)*; **~mama** *(inf)*, **~mutter** *f* mother-in-law; **~papa** *m (inf) siehe* **~vater**; **~sohn** *m* son-in-law; **~tochter** *f* daughter-in-law; **~vater** *m* father-in-law.
Schwiele *f* -, -n callus; *(Vernarbung)* welt.
schwielig *adj Hände* callused.
schwiem(e)lig *adj (dial inf)* dizzy.
schwierig *adj* difficult; *(schwer zu lernen etc auch)* hard. **er ist ein ~er Fall** he is a problem.
Schwierigkeit *f* difficulty. **in ~en geraten** or **kommen** to get into difficulties or trouble; **jdm ~en machen** to make difficulties or trouble for sb; **es macht mir überhaupt keine ~en** it won't be at all difficult for me; **warum mußt du bloß immer ~en machen!** why must you always be difficult or make difficulties!; **jdn in ~en** *(acc)* **bringen** to create difficulties for sb; **mach keine ~en!** *(inf)* don't be difficult, don't make any trouble; **ohne ~en** without any difficulty; **ohne große ~(en)** without any great difficulty.
Schwierigkeitsgrad *m* degree of difficulty.
schwill *imper sing of* **schwellen.**
Schwimm-: **~anzug** *m* swimming costume, swimsuit; **~bad** *nt* swimming pool; *(Hallenbad)* swimming baths *pl*; **~bagger** *m* dredger; **~bahn** *f* lane; **~bassin**, **~becken** *nt* (swimming) pool; **~bewegungen** *pl* swimming action *sing*; *(~züge)* swimming strokes *pl*; **~blase** *f (Zool)* air bladder; **~dock** *nt* floating dock.
schwimmen *pret* **schwamm**, *ptp* **geschwommen** *aux sein* 1 *vi* **(a)** *auch aux haben* to swim. **~ gehen** to go swimming or for a swim; **er ist über den Fluß geschwommen** he swam (across) the river.
(b) *(auf dem Wasser treiben)* to float. **seine Schiffe ~ auf allen Meeren** his ships are afloat on every ocean.
(c) *(inf: überschwemmt sein, triefen) (Boden)* to be swim-

ming (*inf*), to be awash. in Fett (*dat*) ~ to be swimming in fat; in seinem Blut ~ to be soaked in blood; in Tränen ~ to be bathed in tears; in *or* im Geld ~ to be rolling in it *or* in money (*inf*).
  (d) (*fig: unsicher sein*) to be at sea, to flounder.
  (e) es schwimmt mir vor den Augen I feel giddy *or* dizzy, everything's going round.
  2 *vt auch aux haben* (*Sport*) to swim.
Schwimmen nt -s, *no pl* swimming. zum ~ gehen to go swimming; ins ~ geraten *or* kommen (*fig*) to begin to flounder.
schwimmend adj floating. ~es Fett deep fat; im ~en Fett aufbraten to deep-fry; ~e Waren/Frachten goods afloat, floating goods.
Schwimmer m -s, - (a) swimmer. (b) (*Tech, Angeln*) float.
Schwimmerbecken nt swimmer's pool.
Schwimmerin f swimmer.
Schwimm-: s~fähig adj Material buoyant; Fahrzeug, Flugzeug amphibious; Boot, Floß floatable; s~fähig sein to be able to float; (*Material*) to float, to be buoyant; ~fest nt swimming gala; ~flügel m water wing; ~fuß m web-foot, webbed foot; ~gürtel m swimming *or* cork belt; ~halle f swimming bath(s pl), (indoor) swimming pool; ~haut f (*Orn*) web; ~hilfe f swimming aid; ~hose f siehe Badehose; ~käfer m diving beetle; ~kissen nt water wing; ~kran m floating crane; ~lage f swimming position; ~lehrer m swimming instructor; ~schüler(in f) m boy/girl/person who is learning to swim; ~sport m swimming no art; ~stadion nt swimming stadium, international swimming pool; ~stil m stroke; (*Technik*) (swimming) style; ~stoß m stroke; ~trikot nt swimsuit, swimming costume; ~übungen pl swimming exercises pl; ~unterricht m swimming lessons pl; ~verein m swimming club; ~versuch m (*fig*) die ersten ~versuche the/one's first tentative steps; ~vogel m waterbird, waterfowl; ~weste f life jacket.
Schwindel m -s, *no pl* (a) (*Gleichgewichtsstörung*) dizziness; (*esp nach Drehen auch*) giddiness.
  (b) (*Lüge*) lie; (*Betrug*) swindle, fraud; (*Vertrauensmißbrauch*) con (*inf*). die Berichte über das perfekte Haarwuchsmittel sind reiner ~ the reports about this perfect hair-restorer are a complete swindle *or* fraud *or* con (*inf*); mit den Subventionen wird viel ~ getrieben a lot of swindling *or* cheating goes on with the subsidies; das ist alles ~, was er da sagt what he says is all a pack of lies *or* a big con (*inf*); glaub doch nicht an diesen ~! don't be taken in!; den ~ kenne ich! (*inf*), auf den ~ falle ich nicht herein! (*inf*) that's an old trick.
  (c) (*inf: Kram*) der ganze ~ the whole caboodle (*inf*) *or* shoot (*inf*); ich will von dem ganzen ~ nichts mehr wissen! I don't want to hear another thing about the whole damn business (*inf*).
Schwindel|anfall m dizzy turn, attack of dizziness.
Schwindelei f (*inf*) (*leichte Lüge*) fib (*inf*); (*leichter Betrug*) swindle. seine ständige ~ his constant fibbing (*inf*).
Schwindel-: s~erregend adj (a) causing dizziness, vertiginous (*form*); in s~erregender Höhe at a dizzy height; (b) Preise astronomical; ~firma f bogus firm *or* company; s~frei adj Wendy ist nicht s~frei Wendy can't stand heights, Wendy suffers from vertigo; sie ist völlig s~frei she has a good head for heights, she doesn't suffer from vertigo at all; ~gefühl nt feeling of dizziness; (*esp nach Drehen auch*) feeling of giddiness; s~haft adj (a) (*betrügerisch*) fraudulent; (b) (s~erregend) dizzy; in s~hafter Höhe at a dizzy height.
schwind(e)lig adj dizzy; (*esp nach Drehen*) giddy. mir ist *or* ich bin ~ I feel dizzy/giddy; mir wird leicht ~ I get dizzy/giddy easily.
schwindeln 1 vi (a) mir *or* mich (*rare*) schwindelt I feel dizzy *or* (*esp vom Drehen*) giddy; mir schwindelte der Kopf, mein Kopf schwindelte my head was reeling; der Gedanke macht mich ~ (*fig*) my head reels *or* I feel dizzy at the thought; in ~der Höhe at a dizzy height; das Dorf lag in ~der Tiefe unter uns below us there was a dizzy drop to the village; ein ~der Abgrund a yawning abyss *or* chasm.
  (b) (*inf: lügen*) to fib (*inf*), to tell fibs (*inf*).
  2 vt (*inf*) das hat sie geschwindelt she was lying; das ist alles geschwindelt it's all lies.
  3 vr sich durch die Kontrollen/in den Saal ~ to con *or* wangle one's way through the checkpoint/into the hall (*inf*); sich durchs Leben/durch die Schule ~ to con one's way through life/school.
Schwindel-: ~preis m astronomical *or* exorbitant price; ~unternehmen nt siehe ~firma.
schwinden pret schwand, ptp geschwunden vi aux sein (a) (*abnehmen*) to dwindle; (*Schönheit*) to fade, to wane; (*allmählich ver~*) (*Hoffnung auch, Erinnerung, Angst, Zeit*) to fade away; (*Kräfte*) to fade, to fail. im S~ begriffen sein to be dwindling; (*Schönheit*) to be on the wane; ihm schwand der Mut, sein Mut schwand his courage failed him; ihm schwanden die Sinne (*liter*) he grew faint; aus den Augen ~ to fade from view; aus der Erinnerung ~ to fade from (one's) memory.
  (b) (*verblassen: Farben*) to fade; (*leiser werden: Ton auch*) to fade *or* die away; (*sich auflösen: Dunkelheit*) to fade away, to retreat (*liter*).
  (c) (*Tech: Holz, Metall, Ton*) to shrink, to contract.
Schwindler m -s, - swindler; (*Hochstapler*) con-man; (*Lügner*) liar, fibber (*inf*), fraud.
schwindlerisch adj fraudulent.
schwindlig adj siehe schwind(e)lig.
Schwindsucht f (*dated*) consumption. die (galoppierende) ~ haben (*dated*) to have galloping consumption; (*fig hum*) to suffer from a sort of wasting disease.
schwindsüchtig adj (*dated*) consumptive; (*fig hum*) shrinking, ailing.
Schwindsüchtige(r) mf decl as adj (*dated*) consumptive.
Schwingboden m sprung floor.

Schwinge f -, -n (*liter: Flügel*) wing, pinion (*poet*). auf den ~n der Poesie/Begeisterung on wings of poetry/passion.
schwingen pret schwang, ptp geschwungen 1 vt to swing; (*drohend*) Schwert, Stock etc to brandish; Hut, Zauberstab, Fahne to wave. die Gläser *or* den Becher ~ (*hum*) to quaff a glass (*old, hum*); Rahm ~ (*Sw*) to whip cream; siehe geschwungen, Klappe, Rede, Tanzbein.
  2 vr sich auf etw (acc) ~ to leap *or* jump onto sth, to swing oneself onto sth; sich über etw (acc) ~ to vault across *or* over sth, to swing oneself over sth; sich in etw (acc) ~ to vault into sth, to swing oneself into sth; sich in die Luft *or* Höhe ~ (*geh*) to soar (up) into the air; sich auf den Thron ~ (*fig*) to usurp the throne; die Brücke schwingt sich elegant über das Tal the bridge sweeps elegantly over the valley.
  3 vi to swing.
  (b) (*vibrieren: Brücke, Saite*) to vibrate; (*Wellen*) to oscillate.
  (c) (*geh*) (*nachklingen*) to linger. in ihren Worten schwang leichte Kritik her words had a tone of mild criticism; in diesen Volksliedern schwingt etwas von der ... these folksongs are resonant with something of the ... (*liter*).
Schwingen nt -s, *no pl* (*Sw Sport*) (*kind of*) wrestling.
Schwinger m -s, - (*Boxen*) swing; (*Sw*) wrestler.
Schwingfest nt (*Sw*), **Schwinget** m -s, *no pl* (*Sw*) wrestling gala.
Schwing-: ~flügel m casement window; ~hebel m (*Aut*) rocker arm; ~tür f swing door.
Schwingung f (*Phys*) vibration; (*von Wellen*) oscillation; (*fig*) vibration. in ~ kommen to begin to swing *or* (*Saite*) to vibrate *or* (*Wellen*) to oscillate; etw in ~(en) versetzen to set sth swinging; to start sth vibrating; to start sth oscillating.
Schwingungs-: ~dämpfer m (*Tech*) vibration damper; ~dauer f (*Phys*) time of vibration; period (of oscillation); ~kreis m (*Rad*) resonant circuit; ~weite f (*Phys*) amplitude; ~zahl f (*Phys*) frequency of oscillation.
schwipp interj ~, schwapp splish-splash.
Schwipp-: ~schwager m (*inf*) sister-in-law's husband; sister-in-law's/brother-in-law's brother; ~schwägerin f (*inf*) brother-in-law's wife; brother-in-law's/sister-in-law's sister.
Schwips m -es, -e (*inf*) einen (kleinen) ~ haben to be tiddly (*Brit inf*) *or* (slightly) tipsy.
schwirren vi aux sein to whizz; (*Bienen, Fliegen etc*) to buzz. unzählige Gerüchte ~ durch die Presse the press is buzzing with countless rumours; die Gerüchte schwirrten nur so the rumours were really buzzing around; die Gedanken/Zahlen schwirrten mir durch den Kopf thoughts/figures were whirling around in *or* buzzing through my head; mir schwirrt der Kopf my head is buzzing.
Schwitzbad nt Turkish bath; (*Dampfbad*) steam bath.
Schwitze f -, -n (*Cook*) roux.
schwitzen 1 vi (*lit, fig*) to sweat; (*Mensch auch*) to perspire; (*Fenster*) to steam up. Gott sei Dank, daß du kommst, wir haben vielleicht geschwitzt! (*inf*) thank God you've come, we were really in a sweat (*inf*).
  2 vt (a) Harz to sweat; siehe Rippe.
  (b) (*Cook*) Mehl to brown in fat.
  3 vr sich halb tot ~ (*inf*) to get drenched in sweat; sich naß ~ to get drenched in sweat; wir schleppen diese Kisten und ~ uns halb tot we've been sweating away with these crates (*inf*).
Schwitzen nt -s, *no pl* sweating; (*von Mensch auch*) perspiration.
schwitzig adj siehe verschwitzt.
Schwitz-: ~kasten m (*Ringen*) headlock; jdn in den ~kasten nehmen to get sb in a headlock, to put a headlock on sb; ~kur f sweating cure; ~packung f hot pack.
Schwof m -(e)s, -e (*inf*) hop (*inf*), shindig (*dated inf*), dance.
schwofen vi (*inf*) to dance. ~ gehen to go to a hop (*inf*) *or* shindig (*dated inf*) *or* dance.
schwoll pret of **schwellen**.
schwören pret schwor, ptp geschworen vti to swear. ich schwöre es(, so wahr mir Gott helfe) I swear it (so help me God); auf die Bibel/die Verfassung etc ~ to swear on the Bible/the Constitution etc; er schwor bei Gott/seiner Ehre, nichts davon gewußt zu haben he swore by God/by *or* on his honour that he knew nothing about it; ich kann darauf ~, daß ... I could swear to it that ...; ich hätte ~ mögen *or* geschworen, daß ... I could have sworn that ...; jdm/sich etw ~ to swear sth to sb/oneself; ich spreche nie mehr mit ihm, das habe ich mir geschworen I have sworn never to speak to him again; er macht das nie wieder, das hat er ihr geschworen he has sworn to her that he'll never do it again; aber das hast du mir geschworen! but you swore ...!; sie schworen sich (*dat*) ewige Liebe they swore (each other) eternal love; auf jdn/etw ~ (*fig*) to swear by sb/sth.
Schwuchtel f -, -n (*sl*) queer (*sl*).
schwul adj (*inf*) gay, queer (*pej inf*).
schwül adj (*lit, fig*) Tag, Schönheit, Stimmung sultry; Wetter, Tag etc auch close, muggy; (*dumpf-sinnlich*) Träume, Phantasien sensuous; Beleuchtung murky.
Schwüle f -, *no pl* siehe adj sultriness; closeness, mugginess; sensuousness. in dieser ~ in this sultry weather.
Schwulen- (*inf*): ~bar f, ~lokal nt gay bar; ~strich m (*sl*) gay *or* queer (*pej inf*) beat (*inf*).
Schwule(r) mf decl as adj (*inf*) gay, queer (*pej inf*), fag (*US pej sl*).
Schwulität f (*inf*) trouble no indef art, difficulty. in ~en geraten *or* kommen to get into a fix (*inf*); sonst komme ich in ~en *or* I'll be in a fix (*inf*) *or* in trouble; jdn in ~en bringen to get sb into trouble *or* hot water (*inf*).
Schwulst m -(e)s, *no pl* (*pej*) (*in der Sprache*) bombast, fustian, pompousness; (*in der Kunst*) bombast, ornateness, floridness.

schwulstig *adj* (a) *siehe* **geschwollen.** (b) (*esp Aus*) *siehe* **schwülstig.**

schwülstig *adj* (*pej*) *Stil, Redeweise* bombastic, fustian, pompous.

Schwülstigkeit *f* (*pej*) *siehe* **Schwulst.**

schwumm(e)rig *adj* (*inf*) (*nervös*) uneasy, apprehensive; (*dial: schwindelig*) dizzy, giddy; (*unwohl*) funny (*inf*). **mir wird ~** I feel uneasy/dizzy/funny (*inf*).

Schwund *m* -(e)s, *no pl* (a) (*Abnahme, Rückgang*) decrease (*gen* in), decline (*gen* in), dwindling (*gen* of). (b) (*von Material*) shrinkage; (*Tech: Abfall*) waste. **~ machen** (*inf*) to produce scrap. (c) (*Rad*) fading. (d) (*Med*) atrophy. (e) (*Ling: von Vokal etc*) loss.

Schwund-: **~ausgleich** *m* (*Rad*) automatic frequency control, anti-fade device; **~stufe** *f* (*Ling*) zero grade.

Schwung *m* -(e)s, ⸚e (a) *swing*; (*ausholende Handbewegung*) flourish; (*Sprung*) leap. **jdm/etw einen ~ geben** to give sb/sth a push; **etw in ~ setzen** to set sth in motion.
(b) *no pl* (*fig: Elan*) verve, zest; (*von Mensch auch*) go (*inf*); (*lit: Antrieb*) momentum. **in ~ kommen** (*lit: Schlitten etc*) to gather *or* gain momentum; (*fig auch*) to get going; **jdn/etw in ~ bringen** (*lit, fig*) to get sb/sth going; **die Sache *or* den Laden in ~ bringen** (*inf*) to get things going; **~ in die Sache *or* den Laden bringen** (*inf*) to put a bit of life into things, to liven things up; **jdm/etw ~ geben** (*lit*) to give sb/sth momentum; (*fig auch*) to get sb/sth going; **in ~ sein** (*lit: Schlitten etc*) to be going full speed *or* full pelt (*inf*); (*fig*) to be in full swing; **etw mit ~ tun** to do sth with zest; **voller/ohne ~** full of/lacking life *or* verve *or* zest.
(c) (*Linienführung*) sweep.
(d) (*inf: Menge*) (*Sachen*) stack, pile (*inf*); (*Leute*) bunch.

Schwung-: **~brett** *nt* springboard; **~feder** *f* (*Orn*) wing feather; **s~haft** *adj Handel* flourishing, roaring; **sich s~haft entwickeln** to grow hand over fist; **~kraft** *f* centrifugal force; **s~los** *adj* lacking in verve *or* zest, lacking life; *Mensch auch* lacking go (*inf*); **sich s~los fühlen** not to have any get up and go (*inf*); **~rad** *nt* flywheel.

schwungvoll *adj* (a) *Linie, Bewegung, Handschrift* sweeping. (b) (*mitreißend*) *Rede, Aufführung* lively. **es hätte etwas ~er gespielt werden müssen** it should have been played with somewhat more zest *or* verve.

schwupp *interj* in a flash, as quick as a flash. **~!** da ist er hingefallen bang! down he fell; **und ~ hatte der Zauberer ... and hey presto, the conjurer had ...**

Schwupp *m* -s, -e (*inf: Stoß*) push. **in einem ~** in one fell swoop.

schwuppdiwupp, schwups *interj siehe* **schwupp.**

Schwups *m* -es, ⸚e (*inf*) *siehe* **Schwupp.**

Schwur *m* -(e)s, ⸚e (*Eid*) oath; (*Gelübde*) vow.

Schwur-: **~finger** *pl* thumb, first finger and second finger, raised in swearing an oath; **~gericht** *nt* court with a jury; **vor das ~gericht kommen** to be tried by jury; **~gerichtsverfahren** *nt* trial by jury *no def art.*

Schwyzerdütsch, Schwyzertütsch ['ʃviːtsɐtyːtʃ] *nt* -(s), *no pl* (*Sw*) Swiss German.

Science-fiction ['saɪənsfɪkʃən] *f* -, -s science fiction, sci-fi (*inf*).

Scirocco [ʃi'rɔko] *m* -s, -s *siehe* **Schirokko.**

Scotchterrier ['skɔtʃterɪɐ] *m* Scotch terrier, Scottie.

Scriptgirl ['skrɪptgøːɛl, -gœrl] *nt* (*Film*) script girl.

Scrotum *nt* -s, **Scrota** (*Med*) scrotum.

Scylla ['stsyla] *f* -, *no pl* (*Myth*) *siehe* **Szylla.**

SDS [esdeː'es] *m* - *abbr of* **Sozialistischer Deutscher Studentenbund.**

Seal [siːl] *m or nt* -s, -s sealskin.

Sealskin ['siːlskɪn] *m or nt* -s, -s (a) sealskin. (b) imitation sealskin.

Séance [se'ãːsə] *f* -, -n séance.

Seborrhöe [zebo'røː] *f* -, *no pl* dandruff, seborrh(o)ea (*spec*).

sec *abbr of* **Sekunde.**

sechs [zɛks] *num* six; *siehe auch* **vier.**

Sechs- [zɛks-] in *cpds* six; *siehe auch* **vier-;** **~achteltakt** *m* (*Mus*) six-eight time **~eck** *nt* hexagon; **s~eckig** *adj* hexagonal,

Sechser ['zɛksɐ] *m* -s, - (a) (*obs*) six-kreutzer/-groschen *etc* piece; (*dial inf*) five-pfennig piece. **nicht für einen ~ Verstand haben** not to have a scrap *or* a ha'p'orth (*Brit*) of sense; **einen ~ im Lotto haben** to get a six in the German national lottery (*i.e.* the top prize). (b) *siehe* **Sechs.** (c) *siehe auch* **Vierer.**

sechserlei ['zɛksɐ'laɪ] *adj inv* six kinds of; *siehe auch* **viererlei.**

Sechs- [zɛks-]: **s~fach 1** *adj* sixfold; **2** *adv* sixfold, six times; *siehe auch* **vierfach;** **~füßer** *m* -s, - (*Zool*) hexapod; **s~hundert** *num* six hundred; **~kampf** *m* gymnastic competition with six events; **s~mal** *adv* six times; **s~spurig** *adj* six-lane; **~tagerennen** *nt* six-day (bicycle) race; **s~tägig** *adj* six-day; **s~tausend** *num* six thousand; **ein ~tausender** *a* mountain six thousand metres in height.

Sechstel ['zɛkstl] *nt* -s, - sixth; *siehe auch* **Viertel**[1].

sechstens ['zɛkstns] *adv* sixth(ly), in the sixth place.

sechste(r, s) ['zɛkstə] *adj* sixth. **einen ~n Sinn für etw haben, den ~n Sinn haben** to have a sixth sense (for sth); *siehe auch* **vierte(r, s).**

Sechsundsechzig ['zɛksʊnt'zɛçtsɪç] *nt* -, *no pl* (*Cards*) sixty-six.

Sechszylinder ['zɛks-] *m* six-cylinder car/engine.

sechzehn ['zɛçtseːn] *num* sixteen; *siehe auch* **vierzehn.**

Sechzehntel(note *f*) *nt* -s, - (*Mus*) semiquaver (*Brit*), six-teenth note (*US*).

Sechzehntelpause *f* (*Mus*) semiquaver rest (*Brit*), sixteenth note rest (*US*).

sechzig ['zɛçtsɪç] *num* sixty; *siehe auch* **vierzig.**

Sechziger(in *f*) *m* -s, - sixty-year-old, sexagenarian.

SED [ɛsɛeː'deː] *f* - *abbr of* **Sozialistische Einheitspartei Deutschlands.**

Sedativ(um) *nt* (*Pharm*) sedative.

Sedezformat *nt* (*Typ*) sextodecimo.

Sediment *nt* (*Geol*) sediment.

sedimentär *adj* (*Geol*) sedimentary.

Sedimentgestein *nt* (*Geol*) sedimentary rock.

See[1] *f* -, -n [zeːən] sea. **grobe *or* schwere ~** rough *or* heavy seas; **an der ~** by the sea, at the seaside; **an die ~ fahren** to go to the sea(side); **auf hoher ~** on the high seas; **auf ~** at sea; **in ~ gehen** *or* **stechen** to put to sea; **zur ~ fahren** to be a merchant seaman; **zur ~ gehen** to go to sea.

See[2] *m* -s, -n [zeːən] lake; (*in Schottland*) loch; (*Teich*) pond.

See-: **~aal** *m* (a) (*Zool*) conger (eel); (b) (*Comm*) dogfish; **~adler** *m* sea eagle; **~alpen** *pl* (*Geog*) Maritime Alps *pl*; **~amt** *nt* (*Admin*) maritime court; **~anemone** *f* sea anemone; **~bad** *nt* (a) (*Kurort*) seaside resort; (b) (*Bad im Meer*) bathe *or* swim in the sea; **~bär** *m* (a) (*hum inf*) seadog (*inf*); (b) (*Zool*) fur seal; **~beben** *nt* seaquake; **s~beschädigt** *adj* (*form*) *Schiff* damaged at sea; **~boden** *m* bottom *or* bed of a/the sea/lake; **der ~boden des Loch Ness** the bottom *or* bed of Loch Ness; **~-Elefant** *m* sea-elephant; **s~erfahren** *adj Volk* experienced at navigation *or* seafaring; **s~fähig** *adj siehe* **s~tüchtig;** **s~fahrend** *adj attr Volk* seafaring; **~fahrer** *m* seafarer; **Sindbad der ~fahrer** Sinbad the Sailor.

Seefahrt *f* (a) (*Fahrt*) (sea) voyage; (*Vergnügungs~*) cruise. (b) (*Schiffahrt*) seafaring *no art.* **ungeeignet für die ~ in ...** unsuited for navigation *or* sailing in ...; **die ~ lernen** to learn to sail; **die Regeln der ~** the rules of the sea.

Seefahrts-: **~amt** *nt* (*esp DDR*) shipping board; **~buch** *nt* (seaman's) registration book; **~schule** *f* merchant navy training college.

See-: **s~fest** *adj* (*Mensch*) not subject to seasickness; **s~fest sein** to be a good sailor. (b) *siehe* **s~tüchtig;** (c) *Ladung* fit for sea transport; **~fisch** *m* salt-water fish; **~fischerei** *f* sea fishing; **~fracht** *f* sea freight; **~frachtbrief** *m* (*Comm*) bill of lading; **~funk(dienst)** *m* shipping radio service; **~gang** *m* swell; **starker *or* hoher ~gang** heavy *or* rough seas *or* swell; **~gefahr** *f* (*Comm*) sea-risk; **~gefecht** *nt* sea *or* naval battle; **~geltung** *f* (*Hist*) naval prestige; **~gemälde** *nt* seascape; **~gras** *nt* (*Bot*) eelgrass, sea grass *or* hay; **~grasmatratze** *f* sea grass mattress; **s~grün** *adj* sea-green; **~hafen** *m* seaport; **~handel** *m* maritime trade; **~hase** *m* lumpsucker; **~held** *m* naval hero; **~herrschaft** *f* naval *or* maritime supremacy; **~höhe** *f* sea level; **~hund** *m* seal; **~hundsfell** *nt* sealskin; **~igel** *m* sea urchin; **~jungfer** *f* (*Zool*) dragonfly; **~jungfrau** *f* (*Myth*) mermaid; **~kadett** *m* (*Mil*) naval cadet; **~kanal** *m* (maritime) canal; **~karte** *f* sea *or* nautical chart; **~katze** *f* catfish; **s~klar** *adj* ready to sail; **~klima** *nt* maritime climate; **s~krank** *adj* sea-sick; **Paul wird leicht s~krank** Paul is a bad sailor; **~krankheit** *f* seasickness; **~krieg(führung** *f*) *m* naval war(fare); **~kriegsrecht** *nt* laws of naval warfare *pl*; **~kuh** *f* (*Zool*) seacrow, manatee; **~lachs** *m* (*Cook*) pollack.

Seel[amt] *nt* (*Sw Eccl*) *siehe* **Seelenamt.**

Seeland *nt* -s (*Geog*) (a) (*dänisch*) Zealand, Seeland. (b) (*niederländisch*) Zeeland.

Seelchen *nt* (*inf*) dear soul.

Seele *f* -, -n (a) (*Rel, fig*) soul; (*Herzstück, Mittelpunkt*) life and soul. **seine ~ aushauchen** (*euph liter*) to breathe one's last (*liter*); **in tiefster *or* innerster ~** (*geh*) in one's heart of hearts; **mit dieser Bemerkung verletzte sie ihre Mutter in tiefster ~** (*geh*) this remark cut her mother to the quick; **mit ganzer ~** with all one's soul; **von ganzer ~** with all one's heart (and soul); **aus tiefster *or* innerster ~** with all one's heart and with all one's soul; **danken from the bottom of one's heart; jdm aus der ~ *or* aus tiefster ~ sprechen** to express exactly what sb feels; **das liegt mir auf der ~ it weighs heavily on my mind; sich (dat) etw von der ~ reden** to get sth off one's chest; **sich (dat) die ~ aus dem Leib reden** (*inf*) to talk until one is blue in the face (*inf*); **jdm etw auf die ~ binden** (*dated*) to impress sth upon sb; **das tut mir in der ~ weh** I am deeply distressed; **jdm in der ~ lesen können** (*geh*) to be able to see into sb's soul; **zwei ~n und ein Gedanke** (*prov*) two minds with but a single thought; **zwei ~n wohnen in meiner Brust** (*liter*) I am torn; **dann/nun hat die liebe ~ Ruh** (*inf*) that'll put him/us *etc* out of his/our misery; **meiner Seel!** (*old*) upon my soul! (*old*).
(b) (*Mensch*) soul. **eine ~ von Mensch *or* von einem Menschen** an absolute dear.
(c) (*von Feuerwaffen*) bore.
(d) (*von Tau*) core.

Seelen-: **~achse** *f* axis (of the bore); **~adel,** *m* (*liter*) nobility of mind; **~amt** *nt* (*Eccl*) requiem; **~arzt** (*hum*), **~doktor** (*hum inf*) *m* head-shrinker (*hum inf*), shrink (*inf*), trick-cyclist (*hum sl*); **~bräutigam** *m* (*liter*) guardian of one's soul; **~drama** *nt* psychological drama; **~forscher** *m* psychologist; **~freund(in** *f*) *m* (*geh*) soul mate; **~friede(n)** *m* (*geh*) peace of mind; **~größe** *f* (*geh*) greatness of mind, magnanimity; **s~gut** *adj* kind-hearted; **~güte** *f* (*geh*) kind-heartedness; **~heil** *nt* spiritual salvation, salvation of one's soul; (*fig*) spiritual welfare; **~heilkunde** *f* (*dated*) psychiatry; **~hirt(e)** *m* (*geh, iro*) pastor; **~kunde** *f* (*dated*) psychology; **~leben** *nt* inner life; **er versteht ihr ~leben überhaupt nicht** he does not understand her emotions *or* feelings at all; **~lehre** *f* (*dated*) psychology; **s~los** *adj* soulless; **~massage** *f* (*hum inf*) gentle persuasion; **~messe** *f* (*Eccl*) requiem mass; **~not,** **~pein,** **~qual** *f* (*geh*) (mental) anguish; **~regung** *f* sign of emotion, emotional reaction *or* response; **~ruhe** *f* calmness, coolness; **in aller ~ruhe** calmly; (*kaltblütig*) as cool as you please; **s~ruhig** *adv* calmly; (*kaltblütig*) as cool as you please, as cool as a cucumber (*inf*); **~tröster** *m* (*hum*) (*Schnaps*) pick-me-up (*inf*); (*Mensch*) comforter; s~**vergnügt** *adj* as happy as a sandboy; ~**verkäufer** *m* (*Hist*) seller of souls; (*fig pej*) (*Heuerbaas*) press-gang officer; (*Schiff*) death trap; s~**verwandt** *adj* congenial (*liter*); **sie waren** s~**verwandt** they were kindred spirits; ~**verwandtschaft** *f* affinity, congeniality of spirit (*liter*); s~**voll** *adj* soulful; ~**wanderung** *f* (*Rel*) transmigration of souls, metempsychosis; ~**wärmer** *m* -s, - (*hum: Schnaps*) pick-me-up (*inf*); ~**zustand** *m* psychological *or* mental state.

See-: ~**leute** *pl of* ~**mann**; ~**lilie** *f* sea lily.

seelisch *adj* (*Rel*) spiritual; (*geistig*) mental, psychological; *Erschütterung, Belastung* emotional; *Grausamkeit* mental. ~ **bedingt sein** to be psychologically conditioned, to have psychological causes; ~**e Kraft zu etw haben** to have the strength of mind for sth; ~**e Abgründe** the blackest depths of the human soul.

See-: ~**lotse** *m* pilot; ~**löwe** *m* sea lion.

Seelsorge *f*, *no pl* spiritual welfare. **in der** ~ **arbeiten** to do spiritual welfare work with a church.

Seelsorger(in *f*) *m* -s, - pastor.

seelsorgerisch, seelsorg(er)lich *adj* pastoral.

See-: ~**luft** *f* sea air; ~**macht** *f* naval *or* sea *or* maritime power.

Seemann *m*, *pl* -**leute** sailor, seaman, mariner (*esp liter*).

seemännisch 1 *adj Ausbildung, Sprache etc* nautical; *Tradition auch* seafaring. **das ist typisch** ~ that is typical of sailors. **2** *adv* nautically. ~ **heißen sie ...** in nautical *or* sailors' language they are called ...

Seemanns-: ~**amt** *nt* shipping board; ~**ausdruck** *m* nautical *or* sailors' term; ~**brauch** *m* seafaring custom; ~**gang** *m* sailor's walk; ~**garn** *nt*, *no pl* (*inf*) sailor's yarn; ~**garn spinnen** to spin a yarn; ~**heim** *nt* sailors' home; ~**lied** *nt* sea shanty; ~**los** *nt* a sailor's lot; ~**mission** *f* mission to seamen, seamen's mission; ~**sprache** *f* nautical *or* sailors' slang; ~**tod** *m* sailor's death; **den** ~**tod sterben** to die a sailor's death.

See-: ~**meile** *f* nautical *or* sea mile; ~**mine** *f* (sea) mine; ~**nelke** *f* sea anemone.

Seengebiet ['ze:ən-] *nt* lakeland district.

Seenot *f*, *no pl* distress. **in** ~ **geraten** to get into distress.

Seenot-: ~**kreuzer** *m* (motor) lifeboat; ~**(rettungs)dienst** *m* sea rescue service; ~**zeichen** *nt* nautical distress signal.

Seenplatte ['ze:ən-] *f* lowland plain full of lakes.

See-: ~**nymphe** *f* mermaid; ~**otter** *m* sea otter; ~**pferd(chen)** *nt* sea-horse; ~**räuber** *m* pirate; (*in Mittelamerika im 17., 18. Jh. auch*) buccaneer; ~**räuberei** *f* piracy; ~**räuberschiff** *nt* pirate (ship); buccaneer; ~**recht** *nt* maritime law; ~**reise** *f* (sea) voyage; (*Kreuzfahrt*) cruise; ~**rose** *f* waterlily; ~**sack** *m* seabag, sailor's kitbag; ~**salz** *nt* sea *or* bay salt; ~**sand** *m* sea sand; ~**schaden** *m* damage at sea, average (*spec*); ~**schiff** *nt* seagoing *or* ocean-going ship *or* vessel; ~**schiffahrt** *f* maritime *or* ocean shipping; ~**schildkröte** *f* sea turtle; ~**schlacht** *f* naval *or* sea battle; ~**schlange** *f* sea snake; (*Myth*) sea serpent; ~**schwalbe** *f* tern; ~**sieg** *m* naval victory; ~**sperre** *f* naval blockade; ~**stadt** *f* seaside town; ~**stern** *m* (*Zool*) starfish; ~**straßenordnung** *f* rules of the road (at sea) *pl*, international regulations for preventing collisions at sea *pl* (*form*); ~**streitkräfte** *pl* naval forces *pl*, navy; ~**stück** *nt* (*Art*) seascape; ~**tang** *m* seaweed; ~**taucher** *m* (*Orn*) grebe; ~**transport** *m* shipment *or* transport by sea, sea transport; s~**tüchtig** *adj* seaworthy; ~**tüchtigkeit** *f* seaworthiness; ~**ufer** *nt* lakeside; (*von großem See auch*) (lake) shore; ~**ungeheuer** *nt* sea monster; s~**untüchtig** *adj* unseaworthy; ~**verkehr** *m* maritime traffic; ~**versicherung** *f* marine insurance; ~**vogel** *m* sea bird; ~**volk** *nt* (*Nation*) seafaring nation *or* people; (*inf:* ~**leute**) seafaring people *pl*; ~**walze** *f* (*Zool*) sea-cucumber; s~**wärts** *adv* (*in Richtung Meer*) seaward(s), toward(s) the sea; (*in Richtung Binnen*)*see*) toward(s) the lake; ~**wasser** *nt* (*Meerwasser*) sea water; (*Wasser eines Sees*) lake water; ~**weg** *m* sea route; **auf dem** ~**weg reisen** to go *or* travel by sea; ~**wesen** *nt* maritime affairs *pl*, *no art*; ~**wetterdienst** *m* meteorological service, Met Office (*Brit inf*); ~**wind** *m* sea breeze, onshore wind; ~**wolf** *m* (*Zool*) wolf-fish; ~**zeichen** *nt* navigational aid; ~**zunge** *f* sole.

Segel *nt* -s, - sail. **mit vollen** ~**n** under full sail *or* canvas; (*fig*) with gusto; **unter** ~ **gehen** (*Naut*) to set sail; **die** ~ **streichen** (*Naut*) to strike sail; (*fig*) to give in.

Segel-: ~**boot** *nt* sailing boat (*Brit*), sailboat (*US*); ~**fahrt** *f* sail; s~**fliegen** *vi infin only* to glide; s~**fliegen gehen** to go gliding; ~**fliegen** *nt* gliding; ~**flieger** *m* glider pilot; ~**fliegerei** *f* gliding; ~**fliegerohren** *pl* (*hum*) cab-door ears *pl* (*hum*), flappy ears *pl* (*inf*); ~**flug** *m* (*no pl:* ~**fliegerei**) gliding; (*Flug im* ~*flugzeug*) glider flight; ~**flugplatz** *m* gliding field; ~**flugzeug** *nt* glider; (*leichter gebaut auch*) sailplane; ~**flugzeugbau** *m* building gliders/sailplanes, glider/sailplane construction; ~**jacht** *f* (sailing) yacht, sailboat (*US*); ~**karte** *f* chart; s~**klar** *adj pred* ready to sail; ~**klasse** *f* (*Sport*) (yacht) class; ~**klub** *m* sailing club; ~**macher** *m* sailmaker.

segeln *vti* (a) *aux haben or sein* (*lit, fig*) to sail. **eine Strecke** ~ to sail a course; **eine Regatta** ~ to sail in a regatta; **als junger Mensch hat er viel gesegelt** in his younger days he did a lot of sailing *or* he sailed a lot; ~ **gehen** to go for a sail.

(b) *aux sein* (*inf*) **durch eine Prüfung** ~ to flop in an exam (*inf*), to fail (in) an exam.

Segeln *nt* -s, *no pl* sailing.

Segel-: ~**partie** *f* sail, sailing trip; ~**regatta** *f* sailing *or* yachting regatta; ~**schiff** *nt* sailing ship *or* vessel; ~**schulschiff** *nt* training sailing ship; ~**sport** *m* sailing *no art*; ~**tuch** *nt* canvas.

Segen *m* -s, - (a) (*lit, fig*) blessing; (*Eccl: Gnadengebet auch*) benediction. **es ist ein** ~, **daß ...** it is a blessing that ...; **über jdn/etw den** ~ **sprechen** to give sb/sth one's blessing; (*Eccl auch*) to pronounce one's blessing upon sb/sth; **jdm den** ~ **erteilen** *or* **spenden** to give sb one's blessing *or* benediction;

meinen ~ **hat er, er hat meinen** ~ he has my blessing.

(b) (*Heil, Erfolg*) blessing, boon, godsend. **das bringt keinen** ~ no good will come of it; **ein wahrer** ~ a real blessing *or* boon; **zum** ~ **der Menschheit werden** to be for *or* redound to (*liter*) the benefit of mankind.

(c) (*liter: Ertrag, Lohn*) fruits *pl*.

(d) (*inf*) **der ganze** ~ the whole lot *or* shoot (*inf*).

Segen-: s~**bringend** *adj* beneficent; ~**erteilung** *f* (*Eccl*) benediction, blessing; s~**spendend** *adj* beneficent.

Segens-: s~**reich** *adj* beneficial; *Tätigkeit* beneficent; ~**wunsch** *m* (*liter*) blessing; **herzliche** ~**wünsche** congratulations and best wishes.

Segler *m* -s, - (a) (*Segelsportler*) yachtsman, sailor. (b) (*Schiff*) sailing vessel. (c) (*Orn*) swift.

Seglerin *f* yachtswoman.

Seglermütze *f* sailor's cap.

Segment *nt* segment.

segmental *adj* segmental.

segmentär *adj* segmentary.

segmentieren* *vt* to segment.

Segmentierung *f* segmentation.

segnen *vt* (*Rel*) to bless. ~**d die Hände erheben** to raise one's hands in blessing; *siehe* **gesegnet**.

Segnung *f* (*Rel*) blessing, benediction.

Segregation *f* (*Sociol*) segregation.

sehbehindert *adj* partially sighted.

sehen *pret* **sah**, *ptp* **gesehen** 1 *vt* (a) to see; (*an*~ *auch*) to look at; *Fernsehsendung auch* to watch. **gut/schlecht zu** ~ **sein** to be easily seen/difficult to see; **sieht man das?** does it show?; **das kann man** ~ you can see that, you can tell that (just by looking); **siehst du irgendwo mein Buch?** can you see my book anywhere?; **von ihm war nichts mehr zu** ~ he was no longer to be seen; **da gibt es nichts zu** ~ there is nothing to see *or* to be seen; **darf ich das mal** ~? can I have a look at that?, can I see that?; **das muß man gesehen haben** it has to be seen to be believed; (*läßt sich nicht beschreiben*) you have to see it for yourself; **ich kann den Mantel/den Menschen nicht mehr** ~ I can't stand the sight of that coat/him any more; **ich kann ihn nicht** ~ (*fig*) I can't stand the sight of him; **jdn kommen/weggehen** ~ to see sb coming/leaving; **jdn/etw zu** ~ **bekommen** to get to see sb/sth; **Sie** ~ **jetzt eine Direktübertragung ...** we now bring you a live broadcast ...; **Sie sahen eine Direktübertragung ...** that was *or* you have been watching a live broadcast ...; **den möchte ich** ~, **der ...** I'd like to meet the man who ...; **da sieht man es mal wieder!** that's typical!, it all goes to show (*inf*); **hat man so was schon gesehen!** (*inf*) did you ever see anything like it!; **ich sehe was, was du nicht siehst** (*Spiel*) I spy with my little eye.

(b) (*treffen*) to see. **sich** *or* **einander** (*acc*) ~ to see each other; **also, wir** ~ **uns morgen** right, I'll see you tomorrow; **ich freue mich, Sie zu** ~! nice to see you.

(c) (*erkennen, feststellen, glauben*) to see. **sich/jdn als etw** ~ to see oneself/sb as sth; **etw in jdm** ~ to see sth in sb; **das müssen wir erst mal** ~ that remains to be seen; **das sehe ich noch nicht** (*inf*) I still don't see that happening; (*ob er tatsächlich kommt*), **das wird man noch** ~ we'll see (if he actually does come); **das wollen wir** (*doch*) **erst mal** ~! we'll see about that!; **das wollen wir** (**doch**) **erst mal** ~, **ob ...** we'll see if ...

(d) (*betrachten, beurteilen*) to see; (*deuten, interpretieren auch*) to look at. **wie siehst du das?** how do you see it?; **das darf man nicht so** ~ you shouldn't look at it like that, that's not the way to look at it; **du siehst das/ihn nicht richtig** you've got it/him wrong; **das sehe ich anders**, **so sehe ich das nicht** that's not how I see it; **rein menschlich/dienstlich gesehen** looking at it personally/officially, from a purely personal/official point of view; **so gesehen** looked at *or* regarded in this way; **du hast wohl keine Lust, oder wie sehe ich das?** (*inf*) you don't feel like it, do you *or* right (*esp US*)?; **du bist wohl müde, oder wie sehe ich das?** (*inf*) you're tired, aren't you *or* right (*esp US*)?; **neue Krawatte, oder wie sehe ich das?** (*inf*) new tie, eh?

(e) **sich** ~ **lassen** to put in an appearance, to appear; **er hat sich schon lange nicht mehr zu Hause** ~ **lassen** he hasn't shown up at home (*inf*) *or* put in an appearance at home for a long time; **er läßt sich kaum noch bei uns** ~ he hardly comes to see us any more; **lassen Sie sich doch mal wieder** ~! do come again; **er kann sich in der Nachbarschaft nicht mehr** ~ **lassen** he can't show his face in the neighbourhood any more; **kann ich mich in diesem Anzug** ~ **lassen?** can I be seen in this suit?, am I fit to be seen in this suit?; **mit diesem Mann kann sie sich durchaus** ~ **lassen** she needn't be ashamed of being seen with a man like that; **das neue Rathaus kann sich** ~ **lassen** the new town hall is certainly something to be proud of.

2 *vr* **sich betrogen/getäuscht/enttäuscht** ~ to see oneself cheated/deceived/to feel disappointed; **sich genötigt** *or* **veranlaßt** ~, **zu ...** to see *or* find it necessary to ...; **sich gezwungen** ~, **zu ...** to see *or* find oneself obliged to ...; **sich in der Lage** ~, **zu ...** (*form*) to see *or* find oneself in a position to ... (*form*).

3 *vi* (a) to see. **siehe oben/unten** see above/below; **siehe!** (*esp Bibl*)/**sehet!** (*old, liter, Bibl*) lo! (*Bibl*), behold! (*Bibl*); **siehe** da! (*liter*) behold! (*liter*); **siehst du** (**wohl**)!, **siehste!** (*inf*) you see!; **sieh doch!** look (here)!; ~ **Sie mal!** look!; **er sieht gut/schlecht** he can/cannot see very well; **scharf/weit** ~ (**können**) to be able to see clearly/a long way; ~**en Auges** (*geh*) with open eyes, with one's eyes open; **willst du mal** ~? do you want to see *or* look?, do you want to have a look?; **laß mal** ~ let me see *or* look *or* have a look, give us a look (*inf*); **jdm über die Schulter** ~ to look over sb's shoulder; **na siehst du** (there you are,) you see?; **kaum nicht gesehen** (*inf*) in a flash, in the twinkling of an eye; **wie ich sehe ...** I (can) see (that) ...; **Sie sind beschäftigt, wie ich sehe** I can see you're busy; **ich sehe schon, du willst nicht sehen** I can see you don't want to; **wir werden schon** ~

we'll see; **da kann man mal ~, da kannste mal ~** (*inf*) that just shows (you) (*inf*) *or* goes to show (*inf*); **wir wollen ~** we'll have to see; **mal ~, ob ...** (*inf*) let's see if ...; **mal ~** (*inf*) we'll see; **jeder muß ~, wo er bleibt** (it's) every man for himself; **sieh, daß du ... make sure *or* see** (that) you ...

(b) (*herausragen*) **aus etw ~** to be sticking *or* peeping *or* peeking (*inf*) out of sth; **das Boot sah kaum aus dem Wasser** the boat hardly showed above the water.

(c) (*zeigen, weisen*) to look. **das Fenster sieht auf den Garten** the window looks onto the garden; **das Zimmer sieht nach der Straße** the room looks onto *or* faces the street.

(d) nach jdm ~ (*jdn betreuen*) to look after sb; (*jdn besuchen*) to go/come to see sb; **nach etw ~** to look after sth; **ich muß nur mal eben nach den Kartoffeln ~** I've just got to (have a) look at the potatoes; **nach der Post ~** to see if there are any letters.

(e) auf etw (*acc*) **~** to pay attention to sth, to care about sth; **darauf ~, daß ...** to make sure (that) ...

Sehen *nt* **-s**, *no pl* seeing; (*Sehkraft*) sight, vision. **als Photograph muß man richtiges, bewußtes ~ lernen** as a photographer one has to learn to see correctly and consciously; **ich kenne ihn nur vom ~** I only know him by sight.

sehenswürdig, sehenswert *adj* worth seeing. **ein ~es Schloß** a castle (which is) worth seeing.

Sehenswürdigkeit *f* sight. **die Kneipe ist wirklich eine ~!** that pub is really (a sight) worth seeing!; **die ~en (einer Stadt) besichtigen** to go sightseeing (in a city), to see the sights (of a city).

Seher ['ze:ɐ] *m* **-s**, **-** (*liter*) seer; (*Hunt*) eye.

Seher-: **~blick** *m* (*geh*) prophetic eye; **den ~blick haben** to have a prophetic eye; **~gabe** *f* (*geh*) gift of prophecy, prophetic gift.

Seherin ['ze:ərɪn] *f* seer.

seherisch ['ze:ərɪʃ] *adj attr* prophetic.

Seh-: **~fehler** *m* visual *or* sight defect; **~feld** *nt siehe* **Gesichtsfeld;** **~kraft** *f* (eye)sight; **~kreis** *m siehe* **Gesichtskreis;** **~loch** *nt* (*Opt*) pupil.

Sehne *f* **-, -n (a)** (*Anat*) tendon, sinew. **(b)** (*Bogen~*) string. **(c)** (*Math*) chord.

sehnen *vr* **sich nach jdm/etw ~** to long *or* yearn (*liter*) for sb/sth; (*schmachtend*) to pine for sb/sth; **mit ~dem Verlangen** (*geh*) with longing *or* yearning.

Sehnen *nt* **-s**, *no pl siehe* **Sehnsucht.**

Sehnen-: **~reflex** *m* tendon reflex; **~scheidenentzündung** *f* tendovaginitis (*spec*), inflammation of a tendon and its sheath; **~zerrung** *f* pulled tendon.

Sehnerv *m* optic nerve.

sehnig *adj* Gestalt, Mensch sinewy, wiry; Fleisch stringy.

sehnlich *adj* ardent; Erwartung eager. **sein ~ster Wunsch** his fondest *or* most ardent (*liter*) wish; **sich** (*dat*) **etw ~st wünschen** to long for sth with all one's heart; **wir alle hatten sie ~(st) erwartet** we had all been (most) eagerly awaiting her.

Sehnsucht *f* **-, -̈e** longing, yearning (*nach* for); (*schmachtend*) pining. **~ haben** to have a longing *or* yearning.

sehnsüchtig *adj* longing, yearning; Verlangen, Wunsch etc ardent; Erwartung, Ungeduld eager; Brief full of longing *or* yearning. **der dritte Satz hat etwas seltsam S~es** the third movement has a strangely yearning quality.

sehnsuchtsvoll *adj* longing, yearning; Blick, Augen, Brief, Schilderung, Musik wistful.

Sehorgan *nt* visual organ.

sehr *adv, comp* (**noch**) **mehr,** *superl* **am meisten (a)** (*mit adj, adv*) very. **~ verbunden!** (*dated form*) much obliged; **er ist ~ dafür/dagegen** he is very much in favour of it, he is all for it/he is very much against it; **hat er ~ viel getrunken?** did he drink very much?; **er hat ~ viel getrunken** he drank a lot; **~ zu meiner Überraschung** very much to my surprise; **es geht ihm ~ viel besser** he is very much better; **wir haben ~ viel Zeit/Geld** we have plenty of time/money *or* a lot of time/money *or* lots of time/money; **wir haben nicht ~ viel Zeit/Geld** we don't have very much time/money.

(b) (*mit vb*) very much, a lot. **so ~ so much; jdn so ~ schlagen/zusammenschlagen, daß ...** to hit sb so hard that/to beat sb up so much *or* so badly that ...; **sich über etw** (*acc*) **so ~ ärgern/freuen, daß ...** to be so (very) annoyed/pleased about sth that ...; **~ verwurzelt sein** to be very deeply rooted; **wie ~ how much; keiner weiß, wie ~ ich leide** nobody knows how (very) much I suffer; **wie ~ er sich auch ...** however much he ...; **sich ~ vorsehen** to be very careful *or* very much on the lookout; **sich** (*dat*) **etw ~ überlegen** to consider sth very carefully; **sich ~ anstrengen** to try very hard; **es lohnt sich ~** it's very *or* well worthwhile; **~ weinen** to cry a lot *or* a great deal; **hat sie ~ geweint?** did she cry very much *or* a lot?; **es regnet ~** 'it's raining hard *or* heavily; **regnet es ~?** is it raining very much *or* a lot?; **freust du dich? — ja, ~!** are you pleased? — yes, very; **freust du dich darauf? — ja, ~** are you looking forward to it? — yes, very much; **tut es weh? — ja, ~/nein, nicht ~** does it hurt? — yes, a lot/no, not very much *or* not a lot; **~ sogar!** yes, very much so (in fact); **zu ~ too much; nicht zu ~ not too much; man sollte sich nicht zu ~ ärgern** one shouldn't get too annoyed.

sehren *vt* (*old, dial*) *siehe* **verletzen.**

Seh-: **~rohr** *nt* periscope; **~schärfe** *f* keenness of sight, visual acuity; **~schlitz** *m* slit; (*von Panzer etc*) observation slit; **~schwäche** *f* poor eyesight; **~störung** *f* visual defect; **wenn ~störungen auftreten** when the vision becomes disturbed; **~test** *m* eye test; **~vermögen** *nt* powers of vision *pl*; **~weite** *f siehe* **Sichtweite; ~werkzeug** *nt* visual organ, organ of sight; **~winkel** *m siehe* **Gesichtswinkel.**

sei *imper sing*, 1. *and* 3. *pers sing subjunc of* **sein.**

seibern *vi* (*dial*) *siehe* **sabbern.**

Seich *m* **-(e)s**, *no pl*, **Seiche** *f* **-,** *no pl* **(a)** (*dial sl*) piss (*vulg*). **(b)** (*inf: Geschwätz*) *siehe* **Geseich(e).**

seichen *vi* **(a)** (*dial sl*) to piss (*vulg*). **(b)** (*inf*) *siehe* **schwafeln.**

seicht *adj* (*lit, fig*) shallow. **die ~e Stelle** the shallows *pl*.

Seichtheit *f* (*lit, fig*) shallowness.

Seichtigkeit *f* (*fig*) shallowness *no pl*. **er sagte nur ~en** everything he said was so shallow.

seid 2. *pers pl present, imper pl of* **sein.**

Seide *f* **-, -n** silk.

Seidel *nt* **-s**, **- (a)** (*Gefäß*) stein, (beer) mug. **(b)** (*S Ger: altes Maß*) half-litre, ≈ pint.

Seidelbast *m* (*Bot*) daphne.

seiden *adj attr* (*aus Seide*) silk, silken (*liter*).

Seiden- *in cpds* silk; **s~artig** *adj* silky, silk-like; **~atlas** *m* silk satin; **~band** *nt* silk ribbon; **~bau** *m* (*form*) sericulture (*form*), silkworm breeding; **~faden** *m*, **~garn** *nt* silk thread; **~gewebe** *nt* silk fabric; **~glanz** *m* silky *or* silken sheen; **~papier** *nt* tissue paper; **~raupe** *f* silkworm; **~raupenzucht** *f* silkworm breeding; **~schwanz** *m* (*Orn*) waxwing; **~spinner** *m* (a) (*Zool*) silk moth; **(b)** (*als Beruf*) silk spinner; **~spinnerei** *f* (a) silk spinning; **(b)** (*Betrieb*) silk mill; **~stoff** *m* silk cloth *or* fabric; **~straße** *f* (*Hist*) silk road; **~strumpf** *m* silk stocking; **s~weich** *adj* soft as silk, silky soft.

seidig *adj* (*wie Seide*) silky, silken.

Seiende(s) *nt decl as adj* (*Philos*) being *no art*.

Seife *f* **-, -n (a)** soap. **(b)** (*Geol*) alluvial deposit.

seifen *vt* **(a)** (*ein~, ab~*) to soap. **(b)** (*Min*) to wash.

Seifen-: **~blase** *f* soap-bubble; (*fig*) bubble; **~blasen machen** to blow (soap-)bubbles; **~flocken** *pl* soapflakes *pl*; **~kisten-rennen** *nt* soap-box derby; **~lauge** *f* (soap)suds *pl*; **~napf** *m* shaving mug; **~pulver** *nt* soap powder; **~schale** *f* soap dish; **~schaum** *m* lather; **~sieder** *m* **-s**, **-** soap-boiler; **mir ging ein ~sieder auf** (*dated inf*) the penny dropped (*inf*), it suddenly dawned on me; **~wasser** *nt* soapy water.

seifig *adj* soapy.

Seigerschacht *m* (*Min*) perpendicular shaft.

Seihe *f* **-, -n** *siehe* **Seiher.**

seihen *vt* (*sieben*) to sieve; (*S Ger, Aus: Flüssigkeit abgießen von*) to strain.

Seiher *m* **-s**, **-** (*esp S Ger, Aus*) strainer, colander.

Seihtuch *nt* (*muslin*) cloth.

Seil *nt* **-(e)s**, **-e** rope; (*Kabel*) cable; (*Hoch~*) tightrope, highwire. **auf dem ~ tanzen** (*fig*) to be walking a tightrope.

Seil-: **~bahn** *f* cable railway; (*Berg~ auch*) funicular; **~brücke** *f* rope bridge.

Seiler *m* **-s**, **-** ropemaker.

Seilerbahn *f* ropewalk.

Seilerei *f* **(a)** (*Seilerhandwerk*) ropemaking. **(b)** (*Seilerwerkstatt*) ropewalk, ropery (*rare*).

Seilerwaren *pl* rope goods *pl*.

Seil-: **~fähre** *f* cable ferry; **s~hüpfen** *vi sep aux sein* to skip; **~schaft** *f* (*Bergsteigen*) rope, roped party; **~schwebebahn** *f* cable railway; (*Bergseilbahn auch*) funicular; **s~springen** *vi sep irreg aux sein* to skip; **~tanz** *m* tightrope *or* high-wire act; **s~tanzen** *vi sep* to walk the tightrope *or* high-wire; **~tänzer** *m* tightrope walker, high-wire performer; **~winde** *f* winch; **~ziehen** *nt siehe* **Tauziehen.**

Seim *m* **-(e)s**, **-e** viscous *or* glutinous substance.

seimig *adj* viscous, glutinous.

Sein *nt* **-s**, *no pl* being *no art*; (*Philos*) (*Existenz, Da~ auch*) existence *no art*; (*Wesen, So~*) essence, suchness. **~ und Schein** appearance and reality; **~ oder Nichtsein** to be *or* not to be.

sein[1] *pret* **war**, *ptp* **gewesen** *aux sein* 1 *vi* **(a)** to be. **wir waren we were; wir sind gewesen** we have been, we've been; **sei (mir)/seien Sie (mir) nicht böse, aber ...** don't be angry (with me) but ...; **sei/seid so nett und ...** be so kind as to ...; **du bist wohl verrückt!** (*inf*) you must be crazy; **ist das heiß/kalt!** that's really hot/cold!, is that hot/cold!; **das wäre gut** that would *or* that'd (*inf*) be a good thing; **es wäre schön gewesen** it would *or* it'd (*inf*) have been nice; **die Arbeit will sofort erledigt ~** (*geh*) this work must be done immediately; **das will abgewartet ~** (*geh*) that remains to be seen; **er ist Lehrer/Inder/ein Verwandter/der Chef** he is a teacher/(an) Indian/a relative/the boss; **was sind Sie** (*beruflich*)? what do you do?; **er ist immer noch nichts** he still hasn't become anything; **Liverpool ist Fußballmeister/eine große Stadt** Liverpool are football champions/is a large town; **in der Küche sind noch viele** there's (*inf*) *or* there are still plenty in the kitchen; **drei und vier ist *or* sind sieben** three and four is *or* are seven; **x sei 4 let x be *or* equal 4; wenn ich Sie/er wäre** if I were *or* was you/him *or* he (*form*); **er war es nicht** it wasn't him; **das bist natürlich wieder du gewesen** of course it was you again; **niemand will es gewesen ~** nobody admits that it was him/her *or* them (*inf*); **das kann schon ~** that may well be; **und das wäre?** and what would *or* might that be?; **das wär's!** that's all, that's it; **wie war das noch?** what was that again?; **wie war das noch mit dem Witz?** how did that joke go now?; **bist du's/ist er's?** is that you/him?; **wer ist da?** who's there?; **ist da jemand?** is (there) anybody there?; **er ist aus Genf/aus guter Familie** he is *or* comes from Geneva/a good family; **morgen bin ich im Büro/in Rom** I'll *or* I will *or* I'll be in the office/in Rome tomorrow; **waren Sie mal in Rom?** have you ever been to Rome?; **wir waren baden/essen** we went swimming/out for a meal; **wo warst du so lange?** where have you been all this time?, what kept you?; **er war vier Jahre hier, bevor er ...** he had been here for four years before he ...; **es sind über zwanzig Jahre her, daß ...** it is more than twenty years since ...

(b) (*mit infin +zu*) **du bist nicht zu sehen** you cannot be seen; **das war ja vorauszusehen** that was to be expected; **das war nicht vorauszusehen** we couldn't have known that; **der Brief ist persönlich abzugeben** the letter is to be delivered by hand; **wie**

ist das zu verstehen? how is that to be understood?; **er ist nicht zu ersetzen** he cannot be replaced; **ein eigener Garten ist nicht zu unterschätzen** a garden of one's own is not to be underestimated; **mit ihr ist ja nicht zu sprechen** you can't talk to her.

(c) was ist? what's the matter?, what is it?; **ist was?** what is it?; **(paßt dir was nicht)** is something the matter?; **was ist mit dir/ihm?** what or how about you/him?; **(was hast du/hat er?)** what's wrong or the matter or up (inf) with you/him?; **das kann nicht ~** that can't be (true); **wie wäre es mit ...?** how about ...?, what about ...?; **sei es, daß ..., sei es, daß ...** whether ... or ...; nun, **wie ist es?** well, how or what about it?; **wie wäre es, wenn wir ihn besuchen würden?** what about or how about going to see him?, why don't we go to see him?; **das brauchte nicht zu ~ it** need not or never have happened or have been (dial, liter).

(d) (dasein, existieren) to be. **wenn du nicht gewesen wärst ...** if it hadn't been for you ...; **er ist nicht mehr** (euph) he is no more (euph liter); **alles, was (bis jetzt/damals) war** all that has/had been (liter).

(e) (in unpersönlicher Konstruktion) mir ist schlecht or übel I feel ill; **mir ist kalt** I'm cold; **was ist Ihnen?** what's the matter with you?; **mir ist, als wäre ich zehn Jahre jünger** I feel ten years younger; **mir ist, als hätte ich ihn früher schon einmal gesehen** I have a feeling I've seen him before.

2 v aux to have. **er ist/war jahrelang krank gewesen** he has/had been or he's/he'd been ill for years; **sie ist gestern nicht zu Hause gewesen** she was not or wasn't at home yesterday; **er ist verschwunden** he has or he's disappeared; **er ist gestern verschwunden** he disappeared yesterday; **er ist eben/gestern fünf Kilometer gelaufen** he has just run five kilometres/he ran five kilometres yesterday; **er ist geschlagen worden** he has been beaten.

sein² **1 poss pron (a) (adjektivisch) (bei Männern)** his; **(bei Dingen, Abstrakta)** its; **(bei Mädchen)** her; **(bei Tieren)** its, his/her; **(bei Ländern, Städten)** its, her; **(bei Schiffen)** her, its; **(auf „man" bezüglich)** one's (Brit), his (US), your. **wenn man ~ Leben betrachtet** when one looks at one's or his (US) life, when you look at your life; **jeder hat ~e Probleme** everybody has his or their (inf) problems; **~e komische Frau** that peculiar wife of his, his peculiar wife; **mein und ~ Freund** my friend and his; **~e zwanzig Zigaretten** his/her/one's twenty cigarettes; **er wiegt gut ~e zwei Zentner** (inf) he weighs a good two hundred pounds; **er ist gut ~e zwei Meter** (inf) he's a good two metres; **meinem Bruder ~ Auto** (incorrect) my or me (inf) brother's car.

(b) (old: substantivisch) his.

2 pers pron gen of er, es¹ (old, poet) **ich werde ewig ~ gedenken** I shall remember him forever.

seiner pers pron gen of **er, es¹** (geh) **gedenke ~** remember him; **er war ~ nicht mächtig** he was not in command of himself.

seine(r, s) poss pron (substantivisch) his. **der/die/das ~** (geh) his; **das S~ tun** (geh) to do one's (Brit) or his (US) bit; **er hat das S~ getan** (geh) he did his bit; **jedem das S~** each to his own; **sie ist die S~ geworden** (geh) she has become his (liter); **die S~n** (geh) his family, his people; **(auf „man" bezüglich)** one's (Brit) or his (US) family or people; **das S~** (geh: Besitz) what is his; **(auf „man" bezüglich)** what is one's own (Brit) or his (US).

seiner-: **~seits** adv (von ihm) on his part; (er selbst) for his part; **ich bin ~seits noch nie enttäuscht worden** I have never been disappointed by or in him, he has never let me down yet; **~zeit** adv at that time; (rare: künftig) one day; **~zeitig** adj attr (Aus) then attr.

seines poss pron siehe **seine(r, s)**.

seinesgleichen pron inv (gleichgestellt) his equals pl; (auf „man" bezüglich) one's (Brit) or his (US) equals; (gleichartig) his kind pl; of one's own kind, (pej) the likes of him pl. **jdn wie ~ behandeln** to treat sb as an equal or on equal terms; **das hat nicht or sucht ~ it** is unparalleled; (Kunstwerk auch) it has no equal.

seinet-: **~halben** (dated), **~wegen** adv (a) (wegen ihm) because of him, on account of him, on his account; (ihm zuliebe auch) for his sake; (um ihn) about him; (für ihn) on his behalf; **(b) (von ihm aus)** as far as he is concerned; **~willen** adv: **um ~willen** for his sake, for him.

seinige poss pron der/die/das ~ (form, old) siehe **seine(r, s)**.

seinlassen vt sep irreg **etw ~** (aufhören) to stop sth/doing sth; (nicht tun) to drop sth, to leave sth; **jdn/etw ~** to leave sb/sth alone, to let sb/sth be; **laß es sein!** stop that!; **du hättest es ~ sollen** you should have left well alone; **sie kann es einfach nicht ~** she just can't stop herself.

seins poss pron siehe **seine(r, s)**.

Seinslehre f (Philos) ontology.

seismisch adj seismic.

Seismogramm nt seismogram.

Seismograph m seismograph.

Seismologe m, **Seismologin** f seismologist.

Seismologie f seismology.

seit **1 prep +dat** (Zeitpunkt) since; (Zeitdauer) for, in (esp US). **~ wann?** since when?; **~ Jahren** for years; **ich habe ihn ~ Jahren nicht gesehen** I haven't seen him for or in (esp US) years; **ich bin ~ zwei Jahren hier** I have been here for two years; **schon ~ zwei Jahren nicht mehr** not for two years, not since two years ago; **wir warten schon ~ zwei Stunden** we have been or we've been waiting (for) two hours; **~ etwa einer Woche** since about a week ago, for about a week.

2 conj since.

seitdem **1 adv** since then. **~ ist die Strecke nicht mehr in Betrieb** the line has been closed down since then. **2 conj** since.

Seite f -, -n **(a)** (auch Abstammungslinie, Charakterzug) side. **die hintere/vordere ~** the back/front; **zu or auf beiden ~n des Fensters/des Hauses/der Straße** on both sides of the

window/house/street; **mit der ~ nach vorn** sideways on; **~ an ~** side by side; **an jds ~ (dat) gehen** to walk at or by sb's side or beside sb; **halt dich an meiner ~!** stay by my side; **er ging or wich uns nicht von der ~** he never left our side; **ich kann mich nicht an Ihrer ~ zeigen** I can't be seen with you; **jdn von der ~ ansehen** to give sb a sidelong glance; **auf die or zur ~ gehen or treten** to step aside; **an der ~ (einer Reihe)** to sit at the end (of a row); **zur ~ sprechen/sehen** to speak/look to one side; **zur ~** (Theat) aside; **die ~n wechseln** (Sport) to change ends or over; (fig) to change sides; **jdn auf seine ~ bringen or ziehen** to get sb on one's side; **auf einer ~ gelähmt sein** to be paralyzed in one side; **die Hände in die ~n gestemmt** with arms akimbo, with one's hands on one's hips; **jedes Ding or alles hat zwei ~n** there are two sides to everything; **jdm zur ~ stehen** (fig) to stand by sb's side; **auf jds (dat) ~ stehen or sein** (fig) to be on sb's side; **das Recht ist auf ihrer ~** she has right on her side; **jdm zur ~ springen** (fig) to come to sb's aid; **jdn/sich jdm an die ~ stellen** (fig) to put or set sb/oneself beside sb; **etw auf die ~ legen** (lit, fig) to put sth on one side, to put sth aside; (kippen) to put sth on its side; **jdn zur ~ nehmen** to take sb aside or on one side; **auf der einen ~..., auf der anderen (~) ...** on the one hand ..., on the other (hand) ...; **jds starke ~** sb's forte, sb's strong point; **jds schwache ~** sb's weakness, sb's weak spot; **sich von seiner besten ~ zeigen** to show oneself at one's best; **neue ~n an jdm/etw entdecken** to discover new sides to sb/sth; **von dieser ~ kenne ich ihn gar nicht** I didn't know that side of him; **einer Sache (dat) die beste ~ abgewinnen** to make the best or most of sth.

(b) (Richtung) **von allen ~n** (lit, fig) from all sides; **nach allen ~n auseinandergehen** to scatter in all directions; **sich nach allen ~n umsehen/vergewissern** to look around on all sides/to check up on all sides; **das habe ich von einer anderen ~ erfahren** (fig) I heard it from another source or from elsewhere; **er erfuhr es von dritter ~** (fig) he heard it from a third party; **bisher wurden von keiner ~ Einwände erhoben** so far no objections have been voiced from any quarter; **die Behauptung wurde von keiner ~/von allen ~n/von beiden ~n bestritten** nobody challenged the claim/the claim was challenged by all/both parties; **von meiner ~ aus** (fig) on my part; **von kirchlicher ~ (aus)** on the part of the church.

(c) (Buch~, Zeitungs~) page. **die erste/letzte ~** the first/last page; (von Zeitung) the front/back page.

seiten prep +gen **auf/von ~** on the part of.

Seiten- in cpds side; (esp Tech, Sci etc) lateral; **~altar** m side altar; **~angabe** f page reference; **~ansicht** f side view; (Tech) side elevation; **~arm** m branch, feeder; (von Fluß) branch; **~ausgang** m side exit; **~blick** m sidelong glance; **mit einem ~blick auf** (+acc) (fig) with one eye on; **~fläche** f (Tech) lateral face or surface; **~flosse** f (Aviat) fin; **~flügel** m side wing; (von Altar) wing; **~gang** m (Naut) side strake; (Rail) (side) corridor; **~gasse** f side-street, back-street; **~gebäude** nt side building; (auf Hof) outhouse; (Anbau) annex(e); **~gewehr** nt bayonet; **~halbierende** f -n, -n (Math) median; **~hieb** m (Fechten) side cut; (fig) side-swipe; **~kante** f lateral edge; **~lage** f side position; **in ~lage schlafen** to sleep on one's side; **s~lang** adj several pages long, going on for pages; **etw s~lang beschreiben** to devote pages to describing sth; **sich s~lang über etw (acc) auslassen** to go on for pages about sth; **~länge** f length of a/the side; **ein gleichseitiges Dreieck mit der ~länge 4,5 cm** an equilateral triangle whose sides are 4.5 cm long; **~lehne** f arm(rest); **~leitwerk** nt (Aviat) rudder (assembly); **~linie** f **(a)** (Rail) branch line; **(b)** (von Fürstengeschlecht) collateral line; **(c)** (Tennis) sideline; (Ftbl etc) touchline; **~moräne** f (Geol) lateral moraine; **~pfad** m bypath; **~riß** m (Tech) side elevation; **~ruder** nt (Aviat) rudder.

seitens prep +gen (form) on the part of.

Seiten-: **~scheitel** m side parting (Brit), side part (US); **~schiff** nt (Archit) (side) aisle; **~sprung** m (fig) bit on the side (inf) no pl, (little) infidelity; **die Versuchung, ~sprünge zu machen the** temptation to have a bit on the side (inf); **~stechen** nt stitch; **~stechen haben/bekommen** to have/get a stitch; **~straße** f side-street, side road; **~streifen** m verge; (der Autobahn) hard shoulder, shoulder (US); **„~streifen nicht befahrbar"** "soft verges" (Brit), "soft shoulder" (US); **~tal** nt valley; **~tasche** f side pocket; **~teil** m or nt side; **s~verkehrt** adj the wrong way round; **~wagen** m sidecar; **~wand** f side wall; (von Schiff) side; **~wände** pl (Theat) wings pl; **~wechsel** m (Sport) changeover; **~weg** m side road, byway, back road; **~wege gehen** (fig) to indulge in clandestine activities; **~wind** m crosswind; **~zahl** f **(a)** page number; **(b)** (Gesamtzahl) number of pages.

seither [zait'heːɐ] adv since then.

seitherig [zait'heːrɪç] adj siehe **bisherig**.

seitlich **1 adj** lateral (esp Sci, Tech), side attr. **die ~e Begrenzung der Straße wird durch einen weißen Streifen markiert** the side of the road is marked by a white line; **bei starkem ~en Wind** in a strong crosswind.

2 adv at the side; (von der Seite) from the side. **~ von** at the side of; **~ stehen** to stand sideways on; **etw/sich ~ stellen** to put sth/stand sideways on; **die Kisten sind ~ grün bemalt** the sides of the boxes are painted green; **er ist mir ~ ins Auto gefahren** he crashed into the side of my car.

3 prep +gen to or at the side of.

seitlings adv (obs) (zur Seite) sideways; (auf der Seite) on one's side.

seitwärts adv sideways. **sich ~ halten** to keep to the side.

Sek., sek. abbr of **Sekunde** sec.

Sekans m -, - or **Sekanten, Sekante** f -, -n (Math) secant.

sekkant adj (old, Aus) finicky, finical, fastidious.

sekkieren* vt (old, Aus) to torment.

Sekond f -, -en (Fechten) seconde.

Sekret[1] *nt* -(e)s, -e (a) (*Physiol*) secretion. (b) (*rare: Geheimnis*) secret.

Sekret[2] *f* -, *no pl* (*Eccl*) secret (of the mass).

Sekretär *m* (a) secretary. (b) (*Schreibschrank*) bureau, secretaire. (c) (*Orn*) secretary-bird.

Sekretariat *nt* office.

Sekretärin *f* secretary.

Sekretion *f* (*Physiol*) secretion.

Sekt *m* -(e)s, -e sparkling wine, champagne.

Sekte *f* -, -n sect.

Sektenwesen *nt* sectarianism.

Sektierer(in *f*) *m* -s, - sectarian.

sektiererisch *adj* sectarian.

Sektierertum *nt* sectarianism.

Sektion *f* (a) section; (*esp DDR: Abteilung*) department. (b) (*Obduktion*) post-mortem (examination), autopsy.

Sektions-: ~**befund** *m* post-mortem *or* autopsy findings *pl*; ~**chef** *m* (*von Abteilung*) head of department; ~**saal** *m* dissection room; **s**~**weise** *adv* in sections.

Sektor *m* sector; (*Sachgebiet*) field.

Sektorengrenze *f* sector boundary.

Sektschale *f* champagne glass.

Sekund *f* -, -en (*Mus*) *siehe* **Sekunde.**

Sekunda *f* -, **Sekunden** (*Sch*) *sixth and seventh year of German secondary school.*

Sekundakkord *m* (*Mus*) third inversion (of the seventh chord).

Sekundaner(in *f*) *m* -s, - (*Sch*) *pupil in sixth and seventh year of German secondary school.*

Sekundant *m* second.

sekundär *adj* secondary.

Sekundär- in *cpds* secondary.

Sekundärlehrer *m* (*Sw*) secondary *or* high (*esp US*) school teacher.

Sekundärliteratur *f* secondary literature.

Sekundär-: ~**schule** *f* (*Sw*) secondary school; ~**stufe** *f* (*esp Sw Sch*) secondary *or* high (*esp US*) school level.

Sekunde *f* -, -n (*auch Mus, Math*) second. eine ~, bitte! just a *or* one second, please; **auf die** ~ **genau** to the second.

Sekunden *pl of* **Sekunda, Sekunde.**

Sekunden-: ~**bruchteil** *m* split second, fraction of a second; ~**geschwindigkeit** *f siehe* ~**schnelle**; **s**~**lang** 1 *adj* of a few seconds; 2 *adv* for a few seconds; ~**schnelle** *f*: **in** ~**schnelle** in a matter of seconds; ~**zeiger** *m* second hand.

sekundieren* *vi* + *dat* to second; (*unterstützen auch*) to back up. **jdm** (**bei einem Duell**) ~ to act as *or* be sb's second (in a duel).

sekundlich, sekündlich 1 *adj* (*rare*) *Abstand* one-second. 2 *adv* every second.

Sekurit ® *nt* -s, *no pl* Triplex ®.

sel. *abbr of* **selig.**

Sela *nt* -s, -s (*Bibl*) selah.

selber *dem pron siehe* **selbst 1.**

selbe(r, s) *pron siehe* **derselbe, dieselbe, dasselbe.**

Selbermachen *nt* do-it-yourself, DIY (*inf*); (*von Kleidern etc*) making one's own. **Möbel/Spielzeug zum** ~ do-it-yourself furniture/build-it-yourself toys.

selbig *pron* (*obs, Bibl*) the same.

selbst 1 *dem pron* (a) **ich/er/sie/das Haus/die Katze** ~ I myself/he himself/she herself/the house itself/the cat itself; **wir/Sie/sie/die Häuser** ~ we ourselves/you yourselves/they themselves/the houses themselves; **er ist gar nicht mehr er** ~ he's not himself any more; **du Esel!** — ~ **einer** (*inf*) you idiot! — same to you (*inf*); **sie ist die Güte/Tugend** ~ she's kindness/virtue itself; ~ **ist der Mann/die Frau!** self-reliance is the name of the game (*inf*); **er braut sein Bier/bäckt sein Brot** ~ he brews his own beer/bakes his own bread; **er wäscht seine Wäsche** ~ he does his washing himself, he does his own washing; **was man von sich** ~ **hält** what one thinks of oneself; **zu sich** ~ **kommen** to reflect; **eine Sache um ihrer** ~ **willen tun** to do sth for its own sake; **sie tut mir** ~ **leid** I feel very sorry for her myself.

(b) (*ohne Hilfe*) alone, by oneself/himself/yourself *etc*, on one's/his/your *etc* own.

(c) **von** ~ by myself/yourself/himself/itself/ourselves *etc*; **das funktioniert von** ~ it works by itself *or* automatically; **das regelt sich alles von** ~ it'll sort itself out (by itself); **er kam ganz von** ~ he came of his own accord *or* off his own bat (*inf*); **das hat er ganz von** ~ **entschieden** he decided that all by himself.

2 *adv* even. ~ **der Minister/Gott** even the Minister/God (himself); ~ **wenn** even if.

Selbst *nt*, -, *no pl* self.

Selbst-: ~**abholer(in** *f*) *m* -s, - ~**abholer sein** to collect one's own mail; ~**achtung** *f* self-respect, self-esteem; ~**analyse** *f* self-analysis.

selbständig *adj* independent; (*steuerlich*) self-employed; (*rare: getrennt*) separate. ~ **denken** to think for oneself; ~ **arbeiten/handeln** to work/act independently *or* on one's own; **ich suche eine** ~**e Arbeit** I am looking for a job where I can work on my own; ~ **sein** (*beruflich*) to have set up on one's own; **sich** ~ **machen** (*beruflich*) to set up on one's own, to start one's own business; (*hum*) to go off on its own; (*verschwinden*) to grow legs (*hum*); **das entscheidet er** ~ he decides that on his own *or* by himself *or* independently.

Selbständige(r) *mf decl as adj* independent businessman/woman; (*steuerlich*) self-employed person.

Selbständigkeit *f* independence. **in großer** ~ **handeln** (*beruflich*) to act on one's own (initiative) *or* independently; ~ **im Denken lernen** to learn to think for oneself.

Selbst-: ~**anklage** *f* self-accusation; ~**anschluß** *m* (*Telec*)

automatic dial telephone; (*Verbindung*) automatic dialling connection; ~**anzeige** *f* (a) (*steuerlich*) voluntary declaration; (b) ~**anzeige erstatten** to come forward oneself; ~**aufopferung** *f* self-sacrifice; ~**auslöser** *m* (*Phot*) delayed-action shutter release, delay timer; ~**bedienung** *f* self-service; ~**bedienungsladen** *m* self-service shop (*esp Brit*) *or* store; ~**befleckung** *f* (*old, Rel*) self-abuse; ~**befreiung** *f* self-liberation; (*Jur*) prison escape without outside assistance; ~**befriedigung** *f* masturbation; (*fig auch*) self-gratification; ~**befruchtung** *f* (*Biol*) self-fertilization; ~**behauptung** *f* self-assertion; ~**beherrschung** *f* self-control; **die** ~**beherrschung wahren/verlieren** to keep/lose one's self-control *or* temper; ~**bekenntnis** *nt* confession; ~**beköstigung** *f* (*dated*) self-catering; ~**beobachtung** *f* self-observation; ~**bescheidung** *f* (*geh*) self-denial; ~**besinnung** *f* self-contemplation; **zur** ~**besinnung kommen** to reflect; **hier ist es unmöglich, zur** ~**besinnung zu kommen** that there is no opportunity (afforded) here for self-contemplation; **er kam plötzlich zur** ~**besinnung** he had a sudden moment of awareness; **dieses Erlebnis brachte sie endlich zur** ~**besinnung** this experience forced her to take stock of herself at last; ~**bespiegelung** *f* (*pej*) self-admiration; ~**bestätigung** *f* self-affirmation; **das empfand er als** ~**bestätigung** it boosted his ego; **man braucht ab und zu eine** ~**bestätigung** now and then you need something to boost your ego; **Lob dient der** ~**bestätigung der Kinder** praise boosts the children's confidence; ~**bestäubung** *f* (*Bot*) self-pollination; ~**bestimmung** *f* self-determination; ~**bestimmungsrecht** *nt* right of self-determination; ~**beteiligung** *f* (*Insur*) (percentage) excess; ~**betrug** *m* self-deception; ~**beweihräucherung** *f* (*pej*) self-congratulation, self-adulation, self-admiration; ~**bewunderung** *f* self-admiration; **s**~**bewußt** *adj* (a) (**s**~**sicher**) self-assured, self-confident; (*eingebildet*) self-important; (b) (*Philos*) self-aware, self-conscious; ~**bewußtsein** *nt* (a) self-assurance, self-confidence; (*Einbildung*) self-importance; (b) (*Philos*) self-awareness, self-consciousness; ~**bildnis** *nt* self-portrait; ~**binder** *m* (a) (*Krawatte*) tie; (b) (*Mähdrescher*) reaper-binder; ~**biographie** *f* autobiography; ~**bucher** *m* -s, - (*Post*) firm etc with its own franking machine; ~**darstellung** *f* self-portrayal; **Autoren des 20. Jahrhunderts in** ~**darstellungen** self-portraits of 20th century writers; ~**disziplin** *f* self-discipline; ~**einschätzung** *f* self-assessment; **eine gesunde** ~**einschätzung** a healthy self-awareness; ~**entfaltung** *f* self-development; (*Philos*) unfolding; ~**entleibung** *f* (*liter*) suicide; ~**entzündung** *f* spontaneous combustion; ~**erhaltung** *f* self-preservation, survival; ~**erhaltungstrieb** *m* survival instinct, instinct of self-preservation; ~**erkenntnis** *f* self-knowledge; ~**erkenntnis ist der erste Schritt zur Besserung** (*prov*) self-knowledge is the first step towards self-improvement; **s**~**ernannt** *adj* self-appointed; (*in bezug auf Titel*) self-styled; ~**erniedrigung** *f* self-abasement; ~**erziehung** *f* self-discipline; ~**erziehung zur Pünktlichkeit** teaching oneself to be punctual; ~**fahrer** *m* (a) (*Krankenfahrstuhl*) self-propelling wheelchair; (b) (*Aut*) person who drives a hired car himself; **Autovermietung für** ~**fahrer** self-drive car hire; **wir vermieten nur an** ~**fahrer** we only have self-drive; ~**fahrlafette** *f* (*Mil*) self-propelled gun; ~**finanzierung** *f* self-financing; **in** ~**finanzierung** with one's own resources *or* means; **s**~**gebacken** *adj* home-baked, home-made; **s**~**gebaut** *adj* home-made, self-made; *Haus* self-built; **s**~**gebraut** *adj* Bier home-brewed; ~**gedrehte** *f decl as adj* roll-up (*inf*); ~**gedrehte rauchen** to roll one's own; **s**~**gefällig** *adj* self-satisfied, smug, complacent; ~**gefälligkeit** *f* self-satisfaction, smugness, complacency; ~**gefühl** *nt* self-esteem; **ein übertriebenes** ~**gefühl besitzen** to have an exaggerated opinion of oneself, to have an oversized ego (*inf*); **s**~**gemacht** *adj* Möbel etc home-made, self-made; *Marmelade etc* home-made; **s**~**genügsam** *adj* (a) (*bescheiden*) modest (in one's demands); (b) (*sich selbst genug*) self-sufficient; ~**genügsamkeit** *f siehe adj* (a) modesty (in one's demands); (b) self-sufficiency; **s**~**gerecht** *adj* self-righteous; ~**gerechtigkeit** *f* self-righteousness; **s**~**gesponnen** *adj* homespun; ~**gespräch** *nt* ~**gespräche führen** *or* **halten** to talk to oneself; **s**~**gestrickt** *adj* (a) *Pullover etc* hand-knitted; **ist das s**~**gestrickt?** did you knit it yourself?; (b) (*inf*) *Hund* fluffy; *Methode etc* homespun, amateurish; **ein** ~**gestrickter** (*hum*) ball of fluff (*inf*); **s**~**gezogen** *adj* (a) *Rosen etc* home-cultivated; *Kerzen* home-made; **s**~**haß** *m* self-hate, self-hatred; **s**~**herrlich** *adj* (*pej*) (a) (*eigenwillig*) high-handed; (b) (**s**~**gefällig**, **s**~**gerecht**) self-satisfied; ~**herrlichkeit** *f* (*pej*) *siehe adj* (a) high-handedness; (b) self-satisfaction; ~**herrschaft** *f* (*rare*) autocracy; ~**herrscher** *m* (*rare*) autocrat; ~**hilfe** *f* self-help; **zur** ~**hilfe greifen** to take matters into one's own hands; ~**interpretation** *f* image of oneself, self-image; ~**ironie** *f* self-mockery, self-irony.

selbstisch *adj* (*geh*) selfish.

Selbst-: ~**isolierung** *f* self-isolation; ~**justiz** *f* arbitrary law; ~**justiz üben** to take the law into one's own hands; **s**~**klebend** *adj* self-adhesive; ~**kontrolle** *f* check on oneself; (*von Computer*) automatic check; **zur** ~**kontrolle** to keep a check on oneself; **der Computer hat** ~**kontrolle** the computer is self-checking *or* has an automatic check; ~**kosten** *pl* (*Econ*) prime costs *pl*; ~**kostenpreis** *m* cost price; ~**kritik** *f* self-criticism; **s**~**kritisch** *adj* self-critical; ~**lader** *m* -s, - self-loader, semi-automatic weapon *or* firearm; ~**laut** *m* vowel; **s**~**lautend** *adj* vocalic; ~**lob** *nt siehe* **Eigenlob**; **s**~**los** *adj* selfless; ~**losigkeit** *f* selflessness; ~**mitleid** *nt* self-pity; ~**mord** *m* (*lit, fig*) suicide; ~**mörder** *m* suicide; **ich bin doch kein** ~**mörder!** (*inf*) I have no desire to commit suicide; **s**~**mörderisch** *adj* (*lit, fig*) suicidal; **in s**~**mörderischer Absicht** intending to commit suicide; ~**mordgedanken** *pl* suicidal thoughts *pl*; **sich mit**

~**mordgedanken tragen** to contemplate suicide; ~**mordversuch** m suicide attempt, attempted suicide; ~**porträt** nt siehe ~**bildnis**; s~**quälerisch** adj self-tormenting; s~**redend** adv of course, naturally; ~**regierung** f self-government; ~**schuldner** m (Jur) directly suable guarantor; s~**schuldnerisch** adj (Jur) Bürgschaft directly enforceable; Bürge directly suable; ~**schuß** m set-gun, spring-gun; ~**schutz** m self-protection; s~**sicher** adj self-assured, self-confident; ~**sicherheit** f self-assurance, self-confidence; ~**studium** nt private study; etw im ~**studium lernen** to learn sth by studying on one's own; ~**sucht** f egoism; s~**süchtig** adj egoistic; s~**tätig** adj (a) (automatisch) automatic, self-acting; damit sich nicht s~**tätig ein Schuß lösen kann** so that a gun can't fire by itself; (b) (eigenständig) independent; ~**tätigkeit** f siehe adj (a) automatic functioning; (b) independence; ~**täuschung** f self-deception; ~**tor** nt siehe **Eigentor**; ~**tötung** f suicide; ~**überhebung** f arrogance; ~**überschätzung** f over-estimation of one's abilities; das ist eine ~**überschätzung, wenn er meint** ... he's over-estimating himself or his abilities if he thinks ...; ~**überwindung** f will-power; das war echte ~**überwindung** that shows real will-power; selbst bei der größten ~**überwindung könnte ich das nicht tun** I simply couldn't bring or force myself to do it; ~**verachtung** f self-contempt; ~**verbraucher** m Verkauf nur an ~**verbraucher** goods not for resale; ~**verbrennung** f sich durch ~**verbrennung töten** to burn oneself to death; „**zwei** ~**verbrennungen in einem Monat**" "two people burn themselves to death in one month"; s~**verdient** adj s~**verdientes Geld** money one has earned oneself; sein s~**verdientes Motorrad** the motorbike he bought with the money he earned; s~**verfaßt** adj (form) one has own composition; alle seine Reden sind s~**verfaßt** he writes all his speeches himself; s~**vergessen** adj absent-minded; Blick faraway; s~**vergessen dasitzen** to sit there lost to the world; ~**vergessenheit** f absent-mindedness; in seinem Blick lag völlige ~**vergessenheit** he looked totally lost to the world; ~**vergötterung** f self-glorification; ~**verlag** m im ~**verlag erschienen** published oneself or at one's own expense; ~**verleugnung** f self-denial; ~**verliebtheit** f self-love; ~**vernichtung** f self-destruction; ~**verschulden** nt one's own fault; wenn ~**verschulden vorliegt** ... if the claimant is himself at fault ...; s~**verschuldet** adj wenn der Unfall/Verlust s~**verschuldet ist** if the claimant is himself responsible or to blame for the accident/loss; ~**versicherung** f personal insurance; ~**versorger** m (a) ~**versorger sein** to be self-sufficient or self-reliant; (b) (im Urlaub etc) self-caterer; **Appartements/Urlaub für** ~**versorger** self-catering apartments/holiday; ~**versorgung** f self-sufficiency, self-reliance; (in Urlaub etc) self-catering; s~**verständlich** 1 adj Freundlichkeit natural; Wahrheit self-evident; seine s~**verständliche Hilfe/Art zu helfen** his help which was given as a matter of course/his completely natural way of helping; das ist doch s~**verständlich!** that goes without saying, that's obvious; vielen Dank für Ihre Hilfe — aber das ist doch s~**verständlich** thanks for your help — it's no more than anybody would have done; kann ich mitkommen? — aber das ist doch s~**verständlich** can I come too? — but of course; es war für uns s~**verständlich, daß Sie** ... we took it for granted that you ...; das ist keineswegs s~**verständlich** it's by no means a matter of course, it cannot be taken for granted; etw für s~**verständlich halten, etw als** s~**verständlich annehmen** to take sth for granted; 2 adv of course; wie s~**verständlich** as if it were the most natural thing in the world; diese s~**verständlich angebotene Hilfe** this help, so naturally offered; ~**verständlichkeit** f naturalness; (Unbefangenheit) casualness no indef art; (von Wahrheit) self-evidence; (s~**verständliche Wahrheit** etc) self-evident truth etc; nichts zu danken, das war doch eine ~**verständlichkeit** think nothing of it, it was no more than anyone would have done; das war doch eine ~**verständlichkeit, daß wir** ... it was only natural that we ...; etw für eine ~**verständlichkeit halten** to take sth as a matter of course; das sind heute ~**verständlichkeiten** those are things we take for granted today; aber meine Herren, das ist eine ~**verständlichkeit, über die wir nicht zu reden brauchen** but gentlemen, that is obvious or can be taken as read and doesn't need discussion; ~**verständnis** nt jds ~**verständnis** the way sb sees himself/herself; nach seinem eigenen ~**verständnis** as he sees himself; „**das** ~**verständnis der Frau**" "how women see themselves"; ~**verstümmelung** f self-inflicted wound; (das Verstümmeln) self-mutilation; ~**versuch** m experiment on oneself; ~**verteidigung** f self-defence; ~**vertrauen** nt self-confidence; ~**verwaltung** f self-administration; (Verwaltungskörper) self-governing body; ~**verwirklichung** f self-realization; ~**vorwurf** m self-reproach; ~**wählferndienst** m (Telec) automatic dialling service, subscriber trunk dialling (Brit), STD (Brit); ~**wählfernverkehr** m (Telec) automatic dialling, STD system (Brit); ~**wertgefühl** nt feeling of one's own worth or value, self-esteem; s~**zerstörerisch** adj self-destructive; ~**zerstörung** f self-destruction; ~**zucht** f (dated) siehe ~**disziplin**; s~**zufrieden** adj self-satisfied; ~**zufriedenheit** f self-satisfaction; s~**zündend** adj self-igniting; ~**zweck** m end in itself; als ~**zweck** as an end in itself.

selchen vti (S Ger, Aus) Fleisch to smoke.
Selcher m -s, - (S Ger, Aus) (pork) butcher.
Selchfleisch nt (S Ger, Aus) smoked meat.
selektieren* vt to select.
Selektion f selection.
Selektions-: ~**lehre**, ~**theorie** f theory of natural selection.
selektiv adj selective.
Selektivität [zelɛktivi'tɛːt] f (Rad) selectivity; (fig) selectiveness.

Selen nt -s, no pl (Chem) selenium.
Selenzelle f (Phot) selenium cell.
Selfmademan ['sɛlfmeːtmɛn] m -s, **Selfmademen** self-made man.
selig adj (a) (Rel) blessed; (old: verstorben) late. ~ **die Armen im Geiste, denn** ... (Bibl) blessed are the poor in spirit, for ... (Bibl); bis an mein ~**es Ende** (old, hum) until the day I die; mein Vater ~ (old), mein ~**er Vater** (old) my late father; ~ **entschlafen** (liter) departed this life; Gott hab ihn ~ (old) God rest his soul; siehe Angedenken, geben, Gefilde.
(b) (überglücklich) overjoyed; Lächeln auch beatific (liter); Stunden blissful; (inf: beschwipst) tipsy (inf), merry (inf).
Selige(r) mf decl as adj (a) (Eccl) blessed (inf). die ~**n** the Blessed. (b) (old) mein/Ihr ~**r** my/your late husband.
Seligkeit f (a) (Rel) salvation. ewige ~ eternal salvation. (b) (Glück) (supreme) happiness, bliss.
Selig-: s~**preisen** sep irreg 1 vt (a) (Bibl) to bless; (b) (liter: verherrlichen) to glorify; 2 vr to thank one's lucky stars; ~**preisung** f (Bibl) Beatitude; (liter) glorification; s~**sprechen** vt sep irreg (Eccl) to beatify; ~**sprechung** f (Eccl) beatification.
Seller ['sɛlɐ] m -s, - (inf) seller.
Sellerie m -s, -(s), f -, - celeriac; (Stangen~) celery.
selten 1 adj rare; (kaum vorkommend auch) scarce. du bist ja in letzter Zeit ein ~**er Gast** you're a stranger here these days; siehe Erde. 2 adv (nicht oft) rarely, seldom; (besonders) exceptionally. nur/höchst ~ very/extremely rarely or seldom; ~ **so gelacht!** (inf) what a laugh! (inf).
Seltenheit f (a) no pl (seltenes Vorkommen) rareness, rarity. (b) (seltene Sache) rarity. das ist keine ~ bei ihr it's nothing unusual with her.
Seltenheitswert m rarity value.
Selters nt -, - (inf), **Selter(s)wasser** nt soda (water).
seltsam adj strange; (komisch auch) odd, peculiar. ~ berührt strangely moved.
seltsamerweise adv strangely enough.
Seltsamkeit f (a) no pl (Sonderbarkeit) strangeness, oddness, peculiarity. (b) (seltsame Sache) oddity.
Semantik f semantics sing.
semantisch adj semantic.
Semaphor [zema'foːɐ] nt or m -s, -e (Naut, Rail) semaphore.
Semasiologie f (Ling) semasiology.
Semester nt -s, - (Univ) semester (US), term (of a half-year's duration). im 7./8. ~ sein to be in one's 4th year; die älteren ~ the older or senior students; ein älteres ~ a senior student; (hum) an old boy/girl; sie ist auch schon ein älteres ~ she's no chicken (inf).
Semester- (Univ): ~**ferien** pl vacation sing; s~**lang** adj for years; ~**schluß** m end of term, end of the semester (US); ~**zeugnis** nt credit (US), end-of-term certificate.
-semestrig adj suf -term, -semester (US).
Semi- in cpds semi-; ~**finale** [ˈzeːmi-] nt (Sport) semifinal(s); ~**kolon** [zemiˈkoːlon] nt -s, -s or -**kola** semicolon.
Seminar nt -s, -e or (Aus) -**ien** [-iən] (a) (Univ) department; (~**übung**) seminar. (b) (Priester~) seminary. (c) (Lehrer~, Studien~) teacher training college, college of education.
Seminar- (Univ): ~**apparat** m seminar course books pl; ~**arbeit** f seminar paper.
Seminarist m (Eccl) seminarist.
seminaristisch adj (Eccl) seminarian.
Seminar- (Univ): ~**schein** m certificate of attendance for one semester (US) or half-year; ~**übung** f seminar.
Semiologie f semiology.
Semiotik f semiotics sing.
semipermeabel adj semipermeable.
Semit(in f) m -en, -en Semite.
semitisch adj Semitic.
Semitist(in f) m Semitist.
Semitistik f Semitics sing.
Semivokal m semivowel.
Semmel f -, -n (dial) roll. geriebene ~ breadcrumbs pl.
Semmel-: s~**blond** adj (dated) flaxen-haired; ~**brösel(n)** pl breadcrumbs pl; ~**kloß**, ~**knödel** (S Ger, Aus) m bread dumpling; ~**mehl** nt breadcrumbs pl.
sen. abbr of **senior** sen.
Senat m -(e)s, -e (a) (Pol, Univ) senate. (b) (Jur) Supreme Court.
Senator m, **Senatorin** f senator.
senatorisch adj attr senatorial.
Senats- in cpds of the senate; ~**ausschuß** m senate committee; s~**eigen** adj belonging to the senate; ~**präsident** m chairman of the senate.
Send-: ~**bote** m (Hist) emissary, ambassador (old); ~**brief** m (liter) circular letter.
Sende-: ~**anlage** f transmitting installation; ~**antenne** f transmitting aerial; ~**bereich** m transmission range; ~**einrichtung** f transmitting facility; ~**folge** f (a) (Sendung in Fortsetzungen) series sing; (einzelne Folge) episode; (b) (Programmfolge) programmes pl; ~**gebiet** nt area; ~**haus** nt studios pl; ~**leiter** m producer.
senden[1] pret **sandte** or **sendete**, ptp **gesandt** or **gesendet** 1 vt to send (an +acc to). jdm etw ~ to send sb sth, to send sth to sb. 2 vi nach jdm ~ to send for sb.
senden[2] vti (Rad, TV) to broadcast; Signal etc to transmit.
Sendepause f interval; (fig inf) deathly silence. danach tritt eine ~ bis 6 Uhr ein afterwards we shall be going off the air until 6 o'clock; auf meine Frage hin herrschte ~ my question was met by deathly silence.
Sender m -s, - transmitter; (~**kanal**) (Rad) station; (TV) channel (Brit), station (esp US). der ~ Prag Radio Prague.

Sende-: ~raum m studio; ~reihe f (radio/television) series.

Sender-: ~einstellung f tuning; ~-Empfänger m transceiver.

Sende-: ~saal m studio; ~schluß m (Rad, TV) closedown, end of broadcasts; **und nun bis ~schluß** and now until we close down; ~turm m radio tower; ~zeichen nt call sign; ~zeit f broadcasting time; **und damit geht unsere heutige ~zeit zu Ende and** that concludes our programmes for today.

Sendling m (obs) messenger, emissary.

Sendschreiben nt (liter) circular letter.

Sendung f (a) no pl (das Senden) sending. (b) (Post~) letter; (Päckchen) packet; (Paket) parcel; (Comm) consignment. (c) (Rad, TV) programme; (Rad auch) broadcast; (das Senden) broadcasting; (von Signal etc) transmission. (d) (liter: Aufgabe) mission.

Sendungsbewußtsein nt sense of mission.

Senegal[1] m -(s) der ~ the Senegal (River).

Senegal[2] nt -s Senegal.

Senegaler(in f) m -s, -, **Senegalese** m -n, -n, **Senegalesin** f Senegalese.

senegalesisch, senegalisch adj Senegalese.

Senesblätter pl siehe **Sennesblätter**.

Seneschall m -s, -e (Hist) seneschal.

Seneszenz f (Med) senescence.

Senf m -(e)s, -e mustard. **einen langen ~ machen** (inf) to make a great song and dance (inf); **seinen ~ dazugeben** (inf) to get one's three ha'p'orth in (Brit inf), to have one's say.

Senf-: s~farben, s~farbig adj mustard(-coloured); ~früchte pl (Cook) pickles pl; ~gas nt (Chem) mustard gas; ~gurke f gherkin pickled with mustard seeds; ~korn nt mustard seed; ~mehl nt flour of mustard; ~packung f (Med) mustard poultice; ~pflaster nt (Med) mustard plaster; ~soße, ~tunke (dial) f mustard sauce; ~umschlag m (Med) mustard poultice.

Senge pl (dated inf) ~ **kriegen** to get a good hiding.

sengen 1 vt to singe. 2 vi to scorch. **~d und brennend** (old, liter) with fire and sword.

senil adj (pej) senile.

Senilität f, no pl (pej) senility.

senior adj **Franz Schulz ~** Franz Schulz senior.

Senior m (a) (auch ~chef) boss, old boy (inf). **kann ich mal den ~ sprechen?** can I speak to Mr X senior? (b) (Sport) senior player. **die ~en** the seniors, the senior team. (c) ~en pl senior citizens pl; (hum) old folk pl.

Senioren-: ~hotel nt hotel for the elderly; ~karte f pensioner's or senior citizen's ticket; ~mannschaft f senior team; ~paß m senior citizen's travel pass; ~(wohn)haus, ~(wohn)heim nt old people's home.

Seniorpartner m senior partner.

Senkblei nt siehe **Senklot**.

Senke f -, -n valley.

Senkel m -s, - (a) lace. (b) siehe **Senklot**.

senken 1 vt to lower; Lanze, Fahne to dip; Kopf to bow; Preis, Steuern auch to decrease; (Tech) Schraube, Loch, Schacht to sink; (Hort) Schößling, Wurzeln etc to plant.
2 vr to sink; (Decke) to sag; (Grab, Haus, Boden, Straße auch) to subside; (Flugzeug) to descend; (Wasserspiegel auch) to go down, to drop, to fall; (Stimme) to drop; (liter: Nacht) to fall, to descend (über, auf +acc on). **dann senkte sich ihr Blick** then she looked down, then she lowered her eyes or her gaze (liter).

Senk-: ~fuß m (Med) fallen arches pl; ~grube f cesspit; ~kasten m caisson; ~lot nt plumbline; (Gewicht) plummet.

senkrecht adj vertical; (Math) perpendicular. **immer schön ~ bleiben!** (inf) keep your end up (inf); siehe **einzig**.

Senkrechte f decl as adj vertical; (Math) perpendicular.

Senkrechtstarter m (Aviat) vertical take-off aircraft; (fig inf) whizz kid (inf).

Senkung f (a) sinking; (von Boden, Straße) subsidence; (von Wasserspiegel) fall (gen in), drop (gen in); (als Maßnahme) lowering; (von Decke) sag(ging); (von Stimme) lowering; (von Preisen) lowering (von of), decrease (von in).
(b) (Vertiefung) hollow, valley.
(c) (Poet) thesis.
(d) (Med) siehe **Blutsenkung**.

Senkungsgeschwindigkeit f (Med) rate of sedimentation.

Senkwaage f hydrometer.

Senn m -(e)s, -e, **Senne** m -n, -n (S Ger, Aus) siehe **Senner**.

Senne f -, -n (S Ger, Aus) Alpine pasture.

Senner m -s, - (Alpine) dairyman.

Sennerei f (Gebäude) Alpine dairy; (Wirtschaftsform) Alpine dairy farming.

Sennerin f (Alpine) dairymaid.

Sennesblätter pl senna leaves pl.

Sennhütte f Alpine dairy hut.

Sennin f siehe **Sennerin**.

Senn-: ~tum nt (esp Sw) Alpine herd; ~wirtschaft f siehe Sennerei.

Sensation f sensation.

sensationell [zenzatsio'nɛl] adj sensational.

Sensations-: ~bedürfnis nt need for sensation; ~blatt nt sensational paper; ~gier f (pej) sensation-seeking; aus ~gier for the sheer sensation; ~lust f desire for sensation; s~lüstern adj sensation-seeking; s~lustig adj sensation-loving; s~mache f (inf) sensationalism; ~meldung, ~nachricht f sensational news sing; **eine ~nachricht** a sensation, a scoop, a sensational piece of news; ~presse f sensational papers pl, yellow press; ~prozeß m sensational trial.

Sense f -, -n (a) scythe. (b) (inf) **jetzt/dann ist ~!** that's the end!; **es ist nichts mehr da, ~!** there's none left, all gone!

Sensenmann m (liter) Death no art, Reaper (liter).

sensibel adj sensitive.

Sensibilisator m (Phot) sensitizer.

sensibilisieren* vt to sensitize.

Sensibilisierung f sensitization.

Sensibilität f sensitivity; (Feingefühl auch) sensibility.

sensitiv adj (geh) sensitive.

Sensitivität f (geh) sensitivity.

Sensor m sensor.

sensoriell adj siehe **sensorisch**.

Sensorien [zɛn'zoːriən] pl sensoria pl.

sensorisch adj sensory.

Sensualismus m (Philos) sensualism, sensationalism.

Sensualität f sensuality.

sensuell adj siehe **sensorisch**.

Sentenz f aphorism.

sentenziös adj sententious.

Sentiment [sãtiˈmãː] nt -s, -s (liter) siehe **Empfindung**.

sentimental, sentimentalisch (old) adj sentimental.

Sentimentalität f sentimentality.

separat adj separate; (in sich abgeschlossen) Wohnung, Zimmer self-contained.

Separat-: ~(ab)druck m offprint; ~friede(n) m separate peace.

Separatismus m (Pol) separatism.

Separatist(in f) m (Pol) separatist.

separatistisch adj (Pol) separatist.

Séparée [zepa'reː] nt -s, -s private room; (Nische) private booth.

separieren* vt (rare) siehe **absondern** 1 (a).

separiert adj (esp Aus) Zimmer self-contained.

sepia adj inv sepia.

Sepia f -, **Sepien** [-iən] (a) (Zool) cuttle-fish. (b) no pl (Farbstoff) sepia (ink).

Sepia-: ~schale f cuttle-fish shell; ~zeichnung f sepia (drawing).

Sepien ['zeːpiən] pl of **Sepia**.

Sepp(e)lhose f (inf) lederhosen pl, leather shorts pl.

Sepp(l) m -s (S Ger) abbr of **Josef**.

Sepsis f -, **Sepsen** (Med) sepsis.

September m -(s), - September; siehe auch **März**.

Septett nt -(e)s, -e (Mus) septet(te).

Septime f -, -n, **Septim** f -, -en (Aus) (Mus) seventh.

septisch adj septic.

Septuaginta f - (Eccl) Septuagint.

Sequenz f sequence; (Cards auch) flush, run.

sequestrieren* vt (Jur) to sequester, to sequestrate.

Sera pl of **Serum**.

Serail [zeˈraːj, zeˈrai(l)] nt -s, -s seraglio.

Seraph ['zeːraf] m -s, -e or -im [-iːm] seraph.

Serbe m -n, -n Serbian.

Serbien ['zɛrbiən] nt -s Serbia.

Serbin f Serbian (woman/girl).

serbisch adj Serbian.

Serbokroatisch(e) nt decl as adj Serbo-Croat; siehe auch **Deutsch(e)**.

Seren pl of **Serum**.

Serenade f serenade.

Sergeant [zɛrˈʒant] m -en, -en (dated Mil) sergeant.

Serie ['zeːriə] f series sing; (von Waren auch) line; (Billard) break. **in ~ gehen** to go into production, to go onto the production line; **in ~ hergestellt werden** to be mass-produced; **das Gesetz der ~** the law of averages.

seriell adj **Herstellung series** attr. **~ hergestellt werden** to be mass-produced; ~e **Musik** serial music.

Serien- ['zeːriən-]: ~fabrikation, ~fertigung f series production; ~haus nt ordinary or standard house, Wimpey-type house (Brit inf); ~herstellung f series production; s~mäßig 1 adj Autos production attr; Ausstattung standard; Herstellung series attr; 2 adv herstellen in series; **das wird s~mäßig eingebaut** it's a standard fitting; ~nummer f serial number; ~produktion f series production; **in ~produktion gehen** to go into production, to go onto the production line; s~reif adj (Aut) ready to go into production; ~schaltung f (Elec) series connection; s~weise adv one after the other.

Serigraphie f (a) (Verfahren) silk-screen printing, serigraphy (spec). (b) (Bild) silk-screen print, serigraph (spec).

seriös adj serious; (anständig) respectable; Firma sound.

Seriosität f siehe adj seriousness; respectability; soundness.

Sermon m -s, -e (pej) sermon, lecture. **jdm einen langen ~ halten** to preach sb a long sermon, to give sb a long lecture.

Serodiagnostik f serodiagnosis.

Serologie f serology.

serologisch adj serological.

Serpentin m -s, -e (Miner) serpentine.

Serpentine f winding road, zigzag; (Kurve) double bend. **die Straße führt in ~n den Berg hinauf** the road winds or zigzags its way up the mountain.

Serpentinenstraße f winding or serpentine road.

Serum nt -s, **Seren** or **Sera** serum.

Serum-: ~behandlung f siehe ~therapie; ~diagnostik f siehe Serodiagnostik; ~krankheit f serum sickness; ~therapie f serotherapy, serum-therapy.

Service[1] [zɛrˈviːs] nt -(s), - auch [zɛrˈviːsə] (Geschirr) dinner/coffee etc service; (Gläser~) set.

Service[2] ['sɜːvɪs] m or nt -s (Comm, Sport) service; (Sport auch) serve.

Servierbrett [zɛrˈviːɐ-] nt tray.

servieren* [zɛrˈviːrən] 1 vt to serve (jdm etw sb sth, sth to sb); (inf: anbieten) to serve up (inf) (jdm for sb). **jdm den Ball ~** (Ftbl etc) to pass the ball to sb; (Tennis) to hit the ball right to sb; **er bekam den Ball toll serviert** the ball was beautifully set up for him; **du hättest es ihr etwas schonender ~**

können (*fig inf*) you could have dealt it out a little more mercifully.

2 *vi* to serve. **nach 24 Uhr wird nicht mehr serviert** there is no waiter service after midnight; **es ist serviert!** lunch/dinner *etc* is served.

Serviererin [zɛr'viːrərɪn] *f* waitress.

Servier- [zɛr'viːɐ-]: **~fräulein** *nt* (*dated*) waitress; **~tisch** *m* serving table; **~tochter** *f* (*Sw*) waitress; **~wagen** *m* trolley.

Serviette [zɛr'viɛtə] *f* serviette, napkin.

Serviettenring *m* serviette *or* napkin ring.

servil [zɛr'viːl] *adj* (*geh*) servile.

Servilität [zɛrvili'tɛːt] *f* (*geh*) servility.

Servitut [zɛrvi'tuːt] *nt* -(e)s, -e (*Jur*) siehe **Dienstbarkeit**.

Servo- ['zɛrvo-] (*Tech*): **~bremse** *f* power *or* servo(-assisted) brake; **~lenkung** *f* power *or* servo(-assisted) steering; **~motor** *m* servomotor.

Servus ['zɛrvʊs] *interj* (*Aus, S Ger*) (*beim Treffen*) hello; (*beim Abschied*) goodbye, so long (*inf*), cheerio (*Brit inf*). **seinen ~ druntersetzen** (*inf*) to sign, to add one's monicker (*sl*).

Sesam *m* -s, -s sesame. **~, öffne dich!** open Sesame!

Sessel *m* -s, - easy chair; (*Polstersessel*) armchair; (*Aus: Stuhl*) chair.

Sessel-: **~lehne** *f* (chair) arm; **~lift** *m* chairlift.

seßhaft *adj* settled; (*ansässig*) resident. **~ werden, sich ~ machen** to settle down.

Seßhaftigkeit *f, no pl* settled form of existence; (*von Lebensweise*) settledness. **die sprichwörtliche ~ der Holsteiner** the proverbial sedentariness of the Holsteiners.

Session *f* siehe **Sitzungsperiode**.

Set *m or nt* -s, -s (a) set. (b) (*Deckchen*) place mat, tablemat.

Setter *m* -s, - setter.

Setz|ei *nt* fried egg.

setzen 1 *vt* **(a)** (*hintun, hinbringen*) to put, to place, to set; (*sitzen lassen*) to sit, to place, to put. **etw auf die Rechnung/Speisekarte** *etc* ~ to put sth on the bill/menu *etc*; **etw an den Mund/die Lippen** ~ to put sth to one's mouth/lips; **jdn an Land** ~ to put *or* set sb ashore; **jdn über den Fluß** ~ to take sb across the river; **Fische in einen Teich** ~ to stock a pond with fish; **ein Stück auf den Spielplan** ~ to put on a play; **etw auf die Tagesordnung** ~ to put sth on the agenda; **etw in die Zeitung** ~ to put sth in the paper; **jdn in Erstaunen/Schrecken** ~ to astonish/frighten sb; **jdn über andere/jemanden anders** ~ to put *or* set sb above others/somebody else; **sich** (*dat*) **etw in den Kopf** *or* **Schädel** (*inf*) ~ to take sth into one's head; **dann setzt es was** *or* **Hiebe** *or* **Prügel** (*all inf*) there'll be trouble; **seine Hoffnung/sein Vertrauen in jdn/etw** ~ to put *or* place one's hopes/trust in sb/sth; **seine Ehre in etw** (*acc*) ~ to make sth a point of honour; **seinen Ehrgeiz in etw** (*acc*) ~ to make sth one's goal; **sein Leben an etw** (*acc*) ~ (*geh*) to devote one's life to sth; **siehe Druck**[1].

(b) (*Hort: pflanzen*) to set, to plant; (*aufziehen*) *Stander, Laternen* to put up; (*Naut*) *Segel* to set; (*Typ*) to set; (*geh: formulieren*) *Worte* to choose. **ein Gedicht/einen Text in Musik ~** to set a poem/words to music.

(c) *Preis, Summe* to put (*auf* +*acc* on); (*bei Gesellschaftsspielen: spielen, ziehen*) *Stein, Figur* to move. **etw als Pfand ~** to leave sth as a deposit; **Geld auf ein Pferd ~** to put *or* place *or* stake money on a horse; **auf seinen Kopf sind 100.000 Dollar gesetzt** there's 100,000 dollars on his head.

(d) (*errichten, aufstellen*) to build; *Denkmal auch* to erect, to put *or* set up; (*fig*) *Norm etc* to set. **jdm ein Grabmal/Denkmal ~** to put *or* set up *or* build a monument to sb.

(e) (*schreiben*) *Komma, Punkt* to put. **seinen Namen unter etw** (*acc*) ~ to put one's signature to sth.

(f) (*bestimmen*) *Ziel, Grenze, Termin etc* to set; (*annehmen*) *Hypothese etc* to assume, to posit (*form*). **jdm/sich ein Ziel/eine Frist ~** to set sb/oneself a goal/deadline; **den Fall ~** to make the assumption; siehe **gesetzt**.

(g) (*Hunt: gebären*) to bear, to produce.

2 *vr* **(a)** (*Platz nehmen*) to sit down; (*Vogel*) to perch, to alight. **sich auf einen Stuhl/seinen Platz ~** to sit down on a chair/at one's place; **sich ins Auto ~** to get into the car; **sich in die Sonne/ins Licht ~** to sit in the sun/light; **sich jdm auf den Schoß ~** to sit on sb's lap; **sich zu jdm ~** to sit with sb; **wollen Sie sich nicht zu uns ~?** won't you join us?; **darf ich mich zu Ihnen ~?** may I join you?; **bitte ~ Sie sich** please sit down, please take a seat, please be seated (*form*); **setz dich doch** sit yourself down (*inf*).

(b) (*Kaffee, Tee, Lösung*) to settle.

(c) (*sich festsetzen: Staub, Geruch, Läuse*) to get (*in* +*acc* into).

3 *vi* **(a)** (*bei Glücksspiel, Wetten*) to bet. **auf ein Pferd ~** to bet on *or* to place a bet on *or* to back a horse; **auf jdn/etw ~** (*lit, fig*) to put one's money on sb/sth, to back sb/sth; **hoch/niedrig ~** to play for high/low stakes.

(b) (*Typ*) to set.

(c) (*springen*) *Pferd, Läufer* to jump; (*Mil*) to cross. **über einen Graben/Zaun/ein Hindernis ~** to jump (over) *or* clear a ditch/fence/hurdle; **über einen Fluß ~** to cross a river.

Setzer *m* -s, - (*Typ*) compositor, typesetter, comp (*Typ sl*).

Setzerei *f*, **Setzersaal** *m* (*Typ*) composing room, caseroom.

Setz-: **~fehler** *m* (*Typ*) printer's error, literal; **~hase** *m* (*Hunt*) doe hare; **~kasten** *m* case; **~latte** *f* (*Surv*) aligning pole; **~ling** *m* (a) (*Hort*) seedling; (b) (*Fisch*) fry; **~maschine** *f* typesetting machine, typesetter; **~schiff** *nt* (*Typ*) galley; **~waage** *f* spirit level.

Seuche *f* -, -n epidemic; (*fig pej*) scourge. **das ist die reinste ~** (*inf*) it's like an epidemic.

Seuchen-: **s~artig** *adj* epidemic; **sich s~artig ausbreiten** to spread like the plague; **~bekämpfung** *f* epidemic control;

~gebiet *nt* epidemic *or* infested area *or* zone; **~gefahr** *f* danger of epidemic; **~herd** *m* centre of an/the epidemic.

seufzen *vti* to sigh.

Seufzer *m* -s, - sigh.

Seufzerbrücke *f* Bridge of Sighs.

Sex *m* -(es), *no pl* sex. **sie hat viel ~** she's very sexy.

Sex-: **~-Appeal** [-ə'piːl] *m* -s, *no pl* sex appeal; **~bombe** *f* (*inf*) sex bomb (*inf*); **~boutique** *f* sex shop; **~film** *m* sex film, skin flick (*sl*); **~foto** *nt* sexy photo; **~hilfe** *f* sex aid, marital aid (*euph*).

Sexismus *m* sexism.

Sexist(in *f*) *m* sexist.

sexistisch *adj* sexist.

Sex-: **~kontrolle** *f* sex check; **~magazin** *nt* sex magazine; **~muffel** *m* (*hum inf*) sexless person.

Sexologe *m*, **Sexologin** *f* sexologist.

Sexologie *f* sexology.

Sex-: **~protz** *m* (*hum inf*) sexual athlete; **~shop** ['zɛksʃɔp] *m* sex shop.

Sexta *f* -, **Sexten** (*Sch*) ≈ first year in a German secondary school; top year in an Austrian secondary school.

Sextaner(in *f*) *m* -s, - pupil in the first year of a German secondary school; pupil in the top year of an Austrian secondary school.

Sextanerblase *f* (*hum inf*) weak *or* Chinese (*hum sl*) bladder.

Sextant *m* (*Naut*) sextant.

Sexte *f* -, -n (*Mus*) sixth.

Sexten *pl of* **Sexta**.

Sextett *nt* -(e)s, -e (*Mus*) sextet(te).

Sextillion [zɛkstɪ'lioːn] *f* sextillion (*Brit*), undecillion (*US*).

sexual *adj* (*rare*) sexual.

Sexual-: **~atlas** *m* illustrated sex handbook; **~empfinden** *nt* sexual feeling; **~erziehung** *f* sex education; **~ethik** *f* sexual ethics *pl*; **~forscher** *m* sexologist; **~forschung** *f* sexology; **~hormon** *nt* sex hormone; **~hygiene** *f* sex(ual) hygiene.

sexualisieren* *vt* to eroticize.

Sexualisierung *f* eroticization.

Sexualität *f, no pl* sexuality.

Sexual-: **~leben** *nt* sex life; **~mörder** *m* sex murderer; **~neurose** *f* sex neurosis; **~pädagogik** *f* sex education; **~partner** *m* sex partner; **~trieb** *m* sex(ual) drive; **~wissenschaft** *f* sexology.

sexuell *adj* sexual.

Sexus *m* -, - (*geh*) sexuality.

sexy ['zɛksi] *adj pred* (*inf*) sexy (*inf*).

Seychellen [ze'ʃɛlən] *pl* (*Geog*) Seychelles *pl*.

Sezession *f* secession.

Sezessionist(in *f*) *m* secessionist.

sezessionistisch *adj* secessionist.

Sezessionskrieg *m* American Civil War.

sezieren* *vti* (*lit, fig*) to dissect.

Seziersaal *m* dissecting room.

S-förmig ['ɛs-] *adj* S-shaped.

Sgraffito [sgra'fiːto] *nt* -s, -s *or* **Sgraffiti** [sgra'fiːti] (*Art*) sgraffito.

Shag [ʃɛk] *m* -s, -s shag.

Shagpfeife ['ʃɛk-] *f* shag pipe.

Shake [ʃeːk] *m* -(s), -s shake.

Shakehands ['ʃeːkhɛnts] *nt* -, - (*inf*) handshake. **~ machen** to shake hands, to press the flesh (*hum inf*).

Shakespearebühne ['ʃeːkspiːʀə-] *f* Elizabethan stage.

Shakespearesch, Shakespearisch ['ʃeːkspiːʀəʃ, -ɪʃ] *adj* Shakespearean.

Shampoo(n) [ʃamˈpuː(n), ʃamˈpoː(n), ˈʃampoː(n)] *nt* -s, -s shampoo.

shampoonieren* [ʃampuˈniːrən, ʃampoˈn-] *vt* to shampoo.

Shanty ['ʃɛnti, ʃanti] *nt* -s, -s *or* **Shanties** shanty.

Shawisch ['ʃɔːʃ] *adj* Shavian.

Sheriff ['ʃɛrɪf] *m* -s, -s sheriff.

Sherpa ['ʃɛrpa] *m* -s, -s Sherpa.

Sherry ['ʃɛrɪ] *m* -s, -s sherry.

Shetland- ['ʃɛtlant-]: **~inseln** *pl* Shetland Islands *pl*, Shetlands *pl*; **~pony** *nt* Shetland pony; **~wolle** *f* Shetland wool.

Shit [ʃɪt] *nt* -s, *no pl* (*sl: Haschisch*) shit (*sl*).

shocking ['ʃɔkɪŋ] *adj pred* shocking.

Shopping ['ʃɔpɪŋ] *nt* -s, *no pl* shopping. **~ machen** (*inf*) to do some shopping.

Shopping-Center ['ʃɔpɪŋsɛntɐ] *nt* shopping centre.

Shorts [ʃɔːɐts, ʃɔrts] *pl* (pair of) shorts *pl*.

Shorty ['ʃɔːɐti, 'ʃɔrti] *nt* -s, -s *or* **Shorties** shorty pyjamas *pl*.

Show [ʃoː] *f* -, -s show. **eine ~ abziehen** (*inf*) to put on a show (*inf*).

Show-: **~down** [ʃoʊdaʊn] *m or nt* showdown; **~geschäft** *nt* show business; **~man** ['ʃoʊmən] *m* -s, -men showman; **~master** ['ʃoʊmaːstɐ] *m* -s, - compère, emcee (*US*).

Shredder ['ʃredɐ] *m* -s, -, **Shredder|anlage** *f* shredder, shredding machine.

Siam [ziːam] *nt* -s Siam.

Siamese *m* -n, -n, **Siamesin** *f* Siamese.

siamesisch *adj* Siamese. **~e Katze** Siamese cat; **~e Zwillinge** Siamese twins.

Siamkatze *f* Siamese (cat).

Sibirien [zi'biːriən] *nt* -s Siberia.

sibirisch *adj* Siberian. **~e Kälte** Siberian *or* arctic conditions *pl*.

Sibylla [zi'byla], **Sibylle** [zi'bylə] *f* -, **Sibyllen** sibyl.

sibyllinisch [zibyˈliːnɪʃ] *adj* sibylline, sibyllic.

sich *refl pron* **(a)** (*acc*) (+*infin, bei „man"*) oneself; (*3. pers sing*) himself; herself; itself; (*Höflichkeitsform*) yourself; yourselves; (*3. pers pl*) themselves.

(b) (*dat*) (+*infin, bei „man"*) to oneself; (*3. pers sing*) to himself; to herself; to itself; (*Höflichkeitsform*) to yourself/

yourselves; (*3. pers pl*) to themselves. ~ **die Haare waschen/ färben** *etc* to wash/dye *etc* one's hair; **er hat ~ das Bein gebrochen** he has broken his leg; **sie hat ~ einen Pulli gekauft/gestrickt** she bought/knitted herself a pullover, **she bought/knitted a pullover for herself; wann hat sie ~ das gekauft?** when did she buy that?

(c) *acc, dat* (*mit prep*) (+*infin, bei „man"*) one; (*3. pers sing*) him; her; it; (*Höflichkeitsform*) you; (*3. pers pl*) them. **wenn man keinen Paß bei ~** (*dat*) **hat** if one hasn't a passport with one or him (*US*), if you haven't a passport with you; **nur an ~** (*acc*) **denken** to think only of oneself; **wenn er jemanden zu ~** (*dat*) **einlädt** if he invites somebody round to his place.

(d) (*einander*) each other, one another.

(e) (*impers*) **hier sitzt/singt es ~ gut** it's good to sit/sing here; **diese Wolle strickt ~ gut/dieses Auto fährt ~ gut** this wool knits well/this car drives well.

Sichel *f* -, -**n** sickle; (*Mond~*) crescent.

sicher 1 *adj* (a) (*gewiß*) certain, sure. **der ~e Tod/Sieg** certain death/victory; (*sich dat*) **einer Sache** (*gen*) **~ sein** to be sure or certain of sth; **sich** (*dat*) **jds/seiner selbst** (*gen*) **~ sein** to be sure of sb/oneself; (*sich dat*) **seiner Sache** (*gen*) **~ sein** to be sure of what one is doing; **soviel ist ~** that/this much is certain; **ist das ~?** is that certain?; **man weiß nichts S~es** we don't know anything certain; **das ist uns ~** that is for sure; **mit der guten Zeit ist uns der zweite Platz ~** with such a good time we're sure of certain of second place.

(b) (*geschützt, gefahrlos*) safe; (*geborgen*) secure; *Investition auch* secure. **vor jdm/etw ~ sein** to be safe from sb/sth; **~ leben** to live or lead a secure life; **~ ist ~** you can't be too sure.

(c) (*zuverlässig*) reliable; *Methode auch* sure-fire *attr* (*inf*); *Verhütungsmethode auch*, *Fahrer, Schwimmer* sure; (*fest*) *Gefühl, Zusage* certain, definite; *Hand, Einkommen, Job* steady; *Stellung* secure. **ein ~er Schütze** a sure shot; **~ auf den Beinen sein** to be steady on one's legs; **mit ~em Instinkt** with a sure instinct.

(d) (*selbstbewußt*) (self-)confident, (self-)assured. **~ wirken/auftreten** to give an impression of (self-)confidence or (self-)assurance.

2 *adv* (a) *fahren etc* safely.

(b) (*natürlich*) of course. **~!** of course, sure (*esp US*).

(c) (*bestimmt*) **das wolltest du ~ nicht sagen** surely you didn't mean that; **du hast dich ~ verrechnet** you must have counted wrongly; **das weiß ich ganz ~** I know that for certain or for sure; **das ist ganz ~ das Beste** it's quite certainly the best; **aber er kommt ~ noch** I'm sure or certain he'll come; **das hat er ~ vergessen** I'm sure he's forgotten it; (*garantiert*) he's sure to have forgotten it; **er kommt ~ auch** mit he's bound or sure or certain to want to come too.

sichergehen *vi sep irreg aux sein* to be sure; (*sich vergewissern auch*) to make sure.

Sicherheit *f* (a) *no pl* (*Gewißheit*) certainty. **mit an ~ grenzender Wahrscheinlichkeit** almost certainly, probably if not certainly; **das ist mit ~ richtig** that is definitely right; **obwohl die These sich nicht mit ~ beweisen läßt** although the thesis cannot be proved with any degree of certainty.

(b) *no pl* (*Schutz, das Sichersein*) safety; (*als Aufgabe von Sicherheitsbeamten etc*) security. **~ und Ordnung** law and order; **die öffentliche ~** public safety or security; **die ~ der Bevölkerung** the safety or security of the population; **soziale ~** social security; **jdn/etw in ~ bringen** to get sb/sth to safety; **sich in ~ bringen** to get (oneself) to safety; **es gelang mir in letzter Minute, mich im Keller in ~ zu bringen** at the last minute I managed to get to the safety of the cellar; **~ im Straßen-/Flugverkehr** road/air safety; **in ~ sein, sich in ~ befinden** to be safe; **sich in ~ wiegen** or **wähnen** to think oneself safe; **jdn in ~ wiegen/wähnen** to lull sb into a (false) sense of security/to think sb safe; **der ~ (geh) halber** in the interests of safety; (*um sicherzugehen*) to be on the safe side; **schnallen Sie sich zu Ihrer ~ an** fasten your seat belt for your own safety; **lassen Sie sich zu Ihrer ~ eine Quittung geben** make sure you get a receipt, just to be on the safe side.

(c) *no pl* (*Zuverlässigkeit*) (*von Mittel, Methode, Geschmack, Instinkt*) reliability, sureness; (*Festigkeit*) (*der Hand, beim Balancieren etc*) steadiness; (*von Fahrer, Schwimmer*) competence; (*von Hand, Job, Einkommen*) steadiness; (*von Stellung*) security. **mit tödlicher ~** with deadly accuracy.

(d) *no pl* (*Selbstbewußtsein*) (self-)confidence, (self-) assurance. **~ im Auftreten** self-confident *etc* manner.

(e) *no pl* (*Gewandtheit*) confidence, assurance, sureness.

(f) (*Comm*) security; (*Pfand*) surety. **~ leisten** (*Comm*) to offer security; (*Jur*) to stand or go bail.

Sicherheits-: **~abstand** *m* safe distance; **~auto** *nt* safe car; **~beamte(r)** *m* security officer; (*Pol auch*) security agent or man; **das ist ein Problem für unsere ~beamten** it's a problem for security; **~behörde** *f* security service; **~bestimmungen** *pl* safety regulations *pl*; (*betrieblich, Pol etc*) security controls *pl* or regulations *pl*; **~bindung** *f* (*Ski*) security binding; **~direktion** *f* (*Aus*) security service; **~faktor** *m* security factor; **~glas** *nt* safety glass; **~gurt** *m* (*in Flugzeug*) seat belt; (*in Auto auch*) safety belt; **s~halber** *adv* to be on the safe side; **~kette** *f* safety chain; **~kontrolle** *f* security check; **~lampe** *f* (*Min*) safety lamp; **~leistung** *f* (*Comm*) surety; (*Jur*) bail; **~maßnahme** *f* safety precaution or measure; **~maßregel** *f* (*betrieblich, Pol etc*) security measure; **~nadel** *f* safety pin; **~polizei** *f* security police *pl*; **~rad** *nt* (*Hist*) safety bicycle; **~rat** *m* security council; **~risiko** *nt* security risk; **~schloß** *nt* safety or Yale ® lock; **~schlüssel** *m* special key (*for safety locks*), Yale ® key; **~truppen** *pl* security troops *pl*; **~ventil** *nt* safety valve; **~verschluß** *m* safety catch; **~vorkehrung** *f* safety precaution; (*betrieblich, Pol etc*) security precaution; **die ~vorkehrungen waren sehr gut** security

was or the security precautions were very good.

sicherlich *adv siehe* sicher 2 (b, c).

sichern 1 *vt* (a) (*gegen, vor* +*dat* against) to safeguard; (*absichern*) to protect; (*Mil auch*) to protect, to cover; (*sicher machen*) *Tür, Wagen, Fahrrad etc* to secure; (*Bergsteiger etc*) to belay, to secure; (*Mil*) to protect, to cover. **eine Feuerwaffe ~** to put the safety catch of a firearm on.

(b) **jdm/sich etw ~** to get or secure sth for sb/oneself; **~ Sie sich rechtzeitig Ihren Rentenanspruch** make sure of your pension entitlement in good time; **diese beiden Flaschen habe ich extra für mich gesichert** I've made sure of these two bottles for myself.

2 *vr* to protect oneself; (*Bergsteigen*) to belay or secure oneself. **sich vor etw** (*dat*) or **gegen etw ~** to protect oneself against sth, to guard against sth.

3 *vi* (*Hunt*) to scent.

sicherstellen *vt sep* (a) (*in Gewahrsam nehmen*) *Waffen, Haschisch* to take possession of. **das Tatfahrzeug wurde sichergestellt** the vehicle used in the crime was found (and taken in). (b) (*garantieren*) to guarantee.

Sicherstellung *f siehe vt* (a) taking possession; finding. (b) guarantee.

Sicherung *f* (a) *siehe vt* (a) safeguarding; protection; securing; belaying. (b) (*Schutz*) safeguard. (c) (*Elec*) fuse; (*von Waffe*) safety catch. **da ist** (*bei*) **ihm die ~ durchgebrannt** (*fig inf*) he blew a fuse (*inf*).

Sicherungs-: **~übereignung** *f* (*Jur*) transfer of ownership as security on a debt; **~verwahrung** *f* (*Jur*) preventive detention.

sicherwirkend *adj seiner* reliable.

Sicht *f* -, *no pl* (a) (*Sehweite*) visibility. **die ~ betrug teilweise nur 20 Meter** at times visibility was down to 20 metres; **eine ~ von 30 Metern** 30 metres' visibility; **in ~ sein/kommen** to be in/come into sight; **aus meiner/seiner etc ~** (*fig*) as I see/he sees it, from my/his point of view; **auf lange/kurze ~** (*fig*) in the long/short term; *planen* for the long/short term; **auf lange ~ ausgebucht** fully booked for a long time ahead.

(b) (*Ausblick*) view.

(c) (*Comm*) **auf** or **bei ~** at sight; **acht Tage nach ~** one week after sight.

sichtbar *adj* (*lit, fig*) visible. **~ werden** (*fig*) to become apparent; **allmählich wurden Fortschritte ~** it could gradually be seen that progress was being made.

Sichtbarkeit *f, no pl* visibility.

sichtbarlich *adj* (*old*) *siehe* sichtlich.

Sichtbarwerden *nt* (*lit, fig*) appearance. **um das ~ früherer Fehler zu verhindern** to prevent earlier mistakes from becoming apparent.

sichten *vt* (a) (*erblicken*) to sight. (b) (*durchsehen*) to look through, to examine, to inspect; (*ordnen*) to sift through.

Sicht-: **~flug** *m* contact flight; **~gerät** *nt* monitor; (*Computers*) VDU, visual display unit; **~grenze** *f* visibility limit.

sichtig *adj* (*Naut*) *Wetter* clear.

Sichtkartei *f* visible card index.

sichtlich 1 *adj* obvious. 2 *adv* obviously, visibly.

Sichtung *f siehe vt* (a) sighting. (b) looking through (*einer Sache gen*), examination, inspection. (c) sifting.

Sicht-: **~verhältnisse** *pl* visibility *sing*; **~vermerk** *m* endorsement; **~wechsel** *m* (*Fin*) bill payable on demand; **~weite** *f* visibility *no art*; **außer ~weite** out of sight; **~werbung** *f* poster-advertizing.

Sickergrube *f* soakaway.

sickern *vi aux sein* to seep; (*dickere Flüssigkeit auch*) to ooze; (*in Tropfen*) to drip; (*fig*) to leak out. **in die Presse ~** to be leaked to the press.

Sickerwasser *nt* water seeping through the ground.

siderisch *adj* (*Astron*) sidereal.

sie *pers pron 3. pers* (a) *sing gen* **ihrer**, *dat* **ihr**, *acc* **sie** (*von Frau, weiblichem Tier*) (*nom*) she; (*acc*) her; (*von Dingen*) it; (*von Behörde, Polizei*) (*nom*) they *pl*; (*acc*) them *pl*. **wenn ich ~ wäre ...** if I were her or she (*form*) ...; **~ ist es** it's her, it is she (*form*); **wer hat das gemacht? — ~** who did that? — she did or her!; **wer ist der Täter? — ~** who is the person responsible? — she is or her!; **~ war es nicht, ich war's** it wasn't her, it was me; **~ und du/ich** you and she/she and I; **unser Hund ist eine ~** our dog is a she.

(b) *pl gen* **ihrer**, *dat* **ihnen**, *acc* **sie** (*nom*) they; (*acc*) them. **~ sind es** it's them; **~ sind es, die ...** it's them or it is they (*form*) who ...; **wer hat's zuerst bemerkt? — ~** who noticed it first? — they did or them (*inf*).

(c) (*obs: als Anrede*) S~ *sing* you, thee (*obs*); *pl* you.

Sie 1 *pers pron 2. pers sing* or *pl mit 3. pers pl vb gen* **Ihrer**, *dat* **Ihnen**, *acc* **Sie** you; (*im Imperativ*) *nicht übersetzt*. **beeilen ~ sich!** hurry up!; **he, ~!** (*inf*) hey, you!; **~, wissen ~ was ...** (*inf*) do you know what ...

2 *nt* -**s**, *no pl* polite or "Sie" form of address. **jdn per** or **mit ~ anreden** to use the polite form of address to sb, to call sb "Sie".

Sieb *nt* -(**e**)**s**, -**e** sieve; (*für Erde auch*) riddle; (*für Korn, Gold auch*) screen; (*Tee~*) strainer; (*Gemüse~*) colander. **ein Gedächtnis wie ein ~ haben** to have a memory like a sieve.

Sieb-: **~bein** *nt* (*Anat*) ethmoid (bone); **~druck** *m* (silk-)screen print; (*~druckverfahren*) (silk-)screen printing.

sieben[1] 1 *vt* to pass through a sieve; *Korn, Gold* to screen; (*Cook*) to sift, to sieve.

2 *vi* (*fig inf*) **solche Unternehmen ~ sehr** organisations like that pick and choose very carefully or are very selective; **es wird stark gesiebt** they pick and choose or are very selective; **am Ende des Semesters wird gründlich gesiebt** at the end of the term they weed a lot of people out; **bei der Prüfung wird stark gesiebt** the exam will weed a lot of people out.

sieben[2] *num* seven. **die S~ Weisen** the Seven Sages; **die S~**

Weltwunder the seven wonders of the world; **die S~ Welt-meere** the Seven Seas; **die S~ Freien Künste** the humanities, the (seven) liberal arts; **die ~ Todsünden** or **Hauptsünden** the seven deadly sins; **die ~ fetten und die ~ mageren Jahre** (*Bibl*) the seven fat and the seven lean years; *siehe auch* **vier.**

Sieben f -, - or -en seven; *siehe* **Vier, böse.**

Sieben- *in cpds siehe auch* **Vier-;** s~**armig** *adj* **Leuchter** seven-armed; ~**bürgen** nt (*Geog*) Transylvania; ~**eck** nt heptagon; ~**gestirn** nt (*Astron*) Pleiades pl; ~**hügelstadt** f city of the seven hills; s~**hundert** num seven hundred; s~**jährig** *adj* seven-year-old; (*sieben Jahre dauernd*) seven-year *attr*; **der ~jährige Krieg** the Seven-Years' War; s~**mal** *adv* seven times; ~**meilenstiefel** pl (*Liter*) seven-league boots pl; ~**meter** m (*Sport*) penalty; ~**monatskind** nt seven-month baby; ~**sachen** pl (*inf*) belongings pl, things pl; ~**schläfer** m (a) (*Zool*) edible or fat dormouse; (b) 27th June, *day which is said to determine the weather for the next seven weeks*; s~**tausend** num seven thousand.

Siebentel, Siebtel nt -s, - seventh.

siebentens, siebtens *adv* seventh(ly), in seventh place.

siebente(r, s) *adj siehe* **siebte(r, s).**

siebte(r, s) *adj* seventh; *siehe auch* **vierte(r, s).**

siebzehn num seventeen. **S~ und Vier** (*Cards*) pontoon; *siehe auch* **vierzehn.**

siebzig num seventy; *siehe auch* **vierzig.**

Siebziger(in f) m -s, -, **Siebzigjährige(r)** mf decl as adj seventy-year-old, septuagenarian.

siech *adj* (*old, liter*) ailing, infirm.

siechen vi (*rare*) *siehe* **dahinsiechen.**

Siechen-: ~**haus** (*old*), ~**heim** (*old*) nt infirmary.

Siechtum nt, no pl (*liter*) infirmity.

Siede-: s~**heiß** *adj* boiling hot, scalding; ~**hitze** f boiling heat.

Siedelland nt settlement area.

siedeln vi to settle.

sieden pret **siedete** or **sott,** ptp **gesiedet** or **gesotten 1** vi (*Wasser, Zucker etc*) to boil; (*Aus, S Ger*) to simmer. **da siedet einem das Blut** it makes your blood boil.

   2 vt *Seife, Leim* to produce by boiling; (*Aus, S Ger*) to simmer. ~**d heiß/~de Hitze** boiling or scalding hot/heat; (*von Klima auch*) swelteringly hot/sweltering heat; *siehe* **gesotten.**

Siedepunkt m (*Phys, fig*) boiling-point.

Siedler m -s, - settler; (*Bauer*) smallholder.

Siedlerstelle f smallholding.

Siedlung f (a) (*Ansiedlung*) settlement. (b) (*Siedlerstelle*) smallholding. (c) (*Wohn~*) housing scheme or estate.

Siedlungshaus nt house on a housing scheme.

Sieg m -(e)s, -e victory (*über* +acc over); (*in Wettkampf auch*) win (*über* +acc over). **um den ~ kämpfen** to fight for victory; **den ~ davontragen** or **erringen** to be victorious; (*in Wettkampf auch*) to be the winner/winners; **den ~ an seine Fahnen heften** (*geh*) to call victory one's own; **einer Sache** (*dat*) **zum ~ verhelfen** to help sth to triumph; **von ~ zu ~ schreiten** (*geh*) to heap victory upon victory.

Siegel nt -s, - seal. **unter dem ~ der Verschwiegenheit** under the seal of secrecy; *siehe* **Buch, Brief.**

Siegellack m sealing wax.

siegeln vt *Urkunde* to affix a/one's seal to; (*ver~*) *Brief* to seal.

Siegel-: ~**ring** m signet ring; ~**wachs** nt sealing wax.

siegen vi (*Mil*) to be victorious; (*fig auch*) to triumph; (*in Wettkampf*) to win. **über jdn/etw ~** (*Mil*) to vanquish sb/sth; (*fig*) to triumph over sb/sth; (*in Wettkampf*) to beat sb/sth, to win against sb/sth; **ich kam, sah und siegte** I came, I saw, I conquered.

Sieger m -s, - victor; (*in Wettkampf*) winner. **zweiter ~** runner-up; ~ **werden** to be the winner, to win; **als ~ hervorgehen** to emerge victorious.

Siegerehrung f (*Sport*) presentation ceremony.

Siegerin f victress (*liter*); (*in Wettkampf*) winner.

Sieger-: ~**kranz** m victor's laurels pl; **im ~kranz** crowned with the victor's laurels; ~**macht** f usu pl (*Pol*) victorious power; ~**urkunde** f (*Sport*) winner's certificate.

Sieges-: s~**bewußt** *adj* confident of victory; ~**botschaft** f news of victory sing; ~**denkmal** nt victory monument; ~**feier** f victory celebrations pl; (*Sport*) victory celebration; ~**geschrei** nt (*pej*) shouts of victory pl; s~**gewiß** *adj siehe* s~**sicher;** ~**göttin** f goddess of victory; ~**kranz** m victor's laurels pl; ~**palme** f palm (of victory); ~**preis** m winner's prize; (*Boxen*) winner's purse; ~**säule** f victory column; ~**serie** f series sing of victories/wins; s~**sicher** *adj* certain or sure of victory; ~**taumel** m triumphant euphoria; **im ~taumel** euphoric with their etc victory or triumph; s~**trunken** *adj* (*liter*) drunk with victory; ~**zug** m triumphal march.

sieg-: ~**gewohnt** *adj* used to victory/winning; ~**haft** *adj siehe* **siegesbewußt;** ~**reich** *adj* victorious, triumphant; (*in Wettkampf*) winning *attr*, successful.

sieh, siehe *imper sing of* **sehen.**

siehste (*inf*) 2. pers sing present of **sehen** (*inf*) (you) see.

Siel nt or m -(e)s, -e (*Schleuse*) sluice; (*Abwasserkanal*) sewer.

Siele f -, -n trace. **in den ~n sterben** (*fig*) to die in harness.

sielen vr (*dial*) *siehe* **suhlen.**

siena ['ziɛna] *adj inv* sienna.

Sierra [si'ɛra] f -, -s or **Sierren** [si'ɛran] (*Geog*) sierra.

siezen vt jdn/sich ~ to use the formal term of address to sb/each other, to address sb/each other as "Sie".

Sigel nt -s, -, **Sigle** ['ziːgl] f -, -n short form, grammalogue (*spec*).

Sightseeing ['saɪtsiːɪŋ] nt -, no pl sightseeing. **~ machen** to do some sightseeing.

Sigill nt -s, -e (*old*) *siehe* **Siegel.**

sigillieren* vt (*old*) *siehe* **siegeln.**

Signal nt -s, -e signal. **(ein) ~ geben** to give a signal; **mit der Hupe (ein) ~ geben** to hoot (as a signal); **~e setzen** (*fig*) to blaze a trail.

Signalanlage f signals pl, set of signals.

Signalement [zɪgnaləˈmãː] nt -s, -s (*Sw*) (personal) description.

Signal-: ~**flagge** f signal flag; ~**gast** m signalman; ~**horn** nt (*Hunt*) (hunting) horn; (*Mil*) bugle.

signalisieren* vt (*lit, fig*) to signal.

Signal-: ~**kelle** f signalling disc; ~**lampe, ~laterne** f signalling lamp; (*installiert*) signal lamp; ~**mast** m signal mast; ~**pfeife** f whistle; ~**pistole** f Very pistol; ~**technik** f signalling.

Signatar m (*form*) signatory (*gen* to).

Signatarmächte pl signatory powers pl.

Signatur f (a) (*Unterschrift, Buch~*) signature. (b) (*auf Landkarten*) symbol. (c) (*Bibliotheks~*) shelf mark.

Signet [zɪˈgneːt, zɪˈgnet, zɪnˈjeː] nt -s, -s (*Typ*) publisher's mark.

signieren* vt to sign; (*mit Anfangsbuchstaben auch*) to initial.

Signierung f, no pl siehe vt signing; initialling.

signifikant *adj* (*geh*) significant.

Signifikanz f (*geh*) significance.

Sikh [ziːk] m -(s), -s Sikh.

Silage [ziˈlaːʒə] f -, no pl (*Agr*) silage.

Silbe f -, -n syllable. **~ für ~** (*fig*) word for word; **er hat es mit keiner ~ erwähnt/verraten** he didn't say/breathe a word about it; **davon versteh ich keine ~** I don't understand a word (of it).

Silben-: ~**maß** nt (*dated*) *siehe* **Versmaß;** ~**rätsel** nt word game in which the answers are obtained by combining syllables from a given list; ~**schrift** f syllabary; ~**trennung** f syllabification; s~**weise** *adv* in syllables; ~**zahl** f number of syllables.

-silber m -, - in cpds (*Poet*) siehe **-silb(l)er.**

Silber nt -s, no pl silver; (*Tafelbesteck auch*) silverware; (*Her*) argent. **aus ~** made of silver; *siehe* **reden.**

Silber- *in cpds* silver; ~**arbeit** f silverwork no pl; ~**besteck** nt silver(ware), silver cutlery; ~**blick** m (*inf*) squint; ~**distel** f carline thistle; s~**farben,** s~**farbig** *adj* silver(-coloured), (*Her*) argent; ~**fischchen** nt silverfish; ~**folie** f silver foil; ~**fuchs** m silver fox; ~**geld** nt silver; ~**geschirr** nt silver(ware); ~**glanz** m (*Miner, Chem*) silver glance, argentite, silver sulphide; (*poet*) silvery gleam; s~**grau** *adj* silver(y)-grey; ~**haar** nt (*poet*) silver(y) hair; (*von Mann auch*) hoary head (*poet*); s~**haltig** *adj* silver-bearing, argentiferous (*spec*); s~**hell** *adj* Stimme, Lachen silvery.

silberig *adj siehe* **silbrig.**

Silber-: ~**hochzeit** f silver wedding (anniversary); ~**hütte** f silverworks sing or pl; ~**klang** m (*poet*) silvery sound; ~**ling** m (*Bibl*) piece of silver; ~**löwe** m puma; ~**möwe** f herring gull.

silbern *adj* silver; (*liter*) Licht, Stimme, Haare silvery (*liter*), silvern (*poet*). ~**e Hochzeit** silver wedding (anniversary); **das S~e Zeitalter** (*Myth*) the Silver Age.

Silber-: ~**pappel** f white poplar; ~**schmied** m silversmith; ~**stickerei** f (*Kunst*) silver embroidery; (*Produkt*) silver-embroidered garment/cushion etc; ~**streif(en)** m (*fig*) es zeichnete sich ein ~streif(en) am Horizont ab you/they etc could see light at the end of the tunnel; **das war wie ein ~streif(en) am Horizont** that was a ray of sunshine; ~**stück** nt silver coin; ~**tanne** f siehe **Edeltanne;** ~**währung** f currency based on the silver standard; ~**waren** pl silver sing; s~**weiß** *adj* silvery white; ~**zeug** nt silver sing.

-silbig *adj suf* **fünf~/zehn~ sein** to have five/ten syllables; **ein sechs~es Wort** a word with six syllables.

-silb(l)er m -s, - in cpds (*Poet*) -syllable; **ein Fünf~/Acht~** a pentasyllable/an octosyllable.

silbrig *adj* silvery.

Silhouette [ziˈlu̯ɛtə] f silhouette. **sich als ~ gegen etw abheben** or **abzeichnen** to be silhouetted against sth.

Silikat, Silicat (*spec*) nt -(e)s, -e silicate.

Silikon nt -s, -e silicone.

Silikonplättchen nt silicon chip.

Silikose f -, -n (*Med*) silicosis.

Silizium nt -s, no pl silicon.

Silo m -s, -s silo.

Silur nt -s, no pl (*Geog*) Silurian.

Silvaner [zɪlˈvaːnɐ] m -s, - sylvaner (grape/wine).

Silvester [zɪlˈvɛstɐ] m or nt -s, - New Year's Eve, Hogmanay (*esp Scot*).

Silvester-: ~**abend** m New Year's Eve, Hogmanay (*esp Scot*); ~**feier** f New Year's Eve or New Year party; ~**nacht** f night of New Year's Eve or Hogmanay (*esp Scot*).

Simonie f simony.

simpel *adj* simple; *Mensch auch* simple-minded; (*vereinfacht*) simplistic.

Simpel m -s, - (*inf*) simpleton.

Simpelfransen pl (*inf*) fringe sing, bangs pl (*US*).

Simplex nt -, -e or **Simplizia** (*Gram*) simplex.

Simplifikation f (*geh*) simplification.

simplifizieren* vt (*geh*) to simplify.

Simplizität f (*geh*) simplicity.

Sims m or nt -es, -e (*Fenster~*) (window)sill; (*außen auch*) (window)ledge; (*Gesims*) ledge; (*Kamin~*) mantlepiece.

Simulant(in f) m malingerer.

Simulation f simulation.

Simulator m (*Sci*) simulator.

simulieren* 1 vi (a) to feign illness. **er simuliert nur** he's shamming; (*um sich zu drücken auch*) he's malingering. (b) (*inf: nachdenken*) to meditate, to ruminate. 2 vt (a) *Krankheit* to feign, to sham. (b) (*Sci*) to simulate.

simultan *adj* simultaneous.

Simultan-: ~**dolmetschen** nt -s, no pl simultaneous translation; ~**dolmetscher** m simultaneous translator.

Simultaneität [zimʊltanei'tɛːt], **Simultanität** f (geh) simultaneity, simultaneousness.

Simultan-: ~kirche f church used by several denominations; ~schule f siehe Gemeinschaftsschule; ~spiel nt (Chess) simultaneous game.

sin. abbr of Sinus.

Sinai ['ziːnai] m -(s), **Sinaihalbinsel** f Sinai (Peninsula).

sind 1. and 3. pers pl, bei Sie sing and pl present of sein.

Sinekure f -, -n (liter) sinecure.

sine tempore adv abbr s.t. (Univ) punctually.

Sinfonie f symphony.

Sinfonie-: ~konzert nt symphony concert; ~orchester nt symphony orchestra.

Sinfoniker(in f) m -s, - member of a symphony orchestra. **die Bamberger** ~ the Bamberg Symphony Orchestra.

sinfonisch adj symphonic.

Singlakademie f choral society.

Singapur ['zɪŋgapuːɐ] nt -s Singapore.

Sing-: s~bar adj singable; **schwer** s~bar **sein** to be hard to sing; ~drossel f song thrush.

singen pret **sang**, ptp **gesungen** 1 vi (a) (lit, fig) to sing; (esp Eccl: eintönig, feierlich) to chant; (Dynamo auch) to hum; (Telegraphendrähte auch) to buzz, to hum. **zur Gitarre/Mandoline** ~ to sing to the guitar/mandoline; **ein** ~**der Tonfall** a lilt, a lilting accent; **singe, wem Gesang gegeben** (dated prov) if God gave you a good voice you should use it; **siehe Alte(r).**

(b) (sl: gestehen) to squeal (sl), to sing (sl), to talk.

2 vt (lit, fig) to sing; (esp Eccl) Psalmen, Kanon to chant. **jdn in den Schlaf** or **Schlummer** (liter) ~ to sing sb to sleep; **das kann ich schon** ~ (inf) I know it backwards.

3 vr **sich heiser/in den Schlaf** ~ to sing oneself hoarse/to sleep; **sich müde** ~ to sing until one is tired; **hier singt es sich gut** this is a good place to sing (in); **das Lied singt sich leicht** it's an easy song to sing.

Singen nt -s, no pl (a) siehe vi (a) singing; chanting; humming; buzzing, humming. (b) (Sch) singing.

Singerei f (inf) singing.

Singhalese [zɪŋga'leːzə] m -n, -n, **Singhalesin** f Sin(g)halese.

Singhalesisch(e) [zɪŋga'leːzɪʃ(ə)] nt decl as adj Sin(g)halese.

Single[1] ['sɪŋgl] f -, -(s) (Schallplatte) single.

Single[2] ['sɪŋgl] nt -, -(s) (Tennis etc) singles sing.

Single[3] ['sɪŋgl] m -s, -s (Alleinlebender) single. **Urlaub für** ~s singles' holiday.

Sing-: ~sang m -s, -s (a) (Liedchen) ditty; (b) (Gesang) monotonous singing; (c) (singende Sprechweise) singsong; ~spiel nt lyrical drama; ~stimme f vocal part.

Singular m singular.

singulär adj (geh) unique.

singularisch adj (Gram) singular.

Singularität f (geh) uniqueness.

Sing-: ~vogel m song-bird; ~weise f way of singing.

sinister adj (geh) sinister.

sinken pret **sank**, ptp **gesunken** vi aux sein (a) to sink; (Schiff auch) to go down; (Ballon) to descend; (Nebel) to come down, to descend (liter). **auf den Grund** ~ to sink to the bottom; **auf einen Stuhl/zu Boden** ~ to sink into a chair/to the ground; **ins Bett** ~ to fall into bed; **in Schlaf** ~ to sink into a sleep; **an jds Brust** (acc) or **jdm an die Brust** ~ (liter) to fall upon sb's breast; **in Ohnmacht** ~ (geh) to swoon, to fall into a faint; **ich hätte in die Erde** ~ **mögen** I wished the earth would (open and) swallow me up; **bis in die** ~**de Nacht** (liter) until nightfall; **sein Stern ist im** or **am S**~ (geh) his star is waning; **die Arme/den Kopf** ~ **lassen** to let one's arms/head drop.

(b) (Boden, Gebäude) to subside, to sink; (Fundament) to settle. **das Haus war ein Meter tiefer gesunken** the house had sunk one metre; **in Staub** or **Trümmer/in Schutt und Asche** ~ (geh) to fall in ruins/be reduced to a pile of rubble.

(c) (niedriger werden: Wasserspiegel, Temperatur, Preise etc) to fall, to drop.

(d) (schwinden) (Ansehen, Vertrauen) to diminish; (Einfluß auch) to wane, to decline; (Hoffnung, Stimmung) to sink. **den Mut/die Hoffnung** ~ **lassen** to lose courage/hope.

(e) (moralisch) to sink. **tief gesunken sein** to have sunk low; **in jds Meinung/Achtung** (dat) ~ to go down in sb's estimation.

Sinn m -(e)s, -e (a) (Wahrnehmungsfähigkeit) sense. **die** ~**e (sinnliche Begierde) one's desires; seiner** ~**e (gen) nicht mehr mächtig sein, nicht mehr Herr seiner** ~**e (gen) sein** to have lost all control over oneself; **siehe fünf, sechste(r, s).**

(b) ~**e** pl (Bewußtsein) senses pl, consciousness; **er verlor** or **ihn verließen seine** ~**e** he lost consciousness; **er war von** or **nicht bei** ~**en** he was out of his senses or mind; **wie von** ~**en** like one demented; **bist du noch bei** ~**en?** have you taken leave of your senses?

(c) (Gedanken, Denkweise) mind. **sich** (dat) **jdn/etw aus dem** ~ **schlagen** to put sb/(all idea of) sth out of one's mind, to forget all about sb/sth; **es kommt** or **will mir nicht aus dem** ~ (geh) I can't get it out of my mind; **es kam mir plötzlich in den** ~ it suddenly came to me; **das will mir einfach nicht in den** ~ I just can't understand it; **etw im** ~ **haben** to have sth in mind; **anderen** ~**es werden** (geh), **seinen** ~ **ändern** (geh) to change one's mind; **(mit jdm) eines** ~**es sein** (geh) to be of the same mind (as sb), to be of one mind.

(d) (Wunsch) inclination. **ihr** ~ **ist auf ... (acc) gerichtet** (geh) her inclination is to ...; **danach steht ihm der** ~ (geh) that is his wish.

(e) (Verständnis, Empfänglichkeit) feeling. **dafür fehlt ihm der** ~ he has no feeling for that sort of thing; ~ **für Humor/Proportionen/Gerechtigkeit** etc **haben** to have a sense of humour/proportion/justice etc; ~ **für Kunst/Literatur/das Höhere haben** to appreciate art/literature/higher things.

(f) (Geist) spirit. **dem** ~**e des Gesetzes nach, im** ~**e des Gesetzes** according to the spirit of the law; **in jds** ~**e** (dat) **handeln** to act as sb would have wished; **im** ~**e des Verstorbenen** in accordance with the wishes of the deceased; **das ist nicht in meinem/seinem** ~**e** that is not what I myself/he himself would have done/wished etc.

(g) (Zweck) point. **das ist nicht der** ~ **der Sache** that is not the point, that is not the object of the exercise; ~ **und Zweck einer Sache** (gen) the (aim and) object of sth; ~ **und Unsinn dieser Maßnahmen/des Geschichtsunterrichts** reasoning or lack of it behind these measures/behind history teaching; **der** ~ **des Lebens** the meaning of life; **ohne** ~ **und Verstand sein** to make no sense at all; **das hat keinen** ~ there is no point or sense in that; **es hat keinen** ~**, jetzt noch loszugehen** there's no point or sense (in) starting out now; **was hat denn das für einen** ~? what's the point of or in that or the sense in that?

(h) (Bedeutung) meaning; (von Wort, Ausdruck auch) sense. **im übertragenen/weiteren** ~ in the figurative/broader sense; **der Satz (er)gibt keinen** ~ the sentence doesn't make sense.

Sinn-: s~betörend adj (liter) sensuously intoxicating; ~bild nt symbol; s~bildlich adj symbolic(al).

sinnen pret **sann**, ptp **gesonnen** (geh) 1 vi (a) (nachdenken) to meditate, to ponder, to muse; (grübeln) to brood. **über etw** (acc) ~ to reflect on/brood over sth.

(b) (planen) **auf etw** (acc) ~ to devise sth, to think sth up, to think of sth; **auf Verrat/Rache** ~ to plot treason/revenge; **all sein S**~ **und Trachten** all his mind and energies.

2 vt (old liter) Verrat, Rache to plot.

Sinnen-: ~freude f enjoyment of the pleasures of life; s~freudig, s~froh adj ein s~freudiger Mensch a person who enjoys the pleasures of life; ~genuß m sensual pleasure; ~lust f (liter) sensuality; ~mensch m sensuous person; ~rausch m (liter) sensual passion.

sinn-: ~entleert adj bereft of content; ~entstellend adj ~entstellend sein to distort the meaning; ~entstellend übersetzt translated so that the meaning is/was distorted.

Sinnenwelt f (liter) material world.

Sinnes-: ~änderung f change of mind or heart; ~art f (geh) siehe Gesinnung; ~eindruck m sensory impression, impression on the senses; ~nerv m sensory nerve; ~organ nt sense organ; ~reiz m sensory stimulus; ~störung f sensory disorder; ~täuschung f hallucination; ~wahrnehmung f sensory perception no pl; ~wandel m change of mind or heart.

Sinn-: s~fällig adj manifest, obvious; ~gebung f (geh) giving meaning (+gen to); (Sinn) meaning; ~gedicht nt epigram; s~gemäß adj (a) (inhaltlich) etw s~gemäß wiedergeben to give the gist of sth; eine s~gemäße Zusammenfassung a summary which gives the gist (of it); (b) (esp Jur: analog) corresponding, analogous; etw s~gemäß anwenden to apply sth by analogy; s~getreu adj Übersetzung faithful (to the sense or meaning).

sinnieren* vi to brood (über +acc over), to ruminate (über +acc about).

Sinnierer(in f) m -s, - brooder.

sinnig adj apt; Vorrichtung practical.

sinnlich adj (a) (Philos) Empfindung, Eindrücke sensory, sensorial. **die** ~**e Welt** the material world; ~**e Anschauung** perception (by the senses); ~**wahrnehmbar** perceptible by the senses. (b) (vital, sinnenfroh) sensuous; (erotisch) sensual. ~**e Liebe** sensual love.

Sinnlichkeit f (a) (Philos) sensory or sensorial nature. (b) (Vitalität, Sinnenfreude) sensuousness; (Erotik) sensuality.

sinnlos adj (a) (unsinnig) Redensarten, Geschwätz meaningless; Verhalten, Töten senseless.

(b) (zwecklos) pointless, futile, senseless; Hoffnung forlorn. **es ist/wäre** ~**, zu** ... it is/would be pointless or futile to ...; **das ist völlig** ~ there's no sense in that, that's completely pointless.

(c) Wut blind; Hast desperate. ~ **betrunken** blind drunk.

Sinnlosigkeit f (a) siehe adj (a) (Unsinnigkeit) meaninglessness; senselessness. (b) siehe adj (b) (Zwecklosigkeit) pointlessness, futility, senselessness; forlornness.

Sinn-: s~reich adj Deutung meaningful; (zweckdienlich) Einrichtung, Erfindung useful; ~spruch m epigram; s~verwandt adj synonymous; s~verwandte Wörter synonyms; ~verwandtschaft f synonymity; s~voll adj (a) Satz meaningful; (b) (fig) (vernünftig) sensible; (nützlich) useful; s~widrig adj nonsensical, absurd; ~widrigkeit f nonsensicalness, absurdity.

Sinologe m, **Sinologin** f Sinologist.

Sinologie f Sinology.

sintemal(en) conj (obs, hum) because, since.

Sinter m -s, - (Miner) sinter.

Sinterterrasse f sinter terrace.

sintern vti to sinter.

Sintflut f (Bibl) Flood. **nach mir/uns die** ~ (inf) it doesn't matter what happens when I've/we've gone.

sintflutlartig adj ~e Regenfälle torrential rain.

Sinus m -, - or -se (a) (Math) sine. (b) (Anat) sinus.

Sinus-: ~kurve f sine curve; ~satz m sine theorem.

Sioux ['ziːʊks] m -, - Sioux.

Siphon ['ziːfõ] m -s, -s siphon; (Aus inf) soda (water).

Sippe f -, -n (extended) family, kinship group (spec); (inf: Verwandtschaft) family, clan (inf); (Zool) species sing.

Sippen-: ~älteste(r) mf head of the family; ~forschung f genealogy, genealogical research; ~haft (inf), ~haftung (Jur) f liability of all the members of a family for the crimes of one member; ~verband m kinship group.

Sippschaft f (pej inf) (Familie) tribe (inf); (Bande, Gesindel auch) bunch (inf).

Sire [siːr] interj (old liter) Sire (old).

Sirene f -, -n (*Myth, Tech, fig*) siren; (*Zool*) sirenian.
Sirenen-: ~**geheul** nt wail of a/the siren/sirens; ~**gesang** m siren song.
Sirius m - (*Astron*) Sirius.
sirren vi *siehe* **surren**.
Sirup m -s, -e syrup; (*schwarz, aus Zuckerrohr auch*) treacle.
Sisal(hanf) m -s sisal (hemp).
Sisalteppich m sisal mat.
sistieren* vt (*Jur*) *Verdächtigen* to detain; *Verfahren* to adjourn.
Sistierung f (*Jur*) *siehe* vt detention; adjournment.
Sisyphus|arbeit ['zi:zyfʊs-] f Sisyphean task (*liter*), never-ending task.
Sit-in [sɪt'|ɪn] nt -(s), -s sit-in. **ein** ~ **machen** to have or stage or hold a sit-in.
Sitte f -, -n **(a)** (*Brauch*) custom; (*Mode*) practice. ~ **sein** to be the custom/the practice; ~**n und Gebräuche** customs and traditions; **was sind denn das für** ~**n?** what's all this?; **hier reißen ja** ~**n ein!** (*inf*) the things people have started doing!
(b) usu pl (*gutes Benehmen*) manners pl; (*Sittlichkeit*) morals pl. **gegen die (guten)** ~**n verstoßen,** ~ **und Anstand verletzen** to offend common decency; **gute** ~**n** good manners pl; **was sind denn das für** ~**n?** what sort of a way is that to behave!
(c) (sl: **Sittenpolizei**) vice squad.
Sitten-: ~**apostel** m (*pej*) moralizer; ~**bild** nt (*Art*) genre picture; **ein** ~**bild aus dem alten Rußland** a picture or portrayal of the life and customs in the Russia of old; ~**dezernat** nt vice squad; ~**gemälde** nt *siehe* ~**bild**; ~**geschichte** f ~**geschichte Roms** history of Roman life and customs; ~**gesetz** nt moral law; ~**kodex** m moral code; ~**lehre** f ethics sing; ~**lehrer** m moralist; **s~los** adj immoral; ~**losigkeit** f immorality; ~**polizei** f vice squad; ~**prediger** m moralist, sermonizer; ~**richter** m judge of public morals; **s~streng** adj highly moral; ~**strenge** f strict morality; ~**strolch** m (*Press sl*) sex fiend; ~**verderbnis** f (*liter*), ~**verfall** m decline or drop in moral standards; ~**wächter** m (*iro*) guardian of public morals; **s~widrig** adj (*form*) immoral.
Sittich m -s, -e parakeet.
sittig adj (*obs*) *siehe* **sittsam.**
sittlich adj moral. **ihm fehlt der** ~**e Halt/die** ~**e Reife** he lacks moral fibre/he's morally immature; **er verlor jeden** ~**en Halt** he became morally unstable; **das S~e** morality.
Sittlichkeit f, no pl morality.
Sittlichkeits-: ~**delikt** nt sexual offence; ~**verbrechen** nt sex crime; ~**verbrecher** m sex offender.
sittsam adj demure.
Sittsamkeit f demureness.
Situation f situation; (*persönliche Lage auch*) position.
Situations-: ~**bericht** m report on the situation; ~**komik** f comicalness or comedy of the situation/situations; (*Art der Komik*) situation comedy, sitcom (*inf*).
situiert adj **gut/schlecht** ~ **sein** to be well/poorly situated financially; *siehe* **gutsituiert.**
Situierung f (*Aus*) situation.
Sitz m -es, -e **(a)** (~**platz, Parl**) seat. ~ **und Stimme haben** to have a seat and a vote.
(b) (*von Regierung, Graf, Universität, fig*) seat; (*Wohn~*) residence, domicile (*form*); (*von Firma, Verwaltung*) headquarters pl. **diese Stadt ist der** ~ **der Forstverwaltung** the forestry authority has its headquarters in this town.
(c) no pl (*Tech, von Kleidungsstück*) sit; (*von der Größe her*) fit. **einen guten/schlechten** ~ **haben** to sit/fit well/badly.
(d) no pl (*von Reiter*) seat.
(e) **auf einen** ~ (*inf*) in one go (*inf*).
Sitz-: ~**bad** nt sitz or hip bath; ~**badewanne** f sitz or hip bath; ~**bank** f bench.
sitzen vi *insep saß, ptp* **gesessen** *aux haben or* (*Aus, S Ger, Sw*) **sein (a)** to sit; (*auf Mauer, Stuhllehne etc auch, Vogel*) to perch. **bleiben Sie bitte** ~!, **bitte bleiben Sie** ~! please don't get up; ~ **Sie bequem?** are you comfortable?; **hier sitzt man sehr bequem** it's very comfortable sitting here; **auf der Toilette** ~ to be on (*inf*) or in the toilet; **etw im S~ tun** to do sth sitting down; **beim Frühstück/Mittagessen** ~ to be having breakfast/lunch; **beim Wein/Schach** ~ to sit over a glass of wine/a game of chess; **an einer Aufgabe/über den Büchern/einer Arbeit** ~ to sit over a task/one's books/a piece of work.
(b) (*Modell* ~) to sit (*jdm for sb*).
(c) (*seinen Sitz haben*) (*Regierung, Gericht etc*) to sit; (*Firma*) to have its headquarters.
(d) (*Mitglied sein*) (*im Parlament*) to have a seat (*in + dat* in); (*im Vorstand, Aufsichtsrat etc*) to be or sit (*in + dat* on).
(e) (*inf: im Gefängnis* ~) to be inside (*inf*). **gesessen haben** to have done time (*inf*), to have been inside (*inf*); **er mußte zwei Jahre** ~ he had to do two years (*inf*).
(f) (*sein*) to be. **er sitzt in Bulgarien/im Kultusministerium** (*inf*) he's in Bulgaria/the ministry of culture; **er sitzt in der Äußeren Mongolei (und kann nicht weg)** (*inf*) he's stuck in outer Mongolia (*inf*); **die Verfolger saßen uns auf den Fersen** our pursuers were hard on our heels.
(g) (*angebracht sein: Deckel, Schraube etc*) to sit. **der Deckel/die Schraube sitzt fest** the lid is on tightly/the screw is in tightly; **locker** ~ to be loose.
(h) (*stecken*) to be (stuck). **fest** ~ to be stuck tight(ly); **der Splitter saß fest in meinem Fuß** the splinter wouldn't come out of my foot.
(i) (*im Gedächtnis* ~) to have sunk in. **diese Vokabeln wollen nicht** ~ this vocabulary just won't sink in.
(j) (*seinen Herd haben*) (*Infektion, Schmerz*) to be; (*fig: Übel, Haß, Schmerz auch*) to lie.
(k) (*Kleid, Frisur*) to sit. **deine Krawatte sitzt nicht richtig**

your tie isn't straight; **sein Hut saß schief** his hat was (on) crooked.
(l) (*inf: treffen*) to hit home. **das saß** or **hat gesessen!** that hit home.
(m) **einen** ~ **haben** (*inf*) to have had one too many.
sitzenbleiben vi *sep irreg aux sein* (*inf*) **(a)** (*Sch*) to stay down (a year), to have to repeat a year. **(b)** **auf einer Ware** ~ to be left with a product. **(c)** (*Mädchen*) (*beim Tanz*) to be left sitting; (*nicht heiraten*) to be left on the shelf (*inf*).
Sitzenbleiber(in f) m -s, - (*inf*) pupil who has to repeat a year.
sitzend adj attr *Lebensweise etc* sedentary.
sitzenlassen vt *sep irreg ptp* ~ or **sitzengelassen** (*inf*) **(a)** (*Sch: nicht versetzen*) to keep down (a year).
(b) (*hinnehmen*) **eine Beleidigung etc auf sich** (*dat*) ~ to stand for or take an insult etc.
(c) **jdn** ~ (*im Stich lassen*) to leave sb in the lurch; (*warten lassen*) to leave sb waiting; *Freund(in)* (*durch Nichterscheinen*) to stand sb up.
(d) (*nicht heiraten*) to jilt, to walk out on.
-sitzer m -s, - *in cpds* -seater.
Sitzerei f (*inf*) sitting about.
Sitz-: ~**fleisch** nt (*inf*) ability to sit still; ~**fleisch haben** to be able to sit still; (*hum: Besucher*) to stay a long time; **er hat kein** ~**fleisch** (*läßt schnell nach*) he can't stick at anything; (*ist nervös*) he can't sit still; ~**gelegenheit** f seats pl, seating (accommodation); **eine** ~**gelegenheit suchen** to look for somewhere to sit or for a seat; ~**kissen** nt (floor) cushion; ~**ordnung** f seating plan; ~**platz** m seat; ~**reihe** f row of seats; ~**riese** m (*hum*) short person with a long body who looks tall when sitting down; ~**streik** m *siehe* **Sit-in.**
Sitzung f **(a)** (*Konferenz*) meeting; (*Jur: Gerichtsverhandlung*) session; (*Parlaments*~) sitting. **(b)** (*Einzel*~) (*bei Künstler*) sitting; (*bei Zahnarzt*) visit; (*sl: Toilettenbesuch*) session. **spiritistische** ~ séance.
Sitzungs-: ~**bericht** m minutes pl; ~**geld** nt (*Parl*) attendance allowance; ~**periode** f (*Parl*) session; (*Jur*) term; ~**saal** m conference hall; (*Jur*) courtroom; ~**zimmer** nt conference room.
sixtinisch adj Sistine.
Sizilianer(in f) m -s, - Sicilian.
sizilianisch adj Sicilian.
Sizilien [zi'tsi:liən] nt -s Sicily.
Skai ® nt -(s), no pl imitation leather.
Skala f -, **Skalen** or -s (*Gradeinteilung, Mus*) scale; (*Reihe gleichartiger Dinge*) range; (*fig*) gamut, range.
Skalde m -n, -n skald.
Skaldendichtung f skaldic poetry.
Skalp m -s, -e scalp.
Skalpell nt -s, -e scalpel.
skalpieren* vt to scalp.
Skandal m -s, -e scandal; (*inf: Krach*) to-do (*inf*), fuss. **einen** ~ **machen** to create or cause a scandal; **to make a to-do** (*inf*) or fuss; **das ist ein** ~! it's scandalous or a scandal.
Skandal-: ~**blatt** nt (*pej*) scandal sheet; ~**geschichte** f (bit or piece of) scandal; ~**nudel** f (*hum*) **sie ist eine richtige** ~**nudel** she's always involved in some scandal or other; **Lola, diese** ~**nudel** the scandalous Lola.
skandalös adj scandalous.
Skandal-: ~**presse** f (*pej*) gutter press; ~**prozeß** m sensational trial or case; **s~süchtig** adj (*pej*) *Publikum, Leser* fond of scandal; *Klatschtante, Presse etc auch* scandalmongering attr; **s~umwittert** adj (*Press sl*) surrounded by scandal.
skandieren* vti to scan.
Skandinavien [skandi'na:viən] nt -s Scandinavia.
Skandinavier(in f) [skandi'na:viɐ, -iərɪn] m -s, - Scandinavian.
skandinavisch adj Scandinavian.
Skarabäus [skara'bɛːʊs] m -, **Skarabäen** [-'bɛːən] scarab.
Skat m -(e)s, -e (*Cards*) skat. ~ **spielen** or **dreschen** (*inf*) or **kloppen** (*sl*) to play skat.
Skatbrüder pl (*inf*) fellow skat players pl.
skaten vi (*inf*) to play skat.
Skater(in f) m -s, - (*inf*) skat player.
skatologisch adj (*geh*) scatological.
Skatspieler m skat player.
Skeleton ['skɛlətn, -letən] m -s, -s (*Sport*) skeleton.
Skelett nt -(e)s, -e (*lit, fig*) skeleton. **er war bis aufs** ~ **abgemagert, er war nur noch ein** ~ he was like a skeleton.
Skepsis f -, no pl scepticism. **mit/voller** ~ sceptically.
Skeptiker(in f) m -s, - sceptic.
skeptisch adj sceptical.
Skeptizismus m (*esp Philos*) scepticism.
skeptizistisch adj (*esp Philos*) sceptic(al).
Sketch [skɛtʃ] m -es, -(e)s (*Art, Theat*) sketch.
Ski [ʃiː] m -s, - or -er ['ʃiːɐ] -s, - laufen or fahren to ski.
Ski- in cpds ski; ~**ausrüstung** f skiing gear; **eine komplette** ~**ausrüstung** a complete set of skiing gear; ~**bob** m skibob.
Skier ['ʃiːɐ] pl of **Ski.**
Skifahrer m skier.
Skiff nt -(e)s, -e skiff.
Ski- ['ʃiː-]: ~**fliegen** nt, ~**flug** m ski flying; ~**gebiet** nt ski(ing) area; ~**gelände** nt ski(ing) area; ~**hase** m, ~**haserl** nt -s, -n (*hum inf*) girl skier; ~**hose** f (pair of) ski pants pl; ~**hütte** f ski hut or lodge (*US*); ~**kjöring** [-jøːrɪŋ] nt -s, -s skijoring; ~**kurs** m skiing course; ~**lauf** m skiing; ~**läufer** m skier; ~**lehrer** m ski instructor; ~**lift** m ski-lift; ~**piste** f ski-run; ~**sport** m skiing; ~**springen** nt ski jumping; ~**springer** m ski-jumper; ~**stock** m ski stick.
Skizze ['skɪtsə] f -, -n sketch; (*fig: Grundriß*) outline, plan.
Skizzen- ['skɪtsn-]: ~**buch** nt sketchbook; **s~haft** 1 adj *Zeich-*

nung etc roughly sketched; *Beschreibung etc* (given) in broad outline; 2 *auf etw* s~**haft zeichnen/beschreiben** to sketch sth roughly/describe sth in broad outline.

skizzieren* [skı'tsi:rən] *vt* to sketch; *(fig) Plan etc* to outline.

Skizzierung [skı'tsi:rʊŋ] *f* sketching; *(fig: von Plan etc)* outlining.

Sklave ['skla:və, 'skla:fə] *m* -n, -n slave. ~ **einer Sache** *(gen)* **sein** *(fig)* to be a slave to sth; **jdn zum** ~**n machen** to make a slave of sb; *(fig)* to enslave sb, to make sb sb's slave.

Sklaven- ['skla:vn-, 'skla:fn-]: ~**arbeit** *f* slavery; *(Arbeit von Sklaven)* work of slaves; ~**dienst** *m* slavery; ~**galeere** *f* slave galley; ~**halter** *m* slave-holder; ~**haltergesellschaft** *f* slave-owning society; ~**handel** *m* slave trade; ~**handel betreiben** to deal in slaves; ~**händler** *m* slave-trader, slaver; ~**markt** *m* slave market; ~**treiber** *m* *(lit, fig)* slave-driver.

Sklaventum ['skla:vntu:m, -a:fn-] *nt (rare) (lit, fig)* slavery *no art.*

Sklaverei [skla:və'rai, -a:fə'rai] *f no pl (lit, fig)* slavery *no art.* **jdn in die** ~ **führen** to take sb into slavery.

Sklavin ['skla:vın, 'skla:fın] *f (lit, fig)* slave.

sklavisch ['skla:vıʃ, skla:fıʃ] *adj* slavish.

Sklerose *f* -, -n sclerosis.

skontieren* *vt* **jdm etw** ~ to give sb a cash discount on sth.

Skonto *nt or m* -s, -s *or* **Skonti** cash discount. **bei Barzahlung 3%** ~ 3% discount for cash; **jdm** ~ **geben** *or* **gewähren** *(form)* to give *or* allow sb a cash discount *or* a discount for cash.

Skooter ['sku:tɐ] *m* -s, - siehe **Autoskooter.**

Skorbut *m* -(e)s, *no pl* scurvy.

Skorpion *m* -s, -e *(Zool)* scorpion; *(Astrol)* Scorpio.

Skribent *m (dated pej)* hack, scribbler.

Skript *nt* -(e)s, -en (a) *pl usu* -s *(Film)* (film) script. (b) *(Univ)* (set of) lecture notes *pl.* **ein** ~ **anfertigen** to take lecture notes.

Skriptgirl ['skrıptgø:ɐl, -gœrl] *nt* script girl.

Skriptum *nt* -s, **Skripten** *or* **Skripta** *(Univ, esp Aus)* siehe **Skript (b).**

Skrotum *nt* -s, **Skrota** *(Med)* scrotum.

Skrupel *m* -s, - *usu pl* scruple. **keine** ~ **haben** *or* **kennen** to have no scruples; **er hatte keine** ~, **das zu tun** he didn't scruple to do it; **sich** *(dat)* **über etw** *(acc)* ~ **machen** to have scruples about sth; **ohne (jeden)** ~ without (the slightest) scruple.

Skrupel-: s~**los** *adj* unscrupulous; ~**losigkeit** *f* unscrupulousness.

skrupulös *adj (geh)* scrupulous.

Skullboot ['skʊlbo:t] *nt* sculler.

skullen ['skʊlən] *vi (Sport)* to scull.

Skulptur *f* sculpture.

Skunk *m* -s, -s *or* -e skunk.

skurril *adj (geh)* droll, comical.

Skurrilität *f (geh)* drollery.

S-Kurve ['es-] *f* S-bend.

Skyeterrier ['skaiterıɐ] *m* Skye terrier.

Slalom *m* -s, -s slalom. **(im)** ~ **fahren** *(fig inf)* to drive a crazy zig-zag course.

Slang [slɛŋ] *m* -s, *no pl* slang.

Slapstick ['slɛp-stık] *m* -s, -s slapstick.

S-Laut ['es-] *m (stimmlos)* 's'-sound; *(stimmhaft)* 'z'-sound.

Slawe *m* -n, -n Slav.

Slawentum *nt* Slavdom.

Slawin *f* Slav (woman/girl).

slawisch *adj* Slavonic, Slavic.

Slawismus *m* Slavonicism, Slavism.

Slawist(in *f)* *m* Slavonicist, Slavist.

Slawistik *f* Slavonic studies *sing.*

Slibowitz *m* -(e)s, -e slivovitz.

Slip *m* -s, -s (pair of) briefs *pl;* *(Damen*~ *auch)* (pair of) panties *pl.*

Slipper *m* -s, - slip-on shoe.

Slogan ['slo:gn] *m* -s, -s slogan.

Slowake *m* -n, -n Slovak.

Slowakei *f* - **die** ~ Slovakia.

Slowakin *f* Slovak (woman/girl).

slowakisch *adj* Slovakian, Slovak.

Slowene *m* -n, -n Slovene.

Slowenien [slo've:niən] *nt* -s Slovenia.

slowenisch *adj* Slovenian.

Slowfox ['slo:fɔks] *m* -(es), -e slow foxtrot.

Slum [slam] *m* -s, -s slum.

S.M. *abbr of* **Seine(r) Majestät** HM.

sm *abbr of* **Seemeile.**

Smalltalk ['smɔ:ltɔ:k] *m* -(s), *no pl* small talk.

Smaragd *m* -(e)s, -e emerald.

smaragden *adj (liter)* emerald(-green).

smaragdgrün *adj* emerald-green.

smart [sma:ɐt, smart] *adj (inf)* smart.

Smog *m* -(s), -s smog.

Smok|arbeit *f (Sew)* smocking.

smoken *vti (Sew)* to smock.

Smoking ['smo:kıŋ] *m* -s, -s dinner-jacket, dj *(inf)*, tuxedo *(US)*, tux *(US inf)*.

Smutje *m* -s, -s *(Naut)* ship's cook.

Smyrnateppich *m* Smyrna (carpet).

Snack [snɛk] *m* -s, -s snack (meal).

Snackbar ['snɛkba:ɐ] *f* snack bar.

Snob *m* -s, -s snob.

Snobiety [sno'baiəti] *f* -, *no pl (hum)* **die** ~ snob society.

Snobismus *m* snobbery, snobbishness.

snobistisch *adj* snobbish.

SO *abbr of* **Südosten** SE.

s.o. *abbr of* **siehe oben.**

so 1 *adv* (a) *(mit adj, adv)* so; *(mit vb:* ~ **sehr)** so much, ~ **groß**

etc so big *etc;* **eine** ~ **große Frau** such a big woman; **es ist gar nicht** ~ **einfach** it's really not so easy; ~ **groß** *etc* **wie ... as big** *etc* **as ...;** ~ **groß** *etc,* **daß ...** so big *etc* that ...; **sie hat ihn** ~ **geschlagen, daß ...** she hit him so hard that ...; **er ist** ~ **gelaufen** he ran so fast; **ich habe** ~ **gearbeitet** I worked so hard; ~ **gut es geht** as best *or* well as I/he *etc* can; **er ist nicht** ~ **dumm, das zu glauben** he's not so stupid as to believe that, he's not stupid enough to believe that; **sie hat sich** ~ **gefreut** she was so *or* really pleased; **das hat ihn** ~ **geärgert, daß ...** that annoyed him so much that ...; **ich wußte nicht, daß es ihn** ~ **ärgern würde** I didn't know that it would annoy him so *or* that much; **ich freue mich** ~ **sehr, daß du kommst** I'm so pleased you're coming.

(b) *(auf diese Weise, von dieser Art)* like this/that, this/that way, thus *(form)*. **mach es nicht** ~ don't do it like that *or* that way; **du sollst es** ~ **machen, ...** you should do this *or* this way; **mach es** ~, **wie er es vorgeschlagen hat** do it the way *or* as *or* like *(inf)* he suggested; **ist es dort tatsächlich** ~? is it really like that there?; **ist das tatsächlich** ~? is that really so?; ~ **ist sie nun einmal** that's the way she is, that's what she's like; **sei doch nicht** ~ don't be like that; ~ **ist es nicht gewesen** it wasn't like that, that's not how it was; **es ist vielleicht besser** ~ perhaps it's better like that *or* that way; ~ **ist das!** that's the way things are, that's how it is; *(ach)* ~ **ist das!** I see!; **ist das** ~? is that so?; ~ **oder/und** ~ either way; **und** ~ **weiter (und** ~ **fort)** and so on (and so forth); **gut** ~! fine!, good!; **das ist gut** ~ that's fine; **das ist auch gut** ~! (and) a good thing too!; **mir ist (es)** ~, **als ob ...** it seems to me as if ...; ~ **geht es, wenn ...** that's what happens if ...; **... und** ~ **ist es also geschehen** ... and so that is what happened; **das kam** ~: ... this is what happened ..., it happened like this ...; **es verhält sich** ~: ... the facts are thus *(form) or* as follows ...; **das habe ich nur** ~ **gesagt** I didn't really mean it.

(c) *(etwa)* about, *or* so. **ich komme** ~ **um 8 Uhr** I'll come at about 8, I'll come at 8 *or* so *or* or thereabouts; **sie heißt doch Malitzki oder** ~ she's called Malitzki or something.

(d) *(inf: umsonst)* for nothing.

(e) *(als Füllwort)* nicht *übersetzt.* ~ **dann und wann** now and then; ~ **bist du also gar nicht dort gewesen?** *(geh)* so you weren't there after all?; ~ **beeil dich doch!** do hurry up!; ~ **mancher** a number of people *pl,* quite a few people *pl.*

(f) *(solch)* ~ **ein Gebäude/Fehler** a building/mistake like that, such a building/mistake; ~ **ein guter Lehrer/schlechtes Bild** *etc* such a good teacher/bad picture *etc;* ~ **ein Idiot!** what an idiot!; **hast du** ~ **etwas schon einmal gesehen?** have you ever seen anything like it?; ~ **(et)was ist noch nie vorgekommen** nothing like that has ever happened; **sie ist doch Lehrerin, oder** ~ **was** she's a teacher or something like that; **na** ~ **was!** well I never!, no!; ~ **etwas Schönes** something as beautiful as that, such a beautiful thing; ~ **einer wie ich/er** somebody like *or* a person such as myself *or* me/him; **er ist** ~ **einer wie ich** he's like me; *siehe* um 3b.

2 *conj* (a) ~ **daß** so that.

(b) ~ **wie es jetzt ist** as *or* the way things are at the moment.

(c) ~ **klein er auch sein mag** however small he may be; ~ **wahr ich lebe** as true as I'm standing here.

(d) **kaum hatte er ...,** ~ **...** scarcely had he ... when ...; **wenn du ...,** ~ **mußt du ...** if you ..., you have to ...

(e) *(old: falls)* if, provided that. ~ **der Herrgott will, sehen wir uns wieder** God willing, we shall see one another again.

3 *interj* so; *(wirklich)* oh, really; *(abschließend)* well, right. **er ist schon da** — ~ **he's here already** — is he? *or* oh *or* really; **ich kann nicht mitkommen** — ~ I can't come with you — can't you? *or* oh!; ~ **oder** ~, **es wäre es für heute weil** *or* **right** *or* so, that's it for today; ~, **jetzt habe ich die Nase voll** I've had enough; ~, ~! well well; *siehe* ach.

sobald *conj* as soon as.

Söckchen *nt dim of* **Socke.**

Socke *f* -, -n sock. **sich auf die** ~**n machen** *(inf)* to get going *(inf)*; **von den** ~**n sein** *(inf)* to be flabbergasted *(inf)*, to be knocked for six *(inf)*.

Sockel *m* -s, - base; *(von Denkmal, Statue)* plinth, pedestal, socle *(spec)*; *(Elec)* socket; *(für Birne)* holder.

Sockel-: ~**betrag** *m* basic sum; ~**rente** *f* basic pension.

Socken *m* -s, - *(S Ger, Aus)* sock.

Sockenhalter *m (sock)* suspender *(Brit)*, garter.

Soda *f* -, *no pl, nt* -s, *no pl* soda.

sodann *adv (old)* thereupon *(old, form)*, then.

sodaß *conj (Aus)* = **so daß.**

Sodawasser *nt* soda water.

Sodbrennen *nt* heartburn.

Sode *f* -, -n (a) *(Rasenstück, Torfscholle)* turf, sod. (b) *(old: Salzsiederei)* saltworks *sing or pl.*

Sodom ['zo:dɔm] *nt* -s Sodom. ~ **und Gomorrha** *(lit, fig)* Sodom and Gomorrah.

Sodomie *f* buggery, bestiality.

sodomitisch *adj* bestial.

so|eben *adv* just (this moment). ~ **hören wir** *or* **haben wir gehört ... we have just** (this moment) **heard ...;** ~ **erschienen** just out *or* published.

Sofa *nt* -s, -s sofa, settee *(esp Brit)*.

Sofa-: ~**ecke** *f* corner of the/a sofa; ~**kissen** *nt* sofa cushion.

sofern *conj* provided (that). ~ **... nicht** if ... not.

soff *pret of* **saufen.**

Sofia ['zɔfia, 'zo:fia] *nt* -s *(Geog)* Sofia.

Sofioter(in *f)* *m* -s, - Sofian.

sofort *adv* immediately, straight *or* right away, at once. ~ **nach ...** immediately after ...; **komm hierher, aber** *or* **und zwar** ~! come here this instant *or* at once!; **(ich) komme** ~! (I'm) just coming!; *(Kellner etc)* I'll be right with you.

Soforthilfe *f* emergency relief *or* aid.

sofortig *adj* immediate, instant.

Sofortmaßnahme *f* immediate measure.
Softleis, Soft-Eis ['sɔft-] *nt* soft ice-cream.
Software ['sɔftwɛːɐ] *f* -, -s (*Tech*) software.
sog *pret of* **saugen.**
sog. *abbr of* **sogenannt.**
Sog *m* -(e)s, -e (*saugende Kraft*) suction; (*bei Schiff*) wake; (*bei Flugzeug, Fahrzeug*) slipstream; (*von Strudel*) vortex; (*von Brandungswelle*) undertow; (*fig*) maelstrom.
sogar *adv* even. er kam ~ he even came; **jedes Getränk, ja ~ schon ein kleines Bier, kostet sehr viel** every drink, even a small glass of beer *or* a small glass of beer, even, costs a lot; **schön, ~ sehr schön** beautiful, in fact very beautiful; **ich kann sie gut leiden, ich finde sie ~ sehr nett** I like her, in fact I think she's very nice; **ich habe sie nicht nur gesehen, sondern ~ geküßt** I didn't just see her, I actually kissed her (as well).
sogenannt *adj attr* as it/he *etc* is called; (*angeblich*) so-called.
sogleich *adv siehe* **sofort.**
Sohle *f* -, -n (a) (*Fuß~ etc*) sole; (*Einlage*) insole. **auf leisen ~n** (*poet*) softly, noiselessly; **mit nackten ~n** barefoot; **es brennt ihm unter den ~n** he has itchy feet (*inf*), his feet are itching (*inf*); **eine kesse ~ aufs Parkett legen** to put up a good show on the dance floor; *siehe* **heften, Scheitel.**
  (b) (*Boden*) bottom; (*Tal~ auch*) floor; (*Fluß~ auch*) bed.
  (c) (*Min*) (*Grubenboden*) floor; (*Stollen*) level.
sohlen *vt* to sole.
Sohl(en)leder *nt* sole leather.
Sohn *m* -(e)s, ~e (*lit, fig*) son. **Gottes ~, der ~ Gottes** (*Bibl*) the Son of God; **des Menschen ~** (*Bibl*) the Son of Man; **na, mein ~** well, son *or* sonny; *siehe* **verloren.**
Söhnchen *nt dim of* **Sohn.**
Söhnemann *m* (*dial inf*) son, sonny.
Söhnesliebe *f* filial devotion *or* love.
Söhnlein *nt dim of* **Sohn.**
soigniert [soan'jiːɐt] *adj* (*geh*) elegant; (*bei Frauen auch*) soignée; (*bei Männern auch*) soigné.
Soiree [soa're:] *f* -, -n [-ɛːɔn] soirée.
Soja *f* -, **Sojen** soya, soy.
Soja-: ~**bohne** *f* soya bean, soybean; ~**bohnenkeime** *pl* bean sprouts *pl*; ~**soße** *f* soya sauce.
Sokrates ['zo:krates] *m* - Socrates.
Sokratiker *m* -s, - Socratic.
sokratisch *adj* Socratic.
solang(e) *conj* as *or* so long as.
Solar- *in cpds* solar; ~**plexus** *m* -, - (*Anat*) solar plexus.
Solbad *nt* (*Bad*) salt-water *or* brine bath; (*Badeort*) salt-water spa.
solch *adj inv*, **solche(r, s)** *adj* such. **ein ~er Mensch, ~ ein Mensch** such a person, a person like that/this; ~**e Menschen** people like that, such people; ~**es Wetter/Glück** such weather/luck; **wir haben ~en Durst**/~**e Angst** we're so thirsty/afraid; ~ **langer** *or* **ein ~er langer Weg** such a long way; **der Mensch als** ~**er** man as such; ~**es** that kind of thing; ~**e** (*Leute*) such people; **Experten und** ~**e, die es werden wollen** experts and people who would like to be experts; **Rechtsanwälte gibt es** ~**e und** ~**e** there are lawyers and lawyers; **wie sind die Schularbeiten?** — **es gibt** ~**e und** ~**e** what is the homework like? — mixed; **ich hätte gern** ~**e und** ~**e** (*Bonbons*) I'd like some of those (sweets) and some of those.
solcher-: ~**art**, ~**lei** *adj attr inv* (*geh*) such; ~**gestalt** *adv* (*geh*) *siehe* **dergestalt;** ~**maßen** *adv* (*old*) to such an extent, so; ~**maßen erbost, verließ er den Saal** he was so infuriated (that) he left the hall.
Sold *m* -(e)s, *no pl* (*Mil*) pay. **in jds** ~ (*dat*) **stehen** (*old*) to be in sb's employ; (*pej*) to be in sb's pay.
Soldat *m* -en, -en soldier; (*old Chess*) pawn. **bei den** ~**en sein** (*dated*) to be in the army, to be a soldier; **zu den** ~**en kommen** (*dated*), ~ **werden** to join the army, to join up (*inf*), to become a soldier; ~ **spielen** to play soldiers; *siehe* **Grabmal.**
Soldaten-: ~**friedhof** *m* military cemetery; ~**gesetz** *nt* military regulations *pl, no art*; ~**lied** *nt* army *or* soldier's song; ~**rat** *m* soldiers' council; (*Sowjet*) soldiers' soviet; ~**rock** *m* (*old*) military *or* soldier's uniform; ~**sprache** *f* military *or* soldier's slang; ~**stiefel** *m* army *or* soldier's boot; ~**tum** *nt* soldiership *no art*, soldiery *no art*; (*Tradition*) military tradition; ~**verband** *m* ex-servicemen's *or* veterans' (*esp US*) association.
Soldateska *f* -, **Soldatesken** (*pej*) band of soldiers.
soldatisch *adj* (*militärisch*) military; (*soldatengemäß*) soldierly.
Soldbuch *nt* (*Hist*) military passbook.
Söldling *m* (*old pej*) hireling (*old*).
Söldner *m* -s, - mercenary.
Söldner-: ~**heer** *nt* army of mercenaries, mercenary army; ~**truppe** *f* mercenary force.
Sole *f* -, -n brine, salt water.
Solei ['zo:lai] *nt* pickled egg.
Soli *pl of* **Solo.**
solid *adj siehe* **solid(e).**
solidarisch *adj* sich **mit jdm** ~ **erklären** to declare one's solidarity with sb; **eine** ~**e Haltung zeigen** to show (one's) solidarity; **in** ~**er Übereinstimmung** in complete solidarity; **sich mit jdm** ~ **fühlen** to feel solidarity with sb; ~ **mit jdm handeln** to act in solidarity with sb.
solidarisieren* *vr* **sich** ~ **mit** to show (one's) solidarity with.
Solidarität *f* solidarity.
Solidaritäts-: ~**adresse** *f* message of solidarity; ~**gefühl** *nt* feeling of solidarity; ~**streik** *m* sympathy strike.
solid(e) *adj Haus, Möbel etc* solid, sturdy; *Arbeit, Wissen, Mechaniker* sound; *Mensch, Leben, Lokal* respectable; *Firma* solid; *Preise* reasonable.

Solidität *f siehe adj* solidness, sturdiness; soundness; respectability; solidness; reasonableness.
Solipsismus *m* (*Philos*) solipsism.
Solist(in *f*) *m* (*Mus*) soloist.
solistisch *adj, adv* solo.
Solitär *m* solitaire; (*Diamant*) diamond solitaire, solitaire diamond.
Soll *nt* -(s), -(s) (a) (*Schuld*) debit; (*Schuldseite*) debit side. ~ **und Haben** debit and credit. (b) (*Comm: Planaufgabe*) target.
sollen 1 *modal aux vb pret* **sollte,** *ptp* ~ (a) (*bei Befehl, Anordnung, Verpflichtung, Plan*) to be to. **was soll ich/er tun?** what shall *or* should I/should he do?, **what am I/is he to do?;** (*was sind meine etc Aufgaben auch*) what am I/is he meant to do?; **kannst du mir helfen?** — **klar, was soll ich tun?** can you help me? — of course, what shall I do?; **soll ich Ihnen helfen?** shall *or* can I help you?; **soll ich dir mal sagen, wie ...?** shall I tell you how ...?; **du weißt, daß du das nicht tun sollst** you know that you shouldn't do that *or* aren't to do that; (*das ist nicht deine Aufgabe auch*) you know that you're not meant to do that; **er weiß nicht, was er tun soll** he doesn't know what to do *or* what he should do; (*kennt seine Aufgaben nicht auch*) he doesn't know what he's meant to do; **sie sagte ihm, er solle draußen warten** she told him (that he was) to wait *or* that he should wait outside; **er wurde wütend, weil er draußen warten sollte** he was livid that he was told to wait outside; **sie sagte mir, was ich tun sollte/alles tun soll** she told me what to do *or* what I should do/everthing I should do *or* am meant to do; **was ich (nicht) alles tun/wissen soll!** the things I'm meant *or* supposed to do/know!; **es soll nicht wieder vorkommen** it shan't *or* won't happen again; **er soll reinkommen** let him come in, tell him to come in; **der soll nur kommen!** just let him come!; **und da soll man nicht böse werden/nicht lachen!** and then they expect you/me *etc* not to get cross/not to laugh; **niemand soll sagen, daß ... let no-one say that ...,** no-one shall say that ...; **ich soll Ihnen sagen, daß ...** I am to tell you *or* I've been asked to tell you that ...; **ich soll dir schöne Grüße von Renate bestellen** Renate asked me to give you her best wishes; **du sollst nicht töten** (*Bibl*) thou shalt not kill; **so soll es sein** that's how it should be; **das Haus soll nächste Woche gestrichen werden** the house is (meant) to be painted next week; **das Gebäude soll ein Museum werden** the building is (meant) to become a museum.
  (b) (*konjunktivisch*) **was sollte ich/er deiner Meinung nach tun?** what do you think I/he should do *or* ought to do?; **so etwas sollte man nicht tun** one shouldn't do *or* oughtn't to do that; **das hättest du nicht tun** ~ you shouldn't have *or* oughtn't to have done that; **das hättest du sehen** ~**!** you should have seen it!; **du solltest lieber etwas früher kommen/zu Hause bleiben** it would be better if you came early/stayed at home.
  (c) (*bei Vermutung, Erwartung*) to be supposed *or* meant to. **er soll heute kommen** he should come today, he is supposed *or* meant to come today; **sie soll krank/verheiratet sein** I've heard she's ill/married, she's supposed to be ill/married; **Xanthippe soll zänkisch gewesen sein** Xanthippe is supposed *or* said to have been quarrelsome; **das soll gar nicht so einfach sein** they say it's not that easy; **was soll das heißen?** what's that supposed *or* meant to mean?; **wer soll das sein?** who is that supposed *or* meant to be?
  (d) (*können, mögen*) **gut, Sie** ~ **recht haben!** all right, have it your own way (*inf*) *or* whatever you say; **mir soll es gleich sein** it's all the same to me; **so etwas soll es geben** these things happen; **man sollte glauben, daß ...** you would think that ...; **sollte das möglich sein?** is that possible?, can that be possible?
  (e) (*konditional*) **sollte das passieren, ...** if that should happen ..., should that happen ...; **ich soll unrecht haben, tut es mir leid** I'm sorry if I should be wrong, I'm sorry should I be wrong.
  (f) *subjunc* (*geh: jdm beschieden sein*) **er sollte sie nie wiedersehen** he was never to see her again; **Jahre sollten vergehen, bevor ...** years were to pass before ...; **es sollte nicht lange dauern, bis ...** it was not to be long until ...
  2 *vi pret* **sollte,** *ptp* **gesollt** (a) **soll ich?** should I?; **ja, du sollst** yes, you should; **er hätte** ~ he should have.
  (b) **was soll das?** what's all this?; (*warum denn das*) what's that for?; **was soll's?** what the hell (*inf*) *or* heck (*inf*)?; **was soll der Quatsch/Mist** *etc*? (*inf*) what do you think you're playing at? (*inf*); **was soll ich dort?** what would I do there?
  3 *vt pret* **sollte,** *ptp* **gesollt das sollst/solltest du nicht** you shouldn't do that; **das hast du nicht gesollt** you shouldn't have done that; **was man nicht alles soll** *or* **sollte!** (*inf*) the things you're meant to do!
Söller *m* -s, - balcony.
Soll-: ~**seite** *f* (*Fin*) debit-side; ~**stärke** *f* required *or* authorized strength; ~**zinsen** *pl* (*Fin*) interest owing *sing*.
solo *adv* (*Mus*) solo; (*fig inf*) on one's own, alone.
Solo *nt* -s, **Soli** (*alle Bedeutungen*) solo.
Solo- *in cpds* solo; ~**gesang** *m* solo.
solvent [zɔl'vent] *adj* (*Fin*) solvent.
Solvenz [zɔlvɛnts] *f* (*Fin*) solvency.
Somali *m* -(s), -(s) Somali.
Somalia *nt* -s Somalia.
Somalier(in *f*) [-iɐ, -iərɪn] *m* -s, - Somali.
Somalihalblinsel *f*, **Somaliland** *nt* Somaliland.
somalisch *adj* Somali.
somatisch *adj* (*Med*) somatic.
Sombrero *m* -s, -s sombrero.
somit *adv* consequently, therefore.
Sommer *m* -s, - summer. **im** ~, **des** ~**s** (*geh*) in (the) summer; **im nächsten** ~ next summer; **im** ~ **des Jahres 1951** in the summer of 1951; ~ **wie** *or* **und Winter** all year round.
Sommer- *in cpds* summer; ~**abend** *m* summer('s) evening;

~anfang m beginning of summer; ~ferien pl summer holidays pl (Brit) or vacation (esp US); (Jur, Parl) summer recess; in die ~ferien fahren to go away for the or one's summer holidays (Brit) or vacation (US); in die ~ferien gehen to begin one's summer holidays (Brit) or vacation (US); (Sch auch) to break up for the summer (holidays) (Brit); (Univ) to go down for the summer; (Jur, Parl) to go into the summer recess; ~frische f -, -n (dated) (a) no pl (~urlaub) summer holiday or vacation (US) or break; in die ~frische gehen to go away for a summer holiday etc; (b) (Ort) summer resort; ~frischler(in f) m -s, - (dated) summer holidaymaker or vacationist (US); ~gast m summer guest; ~gerste f spring barley; ~getreide nt spring cereal; ~halbjahr nt summer semester, ≈ summer term (Brit); ~haus nt holiday home; ~kleidung f summer clothing; (esp Comm) summerwear.

sommerlich adj (sommerartig, heiter) summery; (Sommer-) summer attr.

Sommer-: ~mantel m summer coat; ~monat m summer month; ~nacht f summer('s) night; ~olympiade f Summer Olympics pl; ~pause f summer break; (Jur, Parl) summer recess; ~regen m summer rain; ~reifen m normal tyre.

sommers adv (geh) in summer. ~ wie winters all year round.

Sommer-: ~saison f summer season; ~schlußverkauf m summer sale; ~semester nt (Univ) summer semester, ≈ summer term (Brit); ~sitz m summer residence; ~spiele pl Summer Games pl; die Olympischen ~spiele the Summer Olympics or Olympic Games; ~sprosse f freckle; s~sprossig adj freckled.

sommersüber adv during summer.

Sommer-: ~tag m summer's day; ~theater nt open-air theatre; ~weizen m spring wheat; ~wetter nt summer weather; ~wohnung f holiday flat (Brit) or apartment; ~zeit f summer time no art; (geh: Sommer) summertime, summertide (liter); zur ~zeit (geh) in summertime.

somnambul adj (spec) somnambulary.

Somnambule(r) mf decl as adj (spec) somnambulist.

Somnambulismus m (spec) somnambulism.

sonach adv (old) siehe somit.

Sonate f -, -n sonata.

Sonatine f sonatine.

Sonde f -, -n (Space, Med: zur Untersuchung) probe; (Med: zur Ernährung) tube; (Met) sonde.

sonder prep +acc (obs) without. ~ allen Zweifel without any doubt.

Sonder- in cpds special; ~abdruck m (Typ) offprint; ~anfertigung f special model; eine ~anfertigung sein to have been made specially; ~angebot nt special offer; ~ausbildung f specialist or special training; ~ausführung f special model or version; (Auto auch) custom-built model; ~ausgabe f (a) special edition; (b) ~ausgaben pl (Fin) additional or extra expenses pl.

sonderbar adj strange, peculiar, odd.

sonderbarerweise adv strangely enough, strange to say.

Sonderbarkeit f siehe adj strangeness, peculiarity, oddness; curiousness.

Sonder-: ~beauftragte(r) mf (Pol) special emissary; ~berichterstatter m (Press) special correspondent; ~botschafter m ambassador extraordinary; ~druck m siehe ~abdruck; ~einsatz m special action; ~fahrt f special excursion or trip; „~fahrt" (auf Schild) "special"; ~fall m special case; (Ausnahme) exception; ~frieden m separate peace; ~genehmigung f special permission; (Schein) special permit; ~gericht nt special court; s~gleichen adj inv eine Frechheit/Geschmacklosigkeit s~gleichen the height of cheek/bad taste; mit einer Frechheit s~gleichen with unparalleled cheek; ~klasse f special class; (von Obst etc) top grade; ~kommando nt special unit; ~konto nt special account.

sonderlich 1 adj attr particular, especial, special. ohne ~e Begeisterung without any particular enthusiasm, without much enthusiasm. **2** adv particularly, especially.

Sonderling m eccentric.

Sonder-: ~marke f special issue (stamp); ~maschine f special plane or aircraft; ~meldung f (Rad, TV) special announcement.

sondern¹ conj but. ~? where/who/what etc then?; wir fahren nicht nach Spanien, ~ nach Frankreich we're not going to Spain, we're going to France, we're not going to Spain but to France; nicht nur ..., ~ auch not only ... but also.

sondern² vt (old, geh) to separate (von from); siehe gesondert.

Sonder-: ~nummer f (Press) special edition or issue; ~preis m special reduced price; ~recht nt (special) privilege; ~regelung f special provision.

sonders adv siehe samt.

Sonder-: ~schicht f special shift; (zusätzlich) extra shift; ~schule f special school; ~schullehrer m teacher at a special school; ~sprache f jargon; eine ~sprache haben to have one's own jargon; ~stellung f special position; ~stempel m (bei der Post) special postmark.

Sonderung f (old, geh) separation.

Sonder-: ~urlaub m (Mil) special leave; (für Todesfall etc) compassionate leave; ~wünsche pl special requests pl; ~ziehungsrechte pl (Fin) special drawing rights pl; ~zug m special train.

sondieren * **1** vt to sound out. das Terrain or Gelände ~ to spy out the land; die Lage ~ to find out how the land lies. **2** vi to sound things out. ~, ob ... to try to sound out whether ...

Sondierung f sounding out no pl. die ~ des Terrains spying out the land; ohne gründliche ~ without sounding things out thoroughly.

Sondierungsgespräch nt exploratory discussion or talk.

Sonett nt -(e)s, -e sonnet.

Song [sɔŋ] m -s, -s song.

Sonnabend m Saturday; siehe auch Dienstag.

sonnabends adv on Saturdays, on a Saturday.

Sonne f -, -n (a) sun; (Sonnenlicht) sunlight. die liebe ~ (poet, inf), Frau ~ (poet) the sun; unter der ~ (fig geh) under the sun; an or in die ~ gehen to go out in the sun(shine); er kommt viel/wenig an die ~ he gets/doesn't get a lot of sun, he goes/doesn't go out in the sun a lot; geh mir aus der ~! (inf) stop blocking my view!, get out of the way!; (aus dem Licht) get out of the or my light!; das Zimmer hat wenig ~ the room doesn't get much sun(light); die ~ bringt es an den Tag (prov) truth will out (prov).
  (b) (Heiz~) electric fire.

sonnen 1 vt Betten to put out in the sun. **2** vr to sun oneself. sich in etw (dat) ~ (fig) to bask in sth.

Sonnen-: ~anbeter m (lit, fig) sun-worshipper; ~aufgang m sunrise, sun-up (inf); den ~aufgang abwarten to wait for the sun to rise; ~bad nt sunbathing no pl; ein fünfstündiges ~bad five hours in the sun, five hours' sunbathing; ein ~bad nehmen to sunbathe, to bask in the sun; s~baden vi sep infin, ptp only to sunbathe; ~bahn f sun's path; ~ball m (liter) fiery orb (liter); ~batterie f solar battery; ~blende f (Phot) lens hood.

Sonnenblume f sunflower.

Sonnenblumen-: ~kern m sunflower seed; ~öl nt sunflower oil.

Sonnen-: ~brand m sunburn no art; ~bräune f suntan; ~bräune ist ... a suntan is ...; ~brille f (pair of) sunglasses pl, shades pl (US); ~dach nt awning, sun-blind; (Aut dated) sun(shine)-roof; ~deck nt (Naut) sundeck; s~durchflutet adj (geh) sunny, with the sun streaming in; ~energie f solar energy; ~ferne f (Astron) aphelion; ~finsternis f solar eclipse, eclipse of the sun; ~fleck m (Astron) sunspot; s~gebräunt adj suntanned; ~geflecht nt (Physiol) solar plexus; ~glanz m (poet), ~glast m (old poet) sunlight, sunshine; ~glut f (geh) blazing heat of the sun; ~gott m sungod; s~halb adv (Sw) siehe sonnseitig; s~hell adj sunny, sunlit; ~hitze f heat of the sun; s~hungrig adj hungry for the sun; ~hungrige pl sun-seekers pl; ~hut m sunhat; ~jahr nt (Astron) solar year; s~klar adj (inf) clear as daylight, crystal-clear; ~könig m (Hist) Sun King, Roi Soleil; ~kult m sun cult; ~licht nt sunlight; ~nähe f (Astron) perihelion; ~öl nt suntan oil; ~rad nt (Hist) (representation of the) sun; ~schein m sunshine; bei ~schein/strahlendem ~schein in the sunshine/in brilliant sunshine; ~schirm m sunshade; (für Frauen auch) parasol; ~schutz m protection against the sun; ~schutzfaktor m protection factor; ~segel nt awning; ~seite f side facing the sun, sunny side (auch fig); ~stand m position of the sun; ~stich m heatstroke no art, sunstroke no art; ich hatte einen leichten ~stich I had a touch of the sun; du hast wohl einen ~stich! (inf) you must have been out in the sun too long!; ~strahl m sunbeam, ray of sunshine; (esp Astron, Phys) sun-ray; ~system nt solar system; ~tag m (Met auch) day of sunshine; (Astron) solar day; ~uhr f sundial; ~untergang m sunset, sundown; den ~untergang abwarten to wait for the sun to set; s~verbrannt adj Vegetation scorched; Mensch sunburnt; ~wende f solstice; ~wendfeier f siehe Sonnwendfeier; ~wind m (Phys) solar wind.

sonnig adj sunny.

Sonn-: ~seite f (Aus) siehe Sonnenseite; s~seitig adv (Aus) s~seitig gelegen facing the sun.

Sonntag m Sunday; siehe auch Dienstag.

sonntägig adj attr Sunday. die gestrigen ~en Verhandlungen ... the negotiations yesterday, Sunday, ...

sonntäglich adj Sunday attr. ~ gekleidet dressed in one's Sunday best.

sonntags adv on Sundays, on a Sunday; siehe auch dienstags.

Sonntags- in cpds Sunday; ~arbeit f Sunday working; ~ausflug m Sunday trip; ~beilage f Sunday supplement; ~dienst m (von Polizist etc) Sunday duty; ~dienst haben (Apotheke) to be open on Sundays; ~fahrer m (pej) Sunday driver; ~jäger m (pej) once-a-month huntsman; ~kind nt (lit) Sunday's child; ein ~kind sein (fig) to have been born under a lucky star; ~kleidung f Sunday clothes pl; ~maler m Sunday painter; ~rede f (iro) ~reden halten to get up on one's soap-box from time to time; ~redner m (iro) soap-box speaker; ~rückfahrkarte f weekend return (ticket) (Brit), weekend round-trip ticket (US); ~ruhe f die ~ruhe stören/einhalten to contravene the observance of/to observe Sunday as a day of rest; ~schule f Sunday school; ~staat m (hum) Sunday best; in vollem ~staat in one's Sunday best; ~zeitung f Sunday paper.

Sonnwend-: ~feier f midsummer/midwinter celebrations pl; ~feuer nt bonfire at midsummer/midwinter celebrations.

sonor adj sonorous.

sonst 1 adv (a) (außerdem) (mit pron, adv) else; (mit n) other. ~ keine Besucher/Zeitungen etc no other visitors/papers etc; ~ noch Fragen? any other questions?; wer/wie etc (denn) ~? who/how etc else?; bringst du all deine Freunde mit? — was denn ~? are you bringing all your friends? — of course; ~ niemand or keiner/(noch) jemand or wer (inf) nobody/somebody else; ~ und ~ keiner nobody else but he, he and nobody else, he and he alone; wenn du ~ irgend jemanden kennst if you know somebody or anybody else or any other person; wenn du ~ irgendwann mal kommen kannst if you can come some or any other time; er denkt, er ist ~ wer (inf) he thinks he's somebody special, he thinks he's the bee's knees (inf) or the cat's whiskers (inf); ~ nichts/noch etwas nothing/something else; ~ noch etwas? is that all?, anything else?; (in Geschäft auch) will there be anything else?, will that be all?; ja ~ noch was! (iro inf) that'd be right! (inf); ~ bist du gesund or geht's dir gut? (iro inf) are you feeling okay? (*inf*); ~ **willst du nichts?** (*iro inf*) anything else you'd like?; **und wer weiß was ~ noch alles and goodness knows what else; wir haben Müllers, Meiers und ~ noch verschiedene Leute besucht** we visited the Müllers, the Meiers and various other people besides; **wo warst du ~ überall?** where else were you?

(b) (*andernfalls, im übrigen*) otherwise. **wie geht's ~?** how are things apart from that or otherwise?

(c) (*in anderen Beziehungen*) in other ways. **wenn ich Ihnen ~ noch behilflich sein kann** if I can help you in any *or* some other way.

(d) (*gewöhnlich*) usually. **genau wie es ~ ist** just as it usually is; **genau wie/anders als ~** the same as/different from usual; **mehr/weniger als ~** more/less than usual; **der ~ so mürrische Herr Grün war heute direkt freundlich** Mr Grün, who is usually so grumpy, was really friendly today.

(e) (*früher*) **alles war wie ~** everything was as it always used to be; **war das auch ~ der Fall?** was that always the case?; **wenn er ~ zu Besuch hier war** when he has visited us before.

2 *conj* otherwise, *or* (else).

sonstig *adj attr* other; *Fragen, Auskünfte etc* further. **aber ihr ~es Verhalten ist/ihre ~en Leistungen sind verhältnismäßig gut** but her behaviour/performance is quite good; „**S~es**" "other".

sonst-: ~**jemand** *indef pron* (*inf*) siehe ~**wer**; ~**wann** *adv* (*inf*) some other time; ~**was** *indef pron* (*inf*) **da kann ja ~was passieren** anything could happen; **von mir aus kannst du ~was machen** as far as I'm concerned you can do whatever you like; **ich habe ~was versucht** I've tried everything; ~**wer** *indef pron* (*inf*) **das kannst du ~wem schenken** you can give that to some other sucker (*sl*) *or* to somebody else; **das kannst du ~wem erzählen!** tell that to the marines! (*inf*); **sei still, da kann ~wer kommen** be quiet, anybody might come; **da kann ~wer kommen, wir machen keine Ausnahmen** it doesn't matter who it is, we're not making any exceptions; ~**wie** *adv* (*inf*) **in some other way; (*sehr*) like mad (*inf*) *or* crazy (*inf*); ~**wo** *adv* (*inf*) somewhere else; ~**wo, nur nicht hier anywhere (else) but here; ~**wohin** *adv* (*inf*) somewhere else; **wo soll ich hingehen? — von mir aus ~wohin** where shall I go? — anywhere you like; **das kannst du dir ~wohin stecken!** (*sl*) you can stuff that! (*sl*), you know where you can put that! (*sl*).

so|oft *conj* whenever.

Soor *m* -(e)s, -e (*Med*) thrush *no art*.

Sophismus *m* sophism.

Sophist(in *f*) *m* sophist.

Sophisterei *f* sophistry.

Sophistik *f* sophistry.

Sophokles ['zo:foklɛs] *m* - Sophocles.

Sopran *m* -s, -e soprano; (*Knaben~, Instrument~ auch*) treble; (*Chorstimmen*) sopranos *pl*; trebles *pl*.

Sopranist *m* treble.

Sopranistin *f* soprano.

Sorbe *m* -n, -n, **Sorbin** *f* Sorb.

Sorbinsäure *f* sorbic acid.

sorbisch *adj* Sorbian.

Sore *f* -, *no pl* (*sl*) loot, swag (*hum*).

Sorge *f* -, -n (a) worry; (*Ärger auch*) trouble; (*Kummer auch*) care. **frei von ~n** free of care *or* worries; **keine ~!** (*inf*) don't (you) worry!; ~ **haben, ob/daß ...** to be worried whether /that ...; **wir betrachten diese Entwicklung mit ~** we view this development with concern; ~**n haben** to have problems; **weniger/ nichts als ~n haben** to have fewer/nothing but worries *or* headaches (*inf*); **ich habe solche ~n** I have so many worries *or* troubles; **ich habe solche ~** I'm so worried; **du hast ~n!** (*iro*) you think you've got troubles! (*inf*); ~**n haben die Leute!** the worries people have!; **mit dem haben wir nichts als ~n** we've had nothing but trouble with him/that; **jdm ~n machen** (*Kummer bereiten*) to cause sb a lot of worry; (*beunruhigen*) to worry sb; **es macht mir ~n, daß ...** it worries me that ...; **in ~ (**dat*) sein** to be worried; **sich** (*dat*) ~**n machen** to worry; **wir haben uns solche ~n gemacht** we were so worried; **machen Sie sich deshalb keine ~n** don't worry about that; **seien Sie ohne ~!** (*geh*) do not fear (*liter*) *or* worry; **lassen Sie das meine ~ sein** let me worry about that; **das ist nicht meine ~** that's not my problem; **für etw ~ tragen** (*geh*) to attend *or* see to sth, to take care of sth; **dafür ~ tragen, daß ...** (*geh*) to see to it that ...

(b) (*Für~, Jur*) care.

sorgen 1 *vr* to worry. **sich ~ um** to be worried *or* to worry about.

2 *vi* ~ **für** (*sich kümmern um*) to take care of, to look after; (*betreuen auch*) to care for; (*vorsorgen für*) to provide for; (*herbeischaffen*) **Proviant, Musik** to provide; (*bewirken*) to ensure; **dafür ~, daß ...** to see to it that ..., to make sure that ...; **für Ruhe/einen reibungslosen Ablauf ~** to make sure that things are quiet/go smoothly; **das reichlich fließende Bier sorgte für Stimmung** the plentiful supply of beer made sure that things went with a swing; **dafür ist gesorgt** that's taken care of.

Sorgen-: ~**brecher** *m* -s, - (*hum*) comforter, drowner of sorrows; **s~frei** *adj* free of care; (*heiter, sich keine ~ machend*) carefree; ~**kind** *nt* (*inf*) problem child; (*fig auch*) biggest headache (*inf*); ~**last** *f* (*geh*) burden of one's cares; **s~los siehe s~frei; s~schwer** *adj* **Stimme, Blick** troubled; **Leben** full of cares; **s~voll** *adj* worried; **Leben** full of worries.

Sorgerecht *nt* (*Jur*) custody.

Sorgfalt *f* -, *no pl* care. **ohne ~ arbeiten** to work carelessly; **viel ~ auf etw** (*acc*) **verwenden** to take a lot of care over sth.

sorgfältig *adj* careful.

Sorgfältigkeit *f* carefulness.

Sorgfaltspflicht *f* (*Jur*) duty of care to a child. **Verletzung der ~** negligence of one's duties as a parent/guardian.

---

sorglos *adj* (*unbekümmert*) carefree; (*leichtfertig, nachlässig*) careless. **jdm ~ vertrauen** to trust sb implicitly.

Sorglosigkeit *f* siehe *adj* carefreeness; carelessness.

sorgsam *adj* careful.

Sorte *f* -, -n (a) sort, type, kind; (*von Waren*) variety, type; (*Qualität, Klasse*) grade; (*Marke*) brand. **beste** *or* **erste ~** top quality *or* grade; **diese Psychiater sind eine ganz komische ~** these psychiatrists are quite a peculiar bunch (*inf*); **du bist mir vielleicht eine ~!** (*inf*) you're a right one! (*inf*).

(b) (*Fin*) *usu pl* foreign currency.

sortieren* *vt* to sort; **Waren** (*nach Qualität, Größe auch*) to grade. **etw in einen Schrank/ein Regal etc ~** to sort sth and put it in a cupboard/bookcase *etc*.

Sortierer(in *f*) *m* -s, - sorter.

Sortiermaschine *f* sorting machine, sorter.

Sortiment *nt* (a) assortment; (*von Waren auch*) range; (*Sammlung auch*) collection. **(b)** (*Buchhandel*) retail book trade.

Sortimenter *m* -s, - retail bookseller, book retailer.

Sortiments-: ~**buchhandel** *m* retail book trade; ~**buchhändler** *m* siehe **Sortimenter;** ~**buchhandlung** *f* retail bookshop (*esp Brit*) *or* bookstore (*esp US*).

SOS [ɛsloː'lɛs] *nt* -, - SOS. ~ **funken** to put out an SOS.

sosehr *conj* however much, no matter how much.

Sosein *nt* (*Philos*) essence.

SOS-Kinderdorf [ɛsloː'lɛs-] *nt* children's home organized into family units.

soso **1** *adv* (*inf: einigermaßen*) so-so (*inf*), middling (*inf*). **2** *interj* ~**!** I see!; (*erstaunt*) well well!; (*indigniert, iro auch*) really!; (*interessiert-gelassen auch*) oh yes?; (*drohend*) well!

SOS-Ruf [ɛsloː'lɛs-] *m* (*lit*) SOS (call), mayday; (*fig*) SOS.

Soße *f* -, -n sauce; (*Braten~*) gravy; (*pej inf*) gunge (*inf*).

Soßenlöffel *m* gravy spoon.

sott *pret of* **sieden.**

Soubrette [zu'brɛtə] *f* soubrette.

Soufflé [zu'fleː] *nt* -s, -s (*Cook*) soufflé.

Souffleur [zu'fløːɐ] *m,* **Souffleuse** [zu'fløːzə] *f* (*Theat*) prompter.

Souffleurkasten [zu'fløːɐ-] *m* (*Theat*) prompt-box.

soufflieren* [zu'fliːrən] *vti* (*Theat*) to prompt. **jdm (den Text) ~** to prompt sb.

Soul ['zøːʊl, zøˈuːl] *nt* -s (*Geog*) Seoul.

so|undso *adv* ~ **lange** for such and such a time; ~ **groß/breit** of such and such a size/width; ~ **oft** *n* (number of) times; ~ **viele** so and so many; **Paragraph ~** article such-and-such *or* so-and-so; **er sagte, mach das ~** he said, do it in such and such a way.

So|undso *m* -s, -s **Herr ~** Mr So-and-so.

so|undsovielte(r, s) *adj* umpteenth. **am/bis zum S~n** (*Datum*) on/by such and such a date; **er ist der S~, der ...** he's the umpteenth person who ... (*inf*).

Souper [zu'peː] *nt* -s, -s (*geh*) dinner.

soupieren* [zu'piːrən] *vi* (*geh*) to dine.

Soutane [zu'taːnə] *f* -, -n (*Eccl*) cassock.

Souterrain [zuteˈrɛ̃, 'zuːterɛ̃] *nt* -s, -s basement.

Souvenir [zuvə'niːɐ] *nt* -s, -s souvenir. ~**jäger** *m* (*inf*) souvenir-hunter; ~**laden** *m* souvenir shop.

souverän [zuvə'rɛːn] *adj* sovereign *no adv;* (*fig*) supremely good; (*überlegen*) (most) superior *no adv.* **das Land wurde ~** the country became a sovereign state; ~ **regieren** to rule as (the) sovereign, to have sovereign power, to be sovereign; ~ **siegen** to win a commanding victory; **sein Gebiet/die Lage ~ beherrschen** to have a commanding knowledge of one's field/to be in full command of a situation; **er hat die Situation ganz ~ gehandhabt** he dealt with the situation supremely well; **er ist ganz ~ darüber hinweggegangen** he blithely ignored it.

Souverän [zuvə'rɛːn] *m* -s, -e sovereign; (*Parlament, Organisation*) sovereign power.

Souveränität [zuvərɛni'tɛːt] *f* sovereignty; (*fig*) (*Überlegenheit*) superiority; (*Leichtigkeit*) supreme ease.

soviel 1 *adv* so much. **halb/doppelt ~** half/twice as much; ~ **als** *or* **wie ...** as much as ...; **nimm dir ~ du willst** take as much as you like; **noch einmal ~** the same again; (*doppelt ~*) twice as much; **das ist ~ wie eine Zusage** that is tantamount to *or* that amounts to a promise; ~ **für heute!** that's all for today!; ~**, was ihn betrifft** so much for him.

2 *conj* as *or* so far as. ~ **ich weiß, nicht!** not as *or* so far as I know; ~ **ich weiß ...** however much I ...

sovielmal 1 *adv* so many times. **2** *conj* ~ **... auch ...** no matter how many times ..., however many times ...

soweit 1 *adv* **(a)** by and large, on the whole; (*bis jetzt*) up to now; (*bis zu diesem Punkt*) thus far. ~ **ganz gut** (*inf*) not too bad; ~ **wie** *or* **als möglich** as far as possible; **ich bin ~ fertig** I'm more *or* less ready.

(b) ~ **sein** to be finished *or* (*bereit*) ready; **seid ihr schon ~, daß ihr anfangen könnt?** are you ready to start?; **es ist/war bald ~** the time has/had nearly come; **wie lange dauert es noch, bis der Film anfängt?** — **es ist gleich ~** how long will it be before the film begins? — it'll soon be time.

2 *conj* as *or* so far as; (*insofern*) in so far as. ~ **ich sehe** as *or* so far as I can tell *or* see.

sowenig 1 *adv* no more, not any more (*wie* than). **sie ist mir ~ sympathisch wie dir** I don't like her any more than you do; ~ **wie** *or* **als möglich** as little as possible. **2** *conj* however little, little as. ~ **ich auch ...** however little I ...

sowie *conj* **(a)** (*sobald*) as soon as, the moment (*inf*). **(b)** (*und auch*) as well as.

sowieso *adv* anyway, anyhow, in any case. **wir sind ~ nicht gegangen** we didn't go anyway *or* anyhow *or* in any case; **das ~!** obviously!, of course!, that goes without saying.

Sowjet *m* -s, -s Soviet. ~**armee** *f* Soviet Army; ~**bürger** *m* Soviet citizen.

sowjetisch adj Soviet.

Sowjet-: ~**macht** f Soviet power no art; ~**mensch** m Soviet citizen; ~**republik** f Soviet Republic; **Union der Sozialistischen** ~**republiken** Union of Soviet Socialist Republics; ~**russe** m Soviet Russian; ~**staat** m Soviet State; ~**stern** m Soviet star, star of the Soviets; ~**union** f Soviet Union; ~**volk** nt Soviet people pl; ~**zone** f (Hist) Soviet zone.

sowohl conj ~ ... als or wie (auch) both ... and, ... as well as.

Sozi m -s, -s (pej inf) Socialist.

Sozia f -, -s (sl) girl pillion-rider.

sozial adj social; (~ bewußt) socially conscious; (an das Gemeinwohl denkend) public-spirited. **die** ~**en Berufe** the caring professions; ~**er Wohnungsbau** ≈ council housing (Brit); ~ **denken** to be socially minded; **ich habe heute meinen** ~**en Tag!** (inf) I'm feeling charitable today.

Sozial-: ~**abgaben** pl (social) welfare contributions pl; ~**amt** nt (social) welfare office; ~**arbeit** f social work; ~**arbeiter** m social worker; ~**beiträge** pl siehe ~**abgaben;** ~**bericht** m (BRD Parl) welfare report; ~**beruf** m caring profession; ~**demokrat** m social democrat; ~**demokratie** f social democracy; **s~demokratisch** adj social-democratic; ~**demokratismus** m (pej) social democracy; ~**einrichtungen** pl social facilities pl; ~**ethik** f (social) ethics; ~**fall** m hardship case; ~**faschismus** m socialist fascism; ~**forschung** f social research; ~**fürsorge** f (dated) siehe ~**hilfe;** ~**gericht** nt (social) welfare tribunal; ~**geschichte** f social history; ~**gesetzgebung** f social welfare legislation; ~**hilfe** f welfare (aid); ~**hygiene** f public health or hygiene; ~**imperialismus** m social imperialism.

Sozialisation f (Psych, Sociol) socialization.

sozialisieren* vt (Psych, Sociol, Ind) to socialize; (Pol: verstaatlichen) to nationalize.

Sozialisierung f siehe vt socialization; nationalization.

Sozialismus m socialism.

Sozialist(in f) m socialist.

sozialistisch adj socialist.

Sozial-: **s~ökonomisch** adj socioeconomic; ~**pädagoge** n social education worker; ~**pädagogik** f social education; ~**politik** f social policy; **s~politisch** adj socio-political; ~**prestige** nt social standing; ~**produkt** nt national product; ~**psychologe** f social psychology; ~**recht** nt social legislation; ~**reform** f social reform; ~**rente** f social security pension; ~**revolutionär** m social revolutionary; ~**staat** m welfare state; ~**struktur** f social structure; ~**tarif** m subsidized rate; ~**versicherung** f national insurance (Brit), social security (US); ~**wissenschaften** pl social sciences pl; ~**wissenschaftler** m social scientist; ~**wohnung** f council flat (Brit); ~**zulage** f (welfare) allowance.

Sozio-: ~**gramm** nt sociogram; ~**linguistik** f sociolinguistics sing; **s~linguistisch** adj sociolinguistic.

Soziologe m, **Soziologin** f sociologist.

soziologisch adj sociological.

Soziometrie f sociometry.

Sozius m -, -se (a) (Partner) partner. (b) (Beifahrer) pillion rider or passenger; (inf: ~sitz) pillion (seat).

Soziussitz m pillion (seat).

sozusagen adv so to speak, as it were.

Spachtel m -s, - or f -, -n (a) (Werkzeug) spatula. (b) (spec: ~masse) filler.

Spachtelmasse f filler.

spachteln 1 vt Mauerfugen, Ritzen to fill (in), to smooth over, to stop. 2 vi to do some filling; (inf: essen) to tuck in.

Spagat[1] m or nt -(e)s, -e splits pl. ~ **machen** to do the splits.

Spagat[2] m -(e)s, -e (S Ger, Aus: Bindfaden) string.

Spaghetti[1] [ʃpa'geti] pl spaghetti sing.

Spaghetti[2] m -(s), -s, **Spaghettifresser** m -s, - (pej sl: Italiener) wop (pej sl), eyetie (sl).

spähen vi to peer; (durch Löcher etc auch) to peep; (vorsichtig auch) to spy; (old Mil) to reconnoitre, to scout. **nach jdm/etw** ~ to look out for sb/sth.

Späher(in f) m -s, - (old Mil) scout; (Posten) lookout.

Spähtrupp m (Mil) reconnaissance or scouting party or patrol.

spakig adj (N Ger) Bettwäsche, Matratze mildewed.

Spalier nt -s, -e (a) (Gitter) trellis; (für Obst auch) espalier. **am** ~ **ziehen** to trellis/espalier, to train on a trellis/an espalier. (b) (von Menschen) row, line; (zur Ehrenbezeigung) guard of honour. ~ **stehen/ein** ~ **bilden** to form a guard of honour.

Spalier|obst nt wall fruit.

Spalt m -(e)s, -e (a) (Öffnung) gap, opening; (zwischen Vorhängen etc auch) chink; (Riß) crack; (Fels~) crevice, fissure. **die Tür stand einen** ~ **offen** the door was slightly ajar; **die Tür/Augen einen** ~ **öffnen** to open the door/one's eyes slightly. (b) (fig: Kluft) split. **ein** ~ **ging durch die Partei** there was a split in the party, the party was split; **der** ~, **der durch die Bevölkerung ging** the split in the population.

spaltbar adj (Phys) Atomkerne fissionable.

Spaltbarkeit f (Phys) fissionability.

Spaltbreit m: **etw einen** ~ **öffnen** etc to open etc sth slightly.

spaltbreit adj **ein** ~**er Schlitz** a narrow crack.

Spalte f -, -n (a) (esp Geol) fissure; (Fels~ auch) cleft, crevice; (Gletscher~) crevasse; (in Wand) crack; (sl: Vagina) hole (sl). (b) (Typ, Press) column.

spalten ptp auch **gespalten** 1 vt (lit, fig) to split; (Chem) Öl to crack (spec); Holz to chop. **bei dieser Frage sind die Meinungen gespalten** opinions are divided on this question; siehe **gespalten, Schädel.** 2 vr to split; (Meinungen) to be split.

Spalt-: ~**material** nt fissionable material; ~**pilz** m (old) usu pl bacterium; ~**produkt** nt fission product.

Spaltung f (lit, fig) splitting; (von Atomkernen auch) fission; (von Öl) cracking (spec); (in Partei) split; (eines Landes) split, division. **die** ~ **der Persönlichkeit/des Bewußtseins** the

split in his etc personality/mind.

Span m -(e)s, ⁻e (Hobel~) shaving; (Bohr~ auch) boring; (zum Feueranzünden) piece of kindling; (Metall~) filing. **arbeiten, daß die** ⁻**e fliegen** (prov) to work furiously.

spänen vt Holzboden to scour with steel wool.

Spanferkel nt sucking pig.

Spange f -, -n clasp; (Haar~) hair slide (Brit), barrette (US); (Schuh~) strap, bar; (Schnalle) buckle; (Arm~) bangle, bracelet.

Spangenschuh m bar shoe.

Spaniel ['ʃpa:niel] m -s, -s spaniel.

Spanien ['ʃpa:niən] nt -s Spain.

Spanier(in f) ['ʃpa:niɐ, -iərin] m -s, - Spaniard. **die** ~ the Spanish, the Spaniards; **stolz wie ein** ~ **sein** (prov) to be (very) proud; siehe **Deutsche(r).**

spanisch adj Spanish. **S~e Fliege** Spanish fly; ~**e Wand** (folding) screen; **das kommt mir** ~ **vor** (inf) that seems odd to me.

Spanisch(e) nt decl as adj Spanish; siehe **Deutsch(e).**

Span-: ~**kiste** f chip basket; ~**korb** m chip basket.

Spann m -(e)s, -e instep.

spann pret of **spinnen.**

Spannbeton m prestressed concrete.

Spanne f -, -n (altes Längenmaß) span; (geh: Zeit~) while; (Verdienst~) margin. **eine** ~ **Zeit** (geh) a space or span of time.

spannen 1 vt (a) Saite, Seil to tighten, to tauten; Bogen to draw; Feder to tension; Muskeln to flex; Strickteile, Wolle to stretch; Gewehr, (Abzugs)hahn, (Kamera)verschluß to cock. **einen Stiefel** ~ to put a boot on a/the boot-tree; **einen Tennisschläger** ~ to put a tennis racket in a/the press.
(b) (straff befestigen) Werkstück to clamp; Wäscheleine to put up; Netz, Plane, Bildleinwand to stretch. **einen Bogen in die Schreibmaschine** ~ to insert or put a sheet in the typewriter.
(c) (anschirren) to hitch (up), to harness (vor +acc to).
(d) **seine Hand ist noch zu klein, um eine Oktave zu** ~ his hand is still too small to stretch or span an octave.
(e) (fig) **seine Erwartungen zu hoch** ~ to pitch one's expectations too high; siehe **Folter.**
(f) (inf: merken) to catch on to (inf), to get wise to (inf).
2 vr (a) (Haut) to go or become taut; (Muskeln auch) to tense.
(b) **sich über etw** (acc) ~ (Regenbogen, Brücke) to span sth; (Haut) to stretch over sth.
3 vi (a) (Kleidung) to be (too) tight; (Haut) to be taut.
(b) (Gewehr) ~ to cock; (Kamera ~) to cock the shutter.
(c) **auf etw** (acc) ~ (inf) (gespannt warten) to look forward excitedly to sth; (gespannt lauschen) to listen intently for sth.

spannend adj exciting; (stärker) thrilling. **mach's nicht so** ~! (inf) don't keep me/us in suspense.

Spanner m -s, - (a) (für Tennisschläger) press; (Hosen~) hanger; (Schuh~) shoetree; (Stiefel~) boot-tree. (b) (Zool) geometer moth; (Raupe) looper. (c) (inf: Voyeur) peeping Tom.

-spänner m -s, - in cpds Vier~ etc four-in-hand etc.

-spännig adj suf vier~ **fahren** to drive a four-in-hand.

Spann-: ~**kraft** f (von Feder, Bremse) tension; (von Muskel) tone, tonus (spec); (fig) vigour; s~**kräftig** adj (fig) vigorous.

Spannung f (a) no pl (von Seil, Feder, Muskel etc) tension, tautness; (Mech: innerer Druck) stress. **wegen der zu großen** ~ **riß das Seil** the rope broke because the strain (on it) was too great.
(b) (Elec) voltage, tension. **unter** ~ **stehen** to be live.
(c) no pl (fig) excitement; (Spannungsgeladenheit) suspense, tension. **mit großer/atemloser** ~ with great/breathless excitement; **in erwartungsvoller** ~ full of excited anticipation, full of excitement; **etw mit** ~ **erwarten** to await sth full of suspense; **seine mit** ~ **erwarteten Memoiren sind endlich erschienen** his eagerly awaited memoirs have appeared at last.
(d) no pl (innerliche, nervliche Anspannung) tension.
(e) usu pl (Feindseligkeit) tension no pl.

Spannungs-: ~**abfall** m voltage drop; ~**feld** nt (lit) electric field; (fig) area of conflict; s~**frei** adj (lit) Metall, Glas unstressed; (fig) relaxed; ~**gebiet** nt (Pol) flashpoint, area of tension; ~**messer** m -s, - (Elec) voltmeter; ~**moment** nt (fig) suspense-creating factor; ~**prüfer** m voltage detector; ~**regler** m voltage regulator.

Spannweite f (Math) range; (Archit) span; (Aviat) (wing)span; (von Vogelflügeln) wingspread, (wing)span.

Span-: ~**platte** f chipboard; ~**schachtel** f small box made from very thin strips of wood.

Spant[1] nt -(e)s, -en (Naut) rib.

Spant[2] m -(e)s, -en (Aviat) frame.

Spar-: ~**buch** nt savings book; (bei Bank auch) bankbook, passbook; ~**büchse** f moneybox; ~**einlage** f savings deposit.

sparen 1 vt to save. **dadurch habe ich (mir) viel Geld/Zeit/Arbeit gespart** I saved (myself) a lot of money/time/work that way; **keine Kosten/Mühe** ~ to spare no expense/effort; **spar' dir deine guten Ratschläge!** (inf) you can keep your advice!; **diese Mühe/diese Kosten/das hätten Sie sich** (dat) ~ **können** you could have saved or spared yourself the trouble/this expense/the bother; **diese Bemerkung hätten Sie sich** (dat) ~ **können!** you should have kept that remark to yourself!
2 vi to save; (sparsam sein, haushalten) to economize, to make savings. **an etw** (dat) ~ to be sparing with sth; (mit etw haushalten) to economize or save on sth; **sie hatte nicht an or mit der Sahne gespart** she wasn't sparing with or of the cream; **er hatte nicht mit Lob gespart** he was unstinting or lavish in his praise; **für or auf etw** (acc) ~ to save up for sth; **am falschen Ort** ~ to make false economies, to make savings in the wrong place; **spare in der Zeit, so hast du in der Not** (Prov) waste not, want not (Prov).

Sparer(in f) m -s, - (bei Bank etc) saver.

Sparflamme f low flame; (Zündflamme) pilot light. **auf ~** (fig inf) just ticking over (inf); **auf ~ kochen** (fig) to soft-pedal (inf), to go easy.

Spargel m -s, -, (Sw) f -, -n asparagus.

Spargelder pl savings pl.

Spargelspitze f asparagus tip.

Spar-: ~**groschen** m nest egg; ~**guthaben** nt savings account; ~**kasse** f savings bank; ~**kassenbuch** nt siehe ~**buch;** ~**konto** nt savings or deposit account.

spärlich adj sparse; Ausbeute, Reste, Einkünfte, Kenntnisse meagre, scanty; Beleuchtung poor; (Be)kleidung scanty, skimpy; Mahl meagre; Nachfrage poor, low. **~ bekleidet** scantily clad or dressed; **~bevölkert** sparsely or thinly populated; **~ beleuchtet** poorly lit; **die Geldmittel fließen nur ~** the money is only coming slowly or in dribs and drabs.

Spärlichkeit f siehe adj sparseness; meagreness, scantiness; poorness; scantiness, skimpiness; meagreness; low level, poorness.

Spar-: ~**maßnahme** f economy measure; ~**packung** f economy size (pack); ~**pfennig** m nest egg; ~**prämie** f savings premium; ~**quote,** ~**rate** f rate of saving.

Sparren m -s, - rafter. **du hast ja einen ~ (zuviel im Kopf)** (inf) you must have a screw loose (inf).

Sparring ['ʃpariŋ, 'spariŋ] nt -s, no pl (Boxen) sparring.

Sparrings-: ~**kampf** m sparring bout; ~**partner** m sparring partner.

sparsam adj thrifty; (haushälterisch, wirtschaftlich) economical. **~ leben** to live economically; **~ im Verbrauch** economical; **mit etw ~ umgehen** or **sein** to be sparing with sth; **~ verwenden** to use sparingly; **von einer Möglichkeit nur ~(en) Gebrauch machen** to make little use of an opportunity.

Sparsamkeit f thrift; (das Haushalten) economizing. **~ im Verbrauch** economicalness.

Sparschwein nt piggy bank.

Spartakiade [ʃpartaˈkiaːdə, sp-] f Spartakiad.

Spartakist [ʃpartaˈkɪst, sp-] m Spartacist.

Spartakusbund ['ʃpartakʊs-, 'sp-] m Spartacus league.

Spartaner [ʃparˈtaːnɐ, sp-] m -s, -, **Spartan.**

spartanisch [ʃparˈtaːnɪʃ, sp-] adj (lit) Spartan; (fig auch) spartan. **~ leben** to lead a Spartan or spartan life.

Sparte f -, -n (a) (Comm) (Branche) line of business; (Teilgebiet) branch, area. **(b)** (Rubrik) column, section.

Spar-: ~**vertrag** m savings agreement; ~**zins** m interest no pl (on a savings account).

spasmisch, spasmodisch adj (Med) spasmodic, spasmic.

Spaß m -es, -̈e (no pl: Vergnügen) fun; (Scherz) joke; (Streich) prank, lark (Brit inf). **laß die dummen ~e!** stop fooling around!; **~ beiseite** joking apart; **viel ~!** have fun (auch iro), have a good time!, enjoy yourself/yourselves!; **wir haben viel ~ gehabt** we had a lot of fun or a really good time, we enjoyed ourselves a lot; **im Urlaub will ich (meinen) ~ haben** I want to enjoy myself or to have fun when I'm on holiday; **an etw** (dat) **~ haben** to enjoy sth; **er hat viel ~ an seinem Garten** his garden gives him a lot of pleasure; **es macht mir ~/keinen ~(, das zu tun)** it's fun/no fun (doing it), I enjoy or like/don't enjoy or like (doing it); **wenn's dir ~ macht** if you want to, if it turns you on (sl); **Hauptsache, es macht ~** the main thing is to have fun or to enjoy yourself; **es macht ~/keinen ~** it's fun/no fun; **ich hab' doch nur ~ gemacht!** I was only joking or kidding (inf)!, it was only (in) fun; **(nur so,) zum** or **aus ~** (just) for fun, (just) for the fun or hell of it (inf); **etw aus** or **im** or **zum ~ sagen** to say sth as a joke or in fun; **das sage ich nicht bloß zum ~** I'm not saying that for the fun of it, I kid you not (hum inf); **da hört der ~ auf, das ist kein ~ mehr** that's going beyond a joke; **aus (dem) ~ wurde Ernst** the fun turned deadly earnest; **~ muß sein** there's no harm in a joke; (als Aufheiterung) all work and no play (makes Jack a dull boy) (prov); **es war ein ~, ihm bei der Arbeit zuzusehen** it was a joy to see him at work; **sich** (dat) **einen ~ daraus machen, etw zu tun** to get enjoyment or a kick (inf) out of doing sth; **seinen ~ mit jdm treiben** to make fun of sb; (sich mit jdm vergnügen) to have one's fun with sb; **laß/gönn ihm doch seinen or den ~!** let him enjoy himself or have his fun; **er versteht keinen ~** he has no sense of humour; (er läßt nicht mit sich spaßen) he doesn't stand for any nonsense; **da verstehe ich keinen ~!** I won't stand for any nonsense; **das war ein teurer ~** (inf) that was an expensive business (inf).

Späßchen nt dim of **Spaß** little joke.

spaßen vi (dated) to joke, to jest. **mit Blutvergiftung/mit radioaktivem Material ist nicht zu ~** blood poisoning is no joke or joking matter/radioactive material is no joke; **mit ihm ist nicht zu ~,** er läßt nicht mit sich ~ he doesn't stand for any nonsense.

spaßeshalber adv for the fun of it, for fun.

spaßhaft, spaßig adj funny, droll.

Späßlein nt siehe **Späßchen.**

Spaß-: ~**macher** m (~**vogel**), (im Zirkus) clown; ~**verderber** m -s, - spoilsport, wet blanket, killjoy; ~**vogel** m joker.

Spastiker(in f) [ʃpastikɐ, -ərɪn, 'sp-] m -s, - spastic.

spastisch [ʃpastɪʃ, 'sp-] adj spastic. **~ gelähmt** suffering from spastic paralysis.

Spat m -(e)s, -e (a) (Miner) spar. **(b)** no pl (Vet) spavin.

spät 1 adj late; Reue, Ruhm, Glück belated. **am ~en Nachmittag** in the late afternoon; **im ~en 18. Jahrhundert** in the late 18th century; **die Werke des ~en Shakespeare, die ~en Werke Shakespeares** the works of the late(r) Shakespeare, Shakespeare's late(r) works; **ein ~es Mädchen** (inf) an old maid.

2 adv late. **~ in der Nacht/am Tage** late at night/in the day; **es ist/wird schon ~** it is/is getting late; **heute abend wird es ~** it'll be a late night tonight; (nach Hause kommen) I/he etc will be

late this evening; **gestern ist es (bei der Arbeit) ~ geworden** I worked late yesterday; **wir hatten gestern eine Party, und da ist es ziemlich ~ geworden** we had a party yesterday and it went on fairly late; **von früh bis ~** from morning till night; **wie ~ ist es?** what's the time?; **zu ~** too late; **er kommt morgens regelmäßig fünf Minuten zu ~** he's always five minutes late in the mornings; **der Zug ist zu ~ angekommen** the train arrived late; **wir sind ~ dran** we're late; **er hat erst ~ mit dem Schreiben angefangen** he only started writing late in life; **besser ~ als nie** (prov) better late than never (prov).

Spät-, spät- in cpds late.

Spatel m -s, - spatula.

Spaten m -s, - spade.

Spatenstich m cut of the spade. **den ersten ~ tun** to turn the first sod.

Spät|entwickler m late developer.

später comp of **spät** **1** adj later; (zukünftig) future. **in der ~en Zukunft** further on in the future; **die S~en** (liter) posterity sing.

2 adv later (on). **das werden wir ~ erledigen** we'll settle that later (on); **ein paar Minuten ~** a few minutes later; **~ als** later than; **das war viel ~ als Augustus** that was much later (on) than Augustus; **was will er ~ (einmal) werden?** what does he want to do later (on)?; **an ~ denken** to think of the future; **bis ~!,** **also dann, auf ~!** see you later!

späterhin adv later (on).

spätestens adv at the latest. **~ morgen/in einer Stunde** tomorrow/in one hour at the latest; **~ um 8 Uhr** not later than 8 o'clock, by 8 o'clock at the latest; **bis ~ in einer Woche** in one week at the latest.

Spät-: ~**geburt** f late birth; ~**gotik** f late Gothic; ~**heimkehrer** m late returnee (from a prisoner-of-war camp); ~**herbst** m late autumn, late fall (US); ~**jahr** nt (liter) autumn, fall (US); ~**kapitalismus** m late capitalism; ~**lese** f late vintage; ~**nachmittag** m late afternoon; ~**obst** nt late fruit; ~**schicht** f late shift; ~**sommer** m late summer.

Spatz m -en, -en (a) sparrow. **wie ein ~ essen** to peck at one's food; **besser ein ~ in der Hand als eine Taube auf dem Dach** (Prov) a bird in the hand is worth two in the bush (Prov); **siehe pfeifen. (b)** (inf: Kind) tot, mite; (Anrede) darling, honey.

Spätzchen nt dim of **Spatz** little sparrow; (inf: Kind) tot, mite; (Anrede) honey-bun (inf), sweetie pie (inf).

Spatzenhirn nt (pej) birdbrain (inf).

Spätzle pl (S Ger Cook) spaetzle (sort of pasta).

Spätzündung f retarded ignition. **~ haben** (inf) to be slow on the uptake.

spazieren* vi aux sein to stroll; (stolzieren) to strut. **wir waren ~ we** went for a walk or stroll.

spazieren-: ~**fahren** sep irreg **1** vi aux sein (im Auto) to go for a drive or ride or run; (mit Fahrrad, Motorrad) to go for a ride; **ich will nur ein bißchen ~fahren** I just want to go for a little drive or ride or run; **2** vt jdn ~**fahren** to take sb for a drive or ride or run; **das Baby** (im Kinderwagen) ~**fahren** to take the baby for a walk in the pram); ~**führen** vt sep jdn ~**führen** to take sb for a walk; **sie hat ihr neues Kleid/ihren Fotoapparat ~geführt** (inf) she paraded her new dress/her camera; ~**gehen** vi sep irreg aux sein to go for a walk or stroll; **ich gehe jetzt ein bißchen ~** I'm going to go for a little walk or stroll now.

Spazier-: ~**fahrt** f (im Auto) ride, drive, run; (mit Fahrrad, Motorrad) ride; **eine ~fahrt machen** to go for a ride etc; ~**gang** m walk, stroll; (fig) child's play no art, doddle (inf); (Match) walkover; **einen ~gang machen** to go for a walk or stroll; ~**gänger** m -s, - stroller; ~**ritt** m ride; ~**stock** m walking stick; ~**weg** m path, walk.

SPD [ɛspeː'deː] f - abbr of **Sozialdemokratische Partei Deutschlands.**

Specht m -(e)s, -e woodpecker.

Speck m -(e)s, -e (Schweine~) bacon fat; (Schinken~, durchwachsener ~) bacon; (Wal~) blubber; (inf: bei Mensch) fat, flab (inf). **mit ~ fängt man Mäuse** (Prov) you have to throw a sprat to catch a mackerel; **~ ansetzen** (inf) to get fat, to put on weight, to put it on (inf); **~ auf den Knochen or drauf haben** (inf) to be fat; (an Hüften) to be broad in the beam (inf); **ran an den ~** (inf) let's get stuck in (inf).

Speck-: ~**bauch** m (inf) potbelly (inf), paunch; s~**bäuchig** adj (inf) potbellied (inf).

speckig adj greasy.

Speck-: ~**nacken** m fat neck; s~**nackig** adj fat-necked; ~**scheibe** f (bacon) rasher; ~**schwarte** f bacon rind; **wie eine ~schwarte glänzen** (inf) to shine greasily; (vor Sauberkeit) to gleam like a new penny; ~**seite** f side of bacon; ~**stein** m (Miner) soapstone, steatite.

spedieren* vt to forward, to ship. **jdn an die frische Luft ~** (inf) to throw sb out.

Spediteur [ʃpediˈtøːɐ] m carrier, haulier, haulage contractor; (Zwischen~) forwarding agent; (von Schiffsfracht) shipper, shipping agent; (Umzugsfirma) furniture remover.

Spedition f **(a)** (das Spedieren) carriage, transporting; (auf dem Wasserweg) shipping. **(b)** (Firma) haulage contractor; (Zwischen~) forwarding agency; (Schiffskontor) shipping agency; (Umzugsfirma) removal firm; (Versandabteilung) forwarding department.

Speditions-: ~**branche** f haulage business; ~**firma** f, ~**geschäft** nt haulage contractor; (Zwischenspediteur) forwarding agency; (Schiffskontor) shipping agency; (Umzugsfirma) removal firm; ~**kosten** pl haulage (costs pl).

Speer m -(e)s, -e spear; (Sport) javelin.

Speer-: ~**spitze** f (lit, fig) spearhead; ~**werfen** nt (Sport) das ~werfen the javelin, throwing the javelin; **im ~werfen** in the javelin; ~**werfer** m (Sport) javelin thrower.

Speiche f -, -n (a) spoke. **dem Schicksal in die ~n greifen** or fallen (fig) to try to stop the wheel of fate. (b) (Anat) radius.

Speichel m -s, no pl saliva, spittle.

Speichel-: ~drüse f salivary gland; ~fluß m salivation; ~lecker m -s, - (pej inf) lickspittle, toady, bootlicker (inf); ~leckerei f (pej inf) toadying, bootlicking (inf).

Speicher m -s, - (Lagerhaus) storehouse; (im Haus) loft, attic; (Wasser~) tank, reservoir; (beim Computer) memory, store. auf dem ~ in the loft or attic.

Speicher-: ~batterie f storage battery, accumulator (Brit); ~becken nt reservoir; ~geld nt storage (charges pl); ~kapazität f storage capacity; (von Computer) memory capacity; ~kraftwerk nt storage power station.

speichern 1 vt Vorräte, Energie, Daten to store; (fig) Gefühle to store up. 2 vr to accumulate.

Speicher|ofen m storage heater.

Speicherung f storing, storage.

speien pret spie, ptp gespie(e)n vti to spit, to expectorate (spec); Lava, Feuer to spew (forth); Wasser to spout; Flammen, Dämpfe to belch (forth or out); (sich übergeben) to vomit. der Drache spie Feuer the dragon breathed fire; siehe Gift.

Speik m -s, -e spikenard.

Speis[1] m -es, no pl (S Ger) mortar.

Speis[2] f -, -en (S Ger, Aus) pantry, larder.

Speise f -, -n (a) (geh: Nahrung) food, fare (liter); (Gericht) dish; (Süß~) sweet (Brit), dessert. ~n und Getränke meals and beverages; vielen Dank für Speis und Trank many thanks for the meal; kalte und warme ~n hot and cold meals; erlesene ~n choice dishes.

(b) no pl (Mörtel) mortar.

(c) (Metal) speiss; (Glocken~) bell metal.

Speise-: ~brei m chyme; ~eis nt icecream; ~fett nt cooking or edible fat; ~haus nt restaurant, eating house; ~kammer f larder, pantry; ~karte f menu; ~leitung f (Elec) feeder, supply main; ~lokal nt restaurant.

speisen (hum) ptp gespiesen 1 vti (geh) to eat, to dine (form). zu Abend ~ to have dinner, to dine (in the evening) (form); zu Mittag ~ to lunch; wünsche wohl zu ~ I hope you enjoy your meal; etw ~ to eat sth, to dine on sth (form); was wünschen Sie zu ~? what do you wish to eat, sir/madam?

2 vt (liter, Tech) to feed; (old) Gast to dine.

Speisen-: ~aufzug m dumb waiter, service lift; ~folge f order of the menu or the courses.

Speise-: ~öl nt salad oil; (zum Braten) cooking or edible oil; ~opfer nt food offering; ~reste pl left-overs pl; (zwischen den Zähnen) food particles pl; ~röhre f (Anat) gullet; ~saal m dining hall; (in Hotel etc) dining room; (auf Schiffen) dining saloon; (in Klöstern, Internaten etc auch) refectory; ~saft m chyle; ~schrank m larder, pantry; ~stärke f cornflour, cornstarch (US); ~wagen m (Rail) dining car, restaurant car, diner (esp US); ~zettel m menu; ~zimmer nt dining room.

Speisung f (geh) feeding; (Tech auch) supply. die ~ der Fünftausend the feeding of the five thousand.

speiübel adj mir ist ~ I think I'm going to be sick or to throw up; da kann einem ~ werden, wenn man das sieht the sight of that is enough to make you feel sick.

Spektabilität [ʃpɛktabiliˈtɛːt, sp-] f (Univ) (Mr) Dean.

Spektakel[1] m -s, - (inf) row, rumpus (inf); (Aufregung) fuss, bother, palaver (inf).

Spektakel[2] [ʃpɛkˈtaːkl, sp-] nt -s, - (old) spectacle, show.

spektakulär [ʃpɛktakuˈlɛːɐ, sp-] adj spectacular.

Spektra pl of **Spektrum**.

Spektral- [ʃpɛkˈtraːl-, sp-]: ~analyse f spectrum analysis; ~farbe f colour of the spectrum.

Spektren pl of **Spektrum**.

Spektroskop [ʃpɛktroˈskoːp, sp-] nt -s, -e spectroscope.

spektroskopisch [ʃp-, sp-] adj spectroscopic.

Spektrum [ˈʃpɛktrum, ˈsp-] nt -s, **Spektren** or **Spektra** spectrum.

Spekulant(in f) m speculator.

Spekulation f (a) (Fin) speculation (mit in). ~ mit Grundstücken property speculation. (b) (Vermutung) speculation. ~en anstellen to make speculations; man stellt schon ~en an, ob ... people are already speculating as to whether ...

Spekulations-: ~geschäft nt speculative transaction or operation; es war ein ~~geschäft, aber es hat sich gelohnt it was a gamble but it was worth it; ~gewinn m speculative gains pl or profit; ~objekt nt object of speculation; ~papier nt speculative security or stock.

Spekulatius [ʃpekuˈlaːtsɪus] m -, - spiced biscuit (Brit) or cookie (US).

spekulativ adj speculative.

spekulieren* vi (a) (Fin) to speculate (mit in); siehe Baisse, Hausse. (b) (Vermutungen anstellen) to speculate. auf etw (acc) ~ (inf) to have hopes of sth.

Spelunke f -, -n (pej inf) dive (inf).

Spelz m -es, -e (Agr) spelt.

Spelze f -, -n (Bot) husk; (von Gras) glume.

spendabel adj (inf) generous, open-handed.

Spende f -, -n donation; (Beitrag) contribution. eine ~ geben or machen to give a donation/contribution, to donate/contribute something; bitte eine kleine ~! please give or donate or contribute something (for charity).

spenden vti Lebensmittel, Blut, Geld to donate, to give; (beitragen) Geld to contribute; Abendmahl, Segen to administer; Schatten to afford, to offer; Trost to give. bitte ~ Sie für das Rote Kreuz! please donate/contribute something to or for the Red Cross; siehe Beifall, Lob.

Spendenkonto nt donations account.

Spender(in f) m -s, - donator; (Beitragleistender) contributor; (Med) donor. wer war der edle ~? (inf) to whom am I indebted?

spendieren* vt to buy, to get (jdm etw sb sth, sth for sb). spendierst du mir einen? (inf) are you going to buy or stand me a drink?; laß mal, das spendiere ich forget it, it's on me.

Spendierhosen pl (inf) seine ~ anhaben to be in a generous mood, to be feeling generous.

Spengler m -s, - (dial: Klempner) plumber.

Spenzer m -s, - long-sleeved vest; (kurze Jacke) short jacket.

Sperber m -s, - sparrowhawk.

Sperenzchen, Sperenzien [-ən] pl (inf) ~ machen (inf) to make trouble, to be difficult.

Sperling m sparrow.

Sperma nt -s, **Spermen** or -ta sperm.

Sperrad nt getrennt Sperr-rad ratchet wheel.

sperr|angelweit adv (inf) ~ offen wide open.

Sperr-: ~ballon m (Mil) barrage balloon; ~bezirk m no-go area, prohibited area.

Sperre f -, -n (a) (Hindernis, Schlagbaum, Bahnsteig~ etc) barrier; (Polizei~) roadblock; (Mil) obstacle; (Tech) locking device.

(b) (Verbot, Sport) ban; (Blockierung) blockade; (Comm) embargo; (Nachrichten~) (news) blackout.

(c) (Psych) mental block. eine psychologische/emotionale ~ a mental/emotional block.

sperren 1 vt (a) (schließen) Grenze, Hafen, Straße, Brücke, Tunnel to close; Platz, Gegend auch to close off; (Tech) to lock. Tunnel gesperrt! tunnel closed; etw für jdn/etw ~ to close sth to sb/sth.

(b) (Comm) Konto to block, to freeze; Scheck to stop.

(c) (Sport: ausschließen) to ban, to bar.

(d) (Sport: behindern) Gegner to obstruct, to block.

(e) (verbieten) Einfuhr, Ausfuhr to ban. jdm den Urlaub/das Gehalt ~ to stop sb's holidays/salary; jdm den Ausgang ~ (Mil) to confine sb to barracks.

(f) (abstellen) Gas, Strom, Telefon to cut off, to disconnect. jdm den Strom/das Telefon ~ to cut off or disconnect sb's electricity/telephone.

(g) (einschließen) jdn in etw (acc) ~ to shut or lock sb in sth.

(h) (Typ) to space out.

2 vr sich (gegen etw) ~ to ba(u)lk or jib (at sth); jetzt laß dir doch auch einmal etwas schenken und sperr dich nicht so accept a present for once, can't you, and don't be so ungracious.

3 vi (a) (nicht schließen: Tür, Fenster) to stick, to jam; (blockiert sein: Räder) to lock.

(b) (Sport) to obstruct. S~ ist nicht zulässig obstruction is not allowed.

Sperr-: ~feuer nt (Mil, fig) barrage; sein Vorschlag geriet ins ~feuer der Kritik his suggestion ran into a barrage of criticism; ~frist f waiting period (auch Jur); (Sport) (period of) suspension; ~gebiet nt no-go area, prohibited area or zone; ~getriebe nt locking mechanism; ~gut nt bulky freight or goods pl; ~holz nt plywood.

sperrig adj bulky; (unhandlich) unwieldy.

Sperr-: ~kette f chain; (an Haustür) safety chain; ~klinke f pawl; ~konto nt blocked account; ~kreis m (Rad) wave trap; ~mauer f wall; ~minorität f (Fin) blocking minority; ~müll m bulky refuse; ~müllabfuhr f removal of bulky refuse; ~rad nt siehe Sperrad; ~sitz m (im Kino) back seats pl; (im Zirkus) front seats pl; (old: im Theater) stalls pl, orchestra; ~stunde f closing time.

Sperrung f (a) siehe vt closing; closing off; locking; blocking; stopping; banning, barring; banning; stopping, stoppage; cutting off, disconnection, disconnecting; spacing. (b) siehe Sperre (b).

Sperr-: ~zoll m prohibitive tariff; ~zone f siehe ~gebiet.

Spesen pl expenses pl. Sie machen zu hohe ~ your expenses are too high; auf ~ reisen/essen to travel/eat on expenses; außer ~ nichts gewesen hardly profitable but enjoyable.

Spesen-: s~frei adj free of charge; ~konto nt expense account; ~ritter m (inf) expense-account type (inf).

Spezerei f usu pl (old) spice; (Delikatesse) exotic delicacy.

Spezereiwaren pl (old) spices pl; (Delikatessen) exotic delicacies pl.

Spezi m -s, -s (S Ger inf) pal (inf), chum (inf).

Spezial-: ~arzt m specialist; ~ausbildung f specialized training; ~ausführung f special model or version; ein Modell in ~ausführung a special version; ~disziplin f special discipline; ~fach nt special subject; ~fahrzeug nt special-purpose vehicle; ~fall m special case; ~gebiet nt special field or topic; ~geschäft nt specialist shop; ein ~geschäft für Sportkleidung a sportswear specialist's.

spezialisieren* 1 vr sich (auf etw acc) ~ to specialize (in sth). 2 vt (old: spezifizieren) to specify, to itemize.

Spezialisierung f specialization.

Spezialist(in f) m specialist (für in).

Spezialistentum nt specialization.

Spezialität f speciality (esp Brit), specialty (esp US).

Spezial-: ~slalom m special slalom; ~vollmacht f special authorization.

speziell 1 adj special; (außerordentlich, individualisierend auch) especial. auf Ihr (ganz) S~es! your good health!; er ist mein ganz ~er Freund he's a very special friend of mine (auch iro). 2 adv (e)specially.

Spezies [ˈʃpeːtsies, ˈsp-] f -, - (Biol) species sing. die ~ Mensch the human species.

Spezifikation f specification; (Aufgliederung) classification.

spezifisch adj specific.

spezifizieren* vt to specify; (einzeln aufführen auch) to itemize.

Spezifizierung f specification, specifying; (Einzelaufführung auch) itemization, itemizing.

Sphäre f -, -n (lit, fig) sphere; siehe schweben.
Sphären-: ~harmonie f harmony of the spheres; ~musik f music of the spheres.
sphärisch adj spherical; Klänge, Musik celestial.
Sphinx f -, -e sphinx.
Spick|aal m smoked eel.
spicken 1 vt (Cook) Braten to lard; (inf: bestechen) to bribe, to square (inf). **eine (gut) gespickte Brieftasche** a well-lined wallet; **mit Fehlern/Zitaten gespickt** peppered with mistakes/quotations, larded with quotations. 2 vi (Sch sl) to copy, to crib (inf) (bei off, from).
Spickzettel m crib.
spie pret of **speien**.
Spiegel m -s, - (a) mirror, glass (old); (Med) speculum; (fig) mirror. **in den ~ schauen** or **sehen** to look in the mirror; **glatt wie ein ~** like glass; **im ~ der Öffentlichkeit** or **der öffentlichen Meinung** as seen by the public, as reflected in public opinion; **das kannst du dir hinter den ~ stecken** (inf) (you can) put that in your pipe and smoke it (inf); **jdm den ~ vorhalten** (fig) to hold up a mirror to sb.
  (b) (Wasser~, Alkohol~, Zucker~) level.
  (c) (Aufschlag) lapel; (Mil: Kragen~) tab.
  (d) (Archit: von Decke, Tür) panel.
  (e) (Hunt) (bei Rotwild) escutcheon; (bei Vögeln) speculum.
  (f) (Liter: Sammlung von Regeln, Gesetzen etc) code.
  (g) (Typ) type area.
Spiegel-: ~bild nt (lit, fig) reflection; (seitenverkehrtes Bild) mirror image; **die Schrift im ~bild** the mirror image of the writing; **s~bildlich** adj Zeichnung etc mirror image; **s~bildlich schreiben** to do mirror writing; **s~blank** adj glossy, shining, bright as a mirror; **sie hat den Herd s~blank geputzt** she polished the cooker until it shone like a mirror.
Spiegel|ei nt fried egg.
Spiegel-: ~fechterei f (fig) (Scheingefecht) shadow-boxing; (Heuchelei, Vortäuschung) sham, bluff; ~fernrohr nt reflector (telescope); ~folie f mirror foil; ~glas nt mirror glass; **s~glatt** adj like glass, glassy, as smooth as glass; **s~gleich** adj symmetrical; ~gleichheit f symmetry; ~heck nt (Naut) square stern; ~karpfen m mirror carp.
spiegeln 1 vi (reflektieren) to reflect (the light); (glitzern) to gleam, to shine. 2 vt to reflect, to mirror. 3 vr to be mirrored or reflected; (sich betrachten) to look at one's reflection.
Spiegel-: ~reflexkamera f reflex camera; ~schrift f mirror writing; **etw in ~schrift schreiben** to write sth backwards.
Spiegelung f reflection; (Luft~) mirage.
Spieker m -s, - (N Ger: Nagel) nail; (Naut) spike.
Spiel nt -(e)s, -e (a) (Unterhaltungs~, Glücks~, Sport, Tennis) game; (Wettkampfs~ auch) match; (Theat: Stück) play; (fig: eine Leichtigkeit) child's play no art. **ein ~ spielen** (lit, fig) to play a game; **im ~ sein** (lit) to be in the game; (fig) to be involved or at work; **die Kräfte, die hier mit im ~ waren** the forces which were at play here; **das Leben ist kein ~** life is not a game; **das ~ verloren geben** to give the game up for lost; (fig) to throw in the towel; **machen Sie ihr ~!** place your bets!, faites vos jeux; **jdn ins ~ schicken** (Sport) to send sb on; **jdn aus dem ~ nehmen** (Sport) to take sb off; **ein ~ im ~** (Theat) a play within a play.
  (b) (das Spielen, Spielweise) play(ing); (Mus, Theat) playing; (Sport) play; (bei Glücksspielen) gambling. **das ~ ist für die Entwicklung des Kindes wichtig** play(ing) is important for children's development; **stör das Kind nicht beim ~** don't disturb the child while he's playing or at play; **stummes ~** miming.
  (c) (Bewegung, Zusammenspiel) play. **~ der Hände** hand movements; **das (freie) ~ der Kräfte** the (free) (inter)play of forces; **~ der Lichter** play of lights; **das ~ der Wellen** the play of the waves.
  (d) **ein (seltsames) ~ der Natur** a (strange) freak of nature; **ein ~ des Schicksals** or **Zufalls** a whim of fate.
  (e) (Spielzubehör) game; (Karten) deck, pack; (Satz) set. **führen Sie auch ~e?** do you have games?; **das Monopoly-~ ist nicht mehr vollständig** the Monopoly set has something missing.
  (f) (von Stricknadeln) set.
  (g) (Tech) (free) play; (~raum) clearance.
  (h) (Hunt) tail.
  (i) (fig) **das ist ein ~ mit dem Feuer** that's playing with fire; **leichtes ~ (mit or bei jdm) haben** to have an easy job of it (with sb); **bei den einfachen Bauern hatten die Betrüger leichtes ~** the simple peasants were easy game for the swindlers; **jdm das ~ verderben** to spoil sb's little game; **das ~ ist aus** the game's up; **die Hand** or **Finger im ~ haben** to be involved in, to have a hand in affairs; **jdn/etw aus dem ~ lassen** to leave or keep sb/sth out of it; **etw mit ins ~ bringen** to bring in or up sth; **etw aufs ~ setzen** to put sth at stake or on the line (inf), to risk sth; **auf dem ~(e) stehen** to be at stake; **sein ~ mit jdm treiben** to play games with sb.
Spiel-: ~alter nt playing stage; ~anzug m playsuit, rompers pl; ~art f variety; ~automat m gambling or gaming machine; (zum Geldgewinnen) fruit machine, one-armed bandit (hum inf); ~bahn f (Golf) fairway; ~ball m (Volleyball) match-ball, game-ball (US); (Tennis) game point; (Billard) cue ball; (fig) plaything; **ein ~ball der Wellen sein** (geh) to be at the mercy of or be tossed about by the waves; ~bank f casino; **s~bar** adj playable; ~beginn m start of play; **gleich nach ~beginn** just after the start of play; ~bein nt free leg; **s~bereit** adj ready to play; ~brett nt board; (Basketball) backboard.
Spielchen nt (inf) little game.
Spieldose f musical box (Brit), music box (US).
spielen 1 vt to play. **jdm einen Streich ~** to play a trick on sb; **Klavier/Flöte ~** to play the piano/the flute; **was wird heute im**

Theater/Kino gespielt? what's on at the theatre/cinema today?, what's playing at the theatre/what's showing at the cinema today?; **sie ~ einen Film von ...** they're showing a film by ...; **das Stück war sehr gut gespielt** the play was very well acted or performed or done; **wir haben den Galileo in Stuttgart gespielt** we played Galileo in Stuttgart; **den Unschuldigen ~** to play the innocent; **den Beleidigten ~** to act all offended; **sie spielt die große Dame** she's playing or acting the grand lady; **am Sonntag mußte ich mal wieder Klempner ~** on Sunday I had to do my plumber's act again; **was wird hier gespielt?** (inf) what's going on here?; siehe Herr, Schicksal.
  2 vi to play; (Theat) (Schauspieler) to act, to play; (Stück) to be on, to play; (Film) to be on, to show; (beim Glücksspiel) to gamble. **die Mannschaft hat gut/schlecht etc gespielt** the team had a good/bad etc game, the team played well/badly etc; **bei ihm spielt das Radio den ganzen Tag** he has the radio on all day; **seine Beziehungen ~ lassen** to bring one's connections to bear or into play; **seine Muskeln ~ lassen** to ripple one's muscles; **der Wind spielt in den Blättern** the wind is playing among the leaves; **na ja, wie das Leben so spielt** life's funny like that; **in der Hauptrolle spielt X X** is playing the lead; **das Stück spielt im 18. Jahrhundert/in Italien** the play is set in the 18th century/in Italy; **nervös spielte er mit dem Bleistift** he played or toyed nervously with the pencil; **mit dem Gedanken ~, etw zu tun** to toy or play with the idea of doing sth; **mit jdm/jds Liebe/Gefühlen ~** to play (around) with sb/sb's affections/feelings; **ein Lächeln spielte um ihre Lippen** a smile played about her lips; **ihr Haar spielt ins Rötliche** her hair has a reddish tinge.
  3 vr **sich müde ~** to tire oneself out playing; **sich in den Vordergrund ~** to push oneself into the foreground; **auf nassem Boden spielt es sich schlecht** (Sport) wet ground isn't very good to play on.
spielend 1 adj playing. 2 adv easily. **das ist ~ leicht** that's very easy.
Spiel|ende nt end of play. **kurz vor ~** just before the end of play.
Spieler(in f) m -s, - player; (Theat auch) actor/actress; (Glücks~) gambler.
Spielerei f (a) no pl (das Spielen) playing; (beim Glücksspiel) gambling; (das Herumspielen) playing or fooling or fiddling (inf) about or around; (Kinderspiel) child's play no art, doddle (inf). **das ist nur ~** I am/he is etc just playing or fooling about; **hör mit der ~ am Fernseher auf!** stop playing or fooling or fiddling about or around with the TV!
  (b) (Gegenstand) frivolity; (Gerät auch) gadget.
spielerisch 1 adj (a) (verspielt) Geste, Katze etc playful.
  (b) **mit ~er Leichtigkeit** with the greatest of ease, with consummate ease.
  (c) (Sport) playing; (Theat) acting. **~es Können** playing/acting ability; **die ~e Leistung** the playing/acting.
  2 adv (a) (verspielt) playfully.
  (b) (mit Leichtigkeit) with the greatest of ease, with consummate ease.
  (c) (Sport) in playing terms; (Theat) in acting terms.
Spielerwechsel m substitution.
Spiel-: ~feld nt field, pitch (Brit); (Tennis, Squash, Basketball) court; ~figur f piece; ~film m feature film; ~fläche f playing area; (bei Gesellschaftsspielen) playing surface; ~folge f (Sport) order of play; (Theat) programme; **s~frei** adj (Theat, Sport) **s~freier Tag** rest-day; **die s~freie Zeit** the close season; **der Sonntag ist s~frei** (Theat) there is no performance on Sundays; (Sport) there is no game on Sundays; **unsere Mannschaft ist heute s~frei** our team has no game today; **s~freudig** adj keen, enthusiastic; ~führer m (team) captain; ~gefährte m playmate, playfellow; ~geld nt (a) (Einsatz) stake; (b) (unechtes Geld) play money, toy money; ~genosse m siehe ~gefährte; ~geschehen nt (Sport) play, action; **das gesamte ~geschehen** all of the play or action; ~hölle f gambling den; ~kamerad m siehe ~gefährte; ~karte f playing card; ~kasino nt (gambling) casino; ~klasse f division; ~leidenschaft f passion for gambling, gambling mania; ~leiter m (a) siehe Regisseur(in); (b) (Sport) organizer; (c) (Conférencier) master of ceremonies, emcee (inf); ~macher m key player; ~mann m, pl -leute (Hist) minstrel; (Mitglied eines ~mannszuges) bandsman; ~mannszug m (brass) band; ~marke f chip, counter; ~minute f minute (of play); ~plan m (Theat, Film) programme; **ein Stück vom ~plan absetzen** to drop a play (from the programme); ~platz m (für Kinder) playground; (Sport) playing-field; ~raum m room to move; (fig) scope; (zeitlich) time; (bei Planung etc) leeway; (Tech) clearance, (free) play; **ich habe 5 Minuten Zeit zum Umsteigen, das ist sehr wenig ~raum** I've got 5 minutes to change, that doesn't leave (me) much time (to play with); **jedes Kind braucht einen gewissen ~raum, um sich frei entwickeln zu können** all children need a certain amount of scope to be able to develop freely; ~rausch m gambling fever; ~regel f (lit, fig) rule of the game; **sich an die ~regeln halten, die ~regeln beachten** (lit, fig) to stick to the rules (of the game), to play the game; **gegen die ~regeln verstoßen** (lit, fig) to break the rules, not to play the game; ~runde f round; ~saal m gaming hall; ~sachen pl toys pl, playthings pl; ~saison f (Theat, Sport) season; ~schuld f gambling debt; ~schule f (dated) siehe Kindergarten; ~stand m score; **bei einem ~stand von ...** with the score (standing) at ...; ~tag m day; ~teufel m gambling urge or bug (inf); **vom ~teufel besessen sein** (inf) to have the gambling bug (inf); ~tisch m games table; (beim Glücksspiel) gaming or gambling table; ~trieb m play instinct; ~uhr f musical box (Brit), music box (US); ~verbot nt (Sport) ban; ~verbot haben to be banned; ~verderber(in f) m -s, - spoilsport;

~verlängerung *f* extra time (*Brit*), overtime (*US*); (*wegen Verletzung auch*) injury time (*Brit*); ~verlängerung (von 30 Minuten) (30 minutes') extra time *etc* was played; ~verlauf *m* action, play; es widersprach dem ~verlauf, daß ... it went against the run of the play that ...; ~waren *pl* toys *pl*; ~warenhandlung *f*, ~warengeschäft *nt* toy shop (*Brit*) or store (*esp US*); ~weise *f* way of playing; offensive/defensive/unfaire ~weise attacking/defensive/unfair play; ~werk *nt* musical mechanism; ~wiese *f* playing field; (*fig*) playground; dieses Bett ist eine richtige ~wiese this bed has plenty of space for fun and games; ~zeit *f* (a) (*Saison*) season; (b) (~*dauer*) playing time; die normale ~zeit (*Sport*) normal time; nach dreimonatiger ~zeit wurde das Stück abgesetzt the play was taken off after a three-month run.
Spielzeug *nt* toy; toys *pl*, playthings *pl*; (*fig auch*) plaything. er hat viel ~ he has a lot of toys.
Spielzeug- in cpds toy; ~eisenbahn *f* toy train set.
Spielzimmer *nt* playroom.
Spier *m* -s, -e blade (of grass).
Spiere *f* -, -n, **Spier** *f* -, -en (*Naut*) spar, boom.
Spierling *m* (a) (*Eberesche*) service tree. (b) (*Fisch*) smelt, sparling.
Spieß *m* -es, -e (a) (*Stich- und Wurfwaffe*) spear; (*Brat~*) spit; (*kleiner*) skewer. am ~ gebraten roasted on the spit, spit-roast(ed); Schaschlik am ~ skewered kebab, kebab on the spit; wie am ~(e) schreien (*inf*), schreien als ob man am ~ steckt (*inf*) to squeal like a stuck pig; den ~ umkehren or umdrehen (*fig*) to turn the tables; *siehe* brüllen.
(b) (*Mil sl*) sarge (*sl*).
(c) (*Hunt*) spike.
(d) (*Typ*) work-up (*US*), spacing mark.
Spieß-: ~bock *m* (*Hunt*) brocket, spike buck; ~braten *m* joint roasted on a spit.
Spießbürger *m* (petit) bourgeois. ihre Eltern sind richtige ~ her parents are typically middle-class.
spießbürgerlich *adj* middle-class, (petit) bourgeois.
Spießbürgertum *nt* (petit-)bourgeois conformism, middle-class values *pl*.
spießen *vt* etw auf etw (*acc*) ~ (*auf Pfahl etc*) to impale sth on sth; (*auf Gabel etc*) to skewer sth on sth; (*auf größeren Bratspieß*) to spit sth on sth; (*auf Nadel*) to pin sth on sth; einen Zettel an die Wand ~ to pin a notice to the wall.
Spießer *m* -s, - (a) (*inf*) *siehe* Spießbürger. (b) (*Hunt*) *siehe* Spießbock.
Spießgeselle *m* (*old*) companion; (*hum: Komplize*) crony (*inf*).
spießig *adj* (*inf*) *siehe* spießbürgerlich.
Spießrute *f* switch. ~n laufen (*fig*) to run the gauntlet.
Spießrutenlauf *m* (*fig*) running the gauntlet. für ihn wird jeder Gang durch die Stadt zum ~ every time he walks through town it's like running the gauntlet.
Spikes [ʃpaiks, sp-] *pl* (*Sportschuhe, Stifte*) spikes *pl*; (*Autoreifen*) studded tyres *pl*; (*Stifte an Reifen*) studs *pl*.
Spike(s)reifen ['ʃpaik(s)-, sp-] *pl* studded tyres *pl*.
Spill *nt* -(e)s, -e (*Naut*) capstan.
spillerig *adj* (*N Ger*) spindly.
spinal *adj* (*Med*) spinal. ~e Kinderlähmung poliomyelitis.
Spinat *m* -(e)s, *no pl* spinach.
Spinatwachtel *f* (*pej inf*) old cow (*inf*) or baggage (*inf*).
Spind *m or nt* -(e)s, -e (*Mil, Sport*) locker; (*old: Vorratskammer*) cupboard.
Spindel *f* -, -n spindle; (*Treppen~*) newel.
spindeldürr *adj* (*pej*) spindly, thin as a rake. ~e Beine spindle-shanks (*inf*), spindly legs.
spindelförmig *adj* spindle-shaped.
Spinett *nt* -s, -e (*Mus*) spinet.
Spinnaker ['ʃpinakɐ] *m* -s, - (*Naut*) spinnaker.
Spinne *f* -, -n spider.
spinnefeind *adj pred* (*inf*) sich or einander (*dat*) ~ sein to be deadly enemies.
spinnen *pret* spann, *ptp* gesponnen 1 *vt* to spin; (*old liter: ersinnen*) Verrat, Ränke to concoct, to invent; Geschichte to spin. ein Netz von Lügen or ein Lügengewebe ~ to weave a web of lies; das ist alles gesponnen (*inf*) it's all fairy-tales; *siehe* Garn, Seemannsgarn.
2 *vi* (a) (*lit*) to spin. es ist nichts so fein gesponnen, es kommt doch ans Licht der Sonnen (*Prov*) truth will out (*inf*).
(b) (*inf*) (*leicht verrückt sein*) to be crazy or nutty (*inf*) or screwy (*inf*); (*Unsinn reden*) to talk rubbish; (*Lügengeschichten erzählen*) to make it up, to tell tall stories. der spinnt in den höchsten Tönen he's completely nuts (*inf*); stimmt das, oder spinnst du? is that true, or are you having me on? (*inf*) or putting me on? (*US inf*); sag mal, spinn' ich, oder ...? am I imagining things or ...?; ich denk' ich spinn' I don't believe it; ich spinn' doch nicht no way (*inf*); spinn doch nicht! come off it! (*inf*); du spinnst wohl!, spinnst du? you must be crazy!, are you crazy!; ich dein Auto waschen?, du spinnst wohl! me clean your car!, you've got to be joking or kidding (*inf*).
Spinnen-: ~faden *m* spider's thread; ~gewebe *nt siehe* Spinngewebe; ~netz *nt* cobweb, spider's web.
Spinner(in *f*) *m* -s, - (a) spinner. (b) (*inf*) nutcase (*inf*), screwball (*esp US inf*). du ~, das stimmt doch nicht! are you crazy?, that's not true at all! (c) (*Zool*) silkworm moth.
Spinnerei *f* (a) (*das Spinnen*) spinning. (b) (*Spinnwerkstatt*) spinning mill. (c) (*inf*) crazy behaviour *no pl*; crazy thing; (*Unsinn*) rubbish, garbage (*inf*). das ist doch eine ~, so was zu machen it's crazy to do that; deine ~en glaubt dir doch kein Mensch! nobody's going to believe all that rubbish.
Spinn-: ~faser *f* spinning fibre; ~gewebe *nt* cobweb, spider's web; ~maschine *f* spinning-machine; ~rad *nt* spinning-wheel; ~rocken *m* -s, - distaff; ~stube *f* spinning-room; ~web *nt or m*

-(e)s, -e (*Aus, S Ger*), ~webe *f* -, -n cobweb, spider's web.
spinös *adj* crackpot *attr* (*inf*).
spintisieren *vi* (*inf*) to ruminate, to muse.
Spion *m* -s, -e spy; (*inf: Guckloch*) spy-hole, peephole; (*Fensterspiegel*) busybody, window mirror.
Spionage [ʃpio'naːʒə] *f* -, *no pl* spying, espionage. ~ treiben to spy, to carry on espionage; unter dem Verdacht der ~ für ... on suspicion of spying for ...
Spionage-: ~abwehr *f* counter-intelligence or counter-espionage (service); ~dienst *m* (*inf*) secret service; ~netz *nt* spy network; ~ring *m* spy-ring.
spionieren* *vi* to spy; (*fig inf: nachforschen*) to snoop or poke about (*inf*).
Spionin *f* (woman) spy.
Spirale *f* -, -n spiral; (*geometrisch, Sci auch*) helix; (*Med*) coil.
Spiralfeder *f* coil spring.
spiralig *adj* (*rare*) spiral, helical.
Spiralnebel *m* (*Astron*) spiral nebula.
Spirans ['ʃpiːrans, sp-] *f* -, **Spiranten, Spirant** [ʃpiˈrant, sp-] *m* (*Ling*) fricative, spirant.
Spiritismus [ʃpiriˈtɪsmʊs, sp-] *m* spiritualism, spiritism.
Spiritist(in *f*) [ʃpiriˈtɪst(ɪn), sp-] *m* spiritualist.
spiritistisch [ʃpiriˈtɪstɪʃ, sp-] *adj* spiritualist.
Spiritual ['spiritjʊəl] *m or nt* -s, -s (negro) spiritual.
Spiritualismus [ʃpiritʊaˈlɪsmʊs, sp-] *m* spiritualism.
spiritualistisch [ʃpiritʊaˈlɪstɪʃ, sp-] *adj* spiritualist.
spirituell [ʃpiriˈtuɛl, sp-] *adj* spiritual.
Spirituosen [ʃpiriˈtuoːzn, sp-] *pl* spirits *pl*.
Spiritus *m* -, *no pl* (a) [ʃp-] (*Alkohol*) spirit. mit ~ kochen to cook with a spirit stove; etw in ~ legen to put sth in alcohol. (b) [sp-] (*Ling*) spiritus.
Spiritus-: ~kocher *m* spirit stove; ~lampe *f* spirit lamp.
Spital *nt* -s, ̈-er (*old, Aus, Sw: Krankenhaus*) hospital, spital (*obs*); (*rare: Altersheim*) old people's home.
Spitals- in cpds (*Aus, Sw*) *siehe* Krankenhaus-.
Spittel¹ *nt* -s, - (*dial*) *siehe* Spital.
Spittel² *m* -s, - (*old*) poor house.
spitz *adj* (a) (*mit einer Spitze*) pointed; (*nicht stumpf*) Bleistift, Nadel *etc* sharp; (*Math*) Winkel acute. die Feder dieses Füllhalters ist nicht ~ genug the nib on this fountain pen is too broad; ~e Schuhen pointed shoes, winkle-pickers (*hum inf*); ~ zulaufen or zugehen to taper (off), to run to a point; etw mit ~en Fingern anfassen (*inf*) to pick sth up gingerly; über einen ~en Stein stolpern to pronounce "sp" and "st" as in English; du bist wohl über einen ~en Stein gestolpert are your false teeth slipping or something? (*hum*).
(b) (*gehässig*) Bemerkung pointed, barbed; Zunge sharp.
(c) (*kränklich*) Aussehen, Gesicht pinched, haggard, peaky.
(d) (*sl: lüstern*) randy (*Brit inf*), horny (*inf*). ~ wie Nachbars Lumpi as randy or horny as (*Frau*) a bitch in heat or (*Mann*) an old goat (*all inf*); jdn ~ machen to turn sb on (*sl*).
Spitz *m* -es, -e (*Hunderasse*) spitz, pomeranian.
Spitz-: ~bart *m* goatee; s~bärtig *adj* with a goatee, goateed; ~bauch *m* potbelly (*inf*); s~bekommen* *vt sep irreg* (*inf*) etw s~bekommen to cotton on to sth (*inf*), to get wise to sth (*inf*); s~bekommen, daß ... to cotton on or get wise to the fact that ... (*inf*); ~bogen *m* pointed arch, ogive (*spec*); ~bub(e) *m* (*old*) villain, rogue; (*dial inf: Schlingel*) scamp (*inf*), scallywag (*inf*); ~bubengesicht *nt* (*old*) villainous or roguish face; ~bubenstreich *m* (*dated*) nasty or knavish (*old*) trick; ~büberei *f* (*old*) knavery (*old*); ~bübin *f siehe* ~bub(e); s~bübisch *adj* roguish, mischievous.
Spitze *f* -, -n (a) (*Schwert~, Nadel~, Pfeil~, Bleistift~, Kinn~*) point; (*Schuh~*) pointed toe; (*Finger~, Nasen~, Bart~, Spargel~*) tip; (*Zigarren~, Haar~*) end; (*Berg~, Fels~*) peak, top; (*Baum~, Turm~, Giebel~*) top; (*Pyramiden~*) top, apex (*form*); (*Dreiecks~*) top, vertex (*form*). auf der ~ stehen to be upside-down; etw auf die ~ treiben to carry sth too far or to extremes; einer Sache (*dat*) die ~ abbrechen/nehmen (*fig*) to take the sting out of sth; jdm/einer Sache die ~ bieten (*fig*) to stand up to sb/sth, to defy sb/sth.
(b) (*fig: Höchstwert*) peak; (*inf: Höchstgeschwindigkeit*) top speed. dieser Sportwagen fährt 200 ~ (*inf*) this sports car has a top speed of 200.
(c) (*Führung*) head; (*vorderes Ende*) front; (*esp Mil: von Kolonne etc*) head; (*Tabellen~*) top. die ~n der Gesellschaft the leading lights of society; an der ~ stehen to be at the head; (*auf Tabelle*) to be (at the) top (of the table); an der ~ liegen (*Sport, fig*) to be in front or in the lead; Ruritanien liegt im Lebensstandard an der ~ Ruritania has the highest standard of living; die ~ halten (*Sport, fig*) to keep the lead; sich an die ~ setzen to put oneself at the head; (*in Wettbewerb etc, Sport*) to go into or take the lead; (*auf Tabelle*) to go to the top (of the table); (*im Pferderennen*) to take up the running; er wurde an die ~ des Unternehmens gestellt he was put at the top or head of the company.
(d) (*Zigaretten-, Zigarrenhalter*) (cigarette/cigar) holder.
(e) (*fig: Stichelei*) dig. das ist eine ~ gegen Sie that's a dig at you, that's directed at you; die ~ zurückgeben to give tit for tat.
(f) (*Comm: Überschuß*) surplus.
(g) (*Gewebe*) lace. Höschen mit ~n panties with lace borders.
(h) (*sl: prima*) great (*inf*).
Spitzel *m* -s, - (*Informant*) informer; (*Spion*) spy; (*Schnüffler*) snooper; (*Polizei~*) police informer, nark (*Brit sl*).
Spitzeldienste *pl* informing *no pl*. für jdn ~ leisten to act as an informer for sb.
spitzeln *vi* to spy; (*Spitzeldienste leisten*) to act as an informer.
spitzen 1 *vt* (*spitz machen*) Bleistift to sharpen; Lippen, Mund to purse; (*zum Küssen*) to pucker; Ohren (*lit, fig*) to prick up.

spitzt doch die Ohren, dann versteht ihr auch, was ich sage! open your ears and then you'll understand what I'm saying! **2** vir (inf) (sich) auf etw (acc) ~ to look forward to sth. **3** vi (dial inf) (aufpassen) to keep a look-out, to keep one's eyes skinned (inf); (heimlich spähen) to peek. ich muß ~, ob er hier entlangkommt I've got to keep a look-out or keep my eyes skinned to see if he comes along this way.

Spitzen- in cpds top; (aus Spitze) lace; ~**belastung** f peak (load); **die Zeit der ~belastung** the peak period; ~**besatz** m lace trimming; ~**bluse** f lace blouse; ~**deckchen** nt, ~**decke** f lace doily; ~**erzeugnis** nt top(-quality) product; ~**feld** nt (Sport) leaders pl, leading group; **im ~feld** amongst the leaders, in the leading group; ~**funktionär** m top official; ~**garnitur** f set of lace underwear; ~**gehalt** nt top salary; ~**geschwindigkeit** f top speed; ~**gremien** pl leading or top committees pl; ~**gruppe** f top group; (Sport: ~**feld**) leading group; ~**höschen** nt lace panties pl; ~**kandidat** m top candidate; ~**klasse** f top class; **Sekt/ ein Auto** etc **der** ~**klasse** top-class champagne/a top-class car etc; **die** ~**klasse der ruritanischen Schachspieler/Skiläufer** the cream or best of the Ruritanian chess-players/skiers; ~**klasse!** (inf) great! (inf); ~**könner** m ace, first-rate or top-class talent; ~**kragen** m lace collar; ~**leistung** f top performance; (von Maschine, Auto) peak performance; (bei der Herstellung von Produkten, Energie) peak output; (fig: ausgezeichnete Leistung) top-class or first-rate performance; (Sport: Rekord) record (performance); ~**lohn** m top wage(s pl); ~**modell** nt top model; ~**organisation** f siehe ~**verband**; ~**position** f leading or top position; ~**preise** pl (Comm) top prices; ~**qualität** f top quality; ~**reiter** m (Sport) leader; (fig) (Kandidat) front-runner; (Ware) top seller; (Film, Stück etc) hit; (Schlager) top of the pops, number one; ~**sportler** m top(-class) sportsman; ~**stellung** f leading position; ~**stickerei** f lace embroidery; ~**strom** m peak current; ~**tanz** m dance on points, toe-dance (US); ~**tuch** nt lace cloth, piece of lace; (Taschentuch) lace handkerchief; ~**verband** m leading organization or group; ~**verdiener** m top earner; ~**verkehrszeit** f peak period; ~**wein** m top-quality wine; ~**wert** m peak; ~**zeit** f (Sport) record time.

Spitzer m -s, - (inf) (pencil-)sharpener.
Spitz-: ~**feile** f taper file; s~**findig** adj over-subtle, over-precise; (haarspalterisch auch) hairsplitting, nit-picking (inf); Unterschied auch over-nice; ~**findigkeit** f over-subtlety, over-precision no pl; (Haarspalterei auch) hairsplitting no pl, nit-picking no pl (inf); (von Unterschied auch) over-nicety; zu behaupten, daß das Wort hier seine Bedeutung ändert, ist eine ~**findigkeit** it's splitting hairs or it's over-subtle or it's nit-picking (inf) to claim that the word changes its meaning here; s~**giebelig** adj with pointed gables; s~**haben** vt sep irreg (inf) etw s~**haben** to have cottoned on to sth (inf), to have got wise to sth (inf); s~**haben, daß ...** to have cottoned on to or have got wise to the fact that ... (inf); ~**hacke** f pick-axe.
spitzig adj (old, dial) siehe **spitz.**
Spitz-: ~**kehre** f (Rail) switchback turn; (Ski) kick-turn; ~**kopf** m pointed head; (inf) swine (inf); s~**kriegen** vt sep (inf) siehe s~**bekommen**; ~**kühler** m (Aut) pointed or V-shaped radiator; (hum inf) pot-belly; ~**marke** f (Typ) sidehead; ~**maus** f shrew; **du bist eine richtige** ~**maus geworden** (inf) you've gone so thin; ~**name** m nickname; **mit dem** ~**namen** nicknamed; ~**wegerich** m ribwort; s~**wink(e)lig** adj (Math) Dreieck acute-angled; Gasse sharp-cornered, angular; s~**züngig** adj sharp-tongued.
Spleen [ʃpliːn] m -s, -s (inf) (Angewohnheit) strange or crazy habit, eccentricity, quirk (of behaviour); (Idee) crazy idea or notion; (Fimmel) obsession. **die Psychologen haben doch alle irgendeinen** ~! these psychologists are all cranks!; **du hast ja einen** ~! you're round the bend (inf) or off your head (inf).
spleenig [ˈʃpliːnɪç] adj (inf) crazy, nutty (inf).
spleißen pret **spliß**, ptp **gesplissen** vt (a) (dial, old) Holz to split. (b) (Naut) Taue, Leinen to splice.
splendid [ʃplɛnˈdiːt, sp-] adj (geh) generous; Behandlung etc auch handsome.
Splint m -(e)s, -e cotter (pin), split pin.
spliß pret of **spleißen.**
Splitt m -(e)s, -e stone chippings pl; (Streumittel) grit.
Splitter m -s, - (Holz~, Metall~, Knochen~) splinter; (Glas~ auch, Granat~) fragment. **der** ~ **in deines Bruders Auge** (Bibl) the mote that is in thy brother's eye (Bibl).
Splitter-: ~**bombe** f (Mil) fragmentation bomb; s~**(faser)nackt** adj (inf) stark-naked, starkers pred (Brit hum inf); ~**fraktur** f (Med) splintered or comminuted (spec) fracture; s~**frei** adj Glas shatterproof; ~**graben** m (Mil) slit trench; ~**gruppe** f (Pol) splinter group.
splitt(e)rig adj splintering.
splittern vi aux sein or haben (Holz, Glas) to splinter.
splitternackt adj siehe **splitter(faser)nackt.**
Splitterpartei f (Pol) splinter party.
Splittingsystem [ˈʃplɪtɪŋ-, sp-] nt (Fin) tax system in which husband and wife each pay income tax on half the total of their combined incomes.
splittrig adj siehe **splitt(e)rig.**
SPÖ [ɛspeːˈʔøː] f - abbr of **Sozialistische Partei Österreichs.**
Spoiler [ˈʃpɔylɐ] m -s, - spoiler.
Spökenkieker m -s, - (N Ger) psychic, clairvoyant, person who has second sight.
Spökenkiekerei f (N Ger) second sight.
Spondeus [ʃpɔnˈdeːʊs, sp-] m -, **Spondeen** [ʃpɔnˈdeːən, sp-] (Poet) spondee.
spontan [ʃpɔnˈtaːn, sp-] adj spontaneous.
Spontaneität [ʃpɔntaneiˈtɛːt, sp-] f spontaneity.
sporadisch [ʃpoˈraːdɪʃ, sp-] adj sporadic.
Spore f -, -n (Biol) spore.
Sporen pl of **Sporn, Spore.**

sporenklirrend adv (old) with a clatter of spurs.
Sporentierchen pl (Biol) sporozoa pl.
Sporn m -(e)s, **Sporen** usu pl (auch Zool, Bot) spur; (Naut auch) ram; (am Geschütz) trail spade; (Aviat: Gleitkufe) tail-skid; (Rad) tail-wheel. **einem Pferd die Sporen geben** to spur a horse, to give a horse a touch of the spurs; **sich** (dat) **die (ersten) Sporen verdienen** (fig) to win one's spurs.
spornen vt (geh) to spur; (fig) to spur on; siehe **gestiefelt.**
spornstreichs adv (old) post-haste, straight away.
Sport m -(e)s, (rare) -e sport; (Zeitvertreib) hobby, pastime. **treiben Sie** ~? do you do any sport?; **er treibt viel** ~ he goes in for or he does a lot of sport; **etw aus** or **zum** ~ **betreiben** to do sth as a hobby or for fun; **sich** (dat) **einen** ~ **aus etw machen** (inf) to get a kick out of sth (inf).
Sport-: ~**abzeichen** nt sports certificate; ~**amt** nt sport authorities pl; ~**angler** m angler; ~**anzug** m sports clothes pl; (Trainingsanzug) track suit; ~**art** f (kind of) sport; ~**artikel** m (a) ~**artikel** pl sports equipment with sing vb; **ein** ~**artikel** a piece of sports equipment; (b) (inf: ~**bericht**) sports report; ~**arzt** m sports physician; s~**begeistert** adj keen on sport, sports-mad (inf); **ein** ~**begeisterter** a sports enthusiast or fan; ~**beilage** f sports section or page(s pl); ~**bericht** m sports report; ~**berichterstattung** f sports reporting.
Sporteln pl (old Admin) fees pl.
Sport-: ~**ereignis** nt sporting event; ~**fechten** nt fencing; **das Fechten, das hier getrieben wird, kann man nicht als** ~**fechten bezeichnen** the fencing practised here cannot be described as a sport; ~**feld** nt sports ground; ~**fest** nt sports festival; ~**flieger** m amateur pilot; ~**flugzeug** nt sporting aircraft; ~**freund** m sport(s)-fan; ~**funk** m sports programmes pl; ~**geist** m sportsmanship; ~**gerät** nt piece of sports equipment; ~**geräte** sports equipment; ~**geschäft** nt sports shop (Brit) or store (esp US); ~**halle** f sports hall; ~**hemd** nt casual or sports or sport (US) shirt; ~**herz** nt (Med) athlete's heart; ~**hochschule** f college of physical education.
sportiv adj (dated) athletic, sporty (inf).
Sport-: ~**jackett** nt sports jacket (Brit), sport coat (US); ~**kanone** f siehe **Sportskanone**; ~**karre** f (N Ger) push-chair (Brit), (baby-)stroller (US); ~**kleidung** f sportswear; ~**klub** m sports club; ~**lehrer(in** f) m sports instructor; (Sch) PE or physical education teacher; (für Sport im Freien) games master/mistress (Brit) or teacher (Brit), sport teacher.
Sportler m -s, - sportsman, athlete.
Sportlerherz nt athlete's heart.
Sportlerin f sportswoman, (woman) athlete.
sportlich adj (a) (den Sport betreffend) Veranstaltung, Wettkampf sporting. ~ **gesehen, ...** from a sporting point of view ...
(b) Mensch sporty; (durchtrainiert) athletic.
(c) (fair) sporting, sportsmanlike no adv.
(d) Kleidung casual; ~(-schick) natty (inf), snazzy (inf), smart but casual; (wie Sportkleidung aussehend) sporty. ~ **gekleidet** casually dressed/wearing smart but casual clothes, smartly but casually dressed; **eine** ~**e Note** a sporty touch.
(e) Auto sporty.
Sportlichkeit f (a) (von Menschen) sportiness; (Durchtrainiertheit) athletic appearance. **er bewies seine** ~, **indem er über den Zaun sprang** he proved how athletic he was by jumping over the fence. (b) (Fairneß) sportsmanship; (von Verhalten auch, um Entscheidung) sporting nature. (c) (von Kleidung) siehe adj (d) casualness; nattiness (inf), snazziness (inf), casual smartness; sportiness. **die** ~ **der neuen Jacke macht sie so vielseitig verwendbar** the clean, simple cut of the new jacket makes it suitable for all occasions.
Sport-: ~**mantel** m casual coat; s~**mäßig** adj siehe s~**smäßig**; ~**medizin** f sports medicine; ~**meldung**, ~**nachricht** f ~**nachrichten** pl sports news with sing vb or reports pl; **eine wichtige** ~**meldung** or ~**nachricht** an important piece of sports news; ~**platz** m sports field; (in der Schule) playing field(s pl); ~**rad** nt sports cycle or bike (inf); ~**redakteur** m sports editor; ~**reportage** f sports reporting; (Bericht) sports report; **die** ~**reportage über die Weltmeisterschaft** the coverage of the world championships; ~**schlitten** m racing toboggan; ~**schuh** m casual shoe.
Sports-: ~**freund** m (fig inf) buddy (inf); **wenn der** ~**freund da ... if this guy ...** (inf); ~**kanone** f (inf) sporting ace (inf); ~**mann** m, pl -**männer** or -**leute** (dated) sportsman; (inf: als Anrede) sport (esp Austral inf), mate (inf); s~**mäßig** adj sporty; **sich** s~**mäßig betätigen** to do sport; **wie sieht's denn dort** s~**mäßig aus?** what sort of sporting facilities are there?
Sport-: ~**unfall** m sporting accident; ~**veranstaltung** f sporting event; ~**verein** m sports club; ~**wagen** m sports (Brit) or sport (US) car; (für Kind) push-chair (Brit), (baby-)stroller (US); ~**zeitung** f sports paper; ~**zeug** nt (inf) sport('s) things pl.
Spot [spɔt] m -s, -s commercial, advertisement, ad (inf).
Spotgeschäft [ˈspɔt-] nt (Fin) spot transaction.
Spotlight [ˈspɔtlait] nt -s, -s spotlight.
Spott m -(e)s, no pl mockery; (höhnisch auch) ridicule, derision. ~ **und Hohn ernten** to earn scorn and derision, to be laughed out of court; **jdn dem** ~ **preisgeben** to hold sb up to ridicule; **dem** ~ **preisgegeben sein** to be held up to ridicule, to be made fun of; **seinen** ~ **mit jdm treiben** to make fun of sb; **Gegenstand des allgemeinen** ~**es** object of general ridicule, laughing-stock; siehe **Schaden.**
Spott-: ~**bild** nt (fig) travesty, mockery; **das** ~**bild eines Präsidenten** a travesty etc of a president; s~**billig** adj dirt-cheap (inf); **das habe ich** s~**billig gekauft** I bought it for a song (inf) or for practically nothing, I bought it dirt-cheap (inf); ~**drossel** f mocking-bird; (dated fig: Spötter) tease, mocker.
Spöttelei f (das Spotten) mocking; (ironische Bemerkung) mocking remark.

spötteln vi to mock (*über jdn/etw* sb/sth), to poke gentle fun (*über jdn/etw* at sb/sth).

spotten vi (a) to mock, to poke fun; (*höhnen auch*) to ridicule, to be derisive. **über jdn/etw ~** to mock sb/sth, to poke fun at sb/sth, to ridicule sb/sth; (*höhnisch auch*) to deride sb/sth, to ridicule sb/sth; **du hast leicht ~!, spotte nur!** it's easy for you to mock or laugh!, it's all very well for you to mock.

(**b**) +*gen* (*old, liter: hohnsprechen*) to mock; (*geh: mißachten*) *der Gefahr* to be contemptuous of, to scorn. **das spottet jeder Beschreibung** that simply defies or beggars description.

Spötter(in f) m **-s**, - (*satirischer Mensch*) wit, satirist; (*jd, der über etw spottet*) mocker.

Spott-: ~**figur** f joke figure, ludicrous character; **eine ~figur sein** to be a figure of fun, to be an object of ridicule; ~**geburt** f (*liter*) freak, monstrosity; ~**gedicht** nt satirical poem, squib, lampoon; ~**gelächter** nt mocking laughter.

spöttisch adj mocking; (*höhnisch auch*) ridiculing, derisive.

Spott-: ~**lied** nt satirical song; ~**lust** f love of mockery, inclination to mock; **s~lustig** adj given to mockery, inclined to mock; ~**name** m derisive nickname; ~**preis** m ridiculously or ludicrously low price; **für einen ~preis** for a song (*inf*); ~**rede** f satirical or lampooning speech; ~**reden führen** to make satirical or lampooning speeches; ~**sucht** f compulsive mocking; **s~süchtig** adj who/which delights in (constant) mockery; ~**vers** m satirical verse.

sprach pret of **sprechen**.

Sprach-: ~**atlas** m linguistic atlas; ~**autonomie** f (*Pol*) linguistic autonomy; ~**barriere** f language barrier; ~**bau** m linguistic structure; **s~begabt** adj good at languages, linguistically talented or gifted; ~**begabung** f talent for languages, linguistic talent; ~**denkmal** nt linguistic monument.

Sprache f **-, -n** language; (*das Sprechen*) speech; (*Sprechweise*) speech, way of speaking; (*Fähigkeit, zu sprechen*) power or faculty of speech. **eine/die ~ sprechen** to (be able to) speak a language/the language or lingo (*inf*); **die ~ analysieren** to analyze language; **die ~ der Musik** the language of music; **in französischer** etc **~** in French etc (*lit, fig*) to speak the same language; **das spricht eine klare** or **deutliche ~** (*fig*) that speaks for itself, it's obvious what that means; **das spricht eine andere ~** (*fig*) that gives a completely different picture; **er spricht jetzt eine ganz andere ~** (*fig*) he's changed his tune now; **heraus mit der ~!** (*inf*) come on, out with it!; **die ~ auf etw** (*acc*) **bringen** to bring the conversation round to sth; **zur ~ kommen** to be mentioned or brought up, to come up; **etw zur ~ bringen** to bring sth up, to mention sth; **die ~ verlieren** to lose the power of speech; **hast du die ~ verloren?** have you lost your tongue?, has the cat got your tongue? (*inf*); **die ~ wiederfinden** to be able to speak again; **es raubt** or **verschlägt einem die ~** it takes your breath away; **mir blieb die ~ weg** I was speechless.

Sprach-: ~**eigentümlichkeit** f linguistic peculiarity or idiosyncrasy; ~**einheit** f (a) (*Ling*) linguistic unit; (b) (*Einheitlichkeit*) linguistic unity.

Sprachen-: ~**frage** f (*Pol*) language question; ~**gewirr** nt babel of tongues (*usu hum*), mixture or welter of languages; ~**kampf** m (*Pol*) language conflict; ~**recht** nt language law; (*Anspruch*) language rights pl; ~**schule** f language school; ~**zentrum** nt (*Univ*) language centre.

Sprach-: ~**erziehung** f (*form*) language education; ~**familie** f family of languages, language family; ~**fehler** m speech defect or impediment; ~**forscher** m linguist(ic researcher); (*Philologe*) philologist; ~**forschung** f linguistic research; (*Philologie*) philology; ~**führer** m phrase-book; ~**gebiet** nt language area; **ein französisches** etc **~gebiet** a French-speaking etc area; ~**gebrauch** m (linguistic) usage; **moderner deutscher ~gebrauch** modern German usage; ~**gefühl** nt feeling for language; ~**gelehrte(r)** mf linguistic scholar; ~**gemeinschaft** f speech community; ~**genie** nt linguistic genius; ~**geschichte** f linguistic history; **die ~geschichte des Mongolischen** the history of the Mongolian language; ~**gesetze** pl linguistic laws pl; ~**gewalt** f power of expression, eloquence; **s~gewaltig** adj eloquent; **ein s~gewaltiger Redner** a powerful speaker; **s~gewandt** adj articulate, fluent; ~**gewissen** nt (*liter*) linguistic consciousness; ~**grenze** f linguistic or language boundary; ~**gut** nt linguistic heritage; **ein Wörterbuch kann nicht das gesamte ~gut widerspiegeln** a dictionary cannot reflect the whole wealth of a language.

-sprachig adj suf -language; (*zwei~, mehr~*) -lingual.

Sprach-: ~**insel** f linguistic enclave or island; ~**kenntnisse** pl linguistic proficiency sing; **mit englischen ~kenntnissen** with a knowledge of English; **haben Sie irgendwelche ~kenntnisse?** do you know any languages?; ~**kenntnisse erwünscht** (knowledge of) languages desirable; ~**kompetenz** f linguistic competence; ~**kritik** f linguistic criticism; **s~kundig** adj (*in mehreren Sprachen*) proficient in or good at (foreign) languages; (*in einer bestimmten Sprache*) linguistically proficient; **es ist schwer, sich in diesem Land zurechtzufinden, wenn man s~kundig ist** it's very difficult to get along in this country if you don't know or are not familiar with the language; ~**kurs(us)** m language course; ~**labor** nt language laboratory or lab (*inf*); ~**lähmung** f paralysis of the organs of speech; ~**landschaft** f linguistic geography; ~**lehre** f (*Grammatik, Grammatikbuch*) grammar; ~**lehrer** m language teacher; ~**lehrgang** m language course.

sprachlich adj linguistic; *Unterricht, Schwierigkeiten* language attr; *Fehler* grammatical. **~ hatten die Einwanderer keine Schwierigkeiten** the immigrants had no language difficulties; **~ falsch/richtig** ungrammatical/grammatical, grammatically incorrect/correct; **eine intelligente Analyse, auch ~ gut** an intelligent analysis, well written too.

sprachlos adj (*ohne Sprache*) speechless; (*erstaunt*) speechless, dumbfounded. **ich bin ~!** I'm speechless; **da ist man (einfach) ~** (*inf*) that's quite or really something (*inf*).

Sprachlosigkeit f speechlessness.

Sprach-: **s~mächtig** adj (*liter*) eloquent; ~**melodie** f intonation, speech melody; ~**mißbrauch** m misuse of language; ~**mittler** m translator and interpreter; ~**pflege** f concern for the purity of language; **aktive ~pflege betreiben** to be actively concerned with the purity of a language; ~**pfleger** m purist; ~**philosophie** f philosophy of language; ~**psychologie** f psychology of language; ~**raum** m siehe ~**gebiet**; ~**regel** f grammatical rule, rule of grammar; (*für Aussprache*) pronunciation rule; (*Ling*) linguistic rule, rule of language; **die einfachsten ~regeln des Lateinischen** the most elementary rules of Latin; ~**regelung** f linguistic ruling; ~**reinheit** f linguistic purity; ~**reiniger** m **-s**, - purist; ~**rohr** nt (*Megaphon*) megaphone; (*fig*) mouthpiece; **sich zum ~rohr einer Sache/Gruppe machen** to become the spokesman for or mouthpiece (*usu pej*) of sth/a group; ~**schäden** pl aphasia sing; ~**schatz** m (*geh*) vocabulary; **dem englischen ~schatz fehlt ein Wort für ...** the English language has no word for ...; ~**schnitzer** m (grammatical) howler; (*stilistisch*) solecism; ~**schönheit** f linguistic beauty, beauty of language; **die ~schönheit von Rimbauds ...** the beauty of the language of Rimbaud's ...; ~**schöpfer** m linguistic innovator; **s~schöpferisch** adj (linguistically) creative; ~**schöpfung** f linguistic innovation; ~**schule** f siehe **Sprachenschule**; ~**silbe** f syllable; ~**soziologie** f sociology of language; ~**stamm** m (language) stock; ~**stil** m style, way one uses language; ~**störung** f speech disorder; ~**struktur** f linguistic structure; ~**studium** nt study of languages/a language, linguistic or language studies pl; ~**talent** nt talent or gift for languages; ~**theorie** f theory of language; ~**übung** f linguistic or language exercise; ~**unterricht** m language teaching or instruction; **der französische ~unterricht** French teaching, the teaching of French; ~**unterricht/französischen ~unterricht erteilen** to give language lessons/French lessons; ~**verein** m language society; ~**verfall** m decay of language; ~**vergleichung** f comparative analysis (of languages); ~**vermögen** nt faculty of language; ~**verwandtschaft** f linguistic relationship or kinship; ~**verwirrung** f confused mixture of languages, confusion of tongues (*Bibl*); siehe **babylonisch**; ~**wissenschaft** f linguistics sing; (*Philologie*) philology; **vergleichende ~wissenschaften** comparative linguistics/philology; ~**wissenschaftler** m linguist; (*Philologe*) philologist; **s~wissenschaftlich** adj linguistic; ~**zentrum** nt (*Univ*) language centre; ~**zweig** m (language) branch.

sprang pret of **springen**.

Spray [ʃpreː, spreː] m or nt **-s**, **-s** spray.

Spraydose [ʃpreː-, ʹspreː-] f aerosol (can), spray.

sprayen [ʃpreːən, sp-] vti to spray.

Sprech-: ~**anlage** f intercom; ~**blase** f balloon; ~**bühne** f theatre, stage; ~**chor** m chorus; (*fig*) chorus of voices; **im ~chor rufen** to shout in unison, to chorus; ~**einheit** f (*Telec*) unit.

sprechen pret **sprach**, ptp **gesprochen** 1 vi to speak (*über +acc, von* about, of); (*reden, sich unterhalten auch*) to talk (*über +acc, von* about). **viel ~** to talk a lot; **frei ~** to extemporize, to speak off the cuff (*inf*); **er spricht wenig** he doesn't say or talk very much; **sprich!** (*liter*) speak! (*liter*); **~ Sie!** (*form*) speak away!; **sprich doch endlich!** say something; also **sprach** ... thus spoke ..., thus spake ... (*liter, Bibl*); **im Traum or Schlaf ~** to talk in one's sleep; **gut/schön ~** to speak well/beautifully; **im Rundfunk/Fernsehen ~** to speak on the radio/on television; **es spricht/es ~ ...** the speaker is/the speakers are ...; **die Vernunft ~ lassen** to listen to reason, to let the voice of reason be heard; **sein Herz ~ lassen** to follow the dictates of one's heart; **schlecht** or **nicht gut auf jdn zu ~ sein** to be on bad terms with sb; **mit jdm ~** to speak or talk with or to sb; **mit sich selbst ~** to talk to oneself; **ich muß mit dir ~** I must talk or speak with you; **ich habe mit dir zu ~** I want to have a word or a few words with you; **wie sprichst du mit mir?** who do you think you're talking to?; **so spricht man nicht mit seinem Großvater** that's no way to talk or speak to your grandfather; **sie spricht nicht mit jedem** she doesn't speak or talk to just anybody; **wir ~ nicht mehr miteinander** we are no longer on speaking terms, we're not speaking any more; **mit wem spreche ich?** to whom am I speaking, please?; **~ wir nicht mehr darüber!** let's not talk about that any more, let's drop the subject; **darüber spricht man nicht** one doesn't talk about or speak of such things; **wovon ~ Sie eigentlich?** what are you talking about?; **ich weiß nicht, wovon Sie ~** I don't know what you're talking about; **~ wir von etwas anderem** let's talk about something else, let's change the subject; **wir haben gerade von dir gesprochen** we were just talking about you; **es wird kaum noch von ihm gesprochen** he's hardly mentioned now; **für jdn/etw ~** to speak for sb/sth, to speak on (*Brit*) or in (*US*) behalf of sb/sth; **es spricht für jdn/etw(, daß ...)** it says something for sb/sth (that ...), it speaks well for sb/sth (that ...); **das spricht für ihn** that's a point in his favour, that says something for him; **es spricht nicht für die Firma, daß so was passieren konnte** it doesn't say much for the firm that something like that could happen; **das spricht für sich (selbst)** that speaks for itself; **es spricht vieles dafür** there's a lot to be said for it; **es spricht vieles dafür, daß ...** there is every reason to believe that ...; **was spricht dafür/dagegen?** what is there to be said for/against it?; **daraus spricht, daß ...** that shows or reveals that ...; **das spricht ihr aus dem Gesicht** (*geh*) it was obvious from the expression on her face; **aus seinen Worten sprach Verachtung/Hoffnung** his words expressed contempt/hope; **er sprach vor den Studenten/dem Ärztekongreß** he spoke to the students/the medical conference; **ganz allgemein gesprochen** generally speaking.

2 *vt* (a) *(sagen)* to say, to speak; *eine Sprache, Mundart* to speak; *(aufsagen) Gebet* to say; *Gedicht* to say, to recite. **es wurde viel gesprochen** a lot of talking was done; **alles, was er sprach ...** everything he said ...; ~ **Sie Japanisch?** do you speak Japanese?; **hier spricht man Spanisch** Spanish spoken, we speak Spanish; *siehe* **Sprache**.

(b) *Urteil* to pronounce; *siehe* **Recht**.

(c) *(mit jdm reden)* to speak to. **kann ich bitte Herrn Kurz ~?** may I speak to Mr Kurz, please?; **er ist nicht zu ~** he can't see anybody; **ich bin für niemanden zu ~** I can't see anybody, I'm not available; **ich hätte gern Herrn Bremer gesprochen** could I speak to Mr Bremer?; **kann ich Sie einen Augenblick or kurz ~?** can I see you for a moment?, can I have a quick word?; **für Sie bin ich jederzeit zu ~** I'm always at your disposal; **wir ~ uns noch!** you haven't heard the last of this!

sprechend *adj Augen, Gebärde* eloquent; *Ähnlichkeit* striking. **jdm ~ ähnlich sehen** to look exactly like sb.

Sprecher(in *f) m* -s, - speaker; *(Nachrichten~)* newscaster, newsreader; *(für Dokumentarfilme, Stücke etc)* narrator; *(Ansager)* announcer; *(Wortführer)* spokesman. **sich zum ~ von jdm/etw machen** to become the spokesman of sb/sth.

Sprech-: ~**erziehung** *f* speech training, elocution; **s~faul** *adj* taciturn; **sei doch nicht so s~faul!** haven't you got a tongue in your head!; **morgens ist sie besonders s~faul** she's not exactly talkative in the mornings; ~**fehler** *m* slip of the tongue; ~**fenster** *nt* grille; ~**funk** *m* radio-telephone system; ~**funkgerät** *nt* radiotelephone; *(tragbar auch)* walkie-talkie; ~**funkverkehr** *m* local radio traffic; **den ~funkverkehr unterbrechen** to interrupt radiotelephone communications; ~**gebühr** *f (Telec)* call charge; ~**gesang** *m (Mus)* speech-song, sprechgesang; ~**kunde** *f* study of speech; ~**melodie** *f siehe* **Sprachmelodie**; ~**muschel** *f (Telec)* mouthpiece; ~**organ** *nt* organ of speech, speech organ; ~**platte** *f* spoken-word record; ~**probe** *f* voice trial; ~**puppe** *f* talking or speaking doll; ~**rolle** *f* speaking part; ~**schulung** *f* voice training; ~**silbe** *f (Ling)* (phonetic) syllable; ~**stimme** *f* speaking voice; *(Mus)* sprechstimme, speech voice; ~**stunde** *f* consultation (hour); *(von Arzt)* surgery *(Brit)*, doctor's office *(US)*; ~**stunden** consultation hours; *(von Arzt)* surgery *(Brit)* or consulting hours; ~**stunde halten** to hold surgery *(Brit)*; ~**stundenhilfe** *f* (doctor's) receptionist; ~**taste** *f* "talk" button or switch; ~**übung** *f* speech exercise; ~**unterricht** *m* elocution lessons *pl*; ~**weise** *f* way of speaking; ~**werkzeuge** *pl* organs of speech; ~**zeit** *f* (a) *(~stunde)* consulting time; *(von Arzt)* surgery time *(Brit)*; (b) *(Besuchszeit: in Gefängnis, Kloster)* visiting time; (c) *(Telec)* call time; ~**zimmer** *nt* consulting room.

Spreißel¹ *m* -s, - *(S Ger)* splinter.

Spreißel² *nt* -s, - *(Aus)* kindling *no pl*.

Spreite *f* -, -n *(leaf)* blade.

Spreize *f* -, -n (a) *(Build)* strut. (b) *(Sport)* straddle.

spreizen 1 *vt Flügel, Gefieder* to spread; *Finger, Zehen auch* to splay (out); *Beine auch* to open; *(Sport)* to straddle.

2 *vr (sich sträuben)* to kick up *(inf)*; *(sich aufplustern)* to give oneself airs, to put on airs. **sich wie ein Pfau ~** to puff oneself up, to put on airs; **sich gegen etw ~** to kick against sth.

Spreiz-: ~**fuß** *m* splayfoot; ~**schritt** *m (Sport)* straddle; **im ~schritt stehen** to stand with one's legs apart.

Spreng-: ~**arbeiten** *pl* blasting operations *pl*; ~**bombe** *f* high-explosive bomb.

Sprengel *m* -s, - *(Kirchspiel)* parish; *(Diözese)* diocese; *(old, rare: Amtsbezirk)* district.

sprengen 1 *vt* (a) to blow up; *Fels* to blast.

(b) *Türschloß, Tor* to force (open); *Tresor* to break open; *Bande, Fesseln* to burst, to break; *Eisdecke, Versammlung* to break up; *(Spiel)bank* to break; *siehe* **Rahmen**.

(c) *(bespritzen)* to sprinkle; *Beete, Rasen auch* to water; *Wäsche* to sprinkle (with water); *(verspritzen) Wasser* to sprinkle, to spray.

2 *vi* (a) to blast.

(b) *aux sein (liter: kraftvoll reiten)* to thunder.

Spreng-: ~**kammer** *f* demolition chamber; ~**kapsel** *f* detonator; ~**kommando** *nt* demolition squad; *(zur Bombenentschärfung)* bomb disposal squad; ~**kopf** *m* warhead; ~**körper** *m* explosive device; ~**kraft** *f* explosive force; ~**ladung** *f* explosive charge; ~**meister** *m (in Steinbruch)* blaster; *(bei Abbrucharbeiten)* demolition expert; *(zur Bombenentschärfung)* bomb-disposal expert; ~**satz** *m* explosive device.

Sprengstoff *m* explosive.

Sprengstoff-: ~**anschlag** *m,* ~**attentat** *nt* bomb attack; *(erfolgreich auch)* bombing; **auf ihn/das Haus wurde ein ~anschlag verübt** he was the subject of a bomb attack/there was a bomb attack on the house.

Sprengung *f siehe vt* (a) blowing-up; blasting. (b) forcing (open); breaking open; bursting, breaking; breaking-up; breaking. (c) sprinkling; watering; sprinkling (with water); sprinkling, spraying.

Spreng-: ~**wagen** *m* water(ing)-cart, street sprinkler; ~**wedel** *m (Eccl)* aspergillum; ~**wirkung** *f* explosive effect.

Sprenkel *m* -s, - (a) *(Tupfen)* spot, speckle. (b) *(Vogelschlinge)* snare.

sprenkeln *vt Farbe* to sprinkle spots of; *siehe* **gesprenkelt**.

Spreu *f* -, *no pl* chaff. **wie (die) ~ im Wind** *(Bibl)* like chaff in the wind *(Bibl)*; **die ~ vom Weizen trennen** or **sondern** *(fig)* to separate the wheat from the chaff.

sprich *imper sing* of **sprechen**.

Sprichwort *nt, pl* -**er** proverb.

sprichwörtlich *adj (lit, fig)* proverbial.

sprießen *pret* **sproß** or **sprießte**, *ptp* **gesprossen** *vi aux sein (aus der Erde)* to come up, to spring up; *(Knospen, Blätter)* to

shoot; *(fig geh: Liebe, Zuneigung)* to burgeon *(liter)*.

Spriet *nt* -(e)s, -e *(Naut)* sprit.

Springbrunnen *m* fountain.

springen *pret* **sprang**, *ptp* **gesprungen 1** *vi aux sein* (a) *(lit, fig, Sport, bei Brettspielen)* to jump; *(mit Schwung auch)* to leap, to spring; *(beim Stabhochsprung)* to vault; *(Raubtier)* to pounce; *(sich springend fortbewegen)* to bound; *(hüpfen, seilhüpfen)* to skip; *(auf einem Bein hüpfen)* to hop; *(Ball etc)* to bounce; *(Wassersport)* to dive; *(S Ger inf: eilen)* to nip *(Brit inf)*, to pop *(inf)*. **singen/tanzen und ~** to sing and leap about/dance and leap about; **jdm an den Hals** or **die Kehle** or **die Gurgel** *(inf)* ~ to leap or fly at sb's throat; *(fig)* to fly at sb, to go for sb; **ich hätte ihm an die Kehle ~ können** I could have strangled him; **aus dem Gleis** or **den Schienen ~** to jump the rails; **ins Aus ~** *(Sport)* to go out (of play); **die Kinder kamen gesprungen** the children came running; *siehe* **Bresche, Klinge**.

(b) **etw ~ lassen** *(inf)* to fork out for sth *(inf)*; *Runde* to stand sth; *Geld* to fork out sth; **für jdn etw ~ lassen** *(inf)* to treat sb to sth; *esp Getränke auch* to stand sb sth; **das hat der Chef ~ lassen!** *(inf)* that was on the boss! *(inf)*.

(c) *(geh: hervorsprudeln)* to spring; *(Wasserstrahl, Quelle auch, Blutstrahl)* to spurt; *(Funken)* to leap.

(d) *(Saite, Glas, Porzellan)* to break; *(Risse bekommen)* to crack; *(sich lösen: Knopf)* to come off *(von etw sth)*.

(e) *(geh: aufplatzen)* to burst (forth).

2 *vt aux haben* **einen (neuen) Rekord ~** *(Sport)* to make a record jump.

Springen *nt* -s, - *(Sport)* jumping; *(Stabhoch~)* vaulting; *(Wassersport)* diving.

springend *adj* **der ~e Punkt** the crucial point.

Springer(in *f) m* -s, - (a) jumper; *(Stabhoch~)* vaulter; *(Wassersport)* diver. (b) *(Chess)* knight. (c) *(Ind)* stand-in.

Spring-: ~**flut** *f* spring tide; ~**form** *f (Cook)* springform.

Springinsfeld *m* -(e)s, -e madcap.

Spring-: ~**kraut** *nt (Bot)* touch-me-not; **s~lebendig** *adj* lively, full of beans *(inf)*; ~**pferd** *nt* jumper; ~**quell** *m (poet)* fountain; ~**reiten** *nt* show jumping; ~**seil** *nt* skipping rope; **über ein ~seil springen** *(seilspringen)* to skip; ~**turnier** *nt* show jumping competition.

Sprinkler *m* -s, - sprinkler.

Sprinkleranlage *f* sprinkler system.

Sprint *m* -s, -s sprint.

sprinten *vti aux sein* to sprint.

Sprinter(in *f) m* -s, - sprinter.

Sprintstrecke *f* sprint distance.

Sprit *m* -(e)s, -e *(inf)* gas *(inf)*, juice *(inf)*; *(Rohspiritus)* neat spirit, pure alcohol.

Spritz-: ~**beutel** *m* icing or piping bag; ~**düse** *f* nozzle; *(Tech)* jet.

Spritze *f* -, -n syringe; *(Feuer~, Garten~)* hose; *(Injektion)* injection, jab *(inf)*. **eine ~ bekommen** to have an injection or a jab *(inf)*; **der Mann an der ~** *(fig inf)* the kingpin.

spritzen 1 *vti* (a) to spray; *(in einem Strahl auch) Wasser* to squirt; *(Cook) Zuckerguß etc* to pipe; *(verspritzen) Wasser, Schmutz etc* to splash; *(Fahrzeug)* to spray, to spatter. **die Feuerwehr spritzte (Wasser) in das brennende Gebäude** the firemen directed their hoses into the burning building; **das vorbeifahrende Auto spritzte mir Wasser ins Gesicht** the passing car sprayed or spattered water in my face.

(b) *(lackieren) Auto* to spray.

(c) *Wein* to dilute with soda water/mineral water. **er trinkt Rotwein gespritzt** he drinks red wine with soda water/mineral water; *siehe* **Gespritzte(r)**.

(d) *(injizieren) Serum etc* to inject; *Heroin etc auch* to shoot *(sl)*; *(eine Injektion geben)* to give injections/an injection. **wir müssen (dem Kranken) Morphium ~** we have to give (the patient) a morphine injection; **er spritzt seit einem Jahr** *(inf)* he has been shooting or mainlining for a year *(sl)*; *(Diabetiker)* he has been injecting himself for a year.

2 *vi* (a) *aux haben* or *sein (Wasser, Schlamm)* to spray, to splash; *(heißes Fett)* to spit; *(in einem Strahl)* to spurt; *(aus einer Tube, Wasserpistole etc)* to squirt. **es spritzte gewaltig, als er ins Wasser plumpste** there was an enormous splash when he fell into the water.

(b) *aux sein (inf: eilen)* to dash, to nip *(Brit inf)*.

Spritzen-: ~**haus** *nt* fire station; ~**wagen** *m (old)* fire engine.

Spritzer *m* -s, - *(Farb~, Wasser~)* splash; *(von Parfüm, Mineralwasser auch)* dash.

Spritz-: ~**fahrt** *f (inf)* spin *(inf)*; **eine ~fahrt machen** to go for a spin *(inf)*; ~**gebäck** *nt (Cook)* ≈ Viennese whirl/whirls *pl*; ~**guß** *m* injection moulding; *(Metal)* die-casting.

spritzig 1 *adj Wein* tangy, piquant; *Auto* lively, nippy *(Brit inf)*; zippy *(inf)*; *Aufführung, Dialog etc* sparkling, lively; *(witzig)* witty. **das Kabarett war ~ und witzig** the cabaret was full of wit and sparkle.

2 *adv aufführen, darstellen* with sparkle; *schreiben* racily; *(witzig)* wittily.

Spritz-: ~**kuchen** *m (Cook)* cruller; ~**lack** *m* spray(ing) paint; ~**lackierung** *f* spraying; ~**pistole** *f* spray-gun; ~**schutz** *m* guard; ~**tour** *f siehe* ~**fahrt**; ~**tülle** *f* nozzle.

spröd(e) *adj Glas, Stein, Haar* brittle; *Haut* rough; *Stimme* thin; *(fig) Material* obdurate, recalcitrant; *(abweisend)* aloof.

Sprödigkeit *f siehe adj* brittleness; roughness; thinness; obdurateness, obduracy, recalcitrancy; aloofness.

sproß *pret* of **sprießen**.

Sproß *m* -sses, -sse shoot; *(fig: Nachkomme)* scion *(liter)*.

Sprosse *f* -, -n *(lit, fig)* rung; *(Fenster~)* *(senkrecht)* mullion; *(waagerecht)* transom; *(Geweih~)* branch, point, tine.

sprossen *vi aux sein (liter) siehe* **sprießen**.

Sprossen-: ~**kohl** m (Aus) (Brussels) sprouts pl; ~**wand** f (Sport) wall bars pl.
Sprößling m shoot; (fig hum) offspring.
Sprossung f budding.
Sprotte f -, -n sprat.
Spruch m -(e)s, ⁼e (a) saying; (Sinn~ auch) aphorism; (Maxime auch) adage, maxim; (Wahl~) motto; (Bibel~) quotation, quote; (Poet: Gedicht) medieval lyric poem. **die ⁼e Salomos** (Bibl) (the Book of) Proverbs; ⁼**e** (inf: Gerede) patter no pl (inf); ⁼**e machen** (inf) or **klopfen** (inf) or **kloppen** (sl) to talk fancy (inf); (angeben) to talk big (inf); (Verkäufer) to give one's patter (inf) or spiel (sl); **mach keine ⁼e!** (inf) come off it! (inf); **das sind doch nur ⁼e!** that's just talk.
(b) (Richter~) judgement; (Frei-/Schuld~) verdict; (Strafurteil) sentence; (Schieds~) ruling.
Spruchband nt banner.
Spruchdichtung f (Poet) medieval lyric poetry.
Sprücheklopfer m (inf) patter-merchant (inf); (Angeber) big talker (inf).
Spruchkammer f (Hist) denazification court.
Sprüchlein nt dim of **Spruch. sein ~ hersagen** to say one's (little) piece.
spruchreif adj (inf) **die Sache ist noch nicht ~** it's not definite yet so we'd better not talk about it; **die Sache wird erst ~, wenn ... we** can only start talking about it definitely when ...
Sprudel m -s, - (saurer ~) mineral water; (süßer~) fizzy drink.
sprudeln 1 vi (a) (schäumen) (Wasser, Quelle) to bubble; (Sekt, Limonade) to effervesce, to fizz; (fig: vor Freude, guten Ideen etc) to bubble. (b) aux sein (hervor~) (Wasser etc) to bubble; (fig: Worte) to pour out. 2 vt (Aus: quirlen) to whisk.
sprudelnd adj (lit) Getränke fizzy, effervescent; (fig) Temperament, Witz bubbling, bubbly (inf), effervescent.
Sprudler m -s, - (Aus) whisk.
Sprühdose f spray (can); (unter Druck stehend auch) aerosol (can).
sprühen 1 vi (a) aux haben or sein to spray; (Funken) to fly. (b) (fig) (vor Witz etc) to bubble over, to effervesce; (Augen) (vor Freude etc) to sparkle; (vor Zorn etc) to glitter, to flash. 2 vt to spray; (fig: Augen) to flash. **er sprühte Lack auf die beschädigte Stelle** he sprayed the damaged spot with paint.
sprühend adj Laune, Temperament etc bubbling, bubbly (inf), effervescent; Witz sparkling, bubbling.
Sprüh-: ~**nebel** m mist; ~**regen** m drizzle, fine rain.
Sprung m -(e)s, ⁼e (a) jump; (schwungvoll, fig: Gedanken~ auch) leap; (Hüpfer) skip; (auf einem Bein) hop; (Satz) bound; (von Raubtier) pounce; (Stabhoch~) vault; (Wassersport) dive. **einen ~/einen kleinen ~ machen** to jump/do a small jump; **zum ~ ansetzen** (lit) to get ready to jump etc; (fig) to get ready to pounce; **sie wagte den ~ nicht** (fig) she didn't dare (to) take the plunge; **ein großer ~ nach vorn** (fig) a great leap forward; **damit kann man keine großen ⁼e machen** (inf) you can't exactly live it up (inf); **auf dem ~ sein** or **stehen, etw zu tun** to be about to do sth; **nun komm schon! — ich bin schon auf dem ~!** come along! — I'm just coming; **immer auf dem ~ sein** (inf) to be always on the go (inf); (aufmerksam) to be always on the ball (inf); **jdm auf die ⁼e helfen** (wohlwollend) to give sb a (helping) hand; (drohend) to show sb what's what; **jdm auf** or **hinter die ⁼e kommen** (inf) to catch on to sb, to get wise to sb (inf).
(b) (inf: kurze Strecke) stone's throw (inf). **bis zum Postamt ist es nur ein ~** the post office is only a stone's throw from here (inf); **auf einen ~ bei jdm vorbeikommen/-gehen** to drop or pop in to see sb (inf).
(c) (Riß) crack. **einen ~ haben/bekommen** to be cracked/to crack.
(d) (Geol) siehe **Verwerfung.**
(e) (Hunt: Rudel) herd.
(f) (Agr: Begattung) mounting. **dieser Hengst eignet sich nicht zum ~** this stallion isn't suitable for stud purposes; **es kam nicht zum ~** they didn't mate.
Sprung-: ~**bein** nt (a) (Anat) anklebone; (b) (Sport) takeoff leg; **s~bereit** adj ready to jump; Katze ready to pounce; (fig hum) ready to go; ~**brett** nt (lit, fig) springboard; ~**deckel** m spring lid; ~**feder** f spring; ~**federmatratze** f spring mattress; ~**gelenk** nt ankle joint; (von Pferd) hock; ~**grube** f (Sport) (landing) pit; **s~haft** 1 adj (a) Mensch, Charakter volatile; Denken disjointed; (b) (rapide) Aufstieg, Entwicklung etc rapid; Preisanstieg auch sharp; 2 adv ansteigen, entwickeln by leaps and bounds; ~**haftigkeit** f siehe adj (a) volatile nature, volatility; disjointedness; (b) rapidity, rapidness; sharpness; ~**kraft** f (Sport) takeoff power, leg power; ~**lauf** m (Ski) ski-jumping; ~**netz** nt (jumping) net, life net (US); ~**schanze** f (Ski) ski-jump; ~**stab** m (vaulting) pole; ~**tuch** nt jumping sheet or blanket, life net (US); ~**turm** m diving platform; **s~weise** adv in bounds or jumps; (fig) by leaps and bounds.
Spucke f -, no pl (inf) spittle, spit. **da bleibt einem die ~ weg!** its flabbergasting (inf); **als ich das hörte, blieb mir die ~ weg** when I heard that I was flabbergasted (inf) or you could have knocked me down with a feather (inf); **mit Geduld und ~** (hum inf) with blood, sweat and tears (hum).
spucken vti to spit; (inf: sich übergeben) to throw up (inf), to be sick; (fig inf) Lava, Flammen to spew (out); (inf: Maschine, Motor etc) to give the occasional hiccup (inf). **in die Hände ~** (lit) to spit on one's hands; (fig) to roll up one's sleeves.
Spucknapf m spittoon.
Spuk m -(e)s, -e (a) (Geistererscheinung) **der ~ fing um Mitternacht an** the ghosts started to walk at midnight; **glaubst du an ~?** do you believe in ghosts?; **ich glaube an diesen ~** I don't believe the place is haunted; **wie ein ~ like** a ghost.
(b) (fig) (Mummenschanz) grotesque charade; (Lärm) din,

racket (inf); (Aufheben) fuss, to-do (inf), palaver (inf). **einen ~ machen** (Lärm) to make a din or racket (inf); (Aufheben) to kick up a fuss (inf).
spuken vi to haunt. **an einem Ort/in einem Schloß ~** to haunt or walk a place/castle; **es spukt auf dem Friedhof/im alten Haus** etc the cemetery/old house etc is haunted; **hier spukt es** this place is haunted; **durch den Film spukten wunderliche Gestalten/eigenartige Ideen** the film was haunted by weird and wonderful apparitions/strange ideas; **das spukt noch immer in den Köpfen** that still has a hold on people's minds; **bei dem spukt es ja im Kopf** (inf) he's a bit wrong in the head (inf).
Spuk-: ~**geschichte** f ghost story; **s~haft** adj eerie; ~**schloß** nt haunted castle.
Spül-: ~**automat** m (automatic) dishwasher; ~**bad** nt rinse.
Spülbecken nt, **Spüle** f -, -n sink.
Spule f -, -n (a) spool, reel; (Nähmaschinen~, Ind) bobbin; (Elec) coil. (b) (Federkiel) quill.
spulen vt to spool, to reel; (auf~ auch) to wind onto a spool or reel/bobbin.
spülen vti (a) (aus~, ab~) to rinse; Wunde to wash; Darm to irrigate; Vagina to douche; (abwaschen) Geschirr to wash up; (auf der Toilette) to flush. **du spülst und ich trockne ab** you wash and I'll dry; **vergiß nicht zu ~** don't forget to flush the toilet.
(b) (Wellen etc) to wash. **etw an Land ~** to wash sth ashore.
Spüler(in f) m -s, - dishwasher, washer-up.
Spülfrau f dishwasher, washer-up, washing-up lady.
Spülicht nt -s, -e (old) dishwater.
Spül-: ~**kasten** m cistern; ~**klosett** nt flush toilet, water closet; ~**lappen** m dishcloth; ~**maschine** f (automatic) dishwasher; ~**mittel** nt washing-up liquid; ~**programm** nt wash programme; (von Waschmaschine) rinse cycle.
Spülrad nt bobbin-winder.
Spül-: ~**schüssel** f washing-up bowl; ~**stein** m sink; ~**tisch** m sink (unit).
Spülung f rinsing; (Wasser~) flush; (Med) (Darm~) irrigation; (Vaginal~) douche; (Aut) scavenging.
Spülwasser nt (beim Abwaschen) dishwater, washing-up water; (beim Wäschewaschen) rinsing water.
Spulwurm m roundworm, ascarid (Med).
Spund m -(e)s, -e (a) bung, spigot; (Holztechnik) tongue. (b) **junger ~** (dated inf) young pup (dated inf).
spunden vt Faß to bung.
Spund-: ~**loch** nt bunghole; ~**wand** f (Build) bulkhead.
Spur f -, -en (a) (Abdruck im Boden etc) track; (Hunt auch) spoor no pl; (hinterlassenes Zeichen) trace, sign; (Brems~) skidmarks pl; (Blut~, Schleim~ etc, Fährte zur Verfolgung) trail. **von den Tätern fehlt jede ~** there is no clue as to the whereabouts of the persons responsible; **der Täter hat keine ~en hinterlassen** the culprit left no traces or marks; **jds ~ aufnehmen** to take up sb's trail; **jdm auf der ~ sein** to be on sb's trail; **auf der richtigen/falschen ~ sein** (lit, fig) to be on the right/wrong track; **jdn auf jds ~ bringen** to put sb onto sb's trail or onto sb; **jdn auf die richtige ~ bringen** (fig) to put sb on(to) the right track; **jdm auf die ~ kommen** to get onto sb; **auf** or **in jds ~en wandeln** to follow in sb's footsteps; **(seine) ~en hinterlassen** (fig) to leave its mark; **ohne/nicht ohne ~(en)** an jdm vorübergehen to have no effect on sb/to leave its mark on sb.
(b) (fig: kleine Menge, Überrest) trace; (von Pfeffer, Paprika etc) touch, soupçon; (von Vernunft, Anstand, Talent etc) scrap, ounce. **sie hat doch eine ~ Vernunft/Takt** these have some sense/talent; **von Anstand/Takt keine ~** (inf) no decency/tact at all; **von Liebe keine ~** (inf) love doesn't/didn't come into it; **keine ~** (inf), **nicht die ~** (inf) not/nothing at all; **keine ~ davon ist wahr** (inf) there's not a scrap or an ounce of truth in it; **eine ~ zu laut/grell** a shade or a touch too loud/garish.
(c) (Fahrbahn) lane. **auf der linken ~ fahren** to drive in the left-hand lane; **in der ~ bleiben** to keep in lane.
(d) (Aut: gerade Fahrtrichtung) tracking. **~ halten** (beim Bremsen etc) to hold its course; (nach Unfall) to track properly; **aus der ~ geraten** or **kommen** (durch Seitenwind etc) to go off course; (beim Bremsen etc) to skid.
(e) (~weite) (Rail) gauge; (Aut) track.
spürbar adj noticeable, perceptible.
Spurbreite f (Rail) gauge.
spuren vi (Ski) to make or lay a track; (Aut) to track; (inf) to obey; (sich fügen) to toe the line; (funktionieren: Maschine, Projekt) to run smoothly, to go well. **jetzt wird gespurt!** (inf) I want a little obedience; **bei dem Lehrer wird gespurt** (inf) he makes you obey, that teacher.
spüren 1 vt to feel; (intuitiv erfassen) jds Haß, Zuneigung, Unwillen etc auch to sense. **sie spürte, daß der Erdboden leicht bebte** she felt the earth trembling underfoot; **sie ließ mich ihr Mißfallen ~** she made no attempt to hide her displeasure, she let me know that she was displeased; **etw in allen Gliedern ~** (lit, fig) to feel sth in every bone of one's body; **davon ist nichts zu ~** there is no sign of it, it's not noticeable; **etw zu ~ bekommen** (lit) to feel sth; (fig) to feel the (full) force of sth; **jds Spott, Anerkennung etc zu ~ bekommen** to meet with sth; (bereuen) to suffer for sth, to regret sth; **es zu ~ bekommen, daß ... to** feel the effects of the fact that ...; **ihr werdet es noch zu ~ bekommen, daß ihr so faul seid** some day you'll regret being so lazy; **sie bekamen es deutlich zu ~, daß sie Weiße waren** they were made very conscious or aware of the fact that they were whites.
2 vti (Hunt) (nach) etw ~ to track sth, to follow the scent of sth.
Spüren-: ~**element** nt trace element; ~**sicherung** f securing of evidence; **die Leute von der ~sicherung** the forensic people.
Spürhund m tracker dog; (inf: Mensch) sleuth.

spurlos adj without trace. ~ verschwinden to disappear or vanish without trace, to vanish into thin air; ~ an jdm vorübergehen to have no effect on sb; (Ereignis, Erfahrung etc auch) to wash over sb; das ist nicht ~ an ihm vorübergegangen it left its mark on him.

Spür-: ~nase f (Hunt) nose; eine ~nase für etw haben (fig inf) to have a (good) nose for sth; ~sinn m (Hunt, fig) nose; (fig: Gefühl) feel.

Spurt m -s, -s or -e spurt; (End~, fig) final spurt. zum ~ ansetzen (lit, fig) to make a final spurt.

spurten vi aux sein (Sport) to spurt; (zum Endspurt ansetzen) to make a final spurt; (inf: rennen) to sprint, to dash.

Spurweite f (Rail) gauge; (Aut) track.

sputen vr (old, dial) to hurry, to make haste (old, liter).

Sputnik [ˈʃputnɪk, sp-] m -s, -s sputnik.

SSO abbr of **Südsüdost** SSE.

SSW abbr of **Südsüdwest** SSW.

st interj (Aufmerksamkeit erregend) psst; (Ruhe gebietend) shh.

s.t. [esˈteː] adv abbr of **sine tempore**.

St. abbr of **Stück**; **Sankt** St.

Staat m -(e)s, -en (a) state; (Land) country. die ~en (inf) the States (inf); im deutschen ~ in Germany; ein ~ im ~e a state within a state; von ~s wegen on a governmental level; im Interesse/zum Wohl des ~es in the national interest or in the interests of the state/for the good of the nation; beim ~ arbeiten or sein (inf) to be employed by the government or state; so wenig ~ wie möglich minimal government; ~ ist ~ the state's the state; der ~ bin ich (prov) l'État, c'est moi.
(b) (Ameisen~, Bienen~) colony.
(c) (fig) (Pracht) pomp; (Kleidung, Schmuck) finery. in vollem ~ in all one's finery; (Soldaten) in full dress; (Würdenträger) in full regalia; (großen) ~ machen to make a show; damit ist kein ~ zu machen, damit kann man nicht gerade ~ machen that's nothing to write home about (inf); ohne großen ~ damit zu machen without making a big thing about it (inf).

Staaten-: ~bund m confederation (of states); s~los adj stateless; ~lose(r) mf decl as adj stateless person; ~losigkeit f statelessness.

staatl. gepr. abbr of **staatlich geprüft**.

staatlich 1 adj state attr; Gelder, Unterstützung etc auch government attr; (staatseigen) Betrieb, Güter auch state-owned; (~ geführt) state-run.
2 adv by the state. ~ subventioniert subsidized by the state, state-subsidized; ~ anerkannt state-approved, government-approved; ~ geprüft state-certified.

staatlicherseits adv on a governmental level.

Staatlichkeit f statehood.

Staats-: ~abgaben pl (government) taxes pl; ~affäre f (a) (lit) affair of state; (b) (fig) siehe ~aktion; ~akt m (lit) state occasion; (fig inf) song and dance (inf); er wurde in or mit einem feierlichen ~akt verabschiedet his farewell was a state occasion; ~aktion f major operation; ~amt nt public office; ~angehörige(r) mf decl as adj national; (einer Monarchie auch) subject; ~angehörigkeit f nationality; ~angehörigkeitsnachweis m proof of nationality; ~anleihe f government bond; ~anwalt m prosecuting attorney (US), public prosecutor; der ~anwalt forderte ... the prosecution called for ...; ~anwaltschaft f prosecuting attorney's office (US), public prosecutor's office; (Anwälte) prosecuting attorneys pl (US), public prosecutors pl; ~apparat m apparatus of state; ~archiv nt state archives pl; ~aufsicht f state or government control; ~ausgaben pl public spending or expenditure sing; ~bahn f state-owned or national railway(s pl); ~bank f national or state bank; ~bankrott m national bankruptcy; ~beamte(r) m public servant; ~begräbnis nt state funeral; ~besitz m state property; (in) ~besitz sein to be state-owned; ~besuch m state visit; ~betrieb m state-owned or nationalized enterprise; ~bibliothek f national library; ~bürger m citizen; ~bürgerkunde f (Sch) civics sing; s~bürgerlich adj attr civic; Rechte civil; ~chef m head of state; ~diener m public servant; ~dienst m civil service; s~eigen adj state-owned; ~eigentum nt state property no art, property of the state; ~empfang m state reception; s~erhaltend adj conducive to the well-being of the state; ~examen nt state exam(ination), ≈ first degree, university degree required for the teaching profession; ~feiertag m national holiday; ~feind m enemy of the state; s~feindlich adj hostile to the state; sich s~feindlich betätigen to engage in activities hostile to the state; ~finanzen pl public finances pl; ~flagge f national flag; ~form f type of state; ~gebiet nt national territory no art; s~gefährdend adj threatening the security of the state; ~gefährdung f threat to the security of the state; ~geheimnis nt (lit, fig hum) state secret; ~gelder pl public funds pl; ~gerichtshof m constitutional court; ~gewalt f authority of the state; ~grenze f state frontier or border; ~haushalt m national budget; ~hoheit f sovereignty; ~idee f conception of a state; ~interesse nt interests pl of the (state); ~kanzlei f state chancellery; ~kapitalismus m state capitalism; ~karosse f state carriage; ~kasse f treasury, public purse; ~kirche f state church; ~klugheit f (liter) statesmanship; ~kommissar m state commissioner; ~kosten pl public expenses pl; auf ~kosten at the public expense; ~kunst f (liter) statesmanship, statecraft; ~lehre f political science; ~lotterie f national or state lottery; ~mann m statesman; s~männisch adj statesmanlike; ~minister m state minister; ~monopol nt state monopoly; ~oberhaupt nt head of state; ~ordnung f system of government; ~-und Gesellschaftsordnung social system and system of government; ~organ nt organ of the state; ~partei f official party; s~politisch adj political; ~polizei f state police, ≈ Special Branch (Brit); die Geheime ~polizei (Hist) the Ge-

stapo; ~präsident m president; ~prüfung f (form) siehe ~examen; ~raison, ~räson f reasons of state; ~rat m (a) (Kollegium) council of state; (Sw) cantonal government; (b) (Hist: Titel) councillor of state; (Sw) member of the cantonal government; ~recht nt (a) national law; (b) (Verfassungsrecht) constitutional law; s~rechtlich adj siehe n (a) Entscheidung, Überlegung of national law; s~rechtlich unterscheiden sich ... in national law there are differences between ...; (b) constitutional; ~regierung f state government; ~religion f state religion; ~rente f state or government pension; ~ruder nt (geh) helm of the state; ~säckel m (old, hum) national coffers pl; ~schatz m national treasury; ~schiff nt (liter) ship of state; ~schuld f (Fin) national debt; ~sekretär m secretary of state (US); (BRD: Beamter) ≈ permanent secretary (Brit); ~sicherheit f national or state security; ~sicherheitsdienst m (DDR) national or state security service; ~sozialismus m state socialism; ~streich m coup (d'état); ~theater nt state theatre; ~unternehmen nt state-owned enterprise; ~verbrechen nt political crime; (fig) major crime; ~verfassung f (national) constitution; ~verleumdung f slander or (schriftlich) libel of the state; ~vermögen nt national or public assets pl; ~vertrag m international treaty; ~verwaltung f administration of the state; ~wald m state-owned forest; ~wesen nt state; ~wissenschaft(en pl) f (dated) political science; ~wohl nt (geh) good or welfare of the state; ~zuschuß m state or government grant.

Stab m -(e)s, ⸚e (a) rod; (Gitter~) bar; (Spazierstock, Wander~) stick; (Bischofs~) crosier; (Hirten~) crook; (Marschall~, Dirigenten~, für Staffellauf, von Majorette etc) baton; (als Amtzeichen) mace; (für ~hochsprung, Zelt~) pole; (Meß~) (measuring) rod or stick; (Aut) dipstick; (Zauber~) wand. den ~ über jdn brechen (Hist) ≈ to put on the black cap when sentencing sb; (fig) to condemn sb; den ~ führen (Mus geh) to conduct.
(b) (Mitarbeiter~, Mil) staff; (von Experten) panel; (Mil: Hauptquartier) headquarters sing or pl.

Stäbchen nt dim of **Stab** (Eß~) chopstick; (Kragen~) (collar) stiffener; (Korsett~) bone; (Anat: der Netzhaut) rod; (beim Häkeln) treble; (inf: Zigarette) ciggy (inf).

Stab-: s~förmig adj rod-shaped; ~führung f (Mus) conducting; unter der ~führung von conducted by or under the baton of; ~heuschrecke f stick insect; ~hochspringer m pole-vaulter; ~hochsprung m pole vault.

stabil [ʃtaˈbiːl, st-] adj Möbel, Schuhe, Kind sturdy, robust; Währung, Beziehung, Charakter stable; Gesundheit sound; (euph: korpulent) well-built, solid.

Stabilisation [ʃtabilizaˈtsioːn, st-] f stabilization.

Stabilisator [ʃtabliˈzaːtor, st-] m stabilizer.

stabilisieren* [ʃtabiliˈziːrən, st-] 1 vt to stabilize. 2 vr to stabilize, to become stable.

Stabilität [ʃtabiliˈtɛːt, st-] f stability.

Stab-: ~kirche f stave church; ~lampe f (electric) torch, flashlight (US); ~magnet m bar magnet; ~reim m alliteration; der ~reim als poetisches Mittel alliteration as a poetic device.

Stabs-: ~arzt m (Mil) captain in the medical corps; ~chef m (Mil inf) chief of staff; ~feldwebel m (Mil) warrant officer class II (Brit), master sergeant (US); ~offizier m (Mil) staff officer; (Rang) field officer.

Stab-: ~spiel nt bell lyra; (mit Klaviatur) celesta; ~wechsel m (Sport) baton change, change-over.

Staccato [staˈkaːto] nt -s, -s or **Staccati** staccato.

stach pret of **stechen**.

Stachel m -s, -n (von Rosen, Ginster etc) thorn, prickle; (von Kakteen, Stachelhäutern, Igel) spine; (von ~schwein) quill, spine; (auf ~draht) barb; (zum Viehantrieb) goad; (Gift~: von Bienen etc) sting; (fig liter) (von Ehrgeiz, Neugier etc) spur; (von Vorwurf, Haß) sting. Tod, wo ist dein ~? (Bibl) Death where now thy sting?; der ~ des Fleisches (liter) the urges of the body pl; ein ~ im Fleisch (liter) a thorn in the flesh or side; einer Sache (dat) den ~ nehmen (geh) to take the sting out of sth; siehe löcken.

Stachel-: ~beere f gooseberry; ~beerstrauch m gooseberry bush.

Stacheldraht m barbed wire.

Stacheldraht-: ~verhau m barbed-wire entanglement; ~zaun m barbed-wire fence.

Stachel-: ~flosser m -s, - (Zool) spiny-finned fish; s~förmig adj spiky; (Biol) spiniform no adv; ~halsband nt spiked (dog) collar; ~häuter m -s, - (Zool) echinoderm (spec).

stach(e)lig adj Rosen, Ginster etc thorny; Kaktus, Igel etc spiny; (sich ~ anfühlend) prickly; Kinn, Bart bristly; Draht spiky, barbed.

stacheln vti siehe **anstacheln**.

Stachel-: ~rochen m stingray; ~schnecke f murex; ~schwein nt porcupine.

stachlig adj siehe **stach(e)lig**.

Stadel m -s, - (S Ger, Aus, Sw) barn.

Stadion nt -s, **Stadien** [-ian] stadium.

Stadium nt -s, **Stadien** [-ian] stage. im vorgerückten/letzten ~ (Med) at an advanced/terminal stage; er hat Krebs im vorgerückten/letzten ~ he has advanced/terminal cancer.

städt. abbr of **städtisch**.

Stadt f -, ⸚e (a) town; (Groß~) city. die ~ Paris the city of Paris; ~ und Land town and country; in ~ und Land throughout the land, the length and breadth of the land; die ganze ~ spricht davon it's all over town, the whole town is talking about it, it's the talk of the town; in die ~ gehen to go into town.
(b) (~verwaltung) (town) council; (von Groß~) corporation. bei der ~ angestellt sein to be working for the council/corporation; die ~ Ulm Ulm Corporation.

Stadt-: ~adel m town nobility; ~amtmann m siehe Amtmann; s~auswärts adv out of town; ~autobahn f urban motorway (Brit) or freeway (US); ~bad nt municipal swimming pool or baths pl; ~bahn f suburban railway (Brit), city railroad (US); ~behörde f municipal authority; s~bekannt adj well-known, known all over town; ~bewohner m town-dweller; (von Groß~) city-dweller; ~bewohner pl townspeople; city-people; ~bezirk m municipal district; ~bild nt urban features pl, townscape; cityscape; das ständig wechselnde ~bild Bonns the constantly changing face of Bonn; ~bücherei f municipal or town/city (lending) library; ~bummel m stroll in the or through town.

Städtchen nt dim of Stadt small town.

Stadt-: ~chronik f town/city chronicles pl; ~direktor m town clerk (Brit), town/city manager (US).

Städte-: ~bau m urban development; s~baulich 1 adj urban development attr; Veränderungen in urban development; 2 adv as regards urban development.

stadt|einwärts adv into town.

Städteplanung f town or urban planning.

Städter(in f) m -s, - town-dweller; (Groß~) city-dweller.

Städtetag m convention or congress of municipal authorities.

Stadt-: ~fahrt f journey within a/the town/city; ~flucht f exodus from the cities; ~gas nt town gas; ~gebiet nt municipal area; (von Groß~ auch) city zone; ~gemeinde f municipality; ~gespräch m a (das) ~gespräch sein to be the talk of the town; (b) (Telec) local call; ~grenze f town/city boundary; ~gue(r)rilla f urban guerrilla; ~haus nt (a) (rare: Rathaus) town hall; (b) (privates) townhouse.

städtisch adj municipal, town/city attr; (nach Art einer Stadt) urban. die ~e Bevölkerung the town/city or urban population; die ~e Lebensweise the urban way of life, town/city life.

Stadt-: ~kämmerer m town/city treasurer; ~kasse f town/city treasury; ~kern m town/city centre; ~kind nt town/city child; ~kommandant m military governor (of a town/city); ~kreis m town/city borough; s~kundig adj with a good knowledge of a/the town/city; ~landschaft f town/city landscape, townscape/cityscape; ~luft f town/city air; ~luft macht frei (Hist) principle whereby a serf became a freeman if he stayed in a town/city for a year and a day; ~mauer f city wall; ~mensch m town/city person; ~mission f city mission; ~mitte f town/city centre; ~oberhaupt nt head of a/the town/city; ~park m town/city or municipal park; ~parlament nt city council; ~plan m (street) map of (a/the town); (Archit) town/city plan; ~planung f town planning; ~rand m outskirts pl (of a/the town/city); am ~rand on the outskirts (of the town/city); ~randsiedlung f suburban housing scheme; ~rat m (a) (Behörde) (town/city) council; (b) (Mitglied) (town/city) councillor; ~recht nt (Hist) town charter; ~rundfahrt f (sightseeing) tour of a/the town/city; eine ~rundfahrt machen to go on a (sightseeing) tour of a/the town/city; ~schreiber m (obs, Sw) town clerk; ~staat m city state; ~streicher(in f) m -s, - town/city tramp; ~streicherei f urban vagrancy; ~teil m district, part of town; ~theater nt municipal theatre; ~tor nt town/city gate; ~väter pl (old, hum) city fathers pl or elders pl; ~verkehr m (a) (Straßenverkehr) town/city traffic; (b) (örtlicher Nahverkehr) local town/city transport; ~verordnete(r) mf decl as adj town/city councillor; ~verwaltung f administration of a/the town/city; (Behörde) (town) council/corporation, municipal authority; ~viertel nt district, part of town; ~wappen nt municipal coat of arms; ~werke pl town's/city's department of works; ~wohnung f town/city apartment or flat (Brit); ~zentrum nt town/city centre.

Stafette f (Hist) courier, messenger.

Stafettenlauf m (Sport) siehe Staffellauf.

Staffage [sta'faːʒə] f -, -n (Art: Beiwerk) staffage; (fig) window-dressing.

Staffel f -, -n (a) (Formation) (Mil, Naut, Aviat) echelon; (Aviat: Einheit) squadron. ~ fliegen to fly in echelon formation. (b) (Sport) relay (race); (Mannschaft) relay team; (fig) relay. ~ laufen/schwimmen to run/swim in a relay (race). (c) (Stufe, Sprosse) rung; (S Ger: Steintreppe) stone steps pl.

Staffelei f easel.

Staffellauf m relay (race).

staffeln vt (a) Gehälter, Tarife, Fahrpreise to grade, to graduate; Anfangszeiten, Startplätze to stagger. nach Dienstalter gestaffelte Gehälter salaries graded according to years of service; die Startplätze gestaffelt anordnen to stagger the starting places.
(b) (in Formation bringen) to draw up in an echelon. gestaffelte Formation (Aviat) echelon formation.

Staffel-: ~schwimmen nt relay swimming; ~tarif m graduated or differential tariff.

Staff(e)lung f siehe staffeln (a) grading, graduating, staggering. (b) drawing up in an echelon.

Stag nt -(e)s, -e(n) (Naut) stay.

Stagflation [ʃtakflaˈtsioːn, st-] f (Econ) stagflation.

Stagnation [ʃtagnaˈtsioːn, st-] f stagnation, stagnancy. es kam zu einer ~ there was a period of stagnation or stagnancy.

stagnieren* [ʃtaˈgniːrən, st-] vi to stagnate.

Stagnierung f siehe Stagnation.

stahl pret of stehlen.

Stahl m -(e)s, -e or ¨e steel; (old liter: Schwert auch) blade. Nerven wie ~ nerves of steel.

Stahl- in cpds steel; ~bau m steel-girder construction; ~beton m reinforced concrete; s~blau adj steel-blue; ~blech nt sheet-steel; (Stück) steel sheet.

stählen 1 vt Körper, Muskeln, Nerven to harden, to toughen. seinen Mut ~ to steel oneself. 2 vr to toughen or harden oneself; (sich wappnen) to steel oneself.

stählern adj Waffen, Ketten steel; (fig) Muskeln, Wille of iron, iron attr; Nerven of steel; Blick steely.

Stahl-: ~feder f steel nib; ~gerüst nt tubular steel scaffolding; (Gerippe) steel-girder frame; s~grau adj steel-grey; s~hart adj (as) hard as steel; ~helm m (Mil) steel helmet; ~hochstraße f temporary (steel) overpass; ~kammer f strong-room; ~mantelgeschoß nt steel jacket bullet; ~rohr nt tubular steel; (Stück) steel tube; ~rohrmöbel pl tubular steel furniture sing; ~roß nt (hum) bike (inf), velocipede (form, hum); ~stich m (Art) steel engraving; ~träger m steel girder; ~waren pl steel goods pl, steelware sing; ~werk nt steelworks sing or pl; ~wolle f steel wool.

stahn vi (obs) siehe stehen.

stak (geh) pret of stecken 1.

Stake f -, -n **Staken** m -s, - (N Ger) (punt/barge) pole.

staken vti (vi: aux sein) to pole; Stocherkahn auch to punt; (fig) to stalk.

Staket nt -(e)s, -e, **Staketenzaun** m paling, picket fence.

Stakkato [ʃtaˈkaːto, st-] nt -s, -s or **Stakkati** staccato.

staksen vi aux sein (inf) to stalk; (unsicher) to teeter; (steif) to hobble. mit ~den Schritten gehen to stalk/teeter/hobble.

staksig adj (unbeholfen) gawky. ~ gehen (steif) to hobble; (unsicher) to teeter.

Stalagmit [ʃtalaˈgmiːt, st-, -mɪt] m -en or -s, -en stalagmite.

Stalaktit [ʃtalakˈtiːt, ʃt-, -tɪt] m -en or -s, -en stalactite.

Stalinismus [ʃtaliˈnɪsmʊs] m Stalinism.

Stalinist(in f) [ʃtaliˈnɪst(ɪn)] m Stalinist.

stalinistisch [ʃtaliˈnɪstɪʃ] adj Stalinist.

Stalin|orgel [ˈstaːlin-, ˈʃt-] f multiple rocket launcher.

Stall m -(e)s, ¨e (a) (Pferde~, Gestüt, Aut: Renn~) stable; (Kuh~) cowshed, (cow) barn (US), byre (Brit); (Hühner~) henhouse, coop; (Kaninchen~) hutch; (Schaf~) (sheep)cote; (Schweine~) (pig)sty, (pig)pen (US). den ~ ausmisten to clean out the stable etc; (fig) to clean out the Augean stables; ein (ganzer) ~ voll Kinder (inf) a (whole) pack of children.
(b) (inf: Zimmer, Büro) hole (inf).
(c) (inf: Hosenschlitz) flies pl.

Stallaterne f getrennt Stall-laterne stable lamp.

Stall-: ~bursche m siehe ~knecht; ~dung, ~dünger m farmyard manure; ~hase m rabbit; ~knecht m farm hand; (für Pferde) stableman, stable lad or hand; (für Kühe) cowhand; ~laterne f siehe Stallaterne; ~magd f farm girl; (für Pferde) stable maid; (Kuhmagd) milkmaid; ~meister m equerry; ~mist m farmyard manure.

Stallung(en pl) f stables pl.

Stamm m -(e)s, ¨e (a) (Baum~) trunk; siehe Apfel.
(b) (Ling) stem.
(c) (Volks~) tribe; (Abstammung) line; (Biol) phylum; (Bakterien~) strain. der ~ der Bourbonen the house of Bourbon; aus königlichem ~ of royal blood or stock or lineage; aus dem ~e Davids of the line of David, of David's line; vom ~e Nimm sein (hum) to be one of the takers of this world.
(d) (Kern, fester Bestand) regulars pl; (Kunden auch) regular customers pl; (von Mannschaft) regular team-members pl; (Arbeiter) regular or permanent workforce; (Angestellte) permanent staff pl. ein fester ~ von Kunden regular customers, regulars; zum ~ gehören to be one of the regulars etc.

Stamm-: ~aktie f (St Ex) ordinary or common (US) share; ~baum m family or genealogical tree; (Biol) phylogenetic tree; (von Zuchttieren) pedigree; (Ling) tree; einen guten ~baum haben (lit, hum) to have a good pedigree; ~belegschaft f permanent or regular workforce; (Angestellte) regular staff pl; ~buch nt (a) siehe Familienbuch; (b) (Gästebuch) visitor's book; jdm etw ins ~buch schreiben (fig) to make sb take note of sth; das kannst du dir ins ~buch schreiben! (fig) take note; ~burg f ancestral castle; ~einlage f (Fin) capital investment in ordinary shares or common stock (US).

stammeln vti to stammer.

Stamm|eltern pl progenitors pl.

stammen vi to come (von, aus from); (zeitlich) to date (von, aus from); (Gram auch) to be derived (von, aus from). woher ~ Sie? where do you come from (originally)?; die Bibliothek/Uhr stammt von seinem Großvater the library/watch originally belonged to his grandfather.

Stammes- in cpds tribal; ~bewußtsein nt tribal spirit; ~genosse m member of a/the tribe, tribesman; ~geschichte f (Biol) phylogeny; s~geschichtlich adj (Biol) phylogenetic; ~kunde f (Hist) ethnology; ~verband m tribal unit; ~zugehörigkeit f tribal membership.

Stamm-: ~form f base form; ~gast m regular; ~gericht nt standard meal; ~gut nt family estate; ~halter m son and heir; ~haus nt (Comm) parent branch; (Gesellschaft) parent company; (Fabrik) parent factory; ~holz nt trunk wood.

stämmig adj (gedrungen) stocky, thickset no adv; (kräftig) sturdy.

Stämmigkeit f siehe adj stockiness; sturdiness.

Stamm-: ~kapital nt (Fin) ordinary share or common stock (US) capital; ~kneipe f (inf) local (Brit inf); ~kunde m regular (customer); ~kundschaft f regulars pl, regular customers pl; ~land nt place of origin.

Stammler m -s, - stammerer.

Stamm-: ~lokal nt favourite café/restaurant etc; (Kneipe) local (Brit); ~mutter f siehe Stammmutter; ~personal nt permanent staff pl; ~platz m usual or regular seat; ~rolle f (Mil) muster roll; ~silbe f radical, root syllable; ~sitz m (von Firma) headquarters sing or pl; (von Geschlecht) ancestral seat; (im Theater etc) regular seat; ~tafel f genealogical table; ~tisch m (Tisch in Gasthaus) table reserved for the regulars; (~tischrunde) group of regulars; er hat mittwochs seinen ~tisch Wednesday is his night for meeting his friends at the pub; ~**tischpolitiker** m (pej) armchair or alehouse politician; ~**tischrunde** f group of regulars.

Stammutter f getrennt Stamm-mutter progenitrix (form).

Stamm-: ~**vater** m progenitor (form); s~**verwandt** adj related; **Wörter** cognate, derived from the same root; ~**vokal** m radical or root vowel; ~**würze** f original wort; ~**zahn** m (dated sl) steady (inf).

Stamokap ['sta:mokap] m -s, no pl (Pol) abbr of staatsmonopolistischer Kapitalismus.

Stamper m -s, -, **Stamperl** nt -s, -n (S Ger, Aus) stemless schnapps glass.

stampfen 1 vi (a) (laut auftreten) to stamp; (auf und nieder gehen: Maschine) to pound. **mit dem Fuß/den Hufen** ~ to stamp one's foot/to paw the ground with its hooves.

   (b) aux sein (gehen) (mit schweren Schritten) to tramp; (wütend) to stamp; (stapfen) to trudge.

   (c) aux haben or sein (Schiff) to pitch, to toss.

2 vt (a) (festtrampeln) Lehm, Sand to stamp; Trauben to press; (mit den Füßen) to tread; siehe **Boden.**

   (b) (mit Stampfer) to mash; (im Mörser) to pound.

Stampfer m -s, - (Stampfgerät) pounder; (Saugkolben) plunger; (sl: Bein) tree-trunk (inf).

Stampfkartoffeln pl (dial) mashed potato(es pl).

stand pret of **stehen.**

Stand m -(e)s, ⁻e (a) no pl (das Stehen) standing position; (~fläche) place to stand; (für Gegenstand) stand. **aus dem** ~ from a standing position; **ein Sprung/Start aus dem** ~ a standing jump/start; **bei jdm** or **gegen jdn einen schweren** ~ **haben** (fig) to have a hard time of it with sb.

   (b) (Markt~ etc) stand; (Taxi~ auch) rank.

   (c) no pl (Lage) state; (Niveau, Fin: Kurs) level; (Zähler~, Thermometer~, Barometer~ etc) reading, level; (Kassen~, Konto~) balance; (von Gestirnen) position; (Sport: Spiel~) score. **jdn in den** ~ **setzen, etw zu tun** to put sb in a position to do sth; **beim jetzigen** ~ **der Dinge** the way things stand or are at the moment; **nach letztem** ~ **der Dinge** from the way things stood or were when we etc last heard; **der neueste** ~ **der Forschung** the latest developments in research; **etw auf den neuesten** ~ **bringen** to bring sth up to date; **im** ~ **der Sklaverei/Knechtschaft** in a state of slavery/bondage.

   (d) (soziale Stellung) station, status; (Klasse) rank, class; (Beruf, Gewerbe) profession; (Reichs~) estate. **Name und** ~ (old) name and profession; **die niederen/vornehmen** or **höheren** ⁻e (old) the lower/upper classes; **ein Mann von (hohem)** ~ (old) a man of (high) rank; **über/unter seinem** ~ **heiraten** (dated) to marry above/below one's station (dated).

   (e) (Sw) siehe **Kanton.**

Standard ['ʃtandart, st-] m -s, -s standard.

Standard- in cpds standard.

standardisieren* [ʃtandardi'zi:rən, st-] vt to standardize.

Standardisierung [ʃt-, st-] f standardization.

Standarte f -, -n (a) (Mil, Pol) standard. (b) (Hunt) brush.

Stand-: ~**bein** nt (Sport) pivot leg; (Art) standing leg; ~**bild** nt statue.

Ständchen nt serenade. **jdm ein** ~ **bringen** to serenade sb.

Stände-: ~**ordnung** f system of estates; ~**organisation** f professional organization; ~**parlament** nt parliament of estates.

Stander m -s, - pennant.

Ständer m -s, - (Hut~, Noten~, Karten~ etc) stand; (Pfeifen~, Schallplatten~ etc auch) rack; (Pfeiler) upright; (Elec) stator; (sl: Erektion) hard-on (sl).

Ständerat ['ʃtendəra:t] m (Sw Parl) upper chamber; (Abgeordneter) member of the upper chamber.

Standes-: ~**amt** nt registry office (Brit); **auf dem** ~**amt** at the registry office; s~**amtlich** adj s~**amtliche Trauung** registry office (Brit) or civil wedding; **sich** s~**amtlich trauen lassen** to get married in a registry office, to have a registry office or civil wedding; ~**beamte(r)** m registrar; ~**bewußtsein** nt status consciousness; ~**dünkel** m snobbishness, snobbery; ~**ehe** f marriage between people of the same rank; ~**ehre** f honour as a nobleman/officer etc; (von Ärzten, Handwerkern etc) professional honour; s~**gemäß** 1 adj befitting one's rank or station (dated); 2 adv in a manner befitting one's rank or station (dated); ~**heirat** f siehe ~**ehe**; ~**herr** m (Hist) mediatized prince; ~**organisation** f professional association; ~**person** f (old) person of quality (old); ~**privileg** nt class privilege; ~**sprache** f professional jargon.

Ständestaat m (Hist) corporate or corporative state.

Standes-: ~**tracht** f (official) robes pl; ~**unterschied** m class difference; s~**widrig** adj socially degrading; (beruflich) unprofessional.

Stand-: s~**fest** adj Tisch, Leiter stable, steady; (fig) steadfast; ~**festigkeit** f stability (auch Sci); (fig auch) steadfastness; ~**foto** nt still (photograph); ~**geld** nt stallage; ~**gericht** nt (Mil) drumhead court martial; **vor ein** ~**gericht kommen** or **gestellt werden** to be summarily court-martialled; s~**haft** adj steadfast, strong; **sie blieb** s~**haft im Glauben** her faith did not falter or swerve; **etw** s~**haft verteidigen** to defend sth staunchly; **er weigerte sich** s~**haft** he staunchly or steadfastly refused; ~**haftigkeit** f steadfastness, staunchness, resolution; s~**halten** vi sep irreg (Mensch) to stand firm; (Gebäude, Brücke etc) to hold; (+dat) to withstand, to stand up to; **Versuchungen** (dat) s~**halten** to resist temptation; **die Soldaten hielten** s~, **bis Verstärkung kam** the soldiers held their ground or held out until reinforcements came; **einer/der Prüfung** s~**halten** to stand up to or bear close examination.

ständig adj (a) (dauernd) permanent; Praxis, Regel established; Korrespondent (Press) resident; Mitglied full; Einkommen regular. ~**er Ausschuß** standing committee.

   (b) (unaufhörlich) constant, continual. **müssen Sie mich** ~

unterbrechen? must you keep (on) interrupting me?, must you continually or constantly interrupt me?; **sie kommt** ~ **zu spät** she's constantly or always late; **sie beklagt sich** ~ she's forever or always complaining; **sie ist** ~ **krank** she's always ill; **passiert das oft?** — ~ does it happen often? — always, all the time.

standisch adj corporate, corporative.

Standl nt -s, -(n) (Aus) market stall.

Standlicht nt sidelights pl. **mit** ~ **fahren** to drive on sidelights.

Stand|ort m location; (von Schütze, Schiff etc) position; (Mil) garrison; (Bot) habitat; (von Pflanzungen) site; (fig) position. **den** ~ **der Schule in der Gesellschaft bestimmen** to define the position or place of the school in society; **die Division hat ihren** ~ **in** ... the division is based or garrisoned in ...

Stand|ort-: ~**älteste(r)** m (Mil) senior officer of a garrison, post senior officer (US); ~**bestimmung** f (fig) definition of the position; ~**faktor** m usu pl (Econ) locational factor; ~**katalog** m shelf catalogue, shelf list; ~**zeichen** nt shelf mark.

Stand-: ~**pauke** f (inf) lecture (inf), telling-off (inf); **jdm eine** ~**pauke halten** to give sb a lecture (inf) or telling-off (inf), to tell sb off (inf); ~**platz** m stand; (für Taxis auch) rank; ~**punkt** m (a) (rare: Beobachtungsplatz) vantage point, viewpoint; (b) (Meinung) point of view, standpoint; **auf dem** ~**punkt stehen** or **den** ~**punkt vertreten, daß** ... to take the view that ...; **jdm seinen** ~**punkt klarmachen** to make one's point of view clear to sb; **von seinem** ~**punkt aus** from his point of view; **das ist doch kein** or **vielleicht ein** (iro) ~**punkt!** what kind of attitude is that!; ~**quartier** nt (Mil) base; ~**recht** nt (Mil) military law (invoked in times of emergency); ~**recht verhängen** to impose military law (über +acc on); s~**rechtlich** adj s~**rechtlich erschießen** to put straight before a firing squad; **eine** s~**rechtliche Erschießung** an on-the-spot execution; s~**sicher** adj stable; Mensch steady (on one's feet/skis etc); ~**sicherheit** f siehe adj stability; steadiness; ~**spur** f (Aut) hard shoulder; ~**uhr** f grandfather clock; ~**vogel** m non-migratory bird.

Stange f -, -n (a) (langer, runder Stab) pole; (Querstab, Ballett~) bar; (Kleider~, Teppich~) rail; (Gardinen~, Leiste für Treppenläufer) rod; (Vogel~) perch; (Hühner~) perch, roost; (Gebiß~) bit; (Hunt: Schwanz) brush; (Geweihteil) branch (of antlers); (fig: dünner Mensch) beanpole (inf).

   (b) (länglicher Gegenstand) stick. **eine** ~ **Zigaretten** a carton of 200 cigarettes.

   (c) (zylinderförmiges Glas) tall glass.

   (d) (Redewendungen) **ein Anzug von der** ~ a suit off the peg; **von der** ~ **kaufen** to buy off the peg; **jdn bei der** ~ **halten** (inf) to keep or hold sb; **bei der** ~ **bleiben** (inf) to stick at it (inf); **jdm die** ~ **halten** (inf) to stick up for sb (inf), to stand up for sb; **eine schöne** ~ **Geld** (inf) a tidy sum (inf); **eine** ~ **angeben** (sl) to show off like crazy (inf), to lay it on thick (inf).

Stangen-: ~**bohne** f runner bean; ~**brot** nt French bread; (Laib) French loaf; ~**spargel** m asparagus spears pl.

stank pret of **stinken.**

Stänkerei f (inf) grousing.

Stänk(er)er m -s, - (inf) grouser.

stänkern vi (inf) (a) (Unfrieden stiften) to stir things up (inf).

   (b) (Gestank verbreiten) to make a stink (inf).

Stanniol [ʃta'nio:l, st-] nt -s, -e silver foil.

Stanniolpapier nt silver paper.

stante pede ['stantə 'pe:də] adv instanter, hotfoot.

Stanze f -, -n (a) (für Prägestempel, Bleche) die, stamp; (Loch~) punch. (b) (Poet) eight-line stanza.

stanzen vt to press; (prägen) to stamp, to emboss; Löcher to punch.

Stanzer(in f) m -s, - press worker.

Stanzmaschine f siehe Stanze (a).

Stapel m -s, - (a) (geschichteter Haufen, fig: Vorrat) stack, pile.

   (b) (Comm) (~platz) store, depot; (Handelsplatz) trading centre, emporium.

   (c) (Naut: Schiffs~) stocks pl. **auf** ~ **legen** to lay down; **auf** ~ **liegen** to be on the stocks; **vom** ~ **laufen** to be launched; **vom** ~ **lassen** to launch; (fig) to come out with (inf).

   (d) (von Wolle, Baumwolle) staple.

Stapellauf m (Naut) launching.

stapeln 1 vt to stack; (lagern) to store. 2 vr to pile up.

Stapel-: ~**platz** m siehe Stapel (b); ~**roller** m fork-lift truck.

Stapelung f siehe stapeln 1 stacking; storing.

Stapelware f staple commodity.

Stapfe f -, -n, **Stapfen** m -s, - footprint.

stapfen vi aux sein to trudge, to plod.

Star[1] m -(e)s, -e (Orn) starling.

Star[2] m -(e)s, -e (Med) grauer/grüner/schwarzer ~ cataract/glaucoma/amaurosis (spec); **jdm den** ~ **stechen** (fig) to tell sb some home truths.

Star[3] [ʃtaːɐ, staːɐ] m -s, -s (Film etc) star; (fig auch) leading light. **er trat wie ein** ~ **auf** he put on a big star act.

Star|allüren pl (inf) airs and graces pl. ~ **an den Tag legen** to put on or give oneself airs and graces.

starb pret of **sterben.**

Star-: ~**besetzung** f star cast; ~**brille** f pair of glasses fitted with cataract lenses.

Star(en)kasten m nesting box (for starlings).

Star- (Press): ~**gage** f top fee; ~**gast** m star guest.

stark 1 adj comp ⁻er, superl ⁻ste(r, s) (a) (kräftig, konzentriert) strong (auch Gram); (mächtig) Stimme, Staat, Partei auch powerful. ~ **bleiben** to be strong; (im Glauben) to hold firm; **sich für etw** ~ **machen** (inf) to stand up for sth; **den** ~**en Mann spielen** or **markieren** or **mimen** (all inf) to play the big guy (inf); **das ist seine** ~**e Seite** that is his strong point or his forte; **das ist** ~ or **ein** ~**es Stück** (inf) or ~**er Tobak!** that's a bit much!; (eine Unverschämtheit auch) that's a bit thick! (inf).

   (b) (dick) thick; (euph: korpulent) Dame, Herr large,

well-built (euph); Arme, Beine large, strong (euph). Kostüme für ~ere Damen costumes for the fuller figure.

(c) (beträchtlich, heftig) Schmerzen, Kälte severe; Frost auch, Regen, Schneefall, Verkehr, Raucher, Trinker, Druck heavy; Sturm violent; Erkältung bad, heavy; Wind, Strömung, Eindruck strong; Appetit, Esser hearty; Beifall hearty, loud; Fieber high; Trauer, Schmerz deep; Übertreibung, Widerhall, Bedenken considerable, great. ~e Abneigung strong dislike.

(d) (leistungsfähig) Motor powerful; Sportler able; Mannschaft strong; Brille, Arznei strong. er ist in Englisch nicht sehr ~ he isn't very strong in English.

(e) (zahlreich) Auflage, Gefolge large; Nachfrage great, big. wir hoffen auf ~e Beteiligung we are hoping that a large number of people will take part; zehn Mann ~ ten strong; das Buch ist 300 Seiten ~ the book is 300 pages long; eine 20 Bände ~e Neuausgabe a new edition of or in 20 volumes.

(f) (inf: hervorragend) Leistung, Werk great (inf). sein ~stes Buch his best book.

2 adv, comp ~er, superl am ~sten **(a)** (mit vb) a lot; (mit adj, ptp) very; regnen, rauchen etc auch heavily; beeindrucken auch greatly, übertreiben auch greatly, grossly; vertreten, dagegen sein strongly; abgenutzt, beschmutzt, beschädigt etc badly; vergrößert, verkleinert greatly. ~ wirken to have a strong effect; ~ gesalzen/gewürzt very salty/highly spiced; ~ verschuldet heavily or deeply in debt; ~ benachteiligt at a great disadvantage; ~ gefragt in great demand; ~ behaart sein to be very hairy, to have a lot of hair; ~er behaart sein to have more hair; ~er befahrene Straßen busier roads; die Ausstellung wurde ~ besucht there were a lot of visitors to the exhibition; das Auto zieht ~ nach links the car is pulling badly to the left; er ist ~ erkältet he has a bad or heavy cold; drück ~er auf die Klingel push the bell harder.

(b) (inf: hervorragend) really well. die singt unheimlich ~ she's a really great singer (inf), she sings really well.

Starkasten m siehe Star(en)kasten.
Starkbier nt strong beer.
Stärke[1] f -, -n **(a)** strength (auch fig); (von Stimme auch) power.

(b) (Dicke, Durchmesser) thickness; (Macht) power.

(c) (Heftigkeit) (von Strömung, Wind, Einfluß) strength; (von Eindruck auch, von Leid) intensity; (von Regen, Frost, Verkehr, Druck) heaviness; (von Sturm, Abneigung) violence; (von Schmerzen, Kälte, Erkältung, Fieber etc) severity; (von Appetit) heartiness.

(d) (Leistungsfähigkeit) (von Motor) power; (von Sportmannschaft, Arznei, Brille) strength.

(e) (Anzahl) (von Gefolge, Heer, Mannschaft) size, strength; (von Beteiligung, Nachfrage) amount; (Auflage) size.

(f) (fig: starke Seite) strength, strong point.

Stärke[2] f -, -n (Chem) starch.
Stärkemehl nt (Cook) thickening agent, ≈ cornflour (Brit), cornstarch (US).
stärken 1 vt **(a)** (kräftigen) (lit, fig) to strengthen; Selbstbewußtsein to boost, to increase; Gesundheit to improve; siehe Rückgrat. **(b)** (erfrischen) to fortify. **(c)** Wäsche to starch. **2** vi to be fortifying. das stärkt it fortifies you; ~des Mittel tonic. **3** vr to fortify oneself.
Stärkezucker m glucose.
stark-: ~gliedrig, ~knochig adj heavy-boned; ~leibig adj (euph) stout, well-built (euph).
Starkstrom m (Elec) heavy current.
Starkstrom- in cpds power; ~kabel nt power cable; ~leitung f power line; (Kabel) power lead; ~technik f branches of electrical engineering not connected with telecommunications.
starktonig adj stressed.
Starkult m star-cult.
Stärkung f **(a)** strengthening (auch fig); (des Selbstbewußtseins) boosting. das dient der ~ der Gesundheit it is beneficial to the health. **(b)** (Erfrischung) refreshment. eine ~ zu sich nehmen to take or have some refreshment.
Stärkungsmittel nt (Med) tonic.
stark-: ~wandig adj Schiff thick-walled; ~wirkend adj attr Medikament, Alkohol potent.
Starlet ['ʃtɑːrlɛt, st-] nt -s, -s (Film) starlet.
Star-: ~matz m starling; ~operation f operation for cataract.
starr adj **(a)** stiff; (unbeweglich) rigid. ~ vor Frost stiff with frost; meine Finger sind vor Kälte ganz ~ my fingers are frozen stiff or stiff with cold; ~ miteinander verbunden joined rigidly; ~ abstehen to stand up stiffly.

(b) (unbewegt) Augen glassy; Blick auch fixed. jdn ~ ansehen to look fixedly at sb, to stare at sb.

(c) (regungslos) paralyzed. ~ vor Schrecken/Entsetzen paralyzed with fear/horror; ~ vor Staunen dumbfounded.

(d) (nicht flexibel) Regelung, Prinzip inflexible, rigid; Haltung auch intransigent. ~ an etw (dat) festhalten to hold rigidly to sth.
Starre f -, no pl stiffness, rigidity.
starren vi **(a)** (starr blicken) to stare (auf +acc at). ins Leere ~ to stare or gaze into space; jdm ins Gesicht ~ to stare sb in the face; vor sich (acc) hin ~ to stare straight ahead; was ~ Sie so? what are you staring at?; siehe Loch.

(b) von Gewehren ~ to bristle with guns; der Stoff starrt von Löchern the fabric is full of or riddled with holes.

(c) (steif sein) to be stiff (von, vor +dat with). Moskau starrt vor Kälte Moscow is in the grip of the cold; vor Dreck ~ to be thick or covered with dirt; (Kleidung) to be stiff with dirt.

(d) (abstehen) to jut up/out.
Starrheit f siehe adj stiffness; rigidity; glassiness; fixedness; paralysis; inflexibility, rigidity; intransigence.
Starr-: ~kopf m (Mensch) stubborn or obstinate mule; einen

~kopf haben to be stubborn or obstinate; s~köpfig adj stubborn, obstinate; ~köpfigkeit f stubbornness, obstinacy; ~krampf m (Med) tetanus, lockjaw; ~sinn m stubbornness, mulishness; s~sinnig adj stubborn, mulish; ~sinnigkeit f siehe ~sinn; ~sucht f (Med) catalepsy.
Start m -s, -s **(a)** (Sport) start; (~platz, ~linie auch) starting line; (Pferderennen auch) starting post; (Autorennen auch) starting grid. am~ sein to be at the start/on or at the starting line/at the starting post/on the starting grid; (Läufer) to be on their blocks; das Zeichen zum ~ geben to give the starting signal; einen guten/schlechten ~ haben (lit, fig) to get (off to) a good/bad start.

(b) (Aviat) take-off; (Raketen~) launch; (~platz) runway. vor ~ der Maschine before take-off; der Maschine den ~ freigeben to clear the plane for take-off.
Start-: ~automatik f (Aut) automatic choke; ~bahn f (Aviat) runway; ~- und Landebahn runway; s~berechtigt adj (Sport) eligible (to enter); s~bereit adj (Sport, fig) ready to start or go, ready for the off (inf); (Aviat) ready for take-off; (Space) ready for lift-off; ~block m (Sport) starting block.
starten 1 vi aux sein to start; (Aviat) to take off; (zum Start antreten) to take part; to run; to swim; (Pferde- or Autorennen) to race; (inf: abreisen) to set off. in die letzte Runde ~ to go into or enter the last lap.

2 vt Satelliten, Rakete to launch; Unternehmen, Kampagne auch, Motor to start; Expedition to get under way.
Starter m -s, - (Aut, Sport) starter.
Starterklappe f (Aut) choke.
Start-: ~erlaubnis f (Sport) permission to take part/run/swim/ race; (Aviat) clearance for take-off; ~flagge f starting flag; ~geld nt (Sport) entry fee; ~hilfe f (Aviat) rocket-assisted take-off; (fig) initial aid; im Winter braucht mein Auto ~hilfe my car won't start on its own in winter; dieses Mittel soll eine wirksame ~hilfe sein this is supposed to be very effective in helping you start your car etc; jdm ~hilfe geben to help sb get off the ground; s~klar adj (Aviat) clear(ed) for take-off; (Sport) ready to start or for the off; ~kommando nt (Sport) starting signal; (Aviat) take-off command; ~linie f (Sport) starting line; ~loch nt (Sport) starting hole; in den ~löchern on their marks; ~maschine f (Sport) starting gate; ~nummer f number; ~platz m (Sport) starting place; (für Läufer) marks pl; (Autorennen) starting grid; ~rampe f (Space) launching pad; ~schleuder f (Aviat) catapult; ~schuß m (Sport) starting signal; (fig) signal (zu for); vor dem ~schuß before the gun; den ~schuß geben to fire the (starting) pistol; (fig) to open the door; (Erlaubnis geben) to give the go-ahead; ~sprung m racing dive; ~verbot nt (Aviat) ban on take-off; (Sport) ban; ~verbot bekommen to be banned or barred; ~zielsieg m (Sport) runaway victory.
Stasi m -, no pl abbr of Staatssicherheitsdienst (DDR).
Statik ['ʃtɑːtɪk, st-] f **(a)** (Sci) statics sing. **(b)** (Build) structural engineering.
Statiker(in f) ['ʃtɑːtɪkɐ, -ərɪn, st-] m -s, - (Tech) structural engineer.
Station f **(a)** station; (Haltestelle) stop; (fig: Abschnitt) (von Reise) stage; (von Leben) phase. ~ machen to stop off. **(b)** (Kranken~) ward. er liegt/arbeitet auf ~ drei he is in/works on ward three. **(c)** freie ~ free board and lodging.
stationär [ʃtatsio'nɛːr] adj (Astron, Sociol) stationary; (Med) in-patient attr. ~er Patient in-patient; ~behandeln to treat in hospital.
stationieren* [ʃtatsio'niːrən] vt Truppen to station.
Stationierung [ʃtatsio'niːruŋ] f stationing.
Stationierungskosten pl stationing costs pl.
Stations-: ~arzt m ward doctor; ~schwester f ward sister; ~vorstand (Aus, Sw), ~vorsteher m (Rail) station-master, station-agent (US).
statisch ['ʃtɑːtɪʃ, st-] adj (lit, fig) static; Gesetze of statics.
stätisch adj Pferd self-willed.
Statist m (Film) extra; (Theat) supernumerary; (fig) cipher. er war nur ein kleiner ~ (fig) he only played a minor role.
Statistenrolle f (lit, fig) minor role; (Film, Theat auch) walk-on part, bit part.
Statisterie f (Film) extras pl; (Theat) supernumeraries pl.
Statistik [ʃta'tɪstɪk, st-] f statistics sing. eine ~ a set of statistics; die ~en the statistics pl.
Statistiker(in f) [ʃta'tɪstɪkɐ, -ərɪn, st-] m -s, - statistician.
Statistin f siehe Statist.
statistisch [ʃta'tɪstɪʃ, st-] adj statistical; siehe erfassen.
Stativ nt tripod.
statt 1 prep +gen or (old, inf, wenn kein Artikel) +dat instead of. ~ dessen instead; ~ meiner/seiner/ihrer etc in my/his/her etc place, instead of me/him/her etc; ~ Urlaub(s) in lieu of or instead of holiday; ~ Karten heading of an announcement expressing thanks for condolences in place of individual replies.

2 conj instead of. ~ zu bleiben instead of staying; ~ zu bleiben, wollte ich lieber ... rather then stay I wanted to ...; ~ ein Wort zu sagen without saying a word.
Statt f -, no pl (form) stead (form), place. an meiner/seiner/ihrer ~ in my/his/her stead (form) or place; an Kindes ~ annehmen (Jur) to adopt; an Zahlungs ~ (Comm) in lieu of payment; siehe Eid.
Stätte f -, -n (liter) place. eine bleibende ~ a permanent home.
Statt-: s~finden vi sep irreg to take place; (Veranstaltung auch) to be held; (Ereignis auch) to occur; s~geben vi sep irreg +dat (form) to grant; siehe Einspruch; s~haben vi sep irreg (rare) siehe s~finden; s~haft adj pred permitted, allowed; ~halter m governor; ~halterschaft f governorship.
stattlich adj **(a)** (hochgewachsen, groß) Tier magnificent;

Bursche strapping, powerfully built; *(eindrucksvoll)* *Erscheinung, Fünfziger* imposing; *(ansehnlich)* *Gebäude, Anwesen, Park* magnificent, splendid. **ein ~er Mann** a fine figure of a man.
(b) *(umfangreich) Sammlung* impressive; *Familie* large; *(beträchtlich) Summe, Anzahl, Einnahmen* handsome, considerable.

Stattlichkeit *f, no pl siehe adj* **(a)** magnificence; powerful build; imposingness; magnificence, splendour; *(von Mann)* imposing figure. **(b)** impressiveness; largeness; handsomeness.

Statue ['ʃtaːtuə, st-] *f* -, **-n** statue.

statuenhaft ['ʃtaːtuən-, st-] *adj* statuesque; *(unbeweglich)* like a statue, statue-like.

Statuette [ʃta'tuɛtə, st-] *f* statuette.

statuieren* [ʃtatu'iːrən, st-] *vt* **ein Exempel an jdm ~** to make an example of sb; **um ein Exempel zu ~** as an example *or* warning to others; **ein Exempel mit etw ~** to use sth as a warning; **wir müssen da ein Exempel ~** we will have to make an example of somebody; **die Firma hat ein Exempel statuiert und ihn entlassen** the company made an example of him and dismissed him.

Statur *f* build.

Status ['ʃtaːtus, st-] *m* -, - status. **~ quo/~ quo ante** status quo.

Statussymbol *nt* status symbol.

Statut [ʃta'tuːt, st-] *nt* -(e)s, **-en** statute.

statutarisch [ʃtatu'taːrɪʃ, st-] *adj* statutory. **das ist ~ nicht möglich** that is excluded by statute.

Stau *m* -(e)s, **-e** *or* **-s (a)** *(Wasserstauung)* build-up; *(Wind~)* barrier effect; *(Verkehrsstauung)* tailback. **die See ist im ~** *(Naut)* the tide is turning *or* on the turn. **(b)** *siehe* **Stauung**.

Stau|anlage *f* dam.

Staub *m* -(e)s, **-e** *or* **Stäube** dust; *(Bot)* pollen. **~ saugen** to vacuum, to hoover ®; **~ wischen** to dust; **zu ~ werden** *(liter)* to turn to dust; *(wieder)* to return to dust *(liter)*; **in ~ und Asche sinken** *(liter)* to crumble into dust and ashes; **sich vor jdm in den ~ werfen** to throw oneself at sb's feet; **vor jdm im ~ kriechen** *(lit, fig)* to grovel before sb *or* at sb's feet; **sich aus dem ~e machen** *(inf)* to clear off *(inf)*; **den ~ (eines Ortes/ Landes) von den Füßen schütteln** *(liter)* to shake the dust (of a place/country) off one's feet; *siehe* **aufwirbeln**.

Staub- *in cpds* dust; **~besen** *m* feather duster; **~beutel** *m* (a) *(Bot)* anther; **(b)** *(von ~sauger)* dust bag; **~blatt** *nt* *(Bot)* stamen.

Stäubchen *nt* speck *or* particle of dust.

Staubecken *nt* reservoir.

stauben *vi* to be dusty; *(Staub machen, aufwirbeln)* to make *or* create a lot of dust. **bei Trockenheit staubt es mehr** there's a lot more dust around when it's dry.

stäuben 1 *vt* **Mehl/Puder etc auf etw** *(acc)* **~** to dust sth with flour/powder *etc*, to sprinkle flour/powder *etc* on sth. 2 *vi aux sein (rare) (zerstieben)* to scatter; *(Wasser)* to spray.

Staub- **~faden** *m* *(Bot)* filament; **~fänger** *m* *(inf)* dust collector; **die vielen Bücher sind bloß ~fänger** all those books just lie around collecting dust; **~fetzen** *m* *(Aus)* duster; **~flocke** *f* piece of fluff; **~geborene(r)** *mf decl as adj (old, liter)* mortal (being); **~gefäß** *nt* *(Bot)* stamen.

staubig *adj* dusty.

Staub- **~korn** *nt* speck of dust, dust particle; **~lappen** *m* duster; **~lunge** *f* *(Med)* dust on the lung; *(von Kohlenstaub)* black lung; **~mantel** *m* *(dated)* dust coat, duster *(US)*; **s~saugen** *vi insep, ptp* **s~gesaugt** to vacuum, to hoover ®; **~sauger** *m* vacuum cleaner, hoover ®; **~saugervertreter** *m* vacuum cleaner salesman; *(pej)* door-to-door salesman; **~schicht** *f* layer of dust; **~tuch** *nt* duster; **~wedel** *m* feather duster.

stauchen *vt* **(a)** *(zusammendrücken)* to compress *(auch Tech)*, to squash *(inf)*; *(rare: ver~)* to sprain. **(b)** *(inf) siehe* **zusammenstauchen**.

Staudamm *m* dam.

Staude *f* -, **-n** *(Hort)* herbaceous perennial (plant); *(Busch)* shrub; *(Bananen~, Tabak~, Rosenkohl~)* plant.

stauen 1 *vt* **(a)** *Wasser, Fluß* to dam (up); *Blut* to stop *or* stem the flow of. **(b)** *(Naut)* to stow (away).
2 *vr (sich anhäufen)* to pile up; *(ins Stocken geraten)* to get jammed; *(Wasser, fig)* to build up; *(Menschen)* to crowd; *(Blut)* to accumulate; *(durch Abbinden)* to be cut off. **die Menschen stauten sich in den Gängen** people were jamming the corridors; **der Verkehr staute sich über eine Strecke von 2 km** there was a 2 km tailback.

Stauer *m* -s, - *(Naut)* stevedore.

Staumauer *f* dam wall.

staunen *vi* to be astonished *or* amazed *(über + acc* at). **~d in** astonishment *or* amazement; **ich staune(, ich staune)!** *(inf)* well, I never!, well well!; **man staunt, wie ... ** it's amazing how ...; **da kann man nur noch** *or* **bloß ~** it's just amazing; **da staunst du, was?** *(inf)* you didn't expect that, did you!; *siehe* **Bauklotz**.

Staunen *nt* -s, *no pl* astonishment, amazement *(über + acc* at). **jdn in ~** versetzen to amaze *or* astonish sb.

staunenswert *adj* astonishing, amazing.

Staupe¹ *f* -, **-n** *(Vet)* distemper.

Staupe², Stäupe *f* -, *no pl (Hist)* flogging.

stäupen *vt (Hist)* to flog.

Stausee *m* reservoir, artificial lake.

Stauung *f* **(a)** *(Stockung)* pile-up; *(in Lieferungen, Post etc)* hold-up; *(von Menschen)* jam; *(von Verkehr)* tailback. **bei einer ~ der Züge im Bahnhof/der Schiffe im Hafen** when the station/harbour gets congested; **eine ~ des Verkehrs** a traffic jam.
(b) *(von Wasser)* build-up (of water). **~en sind hier sehr**

häufig the water often gets blocked here; **zur ~ eines Flusses** to block a river.
(c) *(Blut~)* congestion *no pl*. **bei ~(en)** *(des Blutes)* **in den Venen** when the veins become congested, when blood becomes congested in the veins.

Std., Stde. *abbr of* **Stunde** hr.

stdl. *abbr of* **stündlich**.

Steak [steːk] *nt* -s, **-s** steak.

Stearin [ʃteaˈriːn, st-] *nt* -s, **-e** stearin.

Stearinkerze [ʃteaˈriːn-, st-] *f* stearin candle.

Stech-: **~apfel** *m* *(Bot)* thorn-apple; **~becken** *nt* *(Med)* bedpan; **~beitel** *m* chisel.

stechen *pret* **stach**, *ptp* **gestochen** 1 *vi* **(a)** *(Dorn, Stachel etc)* to prick; *(Insekt mit Stachel)* to sting; *(Mücken, Moskitos)* to bite; *(mit Messer etc)* to stab *(nach* at); *(Sonne)* to beat down; *(mit Stechkarte) (bei Ankunft)* to clock in *or* on; *(bei Weggang)* to clock out *or* off. **die Sonne sticht in die Augen** the sun hurts one's eyes; **der Geruch sticht in die Nase** the smell stings one's nose; **mit etw in etw** *(acc)* **~** to stick sth in(to) sth; **jdm durch die Ohrläppchen ~** to pierce sb's ears.
(b) *(Cards)* to take the trick.
(c) *(Sport)* to have a play-/jump-/shoot-off.
(d) *(Farbe: spielen)* **die Farbe sticht ins Rötliche** the colour has a tinge of red *or* a reddish tinge.
2 *vt* **(a)** *(Dorn, Stachel etc)* to prick; *(Insekt mit Stachel)* to sting; *(Mücken, Moskitos)* to bite; *(mit Messer etc)* to stab; **Löcher ~** to pierce. **die Kontrolluhr ~** to clock on/in/out.
(b) *(Cards)* to take.
(c) *(ausschneiden, herauslösen) Spargel, Torf, Rasen* to cut.
(d) *(ab~) Schwein, Kalb* to stick, to kill; *(Angeln) Aale* to spear. **er machte Augen wie ein gestochenes Kalb** his eyes nearly popped out of his head.
(e) *(gravieren)* to engrave. **wie gestochen schreiben** to write a clear hand.
3 *vr* to prick oneself *(an + dat* on, *mit* with). **sich** *(acc or dat)* **in den Finger ~** to prick one's finger.
4 *vti impers* **es sticht** it is prickly; **es sticht mir** *or* **mich im Rücken** I have a sharp pain in my back.

Stechen *nt* -s, - **(a)** *(Sport)* play-/jump-/shoot-off. **(b)** *(Schmerz)* sharp pain.

stechend *adj* piercing; *(jäh) Schmerz* sharp; *(durchdringend) Augen, Blick auch* penetrating; *(beißend) Geruch* pungent.

Stech-: **~fliege** *f* stable fly; **~kahn** *m* punt; **~karte** *f* clocking-in card; **~mücke** *f* gnat, midge, mosquito; **~palme** *f* holly; **~schritt** *m* *(Mil)* goose-step; **~uhr** *f* time-clock; **~zirkel** *m* (pair of) dividers.

Steck-: **~brief** *m* "wanted" poster; *(fig)* personal description; **s~brieflich** *adv* **jdn s~brieflich verfolgen** to put up "wanted" posters for sb; **s~brieflich gesucht werden** to be wanted *or* on the wanted list; **~dose** *f* *(Elec)* (wall)socket.

Stecken *m* -s, - stick.

stecken 1 *vi pret* **steckte** *or* **stak** *(geh)*, *ptp* **gesteckt (a)** *(festsitzen)* to be stuck; *(an- or eingesteckt sein)* to be; *(Nadel, Splitter etc)* to be sticking; *(Brosche, Abzeichen etc)* to be (pinned). **eine Blume im Knopfloch/einen Ring am Finger ~ haben** to have a flower in one's buttonhole/a ring on one's finger; **der Stecker steckt in der Dose** the plug is in the socket; **er steckte in einem neuen Anzug** *(hum)* he was all done up in a new suit *(inf)*; **der Schlüssel steckt** the key is in the lock.
(b) *(verborgen sein)* to be (hiding). **wo steckt er?** where has he got to?; **wo hast du die ganze Zeit gesteckt?** where have you been (hiding) all this time?; **darin steckt viel Mühe** a lot of work *or* trouble has gone into *or* has been put into that; **da steckt etwas dahinter** *(inf)* there's something behind it; **was steckte hinter ihren Worten?** what was behind her words?; **in ihm steckt etwas** he certainly has it in him; **zeigen, was in einem steckt** to show what one is made of, to show one's mettle.
(c) *(strotzen vor)* **voll** *or* **voller Fehler/Nadeln/Witz etc ~** to be full of mistakes/pins/wit *etc*.
(d) *(verwickelt sein in)* **in Schwierigkeiten/tief in Schulden ~** to be in difficulties/to be deep(ly) in debt; **in einer Krise/der Pubertät ~** to be in the throes of a crisis/to be an adolescent.
2 *vt pret* **steckte**, *ptp* **gesteckt (a)** to put; *Haare* to put up; *Brosche* to pin *(an + acc* onto). **die Hände in die Taschen ~** to put *or* stick *(inf)* one's hands in one's pockets; **das Hemd in die Hose ~** to tuck one's shirt in (one's trousers); **jdn ins Bett ~** *(inf)* to put sb to bed; **jdn ins Gefängnis ~** *(inf)* to stick sb in prison *(inf)*, to put sb away *or* inside *(inf)*; **jdn in Uniform ~** *(inf)* to put sb in uniform; **etw in den Ofen/Briefkasten ~** to put *or* stick *(inf)* sth in the oven/letter-box.
(b) *(Sew)* to pin. **den Saum eines Kleides ~** to pin up the hem of a dress.
(c) *(inf: investieren) Geld, Mühe* to put *(in + acc* into); *Zeit* to devote *(in + acc* to).
(d) **jdm etw ~** *(inf)* to tell sb sth; **es jdm ~** *(inf)* to give sb a piece of one's mind.
(e) *(pflanzen)* to set.

Stecken-: **s~bleiben** *vi sep irreg aux sein* to stick fast, to get stuck; *(Kugel)* to be lodged; *(in der Rede)* to falter; *(beim Gedichtaufsagen)* to get stuck; **etw bleibt jdm im Halse s~** *(lit, fig)* sth sticks in sb's throat; **s~lassen** *vt sep irreg* to leave; **den Schlüssel s~lassen** to leave the key in the lock; **laß dein Geld s~!** leave your money where it is *or* in your pocket!; **~pferd** *nt* *(lit, fig)* hobby-horse; **sein ~pferd reiten** *(fig)* to be on one's hobby-horse.

Stecker *m* -s, - *(Elec)* plug.

Steck-: **~kissen** *nt* papoose; **~kontakt** *m* *(Elec)* plug.

Steckling *m* *(Hort)* cutting.

Stecknadel *f* pin. **keine ~ hätte zu Boden fallen können** there wasn't room to breathe; **man hätte eine ~ fallen hören können**

you could have heard a pin drop; **jdn/etw wie eine ~ suchen** to hunt high and low for sb/sth; **eine ~ im Heuhaufen** or **Heuschober suchen** (*fig*) to look for a needle in a hay-stack.

Steck-: ~**nadelkissen** *nt* pincushion; ~**reis** *nt* (*Hort*) cutting; ~**rübe** *f* swede; turnip; ~**schach** *nt* travelling chess-set; ~**schloß** *nt* bicycle lock; ~**schlüssel** *m* box spanner; ~**schuß** *m* bullet lodged in the body; ~**tuch** *nt* (*esp Aus*) breast-pocket handkerchief; ~**zwiebel** *f* bulb.

Stefan *m* - Stephen.

Steg *m* -(e)s, -e (**a**) (*Brücke*) footbridge; (*Landungs*~) landing stage; (*old: Pfad*) path. (**b**) (*Mus, Brillen*~) bridge; (*Tech: an Eisenträgern*) vertical plate, web. (**c**) (*Hosen*~) strap (*under the foot*). (**d**) (*Typ*) furniture.

Stegreif *m* aus dem ~ **spielen** (*Theat*) to improvise, to ad-lib; **eine Rede aus dem ~ halten** to make an impromptu or off-the-cuff or ad-lib speech; **etw aus dem ~ tun** to do sth just like that.

Stegreif-: ~**dichter** *m* extempore poet; ~**komödie** *f* improvised comedy; ~**rede** *f* impromptu speech; ~**spiel** *nt* (*Theat*) improvisation; ~**vortrag** *m* impromptu lecture.

Steh- *in cpds* stand-up.

Steh|aufmännchen *nt* (*Spielzeug*) tumbler; (*fig*) somebody who always bounces back. **er ist ein richtiges ~** he always bounces back, you can't keep a good man down (*prov*).

Steh-: ~**ausschank** *m* stand-up bar; ~**empfang** *m* stand-up reception.

stehen *pret* **stand**, *ptp* **gestanden** *aux* **haben** or (*S Ger, Aus, Sw*) **sein** 1 *vi* (**a**) (*in aufrechter Stellung sein*) to stand; (*warten auch*) to wait; (*Penis*) to be erect; (*inf: fertig sein*) to be finished; (*inf: geregelt sein*) to be settled. **fest/sicher ~** to stand firm(ly)/securely; (*Mensch*) to have a firm/safe foothold; **gebückt/krumm ~** to slouch; **unter der Dusche ~** to be in the shower; **an der Bushaltestelle ~** to stand or wait at the bus-stop; **neben jdm zu ~ kommen** (*Mensch*) to end up beside sb; **ich kann nicht mehr ~** I can't stand (up) any longer; **der Weizen steht gut** the wheat is growing well; **der Kaffee ist so stark, daß der Löffel drin steht** (*hum*) the coffee is so strong that the spoon will almost stand up in it; **so wahr ich hier stehe as sure as I'm standing here; **hier stehe ich, ich kann nicht anders!** (*Hist*) here I stand, I can do no other; **mit jdm/etw ~ und fallen** to depend on sb/sth; (*wesentlich sein für*) to stand or fall by sb/sth; **seine Hose steht vor Dreck** (*inf*) his trousers are stiff with dirt; **er steht (ihm)** (*sl*), **er hat einen ~** (*sl*) he has a hard-on (*sl*); **das/die Sache steht** (*inf*) that/the whole business is finally settled.

(**b**) (*sich befinden*) to be. **die Vase/die Tasse steht auf dem Tisch** the vase is (standing)/the cup is on the table; **mein Auto steht seit Wochen vor der Tür** my car has been standing or sitting (*inf*) outside for weeks; **meine alte Schule steht noch** my old school is still standing or is still there; **vor der Tür stand ein Fremder** there was a stranger (standing) at the door; **auf der Fahrbahn stand Wasser** there was water on the road; **ihm steht der Schweiß auf der Stirn** his forehead is covered in sweat; **am Himmel ~** to be in the sky; **der Mond steht am Himmel** the moon is shining; **die Sonne steht abends tief/im Westen** the sun in the evening is deep in the sky/in the West; **Geld bei jdm ~ haben** (*inf*) to be owed money by sb; **unter Schock ~** to be in a state of shock; **unter Drogeneinwirkung/Alkohol ~** to be under the influence of drugs/alcohol; **kurz vor dem Krieg ~** to be on the brink of war; **vor einer Entscheidung ~** to be faced with a decision; **die Frage steht vor der Entscheidung** the question is about to be decided; **im 83. Lebensjahr ~** to be in one's 83rd year; **man muß wissen, wo man steht** you have to know where you stand; **ich tue, was in meinen Kräften/meiner Macht steht** I'll do everything I can/in my power; **das steht zu erwarten/fürchten** (*geh*) that is to be expected/feared; *siehe* **Leben**.

(**c**) (*geschrieben, gedruckt sein*) to be; (*aufgeführt sein auch*) to appear. **wo steht das?** (*lit*) where does it say that?; (*fig*) who says so?; **was steht da/in dem Brief/in der Zeitung?** what does it/the letter/the paper say?; **steht etwas von Tante Erna drin?** does it say anything or is there anything about Aunt Erna?; **das steht im Gesetz** the law says so, that is what the law says; **darüber steht nichts im Gesetz** the law says nothing about that; **es stand im „Kurier"** it was in the "Courier"; **das steht bei Nietzsche** it says that in Nietzsche; **das steht in der Bibel (geschrieben)** it says that or so in the Bible, the Bible says so; **es steht geschrieben** (*Bibl*) it is written (*Bibl*).

(**d**) (*angehalten haben*) to have stopped; (*Maschine, Fließband auch*) to be at a standstill. **meine Uhr steht** my watch has stopped; **der ganze Verkehr steht** all traffic is at a complete standstill.

(**e**) (*inf: geparkt haben*) to be parked. **wo ~ Sie?** where are or have you parked?

(**f**) (*anzeigen*) (*Rekord*) to stand (*auf +dat* at); (*Mannschaft etc*) to be (*auf +dat* in). **der Pegel steht auf 3.48 m** the water mark is at or is showing 3.48 m; **der Zeiger steht auf 4 Uhr** the clock says 4 (o'clock); **die Kompaßnadel steht auf** or **nach Norden** the compass needle is indicating or pointing north; **wie steht das Spiel?** what is the score?; **es steht 0:0** neither side has scored, there is still no score; **es steht 2:1 für München** the score is or it is 2-1 to Munich; **die/die Sache steht mir bis hier (oben)** (*inf*) I'm fed up to the back-teeth with it (*inf*), I'm sick and tired of it (*inf*).

(**g**) (*Gram*) (*bei Satzstellung*) to come; (*bei Zeit, Fall, Modus*) to be; (*gefolgt werden von*) to take. **mit dem Dativ/Akkusativ ~** to take or govern the dative/accusative; **Wunschsätze ~ im Konjunktiv** optative clauses take the subjunctive.

(**h**) (*passen zu*) jdm ~ to suit sb.

(**i**) (*Belohnung, Strafe etc*) **auf Betrug steht eine Gefängnisstrafe** the penalty for fraud is imprisonment, fraud is punish-

able by imprisonment; **auf die Ergreifung der Täter steht eine Belohnung** there is a reward for or a reward has been offered for the capture of the persons responsible.

(**j**) (*bewertet werden: Währung, Kurs*) to be or stand (*auf +dat* at). **wie steht das Pfund?** how does the pound stand?; **am besten steht der Schweizerfranken** the Swiss franc is strongest.

(**k**) (*Redewendungen*) **zu seinem Versprechen ~** to stand by or keep one's promise; **zu dem, was man gesagt hat, ~** to stick to what one has said; **zu seinen Behauptungen/seiner Überzeugung ~** to stand by what one says/by one's convictions; **zum Sozialismus ~** to be a staunch socialist; **zu jdm ~** to stand or stick by sb; **wie ~ Sie dazu?** what are your views or what is your opinion on that?; **wie ~ Sie dazu, Angeklagter?** do you have anything to say in reply?; **für etw ~** (*sl*) to stand for sth; **auf jdn/etw ~** (*sl*) to be mad about sb/sth (*inf*), to go for sb/sth (*inf*), to be into sb/sth (*sl*); **hinter jdm/etw ~** to be behind sb/sth; **das steht (ganz) bei Ihnen** (*form*) that is (entirely) up to you.

2 *vr* (**a**) **wie steht man sich in diesem Land?** what are things like in this country?; **wie ~ sich Müllers jetzt?** how are things with the Müllers now?; **sich gut/schlecht ~** to be well-off/badly off; **sich bei** or **mit jdm gut/schlecht ~** to be well-off/badly off with sb/sth; **sich mit jdm gut/schlecht ~** (*sich verstehen*) to get on well/badly with sb.

(**b**) **hier steht es sich nicht gut** this isn't a very good place to stand.

3 *vi impers* **es steht schlecht/gut/besser um jdn** (*bei Aussichten*) things look or it looks bad/good/better for sb; (*gesundheitlich, finanziell*) sb is doing badly/well/better; **es steht schlecht/gut/besser um etw** things look or it looks bad/good/better for sth, sth is doing badly/well/better; **wie steht's?** how are or how's things?; **wie steht es damit?** how about it?; **wie steht es mit ...?** what is the position regarding ...?; **so steht es also!** so that's how it is, so that's the way it is.

4 *vt* **Posten, Wache** to stand. **sich** (*acc*) **müde ~, sich** (*dat*) **die Beine in den Bauch** (*inf*) **~** to stand until one is ready to drop.

Stehen *nt* -s, *no pl* (**a**) standing. **das viele ~** all this standing; **etw im ~ tun** to do sth standing up.

(**b**) (*Halt*) **zum ~ bringen** to stop; **Lokomotive, LKW, Verkehr, Produktion auch** to bring to a standstill or halt or stop; **Produktion, Heer, Vormarsch auch** to halt; **zum ~ kommen** to stop; (*Lokomotive, LKW, Verkehr, Produktion auch*) to come to a standstill or halt or stop.

stehenbleiben *vi sep irreg aux sein* (**a**) (*anhalten*) to stop; (*Zug, LKW, Verkehr, Produktion auch*) to come to a standstill or halt or stop; (*Aut: Motor auch*) to cut out; (*beim Lesen auch*) to leave off. **~! stop!;** (*Mil*) halt!

(**b**) (*nicht weitergehen*) (*Mensch, Tier*) to stay; (*Entwicklung*) to stop; (*Zeit*) to stand still; (*Auto, Zug*) to stand.

(**c**) (*vergessen* or *zurückgelassen werden*) to be left (behind). **mein Regenschirm muß im Büro stehengeblieben sein** I must have left my umbrella in the office.

(**d**) (*im Text unverändert bleiben*) to be left (in). **soll das so ~?** should that stay or be left as it is?

stehend *adj attr* **Fahrzeug** stationary; **Wasser, Gewässer** stagnant; (*ständig*) **Heer** standing, regular; **Start** (*Radfahren*) standing. **~e Redensart** stock phrase; **~en Fußes** (*liter*) instanter, immediately; **~es Gut** (*Naut*) standing rigging.

stehenlassen *ptp* or **stehengelassen** *vt sep irreg* to leave; (*zurücklassen, vergessen auch*) to leave behind; (*Cook*) to let stand; **Essen, Getränk** to leave (untouched); **Fehler** to leave (in). **laßt das (an der Tafel) stehen** leave it (on the board); **alles stehen- und liegenlassen** to drop everything; (*Flüchtlinge etc*) to leave everything behind; **jdn einfach ~** to leave sb standing (there), to walk off and leave sb; **sich** (*dat*) **einen Bart ~** to grow a beard; **jdn vor der Tür/in der Kälte ~** to leave sb standing outside/in the cold.

Steher *m* -s, - (*Pferderennen, fig*) stayer; (*Radfahren*) motor-paced rider.

Steherrennen *nt* (*Radfahren*) motor-paced race.

Steh-: ~**geiger** *m* café violinist; ~**imbiß** *m* stand-up snack-bar; ~**kneipe** *f* stand-up bar; ~**konvent** *m* (*hum*) stand-up do (*inf*); **darf ich mal Ihren ~konvent unterbrechen, meine Herren?** excuse me for interrupting, gentlemen (*iro*); ~**kragen** *m* stand-up collar; (*Vatermörder*) wing collar; (*von Geistlichen auch*) dog collar; ~**kragenproletariat** *nt* (*hum*) white-collar workers *pl*; ~**kragenproletarier** *m* (*hum*) white-collar worker; ~**lampe** *f* standard lamp; ~**leiter** *f* stepladder.

stehlen *pret* **stahl**, *ptp* **gestohlen** 1 *vti* to steal. **hier wird viel gestohlen** there's a lot of stealing around here; **jdm die Ruhe ~** to disturb sb; **jdm die Zeit ~** to waste sb's time; **er stahl ihr einen flüchtigen Kuß** (*liter*) he stole a fleeting kiss (from her); *siehe* **Elster, gestohlen**.

2 *vr* to steal. **sich in das/aus dem Haus ~** to steal into/out of the house; **die Sonne stahl sich durch die Wolken** (*liter*) the sun stole forth from behind the clouds (*liter*).

Stehler *m* -s, - *siehe* **Hehler(in)**.

Steh-: ~**platz** *m* **ich bekam nur noch einen ~platz** I had to stand; **ein ~platz kostet 1 Mark** a ticket for standing room costs 1 mark, it costs 1 mark to stand; **ein guter ~platz ist besser als ein schlechter Sitzplatz** a good place in the standing room is better than a bad seat; ~**plätze** standing room *sing*; **zwei ~plätze, bitte** two standing, please; **die Anzahl der ~plätze ist begrenzt** only a limited number of people are allowed to stand; ~**pult** *nt* high desk; ~**satz** *m* (*Typ*) standing or line type; ~**vermögen** *nt* staying power, stamina.

Steiermark *f* - Styria.

steif *adj* (**a**) stiff; **Grog auch** strong; **Penis** hard, erect. **~ vor Kälte** with cold; **eine ~e Brise** a stiff breeze; **ein ~er Hals** a stiff neck; **ein ~er Hut** a homburg (hat); (*Melone*) a bowler (hat), a derby (*US*); **sich ~ (wie ein Brett) machen** to go rigid; **das Eiweiß ~ schlagen** to beat the egg white until stiff; **~ und fest auf etw** (*dat*) **beharren** to insist stubbornly *or* obstinately on sth; **ein S~er** (*sl*) a hard-on (*sl*). **(b)** (*gestärkt*) starched; *Kragen auch* stiff. **(c)** (*förmlich*) stiff; *Empfang, Konventionen, Begrüßung, Abend* formal. **~ lächeln** to smile stiffly.

Steife *f* -, **-n (a)** *no pl* stiffness. **(b)** (*Stärkemittel*) starch.

steifen *vt* to stiffen; *Wäsche* to starch; *siehe* **Nacken**.

Steifftier ® *nt* soft toy (animal).

Steifheit *f siehe* **steif (a)** stiffness; strength; hardness; erectness. **(b)** starchedness; stiffness. **(c)** stiffness; formality.

Steifleinen *nt* buckram.

Steig *m* -(e)s, -e steep track.

Steigbügel *m* stirrup. **jdm den ~ halten** (*fig*) to help sb on.

Steigbügelhalter *m* (*esp Pol pej*) **jds ~ sein** to help sb to come to power.

Steige *f* -, **-n** (*dial*) **(a)** *siehe* **Steig. (b)** *siehe* **Stiege.**

Steig|**eisen** *nt* climbing iron *usu pl*; (*Bergsteigen*) crampon; (*an Mauer*) rung (in the wall).

steigen *pret* **stieg**, *ptp* **gestiegen** *aux* **sein 1** *vi* **(a)** (*klettern*) to climb. **auf einen Berg/Turm/Baum/eine Leiter ~** to climb (up) a mountain/tower/tree/ladder; **aufs Fahrrad/Pferd ~** to get on(to) the/one's bicycle/get on(to) *or* mount the/one's horse; **ins Bett/in die Straßenbahn ~** to get into bed/on the tram; **ins Wasser/in die Badewanne ~** to climb *or* get into the bath; **in die Kleider ~** (*inf*) to put on one's clothes; **vom Fahrrad/Pferd ~** to get off *or* dismount from the/one's bicycle/horse; **aus dem Wasser/der Badewanne/dem Bett ~** to get out of the water/the bath/bed; **aus dem Zug/Bus/Flugzeug ~** to get off the train/bus/plane; **in die Prüfung ~** (*inf*) to do *or* sit the exam; **wer hoch steigt, fällt tief** (*Prov*) the bigger they come the harder they fall (*prov*). **(b)** (*sich aufwärts bewegen*) to rise; (*Vogel auch*) to soar; (*Flugzeug, Straße*) to climb; (*sich aufbäumen: Pferd*) to rear; (*sich auflösen: Nebel*) to lift; (*sich erhöhen*) (*Preis, Zahl, Gehalt etc*) to increase, to go up, to rise; (*Fieber*) to go up; (*zunehmen*) (*Chancen, Mißtrauen, Ungeduld etc*) to increase; (*Spannung*) to increase, to mount. **Drachen ~ lassen** to fly kites; **der Gestank/Duft stieg ihm in die Nase** the stench/smell reached his nostrils; **das Blut stieg ihm in den Kopf/das Gesicht** the blood rushed to his head/face; **in jds Achtung** (*dat*) **~ to rise** in sb's estimation; **die allgemeine/meine Stimmung stieg** the general mood improved/my spirits rose. **(c)** (*inf: stattfinden*) to be. **steigt die Demonstration/Prüfung oder nicht?** is the demonstration/examination on or not?; **bei Helga steigt Sonnabend eine Party** Helga's having a party on Saturday.
2 *vt Treppen, Stufen* to climb (up).

Steiger *m* -s, - (*Min*) pit foreman.

steigern 1 *vt* **(a)** to increase; *Geschwindigkeit auch* to raise (*auf + acc* to); *Not, Gefahr auch* to intensify; *Wert auch* to add to; *Wirkung auch* to heighten; *Farbe* to intensify, to heighten; (*verschlimmern*) *Übel, Zorn* to aggravate. **(b)** (*Gram*) to compare. **(c)** (*ersteigern*) to buy at an auction.
2 *vi* to bid (*um* for).
3 *vr* **(a)** (*sich erhöhen*) to increase; (*Gefahr auch*) to rise; (*Farben auch*) to be intensified; (*Zorn, Übel*) to be aggravated, to worsen. **sein Ärger steigerte sich zu Zorn** his annoyance turned into rage; **seine Schmerzen steigerten sich ins Unerträgliche** his pain became unbearable. **(b)** (*sich verbessern*) to improve. **(c)** (*hinein~*) **sich in etw** (*acc*) **~** to work oneself (up) into sth.

Steigerung *f* **(a)** *siehe vt* **(a)** (*das Steigern*) increase (*gen* in); rise (*gen* in); intensification; heightening; intensification, heightening; aggravation. **(b)** (*Verbesserung*) improvement. **(c)** (*Gram*) comparative.

Steigerungs-: **~form** *f* (*Gram*) comparative/superlative form; **~stufe** *f* (*Gram*) degree of comparison.

Steig-: **~fähigkeit** *f* (*Aut*) hill-climbing *or* pulling capacity; **~ fähigkeit beweisen** to pull well; **~flug** *m* (*Aviat*) climb, ascent; **~geschwindigkeit** *f* rate of climb *or* ascent.

Steigung *f* (*Hang*) slope; (*von Hang, Straße, Math*) gradient; (*Gewinde~*) pitch. **eine ~ von 10%** a gradient of one in ten *or* of 10%.

Steigungs-: **~grad** *m* gradient; **~winkel** *m* angle of gradient.

steil *adj* **(a)** steep. **eine ~e Karriere** (*fig*) a rapid rise. **(b)** (*senkrecht*) upright. **sich ~ aufrichten** to sit/stand up straight. **(c)** (*Sport*) **~e Vorlage, ~er Paß** through ball. **(d)** (*dated sl*) super (*inf*), smashing (*inf*). **ein ~er Zahn** (*dated sl*) a smasher (*inf*).

Steilheit *f* steepness.

Steil-: **~küste** *f* steep coast; (*Klippen*) cliffs *pl*; **~paß** *m*, **~vorlage** *f* (*Sport*) through ball; **~wand** *f* steep face; **~wandfahrer** *m* wall-of-death rider; **~wandzelt** *nt* frame tent.

Stein *m* -(e)s, -e **(a)** (*auch Bot, Med*) stone; (*Feuer~*) flint; (*Edel~ auch, in Uhr*) jewel; (*Spiel~*) piece. **~e und Erden** minerals; **der ~ der Weisen** (*lit, fig*) the philosophers' stone; **es blieb kein ~ auf dem anderen** everything was smashed to pieces; (*bei Gebäuden, Mauern*) not a stone was left standing; **das könnte einen ~ erbarmen** that would move the stoniest heart; **das könnte einen ~ erweichen** that would move the hardest heart to pity; **mir fällt ein ~ vom Herzen!** (*fig*) that's a load off my mind!; **bei jdm einen ~ im Brett haben** (*fig inf*) to be well in with sb (*inf*); **den ersten ~ (auf jdn) werfen** (*prov*) to cast the first stone (at sb); *siehe* **Anstoß**, **rollen**, **Krone**.

(b) (*Bau~, Natur~*) stone; (*groß, esp Hohlblock*) block; (*kleiner, esp Ziegel~*) brick. **(c)** *no pl* (*Material*) stone. **ein Haus aus ~** a house made of stone, a stone house; **ein Herz aus ~** (*fig*) a heart of stone; **es friert ~ und Bein** (*fig inf*) it's freezing cold outside; **~ und Bein schwören** (*fig inf*) to swear blind (*inf*); **zu ~ erstarren** *or* **werden** to turn to stone; (*fig*) to be as if turned to stone.

Stein-: **~adler** *m* golden eagle; **s~alt** *adj* ancient, as old as the hills; **~bau** *m* **(a)** *no pl* building in stone *no art*; **(b)** (*Gebäude*) stone building; **~bock** *m* **(a)** (*Zool*) ibex; **(b)** (*Astrol*) Capricorn; **~boden** *m* stone floor; **~bohrer** *m* masonry drill; (*Gesteinsbohrer*) rock drill; **~bruch** *m* quarry; **~brucharbeiter** *m* quarryman, quarry worker; **~butt** *m* (*Zool*) turbot; **~druck** *m* (*Typ*) lithography; **~drucker** *m* lithographer; **~eiche** *f* holm oak.

steinern *adj* stone; (*fig*) stony. **ein ~es Herz** a heart of stone.

Stein-: **~erweichen** *nt* **zum ~erweichen weinen** to cry heartbreakingly; **s~erweichend** *adj* heart-rending, heartbreaking; **~frucht** *f* stone fruit; **~fußboden** *m* stone floor; **~garten** *m* rockery, rock garden; **~geiß** *f* female ibex; **s~grau** *adj* stone-grey; **~gut** *nt* stoneware; **~hagel** *m* hail of stones.

Steinhäger ® *m* -s, - Steinhäger, type of schnapps.

steinhart *adj* (as) hard as a rock, rock hard.

steinig *adj* stony. **ein ~er Weg** (*fig*) a path of trial and tribulation.

steinigen *vt* to stone.

Steinigung *f* stoning.

Steinkohle *f* hard coal.

Steinkohlen-: **~bergbau** *m* coal mining; **~bergwerk** *nt* coal mine, colliery; **~revier** *nt* coal-mining area.

Stein-: **~krankheit** *f siehe* **~leiden**; **~krug** *m* (*aus ~ gut/~ zeug*) (*Kanne*) earthenware/stoneware jug; (*Becher*) earthenware/stoneware mug; (*für Bier*) stein; **~leiden** *nt* (*Nieren-/Blasen-/Gallen~e*) kidney/bladder stones *pl*; gallstones *pl*; **ein ~leiden haben** to suffer from kidney *etc* stones; **s~leidend** *adj* suffering from kidney *etc* stones; **~meißel** *m* stone chisel; **~metz** *m* -en, -en stonemason; **~obst** *nt* stone fruit; **~operation** *f* operation to remove kidney *etc* stones; **~pilz** *m* boletus edulis (*spec*); **~platte** *f* stone slab; (*zum Pflastern*) flagstone; **s~reich[1]** *adj* (*inf*) stinking rich (*inf*), rolling in it (*inf*); **s~reich[2]** *adj* (*mit vielen Steinen*) stony; **~salz** *nt* rock salt; **~schlag** *m* (*a*) rockfall; (*zum Straßenbau*) (road-)metal; „Achtung ~schlag" "danger falling stones"; **(b)** *no pl* (*Schotter*) broken stone; (*zum Straßenbau*) (road-)metal; **~schlaggefahr** *f* danger of rockfall(s); **~schleuder** *f* catapult; **~schneider** *m* gem-cutter; **~schnitt** *m* (*a*) cut (gem)stone; (*b*) *no pl* (*Verfahren*) gem cutting; **~setzer** *m* road worker; **~tafel** *f* stone tablet; **~topf** *m* (*aus ~ gut/~ zeug*) earthenware/stoneware pot; **~wild** *nt* (*Hunt*) ibexes *pl*; **~wurf** *m* (*a*) (*fig*) stone's throw; **(b)** (*lit*) **mit einem ~wurf** by throwing a stone; **~wüste** *f* stony desert; (*fig*) concrete jungle; **~zeit** *f* Stone Age; **s~zeitlich** *adj* Stone Age *attr*; **~zeug** *nt* stoneware.

Steirer(in *f*) *m* -s, - Styrian.

steirisch *adj* Styrian.

Steiß *m* -es, -e (*Anat*) coccyx; (*hum inf*) tail (*inf*), behind.

Steiß-: **~bein** *nt* (*Anat*) coccyx; **~geburt** *f* (*Med*) breech birth *or* delivery; **~lage** *f* (*Med*) breech presentation.

Stele ['ste:lǝ, 'ʃte:lǝ] *f* -, **-n** stele.

Stellage [ʃtɛ'la:ʒǝ] *f* -, **-n** (*inf: Gestell*) rack, frame; (*dial inf: Beine*) legs *pl*, pins *pl* (*inf*).

stellar [ʃtɛ'la:ɐ, st-] *adj* (*Astron*) stellar.

Stelldich|**ein** *nt* -(s), -(s) (*dated*) rendezvous, tryst (*old*). **sich** (*dat*) **ein ~ geben** (*fig*) to come together.

Stelle *f* -, **-n (a)** place, spot; (*Standort*) place; (*Fleck: rostend, naß, faul etc*) patch. **an dieser ~** in this place, on this spot; **eine gute ~ zum Parken/Picknicken** a good place *or* spot to park/for a picnic; **das Buch/Auto steht an der üblichen ~** the book/car is in its usual place; **legen Sie das an eine andere ~** put it in a different place; **diese ~ muß repariert werden** this bit needs repairing, it needs to be repaired here; **eine kahle ~ am Kopf** a bald patch on one's head; **eine wunde/entzündete ~ am Finger** a cut/an inflammation on one's finger, a cut/an inflamed finger; **Salbe auf die wunde/aufgeriebene ~ auftragen** apply ointment to the affected area; **eine empfindliche ~** (*lit*) a sensitive spot *or* place; (*fig*) a sensitive point; **eine schwache ~** a weak spot; (*fig auch*) a weak point; **auf der ~ laufen** to run on the spot; **der ~ treten** (*lit*) to mark time; (*fig*) not to make any progress *or* headway; **auf der ~** (*fig: sofort*) on the spot; *kommen, gehen* straight *or* right away; **nicht von der ~ kommen** not to make any progress *or* headway; (*fig auch*) to be bogged down; **etw nicht von der ~ kriegen** (*inf*) *or* **bekommen** to be unable to move *or* shift sth; **sich nicht von der ~ rühren** *or* **bewegen**, **nicht von der ~ weichen** to refuse to budge (*inf*) *or* move; **zur ~ sein** to be on the spot; (*bereit, etw zu tun*) to be at hand; **X zur ~!** (*Mil*) X reporting!; **sich bei jdm zur ~ melden** (*Mil*) to report to sb; *siehe* **Ort[1]**.

(b) (*in Buch etc*) place; (*Abschnitt*) passage; (*Text~, esp beim Zitieren*) reference; (*Text~*) verse; (*Mus*) passage. **an dieser ~** here; **an anderer ~** elsewhere, in another place.

(c) (*Zeitpunkt*) point. **an dieser ~** at this point *or* juncture; **an anderer ~** on another occasion; **an früherer/späterer ~** earlier/later; (*an anderem Tag auch*) on an earlier/ a later occasion; **an passender ~** at an appropriate moment.

(d) (*in Reihenfolge, Ordnung, Liste*) place; (*in Tabelle, Hierarchie auch*) position. **an erster ~** in the first place, first; **an erster/zweiter ~ geht es um ...** in the first instance *or* first/secondly it's a question of ...; (*bei jdm*) **an erster/letzter ~ kommen** to come first/last (for sb); **an erster/zweiter etc ~ stehen** to be first/second *etc*, to be in first/second *etc* place; (*in bezug auf Wichtigkeit*) to come first/second *etc*; **an**

führender/einflußreicher ~ **stehen** to be in or have a leading/an influential position.

(e) (Math) figure, digit; (hinter Komma) place. **drei** ~**n hinter dem Komma** three decimal places; **eine Zahl mit drei** ~**n** a three-figure number.

(f) (Lage, Platz, Aufgabenbereich) place. **an** ~ **von** or (+gen) in place of, instead of; **an jds** ~ (acc)/**an die** ~ **einer Sache** (gen) **treten** to take sb's place/the place of sth; **das erledige ich/ich gehe an deiner** ~ I'll do that for you/I'll go in your place; **ich möchte jetzt nicht an seiner** ~ **sein** I wouldn't like to be in his position or shoes; **an deiner** ~ **würde ich ...** in your position or if I were you I would ...

(g) (Posten) job; (Ausbildungs~) place. **eine freie** or **offene** ~ a vacancy; **ohne** ~ without a job; **wir haben zur Zeit keine** ~**n zu vergeben** we haven't any vacancies at present.

(h) (Dienst~) office; (Behörde) authority. **da bist du bei mir/ihm an der richtigen** ~! (inf) you've come/you went to the right place; **sich an höherer** ~ **beschweren** to complain to somebody higher up or to a higher authority.

stellen 1 vt (a) (hin~) to put; (an bestimmten Platz legen auch) to place. **jdm etw auf den Tisch** ~ to put sth on the table for sb; **jdm etw in den Weg** ~ (lit, fig) to put or place sth in sb's way; **jdn über/unter jdn** ~ (fig) to put or place sb above/below sb; **auf sich** (acc) **selbst gestellt sein** (fig) to have to fend for oneself.

(b) (in senkrechte Position bringen) to stand. **die Ohren** ~ to prick up its ears; **den Schwanz** ~ to lift up its tail; **du solltest es** ~, **nicht legen** you should stand it up, not lay it down.

(c) (Platz finden für) etw nicht ~ **können** (unterbringen) not to have room or space for sth; **etw gut** ~ **können** to have a good place for sth.

(d) (anordnen) to arrange. **das sollten Sie anders** ~ you should put it in a different position.

(e) (er~) (jdm) **eine Diagnose** ~ to provide (sb with) a diagnosis, to make a diagnosis (for sb); **jdm sein Horoskop** ~ to draw up or cast sb's horoscope.

(f) (arrangieren) Szene to arrange; Aufnahme to pose. **eine gestellte Pose** a pose.

(g) (beschaffen, aufbieten) to provide.

(h) (ein~) to set (auf +acc at); Uhr etc to set (auf +acc for). **das Radio lauter/leiser** ~ to turn the radio up/down; **die Heizung höher/kleiner** ~ to turn the heating up/down.

(i) (finanziell) **gut/besser/schlecht gestellt** well/better/badly off.

(j) (erwischen) to catch; (fig inf) to corner; siehe Rede.

(k) in Verbindung mit n siehe auch dort. Aufgabe, Thema, Bedingung, Termin to set (jdm sb); Frage to put (jdm, an jdn to sb); Antrag, Forderung, Bedingung to make.

(l) (in Redewendungen) **etw in jds Belieben** or **Ermessen** (acc) ~ to leave sth to sb's discretion, to leave sth up to sb; **jdn unter jds Aufsicht** (acc) ~ to place or put sb under sb's care; **jdn vor ein Problem/eine Aufgabe** etc ~ to confront sb with a problem/task etc; **jdn vor eine Entscheidung** ~ to put sb in the position of having to make a decision.

2 vr (a) to (go and) stand (an +acc at, by); (sich auf~, sich einordnen) to position oneself; (sich aufrecht hin~) to stand up. **sich auf** (die) **Zehenspitzen** ~ to stand on tip-toe; **sich auf den Standpunkt** ~, ... to take the view ...; **sich gegen jdn/etw** ~ (fig) to oppose sb/sth; **sich hinter jdn/etw** ~ (fig) to support or back sb/sth, to stand by sb/sth; **sich jdm in den Weg/vor die Nase** ~ to stand in sb's way (auch fig)/right in front of sb.

(b) (Gegenstand, Körperteil) **sich senkrecht** ~ to stand or come up; **sich in die Höhe** ~ to stand up; (Ohren) to prick up.

(c) (fig: sich verhalten) **sich positiv/anders zu etw** ~ to have a positive/different attitude towards sth; **wie stellst du dich zu ...?** how do you regard ...?, what do you think of ...?; **sich gut mit jdm** ~ to put oneself on good terms with sb.

(d) (inf: finanziell) **sich gut/schlecht** ~ to be well/badly off.

(e) (sich ein~: Gerät etc) to set itself (auf +acc at). **die Heizung stellt sich von selbst kleiner** the heating turns itself down.

(f) (sich ausliefern, antreten) to give oneself up, to surrender (jdm to sb). **sich der öffentlichen Kritik** ~ to lay oneself open to public criticism; **sich den Journalisten/den Fragen der Journalisten** ~ to make oneself available to the reporters/ to be prepared to answer reporters' questions; **sich** (dem **Militär** or **Wehrdienst**) ~ to report for military service; **sich einer Herausforderung/einem Herausforderer** ~ to take up a challenge/take on a challenger; **sich** (jdm) **zum Kampf** ~ to be prepared to do battle (with sb), to announce one's readiness to fight (sb).

(g) (sich ver~) **sich krank/schlafend** etc ~ to pretend to be ill/asleep etc; **sich tot** ~ to play dead, to pretend to be dead; siehe dumm, taub.

(h) (fig: entstehen) to arise (für for). **es stellten sich uns** (dat) **allerlei Probleme** we were faced or confronted with all sorts of problems.

Stellen-: ~**angebot** nt offer of employment, job offer; „~**angebote**" "situations vacant", "vacancies"; ~**anzeige** f job advertisement or ad (inf); ~**besetzung** f appointment, filling a/the post no art; ~**gesuch** nt advertisement seeking employment, "employment wanted" advertisement; „~**gesuche**" "situations wanted"; ~**markt** m employment or job market; (in Zeitung) appointments section; ~**nachweis** m, ~**vermittlung** f employment bureau or centre; (privat auch) employment agency; **s**~**weise** adv in places, here and there; **s**~**weise Schauer** scattered showers, showers in places; ~**wert** m (Math) place value; (fig) status.

-stellig adj suf (bei Zahlen) -figure, -digit; (hinter Komma) -place. **ein drei**~**er Dezimalbruch** a number with three decimal places.

Stell-: ~**macher** m (N Ger) (Wagenbauer) cartwright; (esp von Wagenrädern) wheelwright; ~**macherei** f cart-making; (Werkstatt) cartwright's/wheelwright's (work-)shop; ~**probe** f (Theat) blocking rehearsal; ~**schraube** f (Tech) adjusting or set screw.

Stellung f (a) (lit, fig, Mil) position. **in** ~ **bringen/gehen** to bring/get into position, to place in position/take up one's position; **die** ~ **halten** (Mil) to hold one's position; (hum) to hold the fort; ~ **beziehen** (Mil) to move into position; (fig) to declare one's position, to make it clear where one stands; **zu etw** ~ **nehmen** to give one's opinion on sth, to comment on sth; **ich möchte dazu nicht** ~ **nehmen** I would rather not comment on that; **für jdn/etw** ~ **nehmen** or **beziehen** to come out in favour of sb/sth; (verteidigen) to take sb's part/to defend sth; **gegen jdn/etw** ~ **nehmen** or **beziehen** to come out against sb/sth.

(b) (Rang) position. **in führender/untergeordneter** ~ in a leading/subordinate position; **in meiner** ~ **als** ... in my capacity as ...; **die rechtliche** ~ **des Mieters** the legal status of the tenant.

(c) (Posten) position, post, situation (dated, form). **bei jdm in** ~ **sein** to be in sb's employment or employ (form); **ohne** ~ **sein** to be without employment or unemployed.

Stellungnahme f -, -n statement (zu on). **sich** (dat) **seine** ~ **vorbehalten, sich einer** ~ (gen) **enthalten** to decline to comment; **eine** ~ **zu etw abgeben** to make a statement on sth; **alle warteten auf die** ~ **des Präsidenten** all were waiting to see what position the president would take (zu on).

Stellungs-: ~**befehl** m siehe **Gestellungsbefehl**; ~**fehler** m (Sport) positional error; ~**krieg** m positional warfare no indef art; **s**~**los** adj without employment, unemployed; ~**spiel** nt (Sport) positional play no indef art; ~**suche** f search for employment; **auf** ~**suche sein** to be looking for employment or a position; ~**wechsel** m change of employment.

stellv. abbr of **stellvertretend**.

Stell-: **s**~**vertretend** adj (von Amts wegen) deputy attr; (vorübergehend) acting attr; **s**~**vertretend für jdn** deputizing or acting for sb; **s**~**vertretend für jdn handeln** to deputize or act for sb; **s**~**vertretend für jdn/etw stehen** to stand in for sb/sth or in place of sb/sth; ~**vertreter** m (acting) representative; (von Amts wegen) deputy; (von Arzt) locum; **der** ~**vertreter Christi** (auf Erden) the Vicar of Christ; ~**vertretung** f (~vertreter) representative; (von Amts wegen) deputy; (von Arzt) locum; **die** ~**vertretung für jdn übernehmen** to represent sb; (von Amts wegen) to stand in or deputize for sb; **in** ~**vertretung** +gen for, on behalf of; ~**werk** nt (Rail) signal box (Brit), signal or switch tower (US).

Stelz-: ~**bein** nt (inf) siehe ~**fuß**; **s**~**beinig** adj wooden-legged; (fig) (steif) stiff.

Stelze f -, -n (a) stilt; (inf: Bein) leg, pin (inf). **auf** ~**n gehen** to walk on stilts; (fig: Lyrik etc) to be stilted. (b) (Orn) wagtail. (c) (Aus: Schweins~) pig's trotter.

stelzen vi aux sein (inf) to stalk.

Stelzen-: ~**laufen** nt walking on stilts no art; ~**laufen lernen** to learn to walk on stilts; ~**läufer** m stilt-walker.

Stelz-: ~**fuß** m wooden leg, peg (inf), peg-leg; (Mensch) peg-leg; ~**vögel** pl (Orn) waders pl.

Stemmbogen m (Ski) stem turn.

Stemmeisen nt crowbar.

stemmen 1 vt (a) (stützen) to press; Ellenbogen to prop. **die Arme in die Seiten** or **Hüften gestemmt** with arms akimbo; **die Arme in die Hüften** ~ to put one's hands on one's hips; **er hatte die Arme in die Hüften gestemmt** he stood with arms akimbo.

(b) (hoch~) to lift (above one's head). **einen** ~ (inf) to have a few (inf).

(c) (meißeln) to chisel; (kräftiger) Loch to knock (in +acc in).

2 vr **sich gegen etw** ~ to brace oneself against sth; (fig) to set oneself against sth, to oppose sth.

3 vi (Ski) to stem.

Stemmschwung m (Ski) stem turn.

Stempel m -s, - (a) (Gummi~) (rubber-)stamp.

(b) (Abdruck) stamp; (Post~) postmark; (Vieh~) brand, mark; (auf Silber, Gold) hallmark. **jdm/einer Sache einen/seinen** ~ **aufdrücken** (fig) to make a/one's mark on sb/sth; **den** ~+gen or **von tragen** to bear the stamp of.

(c) (Tech) (Präge~) die; (stangenförmig, Loch~) punch.

(d) (Tech: von Druckpumpe etc) piston, plunger.

(e) (Min) prop.

(f) (Bot) pistil.

Stempel-: ~**farbe** f stamping ink; ~**geld** nt (inf) dole (money) (inf); ~**kissen** nt ink pad.

stempeln 1 vt to stamp; Brief to postmark; Briefmarke to frank; Gold, Silber to hallmark. **jdn zum Lügner** ~ (fig) to brand sb as a liar. 2 vi (inf) ~ **gehen** to be/go on the dole (inf). (b) (Stempeluhr betätigen) to clock on or in; (beim Hinausgehen) to clock off or out.

Stempel-: ~**schneider** m punch cutter; ~**ständer** m rubber-stamp holder; ~**uhr** f time-clock.

Stempelung f stamping; (von Brief) postmarking; (von Briefmarke) franking; (von Gold, Silber) hallmarking.

Stempelzeichen nt siehe **Stempel** (b).

Stengel m -s, - stem, stalk. **vom** ~ **fallen** (inf) (Schwächeanfall haben) to collapse; (überrascht sein) to be staggered (inf); **fall nicht vom** ~! (inf) prepare yourself for a shock!; **er fiel fast vom** ~ (inf) he almost fell over backwards (inf).

stengellos adj stemless.

Steno f -, no pl (inf) shorthand.

Steno-: ~**block** m shorthand pad; ~**gramm** nt text in shorthand; (Diktat) shorthand dictation; **ein** ~**gramm aufnehmen** to take shorthand; ~**grammblock** m shorthand pad; ~**graph(in** f) m (im Büro) shorthand secretary; (esp in Gericht, bei Konferenz etc) stenographer; ~**graphie** f shorthand, stenography (dated,

form); s~**graphieren*** 1 *vt* to take down in shorthand; 2 *vi* to do shorthand; **können Sie s~graphieren?** can you do shorthand?; s~**graphisch** *adj* shorthand *attr*; **etw s~graphisch notieren** to take sth down in shorthand; ~**kontorist** *m* shorthand typist; ~**sekretär** *m* (*inf*) shorthand secretary; ~**stift** *m* shorthand pencil; ~**typist(in** *f*) *m* shorthand typist.
Stentorstimme *f* (*geh*) stentorian voice.
Stenz *m* **-es, -e** dandy.
Step *m* **-s, -s** tap-dance. ~ **tanzen** to tap-dance.
Step|eisen *nt* tap (*on tap-dancing shoes*).
Stephan, Stephen *m* - Stephen, Steven.
Stepp|anorak *m* quilted anorak.
Steppdecke *f* quilt.
Steppe *f* **-, -n** steppe.
steppen[1] *vti* to (machine-)stitch; **wattierten Stoff** to quilt.
steppen[2] *vi* to tap-dance.
Steppen-: ~**brand** *m* steppe fire; ~**käse** *m* low-fat (hard) cheese; ~**wolf** *m* (*Zool*) prairie wolf, coyote.
Stepp-: ~**fuß** *m* foot; ~**jacke** *f* quilted jacket.
Steppke *m* **-(s), -s** (*N Ger inf*) nipper (*inf*), (little) laddie (*inf*).
Stepp-: ~**naht** *f* (*Sew*) backstitch seam; (*mit Maschine*) straight stitch seam; ~**stich** *m* (*Sew*) backstitch; (*mit Maschine*) straight stitch.
Step-: ~**tanz** *m* tap-dance; ~**tänzer** *m* tap-dancer.
Ster *nt* **-s, -s** *or* **-e** stere.
Sterbe-: ~**alter** *nt* age of death; ~**bett** *nt* death-bed; **auf dem** ~**bett liegen** to be on one's death-bed; ~**buch** *nt* register of deaths; ~**datum** *nt* date of death; ~**fall** *m* death; ~**geld** *nt* death benefit; ~**glocke** *f* funeral bell; **das Läuten der** ~**glocke** the death knell; ~**hemd** *nt* (burial) shroud; ~**hilfe** *f* **(a)** death benefit; **(b)** (*Euthanasie*) euthanasia; **jdm** ~**hilfe geben** *or* **gewähren** to administer euthanasia to sb (*form*); ~**kasse** *f* death benefit fund; ~**lager** *nt* (*geh*) death-bed; ~**monat** *m* month of death.
sterben *pret* **starb,** *ptp* **gestorben** *vti* **aus sein** to die. **jung/als Christ** ~ to die young/a Christian; **einen schnellen/leichten Tod/eines natürlichen Todes** ~ to die quickly/to have an easy death/to die a natural death; **an einer Krankheit/Verletzung** ~ to die of an illness/from an injury; **daran wirst du nicht** ~! (*hum*) it won't kill you!; **vor Angst/Durst/Hunger** ~ to die of fright/thirst/starvation (*auch fig*); **er stirbt vor Angst** (*fig*) he's frightened to death, he's scared stiff (*inf*); **vor Langeweile/Neugierde** ~ to die of boredom/curiosity; **tausend Tode** ~ to die a thousand deaths; **so leicht stirbt man nicht!** (*hum*) you'll/he'll *etc* survive!; **gestorben sein** to be dead *or* deceased (*Jur, form*); **gestorben!** (*Film sl*) print it!, I'll buy it!; **er ist für mich gestorben** (*fig inf*) he might as well be dead *or* he doesn't exist as far as I'm concerned; **"und wenn sie nicht gestorben sind, so leben sie noch heute"** "and they lived happily ever after".
Sterben *nt* **-s,** *no pl* death. **Angst vor dem** ~ fear of death *or* dying; **wenn es ans** ~ **geht** when it comes to dying; **im** ~ **liegen** to be dying; **zum** ~ **langweilig** (*inf*) deadly boring *or* dull, deadly (*inf*); **zum** ~ **gelangweilt** (*inf*) bored to death *or* tears (*inf*), bored stiff (*inf*).
Sterbens-: ~**angst** *f* (*inf*) mortal fear; **s~elend** *adj* (*inf*) wretched, ghastly; **ich fühle mich s~elend** I feel wretched *or* ghastly, I feel like death (*inf*); **s~krank** *adj* mortally ill; **s~langweilig** *adj* (*inf*) deadly boring *or* dull, deadly (*inf*); **s~matt** *adj* utterly exhausted; ~**wort,** ~**wörtchen** *nt* (*inf*) **er hat kein** ~**wort gesagt** *or* **verraten** he didn't say a (single) word; **ich werde kein** ~**wort davon sagen** I won't breathe a word.
Sterbe-: ~**ort** *m* place of death; ~**sakramente** *pl* last rites *pl or* **sacraments** *pl*; ~**stunde** *f* last hour, dying hour; ~**urkunde** *f* death certificate; ~**ziffer** *f* mortality *or* death rate; ~**zimmer** *nt* death chamber (*liter, form*); **Goethes** ~**zimmer** the room where Goethe died.
sterblich 1 *adj* mortal. **jds** ~**e Hülle** *or* (**Über**)**reste** sb's mortal remains *pl*. 2 *adv* (*inf*) terribly (*inf*), dreadfully (*inf*).
Sterbliche(r) *mf decl as adj* mortal.
Sterblichkeit *f* mortality; (*Zahl*) mortality (rate), death-rate.
Stereo ['fteːreo, 'st-] *nt* **in** ~ in stereo.
stereo ['fteːreo, 'st-] *adj pred* (*in*) stereo.
Stereo- ['fteːreo, 'st-] *in cpds* stereo; (**s~skopisch**) stereoscopic; ~**anlage** *f* stereo unit *or* system, stereo (*inf*); ~**aufnahme** *f* stereo recording; ~**bild** *nt* (*von* ~**skop vermittelt*) stereoscopic picture; (*dreidimensional*) 3-D picture; ~**box** *f* speaker; ~**film** *m* 3-D film; ~**gerät** *nt* stereo unit; ~**kamera** *f* stereoscopic camera; ~**metrie** *f* stereometry, solid geometry; **s~phon** 1 *adj* stereophonic; 2 *adv* stereophonically; ~**phonie** *f* stereophony; **s~phonisch** *adj* stereophonic; ~**skop** *nt* -s, -e stereoscope; ~**skopie** *f* stereoscopy; **s~skopisch** *adj* stereoscopic; (*dreidimensional*) 3-D, three-dimensional; **s~typ** 1 *adj* (*fig*) stereotyped, stock *attr*; **Lächeln** (*gezwungen*) stiff; (*unpersönlich*) impersonal; 2 *adv* in stereotyped fashion; stiffly; impersonally; ~**typdruck** *m* stereotype; ~**typeur** [-ty'pøːɐ] *m* stereotyper; ~**typie** *f* (*Psych*) stereotypy; (*Typ auch*) stereotype printing; (*Werkstatt*) stereotype printing shop.
steril [ſteˈriːl, st-] *adj* (*lit, fig*) sterile.
Sterilisation [ſteriliza'tsioːn, st-] *f* sterilization.
sterilisieren* [ſteriliˈziːrən, st-] *vt* to sterilize.
Sterilisierung [ſt-, st-] *f* sterilization.
Sterilität [ſteriliˈtɛːt, st-] *f* (*lit, fig*) sterility.
Sterling ['fterlɪŋ, st-] *m* **-s, -e** sterling. **30 Pfund** ~ 30 pounds sterling.
Stern[1] *m* **-(e)s, -e** **(a)** star. **dieser** ~ (*poet: die Erde*) this earth *or* orb (*poet*); **mit** ~**en übersät** star-spangled *attr*; **Himmel auch** starry *attr*; **unter fremden** ~**en sterben** (*poet*) to die in foreign climes (*liter*); **in den** ~**en lesen** (*Astrol*) to read the stars; **in den** ~**en** (**geschrieben**) **stehen** (*fig*) to be (written) in

the stars; **das steht (noch) in den** ~**en** (*fig*) it's in the lap of the gods; **nach den** ~**en greifen** (*fig*) to reach for the stars; **er wollte die** ~**e vom Himmel holen** he wanted the moon; **für sie holt er die** ~**e vom Himmel** he would do anything for her, he would go to the ends of the earth and back again for her; ~**e sehen** (*inf*) to see stars; **der** ~ **der Weisen** (*Bibl*) the Star of Bethlehem; **sein** ~ **geht auf** *or* **ist im Aufgehen/sinkt** *or* **ist im Sinken** his star is in the ascendant/on the decline; **mein guter** ~ my lucky star; **unter einem guten** *or* **glücklichen** *or* **günstigen** ~ **geboren sein** to be born under a lucky star; **unter einem guten** *or* **glücklichen** *or* **günstigen/ungünstigen** ~ **stehen** to be blessed with good fortune/to be ill-starred *or* ill-fated; **mit ihr ging am Theaterhimmel ein neuer** ~ **auf** with her coming a new star was born in the theatrical world.
(b) (*Abzeichen*) (*von Uniform*) star. **ein Hotel/Cognac mit 3** ~**en** a 3-star hotel/brandy.
(c) (~**kreuzung**) multiple junction.
(d) (*sternförmige Blesse*) star-shaped blaze, star.
Stern[2] *m* **-s, -e** (*Naut*) stern.
Stern-: **s~bedeckt** *adj* starry, star-spangled; ~**bild** *nt* (*Astron*) constellation; (*Astrol*) sign (of the zodiac).
Sternchen *nt* *dim of* **Stern**[1] **(a)** little star. **(b)** (*Typ*) asterisk, star. **(c)** (*Film*) starlet.
Stern-: ~**deuter** *m* astrologer, star-gazer (*hum*); ~**deuterei** *f*, *no pl*, ~**deutung** *f* astrology, star-gazing (*hum*).
Sternen-: ~**banner** *nt* Star-Spangled Banner, Stars and Stripes *sing*; **s~bedeckt** *adj* starry, star-covered; ~**gewölbe** *nt* (*poet*) starry vault (*poet*); ~**glanz** *m* (*poet*) starshine (*liter*); **der Himmel erstrahlte im** ~**glanz** the heavens shone with the light of the stars (*liter*); ~**himmel** *m* starry sky; **Veränderungen am** ~**himmel** changes in the star formation; **s~klar** *adj* starry *attr*, starlit; **s~los** *adj* starless; ~**schein** *m* (*poet*) *siehe* ~**glanz**; ~**zelt** *nt* (*poet*) starry firmament (*liter*).
Stern-: ~**fahrt** *f* (*Mot, Pol*) rally (*where participants commence at different points*); **eine** ~**fahrt nach Ulan Bator** a rally converging on Ulan Bator; **s~förmig** *adj* star-shaped, stellate (*spec*); ~**forscher** *m* astronomer; ~**gewölbe** *nt* (*Archit*) stellar vault; ~**gucker** *m* **-s, -** (*hum*) star-gazer (*hum*); ~**hagelblau,** **s~hagelvoll** *adj* (*inf*) rolling *or* roaring drunk (*inf*), blotto (*sl*) *pred*; ~**haufen** *m* (*Astron*) star cluster; **s~hell** *adj* starlit, starry *attr*; ~**jahr** *nt* sidereal year; ~**karte** *f* (*Astron*) celestial chart, star *or* stellar map *or* chart; **s~klar** *adj* starry *attr*, starlit; ~**konstellation** *f* (*stellar*) constellation; ~**kreuzung** *f* multiple junction; ~**kunde** *f* astronomy; ~**marsch** *m* (*Pol*) protest march with marchers converging on assembly point from different directions; ~**motor** *m* radial engine; ~**schnuppe** *f* shooting star; ~**stunde** *f* great moment; **das war meine** ~**stunde** that was a great moment in my life; ~**system** *nt* galaxy; ~**tag** *m* (*Astron*) sidereal day; ~**warte** *f* observatory; ~**zeichen** *nt* (*Astrol*) sign of the zodiac; **im** ~**zeichen der Jungfrau** under the sign of Virgo; ~**zeit** *f* (*Astron*) sidereal time.
Stert [ſteːrt] *m* **-(e)s, -e** (*N Ger*), **Sterz** *m* **-es, -e** **(a)** (*Schwanzende*) tail; (*Cook*) parson's nose (*inf*). **(b)** (*Pflug*~) handle.
stet *adj attr* constant; **Fleiß** *auch* steady; **Arbeit, Wind** *auch* steady, continuous. ~**er Tropfen höhlt den Stein** (*Prov*) constant dripping wears away the stone.
Stethoskop [ſteto'skoːp, st-] *nt* **-s, -e** stethoscope.
stetig *adj* steady; (*Math*) *Funktion* continuous. ~ **steigende Bedeutung** ever-increasing *or* steadily increasing importance; ~**es Meckern** constant moaning.
Stetigkeit *f* *siehe adj* constancy, steadiness; continuity.
stets *adv* always. ~ **zu Ihren Diensten** (*form*) always *or* ever (*form*) at your service; ~ **der Ihre** (*old form*) yours ever.
Steuer[1] *nt* **-s, -** (*Naut*) helm, tiller; (*Aut*) (steering-)wheel; (*Aviat*) control column, controls *pl*. **am** ~ **stehen** (*Naut*) *or* **sein** (*Naut, fig*) to be at the helm; **am** ~ **sitzen** *or* **sein, hinter dem** ~ **sitzen** (*inf*) (*Aut*) to be at *or* behind the wheel, to drive; (*Aviat*) to be at the controls; **jdn ans** ~ **lassen** to let sb drive, to let sb take the wheel; **das** ~ **übernehmen** (*lit, fig*) to take over; (*lit auch*) to take (over) the helm/wheel/controls; (*fig auch*) to take the helm; **das** ~ **fest in der Hand haben** (*fig*) to be firmly in control, to have things firmly under control; **das** ~ **herumwerfen** *or* **-reißen** (*fig*) to turn the tide of events.
Steuer[2] *f* **-, -n (a)** (*Abgabe*) tax; (*Gemeinde*~) rates *pl* (*Brit*), local tax (*US*). ~**n** tax; (*Arten von* ~) taxes; ~**n zahlen** to pay tax; **ich bezahle 35%** ~**n** I pay 35% tax; **in Schweden zahlt man hohe** ~**n** in Sweden tax is very high *or* people are highly taxed; **die** ~**n herabsetzen** to reduce taxation, to cut tax *or* taxes; **das Auto kostet mich viel** ~(**n**) my car costs me a lot in tax; **der** ~ **unterliegen** (*form*) to be liable *or* subject to tax, to be taxable.
(b) (*inf:* ~**behörde**) **die** ~ the tax people (*inf*) *or* authorities *pl*, the Inland Revenue (*Brit*), the Internal Revenue (*US*).
Steuer-: ~**aufkommen** *nt* tax revenue, tax yield; **s~bar** *adj* taxable, liable *or* subject to tax; ~**beamte(r)** *m* tax officer *or* official; **s~begünstigt** *adj Investitionen, Hypothek* tax-deductible; *Waren* taxed at a lower rate; **s~begünstigtes Sparen** form of saving entitling the saver to tax relief; **Investitionen sind s~begünstigt** you get tax relief on investments; ~**begünstigung** *f* tax concession (*gen on*); ~**behörde** *f* tax authorities *pl*, inland (*Brit*) *or* internal (*US*) revenue authorities *pl*; ~**berater** *m* tax consultant; ~**bescheid** *m* tax assessment; ~**betrug** *m* tax evasion *or* dodging; ~**bevollmächtigte(r)** *mf* tax expert *or* consultant; ~**bord** *nt* **-s,** *no pl* (*Naut*) starboard; **s~bord(s)** *adv* (*Naut*) to starboard; ~**einnahmen** *pl* revenue from taxation; ~**einnehmer** *m* (*Hist*) tax-collector; ~**erhöhung** *f* tax increase; ~**erklärung** *f* tax return *or* declaration; ~**erlaß** *m* tax exemption; ~**erstattung** *f* tax rebate; ~**fahndung** *f* investigation of (suspected) tax evasion; (*Behörde*) commission for investigation of suspected tax

evasion; ~**flucht** f tax evasion (by leaving the country); **s~frei** adj tax-free, exempt from tax; ~**freiheit** f tax exemption, exemption from tax; ~**freiheit genießen** to be exempt from tax; ~**gelder** pl tax money, taxes pl; **warum soll das aus ~geldern finanziert werden?** why should it be paid for with tax-payers' money?, why should the tax-payer have to pay for it?; **Veruntreuung von ~geldern** tax embezzlement; ~**gerät** nt tuner-amplifier; ~**hinterziehung** f tax evasion; ~**hoheit** f right to levy tax(es); ~**inspektor** m tax inspector; ~**jahr** nt tax year; ~**karte** f notice of pay received and tax deducted; ~**klasse** f tax bracket or group; ~**knüppel** m control column; (Aviat auch) joystick.

steuerlich adj tax attr. ~**e Belastung** tax burden; **aus ~en Überlegungen** for tax reasons; **es ist ~ günstiger ...** for tax purposes it is better ...; **das wirkt sich ~ ganz günstig aus** tax-wise or from the tax point of view it works out very well.

steuerlos adj rudderless, out of control; (fig) leaderless.

Steuermann m, pl -**männer** or -**leute** helmsman; (als Rang) (first) mate; (Rowing) cox(swain). **Zweier mit/ohne ~** coxed/coxless pairs.

Steuermannspatent nt (Naut) mate's ticket (inf) or certificate.

Steuer-: ~**marke** f revenue or tax stamp; (für Hunde) dog licence disc, dog tag (US); ~**moral** f tax-payer honesty.

steuern 1 vt (a) Schiff to steer, to navigate; (lotsen auch) to pilot; Flugzeug to pilot, to fly; Auto to steer; (fig) Wirtschaft, Politik to run, to control, to manage. **staatlich gesteuert** state-controlled, under state control; **einen Kurs ~** (lit, fig) to steer a course; (fig auch) to take or follow a line; **eine Diskussion/die Wirtschaft in eine bestimmte Richtung ~** to steer a discussion/the economy in a certain direction.

(**b**) (regulieren) to control.

2 vi (**a**) aux sein to head; (Aut auch) to drive; (Naut auch) to make, to steer. **wohin steuert die Wirtschaft?** where is the economy heading or headed (for)?

(**b**) (am Steuer sein) (Naut) to be at the helm; (Aut) to be at the wheel; (Aviat) to be at the controls.

(**c**) (geh: Einhalt gebieten) **einer Sache** (dat) ~ to put a stop to sth; **einem Übel/Mangel ~** to remedy an evil/a shortage.

Steuer-: ~**oase** f, ~**paradies** nt tax haven; ~**pflicht** f liability to tax; (von Person auch) liability to pay tax; **der ~pflicht unterliegen** to be liable to tax, to be taxable; **s~pflichtig** adj Einkommen taxable, liable to tax; Person auch liable to (pay) tax; ~**pflichtige(r)** mf tax-payer; ~**politik** f tax or taxation policy; **s~politisch** adj relating to tax policy; **s~politische Maßnahmen der Regierung** government tax measures; **aus s~politischen Gründen** for tax or taxation reasons; **es wäre s~politisch unklug ...** it would be unwise tax policy ...; **das wäre s~politisch günstig** it would be good from the tax or taxation point of view; ~**progression** f progressive taxation; ~**prüfer** m tax inspector; ~**prüfung** f tax inspector's investigation; ~**rad** nt (Aviat) control wheel; (Aut) (steering-)wheel; ~**recht** nt tax law; **s~rechtlich** adj relating to tax(ation) law; **s~rechtliche Änderungen** changes in the tax(ation) laws; **ein s~rechtlicher Fachmann** a tax expert; **das ist s~rechtlich unmöglich** the tax laws make that impossible; ~**reform** f tax reform; ~**ruder** nt rudder; ~**sache** f tax matter; **Helfer in ~sachen** tax consultant; ~**satz** m rate of taxation; ~**schraube** f die ~**schraube anziehen** to put the screws on or to squeeze the taxpayer; ~**schuld** f tax(es pl) owing no indef art, tax liability; ~**senkung** f tax cut.

Steuerung f (**a**) no pl (das Steuern) (von Schiff) steering, navigation; (von Flugzeug) piloting, flying; (fig) (von Politik, Wirtschaft) running, control, management; (Regulierung) control, regulation; (Bekämpfung) control.

(**b**) (Steuervorrichtung) (Aviat) controls pl; (Tech) steering apparatus or mechanism. **automatische ~** (Aviat) automatic pilot, autopilot; (Tech) automatic steering (device).

Steuer-: ~**veranlagung** f tax assessment; ~**vergehen** nt tax evasion or dodging no pl; ~**vorteil** m tax advantage or benefit; ~**zahler** m taxpayer; ~**zeichen** nt (form) siehe Banderole.

Steven ['ʃteːvn] m -s, - (Naut) (Vorder~) prow; (Achter~) stern.

Steward ['stjuːɐt, ʃt-] m -s, -s (Naut, Aviat) steward.

Stewardeß, Stewardess ['stjuːɐdɛs, stjuːˈɐˈdɛs, ʃt-] f -, -ssen stewardess.

StGB [esteːgeːˈbeː] nt -s abbr of Strafgesetzbuch.

stibitzen* vt (dated hum) to swipe (inf), to pinch (inf).

stich imper sing of stechen.

Stich m -(e)s, -e (**a**) (das Stechen) (Insekten~) sting; (Mücken~) bite; (Nadel~) prick; (Messer~) stab.

(**b**) (~wunde) (von Messer etc) stab wound; (von Insekten) sting; (von Mücken) bite; (Einstichloch) prick.

(**c**) (stechender Schmerz) piercing or shooting or stabbing pain; (Seiten~) stitch; (fig) pang. ~**e haben** to have a stitch; **es gab mir einen ~ (ins Herz)** I was cut to the quick.

(**d**) (Sew) stitch.

(**e**) (Kupfer~, Stahl~) engraving.

(**f**) (Schattierung) tinge, shade (in +acc of); (Tendenz) hint, suggestion (in +acc of). **ein ~ ins Rote** a tinge of red, a reddish tinge; **ein ~ ins Gewöhnliche/Vulgäre** a hint or suggestion of commonness/vulgarity.

(**g**) (Cards) trick. **einen ~ machen** or **bekommen** to get a trick.

(**h**) **jdn im ~ lassen** to let sb down; (verlassen) to abandon or desert sb, to leave sb in the lurch; **etw im ~ lassen** to abandon sth.

(**i**) ~ **halten** to hold water, to be valid or sound; **das hat einer Prüfung nicht ~ gehalten** it did not hold water on examination.

(**j**) **einen ~ haben** (Eßwaren) to be off or bad, to have gone off or bad; (Butter auch) to be or have gone rancid; (Milch) to be or have gone sour or off; (sl: Mensch: verrückt sein) to be

nuts (inf), to be round the bend (inf).

Stich-: ~**bahn** f (Rail) branch terminal line; ~**blatt** nt (**a**) (von Degen) guard; (**b**) (Cards) trump (card).

Stichel m -s, - (Art) gouge.

Stichelei f (**a**) (Näherei) sewing. (**b**) (pej inf: boshafte Bemerkung) snide (inf) or sneering remark, gibe, dig. **deine ständigen ~en kannst du dir sparen** stop getting at me or making digs at me.

sticheln vi (**a**) to sew; (sticken) to embroider. (**b**) (pej inf: boshafte Bemerkungen machen) to make snide (inf) or sneering remarks. **gegen jdn ~** to make digs at sb.

Stich-: ~**entscheid** m (Pol) result of a/the run-off (US), final ballot; (Sport) result of a/the play-off; **s~fest** adj siehe hiebfest; ~**flamme** f tongue of flame; **s~halten** vi sep irreg (Aus) siehe Stich (i); **s~haltig, s~hältig** (Aus) adj sound, valid; Beweis conclusive; **sein Alibi ist nicht s~haltig** his alibi doesn't hold water; ~**haltigkeit** f, no pl soundness, validity.

stichig adj (rare) Milch off pred, sour.

Stich-: ~**kampf** m (Sport) play-off; ~**kanal** m branch canal.

Stichling m (Zool) stickleback.

Stichprobe f spot check; (Sociol) (random) sample survey. ~**n machen** to carry out or make spot checks; (Sociol) to carry out a (random) sample survey; **bei der ~ wurde festgestellt, daß ...** the spot check/sampling revealed that ...

Stichproben-: ~**erhebung** f (Sociol) (random) sample survey; **s~weise** adv on a random basis; **es werden nur s~weise Kontrollen gemacht** only spot checks are made.

Stich-: ~**säge** f fret-saw; ~**tag** m qualifying date; ~**waffe** f stabbing weapon; ~**wahl** f (Pol) final ballot, run-off (US).

Stichwort nt (**a**) pl -**wörter** (in Nachschlagewerken) headword. (**b**) pl -**worte** (Theat, fig) cue. (**c**) pl -**worte** usu pl notes pl; (bei Nacherzählung etc) key words pl.

Stichwort-: **s~artig** adj abbreviated, shorthand; **eine s~artige Gliederung** an outline; **etw s~artig zusammenfassen/ wiedergeben** to summarize the main points of sth/to recount sth in a shorthand or an abbreviated fashion; **jdn s~artig über etw** (acc) **informieren** to give sb a brief outline of sth; **s~artig den Verlauf des Geschehens festhalten** to note the main points of what happened; ~**katalog** m classified catalogue; ~**verzeichnis** nt index.

Stichwunde f stab wound.

Stick|arbeit f embroidery. **sie saß gerade an einer ~** she was sitting embroidering.

sticken vti to embroider.

Stickerei f (**a**) no pl (das Sticken) embroidery, embroidering. (**b**) (Gegenstand) embroidery.

Stickerin f embroideress, embroiderer.

Stick-: ~**garn** nt embroidery thread or silk; ~**husten** m whooping cough.

stickig adj Luft, Zimmer stuffy, close; Klima sticky, humid; (fig) Atmosphäre stifling, oppressive.

Stick-: ~**luft** f close or stuffy air; ~**maschine** f embroidery machine; ~**muster** nt embroidery pattern; ~**nadel** f embroidery needle; ~**rahmen** m embroidery frame; ~**seide** f embroidery silk.

Stickstoff m nitrogen.

Stickstoff-: ~**dünger** m nitrogen fertilizer; **s~haltig** adj containing nitrogen, nitrogenous (spec).

stieben pret **stob** or **stiebte**, ptp **gestoben** or **gestiebt** vi (geh) (**a**) aux haben or sein (sprühen) (Funken, Staub etc) to fly; (Schnee) to spray, to fly; (Wasser) to spray. (**b**) aux sein (jagen, rennen) to flee; siehe auseinanderstieben.

Stiefbruder m stepbrother.

Stiefel m -s, - (**a**) boot.

(**b**) (inf) **seinen** (alten) ~ **arbeiten** or **weitermachen** to carry on as usual or in the same old way; **einen ~ zusammenreden** to talk a lot of nonsense or a load of rubbish (inf).

(**c**) (Trinkgefäß) large, boot-shaped beer glass holding 2 litres. **einen (ordentlichen) ~ vertragen** (inf) to be able to take one's drink or hold one's liquor.

Stiefel-: ~**absatz** m (boot-)heel; ~**anzieher** m -s, - boot-hook.

Stiefelette f (Frauen~) bootee; (Männer~) half-boot.

Stiefelknecht m boot-jack.

stiefeln vi aux sein (inf) to hoof it (inf). **der stiefelt immer im alten Trott weiter** he keeps plodding along in the same old way; siehe gestiefelt.

Stiefel-: ~**putzer** m -s, - boots sing; ~**schaft** m -(e)s, ~e bootleg, leg of a/the boot.

Stief|eltern pl step-parents pl.

Stiefelwichse f (dated) boot-polish, boot-blacking.

Stief-: ~**geschwister** pl stepbrother(s) and sister(s); ~**kind** nt stepchild; (fig) poor cousin; **sie fühlt sich immer als ~kind des Glücks** she always feels that fortune never smiles upon her; ~**mutter** f stepmother; ~**mütterchen** nt (Bot) pansy; **s~mütterlich** adj (fig) jdn/etw **s~mütterlich behandeln** to pay little attention to sb/sth, to put sb/sth in second place; **die Natur hat ihn s~mütterlich behandelt** Nature has not been kind to him; ~**schwester** f stepsister; ~**sohn** m stepson; ~**tochter** f stepdaughter; ~**vater** m stepfather.

stieg pret of steigen.

Stieg m -(e)s, -e siehe Steig.

Stiege f -, -n (**a**) (schmale Treppe) (narrow) flight of stairs or staircase. (**b**) (old: 20 Stück) score. **eine ~ Eier** a score of eggs. (**c**) (Lattenkiste) crate.

Stiegenhaus nt (S Ger, Aus) staircase.

Stieglitz m -es, -e goldfinch.

stiehl imper sing of stehlen.

Stiel m -(e)s, -e (**a**) (Griff) handle; (Besen~ auch) broomstick; (Pfeifen~, Glas~) stem. (**b**) (Stengel) stalk; (Blüten~) stalk, stem, peduncle (spec); (Blatt~) leafstalk, petiole (spec).

Stiel|augen pl (fig inf) ~ **machen** or **kriegen** to gape, to gawp, to goggle (inf); **er machte** ~ **his eyes** (nearly) popped out of his head; **etw mit** ~ **ansehen** to gape or gawp or goggle at sth.

Stiel-: ~**glas** nt stemmed glass; ~**kamm** m tail comb; s~**los** adj *Gerät* handleless, without a handle; *Blatt* stalkless; *Glas* stemless; ~**pfanne** f frying pan with a (long) handle.

stiemen vi impers (dial) to snow heavily, to blow a blizzard.

stier adj (a) (stumpfsinnig) *Blick* vacant, blank. (b) (*Aus, Sw* inf) *Geschäft* slack, slow; *Mensch* broke (inf).

Stier m -(e)s, -e (a) bull; (junger ~) bullock. **wütend wie ein** ~ (**sein**) (to be) beside oneself with rage or fury; **wütend wie ein** ~ **werden** to fly into a rage; **wie ein** ~ **brüllen** to bawl one's head off (inf), to bellow like a bull; **den** ~ **bei den Hörnern packen** or **fassen** (prov) to take the bull by the horns (prov). (**b**) (*Astrol*) Taurus no art. **ich bin (ein)** ~ I'm (a) Taurus.

stieren vi (auf +acc at) to stare; (neugierig auch) to gape. (lüstern) **auf jdn** ~ to ogle (inf) or eye sb; **sein Blick stierte ins Leere** he stared vacantly into space.

Stier-: ~**kampf** m bull-fight; ~**kampfarena** f bull-ring; ~**kämpfer** m bull-fighter; ~**nacken** m neck like a bull, thick neck; s~**nackig** adj bull-necked; ~**opfer** nt sacrifice of a bull.

Stiesel m -s, - (inf) boor, lout (inf).

sties(e)lig adj (inf) boorish, loutish (inf).

Sties(e)ligkeit f (inf) boorishness, loutishness (inf).

stieß pret of **stoßen**.

Stift[1] m -(e)s, -e (a) (*Metall*~) pin; (*Holz*~ auch) peg; (*Nagel*) tack. (**b**) (*Blei*~) pencil; (*Bunt*~ auch) crayon; (*Filz*~) felt-tip, felt-tipped pen; (*Kugelschreiber*) ball-point (pen), biro ® (Brit). (**c**) (inf: *Lehrling*) apprentice (boy).

Stift[2] nt -(e)s, -e (*Dom*~) cathedral chapter; (*Theologie*~) seminary; (old: *Heim, Anstalt*) home; (in *Namen*) foundation; (old: *Bistum*) diocese.

stiften vt (a) (gründen) *Kirche, Universität* to found, to establish; (spenden, spendieren) to donate; *Geld, Summe* to put up, to donate; *Universität, Stipendium* etc to endow. (**b**) *Verwirrung* to cause; *Unfrieden, Unheil auch, Frieden* to bring about, to stir up; *Ehe* to arrange. **Gutes/Schaden** ~ to do good/damage.

stiftengehen vi sep irreg aux sein (inf) to hop it (inf).

Stifte(n)kopf m (dated inf) crew-cut; (*Mensch*) person with a crew-cut.

Stifter(in f) m -s, - (*Gründer*) founder; (*Spender*) donator.

Stifterreligion f religion founded by a particular person eg *Buddha, Jesus*.

Stifts-: ~**dame** f, ~**fräulein** nt (*Eccl*) canoness; ~**herr** m (*Eccl*) canon; ~**hütte** f (*Bibl*) Tabernacle; ~**kirche** f collegiate church; ~**schule** f cathedral school.

Stiftung f (a) (*Gründung*) foundation, establishment; (*Schenkung*) donation; (von *Universität, Stipendium* etc) endowment. (**b**) (*Organisation*) foundation.

Stiftungs-: ~**fest** nt Founder's Day celebration; ~**urkunde** f foundation charter.

Stiftzahn m post crown.

Stigma['ʃtɪgma, st-] nt -s, -ta (*Biol, Rel, fig*) stigma.

Stigmatisiere(r) [ʃt-, st-] mf decl as adj (*Biol, Rel*) stigmatic; (fig) stigmatized person.

Stil [ʃtiːl, stiːl] m -(e)s, -e style; (*Eigenart*) way, manner. **im großen** ~, **großen** ~**s** in a big way; **schlechter** ~ bad style; **das ist schlechter** ~ (fig) that is bad form; ~ **haben** (fig) to have style; **er fährt einen rücksichtslosen** ~ he drives recklessly or in a reckless manner; **er schwimmt/schreibt einen sehr schwerfälligen** ~ his swimming style is very awkward/his writing style is very clumsy; **nach der Zeitrechnung alten/neuen** ~**s** according to the old/new calendar.

Stil-: ~**analyse** f (*Art, Liter*) stylistic analysis; s~**bildend** adj (für jdn) s~**bildend sein/s~bildend wirken** to improve sb's style; ~**blüte** f (hum) stylistic howler; ~**bruch** m stylistic incongruity or inconsistency; (in *Roman* etc) abrupt change in style; **das ist ein glatter** ~**bruch** (inf) that is really incongruous; ~**ebene** f (*Liter, Ling*) style level; s~**echt** adj period attr; s~**echt eingerichtet** with period furniture; ~**element** nt stylistic element; ~**empfinden** nt siehe ~**gefühl**.

Stilett [ʃti'lɛt, st-] nt -s, -e stiletto.

Stil-: ~**fehler** m stylistic lapse; ~**gefühl** nt feeling for or sense of style; s~**gerecht** adj appropriate to or in keeping with a/the style; s~**getreu** adj in or true to the original style.

stilisieren* [ʃtili'ziːrən, st-] vt to stylize.

Stilisierung [ʃt-, st-] f stylization.

Stilist [ʃti'lɪst, st-] m stylist.

Stilistik [ʃti'lɪstɪk, st-] f (*Liter*) stylistics sing; (*Handbuch*) guide to good style.

stilistisch [ʃti'lɪstɪʃ, st-] adj stylistic. **ich muß meine Vorlesung** ~ **überarbeiten** I must go over my lecture to polish up the style.

Stilkunde f siehe **Stilistik**.

still adj (a) (ruhig) quiet, silent; (lautlos) *Seufzer* quiet; *Gebet* silent; (schweigend) *Vorwurf, Beobachter* silent. ~ **werden** to go quiet, to fall silent; **im Saal wurde es** ~, **der Saal wurde** ~ the room fell silent; **um ihn/darum ist es** ~ **geworden** you don't hear anything about him/it any more; **es blieb** ~ there was no sound, silence reigned; **S~e Nacht** Silent Night; ~ **weinen/leiden** to cry quietly/to suffer in silence; ~ **vor sich hin arbeiten** to work away quietly; **in** ~**em Gedenken** in silent tribute; **in** ~**em Schmerz/in** ~**er Trauer** in silent suffering/grief; **im** ~**en** without saying anything, quietly; **in** ~**em dachte mir im** ~**en** I thought to myself; **sich** (dat) ~ **gegenübersitzen** to sit opposite one another in silence or without speaking; **die S~en im Lande** the quiet ones; **sei doch** ~**!** be or keep quiet; ~**e Messe** silent mass.

(**b**) (unbewegt) *Luft* still; *See auch* calm. **der S~e Ozean** the Pacific (Ocean); ~ **sitzen** to sit or keep still; **den Kopf/die**

Hände/Füße ~ **halten** to keep one's head/hands/feet still; **ein Glas/Tablett** ~ **halten** to hold a glass/tray steady; **vor uns lag** ~ **die Ägäis** before us lay the calm waters of the Aegean; ~**e Wasser sind tief** (Prov) still waters run deep (Prov); **er ist ein** ~**es Wasser** he's a deep one or a dark horse.

(**c**) (einsam, abgeschieden) *Dorf, Tal, Straße* quiet. **ein** ~**es Eckchen** a quiet corner; **ein** ~**es Plätzchen** a quiet spot.

(**d**) (heimlich) secret. **im** ~**en** in secret; **er ist dem** ~**en Suff ergeben** he drinks on the quiet, he's a secret drinker.

(**e**) (*Comm*) *Gesellschafter, Teilhaber* sleeping (Brit), silent (US); *Reserven, Rücklagen* secret, hidden. ~**e Beteiligung** sleeping partnership (Brit), non-active interest.

Stille f -, no pl (a) (*Ruhe*) quiet(ness), peace(fulness); (*Schweigen*) silence. **in der** ~ **der Nacht** in the still of the night; **in aller** ~ quietly, calmly; **die Beerdigung fand in aller** ~ **statt** it was a quiet funeral; **jdn in aller** ~ **begraben** to give sb a quiet burial.

(**b**) (*Unbewegtheit*) calm(ness); (der *Luft*) stillness.

(**c**) (*Einsamkeit, Abgeschiedenheit*) quiet, seclusion.

(**d**) (*Heimlichkeit*) secrecy. **in aller** ~ in secret, secretly.

stille adj (old) siehe **still**.

Stilleben ['ʃtɪleːbn] nt getrennt: **Still-leben** still life.

stillegen vt sep getrennt **still-legen** to close or shut down; *Schiff* to lay up. **stillgelegtes Bergwerk** disused mine.

Stillegung f getrennt **Still-legung** siehe vt closure, shut-down; laying-up.

Stillehre f stylistics sing.

stillen 1 vt a (zum *Stillstand bringen*) *Tränen* to stop; *Schmerzen* to ease, to relieve, to allay; *Blutung auch* to staunch, to check. (**b**) (befriedigen) *Neugier, Begierde, Verlangen, Hunger* to satisfy, to still (liter); *Durst auch* to quench. (**c**) *Säugling* to breast-feed, to nurse. 2 vi to breast-feed.

Stillgeld nt nursing mothers' allowance.

stillgestanden interj (*Mil*) halt.

Stillhalte|abkommen nt (*Fin, fig*) moratorium.

stillhalten vi sep irreg to keep or hold still; (fig) to keep quiet.

stilliegen vi sep irreg aux sein or haben getrennt **still-liegen** (a) (außer *Betrieb* sein) to be closed or shut down. (**b**) (lahmliegen) to be at or have been brought to a standstill, to have come to a halt.

stillos adj lacking in style; (fehl am *Platze*) incongruous. **eine völlig** ~ **Zusammenstellung von Möbelstücken** a collection of furniture completely lacking (in) any sense of style; **völlig** ~ **servierte sie Hummersuppe in Teetassen** showing absolutely no sense of style she served up lobster soup in tea cups.

Stillosigkeit f siehe adj lack of style no pl; incongruity. **solche** ~**en ist man von ihr gewohnt** we're used to her having no sense of style or to such displays of tastelessness from her.

stillschweigen vi sep irreg to remain silent. **zu etw** ~ to stand silently by or remain silent in the face of sth; **schweig still!** be silent or quiet.

Stillschweigen nt silence. **auf sein** ~ **kann man sich verlassen** one can rely on his keeping silent; **jdm** ~ **auferlegen** to swear sb to silence; **über etw** (acc) ~ **bewahren** to observe or maintain silence about sth; **etw mit** ~ **übergehen** to pass over sth in silence.

stillschweigend adj silent; *Einverständnis* tacit. **über etw** (acc) ~ **hinweggehen** to pass over sth in silence.

stillsitzen vi sep irreg aux sein or haben to sit still.

Stillstand m standstill; (von *Betrieb, Produktion, Verhandlungen* etc auch) stoppage; (vorübergehend) interruption; (in *Entwicklung*) halt. **bei** ~ **der Maschine** ... when the machine is stopped ...; **ein** ~ **des Herzens** a cardiac arrest; **seit dem** ~ **der Ölproduktion** since oil production came to a stop or stopped; **Hauptsache ist, daß kein** ~ **in der Produktion eintritt** the main thing is that production is not interrupted; **zum** ~ **kommen** (Verkehr) to come to a standstill or stop; (*Produktion auch, Maschine, Motor, Herz, Blutung*) to stop; **etw zum** ~ **bringen** *Verkehr* to bring sth to a standstill or stop; (*Produktion auch, Maschine, Motor* to stop sth; *Blutung* to stop or check sth; ~ **ist Rückgang** (prov) if you don't go forwards, you go backwards.

stillstehen vi sep irreg aux sein or haben (a) (*Produktion, Handel* etc) to be at a standstill; (*Fabrik, Maschine auch*) to be or stand idle; (*Verkehr auch*) to be stopped; (*Herz*) to have stopped. **die Zeit schien stillzustehen** time seemed to stand still or to stop.

(**b**) (stehenbleiben) to stop; (*Maschine*) to stop working. **keinen Moment** ~ not to stop for a moment; **mein Herz stand still vor Schreck** I was so frightened my heart stood still; **da stand mir der Verstand still** I didn't know what to think.

stillstellen vt sep (liter) **das Denken/seine Sorgen** ~ to stop thinking/worrying.

stillvergnügt adj contented.

Stillzeit f lactation period.

Stil-: ~**mittel** nt stylistic device; ~**möbel** pl period furniture sing; ~**probe** f specimen or sample of written work; s~**rein** adj stylistically correct; ~**übung** f exercise in stylistic composition; s~**voll** adj stylish; s~**widrig** adj (stylistically) incongruous or inappropriate; ~**wörterbuch** nt dictionary of correct usage.

Stimm-: ~**abgabe** f voting; **sie kommen zur** ~**abgabe** they come to vote or cast their votes; **jdn bei der** ~**abgabe beobachten** to watch sb voting or casting his/her vote; ~**aufwand** m vocal effort; **mit** ~**aufwand allein kannst du das nicht erreichen** you won't get it just by raising your voice or by shouting; ~**band** nt usu pl vocal chord; **seine** ~**bänder strapazieren** to strain one's voice; (fig) to talk one's head off; s~**berechtigt** adj entitled to vote; ~**berechtigte(r)** mf decl as adj person entitled to vote; ~**bezirk** m constituency; ~**bildung** f (a) voice production; (**b**)

(Ausbildung) voice training; ~**bruch** *m siehe* ~**wechsel**; ~**bürger** *m* voter, elector.

Stimme *f* -, -**n** **(a)** voice; *(Mus: Part)* part; *(Orgel~)* register; *(fig)* *(Meinungsäußerung)* voice; *(Sprachrohr)* mouthpiece, voice; *(liter: Ruf)* call. **mit leiser/lauter ~** in a soft/loud voice; **gut/nicht bei ~ sein** to be in good/bad voice; **erste/zweite/dritte ~** *(in Chor)* first/second/third part; **bei einem Lied die erste/ zweite ~ singen** to sing the top part *or* melody of/descant to a song; **die ~n mehren sich, die ... there** is a growing body of (public) opinion that ..., there is a growing body of people calling for ...; **die ~ des Donners/des Meeres** *(liter)* the sound of thunder/the sea; **die ~(n) der Glocken/Geigen** *(liter)* the sound of the bells/violins; **die ~ der Öffentlichkeit/des Volkes** *(geh)* public opinion/the voice of the people; **die ~ der Wahrheit** the voice of truth; **eine ~ aus dem Dunkel/Exil** a voice out of the darkness/from exile; **der ~ der Natur folgen** *(euph hum)* *(seine Notdurft verrichten)* to answer the call of nature; *(dem Geschlechtstrieb nachgeben)* to give way to a natural urge; **der ~ des Gewissens folgen** to act on *or* according to one's conscience; **der ~ des Herzens folgen** to follow the leanings or dictates of one's heart; **der ~ der Vernunft folgen** to be guided by reason, to listen to the voice of reason.

(b) *(Wahl~, Votum)* vote. **eine/keine ~ haben** to have the vote/not to be entitled to vote; *(Mitspracherecht)* to have a/ no say *or* voice; **seine ~ abgeben** to cast one's vote, to vote; **jdm/einer Partei seine ~ geben** to vote for sb/a party; **die abgegebenen ~n** the votes cast; *siehe* **enthalten**.

2 stimmen 1 *vi* **(a)** *(richtig sein)* to be right; *(zutreffen auch)* to be correct. **stimmt es, daß ...?** is it true that ...?; **das stimmt** that's right; **das stimmt nicht** that's not right, that's wrong; **hier stimmt was nicht!** there's something wrong here; **mit ihr stimmt etwas nicht** there's something wrong *or* the matter with her; **das stimmt schon, aber ...** that's true, but ...; **stimmt so!** that's all right, keep the change.

(b) *(zusammenpassen)* to go (together).

(c) *(wählen, sich entscheiden)* to vote. **für/gegen jdn/etw ~** to vote for/against sb/sth.

2 *vt* *Instrument* to tune. **etw höher/niedriger ~** to raise/lower the pitch of sth, to tune sth up/down, to sharpen/flatten sth; **jdn froh/traurig ~** to make sb (feel) cheerful/sad; **jdn gegen etw ~** *(geh)* to prejudice *or* turn sb against sth; *siehe* **gestimmt**.

Stimmen-: ~**auszählung** *f* count (of votes); ~**fang** *m* *(inf)* canvassing, vote-getting *(inf)*; **auf ~fang sein/gehen** to be/go canvassing; ~**gewirr** *nt* babble of voices; ~**gleichheit** *f* tie, tied vote; **bei ~gleichheit** in the event of a tie *or* tied vote; ~**hören** *nt* *(Psych, Med)* hearing voices; ~**kauf** *m* vote-buying, buying votes, ~**mehrheit** *f* majority of votes; ~**splitting** [-ʃplɪtɪŋ, -sp-] *nt* -s, *no pl* *(Pol)* splitting one's vote.

Stimm|enthaltung *f* abstention.

Stimmenwerbung *f* canvassing. **auf ~ gehen** to go canvassing.

Stimmer *m* -s, - *(Mus)* tuner.

Stimm-: ~**gabel** *f* tuning fork; **s~gewaltig** *adj* *(geh)* with a strong *or* powerful voice; **s~haft** *adj* *(Ling)* voiced; **s~haft ausgesprochen werden** to be voiced; ~**lage** *f* *(Mus)* voice, register.

stimmlich *adj* vocal. **sie hat ~ nachgelassen** the quality of her voice has declined; **ihre ~en Qualitäten** the quality of her voice; **~ hat er nicht viel zu bieten** he doesn't have much of a voice.

Stimm-: ~**liste** *f* voting list; **s~los** *adj* *(Ling)* voiceless, unvoiced; **s~los ausgesprochen werden** not to be voiced; ~**recht** *nt* right to vote; ~**ritze** *f* glottis; ~**umfang** *m* vocal range.

Stimmung *f* **(a)** *(Gemütszustand)* mood; *(Atmosphäre auch)* atmosphere; *(bei der Truppe, unter den Arbeitern)* morale. **in (guter)/gehobener/schlechter ~** in a good mood/in high spirits/in a bad mood; **wir hatten eine tolle ~** we were in a tremendous mood; **in ~ kommen/sein** to liven up/to be in a good mood; **ich bin nicht in der ~ zum Tanzen** I'm not in the mood for dancing; **sehr von ~en abhängig sein** to be moody, to be subject to changeable moods; **~! enjoy yourselves, have a good time.**

(b) *(Meinung)* opinion. **~ gegen/für jdn/etw machen** to stir up (public) opinion against/in favour of sb/sth.

(c) *(St Ex)* mood.

(d) *(Mus)* *(das Stimmen)* tuning; *(das Gestimmtsein)* pitch.

Stimmungs-: ~**barometer** *nt* *(esp Pol)* barometer of public opinion; ~**bild** *nt* atmospheric picture; **dieser Bericht gibt ein eindrucksvolles ~bild** this report conveys the general atmosphere extremely well; **s~fördernd** *adj* **s~förderndes Mittel** anti-depressant (drug); **bei einer Party/jdm s~fördernd wirken** to liven up the atmosphere/to liven sb up; ~**kanone** *f* *(inf)* life and soul of the party; **eine richtige ~kanone** the life and soul of the party; ~**kapelle** *f* band which plays light music; ~**mache** *f, no pl* *(pej)* cheap propaganda; ~**mensch** *m* moody person; ~**musik** *f* light music; ~**umschwung** *m* change of atmosphere; *(Pol)* swing (in public opinion); *(St Ex)* change in trend; **s~voll** *adj* Bild idyllic; *Atmosphäre* tremendous; *Gedicht, Beschreibung* full of atmosphere, atmospheric; **das war ein s~voller Abend** it was a tremendous evening; **die Schloßkonzerte sind immer sehr s~voll** the concerts in the castle always have a tremendous atmosphere; ~**wandel** *m* change of atmosphere; *(Pol)* change in (public) opinion.

Stimm-: ~**vieh** *nt* *(pej)* gullible voters *pl*; ~**volk** *nt* voters *pl*, electorate; ~**wechsel** *m* **nach dem ~wechsel** after one's voice has broken; **er ist im ~wechsel** his voice is breaking; ~**werkzeuge** *pl* vocal organs *pl*; ~**zettel** *m* ballot paper.

Stimulans [ˈʃtiːmulans, st-] *nt* -, **Stimulantia** [ʃtimuˈlantsia, st-] *or* **Stimulanzien** [ʃtimuˈlantsiən, st-] *(Med, fig)* stimulant.

Stimulation [ʃtimulaˈtsioːn, st-] *f* *(Med, fig)* stimulation.

stimulieren* [ʃtimuˈliːrən, st-] *vt* *(Med, fig)* to stimulate.

Stimulierung [ʃt-, st-] *f* *(Med, fig)* stimulation.

Stimulus [ˈʃtiːmulus, st-] *m* -, **Stimuli** *(Psych)* stimulus; *(fig auch)* stimulant.

Stinkadores¹ *f* -, - *(inf)* smelly cigar.

Stinkadores² *m* -, - *(inf)* smelly cheese.

Stink-: ~**bombe** *f* stink bomb; ~**drüse** *f* *(Zool)* scent gland.

stinken *pret* **stank**, *ptp* **gestunken** *vi* **(a)** *(nach of)* to stink, to reek, to pong *(Brit inf)*. **die Wohnung/er stinkt nach Kneipe** the flat smells like a pub/he smells of drink; **wie ein Bock** *or* **Wiedehopf** *or* **eine Wachtel** *or* **die Pest ~** *(inf)* to stink to high heaven *(inf)*.

(b) *(fig inf)* **er stinkt nach Geld** he's stinking rich *(inf)*; **er stinkt vor Faulheit** he's bone-idle; **das stinkt zum Himmel** it's an absolute scandal *or* absolutely appalling; **an der Sache stinkt etwas** there's something fishy about it *(inf)*; **das stinkt nach Verrat** that smells of treachery; **die Sache stinkt mir** *(sl)*, **mir stinkt's!** *(sl)* I'm fed up to the back teeth (with it) *(inf)*.

stinkend *adj* stinking, foul-smelling.

stinkfaul *adj* *(inf)* bone-idle, bone-lazy.

stinkig *adj* *(inf)* stinking *(inf)*.

Stink-: **s~langweilig** *adj* *(inf)* deadly boring *or* dull; ~**laune** *f* *(inf)* stinking *(inf)* *or* foul mood; ~**morchel** *f* *(Bot)* stinkhorn; **s~normal** *adj* *(inf)* boringly normal *or* ordinary; **s~reich** *adj* *(inf)* stinking rich *(inf)*; ~**stiebel** *(dial)*, ~**stiefel** *m* *(inf)* stinking pig *(inf)*; *(hum: Kumpel)* mate *(inf)*; ~**tier** *nt* skunk; **s~vornehm** *adj* *(inf)* posh *(inf)*, swanky *(inf)*; *Lokal auch* swish *(inf)*; **sie tut so s~vornehm** she acts so posh; ~**wut** *f* *(inf)* raging temper; **eine ~wut (auf jdn) haben** to be livid (with sb).

Stint *m* -(e)s, -e *(Zool)* smelt, sparling. **sich freuen wie ein ~** *(inf)* to be as happy as a sandboy.

Stipendiat(in *f)* *m* -en, -en scholarship holder, person receiving a scholarship/grant.

Stipendium *nt* *(als Auszeichnung etc erhalten)* scholarship; *(zur allgemeinen Unterstützung des Studiums)* grant.

Stippe *f* -, -n *(dial)* siehe **Tunke**.

stippen *vti* *(dial)* siehe **tunken**.

Stippvisite *f* *(inf)* flying visit.

Stipulation [ʃtipulaˈtsioːn, st-] *f* *(Jur)* stipulation.

stipulieren* [ʃtipuˈliːrən, st-] *vti* to stipulate. **von Arbeitgeberseite wurden neue Verhandlungen stipuliert** the employers insisted on new talks.

stirb *imper sing of* **sterben**.

Stirn *f* -, -en forehead, brow *(esp liter)*. **sich/jdm das Haar aus der ~ streichen** to brush one's/sb's hair out of one's/his/her face; **den Hut in die ~ drücken** to pull one's hat down over one's eyes; **es steht ihm auf der ~ geschrieben** *(geh)* it is written in his face; **jdm etw an der ~ ablesen** *(geh)* to tell sth by sb's face *or* expression; **die ~ haben** *or* **besitzen, zu ...** to have the effrontery *or* nerve *or* gall to ...; **jdm/einer Sache die ~ bieten** *(geh)* to stand up to sb/sth, to defy sb/sth; *siehe* **eisern**.

Stirn-: ~**ader** *f* vein in the/one's temple; ~**auge** *nt* *(Zool)* ocellus; ~**band** *nt* headband; ~**bein** *nt* frontal bone.

Stirne *f* -, -n *(liter, dial)* siehe **Stirn**.

Stirn-: ~**falte** *f* wrinkle (on one's forehead); ~**glatze** *f* receding hair-line; ~**höhle** *f* frontal sinus; ~**höhlenkatarrh** *m*, ~**höhlenvereiterung** *f* sinusitis; ~**lage** *f* *(Med)* brow presentation; ~**locke** *f* quiff, cowlick; ~**rad** *nt* *(Tech)* spurwheel; ~**reflektor** *m* *(Med)* forehead mirror; ~**riemen** *m* brow band; ~**runzeln** *nt* -s, *no pl* frown; ~**seite** *f* end wall, gable-end; ~**spiegel** *m* *(Med)* siehe **~reflektor**; ~**wand** *f* end wall.

Stoa [ˈʃtoːa, st-] *f* -, *no pl* *(Philos)* Stoics *pl*, Stoic school.

stob *pret of* **stieben**.

stöbern¹ *vi* to rummage *(in +dat* in, *durch* through).

stöbern² *vi impers* **es stöbert** *(Schnee/Staub)* the snow/dust is blowing hard.

stochern *vi* to poke *(in +dat* at); *(im Essen)* to pick *(in +dat* at). **er stocherte mit einem Schürhaken im Feuer** he poked the fire; **sich** *(dat)* **in den Zähnen ~** to pick one's teeth.

Stock *m* -(e)s, ⸚e **(a)** stick; *(Rohr~)* cane; *(Takt~)* baton; *(Zeige~)* pointer; *(Billard~)* cue. **er stand da (steif) wie ein ~** *or* **als ob er einen ~ verschluckt hätte** he stood there as stiff as a poker; **am ~ gehen** to walk with (the aid of) a stick; *(fig inf)* to be in a bad way; *(nach viel Arbeit)* to be dead-beat *(inf)*; *(finanziell)* to be in difficulties; **da gehst du am ~** *(sl)* you'll be flabbergasted *(inf)*; **~ und Hut** *(dated)* hat and stick.

(b) *(Wurzel~)* roots *pl*.

(c) *(Pflanze)* *(Reb~)* vine; *(Rosen~)* rose-bush; *(Bäumchen)* rose-tree; *(Blumen~)* pot-plant. **über ~ und Stein** up hill and down dale.

(d) *(Bienen~)* hive.

(e) *(Geol: Gesteinsmasse)* massif, rock mass.

(f) *(Hist)* stocks *pl*. **jdn in den ~ legen** to put sb in the stocks.

(g) *pl* - *(~werk)* floor, storey *(Brit)*, story *(US)*. **das Haus hat drei ~** *or* **ist drei ~ hoch** the house is three storeys/stories high; **im ersten ~** on the first floor *(Brit)*, on the second floor *(US)*.

(h) [stɔk] *pl* -s *(Econ)* stock.

Stock- *(inf)* in cpds **ein ~engländer/-bayer** an Englishman/ Bavarian through and through.

Stock-: ~**ausschlag** *m* shoot from a tree stump; **s~besoffen** *(sl)*, **s~betrunken** *(inf)* *adj* blind *or* dead drunk; **ein ~besoffener** a drunk; **s~blind** *adj* *(inf)* as blind as a bat, completely blind.

Stöckchen *nt dim of* **Stock (a, c)**.

stock-: ~**dumm** *adj* *(inf)* thick (as two short planks) *(inf)*; ~**dunkel** *adj* *(inf)* pitch-dark.

Stöckel¹ *m* -s, - *(inf)* stiletto.

Stöckel² *nt* -s, - *(Aus)* outhouse, outbuilding.

Stöckel|absatz *m* stiletto heel.

stöckeln *vi aux sein* *(inf)* to trip, to mince.

Stöckelschuh *m* stiletto, stiletto-heeled shoe.

stocken *vi* **(a)** *(Herz, Puls)* to miss *or* skip a beat; *(Gedanken,*

Worte) to falter; (*nicht vorangehen*) (*Arbeit, Entwicklung*) to make no progress; (*Unterhaltung, Gespräch*) to flag; (*Verkehr*) to be held up *or* halted. **ihm stockte das Herz/der Puls** his heart/pulse missed *or* skipped a beat; **ihm stockte der Atem** he caught his breath; **ins S~ geraten** *or* **kommen** (*Unterhaltung, Gespräch*) to begin to flag.

(b) (*stagnieren*) (*Verhandlungen*) to break off *or* stop (temporarily); (*Geschäfte, Handel*) to slacken *or* drop off.

(c) (*innehalten*) (*in der Rede*) to falter; (*im Satz*) to break off, to stop short.

(d) (*gerinnen*) (*Blut*) to thicken; (*S Ger, Aus: Milch*) to curdle, to go sour. **das Blut stockte ihm in den Adern** (*geh*) the blood froze in his veins.

(e) (*stockig werden*) (*Wäsche, Papier, Bücher*) to become mildewed, to go mouldy.

stockend *adj* faltering, hesitant.

Stock|ente *f* mallard.

Stock-: s~**finster** *adj* (*inf*) pitch-dark, pitch-black; ~**fisch** *m* dried cod; (*pej: Mensch*) dull old stick, stick-in-the-mud; ~**fleck** *m* mark caused by mould or mildew; s~**fleckig** *adj* mouldy, mildewed; ~**haus** *nt* (*Hist*) gaol; ~**hieb** *m* siehe ~**schlag.**

stockig *adj* Geruch, Luft musty; Papier, Wäsche mildewed, mouldy.

-stöckig *adj suf* -storey *attr*, -storeyed (*Brit*), -storied (*US*).

stock-: ~**katholisch** *adj* (*inf*) Catholic through and through; ~**konservativ** *adj* (*inf*) arch-conservative.

Stock-: s~**nüchtern** *adj* (*inf*) stone-cold sober (*inf*); s~**sauer** *adj* (*sl*) pissed-off (*sl*); ~**schirm** *m* walking-stick umbrella; ~**schlag** *m* blow (from a stick); (*mit Rohr~*) stroke of the cane; ~**schnupfen** *m* permanent cold; s~**steif** *adj* (*inf*) as stiff as a poker; **sie bewegt sich s~steif** she moves very stiffly; s~**still** *adj* (*inf*) deathly quiet; Mensch stock-still; s~**taub** *adj* (*inf*) as deaf as a post.

Stockung *f* **(a)** (*vorübergehender Stillstand*) interruption, hold-up (*gen, in + dat* in); (*Verkehrs~*) congestion, traffic-jam, hold-up. **der Verkehr läuft wieder ohne ~en** traffic is flowing smoothly again.

(b) (*von Verhandlungen*) breakdown (*gen* of, in); (*von Geschäften, Handel*) slackening *or* dropping off (*gen* in).

(c) (*Pause, Unterbrechung*) (*im Gespräch*) break, lull; (*in der Rede*) pause, hesitation.

(d) (*Gerinnung*) thickening; (*von Milch*) curdling.

stockvoll 1 *adj* (*sl: betrunken*) blind *or* dead drunk (*inf*), pissed (*sl*). **2** *adv* (*inf: direkt*) straight, head-on (*inf*).

Stockwerk *nt* floor, storey (*Brit*), story (*US*). **im S. ~ on the 5th** (*Brit*) *or* **6th** (*US*) **floor; ein Haus mit vier ~en** a four-storeyed (*Brit*) *or* four-storied (*US*) building.

Stockzahn *m* (*Aus*) molar (tooth).

Stoff *m* -(**e**)**s, -e (a)** material, fabric; (*als Materialart*) cloth.

(b) (*no pl: Materie*) matter. **~ und Form** (*Philos*) matter and form.

(c) (*Substanz, Chem*) substance; (*Papier~*) pulp. **tierische/pflanzliche ~e** animal substance/vegetable matter; **aus härterem ~ gemacht sein** (*fig*) to be made of sterner stuff.

(d) (*Gegenstand, Thema*) subject (matter); (*Unterhaltungs~, Diskussions~*) topic, subject; (*Material*) material. **~ für ein** *or* **zu einem Buch sammeln** to collect material for a book; **der Vortrag bot reichlich ~ für eine Diskussion** the lecture provided plenty of material *or* topics for discussion; **~ zum Lesen/Nachdenken** reading matter/food for thought.

(e) (*inf: Rauschgift*) dope (*sl*), stuff (*sl*).

Stoff-: ~**bahn** *f* length of material; ~**ballen** *m* roll *or* bolt of material *or* cloth; s~**bespannt** *adj* fabric-covered.

Stoffel *m* -s, - (*pej inf*) lout (*inf*), boor.

stoff(e)lig *adj* (*pej inf*) uncouth, boorish.

Stoffetzen *m* getrennt Stoff-fetzen scrap of cloth.

Stoff-: ~**fülle** *f* siehe Stoffülle; ~**handschuh** *m* fabric glove.

stofflich *adj* (*Philos*) material; (*den Inhalt betreffend*) as regards subject matter.

Stofflichkeit *f* (*Philos*) materiality.

stofflig *adj* siehe stoff(e)lig.

Stoff-: ~**puppe** *f* rag doll; ~**rest** *m* remnant.

Stoffülle *f getrennt* Stoff-fülle wealth of material.

Stoffwahl *f* choice of subject.

Stoffwechsel *m* metabolism.

Stoffwechsel-: ~**krankheit** *f* metabolic disease or disorder; ~**störung** *f* metabolic disturbance.

Stoffzugabe *f* extra material.

stöhnen *vi* (*alle Bedeutungen*) to groan; (*klagen auch*) to moan. **~d** with a groan.

Stöhnen *nt* -s, *no pl* (*lit, fig*) groaning *no pl*; (*Stöhnlaut*) groan.

Stoiker(in *f*) ['ʃtɔikɐ, -ərɪn, st-] *m* -s, - (*Philos*) Stoic (philosopher); (*fig*) stoic.

stoisch ['ʃtɔiʃ, st-] *adj* (*Philos*) Stoic; (*fig*) stoic(al).

Stoizismus [ʃtɔiˈtsɪsmʊs, st-] *m* (*Philos*) Stoicism; (*fig*) stoicism.

Stola ['ʃtoːla, st-] *f* -, **Stolen** stole.

Stolle *f* -, -**n** siehe **Stollen (b).**

Stollen *m* -s, - (a) (*Min, Mil*) gallery, tunnel. (b) (*Cook*) fruit loaf (*eaten at Christmas*), stollen (*US*). (c) (*Zapfen*) (*Hufeisen*) calk(in); (*Schuh~*) stud. (d) (*Poet*) stollen, *one of the two equal sections forming the "Aufgesang" in "Minnesang".*

Stolperdraht *m* trip-wire; (*fig*) stumbling-block.

stolp(e)rig *adj* Gang stumbling; Weg uneven, bumpy.

stolpern *vi aux sein* to stumble, to trip (*über + acc* over); (*fig: zu Fall kommen*) to come a cropper (*inf*), to come unstuck (*inf*). **ins S~kommen** *or* **geraten** (*lit*) to come a cropper (*inf*); (*fig auch*) to slip up; **jdn zum S~ bringen** (*lit*) to trip sb up, to make sb trip; (*fig*) to be sb's downfall; **über einen Hinweis ~** (*fig*) to

stumble upon a clue; **über einen Bekannten ~** (*fig*) to bump *or* run into an acquaintance; **über einen Strohhalm ~** (*fig*) to come to grief over a trifle.

stolz *adj* **(a)** proud (*auf + acc* of). **~ wie ein Pfau** as proud as a peacock; **warum so ~?** why so proud?; (*bei Begegnung*) don't you know me any more?; **darauf kannst du ~ sein** that's something to be proud of; **der ~e Besitzer** the proud owner; **ein ~er Tag** a proud day.

(b) (*imposant*) Bauwerk, Schiff majestic, impressive; (*iro: stattlich*) Preis, Summe princely. **~ erhebt sich die Burg über der kleinen Stadt** the castle rises proudly above the little town.

Stolz *m* -**es**, *no pl* pride. **sein Garten/Sohn etc ist sein ganzer ~** his garden/son etc is his pride and joy; **voller ~ auf etw** (*acc*) **sein** to be very proud of sth; **ich habe auch meinen ~** I do have my pride; **aus falschem/verletztem ~ handeln** to act out of false/wounded pride; **seinen ~ in etw** (*acc*) **setzen** to take a pride in sth.

stolzieren* *vi aux sein* to strut, to swagger; (*hochmütig, beleidigt*) to stalk.

stop [ʃtɔp, stɔp] *interj* stop; (*auf Verkehrsschild auch*) halt (*Brit*).

Stopf-: ~**büchse, ~buchse** *f* (*Tech*) stuffing box; ~**ei** *nt* = darning mushroom.

stopfen 1 *vt* **(a)** (*aus~, füllen*) to stuff; Pfeife, Loch, Wurst to fill; (*inf*) Taschen auch to cram. **jdm den Mund** (*inf*) *or* **das Maul** (*sl*) **~** to silence sb.

(b) (*hinein~*) to stuff; Korken auch to ram. **gierig stopfte er alles in sich hinein, was man ihm auftischte** he greedily stuffed down everything they served up.

(c) (*ver~*) Trompete etc to mute; (*mit Stöpsel*) to plug, to stop.

(d) (*ausbessern, flicken*) Loch, Strümpfe etc to darn, to mend; *siehe* **gestopft.**

2 *vi* **(a)** (*Speisen*) (*ver~*) to cause constipation, to constipate; (*sättigen*) to be filling.

(b) (*inf: gierig essen*) to bolt *or* wolf (down) one's food, to stuff oneself (*inf*).

(c) (*flicken*) to darn, to do darning.

Stopfen *m* -s, - (*dial*) stopper; (*Korken*) cork.

Stopfer *m* -s, - (*Pfeifen~*) tamper.

Stopf-: ~**garn** *nt* darning cotton *or* thread; ~**nadel** *f* darning needle; ~**pilz** *m* (*Sew*) darning mushroom.

stopp [ʃtɔp] *interj* stop.

Stopp [ʃtɔp] *m* -**s**, -**s** stop, halt; (*Lohn~*) freeze.

Stoppball *m* (*Tennis etc*) dropshot.

Stoppel¹ *f* -, -**n** (*Getreide~, Bart~*) stubble.

Stoppel² *m* -s, - (*Aus*) siehe **Stöpsel.**

Stoppel-: ~**bart** *m* stubbly beard, stubble; ~**feld** *nt* stubble-field; ~**haar** *nt* bristly hair.

stopp(e)lig *adj* Bart stubbly; Kinn auch bristly.

stoppeln *vti* Ähren to glean.

stoppen 1 *vt* **(a)** to stop; Gehälter, Preise to freeze; (*Ftbl*) Ball auch to trap. **(b)** (*Zeit abnehmen*) to time. **er hat die Laufzeit/Zeit genau gestoppt** he timed exactly how long it took. **2** *vi* **(a)** to stop. **(b)** **ihr beide lauft, und ich stoppe** you two run and I'll time you.

Stopper *m* -s, - **(a)** (*Ftbl*) centre half. **(b)** (*Naut*) stopper. **(c)** (*an Gardinenstange*) curtain stop, end-piece. **(d)** (*Zeitnehmer*) timekeeper.

Stopplicht *nt* stop-light, red light; (*Aut*) brake light.

stopplig *adj* siehe stopp(e)lig.

Stopp-: ~**schild** *nt* stop *or* halt (*Brit*) sign; ~**straße** *f* road with stop signs, secondary road, stop street (*US*); ~**uhr** *f* stop-watch.

Stöpsel *m* -**s**, - (*Aus*) siehe (*Korken*) cork.

Stöpsel *m* -s, - (*von Waschbecken, Badewanne etc*) plug; (*Telec auch*) jack; (*Pfropfen*) stopper; (*Korken*) cork; (*inf: Knirps*) little fellow.

stöpseln *vti* (*Telec*) to connect.

Stöpselzieher *m* -s, - (*Aus*) corkscrew.

Stör¹ *m* -(**e**)**s**, -**e** (*Zool*) sturgeon.

Stör² *f* (*Aus*): **in** *or* **auf die ~ gehen** to work at the customer's home.

Stör-: ~**aktion** *f* disruptive action *no pl*; s~**anfällig** *adj* susceptible to interference.

Storch *m* -(**e**)**s**, **̈e** stork. **wie der ~ im Salat einherstolzieren/gehen** (*inf*) to stalk about/to pick one's way carefully; **der ~ hat sie ins Bein gebissen** (*dated hum*) she's expecting a little stranger (*hum*).

storchbeinig *adj* (*hum inf*) spindle-legged.

Storchennest *nt* stork's nest.

Störchin *f* female stork.

Storchschnabel *m* **(a)** (*Bot*) cranesbill, crane's-bill. **(b)** (*Tech*) pantograph.

Store [ʃtoːɐ, stoːɐ] *m* -**s**, -**s** *usu pl* net curtain; (*Sw*) shutters *pl*.

stören 1 *vt* **(a)** (*beeinträchtigen*) Schlaf, öffentliche Ordnung, Frieden etc to disturb; Verhältnis, Harmonie, Gesamteindruck etc to spoil; Rundfunkempfang to interfere with; (*absichtlich*) to jam. **jds Pläne ~** to interfere with sb's plans.

(b) Handlungsablauf, Prozeß, Vorlesung, Feier to disrupt.

(c) (*unangenehm berühren*) to disturb, to bother. **was mich an ihm/daran stört** what I don't like about him/it; **entschuldigen Sie, wenn ich Sie störe** I'm sorry to bother you, I'm sorry if I'm disturbing you; **störe mich jetzt nicht!** don't bother *or* disturb me now!; **lassen Sie sich nicht ~!** don't let me disturb you, don't mind me; **stört es Sie, wenn ich rauche?** do you mind if I smoke?, does it bother you if I smoke?; **würden Sie bitte aufhören zu rauchen, es stört mich** would you mind not smoking, I find it annoying; **das stört mich nicht** that doesn't bother me, I don't mind; **sie stört uns nicht** she doesn't bother us, we don't mind her; **sie läßt sich durch nichts ~** she doesn't let anything bother her.

2 *vr* **sich an etw** (*dat*) ~ to be bothered about; **ich störe mich an seiner Unpünktlichkeit** I take exception to his unpunctuality; **er stört sich daran, wenn ich zuviel trinke** he takes exception to my drinking too much.

3 *vi* **(a)** (*lästig, im Weg sein*) to get in the way; (*unterbrechen*) to interrupt; (*Belästigung darstellen: Musik, Lärm etc*) to be disturbing. **bitte nicht ~!** please do not disturb!; **ich möchte nicht ~** I don't want to be in the way *or* to be a nuisance, I don't want to interrupt; (*in Privatsphäre etc*) I don't want to intrude; **störe ich?** am I intruding?; **wenn ich nicht störe** if I'm not in the way *or* disturbing you; **stört das sehr, wenn ich jetzt fernsehe?** would it disturb you if I watch television?; **etw als ~d empfinden** to find sth bothersome; **ein ~der Lärm** a disturbing noise; **ein ~der Umstand** a nuisance, an annoyance; **eine ~de Begleiterscheinung** a troublesome side-effect; **sich ~d bemerkbar machen** to be all too noticeable *or* obvious; **ein ~der Besucher** an unwelcome visitor.

(b) (*unangenehm auffallen*) to spoil the effect, to stick out. **ein hübsches Gesicht, aber die große Nase stört doch etwas** a pretty face, though the big nose does spoil the effect.

Störenfried *m* -(e)s, -e, **Störer** *m* -s, - trouble-maker.

Stör-: ~**faktor** *m* source of friction, disruptive factor; **s~frei** *adj* free from interference; ~**geräusch** *nt* (*Rad, TV*) interference; ~**manöver** *nt* disruptive action.

Storni *pl* of **Storno.**

stornieren* [ʃtɔrˈniːrən, st-] *vti* (*Comm*) *Auftrag* to cancel; *Buchungsfehler* to reverse.

Storno [ˈʃtɔrno, ˈst-] *m or nt* -s, **Storni** (*Comm*) (*von Buchungsfehler*) reversal; (*von Auftrag*) cancellation.

störrisch, störrig (*rare*) *adj* stubborn, obstinate; *Kind, Pferd* unmanageable, disobedient, refractory; *Pferd* restive; *Haare* unmanageable; *siehe* **Esel.**

Störsender *m* (*Rad*) jamming transmitter, jammer.

Störung *f* **(a)** disturbance.

(b) (*von Ablauf, Verhandlungen etc*) disruption. **die Demonstranten beschlossen die ~ der Parlamentssitzung** the demonstrators decided to disrupt the parliamentary session; **es kam zu einer schweren ~ der Gerichtsverhandlung, als ...** the court proceedings were seriously disrupted when ...

(c) (*Verkehrs~*) hold-up. **es kam immer wieder zu ~en des Verkehrs** there were continual hold-ups (in the traffic), the traffic was continually held up.

(d) (*Tech*) fault, trouble *no indef art.* **eine ~ trouble, a fault; in der Leitung muß eine ~ sein** there must be a fault on the line.

(e) (*Astron*) perturbation.

(f) (*Met*) disturbance.

(g) (*Rad*) interference; (*absichtlich*) jamming. **atmosphärische ~** atmospherics *pl.*

(h) (*Med*) disorder. **gesundheitliche/geistige/nervöse ~en** physical/mental/nervous disorders, nervous trouble.

Störungs-: ~**feuer** *nt* (*Mil*) harassing fire; **s~frei** *adj* trouble-free; (*Rad*) free from interference; **der Verkehr ist/läuft wieder s~frei** the traffic is moving freely again; ~**stelle** *f* (*Telec*) faults service.

Story [ˈstoːri, ˈstɔri] *f* -, -s *or* **Stories** story; (*sl: von Verkäufer etc*) spiel (*sl*).

Stoß *m* -es, -̈e **(a)** push, shove (*inf*); (*leicht*) poke; (*mit Faust*) punch; (*mit Fuß*) kick; (*mit Ellbogen*) nudge, dig; (*mit Kopf, Hörnern*) butt; (*Dolch~ etc*) stab, thrust; (*Kugelstoßen*) put, throw; (*Fechten*) thrust; (*Schwimm~*) stroke; (*Atem~*) gasp; (*Koitusbewegung*) thrust. **einen ~ vertragen können** (*lit, fig*) to be able to take a knock (*or* two); **sich** (*dat*) *or* **seinem Herzen einen ~ geben** to pluck up *or* take courage; **das gab ihm den letzten ~** (*fig*) that was the last straw *or* final blow (for him).

(b) (*Anprall*) impact; (*Erd~*) tremor; (*eines Wagens*) jolt, bump.

(c) (*Med*) intensive course of drugs.

(d) (*Stapel*) pile, stack.

(e) (*Rail: Schienen~*) (rail) joint.

(f) (*Sew:* ~**band**) selvage; (*Tech: Kante*) butt joint. **auf ~ edge to edge.**

(g) (*Mil: Feuer~*) volley, burst of fire; (*Trompeten~ etc*) blast, blow (*in +acc* on).

(h) (*Min*) stope, face.

(i) (*Hunt*) tail feathers *pl.*

Stoß-: **s~artig** *adj Bewegung, Fahrt* jerky; *Lachen* staccato; (*spasmodisch*) spasmodic; ~**band** *nt* (*Sew*) selvage; ~**dämpfer** *m* (*Aut*) shock absorber.

Stößel *m* -s, - pestle; (*Aut: Ventil~*) tappet.

stoß|empfindlich *adj* susceptible *or* sensitive to shock; *Obst* easily damaged. **diese Uhr ist ~** this watch is not shock-proof.

stoßen *pret* **stieß,** *ptp* **gestoßen 1** *vt* **(a)** (*einen Stoß versetzen*) to push, to shove (*inf*); (*leicht*) to poke; (*mit Faust*) to punch; (*mit Fuß*) to kick; (*mit Ellbogen*) to nudge, to dig; (*mit Kopf, Hörnern*) to butt; (*stechen*) *Dolch* to plunge, to thrust; (*vulg*) to fuck (*vulg*), to shag (*vulg*), to poke (*sl*). **sich** (*dat*) **den Kopf etc** *or* **sich** (*acc*) **an den Kopf etc ~** to hit one's head *etc*; **jdm** *or* **jdn in die Seite ~** to nudge sb, to dig sb in the ribs; **jdn von sich ~** to push sb away; (*fig*) to cast sb aside; **jdn/etw zur Seite ~** to push sb/sth aside; (*mit Fuß*) to kick sb/sth aside *or* to one side; **er stieß den Ball mit dem Kopf ins Tor** he headed the ball into the goal; **ein Loch ins Eis ~** to make *or* bore a hole in the ice.

(b) (*werfen*) to push; (*Sport*) *Kugel* to put. **jdn von der Treppe/aus dem Zug ~** to push sb down the stairs/out of the train; **jdn aus dem Haus ~** (*fig*) to throw *or* turn sb out (of the house); **jdn ins Elend ~** (*liter*) to plunge sb into misery.

(c) (*zerkleinern*) *Zimt, Pfeffer, Zucker* to pound.

2 *vr* to bump *or* bang *or* knock oneself. **sich an etw** (*dat*) ~ (*lit*) to bump *etc* oneself on *or* against sth; (*fig*) to take exception to sth, to disapprove of sth; **er stößt sich daran, wenn Mädchen**

Hosen tragen he takes exception to girls wearing trousers.

3 *vi* **(a)** (*mit den Hörnern*) to butt (*nach* at).

(b) (*Tech*) to butt (*an +acc* against).

(c) (*Gewichtheben*) to jerk.

(d) *aux sein* (*treffen, prallen*) to run *or* bump into (*auch fig*); (*herab~: Vogel*) to swoop down (*auf +acc* on). **an etw** (*acc*) ~ to bump into *or* hit sth, (*grenzen*) to border on sth; **gegen etw ~** to run into sth; **zu jdm ~** to meet up with sb, to join sb; **auf jdn ~** to bump *or* run into sb; **auf etw** (*acc*) ~ (*Straße*) to lead into *or* onto sth; (*Schiff*) to hit sth, to run into *or* against sth; (*fig: entdecken*) to come upon *or* across sth; **auf Erdöl/Grundwasser ~** to strike oil/to discover underground water; **auf Widerstand/Ablehnung/Zustimmung ~** to meet with *or* encounter resistance/to meet with disapproval/approval.

(e) (*old: blasen*) to blow, to sound. **in die Trompete ~** to blow *or* sound the trumpet; *siehe* **Horn.**

Stoß-: **s~fest** *adj* shock-proof; ~**gebet** *nt* quick prayer; **ein ~gebet zum Himmel schicken** to say a quick prayer; ~**geschäft** *nt* business with short periods of peak activity; (*Saisonarbeit*) seasonal business; ~**kraft** *f* force; (*von Aufprall*) impact; (*Mil*) combat strength; ~**seufzer** *m* deep sigh; **s~sicher** *adj* shock-proof; ~**stange** *f* (*Aut*) bumper; ~**therapie** *f* (*Med*) intensive course of drug treatment; ~**trupp** *m* (*Mil*) raiding party; ~**verkehr** *m* rush-hour (traffic); ~**waffe** *f* thrust weapon; **s~weise** *adv* **(a)** (*ruckartig*) spasmodically, by fits and starts; **s~weise atmen** to pant; **die Autoschlange bewegte sich s~weise vorwärts** the line of cars moved forward by fits and starts; **(b)** (*stapelweise*) by the pile; ~**zahl** *f* (*Phys*) impact coefficient; ~**zahn** *m* tusk; ~**zeit** *f* (*im Verkehr*) rush-hour; (*in Geschäft etc*) peak period, busy time.

Stotterei *f* (*inf*) stuttering; (*fig*) stuttering and stammering.

Stotterer *m* -s, -, **Stotterin** *f* stutterer.

stottern *vti* to stutter; (*Motor*) to splutter. **leicht/stark ~** to have a slight/bad stutter, to stutter slightly/badly; **ins S~ kommen** to start stuttering; **etw auf S~ kaufen** (*inf*) to buy sth on the never-never (*Brit inf*) *or* on the cuff (*US inf*).

Stotz *m* -es, -̈e (*S Ger*) (tree-)stump.

Stotzen *m* -s, - (*esp S Ger*) **(a)** (*Baumstumpf*) (tree-)stump. **(b)** (*Bottich*) tub, vat.

Stövchen *nt* (teapot- *etc*) warmer.

StPO [esteːpeːˈʔoː] *f* - *abbr of* **Strafprozeßordnung.**

Str. *abbr of* **Straße** St.

stracks *adv* straight, immediately.

Straf-: ~**androhung** *f* threat of punishment; **unter ~androhung** on *or* under threat of penalty; ~**anstalt** *f* penal institution, prison; ~**antrag** *m* action, legal proceedings *pl*; ~**antrag stellen** to institute legal proceedings; **einen ~antrag zurückziehen** to withdraw an action; ~**antritt** *m* commencement of (prison) sentence; **sein ~antritt** the commencement of his (prison) sentence; ~**anzeige** *f* ~**anzeige gegen jdn erstatten** to bring a charge against sb; ~**arbeit** *f* (*Sch*) lines *pl*, imposition; ~**aufhebungsgrund** *m* (*Jur*) *siehe* ~**ausschließungsgrund;** ~**aufschub** *m* (*Jur*) suspension of sentence; (*von Todesstrafe*) reprieve; ~**ausschließungsgrund** *m* (*Jur*) ground for exemption from punishment; ~**aussetzung** *f* (*Jur*) suspension of sentence; ~**aussetzung zur Bewährung** probation, ~**bank** *f* (*Sport*) penalty bench, sin-bin (*inf*).

strafbar *adj Vergehen* punishable. ~**e Handlung** punishable offence; **das ist ~!** that's an offence; **sich ~ machen** to commit an offence.

Strafbarkeit *f*, *no pl* **er war sich** (*dat*) **der ~ seines Verhaltens nicht bewußt** he didn't realize that what he was doing was against the law *or* was a punishable offence.

Straf-: ~**bataillon** *nt* (*Mil*) punishment battalion; ~**befehl** *m* (*Jur*) order of summary punishment (from a local court, on the application of the DPP); ~**befehl ergeht gegen ... ...** is being prosecuted; ~**bescheid** *m* (*Jur*) notification of penalty for a tax offence; ~**bestimmung** *f* (*Jur*) penal laws *pl*, legal sanction.

Strafe *f* -, -n punishment; (*Jur, Sport*) penalty; (*Geld~*) fine; (*Gefängnis~*) sentence. **etw bei ~ verbieten** to make sth punishable by law, to prohibit sth by law; **... bei ~ verboten ...** forbidden; **es ist bei ~ verboten, ...** it is a punishable *or* prosecutable offence ...; **etw unter ~ stellen** to make sth a punishable offence; **unter ~ stehen** to be a punishable offence; **bei ~ von** on pain *or* penalty of; **eine ~ abbüßen** *or* **absitzen** *or* **abbrummen** (*inf*) to serve one's sentence, to do one's time (*inf*); **eine ~ von drei Jahren Gefängnis** a three-year prison sentence; ~ **zahlen** to pay a fine; **100 Dollar ~ zahlen** to pay a $100 fine, to be fined $100; **zur ~ as** a punishment; ~ **muß sein!** discipline is necessary; **sie hat ~ verdient** she deserves to be punished; **seine verdiente** *or* **gerechte ~ bekommen** to get one's just deserts, to be duly punished; **die ~ folgte auf dem Fuße** punishment was swift to come; **das ist die (gerechte) ~ dafür(, daß du gelogen hast)** that's your punishment (for lying), that's what you get (for lying); **er hat seine ~ weg** (*inf*) he's had his punishment; **etw als ~ empfinden** (*als lästig*) to find sth a bind (*inf*); (*als Bestrafung*) to see sth as a punishment; **es ist eine ~, ihr zuhören zu müssen** it's a pain in the neck having to listen to her (*inf*); **dieses Kind/Wetter ist eine ~** this child/weather is a pain (in the neck) (*inf*).

strafen 1 *vt* **(a)** (*be~*) to punish. **jdn (für etw/mit etw) ~** to punish sb (for sth/with sth); **mit etw gestraft sein** to be cursed with sth; **mit seinen Kindern/dieser Arbeit ist er wirklich gestraft** his children *are* a real trial to him/he finds this work a real bind (*inf*); **sie ist vom Schicksal gestraft** she is cursed by Fate, she has the curse of Fate upon her; **er ist gestraft genug** he has been punished enough; *siehe* **Verachtung.**

(b) (*old Jur*) **jdn an seinem Leib/Leben/Vermögen** *or* **Geld und Gut ~** to sentence sb to corporal punishment/to death/to fine sb; *siehe* **Lüge.**

2 *vi* to punish. **orientalische Richter ~ hart** oriental judges give severe sentences; **das S~** punishment.

strafend *adj attr* punitive; **Blick, Worte** reproachful. **die ~e Gerechtigkeit** (*liter*) avenging justice.

Straf-: **~entlassene(r)** *mf decl as adj* ex-convict, discharged prisoner; **~entlassung** *f* discharge, release (from prison); **~erlaß** *m* remission (of sentence); **s~erschwerend** *adj* **Umstand** aggravating; **(als) s~erschwerend kam hinzu, daß** ... the offence/crime was compounded by the fact that ...; **als s~erschwerend wurde gewertet, daß der Täter keine Reue gezeigt hat** the accused's lack of remorse led to the passing of a heavier sentence/imposition of a heavier fine; **s~exerzieren*** *vi insep* (*Mil*) to do punishment drill; **~expedition** *f* punitive expedition.

straff *adj* **Seil** tight, taut; **Haut** smooth; **Busen** firm; **Haltung, Gestalt** erect; **(~sitzend) Hose** etc tight, close-fitting; (*fig:* **streng**) **Disziplin, Organisation** strict, tight. **~ sitzen** to fit tightly, to be close-fitting *or* tight; **etw ~ spannen** *or* **ziehen** to tighten sth; **Decke, Laken** etc to pull sth tight; **die Leine muß ~ gespannt sein** the line has to be tight; **das Haar ~ zurück-kämmen** to comb one's hair back severely.

2 *vr* to tighten, to become taut; (*Haut*) to become smooth; (*Busen*) to become firm; (*sich aufrichten*) to stiffen.

Straffheit *f, no pl siehe* **straff** tightness, tautness; smoothness; firmness; erectness; tightness; strictness, tautness.

Straf-: **s~frei** *adj* **s~frei bleiben/ausgehen** to go unpunished; **s~frei ausgehen** to get off scot-free (*inf*); **aufgrund seiner s~freien Vergangenheit** because he had no previous convictions; **~freiheit** *f* impunity, exemption from punishment; **~gebühr** *f* surcharge; **~gefangene(r)** *mf decl as adj* detainee, prisoner; **~geld** *nt* fine; **~gericht** *nt* criminal court; **ein ~gericht abhalten** to hold a trial; **das göttliche** *or* **himmlische ~gericht** divine judgement; **das ~gericht Gottes** *or* **des Himmels** (*liter*) the judgement of God; **ein ~gericht brach über ihn herein** (*fig*) the wrath of God descended upon him; **~gerichtsbarkeit** *f* jurisdiction; **~gesetz** *nt* criminal *or* penal law; **~gesetzbuch** *nt* Criminal Code; **~gesetzgebung** *f* penal legislation; **~gewalt** *f* legal *or* penal authority; **~justiz** *f* criminal justice *or* law; **~kammer** *f* division for criminal matters (of a court); **~kolonie** *f* penal colony; **~kompanie** *f* (*Mil*) punishment battalion; **~lager** *nt* disciplinary *or* punishment camp.

sträflich 1 *adj* (*lit, fig*) criminal. 2 *adv* **vernachlässigen** etc criminally. **sich ~ blamieren** to make a terrible fool of oneself, to make a proper charlie of oneself (*inf*).

Sträfling *m* prisoner.

Sträflingskleidung *f* prison clothing.

Straf-: **s~los** *adj siehe* **s~frei**; **~losigkeit** *f siehe* **~freiheit**; **~mandat** *nt* ticket; **~maß** *nt* sentence; **das höchste ~maß** the maximum penalty *or* sentence; **s~mildernd** *adj* extenuating, mitigating; **~milderung** *f* mitigation *or* commutation of the/a sentence; **~minute** *f* (*Sport*) penalty minute; **s~mündig** *adj* of the age of criminal responsibility; **ein kleines Kind ist nicht s~mündig** a small child is under the age of criminal responsibility; **~mündigkeit** *f* age of criminal responsibility; **~nachlaß** *m* remission; **~porto** *nt* excess postage; **~predigt** *f* reprimand, dressing-down; **jdm eine ~predigt halten** to give sb a lecture *or* dressing-down; **~prozeß** *m* criminal proceedings *pl*, criminal action *or* case; **~prozeßordnung** *f* code of criminal procedure; **~punkt** *m* (*Sport*) penalty point; **~rahmen** *m* range of sentences; **~raum** *m* (*Sport*) penalty area *or* (*Ftbl auch*) box; **~recht** *nt* criminal law; **~rechtler** *m* -s, - expert in criminal law, penologist; **s~rechtlich** *adj* criminal; **jdn/etw s~rechtlich verfolgen** to prosecute sb/sth; **das ist aber kein s~rechtliches Problem** but that is not a problem of criminal law; **seine Handlung ist verabscheuenswert, wenn sie auch s~rechtlich irrelevant sein mag** his action is detestable even though of no consequence from the point of view of criminal law; **~rechtspflege** *f* criminal justice; **~rede** *f siehe* **~predigt**; **~register** *nt* police *or* criminal records *pl*; (*hum inf*) record; **ein Eintrag im ~register** an entry in the police *or* criminal records *pl*; **einen Eintrag im ~register haben** to have a record; **er hat ein langes ~register** he has a long (criminal) record; (*hum inf*) he's got a bad record; **~richter** *m* criminal judge; **~sache** *f* criminal matter; **~schuß** *m* (*Sport*) penalty (shot); **~senat** *m* criminal division (of the Court of Appeal and Federal Supreme Court); **~stoß** *m* (*Ftbl etc*) penalty (kick); (*Hockey etc*) penalty (shot); **~tat** *f* criminal offence *or* act; **~tatbestand** *m* (*Jur*) **das erfüllt den ~tatbestand der Verleumdung** etc that constitutes calumny *or* libel etc; **~täter** *m* offender, criminal; **~theorie** *f* theory of punishment, penological theory; **~umwandlung** *f* (*Jur*) commutation of a/the penalty; **~verbüßung** *f* serving of a sentence; **nach seiner ~verbüßung** after serving his sentence; **~verfahren** *nt* criminal proceedings *pl*, criminal action *or* case; **~verfolgung** *f* criminal prosecution; **~verfügung** *f* (*Jur*) *siehe* **~mandat**; **s~verschärfend** *adj siehe* **s~erschwerend**; **~verschärfung** *f* increase in the severity of the/a penalty *or* sentence; **das führte zu einer ~verschärfung** this led to the imposition of a heavier fine/the passing of a heavier sentence; **s~versetzen*** *vt insep* **Beamte** to transfer for disciplinary reasons; **~versetzung** *f* (disciplinary) transfer; **~verteidiger** *m* counsel for the defence, defence counsel *or* lawyer; **~vollstreckung** *f* execution of the/a sentence; **~vollzug** *m* penal system;

~vollzugsanstalt *f* (*form*) penal institution; **s~würdig** *adj* (*form*) criminal; **~wurf** *m* (*Sport*) penalty throw; **~zettel** *m* (*inf*) ticket.

Strahl *m* -(e)s, -en (a) (*lit, fig*) ray; (*Licht~ auch*) shaft *or* beam of light; (*Sonnen~*) shaft of light; (*Radio~, Laser~* etc) beam; (*poet: das Leuchten*) light. **im ~ einer Taschenlampe** by the light *or* in the beam of a torch; **im ~ des Mondes** by the light of the moon; **im ~ der Hoffnung** (*liter*) a ray of hope.

(b) (*Wasser~, Luft~*) jet.

Strahl|antrieb *m* (*Aviat*) jet propulsion.

strahlen *vi* (a) (*Sonne, Licht* etc) to shine; (*Sender*) to beam; (*glühen*) to glow (*vor* + *dat* with); (*Heizofen* etc) to radiate.

(b) (*leuchten*) to gleam, to sparkle; (*fig: Gesicht*) to beam. **der Himmel strahlte** the sky was bright; **das ganze Haus strahlte vor Sauberkeit** the whole house was sparkling clean; **was strahlst du so?** what are you beaming for?; **er/sie strahlte vor Freude** he/she was beaming with happiness, he/she was radiant with happiness; **er strahlte** (**übers ganze Gesicht**) he was beaming all over his face; *siehe* **strahlend**.

strahlen *vt* (*S Ger, Sw*) to comb.

Strahlen-: **~behandlung** *f* (*Med*) ray treatment; **~biologie** *f* radiobiology; **~brechung** *f* refraction; **~bündel** *nt* pencil of rays.

strahlend *adj* radiant; **Wetter, Tag** bright, glorious; **Gesicht auch** beaming. **~es Lachen** beaming smile, beam; **der Tag war ~ schön, es war ein ~ schöner** *or* **strahlendschöner Tag** a glorious day; **mit ~en Augen** with bright *or* shining eyes; **mit ~em Gesicht** with a beaming face; (*von Frau, Kind auch*) with a radiant face; **er sah sie ~ an** he beamed at her; **sie sah ihn ~ an** she looked at him, beaming *or* radiant with happiness.

Strahlen-: **s~förmig** *adj* radial; **sich s~förmig ausbreiten** to radiate out; **s~geschädigt** *adj* suffering from radiation damage; **Organ** damaged by radiation; **die ~geschädigten** the radiation victims; **~heilkunde** *f* radiotherapy; **~krankheit** *f* radiation sickness; **~pilz** *m* ray-fungus; **~quelle** *f* source of radiation; **~schäden** *pl* radiation injuries *pl*; (*von Organ auch*) radiation damage *sing*; **~schutz** *m* radiation protection; **~therapie** *f* radiotherapy; **~tierchen** *nt* radiolarian.

strahlig *adj* (*Bot*) radial.

-strahlig *adj suf* **ein zwei~es/vier~es Düsenflugzeug** a two-/four-engined jet plane.

Strahl-: **~rohr** *nt* jet pipe; **~triebwerk** *nt* jet engine; **~turbine** *f* turbo-jet.

Strahlung *f* radiation.

Strahlungs-: **~energie** *f* radiation *or* radiant energy; **~gürtel** *m* Van Allen belt; **der ~gürtel der Erde** the Van Allen belt; **~intensität** *f* dose of radiation; **~wärme** *f* radiant heat.

Strahlverfahren *nt* (jet-)blasting.

Strähne *f* -, -n, **Strähn** *m* -(e)s, -e (*Aus*) (*Haar~*) strand; (*Längenmaß: Woll~, Garn~*) skein, hank. **ich habe schon eine weiße ~** I already have a white streak.

strähnig *adj* **Haar** straggly. **das Haar fiel ihr ~ auf die Schultern** her hair fell in strands *or* in rats' tails (*pej inf*) on her shoulders.

Stramin *m* -s, -e evenweave (embroidery) fabric.

stramm *adj* (*straff*) **Seil, Hose** tight; **Seil auch** taut; (*schneidig*) **Haltung, Soldat** erect, upright; (*kräftig, drall*) **Mädchen, Junge** strapping; **Junge, Beine** sturdy; **Brust** firm; (*inf: tüchtig*) **Marsch, Arbeit** strenuous, tough, hard; (*überzeugt*) staunch; (*sl: betrunken*) tight (*inf*). **~ sitzen** to be tight *or* close-fitting, to fit tightly; **~e Haltung annehmen** to stand to attention; **~ arbeiten** (*inf*) to work hard, to get down to it (*inf*); **~ marschieren** (*inf*) to march hard; **~ konservativ** etc (*inf*) staunchly *or* dyed-in-the-wool conservative etc; **~er Max** open sandwich of boiled ham and fried egg.

stramm-: **~stehen** *vi sep irreg* (*Mil inf*) to stand to attention; **~ziehen** *vt sep irreg* **Seil, Hose** to pull tight, to tighten; **Socken** to pull up; **jdm den Hosenboden** *or* **die Hosen ~ziehen** (*inf*) to give sb a good hiding (*inf*).

Strampelhöschen [-'høːsçən] *nt* rompers *pl*.

strampeln *vi* (a) to flail *or* thrash about; (*Baby*) to thrash about. **das Baby strampelte mit Armen und Beinen** the baby was kicking its feet and waving its arms about. (b) *aux sein* (*inf: radfahren*) to pedal. (c) (*inf: sich abrackern*) to (sweat and) slave.

Strand *m* -(e)s, ¨e (*Meeres~*) beach, strand (*poet*); (*Seeufer*) shore; (*poet: Flußufer*) bank. **am ~** on the beach; **auf ~ geraten** *or* **laufen** to run aground; **auf ~ setzen** to beach.

Strand-: **~anzug** *m* beach suit; **~bad** *nt* (seawater) swimming pool; (*Badeort*) bathing resort; **~binse** *f* sea club-rush; **~distel** *f* sea-holly.

stranden *vi aux sein* to run aground, to be stranded; (*fig*) to fail; (*Mädchen*) to go astray. **Gestrandete der Wohlstandsgesellschaft** wrecks *or* the flotsam of the affluent society, those who have run aground on the shores of the affluent society.

Strand-: **~gerste** *f* sea barley; **~gut** *nt* (*lit, fig*) flotsam and jetsam; **~hafer** *m* marram (grass); **~haubitze** *f:* **blau** *or* **voll wie eine ~haubitze** (*inf*) as drunk as a lord (*inf*), rolling drunk (*inf*); **~hotel** *nt* seaside hotel; **~kiefer** *f* (*Bot*) maritime pine, cluster pine; **~kleidung** *f* beachwear; **~korb** *m* wicker beach chair with a hood; **~läufer** *m* (*Orn*) sandpiper; **~nixe** *f* (*inf*) bathing-beauty; **~promenade** *f* promenade; **~raub** *m* beachcombing; **~räuber** *m* beachcomber; **~recht** *nt* right of salvage.

Strandung *f* running aground. **die ~ wurde absichtlich herbeigeführt** the ship was deliberately run aground.

Strand-: **~vogt** *m* beach warden; **~wache** *f* lifeguard; (*Dienst*) lifeguard duty; **~wächter** *m* lifeguard; **~weg** *m* beach path.

Strang *m* -(e)s, ¨e (*Nerven~, Muskel~*) cord; (*Strick auch*) rope; (*Woll~, Garn~*) hank, skein; (*am Pferdegeschirr*) trace, tug; (*Rail: Schienen~*) track. **jdn zum Tod durch den ~ verurteilen** to sentence sb to be hanged; **der Tod durch den ~** death by hanging; **am gleichen** *or* **an demselben ~ ziehen** (*fig*) to be in the same boat; **über die ~e schlagen** *or* **hauen** (*inf*) to run riot (*inf*), to get carried away (*inf*); *siehe* **reißen.**

Strangulation *f* strangulation.

strangulieren* *vt* to strangle.

Strapaze *f* -, -n strain.

strapazfähig *adj* (*Aus*) *siehe* **strapazierfähig.**

strapazieren* **1** *vt* to be a strain on, to take a lot out of; *Schuhe, Kleidung* to be hard on, to give a lot of hard wear to; (*fig inf*) *Redensart, Begriff* to flog (to death) (*inf*); *Nerven* to strain, to try. **er sah strapaziert aus** he looked worn out *or* exhausted. **2** *vr* to tax oneself.

strapazierfähig *adj Schuhe, Kleidung* hard-wearing, durable; (*fig inf*) *Nerven* strong, tough.

strapaziös *adj* (*lit, fig*) wearing, exhausting.

Straps *m* -es, -e suspender belt (*Brit*), garter belt (*US*).

Straß *m* - *or* -sses, *no pl* paste.

straß|auf *adv*: ~, **straßab** up and down the street.

Straßburg *nt* -s Strasbourg, Strassburg.

Sträßchen *nt* dim of **Straße.**

Straße *f* -, -n (a) road; (*in Stadt, Dorf*) street, road (*Brit*); (*kleine Land~*) lane. **an der ~** by the roadside; **auf die ~ gehen** (*lit*) to go out on the street; (*als Demonstrant*) to take to the streets, to go out into the streets; (*als Prostituierte*) to go on *or* walk the streets; **auf der ~ liegen** (*fig inf*) to be out of work; (*als Wohnungsloser*) to be on the streets; (*als Faulenzer, Asozialer etc*) to hang around the streets *or* around street corners; (*Kraftfahrer*) to have broken down; **auf die ~ gesetzt werden** (*inf*) to be turned out (onto the streets); (*als Arbeiter*) to be sacked (*inf*), to get the sack (*inf*); **über die ~ gehen** to cross (the road/street); **er wohnt drei ~n weiter** he lives three blocks further on; **mit etw auf die ~ gehen** to take to the streets about sth; **er ist aus unserer ~** he's from our street; **davon spricht die ganze ~** the whole street's talking about it; **die ~n der Großstadt** the city streets; **Verkauf über die ~** take-away (*Brit*) or take-out (*US*) sales; (*von Getränken*) off-licence sales *pl* (*Brit*), package store sales *pl* (*US*); **etw über die ~ verkaufen** to sell sth to take away (*Brit*) *or* to take out (*US*); **das Geld liegt/liegt nicht auf der ~** money is there for the asking/money doesn't grow on trees; **ein Mädchen von der ~** a lady of pleasure; **der Mann von der ~** (*fig*) the man in the street.

(b) (*Meerenge*) strait(s *pl*). **die ~ von Dover/Gibraltar/Messina etc** the Straits of Dover/Gibraltar/Messina *etc*.

(c) (*Mob, Pöbel*) **die ~** the masses *pl*, the rabble; **die Herrschaft der ~** mob-rule.

(d) (*Tech*) (*Fertigungs~*) (production) line; (*Walz~*) train.

Straßen-: **~anzug** *m* lounge suit (*Brit*), business suit (*US*); **~arbeiten** *pl* roadworks *pl*; **~arbeiter** *m* roadmender.

Straßenbahn *f* (*Wagen*) tram (*Brit*), streetcar (*US*); (*Netz*) tramway(s) (*Brit*), streetcar system (*US*). **mit der ~** by tram *or* streetcar.

Straßenbahner *m* -s, - (*inf*) tramway (*Brit*) *or* streetcar (*US*) employee.

Straßenbahn-: **~fahrer, ~führer** *m* tram/streetcar driver, motorman (*US*); **~haltestelle** *f* tram/streetcar stop; **~linie** *f* tramline (*Brit*), tram route (*Brit*), streetcar line (*US*); **mit der ~linie 11 fahren** to take the number 11 tram/streetcar; **~schaffner** *m* tram/ streetcar conductor; **~schiene** *f* tramline (*Brit*), tram (*Brit*) *or* streetcar (*US*) rail; **~wagen** *m* tram, streetcar.

Straßen-: **~bau** *m* road construction; **~bauamt** *nt* highways *or* (*städtisch*) roads department; **~bauarbeiten** *pl* roadworks *pl*; **~bekanntschaft** *f* passing *or* nodding acquaintance; **eine nette ~bekanntschaft schließen** to meet a nice person on the street; **sie lebt von ~bekanntschaften** (*Prostituierte*) she depends on street pick-ups (*inf*); **~belag** *m* road surface; **~beleuchtung** *f* street lighting; **~benutzungsgebühr** *f* (road) toll; **~bild** *nt* street scene; **~böschung** *f* embankment; **~breite** *f* width of a/the road; **~decke** *f* road surface; **~dirne** *f* (*dated, form*) common prostitute, street-walker; **~dorf** *nt* linear village; **~dreieck** *nt* triangular junction, triangle; **~ecke** *f* street corner; **ein paar ~ecken weiter** a few blocks further; **~einmündung** *f* road junction; **~feger** *m* -s, - road sweeper; **~führung** *f* route; **~gabelung** *f* fork (in a/the road); **~glätte** *f* slippery road surface; **~graben** *m* ditch; **~handel** *m* street trading; **~händler** *m* street trader; (*mit Obst, Fisch etc auch*) costermonger; **~junge** *m* (*pej*) street urchin, street arab; **~kampf** *m* street fighting *no pl*; **ein ~kampf** a street fight *or* battle; **~karte** *f* road map; **~kehrer** *m* -s, - road sweeper; **~kleid** *nt* outdoor dress; **~kreuzer** *m* -s, - (*inf*) limousine; **~kreuzung** *f* crossroads *sing or pl*, intersection (*US*); **~lage** *f* (*Aut*) road holding; **dieses Auto hat eine gute ~lage** this car holds the road well *or* has good road holding; **~lärm** *m* street noise; **~laterne** *f* street lamp; **~mädchen** *nt* streetwalker, prostitute; **~musikant** *m* street musician; **~name** *m* street name; **~netz** *nt* road network *or* system; **~rand** *m* roadside; **~raub** *m* mugging (*inf*), street robbery; (*durch Wegelagerer*) highway robbery; **~räuber** *m* mugger (*inf*), thief, footpad (*old*); (*Wegelagerer*) highwayman; **~reinigung** *f* street cleaning; **~rennen** *nt* road race; **~sammlung** *f* street collection; **~sänger** *m* street singer; **~schild** *nt* street sign; **~schuh** *m* walking shoe; **~seite** *f* side of a/the road; **~sperre** *f* road-block; **~sperrung** *f* closing (off) of a/the road; **eine ~sperrung vornehmen** to close (off) the road; **~strich** *m* (*inf*) walking the streets, street-walking; (*Gegend*) red-light district; **auf den ~strich gehen** to walk the streets; **~theater** *nt* street theatre; **~tunnel** *m* (road) tunnel; **~überführung** *f* footbridge, pedestrian bridge; **~unterführung** *f* underpass, subway;

~verhältnisse *pl* road conditions *pl*; **~verkauf** *m* street-trading; take-away (*Brit*) or take-out (*US*) sales *pl*; (*Außer-Haus-Verkauf*) (*von alkoholischen Getränken*) off-licence sales *pl* (*Brit*), package store sales *pl* (*US*); (*Verkaufsstelle*) take-away (*Brit*), take-out (*US*); (*für alkoholische Getränke*) off-licence (*Brit*), package store (*US*); **Zeitungen werden im ~verkauf angeboten** newspapers are sold on the streets; **~verkäufer** *m* street seller *or* vendor; (*von Obst, Fisch etc auch*) costermonger; **~verkehr** *m* traffic; **~verkehrsordnung** *f* (*Jur*) Road Traffic Act; **~verzeichnis** *nt* index of street names; (*in Buchform auch*) street directory; **~wacht** *f* road patrol; **~walze** *f* road-roller, steam roller; **~zug** *m* street; **~zustand** *m* road conditions *pl*; **~zustandsbericht** *m* road report.

Sträßlein *nt* dim of **Straße.**

Stratege *m* -n, -n strategist. **na, alter ~** (*fig inf*) well, you old fox (*inf*).

Strategie *f* strategy.

strategisch *adj* strategic.

Stratifikation *f* stratification.

stratifizieren* *vt* (*Geol, Agr*) to stratify.

Stratosphäre *f* -, *no pl* stratosphere.

Stratosphärenflug *m* flight in the stratosphere.

stratosphärisch *adj* stratospheric.

Stratus *m* -, **Strati, Stratuswolke** *f* (*Met*) stratus (cloud).

sträuben 1 *vr* (a) (*Haare, Fell*) to stand on end; (*Gefieder*) to become ruffled. **der Katze sträubt sich das Fell** (*aggressiv*) the cat raises its hackles; **da ~ sich einem die Haare** it's enough to make your hair stand on end.

(b) (*fig*) to struggle (*gegen* against). **die Feder/die Zunge sträubt sich, das zu schildern** (*geh*) one hesitates to put it down on paper/to say it; **es sträubt sich alles in mir, das zu tun** I am most reluctant to do it.

2 *vt Gefieder* to ruffle.

Strauch *m* -(e)s, **Sträucher** bush, shrub.

Strauchdieb *m* (*old*) footpad (*old*). **du siehst aus wie ein ~!** you look like a tramp.

straucheln *vi aux sein* (a) (*geh: stolpern*) to stumble, to trip.

(b) (*fig*) (*auf die schiefe Bahn geraten*) to transgress; (*Mädchen*) to go astray. **an etw** (*dat*) **~** to come to grief over sth; **die Gestrauchelten** the reprobates.

Strauchritter *m* (*old*) footpad (*old*).

Strauchwerk *nt, no pl* (*Gebüsch*) bushes *pl*, shrubs *pl*; (*Gestrüpp*) undergrowth.

Strauß[1] *m* -es, -e ostrich. **wie der Vogel ~** like an ostrich.

Strauß[2] *m* -es, **Sträuße** (a) bunch; (*Blumen~*) bunch of flowers; (*als Geschenk*) bouquet, bunch of flowers; (*kleiner ~, Biedermeier~*) posy. **einen ~ binden** to tie flowers/twigs *etc* into a bunch; (*Blumen~ auch*) to make up a bouquet.

(b) (*old: Kampf, fig*) struggle, battle. **mit jdm einen harten ~ ausfechten** (*lit, fig*) to have a hard struggle *or* fight with sb.

Sträußchen *nt* dim of **Strauß**[2].

Straußenfeder *f* ostrich feather *or* plume.

Strauß(en)wirtschaft *f* (*Aus*) place which sells home-grown wine when a broom is displayed outside.

Straußvögel *pl* struthionidae *pl* (*spec*), struthioids *pl* (*spec*).

Streb *m* -(e)s, -e (*Min*) coal face. **im ~ arbeiten** to work on the coal face.

Strebe *f* -, -n brace, strut; (*Decken~*) joist; (*von Flugzeug*) strut.

Strebe-: **~balken** *m* diagonal brace or strut; **~bogen** *m* flying buttress.

streben *vi* (*geh*) (a) (*den Drang haben, sich bemühen*) to strive (*nach*, an + *acc, zu* for); (*Sch pej*) to swot (*inf*). **danach ~, etw zu tun** to strive to do sth; **die Pflanze strebt nach Licht** the plant seeks the light; **der Fluß strebt zum Meer** the river flows towards the sea; **in die Ferne ~** to be drawn to distant parts; **sich ~d bemühen** to strive one's hardest.

(b) *aux sein* (*sich bewegen*) **nach** *or* **zu etw ~** to make one's way to sth; (*Armee*) to push towards sth; **aus etw ~** to make one's way out of sth.

(c) *aux sein* **in die Höhe/zum Himmel ~** to rise *or* soar aloft.

Streben *nt* -s, *no pl* (a) (*Drängen, Sinnen*) striving (*nach* for); (*nach Ruhm, Geld*) aspiration (*nach* to); (*Bemühen*) efforts *pl*.

(b) (*Tendenz*) shift, movement.

Strebepfeiler *m* buttress.

Streber *m* -s, - (*pej inf*) pushy person; (*Sch*) swot (*inf*).

Streberei *f* (*pej inf*) pushiness (*inf*); (*Sch*) swotting (*inf*).

streberhaft, streberisch *adj* (*pej*) pushy (*inf*), pushing. **ein ~er Schüler** a swot (*inf*).

Streber-: **~leiche** *f* (*Sch sl*) swot(ter) (*inf*); **~natur** *f* (*pej*) pushy nature; (*Sch*) swotting; (*Mensch*) pushy person; (*Sch*) swot (*inf*); **~tum** *nt, no pl* pushiness; (*Sch*) swotting.

strebsam *adj* assiduous, industrious.

Strebsamkeit *f, no pl* assiduity, industriousness.

Strebung *f* (*esp Psych*) tendency.

Streckbett *nt* (*Med*) orthopaedic bed *with traction facilities*.

Strecke *f* -, -n (a) (*Entfernung zwischen zwei Punkten, Sport*) distance; (*Math*) line (*between two points*). **eine ~ zurücklegen** to cover a distance; **eine ziemliche** *or* **gute ~ entfernt sein** (*lit, fig*) to be a long way away; **bis zum Ende des Projekts ist es noch eine ziemliche** *or* **lange ~** there is still quite a good way to go until the end of the project.

(b) (*Abschnitt*) (*von Straße, Fluß*) stretch; (*von Bahnlinie*) section.

(c) (*Weg, Route*) route; (*Straße*) road; (*Bahnlinie, Sport: Bahn*) track; (*fig: Passage*) passage. **welche ~ bist du gekommen?** which way *or* route did you come?; **für die ~ London-Glasgow brauchen wir 5 Stunden** the journey from London to Glasgow will take us 5 hours; **auf der ~ sein** to be in the race; **auf** *or* **an der ~ Paris-Brüssel** on the way from Paris to Brussels; **die ~ Wien-München führt durch ... the** road/track *etc* between Vienna and Munich goes through ...; **in einer ~** in one go (*inf*), without stopping; **auf der ~ arbeiten** (*Rail*) to work on the track; **auf freier** *or* **offener ~** (*esp Rail*) on the open line, between stations; **auf weite ~n (hin)** (*lit, fig*) for long stretches; **auf der ~ bleiben** (*bei Rennen*) to drop out of the running; (*in Konkurrenzkampf*) to fall by the wayside.

(d) (*Hunt*) (*Jagdbeute*) bag, kill. **zur ~ bringen** to bag, to kill; (*fig*) **Verbrecher** to hunt down.

(e) (*Min*) gallery.

strecken 1 *vt* (a) **Arme, Beine, Oberkörper** to stretch; **Hals** to crane; (*Sch: sich melden*) **Finger, Hand** to raise, to put up. **die Zunge aus dem Mund ~** to stick out one's tongue; **die Beine seitwärts ~/gemütlich von sich ~** to stretch (out) one's legs sideways/to stretch out one's legs; **den Kopf aus dem Fenster/ durch die Tür ~** to stick one's head out of the window/through the door; **jdn zu Boden ~** to knock sb to the floor.

(b) (*im Streckverband*) **Bein, Arm** to straighten.

(c) (*Metal*) **Blech, Eisen** to hammer out.

(d) (*inf: absichtlich verlängern*) **Vorräte, Geld** to eke out, to stretch; **Arbeit** to drag out (*inf*); **Essen** to make go further; (*verdünnen*) to thin down, to dilute.

2 *vr* (a) (*sich recken*) to have a stretch, to stretch; (*inf: wachsen*) to shoot up (*inf*). **sich ins Gras/aufs Bett ~** to stretch out on the grass/the bed.

(b) (*sich hinziehen*) to drag on.

Strecken-: **~abschnitt** *m* (*Rail*) section of the line or track, track section; **~arbeiter** *m* (*Rail*) plate-layer; **~begehung** *f* (*Rail*) track inspection; **~führung** *f* (*Rail*) route; **~netz** *nt* rail network; **~rekord** *m* (*Sport*) track record; **~wärter** *m* (*Rail*) track inspector; **s~weise** *adv* in parts or places.

Strecker *m* -s, -, **Streckmuskel** *m* (*Anat*) extensor (muscle).

Streckverband *m* (*Med*) bandage used in traction.

Streich *m* -(e)s, -e (a) (*Schabernack*) prank, trick. **jdm einen ~ spielen** (*lit*) to play a trick on sb; (*fig: Gedächtnis etc*) to play tricks on sb; **immer zu ~en aufgelegt sein** to be always up to pranks or tricks.

(b) (*old, liter*) blow; (*mit Rute, Peitsche*) stroke, lash. **jdm einen ~ versetzen** to strike sb; **auf einen ~** at one blow; (*fig auch*) **in one go** (*inf*).

streicheln *vti* to stroke; (*liebkosen*) to caress. **jdm die Wange/das Haar ~** to stroke/caress sb's cheek/hair.

streichen *pret* **strich**, *ptp* **gestrichen 1** *vt* (a) to stroke. **etw glatt~** to smooth sth (out); **sich** (*dat*) **die Haare aus dem Gesicht/der Stirn ~** to push one's hair back from one's face/forehead; *siehe* **gestrichen.**

(b) (*auftragen*) **Butter, Brot** *etc* to spread; **Salbe, Farbe** *etc* to apply, to put on. **sich** (*dat*) **ein Brot (mit Butter) ~** to butter oneself a slice of bread; **sich ~ lassen** to spread easily.

(c) (*an~: mit Farbe*) to paint. **frisch gestrichen!** wet paint.

(d) **Geige, Cello** to bow.

(e) (*tilgen*) **Zeile, Satz** to delete, to cross out; **Auftrag, Plan, Zug** *etc* to cancel; **Schulden** to write off; **Zuschuß** *etc* to cut. **etw aus dem Protokoll ~** to delete sth from the minutes; **jdn/etw von** *or* **aus der Liste ~** to take sb/sth off the list, to delete sb/sth from the list; **etw aus seinem Gedächtnis ~** (*geh*) to erase sth from one's memory.

(f) (*Naut*) **Segel, Flagge, Ruder** to strike.

2 *vi* (a) (*über etw hinfahren*) to stroke. **mit der Hand über etw** (*acc*) **~** to stroke sth (with one's hand); **sie strich ihm über die Hand/das Haar** she stroked his hand/hair.

(b) *aux sein* (*streifen*) to brush past (*an etw* (*dat*) sth); (*Wind*) to waft. **um/durch etw ~ (herum~)** to prowl around/through sth; **die Katze strich mir um die Beine** the cat rubbed against my legs; **durch den Wald/die Felder ~** (*old, geh*) to ramble or wander through the woods/fields.

(c) *aux sein* (*Vögel*) to sweep (*über* +*acc* over).

(d) (*schmieren*) to spread.

(e) (*malen*) to paint.

(f) (*sl*) **einen ~ lassen** to let one off (*sl*), to fart (*vulg*).

Streicher *pl* (*Mus*) strings *pl.*

Streich-: **s~fähig** *adj* easy to spread; **s~fertig** *adj* ready to use or apply; **~holz** *nt* match; **~holzschachtel** *f* matchbox; **~instrument** *nt* string(ed) instrument; **die ~instrumente** the strings; **~käse** *m* cheese spread; **~musik** *f* music for strings; **~orchester** *nt* string orchestra; **~quartett** *nt* string quartet; **~quintett** *nt* string quintet; **~riemen** *m* strop.

Streichung *f* (*Tilgung*) (*von Zeile, Satz*) deletion; (*Kürzung*) cut; (*von Auftrag, Plan, Zug*) cancellation; (*von Schulden*) writing off; (*von Zuschüssen etc*) cutting. **die drastischen ~en bei den Subventionen** the drastic cuts in subsidies.

Streichwurst *f* sausage for spreading, ≈ meat paste.

Streifband *nt* wrapper. **im** or **unter** (*Sw*) **~ posted** *in a wrapper at reduced rate.*

Streifbandzeitung *f* newspaper sent at printed paper rate.

Streife *f* -, -n (a) (*Patrouille*) patrol. **auf ~ gehen/sein** to go/be on patrol; **seine ~ machen** to do one's rounds, to patrol; **ein Polizist auf ~** a policeman on his beat. (b) (*Hunt*) *siehe* **Streifjagd.**

streifen 1 *vt* (a) (*flüchtig berühren*) to touch, to brush (against); (*Kugel*) to graze; (*Billardkugel*) to kiss; (*Auto*) to scrape. **jdn an der Schulter ~** to touch sb on the shoulder; **jdn mit einem Blick ~** to glance fleetingly at sb; **ein flüchtiger Blick streifte mich** he/she glanced fleetingly at me; **eine Stadt ~** to visit a town briefly.

(b) (*fig: flüchtig erwähnen*) to touch (up)on.

(c) (*ab~, überziehen*) **die Butter vom Messer ~** to scrape the butter off the knife; **die Schuhe von den Füßen ~** to slip one's shoes off; **den Ring vom Finger ~** to slip or take the ring off

one's finger; **ein Insekt von der Schulter ~** to brush an insect off one's shoulder; **sich** (*dat*) **die Handschuhe über die Finger ~** to pull on one's gloves; **er streifte sich** (*dat*) **den Pullover über den Kopf** (*an-/ausziehen*) he slipped the pullover on/off over his head; **die Blätter von den Zweigen ~** to strip the leaves from the twigs; **die Ärmel in die Höhe ~** to pull up one's sleeves.

2 *vi* (a) *aux sein* (*wandern*) to roam, to wander; (*Fuchs*) to prowl. **(ziellos) durch das Land/die Wälder ~** to roam the country/the forests.

(b) *aux sein* (*flüchtig berühren: Blick etc*) **sie ließ ihren Blick über die Menge ~** she scanned the crowd; **sein Blick streifte über seine Besitztümer** he gazed at his possessions.

(c) (*fig: grenzen*) to border (*an* +*acc* on).

Streifen *m* -s, - (a) (*Stück, Band*) strip; (*Speck~*) rasher. **ein ~ Land** *or* **Landes** (*geh*)/**Speck** a strip of land/bacon.

(b) (*Strich*) stripe; (*Farb~*) streak.

(c) (*Loch~, Klebe~ etc*) tape.

(d) (*Tresse*) braid; (*Mil*) stripe.

(e) (*Film*) film; (*Abschnitt*) strip of film.

(f) (*Linie*) line.

(g) **das paßt mir nicht in den ~** (*dated inf*) that's a confounded nuisance; **er paßt nicht/paßt in den ~** (*dated inf*) he does not fit in/fits in; *siehe* **geziemend.**

Streifen-: **~dienst** *m* patrol duty; **~muster** *nt* stripy design or pattern; **ein Anzug mit ~muster** a striped suit; **~polizei** *f* patrol police; **~polizist** *m* policeman on patrol; **~wagen** *m* patrol car.

streifig *adj* streaky.

Streif-: **~jagd** *f* walk-up, *hunt where beaters and guns walk together flushing out game;* **~licht** *nt* (*fig*) highlight; **ein ~licht auf etw** (*acc*) **werfen** to highlight sth; **~schuß** *m* graze; **~zug** *m* raid; (*Bummel*) expedition; (*fig: kurzer Überblick*) brief survey (*durch* of).

Streik *m* -(e)s, -s *or* (*rare*) -e strike. **zum ~ aufrufen** to call a strike; **jdn zum ~ aufrufen** to call sb out on strike; **in den ~ treten** to come out or go on strike.

Streik-: **~aufruf** *m* strike call; **~brecher** *m* -s, - strikebreaker, blackleg (*pej*), scab (*pej*).

streiken *vi* to be on strike, to strike; (*in den Streik treten*) to come out on or go on strike, to strike; (*hum inf*) (*nicht funktionieren*) to pack up (*inf*); (*Magen*) to protest; (*Gedächtnis*) to fail. **der Kühlschrank streikt schon wieder** (*inf*) the fridge has packed up again (*inf*) or is on the blink again (*inf*); **als er noch einen Schnaps eingoß, habe ich gestreikt** (*inf*) when he poured out another schnapps I refused to drink any more; **wenn ich heute abwaschen soll, streike ich** (*inf*) if I have to do the washing up today, I'll go on strike (*inf*); **da streike ich** (*inf*) I refuse!, count me out (*inf*).

Streikende(r) *mf decl as adj* striker.

Streik-: **~geld** *nt* strike pay; **~kasse** *f* strike fund; **~posten** *m* picket; **~posten aufstellen** to put up pickets; **~posten stehen** to picket; **~recht** *nt* right or freedom to strike; **~welle** *f* wave or series of strikes.

Streit *m* -(e)s, -e (a) argument (*über* +*acc* about); (*leichter*) quarrel, squabble; (*zwischen Eheleuten, Kindern auch*) fight; (*Fehde*) feud; (*Auseinandersetzung*) dispute. **~ haben** to be arguing or quarrelling; **wegen etw mit jdm (einen) ~ haben** to argue with sb about sth, to have an argument with sb about sth; **die Nachbarn haben seit Jahren ~** the neighbours have been arguing or fighting for years; **wegen einer Sache ~ bekommen** to get into an argument over sth; **in ~ geraten** to get involved in an argument; **~ anfangen** to start an argument; **~ suchen** to be looking for an argument or a quarrel; **in ~ liegen** (*Gefühle*) to conflict; **mit jdm in ~ liegen** to be at loggerheads with sb; **ein ~ mit Waffen/Fäusten** a fight with weapons/a fistfight.

(b) (*old, liter: Kampf*) battle. **zum ~(e) rüsten** to arm oneself for battle.

Streit|axt *f* (*Hist*) battleaxe. **die ~ begraben** (*fig*) to bury the hatchet.

streitbar *adj* (a) (*streitlustig*) pugnacious. (b) (*old: tapfer*) valiant.

Streitbarkeit *f siehe adj* (a) pugnacity. (b) valour.

streiten *pret* **stritt**, *ptp* **gestritten 1** *vi* (a) to argue; (*leichter*) to quarrel, to squabble; (*Eheleute, Kinder auch*) to fight; (*Gefühle*) to conflict; (*Jur: prozessieren*) to take legal action. **mit Waffen/Fäusten ~** to fight with weapons/one's fists; **Scheu und Neugier stritten in ihr** she had conflicting feelings of shyness and curiosity; **die S~den** the arguers, the people fighting; **es wird immer noch gestritten, ob ... the** argument about whether ... is still going on.

(b) **über etw** (*acc*) **~** to dispute or argue about or over sth; (*Jur*) to go to court over sth; **darüber kann man** or **läßt sich ~** that's a debatable or moot point; **die ~den Parteien** (*Jur*) the litigants.

(c) (*old, liter*) (*kämpfen*) to fight; (*in Wettbewerb*) to compete (*um* for).

2 *vr* to argue, to quarrel, to squabble; (*Eheleute, Kinder auch*) to fight. **habt ihr euch schon wieder gestritten?** have you been fighting again?; **wir wollen uns deswegen nicht ~!** don't let's fall out over that!; **man streitet sich, ob ... there** is argument as to whether ...

Streiter(in *f*) *m* -s, - (*geh*) fighter (*für* for); (*für Prinzip etc auch*) champion (*für* of).

Streiterei *f* (*inf*) arguing *no pl*; quarrelling *no pl*; (*zwischen Eheleuten, Kindern auch*) fighting *no pl.* **eine ~** an argument.

Streit-: **~fall** *m* dispute, conflict; (*Jur*) case; **im ~fall** in case of dispute or conflict; **im ~fall Müller gegen Braun** in the case of Müller versus Braun; **~frage** *f* dispute; **~gegenstand** *m* matter in dispute; (*strittiger Punkt*) matter of dispute; **~gespräch** *nt* debate, discussion; (*Liter, Univ auch*) disputation; **~grund** *m* cause of the/an argument; **~hahn** *m* (*inf*) squabbler; **~hammel** *m* (*S Ger inf*), **~hans(e)l** *m* **-s, -** (*Aus inf*) quarrelsome person.

streitig *adj* **jdm das Recht auf etw** (*acc*) **~ machen** to dispute sb's right to sth; **das/seine Kompetenz kann man ihm nicht ~ machen** that/his competence is indisputable.

Streitigkeiten *pl* quarrels *pl*, squabbles *pl*.

Streit-: **~kräfte** *pl* forces *pl*, troops *pl*; **~lust** *f* (*liter*) argumentative disposition; (*Aggressivität*) aggressive disposition; **s~lustig** *adj* (*geh*) argumentative; (*aggressiv*) aggressive; **~macht** *f* armed forces *pl*; **~objekt** *nt siehe* **~gegenstand;** **~punkt** *m* contentious issue; **~roß** *nt* war-horse; **~sache** *f* dispute; (*Jur*) case; **~schrift** *f* polemic; **~sucht** *f* quarrelsomeness; **s~süchtig** *adj* quarrelsome; **~wagen** *m* (*Hist*) chariot; **~wert** *m* (*Jur*) amount in dispute.

stremmen *vi* (*dial*) to be too tight.

streng *adj* (**a**) strict; *Regel, Kontrolle auch, Maßnahmen* stringent; *Bestrafung* severe; *Anforderungen* rigorous; *Ausdruck, Blick, Gesicht* stern; *Sitten, Disziplin auch* rigid; *Stillschweigen, Diskretion* absolute; *Mode, Schnitt* severe; *Kritik, Urteil* harsh, severe; *Richter* severe, stern; *Lebensführung, Schönheit, Form* austere; *Examen* stiff. **~ gegen jdn/etw vorgehen** to deal severely with sb/sth; **~ durchgreifen** to take rigorous *or* stringent action; **~ gegen sich selbst sein** to be strict *or* severe on *or* with oneself; **~ aber gerecht** severe but just; **etw ~ befolgen, sich ~ an etw halten** to keep strictly *or* rigidly to sth, to observe sth strictly *or* rigidly; **~ geheim** top secret; **~ vertraulich/wissenschaftlich** strictly confidential/scientific; **~ nach Vorschrift** strictly according to regulations; **~(stens) verboten!** strictly prohibited; **sie kleidet sich sehr ~** she wears very severe clothes.

(**b**) (*durchdringend*) *Geruch, Geschmack* pungent; *Frost, Kälte, Winter* intense, severe.

(**c**) (*~gläubig*) *Katholik, Moslem* strict.

Strenge *f* **-,** *no pl siehe adj* (**a**) strictness; stringency; severity; rigorousness; sternness; rigidity; absoluteness; severity; harshness, severity; severity; sternness; austerity; stiffness. **mit ~ regieren** to rule strictly. (**b**) pungency; intensity; severity. (**c**) strictness.

Streng-: **s~genommen** *adv* strictly speaking; (*eigentlich*) actually; **s~gläubig** *adj* strict; **~gläubigkeit** *f* strictness; **s~nehmen** *vt sep irreg* to take seriously; **es mit jdm s~nehmen** to be hard on sb; **es mit etw s~nehmen** to be strict about sth; **wenn man es s~nimmt** strictly speaking.

Streptokokken [ʃtrepto'kɔk(ə)n, ʃt-] *pl* (*Med*) streptococci *pl*.

Streptomycin [ʃtreptomy'tsiːn, ʃt-] *nt* **-s,** *no pl* (*Med*) streptomycin.

Stresemann *m* **-s,** *no pl formal, dark suit with striped trousers.*

Streß [ʃtres, ʃt-] *m* **-sses, -sse** (*alle Bedeutungen*) stress. **im ~ sein** to be under stress.

stressen *vt* to put under stress. **gestreßt sein** to be under stress.

Streß-: **s~geplagt** *adj* under stress; **~krankheit** *f* stress disease; **~situation** *f* stress situation.

Streu *f* **-,** *no pl* straw; (*aus Sägespänen*) sawdust.

streuen **1** *vt* *Futter, Samen* to scatter; *Blumen auch* to strew; *Dünger, Stroh, Sand, Kies* to spread; *Gewürze, Zucker etc* to sprinkle; *Straße, Gehweg etc* to grit; to salt. **2** *vi* (**a**) (*Streumittel anwenden*) to grit; to put down salt. (**b**) (*Salzstreuer etc*) to sprinkle. (**c**) (*Linse, Gewehr etc*) to scatter.

Streuer *m* **-s, -** shaker; (*Salz~*) cellar; (*Pfeffer~*) pot; (*Zucker~ auch*) castor; (*Mehl~ auch*) dredger.

Streufahrzeug *nt* gritter, sander.

streunen *vi* (**a**) to roam about, to wander about *or* around; (*Hund, Katze*) to stray. (**b**) *aux sein durch etw/in etw* (*dat*) **~** to roam *or* wander through/around sth.

Streu-: **~pflicht** *f* obligation *on householder to keep area in front of house gritted in icy weather*; **~pulver** *nt* grit/salt (*for icy roads*); **~sand** *m* sand; (*für Straße*) grit.

Streusel *nt* **-s, -** (*Cook*) crumble (mixture).

Streuselkuchen *m* thin sponge cake with crumble topping.

Streuung *f* (*Statistik*) mean variation; (*Phys*) scattering.

Streuzucker *m* (*grob*) granulated sugar; (*fein*) caster sugar.

strich *pret* von **streichen.**

Strich *m* **-(e)s, -e** (**a**) line; (*Quer~*) dash; (*Schräg~*) oblique, slash (*esp US*); (*Feder~, Pinsel~*) stroke; (*von Land*) stretch. **etw mit (ein paar) knappen ~en zeichnen** (*lit, fig*) to sketch *or* outline sth with a few brief strokes; **jdm einen (dicken) ~ durch etw machen** (*lit*) to cross sth out for sb; (*fig inf*) to knock sb's plans on the head (*inf*); **jdm einen ~ durch die Rechnung/einen Plan machen** to thwart sb's plans/plan; **einen ~ (unter etw** *acc*) **machen** *or* **ziehen** (*fig*) to forget sth; **unterm ~ sein** (*inf*) not to be up to scratch; **er kann noch auf dem ~ gehen** (*inf*) he can still walk along a straight line; **dünn wie ein ~** (*inf*) as thin as a rake (*inf*); **sie ist nur noch ein ~** (in der Landschaft *hum*) (*inf*) she's as thin as a rake now; **den habe ich auf dem ~** (*inf*) I've got it in for him; **keinen ~ tun** (*inf*) not to do a stroke (of work).

(**b**) *no pl* (*Kompaß~*) point.

(**c**) (*von Teppich*) pile; (*von Samt auch, von Gewebe*) nap; (*von Fell, Haar*) direction of growth. **gegen den ~ bürsten** (*lit*) to brush the wrong way; **es geht (mir) gegen den ~** (*inf*) it goes against the grain; **nach ~ und Faden** (*inf*) good and proper (*inf*), thoroughly; **jdn nach ~ und Faden versohlen** (*inf*) to give sb a thorough *or* good hiding.

(**d**) (*Mus: Bogen~*) stroke, bow. **einen harten/weichen ~ haben** to bow heavily/lightly.

(**e**) (*inf*) (*Prostitution*) prostitution *no art*; (*Bordellgegend*) red-light district. **auf den ~ gehen** to be/go on the game (*sl*), to be/become a prostitute.

(**f**) (*von Schwalben etc*) flight.

Strich-: **~ätzung** *f* (*Typ*) line etching; **~biene** *f* (*sl*) hooker (*esp*

US sl); **~dame** *f* (*inf*) tart (*inf*), hooker (*esp US sl*), streetwalker.

stricheln, strichlieren* (*Aus*) **1** *vi* to sketch it in; (*schraffieren*) to hatch. **2** *vt* to sketch in; to hatch. **eine gestrichelte Linie** a broken line.

Strich-: **~junge** *m* (*inf*) male prostitute; **~mädchen** *nt* (*inf*) tart (*inf*), hooker (*esp US sl*); **~punkt** *m* semi-colon; **~vögel** *pl* (*Orn*) migratory birds *pl*; (*hum sl*) tarts *pl* (*inf*), hookers *pl* (*esp US sl*); **s~weise** *adv* (*Met*) here and there; **s~weise Regen** rain in places; **~zeichnung** *f* line drawing.

Strick[1] *m* **-(e)s, -e** (**a**) rope; (*dünner, als Gürtel*) cord. **jdm aus etw einen ~ drehen** to use sth against sb; **zum ~ greifen** (*inf*) to hang oneself; **dann kann ich mir einen ~ nehmen** *or* **kaufen** (*inf*) I may as well pack it all in (*inf*); *siehe* **reißen.**

(**b**) (*inf: Schelm*) rascal. **fauler ~** lazybones *sing* (*inf*), lazy so-and-so (*inf*).

Strick[2] *no art* (*inf*) knitwear.

Strick-: **~arbeit** *f* knitting *no pl*; **eine ~arbeit** a piece of knitting; **~beutel** *m* knitting bag.

stricken *vti* to knit.

Stricker(in *f*) *m* **-s, -** - knitter.

Strickerei *f* knitting *no indef art, no pl.*

Strick-: **~garn** *nt* knitting wool; **~handschuhe** *pl* knitted gloves *pl*; **~jacke** *f* cardigan; **~kleid** *nt* knitted dress; **~leiter** *f* rope ladder; **~maschine** *f* knitting machine; **~muster** *nt* (*lit*) knitting pattern; (*fig*) pattern; **~nadel** *f* knitting needle; **~waren** *pl* knitwear *sing*; **~weste** *f* knitted waistcoat; (*mit Ärmeln*) cardigan; **~wolle** *f* knitting wool; **~zeug** *nt* knitting.

Striegel *m* **-s, -** currycomb.

striegeln **1** *vt* (**a**) to curry(comb); (*fig inf: kämmen*) to comb. (**b**) (*fig: hart behandeln*) **jdn ~** to put sb through the hoop (*inf*). **2** *vr* (*inf*) to spruce oneself up.

Strieme *f* **-, -n, Striemen** *m* **-s, -** weal.

striemig *adj* *Haut* marked with weals.

Striezel *m* **-s, -** (*dial Cook*) plaited Danish pastry.

strikt [ʃtrikt, ʃt-] *adj* strict.

Strip [ʃtrɪp, strɪp] *m* **-s, -s** (*inf*) strip(tease).

Strippe *f* **-, -n** (*inf*) (*Bindfaden*) string. (**b**) (*Telefonleitung*) phone, blower (*Brit inf*). **an der ~ hängen/sich an die ~ hängen** to be/get on the phone *or* blower (*Brit sl*); **jdn an der ~ haben** to have sb on the line *or* phone *or* blower (*Brit sl*).

strippen [ʃtrɪpn, strɪpn] *vi* to strip, to do a striptease act.

Stripper(in *f*) [ʃtrɪpɐ, -ərɪn, ʃt-] *m* **-s, -** (*inf*) stripper.

Striptease [ʃtrɪptiːs, ʃt-] *m or nt* **-,** *no pl* striptease.

Stripteasetänzer(in *f*) [ʃtrɪptiːs-, ʃt-] *m* stripper.

stritt *pret* von **streiten.**

strittig *adj* contentious, controversial. **noch ~** still in dispute.

Strizzi *m* **-s, -s** (*Aus inf*) pimp.

Stroh *nt* **-(e)s,** *no pl* straw; (*Dach~*) thatch. **~ im Kopf haben** (*inf*) to have sawdust between one's ears (*inf*); *siehe* **dreschen.**

Stroh-: **~ballen** *m* bale of straw; **s~blond** *adj* *Mensch* flaxenhaired; *Haare* flaxen, straw-coloured; **~blume** *f* strawflower; **~bund** *nt* bundle of straw; **~dach** *nt* thatched roof; **s~dumm** *adj* thick (*inf*); **s~farben** *adj* straw-coloured; *Haare auch* flaxen; **~feuer** *nt*: **ein ~feuer sein** (*fig*) to be a passing fancy; **s~gedeckt** *adj* thatched; **s~gelb** *adj* straw-coloured; *Haare auch* flaxen; **~halm** *m* straw; **sich an einen ~halm klammern, nach einem ~halm greifen** to clutch at a straw; **~hut** *m* straw hat; **~hütte** *f* thatched hut.

strohig *adj* *Gemüse* tough; *Orangen etc* dry; *Haar* dull and lifeless.

Stroh-: **~kopf** *m* (*inf*) blockhead (*inf*); **~lager** *nt* pallet, straw mattress; **~mann** *m, pl* **-männer** (*~puppe*) scarecrow; (*fig*) front man; (*Cards*) dummy; **~matte** *f* straw mat; **~puppe** *f* scarecrow; **~sack** *m* palliasse; **heiliger ~sack!** (*dated inf*) good(ness) gracious (me)!; **~wisch** *m* (*old*) broom; **~witwe** *f* grass widow; **~witwer** *m* grass widower.

Strolch *m* **-(e)s, -e** (*dated pej*) rogue, rascal.

strolchen *vi aux sein* to roam about. **durch etw/in etw** (*dat*) **~ to** roam through/around sth.

Strom *m* **-(e)s, ⁻e** (**a**) (large) river; (*Strömung*) current; (*von Schweiß, Blut*) river; (*von Besuchern, Flüchen etc*) stream. **ein reißender ~** a raging torrent; **⁻e und Flüsse Europas** rivers of Europe; **ein ~ von Tränen** (*geh*) floods of tears *pl*; **in dem** *or* **im ~ der Vergessenheit versinken** (*geh*) to sink *or* pass into oblivion; **in ⁻en regnen** to be pouring with rain; **der Wein floß in ⁻en** the wine flowed like water; **der ~ seiner Rede** (*geh*) the torrent *or* flood of his words; **der ~ der Zeit/Geschichte** (*geh*) the flow of time/the course of history; **sich vom ~ der Menge treiben lassen** (*geh*) to be carried along by the crowd; **mit dem/gegen den ~ schwimmen** (*lit*) to swim with/against the current; (*fig*) to swim *or* go with/against the tide.

(**b**) (*Elec*) current; (*Elektrizität*) electricity. **~ führen** to be live; **unter ~ stehen** (*lit*) to be live; (*fig*) to be high (*inf*); **mit ~ heizen** to have electric heating; **der ~ ist ausgefallen** the power *or* electricity is off.

Strom-: **s~ab** *adv* downstream; **~abnehmer** *m* (**a**) (*Tech*) pantograph; (**b**) (*~verbraucher*) user *or* consumer of electricity; **s~abwärts** *adv* downstream; **~anschluß** *m* **~anschluß haben** to be connected to the electricity mains; **s~auf(wärts)** *adv* upstream; **~ausfall** *m* power failure; **~bett** *nt* riverbed.

strömen *vi aux sein* to stream; (*Blut auch, Gas*) to flow; (*heraus~*) to pour (*aus* from); (*Menschen auch*) to flock (*aus* out of). **bei ~dem Regen** in (the) pouring rain.

Stromer *m* **-s, -** (*inf*) rover; (*Landstreicher*) tramp, hobo (*esp US*).

stromern *vi aux sein* (*inf*) to roam *or* wander about.

Strom-: **s~führend** *adj attr* (*Elec*) *Leitung* live; **~gebiet** *nt* river basin; **das ~gebiet der Elbe** the Elbe basin; **~kabel** *nt* electric *or* power cable; **~kreis** *m* (electrical) circuit; **~leitung**

f electric cables *pl*; ~**linienform** [-li:niən-] *f* streamlined design; (*von Auto auch*) streamlined body; **s~linienförmig** [-li:niən-] *adj* streamlined; ~**messer** *m* -s, - (*Elec*) ammeter; ~**netz** *nt* electricity *or* power supply system; ~**quelle** *f* source of power *or* electricity; ~**richter** *m* transformer; ~**schiene** *f* (*Rail*) live *or* conductor rail; ~**schnelle** *f* rapids *pl*; ~**speicher** *m* (storage) battery; ~**sperre** *f* power cut; ~**stärke** *f* strength of the/an electric current; ~**stoß** *m* electric shock.

Strömung *f* current; (*fig auch*) trend.

Strömungslehre *f* (*von Flüssigkeiten*) hydrodynamics *sing*; (*von Luft und Gasen*) aerodynamics *sing*.

Strom-: ~**verbrauch** *m* electricity *or* power consumption; ~**versorgung** *f* electricity *or* power supply; ~**wender** *m* -s, - commutator; ~**zähler** *m* electricity meter.

Strontium [ˈʃtrɔntsiʊm, st-] *nt* -s, *no pl* strontium.

Strophe *f* -, -n verse; (*in Gedicht auch*) stanza.

-**strophig** *adj suf* drei-/vier-~ of three/four stanzas *or* verses.

strophisch 1 *adj* stanzaic. **2** *adv* in stanzas.

strotzen *vi* to be full (*von, vor* + *dat* of), to abound (*von, vor* + *dat* with); (*von Kraft, Gesundheit, Lebensfreude*) to be bursting (*von* with); (*vor Ungeziefer*) to be teeming *or* crawling (*vor* + *dat* with); (*von Waffen*) to be bristling (*von, vor* + *dat* with); **von Schmutz** ~ to be thick *or* covered with dirt; **sie/das Kleid strotzte von Juwelen** she/the dress was dripping with jewellery; ~**de Euter** brimming udders.

strubb(e)lig *adj* (*inf*) Haar, Fell tousled.

Strubbelkopf *m* (*inf*) tousled hair; (*Mensch*) tousle-head. **einen** ~ **haben, ein** ~ **sein** to have tousled hair.

Strudel *m* -s, - (**a**) (*lit, fig*) whirlpool; (*von Ereignissen, Vergnügen*) whirl. (**b**) (*Cook*) strudel.

strudeln *vi* to whirl, to swirl.

Strudelteig *m* (*esp S Ger, Aus: Cook*) strudel pastry.

Struktur *f* structure; (*von Stoff etc*) texture; (*Webart*) weave.

Strukturalismus *m* structuralism.

strukturalistisch *adj* structuralist. **etw** ~ **interpretieren** to interpret sth according to structuralist methods.

Struktur|analyse *f* structural analysis.

strukturell *adj* structural.

Strukturformel *f* (*Chem*) structural formula.

strukturieren* *vt* to structure.

Strukturierung *f* structuring.

Struktur-: ~**krise** *f* structural crisis; ~**politik** *f* structural policy; ~**reform** *f* structural reform; ~**wandel** *m* structural change (*gen* in).

Strumpf *m* -(e)s, ⸚e (**a**) sock; (*Damen~*) stocking. **ein Paar ⸚e** a pair of socks/stockings; **auf** ~**en** in one's stockinged feet; **sich auf die ⸚e machen** (*inf*) to get going (*inf*). (**b**) (*Spar-*) **sein Geld im** ~ **haben** = to keep one's money under the mattress. (**c**) (*Glüh~*) mantle.

Strumpf-: ~**band** *nt* garter; ~**fabrik** *f* hosiery factory; ~**geschäft** *nt* hosiery shop (*esp Brit*) *or* store (*esp US*); ~**halter** *m* -s, - suspender (*Brit*), garter (*US*); ~**haltergürtel** *m* suspender belt (*Brit*), garter belt (*US*); ~**hose** *f* tights *pl* (*esp Brit*) *or* panty-hose; **panty-hose**; **eine** ~**hose** a pair of tights (*esp Brit*) *or* panty-hose; ~**waren** *pl* hosiery *sing*; ~**wirker(in** *f*) *m* -s, - hosiery worker.

Strunk *m* -(e)s, ⸚e stalk.

struppig *adj* unkempt; Tier shaggy.

Struwwelkopf [ˈʃtrʊvl-] *m* (*inf*) *siehe* **Strubbelkopf**.

Struwwelpeter [ˈʃtrʊvl-] *m* tousle-head. **der** ~ (*Liter*) shock-headed Peter, Struwwelpeter.

Strychnin [ʃtrʏçˈniːn, st-] *nt* -s, *no pl* strychnine.

Stubben *m* -s, - (*N Ger*) tree stump.

Stübchen *nt dim of* **Stube** little room.

Stube *f* -, -n (*dated, dial*) room; (*dial: Wohnzimmer*) lounge; (*in Kaserne*) barrack room; (*Sch*) study; (*Schlafsaal*) dormitory. ~ **und Küche** (*dial*) one-room flat (*Brit*) *or* apartment with kitchen; **auf der** ~ (*Mil*) in one's barrack room, in one's quarters; (*Sch*) in one's study/dormitory; **die gute** ~ the parlour (*dated*); (*immer*) **herein in die gute** ~! (*hum inf*) come right in; **in der** ~ **hocken** (*inf*) to sit around indoors.

Stuben-: ~**älteste(r)** *mf* (*Mil*) senior soldier in a/the barrack room; (*Sch*) study/dormitory prefect; ~**appell** *m* (*Mil*) barrack room inspection; (*Sch*) study/dormitory inspection; ~**arrest** *m* confinement to one's room *or* (*Mil*) quarters; ~**arrest haben** to be confined to one's room/quarters; ~**dienst** *m* (*Mil*) fatigue duty, barrack room duty; (*Sch*) study/dormitory cleaning duty; ~**dienst haben** to be on fatigue duty *etc*; ~**fliege** *f* (common) housefly; ~**gelehrte(r)** *mf* (*pej*) armchair scholar; ~**hocker** *m* -s, - (*pej inf*) house-mouse (*inf*); ~**kamerad** *m* (*esp Mil*) room-mate; ~**mädchen** *nt* (*dated*) chambermaid; **s~rein** *adj* Katze, Hund house-trained; (*hum*) Witz clean; ~**vogel** *m* cage bird.

Stübe(r)l *nt* -s, - (*Aus*) small room.

Stück *m* -(e)s, *no pl* stucco; (*zur Zimmerverzierung*) moulding.

Stück *nt* -(e)s, -e *or* (*nach Zahlenangaben*) - (**a**) piece; (*von Vieh, Wild*) head; (*von Zucker*) lump; (*Ausstellungs~ auch*) item; (*Seife*) bar, cake; (*von abgegrenztem Land*) plot. **ich nehme fünf** ~ I'll take five; **12** ~ (*Eier*) twelve *or* a dozen (eggs); **20** ~ **Vieh** 20 head of cattle; **sechs** ~ **von diesen Apfelsinen** six of these oranges; **12** ~, ~**er 12** 12 all told; **10 Pfennig das** ~, **pro** ~ 10 Pfennig each; **im** *or* **am** ~ in one piece; **Käse, Wurst auch** unsliced; **aus einem** ~ in one piece; ~ **für** ~ (*ein Exemplar nach dem andern*) one by one; **etw nach** ~ **verkaufen** to sell sth by the piece; **bezahlt werden to do** piecework; **das größte/beste** ~ (*Fleisch etc*) the biggest/best piece (of meat *etc*); **ein** ~ **Garten** a patch of garden; **das ist unser bestes** ~ (*hum*) that is our pride and joy.

(**b**) (*Teil, Abschnitt*) piece, bit; (*von Buch, Rede, Reise etc*) part; (*von Straße etc*) stretch. **ich möchte nur ein kleines** ~ I only want a little bit *or* a small piece; ~ **für** ~ (*einen Teil um den andern*) bit by bit; **in** ~**e gehen/zerspringen** to be broken/

smashed to pieces; **etw in** ~**e schlagen** to smash sth to pieces *or* smithereens; **etw in** ~**e reißen** to tear sth to pieces *or* shreds; **sich für jdn in** ~**e reißen lassen** to do anything for sb; **ein** ~ **Heimat** a piece of home; **in allen** ~**en** on every matter; **übereinstimmen auch** in every detail; **in vielen** ~**en** on many matters *or* things; **ich komme ein** ~ (**des Weges**) **mit** I'll come some *or* part of the way with you.

(**c**) **ein** ~ **spazierengehen** to go for a walk; **ein gutes** ~ **weiterkommen** to make considerable progress *or* headway; **ein schweres** ~ **Arbeit** a tough job; **ein schönes** ~ **Geld** (*inf*) a tidy sum, a pretty penny (*inf*); **das ist (doch) ein starkes** ~! (*inf*) that's a bit much *or* thick (*inf*); **große** ~**e auf jdn halten** to think much *or* highly of sb, to have a high opinion of sb; **große** ~**e auf etw** (*acc*) **halten** to be very proud of sth; **aus freien** ~**en** of one's own free will.

(**d**) (*Fin*) share.

(**e**) (*Bühnen~*) play; (*Musik~*) piece.

(**f**) (*inf: Mensch*) beggar (*inf*), so-and-so (*inf*). **mein bestes** ~ (*hum inf*) my pride and joy; **ein** ~ **Dreck** *or* **Mist** (*sl*) a bitch (*inf*), a cow (*inf*); (*Mann*) a bastard (*sl*).

Stück-: ~**akkord** *m*, ~**arbeit** *f* piecework; ~**arbeiter** *m* pieceworker.

Stuck|arbeit *f* stucco work *no pl*; (*in Zimmer*) moulding.

Stückchen *nt dim of* **Stück** (a, b, e).

Stuckdecke *f* stucco(ed) ceiling.

stücke(l)n 1 *vt* to patch. **2** *vi* to patch it together.

stucken *vi* (*Aus inf*) to swot (*inf*), to cram (*inf*).

Stückeschreiber *m* dramatist, playwright.

Stückfaß *nt* (*Weinmaß*) measure of wine containing 1,200 litres.

Stück-: ~**gut** *nt* (*Rail*) parcel service; **etw als** ~**gut schicken** to send sth as a parcel; ~**leistung** *f* production capacity; ~**lohn** *m* piece(work) rate; ~**notierung** *f* quotation per unit; ~**preis** *m* unit price; (*Comm auch*) price for one; **s~weise** *adv* bit by bit, little by little; **s~weise verkaufen** to sell individually; ~**werk** *nt, no pl* incomplete *or* unfinished work; ~**werk sein/bleiben** to be/remain incomplete *or* unfinished; **das Buch ist ein** ~**werk einzelner Gedanken** the book is a patchwork of individual thoughts; ~**zahl** *f* number of pieces *or* items; ~**zeit** *f* production time per piece *or* item.

stud. *abbr of* **studiosus**. **stud. med./phil.** *etc* student of medicine/humanities *etc*.

Student *m* student; (*Aus: Schüler*) schoolboy; (*einer bestimmten Schule*) pupil.

Studenten-: ~**ausweis** *m* student card; ~**bewegung** *f* student movement; ~**blume** *f* French marigold; ~**bude** *f* (*inf*) student digs *pl*; ~**ehe** *f* student marriage; ~**futter** *nt* nuts and raisins; ~**gemeinde** *f* student religious society; ~**heim** *nt* hall of residence, student hostel; ~**leben** *nt* student life; ~**liebe** *f* student romance; ~**lied** *nt* student song; ~**lokal** *nt* students' pub; ~**pfarrer** *m* university/college chaplain; ~**rabatt** *m* student discount; ~**revolte** *f* student revolt; ~**schaft** *f* students *pl*, student body; ~**sprache** *f* student slang; ~**verbindung** *f* students' society *or* association; (*für Männer auch*) fraternity (*US*); (*für Frauen auch*) sorority (*US*); ~**werk** *nt* student administration; ~**wohnheim** *nt* hall of residence, student hostel.

Studentin *f* student; (*Aus: Schülerin*) schoolgirl; (*einer bestimmten Schule*) pupil.

studentisch *adj attr* student *attr*.

Studie [ˈʃtuːdiə] *f* study (*über* + *acc* of); (*Entwurf auch*) sketch; (*Abhandlung*) essay (*über* + *acc* on).

Studien- [ˈʃtuːdiən-] : ~**abbrecher(in** *f*) *m* -s, - student who fails to complete his/her course of study; ~**abschluß** *m* completion of a course of study; **Volkswirtschaftler mit** ~**abschluß** graduate economist; **die Universität ohne** ~**abschluß verlassen** to leave university without graduating; ~**assessor** *m* graduate teacher who has recently completed his/her training; ~**aufenthalt** *m* study visit ~**beratung** *f* course guidance service; ~**buch** *nt* book in which the courses one has attended are entered; ~**direktor** *m* (*von Fachschule*) principal; (*in Gymnasium*) ~ deputy principal; ~**fach** *nt* subject; ~**fahrt** *f* study trip; (*Sch*) educational trip; ~**förderung** *f* study grant; (*an Universität*) university grant; ~**freund** *m* university/college friend; ~**gang** *m* course of studies; ~**gebühren** *pl* tuition fees *pl*; **s~halber** *adv* for the purpose of study *or* studying; ~**inhalte** *pl* course contents *pl*; ~**jahr** *nt* academic year; ~**jahre** *pl* university/college years *pl*; ~**plan** *m* course of study; ~**platz** *m* university/college place; **ein** ~**platz in Medizin** a place to study medicine; ~**professor** *m* (*S Ger, obs*) secondary school *or* high school (*US*) teacher; ~**rat** *m*, ~**rätin** *f* teacher at a secondary school; ~**referendar** *m* student teacher; ~**reform** *f* university/college reform; ~**reise** *f siehe* ~**fahrt**; ~**zeit** *f* (**a**) student days *pl*; (**b**) (*Dauer*) duration of a/one's course of studies; ~**zeitbegrenzung** *f* limitation on the length of courses of studies; ~**zweck** *m* **für** ~**zwecke, zu** ~**zwecken** for the purposes of study, for study purposes.

studieren* 1 *vi* to study; (*Student sein*) to be a student, to be at university/college, to be at school (*US inf*). **ich studiere an der Universität Bonn** I am (a student) at Bonn University; **nicht jeder kann** ~ not everyone can go to university/college; **wo haben Sie studiert?** what university/college did you go to?; **bei jdm** ~ to study under sb; **jdn** ~ **lassen** to send sb to university/college.

2 *vt* to study; (*an Uni auch*) to read; (*genau betrachten*) to scrutinize. **sie hat vier Semester Jura studiert** she has studied law for two years.

Studierende(r) *mf decl as adj* student.

Studierstube *f* (*dated, dial*) study.

studiert *adj* (*inf*) educated. ~ **sein** to have been at university/college; **ein S~er/eine S~e** an intellectual.

Studierzimmer *nt* study.

Studiker m -s, - (dated hum) student.
Studio nt -s, -s studio.
Studiobühne f studio theatre.
Studiosus m -s, **Studiosi** (old, hum) student.
Studium nt study; (Hochschul~) studies pl; (genaue Betrachtung auch) scrutiny. sein ~ beginnen or aufnehmen (form) to begin one's studies, to go to university/college; das ~ hat fünf Jahre gedauert the course of study lasted five years; während seines ~s while he is/was etc a student or at university/college; er ist noch im ~ he is still a student; das ~ der Mathematik, das mathematische ~ the study of mathematics, mathematical studies pl; archäologische/psychologische Studien betreiben to study archaeology/psychology; er war gerade beim ~ des Börsenberichts, als ... he was just studying the stock exchange report when ...; zu kann man seine Studien machen it's very enlightening; seine Studien zu etw machen to study sth.
Studium generale nt --, no pl general course of studies. ein ~ machen to do a general degree.
Stufe f -, -n (a) step; (Gelände~ auch) terrace; (Mus: Ton~) degree; (bei Rock etc) tier; (zum Kürzen) tuck; (im Haar) layer. mehrere ~n auf einmal nehmen to run up the stairs two or three at a time.
(b) (fig) stage; (Niveau) level; (Rang) grade; (Gram: Steigerungs~) degree. eine ~ höher als ... a step up from ...; die höchste/tiefste ~ the height or pinnacle/the depths pl; mit jdm auf gleicher ~ stehen to be on a level with sb; mit jdm/etw auf die gleiche or eine ~ stellen to put or place sb/oneself on a level or par with sb/sth.
stufen vt Schüler, Preise to grade; Haare to layer; Land etc to terrace.
Stufen-: ~barren m asymmetric bar; ~dach nt stepped roof; s~förmig 1 adj (lit) stepped; Landschaft terraced; (fig) gradual; 2 adv (lit) in steps; angelegt in terraces; (fig) in stages, gradually; ~leiter f (fig) ladder (gen to); s~los adj Schaltung, Übergang direct; (fig: gleitend) smooth; ~ordnung f successive order; ~plan m graduated plan (zu for); ~rakete f multistage rocket; ~schalter m (Elec) sequence switch; ~tarif m (Econ) graduated tariff; s~weise 1 adv step by step, gradually; 2 adj attr gradual.
stufig adj stepped; Land etc terraced; Haar layered. das Haar ~ schneiden to layer sb's hair.
-stufig adj suf drei~e Rakete three-stage rocket.
Stufung f gradation.
Stuhl m -(e)s, -e (a) chair. ist dieser ~ noch frei? is this chair taken?, is this somebody's chair?; sich zwischen zwei ~e setzen, zwischen zwei ~en sitzen (fig) to fall between two stools; ich wäre fast vom ~ gefallen (inf) I nearly fell off my chair (inf); jdm den ~ vor die Tür setzen (fig) to kick sb out (inf); das haut einen vom ~ (sl) it knocks you sideways (inf).
(b) (Königs~) throne. der Apostolische or Heilige or Päpstliche ~ the Apostolic or Holy or Papal See; der ~ Petri the See of Rome; vor den ~ des Richters treten to go before the judge; (vor Gott) to go before one's Maker; vor Gottes ~ gerufen werden to be called before one's Maker.
(c) (Lehramt) chair (gen of, für of, in).
(d) (~gang) bowel movement; (Kot) stool. ~ haben/keinen ~ haben to have had/not to have had a bowel movement.
Stuhl-: ~bein nt chair leg; ~drang m (form) urgent need to empty the bowels; ~entleerung f (form) evacuation of the bowels; ~gang m, no pl bowel movement; regelmäßig ~gang haben to have regular bowels; ~gang/keinen ~gang haben to have had/not to have had a bowel movement; ~lehne f back of a chair; ~verhaltung f (form) retention of faeces.
Stuka ['ʃtuːka, 'ʃtuka] m -s, -s abbr of **Sturzkampfflugzeug** stuka, dive bomber.
Stukkateur [ʃtukaˈtøːɐ] m plasterer (who works with stucco).
Stukkatur f stucco (work), ornamental plasterwork.
Stulle f -, -n (N Ger) slice of bread and butter; sandwich.
Stulpe f -, -n cuff; (von Handschuh) gauntlet.
stülpen vt den Kragen nach oben ~ to turn up one's collar; etw auf/über etw (acc) ~ to put sth on/over sth; etw nach innen/außen ~ to turn sth to the inside/outside; sich (dat) den Hut auf den Kopf ~ to clap or slap on one's hat.
Stulpen-: ~handschuh m gauntlet; ~stiefel m top boot.
Stülpnase f snub or turned-up nose.
stumm adj (a) (lit, fig) dumb. die ~e Kreatur (geh) the dumb creatures pl; ~ vor Schmerz in silent agony; ~ vor Zorn speechless with anger; ~er Diener (Servierwagen) dumb waiter; (Kleiderständer) valet; jdn ~ machen (töten) to silence sb.
(b) (schweigend) mute; Anklage, Blick, Gebet auch silent. sie sah mich ~ an she looked at me without speaking or without saying a word; ~ bleiben to stay silent; siehe Fisch.
(c) (Gram) mute, silent.
(d) Rolle non-speaking; Film, Szene silent.
Stummel m -s, - (a) (Zigatten~, Zigarren~) end, stub, butt; (Kerzen~) stub; (von Gliedmaßen, Zahn) stump. (b) (Stummelschwanz) dock.
Stummel-: ~pfeife f short-stemmed pipe; ~wort nt abbreviation; (Akronym) acronym.
Stumme(r) mf decl as adj dumb or mute person. die ~n the dumb.
Stummfilm m silent film.
Stummfilmzeit f silent film era.
Stumpen m -s, - cheroot.
Stümper(in f) m -s, - (pej) (a) amateur. (b) (Pfuscher) bungler.
Stümperei f (pej) (a) amateur work. (b) (Pfuscherei) bungling; (stümperhafte Arbeit) botched or bungled job.
stümperhaft adj (pej) (nicht fachmännisch) amateurish;

(schlecht auch) botched no adv, bungled no adv.
stümpern vi (auf Klavier, bei Schach etc) to play in an amateurish way (auf + dat on). bei einer Arbeit ~ to do a job in an amateur way; er stümpert nur he's just an amateur; (pfuschen) he's just a bungler.
stumpf adj (a) blunt; Nase snub, turned-up. **Rhabarber macht die Zähne** ~ rhubarb sets one's teeth on edge.
(b) (fig) Haar, Farbe, Mensch dull; Blick, Sinne auch dulled. ~ vor sich hin brüten to sit brooding impassively; einer Sache gegenüber ~ sein to remain impassive about sth.
(c) (Math) Winkel obtuse; Kegel etc truncated.
(d) (Poet) Reim masculine.
Stumpf m -(e)s, -e stump; (Bleistift~) stub. etw mit ~ und Stiel ausrotten to eradicate sth root and branch.
Stumpfheit f (a) bluntness. (b) (fig) dullness.
Stumpf-: ~nase f (dial) snub nose; ~sinn m mindlessness; (Langweiligkeit) monotony, tedium; das ist doch ~sinn that's a tedious business; s~sinnig adj mindless; (langweilig) monotonous, tedious; ~sinnigkeit f siehe ~sinn; s~wink(e)lig adj (Math) Winkel, Dreieck obtuse.
Stündchen nt dim of Stunde. ein paar ~ an hour or so.
Stunde f -, -n (a) hour. eine viertel/halbe/dreiviertel ~ a quarter of an hour/half an hour/three-quarters of an hour; in einer dreiviertel ~ in three-quarters of an hour; eine ganze/gute/knappe ~ a whole/good hour/barely an hour; eine halbe ~ Pause a half-hour break, a break of half an hour; eine ~ entfernt an hour away; eine Reise von zwei ~n a two-hour journey; jede ~ every hour; ~ um ~, ~n um ~n hour after hour; von ~ zu ~ hourly, from hour to hour; sein Befinden wird von ~ zu ~ schlechter his condition is becoming worse hour by hour or worse every hour; acht-/~n-Tag eight-hour day; 90 Meilen in der ~ 90 miles per or an hour.
(b) (Augenblick, Zeitpunkt) time. zu dieser ~ at this/that time; zu jeder ~ at any time; zu später ~ at a late hour; bis zur ~ up to the present moment, as yet; von Stund an (old) from henceforth; die ~ X (Mil) the impending onslaught; sich auf die ~ X vorbereiten (fig) to prepare for the inevitable; eine schwache/schwere ~ a moment of weakness/a time of difficulty; seine ~ kommen or nahen fühlen (geh: Tod) to feel one's hour (of death) approaching; seine ~ hat geschlagen (fig) his hour has come; ihre (schwere) ~ ist gekommen (Entbindung) her time has come; seine schwerste ~ his darkest hour; die ~ der Entscheidung/Wahrheit the moment of decision/truth.
(c) (Unterricht) lesson; (Unterrichts~ auch) class, period. sonnabends haben wir vier ~n on Saturday we have four lessons; in der zweiten ~ haben wir Latein in the second period we have Latin; ~n geben/nehmen to give/have or take lessons.
stunden vt jdm etw ~ to give sb time to pay sth; jdm etw zwei Wochen/bis Mittwoch ~ to give sb two weeks/until Wednesday to pay sth.
Stunden-: ~buch nt (Hist Liter) book of hours; ~frau f (dated) charwoman (Brit) (paid by the hour); ~gebet nt prayer said at any of the canonical hours eg matins, vespers; ~geschwindigkeit f speed per hour; eine ~geschwindigkeit von 90 km a speed of 90 km per hour; ~glas nt hour-glass; ~hotel nt hotel where rooms are rented by the hour; ~kilometer pl kilometres per or an hour pl.
stundenlang 1 adj lasting several hours. eine ~e Verspätung a delay of several hours; nach ~em Warten after hours of waiting. 2 adv for hours.
Stunden-: ~lohn m hourly wage; ~lohn bekommen to be paid by the hour; ~plan m (Sch) time-table; ~schlag m striking of the hour; s~weise adv (pro Stunde) by the hour; (stündlich) every hour; Kellner s~weise gesucht part-time waiters required; der Patient darf s~weise aufstehen the patient may get up for an hour at a time; ~zeiger m hour-hand.
-stündig adj suf eine halb/zwei~e Fahrt a half-hour/two-hour journey, a journey of half an hour/two hours.
Stündlein nt ein ~ a short while; sein letztes ~ hat geschlagen (stirbt) his last hour has come; (fig inf) he's had it (inf).
stündlich 1 adj hourly. 2 adv hourly, every hour.
-stündlich adv suf zwei/drei~ every two/three hours.
Stundung f deferment of payment.
Stunk m -s, no pl (inf) stink (inf), row (inf). ~ machen to kick up a stink (inf); dann gibt es ~ then there'll be a stink (inf).
stupend adj (geh) astounding, tremendous.
stupfen vt (esp S Ger) siehe stupsen.
stupid(e) adj (geh) mindless.
Stupidität f (geh) mindlessness.
Stups m -es, -e nudge.
stupsen vt to nudge.
Stupsnase f snub nose.
stur adj stolid; (unnachgiebig) obdurate; Nein, Arbeiten dogged; (hartnäckig) pig-headed, stubborn; (querköpfig) cussed. ~ weitermachen/~reden/~gehen etc to carry on regardless or doggedly; er fuhr ~ geradeaus/in der Mitte der Straße he just carried straight on/he just carried on driving in the middle of the road; sich ~ stellen, auf ~ stellen (inf) to dig one's heels in; ein ~er Bock (inf) a pig-headed fellow; ~ wie ein Panzer (inf) bull-headed.
Sturheit f siehe adj stolidness; obdurateness; doggedness; pig-headedness, stubbornness; cussedness.
Sturm m -(e)s, -e (a) (lit, fig) storm; (Orkan auch) gale. in ~ und Regen in wind and rain; das Barometer steht auf ~ (lit) the barometer is indicating stormy weather; (fig) there's a storm brewing; die Ruhe or Stille vor dem ~ the calm before the storm; ein ~ im Wasserglas (fig) a storm in a teacup; ~ läuten to keep one's finger on the doorbell; (Alarm schlagen) to ring or sound the alarm bell; die ~e des Lebens the storms or the ups and downs of life; ein ~ der Begeisterung/des Gelächters a

wave of enthusiasm/roars of laughter; im ~ der Leidenschaft (geh) in the throes of passion; ~ und Drang (Liter) Storm and Stress, Sturm und Drang; (fig) emotion; im ~ und Drang sein (fig) to be going through an emotional phase; „Der ~" "The Tempest".

(b) (Angriff) attack; (Mil auch) assault; (Sport: Stürmerreihe) forward line. etw im ~ nehmen (Mil, fig) to take sth by storm; zum ~ blasen (Mil, fig) to sound the attack; gegen etw ~ laufen (fig) to be up in arms against sth; ein ~ auf die Banken/Aktien a run on the banks/shares; ein ~ auf die Karten/Plätze a rush for tickets/seats; der ~ auf die Festung/Bastille the storming of the stronghold/Bastille; siehe erobern.

Sturm-: ~abteilung f (NS) Storm Troopers pl; ~angriff m (Mil) assault (auf+acc on); ~band nt (Mil) chin-strap; s~bewegt adj stormy, storm-tossed (liter); ~bö f squall; ~bock m (Mil) battering-ram; ~boot nt (Mil) assault boat; ~deck nt hurricane deck.

stürmen 1 vi (a) (Meer) to rage; (Wind auch) to blow; (Sport) to attack; (Mil) to attack, to assault (gegen etw sth).

(b) (Sport) (als Stürmer spielen) to play forward; (angreifen) to attack.

(c) aux sein (rennen) to storm.

2 vi impers to be blowing a gale. es stürmte in ihr (geh) she was in a turmoil.

3 vt (Mil, fig) to storm; Bank etc to make a run on.

Stürmer m -s, - (Sport) forward; (fig: Draufgänger) go-getter (inf). ~ und Dränger (Liter) writer of the Storm and Stress period; (fig) ~ angry young man.

Stürmerreihe f (Sport) forward line.

Sturmesbrausen nt (poet) raging of the storm (liter).

Sturm-: ~fahne f warning flag; (Hist Mil) standard; s~fest adj (lit) stormproof; (fig) steadfast; ~flut f storm tide; s~frei adj (Mil) unassailable; eine s~freie Bude a room where visitors may enter unobserved; das Haus ist s~frei there's open house; ~gepäck nt combat or light pack; s~gepeitscht adj (geh) storm-lashed (liter); ~haube f (a) (Hist) helmet, morion; (b) (Zool) whelk shell; ~hut m (Bot) aconite.

stürmisch adj (a) Meer, Überfahrt rough, stormy; Wetter, Tag blustery; (mit Regen) stormy. **(b)** (fig) tempestuous; (aufregend) Zeit, Jugend stormy, turbulent; Entwicklung rapid; Liebhaber passionate, ardent; Jubel, Beifall tumultuous, frenzied. ~e Heiterkeit gales of laughter; nicht so ~ take it easy.

Sturm-: ~laterne f hurricane lamp; ~lauf m trot; im ~lauf at a trot; ~leiter f scaling ladder; ~reif adj (Mil) s~reif sein to be ripe for attack (für by); etw s~reif machen to lay sth open for attack (für by); ~riemen m chin-strap; ~schaden m storm damage no pl; ~schritt m (Mil, fig) double-quick pace; im ~schritt at the double; ~segel nt storm sail; ~spitze f (Mil, Sport) spearhead; s~stark adj (Sport) eine s~starke Mannschaft a team with a strong forward line; ~trupp m (Mil) assault troop; ~-und-Drang-Zeit f (Liter) Storm and Stress or Sturm und Drang period; ~vogel m petrel; (Albatros) albatross; ~warnung f gale warning; ~wind m whirlwind.

Sturz m -es, ̈e (a) (von from, off, aus out of) fall. einen ~ tun to have a fall. **(b)** (in Temperatur, Preis) drop, fall; (von Börsenkurs) slump. **(c)** (von Regierung, Minister) fall; (durch Coup, von König) overthrow. **(d)** (Archit) lintel. **(e)** (Rad~) camber. **(f)** (S Ger, Aus: Glas~) cover.

Sturz-: ~acker m (Agr) newly ploughed field; ~bach m (lit) fast-flowing stream; (fig) stream, torrent.

stürzen 1 vi aux sein **(a)** to fall (von from, off); (geh: steil abfallen) to plunge; (hervor~) to stream. ins Wasser ~ to plunge into the water; vom Pferd ~ to fall off a/one's horse; er ist schwer or heftig/unglücklich gestürzt he had a heavy/bad fall; die Tränen stürzten ihm aus den Augen (geh) tears streamed from his eyes.

(b) (fig: abgesetzt werden) to fall.

(c) (rennen) to rush, to dash. sie kam ins Zimmer gestürzt she burst or came bursting into the room; jdm in die Arme ~ to fling oneself into sb's arms.

2 vt (a) (werfen) to fling, to hurl; jdn aus dem Fenster ~ to fling or hurl sb out of the window; jdn ins Unglück or Verderben ~ to bring disaster to sb.

(b) (kippen) to turn upside down; Pudding to turn out. „nicht ~!" "this side up"; etw über etw (acc) ~ to put sth over sth.

(c) (absetzen) Regierung, Minister to bring down; (durch Coup) to overthrow; König to depose.

(d) (old) die Kasse ~ to cash up.

(e) (Agr) Acker to plough.

3 vr sich zu Tode ~ to fall to one's death; (absichtlich) to jump to one's death; sich auf jdn/etw ~ to pounce on sb/sth; auf Essen to fall on sth; auf Zeitung etc to grab sth; auf den Feind to attack sb/sth; sich ins Wasser ~ to fling or hurl oneself into the water; (sich ertränken) to drown oneself; sich in die Arbeit ~ to throw oneself into one's work; sich in Schulden ~ to plunge into debt; sich ins Unglück/Verderben ~ to plunge headlong into disaster/ruin; sich ins Vergnügen ~ to fling oneself into a round of pleasure; sich in Unkosten ~ to go to great expense.

Sturz-: ~flug m (nose)dive; etw im ~flug angreifen to dive and attack sth; ~geburt f (Med) precipitate delivery; ~gut nt (form) goods unloaded by tipping; ~helm m crash helmet; ~kampfflugzeug nt dive bomber; ~see f (Naut) breaker.

Stuß m -sses, no pl (inf) nonsense, rubbish (inf), codswallop (Brit inf). was für ein ~ what a load of nonsense etc (inf).

Stutbuch nt studbook.

Stute f -, -n mare.

Stuten-: ~fohlen, ~füllen nt filly; ~zucht f studfarm; (Züchtung) stud farming.

Stütz-: ~apparat m calliper, brace; (für Kopf) collar; ~balken m beam; (in Decke) joist; (quer) crossbeam.

Stütze f -, -n (a) support; (Pfeiler) pillar; (für Wäscheleine etc) prop; (Buch~) rest.

(b) (Halt) support; (Fuß~) foot-rest.

(c) (fig) (Hilfe) help, aid (für to); (Beistand) support; (wichtiger Mensch) mainstay; (dated: Hausgehilfin) (domestic) help. seine Tochter war die ~ seines Alters his daughter was his support in his old age; als ~ für seinen Kreislauf as an aid for or to aid his circulation; die ~n der Gesellschaft the pillars of society.

stutzen¹ vi to stop short; (zögern) to hesitate.

stutzen² vt to trim; Baum auch to prune; Flügel, Ohren, Hecke to clip; Schwanz to dock.

Stutzen m -s, - (a) (Gewehr) carbine. **(b)** (Rohrstück) connecting piece; (Endstück) nozzle. **(c)** (Strumpf) woollen gaiter.

stützen 1 vt (Halt geben) to support; Gebäude, Mauer to shore up; Währung auch to back; (fig: untermauern auch) to back up. einen Verdacht durch etw ~ to back up or support a suspicion with sth; einen Verdacht auf etw (acc) ~ to base or found a suspicion on sth; die Ellbogen auf den Tisch ~ to prop or rest one's elbows on the table; den Kopf in die Hände ~ to hold one's head in one's hands.

2 vr sich auf jdn/etw ~ (lit) to lean on sb/sth; (fig) to count on sb/sth; (Beweise, Verteidigung, Theorie) to be based on sb/sth; können Sie sich auf Fakten ~? can you produce facts to bear out what you're saying?; in seiner Dissertation stützte er sich weitgehend auf diese Theorie he based his thesis closely on this theory.

Stutzer m -s, - (a) (pej) fop, dandy. **(b)** (Mantel) three-quarter length coat.

stutzerhaft adj foppish, dandified.

Stutzertum nt foppishness, dandyism.

Stutzflügel m baby grand (piano).

Stützgewebe nt (Med) stroma (spec).

stutzig adj pred ~ werden (argwöhnisch) to become or grow suspicious; (verwundert) to begin to wonder; jdn ~ machen to make sb suspicious; das hat mich ~ gemacht that made me wonder; (argwöhnisch) that made me suspicious.

Stütz-: ~korsett nt support corset; ~mauer f retaining wall; ~pfeiler m supporting pillar or column; (von Brücke auch) pier; ~punkt m (Mil, fig) base; (Ausbildungsstätte) centre; ~rad nt (an Fahrrad) stabilizer; ~stange f supporting pole.

Stützung f support.

Stützungs-: ~käufe pl purchases to support share prices, currency rate etc; ~maßnahme f supporting measure.

StVO abbr of Straßenverkehrsordnung.

stygisch ['ʃtyːgɪʃ, st-] adj (Myth, liter) Stygian.

Styling ['stailɪŋ] nt -s, no pl styling.

Styx [ʃtyks, st-] m - (Myth) Styx.

s.u. abbr of siehe unten.

SU [ɛs'uː] f - abbr of Sowjetunion.

Suada, Suade f -, Suaden (liter) torrent of words.

Suaheli¹ [zua'heːli] m -(s), -(s) Swahili.

Suaheli² [zua'heːli] nt -(s), no pl (Sprache) Swahili.

sub-, Sub- in cpds sub-.

sub|altern adj (pej) Stellung, Beamter subordinate; Gesinnung obsequious, subservient; (unselbständig) unselfreliant.

Sub|alternbeamte(r) m subordinate official; (pej) underling.

Subdominante f -, -n (Mus) subdominant.

Subjekt nt -(e)s, -e a subject. **(b)** (pej: Mensch) customer (inf), character (inf).

subjektiv adj subjective.

Subjektivismus [-'vɪsmus] m, no pl (Philos) subjectivism.

Subjektivität [-vɪ'tɛːt] f subjectivity.

Subjektsatz m (Gram) noun clause as subject.

Sub-: ~kontinent m subcontinent; ~kultur f subculture; s~kutan adj (Med) subcutaneous.

sublim adj (geh) sublime, lofty; Einfühlungsvermögen, Charakter refined; Interpretation eloquent.

Sublimat nt (Chem) (a) (Niederschlag) sublimate. **(b)** (Quecksilberverbindung) mercuric chloride.

Sublimation f (Chem) sublimation.

sublimieren* vt (a) (Psych) to sublimate. **(b)** (Chem) to sublimate, to sublime.

Sublimierung f sublimation.

Sublimität f (geh) siehe sublim sublimeness, loftiness; refinement; eloquence.

submarin adj marine.

Sub|ordination f subordination.

sub|ordinierend adj subordinating.

subsidiär adj subsidiary.

Subskribent(in f) m subscriber.

subskribieren* vti (auf) etw (acc) ~ to subscribe to sth.

Subskription f subscription (gen, auf+acc to).

Subskriptionspreis m subscription price.

Subspezies ['zup-speːtsiːs] f subspecies.

substantiell [zupstan'tsiel] adj (a) (Philos) (stofflich) material; (wesenhaft) essential.

(b) (fig geh: bedeutsam, inhaltlich) fundamental.

(c) (nahrhaft) substantial, solid.

Substantiv ['zupstantiːf] nt -s, -e or (rare) -a noun.

substantivieren* [zupstanti'viːrən] vt to nominalize.

substantivisch ['zupstantiːvɪʃ] adj nominal.

Substanz [zup'stants] f (a) substance; (Wesen) essence. die ~ des Volkes the (essential) character of the people; etw in seiner ~ ~ treffen to affect the substance of sth. **(b)** (Fin) capital assets pl. von der ~ zehren or leben to live on one's capital.

Substanz-: s~los adj insubstantial; s~reich adj solid; Aufsatz auch meaty (inf); ~verlust m loss of volume; (Gewichtsver-

lust) loss of weight; (*fig*) loss of significance *or* importance.

substituierbar [zʊpstituˈiːɐ̯baːɐ̯] *adj* (*geh*) ist A durch B ~? can B be substituted for A?, can A be replaced by B?

substituieren* [zʊpstituˈiːrən] *vt* (*geh*) A durch B ~ to substitute B for A, to replace A with B.

Substitut(in *f*) [zʊpstiˈtuːt(ɪn)] *m* -en, -en deputy *or* assistant departmental manager.

Substitution [zʊpstituˈtsjoːn] *f* (*geh*) die ~ von A durch B the substitution of B for A, the replacement of A by B.

Substrat [zʊpˈstraːt] *nt* substratum.

subsumieren* *vti* to subsume (*unter* +*dat* to).

Subsumtion [zʊpzʊmˈtsjoːn] *f* (*geh*) subsumption (*form*).

subsumtiv *adj* (*geh*) subsumptive (*form*).

subtil *adj* (*geh*) subtle.

Subtilität *f* (*geh*) subtlety.

Subtrahend [zʊptraˈhɛnt] *m* -en, -en (*Math*) subtrahend.

subtrahieren* [zʊptraˈhiːrən] *vti* to subtract.

Subtraktion *f* subtraction.

Subtraktionszeichen *nt* subtraction sign.

Subtropen [ˈzʊptroːpn̩] *pl* subtropics *pl*.

subtropisch [ˈzʊptroːpɪʃ] *adj* subtropical.

Subvention [zʊpvɛnˈtsjoːn] *f* subsidy; (*von Regierung, Behörden auch*) subvention.

subventionieren* [zʊpvɛntsjoˈniːrən] *vt* to subsidize.

Subversion [zʊpvɛrˈzjoːn] *f* (*Pol*) subversion.

subversiv [zʊpvɛrˈziːf] *adj* subversive. sich ~ betätigen to engage in subversive activities.

Such-: ~aktion *f* search operation; ~anzeige *f* missing person/dog *etc* report; eine ~anzeige aufgeben to report sb/sth missing; ~bild *nt* (*form*) searching image; (*Rätsel*) picture puzzle; ~dienst *m* missing persons tracing service.

Suche *f* -, *no pl* search (*nach* for). auf die ~ nach jdm/etw gehen, sich auf die ~ nach jdm/etw machen to go in search of sb/sth; auf der ~ nach etw sein to be looking for sth.

-suche *f in cpds* auf ...~ sein to be looking for a ...

suchen 1 *vt* (a) to look for; (*stärker, intensiv*) to search for. Abenteuer ~ to go out in search of adventure; die Gefahr ~ to look for *or* seek danger; sich (*dat*) einen Mann/eine Frau ~ to look for a husband/wife (for oneself); Verkäufer(in) gesucht sales person wanted; Streit/Ärger (mit jdm) ~ to be looking for trouble/a quarrel (with sb); Schutz vor etw (*dat*) ~ to seek shelter from sth; etw zu tun ~ (*geh*) to seek *or* strive to do sth; was suchst du hier? what are you doing here?; du hast hier nichts zu ~ you have no business being here; er sucht in allem etwas he always has to see a meaning in everything; seinesgleichen ~ to be unparalleled.

(b) (*wünschen, streben nach*) to seek; (*versuchen auch*) to strive, to try. er sucht, die tragischen Erlebnisse zu vergessen he is trying to forget the tragic events; sein Recht/seinen Vorteil ~ to be out for one's rights/one's own advantage; ein Gespräch ~ to try to have a talk.

2 *vi* to search, to hunt. nach etw ~ to look for sth; (*stärker*) to search *or* hunt for sth. nach Worten ~ to search for words; (*sprachlos sein*) to be at a loss for words; such! (*zu Hund*) seek!, find!; gesucht! wanted (*wegen* for); suchet, so werdet ihr finden! (*Bibl*) seek and ye shall find (*Bibl*).

Sucher *m* -s, - (a) (*geh*) seeker. (b) (*Phot*) viewfinder; (*Astron*) finder.

Sucherei *f* (*inf*) searching.

Such-: ~kind *nt* child separated from its parents in war and registered with the Red Cross tracing service; ~mannschaft *f* search party; ~meldung *f* SOS message; (*von* ~dienst) missing person announcement; ~scheinwerfer *m* searchlight.

Sucht *f* -, ̈-e addiction (*nach* to); (*fig*) obsession (*nach* with). eine krankhafte ~ haben, etw zu tun (*fig*) to be obsessed with doing sth; das kann zur ~ werden you'll get *or* become addicted to that; das Trinken ist bei ihm zur ~ geworden he has become addicted to drink; an einer ~ leiden to be an addict.

-sucht *f in cpds* Drogen-/Trink~ addiction to drugs/drink.

süchtig *adj* addicted (*nach* to). von *or* nach etw ~ werden/sein to get *or* become/be addicted to sth; ~ machen (*Droge*) to be addictive; davon wird man nicht ~ that's not addictive.

Süchtige(r) *mf decl as adj* addict.

Süchtigkeit *f* addiction (*nach* to).

Suchtmittel *nt* addictive drug.

Sud *m* -(e)s, -e liquid; (*esp von Fleisch, für Suppe*) stock. der ~ des Gemüses/der Kartoffeln/des Fleisches the vegetable water/potato water/meat stock.

Süd *m* -(e)s, (*rare*) -e (a) (*Naut, Met, liter*) south. aus *or* von/nach ~ from/to the south. (b) (*liter: Wind*) south wind, southerly (wind).

Süd- *in cpds* (*in Ländernamen, politisch*) South; (*geographisch auch*) the South of ..., Southern; ~afrika *nt* South Africa; ~amerika *nt* South America.

Sudan [zuˈdaːn, ˈzuːdan] *m* -s der ~ the Sudan.

Sudaner(in *f*) *m* -s, -, **Sudanese** *m* -n, -n, **Sudanesin** *f* Sudanese.

sudanesisch, sudanisch *adj* Sudanese.

Süd-: s~deutsch *adj* South German; *Dialekt, Spezialität, Mentalität auch* Southern German; die ~deutschen the South Germans; ~deutschland *nt* South(ern) Germany, the South of Germany.

Sudelei *f* (*geschrieben*) scrawling; (*gezeichnet*) daubing; (*an Mauern etc*) graffiti.

sudeln *vti* (*schreiben*) to scrawl; (*zeichnen*) to daub.

Süden *m* -s, *no pl* south; (*von Land*) South. aus dem ~, vom ~ her from the south; gegen *or* gen (*liter*) *or* nach ~ south(wards), to the south; nach ~ hin to the south; im ~ der Stadt/des Landes in the south of the town/country; im tiefen ~ in the deep *or* far south; weiter *or* tiefer im ~ further south; im

~ Frankreichs in the South of France.

Süd|england *nt* the South of England.

Sudeten *pl* (*Geog*) die ~ the Sudeten (land).

Sudetenland *nt* das ~ the Sudetenland.

Süd-: ~europa *nt* Southern Europe; ~frankreich *nt* the South of France; ~früchte *pl* citrus and tropical fruit(s *pl*).

Sudhaus *nt* (*in Brauerei*) brewing room.

Süd-: ~italien *nt* Southern Italy; ~küste *f* south(ern) coast; die ~küste Englands the south coast of England; ~lage *f* southern aspect; ~länder *m* -s, - southerner; (*Italiener, Spanier etc*) Mediterranean *or* Latin type; s~ländisch *adj* southern; (*italienisch, spanisch etc*) Mediterranean, Latin; *Temperament* Latin.

Südler(in *f*) *m* -s, - scrawler; (*von Bild*) dauber.

südlich 1 *adj* (a) southern; *Kurs, Wind, Richtung* southerly. der ~e Polarkreis the Antarctic Circle; der ~e Wendekreis the Tropic of Capricorn; 52 Grad ~er Breite 52 degrees south; ~es Eismeer Antarctic Ocean.

(b) (*mediterran*) Mediterranean, Latin; *Temperament* Latin.

2 *adv* (to the) south. ~ von Wien (gelegen) (to the) south of Vienna; es liegt ~er *or* weiter ~ it is further (to the) south.

3 *prep* +*gen* (to the) south of.

Südlicht *nt* southern lights *pl*, aurora australis.

Süd|ost *m* (a) (*Met, Naut, liter*) south-east, sou'-east (*Naut*). aus *or* von ~ from the south-east; nach ~ to the south-east, south-east(wards). (b) (*liter: Wind*) south-east(erly) (wind), sou'-easterly (*Naut*).

Süd|ost- *in cpds* south-east; (*bei Namen*) South-East.

Süd|osten *m* south-east; (*von Land*) South East. aus *or* von ~ from the south-east; nach ~ to the south-east, south-east(wards).

Süd|ost|europa *nt* South-East(ern) Europe.

süd|östlich 1 *adj* *Gegend* south-eastern; *Wind* south-east(erly). 2 *adv* (to the) south-east. 3 *prep* +*gen* (to the) south-east of.

Süd-: ~pol *m* South Pole; ~polargebiet *nt* Antarctic (region), area of the South Pole; ~polarmeer *nt* Antarctic Ocean; ~polexpedition *f* South Pole *or* Antarctic expedition; ~see *f* South Seas *pl*, South Pacific; ~seeinsulaner *m* South Sea Islander; ~seite *f* south(ern) side; (*von Berg*) south(ern) face; ~slawe *m* Yugoslav; ~staat *m* southern state.

Südsüd-: ~ost *m* (a) (*Naut, Met, liter*) south-south-east, sou'-sou'-east (*Naut*). (b) (*liter: Wind*) sou'-sou'-easterly; ~osten *m* south-south-east, sou'-sou'-east (*Naut*); s~östlich *adj* south-south-east(erly) (*Naut*); ~west *m* (a) (*Naut, Met, liter*) south-south-west, sou'-sou'-west (*Naut*); (b) (*liter: Wind*) sou'-sou'-westerly; ~westen *m* south-south-west, sou'-sou'-west (*Naut*); s~westlich *adj* south-south-west(erly), sou'-sou'-west(erly) (*Naut*).

Südtirol *nt* South(ern) Tyrol.

südwärts *adv* south(wards). der Wind dreht ~ the wind is moving round to the south.

Südwein *m* Mediterranean wine.

Südwest *m* (a) (*Naut, Met, liter*) south-west. aus ~ from the south-west. (b) (*liter: Wind*) south-west(erly) wind, south-wester(ly), sou'-wester (*Naut*).

Südwest- *in cpds* south-west; (*bei Namen*) South-West.

Südwesten *m* south-west; (*von Land*) South West. aus *or* von ~ from the south-west; nach ~ to the south-west, south-west(wards).

Südwester *m* -s, - (*Hut*) sou'wester.

südwestlich 1 *adj* *Gegend* south-western; *Wind* south-west(erly). 2 *adv* (to the) south-west. 3 *prep* +*gen* (to the) south-west of.

Südwind *m* south wind.

Suez-Kanal *m* Suez Canal.

Suff *m* -(e)s, *no pl* (*inf*) dem ~ verfallen to hit the bottle (*inf*); dem ~ ergeben *or* verfallen sein to be on the bottle (*inf*); etw im ~ sagen to say sth when one is tight (*inf*) *or* plastered (*sl*).

Süffel *m* -s, - (*inf*) tippler (*inf*).

süffeln *vi* (*inf*) to tipple (*inf*).

süffig *adj* light and sweet.

Süffisance [zyfiˈzãːs] *f* -, *no pl* (*geh*) smugness, complacency.

süffisant *adj* smug, complacent.

Suffix *nt* -es, -e suffix.

Suffragette *f* suffragette.

suggerieren* *vt* to suggest. jdm etw ~ to influence sb by suggesting sth; jdm ~, daß ... to get sb to believe that ...; jdm Zweifel an seinen Fähigkeiten ~ to get sb to doubt his own abilities; das hat er sich (*dat*) von seiner Frau ~ lassen his wife persuaded him of that.

suggestibel *adj* suggestible.

Suggestibilität *f* suggestibility.

Suggestion *f* suggestion.

suggestiv *adj* suggestive.

Suggestivfrage *f* suggestive question.

Suhle *f* -, -n muddy pool.

suhlen *vr* (*lit, fig*) to wallow.

Sühne *f* -, -n (*Rel, geh*) atonement; (*von Schuld*) expiation. als ~ für etw to atone for sth; das Verbrechen fand seine ~ the crime was atoned for; ~ leisten to atone (*für* for).

sühnen 1 *vt* *Unrecht, Verbrechen* to atone for; *Schuld* to expiate. 2 *vi* to atone.

Sühne-: ~opfer *nt* (*Rel*) expiatory sacrifice; ~termin *m* (*Jur*) conciliatory hearing; ~versuch *m* (*Jur*) attempt at conciliation.

Sühnung *f* (a) (*Rel, geh*) atonement. (b) (*Jur*) conciliation.

Suite [ˈsviːtə, ˈzuːitə] *f* -, -n suite; (*Gefolge*) retinue.

Suizid [zuiˈtsiːt] *m or nt* -(e)s, -e (*form*) suicide.

suizid [zuiˈtsiːt] *adj* (*form*) suicidal. ~gefährdet suicide-prone.

Suizidtäter [zui'tsi:t-] *m (form)* suicide.
Sujet [sy'ʒeː] *nt* -s, -s *(geh)* subject.
Sukkade *f* candied peel.
sukzessiv(e) *adj* gradual.
Sulfat *nt* sulphate.
Sulfid *nt* -(e)s, -e sulphide.
Sulfit *nt* -s, -e sulphite.
Sulfonamid *nt* -(e)s, -e sulphonamide.
Sulky ['zulki, 'zalki] *nt* -s, -s sulky.
Süll *m* or *nt* -(e)s, -e, **Süllbord, Süllrand** *m (Naut)* coaming.
Sultan ['zultaːn] *m* -s, -e sultan.
Sultanat *nt* sultanate.
Sultanin *f* sultana.
Sultanine *f (Rosine)* sultana.
Sülze *f* -, -n, **Sulz** *f* -, -en *(esp S Ger, Aus, Sw)* brawn.
sülzen *(dial)* **1** *vt* to go on and on about *(inf)*. **2** *vi* to go on and on *(inf)*.
Sülzkotelett *nt* cutlet in aspic.
Sumatra[1] [zu'maːtra, 'zuːmatra] *nt* -s Sumatra.
Sumatra[2] *f* -, -s mild cigar originally from Sumatra.
Sumerer *m* -s, - *(Hist)* Sumerian.
sumerisch *adj (Hist)* Sumerian.
summ *interj* buzz. ~ **machen** to buzz.
summa cum laude *adv (Univ)* summa cum laude *(US)*, with distinction.
Summand *m* -en, -en *(Math)* summand.
summarisch **1** *adj (auch Jur)* summary; *Zusammenfassung* summarizing. **2** *adv* etw ~ **zusammenfassen** to summarize sth; ~ **läßt sich sagen, daß** ... to summarize, we can say that ...
summa summarum *adv* all in all, on the whole.
Sümmchen *nt dim of* **Summe**. **ein nettes ~** *(hum)* a tidy sum, a pretty penny *(inf)*.
Summe *f* -, -n sum; *(Gesamt~ auch)* total; *(fig)* sum total. **die ~ aus etw ziehen** to sum up *or* evaluate sth; **die ~, die ich daraus ziehe** ... my evaluation of that ...
summen **1** *vt Melodie etc* to hum. **2** *vi* to buzz; *(Mensch, Motor)* to hum. **3** *vi impers* **es summt** there is a buzzing/humming noise.
Summer *m* -s, - buzzer.
summieren* **1** *vt* to sum up. **2** *vr* to mount up. **das summiert sich** it (all) adds *or* mounts up.
Summton *m*, **Summzeichen** *nt* buzz, buzzing sound.
Sumpf *m* -(e)s, ⸚e marsh; *(Morast)* mud; *(in tropischen Ländern)* swamp. **im ~ der Großstadt** in the squalor and corruption of the big city.
Sumpf-: **~blüte** *f sb who or sth which flourishes in a decaying society*; **~boden** *m* marshy ground; **~dotterblume** *f* marsh marigold.
sumpfen *vi (inf)* to live it up *(inf)*.
Sumpf-: **~fieber** *nt* malaria; **~huhn** *nt* moorhen; *(inf: unsolider Mensch)* fast-liver *(inf)*.
sumpfig *adj* marshy, swampy.
Sumpf-: **~land** *nt* marshland; *(in tropischen Ländern)* swampland; **~otter** *m* mink; **~pflanze** *f* marsh plant; **~vogel** *m* wader; **~zypresse** *f* deciduous cypress.
Sums *m* -es, *no pl (inf)* **viel** *or* **einen großen ~ machen** to make a great to-do *(inf)*.
Sund *m* -(e)s, -e sound, straits *pl*.
Sünde *f* -, -n sin. **eine ~ begehen** to sin, to commit a sin; **jdm seine ~n vergeben** to forgive sb his sins; **es ist eine ~ und Schande** *(inf)* it's a crying shame; **es ist doch keine ~, ihn zu fragen** it's not a sin *or* crime to ask him; **jdn wie die ~ hassen** *(inf)* to hate sb like poison.
Sünden-: **~babel** *nt* hotbed of vice; **~bekenntnis** *nt* confession of one's sins; *(Gebet)* confession (of sins); **~bock** *m (inf)* scapegoat, whipping boy; **jdn zum ~bock machen** to make sb one's scapegoat; **~fall** *m (Rel)* Fall (of Man); **s~frei** *adj* free from sin, without sin; **~geld** *nt* **(a)** *(fig)* ill-gotten gains *pl*; **wirf das Geld weg, das ist ~geld!** throw that away, that's dirty money!; **(b)** *(inf: viel Geld)* packet *(inf)*, mint (of money) *(inf)*; **(c)** *(old: Ablaßgeld)* indulgence money; **~lohn** *m (a)* penalty for one's sins; **seinen gerechten ~lohn bekommen** to pay the penalty for one's sins; **(b)** *siehe* **~geld (a)**; **~pfuhl** *m* den of iniquity; **~register** *nt (fig)* list of sins; **jds ~register vorhalten** to list all sb's sins; **jdm ein langes/sein ~register** to list all sb's sins; **~vergebung** *f* forgiveness *or* remission of sins.
Sünder *m* -s, - sinner. **armer ~** *(Eccl)* miserable sinner; *(old)* criminal under sentence of death; *(fig)* poor wretch; **na, alter ~!** *(dated inf)* well, you old rogue! *(inf)*.
Sünderin *f* sinner.
Sündermiene *f* shame-faced expression. **jdn mit einer ~ ansehen** to look at sb shamefaced(ly).
Sündflut *f*, *no pl siehe* **Sintflut**.
sündhaft *adj (lit)* sinful; *(fig inf)* Preise wicked. **ein ~es Geld** *(inf)* a ridiculous amount of money; **~ teuer** *(inf)* wickedly expensive.
Sündhaftigkeit *f* sinfulness.
sündig *adj* sinful. **~ werden** to sin *(an +dat* against).
sündigen *vi* to sin *(an +dat* against); *(hum)* to indulge. **gegen Gott/die Natur ~** to sin against God/to commit a crime against nature; **gegen seine Gesundheit ~** to jeopardize one's health.
sündteuer *adj (Aus)* wickedly expensive.
Super[1] *nt* -s, *no pl (Benzin)* four-star (petrol) *(Brit)*, premium *(US)*, super.
Super[2] *m* -s, - *(Rad)* superhet (radio set).
super *(inf)* **1** *adj inv* super, smashing, great *(all inf)*. **2** *adv* *(mit adj)* really, incredibly *(inf)*; *(mit vb)* really *or* incredibly *(inf)* well.
Super- *in cpds* super-; *(sehr)* ultra-; **~-8-Film** *m* super-8 film.

superb [zu'pɛrp], **süperb** *(dated geh)* *adj* splendid, superb, superlative.
superfein *adj Qualität* top *attr*; *Eßwaren etc* top-quality; *(inf)* posh *(inf)*.
Superintendent *m (Eccl)* superintendent.
Superior *m*, **Superiorin** *f* superior.
Superiorität *f*, *no pl (geh)* superiority.
superklug *adj (iro inf)* brilliant. **du bist ein S~er** *(Besserwisser)* you are a (real) knowall *(inf)*; *(Dummkopf)* you're brilliant, you are *(iro)*; *(das ist nichts Neues)* you're not telling us anything new.
Superlativ ['zuːpɛlatiːf, zuːpɛla'tiːf] *m (Gram, fig)* superlative.
superlativisch *adj (Gram)* superlative; *(fig)* grand. **ins S~e geraten** to assume massive proportions, to snowball in a big way *(inf)*; **er bedient sich einer ~en Ausdrucksweise** his speech is full of superlatives.
Super-: **s~leicht** *adj (inf)* Zigaretten extra mild; *(kinderleicht)* dead easy *(inf)*; **~macht** *f* superpower; **~mann** *m*, *pl* -männer superman; **~markt** *m* supermarket; **s~modern** *adj (inf)* ultramodern; **s~schnell** *adj (inf)* ultrafast; **~star** *m (inf)* superstar.
Süppchen *nt dim of* **Suppe**. **sein ~ am Feuer anderer kochen** to exploit *or* use other people.
Suppe *f* -, -n soup; *(sämig mit Einlage)* broth; *(klare Brühe)* bouillon; *(fig inf: Nebel)* pea-souper *(inf)*. **klare ~** consommé; **jdm ein schöne ~ einbrocken** *(inf)* to get sb into a pretty pickle *(inf)* or nice mess; **du mußt die ~ auslöffeln, die du dir eingebrockt hast** *(inf)* you've made your bed, now you must lie on it *(prov)*; **jdm die ~ versalzen, jdm in die ~ spucken** *(inf)* to put a spoke in sb's wheel *(inf)*, to queer sb's pitch *(inf)*; **du siehst aus, als ob dir jemand in die ~ gespuckt hätte** you look as though you've lost a pound and found sixpence; *siehe* **Haar, Salz**.
Suppen- *in cpds* soup; **~fleisch** *nt* meat for making soup; *(gekocht)* boiled beef/pork *etc*; **~gemüse** *nt* vegetables *pl* for making soup; **~grün** *nt* herbs and vegetables *pl* for making soup; **~huhn** *nt* boiling fowl; **~kaspar, ~kasper** *m (inf)* poor eater; *(~freund)* soup-fan *(inf)*; **~kelle** *f* soup ladle; **~löffel** *m* soup spoon; **~nudel** *f* vermicelli *nt*, noodles *pl*; **~schüssel** *f* tureen; **~tasse** *f* soup bowl; **~teller** *m* soup plate; **~würfel** *m* stock cube; **~würze** *f* soup seasoning.
suppig *adj* creamy; *(pej)* thin, watery.
Supplement [zuple'ment] *nt (geh)* supplement.
Supplement-: **~band** *m* supplementary volume; **~winkel** *m* supplementary angle.
Suppositorium *nt (Med)* suppository.
Supra-: **~leiter** *m (Phys)* superconductor; **s~national** *adj* supranational; **~naturalismus** *m* supernaturalism.
Supremat *m* or *nt* -(e)s, -e, **Suprematie** *f (geh)* supremacy.
Sure *f* -, -n *(im Koran)* sura(h).
Surfing ['zøːɐfɪŋ, 'zœr-] *nt* -s, *no pl (Sport)* surfing.
Surinam [zuri'nam] *nt* -s Dutch Guiana.
surreal *adj* surreal.
Surrealismus *m*, *no pl* surrealism.
surrealistisch *adj* surrealist(ic).
surren *vi* **(a)** to hum; *(Insekt auch)* to buzz; *(Motor auch, Kamera, Insektenflügel)* to whirr. **(b)** *aux sein (sich bewegen: Insekt)* to buzz.
Surrogat *nt* surrogate.
Suse, Susi *f* - *abbr of* **Susanne**.
suspekt [zus'pekt] *adj* suspicious. **jdm ~ sein** to seem suspicious to sb.
suspendieren* [zuspɛn'diːrən] *vt* to suspend *(von* from).
Suspension [zuspɛn'zioːn] *f (alle Bedeutungen)* suspension.
suspensiv [zuspɛn'ziːf] *adj (Jur)* suspensory.
Suspensorium [zuspɛn'zoːrium] *nt (Med)* suspensory.
süß *adj (lit, fig)* sweet. **etw ~ machen** to sweeten sth; *Tee, Kaffee (mit Zucker)* to sugar sth; **gern ~ essen** to have a sweet tooth, to be fond of sweet things; **sie ist eine S~e** *(inf)* *(ißt gerne ~)* she has a sweet tooth; *(ist nett)* she's a sweetie(-pie) *(inf)*; **das Leben die good life; **es auf die ~e Tour** *or* **auf die S~e versuchen** *(inf)* to turn on the charm; **(mein) S~er/meine S~e** *(inf)* my sweetheart; *(als Anrede auch)* my sweet, sweetie (-pie) *(inf)*; *siehe* **Geheimnis**.
Süße *f* -, *no pl (lit, fig)* sweetness.
süßen 1 *vt* to sweeten; *(mit Zucker)* Tee, Kaffee to sugar. **2** *vi* **mit Honig etc ~** to use honey *etc* as a sweetener.
Süßholz *nt* liquorice. **~ raspeln** *(fig)* to turn on the blarney; **du kannst aufhören, ~ zu raspeln** you can stop soft-soaping me/him *etc (inf)*.
Süßholzraspler *m* -s, - *(hum)* soft-soaper *(inf)*.
Süßigkeit *f* **(a)** *no pl (lit, fig)* sweetness. **(b)** **~en** *pl* sweets *pl (Brit)*, candy *(US)*.
Süß-: **~kartoffel** *f* sweet potato; **~kirsche** *f* sweet cherry; **~klee** *m* hedysarum *(spec)*.
süßlich *adj* **(a)** *(leicht süß)* sweetish, slightly sweet; *(unangenehm süß)* sickly (sweet), cloying. **(b)** *(fig)* Töne, Miene terribly sweet; *Lächeln auch* sugary; *Worte auch* honeyed; *Farben, Geschmack* pretty-pretty *(inf)*; *(kitschig)* mawkish.
Süßlichkeit *f siehe adj* **(a)** slight sweetness; sickly sweetness. **(b)** sweetness; sugariness; pretty-prettiness *(inf)*; mawkishness.
Süß-: **~most** *m* unfermented fruit juice; **~rahmbutter** *f* creamery butter; **s~sauer** *adj* sweet-and-sour; *Gurken etc* pickled; *(fig: gezwungen freundlich)* Lächeln forced; *Miene* artificially friendly; **~speise** *f* sweet dish; **~stoff** *m* sweetener; **~waren** *pl* confectionery *sing*; **~warengeschäft** *nt* sweetshop *(Brit)*, candy store *(US)*, confectioner's; **~wasser** *nt* freshwater; **~wasserfisch** *m* freshwater fish; **~wein** *m* dessert wine.

Sutane f -, -n siehe **Soutane**.
Sütterlinschrift f old-fashioned style of German hand-writing.
SW abbr of **Südwesten** SW.
Swasiland nt -s Swaziland.
Swastika ['svastika] f -, **Swastiken** swastika.
Swimming-pool ['svimɪŋpuːl] m -s, -s swimming pool.
Swinegel m -s, - (dial) hedgehog.
Swing m -s, no pl (Mus, Fin) swing.
swingen vi (Mus) to swing.
syllabisch adj syllabic.
Syllogismus m (Philos) syllogism.
Sylphe m -n, -n, f -, -n (Myth) sylph.
Sylvaner [zyl'vaːnɐ] m -s, - Sylvaner (wine/grape).
Sylvester [zyl'vɛstɐ] nt -s, - siehe **Silvester**.
Symbiose f -, -n symbiosis.
symbiotisch adj symbiotic.
Symbol nt -s, -e symbol.
symbolhaft adj symbolic(al).
Symbolik f symbolism.
symbolisch adj symbolic(al) (für of).
symbolisieren* vt to symbolize.
Symbolismus m symbolism.
Symbolist(in f) m symbolist.
symbolistisch adj symbolist(ic).
Symbol-: ~kraft f symbolic force or power; s~kräftig adj strongly or richly symbolic; s~trächtig adj heavily symbolic, full of symbolism.
Symmetrie f symmetry.
Symmetrie-: ~achse f axis of symmetry; ~ebene f plane of symmetry.
symmetrisch adj symmetric(al).
Sympathie [zympa'tiː] f (Zuneigung) liking; (Mitgefühl, Solidaritätsgefühl) sympathy. **für jdn/etw ~ haben** to have a liking for/a certain amount of sympathy with sb/sth; **diese Maßnahmen haben meine volle ~** I sympathize completely with these measures; **durch seine Unverschämtheit hat er meine ~/hat er sich** (dat) **alle ~(n) verscherzt** he has turned me/everyone against him with his rudeness; **seine ~n gelten nicht der extremen Rechten** he isn't sympathetic towards the extreme right.
Sympathie-: ~äußerung f expression of support; ~kundgebung f demonstration of support; ~streik m sympathy strike; **in ~streik (mit jdm) treten** to come out in sympathy (with sb).
Sympathikus m -, no pl (Physiol) sympathetic nerve.
Sympathisant(in f) m sympathizer.
sympathisch adj (a) pleasant, nice, simpatico (esp US inf). **er/es ist mir ~** I like him/it; **er/es war mir gleich ~** I liked him/it at once, I took to him/it at once, I took an immediate liking to him/it; **das ist mir gar nicht ~** I don't like it at all; **es wäre mir ~, wenn du das machen würdest** I would appreciate it if you would do that.
(b) (Anat, Physiol) sympathetic.
sympathisieren* vi to sympathize (mit with).
Symphonie [zymfo'niː] f symphony.
Symphonie- in cpds siehe **Sinfonie-**.
Symphoniker(in f) m -s, - siehe **Sinfoniker(in)**.
symphonisch adj symphonic.
Symposion [zym'poːziɔn], **Symposium** [zym'poːziʊm] nt -s, **Symposien** [zym'poːziən] symposium.
Symptom nt -s, -e symptom.
symptomatisch adj symptomatic (für of).
Synagoge f -, -n synagogue.
Synästhesie [zyneste'ziː] f synaesthesia.
synchron [zyn'kroːn] adj synchronous; (Ling) synchronic.
Synchrongetriebe [zyn'kroːn-] nt (Aut) synchromesh gearbox.
Synchronisation [zynkroniza'tsioːn] f (Film, TV) synchronization; (Übersetzung) dubbing.
synchronisieren* [zynkroni'ziːrən] vt to synchronize; (übersetzen) Film to dub.
Synchron- [zyn'kroːn-]: ~uhr f synchronous or mains-synchronized clock; ~verschluß m (Phot) flash-synchronized shutter.
Syndikalismus m, no pl syndicalism.
syndikalistisch adj syndicalist(ic).
Syndikat nt (Kartell) syndicate.
Syndikus m -, **Syndiken** or **Syndizi** (Geschäftsführer) syndic; (Justitiar) (company etc) lawyer.

Syndrom nt -s, -e syndrome.
Synkope f -, -n (a) ['zynkɔpə] syncope, syncopation. (b) [zyn'koːpə] (Mus) syncopation.
synkopieren* vt to syncopate.
synkopisch adj syncopic, syncopated (esp Mus).
Synkretismus m, no pl syncretism.
Synodale(r) mf decl as adj (Eccl) synod member.
Synode f -, -n (Eccl) synod.
Synonym [zyno'nyːm] nt -s, -e synonym.
synonym(isch) [zyno'nyːm(ɪʃ)] adj synonymous.
Synonymwörterbuch nt dictionary of synonyms, thesaurus.
Synopse f -, -n, **Synopsis** f -, **Synopsen** synopsis; (Bibl) synoptic Gospels pl.
Synoptiker pl (Bibl) Synoptics pl; (Apostel) Synoptists pl.
Syntagma nt -s, **Syntagmen** or -ta (Ling) syntactic construction.
syntaktisch adj syntactic(al).
Syntax f -, -en syntax.
Synthese f -, -n synthesis.
Synthetics pl synthetics pl.
Synthetik f, no pl (Math) synthesis.
synthetisch adj synthetic; Stoff, Faser auch man-made. **etw ~ herstellen** to make or produce sth synthetically.
Syphilis ['zyːfilɪs] f -, no pl syphilis.
syphiliskrank adj syphilitic, suffering from syphilis. **~ sein** to have syphilis.
Syphilitiker(in f) m -s, - syphilitic.
syphilitisch adj syphilitic.
Syrakus nt - Syracuse.
Syrer(in f) m -s, - Syrian.
Syrien ['zyːriən] nt -s Syria.
Syrier(in f) [-iɐ, -iərɪn] m -s, - Syrian.
syrisch adj Syrian. **das S~e** Syriac, the Syriac language.
System [zys'teːm] nt -s, -e system; (Ordnung, Ordnungsprinzip auch) method. **etw mit ~ machen** to do sth systematically; **etw mit einem ~ machen** to do sth according to a system; **hinter dieser Sache steckt ~** there's method behind it; **~ in etw** (acc) **bringen** to get or bring some system into sth; **Apparate verschiedener ~e** machinery of different designs; **ein ~ von Straßen/Kanälen** a road/canal system.
System-: ~analyse f systems analysis; ~analytiker m systems analyst.
Systematik f, no pl (a) (systematisches Ordnen) system. (b) (Lehre, Klassifikation) systematology.
Systematiker(in f) m -s, - systematist; (fig) systematic person.
systematisch adj systematic.
systematisieren* vt to systematize.
system-: ~bedingt adj determined by the system; ~gerecht adj in accordance with the system; ~immanent adj inherent in the system; **dem Kapitalismus ~immanent sein** to be inherent in the capitalist system.
systemisch adj systemic.
System-: s~konform adj in conformity with the system; ~kritiker m critic of the system; s~kritisch adj critical of the system; s~los adj unsystematic; ~treue f loyalty to the system; ~veränderung f change in the system; ~zwang m obligation to conform to the system.
Systole ['zystolə, -'toːlə] f -, -n (Med) systole.
Szenar nt -s, -e, **Szenario** nt -s, -s, **Szenarium** nt -s scenario.
Szene ['stseːnə] f -, -n (a) (Theat, fig) scene; (Theat: Bühnenausstattung) set. **Beifall auf offener ~** applause during the performance; **hinter der ~** backstage; (fig) behind the scenes; **in ~** (acc) **gehen** to be staged; **etw in ~ setzen** (lit, fig) to stage sth; **sich in ~ setzen** to play to the gallery; **die ~ beherrschen** (fig) to dominate the scene (gen in); (meistern) to control things; **sich in der ~ auskennen** (sl) to know the scene.
(b) (fig: Zank, Streit) scene. **jdm eine ~ machen** to make a scene in front of sb; **mach bloß keine ~** don't go making a scene, I don't want a scene.
-szene f in cpds (sl) scene (sl).
Szenen-: ~folge f sequence of scenes; ~wechsel m scene change.
Szenerie f (Theat, fig) scenery.
szenisch adj (Theat) scenic.
Szepter ['stsɛptɐ] nt -s, - sceptre.
Szientismus [stsiɛn'tɪsmʊs] m, no pl scientism.
Szilla f -, **Szillen** (Bot) scilla.
Szylla ['stsyla] f - (Myth) Scylla. **zwischen ~ und Charybdis** (liter) between Scylla and Charybdis.

T

T, t [te:] *nt* -, - T, t.

t *abbr of* **Tonne.**

Tab *m* -(s), -e *or* -s tab.

Tabak ['ta:bak, 'tabak, (*Aus*) ta'bak] *m* -s, -e tobacco; (*Schnupf~*) snuff.

Tabak- *in cpds* tobacco; **~beutel** *m siehe* **Tabaksbeutel**; **~dose** *f siehe* **Tabaksdose**; **~genuß** *m* (tobacco) smoking; **~händler** *m* (*im Großhandel*) tobacco merchant; (*im Einzelhandel*) tobacconist; **~laden** *m* tobacconist's, tobacco shop; **~mischung** *f* blend (of tobaccos), (tobacco) mixture; **~monopol** *nt* tobacco monopoly, monopoly on tobacco; **~pfeife** *f siehe* **Tabakspfeife**; **~qualm** *m* (*pej*) fug; **~rauch** *m* tobacco smoke.

Tabaks-: **~beutel** *m* tobacco pouch; **~dose** *f* tobacco tin; (*für Schnupftabak*) snuff-box; **~pfeife** *f* pipe.

Tabak-: **~steuer** *f* duty on tobacco; **~trafik** [ta'bak-] *f* (*Aus*) tobacconist's, tobacco shop; **~trafikant** [ta'bak-] *m* (*Aus*) tobacconist; **~vergiftung** *f* nicotine poisoning; **~waren** *pl* tobacco; „**~waren**" tobacconist's.

Tabatiere [taba'tie:rə] *f* -, -n (*Aus*) tobacco tin; (*old: Schnupftabakdose*) snuff-box.

tabellarisch 1 *adj* tabular. **bitte fügen Sie einen ~en Lebenslauf bei** please write out your curriculum vitae in tabular form. **2** *adv* in tabular form, in tables/a table.

tabellarisieren* *vt* to tabulate.

Tabelle *f* table; (*Diagramm*) chart; (*Sport*) (league) table.

Tabellen-: **~form** *f*: **in ~form** in tabular form, in tables/a table; **as a chart**, in chart form; **t~förmig** *adj* tabular, in tabular form, in the form of a table; **as a chart**, in chart form; **~führer** *m* (*Sport*) league leaders *pl*; **~führer sein** to be at the top of the (league) table; **~platz** *m* (*Sport*) place *or* position in the league; **auf den letzten ~platz** fallen to drop to the bottom of the table; **~stand** *m* (*Sport*) league situation; **~stand auf Seite 15** league tables on page 15.

Tabelliermaschine *f* tabulator, tabulating machine.

Tabernakel *nt or m* -s, - tabernacle.

Taberne *f* -, -n (*obs*) *siehe* **Taverne.**

Tablett *nt* -(e)s, -s *or* -e tray. **jdm etw auf einem silbernen ~ servieren** (*fig: einfach machen*) to hand sb sth on a plate; **muß man dir alles/die Einladung auf einem silbernen ~ servieren?** do you have to have everything done for you/do you want an official invitation?

Tablette *f* tablet, pill.

Tabletten-: **~form** *f*: **in ~form** in tablet form; **~röhre** *f* tablet tube; tube of tablets; **~sucht** *f* addiction to pills, compulsive pill-taking; **t~süchtig** *adj* addicted to pills.

Tabu *nt* -s, -s taboo.

tabu *adj pred* taboo.

tabuieren* *vt* to make taboo, to taboo.

Tabuierung *f* taboo(ing).

tabuisieren* *vt siehe* **tabuieren.**

Tabula rasa *f* - -, *no pl* (*Philos*) tabula rasa. **t~ ~ machen** (*inf*) to make a clean sweep.

Tabulator *m* tabulator, tab (*inf*).

Taburett *nt* -(e)s, -e (*obs, Sw*) stool, taboret (*obs*).

Tabu-: **~schranke** *f* taboo; **~wort** *nt* taboo word *or* expression.

Tach(e)les *no art* (*sl*) (**mit jdm**) **~ reden** to have a talk with sb; **nun wollen wir beide mal ~ reden**—let's do some straight talking, let's talk turkey (*US inf*).

tachinieren* *vi* (*Aus inf*) to laze *or* loaf about (*inf*).

Tachinierer(in *f*) *m* -s, - (*Aus inf*) layabout (*inf*), loafer (*inf*).

Tacho *m* -s, -s (*inf*) speedo (*Brit inf*), speedometer.

Tachometer *m or nt* -s, - speedometer.

Tadel *m* -s, - (*Verweis*) reprimand; (*Vorwurf*) reproach; (*Kritik*) criticism, censure; (*geh: Makel*) blemish, taint; (*Sch: Eintragung ins Klassenbuch*) black mark. **ein Leben ohne jeden ~** (*geh*) an unblemished *or* spotless *or* blameless life; **ihn trifft kein ~** (*geh*) he is above *or* beyond reproach.

tadel-: **~frei** *adj* (*geh*) irreproachable; **~los 1** *adj* perfect; *Deutsch etc auch* faultless; *Benehmen auch* faultless, irreproachable; *Leben* blameless; (*inf*) splendid, first-class; **2** *adv* perfectly; faultlessly; irreproachably; *gekleidet* immaculately.

tadeln *vt* jdn to rebuke, to reprimand; *jds Benehmen* to criticize, to express one's disapproval of.

tadelnd *adj attr* reproachful. **ein ~er Blick** a reproachful look, a look of reproach.

tadelnswert, tadelnswürdig *adj* (*geh*) reprehensible, blameworthy.

Tadels|antrag *m* (*Parl*) motion of censure, censure motion.

Tafel *f* -, -n (**a**) (*Platte*) slab; (*Holz~*) panel; (*~ Schokolade etc*) bar; (*Gedenk~*) plaque; (*Wand~*) (black)board; (*Schreib~*) slate; (*Elec: Schalt~*) control panel, console; (*Anzeige~*) board; (*Verkehrs~*) sign.

(**b**) (*Bildseite*) plate.

(**c**) (*form: festlicher Speisetisch*) table; (*Festmahl*) meal; (*mittags*) luncheon (*form*); (*abends*) dinner. **jdn zur ~ bitten** to ask sb to table; **die ~ aufheben** to officially end the meal; **eine Dame zur ~ führen** to take a lady in to luncheon/dinner.

Tafel-: **~apfel** *m* eating apple; **~aufsatz** *m* centrepiece; **~berg** *m* (*Geog*) table mountain; **~besteck** *nt* (best) silver; **~bild** *nt* panel; **t~fertig** *adj* ready to serve; **t~förmig** *adj* slab-like; *Hochplateau* table-shaped; **~freuden** *pl* delicacies *pl*, culinary delights *pl*; (*Freude am Essen*) pleasures of the table *pl*; **~geschirr** *nt* tableware; **~glas** *nt* sheet glass, plate glass; **~land** *nt* plateau, tableland; **~lappen** *m* (blackboard) duster; **~malerei** *f* panel painting; **~musik** *f* musical entertainment.

tafeln *vi* (*geh*) to feast. **mit jdm ~** to dine with sb.

täfeln *vt Wand* to wainscot; *Decke* to panel, to line with wooden panels.

Tafel-: **~obst** *nt* (dessert) fruit; **~öl** *nt* cooking/salad oil; **~runde** *f* company (at table); (*Liter*) Round Table; **die ganze ~runde applaudierte** the whole table applauded; **eine festliche ~runde saß beisammen** a banquet/dinner party was in progress; **~salz** *nt* table salt; **~silber** *nt* silver; **~tuch** *nt* tablecloth.

Täf(e)lung *f siehe* **täfeln** wainscoting; (wooden) panelling.

Tafel-: **~wasser** *nt* mineral water; **~wein** *m* table wine.

Taferl- (*Aus inf*): **~klasse** *f* first year at junior school; **~klaßler(in** *f*) *m* -s, - *siehe* **Erstkläßler(in).**

Täferung (*Sw*), **Täflung** *f siehe* **Täf(e)lung.**

Taft *m* -(e)s, -e taffeta.

taften *adj* taffeta.

Tag *m* -(e)s, -e (**a**) day. **am ~(e) des/der ...** (on) the day of ...; **am ~ during the day; alle ~e** (*inf*), **jeden ~** every day; **am vorigen ~(e), am ~(e) vorher** the day before, the previous day; **auf den ~ (genau)** to the day; **auf ein paar ~e** for a few days; **auf seine alten ~e** at his age; **bei ~ und Nacht** night and day, day and night; **bis in unsere ~e** up to the present day; **bis die ~e!** (*sl*) so long (*inf*), cheerio (*inf*); **diese** (*inf*) *or* **dieser ~e** (*bald*) in the next few days; **den ganzen ~ (lang)** (*lit, fig*) all day long, the whole day; **eines ~es** one day; **eines ~es wirst du ... one day** *or* **one of these days you'll ...; eines (schönen** *or* **guten) ~es** one (fine) day; **sich** (*dat*) **einen schönen/faulen ~ machen** to have a nice/lazy day; **ein Gedicht, für den ~ geschrieben** a casual poem; **~ für** *or* **um ~** day by day; **in unseren** *or* **den heutigen ~en** these days, nowadays; **unter ~s** (*dial*) during the daytime; **von ~ zu ~** from day to day, every day; **~ der Arbeit** Labour Day; **~ der Republik/Befreiung** (*DDR*) Republic/Liberation Day; **der ~ des Herrn** (*Eccl*) the Lord's Day; **welcher ~ ist heute?** what day is it today?, what's today?; **ein ~ wie jeder andere** a day like any other; **guten ~!** hello (*inf*), good day (*dated form*); (*esp bei Vorstellung*) how-do-you-do; (*vormittags auch*) good morning; (*nachmittags auch*) good afternoon; **~! (**inf**)** hello, hi (*inf*); morning (*inf*); afternoon (*inf*); **ich wollte nur guten ~ sagen** I just wanted to have a chat; **zweimal am ~(e)** *or* **pro ~** twice daily *or* a day; **von einem ~ auf den anderen** overnight; **der Lärm des ~es** the bustle of the world; **der ~ X** D-Day (*fig*); **er erzählt** *or* **redet viel, wenn der ~ lang ist** (*inf*) he'll tell you anything if you let him; **seinen guten/schlechten ~ haben** to have a good/bad *or* off day, to have one of one's good/bad *or* off days; **das war heute wieder ein ~!** (*inf*) what a day!; **mein ~ kommt noch!** my day will come!; **das Thema/Ereignis des ~es** the talking-point/event of the day; **Sie hören jetzt die Nachrichten des ~es** and now the ~ of today's news; **die Aufgaben des ~es** the daily tasks; **in den ~ hinein leben** to take each day as it comes, to live from day to day; **~ und Nacht** night and day, day and night; **das ist ein Unterschied wie ~ und Nacht** they are as different as chalk and cheese; **~ und Stunde bestimmen** to fix a precise time.

(**b**) (*Tageslicht*) **bei ~(e) ankommen** while it's light; *arbeiten, reisen* during the day; **es wird schon ~** it's getting light already; **es ist ~** it's light; **solange (es) noch ~ ist** while it's still light; **an den ~ kommen** (*fig*) to come to light; **etw an den ~ bringen** to bring sth to light; **er legte großes Interesse an den ~** he showed great interest.

(**c**) (*inf: Menstruation*) **meine/ihre ~e** my/her period; **sie hat ihre ~e (bekommen)** it's that time of the month for her.

(**d**) (*Min*) **über/unter ~e** arbeiten to work above/below ground *or* underground, to work on *or* at/below the surface.

-tag *m in cpds* (*Konferenz*) convention, congress.

Tag- (*S Ger, Aus, Sw*) *in cpds siehe* **Tage-.**

tag|aus *adv* **~, tagein** day in, day out, day after day.

Tagchen ['taxçən] *interj* (*hum*) hello there, hi(ya) (*inf*).

Tagdienst *m* day duty.

Tage-: **~arbeit** *f* (*old*) day labour; **~bau** *m*, *pl* -e (*Min*) open-cast mining; **~blatt** *nt* daily (news)paper, local rag (*inf*); **Göttinger ~blatt** Göttingen Daily News; **~buch** *nt* diary, journal (*liter, form*); (*über etw acc*) **~buch führen** to keep a diary (of sth); **~dieb** *m* (*dated*) idler, wastrel; **~geld** *nt* daily allowance.

tag|ein *adv siehe* **tagaus.**

Tage-: **t~lang** *adj* lasting for days; **nach t~langer Unterbrechung** after an interruption of several days, after an interruption lasting several days; **t~lange Regenfälle** several days' rain; **er war t~lang verschwunden** he disappeared for (several) days; **sie hat t~lang geheult** she cried for days (on end); **~lohn** *m* (*dated*) daily wage(s); **im ~lohn arbeiten** *or*

stehen to be paid by the day; ~**löhner(in** f) m -s, - day labourer; ~**marsch** m siehe **Tagesmarsch.**

tagen 1 vi impers (geh) **es tagt** day is breaking or dawning; **es begann schon zu ~** day was breaking or dawning, (the) dawn was breaking.

2 vi (konferieren) to sit. **wir haben noch bis in den frühen Morgen getagt** (inf) we had an all-night sitting (inf).

Tagereise f day's journey.

Tages-: ~**ablauf** m day; ~**anbruch** m daybreak, dawn; ~**anzug** m lounge suit (Brit), business suit (US); ~**arbeit** f day's work; ~**ausflug** m day trip or excursion, day's outing; ~**bedarf** m daily requirement; ~**befehl** m (Mil) order of the day; ~**creme** f day cream; ~**decke** f bedspread; ~**dienst** m duty day; **jeder Kollege hat monatlich sieben** ~**dienste** each colleague is on duty for seven days a month; ~**einnahmen** pl day's takings pl; ~**ereignis** nt event of the day; ~**fragen** pl issues of the day, day-to-day matters; ~**gespräch** nt talk of the town; ~**grauen** nt (geh) dawn; ~**hälfte** f half of the day; **t**~**hell** adj siehe **taghell**; ~**helle** f light of day; ~**karte** f (a) (Speisekarte) menu of the day; (b) (Fahr-, Eintrittskarte) day ticket; ~**kasse** f (a) (Theat) box-office; (b) (Econ) day's takings pl; ~**klinik** f day clinic; ~**kurs** m (St Ex) (von Effekten) current price; (von Devisen) current rate; ~**lauf** m day; ~**leistung** f daily workload; (von Maschine, Schriftsteller etc) daily output; (von Milchkuh auch) daily yield; (Sport) performance of the day; ~**licht** nt, no pl daylight; **ans** ~**licht kommen** (fig) to come to light; **das** ~**licht scheuen** to be a creature of the night, to shun the daylight; ~**lohn** m day's wages; ~**losung** f (Mil) password of the day; ~**marsch** m day's march; **zwei** ~**märsche entfernt** two days' march away; ~**mutter** f child minder; ~**nachrichten** pl (today's) news; **die wichtigsten** ~**nachrichten** (main) headlines; ~**ordnung** f agenda, order of the day (form); **zur** ~**ordnung!** keep to the agenda!; **etw auf die** ~**ordnung setzen** to put sth on the agenda; **auf der** ~**ordnung stehen** to be on the agenda; **zur** ~**ordnung übergehen** to proceed to the agenda; (an die Arbeit gehen) to get down to business; (wie üblich weitermachen) to carry on as usual; **an der** ~**ordnung sein** (fig) to be the order of the day; ~**ordnungspunkt** m item on the agenda; ~**preis** m (Comm) current price; **gestern betrug der** ~**preis ...** yesterday's price was ...; ~**- und Abendpreise** daytime and night prices; ~**presse** f daily (news)papers or press; ~**ration** f daily rations; ~**raum** m day room; ~**reise** f (a) (Entfernung) day's journey; (b) (Ausflug) day trip; ~**satz** m daily rate; ~**schau** f (TV) news sing; ~**zeit** f time (of day); **zu jeder** ~**- und Nachtzeit** at all hours of the day and night; **zu dieser** ~**zeit kommst du nach Hause?!** what sort of time do you call this to come home!; ~**zeitung** f daily (paper); ~**zug** m day train.

Tage-: **t**~**weise** adv on a daily basis; ~**werk** nt (geh) day's work.

Tag-: ~**fahrt** f (Min) ascent; **t**~**hell** adj (as) bright as day; **es war schon** ~**hell** it was already broad daylight.

-tägig adj suf -day.

tägl. abbr of **täglich.**

täglich 1 adj daily; (attr: gewöhnlich) everyday. ~**e Gelder** (Comm) call-money; ~**e Zinsen** (Comm) daily interest; **das reicht gerade fürs** ~**e Leben** it's just about enough to get by on; **sein** ~**(es) Brot verdienen** to earn a living; **das ist unser** ~**(es) Brot** (fig: Ärger etc) it is our stock-in-trade; **das ist so wichtig wie das** ~**e Brot** it's as important as life itself; **unser** ~ **Brot gib uns heute** (Bibl) give us this day our daily bread.

2 adv every day. **einmal** ~ once a day or daily.

-täglich adj suf **sechs**~ every six days.

Tag- (Aus): ~**raum** m siehe **Tagesraum;** ~**reise** f siehe **Tagesreise.**

tags adv (a) ~ **zuvor** the day before, the previous day; ~ **darauf** or **danach** the next or following day. (b) (bei Tag) in the daytime, by day.

Tagschicht f day shift. ~ **haben** to be on (the) day shift.

tags|über adv during the day.

Tag-: **t**~**täglich** 1 adj daily; 2 adv every (single) day; ~**traum** m daydream; ~**träumer** m daydreamer; ~**undnachtgleiche** f equinox.

Tagung f conference; (von Ausschuß) sitting, session.

Tagungs-: ~**ort** m venue (of a/the conference); ~**teilnehmer** m conferee, person attending a conference.

Tag-: ~**wache**[1] f (Aus, Sw Mil) (a) reveille; (b) ~**wache! rise and shine!;** ~**wache**[2], ~**wacht** f (Aus, Sw) day guard.

Tahiti [ta'hi:ti] nt -s Tahiti.

Tahitianer(in f) [tahi:tia:nɐ, -ərɪn] m -s, -, **Tahitier(in** f) [ta'hi:tiɐ, -ərɪn] m -s, - Tahitian.

tahitisch [ta'hi:tiʃ] adj Tahitian.

Taifun m -s, -e typhoon.

Taiga f -, no pl taiga.

Taille ['taljə] f -, -n waist; (bei Kleidungsstücken auch) waistline. **auf seine** ~ **achten** to watch one's waistline; **zu eng in der** ~ too tight at the waist; **ein Kleid auf** ~ a fitted dress.

Taillenweite ['taljən-] f waist measurement.

taillieren* [ta'ji:rən] vt to fit (at the waist).

tailliert [ta'ji:ɐt] adj waisted, fitted; **Hemd** auch slimfit.

Taiwan nt -s Taiwan.

Taiwanese m -n, -n, **Taiwanesin** f Taiwanese.

taiwanesisch adj Taiwan(ese).

Take [te:k] nt or m -, -s (Film, TV) take.

Takel nt -s, - (Naut) tackle.

Takelage [takə'la:ʒə] f -, -n (Naut) rigging, tackle.

takeln vt (Naut) to rig.

Takelung f rigging.

Takelwerk nt siehe **Takelage.**

Takt m -(e)s, -e (a) (Einheit) (Mus) bar; (Phon, Poet) foot. (b) (Rhythmus) time. **den** ~ **schlagen** to beat time; (den) ~ **halten** to keep time; **im** ~ **bleiben** to stay in time; **den** ~

verlieren/wechseln to lose/change the beat, to change (the) time; **im** ~ **singen/tanzen** to sing/dance in time (to the music); **gegen den** ~ **out of time; im/gegen den** ~ **marschieren** to be in/out of step; **den** ~ **angeben** to give the beat or time; **im** ~ **der Musik** in time to or with music; **das Publikum klatschte den** ~ **dazu** the audience clapped in time to the music; **der Zug ratterte in eintönigem** ~ the train rattled along with a monotonous rhythm; **wenn alle Kolben im** ~ **arbeiten** if all the pistons are in phase.

(c) (Aut) stroke.

(d) (Ind) phase.

(e) no pl (Taktgefühl) tact. **mit dem ihm eigenen** ~ with his great tact(fulness); **er hat keinen** ~ **im Leibe** (inf) he hasn't an ounce of tact in him.

Taktbezeichnung f time signature.

Takt-: **t**~**fest** adj (Mus) (a) able to keep time; (b) (inf) (gesundheitlich) fighting fit (inf); (sicher) sure of his etc stuff (inf); ~**gefühl** nt (a) sense of tact; (b) (rare: Mus) sense of rhythm or time.

taktieren* vi (a) to manoeuvre. **so kann man nicht** ~ you can't use those tactics. (b) (rare: Mus) to beat time.

Taktik f tactics pl. **eine** ~ tactics pl, a tactical approach; **man muß mit** ~ **vorgehen** you have to use tactics; ~ **der verbrannten Erde** (Mil) scorched earth policy.

Taktiker m -s, - tactician.

taktisch adj tactical. ~ **vorgehen** to use tactics; ~ **klug** good tactics.

Takt-: **t**~**los** adj tactless; ~**losigkeit** f tactlessness; **es war eine** ~**losigkeit sondergleichen** it was a particularly tactless thing to do/say; ~**maß** nt (Mus) time; ~**messer** m -s, - siehe Metronom; ~**stock** m baton; **den** ~**stock schwingen** (inf) to wield the baton; ~**straße** f (Ind) assembly line; ~**strich** m (Mus) bar (line); **t**~**voll** adj tactful; ~**wechsel** m (Mus) change of time, time change.

Tal nt -(e)s, ⸚er valley, vale (poet). **zu** ~**e** into the valley.

tal|ab(wärts) adv (a) down into the valley. (b) (flußabwärts) downriver, downstream.

Talar m -s, -e (Univ) gown; (Eccl auch) cassock; (Jur) robe(s).

tal|aufwärts adv (a) up the valley. (b) (flußaufwärts) upriver, upstream.

Tal-: ~**brücke** f bridge over a valley; ~**enge** f narrow part of a/the valley, gorge.

Talent nt -(e)s, -e (a) (Begabung) talent (zu for). **ein großes** ~ **haben** to be very talented; **sie hat viel** ~ **zum Singen/zur Schauspielerin** she has a great talent or gift for singing/acting; **da saß** or **stand er nun mit seinem** ~ (inf) he was left looking a right charlie (Brit inf).

(b) (begabter Mensch) talented person. **junge** ~**e** young talent; **er ist ein großes** ~ he is very talented.

(c) (Hist: Geld) talent.

talentiert adj talented, gifted. **die Mannschaft lieferte ein** ~**es Spiel** the team played a game of great skill or a brilliant game.

Talent-: **t**~**los** adj untalented; ~**probe** f audition; ~**suche** f search for talent; **wir sind auf** ~**suche** we are looking for new talent; **t**~**voll** adj talented; **das war nicht sehr t**~**voll** (inf) that wasn't very clever or bright.

Taler m -s, - (Hist) Thaler; (inf) mark, ≈ quid (inf), ≈ buck (US inf).

Talfahrt f (bergabwärts) descent; (flußabwärts) downriver trip; (fig) decline.

Talg m -(e)s, -e tallow; (Cook) suet; (Hautabsonderung) sebum.

Talg-: ~**drüse** f (Physiol) sebaceous gland; ~**licht** nt tallow candle.

Talisman m -s, -e talisman, (lucky) charm; (Maskottchen) mascot.

Talje f -, -n (Naut) block and tackle.

Talk m -(e)s, no pl talc(um).

Talkessel m basin, hollow.

Talkpuder m or nt talcum powder.

Talk-Show ['tɔːkʃoː] f -, -s (TV) talk show, chat show (Brit).

Talkum nt (a) siehe **Talk.** (b) (Puder) talc, talcum powder.

Tallandschaft f valley; valleys pl.

Talmi nt -s, no pl (geh) pinchbeck; (fig) rubbish, trash. ~**Religion** sham religion; ~**Villen** showy villas; **mit dem** ~ **hochtrabender Phrasen** with the tinsel of pompous phrases.

Talmigold nt pinchbeck gold.

Talmud m -(e)s, -e Talmud.

Tal-: ~**mulde** f basin, hollow; ~**schaft** f (Sw, Aus) valley inhabitants pl or dwellers pl or folk; ~**senke** f hollow (of a/the valley); ~**sohle** f bottom of a/the valley, valley bottom; (fig) rock bottom; **in der** ~**sohle** (fig) at rock bottom, in the doldrums; ~**sperre** f dam; **t**~**wärts** adv down to the valley; ~**weg** m (a) valley path; (b) (Geog) t(h)alweg.

Tamarinde f -, -n tamarind.

Tamariske f -, -n tamarisk.

Tambour ['tambuːɐ] m -s, -e drummer.

Tambourmajor ['tambuːɐ-] m drum-major.

Tamburin nt -s, -e tambourine.

Tamp m -s, -e, **Tampen** m -s, - (Naut) rope end.

Tampon ['tampɔn, tam'poːn] m -s, -s tampon; (für Wunde auch) plug.

tamponieren* vt to plug, to tampon.

Tamtam nt -s, -s (a) (Mus) tomtom. (b) (inf: Wirbel) fuss, todo (inf), ballyhoo (inf); (Lärm) din (inf). **der Faschingszug zog mit großem** ~ **durch die Straßen** the Fasching procession paraded loudly through the streets.

Tand m -(e)s, no pl (liter) trinkets pl, knick-knacks pl. **alles Menschenwerk ist doch nur** ~ all human works are but dross (liter).

Tändelei f (liter) (Spielerei) (dilly-)dallying, trifling; (Liebelei) dalliance (liter).

Tandelmarkt (Aus), **Tändelmarkt** (dial) m flea market.

tändeln vi (liter) (liebeln) to dally (liter); (trödeln) to (dilly-)dally, to trifle.

Tandem nt -s, -s tandem.

Tandler(in f) m -s, - (Aus) (a) (Trödler) second-hand dealer. (b) (langsamer Mensch) slowcoach (Brit inf), slowpoke (US inf).

Tang m -(e)s, -e seaweed.

Tanganjika [taŋganˈjiːka] nt -s Tanganyika.

Tangens [ˈtaŋgɛns] m -, - (Math) tan(gent).

Tangenskurve [ˈtaŋgɛns-] f (Math) tan wave.

Tangente [taŋˈgɛntə] f -, -n (Math) tangent; (Straße) ring-road, express-way.

tangential [taŋgɛnˈtsiaːl] adj tangential.

Tanger [ˈtaŋɐ, ˈtandʒɐ] nt -s Tangier(s).

tangieren* [taŋˈgiːrən] vt (a) (Math) to be tangent to. (b) (berühren) Problem to touch on; Stadt, Gebiet to skirt. das tangiert das Problem nur that is merely tangential or peripheral to the problem. (c) (betreffen) to affect; (inf: kümmern) to bother.

Tango [ˈtaŋgo] m -s, -s tango.

Tangojüngling [ˈtaŋgo-] m (pej dated) beau, dandy.

Tank m -(e)s, -s or -e (Behälter, Panzer) tank.

Tank|anzeige f fuel gauge.

tanken vti (a) (bei Auto) to tank up; (bei Rennwagen, Flugzeug) to refuel. wo kann man hier ~? where can I get petrol (Brit) or gas (US) round here?; ich muß noch ~ I have to get some petrol/gas; wir hielten an, um zu ~ we stopped for petrol/gas; was tankst du? — ich tanke nur Super what grade (of petrol/gas) do you use? — I only use 4 star; ich tanke nur für 10 DM I'll just put 10 marks' worth in; ich habe 30 l getankt I put 30 litres in (the tank); hast du getankt? have you tanked up?, have you put petrol/gas in?
(b) (inf) (viel trinken) to have a few; frische Luft to get, to fill one's lungs with; neue Kräfte to get. er hat ganz schön or einiges getankt he's had a few, he's really tanked up (inf).

Tanker m -s, - (Naut) tanker.

Tankerflotte f tanker fleet, fleet of tankers.

Tankfahrzeug nt (Aut) tanker.

Tank-: ~inhalt m content(s) of the tank pl; der ~inhalt beträgt ... the tank holds ..., the tank capacity is ... (form); ~lager nt oil or petrol depot; ~laster m tanker; ~möglichkeit f letzte ~möglichkeit vor ... last filling station before ...; wie sind dort die ~möglichkeiten? what's the petrol (Brit) or gas (US) situation like there?; ~säule f petrol pump (Brit), gas(oline) pump (US); ~schiff nt tanker; ~stelle f filling or petrol (Brit) or gas(oline) (US) station; ~uhr f fuel gauge; ~verschluß m petrol (Brit) or gas (US) cap; ~wagen m tanker; (Rail) tank wagon or car; ~wart m petrol pump (Brit) or gas station (US) attendant.

Tann m -(e)s, -e (poet) pine forest.

Tännchen nt dim of **Tanne.**

Tanne f -, -n fir, pine; (Holz) pine, deal. sie ist schlank wie eine ~ she is as slender as a reed.

tannen adj (rare) pine.

Tannen-: ~baum m (a) fir-tree, pine-tree; (b) (Weihnachtsbaum) Christmas tree; ~nadel f (pine) needle; ~wald m pine forest; ~zapfen m fir cone, pine cone.

Tannicht, Tännicht nt -(e)s, -e (obs) fir thicket.

Tannin nt -s, no pl tannin.

Tannzapfen siehe **Tannenzapfen.**

Tansania nt -s Tanzania.

Tansanier(in f) [tanˈzaːniɐ, -ərɪn] m -s, - Tanzanian.

tansanisch adj Tanzanian.

Tantalusqualen pl torments of Tantalus (liter). ich litt ~ it was tantalizing, I suffered torments (liter); jdm ~ bereiten to tantalize sb.

Tantchen nt (inf) (a) (Verwandte) auntie, aunty. (b) (alte Dame) old dear (inf).

Tante f -, -n (a) (Verwandte) aunt, aunty, auntie. (b) (pej inf: Frau) old girl (inf), old dear (inf). (c) (baby-talk: Frau) lady. ~ Schneider/Monika aunty or auntie Schneider/Monika; ~ Meyer besuchen (hum inf) to spend a penny (hum inf). (d) (Kindergartenschwester etc) teacher; (Krippenschwester) nurse. (e) (sl: Homosexueller) queer (sl), poof (sl), fag (US sl).

Tante-Emma-Laden m (inf) corner shop.

tantenhaft adj (a) (inf) old-maidish. sie benimmt sich so richtig ~ she acts like a real old maid or maiden aunt. (b) (pej: betulich) Ausdruck(sweise) twee. (c) (sl: homosexuell) queer (inf), poofy (sl).

Tantieme [tãˈtieːmə, ˈtiːmə] f -, -n percentage (of the profits); (für höhere Angestellte) director's fee; (für Künstler) royalty.

Tanz m -es, ⁻e (a) dance. dort ist heute abend ~ there's a dance or (für Jugendliche) disco there this evening; im Goldenen Ochsen ist neuerdings auch ~ they now have dancing too at the Golden Ox; zum ~ aufspielen (dated) to strike up a dance (tune); jdn zum ~ auffordern to ask sb to dance or for a dance. (b) (fig geh: von Licht, Schatten) play. der ~ der Boote auf den Wellen the boats' dancing (liter) or bobbing on the waves; ein ~ auf dem Vulkan (fig) playing with fire. (c) (inf: Aufheben) fuss. einen ~ um jdn machen to make a fuss of sb; das war wieder ein ~! what a to-do or carry-on (inf) that was!

Tanz-: ~abend m dance; ~bar f bar with dancing; ~bär m dancing bear; ~bein nt: das ~bein schwingen (hum) to trip the

light fantastic (hum), to shake a leg (hum); ~boden m (~fläche) dance floor; (Saal) dance hall; (dated: Veranstaltung) dance; ~café nt restaurant with dancing.

Tänzchen nt dim of Tanz (dated hum) dance. ein ~ wagen to venture onto the floor.

Tanzdiele f (dated) (Raum) dance hall; (~fläche) dance floor.

tänzeln vi aux haben or (bei Richtungsangabe) sein to mince, to sashay (esp US), to trip; (Boxer) to skip; (Pferd) to step delicately.

tanzen vti aux haben or (bei Richtungsangabe) sein to dance; (Boot auch) to bob; (Kreisel) to spin; (hüpfen) to hop. ~ gehen, zum T~ gehen to go dancing; siehe Pfeife.

Tänzer(in f) m -s, - dancer; (Partner) (dancing) partner; (Ballett~) ballet dancer.

Tanzerei f (a) dancing; (pej) prancing about. (b) (Aus) dancing party.

tänzerisch adj dance-like. ~ veranlagt sein to have a talent for dancing; ~ausgebildet trained as a dancer; der ~e Aspekt der Operette the dance or choreographic aspect of the operetta; eine große ~e Leistung a tremendous piece of dancing; ~ gestaltete Gymnastik gymnastics done in a dance-like way or as a dance; ~e Darbietungen dance acts; sein ~es Können his dancing ability.

Tanz-: ~fläche f dance floor; ~gruppe f dance group; (bei Revue, TV-Show auch) chorus; ~kapelle f dance band; ~kränzchen nt (dated) dancing party; ~kunst f art of dancing, dance; ~kurs(us) m dancing course; ~lehrer m dancing teacher; ~lied nt dance tune; ~lokal nt café with dancing; t~lustig adj fond of or keen on dancing; einige t~lustige Paare blieben noch a few couples who wanted to dance stayed on; ~musik f dance music; ~orchester nt dance orchestra; ~partner m dancing partner; ~platte f record of dance music; ~saal m dance hall; (in Hotel etc) ballroom; ~schritt m (dance) step; ~schuh m dancing shoe; ~schule f dancing school, school of dancing; ~sport m competitive dancing; ~sprache f (Zool) dance language; ~stunde f dancing lesson or class; sie haben sich in der ~stunde kennengelernt they met at dancing lessons or classes; ~tee m thé dansant, tea-dance; ~turnier nt dancing contest or competition; ~veranstaltung f, ~vergnügen nt dance.

Taoismus [taoˈɪsmʊs, tau-] m Taoism.

Tapergreis m (pej inf) old dodderer (pej inf).

tap(e)rig adj (pej inf) doddering, doddery.

Tapet nt: (inf) etw aufs ~ bringen to bring sth up; aufs ~ kommen to be brought up, to come up.

Tapete f -, -n wallpaper. ohne ~ without wallpaper; die ~n wechseln (fig inf) to have a change of scenery or surroundings.

Tapeten-: ~bahn f strip of wallpaper; ~rolle f roll of wallpaper; ~tür f concealed door; ~wechsel m (inf) change of scenery or surroundings.

Tapezier m -s, -e (esp S Ger), **Tapezierer** m -s, - (a) paperhanger, decorator. (b) (Polsterer) upholsterer.

Tapezier|arbeit f wallpapering.

tapezieren* vt to (wall)paper; (inf: mit Bildern) to plaster (inf). neu ~ to repaper.

Tapeziernagel m tack.

tapfer adj brave, courageous; (wacker) steadfast; Soldat, Versuch auch bold. wir marschierten immer ~ weiter, ohne zu merken ... we marched on blithely, not realizing ...; halt dich or bleib ~! (inf) be brave; sich ~ schlagen (inf) to put on a brave show.

Tapferkeit f siehe adj bravery, courage; steadfastness; boldness.

Tapferkeitsmedaille f medal for bravery.

Tapioka f -, no pl tapioca.

Tapir m -s, -e (Zool) tapir.

Tapisserie [tapɪsəˈriː] f (a) tapestry. (b) (old, Sw) drapery.

tapp interj tap.

tappen vi (a) aux sein (tapsen) to go/come falteringly; (Bär) to lumber, to lollop (inf); (dial: gehen) to wander. ~de Schritte faltering steps; er ist in eine Pfütze getappt (inf) he walked smack into a puddle (inf).
(b) (tasten) nach etw ~ to grope for sth; im finstern or dunkeln ~ (fig) to grope in the dark.

täppisch, tappig adj (dial) adj awkward, clumsy.

tap(p)rig adj (dial) siehe **tap(e)rig.**

Taps m -es, -e (dial) clumsy oaf (inf).

tapsen vi aux sein (inf) (Kind) to toddle; (Bär) to lumber, to lollop (inf); (Kleintier) to waddle.

tapsig adj (inf) awkward, clumsy.

Tara f -, **Taren** (Comm) tare.

Tarantel f -, -n tarantula. wie von der ~ gestochen as if stung by a bee, as if bitten by a snake.

Tarantella f -, -s or **Tarantellen** tarantella.

tarieren* vt to tare.

Tarif m -(e)s, -e rate; (Wasser~, Gas~, Verkehrs~ etc auch) tariff; (Gebühr auch) charge. die ~e für Telefonanschlüsse telephone rental; neue ~e für Löhne/Gehälter new wage rates/ salary scales; die Gewerkschaft hat die ~e für Löhne und Gehälter gekündigt the union has put in a new wage claim; nach/über/unter ~ bezahlen to pay according to/above/below the (union) rate(s).

Tarif-: ~autonomie f (right to) free collective bargaining; ~gruppe f grade; ~kommission f joint working party on pay.

tariflich adj agreed, union. der ~e Mindestlohn the agreed minimum wage; die Gehälter sind ~ festgelegt there are fixed rates for salaries.

Tarif-: ~lohn m standard wage; t~los adj t~loser Zustand period when new rates are being negotiated; t~mäßig adj siehe t~lich; ~ordnung f wage/salary scale; ~partner m party to the wage/salary agreement; die ~**partner** union and management; (*Sozialpartner*) both sides of industry; ~**verhandlungen** *pl* wage/salary negotiations *pl*, negotiations on pay *pl*; ~**vertrag** *m* wage/pay agreement.

Tarn-: ~**anstrich** *m* camouflage; ~**anzug** *m* (*Mil*) camouflage battledress.

tarnen 1 *vti* to camouflage; (*fig*) *Absichten, Identität etc* to disguise. **Massagesalons sind meist getarnte Bordelle** massage parlours are usually a cover for brothels; **als Polizist getarnt** disguised as a policeman.

2 *vr* (*Tier*) to camouflage itself; (*Mensch*) to disguise oneself.

Tarn-: ~**farbe** *f* camouflage colour/paint; ~**kappe** *f* magic hat; ~**kleid** *nt* (*Zool*) protective camouflage; ~**name** *m* cover name; ~**netz** *nt* (*Mil*) camouflage netting.

Tarnung *f* camouflage; (*von Agent etc*) disguise. **die Arztpraxis ist nur eine ~** the doctor's practice is just a cover; **er fuhr zur ~ erst eine Station mit der U-Bahn** as a cover he first travelled one stop on the subway; **zur ~ der Inhaltsarmut dieses Essays** to camouflage the essay's lack of content.

Tarock *m or nt* -s, -s tarot.

Tartanbahn *f* (*Sport*) tartan track.

Tartar *m* -en, -en *siehe* **Tatar**[1].

Tartüff *m* -s, -e (*liter*) Tartuffe.

Täschchen ['tɛʃçən] *nt dim of* **Tasche**.

Tasche *f* -, -n (a) (*Hand~*) bag (*Brit*), purse (*US*); (*Reise~ etc*) bag; (*Backen~*) pouch; (*Akten~*) case.

(b) (*bei Kleidungsstücken, Billard~*) pocket; (*Zahn~*) cavity. **sich** (*dat*) **die ~n füllen** (*fig*) to line one's own pockets; **in die eigene ~ arbeiten** *or* **wirtschaften** to line one's own pockets; **etw in der ~ haben** (*inf*) to have sth in the bag (*inf*); **die Hand auf die ~ halten** (*dated inf*), **die ~ zuhalten** (*dated inf*) to keep a tight grip on the purse strings; **jdm das Geld aus der ~ locken** *or* **ziehen** *or* **lotsen** to get sb to part with his money; **etw aus der eigenen ~ bezahlen** to pay for sth out of one's own pocket; **etw in die eigene ~ stecken** (*fig*) to put sth in one's own pocket, to pocket sth; **jdm auf der ~ liegen** (*inf*) to live off sb *or* at sb's expense; **die Hände in die ~n stecken** (*lit*) to put one's hands in one's pockets; (*fig*) to stand idly by; **jdn in die ~ stecken** (*inf*) to put sb in the shade (*inf*); *siehe* **tief**.

Taschen-: ~**ausgabe** *f* pocket edition; ~**buch** *nt* paperback (book); ~**buchausgabe** *f* paperback (edition); ~**dieb** *m* pickpocket; ~**diebstahl** *m* pickpocketing; ~**fahrplan** *m* (pocket) timetable; ~**feitel** *m* (*Aus inf*) penknife, pocket-knife; ~**format** *nt* pocket size; **Transistorradio im ~format** pocket-size(d) transistor; ~**geld** *nt* pocket-money; ~**kalender** *m* pocket diary; ~**kamm** *m* pocket comb; ~**krebs** *m* edible crab; ~**lampe** *f* pocket torch, flashlight (*US*); ~**messer** *nt* pocketknife, penknife; **wie ein ~messer zusammenklappen** (*inf*) to double up; ~**rechner** *m* pocket calculator; ~**schirm** *m* collapsible umbrella; ~**spiegel** *m* pocket mirror; ~**spieler** *m* conjurer; ~**spielerei** *f* sleight of hand *no pl*; **t~spielern** *vi insep* to do conjuring tricks; ~**spielertrick** *m* (*fig*) sleight of hand *no indef art, no pl*; ~**tuch** *nt* handkerchief, hanky (*inf*); ~**uhr** *f* pocket watch; ~**veitel** *m* (*Aus inf*) *siehe* ~**feitel**; ~**wörterbuch** *nt* pocket dictionary.

Täschner, Täschner *m* -s, - bag-maker.

Tasmanien [-iən] *nt* -s Tasmania.

Tasmanier(in *f*) [tas'ma:niɐ, -ərɪn] *m* -s, - Tasmanian.

tasmanisch *adj* Tasmanian.

Täßchen *nt dim of* **Tasse** (little) cup. **ein ~ Tee** a quick cup of tea.

Tasse *f* -, -n cup; (*mit Untertasse*) cup and saucer; (*Suppen~*) bowl. **eine ~ Kaffee** a cup of coffee; **er hat nicht alle ~n im Schrank** (*inf*) he's not all there (*inf*); **eine trübe ~** (*inf*) a wet blanket (*inf*); **hoch die ~n!** (*inf*) bottoms up (*inf*).

Tastatur *f* keyboard.

tastbar *adj* palpable. **eine ~e Beule** a bump you can feel.

Taste *f* -, -n key; (*Knopf an Gerät auch*) button. **in die ~n greifen** (*hum*) to strike up a tune; **auf die ~n hauen** *or* **hämmern** (*inf*) to hammer away at the keyboard.

Tast-: ~**empfinden** *nt siehe* ~**sinn**; ~**empfindung** *f* tactual sensation.

tasten 1 *vi* to feel. **nach etw ~** (*lit, fig*) to feel *or* grope for sth; **Scheinwerfer tasteten nach dem Boot** searchlights scanned (the water) for the boat; **vorsichtig ~d** feeling *or* groping one's way carefully; ~**de Schritte** (*lit, fig*) tentative steps.

2 *vr* to feel *or* grope one's way.

3 *vti* (*drücken*) to press, to punch; *Nummer auch* to punch out; *Telex etc* to key; (*Typ: setzen*) to key(board).

Tasten|instrument *nt* (*Mus*) keyboard instrument.

Taster *m* -s, - (a) (*Zool*) *siehe* **Tastorgan**. (b) (*Typ: Tastatur*) keyboard. (c) (*Typ: Setzer*) keyboard operator, keyboarder.

Tasterin *f siehe* **Taster** (c).

Tast-: ~**organ** *nt* organ of touch, tactile organ; ~**sinn** *m* sense of touch; ~**werkzeug** *nt siehe* ~**organ**.

Tat *f* -, -en (*das Handeln*) action; (*Einzel~ auch*) act; (*Helden~, Un~*) deed; (*Leistung*) feat; (*Verbrechen*) crime. **ein Mann der ~** a man of action; **keine Worte sondern ~en** not words but deeds *or* actions; **eine ~ der Verzweiflung/Nächstenliebe** an act of desperation/charity; **als er sah, was er mit dieser ~ angerichtet hatte** when he saw what he had done by this; **eine geschichtliche/verbrecherische ~** an historic/a criminal act *or* deed; **eine gute/böse ~** a good/wicked deed; **eine eindrucksvolle ~ vollbringen** to do something impressive; **Leben und ~en des ...** the life and exploits of ...; **etw in die ~ umsetzen** to put sth into action; **das war eine ~!** what a feat!; (*erleichtert*) **well done!**; **zur ~ schreiten** to proceed to action; (*hum*) to get on with it; **in der ~ indeed**; (*wider Erwarten, erstaunlicherweise etc*) actually.

tat *pret of* **tun**.

Tatar[1] *m* -en, -en (*Volksstamm*) Tartar.

Tatar[2] *nt* -(s), *no pl*, **Tatarbeefsteak** *nt* steak tartare.

Tataren-: ~**meldung**, ~**nachricht** *f* (*hum*) scare story.

tatauieren* *vti siehe* **tätowieren**.

Tat-: ~**bestand** *m* (*Jur*) facts (of the case) *pl*; (*Sachlage*) facts (of the matter) *pl*; **den ~bestand des Betrugs erfüllen** (*Jur*) to constitute fraud; ~**einheit** *f* (*Jur*) commission of two or more offences in one act; **in ~einheit mit** concomitantly with.

Taten-: ~**drang** *m* thirst for action, energy; ~**durst** *m* (*old, hum*) thirst for action; **t~durstig** *adj* (*old, hum*) eager for action; **t~froh** *adj* (*dated*) enthusiastic; **t~los** *adj* idle; **t~los herumstehen** to stand idly by, to stand by and do nothing; **wir mußten t~los zusehen** we could only stand and watch.

Täter(in *f*) *m* -s, - culprit; (*Jur*) perpetrator (*form*). **als ~ verdächtigt werden** to be a suspect; **als ~ in Frage kommen** to be a possible suspect; **nach dem ~ wird noch gefahndet** the police are still searching for the person responsible *or* the person who committed the crime; **wer war der ~?** who did it?; **unbekannte ~** person or persons unknown; **jugendliche ~** young offenders.

Täterschaft *f* guilt. **die Frage (nach) der ~** (*form*) the question of who was responsible *or* of who committed the crime; **die ~ leugnen/zugeben** to deny/admit one's guilt; (*vor Gericht*) to plead innocent/guilty.

Tat-: ~**form** *f* (*Gram*) active (voice); **t~froh** *adj siehe* **tatenfroh**.

tätig *adj* (a) *attr* active. **dadurch hat er ~e Reue bewiesen** he showed his repentance in a practical way; ~**e Nächstenliebe** practical charity; **in einer Sache ~ werden** (*form*) to take action in a matter.

(b) (*arbeitend*) ~ **sein** to work; **als was sind Sie ~?** what do you do?; **er ist im Bankwesen ~** he's in banking.

tätigen *vt* (*Comm*) to conclude, to effect; *Geschäft auch* to transact; (*geh*) *Einkäufe* to carry out; (*geh*) *Anruf* to make.

Tätigkeit *f* activity; (*Beschäftigung*) occupation; (*Arbeit*) work; (*Beruf*) job. **während meiner ~ als Lehrer** while I was working as a teacher; **zur Zeit übt er eine andere ~ aus** at present he's doing a different job; **auf eine langjährige ~ zurückblicken** to look back on many years of work; **eine hektische** *or* **fieberhafte ~ entfalten** to go into a frenzy of activity; **in ~ treten** to come into operation; (*Mensch*) to act, to step in; **in ~ sein** (*Maschine*) to be operating *or* running; **in/außer ~ setzen** *Maschine* to set going *or* in motion/to stop; *Alarmanlage* to activate/to put out of action; **der Vulkan ist außer ~** the volcano is not active.

Tätigkeits-: ~**bereich** *m* field of activity; ~**bericht** *m* progress report; ~**drang** *m siehe* **Tatendrang**; ~**form** *f* (*Gram*) *siehe* **Tatform**; ~**wort** *nt* (*Gram*) verb.

Tätigung *f siehe* **tätigen** *vt* conclusion, effecting; transaction; carrying out; making.

Tat-: ~**kraft** *f, no pl* energy, vigour, drive; **t~kräftig** *adj* energetic; *Hilfe* active.

tätlich *adj* violent. ~**e Beleidigung** (*Jur*) assault (and battery); ~ **werden** to become violent; **gegen jdn ~ werden** to assault sb; **jdn ~ angreifen** to attack sb physically, to assault sb.

Tätlichkeiten *pl* violence *sing*. **es kam zu ~** there was violence.

Tat-: ~**mensch** *m* man of action; ~**motiv** *nt* motive (for the crime); ~**ort** *m* scene of the crime.

tätowieren* *vt* to tattoo. **sich ~ lassen** to have oneself tattooed.

Tätowierung *f* (a) *no pl* (*das Tätowieren*) tattooing. (b) (*Darstellung*) tattoo.

Tatsache *f* fact. ~ **ist aber, daß ...** but the fact of the matter *or* the truth is that ...; ~? (*inf*) really?, no!; **das stimmt, ~!** (*inf*) it's true, really; **das ist ~** (*inf*) that's a fact; **nackte ~n** (*inf*) the hard facts; (*hum*) girlie pictures; **jdn vor vollendete ~n stellen** to present sb with a fait accompli; **vor der vollendeten ~ stehen** to be faced with a fait accompli; (*unter*) **Vorspiegelung falscher ~n** (under) false pretences.

Tatsachen-: ~**bericht** *m* documentary (report); ~**material** *nt siehe* **Faktenmaterial**.

tatsächlich 1 *adj attr* real, actual.

2 *adv* (a) (*in Wirklichkeit, objektiv*) actually, really, in fact. ~ **war es aber ganz anders** in (actual) fact *or* actually *or* really it was quite different.

(b) (*sage und schreibe*) really, actually. **willst du das ~ tun?** are you really *or* actually going to do it?; ~? really?; ~! oh yes, so it/he *etc* is/was *etc*; **da kommt er!** — ~! he's coming! — so he is!

Tatsächlichkeit *f* (*geh*) actuality, fact.

tätscheln *vt* to pat.

tatschen *vi* (*pej inf*) **auf etw** (*acc*) ~ to paw sth.

Tattergreis *m* (*pej inf*) old dodderer, doddering old man (*pej*).

Tatterich *m* (*inf*): **den ~ haben/bekommen** to have/get the shakes (*inf*).

tatt(e)rig *adj* (*inf*) *Mensch* doddering, doddery; *Hände, Schriftzüge* shaky, quivery.

tatütata *interj* ~! **die Feuerwehr ist da!** dingalingaling! here comes the fire brigade!

Tat-: ~**verdacht** *m* suspicion (*of having committed a crime*); **unter ~verdacht stehen** to be under suspicion; **t~verdächtig** *adj* suspected; ~**verdächtige(r)** *mf* suspect; ~**waffe** *f* weapon (used in the crime); (*bei Mord*) murder weapon.

Tatze *f* -, -n (*lit, fig*) paw. **eine ~ bekommen** (*S Ger: Sch sl*) to get the cane.

Tat-: ~**zeit** *f* time of the incident *or* crime; ~**zeuge** *m* witness (to the incident *or* crime).

Tau[1] *m* -(e)s, *no pl* dew. **vor ~ und Tag** (*poet*) at break of day (*poet*).

Tau[2] *nt* -(e)s, -e (*Seil*) rope; (*Naut auch*) hawser.

taub *adj* deaf; *Glieder* numb; *Gestein* dead; *Metall* dull; *Ähre* unfruitful; *Nuß* empty. **sich ~ stellen** to pretend not to hear; **gegen** *or* **für etw ~ sein** *(fig)* to be deaf to sth.

Täubchen *nt dim of* **Taube. mein ~!** my little dove.

Taube *f* -, **-n** (a) *(Zool)* pigeon; *(Turtel~ auch)* dove. **hier fliegen einem die gebratenen ~n nicht in den Mund** this isn't exactly the land of milk and honey. (b) *(fig, als Symbol)* dove. **~n und Falken** *(Pol inf)* hawks and doves.

Tauben-: t~blau *adj* blue-grey; **~ei** *nt* pigeon's/dove's egg; **t~eigroß** *adj* the size of a golf ball/golf balls.

taubenetzt *adj (liter)* dewy, dew-covered.

Tauben-: t~grau *adj* dove grey; **~haus** *nt* dovecot(e); *(für Brieftauben)* pigeon loft; **~post** *f:* **mit der ~post** by pigeon post; **~schießen** *nt (Sport)* pigeon shooting; **~schlag** *m* (a) *(lit)* **siehe ~haus;** (b) *(fig)* **hier geht es zu wie im ~schlag** it's like Waterloo Station here *(inf);* **~sport** *m* pigeon racing; **~zucht** *f* pigeon breeding *or* fancying.

Taube(r) *mf decl as adj* deaf person *or* man/woman *etc.* **die ~n** the deaf.

Tauber, Täuber *m* **-s, -, Täuberich** *m* cock pigeon.

Taubheit *f* (a) deafness. (b) *(von Körperteil)* numbness.

Täubling *m (Bot)* russula (toadstool).

Taub-: ~nessel *f* deadnettle; **t~stumm** *adj* deaf and dumb, deaf-mute *attr;* **~stumme(r)** *mf* deaf-mute; **~stummheit** *f* deaf-muteness, deaf-mutism.

Tauchboot *nt siehe* **Unterseeboot.**

tauchen 1 vi (a) *aux haben or sein* to dive *(nach* for); *(als Sport auch)* to skin-dive; *(kurz ~)* to duck under; *(unter Wasser sein)* to stay under water; *(U-Boot auch)* to submerge. (b) *aux sein (fig)* to disappear *(in + acc* into); *(aus etw auf~)* to emerge, to appear *(aus* out of, from); *(Boxen: abducken)* to duck. **die Sonne tauchte langsam ins Meer/hinter den Horizont** the sun sank slowly into the sea/beneath the horizon. 2 vt *(kurz ~)* to dip; *Menschen, Kopf* to duck; *(ein~, bei Taufe)* to immerse. **in Licht getaucht** *(geh)* bathed in light.

Tauchen *nt* **-s,** *no pl* diving; *(Sport~ auch)* skin-diving.

Taucher *m* **-s, -** diver.

Taucher-: ~anzug *m* diving suit; **~ausrüstung** *f* diving equipment *or* gear; **~brille** *f* diving goggles *pl;* **~glocke** *f* diving bell; **~helm** *m* diving *or* diver's helmet.

Taucherin *f* diver.

Tauch-: ~maske *f* diving mask; **~sieder** *m* **-s, -** immersion coil *(for boiling water);* **~sport** *m* (skin-)diving; **~station** *f* **auf ~station gehen** *(U-Boot)* to dive; *(hum: in Schützengraben etc)* to duck, to get one's head down; *(fig: sich verstecken)* to make oneself scarce; **auf ~station sein** *(U-Boot)* to be submerged; **~tiefe** *f* depth; *(Naut: von Fluß)* navigable depth.

tauen¹ *vti (vi: aux haben or sein) (Eis, Schnee)* to melt, to thaw. **es taut** it is thawing; **der Schnee taut von den Bergen/Dächern** the snow on the mountains/roofs is melting *or* thawing.

tauen² *vt (N Ger, Naut)* to tow.

Tauende *nt (Naut)* end of a piece of rope.

Tauf-: ~akt *m* baptism *or* christening (ceremony); **~becken** *nt* font; **~buch** *nt* baptismal register.

Taufe *f* -, **-n** baptism; *(christliche auch)* christening; *(Schiffs~)* launching (ceremony). **die ~ empfangen** to be baptized *or* christened; **jdm die ~ spenden** to baptize *or* christen sb; **ein Kind aus der ~ heben** *(old)* to stand sponsor to a child *(old);* **etw aus der ~ heben** *(hum)* Verein to start sth up; Plan to launch sth.

taufen *vt* to baptize; *(bei Äquatortaufe)* to duck; *(nennen)* Kind, Schiff, Hund etc to christen. **sich ~ lassen** to be baptized; **jdn auf den Namen Rufus ~** to christen sb Rufus.

Täufer *m* **-s, -: Johannes der ~** John the Baptist; **die ~** *(Eccl)* the Baptists.

taufeucht *adj* dewy, wet with dew.

Tauf-: ~formel *f* baptism formula; **~gelübde** *nt* baptismal vows *pl;* **~kapelle** *f* baptistry; **~kleid** *nt* christening robe.

Täufling *m* child/person to be baptized.

Tauf-: ~name *m* Christian name; **~pate** *m* godfather; **~patin** *f* godmother; **~register** *nt* baptismal register.

taufrisch *adj (geh)* dewy; *(fig)* fresh; *(nicht müde)* sprightly.

Tauf-: ~schein *m* certificate of baptism; **~stein** *m* (baptismal) font; **~zeuge** *m* godparent.

taugen *vi* (a) *(geeignet sein)* to be suitable *(zu, für* for). **wozu soll denn das ~?** what is that supposed to be for?; **er taugt zu gar nichts** he is useless; **er taugt nicht zum Arzt** he wouldn't make a good doctor; **in der Schule taugt er nichts** he's useless *or* no good at school; **er taugt nicht zu harter Arbeit** he's not much good at hard work; *(wegen Faulheit)* he's not keen on hard work. (b) *(wert sein)* **etwas/nicht viel** *or* **nichts ~** to be good *or* all right/to be not much good *or* no good *or* no use; **taugt der Neue etwas?** is the new bloke any good *or* use?; **der Bursche taugt nicht viel/gar nichts** that bloke is a (real) bad lot *(inf);* **als Mensch taugt er gar nichts** he is worthless as a person; **ob der billige Kaffee wohl etwas taugt?** I wonder if the cheap coffee is any good?

Taugenichts *m* **-(es), -e** *(dated)* good-for-nothing, ne'er-do-well *(old).*

tauglich *adj* Kandidat, Bewerber, Material suitable *(zu* for); *(Mil)* fit *(zu* for). **jdn für ~ erklären** *(Mil)* to declare *or* certify sb fit for service.

Tauglichkeit *f* suitability; *(Mil)* fitness (for service).

Tauglichkeitsgrad *m (Mil)* physical fitness rating (for military service).

Taumel *m* **-s,** *no pl (geh: Schwindel)* (attack of) dizziness *or* giddiness; *(liter: Rausch)* frenzy. **im ~ der Ereignisse sein** *(liter)* to be caught up in the whirl of events; **im ~ der Freude/des Glücks** *(liter)* in a transport of joy/happiness *(liter);* **im ~ der Sinne** *or* **Leidenschaft** *(liter)* in the fever of his/her *etc* passion; **wie im ~ sein** in a daze.

taum(e)lig *adj* dizzy, giddy.

taumeln *vi aux sein* to stagger; *(zur Seite)* to sway.

taumlig *adj siehe* **taum(e)lig.**

Tau-: ~perle *f (liter)* dewdrop; **~punkt** *m* dewpoint.

Tausch *m* **-(e)s, -e** exchange, swap; *(~handel)* barter. **im ~ gegen** *or* **für etw** in exchange for sth; **etw im ~ geben** to exchange *or* swap/barter sth; *(bei Neukauf)* to give in part-exchange; **jdm etw zum ~ für etw anbieten** to offer to exchange *or* swap sth for sth; **etw im ~ nehmen** to take sth in exchange; **einen guten/schlechten ~ machen** to get a good/bad deal.

tauschen 1 vt to exchange, to swap; Güter to barter; *(aus~)* Briefmarken, Münzen etc to swap; Geld to change *(in + acc* into); *(inf: um~)* Gekauftes to change. **einen Blick mit jdm ~** *(geh)* to exchange glances with sb; **Küsse ~** *(geh)* to kiss; **wollen wir die Plätze ~?** shall we change *or* swap places? 2 vi to swap; *(in Handel)* to barter; *(Geschenke aus~)* to exchange presents. **wollen wir ~?** shall we swap (places etc)?; **wir haben getauscht** we swapped, we did a swap; **ich möchte nicht mit ihm ~** I wouldn't like to change places with him.

täuschen 1 vt *(irreführen)* Vertrauen to betray. **mit dieser Fälschung täuschte er sogar die Experten** he even deceived *or* fooled the experts with his forgery; **man kann ihn nicht ~** you can't fool him; **er wurde in seinen Erwartungen/Hoffnungen getäuscht** his expectations/hopes were disappointed; **wenn mich mein Gedächtnis nicht täuscht** if my memory serves me right; **wenn mich nicht alles täuscht** unless I'm completely wrong; **sie läßt sich leicht/nicht ~** she is easily/not easily fooled *(durch* by). 2 vr to be wrong *or* mistaken *(in + dat, über + acc* about). **darin ~ Sie sich** you are mistaken there, that's where you're wrong; **dann hast du dich getäuscht!** then you are mistaken. 3 vi (a) *(irreführen) (Aussehen etc)* to be deceptive; *(Sport)* feint. **das täuscht** that is deceptive. (b) *(Sch form: betrügen)* to cheat.

täuschend 1 adj Nachahmung remarkable; Ähnlichkeit auch striking. **eine ~e Ähnlichkeit mit jdm haben** to look remarkably like sb. 2 adv **sich** *(dat)* **~ ähnlich sehen/sein** to look/be remarkably alike *or* almost identical; **jdm ~ ähnlich sehen** to look remarkably like sb, to be the spitting image of sb.

Täuscher *m* **-s, -** *(sl)* phoney *(inf).*

Täuscherei *f (inf)* exchanging, swapping.

Tausch-: ~geschäft nt exchange, swap; *(Handel)* barter (deal). **mit etw ein ~geschäft machen** to exchange/barter sth; **~gesellschaft** *f* barter society; **~handel** *m* barter; **~handel treiben** to barter; **~mittel** *nt* medium of exchange; **~objekt** *nt* barter *no pl,* barter object; **zum ~objekt werden** to be bartered; **~partner** *m* **~partner für 2-Zimmer-Wohnung gesucht** exchange wanted for 2 room flat.

Täuschung *f* (a) *(das Täuschen)* deception. **das tat er zur ~** he did that in order to deceive. (b) *(Irrtum)* mistake, error; *(falsche Wahrnehmung)* illusion; *(Selbst~)* delusion. **er gab sich einer ~** *(dat)* **hin** he was deluding himself; **darüber darf man sich keiner ~** *(dat)* **hingeben** one must not delude oneself (about that).

Täuschungs-: ~absicht *f* intention to deceive/of cheating; **~manöver** *nt (Sport)* feint; *(inf)* ploy; **~versuch** *m* attempted deception/cheating.

Tausch-: ~wert *m (Sociol)* exchange value, value in exchange; **~wirtschaft** *f (Sociol)* barter economy.

tausend *num* a *or* one thousand; **~ Dank/Grüße/Küsse** thousand thanks/greetings/kisses; *siehe auch* **hundert.**

Tausend¹ *f* -, **-en** *(Zahl)* thousand.

Tausend² *nt* **-s, -e** thousand. **vom ~** in a *or* per thousand; **ei der ~!** *(obs)* zounds! *(obs); siehe auch* **Hundert².**

Tausend- *in cpds* a thousand; *siehe auch* **Hundert-.**

Tausender *m* **-s, -** (a) *(Zahl)* **ein ~** a figure in the thousands; **die ~** the thousands. (b) *(Geldschein)* thousand (mark/dollar *etc* note *or* bill).

tausenderlei *adj inv* a thousand kinds of.

Tausend-: ~füßer *(form),* **~füßler** *m* **-s, -** centipede; *(Zool auch)* millipede; **die ~füß(l)er** the myriapods *(spec);* **~jahrfeier** *f* millenary; **t~jährig** *adj attr* thousand year old; *(t~ Jahre lang)* thousand year (long); **nach mehr als t~jähriger Unterdrückung** after more than a thousand years of oppression; **das t~jährige Reich** *(Bibl)* the millennium; Hitlers „**~jähriges Reich**" Hitler's thousand-year empire"; **~künstler** *m* jack-of-all-trades; **t~mal** *adv* a thousand times; **ich bitte t~mal um Entschuldigung** a thousand pardons; **viel t~mal** *(old)* times without number; *siehe auch* **hundertmal;** **~sas(s)a** *m* **-s, -s** *(dated inf)* hell of a chap *(dated inf);* **~schön** *nt* **-s, -e, ~schönchen** *nt* daisy.

Tausendstel *nt* **-s, -** thousandth; *siehe auch* **Hundertstel.**

tausendste(r, s) *adj* thousandth; *siehe auch* **hundertste(r, s).**

Tausend-: t~undein(e, er, es) *adj* a thousand and one; **Märchen aus ~undeiner Nacht** Tales of the Thousand and One Nights, the Arabian Nights; **t~(und)eins** *num* one thousand and one.

Tautologie *f* tautology.

tautologisch *adj* tautological, tautologous.

Tau-: ~tropfen *m* dewdrop; **~werk** *nt, no pl (Naut)* rigging; **~wetter** *nt* thaw; *(fig auch)* relaxation; **wir haben** *or* **es ist ~wetter** it is thawing; **bei ~wetter** during a thaw, when it thaws; **es herrschte ein kulturelles/politisches ~wetter** there was a period of cultural/political relaxation; **~wind** *m* warm spring wind; **~ziehen** *nt* **-s,** *no pl (lit, fig)* tug-of-war.

Taverne [ta'vɛrnə] *f* -, **-n** *(old)* tavern *(old),* inn; *(in Italien)* taverna.

Taxameter *m* **-s, -** taximeter, clock *(inf).*

Taxator *m (Comm)* valuer.

Taxe *f* -, **-n** (a) *(Schätzung)* valuation, estimate. (b) *(Gebühr)* charge; (*Kur~etc*) tax; (*Gebührenordnung*) scale of charges. (c) (*dial*) *siehe* **Taxi.**

taxfrei *adj* (*esp Sw*) *siehe* **abgabenfrei.**

Taxi *nt* -s, -s taxi, cab, taxicab (*form*). **sich** (*dat*) **ein ~ nehmen** to take a taxi, to go by taxi; **~ fahren** to drive a taxi; (*als Fahrgast*) to go by taxi.

Taxichauffeur *m* taxi *or* cab driver.

taxieren* *vt* Preis, Wert to estimate (*auf +acc* at); Haus, Gemälde etc to value (*auf +acc* at). **etw zu hoch ~** to overestimate/overvalue sth; **etw zu niedrig ~** to underestimate/undervalue sth.

Taxi-: **~fahrer** *m* taxi *or* cab driver, cabby (*inf*); **~fahrt** *f* taxi ride; **~girl** [-gøːɐl, -gœrl] *nt* taxi dancer (*US*); **~stand** *m* taxi rank.

Taxler *m* -s, - (*Aus inf*) cabby (*inf*).

Taxpreis *m* estimated price (*according to valuation*).

Taxus *m* -, - yew (tree).

Taxwert *m* estimated value.

Tb(c) [teː(ˈ)beː (ˈtseː)] *f* -, -s *abbr of* **Tuberkulose** TB.

Tb(c)-krank [teː(ˈ)beː(ˈtseː)-] *adj* **~ sein** to have TB; **die ~en** Patienten patients with TB, TB patients *or* cases.

Teach-in [tiːtʃˈɪn] *nt* -(s), -s teach-in.

Teakholz [ˈtiːk-] *nt* teak. **ein Tisch aus ~** a teak table.

Team [tiːm] *nt* -s, -s team.

Team- [ˈtiːm-]: **~arbeit** *f* teamwork; **etw in ~arbeit machen** to do sth as a team *or* by teamwork; **das wird in ~arbeit gemacht** it's done by teamwork; **~leader** [-liːdɐ] *m* (*Sport: Aus, Sw*) *siehe* Tabellenführer; **~work** [-wɔːk] *nt* -s, *no pl siehe* **~arbeit.**

Tea-Room [ˈtiːruːm] *m* -s, -s (*esp Sw*) tea room.

Technik *f* (a) (*no pl: Technologie*) technology; (*als Studienfach auch*) engineering. **der Mensch und die ~** man and technology; **das Zeitalter der ~** the technological age, the age of technology; **verfluchte ~!** stupid technology!
(b) (*Arbeitsweise, Verfahren*) technique. **jdn mit der ~ von etw vertraut machen** to familiarize sb with the techniques *or* skills of sth; **die ~ des Dramas/der Musik** dramatic/musical techniques.
(c) (*no pl: Funktionsweise und Aufbau*) (*von Auto, Motor etc*) mechanics *pl*.
(d) (*inf: technische Abteilung*) technical department, backroom boys *pl* (*inf*).
(e) (*Aus inf: Technische Hochschule*) institute of technology.

Techniker(in *f*) *m* -s, - engineer; (*Beleuchtungs~, Labor~*) technician; (*fig: Fußballspieler, Künstler*) technician. **ich bin kein ~, ich verstehe das nicht** I am not technically minded, I don't understand that; **er ist mehr Theoretiker als ~** he is more concerned with theoretical than practical matters.

Technikum *nt* -s, **Technika** college of technology.

technisch *adj* (a) (*technologisch*) technological; *Studienfach* technical. **T~e Hochschule/Universität** technological university, Institute of (Science and) Technology; **~e Chemie/Medizin** chemical/medical engineering; **er ist ~ begabt** he is technically minded; **das ~e Zeitalter** the technological age, the age of technology.
(b) (*die Ausführung betreffend*) Schwierigkeiten, Gründe technical; (*mechanisch*) mechanical. **~er Zeichner** engineering draughtsman; **~er Leiter** technical director; **das ist ~ unmöglich** it is technically impossible; (*inf: das geht nicht*) it is absolutely impossible; **~e Einzelheiten** (*fig*) technicalities, technical details.

technisieren* *vt* to mechanize.

Technisierung *f* mechanization.

Technokrat *m* -en, -en technocrat.

Technokratie *f* technocracy.

technokratisch *adj* technocratic.

Technologe *m*, **Technologin** *f* technologist.

Technologie *f* technology.

technologisch *adj* technological.

Techtelmechtel *nt* -s, - (*inf*) affair, carry-on (*inf*). **ein ~ mit jdm haben** to be carrying on with sb (*inf*).

Teckel *m* -s, - dachshund.

Teddy [ˈtɛdi] *m* -s, -s (a) (*auch ~bär*) teddy (bear). (b) (*auch ~stoff*) fur fabric.

Teddyfutter [ˈtɛdi-] *nt* fleecy *or* fur-fabric lining.

Tedeum [teˈdeːʊm] *nt* -s, -s Te Deum.

TEE [teːeːˈeː] *m* -, -(s) (*Rail*) *abbr of* **Trans-Europ(a)-Express.**

Tee *m* -s, -s tea. **einen im ~ haben** (*inf*) to be tipsy (*inf*); **einen ~ geben** (*dated*) to give a tea party.

Tee-: **~bäckerei** *f* (*Aus*) *siehe* **~gebäck;** **~beutel** *m* tea bag; **~blatt** *nt* tea-leaf; **~-Ei** *nt* (*tea*) infuser, tea ball (*esp US*); **~gebäck** *nt, no pl* sweet biscuits *pl*; **~glas** *nt* tea-glass; **~haube** *f* *siehe* **~wärmer;** **~haus** *nt* tea-house; **~kanne** *f* teapot; **~kessel** *m* kettle; (b) (*Gesellschaftsspiel*) guessing-game based on puns; **~licht** *nt* night-light; **~löffel** *m* teaspoon; **~löffelweise** *adv* by the teaspoonful; **t~löffelweise** *adv* by the teaspoonful; **~maschine** *f* tea-urn; **~mischung** *f* blend of tea.

Teen [tiːn] *m* -s, -s (*Press sl*) teenager.

Teenager [ˈtiːneːdʒɐ] *m* -s, - teenager.

Teepause *f* tea break.

Teer *m* -(e)s, -e tar.

Teer-: **~(dach)pappe** *f* (bituminous) roofing felt; **~decke** *f* tarred (road) surface.

teeren *vt* to tar. **~ und federn** to tar and feather.

Teer-: **~farben, ~farbstoffe** *pl* aniline dyes *pl*; **~gehalt** *m* tar content; **t~haltig** *adj* **eine wenig/stark ~haltige Zigarette** a low/high tar cigarette; **t~haltig sein** to contain tar.

Teerose *f* tea-rose.

Teer-: **~pappe** *f* *siehe* **~(dach)pappe;** **~straße** *f* tarred road.

Teerung *f* tarring.

Tee-: **~service** *nt* tea-set; **~sieb** *nt* tea-strainer; **~sorte** *f* (type or sort of) tea; **~strauch** *m* tea bush; **~stube** *f* tea-room; **~stunde** *f* afternoon tea (time); **~tasse** *f* teacup; **~wagen** *m* tea-trolley; **~wärmer** *m* -s, - tea-cosy; **~wurst** *f* smoked German sausage for spreading.

Teflon ® *nt* -s teflon.

Teheran [ˈteːhəraːn, tehəˈraːn] *nt* -s Teh(e)ran.

Teich *m* -(e)s, -e pond. **der große ~** (*dated inf*) the (herring) pond (*hum*).

Teich-: **~molch** *m* smooth newt; **~rose** *f* yellow water-lily.

Teig *m* -(e)s, -e (Hefe~, Knet~, Nudel~) dough; (Mürb~, Blätter~ etc) pastry; (Pfannkuchen~) batter; (esp in Rezepten auch) mixture.

teigig *adj* doughy; (voller Teig) Hände covered in dough/pastry.

Teig-: **~masse** *f* (Cook) dough/pastry/batter/mixture; **~waren** *pl* (Nudeln) pasta *sing*.

Teil¹ *m* -(e)s, -e (a) part; (von Strecke auch) stretch; (von Stadt auch) district, area; (von Gebäude auch) area, section; (von Zeitung) section. **der Bau/das Projekt ist zum ~ fertig** the building/project is partly finished; **wir hörten zum ~ interessante Reden** some of the speeches we heard were interesting; **zum ~ ..., zum ~ ...** partly ..., partly ...; **zum großen/größten ~** for the most part, mostly; **die Inder essen zum größten ~ Reis** for the most part Indians eat rice; **er hat die Bücher darüber zum großen/größten ~ gelesen** he has read many/most of the books about that; **die Studenten wohnen zum größten ~ bei ihren Eltern** for the most part the students live with their parents; **der größere ~ ihres Einkommens** the bulk of her income; **ein großer ~ stimmte dagegen** a large number (of people) voted against it; **der dritte/vierte/fünfte ~ etc** a third, a quarter, a fifth *etc* (von of); **in zwei ~e zerbrechen** to break in two *or* half.
(b) (Jur: Partei, Seite) party.
(c) (auch nt: An~) share. **ein gut ~ Arbeit/Frechheit/der Leute** (dated) quite a bit of work/cheek/many *or* a lot of people; **zu gleichen ~en erben/beitragen** to get an equal share *or* an inheritance/to make an equal contribution; **er hat seinen ~ dazu beigetragen** he did his bit *or* share; **er hat sein(en) ~ bekommen** *or* **weg** (inf) he has (already) had his due; **sich** (dat) **sein(en) ~ denken** (inf) to draw one's own conclusions; **einem jeden ward sein ~** (old liter) everyone received his (fair) share; **das bessere ~ erwählen** (liter) to come off better.
(d) (auch nt) **ich für mein(en) ~** for my part, I ..., I, for my part ...

Teil² *nt* -(e)s, -e (a) part; (Bestand~) component; (Ersatz~) spare, (spare) part; (sl: großer Gegenstand) thing. **etw in seine ~e zerlegen** Tier, Leiche to cut sth up; Motor, Möbel etc to take sth apart *or* to bits *or* to pieces; **... das waren vielleicht ~e** (sl) ... they were real whoppers (inf).
(b) *siehe* **Teil¹** (c, d).

Teil-: **~abkommen** *nt* partial agreement/treaty; **~ansicht** *f* partial view; **~aspekt** *m* aspect, part; **t~bar** *adj* divisible, which can be divided (durch by); **~barkeit** *f* divisibility; **~bereich** *m* part; (in Abteilung) section; **~betrag** *m* part (of an amount); (auf Rechnung) item; (Rate) instalment; (Zwischensumme) subtotal.

Teilchen *nt* particle; (dial: Gebäckstück) cake.

Teilchenbeschleuniger *m* (Phys) particle accelerator.

Teilefertigung *f* (Ind) manufacture of parts *or* components.

teilen 1 *vt* (a) (zerlegen, trennen) to divide (up); (Math) to divide (durch by). **27 läßt sich durch 9 ~** 27 can be divided by 9; **der Fluß teilt das Land in der Mitte** the river divides the country down the middle; (politisch) geteilter Meinung sein to have different (political) opinions; **darüber sind die Meinungen geteilt** opinions differ on that; **darüber kann man geteilter Meinung sein** one can disagree about that; **etw in drei Teile ~** to divide sth in(to) three (parts); **das Schiff teilte die Wellen** *or* **Wogen** (liter) the ship forged its way through the waves.
(b) (auf~) to share (out) (unter +dat amongst). **etw mit jdm ~** to share sth with sb.
(c) (an etw teilhaben) to share. **sie haben Freud und Leid miteinander geteilt** they shared the rough and the smooth; **geteilte Freude ist doppelte Freude** (prov) a joy shared is a joy doubled (prov); **geteilter Schmerz ist halber Schmerz** (prov) a trouble shared is a trouble halved (prov); **sie teilten unser Schicksal** *or* **Los** they shared the same fate as us.
2 *vr* (a) (in Gruppen) to split up.
(b) (Straße, Fluß) to fork, to divide; (Vorhang) to part.
(c) **sich** (dat) **etw ~** to share *or* split sth; **teilt euch das!** share *or* split that between you; **sich in etw** (acc) **~** (geh) to share sth.
(d) (fig: auseinandergehen) **in diesem Punkt ~ sich die Meinungen** opinion is divided on this.
3 *vi* to share. **er teilt nicht gern** he doesn't like sharing.

Teiler *m* -s, - (Math) factor.

Teil-: **~erfolg** *m* partial success; **~ergebnis** *nt* partial result; **einige ~ergebnisse sind schon bekannt** we already know some of the results; **~fabrikat** *nt* component; **~frage** *f* part (of a question); **~gebiet** *nt* (a) (Bereich) branch; (b) (räumlich) area; **~habe** *f* (liter) participation, sharing (an +dat in); (esp an Gott) communion (an +dat with); **t~haben** *vi sep irreg* (geh) (an +dat in) (mitwirken) to have a part, to participate; (liter: t~nehmen) to share; **~haber(in** *f*) *m* -s, - (Comm) partner; **~haberschaft** *f* (Comm) partnership; **t~haftig** *adj* (old) **eines großen Glücks/einer großen Ehre t~haftig werden** to be blessed with great good fortune/a great honour (liter).

-teilig *adj suf* -piece.

Teilkasko-: **t~versichert** *adj* insured with **~versicherung;** **~versicherung** *f* insurance covering more than third party lia-

bility but giving less than fully comprehensive coverage.
Teil-: ~**menge** f (*Math*) subset; t~**möbliert** adj partially furnished.
Teilnahme f -, no pl **(a)** (*Anwesenheit*) attendance (*an* + *dat* at); (*Beteiligung an Wettbewerb etc*) participation (*an* + *dat* in). jdn zur ~ an etw (*dat*) aufrufen to urge sb to take part *or* participate in sth; ~ am Straßenverkehr (*form*) road use; ~ an einer Straftat (*Jur*) complicity in an offence.
(b) (*Interesse*) interest (*an* + *dat* in); (*Mitgefühl*) sympathy. jdm seine herzliche/aufrichtige ~ aussprechen to offer sb one's heartfelt condolences.
Teilnahme-: t~**berechtigt** adj eligible; ~**berechtigung** f eligibility; von der ~**berechtigung** ausgeschlossen sein to be ineligible, not to be eligible.
Teilnahms-: t~**los** adj (*gleichgültig*) indifferent, apathetic; (*stumm leidend*) listless; ~**losigkeit** f siehe adj indifference, apathy; listlessness; t~**voll** adj compassionate, sympathetic.
teilnehmen vi sep irreg **(a)** an etw (*dat*) ~ (*sich beteiligen*) to take part *or* participate in sth; (*anwesend sein*) to attend sth; an Wettkampf, Preisausschreiben etc to take part in sth, to enter sth, to go in for sth; an Wettkampf auch to compete in sth; an Gespräch auch to join in sth; er hat nicht teilgenommen he did not take part etc; an einem Ausflug ~ to go on an outing; an der Wahl ~ to vote in the election; am Krieg ~ to fight in the war; am Unterricht ~ to attend school; an einem Kurs ~ to do a course; am Straßenverkehr ~ (*form*) to use the road.
(b) (*Anteil nehmen*) to share (*an* + *dat* in).
teilnehmend adj compassionate, sympathetic. ~e Beobachtung (*Sociol*) participatory observation.
Teilnehmer(in f) m -s, - **(a)** (*Beteiligter bei Kongreß etc*) participant; (*Kriegs*~) combatant; (*bei Wettbewerb, Preisausschreiben etc*) competitor, contestant; (*Kurs*~) student; (*bei Ausflug etc*) member of a party. er war ~ beider Weltkriege he fought in both world wars; alle ~ an dem Ausflug all those going on the outing.
(b) (*Mittäter*) accomplice.
(c) (*Telec*) subscriber. der ~ meldet sich nicht there is no reply.
Teilnehmerzahl f attendance.
Teilperücke f toupee; (*für Damen*) hair-piece.
teils adv partly. ~ ... ~ ... partly ... partly ...; (*inf: sowohl ... als auch*) both ... and ...; die Demonstranten waren ~ Arbeiter, ~ Studenten some of the demonstrators were workers and the others were students; ~ heiter, ~ wolkig cloudy with sunny periods; ~, ~ (*als Antwort*) half and half; (*inf*) sort of (*inf*); wie geht es dir? — ~, ~ how are you? — so-so.
Teil-: ~**schuldverschreibung** f (*Fin*) bond (forming part of a loan issue); ~**staat** m region, state; ~**strecke** f stretch (of road/ railway etc); (*bei Rennen*) leg, stage; (*bei Rennen*) leg, stage; (*bei öffentlichen Verkehrsmitteln*) (fare-)stage; ~**strich** m secondary graduation line; ~**stück** nt part; (~**strecke** auch) stretch.
Teilung f division.
Teilungsartikel m (*Gram*) partitive article.
Teilverlust m partial loss.
teilweise 1 adv partly; (*manchmal*) sometimes. nicht alle Schüler sind so faul, ~ sind sie sehr interessiert not all the pupils are so lazy, some of them are very interested; der Film war ~ gut the film was good in parts; ~ bewölkt cloudy in parts; morgen tritt ~ eine Wetterbesserung ein there will be a partial improvement in the weather tomorrow.
2 adj attr partial.
Teil-: ~**zahlung** f hire-purchase; (*Rate*) instalment; auf ~**zahlung** on hire-purchase; ~**zahlungspreis** m hire-purchase price; ~**zeitarbeit** f, ~**zeitbeschäftigung** f part-time job/work.
Tein [te'i:n] nt -s, -e tannin.
Teint [tɛ̃:] m -s, -s complexion.
T-Eisen ['te:-] nt t- *or* tee-iron.
Tektonik f (*Archit, Geol*) tectonics pl.
tektonisch adj tectonic.
Tel. abbr of **Telefon**.
Telefon [tele'fo:n, 'te:lefo:n] nt -s, -e (tele)phone. am ~ (*verlangt werden*) (to be wanted) on the phone; ~ haben to be on the phone; jdn ans ~ rufen to get sb (to come) to the phone; ans ~ gehen to answer the phone.
Telefon- in cpds (tele)phone; siehe auch **Fernsprech-**; ~**anruf** m (tele)phone call; ~**apparat** m telephone.
Telefonat nt (tele)phone call.
Telefon-: ~**buch** nt (tele)phone book; ~**draht** m telephone line; ~**gebühr** f call charge; (*Grundgebühr*) telephone rental; ~**gespräch** nt (tele)phone call; (*Unterhaltung*) telephone conversation; ~**häuschen** nt (*inf*) phone box (*Brit*) *or* booth.
telefonieren* 1 vi to make a (tele)phone call. wir haben stundenlang telefoniert we talked *or* were on the phone for hours; bei jdm ~ to use sb's phone; es wird entschieden zuviel telefoniert the phones are definitely used too much; ins Ausland/nach Amerika/Hamburg ~ to make an international call/to call America/Hamburg; er telefoniert den ganzen Tag he is on the phone all day long; mit jdm ~ to speak to sb on the phone. 2 vt (*inf, Sw*) to phone, to ring (up), to call. jdm etw ~ to call *or* phone and tell sb sth.
telefonisch adj telephone. ~e Auskunft/Beratung telephone information/advice service; eine ~e Mitteilung a (tele)phone message; jdm etw ~ mitteilen to tell sb sth over the phone; er hat sich ~ entschuldigt he phoned to apologize; ich bin ~ erreichbar *or* zu erreichen I can be contacted by phone; die ~e Zeitansage the Speaking Clock.
Telefonist(in f) m telephonist; (*in Betrieb auch*) switchboard operator.
Telefonitis f -, no pl (*hum inf*) die ~ haben to be telephone-mad (*inf*).

Telefon-: ~**leitung** f telephone line; ~**marder** m (*Press sl*) telephone vandal; ~**netz** nt telephone network; ~**nummer** f (tele)phone number; ~**rechnung** f (tele)phone bill pl; ~**seelsorge** f ≃ Samaritans pl; ~**überwachung** f telephone tapping; ~**verbindung** f telephone line; (*zwischen Orten*) telephone link; siehe auch **Verbindung (c)**; ~**zelle** f (tele)phone box (*Brit*) *or* booth; ~**zentrale** f (telephone) switchboard.
telegen adj telegenic.
Telegraf m -en, -en telegraph.
Telegrafen-: ~**amt** nt telegraph office; ~**apparat** m telegraph; ~**büro** nt (*dated*) news agency; ~**mast** m telegraph pole.
Telegrafie f telegraphy.
telegrafieren* vti to telegram, to cable, to wire.
telegrafisch adj telegraphic. jdm ~ Geld überweisen to wire sb money.
Telegramm nt -s, -e telegram; (*Auslands*~ auch) cable.
Telegramm-: ~**adresse** f telegraphic address; ~**bote** m telegram boy; ~**formular** nt telegram form; ~**stil** m staccato *or* telegram style, telegraphese.
Telegraph m siehe **Telegraf**.
Telegraphen- in cpds siehe **Telegrafen-**.
Telegraphie f siehe **Telegrafie**.
telegraphieren* vti siehe **telegrafieren**.
telegraphisch adj siehe **telegrafisch**.
Tele- ['tele-]: ~**kinese** f -, no pl telekinesis; t~**kinetisch** adj telekinetic; ~**kolleg** nt ≃ Open University (*Brit*).
Telemark m -s, -s (*Ski*) telemark.
Teleobjektiv nt (*Phot*) telephoto lens.
Teleologie f (*Philos*) teleology.
teleologisch adj (*Philos*) teleological.
Telepath(in f) m -en, -en telepathist.
Telepathie f telepathy.
telepathisch adj telepathic.
Telephon nt -s, -e, **Telephon-** in cpds siehe **Telefon, Telefon-**.
Teleskop nt -s, -e telescope.
Teleskopauge nt telescope eye.
teleskopisch adj telescopic.
Television [televi'zio:n] f siehe **Fernsehen**.
Telex nt -, -e telex.
Teller m -s, - **(a)** plate. ein ~ Suppe a plate of soup. **(b)** (*sl: Platten*~) turntable. **(c)** (*Ski*) basket.
Teller-: ~**eisen** nt (*Hunt*) steel trap; t~**förmig** adj plate-shaped; ~**gericht** nt (*Cook*) one course meal; ~**lippe** f platter lip; ~**mine** f (*Mil*) flat anti-tank mine; ~**mütze** f beret; ~**rand** m rim *or* edge of a/the plate; nicht zum Blick über den ~**rand** fähig sein (*fig*) to be unable to see beyond the end of one's own nose; ~**wärmer** m -s, - plate warmer; ~**wäscher** m dishwasher.
Tellur nt -s, no pl (*Chem*) tellurium.
tellurisch adj (*Geol, liter*) terrestrial, tellurian (*rare*).
Tempel m -s, - temple (*auch fig*).
Tempel-: ~**bau** m (*Gebäude*) temple; ~**herr**, ~**ritter** m (*Hist*) (Knight) Templar; ~**schändung** f desecration of a temple; ~**tanz** m temple dance; ~**tänzerin** f temple dancer.
Tempera-: ~(**farbe**) f tempera (colour); ~**malerei** f (*Maltechnik*) painting in tempera; (*Gemälde*) tempera painting(s).
Temperament nt **(a)** (*Wesensart*) temperament. die vier ~ (*old*) the four humours (*old*); ein hitziges ~ haben to be hot-tempered.
(b) no pl (*Lebhaftigkeit*) vitality, vivacity. viel/kein ~ haben to be very/not to be vivacious *or* lively; sie hat vielleicht ein ~ she's hot-blooded; sein ~ ist mit ihm durchgegangen he lost his temper; sie konnte ihr ~ nicht mehr zügeln she could control herself *or* her temper no longer.
Temperament-: t~**los** adj lifeless, spiritless; ~**losigkeit** f lifelessness, spiritlessness.
Temperamentsausbruch m temperamental fit *or* outburst.
temperamentvoll adj vivacious, lively; *Aufführung auch* spirited; *Auto, Fahrer* nippy (*inf*). ein Lied ~ vortragen to give a spirited rendering of a song.
Temperatur f temperature. erhöhte ~ haben to have a *or* be running a temperature; die ~en sind angestiegen/gesunken the temperature has risen/fallen; bei diesen/solchen ~en in these/such temperatures.
Temperatur-: ~**abfall** m drop *or* fall in temperature; ~**anstieg** m rise in temperature; ~**regler** m thermostat; ~**rückgang** m fall in temperature; ~**schwankung** f variation in temperature; ~**skala** f temperature scale; ~**sturz** m sudden drop *or* fall in temperature.
Temperenzler(in f) m -s, - member of a/the temperance league.
temperieren* vt etw ~ (*auf die richtige Temperatur bringen*) to make sth the right temperature; (*anwärmen*) to warm sth up; der Raum ist angenehm temperiert the room is at a pleasant temperature *or* is pleasantly warm; Rotwein leicht temperiert trinken to drink red wine at room temperature.
Templer m -s, - Templar.
Templerorden m Order of the Knights Templar.
Tempo nt -s, -s **(a)** (*Geschwindigkeit*) speed; (*Arbeits*~, *Schritt*~ auch) pace. ~! (*inf*) hurry up!; ~ dahintermachen (*inf*) to get a move on (*inf*); bei jdm ~ dahintermachen/hinter etw (*acc*) machen (*inf*) to make sb get a move on (with sth) (*inf*); nun mach mal ein bißchen ~! (*inf*) get a move on! (*inf*); ~ 100 speed limit (of) 100 km/h; mit vollem/hohem ~ at full/a high speed; im ~ zulegen/nachlassen to speed up/slow down.
(b) (*Mus*) pl **Tempi** tempo. das ~ einhalten to keep time; das ~ angeben to set the tempo; (*fig*) to set the pace.
Tempora pl of **Tempus**.
temporal adj (*Gram*) temporal.

Temporalsatz *m* temporal clause.

temporär *adj (geh)* temporary.

Tempus *nt* -, **Tempora** *(Gram)* tense.

Tendenz *f* trend *(auch St Ex)*; *(Neigung)* tendency; *(Absicht)* intention; *(no pl: Parteilichkeit)* bias, slant. **die ~ haben, zu ...** to tend to ..., to have a tendency to ...; **die ~ zeigen, zu ...** to show a tendency to ...; **er hat nationalistische ~en** he has nationalist leanings.

Tendenz-: **~betrieb** *m (Ind)* church or charitable, political etc organization in W. Germany exempt from provisions of industrial relations legislation; **~dichtung** *f* tendentious literature.

tendenziell *adj* **eine ~e Veränderung** a change in direction; **~ ist Ruritanien ein faschistischer Staat** Ruritania is a country which shows fascist tendencies; **die Ziele der beiden Parteien unterscheiden sich ~ kaum voneinander** the aims of the two parties are broadly similar (in direction).

tendenziös *adj* tendentious.

Tendenz-: **~stück** *nt* tendentious play; **~wende** *f* change of direction; *(Wendepunkt)* turning point.

Tender *m* -s, - *(Naut, Rail)* tender.

tendieren* *vi* **(a)** *(Fin, St Ex)* to tend. **(b)** **dazu ~, etw zu tun** *(neigen)* to tend to do sth; *(beabsichtigen)* to be moving towards doing sth; **zum Kommunismus/Katholizismus ~** to have leanings towards communism/Catholicism, to have communist/Catholic leanings or tendencies; **zu Erkältungen/Wutausbrüchen ~** to tend to have colds/fits of anger; **seine Begabung tendiert mehr ins Künstlerische** his talents tend more towards the artistic.

Teneriffa *nt* -s Tenerife.

Tenne *f* -, -n, **Tenn** *m* -s, -e *(Sw)* threshing floor.

Tennis *nt* -, *no pl* tennis.

Tennis- in *cpds* tennis; **~platz** *m* tennis court; **~schläger** *m* tennis racquet; **~schuh** *m* tennis shoe.

Tenno *m* -s, -s Emperor of Japan.

Tenor[1] *m* -s, *no pl* tenor.

Tenor[2] *m* -s, -̈e *(Mus)* tenor.

Tenorbuffo *m* tenor buffo.

Tenorist *m* tenor (singer).

Tenorschlüssel *m* tenor clef.

Tentakel *m or nt* -s, - tentacle.

Tenü *nt* -s, -s *(Sw)* garb, dress.

Tenuis ['te:nuis] *f* -, **Tenues** ['te:nueːs] *(Phon)* tenuis.

Teppich *m* -s, -e **(a)** carpet *(auch fig)*; *(Gobelin)* tapestry; *(inf: Wandbehang)* wall-hanging; *(inf: Brücke auch)* rug; *(Öl~)* slick. **etw unter den ~ kehren or fegen** *(lit, fig)* to sweep sth under the carpet; **bleib auf dem ~** *(inf)* be realistic!, be reasonable!; **den roten ~ ausrollen** to bring out the red carpet. **(b)** *(dial inf)* siehe **Decke.**

Teppich-: **~boden** *m* carpet(ing); **das Zimmer ist mit ~boden ausgelegt** the room has wall-to-wall carpeting; **~fliese** *f* carpet tile; **~kehrer** *m* -s, -, **~kehrmaschine** *f* carpet-sweeper; **~klopfer** *m* carpet-beater; **~reinigung** *f* carpet cleaning/cleaner's; **~schnee** *m* carpet foam; **~stange** *f* frame for hanging carpets over for beating.

Terenz *m* - Terence.

Term *m* -s, -e *(Math, Phys, Ling)* term.

Termin *m* -s, -e date; *(für Fertigstellung)* deadline; *(Comm: Liefertag)* delivery date; *(bei Arzt, Besprechung etc)* appointment; *(Sport)* fixture; *(Jur: Verhandlung)* hearing. **der letzte ~** the deadline, the last date; *(bei Bewerbung etc)* the closing date; **sich (dat) einen ~ geben lassen** to make an appointment; **schon einen anderen ~ haben** to have a prior engagement.

Terminal ['tœːrminəl, 'tœr-] *nt or m* -s, -s terminal.

Termin-: **t~gerecht**, **t~gemäß**, *adj* on schedule, according to schedule; **~geschäft** *nt* deal on the forward market; **~geschäfte** futures.

Termini *pl of* **Terminus.**

Terminkalender *m* (appointments or engagements) diary.

terminlich, terminmäßig *adj* **etw ~ einrichten** to fit sth in (to one's schedule); **~e Verpflichtungen** commitments; **ich habe schon zu viele ~e Verpflichtungen** I have too many prior commitments.

Terminologie *f* terminology.

terminologisch *adj* terminological.

Terminus *m* -, **Termini** term. **~ technicus** technical term.

Termite *f* -, -n termite, white ant.

Termiten-: **~hügel** *m* termites' nest, termitarium *(form)*; **~staat** *m* colony of termites.

Terpentin *nt or (Aus)* m -s, -e turpentine; *(inf: ~öl)* turps *(inf)*.

Terpentinöl *nt* oil of turpentine, turps *(inf)*.

Terrain [tɛˈrɛː] *nt* -s, -s land, terrain; *(fig)* territory. **das ~ sondieren** *(Mil)* to reconnoitre the terrain; *(fig)* to see how the land lies; **sich auf neuem ~ bewegen** to be exploring new ground; **sich auf unsicheres ~ begeben** to get onto shaky ground.

Terrakotta *f* -, **Terrakotten** terracotta.

Terrarium *nt* terrarium.

Terrasse *f* -, -n **(a)** *(Geog)* terrace. **(b)** *(Veranda)* terrace, patio; *(Dach~)* roof garden.

Terrassen-: **t~artig**, **t~förmig** **1** *adj* terraced; **2** *adv* in terraces; **~garten** *m* terraced garden; **~haus** *nt* house built on a terraced slope; *(modern)* split-level house.

Terrazzo *m* -s, **Terrazzi** terrazzo.

terrestrisch *adj* terrestrial.

Terrier ['teriɐ] *m* -s, - terrier.

Terrine *f* tureen.

territorial *adj* territorial.

Territorial-: **~armee** *f* territorial army; **~gewässer** *pl* territorial waters *pl*; **~hoheit** *f* territorial sovereignty.

Territorium *nt* territory.

Terror *m* -s, *no pl* terror; *(Terrorismus)* terrorism;

(~herrschaft) reign of terror; *(brutale Einschüchterung)* intimidation; *(Belästigung)* menace. **die Stadt steht unter dem ~ der Mafia** the town is being terrorized by the Mafia; **blutiger ~** terrorism and bloodshed; **organisierter ~** organized terrorism/intimidation; **~ machen** *(inf)* to raise hell *(inf)*.

Terror-: **~akt** *m* act of terrorism, terrorist act; **~angriff** *m* terrorist raid; **~anschlag** *m* terrorist attack; **~herrschaft** *f* reign of terror.

terrorisieren* *vt* to terrorize; *Untergebene etc auch* to intimidate.

Terrorismus *m* terrorism.

Terrorist(in *f)* *m* terrorist.

terroristisch *adj* terrorist *attr*.

Terror-: **~justiz** *f* brutal, intimidatory justice; **~organisation** *f* terrorist organization; **~urteil** *nt* brutal, intimidatory sentence.

Tertia ['tɛrtsia] *f* -, **Tertien** ['tɛrtsiən] **(a)** *(Sch) (Unter-/Ober~)* fourth/fifth year of German secondary school. **(b)** *no pl (Typ)* 16 point type.

Tertianer(in *f)* [tɛrtsiˈaːnɐ, -ərɪn] *m* -s, - *(Sch)* pupil in fourth/fifth year of German secondary school.

Tertiär [tɛrˈtsiɛːɐ] *nt* -s, *no pl (Geol)* tertiary period.

tertiär [tɛrˈtsiɛːɐ] *adj* tertiary.

Tertiärbereich [tɛrˈtsiɛːɐ-] *m* tertiary education.

Tertien *pl of* **Tertia.**

Terz *f* -, **-en** *(Mus)* third; *(Fechten)* tierce. **große/kleine ~** *(Mus)* major/minor third.

Terzett *nt* -(e)s, -e *(Mus)* trio.

Terzine *f (Poet)* tercet.

Tesafilm ® *m* Sellotape ® *(Brit)*, Scotch tape ® *(esp US)*.

Tesching *nt* -s, -s *or* -e *siehe* **Kleinkalibergewehr.**

Tessin *nt* -s **das ~** Ticino.

Test *m* -(e)s, -s *or* -e test.

Testament *nt* **(a)** *(Jur)* will; *(fig)* legacy. **das ~ eröffnen** to read the will; **sein ~ machen** to make one's will; **du kannst dein ~ machen!** you'd better make your will! *(inf)*; **ohne Hinterlassung eines ~s** intestate. **(b)** *(Bibl)* Testament. **Altes/Neues ~** Old/New Testament.

testamentarisch *adj* testamentary. **eine ~e Verfügung** an instruction in the will; **etw ~ festlegen** to write sth in one's will; **~ festgelegt** (written) in the will.

Testaments-: **~eröffnung** *f* reading of the will; **~vollstrecker** *m* executor; *(Frau auch)* executrix.

Testat *nt (Univ)* course attendance certificate.

Testator *m (Erblasser)* testator.

Test-: **~bild** *nt (TV)* testcard; **~bogen** *m* test paper.

testen *vt* to test *(auf + acc for)*. **jdn auf seine Intelligenz ~** to test sb's intelligence.

Tester(in *f)* *m* -s, - tester.

Test-: **~fahrer** *m* test driver; **~fall** *m* test case; **~frage** *f* test question.

testieren* *vt* **(a)** *(bescheinigen)* to certify. **sich (dat) etw ~ lassen** to get oneself a certificate of sth; **jdm etw ~** to certify sth for sb. **(b)** *(Jur: letztwillig verfügen)* to will.

Testikel *m* -s, - testicle.

Testosteron *nt* -s testosterone.

Test-: **~person** *f* subject (of a test); **~pilot** *m* test-pilot; **~reihe, ~serie** *f* series of tests; **~verfahren** *nt* method of testing; **~wahl** *f (inf)* test election; **Kommunalwahlen kann man häufig als ~wahlen ansehen** local elections can often be regarded as a test of electoral feeling.

Tetanus *m* -, *no pl* tetanus.

Tete ['teːtə, 'tɛːtə] *f* -, -n *(Mil)* head of a column.

Tetra-: **~eder** [tetraˈeːdɐ] *nt* -s, - *(Math)* tetrahedron; **~gon** [tetraˈgoːn] *nt* -s, -e *(Math)* tetragon; **~logie** *f* tetralogy.

teuer *adj* expensive, dear *usu pred*; *(fig)* dear. **etw ~ kaufen/verkaufen** to buy/sell sth for or at a high price; **etw zu ~ kaufen** to pay too much for sth; **etw für teures Geld kaufen** to pay good money for sth; **teurer werden** to go up (in price); **Brot wieder teurer!** bread up again; **in Tokio lebt man ~/ist das Leben ~** life is expensive in Tokyo, Tokyo is expensive; **~ aber gut** expensive but well worth the money; **das ist mir (lieb und) ~** *(liter)* that's very dear or precious to me; **das wird ihn ~ zu stehen kommen** *(fig)* that will cost him dear; **einen Sieg ~ erkaufen** to pay dearly for victory; **~ erkauft** dearly bought; **sich (dat) etw ~ bezahlen lassen** to expect a high payment for sth; **mein Teurer** or **~ster/meine Teure** or **T~ste** *(old, hum)* my dearest; *(von Mann zu Mann)* my dearest friend.

Teuerung *f* rise in prices, rising prices *pl*.

Teuerungs-: **~rate** *f* rate of price increases; **~welle** *f* wave or round of price increases; **~zulage** *f* cost of living bonus or supplement; **~zuschlag** *m* surcharge.

Teufel *m* -s, - *(lit, fig)* devil. **den ~ durch Beelzebub austreiben** to replace one evil with another; **den ~ im Leib haben** to be possessed by the devil; **der ~ der Eifersucht** etc a jealous etc devil; **ein ~ von einem Mann/einer Frau** *(old)* a devil of a man/woman.

(b) *(inf: Redewendungen)* **~ nochmal** or **(noch mal** or **aber auch)!** damn it (all)! *(sl)*, confound it! *(inf)*; **~ auch** *(bewundernd)* well I'll be damned *(sl)* or blowed *(inf)*; **scher dich** or **geh zum ~, hol dich der ~** go to hell *(sl)* or blazes *(inf)*!; **der ~ soll ihn/es holen!, hol ihn/es der ~** damn *(sl)* or blast *(inf)* him/it!, to hell with him/it *(sl)*; **jdn zum ~ wünschen** to wish sb in hell; **jdn zum ~ jagen** or **schicken** to send sb packing *(inf)*; **zum ~!** damn! *(sl)*, blast! *(inf)*; **wer zum ~?** who the devil *(inf)* or the hell? *(sl)*; **zum ~ mit dem Ding!** damn *(sl)* or blast *(inf)* the thing!, to hell with the thing! *(sl)*; **zum ~ sein** *(kaputt sein)* to have had it *(inf)*; *(verloren sein)* to have gone west *(inf)*; **den ~ an die Wand malen** *(schwarzmalen)* to think or imagine the worst; *(Unheil heraufbeschwören)* to tempt fate or providence; **wenn**

man vom ~ spricht(, dann ist er nicht weit) (*prov*) talk of the devil (and he's sure to appear) (*inf*); das müßte schon mit dem ~ zugehen that really would be a stroke of bad luck; ihn muß der ~ geritten haben he must have had a devil in him; da soll doch der ~ dreinschlagen it makes your blood boil (*inf*); das soll der ~ verstehen God only knows why/how *etc*; dann kommst *or* gerätst du in ~s Küche then you'll be in a hell of a mess (*sl*); wie der ~ like hell (*sl*), like the devil (*inf*); er ist hinter dem Geld her wie der ~ hinter der armen Seele he's money mad (*inf*); auf ~ komm raus like crazy (*inf*); ich mache das auf ~ komm raus I'll do that come hell or high water; da ist der ~ los all hell's been let loose (*inf*); bist du des ~s? (*old*) have you taken leave of your senses?; ich frage den ~ danach I don't give a damn (*sl*) *or* a fig (*inf*) (about it); sich den ~ um etw kümmern *or* scheren not to give a damn (*sl*) *or* a fig (*inf*) about sth; den ~ werde ich (tun)! I'll be damned if I will! (*sl*), like hell I will! (*sl*).

Teufelei *f* (*inf*) devilish trick; (*Streich*) piece of devilry.

Teufels-: ~arbeit *f* (*inf*) hell of a job (*sl*); ~austreibung *f* casting out of devils *no pl*, exorcism; ~beschwörung *f* exorcism; (*Anrufen*) invocation of/to the devil; ~braten *m* (*old inf*) devil; ~brut *f* (*old*) devil's *or* Satan's brood; ~kerl *m* (*dated*) devil of a fellow (*dated*); ~kirsche *f* (*Bot*) deadly nightshade, belladonna; ~kreis *m* vicious circle; ~kult *m* devil-worship; ~messe *f* black mass; ~weib *nt* (*dated*) devil of a woman.

teuflisch *adj* fiendish, devilish, diabolical.

Teutone *m* -n, -n Teuton.

teutonisch *adj* Teutonic.

Text *m* -(e)s, -e text; (*einer Urkunde auch, eines Gesetzes*) wording; (*von Lied*) words *pl*; (*von Schlager*) lyrics *pl*; (*von Film, Hörspiel, Rede etc*) script; (*Mus: Opern~*) libretto; (*unter Bild*) caption; (*auf Plakat*) words *pl*. weiter im ~ (*inf*) (let's) get on with it; jdn aus dem ~ bringen to put sb off, to make sb lose the thread; ein Telegramm mit folgendem ~ ... a telegram which said *or* read ...

Text-: ~aufgabe *f* problem; ~buch *nt* script; (*für Lieder*) textbook; ~dichter *m* (*von Liedern*) songwriter; (*bei Oper*) librettist.

texten 1 *vt* to write. 2 *vi siehe* Texter(in) to write songs/copy.

Texter(in *f*) *m* -s, - (*für Schlager*) songwriter; (*für Werbesprüche*) copywriter.

Textil- *in cpds* textile; ~arbeiter *m* textile worker; ~branche *f* textile trade; ~fabrik *f* textile factory; (*für Textilien aus Naturfasern auch*) textile mill.

Textilien [-iən] *pl* linen, clothing, fabrics *etc*; (*Ind*) textiles *pl*.

Textil-: ~industrie *f* textile industry; ~waren *pl siehe* Textilien.

Text-: ~kritik *f* textual criticism; ~linguistik *f* (*Ling*) text linguistics *sing*; ~semantik *f* (*Ling*) textual semantics *sing*; ~stelle *f* passage.

Textur *f* texture.

texturieren* *vt* to texture.

Tezett *nt* (*inf*) jdn/etw bis ins *or* zum ~ kennen to know sb/sth inside out (*inf*).

TH [te:'ha:] *f* -, -s *abbr of* Technische Hochschule.

Thailand *nt* -s Thailand.

Thailänder(in *f*) *m* -s, - Thai.

thailändisch *adj* Thai.

Theater *nt* -s, - (a) theatre (*Brit*), theater (*US*); (~kunst *auch*) drama; (*Schauspielbühne*) theatre company; (*Zuschauer*) audience. beim *or* am/im ~ arbeiten to be on the stage/work in the theatre; er ist *or* arbeitet beim Ulmer ~ he's with the Ulm theatre company; heute abend wird im ~ „Othello" gezeigt *or* gegeben "Othello" is on *or* is playing at the theatre tonight; das ~ fängt um 8 Uhr an the performance begins at 8 o'clock; zum ~ gehen to go on the stage; ins ~ gehen to go to the theatre; das französische ~ French theatre; ~ spielen (*lit*) to act; (*Stück aufführen*) to put on a play; (*fig*) to put on an act, to play-act; jdm ein ~ vormachen *or* vorspielen (*fig*) to put on an act for sb's benefit; das ist doch alles nur ~ (*fig*) it's all just play-acting.
(b) (*fig*) to-do (*inf*), fuss. das war vielleicht ein ~, bis ich ... what a palaver *or* performance *or* carry-on I had to ... (*inf*); das ist vielleicht immer ein ~, wenn er kommt there's always a big fuss when he comes; (ein) ~ machen (*Umstände*) to make a (big) fuss (mit jdm *or* sb); (*Szene auch*) to make a scene *or* a song and dance (*inf*); jdm ein ~ machen to make a scene (with sb).

Theater- *in cpds* theatre (*Brit*), theater (*US*); ~abonnement *nt* theatre subscription; ~aufführung *f* stage production; (*Vorstellung, Darbietung*) performance; ~beruf *m* career in the theatre; ~besuch *m* visit to the theatre; ~besucher *m* theatregoer; ~dichter *m* dramatist, playwright; ~gebäude *nt* theatre; ~karte *f* theatre ticket; ~kasse *f* theatre box office; ~kritiker *m* theatre *or* drama critic; ~probe *f* rehearsal; ~stück *nt* (stage) play.

theatralisch *adj* theatrical, histrionic.

Theismus *m* theism.

Theke *f* -, -n (*Schanktisch*) bar; (*Ladentisch*) counter. etw unter der ~ verkaufen to sell sth under the counter.

Thema *nt* -s, Themen *or* -ta (*Gegenstand*) subject, topic; (*Leitgedanke, Mus*) theme. interessant vom ~ her interesting as far as the subject matter is concerned; beim ~ bleiben/vom ~ abschweifen to stick to/stray from *or* wander off the subject *or* point; das ~ wechseln to change the subject; wir wollen das ~ begraben (*inf*) let's not talk about it any more, let's forget the whole subject; das ~ ist (für mich) erledigt (*inf*) as far as I'm concerned the matter's closed; ~ Nr. 1 (*hum inf*) sex.

Themamusik *f* theme music.

Themata *pl of* Thema.

Thematik *f* topic.

thematisch *adj* thematic; (*vom Thema her*) as regards subject matter. ~es Verzeichnis subject index.

thematisieren* *vt* (*geh*) to pick out as a central theme.

Themen *pl of* Thema.

Themen-: ~bereich *m*, ~kreis *m* topic; in den ~bereich „Tiere" gehören to come under the heading of "animals"; ~stellung *f* subject; ~wahl *f* choice of subject *or* topic.

Theologe *m*, **Theologin** *f* theologian.

Theologie *f* theology. Doktor der ~ Doctor of Divinity.

theologisch *adj* theological.

Theorem *nt* -s, -e theorem.

Theoretiker(in *f*) *m* -s, - theorist, theoretician.

theoretisch *adj* theoretical. ~ gesehen in theory, theoretically.

theoretisieren* *vi* to theorize.

Theorie *f* theory; *siehe* grau.

Theosophie *f* theosophy.

Therapeut(in *f*) *m* -en, -en therapist.

Therapeutik *f* therapeutics *sing*.

therapeutisch *adj* therapeutic(al).

Therapie *f* therapy (*auch fig*), treatment; (*Behandlungsmethode*) (method of) treatment (*gegen* for).

Thermal-: ~bereich *m* (*Phys*) thermal region; ~bad *nt* thermal bath; (*Gebäude*) thermal baths *pl*; (*Badeort*) spa, watering-place (*old*); jdm ~bäder verschreiben to prescribe hydrotherapy for sb; ~quelle *f* thermal spring.

Therme *f* -, -n (*Quelle*) thermal *or* hot spring. die ~n the thermals; (*Hist*) the (thermal) baths.

thermisch *adj attr* (*Phys*) thermal.

Thermo- *in cpds* thermo-; ~chemie *f* thermochemistry; ~dynamik *f* thermodynamics *sing*; t~elektrisch *adj* thermoelectric(al).

Thermometer *nt* -s, - thermometer.

Thermometerstand *m* temperature. bei ~ 60° when the temperature reaches 60°, when the thermometer reads 60°.

thermometrisch *adj attr* thermometric(al).

thermonuklear *adj* thermonuclear.

Thermosflasche *f* thermos (flask) ®, vacuum flask *or* bottle (*US*).

Thermostat *m* -(e)s, -e thermostat.

Thesaurus *m* -, **Thesauri** *or* **Thesauren** thesaurus.

These *f* -, -n hypothesis, thesis; (*inf: Theorie*) theory. Luthers 95 ~n Luther's 95 propositions.

Thing *nt* -(e)s, -e (*Hist*) thing.

Thingplatz *m* (*Hist*) thingstead.

Thomas *m siehe* ungläubig.

Thriller ['θrɪlə] *m* -s, - thriller.

Thrombose *f* -, -n thrombosis.

thrombotisch *adj* thrombotic.

Thron *m* -(e)s, -e throne; (*hum inf: Nachttopf*) pot. von seinem ~ herabsteigen (*fig*) to come down off one's high horse.

Thron-: ~anwärter *m* claimant to the throne; (*Thronfolger*) heir apparent; ~besteigung *f* accession (to the throne).

thronen *vi* (*lit: auf dem Thron sitzen*) to sit enthroned; (*fig: in exponierter Stellung sitzen*) to sit in state; (*liter: überragen*) to stand in solitary splendour.

Thron-: ~erbe *m*, ~erbin *f* heir to the throne; ~folge *f* line of succession; die ~folge antreten to succeed to the throne; ~folger(in *f*) *m* -s, - heir to the throne, heir apparent; ~himmel *m* canopy; ~räuber *m* usurper; ~rede *f* King's/Queen's speech at the opening of parliament; ~saal *m* throne room.

Thuja *f* -, **Thujen** arborvitae, Thuja.

Thunfisch *m* tuna (fish).

Thüringen *nt* -s Thuringia.

Thüringer(in *f*) *m* -s, - Thuringian.

thüringisch *adj* Thuringian.

Thusnelda *f* -, (*inf*) bird (*Brit inf*), chick (*inf*).

Thymian *m* -s, -e thyme.

Thymusdrüse *f* thymus (gland).

Tiara *f* -, **Tiaren** tiara, triple crown.

Tibet *nt* -s Tibet.

Tibetaner(in *f*) *m* -s, - Tibetan.

tibetanisch *adj* Tibetan.

tick *interj* tick. ~ tack! tick-tock!

Tick *m* -(e)s, -s tic; (*inf: Schrulle*) quirk (*inf*). Uhren sind sein ~ he has a thing about clocks (*inf*); einen ~ haben (*inf*) to be crazy; er hat einen ~ mit seiner Ordnung he has this thing about tidiness (*inf*).

-tick *m in cpds* (*inf*) ein Auto~ a thing about cars (*inf*).

ticken *vi* to tick (away). du tickst ja nicht richtig you're off your rocker! (*inf*).

Ticket *nt* -s, -s (plane) ticket.

Tide *f* -, -n (*N Ger*) tide.

tief 1 *adj* (a) (*weit reichend*) Tal, Wasser, Wurzeln, Schnee, Wunde, Seufzer deep; Verbeugung auch, Ausschnitt low. ~er Teller soup plate; ein ~er Eingriff in jds Rechte (*acc*) a gross infringement of sb's rights; die ~eren Ursachen the underlying causes; aus ~stem Herzen/~ster Seele from the bottom of one's heart/the depths of one's soul.
(b) (*sehr stark, groß*) Ohnmacht, Schlaf, Erröten, Gefühl deep; Haß auch, Schmerz intense; Not dire; Verlassenheit, Einsamkeit, Elend utter. bis in den ~sten Winter/die ~ste Nacht, bis ~ in den Winter/die Nacht hinein (till) well into winter/late into the night.
(c) *auch adv* (*mitten in etwas liegend*) er wohnt ~ in den Bergen he lives deep in the mountains; ~ im Wald, im ~en Wald deep in the forest, in the depths of the forest; ~ im Winter, im ~en Winter in the depths of winter; ~ in der Nacht, in der ~en Nacht at dead of night; ~ in Afrika, im ~sten Afrika in darkest Africa; ~ im Innern, im ~sten Innern in one's heart of hearts.

(d) *(tiefgründig)* deep, profound. der ~ere Sinn the deeper meaning.

(e) *(niedrig)* *Lage, Stand, Temperatur* low.

(f) *(dunkel)* *Farbton, Stimme* deep; *(Mus)* low; *Ton* low. in ~es Schwarz gekleidet sein to be in deep mourning; etw zu ~ singen to sing sth flat; ~ sprechen to talk in a deep voice; ~er spielen to play in a lower key *or* lower; ~er stimmen to tune down; das Tonbandgerät ~er stellen to turn up the bass on the tape recorder.

2 *adv* **(a)** *(weit nach unten, innen, hinten)* a long way; *bohren, graben, eindringen, tauchen auch* deep; *sich bücken* low; *untersuchen* in depth. ~ in etw *(acc)* einsinken to sink deep into sth, to sink down a long way into sth; 3 m ~ fallen to fall 3 metres; ~ sinken *(fig)* to sink low; ~ fallen *(fig)* to go downhill; bis ~ in etw *(acc)* hinein *(örtlich)* a long way down/deep into sth; *(ganz)* ~ unter uns a long way below us, far below us; der Schmerz sitzt ~er unten the pain is lower down; seine Augen liegen ~ in den Höhlen his eyes are like hollows in his face; ~ verschneit deep *or* thick with snow; wir müssen die Ursache ~er suchen we must search deeper for the reason; ~ in Gedanken (versunken) deep in thought; ~ in Schulden stecken to be deep in debt; jdm ~ in die Augen sehen to look deep into sb's eyes; ~ in die Tasche *or* den Beutel greifen müssen *(inf)* to have to reach *or* dig deep in one's pocket; das greift ~ in unsere Rechte ein that represents a gross infringement of our rights; das geht bei ihm nicht sehr ~ *(inf)* it doesn't go very deep with him.

(b) *(sehr stark)* *verletzen, atmen, erröten, schockieren, erschüttern* deeply; *schlafen auch* soundly; *fühlen, empfinden auch* acutely; *bedauern auch* profoundly; *erschrecken* terribly.

(c) *(mitten in)* siehe 1 (c).

(d) *(tiefgründig)* nachdenken deeply. etw ~er begründen to find a deeper reason for sth.

(e) *(niedrig)* low. ein Stockwerk ~er one floor down *or* lower, on the floor below; Hanau liegt ~er als Schlüchtern Hanau is lower-lying than Schlüchtern; das Haus liegt ~er als die Straße the house lies below (the level of) the road; im Winter steht die Sonne ~er the sun is lower in the sky) in winter.

Tief *nt* -(e)s, -e **(a)** *(Met)* depression; *(im Kern, fig)* low. ein moralisches ~ *(fig)* a low. **(b)** *(Naut: Rinne)* deep *(spec)*, channel.

Tief-: ~bau *m* civil engineering *(excluding the construction of building)*; siehe Hoch-und-Tiefbau; t~betrübt *adj attr* deeply distressed; t~bewegt *adj attr* deeply moved; t~blau *adj attr* deep blue; t~blickend *adj attr* *(fig)* perceptive, astute; ~decker *m* -s, - *(Aviat)* low-winged (mono)plane.

Tiefdruck *m* **(a)** *(Met)* low pressure. **(b)** *(Typ)* gravure.

Tiefdruck-: ~gebiet *nt* *(Met)* area of low pressure, depression; ~keil *m* *(Met)* trough of low pressure.

Tiefe *f* -, -n siehe tief **(a)** depth; *(von Verbeugung, Ausschnitt)* lowness. unten in der ~ far below; in die ~ blicken to look down into the depths *or* a long way; in die ~ versinken to sink into the depths; das U-Boot ging auf ~ the submarine dived; aus der ~ meines Herzens from the depths of my heart. **(b)** deepness; intensity; direness; depths *pl*. **(c)** *(von Wald)* depths *pl*. **(d)** deepness, profundity. **(e)** lowness. **(f)** deepness, lowness. **(g)** *(Art, Phot)* depth.

Tief-: ~ebene *f* lowland plain; die Oberrheinische ~ebene the Upper Rhine Valley; t~empfunden *adj attr* deep(ly)-felt.

Tiefen-: ~bestrahlung *f* deep ray therapy; ~gestein *nt* plutonic rock, pluton; ~heini *m* *(hum inf)* shrink *(inf)*, head-shrinker *(inf)*; ~psychologe *m* depth psychologist; psychoanalyst; ~psychologie *f* depth psychology; psychoanalysis; ~rausch *m* nitrogen narcosis *(form)*; ~schärfe *f* *(Phot)* depth of field; ~wirkung *f* deep action; *(Art, Phot)* effect of depth.

Tief-: t~ernst *adj* deadly serious; t~erschüttert *adj attr* deeply disturbed; ~flieger *m* low-flying aircraft, hedgehopper *(inf)*; geistiger ~flieger *(pej inf)* numskull *(inf)*, dummy *(inf)*; ~flug *m* low-level *or* low-altitude flight; er überquerte den Kanal im ~flug he crossed low over the Channel; ~gang *m* *(Naut)* draught; *(fig inf)* depth; ~garage *f* underground car park; t~gefroren *adj* frozen; t~gehend *adj* *(lit, fig)* deep; *Schmerz* extreme, acute; *Kränkung* extreme; t~gekühlt *adj* *(gefroren)* frozen; *(sehr kalt)* chilled; t~greifend *adj* far-reaching; t~gründig *adj* profound, deep; *(durchdacht)* well-grounded.

Tiefkühl-: ~fach *nt* freezer compartment; ~kost *f* frozen food; ~truhe *f* (chest-type) deep-freeze *or* freezer.

Tief-: ~lader *m* -s, - ~ladewagen *m* low-loader; ~land *nt* lowlands *pl*; t~liegend *adj attr* *Gegend, Häuser* low-lying; *Augen* deep-set; *(nach Krankheit)* sunken; ~punkt *m* low; ~schlag *m* *(Boxen, fig)* hit below the belt; jdm einen ~schlag verpassen *(lit, fig)* to hit sb below the belt; das war ein ~schlag *(lit, fig)* that was below the belt; t~schürfend *adj* profound.

Tiefsee *f* deep sea.

Tiefsee- *in cpds* deep-sea.

Tief-: ~sinn *m* profundity; t~sinnig *adj* profound, ~sinnigkeit *f* profundity; ~stand *m* low; ~stapelei *f* understatement; *(auf eigene Leistung bezogen)* modesty; die sprichwörtliche ~stapelei der Briten the British art of understatement; t~stapeln *vi sep* to understate the case; to be modest; ~start *m* crouch start.

Tiefst-: ~preis *m* lowest price; „~preise" "rock bottom prices"; ~temperatur *f* lowest temperature; ~wert *m* lowest value.

tieftraurig *adj* very sad.

Tiegel *m* -s, - *(zum Kochen)* (sauce)pan; *(in der Chemie)* crucible; *(~druckpresse)* platen (press).

Tier *nt* -(e)s, -e animal; *(großes ~ auch)* beast; *(Haus~ auch)* pet; *(inf: Ungeziefer)* bug *(inf)*; *(inf: Mensch)* brute; *(grob)* animal; *(gefräßig)* pig *(inf)*. großes *or* hohes ~ *(inf)* big shot *(inf)*; das ~ im Menschen the beast in man; da wird der Mensch zum ~ it brings out man's bestiality; dann kommt das ~ im Manne bei ihm heraus that brings out the caveman in him; sich wie die ~e benehmen to behave like animals.

Tier- *in cpds* animal; *(Med)* veterinary; *(für Haustiere)* pet; ~arzt *m* vet, veterinary surgeon *(form)*, veterinarian *(US)*; ~asyl *nt* (animal) pound.

Tierchen *nt dim of* Tier little animal. ein niedliches ~ a sweet little creature; siehe Pläsierchen.

Tier-: ~freund *m* animal/pet lover; ~garten *m* zoo; ~halter *m* *(von Haustieren)* pet-owner; *(von Nutztieren)* livestock owner; ~handlung *f* pet shop; ~heilkunde *f* veterinary medicine; ~heim *nt* animal home.

tierisch *adj* animal *attr*; *(fig)* *Roheit, Grausamkeit* bestial; *(unzivilisiert)* *Benehmen, Sitten* animal *attr*; *(fig inf: unerträglich)* deadly *no adv* *(inf)*, terrible. ~er Ernst *(inf)* deadly seriousness; sich ~ betragen to behave like an animal.

Tier-: ~kämpfe *pl* animal fights *pl*; ~kreis *m* zodiac; ~kreiszeichen *nt* sign of the zodiac; im ~kreiszeichen des Skorpions geboren sein to be born under Scorpio; ~kunde *f* zoology; ~liebe *f* love of animals; t~liebend *adj* fond of animals, animal-loving *attr*; pet-loving *attr*; ~medizin *f* veterinary medicine; ~park *m* zoo; ~pfleger *m* zoo-keeper; ~quäler *m* -s, - person who is cruel to animals; ein ~quäler sein to be cruel to animals; ~quälerei *f* cruelty to animals; *(fig inf)* cruelty to dumb animals; ~reich *nt* animal kingdom; ~schutz *m* protection of animals; ~schutzverein *m* society for the prevention of cruelty to animals; ~versuch *m* animal experiment; ~welt *f* animal kingdom; ~zucht *f* stockbreeding.

Tiger *m* -s, - tiger.

Tiger-: ~auge *nt* tiger's-eye; ~fell *nt* tiger skin.

Tigerin *f* tigress.

tigern **1** *vt* siehe getigert. **2** *vi aux sein* *(inf)* to mooch.

Tilde *f* -, -n tilde.

tilgbar *adj* *Schulden* repayable.

tilgen *vt* *(geh)* **(a)** *Schulden* to pay off. **(b)** *(beseitigen)* *Sünde, Unrecht, Spuren* to wipe out; *Erinnerung, Druckfehler* to erase; *Strafe* to set aside; *Posten* *(Typ, Ling)* to delete. ein Volk vom Erdboden ~ to wipe a nation off the face of the earth.

Tilgung *f* siehe vt **(a)** repayment. **(b)** wiping out; erasure; setting aside; deletion.

Tilsiter *m* -s, - Tilsit cheese.

Timbre [tɛ̃ːbr] *nt* -s, -s *(geh)* timbre.

Timpani *pl* *(Mus)* timpani *pl*.

tingeln *vi* *(inf)* to appear in small night-clubs/theatres etc.

Tingeltangel *nt or m* -s, - *(dated)* *(Veranstaltung)* hop *(inf)*; *(Lokal)* second-rate night-club, honky-tonk *(US inf)*.

Tinktur *f* tincture.

Tinnef *m* -s *no pl* *(inf)* rubbish, trash *(inf)*.

Tinte *f* -, -n ink. ~ verspritzen *(fig)* to write; sich in die ~ setzen, in die ~ geraten *(fig)* to get (oneself) into a pickle *(inf)*; in der ~ sitzen *(inf)* to be in the soup *(inf)*.

Tinten-: ~faß *nt* inkpot; *(eingelassen)* inkwell; ~fisch *m* cuttlefish; *(Kalmar)* squid; *(achtarmig)* octopus; ~fleck *m* *(auf Kleidung)* ink stain; *(auf Papier)* ink blot; ~klecks *m* ink blot; ~pilz *m* ink-cap; ~stift *m* indelible pencil.

Tip *m* -s, -s *(Sport, St Ex)* tip; *(Andeutung)* hint; *(an Polizei)* tip-off. ich gebe dir einen ~, wie du ... I'll give you a tip how to ...; ich gebe dir einen ~, was du ihm/mir schenken kannst I'll tell you what you could give him/I'll give you a hint as to what you could give him/I'll give you a hint as to what you could give me; unser ~ für diesen Sommer: ... this summer we recommend ...

Tippelbruder *m* *(dated inf)* gentleman of the road.

tippeln *vi aux sein* *(inf)* *(gehen)* to foot it *(inf)*; *(mit kurzen Schritten)* to trip; *(auf Zehenspitzen)* to tiptoe; *(Maus, Kinder)* to patter.

tippen *vti* **(a)** *(klopfen)* to tap *(an/auf/gegen etw (acc)* sth). *(zeigen)* to touch *(auf or an etw (acc)* sth). jdn *or* jdm auf die Schulter ~ to tap sb on the shoulder; sich *(dat)* an die Stirn ~ to tap one's forehead; an den Hut ~ to touch *or* tip one's hat; an einen Punkt/eine Frage ~ *(fig)* to touch on a point/question. **(b)** *(inf: auf der Schreibmaschine)* to type *(an etw (dat)* sth). **(c)** *(wetten)* to fill in one's coupon; *(im Toto auch)* to do the pools. im Lotto ~ to do the lottery; eine bestimmte Zahl ~ to put a particular number on one's coupon. **(d)** nur *vi* *(inf: raten)* to guess. auf jdn/etw ~ to put one's money on sb/sth *(inf)*; ich tippe darauf, daß ... I bet (that) ...; auf jds Sieg *(acc)* ~ to back sb to win *(inf)*.

Tippfehler *m* *(inf)* typing mistake *or* error.

Tippfräulein *nt* *(inf)*, **Tippse** *f* -, -n *(pej)* typist.

tipptapp *interj* pitter-patter.

tipptopp *(inf)* **1** *adj* immaculate; *(prima)* first-class, tip-top *(dated inf)*. **2** *adv* immaculately; *(prima)* really well. ~ sauber spotless.

Tippzettel *m* *(im Toto)* football *or* pools coupon; *(im Lotto)* lottery coupon.

Tirade *f* tirade, diatribe.

tirilieren* *vi* *(geh)* to warble, to trill.

Tirol *nt* -s the Tyrol.

Tiroler(in *f)* *m* -s, - Tyrolese, Tyrolean.

Tirolerhut *m* Tyrolean hat.

Tisch *m* -(e)s, -e table; *(Schreib~)* desk; *(Werk~)* bench; *(Mahlzeit)* meal. bei ~ at (the) table; vom ~ aufstehen to leave the table; sich zu *or* an den ~ setzen to sit down at the table; zu ~ kommen to come to the table; die Gäste zu ~ bitten to ask the guests to take their places; bitte zu ~! lunch/dinner is served!; vor/nach ~ before/after the meal; zu ~ sein/gehen to be having one's lunch/dinner/to go to lunch/dinner; er zahlte bar auf den ~ he paid cash down or cash on the nail (inf); etw auf den ~ des Hauses legen (fig) to produce sth for all to see; etw auf den ~ bringen (inf) to serve sth (up); die Beine or Füße unter jds ~ strecken (inf) to eat at sb's table; unter den ~ fallen (inf) to go by the board; jdn unter den ~ trinken or saufen (inf) to drink sb under the table; es wird gegessen, was auf den ~ kommt! you'll eat what you're given; zwei Parteien an einen ~ bringen (fig) to get two parties round the conference table; getrennt von ~ und Bett leben to be separated; vom ~ sein (fig) to be cleared out of the way; siehe rund, grün, rein².

Tisch- in cpds ~besen m crumb brush; ~dame f dinner partner; ~decke f tablecloth; ~ende nt end of a table; am oberen/unteren ~ende to sit at the head/the foot of the table; ~feuerzeug nt table lighter; ~gast m (luncheon/dinner) guest; ~gebet nt grace; ~gesellschaft f dinner party; ~gespräch nt table talk; ~herr m dinner partner; ~karte f place card; ~kasten m drawer in the table; ~lampe f table lamp; ~läufer m table runner.

Tischleindeckdich nt -(s) ein ~ gefunden haben (fig) to be onto a good thing (inf).

Tischler m -s - joiner, carpenter; (Möbel~) cabinet-maker.

Tischlerei f (a) (Werkstatt) joiner's or carpenter's/cabinet-maker's workshop. (b) no pl (inf) siehe **Tischlerhandwerk**.

Tischlerhandwerk nt joinery, carpentry; cabinetmaking.

tischlern vi (inf) to do woodwork.

Tischlerwerkstatt f siehe **Tischlerei (a).**

Tisch-: ~nachbar m neighbour (at table); ~ordnung f seating plan; ~platte f tabletop; ~rechner m desk calculator; ~rede f after-dinner speech; (Unterhaltung) table talk; ~redner m after-dinner speaker; ~rücken nt -s, no pl table-turning; ~telefon nt table telephone (in night-club).

Tischtennis nt table tennis.

Tischtennis- in cpds table-tennis; ~platte f table-tennis table; ~schläger m table-tennis bat.

Tisch-: ~tuch nt tablecloth; ~wäsche f table linen; ~wein m table wine; ~zeit f mealtime; zur ~zeit at mealtimes.

Titan¹ m -en, -en (Myth) Titan.

Titan² nt -s, no pl (Chem) titanium.

titanenhaft, titanisch adj titanic.

Titel m -s, - (a) title. jdn mit ~ ansprechen to address sb by his/her title, to give sb his/her title; unter dem ~ under the title; (fig: Motto) under the slogan. (b) (~blatt) title page. (c) (von Gesetz, Etat) section.

Titel-: ~anwärter m (main) contender for the title; ~bild nt cover (picture); ~blatt nt title page.

Titelei f (Typ) prelims pl.

Titel-: ~held m eponymous hero, hero (mentioned in the title); ~kampf m (Sport) finals pl; (Boxen) title fight; ~rolle f title role; ~schutz m copyright (of a title); ~seite f cover, front page; ~sucht f mania for titles; ~träger m person with a title; ~verteidiger m title holder; ~zeile f title line.

Titte f -, -n (vulg) tit (sl), boob (inf), knocker (sl).

Titularbischof m titular bishop.

Titulatur f title, form of address.

titulieren* vt Buch, Werk etc to entitle (mit etw sth); jdn to call (mit etw sth), to address (mit as).

tizianrot adj Haare titian (red).

tja interj well.

Toast [to:st] m -(e)s, -e (a) (Brot) toast. ein ~ some toast. (b) (Trinkspruch) toast. einen ~ auf jdn ausbringen to propose a toast to sb.

Toastbrot ['to:st-] nt sliced white bread for toasting.

toasten ['to:stn] 1 vi to drink a toast (auf + acc to). 2 vt Brot to toast.

Toaster ['to:stɐ] m -s, - toaster.

Tobak m: das ist starker ~! (inf) that's a bit thick! (inf); siehe Anno.

Tobel m or nt -s, - (S Ger, Sw, Aus) siehe **Klamm.**

toben vi (a) (wüten) (Elemente, Leidenschaften, Kämpfe etc) to rage; (Mensch) to throw a fit; (vor Wut, Begeisterung etc) to go wild (vor with). (b) (ausgelassen spielen) to rollick (about); aux sein (inf: laufen) to charge about.

Toberei f (inf) rollicking about.

Tobsucht f (bei Tieren) madness; (bei Menschen) maniacal rage.

tobsüchtig adj mad; Mensch auch raving mad.

Tobsuchtsanfall m (inf) fit of rage. einen ~ bekommen to blow one's top (inf), to go stark raving mad (inf).

Tochter f -, ¨ daughter; (~firma) subsidiary; (Sw: Bedienstete) girl. die ~ des Hauses (form) the daughter or young lady of the house; das Fräulein ~ (iro, form) mademoiselle; siehe höher.

Töchterchen nt baby daughter.

Tochter-: ~firma f subsidiary (firm); ~geschwulst f secondary growth or tumour; ~gesellschaft f subsidiary (company).

töchterlich adj attr daughterly; Pflicht, Gehorsam, Liebe filial.

Tod m -(e)s, -e death. der ~ als Schnitter Death the Reaper; ~ durch Erschießen/Ersticken death by firing squad/suffocation; auf den ~ krank sein to be dangerously or critically ill; jdn auf den ~ verwunden to wound sb fatally or mortally; eines natürlichen/gewaltsamen ~es sterben to die of natural causes/a violent death; er muß des ~es sterben he will have to die; sich zu ~e trinken/trinken to fall to one's death/drink oneself to death; des ~es/ein Kind des ~es sein to be doomed; sich (dat) den ~ holen to catch one's death (of cold); in den ~ gehen to go to one's death; für jdn in den ~ gehen to die for sb; bis in den ~ until death; jdm in den ~ folgen to follow sb; ~ und Teufel! (old) by the devil! (old); weder ~ noch Teufel werden

mich davon abhalten! I'll do it, come hell or high water!; jdn/etw auf den ~ nicht leiden or ausstehen können (inf) to be unable to abide or stand sb/sth; etw zu ~e hetzen or reiten (fig) to flog sth to death; sich zu ~(e) langweilen to be bored to death; sich zu ~(e) schämen to be utterly ashamed; zu ~e betrübt sein to be in the depths of despair; siehe Leben, bleich.

tod-: ~bringend adj (geh) Gift deadly, lethal; Krankheit fatal; ~elend adj (inf) as miserable as sin (inf), utterly miserable; ~ernst adj (inf) deadly or absolutely serious; es ist mir ~ernst (damit) I'm deadly or absolutely serious (about it).

Todes-: ~angst f mortal agony; eine ~angst haben/~ängste ausstehen (inf) to be scared to death (inf); ~anzeige f (als Brief) letter announcing sb's death; (Annonce) obituary (notice); „~anzeigen" Deaths; ~art f death, way to die; ~erklärung f die ~erklärung aussprechen to pronounce death; ~fall m death; (in der Familie auch) bereavement; ~furcht f fear of death; ~gefahr f mortal danger; ~jahr nt year of sb's death; ~kampf m death throes pl; ~kandidat m condemned man/woman etc; t~mutig adj absolutely fearless; ~nachricht f news of sb's death; ~not f mortal anguish; in ~nöten sein (fig) to be in a desperate situation; ~opfer nt death, casualty, fatality; ~qualen pl final or mortal agony; ~qualen ausstehen (fig) to suffer agony or agonies; ~schuß m fatal shot; der ~schuß auf jdn the shot which killed sb; ~schütze m person who fires/fired the fatal shot; (Attentäter) assassin; ~spirale f death spiral; ~stoß m deathblow; jdm/einer Sache den ~stoß geben or versetzen (lit, fig) to deal sb the deathblow/deal the deathblow to sth; ~strafe f death penalty; ~stunde f hour of death; (Jahrestag) anniversary of sb's death; ~tag m day of sb's death; ~ursache f cause of death; ~urteil nt death sentence; ~verachtung f (inf) mit ~verachtung with utter disgust or repugnance; jdn mit ~verachtung strafen to scorn to notice sb; ~wunde f fatal injury; ~zeit f time of death.

Tod-: ~feind m deadly or mortal enemy; t~geweiht adj doomed; t~krank adj dangerously or critically ill.

tödlich adj fatal; Gefahr mortal, deadly; Gift deadly, lethal; Dosis lethal; (inf) Langeweile, Ernst, Sicherheit deadly; Beleidigung mortal. ~ verunglücken to be killed in an accident.

Tod-: t~müde adj (inf) dead tired (inf); t~schick adj (inf) dead smart (inf); t~sicher (inf) 1 adj dead certain (inf); Methode, Tip sure-fire (inf); eine t~sichere Angelegenheit or Sache a dead cert (inf), a cinch (esp US inf); das ist doch t~sicher, daß ... it's a dead cert that ... (inf); 2 adv for sure or certain; ~sicherheit f (inf) mit ~sicherheit for sure or certain; ~sünde f mortal or deadly sin; t~unglücklich adj (inf) desperately unhappy.

Toga f -, Togen toga.

Tohuwabohu [to:huva'bo:hu] nt -(s), -s chaos no pl. das war ein ~ it was utter or complete chaos.

Toilette [toa'lɛtə] f (a) (Abort) toilet, lavatory (Brit); (im Privathaus auch) bathroom (euph). öffentliche ~ public conveniences pl (Brit), comfort station (US); auf die ~ gehen/auf der ~ sein to go to/be in the toilet. (b) no pl (geh: Ankleiden, Körperpflege) toilet. ~ machen to do one's toilet (old). (c) (geh: Kleidung) outfit. in großer ~ in full dress.

Toiletten- [toa'lɛtn-] in cpds toilet; ~artikel m usu pl toiletry; ~beutel m sponge (Brit) or toilet bag; ~frau f toilet or lavatory (Brit) attendant; ~garnitur f (a) toilet or bathroom set; (b) (für ~tisch) dressing table set; ~papier nt toilet paper; ~schrank m bathroom cabinet; ~seife f toilet soap; ~sitz m toilet or lavatory (Brit) seat; ~tasche f toilet bag; ~tisch m dressing table; ~wasser nt toilet water.

toi, toi, toi interj (inf) (vor Prüfung etc) good luck; (unberufen) touch wood.

Tokaier(wein) m -s, - Tokay.

Töle f -, -n (dial pej) cur.

tolerant adj tolerant (gegen of).

Toleranz f tolerance (gegen of).

Toleranz-: ~dosis f tolerance dose; ~grenze f limit of tolerance; ~schwelle f tolerance level or threshold.

tolerieren* vt to tolerate.

Tolerierung f toleration.

toll adj (a) (old: irr, tollwütig) mad. (b) (wild, ausgelassen) wild; Streiche, Gedanken, Treiben auch mad. es ging ~ her or zu this was pretty wild (inf); (drei) ~en Tage the (last three) days of Fasching. (c) (inf: verrückt) mad, crazy. das war ein ~es Ding that was mad or madness; (wie) ~ regnen/fahren etc to rain like mad (inf) or crazy (inf)/drive etc like a madman or maniac. (d) (inf: schlimm) terrible. es kommt noch ~er! there's more or worse to come; es zu ~ treiben to go too far. (e) (inf: großartig) fantastic (inf), great (inf) no adv.

tolldreist adj bold, (as) bold as brass.

Tolle f -, -n quiff.

tollen vi (a) to romp or rollick about. (b) aux sein (laufen) to rush about.

Toll-: ~haus nt (old) lunatic asylum; ~heit f (a) no pl (old) madness; (b) (Tat) mad act.

Tollität f form of address for Royal Fasching Couple.

Toll-: ~kirsche f deadly nightshade, belladonna; t~kühn adj daredevil attr, daring; ~kühnheit f daring; in seiner ~kühnheit daringly; ~wut f rabies; ~wutgefahr f danger of rabies; t~wütig adj rabid.

Tolpatsch m -es, -e (inf) clumsy or awkward creature.

tolpatschig adj (inf) awkward, ungainly, clumsy.

Tölpel m -s, - (inf) fool.

tölpelhaft adj foolish, silly.

Tomahawk ['tɔmahaːk, -hoːk] m -s, -s tomahawk.

Tomate f -, -n tomato. du treulose ~! (inf) you're a fine friend!

Tomaten- *in cpds* tomato; ~**mark**, ~**püree** *nt* tomato puree.
Tombola *f* -, -s *or* **Tombolen** tombola.
Tommy ['tɔmi] *m* -s, -s (*inf*) tommy.
Ton[1] *m* -(e)s, -e (*Erdart*) clay.
Ton[2] *m* -(e)s, ⸚e (a) (*Laut*) sound (*auch Rad, Film*); (*von Zeitzeichen, im Telefon*) pip; (*Klangfarbe*) tone; (*Mus: Note*) note. halber/ganzer ~ semitone/tone; den ~ **angeben** (*lit*) to give the note; (*fig*) (*Mensch*) to set the tone; (*Thema, Farbe etc*) to be predominant; keinen ~ **heraus-** *or* **hervorbringen** not to be able to say a word; keinen ~ **sagen** *or* von sich geben not to make a sound; er hat keinen ~ **von sich hören lassen** (*fig*) we haven't heard a word *or* a peep (*inf*) from him; keinen ~ (**über etw** *acc*) **verlauten lassen** (*fig*) not to say a word (about sth); hast du *or* hat der Mensch ⸚e! (*inf*) did you ever! (*inf*); dicke *or* große ⸚e **spucken** *or* **reden** (*inf*) to talk big; in großen ⸚**en** grandiosely; jdn in höchsten ⸚**en loben** (*inf*) to praise sb to the skies *or* highly.
  (**b**) (*Betonung*) stress; (*Tonfall*) intonation; (*im Chinesischen etc*) tone.
  (**c**) (*Redeweise, Umgangston*) tone; (*Atmosphäre*) atmosphere. den richtigen ~ **finden** to strike the right note; ich verbitte mir diese ⸚**e** *or* **diesen** ~ I will not be spoken to like that; einen anderen ~ *or* **andere** ⸚**e anschlagen** to change one's tune; der ~ **macht die Musik** (*Prov*) it's not what you say but the way that you say it; der **gute** ~ good form.
  (**d**) (*Farb*~) tone; (*Nuance*) shade.
Ton|abnehmer *m* cartridge, pick-up.
tonal *adj* tonal.
Ton-: t~**angebend** *adj* who/which sets the tone; t~**angebend sein** to set the tone; ~**arm** *m* pick-up arm; ~**art** *f* (*Mus*) key; (*fig: Tonfall*) tone; **eine andere** ~**art anschlagen** to change one's tune; ~**assistent** *m* sound operator; ~**assistenz** *f* sound; ~**atelier** *nt* recording studio.
Tonband *nt* tape (*mit of*); (*inf: Gerät*) tape recorder.
Tonband-: ~**aufnahme** *f* tape recording; ~**gerät** *nt* tape recorder.
Ton-: ~**blende** *f* tone control; ~**dichter** *m* composer; ~**dichtung** *f* tone poem.
tonen *vt* (*Phot*) to tone.
tönen[1] *vi* (*lit, fig: klingen*) to sound; (*schallen auch*) to resound; (*großspurig reden*) to boast. nach etw ~ (*fig*) to contain (over)tones of sth; von unten tönten Kinderstimmen children's voices could be heard from below.
tönen[2] *vt* to tint. die Sonne hat ihre Haut schon goldbraun getönt the sun has bronzed her skin; der Herbst tönt alle Blätter autumn makes all the leaves change colour; etw leicht rot etc ~ to tinge sth (with) red *etc*.
Ton|erde *f* aluminium oxide; *siehe* essigsauer.
tönern *adj attr* clay. auf ~**en Füßen stehen** (*fig*) to be shaky.
Ton-: ~**fall** *m* tone of voice; (*Intonation*) intonation; ~**film** *m* sound film, talkie (*inf*); ~**filmgerät** *nt* sound film projector; ~**folge** *f* sequence of notes/sounds; (*bei Film*) sound sequence; ~**frequenz** *f* audio frequency; ~**gefäß** *nt* earthenware vessel; ~**geschirr** *nt* earthenware; ~**geschlecht** *nt* scale; t~**haltig** *adj* clayey, argillaceous (*spec*), argilliferous (*spec*); ~**höhe** *f* pitch.
Tonika *f* -, **Toniken** (*Mus*) tonic.
Tonikum *nt* -s, **Tonika** tonic.
Ton-: ~**ingenieur** *m* sound engineer; ~**kabine** *f* sound booth; ~**kamera** *f* sound camera; ~**kopf** *m* recording head; ~**lage** *f* pitch (level); (~**umfang**) register; **eine** ~**lage höher one note higher**; ~**leiter** *f* scale; t~**los** *adj* toneless; *Stimme auch* flat; ... **sagte er** t~**los** ... he said in a flat voice; ~**malerei** *f* (*Mus*) tone painting; ~**meister** *m* sound mixer.
Tonnage [tɔ'naːʒə] *f* -, -n (*Naut*) tonnage.
Tönnchen *nt* little barrel, tub; (*fig hum: Mensch*) roly-poly (*inf*), dumpling (*inf*).
Tonne *f* -, -n (**a**) (*Behälter*) barrel, cask; (*aus Metall*) drum; (*für Regen auch*) butt; (*Müll*~) bin (*Brit*), trash can (*US*); (*inf: Mensch*) fatty (*inf*). (**b**) (*Gewicht*) metric ton(ne). (**c**) (*Register*~) (register) ton. (**d**) (*Naut: Boje*) buoy.
Tonnen-: ~**gewölbe** *nt* (*Archit*) barrel vaulting; t~**weise** *adv* by the ton, in tons; t~**weise Fische fangen** (*fig*) to catch tons (and tons) of fish.
Ton-: ~**setzer** *m* (*geh*) composer; ~**silbe** *f* tonic *or* stressed syllable; ~**sprache** *f* tone language; ~**spur** *f* soundtrack; ~**störung** *f* sound interference; ~**streifen** *m* soundtrack.
Tonsur *f* tonsure.
Ton-: ~**taube** *f* clay pigeon; ~**taubenschießen** *nt* clay pigeon shooting; ~**techniker** *m* sound technician; ~**träger** *m* soundcarrier; ~**umfang** *m* register.
Tonung *f* (*Phot*) toning.
Tönung *f* (*das Tönen*) tinting; (*Farbton*) shade, tone.
Ton-: ~**waren** *pl* earthenware *sing*; ~**zeichen** *nt* call signal; ~**ziegel** *m* brick; (*Dachziegel*) tile.
Top- *in cpds* top.
Topas *m* -es, -e topaz.
Topf *m* -(e)s, ⸚e pot; (*Koch*~ *auch*) (sauce)pan; (*Nacht*~) jerry (*inf*); (*fig hum: Hut*) hat; (*sl: Toilette*) loo (*Brit inf*), john (*US inf*). **allen Leuten in die** ⸚**e gucken** (*inf*) to poke one's nose into everything *or* everybody's affairs; alles in einen ~ **werfen** (*fig*) to lump everything together; im ~ **sein** (*fig*) to be in the bag (*inf*); **jeder** ~ **findet seinen Deckel** (*fig inf*) every Jack will find his Jill (*prov*).
Topfblume *f* potted flower.
Töpfchen *nt dim of* Topf.
Topfen *m* -s, - (*Aus, S Ger*) *siehe* Quark.
Töpfer(in *f*) *m* -s, - potter; (*dial: Ofensetzer*) stove fitter.
Töpferei *f* pottery.
Töpferhandwerk *nt* potter's trade.
töpfern 1 *vi* to do pottery. **2** *vt* to make (in clay). wir sahen zu,

wie er auf der Scheibe eine Vase töpferte we watched him throwing a vase.
Töpfer-: ~**ofen** *m* kiln; ~**scheibe** *f* potter's wheel; ~**waren** *pl* pottery *sing*; (*irden*) earthenware *sing*.
Topfgucker *m* -s, - (*inf*) nos(e)y parker (*inf*).
Topfhandschuh *m* ovenglove.
topfit ['tɔp'fɪt] *adj pred* in top form; (*gesundheitlich*) as fit as a fiddle.
Topf-: ~**kuchen** *m siehe* Gugelhupf; ~**lappen** *m* ovencloth; (*kleiner*) panholder; ~**markt** *m market where pots and pans are sold*; ~**pflanze** *f* potted plant.
Topograph(in *f*) *m* topographer.
Topographie *f* topography.
topographisch *adj* topographic(al).
Topologie *f* (*Math*) topology.
Topos *m* -, **Topoi** (*Liter*) topos.
topp *interj* done, it's a deal.
Topp *m* -s, -e *or* -s (*Naut*) masthead. **über die** ~**en geflaggt sein** *or* **haben** to be dressed overall.
Toppsegel *nt* topsail.
Tor[1] *m* -en, -en (*old, liter*) fool.
Tor[2] *nt* -(e)s, -e (**a**) (*lit, fig: Himmels*~, *Höllen*~) gate; (*Durchfahrt, fig: zum Glück etc*) gateway; (~*bogen*) archway; (*von Garage, Scheune*) door. jdm das ~ **zu etw öffnen** to open sb's eyes to sth; **zu Karriere** *etc* to open the door to sth for sb; *siehe* Felsentor, Gletschertor, Tür. (**b**) (*Sport*) goal; (*bei Skilaufen*) gate. **im** ~ **stehen** to be in goal, to be the goalkeeper.
Tor-: ~**bogen** *m* arch, archway; ~**einfahrt** *f* entrance gate.
Torero *m* -(s), -s torero.
Toresschluß *m siehe* Torschluß.
Torf *m* -(e)s, *no pl* peat.
Torf-: ~**boden** *m* peat; ~**erde** *f* peat; ~**feuerung** *f* peat fire(s).
torfig *adj* peaty.
Torflügel *m* gate (*of a pair of gates*).
Torf-: ~**moor** *nt* peat bog *or* (*trocken*) moor; ~**moos** *nt* sphagnum (moss); ~**mull** *m* (loose) garden peat; ~**stecher** *m* -s, - peat-cutter; ~**stich** *m* patch *or* plot of peat.
Torheit *f* foolishness, stupidity; (*törichte Handlung*) foolish *or* stupid action. er hat die ~ **begangen, zu ...** he was foolish *or* stupid enough to ...
Torhüter *m siehe* Torwart.
töricht *adj* foolish, stupid; *Wunsch, Hoffnung* idle.
törichterweise *adv* foolishly, stupidly.
Törin *f* (*old, liter*) fool, foolish woman.
Torjäger *m siehe* Torschütze.
torkeln *vi aux sein* to stagger, to reel.
Tor-: ~**latte** *f* crossbar; ~**lauf** *m* slalom; ~**linie** *f* goal-line; t~**los** *adj* goalless; **das Spiel blieb** t~**los** *or* **ging** t~**los aus** it was a goalless draw, there was no score; ~**mann** *m, pl* -**männer** goalkeeper, goalie (*inf*).
Tornado *m* -s, -s tornado.
Tornister *m* -s, - (*Mil*) knapsack; (*dated: Schulranzen*) satchel.
torpedieren* *vt* (*Naut, fig*) to torpedo.
Torpedo *m* -s, -s torpedo.
Torpedoboot *nt* torpedo-boat.
Tor-: ~**pfosten** *m* gatepost; (*Sport*) goalpost; ~**schluß** *m* (*fig*) kurz vor ~**schluß** at the last minute *or* the eleventh hour; nach ~**schluß** too late; ~**schlußpanik** *f* (*fig*) last minute panic; (*von Unverheirateten*) fear of being left on the shelf; ~**schrei** *m* cry of "goal!"; ~**schütze** *m* (goal) scorer.
Torsion *f* torsion.
Torsions-: ~**festigkeit** *f* torsional strength; ~**stab** *m* torsion bar.
Torso *m* -s, -s *or* **Torsi** torso; (*fig*) skeleton.
Torszene *f* action in the goal area *no pl*.
Tort [tɔrt] *m* -(e)s, *no pl* (*geh*) wrong, injustice. jdm etw zum ~ **tun** to do sth to vex sb.
Törtchen *nt dim of* Torte (small) tart, tartlet.
Torte *f* -, -n gâteau; (*Obst*~) flan.
Tortelett *nt* -s, -s, **Tortelette** *f* (small) tart, tartlet.
Torten-: ~**boden** *m* flan case *or* (*ohne Seiten*) base; ~**guß** *m* glaze; ~**heber** *m* -s, - cake slice; ~**platte** *f* cake plate; ~**schaufel** *f* cake slice.
Tortur *f* torture; (*fig auch*) ordeal.
Tor-: ~**verhältnis** *nt* score; ~**wächter**, ~**wart** *m* goalkeeper.
tosen *vi* (**a**) to roar, to thunder; (*Wind, Sturm*) to rage. ~**der Beifall** thunderous applause. (**b**) *aux sein* (*mit Ortsangabe*) to thunder.
tot *adj* (**a**) (*gestorben*) (*lit, fig*) dead; (*inf: erschöpft*) dead (beat) (*inf*), whacked (*inf*). mehr ~ **als lebendig** (*fig inf*) more dead than alive; ~ **geboren werden** to be stillborn; ~ **umfallen** *or* zu Boden fallen to drop dead; **ich will** ~ **umfallen, wenn das nicht wahr ist** cross my heart and hope to die (if it isn't true) (*inf*); ~ **zusammenbrechen** to collapse and die; er war auf der Stelle ~ he died instantly; den ~**en Mann machen** (*inf*) to float on one's back; ein ~**er Mann sein** (*fig inf*) to be a goner (*inf*).
  (**b**) (*leblos*) *Ast, Pflanze, Geschäftszeit, Sprache, Leitung* dead; *Augen* sightless, blind; *Haus, Stadt* deserted; *Gegend auch, Landschaft etc* bleak; *Wissen* useless; *Vulkan auch* extinct; *Farbe* dull, drab; (*Rail*) *Gleis* disused. ~**er Flußarm** backwater; (*Schleife*) oxbow (lake); ein ~**er Briefkasten** a dead-letter box; der ~**e Winkel** the blind spot; (*Mil*) dead angle; das T~**e Meer** the Dead Sea; ein ~**er Punkt** (*Stillstand*) a standstill *or* halt; (*in Verhandlungen*) deadlock; (*körperliche Ermüdung*) low point (*of energy/stamina*); ich habe im Moment meinen ~**en Punkt** I'm at a low ebb just now; an einen ~**en Punkt gelangen** to come to a standstill/to reach (a) deadlock; den ~**en Punkt überwinden** to break the deadlock; (*körperlich*) to get one's second wind; der ~**e Buchstabe** dead *or* empty words *pl*.

(c) *(nutzlos) Last, Gewicht* dead; *(bei Fahrzeug auch)* unladen; *Kapital* dead. **ein** ~es **Rennen** *(lit, fig)* a dead heat; ~er **Gang** *(Tech)* play.
(d) *(Min)* **ein** ~er **Mann** *a worked-out part of a mine.*
total 1 *adj* total; *Staat* totalitarian. **2** *adv* totally.
Total *nt* -s, -e *(Sw)* total.
Total-: ~ansicht *f* complete view; ~ausverkauf *m* clearance sale.
Totalisator *m* totalizator, tote *(inf)*.
totalitär 1 *adj* totalitarian. **2** *adv* in a totalitarian way.
Totalitarismus *m* totalitarianism.
Totalität *f* totality, entirety.
Total-: ~operation *f* extirpation; *(von Gebärmutter)* hysterectomy; *(mit Eierstöcken)* hysterosaphorectomy; ~schaden *m* write-off; ~schaden machen *(inf)* to write a car *etc* off.
tot-: ~arbeiten *vr sep (inf)* to work oneself to death; ~ärgern *vr sep (inf)* to be/become livid.
Totem *nt* -s, -s totem.
Totemismus *m* totemism.
Totempfahl *m* totem pole.
töten *vti (lit, fig)* to kill; *Nerv* to deaden. **er/das kann einem den Nerv** ~ *(fig inf)* he/that really gets on my/one's *etc* nerves or wick *(inf)*; **siehe Blick.**
Toten-: ~acker *m (liter)* graveyard; ~amt *nt* requiem mass; ~bestattung *f* burial of the dead; ~bett *nt* deathbed; t~blaß *adj* deathly pale, pale as death; ~blässe *f* deathly pallor; t~bleich *adj siehe* t~blaß; ~feier *f* funeral or burial ceremony; ~flecke *pl* post-mortem or cadaveric *(spec)* lividity *sing*; ~glocke *f* (death) knell; ~gräber *m* gravedigger; ~hemd *nt* shroud; **ich glaubte schon, ich hätte mein** ~hemd an *(fig)* I thought my hour or time had come; ~klage *f* lamentation of the dead; *(Liter)* dirge, lament; ~kopf *m* **(a)** skull; *(als Zeichen)* death's-head; *(auf Piratenfahne, Arzneiflasche etc)* skull and crossbones; **(b)** *(Zool)* death's-head moth; ~kult *nt* cult of the dead; ~maske *f* death mask; ~messe *f* requiem mass; ~reich *nt (Myth)* kingdom of the dead; ~schein *m* death certificate; ~sonntag *m* Sunday before Advent, on which the dead are commemorated; ~stadt *f* necropolis; ~starre *f* rigor mortis; t~still *adj* deathly silent or quiet; ~stille *f* deathly silence or quiet; ~tanz *m* dance of death, danse macabre; ~wache *f* wake.
Tote(r) *mf decl as adj* dead person, dead man/woman; *(bei Unfall etc)* fatality; *(Mil)* casualty. **die** ~n the dead; **es gab 3** ~ **3 people died** or **were killed; das ist ein Lärm, um** ~ **aufzuwecken** the noise is enough to waken the dead.
Tot-: ~erklärte(r) *mf decl as adj* person or man/woman *etc* declared to be dead; t~fahren *vt sep (inf)* to knock down and kill; t~geboren *adj attr* stillborn; **ein** t~geborenes **Kind sein** *(fig)* to be doomed (to failure); ~geburt *f* stillbirth; *(Kind)* stillborn child or baby; ~geglaubte(r) *mf decl as adj* person or man/woman *etc* believed to be dead; ~gesagte(r) *mf decl as adj* person or man/woman *etc* who has been declared dead; t~kriegen *vt sep (inf)* **nicht** t~zukriegen **sein** to go on for ever; t~küssen *vt sep (inf)* to smother in kisses; t~lachen *vr sep (inf)* to kill oneself (laughing) *(inf)*; **es ist zum** t~lachen it is killingly funny or killing *(inf)*; t~laufen *vr sep irreg (inf)* to peter out; t~machen *sep (inf)* **1** *vt* to kill; **2** *vr (fig)* to kill oneself.
Toto *m or (inf, Aus, Sw) nt* -s, -s *(football)* pools. **(im)** ~ **spielen** to do the pools; **etw im** ~ **gewinnen** to win sth on the pools; **im** ~ **gewinnen** *(Hauptgewinn)* to win the pools; **er hat vier Richtige im** ~ four of his matches came up.
Toto- *in cpds* pools; ~schein, ~zettel *m* pools coupon.
Tot-: t~schießen *vt sep irreg (inf)* to shoot dead; ~schlag *m (Jur)* manslaughter; *(US)* homicide; *siehe* **Mord;** t~schlagen *vt sep irreg (lit, fig)* to kill; *(inf) Menschen auch* to beat to death; **du kannst mich** t~schlagen, **ich weiß es nicht/habe es nicht for the life of me** I don't know/haven't got it; ~schläger *m* cudgel, club; t~schweigen *vt sep irreg* to hush up *(inf)*; t~stellen *vr sep* to pretend to be dead, to play dead; *(Mensch auch)* to play possum *(inf)*; t~stürzen *vr sep* to fall to one's death; t~treten *vt sep irreg* to trample to death; *Insekt etc* to tread on and kill.
Tötung *f* killing. **fahrlässige** ~ manslaughter through culpable negligence.
Tötungs-: ~absicht *f* intention to kill; ~versuch *m* attempted murder.
Touch [tatʃ] *m* -s, -s *(Atmosphäre)* air, tone, flavour; *(Flair)* touch; *(Tendenz)* leanings *pl*.
Toupet [tu'pe:] *nt* -s, -s toupée.
toupieren* [tu'pi:rən] *vt* to backcomb.
Tour [tu:r] *f* -, -en **(a)** *(Fahrt)* trip, outing; *(Ausflugs~)* tour; *(Spritz~)* *(mit Auto)* drive; *(mit Rad)* ride; *(Wanderung)* walk, hike; *(Berg~)* climb. **auf** ~ **gehen** to go on or for a trip or outing/on a tour/for a drive/ride/walk or hike/climb; **auf** ~ **sein** to be away on a trip or outing/tour; to be out for a drive/ride/walk; to be off climbing; **eine** ~ **machen** to go on a trip or outing/tour; to go for a drive/ride/walk/climb.
(b) *(Umdrehung)* revolution, rev *(inf)*; *(beim Tanz)* figure; *(beim Stricken)* two rows; *(mit Rundnadeln)* round. **auf** ~en **kommen** *(Auto)* to reach top speed; *(fig inf)* to get into top gear; *(sich aufregen)* to get worked up *(inf)*; **auf vollen** ~en **laufen** *(lit)* to run at full or top speed; *(fig)* to be in full swing; **in einer** ~ *(inf)* incessantly, the whole time.
(c) *(inf: Art und Weise)* ploy. **mit der** ~ **brauchst du mir gar nicht zu kommen** don't try that one on me; **etw auf die langsame** ~ **machen** to do sth the slow way; **auf die krumme** or **schiefe** or **schräge** ~ by dishonest means; **etw auf die weiche** ~ **versuchen** to try using soft soap to get sth; **er hat wieder seine** ~(en) **he** is in one of his moods again.
Touren- ['tu:rən-]: ~rad *nt* tourer; ~wagen *m (im Motorsport)* saloon (car); ~zahl *f* number of revolutions or revs *pl (inf)*; ~zähler *m* rev counter.

Tourismus [tu'rɪsmʊs] *m* tourism.
Tourist [tu'rɪst] *m* tourist.
Touristenklasse [tu'rɪst(ə)n-] *f* tourist class.
Touristik [tu'rɪstɪk] *f* tourism, tourist industry.
Tournedos [tʊrnə'do:] *nt* -, - [-'do:s] *usu pl (Cook)* tournedos.
Tournee [tʊr'ne:] *f* -, -n [-e:ən] or -s tour. **auf** ~ **gehen/sein** to go on tour/be on tour or touring.
tour-retour [tu:rre'tu:r] *adv (Aus)* return.
Tower ['tauə] *m* -s, - *(Aviat)* control tower.
Trab *m* -(e)s, *no pl* trot. **im** ~ **at a trot; (im)** ~ **reiten** to trot; **sich in** ~ **setzen** *(inf)* to get going or cracking *(inf)*; **auf** ~ **sein** *(inf)* to be on the go *(inf)*; **jdn in** ~ **halten** *(inf)* to keep sb on the go; **jdn auf (den)** ~ **bringen** *(inf)* to make sb get a move on *(inf)*.
Trabant *m* **(a)** *(Astron)* satellite. **(b)** *(Hist)* bodyguard; *(fig)* satellite. **(c)** *usu pl (dated inf)* kiddie-wink *(inf)*.
Trabantenstadt *f* satellite town.
traben *vi* **(a)** *aux haben or sein* to trot. **mit dem Pferd** ~ to trot one's horse. **(b)** *aux sein (inf: laufen)* to trot. **ich mußte noch einmal in die Stadt** ~ I had to go traipsing back into town.
Traber *m* -s, - trotter.
Trab-: ~rennbahn *f* trotting course; ~rennen *nt* trotting; *(Veranstaltung)* trotting race.
Tracht *f* -, -en **(a)** *(Kleidung)* dress, garb; *(Volks~ etc)* costume; *(Schwestern~)* uniform. **(b)** *(obs: Traglast)* load. **jdm eine** ~ **Prügel verabfolgen** or **verabreichen** *(inf)* to give sb a beating or thrashing.
trachten *vi (geh)* to strive *(nach for, after)*. **danach** ~, **etw zu tun** to strive or endeavour to do sth; **jdm nach dem Leben** ~ to be after sb's blood.
Trachten-: ~fest *nt festive occasion where traditional/national costume is worn;* ~gruppe *f group dressed in traditional/national costume;* ~jacke *f traditionally styled jacket made of thick woollen material;* *(von Volkstracht) jacket worn as part of traditional/national costume;* ~kostüm *nt suit made of thick woollen material.*
trächtig *adj (lit) Tier* pregnant; *(fig geh)* laden *(von* with); *Gedanke etc* meaningful, significant.
Trächtigkeit *f* pregnancy; *(fig)* meaningfulness, significance.
tradieren* *vt (geh)* to hand down.
Tradition [tradi'tsio:n] *f* tradition.
Traditionalismus [traditsiona'lɪsmʊs] *m* traditionalism.
Traditionalist [traditsiona'lɪst] *m* traditionalist.
traditionalistisch [traditsiona'lɪstɪʃ] *adj* traditionalistic.
traditionell [traditsio'nɛl] *adj usu attr* traditional.
Traditions-: t~bewußt *adj* tradition-conscious; ~bewußtsein *nt* tradition-consciousness, consciousness of tradition; t~gebunden *adj* bound by tradition; t~gemäß *adv* traditionally, according to tradition; t~reich *adj* rich in tradition.
traf *pret of* **treffen.**
Trafik *f* -, -en *(Aus)* tobacconist's (shop).
Trafikant(in *f) m (Aus)* tobacconist.
Trafo *m* -(s), -s *(inf)* transformer.
träg *adj siehe* **träge.**
Trag-: ~bahre *f* stretcher; t~bar *adj* **(a)** *Apparat, Gerät* portable; *Kleid* wearable; **(b)** *(annehmbar)* acceptable *(für* to); *(erträglich)* bearable.
Trage *f* -, -n *(Bahre)* litter; *(Tragkorb)* pannier.
träge *adj* **(a)** *(sluggish; Mensch, Handbewegung etc auch* lethargic. **geistig** ~ mentally lazy. **(b)** *(Phys) Masse* inert.
tragen *pret* **trug,** *ptp* **getragen 1** *vt* **(a)** *(durch Hochheben, befördern, dabeihaben)*, *(fig) Schall* to carry; *(an einen Ort bringen)* to take; *(Wellen etc auch)* to bear; *(fig) Gerücht etc* to pass on, to spread. **etw mit** or **bei sich** ~ to carry sth with one; **den Brief zur Post** ~ to take the letter to the post office; **den Arm in der Schlinge** ~ to have one's arm in a sling.
(b) *(am Körper* ~) *Kleid, Brille, Rot etc, Perücke* to wear; *(im Moment auch)* to have on; *Bart, Gebiß* to have; *Waffen* to carry. **wie trägt sie zur Zeit ihre Haare?** how is she wearing her hair now?; **getragene Kleider** second-hand clothes; *(abgelegt)* cast-offs; *siehe* **Trauer.**
(c) *(stützen, halten, fig)* to support; *(fig: Vertrauen, Hoffnung auch)* to sustain. **das Gespräch war von Ernst getragen** *(geh)* the conversation was conducted in earnest tones; *siehe* **tragend, getragen.**
(d) *(aushalten, Tragfähigkeit haben)* to take (the weight of), to carry.
(e) *(hervorbringen) Zinsen* to yield; *Ernte auch* to produce; *(lit, fig) Früchte* to bear. **der Baum/Acker trägt viele Früchte/viel Weizen** the tree/field produces a good crop of fruit/wheat; *(in dieser Saison)* the tree/field is full of fruit/wheat.
(f) *(trächtig sein)* to be carrying.
(g) *(ertragen) Schicksal, Leid etc* to bear, to endure; *Kreuz* to bear.
(h) *(übernehmen) Verluste* to defray; *Kosten auch* to bear, to carry; *Risiko* to take; *Folgen* to take, to bear; *(unterhalten) Verein, Organisation* to support, to back. **Initiative** ~ to take the initiative; **die Verantwortung/Schuld für etw** ~ to be responsible for sth/to be to blame for sth.
(i) *(haben) Titel, Namen, Aufschrift etc* to bear, to have; *Vermerk* to contain; *Etikett* to have. **der Brief trägt das Datum vom ... the letter is dated ...**
2 *vi* **(a)** *(Baum, Acker etc)* to crop, to produce a crop. **gut/schlecht** ~ to crop well/badly, to produce a good/bad crop; *(in dieser Saison)* to have a good/bad crop.
(b) *(schwanger sein)* to be pregnant.
(c) *(reichen: Geschütz, Stimme)* to carry.
(d) *(Eis)* to take weight. **das Eis trägt noch nicht** the ice won't take anyone's weight yet.
(e) **schwer an etw** *(dat)* ~ to have a job carrying or to carry sth; *(fig)* to find sth hard to bear; **schwer zu** ~ **haben** to have a

lot to carry; (*fig*) to have a heavy cross to bear.

(f) zum T~ kommen to come to fruition; (*nützlich werden*) to come in useful; etw zum T~ bringen to bring sth to bear (*in +dat on*).

3 *vr* **(a)** sich gut *or* leicht/schwer *or* schlecht ~ to be easy/difficult *or* hard to carry; schwere Lasten ~ sich besser auf dem Rücken it is better to carry heavy loads on one's back.

(b) (*Kleid, Stoff*) to wear.

(c) (*geh: gekleidet sein*) to dress.

(d) sich mit etw ~ (*geh*) to contemplate sth.

(e) (*ohne Zuschüsse auskommen*) to be self-supporting.

tragend *adj* **(a)** (*stützend*) Säule, Bauteil, Chassisteil weight- or load-bearing; (*fig: bestimmend*) Idee, Motiv fundamental, basic. **(b)** (*Theat*) Rolle major, main. **(c)** Stimme resonant. **(d)** (*trächtig*) pregnant.

Träger *m* -s, - **(a)** (*an Kleidung*) strap; (*Hosen~*) braces *pl*. **(b)** (*Build*) (*Holz~, Beton~*) (supporting) beam; (*Stahl~, Eisen~*) girder. **(c)** (*Tech: Stütze von Brücken etc*) support. **(d)** (*Flugzeug~*) carrier. **(e)** (*Mensch*) (*von Lasten*) bearer, porter; (*Aus~ von Zeitungen*) delivery boy; (*von Namen*) bearer; (*rare: von Orden, Amt, Titel*) bearer, holder; (*von Kleidung*) wearer; (*eines Preises*) winner; (*von Krankheit*) carrier. **(f)** (*fig*) (*der Kultur, Staatsgewalt etc*) representative; (*einer Bewegung, Entwicklung*) upholder, supporter; (*einer Veranstaltung*) sponsor; (*Mittel*) vehicle. als ~ dieser Entwicklung kommen mehrere Faktoren in Frage several factors may further this development; ~ des Vereins/der Universitäten those who support *or* back the club/are responsible for the universities.

Trägerhose *f* trousers *pl* with straps.

Trägerin *f* siehe **Träger** (e).

Träger-: ~kleid *nt* pinafore dress (*Brit*), jumper (*US*); (*sommerlich*) sundress; ~lohn *m* porterage; ~rakete *f* carrier rocket; ~rock *m* pinafore dress (*Brit*), jumper (*US*); (*für Kinder*) skirt with straps; ~schürze *f* pinafore.

Trage-: ~tasche *f* carrier bag; ~zeit *f* gestation period.

Trag-: t~fähig *adj* able to take a load/weight; ~fähigkeit *f* load-/weight-bearing capacity; (*von Brücke*) maximum load; ~fläche *f* wing; (*von Boot*) hydrofoil; ~flächenboot *nt* hydrofoil; ~flügel *m* siehe ~fläche; ~flügelboot *nt* siehe ~flächenboot.

Trägheit *f* siehe **träge** *adj* sluggishness; lethargy; (*Faulheit*) laziness; (*Phys*) inertia.

Trägheits-: ~gesetz *nt* law of inertia; ~moment *nt* moment of inertia.

Traghimmel *m* canopy, baldachin.

Tragik *f* tragedy. das ist die ~ der Sache, daß ... what's tragic about it is that ...

Tragiker *m* -s, - tragedian.

Tragi-: ~komik *f* tragicomedy; t~komisch *adj* tragicomical; ~komödie *f* tragicomedy.

tragisch *adj* tragic. etw ~ nehmen (*inf*) to take sth to heart; das ist nicht so ~ (*inf*) it's not the end of the world.

Trag-: ~korb *m* pannier; ~kraft *f* siehe ~fähigkeit; ~last *f* load; (*Gepäck*) heavy luggage (*esp Brit*) *or* baggage; ~lufthalle *f* air hall.

Tragöde *m* -n, -n tragedian.

Tragödie [-iə] *f* (*Liter, fig*) tragedy. es ist eine ~ mit ihm/dieser Maschine this machine is a disaster.

Tragödien- [-iən-]: ~darsteller *m* tragedian; ~dichter *m* tragedian.

Tragödin *f* tragedienne.

Trag-: ~pfeiler *m* weight- *or* load-bearing pillar; (*von Brücke*) support; ~riemen *m* strap; (*von Gewehr*) sling; ~schicht *f* base course; ~sessel *m* sedan chair; ~weite *f* (*von Geschütz etc*) range; (*fig*) consequences *pl*; (*von Gesetz*) scope; sind Sie sich der ~weite dieses Schritts/Ihres Handelns bewußt? are you aware of the possible consequences *or* of the implications of this step/of your action?, are you aware of what this step/your action could mean?; von großer ~weite sein to have far-reaching consequences *or* implications; ~werk *nt* (*Aviat*) wing assembly.

Trainer(in *f*) [ˈtrɛːnɐ, ˈtrɛː-] *m* -s, - coach, trainer; (*von Rennpferd*) trainer; (*von Schwimmer, Tennisspieler*) coach; (*bei Fußball*) manager; (*Sw: Trainingsanzug*) track-suit.

trainieren* [trɛˈniːrən, trɛˈniː-] **1** *vt* to train; Mannschaft, Sportler *auch* to coach; Sprung, Übung, Weitsprung to practise; Muskel to exercise. Fußball/Tennis ~ to do some football/tennis practice; ein (gut) trainierter Sportler an athlete who is in training; auf etw (*acc*) trainiert sein to be trained to do sth; jdn auf *or* für etw (*acc*) ~ to train *or* coach sb for sth; er hat Tennis mit mir trainiert he helped me practise my tennis; er trainiert Fußball mit der Mannschaft he does football training with the team.

2 *vi* (*Sportler*) to train; (*Rennfahrer*) to practise; (*Übungen machen*) to exercise; (*üben*) to practise. auf *or* für etw (*acc*) ~ to train/practise for sth; da mußt du schon noch etwas ~ you'll have to practise that a bit more.

3 *vr* to train (*auf +acc* for); (*üben*) to practise; (*um fit zu werden*) to get some exercise, to get into training.

Training [ˈtrɛːnɪŋ] *nt* -s, -s training *no pl*; (*Fitneß~*) exercise *no pl*; (*Autorennen*) practice; (*fig: Übung*) practice. er geht jeden Abend zum ~ he goes training every evening; ein 2-stündiges ~ a 2-hour training session *or* bout; die verschiedenen ~s the various types of training; er übernimmt das ~ der Mannschaft he's taking over the training *or* coaching of the team; im ~ stehen to be in training; durch regelmäßiges ~ lernen die Schüler ... by regular practice the pupils learn ...

Trainings-: ~anzug *m* track-suit; ~hose *f* track-suit trousers *pl*; ~jacke *f* track-suit top; ~lager *nt* training camp; ~methode *f* training method; ~möglichkeit *f* training facilities *pl*; ~runde *f* practice lap; ~schuh *m* training shoe; ~zeit *f* practice time.

Trakehner *m* -s, - type of riding horse from Prussia.

Trakt *m* -(e)s, -e (*Gebäudeteil*) section; (*Flügel*) wing; (*von Autobahn auch*) stretch.

Traktat *m or nt* -(e)s, -e **(a)** (*Abhandlung*) treatise; (*Flugschrift, religiöse Schrift*) tract. **(b)** (*obs: Vertrag*) treaty.

Traktätchen *nt* (*pej*) tract.

traktieren* *vt* **(a)** (*inf*) (*schlecht behandeln*) to maltreat; Menschen *auch* to give a rough time (to); (*quälen*) kleine Schwester, Tier *etc* to torment. jdn mit Vorwürfen ~ to keep on at sb (*inf*); Fußballer, die sich gegenseitig ~ football players who go in for rough stuff; er hat ihn mit Tritten gegen das Schienbein traktiert he kicked him on the shin. **(b)** (*obs: bewirten*) to treat (*mit* to).

Traktor *m* -s, -en tractor.

Traktorist(in *f*) *m* (*DDR*) tractor-driver.

trällern *vti* to warble; (*Vogel auch*) to trill. vor sich hin ~ to warble away to oneself.

Tram *f* -, -s (*dial, Sw*), **Trambahn** *f* (*S Ger*) siehe **Straßenbahn**.

Traminer *m* -s, - Traminer (wine).

Tramp [trɛmp, tramp] *m* -s, -s tramp.

Trampel *m or nt* -s, - *or f* -, -n clumsy clot (*inf*), clumsy oaf (*inf*). ~ vom Land (*country*) bumpkin *or* cousin.

trampeln 1 *vi* **(a)** (*mit den Füßen stampfen*) to stamp. die Zuschauer haben getrampelt the audience stamped their feet. **(b)** *aux sein* (*schwerfällig gehen*) to stamp *or* tramp along. über die Wiese/das Gras ~ to tramp across the meadow/grass.

2 *vt* **(a)** (*mit Füßen bearbeiten*) Weg to trample. jdn zu Tode ~ to trample sb to death; etw platt ~ to trample sth flat, to flatten sth underfoot. **(b)** (*abschütteln*) to stamp (*von* from).

Trampel-: ~pfad *m* track, path; ~tier *nt* **(a)** (*Zool*) (Bactrian) camel; **(b)** (*inf*) clumsy oaf (*inf*).

trampen [ˈtrɛmpn, ˈtram-] *vi* to hitch-hike, to hitch (*inf*).

Tramper(in *f*) [ˈtrɛmpɐ, -ərɪn] *m* -s, - hitch-hiker, hitcher (*inf*).

Trampfahrt *f* **(a)** (*Naut*) tramp voyage. auf ~ sein to be tramping. **(b)** (*Reise per Anhalter*) hitch-hiking tour. auf ~ sein to be away hitch-hiking.

Trampolin *nt* -s, -e trampoline.

Trampolinspringen *nt* -s, *no pl* trampolining.

Tramp-: ~schiff *nt* tramp (ship); ~schiffahrt *f* tramp shipping.

Tramway [ˈtramveː] *f* -, -s (*Aus*) siehe **Straßenbahn**.

Tran *m* -(e)s, -e **(a)** (*von Fischen*) train oil. **(b)** (*inf*) im ~ dop(e)y (*inf*); (*leicht betrunken*) tipsy, merry (*inf*); ich lief wie im ~ durch die Gegend I was running around in a dream *or* a daze; das habe ich im ~ ganz vergessen it completely slipped my mind.

Trance [ˈtrɑ̃ːs(ə)] *f* -, -n trance.

Trance-: t~artig *adj* trance-like; ~zustand *m* (state of) trance.

Tranchierbesteck [trãˈʃiːr-] *nt* carving set, set of carvers.

tranchieren* [trãˈʃiːrən] *vt* to carve.

Tranchier-: ~gabel *f* carving-fork; ~messer *nt* carving-knife.

Träne *f* -, -n tear; (*einzelne* ~) tear(drop); (*inf: Mensch*) drip (*inf*). den ~n nahe sein to be near to *or* on the verge of tears; unter ~n lächeln to smile through one's tears; unter ~n gestand er seine Schuld/Liebe in tears he confessed his fault/love; ~n lachen to laugh till one cries *or* till the tears run down one's cheeks; deswegen vergieße ich keine ~n (*fig*) I'll shed no tears over that; die Sache/der Mann ist keine ~ wert the matter/man isn't worth crying over; bittere ~n weinen to shed bitter tears; jdm/sich die ~n trocknen/abwischen to dry sb's/one's eyes, to wipe away sb's/one's tears; ich danke mit einer ~ im Knopfloch (*hum inf*) I really appreciate it.

tränen *vi* to water.

Tränen-: ~drüse *f* lachrymal gland; er drückt mit seinen Liedern immer auf die ~drüsen (*inf*) his songs are real tear-jerkers (*inf*); der Film drückt sehr auf die ~drüsen the film is a real tear-jerker (*inf*); im Schlußakt drückt der Autor kräftig auf die ~drüsen (*inf*) the author has written a real tear-jerker of a final act; t~feucht *adj* wet with tears; Augen tear-filled; ~fluß *m* flood of tears; ~gas *nt* tear gas; t~reich *adj* tearful; ~sack *m* lachrymal sac.

Tran-: ~funsel, ~funzel *f* (*inf*) slowcoach (*Brit inf*), slowpoke (*US inf*); t~funzlig *adj* (*inf*) slow, sluggish.

tranig *adj* like train oil; (*inf*) slow, sluggish.

Trank *m* -(e)s, -̈e (*liter*) drink, draught (*liter*), potion (*liter*).

trank *pret of* trinken.

Tränke *f* -, -n drinking trough.

tränken *vt* **(a)** Tiere to water. **(b)** (*durchnässen*) to soak. seine Antwort war mit Hohn getränkt (*geh*) his answer brimmed with scorn.

Trans- *in cpds* trans-.

Trans|aktion *f* transaction.

trans|atlantisch *adj* transatlantic.

tranchieren* *vt* (*Aus*) siehe **tranchieren**.

Trans-Europ(a)-Express *m* Trans-Europe Express.

Transfer *m* -s, -s transfer; (*Psych*) transference.

transferieren* *vt* to transfer.

Transformation *f* transformation.

Transformations-: ~grammatik *f* transformational grammar; ~regel *f* transformation rule.

Transformator *m* transformer.

Transformatorenhäuschen *nt* transformer.

transformieren* vt to transform.
Transfusion f transfusion.
Transistor m transistor.
Transistorradio nt transistor (radio).
Transit m -s, -e transit.
Transit-: ~abkommen nt transit agreement; ~halle f (Aviat) transit area; ~handel m transit trade.
transitiv adj (Gram) transitive.
Transit-: ~raum m (Aviat) transit lounge; ~sperre f, ~verbot nt ban on the transit of goods, people etc through neighbouring country; ~verkehr m transit traffic; (~handel) transit trade; Passagiere im ~verkehr transit passengers pl.
transkribieren* vt to transcribe; (Mus) to arrange.
Transmission f (Mech) transmission.
Trans|ozean- in cpds transoceanic.
transparent [transpa'rɛnt] adj transparent; Gewebe etc diaphanous (liter); (fig geh) Argument lucid, clear.
Transparent [transpa'rɛnt] nt -(e)s, -e (Reklameschild etc) neon sign; (Durchscheinbild) transparency; (Spruchband) banner.
Transparentpapier nt waxed tissue paper; (zum Pausen) tracing paper.
Transparenz [transpa'rɛnts] f siehe adj transparency; diaphaneity (liter); lucidity, clarity. sie fordern mehr ~ bei allen Vorgängen in der Politik they demand more openness in all political matters.
Transpiration [transpira'tsio:n] f (geh) perspiration; (von Pflanze) transpiration.
transpirieren* [transpi'ri:rən] vi (geh) to perspire; (Pflanze) to transpire.
Transplantat [transplan'ta:t] nt (Haut) graft; (Organ) transplant.
Transplantation [transplanta'tsio:n] f (a) (Med) transplant; (von Haut) graft; (Vorgang) transplantation; grafting. (b) (Bot) grafting.
transplantieren* [transplan'ti:rən] vti (a) (Med) Organ to transplant; Haut to graft. (b) (Bot) to graft.
transponieren* [transpo'ni:rən] vt (Mus) to transpose.
Transport [trans'pɔrt] m -(e)s, -e (a) (das Transportieren) transport. ein ~ auf dem Landweg road transport; ein ~ des Kranken ist ausgeschlossen moving the patient is out of the question; beim ~ beschädigte/verlorengegangene Waren goods damaged/lost in transit; für den ~ meiner Möbel mußte ich viel bezahlen I had to pay a lot to have my furniture transported.
(b) (Fracht) consignment, shipment; (von Soldaten etc) load, transport; (von Gefangenen) transport.
transportabel [transpɔr'ta:bl] adj transportable.
Transport-: [trans'pɔrt-]: ~arbeiter m transport worker; ~band nt conveyor belt; ~behälter m container.
Transporter [trans'pɔrtɐ] m -s, - (Schiff) cargo ship; (Flugzeug) transport plane; (Auto) van; (Auto~) transporter.
Transporteur [transpɔr'tø:ɐ] m (a) (Mensch) removal man. (b) (an Nähmaschine) fabric guide, feed dog. (c) (Winkelmesser) protractor.
Transport-: [trans'pɔrt-]: t~fähig adj moveable; ~flugzeug nt transport plane or aircraft.
transportieren* [transpɔr'ti:rən] 1 vt to transport; Güter, Sauerstoff auch to carry; Patienten to move; Film to wind on; (Nähmaschine) to feed. 2 vi (Förderband) to move; (Nähmaschine) to feed; (Kamera) to wind on.
Transport-: [trans'pɔrt-]: ~kosten pl carriage sing; ~mittel nt means of transport sing; ~schiff nt cargo ship; (Mil) transport ship; ~unternehmen nt haulier, haulage firm; ~wesen nt transport.
Transsexuelle(r) mf decl as adj transsexual.
Transuse f -, -n (inf) slowcoach (Brit inf), slowpoke (US inf).
Transvestismus [transvɛs'tısmʊs] m transvestism.
Transvestit [transvɛs'ti:t] m -en, -en transvestite.
Transvestitismus [transvɛsti'tısmʊs] m transvestism.
transzendent adj transcendent(al); (Math) transcendental.
transzendental adj transcendental.
Transzendenz f transcendency, transcendence.
Trantüte f (inf) slowcoach (Brit inf), slowpoke (US inf).
Trapez nt -es, -e (a) (Math) trapezium. (b) (von Artisten) trapeze.
Trapez-: ~akt m trapeze act; t~förmig adj trapeziform; ~künstler m trapeze artist.
Trapezoeder nt -s, - trapezohedron.
Trapezoid nt -(e)s, -e trapezoid.
Trappist m (Eccl) trappist.
trapp, trapp interj (von Kindern etc) clitter clatter; (von Pferd) clip clop.
trappeln vi aux sein to clatter; (Pony) to clip-clop.
trapsen vi aux sein (inf) to galumph (inf); siehe Nachtigall.
Trara nt -s, -s (von Horn) tantara; (fig inf) hullabaloo (inf), to-do (inf) (um about).
Trassant m (Fin) drawer.
Trassat m -en, -en (Fin) drawee.
Trasse f -, -n (Surv) marked-out route.
trat pret of treten.
Tratsch m -(e)s, no pl (inf) gossip, scandal, tittle-tattle (inf).
Tratsche f -, -n (pej inf) scandalmonger, gossip.
tratschen vi (inf) to gossip.
Tratscherei f (inf) gossip(ing) no pl, scandalmongering no pl.
Tratsch-: ~maul nt ~tante f (pej inf) scandalmonger, gossip.
Tratte f -, -n (Fin) draft.
Trau|altar m altar.
Traube f -, -n (einzelne Beere) grape; (ganze Frucht) bunch of grapes; (Blütenstand) raceme (spec); (fig) (von Bienen)

cluster; (Menschen~) bunch, cluster. ~n (Fruchtart) grapes; die ~n sind sauer (prov) that's sour grapes.
Trauben-: ~lese f grape harvest; ~saft m grape juice; ~zucker m glucose, dextrose.
trauen 1 vi + dat to trust. einer Sache (dat) nicht ~ to be wary of sth; ich traute meinen Augen/Ohren nicht I couldn't believe my eyes/ears; ich traue dem Frieden nicht (I think) there must be something afoot, it's too good to be true; siehe Weg.
2 vr to dare. sich (acc or rare) dat) ~, etw zu tun to dare (to) do sth; ich trau' mich nicht I daren't, I dare not; sich auf die Straße/nach Hause/zum Chef ~ to dare to go out (of doors)/ home/to one's boss.
3 vt to marry. sich standesamtlich/kirchlich ~ lassen to get married in a registry office (Brit)/in church.
Trauer f -, no pl (das Trauern, ~zeit, ~kleidung) mourning; (Schmerz, Leid) sorrow, grief. ~ haben/tragen to be in mourning; in tiefer ~ ... (much loved and) sadly missed by ...
Trauer-: ~anzeige f obituary, death notice; ~binde f black armband; ~botschaft f sad news sing, no indef art; ~brief m letter announcing sb's death; ~fall m bereavement, death; ~feier f funeral service; ~flor m black ribbon; ~gefolge nt funeral procession; ~gemeinde f mourners pl; ~haus nt house of mourning; ~jahr nt year of mourning; ~karte f card announcing sb's death; ~kleidung f mourning; ~kloß m (inf) wet blanket (inf); ~mantel m (Zool) Camberwell beauty; ~marsch m funeral march; ~miene f (inf) long face.
trauern vi to mourn (um jdn (for) sb, um etw sth); (Trauerkleidung tragen) to be in mourning. die ~den Hinterbliebenen his/her bereaved family.
Trauer-: ~nachricht f sad news sing, no indef art; ~parte f (Aus) siehe ~anzeige; ~rand m black edge or border; ~ränder (inf) dirty fingernails; ~schleier m black or mourning veil; ~spiel nt tragedy; (fig inf) fiasco; was hier passiert, ist das reinste ~spiel it's really pathetic what's going on here; es ist ein ~spiel mit ihm/dem Projekt he's really pathetic/the project is in a bad way (inf); ~weide f weeping willow; ~zeit f (period of) mourning; ~zug m funeral procession.
Traufe f -, -n eaves pl; siehe Regen.
träufeln 1 vt to dribble. 2 vi aux haben or sein (old, geh: Wasser) to trickle.
Trauformel f marriage vows pl.
traulich adj cosy. im ~en Heim in the cosiness or the cosy surroundings of one's home; ~ zusammenleben to live together harmoniously or in harmony.
Traulichkeit f cosiness.
Traum m -(e)s, Träume (lit, fig) dream; (Tag~ auch) daydream, reverie. sie lebt wie im ~ she is living (as if) in a dream or (nach Schock) daze; er fühlte sich wie im ~ he felt as if he were dreaming; es war immer sein ~, ein großes Haus zu besitzen he had always dreamed of owning a large house; aus der ~!, der ~ ist aus! it's all over; aus der ~ vom neuen Auto that's put paid to your/my etc dreams of a new car; dieser ~ ist ausgeträumt this dream is over; der ~ meiner schlaflosen Nächte (hum inf) the man/woman of my dreams; Träume sind Schäume dreams are but shadows; siehe einfallen.
Trauma nt -s, Traumen or -ta (Med, Psych) trauma; (fig auch) nightmare.
traumatisch adj (Psych) traumatic; (fig auch) nightmarish.
Traum-: ~beruf m dream job, job of one's dreams; ~bild nt vision; ~deuter m interpreter of dreams; ~deutung f dream interpretation, interpretation of dreams.
Traumen pl of Trauma.
träumen 1 vi to dream; (tag~ auch) to daydream; (inf: nicht aufpassen) to (day)dream, to be in a dream. von jdm/etw ~ to dream about sb/sth; (sich ausmalen) to dream of sb/sth; mir träumte, daß ... I dreamed or dreamt that ...; träume süß! sweet dreams!; vor sich hin ~, mit offenen Augen ~ to daydream; du träumst wohl! (inf) you must be joking!; das hätte ich mir nicht ~ lassen I'd never have thought it possible.
2 vt to dream; Traum to have. etwas Schönes/Schreckliches ~ to have a pleasant/an unpleasant dream.
Träumer(in f) m -s, - (day)dreamer; (Phantast) dreamer, visionary.
Träumerei f (a) no pl (das Träumen) (day)dreaming. (b) (Vorstellung) daydream, reverie.
träumerisch adj dreamy; (schwärmerisch) wistful.
Traum-: ~fabrik f (pej) dream factory; ~gesicht nt (geh) vision; ~gesichte haben to see visions; t~haft adj (phantastisch) fantastic; (wie im ~) dreamlike.
Traumined m -s, -e (Aus) coward.
traum-: ~verloren 1 adj dreamy; 2 adv dreamily, as if in a dream; ~wandlerisch adj mit ~wandlerischer Sicherheit with instinctive sureness.
Traurede f marriage sermon; (im Standesamt) marriage address.
traurig adj sad; (unglücklich) Verhältnisse, Leben auch unhappy; Blick auch sorrowful; (beklagenswert) Zustand sad, sorry; Leistung, Erfolg, Rekord pathetic, sorry; Wetter miserable; Berühmtheit notorious. mit meinen Finanzen/der Wirtschaft steht es sehr ~ aus my finances are/the economy is in a very sorry state; ~, ~ dear, dear; wie sieht es damit aus? — ~(, ~) what are the prospects for that? — not at all good or pretty bad; um meine Zukunft sieht es ~ aus my future doesn't look too bright; das ist doch ~, was er da geleistet hat what he's done is pathetic; das sind ja ~e Verhältnisse, wenn ... it is a sorry or sad state of affairs when ...; ~, daß ... it is sad that; es ist ~, wenn it is sad if ...; ~ weggehen to go away sadly or feeling sad.
Traurigkeit f sadness. allgemeine ~ a general feeling of sadness.

Trau-: ~ring m wedding ring; ~schein m marriage certificate.

traut adj (liter, hum) (gemütlich) cosy; (vertraut) familiar; Freund close. im ~en Kreise among one's family and friends; ein Abend im ~en Heim an evening at home; ~es Heim Glück allein (prov) home sweet home.

Traute f: ~ haben/keine ~ haben (inf) to have/not to have the guts (inf).

Trauung f wedding, wedding or marriage ceremony.

Trauzeuge m witness (at marriage ceremony).

Travellerscheck ['trɛvəlɐ-] m traveller's cheque (Brit), traveler's check (US).

Travestie [travɛs'tiː] f travesty.

travestieren* [travɛs'tiːrən] vt to travesty, to make a travesty of.

Treber pl (Bier~) spent hops pl; (Wein~) marc sing; (Frucht~) pomace sing.

Treck m -s, -s trek, trail; (Leute) train; (die Wagen etc) wagon train.

Trecker m -s, - tractor.

Treff¹ nt -s, -s (Cards) club. die ~sieben the seven of clubs; das ~-As the ace of clubs.

Treff² m -s, -s (inf) (Treffen) meeting, get-together (inf); (~punkt) haunt, rendezvous.

treffen pret traf, ptp getroffen 1 vt (a) (durch Schlag, Schuß etc) to hit (an/in + dat on, in + acc in); (Blitz, Faust auch, Unglück) to strike. auf dem Photo bist du gut getroffen (inf) that's a good photo or picture of you; siehe Schlag.
(b) (fig: kränken) to hurt.
(c) (betreffen) to hit, to affect. es trifft immer die Falschen it's always the wrong people who are hit or affected; ihn trifft keine Schuld he's not to blame.
(d) (finden) to hit upon, to find; (lit, fig) Ton to hit. du hast's getroffen (mit Antwort) you've hit the nail on the head; (mit Geschenk) that's the very thing.
(e) (jdm begegnen, mit jdm zusammenkommen) to meet; (an~) to find.
(f) es gut/schlecht ~ to be fortunate or lucky/unlucky (mit with); es mit dem Wetter/der Unterkunft gut/schlecht ~ to have good/bad weather/accommodation; ich hätte es schlechter ~ können it could have been worse.
(g) Anstalten etc to make; Vereinbarung to reach; Entscheidung auch, Vorsorge, Maßnahmen to take.
2 vi (a) (Schlag, Schuß etc) to hit. der Schuß/er hat getroffen the shot/he hit it/him etc; nicht ~ to miss; gut/schlecht ~ to aim well/badly; getroffen! a hit; siehe Schwarze(s).
(b) aux sein (stoßen) auf jdn/etw ~ to meet sb/sth.
(c) (verletzen) to hurt. sich getroffen fühlen to feel hurt; (auf sich beziehen) to take it personally.
3 vr (zusammen~) to meet. unsere Interessen ~ sich im Sport we are both interested in sport.
4 vr impers es trifft sich, daß ... it (just) happens that ...; das trifft sich gut/schlecht, daß ... it is convenient/inconvenient that ...

Treffen nt -s, - meeting; (Sport, Mil) encounter. ins ~ führen (Mil) to send into battle; (fig) to put forward.

treffend adj apt; Ähnlichkeit striking. jdn ~ nachahmen to do a brilliant imitation of sb.

Treffer m -s, - hit; (Tor) goal; (fig: Erfolg) hit; (Gewinnlos) winner. das Geschenk/das Auto war ein ~ the present/car was just the right thing; einen ~ erzielen to score a hit; (Fibl) to shoot a goal.

trefflich adj (liter) splendid, excellent.

Trefflichkeit f (liter) excellence.

Treff-: ~punkt m rendezvous, meeting place; einen ~punkt ausmachen to arrange where or somewhere to meet; t~sicher adj accurate; (fig) Bemerkung apt; Urteil sound, unerring; ~sicherheit f accuracy; aptness; soundness, unerringness.

Treibeis nt drift ice.

treiben pret trieb, ptp getrieben 1 vt (a) (lit, fig) to drive; (Tech: an~ auch) to propel; (auf Treibjagd) Wild to beat; Teig to make rise; (fig: drängen) to rush; (an~) to push. jdn zum Wahnsinn/zur Verzweiflung/zum Selbstmord ~ to drive sb mad/to despair/to (commit) suicide; jdn zur Eile/Arbeit ~ to make sb hurry (up)/work; jdn zum Äußersten ~ to push sb too far; du treibst mich noch so weit, daß ich ... you're pushing me too far, I ...; die ~de Kraft bei etw sein to be the driving force behind sth.
(b) (Reaktion erzeugen) to bring. jdm den Schweiß/das Blut ins Gesicht ~ to make sb sweat/blush; der Wind/der Gedanke treibt mir Tränen in die Augen the wind makes my eyes water/the thought brings tears to my eyes.
(c) (einschlagen) Nagel, Pfahl etc to drive.
(d) (bearbeiten, formen) Metall to beat.
(e) (ausüben, betreiben) Handel, Geschäfte to do; Studien, Politik to pursue; Gewerbe to carry on; Sport to do; (machen) to do; Schabernack, Unfug, Unsinn to be up to; Spaß to have; Aufwand to make, to create; Unzucht to commit. was treibst du? what are you up to?; Schiffahrt ~ to sail; Mißbrauch mit etw ~ to abuse sth; Handel mit etw/jdm ~ to trade in sth/with sb; Wucher ~ to profiteer.
(f) wenn du es weiter so treibst ... if you go or carry on like that ...; es toll ~ to have a wild time; es zu toll ~ to overdo it; es schlimm ~ to behave badly; in seiner Jugend hat er es schlimm getrieben he was quite a lad in his youth (inf); es zu bunt or weit ~ to go too far; er treibt es noch so weit, daß er hinausgeworfen wird if he goes on like that, he'll get thrown out; es mit jdm ~ (sl) to have it off with sb (Brit inf), to have sex with sb.
(g) (hervorbringen) Blüten, Knospen etc to sprout, to put forth; (im Treibhaus) to force; siehe Blüte.
2 vi (a) aux sein (sich fortbewegen) to drift. sich ~ lassen (lit,

fig) to drift; sich von der Stimmung ~ lassen to let oneself be carried along by the mood.
(b) (wachsen) to sprout.
(c) (Bier, Kaffee, Medizin etc) to have a diuretic effect; (Hefe) to make dough etc rise. ~de Medikamente diuretics.

Treiben nt -s, - (a) (Getriebe) hustle and bustle; (von Schneeflocken) swirling. ich schaute dem munteren ~ der Kinder zu I watched the children playing happily; ich beobachte dein ~ schon lange I've been watching what you've been getting up to for a long time. (b) (Treibjagd) battue (spec).

Treiber m -s, - (Vieh~) drover; (Hunt) beater.

Treib-: ~gas nt (bei Sprühdosen) propellant; ~gut nt flotsam and jetsam pl.

Treibhaus nt hothouse.

Treibhaus-: ~luft f (a) hothouse air; (b) (fig) hot, humid atmosphere; (im Freien auch) sultry atmosphere; ~pflanze f hothouse plant; ~temperatur f hothouse temperature; hier herrscht die reinste ~temperatur! it's like a hothouse here.

Treib-: ~holz nt driftwood; ~jagd f battue (spec), shoot (in which game is sent up by beaters); ~mittel nt (in Sprühdosen) propellant; (Cook) raising agent; ~netz nt driftnet; ~sand m siehe Triebsand; ~schlag m (Sport) drive; ~stoff m fuel; (Raketen~ auch) propellant.

treideln vt to tow.

Trema nt -s, -s or -ta dieresis.

tremolieren* vi to quaver.

Tremolo nt -s, -s or **Tremoli** tremolo.

Trenchcoat ['trɛntʃkoːt] m -(s), -s trenchcoat.

Trend m -s, -s trend.

trennbar adj separable. ein nicht ~es Wort an inseparable word.

Trennbarkeit f separability.

trennen 1 vt (a) (entfernen) Mensch, Tier to separate (von from); (Tod) to take away (von from); (in Teile teilen, ab~) to separate; Kopf, Glied etc to sever; (abmachen) to detach (von from); Aufgenähtes to take off, to remove; Saum, Naht to unpick, to undo. zwei Teile voneinander ~ to separate two parts; etw in zwei Hälften ~ to divide or split sth into two halves.
(b) (aufspalten, scheiden) Bestandteile, Eier, Raufende to separate; Partner, Freunde to split up; (räumlich) to separate; Begriffe to differentiate, to distinguish (between); Ehe to dissolve; (nach Rasse, Geschlecht) to segregate. voneinander getrennt werden to be separated; Ursache und Folge ~ to make or draw a distinction between cause and results; Gut von Böse ~ to distinguish between good and evil, to differentiate or distinguish good from evil; uns trennt zu vieles we have too little in common; jetzt kann uns nichts mehr ~ now nothing can ever come between us; alles T~de (zwischen uns/den beiden) all our/their differences; das Radio trennt die Sender gut/schlecht the radio has good/bad selectivity; siehe getrennt.
(c) (in Bestandteile zerlegen) Kleid to take to pieces; (Ling) Wort to divide, to split up; (Chem) Gemisch to separate (out).
2 vr (a) (auseinandergehen) to separate; (Partner, Eheleute etc auch) to split up; (Abschied nehmen) to part. sich von jdm/der Firma ~ to leave sb/the firm; die zwei Mannschaften trennten sich 2:0/1:1 the final score was 2-0/the two teams drew one-all; sich im guten/bösen ~ to part on good/bad terms.
(b) (weggeben, verkaufen etc) sich von etw ~ to part with sth; er konnte sich davon nicht ~ he couldn't bear to part with it; (von Plan) he couldn't give it up; (von Anblick) he couldn't take his eyes off; (von Party) he couldn't tear himself away.
(c) (sich teilen) (Wege, Flüsse) to divide. hier ~ sich unsere Wege (fig) now we must go our separate ways.
3 vi (zwischen Begriffen) to draw or make a distinction. das Radio trennt gut/scharf the radio has good selectivity.

Trenn-: ~messer nt (Sew) unpicker; ~punkt m (Ling) dieresis; t~scharf adj t~scharf sein to have good selectivity; ~schärfe f selectivity.

Trennung f (a) (Abschied) parting.
(b) (Getrenntwerden, Getrenntsein) separation; (das Trennen auch) separating; (in Teile) division; (von Begriffen) distinction; (von Eheleuten) separation; (der Ehe) dissolution; (von Sender) selectivity; (von Wort) division; (Rassen~, Geschlechter~) segregation. die Partner entschlossen sich zu einer ~ the partners decided to separate or split up.

Trennungs-: ~entschädigung f, ~geld nt separation allowance; ~schmerz m pain of parting; ~strich m hyphen; einen ~strich ziehen (fig) to make a clear distinction (zwischen between).

Trenn(ungs)-: ~wand f partition (wall); ~zeichen nt hyphen.

Trense f -, -n snaffle.

treppauf adv: ~, treppab up and down stairs.

Treppe f -, -n (a) (Aufgang) (flight of) stairs pl, staircase; (im Freien) (flight of) steps pl. eine ~ a staircase, a flight of stairs/ steps; wir haben die ~ (inf), wir sind mit der ~ an der Reihe (inf) it's our turn to clean or do the stairs; die ~ hinaufgehen/hinuntergehen to go up/down the stairs, to go upstairs/downstairs; du bist wohl die ~ hinuntergefallen (fig inf) what's happened to your hair?; siehe hinauffallen.
(b) (inf: Stufe) step.
(c) (inf: Stockwerk) floor.

Treppen-: ~absatz m half-landing; ~geländer nt banister; ~haus nt stairwell; im ~haus on the stairs; ~stufe f step, stair; ~witz m: der ~witz der Weltgeschichte an irony of history.

Tresen m -s, - (Theke) bar; (Ladentisch) counter.

Tresor m -s, -e (Raum) strongroom, vault; (Schrank) safe.

Tresorknacker m -s, - (inf) safebreaker.

Tresse f -, -n gold/silver braid.

Trester pl siehe Treber.

Tret-: ~**auto** nt pedal car; ~**boot** nt pedal boat, pedalo; ~**eimer** m pedal bin.

treten pret **trat**, ptp **getreten** 1 vi (a) (ausschlagen, mit Fuß anstoßen) to kick (gegen etw sth, nach out at).
  (b) aux sein (mit Raumangabe) to step. **hier kann man nicht mehr** ~ there is no room to move here; **vom Schatten ins Helle** ~ to move out of the shadow into the light; **etwas näher an etw** (acc) ~ to move or step closer to sth; **vor die Kamera** ~ to appear on TV/in a film or on the screen; **in den Vordergrund/Hintergrund** ~ to step forward/back; (fig) to come to the forefront/to recede into the background; **an jds Stelle** ~ to take sb's place; siehe **nah(e)**.
  (c) aux sein or haben (in Loch, Pfütze, auf Gegenstand etc) to step, to tread. **jdm auf den Fuß** ~ to step on sb's foot, to tread on sb's toe; **jdm auf die Füße** ~ (fig) to tread on sb's toes; **jdm auf den Schlips** (inf) or **Schwanz** (sl) ~ to offend sb; **sich auf den Schlips** (inf) or **Schwanz** (sl) **getreten fühlen** to feel offended; siehe **Stelle**.
  (d) aux sein or haben (betätigen) **in die Pedale** ~ to pedal hard; **aufs Gas(pedal)** ~ (Pedal betätigen) to press the accelerator; (schnell fahren) to put one's foot down (inf), to step on it (inf); **auf die Bremse** ~ to brake, to put one's foot on the brake.
  (e) aux sein (hervor~, sichtbar werden) **Wasser trat aus allen Ritzen und Fugen** water was coming out of every crack and cranny; **der Schweiß trat ihm auf die Stirn** sweat appeared on his forehead; **Tränen traten ihr in die Augen** tears came to her eyes, her eyes filled with tears; **der Fluß trat über die Ufer** the river overflowed its banks; **der Mond trat aus den Wolken/hinter die Wolken** the moon appeared from behind/went or disappeared behind the clouds; **der Saft tritt in die Bäume** the sap is rising in the trees; **es trat plötzlich wieder in mein Bewußtsein** it suddenly came back to me.
  (f) aux sein (Funktionsverb) (beginnen) to start, to begin; (ein~) to enter. **in jds Leben** (acc) ~ to come into or enter sb's life; **ins Leben or Dasein** ~ to come into being; **die Sonne tritt in das Zeichen des Stiers** the sun is entering the sign of Taurus; **in den Ruhestand** ~ to retire; **in den Streik or Ausstand** ~ to go on strike; **in den Staatsdienst/Stand der Ehe or Ehestand** ~ to enter the civil service/into the state of matrimony; **mit jdm in Verbindung** ~ to get in touch with sb; **sie tritt heute ins 50. Lebensjahr** she celebrates her 49th birthday today; siehe **Erscheinung, Kraft** etc.

  2 vt (a) (einen Fußtritt geben, stoßen) to kick; (Sport) **Ecke, Freistoß** to take. **jdn ans Bein** ~ to kick sb's leg or sb on the leg; **jdn mit dem Fuß** ~ to kick sb; **sich** (dat) **in den Hintern** ~ (fig inf) to kick oneself.
  (b) (mit Fuß betätigen) **Spinnrad, Webstuhl, Blasebalg** to operate (using one's foot). **die Bremse** ~ to brake, to put on the brakes; **die Pedale** ~ to pedal; **den Takt** ~ to tap one's foot in time to the music.
  (c) (trampeln) **Pfad, Weg, Bahn** to tread. **sich** (dat) **einen Splitter in den Fuß** ~ to get a splinter in one's foot; siehe **Wasser**.
  (d) (fig) (schlecht behandeln) to shove around (inf). **jdn** ~ (inf: antreiben) to get at sb.
  (e) (begatten) to tread, to mate with.

Treter m -s, - (inf) comfortable shoe.

Tret-: ~**mine** f (Mil) (anti-personnel) mine; ~**mühle** f (lit, fig) treadmill; **in der** ~**mühle sein** to be in a rut (inf); **die tägliche** ~**mühle** the daily grind; ~**rad** nt treadmill; ~**roller** m scooter.

treu 1 adj **Freund, Sohn, Kunde** etc loyal; **Diener** auch devoted; **Seele** auch, **Hund, Gatte** etc faithful; **Abbild** true; **Gedenken** respectful; (~herzig) trusting; **Miene** innocent. **jdm in** ~**er Liebe verbunden sein** to be bound to sb by loyalty and love; **jdm** ~ **sein/bleiben** to be/remain faithful; (nicht betrügen auch) to be/remain true to sb; **sich** (dat) **selbst** ~ **bleiben** to be true to oneself; **seinen Grundsätzen** ~ **bleiben** to stick to or remain true to one's principles; **der Erfolg/das Glück ist ihr** ~ **geblieben** success kept coming her way/her luck held (out); ~ **wie Gold** faithful and loyal; (Diener etc auch) faithful as a dog; **Dein** ~**er Freund** (old) yours truly; **jdm etw zu** ~**en Händen übergeben** to give sth to sb for safekeeping.
  2 adv faithfully; **dienen** auch loyally; **sorgen** devotedly; (~herzig) trustingly; **ansehen** innocently. ~ **und brav** (Erwachsener) dutifully; (Kind) like a good boy/girl, as good as gold; siehe **ergeben**.

Treu-: ~**bruch** m breach of faith; t~**brüchig** adj faithless, false; (jdm) t~**brüchig werden** to break faith (with sb); t~**deutsch** adj truly German; (pej) typically German; t~**doof** adj (inf) guileless, artless, naive.

Treue f -, no pl siehe **treu** loyalty; devotion, devotedness; faithfulness; (eheliche ~) faithfulness, fidelity. **einer Flagge** ~ **geloben** to pledge allegiance to a flag; **sie gelobten einander ewige** ~ they vowed to be eternally faithful to one another; **jdm die** ~ **halten** to keep faith with sb; (Ehegatten etc) to remain faithful to sb; **meiner Treu!** (old) my word!; **auf Treu und Glauben in good faith; in alter** ~ for old times' sake; **in alter** ~ **Dein** as ever, yours; siehe **brechen**.

Treu|eid m oath of loyalty or allegiance.

Treu(e)pflicht f loyalty (owed by employee to employer and vice versa).

Treueprämie f long-service bonus.

treu|ergeben adj attr devoted, loyal, faithful.

Treueschwur m oath of loyalty or allegiance; (von Geliebtem etc) vow to be faithful.

Treu-: ~**hand** f -, no pl trust; ~**händer(in** f) m -s, - trustee, fiduciary (form); ~**handgesellschaft** f trust company; t~**herzig** adj innocent, trusting; ~**herzigkeit** f innocence; t~**lich** adv loyally, faithfully; t~**los** adj disloyal, faithless;

t~**los an jdm handeln** to fail sb; **du** t~**loses Stück** (inf) you wretch; siehe **Tomate**; ~**losigkeit** f disloyalty, faithlessness; t~**sorgend** adj attr devoted.

Triangel m -s, - triangle.

Trias f -, no pl Triassic (Period).

Tribun m -s or -en, -e(n) tribune.

Tribunal nt -s, -e tribunal.

Tribunat nt -(e)s, -e tribunate.

Tribüne f -, -n (Redner~) platform, rostrum; (Zuschauer~, Zuschauer) stand; (Haupt~) grandstand.

Tribut m -(e)s, -e (Hist) tribute, dues pl; (fig) tribute; (Opfer) toll. **jdm** ~ **entrichten** or (fig) **zollen** to pay tribute to sb.

tributpflichtig adj tributary (rare), obliged to pay tribute.

Trichine f trichina.

Trichinen-: t~**haltig** adj trichinous; ~**schau** f meat inspection (to check for trichinae); ~**schauer(in** f) m -s, - meat inspector.

Trichter m -s, - funnel; (Bomben~) crater; (von Grammophon) horn; (von Trompete, Megaphon etc) bell; (von Hörgerät) trumpet; (von Lautsprecher) cone; (Einfüll~) hopper. **jdn auf den** ~ **bringen** (inf), **jdm auf den** ~ **helfen** (inf) to give sb a clue; **auf den** ~ **kommen** (inf) to catch on (inf).

trichterförmig adj funnel-shaped, funnel-like.

Trick m -s, -s or (rare) -e trick; (betrügerisch auch, raffiniert) ploy, dodge; (Tip, Rat) tip. **ein fauler/gemeiner** ~ a mean or dirty trick; **keine faulen** ~**s!** no funny business! (inf); **das ist der ganze** ~ that's all there is to it; **den** ~ **raushaben, wie man etw macht** (inf) to have got the knack of doing sth; **der** ~ **dabei ist, ...** the trick is to ...; **da ist doch ein** ~ **dabei** there is a trick to (doing) it; **ich habe einen** ~ **angewendet, daß sie mich doch gehen ließ** I tricked her into letting me go after all; **jdm einen** ~ **verraten** to give sb a tip.

Trick-: ~**betrug** m confidence trick; ~**betrüger** m confidence trickster; ~**film** m trick film; (Zeichen~) cartoon (film); ~**kiste** f (von Zauberer) box of tricks; (fig inf) bag of tricks; t~**reich** adj (inf) tricky; (raffiniert) clever.

tricksen (inf) 1 vt to fiddle; (Sport) to feint. **phantastisch, wie er mit den Karten trickst** it's amazing what he can do with cards. 2 vt to trick.

Tricktaste f trick or superimpose button.

trieb pret of **treiben**.

Trieb m -(e)s, -e (a) (Psych, Natur~) drive; (Drang) urge; (Verlangen) desire, urge; (Neigung, Hang) inclination; (Selbsterhaltungs~, Fortpflanzungs~) instinct. **sie ist von ihren** ~**en beherrscht** she is guided completely by her physical urges or desires; **du mußt lernen, deine** ~**e zu beherrschen** you must learn to control your physical urges or desires; **einen** ~ **zum Verbrechen haben** to have criminal urges.
  (b) (Bot) shoot.
  (c) (Tech) drive.

Trieb-: t~**artig** adj attr **Verhalten** instinctive; (von Sexualverbrecher etc) compulsive; ~**befriedigung** f gratification of a physical urge; ~**feder** f (fig) motivating force (gen behind); t~**haft** adj **Handlungen** compulsive; **ein** ~ **haftes Instinkt** an instinctive urge; **sie hat ein sehr** t~**haftes Wesen, sie ist ein** t~**hafter Mensch** she is ruled by her physical urges or desires; ~**haftigkeit** f domination by one's physical urges; ~**handlung** f act motivated by one's physical urges; ~**kraft** f (Mech) motive power; (Bot) germinating power; (fig) driving force; ~**leben** nt physical activities pl; (Geschlechtsleben) sex life; ~**mensch** m creature of instinct; ~**mittel** nt siehe **Treibmittel**; ~**rad** nt driving wheel; ~**sand** m quicksand; ~**täter**, ~**verbrecher** m sexual offender; ~**wagen** m (Rail) railcar; ~**werk** nt power plant; (in Uhr) mechanism.

Trief-: ~**auge** nt (Med) bleary eye; ~**augen** (pej) watery eyes; (von Mensch) sheep-like eyes; t~**äugig** adj watery-eyed; **er schaute mich** t~**äugig an** (pej) he looked at me with dumb devotion.

Triefel m -s, - (inf) drip (inf).

trief(e)lig adj (inf) **Mensch** drippy (inf); **Entschuldigung, Vorführung** etc pathetic, feeble.

triefen pret **triefte** or (geh) **troff**, ptp **getrieft** or (rare) **getroffen** vi (a) to be dripping wet; (Nase) to run; (Auge) to water. ~ **vor** to be dripping with; (fig pej) to gush with; ~**d vor Nässe**, ~**d naß** dripping wet, wet through; ~**d** soaking (wet).
  (b) aux sein (rinnen) to drip.

Triefnase f (inf) runny nose (inf).

triezen vt (inf) **jdn** ~ to pester sb; (schuften lassen) to drive sb hard.

triff imper sing of **treffen**.

Trift f -, -en (Weide) pasture; (Weg) cattle/sheep track.

triftig adj convincing; **Entschuldigung, Grund** auch good.

Triftigkeit f, no pl convincingness.

Trigonometrie f trigonometry.

trigonometrisch adj trigonometric(al).

Trikolore f -, -n tricolour.

Trikot[1] [tri'ko:, 'triko] m or nt -s, no pl (~stoff) cotton jersey.

Trikot[2] [tri'ko:, 'triko] nt -s, -s (Hemd) shirt, jersey; (dated: Turnanzug) leotard; (old: Badeanzug) bathing costume. **das gelbe** ~ (bei Tour de France) the yellow jersey.

Trikotage [triko'ɑ:ʒə] f -, -n cotton jersey underwear no pl.

Triller m -s, - (Mus) trill; (von Vogel auch) warble.

trillern vti to warble, to trill. **du trillerst wie eine Lerche** you sing like a lark.

Trillerpfeife f (pea-)whistle.

Trillion f -, -en trillion (Brit), quintillion (US).

Trilogie f trilogy

Trimester nt -s, - term.

Trimm-: ~-**Aktion** f keep-fit campaign; ~-**dich-Gerät** nt keep-fit apparatus; ~-**dich-Pfad** m keep-fit trail.

trimmen 1 vt **Hund, Schiff, Flugzeug** to trim; (inf) **Mensch, Tier**

to teach, to train; *Funkgerät* to tune. **den Motor/das Auto auf Höchstleistung** ~ (*inf*) to soup up the engine/car (*inf*); **jdn auf tadelloses Benehmen** ~ to teach *or* train sb to behave impeccably; **etw auf alt** ~ to make sth look old; **auf alt getrimmt** done up to look old; **auf rustikal getrimmtes Restaurant** restaurant done up in rustic style; **jdn auf einen bestimmten Typ** ~ to make *or* mould sb into a certain type.
  2 *vr* to do keep-fit (exercises). **trimm dich durch Sport** keep fit with sport.
Trimm-: ~**gerät** *nt* keep-fit apparatus; ~**pfad** *m* keep-fit trail.
Trinität *f* (*geh*) trinity.
Trink-: t~**bar** *adj* drinkable; ~**branntwein** *m* spirit *usu pl*; ~**ei** *nt* new-laid egg.
trinken *pret* **trank**, *ptp* **getrunken** **1** *vt* to drink; *ein Bier, Tasse Tee, Flasche Wein auch* to have. **alles/eine Flasche leer** ~ to finish off all the drink/a bottle; **ich habe nichts zu** ~ **im Haus** I haven't any drink in the house; **er trinkt gern einen** (*inf*) he likes his drink; (**schnell**) **einen** ~ **gehen** (*inf*) to go for a (quick) drink; *siehe* **Tisch**.
  2 *vi* to drink. **jdm zu** ~ **geben** to give sb a drink *or* something to drink; **laß mich mal** ~ let me have a drink; **auf jds Wohl/jdn/etw** ~ to drink sb's health/to sb/to sth.
  3 *vr* **sich voll/satt** ~ to drink one's fill; (*mit Alkohol*) to get drunk; **sich arm** ~ to drink one's money away.
  4 *vr impers* **es trinkt sich gut/schlecht daraus** it is easy/difficult to drink from; **dieser Wein trinkt sich gut** this is a pleasant *or* palatable wine.
Trinker(in *f*) *m* **-s,** - drinker; (*Alkoholiker*) alcoholic.
Trinkerheilanstalt *f* detoxification centre.
Trink-: t~**fest** *adj* so ~**fest bin ich nicht** I can't hold my drink very well; **seine t~festen Freunde** his hard-drinking friends; ~**festigkeit** *f* ability to hold one's drink; t~**freudig** *adj* fond of drinking; ~**gefäß** *nt* drinking vessel; ~**gelage** *nt* drinking session; ~**geld** *nt* tip; **von ihm/heute hat sie wenig** ~**geld bekommen** she got a small tip from him/she didn't get much in the way of tips today; **jdm** ~**geld geben** to tip sb, to give sb a tip; ~**glas** *nt* (drinking) glass; ~**halle** *f* (*in Heilbädern*) pump room; (*Kiosk*) refreshment kiosk; ~**halm** *m* drinking straw; ~**lied** *nt* drinking song; ~**milch** *f* milk; ~**schale** *f* drinking bowl; ~**schokolade** *f* drinking chocolate; ~**spruch** *m* toast; ~**wasser** *nt* drinking water; „**kein** ~**wasser**" "not for drinking", "no drinking water".
Trio *nt* **-s,** -s trio.
Triole *f* -, **-n** (*Mus*) triplet.
Triolett *nt* **-(e)s,** -e triolet.
Trip *m* **-s,** -s (*inf*) trip.
trippeln *vi aux haben or* (*bei Richtungsangabe*) *sein* to trip; (*Kind, alte Dame*) to toddle; (*geziert*) to mince; (*Boxer*) to dance around; (*Pferd*) to frisk. **mit dem Ball** ~ to dribble the ball.
Tripper *m* **-s,** - gonorrhoea *no art*. **sich** (*dat*) **den** ~ **holen** (*inf*) to get a dose of the clap) (*inf*).
trist *adj* dreary, dismal; *Farbe* dull.
Triste *f* **-, -n** (*Aus*) haystack.
tritt *imper sing of* **treten**.
Tritt *m* **-(e)s,** -e **(a)** (*Schritt*) step; (*Gang auch*) tread. **einen falschen** ~ **machen** to take a wrong step; **ich hörte** ~**e** I heard footsteps.
  (b) (*Gleichschritt*) step. **im** ~ **marschieren,** ~ **halten** to march in step, to keep in step.
  (c) (*Fuß*~) kick. **jdm einen** ~ **geben** to give sb a kick, to kick sb; (*fig*) (*entlassen etc*) to kick sb out (*inf*); (*inf: anstacheln*) to give sb a kick in the pants (*inf*) *or* up the backside (*inf*); **einen** ~ **in den Hintern kriegen** (*inf*) to get a kick in the pants (*inf*) *or* up the backside (*inf*); (*fig*) to get kicked out (*inf*).
  (d) (*bei* ~**leiter, Stufe*) step; (*Gestell*) steps *pl*; (~**brett**) step; (*an Auto*) running board.
  (e) (*Fußspur*) footprint; (*von Tier*) track.
  (f) (*Hunt: Fuß*) foot.
  (g) (*bei Vögeln*) mating.
Tritt-: ~**brett** *nt* step; (*an Auto*) running board; (*an Nähmaschine*) treadle; ~**brettfahrer** *m* (*inf*) fare-dodger; (*fig*) free-rider (*inf*); ~**leiter** *f* stepladder; ~**roller** *m siehe* **Tretroller**.
Triumph *m* **-(e)s,** -e triumph. **im** ~ in triumph; ~**e feiern** to be a great success *or* very successful.
triumphal *adj* triumphant.
Triumph-: ~**bogen** *m* triumphal arch; ~**geschrei** *nt* triumphant cheer, cheer of triumph.
triumphieren* *vi* (*frohlocken*) to rejoice, to exult. **über jdn/etw** ~ (*geh*) to triumph over *or* overcome sb/sth.
triumphierend *adj* triumphant.
Triumphzug *m* triumphal procession.
Triumvirat [triumvi'ra:t] *nt* triumvirate.
trivial [tri'via:l] *adj* trivial; *Gespräch auch* banal, trite.
Trivialität [triviali'tɛːt] *f siehe adj* triviality; banality, triteness.
Trivialliteratur [tri'via:l-] *f* (*pej*) light fiction.
Trochäus [trɔ'xɛːʊs] *m* -, **Trochäen** [trɔ'xɛːən] (*Poet*) trochee.
trocken *adj* **(a)** dry; *Gebiet auch* arid; *Gedeck* without wine *etc*. ~**er Dunst** (*Met*) haze; ~ **werden** to dry; (*Brot*) to go *or* get *or* become dry; **das Schiff liegt** ~ the ship is high and dry; **noch** ~ **nach Hause kommen** to get home dry *or* without getting wet; **ins T~e kommen/gehen** to come/go into the dry; **im T~en sein** to be somewhere dry *or* sheltered; **da bleibt kein Auge** ~ everyone is moved to tears; (*vor Lachen*) everyone laughs till they cry, everyone falls about laughing (*inf*); ~**en Auges/Fußes** (*liter*) dry-eyed/without getting one's feet wet; ~ **Brot essen** (*liter*) to eat dry bread; **sie hatten keinen** ~**en Faden mehr am Leib** they were soaked to the skin *or* wet through; ~ **aufbewahren/lagern** to keep/store in a dry place; **sich** ~

rasieren to use an electric razor; **die Haare** ~ **schneiden** to cut one's/sb's hair dry; **die Gäste** ~ **sitzen lassen** to leave one's guests without a drink; **auf dem** ~**en sitzen** (*inf*) to be in a tight spot (*inf*) *or* in difficulties; *siehe* **Schäfchen, Ohr**.
  (b) (*langweilig*) dry.
  (c) (*herb*) *Sekt, Sherry,* (*fig*) *Humor, Art etc* dry.
Trocken-: ~**automat** *m* tumble dryer; ~**beerenauslese** *f* wine made from choice grapes left on the vine to dry out at the end of the season; ~**boden** *m* drying room (*in attic*); t~**bügeln** *vt sep* to iron dry; ~**dock** *nt* dry dock; ~**ei** *nt* dried egg; ~**futter** *nt* dried *or* dehydrated food; ~**gebiet** *nt* arid region; t~**gefrieren*** *vt insep irreg* to freeze-dry; ~**gestell** *nt* drying rack; ~**haube** *f* (*salon*) hairdryer; ~**hefe** *f* dried yeast.
Trockenheit *f* (*lit, fig*) dryness; (*von Gebiet auch*) aridness; (*Trockenperiode*) drought. **es herrschte letzten Sommer große** ~ last summer was very dry.
Trocken-: ~**kurs** *m* (*Sport, fig: beim Autofahren etc*) course in which a beginner learns the basic techniques/skills out of the normal element; **einen** ~**kurs machen** to learn the basics; t~**legen** *vt sep* (*a*) *Baby* to change; (*inf*) *Trinker* to dry out; **(b)** *Sumpf, Gewässer* to drain; ~**legung** *f* draining; ~**maß** *nt* dry measure; ~**milch** *f* dried milk; ~**platz** *m* drying area; ~**rasierer** *m* **-s,** - (*inf*) user of electric shaver *or* razor; (*Rasierapparat*) electric shaver *or* razor; ~**rasur** *f* dry *or* electric shave; (*das Rasieren*) shaving with an electric razor *no art*; t~**reiben** *vt sep irreg* to rub dry; ~**shampoo** *nt* dry shampoo; t~**sitzen** *vi sep irreg* (*inf*) to sit there without a drink/with one's glass empty; ~**spiritus** *m* solid fuel (*for camping stove etc*); ~**starre** *f* aestivation; t~**stehen** *vi sep irreg* (*Kuh*) to be dry; ~**wäsche** *f* dry weight (of washing); ~**zeit** *f* (*a*) (*Jahreszeit*) dry season; **(b)** (*von Wäsche etc*) drying time.
trocknen 1 *vt* to dry. **2** *vi aux sein* to dry.
Troddel *f* **-, -n** tassel.
Trödel *m* **-s,** *no pl* (*inf*) junk.
Trödelei *f* (*inf*) dawdling.
Trödel-: ~**kram** *m siehe* **Trödel**; ~**laden** *m* junk shop.
trödeln *vi* to dawdle.
Trödler *m* **-s,** - **(a)** (*Händler*) junk dealer. **(b)** (*inf: langsamer Mensch*) dawdler, slowcoach (*Brit inf*), slowpoke (*US inf*).
troff *pret of* **triefen**.
Trog *m* **-(e)s,** -e trough; (*Wasch*~) tub.
trog *pret of* **trügen**.
Trogtal *nt* glaciated *or* U-shaped valley.
Trojaner(in *f*) *m* **-s,** - Trojan.
trojanisch *adj* Trojan. **das T~e Pferd** the Trojan Horse.
trölen *vi* (*Sw*) to dawdle.
Troll *m* **-s,** -e troll.
trollen *vr* (*inf*) to push off (*inf*).
Trommel *f* **-, -n (a)** (*Mus*) drum. **die** ~ **rühren** (*fig inf*) to drum up (some) support. **(b)** (*Tech*) (*in Maschine*) drum; (*in Revolver*) revolving breech.
Trommel-: ~**bremse** *f* drum brake; ~**fell** *nt* eardrum; **da platzt einem ja das** ~**fell** (*fig*) the noise is earsplitting; ~**feuer** *nt* drumfire, heavy barrage.
trommeln 1 *vi* to drum; (*Regen*) to bear (down). **gegen die Brust** ~ to beat one's chest; **mit den Fingern** ~ to drum one's fingers. **2** *vt Marsch, Lied* to play on the drum/drums, to drum. **jdn aus dem Schlaf** ~ to knock sb up (*Brit inf*), to wake sb up (by hammering on the door).
Trommel-: ~**revolver** *m* revolver; ~**schlag** *m* drum beat; (*das Trommeln*) drumming; ~**schlegel** *m* drumstick; ~**sprache** *f* bush telegraph; ~**stöcke** *pl* drumsticks *pl*; ~**waschmaschine** *f* drum washing machine; ~**wirbel** *m* drum-roll.
Trommler(in *f*) *m* **-s,** - drummer.
Trompete *f* **-, -n** trumpet; *siehe* **Pauke**.
trompeten* **1** *vi* to trumpet; (*sich schneuzen*) to blow one's nose loudly. **2** *vt Marsch* to play on the trumpet.
Trompetengeschmetter *nt* blare *or* blast of trumpets.
Trompeter(in *f*) *m* **-s,** - trumpeter.
Tropen *pl* tropics *pl*.
Tropen- in *cpds* tropical; ~**anzug** *m* tropical suit; ~**fieber** *nt* malaria; ~**helm** *m* pith-helmet, topee; ~**klima** *nt* tropical climate; ~**koller** *m* tropical madness; ~**krankheit** *f* tropical disease; ~**tag** *m* scorcher (*inf*); ~**tauglichkeit** *f* fitness for service in the tropics.
Tropf *m* **-(e)s,** -e (*inf*) **(a)** (*Schelm*) rogue, rascal. **einfältiger** ~ twit (*Brit inf*), dummy (*inf*); **armer** ~ poor beggar (*inf*) *or* devil. **(b)** *no pl* (*Infusion*) drip (*inf*).
tropf *interj* drip.
Tröpfchen-: ~**infektion** *f* airborne infection; t~**weise** *adv* in dribs and drabs.
tröpfeln 1 *vi* **(a)** (*Leitung, Halm*) to drip; (*Nase*) to run. **(b)** *aux sein* (*Flüssigkeit*) to drip. **2** *vi impers* **es tröpfelt** it is spitting. **3** *vt* to drip.
tropfen 1 *vi* to drip; (*Nase*) to run. **es tropft durch die Decke/von den Bäumen/aus der Leitung** there is water dripping through the ceiling/the rain is dripping from the trees/the pipe is dripping. **2** *vt* to drop, to drip.
Tropfen *m* **-s,** - drop; (*Schweiß*~ *auch*) bead; (*einzelner* ~ *an Kanne, Nase etc*) drip; (*inf: kleine Menge*) drop. ~ *pl* (*Medizin*) drops; **ein guter** *or* **edler** ~ (*inf*) a good wine; **bis auf den letzten** ~ to the last drop; **alles bis auf den letzten** ~ **trinken** to drink every drop; **ein** ~ **auf den heißen Stein** (*fig inf*) a drop in the ocean.
-tropfen *pl in cpds* (*Med*) drops *pl*.
Tropfenfänger *m* **-s,** - drip-catcher.
tropfenweise *adv* drop by drop.
Tropf-: ~**infusion** *f* intravenous drip; t~**naß** *adj* dripping wet; ~**stein** *m* dripstone; (*an der Decke*) stalactite; (*am Boden*)

stalagmite; ~steinhöhle f dripstone cave.
Trophäe [tro'fɛ:ə] f -, -n trophy.
tropisch adj tropical.
Troß m -sses, -sse (old) baggage train. er gehört zum ~ (fig) he's a hanger-on; (hat untergeordnete Rolle) he's an underling.
Trosse f -, -n cable, hawser.
Trost m -(e)s, no pl consolation, comfort. jdm ~ zusprechen/bringen to console or comfort sb; das Kind war ihr einziger ~ the child was her only comfort; ~ im Alkohol/in der Religion suchen to seek solace in alcohol/religion; ein ~, daß jetzt alles vorbei ist it is a relief that everything is over; zum ~ kann ich Ihnen sagen, daß ... it may comfort you to know that ...; das ist ein schwacher or schlechter/schöner (iro) ~ that's pretty cold comfort/some comfort that is!; du bist wohl nicht ganz or recht bei ~(e)! (inf) you must be out of your mind!
trösten vt to comfort; (Trost zusprechen auch) to console. jdn/sich mit etw ~ to console sb/oneself with sth; sich/jdn über etw (acc) ~ to get over sth/to help sb to get over sth; ~ Sie sich! never mind.
Tröster(in f) m -s, - comforter.
tröstlich adj cheering, comforting. das ist ja sehr ~ (iro) that's some comfort.
trostlos adj hopeless; Jugend, Verhältnisse miserable, wretched; (verzweifelt) inconsolable; (öde, trist) dreary. ~ langweilig desperately boring.
Trostlosigkeit f, no pl siehe adj hopelessness; misery, wretchedness; inconsolability; dreariness.
Trost-: ~pflaster nt consolation; als ~pflaster by way of consolation; ~preis m consolation prize; t~reich adj comforting; ~worte pl words of consolation pl.
Tröstung f comfort; (das Trösten) comforting.
Trott m -s, no pl (slow) trot; (fig) routine. im ~ at a (slow) trot; aus dem alten ~ herauskommen to get out of one's rut.
Trottel m -s, - (inf) idiot, dope (inf).
trottelig adj (inf) stupid, dopey (inf).
trotten vi aux sein to trot along; (Pferd) to trot slowly.
Trotteur [trɔ'tøːr] m -s, -s casual (shoe).
Trottoir [trɔ'toaːr] nt -s, -s or -e (dated, S Ger) pavement.
trotz prep + gen (geh) or + dat (inf) in spite of, despite. ~ allem or alledem in spite of everything, for all that.
Trotz m -es, no pl defiance; (trotziges Verhalten) contrariness. jdm/einer Sache zum ~ in defiance of sb/sth; jdm/einer Sache ~ bieten (geh) to defy or flout sb/sth.
Trotz|alter nt defiant age. sich im ~ befinden, im ~ sein to be going through a defiant phase; ins ~ kommen to get to or reach a defiant age.
trotzdem 1 adv nevertheless. (und) ich mache das ~! I'll do it all the same. 2 conj (strictly incorrect) even though.
trotzen vi (a) +dat to defy; der Kälte, Klima etc to withstand; der Gefahr auch to brave. (b) (trotzig sein) to be awkward or difficult or contrary.
trotzig adj defiant; Kind etc difficult, awkward; (widerspenstig) contrary.
Trotzkismus m Trotskyism.
Trotzkist m Trotskyite, Trotskyist.
Trotz-: ~kopf m (inf) (Einstellung) defiant streak; (widerspenstig) contrary streak; (Mensch) contrary so-and-so (inf); sei doch nicht so ein ~kopf don't be so difficult; seinen ~kopf haben to be in a defiant/contrary mood; t~köpfig adj contrary; ~phase f phase of defiance; ~reaktion f act of defiance; das war eine reine ~reaktion he/she just reacted like that out of defiance; ... dann kommt bei ihm die ~reaktion ... then he starts being difficult.
Troubadour ['truːbaduːr, trubaˈduːr] m -s, -s or -e troubadour.
Trouble ['trabl] m -s, no pl (sl) trouble. ~ kriegen/machen to make trouble; ~ haben to have problems.
trüb(e) adj (a) (unklar) Flüssigkeit cloudy; (glanzlos, matt) Glas, Augen, Himmel, Tag dull; Sonne, Mond, Licht dim. in ~en Wassern or im ~en fischen (inf) to fish in troubled waters. (b) (fig: bedrückend, unerfreulich) cheerless; Zeiten bleak; Stimmung, Aussichten, Vorahnung, Miene gloomy; Erfahrung grim. es sieht trüb aus things are looking pretty bleak; ~e Tasse (inf) drip (inf); (Spielverderber) wet blanket (inf).
Trubel m -s, no pl hurly-burly.
trüben 1 vt (a) Flüssigkeit to make cloudy, to cloud; Glas, Metall to dull; (geh) Himmel to overcast; Wasseroberfläche to ruffle; Augen, Blick to dull, to cloud. sie sieht aus, als könnte sie kein Wässerlein ~ (inf) she looks as if butter wouldn't melt in her mouth; kein Wölkchen trübte den Himmel there wasn't a cloud in the sky. (b) (fig) Glück, Freude, Verhältnis to spoil, to mar; Beziehungen to strain; Laune to dampen; Bewußtsein, Erinnerung to dull, to dim; (geh) Verstand to dull; Urteilsvermögen to dim, to cloud over. 2 vr (Flüssigkeit) to go cloudy; (Spiegel, Metall) to become dull; (geh) (Verstand) to become dulled; (Augen) to dim, to cloud; (Himmel) to cloud over; (fig) (Stimmung, Laune) to be dampened; (Beziehungen, Verhältnis) to become strained; (Glück, Freude) to be marred.
Trüb-: ~heit f no pl cloudiness; dullness; ~sal f -, -e (liter) afflictions pl; (no pl: Stimmung) sorrow; ~sal blasen (inf) to mope; t~selig adj (betrübt, verzagt) gloomy, miserable; (öde, trostlos) Gegend, Zeiten depressing, bleak; Behausung, Wetter miserable; ~seligkeit f siehe adj gloom, misery; depressingness, bleakness; gloominess, miserableness; ~sinn m, no pl gloom, melancholy; t~sinnig adj gloomy, melancholy.
Trübung f siehe vt (a) clouding; dulling; overcasting; ruffling. (b) spoiling, marring; straining; dampening; dulling.
trudeln vi (a) aux sein or haben (Aviat) to spin. ins T~

kommen or geraten to go into a spin. (b) (dial: würfeln) to play dice.
Trüffel¹ f -, -n (Pilz) truffle.
Trüffel² m -s, - truffle.
Trug m -(e)s, no pl (liter) deception; (der Sinne) illusion; (der Phantasie) delusion; siehe Lug.
trug pret of **tragen**.
Trugbild nt delusion; (der Sinne) illusion.
trügen pret **trog**, ptp **getrogen** 1 vt to deceive. wenn mich nicht alles trügt unless I am very much mistaken. 2 vi to be deceptive.
trügerisch adj (liter: betrügerisch) deceitful, false; (irreführend) deceptive.
Trug-: ~gebilde nt (liter) delusion; (der Sinne) illusion; ~schluß m fallacy, misapprehension; einem ~schluß unterliegen to be labouring under a misapprehension.
Truhe f -, -n chest.
Trumm nt -(e)s, ̈-er (dial) (großer Brocken) lump; (großes Exemplar) whopper (inf). die Emma ist vielleicht ein ~! (inf) Emma isn't half a big lass (inf).
Trümmer pl rubble sing; (Ruinen, fig: von Glück etc) ruins pl; (von Schiff, Flugzeug etc) wreckage sing; (Überreste) remnants pl; (inf: von Essen) remains pl. in ~n liegen to be in ruins; in ~ gehen to be ruined (auch fig)/wrecked; etw in ~ schlagen to smash sth to pieces or up.
Trümmer-: ~beseitigung f clearance of rubble; ~feld nt expanse of rubble/ruins; (fig) scene of devastation or destruction; ~frau f woman who clears away rubble after bombing; t~haft 1 adj ruined; Überreste (eines Flugzeugs etc) wrecked; 2 adv in ruins; (bei Gefäß etc) in pieces; ~haufen m heap of rubble.
Trumpf m -(e)s, ̈-e (Cards) (~karte) trump (card); (Farbe) trumps pl; (fig) trump card. ~ sein to be trumps; (fig inf: modisch sein) to be in (inf); den ~ in der Hand haben/aus der Hand geben (fig) to hold the/waste one's trump card; noch einen ~ in der Hand haben to have an ace up one's sleeve; jdm den ~ aus der Hand nehmen (fig) to trump sb.
Trumpf|as nt ace of trumps.
trumpfen 1 vt to trump. 2 vi to play a trump (card). mit dem König ~ to play the king of trumps.
Trumpf-: ~farbe f trumps pl; ~karte f trump (card).
Trunk m -(e)s, ̈-e (old, liter) draught (old, liter); (Zauber~ auch) potion; (das Trinken) drink. jdm etw/das Glas zum ~ reichen to pass sb sth to drink/a glass or drink. (b) (~sucht) dem ~ ergeben or verfallen sein to have taken to drink.
trunken (liter) 1 adj inebriated, intoxicated; (vor Freude, Glück etc) drunk (vor with). 2 adv drunkenly.
Trunken-: ~bold m -(e)s, -e (pej) drunkard; ~heit f drunkenness, inebriation, intoxication; ~heit am Steuer drunken driving; im Zustand der ~heit in a state of inebriation or intoxication.
Trunk-: ~sucht f alcoholism; t~süchtig adj alcoholic; t~süchtig werden to become an alcoholic; ~süchtige(r) mf alcoholic.
Trupp m -s, -s bunch; (Einheit) group; (Mil) squad; (esp beritten) troop.
Truppe f -, -n (a) (Mil) army, troops pl; (Panzer~ etc) corps sing. ~n pl troops; zur ~ zurückkehren to report back; nicht von der schnellen ~ sein (inf) to be slow. (b) (Künstler~) troupe, company.
Truppen-: ~abzug m withdrawal of troops; ~arzt m (army) medical officer; ~bewegung f usu pl troop movement; ~einheit f unit; (bei der Kavallerie) troop; ~führer m unit/troop commander; ~gattung f corps sing; ~parade f military parade or review; ~schau f troop inspection; ~stationierung f stationing of troops; ~teil m unit; ~übung f field exercise; ~übungsplatz m military training area; ~verbandsplatz m field dressing station.
truppweise adv in bunches/groups; (Mil) in squads/troops.
Trust [trast] m -(e)s, -s or -e trust.
Trut-: ~hahn m turkey(cock); ~henne f turkey(hen); ~huhn nt usu pl turkey.
Trutz m -es, no pl (obs) siehe Schutz.
trutzen vi (obs) to defy.
Tschapperl nt -s, -n (Aus) dolt (inf). armes ~ poor devil (inf).
tschau interj (inf) cheerio (Brit inf), so long (inf), ciao (inf).
Tscheche m -n, -n, **Tschechin** f Czech.
Tschechei f - die ~ (dated inf) Czechoslovakia.
tschechisch adj Czech.
Tschechisch(e) nt decl as adj Czech; siehe auch Deutsch(e).
Tschechoslowake m -n, -n, **Tschechoslowakin** f Czechoslovak.
Tschechoslowakei f - die ~ Czechoslovakia.
tschechoslowakisch adj Czechoslovak(ian).
Tschik m -s, - (Aus) (inf: Stummel) fag-end (Brit inf); (sl: Zigarette) fag (Brit inf).
tschilpen vi to chirp.
Tschinelle f (Aus Mus) cymbal.
tschüs interj (inf) cheerio (Brit inf), 'bye (inf), so long (inf).
Tschusch m -en, -en (Aus pej) ≈ wog (pej sl).
Tsd. abbr of **Tausend.**
Tsetsefliege f tsetse fly.
T-Shirt ['tiːʃɔːt] nt -s, -s T-shirt, tee-shirt.
T-Träger ['teː-] m T-bar, T-girder.
TU [teːˈʔuː] f - abbr of **Technische Universität.**
TÜ(A) ['teːˑ(ˈ)yːˈ(aː)] nt - abbr of **Technisches Überwachungsamt.**
Tuba f -, **Tuben** (a) (Mus) tuba. (b) (Anat) tube.
Tube f -, -n tube. auf die ~ drücken (inf) to get a move on (inf); (im Auto auch) to put one's foot down (inf).

Tuberkel m -s, - or (Aus auch) f -, -n tubercle.
Tuberkelbazillus m tuberculosis bacillus.
tuberkulös adj tubercular, tuberculous.
Tuberkulose f -, -n tuberculosis.
Tuberkulose-: t~krank adj tubercular, tuberculous; ~kranke(r) mf TB case.
Tuch nt -(e)s, ¨-e (a) pl -e (old: Stoff) cloth, fabric.
  (b) (Stück Stoff) cloth; (Tisch~) cloth; (Hals~, Kopf~) scarf; (Schulter~) shawl; (Hand~) towel; (Geschirr~) cloth, towel; (Taschen~) handkerchief; (zum Abdecken von Möbeln) dustsheet. das rote ~ (des Stierkämpfers) the bullfighter's cape; das wirkt wie ein rotes ~ auf ihn it makes him see red, it's like a red rag to a bull (to him).
Tuch-: ~art f type of cloth or fabric; ~fabrik f textile factory or mill; ~fühlung f physical or body contact; in ~fühlung in physical contact; (Mil) shoulder to shoulder; (fig) cheek by jowl; ~fühlung haben to be in physical contact (with sb); (fig) to be close to sb; auf ~fühlung gehen to move closer (to sb/together); mit jdm in ~fühlung kommen to come into physical or (fig) actual contact with sb; ~händler m cloth merchant; ~macher m clothworker.
tüchtig 1 adj (a) (fähig) capable, competent (in +dat at); (fleißig) efficient; Arbeiter good. etwas T~es lernen/werden (inf) to get a proper training/job; ~, ~! not bad!
  (b) (inf: groß) Portion big, huge; Stoß, Schlag hard; Appetit, Esser big. eine ~e Tracht Prügel a good hiding; eine ~e Portion Frechheit etc a fair amount of cheek etc.
  2 adv **(a)** (fleißig, fest) hard; essen heartily. hilf ~ mit lend or give us a hand.
  (b) (inf: sehr) good and proper (inf). ~ regnen to pelt (inf); jdm ~ die Meinung sagen to give sb a piece of one's mind; ~ ausschimpfen to scold thoroughly; ~ zulangen to tuck in (inf); jdn ~ anschmieren/betrügen to take sb for a ride (inf); jdn ~ belügen to tell sb a pack of lies; sich ~ ausruhen to have a good rest.
Tüchtigkeit f (Fähigkeit) ability, competence; (von Arbeiter etc) efficiency.
Tuchwaren pl cloth goods pl.
Tücke f -, -n (a) (no pl: Bosheit) malice, spite; (böswillige Handlung) malicious or spiteful action.
  (b) (Gefahr) danger, peril; (von Krankheit) perniciousness. voller ~n stecken to be difficult; (gefährlich) to be dangerous or (Berg, Fluß auch) treacherous; das ist die ~ des Objekts these things have a will of their own!; seine ~n haben (Maschine etc) to be temperamental; (schwierig sein) to be difficult; (gefährlich sein) to be dangerous or (Berg, Fluß auch) treacherous; siehe List.
  (c) (des Glücks etc) vagary usu pl; (des Schicksals auch) fickleness no pl.
tuckern vi aux haben or (bei Richtungsangabe) sein to put-put, to chug.
tückisch adj (boshaft) Mensch, Blick, Lächeln malicious, spiteful; Zufall unhappy; (bösartig, gefährlich) Berge, Strom etc treacherous; Krankheit pernicious.
tu(e) imper sing of tun.
Tuerei [tu:ə'rai] f (inf) antics pl.
Tuff m -s, -e, **Tuffstein** m tuff.
Tüftelarbeit f (inf) fiddly or finicky job.
Tüftelei f (inf) fiddly or finicky job. das ist eine ~ that's fiddly or finicky.
tüftelig adj (inf) fiddly, finicky.
tüfteln vi (inf) to puzzle; (basteln) to fiddle about (inf). an etw (dat) ~ to fiddle about with sth; (geistig) to puzzle over sth; er tüftelt gern he likes doing fiddly or finicky things.
Tüftler(in f) m -s, - (inf) person who likes doing fiddly or finicky things.
Tugend f -, -en virtue. seine ~ bewahren to remain virtuous; (Unschuld auch) to keep one's virtue; siehe Not.
Tugend-: ~bold m -(e)s, -e (pej) paragon of virtue; t~haft adj virtuous; ~haftigkeit f virtuousness; ~held m (inf) siehe ~bold; t~lich adj (old) virtuous; t~los adj unvirtuous; t~sam adj virtuous; ~wächter m (iro) guardian of his/her etc virtue.
Tukan m -s, -e toucan.
Tüll m -s, -e tulle (für Gardinen) net.
Tülle f -, -n spout; (Spritzdüse) pipe.
Tüllgardine f net curtain.
Tulpe f -, -n (a) (Bot) tulip. (b) (Glas) tulip glass.
Tulpenzwiebel f tulip bulb.
tumb adj (obs, hum) stupid, dim.
Tumbler ['tamblɐ, 'tomblɐ] m -s, - (a) (esp Sw) tumble-drier. (b) (Glas) tumble.
tummeln vr (a) (Hunde, Kinder etc) to romp (about). (b) (sich beeilen) to hurry (up).
Tummelplatz m play area; (fig) hotbed.
Tümmler m -s, - (bottle-nosed) dolphin.
Tumor m -s, -en [tu'mo:rən] tumour.
Tümpel m -s, - pond.
Tumult m -(e)s, -e commotion; (Aufruhr auch) disturbance; (der Gefühle) tumult, turmoil.
tun pret tat, ptp getan **1** vt **(a)** (machen, ausführen) to do. etw aus Liebe/Bosheit etc ~ to do sth out of love/malice etc; jdm etw zu ~ geben to give sb sth to do; was kann ich für Sie ~? what can I do for you?; was tut man in dieser Situation? what should one do in this situation?; wir haben getan, was wir konnten we did what we could; sie wußte nicht, was ~ or was sie ~ sollte she didn't know what to do; was ~? what can be done?, what shall we do?; mal sehen, was sich (für Sie) ~ läßt let's see what we can do (for you); du kannst ~ und lassen, was du willst you can do as you please; er bestimmt, was wir zu ~ und zu lassen haben he tells us what to do and what not to do; tu, was du

nicht lassen kannst well, if you must; ... aber er tut es einfach nicht ... but he just won't (do it); damit ist es noch nicht getan and that's not all; was tut das Buch unterm Bett? (inf) what is the book doing under the bed?; etwas/nichts gegen etw ~ to do something/nothing about sth; Sie müssen etwas für sich ~ you should treat yourself; (sich schonen) you should take care of yourself; er tut nichts als faulenzen/unsere Zeit vergeuden he does nothing but laze around/waste our time; so etwas tut man nicht! that is just not done; so etwas tut man als anständige Frau nicht! a decent woman doesn't do such things; es mit jdm ~ (sl) to do it with sb (inf).
  (b) (Funktionsverb) Arbeit, Pflicht to do; Blick, Schritt, Gelübde to take; Reise to go on. einen Schrei ~ to cry or shout (out); einen Fall ~ to fall; es tat einen Knall there was a bang.
  (c) (angehen, beteiligt sein) das hat etwas/nichts mit ihm/ damit zu ~ that is something/nothing to do with him; das hat doch damit gar nichts zu ~ that is nothing to do with it; das tut nichts zur Sache that's beside the point; damit/mit ihm habe ich nichts zu ~/will ich nichts zu ~ haben I have/want nothing to do with it/him; ich habe mit mir (selbst) zu ~ I have problems (myself or of my own); es mit jdm zu ~ bekommen or kriegen (inf) to get into trouble with sb; er hat es mit der Leber/dem Herzen etc zu ~ (inf) he has liver/heart etc trouble.
  (d) (ausmachen) was tut's? what does it matter?, what difference does it make?; das tut nichts it doesn't matter; das tut dir/ihm nichts it won't do you/him any harm; darum ist es mir sehr getan or zu ~ (geh) I am very concerned about it.
  (e) (an~, zuteil werden lassen) jdm etwas ~ to do something to sb; (stärker) to harm or hurt sb; er hat mir nichts getan he didn't do anything (to me); (stärker) he didn't hurt or harm me; der Hund tut dir schon nichts the dog won't hurt or harm you; hat der Mann/der Lehrer/dein Chef dir was getan? did the man/ teacher/your boss do anything (to you)?; jdm Böses or ein Leid (old)/einen Gefallen ~ to harm sb/do sb a favour; was du nicht willst, daß man dir tu', das füg' auch keinem andern zu (Prov) do as you would be done by (prov).
  (f) (inf: an einen bestimmten Ort legen, geben etc) to put. jdn in eine andere Schule ~ to put sb in a different school.
  (g) (inf: ausreichen, genügen) to do. das tut's für heute that'll do for today; unser Auto muß es noch ein Weilchen ~ we'll have to make do with our car a little while longer.
  (h) (inf: funktionieren) die Uhr/das Auto tut es nicht mehr the watch/car has had it (inf).
  (i) +infin (inf: zur Betonung, old: zur Bildung der Vergangenheit) dann tat er sich waschen then he washed or did wash (obs) himself; sie ~ jetzt essen (inf) they're eating; und dann tut er schwimmen (inf) and then he goes swimming.
  2 vr **(a)** (geschehen) es tut sich etwas/nichts there is something/nothing happening, something/nothing is happening; hat sich in dieser Hinsicht schon etwas getan? has anything been done about this?; hat sich bei euch etwas getan? have things changed (with you)?; hier hat sich einiges getan there have been some changes here.
  (b) (mit adj) sich (mit etw) dicke ~ (inf) to show off (about sth); sich (acc or dat) mit etw schwer ~ to have difficulty or problems with sth.
  3 vi **(a)** zu ~ haben (beschäftigt sein) to be busy, to have work to do; in der Stadt/auf dem Finanzamt zu ~ haben to have things to do in town/business at the tax office; ich hatte zu ~, das wieder in Ordnung zu bringen I had my work cut out putting or to put it back in order; mit jdm zu ~ haben to deal with sb.
  (b) (sich benehmen) to act. so ~, als ob ... to pretend that ...; tu doch nicht so stupid; tust du nur so dumm? are you just acting stupid?; sie tut nur so she's only pretending.
  (c) Sie täten gut daran, früh zu kommen you would do well to come early; Sie haben recht getan you did right.
Tun nt -s, no pl conduct. sein ganzes ~, sein ~ und Lassen everything he does; heimliches/verbrecherisches ~ secret/criminal actions; erzählen Sie mir etwas von Ihrem ~ tell me what you've been doing.
Tünche f -, -n whitewash; (getönt) distemper, wash; (fig) veneer; (inf: Schminke) make-up.
tünchen vt to whitewash/distemper.
Tundra f -, **Tundren** tundra.
Tunell nt -s, -e (dial, S Ger, Aus) tunnel.
Tuner ['tju:nɐ] m -s, - tuner.
Tuneser(in f) m, **Tunesier(in** f) [-iɐ, -iərɪn] m -s, - Tunisian.
Tunesien [-iən] nt -s Tunisia.
tunesisch adj Tunisian.
Tunichtgut m -(e)s, -e ne'er-do-well, good-for-nothing.
Tunika f -, **Tuniken** tunic.
Tunke f -, -n sauce; (Braten~) gravy.
tunken vt to dip; (stippen auch) to dunk (inf); jdn to duck.
tunlich adj possible, feasible; (ratsam) advisable.
tunlichst adv if possible. ~ bald as soon as possible; ich werde es ~ vermeiden, ihm meine Meinung zu sagen I'll do my best to avoid telling him what I think; das wirst du ~ bleiben lassen you'll do nothing of the kind or sort.
Tunnel m -s, - or -s tunnel.
tunnelieren* vt (Aus) to tunnel.
Tunte f -, -n (inf) (a) (dated) sissy (inf). (b) (Homosexueller) fairy (pej inf).
tuntenhaft adj (inf) fussy; Homosexueller etc effeminate.
tuntig adj (inf) (a) (dated: albern, zimperlich) sissy (inf). (b) (weibisch) effeminate, poofy (sl).
Tupf m -(e)s, -e (Aus) siehe Tupfen.
Tüpfel m or nt -s, -, **Tüpfelchen** nt dot.
tüpfeln vt to spot. getüpfelt spotted; (mit kleinen Tupfen) dotted.
tupfen vt to dab. getupft spotted.

Tupfen m -s, - spot; (klein) dot.

Tupfer m -s, - swab.

Tür f -, -en door; (Garten~) gate. in der ~ in the doorway; ~ an ~ mit jdm wohnen to live next door to sb; an die ~ gehen to answer the door, to go/come to the door; Weihnachten steht vor der ~ Christmas is just (a)round the corner; jdn vor die ~ setzen (inf) to throw or kick (inf) sb out; jdm die ~ weisen to show sb the door; jdm die ~ vor der Nase zumachen to shut the door in sb's face; ein jeder kehre vor seiner ~ (prov) everyone should set his own house in order; die Leute haben ihm fast die ~ eingerannt (nach Anzeige etc) he was snowed under with replies; mit der ~ ins Haus fallen (inf) to blurt it/things out; die ~ für etw offenhalten or nicht zuschlagen (fig) to keep the way open for sth; zwischen ~ und Angel in passing; einer Sache (dat) ~ und Tor öffnen (fig) to open the way to sth; ach, du kriegst die ~ nicht zu! (inf) well I never!

Tür|angel f (door) hinge.

Turban m -s, -e turban.

Türbeschlag m (ornamental) mounting (on a door).

Turbine f turbine.

Turbinen-: ~antrieb m turbine drive; (an Flugzeug) turbo-jet propulsion; ~flugzeug nt turbo-jet; ~triebwerk nt turbine engine; (an Flugzeug) turbo-jet, jet turbine engine.

Turbo-: ~generator m turbogenerator; ~-Prop-Flugzeug nt turboprop aircraft.

turbulent adj turbulent, tempestuous. dort geht's ~ zu things are in turmoil there.

Turbulenz f (a) no pl turbulence, turmoil. (b) (turbulentes Ereignis) excitement, turmoil no pl. (c) (Wirbel, Luftstrom) turbulence.

Türchen nt small door.

Türdrücker m (Knauf) doorknob; (inf: Öffner) buzzer (for opening the door).

Türe f -, -n (dial) siehe Tür.

Turf [turf] m -s, -s (a) (Rennbahn) racecourse. (b) (no pl: Sportart) turf.

Tür-: ~flügel m door (of a pair of doors); ~füllung f door panel; ~griff m door handle; ~hüter m (obs) doorman.

-türig adj suf ein~/zwei~ etc with one door/two doors etc; ein vier~es Auto a four-door car.

Türke m -n, -n Turk. einen ~n bauen (inf) (etwas vortäuschen) to fiddle the figures (inf); (Mist machen) to make a blunder or boob (Brit inf).

Türkei f - die ~ Turkey.

Türken m -s, no pl (Aus inf) maize.

türken vt (sl) jdn to diddle (inf); etw to fiddle (inf).

Türkenbund m -(e)s, Türkenbünde (Bot) Turk's cap lily.

Türkette f (door) chain.

Türkin f Turk, Turkish woman/girl.

Türkis¹ m -es, -e (Edelstein) turquoise.

Türkis² nt -, no pl (Farbe) turquoise.

türkis adj turquoise.

türkisch adj Turkish. T~er Honig nougat; ~er Weizen maize.

Türkisch(e) nt decl as adj Turkish; siehe auch Deutsch(e).

türkisfarben, türkisgrün adj turquoise(-coloured).

Tür-: ~klinke f door handle; ~klopfer m doorknocker.

Turm m -(e)s, "e (a) tower; (spitzer Kirch~) spire; (im Schwimmbad) diving tower. (b) (Chess) castle, rook.

Turmbau m (das Bauen) building a tower. der ~ zu Babel the building of the Tower of Babel.

Türmchen nt dim of Turm turret.

türmen 1 vt to pile (up). 2 vr to pile up; (Wolken) to build up, to bank; (Wellen) to tower up. 3 vi aux sein (inf: davonlaufen) to skedaddle (inf), to take to one's heels, to run off.

Turm-: ~falke m kestrel; t~hoch adj towering, lofty; ~schwalbe f swift; ~springen nt high diving; ~uhr f clock (on a/the tower); (Kirch~) church clock.

Turn-: ~anzug m leotard; ~bruder m member of a gymnastics club.

turnen 1 vi (a) (an Geräten) to do gymnastics; (Sch) to do gym or PE or PT. am Reck/an den Ringen/auf der Matte etc ~ to work on or do exercises on the horizontal bar/rings/mat etc; sie kann gut ~ she is good at gym or PE or PT.
(b) aux sein (herumklettern) to climb about; (Kind) to romp.
2 vt Reck etc to work on, to do exercises on; Übung to do.

Turnen nt -s, no pl gymnastics sing; (inf: Leibeserziehung) gym, PE (inf), PT (inf).

Turner(in f) m -s, - gymnast.

Turnerei f (inf) sporting activities pl; (fig) acrobatics pl.

turnerisch adj gymnastic. ~ hervorragend Mensch excellent at gymnastics; Übung excellent gymnastically.

Turnerschaft f (a) (die Turner) gymnasts pl; (Vereinigung der Turnvereine) gymnastic association. (b) (Studentenverbindung) student organization.

Turn-: ~fest nt gymnastics display or festival; (von Schule) sports day; ~gerät nt (Reifen, Ball etc) piece(s) of gymnastic equipment; (Reck, Barren etc) (piece of) gymnastic apparatus; ~halle f gym(nasium); (Gebäude auch) sports hall; ~hemd nt gym or PE or PT shirt; ~hose f gym or PE or PT shorts pl.

Turnier nt -s, -e (Ritter~, sportliche Veranstaltung) tournament; (Tanz~) competition; (Reit~) show.

Turnier-: ~pferd nt show or competition horse; ~reiter m show or competition rider; ~tanz m (competition) ballroom dance/dancing.

Turn-: ~kleidung f gym or PE or PT clothes pl or kit; ~kunst f gymnastic skills pl; ~lehrer m gym or PE or PT teacher; ~riege f gymnastics team; ~saal m (Aus) siehe ~halle; ~schuh m gym shoe; ~schwester f member of a gymnastics club; ~stunde f gym or PE or PT lesson; (im Verein) gymnastics lesson; ~übung f gymnastic exercise; ~unterricht m gymnastic instruction; (~stunde) gym, PE, PT.

Turnüre f -, -n bustle.

Turnus m -, -se (a) rota. im (regelmäßigen) ~ in rotation. (b) (Aus) (Arbeitsschicht) shift; (Med) housemanship (Brit), internship (US).

Turn-: ~vater m: ~vater Jahn Jahn, the father of gymnastics; ~verein m gymnastics club; ~wart m gymnastics supervisor; ~zeug nt gym or PE or PT things pl or kit.

Tür-: ~öffner m (im Hotel) doorman, commissionaire; elektrischer ~öffner buzzer (for opening the door); ~pfosten m doorpost; ~rahmen m doorframe; ~schild nt doorplate; ~schloß nt door lock; ~schnalle f (Aus) siehe ~klinke; ~schwelle f threshold; ~spalt m crack (of a/the door); ~steher m -s, - bouncer; ~sturz m lintel.

turteln vi to bill and coo; (fig auch) to whisper sweet nothings.

Turteltaube f turtle-dove. ~n (inf: Verliebte) lovebirds, turtle-doves.

Türvorleger m doormat.

Tusch m -es, -e (a) (Mus) flourish; (von Blasinstrumenten auch) fanfare. (b) (Aus) siehe Tusche.

Tusche f -, -n (Auszieh~) Indian ink; (~farbe) water colour; (Wimpern~) mascara.

tuscheln vti to whisper. hinter seinem Rücken über jdn ~ to say things (inf) or talk behind sb's back.

tuschen vt (mit Farbe) to paint in water colour(s); (mit Ausziehtusche) to draw in Indian ink. sich (dat) die Wimpern ~ to put one's mascara on.

Tusch-: ~farbe f water colour; ~kasten m paintbox; ihr Gesicht sieht aus wie ein ~kasten (fig inf) she's made up to the eyeballs (inf); ~zeichnung f pen-and-ink drawing.

tut interj toot.

Tüte f -, -n (aus Papier, Plastik) bag; (Eis~) cornet, cone; (von Suppenpulver etc) packet; (inf: für Alkoholtest) breathalyzer; (inf: Mensch) drip (inf). in die ~ blasen (inf) to be breathalyzed, to blow in the bag (inf); ~n kleben (inf) to be in clink (inf); das kommt nicht in die ~! (inf) no way! (inf).

tuten vti to toot; (Schiff) to sound its hooter/foghorn. von T~ und Blasen keine Ahnung haben (inf) not to have a clue (inf).

Tutor m (rare) tutor.

TÜV [tyf] m -s, -s abbr of Technischer Überwachungs-Verein = MOT (Brit) das Auto ist durch den ~ gekommen the car got through or passed its MOT.

Tuwort nt, pl Tuwörter doing-word.

TV [te:'fau] abbr of (a) Television. (b) Turnverein.

TV- [te:'fau-] in cpds TV; ~-Programm nt TV programmes pl; ~-Sendung f TV broadcast.

Tweed [tvi:t] m -s, -s or -e tweed.

Twen m -(s), -s person in his/her twenties.

Twinset nt or m -(s), -s twin-set.

Twist¹ m -es, -e (Garn) twist.

Twist² m -s, -s (Tanz) twist.

twisten vi to twist, to do the twist.

Tympanon nt -s, Tympana (Archit) tympanum.

Typ m -s, -en (a) (Modell) model. (b) (Menschenart) type. er ist nicht mein ~ (inf) he's not my type (inf). (c) (inf: Mensch) person, character; (sl: Mann, Freund) bloke (Brit inf), guy (inf). dein ~ wird verlangt (inf) you're wanted; dein ~ ist nicht gefragt (inf) you're not wanted round here.

Type f -, -n (a) (Typ) (Schreibmaschinen~) type bar; (Druckbuchstabe) character. ~n (Schrift) type sing; ~n gießen to set type. (b) (inf: Mensch) character. (c) (bei Mehl) grade.

Typen pl of Typus, Type.

Typhus m -, no pl typhoid (fever).

Typhus-: ~epidemie f typhoid (fever) epidemic; ~impfung f typhoid inoculation; ~kranke(r) mf typhoid case.

typisch adj typical (für of). ~ deutsch/Mann/Frau typically German/male/female; (das ist ein) ~er Fall von denkste! no such luck! (inf).

typisieren* vt Charakter to stylize; Erzeugnisse etc to standardize.

Typograph m (geh) typographer.

Typographie f typography.

typographisch adj typographic(al).

Typologie f typology.

Typus m -, Typen type.

Tyrann m -en, -en (lit, fig) tyrant.

Tyrannei f tyranny.

Tyrannen-: ~mord m tyrannicide; ~mörder m tyrannicide.

Tyrannin f tyrant.

tyrannisch adj tyrannical.

tyrannisieren* vt to tyrannize.

Tz ['te:tset, te'tset] nt: bis ins or zum ~ completely, fully.

U

U, u [u:] *nt* -, - U, u; *siehe* X.
u. *abbr of* und.
u.a. *abbr of* und andere(s); unter anderem/anderen.
U.A.w.g. *abbr of* Um Antwort wird gebeten RSVP.
UB [u:'be:] *f* -, -s *abbr of* Universitätsbibliothek.
U-Bahn ['u:-] *f* underground, subway (*US*); (*in London*) tube.
U-Bahnhof ['u:-] *m* underground *etc* station.

übel 1 *adj* (a) (*schlimm, unangenehm*) bad; *Kopfweh, Erkältung etc auch* nasty. er war übler Laune he was in a bad *or* nasty mood; das ist gar nicht so ~ that's not so bad at all.
(b) (*moralisch, charakterlich schlecht*) wicked, bad; *Eindruck, Ruf* bad; *Tat auch* evil. ein übler Bursche *or* Kunde (*inf*) a nasty piece of work (*inf*), a bad lot (*inf*); das ist eine üble Sache! it's a bad business; ein übler Streich a nasty trick; auf üble *or* in der ~sten Weise, in übler *or* ~ster Weise in a most unpleasant way; jdm Übles antun (*geh*) to be wicked to sb, to do wicked things to sb.
(c) (*physisch schlecht, eklig*) *Geschmack, Geruch, Gefühl* nasty; (*fig*) *Geschmack auch* bad. mir wird ~ I feel ill *or* sick; es kann einem ~ werden it's enough to make you feel ill *or* sick.
(d) (*verkommen, ~beleumdet*) *Stadtviertel* evil, bad; *Kaschemme* evil, low.
2 *adv* (a) (*schlimm, unangenehm, schlecht*) badly. etw ~ aufnehmen to take sth badly; das ist ihm ~ bekommen it did him no good at all; ~ dran sein to be in a bad way; es steht ~ mit ihm he's in a bad way; das schmeckt gar nicht so ~ it doesn't taste so bad; der Hut steht dir nicht ~ that hat doesn't look bad on you at all; wie geht's? — danke, nicht ~ how's things? — not bad, thanks; **ich hätte nicht ~ Lust, jetzt nach Paris zu fahren** I wouldn't mind going to Paris now.
(b) (*moralisch, charakterlich schlecht*) badly. über jdn ~ reden to say bad things about sb; jdm etw ~ vermerken to hold sth against sb, to take sth amiss; jdm etw ~ auslegen to take sth amiss.
(c) (*physisch schlecht*) ill, poorly. das Essen ist ihm ~ bekommen the food disagreed with him.
Übel *nt* -s, - (a) (*geh: Krankheit, Leiden*) illness, malady (*old*).
(b) (*Mißstand*) ill, evil. ein notwendiges/das kleinere ~ a necessary/the lesser evil; alles ~s ist, daß ... the cause *or* root of all the trouble is that ...; die Gleichgültigkeit ist die Wurzel alles *or* allen ~s indifference is the root of all evil; das ~ bei der Sache the trouble.
(c) (*Plage, Schaden*) evil. von ~ sein to be a bad thing, to be bad; zu allem ~ ... to make matters worse ...; ein ~ kommt selten allein (*Prov*) misfortunes seldom come alone.
übel-: ~beleumdet *adj attr* disreputable, of ill repute; ~beraten *adj attr* (*geh*) ill-advised; ~gelaunt *adj attr* (*geh*) ill-humoured, sullen, morose; ~gesinnt *adj attr* (*geh*) ill-disposed.
Übelkeit *f* (*lit, fig*) nausea. eine plötzliche ~ a sudden feeling of nausea; ~ erregen to cause nausea.
Übel-: ü~launig *adj* ill-tempered, cantankerous; ~launigkeit *f* ill temper, cantankerousness; ü~nehmen *vt sep irreg* to take amiss *or* badly *or* in bad part; jdm etw ü~nehmen to hold sth against sb, to take sth amiss *or* badly *or* in bad part; **bitte nehmen Sie es (mir) nicht ü~, aber ...** please don't take it amiss *or* take offence, but ...; **ich habe ihm gar nicht einmal ü~genommen, daß er gelogen hat, aber ...** I didn't even mind him lying but ..., I didn't even take it amiss that he lied but ...; ü~nehmerisch *adj* (*schnell beleidigt*) touchy; (*nachtragend*) resentful; ü~riechend *adj* foul-smelling, evil-smelling; ~sein *nt* nausea; ~stand *m* (*social*) evil *or* ill; ~tat *f* (*dated, liter*) evil *or* wicked act *or* deed, misdeed; ~täter *m* (*geh*) wrongdoer; ü~tun *vi sep irreg* (*dated, liter*) jdm ü~tun to be wicked to sb; ü~wollen *vi sep* (*geh*) jdm ü~wollen to wish sb harm *or* ill, to be ill-disposed towards sb; ~wollen *nt* (*geh*) ill will.
üben 1 *vt* (a) (*praktisch erlernen*) *Aussprache, Musik, Sport* to practise; (*Mil*) to drill.
(b) (*schulen, trainieren*) *Gedächtnis, Muskeln etc* to exercise. mit geübtem Auge with a practised eye; geübt sein to be experienced.
(c) (*tun, erkennen lassen*) to exercise. Gerechtigkeit ~ (*geh*) to be just (*gegen* to), to show fairness (*gegen* to); Kritik an etw (*dat*) ~ to criticize sth; Geduld ~ to be patient; *siehe* Barmherzigkeit.
2 *vr* sich in etw (*dat*) ~ to practise sth; sich in Geduld (*dat*) ~ (*geh*) to have patience, to possess one's soul in patience.
3 *vi* (*praktisch lernen*) to practise.
über 1 *prep* (a) +*acc* (*räumlich*) over; (*quer* ~ *auch*) across; (*weiter als*) beyond. etw ~ etw hängen/stellen to hang/put sth over *or* above sth; es wurde ~ alle Sender ausgestrahlt it was broadcast over all transmitters; er lachte ~ das ganze Gesicht he was beaming all over his face.
(b) +*dat* (*räumlich*) (*Lage, Standort*) over, above; (*jenseits*) over, across. zwei Grad ~ Null two degrees (above zero); ~ der Stadt lag dichter Nebel a thick mist hung over the town; ~ uns lachte die Sonne the sun smiled above us; er trug den Mantel ~ dem Arm he was carrying his coat over his arm; ~ jdm stehen *or* sein (*fig*) to be over *or* above sb; er steht ~ der Situation (*fig*)

he is above it all.
(c) +*dat* (*zeitlich: bei, während*) over. ~ der Arbeit einschlafen to fall asleep over one's work; etw ~ einem Glas Wein besprechen to discuss sth over a glass of wine; ~ all der Aufregung/unserer Unterhaltung habe ich ganz vergessen, daß ... in all the *or* what with all the excitement/what with all this chatting I quite forgot that ...; ~ Mittag geht er meist nach Hause he usually goes home over lunch *or* at midday.
(d) +*acc* Cäsars Sieg ~ die Gallier Caesar's victory over the Gauls; Gewalt ~ jdn haben to have power over sb; es kam plötzlich ~ ihn it suddenly came over him; Schweinebraten geht ihm ~ alles he likes roast pork more than anything; sie liebt ihn ~ alles she loves him more than everything; das geht mir ~ den Verstand that's beyond my understanding; Fluch ~ dich! (*obs*) a curse upon you! (*obs*).
(e) +*acc* (*vermittels, auf dem Wege* ~) via. das habe ich ~ seine Frau erfahren I heard it from *or* via *or* through his wife; die Nummer erfährt man ~ die Auskunft you'll get the number from *or* through *or* via Information; wir sind ~ die Autobahn gekommen we came by *or* via the autobahn; nach Köln ~ Aachen to Cologne via Aachen; Zug nach Frankfurt ~ Wiesbaden und Mainz train to Frankfurt via *or* stopping at *or* calling at Wiesbaden and Mainz.
(f) +*acc* (*zeitlich*) (*innerhalb eines Zeitraums, länger als*) over. ~ Weihnachten over Christmas; bis ~ Ostern until after Easter; den ganzen Sommer ~ all summer long; ~ Wochen (*ausgedehnt*) for weeks on end; die ganze Zeit ~ all the time; das ganze Jahr ~ all through the year, all year round; ~ kurz oder lang sooner *or* later; es ist ~ vierzehn Tage her, daß ... it's over fourteen days since ...
(g) +*acc* (*bei Zahlenangaben*) (*in Höhe von*) for; (*mehr als*) over. ein Scheck ~ DM 20 a cheque for 20 DM; eine Rechnung von ~ £ 100 a bill for over *or* of over £100; Kinder ~ 14 Jahre/Städte ~ 50.000 Einwohner children over 14 years *or* of 14 (years of age) and over/towns of over 50,000 inhabitants; Pakete ~ 10 kg parcels over 10 kgs.
(h) +*acc* (*wegen*) over; (*betreffend*) about. ein Buch/Film/Vortrag *etc* ~ ... a book/film/lecture *etc* about *or* on ...; was wissen Sie ~ ihn? what do you know about him?; ~ welches Thema schreiben Sie Ihr neues Buch? what's the subject of your new book?, what's your new book about?; ~ Politik/Wörterbücher/Fußball *etc* reden to talk (about) politics/dictionaries/football *etc*; ~ jdn/etw lachen to laugh about *or* at sb/sth; sich ~ etw freuen/ärgern to be pleased/angry about *or* at sth.
(i) +*acc* (*steigernd*) upon. Fehler ~ Fehler mistake upon *or* after mistake, one mistake after another; einmal ~ das andere (*old, liter*) time after time.
2 *adv* ~ und ~ all over; er wurde ~ und ~ rot he went red all over; ich stecke ~ und ~ in Schulden I am up to my ears in debt; (*das*) Gewehr ~! (*Mil*) shoulder arms!; jdm in etw (*dat*) ~ sein (*inf*) to be better than sb at sth.
überaktiv *adj* hyperactive, overactive.
überall *adv* everywhere. ich habe dich schon ~ gesucht I've been looking everywhere *or* all over (*inf*) for you; ich habe ~ deinetwegen angerufen I've been telephoning all over the place *or* everywhere for you; ~ herumliegen to be lying all over the place *or* shop (*inf*); ~ in London/der Welt everywhere in *or* all over London/the world; ~ wo wherever; ~ Bescheid wissen (*wissensmäßig*) to have a wide-ranging knowledge; (*an Ort*) to know one's way around; sie ist ~ zu gebrauchen she can do everything; es ist ~ dasselbe it's the same wherever you go; so ist es ~ it's the same everywhere; ~ und nirgends zu Hause sein to be at home everywhere and nowhere; er ist immer ~ und nirgends, den erreichst du nie he's always here, there and everywhere, you'll never find him.
überall-: ~her *adv* from all over; ~hin *adv* everywhere.
Über-: ü~altert *adj* (a) (*Sociol*) having a disproportionate number of *or* too high a percentage of old people; (b) (*rare*) *siehe* veraltet; ~alterung *f* (*Sociol*) increase in the percentage of old people; ~angebot *nt* surplus (*an* + *dat* of); ü~ängstlich *adj* overanxious; ü~anstrengen* *insep* 1 *vt* to overstrain, to overexert; Kräfte to overtax; Augen to strain; 2 *vr* to overstrain *or* overexert oneself; ü~anstrenge dich nicht (*iro*) don't strain yourself! (*iro*); ~anstrengung *f* overexertion; eine ~anstrengung der Nerven/Augen a strain on the *or* one's nerves/eyes; ü~antworten* *vt insep* (*geh*) jdm etw ü~antworten to hand sth over to sb, to place sth in sb's hands; etw dem Feuer ü~antworten (*liter*) to commit sth to the flames; ü~arbeiten* *insep* 1 *vt* to rework, to go over; in einer ü~arbeiteten Fassung published in a revised edition; 2 *vr* to overwork; ~arbeitung *f*, *no pl* (a) (*Vorgang*) reworking; (*Ergebnis*) revision, revised version; (b) (~anstrengung) overwork; ~ärmel *m* oversleeve; ü~aus *adv* extremely, exceedingly; ü~backen* *vt insep irreg* to put in the oven/under the grill; mit Käse ü~backen au gratin; ü~backene Käseschnitten cheese on toast.
Überbau *m, pl* -e *or* (*Build auch*) -ten (*Build, Philos*) superstructure.

überbauen* *vt insep* to build over; (*mit einem Dach*) to roof over, to build a roof over.

Über-: **ü~beanspruchen*** *vt insep* (a) *Menschen, Körper* to overtax, to make too many demands on; (*arbeitsmäßig*) **ü~beansprucht sein** to be overworked; (b) *Einrichtungen, Dienste* to overburden; (c) *Maschine, Auto etc* to overtax, to overstrain; (d) *Werkstoffe, Materialien* to overstrain; (*durch Gewicht auch*) to overload; **~beanspruchung** *f* (a) (*von Menschen*) overtaxing; (*arbeitsmäßig*) overworking; (b) overburdening; (c) overtaxing, overstraining; (d) overstraining; overloading; **ü~behalten*** *vt insep irreg* (a) *siehe* **übrigbehalten**; (b) (*nicht auszuziehen*) *Mantel* to keep on; **~bein** *nt* (*an Gelenk*) ganglion; **ü~bekommen*** *vt sep irreg* (*inf*) **jdn/etw ü~bekommen** to get sick of *or* fed up with sb/sth (*inf*); **ü~belasten*** *vt insep siehe* **ü~lasten**; **~belastung** *f siehe* **~lastung**; **ü~belegen*** *vt insep usu ptp* to overcrowd; *Kursus, Fach etc* to oversubscribe; **~belegung** *f siehe vt* overcrowding; oversubscription; **ü~belichten*** *vt insep* (*Phot*) to overexpose; **~belichtung** *f* (*Phot*) overexposure; **~beschäftigung** *f* overemployment; **ü~besetzt** *adj Behörde, Abteilung* overstaffed; **ü~betonen*** *vt insep* (*fig*) to overstress, to overemphasize; *Hüften, obere Gesichtshälfte etc* to overaccentuate, to overemphasize; **ü~betrieblich** *adj* industry-wide; **~bevölkerung** *f* overspill population; **ü~bewerten*** *vt insep* (*lit*) to overvalue; (*fig auch*) to overrate; *Schulleistung etc* to mark too high; **wollen wir doch diese so vereinzelte Äußerung nicht ü~bewerten** let's not attach too much importance to such an isolated remark; **~bewertung** *f* (*lit*) overvaluing; (*fig auch*) overrating; **die ~bewertung einer einzelnen Äußerung** attaching too much importance to an isolated statement; **diese Eins ist eine klare ~bewertung** this grade one is clearly too high; **~bezahlung** *f* overpayment.

überbietbar *adj* (*fig*) **kaum noch ~** sein to take some beating; **ein an Vulgarität nicht mehr ~er Pornofilm** a porn film of unsurpassed *or* unsurpassable vulgarity.

überbieten* *insep irreg* **1** *vt* (*bei Auktion*) to outbid (*um* by); (*fig*) to outdo; *Leistung, Rekord* to beat. **das ist kaum noch zu ~** it's outrageous. **2** *vr* **sich in etw** (*dat*) (*gegenseitig*) **~** to vie with one another *or* each other in sth; **sich** (*selber*) **~** to surpass oneself.

Überbietung *f siehe vt* outbidding; outdoing; beating. **eine ~ dieses Rekordes** to beat this record.

über-: **~binden** *vt sep irreg* (*Mus*) to join up; **~blasen*** *vt insep irreg* (*Mus*) to overblow; **~blättern*** *vt insep Buch* to leaf *or* flick *or* glance through; *Stelle* to skip over *or* past, to miss; **~bleiben** *vi sep irreg aux sein* (*inf*) *siehe* **übrigbleiben**.

Überbleibsel *nt* -s, - remnant; (*Speiserest*) leftover *usu pl*, remains *pl*; (*Brauch, Angewohnheit etc*) survival, hangover; (*Spur*) trace.

überblenden[1] *vi sep* (*Film, Rad: Szene etc*) to dissolve; (*plötzlich*) to cut. **wir blenden über zu ...** we now go over to ...

überblenden[2]* *vt insep* (*ausblenden*) to fade out; (*überlagern*) to superimpose.

Überblendung[1] *f siehe vi* fade; dissolve; cut; (*das Überblenden*) fading; dissolving; cutting. **ist das Studio bereit zur ~ zu ...?** is the studio ready to go over to ...?

Überblendung[2] *f siehe vt* fading out; superimposition.

Überblick *m* (*über* +*acc* of) (a) (*freie Sicht*) view. (b) (*Einblick*) perspective, overall *or* broad view, overview. **er hat keinen ~, es fehlt ihm an ~** (*dat*) he lacks an overview, he has no overall picture; **den ~ verlieren** to lose track (of things). (c) (*Abriß*) survey; (*Übersicht, Zusammenhang*) synopsis, summary. **sich** (*dat*) **einen ~ verschaffen** to get a general idea; **Weltgeschichte im ~** compendium of world history.

überblicken* *vt insep* (a) (*lit*) *Platz, Stadt* to overlook, to have *or* command a view of. (b) (*fig*) to see; *Lage etc auch* to grasp. **die Entwicklung läßt sich leicht ~** the development can be seen at a glance; **bis ich die Lage besser überblicke** until I have a better view of the situation; **das läßt sich noch nicht ~** I/we *etc* cannot tell *or* say as yet.

über-: **~borden*** *vi insep aux haben or sein* (*fig geh*) to be overextravagant; **~bordende Metapher** overextravagant metaphors; **~braten[1]*** *vt insep irreg* (*Cook*) to fry lightly; **~braten[2]** *vt sep irreg jdm eins ~braten** (*sl*) to land sb one (*inf*).

Überbreite *f* excess width. **Vorsicht, ~!** caution, wide load.

überbringen* *vt insep irreg jdm etw ~** to bring sb sth, to bring sth to sb; *Brief etc auch* to deliver sth to sb.

Überbringer(in *f*) *m* -s, - bringer, bearer; (*von Scheck etc*) bearer.

überbrückbar *adj Gegensätze* reconcilable. **schwer ~e Gegensätze** differences which are difficult to reconcile.

überbrücken* *vt insep* (a) (*old*) *Fluß* to bridge (over). (b) (*fig*) *Kluft, Zeitraum* to bridge; *Krisenzeiten* to get over *or* through; *Gegensätze* to reconcile. **die Gegensätze zwischen ... ~** to bridge the gap between ...

Überbrückung *f siehe vt* (b) bridging; getting over *or* through; reconciliation. **100 Mark zur ~** 100 marks to tide one over.

Überbrückungs-: **~beihilfe** *f*, **~geld** *nt* interim aid, money to tide one over; **~kredit** *m* bridging loan.

Über-: **ü~bürden*** *vt insep* (*geh*) to overburden; **~dach** *nt* roof; **ü~dachen*** *vt insep* to roof over, to cover over; **ü~dachte Fahrradständer/Bushaltestelle** covered bicycle stands/bus shelter; **ü~dauern*** *vt insep* to survive; **das alte Gemäuer hat schon viele Generationen ü~dauert** the old walls have already survived *or* outlasted many generations; **~decke** *f* bedspread, bedcover, counterpane; **ü~decken[1]** *vt sep* to cover up *or* over; (*inf: auflegen*) *Tischtuch* to put on; **ü~decken[2]*** *insep* **1** *vt Riß*,

---

Geschmack to cover up, to conceal; **2** *vr* (*sich ü~schneiden*) to overlap; **ü~dehnen*** *vt insep Sehne, Muskel etc* to strain; *Gummi*, (*fig*) *Begriff* to overstretch; **ü~denken*** *vt insep irreg* to think over, to consider; **etw noch einmal ü~denken** to reconsider sth; **ü~deutlich** *adj* all too obvious.

überdies *adv* (*geh*) (a) (*außerdem*) moreover, furthermore, what is more. (b) (*ohnehin*) in any case, anyway.

Über-: **ü~dimensional** *adj* colossal, huge, oversize(d); **ü~dimensioniert** *adj* oversize(d); **ü~dosieren*** *insep infin auch* **ü~zudosieren** *vt insep* dieses Mittel wird oft **ü~dosiert** an excessive dose of this medicine is often given/taken; **nicht ü~dosieren** do not exceed the dose; **~dosis** *f* overdose, OD (*inf*); (*zu große Zumessung*) excessive amount; **sich** (*dat*) **eine ~dosis Heroin spritzen** to give oneself an overdose of heroin, to OD on heroin (*inf*); **ü~drehen*** *vt insep Uhr etc* to overwind; *Motor* to overrev; *Gewinde, Schraube* to strip; **ü~dreht** *adj* (*inf*) overexcited; (*ständig*) highly charged, hyped(-up) (*sl*); (*ü~kandidelt*) weird; **ein ü~drehter Typ** a weirdo (*inf*).

Überdruck[1] *m* -s, ¨-e overprint.

Überdruck[2] *m* -s, *no pl* (*Tech*) excess pressure *no pl*.

überdrucken* *vt insep* to overprint.

Überdruck-: **~kabine** *f* (*Aviat*) pressurized cabin; **~ventil** *nt* pressure relief valve, blow-off valve.

Überdruß *m* -sses, *no pl* (*Übersättigung*) surfeit, satiety (*liter*) (*an* +*dat* of); (*Widerwille*) aversion (*an* +*dat* to), antipathy (*an* +*dat* to). **bis zum ~** ad nauseam; **er aß Kaviar bis zum ~** he ate caviar until he wearied of it *or* had had a surfeit of it; **~ am Leben** weariness of living *or* life.

überdrüssig *adj* **jds/einer Sache** (*gen*) **~ sein/werden** to be weary of sb/sth/to (*grow*) weary of sb/sth.

Über-: **ü~durchschnittlich 1** *adj* above-average; **2** *adv* exceptionally, outstandingly; **er arbeitet ü~durchschnittlich gut** he works better than average; **sie verdient ü~durchschnittlich gut** she earns more than the average, she has an above-average salary; **~eck** *adv* at right angles to each other *or* one another); **~eifer** *m siehe adj* overenthusiasm, overeagerness, overzealousness; officiousness; **ü~eifrig** *adj* overenthusiastic, overeager, overzealous; (*pej: wichtigtuerisch*) officious; **ü~eignen*** *vt insep* (*geh*) **jdm etw ü~eignen** to make sth over to sb, to transfer sth to sb; **~eignung** *f* (*geh*) transference; **~eile** *f* haste; **ü~eilen*** *insep* **1** *vt* to rush; **ü~eilen Sie nichts!** don't rush things!; **2** *vr* to rush; **ü~eil dich bloß nicht!** (*iro*) don't rush yourself (*iro*); **ü~eilt** *adj* hasty, precipitate; **~eilung** *f*, *no pl* haste, precipitateness; **nur keine ~eilung!** take your time!

über|einander *adv* (a) (*räumlich*) on top of each other *or* one another, one on top of the other; **hängen** one above the other. **wir wohnen ~** we live one above the other, we live on top of each other. (b) (*über sich gegenseitig*) about each other *or* one another.

über|einander-: **~legen** *vt sep* to put *or* lay one on top of the other, to put *or* lay on top of each other *or* one another; **~liegen** *vi sep irreg* to lie one on top of the other, to lie one on top of each other *or* one another; **~schlagen** *vt sep irreg* **die Beine/Arme ~schlagen** to cross one's legs/to fold one's arms.

über|einkommen *vi sep irreg aux sein* to agree. **wir sind darin übereingekommen, daß ...** we have agreed that ...

Übereinkommen *nt* -s, -, **Über|einkunft** *f* -, ¨-e arrangement, understanding, agreement; (*Vertrag*) agreement. **ein Übereinkommen *or* eine Übereinkunft treffen** to enter into *or* make an agreement; **ein Übereinkommen *or* eine Übereinkunft erzielen** to reach *or* come to an agreement, to reach agreement.

über|einstimmen *vi sep* to agree, to concur (*form*); (*Meinungen*) to tally, to concur (*form*); (*Angaben, Meßwerte, Rechnungen etc*) to correspond, to tally, to agree; (*zusammenpassen: Farben, Stile etc*) to match; (*Gram*) to agree; (*Dreiecke*) to be congruent. **mit jdm in etw** (*dat*) **~** to agree with sb on sth; **wir stimmen darin überein, daß ...** we agree *or* are agreed that ...

über|einstimmend 1 *adj* corresponding; *Meinungen* concurring, concurrent; *Farben etc* matching. **nach ~en Meldungen/Zeugenaussagen** according to all reports/according to mutually corroborative testimonies. **2** *adv* **alle erklärten ~, daß ...** everybody agreed that ..., everybody unanimously stated that ...; **wir sind ~ der Meinung, daß ...** we are unanimously of the opinion that ..., we unanimously agree that ...; **~ mit** in agreement with.

Über|einstimmung *f* (a) (*Einklang, Gleichheit*) correspondence, agreement. **sein Handeln steht nicht mit seiner Theorie in ~** there's a disparity *or* no correspondence between his actions and his theory; **bei den Zeugenaussagen gab es nur in zwei Punkten ~** the testimonies only agreed *or* corresponded *or* tallied in two particulars; **zwei Dinge in ~ bringen** to bring two things into line; **es besteht keine ~ zwischen x und y und y do not agree. (b) (*von Meinung*) agreement. **darin besteht bei allen Beteiligten ~** all parties involved are agreed on that; **in ~ mit jdm/etw** in agreement with sb/in accordance with sth. (c) (*Gram*) agreement.

Über-: **ü~empfindlich** *adj* (*gegen* to) oversensitive, hypersensitive (*auch Med*); **~empfindlichkeit** *f* (*gegen* to) oversensitivity, hypersensitivity (*auch Med*); **sie ist von einer unglaublichen ~empfindlichkeit** she is incredibly oversensitive *or* hypersensitive; **ü~erfüllen*** *vt insep infin auch* **ü~zuerfüllen** *Norm, Soll* to exceed (*um* by); **~erfüllung** *f no pl*: **das ~erfüllen** exceeding; **bei ~erfüllung des Plansolls werden Sonderprämien gezahlt** anyone who exceeds the target *or* quota is paid special premiums; **das kommt einer ~erfüllung des Solls um 3% gleich** this is equivalent to exceeding the target by 3%; **ü~ernähren*** *vt insep infin auch* **ü~zuernähren** to overfeed; **~ernährung** *f* (*no pl: das ~ernähren*) overfeeding; (*Krankheit*) overeating; **ü~essen¹** *vt sep irreg* sich (*dat*) etw ü~essen to grow sick of sth; Spargel kann ich mir gar nicht ü~essen I can't eat enough asparagus; **ü~essen²** *pret* ü~aß, *ptp* ü~gessen *vr insep* to overeat; ich habe mich an Käse ü~gessen I've eaten too much cheese.

überfahren¹ *sep irreg* **1** *vt* (*mit Boot etc*) to take *or* ferry across. **2** *vi aux sein* to cross over.

überfahren²* *vt insep irreg* (a) jdn, Tier to run over, to knock down. (b) (*hinwegfahren über*) to go *or* drive over; Fluß *etc auch* to cross (over). (c) (*übersehen und weiterfahren*) Ampel *etc* to go through. (d) (*inf: übertölpeln*) jdn ~ to stampede sb into it. (e) (*plötzlich über einen kommen*) to come over.

Überfahrt *f* crossing.

Überfall *m* (a) (*Angriff*) attack (*auf* +*acc* on); (*auf jdn auch*) assault (*auf* +*acc* on); (*auf offener Straße auch*) mugging (*auf* +*acc* of); (*auf Bank etc*) raid (*auf* +*acc* on), holdup; (*auf Land*) invasion (*auf* +*acc* of). einen ~ auf jdn/etw verüben *or* ausführen to carry out an attack *etc* on sb/sth; dies ist ein ~, keine Bewegung! this is a holdup *or* stick-up (*inf*), freeze! (b) (*hum: unerwartetes Erscheinen*) invasion. er hat einen ~ auf uns vor he's planning to descend on us.

überfallen* *vt insep irreg* (a) (*angreifen*) to attack; jdn *auch* to assault; (*auf offener Straße auch*) to mug; Bank *etc* to raid, to hold up, to stick up (*inf*); Land *auch* to invade; (*Mil*) Hauptquartier, Lager to raid. (b) (*fig geh: überkommen*) (*Gefühle, Schlaf, Müdigkeit, Krankheit etc*) to come over *or* upon; (*überraschen: Nacht*) to overtake, to come upon suddenly. plötzlich überfiel ihn heftiges Fieber he suddenly had a bad attack of fever. (c) (*fig inf: überraschend besuchen*) to descend (up)on; (*bestürmen*) to pounce upon. jdn mit Fragen/Wünschen ~ to bombard sb with questions/requests.

Über-: **ü~fällig** *adj* overdue *usu pred*; seit einer Woche ü~fällig sein to be a week overdue; **~fallkommando**, **~fallskommando** (*Aus*) *nt* flying squad, riot squad; **ü~feinert** *adj* overrefined; **~feinerung** *f* overrefinement; **ü~fischen*** *vt insep* to overfish; **~fischung** *f* overfishing; **ü~fliegen*** *vt insep irreg* (a) (*lit*) to fly over, to overfly; (b) (*fig*) ein Lächeln/eine leichte Röte ü~flog ihr Gesicht a smile/a faint blush flitted across her face; (c) (*flüchtig ansehen*) Buch *etc* to take a quick look at, to glance through *or* at *or* over; **ü~fließen¹*** *vt insep irreg* (*rare*) to inundate, to flood; **ü~fließen²** *vi sep irreg aux sein* (a) (*Gefäß*) to overflow; (*Flüssigkeit auch*) to run over; ineinander ~fließen (*Farben*) to run; (c) (*fig: vor Dank, Höflichkeit etc*) to overflow, to gush (*vor* +*dat* with); **ü~flügeln*** *vt insep* to outdistance, to outstrip; (*in Leistung, bei Wahl*) to outdo; Erwartungen *etc* to surpass.

Überfluß *m* **-sses**, *no pl* (a) (super)abundance (*an* +*dat* of); (*Luxus*) affluence. Arbeit/Geld im ~ plenty of work/money, an abundance of work/money; das Land des ~sses the land of plenty; im ~ leben to live in luxury; im ~ vorhanden sein to be in plentiful supply; ~ an etw (*dat*) haben, etw im ~ haben to have plenty *or* an abundance of sth, to have sth in abundance. (b) zu allem *or* zum ~ (*unnötigerweise*) superfluously; (*obendrein*) to crown it all (*inf*), into the bargain; zu allem *or* zum ~ fing es auch noch an zu regnen and then, to crown it all, it started to rain, and then it started to rain into the bargain.

Überflußgesellschaft *f* affluent society.

überflüssig *adj* superfluous; (*frei, entbehrlich*) spare; (*unnötig*) unnecessary; (*zwecklos*) futile, useless. ~ zu sagen, daß ... it goes without saying that ...

überflüssigerweise *adv* superfluously.

Über-: **ü~fluten¹** *vi sep aux sein* (ü~fließen²) to overflow; **ü~fluten²*** *vt insep* (*lit, fig*) to flood; (*fig auch*) to inundate; **~flutung** *f* (a) (*lit*) flood; (*das ~fluten*) flooding *no pl*; (b) (*fig*) flooding *no pl*, inundation; **ü~fordern*** *vt insep* to overtax; jdn auch to ask *or* expect too much of; damit ist er ü~fordert that's asking *or* expecting too much of him; als Abteilungsleiter wäre er doch etwas ü~fordert being head of department would be too much for him *or* would stretch him too far; **~forderung** *f* excessive demand(s) (*für* on); (*no pl: das ~fordern*) overtaxing; **~fracht** *f* excess freight; **ü~frachtet** *vt insep* (*fig*) to overload; ein mit Emotionen ü~frachteter Begriff a concept fraught with emotions, an emotionally loaded concept; **ü~fragt** *adj pred* stumped (for an answer); da bin ich ü~fragt there you've got me, there you have me, that I don't know; **ü~fremden*** *vt insep* to infiltrate with too many foreign influences; (*Econ*) to swamp; **ü~fremdet werden** to be swamped by foreigners/foreign capital; **~fremdung** *f, no pl* foreign infiltration; (*Econ*) swamping; **ü~fressen*** *vr insep irreg* (*inf*) to overeat, to eat too much; sich an etw (*dat*) ü~fressen to gorge oneself on sth; **~fuhr** *f* -, -en (*Aus*) ferry; **ü~führen¹** *vt sep* to transfer; Leichnam to transport; Wagen to drive; **ü~führen²*** *vt insep* (a) siehe ü~führen¹; (b) Täter to convict (*gen* of); ein ü~führter Verbrecher a convicted criminal; (c) (ü~bauen) eine Straße/einen Fluß mit einer Brücke ü~führen to build a footbridge/bridge over a street/river; **~führung** *f* (a) transportation; (b) *no pl* (*Jur*) conviction; der Polizei gelang die ~führung des Täters the police managed to secure a conviction; (c) (*Brücke über Straße etc*) bridge (*auch Rail*), overpass; (*Fußgänger~*) footbridge; **~fülle** *f* profusion, superabundance; **ü~füllen*** *vt insep* Glas *etc* to overfill; sich (*dat*) den Magen ü~füllen to eat too much; **ü~füllt** *adj* overcrowded; Kurs oversubscribed; (*Comm*) Lager overstocked, overfilled; **~füllung** *f, no pl* overcrowding; (*von Kursus, Vorlesung*) oversubscription; **~funktion** *f* hyperactivity, hyperfunction(ing); **ü~füttern*** *vt insep* to overfeed; **~fütterung** *f* overfeeding.

Übergabe *f* -, *no pl* handing over *no pl*; (*von Neubau*) opening; (*Mil*) surrender. die ~ der Zeugnisse findet am Ende des Schuljahres statt reports are handed out at the end of the school year; die ~ des neuen Schwimmbads an die Öffentlichkeit wird durch den Bürgermeister vorgenommen the mayor will open the new swimming pool to the public.

Übergang *m* (a) (*das Überqueren*) crossing. (b) (*Fußgänger~*) crossing, crosswalk (*US*); (*Brücke*) footbridge; (*Bahn~*) level crossing (*Brit*), grade crossing (*US*). (c) (*Grenzübergangsstelle*) checkpoint. (d) (*fig: Wechsel, Überleitung*) transition. dies soll nur ein ~ und keine endgültige Lösung sein this is meant to be merely an interim and not a definitive solution.

Übergangs-: **~bestimmung** *f* interim *or* temporary regulation; **~erscheinung** *f* temporary phenomenon; **ü~los** *adj* without a transition; (*zeitlich auch*) without a transitional period; **~lösung** *f* interim *or* temporary solution; **~mantel** *m* between-seasons coat; **~phase** *f* transitional phase; **~regelung** *f* interim arrangement; **~stadium** *nt* transitional stage; **~zeit** *f* (a) transitional period, period of transition; (b) (*zwischen Jahreszeiten*) in-between season/weather; **~zustand** *m* transitional state.

Übergardinen *pl* curtains *pl*, drapes *pl* (*US*).

übergeben* *insep irreg* **1** *vt* (a) to hand over; (*überreichen*) Dokument, Zettel, Einschreiben to hand (jdm sb); Diplom *etc* to hand over (jdm to sb), to present (jdm to sb); (*vermachen*) to bequeath (jdm to sb); (*Mil auch*) to surrender. ein Gebäude der Öffentlichkeit/eine Straße dem Verkehr ~ to open a building to the public/a road to traffic; eine Angelegenheit einem Rechtsanwalt ~ to place a matter in the hands of a lawyer. (b) (*weiterreichen, verleihen*) Amt, Macht to hand over. (c) etw dem Druck ~ (*geh*) to send sth to the printer's; einen Leichnam der Erde/dem Wasser ~ (*liter*) to commit a body to the earth/water. **2** *vr* (*sich erbrechen*) to vomit, to be sick. ich muß mich ~ I'm going to be sick.

übergehen¹ *vi sep irreg aux sein* (a) in etw (*acc*) ~ (*in einen anderen Zustand*) to turn *or* change into sth; (*Farben*) to merge into sth; in jds Besitz (*acc*) ~ to become sb's property; in Schreien ~ to degenerate into shouting; in andere Hände/in Volkseigentum ~ to pass into other hands/into public ownership. (b) auf jdn ~ (*geerbt, übernommen werden*) to pass to sb. (c) zu etw ~ to go over to sth; zum Feinde/zur Gegenpartei ~ to go over to the enemy/the opposition.

übergehen²* *vt insep irreg* to pass over; Kapitel, Abschnitt *etc auch* to skip; Einwände *etc auch* to ignore.

Über-: **ü~genau** *adj* overprecise, pernickety (*inf*); **ü~genug** *adv* more than enough; von seiner Arroganz haben wir ü~genug we have had more than enough of his arrogance; **ü~geordnet** *adj* (a) Behörde, Dienststelle higher; die uns ü~geordnete Behörde the next authority above us; (b) (*Gram*) Satz superordinate; (*Ling, Philos*) Begriff generic; (c) (*fig*) von ü~geordneter Bedeutung sein to be of overriding importance; **~gepäck** *nt* (*Aviat*) excess baggage; **ü~gescheit** *adj* (*iro*) know-all, know-it-all (*US*), smart-ass (*sl*) *all attr*; so ein **~gescheiter** some clever dick (*inf*) *or* smart-ass (*sl*) *or* know-all; **ü~geschnappt 1** *ptp of* ü~schnappen; **2** *adj* (*inf*) crazy; **~gewicht** *nt* overweight; (*fig*) predominance; **~gewicht haben** (*Paket etc*) to be overweight; an ~gewicht leiden, ~gewicht haben (*Mensch*) to be overweight; **5 Gramm ~gewicht** 5 grammes excess weight; das ~gewicht bekommen/haben (*fig*) to become predominant/to predominate; wenn sie das militärische ~gewicht bekommen if they gain military dominance; **ü~gewichtig** *adj* overweight; **ü~gießen¹** *vt sep irreg* jdm etw ü~gießen to pour sth over sb; **ü~gießen²*** *vt insep irreg* to pour over; jdn to douse; Braten to baste; jdn/sich mit etw ü~gießen to pour sth over sb/oneself; (*absichtlich auch*) to douse sb/oneself with sth; mit Licht ü~gossen (*liter*) bathed in light, suffused with light (*liter*); **ü~glücklich** *adj* overjoyed; **ü~greifen** *vi sep irreg* (a) (*beim Klavierspiel*) to cross one's hands (over); (b) (*auf Rechte etc*) to encroach *or* infringe (*auf* +*acc* on); (*Feuer, Streik, Krankheit etc*) to spread (*auf* +*acc* to); ineinander ü~greifen to overlap; **ü~greifend** *adj* (*fig*) Gesichtspunkte, Überlegungen general, comprehensive; **~griff** *m* (*Einmischung*) infringement (*auf* +*acc* of), encroachment (*auf* +*acc* on), interference *no pl* (*auf* +*acc* with *or* in); (*Mil*) attack (*auf* +*acc* upon), incursion (*auf* +*acc* into); **ü~groß** *adj* oversize(d), huge, enormous; **~größe** *f* (*bei Kleidung etc*) outsize; **62 ist eine ~größe** 62 is outsize; **ü~haben** *vt sep irreg* (*inf*) (a) (*satt haben*) to be sick (and tired) of (*inf*), to be fed up *or* with (*inf*); (b) (*übrig haben*) to have left (over); für etw nichts ü~haben not to like sth; (c) Kleidung to have on.

überhandnehmen *vi sep irreg* to get out of control *or* hand; (*schlechte Sitten, massive Lohnforderungen, Laxheit etc auch*) to become rife *or* rampant; (*Meinungen, Ideen etc*) to become rife *or* rampant, to gain the upper hand.

Über-: **~hang** *m* (a) (*Fels~*) overhang, overhanging rock; (*Baum~*) overhanging branches *pl*; (b) (*Vorhang*) helmet; (*von Bettdecke etc*) valance; (c) (*Comm: Überschuß*) surplus (*an* +*dat* of); **ü~hängen 1** *vi sep irreg aux haben or sein* to overhang; (*hinausragen auch*) to jut out; **2** *vt sich* (*dat*) ein Gewehr ü~hängen to sling a rifle over one's shoulder; sich (*dat*) einen Mantel ü~hängen to put *or* hang a coat round *or* over one's shoulders; **~hangsmandat** *nt* (*Pol*) seat gained as a result of votes for a specific candidate over and above the seats to which a party is entitled by the number of votes cast for the party; **ü~hasten*** *vt insep* to rush; **ü~hastet** *adj* overhasty, hurried; **ü~hastet sprechen** to speak too fast; **ü~häufen*** *vt* *insep jdn* to overwhelm, to inundate; *Schreibtisch etc* to pile high; **jdn mit Geschenken/Glückwünschen/Titeln ü~häufen** to heap presents/congratulations/titles (up)on sb; **ich bin völlig mit Arbeit ü~häuft** I'm completely snowed under *or* swamped (with work); **jdn mit Vorwürfen ü~häufen** to heap reproaches (up)on sb('s head).

überhaupt *adv* (a) (*sowieso, im allgemeinen*) in general; (*überdies, außerdem*) anyway, anyhow. **und ~, warum nicht?** and anyway *or* after all, why not?; **er sagt ~ immer sehr wenig** he never says very much at the best of times *or* anyway *or* anyhow; **nicht nur Rotwein, sondern Wein ~ mag ich nicht** it's not only red wine I don't like, I don't like wine at all *or* full stop (*esp Brit*) *or* period.
  (b) (*in Fragen, Verneinungen*) at all. **~ nicht** not at all; **ich denke ~ nicht daran, mitzukommen** I've (absolutely) no intention whatsoever of coming along; **~ nie** never (ever), never at all; **~ kein Grund** no reason at all *or* whatsoever; **hast du denn ~ keinen Anstand?** have you no decency at all?; **ich habe die ganze Nacht ~ nicht geschlafen** I didn't sleep at all the whole night; **das habe ich ja ~ nicht geweußt** I had no idea at all; **ich habe ~ nichts gehört** I didn't hear anything at all, I didn't hear a thing; **das steht in ~ keinem Verhältnis zu ...** that bears no relationship at all *or* whatsoever to ...
  (c) (*erst, eigentlich*) **dann merkt man ~ erst, wie schön ...** then you really notice for the first time how beautiful ...; **waren Sie ~ schon in dem neuen Film?** have you actually been to the latest film?; **da fällt mir ~ ein, ...** now I remember ...; **wenn ~ it at all; wie ist das ~ möglich?** how is that possible?; **gibt es das ~?** is there really such a thing?, is there really any such thing?; **was wollen Sie ~ von mir?** (*herausfordernd*) what do you want from me?; **wer sind Sie ~?** who do you think you are?; **was will der Verfasser ~?** what on earth is the author getting at?; **wissen Sie ~, wer ich bin?** do you realize who I am?

Über-: **ü~heben*** *vr insep irreg* (*lit*) to (over)strain oneself; (*fig geh: hochmütig sein*) to be arrogant; **sich über jdn ü~heben** to consider oneself superior to sb; **ü~heblich** *adj* arrogant; **~heblichkeit** *f, no pl* arrogance; **~hebung** *f* (*fig geh*) presumption; **ü~heizen*** *vt insep* to overheat; **ü~hitzen*** *vt insep* to overheat; **ü~hitzt** *adj* (*fig*) *Gemüter, Diskussion* too heated *pred*; *Phantasie* wild; **ü~höhen*** *vt insep Preise* to raise *or* increase excessively; *Kurve* to bank, to superelevate (*spec*); **ü~höht** *adj Kurve* banked, superelevated (*spec*); *Forderungen, Preise* exorbitant, excessive.

überholen¹* *vti insep* (a) *Fahrzeug* to overtake (*esp Brit*), to pass; (*fig: übertreffen*) to overtake. (b) (*Tech*) *Maschine, Motor etc* to overhaul.

überholen² *sep 1 vti* (*old*) to ferry. **hol über!** ferry! **2 vi** (*Naut: Schiff*) to keel over.

Überhol- (*Aut*): **~fahrbahn** *f siehe* **~spur**; **~manöver** *nt* overtaking (*esp Brit*) *or* passing manoeuvre; **~spur** *f* overtaking (*esp Brit*) *or* fast lane.

Überhol-: **~verbot** *nt* restriction on overtaking (*esp Brit*) *or* passing; (*als Schild etc*) no overtaking (*Brit*), no passing; **auf dieser Strecke besteht ~verbot** no overtaking *etc* on this stretch; **nach der nächsten Kurve ist das ~verbot wieder aufgehoben** the restriction on overtaking *etc* ends after the next bend; **~vorgang** *m* (*form*) overtaking (*esp Brit*), passing; **vor Beginn des ~vorganges** before starting *or* beginning to overtake *etc*; **der ~vorgang war noch nicht abgeschlossen, als das Fahrzeug ...** the vehicle had not finished overtaking *etc* when it ...

überhören¹* *vt insep* not to hear; (*nicht hören wollen*) to ignore. **das möchte ich überhört haben!** (I'll pretend) I didn't hear that!

überhören² *vr sep sich* (*dat*) **etw ~** to be tired *or* sick (*inf*) of hearing sth.

Über-Ich *nt* superego.

über|interpretieren* *vt insep infin auch* **überzuinterpretieren** to overinterpret.

Über-: **ü~irdisch** *adj* celestial, heavenly; **ü~kandidelt** *adj* (*inf*) eccentric; **ü~kippen** *vi sep aux sein* to topple *or* keel over; (*Stimme*) to crack; **ü~kleben¹*** *vt insep* **die Kiste ü~kleben** to stick something over the box; **etw mit Papier ü~kleben** to stick paper over sth; **ü~kleben²** *vt sep* **etwas ü~kleben** to stick something over it; **ü~klug** *adj* (*pej*) too clever by half, know-all *attr*, know-it-all (*US*) *attr*, smart-ass (*sl*) *attr*; **sei doch nicht so ü~klug!** don't be so clever *or* such a know-all; **ü~kochen** *vi sep aux sein* (*lit, fig*) to boil over.

überkommen¹* *insep irreg 1 vt* (*überfallen, ergreifen*) to come over. **ein Gefühl der Verlassenheit überkam ihn** a feeling of desolation came over him, he was overcome by a feeling of desolation; **Furcht** *etc* **überkam ihn** he was overcome with fear *etc*; **was überkommt dich denn?** what's come over you?
  2 vi aux sein *ptp only* (*überliefern*) **es ist uns** (*dat*) **~** (*old*) it has come down to us, it has been handed down to us.

überkommen² *vt sep irreg* (*Sw*) to get handed down.

Über-: **~kompensation** *f* overcompensation; **ü~kompensieren*** *vt insep infin auch* **ü~zukompensieren** to overcompensate for; **ü~kreuz** *adv siehe* **Kreuz¹**; **ü~kriegen** *vt sep* (*inf*) (a) (*ü~drüssig werden*) to get tired *or* sick (and tired) (*inf*) of, to get fed up of *or* with (*inf*); (b) **eins ü~kriegen** to get landed one (*inf*); **ü~krusten*** *vt insep* (*with a layer *or* crust of*); **mit Dreck ü~krustet** caked with mud; **ü~kühlen*** *vt insep* (*Aus Cook*) to cool down; **ü~laden¹** *vt insep irreg* (*zu stark belasten*) to overload; (*mit Arbeit auch*) to overburden; (*reichlich geben*) to shower; (*zu voll packen*) *Schreibtisch, Wand etc auch* to clutter, to cover; (*zu stark verzieren auch*) to clutter; **sich** (*dat*) **den Magen ü~laden** to overeat, to gorge oneself; **2 adj** *Wagen* overloaded, overladen; (*fig*) *Stil* ornate, flowery; *Bild* cluttered; **ü~lagern***

insep 1 vt (a) **diese Schicht wird von einer anderen ü~lagert** another stratum overlies this one; **am Abend ist dieser Sender von einem anderen ü~lagert** in the evenings this station is blotted out by another one; (b) *Thema, Problem, Konflikt etc* to eclipse; **2 vr** (*sich überschneiden*) to overlap; **~lagerung** *f* (*von Themen, Problemen etc*) eclipsing; (*~schneidung*) overlapping; **das führt zu ~lagerung von zwei Schichten/Sendern** that leads to one stratum overlying another/one station blotting out another.

Überland-: **~bus** *m* country bus; **~leitung** *f* (*Elec*) overhead power line *or* cable; **~zentrale** *f* (*Elec*) rural power station.

Über-: **ü~lang** *adj Oper, Stück etc* overlength; *Arme, Mantel* too long; **~länge** *f* excessive length; **~länge haben** to be over-length; **ü~lappen*** *vir insep* to overlap.

überlassen¹* *vt insep irreg* (a) (*haben lassen, abgeben*) **jdm etw ~** to let sb have sth.
  (b) (*anheimstellen*) **es jdm ~, etw zu tun** to leave it (up) to sb to do sth; **das bleibt (ganz) Ihnen ~** that's (entirely) up to you; **das müssen Sie schon mir ~** you must leave that to me; **es bleibt Ihnen ~, zu ...** it's up to you to ...; **jdm die Initiative/Wahl ~** to leave the initiative/choice (up) to sb.
  (c) (*in Obhut geben*) **jdm etw ~** to leave sth with sb *or* in sb's care, to entrust sth to sb's care; **sich** (*dat*) **selbst ~ sein** to be left to one's own devices, to be left to oneself; (*ohne Anleitung*) to be left to one's own resources; **jdn sich** (*dat*) **selbst ~** to leave sb to his/her own devices/resources.
  (d) (*preisgeben*) **sich seinem Schmerz/seinen Gedanken/Gefühlen ~** to abandon oneself to one's pain/thoughts/feelings; **jdn seinem Schicksal ~** to leave *or* abandon sb to his fate; **jdn seinem Kummer ~** to offer sb no comfort in his/her grief.

überlassen² *vt sep irreg* (*inf*) *siehe* **übriglassen.**

Überlassung *f, no pl* (*von Recht, Anspruch*) surrender. **die käufliche ~ eines Gegenstandes** (*form*) the sale of an article.

überlasten* *vt insep* to put too great a strain on; *jdn* to overload; (*Elec*) *Telefonnetz*, (*durch Gewicht*) to overload. **überlastet sein** to be under too great a strain; (*überfordert sein*) to be overtaxed; (*Elec etc*) to be overloaded.

Überlastung *f* (*von Mensch*) overtaxing, (*Überlastetsein*) strain; (*Elec, durch Gewicht*) overloading. **bei ~ der Leber** when there is too much strain on the liver.

Überlauf *m* overflow.

überlaufen¹* *vt insep irreg* (a) *Gegner, Abwehr* to overrun.
  (b) (*fig: ergreifen: Angst etc*) to seize. **es überlief ihn heiß** he felt hot under the collar; **es überlief ihn kalt** a cold shiver ran down his back *or* up and down his spine; **es überlief mich heiß und kalt** I went hot and cold all over.

überlaufen² *vi sep irreg aux sein* (a) (*Wasser, Gefäß*) to overflow; (*überkochen*) to boil over. **ineinander ~** (*Farben*) to run (into one another); **zum Ü~ voll** full to overflowing; **jetzt läuft das Maß über** (*fig*) my patience is at an end; *siehe* **Galle.**
  (b) (*Mil: überwechseln*) to desert. **zum Feind ~** to go over *or* desert to the enemy.

überlaufen³ *adj* overcrowded; *Stadt, Ort, Insel etc auch* overrun.

Überläufer *m* (*Mil*) deserter; (*Mil auch, Pol*) turncoat.

Überlaufrohr *nt* overflow pipe.

überlaut **1** *adj* (a) (*zu laut*) overloud. (b) (*aufdringlich*) *Mensch* obtrusive, loud; *Farben* loud, garish; (*flegelhaft*) *Benehmen* brash, loud. **2** *adv* too loudly.

überleben* *insep 1 vti* (a) *Unglück, Operation etc* to survive; *die Nacht auch* to last, to live through. **das überlebe ich nicht!** (*inf*) it'll be the death of me (*inf*); **Sie werden es sicher ~** (*iro*) it won't kill you, you'll survive.
  (b) (*länger leben als*) to outlive, to survive (*um* by).
  2 vr das hat sich überlebt/wird sich ganz schnell überlebt haben that's had its day/will very soon have had its day; **diese Mode überlebt sich ganz schnell** this fashion will soon be a thing of the past.

Überlebende(r) *mf decl as adj* survivor.

Überlebenschance *f* chance of survival.

überlebensgroß *adj* larger-than-life.

Überlebensgröße *f* **in ~** larger than life.

überlebt *adj* outmoded, out-of-date.

überlegen¹* *insep 1 vti* (*nachdenken*) to think. **störe ihn nicht, solange er überlegt** don't disturb him while he's thinking; **ihn und her ~** to deliberate; **überleg doch mal!** think!; **hin und her ~** to deliberate; **ich habe hin und her überlegt** I've thought about it a lot; **ohne zu ~** without thinking; (*ohne zu zögern*) without thinking twice.
  2 vt (*überdenken, durchdenken*) to think over *or* about, to consider. **das werde ich mir ~** I'll think it over, I'll think about it, I'll give it some thought; **ich habe es mir anders/noch mal überlegt** I've changed my mind/I've had second thoughts about it; **wenn man es sich** (*dat*) **recht überlegt** when you think about it; **wollen Sie es sich** (*dat*) **nicht noch einmal ~?** won't you think it over again?, won't you reconsider?; **das muß ich mir noch sehr ~** I'll have to think it over *or* consider it very carefully; **das hätten Sie sich** (*dat*) **vorher ~ müssen** you should have thought of *or* about that before *or* sooner; **es wäre zu ~** it should be considered.

überlegen² *sep 1 vt* **jdm etw ~** to put *or* lay sth over sb; **ein Kind ~** (*inf*) to put a child over one's knee. **2 vr** (*sich zur Seite legen*) to lean over, to tilt.

überlegen³ **1** *adj* superior; (*hochmütig auch*) supercilious. **jdm ~ sein** to be superior to sb; **das war ein ~er Sieg** that was a good *or* convincing victory. **2** *adv* in a superior manner *or* fashion. **Bayern München hat ~ gesiegt** Bayern Munich won convincingly.

Überlegenheit *f, no pl* superiority; (*Hochmut auch*) superciliousness.

überlegt **1** *adj* (well-)considered. **2** *adv* in a considered way.

Überlegung f (a) (Nachdenken) consideration, thought, reflection. bei näherer/nüchterner ~ on closer examination/on reflection; das wäre wohl einer ~ wert that would be worth thinking about or over, that would be worth considering or worthy of consideration; ohne ~ without thinking; da können wir ohne ~ zusagen we can say yes quite happily.
(b) (Bemerkung) observation. ~en anstellen to make observations (zu about or on); ~en vortragen to give one's views (zu on or about).

überleiten sep 1 vt Thema, Abschnitt etc to link up (in + acc to, with). 2 vi zu etw ~ to lead up to sth; in eine andere Tonart ~ (Mus) to change key.

Überleitung f connection; (zur nächsten Frage, Mus) transition. gut gegliedert, aber ~ fehlt (Sch) well organized, but disjointed.

überlesen* vt insep irreg (a) (flüchtig lesen) to glance through or over or at. (b) (übersehen) to overlook, to miss.

überliefern* vt insep Brauch, Tradition to hand down. das Manuskript ist nur als Fragment überliefert the manuscript has only come down to us in fragmentary form.

Überlieferung f (a) tradition. schriftliche ~en (written) records. (b) (Brauch) tradition, custom. an der ~ festhalten to hold on to tradition; nach alter ~ according to tradition.

überlisten* vt insep to outwit.

überm contr of über dem.

übermachen* vt insep (old: vermachen) to make over (dat to).

Übermacht f, no pl superior strength or might; (fig: von Gefühlen, Ideologie etc) predominance. in der ~ sein to have the greater strength.

übermächtig adj Gewalt, Stärke superior; Feind, Opposition powerful, strong; Wunsch, Bedürfnis overpowering; (fig) Institution, Rauschgift all-powerful.

übermalen¹ vt sep to paint over.

übermalen²* vt insep to paint over or on top of.

übermannen* vt insep (geh) to overcome.

Übermaß nt, no pl excess, excessive amount (an + acc of). im ~ to or in excess; er hat Zeit im ~ he has more than enough time.

übermäßig 1 adj (a) excessive; Schmerz, Sehnsucht violent; Freude intense. das war nicht ~ that was not too brilliant. (b) (Mus) ~es Intervall augmented interval.
2 adv excessively; essen/trinken auch to excess. sich ~ anstrengen to overdo things; er hat sich nicht ~ bemüht he didn't exactly overexert himself; sie haben nicht ~ gut gespielt they didn't exactly play brilliantly.

Übermensch m superman.

übermenschlich adj superhuman. Ü~es leisten to perform superhuman feats.

übermitteln* vt insep to convey (jdm to sb); (telephonisch etc) Meldung to transmit, to send.

Übermitt(e)lung f siehe vt conveyance; transmission; sending.

übermorgen adv the day after tomorrow. ~ abend/früh the day after tomorrow in the evening/morning.

übermüden* vt insep usu ptp to overtire; (erschöpfen auch) to overfatigue.

Übermüdung f overtiredness; (Erschöpfung auch) overfatigue.

Übermüdungs|erscheinung f sign of overtiredness/fatigue.

Übermut m high spirits pl. vor lauter ~ wußten die Kinder nicht, was sie tun sollten the children were so full of high spirits that they didn't know what to do with themselves; ~ tut selten gut (prov) pride goes before a fall (Prov); (zu Kindern) it'll end in tears.

übermütig adj (a) (ausgelassen) high-spirited, boisterous. (b) (zu mutig) cocky (inf). werd bloß nicht ~! don't be cocky (inf). (c) (dated: überheblich) arrogant.

übern contr of über den.

übernächste(r, s) adj attr next ... but one. das ~ Haus the next house but one; die ~ Woche the week after next; am ~n Tag war er ... two days later or the next day but one he was ...; er kommt ~en Freitag he's coming a week on Friday or (on) Friday week.

übernachten* vi insep to sleep; (in Hotel, Privathaus etc auch) to stay; (eine Nacht) to spend or stay the night. bei jdm ~ to stay with sb, to sleep or stay at sb's place; wie viele Leute können bei dir ~? how many people can you put up?

übernächtigt, übernächtig (esp Aus) adj bleary-eyed.

Übernachtung f overnight stay. ~ und Frühstück bed and breakfast.

Übernachtungsmöglichkeit f overnight accommodation no pl. sich nach einer ~ umsehen to look around for somewhere to stay the night.

Übernahme f -, -n (a) takeover; (das Übernehmen) taking over; (von Ausdruck, Ansicht) adoption; (von Zitat, Wort) borrowing. seit der ~ des Geschäfts durch den Sohn since the son took over the business.
(b) (von Amt) assumption; (von Verantwortung auch) acceptance. durch ~ dieser Aufgabe by taking on or undertaking this task; er hat sich zur ~ der Kosten/Hypothek verpflichtet he has undertaken to pay the costs/mortgage; bei ~ einer neuen Klasse when taking charge of a new class; er konnte Rechtsanwalt Mayer zur ~ seines Falles bewegen he persuaded Mr Mayer, the barrister, to take (on) his case.

Übernahmsstelle f (Aus) siehe Annahmestelle.

übernational adj supranational.

übernatürlich adj supernatural.

übernehmen¹* insep irreg 1 vt (a) to take; Aufgabe, Arbeit to take on, to undertake; Verantwortung to take on, to assume, to accept; Kosten, Hypothek to agree to pay; (Jur) Fall to take

(on); jds Verteidigung to take on; (kaufen) to buy. den Befehl or das Kommando ~ to take command or charge; seit er das Amt übernommen hat since he assumed office; er übernimmt Ostern eine neue Klasse he's taking charge of a new class at Easter; lassen Sie mal, das übernehme ich! let me take care of that; es ~, etw zu tun to take on the job of doing sth, to undertake to do sth; etw kostenlos von jdm ~ to get sth free from sb.
(b) (stellvertretend, ablösend) to take over (von from); Ausdruck, Ansicht auch to adopt; Zitat, Wort to take, to borrow.
(c) Geschäft, Praxis etc to take over.
(d) (Aus inf: übertölpeln) to put one over on (inf).
2 vr to take on or undertake too much; (sich überanstrengen) to overdo it; (beim Essen) to overeat. ~ Sie sich nur nicht! (iro) don't strain yourself! (iro).

übernehmen² vt sep irreg Cape etc to put on. das Gewehr ~ (Mil) to slope arms.

übernervös adj highly strung.

über|ordnen vt sep jdn jdm ~ to put or place or set sb over sb; siehe übergeordnet. (b) etw einer Sache (dat) ~ to give sth precedence over sth; einer Sache (dat) übergeordnet sein to have precedence over sth, to be superordinate to sth.

Über|ordnung f superiority (über + acc to). wir müssen eine ~ der Verwaltung über die ärztliche Tätigkeit verhindern we must prevent administration being given precedence over medical practice.

überparteilich adj non-party attr, non-partisan; (Parl) Problem all-party attr, crossbench attr (Brit); Amt, Präsident etc above party politics.

Überparteilichkeit f non-partisanship.

überpinseln¹ vt sep (inf) Wand to paint over.

überpinseln²* vt insep Fleck to paint over.

Überpreis m exorbitant price. zu ~en at exorbitant prices.

Überproduktion f overproduction.

überprüfbar adj checkable.

überprüfen* vt insep (auf + acc for) to check; Gepäck auch, Maschine, Waren, (Fin) Bücher to inspect, to examine; Entscheidung, Lage, Frage to examine, to review; Ergebnisse, Teilnehmer etc to scrutinize; (Pol) jdn to screen. etw erneut ~ to re-check/re-examine sth/scrutinize sth again; die Richtigkeit von etw ~ to check (the correctness of) sth.

Überprüfung f (a) no pl siehe vt checking; inspection; examination; review; scrutiny; (Pol) screening. nach ~ der Lage after reviewing the situation, after a review of the situation. (b) (Kontrolle) check, inspection.

überquellen vi sep irreg aux sein to overflow (von, mit with); (Cook) (Teig) to rise over the edge; (Reis) to boil over. die Augen quollen ihm über his eyes grew as big as saucers; vor Freude/Dankbarkeit ~ to be overflowing with joy/gratitude.

überqueren* vt insep to cross.

überragen¹* vt insep jdn (lit: größer sein) to tower above. (b) (fig: übertreffen) to outshine (an + dat, in + dat in).

überragen² vi sep (senkrecht) to protrude; (waagerecht) to jut out, to project.

überragend adj (fig) outstanding; Bedeutung auch paramount.

überraschen* vt insep to surprise; (überrumpeln auch) to catch or take unawares, to take by surprise. jdn bei etw ~ to surprise or catch sb doing sth; von einem Gewitter überrascht werden to be caught in a storm; lassen wir uns ~! let's wait and see!

überraschend adj surprising; Besuch surprise attr; Tod, Weggang unexpected. eine ~e Wendung nehmen to take an unexpected turn; das kam (für uns) völlig ~ that came as a complete surprise or (Sterbefall etc) shock (to us); er mußte ~ nach Köln fahren he had to go to Cologne unexpectedly.

überraschenderweise adv surprisingly.

überrascht adj surprised (über + acc at). jdn ~ ansehen to look at sb in surprise; sich von etw (nicht) ~ zeigen to show (no) surprise at sth; da bin ich aber ~! that's quite a surprise.

Überraschung f surprise. zu meiner (größten) ~ to my (great) surprise, much to my surprise; Mensch, ist das eine ~! (inf) well, that's a surprise (and a half inf)!; jdm eine kleine ~ kaufen to buy a little something for sb as a surprise; für eine ~ sorgen to have a surprise in store; mit ~ mußte ich sehen or feststellen, daß ... I was surprised to see that ...

Überraschungs-: ~angriff m surprise attack; ~moment nt moment of surprise; ~sieger m (Sport) surprise winner.

überrechnen* vt insep to calculate roughly, to estimate (roughly).

überreden* vt insep to persuade, to talk round. jdn ~, etw zu tun to persuade sb to do sth, to talk sb into doing sth; jdn zu etw ~ to talk sb into sth; ich habe mich zum Kauf ~ lassen I let myself be talked or persuaded into buying it/them; laß dich nicht ~ don't (let yourself) be talked into anything.

Überredung f persuasion.

Überredungskunst f persuasiveness. all ihre Überredungskünste all her powers of persuasion.

überregional adj national; Zeitung, Sender auch nationwide.

überreich adj lavish, abundant; (zu reich) overabundant. ~ an etw (dat) overflowing with sth; Dummköpfe sind auf der Welt in ~em Maße vorhanden there are idiots galore in the world; jdn ~ beschenken to lavish presents on sb.

überreichen* vt insep (jdm) etw ~ to hand sth over (to sb); (feierlich) to present sth (to sb).

überreichlich adj ample, abundant; (zu reichlich) overabundant. in ~em Maße in abundance; ~ essen/trinken to eat/drink more than ample.

Überreichung f presentation.

überreif adj overripe.

Überreife f overripeness.

überreizen* insep 1 vt to overtax; Phantasie to overexcite;

Nerven, Augen to overstrain. **2** *vr* (*Cards*) to overbid.

überreizt *adj* overtaxed; *Augen* overstrained; (*nervlich*) over-wrought; (*zu erregt*) overexcited.

Überreiztheit *f siehe adj* overtaxed state; overstrain; over-wrought state; overexcitedness.

Überreizung *f siehe vt* overtaxing; overexcitement, overstimulation; overstraining.

überrennen* *vt insep irreg* to run down; (*Mil*) to overrun; (*fig*) to overwhelm.

Überrepräsentation *f* overrepresentation.

überrepräsentiert *adj* overrepresented.

Überrest *m* remains *pl*; (*letzte Spur: von Ruhm, Selbstachtung etc auch*) remnant, vestige. ein Häufchen Asche war der kläg-liche ∼ the only remains were a sorry heap of ashes.

überrieseln* *vt insep Wiese* to water, to spray; (*mit Gräben zu*) irrigate. eine Schauer überrieselte ihn a shiver ran down his spine; es überrieselt mich kalt, wenn ... it makes my blood run cold *or* sends a shiver down my spine when ...

Überrock *m* (*dated: Mantel*) greatcoat, overcoat; (*old: Gehrock*) frock-coat.

Überrollbügel *m* (*Aut*) roll bar.

überrollen¹* *vt insep* to run down; (*Mil, fig*) to overrun. wir dürfen uns von ihnen nicht ∼ lassen we mustn't let them steam-roller us.

überrollen² *vt sep* (*inf*) to paint over (with a roller).

überrumpeln* *vt insep* (*inf*) to take by surprise, to take *or* catch unawares; (*überwältigen*) to overpower. jdn mit einer Frage ∼ to throw sb with a question.

Überrump(e)lung *f* surprise attack; (*Überwältigung*) overpowering. durch ∼ with a surprise attack.

Überrump(e)lungstaktik *f* surprise tactics *pl*.

überrunden* *vt insep* (*Sport*) to lap; (*fig*) to outstrip.

übers *prep* +*acc* (a) *contr of* über das. (b) (*old*) ∼ Jahr in a year.

übersäen* *vt insep* to strew; (*mit Abfall etc auch*) to litter. übersät strewn; (*mit Abfall etc auch*) littered; (*mit Sternen*) *Himmel* studded; (*mit Narben etc*) covered; ein mit Fehlern übersäter Aufsatz an essay strewn *or* littered with mistakes.

übersatt *adj* more than full *or* replete (*von* with).

übersättigen* *vt insep* to satiate; *Markt* to glut, to oversatu-rate; (*Chem*) to supersaturate. übersättigt sein (*Menschen*) to be sated with luxuries; das reizt ihn nicht mehr, er ist schon übersättigt that doesn't hold any attraction for him any more, he has had a surfeit.

Übersättigung *f* satiety; (*des Marktes*) glut, oversaturation; (*Chem*) supersaturation.

Überschall- *in cpds* supersonic; ∼flugzeug *nt* supersonic air-craft, SST (*US*); ∼geschwindigkeit *f* supersonic speed; mit ∼geschwindigkeit fliegen to fly supersonic *or* at supersonic speeds; ∼knall *m* sonic boom.

überschatten* *vt insep* (*geh*) (*lit, fig*) to overshadow; (*fig: trüben*) to cast a shadow *or* cloud over.

überschätzen* *vt insep* to overrate, to overestimate; *Entfer-nung, Zahl etc* to overestimate.

Überschätzung *f* overestimation.

Überschau *f* (*geh*) overview (*über* +*acc* of).

überschaubar *adj Plan, Gesetzgebung etc* easily comprehen-sible, clear. damit die Abteilung ∼ bleibt so that one can keep a general overview of *or* keep track of (*inf*) the department; die Folgen sind noch nicht ∼ the consequences cannot yet be clearly seen.

Überschaubarkeit *f* comprehensibility, clarity. zum Zwecke der besseren ∼ to give (you) a better idea.

überschauen* *vt insep siehe* **überblicken**.

überschäumen *vi sep aux sein* to froth *or* foam over; (*fig*) to brim *or* bubble (over) (*vor* +*dat* with); (*vor Wut*) to boil (over). ∼de Begeisterung *etc* exuberant *or* effervescent *or* bubbling enthusiasm *etc*.

Überschicht *f* (*Ind*) extra shift.

überschießen *vi sep irreg aux sein* (a) (*Wasser*) to gush *or* pour over. (b) der ∼de Betrag the remaining amount, the remainder.

überschlächtig *adj Wasserrad* overshot.

überschlafen* *vt insep irreg Problem etc* to sleep on.

Überschlag *m* (a) (*Berechnung*) (rough) estimate. (b) (*Dre-hung*) somersault (*auch Sport*); (*Aviat: Looping*) loop. einen ∼ machen to turn *or* do a somersault; (*Aviat*) to loop the loop.

überschlagen¹* *insep irreg* **1** *vt* (a) (*auslassen*) to skip, to miss.
    (b) (*berechnen*) *Kosten etc* to estimate (roughly).
    2 *vr* (a) to somersault; (*Auto auch*) to turn over; (*Mensch: versehentlich auch*) to go head over heels; (*fig: Ereignisse*) to come thick and fast. sich vor Hilfsbereitschaft/Freundlichkeit (*dat*) ∼ to fall over oneself to be helpful/friendly; nun überschlag dich mal nicht! don't get carried away.
    (b) (*Stimme*) to crack.

überschlagen² *sep irreg* **1** *vt Beine* to cross; *Arme* to fold; *Decke* to fold *or* turn back. mit übergeschlagenen Beinen/Armen with one's legs crossed/arms folded. **2** *vi aux sein* (a) (*Wellen*) to break. (b) (*Stimme etc*) in etw (*acc*) ∼ to turn into sth.

überschlagen³ *adj Flüssigkeit* lukewarm, tepid; *Zimmer* slightly warm.

Über-: ü∼schlägig *adj siehe* ü∼schläglich; ∼schlaglaken *nt* top sheet; ü∼schläglich *adj* rough, approximate; ü∼schlank *adj* too thin; ü∼schlau *adj* (*inf*) too clever by half, clever-clever (*inf*), smart-aleck *attr* (*inf*).

überschnappen *vi sep aux sein* (a) (*Riegel etc*) to clip *or* snap on. (b) (*Stimme*) to crack, to break; (*inf: Mensch*) to crack up (*inf*); *siehe* **übergeschnappt**.

überschneiden* *vr insep irreg* (*Linien*) to intersect; (*Flächen, fig: Themen, Interessen, Ereignisse etc*) to overlap; (*völlig*) to coincide; (*unerwünscht*) to clash.

Überschneidung *f siehe vr* intersection; overlap *no pl*; coinci-dence; clash.

überschnell *adj* overhasty.

überschreiben* *vt insep irreg* (a) (*betiteln*) to head. (b) (*übertragen*) etw jdm *or* auf jdn ∼ to make *or* sign sth over to sb.

überschreien* *vt insep irreg* to shout down.

überschreiten* *vt insep irreg* to cross; (*fig*) to exceed; *Höhepunkt, Alter* to pass. „Ü∼ der Gleise verboten" "do not cross the line"; er hat die Sechzig schon überschritten he is over *or* past *or* he has passed sixty already; die Grenze des Erlaubten/des Anstands ∼ to go beyond what is permissible/decent.

Überschrift *f* heading; (*Schlagzeile*) headline.

Überschuh *m* overshoe, galosh *usu pl*.

überschuldet *adj* heavily in debt; *Grundstück* heavily mort-gaged.

Überschuldung *f* excessive debts *pl*; (*von Grundstück*) heavy mortgaging.

Überschuß *m* surplus (*an* +*dat* of). seinen ∼ an Kraft austoben to work off one's surplus energy.

überschüssig *adj* surplus.

überschütten¹* *vt insep* (a) (*bedecken*) jdn/etw mit etw ∼ to tip sth onto sb/sth, to cover sb/sth with sth; (*mit Flüssigkeit*) to pour sth onto sb/sth.
    (b) (*überhäufen*) jdn mit etw ∼ to shower sb with sth, to heap sth on sb; mit Vorwürfen to heap sth on sb; er wurde mit Lob überschüttet he was showered with praise, praise was heaped on him.

überschütten² *vt sep* (*vergießen*) to slop.

Überschwang *m* -(e)s, *no pl* exuberance. im ∼ der Freude/der Gefühle in one's joyful exuberance/in exuberance; im ersten ∼ in the first flush of excitement.

überschwappen *vi sep aux sein* to splash over; (*aus Tasse etc auch*) to slop over.

überschwemmen* *vt insep* (*lit, fig*) to flood; (*Touristen*) *Land etc auch* to overrun, to inundate *usu pass*; (*Angebote, Anträge*) *Inserenten, Behörde etc auch* to inundate *usu pass*, to deluge *usu pass*, to swamp; *Verbraucher, Leser etc* to swamp.

Überschwemmung *f* (*lit*) flood; (*das Überschwemmen*) flooding *no pl*; (*fig*) inundation; (*von Verbrauchern, Lesern*) swamping. es kam zu ∼en there was a lot of flooding *or* were a lot of floods.

Überschwemmungs-: ∼gebiet *nt* (*überschwemmtes Gebiet*) flood area; (*Geog*) floodplain; ∼gefahr *f* danger of flooding; ∼katastrophe *f* flood disaster.

überschwenglich *adj* effusive, gushing *no adv* (*pej*).

Überschwenglichkeit *f* effusiveness.

Übersee *no art* in/nach ∼ overseas; aus/von ∼ from overseas; Briefe für ∼ overseas letters, letters to overseas destinations; Besitzungen in ∼ haben to have overseas territories *or* ter-ritories overseas.

Übersee-: ∼dampfer *m* ocean liner; ∼hafen *m* international port; ∼handel *m* overseas trade.

überseeisch [ˈyːbɐzeːɪʃ] *adj* overseas *attr*.

Übersee-: ∼kabel *nt* transoceanic cable; (*im Atlantik*) trans-atlantic cable; ∼koffer *m* trunk; ∼land *nt* overseas country; ∼verkehr *m* overseas traffic.

übersehbar *adj* (a) (*lit*) *Gegend etc* visible. das Tal ist von hier schlecht ∼ you don't get a good view of the valley from here.
    (b) (*fig*) (*erkennbar*) *Folgen, Zusammenhänge etc* clear; (*abschätzbar*) *Kosten, Angebote* etc assessable. dieses Fach-gebiet ist nicht mehr ∼ it is no longer possible to have an overall view of this subject; die Folgen sind klar/schlecht ∼ the consequences are quite/not very clear; der Schaden ist noch gar nicht ∼ the damage cannot be assessed yet.
    (c) solche Druckfehler sind leicht ∼ misprints like that are easily overlooked *or* are easy to overlook *or* miss; dieses grelle Orange ist wirklich nicht ∼ you couldn't miss *or* overlook *or* fail to see this bright orange.

übersehen¹* *vt insep irreg* (a) (*lit*) *Gegend etc* to look over, to have a view of.
    (b) (*erkennen, Bescheid wissen über*) *Folgen, Zusam-menhänge, Sachlage* to see clearly; *Fachgebiet* to have an overall view of; (*abschätzen*) *Schaden, Kosten, Dauer etc* to assess. dieses Fach ist nicht mehr zu ∼ it is no longer possible to have an overall view of this subject.
    (c) (*ignorieren, nicht erkennen*) to overlook; (*nicht bemerken*) to miss, to fail to see *or* notice. ∼, daß ... to overlook the fact that ...; dieses Problem ist nicht mehr zu ∼ this problem cannot be overlooked any longer; etw stillschweigend ∼ to pass over sth in silence.

übersehen² *vt sep irreg* sich (*dat*) etw ∼ to get *or* grow tired *or* to tire of seeing sth.

übersein *vi sep irreg aux sein* (*Zusammenschreibung nur bei infin und ptp*) (*inf*) jdm ist etw über sb is fed-up with sth (*inf*); mir ist diese Arbeit schon lange über I've been fed up with this work for a long time (*inf*).

übersenden* *vt insep irreg* to send; *Geld auch* to remit (*form*). hiermit ∼ wir Ihnen ... please find enclosed ...

Übersendung *f siehe vt* sending; remittance (*form*).

übersetzbar *adj* translatable. leicht/schwer ∼ easy/hard to translate.

übersetzen¹* *vti insep* (a) (*lit*) to translate. aus dem *or* vom Engli-schen ins Deutsche ∼ to translate from English into German; ein Buch aus dem Englischen ∼ to translate a book from (the) English; etw falsch ∼ to mistranslate sth; sich leicht/schwer ∼

lassen to be easy/hard to translate; sich gut/schlecht ~ lassen to translate well/badly. (b) (*Tech*) (*umwandeln*) to translate; (*übertragen*) to transmit.

übersetzen² sep 1 vt (a) (*mit Fähre*) to take or ferry across. (b) den Fuß ~ to put one's leg over. 2 vi aux sein to cross over.

Übersetzer(in f) m -s, - translator.·

Übersetzung f (a) translation. (b) (*Tech*) (*Umwandlung*) translation; (*Übertragung*) transmission; (*Herab~, Herauf~*) change in the transmission ratio; (*~sverhältnis*) transmission or gear ratio.

Übersetzungs-: ~büro nt translation bureau or agency; ~fehler m translation error, error in translation; ~verhältnis nt (*Tech*) transmission or gear ratio.

Übersicht f (a) no pl (*Überblick*) overall view. die ~ verlieren to lose track of things or of what's going on. (b) (*Abriß, Resümee*) survey; (*Tabelle*) table.

übersichtig adj (old) long-sighted, far-sighted (esp US).

übersichtlich adj Gelände etc open; (*erfaßbar*) Darstellung etc clear. eine Bibliothek muß ~ sein a library should be clearly laid out.

Übersichtlichkeit f siehe adj openness; clarity.

Übersichtskarte f general map.

übersiedeln sep, **übersiedeln*** insep vi aux sein to move (von from, nach, in +acc to).

Übersied(e)lung [auch 'y:bə-] f (*das Übersiedeln*) moving; (*Umzug*) move, removal (form).

übersinnlich adj supersensory; (*übernatürlich*) supernatural. die ~e Welt the world beyond the senses.

überspannen* vt insep (a) (*Brücke, Decke etc*) to span. etw mit Leinwand/Folie etc ~ to stretch canvas/foil etc over sth, to cover sth with canvas/foil etc. (b) (*zu stark spannen*) to put too much strain on; (fig) Forderungen to push too far; siehe Bogen.

überspannt adj Ideen, Forderungen wild, extravagant; (*exaltiert*) eccentric; (*hysterisch*) hysterical; Nerven overexcited.

Überspanntheit f siehe adj wildness, extravagance; eccentricity; hysteria; overexcited state.

Überspannung f (*Elec*) overload.

überspielen* vt insep (a) (*verbergen*) to cover (up). (b) (*übertragen*) Aufnahme to transfer. ein Platte (auf Band) ~ to tape a record, to put a record on or transfer a record to tape. (c) (Sport) to pass; (*ausspielen, klar besiegen*) to outplay.

überspielt adj (a) (Sport) played out, stale. (b) (Aus) Klavier overplayed.

überspitzen vt insep to carry too far, to exaggerate; Argument to overstate.

überspitzt 1 adj (*zu spitzfindig*) oversubtle, fiddly (inf); (*übertrieben*) exaggerated; Argument overstated. 2 adv oversubtly; in an exaggerated fashion. ~ argumentieren to overstate one's argument(s) or case.

übersprechen* vt insep irreg to speak over. etw mit einem Kommentar ~ to speak a commentary over sth, to do a voice-over for sth.

überspringen¹* vt insep irreg (a) Hindernis, Höhe to jump to, to clear. (b) (*weiter springen als*) to jump more than. die 2-m-Marke ~ to jump more than 2 metres. (c) (*auslassen*) Klasse to miss (out), to skip; Kapitel, Lektion auch to leave out.

überspringen² vi sep irreg aux sein (lit, fig) to jump (auf +acc to); (Begeisterung) to spread quickly (auf +acc to); siehe Funke.

übersprudeln vi sep aux sein (lit, fig) to bubble over (vor with); (beim Kochen) to boil over. ~d (fig) bubbling, effervescent.

überspülen* vt insep to flood; (Wellen auch) to wash over. überspült sein to be awash.

überstaatlich adj supranational.

überstehen¹* vt insep irreg (*durchstehen*) to come or get through; (*überleben*) to survive; (*überwinden*) to overcome; Gewitter to weather, to ride out; Krankheit to get over, to recover from. wenn du deine Prüfung überstanden hast when you've got your exam over and done with; etw lebend ~ to survive sth, to come out of sth alive; das Schlimmste ist jetzt überstanden the worst is over now; nach überstandener Gefahr when the danger was past; das wäre überstanden! thank heavens that's over; er hat es überstanden (euph) he has gone to rest (euph) or has passed away (euph).

überstehen² vi sep irreg aux haben or sein to jut or stick out, to project. um 10 cm ~ to jut out etc 10cm.

übersteigen* vt insep irreg (a) (*klettern über*) to climb over. (b) (*hinausgehen über*) to exceed, to go beyond; (*Philos, Liter: transzendieren*) to transcend; siehe Fassungsvermögen.

übersteigern* insep 1 vt Preise, Tempo to force up; Forderungen to push too far. 2 vr to get carried away.

übersteigert adj excessive. an einem ~en Selbstbewußtsein leiden to have an inflated view of oneself.

Übersteigerung f (*von Emotionen*) excess; (*von Forderungen*) pushing too far.

überstellen* vt insep (Admin) to hand over.

überstempeln* vt insep to stamp over. ein überstempeltes Paßbild a passport photograph which has been stamped (over).

übersteuern* insep 1 vi (Aut) to oversteer. 2 vt (Elec) to overmodulate.

überstimmen* vt insep to outvote; Antrag to vote down.

überstrahlen* vt insep (lit) to illuminate; (fig) to outshine.

überstrapazieren* insep infin auch überzustrapazieren 1 vt to wear out; Ausrede etc to wear thin. überstrapaziert worn out, outworn; thin. 2 vr to wear oneself out.

überstreichen* vt insep irreg to paint/varnish over.

überstreifen vt sep (sich dat) etw ~ to slip sth on.

überströmen¹* vt insep (*überfluten*) to flood. von Schweiß/Blut überströmt sein to be streaming or running with sweat/blood.

überströmen² vi sep aux sein (a) (lit, fig: überlaufen) to overflow. er sprach mit ~der Freude/Dankbarkeit he spoke in a voice overflowing with joy/gratitude. (b) (*hinüberströmen*) to spread, to communicate itself (auf +acc to).

überstülpen vt sep sich (dat) etw ~ to put on sth; jdm/einer Sache etw ~ to put sth on sb/sth.

Überstunde f hour of overtime. ~n overtime sing; ~n/zwei ~n machen to do or work overtime/two hours overtime.

Überstundenzuschlag m overtime allowance. der ~ beträgt 50% overtime is paid at time and a half.

überstürzen* insep 1 vt to rush into; Entscheidung auch to rush. man soll nichts ~ (prov) look before you leap (Prov). 2 vr (*Ereignisse etc*) to happen in a rush; (*Nachrichten*) to come fast and furious; (*Worte*) to come tumbling out. sich beim Sprechen ~ to speak all in a rush; sich beim Essen ~ to bolt one's food.

überstürzt adj overhasty, precipitate.

Überstürzung f (*das Überstürzen*) rushing (+gen into); (Hast) rush.

übersüß adj too sweet, oversweet; Kuchen etc auch sickly.

übertariflich adj, adv above the agreed or union rate.

übertäuben* vt insep (geh) to dull.

übertauchen* vt insep (Aus inf) to get over.

überteuern* vt insep Waren to overcharge for; Preis to inflate, to force up.

überteuert adj overexpensive; Preise inflated, excessive.

Überteuerung f (a) (*das Überteuern*) overcharging (+gen for); (*von Preisen*) forcing up, (over)inflation. (b) (*Überteuertsein*) expensiveness; excessiveness.

übertippen* vt insep to type over.

übertölpeln* vt insep to take in, to dupe.

Übertölpelung f taking-in.

übertönen* vt insep to drown.

Übertrag m -(e)s, -̈e amount carried forward or over.

übertragbar adj transferable (auch Jur); Methode, Maßstab applicable (auf +acc to); Ausdruck translatable (in +acc into); Krankheit communicable (form) (auf +acc to), infectious; (*durch Berührung*) contagious.

übertragen¹* insep irreg 1 vt (a) (*an eine andere Stelle bringen, an jdn übergeben*) to transfer (auch Jur, Psych); Krankheit to pass on, to transmit, to communicate (auf +acc to); (Tech) Bewegung to transmit. (b) (*an eine andere Stelle schreiben*) to transfer; (*kopieren*) to copy (out); (*transskribieren*) to transcribe. (c) (*übersetzen*) Text to render (in +acc into). (d) (*anwenden*) Methode, Maßstab to apply (auf +acc to). (e) (Mus: in andere Tonart) to transpose. (f) etw auf Band ~ to tape sth, to record sth (on tape); eine Platte auf Band ~ to transfer a record to tape, to tape a record. (g) (*verleihen*) Auszeichnung, Würde to confer (jdm on sb); Vollmacht, Verantwortung to give (jdm sb). (h) (*auftragen*) Aufgabe, Mission to assign (jdm to sb). (i) (TV, Rad) to broadcast, to transmit. etw im Fernsehen ~ to televise sth, to broadcast sth on television; durch Satelliten ~ werden to be broadcast or sent by satellite. 2 vr (*Eigenschaft, Krankheit etc*) to be passed on or communicated or transmitted (auf +acc to); (Tech) to be transmitted (auf +acc to); (*Heiterkeit etc*) to communicate itself, to spread (auf +acc to). diese Krankheit überträgt sich auf Menschen this disease can be passed on etc to humans; seine Fröhlichkeit hat sich auf uns ~ we were infected by his happiness.

übertragen² adj (a) Bedeutung etc figurative. (b) (Aus) worn; (*gebraucht*) secondhand, used. etw ~ kaufen to buy sth secondhand.

Überträger m (Med) carrier.

Übertragung f siehe vt (a) transference; passing on, transmission, communication; transmission. (b) transference; copying (out); transcription. (c) rendering. (d) application. (e) transposition. (f) ~ auf andere Tonträger verboten" "recording forbidden in any form"; die ~ von Platten auf Tonband the taping of records, the transfer of records to tape. (g) conferral; giving. (h) assignment. (i) broadcasting, transmission; (Sendung) broadcast, transmission.

Übertragungswagen m outside broadcast unit.

übertrainiert adj overtrained.

übertreffen* insep irreg 1 vt to surpass (an +dat in); (mehr leisten als auch) to do better than, to outdo, to outstrip; (*übersteigen auch*) to exceed; Rekord to break. jdn an Intelligenz/Schönheit ~ to be more intelligent/beautiful etc than sb; jdn um vieles or bei weitem ~ to surpass sb by far; (bei Leistung auch) to do far better than sb, to outstrip sb by a long way; alle Erwartungen ~ to exceed or surpass all expectations; er ist nicht zu ~ he is unsurpassable. 2 vr sich selbst ~ to surpass or excel oneself.

übertreiben* vt insep irreg (a) (auch vi: aufbauschen) to exaggerate. der „Macbeth" übertrieb stark Macbeth over-acted a lot. (b) (*zu weit treiben*) to overdo, to carry or take too far or to extremes. es mit der Sauberkeit ~ to carry cleanliness too far; man kann es auch ~ you can overdo things, you can go too far.

Übertreibung f (a) exaggeration; (*theatralisch*) overacting no pl. man kann ohne ~ sagen ... it's no exaggeration to say ... (b) die ~ des Sports/der Arbeit etc ist ungesund it's not healthy to do too much sport/work; ihre ~ der Sparsamkeit/Sauberkeit the way she carries economy/cleanliness too far *or* to extremes; etw ohne ~ tun to do sth without overdoing it *or* carrying it too far *or* to extremes.

übertreten[1] *vi sep irreg aux sein* (a) *(Fluß)* to break its banks, to flood. (b) *(zu anderer Partei etc)* to go over *(zu* to); *(in andere Schule)* to move *(in* +acc to). (c) *(im Sport)* to overstep.

übertreten[2*] *vt insep irreg Grenze etc* to cross; *(fig) Gesetz, Verbot* to break, to infringe, to violate.

Übertretung *f (von Gesetz etc)* violation, infringement; *(Jur: strafbare Handlung)* misdemeanour.

übertrieben 1 *ptp of* **übertreiben.** 2 *adj* exaggerated; *(zu stark, übermäßig)* Vorsicht, Training excessive.

Übertriebenheit *f* exaggeratedness; *(Übermäßigkeit)* excessiveness.

Übertritt *m (über Grenze)* crossing *(über* +acc of); *(zu anderem Glauben)* conversion; *(von Abtrünnigen, esp zu anderer Partei)* defection; *(in andere Schule)* move *(in* +acc to). die Zahl der ~e zur demokratischen Partei the number of people going over to the democratic party.

übertrocknen* *vi insep aux sein (Aus)* to dry.

übertrumpfen* *vt insep (Cards)* to overtrump; *(fig)* to outdo.

übertun[1] *vt sep irreg sich (dat)* einen Mantel *etc* ~ *(inf)* to put a coat on; jdm einen Schal *etc* ~ to put a scarf *etc* on sb.

übertun[2*] *vr insep irreg (dial)* to overdo it *(inf).*

übertünchen[1*] *vt insep* to whitewash; *(mit Farbton)* to distemper; *(fig)* to cover up.

übertünchen[2] *vt sep* to whitewash (over); *(mit Farbton)* to distemper (over).

überübermorgen *adv (inf)* in three days, the day after the day after tomorrow. ~ abend/früh in three days in the evening/ morning.

überversichern* *vt insep infin auch* **überzuversichern** to overinsure.

Überversicherung *f* overinsurance.

übervölkern* *vt insep* to overpopulate.

Übervölkerung *f* overpopulation.

übervoll *adj* overfull *(von* with), too full; *(von Menschen, Sachen auch)* crammed *(von* with); Glas full to the brim or to overflowing.

übervorsichtig *adj* overcautious.

übervorteilen* *vt insep* to cheat, to do down *(inf).*

Übervorteilung *f* cheating.

überwach *adj* (too) wide-awake; *(fig)* alert.

überwachen* *vt insep (kontrollieren)* to supervise; *(beobachten)* to keep a watch on, to observe; Verdächtigen to keep under surveillance, to keep a watch on, to watch; *(auf Monitor, mit Radar, fig)* to monitor.

Überwachung *f siehe vt* supervision; observation; surveillance; monitoring.

überwältigen* *vt insep* (a) *(lit)* to overpower; *(zahlenmäßig)* to overwhelm; *(bezwingen)* to overcome. (b) *(fig) (Schlaf, Mitleid, Angst etc)* to overcome; *(Musik, Schönheit etc)* to overwhelm.

überwältigend *adj* overwhelming; Schönheit stunning; Gestank, Gefühl auch overpowering. nicht gerade ~ nothing to write home about *(inf).*

Überwältigung *f siehe vt* (a) overpowering; overwhelming; overcoming.

überwälzen* *vt insep (esp Aus) siehe* **abwälzen.**

überwechseln *vi sep* to move *(in* +acc to); *(zu Partei etc)* to go over *(zu* to); *(zu Partei etc)* to cross over.

Überweg *m* ~ für Fußgänger pedestrian crossing.

überweisen* *vt insep irreg Geld* to transfer *(an* +acc, auf +acc to); *(weiterleiten)* Vorschlag etc, Patienten to refer *(an* +acc to). mein Gehalt wird direkt auf mein Bankkonto überwiesen my salary is paid directly into my bank account.

Überweisung *f (Geld~)* (credit) transfer; *(von Patient, Vorschlag etc)* referral.

Überweisungs-: ~auftrag *m* (credit) transfer order; ~formular *nt* (credit) transfer form; ~schein *m (von Arzt)* letter of referral; *(für Bank)* (credit) transfer form.

überweit *adj* loose-fitting, too big.

Überweite *f* large size. Kleider in ~(n) outsize dresses, dresses in the larger sizes.

überwerfen[1*] *vr insep irreg* sich (mit jdm) ~ to fall out (with sb).

überwerfen[2] *vt sep irreg* to put over; Kleidungsstück to put on; *(sehr rasch)* to throw on.

Überwesen *nt* preterhuman being.

überwiegen* *insep irreg* 1 *vt* to outweigh. 2 *vi (das Übergewicht haben)* to be predominant, to predominate; *(das Übergewicht gewinnen)* to prevail.

überwiegend 1 *adj* predominant, mainly. 2 *adv* Mehrheit vast. 2 *adv* predominantly, mainly.

überwindbar *adj* Schwierigkeiten, Hindernis surmountable. diese Angst ist nur schwer ~ it is hard to overcome this fear.

überwinden* *insep irreg* 1 *vt* to overcome; Hindernis auch to surmount, to get over; Enttäuschung, Angst, Scheu auch to get over; *(hinter sich lassen)* to outgrow; *siehe* **überwunden.**
2 *vr* to overcome one's inclinations. sich ~, etw zu tun to force oneself to do sth; ich konnte mich nicht ~, das zu tun *or* nicht dazu ~ I couldn't bring myself to do it.

Überwinder *m* -s, - *(liter)* conqueror, vanquisher.

Überwindung *f* overcoming; *(von Schwierigkeiten, Hindernis auch)* surmounting; *(Selbst~)* will power. das hat mich viel ~ gekostet that was a real effort of will for me, that took me a lot of will power; selbst bei der größten ~ könnte ich das nicht tun I simply couldn't bring myself to do it.

überwintern* *vi insep* to (spend the) winter; *(Pflanzen)* to overwinter; *(inf: Winterschlaf halten)* to hibernate.

Überwinterung *f* wintering, spending the winter; *(von Pflanzen)* overwintering; *(inf: Winterschlaf)* hibernation.

überwölben* *vt insep* to vault.

überwölken* *vr insep siehe* **bewölken.**

überwuchern* *vt insep* to overgrow, to grow over; *(fig)* to obscure.

überwunden 1 *ptp of* **überwinden.** 2 *adj* Standpunkt, Haltung etc of the past; Angst conquered. ein bis heute noch nicht ~es Vorurteil a prejudice which is still prevalent today.

Überwurf *m (Kleidungsstück)* wrap; *(Ringen)* shoulder throw; *(Aus: Bett~)* bedspread, counterpane.

Überzahl *f, no pl* in der ~ sein to be in the majority; *(Feind)* to be superior in number; die Frauen waren in der ~ the women outnumbered the men *or* were in the majority.

überzahlen* *vt insep Waren* to pay too much for. das Auto ist überzahlt you/he etc paid too much for the car, the car cost too much.

überzählen* *vt insep* to count (through).

überzählig *adj (überschüssig)* surplus; *(überflüssig)* superfluous; *(übrig)* spare.

überzeichnen* *vt insep* (a) *(Fin)* Anleihe to oversubscribe. (b) *(fig: übertrieben darstellen)* to exaggerate, to overdraw.

Überzeit *f (Sw)* overtime.

überzeugen* *insep* 1 *vt* to convince; *(umstimmen auch)* to persuade; *(Jur)* to satisfy. er ließ sich nicht ~ he would not be convinced *or* persuaded, there was no convincing *or* persuading him; ich bin davon überzeugt, daß ... I am convinced *or* certain that ...; Sie dürfen überzeugt sein, daß ... you may rest assured *or* be certain that ...; er ist sehr von sich überzeugt he is very sure of himself.
2 *vi* to be convincing, to carry conviction. er konnte nicht ~ he wasn't convincing, he was unconvincing.
3 *vr* sich (selbst) ~ to convince oneself *(von* of), to satisfy oneself *(von* as to); *(mit eigenen Augen)* to see for oneself; ~ Sie sich selbst! see for yourself!

überzeugend *adj* convincing.

überzeugt *adj attr* Anhänger, Vegetarier etc dedicated, convinced; Christ, Moslem devout, convinced.

Überzeugung *f* (a) *(das Überzeugen)* convincing. (b) *(Überzeugtsein)* conviction; *(Prinzipien)* convictions pl, beliefs pl. meiner ~ nach ... I am convinced (that) ..., it is my conviction that ...; ich bin der festen ~, daß ... I am firmly convinced *or* of the firm conviction that ...; zu der ~ gelangen *or* kommen, daß ..., die ~ gewinnen, daß ... to become convinced that ..., to arrive at the conviction that ...; *siehe* **Brusston.**

Überzeugungs-: ~kraft *f* persuasiveness, persuasive power; ~täter *m* political/religious criminal.

überziehen[1*] *insep irreg* 1 *vt* (a) *(bedecken)* to cover; *(mit Schicht, Belag)* to coat; *(mit Metall)* to plate; *(mit Zuckerguß)* to ice, to frost *(esp US).* ein Bett ~/frisch ~ to make up a bed/to change a bed *or* the bedlinen *or* the linen on a bed; Polstermöbel neu ~ lassen to have furniture re-covered; von Rost überzogen covered in *or* coated with rust; mit Gold/Silber überzogen gold-/silver-plated.
(b) Konto to overdraw. er hat sein Konto (um 500 Mark) überzogen he has overdrawn his account (by 500 marks), he is (500 marks) overdrawn.
(c) *(geh: heimsuchen)* to invade. ein Land mit Krieg ~ to turn a country into a battlefield.
(d) Redezeit etc to overrun.
2 *vi (Fin)* to overdraw one's account.
3 *vr* (a) *(sich bedecken: Himmel)* to cloud over, to become overcast. der Himmel ist überzogen the sky is overcast.
(b) *(mit Schicht etc)* to become covered *or* coated.

überziehen[2] *vt sep irreg* (a) *(sich dat)* etw ~ to put sth on. (b) jdm eins ~ *(inf)* to give sb a clout *(inf),* to clout *or* clobber sb *(inf).*

Überzieher *m* -s, - *(dated)* (a) *(Mantel)* greatcoat. (b) *(inf: Kondom)* sheath, French letter *(inf).*

Überziehungskredit *m* overdraft provision.

überzüchten* *vt insep* to overbreed; Motor to overdevelop.

überzuckern* *vt insep* (a) *(mit Zucker überstreuen)* to (sprinkle with) sugar. (b) *(zu stark zuckern)* to put too much sugar in/on. das Kompott ist überzuckert the stewed fruit has too much sugar in it.

Überzug *m* (a) *(Beschichtung)* coat(ing); *(aus Metall)* plating; *(für Kuchen, esp aus Zuckerguß)* icing, frosting *(esp US).* (b) *(Bett~, Sessel~ etc)* cover; *(Kopfkissen~ auch)* (pillow)slip.

Üble(s) *nt decl as adj siehe* **übel.**

üblich *adj* usual; *(herkömmlich)* customary; *(typisch, normal)* normal. wie ~ as usual; es ist bei uns/hier ~ *or* das ~e, daß ... it's usual for us/here to ..., it's the custom with us/here that ...; das ist bei ihm so ~ that's usual for him; allgemein ~ sein to be common practice; die allgemein ~en Bedingungen/Methoden the usual conditions/methods.

üblicherweise *adv* usually, generally, normally.

Übliche(s) *nt decl as adj* das ~ the usual things pl, the usual.

U-Bogen *m* loop which some Germans write over "u".

U-Boot *nt* submarine, sub *(inf); (esp Hist: der deutschen Marine)* U-boat.

U-Boot-Krieg *m* submarine warfare *no art.*

übrig *adj* (a) *attr (verbleibend)* rest of, remaining, *(andere auch)* other. meine/die ~en Sachen the rest of my/the things; alle ~en Bücher all the rest of the books, all the other *or* remaining books; der ~e Teil des Landes the rest of *or* remaining part *or* remainder of the country.
(b) *pred* left, left over; *(zu entbehren)* spare. etw ~ haben to have sth left/to spare; haben Sie vielleicht eine Zigarette (für mich) ~? could you spare (me) a cigarette?
(c) *(mögen)* für jdn/etw wenig/nichts ~ haben not to have

much/to have no time for sb/sth; **für jdn/etw etwas/viel ~ haben** to have a soft spot for or to be fond/very fond of sb/sth, to have a liking/a great liking for sb/sth.

(d) (*substantivisch*) **das ~e** the rest, the remainder; **alles ~e** all the rest, everything else; **die/alle ~en** the/all the rest or others; **im ~en** incidentally, by the way; **ein ~es tun** (*geh*) to do one more thing.

übrig-: **~behalten** vt sep irreg to have left over; **~bleiben** vi sep irreg aux sein to be left over, to remain; **wieviel ist ~geblieben?** how much is left?; **da wird ihm gar nichts anderes ~bleiben** he won't have any choice or any other alternative; **was blieb mir anderes ~ als ...?** what choice did I have but ...?, there was nothing left for it but to ...

übrigens adv incidentally, by the way.

übriglassen vt sep irreg to leave (jdm for sb). **(einiges)/viel zu wünschen ~** (*inf*) to leave something/a lot to be desired.

Übung f **(a)** no pl (das Üben, Geübtsein) practice. **das macht die ~, das ist alles nur ~** it's a question of practice, it comes with practice; **aus der ~ kommen/außer ~ sein** to get/be out of practice; **in ~ bleiben** to keep in practice, to keep one's hand in (*inf*); **zur ~** for or as practice; **(richtig) ~ in etw** (*dat*) **haben/bekommen** to have/get (quite) a bit of practice in sth; **~ macht den Meister** (*Prov*) practice makes perfect (*Prov*).

(b) (*Veranstaltung*) practice; (*Mil, Sport, Sch*) exercise; (*Feuerwehr~*) exercise, drill; (*Univ: Kursus*) seminar.

Übungs-: **~arbeit** f (Sch) practice or mock test; **~aufgabe** f (Sch) exercise; **~buch** nt (Sch) book of exercises; **~flug** m practice flight; **ü~halber** adv for practice; **~heft** nt (Sch) exercise book; **~munition** f blank ammunition; **~platz** m training area or ground; (*Exerzierplatz*) drill ground; **~schießen** nt shooting practice; **~stück** nt (Sch, Mus) exercise.

UdSSR [uːdeːʔɛsʔɛsˈʔɛr] f - abbr of **Union der Sozialistischen Sowjetrepubliken**. **die ~** the USSR.

u.E. abbr of **unseres Erachtens**.

U-Eisen nt U-iron.

Ufer nt -s, - (*Fluß~*) bank; (*See~*) shore; (*Küstenlinie*) shoreline. **direkt am ~ gelegen** right on the water's edge or waterfront; **etw ans ~ spülen** to wash sth ashore; **der Fluß trat über die ~** the river broke or burst its banks; **das sichere ~ erreichen** to reach dry land or terra firma.

Ufer-: **~bau** m bank and shoreline construction; **~befestigung** f bank reinforcement; **~böschung** f embankment; **~land(schaft** f) nt shoreland; **u~los** adj (endless) endless; (*grenzenlos*) boundless; **ins u~lose gehen** (*Debatte etc*) to go on forever or interminably, to go on and on; (*Kosten*) to go up and up; **sonst geraten wir ins u~lose** otherwise things will get out of hand; **ans ~lose grenzen** (*Verleumdungen etc*) to go beyond all bounds; **~mauer** f sea wall; **~staat** m riparian state (*form*), country which borders onto a lake or river; **~straße** f lakeside/riverside road.

uff interj (*inf*) phew. **~, das wäre geschafft!** phew, that's that done!

Uffz. m -, -e abbr of **Unteroffizier** NCO.

UFO, Ufo [ˈuːfoː] nt -(s), -s UFO, Ufo.

U-förmig adj U-shaped. **~ gebogen** with a U-shaped bend, bent into a U.

Uganda nt -s Uganda.

Ugander(in f) m -s, - Ugandan.

ugandisch adj Ugandan.

uh interj oh; (*angeekelt*) ugh, yuck (*inf*).

U-Haft f (*inf*) custody.

U-Haken m U-shaped hook.

Uhl f -, -en (N Ger) siehe **Eule**.

Uhlenspiegel m (N Ger) siehe **Eulenspiegel**.

Uhr f -, -en **(a)** clock; (*Armband~, Taschen~*) watch; (*Anzeigeinstrument*) gauge, dial, indicator; (*Wasser~, Gas~*) meter. **nach der or auf die or zur ~ sehen** to look at the clock etc; **Arbeiter, die ständig auf die or nach der ~ sehen** clock-watchers; **nach meiner ~** by my watch; **wie nach der ~** (*fig*) like clockwork; **rund um die ~** round the clock; **seine ~ ist abgelaufen** (*fig geh*) the sands of time have run out for him.

(b) (*bei Zeitangaben*) **um drei (~) at three** (o'clock); **ein ~ dreißig, (in Ziffern)** 1³⁰ **~** half past one, 1.30 (*ausgesprochen "one-thirty"*); **wieviel ~ ist es?** what time is it?, what's the time?; **um wieviel ~?** (at) what time?

Uhr(arm)band nt watch strap; (*aus Metall*) watch bracelet.

Uhrchen nt dim of **Uhr** little clock etc.

Uhren-: **~industrie** f watch-and-clock(-making) industry; **~vergleich** m comparison of watch/clock times; **einen ~vergleich machen** to check or synchronize watches.

Uhr-: **~feder** f watch spring; **~glas** nt (auch Sci) watch-glass; **~kette** f watch chain, fob (chain); **~macher(in** f) m watch-maker; clock-maker, horologist (*form*); **~macherhandwerk** nt watch-making; clock-making, horology (*form*); **~werk** nt clockwork mechanism (auch fig), works pl (of a watch/clock), movements pl; **~zeiger** m (clock/watch) hand; **~zeigersinn** m im **~zeigersinn** clockwise; **entgegen dem ~zeigersinn** anti-or counter-clockwise; **~zeit** f time (of day); **haben Sie die genaue ~zeit?** do you have the correct time?

Uhu [ˈuːhu] m -s, -s eagle-owl.

Ukas m -ses, -se (Hist, pej) ukase.

Ukraine [auch uˈkraɪnə] f - **die ~** the Ukraine.

Ukrainer(in f) [auch uˈkraɪnɐ, -ərɪn] m -s, - Ukrainian.

ukrainisch [auch uˈkraɪnɪʃ] adj Ukrainian.

Ukulele f -, -n ukulele.

UKW [uːkaːˈveː] abbr of **Ultrakurzwelle** ≈ VHF.

Ul f -, -en (N Ger) siehe **Eule**.

Ulan m -en, -en (Hist) u(h)lan.

Ulensp(i)egel m siehe **Eulenspiegel**.

Ulfilasbibel f Gothic bible, Ulfilas' translation of the bible.

Ulk m -(e)s, -e (*inf*) lark (*inf*); (*Streich*) trick, practical joke; (*Spaß*) fun no pl, no indef art. **~ machen** to clown or play about or around; **etw aus ~ sagen/tun** to say/do sth as a joke or in fun; **mit jdm seinen ~ treiben** (*Spaß machen*) to have a bit of fun with sb; (*Streiche spielen*) to play tricks on sb.

ulken vi (*inf*) to joke, to clown around. **über ihn wurde viel geulkt** they often had a bit of fun with him.

ulkig adj (*inf*) funny; (*seltsam auch*) odd, peculiar.

Ulkus nt -, **Ulzera** (Med) ulcer.

Ulme f -, -n elm.

Ulmen-: **~krankheit** f, **~sterben** nt Dutch elm disease.

Ultima f -, **Ultimä** or **Ultimen** (Ling) final syllable.

Ultima ratio [ˈʊltima ˈraːtsio] f --, no pl (geh) final or last resort.

Ultimaten pl of **Ultimatum**.

ultimativ adj Forderung etc given as an ultimatum. **wir fordern ~ eine Lohnerhöhung von 9%** we demand a pay rise of 9% and this is an ultimatum; **jdn ~ zu etw auffordern** to give sb an ultimatum to do sth.

Ultimatum nt -s, -s or **Ultimaten** ultimatum. **jdm ein ~ stellen** to give sb an ultimatum.

Ultimen pl of **Ultima**.

Ultimo m -s, -s (Comm) last (day) of the month. **per ~** by the end of the month; **bis ~** (*fig*) till the last minute.

Ultra m -s, -s (pej) extremist.

Ultra- in cpds ultra; **u~kurz** adj (Phys) ultra-short.

Ultrakurzwelle f (Phys) ultra-short wave; (Rad) ≈ very high frequency, ≈ frequency modulation.

Ultrakurzwellen-: **~empfänger** m VHF receiver; **~sender** m VHF station; (*Apparat*) VHF transmitter.

Ultra-: **~marin** m, no pl ultramarine; **u~marin(blau)** adj ultramarine; **u~modern** adj ultramodern; **u~montan** adj (pej geh) papist (pej); **u~rot** adj siehe infrarot; **~schall** m (Phys) ultrasound; **~schallwellen** pl ultrasonic waves pl; **~strahlung** f (Phys) cosmic rays pl; **u~violett** adj ultraviolet.

Ulzera pl of **Ulkus**.

um 1 prep +acc **(a)** **~ ...** (herum) round (esp Brit), around; (*unbestimmter, in der Gegend von*) around, about; **er hat gern Freunde ~ sich** he likes to have friends around him.

(b) (*nach allen Seiten*) **~ sich schauen** to look around (one) or about one; **~ sich schlagen** to hit out in all directions; **etw ~ sich werfen** to throw sth around or about.

(c) (*zur ungefähren Zeitangabe*) **~ ...** (herum) around about; (*bei Uhrzeiten auch*) at about; **die Tage ~ die Sommersonnenwende** (herum) the days either side of the summer solstice; **~ Weihnachten/Ostern** etc around Christmas/Easter etc.

(d) (*zur genauen Angabe der Uhrzeit*) at. **bitte kommen Sie** (genau) **~ acht** please come at eight (sharp).

(e) (*betreffend, über*) about. **es geht ~ das Prinzip** it's a question of principles, it's the principle of the thing; **es geht ~ alles** it's all or nothing; **es steht schlecht ~ seine Gesundheit** his health isn't very good.

(f) (*für, Ergebnis, Ziel bezeichnend*) for. **der Kampf ~ die Stadt/den Titel** the battle for the town/the title; **~ Geld spielen** to play for money; **~ etw rufen/bitten** etc to cry/ask etc for sth.

(g) (*wegen*) **die Sorge ~ die Zukunft** concern for or about the future; **(es ist) schade ~ das schöne Buch** (it's a) pity or shame about that nice book; **sich ~ etw sorgen** to worry about sth; **es tut mir leid ~ ihn** I'm sorry for him.

(h) (*bei Differenzangaben*) by. **~ 10% teurer** 10% more expensive; **er ist ~ zwei Jahre jünger als sie** he is two years younger than she is, he is younger than her by two years; **~ vieles besser** far better, better by far; **~ einiges besser** quite a bit better; **~ nichts besser/teurer** etc no better/dearer etc; **etw ~ 4 cm verkürzen** to shorten sth by 4 cm.

(i) (*bei Verlust*) **jdn ~ etw bringen** to deprive sb of sth; **~ etw kommen** to be deprived of sth, to miss out on sth.

(j) (*nach*) after, upon. **Stunde ~ Stunde** hour after or upon hour; **einer ~ den anderen/eine ~ die andere** one after the other; **einen Tag ~ den anderen** day after day.

2 prep +gen **~ ... willen** for the sake of; **~ Gottes willen!** for goodness or (*stärker*) God's sake!

3 conj **(a)** **~ ... zu** (*final*) (in order) to; **er spart jeden Pfennig, ~ sich später ein Haus kaufen zu können** he is saving every penny in order to be able to buy a house later; **intelligent genug/zu intelligent, ~ ... zu intelligent** enough/too intelligent to ...; **der Fluß schlängelt sich durch das enge Tal, ~ dann in der Ebene zu einem breiten Strom anzuwachsen** the stream winds through the narrow valley and then broadens out into a wide river in the plain; **er studierte jahrelang Jura, ~ dann Taxifahrer zu werden** he studied law for several years only to become a taxi-driver.

(b) (*desto*) **~ so besser/schlimmer!** so much the better/worse!, all the better/that's even worse!; **je mehr ..., ~ so weniger/eher kann man ...** the more ... the less/sooner one can ...; **~ so mehr**, als ... all the more considering or as; **unser Urlaub ist sehr kurz, ~ so besser muß er geplant werden** as our holiday is so short, we have to plan it all the better.

4 adv **(a)** (*ungefähr*) **~ (die) 30 Schüler** etc about or around or round about 30 pupils etc, 30 pupils etc or so.

(b) (*rare*) **~ und ~** all around.

um|ackern vt sep to plough up.

um|adressieren* vt sep to readdress; (*und nachschicken*) to redirect.

um|ändern vt sep to alter; (*modifizieren auch*) to modify.

um|arbeiten vt sep to alter; Buch etc to revise, to rewrite, to rework; Metall etc to rework. **einen Roman zu einem Drama/Drehbuch ~** to adapt a novel for the stage/screen.

Um|arbeitung f alteration; (von Buch etc) revision, rewriting, reworking; (zu Drama etc) adaptation; (von Metall) reworking.

um|armen* vt insep to embrace (auch euph); (fester) to hug.
Um|armung f siehe vt embrace; hug.
Um|armungsversuch m (fig) overture.
um|arrangieren* ['ʊmarãʒiːrən] vt sep or insep to rearrange.
Umbau m siehe vt rebuilding, renovation; conversion; alterations pl (+ gen, von to); modification; reorganization; changing. **das Gebäude befindet sich im** ~ the building is being rebuilt.
umbauen¹ sep 1 vt Gebäude (gründlich renovieren) to rebuild, to renovate; (zu etw anderem) to convert (zu into); (umändern) to alter; Maschine etc to modify; (fig: Organisation) to reorganize; (Theat) Kulissen to change. **2** vi to rebuild.
umbauen²* vt insep to enclose. **der Dom ist völlig umbaut** the cathedral is completely surrounded by buildings; **umbauter Raum** enclosed or interior area.
umbehalten* vt sep irreg Schal etc to keep on.
umbenennen* vt sep irreg to rename (in etw sth).
Umbenennung f renaming.
umbesetzen* vt sep (Theat) to recast; Mannschaft to change, to reorganize; Posten, Stelle to reassign.
Umbesetzung f siehe vt recasting; change, reorganization; reassignment. **eine** ~ **vornehmen** (Theat) to alter the cast; ~en **vornehmen** (Theat) to recast roles; ~en **im Kabinett vornehmen** to reshuffle the cabinet.
umbestellen* sep 1 vi to change one's order. **2** vt Patienten etc to give another or a new appointment to.
umbetten vt sep Kranken to move or transfer (to another bed); Leichnam to rebury, to transfer; Fluß to rechannel.
umbiegen sep irreg 1 vt to bend. **2** vt to curl. **3** vi aux sein (Weg) to bend, to turn; (zurückgehen) to turn round or back.
umbilden vt sep (fig) to reorganize, to reconstruct; (Pol) Kabinett to reshuffle (Brit), to shake up (US).
Umbildung f siehe vt reorganization, reconstruction; reshuffle, shake-up.
umbinden¹ vt sep irreg to put on; (mit Knoten auch) to tie on. **sich** (dat) **einen Schal** ~ to put a scarf on.
umbinden²* vt insep irreg siehe **umwickeln²**.
umblasen¹ vt sep irreg to blow down.
umblasen²* vt insep irreg **von den Winden** ~ **werden** (liter) to be buffeted by the winds (liter).
umblättern vti sep to turn over.
Umblick m siehe **Rundblick**.
umblicken vr sep to look round. **sich nach jdm/etw** ~ to turn round to look at sb/sth.
Umbra f -, no pl (Astron) umbra; (Farbe) umber.
Umbralglas ® nt photochrom(at)ic glass.
umbranden* vt insep to surge around. **von der See umbrandet** surrounded by the surging sea.
umbrausen* vt insep to surge around. **vom Sturm umbraust** buffeted by the storm.
umbrechen¹ sep irreg 1 vt (a) (umknicken) to break down. (b) (umpflügen) Erde to break up. **2** vi aux sein to break.
umbrechen²* vti insep irreg (Typ) to make up.
umbringen sep irreg 1 vt to kill (auch fig inf), to murder. **das ist nicht umzubringen** (fig inf) it's indestructible; **das bringt mich noch um!** (inf) it'll be the death of me! (inf).
2 vr to kill oneself. **bringen Sie sich nur nicht um!** (fig inf) you'll kill yourself (if you go on like that)!; **er bringt sich fast um vor Höflichkeit** (inf) he falls over himself to be polite.
Umbruch m (a) radical change. (b) (Typ) makeup. (c) (Agr) ploughing (Brit) or plowing (US) up.
umbuchen sep 1 vt (a) Reise, Termin to alter one's booking for. (b) (Fin) Betrag to transfer. **2** vi (a) to alter one's booking (auf + acc for). (b) to transfer (auf + acc to).
Umbuchung f siehe vb (a) rebooking. (b) transfer.
umdenken vi sep irreg to change one's ideas or views. **darin müssen wir** ~ we'll have to rethink that.
umdeuten vt sep to change the meaning of; (Liter) to reinterpret, to give a new interpretation to.
umdichten vt sep to rework, to recast.
umdirigieren* vt sep to redirect.
umdisponieren* vi sep to change one's arrangements or plans.
umdrängen* vt insep to throng or crowd around; (stärker) to mob. **sie wurde so umdrängt, daß** ... there was such a crowd around her that ...
umdrehen sep 1 vt (a) to turn over; (auf den Kopf) to turn up (the other way); (mit der Vorderseite nach hinten) to turn round, to turn back to front; (von innen nach außen) Strumpf etc to turn inside out; Tasche to turn (inside) out; (von außen nach innen) to turn back the right way; (um die Achse) to turn round; Schlüssel to turn; siehe **Pfennig, Spieß**.
(b) **einem Vogel/jdm den Hals** ~ to wring a bird's/sb's neck.
(c) (verrenken) **jdm den Arm** ~ to twist sb's arm; siehe **Wort**.
2 vr to turn round (nach to look at); (im Bett etc) to turn over. **dabei drehte sich ihm der Magen um** (inf) it turned his stomach.
3 vi to turn round or back.
Umdrehung f turn; (Phys) revolution, rotation; (Mot) revolution, rev.
Umdrehungszahl f (number of) revolutions pl per minute/second.
umdüstern* vr insep (liter) to become melancholy or sombre. **seine Stirn umdüsterte sich** his brow darkened (liter).
um|einander (emph **umeinander**) adv about each other or one another; (räumlich) (a)round each other.
um|erziehen* vt sep irreg (Pol euph) to re-educate (zu to become).
Um|erziehungslager nt (Pol euph) re-education centre.
umfächeln* vt insep (geh) to fan; (Luftzug auch) to caress (liter).

umfahren¹ sep irreg 1 vt to run over or down, to knock down. **2** vi aux sein (inf) to go out of one's way (by mistake). **er ist 5 Kilometer umgefahren** he went 5 kilometres out of his way.
umfahren²* vt insep irreg to travel or go round; (mit dem Auto) to drive round; (auf Umgehungsstraße) to bypass; (um etw zu vermeiden) to make a detour round, to detour; Kap to round, to double; die Welt to sail round, to circumnavigate.
Umfahrung f (a) siehe **umfahren²** travelling round; driving round; bypassing; detour; rounding, doubling; sailing (round), circumnavigation. (b) (Aus) siehe **Umgehungsstraße**.
Umfahrungsstraße f (Aus) siehe **Umgehungsstraße**.
Umfall m (Pol inf) turnaround (inf).
umfallen vi sep irreg aux sein (Mensch) to fall over or down; (Baum, Gegenstand) to fall (down); (vornüber kippen) to fall or topple over; (inf: ohnmächtig werden) to pass out, to faint; (fig inf: nachgeben) to give in. **vor Müdigkeit fast** ~, **zum U**~ **müde sein** to be (almost) dead on one's feet (inf), to be ready or fit to drop; **vor Schreck fast** ~ (inf) to almost die with fright, to almost have a heart attack (inf); ~ **wie die Fliegen** (inf) to drop like flies; siehe **tot**.
umfalzen vt sep to fold over.
Umfang m -(e)s, **Umfänge** (a) (von Kreis etc) perimeter, circumference (auch Geom); (von Baum auch, Bauch~) girth.
(b) (Fläche) area; (Rauminhalt) capacity; (Größe) size; (von Gepäck etc) amount. **das Buch hat einen** ~ **von 800 Seiten** the book contains or has 800 pages.
(c) (fig) (Ausmaß) extent; (Reichweite) range; (Stimm~) range, compass; (von Untersuchung, Arbeit etc) scope; (von Verkehr, Verkauf etc) volume. **in großem** ~ on a large scale; **in vollem** ~ fully, entirely, completely; **größeren/erschreckenden** ~ **annehmen** to assume greater/alarming proportions; **das hat einen solchen** ~ **angenommen, daß** ... it has assumed such proportions that ...; **etw in vollem** ~ **übersehen können** to be able to see the full extent of sth.
umfangen* vt insep irreg (a) **jdn mit seinen Blicken** ~ (fig) to fix one's eyes upon sb. (b) (fig: umgeben) to envelop. (c) (geh: umarmen) to embrace.
umfänglich, umfangreich adj extensive; (fig: breit) Wissen etc auch wide; (geräumig) spacious; Buch thick.
umfärben vt sep to dye a different colour.
umfassen* vt insep (a) to grasp, to clasp; (umarmen) to embrace. **ich konnte den Baum nicht mit den Armen** ~ I couldn't get my arms (a)round the tree; **er hielt sie umfaßt** he held her close or to him, he held her in an embrace; **einander or sich** ~ to embrace (each other).
(b) (Mil) to encircle, to surround.
(c) (fig) (einschließen) Zeitperiode to cover; (enthalten) to contain, to include; Seiten to contain.
umfassend adj (umfangreich, weitreichend) extensive; (vieles enthaltend) comprehensive; Vollmachten, Maßnahmen auch sweeping; Vorbereitung thorough; Geständnis full, complete.
Umfassung f (Mil) encirclement.
Umfassungsmauer f exterior wall.
Umfeld nt (associated) area or field. **zum** ~ **von etw gehören** to be associated with sth.
umflechten* vt insep irreg eine Flasche etc mit etw ~ to weave sth around a bottle etc; **eine umflochtene Flasche** a raffia-covered bottle.
umfliegen¹* vt insep irreg to fly (a)round.
umfliegen² vi sep irreg aux sein (inf) to go flying (inf).
umfließen* vt insep irreg (lit, fig) to flow around; (fig poet: Licht) to flood around. **von einem Strom umflossen sein** to be surrounded by a river.
umflort adj (liter) Augen misty, misted over.
umfluten* vt insep to surge around.
umformen vt sep (a) to remodel, to reshape (in + acc into). (b) (Elec) to convert. (c) (Ling) to transform.
Umformer m -s, - (Elec) converter.
Umformung f siehe vt remodelling, reshaping; conversion; transformation.
Umfrage f (a) (Sociol) survey; (esp Pol) (opinion) poll. **eine** ~ **halten** or **machen** or **veranstalten** to carry out or hold a survey/a poll or an opinion poll. (b) ~ **halten** to ask around; **unter** or **bei den Mitgliedern** ~ **halten** to ask (around) the members.
Umfrage|ergebnis nt survey/poll result(s pl).
umfried(ig)en* vt insep to enclose; (mit Zaun auch) to fence in; (mit Mauer auch) to wall in.
Umfried(ig)ung f (a) (das Umfrieden) **die** ~ **der Burg dauerte Jahrzehnte** enclosing/walling in the castle took years. (b) (Zaun, Mauer etc) enclosing fence/wall etc. **als** ~ **für den Park dient eine Hecke** the park is enclosed by a hedge.
Umfriedungsmauer f enclosing wall.
umfrisieren* vt sep (inf) (a) Nachrichten etc to doctor (inf). (b) **sich** (dat) **die Haare** ~ **lassen** to have one's hair restyled.
umfüllen vt sep to transfer into another bottle/container etc.
umfunktionieren* vt sep to change or alter the function of. **etw in** (+ acc) or **zu etw** ~ to change or turn sth into sth; **ein Wohnzimmer** ~ (hum) to use a living-room for a different purpose.
Umfunktionierung f **die** ~ **einer Sache** (gen) changing the function of sth; **die** ~ **der Versammlung zu einer Protestkundgebung** changing the function of the meeting and making a protest rally out of it.
Umgang¹ m -s no pl (a) (gesellschaftlicher Verkehr) contact, dealings pl; (Bekanntenkreis) acquaintances pl, friends pl. **schlechten** ~ **haben** to keep bad company; **das sieht man schon/das liegt an seinem** ~ you can tell that from/that's because of the company he keeps; ~ **mit jdm/einer Gruppe haben** or **pflegen** to associate with sb/associate or mix with a group; **keinen/so gut wie keinen** ~ **mit jdm haben** to have

nothing/little to do with sb; **sie hat nur ~ mit den besten gesellschaftlichen Kreisen** she only mixes in the best social circles; **er ist kein ~ für dich** he's not fit company or no company for you.

(b) im ~ mit Tieren/Jugendlichen/Vorgesetzten muß man ... in dealing with animals/young people/one's superiors one must ...; **durch ständigen ~ mit Autos/Büchern/Kindern** through having a lot to do with cars/books/children; **an den ~ mit Tieren/Kindern gewöhnt sein** to be used to animals/children; **an den ~ mit Büchern/Nachschlagewerken gewöhnt sein** to be used to having books around (one)/to using reference books; **der ~ mit Tieren/Kindern muß gelernt sein** you have to learn how to handle animals/children.

Umgang² m -(e)s, **Umgänge (a)** (Archit: Säulen~) ambulatory. **(b)** (Feld~, Flur~) procession.

umgänglich adj (entgegenkommend) obliging; (gesellig) sociable, friendly; (verträglich) affable, pleasant-natured.

Umgänglichkeit f siehe adj obliging nature; sociability, friendliness; affability, pleasant nature.

Umgangs-: ~formen pl manners pl; ~sprache f colloquial language or speech; **die deutsche ~sprache** colloquial German; **u~sprachlich** adj colloquial.

umgarnen* vt insep to ensnare, to beguile.

Umgarnung f beguilement.

umgaukeln* vt insep (geh) to flutter about or around; (fig: mit Schmeicheleien etc) to ensnare, to beguile.

umgeben* insep irreg 1 vt to surround (auch fig). **mit einer Mauer/einem Zaun ~ sein** to be walled/fenced in, to be surrounded by a wall/fence; **das von Weinbergen ~e Stuttgart** the town of Stuttgart, surrounded by vineyards. **2** vr **sich mit jdm/etw ~** to surround oneself with sb/sth.

Umgebung f (Umwelt) surroundings pl; (von Stadt auch) environs pl, surrounding area; (Nachbarschaft) vicinity, neighbourhood; (gesellschaftlicher Hintergrund) background; (Freunde, Kollegen etc) people pl about one. **Hamburg und ~** Hamburg and the Hamburg area, Hamburg and its environs or the surrounding area; **in der näheren/weiteren ~ Münchens** on the outskirts/in the environs of Munich; **zu jds (näherer) ~ gehören** (Menschen) to be one of the people closest to sb; **in seiner ~ fühle ich mich unwohl** I feel uneasy in his company.

Umgegend f surrounding area. **die ~ von London** the area around London.

umgehen¹ vi sep irreg aux sein **(a)** (Gerücht etc) to circulate, to go (a)round or about; (Grippe) to be about; (Gespenst) to walk. **in diesem Schloß geht ein Gespenst um** this castle is haunted (by a ghost).

(b) mit jdm/etw ~ können (behandeln, handhaben) to know how to handle or treat sb/sth; **mit Geld** to know how to handle sth; (mit jdm/etw verfahren) to know how to deal with or handle sb/sth; **mit jdm grob/behutsam ~** to treat sb roughly/gently; **wie der mit seinen Sachen umgeht!** you should see how he treats his things!; **sorgsam/verschwenderisch mit etw ~** to be careful/lavish with sth; **sage mir, mit wem du umgehst, und ich sage dir, wer du bist** (Prov) you can tell the sort of person somebody is from or by the company he keeps; **mit einer Idee ~** to turn an idea over in one's mind; **mit dem Gedanken ~, etw zu tun** to be thinking about doing sth.

(c) (inf: Umweg machen) to go out of one's way (by mistake).

umgehen²* vt insep irreg **(a)** to go round; (vermeiden) to avoid; (Straße) to by-pass; (Mil) to outflank.

(b) (fig) to avoid; Schwierigkeit auch, Gesetz to circumvent, to get round, to by-pass; Frage, Thema auch to evade. **die Antwort auf etw** (acc) ~ to avoid answering sth.

umgehend 1 adj immediate, prompt. **mit ~er Post** (dated) by return of post (Brit) or mail (US). **2** adv immediately.

Umgehung f, no pl **(a)** siehe **umgehen²** going round; avoidance; by-passing; outflanking; avoidance; circumvention, getting round, by-passing; evasion. **die ~ des Geländes** going round the grounds; **unter ~ der Vorschriften** by getting round or circumventing the regulations. **(b)** (inf: ~sstraße) by-pass.

Umgehungsstraße f by-pass.

umgekehrt 1 ptp of **umkehren**.

2 adj reversed; Reihenfolge reverse; (gegenteilig) opposite, contrary; (anders herum) the other way around. **nein, ~!** no, the other way round; **mit ~em Vorzeichen** (Math) with the opposite sign; (fig) with the roles reversed; **gerade or genau ~!** quite the contrary!, just the opposite!; **die Sache war genau ~ und nicht so, wie er sie erzählte** the affair was exactly the reverse of what he said; **im ~en Verhältnis zu etw stehen** or **sein** to be in inverse proportion to sth.

3 adv (anders herum) the other way round; (am Satzanfang: dagegen) conversely; proportional inversely. **... und/oder ~ ...** and/or vice versa; **~ als or wie** (inf) **...** the other way round to what ...; **es kam ~** (inf) the opposite happened.

umgestalten* vt sep to alter; (reorganisieren) to reorganize; (umbilden) to remodel; (umordnen) to rearrange. **etw in etw** (acc) or **zu etw ~** to redesign sth as sth; Werk, Buch to rewrite or recast sth as sth.

Umgestaltung f siehe vt alteration; reorganization; remodelling; rearrangement.

umgewöhnen* vr sep to re-adapt.

umgießen vt sep irreg **(a)** to transfer (in +acc into); (verschütten) to spill. **(b)** (Metal) to recast.

umgittern* vt insep to put a railing (a)round.

umglänzen* vt insep (poet) (Sonne etc) to bathe in light. **von der Morgensonne/von Ruhm umglänzt** bathed in the morning sunlight/resplendent with glory.

umgraben vt sep irreg to dig over; Erde to turn (over).

umgrenzen* vt insep to bound, to surround; (umfassen auch) to enclose; (fig) to delimit, to define.

Umgrenzung f **(a)** boundary. **(b)** (das Umgrenzen) (mit Mauer etc) enclosing; (fig) delimitation, definition.

umgruppieren* vt sep Möbel etc to rearrange; Mitarbeiter to redeploy; (auf andere Gruppen verteilen), (Mil) Truppen to regroup.

Umgruppierung f siehe vt rearrangement; redeployment; regrouping.

umgucken vr sep siehe **umsehen.**

umgürten¹ vt sep to fasten (dat around).

umgürten²* vr insep **sich mit einem Schwert ~** (liter) to gird on a sword (liter).

umhaben vt sep irreg (inf) to have on.

umhacken vt sep to break up.

umhalsen* vt sep **jdn ~** (inf) to throw one's arms around sb's neck.

Umhang m -(e)s, **Umhänge** cape; (länger) cloak; (Umhängetuch) shawl, wrap (esp US).

Umhängemikrophon nt neck or lavalier (spec) microphone.

umhängen vt sep **(a)** Rucksack etc to put on; Jacke, Schal etc to drape round; Gewehr auch to sling on. **sich** (dat) **etw ~** to put sth on; to drape sth round one; **jdm etw ~** to put sth on sb; to drape sth around sb. **(b)** Bild to rehang.

Umhängetasche f shoulder bag.

umhauen vt sep irreg **(a)** to chop or cut down, to fell. **(b)** (inf: umwerfen) to knock flying (inf) or over. **(c)** (inf) (erstaunen) to bowl over (inf); (Gestank etc) to knock out.

umhegen* vt insep (geh) to look after or care for lovingly.

umher adv around, about. **weit ~** all around.

umher- pref siehe auch **herum-** around, about; ~fahren sep irreg 1 vt (mit Auto) to drive around or about; (in Kinderwagen) to walk around or about; **jdn in der Stadt ~fahren** to drive/walk sb around or about the town; **2** vi aux sein to travel around or about; (mit Auto) to drive around or about; (mit Kinderwagen) to walk around or about; ~gehen vi sep irreg aux sein to walk around or about; **im Zimmer/Garten ~gehen** to walk (a)round the room/garden; ~getrieben adj (liter) wandering attr; **U~getriebene(r)** mf decl as adj (liter) wanderer, wandering soul (liter); ~irren vi sep aux sein (in etw (dat) sth) to wander around or about; (Blick, Augen) to roam about; **ängstlich irrte ihr Blick im Zimmer ~** her eyes anxiously scanned the room; **nach langen Jahren des U~irrens** after many years of wandering (around); ~jagen vi sep (vi: aux sein) to chase about or around; ~laufen vi sep irreg aux sein to walk about or around; (rennen) to run about or around; **im Garten ~laufen** to walk/run about or (a)round the garden; ~schleichen vi sep irreg aux sein to creep about or around (in etw (dat) sth); ~schlendern vi sep aux sein to stroll about or around (in etw (dat) sth); ~spähen vi sep to look about or around; ~streifen vi sep aux sein to wander or roam about or around (in etw (dat) sth); ~streunen vi sep aux sein (geh) siehe **herumstreunen**; ~wandern vi sep aux sein to wander or roam about or around (in etw (dat) sth); ~ziehen sep irreg 1 vi aux sein to move or travel around (in etw (dat) sth); **2** vt to pull about or around.

umhinkönnen vi sep irreg **ich/er etc kann nicht umhin, das zu tun** I/he etc can't avoid doing it; (einem Zwang folgend) I/he etc can't help doing it; **ich konnte nicht umhin I couldn't avoid it; I couldn't help it; ..., so daß sie einfach nicht umhinkonnten, mir zu glauben ...** so that they simply couldn't help but believe me.

umhören vr sep to ask around. **sich unter seinen Kollegen ~** to ask around one's colleagues.

umhüllen* vt insep to wrap (up) (mit in). **von einem Geheimnis umhüllt** shrouded in secrecy or mystery.

uminterpretieren* vt sep to interpret differently; (Liter) to reinterpret.

umjubeln* vt insep to cheer. **ein umjubelter Popstar** a wildly acclaimed pop idol.

umkämpfen* vt insep Entscheidung, Stadt to dispute; Wahlkreis, Sieg to contest.

Umkehr f -, no pl **(a)** (lit) turning back. **jdn zur ~ zwingen** to force sb to turn back. **(b)** (fig geh) (Änderung) change; (zur Religion etc) changing one's ways. **zur ~ bereit sein** to be ready to change one's ways; ~ **geloben** to vow to change one's ways.

Umkehr|anstalt f (Phot) reversal film processing laboratory.

umkehrbar adj reversible.

umkehren sep **1** vi aux sein to turn back; (auf demselben Weg zurückgehen) to retrace one's steps; (fig) to change one's ways.

2 vt Kleidungsstück (von innen nach außen) to turn inside out; (von außen nach innen) to turn the right way out; Tasche to turn (inside) out; Reihenfolge to invert; to invert (auch Gram, Math, Mus); Verhältnisse (umstoßen) to overturn; (auf den Kopf stellen) to turn upside down, to invert. **das ganze Zimmer ~** (inf) to turn the whole room upside down (inf); siehe auch **umgekehrt.**

3 vr (Verhältnisse) to become inverted or reversed. **dabei kehrt sich mir der Magen um** it turns my stomach, my stomach turns (over) at the sight/smell etc of it; **mein Inneres kehrt sich um, wenn ...** my gorge rises when ...

Umkehrfilm m (Phot) reversal film.

Umkehrlinse f inverting lens.

Umkehrung f (von Gesagtem, Reihenfolge etc) reversal, inversion (auch Gram, Math, Mus). **das ist eine ~ dessen, was ich gesagt habe** that's the opposite or reverse of what I said; **die ~ unserer Gesellschaftsordnung** turning society upside down.

umkippen sep **1** vt to tip over, to upset; Auto, Boot to overturn, to turn over; Leuchter, Vase to knock over; volles Gefäß to upset.

2 vi aux sein **(a)** to tip or fall over; (Auto, Boot) to overturn, to turn over; (volles Gefäß, Bier) to be spilled or upset. **(b)** (inf: ohnmächtig werden) to pass out. **(c)** (es sich anders überlegen) to come round.

(d) (*Fluß, See*) to be(come) polluted.

umklammern* *vt insep* to wrap one's arms/legs around; (*umarmen auch*) to hug, to embrace; (*mit Händen*) to clasp; (*festhalten*) to cling to; (*Ringen*) to hold, to clinch; (*Mil*) to trap in a pincer movement. **sie hielt ihn/meine Hand umklammert** she held him/my hand tight, she clung (on) to him/my hand; **einander** *or* **sich ~** (*Ringen*) to go into a/be in a clinch.

Umklammerung *f* clutch; (*Umarmung*) embrace; (*Ringen*) clinch; (*Mil*) pincer movement.

umklappbar *adj* folding *attr*, collapsible.

umklappen *sep* 1 *vt* to fold down. 2 *vi aux sein* (*inf*) to pass out.

Umkleidekabine *f* changing cubicle; (*in Kleidungsgeschäft auch*) changing *or* fitting room.

umkleiden¹ *vr sep* to change (one's clothes). **sie ist noch nicht umgekleidet** she isn't changed yet.

umkleiden²* *vt insep* to cover. **die Wahrheit mit schönen Worten ~** (*fig*) to gloss over *or* varnish the truth.

Umkleideraum *m* changing room; (*esp mit Schließfächern*) locker room; (*Theat*) dressing room.

umknicken *sep* 1 *vt Ast* to snap; *Gras, Strohhalm* to bend over; *Papier* to fold (over). 2 *vi aux sein* (*Ast*) to snap; (*Gras, Strohhalm*) to get bent over. **mit dem Fuß ~** to twist one's ankle.

umkommen *vi sep irreg aux sein* **(a)** (*sterben*) to die, to be killed, to perish (*liter*). **vor Lange(r)weile ~** (*inf*) to be bored to death (*inf*), to nearly die of boredom; **da kommt man ja um!** (*inf*) (*vor Hitze*) the heat is killing (*inf*); (*wegen Gestank*) it's enough to knock you out (*inf*); **ich komme um vor Hitze** (*inf*) the heat is killing me (*inf*).

(b) (*inf: verderben: Lebensmittel*) to go off *or* bad.

umkränzen* *vt insep* (*liter*) to wreathe, to garland.

Umkreis *m* (*Umgebung*) surroundings *pl*; (*Gebiet*) area; (*Nähe*) vicinity; (*Geom*) circumcircle. **im näheren ~** in the vicinity; **im ~ von 20 Kilometern** within a radius of 20 kilometres.

umkreisen* *vt insep* to circle (around); (*Astron*) to orbit, to revolve around; (*Space*) to orbit.

Umkreisung *f* (*Space, Astron*) orbiting. **drei ~en der Erde** three orbits of the Earth; **die ~ des Feindes** circling the enemy.

umkrempeln *vt sep* **(a)** to turn up; (*mehrmals*) to roll up. **(b)** (*umwenden*) to turn inside out; (*inf*) *Zimmer* to turn upside down; (*inf*) *Betrieb* to shake up (*inf*). **jdn ~** (*fig inf*) to change sb *or* sb's ways.

umkucken *vr sep* (*N Ger inf*) *siehe* **umsehen**.

umladen *vt sep irreg* to transfer, to reload; (*Naut*) to transship.

Umladung *f* transfer, reloading; (*Naut*) transshipping.

Umlage *f* **eine ~ machen** to split the cost; **sie beschlossen eine ~ der Kosten** they decided to split the costs.

umlagern¹* *vt insep* to surround; (*sich drängen um, Mil*) to besiege, to beleaguer.

umlagern² *vt sep* to transfer (*in +acc* into); (*in anderes Lager bringen*) *Waren etc* to re-store.

Umland *nt, no pl* surrounding countryside.

Umlandgemeinde *f* surrounding community.

Umlauf *m* **-s, Umläufe** **(a)** (*von Erde etc*) revolution; (*das Kursieren*) circulation (*auch fig*). **im ~ sein** to be circulating, to be in circulation; **in ~ bringen** to circulate; **Geld auch** to put in circulation; **Gerücht auch** to put about, to spread. **(b)** (*Rundschreiben*) circular. **(c)** (*Med: Fingerentzündung*) whitlow.

Umlaufbahn *f* orbit. **die ~ um den Mond/die Erde** lunar/earth orbit; **auf der ~ um die Erde sein** to be orbiting the earth.

umlaufen¹ *sep irreg* 1 *vt* to (run into and) knock over. 2 *vi aux sein* to circulate.

umlaufen²* *vt insep irreg* to orbit.

Umlauf-: **~schreiben** *nt* circular; **~zeit** *f* (*Astron*) period; (*Space*) orbiting time.

Umlaut *m* **(a)** *no pl* umlaut, vowel mutation. **(b)** (*Laut*) vowel with umlaut, mutated vowel.

umlauten *vt sep* to mutate, to modify (*zu* into).

umlegen *sep* 1 *vt* **(a)** (*umhängen, umbinden*) to put round; *Verband* to put on, to apply. **jdm/sich eine Stola ~** to put a stole round sb's/one's shoulders.

(b) *Mauer, Baum* to bring down; (*sl: zu Boden schlagen*) *Gegner* to knock down, to floor.

(c) (*umklappen*) to tilt (over); *Kragen* to turn down; *Manschetten* to turn up; (*Cards*) to turn (over); *Hebel* to turn.

(d) (*verlegen*) *Kranke* to transfer, to move; *Leitung* to re-lay.

(e) *Termin* to change (*auf +acc* to).

(f) (*verteilen*) **die 20 Mark wurden auf uns fünf umgelegt** the five of us each paid a contribution towards the 20 marks.

(g) (*sl: ermorden*) to do in (*inf*), to bump off (*sl*).

(h) (*sl*) *Mädchen* to lay (*sl*), to screw (*sl*).

2 *vr* **(a)** (*Boot*) to capsize, to turn over; (*Getreide*) to be flattened.

(b) (*sl: sich umbringen*) to do oneself in (*inf*).

umleiten *vt sep* to divert.

Umleitung *f* diversion; (*Strecke auch*) detour.

umlernen *vi sep* to retrain; (*fig*) to change one's ideas.

umliegend *adj* surrounding.

umlodern* *vt insep* (*liter*) to light up. **von Fackeln umlodert** lighted up by blazing torches.

Umluft *f* (*Tech*) circulating air.

ummauern* *vt insep* to wall in (*mit* by).

ummelden *vtr sep* **jdn/sich ~** to notify (the police of) a change in sb's/one's address.

Ummeldung *f* notification of (one's) change of address.

ummi *adv* (*Aus inf*) *siehe* **hinüber**.

ummodeln *vt sep* (*inf*) to change.

umnachtet *adj* (*geh*) *Geist* clouded over *pred*. **geistig ~ men- tally** deranged.

Umnachtung *f* **geistige ~** mental derangement; **da muß ich in geistiger ~ gewesen sein** (*iro*) I must have had a brainstorm.

umnähen *vt sep* *Saum* to stitch up.

umnebeln* *insep* 1 *vt* (*mit Tabakrauch*) to surround with smoke. 2 *vr* (*Blick*) to cloud *or* mist over. **mit umnebeltem Blick** with misty eyes.

umnehmen *vt sep irreg* *Mantel, Schal* to put on.

umnumerieren* *vt sep* to renumber.

umordnen *vt sep* to rearrange; (*in andere Reihenfolge bringen auch*) to re-order.

Umorganisation *f* reorganization.

umorganisieren* *vt sep* to reorganize.

umorientieren* *vr sep* (*fig*) to reorientate oneself.

Umorientierung *f* reorientation.

umpacken *vt sep* to repack.

umpflanzen¹ *vt sep* to transplant; *Topfpflanze* to repot.

umpflanzen²* *vt insep* **einen Platz mit Bäumen ~** to plant trees around a square.

umpflügen *vt sep* to plough up.

umpolen *vt sep* (*Elec*) to reverse the polarity of; (*inf: ändern*) to convert (*auf +acc* to).

umprägen *vt sep* *Münzen* to re-mint.

umquartieren* *vt sep* to move; *Truppen* (*in andere Kaserne etc*) to re-quarter; (*in anderes Privathaus*) to rebillet.

umrahmen¹* *vt insep* to frame. **die Ansprache war von musikalischen Darbietungen umrahmt** the speech was accompanied by musical offerings (before and after).

umrahmen² *vt sep* to reframe.

Umrahmung *f* setting (*-gen, von* for); (*das Umrahmen*) framing. **mit musikalischer ~** with music before and after.

umranden* *vt insep* to edge, to border.

umrandet *adj* *Augen* red-rimmed.

Umrandung *f* border, edging.

umranken* *vt insep* to climb *or* twine (a)round. **von** *or* **mit Efeu umrankt** twined around with ivy.

umräumen *sep* 1 *vt* (*anders anordnen*) to rearrange, to change (a)round; (*an anderen Platz bringen*) to shift, to move. 2 *vi* to change the furniture (a)round, to rearrange the furniture.

umrechnen *vt sep* to convert (*in -acc* into).

Umrechnung *f* conversion.

Umrechnungs-: **~kurs** *m* exchange rate, rate of exchange; **~tabelle** *f* conversion table.

umreisen* *vt insep* to travel (a)round.

umreißen¹ *vt sep irreg* to tear down; (*umwerfen*) to knock over.

umreißen²* *vt insep irreg* to outline. **scharf umrissen** clear-cut, well defined; *Züge auch* sharply defined.

umrennen *vt sep irreg* to (run into and) knock down.

umringen* *vt insep* to surround, to gather around; (*drängend*) to throng *or* crowd around. **von neugierigen Passanten umringt** surrounded/thronged by curious passers-by.

Umriß *m* outline; (*Kontur*) contour(s *pl*). **etw in Umrissen zeichnen/erzählen** to outline sth, to draw/tell sth in outline; **„Geschichte in Umrissen"** "History – A Brief Outline".

umrißhaft *adj* in outline.

Umrißzeichnung *f* outline drawing.

umrühren *vt sep* to stir. **etw unter ständigem U~ kochen** to boil sth stirring constantly *or* continually.

umrüsten *vt sep* **(a)** (*Tech*) to adapt. **etw auf etw** (*acc*) **~** to adapt *or* convert sth to sth. **(b)** (*Mil*) to re-equip.

ums *contr of* **um das**.

umsatteln *sep* 1 *vt Pferd* to resaddle. 2 *vi* (*inf*) (*beruflich*) to change jobs; (*Univ*) to change courses. **von etw auf etw** (*acc*) **~** to switch from sth to sth.

Umsatz *m* (*Comm*) turnover. **500 Mark ~ machen** (*inf*) to do 500 marks' worth of business.

Umsatz-: **~anstieg** *m* increase in turnover; **~beteiligung** *f* commission; **~rückgang** *m* drop in turnover; **~steuer** *f* sales tax.

umsäumen¹ *vt sep* *Stoffrand* to hem.

umsäumen²* *vt insep* to line; (*Sew*) to edge. **von Bäumen umsäumt** tree-lined.

umschaffen *vt sep irreg* (*geh*) to re-create, to transform.

umschalten *sep* 1 *vt* (*auf +acc* to) *Schalter* to flick; *Hebel* to turn; *Strom* to convert; *Gerät* to switch over. **den Schalter auf „heiß" ~** to put the switch to "hot".

2 *vi* to flick the/a switch; to push/pull a/the lever; (*auf anderen Sender*) to turn *or* change over (*auf +acc* to); (*im Denken, sich gewöhnen*) to change (*auf +acc* to); (*Aut*) to change (*Brit*), to shift (*in +acc* to). **„wir schalten jetzt um nach Hamburg"** "and now we go over *or* we're going over to Hamburg".

Umschalter *m* (*Elec*) (change-over) switch; (*von Schreibmaschine*) shift-key.

Umschalt-: **~pause** *f* (*Rad, TV*) intermission, break (*before going over to somewhere else*); **~taste** *f* shift-key.

Umschaltung *f* (*auf +acc* to) change-over; (*im Denken, Umgewöhnung*) change.

umschatten* *vt insep* (*geh*) **seine Augen waren umschattet** he had shadows *or* rings under his eyes.

Umschau *f, no pl* (*fig*) review; (*TV, Rad*) magazine programme. **~ halten** to look around (*nach* for).

umschauen *vr sep* *siehe* **umsehen**.

umschichten *sep* 1 *vt* to restack. 2 *vr* (*Sociol*) to restructure itself.

umschichtig *adv* on a shift basis. **~ arbeiten** to work in shifts.

Umschichtung *f* **(a)** restacking. **(b)** (*Sociol*) restructuring. **soziale ~** change of social stratification, social regrouping *or* restructuring.

umschießen *vt sep irreg* to (shoot at and) knock over.

umschiffen¹* *vt insep* to sail (a)round; *Kap auch* to round, to double (*spec*); *Erde auch* to circumnavigate; *siehe* **Klippe**.

umschiffen² *vt sep* to transfer; *Fracht auch* to transship.

Umschiffung¹ *f siehe* **umschiffen¹** sailing (a)round; rounding, doubling; circumnavigation. **die ~ einer gefährlichen Klippe** (*fig*) getting over a dangerous obstacle.

Umschiffung² *f siehe* **umschiffen²** transfer; transshipping, transshipment.

Umschlag *m* (a) (*Veränderung*) (sudden) change (+*gen* in, *in* +*acc* into).

(b) (*Hülle*) cover; (*Brief~*) envelope; (*als Verpackung*) wrapping; (*Buch~*) jacket.

(c) (*Med*) compress; (*Packung*) poultice.

(d) (*Ärmel~*) cuff; (*Hosen~*) turn-up (*Brit*), cuff (*US*).

(e) (*umgeschlagene Gütermenge*) volume of traffic. **einen hohen ~ an Baumwolle** *etc* **haben** to handle a lot of cotton *etc*.

(f) (*Umladung*) (*auf* +*acc* to) transfer, transshipment.

umschlagen *sep irreg* 1 *vt* (a) *Seite etc* to turn over; *Ärmel, Hosenbein, Saum* to turn up; *Teppich, Decke* to fold *or* turn back; *Kragen* to turn down.

(b) (*um die Schultern*) *Schal* to put on.

(c) (*umladen*) *Güter* to transfer, to transship. **etw vom Schiff auf die Bahn ~** to unload sth from the ship onto the train.

(d) (*absetzen*) *Güter* to handle.

2 *vi aux sein* (a) (*sich ändern*) to change (suddenly); (*Wind auch*) to veer round; (*Stimme*) to break, to crack. **in etw** (*acc*) **~** to change *or* turn into sth; **ins Gegenteil ~** to become the opposite.

(b) (*sauer werden*) to go off; (*Milch auch*) to turn.

Umschlag-: **~entwurf** *m* jacket design; **~hafen** *m* port of transshipment; **~klappe** *f* jacket flap (*of book*); **~platz** *m* trade centre; **~tuch** *nt* shawl, wrap (*esp US*).

umschleichen* *vt insep irreg* to creep *or* prowl around.

umschließen* *vt insep irreg* to surround (*auch Mil*), to enclose; (*mit den Armen*) to embrace (*mit* in); (*fig: Plan, Entwurf etc*) to include, to encompass.

umschlingen* *vt insep irreg* (a) (*Pflanze*) to twine (a)round.

(b) (*geh*) *jdn* (*mit den Armen*) **~** to enfold (*liter*) *or* clasp sb in one's arms, to embrace sb.

Umschlingung *f* (*geh*) embrace.

umschlungen *adj* **eng ~** with their *etc* arms tightly round each other.

Umschluß *m* (*in Strafanstalt*) recreation.

umschmeicheln* *vt insep* to flatter; (*fig*) to caress.

umschmeißen *vt sep irreg* (*inf*) (a) *siehe* **umhauen** (b, c). (b) **das schmeißt meine Pläne um** that mucks my plans up (*inf*).

umschmelzen *vt sep irreg* to recast.

umschnallen *vt sep* to buckle on.

umschreiben¹ *vt sep irreg* (a) *Text etc* to rewrite; (*in andere Schrift*) to transcribe (*auch Phon*), to transliterate; (*bearbeiten*) *Theaterstück etc* to adapt (*für* for).

(b) (*umbuchen*) to alter, to change (*auf* +*acc* for).

(c) *Hypothek etc* to transfer. **etw auf jdn ~/~ lassen** to transfer sth/have sth transferred to sb or sb's name.

umschreiben²* *vt insep irreg* (a) (*mit anderen Worten ausdrücken*) to paraphrase; (*darlegen*) to outline, to describe; (*abgrenzen*) to circumscribe; (*verhüllen*) *Sachverhalt* to refer to obliquely, to skate around (*inf*). (b) (*Ling*) *Verneinung etc* to construct.

Umschreibung¹ *f siehe* **umschreiben¹** rewriting; transcription (*auch Phon*), transliteration; adaptation; altering, changing; transfer.

Umschreibung² *f siehe* **umschreiben²** (a) *no pl* paraphrasing; outlining, description; circumscribing, circumscription; oblique reference (*gen* to). (b) *no pl* construction. (c) (*das Umschriebene*) paraphrase; outline, description; circumscription; oblique reference (*gen* to); circumlocution.

Umschrift *f* (a) (*auf Münze*) inscription, circumscription. (b) (*Ling: Transkription*) transcription (*auch Phon*), transliteration.

umschulden *vt sep* (*Comm*) *Kredit* to convert, to fund. **ein Unternehmen ~** to change the terms of a firm's debt(s).

Umschuldung *f* funding *no pl*.

umschulen *vt sep* (a) to retrain; (*Pol euph*) to re-educate. (b) (*auf andere Schule*) to transfer (to another school).

Umschüler *m* student for retraining.

Umschulung *f* retraining; re-education; transfer.

umschütten *vt sep* to spill, to upset. **etw aus einer Dose in eine Kanne ~** to pour sth from a can into a jug.

umschwärmen* *vt insep* to swarm (a)round; (*Menschen auch*) to flock (a)round; (*verehren*) to idolize. **von Verehrern umschwärmt werden** (*fig*) to be besieged *or* surrounded by admirers; **eine umschwärmte Schönheit** a much-courted beauty.

umschweben* *vt insep* (*geh*) to float *or* hover about.

Umschweife *pl* **ohne ~** straight out, plainly; **mach keine ~!** don't beat about the bush, come (straight) to the point.

umschwenken *vi sep* (a) *aux sein or haben* (*Anhänger, Kran*) to swing out; (*fig*) to do an about-face *or* about-turn. **der Kran schwenkte nach rechts um** the crane swung to the right. (b) (*Wind*) to veer (round).

umschwirren* *vt insep* (*lit, fig*) to buzz (a)round.

Umschwung *m* (a) (*Gymnastik*) circle. (b) (*fig*) (*Veränderung*) drastic change; (*ins Gegenteil*) reversal, about-turn. **ein ~ zum Besseren** a drastic change for the better.

umsegeln* *vt insep* to sail round; *Kap auch* to round, to double (*spec*); *Erde auch* to circumnavigate.

Umseg(e)lung *f siehe vt* sailing round; rounding, doubling (*spec*); circumnavigation.

umsehen *vr sep irreg* to look around (*nach* for); (*rückwärts*) to look round *or* back. **sich in der Stadt ~** to have a look (a)round the town; **sich in der Welt ~** to see something of the world; **ich möchte mich nur mal ~** (*in Geschäft*) I'm just looking, I just wanted to have a look (around); **ohne mich wird er sich noch ~**

(*inf*) he'll just have to see how he manages without me.

umsein *vi sep irreg aux sein* (*Zusammenschreibung nur bei infin und ptp*) (*Frist, Zeit*) to be up.

Umseite *f* (*Press*) page two. **auf der ~** on page two.

umseitig *adj* overleaf. **die ~e Abbildung** the illustration overleaf.

umseits *adv* (*form*) overleaf.

umsetzen *sep* 1 *vt* (a) *Pflanzen* to transplant; *Topfpflanze* to repot; *Schüler* to move (to another seat).

(b) *Waren* to turn over.

(c) (*Typ*) to re-set.

(d) **etw in etw** (*acc*) **~** to convert sth into sth; (*Mus: transponieren*) to transpose sth into sth; (*in Verse etc*) to render *or* translate sth into sth; **sein Geld in Briefmarken/Alkohol ~** to spend all one's money on stamps/alcohol; **etw in die Tat ~** to translate sth into action.

2 *vr* (*Schüler*) to change seats *or* places. **sich in etw** (*acc*) **~** to be converted into sth.

Umsichgreifen *nt* **-s**, *no pl* spread.

Umsicht *f siehe* **umsichtig** circumspection, prudence; judiciousness.

umsichtig *adj* circumspect, prudent; *Handlungsweise etc auch* judicious.

Umsichtigkeit *f siehe* **Umsicht**.

umsiedeln *vti sep* (*vi: aux sein*) to resettle. **von einem Ort an einen anderen ~** to move from one place and settle in another.

Umsied(e)lung *f* resettlement.

Umsiedler *m* resettler.

umsinken *vi sep irreg aux sein* (*geh*) to sink to the ground. **vor Müdigkeit ~** to drop with exhaustion.

umso *conj* (*Aus*) = **um so**.

umsomehr *adv* (*Aus*) = **um so mehr**.

umsonst *adv* (a) (*unentgeltlich*) free, for nothing, free of charge (*esp Comm*). **~ sein** to be free (of charge); **das hast du nicht ~ getan!** you'll pay for that, I'll get even with you for that; **~ ist nur der Tod(, und der kostet das Leben)** (*Prov*) you don't get anything for nothing in this world.

(b) (*vergebens*) in vain, to no avail; (*erfolglos*) without success.

(c) (*ohne Grund*) for nothing. **nicht ~** not for nothing, not without reason.

umsorgen* *vt insep* to care for, to look after.

umsoweniger *adv* (*Aus*) = **um so weniger**.

umspannen¹* *vt insep* (a) **etw mit beiden Armen/der Hand ~** to get both arms/one's hand (all the way) round sth. (b) (*fig*) *Bereich* to encompass, to embrace.

umspannen² *vt sep* (a) *Pferde* to change. (b) (*Elec*) to transform.

Umspanner *m* **-s**, **-** (*Elec*) transformer.

Umspann-: **~station** *f*, **~werk** *nt* (*Elec*) transformer (station).

umspielen* *vt insep* (a) (*geh*) (*Rock etc*) to swirl about; (*Lächeln*) to play about; (*Wellen*) to lap about. (b) (*Ftbl*) to dribble round, to take out (*inf*).

Umspringbild *nt* (*Psych*) dual-aspect picture.

umspringen¹ *vi sep irreg aux sein* (a) (*Wind*) to veer round (*nach* to), to change; (*Bild*) to change. (b) (*Ski*) to jump-turn. (c) **mit jdm grob** *etc* **~** (*inf*) to treat sb roughly *etc*, to be rough with sb; **so kannst du nicht mit ihr ~!** (*inf*) you can't treat her like that!

umspringen²* *vt insep irreg* to jump about, to leap around.

umspulen *vt sep* to rewind.

umspülen* *vt insep* to wash round.

Umstand *m* **-(e)s**, **Umstände** (a) (*circumstance*); (*Tatsache*) fact. **ein unvorhergesehener ~** something unforeseen, unforeseen circumstances; **den Umständen entsprechend** much as one would expect (under the circumstances); **es geht ihm den Umständen entsprechend (gut)** he is as well as can be expected (under the circumstances); **nähere/die näheren Umstände** further details; **in anderen Umständen sein** to be expecting, to be in the family way; **je nach den Umständen as circumstances dictate**; **unter diesen/keinen/anderen Umständen** under these/no/any other circumstances; **unter Umständen** possibly; **unter allen Umständen** at all costs; **wenn es die Umstände erlauben** ... if circumstances permit *or* allow ...

(b) **Umstände** *pl* (*Mühe, Schwierigkeiten*) bother *sing*, trouble *sing*; (*Förmlichkeit*) fuss *sing*; **ohne (große) Umstände** without (much) fuss, without a (great) fuss; **das macht gar keine Umstände** it's no bother *or* trouble at all; **jdm Umstände machen** *or* **bereiten** to cause sb bother *or* trouble, to put sb out; **machen Sie bloß keine Umstände!** please don't go to any bother *or* trouble, please don't put yourself out; **einen ~ machen** to make a fuss (*mit* over).

umständehalber *adv* owing to circumstances. „**~ zu verkaufen**" "forced to sell".

umständlich *adj* *Arbeitsweise, Methode* (awkward and) involved; (*langsam und ungeschickt*) ponderous; *Vorbereitung* elaborate; *Erklärung, Übersetzung, Anleitung* long-winded; *Abfertigung* laborious, tedious; *Arbeit, Reise* awkward. **sei doch nicht so ~!** don't make such heavy weather of everything!, don't make everything twice as hard as it really is!; **er ist fürchterlich ~** he always makes such heavy weather of everything; **etw ~ machen** to make heavy weather of doing sth; **etw ~ erzählen/erklären/beschreiben** *etc* to tell/explain/describe *etc* sth in a roundabout way; **das ist vielleicht ~ what a palaver** (*inf*); **das ist mir zu ~** that's too much palaver (*inf*) *or* trouble *or* bother; **sich ~ von jdm verabschieden** to take one's leave of sb very ceremoniously.

Umständlichkeit *f siehe adj* involvedness; ponderousness; elaborateness; long-windedness; laboriousness, tediousness; awkwardness. **ihre ~** the way she makes such heavy weather of everything.

Umstands-: ~bestimmung *f* adverbial phrase; ~kandidat, ~kasten (*inf*) *m* fusspot (*inf*), fussbudget (*US inf*); ~kleid *nt* maternity dress; ~kleidung *f* maternity wear; ~kommissar, ~krämer *m* (*inf*) fusspot (*inf*), fussbudget (*US inf*); ~moden *pl* maternity fashions *pl*; ~wort *nt* adverb.

umstecken *vt sep* (a) (*Elec*) *Kontakt etc* to move; *Gerät etc auch* to plug into another socket. (b) *Kleid, Saum* to pin up. (c) *Pflanzen* to transplant.

umstehen* *vt insep irreg* to surround, to stand round. **ein von Bäumen umstandener Teich** a pond surrounded by trees.

umstehend 1 *adj attr* (a) (*in der Nähe stehend*) standing round about. **die U~en** the bystanders, the people standing round about. (b) (*umseitig*) overleaf. **die ~e Erklärung** the explanation overleaf; **im ~en** overleaf; **beachten Sie bitte auch ~es** *or* **das U~e** see also overleaf. **2** *adv* overleaf.

Umsteige-: ~bahnhof *m* interchange (station); ~berechtigung *f* **mit diesem Fahrschein haben Sie keine ~berechtigung** you can't change (buses/trains) on this ticket; ~fahrschein *m* transfer ticket; ~möglichkeit *f* **dort haben Sie ~möglichkeit** you can change there (*nach* for).

umsteigen *vi sep irreg aux sein* (a) to change (*nach* for); (*in Bus, Zug etc*) to change (buses/trains *etc*). **bitte hier ~ nach Eppendorf** (all) change here for Eppendorf; **in einen anderen Wagen/von einem Auto ins andere ~** to change *or* switch carriages/cars; **bitte beim U~ beeilen!** will those passengers changing here please do so quickly. (b) (*fig inf*) to change over, to switch (over) (*auf* + *acc* to).

Umsteiger *m -s, -* (*inf*) transfer (ticket).

umstellen¹ *sep 1 vti* (a) *Möbel etc* to rearrange, to change round; (*Gram*) *Wörter, Satz auch* to reorder; *Subjekt und Prädikat* to transpose.
(b) (*anders einstellen*) *Hebel, Telefon, Fernsehgerät, Betrieb* to switch over; *Radio* to tune *or* switch to another station; *Uhr* to alter, to put back/forward. **auf etw (*acc*) ~ (*Betrieb*)** to go or switch over to sth; *auf Erdgas etc* to convert *or* be converted to sth; **etw auf Computer ~** to computerize sth; **der Betrieb wird auf die Produktion von Turbinen umgestellt** the factory is switching over to producing turbines.
2 *vr* to move *or* shift about; (*fig*) to get used to a different lifestyle. **sich auf etw (*acc*) ~** to adapt or adjust to sth.

umstellen²* *vt insep* to surround.

Umstellung *f siehe* umstellen¹ 1 (a) rearrangement, changing round; reordering; transposition.
(b) switch-over; tuning to another station; alteration, putting back/forward. **~ auf Erdgas** conversion to natural gas; **~ auf Computer** computerization.
(c) (*fig: das Sichumstellen*) adjustment (*auf* + *acc* to). **das wird eine große ~ für ihn sein** it will be a big change for him.

umsteuern¹ *vt sep Satelliten etc* to alter the course of.

umsteuern²* *vt insep Hindernis* to steer round.

umstimmen *vt sep* (a) *Instrument* to tune to a different pitch, to retune. (b) **jdn ~** to change sb's mind; **er war nicht umzustimmen, er ließ sich nicht ~** he was not to be persuaded.

umstoßen *vt sep irreg Gegenstand* to knock over; (*fig*) (*Mensch*) *Plan, Testament, Bestimmung etc* to change; (*Umstände etc*) *Plan, Berechnung* to upset.

umstrahlen* *vt insep* (*liter*) to shine around. **von einem Heiligenschein umstrahlt** surrounded *or* illuminated by a halo.

umstritten *adj* (*fraglich*) controversial; (*wird noch debattiert*) disputed.

umstrukturieren* *vt sep* to restructure.

Umstrukturierung *f* restructuring.

umstülpen *vt sep* to turn upside down; *Tasche* to turn out; *Manschetten etc* to turn up *or* back.

Umsturz *m* coup (d'état), putsch.

Umsturzbewegung *f* subversive movement.

umstürzen *sep 1 vt Puddingform etc* to turn upside down; (*fig*) *Regierung, Staat, Verfassung* to overthrow; *Demokratie* to destroy. **~de Veränderungen** revolutionary changes. **2** *vi aux sein* to fall; (*Möbelstück, Wagen etc*) to overturn.

Umstürzler(in *f*) *m -s, -* subversive.

umstürzlerisch *adj* subversive. **sich ~ betätigen** to engage in subversive activities.

Umsturzversuch *m* attempted coup *or* putsch.

umtanzen* *vt insep* to dance round.

umtaufen *vt sep* to rebaptize; (*umbenennen*) to rename, to rechristen.

Umtausch *m* exchange. **diese Waren sind vom ~ ausgeschlossen** these goods cannot be exchanged; **beim ~ bitte den Kassenzettel vorlegen** please produce the receipt when exchanging goods.

umtauschen *vt sep* to (ex)change; *Geld* to change, to convert (*form*) (*in* + *acc* into).

umtopfen *vt sep Blumen etc* to repot.

umtost *adj* (*liter*) buffeted (*von* by).

umtreten *vt sep irreg* to tread down.

Umtriebe *pl* machinations *pl*. **umstürzlerische ~** subversive activities.

Umtrunk *m* drink.

umtun *vr sep irreg* (*inf*) to look around (*nach* for).

U-Musik *f abbr of* Unterhaltungsmusik.

umverteilen* *vt sep or insep* to redistribute.

Umverteilung *f* redistribution.

umwachsen* *vt insep irreg* to grow round. **ein von Bäumen ~er Teich** a pond with trees growing all round it.

Umwallung *f* ramparts *pl*.

Umwälz\anlage *f* circulating plant.

umwälzen *vt sep Luft, Wasser* to circulate; (*fig*) to change radically, to revolutionize.

umwälzend *adj* (*fig*) radical; *Veränderungen auch* sweeping; *Ereignisse* revolutionary.

Umwälzpumpe *f* circulating pump.

Umwälzung *f* (*Tech*) circulation; (*fig*) radical change.

umwandelbar *adj* (*in* + *acc* to) convertible; *Strafe* commutable.

umwandeln¹ *sep 1 vt* to change (*in* + *acc* into); (*Comm, Fin, Sci*) to convert (*in* + *acc* to); (*Jur*) *Strafe* to commute (*in* + *acc* to); (*fig*) to transform (*in* + *acc* into). **er ist wie umgewandelt** he's a changed man *or* a (completely) different person. **2** *vr* to be converted (*in* + *acc* into).

umwandeln*² *vt insep* (*liter*) to walk round.

Umwandlung *f siehe* unwandeln¹ change; conversion; commutation; transformation.

umweben* *vt insep irreg* (*liter*) to envelop. **viele Sagen umwoben das alte Schloß** many legends had been woven round the old castle; **ein von Sagen umwobener Ort** a place around which many legends have been woven.

umwechseln *vt sep Geld* to change (*in* + *acc* to, into).

Umwechslung *f* exchange (*in* + *acc* for).

Umweg ['ʊmveːk] *m* detour; (*fig*) roundabout way. **einen ~ machen/fahren** to go a long way round; (*absichtlich auch*) to make a detour; **wenn das für Sie kein ~ ist** if it doesn't take you out of your way; **auf ~en** (*ans Ziel kommen*) (to get there) by a roundabout *or* circuitous route; (*fig*) (to get there) in a rather roundabout way; **er ist auf ~en in den Schuldienst gekommen** he didn't go straight into teaching by any means; **auf dem ~ über jdn** (*fig*) indirectly via sb; **etw auf ~en erfahren** (*fig*) to find sth out indirectly.

umwehen¹* *vt insep* to fan, to blow round. **sich vom Wind ~ lassen** to be fanned by the breeze.

umwehen² *vt sep* to blow over.

Umwelt *f, no pl* environment.

Umwelt- *in cpds* environmental; **u~bedingt** *adj* caused by the environment; ~belastung *f* ecological damage, damage to the environment; ~erziehung *f* education in environmental problems; **u~feindlich** *adj* ecologically harmful, damaging to the environment; **u~freundlich** *adj* ecologically harmless, harmless to the environment; **u~geschädigt** *adj* environmentally deprived; **u~gestört** *adj* (*Psych*) maladjusted (*due to adverse social factors*); ~krankheiten *pl* diseases *pl* caused by pollution; ~kriminalität *f* environmental crimes *pl*; ~krise *f* ecological crisis; ~planung *f* ecological planning; ~politik *f* ecological policy; **u~schädlich** *adj* ecologically harmful, harmful to the environment; ~schutz *m* conservation *no art*; ~schützer *m* conservationist, environmentalist; ~sünder *m* (*inf*) pollutionist (*hum*); ~verschmutzung *f* pollution (of the environment); ~verseuchung *f* contamination of the environment; ~verstöße *pl* environmental offences *pl*.

umwenden *sep irreg 1 vt* to turn over. **2** *vr* to turn (round) (*nach* to).

umwerben* *vt insep irreg* to court.

umwerfen *vt sep irreg* (a) *Gegenstand* to knock over; *Möbelstück etc* to overturn.
(b) (*fig: ändern*) to upset, to knock on the head (*inf*).
(c) *jdn* (*körperlich*) to knock down; (*Ringen*) to throw down; (*fig inf*) to stun, to bowl over. **ein Whisky wirft dich nicht gleich um** one whisky won't knock you out.
(d) **sich** (*dat*) **etw ~** to throw *or* put sth round one's shoulders.

umwerfend *adj* fantastic. **von ~er Komik** hilarious, a scream (*inf*).

Umwertung *f* re-evaluation.

umwickeln¹* *vt insep* to wrap round; (*mit Band, Verband auch*) to swathe (*liter*) (*mit* in); (*mit Schnur, Draht etc*) to wind round. **etw mit Stoff/Draht ~** to wrap cloth/wind wire round sth.

umwickeln² *vt sep* to wrap round; (*Garn etc*) to rewind. **jdm/sich etw ~** to wrap sth round sb/oneself.

umwidmen *vt sep* (*Admin*) to re-allocate.

umwinden* *vt insep irreg* (*geh*) to wind round (*mit* with). **etw mit Blumen ~** to entwine sth with flowers.

umwittert *adj* (*geh*) surrounded (*von* by). **von Geheimnissen ~** shrouded in mystery.

umwogen* *vt insep* (*liter*) to wash round.

umwohnend *adj* neighbouring. **die U~en** the local residents.

Umwohner *pl* local residents *pl*.

umwölken* *vr insep* (*geh*) to cloud over; (*Sonne, Mond auch*) to become veiled in cloud (*liter*), to darken; (*Berggipfel*) to become shrouded in cloud; (*fig: Stern*) to cloud.

umwühlen *vt sep* to churn up.

umzäunen* *vt insep* to fence round.

Umzäunung *f* (*das Umzäunen*) fencing round; (*Zaun*) fence, fencing.

umziehen¹ *sep irreg 1 vi aux sein* to move (house); (*Firma etc*) to move. **nach Köln ~** to move to Cologne. **2** *vt* (a) **die Kinder ~** to get the children changed. (b) (*hum: den Umzug für jdn durchführen*) to move. **3** *vr* to change, to get changed.

umziehen²* *insep irreg* (*geh*) **1** *vt* to surround. **2** *vr* (*Himmel*) to cloud over (*auch fig*), to become overcast *or* cloudy.

umzingeln* *vt insep* to surround, to encircle.

Umzingelung *f* encirclement.

Umzug ['ʊmtsuːk] *m* (a) (*Wohnungs~*) move, removal. **wann soll euer ~ sein?** when are you moving? (b) (*Festzug*) procession; (*Demonstrationszug*) parade.

Umzugskosten *pl* removal costs *pl*.

UN [uːˈʔɛn] *pl* UN *sing*, United Nations *sing*.

un\abänderlich *adj* (a) (*unwiderruflich*) unalterable; *Entschluß, Urteil auch* irrevocable, irreversible. **~ feststehen** to be absolutely certain. (b) (*ewig*) *Gesetze, Schicksal* immutable.

Un|ab|änderlichkeit *f siehe adj* (a) unalterability; irrevocability, irreversibility. (b) immutability.

un|abdingbar, un|abdinglich *adj Voraussetzung, Forderung* indispensable; *Recht* inalienable.

Un|abdingbarkeit *f siehe adj* indispensability; inalienability.

un-: ~abgelegt *adj* unfiled; ~abgeschlossen *adj* (*nicht verschlossen*) unlocked; (*nicht fertiggestellt*) unfinished.

un|abhängig *adj* independent (*von* of); *Journalist* freelance. das ist ~ davon, ob/wann *etc* that does not depend on *or* is not dependent on whether/when *etc*; ~ davon, was Sie meinen irrespective of *or* regardless of what you think; sich ~ machen to go one's own way; sich von jdm/etw ~ machen to become independent of sb/sth.

Un|abhängigkeit *f* independence.

Un|abhängigkeits-: ~bewegung *f* independence movement; ~erklärung *f* declaration of independence; ~krieg *m* war of independence.

un|abkömmlich *adj* (*geh*) busy, engaged *pred* (*form*).

un|ablässig *adj* continual; *Regen, Lärm etc auch* incessant; *Versuche, Bemühungen auch* unremitting, unceasing. ~ für den Frieden kämpfen to fight unceasingly for peace.

un|absehbar *adj* (a) (*fig*) *Folgen etc* unforeseeable; *Schaden* incalculable, immeasurable. der Schaden/die Zahl der Toten ist noch ~ the amount of damage/the number of dead is not yet known; auf ~e Zeit for an indefinite period.
(b) (*lit*) interminable; *Weite* boundless. ~ lang sein to seem to be interminable; in ~er Weite boundlessly; in ~er Ferne in the far far distance.

Un|absehbarkeit *f siehe adj* (a) unforeseeability; incalculability, immeasurability. (b) interminability; boundlessness.

Un-: u~absichtlich *adj* unintentional; (*aus Versehen auch*) accidental; u~abwählbar *adj* er ist u~abwählbar he cannot be voted out of office; u~abweisbar, u~abweislich *adj* irrefutable; u~abwendbar *adj* inevitable; ~abwendbarkeit *f* inevitability; u~achtsam *adj* (*unaufmerksam*) inattentive; (*nicht sorgsam*) careless; (*unbedacht*) thoughtless; ~achtsamkeit *f siehe adj* inattentiveness; carelessness; thoughtlessness.

un|ähnlich *adj* dissimilar. einer Sache (*dat*) ~ sein to be unlike sth *or* dissimilar to sth; einander ~ unlike each other, dissimilar.

Un|ähnlichkeit *f* dissimilarity.

Un-: u~anfechtbar *adj Urteil, Entscheidung, Gesetz* unchallengeable, incontestable; *Argument etc* unassailable; *Beweis* irrefutable; ~anfechtbarkeit *f siehe adj* unchallengeability, incontestability; unassailability; irrefutability; u~angebracht *adj Bescheidenheit, Bemerkung* uncalled-for; *Sorge, Sparsamkeit, Bemühungen auch* misplaced; (*für Kinder, Altersstufe etc*) unsuitable; (*unzweckmäßig*) *Maßnahmen* inappropriate; u~angefochten *adj* unchallenged *no adv*; *Testament, Wahlkandidat* uncontested; *Urteil, Entscheidung auch* undisputed, uncontested; Liverpool führt u~angefochten die Tabelle Liverpool are unchallenged at the top of the league; u~angemeldet *adj* unannounced *no adv*; *Besucher* unexpected; *Patient etc* without an appointment.

un|angemessen *adj* (*zu hoch*) unreasonable, out of all proportion; (*unzulänglich*) inadequate. einer Sache (*dat*) ~ sein to be inappropriate to sth; dem Ereignis ~ sein to be unsuitable for *or* inappropriate to the occasion, to ill befit the occasion.

un|angenehm *adj* unpleasant; *Mensch, Arbeit, Geschmack, Geruch auch* disagreeable; (*peinlich*) *Situation auch* awkward, embarrassing; *Zwischenfall, Begegnung* embarrassing. das ist mir immer so ~ I never like that, I don't like that at all; es war mir ~, das tun zu müssen I didn't like having to do it; es ist mir ~, daß ich Sie gestört habe I feel bad about having disturbed you; mein ständiges Husten war mir ~ I felt bad *or* embarrassed about coughing all the time; ~ berührt sein to be embarrassed (*von* by); er kann ~ werden he can get quite nasty.

un-: ~angepaßt *adj* non-conformist; ~angetastet *adj* untouched; ~angetastet bleiben (*Rechte*) not to be violated; ~angezogen *adj* not dressed; so ~angezogen kann ich doch nicht ins Theater gehen I can't go to the theatre like this – I'm not dressed decently; ~angreifbar *adj Macht, Herrscher* unassailable; *Argument auch* irrefutable, unchallengeable; *Festung, Land* impregnable; ~annehmbar *adj* unacceptable.

Un|annehmlichkeit *f usu pl* trouble *no pl*; (*lästige Mühe auch*) bother *no pl*. ~en haben/bekommen *or* kriegen to be in/to get into trouble; das macht mir nicht die geringste ~ it's no trouble *or* bother at all; mit etw ~en haben to have a lot of trouble with sth; mit den Behörden ~en haben to get into trouble with the authorities.

un|ansehnlich *adj* unsightly; *Frau etc* plain; *Tapete, Möbel* shabby; *Nahrungsmittel* unappetizing.

un|anständig *adj* (a) (*unkultiviert, unerzogen*) ill-mannered, bad-mannered; (*frech, unverschämt*) rude; (*charakterlich minderwertig*) unprincipled. so was U~es! how rude!
(b) (*obszön, anstößig*) dirty; *Witz, Lied auch* rude; *Wörter auch* four-letter *attr*, rude; (*vulgär*) *Kleidung* indecent. ~e Reden führen to talk smut.

Un|anständigkeit *f siehe adj* (a) bad *or* ill manners *pl*; rudeness *no pl*; unprincipledness *no pl*. (b) dirtiness; rudeness; indecency. ~en erzählen to tell dirty jokes/stories.

Un-: u~antastbar *adj* (*nicht zu verletzen*) inviolable, sacrosanct; (*über Zweifel erhaben*) unimpeachable; ~antastbarkeit *f siehe adj* inviolability; unimpeachability; u~appetitlich *adj* (*lit, fig*) unappetizing.

un|art *f* bad habit; (*Ungezogenheit*) rude habit.

un|artig *adj* naughty.

Un|artigkeit *f* (a) *no pl* (*Unartigsein*) naughtiness. (b) (*Handlungsweise*) naughty behaviour *no pl* or trick.

Un-: u~artikuliert *adj* inarticulate; (*undeutlich*) unclear, indistinct; u~ästhetisch *adj* unappetizing; u~aufdringlich *adj* unobtrusive; *Parfüm auch* discreet; *Mensch* unassuming; ~aufdringlichkeit *f siehe adj* unobtrusiveness; discreetness; unassuming nature.

un|auffällig 1 *adj* inconspicuous; (*unscheinbar, schlicht*) unobtrusive. die Narbe/sein Hinken ist ziemlich ~ the scar/his limp isn't very noticeable; er ist ein ziemlich ~er junger Mann he's not the kind of young man you notice particularly. 2 *adv* unobtrusively, discreetly; *siehe* folgen.

Un|auffälligkeit *f siehe adj* inconspicuousness; unobtrusiveness.

un|auffindbar *adj* nowhere to be found; *Verbrecher, vermißte Person* untraceable.

un|aufgefordert 1 *adj* unsolicited (*esp Comm*). seine ~e Schadensersatzzahlung the fact that he paid for the damage without being asked.
2 *adv* without being asked. ~ anfallende Arbeiten erledigen können to be able to work on one's own initiative; jdm ~ Prospekte zuschicken to send sb unsolicited brochures; ~ zugesandte Manuskripte unsolicited manuscripts.

Un-: u~aufgeklärt *adj* (a) unexplained; *Verbrechen* unsolved; (b) *Mensch* ignorant; (*sexuell*) ignorant of the facts of life; u~aufgeräumt *adj* untidy; u~aufgeschlossen *adj* (*engstirnig*) narrow-minded; (*nicht empfänglich*) hidebound; einer Sache gegenüber u~aufgeschlossen sein to be closed *or* not to be receptive to sth; ~aufgeschlossenheit *f siehe adj* narrow-mindedness; hidebound nature; seine ~aufgeschlossenheit gegenüber allem Neuen the way he's closed to anything new; u~aufhaltbar *adj* unstoppable; u~aufhaltsam *adj* (a) (*unaufhaltbar*) unstoppable; (b) (*unerbittlich*) inexorable; u~aufhörlich *adj* continual, constant, incessant; u~auflösbar, u~auflöslich *adj* (*Math*) insoluble; (*Chem auch*), *Ehe* indissoluble; ~auflösbarkeit, ~auflöslichkeit *f siehe adj* insolubility; indissolubility; u~aufmerksam *adj* inattentive; (*flüchtig*) *Leser etc* unobservant; da war ich einen Augenblick u~aufmerksam I didn't pay attention for a moment; ~aufmerksamkeit *f siehe adj* inattentiveness; unobservance; u~aufrichtig *adj* insincere; ~aufrichtigkeit *f* insincerity; u~aufschiebbar *adj* urgent; es ist u~aufschiebbar it can't be put off *or* delayed *or* postponed; u~ausbleiblich *adj* inevitable, unavoidable; u~ausdenkbar *adj* unimaginable, unthinkable; u~ausführbar *adj* impracticable, unfeasible; u~ausgefüllt *adj* (a) *Formular etc* blank; (b) *Leben, Mensch* unfulfilled.

un|ausgeglichen *adj* unbalanced; *Verhältnis auch*, *Vermögensverteilung etc* unequal; *Stil auch* disharmonious; *Mensch* (*launisch*) moody; (*verhaltensgestört*) unstable. ein Mensch mit ~em Wesen a person of uneven temper.

Un|ausgeglichenheit *f siehe adj* imbalance; inequality; disharmony; moodiness; instability. die ~ seines Wesens the unevenness of his temper.

Un-: u~ausgegoren *adj* immature; *Idee, Plan auch* half-baked (*inf*); *Jüngling auch* callow; ~ausgegorenheit *f siehe adj* immaturity; callowness; u~ausgeschlafen *adj* tired; er ist u~ausgeschlafen/sieht u~ausgeschlafen aus he hasn't had/ looks as if he hasn't had enough sleep; u~ausgesetzt *adj* incessant, constant, continual; u~ausgesprochen *adj* unsaid *pred*, unspoken; u~ausgewogen *adj* unbalanced; ~ausgewogenheit *f* imbalance; u~auslöschlich *adj* (*geh*) (*lit, fig*) indelible; u~ausrottbar *adj Unkraut* indestructible; (*fig*) *Vorurteile, Vorstellung etc* ineradicable; ~ausrottbarkeit *f* (*fig*) ineradicability; u~aussprechbar *adj* unpronounceable.

unaussprechlich *adj* (a) *Wort, Laut* unpronounceable. (b) *Schönheit, Leid etc* inexpressible. er verehrt sie ~ he absolutely worships her. (c) (*liter: ungeheuerlich*) *Tat, Verbrechen* unspeakable. (d) die U~en (*hum*) one's unmentionables (*inf*).

Un-: u~ausstehlich *adj* intolerable; *Mensch, Art, Eigenschaft auch* insufferable; u~ausweichlich *adj* unavoidable, inevitable; *Folgen auch* inescapable; ~ausweichlichkeit *f* inevitability; (*Dilemma*) dilemma.

unbändig *adj* (a) (*ausgelassen, ungestüm*) *Kind* boisterous. sie freuten sich ~ they were dancing around (with joy). (b) (*ungezügelt*) unrestrained *no adv*; *Haß, Zorn etc auch* unbridled *no adv*; *Hunger* enormous.

Un-: u~bar *adj* (*Comm*) etw u~bar bezahlen not to pay sth in cash, to pay sth by cheque/credit card *etc*; u~bare Zahlungsweise non-cash payment; u~barmherzig *adj* merciless; *Mensch auch* pitiless; ~barmherzigkeit *f siehe adj* mercilessness; pitilessness; u~beabsichtigt *adj* unintentional.

unbe|achtet *adj* unnoticed; *Warnung, Vorschläge* unheeded. jdn/etw ~ lassen not to take any notice of sb/sth; wollen wir die weniger wichtigen Punkte zunächst ~ lassen let's leave aside the less important points for the time being; das dürfen wir nicht ~ lassen we mustn't overlook that, we mustn't leave that out of account.

Un-: u~beachtlich *adj* insignificant; u~beanstandet 1 *adj* not objected to; etw u~beanstandet lassen to let sth pass *or* go; 2 *adv* without objection; das Paket wurde u~beanstandet weitergeleitet the parcel got through without any problems; u~beantwortet *adj* unanswered; u~bebaut *adj Land* undeveloped; *Grundstück* vacant; *Feld* uncultivated; u~bedacht *adj* (*hastig*) rash; (*unüberlegt*) thoughtless; ~bedachtheit *f* rashness; thoughtlessness; u~bedachtsam *adj* siehe u~bedacht; u~bedarft *adj* (*inf*) simple-minded; *Mensch* (*auf bestimmtem Gebiet*) green (*inf*), clueless (*inf*); (*dumm*) dumb (*inf*); u~bedeckt *adj* bare; u~bedeckten Hauptes (*geh*) with u~bedecktem Haupt (*geh*) bare-headed.

unbedenklich 1 *adj* (*ungefährlich*) completely harmless, quite safe; (*sorglos*) thoughtless. 2 *adv* (*ungefährlich*) quite safely, without coming to any harm; (*ohne zu zögern*) without thinking (twice *inf*).

Unbedenklichkeit f siehe adj harmlessness; thoughtlessness.

Unbedenklichkeitsbescheinigung f (Jur) document certifying that one has no taxes, loans etc outstanding.

Un-: u~bedeutend adj (unwichtig) insignificant, unimportant; (geringfügig) Rückgang, Änderung etc minor, minimal; ~bedeutendheit f insignificance.

unbedingt 1 adj attr (absolut) Ruhe, Verschwiegenheit absolute; (bedingungslos) Gehorsam, Treue auch implicit, unconditional; Anhänger etc unreserved; Reflex unconditioned.

2 adv (auf jeden Fall) really; wichtig, erforderlich absolutely. ich muß ~ mal wieder ins Kino gehen I really must go to the cinema again; ich mußte sie ~ sprechen I really or absolutely had to speak to her; (äußerst wichtig) it was imperative that I spoke to her; müßt ihr denn ~ in meinem Arbeitszimmer spielen? do you have to play in my study?; das ist nicht meine Schuld, du wolltest ja ~ ins Kino gehen! it's not my fault, you would go to the cinema or you were (hell-)bent on going to the cinema; er wollte ~ mit Renate verreisen he was (hell-)bent on going away with Renate; ~! of course!, I should say so!; nicht ~ not necessarily; nicht ~ nötig not absolutely or strictly necessary.

Unbedingtheit f (Bedingungslosigkeit) unconditionalness; (von Treue, Vertrauen auch) absoluteness.

Un-: u~beeidigt adj (Jur) unsworn usu attr, not on oath; u~beeindruckt adj unimpressed; u~beeinflußbar adj Entwicklung unalterable; Mensch unswayable, uninfluenceable; u~beeinflußt adj uninfluenced (von by); u~befahrbar adj Straße, Weg impassable; Gewässer unnavigable; „Seitenstreifen/Bankette u~befahrbar" "soft verges (Brit) or shoulder (US)"; u~befahren adj Straße, Weg unfrequented; Seeweg, Fluß unused; u~befangen adj (a) (unparteiisch) impartial, unbiased no adv, objective; (b) (natürlich) natural; (ungehemmt) uninhibited; u~befangenheit f siehe adj (a) impartiality, objectiveness; (b) naturalness; uninhibitedness; u~befleckt adj (liter) spotless, unsullied, untarnished; Jungfrau undefiled; die ~befleckte Empfängnis the Immaculate Conception; u~befriedigend adj unsatisfactory; u~befriedigt adj (frustriert) unsatisfied; (unerfüllt auch) unfulfilled; (unzufrieden) dissatisfied; u~befristet adj Arbeitsverhältnis, Vertrag for an indefinite period; Aufenthaltserlaubnis, Visum permanent; etw u~befristet verlängern to extend sth indefinitely or for an indefinite period; u~befruchtet adj unfertilized; u~befugt adj unauthorized; Eintritt für ~befugte verboten, kein Zutritt für ~befugte no admittance to unauthorized persons; u~begabt adj untalented, ungifted; für etw u~begabt sein to have no talent for sth; er ist handwerklich völlig u~begabt he's no handyman; ~begabtheit f lack of talent; u~beglichen adj unpaid, unsettled.

unbegreiflich adj (unverständlich) incomprehensible; Leichtsinn, Irrtum, Dummheit inconceivable; (unergründlich) Menschen, Länder inscrutable. es wird mir immer ~ bleiben, wie/daß ... I shall never understand how/why ...; es ist uns allen ~, wie das passieren konnte none of us can understand how it happened; das U~e (Rel) the Unknowable.

unbegreiflicherweise adv inexplicably.
Unbegreiflichkeit f siehe adj incomprehensibility; inconceivability; inscrutability.

unbegrenzt adj unlimited; Möglichkeiten, Energie, Vertrauen etc auch limitless, boundless, infinite; Land, Meer etc boundless; Zeitspanne, Frist indefinite. zeitlich ~ indefinite; ~, auf ~e Zeit indefinitely; er hat ~e Zeit he has unlimited time; in ~er Höhe of an unlimited or indefinite amount; es ist nach oben ~ there's no upper limit (on it), the sky's the limit (inf); „~ haltbar" "will keep indefinitely".

unbegründet adj Angst, Verdacht, Zweifel unfounded, groundless, without foundation; Maßnahme unwarranted. eine Klage als ~ abweisen to dismiss a case.

unbehaart adj hairless; (auf dem Kopf) bald.

Unbehagen nt (feeling of) uneasiness or disquiet, uneasy feeling; (Unzufriedenheit) discontent (an +dat with); (körperlich) discomfort.

unbehaglich adj uncomfortable; Gefühl auch uneasy. sich in jds Gesellschaft (dat) ~ fühlen to feel uncomfortable or ill at ease in sb's company.

Un-: u~behauen adj unhewn; u~behaust adj (liter) homeless; u~behelligt adj (unbelästigt) unmolested; (unkontrolliert) unchecked; jdn u~behelligt lassen to leave sb alone; (Polizei etc) not to stop sb; u~beherrscht adj uncontrolled; Mensch lacking self-control; (gierig) greedy; u~beherrscht reagieren to react in an uncontrolled way or without any self-control; ~beherrschtheit f siehe adj lack of self-control; greediness; u~behindert adj unhindered, unimpeded; Sicht clear, uninterrupted.

unbeholfen adj clumsy, awkward; (hilflos) helpless; (plump) Annäherungsversuch clumsy. mit seinem verletzten Bein geht er sehr ~ he walks very awkwardly with his injured leg.

Unbeholfenheit f, no pl siehe adj clumsiness, awkwardness; helplessness; clumsiness.

Un-: u~beirrbar adj unwavering, ~beirrbarkeit f unwaveringness; u~beirrt adj (a) (ohne sich irritieren zu lassen) unflustered; (b) siehe u~beirrbar.

unbekannt adj unknown; Gesicht auch unfamiliar; Flugzeug, Flugobjekt etc unidentified. eine (mir) ~e Stadt/Stimme a town/voice I don't know, a town/voice unknown to me; das war mir ~ I didn't know that, I was unaware of that; dieser Herr/diese Gegend ist mir ~ I don't know or I'm not acquainted with this gentleman/area; Angst ist ihm ~ he doesn't know what fear is or the meaning of (the word) fear; es wird Ihnen nicht ~ sein, daß ... you will no doubt be aware that ...; ~e Größe

(Math) unknown quantity; (fig) little-known genius; aus ~er Ursache for some unknown reason; nach ~ verzogen moved-address unknown; ich bin hier ~ (inf) I'm a stranger here; ~e Täter person or persons unknown; Strafanzeige gegen U~ charge against person or persons unknown.

Unbekannte f -n, -n (Math) unknown.

Unbekannte(r) mf decl as adj stranger. der große ~ (hum) the mystery man/person etc.

unbekannterweise adv grüße sie/ihn ~ von mir give her/him my regards although I don't know her/him.

Unbekanntheit f (von Dichter, Buch etc) obscurity. die ~ dieses Dorfes/dieser Fakten (the fact) that this village/these facts are so little known.

unbekleidet adj bare. sie war ~ she had nothing or no clothes on, she was bare.

unbekümmert adj (a) (unbesorgt) unconcerned. sei ganz ~ don't worry; das kannst du ~ tun you needn't worry about doing that. (b) (sorgenfrei) carefree.

Unbekümmertheit f siehe adj (a) lack of concern. (b) carefreeness.

unbelastet adj (a) (ohne Last) unloaded, unladen. das linke Bein ~ lassen to keep one's weight off one's left leg. (b) (ohne Schulden) unencumbered. (c) (Pol: ohne Schuld) guiltless. (d) (ohne Sorgen) free from care or worries. von Hemmungen/Ängsten etc ~ free from inhibitions/fears etc; er ging ~ in die Prüfung he went into the exam with no worries on his mind.

Un-: u~belebt adj Straße, Gegend quiet; die u~belebte Natur the inanimate world, inanimate nature; u~beleckt adj u~beleckt von aller Kultur sein (inf) to be completely uncultured; u~belehrbar adj fixed in one's views; Rassist etc dyed-in-the-wool attr; er ist u~belehrbar you can't tell him anything; wenn du so u~belehrbar bist if you won't be told; ~belehrbarkeit f seine ~belehrbarkeit the fact that you just can't tell him anything; u~belesen adj unread, unlettered; u~beleuchtet adj unlit; Fahrzeug without lights; u~belichtet adj (Phot) unexposed; u~beliebt adj unpopular (bei with); sich u~beliebt machen to make oneself unpopular; ~beliebtheit f unpopularity (bei with); u~belohnt adj unrewarded; u~bemannt adj Raumflug, Station unmanned; Fahrzeug driverless; Flugzeug pilotless; (inf: ohne Mann) without a man; u~bemerkbar adj imperceptible; u~bemerkt adj unnoticed; (nicht gesehen auch) unobserved; u~bemerkt bleiben to escape attention, to go unnoticed.

unbemittelt adj without means. ~e Studenten erhalten vom Staat eine Beihilfe students without (any) means of their own receive state aid; ein ~er Nichtsnutz a penniless good-for-nothing.

unbenommen adj pred (form) es bleibt or ist Ihnen ~, zu ... you are (quite) free or at liberty to ...; das bleibt or ist dir ~ you're quite free or at liberty to do so.

un-: ~benutzbar adj unusable; ~benutzt adj unused.

unbeobachtet adj unobserved, unnoticed. in einem ~en Moment when nobody was looking; wenn er sich ~ fühlt ... when he thinks nobody is looking ...

unbequem adj (ungemütlich) uncomfortable, uncomfy; (lästig) Mensch, Frage, Situation awkward, inconvenient; Aufgabe unpleasant; (mühevoll) difficult. diese Schuhe sind mir zu ~ these shoes are too uncomfortable; der Regierung/den Behörden etc ~ sein to be an embarrassment to the government/authorities etc.

Unbequemlichkeit f siehe adj uncomfortableness, uncomfiness; awkwardness, inconvenience; unpleasantness; difficulty.

Un-: u~berechenbar adj unpredictable; ~berechenbarkeit f unpredictability; u~berechtigt adj (ungerechtfertigt) unwarranted; Sorge, Kritik etc unfounded; (unbefugt) unauthorized; u~berechtigterweise adv siehe adj without justification; without reason; without authority.

unberücksichtigt adj unconsidered. etw ~ lassen not to consider sth, to leave sth out of consideration; die Frage ist ~ geblieben this question has not been considered; ein bisher ~er Punkt a point which has not yet been considered.

unberufen adj ~ (toi, toi, toi)! touch wood!

unberührbar adj untouchable. die U~en the untouchables.

unberührt adj (a) (unangetastet, neu) untouched; Bett not slept in; (fig) Wald etc virgin; Natur unspoiled. ~ sein (Mädchen) to be a virgin; ~ in die Ehe gehen to be a virgin when one marries; das Essen ~ stehenlassen to leave one's food untouched. (b) (mitleidlos) unmoved. das kann ihn nicht ~ lassen he can't help but be moved by that. (c) (unbetroffen) unaffected.

Unberührtheit f (von Mädchen) virginity. jahrtausendelange ~ (fig) thousands of years of being left completely unspoiled; wo finden Sie sonst noch diese ~ der Natur? where else will you find nature so completely unspoiled?

unbeschadet prep +gen (form) regardless of. ~ dessen, daß ... regardless of the fact that ...

unbeschädigt adj undamaged; Geschirr, Glas etc auch intact, unbroken; Siegel unbroken; (inf) Mensch intact (inf), unharmed, in one piece (inf). ~ bleiben not to be damaged/broken; (seelisch etc) to come off unscathed.

unbeschäftigt adj (müßig) idle; (arbeitslos) not working; Schauspieler(in) resting pred.

unbescheiden adj presumptuous. darf ich mir die ~e Frage erlauben, ...? I hope you don't think me impertinent but might I ask ...?, I hope you don't mind my asking, but ...?

Unbescheidenheit f presumptuousness; (von Mensch auch) presumption.

Un-: u~**bescholten** adj (geh) respectable; Ruf spotless; (Jur) with no previous convictions; ~**bescholtenheit** f (geh) siehe adj respectability; spotlessness; lack of previous convictions; u~**beschrankt** adj Bahnübergang without gates, unguarded.

unbeschränkt adj unrestricted; Macht absolute; Geldmittel, Haftung, Zeit, Geduld unlimited; Vertrauen unbounded, boundless; Freiheit, Vollmacht auch limitless. wieviel darf ich mitnehmen? — ~ how much can I take? — there's no limit or restriction; jdm ~e Vollmacht geben to give sb carte blanche.

unbeschreiblich adj indescribable; Frechheit tremendous, enormous. ~ zunehmen (zahlenmäßig) to show a staggering increase.

un-: ~**beschrieben** adj blank; siehe Blatt; ~**beschwert** adj (a) (sorgenfrei) carefree; Melodien light; Unterhaltung, Lektüre light-hearted; (b) (ohne Gewicht) unweighted; ~**beseelt** adj (liter) siehe ~**belebt**.

unbesehen adv indiscriminately; (ohne es anzusehen) without looking at it/them. das glaube ich dir ~ I believe it if you say so; das glaube ich dir nicht ~ I'll believe that when I see it.

Un-: u~**besetzt** adj vacant; Stuhl, Platz auch unoccupied; Bus, Zug empty; Schalter closed; u~**besiegbar** adj Armee etc invincible; Mannschaft, Sportler etc auch unbeatable; ~**besiegbarkeit** f invincibility; u~**besiegt** adj undefeated; u~**besonnen** adj rash; ~**besonnenheit** f rashness.

unbesorgt 1 adj unconcerned. Sie können ganz ~ sein you can set your mind at rest or ease. 2 adv without worrying. das können Sie ~ tun you don't need to worry about doing that.

Un-: u~**beständig** adj Wetter (immer) changeable; (zu bestimmten Zeitpunkt auch) unsettled; Mensch unsteady; (in Leistungen) erratic; (launisch) moody; Liebhaber inconstant; Liebe transitory; ~**beständigkeit** f siehe adj changeableness, changeability; unsettledness; unsteadiness; erraticness; moodiness; inconstancy; transitoriness; u~**bestätigt** adj unconfirmed; u~**bestechlich** adj (a) Mensch incorruptible; (b) Urteil, Blick unerring; ~**bestechlichkeit** f siehe adj (a) incorruptibility; (b) unerringness; u~**bestimmbar** adj indeterminable; ~**bestimmbarkeit** f non-determinability.

unbestimmt adj (a) (ungewiß) uncertain; (unentschieden auch) undecided. (b) (unklar, undeutlich) Gefühl, Erinnerung etc vague. etw ~ lassen to leave sth open; auf ~e Zeit for an indefinite period, indefinitely. (c) (Gram) indefinite.

Unbestimmtheit f, no pl siehe adj (a) uncertainty. (b) vagueness.

unbestreitbar adj Tatsache indisputable; Verdienste, Fähigkeiten unquestionable.

unbestritten adj undisputed no adv, indisputable. es ist ja ~, daß ... nobody denies or disputes that ...

unbeteiligt adj (a) (uninteressiert) indifferent; (bei Diskussion) uninterested. (b) (nicht teilnehmend) uninvolved no adv (an +dat, bei in); (Jur, Comm) disinterested. es kamen auch U~e zu Schaden innocent bystanders were also injured.

un-: ~**betont** adj unstressed; ~**beträchtlich** adj insignificant; Unannehmlichkeiten etc minor; Aufpreis, Verbilligung slight; ~**beträchtlich** mehr/teurer slightly more/dearer; nicht ~**beträchtlich** not inconsiderable; ~**beugsam** adj uncompromising, unbending; Wille unshakeable; ~**bewacht** adj (lit, fig) unguarded; Parkplatz unattended; ~**bewaffnet** adj unarmed; ~**bewältigt** adj unconquered, unmastered; Deutschlands ~**bewältigte** Vergangenheit the past with which Germany has not yet come to terms.

unbeweglich adj (a) (nicht zu bewegen) immovable; (steif) stiff; (geistig ~) rigid, inflexible. ohne Auto ist man ziemlich ~ you're not very mobile or you can't get around much without a car; ~e Güter (Jur) immovable property. (b) (bewegungslos) motionless. ~ dastehen/daliegen to stand/lie there without moving or motionless.

Unbeweglichkeit f siehe adj (a) immovability; stiffness; rigidity, inflexibility. (b) motionlessness.

un-: ~**bewegt** adj motionless, unmoving; Meer unruffled; (fig: unberührt) unmoved; ~**beweibt** adj (inf) unmarried, wifeless (inf); ~**bewiesen** adj unproven; ~**bewohnbar** adj uninhabitable; ~**bewohnt** adj Gegend, Insel, Planet uninhabited; Wohnung, Haus unoccupied, empty; ~**bewußt** adj unconscious; Reflex involuntary; das U~**bewußte** (Psych) the unconscious; ~**bezahlbar** adj (a) (lit: zu teuer) prohibitive, impossibly dear; Luxus, Artikel which one couldn't possibly afford; (fig: komisch) priceless. (b) (fig: praktisch, nützlich) invaluable; ~**bezahlt** adj Urlaub unpaid; Rechnung, Schuld etc auch unsettled, outstanding; sein noch ~**bezahltes** Auto the car he hasn't finished paying for yet; ~**bezähmbar** adj Optimismus, heiteres Gemüt, Neugier etc irrepressible, indomitable; Verlangen, Lust uncontrollable; Hunger insatiable; Durst unquenchable; ~**bezweifelbar** adj undeniable; Tatsache auch unarguable; ~**bezwingbar**, ~**bezwinglich** adj unconquerable; Gegner invincible; Festung impregnable; Drang uncontrollable.

Unbilden pl (liter) (a) (des Wetters) rigours pl. (b) (einer schweren Zeit etc) trials pl, (trials and) tribulations pl.

Unbildung f lack of education.

Unbill f -, no pl (old, liter) injustice, wrong.

unbillig adj (Jur: ungerecht) unjust; (unangemessen) unreasonable. ~e Härte (Jur) undue hardship.

Unbilligkeit f siehe adj injustice; unreasonableness.

Un-: u~**blutig** 1 adj bloodless; (Med) non-operative; 2 adv without bloodshed; u~**botmäßig** adj (geh) insubordinate; Kind unruly; ~**botmäßigkeit** f (geh) insubordination; unruliness; u~**brauchbar** adj (nutzlos) useless, (of) no use pred; (nicht zu verwenden) unusable; ~**brauchbarkeit** f siehe adj uselessness; unusability; u~**bürokratisch** 1 adj unbureaucratic; 2 adv without a lot of red tape, unbureaucratically; u~**christlich** adj

unchristian; eine u~**christliche** Zeit (inf) an ungodly hour.

und conj (a) and. ~? well?; ~ dann? (and) what then or then what?; (danach) and then?, and after that?; ~ ähnliches and things like that, and suchlike; ~ anderes and other things; er kann es nicht, ~ ich auch nicht he can't do it, (and) nor or neither can I; ~ ihm Geld leihen? (inf) me, lend him money?; du ~ tanzen können? (inf) you dance?; immer zwei ~ zwei two at a time; Gruppen zu fünf ~ fünf groups of five; er aß ~ aß he ate and ate, he kept on (and on) eating; er konnte ~ konnte nicht aufhören he simply couldn't stop.

(b) (konzessiv) even if. ..., ~ wenn ich selbst bezahlen muß ... even if I have to pay myself; ~ ... (auch) noch no matter how ...; ..., ~ wenn du auch noch so bettelst ... no matter how much you beg; ~ selbst even; ~ selbst dann even then.

undamenhaft adj unladylike.

Undank m ingratitude. ~ ernten to get little thanks; ~ ist der Welt Lohn (Prov) never expect thanks for anything.

undankbar adj (a) Mensch ungrateful. sich jdm gegenüber ~ zeigen or erweisen to be ungrateful to sb. (b) (unerfreulich) Aufgabe, Arbeit etc thankless.

Undankbarkeit f siehe adj (a) ingratitude, ungratefulness. (b) thanklessness.

un-: ~**datiert** adj undated; ~**definierbar** adj Begriff indefinable; das Essen war ~**definierbar** nobody could say what the food was; ~**dehnbar** adj inelastic; ~**deklinierbar** adj indeclinable; ~**demokratisch** adj undemocratic.

undenkbar adj unthinkable, inconceivable. es/diese Möglichkeit ist nicht ~ it/the possibility is not inconceivable.

undenklich adj: seit ~en Zeiten (geh) since time immemorial.

undeutlich adj indistinct; (wegen Nebel etc auch) hazy; Foto auch blurred; Erinnerung auch vague, hazy; Schrift illegible; Ausdrucksweise, Erklärung unclear, muddled. ~ sprechen to speak indistinctly, to mumble; ich konnte es nur ~ verstehen I couldn't understand it very clearly; bemüh dich mal, nicht so ~ zu schreiben try to write more clearly; sie/es war nur ~ erkennbar or zu erkennen you couldn't see her/it at all clearly.

undeutsch adj un-German.

undicht adj Dose, Gefäß not air-/water-tight. das Rohr ist ~ the pipe leaks; das Fenster ist ~ the window lets in a draught; er/sie/es muß eine ~e Stelle haben (Rohr etc) it must have a leak; (Reifen etc) it must have a hole in it; (Flasche etc) the seal must be broken; im Geheimdienst muß eine ~e Stelle sein the secret service must have a leak somewhere.

undifferenziert adj simplistic; (nicht analytisch) undifferentiated; (gleichartig) uniform; Warenangebot uncomprehensive.

Unding nt, no pl absurdity. es ist ein ~, zu ... it is preposterous or absurd to ...

Un-: u~**diplomatisch** adj undiplomatic; u~**diszipliniert** adj undisciplined; ~**diszipliniertheit** f lack of discipline; u~**dramatisch** adj (fig) undramatic, unexciting; u~**duldsam** adj intolerant (gegen of); ~**duldsamkeit** f, no pl intolerance (gegen of); u~**durchdringbar**, u~**durchdringlich** adj Gebüsch, Urwald impenetrable; Gesicht, Miene inscrutable; u~**durchführbar** adj impracticable, unworkable; ~**durchführbarkeit** f impracticability, unworkability; u~**durchlässig** adj impermeable, impervious (gegen to); ~**durchlässigkeit** f impermeability, imperviousness; u~**durchschaubar** adj unfathomable; Exot, Volk etc inscrutable; er ist ein u~**durchschaubarer** Typ (inf) you never know what game he's playing (inf); ~**durchschaubarkeit** f siehe adj unfathomability; inscrutability; u~**durchsichtig** adj (a) Fenster opaque; Papier non-transparent; Stoff etc non-transparent, not see-through (inf); (b) (fig pej) Mensch, Methoden devious; Motive obscure; Vorgänge, Geschäfte dark; es ist eine ganze u~**durchsichtige** Angelegenheit you can't tell what's going on in that business; ~**durchsichtigkeit** f, no pl siehe adj (a) opacity; non-transparency; (b) deviousness; obscureness; darkness.

un|eben adj (a) Oberfläche, Fußboden, Wand etc uneven; Straße auch bumpy; Gelände rough, bumpy. (b) (dial inf) bad. gar kein so ~er Typ, dieser Otto not a bad sort, this Otto.

Un|ebenheit f siehe adj unevenness; bumpiness; roughness. kleine ~en uneven patches.

Un-: u~**echt** adj false; (vorgetäuscht) fake; Schmuck, Edelstein, Blumen etc artificial, fake (usu pej); Bruch improper; u~**edel** adj Metalle base; u~**egal** adj (sl) unequal; u~**ehelich** adj illegitimate; u~**ehelich** geboren sein to be illegitimate, to have been born out of wedlock (old, form); ~**ehelichkeit** f illegitimacy; ~**ehre** f, no pl dishonour; jdm ~**ehre** machen or zur ~**ehre** gereichen (geh) to disgrace sb; u~**ehrenhaft** adj dishonourable; u~**ehrenhaft** (aus der Armee) entlassen werden to be given a dishonourable discharge; ~**ehrenhaftigkeit** f, no pl dishonesty; u~**ehrerbietig** adj disrespectful; ~**ehrerbietigkeit** f disrespectfulness, disrespect; (Benehmen) sign of disrespect; u~**ehrlich** adj dishonest; u~**ehrlich** spielen to cheat; auf u~**ehrliche** Weise by dishonest means; ~**ehrlichkeit** f dishonesty; u~**eidlich** adj u~**eidliche** Falschaussage (Jur) false statement made while not under oath; u~**eigennützig** adj unselfish, selfless, altruistic; ~**eigennützigkeit** f unselfishness, selflessness, altruism; u~**eigentlich** adj (Math) improper; (b) (übertragen) figurative; u~**eingeladen** adj uninvited; u~**eingeladen** kommen to come uninvited or without an invitation; u~**eingeladen** erscheinen to gatecrash (bei etw sth); u~**eingelöst** adj unredeemed; Wechsel dishonoured; Versprechen etc unfulfilled.

un|eingeschränkt 1 adj absolute, total; Freiheit, Rechte unlimited, unrestricted; Annahme, Zustimmung unqualified; Vertrauen auch, Lob unreserved; Handel free, unrestricted; Vollmachten plenary.

2 *adv siehe adj* absolutely, totally; without limitation *or* restriction; without qualification; without reservation, unreservedly; freely, without restriction.

Un-: u~eingeweiht *adj* uninitiated; u~einheitlich *adj* nonuniform; *Öffnungs-, Arbeitszeiten, Systeme, Reaktion* varied; *(nicht für alle gleich) Arbeitszeiten, Schulferien* different; *Qualität* inconsistent; *Börse* irregular; *Preise* unsteady; u~einig *adj* (a) *(verschiedener Meinung)* in disagreement; über etw *(acc)* u~einig sein to disagree *or* to be in disagreement about sth; ich bin mit mir selbst noch u~einig I haven't made up my mind yet. (b) *(zerstritten)* divided; ~einigkeit *f* disagreement *(gen* between); ~einigkeit in der Partei division within the party; u~einnehmbar *adj* impregnable.

un|eins *adj pred* disagreed; *(zerstritten)* divided. (mit jdm) ~ sein/werden to disagree with sb; ich bin mit mir selbst ~ I cannot make up my mind; die Mitglieder sind (untereinander) ~ the members are divided amongst themselves.

Un-: u~elastisch *adj* inelastic; *(fig: nicht anpassungsfähig)* inflexible, unadaptable; u~elegant *adj* inelegant; u~empfänglich *adj (für* to) insusceptible, unsusceptible; *(für Eindrücke auch, Atmosphäre)* insensitive; ~empfänglichkeit *f siehe adj* insusceptibility, unsusceptibility; insensitiveness.

un|empfindlich *adj (gegen* to) insensitive; *(durch Übung, Erfahrung)* inured; *Bazillen etc* immune; *Pflanzen* hardy; *Baustoffe* which weather well; *Textilien* practical. gegen Kälte ~e Pflanzen plants which aren't sensitive to the cold.

Un|empfindlichkeit *f siehe adj* insensitiveness, insensitivity; inurement; immunity; hardiness. dieser Baustoff ist wegen seiner ~ gegen Witterungseinflüsse besonders gut geeignet this building material is particularly suitable because it weathers so well; die ~ dieses Stoffs the fact that this material is so practical.

un|endlich 1 *adj* infinite; *(zeitlich)* endless; *Universum* infinite, boundless. das U~e infinity; im U~en at infinity; (bis) ins U~e *(lit, Math)* to infinity; bis ins ~e *(~ lange)* forever; auf ~ einstellen *(Phot)* to focus at infinity. **2** *adv* endlessly; infinitely; *(fig: sehr)* terribly. ~ lange diskutieren to argue endlessly; ~ viele Dinge/Leute *etc* no end of things/people *etc*.

un|endlichemal, un|endlichmal *adv* endless times.

Un|endlichkeit *f* infinity; *(zeitlich)* endlessness; *(von Universum)* boundlessness. ~ von Raum und Zeit infinity of time and space.

Un-: u~entbehrlich *adj* indispensable; *Kenntnisse* essential; ~entbehrlichkeit *f siehe adj* indispensability; essentiality; u~entdeckt *adj* undiscovered; u~entgeltlich *adj* free of charge; etw u~entgeltlich tun to do sth free of charge; u~entrinnbar *adj (geh)* inescapable.

un|entschieden *adj (nicht entschieden)* undecided; *(entschlußlos)* indecisive; *(Sport)* drawn. das Spiel steht immer noch 2:2 ~ the score is still level at 2 all; ~ enden *or* ausgehen to end in a draw; ~ spielen to draw; ein ~es Rennen a dead heat.

Un|entschieden *nt* -s, - *(Sport)* draw. mit einem ~ enden to end in a draw.

un|entschlossen *adj (nicht entschieden)* undecided; *(entschlußlos) Mensch* indecisive, irresolute. ich bin noch ~ I haven't decided *or* made up my mind yet; ~ stand er vor dem Haus he stood hesitating in front of the house.

Un|entschlossenheit *f siehe adj* undecidedness; indecision, irresoluteness.

un|entschuldbar *adj* inexcusable.

un|entschuldigt 1 *adj* unexcused. ~es Fernbleiben von der Arbeit/Schule absenteeism/truancy. **2** *adv* without an excuse.

un|entwegt 1 *adj (mit Ausdauer)* continuous, constant; *(ohne aufzuhören auch)* incessant; *Kämpfer* untiring. einige U~e a few stalwarts. **2** *adv* constantly; incessantly; without tiring. ~ weitermachen to continue unceasingly.

Un|entwegtheit *f siehe adj* continuousness, constancy; incessancy; tirelessness.

un-: ~entwirrbar *adj* which can't be disentangled; *Zusammenhänge* involved, complex; ~entzifferbar *adj* indecipherable; ~entzündbar *adj* non-inflammable, non-flammable; ~erachtet *prep* +*gen (old) siehe* ~geachtet.

un|erbittlich *adj* relentless; *Mensch auch* inexorable, pitiless. ~ auf jdn einschlagen to hit sb pitilessly *or* mercilessly.

Un|erbittlichkeit *f siehe adj* relentlessness; inexorableness, pitilessness.

Un-: u~erfahren *adj* inexperienced; ~erfahrene(r) *mf decl as adj* inexperienced person/man/woman *etc*; ~erfahrenheit *f* inexperience, lack of experience; u~erfindlich *adj* incomprehensible; *Grund* obscure; aus u~erfindlichen Gründen for some obscure reason; u~erforschbar, u~erforschlich *adj* impenetrable; *Wille* unfathomable; u~erfreulich *adj* unpleasant; ~erfreuliches *(schlechte Nachrichten)* bad news *sing; (Übles)* bad things *pl*; u~erfüllbar *adj* unrealizable; *Wunsch, Ziel auch* unattainable; u~erfüllt *adj* unfulfilled; u~ergiebig *adj Quelle, Thema* unproductive; *Boden, Ernte, Nachschlagewerk* poor; *Kaffee, Trauben* uneconomical; u~ergründbar, u~ergründlich *adj* unfathomable; u~erheblich *adj (geringfügig)* insignificant; *(unwichtig auch)* unimportant, irrelevant; nicht u~erheblich verbessert considerably improved; u~erhofft *adj* unexpected.

un|erhört[1] *adj* (a) *attr (ungeheuer, gewaltig)* enormous; *(empörend)* outrageous; *Frechheit* incredible. das ist ja ~! that's quite outrageous.
2 *adv* incredibly. ~ viel a tremendous amount (of); ~ viel wissen/arbeiten to know a tremendous amount/to work tremendously hard; sich ~ beeilen to hurry tremendously; ~ aufpassen to watch very carefully.

un|erhört[2] *adj Bitte, Gebet* unanswered; *Liebe* unrequited; *Liebhaber* rejected.

un-: ~erkannt *adj* unrecognized; ~erkannt entkommen to get away without being recognized; ~erkennbar *adj* unrecognizable; ~erkenntlich *adj* ungrateful; ~erklärbar, ~erklärlich *adj* inexplicable; das ist mir ~erklärbar *or* ~erklärlich I can't understand it; ~erklärt *adj Phänomen, Sachverhalt* unexplained; *Krieg, Liebe* undeclared; ~erläßlich *adj* imperative.

un|erlaubt *adj* forbidden; *Betreten, Parken* unauthorized; *(ungesetzlich)* illegal. etw ~ tun to do sth without permission; ~e Handlung *(Jur)* tort; ~er Waffenbesitz illegal possession of firearms; *siehe* entfernen, Entfernung.

un|erlaubterweise *adv* without permission.

un|erledigt *adj* unfinished; *Post* unanswered; *Rechnung* outstanding; *Auftrag* unfulfilled; *(schwebend)* pending. auf dem Aktenordner stand „~" the file was marked "pending".

Un-: u~ermeßlich *adj* immense; *Weite, Himmel, Ozean* vast; ~ermeßlichkeit *f siehe adj* immensity; vastness; u~ermüdlich *adj Bestrebungen, Fleiß* untiring, tireless; *Versuche* unceasing; ~ermüdlichkeit *f* tirelessness; u~ernst *adj* frivolous; u~erprobt *adj* untested, untried; u~erquicklich *adj (unerfreulich)* unedifying; *(nutzlos)* unproductive, fruitless; u~erreichbar *adj Ziel, Leistung, Qualität* unattainable; *Ort, Ferne* inaccessible; *(telefonisch)* unobtainable; u~erreicht *adj Ziel* unequalled; *Ziel* unattained.

un|ersättlich *adj* insatiable; *Wissensdurst auch* inexhaustible.

Un|ersättlichkeit *f siehe adj* insatiability; inexhaustibility.

Un-: u~erschlossen *adj Land* undeveloped; *Boden* unexploited; *Vorkommen, Markt, Erdöllager* untapped; u~erschöpflich *adj* inexhaustible; u~erschrocken *adj* intrepid, courageous; ~erschrockenheit *f* intrepidity, courage; u~erschütterlich *adj* unshakeable; *Ruhe* imperturbable.

un|erschwinglich *adj* exorbitant, prohibitive. für jdn ~ sein to be beyond sb's means; ein für uns ~er Luxus a luxury beyond our means; ~ (teuer) sein to be prohibitively expensive *or* prohibitive.

un-: ~ersetzbar, ~ersetzlich *adj* irreplaceable; *Mensch auch* indispensable; ~ersprießlich *adj (unerfreulich)* unedifying; *(nutzlos)* unproductive, fruitless; ~erträglich *adj* unbearable; ~erwähnt *adj* unmentioned; ~erwartet *adj* unexpected; ~erwidert *adj Brief, Behauptung* unanswered; *Liebe* unrequited; *Sympathie* one-sided; ~erwünscht *adj Kind* unwanted; *Besuch, Effekt* unwelcome; du bist hier ~erwünscht you're not welcome here; ein ~erwünschter Ausländer *(Pol)* an undesirable alien; ~erziehbar *adj* ineducable; ~erzogen *adj* ill-bred, ill-mannered; *Kind auch* badly brought up.

UNESCO [u'nɛsko] *f* - die ~ UNESCO.

unfachgemäß, unfachmännisch *adj* unprofessional.

unfähig *adj* (a) *attr* incompetent. (b) ~ sein, etw zu tun to be incapable of doing sth; *(vorübergehend)* to be unable to do sth; einer Sache *(gen)* or zu etw ~ sein to be incapable of sth.

Unfähigkeit *f* (a) *(Untüchtigkeit)* incompetence. (b) *(Nichtkönnen)* inability.

Un-: u~fair *adj* unfair *(gegenüber* to); ~fairneß, ~fairness *f* unfairness.

Unfall *m* -s, Unfälle accident. er ist bei einem ~ ums Leben gekommen he died in an accident; gegen ~ versichert insured against accidents.

Unfall-: ~arzt *m* specialist for accident injuries; ~beteiligte(r) *mf* person/man/woman *etc* involved in an/the accident; ~bilanz *f* accident figures *pl or* statistics *pl*; ~fahrer *m* driver at fault in an/the accident; ~flucht *f* failure to stop after *or (nicht melden)* report an accident; *(bei Verletzung von Personen auch)* hit-and-run driving; ~flucht begehen to fail to stop after/report an accident; to commit a hit-and-run offence; u~flüchtig *adj Fahrer* who fails to stop after/report an accident; hit-and-run *attr*; u~flüchtig werden to fail to stop after/report an accident; ~flüchtige *pl* drivers *pl* who fail to stop after/report an accident; hit-and-run drivers *pl*; ~folge *f* result of an/the accident; u~frei **1** *adj* accident-free; **2** *adv* without an accident; ~hilfe *f* help at the scene of an/the accident; *(Erste Hilfe)* first aid; ~klinik *f*, ~krankenhaus *nt* accident hospital; ~opfer *nt* casualty; ~ort *m* scene of an/the accident; ~quote, ~rate *f* accident rate; ~risiko *nt* accident risk; ~schutz *m (Versicherung)* accident insurance; *(Maßnahmen)* accident prevention; ~skizze *f* diagram *or* sketch of an/the accident; ~station *f* accident *or* emergency ward; ~statistik *f* accident statistics *pl*; ~stelle *f* scene of an/the accident; ~tod *m* accidental death; bei ~tod in the event of death by misadventure; ~tote(r) *mf siehe* Verkehrstote(r); ~ursache *f* cause of an/the accident; ~verhütung *f* accident prevention; ~verletzte(r) *mf* casualty; ~versicherung *f* accident insurance; ~wagen *m* car involved in an/the accident; *(inf: Rettungswagen)* ambulance; der Wagen ist so billig, weil es ein ~wagen ist the car is so cheap because it has been involved in an accident; ~zahl, ~ziffer *f* number of accidents; steigende ~ziffern rising accident rates; ~zeuge *m* witness to an/the accident.

unfaßbar, unfaßlich *adj* incomprehensible. es ist mir *or* für mich ~, wie ... I (simply) cannot understand how ...

Un-: u~fehlbar **1** *adj* infallible; *Instinkt* unerring; **2** *adv* without fail; ~fehlbarkeit *f* infallibility; ~fehlbarkeitsglaube *m* infallibilism; u~fein *adj* unrefined *no adv*, indelicate; das ist u~fein/mehr als u~fein that's bad manners/most ungentlemanly/unladylike; u~fern *(geh)* **1** *prep* +*gen* not far from, near; **2** *adv* u~fern von not far from, near; u~fertig *adj (unvollendet)* unfinished; *(nicht vollständig)* incomplete; *(unreif) Mensch* immature.

Unflat ['unfla:t] *m* -(e)s, *no pl (lit old)* feculence *(form); (fig geh)* vituperation. jdn mit ~ bewerfen *(fig)* to inveigh against *or* vituperate sb.

unflätig *adj (geh)* offensive. sich ~ ausdrücken to use obscene language.

Unflätigkeit f offensiveness; (von Ausdrucksweise) obscenity.

Un-: u~flektiert adj (Gram) uninflected; u~flott adj (inf) not nice; das ist gar nicht so u~flott that's not bad; er/sie ist gar nicht so u~flott he's/she's a bit of all right (inf); u~folgsam adj disobedient; ~folgsamkeit f disobedience; u~formell adj informal.

unförmig adj (formlos) shapeless; Möbel, Auto inelegant; (groß) cumbersome; Füße, Gesicht unshapely.

Unförmigkeit f siehe adj shapelessness; inelegance; cumbersomeness; unshapeliness.

Un-: u~förmlich adj informal; ~förmlichkeit f informality; u~frankiert adj unstamped; u~fraulich adj unfeminine.

unfrei adj (a) (politisch, Hist: leibeigen) not free. ~ sein (Hist) to be a bondman or in bondage or a serf. (b) (befangen, eingeengt) constrained, uneasy. (c) Brief etc unfranked.

Unfreie(r) mf decl as adj (Hist) serf.

Unfreiheit f lack of freedom; (Hist) bondage.

unfreiwillig adj (gezwungen) compulsory. ich mußte ~ zuhören/war ~er Zeuge I was forced to listen/was an unwilling witness. (b) (unbeabsichtigt) Witz, Fehler unintentional.

unfreundlich adj unfriendly (zu, gegen to); Wetter inclement; Landschaft, Zimmer, Farbe cheerless. jdn ~ behandeln to be unfriendly to sb; jdn ~ begrüßen/ansehen to give sb an unfriendly welcome/look; ~ reagieren to react in an unfriendly way; ein ~er Akt (Pol) a hostile act.

Unfreundlichkeit f (a) siehe adj unfriendliness; inclemency; cheerlessness. (b) (unfreundliche Bemerkung) unpleasant remark.

Unfriede(n) m strife. in ~n (mit jdm) leben to live in conflict (with sb).

un-: ~frisiert adj (lit) Haare uncombed; Mensch with one's hair not done; (fig inf) (nicht verfälscht) undoctored; Auto not souped-up (sl); ~fromm adj impious.

unfruchtbar adj infertile; Boden auch barren; Frau auch barren (old, liter); (fig: Debatte etc) fruitless; Schaffenszeit unproductive. ~ machen to sterilize; die ~en Tage (Med) the days of infertility.

Unfruchtbarkeit f siehe adj infertility; barrenness; fruitlessness.

Unfruchtbarmachung f sterilization.

Unfug ['ʊnfuːk] m -s, no pl nonsense. ~ treiben or anstellen or machen to get up to mischief; laß den ~! stop that nonsense!; wegen groben ~s for causing a public nuisance.

un-: ~fundiert adj unfounded; ~galant (geh) adj discourteous, ungentlemanly no adv; ~gangbar adj Pfad, Weg impassable; ~gar adj underdone.

Ungar(in f) ['ʊŋgar(ɪn)] m -n, -n Hungarian.

ungarisch ['ʊŋgarɪʃ] adj Hungarian.

Ungarisch(e) ['ʊŋgarɪʃ(ə)] nt decl as adj Hungarian; siehe auch Deutsch(e).

Ungarn ['ʊŋgarn] nt -s Hungary.

Un-: u~gastlich adj inhospitable; ~gastlichkeit f inhospitableness.

ungeachtet prep +gen in spite of, despite. ~ dessen, daß es regnet in spite of it raining or of the fact that it is raining; ~ aller Ermahnungen, aller Ermahnungen ~ despite all warnings; er ist sehr stark, ~ dessen, daß er so klein ist he's very strong, in spite of being so small.

un-: ~geahndet adj (Jur) unpunished; ~geahnt adj undreamt-of; ~gebacken adj unbaked; ~gebärdig adj unruly; ~gebeten adj uninvited; er kam ~gebeten he came uninvited or unasked or without an invitation; ~gebeugt adj (a) unbent, unbowed; (b) (Gram) uninflected; ~gebildet adj uncultured; (ohne Bildung) uneducated; U~gebildete uneducated or ignorant people; ~gebleicht adj unbleached; ~geboren adj unborn; ~gebrannt adj Kaffee unroasted; Ton etc unfired; ~gebräuchlich adj uncommon; ~gebraucht adj unused; ~gebrochen adj unbroken; (Phys) Licht unrefracted.

Ungebühr f, no pl (old, form) impropriety. ~ vor Gericht contempt of court.

ungebührlich adj improper. sich ~ aufregen to get unduly excited.

ungebunden adj (a) Buch unbound; Blumen loose. (b) in ~er Rede in prose. (c) (unabhängig) Leben (fancy-)free; (unverheiratet) unattached; (Pol) independent. frei und ~ footloose and fancy-free; parteipolitisch ~ (politically) independent, not attached to any political party.

Ungebundenheit f independence.

Un-: u~gedeckt adj (a) (schutzlos) Schachfigur etc unprotected, unguarded; (Sport) Tor undefended; Spieler unmarked, uncovered; Scheck, Kredit uncovered; (b) Tisch unlaid; u~gedient adj (dated Mil) with no prior service; ~gediente(r) m decl as adj (dated) person with no prior service; u~gedruckt adj unprinted; (nicht veröffentlicht) unpublished.

Ungeduld f impatience. vor ~ with impatience; voller ~ impatiently.

ungeduldig adj impatient.

ungeeignet adj unsuitable; (für Beruf, Stellung auch) unsuited (für to, for).

ungefähr 1 adj attr approximate, rough. nach ~en Schätzungen at a rough guess or estimate.
2 adv roughly; (bei Zahlen-, Maßangaben auch) approximately. (so) ~ dreißig about or approximately thirty; ~ 12 Uhr about or approximately 12 o'clock; von ~ from nowhere; (zufällig) by chance; diese Bemerkung kommt doch nicht von ~ he etc didn't make this remark just by chance; wo ~? whereabouts?; wie ~? approximately how?; so ~ more or less!; können Sie mir (so) ~ sagen, wieviel das kosten soll/wie Sie sich das vorgestellt haben? can you give me a rough idea

of or tell me roughly how much it will cost/how you imagined it?; ~ (so) wie a bit like; können Sie den Mann ~ beschreiben? can you give me/us etc a rough description of the man?; etw (so) ~ wissen to know sth roughly or have a rough idea of sth; dann weiß ich ~ Bescheid then I've got a rough idea; so ~ habe ich mir das gedacht I thought it would be something like this; so ~, als wären wir kleine Kinder a bit as if we were little children; das hat sich ~ so abgespielt it happened something like this.

Un-: u~gefährdet adj safe, unendangered no adv; (b) (Sport) not in danger; u~gefährdet siegen to win comfortably; u~gefährlich adj safe; Tier, Krankheit, Arzneimittel etc harmless; nicht ganz u~gefährlich not altogether safe/harmless; (Expedition) not altogether without its dangers; ~gefährlichkeit f siehe adj safeness; harmlessness; u~gefällig adj Mensch unobliging; ~gefälligkeit f unobligingness; u~gefärbt adj Haare, Stoff undyed, natural; Lebensmittel without (added) colouring; u~gefedert adj springless, without springs; u~gefiltert adj unfiltered; u~geformt adj unformed; (gestaltlos) amorphous; u~gefragt adv unasked; u~gefrühstückt adv (hum) without having had breakfast; u~gefüge adj (geh) cumbersome; u~gefüttert[1] adj Tier unfed; u~gefüttert[2] adj Kleidung, Briefumschlag unlined; u~gegenständlich adj abstract; u~gegerbt adj untanned; u~gegessen adv (hum) on an empty stomach; u~gegliedert adj Körper, Stengel unjointed; (fig) disjointed; Satz, Aufsatz etc unstructured.

ungehalten adj indignant (über +acc about).

Ungehaltenheit f indignation.

un-: ~gehärtet adj Stahl untempered; ~geheißen adv (geh) voluntarily; ~geheizt adj unheated; ~gehemmt adj unrestrained.

Ungeheuer nt -s, - monster; (fig auch) ogre.

ungeheuer 1 adj (a) siehe ungeheuerlich.
(b) (riesig) enormous, immense; (in bezug auf Länge, Weite) vast. sich ins ~e steigern to take on enormous dimensions.
(c) (genial, kühn) tremendous.
(d) (frevelhaft, vermessen) outrageous, dreadful.
2 adv (sehr) enormously, tremendously; (negativ) terribly, awfully. ~ groß tremendously big; ~ viele Menschen an enormous number of people.

ungeheuerlich adj monstrous; Tat auch atrocious; Verleumdung outrageous; Verdacht, Dummheit dreadful; Leichtsinn outrageous, appalling.

Ungeheuerlichkeit f siehe adj monstrosity; atrocity; atrociousness; outrageousness; dreadfulness; outrageousness. so eine ~! how outrageous!; ~en (Verbrechen etc) atrocities; (Behauptungen etc) outrageous claims.

Un-: u~gehindert adj unhindered; u~gehobelt adj Brett etc unplaned; Mensch, Benehmen boorish; u~gehörig adj impertinent; ~gehörigkeit f impertinence; u~gehorsam adj disobedient; ~gehorsam m disobedience; (Mil) insubordination; u~gehört adv unheard; u~gehört verhallen (fig) to fall on deaf ears.

Ungeist m, no pl (geh) demon.

un-: ~geistig adj unintellectual; ~gekämmt adj Haar uncombed; ~gekämmt aussehen to look unkempt; ~geklärt adj (a) Abwasser etc untreated; (b) Frage, Verbrechen unsolved; Ursache unknown; ~gekocht adj raw; Flüssigkeit unboiled; Obst etc uncooked; ~gekrönt adj uncrowned; ~gekühlt adj unchilled; ~gekündigt adj: in ~gekündigter Stellung not under notice (to leave); ~gekünstelt adj natural, genuine; Sprechweise unaffected; ~gekürzt adj not shortened; Buch unabridged; Film uncut; Ausgaben not cut back; ~geladen adj (a) Kamera, Gewehr etc unloaded; (b) Gäste etc uninvited; ~geläufig adj unfamiliar.

ungelegen adj inconvenient. komme ich (Ihnen) ~? is this an inconvenient time for you?; etw kommt jdm ~ sth is inconvenient for sb; das kam (mir) gar nicht so ~ that was really rather convenient.

Ungelegenheiten pl inconvenience sing. jdm ~ bereiten or machen to inconvenience sb.

Un-: u~gelegt adj siehe Ei; u~gelehrig adj unteachable; u~gelenk adj awkward; Bewegungen auch clumsy; u~gelenkig adj not supple, stiff; (fig inf: nicht flexibel) inflexible, unbending; ~gelenkigkeit f siehe adj stiffness; inflexibility; u~gelernt adj unskilled; u~gelesen adj unread; u~geliebt adj unloved; u~gelogen adv honestly; u~gelöst adj unsolved; (Chem) undissolved; u~gelüftet adj unaired.

Ungemach ['ʊngəmaːx] nt -s, no pl (liter) hardship.

un-: ~gemacht adj Bett unmade; ~gemahlen adj unground.

ungemein adj immense, tremendous.

un-: ~gemildert adj undiminished; ~gemildert fortbestehen to continue undiminished; ~gemustert adj plain.

ungemütlich adj uncomfortable; Mensch uncomfortable to be with; Land, Wetter, Wochenende unpleasant. mir wird es hier ~ I'm getting a bit uncomfortable or uneasy; sei doch nicht so ~ don't be so unsociable; er kann ~ werden he can get nasty; ich kann auch ~ werden I can be very unpleasant if I choose; hier kann es gleich sehr ~ werden things could get very nasty here in a moment.

Ungemütlichkeit f siehe adj uncomfortableness; unpleasantness.

ungenannt adj anonymous. ~ bleiben to remain anonymous.

ungenau adj (nicht fehlerfrei) inaccurate; (nicht wahrheitsgetreu) inexact; (vage) vague; (ungefähr) rough, approximate. ~ arbeiten/messen/rechnen to work inaccurately/measure approximately/calculate roughly.

Ungenauigkeit f siehe adj inaccuracy; inexactness; vagueness; roughness.

ungeneigt adj disinclined.

ungeniert ['unʒeni:ɐt] 1 adj (frei, ungehemmt) unembarrassed, free and easy; (bedenkenlos, taktlos) uninhibited. 2 adv openly; (bedenkenlos, taktlos) without any inhibition. **greifen Sie bitte ~ zu** please feel free to help yourself/yourselves.

Ungeniertheit ['unʒeni:ɐthait] f siehe adj lack of embarrassment; lack of inhibition.

ungenießbar adj (nicht zu essen) inedible; (nicht zu trinken) undrinkable; (unschmackhaft) unpalatable; (inf) Mensch unbearable.

Ungenügen ['ungəny:gn] nt -s, no pl discontent.

ungenügend ['ungəny:gnt] adj inadequate, insufficient; Schulnote unsatisfactory. **ein U~** an "unsatisfactory", the lowest mark.

Un-: u~genutzt, u~genützt adj unused; Energien unexploited, eine Chance u~genutzt or u~genützt lassen to miss an opportunity; u~geöffnet adj unopened; u~geordnet adj Bücher, Papiere etc untidy, disordered; (fig) disordered; u~geordnet herumliegen to lie (about) in disorder or disarray; u~gepflastert adj unpaved; u~gepflegt adj Mensch untidy, unkempt; Park, Rasen, Hände etc neglected; sich u~gepflegt ausdrücken to talk in a common way; u~geprüft adj untested; etw u~geprüft übernehmen to accept sth without testing it; Zahlen to accept sth without checking; (unkritisch) to accept sth at face value; u~geputzt adj uncleaned; Zähne unbrushed; Schuhe unpolished; u~gerächt adj unavenged; u~gerade adj odd; u~geraten adj Kind ill-bred; u~gerechnet prep + gen not including, excluding; u~gerecht adj unjust, unfair; u~gerechterweise adv unjustly, unfairly; u~gerechtfertigt 1 adj unjustified; Behauptung auch unwarranted; 2 adv unjustly, unduly; ~gerechtigkeit f injustice; so eine ~gerechtigkeit! how unjust!; u~geregelt adj Zeiten irregular; Leben disordered; u~gereimt adj Verse unrhymed; (fig) inconsistent; u~gereimte Verse blank verse sing; ~gereimtheit f (fig) inconsistency.

ungern adv reluctantly. (höchst) ~! if I/we really have to!; etw höchst ~ tun to do sth very reluctantly or with the greatest reluctance; das tue ich gar nicht ~ I don't mind doing that at all.

un-: ~gerufen adj uncalled, without being called; ~gerührt adj unmoved; ~gesagt adj unsaid; etw ~gesagt machen to pretend sth has never been said; ~gesalzen adj unsalted; ~gesattelt adj unsaddled; ~gesättigt adj Hunger etc unsatisfied; (Chem) unsaturated; ~gesäuert adj Brot unleavened; ~geschält adj Obst, Gemüse unpeeled; Getreide, Reis unhusked; Baumstämme unstripped; ~geschehen adj undone; etw ~geschehen machen to undo sth.

Ungeschick nt -s, no pl, **Ungeschicklichkeit** f clumsiness. ~, verlaß mich nicht! butter-fingers!

ungeschickt adj clumsy, awkward; (unbedacht) careless, undiplomatic. **U~ läßt grüßen!** (inf) butter-fingers!

Ungeschicktheit f siehe Ungeschick.

ungeschlacht adj (pej) hulking great; Sitten barbaric.

Un-: u~geschlechtlich adj asexual; u~geschliffen adj Edelstein, Glas uncut; Messer etc blunt; (fig) Benehmen, Mensch uncouth; ~geschliffenheit f (fig) uncouthness; u~geschmälert adj undiminished; u~geschmeidig adj Stoff, Leder rough; Haar coarse; u~geschminkt adj without make-up; (fig) Wahrheit unvarnished; etw u~geschminkt berichten to give an unvarnished report of sth.

ungeschoren adj unshorn; (fig) spared. jdn ~ lassen (inf) to spare sb; (ungestraft) to let sb off (scot-free); ~ davonkommen (inf) to get off (scot-free).

Un-: u~geschrieben adj attr unwritten; u~geschult adj untrained; u~geschützt adj unprotected; Schachfigur auch unguarded; (Mil) Einheit exposed; Anlagen undefended; (Sport) Tor undefended; u~gesehen adj unseen; u~gesellig adj unsociable; Tier non-gregarious; ~geselligkeit f siehe adj unsociableness; non-gregariousness; u~gesetzlich adj unlawful, illegal; ~gesetzlichkeit f unlawfulness, illegality; u~gesichert adj unsecured, not secured; Schußwaffe cocked, with the safety catch off; u~gesittet adj uncivilized; u~gestalt adj (geh) Mensch misshapen, deformed; u~gestempelt adj unstamped; Briefmarke unfranked; (für Sammler) mint; u~gestillt adj Durst unquenched; Hunger unappeased; Blutung unstaunched; Schmerz unrelieved; Verlangen unfulfilled; Neugier unsatisfied; u~gestört adj undisturbed; (Rad, TV etc) without interference; u~gestraft adv with impunity.

ungestüm ['ungəʃty:m] adj impetuous.

Ungestüm ['ungəʃty:m] nt -(e)s, no pl impetuousness.

un-: ~gesühnt adj unexpiated, unatoned; ~gesund adj unhealthy; (schädlich) harmful; ~gesüßt adj unsweetened; ~getan adj undone; etw ~getan machen to undo sth; ~getauft adj unchristened; (inf: unverwässert) undiluted; ~geteilt adj undivided; ~getilgt adj Schulden uncleared; ~getragen adj Kleidung new, unworn; ~getreu adj (liter) disloyal, faithless (liter); ~getrübt adj clear; Glück, Freude perfect, unspoilt.

Ungetüm ['ungəty:m] nt -(e)s, -e monster.

un-: ~geübt adj unpractised; Mensch out of practice; ~gewandt adj awkward; ~gewarnt adj unwarned; ~gewaschen adj unwashed.

ungewiß adj uncertain; (vage) vague. **ein Sprung/eine Reise ins Ungewisse** (fig) a leap/a journey into the unknown; **jdn (über etw acc) im ungewissen lassen** to leave sb in the dark (about sth); **im ungewissen bleiben/sein** to stay/be in the dark.

Ungewißheit f uncertainty.

Ungewitter nt (obs) siehe Unwetter.

ungewöhnlich 1 adj unusual. 2 adv unusually; (äußerst auch) exceptionally.

Ungewöhnlichkeit f unusualness.

ungewohnt adj (fremdartig) strange, unfamiliar; (unüblich) unusual. **das ist mir ~** I am unaccustomed or not used to it.

ungewollt adj unintentional. **er mußte ~ lachen** he couldn't help laughing.

un-: ~gewürzt adj unseasoned; ~gezählt adj (unzählbar) countless; (nicht gezählt) uncounted; ~gezähmt adj untamed; (fig) uncurbed; ~gezeichnet adj unsigned.

Ungeziefer nt -s, no pl pests pl, vermin; (old fig) vermin.

ungezielt adj unaimed. **~ schießen** to shoot without taking aim.

ungezogen adj naughty, ill-mannered.

Ungezogenheit f (a) no pl naughtiness, unmannerliness. **(b)** (ungezogene Handlung) bad manners no indef art. **so eine ~ von dir!** what bad manners!; **noch mehr solche ~en, und es setzt was!** if you don't stop being naughty you'll catch it.

Un-: u~gezügelt 1 adj (unbeherrscht) unbridled; (ausschweifend) dissipated; 2 adv without restraint; u~gezwungen adj casual, informal; sich u~gezwungen bewegen to feel quite free; ~gezwungenheit f casualness, informality; u~giftig adj nonpoisonous.

Unglaube m unbelief, lack of faith; (esp Philos) scepticism.

unglaubhaft adj incredible, unbelievable.

ungläubig 1 adj unbelieving; (Rel) infidel; (zweifelnd) doubting, disbelieving. **~er Thomas** (Bibl, fig) doubting Thomas. 2 adv doubtingly, doubtfully, in disbelief.

Ungläubige(r) mf unbeliever; (Rel) infidel.

unglaublich adj unbelievable, incredible. **das grenzt ans U~e** that's almost incredible.

unglaubwürdig adj implausible; Dokument dubious; Mensch unreliable. **diese Regierung wirkt völlig ~** this government lacks credibility; **sich ~ machen** to lose credibility.

Unglaubwürdigkeit f siehe adj implausibility; dubiousness; unreliability.

ungleich 1 adj (nicht gleichartig) Charaktere dissimilar, unlike pred; Größe, Farbe different; (nicht gleichwertig, nicht vergleichbar) Mittel, Waffen unequal; (Math) not equal. **fünf plus fünf ~ neun** five plus five does not equal nine; **sie sind ein ~es Paar** they are very different; **das Zeichen für ~** the not-equals sign. 2 adv much, incomparably.

Ungleich-: u~artig adj dissimilar; ~gewicht nt (fig) imbalance.

Ungleichheit f siehe adj dissimilarity; difference; inequality; difference.

Ungleichheitszeichen nt (Math) not-equals sign.

Ungleich-: u~mäßig adj uneven; Atemzüge, Gesichtszüge, Puls irregular; u~mäßig lang of uneven length; ~mäßigkeit f siehe adj unevenness; irregularity; u~namig adj (Math) of different denominations; (Phys) opposite, unlike; u~seitig adj (Math) Vieleck irregular.

Ungleichung f (Math) inequation.

Unglück nt -(e)s, -e (Unfall, Vorfall) accident; (Mißgeschick auch) mishap; (Schicksalsschlag) disaster, tragedy; (Unheil) misfortune; (Pech, im Aberglauben, bei Glücksspiel) bad luck; (Unglücklichsein) unhappiness. **in sein ~ rennen** to head for disaster; **sich ins ~ stürzen** to rush headlong into disaster; **du stürzt mich noch ins ~!** you'll be my undoing!; **das ist auch kein ~ that is not a disaster;** so or **welch ein ~!** what a disaster!; **er hat im Leben viel ~ gehabt** he has experienced a great deal of misfortune in life; **er hatte das ~, dabeizusein** he had the misfortune to be present; **es ist ein ~, daß ...** it is bad luck that ...; **das ~ wollte es, daß ...** as (bad) luck would have it, ...; **das bringt ~** that brings bad luck, that's unlucky; **zum ~, zu allem ~** to make matters worse; **ein ~ kommt selten allein** (Prov) it never rains but it pours (Prov); **~ im Spiel, Glück in der Liebe** (prov) unlucky at cards, lucky in love; siehe Glück, Häufchen.

unglückbringend adj (geh) ominous, unpropitious.

unglücklich adj (a) (traurig) Mensch, Gesicht etc unhappy; Liebe unrequited; Liebesgeschichte unhappy. **~ verliebt sein** to be crossed in love.

(b) (bedauerlich) sad, unfortunate. **~ enden** or **ausgehen** to turn out badly, to end in disaster; **eine ~e Figur abgeben** to cut a sorry figure.

Unglückliche(r) mf unhappy person, unhappy man/woman etc. **ich ~(r)!** poor me!; **der ~!** the poor man!

unglücklicherweise adv unfortunately.

Unglücks-: ~bote m bringer of bad tidings; ~botschaft f bad tidings pl.

Unglücks-: u~selig adj (liter) (a) (Unglück habend) unfortunate, hapless; (armselig) miserable; (bedauernswert) lamentable; (b) (u~bringend) disastrous; ~selige(r) mf (liter) (poor) wretch; **ich ~selige(r)** woe is me! (liter); u~seligerweise adv (liter) unfortunately.

Unglücks-: ~fahrer m driver who caused an/the accident; ~fall m accident, mishap; **ein tragischer ~fall** a tragic accident; ~kind nt, ~mensch m unlucky person, unlucky man/woman etc; **du ~mensch** you unlucky man/woman; **ich war schon immer ein ~mensch/~kind** I've always been unlucky; ~rabe m (inf) unlucky thing (inf); ~tag m fateful day; ~vogel m (inf) unlucky thing (inf); ~wagen m accident car; ~wurm m (inf) poor soul; **du ~wurm!** you poor old thing! (inf); ~zahl f unlucky number.

Ungnade f disgrace, disfavour. **bei jdm in ~ fallen** to fall out of favour with sb.

ungnädig adj ungracious; (hum) unkind, harsh. **etw ~ aufnehmen** to take sth with bad grace.

un-: ~grammatisch adj ungrammatical; ~graziös adj ungraceful, inelegant.

Ungulaten [ungu'la:tn] pl (Zool) ungulates pl.

ungültig adj (nicht gültig) invalid; (nicht mehr gültig) no longer valid; (nichtig) void; Stimmzettel spoilt; (Sport) Tor disallowed. „~" (in Paß) "cancelled"; ~er Sprung no-jump; etw für ~ erklären to declare sth null and void; eine Ehe für ~ erklären to annul a marriage.

Ungültigkeit f invalidity; (Nichtigkeit) voidness; (von Ehe) nullity; (von Tor) disallowing.

Ungültigmachung f (Admin) invalidation.

Ungunst f (liter) disfavour; (von Umständen, Lage) adversity; (von Witterung) inclemency. zu jds ~en to sb's disadvantage.

ungünstig adj unfavourable, disadvantageous; Termin inconvenient; Augenblick, Wetter bad; Licht unflattering; (nicht preiswert) expensive.

ungünstigstenfalls adv if the worst comes/came to the worst.

ungustiös ['uŋgʊstɨoːs] adj (esp Aus) siehe **unappetitlich**.

ungut adj bad; Verhältnis auch strained. ein ~es Gefühl haben to have an uneasy or bad feeling; nichts für ~! no offence!

un-: ~haltbar adj Zustand intolerable; Vorwurf, Behauptung etc untenable; Torschuß unstoppable; ~handlich adj unwieldy; ~harmonisch adj unharmonious; ~häuslich adj (inf) unhomely.

Unheil nt -s, no pl disaster. ~ stiften or anrichten to do damage.

unheilbar adj incurable. ~ krank sein to have a terminal illness.

Unheilbarkeit f incurability.

unheil-: ~bringend adj fateful, ominous; ~drohend, ~schwanger adj (liter) portentous.

Unheilsprophet m prophet of doom.

Unheilstifter m mischief-maker.

unheil-: ~verkündend adj (liter) ominous, fateful; ~voll adj disastrous.

unheimlich 1 adj (a) (angsterregend) frightening, eerie, sinister. das/er ist mir ~ it/he gives me the creeps (inf); mir ist ~ (zumute) it is uncanny.
(b) (inf) tremendous (inf).
2 adv [auch ʊnˈhaɪmlɪç] (inf: sehr) incredibly (inf). ~ viel Geld/viele Menschen a tremendous (inf) or an incredible (inf) amount of money/number of people.

Un-: u~heizbar adj unheatable; u~historisch adj unhistoric; u~höflich adj impolite; ~höflichkeit f impoliteness.

Unhold m -(e)s, -e (a) (old: Böser) fiend. (b) (Press sl) monster, fiend.

un-: ~hörbar adj silent; Frequenzen inaudible; ~hygienisch adj unhygienic.

Uni f -, -s (inf) varsity (dated Brit inf), "U" (US inf), university; siehe auch **Universität**.

uni [yˈniː] adj pred self-coloured, plain. in U~blau in plain blue.

UNICEF ['uːnitsɛf] f - (die) UNICEF.

un-: ~idealistisch adj unidealistic; ~idiomatisch adj unidiomatic.

uniert adj (Eccl) Kirche uniate.

Unierte(r) mf decl as adj (Eccl) member of a uniate church.

unifarben [yˈniː-] adj siehe **uni**.

Uniform f -, -en uniform; siehe **ausziehen**.

uniform adj uniform.

uniformieren* vt (a) (mit Uniform ausstatten) to uniform. (b) (einheitlich machen) to make uniform.

uniformiert adj uniformed.

Uniformierte(r) mf decl as adj person etc in uniform.

Uniformität f uniformity.

Uniformrock m tunic.

Unikum nt -s, -s or **Unika** a (Einmaliges) unique thing etc. ein ~ a curiosity; (Seltenheit) a rarity. (b) (inf) real character.

unilateral adj unilateral.

un-: ~intellektuell adj unintellectual; ~intelligent adj unintelligent; ~interessant adj uninteresting; sein Angebot ist für uns ~interessant his offer is of no interest to us; das ist doch völlig ~interessant that's of absolutely no interest; ~interessiert adj (neutral) disinterested; (nicht interessiert) uninterested.

Union f -, -en union. die ~ (BRD Pol) the CDU and CSU.

Unionsparteien pl (BRD Pol) CDU and CSU parties pl.

Unisono nt -s, -s or **Unisoni** (Mus) unison.

unisono adv (Mus, fig) in unison.

Unitarier(in f) [-ɪɐ, -ɪɐɪn] m -s, - Unitarian.

Unitarismus m Unitarianism.

Unität f (a) siehe **Einheit**. (b) siehe **Einzigkeit**. (c) (hum: Universität) varsity (dated Brit inf), "U" (US inf), university.

Univ. abbr of **Universität**.

universal, universell [univɛr-] adj universal.

Universal- [univɛrˈzaːl-] in cpds all-purpose, universal; (Mech) universal; Bildung etc general; ~entwickler m (Phot) universal developer; ~erbe m universal successor, sole heir; ~genie nt universal genius; ~geschichte f world history.

Universalien [univɛrˈzaːliən] pl (Philos, Ling) universals.

Universalität [univɛrzaliˈtɛːt] f universality.

Universal- [univɛrˈzaːl-]: ~mittel nt universal remedy, cureall; ~reiniger m general-purpose cleaner; ~religion f universal religion.

universell [univɛr-] siehe **universal**.

Universität [univɛrziˈtɛːt] f university. die ~ Freiburg, die Freiburger ~ the university of Freiburg, Freiburg university; auf die ~ gehen, die ~ besuchen to go to university; die ~ verlassen to leave university; (das Gebäude) to leave the university; an eine ~ berufen werden to be appointed to a professorship or given a chair.

Universitäts- in cpds university; siehe auch **Hochschul-**; ~bibliothek f university library; ~buchhandlung f university bookshop (Brit) or bookstore (esp US); ~dozent m senior lecturer (Brit), associate professor (US); ~gelände nt university campus; ~institut nt university institute; ~klinik f university clinic or hospital; ~laufbahn f university career; ~stadt f university town; ~studium nt (Ausbildung) university

training; dazu ist ein ~studium erforderlich you need a degree for that; ~zeit f university years pl.

Universum [uniˈvɛrzʊm] nt -s, no pl universe.

unkameradschaftlich adj uncomradely; Schüler, Verhalten unfriendly.

Unke f -, -n toad; (inf: Schwarzseher) Jeremiah.

unken vi (inf) to foretell gloom.

unkenntlich adj unrecognizable; Inschrift etc indecipherable.

Unkenntlichkeit f siehe adj unrecognizableness; indecipherability. bis zur ~ beyond recognition.

Unkenntnis f, no pl ignorance. jdn in ~ über etw (acc) lassen to leave sb in ignorance about sth; in ~ über etw (acc) sein to be ignorant about sth; ~ schützt vor Strafe nicht (Prov) ignorance is no excuse.

Unkenruf m (fig) prophecy of doom.

Un-: u~keusch adj unchaste; ~keuschheit f unchastity; u~kindlich adj unchildlike; u~kirchlich adj secular.

unklar adj (unverständlich) unclear; (ungeklärt) unclarified; (undeutlich) blurred, indistinct; Wetter hazy. es ist mir völlig ~, wie das geschehen konnte I (just) can't understand how that could happen; ich bin mir darüber noch im ~en I'm not quite clear about that yet; über etw (acc) völlig im ~en sein to be completely in the dark about sth; jdn über etw (acc) im ~en lassen to leave sb in the dark about sth; nur ~ zu erkennen sein not to be easily discernible, not to be easy to make out.

Unklarheit f lack of clarity; (über Tatsachen) uncertainty. darüber herrscht noch ~ it is still uncertain or unclear.

Un-: u~kleidsam adj unflattering; u~klug adj unwise, imprudent, ill-advised; ~klugheit f imprudence; (Handlung) imprudent act; u~kollegial adj uncooperative; u~kompliziert adj straightforward, uncomplicated; u~komplizierter more straightforward, less complicated; ~kompliziertheit f straightforwardness; u~kontrollierbar adj uncontrollable; u~kontrollierbar werden (Mißbrauch etc) to get out of hand; u~kontrolliert adj unchecked; u~konventionell adj unconventional; u~korrekt adj (a) improper; (b) siehe **inkorrekt**; ~korrektheit f impropriety.

Unkosten pl costs pl; (Ausgaben) expenses pl. die ~ (für etw) tragen to bear the cost(s) (of sth); to pay the expenses (for sth); das ist mit großen ~ verbunden that involves a great deal of expense; (mit etw) ~ haben to incur expense (with sth); sich in ~ stürzen (inf) to go to a lot of expense; sich in geistige ~ stürzen (hum) to strain oneself (hum, iro).

Unkosten-: ~beitrag m contribution towards costs/expenses; ~vergütung f reimbursement of expenses.

Unkraut nt weed. ~, Unkräuter weeds; ~ vergeht nicht (Prov) it would take more than that to finish me/him etc off! (hum).

Unkraut-: ~bekämpfung f weed control; ~bekämpfungsmittel nt weed killer, herbicide (form); ~vertilgung f weed killing; ~vertilgungsmittel nt weed killer, herbicide (form).

Un-: u~kriegerisch adj unwarlike; u~kritisch adj uncritical; u~kultiviert 1 adj uncultivated; Mensch auch uncultured; 2 adv in an uncultivated or uncultured manner; ~kultur f (geh) lack of culture; u~kündbar adj permanent; Vertrag binding, not terminable; Anleihe irredeemable; in u~kündbarer Stellung in a permanent position; ~kündbarkeit f permanence; binding nature; irredeemability.

unkundig adj ignorant (+gen of). einer Sprache ~ sein to be unacquainted with or to have no knowledge of a language; des Lesens/Schreibens ~ sein to be illiterate, not to be able to read/write.

Un-: u~künstlerisch adj unartistic; u~längst adv (geh) recently; u~lauter adj dishonest; Wettbewerb unfair; u~leidlich adj disagreeable, unpleasant; u~lenkbar adj uncontrollable; Fahrzeug unsteerable; u~lesbar, u~leserlich adj unreadable; Handschrift etc auch illegible; ~leserlichkeit f siehe adj unreadableness; illegibility; u~leugbar adj undeniable, indisputable; u~lieb adj: es ist mir nicht u~lieb, daß ... I am quite glad that ...; u~liebenswürdig adj not very pleasant.

unliebsam adj unpleasant. er ist dem Lehrer ~ aufgefallen his behaviour brought him to the teacher's notice; das ist mir noch in ~er Erinnerung that's still an unpleasant memory.

Un-: u~liniert adj Papier unruled, unlined; ~logik f illogicality, lack of logic; u~logisch adj illogical; u~lösbar adj (a) (fig) (untrennbar) indissoluble; (nicht lösbar) Problem etc insoluble; Widerspruch irreconcilable; (b) (lit) (Chem) insoluble; Knoten etc inextricable; u~löslich adj (Chem) insoluble.

Unlust f, no pl (a) (Widerwille) reluctance. etw mit ~ tun to do sth reluctantly or with reluctance.
(b) (Lustlosigkeit, Langeweile) listlessness; (St Ex) slackness.

Unlustgefühl nt siehe Unlust (a) feeling of reluctance. (b) listlessness no pl.

unlustig adj (gelangweilt) bored; (widerwillig) reluctant. ich bin heute ausgesprochen ~ I just can't find any enthusiasm today.

Un-: u~mädchenhaft adj Kleidung unfeminine, ungirlish; Benehmen unladylike; (rauhbeinig) tomboyish; u~magnetisch adj non-magnetic; u~maniert adj (liter) unmannered (liter), unaffected; u~manierlich adj (dated) unmannerly auch; u~männlich adj unmanly; ~männlichkeit f unmanliness; u~marxistisch adj non-marxist; u~maskiert adj Ballbesucher etc undisguised; Bankräuber etc unmasked.

Unmasse f (inf) load (inf). eine ~ Leute/Bücher or an Büchern, ~n von Leuten/Büchern a load of people/books (inf), loads or masses of people/books (inf).

unmaßgeblich adj (nicht entscheidend) Urteil unauthoritative; (unwichtig) Äußerung, Mensch inconsequential, of no consequence. nach meiner ~en Meinung (hum) in my humble opinion (hum).

unmäßig adj excessive, immoderate. ~ **essen/trinken** to eat/drink to excess; **er hat gestern ~ getrunken** he drank far too much or an excessive amount yesterday.

Unmäßigkeit f excessiveness, immoderateness. ~ **im Essen/Trinken** excessive eating/drinking.

un-: ~**materialistisch** adj unmaterialistic; ~**medizinisch** adj unmedical; ~**melodisch** adj unmelodious.

Unmenge f vast number; (bei unzählbaren Mengenbegriffen) vast amount. ~**n von Leuten, eine ~ Leute** a vast number or vast numbers of people; ~**n essen** to eat an enormous amount, to eat masses (inf).

Unmensch m brute, monster. **ich bin ja kein ~** I'm not an ogre.

unmenschlich adj (a) inhuman. (b) (inf: ungeheuer) tremendous, terrific.

Unmenschlichkeit f inhumanity.

un-: ~**merklich** adj imperceptible; ~**meßbar** adj unmeasurable; ~**methodisch** adj unmethodical; ~**militärisch** adj unmilitary; ~**militaristisch** adj unmilitaristic; ~**mischbar** adj unmixable, immiscible (form); ~**mißverständlich** adj unequivocal, unambiguous; **jdm etw ~mißverständlich zu verstehen geben** to tell sb sth in no uncertain terms.

unmittelbar 1 adj Nähe, Nachbarschaft etc immediate; (direkt) direct; (Jur) Besitz, Besitzer direct, actual. **aus ~er Nähe schießen** to fire at close range.
2 adv immediately; (ohne Umweg) directly. ~ **danach** or **darauf** immediately or straight afterwards; ~ **vor** (+ dat) (zeitlich) immediately before; (räumlich) right or directly in front of; **das berührt mich ~** it affects me directly.

un-: ~**möbliert** adj unfurnished; ~**modern** adj old-fashioned; ~**modern werden** to go out of fashion; **es gilt als ~modern, das zu tun** it's considered old-fashioned to do that; ~**modisch** adj unfashionable.

unmöglich 1 adj impossible; (pej inf: unpassend auch) ridiculous. **das ist mir ~** that is impossible for me; **U~es/das U~e** the impossible; **etw ~ machen** to make sth impossible; **jdm etw ~ machen** to make it impossible for sb to do sth; ~ **aussehen** (inf) to look ridiculous; **jdn/sich ~ machen** to make sb/oneself (look) ridiculous, to make sb look a fool/to make a fool of oneself.
2 adv (keinesfalls) not possibly; (pej inf: unpassend) impossibly. **ich kann es ~ tun** I cannot possibly do it.

Unmöglichkeit f impossibility.

Un-: ~**moral** f immorality; **u~moralisch** adj immoral; **u~motiviert** 1 adj unmotivated; 2 adv without motivation; **u~mündig** adj underage; (fig: geistig unselbständig) sheeplike; ~**mündige(r)** mf decl as adj minor; ~**mündigkeit** f minority; (fig: geistige Unselbständigkeit) mental immaturity; **u~musikalisch** adj unmusical; ~**musikalität** f lack of musicality, unmusicalness.

Unmut m ill-humour; (Unzufriedenheit) displeasure (über + acc at).

unmutig adj ill-humoured; (unzufrieden) displeased (über + acc at).

Un-: **u~nachahmlich** adj inimitable; **u~nachgiebig** adj Material etc inflexible; (fig) Haltung, Mensch auch intransigent, unyielding; **sich u~nachgiebig verhalten** to be obstinate or adamant; ~**nachgiebigkeit** f inflexibility; intransigence; **u~nachsichtig** 1 adj (stärker) merciless, pitiless, Strenge unrelenting; 2 adv hinrichten mercilessly, pitilessly; bestrafen severely; ~**nachsichtigkeit** f severity; mercilessness, pitilessness; **u~nachsichtlich** adj siehe **u~nachsichtig**; **u~nahbar** adj unapproachable, inaccessible; ~**nahbarkeit** f unapproachableness, inaccessibility; **u~natürlich** adj unnatural; (abnorm auch) abnormal; **er ißt u~natürlich viel** he eats an abnormal amount; ~**natürlichkeit** f unnaturalness; abnormality; **u~nennbar** adj (liter) unspeakable, unutterable (liter); **u~normal** adj abnormal; **u~nötig** adj unnecessary, needless; **sich u~nötig aufregen** to get unnecessarily or needlessly excited; **u~nötigerweise** adv unnecessarily, needlessly.

unnütz adj useless; (umsonst auch) pointless. ~ **Geld ausgeben** to spend money unnecessarily or needlessly.

unnützerweise adv unnecessarily, needlessly.

UNO ['uːno] f -, no pl **die ~** the UN sing.

Un-: **u~ökonomisch** adj uneconomic; Fahrweise, Konsumverhalten uneconomical; **u~ordentlich** adj untidy; Lebenswandel disorderly; ~**ordentlichkeit** f untidiness; disorderliness.

Un|ordnung f disorder no indef art; (in Zimmer etc auch) untidiness no indef art; (Durcheinander) muddle, mess. **in ~ geraten** to get into (a state of) disorder/become untidy/get into a muddle or mess; **etw in ~ bringen** to get sth in a mess, to mess sth up; ~ **machen** or **schaffen** to put or throw everything into disorder, to turn everything upside down.

Un-: **u~organisch** adj inorganic; **u~organisiert** 1 adj (a) disorganized; (b) siehe **nichtorganisiert**; 2 adv in a disorganized fashion or way; **u~orthodox** adj unorthodox; ~**paarhufer** pl (Zool) odd-toed ungulates pl; **u~paar(ig)** adj unpaired; (Med) azygous (spec); **u~pädagogisch** adj educationally unsound; Lehrer etc bad (as a teacher).

unparlamentarisch adj unparliamentary.

unparteiisch adj impartial, neutral; Meinung, Richter, Urteil impartial, unbiased.

Unparteiische(r) mf decl as adj impartial or neutral person. **die Meinung eines ~n einholen** to get an impartial opinion; **der ~** (Sport) the referee.

Un-: **u~parteilich** adj (esp Pol) neutral; ~**parteilichkeit** f neutrality; **u~passend** adj (esp Pol) (unangebracht) unsuitable, inappropriate; Zeit auch inconvenient; Augenblick inconvenient, inopportune; **u~passierbar** adj impassable.

unpäßlich adj (geh) indisposed (form), unwell (auch euph). **sich**

~ **fühlen** to be indisposed/feel unwell.

Unpäßlichkeit f (geh) indisposition (form). **sie mußte die Vorstellung wegen ~ leider absagen** unfortunately she had to cancel the performance because she was indisposed.

Un-: **u~patriotisch** adj unpatriotic; ~**person** f (Pol) unperson; **u~persönlich** adj impersonal (auch Ling); Mensch distant, aloof; **jdn mit u~persönlichem Abstand behandeln** to be aloof with sb, to treat sb with aloofness; ~**persönlichkeit** f siehe adj impersonality; distance, aloofness; **u~pfändbar** adj (Jur) unseizable; **u~poetisch** adj unpoetic(al); **u~politisch** adj unpolitical; **u~populär** adj unpopular; **u~praktisch** adj Mensch unpractical; Maschine, Lösung impractical; **u~prätentiös** adj (geh) unpretentious; **u~präzis(e)** adj imprecise; **u~problematisch** adj (ohne Probleme) unproblematic; (einfach, leicht) uncomplicated; **das wird nicht ganz u~problematisch sein** it won't be without its problems; **u~produktiv** adj unproductive; Kapital auch idle; ~**produktivität** f siehe adj unproductiveness; idleness; **u~proportioniert** adj out of proportion, disproportionate; Körper out of proportion, ill-proportioned.

unpünktlich adj Mensch unpunctual; Zug not on time. ~ **kommen/abfahren** to come/leave late; **er ist immer ~** he's never punctual or on time; **die Züge dort fahren immer ~** the trains there never run to time.

Unpünktlichkeit f unpunctuality. **er kommt wegen der ~ der Züge oft zu spät** he's often late because the trains don't run to time.

un-: ~**qualifiziert** adj unqualified; Äußerung incompetent; ~**quittiert** adj unreceipted; ~**rasiert** adj unshaven; siehe **fern**.

Unrast f -, no pl (geh) restlessness.

Unrat ['uːnraːt] m -(e)s, no pl (geh) refuse; (fig) filth. ~ **wittern** to suspect something.

un-: ~**rationell** adj inefficient; ~**ratsam** adj inadvisable, unadvisable; ~**realistisch** adj unrealistic; ~**recht** adj wrong; **auf ~rechte Gedanken kommen** (dated) to get naughty or wicked ideas; **das ist mir gar nicht so ~recht** I don't really mind.

Unrecht nt -s, no pl wrong, injustice. **zu ~** verdächtigt wrongly, unjustly; **diese Vorurteile bestehen ganz zu ~** these prejudices are quite unfounded; **nicht zu ~** not without good reason; **im ~ sein** to be wrong; **jdn/sich ins ~ setzen** to put sb/oneself in the wrong; **ihm ist im Leben viel ~ geschehen** he has suffered many injustices or he has often been wronged in life; **u~ bekommen** to be shown to be wrong; **u~ haben** to be wrong; **jdm u~ geben** to contradict sb; **u~ handeln/tun** to do wrong; **jdm u~ tun** to do sb an injustice, to do wrong by sb; **Sie haben nicht ganz u~** you're not entirely wrong.

Unrecht-: **u~mäßig** adj illegitimate, unlawful, illegal; Thronfolger wrongful; **sich etw u~mäßig aneignen** to misappropriate sth; **u~mäßigerweise** adv illegitimately, unlawfully, illegally; wrongfully; ~**mäßigkeit** f unlawfulness, illegality; wrongfulness.

Un-: **u~redlich** adj dishonest; ~**redlichkeit** f dishonesty; **u~reell** adj unfair; (unredlich) dishonest; Preis, Geschäft unreasonable; **u~reflektiert** adj Strahlen unreflected; Bemerkung spontaneous; Mensch who acts/speaks without thinking; **etw u~reflektiert wiedergeben** to repeat sth without thinking.

unregelmäßig adj irregular (auch Ling); Zähne, Gesicht, Handschrift auch uneven. ~ **essen/schlafen** not to eat/sleep regularly.

Unregelmäßigkeit f siehe adj irregularity; unevenness. **ihm wurden (finanzielle) ~en vorgeworfen** he was accused of (financial) irregularities.

Un-: **u~reif** adj Obst unripe; Mensch, Plan, Gedanke, Werk immature; ~**reife** f siehe adj unripeness; immaturity.

unrein adj (schmutzig) not clean, dirty; Klang, Ton impure; Atem, Haut bad; (Rel) Speise, Tier, Mensch unclean; Gedanken, Taten unchaste, impure. **etw ins ~e sprechen** to say sth off the record; **etw ins ~e schreiben** to write sth out in rough.

Unreinheit f siehe adj dirtiness; impurity; (von Atem) unpleasantness; uncleanness, unchasteness, impurity. **die ~ ihrer Haut** her bad skin.

Un-: **u~reinlich** adj not clean; ~**reinlichkeit** f uncleanliness; **u~rentabel** adj unprofitable.

Unrentabilität f, no pl unprofitableness.

unrettbar adv ~ **verloren** irretrievably lost; (wegen Krankheit) beyond all hope; **die ~ Verdammten** those damned beyond redemption or salvation.

Un-: **u~richtig** adj incorrect; (Admin) Angaben etc false; **u~richtigerweise** adv incorrectly; falsely; ~**richtigkeit** f incorrectness; (Admin: von Angaben etc) falseness; (Fehler) error, mistake; **u~ritterlich** adj unchivalrous; ~**ritterlichkeit** f lack of chivalry, unchivalrousness; **u~romantisch** adj unromantic.

Unruh f -, -en (von Uhr) balance spring.

Unruhe f -, -n (a) no pl restlessness; (Nervosität) agitation; (Besorgnis) agitation, disquiet. **in ~ sein** to be restless; (besorgt) to be agitated or uneasy.
(b) no pl (Lärm) noise, disturbance; (Geschäftigkeit) (hustle and) bustle.
(c) no pl (Unfrieden) unrest no pl, trouble. ~ **stiften** to create unrest; (in Familie, Schule) to make trouble.
(d) (politische) ~**n** (political) disturbances or unrest no pl.

Unruhe-: ~**herd** m trouble spot; ~**stifter(in** f) m -s, - troublemaker.

unruhig adj restless; (nervös auch) fidgety no adv; (laut, belebt) noisy; Schlaf troubled no adv, fitful, uneasy; Zeit etc troubled, uneasy; Bild, Muster busy; Meer troubled. **ein ~er Geist** (inf) a restless creature.

unrühmlich adj inglorious. ein ~es Ende nehmen to have an inglorious end.

uns 1 pers pron acc, dat of wir us; (dat auch) to/for us. bei ~ (zu Hause, im Betrieb etc) at our place; (in unserer Beziehung) between us; (in unserem Land) in our country; bei ~ zu Hause/im Garten at our house/in our garden; einer von ~ one of us; Freund von ~ a friend of ours; das gehört ~ that is ours or belongs to us; viele Grüße von ~ beiden/allen best wishes from both/all of us.
2 refl pron acc, dat ourselves; (einander) each other, one another. wir freuten ~ we were glad; wir wollen ~ ein neues Auto kaufen we want to buy (ourselves) a new car; ~ selbst ourselves; wann sehen wir ~ wieder? when will we see each other again?; unter ~ gesagt between ourselves, between you and me; mitten unter ~ in our midst; hier sind wir unter ~ we are alone here; das bleibt unter ~ it won't go any further.

unsachgemäß adj improper. ein Gerät ~ behandeln to put an appliance to improper use.

unsachlich adj (a) (nicht objektiv) unobjective. (b) (fehl am Platz) uncalled-for. ~ werden to become personal.

Unsachlichkeit f lack of objectivity, unobjectiveness. diese Bemerkung zeugt von ~ this remark is/was uncalled-for.

unsagbar, unsäglich adj (liter) unspeakable, unutterable (liter).

unsanft adj rough; Druck ungentle; (unhöflich) rude. ~ aus dem Schlaf gerissen werden to be rudely awakened.

unsauber adj (a) (ungewaschen, schmutzig) dirty, not clean. (b) (unordentlich) Handschrift, Arbeit untidy; (nicht exakt) Schuß, Schlag, Schnitt inaccurate; Ton, Klang impure. (c) (unmoralisch) shady, underhand; Spielweise dirty (inf), unfair.

Unsauberkeit f siehe adj (a, b) (a) dirtiness. (b) untidiness; inaccuracy; impurity.

unschädlich adj harmless; Genußmittel, Medikament auch safe, innocuous; Bombe auch safe. jdn/etw ~ machen (inf) to take care of sb/sth (inf).

Unschädlichkeit f siehe adj harmlessness; safeness, innocuousness; safeness.

unscharf adj blurred, fuzzy; Foto auch out of focus; Justierung unsharp; (Rad) indistinct, unclear; Erinnerung, Vorstellung indistinct, hazy. der Sender/das Radio ist ~ eingestellt the station/the radio is not clearly tuned. (b) Munition blank; Bomben etc unprimed.

Unschärfe f siehe adj (a) blurredness, fuzziness; unsharpness; indistinctness; haziness. begriffliche ~ lack of conceptual clarity.

unschätzbar adj incalculable, inestimable; Hilfe invaluable. von ~em Wert invaluable; Schmuck etc priceless.

unscheinbar adj inconspicuous; (unattraktiv) Aussehen, Mensch unprepossessing.

Unscheinbarkeit f siehe adj inconspicuousness; unprepossessing nature.

unschicklich adj unseemly, improper. es ist ~ für eine junge Dame, das zu tun it ill becomes a young lady or it is unseemly or improper for a young lady to do that.

Unschicklichkeit f siehe adj unseemliness no indef art, impropriety.

unschlagbar adj unbeatable.

Unschlagbarkeit f unbeatability.

Unschlitt nt -(e)s, -e (old) tallow.

unschlüssig adj (unentschlossen, zögernd) irresolute, hesitant. sich (dat) ~ (über etw acc) sein to be undecided (about sth); to be hesitant about sth.

Unschlüssigkeit f siehe adj indecision; irresoluteness, hesitancy.

unschön adj (häßlich) unsightly; (stärker) ugly; Gesicht plain; (unangenehm) unpleasant. ~e Szenen ugly scenes.

Unschuld f, no pl (a) (Schuldlosigkeit) innocence. (b) (Jungfräulichkeit) virginity. (c) (Naivität, Unverdorbenheit) innocence; (fig: Mädchen) innocent. die ~ vom Lande (inf) a real innocent; in aller ~ in all innocence.

unschuldig adj (a) (nicht schuldig) innocent. an etw (dat) ~ sein not to be guilty of sth; er war völlig ~ an dem Unfall he was completely without blame in the accident, he was in no way responsible for the accident; sind Sie schuldig oder ~? — how do you plead, guilty or not guilty? — not guilty; jdn ~ verurteilen to convict sb when he is innocent; er sitzt ~ im Gefängnis he is being held, an innocent man, in prison.
(b) (jungfräulich) innocent, virginal. ~ in die Ehe gehen to be married a virgin; er/sie ist noch ~ he/she is still a virgin.
(c) (harmlos, unverdorben) innocent. ~ tun to act the innocent.

Unschuldige(r) mf decl as adj innocent (man/child etc). die ~n the innocent.

unschuldigerweise adv unjustly, despite one's innocence.

Unschulds-: ~beteuerung f protest of innocence; ~engel m (inf), ~lamm nt (inf) little innocent; ~miene f innocent face or expression; mit ~miene with an air of innocence; u~voll adj innocent; mit u~voller Miene with an air of innocence.

unschwer adv easily, without difficulty. das dürfte ja wohl ~ zu erraten sein that shouldn't have been too hard to guess.

Unsegen m (Unglück) misfortune; (Fluch) curse (für (up)on). sich zum ~ auswirken to become a curse.

unselbständig 1 adj Denken, Handeln lacking in independence, unindependent; Mensch auch dependent, unable to stand on one's own two feet. Einkünfte aus ~er Arbeit income from (salaried) employment; manche Menschen bleiben ihr Leben lang ~ some people never manage to stand on their own two feet; sei doch nicht immer so ~! show a bit of independence once in a while!
2 adv (mit fremder Hilfe) not independently. diese Scholar-

beit ist ~ angefertigt worden this exercise was not done independently.

Unselbständige(r) mf (Fin) employed person.

Unselbständigkeit f lack of independence, dependence.

unselig adj (unglücklich) unfortunate; (verhängnisvoll) ill-fated. Zeiten ~en Angedenkens! unhappy memories!; ich U~er! (old liter) oh unhappy wretch! (old liter), woe is me! (old liter); siehe Angedenken.

unser 1 poss pron (a) (adjektivisch) our. ~e or unsre Bücher our books.
(b) (old: substantivisch) ours.
2 pers pron gen of wir (old, Bibl, geh) of us. ~ beider gemeinsame Zukunft our common future; Herr, erbarme dich ~ Lord, have mercy upon us; ~ aller heimlicher Wunsch the secret wish of all of us.

unser|einer, unser|eins indef pron (inf) the likes of us (inf).

uns(e)re(r, s) poss pron, nt auch unsers (substantivisch) ours. der/die/das ~ (geh) ours; wir tun das U~ (geh) we are doing our bit; die U~n (geh) our family; das U~ (geh: Besitz) what is ours.

unser(er)seits adv (auf unserer Seite) for our part; (von unserer Seite) from or on our part. den Vorschlag haben wir ~ gemacht we made the suggestion ourselves.

uns(e)resgleichen indef pron people like us or ourselves. Menschen ~ people like us or ourselves.

uns(e)resteils adv siehe unser(er)seits.

uns(e)rige(r, s) poss pron (old, geh) der/die/das ~ ours; die U~n our families; das ~ (Besitz) what is ours; wir haben das U~ getan we have done our part.

unseriös adj Mensch slippery, not straight; Auftreten, Aussehen, Kleidung, Bemerkung frivolous; Firma, Bank untrustworthy, shady; Zeitung not serious; Verlag low-brow; Schriftsteller, Wissenschaftler not to be taken seriously, not serious, frivolous. das Geschäft war keineswegs ~ the deal was strictly above board.

unserseits adv siehe unser(er)seits.

unsersgleichen indef pron siehe uns(e)resgleichen.

unserthalben, unsertwegen adv on our behalf.

unsertwillen adv: um ~ for our sake.

Unservater nt -s, - (Sw) siehe Vaterunser.

unsicher adj (a) (gefährlich) dangerous, unsafe. die Gegend ~ machen (fig inf) to knock about the district (inf); sich ~ fühlen to feel unsafe.
(b) (nicht selbstbewußt, verunsichert) insecure, unsure (of oneself). jdn ~ machen to make sb feel unsure of himself/herself; sie blickte ~ im Kreise umher she looked round timidly.
(c) (ungewiß, zweifelhaft) unsure, uncertain; (unstabil) uncertain, unstable, unsettled.
(d) (ungeübt, ungefestigt) unsure; Hand unsteady; Kenntnisse shaky. ~ auf den Beinen unsteady on one's feet; mit ~er Hand with an unsteady hand.

Unsicherheit f siehe adj (a—c) (a) danger. (b) unsureness. (c) unsureness, uncertainty; uncertainty, instability.

Unsicherheitsfaktor m element of uncertainty.

unsichtbar adj (lit, fig) invisible.

Unsichtbarkeit f, no pl invisibility.

Unsinn m, no pl nonsense no indef art, rubbish no indef art. ~ machen or treiben to do silly things; ~ reden to talk nonsense; laß den ~! stop fooling about!; mach keinen ~, Hände hoch! (inf) no clever stuff – put your hands up! (inf); wirklich? mach keinen ~! (inf) really? – stop messing about! (inf); siehe Sinn.

unsinnig 1 adj (sinnlos) nonsensical, foolish; (ungerechtfertigt) unreasonable; (stärker) absurd. 2 adv nonsensically, foolishly; unreasonably; absurdly. ~ viel (inf) an incredible amount (inf); ~ hohe Preise (inf) ridiculously high prices (inf).

Unsinnigkeit f siehe adj foolishness; unreasonableness; absurdity.

Unsitte f (schlechte Gewohnheit) bad habit; (dummer Brauch) silly custom.

unsittlich adj immoral; (in sexueller Hinsicht) indecent.

Unsittlichkeit f siehe adj immorality; indecency.

unsoldatisch adj unsoldierly.

unsolid(e) adj Mensch free-living; (unredlich) Firma, Angebot, Geschäftsmann unreliable. ~ leben to have an unhealthy lifestyle; ein ~es Leben führen to be free-living; an dem Angebot war nichts U~es the offer was strictly above board.

Un-: u~sortiert adj unsorted; u~sozial adj Verhalten, Mensch antisocial; Maßnahmen, Politik unsocial; u~spezifisch adj non-specific; u~sportlich adj (a) (ungelenkig) unathletic; (b) (unfair) unsporting; ~sportlichkeit f (~fairness) lack of sportsmanship; und das bei seiner ~sportlichkeit! and he being so unathletic!

unsre pron siehe unser.

unsrerseits adv siehe uns(er)erseits.

unsresgleichen indef pron siehe uns(e)resgleichen.

unsresteils adv siehe uns(e)resteils.

unsretwegen adv siehe unsertwegen.

unsretwillen adv siehe unsertwillen.

unsrige(r, s) poss pron siehe uns(e)rige(r, s).

un-: ~stabil adj unstable; ~statthaft adj (form) inadmissible; (~gesetzlich) illegal; (Sport) not allowed.

unsterblich adj (a) immortal; Liebe undying. jdn ~ machen to immortalize sb. 2 adv (inf) utterly. sich ~ blamieren to make an utter fool or a complete idiot of oneself; ~ verliebt sein to be head over heels or madly in love (inf).

Unsterbliche(r) mf immortal.

Unsterblichkeit f immortality. die ~ seiner Liebe his undying love.

Unsterblichkeitsglaube m belief in immortality.

Unstern m, no pl (liter) unlucky star. die Liebe der beiden stand unter einem ~ their love was followed by an unlucky star.

unstet adj Glück, Liebe fickle; Mensch restless; (wankelmütig) changeable; Entwicklung unsteady; Leben unsettled.

Unstete f -, no pl siehe **Unstetigkeit.**

Unstetigkeit f siehe adj fickleness; restlessness; changeability; unsteadiness; unsettled nature.

Un-: u~stillbar adj (a) Durst, Wissensdurst unquenchable; Verlangen, Sehnsucht, Hunger insatiable; (b) Blutstrom uncontrollable; u~stimmig adj Aussagen etc at variance, differing attr; in einem Punkt sind wir noch u~stimmig we still disagree or differ on one point; ~stimmigkeit f (~genauigkeit, Fehler) discrepancy, inconsistency; (Streit) difference; u~stofflich adj immaterial; Seele auch incorporeal; u~streitig adv indisputably, incontestably; ~summe f vast sum; u~symmetrisch adj asymmetric(al).

unsympathisch adj unpleasant, disagreeable. er ist ~ he's unpleasant or a disagreeable type; das/er ist mir ~ I don't like that/him; am ~sten an diesen Leuten ist mir ... what I find most unpleasant about or what I like least about these people is ...

unsystematisch adj unsystematic.

untad(e)lig, untadelhaft (rare) adj impeccable; Verhalten auch irreproachable; Mensch beyond reproach.

untalentiert adj untalented.

Untat f atrocity, atrocious deed. ~en begehen (im Krieg etc) to commit atrocities.

untätig adj (müßig) idle; (nicht handelnd) passive; Vulkan inactive, dormant.

Untätigkeit f siehe adj idleness; passivity; dormancy.

Un-: u~tauglich adj (zu, für for) unsuitable; (für Wehrdienst) unfit; ~tauglichkeit f siehe adj unsuitability; unfitness; u~teilbar adj indivisible.

unten adv (im unteren Teil, am unteren Ende, in Rangfolge) at the bottom; (tiefer, drunten) (down) below; (an der Unterseite) underneath; (in Gebäude) (down) below, downstairs; (inf: geographisch) down south; (flußab) downstream; (tiefer gelegen) down there/here. von ~ from below; die Frau von ~ war gekommen the woman from downstairs or down below had come; nach ~ down; die Säule wird nach ~ hin breiter the column broadens out towards the base or bottom; bis ~ to the bottom; bis ~ ist es noch eine Stunde zu Fuß it's another hour's walk to the bottom; der Schneefall kam nicht bis ~ ins Tal the snow did not reach as far down as the valley; ~ am Berg/Fluß at the bottom of the hill/down by the river(side); ~ im Tal/Wasser/Garten down in the valley/water/garden; ~ im Glas at the bottom of the glass; ~ auf dem Bild at the bottom of the picture; ~ auf der Straße down on the street; dort or da/hier ~ down there/here; weiter ~ further down; ~ bleiben to stay down; sich ~ waschen (euph inf) to wash oneself down below (inf); rechts/links ~ down on the right/left; siehe ~ see below; er ist bei mir ~ durch (inf) I'm through or I've finished with him (inf); ich weiß schon nicht mehr, was oben und ~ ist (inf) I don't know whether I'm coming or going (inf) or whether I'm on my head or my heels (inf); ~ wohnen to live downstairs.

Unten-: u~an adv (am unteren Ende) at the far end; (in Reihenfolge: lit, fig) at the bottom; (bei jdm) u~an stehen (fig) not to be a priority (with sb), to be at the bottom of sb's list; u~drunter adv (inf) underneath; u~erwähnt, u~genannt adj attr mentioned below; der/die ~erwähnte or ~genannte the undermentioned (person) (form), the person mentioned below; bitte lesen Sie auch das u~erwähnte please also see below; u~herum adv (inf) down below (inf); u~liegend adj attr bottom; u~stehend adj following; (lit) standing below; im u~stehenden given below; u~stehendes the following; das U~stehende what follows.

unter prep (a) +dat (~halb von) under; (drunter) underneath, below; (U~ordnung ausdrückend) under; (zwischen, innerhalb) among(st); (weniger, geringer als) under, below. ~ 18 Jahren/DM 50 under 18 years (of age)/DM 50; ~ dem Durchschnitt below average; Temperaturen ~ 25 Grad temperatures below 25 degrees; Städte ~ 10.000 Einwohner(n) towns with a population of under or below 10,000; ~ sich (dat) sein to be by themselves; jdn ~ sich haben to have sb under one; ~ etw leiden to suffer from sth; ~ Mittag (dial) in the morning; ~ der Woche (dial) within the (working) week; ~ anderem inter alia, among other things.

(b) +acc under. bis ~ das Dach up to the bottom of the roof; ~ Verbrecher geraten to fall in with criminals.

Unter-: ~abteilung f subdivision; ~angebot nt lack (an + dat of); ~arm m forearm; ~art f (esp Biol) subspecies; ~ausschuß m subcommittee; ~bau m, pl -ten (von Gebäude) foundations pl; (von Brücke, Bahnstrecke, fig) substructure; (bei Straßen) (road)bed; ~begriff m member of a conceptual class, subsumable concept; u~belegt adj Hotel etc not full; Fortbildungskurs under-subscribed; das Hotel ist ziemlich u~belegt the hotel is not very full; u~belichten* vti insep (Phot) to underexpose; u~belichtet adj (Phot) underexposed; geistig u~belichtet sein (hum) to be a bit dim (inf); ~belichtung f underexposure; u~bemannt adj undermanned; u~besetzt adj understaffed; ~besetzung f understaffing; ~bett nt feather bed; u~bewerten* vt insep to underrate, to undervalue; ~bewertung f underrating no pl, undervaluation; u~bewußt adj subconscious; das ~bewußte the subconscious; ~bewußtsein nt subconscious; im ~bewußtsein subconsciously; u~bezahlen* vt insep to underpay; u~bezahlt adj underpaid; ~bezahlung f underpayment; u~bieten* vt insep irreg Konkurrenten to undercut; (fig) to surpass; sich gegenseitig u~bieten to undercut each other; eine kaum noch zu u~bietende Leistung an unsurpassable achievement (iro); ~bilanz f deficit balance; u~binden[1]* vt insep irreg to stop, to prevent; (Med) Blutung to ligature; u~binden[2] vt sep irreg to

tie (on) underneath; ~bindung f, no pl ending; (Med) ligature; u~bleiben* vi insep irreg aux sein (a) (aufhören) to cease, to stop; das hat zu u~bleiben that will have to cease or stop; (b) (nicht geschehen) not to occur or happen; das wäre besser u~blieben (Vorfall) it would have been better if it had never happened; (Bemerkung) it would have been better left unsaid; (c) (versäumt werden) to be omitted; ~bodenschutz m (Mot) underseal; u~brechen* insep irreg 1 vt to interrupt; Stille, Reise, Eintönigkeit, Langeweile, Gleichförmigkeit to break; (langfristig) to break off; Telefonverbindung to disconnect; Spiel to suspend, to stop; entschuldigen Sie bitte, wenn ich Sie u~breche forgive me for interrupting; wir sind u~brochen worden (am Telefon) we've been cut off; 2 vr to break off; ~brecher m -s, - (Elec) interrupter; (Aut) contact breaker; ~brecherkontakt m (Elec, Aut) (contact-breaker) point; ~brechung f interruption; break (+gen in); (von Telefonverbindung) disconnection; (von Spiel) stoppage; bei ~brechung der Reise when breaking the journey; ohne ~brechung without a break; nach einer kurzen ~brechung (Rad, TV) after a short break or intermission; mit ~brechungen with a few breaks in between; u~breiten* vt insep Plan to present; (jdm) einen Vorschlag u~breiten to make a proposal (to sb), to put a suggestion (to sb).

unterbringen vt sep irreg (a) (verstauen, Platz geben) to put; (in Heim, Krankenhaus etc) to put; Arbeitslose etc to fix up (bei with); Zitat (in Text etc) to get in (in etw (acc) sth). ich kann in meinem Auto noch einen ~ I can get one more or I have room for one more in my car; das Krankenhaus kann keine neuen Patienten ~ the hospital has room for or can accommodate no new patients; wir können noch zwei Lehrlinge ~, aber nicht mehr we can accommodate or find room for another two apprentices but no more; etw bei jdm ~ to leave sth with sb; ich kenne ihn, aber ich kann ihn nirgends ~ (inf) I know him, but I just can't place him.

(b) (Unterkunft geben) Menschen to accommodate; (in Haus, Hotel, Krankenhaus etc auch) to put up; Ausstellung, Sammlung auch to house. gut/schlecht untergebracht sein to have good/bad accommodation; (versorgt werden) to be well/badly looked after; wie sind Sie untergebracht? what's your accommodation like?; how are you looked after?

Unterbringung f accommodation.

Unterbruch m (Sw) siehe **Unterbrechung.**

unterbuttern vt sep (inf) (a) to sneak in (inf); (zuschießen) to throw in. (b) (unterdrücken) to ride roughshod over; (opfern) to sacrifice. er wird von ihr untergebuttert she dominates him.

Unterdeck nt (Naut) lower deck. im ~ below deck.

unterderhand adv secretly; verkaufen privately.

unterdes(sen) adv (in the) meantime, meanwhile.

Unterdruck m (Phys) below atmospheric pressure; (Med) low blood pressure, hypotension (spec).

unterdrücken* vt insep (a) (zurückhalten) Neugier, Gähnen, Lachen to suppress; Gefühle, Tränen auch to hold back, to restrain; Antwort, Bemerkung to hold back. (b) (beherrschen) Volk, Sklaven to oppress, to repress; Freiheit to suppress; Revolution to suppress, to put down. die Unterdrückten the oppressed.

Unterdrücker(in f) m -s, - oppressor.

Unterdrückung f siehe vt (a) suppression; restraining; holding back. (b) oppression, repression; suppression.

unterdurchschnittlich adj below average. er verdient ~ he has a below average income, he earns below the average.

untereinander adv (a) (gegenseitig) each other; (miteinander) among ourselves/themselves etc. Familien, die ~ heiraten families that intermarry. (b) (räumlich) one below or underneath the other.

untereinander- pref (a) (durcheinander-) together. (b) (örtlich) one below or underneath the other.

Unter-: u~entwickelt adj underdeveloped; (inf: geistig ~) thick (inf); ~entwicklung f underdevelopment.

untere(r, s) adj, superl **unterste(r, s)** lower.

Unter-: u~ernährt adj undernourished, suffering from malnutrition; ~ernährung f malnutrition.

unterfangen* vr insep irreg (geh) to dare, to venture. sich einer Sache (gen) ~ to dare to do sth, to venture (to do) sth.

Unterfangen nt -s, - (geh) venture, undertaking. ein schwieriges ~ a difficult undertaking.

unterfassen vt sep jdn ~ to take sb's arm; sie gingen untergefaßt they walked along arm in arm or with arms linked.

unterfliegen* vt insep irreg to fly underneath.

Unterfranken nt (Geog) Lower Franconia.

unterführen* vt insep to pass underneath. die Autobahn wird hier von einer Landstraße unterführt a highway passes underneath the motorway at this point.

Unterführung f (a) underpass; (für Fußgänger auch) subway. (b) (Typ etc) siehe **Unterführungszeichen.**

Unterführungszeichen nt (Typ) ditto (mark).

Unter-: ~funktion f insufficient function no indef art, hypofunction (spec); (eine) ~funktion der Schilddrüse thyroid insufficiency, hypothyroidism (spec); ~futter nt interfacing; u~füttern* vt insep to interface.

Untergang m (a) (von Schiff) sinking. (b) (von Gestirn) setting. (c) (das Zugrundegehen) (allmählich) decline; (völlig) destruction; (der Welt) end; (von Individuum) downfall, ruin. die Propheten des ~s the prophets of doom; dem ~ geweiht sein to be doomed; du bist noch mal mein ~! you'll be the death of me! (inf).

Untergangsstimmung f feeling of doom.

Unter-: u~gärig adj Bier bottom-fermented; ~gattung f subgenus.

untergeben *adj* subordinate.

Untergebene(r) *mf decl as adj* subordinate; (*pej: Subalterner auch*) underling.

untergegangen *adj Schiff* sunken; *Gestirn* set; *Volk etc* extinct; *Zivilisation, Kultur* extinct, lost.

untergehen *vi sep irreg aux sein* (a) (*versinken*) to sink; (*Schiff auch*) to go down; (*fig: im Lärm etc*) to be submerged *or* drowned.
(b) (*Gestirn*) to set. **sein Stern ist im U~** his star is waning *or* on the wane.
(c) (*zugrundegehen*) (*Kultur*) (*allmählich*) to decline; (*völlig*) to be destroyed; (*Welt*) to come to an end; (*Individuum*) to perish. **dort muß man sich durchsetzen, sonst geht man unter** you've got to assert yourself there or you'll go under.

Unter-: u~**geordnet** 1 *ptp of* u~**ordnen**; 2 *adj Dienststelle, Stellung* subordinate; *Rolle auch* secondary; *Bedeutung* secondary; ~**geschoß** *nt* basement; ~**gestell** *nt* (a) base; (*Mot*) subframe; (b) (*inf*) (*Unterleib*) lower regions; (*Beine*) pins *pl* (*inf*); ~**gewicht** *nt* underweight; ~**gewicht haben** to be underweight; u~**gewichtig** *adj* underweight; u~**gliedern*** *vt insep* to subdivide; u~**graben¹*** *vt insep irreg* to undermine; u~**graben²** *vt sep irreg* to dig in.

Untergrund *m, no pl* (a) (*Geol*) subsoil. (b) (*Farbschicht*) undercoat; (*Hintergrund*) background. (c) (*Liter, Pol etc*) underground. **er lebt seit Jahren im ~** he's been living underground for years; **in den ~ gehen** to go underground.

Untergrund- *in cpds* (*Liter, Pol*) underground; ~**bahn** *f* underground, subway (*US*).

Unter-: ~**gruppe** *f* subgroup; u~**haben** *vt sep irreg* (*inf*) to have (on) underneath; u~**haken** *sep* 1 *vt* jdn u~**haken** to link arms with sb; 2 *vr* **sich bei jdm** u~**haken** to link arms with sb; u~**gehakt gehen** to walk arm in arm.

unterhalb 1 *prep* +*gen* below; (*bei Fluß auch*) downstream from. 2 *adv* below; downstream. ~ **von** below; downstream from.

Unterhalt *m* -(*e*)*s, no pl* (a) (*Lebens~*) keep, maintenance (*esp Jur*). **für jds ~ aufkommen** to pay for sb's keep; **seinen ~ verdienen** to earn one's living; **seinen ~ haben** to earn enough. (b) (*Instandhaltung*) upkeep.

unterhalten¹* *insep irreg* 1 *vt* (a) (*versorgen, ernähren*) to support; *Angestellten* to maintain.
(b) (*halten, betreiben*) *Geschäft, Gaststätte* to keep, to run; *Konto* to have; *Kfz* to run.
(c) (*instand halten*) *Gebäude, Fahrzeug etc* to maintain.
(d) (*pflegen, aufrechterhalten*) *Kontakte, Beziehungen* to maintain.
(e) *Gäste, Publikum* to entertain.
2 *vr* (a) (*sprechen*) to talk (*mit* to, with). **man kann sich mit ihm gut/schlecht/glänzend ~** he's easy/not easy/really easy to talk to; **man kann sich mit ihm nicht ~** he's impossible to talk to, you can't talk to him; **sich mit jdm (über etw** *acc*) ~ to (have a) talk or chat with sb (about sth); **er war nur gekommen, um sich ein bißchen zu ~** he only came for a bit of a chat or talk; **Herr Schmidt, ich hätte mich mal gerne mit Ihnen ein bißchen ~** Herr Schmidt I should like (to have) a little talk or chat with you; **wir ~ uns noch!** (*drohend, begütigend*) we'll talk about that later.
(b) (*sich vergnügen*) to enjoy oneself, to have a good time. **habt ihr Euch gut ~?** did you enjoy yourselves or have a good time?; **sich mit etw ~** to amuse or entertain oneself with sth; **wir hoffen, liebe Zuhörer, daß Sie sich bei unserem Programm gut ~ haben** we hope you have enjoyed our programme.

unterhalten² *vt sep irreg* to hold underneath. **ein Tuch ~** to hold a cloth underneath.

Unterhalter(in *f*) *m* -*s*, - (a) entertainer; (*unterhaltsamer Mensch*) conversationalist. (b) (*Verdiener*) breadwinner.

unterhaltsam *adj* entertaining.

Unterhalts-: u~**berechtigt** *adj* entitled to maintenance; ~**klage** *f* action for maintenance; (**gegen jdn**) ~**klage erheben** to file a suit for maintenance (against sb); ~**kosten** *pl* (*von Gebäude, Anlage*) maintenance (costs *pl*); (*von Kfz*) running costs *pl*; ~**leistung** *f* payment of maintenance; ~**pflicht** *f* obligation to pay maintenance; u~**pflichtig** *adj* under obligation to pay maintenance; u~**pflichtige(r)** *mf decl as adj* person obliged to pay maintenance.

Unterhaltung *f* (a) (*Gespräch*) talk, chat, conversation. **eine ~ (mit jdm) führen** to have a talk or conversation (with sb); **hier kann man keine ~ führen** we can't talk here.
(b) (*Amüsement*) entertainment. **wir wünschen gute or angenehme ~** we hope you enjoy the programme.
(c) *no pl* (*Instandhaltung*) upkeep; (*von Gebäuden auch, Kfz, Maschinen*) maintenance.

Unterhaltungs-: ~**elektronik** *f* (*Industrie*) entertainment electronics *sing*; (*Geräte*) audio systems *pl*; ~**film** *m* light entertainment film; ~**kosten** *pl siehe* **Unterhaltskosten**; ~**lektüre** *f* light reading; ~**literatur** *f* light fiction; ~**musik** *f* light music; ~**programm** *nt* light entertainment programme; ~**roman** *m* light novel; ~**sendung** *f* light entertainment programme.

unterhandeln* *vi insep* **über etw** (*acc*) ~ to negotiate on sth.

Unterhändler *m* negotiator.

Unterhandlung *f* negotiation.

Unterhaus *nt* Lower House, House of Commons (*Brit*), Commons *sing* (*Brit*). **Mitglied des ~es** member of parliament, MP.

Unterhaus-: ~**abgeordnete(r)** *mf*, ~**mitglied** *nt* member of parliament, MP; ~**sitzung** *f* session of the House.

Unterhaut *f* (*Anat*) subcutis.

Unterhemd *nt* vest (*Brit*), undershirt (*US*).

unterhöhlen* *vt insep* (a) to hollow out. (b) (*fig*) to undermine.

Unterholz *nt, no pl* undergrowth.

Unterhose *f* (*Herren~*) (under)pants *pl*, pair of (under)pants, briefs *pl*; (*Damen~*) (pair of) pants *pl* or briefs *pl*. **lange ~n** long johns *pl*.

unterirdisch *adj* underground; *Fluß etc auch* subterranean. ~ **verlaufen** to run underground.

unterjochen* *vt insep* to subjugate.

Unterjochung *f* subjugation.

unterjubeln *vt sep* (*inf*) (a) (*andrehen*) **jdm etw ~** to palm sth off on sb (*inf*). (b) (*anlasten*) **jdm etw ~** to pin sth on sb (*inf*).

unterkellern* *vt insep* to build with a cellar. **das Haus ist nicht unterkellert** the house doesn't have a cellar; **ein ganz/teilweise unterkellertes Haus** a house with a cellar underneath the whole of it/underneath part of it.

Unter-: ~**kiefer** *m* lower jaw; ~**klasse** *f* (a) subclass; (b) (*Sociol*) lower class; ~**kleid** *nt* full-length slip *or* petticoat; ~**kleidung** *f* underwear, underclothes *pl*.

unterkommen *vi sep irreg aux sein* (a) (*Unterkunft finden*) to find accommodation; (*inf: Stelle finden*) to find a job (*als as, bei* with, at). **bei jdm ~** to stay at sb's (place). (b) (*inf*) **so etwas ist mir noch nie untergekommen!** (*inf*) I've never come across anything like it!

Unterkommen *nt* -*s*, - (*Obdach*) accommodation. **bei jdm ein ~ finden** to be put up at sb's (place).

Unter-: ~**körper** *m* lower part of the body; u~**kötig** *adj* (*N Ger*) festering; u~**kriechen** *vi sep irreg aux sein* (*inf*) to shack up (*bei jdm* with) (*inf*); u~**kriegen** *vt sep* (*inf*) to bring down; (*deprimieren*) to get down; **sich nicht** u~**kriegen lassen** not to let things get one down; **laß dich von ihnen nicht** u~**kriegen** don't let them get you down; u~**kühlen*** *vt insep Flüssigkeit, Metalle, Gas* to supercool, to undercool; *Körper* to expose to subnormal temperatures; u~**kühlt** *adj* supercooled, undercooled; *Körper* affected by hypothermia; (*fig*) *Atmosphäre* chilly; *Mensch* cool; *Musik, Spielweise* subdued, reserved; ~**kühlung** *f, no pl* (*von Flüssigkeit, Metall, Gas*) supercooling, undercooling; (*im Freien*) exposure; (*Med*) hypothermia; **die** ~**kühlung des Körpers** hypothermia.

Unterkunft *f* -, **Unterkünfte** (a) accommodation *no pl*, lodging. **eine ~ suchen** to look for accommodation *or* lodging; ~ **und Verpflegung** board and lodging. (b) (*von Soldaten etc*) quarters *pl*; (*esp in Privathaus*) billet.

Unterkunfts-: ~**möglichkeit** *f* accommodation *no pl*; **habt ihr dort eine** ~**möglichkeit?** have you any accommodation *or* somewhere to stay there?; ~**raum** *m* quarters *pl*.

Unterlage *f* (a) base; (*Schreib~, Tuch, Decke zum Bügeln auch*) pad; (*für Teppich*) underlay; (*im Bett*) drawsheet. **du brauchst eine ~** (*zum Schreiben*) you need something to rest on; (*zum Schlafen*) you need something to lie on. (b) *usu pl* (*Belege, Urkunden, Papiere*) document, paper. (c) (*Hort*) rootstock.

Unter-: ~**land** *nt, no pl* lowland; ~**länder(in** *f*) *m* -*s*, - lowlander; u~**ländisch** *adj attr* lowland; ~**länge** *f* tail (of letters), descender (*spec*); ~**laß** *m*: **ohn(e)** ~**laß** (*old*) incessantly, continuously; *arbeiten auch* without respite.

unterlassen* *vt insep irreg* (*nicht tun*) to refrain from; (*nicht durchführen*) not to carry out; (*auslassen*) to omit; *Bemerkung, Zwischenrufe* to refrain from making; *etwas Dummes etc* to refrain from doing; *Trinken auch* to abstain from. **kurz vor der Niederkunft sollten Sie lange Reisen ~** you should refrain from making long journeys just before your confinement; **keine Anstrengung** *or* **nichts ~** to spare no effort; ~ **Sie das!** don't do that, stop that!; **er hat es ~, mich zu benachrichtigen** he failed or omitted to notify me; **warum wurde das ~?** why was it not done?; ~ **Hilfeleistung** (*Jur*) failure to give assistance.

Unterlassung *f* (a) (*Versäumnis*) omission (of sth), failure (to do sth). **bei ~ (der Zahlung)** in case of default (of payment); **auf ~ klagen** (*Jur*) to ask for an injunction. (b) (*Gram*) ~ **der Deklination** non-declension.

Unterlassungs-: ~**delikt** *nt siehe* ~**straftat**; ~**fall** *m* (*Admin*) case of default; **im** ~**falle** in case of default; ~**klage** *f* (*Jur*) injunction suit; ~**straftat** *f* (*Jur*) (offence of) default; ~**sünde** *f* sin of omission; ~**urteil** *nt* injunction.

Unterlauf *m* lower reaches (of a river).

unterlaufen¹* *insep irreg* 1 *vi* +*dat aux sein* (*Fehler, Irrtum, Versehen*) to occur. **mir ist ein Fehler/Fauxpas ~** I made a mistake/faux pas. 2 *vt Bestimmungen, Maßnahmen* to get round; *Steuergesetze* to avoid. **jdn ~** (*Sport*) to slip under sb's guard.

unterlaufen² *adj* suffused with blood. **ein mit Blut ~es Auge** a bloodshot eye.

Unterleder *nt* sole leather.

unterlegen¹ *vt sep* to put underneath; (*fig*) to attribute, to ascribe. **einer Sache** (*dat*) **einen anderen Sinn ~** to put a different interpretation or construction on sth, to read another meaning into sth.

unterlegen²* *vt insep* to underlay; (*mit Stoff, Watte etc*) to line; (*mit Watte*) to pad. **einer Melodie** (*dat*) **einen Text ~** to put or set words to a tune.

unterlegen³ 1 *ptp of* **unterliegen**. 2 *adj* inferior; (*besiegt*) defeated. **jdm ~ sein** to be inferior to sb, to be sb's inferior; **zahlenmäßig ~ sein** to be outnumbered, to be numerically inferior.

Unterlegene(r) *mf decl as adj* underdog. **der ~ sein** to be in the weaker position.

Unterlegenheit *f, no pl* inferiority.

Unterlegscheibe *f* (*Tech*) washer.

Unterleib *m* abdomen; (*im engeren Sinne: Geschlechtsorgane*) lower abdomen.

Unterleibs- *in cpds* abdominal; (*in bezug auf weibliche Geschlechtsorgane*) gynaecological; ~**krebs** *m* cancer of the abdomen; cancer of the womb; ~**organ** *nt* abdominal organ; ~**schmerzen** *pl* abdominal pains.

Unter-: ~leutnant m (Mil) second lieutenant; ~lid nt lower lid.
unterliegen* vi insep irreg aux sein (a) (besiegt werden) to be defeated (+dat by), to lose (+dat to); (fig) einer Versuchung etc to succumb (+dat to), to give away (+dat to).
  (b) +dat (unterworfen sein) to be subject to; einer Gebühr, Steuer to be liable to. es unterliegt keinem Zweifel, daß ... it's not open to any doubt that ...; siehe unterlegen³.
Unterlippe f bottom or lower lip.
unterm contr of unter dem.
untermalen* vt insep (a) (Art) Bild to prime. (b) (mit Musik) to provide with background or incidental music; Film to provide a soundtrack for; (fig) to underlie. eine Ansage mit leiser Musik ~ to play soft background music with an announcement.
Untermalung f siehe vt (a) preparatory or priming coat. (b) background music.
untermauern* vt insep (Build) to underpin; (fig auch) Behauptung, Theorie to back up, to substantiate, to support.
Untermauerung f siehe vt underpinning; support. zur ~ seiner These in support of his thesis, to back up or substantiate his thesis.
Untermenge f (Math) subset.
untermengen vt sep to mix in, to add.
Untermensch m (esp NS) subhuman creature.
Untermiete f tenancy. bei jdm zur or in ~ wohnen to be sb's tenant; (als Zimmerherr etc auch) to lodge with sb; zur or in ~ wohnen to live in rented accommodation/lodgings.
Untermieter m tenant; (Zimmerherr etc auch) lodger.
Untermiet-: ~verhältnis nt subtenancy; ~zimmer nt (Aus) sublet room.
unterminieren* vt insep (lit, fig) to undermine.
Unterminierung f undermining.
untermischen vt sep to mix in, to add.
Untermittelschüler m (Aus inf) middle school pupil.
untern contr of unter den.
unternehmen* vt insep irreg to do; (durchführen auch) to undertake; Versuch, Vorstoß, Reise to make. einen Ausflug ~ to go on an outing; Schritte ~ to take steps; etwas/nichts gegen jdn/etw ~ to do something/nothing about sb/sth, to take some/no action against sb/sth; zu viel ~ to do too much, to take on too much.
Unternehmen nt -s, - (a) (Firma) business, concern, enterprise. (b) (Aktion, Vorhaben) undertaking, enterprise, venture; (Mil) operation.
unternehmend 1 prp of unternehmen. 2 adj enterprising.
Unternehmens-: ~berater m management consultant; ~form f form or type of enterprise; ~leitung f management; die Herren in der ~leitung management; ~planung f business planning; ~vorstand m board of directors.
Unternehmer(in) f) m -s, - (business) employer; (alten Stils) entrepreneur; (Industrieller auch) industrialist. die ~ the employers.
Unternehmer-: ~geist m entrepreneurial spirit; ~gewinn m (business) profit.
unternehmerisch adj entrepreneurial.
Unternehmer-: ~kreise pl in/aus ~kreisen in/from business circles; ~organisation f siehe ~verband; ~tum nt (die Unternehmer) management no art, employers pl; (~geist) entrepreneurship; ein freies/das freie ~tum free enterprise; ~verband m employers' association.
Unternehmung f (a) siehe Unternehmen. (b) (Transaktion) undertaking.
Unternehmungs-: ~geist m, no pl enterprise; ~lust f, no pl enterprise; ~lustig adj (tatendurstig) enterprising; (abenteuerlustig auch) adventurous.
Unteroffizier m (a) (Rang) non-commissioned officer, NCO. ~ vom Dienst duty NCO. (b) (Dienstgrad) (bei der Armee) sergeant; (bei der Luftwaffe) corporal (Brit), airman first class (US).
Unteroffiziers-: ~anwärter m NCO candidate; ~rang m non-commissioned rank.
Unter-: u~ordnen sep 1 vt to subordinate (+dat to); siehe u~geordnet; 2 vr to subordinate oneself (+dat to); u~ordnend adj (Gram) Konjunktion subordinating; ~ordnung f (a) no pl subordination; (b) (Biol) suborder; ~organisation f subsidiary organization.
Unterpfand nt (old, liter) pledge.
Unterpflaster(straßen)bahn f underground tramway.
unterpflügen vt sep to plough under or in.
Unterprima f(Sch) eighth year of German secondary school, ≈ lower sixth (Brit).
Unterprimaner m (Sch) pupil in eighth year of German secondary school, ≈ sixth-former (Brit).
unterprivilegiert adj underprivileged. U~e/die U~en underprivileged people/the underprivileged.
Unterproduktion f underproduction.
Unterputzleitung f (Elec) concealed cable.
unterqueren* vt insep to underrun.
unterreden* vr insep sich (mit jdm) ~ to confer (with sb), to have a discussion (with sb).
Unterredung f discussion; (Pol auch) talks pl.
unterrepräsentiert adj under-represented.
Unterricht m -(e)s, no pl lessons pl, classes pl. theoretischer/praktischer ~ theoretical/practical instruction or classes; ~ in Mathematik/Englisch maths/English lessons or classes; heute fällt der ~ in Englisch aus there will be no English lesson today; (jdm) ~ geben or erteilen to teach (sb) (in etw (dat) sth); (bei jdm) ~ nehmen or haben to take or have lessons (with sb); es klingelt zum ~ the lesson bell is ringing; am ~ teilnehmen to attend classes; im ~ sein (Lehrer) to be in class, to be teaching; zu spät zum ~ kommen to be late for

class; im ~ aufpassen to pay attention in class; den ~ vorbereiten to prepare one's lessons; der ~ beginnt um 8 Uhr lessons or classes start at 8 o'clock; ~ in Fremdsprachen foreign language teaching; fortschrittlicher ~ progressive teaching (methods pl).
unterrichten* insep 1 vt (a) (Unterricht geben) Schüler, Klasse, Fach to teach. jdn in etw (dat) ~ to teach sb sth. (b) (informieren) to inform (von, über +acc about). 2 vi to teach.
3 vr sich über etw (acc) ~ to obtain information about sth, to inform oneself about sth; sich von jdm über etw (acc) ~ lassen to be informed by sb about sth.
unterrichtet adj informed. gut ~e Kreise well-informed circles.
unterrichtlich adj teaching.
Unterrichts-: ~betrieb m, no pl lessons pl, classes pl; (~routine) teaching no art; ~brief m correspondence lesson; ~einheit f teaching unit; ~fach nt subject; Geschichte ist ~fach history is on the curriculum; ~film m educational film; u~frei adj Stunde, Tag free; der Montag ist u~frei there are no classes on Monday; ~gegenstand m (a) topic, subject; (b) (Aus) siehe ~fach; ~methode f teaching method; ~ministerium nt Ministry of Education; ~mittel nt teaching aid; ~raum m teaching room; ~sprache f language in which lessons are conducted; ~stoff m subject matter, teaching subject; ~stunde f lesson, period; während der ~stunden during lessons; ~veranstaltung f lesson; (Univ) lecture; ~vorbereitung f teaching preparation; ~wesen nt educational system; ~ziel nt teaching objective; ~zwecke pl zu ~zwecken for teaching purposes.
Unterrichtung f, no pl (Belehrung) instruction; (Informierung) information.
Unterrock m underskirt, slip.
unterrühren vt sep to stir or mix in.
unters contr of unter das.
untersagen* vt insep to forbid, to prohibit. jdm etw ~ to forbid sb sth, to prohibit sb from doing sth; (das) Rauchen (ist hier) strengstens untersagt smoking (is) strictly prohibited or forbidden (here); jdm etw gerichtlich ~ to enjoin sb to do sth.
Untersatz m (a) mat; (für Gläser, Flaschen etc) coaster; (für Blumentöpfe etc) saucer. etw als ~ verwenden to use sth to put underneath; siehe fahrbar. (b) (Philos) minor premise.
Unterschall-: ~flug m subsonic flight; ~geschwindigkeit f subsonic speed.
unterschätzen* vt insep to underestimate.
Unterschätzung f underestimation.
unterscheidbar adj distinguishable.
unterscheiden* insep irreg 1 vt (einen Unterschied machen, trennen) to distinguish; (auseinanderhalten auch) to tell apart. A nicht von B ~ können to be unable to tell the difference between A and B, to be unable to tell A from B; zwei Personen (voneinander) ~ to tell two people apart; kannst du die beiden ~? can you tell which is which?; das ~de Merkmal the distinguishing feature; nach verschiedenen Merkmalen ~ to classify or divide according to various characteristics.
2 vi to differentiate, to distinguish.
3 vr sich von etw ~ to differ (from) sth; worin unterscheidet sich eine Amsel von einer Drossel? what is the difference between a blackbird and a thrush?
Unterscheidung f differentiation; (Unterschied) difference, distinction. eine ~ treffen to make a distinction.
Unterscheidungs-: ~merkmal nt distinctive or distinguishing feature; ~vermögen nt discernment; das ~vermögen the power of discernment.
Unterschenkel m lower leg.
Unterschicht f (Sociol) lower stratum (Sociol), lower class.
unterschieben¹* vt insep irreg (inf: unterstellen) jdm etw ~ to attribute sth to sb; du unterschiebst mir immer, daß ich schwindle you're always accusing me of cheating; einer Äußerung einen ganz falschen Sinn ~ to twist the meaning of a statement completely.
unterschieben² vt sep irreg (a) (lit) to push underneath. etw unter etw (acc) ~ to push sth under(neath) sth.
  (b) (fig) jdm etw ~ to foist sth on sb; er wehrte sich dagegen, daß man ihm das Kind ~ wollte he defended himself against the charge that the child was his; ein untergeschobenes Kind a child foisted on sb.
  (c) siehe unterschieben¹.
Unterschiebung [auch 'untɐ-] f (a) siehe unterschieben¹ imputation, attribution. das eine ~ that is a misrepresentation. (b) siehe unterschieben² (b) foisting. die ~ eines Kindes the foisting of a child on sb.
Unterschied m -(e)s, -e difference (auch Math); (Unterscheidung auch) distinction. einen ~ (zwischen zwei Dingen) machen to make a distinction (between two things); es besteht ein ~ (zwischen ...) there's a difference or distinction (between ...); das macht keinen ~ that makes no difference; es ist ein großer ~, ob ... it makes a big difference whether ...; ein feiner ~ a slight difference, a fine distinction; zum ~ von (rare) or im ~ zu (jdm/etw) in contrast to (sb/sth), unlike (sb/sth); mit dem ~, daß ... with the difference that ...; alle ohne ~ halfen mit everyone without exception lent a hand; es wurden alle ohne ~ getötet everyone was killed indiscriminately; das ist ein gewaltiger ~! there's a vast difference!
unterschiedlich adj different; (veränderlich) variable; (gemischt) varied, patchy. das ist sehr ~ it varies a lot; ~ gut/lang of varying quality/length; sie haben ~ reagiert their reactions varied.
Unterschiedlichkeit f siehe adj difference; variability; variedness, patchiness.

Unterschieds-: ~betrag *m* difference, balance; u~los *adj* indiscriminate.

unterschlächtig *adj Wasserrad* undershot.

unterschlagen¹* *vt insep irreg Geld* to embezzle, to misappropriate; *Brief, Beweise* to withhold, to suppress; (*inf*) *Neuigkeit, Nachricht, Wort etc* to keep quiet about. das hast du mir die ganze Zeit ~ and you've kept quiet about it all this time.

unterschlagen² *vt sep irreg* (a) (*verschränken*) *Beine* to cross. mit untergeschlagenen Beinen dasitzen to sit cross-legged. (b) *Bettuch* to tuck in *or* under.

Unterschlagung *f* (*von Geld*) embezzlement, misappropriation; (*von Briefen, Beweisen etc*) withholding, suppression.

Unterschleif *m* -(e)s, -e (*rare*) *siehe* **Unterschlagung.**

Unterschlupf *m* -(e)s, **Unterschlüpfe** (*Obdach, Schutz*) cover, shelter; (*Versteck*) hiding-place, hide-out.

unterschlüpfen (*dial*), **unterschlupfen** *vi sep aux sein* (*inf*) (*Obdach or Schutz finden*) to take cover *or* shelter; (*Versteck finden*) to hide out (*inf*) (bei jdm at sb's).

unterschreiben* *insep irreg* **1** *vt* to sign. der Brief ist mit „Müller" unterschrieben the letter is signed "Müller"; das kann *or* würde ich ~! (*fig*) I'll subscribe to that! **2** *vi* to sign. mit vollem Namen ~ to sign one's full name.

unterschreiten* *vt insep irreg* to fall short of; *Temperatur, Zahlenwert* to fall below.

Unterschrift *f* (a) signature. seine ~/fünf ~en leisten to give one's signature/one's signature five times; jdm etw zur ~ vorlegen to give sb sth to sign; eigenhändige ~ personal signature; seine ~ unter etw (*acc*) setzen to put one's signature to sth, to sign sth. (b) (*Bild~*) caption.

Unterschriften-: ~mappe *f* signature folder; ~sammlung *f* collection of signatures.

unterschriftlich *adj, adv* by signature.

Unterschrifts-: u~berechtigt *adj* authorized to sign; ~berechtigte(r) *mf decl as adj* authorized signatory; ~fälschung *f* forging of a/the signature; ~leistung *f* signing of a/the document *etc*; ~probe *f* specimen signature; u~reif *adj Vertrag* ready to be signed.

unterschwellig *adj* subliminal.

Unterseeboot *nt* submarine. (*ehemaliges deutsches auch*) U-boat.

unterseeisch [-zeːɪʃ] *adj* underwater, undersea, submarine.

Unter-: ~seite *f* underside; (*von Topf, Teller, Kuchen auch*) bottom; (*von Blatt*) undersurface; an der ~seite on the underside/bottom/undersurface; ~sekunda *d* (*Sch*) sixth year of German secondary school; ~sekundaner(in *f*) *m* (*Sch*) pupil in sixth year of German secondary school; u~setzen *vt sep* to put underneath; ~setzer *m* -s, - *siehe* Untersatz (a).

untersetzt *adj* stocky.

untersinken *vi sep irreg aux sein* to sink, to go under, to submerge.

unterspülen* *vt insep* to undermine, to wash away the base of.

Unter-: ~staatssekretär *m* Undersecretary of State; ~stadt *f* lower part of a/the town; ~stand *m* shelter; (*Mil*) dugout.

unterständig *adj* (*Bot*) inferior, hypogynous (*spec*).

unterstandslos *adj* (*Aus*) homeless.

unterstehen¹* *insep irreg* **1** *vi + dat* to be under (the control of); jdm to be subordinate to; *einer Behörde, dem Ministerium auch* to come under (the jurisdiction of); *dem Gesetz* to be subject to. dem Verkaufsdirektor ~ sechs Abteilungsleiter the sales director is in charge of six department heads.

   2 *vr* to dare, to have the audacity. untersteh dich (ja nicht)! (don't) you dare!; was ~ Sie sich! how dare you!

unterstehen² *vi sep irreg* to take shelter *or* cover.

unterstellen¹* *insep* **1** *vt* (a) (*unterordnen*) to (make) subordinate (*dat* to); *Abteilung, Ministerium etc auch* to put under the control (*dat* of). jdm/etw unterstellt sein to be under sb/sth, to be answerable to sb/sth; ihm sind vier Mitarbeiter unterstellt he is in charge of four employees, he has four employees subordinate to him; jdm etw ~ to put sb in charge of sth; (*Mil*) to put sth under the command of sb *or* under sb's command. (b) (*annehmen*) to assume, to suppose. einmal unterstellt, es sei so gewesen supposing *or* let us suppose (that) it was so. (c) (*pej: unterschieben*) jdm etw ~ to insinuate *or* imply that sb has done/said sth; jdm Nachlässigkeit ~ to insinuate that sb has been negligent; ihm wurde unterstellt, gesagt zu haben, ... he was purported to have said ...

   2 *vr* to subordinate oneself (+ *dat* to).

unterstellen² *sep* **1** *vt* (*abstellen, unterbringen*) to keep; *Möbel auch* to store. **2** *vr* to take shelter *or* cover.

Unterstellung *f* (a) (*falsche Behauptung*) misrepresentation; (*Andeutung*) insinuation; (*Annahme*) assumption, presumption. (b) *no pl* (*Unterordnung*) subordination (*unter* + *acc* to).

unterste(r, s) *adj superl of* **untere(r, s)** lowest; (*tiefste auch*) bottom; (*rangmäßig*) lowest; (*letzte*) last. das U~ zuoberst kehren to turn everything upside down.

untersteuern* *vi insep* to understeer.

untersteuert *adj Auto* with understeer.

unterstreichen* *vt insep irreg* (*lit, fig*) to underline; (*fig: betonen auch*) to emphasize.

Unterstreichung *f siehe vt* underlining; emphasizing.

Unterströmung *f* (*lit, fig*) undercurrent.

Unterstufe *f* (*Sch*) lower school, lower grade (*US*).

unterstützen* *vt insep* to support (*auch fig*); (*aus öffentlichen Mitteln auch*) to subsidize; (*finanziell fördern auch*) to back, to sponsor. jdn (*moralisch*) ~ to give sb (moral) support.

Unterstützung *f* (a) *no pl* (*Tätigkeit*) support (*zu, für* for). zur ~ seiner Behauptung in support of his statement. (b) (*Zuschuß*) assistance, aid; (*inf: Arbeitslosen~*) (unemployment) benefit. staatliche ~ state aid; ~ beziehen to be on social security *or* on welfare (*US*).

Unterstützungs-: u~bedürftig *adj* needy; ~bedürftige the needy; ~empfänger *m* person on relief.

Untersuch *m* -s, -e (*Sw*) *siehe* **Untersuchung.**

untersuchen* *vt insep* (a) to examine (*auf* + *acc* for); (*erforschen*) to look into, to investigate; (*genau*) *Dokumente etc* to scrutinize; (*statistisch, soziologisch etc*) to sound (out), to survey; (*chemisch, technisch etc*) to test (*auf* + *acc* for). sich ärztlich ~ lassen to have a medical (examination) *or* a check-up; etw gerichtlich ~ to try sth (in court); etw chemisch ~ to test *or* analyze sth (chemically). (b) (*nachprüfen*) to check, to verify.

Untersuchung *f siehe vt* (a) examination; investigation (*gen, über* + *acc* into); scrutiny; sounding, survey; test; (*ärztlich*) examination, check-up. (b) check, verification.

Untersuchungs-: ~ausschuß *m* investigating *or* fact-finding committee; (*nach Unfall etc*) committee of inquiry; ~befund *m* (*Med*) result of an/the examination; (*Bericht*) examination report; ~ergebnis *nt* (*Jur*) findings *pl*; (*Med*) result of an/the examination; (*Sci*) test result; ~gefangene(r) *mf* prisoner awaiting trial; ~gefängnis *nt* prison (*for people awaiting trial*); ~haft *f* custody, (period of) imprisonment *or* detention while awaiting trial; in ~haft sein *or* sitzen (*inf*) to be in prison *or* detention awaiting trial; jdn in ~haft nehmen to commit sb for trial; die ~haft verlängern to remand sb in custody; ~häftling *m siehe* ~gefangene(r); ~kommission *f siehe* ~ausschuß; ~methode *f* examination/investigation/research method; ~richter *m* examining magistrate; ~station *f* research station; ~zimmer *nt* (*Med*) examination room; (*in Praxis*) surgery.

Untertage- *in cpds siehe* **Untertage-.**

untertage *adv siehe* **Tag.**

Untertage- *in cpds siehe* **Tag.** ~arbeiter *m* (coal)face worker; ~bau *m, no pl* underground mining.

untertags *adv* (*Aus, dial*) *siehe* **tagsüber.**

Untertan *m* -en, -en (*old: Staatsbürger*) subject; (*pej*) underling (*pej*).

untertan *adj pred* (+ *dat* to) subject; (*dienstbar, hörig*) subservient. sich (*dat*) ein Volk ~ machen to subjugate a nation.

Untertanen-: ~geist *m*, ~gesinnung *f* servile *or* subservient spirit.

untertänig *adj* subservient, submissive. Ihr ~ster Diener (*obs*) your most obedient *or* humble servant; jdn ~st bitten to ask sb most humbly.

Untertänigkeit *f* subservience, submissiveness.

Unter-: u~tariflich *adj Bezahlung* below an/the agreed rate; ~tasse *f* saucer; fliegende ~tasse flying saucer.

untertauchen¹ *sep* **1** *vi aux sein* to dive (under); (*U-Boot auch*) to submerge; (*fig*) to disappear. **2** *vt* to immerse; jdn to duck.

untertauchen²* *vt insep* to dive under.

Unterteil *nt or m* bottom *or* lower part.

unterteilen* *vt insep* to subdivide (*in* + *acc* into).

Unterteilung *f* subdivision (*in* + *acc* into).

Unter-: ~teller *m siehe* ~tasse; ~temperatur *f* low (body) temperature; ~tertia *f* (*Sch*) fourth year of German secondary school; ~tertianer(in *f*) *m* (*Sch*) pupil in fourth year of German secondary school; ~titel *m* subtitle; (*für Bild*) caption; u~titeln* *vt insep Film* to subtitle; *Bild* to caption; ~ton *m* (*Mus, fig*) undertone; u~tourig [-tuːrɪç] *adj* with low revs; u~tourig fahren to drive with low revs; u~treiben* *insep irreg* **1** *vt* to understate; **2** *vi* to play things down; ~treibung *f* (a) understatement; (b) (*das* ~treiben) playing things down *no art*; u~tunneln* *vt insep* to tunnel under; *Berg auch* to tunnel through; ~tunnelung *f* tunnelling; u~vermieten* *vti insep* to sublet, to sublease; ~versichert *adj* underinsured; ~versicherung *f* underinsurance; u~wandern* *vt insep* to infiltrate; ~wanderung *f* infiltration; u~wärts *adv* (*dial*) underneath.

Unterwäsche *f* (a) *no pl* underwear *no pl*. (b) (*für Autos*) underbody cleaning.

Unterwasser-: ~behandlung *f* (*Med*) underwater treatment; ~fotografie *f* underwater photography; ~gymnastik *f* underwater exercises *pl*; ~jagd *f* scuba *or* aqualung fishing; ~jäger *m* spear fisherman, underwater fisherman; ~kamera *f* underwater camera; ~labor *nt* underwater laboratory, sealab; ~massage *f* (*Med*) underwater massage; ~photographie *f siehe* ~fotografie; ~station *f siehe* ~labor.

unterwegs *adv* on the *or* one's/its way (*nach, zu* to); (*auf Reisen*) away. eine Karte von ~ schicken to send a card while one is away; bei denen ist wieder ein Kind ~ they've got another child on the way; bei ihr ist etwas (Kleines) ~ she's expecting.

unterweisen* *vt insep irreg* (*geh*) to instruct (*in* + *dat* in).

Unterweisung *f* (*geh*) instruction.

Unterwelt *f* (*lit, fig*) underworld.

unterweltlich *adj* underworld.

unterwerfen* *insep irreg* **1** *vt* (a) *Volk, Land* to subjugate, to conquer. (b) (*unterziehen*) to subject (*dat* to). einer Sache (*dat*) unterworfen sein to be subject to sth. **2** *vr* (*lit, fig*) sich jdm/einer Sache ~ to submit to sb/sth.

Unterwerfung *f siehe vtr* (a) subjugation, conquest. (b) subjection. (c) submission.

unterwinden* *vr insep irreg* (*old, liter*) sich einer Sache (*gen*) ~ to undertake to do sth.

unterworfen 1 *ptp of* **unterwerfen.** **2** *adj* der Mode/dem Zeitgeschmack ~ sein to be subject to fashion/prevailing tastes.

unterwürfig *adj* (*pej*) obsequious.

Unterwürfigkeit *f* (*pej*) obsequiousness.

unterzeichnen* *vt insep* (*form*) to sign.

Unterzeichner *m* -s, - signatory.

Unterzeichnerstaat *m* signatory state.

Unterzeichnete(r) mf decl as adj (form) undersigned. **der rechts/links** ~ the right/left signatory.
Unterzeichnung f signing.
Unterzeug nt (inf) underclothes pl; (von Frau auch) undies pl (inf).
unterziehen[1]* insep irreg 1 vr **sich einer Sache** (dat) ~ (müssen) to (have to) undergo sth; **sich einer Operation** (dat) ~ to undergo or have an operation; **sich einer Prüfung** (dat) ~ to take an examination; **sich der Mühe** (dat) ~, etw zu tun (geh) to take the trouble to do sth.
2 vt to subject (dat to). **jdn/etw einer Prüfung** ~ to subject sb/sth to an examination; **jdn einer Operation** ~ to perform an operation on sb.
unterziehen[2] vt sep irreg (a) Unterwäsche, Kleidung to put on underneath. **sich** (dat) **etw** ~ to put sth on underneath. (b) (Cook) Eischnee, Sahne to fold in.
untief adj shallow.
Untiefe f (a) (seichte Stelle) shallow, shoal. (b) (liter: große Tiefe) depth.
Untier nt monster.
untilgbar adj (geh) (nicht rückzahlbar) irredeemable; (fig) indelible.
Untote(r) mf die ~n the undead.
Un-: **u~tragbar** adj Zustände, Belastung intolerable, unbearable; **~tragbarkeit** f intolerability, unbearableness; **u~trainiert** adj untrained; **u~trennbar** adj inseparable; **u~trennbar zusammengesetzte Verben** inseparable verbs.
untreu adj Liebhaber etc unfaithful; (einem Prinzip etc) disloyal (dat to). **sich** (dat) **selbst** ~ **werden** to be untrue to oneself; **jdm** ~ **werden** to be unfaithful to sb.
Untreue f siehe adj unfaithfulness; disloyalty.
untrinkbar adj undrinkable.
untröstlich adj inconsolable (über - acc about). **er war** ~, **daß er es vergessen hatte** he was inconsolable about having forgotten it.
untrüglich adj Gedächtnis infallible; Zeichen unmistakable.
Untugend f (Laster) vice; (schlechte Angewohnheit) bad habit; (Schwäche) weakness.
untunlich adj (dated) (unzweckmäßig) impractical; (unklug) imprudent.
Un-: **u~übel** adj: **(gar) nicht (so) u~übel** not bad (at all); **u~überbietbar** adj Preis, Rekord etc unbeatable; Frechheit, Virtuosität, Eifer unparalleled; **u~überbrückbar** adj (fig) Gegensätze etc irreconcilable; Kluft unbridgeable; **u~überdacht** adj open, uncovered; **u~überlegt** adj Mensch rash; Entschluß, Maßnahmen etc auch ill-considered; **u~überlegt handeln** to act rashly; **~überlegtheit** f rashness; **u~überschreitbar** adj Termin, Preis final; Grenze, Fluß uncrossable; Gebirge unclimbable; **u~übersehbar** adj **(a)** (nicht abschätzbar) Schaden, Schwierigkeiten, Folgen inestimable, incalculable; (nicht übersehbar) Menge, Häusermeer etc vast, immense; **(b)** (auffällig) Fehler etc obvious, conspicuous; **u~übersetzbar** adj untranslatable; **u~übersichtlich** adj **(a)** Gelände broken; Kurve, Stelle blind; **(b)** (durcheinander) System, Plan confused; **u~übertrefflich** 1 adj matchless, unsurpassable; Rekord unbeatable; 2 adv superbly, magnificently; **u~übertroffen** adj unsurpassed; **u~überwindbar** (rare), **u~überwindlich** adj Gegner, Heer invincible; Festung impregnable; Hindernis, Gegensätze, Abneigung etc insuperable, insurmountable; **u~üblich** adj not usual, not customary.
un|umgänglich adj essential, absolutely necessary; (unvermeidlich) inevitable. ~ **notwendig werden** to become absolutely essential/quite inevitable.
un|umkehrbar adj irreversible.
Un|umkehrbarkeit f irreversibility.
un|umschränkt adj unlimited; Freiheit, Gewalt, Macht auch absolute. ~ **herrschen** to have absolute rule.
un|umstößlich adj Tatsache irrefutable, incontrovertible; Entschluß irrevocable. ~ **feststehen** to be absolutely definite.
Un|umstößlichkeit f siehe adj irrefutability, incontrovertibility; irrevocability.
un-: **~umstritten** adj indisputable, undisputed; **~umwunden** adv frankly; **~unterbrochen** adj **(a)** (nicht unterbrochen) unbroken, uninterrupted; **(b)** (unaufhörlich) incessant, continuous.
unver|änderlich adj (gleichbleibend) unchanging, invariable; (unwandelbar) unchangeable. **eine** ~**e Größe, eine U~e** (Math) a constant, an invariable.
Unver|änderlichkeit f siehe adj unchangingness, invariability; unchangeableness.
unver|ändert adj unchanged. **er ist immer** ~ **freundlich** he is always friendly; **du siehst** ~ **jung aus** you look as young as ever; **unsere Weine sind immer von** ~**er Güte** our wines are always consistently good.
Un-: **u~verantwortlich** adj irresponsible; **~verantwortlichkeit** f irresponsibility; **u~verarbeitet** 1 adj Material unprocessed, raw; (fig) Eindruck raw, undigested; 2 adv in a raw state; **u~veräußerlich** adj **(a)** Rechte inalienable; **(b)** Besitz unmarketable, unsaleable; **u~verbesserlich** adj incorrigible; **u~verbildet** adj Charakter, Wesen unspoilt.
unverbindlich adj **(a)** (nicht bindend) Angebot, Preisangabe not binding; Besichtigung free. **sich** (dat) **etw** ~ **schicken lassen** to have sth sent without obligation. **(b)** (vage, allgemein) non-committal; (nicht entgegenkommend) abrupt, curt.
Unverbindlichkeit f **(a)** no pl (von Auskunft, Beratung etc) freedom from obligation. **(b)** no pl (Vagheit, Allgemeinheit) non-commitment, vagueness; (mangelndes Entgegenkommen) abruptness, curtness. **(c)** (unverbindliche Äußerung) non-committal remark.

un-: **~verblümt** adj blunt; **das kommt einer** ~**verblümten Erpressung gleich!** that's downright blackmail!; **~verbraucht** adj (fig) unspent; **~verbrennbar** adj incombustible.
unverbrüchlich adj (geh) steadfast. ~ **zu etw stehen** to stand by sth unswervingly.
unverbürgt adj unconfirmed.
unverdächtig adj unsuspicious; (nicht unter Verdacht stehend) unsuspected, above suspicion. **sich möglichst** ~ **benehmen** to arouse as little suspicion as possible; **das ist doch völlig** ~ there's nothing suspicious about that.
Un-: **u~verdaulich** adj (lit, fig) indigestible; **u~verdaut** adj undigested; (fig auch) unassimilated; **u~verderblich** adj unperishable, non-perishable; **u~verdient** adj undeserved; **u~verdientermaßen, u~verdienterweise** adv undeservedly, unjustly; **u~verdorben** adj (lit, fig) unspoilt, pure; **~verdorbenheit** f (fig) purity; **u~verdrossen** adj undeterred; (unermüdlich) untiring, indefatigable; (unverzagt) undaunted; **~verdrossenheit** f, no pl siehe adj undeterredness; indefatigability; undauntedness; **u~verdünnt** adj undiluted; Spirituosen **u~verdünnt trinken** to drink spirits neat.
unver|ehelicht adj (old, form) unwedded, unwed. **„~"** adj (auf Urkunde) (Frau) "spinster"; (Mann) "bachelor"; **die** ~**e Eleanor X** Eleanor X, spinster.
Un-: **u~vereinbar** adj incompatible; **miteinander u~vereinbar sein** to be incompatible; **~vereinbarkeit** f incompatibility; **u~verfälscht** adj (lit, fig) unadulterated; Dialekt pure; Natürlichkeit unaffected; Natur unspoilt; **~verfälschtheit** f siehe adj unadulterated quality or character; purity; unaffectedness; unspoilt quality or character; **u~verfänglich** adj harmless; **das ist u~verfänglich** it doesn't commit you to anything; **~verfänglichkeit** f harmlessness.
unverfroren adj insolent.
Unverfrorenheit f insolence.
unvergänglich adj Kunstwerk, Werte, Worte, Ruhm immortal; Eindruck, Erinnerung, Reiz everlasting.
Unvergänglichkeit f siehe adj immortality; everlastingness.
unvergessen adj unforgotten. **August wird (uns allen)** ~ **bleiben** we'll (all) remember August.
unvergeßlich adj unforgettable; Erlebnis auch memorable. **das wird mir** ~ **bleiben, das bleibt mir** ~ I'll always remember that, I'll never forget that.
Un-: **u~vergleichbar** adj incomparable; **~vergleichbarkeit** f incomparability; **u~vergleichlich** 1 adj unique, incomparable; 2 adv incomparably, immeasurably; **u~vergoren** adj unfermented; **u~verhältnismäßig** adv disproportionately; (übermäßig) excessively; **~verhältnismäßigkeit** f disproportion; (Übermäßigkeit) excessiveness; **ihm wurde ~verhältnismäßigkeit der Strafe vorgeworfen** he was accused of imposing a disproportionate punishment; **u~verheiratet** adj unmarried, single.
unverhofft adj unexpected. **das kam völlig** ~ it was quite unexpected, it came out of the blue.
Unverhofftheit f unexpectedness.
unverhohlen adj open, unconcealed.
Unverhohlenheit f openness.
Un-: **u~verhüllt** adj **(a)** Tatsachen undisguised, naked; Wahrheit auch unveiled; **(b)** (liter, iro: nackt) unclad; **(c)** siehe **u~verhohlen**; **u~verjährbar** adj (Jur) not subject to a statute of limitations; **u~verkäuflich** adj (abbr **unverk.**) unmarketable, unsaleable; **u~verkäufliches Muster** free sample; **„u~verkäuflich"** "not for sale"; **u~verkennbar** adj unmistakable; **u~verlangt** adj unsolicited; **u~verlangt eingesandte Manuskripte** unsolicited manuscripts; **u~verläßlich** adj unreliable; **u~verletzbar** adj siehe **u~verwundbar**; **u~verletzlich** adj **(a)** (fig) Rechte, Grenze inviolable; **(b)** (lit) invulnerable; **~verletzlichkeit** f (fig) inviolability; (lit) invulnerability; **u~verletzt** adj uninjured, unhurt, unharmed; Körperteil undamaged; Siegel unbroken; **u~verlierbar** adj (ever)lasting; **u~vermählt** adj (geh) unwedded, unwed; **u~vermeidbar** adj inevitable; **u~vermeidlich** adj inevitable; (nicht zu umgehen) unavoidable; **der u~vermeidliche Herr X** the inevitable Mr X; **~vermeidlichkeit** f inevitability; unavoidable nature; **u~vermietet** adj unlet, unrented; **u~vermindert** adj undiminished; **u~vermischt** adj separate, unmixed; (rein) pure; Tee, Wein etc pure, unadulterated.
unvermittelt adj **(a)** (plötzlich) sudden, unexpected. **(b)** (Philos) immediate.
Unvermitteltheit f, no pl **(a)** suddenness, unexpectedness. **(b)** (Philos) immediacy.
Unvermögen nt, no pl inability; (Machtlosigkeit) powerlessness.
unvermögend adj **(a)** (arm) without means. **(b)** (old, liter) (unfähig) helpless. ~ **sein, etw zu tun** not to be able to do sth.
unvermutet adj unexpected.
Unvernunft f (Torheit) stupidity; (mangelnder Verstand) irrationality; (Uneinsichtigkeit) unreasonableness.
unvernünftig adj siehe n stupid; irrational; unreasonable.
un-: **~veröffentlicht** adj unpublished; **~verpackt** adj unpackaged, loose; **~verputzt** adj unplastered.
unverrichtet adj: **~er Dinge or Sache** (Aus) without having achieved anything, empty-handed.
unverrichteterdinge, unverrichtetersache adv without having achieved anything.
unverrückbar adj (fig) unshakeable, unalterable; Entschluß auch firm, definite; Gewißheit absolute. ~ **feststehen** to be absolutely definite.
unverschämt adj outrageous; Mensch, Frage, Benehmen etc impudent, impertinent; Lüge, Verleumdung etc auch blatant, barefaced. **grins/lüg nicht so** ~! take that cheeky grin off your face/don't tell such barefaced lies!

Unverschämtheit f (a) no pl siehe adj outrageousness; impudence, impertinence; blatancy, barefacedness. **die ~ besitzen, etw zu tun** to have the impertinence or impudence to do sth. (b) (Bemerkung) impertinence; (Tat) outrageous thing. **das ist eine ~!** it's outrageous!

un-: ~**verschleiert** adj unveiled; (b) (fig) Wahrheit unvarnished; ~**verschlossen** adj unlocked; Briefumschlag unsealed.

unverschuldet adj (a) ein ~er Unfall an accident which was not his/her etc fault or which happened through no fault of his/her etc own; ~ **in eine Notlage geraten** to get into difficulties through no fault of one's own. (b) (ohne Schulden) free from or of debt; Grundstück auch unencumbered.

unverschuldetermaßen, unverschuldeterweise adv through no fault of one's own.

unversehens adv all of a sudden, suddenly; (überraschend) unexpectedly.

Un-: u~**versehrt** adj Mensch (lit, fig) unscathed; (unbeschädigt) intact pred; ~**versehrtheit** f (ohne Verletzung) freedom from injury; (ohne Beschädigung) intactness; körperliche ~**versehrtheit** freedom from bodily harm; **seine seelische ~versehrtheit** the fact that he was mentally unscathed; u~**versiegbar**, u~**versieglich** adj inexhaustible; u~**versiegelt** adj unsealed; u~**versöhnlich** adj irreconcilable; ~**versöhnlichkeit** f irreconcilability; u~**versorgt** adj Familie, Kinder unprovided-for.

Unverstand m lack of judgement; (Torheit) folly, foolishness. **etw im ~ tun** to do sth to excess.

unverstanden adj not understood; (mißverstanden) misunderstood. **der Arme fühlt sich ~** the poor man feels that his wife doesn't understand him/nobody understands him.

unverständig adj lacking understanding, ignorant.

Unverständigkeit f lack of understanding, ignorance.

unverständlich adj (nicht zu hören) inaudible; (unbegreifbar) incomprehensible.

Unverständnis nt, no pl lack of understanding; (Nichterfassen, für Kunst etc) lack of appreciation.

un-: ~**verstellt** adj (a) Stimme undisguised; (b) (echt) unfeigned, genuine; u~**versteuert** adj untaxed; u~**versucht** adj: **nichts u~versucht lassen** to try everything.

unverträglich adj (a) (streitsüchtig) cantankerous, quarrelsome. (b) (unverdaulich) indigestible; (Med) intolerable; (Med: mit anderer Substanz etc) incompatible.

Unverträglichkeit f, no pl siehe adj (a) cantankerousness, quarrelsomeness. (b) indigestibility; intolerance; incompatibility.

unverwandt 1 adj ~**en Blickes** (liter) with a steadfast gaze. 2 adv fixedly, steadfastly.

Un-: u~**verwechselbar** adj unmistakable, distinctive; ~**verwechselbarkeit** f unmistakableness, distinctiveness; u~**verwehrt** adj: **das sei dir u~verwehrt** (old, geh) you are at liberty to do this (form); u~**verweslich** adj imperishable; u~**verwindbar** adj insurmountable; u~**verwirklicht** adj unrealized; u~**verwischbar** adj (lit, fig) indelible; u~**verwundbar** adj (lit, fig) invulnerable; ~**verwundbarkeit** f (lit, fig) invulnerability.

unverwüstlich adj indestructible; Stoff, Teppich etc auch tough, durable; Gesundheit robust; Humor, Mensch irrepressible.

un-: ~**verzagt** adj undaunted; ~**verzeihbar** (rare), ~**verzeihlich** adj unpardonable, unforgivable; ~**verzerrt** adj Fernsehbild etc, (fig: objektiv) undistorted; ~**verzichtbar** adj attr Recht inalienable; Anspruch undeniable, indisputable; Bedingung indispensible; ~**verzinslich** adj interest-free; ~**verzollt** adj duty-free.

unverzüglich 1 adj immediate, prompt. 2 adv immediately, without delay, at once.

unvollendet adj unfinished. **Die „U~e" von Schubert** Schubert's Unfinished (Symphony).

unvollkommen adj (unvollständig) incomplete; (fehlerhaft, mangelhaft) imperfect. **er kann zwar Englisch, aber doch recht ~** he can speak English, but his knowledge is rather limited.

Unvollkommenheit f siehe adj incompleteness; imperfection.

unvollständig adj incomplete; Hilfsverb defective. **er hat das Formular ~ ausgefüllt** he didn't fill the form out properly or correctly.

Unvollständigkeit f incompleteness; defectiveness.

unvorbereitet adj unprepared (auf +acc for). **eine ~e Rede halten** to make an impromptu speech, to speak off the cuff; **der Tod des Vaters traf sie ~** her father's death came unexpectedly.

unvordenklich adj: **seit ~en Zeiten** (liter) from time immemorial.

Un-: u~**voreingenommen** adj unbiased, unprejudiced, impartial; ~**voreingenommenheit** f, no pl impartiality; u~**vorhergesehen** adj unforeseen; Besuch unexpected; **wir bekamen u~vorhergesehen or u~vorhergesehenen Besuch** we had visitors unexpectedly, we had unexpected visitors; u~**vorsätzlich** adj (Jur) unpremeditated; u~**vorschriftsmäßig** adj not in keeping with the regulations; **ein u~vorschriftsmäßig geparktes Fahrzeug** an improperly parked vehicle; u~**vorsichtig** adj careless; (voreilig) rash; u~**vorsichtigerweise** adv carelessly; (voreilig) rashly; ~**vorsichtigkeit** f carelessness; rashness; **so eine ~vorsichtigkeit von dir!** how reckless or rash of you!; u~**vorstellbar** adj inconceivable; u~**vorteilhaft** adj unfavourable, disadvantageous; Kleid, Frisur etc unbecoming; u~**vorteilhaft aussehen** not to look one's best.

unwägbar adj Umstand, Unterschied imponderable; Risiko auch incalculable, inestimable.

Unwägbarkeit f (a) no pl siehe adj imponderability; incalculability. (b) imponderable.

Un-: u~**wahr** adj untrue; u~**wahrhaftig** adj untruthful; Gefühle insincere; ~**wahrhaftigkeit** f untruthfulness; insincerity; ~**wahrheit** f untruth.

unwahrscheinlich 1 adj (nicht zu erwarten, kaum denkbar) unlikely, improbable; (unglaubhaft) implausible, improbable; (inf: groß) incredible (inf).
2 adv (inf) incredibly (inf). **wir haben uns ~ beeilt** we hurried as much as we possibly could; **er gab sich ~ Mühe** he took an incredible amount of trouble (inf).

Unwahrscheinlichkeit f siehe adj unlikeliness, improbability; implausibility; incredibleness.

unwandelbar adj (geh) (a) (unveränderlich) unalterable, immutable. (b) Treue, Liebe unwavering, steadfast.

Unwandelbarkeit f (geh) siehe adj (a) unalterableness, immutability. (b) steadfastness.

unwegsam adj Gelände etc rough.

Unwegsamkeit f roughness.

unweiblich adj unfeminine.

Unweiblichkeit f, no pl unfemininity.

unweigerlich 1 adj attr Folge inevitable. 2 adv inevitably; (fraglos) undoubtedly; (grundsätzlich) invariably.

unweit prep +gen, adv not far from.

unwert adj (rare) siehe **unwürdig**.

Unwert m (a) siehe **Unwürdigkeit**. (b) demerits pl. **über Wert und ~ einer Sache diskutieren** to discuss the merits and demerits of sth.

Unwesen nt, no pl (übler Zustand) terrible state of affairs. **dem ~ (der Rauschgiftsucht) steuern** (geh) to combat the problem (of drug addiction); **sein ~ treiben** to be up to mischief; (Landstreicher etc) to make trouble; (Gespenst) to walk abroad; (Vampir etc) to strike terror into people's hearts.

unwesentlich adj (nicht zur Sache gehörig) irrelevant; (unwichtig) unimportant, insignificant. **sich von einer Sache nur ~ unterscheiden** to differ only negligibly or marginally from sth; **zu einer Sache nicht/nur ~ beitragen** to make a not insignificant/any an insignificant contribution to sth.

Unwetter nt (thunder)storm. **ein ~ brach los** a storm broke.

Un-: u~**wichtig** adj unimportant, insignificant; (belanglos) irrelevant; (verzichtbar) non-essential; ~**wichtigkeit** f siehe adj unimportance, insignificance; irrelevance; non-essentiality; (unwichtige Angelegenheit) triviality; u~**widerlegbar**, u~**widerleglich** adj irrefutable; u~**widerruflich** adj irrevocable; **die u~widerruflich letzte Vorstellung** positively or definitely the last or final performance; **es steht u~widerruflich fest, daß** ... it is absolutely definite that ...; ~**widerruflichkeit** f irrevocability, irrevocableness; u~**widersprochen** adj uncontradicted; Behauptung auch unchallenged; **das darf nicht u~widersprochen bleiben** we can't let this pass unchallenged; u~**widerstehlich** adj irresistible; u~**wiederbringlich** adj (geh) irretrievable.

Unwille(n) m, no pl displeasure, indignation (über +acc at); (Ungeduld) irritation. **jds ~n erregen** to incur sb's displeasure; **seinem ~n Luft machen** to give vent to one's indignation; **etw nur mit ~n tun** to do sth only with reluctance.

unwillig adj indignant (über +acc about); (widerwillig) unwilling, reluctant.

Unwilligkeit f siehe adj indignation; unwillingness, reluctance.

unwillkommen adj unwelcome.

unwillkürlich adj spontaneous; (instinktiv) instinctive; (Physiol, Med) involuntary. **ich mußte ~ lachen** I couldn't help laughing.

Un-: u~**wirklich** adj unreal; ~**wirklichkeit** f unreality; u~**wirksam** adj (wirkungslos, auch Med) ineffective; Vertrag, Rechtsgeschäft inoperative; (nichtig) null, void; (Chem) inactive; ~**wirksamkeit** f ineffectiveness; inoperativeness; nullity; inactivity; u~**wirsch** adj Mensch, Benehmen surly, gruff; Bewegung brusque; u~**wirtlich** adj inhospitable; ~**wirtlichkeit** f inhospitableness; u~**wirtschaftlich** adj uneconomic; ~**wirtschaftlichkeit** f uneconomicalness; ~**wissen** nt ignorance; u~**wissend** adj ignorant; (ahnungslos) unsuspecting; (unerfahren) inexperienced; ~**wissenheit** f, no pl siehe adj ignorance; unsuspectingness; inexperience; ~**wissenheit schützt vor Strafe nicht** ignorance is no excuse or (Jur) is no defence in law; u~**wissenschaftlich** adj unscientific; Textausgabe unscholarly; Essay, Ausdrucksweise unacademic; ~**wissenschaftlichkeit** f siehe adj unscientific nature/character etc; unscholarliness; unacademic nature/character etc; u~**wissentlich** adv unwittingly, unknowingly.

unwohl adj (unpäßlich) unwell, indisposed (form); (unbehaglich) uneasy. **mir ist ~, ich fühle mich ~** I don't feel well; **in ihrer Gegenwart fühle ich mich ~** I'm ill at ease or I feel uneasy in her presence.

Unwohlsein nt disposition; (unangenehmes Gefühl) unease. **von einem (plötzlichen) ~ befallen werden** to be taken ill suddenly.

Un-: u~**wohnlich** adj Zimmer etc uncomfortable, cheerless; u~**würdig** adj unworthy (+gen of); Verhalten undignified; (schmachvoll) degrading, shameful; ~**würdigkeit** f siehe adj unworthiness; lack of dignity; degradation, shame.

Unzahl f **eine ~ von** a host of.

unzählbar adj innumerable, countless; (Ling) uncountable. **~ viele huge numbers; ~ viele Bücher/Mädchen** innumerable books/girls.

unzählig 1 adj innumerable, countless. **~e Male** countless times, time and again. 2 adv **~ viele** huge numbers; **~ viele Bücher/Mädchen** innumerable books/girls.

unzähligemal adv countless times, time and again.

un-: ~**zähmbar** *adj* untamable; (*fig auch*) indomitable; ~**zart** *adj* ungentle.

Unze *f* -, -**n** ounce.

Unzeit *f:* **zur** ~ (*geh*) at an inopportune moment, inopportunely.

Un-: u~**zeitgemäß** *adj* (*altmodisch*) old-fashioned, outmoded; (*nicht in die Zeit passend*) untimely; u~**zensiert** *adj* uncensored; (*Sch*) ungraded; u~**zerbrechlich** *adj* unbreakable; u~**zeremoniell** *adj* unceremonious; u~**zerkaut** *adj* unchewed; u~**zerreißbar** *adj* untearable; u~**zerstörbar** *adj* indestructible; ~**zerstörbarkeit** *f* indestructibility; u~**zertrennlich** *adj* inseparable.

Unziale *f* -, -**n** (*Typ*) (a) (*Schrift*) uncial (writing). (b) (*Buchstabe*) uncial (letter).

Unzialschrift *f* (*Typ*) uncial writing.

Un-: u~**ziemend** (*old*), u~**ziemlich** *adj* unseemly, unbecoming, indecorous; ~**ziemlichkeit** *f* (a) *no pl* unseemliness, indecorousness; (b) (*Benehmen*) impropriety; u~**zivilisiert** *adj* (*lit, fig*) uncivilized.

Unzucht *f, no pl* (*esp Jur*) sexual offence. **das gilt als** ~ that's regarded as a sexual offence; ~ **treiben** to fornicate; ~ **mit** **Abhängigen/Kindern/Tieren** (*Jur*) illicit sexual relations with dependants/children/animals; **gewerbsmäßige** ~ prostitution; **widernatürliche** ~ unnatural sexual act(s *pl*); ~ **zwischen** **Männern** sodomy; ~ **mit jdm treiben** to fornicate with sb; (*Jur*) to commit a sexual offence/sexual offences with sb; **jdn zur** ~ **verleiten** *or* **verführen** to seduce sb; **jdn zur** ~ **mißbrauchen** to abuse sb (for sexual purposes).

unzüchtig *adj* (*esp Jur*) indecent; *Reden, Schriften* obscene; *Gedanken auch* unchaste. ~**e Handlungen** obscene acts; (*Jur*) illicit sexual acts; ~ **leben** to live licentiously.

Unzüchtigkeit *f siehe adj* indecency; obscenity; unchastity; licentiousness.

Un-: u~**zufrieden** *adj* dissatisfied, discontent(ed); (*mißmutig*) unhappy; **manche Leute sind immer** u~**zufrieden** some people are never content *or* happy; ~**zufriedenheit** *f, no pl siehe adj* dissatisfaction, discontent; unhappiness; discontent(ment); u~**zugänglich** *adj Gegend, Gebäude etc* inaccessible; *Charakter, Mensch* inapproachable; (*taub, unaufgeschlossen gegen*) deaf, impervious (+*dat* to); ~**zugänglichkeit** *f siehe adj* inaccessibility; unapproachability; deafness, imperviousness; u~**zukömmlich** *adj* (*Aus*) insufficient, inadequate; (*nicht zukommend*) undue; ~**zukömmlichkeit** *f* (*Aus*) unpleasantness; (*Unzulänglichkeit*) inadequacy; u~**zulänglich** *adj* (*nicht ausreichend*) insufficient; (*mangelhaft*) inadequate; ~**zulänglichkeit** *f* (a) *siehe adj* insufficiency; inadequacy; (b) *usu pl* shortcomings *pl*; u~**zulässig** *adj* (*auch Jur*) inadmissible; *Gebrauch* improper; *Beeinflussung* undue; *Belastung, Geschwindigkeit* excessive; **für** u~**zulässig erklären** (*Jur*) to rule out; u~**zumutbar** *adj* unreasonable; u~**zurechnungsfähig** *adj* not responsible for one's actions, of unsound mind; **jdn für** u~**zurechnungsfähig erklären lassen** (*Jur*) to have sb certified (insane); **geistig** u~**zurechnungsfähig** non compos mentis (*Jur*), of unsound mind; ~**zurechnungsfähigkeit** *f* unsoundness of mind; ~**zurechnungsfähigkeit geltend machen** to enter *or* put forward a plea of insanity; u~**zureichend** *adj* insufficient, inadequate; u~**zusammenhängend** *adj* incoherent, disjointed; u~**zuständig** *adj* (*Admin, Jur*) incompetent, not competent; **sich für** u~**zuständig erklären** to disclaim competence; u~**zustellbar** *adj* undeliverable; *Postsendung* dead; **falls** u~**zustellbar bitte zurück an Absender** if undelivered, please return to sender; ~**zustellbarkeit** *f* undeliverability; u~**zuträglich** *adj* unhealthy; **jdm (gesundheitlich)** *or* **jds** **Gesundheit** u~**zuträglich sein** not to agree with sb, to be bad for sb's health; u~**zutreffend** *adj* inappropriate, inapplicable; (*unwahr*) incorrect; ~**zutreffendes bitte streichen** delete as applicable; u~**zuverlässig** *adj* unreliable; ~**zuverlässigkeit** *f* unreliability; u~**zweckmäßig** *adj* (*nicht ratsam*) inexpedient; (*unpraktisch*) impractical; (*ungeeignet*) unsuitable, inappropriate; ~**zweckmäßigkeit** *f siehe adj* inexpediency; impracticality; unsuitableness, inappropriateness; u~**zweideutig** *adj* unambiguous, unequivocal; (*fig: unanständig*) explicit; **er sagte mir** u~**zweideutig, daß** ... he told me in no uncertain terms that ...; u~**zweifelhaft** **1** *adj* undoubted, indubitable, unquestionable; **2** *adv* without doubt, undoubtedly, indubitably.

üppig *adj Wachstum* luxuriant; *Vegetation auch* lush; *Haar* thick; *Mahl, Ausstattung* sumptuous, opulent; *Rente, Gehalt* lavish; *Figur, Frau, Formen* voluptuous; *Busen* ample; *Leben* luxurious; *Phantasie* rich. **nun werd mal nicht zu** ~! (*inf*) let's have no more of your cheek! (*inf*); ~ **leben** to live in style; ~ **wuchernde Vegetation** rampant vegetation.

Üppigkeit *f siehe adj* luxuriance; lushness; thickness; sumptuousness, opulence; lavishness; voluptuousness; ampleness; luxury; richness.

up to date ['ʌp tə 'deɪt] *adj pred* (*inf*) up to date; *Kleidung* modern.

Ur *m* -(**e**)**s**, -**e** (*Zool*) aurochs.

Ur- *in cpds* (*erste*) first, prime; (*ursprünglich*) original; ~**abstimmung** *f* strike ballot; ~**adel** *m* ancienne noblesse, ancient nobility; ~**ahn(e)** *m* (*Vorfahr*) forefather, forebear; (~*großvater*) great-grandfather; ~**ahne** *f* (*Vorfahr*) forebear; (~*großmutter*) great-grandmother.

Ural *m* -**s** (*Geog*) (a) (*Fluß*) Ural. (b) (*Gebirge*) **der** ~ the Urals *pl*, the Ural mountains *pl*.

Ur-: ~**alt** *adj* ancient; *Problem, Brauch auch* age-old; **seit** u~**alten Zeiten** from time immemorial; **aus** u~**alten Zeiten** from long (long) ago; u~**alters** *adv* (*old*) **von** u~**alters her** from time immemorial.

Uran *nt* -**s**, *no pl* uranium.

Uranbrenner *m* uranium pile.

Ur-: ~**anfang** *m* first beginning; u~**anfänglich** *adj* primeval; ~**angst** *f* primeval fear; ~**anlage** *f* genetic predisposition; u~**aufführen** *vt ptp* u~**aufgeführt** *infin, ptp only* to give the first performance (of), to play for the first time; *Film is* premiere *usu pass.*

Uraufführung *f* premiere; (*von Theaterstück etc auch*) first night *or* performance; (*von Film auch*) first showing.

Uraufführungs-: ~(**film**)**theater**, ~**kino** *nt* premiere cinema.

Urausgabe *f* first edition.

urban *adj* (*geh*) urbane.

urbanisieren* *vtr* (*Sociol*) to urbanize.

Urbanisierung *f* (*Sociol*) urbanization.

Urbanität *f* (*geh*) urbanity.

urbar *adj* **einen Wald/die Wüste/Land** ~ **machen** to clear a forest/to reclaim the desert/to cultivate land.

urbarisieren* *vti* (*Sw*) **urbar machen.**

Urbarisierung *f* (*Sw*), **Urbarmachung** *f siehe adj* clearing; reclamation; cultivation.

Ur-: ~**bayer** *m* (*inf*) typical Bavarian; ~**bedeutung** *f* (*Ling*) original meaning; ~**beginn** *m* very *or* first beginning; **seit** ~**beginn** *or* **von** ~**beginn an** from the beginning(s) of time; ~**berliner** *m* (*inf*) typical Berliner; ~**bevölkerung** *f* natives *pl*, original inhabitants *pl*; (*in Australien und Neuseeland*) Aborigines *pl*; ~**bewohner** *m* native, original inhabitant; (*in Australien und Neuseeland*) Aborigine; ~**bild** *nt* prototype, archetype; (*Philos*) idea.

urchig *adj* (*Sw*) *siehe* **urwüchsig.**

Ur-: ~**christen** *pl* (*Eccl Hist*) early Christians *pl*; ~**christentum** *nt* early Christianity; u~**christlich** *adj* early Christian; u~**deutsch** *adj* essentially German.

Urdu *nt* -(**s**) (*Ling*) Urdu.

Ur-: u~**eigen** *adj* very own; **es liegt in seinem** u~**eigensten** **Interesse** it's in his own best interests; **ein dem Menschen** u~**eigener Hang** an inherent human quality; ~**einwohner** *m* native, original inhabitant; (*in Australien und Neuseeland*) Aborigine; ~**eltern** *pl* (*Vorfahren*) forebears *pl*; (~*großeltern*) great-grandparents *pl*; ~**enkel** *m* great-grandchild, great-grandson; ~**enkelin** *f* great-granddaughter; ~**fassung** *f* original version; ~**fehde** *f* (*Hist*) oath of truce; ~**fehde schwören** to abjure all vengeance; ~**form** *f* prototype; ~**gemeinde** *f* (*Eccl Hist*) early Christian community; u~**gemütlich** *adj* (*inf*) really comfortable/cosy etc; *siehe* **gemütlich**; u~**germanisch** *adj* (*Ling*) Proto-Germanic; (*fig*) essentially Germanic; **das** ~**germanische** Proto-Germanic; ~**geschichte** *f* prehistory; ~**gestalt** *f siehe* ~**form**; ~**gesellschaft** *f* primitive society; ~**gestein** *nt* primitive rocks *pl*; **politisches** ~**gestein** (*fig*) a dyed-in-the-wool politician; ~**gewalt** *f* elemental force.

urgieren* (*Aus form*) **1** *vt* to expedite matters. **2** *vt* to expedite matters.

Urgroß-: ~**eltern** *pl* great-grandparents *pl*; ~**mutter** *f* great-grandmother; ~**vater** *m* great-grandfather.

Ur-: ~**grund** *m* very basis, source; ~**heber(in** *f*) *m* -**s**, - originator; (*liter: Schöpfer*) creator; (*Jur: Verfasser*) author; **der geistige** ~**heber** the spiritual father.

Urheber-: ~**recht** *nt* copyright (*an* +*dat* on); u~**rechtlich** *adj, adv* on copyright *attr*; u~**rechtlich geschützt** copyright(ed); ~**schaft** *f* authorship; ~**schutz** *m* copyright.

Urheimat *f* original home(land).

urig *adj* (*inf*) *Mensch* earthy; *Lokal etc* ethnic.

Urin *m* -**s**, -**e** urine. **etw im** ~ **haben** (*sl*) to have a gut feeling about sth (*inf*).

Urinal *nt* -**s**, -**e** (*Med*) urinal.

Urinalbecken *nt* (bowl) urinal.

urinieren* *vti* to urinate.

Ur-: ~**instinkt** *m* primary *or* basic instinct; ~**kanton** *m* (*Sw*) original canton; ~**kirche** *f* early Church; ~**knall** *m* (*Astron*) big bang; u~**komisch** *adj* (*inf*) screamingly funny (*inf*); ~**kommunismus** *m* early *or* primitive communism; ~**kraft** *f* elemental force.

Urkunde *f* -, -**n** document; (*Kauf*~) deed, titledeed; (*Gründungs*~ etc) charter; (*Sieger*~, *Diplom*~, *Bescheinigung etc*) certificate. **eine** ~ (**über etw** *acc*) **ausstellen** *or* **ausfertigen** (*Jur*) to draw up a document about sth; **eine** ~ **bei jdm hinterlegen** to lodge a document with sb.

Urkundenfälschung *f* forgery *or* falsification of a/the document/documents.

urkundlich *adj* documentary. ~ **verbürgt** *or* **bestätigt** authenticated; ~ **beweisen** *or* **belegen** to give documentary evidence; ~ **erwähnt** mentioned in a document.

Urkundsbeamte(r) *m*, **Urkundsperson** *f* registrar.

Urlandschaft *f* primitive *or* primeval landscape.

Urlaub *m* -(**e**)**s**, -**e** (*Ferien*) holiday(s), vacation (*esp US*); (*esp Mil*) leave (of absence). ~ **haben** to have a holiday *or* vacation/to have leave; **in** *or* **im** *or* **auf** (*inf*) ~ **sein** to be on holiday *or* vacation/on leave; **er macht zur Zeit (in Italien)** ~ he's on holiday *or* he's vacationing (*esp US*) (in Italy) at the moment; **in** ~ **fahren** to go on holiday *or* vacation/on leave; **zwei Wochen** ~ two weeks' holiday *or* vacation/leave; (**sich** *dat*) **einen Tag** ~ **nehmen** to take a day off *or* a day's holiday; ~ **bis zum Wecken** (*Mil*) night leave.

urlauben *vi* (*inf*) to holiday, to vacation (*esp US*).

Urlauber(in *f*) *m* -**s**, - holiday-maker, vacationist (*US*); (*Mil*) soldier on leave.

Urlaubs-: ~**geld** *nt* holiday pay, holiday money; u~**reif** *adj* (*inf*) ready for a holiday *or* vacation (*esp US*); ~**reise** *f* holiday *or* vacation (*esp US*) trip; **eine** ~**reise machen** to go on a trip; ~**plan** *m usu pl* holiday *or* vacation (*esp US*) plan; ~**schein** *m* (*Mil*) pass; ~**sperre** *f* (*Mil*) ban on leave; ~**stimmung** *f* holiday mood; ~**tag** *m* (one day of) holiday *or* vacation (*esp US*); **die ersten drei** ~**tage hat es geregnet** it rained on the first three days of the/my/his etc holiday; **ich habe noch drei** ~**tage gut**

I've still got three days' holiday to come; ~**woche** f (one week of) holiday or vacation (esp US); ~**zeit** f holiday or vacation (esp US) period or season.

Ur-: ~**laut** m elemental cry; ~**mensch** m primeval man; (inf) caveman (inf); ~**meter** nt standard metre; ~**mund** m (Biol) blastopore; ~**mutter** f first mother.

Urne f -, -n urn; (Los~) box; (Wahl~) ballot-box. **zur** ~ **gehen** to go to the polls.

Urnen-: ~**feld** nt (Archeol) urnfield, urnsite; ~**friedhof** m urn cemetery, cinerarium; ~**gang** m (Pol) going to the polls no art; ~**grab** nt urn grave.

Urogenital- (Anat): ~**system** nt urogenital system; ~**trakt** m urogenital tract.

Urologe m, **Urologin** f urologist.

Urologie f urology.

urologisch adj urological.

Ur-: ~**oma** f (inf) great-granny (inf); ~**opa** m (inf) great-grandpa (inf); ~**pflanze** f primordial plant; **u~plötzlich** (inf) 1 adj attr very sudden; 2 adv all of a sudden; ~**quell** m, ~**quelle** f (geh) primary source, fountainhead.

Ursache f -, -n cause (auch Philos); (Grund) reason; (Beweggrund) motive; (Anlaß) occasion. ~ **und Wirkung** cause and effect; **kleine** ~, **große Wirkung** (prov) big oaks from little acorns grow (prov); **keine** ~! (auf Dank) don't mention it, you're welcome; (auf Entschuldigung) that's all right; **ohne** (**jede**) ~ for no reason (at all); **aus nichtiger** ~ for a trifling reason/trifling reasons; **aus unbekannter/ungeklärter** ~ for no apparent reason/for reasons unknown; **jdm** ~ **geben, etw zu tun** to give sb cause to do sth; **ich habe alle** ~ **anzunehmen, daß** ... I have every reason to suppose that ...; **alle/keine** ~ **zu etw haben** to have every/no reason for sth; **alle/keine** ~ **haben, etw zu tun** to have every/no reason to do sth; **die** ~ **für etw** or **einer Sache** (gen) **sein** to be the cause of/reason for sth.

ursächlich adj (esp Philos) causal. ~ **für etw sein** to be the cause of sth; **in** ~**em Zusammenhang stehen** to be causally related.

Ursächlichkeit f (esp Philos) causality.

Ur-: ~**schlamm** m primeval mud; ~**schleim** m (a) protoplasm; (b) (inf) **beim** ~**schleim anfangen** (fig inf) to go back to the flood or the ark; ~**schrei** m (Psych) primal scream; ~**schrift** f original (text or copy); **u~schriftlich** 1 adj original; 2 adv in the original; **u~senden** vt sep infin, ptp only (Rad) to broadcast for the first time; **das wurde im April u~gesendet** that was first broadcast in April; ~**sendung** f (Rad) first broadcast.

urspr. abbr of **ursprünglich**.

Ursprache f (a) proto-language. (b) (bei Übersetzungen) original (language), source language.

Ursprung m -s, **Ursprünge** (a) origin; (Anfang auch) beginning; (Abstammung) extraction. **er/dieses Wort ist keltischen** ~**s** he is of Celtic extraction/this word is Celtic in origin or of Celtic origin; **seinen** ~ **in etw** (dat) **haben, einer Sache** (dat) **seinen** ~ **verdanken** to originate in or to have one's/its origins in sth.

(b) (old: lit, fig: Quelle) source.

ursprünglich 1 adj (a) attr original; (anfänglich) initial, first. (b) (urwüchsig) natural; Natur unspoilt. 2 adv originally; (anfänglich) initially, at first, in the beginning.

Ursprünglichkeit f naturalness, simplicity.

Ursprungsland nt (Comm) country of origin.

Urständ f: (fröhliche) ~ **feiern** (hum) to come back with a vengeance, to come to life again.

Urstromtal nt (Geol, Geog) glacial valley (in North Germany).

Urteil nt -s, -e (a) judgement (auch Philos); (Entscheidung) decision; (Meinung) opinion. **nach meinem** ~ in my judgement/opinion; **ich habe darüber kein** ~, **ich kann darüber kein** ~ **abgeben** I am no judge of this; **sich** (dat) **ein** ~ **über etw** (acc) **erlauben/ein** ~ **über etw fällen** to pronounce or pass judgement on sth; **sich** (dat) **kein** ~ **über etw** (acc) **erlauben können** to be in no position to judge sth; **in seinem** ~ **unsicher werden** to become unsure or uncertain of one's judgement; **nach dem** ~ **von Sachverständigen** according to expert opinion; **jdn in seinem** ~ **bestärken** to strengthen sb in his opinion; **mit seinem** ~ **zurückhalten** to be reticent about giving one's opinion(s); **zu dem** ~ **kommen, daß** ... to come to the conclusion that ...; **sich** (dat) **ein** ~ **über jdn/etw bilden** to form an opinion about sb/sth.

(b) (Jur: Gerichts~) verdict; (Richterspruch) judgement; (Strafmaß) sentence; (Schiedsspruch) award; (Scheidungsspruch) decree. **das** ~ **über jdn sprechen** (Jur) to pass or to pronounce judgement on sb; **jdm/sich selber sein** ~ **sprechen** (fig) to pronounce sb's/one's own sentence.

urteilen vi to judge (nach by). **über etw** (acc) ~ to judge sth; (seine Meinung äußern) to give one's opinion on sth; **hart/abfällig über jdn** ~ to judge sb harshly/to be disparaging about sb; **nach seinem Aussehen zu** ~ judging by or to judge by his appearance; **vorschnell** ~ to make a hasty judgement.

Urteils-: ~**begründung** f (Jur) opinion; **u~fähig** adj competent or able to judge; (umsichtig) discerning, discriminating; **dazu ist er u~fähig genug** his judgement is sound enough for that; ~**fähigkeit** f siehe adj competence or ability to judge; discernment, discrimination; ~**findung** f (Jur) reaching a verdict no art; ~**kraft** f, no pl power or faculty of judgement; (Umsichtigkeit) discernment, discrimination; „**Kritik der** ~**kraft**" "Critique of Judgement"; ~**schelte** f attack on a/the court's ruling; ~**spruch** m (Jur) judgement; (von Geschworenen) verdict; (von Strafgericht) sentence; (von Schiedsgericht) award; ~**verkündung** f (Jur) pronouncement of judgement; ~**vermögen** nt siehe ~**kraft**.

Ur-: ~**text** m original (text); ~**tiefe** f (liter) depth(s); ~**tier** nt, ~**tierchen** nt protozoon; (in der Morphologie) primordial animal; ~**trieb** m basic drive or instinct; **u~tümlich** adj siehe **u~wüchsig**; ~**tümlichkeit** f siehe ~**wüchsigkeit**; ~**typ(us)** m -s, -typen prototype.

Ur|ur- in cpds great-great-.

Ur-: ~**vater** m forefather; ~**väterzeit** f olden times pl; **seit** ~**väterzeiten** from time immemorial; **schon zur** ~**väterzeit** even in olden times; **u~verwandt** adj Wörter, Sprachen cognate; ~**viech** or ~**vieh** nt (inf) real character; ~**vogel** m archaeopteryx; ~**volk** nt first people; ~**wahl** f (Pol) primary (election); ~**wähler** m (Pol) primary elector or voter.

Urwald m primeval forest; (in den Tropen) jungle.

Urwaldlaute pl (inf) jungle noises pl.

Ur-: ~**weib** nt (inf) real woman; ~**welt** f primeval world; **u~weltlich** adj primeval, primordial; **u~wüchsig** adj (unverbildet, naturhaft) natural; Natur unspoilt; (urweltlich) Flora, Fauna primeval; (ursprünglich) original, native; (bodenständig) rooted to the soil; (unberührt) Land etc untouched; (urgewaltig) Kraft elemental; (derb, kräftig) sturdy; Mensch rugged; Humor, Sprache earthy; ~**wüchsigkeit** f siehe adj naturalness, unaffectedness; primeval character; originality, nativeness; nativeness; untouched nature; elemental nature; sturdiness; ruggedness; earthiness; ~**zeit** f primeval times pl; **seit** ~**zeiten** since primeval times; (inf) for donkey's years (inf); **vor** ~**zeiten** in primeval times; (inf) ages ago; **u~zeitlich** adj primeval; ~**zelle** f (Biol) primordial cell; ~**zeugung** f abiogenesis; ~**zustand** m primordial or original state.

USA [u:|ɛs'|a:] pl **die** ~ the USA sing; **in die** ~ **fahren** to travel to the USA.

Usambaraveilchen nt African violet.

US-amerikanisch [u:'|ɛs-] adj US-American.

Usance [y'zã:s] f -, -n usage, custom; (Comm) practice.

usf. abbr of **und so fort**.

Usurpation f (liter) usurpation.

Usurpator m (liter) usurper.

usurpatorisch adj (liter) usurpatory, usurpative.

usurpieren* vt (liter) to usurp.

Usus m -s, no pl custom. **das ist hier so** ~ it's the custom here.

usw. abbr of **und so weiter** etc.

Utensil nt -s, -ien [-iən] utensil, implement.

Uterus m -, **Uteri** uterus.

Utilitarismus m Utilitarianism.

Utilitarist(in f) m Utilitarian.

utilitaristisch adj utilitarian.

Utopia nt -s, -s Utopia.

Utopie f utopia; (Wunschtraum) utopian dream.

utopisch adj utopian; (von Utopia) Utopian.

Utopismus m utopianism.

Utopist(in f) m utopian.

utopistisch adj (pej) utopian.

u.U. abbr of **unter Umständen**.

UV [u:'fau] abbr of **ultraviolett**.

UV- [u:'fau-] in cpds ultraviolet.

u.v.a.(m.) abbr of **und vieles andere (mehr)**.

U.v.D. [u:fau'de:] m -s, -s abbr of **Unteroffizier vom Dienst** (Mil).

Ü-Wagen m (Rad, TV) outside broadcast vehicle.

Uz m -(e)s, -e (dated, inf) siehe **Uzerei**.

uzen vti (inf) to tease, to kid (inf).

Uzerei f (dial, inf) teasing, kidding (inf).

Uzname m (inf) nickname.

V, v [fau] *nt* -, - V, v.

V *abbr of* Volt; Volumen.

va banque [va'bãːk]: ~ ~ spielen (*geh*) to play vabanque; (*fig*) to put everything at stake.

Vabanquespiel [va'bãːk-] *nt* (*fig*) dangerous game.

Vademekum [vade'meːkʊm] *nt* -s, -s (*geh*) vade mecum.

vag [vaːk] *adj siehe* vag(e).

Vagabund [vaga'bʊnt] *m* -en, -en vagabond.

Vagabundenleben [va-] *nt* vagabond life; (*fig auch*) roving life.

vagabundieren* [vagabʊn'diːrən] *vi* (**a**) (*als Landstreicher leben*) to live as a vagabond/as vagabonds. das V~ vagabondage; ein ~des Volk a nomadic people. (**b**) *aux sein* (*umherziehen*) to rove around, to lead a vagabond life. durch die Welt ~ to rove *or* wander all over the world.

vag(e) [vaːk, 'vaːgə] *adj* vague.

Vagheit ['vaːkhait] *f* vagueness.

Vagina [va'giːna] *f* -, **Vaginen** vagina.

vaginal [vagi'naːl] *adj* vaginal.

vakant [va'kant] *adj* (*old, form*) vacant.

Vakanz [va'kants] *f* (*old, form: Stelle*) vacancy; (*old, dial: Ferien*) vacation. in die ~ gehen (*old, dial*) to go on vacation.

Vakuum ['vaːkuʊm] *nt* -s, **Vakuen** ['vaːkuən] *or* **Vakua** (*lit, fig*) vacuum. unter/im ~ in a vacuum.

Vakuum- ['vaːkuʊm-] *in cpds* vacuum; ~**pumpe** *f* vacuum pump; ~**röhre** *f* vacuum tube; **v~verpackt** *adj* vacuum-packed; ~**verpackung** *f* vacuum pack; (*das Verpacken*) vacuum packaging; **v~versiegelt** *adj* vacuum-sealed.

Valentinstag ['vaːlentiːns-] *m* (*St*) Valentine's Day.

Valenz [va'lɛnts] *f* valency.

valleri, vallera [falə'riː, falə'raː] *interj* falderal, folderol.

Valuta [va'luːta] *f* -, **Valuten** (**a**) (*Währung*) foreign currency. (**b**) (*im Zahlungsverkehr*) value; (*Datum*) value date.

Vamp [vɛmp] *m* -s, -s vamp.

Vampir ['vampiːɐ, vam'piːɐ] *m* -s, -e vampire; (*Zool*) vampire (bat).

Van-Allen-Gürtel [vɛn'ɛln-] *m* Van Allen belt.

Vandale [van'daːlə] *m* -n, -n (*Hist*) Vandal.

vandalisch [van'daːlɪʃ] *adj* (*Hist*) Vandal *attr*; (*fig*) vandalistic.

Vandalismus [vanda'lɪsmʊs] *m, no pl* vandalism.

Vanille [va'nɪljə, va'nɪlə] *f* -, *no pl* vanilla.

Vanille(n)- [va'nɪljə(n)-, va'nɪlə(n)-]: ~**eis** *nt* vanilla ice-cream; ~**geschmack** *m* vanilla flavour; mit ~**geschmack** vanilla-flavoured; ~**stange** *f* vanilla pod; ~**zucker**, **Vanillinzucker** *m* vanilla sugar.

variabel [va'riaːbl] *adj* variable.

Variabilität [variabili'tɛːt] *f* variability.

Variable [va'riaːblə] *f* -n, -n variable.

Variante [va'riantə] *f* -, -n variant (*zu* on).

Variation [varia'tsioːn] *f* (*alle Bedeutungen*) variation. ~en zu einem Thema variations on a theme.

Variations- [varia'tsioːns-]: **v~fähig** *adj* capable of variation; ~**möglichkeit** *f* possibility of variation.

Varietät [varie'tɛːt] *f* (*auch Bot, Zool*) variety.

Varieté [varie'teː] *nt* -s, -s (**a**) variety (entertainment), vaudeville (*esp US*). (**b**) (*Theater*) variety theatre, music hall (*Brit*), vaudeville theater (*US*).

variieren* [vari'iːrən] *vti* to vary.

Vasall [va'zal] *m* -en, -en (*Hist, fig*) vassal.

Vasallen- [va'zalən-]: ~**pflicht** *f* (*Hist*) vassalage, feudal service; ~**staat** *m* (*Hist*) vassal state; (*fig*) client *or* satellite state; ~**tum** *nt, no pl* vassalage.

Väschen ['vɛːsçən] *nt* little vase.

Vase ['vaːzə] *f* -, -n vase.

Vasektomie [vazɛkto'miː] *f* (*spec*) vasectomy.

Vaselin [vaze'liːn] *nt* -s, *no pl*, **Vaseline** *f* -, *no pl* Vaseline ®.

vasomotorisch [vazomo'toːrɪʃ] *adj* vasomotor *attr*, vasomotory. ~ gestört sein to have a vasomotory disorder.

Vater *m* -s, ̈ (*lit fig*) father; (*Gott, bei Namen*) Father; (*von Zuchttieren*) sire. ~ von zwei Kindern sein to be the father of two children; ~ unser (*Rel*) Our Father; unsere ̃ *pl* (*geh: Vorfahren*) our (fore)fathers *or* forebears; die ̃ der Stadt the town/city fathers; wie der ~, so der Sohn (*prov*) like father, like son (*prov*); sich zu den ̃n versammeln (*fig liter*) to go to join one's fathers *or* ancestors; wer war der ~ dieses Kindes? (*fig hum*) whose idea was that?; ach du dicker ~! (*inf*) oh my goodness!, oh heavens!; ~ Staat (*hum*) the State.

Väterchen *nt dim of* Vater (*Vater*) dad(dy) (*inf*); (*alter Mann*) grandad (*inf*). ~ Staat the State.

Vater-: ~**figur** *f* father figure; ~**freuden** *pl* joys of fatherhood *pl*; ~**haus** *nt* parental home.

Vaterland *nt* native country; (*esp Deutschland*) Fatherland. dem ~ dienen/sein ~ lieben to serve/love one's country.

vaterländisch [-lɛndɪʃ] *adj* (*national*) national; (*patriotisch*) patriotic.

Vaterlands-: ~**liebe** *f* patriotism, love of one's country; **v~liebend** *adj* patriotic; **v~los** *adj* without a native land (*esp poet*); (*staatenlos*) stateless; ~**verräter** *m* traitor to one's country; (*in Deutschland auch*) traitor to the Fatherland.

väterlich *adj* (*vom Vater*) paternal; (*wie ein Vater auch*) fatherly. er klopfte ihm ~ auf die Schulter he gave him a fatherly pat on the shoulder.

väterlicherseits *adv* on one's father's side. meine Großeltern ~ my paternal grandparents.

Väterlichkeit *f* fatherliness.

Vater-: ~**liebe** *f* paternal *or* fatherly love; ~**liebe ist unersetzbar** a father's love is irreplaceable; **v~los** *adj* fatherless; ~**mord** *m* patricide; ~**mörder** *m* (**a**) patricide, father-killer (*inf*); (**b**) (*hum: Kragen*) stand-up collar, choker (*dated*); ~**recht** *nt* patriarchy.

Vaterschaft *f* fatherhood *no art*; (*esp Jur*) paternity. gerichtliche Feststellung der ~ (*Jur*) affiliation.

Vaterschafts-: ~**bestimmung** *f* determination of paternity; ~**klage** *f* paternity suit.

Vätersitte *f* tradition of one's forefathers.

Vater(s)name *m* (*old*) surname.

Vater-: ~**stadt** *f* home town; ~**stelle** *f* bei jdm ~**stelle** vertreten/an ~**stelle** stehen to act *or* be a father to sb/take the place of sb's father; ~**tag** *m* Father's Day; ~**unser** *nt* -s, - Our Father; das ~**unser** the Lord's Prayer.

Vati *m* -s, -s (*inf*) dad(dy) (*inf*).

Vatikan [vati'kaːn] *m* -s Vatican.

vatikanisch [vati'kaːnɪʃ] *adj attr* Vatican.

Vatikanstadt [vati'kaːn-] *f* Vatican City.

V-Ausschnitt ['fau-] *m* V-neck. ein Pullover mit ~ a V-neck jumper (*Brit*) *or* sweater.

v. Chr. *abbr of* vor Christus BC.

VDE ['faudeː'eː] *m* -s, *no pl abbr of* Verband Deutscher Elektrotechniker.

VEB ['fau|eː'beː] *m* -s, -s *abbr of* Volkseigener Betrieb.

Vegetarier(in *f*) [vege'taːriɐ, -ərɪn] *m* -s, - vegetarian.

vegetarisch [vege'taːrɪʃ] *adj* vegetarian. sich ~ ernähren to live on a vegetarian diet.

Vegetarismus [vegeta'rɪsmʊs] *m, no pl* vegetarianism.

Vegetation [vegeta'tsioːn] *f* vegetation.

vegetativ [vegeta'tiːf] *adj* (*pflanzlich*) vegetative; *Nervensystem* autonomic.

vegetieren* [vege'tiːrən] *vi* to vegetate; (*kärglich leben*) to eke out a bare *or* miserable existence.

vehement [vehe'ment] *adj* (*geh*) vehement.

Vehemenz [vehe'mɛnts] *f* (*geh*) vehemence.

Vehikel [ve'hiːkl] *nt* -s, - (**a**) (*pej inf*) boneshaker (*inf*). (**b**) (*Pharm, fig geh*) vehicle.

Veilchen *nt* violet; (*inf: blaues Auge*) shiner (*inf*), black eye. sie ist bescheiden wie das ~ im Moose *or* wie ein ~, das im verborgenen blüht she is modesty itself; blau wie ein ~ (*inf*) drunk as a lord (*inf*), roaring drunk (*inf*).

veilchenblau *adj* violet; (*inf: betrunken*) roaring drunk (*inf*).

Veitstanz *m* (*Med*) St Vitus's dance. einen ~ aufführen (*fig inf*) to jump *or* hop about like crazy (*inf*).

Vektor ['vɛktɔr] *m* vector.

Velar(laut) [ve'laːɐ-] *m*, -s, -e velar (sound).

Velo ['veːlo] *nt* -s, -s (*Sw*) bicycle, bike (*inf*); (*motorisiert*) moped.

Velour *nt* -s, -s *or* -e, **Velours** *nt* -, - [və'luːɐ, ve'luːɐ] (*auch* ~**leder**) suede.

Velours [və'luːɐ, ve'luːɐ] *m* -, - (*Tex*) velour(s).

Veloursteppich [və'luːɐ-, ve'luːɐ-] *m* velvet carpet.

Vendetta [vɛn'dɛta] *f* -, **Vendetten** vendetta.

Vene ['veːnə] *f* -, -n vein.

Venedig [ve'neːdɪç] *nt* -s Venice.

Venen|entzündung ['veːnən-] *f* phlebitis.

venerisch [ve'neːrɪʃ] *adj* (*Med*) venereal.

Venezianer(in *f*) [vene'tsiaːnɐ, -ərɪn] *m* -s, - Venetian.

venezianisch [vene'tsiaːnɪʃ] *adj* Venetian.

Venezolaner(in *f*) [venetso'laːnɐ, -ərɪn] *m* -s, - Venezuelan.

venezolanisch [venetso'laːnɪʃ] *adj* Venezuelan.

Venezuela [vene'tsueːla] *nt* -s Venezuela.

Venia legendi ['veːnia leːgɛndi] *f* -, *no pl* (*Univ*) authorization to teach at a university.

venös [ve'nøːs] *adj* venous.

Ventil [vɛn'tiːl] *nt* -s, -e (*Tech, Mus*) valve; (*fig*) outlet.

Ventilation [vɛntila'tsioːn] *f* ventilation; (*Anlage*) ventilation system.

Ventilator [vɛnti'laːtɔr] *m* ventilator.

ventilieren* [vɛnti'liːrən] *vt* (*fig*) to ventilate; (*fig*) (*äußern*) to air; (*erwägen*) to examine, to consider carefully.

Venus ['veːnʊs] *f* -, *no pl* (*Myth, Astron*) Venus.

ver|abfolgen* *vt* (*form*) Medizin etc to administer (*form*) (*jdm* to sb); (*verordnen*) to prescribe (*jdm* for sb).

ver|abreden* **1** *vt* to arrange; *Termin auch* to fix, to agree upon; *Straftat* to collude in; *Mord, Hochverrat, Meuterei* to conspire in. es war eine verabredete Sache it was arranged beforehand; ein vorher verabredetes Zeichen a prearranged signal; zum verabredeten Zeitpunkt/Ort at the agreed time/place, at the time/place arranged; eine verabredete Straftat an act of collusion/conspiracy; wir haben verabredet, daß wir uns um 5 Uhr treffen we have arranged to meet at 5 o'clock; wie verabredet as arranged; schon verabredet sein (*für* on) to have a previous or prior engagement (esp form), to have something else on (inf); **mit jdm verabredet sein** to have arranged to meet sb; (geschäftlich, formell) to have an appointment with sb; (esp mit Freund) to have a date with sb.

2 vr **sich mit jdm/miteinander** ~ to arrange to meet sb/to meet; (geschäftlich, formell) to arrange an appointment with sb/an appointment; (esp mit Freund) to make a date with sb/a date; (Jur) to collude with sb/collude.

Ver|abredung f (Vereinbarung) arrangement, agreement; (Treffen) engagement (form); (geschäftlich, formell) appointment; (esp mit Freund) date; (Jur) collusion; (von Mord, Hochverrat, Meuterei) conspiracy. **ich habe eine** ~ I'm meeting somebody; ~ **einer Straftat** (Jur) collusion/conspiracy to commit a criminal offence.

ver|abreichen* vt Tracht Prügel etc to give; Arznei auch to administer (form) (jdm to sb); (verordnen) to prescribe (jdm for sb); (old) Speise to serve.

Ver|abreichung f (form) siehe vt giving; administering; prescription; serving.

ver|absäumen* vt (form) to neglect, to omit.

ver|abscheuen* vt to detest, to abhor, to loathe.

ver|abscheuung f detestation, abhorrence, loathing.

ver|abscheuenswert adj detestable, abhorrent, loathsome.

ver|abscheuungswürdig adj siehe verabscheuenswert.

ver|abschieden* **1** vt to say goodbye to; (Abschiedsfeier veranstalten für) to hold a farewell ceremony for; (entlassen) Beamte, Truppen to discharge; (Pol) Haushaltsplan to adopt; Gesetz to pass. **wie bist du von deinen Kollegen/bei deiner Stelle verabschiedet worden?** what sort of a farewell did your colleagues arrange for you/did you receive at work?

2 vr **sich (von jdm)** ~ to say goodbye (to sb), to take one's leave (of sb) (form), to bid sb farewell (liter); **er ist gegangen, ohne sich zu** ~ he left without saying goodbye.

Ver|abschiedung f (von Beamten etc) discharge; (Pol) (von Gesetz) passing; (von Haushaltsplan) adoption.

ver|absolutieren* vt to make absolute.

ver|achten* vt to despise; jdn auch to hold in contempt; (liter) Tod, Gefahr to scorn. **nicht zu** ~ (inf) not to be despised, not to be scoffed at, not to be sneezed at (inf); **einen guten Whisky hat er nie verachtet** (inf) he never said no to a good drop of whisky.

ver|achtenswert adj despicable, contemptible.

Ver|ächter m: **kein** ~ **von etw sein** to be quite partial to sth.

ver|ächtlich adj contemptuous, scornful; (verachtenswert) despicable, contemptible. **jdn/etw** ~ **machen** to run sb down/belittle sth.

Ver|achtung f, no pl contempt (von for). **jdn mit** ~ **strafen** to treat sb with contempt.

ver|albern* vt (inf) to make fun of. **jdn** ~ to pull sb's leg (inf).

ver|allgemeinern* vti to generalize.

Ver|allgemeinerung f generalization.

ver|alten* vi aux sein to become obsolete; (Ansichten, Methoden) to become antiquated; (Mode) to go out of date.

ver|altet adj obsolete; Ansichten antiquated; Mode out-of-date.

Veranda [ve'randa] f -, **Veranden** veranda, porch.

ver|änderbar adj (rare) changeable.

ver|änderlich adj variable; Wetter, Mensch variable.

Ver|änderlichkeit f siehe adj variability; changeability.

ver|ändern* **1** vt to change. **2** vr to change; (Stellung wechseln) to change one's job; (Wohnung wechseln) to move. **sich zu seinem Vorteil/Nachteil** ~ (im Aussehen) to look better/worse; (charakterlich) to change for the better/worse; **verändert aussehen** to look different.

Ver|änderung f change. **eine berufliche** ~ a change of job.

ver|ängstigen* vt (erschrecken) to frighten, to scare; (einschüchtern) to intimidate.

ver|ankern* vt (Naut, Tech) to anchor; (fig) (in + dat in) Rechte etc (in Gesetz) to establish, to ground; Gedanken (in Bewußtsein) to embed, to fix.

Ver|ankerung f (Naut, Tech) (das Verankern) anchoring; (das Verankertsein) anchorage; (fig) (von Rechten) (firm) establishment; (von Gedanken) embedding, fixing.

ver|anlagen* vt to assess (mit at).

ver|anlagt adj melancholisch/tuberkulös ~ **sein** to have a melancholy/tubercular disposition; **technisch/mathematisch/praktisch** ~ **sein** to be technically/mathematically/practically minded; **künstlerisch/musikalisch** ~ **sein** to have an artistic/a musical bent; **zu** or **für etw** ~ **sein** to be cut out for sth; **er ist so** ~, **daß** ... it's his nature to ...; **er ist eben so** ~ that's just the way he is, that's just his nature.

Ver|anlagung f (a) (körperlich, esp Med) predisposition; (charakterlich) nature, disposition; (Hang) tendency; (allgemeine Fähigkeiten) natural abilities pl; (künstlerisches, praktisches etc Talent) bent. **eine** ~ **zum Dickwerden/zur Kriminalität haben** to have a tendency to put on weight/to have criminal tendencies.

(b) (von Steuern) assessment.

ver|anlassen* vt **(a) etw** ~ to arrange for sth, to see to it that sth is done/carried out etc; (befehlen) to order sth; **eine Maßnahme** ~ to arrange for/order a measure to be taken; **ich werde das Nötige** ~ I will see (to it) that the necessary steps are taken; **wir werden alles Weitere** ~ we will take care of or see to everything else.

(b) auch vi (bewirken) to give rise (zu to). **jdn zu etw** ~ (Ereignis etc) to lead sb to sth; (Mensch) to cause or induce sb to do sth; **jdn (dazu)** ~, **etw zu tun** (Ereignis etc) to lead sb to do sth; (Mensch) to cause or induce sb to do sth; **das veranlaßt zu der Annahme, daß** ... that leads one to assume that ...; **sich (dazu) veranlaßt fühlen**, **etw zu tun** to feel compelled or obliged to do sth.

Ver|anlassung f cause, reason. **auf** ~ **von** or + gen **at the**

instigation of; **keine** ~ **zu etw haben/keine** ~ **haben, etw zu tun** to have no cause or reason for sth/to do sth or for doing sth; ~ **zu etw geben** to give cause for sth.

ver|anschaulichen* vt to illustrate (+ dat to, an + dat, mit with). **sich** (dat) **etw** ~ to picture sth (to oneself), to visualize sth; **sich** (dat) ~, **daß** ... to see or realize that ...

Ver|anschaulichung f illustration. **zur** ~ as an illustration, to illustrate sth.

ver|anschlagen* vt to estimate (auf + acc at). **etw zu hoch/niedrig** ~ to overestimate/underestimate sth.

Ver|anschlagung f estimate; (das Veranschlagen) estimation.

ver|anstalten* vt to organize, to arrange; Wahlen to hold; Umfrage to do; (kommerziell) Wettkämpfe, Konzerte etc to promote; Party etc to hold, to give; (inf) Szene to make.

Ver|anstalter(in f) m -s, - organizer; (Comm: von Wettkämpfen, Konzerten etc) promoter.

Ver|anstaltung f **(a)** event (von organized by); (feierlich, öffentlich) function. **(b)** no pl (das Veranstalten) organization.

ver|antworten* **1** vt to accept (the) responsibility for; die Folgen auch, sein Tun to answer for (vor + dat to). **(es)** ~, **daß jd etw tut** to accept the responsibility for sb doing sth; **wie könnte ich es denn** ~, ...? it would be most irresponsible of me ...; **ein weiterer Streik/eine solche Operation wäre nicht zu** ~ another strike/such an operation would be irresponsible; **eine nicht zu** ~**de Fahrlässigkeit/Schlamperei** inexcusable negligence/slackness; **etw sich selbst gegenüber** ~ to square sth with one's own conscience.

2 vr **sich für** or **wegen etw** ~ to justify sth (vor + dat to); (für Missetaten etc) to answer for sth (vor + dat before); **sich vor Gericht/Gott etc** ~ **müssen** to have to answer to the courts/God etc (für, wegen for).

ver|antwortlich adj responsible; (haftbar) liable. **jdm (gegenüber)** ~ **sein** to be responsible or answerable or accountable to sb; **jdn für etw** ~ **machen** to hold sb responsible for sth; **für etw** ~ **zeichnen** (form) (lit) to sign for sth; (fig) to take responsibility for sth; **der** ~**e Leiter des Projekts** the person in charge of the project.

Ver|antwortliche(r) mf decl as adj person responsible. **die** ~**n** jd those responsible.

Ver|antwortlichkeit f, no pl responsibility; (Haftbarkeit) liability.

Ver|antwortung f responsibility (für for). **auf eigene** ~ on one's own responsibility; **auf deine** ~! you take the responsibility!, on your own head be it!; **die** ~ **übernehmen** to take or accept or assume (esp form) responsibility; **jdn zur** ~ **ziehen** to call sb to account.

Ver|antwortungs-: v~**bewußt** adj responsible; ~**bewußtsein** nt sense of responsibility; v~**freudig** adj willing to take responsibility; v~**los** adj irresponsible; ~**losigkeit** f, no pl irresponsibility; v~**voll** adj responsible.

ver|äppeln* vt (inf) **jdn** ~ to make fun of sb; (auf den Arm nehmen) to pull sb's leg (inf).

ver|arbeitbar adj workable. **leicht/schwer** ~ easy/hard to work.

ver|arbeiten* vt to use (zu etw to make sth); (Tech, Biol etc) to process; Ton, Gold etc to work; (verbrauchen) to consume; (verdauen) to digest; (fig) to use (zu for); Stoff to treat; Daten to process; Erlebnis etc to assimilate, to digest; (bewältigen) to overcome. ~**de Industrie** processing industries pl; **etw geistig** ~ to assimilate or digest sth.

ver|arbeitet adj **(a)** gut/schlecht ~ Rock etc well/badly finished. **(b)** (dial: abgearbeitet) worn.

Ver|arbeitung f **(a)** siehe vt use, using; processing; working; digestion; using; treating; processing; assimilation, digestion; overcoming. **(b)** (Aussehen) finish; (Qualität) workmanship no indef art.

ver|argen* vt **jdm etw** ~ to hold sth against sb; **jdm** ~, **daß** ... to hold it against sb that ...; **ich kann es ihm nicht** ~, **wenn er** ... I can't blame him if he ...

ver|ärgern* vt **jdn** ~ to annoy sb; (stärker) to anger sb.

ver|ärgert adj annoyed; (stärker) angry.

Ver|ärgerung f annoyance; (stärker) anger.

ver|armen* vi aux sein (lit, fig) to become impoverished. **ver|armt** impoverished.

Ver|armung f, no pl impoverishment.

ver|arschen* vt (sl) to take the piss out of (sl); (für dumm verkaufen) to mess or muck around (inf).

ver|arzten* vt (inf) to fix up (inf); (mit Verband) to patch up (inf); (fig hum) to sort out (inf).

ver|ästeln* vr to branch out; (fig) to ramify. **eine verästelte Organisation** a complex organization; **ein verästelter Baum** a branched or ramose (spec) tree.

Ver|ästelung f branching; (fig) ramifications pl.

ver|auktionieren* vt to auction off.

ver|ausgaben* vr to overexert or overtax oneself; (finanziell) to overspend. **ich habe mich total verausgabt** (finanziell) I'm completely spent out.

Ver|ausgabung f, no pl (finanziell) overspending; (fig) overexertion.

ver|auslagen* vt (Comm) to lay out, to disburse (form).

ver|äußerlich adj (form: verkäuflich) saleable, for sale.

ver|äußerlichen* **1** vt to trivialize. **2** vi aux sein to become superficial.

ver|äußern* vt (form: verkaufen) to dispose of; Rechte, Land to alienate.

Ver|äußerung f siehe vt disposal; alienation.

Verb [verp] nt -s, -en verb.

verbal [ver'baːl] adj verbal (auch Gram).

Verbalinjurie [ver'baːlinjuːriə] f (Jur) verbal injury.

verballhornen* vt to parody; (unabsichtlich) to get wrong.

Verballhornung f parody; (*unabsichtlich*) ≈ spoonerism.
Verband m -(e)s, -e (a) (*Med*) dressing; (*mit Binden*) bandage. (b) (*Bund*) association. (c) (*Mil*) unit. im ~ fliegen to fly in formation. (d) (*Archit*) bond.
Verband(s)-: ~kasten m first-aid box; ~material nt dressing material; ~päckchen nt first-aid packet; ~stoff m dressing; ~watte f surgical cottonwool (*Brit*), absorbent cotton (*US*), cotton batting (*US*); ~zeug nt dressing material.
verbannen* vt to banish (*auch fig*), to exile (*aus* from, *auf* to).
Verbannte(r) mf decl as adj exile.
Verbannung f banishment no art, exile no art; (*das Verbannen*) banishment, exiling.
Verbannungs|ort m place of exile.
verbarrikadieren* 1 vt to barricade. 2 vr to barricade oneself in (*in etw* (*dat*)) sth.
verbaseln* vt (*dial*) to mislay.
verbat pret of **verbitten**.
verbauen* vt (a) (*versperren*) to obstruct, to block. sich (*dat*) alle Chancen/die Zukunft ~ to spoil one's chances/one's prospects for the future; jdm die Möglichkeit ~, etw zu tun to ruin or spoil sb's chances of doing sth.
(b) (*verbrauchen*) Holz etc to use in building; Geld to use for building.
(c) (*schlecht bauen*) to construct badly.
(d) (*inf: verderben*) Text, Arbeit etc to botch (*inf*).
verbeißen* irreg 1 vt (*fig inf*) sich (*dat*) etw ~ Zorn etc to stifle sth, to suppress sth; Bemerkung to bite back sth; Schmerz to hide sth; sich (*dat*) das Lachen ~ to keep a straight face. 2 vr sich in etw (*acc*) ~ (*lit*) to bite into sth; (*Hund*) to sink its teeth into sth; (*fig*) to become set or fixed on sth; siehe **verbissen**.
verbergen* irreg 1 vt (+dat, vor + dat from) (*lit, fig*) to hide, to conceal; (*vor der Polizei auch*) to harbour. sein Gesicht in den Händen ~ to bury one's face in one's hands; jdm etw ~ (*verheimlichen*) to keep sth from sb; siehe **verborgen**². 2 vr to hide (oneself), to conceal oneself.
Verbesserer m -s, - improver; (*Welt~*) reformer; (*sprachlicher* ~, *pej*) pedant.
verbessern* 1 vt (a) (*besser machen*) to improve; Leistung, Bestzeit to improve (up)on, to better; die Welt to reform. eine neue, verbesserte Auflage a new revised edition.
(b) (*korrigieren*) to correct.
2 vr (*Lage etc*) to improve, to get better; (*Mensch*) (*in Leistungen*) to improve, to do better; (*beruflich, finanziell*) to better oneself; (*sich korrigieren*) to correct oneself.
Verbesserung f (a) improvement (*von* in); (*von Leistung, Bestzeit*) improvement (*von* on); (*von Buch*) revision; (*berufliche, finanzielle* ~) betterment. (b) (*Berichtigung*) correction.
Verbesserungs-: v~fähig adj capable of improvement; ~vorschlag m suggestion for improvement.
verbeten ptp of **verbitten**.
verbeugen* vr to bow (*vor* +dat to).
Verbeugung f bow. eine ~ vor jdm machen to (make a) bow to sb.
verbeulen* vt to dent.
verbiegen* irreg 1 vt to bend (out of shape); siehe **verbogen**. 2 vr to bend; (*Holz*) to warp; (*Metall*) to buckle.
verbiestern* (*inf*) 1 vt (*verstören*) to throw (*inf*); (*störrisch machen*) to make pig-headed (*inf*). 2 vr sich in etw (*acc*) ~ to become fixed on sth.
verbiestert adj (*inf*) (*mißmutig*) crotchety (*inf*); (*verstört*) disturbed no adv.
verbieten pret **verbot**, ptp **verboten** vt to forbid; (*amtlich auch*) to prohibit; Zeitung, Partei to ban, to prohibit. jdm ~, etw zu tun to forbid sb to do sth; (*amtlich auch*) to prohibit sb from doing sth; jdm das Rauchen/den Zutritt/den Gebrauch von etw ~ to forbid sb to smoke/to enter/the use of sth; (*amtlich auch*) to prohibit sb from smoking/entering/using sth; meine Situation verbietet (es) mir, mich dazu zu äußern my position doesn't allow me to comment on that; mein Taktgefühl/die Höflichkeit verbietet mir eine derartige Bemerkung tact/politeness prevents me from making such a remark; das verbietet sich von selbst that has to be ruled out; siehe **verboten**.
verbilden* vt (*fig*) jdn to bring up badly, to miseducate; Geschmack, Charakter to spoil, to deform.
verbildlichen* vt siehe **veranschaulichen**.
Verbildung f siehe vt miseducation; spoiling, deformation.
verbilligen* 1 vt to reduce the cost of; Kosten, Preis to reduce. verbilligte Waren/Karten reduced goods/tickets at reduced prices; etw verbilligt abgeben to sell sth at a reduced price.
2 vr to get or become cheaper; (*Kosten, Preise auch*) to go down.
verbimsen* vt (*inf*) to bash up (*inf*).
verbinden* irreg 1 vt (a) (*Med*) to dress; (*mit Binden*) to bandage. jdm die Augen ~ to blindfold sb; mit verbundenen Augen blindfold(ed).
(b) (*verknüpfen, in Kontakt bringen*) (*lit, fig*) to connect, to link; Punkte to join (up).
(c) (*Telec*) jdn (*mit jdm*) ~ to put sb through (to sb); ich verbinde! I'll put you through, I'll connect you; (Sie sind hier leider) falsch verbunden! (I'm sorry, you've got the) wrong number!; mit wem bin ich verbunden? who am I speaking to?
(d) (*gleichzeitig haben or tun, anschließen*) to combine.
(e) (*assoziieren*) to associate.
(f) (*mit sich bringen*) mit etw verbunden sein to involve sth, to be bound up with sth; die damit verbundenen Kosten/Gefahren etc the costs/dangers etc involved.
(g) (*emotional*) Menschen to unite, to join together. freundschaftlich/in Liebe verbunden sein (*geh*) to be united or joined together in friendship/love; jdn mit etw ~ to make sb feel attached to sth.
2 vr (a) to combine (*auch Chem*) (*mit* with, *zu* to form), to join

(together), to join forces (*zu* in, to form). sich ehelich/in Liebe/Freundschaft ~ (*geh*) to join together in marriage/love/friendship; in ihrer Person ~ sich Klugheit und Schönheit she combines both intelligence and beauty.
(b) (*assoziiert werden*) to be associated; (*hervorgerufen werden*) to be evoked (*mit* by).
3 vi (*emotional*) to form a bond; siehe **verbunden**.
verbindlich adj (a) obliging. ~sten Dank! (*form*) thank you kindly!, I/we thank you! (b) (*verpflichtend*) obligatory, compulsory; Regelung, Zusage binding; (*verläßlich*) Auskunft reliable. ~ zusagen to accept definitely.
Verbindlichkeit f siehe adj (a) obligingness; (*höfliche Redensart*) civility usu pl, courtesy usu pl, polite word(s pl).
(b) no pl obligatory or compulsory nature, compulsoriness; binding nature or force; reliability.
(c) ~en pl (*Comm, Jur*) obligations pl, commitments pl; (*finanziell auch*) liabilities pl; seine ~en erfüllen to fulfil one's obligations or commitments; to meet one's liabilities; ~en gegen jdn haben to have (financial) commitments to sb.
Verbindung f (a) connection; (*persönliche, einflußreiche Beziehung auch, Kontakt*) contact (*zu, mit* with). in ~ mit (*zusammen mit*) in conjunction with; (*im Zusammenhang mit*) in connection with; jdn/etw mit etw in ~ bringen to connect sb/sth with sth; (*assoziieren*) to associate sb/sth with sth; er/sein Name wurde mit dem Mord/der Affäre in ~ gebracht he/his name was mentioned in connection with the murder/the affair; eine ~ zwischen Vorkommnissen herstellen to establish a connection between occurrences; seine ~en spielen lassen to use one's connections, to pull a few strings (*inf*); ~en anknüpfen or aufnehmen to get contacts; ~ mit jdm aufnehmen to contact sb; die ~ aufrechterhalten to maintain contact; (*esp zwischen Freunden*) to keep in touch or contact; sich (mit jdm) in ~ setzen, (mit jdm) in ~ treten to get in touch or contact (with sb), to contact sb; mit jdm in ~ stehen to be in touch or contact with sb; mit etw in ~ stehen to be connected with sth.
(b) (*Verkehrs~*) connection (*nach* to). die ~ von Berlin nach Warschau the connections pl from Berlin to Warsaw; es besteht direkte ~ nach München there is a direct connection to Munich.
(c) (*Telec: Anschluß*) line. telefonische ~/~ durch Funk telephonic/radio communication; eine ~ (zu einem Ort) bekommen to get through (to a place); unsere ~ wurde unterbrochen we were cut off.
(d) (*Mil*) contact; (*durch Funk etc*) communication; (*Zusammenarbeit*) liaison. ~ aufnehmen to make contact; to establish communication.
(e) (*Kombination*) combination.
(f) (*Vereinigung, Bündnis*) association; (*ehelich*) union; (*Univ*) society; (*für Männer*) fraternity (*US*); (*für Frauen*) sorority (*US*). eine ~ mit jdm eingehen to join together with sb; eine schlagende/nicht schlagende ~ (*Univ*) a duelling/non-duelling fraternity.
(g) (*Chem*) (*Prozeß*) combination; (*Ergebnis*) compound (*aus* formed out of). eine ~ mit etw eingehen to form a compound with sth, to combine with sth.
Verbindungs- in cpds (*esp Tech, Archit*) connecting; (*Univ*) fraternity; ~mann m, pl -leute or -männer intermediary; (*Agent*) contact; ~offizier m liaison officer; ~stelle f (*von Gleisen, Kabeln*) junction (point); (*von Rohren, Gekkiebtem etc*) join; (*Amt*) liaison office; ~straße f connecting road; ~stück nt connecting piece; ~student m member of a fraternity; ~tür f connecting door.
verbissen 1 ptp of **verbeißen**. 2 adj grim; Arbeiter dogged, determined; Gesicht, Miene determined.
Verbissenheit f, no pl siehe adj grimness; doggedness, determination.
verbitten* pret **verbat**, ptp **verbeten** vr sich (*dat*) etw (*schwer/sehr etc*) ~ to refuse (absolutely) to tolerate sth; das verbitte ich mir!, das will ich mir verbeten haben! I won't have it!
verbittern* 1 vt to embitter, to make bitter. jdm das Leben ~ to make sb's life a misery. 2 vi aux sein to become embittered or bitter. verbittert embittered, bitter.
Verbitterung f bitterness, embitterment.
verblassen* vi aux sein (*lit, fig*) to fade; (*Mond*) to pale. alles andere verblaßt daneben (*fig*) everything else pales into insignificance beside it.
Verbleib m -(e)s, no pl (*form*) whereabouts pl.
verbleiben* vi irreg aux sein to remain. bei seiner Meinung ~ to persist in one's opinion; etw verbleibt jdm sb has sth left; ... verbleibe ich Ihr ... (*form*) ... I remain, Yours sincerely ...; wir sind so verblieben, daß wir ... we agreed or arranged to ..., it was agreed or arranged that we ...; sein V~ in dieser Position ist unmöglich geworden it has become impossible for him to remain in this post.
verbleichen pret **verblich**, ptp **verblichen** vi aux sein (*lit, fig*) to fade; (*Mond*) to pale; (*liter: sterben*) to pass away, to expire (*liter*). verblichen (*lit, fig*) faded.
verbleien* vt (a) Benzin to lead, to put a lead additive in. (b) (*mit Blei überziehen*) to lead-coat, to coat with lead.
verblenden* vt (a) (*fig*) to blind. verblendet sein to be blind. (b) (*Archit*) to face.
Verblendung f (a) (*fig*) blindness. (b) (*Archit*) facing.
verbleuen* vt (*inf*) to bash up (*inf*).
verblich pret of **verbleichen**.
verblichen ptp of **verbleichen**.
Verblichene(r) mf decl as adj (*liter*) deceased.
verblöden* vi aux sein (*inf*) to become a zombi(e) (*inf*).
Verblödung f (*inf*) stupefaction. diese Arbeit führt noch zu meiner völligen ~ this job will turn me into a zombi(e)

(inf); **die dauernde Reklame führt noch zu unserer völligen** ~ the long-term effect of advertising is to make us totally uncritical.

verblüffen* vt (erstaunen) to stun, to amaze; (verwirren) to baffle. **sich durch** or **von etw** ~ **lassen** to be taken in by sth.

Verblüffung f, no pl siehe vt amazement; bafflement.

verblühen* vi aux sein (lit, fig) to fade. **der Baum ist verblüht** the blossom has fallen from the tree; **sie sieht verblüht aus** her beauty has faded.

verblümt adj oblique. **etw/sich** ~ **ausdrücken** to say sth/express oneself in a roundabout way.

verbluten* 1 vi aux sein to bleed to death. 2 vr (fig) to spend oneself.

Verblutung f fatal haemorrhage; (das Verbluten) bleeding to death. **Tod durch** ~ death caused by (a) haemorrhage.

verbocken* vt (inf) (verpfuschen) to botch (inf), to bungle (inf); (anstellen) to get up to (inf).

verbockt adj (inf) pig-headed (inf); **Kind** headstrong.

verbogen 1 ptp of **verbiegen**. 2 adj bent; **Rückgrat** curved; (fig) twisted.

verbohren* vr (inf) **sich in etw** (acc) ~ to become obsessed with sth; (unbedingt wollen) to become (dead) set on sth (inf).

verbohrt adj **Haltung** stubborn, obstinate; **Politiker** auch, **Meinung** inflexible.

Verbohrtheit f inflexibility.

verborgen[1]* vt to lend out (an +acc to).

verborgen[2] 1 ptp of **verbergen**.
2 adj hidden. **etw/sich** ~ **halten** to hide sth/to hide; **im V~en leben** to live hidden away; **so manches schöne Mädchen/große Talent blüht im** ~**en** many beautiful girls/great talents flourish in obscurity; **im** ~**en wachsen/blühen** (lit) to grow/bloom in places hard to find; **im** ~**en liegen** to be not yet known; **Gott sieht ins V~e** God sees into the hidden reaches of the soul.

Verborgenheit f, no pl seclusion.

verbot pret of **verbieten**.

Verbot nt -(e)s, -e ban. **er ging trotz meines** ~**s** he went even though I had forbidden him to do so; **trotz des ärztlichen** ~**es** against doctor's orders, in spite of doctor's orders; **gegen ein** ~ **verstoßen** to ignore a ban; **das** ~ **der Eltern, zu rauchen/einen Freund mitzubringen** the parents' ban on smoking/on bringing a friend; **ich bin gegen das** ~ **irgendeiner Partei/Zeitung** I'm opposed to a ban on or to banning any party/newspaper.

verboten 1 ptp of **verbieten**. 2 adj forbidden; (amtlich) prohibited; (gesetzeswidrig) **Handel** illegal; **Zeitung, Partei, Buch** etc banned. **jdm ist etw** ~ sb is forbidden to do sth; **Rauchen/Parken** ~ no smoking/parking; **er sah** ~ **aus** (inf) he looked a real sight (inf).

verbotenerweise adv against orders; (gesetzeswidrig) illegally. **er hat** ~ **geraucht** he smoked even though it was forbidden or (amtlich) prohibited.

Verbots-: ~**schild** nt, ~**tafel** f (allgemein) notice or sign (prohibiting something); (im Verkehr) prohibition sign.

verbrach pret of **verbrechen**.

verbracht ptp of **verbringen**.

verbrachte pret of **verbringen**.

verbrämen* vt (geh) **Kleidungsstück** to trim; (fig) **Rede** to pad; **Wahrheit** to gloss over; **Kritik** to veil (mit in).

verbrannt 1 ptp of **verbrennen**. 2 adj burnt; (fig) **Erde** scorched.

Verbrauch m -(e)s, no pl consumption (von, an +dat of); (von Geld) expenditure; (von Kräften) drain (von, an +dat on). **einen enormen** ~ **an Benzin haben** to have an enormous petrol consumption, to use an enormous amount of petrol; **im Winter ist der** ~ **an Kalorien/Energie höher** we use up more calories/energy in winter; **sparsam im** ~ economical; **zum baldigen** ~ **bestimmt** to be used immediately; **der** ~ **von öffentlichen Geldern** public expenditure.

verbrauchen* vt (a) (aufbrauchen) to use; **Vorräte** to use up; **Benzin, Wasser, Nahrungsmittel** etc auch to consume. **der Wagen verbraucht 10 Liter Benzin auf 100 km** the car does 10 kms to the litre.
(b) (abnützen) **Kräfte** etc to exhaust; **Kleidung** etc to wear out. **sich** ~ to wear oneself out; **verbrauchte Luft/Nerven** stale or stuffy air/frayed or tattered nerves; **sie ist schon völlig verbraucht** she is already completely spent.

Verbraucher m -s, - consumer.

Verbraucher- in cpds consumer; ~**genossenschaft** f consumer cooperative; ~**preis** m consumer price; ~**schutz** m consumer protection; ~**verband** m consumer council.

Verbrauchs-: ~**güter** pl consumer goods pl; ~**lenkung** f control of consumption; ~**steuer** f excise.

Verbrechen nt -s, - (lit, fig) crime (gegen, an +dat against).

verbrechen pret **verbrach**, ptp **verbrochen** vt (a) **Straftat, Greueltat** to commit. **etwas** ~ to commit a crime.
(b) (inf: anstellen) **etwas** ~ to be up to something (inf); **was habe ich denn jetzt schon wieder verbrochen?** what on earth have I done now?
(c) (hum inf) **Gedicht, Kunstwerk, Übersetzung** etc to be the perpetrator of (hum).

Verbrechensbekämpfung f combating crime no art.

Verbrecher m -s, - criminal.

Verbrecher-: ~**album** nt rogues' gallery (hum); ~**bande** f gang of criminals; ~**gesicht** nt (pej) criminal face.

Verbrecherin f criminal.

verbrecherisch adj criminal. **in** ~**er Absicht** with criminal intent.

Verbrecher-: ~**jagd** f chase after a/the criminal/criminals; ~**kartei** f criminal records pl; ~**kolonie** f penal colony; ~**tum** nt criminality; ~**viertel** nt (pej inf) shady part of town; ~**visage** f (pej inf) criminal face; ~**welt** f underworld.

verbreiten* 1 vt to spread; **Ideen, Lehre** auch to disseminate;

Zeitung to distribute, to circulate; (ausstrahlen) **Wärme** to radiate; **Licht** to shed; **Ruhe** to radiate. **eine (weit) verbreitete Ansicht** a widely or commonly held opinion; **eine verbreitete Zeitung** a newspaper with a large circulation or a wide distribution.
2 vr (a) to spread.
(b) **sich über ein Thema** ~ to expound on or hold forth on a subject.

verbreitern* 1 vt to widen. 2 vr to get wider, to widen out.

Verbreiterung f widening.

Verbreitung f, no pl siehe vt spreading; dissemination; distribution, circulation; radiation; shedding; radiation.

verbrennbar adj combustible.

verbrennen* irreg 1 vt (a) to burn; **Müll** auch to incinerate; (einäschern) **Tote** to cremate; (verbrauchen) **Gas, Kerzen** to burn; **Strom** to use.
(b) (versengen) to scorch; **Finger, Haut** etc to burn; **Haar** to singe; (verbrühen) to scald. **sich** (dat) **die Zunge/den Mund** or **den Schnabel** ~ (lit) to burn one's tongue/mouth; (fig) to say too much; siehe **Finger**.
2 vr to burn oneself; (sich verbrühen) to scald oneself.
3 vi aux sein to burn; (Mensch, Tier) to burn (to death); (niederbrennen: Haus etc) to burn down; (durch Sonne, Hitze) to be scorched. **das Fleisch** ~ **lassen** to burn the meat; **alles verbrannte** or **war verbrannt** everything was destroyed in the fire; **alle verbrannten** everyone died in the fire; **die verbrannten Leichen/Bücher** the bodies of the people burnt to death in the fire/the books destroyed in or by the fire; siehe auch **verbrannt**.

Verbrennung f (a) no pl (das Verbrennen) burning; (von Müll auch) incineration; (von Treibstoff) combustion; (von Leiche) cremation. (b) (Brandwunde) burn; (Verbrühung) scald. **starke/leichte** ~**en davontragen** to be badly/not seriously burned.

Verbrennungs-: ~**anlage** f incineration plant; ~**kraftmaschine** f internal combustion vehicle; ~**motor** m internal combustion engine; ~**ofen** m furnace; (für Müll) incinerator; ~**produkt** nt waste product (of combustion); ~**wärme** f heat of combustion.

verbriefen* vt to document. **verbriefte Rechte** attested rights.

verbringen pret **verbrachte**, ptp **verbracht** vt (a) **Zeit** etc to spend. (b) (obs, Jur: bringen) to take.

verbrochen ptp of **verbrechen**.

Verbr. Pr. abbr of **Verbraucherpreis**.

verbrüdern* vr to swear eternal friendship (mit to); (politisch) to ally oneself (mit to, with). **Menschen aller Rassen sollten sich** ~ people of all races should be brothers.

Verbrüderung f avowal of friendship; (politisch) alliance.

verbrühen* 1 vt to scald. 2 vr to scald oneself.

Verbrühung f (no pl: das Verbrühen) scalding; (Wunde) scald.

verbuchen* vt to enter (up) (in a/the book). **einen Betrag auf ein Konto** ~ to credit a sum to an account; **Erfolge (für sich)** ~ to notch up or chalk up successes (inf); **etw für sich** or **auf sein Konto** ~ **können** (fig) to be able to credit oneself with sth.

Verbuchung f entering (up).

verbuddeln* vt (inf) to bury.

Verbum [ˈvɛrbʊm] nt -s, **Verba** (geh) verb.

verbummeln* (inf) 1 vt (verlieren) to lose; (vertrödeln, vergeuden) **Nachmittag, Wochenende, Zeit** to waste, to fritter away; (verpassen) **Verabredung** to miss. 2 vi aux sein (a) (herunterkommen) to go to seed. (b) (faul werden) to get lazy. **verbummelt sein** to be lazy.

Verbund m -(e)s, no pl (Econ) combine. **im** ~ **arbeiten** to cooperate.

Verbundbau m composite (method of) building.

verbunden 1 ptp of **verbinden**. 2 adj (form: dankbar) **jdm (für etw)** ~ **sein** to be obliged to sb (for sth).

verbünden* vr to ally oneself (mit to); (Staaten) to form an alliance. **alle haben sich gegen mich verbündet** everyone is against me or has sided against me; **verbündet sein** to be allies or allied.

Verbundenheit f, no pl (von Völkern) solidarity; (von Menschen) (mit Menschen, Natur) closeness (mit to); (mit Land, Tradition) attachment (mit to). **in tiefer** ~, ... very affectionately yours, ...

Verbündete(r) mf decl as adj ally.

Verbund-: ~**glas** nt laminated glass; ~**(loch)karte** f dual(-purpose) card; ~**netz** nt (Elec) (integrated) grid system; ~**platte** f sandwich panel; ~**stahl** m laminated steel; ~**werbung** f joint advertising; ~**wirtschaft** f integrated economy.

verbürgen* vtr to guarantee. **sich für jdn/etw** ~ to vouch for sb/sth; **verbürgte Nachricht** authenticated information; **ein verbürgtes Recht** an established right.

verbürgerlichen* vi aux sein to become bourgeois.

verbüßen* vt to serve.

Verbüßung f, no pl serving. **zur** ~ **einer Haftstrafe von zwei Jahren verurteilt werden** to be sentenced to serve two years in prison.

verbuttern* vt (a) to make into butter. (b) (inf) **Geld** to spend. **er hat beim Bau des Hauses viel Geld verbuttert** he sank a lot of money into building the house (inf).

verchromen* [fɛɐ̯ˈkroːmən] vt to chromium-plate.

Verchromung [fɛɐ̯ˈkroːmʊŋ] f chromium-plating.

Verdacht m -(e)s, no pl suspicion; (hum: Vermutung) hunch. **jdn in** or **im** ~ **haben** to suspect sb; **ich habe sie im** ~, **daß sie die Blumen geschickt hat** (hum) I've got a hunch that she sent the flowers; **im** ~ **stehen, etw getan zu haben** to be suspected of having done sth; **jdn in** ~ **bringen** to make sb look guilty; **den** ~ **auf jdn lenken** to throw or cast suspicion on sb; **jdn wegen** ~**s einer Sache** (gen) **festnehmen** to arrest sb on suspicion of sth; **(gegen jdn)** ~ **schöpfen** to become suspicious (of sb); **es besteht** ~ **auf Krebs** (acc) cancer is suspected; **bei** ~

auf Krebs in the case of suspected cancer; **etw auf ~ tun** (*inf*) to do sth on spec (*inf*).

verdächtig *adj* suspicious; (~ *aussehend*) suspicious-looking. ~ **aussehen** to look suspicious; **sich ~ machen** to arouse suspicion; **die drei ~en Personen** the three suspects; **einer Sache** (*gen*) ~ **sein** to be suspected of sth.

verdächtigen* *vt* to suspect (*gen* of). **ich will niemanden ~, aber ...** I don't want to cast suspicion on anyone, but ...; **er wird verdächtigt, gestohlen zu haben, er wird des Diebstahls verdächtigt** he is suspected of theft.

Verdächtige(r) *mf decl as adj* suspect.

Verdächtigung *f* suspicion. **die ~ eines so integren Mannes käme mir nie in den Sinn** it would never occur to me to suspect a man of his integrity.

Verdachts-: **~grund** *m* grounds *pl* for suspicion; **~moment** *nt* suspicious circumstance.

verdammen* *vt* (*esp Rel: verfluchen*) to damn; (*verurteilen*) to condemn; *siehe auch* **verdammt, Scheitern.**

verdammenswert *adj* damnable, despicable.

Verdammnis *f* (*Rel*) damnation *no art.*

verdammt 1 *adj*, *adv* (*inf*) damned (*inf*), bloody (*Brit sl*). **~er Mist!** (*sl*) sod it! (*Brit sl*); **~e Scheiße!** (*sl*) shit! (*sl*); **~ hübsch** damned pretty (*inf*); **das tut ~ weh** that hurts like hell (*sl*); **~ viel Geld** a hell of a lot of money (*sl*); **mir geht's ~ gut/schlecht** I'm on top of the world (*inf*)/in a bad way.

2 *interj* (*sl*) **~!** damn or blast (*it*) (*inf*); **~ noch mal!** bloody hell (*Brit sl*), damn it all (*inf*); **du wirst dich ~ noch mal entschuldigen!** apologize, damn you! (*inf*).

Verdammte(r) *mf decl as adj* (*Rel*) **die ~n** the damned *pl.*

Verdammung *f* condemnation; (*Rel*) damnation.

verdampfen* *vti* (*vi: aux sein*) to vaporize; (*Cook*) to boil away.

Verdampfer *m* -s, - vaporizer.

Verdampfung *f* vaporization.

verdanken* *vt* **jdm etw ~** to owe sth to sb; **es ist jdm/einer Sache zu ~(, daß ...)** it is thanks or due to sb/sth (that ...); **das verdanke ich dir** (*iro*) I've got you to thank for that.

verdarb *pret of* **verderben.**

verdattert *adj*, *adv* (*inf*) flabbergasted (*inf*).

verdauen* **1** *vt* (*lit, fig*) to digest. **2** *vi* (*Mensch*) to digest one's food; (*Magen etc*) to digest the food. **um besser ~ zu können ...** in order to improve one's digestion ...

verdaulich *adj* digestible. **leicht ~** easily digestible, easy to digest; **schwer ~** hard to digest.

Verdaulichkeit *f*, *no pl* digestibility.

Verdauung *f* digestion. **eine gute/schlechte ~ haben** to have good/poor digestion.

Verdauungs-: **~apparat** *m* digestive system; **~beschwerden** *pl* digestive trouble *sing*; **~kanal** *m* alimentary canal, digestive tract; **~organ** *nt* digestive organ; **~saft** *m* gastric juice; **~spaziergang** *m* constitutional; **~störung** *f usu pl* indigestion *no pl*; **~trakt** *m* digestive or alimentary tract.

Verdeck *nt* -(e)s, -e (a) (*Dach*) (*von Kutsche, Kinderwagen*) hood (*Brit*), canopy; (*von Auto*) soft top, hood (*Brit*); (*hart*) roof; (*von Flugzeug*) canopy. (b) (*von Passagierdampfer*) sundeck; (*von doppelstöckigem Bus*) open top deck.

verdecken* *vt* to hide, to conceal; (*zudecken*) to cover (up); *Sicht* to block; (*fig*) *Absichten, Widerspruch, Symptome* to conceal; *Unterschlagungen etc* to conceal, to cover up. **eine Wolke verdeckte die Sonne** a cloud hid or covered the sun; **sie verdeckte ihr Gesicht mit den Händen** she covered her face with her hands, she hid her face in her hands; **verdeckt** concealed; *Widerspruch* hidden; *siehe* **Karte.**

verdenken* *vt irreg* **jdm etw ~** to hold sth against sb; **ich kann es ihm nicht ~(, daß er es getan hat)** I can't blame him (for doing it).

Verderb *m* -(e)s, *no pl* (*geh: Untergang*) ruin. **sein ~** his ruin, the ruin of him; *siehe* **Gedeih.**

verderben *pret* **verdarb,** *ptp* **verdorben 1** *vt* to spoil; (*stärker*) to ruin; *Plan auch* to wreck; *Luft* to pollute; *jdn* (*moralisch*) to corrupt; (*sittlich*) to deprave, to corrupt; (*verwöhnen*) to spoil. **jdm etw ~** *Abend, Urlaub* to spoil or ruin sth for sb; *Chancen, Leben, Witz* to ruin sth for sb; **sich** (*dat*) **das Leben ~** to ruin one's life; **sich** (*dat*) **den Magen/Appetit ~** to give oneself an upset stomach/to spoil one's appetite; **sich** (*dat*) **die Augen/Stimme/Lungen ~** to ruin or damage one's eyes or eyesight/voice/lungs; **die Preise ~** to force prices down/up; **jds Laune** or **jdm die Laune ~** to put sb in a bad mood; **jdm die Freude** or **den Spaß/die Lust an etw** (*dat*) **~** to spoil sb's enjoyment of sth; **es** (*sich dat*) **mit jdm ~** to fall out with sb.

2 *vi aux sein* (*Material*) to become spoiled/ruined; (*Nahrungsmittel*) to go bad or off; (*Ernte*) to be ruined; (*Mensch*) to become depraved or corrupted. **da** or **daran ist nichts mehr zu ~** it or things couldn't get any worse; **an dem Kuchen/Hemd ist nichts mehr zu ~** the cake/shirt is absolutely ruined anyway; *siehe* **verdorben.**

Verderben *nt* -(e)s, *no pl* (a) (*Untergang, Unglück*) undoing, ruin. **in sein ~ rennen** to rush headlong towards ruin; **jdn ins ~ stürzen** to bring ruin or disaster (up)on sb; **jdn ins ~ führen** to lead sb to disaster; (*moralisch*) to corrupt sb.
(b) (*von Material*) spoiling, ruining; (*von Nahrungsmittel*) going off; (*von Luft, Wasser*) pollution.

verderbenbringend *adj* disastrous.

verderblich *adj* pernicious; *Einfluß auch* corrupting; *Lebensmittel* perishable.

Verderblichkeit *f*, *no pl* perniciousness; perishableness. **die leichte ~ von Fisch** the extreme perishableness of fish.

Verderbnis *f* corruption, depravity; (*Verderbtheit*) corruptness, depravity.

verderbt *adj* (a) (*dated: moralisch*) corrupt(ed), depraved. (b) (*Typ*) corrupt.

Verderbtheit *f* (*dated*) corruptness, depravity.

verdeutlichen* *vt* to show clearly; (*deutlicher machen*) to clarify, to elucidate; (*erklären*) to explain. **er versuchte seinen Standpunkt an einem Beispiel zu ~** he tried to clarify his position by means of an example; **sich** (*dat*) **etw ~** to think sth out for oneself; **etw besser/näher ~** to clarify sth further.

Verdeutlichung *f* clarification. **zur ~ seiner Absichten** in order to show his intentions clearly.

verdeutschen* *vt* to translate into German; (*fig inf*) to translate (into normal language).

verdichten* **1** *vt* (*Phys*) to compress; (*fig: komprimieren*) to condense; *Gefühle* to intensify, to heighten.
2 *vr* to thicken; (*Schneetreiben*) to worsen; (*Gas*) to become compressed; (*fig: häufen*) to increase; (*Verdacht, Eindruck*) to deepen. **die Handlung verdichtet sich** the plot thickens; **die Gerüchte ~ sich, daß ...** the rumours that ... are increasing; **mein Eindruck verdichtete sich zur Gewißheit** my impression hardened into certainty.

Verdichter *m* -s, - (*Tech*) compressor.

Verdichtung *f* (a) *siehe* *vt* compression; condensing; intensification, heightening. (b) *siehe* *vr* thickening; worsening; compression; increase (*gen* in); deepening; (*der Handlung*) thickening.

verdicken* **1** *vt* to thicken; *Blut* to coagulate; (*verbreitern*) to widen; (*gelieren lassen*) to make set; (*verstärken*) to strengthen.
2 *vr* to thicken; (*Gelee*) to set; (*Blut*) to coagulate; (*Milch*) to curdle; (*weiter werden*) to become thicker; (*Rohr, Flasche*) to become wider, to widen out; (*anschwellen*) to swell.

Verdickung *f* (*das Verdicken*) thickening; (*von Blut*) coagulation; (*von Gelee*) setting; (*von Milch*) curdling; (*von Rohr, Flasche*) widening; (*Schwellung*) swelling; (*Verstärkung*) strengthening; (*verdickte Stelle*) bulge.

verdienen* **1** *vt* (a) (*einnehmen*) to earn; (*Gewinn machen*) to make. **sein Brot** or **seinen Unterhalt ~** to earn or make one's living; **er hat an dem Auto DM 200 verdient** he made DM200 on the car; **dabei ist nicht viel zu ~** there's not much money in that; **sich** (*dat*) **etw ~** to earn the money for sth; **sich** (*dat*) **das Studium ~** to pay for or finance one's own studies.
(b) (*fig*) *Lob, Strafe* to deserve. **sich** (*dat*) **etw (redlich) verdient haben** to deserve sth, to have earned sth; *Schläge auch* to have had sth coming to one (*inf*); **er verdient es nicht anders/besser** he doesn't deserve anything else/any better; *siehe* **verdient.**
2 *vi* to earn; (*Gewinn machen*) to make (a profit) (*an* + *dat* on). **in dieser Familie ~ drei Personen** there are three wage-earners in this family; **er verdient gut/besser** he earns a lot/more; **er verdient schlecht** he doesn't earn much; **am Krieg ~** to profit from war.

Verdiener *m* -s, - wage-earner. **der einzige ~** the sole breadwinner.

Verdienst¹ *m* -(e)s, -e (*Einkommen*) income, earnings *pl*; (*Profit*) profit. **einen besseren ~ haben** to earn more.

Verdienst² *nt* -(e)s, -e (a) (*Anspruch auf Anerkennung*) merit; (*Dank*) credit. **es ist sein ~/das ~ der Wissenschaftler(, daß ...)** it is thanks to him/the scientists (that ...); **nach ~** on merit; **ein Mann von hohem ~** a man of great merit; **das ~ gebührt ihm allein** the credit is entirely his; **sich** (*dat*) **etw als** or **zum** (*rare*) **~ anrechnen** to take the credit for sth.
(b) *usu pl* (*Leistung*) contribution; (*wissenschaftlich auch, national*) service. **ihre ~e um die Wissenschaft/als Wissenschaftlerin** her services or contribution to science; **seine ~e um das Vaterland/die Stadt** his services to his country/town; **seine ~e um die Dichtung/den Weltfrieden** his contribution to poetry/world peace; **hohe ~e erwerben** to make a great contribution (*um* to); **er hat sich** (*dat*) **große ~e um das Vaterland erworben** he has rendered his country great service.

Verdienst-: **~adel** *m* = life peerage; (*Angehörige des ~adels*) = life peers *pl*; **~ausfall** *m* loss of earnings; **~kreuz** *nt* highest decoration awarded for military or other service; **v~lich** *adj* commendable; **~möglichkeit** *f* opportunity for earning money; **~orden** *m* order of merit; **~spanne** *f* profit margin; **v~voll** *adj* commendable.

verdient **1** *ptp of* **verdienen. 2** *adj* (a) *Lohn, Strafe* rightful; *Ruhe, Lob* well-deserved. (b) *Wissenschaftler, Politiker, Sportler* of outstanding merit. **sich um etw ~ machen** to render outstanding services to sth.

verdientermaßen, verdienterweise *adv* deservedly.

Verdikt [vɛrˈdɪkt] *nt* -(e)s, -e (*geh*) verdict.

verdingen *pret* **verdingte,** *ptp* **verdungen** or **verdingt** (*old*) **1** *vt* **jdn** to put into service (*bei* with); *Arbeit* to give. **2** *vr* **sich** (*bei jdm*) **~** to enter service (with sb).

verdinglichen* *vt* (*konkretisieren*) to put into concrete terms, to concretize; (*Philos*) *Ideen* to reify; *Menschen* to objectify.

Verdinglichung *f* *siehe* *vt* concretization; reification; objectification.

verdirb *imper sing of* **verderben.**

verdolmetschen* *vt* to translate, to interpret.

Verdolmetschung *f* translation.

verdonnern* *vt* (*inf*) (*zu Haft etc*) to sentence, to condemn (*zu* to). **jdn zu etw ~, jdn dazu ~, etw zu tun** to order sb to do sth as a punishment; **jdn zu einer Geldstrafe/Gefängnisstrafe von ... ~** to fine sb .../to sentence sb to a term of ... imprisonment.

verdoppeln* **1** *vt* to double; (*fig*) *Anstrengung etc* to redouble. **2** *vr* to double.

Verdopp(e)lung *f* *siehe* *vt* doubling; redoubling.

verdorben 1 *ptp of* **verderben. 2** *adj* (a) *Lebensmittel* bad, off *pred*; *Wasser, Luft* polluted; *Magen* upset. (b) *Stimmung, Urlaub, Freude* spoiled, ruined. (c) (*moralisch*) corrupt; (*sittlich*) depraved; (*verzogen*) *Kind* spoiled.

Verdorbenheit *f* depravity.

verdorren* *vi aux sein* to wither.

verdösen* *vt* (*inf*) to doze away.

verdrahten* *vt* to wire (up).

verdrängen* *vt jdn* to drive out; *Gegner auch* to oust; (*ersetzen*) to supersede, to replace; (*Phys*) *Wasser, Luft* to displace; (*Met*) to drive; (*fig*) *Sorgen* to dispel, to drive away; (*Psych*) to repress, to suppress. **er hat sie aus seinem Herzen verdrängt** he has forced himself to forget her; **das jüngste Kind hat die älteren aus dem Herzen der Eltern verdrängt** the youngest child has replaced the older ones in the parents' affections; **jdn aus dem Amt/von der Macht ~** to oust sb; **das habe ich völlig verdrängt** (*hum: vergessen*) it completely slipped my mind (*inf*); **jdn/etw aus dem Bewußtsein ~** to repress *or* suppress all memory of sb/sth.

Verdrängung *f siehe vt* driving out; ousting; superseding, replacing; displacement; driving; dispelling; repression, suppression.

verdrecken* *vti* (*vi: aux sein*) (*inf*) to get dirty *or* filthy. **verdreckt** filthy (dirty).

verdrehen* *vt* to twist; *Gelenk auch* to wrench; (*anders einstellen*) *Radio, Regler, Lampe* to adjust; (*verknacksen*) to sprain; *Hals* to crick; *Augen* to roll; *jds Worte, Tatsachen auch* to distort. **das Recht ~** to pervert the course of justice; **sich (*dat*) den Hals ~** (*fig inf*) to crane one's neck; *siehe* **Kopf.**

verdreht *adj* (*inf*) crazy (*inf*); *Bericht* confused, garbled; (*psychisch durcheinander*) screwed-up (*sl*).

Verdrehtheit *f* (*inf*) craziness; (*von Bericht etc*) confusion, garbledness; (*psychisch*) screwed-up behaviour *no pl* (*sl*).

Verdrehung* *f siehe vt* twisting; adjusting; wrenching; spraining; cricking; rolling; distortion; perversion.

verdreifachen* *vtr* to treble, to triple.

Verdreifachung *f* trebling, tripling.

verdreschen* *vt irreg* (*inf*) to beat up; (*als Strafe*) to thrash.

verdrießen *pret* **verdroß**, *ptp* **verdrossen** *vt jdn* to irritate, to annoy. **sich (*dat*) den Abend/den Urlaub etc durch etw ~ lassen** to let sth spoil one's evening/holiday *etc*; **lassen Sie es sich nicht ~!** to be put off *or* worried by it; **sich keine Mühe ~ lassen** to spare no effort; *siehe* **verdrossen.**

verdrießlich *adj* morose; *Arbeit, Angelegenheit* irksome.

Verdrießlichkeit *f siehe adj* moroseness; irksomeness.

verdroß *pret of* **verdrießen.**

verdrossen 1 *ptp of* **verdrießen.** 2 *adj* (*schlechtgelaunt*) morose; (*unlustig*) *Mensch, Gesicht* unwilling, reluctant.

Verdrossenheit *f* (*schlechte Laune*) moroseness; (*Lustlosigkeit*) unwillingness, reluctance. **mit ~ arbeiten** to work unwillingly *or* reluctantly.

verdrucken* 1 *vt* to make a misprint. 2 *vt* to misprint.

verdrücken* 1 *vt* (a) *Kleider* to crumple. (b) (*dial: zerdrücken*) to crush, to squash. (c) (*inf*) *Essen* to polish off (*inf*). 2 *vr* (*inf*) to beat it (*inf*). **sich heimlich ~** to slip away (unnoticed).

Verdruß *m* **-sses, -sse** frustration. **~ mit jdm haben** to get frustrated with sb; **zu jds ~** to sb's annoyance; **jdm zum ~** to spite sb.

verduften* *vi aux sein* (a) to lose its smell; (*Parfüm*) to lose its scent; (*Tee, Kaffee*) to lose its aroma. (b) (*inf: verschwinden*) to beat it (*inf*).

verdummen* 1 *vt jdn* ~ (*für dumm verkaufen*) to make sb out to be stupid; (*dumm machen*) to dull sb's mind. 2 *vi aux sein* to stultify, to become stultified.

Verdummung *f* (a) *siehe vt* treating as stupid; dulling (of sb's mind). (b) *siehe vi* stultification.

verdungen *ptp of* **verdingen.**

verdunkeln* 1 *vt* to darken; *Bühne auch*, (*im Krieg*) to black out; *Farbe auch* to deepen, to make darker; (*fig*) *Zusammenhänge, Motive etc* to obscure; *jds Glück* to dim; *jds Ruf* to damage, to harm. *Tatbestände* ~ to suppress evidence; **die Sonne ~** (*Mond*) to eclipse the sun; (*Wolken*) to obscure the sun.
    2 *vr* to darken; (*Himmel auch*) to grow darker; (*Verstand*) to become dulled.

Verdunk(e)lung *f* (a) *siehe vt* darkening; blacking out; deepening; obscuring; dimming; damaging, harming. **die ~ nicht einhalten** not to keep to the blackout. (b) (*das Dunkelwerden*) *siehe vr* darkening; dulling. (c) (*inf*) (*Vorhang*) curtain; (*Jalousie*) blind (*sl*). (d) (*Jur*) suppression of evidence.

Verdunk(e)lungsgefahr *f* (*Jur*) danger of suppression of evidence.

verdünnen* 1 *vt* to thin (down); (*mit Wasser*) to water down; *Lösung* to dilute; *Gas* to rarefy. **den Teig mit Wasser ~** to add water to the dough. 2 *vr* (*Lösung*) to become diluted; (*Luft*) to become rarefied; (*Vegetation*) to become thinner; (*schmaler werden*) to become thinner; (*Rohr*) to become narrower. **verdünnte Luft** rarefied air.

Verdünner *m* **-s, -** thinner.

verdünnisieren* *vr* (*hum inf*) to beat a hasty retreat.

Verdünnung *f* (a) thinning; (*von Lösung*) dilution; (*mit Wasser*) watering down; (*von Luft*) rarefaction (*form*); (*Verengung*) narrowing. (b) (*Flüssigkeit zum Verdünnen*) thinner.

verdunsten* *vi aux sein* to evaporate.

Verdunster *m* **-s, -** humidifier.

Verdunstung *f* evaporation.

verdursten* *vi aux sein* to die of thirst.

verdusseln* *vt* (*inf*) *etw* ~ to forget all about sth.

verdüstern* *vtr* to darken.

verdutzen* *vt* (*inf*) to take aback, to nonplus; (*verwirren*) to baffle.

verdutzt *adj, adv* (*inf*) taken aback, nonplussed; (*verwirrt*) baffled.

Verdutztheit *f* (*inf*) bafflement.

ver|ebben* *vi aux sein* to subside.

ver|edeln* *vt Metalle, Erdöl* to refine; *Fasern* to finish; (*Bot*) to graft; *Boden, Geschmack* to improve; *jdn, Charakter* to ennoble.

Ver|ed(e)lung *f siehe vt* refining; finishing; grafting; improving; ennoblement.

ver|ehelichen* *vr* (*form*) **sich (mit jdm)** ~ to marry (sb).

ver|ehelicht *adj* (*form*) married. **Eva Schmidt, ~e Meier** Eva Meier née Schmidt; **seine V~e** his wife.

Ver|ehelichung *f* (*form*) marriage.

ver|ehren* *vt* (a) (*hochachten*) to admire; *Gott, Maria, Heiligen* to honour; (*ehrerbietig lieben*) to worship, to adore; *siehe* **verehrt.** (b) (*schenken*) **jdm etw ~** to give sb sth.

Ver|ehrer(in *f*) *m* **-s, -** admirer.

ver|ehrt *adj* (*in Anrede*) (**sehr**) ~**e Anwesende/Gäste/~es Publikum** Ladies and Gentlemen; (**sehr**) ~**e gnädige Frau** (*in Brief*) (dear) Madam; **mein V~ester/meine V~este** (*iro, form*) (my) dear Sir/Madam.

Ver|ehrung *f* (*Hochachtung*) admiration; (*von Heiligen*) worship; (*Liebe*) adoration.

ver|ehrungs-: ~**voll** *adv* (*geh*) reverentially, in reverence; ~**würdig** *adj* (*geh*) *Mensch, Güte* commendable, praiseworthy; *Künstlerin* admirable.

ver|eiden* (*dated*), **ver|eidigen*** *vt* to swear in. **jdn auf etw** (*acc*) ~ to make *or* have sb swear on sth; **vereidigter Übersetzer** *etc* sworn translator *etc*.

Ver|eidigung, Ver|eidung *f* (*dated*) *f* swearing in.

Ver|ein *m* **-(e)s, -e** organization; (*esp Tier~, Landschaftsschutz~ etc auch*) society; (*kulturell auch*) association; (*Sport~*) club; (*inf*) crowd. **ein wohltätiger ~** a charity; **ihr seid vielleicht ein ~!** (*inf*) what a bunch you are! (*inf*); **eingetragener ~** registered society *or* (*wohltätig*) charity; **im ~ mit** in conjunction with; **im ~ rufen** to shout *or* chant in unison.

ver|einbar *adj* compatible; *Aussagen* consistent. **nicht (miteinander) ~** incompatible; *Aussagen* inconsistent; **eine mit meinem Gewissen nicht ~e Tat** a deed which I cannot reconcile with my conscience.

ver|einbaren* *vt* (a) (*miteinander absprechen*) to agree; *Zeit, Treffen, Tag* to arrange. **(es)** ~, **daß ...** to agree/arrange that ... (b) **etw mit etw ~** to reconcile sth with sth; **sich mit etw ~ lassen** to be compatible with sth; **mit etw zu ~ sein** to be compatible with sth; (*Aussagen*) to be consistent with sth; (*Ziele, Ideale*) to be reconcilable with sth.

Ver|einbarkeit *f, no pl siehe adj* compatibility; consistency.

ver|einbartermaßen *adv* as agreed; (*in bezug auf Zeit, Treffen*) as arranged.

Ver|einbarung *f siehe vt* (a) (*das Vereinbaren*) agreeing; arranging; (*Abmachung*) agreement; arrangement. **laut ~ as** agreed; **nach ~** by arrangement.

ver|einbarungsgemäß *adv* as agreed.

ver|einen* 1 *vt* to unite; (*miteinander vereinbaren*) *Ideen, Prinzipien* to reconcile. **eine Familie wieder ~** to reunite a family; **vereint rufen** to shout in unison; **vereint handeln** to act together *or* as one; **sich nicht mit etw ~ lassen** to be irreconcilable with sth; **sie vereint Tugend und Schönheit in sich** (*dat*) she combines virtue and beauty; **Vereinte Nationen** United Nations *sing*.
    2 *vr* to join together. **in ihr ~ sich Schönheit und Tugend** she combines beauty and virtue.

ver|einfachen* *vt* to simplify; (*Math*) to reduce. **etw vereinfacht darstellen** to portray sth in simplified terms.

Ver|einfachung *f* simplification; (*Math*) reduction.

ver|einheitlichen* *vt* to standardize.

Ver|einheitlichung *f* standardization.

ver|einigen* 1 *vt* to unite; *Kräfte auch* to combine; *Eigenschaften* to bring together; (*Comm*) *Firmen* to merge (*zu* into); *Kapital* to pool; *Aktion* to coordinate. **etw mit etw ~** (*vereinbaren*) to reconcile sth with sth; **Schönheit mit Intelligenz (in sich *dat*) ~** to combine beauty with intelligence; **die beiden Standpunkte lassen sich nicht ~** the two points of view are incompatible; **in einer Hand vereinigt sein** to be held by the same person; **Freunde um sich ~** to gather friends around one; **alle Stimmen auf sich** (*acc*) ~ to collect all the votes; **Vereinigtes Königreich** United Kingdom; **Vereinigte Staaten** United States; **Vereinigte Arabische Emirate** United Arab Emirates.
    2 *vr* to unite; (*sich verbünden auch*) to join forces; (*Firmen*) to merge; (*zusammenkommen*) to combine; (*Töne*) to blend; (*Flüsse*) to meet; (*Zellen etc*) to fuse; (*sich versammeln*) to assemble; (*geh: geschlechtlich*) to come together. **sich zu einem harmonischen Ganzen ~** to merge into a harmonious whole; **sich zu einer Koalition ~** to form a coalition.

Ver|einigung *f* (a) *siehe vt* uniting; combining; bringing together; merging; pooling; coordination; (*Math, geh: körperliche, eheliche* ~) union. (b) (*Organisation*) organization.

Ver|einigungs-: ~**freiheit** *f* freedom of association; ~**menge** *f* (*Math*) union *or* join of sets.

ver|einnahmen* *vt* (*form*) to take. **jdn ~** (*fig*) to make demands on sb; *Beruf* to occupy sb; **sie versucht, ihn völlig zu ~** she wants him all to herself.

ver|einsamen* *vi aux sein* to become lonely *or* isolated. **vereinsamt sterben** to die lonely.

Ver|einsamung *f* loneliness, isolation.

Ver|eins-: ~**freiheit** *f siehe* **Vereinigungsfreiheit;** ~**haus** *nt* club house; ~**kamerad** *m* fellow club member; ~**leitung** *f* (a) (*Amt*) chairmanship of an organization/association/a club; (b) (*Personen*) club *etc* committee; ~**meier** *m* **-s, -** (*inf*) clubbable person (*inf*); ~**meierei** *f* (*inf*) clubbableness (*inf*); ~**mitglied** *nt* club member; ~**wesen** *nt* clubs, organizations and societies *pl*.

ver|eint *ptp, adj siehe* **vereinen.**

ver|einzeln* *vt* (*Agr*) to thin (out).

ver|einzelt 1 *adj* occasional; (*Met auch*) isolated. **die Faulheit**

~er Schüler the laziness of the occasional or odd pupil. 2 adv occasionally; (zeitlich auch) now and then; (örtlich auch) here and there. ... ~ bewölkt ... with cloudy patches.

ver|eisen* 1 vt (Med) to freeze. 2 vi aux sein to freeze; (Straße) to freeze or ice over; (Fensterscheibe) to ice over; (Tragfläche auch) to ice up.

ver|eist adj Straßen, Fenster icy; Bäche frozen; Türschloß, Tragfläche iced-up; Land covered in ice.

Ver|eisung f (a) (Med) freezing. (b) siehe vi freezing; freezing or icing over; icing over; icing (up).

ver|eiteln* vt Plan etc to thwart, to foil; Verbrechen, Attentat to foil, to prevent; Versuch auch to frustrate.

Ver|eit(e)lung f siehe vt thwarting, foiling; prevention; frustration.

ver|eitern* vi aux sein to go septic; (Wunde auch) to fester. vereitert sein to be septic; vereiterte Wunde septic wound; vereiterter Zahn abscess; vereiterte Mandeln haben to have tonsillitis.

Ver|eiterung f sepsis. ~ der Wunde/des Zahns/der Mandeln septic wound/dental sepsis/tonsillitis.

ver|ekeln* vt (inf) jdm etw ~ to put sb off sth (inf).

ver|elenden* vi aux sein to become impoverished or (Mensch auch) destitute.

Ver|elendung f impoverishment.

ver|enden* vi aux sein to perish, to die.

ver|engen* 1 vr to narrow, to become narrow; (Gefäße, Pupille) to contract; (Kleid, Taille) to go in; (fig: Horizont) to narrow. 2 vt to make narrower; Pupille etc to make contract; Kleid to take in; Horizont to narrow.

ver|engern* 1 vt (a) Kleidung to take in. (b) siehe verengen 2. 2 vr (a) (Ärmel, Hose) to go in; (spitz zulaufen) to become narrower. (b) siehe verengen 1.

Ver|engung f (a) narrowing; (von Pupille, Gefäß) contraction. (b) (verengte Stelle) narrow part (in + dat of); (in Adern) stricture (in + dat of).

ver|erbbar adj (a) Anlagen hereditary. (b) Besitz heritable.

ver|erben* 1 vt (a) Besitz to leave, to bequeath (dat, an + acc to); (hum) to hand on (jdm to sb), to bequeath (jdm sb). (b) Anlagen to pass on (dat, auf + acc to); Krankheit to transmit. 2 vr to be passed on/transmitted (auf + acc to).

ver|erblich adj siehe vererbbar.

Ver|erbung f (a) (das Vererben) (von Besitz) leaving, bequeathing; (von Anlagen) passing on; (von Krankheit) transmission. (b) (Lehre) heredity. das ist ~ (inf) it's hereditary.

Ver|erbungs-: ~forschung f genetics sing; ~lehre f genetics sing.

ver|ewigen* 1 vt to immortalize; Zustand, Verhältnisse to perpetuate. seine schmutzigen Finger auf der Buchseite ~ to leave one's dirty fingermarks on the page for posterity; der Verewigte (geh) the deceased. 2 vr (lit, fig) to immortalize oneself.

Ver|ewigung f siehe vt immortalization; perpetuation.

Verf., Vf. abbr of Verfasser.

verfahren[1]* vi irreg aux sein (vorgehen) to act, to proceed. mit jdm/etw streng/schlecht ~ to deal strictly/badly with sb/sth.

verfahren[2]* irreg 1 vt Geld, Zeit to spend in travelling; Benzin to use up. 2 vr to lose one's way; (fig) (Angelegenheit) to get muddled; (Mensch) to get into a muddle.

verfahren[3] adj Angelegenheit muddled. eine ~e Sache a muddle.

Verfahren nt -s, - (Vorgehen) actions pl; (~sweise) procedure; (Tech) process; (Methode) method; (Jur) proceedings pl. ein ~ gegen jdn einleiten or anhängig machen to take or initiate legal proceedings against sb.

Verfahrens-: v~rechtlich adj (form) procedural; ~technik f process engineering; ~weise f procedure, modus operandi.

Verfall m -(e)s, no pl (a) (Zerfall) decay; (von Gebäude) dilapidation; (gesundheitlich, geistig) decline. etw dem ~ preisgeben to let sth go to (rack and) ruin; in ~ geraten (Gebäude) to become dilapidated; (stärker) to fall into ruins. (b) (Niedergang: von Kultur, der Sitten, sittlich) decline; (des Römischen Reichs auch) fall; (von Reichtum, Vermögen) fall (von in). (c) (das Ungültigwerden) (von Schuldansprüchen, Rechnung etc) lapsing; (von Scheck, Karte) expiry.

verfallen[1]* vi irreg aux sein (a) (zerfallen) to decay; (Bauwerk) to fall into disrepair, to become dilapidated; (Zellen) to die; (körperlich und geistig) to deteriorate; (Sitten, Kultur, Reich) to decline. der Patient verfällt zusehends the patient has gone into a rapid decline. (b) (ungültig werden) (Briefmarken, Geldscheine, Gutschein) to become invalid; (Scheck, Fahrkarte) to expire; (Strafe, Recht, Termin, Anspruch, Patent) to lapse. (c) (in jds Besitz übergehen) to be forfeited. jdm ~ to be forfeited to sb, to become the property of sb. (d) (abhängig werden) jdm/einer Sache ~/~ sein to become/be a slave to sb/sth; dem Alkohol etc to become/be addicted to sth; jds Zauber etc to become/be enslaved by sth; jdm völlig ~ sein to be completely under sb's spell; einem Irrtum ~ to make a mistake, to be mistaken; dem Tod ~ (sein) (geh) to be destined to die. (e) auf etw (acc) ~ to think of sth; (aus Verzweiflung) to resort to sth; auf abstruse Gedanken ~ to start having abstruse thoughts; wie konntest du nur darauf ~, nach Glasgow zu gehen? whatever made you go to Glasgow?; wer ist denn bloß auf diesen Gedanken ~? whoever thought this up?; wie sind Sie bloß darauf ~? whatever gave you that idea? (f) in etw (acc) ~ to sink into sth; in einen tiefen Schlaf ~ to fall into a deep sleep; in einen ganz anderen Ton ~ to adopt a completely different tone; in einen Fehler ~ to make a mistake.

verfallen[2] adj Gebäude dilapidated, ruined; Mensch (körperlich) emaciated; (geistig) senile; (abgelaufen) Karten, Briefmarken invalid; Strafe lapsed; Scheck expired.

Verfalls-: ~datum nt expiry date; (der Haltbarkeit) eat-by date; ~erscheinung f symptom of decline (gen in); ~tag m expiry date; (von Strafe etc) date of lapsing.

verfälschen* vt to distort; Wahrheit, Aussage auch, Daten to falsify; Lebensmittel, Wein, Geschmack to adulterate.

Verfälschung f siehe vt distortion; falsification; adulteration.

verfangen* irreg 1 vr to get caught. sich in Lügen ~ to get entangled in a web of lies; sich in Widersprüchen ~ to contradict oneself. 2 vi to be accepted. bei jdm nicht ~ not to cut any ice with sb (inf).

verfänglich adj Situation awkward, embarrassing; Aussage, Beweismaterial, Blicke, Andeutungen incriminating; (gefährlich) dangerous; Angewohnheit insidious; Frage tricky.

Verfänglichkeit f siehe adj awkwardness; incriminating nature; dangerousness; insidiousness; trickiness.

verfärben* 1 vt to discolour. etw rot ~ to turn sth red; wenn der Herbst die Blätter verfärbt when autumn turns the leaves. 2 vr to change colour; (Blätter auch) to turn; (Metall, Wäsche, Stoff) to discolour. sich grün/rot ~ to turn or go green/red; sie verfärbte sich she went red/white.

Verfärbung f siehe vr change in colour; turning; discolouring.

verfassen* vt to write; Gesetz, Urkunde to draw up.

Verfasser(in f) m -s, - writer; (von Buch, Artikel etc auch) author.

Verfasserschaft f authorship.

Verfassung f (a) (Pol) constitution. gegen die ~ handeln to act unconstitutionally. (b) (körperlich) state (of health); (seelisch) state of mind. sie ist in guter/schlechter ~ she is in good/bad shape; seine seelische ~ ist gut/schlecht he is in good/poor spirits; sie ist nicht in der ~ zu arbeiten she is in no fit state to work; ich befinde mich or bin nicht in der ~, auf die Party zu gehen I am in no fit state to go to the party. (c) (Zustand) state.

verfassunggebend adj attr constituent.

Verfassungs-: ~änderung f constitutional amendment; ~beschwerde f complaint about infringement of the constitution; ~feind m enemy of the constitution (being declared as such disbars sb from working in the public service); v~feindlich adj anticonstitutional; ~gericht nt constitutional court; v~mäßig adj constitutional; etw v~mäßig garantieren to guarantee sth in the constitution; eine v~mäßige Ordnung a constitutional law; ~recht nt constitutional law; ~schutz m (Aufgabe) defence of the constitution; (Organ, Amt) office responsible for defending the constitution; v~treu adj loyal to the constitution; ~treue f loyalty to the constitution; ~urkunde f constitution, constitutional charter; v~widrig adj unconstitutional; ~wirklichkeit f constitutional reality.

verfaulen* vi aux sein to decay; (Fleisch, Gemüse auch) to rot; (Körper, organische Stoffe) to decompose; (fig) to degenerate.

verfault adj decayed; Fleisch, Obst etc rotten; Zähne auch bad; Körper decomposed; Mensch (innerlich) degenerate.

verfechten* vt irreg to defend; Lehre to advocate, to champion; Meinung auch to maintain.

Verfechter(in f) m -s, - advocate, champion.

Verfechtung f siehe vt defence; advocacy, championing; maintaining. eine weitere ~ dieser Meinung ist nicht mehr gerechtfertigt it is no longer possible to maintain this view.

verfehlen* vt (a) (verpassen, nicht treffen) to miss. seine Worte hatten ihre Wirkung verfehlt/nicht verfehlt his words had missed/hit their target; den Zweck ~ not to achieve its purpose; das Thema ~ to be completely off the subject. (b) (versäumen) nicht ~, etw zu tun not to fail to do sth.

verfehlt adj (unangebracht) inappropriate; (mißraten) Leben, Angelegenheit, Planung unsuccessful. es ist ~, das zu tun you are mistaken in doing that.

Verfehlung f (a) (des Ziels) missing. bei ~ des Themas bekommt der Schüler ... if the essay is off the subject the pupil will get ... (b) (Vergehen) misdemeanour; (Sünde) transgression.

verfeinden* 1 vr to quarrel. sich mit jdm ~ to make an enemy of sb; mit Nachbarn to quarrel with sb; verfeindet sein to have quarrelled; (Familie etc) to be estranged; (Staaten) to be on bad terms; die verfeindeten Schwestern/Staaten the estranged sisters/the enemy states. 2 vt die beiden Völker ~ to set the two countries against one another; warum versuchst sie, ihren Mann und seine Familie zu ~? why is she trying to set her husband against his family?

verfeinern* 1 vt to improve; Methode auch to refine. 2 vr to improve; (Methoden auch) to become refined.

verfeinert adj Methode, Geräte sophisticated.

Verfeinerung f siehe vb improvement; refining; (von Geschmack auch) refinement. die zunehmende ~ technischer Geräte the increasing sophistication of technical equipment.

verfemen* vt (Hist) to outlaw; (fig) jdn to ostracize; Künstler, Ideologie, Methode, Kunstrichtung to condemn.

Verfemte(r) mf decl as adj (Hist) outlaw; (fig) persona non grata.

Verfemung f siehe vt outlawing; ostracizing; condemnation.

verfertigen* vt to manufacture, to produce; Liste to draw up; (usu iro) Brief, Aufsatz to compose.

verfestigen* 1 vt to harden; Flüssigkeit to solidify; (verstärken) to strengthen, to reinforce. 2 vr to harden; (Flüssigkeit) to solidify; (fig) (Haß, Feindschaft) to harden; (Kenntnisse) to be reinforced; (Ideen, Gewohnheiten) to become fixed or set; (Demokratie, Strukturen) to be strengthened or reinforced.

verfetten* vi aux sein (Med) (Mensch) to become fat or obese;

(*Herz, Leber*) to become fatty *or* adipose (*spec*).

Verfettung *f* (*Med*) (*von Körper*) obesity; (*von Organ, Muskeln*) fattiness, adiposity (*spec*).

verfeuern* *vt* to burn; *Munition* to fire. **die ganze Munition/das ganze Öl ~** to use up all the ammunition/oil.

verfilmen* *vt* to film, to make a film of; (*aufbrauchen*) *Film* to use up.

Verfilmung *f* (*das Verfilmen*) filming; (*Film*) film (version).

verfilzen* **1** *vi aux sein* (*Wolle, Pullover*) to become felted; (*Haare*) to become matted. **verfilzt** felted/matted. **2** *vr* to become matted.

verfinstern* **1** *vt* to darken; *Sonne, Mond* to eclipse. **2** *vr* (*lit, fig*) to darken.

Verfinsterung *f* darkening; (*von Sonne etc*) eclipse.

verfitzen* (*inf*) **1** *vt* to tangle. **2** *vr* to become tangled.

verflachen* **1** *vi aux sein* to flatten *or* level out; (*fig: Diskussion, Gespräch, Mensch*) to become superficial *or* trivial. **2** *vr* (*Gelände*) to flatten *or* level out.

Verflachung *f siehe vi* flattening *or* levelling out; superficiality. **um einer ~ der Diskussion vorzubeugen** to stop the conversation becoming superficial *or* trivial.

verflechten* *irreg* **1** *vt* to interweave, to interlace; *Bänder* to interlace; (*auch fig*) *Methoden* to combine; *Firmen* to interlink. **die Hände ~** to lace one's fingers; **Zweige zu einem Korb ~** to weave twigs into a basket; **eng mit etw verflochten sein** (*fig*) to be closely connected *or* linked with sth; **jdn in etw** (*acc*) **~ in** *Gespräch, Unternehmen* to involve sb in sth; **in dunkle Geschäfte** to entangle *or* embroil sb in sth.
  2 *vr* to interweave, to intertwine; (*Bänder*) to interlace; (*sich verwirren*) to become entangled (*mit in*); (*Themen*) to interweave; (*Methoden*) to combine. **sich mit etw ~** to become linked *or* connected with sth.

Verflechtung *f* **(a)** *siehe vb* interweaving, intertwining; interlacing; entanglement; interweaving; combining.
  (b) (*das Verflochtensein*) interconnection (*gen* between); (*Pol, Econ*) integration.

verfleckt *adj* (*inf*) stained.

verfliegen* *irreg* **1** *vi aux sein* **(a)** (*fig*) (*Stimmung, Zorn etc*) to blow over (*inf*), to pass; (*Heimweh, Kummer etc*) to vanish.
  (b) (*sich verflüchtigen*) to vanish; (*Alkohol*) to evaporate; (*Duft*) to fade (away); (*Zeit*) to fly.
  2 *vr* to stray; (*Pilot, Flugzeug*) to lose one's/its bearings.

verfließen* *vi irreg aux sein* **(a)** (*geh: vergehen*) to go by, to pass; *siehe* **verflossen. (b)** (*verschwimmen*) (*Farben*) to run; (*fig*) to become blurred.

verflixt (*inf*) **1** *adj* blessed (*inf*), darned (*inf*); (*kompliziert*) tricky. **du ~er Kerl!** you devil; **das ~e siebte Jahr** = the seven-year itch. **2** *adv* darned (*inf*). **3** *interj* ~! blow! (*inf*).

Verflochtenheit *f, no pl* (*fig*) interconnections *pl* (*von* between).

verflossen **1** *ptp of* **verfließen. 2** *adj* **(a)** *Jahre, Tage* bygone; (*letzte*) last. **(b)** (*inf*) one-time *attr* (*inf*). **ihr V~er** her former *or* ex-boyfriend/-fiancé/-husband.

verfluchen* *vt* to curse. **sei verflucht** curses on you.

verflucht 1 *adj* (*inf*) damn (*inf*), bloody (*Brit sl*). **~ (noch mal)!** damn (it) (*inf*); **diese ~e Tat** (*liter*) this cursed deed; **~e Tat!** (*inf*) damn! (*inf*). **2** *adv* (*sl*) (*bei englischem adj, n*) damn (*inf*), bloody (*Brit sl*); (*bei englischem vb*) like hell (*sl*). **ich habe mich ~ vertan** I made one hell of a mistake (*sl*).

verflüchtigen* **1** *vt* to evaporate. **2** *vr* (*Alkohol, Kohlensäure etc*) to evaporate; (*Duft*) to disappear; (*Gase*) to volatilize; (*fig*) (*Bedenken, Ärger*) to be dispelled; (*hum*) (*Mensch, Gegenstand, Hoffnungen etc*) to vanish; (*Geld*) to go up in smoke (*inf*).

Verflüchtigung *f siehe vr* evaporation; disappearance; volatilization.

Verfluchung *f* cursing; (*Fluch*) curse.

verflüssigen* *vtr* to liquefy.

Verflüssigung *f* liquefaction.

Verfolg *m* -s, *no pl* (*form*) (*Ausübung*) pursuance; (*Verlauf*) course. **im ~ des Schreibens vom ...** further to our letter of ...

verfolgen* *vt* *Ziel, Idee, Karriere etc* to pursue; *jdn auch* to follow; (*jds Spuren folgen*) *jdn* to trail; *Tier* to track; (*mit Hunden etc*) to hunt; *Unterricht, Entwicklung, Geschichte, Spur* to follow; *Idee, Gedanken* to follow up; (*politisch, religiös*) to persecute; (*Gedanke, Erinnerung etc*) *jdn* to haunt. **vom Unglück/Schicksal etc verfolgt werden** *or* **sein** to be dogged by ill fortune/by fate etc; **jdn politisch ~** to persecute sb for political reasons; **jdn gerichtlich ~** to prosecute sb; **jdn mit den Augen** *or* **Blicken ~** to follow sb with one's eyes; **jdn mit Bitten/Forderungen ~** to badger sb with requests/demands; **jdn mit Haß ~** to pursue sb in hate; **welche Absicht verfolgt er?** what is his intention?; *siehe* **strafrechtlich.**

Verfolger(in *f*) *m* -s, - **(a)** pursuer. **(b)** (*politisch, wegen Gesinnung*) persecutor.

Verfolgte(r) *mf decl as adj* **(a)** quarry. **(b)** (*politisch, wegen Gesinnung*) victim of persecution.

Verfolgung *f siehe vt* pursuit; following; trailing; tracking; (*politische ~*) persecution *no pl*. **die ~ aufnehmen** to take up the chase; **gerichtliche ~** court action; **strafrechtliche ~** prosecution; **bei der weiteren ~ der Frage** when this question was/is pursued further; **~ eines Ziels** pursuance of an aim.

Verfolgungs-: **~jagd** *f* chase, pursuit; **~rennen** *nt* (*Sport*) pursuit race; **~wahn** *m* persecution mania.

verformen* **1** *vt* to make go out of shape, to distort (*zu* into); (*umformen*) to work. **verformt sein** to be out of shape; (*Mensch, Gliedmaßen*) to be deformed. **2** *vr* to go out of shape.

Verformung *f* **(a)** distortion. **(b)** (*veränderte Form*) distortion; (*von Mensch, Gliedmaßen*) deformity.

verfrachten* *vt* (*Comm*) to transport; (*Naut*) to ship; (*inf*) *jdn* to bundle off (*inf*). **etw in den Keller/eine Kiste ~** (*inf*) to dump sth in the cellar/a crate.

Verfrachter *m* -s, - transport agent; (*Naut*) freighter; shipper.

Verfrachtung *f* transporting; (*Naut*) shipping.

verfranzen* *vr* (*inf*) to lose one's way; (*Aviat sl*) to lose one's bearings; (*fig*) to get in a muddle *or* tangle.

verfremden* *vt* *Thema, Stoff* to make unfamiliar, to defamiliarize; *Werkstoffe* to use in an unusual way.

Verfremdung *f* defamiliarization; (*Theat, Liter*) alienation, distancing. **die ~ vertrauter Formen** using familiar forms in an unfamiliar way.

Verfremdungs|effekt *m* distancing effect; (*Theat, Liter*) alienation *or* estrangement effect.

verfressen* (*sl*) **1** *vt irreg* to spend *or* blow (*inf*) on food. **2** *adj* greedy.

Verfressenheit *f* (*sl*) greediness.

verfrieren* *vi irreg aux sein* (*dial*) *siehe* **erfrieren.**

verfroren *adj* (*inf*) sensitive to cold; (*durchgefroren*) frozen, freezing cold. **~ sein** (*kälteempfindlich*) to feel the cold.

verfrühen* *vr* (*Winter, Entwicklung, Zug*) to come *or* arrive early; (*Gäste*) to be *or* come too early.

verfrüht *adj* (*zu früh*) premature; (*früh*) early. **solche Aufgaben sind für dieses Alter ~** exercises like this are too advanced for this age group.

Verfrühung *f* premature *or* early arrival *or* onset; (*von Bus, Besucher etc*) early arrival.

verfügbar *adj* available.

verfügen* *vt* to fit flush.

verfügen* **1** *vi* **über etw** (*acc*) **~** to have sth at one's disposal; (*besitzen*) to have sth; **über jdn/etw ~** (*bestimmen über*) to be in charge of sb/sth; **die Art und Weise wie er über seine Untergebenen/meine Zeit/mein Geld verfügt** the way in which he orders his inferiors around/tells me how to spend my time/money; **Gott verfügt über das Schicksal der Menschen** God determines man's fate; **du kannst über mein Auto ~, wenn ich in Urlaub bin** you can use my car while I'm on holiday; **du kannst doch nicht über mein Geld ~** you can't tell me how to spend my money; **du kannst doch nicht über deinen Bruder ~** you can't tell your brother what to do; **über etw** (*acc*) **frei ~ können** to be able to do as one wants with sth; **ich kann im Moment über meine Zeit nicht frei ~** I am not master of my own time just now; **~ Sie über mich** I am at your disposal.
  2 *vt* to order; (*gesetzlich*) to decree; *siehe* **letztwillig.**
  3 *vr* (*form*) to proceed (*form*).

Verfügung *f* **(a)** *no pl* (*das Verfügen*) possession. **freie ~** (*Jur*) free disposal (*über* +*acc* of); **jdm etw zur ~ stellen** to put sth at sb's disposal; (*leihen*) to lend sb sth; **jdm zur ~** *or* **zu jds ~ stehen** to be at sb's disposal; (*jdm*) **zur ~ stehen** (*verfügbar sein*) to be available (to sb); **sich zur ~ halten** to be available (to sb); **halte dich ab 7 Uhr zur ~** be ready from 7 o'clock; **etw zur ~ haben** to have sth at one's disposal.
  (b) (*behördlich*) order; (*von Gesetzgeber*) decree; (*testamentarisch*) provision; (*Anweisung*) instruction; *siehe* **letztwillig.**

Verfügungs-: **~befugnis** *f* right of disposal (*über* +*acc* of); **~gewalt** *f* (*Jur*) right of disposal; **die ~gewalt über Atomwaffen** the power to use atomic weapons; **~recht** *nt* (*Jur*) right of disposal (*über* +*acc* of).

verführen* *vt* to tempt; (*esp sexuell*) to seduce; *die Jugend, das Volk etc* to lead astray. **jdn zu etw ~, jdn ~, etw zu tun** to encourage sb to do sth; **ich lasse mich gern ~** you can twist my arm (*inf*); **diese offenen Kisten ~ ja direkt zum Diebstahl** these open boxes are an encouragement *or* invitation to steal.

Verführer *m* -s, - seducer.

Verführerin *f* seductress, temptress.

verführerisch *adj* seductive; (*verlockend*) tempting.

Verführung *f* seduction; (*von Jugend, Volk*) tempting; (*Verlockung*) enticement, temptation.

Verführungskunst *f* seductive manner; (*von Werbung*) persuasiveness. **ein Meister der ~** a master of seduction *or* (*Werber*) persuasion; **Verführungskünste** seductive *or* (*von Werber*) persuasive charms *or* ways.

verfünffachen* **1** *vt* *Zahl* to multiply by five, to quintuple (*form*). **2** *vr* to increase fivefold *or* five times; (*Zahl auch*) to multiply by five.

verfuttern* *vt* (*inf*) to spend on food.

verfüttern* *vt* to use as animal/bird food; (*aufbrauchen*) to feed (*an* +*acc* to). **etw an die Schweine/Vögel ~** to feed sth to the pigs/birds.

Vergabe *f* -, (*rare*) -n (*von Arbeiten*) allocation; (*von Stipendium, Auftrag etc*) award.

vergack|eiern* *vt* (*inf*) **jdn ~** to pull sb's leg (*inf*), to have sb on (*inf*).

vergaffen* *vr* (*dated inf*) **sich in jdn ~** to fall for sb (*inf*).

vergagt [fɛɐ'gɛ(:)kt] *adj* (*inf*) gimmicky (*inf*).

vergällen* *vt* *Alkohol* to denature; (*fig*) *jdn* to embitter, to sour; *Freude* to spoil; *Leben etc* to sour. **jdm die Freude/das Leben ~** to spoil sb's joy/to sour sb's life.

Vergällung *f siehe vt* denaturation; embitterment, souring; spoiling; souring.

vergaloppieren* *vr* (*inf*) (*sich irren*) to be on the wrong track; (*übers Ziel hinausschießen*) to go too far.

vergalt *pret of* **vergelten.**

vergammeln* (*inf*) **1** *vi aux sein* **(a)** (*verderben*) to get spoilt; (*Speisen*) to go bad. **(b)** (*verlottern*) to go to the dogs (*inf*). **vergammelt aussehen** to look scruffy; **vergammelte Studenten** scruffy(-looking) students.
  2 *vt* to waste. **ich möchte mal wieder einen Tag ~** I'd like to have a day doing nothing.

vergangen 1 *ptp of* **vergehen. 2** *adj* **(a)** (*letzte*) last. **(b)** *Jahre* past; *Zeiten, Bräuche* bygone, former; *Größe auch* former. **das V~e** the past; **das ist alles ~ und vergessen** that is all in the past now.

Vergangenheit f past; (von Stadt, Staat etc auch) history; (Gram) past (tense). **die erste** or **einfache/zweite** or **vollendete/dritte ~** (Gram) the simple past/perfect/pluperfect (tense); **eine Frau mit ~** a woman with a past; **der ~ angehören** to be a thing of the past.

vergänglich adj transitory.

Vergänglichkeit f, no pl transitoriness.

vergären* irreg **1** vi aux sein to ferment. **2** vt to ferment (zu into).

vergasen* vt (Tech: in Motor) to carburet; (durch Gas töten) jdn, Ungeziefer to gas; Kohle to gasify.

Vergasen nt, no pl gassing.

Vergaser m -s, - (Aut) carburettor.

Vergaserbrand m fire in the carburettor.

vergaß pret of vergessen.

Vergasung f siehe vt carburation; gassing; gasification. **etw bis zur ~ diskutieren/lernen** (inf) to discuss sth till one is blue in the face (inf)/to study sth ad nauseam; **das habe ich bis zur ~ gehört** (inf) I've heard that ad nauseam.

vergattern* vt **(a)** Garten etc to fence off; Tiere to fence in. **(b)** (Mil) to instruct. **(c)** (inf) to punish. **jdn zu etw ~** to give sb sth as a punishment.

vergeben* irreg **1** vt **(a)** (weggeben) Auftrag, Stipendium, Preis to award (an +acc to); Plätze, Studienplätze, Stellen to allocate; Karten to give away; Arbeit to assign; (fig) Chance, Möglichkeit to throw away. **ein Amt an jdn ~** to appoint sb to an office; **zu ~ sein** to be available; (Stelle auch) to be open; **~ sein** (Gewinn) to have been awarded or won; (Wohnung, Karten, Plätze) to have been taken; (Stelle) to have been filled; **er/sie ist schon ~** (inf) he/she is already spoken for (inf) or (verheiratet auch) married; **ich bin heute abend schon ~** (inf) I've got something else on this evening; **mein Herz ist schon ~** (liter) my heart belongs to another (liter); **der nächste Tanz ist schon ~** I've already promised the next dance.
(b) (verzeihen) to forgive; Sünde auch to pardon. **jdm etw ~** to forgive sb (for) sth; **das ist ~ und vergessen** that is over and done with or forgiven and forgotten.
2 vr **(a)** sich (dat) etwas/nichts ~ to lose/not to lose face; **was vergibst du dir, wenn du ein bißchen netter bist?** what have you got to lose by being a bit friendlier?
(b) (Cards) to misdeal.

vergebens **1** adj pred in vain, of no avail. **2** adv in vain, vainly.

vergeblich **1** adj futile; Bitten, Mühe auch vain attr. **alle Bitten/Versuche waren ~** all requests/attempts were in vain or of no avail. **2** adv in vain.

Vergeblichkeit f, no pl futility.

Vergebung f, no pl forgiveness.

vergegenständlichen* vt to concretize; (Philos) to reify, to hypostatize.

vergegenwärtigen* vr sich (dat) etw ~ (vor Augen rufen) to visualize sth; (sich vorstellen) to imagine sth; (erinnern) to recall sth; **vergegenwärtige dir doch einmal die Folgen** think of the consequences.

Vergegenwärtigung f siehe vr visualizing; imagining; recalling. **erst bei ~ der Situation wurde mir klar ...** I only realized ... when I visualized/recalled the situation.

Vergehen nt -s, - **(a)** (Verstoß) offence, misdemeanour. **~ im Amt** professional misconduct no pl; **das ist doch kein ~, oder?** that's not a crime, is it? **(b)** no pl (geh: Schwinden) passing; (von Zeit auch) passage; (von Schönheit, Glück) fading.

vergehen* irreg **1** vi aux sein **(a)** (vorbeigehen) to pass; (Liebe, Leidenschaft auch) to die; (Zeit, Jahre etc auch) to go by; (Hunger, Schmerzen auch) to wear off; (Schönheit, Glück) to fade; (Duft) to go, to wear off. **wie doch die Zeit vergeht** how time flies; **mir ist die Lust/Laune dazu vergangen** I don't feel like it any more; **mir ist der Appetit vergangen** I have lost my appetite; **das vergeht wieder** that will pass; **es werden noch Monate ~, ehe ...** it will be months before ...; **damit die Zeit vergeht** in order to pass the time; siehe **vergessen, Hören, Lachen**.
(b) vor etw (dat) **~** to be dying of sth; **vor Angst ~** to be scared to death; **vor Hunger ~** to be dying of hunger, to be starving; **vor Kälte ~** to be frozen; **vor Sehnsucht ~** to pine away; **sie wollte vor Scham ~** she nearly died of shame.
2 vr sich **an jdm ~** to do sb wrong; (unsittlich) to assault sb indecently; **sich an Gott/der Natur ~** to go against God/to defile nature; **sich gegen das Gesetz/die guten Sitten/die Moral ~** to violate the law/violate or outrage propriety/morality.

vergeigen* vt (inf) to lose.

vergeistigt adj cerebral, spiritual.

Vergeistigung f, no pl spiritualization.

vergelten pret vergalt, ptp vergolten vt to repay. **jdm etw ~** to repay sb for sth; (lohnen auch) to reward sb's sth; **vergelt's Gott** (old, dial) God bless you; siehe **gleich**.

Vergeltung f (Rache) retaliation.

Vergeltungs-: ~maßnahme f retaliatory measure; ~schlag m act of reprisal; ~waffen pl retaliatory weapons.

vergesellschaften* vt (Pol) to nationalize; Privatbesitz to take into public ownership; (ins Arbeitereigentum überführen) to hand over to the workers; (rare: Sociol) to socialize.

Vergesellschaftung f, no pl siehe vt nationalization; taking into public ownership; handing over to the workers; socialization.

vergessen pret vergaß, ptp vergessen **1** vti to forget; (liegenlassen) to leave (behind). **... und nicht zu ~ seine Ehrlichkeit ...** and not forgetting his honesty; **daß es nicht vergesse before I forget; das werde ich dir nie ~** (Gutes) I will always remember you for that; (Schlechtes) I will never forget that; **auf jdn/etw ~** (Aus) to forget sb/sth; **vergiß mein nicht** (poet) forget me not (poet); **er vergißt noch mal seinen Kopf** (inf) he'd forget his head if it wasn't screwed on (inf).
2 vr (Mensch) to forget oneself. **Zahlen ~ sich leicht** numbers

are easy to forget or easily forgotten.

Vergessenheit f, no pl oblivion. **in ~ geraten, der ~ anheimfallen** (geh) to be forgotten, to fall into oblivion; **etw aus der ~ hervorholen** to rescue sth from oblivion.

vergeßlich adj forgetful.

Vergeßlichkeit f forgetfulness.

vergeuden* vt to waste; Geld, Talente auch to squander.

Vergeudung f siehe vt wasting; squandering. **das ist die reinste ~** that is (a) sheer waste; **diese ~!** what a waste!

vergewaltigen* **1** vt to rape; (fig) Sprache etc to murder, to mutilate; Volkswillen to violate. **2** vr to force oneself.

Vergewaltigung f siehe vt rape; murder(ing), mutilation; violation.

vergewissern* vr to make sure. **sich einer Sache** (gen) or **über etw** (acc) **~** to make sure of sth.

vergießen* vt irreg Kaffee, Wasser to spill; Blut auch, Tränen to shed. **ich habe bei der Arbeit viel Schweiß vergossen** I sweated blood over that job.

vergiften* **1** vt (lit, fig) to poison; Luft auch to pollute. **2** vr to poison oneself (mit, durch, an +dat with).

Vergiftung f poisoning no pl; (der Luft) pollution. **bei ~en wird der Magen ausgepumpt** the stomach is pumped in cases of poisoning; **an einer ~ sterben** to die of poisoning.

Vergiftungs|erscheinung f symptom of poisoning.

vergilben* vi aux sein to go or become yellow. **vergilbt** yellowed.

vergiß imper sing of vergessen.

Vergißmeinnicht nt -(e)s, -(e) forget-me-not.

vergittern* vt to put a grille on/over; (mit Stangen) to put bars on/over. **vergitterte Fenster** barred windows/windows with grilles over them.

Vergitterung f (Gitter) grille, grating; (Stangen) bars pl. **die ~ der Fenster** putting grilles/bars on the windows.

verglasen* vt to glaze.

verglast adj Augen glazed.

Verglasung f glazing.

Vergleich m -(e)s, -e **(a)** comparison; (Liter) simile. **~e ziehen** or **anstellen** to make or draw comparisons; **im ~ zu** or **mit** in comparison with, compared with or to; **das ist doch gar kein ~!** there is no comparison; **in keinem ~ zu etw stehen** to be out of all proportion to sth; (Leistungen) not to compare with sth; **dem ~ mit jdm standhalten/den ~ mit jdm aushalten** to stand or bear comparison with sb; **sie hält den ~ mit ihrer Vorgängerin nicht aus** she doesn't compare with her predecessor.
(b) (Jur) settlement. **einen gütlichen/außergerichtlichen ~ schließen** to reach an amicable settlement/to settle out of court.

vergleichbar adj comparable.

Vergleichbarkeit f comparability.

vergleichen* irreg **1** vt to compare. **etw mit etw ~** (prüfend) to compare sth with sth; (einen Vergleich herstellen zwischen) to compare or liken sth to sth; **vergleiche oben** compare above; **sie sind nicht (miteinander) zu ~** they cannot be compared (to one another); **die kann man nicht (miteinander) ~** they cannot be compared (with one another), they are not comparable.
2 vr **(a)** sich mit jdm ~ to compare oneself with sb; **wie könnte ich mich mit ihm ~?** how could I compare myself to him? **(b)** (Jur) to reach a settlement, to settle (mit with).

vergleichend adj comparative.

Vergleichs-: ~form f (Gram) comparative form; ~gläubiger m creditor in insolvency proceedings; ~satz m (Gram) comparative clause; ~schuldner m debtor in insolvency proceedings; ~verfahren nt insolvency proceedings pl; ~weg m (Jur) auf dem ~weg by reaching a settlement; v~weise adv comparatively; ~zahl f usu pl comparative figure.

Vergleichung f (rare) comparison.

vergletschern* vi aux sein to become glaciated.

Vergletscherung f glaciation.

verglimmen* vi irreg aux sein (Zigarette) to go out; (Licht, Feuer auch) to die out or away; (fig liter) (Leben) to be extinguished; (Hoffnung, Liebe, Tageslicht) to fade. **~de Kohle** dying cinders.

verglühen* vi aux sein (Feuer, Feuerwerk) to die away; (Draht) to burn out; (Raumkapsel, Meteor etc) to burn up; (liter: Leidenschaft) to fade (away), to die down.

vergnügen* **1** vt to amuse. **2** vr to enjoy oneself. **sich mit jdm/etw ~** to amuse oneself with sb/sth; **sich mit Lesen/Tennis ~** to amuse or entertain oneself by reading/playing tennis; **sich an etw** (dat) **~** to be amused or entertained by sth.

Vergnügen nt -s, - **(a)** (Freude, Genuß) pleasure; (Spaß) fun no indef art; (Erheiterung) amusement. **~ an etw** (dat) **finden** to find enjoyment or pleasure in (doing) sth; **das macht** or **bereitet mir ~** I enjoy it, it gives me pleasure; **sich** (dat) **ein ~ aus etw machen** to get pleasure from (doing) sth; **für viele Leute ist es ein ~, den Verkehr auf der Autobahn zu beobachten** a lot of people enjoy watching the traffic on the motorway; **zu meinem ~ konnte er das auch nicht** to my great delight, he couldn't do it either; **ich laufe jeden Tag eine halbe Stunde nur zum ~** I run for half an hour each day just for pleasure or for the fun of it; **das war ein teures ~** (inf) that was an expensive bit of fun; **ich höre ihn mit großem ~ singen** it gives me great pleasure to hear him sing; **mit ~/großem ~/größtem ~ oder dem größten ~** with pleasure/great pleasure/the greatest of pleasure; **viel ~!** enjoy yourself/yourselves (auch iro); **er hat mir viel ~ gewünscht** he said he hoped I would enjoy myself; **wir wünschen Ihnen bei der Sendung viel ~** we hope you enjoy the programme; **mit wem habe ich das ~?** (form) with whom do I have the pleasure of speaking? (form); **es ist mir ein ~** it is a pleasure for me.
(b) (dated: Veranstaltung) entertainment.

vergnügenshalber adv for pleasure or fun.

vergnüglich adj enjoyable; Stunden auch pleasurable; (erheiternd) amusing.

vergnügt adj Abend, Stunden enjoyable; Mensch, Gesichter, Gesellschaft cheerful; Lachen, Stimmung happy. ~ **aussehen/ lachen** to look cheerful/laugh happily; **über etw** (acc) ~ **sein** to be pleased or happy about sth.

Vergnügtheit f (von Mensch, Gesicht) cheerfulness; (von Stimmung) happiness.

Vergnügung f pleasure; (Veranstaltung) entertainment.

Vergnügungs-: ~**dampfer** m pleasure steamer; ~**fahrt** f pleasure trip; ~**industrie** f entertainment industry; ~**park** m amusement park; ~**reise** f pleasure trip; ~**steuer** f entertainment tax; ~**sucht** f craving for pleasure; **v~süchtig** adj pleasure-craving, sybaritic (liter pej); ~**viertel** nt entertainments district.

vergolden* 1 vt (mit Gold bemalen) Nüsse etc to paint gold; (mit Blattgold) Statue, Buchkante to gild; (mit Gold überziehen) Schmuck to gold-plate; (liter: Sonne, Schein) to bathe in gold, to turn golden; (fig: verschönern) Zeit, Alter, Erinnerung to enhance. **der Herbst vergoldet die Natur** autumn turns nature golden. 2 vr (liter) to turn to gold.

Vergolder(in f) m -s, - gilder.

vergoldet adj Nüsse gold-painted; Buchseiten gilded; Schmuck gold-plated; Natur, Stadt, Erinnerung etc golden.

Vergoldung f (von Nüssen) painting gold; (von Buchseiten) gilding; (von Schmuck) gold-plating; (Überzug) (auf Nüssen) gold paint; (auf Buchseiten) gilt; (auf Schmuck) gold plate.

vergolten ptp of **vergelten.**

vergönnen* vt (geh) jdm etw ~ not to begrudge sb sth; **es war ihr noch vergönnt, das zu sehen** she was granted the privilege of seeing that; **diese Freude war ihm noch/nicht vergönnt** fate granted/did not grant him this pleasure.

vergöttern* vt to idolize.

Vergötterung f idolization.

vergraben* irreg 1 vt to bury. 2 vr (Maulwurf etc) to bury oneself; (fig: zurückgezogen leben) to hide oneself (away). **sich hinter seinen Büchern/in Arbeit** ~ to bury oneself in one's books/in work.

vergrämen* vt (a) (verärgern, beleidigen) to antagonize; (vertreiben) to alienate; (verletzen) to grieve. **jdm das Leben** ~ to make life a misery for sb. (b) (Hunt) Wild to frighten, to scare.

vergrämt adj (kummervoll, bitter) Gesicht etc troubled; (verärgert) angered.

vergrätzen* vt (inf) to vex.

vergraulen* vt (inf) to put off; (vertreiben) to scare off.

vergreifen* vr irreg (a) (danebengreifen) to make a mistake; (Musiker auch) to play a wrong note; (auf Schreibmaschine etc auch) to hit the wrong key; (Sport: bei Gerät) to miss one's grip. **sich im Ton/Ausdruck** ~ (fig) to adopt the wrong tone/use the wrong expression; siehe **vergriffen.**
(b) **sich an etw** (dat) ~ (an fremdem Eigentum) to misappropriate sth; (euph: stehlen) to help oneself to sth (euph); (an Geld auch) to embezzle sth; (an Heiligem) to desecrate or profane sth; **sich an jdm** ~ (angreifen) to lay hands on sb; (geschlechtlich mißbrauchen) to assault sb (sexually); **ich vergreife mich doch nicht an kleinen Kindern** (hum inf) that would be baby snatching (inf).

vergreisen* vi aux sein (Bevölkerung) to age; (Mensch) to become senile. **vergreist** aged; senile.

Vergreisung f (von Bevölkerung) ageing; (von Organismen) senescence; (von Mensch) senility.

vergriffen 1 ptp of **vergreifen.** 2 adj unavailable; Buch out of print.

vergröbern* 1 vt to coarsen. 2 vr to become coarse.

vergrößern 1 vt (räumlich) Raum, Gebäude, Fläche, Gebiet to extend; Abstand auch to increase; (größenmäßig, umfangmäßig) Maßstab, Wissen to enlarge, to increase; Bekanntenkreis to enlarge, to extend; Firma, Absatzmarkt to expand; Produktion to increase; Vollmachten to extend; (zahlenmäßig) Kapital, Mitgliederzahl, Anzahl to increase; (verstärken) Einfluß, Not, Probleme, Schmerz etc to increase; Fotografie to enlarge, to blow up; (Lupe, Brille) to magnify.
2 vr (räumlich) to be extended; (Abstand) to increase; (größenmäßig, umfangmäßig) (Maßstab) to be enlarged, to increase; (Wissen) to increase, to expand; (Bekanntenkreis) to be enlarged, to be extended; (Firma, Absatzmarkt) to expand; (Produktion) to increase; (Vollmachten) to be extended; (zahlenmäßig) to increase; (sich verstärken) to increase; (Pupille, Gefäße) to dilate; (Organ) to become enlarged. **wir wollen uns** ~ (inf) we want to move to a bigger place.
3 vi (Lupe, Brille) to magnify; (Mensch) to do enlarging.

Vergrößerung f (a) siehe vb extension; increase; enlargement; extension; expansion; magnification. **in 1.000facher** ~ magnified 1,000 times. (b) (von Pupille, Gefäß) dilation; (von Organ) enlargement. (c) (vergrößertes Bild) enlargement.

Vergrößerungs-: ~**apparat** m enlarger; **v~fähig** adj Gebäude extendable; Firma, Absatzmarkt expandable, able to expand; Bekanntenkreis to be enlarged; Kapital, Produktion able to be increased; ~**glas** nt magnifying glass.

vergucken* vr (inf) to see wrong (inf). **sich in jdn/etw** ~ to fall for sb/sth (inf).

vergülden* vt (poet) siehe **vergolden.**

vergünstigen* 1 vt Lage to improve; 2 vr (Lage) to improve; (Preise) to come down.

vergünstigt adj Lage improved; Preis reduced. **etw** ~ **kaufen** to buy sth at a reduced price.

Vergünstigung f (Vorteil) privilege; (Preisermäßigung) reduction. **besondere** ~**en für Rentner** special rates for pensioners.

vergüten* vt (a) jdm etw ~ Unkosten to reimburse sb for sth; Preis to refund sb sth; Verlust, Schaden to compensate sb for sth; Arbeit, Leistung to pay or recompense (form) sb for sth. (b) (verbessern) Stahl to temper; Linse to coat.

Vergütung f siehe vt (a) reimbursement; refunding; compensation; payment, recompense. (b) tempering; coating.

verh. abbr of **verheiratet.**

verhackstücken* vt (inf) (kritisieren) to tear apart, to rip to pieces (inf); Musikstück to murder (inf).

verhaften* vt to arrest. **unschuldig verhaftet werden** to be arrested and later proved innocent; **Sie sind verhaftet!** you are under arrest!

verhaftet adj (geh) einer Sache (dat) or mit etw ~ **sein** to be (closely) attached to sth; **einem Irrtum** ~ **sein** to be under a misapprehension.

Verhaftete(r) mf decl as adj person under arrest. **der** ~ **wurde abgeführt** the arrested man was taken away; **die zehn** ~**n** the ten people under arrest.

Verhaftung f arrest.

Verhaftungswelle f wave of arrests.

verhageln* vi aux sein to be damaged by hail. **er sieht verhagelt aus** (inf) he looks rather the worse for wear.

verhallen* vi aux sein (Geräusch etc) to die away. **ihr Ruf/ihre Warnung verhallte ungehört** (fig) her call/her warning went unheard or unheeded.

verhalten[1]* irreg 1 vt (geh: zurückhalten, unterdrücken) Atem to hold; Tränen, Urin to hold back; seine Schritte to curb; Zorn to restrain; Lachen to contain; Schmerz to control.
2 vi to stop. **im Laufen/Sprechen** ~ to stop running/speaking.
3 vr (a) (sich benehmen: Mensch, Maschine, Preise etc) to behave; (handeln) to act. **wie** ~ **Sie sich dazu?** what is your attitude to that?; **sich ruhig** ~ to keep quiet; (sich nicht bewegen) to keep still; **wie man sich bei Hof verhält** how one conducts oneself at court.
(b) (Sachen, Marktlage) to be; (Chem) to react. **wie verhält sich die Sache?** how do things stand?; **2 verhält sich zu 4 wie 1 zu 2** 2 is to 4 as 1 is to 2.
4 vr impers **wie verhält es sich damit?** (wie ist die Lage?) how do things stand?; (wie wird das gehandhabt?) how do you go about it?; **wie verhält es sich eigentlich mit ihm?** (was meint er?) what is his attitude to this?; (was macht er?) what is he doing?; **damit verhält es sich anders** the situation is different; **mit den anderen verhält es sich genauso** the others feel exactly the same; **wenn sich das so verhält, ...** if that is the case ...

verhalten[2] 1 adj restrained; Stimme muted; Atem bated; Wut suppressed; Tempo, Schritte, Rhythmus measured. 2 adv sprechen in a restrained manner; kritisieren, sich äußern, lachen, weinen with restraint; laufen at a measured pace.

Verhalten nt -s, no pl (Benehmen) behaviour; (Vorgehen) conduct; (Chem) reaction. **falsches Parken ist rechtswidriges** ~ unauthorized parking is an offence; **faires** ~ fair conduct.

Verhaltenheit f restraint. **die** ~ **des Rhythmus** the measured rhythm.

Verhaltens-: ~**forscher** m behaviourist; ~**forschung** f behaviourism; **v~gestört** adj disturbed; ~**maßregel** f rule of conduct; ~**muster** nt behaviour pattern; ~**psychologie** f behaviourism; ~**störung** f behavioural disturbance; ~**weise** f behaviour; **du hast or zeigst neuerdings eine merkwürdige** ~**weise** you have been behaving strangely recently.

Verhältnis nt (a) (Proportion) proportion; (Math, Mischungs~) ratio. **im** ~ **zu** in relation or proportion to; **im** ~ **zu früher** (verglichen mit) in comparison with earlier times; **in einem/keinem** ~ **zu etw stehen** to be in/out of all proportion or to bear no relation to sth; **außer** ~ **zu etw stehen** to be out of proportion to sth; **das ist im** ~ **wenig** (im Vergleich mit anderem) this is proportionately very little; (relativ wenig) that is comparatively or relatively little.
(b) (Beziehung) relationship (mit jdm/etw with sb/to sth); relations pl (zu with); (zwischen Ländern, innerhalb einer Gruppe) relations pl (zu with); (Einstellung) attitude (zu to). **ein freundschaftliches** ~ **zu jdm haben, mit jdm in freundschaftlichem** ~ **stehen** to be on friendly terms with sb; **zu jdm/etw kein** ~ **finden können** not to be able to relate to sb/sth.
(c) (Liebes~) affair; (inf) (Geliebte) lady-friend (inf); (Geliebter) friend. **ein** ~ **mit jdm haben** to have an affair with sb.
(d) ~**se** pl (Umstände, Bedingungen) conditions pl; (finanzielle) circumstances pl; **unter or bei normalen** ~**sen** under normal circumstances; **so wie die** ~**se liegen ...** as things stand ...; **die akustischen** ~**se** the acoustics pl; **in ärmlichen** ~**sen leben/aus ärmlichen** ~**sen kommen** to live in poor conditions/come from a poor background; **über seine** ~**se leben** to live beyond one's means; **das geht über meine** ~**se** that is beyond my means; **ich bin für klare** ~**se** I want to know how we stand; **für klare** ~**se sorgen, klare** ~**se schaffen** to get things straight.

Verhältnis-: **v~mäßig** 1 adj (a) (proportional) proportional; (esp Jur: angemessen) proportionate, commensurate; (b) (relativ) comparative, relative; (inf: ziemlich) reasonable; 2 adv (a) (proportional) proportionally; (b) (relativ, inf: ziemlich) relatively; ~**wahl** f proportional representation no art; **jdn durch** ~**wahl ermitteln** to elect sb by proportional representation; **eine** ~**wahl abhalten** to hold a proportional election; ~**wahlrecht** nt (system of) proportional representation; ~**wort** nt preposition.

verhandeln* 1 vt (a) to negotiate. (b) (Jur) Fall to hear. 2 vi (a) to negotiate (über +acc about); (inf: diskutieren) to argue. **da gibt's doch nichts zu** ~ (inf) there's nothing to argue about; **über den Preis läßt sich** ~ (inf) we can discuss the price. (b) (Jur) to hear a/the case. **gegen jdn/in einem Fall** ~ to hear sb's/a case.

Verhandlung f (a) negotiations pl; (das Verhandeln) negotiation. **die zur** ~ **stehende Frage** the question under negotiation; **mit jdm in** ~(en) **stehen** to be negotiating with sb, to be engaged in negotiations with sb; **(mit jdm) in** ~(en) **treten** to enter into negotiations (with sb); ~**en führen** to negotiate; **ich**

lasse mich auf keine ~**(en) ein** (*inf*) I don't propose to enter into any long debates.
(b) (*Jur*) hearing; (*Straf*~) trial.
Verhandlungs-: ~**basis** *f* basis for negotiation(s); ~**basis DM 2.500** (price) DM 2,500 or near offer; **v~bereit** *adj* ready *or* prepared to negotiate; ~**bereitschaft** *f* readiness to negotiate; **die mangelnde** ~**bereitschaft der Regierung** the government's reluctance to negotiate; **v~fähig** *adj* (*Jur*) able to stand trial; ~**fähigkeit** *f* (*Jur*) ability to stand trial; ~**grundlage** *f* basis for negotiation(s); ~**partner** *m* negotiating party; ~**tisch** *m* negotiating table; **v~unfähig** *adj* (*Jur*) unable to stand trial; ~**unfähigkeit** *f* (*Jur*) inability to stand trial.
verhangen *adj* overcast.
verhängen* *vt* **(a)** *Embargo, Strafe, Hausarrest etc* to impose (*über* +*acc* on); *Ausnahmezustand, Notstand* to declare (*über* +*acc* in); (*Sport*) *Elfmeter etc* to award, to give.
    (b) (*zuhängen*) to cover (*mit* with); *Kruzifix, Statue* to veil; (*an den falschen Platz hängen*) to hang up in the wrong place; **mit verhängtem Zügel** *or* **verhängten Zügeln** at full speed.
Verhängnis *nt* (*schlimmes Schicksal*) undoing; (*Katastrophe*) disaster. **jdm zum** *or* **jds** ~ **werden** to prove *or* be sb's undoing; **er entging seinem** ~ **nicht** he could not escape his fate.
verhängnisvoll *adj* disastrous; *Irrtum, Fehler auch, Zögern, Entschlußlosigkeit* fatal; *Tag* fateful.
Verhängung *f siehe vt* **(a)** imposition; declaration; awarding, giving. **(b)** covering; veiling.
verharmlosen* *vt* to play down.
verhärmt *adj Mensch, Gesicht* careworn; *Ausdruck* worried.
verharren* *vi aux haben* *or sein* to pause; (*in einer bestimmten Stellung*) to remain. **auf einem Standpunkt/in** *or* **bei einem Entschluß** ~ to adhere to a viewpoint/to a decision; **in seinem Stillschweigen** ~ to maintain one's silence; (*hartnäckig*) to persist in one's silence.
verharschen* *vi aux sein* (*Schnee, Piste*) to crust.
verhärten* *vtr* (*alle Bedeutungen*) to harden. **sich** *or* **sein Herz gegen jdn/etw** ~ to harden one's heart against sb/sth.
Verhärtung *f* hardening.
verhaspeln* *vr* (*inf*) to get into a muddle *or* tangle.
verhaßt *adj* hated; *Arbeit auch, Pflicht* hateful. **sich** ~ **machen** to make oneself hated (*bei* by); **das ist ihm** ~ he hates that.
verhätscheln* *vt* to spoil, to pamper.
Verhätschelung *f* spoiling, pampering.
Verhau *m* -(e)s, -e (*zur Absperrung*) barrier; (*Käfig*) coop; (*Bretterbude etc*) shack; (*inf: Unordnung*) mess.
verhauen* *irreg* (*inf*) **1** *vt* (*a*) (*verprügeln*) to beat up; (*zur Strafe*) to beat. **(b)** *Klassenarbeit, Prüfung etc* to muff (*inf*). **2** *vr* (**a**) (*sich verprügeln*) to have a fight. **(b)** (*beim Schreiben etc*) to make a mistake; (*beim Tippen auch*) to hit the wrong key; (*beim Klavierspielen auch*) to play a bum note (*inf*). **(c)** (*sich irren*) to slip up (*inf*).
verheben* *vr irreg* to hurt oneself lifting something.
verheddern* *vr* (*inf*) to get tangled up; (*beim Sprechen*) to get in a muddle *or* tangle.
verheeren* *vt* to devastate; (*Truppen auch*) to lay waste.
verheerend **1** *adj* (**a**) *Sturm, Folgen* devastating, disastrous; *Anblick* ghastly. **(b)** (*inf: schrecklich*) frightful, fearful, ghastly (*all inf*). **2** *adv* (*inf: schrecklich*) frightfully (*inf*).
Verheerung *f* devastation *no pl.* ~**(en) anrichten** to cause devastation.
verhehlen* *vt* to conceal to hide. **jdm etw** ~ to conceal *or* hide sth from sb; **ich möchte Ihnen nicht** ~, **daß** ... I have no wish to conceal the fact that ...
verheilen* *vi aux sein* (*Wunde*) to heal (up); (*fig*) to heal.
verheimlichen* *vt* to keep secret, to conceal (*jdm* from sb). **es läßt sich nicht** ~, **daß** ... it is impossible to conceal the fact that ...; **ich habe nichts zu** ~ I have nothing to hide.
Verheimlichung *f* concealment; (*von Tatsache*) suppression.
verheiraten* **1** *vt* to marry (*mit, an* +*acc* to). **2** *vr* to get married, to marry. **sich mit jdm** ~ to marry sb, to get married to sb.
verheiratet *adj* married. **glücklich** ~ **sein** to be happily married; **mit jdm/etw** (*hum inf*) ~ **sein** to be married to sb/sth.
Verheiratung *f* marriage.
verheißen* *vt irreg* to promise. **jdm eine große Karriere** ~ to predict a great career for sb; **seine Miene verhieß nichts Gutes** his expression did not augur well; **das verheißt schönes Wetter** that heralds good weather.
Verheißung *f* promise. **das Land der** ~ the Promised Land.
verheißungsvoll *adj* promising; *Anfang auch* auspicious; *Blicke* alluring. **wenig** ~ unpromising; **mit** ~**en Worten** with promises.
verheizen* *vt* to burn, to use as fuel; (*fig inf*) *Sportler* to burn out; *Minister, Untergebene* to crucify. **Soldaten im Kriege** ~ (*inf*) to send soldiers to the slaughter.
verhelfen* *vi irreg* **jdm zu etw** ~ to help sb to get sth; **jdm zu seinem Glück** ~ to help to make sb happy; **jdm zum Sieg** ~ to help sb to victory.
verherrlichen* *vt* *Gewalt, Krieg, Taten* to glorify; *Gott* to praise; *Tugenden* to extol; (*in Gedichten*) to celebrate.
Verherrlichung *f siehe vt* glorification; praising; extolment; celebration.
verhetzen* *vt* to stir up, to incite (*to* violence *etc*).
Verhetzung *f* incitement, stirring up.
verheult *adj Augen, Gesicht* puffy, swollen from crying. **du siehst so** ~ **aus** you really look as if you have been crying.
verhexen* *vt* to bewitch; (*Fee, Zauberer etc auch*) to cast a spell over; (*inf*) *Maschine etc* to put a jinx on (*inf*). **jdn in etw** (*acc*) ~ to turn sb into sth (by magic); **der verhexte Prinz** the enchanted prince; **das verhexte Schloß** the bewitched castle; **heute ist alles wie verhext** (*inf*) there's a jinx on everything today (*inf*); **das ist doch wie verhext** (*inf*) it's maddening (*inf*).
verhimmeln* *vt* (*inf*) to dote on.

verhindern* *vt* to prevent; *Unglück auch* to avert; *Versuch, Plan* to foil, to stop. **ich konnte es nicht** ~, **daß er die Wahrheit erfuhr** I couldn't prevent him from finding out the truth; **das läßt sich leider nicht** ~ it can't be helped, unfortunately; **er war an diesem Abend** (*dienstlich or geschäftlich*) **verhindert** he was unable to come that evening (for reasons of work); **ein verhinderter Politiker** (*inf*) a would-be politician.
Verhinderung *f siehe vt* prevention; avertion; foiling, stopping. **im Falle seiner** ~ if he is unable to come.
verhohlen *adj* concealed, secret; *Gelächter, Schadenfreude auch, Gähnen* suppressed. **kaum** ~ barely concealed/suppressed.
verhöhnen* *vt* to mock, to deride.
verhohnepipeln* *vt* (*inf*) (*verspotten*) to send up (*inf*); (*zum besten haben*) to have on (*inf*).
Verhohnepipelung *f* send-up (*inf*).
Verhöhnung *f* mocking, ridiculing; (*Bemerkung*) gibe.
verhökern* *vt* (*inf*) to get rid of (*inf*).
verholen* *vt* (*Naut*) to haul away.
verholzen* *vi aux sein* (*Bot*) to lignify.
Verhör *nt* -(e)s, -e questioning, interrogation; (*bei Gericht*) examination. **jdn ins** ~ **nehmen** to question *or* interrogate sb; (*bei Gericht*) to examine sb; (*inf*) to take sb to task; **jdn einem** ~ **unterziehen** (*form*) to subject sb to questioning *or* interrogation/examination.
verhören* **1** *vt* to question, to interrogate; (*bei Gericht*) to examine; (*inf*) to quiz (*inf*). **2** *vr* to mishear, to hear wrongly.
verhornt *adj Haut* horny.
verhudeln* *vt* (*inf*) to botch.
verhüllen* **1** *vt* to veil; *Haupt, Körperteil* to cover; (*fig auch*) to mask, to disguise. **2** *vr* (*Frau*) to veil oneself; (*Berge etc*) to become veiled.
verhüllend *adj Ausdruck* euphemistic.
Verhüllung *f* **(a)** *siehe vt* veiling; covering; masking, disguising. **(b)** (*die Bedeckung*) veil; cover; mask, disguise. **(c)** (*Ausdruck*) euphemism.
verhundertfachen* *vtr* to increase a hundredfold.
verhungern* *vi aux sein* to starve, to die of starvation; (*inf: Hunger haben*) to be starving (*inf*). **er sah völlig verhungert aus** he looked half-starved; (*inf*) he looked absolutely famished (*inf*); **ich bin am V~** (*inf*) I'm starving (*inf*); **jdn ~ lassen** (*lit*) to let sb starve (to death); (*beim Spielen*) to leave sb out of the game; *siehe* Arm.
Verhungernde(r) *mf decl as adj* starving person/man/woman.
Verhungerte(r) *mf decl as adj* person/man/woman *etc* who has starved to death.
verhunzen* *vt* (*inf*) to ruin; *Sprache, Lied auch* to murder.
verhurt *adj* (*pej*) whorish; *Mann* loose-living. **ein** ~**es Frauenzimmer** a whore.
verhüten* *vt* to prevent. **das verhüte Gott!** God forbid!; **möge Gott** ~, **daß ...** God forbid that ...; ~**de Maßnahmen** preventive measures; (*zur Empfängnisverhütung*) precautions.
verhütten* *vt* to smelt.
Verhüttung *f* smelting.
Verhütung *f* prevention; (*Empfängnis~*) contraception.
Verhütungsmittel *nt* contraceptive.
verhutzelt *adj Gesicht, Männlein* wizened; *Haut auch* wrinkled; *Obst* shrivelled.
Verifikation [verifikaˈtsjoːn] *f* verification.
verifizierbar [verifiˈtsiːɐbaːɐ] *adj* verifiable.
verifizieren* [verifiˈtsiːrən] *vt* to verify.
ver|innerlichen* *vt* to internalize; *jdn* to spiritualize.
ver|innerlicht *adj Wesen, Gesichtsausdruck* spiritualized.
Ver|innerlichung *f* internalization; (*von Mensch, in Literatur*) spiritualization.
ver|irren* *vr* to get lost, to lose one's way; (*fig*) to go astray; (*Tier, Kugel*) to stray. **ein verirrtes Schaf** (*lit, fig*) a lost sheep.
Ver|irrung *f* losing one's way *no art*; (*fig*) aberration.
verjagen* **1** *vt* (*lit, fig*) to chase away; *trübe Gedanken, Kummer auch* to dispel. **2** *vr* (*N Ger*) to get out of the way.
verjähren* *vi aux sein* to come under the statute of limitations; (*Anspruch*) to be in lapse. **verjährtes Verbrechen** statute-barred crime; **das ist schon längst verjährt** (*inf*) that's all over and done with.
Verjährung *f* limitation; (*von Anspruch*) lapse.
Verjährungsfrist *f* limitation period.
verjazzen* [fɛɐˈdʒɛsn] *vt* to jazz up.
verjubeln* *vt* (*inf*) *Geld* to blow (*inf*).
verjüngen* **1** *vt* to rejuvenate; (*jünger aussehen lassen*) to make look younger; *Baumbestand* to regenerate. **eine Mannschaft/das Personal** ~ to build up a younger team/staff; **die neue Stelle hat ihn um Jahre verjüngt** the new job gave him a new lease of life; **er kam (um Jahre) verjüngt aus dem Urlaub zurück** he came back from holiday looking years younger. **2** *vr* (**a**) to become younger; (*Haut, Erscheinung*) to become rejuvenated; (*jünger aussehen*) to look younger. **du hast dich verjüngt** (*inf*) you look (much) younger. **(b)** (*dünner werden*) to taper; (*Tunnel, Rohr*) to narrow.
Verjüngung *f* **(a)** rejuvenation; (*von Baumbestand*) regeneration. **(b)** *siehe vr* **(b)** tapering; narrowing.
Verjüngungskur *f* rejuvenation cure. **hast du eine** ~ **gemacht?** (*hum*) have you had a face-lift? (*hum*).
verjuxen* *vr* (*inf*) *Geld* to blow (*inf*).
verkalken* *vi aux sein* (*Arterien*) to become hardened; (*Gewebe*) to calcify; (*Kessel, Wasserleitung etc*) to fur up, to become furred; (*inf: Mensch*) to become senile.
verkalkt *adj* (*inf*) senile.
verkalkulieren* *vr* to miscalculate.
Verkalkung *f siehe vi* hardening; calcification; furring; (*inf*) senility.

verkälten* *vr (dial) siehe* **erkälten.**

verkamisolen*, verkamisölen* *vt (dated inf)* **jdn** ~ to give sb a tanning *(dated inf)*.

verkannt 1 *ptp of* **verkennen. 2** *adj* unrecognized.

verkappt *adj attr* hidden; *Lungenentzündung* undiagnosed. **~er Nebensatz** *(Gram)* subordinate clause *without an introductory word.*

verkapseln* *vr (Med) (Bakterien)* to become encapsulated; *(Parasit)* to become encysted.

Verkapselung *f (Med)* encapsulation; encystment.

verkarsten* *vi aux sein* to develop to karst *(spec)*.

Verkarstung *f* karst development *(spec)*.

verkatert *adj (inf)* hung-over *usu pred (inf)*. **einen ~en Eindruck machen** to look hung-over *(inf)*.

Verkauf *m* -(e)s, **Verkäufe (a)** sale; *(das Verkaufen)* selling. **zum ~ stehen** to be up for sale; **beim ~ des Hauses** when selling the house. **(b)** *(Abteilung)* sales *sing, no art.*

verkaufen* 1 *vt (lit, fig)* to sell *(für, um* for). **"zu ~"** "for sale"; **jdm etw** *or* **etw an jdn ~** to sell sb sth, to sell sth to sb; **sie haben ihr Leben so teuer wie möglich verkauft** they sold their lives as dearly as possible; **er würde sogar seine Großmutter ~** he'd even sell his own grandmother; *siehe* **Straße, verraten, dumm. 2** *vr* **(a)** *(Ware)* to sell; *(Mensch)* to sell oneself. **er hat sich ganz und gar an die Partei verkauft** he is committed body and soul to the party.

(b) *(einen schlechten Kauf machen)* to make a bad buy. **damit habe ich mich verkauft** that was a bad buy.

(c) *(fig: sich anpreisen)* to sell oneself.

Verkäufer(in *f) m* -s, - seller; *(in Geschäft)* sales *or* shop assistant, salesperson; *(im Außendienst)* salesman/ saleswoman/salesperson; *(Jur: von Grundbesitz etc)* vendor.

verkäuflich *adj* sal(e)able, marketable; *(zu verkaufen)* for sale. **leicht** *or* **gut/schwer ~** easy/hard to sell.

Verkäuflichkeit *f, no pl* sal(e)ability, marketability.

Verkaufs- *in cpds* sales; **~abteilung** *f* sales department; **~automat** *m* vending machine; **~bedingungen** *pl* conditions of sale *pl*; **~berater** *m* sales consultant; **~büro** *nt* sales office; **~förderung** *f* sales promotion; *(Abteilung)* sales promotion department; **~genie** *nt* **ein ~genie sein** to be a genius at selling things; **~leiter** *m* sales manager; **v~offen** *adj* open for business; **v~offener Samstag** Saturday on which the shops are open all day; **~personal** *nt* sales personnel *or* staff; **~preis** *m* retail price; **~schlager** *m* big seller.

Verkehr *m* -(e)s, *no pl* traffic; *(Beförderung, Verkehrsmittel)* transport. **für den ~ freigeben, dem ~ übergeben** *Straße etc* to open to traffic; *Transportmittel* to bring into service; **den ~ regeln** to regulate the (flow of) traffic; **der ~ im Suezkanal ist folgendermaßen geregelt ...** for the passage of ships in the Suez Canal the following rules and regulations apply ...; **aus dem ~ ziehen** to withdraw from service.

(b) *(Verbindung)* contact, communication; *(Umgang)* company; *(Geschlechts~)* intercourse. **in brieflichem ~ stehen** to correspond; **die Leute sind dir doch kein ~ für dich** those people aren't the right kind of company for you; **in seinem ~ mit Menschen** in his dealings with people; **seine Eltern sind gegen seinen ~ mit Drogensüchtigen** his parents are against his mixing with drug addicts; **den ~ mit jdm pflegen** *(form)* to associate with sb; **den ~ mit jdm abbrechen** to break off relations *or* contact with sb.

(c) *(Geschäfts~, Handels~)* trade; *(Umsätze, Zahlungs~)* business; *(Post~)* service; *(Umlauf)* circulation. **etw in den ~ bringen/aus dem ~ ziehen** to put sth into/withdraw sth from circulation; **jdn aus dem ~ ziehen** *(töten)* to do sb in *(sl)*; *(ins Gefängnis werfen)* to put sb in jug *(sl)*.

verkehren* 1 *vi* **(a)** *aux haben or sein (fahren)* to run; *(Flugzeug)* to fly. **der Bus/das Flugzeug verkehrt regelmäßig zwischen A und B** the bus runs *or* goes *or* operates regularly/the plane goes *or* operates regularly between A and B.

(b) *(Gast, sein, Kontakt pflegen)* **bei jdm ~** to frequent sb's house, to visit sb (regularly); **mit jdm ~** to associate with sb; **in einem Lokal ~** to frequent a pub; **in Künstlerkreisen ~** to move in artistic circles, to mix with artists; **mit jdm brieflich/schriftlich ~** *(form)* to correspond with sb; **mit jdm (geschlechtlich) ~** to have (sexual) intercourse with sb.

2 *vt* to turn *(in + acc* into). **etw ins Gegenteil ~** to reverse sth.

3 *vr* to turn *(in + acc* into). **sich ins Gegenteil ~** to become reversed.

Verkehrs- *in cpds* traffic; **~abwicklung** *f* traffic handling; **~ader** *f* artery, arterial road; **~ampel** *f* traffic lights *pl; siehe* **Ampel; ~amt** *nt* divisional railway office; *(~büro)* tourist information office; **v~arm** *adj Zeit, Straße* quiet; **ein v~armes Gebiet** an area with little traffic; **~aufkommen** *nt* volume of traffic; **~behinderung** *f (Jur)* obstruction (of traffic); **~betriebe** *pl* transport services *pl;* **~büro** *nt* tourist information office; **~chaos** *nt* chaos on the roads; **~delikt** *nt* traffic offence; **~erziehung** *f* road safety training; **~flughafen** *m* (commercial) airport; **~flugzeug** *nt* commercial aircraft; **~funk** *m* radio traffic service; **v~gefährdend** *adj* dangerous; **~gefährdung** *f (Jur: v~widriges Fahren)* dangerous driving; **eine ~gefährdung darstellen** to be a hazard to other traffic; **v~günstig** *adj Lage* convenient; *Ort, Viertel* conveniently situated; **~hindernis** *nt* (traffic) obstruction; **ein ~hindernis sein** to cause an obstruction; **~insel** *f* traffic island; **~knotenpunkt** *m* traffic junction; **~kontrolle** *f* traffic check; **bei jdm eine ~kontrolle machen** *(Polizei)* to stop sb; **verstärkte ~kontrollen machen** to increase traffic checks; **~lärm** *m* traffic noise; **~minister** *m* minister of transport; **~ministerium** *nt* ministry of transport, department of transportation *(US)*; **~mittel** *nt* means of transport *sing;* **öffentliche/private ~mittel** public/private transport; **~netz** *nt* traffic network; **~opfer** *nt* road casualty; **~ordnung** *f siehe*

Straßenverkehrsordnung; ~polizei *f* traffic police *pl;* **~polizist** *m* traffic policeman; **~regel** *f* traffic regulation; **~regelung** *f* traffic control; **v~reich** *adj Straße, Gegend* busy; **v~reiche Zeit** peak (traffic) time; **~rowdy, ~rüpel** *m* roadhog; **~schild** *nt* road sign; **~schutzmann** *m siehe* **~polizist; v~schwach** *adj Zeit* off-peak; *Gebiet* with little traffic; **die Nachmittagsstunden sind sehr v~schwach** there is very light traffic in the afternoons; **v~sicher** *adj Fahrzeug* roadworthy; *Straße, Brücke* safe (for traffic); **~sicherheit** *f siehe adj* roadworthiness; safety; **~sprache** *f* lingua franca; **~stau** *m,* **~stauung** *f* traffic jam; **~steuern** *pl* transfer taxes *pl;* **~stockung** *f* traffic hold-up; **~straße** *f* road open to traffic; **~strom** *m* flow of traffic; **~sünder** *m (inf)* traffic offender; **~sünderkartei** *f (inf)* central index of road traffic offenders; **~teilnehmer** *m* road-user; **~tote(r)** *mf* road casualty; **die Zahl der ~toten** the number of deaths on the road; **v~tüchtig** *adj Fahrzeug* roadworthy; *Mensch* fit to drive; **~unfall** *m* road accident; *(hum inf)* accident; **~unternehmen** *nt* transport company; **~unterricht** *m* traffic instruction; **v~untüchtig** *adj Fahrzeug* unroadworthy; *Mensch* unfit to drive; **~verbindung** *f* link; *(Anschluß)* connection; **~verbund** *m* transport authority; **~verein** *m* tourist information office; **~verhältnisse** *pl* traffic situation *sing;* *(Straßenzustand)* road conditions *pl;* **~vertrag** *m* traffic treaty between the two Germanys; **~volumen** *nt* volume of traffic; **~vorschrift** *f* (road) traffic regulation; **~wacht** *f* road safety organization; **~weg** *m* highway; **~wesen** *nt* transport and communications *no art;* **v~widrig** *adj* contrary to road traffic regulations; **sich v~widrig verhalten** to break the road traffic regulations; **~zählung** *f* traffic census; **~zeichen** *nt* road sign; **~zentralkartei** *f* central index of traffic offenders.

verkehrt 1 *ptp of* **verkehren.**

2 *adj* wrong; *Vorstellung auch, Welt* topsy-turvy.

3 *adv* wrongly. **etw ~ (herum) anhaben** *(linke Seite nach außen)* to have sth on inside out; *(vorne nach hinten)* to have sth on back to front; **etw ~ halten** to hold sth wrongly; *(falsch herum)* to hold sth the wrong way round; *(oben nach unten)* to hold sth upside down; **die Möbel alle ~ stellen** *(an den falschen Platz)* to put all the furniture in the wrong place; **er ist ~ herum** *(inf: homosexuell)* he's bent *(inf)*; **das ist gar nicht (so) ~** *(inf)* that can't be bad *(inf)*; **der ist gar nicht (so) ~** *(inf)* he's not such a bad sort; **das V~e** the wrong thing; **das V~este, was du tun könntest** the worst thing you could do; **der/die V~e** the wrong person; **eines Tages wirst du an den V~en geraten** one day you'll get your fingers burned; *siehe* **Kaffee¹, Adresse.**

Verkehrtheit *f* wrongness.

Verkehrung *f* reversal; *(von Rollen auch)* switching. **eine ~ ins Gegenteil** a complete reversal.

verkeilen* 1 *vt* **(a)** *(festmachen)* to wedge tight. **(b)** *(inf: verprügeln)* to thrash. **2** *vr* to become wedged together.

verkennen* *vt irreg Lage, jdn etc* to misjudge; *(unterschätzen auch)* to underestimate. **ein Dichter, der zeit seines Lebens verkannt wurde** a poet who remained unrecognized in his lifetime; **ich will nicht ~, daß ...** I would not deny that ...; **es ist nicht zu ~, daß ...** it is undeniable *or* cannot be denied that ...; **seine schlechte Laune/seine Absicht war nicht zu ~** his bad temper/his intention was unmistakable; *siehe* **verkannt.**

Verkennung *f siehe vt* misjudgement; underestimation; *(von Genie, Künstler)* failure to appreciate *(jds* sb). **in ~ der wahren Sachlage ...** misjudging the real situation ...

verketten* 1 *vt (lit)* to chain (up); *Tür, Kiste* to put chains/a chain on; *(fig)* to link. **2** *vr* to become interlinked; to become bound up together. **verkettet sein** *(fig)* to be interlinked *or* bound up (together).

Verkettung *f (das Verketten)* chaining; *(Ketten)* chains *pl;* *(fig)* interconnection.

verketzern* *vt* to denounce.

Verketzerung *f* denunciation.

verkitschen* *vt (inf)* **(a)** *Gemälde, Literatur* to make kitschy; *Lied* to sentimentalize. **(b)** *(verkaufen)* to flog *(Brit inf)*, to sell.

verkitten* *vt* to cement; *Fenster* to put putty round.

verklagen* *vt* to sue *(wegen* for), to take proceedings against *(wegen* for). **jdn auf etw** *(acc)* **~** to take sb to court for sth; **die verklagte Partei, der/die Verklagte** the defendant.

verklammern* 1 *vt* to staple together; *(Med) Wunde* to apply clips to; *(Tech) Bauteile* to brace, to put braces round; *(fig)* to link. **2** *vr (Menschen)* to embrace; *(Hände)* to interlock.

Verklammerung *f siehe vb* **(a)** *(das Verklammern)* stapling; applying of clips *(gen* to); bracing; linking; embracing; interlocking. **(b)** *(die Klammern)* staples *pl;* clips *pl;* braces *pl;* links *pl;* embrace; clasp.

verklären* 1 *vt* to transfigure. **2** *vr* to become transfigured.

verklärt *adj* transfigured.

Verklärung *f (Naut)* ship's protest.

Verklärung *f* transfiguration.

verklatschen* *vt (inf)* **(a)** *(verpetzen)* to tell on *(inf)*. **(b)** *Zeit* to spend chatting.

verklauseln* *(rare)*, **verklausulieren*** *vt Vertrag* to hedge in *or* around with (restrictive) clauses. **der Vertrag ist zu verklausuliert** the contract has too many qualifying clauses.

Verklausulierung *f (von Vertrag)* overqualification.

verkleben* 1 *vt (zusammenkleben)* to stick together; *(zukleben)* to cover *(mit* with); *Tapeten* to stick; *Haare, Verband* to make sticky; *Wunde (mit Pflaster)* to put a plaster on; *(verbrauchen)* to use up.

2 *vi aux sein (Wunde, Eileiter)* to close; *(Augen)* to get gummed up; *(Mehl, Briefmarken, Bonbons)* to stick together; *(Haare)* to become matted. **mit etw ~** to stick to sth.

verklebt *adj Verband, Wunde* sticky; *Augen* gummed up; *Haare* matted; *Eileiter* blocked.

verkleckern* *vt (inf)* to spill; *(fig) Zeit, Energie, Geld* to waste.

verkleiden* 1 vt (a) to disguise; (kostümieren) to dress up, to put into fancy dress; (fig) Ideen, Absicht to disguise, to mask. alle waren verkleidet everyone was dressed up or was in fancy dress.
  (b) (verschalen) Wand, Schacht, Tunnel to line; (vertäfeln) to panel; (bedecken) to cover; (ausschlagen) Kiste etc to line; (verdecken) Heizkörper to cover, to mask.
  2 vr to disguise oneself; (sich kostümieren) to dress (oneself) up. muß man sich ~? do you have to wear fancy dress?
Verkleidung f (a) (das Verkleiden von Menschen) disguising; (Kostümierung) dressing up, putting into fancy dress; (Kleidung) disguise; (Kostüm) fancy dress. (b) siehe vt (b) (das Verkleiden, Material) lining; panelling; covering; lining; covering, masking.
verkleinern* 1 vt to reduce; Raum, Gebiet, Firma, (Lupe, Brille) to make smaller; Fotografie to reduce (in size); Maßstab to scale down; Abstand to decrease; Not, Probleme, Schuld to minimize; jds Leistungen, Verdienste to belittle; Wort to form the diminutive of.
  2 vr to be reduced; (Raum, Gebiet, Firma) to become smaller; (Maßstab) to be scaled down; (Abstand) to decrease; (Not, Probleme, Schuld) to become less. durch den großen Schrank verkleinert sich das Zimmer the big cupboard makes the room (seem) smaller.
  3 vi (Linse etc) to make everything seem smaller.
Verkleinerung f (a) siehe vt reduction; making smaller; reduction (in size); scaling down; decreasing; minimizing; belittling; formation of the diminutive.
  (b) siehe vr reduction; becoming smaller; scaling down; decreasing; lessening.
  (c) (Bild) reduced size reproduction; (Foto) reduction; (Wort) diminutive (form); (Mus) diminution.
Verkleinerungsform f diminutive form.
verkleistern* vt (zusammenkleben) to stick together; (zukleben) to cover; (inf) (mit Kleister beschmieren) to get glue on; (verbrauchen) to use up.
verklemmen* vr to get or become stuck.
verklemmt adj (inf) Mensch inhibited; Beine crossed.
verklickern* vt (inf) jdm etw ~ to make sth clear to sb.
verklingen* vi irreg aux sein to die or fade away; (fig: Begeisterung, Interesse) to fade.
verklopfen*, verklopfen* vt (inf) (a) jdn ~ to give sb whatfor (inf). (b) (verkaufen) to flog (Brit inf), to sell.
verklumpen* vi aux sein to get lumpy.
verknacken* vt (inf) jdn zu zwei Jahren/einer Geldstrafe ~ to do sb for (inf) or give sb two years/stick a fine on sb (inf); verknackt werden to be done (inf).
verknacksen* vt (sich dat) den Knöchel or Fuß ~ to twist one's ankle.
verknallen* (inf) 1 vr sich (in jdn) ~ to fall for sb (inf); ich war damals unheimlich (in ihn) verknallt I was head over heels in love (with him) then. 2 vt Feuerwerkskörper to let off; Munition to use up; Geld (mit Feuerwerkskörpern) to waste on fireworks.
verknappen* 1 vt to cut back; Rationen to cut down (on). 2 vr to run short.
verknautschen* 1 vt to crush, to crumple. 2 vir (vi: aux sein) to crease.
verkneifen* vr irreg (inf) sich (dat) etw ~ to stop oneself (from) saying/doing etc sth; Schmerzen to hide sth; Lächeln to keep back sth; Bemerkung to bite back sth; ich konnte mir das Lachen nicht ~ I couldn't help laughing; das kann ich mir ~ I can manage without that (iro).
verkneten* vt to knead together.
verkniffen 1 ptp of verkneifen. 2 adj Gesicht, Miene (angestrengt) strained; (verbittert) pinched.
verknöchern* vi aux sein (lit, fig) to ossify. **verknöchert** (fig) ossified, fossilized.
Verknöcherung f (lit, fig) ossification.
verknorpeln* vi aux sein to become cartilaginous.
verknorzt adj (dial) fossilized.
verknoten* 1 vt to tie, to knot; (inf) Paket to tie up. 2 vr to become knotted.
verknüpfen* vt (a) (verknoten) to knot or tie (together). (b) (fig) to combine; (in Zusammenhang bringen) to link, to connect; Gedanken, Geschehnisse to associate. mit diesem Ort sind für mich schöne Erinnerungen verknüpft this place has happy memories for me; so ein Umzug ist immer mit großen Ausgaben verknüpft moving house always involves a lot of expense.
Verknüpfung f siehe vt knotting or tying (together); combining, combination; linking, connecting; association.
verknusen* vt (inf) ich kann ihn/das nicht ~ I can't stick him/that (inf).
verkochen* vti (vi: aux sein) (Flüssigkeit) to boil away; (Kartoffeln, Gemüse) to overboil.
verkohlen* 1 vi aux sein to char, to become charred; (Braten) to burn to a cinder. 2 vt (a) Holz to char; (Tech) to carbonize. (b) (inf) jdn ~ to have sb on (inf).
Verkohlung f carbonization.
verkoken* vt to carbonize.
Verkokung f carbonization.
verkommen[1] vi irreg aux sein (a) (Mensch) to go to the dogs, to go to pieces; (moralisch) to become dissolute, to go to the bad; (Kind) to run wild. zu etw ~ to degenerate into sth. (b) (Gebäude, Auto) to become dilapidated, to fall to pieces; (Stadt) to become run-down; (Gelände, Anlage etc) to run wild. (c) (nicht genutzt werden: Lebensmittel, Begabung, Fähigkeiten etc) to go to waste; (verderben: Lebensmittel) to go bad.
verkommen[2] adj Mensch depraved; Frau auch abandoned; Auto, Gebäude dilapidated; Garten wild.

Verkommenheit f, no pl siehe adj depravity; dilapidation, dilapidated state; wildness.
verkonsumieren* vt (inf) to get through; Essen, Getränke auch to consume.
verkoppeln* vt to connect, to couple; Grundbesitz to combine, to pool; (Space) to link (up).
Verkopp(e)lung f siehe vt connection, coupling; pooling; link-up.
verkorken* vt to cork (up).
verkorksen* vt (inf) to make a mess or cock-up (Brit sl) of, to mess up (inf); Kind to screw up (sl). sich (dat) den Magen ~ to upset one's stomach; jdm etw ~ to mess sth up for sb (inf), to wreck sth for sb.
verkorkst adj (inf) ruined; Magen upset; Kind, Mensch screwed up (sl). eine völlig ~e Sache a real mess.
verkörpern* vt to embody, to personify; (Theat) to play (the part of), to portray. jener Staat verkörperte die Idee der Demokratie that state was the embodiment of the democratic idea.
Verkörperung f embodiment; (Mensch auch) personification; (Theat) playing, portrayal.
verkosten* vt to taste.
verköstigen* vt to feed.
Verköstigung f feeding. ihr müßt für eure eigene ~ sorgen you'll have to get your own food.
verkrachen* vr (inf) sich (mit jdm) ~ to fall out (with sb).
verkracht adj (inf) Leben ruined; Typ, Mensch dead-beat (inf); (zerstritten) Nachbarn, Freunde who have fallen out with each other; siehe Existenz.
verkraften* vt to cope with; (seelisch) Schock, jds Tod etc auch to take; (finanziell) to afford, to manage; (inf: essen, trinken können) to manage. Straßen, die das Verkehrsvolumen nicht ~ streets which can't cope with the volume of traffic.
verkrallen* vr (Katze) to dig or sink its claws in; (Hände) to clench up. sich in etw (dat) ~ (Katze) to dig or sink its claws into sth; (Mensch) to dig or sink one's fingers into sth; der Ertrinkende hatte sich in das Holz verkrallt the drowning man was clutching desperately at the wood; sich in ein Problem ~ (fig) to get stuck into a problem.
verkramen* vt (inf) to mislay.
verkrampfen* vr to become cramped; (Hände) to clench up; (Mensch) to go tense, to tense up. verkrampft (fig) tense.
Verkrampfung f (lit, fig) tenseness, tension. seelische ~ mental tension.
verkriechen* vr irreg to creep away; (fig) to hide (oneself away). sich unter den or dem Tisch ~ to crawl or creep under the table; sich ins Bett ~ (inf) to run off to bed, to retreat to one's bed; vor ihm brauchst du dich nicht zu ~ (inf) you don't have to worry about him; am liebsten hätte ich mich vor Scham verkrochen I wanted the ground to open up and swallow me.
verkrümeln* 1 vr (inf) to disappear. 2 vt to crumble.
verkrümmen* 1 vt to bend. 2 vr to bend; Rückgrat to become curved; (Holz) to warp; (Baum, Pflanze) to grow crooked.
verkrümmt adj bent; Wirbelsäule curved; Finger, Knochen, Bäume crooked; Holz warped.
Verkrümmung f bend (gen in), distortion (esp Tech); (von Holz) warp; (von Fingern, Knochen, Bäumen) crookedness no pl. ~ der Wirbelsäule curvature of the spine; starke Winde führen zu ~en bei den Bäumen strong winds make the trees grow crooked; ~ der Hornhaut (nach innen) incurvation of the cornea; (nach außen) excurvation of the cornea.
verkrumpeln* (dial) 1 vt to crumple up. 2 vi aux sein to get crumpled up.
verkrüppeln* 1 vt to cripple. 2 vi aux sein to become crippled; (Zehen, Füße) to become deformed; (Baum etc) to grow stunted.
Verkrüpp(e)lung f siehe vb crippling; deformity; stunted growth.
verkrusten* vir (vi: aux sein) to become encrusted.
verkühlen* vr (inf) to catch a cold, to get a chill. sich (dat) die Nieren ~ to get a chill on the kidneys.
Verkühlung f (inf) chill. ~ der Blase chill on the bladder.
verkümmeln* vt (inf) to sell off, to flog (Brit inf).
verkümmern* vi aux sein (Glied, Organ) to atrophy; (eingehen: Pflanze) to die; (Talent) to go to waste; (Schönheitssinn, Interesse etc) to wither away; (Mensch) to waste away. emotionell/geistig ~ to become emotionally/intellectually stunted; wenn die natürlichen Instinkte im Menschen ~ if man's natural instincts become stunted.
Verkümmerung f (von Organ, Muskel, Glied etc) atrophy; (fig) (von Talent) wasting away, atrophy; (von Gerechtigkeitssinn, Instinkten etc) atrophy.
verkünden* vt to announce; Urteil to pronounce; Evangelium to preach; Gesetz to promulgate; nichts Gutes, Unwetter etc to forebode, to presage (liter); Frühling, neue Zeit to herald.
Verkünder(in f) m -s, - ein ~ des Evangeliums a preacher of the gospel; der ~ einer Friedensbotschaft a harbinger or herald of peace.
verkündigen* vt to proclaim; (iro) to announce; Evangelium auch to preach, to propagate. ich verkündige euch große Freude (Bibl) I bring you tidings of great joy (Bibl).
Verkündiger m -s, - siehe Verkünder(in).
Verkündigung f proclamation; (von Evangelium, von christlicher Lehre auch) preaching, propagation. Mariä ~ the Annunciation; (Tag auch) Lady Day.
Verkündung f siehe vt announcement; pronouncement; preaching; promulgation.
verkünsteln* vr (inf) to overdo it, to go to town (inf). sich an etw (dat) ~ to go to town on sth (inf), to overdo sth.
verkupfern* vt to copper(-plate). **verkupfert** copper-plated.

verkuppeln* vt (pej) to pair off, to get paired off. **jdn an jdn ~** (Zuhälter) to procure sb for sb.

Verkupp(e)lung f pairing off; (durch Zuhälter) procuring. **die ~ der beiden ging daneben** the attempt to pair them off was unsuccessful.

verkürzen* 1 vt to shorten; (Art) to foreshorten; Strecke, Wege etc auch to cut; Abstand, Vorsprung to narrow; Zeit auch to reduce, to cut down; Aufenthalt to cut short; Lebenserwartung auch, Haltbarkeit to reduce; Schmerzen, Leiden to end, to put an end to. **den Spielstand ~** to narrow the gap (between the scores); **sich** (dat) **die Zeit ~** to pass the time, to make the time pass more quickly; **jdm die Zeit ~** to help sb pass the time; **verkürzte Arbeitszeit** shorter working hours; **verkürzter Nebensatz** (Gram) elliptical subordinate clause.
2 vr to be shortened; (Art) to become foreshortened; (Strecke, Zeit auch) to be cut; (Abstand) to be narrowed; (Muskel) to contract; (Haltbarkeit) to be reduced; (Leiden) to be ended; (Urlaub, Aufenthalt) to be cut short.

Verkürzung f **(a)** siehe vb shortening; foreshortening; narrowing; reduction; cutting short; reduction; ending. **(b)** (abgekürztes Wort) contraction, shortened form.

Verl. abbr of **Verlag**; **Verleger**.

verlachen* vt to ridicule, to deride, to laugh at.

Verladebrücke f loading bridge, gantry.

verladen* vt irreg to load; (Mil) (in Eisenbahn) to entrain; (auf Schiff) to embark; (in Flugzeug) to emplane. **die Güter vom Eisenbahnwaggon aufs Schiff ~** to offload the goods from the train onto the ship.

Verladerampe f loading platform.

Verladung f siehe vt loading; entrainment; embarkation; emplaning.

Verlag m -(e)s, -e **(a)** (Buch~) publishing house or company; (Zeitungs~) newspaper publisher's sing. **~ Collins** Collins Publishers; **einen ~ finden** to find a publisher; **in or bei welchem ~ ist das erschienen?** who published it?; **der ~ zahlt nicht viel** the publishers do not pay much; **ein Buch in ~ nehmen** to publish a book; **ein Buch in ~ geben** to have a book published. **(b)** (Zwischenhandelsgeschäft) (firm of) distributors pl.

verlagern* 1 vt (lit, fig) Gewicht, Schwerpunkt, Betonung to shift; Interessen auch to transfer; (lit: an anderen Ort) to move.
2 vr (lit, fig) to shift; (Met: Tief, Hoch etc) to move; (fig: Problem, Frage) to change in emphasis (auf +acc to).

Verlagerung f siehe vb shift; transfer; moving, movement; change in emphasis.

Verlags-: ~**anstalt** f publishing firm; ~**buchhandel** m publishing trade; ~**buchhändler** m publisher; ~**buchhandlung** f publishing firm, publisher; ~**haus** nt publishing house; ~**programm** nt list; ~**recht** nt publishing rights pl; ~**system** nt cottage industry; ~**wesen** nt publishing nt sing.

verlanden* vi aux sein to silt up; (durch Austrocknen) to dry up.

Verlandung f siehe vi silting up; drying up.

verlangen* 1 vt **(a)** (fordern) to demand; (wollen) to want; Preis to ask; Qualifikationen, Erfahrung to require. **was verlangt der Kunde/das Volk?** what does the customer/do the people want?; **wieviel verlangst du für dein Auto?** how much are you asking for or do you want for your car?
(b) (erwarten) to ask (von of). **ich verlange nichts als Offenheit und Ehrlichkeit** I am asking nothing but frankness and honesty; **es wird von jdm verlangt, daß ...** it is required or expected of sb that ...; **das ist nicht zuviel verlangt** it's not asking too much; **das ist ein bißchen viel verlangt** that's asking rather a lot, that's rather a tall order.
(c) (erfordern) to require, to call for.
(d) (fragen nach) to ask for; Paß, Ausweis auch to ask to see. **Sie werden am Telefon verlangt** you are wanted on the phone; **ich verlange/ich verlangte den Geschäftsführer (zu sprechen)** I want or demand to see the manager/I demanded or asked to see the manager.
2 vi ~ **nach** to ask for; (sich sehnen nach) to long for; (stärker) to crave.
3 vt impers (liter) **es verlangt jdn nach jdm/etw** sb craves sth; (nach der Heimat, Geliebten) sb yearns for sb/sth.

Verlangen nt -s, - (nach for) desire; (Sehnsucht) yearning, longing; (Begierde) craving; (Forderung) request. **kein ~ nach etw haben** to have no desire or wish for sth; **auf ~** on demand; **auf ~ des Gerichts** by order of the court; **auf ~ der Eltern** at the request of the parents; **auf sein eigenes ~ hin** at his own request.

verlangend adj longing.

verlängern* 1 vt **(a)** to extend; (räumlich auch) to lengthen, to make longer; (Math) Strecke auch to produce; (zeitlich) Wartezeit, Aufenthalt auch, Leben, Schmerzen, Leiden etc to prolong; Hosenbein, Ärmel etc to lengthen; Paß, Abonnement etc to renew. **die Suppe/Soße ~** (fig inf) to make the soup/gravy go further or stretch; **ein verlängertes Wochenende** a long weekend; siehe **Rücken**.
(b) (Sport) Ball, Paß to touch or play on (zu jdm to sb).
2 vr to be extended; (räumlich auch) to be lengthened; (zeitlich auch, Leiden etc) to be prolonged.
3 vi (Sport) to play on.

Verlängerung f **(a)** siehe vt **(a)** extension; lengthening; prolonging, prolongation; lengthening; renewal.
(b) (Gegenstand) extension.
(c) (Sport) (von Ball) first-time pass; (von Paß) play-on (zu to); (von Spielzeit) extra time (Brit), overtime (US); (nachgespielte Zeit) injury time (Brit). **das Spiel geht in die ~** they're going to play extra time etc, they're going into extra time etc; **eine ~ von fünf Minuten** five minutes' extra time etc.

Verlängerungs-: ~**kabel** nt, ~**schnur** f (Elec) extension lead.

verlangsamen* 1 vt to slow down or up; Geschwindigkeit

auch to reduce, to decelerate; Produktion auch to decelerate; Entwicklung auch to retard. **das Tempo/seine Schritte/die Fahrt ~** to slow down or up. 2 vr to slow down or up; to decelerate; to be retarded.

Verlangsamung f siehe vb slowing down or up; deceleration; retarding, retardation.

verläppern* vr to be or get lost; (Geld) to disappear, to vanish.

Verlaß m -sses, no pl **auf jdn/etw ist kein ~, es ist kein ~ auf jdn/etw** there is no relying on sb/sth, you can't rely on sb/sth.

verlassen¹* irreg 1 vt **(a)** to leave; (fig: Mut, Kraft, Hoffnung) jdn to desert; (im Stich lassen) to desert, to abandon, to forsake (liter). **... und da verließen sie ihn** (iro) ... that's as far as it goes; (bei Arbeit, Reparatur etc) ... that's as far as I/he etc got; **(böswilliges) V~** desertion; siehe **Geist**.
2 vr **sich auf jdn/etw ~** to rely or depend on sb/sth; **darauf können Sie sich ~** you can be sure of that, you can depend on that, take my word for it.

verlassen² adj **(a)** Gegend, Ort, Straßen deserted; (öd) desolate. **eine Tanne, einsam und ~** a solitary fir tree. **(b)** Mensch (allein gelassen) deserted; (einsam) lonely, solitary. **einsam und ~** so all alone. **(c)** (ohne Besitzer) Haus, Fabrik deserted; Auto abandoned.

Verlassenheit f, no pl siehe adj **(a)** desertedness; desolateness.

Verlassenschaft f (Aus, Sw) estate; (literarisch) legacy.

Verlassenschafts|abhandlung f (Aus, Sw) negotiation on inheritance.

verläßlich, verlässig (old) adj reliable; Mensch auch dependable.

Verläßlichkeit f siehe adj reliability; dependability.

verlatschen* vt (inf) to wear out.

Verlaub m: **mit ~** (old) by your leave, with your permission; **mit ~ (zu sagen)** if you will pardon or forgive my saying so.

Verlauf m -(e)s, **Verläufe** course; (Ausgang) end, issue. **im ~ der Zeit** in the course of time; **im ~ des Tages/der Jahre/Monate** in or during the course of the day/over the (course of the) years/months; **im ~ der Verhandlung/Arbeit** in or during the course of the negotiations/work; **einen guten/schlechten ~ nehmen** to go well/badly; **den ~ einer Sache verfolgen/beobachten** to follow/observe the course (which) sth takes; **im weiteren ~ der Sache zeichnete sich folgende Tendenz ab as** things developed the following tendency became apparent.

verlaufen* irreg 1 vi aux sein **(a)** (ablaufen) (Tag, Prüfung) to go; (Feier, Demonstration) to go off; (Kindheit) to pass; (Untersuchung) to proceed. **beschreiben Sie, wie diese Krankheit normalerweise verläuft** describe the course this illness usually takes; **die Verhandlung verlief in angespannter Atmosphäre** the negotiations took place in a tense atmosphere.
(b) (sich erstrecken) to run.
(c) (auseinanderfließen, dial: schmelzen) to run. **die Spur verlief im Sand/Wald** the track disappeared in the sand/forest; ~**e Farben** runny colours; siehe **Sand**.
2 vr **(a)** (sich verirren) to get lost, to lose one's way. **sich zu jdm ~** (iro) to find one's way to sb.
(b) (verschwinden) (Menschenmenge) to disperse; (Wasser auch) to drain away; (sich veriieren: Spur, Weg) to disappear.

Verlaufsform f (Gram) progressive or continuous form.

verlaust adj lice-ridden.

verlautbaren* (form) 1 vti to announce. **es wird amtlich verlautbart, daß ...** it is officially announced that ..., a statement has been issued to the effect that ...; **etw ~ lassen** to let sth be announced or made known. 2 vi impers **es hat verlautbart, daß ...** it has been reported that ...

Verlautbarung f announcement; (inoffiziell) report.

verlauten* 1 vi **etwas/nichts ~ lassen** to give an/no indication, to say something/nothing; **er hat ~ lassen, daß ...** he indicated that ...; **er hat keinen Ton or kein Wort ~ lassen** he hasn't said a word.
2 vi impers aux sein or haben **es verlautet, daß ...** it is reported that ...; **wie aus Bonn verlautet** according to reports from Bonn.

verleben* vt to spend. **eine schöne Zeit ~** to have a nice time.

verlebendigen* vt to liven up, to make more lively.

verlebt adj worn-out, dissipated.

verlegen¹* 1 vt **(a)** (an anderen Ort) to transfer, to move; Schauplatz auch to transpose, to shift.
(b) (verschieben) to postpone (auf +acc until); (vorverlegen) to bring forward (auf +acc to).
(c) (an falschen Platz legen) to mislay, to misplace.
(d) (anbringen) Kabel, Fliesen etc to lay.
(e) (drucken lassen) to publish.
2 vr **sich auf etw** (acc) ~ to resort to sth; **er hat sich neuerdings auf Golf verlegt** he has taken to golf recently; **sich aufs Unterrichten ~** to take up teaching.

verlegen² adj **(a)** embarrassed no adv. ~ **sah er zu Boden** he looked at the floor in embarrassment. **(b)** um **Worte/eine Antwort ~ sein** to be lost or at a loss for words/an answer; um **Geld ~ sein** to be financially embarrassed.

Verlegenheit f **(a)** no pl (Betretenheit, Befangenheit) embarrassment. **jdn in ~ bringen** to embarrass sb; **so ein wunderschöner Strauß, du bringst mich ja ganz in ~** such a lovely bouquet, you really shouldn't have; **in ~ kommen or geraten** to get or become embarrassed.
(b) (unangenehme Lage) embarrassing or awkward situation. **wenn er in finanzieller ~ ist** when he's in financial difficulties, when he's financially embarrassed; **ich bin (finanziell) zur Zeit leider etwas in ~** I'm afraid I'm short of (funds) at the moment; **sich (mit etw) aus der ~ ziehen** to get out of an embarrassing or awkward situation.

Verleger m -s, - publisher; (Händler) distributor.

Verlegung f **(a)** (räumlich) siehe **verlegen¹** **(a)** transfer, moving; transposition, shifting. **(b)** (zeitlich) postponement (*auf* +*acc* until); (*Vor~*) bringing forward (*auf* +*acc* to). (c) (*von Kabeln etc*) laying.

verleiden* *vt* jdm etw ~ to spoil sth for sb, to put sb off sth; **das ist mir jetzt schon verleidet** you've/he's put me off it.

Verleih *m* -(e)s, -e (a) (*Unternehmen*) rental *or* hire company; (*Auto~*) car rental *or* hire; (*Film~*) distributor(s). **gibt es hier einen ~ für Teppichreiniger?** is there anyone who rents *or* hires (out) carpet cleaners round here?; **die meisten Pfarreien haben einen ~ für Bücher** most parishes have a book lending scheme.

(b) (*das Verleihen*) renting (out), hiring (out); (*Film~*) distribution. **der ~ von Büchern** the lending *or* loan of books.

verleihen* *vt* *irreg* (a) (*verborgen*) to lend, to loan (*an jdn* to sb); (*gegen Gebühr*) to rent (out), to hire (out).

(b) (*zuerkennen*) to award (*jdm* (to) sb); *Titel, Ehrenbürgerrechte* to confer, to bestow (*jdm* on sb); *Amt* to bestow (*jdm* upon sb).

(c) (*geben, verschaffen*) to give; *Eigenschaft, Klang, Note auch* to lend. **Gott hat ihr Schönheit verliehen** God gave *or* granted her beauty; **ihre Anwesenheit verlieh der Veranstaltung einen gewissen Glanz** her presence gave *or* lent a certain splendour to the occasion.

Verleiher *m* -s, - hire *or* rental firm; (*von Kostümen etc*) renter, hirer; (*von Filmen*) distributor, (firm of) distributors *pl*; (*von Büchern*) lender.

Verleihung *f* *siehe* vt (a, b) (a) lending, loan(ing); renting, rental, hire, hiring. (b) award(ing); conferment, conferring, bestowal, bestowment.

verleimen* *vt* to glue.

verleiten* *vt* (a) (*verlocken*) to tempt; (*verführen*) to lead astray. **die Sonne hat mich verleitet, schwimmen zu gehen** the sun tempted *or* enticed me to go swimming; **jdn zur Sünde ~** to lead sb into sin; **jdn zum Stehlen/Lügen ~** to lead *or* encourage sb to steal/lie; **jdn zu einem Verbrechen ~** to lead *or* encourage sb to commit a crime; **jdn zum Ungehorsam ~** to encourage sb to be disobedient; **jdn dazu ~, die Schule zu schwänzen** to encourage sb to play truant.

(b) (*veranlassen*) **jdn zu etw ~** to lead sb to sth; **jdn zu einem Irrtum ~** to lead sb to make *or* into making a mistake.

Verleitung *f* (a) (*Verführung*) leading astray; (*zum Lügen, Stehlen*) encouragement. **die ~ der Menschen zur Sünde** leading people into sin. (b) (*Veranlassung*) **die ~ zu einer vorschnellen Äußerung** leading him/one *etc* to make a hasty comment.

verlernen* *vt* to forget, to unlearn. **das Tanzen ~** to forget how to dance.

verlesen* *irreg* 1 *vt* (a) (*vorlesen*) to read (out); *Namen auch* to call out. (b) *Gemüse, Früchte etc* to sort; *Feldsalat* to clean. 2 *vr* (*beim Vorlesen*) to make a slip. **ich habe mich wohl ~** I must have read it wrong(ly), I must have misread it.

Verlesung *f* *siehe* vt (a) reading (out); calling out.

verletzbar *adj* (*lit, fig*) vulnerable.

Verletzbarkeit *f* (*lit, fig*) vulnerability.

verletzen* 1 *vt* (a) (*verwunden*) to injure; (*in Kampf etc, mit Kugel, Messer*) to wound; (*fig*) jdn to hurt, to wound; *jds Stolz, Gefühle* to hurt, to wound, to injure; *jds Ehrgefühl* to injure, to offend; *jds Schönheitssinn, zarte Ohren* to offend. **das verletzt den guten Geschmack** it offends against good taste.

(b) *Gesetz* to break; *Pflicht, Rechte, Intimsphäre* to violate. 2 *vr* to injure oneself.

verletzend *adj Bemerkung* hurtful.

verletzlich *adj* vulnerable.

Verletzlichkeit *f* vulnerability.

Verletzte(r) *mf decl as adj* injured person; (*Unfall~ auch*) casualty; (*bei Kampf*) wounded man. **die ~n** the injured/the wounded; **es gab drei ~** three people were injured *or* hurt/wounded.

Verletzung *f* (a) (*Wunde*) injury. (b) *siehe* vt (*das Verletzen*) injuring; wounding, (*fig*) hurting, wounding; offending *etc*. **zur ~ des Knies führen** to cause a knee injury.

verleugnen* *vt* to deny; *Kind auch* to disown. **ich kann es nicht ~, daß ...** I cannot deny that ...; **es läßt sich nicht ~, daß ...** there is no denying that ...; **er läßt sich immer vor ihr ~** he is never there to her, he always pretends not to be there when she calls; **sich (selbst) ~** to deny one's own self.

Verleugnung *f* *siehe* vt denial; disownment.

verleumden* *vt* to slander, to calumniate (*form*); (*schriftlich*) to libel.

Verleumder(in *f*) *m* -s, - *siehe* vt slanderer; libeller.

verleumderisch *adj siehe* vt slanderous; libellous.

Verleumdung *f* slandering; (*schriftlich*) libelling; (*Bemerkung*) slander, calumny; (*Bericht*) libel.

verlieben* *vr* to fall in love (*in* +*acc* with). **das Kleid ist zum V~ (schön)** the dress is lovely.

verliebt *adj Benehmen, Blicke, Worte* amorous. (**in jdn/etw**) ~ **sein** to be in love (with sb/sth); **ein immer noch stark ~es älteres Ehepaar** an elderly couple still very much in love; **die V~en** the courting couple/couples, the lovers; *siehe* **Ohr.**

Verliebtheit *f* being in love. **seine ~ dauert nie lange** he is never in love for very long; **in einem Moment großer ~** feeling (all at once) tremendously in love.

verlieren *pret* verlor, *ptp* verloren 1 *vt* to lose; *Blätter auch* to shed. **jdn/etw aus dem Gedächtnis ~** to lose all memory of sb/sth, to forget sb/sth; **kein Wort über jdn/etw ~** not to say a word about sb/sth; **wir brauchen kein Wort darüber zu ~** we don't need to waste any words on it; **an ihm hast du nichts verloren** he's no (great) loss; **das/er hat hier nichts verloren** (*inf*) that/he has no business to be here; **diese Bemerkung hat hier nichts verloren** (*inf*) that remark is out of place.

2 *vi* to lose. **sie hat an Schönheit/Charme verloren** she has lost some of her beauty/charm; **sie/die Altstadt** *etc* **hat sehr ver-**

loren she/the old town *etc* is not what she/it *etc* used to be; **durch etw ~** to lose (something) by sth; **sie verliert durch das auffällige Kleid** that conspicuous dress detracts from her looks; **bei jdm ~** to go down in sb's eyes *or* estimation.

3 *vr* (a) (*Menschen*) to lose each other; (*Mensch: sich verirren*) to get lost, to lose one's way.

(b) (*verschwinden*) to disappear; (*verhallen*) to fade away, to die. **der Klang verlor sich in dem riesigen Saal/in den Bergen** the sound was lost in the enormous room/faded away *or* died among the mountains.

(c) (*fig*) (*geistesabwesend sein*) to become lost to the world; (*abschweifen*) to lose one's train of thought. **sich in etw** (*acc*) ~ to become absorbed in sth; **sich in etw** (*dat*) ~ to get *or* become lost in sth; *siehe* **verloren.**

Verlierer(in *f*) *m* -s, - loser.

Verlies *nt* -es, -e dungeon.

verloben* 1 *vr* (*mit* to) to become *or* get engaged, to become betrothed (*old*). 2 *vt* **jdn mit jdm ~** to betroth sb to sb (*old*); **verlobt sein** to be engaged *or* betrothed (*old*) (*mit* to).

Verlöbnis *nt* (*old*) *siehe* **Verlobung.**

Verlobte(r) *mf decl as adj* **mein ~r** my fiancé, my betrothed (*old*); **meine ~** my fiancée, my betrothed (*old*); **die ~n** the engaged couple, the betrothed (*old*).

Verlobung *f* engagement, betrothal (*old*).

Verlobungs- *in cpds* engagement; **~anzeige** *f* engagement announcement; **~zeit** *f* engagement.

verlocken* *vti* to entice, to tempt.

verlockend *adj* enticing, tempting.

Verlockung *f* enticement, temptation; (*Reiz*) allure.

verlodern* *vi aux sein* (*geh*) to flare up and die.

verlogen *adj Mensch* lying, mendacious; *Komplimente, Versprechungen* false; *Moral, Freundlichkeit, Gesellschaft* hypocritical. **die ganze Geschichte war völlig ~** the whole story was a pack of lies.

Verlogenheit *f* *siehe adj* mendacity; falseness; hypocrisy.

verlohnen* *vir impers* (*rare*) to be worthwhile. **es verlohnt die** *or* **der Mühe** *or* **sich der Mühe nicht** it is not worth the trouble.

verlor *pret of* verlieren.

verloren 1 *ptp of* verlieren.

2 *adj* (a) lost; (*einsam auch*) forlorn; (*Cook*) *Eier* poached. **in den Anblick ~ sein** to be lost in contemplation.

(b) vain. **der ~e Sohn** (*Bibl*) the prodigal son; **jdn/etw geben** to give sb/sth up for lost; **auf ~em Posten kämpfen** *or* **stehen** to be fighting a losing battle *or* a lost cause.

verlorengehen *vi sep irreg aux sein* to get *or* be lost; (*Zeit, Geld*) to be lost *or* wasted. **an ihm ist ein Sänger verlorengegangen** he would have made a (good) singer, he ought to have been a singer.

Verlorenheit *f* forlornness.

verlöschen* 1 *pret* verlosch, *ptp* verloschen *vi aux sein* to go out; (*Inschrift, Farbe, Tinte*) to fade; (*Mond, Sterne*) to set; (*Erinnerung, Ruhm*) to fade (away). **sein Leben(slicht) ist verloschen** (*liter*) he has departed this life (*liter*). 2 *vt reg* (*geh*) *siehe* **auslöschen.**

verlosen* *vt* to raffle (off). **wir ~ das letzte Stück Kuchen** we'll draw lots for the last piece of cake.

Verlosung *f* (*das Verlosen*) raffling; (*Lotterie*) raffle, draw; (*Ziehung*) draw.

verlöten* *vt* to solder. **einen ~** (*sl: trinken*) to have a quickie (*inf*) *or* a quick one (*inf*).

verlottern* *vi aux sein* (*inf*) (*Stadt, Restaurant*) to get *or* become run down; (*Garten*) to run wild; (*Mensch*) to go to the dogs; (*moralisch*) to go to the bad. **er verlottert immer mehr** he is sliding further and further downhill; **die Wohnung ist ganz verlottert** the flat is a complete shambles.

verlottert *adj* (*inf*) *Stadt* run-down; *Garten* wild; *Mensch, Aussehen* scruffy; (*moralisch*) dissolute.

verludern* (*inf*) 1 *vi aux sein* to go to the bad. 2 *vt Geld* to squander, to fritter away.

verlumpen* (*inf*) 1 *vt Geld* to chuck away (*inf*). 2 *vi aux sein* to go to the dogs; (*moralisch*) to go downhill.

verlumpt *adj* (*dial*) down and out; *Kleider* worn-out. **~ herumlaufen** to go about in rags.

Verlust *m* -(e)s, -e loss. **~e** *pl* losses *pl*; (*Tote auch*) casualties *pl*; (*bei Glücksspiel*) losses *pl*; **schwere ~e haben/machen** to sustain/make heavy losses; **mit ~ verkaufen** to sell at a loss; **in ~ geraten** (*form*) to be lost; *siehe* **Rücksicht.**

Verlust-: **~anzeige** *f* "lost" notice; **~betrieb** *m* (*inf*) lossmaking business, loss-maker, lame duck (*inf*); **v~bringend** *adj* loss-making; **v~bringend arbeiten** to work at a loss; **~geschäft** *nt* (*Firma*) loss-making business, loss-maker; **ich habe es schließlich verkauft, aber das war ein ~geschäft** I sold it eventually, but I made a loss *or* but at a loss.

verlustieren* *vr* (*hum*) to amuse oneself.

verlustig *adj* (*form*) **einer Sache** (*gen*) ~ **gehen** *or* **werden** to forfeit *or* lose sth; **jdn seiner Rechte für ~ erklären** to declare sb's rights forfeit.

Verlust-: **~liste** *f* (*Mil*) casualty list, list of casualties; **~meldung** *f* (a) report of the loss; **der Absender muß eine ~meldung machen** the sender must report the loss; (b) (*Mil*) casualty report, casualty figures *pl*; **v~reich** *adj* (a) (*Comm*) *Firma* heavily loss-making; **ein v~reiches Jahr** a year in which heavy losses were made, a year of heavy losses; **ein v~reiches Geschäft** a deal on which heavy losses were made; (b) (*Mil*) *Schlacht* involving heavy losses *or* casualties.

Verm. *abbr of* **Vermerk.**

vermachen* *vt* jdm etw ~ to leave *or* bequeath sth to sb; (*inf: gehen*) to bequeath sth to sb; **jdm etw als Schenkung ~** to bequeath sth to sb.

Vermächtnis *nt* bequest, legacy; (*fig*) legacy.

Vermächtnis- (*Jur*) **~geber** *m* legator; **~nehmer** *m* legatee.

vermahlen* vt to grind.

vermählen* (form) **1** vt to marry, to wed. **frisch vermählt sein** to be newly married or wed(ded). **2** vr **sich (mit jdm) ~** to marry or wed (sb); „**wir haben uns vermählt ...**" "the marriage is announced of ...".

Vermählte(r) mf decl as adj **die beiden ~n** the newly-married couple; **die/der soeben ~** the bride/(bride)groom.

Vermählung f (form) marriage.

Vermählungsanzeige f marriage announcement.

vermahnen* vt to warn.

Vermahnung f warning.

vermaledeien* vt (old) to curse.

vermaledeit adj (old) (ac)cursed (old), damned.

vermalen* vt Farben to use up.

vermännlichen* 1 vt to masculinize, to make masculine. **2** vi aux sein (Frauen) to become masculine or like men, to adopt male characteristics; (Gesellschaft) to become male-dominated.

Vermännlichung f masculinization.

vermanschen* vt (inf) to mash up.

vermarkten* vt to market; (fig) to commercialize.

Vermarktung f marketing; (fig) commercialization.

vermasseln* vt (inf) to ruin, to mess up (inf); Prüfung, Klassenarbeit to make a mess or cock-up (Brit sl) of.

vermassen* 1 vi aux sein to lose one's identity or individuality, to become stereotyped. **die Gesellschaft vermaßt immer mehr** society is becoming more and more uniform. **2** vt **die Gesellschaft ~** to make uniform. **jdn ~** to make sb lose his/her identity or individuality, to de-individualize sb.

Vermassung f loss of identity or individuality, stereotyping, de-individualization. **die ~ der Gesellschaft** the stereotyping of society.

vermatscht adj (dial) squashy.

vermauern* vt to wall or brick up.

vermehren* 1 vt to increase; (fortpflanzen) to breed; Bakterien to multiply. **vermehrt increased; diese Fälle treten vermehrt auf** these cases are occurring with increased or increasing frequency or are happening increasingly often.

2 vr to increase; (sich fortpflanzen) to reproduce, to breed; (Bakterien) to multiply; (Pflanzen) to propagate.

Vermehrung f siehe vb increase; reproduction, breeding; multiplying; propagation.

vermeidbar adj avoidable.

vermeiden* vt irreg to avoid; Frage auch to evade. **~, daß eine Sache an die Öffentlichkeit dringt** to avoid letting a matter become public; **es läßt sich nicht ~** it cannot be avoided or helped, it is inevitable or unavoidable; **es läßt sich nicht ~, daß ...** it is inevitable or unavoidable that ...; **nicht, wenn ich es ~ kann** not if I can avoid or help it; **er vermeidet keinen Streit** he's not one to avoid an argument.

vermeidlich adj avoidable.

Vermeidung f avoidance. **die ~ eines Skandals ist nur dann möglich, wenn ...** a scandal can only be avoided if ...; **zur ~ to** avoid.

vermeil [vɛr'mɛːj] adj vermilion.

Vermeil [vɛr'mɛːj] nt -s, no pl gilded silver.

vermeinen* vt (geh) to think. **ich vermeinte, eine Stimme zu hören** I thought I heard a voice.

vermeintlich adj attr putative, supposed; Täter, Vater eines Kindes putative.

vermelden* vt (a) (liter: mitteilen) to announce. **was hast du Neues zu ~?** (hum) what news do you have to announce or report? **(b)** Erfolg to report.

vermengen* vt to mix; (fig inf: durcheinanderbringen) Begriffe etc to mix up, to confuse.

Vermengung f mixing.

vermenschlichen* vt to humanize; (als Menschen darstellen auch) to anthropomorphize.

Vermenschlichung f siehe vt humanization; anthropomorphization.

Vermerk m -(e)s, -e note, remark; (im Kalender auch) entry; (in Paß) observation; (postalisch) remark; (Stempel) stamp.

vermerken* vt (a) to make a note of, to note (down), to write down; (in Paß, Karte) Namen, Datum etc to record. **alle Verkehrssünder werden in Flensburg vermerkt** a record of (the names of) all traffic offenders is kept in Flensburg; **sich (dat) etw ~** to make a note of sth, to note or write sth down.

(b) (zur Kenntnis nehmen) to note, to make a (mental) note of. **jdm etw übel ~** to take sth amiss; **der Vorfall wurde peinlich vermerkt** the incident was noted with some embarrassment.

vermessen[1]***** irreg **1** vt to measure; Land, Gelände to survey. **2** vr (a) (geh) (sich anmaßen) to presume, to dare. **wie kann er sich ~, ...?** how dare he ...? **(b)** (falsch messen) to measure wrongly.

vermessen[2] adj (anmaßend) presumptuous; Diener impudent; (kühn) Unterfangen bold.

Vermessenheit f, no pl siehe adj presumption, presumptuousness; impudence; boldness. **es wäre eine ~, das zu tun that** would be an act of some temerity.

Vermessung f measurement; (von Land, Gelände) survey.

Vermessungs-: ~amt nt land survey(ing) office; ~ingenieur m land surveyor; ~schiff nt survey ship.

vermickert, vermiekert adj (dial) siehe **mick(e)rig.**

vermiesen* vt (inf) **jdm etw ~** to spoil sth for sb; **das hat mir den Urlaub vermiest** that spoiled my holiday.

vermietbar adj rentable. **schlecht ~** difficult to rent (out) or let (out) (esp Brit); **es ist nur als Büroraum ~** it can only be rented (out) or let (out) (esp Brit) as office premises.

vermieten* 1 vt to rent (out), to let (out) (esp Brit), to lease (Jur); Boot, Auto to rent (out), to hire (out), to lease (Jur); Zimmer zu ~ room to let (esp Brit) or for rent. **2** vi to rent (out)

or let (out) (esp Brit) a room/rooms.

Vermieter m -s, - lessor; (von Wohnung etc) landlord, lessor (Jur).

Vermieterin f landlady.

Vermietung f siehe vt renting (out), letting (out) (esp Brit); renting (out), rental, hiring (out).

vermindern* 1 vt to reduce, to decrease; Gefahr, Anfälligkeit, Einfluß etc auch, Ärger, Zorn to lessen; Widerstandsfähigkeit, Reaktionsfähigkeit to diminish, to reduce; Schmerzen to ease, to lessen, to reduce; (Mus) to diminish. **verminderte Zurechnungsfähigkeit** (Jur) diminished responsibility.

2 vr siehe vt to decrease; to lessen; to diminish; (Schmerzen) to ease off, to lessen, to decrease.

Verminderung f siehe vb reduction (gen of), decrease (gen in); lessening; diminution, reduction; easing, lessening, reduction.

verminen* vt to mine.

Verminung f mining.

vermischen* 1 vt to mix; Tabaksorten, Teesorten etc to blend. **vermischte Schriften** miscellaneous writings; „**Vermischtes**" "miscellaneous".

2 vr to mix; (Rassen auch) to interbreed; (Elemente, Klänge, Farben) to blend, to mingle. **Freude vermischt sich mit Leid** joy mingles or is mingled with sorrow; **wo sich Tradition und Fortschritt ~** where tradition and progress are blended (together) or combined.

Vermischung f siehe vb mixing, mixture; blending; interbreeding; blending, mingling; (von Gefühlen, Stilebenen, Metaphern) mixture.

vermissen* vt to miss. **vermißt werden** to be missing; **vermißt sein, als vermißt gemeldet sein** to be reported missing; **ich vermisse zwei silberne Teelöffel** two (of my) silver teaspoons are missing, I'm missing two silver teaspoons; **ich vermisse die Blumen auf den Tischen** I see you don't have the flowers on the tables; **etw an jdm/etw ~** to find sb/sth lacking in sth; **ich vermisse bei diesen Leuten die Freundlichkeit** what I find lacking in these people is kindness; **was ich bei dieser Beschreibung vermisse, ist ...** what I miss in this description is ...; **wir haben dich bei der Party vermißt** we didn't see you at the party; **entschuldige, daß ich zu spät komme — wir hatten dich noch gar nicht vermißt** sorry I'm late — we hadn't even noticed you weren't here; **etw ~ lassen** to lack sth, to be lacking in sth.

Vermißten|anzeige f missing persons report. **eine ~ aufgeben** to report someone (as) missing.

Vermißte(r) mf decl as adj missing person.

vermitteln* 1 vt to arrange (jdm for sb); Stelle, Briefpartner, Privatschüler to find (jdm for sb); Aushilfskräfte, Lehrer etc to find jobs or positions for, to place; (Telec) Gespräch to put through, to connect; Hypotheken, Kredite, Geschäfte to arrange, to negotiate (jdm for sb); Wertpapiere to negotiate; Lösung, Kompromiß, Waffenstillstand to arrange, to negotiate, to mediate; Gefühl, Bild, Idee, Einblick to convey, to give (jdm to sb); Verständnis to give (jdm (to) sb); Wissen to impart (jdm to sb). **jdm etw ~** to get sth for sb; **eine Stelle, die Hotelunterkunft vermittelt** an office which finds hotel accommodation; **kennen Sie jemanden, der Wohnungen vermittelt?** do you know (anybody who acts as) an agent for renting/buying flats?; **ich kann dir eine billige Ferienwohnung ~** I can get you a cheap holiday flat; **wir ~ Wohnungen** we are agents for flats.

2 vi to mediate, to act as mediator or a go-between. **~d eingreifen** to intervene; **~de Worte** conciliatory words.

vermittels(t) prep +gen (form) by means of.

Vermittler(in f) m -s, - **(a)** mediator, go-between. **(b)** (Comm) agent; (Fin, Heirats~) broker; (von Anleihe) negotiator; (Stellen~) clerk in/manager of/person who works in an employment agency or bureau.

Vermittler-: ~gebühr f commission; (Fin auch) brokerage; ~rolle f role of mediator.

Vermittlung f **(a)** siehe vt arranging, arrangement; finding; finding of jobs or positions (+gen for), placing; connection; negotiation; mediating; conveying; giving; imparting. **sie haben sich durch die ~ einer Agentur kennengelernt** they met through an agency; **ich habe das Zimmer/die Stelle durch ~ eines Freundes bekommen** I got the room/job through (the agency of form) or via a friend; **durch seine freundliche ~ with** his kind help; **zur ~ eines besseren Verständnisses** to give a better understanding; **zur ~ eines besseren Eindrucks** to give or convey a better impression; **heute geht die telefonische ~ automatisch vor sich** nowadays telephone calls are put through or connected automatically.

(b) (Schlichtung) mediation. **eine ~ zwischen den beiden ist mir leider nicht gelungen** unfortunately I was unable to reconcile them or to bring about a reconciliation between them.

(c) (Stelle, Agentur) agency; (Heirats~) marriage bureau or agency; (Wohnungs~) estate agent's or agency (Brit), realtor (US); (Arbeits~) employment agency.

(d) (Telec) (Amt) exchange; (in Firma etc) switchboard; (Mensch) operator.

Vermittlungs-: ~amt nt (Telec) telephone exchange; ~ausschuß m mediation committee; ~bemühungen pl efforts to mediate pl; ~gebühr f commission; ~schrank m switchboard; ~stelle f agency; (Telec) (telephone) exchange; (in Firma etc) switchboard; ~versuch m attempt at mediation.

vermöbeln* vt (inf) to beat up; (als Strafe) to thrash.

vermocht ptp of **vermögen.**

vermodern* vi aux sein to moulder, to decay.

Vermod(e)rung f decay.

vermöge prep +gen (liter) by dint of.

vermögen pret **vermochte**, ptp **vermocht** vt, v aux (geh) **etw zu tun ~, (es) ~, etw zu tun** to be able to do sth, to be capable of doing sth; **er vermochte es nicht, sich von den Fesseln zu be-**

freien he was unable or was not able to free himself from the chains; **viel/wenig ~** to be capable of a lot/not to be capable of very much; **etwas Verständnis vermag bei den Schülern viel** a little understanding is capable of achieving a lot with students; **Geduld vermag viel bei ihm** patience works wonders with him.

Vermögen nt -s, - **(a)** (Reichtum, viel Geld) fortune. **das ist ein ~ wert** it's worth a fortune; **das ist ja nicht gerade ein ~** it's not exactly a fortune; **eine Frau, die ~ hat** a woman who has money, a woman of means; **die erste Frage war, ob ich ~ hatte** the first question was whether I had private means.

(b) (Besitz) property. **mein ganzes ~ besteht aus ...** my entire assets consist of ...; **die Verteilung des ~s in einem Land** the distribution of wealth within a country.

(c) (Können) ability, capacity; (Macht) power.

vermögend adj (reich) wealthy, well-off. **ein ~er Mann** a man of means, a wealthy man.

Vermögens-: **~abgabe** f property levy; **~bildung** f wealth creation or formation; (durch Prämiensparen) wealth formation by long-term saving with tax concessions; **~erklärung** f statement of property; (Wertpapiere) statement of assets; **~konzentration** f concentration of wealth; **~politik** f policy on the distribution of wealth; **~steuer** f wealth tax; **~verhältnisse** pl financial or pecuniary circumstances pl; **~verteilung** f distribution of wealth; **~werte** pl assets pl; **v~wirksam** adj profitable, profit-yielding; **Geld v~wirksam investieren** to invest money profitably; **v~wirksame Leistungen** employer's contributions to tax-deductible savings scheme; **~zuwachs** m increase of wealth.

vermorschen* vi aux sein to rot.

vermottet adj (lit, fig) moth-eaten.

vermummen* 1 vt to wrap up (warm). 2 vr **(a)** to wrap (oneself) up (warm). **vermummte Gestalten in einer Winterlandschaft** muffled-up figures in a winter landscape. **(b)** (sich verkleiden) to disguise. **eine vermummte Gestalt betrat den Raum** a cloaked figure entered the room; **tief vermummt** heavily disguised.

Vermummung f disguise.

vermurksen* vt (inf) etw **~/sich** (dat) etw **~** to mess sth up (inf), to make a mess of sth.

vermuten* vt to suspect. **ich vermute es nur** that's only an assumption, I'm only assuming that, that's only what I suspect to be the case; **wir haben ihn dort nicht vermutet** we did not expect or think to find/see etc him there; **ich hatte dich nicht so früh vermutet** I didn't suspect you would be so early; **es ist zu ~, daß ...** it may be supposed that ..., we may assume or presume that ...; **Wissenschaftler ~ Leben auf der Venus** scientists suspect that there is life on Venus; **die Entwicklung läßt ~, daß ...** developments lead one to assume that or give rise to the suspicion or supposition that ...

vermutlich 1 adj attr presumable; Täter suspected. 2 adv presumably.

Vermutung f (Annahme) supposition, assumption; (Mutmaßung) conjecture; (Verdacht) suspicion. **die ~ liegt nahe, daß ...** there are grounds for the supposition or assumption that ...; **das sind alles nur ~en** that is pure conjecture, those are purely suppositions or assumptions; **wir sind nur auf ~en angewiesen** we have to rely on suppositions or assumptions or guesswork; **meine ~en waren doch richtig** my guess or suspicion was right.

vernachlässigen* 1 vt to neglect; (Schicksal) jdn to be unkind or harsh to. **Journalisten, die die Sprache ~** journalists who write bad or sloppy German etc; **das können wir ~** (nicht berücksichtigen) we can ignore that. 2 vr to neglect oneself or one's appearance.

Vernachlässigung f siehe vt neglect; (Nichtberücksichtigung) ignoring, disregarding.

vernageln* vt to nail up. **etw mit Brettern ~** to board sth up.

vernagelt adj (fig inf) thick no adv (inf), wooden-headed (inf); (engstirnig) small-minded. **ich war wie ~** I couldn't think straight; **der Prüfling sah mich ~ an** the examinee looked at me blankly or stupidly.

vernähen* vt to neaten; Wunde to stitch (up); (verbrauchen) to use up.

vernarben* vi aux sein to heal or close (up).

Vernarbung f healing. **leichte Massagen sorgen für schöne ~en** gentle massages help the skin to scar over nicely; **eine gute ~** a good heal.

vernarren* vr (inf) **sich in jdn/etw ~** to fall for sb/sth, to be smitten by sb/sth; **in jdn/etw vernarrt sein** to be crazy (inf) or nuts (sl) about sb/sth, to be infatuated with sb.

Vernarrtheit f, no pl infatuation (in +acc with).

vernaschen* vt Süßigkeiten to eat up; Geld to spend on sweets; (inf) Mädchen, Mann to make it with (inf).

vernebeln* vt (Mil) to cover with a smoke screen; (fig) Tatsachen to obscure, to obfuscate (form); (inf) Zimmer to fug up. **die Dinge ~** to confuse the issue, to muddy the waters.

Verneb(e)lung f, no pl (Mil) screening; (fig: von Tatsachen) obscuring.

vernehmbar adj (a) (hörbar) audible, perceptible. **(b)** (vernehmungsfähig) able to be questioned.

vernehmen* vt irreg **(a)** (hören) to hear.
(b) (erfahren) to hear, to learn. **das Presseamt hat ~ lassen, daß ...** the press agency has given to understand that ...; **er hat über seine Pläne nichts ~ lassen** he has let nothing be known about his plans.
(c) (Jur) Zeugen, Angeklagte to examine; (Polizei) to question. **zu diesem Fall wurden fünfzig Zeugen vernommen** fifty witnesses were heard in connection with this case.

Vernehmen nt: **dem ~ nach** from what I/we etc hear; **gutem/sicherem ~ nach** according to well-informed/reliable sources.

vernehmlich adj clear, audible. **es tönte laut und ~ ...** it sounded loud and clear ..., we heard loud and clear ...; **sich ~ räuspern** to clear one's throat audibly or loudly.

Vernehmung f (Jur: von Zeugen, Angeklagten) examination; (durch Polizei) questioning.

Vernehmungs-: **~beamte(r)** m police interrogator; **v~fähig** adj able to be examined/questioned.

verneigen* vr to bow. **sich vor jdm/etw ~** (lit) to bow to sb/sth; (fig) to bow down before sb/sth.

Verneigung f bow, obeisance (form) (vor +dat before). **eine ~ machen** to bow.

verneinen* vti Frage to answer in the negative; (leugnen) Tatsache, Existenz Gottes etc to deny; These, Argument to dispute; (Gram, Logik) to negate. **die verneinte Form** the negative (form); **eine Seite seines Wesens, die stets verneint** a side of his nature that always denies (liter) or that is always negative.

verneinend adj (auch Gram) negative. **er schüttelte ~ den Kopf** he shook his head.

Verneinung f (Leugnung) denial; (von These etc) disputing; (Gram, Philos) negation; (verneinte Form) negative. **die ~ meiner Frage** the negative answer to my question.

vernichten* vt (lit, fig) to destroy; Schädlinge, Menschheit auch to exterminate; Menschheit, Feind auch to annihilate.

vernichtend adj devastating; Blick auch withering; Niederlage crushing. **~ über jdn urteilen** to make a devastating appraisal of sb; **jdn ~ schlagen** (Mil) to destroy sb utterly; (Sport) to beat sb hollow.

Vernichtung f siehe vt destruction; extermination; annihilation.

Vernichtungs-: **~krieg** m war of extermination; **~lager** nt extermination camp; **~mittel** nt insecticide; (Unkraut~) weedkiller; **~schlag** m devastating blow; **das war der ~schlag für die Regierung** that was the final blow for the government; **zum ~schlag ausholen** (Mil, fig) to prepare to deliver the final blow; **~waffe** f destructive or doomsday weapon.

vernickeln* vt to nickel-plate.

Vernickelung f, no pl nickel plating no pl.

verniedlichen* vt to trivialize.

vernieten* vt to rivet.

Vernietung f riveting.

Vernissage [vɛrnɪˈsaːʒə] f -, -n **(a)** (von Gemälde) varnishing. **(b)** (Eröffnung) opening day.

Vernunft f -, no pl reason (auch Philos), good sense. **zur ~ kommen** to come to one's senses; **~ annehmen** to see reason; **nimm doch ~ an!** why don't you see reason?; **jdm ~ predigen** to reason with sb; **gegen alle (Regeln der) ~** against all (the laws of) reason; **~ walten lassen** (geh) to let reason prevail; **~ beweisen** to show (good) sense or common sense; **etw mit/ohne ~ tun** to do sth sensibly/foolishly; **etw mit ~ essen/trinken** to eat/drink sth with appreciation; **Kinder zur ~ erziehen** to bring children up to be sensible; siehe **bringen**.

Vernunft-: **v~begabt** adj rational, endowed with reason; **~begriff** m concept of reason; **~ehe** f (lit, fig) marriage of convenience; **v~geleitet** adj rational; **v~gemäß** rationally, from a rational point of view; **v~glaube(n)** m rationalism; **~gründe** pl rational grounds pl; **~heirat** f marriage of convenience.

vernünftig 1 adj sensible; (logisch denkend) rational; (inf) (ordentlich, anständig) decent; (annehmbar) reasonable. **sei doch ~!** be sensible or reasonable!; **ich kann keinen ~en Gedanken fassen** I can't think properly.
2 adv siehe adj sensibly; rationally; decently; reasonably; (tüchtig) properly (inf). **~ reden** (inf) to speak properly; **er kann ganz ~ kochen** (inf) he can cook reasonably well.

vernünftigerweise adv etw **~ tun** to have the (good) sense to do sth; **du solltest dich ~ ins Bett legen** you should be sensible and go to bed.

Vernünftigkeit f sensibleness; (von Mensch auch) sense.

Vernunft-: **v~los** adj irrational; **~mensch** m rational person; **v~widrig** adj irrational.

veröden* 1 vt (Med) Krampfadern to sclerose. 2 vi aux sein to become desolate; (sich entvölkern auch) to become deserted; (fig: geistig ~) to become stultified.

Verödung f (a) (von Landschaft) desolation; (Entvölkerung) depopulation; (fig) stultification. **(b)** (Med: von Krampfadern) sclerosis.

veröffentlichen* vti to publish.

Veröffentlichung f publication.

verordnen* vt **(a)** to prescribe, to order; Medikament to prescribe (jdm etw sth for sb). **(b)** (old: verfügen) to decree, to ordain.

Verordnung f **(a)** (Med) prescription. **nach ~ des Arztes einzunehmen** to be taken as directed by the doctor. **(b)** (form: Verfügung) decree, ordinance.

verpachten* vt to lease, to rent out (an +acc to).

Verpächter m -s, - lessor.

Verpachtung f lease.

verpacken* vt to pack; (verbrauchergerecht) (fig) Gedanken etc to package; (einwickeln) to wrap.

Verpackung f siehe vt packing; packaging; wrapping.

Verpackungsgewicht nt weight of packaging, tare (weight).

verpäppeln* vt (inf) to mollycoddle (inf), to pamper (inf).

verpaschen* vt (Aus) to sell (off), to flog (Brit inf).

verpassen* vt **(a)** (versäumen) to miss; Gelegenheit auch to waste; siehe **Anschluß**.
(b) (inf: zuteilen) jdm etw **~** to give sb sth; (aufzwingen) to make sb have sth; jdm eine oder eine Ohrfeige/eine Tracht Prügel **~** to clout sb one (inf)/give sb a good hiding (inf); jdm einen Denkzettel **~** to give sb something to think about (inf).

verpatzen* vt (inf) to spoil; Vereinbarung auch to mess up (inf); (Mensch) Vortrag auch, Examen to make a mess of. **sich** (dat) etw **~** to spoil sth/mess sth up (inf)/make a mess of sth.

verpennen* *(inf)* **1** *vt* (*verpassen*) *Termin, Zeit* to miss by oversleeping; (*schlafend verbringen*) *Tag, Morgen etc* to sleep through; *Leben* to sleep away; (*fig: nicht bemerken*) to sleep through. **2** *vir* to oversleep.

verpennt *adj (inf)* sleepy; (*trottelig: Mensch*) dozy. **ein ~er Typ** (*Vielschläfer*) a sleepy-head *(inf)*; (*Trottel*) a dummy *(inf)*.

verpesten* *vt* to pollute, to contaminate. **die Luft im Büro ~** *(inf)* to stink out the office.

Verpestung *f* pollution, contamination.

verpetzen* *vt (inf)* to tell or sneak on *(inf)* (*bei* to).

verpfänden* *vt* to pawn, to (put in) hock *(inf)*; (*Jur*) to mortgage. (**jdm**) **sein Wort ~** (*obs*) to pledge one's word (to sb).

Verpfändung *f* pawning; (*Jur*) mortgage. **etw zur ~ ins Leihhaus bringen** to take sth to be pawned (in a pawnshop), to put sth in pawn or hock *(inf)*.

verpfeifen* *vt irreg (inf)* to grass on (*bei* to) *(inf)*.

verpflanzen* *vt* (*Bot, Med, fig*) to transplant; *Topfpflanzen* to repot; *Haut* to graft.

Verpflanzung *f siehe vt* transplantation; repotting; grafting; (*Med*) transplant.

verpflegen* **1** *vt* to feed; (*Mil*) *Heer auch* to ration. **2** *vr* **sich** (*selbst*) **~** to feed oneself; (*selbst kochen*) to cook for oneself.

Verpflegung *f* (a) (*das Verpflegen*) catering; (*Mil*) rationing. **die ~ von 4 Leuten** feeding 4 people, catering for 4 people. (b) (*Essen*) food; (*Mil*) rations *pl*, provisions *pl*. **mit voller ~** including food; (*mit Vollpension*) with full board.

Verpflegungskosten *pl* cost of food *sing*.

verpflichten* **1** *vt* (a) (*moralische Pflicht auferlegen*) to oblige, to place under an obligation. **verpflichtet sein, etw zu tun, zu etw verpflichtet sein** to be obliged to do sth; **sich zu etw pflichtet fühlen, etw zu tun, sich zu etw verpflichtet fühlen** to feel obliged to do sth; **jdm verpflichtet sein** to be under an obligation to sb; **sich jdm verpflichtet fühlen** to feel under an obligation to sb. (b) (*binden*) to commit; (*vertraglich, durch Eid, durch Handschlag etc*) to bind. **verpflichtet sein, etw zu tun** to be committed to doing sth; **jdn auf die Verfassung ~** to make sb swear to uphold the constitution; **auf die Verfassung verpflichtet werden** to be sworn to uphold the constitution; **~d** *Zusage, Unterschrift, Versprechen* binding. (c) (*einstellen*) to engage; *Sportler* to sign on; (*Mil*) to enlist.
2 *vi* (*moralische Pflicht darstellen*) to carry an obligation (*zu etw* to do sth); (*bindend sein*) to be binding. **das verpflichtet zu nichts** there is no obligation involved; **siehe Adel**.
3 *vr* (*moralisch*) to make a commitment; (*eidlich, vertraglich*) to commit oneself; (*Mil*) to enlist, to sign up. **sich zu etw ~** to undertake to do sth; (*vertraglich, eidlich*) to commit oneself to doing sth.

Verpflichtung *f* (a) (*das Verpflichten*) obligation (*zu etw* to do sth); (*Pflicht auch, finanzielle ~*) commitment (*zu etw* to do sth); (*Aufgabe*) duty. **dienstliche ~en** official duties; **~en gegen jdn haben** to be in sb's debt (*auch finanziell*); **~en nachkommen** to fulfil one's obligations. (b) (*Einstellung*) engaging; (*von Sportlern*) signing on; (*Mil*) enlistment. (c) (*das Sich-Verpflichten*) (*für, auf* +acc for) signing on; (*Mil*) signing up. **ich habe meine ~ auf sechs Monate bereut** I regret having signed on or committed myself/signed up for six months.

verpfuschen* *vt (inf)* *Arbeit etc* to bungle; *Leben, Erziehung, Urlaub etc* to muck up *(inf)*, to ruin; *Mensch* to ruin; *Kind* to spoil. **jdm/sich den Abend etc ~** to ruin sb's/one's evening etc.

verpiepelt, verpimpelt *adj (dial)* soft *(inf)*. **tu nicht so ~** don't act or be so soft *(inf)*.

verplanen* **1** *vt Zeit* to book up; *Geld* to budget. **jdn ~** *(inf)* to fill up all sb's spare time (for him/her). **2** *vr* to plan badly or wrongly; (*falsch berechnen*) to miscalculate.

verplappern* *vr (inf)* to open one's mouth too wide *(inf)*.

verplaudern* **1** *vt Zeit* to talk or chat away. **2** *vr (inf)* to forget the time talking or chatting.

verplauschen* *vr (Aus)* to forget the time chatting or talking.

verplempern* **1** *vt (inf) Zeit* to waste, to fritter away; *Geld auch* to squander. **2** *vr* to waste oneself.

verplomben* *vt* to seal.

verpönt *adj* frowned (up)on (*bei* by).

verpoppen* *vt* to jazz up.

verprassen* *vt* to blow *(inf)* (*für* on). **etw sinnlos ~** to fritter sth away.

verprellen* *vt* to put off, to intimidate.

verproviantieren* **1** *vt* to supply with food. **2** *vr* to get a food supply.

verprügeln* *vt* to thrash, to beat up.

verpuffen* *vi aux sein* to (go) pop; (*fig*) to fall flat.

verpulvern* *vt (inf)* to fritter away.

verpumpen* *vt (inf)* to lend out, to loan (*an* +acc to).

verpuppen* *vr* to pupate.

Verpuppung *f* pupation.

verpusten* *vir (inf)* to get one's breath back.

Verputz *m* -es, *no pl* plaster, plasterwork; (*Rauhputz*) roughcast; (*hum: Make-up*) warpaint. **über/unter ~** on top of/under plaster.

verputzen* *vt* (a) *Gebäude, Wand* to plaster; (*mit Rauhputz*) to roughcast. (b) (*inf: aufessen*) to polish off *(inf)*, to demolish *(inf)*. **ich kann ihn/das nicht ~** *(inf)* I can't stomach him/it.

verqualmen* *vt Zimmer* to fill with smoke; *(inf) Zigaretten etc* to smoke; *Geld* to spend on smoking. **ein verqualmtes Zimmer** a room full of smoke.

verquält *adj* careworn, troubled.

verquatschen* *(inf)* **1** *vt* to chat away. **2** *vr* (a) (*lange plaudern*) to forget the time chatting. (b) (*Geheimnis aus-*

plaudern) to open one's mouth too wide *(inf)*.

verquellen* *vi irreg aux sein* to swell; (*Holz auch*) to warp. **verquollene Augen** puffy or swollen eyes.

verquer *adv (inf)* (*jdm*) **~ gehen** (*schiefgehen*) to go wrong (for sb); **das kommt mir jetzt etwas ~** that could have come at a better time; **etwas geht mir ~** that goes against the grain.

verquicken* **1** *vt* (a) (*Chem*) to amalgamate. (b) (*fig*) to bring together, to combine; (*vermischen*) to mix. **eng miteinander verquickt** closely related. **2** *vr* **sich (miteinander) ~** to combine.

Verquickung *f* (a) amalgamation. (b) (*fig*) combination.

verquirlen* *vt* to whisk.

verrammeln* *vt* to barricade.

verramschen* *vt (Comm)* to sell off cheap; (*inf auch*) to flog (*Brit inf*).

Verrat *m* -(e)s, *no pl* betrayal (*an* +dat of); (*Jur*) treason (*an* +dat against). **~ an jdm üben** to betray sb.

verraten *pret* **verriet**, *ptp* **verraten** **1** *vt* (a) *Geheimnis, Absicht, jdn* to betray, to give away; (*bekanntgeben, ausplaudern*) to tell; (*fig: erkennen lassen*) to reveal, to show. **nichts ~!** don't say a word!; **er hat es ~** he let it out. (b) *Freunde, Vaterland, gute Sache etc* to betray (*an* +acc to). **~ und verkauft** *(inf)* well and truly sunk *(inf)*.
2 *vr* to give oneself away, to betray oneself.

Verräter(in *f)* *m* -s, - traitor (+gen to).

verräterisch *adj* treacherous, perfidious (*liter*); (*Jur*) treasonable; (*verdächtig*) *Blick, Lächeln etc* telling, telltale *attr*.

verrauchen* **1** *vi aux sein* (*fig: Zorn*) to blow over, to subside. **2** *vt Tabak, Zigarren etc* to smoke; *Geld* to spend on smoking.

verräuchern* *vt* to fill with smoke.

verraucht *adj* smoky, filled with smoke.

verräumen* *vt (S Ger, Aus, Sw)* to put away somewhere.

verrauschen* *vi aux sein* (*fig*) to die or fade away.

verrechnen* **1** *vt* (*begleichen*) to settle; *Scheck* to clear; *Lieferung, Leistungen, Guthaben* to credit/debit to an account; (*auszahlen*) to pay out; *Gutschein* to redeem. **die Spesen von der Firma ~ lassen** to have one's expenses paid by the firm; **etw mit etw ~** (*zusammen abrechnen*) to settle sth (together) with sth; (*gegeneinander aufrechnen*) to balance sth with sth, to offset sth against sth.
2 *vr* to miscalculate; (*Rechenfehler machen*) to make a mistake/mistakes; (*inf: sich täuschen*) to be mistaken. **sich um eine Mark ~** to be out by one mark.

Verrechnung *f siehe vt* settlement; clearing; crediting/debiting to an account; paying out; redemption. „nur zur ~" "A/C payee only".

Verrechnungs-: **~einheit** *f* clearing unit; **~preise** *pl* (*Comm*) internal prices; **~scheck** *m* crossed (*Brit*) or non-negotiable cheque; voucher check (*US*); **~stelle** *f* clearing house.

verrecken* *vi aux sein (vulg)* to die; (*elend sterben*) to die a wretched death. **er ist elend verreckt** he died like a dog *(inf)*; **soll er doch ~!** let him bloody well die!; **jetzt ist der Alte endlich verreckt** he's finally kicked the bucket *(sl)* or snuffed it *(sl)*; **zu Tausenden ~** to perish in their thousands; **es ist zum V~** *(sl)* it's damn awful *(inf)*, it's bloody terrible (*Brit sl*); **etw nicht ums V~ oder ums V~ nicht tun** *(sl)* to damn well *(inf)* or bloody well (*Brit sl*) refuse to do sth.

verregnen **1** *vi aux sein* to be spoilt or spoiled or ruined by rain. **2** *vt impers* **es hat den ganzen Urlaub verregnet** the whole holiday was spoilt etc by rain.

verregnet *adj* rainy, wet.

verreiben* *vt irreg* to rub (*auf* +dat into); *Salbe* to massage (*auf* +dat into).

verreisen* *vi aux sein* to go away (on a trip or journey). **er ist verreist/geschäftlich verreist** he's away, he's out of town/away on business; **wohin ~ Sie in diesem Jahr?** where are you going (on holiday) this year?; **mit dem Auto/der Bahn ~** to go on a car/train journey; (*in Urlaub*) to go on holiday by car/train.

verreißen* *vt irreg* (a) (*kritisieren*) to tear to pieces. (b) (*dial*) **siehe zerreißen.** (c) (*dial*) *Schuß, Lenkrad* to jerk; *Wagen* to make swerve.

verrenken* **1** *vt* to dislocate, to put out of joint; *Hals* to crick. **sich** (*dat*) **die Zunge ~** to twist one's tongue; **lieber sich den Bauch or Magen ~, als dem Wirt was schenken** (*prov*) waste not, want not (*prov*); **siehe Hals¹**. **2** *vr* to contort oneself.

Verrenkung *f* (a) contortion. **~en machen** to contort oneself. (b) (*Med: das Verrenken*) dislocation.

verrennen* *vr irreg* to get carried away. **sich in etw** (*acc*) **~** to get stuck on sth.

verrichten* *vt Arbeit* to perform, to carry out; *Andacht* to perform; *Gebet* to say; **siehe Geschäft, Notdurft.**

Verrichtung *f siehe vt* performing, carrying out; performing; saying. **alltägliche/häusliche ~en** routine or daily/domestic or household tasks.

verriegeln* *vt* to bolt.

verriet *pret* of **verraten**.

verringern* **1** *vt* to reduce; *Leistungen* to make deteriorate. **2** *vr* to decrease; (*Qualität auch, Leistungen*) to deteriorate; (*Abstand, Vorsprung auch*) to lessen, to diminish.

Verringerung *f siehe vb* reduction; decrease; deterioration; lessening, diminution.

verrinnen* *vi irreg aux sein* (*Wasser*) to trickle away (*in* +dat into); (*Zeit*) to elapse.

Verriß *m* -sses, -sse slating review.

verrohen* **1** *vt* to brutalize. **2** *vi aux sein* (*Mensch, Gesellschaft*) to become brutalized; (*Sitten*) to coarsen.

Verrohung *f* brutalization.

verrosten* *vi aux sein* to rust; (*fig: steif werden*) to get rusty. **verrostet** rusty.

verrotten* *vi aux sein* to rot; (*sich organisch zersetzen*) to decompose.

verrucht *adj* despicable, loathsome; *Tat auch* heinous; (*verrufen*) disreputable.

Verruchtheit *f, no pl siehe adj*; despicable nature, loathsomeness; disreputableness.

verrücken* *vt* to move, to disarrange.

verrückt *adj* (a) (*geisteskrank*) mad, insane.
  (b) (*inf*) crazy, mad. ~ **auf** (+*acc*) *or* **nach** crazy *or* mad about (*inf*); **wie** ~ like mad *or* crazy (*inf*); **loads of people came** (*inf*); **so etwas V~es!** what a crazy idea!; **jdn** ~ **machen** to drive sb crazy *or* mad *or* wild; ~ **werden** to go crazy; **bei dem Lärm kann man ja** ~ **werden** this noise is enough to drive you round the bend (*inf*); **ich werd'** ~, (**ich zieh aufs Land**)! (well,) I'll be blowed! (*inf*); **du bist wohl** ~! you must be crazy *or* mad!; ~ **spielen** to play up.

Verrückte(r) *mf decl as adj* (*inf*) lunatic.

Verrücktheit *f* (*inf*) madness, craziness; (*Handlung*) mad *or* crazy thing.

Verrücktwerden *nt*: **zum** ~ enough to drive one mad *or* crazy *or* round the bend (*inf*) *or* up the wall (*inf*).

Verruf *m* -(*e*)**s**, *no pl* **in** ~ **kommen** *or* **geraten** to fall into disrepute; **jdn/etw in** ~ **bringen** to bring sb/sth into disrepute.

verrufen *adj* disreputable.

verrühren* *vt* to mix, to stir.

verrußen* *vi aux sein* to get *or* become sooty.

verrutschen* *vi aux sein* to slip.

Vers [fɛrs] *m* -**es**, -**e** verse (*auch Bibl*); (*Zeile*) line. **etw in** ~**e bringen** *or* **setzen** to put sth into verse; ~**e machen** *or* **schmieden** (*inf*) to make up poems; **ich kann mir keinen** ~ **darauf machen** (*fig*) there's no rhyme or reason in it.

versachlichen* *vt* to objectify.

Versachlichung *f* objectification.

versacken* *vi aux sein* **(a)** (*lit*) to sink, to become submerged. **(b)** (*fig inf*) (*nicht wegkommen*) to stay on; (*herunterkommen*) to go downhill.

versagen* **1** *vt* **jdm/sich etw** ~ to deny sb/oneself sth; (*verweigern*) to refuse sb sth; **ich kann es mir nicht** ~, **eine Bemerkung zu machen** I can't refrain from making a comment; **sich jdm** ~ (*geh*) to refuse to give oneself to sb; **etw bleibt** *or* **ist jdm versagt** sth is denied sb, sb is denied sth; *siehe Dienst*.
  2 *vi* to fail; (*Mensch: im Leben auch*) to be a failure; (*Gewehr*) to fail; to function; (*Maschine auch*) to break down. **die Beine/Nerven etc versagten ihm** his legs/nerves etc gave way; **da versagt diese Methode** this method doesn't work there.

Versagen *nt* -**s**, *no pl* failure; (*von Maschine*) breakdown. **menschliches** ~ human error.

Versager *m* -**s**, - failure, flop (*inf*); (*Blindgänger, Sprengladung*) dud. **das Auto hat die Fahrt ohne** ~ **überstanden** (*inf*) the car made the journey without breaking down.

Versagung *f* denial; (*Entbehrung*) privation.

Versailler Vertrag [vɛr'zai̯ɐ] *m* Treaty of Versailles.

versalzen* *vt* to put too much salt in/on, to oversalt; (*inf: verderben*) to spoil; *siehe Suppe*.

versammeln* **1** *vt* to assemble (*auch Mil*), to gather together; **Truppen** *auch* to rally, to muster. **Leute um sich** ~ to gather people around *or* about one; **vor versammelter Mannschaft** (*inf*) in front of *or* before the assembled company.
  2 *vr* to assemble; (*Parlament*) to sit; (*Ausschuß, Verein, Mitglieder*) to meet; (*Tagung*) to convene.

versammelt *adj* (*Reitsport*) collected.

Versammlung *f* **(a)** (*Veranstaltung*) meeting; (*versammelte Menschen*) assembly. **verfassunggebende** ~ legislative assembly. **(b)** *siehe vt* assembly, gathering (together); rallying, mustering. **(c)** *siehe vr* assembly; sitting; meeting; convening. **(d)** (*Reitsport*) collection.

Versammlungs-: ~**freiheit** *f* freedom of assembly; ~**lokal** *nt* meeting place; ~**raum** *m* (*in Hotel etc*) conference room; (*form: allgemein*) assembly room; ~**recht** *nt* right of assembly; ~**verbot** *nt* prohibition of assembly.

Versand *m* -(*e*)**s**, *no pl* **(a)** (*das Versenden*) dispatch; (*das Vertreiben*) distribution. **der** ~ **per Land/Schiene** shipment by land/rail; **alleiniger** ~ sole distributor. **(b)** (*Abteilung*) dispatch department. **(c)** (*inf*: ~*kaufhaus*) mail order firm.

Versand-: ~**abteilung** *f* dispatch department; ~**artikel** *m* article for dispatch; ~**bahnhof** *m* dispatch station; ~**bereit** *adj* ready for dispatch; ~**buchhandel** *m* mail order book business.

versanden* *vi aux sein* to silt (up); (*fig*) to peter out, to fizzle out (*inf*).

Versand-: **v~fertig** *adj siehe* **v~bereit**; ~**geschäft** *nt* **(a)** mail order firm; **(b)** *siehe* ~**handel**; ~**gut** *nt* goods *pl* for dispatch; ~**handel** *m* mail order business; ~**haus** *nt* mail order firm *or* house; ~**kosten** *pl* transport(ation) costs *pl*; ~**papiere** *pl* transport(ation) documents *pl*.

Versandung *f* silting (up); (*fig*) petering out, fizzling out (*inf*).

Versand-: ~**unternehmen** *nt* mail order business; ~**weg** *m* **auf dem** ~**weg** by mail order.

Versatz *m* -**es**, *no pl* **(a)** (*das Versetzen*) pawning. **(b)** (*Min*) packing, stowing.

Versatz-: ~**amt** *nt* (*dial*) pawnshop; ~**stück** *nt* **(a)** (*Theat*) set piece; **(b)** (*fig*) setting, background; **(c)** (*Aus: Pfandstück*) pledge.

versaubeuteln* *vt* (*inf*) **(a)** (*verschlampen*) to go and lose (*inf*). **(b)** (*verderben*) to mess up (*inf*).

versauen* *vt* (*sl*) to mess up (*inf*).

versauern* (*inf*) **1** *vi aux sein* to stagnate. **eine versauerte alte Jungfer** an embittered old spinster. **2** *vt* **jdm etw** ~ to mess sth up (*inf*) *or* to ruin sth (for sb).

versaufen* *irreg* (*inf*) **1** *vt* **Geld** to spend on booze (*inf*). **seinen Verstand** ~ to drink oneself silly; *siehe Fell*. **2** *vi aux sein* (*dial*) **(a)** (*ertrinken*) to drown. **(b)** (*Motor*) to flood.

versäumen* **1** *vt* to miss; **Zeit** to lose; **Pflicht** to neglect; (*Sw:*

---

aufhalten) **jdn** to delay, to hold up. (**es**) ~, **etw zu tun** to fail to do sth; **nichts** ~, **um jdn glücklich zu machen** to do everything to make sb happy; **das Versäumte** what one has missed; **die versäumte Zeit aufholen** to make up for lost time.
  2 *vr sich bei jdm* ~ to stay too long at sb's house; **wir haben uns in dem Geschäft/bei dieser Arbeit versäumt** we spent too much time in that shop/on this piece of work.

Versäumnis *nt* (*Fehler, Nachlässigkeit*) failing; (*Unterlassung*) omission; (*versäumte Zeit, Sch*) absence (*gen* from); (*Jur*) default (*gen* in). **bei** ~ **rechtzeitiger Bezahlung** failing punctual payment.

Versäumnisurteil *nt* (*Jur*) judgement by default.

Versbau *m* versification, metrical structure.

verschachern* *vt* to sell off.

verschachtelt *adj* **Satz** encapsulated, complex. **ineinander** ~ interlocking.

verschaffen **1** *vt* **jdm etw** ~ *Geld, Kapital, Arbeit, Stelle, Alibi* to provide *or* supply sb with sth *or* sth for sb; *Arbeit, Stelle auch* to find sth for sb; *Erleichterung, Genugtuung, Vergnügen* to give sb sth; *Ansehen, Respekt* to earn sb sth; *siehe Ehre*.
  2 *vr sich* (*dat*) **etw** ~ to obtain sth; *Kenntnisse* to acquire sth; *Ansehen, Vorteil* to gain sth; *Ruhe, Respekt* to get sth; **sich mit Gewalt Zutritt** ~ to force an entry *or* one's way in; **ich muß mir darüber Gewißheit/Klarheit** ~ I must be certain about it/I must clarify the matter.

verschalen* **1** *vt* **Wand** to panel; **Heizung etc** to box in, to encase; (*für Beton*) to build a framework *or* mould for. **2** *vi* (*für Beton*) to build a framework *or* mould.

Verschalung *f siehe vb* panelling; casing; building a framework *or* mould; (*Bretter*) framework, mould.

verschämt *adj* coy.

Verschämtheit *f* coyness.

verschandeln* *vt* to ruin. **jdm/sich etw** ~ to ruin sth for sb/oneself.

Verschand(e)lung *f* ruining.

verschanzen* **1** *vt* (*Mil*) to fortify. **2** *vr* (*Mil, fig*) to entrench oneself (*hinter* +*dat* behind); (*sich verbarrikadieren*) to barricade oneself in (*in etw* (*dat*) sth); (*Deckung suchen*) to take cover (*hinter* +*dat* behind).

Verschanzung *f* **(a)** *siehe vb* fortification; entrenchment; barricading; taking cover. **(b)** (*Mil: Befestigung*) fortification.

verschärfen* **1** *vt* (*erhöhen*) *Tempo, Aufmerksamkeit* to increase; *Gegensätze* to intensify; (*verschlimmern*) *Lage* to aggravate; *Spannungen* to heighten; (*strenger machen*) *Kontrollen, Strafe, Gesetze, Maßnahmen, Prüfungen* to tighten.
  2 *vr siehe vt* to increase; to intensify; to become aggravated; to heighten, to mount; to become tighter.

verschärft **1** *adj siehe vb* increased; intensified; aggravated; heightened; tightened; *Arrest* close.
  2 *adv* (*intensiver*) more intensively; (*strenger*) more severely; *prüfen* more closely. ~ **aufpassen** to keep a closer watch; ~ **kontrollieren** to keep a tighter control; ~ **vorgehen** to take more stringent measures.

Verschärfung *f siehe vb* increase; intensification; aggravation; heightening; mounting; tightening.

verscharren* *vt* to bury.

verschätzen * *vr* to misjudge, to miscalculate (*in etw* (*dat*) sth). **sich um zwei Monate** ~ to be out by two months.

verschauen* *vr* (*Aus*) **(a)** to make a mistake. **(b)** **sich in jdn** ~ to fall for sb.

verschaukeln* *vt* (*inf*) to take for a ride (*inf*).

verscheiden* *vi irreg aux sein* (*geh*) to pass away, to expire.

verscheißen* *vt irreg* (*vulg*) to cover with shit (*vulg*); *siehe* **verschissen**.

verschenken* **1** *vt* (*lit, fig*) to give away. **sein Herz an jdn** ~ (*liter*) to give sb one's heart. **2** *vr sich an jdn* ~ to throw oneself away on sb.

verscherbeln* *vt* (*inf*) to get rid of.

verscherzen* *vr sich* (*dat*) **etw** ~ to lose *or* forfeit sth; **sich** (*dat*) **seine Chancen/jds Gunst** *or* **Wohlwollen** ~ to throw away one's chances/lose *or* forfeit sb's favour; **es sich** (*dat*) **mit jdm** ~ to spoil things (for oneself) with sb.

verscheuchen* *vt* to scare *or* frighten off *or* away; (*fig*) *Sorgen, Gedanken etc* to drive away.

verscheuern* *vt* (*inf*) to sell off.

verschicken* *vt* **(a)** (*versenden*) to send out *or* off. **(b)** (*zur Kur etc*) to send away. **(c)** (*deportieren*) to deport.

Verschickung *f siehe vt* sending out *or* off; sending away; deportation.

verschiebbar *adj* **Möbel etc** movable; **Regler, Spange, Teil** sliding. **leicht** ~**e Gegenstände** objects which are easy to move; **der Termin ist** ~ this appointment can be changed.

Verschiebe- (*Rail*): ~**bahnhof** *m* shunting yard; ~**gleis** *nt* shunting track; ~**lokomotive** *f* shunter.

verschieben* *irreg* **1** *vt* **(a)** (*verrücken*) to move, to shift; **Truppen** to displace; (*Rail*) **Eisenbahnwagen** to shunt; **Perspektive** to alter, to shift.
  (b) (*aufschieben*) to change; (*auf später*) to postpone, to put off, to defer (*um* for).
  (c) (*inf*) **Waren, Devisen** to traffic in.
  2 *vr* **(a)** to move out of place; (*fig: Perspektive, Schwerpunkt*) to alter, to shift.
  (b) (*zeitlich*) to be postponed *or* put off *or* deferred.
  (c) (*Med*) (*bei Knochenbruch*) to become displaced; (*Kniescheibe*) to slip.
  (d) (*Ling: Laute*) to shift.

Verschiebung *f siehe vt* **(a)** moving, shifting; displacement; shunting; alteration, shifting.
  (b) postponement, deferment.
  (c) trafficking.
  (d) (*Geol*) displacement, heave.

(e) (*Ling: von Lauten*) shift.

(f) (*Med*) (*bei Knochenbruch*) displacement; (*von Kniescheibe*) slip.

(g) (*Psych*) displacement.

verschieden 1 *adj* **(a)** (*unterschiedlich*) different; (*unähnlich auch*) dissimilar; *Meinungen etc auch* differing. **die ~sten Sorten** many different kinds, all sorts; **das ist ganz ~** (*wird ~ gehandhabt*) that varies, that just depends; **das sind doch V~e** they are different.

(b) *attr* (*mehrere, einige*) various, several. **da hört doch ~es auf!** (*inf*) that's a bit much (*inf*).

(c) (*substantivisch*) **~e** *pl* various *or* several people; **~es** several things; **V~es** different things; (*in Zeitungen, Listen*) miscellaneous.

2 *adv* differently. **die Häuser sind ~ lang/breit/hoch** the houses vary *or* are different in length/breadth/height.

verschieden|artig *adj* different; (*mannigfaltig*) various, diverse. **die ~sten Dinge** all sorts *or* manner of things.

Verschieden|artigkeit *f* different nature; (*Mannigfaltigkeit*) variety, diversity.

verschiedenemal *adv* several times.

verschiedenerlei *adj inv* **(a)** *attr* many different, various. **(b)** (*substantivisch*) many different things, various things.

verschieden-: **~farbig, ~färbig** (*Aus*) *adj* different-coloured; **die Kostüme waren ~farbig** the costumes were many different colours; **~gestaltig** *adj* various kinds of, of various kinds.

Verschiedenheit *f* difference (*gen* of, in); (*Unähnlichkeit*) dissimilarity; (*Vielfalt*) variety.

verschiedentlich *adv* (*mehrmals*) on several occasions, several times; (*vereinzelt*) occasionally.

verschießen* *irreg* **1** *vt* **(a)** *Munition* to use up; *Pfeile* to shoot off; (*inf*) *Fotos, Film auch* to take; *siehe* **Pulver. (b)** (*Sport*) to miss. **2** *vr* (*inf*) **sich in jdn ~** to fall for sb (*inf*); **in jdn verschossen sein** to be crazy about sb (*inf*). **3** *vi aux sein* (*Stoff, Farbe*) to fade.

verschiffen* *vt* to ship; *Sträfling* to transport.

Verschiffung *f* shipment; (*von Sträflingen*) transportation.

verschilfen* *vi aux sein* to become overgrown with reeds.

verschimmeln* *vi aux sein* (*Nahrungsmittel*) to go mouldy; (*Leder, Papier etc*) to become mildewed, to go mildewy. **verschimmelt** (*lit*) mouldy; mildewed, mildewy; (*fig*) *Ansichten etc* fusty.

Verschiß *m* **-sses, -sse** (*Univ sl*) **in ~ geraten** to fall out of favour; **jdn in ~ tun** to send sb to Coventry, to shun sb.

verschissen 1 *ptp of* **verscheißen. 2** *adj* (*vulg*) *Unterhose* shitty (*sl*). **du hast bei mir ~** (*sl*) I'm through with you (*inf*).

verschlacken* *vi aux sein* (*Ofen*) to become clogged (up) with slag; (*Med: Gewebe*) to become clogged.

Verschlackung *f siehe vi* slag(ging); clogging.

verschlafen* *irreg* **1** *vir* to oversleep. **2** *vt Termin* to miss by oversleeping; (*schlafend verbringen*) *Tag, Morgen* to sleep through; *Leben* to sleep away. **3** *adj* sleepy; (*trottelig*) *Mensch* dozy (*inf*). **~ sein** (*Vielschläfer sein*) to like one's sleep.

Verschlafenheit *f siehe adj* sleepiness; doziness (*inf*).

Verschlag *m* **-(e)s, -e** (*abgetrennter Raum*) partitioned area; (*Schuppen*) shed; (*grob gezimmert*) shack; (*esp für Kaninchen*) hutch; (*ans Haus angebaut*) lean-to; (*unter der Treppe*) gloryhole; (*elende Behausung*) hovel; (*Verpackung*) crate.

verschlagen¹* *vt irreg* **(a)** *etw mit Brettern ~* to board sth up; *etw mit Nägeln ~* to nail sth up.

(b) (*nehmen*) *Atem* to take away. **das hat mir die Sprache ~** it left me speechless.

(c) (*geraten lassen*) to bring. **auf eine einsame Insel ~ werden** to be cast up on a lonely island; **an einen Ort ~ werden** to end up somewhere.

(d) (*Sport*) *Ball* to mishit.

(e) (*verblättern*) *Seite, Stelle* to lose.

(f) (*dial: verprügeln*) to wallop (*inf*), to thrash.

verschlagen² *adj* **(a)** *Mensch, Blick, Tier etc* sly, artful. **(b)** (*dial: lauwarm*) tepid, lukewarm.

Verschlagenheit *f siehe adj* **(a)** slyness, artfulness. **(b)** (*dial*) tepidness.

verschlammen* *vi aux sein* to silt up.

verschlampen* (*inf*) **1** *vt* **(a)** (*verlieren*) to go and lose (*inf*). **(b)** (*verkommen lassen*) to spoil. **2** *vi aux sein* (*Mensch*) to go to seed (*inf*).

verschlechtern* **1** *vt* to make worse, to worsen; *Zustand, Lage auch* to aggravate; *Qualität* to impair; *Aussicht* to diminish, to decrease. **2** *vr* to get worse, to worsen, to deteriorate; (*Leistungen auch*) to decline. **sich finanziell/beruflich ~** to be worse off financially/to take a worse job.

Verschlechterung *f siehe vr* worsening, deterioration; decline. **eine finanzielle/berufliche ~** a financial setback/a retrograde step professionally.

verschleiern* **1** *vt* to veil; (*fig auch*) to disguise, to cover up; *Blick* to blur. **Nebel verschleiert die Aussicht/die Berge** the view is/the mountains are hidden by *or* under a veil of mist. **2** *vr* (*Frau*) to veil oneself; (*Himmel*) to become hazy; (*Blick*) to become blurred; (*träumerisch werden*) to become hazy; (*Stimme*) to become husky.

verschleiert *adj Frau* veiled; *Augen, Aussicht* misty; *Berge* misty, veiled in mist; *Stimme* husky; *Blick* blurred; (*träumerisch*) hazy; (*Phot*) foggy. **etw nur ~ sehen** to see sth only hazily.

Verschleierung *f siehe vt* veiling; disguising, covering up; blurring.

Verschleierungs-: **~taktik** *f* cover-up (*gen* by); **~versuch** *m* attempt at covering up.

verschleifen* *vt irreg* to slur.

Verschleifung *f* slurring.

---

verschleimen* **1** *vt* to block *or* congest with phlegm. **verschleimt sein** (*Patient*) to be congested with phlegm. **2** *vi aux sein* to become blocked *or* congested with phlegm.

Verschleimung *f* mucous congestion.

Verschleiß *m* **-es, -e** (*lit, fig*) wear and tear; (*Verbrauch*) consumption; (*Verluste*) loss. **ein ~ deiner Kräfte** a drain on your strength; **eingeplanter ~** built-in obsolescence; **ihr ~ an Männern** (*hum*) the rate she gets through men. **(b)** (*Aus: Kleinverkauf*) retail trade.

verschleißen *pret* **verschliß,** *ptp* **verschlissen 1** *vt* **(a)** to wear out; (*verbrauchen*) to use up. **(b)** (*Aus*) to retail. **2** *vi aux sein* to wear out; *siehe* **verschlissen. 3** *vr* to wear out; (*Menschen*) to wear oneself out.

Verschleißer(in *f*) *m* **-s, -** (*Aus*) retailer.

Verschleiß-: **~erscheinung** *f* sign of wear; **~prüfung** *f* wear test; **~teil** *nt* part subject to wear and tear.

verschleppen* *vt* **(a)** (*entführen*) *jdn* to abduct; *Kunstschätze etc* to carry off; (*inf*) *etw* to go off with. **(b)** (*verbreiten*) *Seuche* to spread, to carry. **(c)** (*hinauszögern*) *Prozeß, Verhandlung* to draw out, to protract; (*Pol*) *Gesetzesänderung etc* to delay; *Krankheit* to protract.

Verschleppte(r) *mf decl as adj* displaced person.

Verschleppung *f siehe vt* **(a)** abduction; carrying off. **(b)** spreading, carrying. **(c)** protraction; delay; protraction.

Verschleppungstaktik *f* delaying tactics *pl*.

verschleudern* *vt* (*Comm*) to dump; (*vergeuden*) *Vermögen, Geld* to squander.

verschließbar *adj Dosen, Gläser etc* closeable, sealable; *Tür, Schublade, Zimmer etc* lockable.

verschließen* *irreg* **1** *vt* **(a)** (*abschließen*) to lock (up); (*fig*) to close, to shut; (*versperren*) to bar; (*mit Riegel*) to bolt. **jdm die Tür zum Elternhaus ~** (*fig*) to turn sb away from home; **jdm etw ~** (*fig*) to deny sb sth; *siehe* **verschlossen.**

(b) (*wegschließen*) to lock up *or* away.

(c) (*zumachen*) to close; *Glas auch, Karton auch, Brief* to seal; (*mit Pfropfen*) *Flasche* to cork. **die Augen/Ohren/sein Herz (vor etw** *dat*) **~** to shut one's eyes/ears/heart (to sth); **seine Gedanken/seinen Kummer in sich** (*dat*) **~** to keep one's thoughts/one's worries to oneself.

2 *vr* (*Reize, Sprache, Möglichkeit*) to be closed (*dat* to); (*Mensch: reserviert sein*) to shut oneself off (*dat* from). **sich vor jdm ~** to shut oneself off from sb; **sich einer Sache** (*dat*) *or* **gegen etw ~** to close one's mind to sth; **ich kann mich der Tatsache nicht ~, daß ...** I can't close my eyes to the fact that ...

verschlimmbessern* *vt insep* (*hum*) to make worse.

Verschlimmbesserung *f* (*hum*) worsening.

verschlimmern* **1** *vt* to make worse, to aggravate; *Schmerzen auch* to increase. **2** *vr* to get worse, to worsen.

Verschlimmerung *f* worsening; (*von Schmerzen auch*) increase.

verschlingen* *irreg* **1** *vt* **(a)** to entwine, to intertwine. **er stand mit verschlungenen Armen da** he stood there with his arms folded; **ein verschlungener Pfad** a winding path.

(b) (*fressen, gierig essen*) to devour; (*auffressen auch*) to swallow up; (*fig: Welle, Dunkelheit*) to engulf; (*verbrauchen*) *Geld, Strom etc* to eat up, to consume; (*inf*) *Buch, jds Worte* to devour. **jdn mit den Augen** *or* **Blicken ~** to devour sb with one's eyes.

2 *vr* to become entwined *or* intertwined; (*zu einem Knoten etc*) to become entangled; (*Därme*) to become twisted.

Verschlingung *f* **(a)** (*von Fäden etc*) tangle; (*von Muster, Arabeske*) interlacing. **(b)** (*von Darm*) twisting.

verschliß *pret of* **verschleißen.**

verschlissen 1 *ptp of* **verschleißen. 2** *adj* worn (out); *Kleidung, Teppich, Material auch* threadbare.

verschlossen 1 *ptp of* **verschließen.**

2 *adj* closed; (*mit Schlüssel*) *Tür, Fach etc* locked; (*mit Riegel*) bolted; (*Dose auch, Briefumschlag*) sealed; (*fig*) (*unzugänglich*) reserved. **gut ~ aufbewahren** keep tightly closed; **etw bleibt jdm ~** sth is (a) closed (book) to sb; **ihr Wesen bleibt mir ~** she's a mystery to me; **hinter ~en Türen** behind closed doors; **wir standen vor ~er Tür** we were left standing on the doorstep.

Verschlossenheit *f* (*von Mensch*) reserve, reticence.

verschlucken* **1** *vt* to swallow; (*fig auch*) *Wörter, Silben, Buchstaben* to slur; *Geld* to consume; *Schall* to deaden; *siehe* **Erdboden. 2** *vr* to swallow the wrong way; (*fig*) to splutter.

verschludern* (*inf*) **1** *vt* to go and lose (*inf*). **2** *vi aux sein* to let oneself go.

Verschluß *m* **-sses, ¨sse (a)** (*Schloß*) lock; (*luft-, wasserdicht, für Zoll*) seal; (*Deckel, Klappe*) top, lid; (*Pfropfen, Stöpsel*) stopper; (*an Kleidung*) fastener; (*an Schmuck*) catch; (*an Tasche, Buch, Schuh*) clasp. **etw unter ~ halten** to keep sth under lock and key. **(b)** (*Phot*) shutter; (*an Waffe*) breechblock. **(c)** (*Med, Phon*) occlusion.

verschlüsseln* *vt* to (put into) code, to encode.

Verschlüsselung, Verschlüßlung *f* coding.

Verschluß-: **~laut** *m* (*Phon*) plosive; **~sache** *f* item of classified information; **~sachen** *pl* classified information *sing*.

verschmachten* *vi aux sein* to languish (*vor* +*dat* for). **(vor Durst/Hitze) ~** (*inf*) to be dying of thirst/heat (*inf*).

verschmähen* *vt* to spurn, to scorn; *Liebhaber* to spurn, to reject. **verschmähte Liebe** unrequited love; **einen Whisky verschmähe ich nie** I never say no to a whisky.

Verschmähung *f siehe vt* spurning, scorning; rejection.

verschmälern* **1** *vt* to make narrower. **2** *vr* to become narrower, to narrow.

verschmausen* *vt* (*inf*) to feast on.

verschmelzen* *irreg* **1** *vi aux sein* to melt together; (*Metalle*) to fuse; (*Farben*) to blend; (*Betriebe etc*) to merge; (*fig*) to blend (*zu* into). **2** *vt* **(a)** (*verbinden*) *Metalle* to fuse; *Farben* to

blend; *Betriebe, Firmen* to merge. **(b)** *Bruchflächen* to smooth, to round off. **(c)** *(fig)* to unify *(zu into)*.
Verschmelzung f **(a)** *(Verbindung)* fusion; *(von Reizen, Eindrücken)* blending; *(von Farben)* blending. **(b)** *(von Bruchflächen)* smoothing, rounding off. **(c)** *(fig)* *(von Völkern, Begriffen etc)* fusion. **(d)** *(Comm)* merger.
verschmerzen* *vt* to get over.
verschmieren* 1 *vt* **(a)** *(verstreichen)* *Salbe, Schmiere, Creme, Fett* to spread *(in + dat onto)*. **(b)** *(verputzen)* *Löcher* to fill in. **(c)** *(verwischen)* *Fenster, Gesicht* to smear; *Geschriebenes, Lippenstift, Schminke* to smudge. 2 *vi* to smudge.
verschmiert *adj* *Hände, Gesicht* smeary; *Schminke* smudged.
verschmitzt *adj* mischievous.
Verschmitztheit f, *no pl* mischievousness.
verschmutzen* 1 *vt* to dirty, to soil; *Luft, Wasser, Umwelt* to pollute; *Gewehr, Zündkerze* to foul; *Fahrbahn* to make muddy; *(Hund)* *Bürgersteig* to foul. 2 *vi aux sein* to get dirty; *(Luft, Wasser, Umwelt)* to become polluted.
verschmutzt *adj* dirty, soiled; *Luft etc* polluted. **stark ~** very dirty, badly soiled; „~e Fahrbahn" "mud on road".
Verschmutzung f **(a)** *no pl siehe vt* dirtying, soiling; pollution; fouling; making muddy; fouling. **(b)** *(das Verschmutztsein)* dirtiness *no pl*; *(von Luft etc)* pollution. **starke ~en auf der Autobahn** a great deal of mud or dirt on the motorway.
verschnappen* *vr* *(inf)* to open one's big mouth *(inf)*.
verschnaufen* *vir* *(inf)* to have a breather, to have a rest.
Verschnaufpause f breather.
verschneiden* *vt irreg* **(a)** *Wein, Rum, Essigsorten* to blend. **(b)** *(stutzen)* *Flügel* to clip; *Hecke auch* to cut. **(c)** *(falsch schneiden)* *Kleid, Stoff* to cut wrongly; *Haar* to cut badly. **(d)** *Tiere* to geld, to castrate.
verschneit *adj* snow-covered. **tief ~** thick with snow.
Verschnitt m **(a)** *(von Rum, Wein, Essig)* blend. **(b)** *(Abfall)* waste material, clippings *pl*.
verschnörkeln* *vt* to adorn with flourishes.
verschnörkelt *adj* ornate.
Verschnörkelung f **(a)** *(das Verschnörkeln)* embellishing (with flourishes). **(b)** *(Schnörkel)* flourish.
verschnupfen* *vt* *(inf)* to peeve *(inf)*.
verschnupft *adj* *(inf)* **(a)** *(erkältet)* *Mensch* with a cold; *Nase* bunged up *(inf)*. **(b)** *(usu pred: beleidigt)* peeved *(inf)*.
verschnüren* *vt* to tie up; *Schuhe auch* to lace.
Verschnürung f **(a)** *(das Verschnüren)* *siehe vt* tying (up); lacing. **(b)** *(Schnur)* string; *(Schnürband)* lace.
verschollen *adj* *Schiff, Flugzeug, Mensch etc* missing, lost without trace; *Literaturwerk* forgotten. **ein lange ~er Freund** a long-lost friend; **er ist ~** *(im Krieg)* he is missing, presumed dead; **V~e(r)** missing person; *(Jur)* person presumed to be dead.
verschonen* *vt* to spare *(jdn von etw sb sth)*; *(von Steuern auch)* to exempt. **verschone mich mit deinen Reden!** spare me your speeches; **verschone mich damit!** spare me that!; **von etw verschont bleiben** to escape sth.
verschöne(r)n* *vt* to improve (the appearance of); *Wohnung, Haus, Zimmer* to brighten (up).
Verschönerung, Verschönung f *siehe vt* improvement; brightening up.
Verschonung f sparing; *(von Steuern)* exemption.
verschorfen* *vi aux sein* to (form a) scab. **die verschorfte Wunde** the encrusted wound.
Verschorfung f encrustation, scabbing.
verschrammen* 1 *vt* to scratch. 2 *vi aux sein* to become or get scratched.
verschränken* *vt* to cross over; *Arme* to fold; *Beine* to cross; *Hände* to clasp; *Hölzer* to joggle; *(Stricken)* to cable. **verschränkter Reim** embracing rhyme.
Verschränkung f **(a)** *(das Verschränktsein)* fold. **(b)** *siehe vt* crossing over; folding; crossing; clasping; jogging; cabling.
verschrauben* *vt* to screw together.
verschrecken* *vt* to frighten or scare off or away.
verschreckt *adj* frightened, scared.
verschreiben* *irreg* 1 *vt* **(a)** *(verordnen)* to prescribe. **(b)** *(old: übereignen)* to make over, to transfer. **seine Seele dem Teufel ~** to sign away one's soul to the devil. **(c)** *Papier* to use up; *(rare)* *Wort* to write incorrectly. 2 *vr* **(a)** *(falsch schreiben)* to make a slip (of the pen). **(b)** **sich einer Sache** *(dat)* **~** to devote or dedicate oneself to sth; **sich dem Teufel ~** to sell oneself to the devil.
Verschreibung f **(a)** *(Verordnung)* prescription. **(b)** *(old: Übertragung)* making over, transference. **(c)** *(Schreibfehler)* mistake, error.
verschreibungspflichtig *adj* only available on prescription; ethical.
verschrie(e)n *adj* notorious.
verschroben *adj* eccentric, odd.
Verschrobenheit f, *no pl* eccentricity.
verschroten* *vt* to grind coarsely.
verschrotten* *vt* to scrap.
Verschrottung f scrapping. **etw zur ~ geben** to send sth to be scrapped.
verschrumpeln* *vi aux sein* to shrivel.
verschüchtern* *vt* to intimidate.
Verschüchterung f intimidation.
verschulden* 1 *vt* *(schuldhaft verursachen)* to be to blame for, to be responsible for; *Unfall, Unglück* to cause. 2 *vi aux sein (in Schulden geraten)* to get into debt. **immer mehr ~** to get deeper and deeper into debt; **verschuldet sein** to be in debt.
Verschulden nt *-s, no pl* fault. **durch eigenes ~** through one's own fault; **ohne sein/mein ~** through no fault of his (own)/of my own or of mine.
Verschuldung f **(a)** *(Schulden)* indebtedness. **(b)** *(schuld-*

hafte Verursachung) blame *(gen* for*)*. **bei eigener ~ eines Schadens** if one is (oneself) to blame for damage caused.
verschusseln* *vt* *(inf)* *(vermasseln)* to mess or muck up *(inf)*; *(vergessen)* to forget; *(verlegen)* to mislay, to lose.
verschusselt *adj siehe* **schusselig**.
verschütten* *vt* **(a)** *Flüssigkeit* to spill. **(b)** *(zuschütten)* *Brunnen, Flußarm* to fill in. **(c)** *(begraben)* **verschüttet werden** *(Mensch)* to be buried (alive); *(fig)* to be submerged.
verschüttet *adj* buried (alive); *(fig)* submerged.
Verschüttete(r) *mf decl as adj* buried man/woman *(in an accident)*.
verschüttgehen *vi sep irreg aux sein (inf)* to get lost.
verschwägert *adj* related (by marriage) *(mit* to*)*.
Verschwägerung f relationship by marriage *(mit* to*)*.
verschweigen* *vt irreg* *Tatsachen, Wahrheit etc* to hide, to conceal, to withhold *(jdm etw sth from sb)*. **ich habe nichts zu ~** I've nothing to hide.
Verschweigen nt *-s, no pl* concealment, hiding, withholding. **das ~ der Wahrheit** concealing or withholding the truth.
verschweißen* *vt* to weld (together).
verschwenden* *vt* to waste *(auf or an - acc, für on)*; *(leichtsinnig vertun)* *Geld* to squander.
Verschwender(in f*)* m *-s, -* spendthrift, squanderer.
verschwenderisch *adj* wasteful; *Leben* extravagant; *(üppig)* lavish, sumptuous; *Fülle* lavish. **mit etw ~ umgehen** to be lavish with sth.
Verschwendung f wastefulness. **~ von Geld/Zeit** waste of money/time.
Verschwendungs-: **~sucht** f, *no pl* extravagance; **v~süchtig** *adj* (wildly) extravagant.
verschwiegen 1 *ptp of* **verschweigen**. 2 *adj* *Mensch* discreet; *Ort* secluded; *siehe* **Grab**.
Verschwiegenheit f, *no pl (von Mensch)* discretion; *(von Ort)* seclusion. **zur ~ verpflichtet** bound to secrecy; *siehe* **Siegel**.
verschwiemelt *adj (N Ger inf) siehe* **verschwollen**.
verschwimmen* *vi irreg aux sein* to become blurred or indistinct. **es verschwamm ihr alles vor den Augen** everything went fuzzy or hazy; **ineinander ~** to melt into one another, to merge (into one another); *siehe* **verschwommen**.
verschwinden* *vi irreg aux sein* to disappear, to vanish. **verschwinde!** clear off! *(inf)*, away! *(liter)*; **etw ~ lassen** *(Zauberer)* to make sth disappear or vanish; *(verstecken)* to dispose of sth; *(stehlen)* to steal or filch sth; **etw in etw** *(dat)* **~ lassen** to slip sth into sth; **neben jdm/etw ~** to pale into insignificance beside sb/sth, to be eclipsed by sb/sth; *(in bezug auf Größe)* to look minute beside sb/sth; *(mal)* **~ müssen** *(euph inf)* to have to spend a penny *(inf)*.
Verschwinden nt *-s, no pl* disappearance.
verschwindend *adj* *Anzahl, Menge* insignificant. **~ wenig** very, very few; **~ klein** minute.
verschwistern* *vr (fig)* to form a close union; *(Städte)* to become twinned; *(liter: Seelen)* to become closely united.
verschwistert *adj* *(miteinander)* **~ sein** to be brother and sister, to be siblings *(Sociol, Med etc)*; *(Brüder)* to be brothers; *(Schwestern)* to be sisters; *(fig)* to be close; *(Städte)* to be twinned, to be twin towns; **~e Seelen** *(liter)* kindred spirits.
verschwitzen* *vt* **(a)** *Kleidung* to make sweaty. **(b)** *(fig inf)* to forget.
verschwitzt *adj* sweat-stained; *(feucht)* sweaty; *Mensch* sweaty.
verschwollen *adj* swollen.
verschwommen 1 *ptp of* **verschwimmen**. 2 *adj* *Foto, Umrisse* blurred, fuzzy; *Berge* hazy, indistinct; *Erinnerung, Vorstellung* vague, hazy; *Argumente, Begriffe* woolly *no adv*, vague. **ich sehe alles ~** everything looks hazy to me.
Verschwommenheit f *siehe adj* blurredness, fuzziness; haziness, indistinctness; vagueness, haziness; woolliness, vagueness.
verschworen 1 *ptp of* **verschwören**. 2 *adj* **(a)** *Gesellschaft* sworn. **(b)** **einer Sache** *(dat)* **~ sein** to have given oneself over to sth.
verschwören* *vr irreg* **(a)** to conspire, to plot *(mit* with, *gegen* against*)*. **sich zu etw ~** to plot sth, to conspire to do sth; **sie haben sich zu einem Attentat gegen den Diktator verschworen** they are conspiring or plotting to assassinate the dictator; **alles hat sich gegen mich verschworen** *(fig)* there's a conspiracy against me.
(b) *(sich verschreiben)* **sich einer Sache** *(dat)* **~** to give oneself over to sth.
Verschworene(r) *mf decl as adj* conspirator, plotter; *(fig)* ally, accomplice.
Verschwörer(in f*)* m *-s, -* conspirator.
Verschwörung f conspiracy, plot.
verschwunden 1 *ptp of* **verschwinden**. 2 *adj* missing, who/that has/had disappeared.
versechsfachen* [-'zɛks-] 1 *vt* to multiply by six. 2 *vr* to increase sixfold.
versehen* *irreg* 1 *vt* **(a)** *(ausüben)* *Amt, Stelle etc* to occupy, to hold; *Dienst* to perform, to discharge *(form)*; *(sich kümmern um)* to look after, to take care of; *Küche* to see to, to do; *(Bus, Schiff etc)* *Route* to provide the/a service on; *Dienst* to provide. **den Dienst eines Kollegen ~** to take a colleague's place, to perform a colleague's duties.
(b) *(ausstatten)* **jdn mit etw ~** to provide or supply sb with sth; *(ausrüsten auch)* to equip sb with sth; **etw mit etw ~** to put sth on/in sth; *(montieren)* to fit sth with sth; **ein Zimmer mit Teppichen ~** to carpet a room, to furnish a room with carpets; **ein Buch mit einem Umschlag ~** to provide a book with a dustjacket; **mit etw ~ sein** to have sth; **mit Blättern/Wurzeln/Haaren etc ~ sein** to have leaves/roots/hairs etc; **mit Etiketten/Wegweisern ~ sein** to be labelled/sign-posted; **mit**

allem reichlich/wohl ~ sein to be well provided for; die Bücherei ist gut (mit Fachliteratur) ~ the library is well stocked (with specialist literature).

(c) (*Eccl*) jdn (mit den Sterbesakramenten) ~ to administer the last rites *or* sacraments to sb; sich ~ lassen to receive the last sacrament(s).

(d) (*geben*) to give. jdn mit einer Vollmacht ~ to invest sb with full powers; etw mit seiner Unterschrift ~ to affix one's signature to sth (*form*), to sign sth; etw mit einem Stempel/ Siegel ~ to stamp sth/to affix a seal to sth; etw mit Akzept ~ (*Fin*) to accept sth.

(e) (*vernachlässigen*) to omit, to overlook.

2 *vr* (a) (*sich irren*) to be mistaken, to make a mistake.

(b) sich mit etw ~ (*sich versorgen*) to provide oneself with sth; (*sich ausstatten*) to equip oneself with sth.

(c) ehe man sich's versieht before you could turn round, before you could say Jack Robinson (*inf*); sich einer Sache (*gen*) ~ (*obs*) to be prepared for sth.

Versehen *nt* -s, - (*Irrtum*) mistake, error; (*Unachtsamkeit*) inadvertence, oversight. aus ~ by mistake, inadvertently.

versehentlich 1 *adj attr* inadvertent; (*irrtümlich*) erroneous. 2 *adv* inadvertently, by mistake.

Versehgang *m* (*Eccl*) visit to a/the dying man/woman.

versehren* *vt* (*verletzen*) to injure, to hurt; (*zum Invaliden machen*) to disable; (*beschädigen*) to damage.

Versehrten-: ~rente *f* disability *or* invalidity pension; ~sport *m* sport for the disabled.

Versehrte(r) *mf decl as adj* disabled person/man/woman *etc*. Platz für ~ seat for the disabled *or* for disabled persons.

verseifen* *vt* (*Chem*) to saponify.

Verseifung *f* (*Chem*) saponification.

verselbständigen* *vr* to become independent; (*beruflich auch*) to become self-employed.

Verselbständigung *f* die ~ der Kinder children's becoming independent; er hatte zu einer ~ nicht genügend Startkapital he hadn't sufficient capital to become independent.

versenden* *vt irreg or reg* to send; (*Comm auch*) to forward; *Kataloge, Heiratsanzeige etc* to send (out); (*verfrachten auch*) to ship.

Versendung *f siehe vt* sending; forwarding; sending out; shipment. die ~ der Kataloge sending (out) the catalogues.

versengen* *vt* (a) (*Sonne, mit Bügeleisen*) to scorch; (*Feuer*) to singe. (b) (*inf: verprügeln*) to thrash, to wallop (*inf*).

versenkbar *adj* that can be lowered; *Nähmaschine, Tischplatte* fold-away *attr*. nicht ~ *Schiff* unsinkable.

versenken* 1 *vt* (a) *Schatz, Behälter* to sink; *Leiche, Sarg* to lower; *Schiff auch* to send to the bottom; *das eigene Schiff* to scuttle. die Hände in die Taschen ~ to thrust one's hands into one's pockets; den Kopf in ein Buch ~ to bury one's head *or* to immerse oneself in a book.

(b) *Schraube* to countersink; *Tischplatte* to fold away; (*Theat*) to lower. eine Nähmaschine, die man ~ kann a fold-away sewing-machine.

2 *vr* sich in etw (*acc*) ~ to become immersed in sth; *in Gedanken auch, in Anblick* to lose oneself in sth.

Versenkung *f* (a) *siehe vt* (a) sinking; lowering; scuttling.

(b) (*Theat*) trap(door).

(c) (*das Sichversenken*) immersion. jdn aus seiner ~ reißen to tear sb from (his absorption *or* immersion in) his book/work *etc*; seine ~ in diesen Anblick his rapt contemplation of this sight; innere/mystische ~ inner/mystic contemplation.

(d) (*inf*) in der ~ verschwinden to vanish; (*berühmter Mensch, Buch etc*) to vanish *or* disappear from the scene, to sink into oblivion; aus der ~ auftauchen to re-appear; (*Mensch auch*) to re-emerge (on the scene).

Verseschmied *m* (*pej*) rhymester (*pej*), versifier (*pej*).

versessen 1 *ptp of* versitzen. 2 *adj* (*fig*) auf etw (*acc*) ~ sein to be very keen on sth, to be mad *or* crazy about sth (*inf*).

Versessenheit *f* keenness (*auf +acc* on).

versetzen* 1 *vt* (a) (*an andere Stelle setzen*) *Gegenstände, Möbel, Schüler* to move, to shift; *Pflanzen auch* to transplant; (*nicht geradlinig anordnen*) to stagger.

(b) (*beruflich*) to transfer, to move. jdn in einen höheren Rang ~ to promote sb, to move sb up; *siehe* Ruhestand.

(c) (*Sch: in höhere Klasse*) to move *or* put up.

(d) (*Typ, Mus*) to transpose.

(e) (*inf*) (*verkaufen*) to flog (*Brit inf*), to sell; (*verpfänden*) to pawn, to hock (*inf*).

(f) (*inf: nicht erscheinen*) jdn ~ to stand sb up (*inf*).

(g) (*in bestimmten Zustand bringen*) etw in Bewegung/ Schwingung ~ to set sth in motion/to set sth swinging; jdn in Wut/in fröhliche Stimmung ~ to send sb into a rage/to put sb in a cheerful mood; jdn in Sorge/Unruhe ~ to worry/disturb sb; jdn in Angst ~ to frighten sb, to make sb afraid; jdn in die Lage ~, etw zu tun to put sb in a position to do sth; jdn in seine Jugend/in frühere Zeiten ~ to take *or* transport sb back to his youth/times gone by.

(h) (*geben*) *Stoß, Schlag, Tritt etc* to give. jdm eins ~ (*inf*) to belt *or* land sb one (*inf*); jdm einen Stich ~ (*fig*) to cut sb to the quick, to wound sb (deeply); *siehe* Todesstoß.

(i) (*mischen*) to mix.

(j) (*antworten*) to retort.

2 *vr* (a) (*sich an andere Stelle setzen*) to move (to another place), to change places.

(b) sich in jdn/in jds Lage/Gefühle ~ to put oneself in sb's place *or* position.

(c) sich in eine frühere Zeit/seine Jugend *etc* ~ to take oneself back to *or* imagine oneself back in an earlier period/one's youth *etc*.

Versetzung *f* (a) (*beruflich*) transfer. seine ~ in einen höheren Rang his promotion (to a higher grade/rank). (b) (*Sch*)

moving up, being put up. bei nicht erfolgter ~ when the pupil isn't moved *or* put up. (c) (*Mus, Typ*) transposition. (d) (*nicht geradlinige Anordnung*) staggering. (e) (*Vermischung*) mixing.

Versetzungs-: ~konferenz *f* end of year staff meeting (*to decide whether pupils should be put up to next class*); ~zeichen *nt* (*Mus*) accidental; ~zeugnis *nt* end-of-year report.

verseuchen* *vt* (*mit Bakterien*) to infect; (*mit Gas, Giftstoffen*) to contaminate; (*fig*) to contaminate, to poison.

Verseuchung *f siehe vt* infection; contamination *no pl*; poisoning *no pl*.

Vers-: ~form *f* (*Poet*) verse form; ~fuß *m* (*Poet*) (metrical) foot.

Versicherer *m* -s, - insurer; (*bei Lebensversicherung auch*) assurer; (*bei Schiffen*) underwriter.

versichern* 1 *vt* (a) (*bestätigen*) to assure; (*beteuern*) to affirm, to protest. jdm ~, daß ... to assure sb that ...; jdm etw ~ to assure sb of sth; *seine Unschuld* to affirm *or* protest sth to sb.

(b) (*geh*) jdn einer Sache (*gen*) ~ to assure sb of sth; seien Sie versichert, daß ... (you can *or* may) rest assured that ...

(c) (*gegen Betrag*) to insure; *Leben auch* to assure.

2 *vr* (a) (*Versicherung abschließen*) to insure oneself (*mit* for); (*Lebensversicherung auch*) to take out a life insurance *or* assurance policy (*mit* of).

(b) (*sich vergewissern*) to make sure *or* certain.

(c) sich jds/einer Sache ~ (*geh*) to secure sb/sth.

Versicherte(r) *mf decl as adj* insured/assured (party).

Versicherung *f* (a) (*Bestätigung*) assurance; (*Beteuerung*) affirmation, protestation. (b) (*Feuer~ etc*) insurance; (*Lebens~ auch*) assurance.

Versicherungs-: ~agent *m* (*Aus*) insurance agent; ~anstalt *f* insurance company; ~beitrag *m* (a) (*bei staatlicher Versicherung etc*) insurance contribution; (b) (*bei Haftpflichtversicherung etc*) insurance premium; ~betrug *m* insurance fraud; ~dauer *f* period of insurance; ~fall *m* event of loss/ damage; ~gesellschaft *f* insurance/assurance company; ~karte *f* insurance card; die grüne ~karte (*Mot*) the green card; ~mathematik *f* actuarial theory; ~nehmer *m* (*form*) policy holder, insurant (*form*); ~pflicht *f* compulsory insurance; jeder Autofahrer unterliegt der ~pflicht insurance is compulsory for every driver; v~pflichtig *adj* subject to compulsory insurance; ~police *f* insurance/assurance policy; ~prämie *f* insurance premium; ~satz *m* rate of insurance; ~schutz *m* insurance cover; ~summe *f* sum insured/assured; ~träger *m siehe* Versicherer; ~vertreter *m* insurance agent; ~wert *m* insurance value; ~wesen *nt* insurance (business); ~zwang *m* compulsory insurance.

versickern* *vi aux sein* to seep away; (*fig*) (*Gespräch, Unterstützung*) to dry up; (*Interesse, Teilnahme*) to peter out.

versieben* *vt* (*inf*) (*vergessen*) to forget; (*verlieren*) to lose; (*verpfuschen*) to make a mess of (*inf*).

versiebenfachen* 1 *vt* to multiply by seven. 2 *vr* to increase sevenfold.

versiegeln* *vt* *Brief, Tür* to seal (up); *Parkett etc* to seal. mein Mund ist versiegelt my lips are sealed.

Versiegelung *f* (*Vorgang*) sealing; (*Siegel*) seal.

versiegen* *vi aux sein* (*Fluß, Quelle*) to dry up, to run dry; (*fig*) (*Gespräch, Unterstützung*) to dry up; (*Interesse*) to peter out; (*Tränen*) to dry up; (*gute Laune, Humor, Kräfte*) to fail. nie ~der Humor never-failing *or* irrepressible humour; nie ~de Hoffnung never-failing *or* undying hope.

versiert [vɛr-] *adj* experienced, practised. in etw (*dat*) ~ sein to be experienced *or* (*in bezug auf Wissen*) (well) versed in sth.

Versiertheit [vɛr-] *f* experience (*in* -*dat* in); (*in bezug auf Wissen*) knowledge (*in* -*dat* of).

versilbern* *vt* (*silbern bemalen*) to paint silver; (*mit Silber überziehen*) to silver(-plate); (*fig inf: verkaufen*) to flog (*Brit inf*), to sell; (*fig liter: Mond*) to silver.

Versilberung *f* (*Vorgang*) silvering, (silver-)plating; (*Silberschicht*) silver-plate.

versimpeln* (*inf*) 1 *vt* (*vereinfachen*) to make easier *or* simpler. 2 *vi aux sein* (*einfältig werden*) sie ist völlig versimpelt her mind has completely gone to seed.

versinken* *vi irreg aux sein* (*untergehen*) to sink; (*Schiff auch*) to founder. ich hätte im Boden *or* in der Erde/vor Scham ~ mögen I wished the ground would (open and) swallow me up; im Laster/Morast der Großstadt ~ to sink into vice/into the mire of the big city; in etw (*acc*) ~ (*fig*) in Trauer, Melancholie to sink into sth; in Anblick to lose oneself in sth; in Gedanken, Musik to become immersed in sth, to lose oneself in sth; alles versinkt um ihn (herum) (*fig*) he becomes totally oblivious to everything (around him); *siehe* versunken.

versinnbildlichen* *vt* to symbolize, to represent.

Versinnbildlichung *f* symbolization, representation.

Version [vɛr'zio:n] *f* version.

versippt *adj* (*pej*) interrelated.

versitzen* *vt irreg* (*inf*) *Kleidung* to crease, to crush. ich habe heute morgen meine ganze Zeit beim Arzt versessen I sat about (waiting) the whole morning at the doctor's.

versklaven* [fɛr'skla:vn, -a:fn] *vt* (*lit, fig*) to enslave.

Versklavung *f* enslavement.

Vers-: ~kunst *f* versification; ~lehre *f* study of verse; ~maß *nt* metre.

versnoben* *vi aux sein* (*pej*) to become snobbish *or* a snob. versnobt snobbish, snobby (*inf*).

versoffen *adj* (*sl*) boozy (*inf*). ein ~es Genie a drunken genius.

versohlen* *vt* (*inf*) to belt (*inf*); (*zur Strafe auch*) to leather.

versöhnen* 1 *vt* to reconcile; (*besänftigen*) jdn, Götter to placate, to appease; (*fig*) *Unterschiede*, jdn to reconcile. ~de Worte conciliatory/placatory words; das versöhnt einen dann wieder it almost makes up for it.

2 vr to be(come) reconciled; (Streitende) to make it up. **sich mit Gott** ~ to make one's peace with God; **sich mit etw** ~ to reconcile oneself to sth.

versöhnlich adj Mensch conciliatory; Laune, Ton auch placatory; (nichts nachtragend) forgiving. **die Götter** ~ **stimmen** to placate or appease the gods.

Versöhnlichkeit f siehe adj conciliatory/placatory/forgiving nature.

Versöhnung f reconciliation; (Beschwichtigung) appeasement. **zur** ~ **opferte er den Göttern ...** to appease or placate the gods he sacrificed ...

Versöhnungs-: ~fest nt, ~tag m (Rel) Day of Atonement, Yom Kippur no def art; ~politik f policy of reconciliation.

versonnen adj (in Gedanken verloren) Gesichtsausdruck pensive, thoughtful; Mensch auch lost in thought; (träumerisch) Blick dreamy.

Versonnenheit f siehe adj pensiveness, thoughtfulness; dreaminess.

versorgen* **1** vt (a) Kinder, Tiere, Pflanzen, Haushalt, finanzielle Angelegenheiten to look after, to take care of; (bedienen) Maschine, Lift, Heizung to look after.
(b) (beliefern) to supply. **jdn mit etw** ~ (versehen) to provide or supply sb with sth.
(c) (unterhalten) Familie to provide for, to support. **versorgt sein** to be provided for or taken care of.
(d) (dial: wegräumen) to put away.
2 vr (a) **sich mit etw** ~ to provide oneself with sth.
(b) **sich selbst** ~ to look after or take care of oneself.

Versorger(in f) m -s, - (a) (Ernährer) provider, breadwinner.
(b) (Belieferer) supplier.

Versorgung f siehe vt (a - c) (a) care. **vielen Dank für die gute** ~ **meiner Katze/Pflanzen** many thanks for taking such good care of my cat/plants.
(b) supply. **die** ~ **dieses Gebiets mit Bussen** the supply of buses to or provision of buses for this district; **die** ~ **der Truppen (mit Munition)** supplying the troops (with ammunition); **Probleme mit der** ~ **haben** to have supply problems; **auf Grund der schlechten** ~ **der Truppen** because the troops were being poorly supplied.
(c) (Unterhalt) **die** ~ **im Alter/einer sechsköpfigen Familie** providing for one's old age/a family of six; **der Staat übernimmt die** ~ **von Witwen und Waisen** the state undertakes to provide for widows and orphans.

Versorgungs-: v~berechtigt adj entitled to maintenance; (durch Staat) entitled to (state) benefit; ~betrieb m public utility; ~empfänger m recipient of state benefit; ~fahrzeug nt (Mil) supply vehicle; ~flugzeug nt supply plane; ~güter pl supplies pl; ~netz nt (Wasser~, Gas~ etc) (supply) grid; (von Waren) supply network; ~schwierigkeiten pl supply problems pl; ~truppen pl supply troops pl; ~weg m supply channel; ~wirtschaft f public utilities pl.

verspachteln* vt (a) to fill in. (b) (fig inf: aufessen) to put or tuck away (inf).

verspannen* **1** vt to brace, to stay, to guy. **2** vr (Muskeln) to tense up. **verspannt** tense (d up).

Verspannung f (a) (Seile etc) bracing, stays pl. (b) (von Muskeln) tenseness no pl.

verspäten* vr (a) (zu spät kommen) to be late. **der Frühling hat sich verspätet** spring is late. (b) (nicht rechtzeitig wegkommen) to be late leaving; (aufgehalten werden) to be delayed, to be held up.

verspätet adj Zug, Flugzeug delayed, late pred; Ankunft, Eintreten, Frühling, Entwicklung late; Glückwunsch belated; Bewerbung late, belated. **er hat** ~ **sprechen gelernt** he learnt to talk late.

Verspätung f (von Verkehrsmitteln) delay; (von Mensch) late arrival; (von Glückwunsch etc) belatedness. **eine** ~ **der Pubertät/des Frühlings** late puberty/a late spring; **(10 Minuten)** ~ **haben** to be (10 minutes) late; **eine zweistündige** ~ **a delay of two hours**, a two-hour delay; **die** ~ **aufholen** to catch up lost time; **mit** ~ **abfahren/ankommen** to leave/arrive late; **ohne** ~ **ankommen** to arrive on time; **mit zwanzig Minuten** ~ twenty minutes late or (von Verkehrsmitteln auch) behind schedule; **mit sechsmonatiger** etc ~ six months etc late; (nach Ablauf der Frist auch) six months etc too late.

verspeisen* vt (geh) to consume.

verspekulieren* **1** vt to lose through speculation. **2** vr to ruin oneself by speculation; (fig) to miscalculate, to be out in one's speculations.

versperren* vt (a) to block; Weg auch to bar; Aussicht auch to obstruct. (b) (dial: verschließen) to lock or close up.

verspielen* **1** vt (lit, fig) Geld, Chancen to gamble away; Vorteile to bargain away. **den ganzen Abend** ~ to spend the whole evening playing.
2 vi (fig) **jetzt hast du verspielt** it's all up with you now, you've had it now (inf); **er hatte bei ihr verspielt** he was finished or he had had it (inf) as far as she was concerned.

verspielt adj Kind, Katze etc playful; Frisur pretty; Muster, Kleid pretty, dainty; Verzierung dainty.

verspinnen* irreg **1** vt (zu Faden) to spin; (verbrauchen) to use. **2** vr die Larve verspinnt sich (zur Puppe)** the larva spins itself into or forms a cocoon; **sich in etw** (dat) ~ (fig) in Ideen to become immersed in sth; in Lügen to become embroiled or enmeshed in sth.

versponnen adj airy-fairy; Ideen auch wild attr; Mensch head-in-the-clouds pred.

verspotten* vt to mock; (höhnisch) to jeer at, to deride.

Verspottung f (a) siehe vt mocking; jeering, derision all no indef art. (b) (spöttische Rede) mockery no indef art, no pl; jeer, derision no indef art, no pl.

versprechen* irreg **1** vt (a) to promise (jdm etw sb sth). **aber**

er hat es doch versprochen! but he promised!; **jdm/einander versprochen sein** (obs) to be betrothed (old) or promised to sb/to be betrothed (old); siehe hoch, Blaue.
(b) (erwarten lassen) to promise. **das verspricht interessant zu werden** it promises to be interesting; **das Wetter verspricht schön zu werden** the weather looks promising or promises to be good; **nichts Gutes** ~ to be ominous, to bode ill (liter).
2 vr (a) (erwarten) **sich** (dat) **viel/wenig von jdm/etw** ~ to have high hopes/no great hopes of sb/sth; **was versprichst du dir davon?** what do you expect to achieve or gain (by that)?
(b) (falsch sagen, aussprechen) to pronounce a word/words wrong(ly); (etwas Nicht-Gemeintes sagen) to make a slip (of the tongue) or a mistake. **bei dem Wort verspreche ich mich noch immer** I still can't pronounce that word properly.

Versprechen nt -s, - promise.

Versprecher m -s, - (inf) slip (of the tongue). **ein Freudscher** ~ a Freudian slip.

Versprechung f promise.

versprengen* vt (a) Truppen, Soldaten to disperse, to scatter. **versprengte Soldaten** scattered soldiers. (b) Wasser to sprinkle.

verspritzen* **1** vt (a) (versprühen, verteilen) to spray; (versprengen) to sprinkle; Farbe to spray on; (zuspritzen) Fugen to seal by injection moulding; (fig) Tinte to use up; siehe Gift.
(b) (beim Planschen) Wasser to splash, to sp(l)atter; (verkleckern) Farbe, Boden, Heft, Kleidung to sp(l)atter.
(c) (verbrauchen) Wasser, Farbe etc to use.
2 vi aux sein (Wasser) to spray; (Fett) to sp(l)atter.

versprochenermaßen adv as promised.

versprühen* vt to spray; Funken auch to send up or out; (verbrauchen) to use. Witz/Geist ~ (fig) to scintillate.

verspüren* vt to feel, to be conscious of. **er verspürte keine Lust, zur Arbeit zu gehen** he felt no desire to go to work.

verstaatlichen* vt to nationalize; Schulen to put under state control; Kirchen to secularize.

Verstaatlichung f siehe vt nationalization; putting under state control; secularization.

verstädtern* **1** vt to urbanize. **2** vi aux sein to become urbanized.

Verstädterung f urbanization.

verstand pret of verstehen.

Verstand m -(e)s, no pl (Fähigkeit zu denken) reason; (Intellekt) mind, intellect; (Vernunft) (common) sense; (Urteilskraft) (powers pl of) judgement. **das müßte dir dein** ~ **sagen** your common sense should tell you that; **den** ~ **verlieren** to lose one's mind; **hast du denn den** ~ **verloren?** have you taken leave of your senses?, are you out of your mind?; **jdn um den** ~ **bringen** to drive sb out of his mind; **nicht recht or ganz bei** ~ **sein** not to be in one's right mind; **zu** ~ **kommen** to come to one's senses; **mit seinem** ~ **am Ende sein** to be at one's wits' end; **das geht über meinen** ~ it's beyond me, it beats me (inf); **da steht einem der** ~ **still** (fig inf), **da bleibt einem der** ~ **stehen** (fig inf) the mind boggles (inf); **etw ohne** ~ **tun** to do sth mindlessly; **etw ohne** ~ **essen/trinken** not to pay attention to what one is eating/drinking; **etw mit** ~ **genießen/essen/trinken** to savour or relish sth.

verstanden ptp of verstehen.

Verstandes-: ~ehe f siehe Vernunftehe; ~kraft f mental or intellectual faculties pl or powers pl; v~mäßig adj rational; v~mäßig leuchtet das mir ein it makes (rational) sense to me; ~mensch m rational person; ~schärfe f acuteness or sharpness of mind or intellect.

verständig adj (vernünftig) sensible; (einsichtig) understanding.

verständigen* **1** vt to notify, to advise (von of, about). **2** vr to communicate (with each other); (sich einigen) to come to an understanding or agreement. **sich mit jdm** ~ to communicate with sb.

Verständigkeit f siehe adj sensibleness; understanding (für of).

Verständigung f, no pl (a) (Benachrichtigung) notification, advising. (b) (das Sichverständigen) communication no indef art. **die** ~ **am Telephon war schlecht** the (telephone) line was bad. (c) (Einigung) understanding, agreement.

Verständigungs-: ~bereitschaft f willingness or readiness to negotiate; ~schwierigkeiten pl communication difficulties pl; ~versuch m attempt at rapprochement.

verständlich adj (begreiflich) Reaktion etc understandable; (intellektuell erfaßbar) comprehensible; (hörbar) audible; (klar) Erklärung, Ausdruck intelligible. **allgemein** ~ readily comprehensible; **eine schwer** ~e **Unterscheidung** a distinction that is difficult to grasp or understand; **jdm etw** ~ **machen** to make sb understand sth; **sich** ~ **machen** to make oneself understood; (sich klar ausdrücken) to make oneself clear, to express oneself intelligibly; (gegen Lärm) to make oneself heard; **nicht** ~ incomprehensible; inaudible; unintelligible.

verständlicherweise adv understandably (enough).

Verständlichkeit f, no pl comprehensibility; (Hörbarkeit) audibility.

Verständnis nt, no pl (a) (das Begreifen) understanding (für of), comprehension (für of); (Einfühlungsvermögen, Einsicht) understanding (für for); (Mitgefühl) sympathy (für for). **solche Grausamkeiten gehen über menschliches/mein** ~ such cruelty is beyond human/my comprehension; **für etw kein** ~ **haben** to have no understanding/sympathy for sth; **für Probleme, Lage auch** to have no feeling for sth; **für so was habe ich kein** ~ I have no time for that kind of thing; **dafür hast du mein vollstes** ~ you have my fullest sympathy.
(b) (intellektuelles Erfassen) (für of) understanding, comprehension. **mit** ~ **lesen/zuhören** to read/listen with understanding.

(c) (Kunst~ etc) appreciation (für of).

(d) (Verständigung) understanding.

Verständnis-: v~innig adj knowing attr, meaningful; v~los adj uncomprehending; Gesicht, Blick auch blank; (ohne Mitgefühl) unsympathetic (für towards); (für Kunst) unappreciative (für of); ~losigkeit f siehe adj lack of understanding; blankness; lack of sympathy; lack of appreciation; v~voll adj understanding; (mitfühlend auch) sympathetic (für towards); Blick knowing no pred.

verstänkern* vt (inf) Zimmer to make a stink in (inf); Stadt to pollute.

verstärken 1 vt Eindruck, Truppen, (Sport) to reinforce; Argumente, Mauer auch to strengthen; Spannung, Zweifel to intensify, to increase; (Chem) to concentrate; (Phot) to intensify; (Elec) Signal, Strom, Spannung to boost, to amplify; Stimme, Musik, Musikinstrument to amplify.

2 vr (fig) to intensify; (sich vermehren) to increase.

Verstärker m -s, - (Rad, Elec) amplifier; (Telec) repeater; (von Signalen etc) booster; (Phot) intensifier.

Verstärkerröhre f (Elec) amplifier valve.

Verstärkung f siehe vt reinforcement; strengthening; intensification, increase; concentration; intensification; boosting; amplification.

verstauben* vi aux sein to get dusty or covered in dust; (Möbel, Bücher auch, fig) to gather dust. **verstaubt** dusty, covered in dust; (fig) Ideen, Ansichten fuddy-duddy (inf).

verstauchen* vt to sprain. sich (dat) die Hand/den Fuß etc ~ to sprain one's hand/foot etc.

Verstauchung f sprain; (das Verstauchen) spraining.

verstauen* vt (in + dat in(to)) Gepäck to load, to pack; (Naut) to stow; (hum) Menschen to pile, to pack.

Versteck nt -(e)s, -e hiding-place; (von Verbrechern) hideout. ~ spielen to play hide-and-seek.

verstecken* 1 vt to hide, to conceal (vor from).

2 vr to hide, to conceal oneself. sich vor or neben jdm ~ können/müssen (fig) to be no match for sb; sich vor jdm ~ to hide from sb; sich vor or neben jdm nicht zu ~ brauchen (fig) not to need to fear comparison with sb; sich hinter etw (dat) ~ (fig) hinter Pseudonym to write under sth; hinter falschem Namen, Maske to hide behind sth; hinter Andeutungen to be behind sth; V~ spielen to play hide-and-seek.

Versteckspiel nt (lit, fig) hide-and-seek.

versteckt adj (a) (lit: verborgen) hidden; (nicht leicht sichtbar) Eingang, Tür, Winkel concealed; (abgelegen auch) Ort secret. (b) (fig) Lächeln, Blick furtive; Gähnen auch disguised; Bemerkung, Andeutung veiled; Bedeutung hidden, concealed.

verstehen pret verstand ptp verstanden 1 vti (a) to understand; (einsehen auch) to see. jdn/etw falsch or nicht recht ~ to misunderstand sb/sth; versteh mich recht don't misunderstand me, don't get me wrong; jdm zu ~ geben, daß ... to give sb to understand that ...; ein ~der Blick a knowing look; (ist das) verstanden? (is that) understood?; siehe Bahnhof, Spaß.

(b) (hören) to hear, to understand; siehe Wort.

(c) (können, beherrschen) to know; Sprache auch to understand. es ~, etw zu tun to know how to do sth; er versteht die Kunst, etw zu tun he has the art or knack of doing sth; es mit Kindern ~ to be good with or have a way with children; es mit seinen Kollegen ~ to know how to get on with one's colleagues; etwas/nichts von etw ~ to know something/nothing about sth; etw machen, so gut man es versteht to do sth to the best of one's ability or as well as one can; siehe Handwerk.

(d) (auslegen) to understand, to interpret, to see. etw unter etw (dat) ~ to understand sth by sth; wie soll ich das ~? how am I supposed to take that?; das ist bildlich or nicht wörtlich zu ~ that isn't to be taken literally.

2 vr (a) to understand each other.

(b) (miteinander auskommen) to get on or along (with each other or together). sich mit jdm ~ to get on with sb; wir ~ uns (schon) (sind einer Meinung) we understand each other.

(c) (klar sein) to go without saying. versteht sich! (inf) of course!, naturally!; das versteht sich von selbst that goes without saying.

(d) (auffassen) sich als etw ~ to think of or see oneself as sth.

(e) sich auf etw (acc) ~ to be (an) expert at sth, to be a dab hand (inf) or very good at sth.

(f) sich zu etw ~ (form) to agree to sth.

(g) (Comm) to be. die Preise ~ sich einschließlich Lieferung prices are inclusive of delivery.

versteifen* 1 vt to strengthen, to reinforce; (Comm) to tighten; (Sew) to stiffen.

2 vr to stiffen up; (fig) Haltung, Gegensätze to harden; (Maßnahmen) to tighten (up). sich auf etw (acc) ~ (fig) to become set on sth; er hat sich darauf versteift he is set on it.

Versteifung f (a) no pl siehe vt strengthening, reinforcement; strutting; tightening; stiffening.

(b) (Verstärkung) stiffener.

(c) (Med) stiffening no pl.

(d) (fig) (von Haltung) hardening; (von Maßnahmen) tightening (up); (von Gegensätzen) increasing intractability. jds ~ auf etw (acc) sb's being set on sth.

versteigen* vr irreg (lit) to get into difficulties (while climbing). er hat sich zu der Behauptung verstiegen, daß ... he presumed to claim that ...; er verstieg sich zu völlig übertriebenen Forderungen he had the presumption to make quite excessive demands; siehe verstiegen.

versteigern* vt to auction (off). etw ~ lassen to put sth up for auction.

Versteigerung f (sale by) auction. zur ~ kommen to be put up for auction.

versteinern* 1 vi aux sein (Geol) (Pflanzen, Tiere) to fossilize;

(Holz) to petrify; (fig: Miene) to harden. versteinerte Pflanzen/Tiere fossilized plants/animals; wie versteinert (da)stehen to stand there petrified. 2 vr (fig) Miene to harden; (Lächeln) to become fixed or set.

Versteinerung f (Vorgang) fossilization; petrifaction, petrification; (versteinertes Tier etc) fossil; (fig: von Miene) hardening.

verstellbar adj adjustable. in der Höhe ~ adjustable for height.

Verstellbarkeit f adjustability.

verstellen* 1 vt (a) (anders einstellen, regulieren) to adjust; Signal, Zahlen to alter, to change; Möbel, Gegenstände to move or shift (out of position or place); (in Unordnung bringen) to put in the wrong place, to misplace; (falsch einstellen) to adjust wrongly; Radio to alter the tuning of; Uhr to put wrong. meine Sachen sind verstellt my things are in the wrong place.

(b) Stimme to disguise.

(c) (versperren) to block, to obstruct; (vollstellen) Zimmer to clutter up. das verstellt den Blick auf das Wesentliche that obscures one's view of the essential.

2 vr to move (out of position); (fig) to act or play a part; (Gefühle verbergen) to hide one's (true) feelings. er kann sich gut ~ he's good at playing or acting a part.

Verstellung f siehe vt (a) adjustment; alteration; moving or shifting (out of position) no indef art; misplacing no indef art.

(b) disguise. (c) blockage, obstruction; cluttering up. (d) (Vortäuschung) pretending, feigning.

Verstellungs-: ~kunst f ability to pretend or feign; ~künstler(in f) m poseur, phoney (inf).

versterben* vi irreg aux sein to die, to pass away or on.

versteuern* vt to pay on. versteuerte Waren/das versteuerte Einkommen taxed goods/income; das zu versteuernde Einkommen taxable income.

Versteuerung f, no pl taxation.

verstiegen 1 ptp of versteigen. 2 adj (fig: überspannt) extravagant, fantastic; Pläne, Ideen auch high-flown.

Verstiegenheit f extravagance.

verstimmen* vt (lit) to put out of tune; (fig) to put out, to disgruntle.

verstimmt adj Klavier etc out of tune; (fig) (verdorben) Magen upset; (verärgert) put out, disgruntled.

Verstimmung f disgruntlement; (zwischen Parteien) ill-feeling, ill-will.

verstockt adj Kind, Wesen obstinate, stubborn; Sünder unrepentant, unrepenting.

Verstocktheit f, no pl siehe adj obstinacy, stubbornness; unrepentance.

verstohlen adj furtive, surreptitious.

verstopfen* vt to stop up; Ohren auch to plug; Ausguß auch to block (up); Straße to block, to jam.

verstopft adj blocked; Straßen auch jammed; Nase stuffed up, blocked (up); Mensch constipated.

Verstopfung f blockage; (Verkehrsstauung) jam; (Med) constipation.

Verstorbene(r) mf decl as adj deceased.

verstören* vt to disturb.

verstört adj disturbed; (vor Angst) distraught.

Verstörtheit f, no pl disturbed state; (vor Angst) distraction; (Verwirrung) confusion.

Verstoß m -es, ¨e violation (gegen of); (gegen Gesetz auch) offence.

verstoßen* irreg 1 vt jdn to disown, to repudiate. jdn aus einem Verein/einer Gruppe ~ to expel sb from or throw sb out of a club/group. 2 vi gegen etw ~ to offend against sth; gegen Gesetz, Regel auch to contravene sth.

Verstoßene(r) mf decl as adj outcast.

verstreben* vt to brace, to strut.

Verstrebung f supporting no pl; (Strebebalken) support(ing beam).

verstreichen* irreg 1 vt Salbe, Farbe to put on, to apply (auf +dat to); Butter to spread (auf +dat on); Riß to fill in; (verbrauchen) to use. 2 vi aux sein (Zeit) to pass (by), to elapse; (Frist) to expire.

verstreuen* vt to scatter; (versehentlich) to spill. seine Kleider/Spielsachen im ganzen Zimmer ~ to scatter or strew one's clothes/toys over the (whole) room.

verstricken* 1 vt (a) Wolle to use. (b) (fig) to involve, to embroil, to mix up. in eine Angelegenheit verstrickt sein to be mixed up or involved or embroiled in an affair. 2 vr (a) (Wolle) to knit (up). (b) (fig) to become entangled, to get tangled up.

Verstrickung f entanglement.

verströmen* vt (lit, fig) to exude; (liter) sein Blut to shed.

verstümmeln* vt to mutilate, to maim; (fig) Nachricht, Bericht to garble, to distort; Namen to mutilate. sich selbst ~ to mutilate oneself.

Verstümmelung f siehe vt mutilation, maiming no pl; garbling no pl, distortion; mutilation.

verstummen* vi aux sein (Mensch) to go or fall silent, to stop talking; (Geräusch, Gespräch, Musik, Beifall) to cease, to stop; (Wind, Glocken, Instrumente) to become silent or still (liter); (langsam verklingen) to die away; (fig: Kritik, Stimmen der Opposition) to become silent or still; (sich langsam legen) to subside; (Gewissen) to become silent; (Gerüchte) to subside. jdn ~ lassen (Bemerkung, Einwurf) to silence sb; der plötzliche Schock ließ ihn ~ he was struck dumb by the sudden shock; jdn/etw zum V~bringen to silence sb/sth; vor Entsetzen ~ to be struck dumb or to be speechless with terror.

Versuch m -(e)s, -e attempt (zu tun at doing, to do); (wissenschaftlich) experiment, test; (Test) trial, test; (Essay) essay; (Rugby) try. einen ~ machen to make an attempt; to do or carry out an experiment/a trial; mit jdm/etw einen ~

machen to give sb/sth a try or trial; (Forscher) to do a trial/an experiment with sb/sth; **das käme auf einen ~ an** we'll have to have a try; **sie unternahm den ~, ihn umzustimmen** she made an attempt at changing or to change his mind, she had a try at changing his mind; **wir sollten es auf einen ~ ankommen lassen** we should give it a try; **das wollen wir doch auf einen ~ ankommen lassen!** we'll see about that!

versuchen* 1 vt (a) (auch vi: probieren, kosten) to try; (sich bemühen auch) to attempt. **es mit etw ~** to try sth; **versuch's doch!** try, have a try; **es mit jdm ~** to give sb a try; **versuchter Mord/Diebstahl** attempted murder/theft.
(b) (in Versuchung führen) to tempt. **sich versucht fühlen** to feel tempted; **versucht sein** to be tempted.
2 vr **sich an or in etw** (dat) ~ to try one's hand at sth.

Versucher(in f) m -s, - tempter, temptress. **der ~** (Rel) the Tempter.

Versuchs-: ~abteilung f experimental department; ~anlage f experimental plant; ~anstalt f research institute; ~ballon m sounding balloon; **einen ~ballon steigen lassen, es mit einem ~ballon probieren** (fig) to fly a kite; ~bedingungen pl test conditions pl; ~bohrung f experimental drilling; ~kaninchen nt (lit) laboratory rabbit; (fig) guinea-pig; ~karnickel nt (fig, inf) guinea-pig; ~objekt nt test object; (fig: Mensch) guinea-pig; ~person f test or experimental subject; ~reihe f series of experiments; ~stadium nt experimental stage; ~strecke f test track; ~tier nt laboratory animal; v~weise adv as a trial, on a trial basis; **einstellen, engagieren** on probation, on trial.

Versuchung f temptation (auch Rel). **jdn in ~ führen** to lead sb into temptation; **„und führe uns nicht in ~"** "and lead us not into temptation"; **in ~ geraten or kommen** to be tempted.

versudeln* vt to scribble on.

versumpfen* vi aux sein (a) (Gebiet) to become marshy or boggy. (b) (fig inf) (verwahrlosen) to go to pot (inf); (lange zechen) to get involved in a booze-up (inf).

Versumpfung f (lit) increasing marshiness.

versündigen* vr (geh) **sich an jdm/etw ~** to sin against sb/sth; **sich an seiner Gesundheit ~** to abuse one's health.

Versündigung f sin (an + dat against). **eine ~ an der Gesundheit** an abuse of one's health.

versunken 1 ptp of **versinken**. 2 adj sunken, submerged; Kultur submerged; (fig) engrossed, absorbed. **in Gedanken ~** lost or immersed in thought; **völlig in diesen Anblick ~** completely lost or caught up in this sight.

Versunkenheit f, no pl (fig) engrossment. **jdn aus seiner ~ reißen** to tear sb from his (immersion in his) book/thoughts etc; **seine ~ in diesen Anblick** his rapt contemplation of this sight.

versüßen* vt (fig) to sweeten. **jdm etw ~** to sweeten sth for sb; siehe **Pille**.

Vertäfelung f panelling no pl, no indef art.

vertagen* 1 vti to adjourn; (verschieben) to postpone, to defer (auf + acc until, till); (Parl auch) to prorogue (form). 2 vr to be adjourned, to adjourn.

Vertagung f siehe vti adjournment; postponement; prorogation (form).

vertändeln* vt to fritter away.

vertäuen* vt (Naut) to moor.

vertauschbar adj exchangeable (gegen for); (miteinander) interchangeable.

vertauschen* vt (a) (austauschen) to exchange (gegen or mit for); (miteinander) to interchange; Auto, Plätze to change (gegen or mit for); (Elec) Pole to transpose. **vertauschte Rollen** reversed roles.
(b) (verwechseln) Hüte, Mäntel etc to mix up. **seinen Mantel mit einem anderen ~** to mistake another coat for one's own, to mix one's coat up with another; **ich habe meinen Platz mit seinem vertauscht** I took his place by mistake.

Vertauschung f (a) (Austausch) exchange; (von Auto, von Plätzen) changing no pl; (Elec: von Polen) transposition. (b) (Verwechslung) mix-up; (das Vertauschen) mixing up.

Vertäuung f (das Vertäuen) mooring; (die Taue) moorings pl.

verteidigen* 1 vt to defend. 2 vr to defend oneself (auch Sport); (vor Gericht) to conduct one's own defence. 3 vi (Sport) to defend; (als Verteidiger spielen) to be a or play as a defender; (defensiv spielen) to play a defensive game, to play defensively.

Verteidiger(in f) m -s, - defender (auch Sport); (Fürsprecher auch) advocate; (Anwalt) defence lawyer. **der ~ des Angeklagten** the counsel for the defence, the defence counsel.

Verteidigung f (alle Bedeutungen) defence, defense (US). **zur ~ von or gen** in defence of; **zu ihrer/seiner eigenen ~** in her/one's own defence; **er ist immer zur ~ seiner Meinung bereit** he is always ready to defend his opinion; **jdn in die ~ drängen** to force sb onto the defensive; **in die ~ gehen** to go onto the defensive.

Verteidigungs- in cpds defence; ~beitrag m defence contribution; ~bündnis nt defence alliance; v~fähig adj able to defend itself/oneself; ~fall m case of defence; ~gemeinschaft f defence community; ~krieg m defensive war; ~minister m Minister of Defence; ~ministerium nt Ministry of Defence; ~rede f (Jur) speech for the defence; (fig) apologia; ~schlacht f defensive battle; ~schrift f (Jur) (written) defence statement; (fig) apologia; ~spieler m defence player, defender; ~stellung f defensive position; **in ~stellung gehen** to adopt a defensive position; ~system nt defence system, defences pl; **das ~system der Nato** the Nato defence system; v~unfähig adj defenceless; ~waffe f defensive weapon; ~wille m spirit of resistance; ~zustand m defence alert; **im ~zustand** in a defence alert; **im ~zustand sein** on the defence alert; ~zweck m für ~zwecke, zu ~zwecken for defence purposes, for purposes of defence.

verteilen* 1 vt (a) (austeilen) (an + acc to, unter + acc among)

to distribute; Flugblätter auch to hand out; Essen to dish out; Süßigkeiten etc auch to share or divide out; Preise auch to give out; (Theat) Rollen to allot, to allocate.
(b) (anordnen, aufteilen) to distribute; Investitionen, Lehrstoff to spread (über + acc over); (Mil) to deploy; (verstreuen) to spread out; (streichen) Aufstrich, Farbe etc to spread; (streuen) Sand, Zucker, Puder to sprinkle. **Blumen im Zimmer/auf verschiedene Vasen ~** to arrange flowers around the room/in different vases.
2 vr (Zuschauer, Polizisten etc) to spread (themselves) out; (Bevölkerung ~) to spread (itself) out; (Mil: Truppen auch) to deploy; (Farbe, Wasser) to spread (itself) out; (Med: Bakterien, Metastasen) to spread; (Reichtum etc) to be spread or distributed; (zeitlich) to be spread (über + acc over). **auf dem ganzen Platz verteilt** spread out over the square; **übers ganze Land verteilt** spread throughout the country.

Verteiler m -s, - (a) (Comm, Aut) distributor. (b) siehe **Verteilerschlüssel**.

Verteiler-: ~kopf m (Aut) distributor head; ~netz nt (Elec) distribution system; (Comm) distribution network; ~schlüssel m list of people to receive a copy.

Verteilung f distribution; (Zuteilung) allocation; (Mil) deployment; (Theat) casting.

vertellen* vt (N Ger inf) to tell; Unsinn to talk.

verteuern* 1 vt to make dearer or more expensive, to increase or raise the price of. 2 vr to become dearer or more expensive, to increase in or go up in price.

Verteuerung f rise or increase in price.

verteufeln* vt to condemn.

verteufelt (inf) 1 adj Lage, Angelegenheit devilish (inf), tricky, awkward. ~es Glück haben to be damned or darned or deuced (dated) lucky (inf). 2 adv (mit adj) damned (inf), darned (inf), deuced (dated inf); devilish (dated inf); (mit vb) a lot.

Verteufelung f condemnation.

vertiefen* 1 vt Graben, Loch etc to deepen; (fig) Eindruck auch to heighten; Kenntnis, Wissen auch to extend; (Sch) Unterrichtsstoff to consolidate, to reinforce; (Mus) to flatten.
2 vr (lit, fig) to deepen; (fig: Lehrstoff) to be consolidated or reinforced. **sich in etw** (acc) ~ (fig) to become engrossed or absorbed in sth; **in etw** (acc) **vertieft sein** (fig) to be engrossed or absorbed in sth; siehe **Gedanke**.

Vertiefung f (a) siehe vt deepening; heightening; extension; consolidation, reinforcement; flattening. (b) (in Oberfläche) depression; (im Boden auch) dip, hollow. (c) (vertieft sein) engrossment, absorption. **jdn aus seiner ~ reißen** to tear sb away from his book/newspaper etc.

vertieren* vi aux sein to become brutalized, to brutalize.

vertiert adj brutish.

vertikal [verti'ka:l] adj vertical.

Vertikale [verti'ka:lə] f -, -n vertical line. **in der ~n** vertically, in a vertical plane.

vertilgen* vt (a) Unkraut etc to destroy, to eradicate, to kill off; Ungeziefer auch to exterminate. (b) (inf: aufessen) to demolish (inf), to polish off (inf).

Vertilgung f siehe vt destruction, eradication; extermination.

Vertilgungsmittel nt weed-killer; (Insekten~) pesticide.

vertippen* (inf) 1 vr (a) to make a typing error. (b) (beim Lotto, Toto etc) to slip up (inf). 2 vt to mistype, to type wrongly.

vertobacken* vt (dated inf) to thrash.

vertonen* vt to set to music; Theaterstück auch to make a musical version of; Film etc to add a sound-track to.

vertönen* vi aux sein to fade or die away.

Vertonung f siehe vt setting (to music); (vertonte Fassung) musical version, setting; adding a sound-track (gen to).

vertorfen* vi aux sein to turn into peat.

Vertorfung f conversion into peat.

vertrackt adj (inf) awkward, tricky; (verwickelt) complicated, complex.

Vertracktheit f (inf) awkwardness, trickiness; (Verwickeltheit) complexity.

Vertrag m -(e)s, ⁻e contract; (Abkommen) agreement; (Pol: Friedens~) treaty. **mündlicher ~** verbal or oral agreement; **laut ~** under the terms of the contract; **jdn unter ~ nehmen** to contract sb; **unter ~ stehen** to be under contract.

vertragen* irreg 1 vt (a) to take; (aushalten auch) to stand; (dulden auch) to tolerate, to endure, to stand for. **Eier vertrage ich nicht or kann ich nicht ~** I can't take eggs, eggs don't agree with me; **ein Automotor, der viel verträgt** an engine that can stand (up to) a lot or can take a lot; **synthetische Stoffe vertrage ich nicht or kann ich nicht ~** I can't wear synthetics; **so etwas kann ich nicht ~** I can't stand that kind of thing; **er verträgt keinen Spaß** he can't take a joke; **viel ~ können** (inf: Alkohol) to be able to hold one's drink; **er verträgt nichts** (inf) he can't take his drink; **jd/etw könnte etw ~** (inf) sb/sth could do with sth.
(b) (dial) Kleider to wear out. **~ sein** to be (well) worn.
(c) (Sw) to deliver.
2 vr **sich (mit jdm) ~** to get on or along (with sb); **sich wieder ~** to be friends again; **sich mit etw ~** (Nahrungsmittel, Farbe) to go with sth; (Aussage, Verhalten) to be consistent with sth; **diese Farben/Aussagen ~ sich nicht** these colours don't go together/these statements are inconsistent or not consistent.

Verträger m (Sw) delivery man; (Zeitungs~) paper boy/man.

verträglich 1 adj contractual. 2 adv by contract; **festgelegt in** the/a contract. **ein ~ zugesichertes Recht** a contractual right.

verträglich adj (friedlich, umgänglich) peaceable, easy-going, amicable; Speise digestible; (bekömmlich) wholesome; Medikament well tolerated (für by). **gut ~** easily digestible.

Verträglichkeit f, no pl siehe adj amicability; digestibility; wholesomeness. **die ~ dieses Medikaments** the fact that this medicine is well tolerated.

Vertrags- in cpds of the/a contract/an agreement/a treaty; **~bruch** m breach of contract; breaking of an/the agreement; breaking of a/the treaty; **v~brüchig** adj who is in breach of contract; who has broken an/the agreement; who has broken a/the treaty; **v~brüchig werden** to be in breach of contract; to break an/the agreement; to break a/the treaty; **~entwurf** m draft contract/agreement/treaty; **~gaststätte** f tied house; **~gegenstand** m object of the contract/agreement/treaty; **v~gemäß 1** adj (as) stipulated in the contract/agreement/treaty; **2** adv as stipulated in the contract/agreement/treaty; **~hafen** m treaty port; **~händler** m concessionary, appointed retailer; **~partner** m party to a/the contract/treaty; **v~schließend** adj contracting; **~spieler** m player under contract; **~strafe** f penalty for breach of contract; **~verletzung** f breach of contract; infringement of the agreement/treaty; **~werk** nt contract; treaty; **~werkstätte** f authorized repair shop; **v~widrig 1** adj contrary to (the terms of) the contract/agreement/treaty; **2** adv in breach of contract/the agreement/the treaty.

vertrauen* vi jdm/einer Sache ~ to trust sb/sth, to have trust in sb/sth; **auf jdn/etw** ~ to trust in sb/sth; **auf sein Glück** ~ to trust to luck; **sich** (dat) **selbst** ~ to have confidence in oneself.

Vertrauen nt -s, no pl trust, confidence (zu, in +acc, auf +acc in); (Pol) confidence. **voll** ~ full of confidence; **im** ~ (gesagt) strictly in confidence; **ich habe dir das im** ~ **gesagt** that's strictly in confidence, that's strictly between you and me; **im** ~ **darauf, daß** ... confident that ..., in the confidence that ...; ~ **zu jdm fassen** to gain confidence in sb; **jdn ins** ~ **ziehen** to take sb into one's confidence.

vertrauen|erweckend adj ein **~er Mensch/Arzt** etc a person/doctor etc who inspires confidence; **einen ~en Eindruck machen/~ aussehen** to inspire confidence.

Vertrauens-: **~arzt** m doctor who examines patients signed off sick for a lengthy period by their private doctor; **~bruch** m breach of confidence or trust; **~frage** f question or matter of trust; **die ~frage stellen** (Parl) to ask for a vote of confidence; **~lehrer** m liaison teacher (between pupils and staff); **~mann** m, pl **~leute** or **-männer** intermediary agent; (Gewerkschaft) (union) negotiator or representative; (Gewerkschaft) **~person** f someone to confide in, confidant(e); **~posten** m position of trust; **~sache** f (vertrauliche Angelegenheit) confidential matter; (Frage des Vertrauens) question or matter of trust; **~schüler** m class spokesman; **v~selig** adj trusting; (leichtgläubig auch) credulous; **~seligkeit** f trustfulness; credulity; **~stellung** f position of trust; **~verhältnis** nt mutual trust no indef art; **persönliches ~verhältnis** relationship of personal trust; **v~voll** adj trusting; **wende dich v~voll an mich** you know you can always turn to me (for help); **~votum** nt (Parl) vote of confidence; **v~würdig** adj trustworthy; **~würdigkeit** f trustworthiness.

vertrauern* vt to spend (in) moping, to mope away.

vertraulich 1 adj (a) (geheim) Angelegenheit, Ton, Gespräch confidential. (b) (freundschaftlich) friendly, matey (inf), pally (inf); (plump ~) familiar. ~ **werden** to take liberties. **2** adv (a) confidentially, in confidence. (b) in a friendly/familiar way.

Vertraulichkeit f confidentiality; (vertrauliche Mitteilung) confidence; (Aufdringlichkeit) familiarity. **mit aller** ~ in strict(est) confidence; **plumpe/dreiste** ~ familiarity.

verträumen* vt to dream away.

verträumt adj dreamy; (idyllisch) Städtchen etc auch sleepy.

Verträumtheit f siehe adj dreaminess; sleepiness.

vertraut adj intimate; Freund auch close; (bekannt) Gesicht, Umgebung familiar, well-known. **eine ~e Person** a close or an intimate friend; **sich mit etw** ~ **machen** to familiarize or acquaint oneself with sth; **sich mit dem Gedanken** ~ **machen, daß** ... to get used to the idea that ...; **mit etw** ~ **sein** to be familiar or well acquainted with sth; **mit jdm** ~ **werden** to become friendly with sb; **mit jdm sehr** ~ **werden** to get on intimate terms with sb, to become close friends with sb.

Vertraute(r) mf decl as adj close or intimate friend, confidant(e).

Vertrautheit f, no pl siehe adj intimacy; closeness; familiarity.

vertreiben* vt irreg Tiere, Wolken, Einbrecher to drive away; (aus Haus etc) to drive or turn out (aus of); (aus Land) to drive out (aus of), to expel (aus from); (aus Amt, von Stellung) to oust; Feind to drive off, to repulse; (fig) Sorgen, Schmerzen to drive away, to banish; (Comm) Waren to sell. **ich wollte Sie nicht ~, bleiben Sie doch noch ein wenig** I don't mean to chase or drive you away – do stay a bit longer; **ich wollte Sie nicht von Ihrem Stuhl/Platz ~** I didn't mean to take your chair/seat; **jdn vom Thron/aus seinem Amt** ~ to oust sb from the throne/his office; **jdm/sich die Zeit mit etw** ~ to help sb pass the time/to pass (away) or while away the time with sth.

Vertreibung f (aus from) expulsion; (aus Amt etc) ousting; (von Feind) repelling. **die** ~ **aus dem Elternhaus** being turned out of one's parental home.

vertretbar adj justifiable; Theorie, Argument defensible, tenable. **nicht** ~ unjustifiable; indefensible, untenable.

vertreten* vt irreg (a) (jds Stelle, Dienst übernehmen) Kollegen, Arzt etc to replace, to stand in for, to deputize for; Schauspieler to replace, to stand in for; (fig: Funktion einer Sache übernehmen) to replace, to take the place of.
(b) jds Interessen, Firma, Land, Wahlkreis to represent; Sache to look after, to attend to; (Rechtsanwalt) Klienten auch to appear for; Fall to plead.
(c) (Comm: Waren vertreiben für) (Firma) to be the agent for; (Angestellter) to represent.
(d) (verfechten, angehören) Standpunkt, Doktrin, Theorie to support; Meinung to hold, to be of; Ansicht to take, to hold; Kunstrichtung to represent; (rechtfertigen) to justify (vor to).
(e) ~ **sein** to be represented.
(f) **jdm den Weg** ~ to bar sb's way.

(g) **sich** (dat) **den Fuß** ~ to twist or strain one's ankle; **sich** (dat) **die Beine** or **Füße** ~ (inf) to stretch one's legs.

Vertreter(in f) m -s, - (a) (von Land, Firma etc) representative; (Comm) (Firma) agent; (Angestellter) (sales) representative, rep (inf). ~ **für Damenkleider** (sales) representative in ladies' wear; ~ **einer Versicherung** insurance representative or rep (inf); **ein übler** ~ (fig inf) a nasty piece of work (inf).
(b) (Ersatz) replacement; (im Amt) deputy; (von Arzt) locum.
(c) (Verfechter) (von Doktrin) supporter, advocate; (von Meinung) holder; (von Kunstrichtung) representative.

Vertretung f siehe vt (a-d) (a) replacement. **die** ~ (für jdn) **übernehmen** to replace sb, to stand in (for sb); **die** ~ (für jdn) **haben** to stand in (for sb), to deputize (for sb); **X steht in** ~ **X is appearing** in his/her place; **in** ~ (in Briefen) on behalf of.
(b) representation. **X übernimmt die** ~ **des Klienten/Falles** X is appearing for the client/pleading the case; **die** ~ **meiner Interessen** representing my interests.
(c) (Comm) agency; representation.
(d) supporting; holding; representation.
(e) siehe **Vertreter(in)** (a, b).

Vertretungs-: **~stunde** f (Sch) class where one stands in for another teacher, stand-in class; **~stunden geben** to stand in for another teacher; **v~weise** adv as a replacement; (bei Amtsperson) as a deputy; **er übernimmt heute v~weise meine Deutschstunde** he's taking my German lesson for me today.

Vertrieb m -(e)s, -e (a) no pl sales pl. **der** ~ **eines Produktes** the sale of a product; **den** ~ **für eine Firma haben** to have the (selling) agency for a firm. (b) (Abteilung einer Firma) sales department.

Vertriebenen-: **~treffen** nt reunion of exiles; **~verband** m association of exiles.

Vertriebene(r) mf decl as adj exile.

Vertriebs-: **~abteilung** f sales department; **~gesellschaft** f marketing company; **~kosten** pl marketing costs pl; **~leiter** m sales manager.

vertrimmen* vt (inf) to belt (inf), to wallop (inf).

vertrinken* vt irreg to drink away, to spend on drink.

vertrocknen* vi aux sein to dry out; (Eßwaren) to go dry; (Pflanzen) to wither, to shrivel; (Quelle) to dry up. **er ist ein vertrockneter Mensch** he's a dry old stick (inf).

vertrödeln* vt (inf) to fritter away.

vertrösten* vt to put off. **jdn auf ein andermal/auf später** ~ to put sb off. **2** vr to be content to wait (auf +acc for).

vertrotteln* vi (inf) aux sein to vegetate.

vertrusten* [fɛɐˈtrastn] vt (Comm) to form into a trust.

vertüdern* (N Ger) **1** vr to get tangled up. **2** vt to tangle up, to get tangled up.

vertun* irreg **1** vt to waste. **2** vr (inf) to make a mistake or slip, to slip up (inf).

vertuschen* vt to hush up. ~, **daß** ... to hush up the fact that ...; **etw vor jdm** ~ to keep sth from sb.

verübeln* vt jdm etw ~ not to be at all pleased with sb for doing sth, to take sth amiss; **ich hoffe, Sie werden mir die Frage nicht** ~ I hope you won't mind my asking (this); **das kann ich dir nicht** ~ I can't blame you for that.

verüben* vt to commit, to perpetrate (form).

verulken* vt (inf) to make fun of, to take the mickey out of (inf).

verunfallen* vi aux sein (Sw) to have an accident.

verunglimpfen* vt jdn to disparage; Ruf, Ehre, Worte auch to decry.

Verunglimpfung f disparagement.

verunglücken* vi aux sein (Mensch) to have an accident; (Fahrzeug) to crash. (fig inf: mißlingen) to go wrong. **mit dem Flugzeug** ~ to be in a plane crash; **mit dem Auto** ~ to be in a car crash, to have a car accident; siehe **tödlich**.

verunglückt adj (fig) Versuch, Aufführung etc unsuccessful.

Verunglückte(r) mf decl as adj casualty, victim. **10 Tote, 20** ~ 10 dead, 20 injured.

verunreinigen* vt Fluß, Luft, Wasser to pollute; (beschmutzen) to dirty, to soil; (euph: Hund etc) to foul.

Verunreinigung f siehe vt pollution; dirtying, soiling; fouling; (verunreinigter Zustand: von Wasser, Luft) pollution.

verunsichern* vt to make unsure or uncertain (in +dat of). **jetzt hast du mich völlig verunsichert** I just don't know at all any more; **sie versuchten, ihn zu** ~ they tried to throw him; **verunsichert** uncertain.

Verunsicherung f (mangelnde Gewißheit) uncertainty. **das führte zur** ~ **der Wähler/Schüler** it put the electors/pupils into a state of uncertainty.

verunstalten* vt to disfigure; Landschaft auch to scar. **jdn** or **jds Gesicht** ~ to spoil or mar sb's looks.

Verunstaltung f disfigurement. **dieses übertriebene Make-up ist doch eine** ~ **deines Gesichts** you spoil your looks by overdoing the make-up.

veruntreuen* vt to embezzle, to misappropriate.

Veruntreuung f embezzlement, misappropriation.

verunzieren* vt Landschaft, Kunstwerk, Zimmer to spoil. **jdn** or **jds Gesicht** ~ to spoil sb's looks.

verursachen* vt to cause; Schwierigkeiten auch to create (dat for); to give rise to (dat for); Entrüstung, Zorn auch to provoke. **jdm große Kosten** ~ to cause sb a lot of expense; **jdm Umstände** ~ to put sb to or cause sb trouble.

Verursacher(in f) m -s, - cause.

Verursachung f siehe vt causing; creation; provocation.

verurteilen* vt to condemn; (Jur) (für schuldig befinden) to convict (für of); (zu Strafe) to sentence. **jdn zu einer Geldstrafe von 1.000 DM** ~ to fine sb 1,000 DM, to impose a fine of 1,000 DM on sb; **jdn zum Tode** ~ to condemn or sentence (Jur) sb to death; **jdn zu einer Gefängnisstrafe** ~ to give sb a prison sentence.

ver|urteilt *adj* zu etw ~ sein (*Jur*) to be sentenced to sth; (*fig*) to be condemned to sth; zum Tode ~ condemned *or* sentenced (*Jur*) to death; *siehe* Scheitern.

Ver|urteilte(r) *mf decl as adj* convicted man/woman, convict (*Jur*). der zum Tode ~ the condemned man.

Ver|urteilung *f siehe vt* condemnation; conviction; sentencing. seine ~ zu 5 Jahren his being sentenced to 5 years; seine ~ zum Tode his being condemned/sentenced to death.

ver|uzen* *vt* (*inf*) *siehe* verulken.

Verve ['vɛrvə] *f* -, *no pl* (*geh*) verve, spirit.

vervielfachen* *vtr* to multiply.

Vervielfachung *f* multiplication.

vervielfältigen* *vt* to duplicate; (*hektographieren auch*) to mimeograph; (*photokopieren auch*) to photocopy.

Vervielfältigung *f* (a) *siehe vt* duplication; mimeographing; photocopying. (b) (*Abzug*) copy; mimeograph; photocopy.

Vervielfältigungs-: ~apparat *m* duplicating *or* copying machine, duplicator; ~arbeit *f* duplicating; ~gerät *nt*, ~maschine *f siehe* ~apparat; ~papier *nt* duplicating paper; ~recht *nt* right of reproduction, copyright; ~verfahren *nt* duplicating process, copying process.

vervierfachen* *vtr* to quadruple.

vervollkommnen* 1 *vt* to perfect. 2 *vr* to perfect oneself.

Vervollkommnung *f* perfection.

vervollständigen* 1 *vt* to complete; Kenntnisse, gutes Essen *auch* to round off; Erlebnis to make complete. 2 *vr* to be completed.

Vervollständigung *f siehe vt* completion; rounding off; completion.

verwachsen¹* *vi irreg aux sein* (a) (*zusammenwachsen*) to grow (in) together, to grow into one; (*Narbe*) to heal over; (*Knochen*) to knit; (*Wunde*) to heal, to close (over). mit etw ~ to grow into sth.
(b) (*fig: Menschen, Gemeinschaft*) to grow closer (together). zu etw ~ to grow into sth; mit etw ~ mit Arbeit, Aufgabe, Traditionen to become caught up in sth; mit etw ~ sein to have very close ties with sth; ein Volk, das mit seinen Traditionen/ seiner Kultur ~ ist a nation whose traditions are/culture is deeply rooted within it; mit jdm ~ sein to have become very close to sb.

verwachsen²* *adj* (a) Mensch, Tier deformed; Glied *auch*, Pflanze malformed; (*verkümmert*) stunted. (b) (*überwuchert*) overgrown.

verwachsen³* *vir* (Ski) to use the wrong wax.

Verwachsung *f* (*Med*) deformation; malformation; (*verwachsenes Glied auch*) deformity; (*Biol, Min*) adhesion.

verwackeln* *vt* to blur.

verwählen* *vr* to misdial, to dial the wrong number.

verwahren* 1 *vt* (*aufbewahren*) to keep (safe). jdm etw zu ~ geben to give sth to sb for safekeeping. 2 *vr* sich gegen etw ~ to protest against sth.

verwahrlosen* *vi aux sein* to go to seed, to go to pot (*inf*). (*Gebäude auch*) to fall into disrepair, to become dilapidated; (*Mensch*) to let oneself go, to neglect oneself; (*verwildern*) to run wild; (*auf die schiefe Bahn geraten*) to fall into bad ways.

verwahrlost *adj* neglected; Mensch, Äußeres *auch* unkempt. sittlich ~ decadent.

Verwahrlosung *f, no pl siehe vi* neglect; dilapidation; neglect (of oneself); wildness; (*moralisch*) waywardness.

Verwahrsam *m* -s, *no pl* etw in jds ~ geben to give sth to sb for safekeeping; etw in ~ haben/nehmen to keep sth safe/to take sth into safekeeping.

Verwahrung *f* (a) *no pl* (*von Geld etc*) keeping; (*von Täter*) custody, detention. die ~ eines Menschen in einem Heim putting/keeping a person in a home; jdm etw in ~ geben, etw bei jdm in ~ geben to give sth to sb for safekeeping; etw in ~ nehmen to take into safekeeping; (*Behörde*) to take possession of sth; jdn in ~ nehmen to take sb into custody.
(b) (*Einspruch*) protest. gegen etw ~ einlegen to make *or* lodge a protest against sth.

verwaisen* *vi aux sein* to become an orphan, to be orphaned, to be made an orphan; (*fig*) to be deserted *or* abandoned. verwaist orphaned; (*fig*) deserted, abandoned.

verwalten* *vt* to manage; Firma *auch* to run; Angelegenheiten *auch* to conduct; Erbe, Vermögen *auch* to administer; Treuhandsgut to hold in trust; Amt to hold; (*Pol*) Provinz etc to govern; (*Beamte*) to administer; (*Rel*) to administer. er verwaltet das Amt des Oberinspektors gewissenhaft he conscientiously carries out *or* performs his duties as senior inspector; sich selbst ~ (*Pol*) to be self-governing.

Verwalter(in) *f* *m* -s, - administrator; (*Treuhänder*) trustee, custodian. der Papst als ~ Gottes the Pope as God's steward.

Verwaltung *f* (a) *siehe vt* management; running; conducting; administration; holding in trust; holding; government; administration. jdm etw zur ~ übergeben to put sb in charge of (the management/running etc of) sth.
(b) (*Behörde, Abteilung*) administration; (*Haus~*) management. städtische ~ municipal authorities *pl*.

Verwaltungs-: ~angestellte(r) *mf* admin(istration) employee; ~apparat *m* administrative machinery; ~beamte(r) *m* government (administration) official; ~behörde *f* administration; ~bezirk *m* administrative district; ~dienst *m* admin(istration) building *or* block; ~gebäude *nt* admin(istration) building *or* block; ~gebühr *f* administrative charge; ~gericht *nt* Administrative Court; ~kosten *pl* administrative expenses *pl*; ~weg *m* administrative channels *pl*; auf dem ~wege through (the) administrative channels.

verwamsen* *vt* (*inf*) to belt (*inf*), to clobber (*inf*).

verwandelbar *adj* (*Math, Econ*) convertible.

verwandeln* 1 *vt* (*umformen*) to change, to transform; Bett,

---

Zimmer, (*Math, Econ, Chem*) to convert; (*Theat*) Szene to change; (*Jur*) Strafe to commute; (*Rel*) Brot, Wein auch to transubstantiate. jdn/etw in etw (*acc*) ~ to turn sb/sth into sth; (*verzaubern auch*) to change *or* transform sb/sth into sth; die Vorlage ~ (*Ftbl*) to score off the pass; Müller verwandelte den Paß zum 2:0 Müller put the pass away to make it 2-0; ein Gebäude in einen Trümmerhaufen ~ to reduce a building to a pile of rubble; er ist wie verwandelt he's a changed man.
2 *vi* (Sport *sl*) zum 1:0 ~ to make it 1-0.
3 *vr* to change; (*Zool*) to metamorphose. sich in etw (*acc*) *or* zu etw ~ to change or turn into sth; Zeus hat sich in einen Stier verwandelt Zeus turned *or* transformed himself into a bull.

Verwandlung *f* (a) *siehe vt* transformation; conversion; change, changing; commuting; transubstantiation.
(b) *siehe vr* change; metamorphosis; (*von Göttern, von der Natur*) transformation. eine ~ durchmachen to undergo a change *or* transformation; seine erstaunliche ~ the remarkable change in him; „die ~" (Liter) "the Metamorphosis".

Verwandlungs-: ~künstler *m* quick-change artist; ~szene *f* (*Theat*) transformation scene.

verwandt 1 *ptp of* verwenden.
2 *adj* (a) related (mit to); (Ling *auch*) cognate; *siehe* Ecke.
(b) (*fig*) (mit to) Probleme, Methoden, Fragen, Wissenschaften related, allied; Philosophien, Kultur, Gefühle *auch* kindred *attr*; Denker, Geister kindred *attr*. ~e Seelen (*fig*) kindred spirits; geistig ~ sein (*fig*) to be kindred spirits; sie sind einander sehr ~ they are kindred souls, they are very much akin to each other; wir sind uns darin ~, daß ... we're akin to each other in that ...

verwandte *pret of* verwenden.

Verwandte(r) *mf decl as adj* relation, relative.

Verwandtschaft *f* relationship; (*die Verwandten*) relations *pl*, relatives *pl*; (*fig*) affinity, kinship. er leugnete die ~ zu mir he denied being related to me, he denied any relationship with me.

verwandtschaftlich *adj* family *attr*.

Verwandtschaftsgrad *m* degree of relationship. wir kennen ihren ~ nicht we don't know how closely they are related.

verwanzt *adj* Betten, Kleider bug-ridden, bug-infested; (*inf: mit Abhörgeräten*) bugged.

verwarnen* *vt* to caution, to warn.

Verwarnung *f* caution, warning; *siehe* gebührenpflichtig.

verwaschen *adj* faded (in the wash); (*verwässert*) Farbe watery; (*fig*) wishy-washy (*inf*), woolly (*inf*).

verwässern* *vt* to water down; (*fig auch*) to dilute.

Verwässerung *f* watering down; (*fig auch*) dilution.

verweben* *vt irreg* (a) *auch reg* Garne to weave; (*verbrauchen*) to use. (b) (*lit, fig: verflechten*) to interweave (mit, in + *acc* with).

verwechseln* *vt* Gegenstände to mix up, to get muddled *or* mixed up; Begriffe, Menschen auch to confuse. jdn (mit jdm) ~ to confuse sb with sb; (*für jdn halten auch*) to mistake sb for sb; entschuldigen Sie, ich habe Sie verwechselt sorry – I thought you were *or* I (mis)took you for someone else; zum V~ ähnlich sein to be the spitting image of each other, to be as like as two peas in a pod; ich habe meinen Schirm verwechselt I took somebody else's umbrella by mistake; sie verwechselt mir und mich (*lit*) she mixes up *or* confuses "mir" and "mich"; (*fig*) he doesn't know her grammar; *siehe* mein.

Verwechslung *f* confusion; (*Irrtum*) mistake. die Polizei ist sicher, daß eine ~ (des Täters) völlig ausgeschlossen ist the police are certain that there can be absolutely no mistake (about the culprit); es kam deshalb zu einer ~, weil ... there was a mix-up *or* confusion because ...; das muß eine ~ sein, da muß es sich um eine ~ handeln there must be some mistake.

verwegen *adj* daring, bold; (*tollkühn*) foolhardy, rash; (*keck*) cheeky, saucy. den Hut ~ aufsetzen to set one's hat at a jaunty *or* rakish angle; darf ich so ~ sein, und Sie zum Essen einladen? may I make so bold as to invite you for a meal?

Verwegenheit *f siehe adj* daring, boldness; foolhardiness, rashness; cheek(iness), sauciness.

verwehen* 1 *vt* Blätter to blow away, to scatter; Spur, Pfad to cover over, to obliterate. vom Winde verweht gone with the wind. 2 *vi aux sein* (*geh*) (Worte, Musik) to be carried away, to drift away; (Spur, Pfad) to be obliterated, to be covered over.

verwehren* *vt* (*geh*) jdm etw ~ to refuse *or* deny sb sth; die neugebauten Häuser ~ ihnen jetzt den Blick auf ... the newly built houses now bar their view of ...; jdm ~, etw zu tun to bar sb from doing sth; es war ihm verwehrt, seine Kinder erwachsen zu sehen he was denied seeing his children as adults.

Verwehung *f* (Schnee~) (snow)drift; (Sand~) (sand) drift.

verweichlichen* 1 *vt* jdn ~ to make sb soft; ein verweichlichter Mensch a weakling; ein verweichlichtes Muttersöhnchen a mollycoddled mother's boy. 2 *vi aux sein* to get *or* grow soft.

Verweichlichung *f* softness. willst du mir vielleicht ~ der Kinder vorwerfen? are you accusing me of making the children soft?; Zentralheizung führt zur ~ central heating makes you soft.

verweigern* *vt* to refuse; Befehl to refuse to obey; Kriegsdienst to refuse to do. jdm etw ~ to refuse *or* deny sb sth; er kann ihr keinen Wunsch ~ he can refuse *or* deny her nothing; es war ihr verweigert, ihren Sohn wiederzusehen she was denied seeing her son; die Annahme eines Briefes ~ to refuse (to accept *or* to take delivery of) a letter; das Pferd hat (das Hindernis) verweigert the horse refused (at the fence *or* jump); sich jdm ~ (*euph*) to refuse (to have) intimacy with sb.

Verweigerung *f* refusal; (*von Hilfe, Auskunft etc auch*) denial. die ~ einer Aussage (*Jur*) refusal to make a statement; ~ des Kriegsdienstes refusal to do (one's) military service; ~ des Gehorsams disobedience.

Verweigerungsfall m (Jur): im ~ in case of refusal to make a statement.

verweilen* **1** vi (geh) (Mensch) to stay; (Blick) to rest; (Gedanken) to dwell, to linger. **bei einer Sache** ~ to dwell on sth; **verweile doch** tarry or stay awhile (liter); **hier laßt uns** ~ let us linger or tarry (liter) here. **2** vr to linger, to tarry (liter).

Verweilen nt -s, no pl (geh) stay. **sein ~ bei dem Gedanken/ Thema** his dwelling on the thought/theme; **hier ist meines ~s nicht mehr** (liter) I can no longer tarry here (liter).

verweint adj Augen tear-swollen; Gesicht tear-stained; Mensch with (a) tear-stained face. ~ **aussehen** to look as though one has just been crying.

Verweis m -es, -e **(a)** (Rüge) reprimand, rebuke, admonishment. **jdm einen ~ erteilen** or **aussprechen** to reprimand or rebuke or admonish sb. **(b)** (Hinweis) reference (auf + acc to).

verweisen* irreg **1** vt **(a)** (hinweisen) jdn auf etw (acc)/an jdn ~ to refer sb to sth/sb.
(b) (von der Schule) to expel. **jdn des Landes** or **aus dem Lande** ~ to expel sb (from the country); **jdn vom Platz** or **des Spielfeldes** ~ to send sb off; **jdn auf den zweiten Platz** ~ (Sport) to relegate sb to second place.
(c) (zur) to refer (an + acc to).
(d) (dated: rügen) jdn ~ to rebuke or reprove or admonish sb; **jdm etw** ~ (tadeln) to rebuke or reprove or admonish sb for sth; (verbieten) to forbid sb (to) sth.
2 vi **auf etw** (acc) ~ to refer to sth.

Verweisung f **(a)** expulsion. **(b)** (Hinweis) siehe **Verweis (b)**. **(c)** (Jur) referral (an + acc to).

verwelken* vi aux sein (Blumen) to wilt; (fig) to fade. **ein verwelktes Gesicht** a worn face; **eine verwelkte Schönheit** a faded beauty.

verweltlichen* vt to secularize.

Verweltlichung f secularization.

verwendbar adj usable (zu for). **das ist nur einmal ~** it can be used once only.

Verwendbarkeit f, no pl usability.

verwenden pret **verwendete** or **verwandte**, ptp **verwendet** or **verwandt 1** vt to use; Methode, Mittel auch to employ; (verwerten auch) to make use of, to utilize. **Mühe/Fleiß auf etw** (acc) ~ to put effort/hard work into sth; **Zeit auf etw** (acc) ~ to spend time on sth, to put time into sth.
2 vr **sich** (bei jdm) **für jdn** ~ to intercede (with sb) or to approach sb on sb's behalf.

Verwendung f **(a)** use; (von Mitteln etc auch) employment; (von Zeit, Geld) expenditure (auf + acc on). **keine ~ für etw haben** to have no use for sth; **für alles ~ haben** (inf) to have a use for everything; ~ **finden** to have a use, to come in handy or useful; **für jdn/etw ~ finden** to find a use for sb/sth; **in ~ stehen** (Aus) to be in use; **etw in ~ nehmen** (Aus) to put in service. **(b)** (old: Fürsprache) intercession (bei with). **auf jds ~** (acc) **hin** through the intercession of sb.

Verwendungs-: v~**fähig** adj usable; **für etw** v~**fähig sein** to be suitable for sth; ~**möglichkeit** f (possible) use; ~**weise** f manner of use; **die** ~**weise von etw** the way in which sth is used; ~**zweck** m use, purpose.

verwerfen* irreg **1** vt **(a)** (ablehnen) to reject; eigene Meinung, Ansicht to discard; (Jur) Klage, Antrag to dismiss; Urteil to quash; (kritisieren) Handlungsweise, Methode to condemn. **(b)** Ball to lose. **2** vr **(a)** (Holz) to warp; (Geol) to fault. **(b)** (Cards) to misdeal. **3** vi Tier to abort.

verwerflich adj reprehensible.

Verwerflichkeit f reprehensibleness.

Verwerfung f **(a)** siehe vt **(a)** rejection; discarding; dismissal; quashing; condemnation. **(b)** (Geol) fault; (von Holz) warping.

verwertbar adj usable.

Verwertbarkeit f usability.

verwerten* vt (verwenden) to make use of, to utilize; Reste to use, to make use of; Kenntnisse auch to exploit, to put to (good) use; Erfahrungen auch to turn to (good) account; (kommerziell) Erfindung, Material etc to exploit. **dieser Stoff wird sich gut für ein Kleid ~ lassen** this material will make a nice dress.

Verwertung f siehe vt utilization; using; exploitation.

verwesen* **1** vi aux sein to decay; (Fleisch) to rot. **2** vt (obs) to administer; **jds Amt** ~ to deputize for sb.

Verweser m -s, - administrator; (Amts~) deputy; (Pfarr~) locum (tenens).

Verwesung f, no pl decay. **in ~ übergehen** to start to decay.

verwetten* vt to gamble away.

verwichsen* [vɛɐˈviksn] vt (inf) **(a)** siehe **verwamsen**. **(b)** Geld to squander.

verwickeln* **1** vt Fäden etc to tangle (up), to get tangled up. **jdn in etw** (acc) ~ to involve sb in sth; **in Kampf, in dunkle Geschäfte** auch to get sb mixed up in sth; **in Skandal** auch to get sb mixed up in sth, to embroil sb in sth.
2 vr (Fäden etc) to tangle (up), to become tangled. **sich in etw** (acc) ~ (lit) to become entangled in sth, to get caught up in sth; (fig) **in Widersprüche** to get oneself tangled up in sth; **in Skandal** to get mixed up or involved or embroiled in sth.

verwickelt adj (fig inf) (schwierig) involved, complicated, intricate; (verwirrt) Mensch fuddled, confused.

Verwick(e)lung f involvement (in + acc in); (in Skandal auch) embroilment; (Komplikation) complication; (Verwirrung) confusion; (Theat, Liter) intrigue, intricacy (of plot).

verwildern* vi aux sein (Garten) to become overgrown, to overgrow; (Pflanzen) to grow wild; (Haustier) to become wild; (hum inf: Mensch) to run wild.

verwildert adj wild; Garten overgrown; Aussehen unkempt.

Verwilderung f (von Garten) overgrowing. **Zustand der ~** state of neglect; **mangelnde Sorge führte zur ~ des Tieres/der Kinder** as a result of negligence the animal became wild/the children ran wild.

verwinden* vt irreg to get over.

verwinkelt adj full of corners.

verwirken vt (geh) to forfeit.

verwirklichen* **1** vt to realize; Hoffnung auch to fulfil; Idee, Plan auch to put into effect, to translate into action; Wunsch, Traum auch to make come true, to turn into a reality.
2 vr to be realized; to be fulfilled; to be put into effect, to be translated into action; to come true, to become a reality; (Mensch) to fulfil oneself.

Verwirklichung f, no pl realization; (von Hoffnung, Selbst~) fulfilment.

Verwirkung f forfeit(ure). ~ **einer Strafe** (Jur) incurrence of a penalty.

verwirren* **1** vt **(a)** Haar to tousle; to ruffle (up); Fäden etc to tangle (up), to get tangled up.
(b) (durcheinanderbringen) to confuse; (konfus machen) to bewilder; (aus der Fassung bringen auch) to fluster; Sinne, Verstand auch to (be)fuddle.
2 vr (Fäden etc) to become tangled (up) or snarled up; (Haare) to become tousled or dishevelled; (fig) to become confused.

Verwirrung f **(a)** (Durcheinander, Verlegenheit) confusion; (Fassungslosigkeit auch) bewilderment. **jdn in ~ bringen** to confuse/bewilder sb; (verlegen machen) to fluster sb. **(b)** (von Haaren) dishevelment; (von Fäden) entanglement.

verwirtschaften* vt to squander away.

verwischen* **1** vt (verschmieren) to smudge, to blur; (lit, fig) Spuren to cover over; (fig) Eindrücke, Erinnerungen to blur. **2** vr (lit, fig) to become blurred; (Schrift etc auch) to become smudged; (Erinnerung auch) to fade.

verwittern* vi aux sein to weather.

verwittert adj Gestein weathered; Gesicht auch weather-beaten.

Verwitterung f weathering.

verwitwet adj widowed. **Frau Meier, ~e Schulz** Mrs Meier, the widow of Mr Schulz.

verwohnen* vt Wohnung to run down; Möbel to wear out.

verwöhnen* **1** vt to spoil; (Schicksal) to smile upon, to be good to. **2** vr to spoil oneself.

verwohnt adj Wohnung lived-in pred; Möbel battered.

verwöhnt adj spoilt, spoiled; Kunde, Geschmack discriminating. **vom Schicksal/von den Göttern** ~ smiled upon by fate/the gods.

Verwöhntheit f, no pl siehe adj spoiltness; discriminating-ness.

Verwöhnung f, no pl spoiling.

verworfen **1** ptp **of** **verwerfen**. **2** adj (geh) depraved, degenerate; Blick depraved.

Verworfenheit f, no pl depravity, degeneracy.

verworren adj confused, muddled; (verwickelt) complicated, involved, intricate.

Verworrenheit f, no pl siehe adj confusion; complicatedness, intricacy.

verwundbar adj (lit, fig) vulnerable.

Verwundbarkeit f (lit, fig) vulnerability.

verwunden* vt to wound; (lit auch) to injure.

verwunderlich adj surprising; (stärker) astonishing, amazing; (sonderbar) strange, odd. **es ist sehr ~, daß ... it's** most amazing or surprising that ...; **es ist nicht ~, daß ...** it is no wonder or not surprising that ...

verwundern* **1** vt to astonish, to amaze. **2** vr (über + acc at) to be amazed or astonished, to wonder. **sich über etw** (acc) **sehr ~ müssen** to be most amazed at sth.

Verwunderung f, no pl astonishment, amazement. **zu meiner größten ~** to my great astonishment or amazement; **jdn in ~ setzen** to astonish or amaze sb.

verwundet adj (lit, fig) wounded.

Verwundete(r) mf decl as adj casualty. **die ~n** (Mil) the wounded.

Verwundung f wound.

verwunschen adj enchanted.

verwünschen* vt **(a)** (verfluchen) to curse. **verwünscht** cursed, confounded. **(b)** (in Märchen) (verzaubern) to enchant, to put or cast a spell on or over; (verhexen) to bewitch.

Verwünschung f **(a)** (Fluch) curse, oath. **(b)** no pl (Verzauberung) enchantment; (Verhexung) bewitchment.

verwursteln* vt (inf) to mess up (inf), to make a mess of.

verwurzelt adj ~ **sein** (Pflanze) to be rooted; (fest) in or mit etw (dat) ~ **sein** (fig) to be deeply rooted in sth.

Verwurzelung f (lit) rooting; (fig) rootedness.

verwüsten* vt to devastate, to ravage; (fig) Gesicht to ravage.

Verwüstung f devastation no pl, ravaging no pl; (von Gesicht) ravages pl. **die ~en durch den Sturm** the devastation caused by or the ravages of the storm; **~en anrichten** to inflict devastation.

verzagen* vi (geh) to become disheartened, to lose heart. **an etw** (dat) ~ to despair of sth; **nicht ~!** don't despair.

verzagt adj disheartened, despondent.

Verzagtheit f, no pl despondency.

verzählen* **1** vr to miscount, to count wrongly. **2** vti (dial inf) siehe **erzählen**.

verzahnen* vt Bretter to dovetail; Zahnräder to cut teeth or cogs in, to gear; (fig auch) to (inter)link. **ineinander verzahnt sein** to mesh.

Verzahnung f (von Brettern) (das Verzahnen) dovetailing; (das Verzahntsein) dovetail; (von Zahnrädern) gearing; (fig) dovetailing.

verzanken* vr to quarrel, to fall out.

verzapfen* vt **(a)** Getränke to serve or sell on draught. **(b)** Holzstücke to mortice and tenon; (mit Dübel) to dowel. **(c)** (inf) Unsinn to come out with; (pej) Gedichte, Artikel to concoct.

verzärteln vt (pej) to mollycoddle, to pamper.

Verzärtelung f, no pl (pej) mollycoddling, pampering.

verzaubern* vt (lit) to cast a spell on or over, to put a spell on; (fig) Mensch auch to enchant. jdn in etw (acc) ~ to turn sb into sth; eine verzauberte Prinzessin an enchanted princess.

Verzauberung f (lit, fig) enchantment; (Verhexung) bewitchment. die ~ des Prinzen in einen Frosch turning the prince into a frog.

verzehnfachen* vtr to increase ten-fold.

Verzehr m -(e)s, no pl consumption.

verzehren* 1 vt (form: lit, fig) to consume. 2 vr (geh) to languish (liter), to eat one's heart out. sich vor Gram/Sorgen ~ to be consumed by or with grief/worries; sich nach jdm ~ to pine for sb.

verzeichnen* 1 vt (a) to record; (aufzeichnen auch) to note; (in einer Liste auch) to enter; (St Ex) Kurse to quote. gewaltige Änderungen sind zu ~ enormous changes are to be noted; Todesfälle waren nicht zu ~ there were no fatalities; einen Erfolg zu ~ haben to have scored a success; das kann die Regierung als einen Erfolg ~ the government can mark this up as a success; in einer Liste ~ to list.
(b) (falsch zeichnen) to draw wrong(ly); (fig) to misrepresent, to distort.
2 vr to make mistakes/a mistake in one's drawing.
3 vti (Opt) to distort.

Verzeichnis nt index; (Tabelle) table; (Namens~, esp amtlich) register; (Aufstellung) list.

verzeihen pret verzieh, ptp verziehen vti (vergeben) to forgive; (Gott, Gebieter) to pardon; (entschuldigen) to excuse, to pardon. jdm (etw) ~ to forgive sb (for sth); ich kann es mir nicht ~, daß ich sie geschlagen habe I'll never forgive myself for hitting her; das ist nicht zu ~ that's unforgivable; (nicht zu entschuldigen auch) that's inexcusable or unpardonable; es sei dir noch einmal verziehen you're forgiven or excused!, we'll forgive you!; ~ Sie! excuse me!; (als Entschuldigung auch) I beg your pardon!; ~ Sie die Störung, ~ Sie, daß ich stören muß excuse me for disturbing her.

verzeihlich adj forgivable; (zu entschuldigen) excusable, pardonable.

Verzeihung f, no pl forgiveness; (Entschuldigung) pardon. ~! excuse me!; (als Entschuldigung auch) sorry!; (jdn) um ~ bitten (sich entschuldigen) to apologize (to sb); ich bitte vielmals um ~ I do apologize (für for), I'm terribly sorry (für about).

verzerren* 1 vt (lit, fig) to distort, to contort; Sehne, Muskel to strain, to pull. etw verzerrt darstellen (fig) to present a distorted picture of sth. 2 vi (Lautsprecher, Spiegel etc) to distort. 3 vr to become distorted; (Gesicht etc) to become contorted (zu in.)

Verzerrung f (lit, fig) distortion; (von Gesicht etc) contortion; (von Muskel, Sehne) straining, pulling; (Statistik) bias.

verzetteln* 1 vt (a) to waste; Geld, Zeit etc auch to fritter away; Energie auch to dissipate. (b) Wörter, Bücher to catalogue. 2 vr to waste a lot of time; (bei Aufgabe, Diskussion) to get bogged down.

Verzicht m -(e)s, -e renunciation (auf +acc of); (auf Anspruch) abandonment (auf +acc of); (Opfer) sacrifice; (auf Recht, Eigentum, Amt) relinquishment (auf +acc of); (auf Thron) abdication (auf +acc of). der ~ auf Zigaretten fällt ihm schwer he finds it hard to give up cigarettes; ein ~, der mir nicht schwerfällt that's something I can easily do without; ~ ist ein Fremdwort für sie doing without is foreign to her; ~ leisten or üben (auf +acc) (form) siehe verzichten.

verzichten vi to do without; (Opfer bringen) to make sacrifices. einer muß leider ~ somebody has to do without, I'm afraid; es war nur ein Apfel vorhanden, da hat sie zugunsten ihrer Schwester verzichtet there was only one apple, so she let her sister have it; der Kandidat hat zugunsten eines Jüngeren verzichtet the candidate stepped down in favour of a younger man; danke, ich verzichte (iro) not for me, thanks; auf jdn/etw ~ (ohne auskommen müssen) to do without sb/sth; auf Alkohol, Süßigkeiten etc auch to abstain from sth; (aufgeben) to give up sb/sth; auf Erbschaft, Eigentum to renounce sth; auf Anspruch to waive sth; auf Recht to relinquish sth; (von etw absehen) auf Kommentar, Anzeige etc to abstain from sth; auf Kandidatur, Wiederwahl, Amt to refuse sth; auf den Thron ~ to abdicate; auf jdn/etw ~ können to be able to do without sb/sth; auf Einzelheiten/eine förmliche Vorstellung ~ können to be able to dispense with details/a foreal introduction.

Verzicht-: ~erklärung f (auf +acc of) renunciation; (auf finanzielle Leistungen) disclaimer; (auf Rechte) waiver; ~leistung f (Jur) renunciation; ~politik f (pej) policy of surrender; ~politiker m (pej) politician supporting a policy of surrender.

verzieh pret of **verzeihen.**

verziehen¹ᵃ irreg 1 vt (a) Mund, Züge etc to twist (zu into). das Gesicht ~ to pull or make a face, to grimace; den Mund ~ to turn up one's mouth; keine Miene ~ not to turn a hair.
(b) Stoff to pull out of shape, to stretch; Chassis, Gestell to bend out of shape; Holz to warp.
(c) Kinder to bring up badly; (verwöhnen) to spoil; Tiere to train badly.
(d) Pflanzen to thin out.
2 vr (a) (Stoff) to go out of shape, to stretch; (Chassis) to be bent out of shape; (Holz) to warp.
(b) (Mund, Gesicht etc) to twist (zu into), to contort.
(c) (verschwinden) to disappear (auch inf); (Gewitter) to pass; (Nebel, Wolken) to disperse; (inf: schlafengehen) to be off to bed (inf).
3 vi aux sein to move (nach to). verzogen (Vermerk) no longer at this address; falls Empfänger verzogen in case of change of address.

verziehen² ptp of **verzeihen.**

verzieren* vt to decorate; (verschönern) to embellish; (Mus) to ornament.

Verzierung f siehe vt decoration; embellishment; ornamentation; (Mus: verzierende Noten) ornament; siehe abbrechen.

verzinken* vt (a) Metalle to galvanize. (b) (sl: verraten) to grass or squeal on (sl).

verzinsbar adj siehe **verzinslich.**

verzinsen* 1 vt to pay interest on. jdm sein Kapital (mit or zu 5%) ~ to pay sb (5%) interest on his/her capital; das Geld wird mit 3% verzinst 3% interest is paid on the money, the money yields or bears 3% interest. 2 vr sich (mit 6%) ~ to yield or bear (6%) interest.

verzinslich adj interest-bearing attr, yielding or bearing interest. ~/fest ~ sein to yield or bear interest/a fixed rate of interest; zu 3%/einem hohen Satz ~ yielding or bearing 3% interest/a high rate of interest; nicht ~ free of interest; das ist vom ersten Mai the interest on that is payable from the 1st of May; Kapital ~ anlegen to put capital out at interest.

Verzinsung f (das Verzinsen) payment of interest (+gen, von on); (Zinsertrag) interest (yield or return) (+gen, von on); (Zinssatz) interest rate.

verzogen 1 ptp of **verziehen.** 2 adj Kind badly brought up; (verwöhnt) spoilt; Tier badly trained.

verzögern* 1 vt to delay; (verlangsamen) to slow down. 2 vr to be delayed.

Verzögerung f (a) delay, hold-up. (b) no pl (das Verzögern) delaying; (Verlangsamung) slowing down; (Phys) deceleration; (Mil) holding action.

Verzögerungstaktik f delaying tactics pl.

verzollen* vt to pay duty on. diese Waren müssen verzollt werden you must pay duty on these articles; haben Sie etwas zu ~? have you anything to declare?; verzollt duty-paid.

Verzollung f payment of duty (+gen on).

verzücken* vt to enrapture, to send into raptures or ecstasies.

verzuckern* 1 vi aux sein (Honig etc) to crystallize. 2 vt (zu stark zuckern) to put too much sugar on/in etc, to oversweeten. (b) (fig) siehe **versüßen.**

verzückt adj enraptured, ecstatic. ~ lauschte er der Musik he listened enraptured to the music.

Verzückung f, no pl rapture, ecstasy. in ~ geraten to go into raptures or ecstasies (wegen over).

Verzug m (a) delay; (Rückstand von Zahlung) arrears pl. ohne ~ without delay, forthwith; bei ~ (der Zahlungen) on default of payment; im ~ in arrears pl; mit etw in ~ geraten to fall behind with sth; mit Zahlungen to fall into arrears with sth.
(b) es ist Gefahr im ~ there's danger ahead.
(c) (form: aus Stadt) moving away.

Verzugszinsen pl interest payable on arrears sing.

verzupfen* vr (Aus inf) to be off (inf).

verzwackt adj (inf) tricky.

verzweifeln* vi aux sein to despair (an +dat of). am Leben ~ to despair of life; nur nicht ~! don't despair!, don't give up!; es ist zum V~! it makes you despair!, it drives you to despair!

verzweifelt adj Blick, Stimme etc despairing attr, full of despair; Lage, Versuch, Kampf etc desperate. ich bin (völlig) ~ I'm in (the depths of) despair; (ratlos) I just don't know what to do, I'm at my wits' end; ..., sagte er ~ ... he said despairingly.

Verzweiflung f (Gemütszustand) despair; (Ratlosigkeit) desperation. etw in seiner or aus ~ tun to do sth in desperation; in ~ geraten to despair; jdn zur or in die ~ treiben to drive sb to despair; siehe bringen.

Verzweiflungstat f act of desperation.

verzweigen* vr (Bäume) to branch (out); (Straße) to branch (off); (Leitung) to branch; (Firma) to establish branches; (Anat, fig) to ramify.

verzweigt adj Baum, Familie, Firma, Straßennetz branched; (Anat, fig) ramified.

Verzweigung f siehe vr branching (out); branching (off); branching; establishment of branches; ramification.

verzwickt adj (inf) tricky.

Verzwicktheit f (inf) trickiness.

Vesper¹ f -, -n (Eccl) vespers pl.

Vesper² nt -s, - (dial) (auch ~pause, ~zeit) break; (auch ~brot) sandwiches pl.

vespern (dial) 1 vt to guzzle (inf). 2 vi (essen) to guzzle things (inf); (Pause machen) to have a break. er vespert gerade he's just having his break.

Vestibül [vɛstiˈbyːl] nt -s, -e (dated, geh) vestibule.

Veteran [veteˈraːn] m -en, -en (Mil, fig) veteran; (Aut) vintage car.

Veterinär [veteriˈnɛːɐ] m (old, form) veterinary surgeon.

Veterinärmedizin [veteriˈnɛːɐ-] f veterinary medicine.

Veto [ˈveːto] nt -s, -s veto; siehe einlegen.

Vetorecht [ˈveːto-] nt right of veto.

Vettel f -, -n (old pej) hag.

Vetter m -s, -n cousin; (in Märchen) Brother, Brer.

Vettern-: ~ehe f marriage between (first) cousins; ~wirtschaft f (inf) nepotism.

Vexierbild [vɛˈksiːɐ-] nt picture puzzle.

vexieren* [vɛˈksiːrən] vt (old) to vex.

V-Form [ˈfau-] f V-shape. in ~ in a V-shape, in the shape of) a V.

v-förmig [ˈfau-] adj V-shaped, in the shape of) a V. ~ aussehen to look like a V, to be V-shaped.

vgl. abbr of **vergleiche** cf.

v.H. abbr of **vom Hundert** per cent.

via [ˈviːa] adv via.

Viadukt [viaˈdʊkt] m -(e)s, -e viaduct.

Vibraphon [ˈvibrafoːn] nt -s, -e vibraphone, vibraharp (US).

Vibration [vibraˈtsioːn] f vibration.

Vibrator [viˈbraːtɔr] m vibrator.

vibrieren* [viˈbriːrən] *vi* to vibrate; (*Stimme*) to quiver, to tremble; (*schwanken: Ton*) to vary, to fluctuate.

Video [ˈviːdeo] *nt* -s, no *pl* video.

Video- [ˈviːdeo-] *in cpds* video; **~aufnahme** *f* video recording; **~band** *nt* video-tape.

Videothek [videoˈteːk] *f* -, -en video-tape library.

Videoverfahren [ˈviːdeo-] *nt* video *no art.*

vidieren* [viˈdiːrən] *vt* (*Aus, obs*) to sign.

Viech *nt* -(e)s, -er (*inf*) creature.

Viecherei *f* (*inf*) (a) (*Quälerei*) torture *no indef art* (*inf*). (b) (*grober Scherz*) rotten trick.

Vieh *nt* -(e)s, no *pl* (a) (*Nutztiere*) livestock; (*Rinder auch*) cattle *pl*. **10 Stück ~** 10 head of livestock/cattle. (b) (*inf: Tier*) animal, beast (*usu hum*). (c) (*pej inf: Mensch*) swine.

Vieh-: **~bestand** *m* livestock; **~futter** *nt* (animal) fodder *or* feed; **~handel** *m* livestock/cattle trade; **er hat einen ~handel** he deals in livestock/cattle; **~händler** *m* livestock/cattle dealer.

viehisch *adj* brutish; *Schmerzen* beastly; (*unzivilisiert*) *Benehmen* swinish. **~ essen** to eat like a pig; **~ hausen** to live like an animal/animals.

Vieh-: **~markt** *m* livestock/cattle market; **~salz** *nt* (*für Tiere*) cattle salt; (*zum Streuen*) road salt; **~seuche** *f* livestock disease; **~treiber** *m* drover; **~wagen** *m* cattle truck; **~weide** *f* pasture; **~zeug** *nt* (*inf*) animals *pl*, creatures *pl*; **~zucht** *f* (live)stock/cattle breeding.

viel *indef pron, adj, comp* **mehr**, *superl* **meiste(r, s)** *or adv* **am meisten** (a) *sing* (*adjektivisch*) a lot of, a great deal of; (*fragend, verneint auch*) much; (*substantivisch*) a lot, a great deal; (*fragend, verneint auch*) much. **~es** a lot of things; **~(es)**, **was ...**, **~(es) von dem, was ...** a lot *or* great deal of what ...; **in ~em, in ~er Hinsicht** *or* **Beziehung** in many respects; **mit ~em** with a lot of things; **um ~es besser** *etc* a lot *or* much *or* a great deal better *etc*; **sehr ~ (Geld** *etc*) a lot *or* a great deal (of money *etc*); **nicht sehr ~ (Geld** *etc*) not very much (money *etc*); **so ~ (Arbeit** *etc*) so much *or* such a lot (of work *etc*); **noch (ein)mal so ~ (Zeit** *etc*) as much (time *etc*) again; **zweimal so ~ (Arbeit** *etc*) twice as much (work *etc*); **gleich ~ (Gewinn** *etc*) the same amount (of profit *etc*); **ziemlich ~ (Schmutz** *etc*) rather a lot (of dirt *etc*); **ein bißchen ~ (Regen** *etc*) a bit too much (rain *etc*); **furchtbar ~ (Regen** *etc*) an awful lot (of rain *etc*); **zu ~ (Brot** *etc*) too much (bread *etc*); **einer zu ~** one too many; **~ Erfolg!** good luck!, I wish you every success!; **~ Spaß!** have fun!, enjoy yourself/yourselves!; **~ Neues/Schönes** *etc* a lot of *or* many new/beautiful *etc* things; **~ Volk** a lot of people; **das ~e/sein ~es Geld** all that/all his money; **das ~e Geld/Lesen** *etc* all this money/reading *etc*; **~ zu tun haben** to have a lot to do; **er hält ~/nicht ~ von ihm/davon** he thinks a lot *or* a great deal/doesn't think much of him/it; **das will ~/nicht ~ heißen** *or* **sagen** that's saying a lot *or* a great deal/not saying much.

(b) **~e** *pl* (*adjektivisch*) many, a lot of, a great number of; (*substantivisch*) many, a lot; **es waren nicht ~e auf der Party/in der Schule** there weren't many (people) *or* a lot (of people) at the party/many (children) *or* a lot (of children) at school; **da wir so ~e sind** since there are so many *or* such a lot of us; **davon gibt es nicht ~e/nicht mehr ~e** there aren't many *or* a lot about/many *or* a lot left; **furchtbar ~e (Kinder/Bewerbungen** *etc*) a tremendous number *or* an awful lot (of children/applications *etc*); **gleich ~e (Angestellte/Anteile** *etc*) the same number (of employees/shares *etc*); **so/zu ~e (Menschen/Fehler** *etc*) so/too many (people/mistakes *etc*); **er hat ~e(e) Sorgen/Probleme** *etc* he has a lot of worries/problems *etc*; **~e hundert Menschen** many hundreds of people; **die/seine ~en Fehler** *etc* the/his many mistakes *etc*; **die ~en Leute/Bücher!** all these people/books!; **~e glauben, ...** many (people) *or* a lot of people believe ...; **und ~e andere** and many others; **es waren derer** *or* **ihrer ~e** (*liter*) there were many of them.

(c) (*adverbial: mit vb*) a lot, a great deal; (*fragend, verneint auch*) much. **er arbeitet ~/nicht ~** he works a lot/doesn't work much; **er arbeitet zu/so ~** he works too/so much *or* such a lot; **sie ist ~ krank/von zu Hause weg** she's ill/away a lot; **die Straße wird (sehr/nicht) ~ befahren** this street is (very/not very) busy; **dieses Thema wird ~ diskutiert** this subject is much debated; **sich ~ einbilden** to think a lot of oneself.

(d) (*adverbial: mit adj, adv*) much, a lot. **~ größer** *etc* much *or* a lot bigger *etc*; **nicht ~ anders** not very *or* much *or* a lot different; **~ zu ... much too ...**; **~ zu ~** much *or* far too much; **~ zu ~e** far too many; **ich ginge ~ lieber ins Kino** I'd much rather go *or* I'd much prefer to go to the cinema.

Viel-: **v~bändig** *adj* multivolumed, in many volumes; **v~beschäftigt** *adj attr* very busy; **v~deutig** *adj* ambiguous; **~deutigkeit** *f* ambiguity; **v~diskutiert** *adj attr* much discussed; **~eck** *nt* polygon; **v~eckig** *adj* polygonal (*Math*), many-sided; **~ehe** *f* polygamy.

vielen|orts *adv siehe* **vielerorts**.

vielerlei *adj inv* (a) various, all sorts of, many different. (b) (*substantivisch*) all kinds *or* sorts of things.

viel|er|örtert *adj attr* much discussed.

vieler|orts *adv* in many places.

vielfach 1 *adj* multiple *attr*, manifold. **ein ~er Millionär** a multimillionaire; **auf ~e Weise** in many various ways; **auf ~en Wunsch** at the request of many people; **um ein ~es besser** *etc* many times better *etc*.

2 *adv* many times; (*in vielen Fällen*) in many cases; (*auf ~e Weise*) in many ways; (*inf: häufig*) frequently. **~ bewährt** tried and tested many times; **einen Faden ~ nehmen** to take several strands.

Vielfache(s) *nt decl as adj* (*Math*) multiple. **das kleinste gemeinsame ~** (*Math*) the least *or* lowest common multiple; **um ein ~s** many times over; **der Gewinn hat sich um ein ~s vermehrt/ist um ein ~s gestiegen** the profit has been multi-

plied several times; **er verdient ein ~s von dem, was ich verdiene** his salary is many times larger than mine.

Vielfalt *f* (great) variety.

vielfältig *adj* varied, diverse.

Vielfältigkeit *f, no pl* variety, diversity.

Viel-: **v~farbig**, **v~färbig** (*Aus*) *adj* multicoloured; (*Tech*) polychrome *attr*, polychromatic; **v~flächig** *adj* many-faced, polyhedral (*Math*); **~flächner** *m* -s, - (*Math*) polyhedron; **~fraß** *m* -es, -e (*Zool, fig*) glutton; (*amerikanischer ~fraß auch*) wolverine; **v~gehaßt** *adj attr* much-hated; **v~gekauft** *adj attr* frequently bought, much-purchased; **v~geliebt** *adj attr* much-loved; **v~genannt** *adj attr* much-cited, frequently mentioned; **v~geprüft** *adj attr* (*hum*) sorely tried; **v~gereist** *adj attr* much-travelled; **v~geschmäht** *adj attr* much-maligned; **v~gestaltig** *adj* variously shaped, varied in shape and form, multiform (*form*); (*fig: mannigfaltig*) varied; **in v~gestaltiger Weise** in multifarious ways; **~gestaltigkeit** *f* multiformity; (*Sci*) polymorphism; (*fig*) variety; **v~glied(e)rig** *adj* having *or* with many parts; (*Math*) polynomial; **~götterei** *f* polytheism; **~heit** *f, no pl* (*rare*) multiplicity; **v~hundertmal** *adv* (*liter*) hundreds upon hundreds of times, many hundreds of times; **v~köpfig** *adj* many-headed, polycephalous (*Sci, form*); (*inf*) *Familie, Schar* large.

vielleicht *adv* (a) perhaps; (*in Bitten auch*) by any chance. **ja, ~** yes, perhaps *or* maybe; **haben Sie ~ meinen Hund gesehen?** have you seen my dog by any chance?; **könnten Sie mir ~ sagen, wie spät es ist?** could you possibly tell me the time?; **~ könnten Sie so freundlich sein und ...?** perhaps you'd be so kind as to ...?; **~ sagst du mir mal, warum** you'd better tell me why; **~ hältst du mal den Mund!** keep your mouth shut; **hat er sich ~ verirrt/weh getan?** maybe he has got lost/hurt himself; **hast du ihm das ~ erzählt?** did you perhaps tell him that?; (*entsetzt: denn etwa*) you didn't tell him that, did you?; **~ hast du recht** perhaps you're right, you may be right, maybe you're right; **~, daß ...** it could be that ...

(b) (*wirklich, tatsächlich, inf: verstärkend*) really. **soll ich ~ 24 Stunden arbeiten?!** am I supposed to work 24 hours then?; **erwartet sie ~ von uns, daß wir ...?!** does she really expect us to ...?; **willst du mir ~ erzählen, daß ...?!** do you really mean to tell me that ...?; **du bist ~ ein Idiot!** you really are an idiot!; **ich war ~ nervös!** I wasn't half nervous! (*inf*), was I nervous!, I was as nervous as anything (*inf*); **das ist ~ ein Haus!** that's what I call a house! (*inf*), that's some house! (*inf*); **das war ~ eine Katastrophe** that was a real disaster.

(c) (*ungefähr*) perhaps, about.

vielmal *adv* (*Sw*) *siehe* **vielmals**.

vielmalig *adj attr* repeated.

vielmals *adv* (a) (*in bestimmten Wendungen*) **danke ~!** thank you very much!, many thanks!; **ich bitte ~ um Entschuldigung!** I do apologize!; **er läßt ~ grüßen** he sends his best regards. (b) (*liter: häufig*) many times, oft-times (*liter*).

Vielmännerei *f* polygamy, polyandry.

vielmehr *adv* rather; (*sondern, nur*) just. **ich glaube ~, daß ...** rather I *or* I rather think that ...; **nicht dumm, ~ faul** lazy rather than stupid, not stupid just lazy.

Viel-: **v~sagend** *adj* meaningful, significant; **jdn v~sagend ansehen** to give sb a meaningful look; **v~schichtig** *adj* (*lit rare*) multilayered; (*fig*) complex; **~schreiber** *m* prolific writer; **er ist ein richtiger ~schreiber** (*pej*) he really churns out the stuff (*inf*); **v~seitig** *adj* (*lit*) many-sided; *Mensch, Gerät, Verwendung* versatile; *Interessen* varied; *Ausbildung* broad, all-round *attr*; **diese Beruf ist sehr v~seitig** there are many different sides to this job; **v~seitig interessiert/anwendbar** *etc* to have varied interests/many uses *etc*; **auf v~seitigen Wunsch** by popular request; **~seitigkeit** *f siehe adj* many-sidedness; versatility; variedness; broadness, all-round nature; **v~sprachig** *adj* multilingual, polyglot; **er ist v~sprachig** he is multilingual *or* a polyglot; **~staaterei** *f* particularism; **v~stimmig** *adj* many-voiced; **v~tausendmal** *adv* (*liter*) thousands upon thousands of times, many thousands of times; **v~umworben** *adj attr* much-sought-after; *Frau* much-courted; **v~versprechend** *adj* promising, full of promise; **v~versprechend** *adj* promising, encouraging; **~völkerstaat** *m* multinational state; **~weiberei** *f* polygamy, polygyny; **~zahl** *f* multitude; **eine ~zahl von Abbildungen** a wealth of illustrations.

Vielzweck- *in cpds* multipurpose.

vier *num* (a) four. **die ersten/nächsten/letzten ~** the first/next/last four; **sie ist ~ (Jahre)** she's four (years old); **mit ~ (Jahren)** at the age of four; **~ Millionen** four million; **es ist ~ (Uhr)** it's four (o'clock); **um/gegen ~ (Uhr)** *or* **~e** (*inf*) at/around four (o'clock); **~ Uhr ~** four minutes past four; **~/fünf Minuten vor/nach ~** four minutes/five (minutes) to/past four; **halb ~** half past three; **~ Minuten vor/nach halb ~** twenty-six minutes past/three/twenty-six minutes to four; **für** *or* **auf ~ Tage** for four days; **in ~ Tagen** in four days, in four days' time; **~ zu drei** (*geschrieben* 4:3) four-three, four to three, 4-3; **wir waren** *or* **unser zu ~t** *or* **zu ~en** *or* **unser ~** (*geh*) there were four of us, we were four in number (*form*); **wir fahren zu ~t** *or* **mit ~en in Urlaub** there are four of us going on holiday together, we are going on holiday as a foursome; **sie kamen zu ~t** *or* **~en** four of them came; **stellt euch ~ und ~** *or* **zu je ~** *or* **zu ~t** *or* **zu ~en auf** line up in fours; **eine Familie von ~en** (*inf*) a family of four; **Vater ~er Töchter** *or* **von ~ Töchtern** father of four daughters.

(b) **jdn unter ~ Augen sprechen** to speak to sb in private *or* privately; **ein Gespräch unter ~ Augen** a private conversation *or* talk, a tête-à-tête; **jdn um ein Gespräch unter ~ Augen bitten** to ask to speak to sb privately *or* in private; **~ Augen sehen mehr als zwei** (*prov*) two heads are better than one (*prov*); **alle ~e von sich strecken** (*inf*) (*ausgestreckt liegen*) to stretch out; (*tot sein*) to have given up the ghost; **auf allen ~en** (*inf*) on all fours; **sich auf seine ~ Buchstaben setzen** (*hum inf*) to sit oneself down; *siehe* Wind, Wand, Hand.

Vier *f* -, -en four; (*Buslinie etc*) (number) four. **die** ~ *pl* (*Pol*) the (Big) Four; **die Herz-** ~ the four of hearts.

Vier-: ~**achser, 4achser** *m* -s, - (*Aut*) four-axle vehicle; **v**~**armig** *adj* with four arms; *Leuchter* with four branches; **v**~**bändig** *adj* four-volume *attr*, in four volumes; ~**beiner** *m* -s, - (*hum*) four-legged friend (*hum*); **v**~**beinig** *adj* four-legged; **v**~**blätt(e)rig** *adj* four-leaf *attr*, four-leaved; **v**~**dimensional** *adj* four-dimensional; ~**eck** *nt* four-sided figure, quadrilateral (*Math*); (*Rechteck*) rectangle; **v**~**eckig** *adj* square; (*esp Math*) four-sided, quadrangular, quadrilateral; (*rechteckig*) rectangular; **v**~**einhalb** *num* four and a half.

Vierer *m* -s, - (*Rudern, Sch*) four; (*Golf*) foursome; (*inf: Linie*) (number) four; (*inf: Lotto*) score of 4 correct; (*Aus, S Ger*) (*Ziffer*) four.

Vierer-: ~**bande** *f* gang of four; ~**bob** *m* four-man bob; ~**gruppe** *f* group of four; **v**~**lei** *adj inv* (a) *attr* Brot, Käse, Wein four kinds *or* sorts of; *Möglichkeiten, Fälle, Größen* four different; (b) (*substantivisch*) four different things; (*vier Sorten*) four different kinds; ~**pasch** *m* (all) fours *no indef art*; ~**reihe** *f* row of four; ~**treffen** *nt* (*Pol*) (*der vier Mächte*) four-power conference, meeting of the four powers; (*von Politikern*) meeting of four politicians.

vierfach, vierfältig (*geh*), **4fach 1** *adj* fourfold, quadruple (*esp Math*). **die** ~**e Größe/Menge/Anzahl** four times the size/amount/number; **in** ~**er Ausfertigung** in quadruplicate; **in** ~**er Vergrößerung** enlarged four times.

2 *adv* four times, fourfold. **das Papier** ~ **legen** *or* **nehmen** to fold the paper in four; **den Faden** ~ **nehmen** to take four threads together; **er hat den Band** ~ he has four copies of the book; **das Produkt wird** ~ **geprüft** this product is checked four times, there's a quadruple *or* fourfold check on this product.

Vierfache(s) *nt decl as adj* four times the amount, quadruple (*Math*). **das** ~ **von jdm verdienen** to earn four times as much as sb; **das** ~ **von 3 ist 12** four times 3 is 12; **zwei um das** ~ **vermehren** to add two to the quadruple of two; **um das** ~ **zunehmen** to quadruple.

Vier-: ~**farbendruck** *m* (*Verfahren*) four-colour printing; (*Erzeugnis*) four-colour print; ~**farb(en)stift** *m* four-colour pen; ~**felderwirtschaft** *f* four-course rotation; ~**flach** *nt* -(e)s, -e (*Math*) tetrahedron; **v**~**flächig** *adj Körper, Gebilde* tetrahedral; ~**fruchtmarmelade** *f* four-fruit jam; ~**füßer** *m* -s, - *siehe* ~**füßler**; **v**~**füßig** *adj* four-legged, quadruped(al) (*spec*); (*Poet*) tetrameter *attr*, with four feet; ~**füßler** *m* -s, - (*Zool*) quadruped, tetrapod (*spec*); ~**ganggetriebe** *nt* four-speed gearbox; **v**~**geschossig** *adj* four-storey *attr*, four storeyed; **v**~**geschossig bauen** to build houses/offices *etc* with four storeys; ~**gespann** *nt* (*vier Tiere, Wagen mit vier Tieren*) four-in-hand; (*Hist: Quadriga*) quadriga; (*vier Menschen*) foursome; **v**~**händig** *adj* (*Mus*) four-handed; **v**~**händig spielen** to play something for four hands; **v**~**hebig** *adj* (*Poet*) tetrameter; **v**~**hebig sein** to be a tetrameter.

vierhundert *num* four hundred.

Vierhundertjahrfeier *f* quatercentenary, quadricentennial (*US*).

vierhundertste(r, s) *adj* four hundredth.

vierhunderttausend *num* four hundred thousand.

Vier-: ~**jahresplan** *m* (*Econ*) four-year plan; **v**~**jährig, 4jährig** *adj* (4 Jahre alt) four-year-old *attr*; (4 Jahre dauernd) four-year *attr*, quadrennial; **ein v**~**jähriges Kind** a four-year-old child, a child of four; ~**jährige(r)** *mf decl as adj* four-year-old; ~**kampf** *m* (*Sport*) four-part competition; **v**~**kant** *adj, adv* (*Naut*) square; ~**kant** *m or nt* -(e)s, -e (*Tech*) square; (*Math*) tetrahedron; ~**kanteisen** *nt* square steel bar; ~**kantholz** *nt* squared timber; **v**~**kantig** *adj* square(-headed); **eine achtkantig;** ~**kantschlüssel** *m* square box spanner (*Brit*) *or* wrench; **v**~**köpfig** *adj* Ungeheuer four-headed; **eine v**~**köpfige Familie** a family of four.

Vierling *m* quadruplet, quad (*inf*).

Viermächte-: ~**abkommen** *nt* quadripartite *or* four-power agreement; ~**stadt** *f* city occupied by the four powers.

Vier-: **v**~**mal** *adv* four times; **v**~**mal so viele** four times as many; **v**~**malig** *adj* done *or* repeated four times; **v**~**maliges Klingeln/v**~**malige Vorstellungen** four rings/performances; **nach v**~**maligem Versuch** after the fourth attempt; **nach v**~**maliger Aufforderung** after the fourth time of asking, after four repeated requests; ~**master** *m* -s, - (*Naut*) four-master; ~**mastzelt** *nt* four-poled tent; **v**~**monatig** *adj attr Säugling* four-month-old; *Abstände* four-monthly; *Lieferungsfrist, Aufenthalt* four months; **v**~**monatlich 1** *adj attr Erscheinen* four-monthly; **2** *adv* erscheinen, sich wiederholen every four months; **v**~**motorig** *adj* four-engined; ~**pfünder** *m* four-pounder; **v**~**phasig** *adj* (*Elec*) four-phase.

Vierrad- (*Aut*): ~**antrieb** *m* four-wheel drive; ~**bremse** *f* four-wheel braking system.

Vier-: **v**~**räd(e)rig** *adj* four-wheel *attr*, four-wheeled; **das Auto ist v**~**räd(e)rig** that car is a four-wheeler; **v**~**saitig** *adj* four-stringed; **v**~**saitig sein** to have four strings; **v**~**schrötig** *adj* burly; **v**~**seitig** *adj* four-sided; *Abkommen, Verhandlungen etc* quadripartite; *Brief, Broschüre* four-page *attr*; ~**sektorenstadt** *f* city divided into four sectors; ~**silber** *m* -s, - (*Poet*) tetrasyllable; **v**~**silbig** *adj* four-syllable *attr*, quadrisyllabic, tetrasyllabic; ~**sitzer** *m* -s, - four-seater; **v**~**sitzig** *adj* four-seater *attr*, with four seats; **v**~**sitzig sein** to be a four-seater, to have four seats; **v**~**spaltig** *adj* four-column *attr*; **v**~**spaltig sein** to have four columns; ~**spänner** *m* -s, - four-in-hand; **v**~**spännig** *adj* Wagen four-horse *attr*; **v**~**spännig fahren** to drive a team of four horses *or* a four-in-hand; **v**~**sprachig** *adj* Mensch, Wörterbuch quadrilingual; *Speisekarte* in four languages; **v**~**sprachig aufwachsen** to grow up speaking four languages; **das Buch wird v**~**sprachig**

angeboten the book is available in four languages; **v**~**spurig** *adj* four-lane *attr*; **v**~**spurig sein** to have four lanes; **v**~**stellig** *adj* four-figure *attr*; (*Math*) *Funktion, Dezimalbruch* four-place *attr*; **v**~**stellig sein** to have four figures/places; **v**~**stimmig** *adj* four-part *attr*, for four voices; **v**~**stimmig singen** to sing a song for four voices; **v**~**stöckig** *adj* Haus four-storey *attr*, four-storeyed, four storeys high; **v**~**strahlig** *adj* Flugzeug four-jet *attr*, four-engined; **v**~**strophig** *adj* Gedicht four-verse *attr*, four-stanza *attr*; **v**~**strophig sein** to have four verses *or* stanzas; ~**stufenrakete** *f* four-stage rocket; **v**~**stufig** *adj* four-stage *attr*; **v**~**stufig sein** to have four stages; **v**~**stündig** *adj attr* Reise, Vortrag four-hour; **v**~**stündlich 1** *adj attr* four-hourly; **2** *adv* every four hours.

viert *adj* (a) **zu** ~ *siehe* vier. (b) *siehe* vierte(r, s).

Vier-: ~**tagewoche** *f* four-day week; **v**~**tägig** *adj attr* (4 Tage dauernd) four-day; (4 Tage alt) four-day old; **v**~**täglich** *adj, adv* every four days; ~**takter** *m* -s, - (*inf*), ~**taktmotor** *m* four-stroke (engine); **v**~**tausend** *num* four thousand; ~**tausender** *m* -s, - (*Berg*) four-thousand-metre mountain.

vierte *adj siehe* vierte(r, s).

vier-: ~**teilen** *vt* (a) *insep* (*Hist*) to quarter; **sie würden sich für ihn** ~**teilen lassen** they would die for him; (b) *sep siehe* vierteln; ~**teilig** *adj* (*mit vier einzelnen Teilen*) four-piece *attr*; *Roman* four-part *attr*, in four parts; ~**teilig sein** to have four pieces/parts; **ich habe dieses Service nur** ~**teilig** I only have four settings of this dinner service.

Viertel[1] ['fɪrtl] *nt* (*Sw auch m*) -s, - (a) (*Bruchteil*) quarter; (*inf*) (~**pfund**) = quarter; (~**liter**) quarter-litre. **der Mond ist im ersten/letzten** ~ the moon is in the first/last quarter; **ein** ~ **Wein/Butter** *etc* a quarter-litre of wine/quarter of butter *etc*. (b) (*Uhrzeit*) (ein) ~ **nach/vor sechs** (a) quarter past/to six; (ein) ~ **sechs** (a) quarter past five; **drei** ~ **sechs** (a) quarter to six; **es ist** ~ **it's** (a) quarter past; **die Uhr schlug** ~ the clock struck (a) quarter past *or* the quarter; *siehe* akademisch.

Viertel[2] ['fɪrtl] *nt* -s, - (*Stadtbezirk*) quarter, district.

viertel ['fɪrtl] *adj inv* quarter. **ein** ~ **Liter/Pfund** a quarter (of a) litre/pound; **drei** ~ **Liter** three quarters of a litre.

Viertel- ['fɪrtl-]: ~**drehung** *f* quarter-turn; ~**finale** *nt* quarter-finals *pl*; ~**finalspiel** *nt* quarter-final.

Vierteljahr *nt* three months *pl*, quarter (*Comm, Fin*).

Vierteljahres- in *cpds* quarterly; ~**schrift** *f* quarterly.

Viertel- ['fɪrtl-]: ~**jahrhundert** *nt* quarter of a century; **v**~**jährig** *adj attr* Kind *etc* three-month-old; *Aufenthalt, Frist* three months'; **v**~**jährlich 1** *adj* quarterly; *Kündigung* three months' *attr*; **2** *adv* quarterly, every three months; **v**~**jährlich kündigen** to give three months' notice; ~**kreis** *m* quadrant; ~**liter** *m or nt* quarter of a litre, quarter-litre.

vierteln ['fɪrtln] *vt* (*in vier Teile teilen*) to divide into four; *Kuchen, Apfel etc auch* to divide into quarters; (*durch vier teilen*) to divide by four; *Summe, Gewinn* to quarter, to divide by four.

Viertel- ['fɪrtl-]: ~**note** *f* crotchet (*Brit*), quarter note (*US*); ~**pause** *f* crotchet/quarter-note rest; ~**pfund** *nt* = quarter of a pound, quarter(-pound); ~**stunde** *f* quarter of an hour; **v**~**stündig** *adj attr* Abstand quarter-hour, of a quarter of an hour; *Vortrag* lasting *or* of a quarter of an hour; **v**~**stündlich 1** *adj attr* Abstand quarter-hour, of a quarter of an hour; **eine v**~**stündliche Einnahme des Medikaments anordnen** to order the medicine to be taken every quarter of an hour; **2** *adv* every quarter of an hour, quarter-hourly; ~**ton** *m* quarter tone.

viertens *adv* fourth(ly), in the fourth place.

Vierte(r) *mf decl as adj* fourth. ~**r werden** to be *or* come fourth; **am V**~**n** (des Monats) on the fourth (of the month); **Karl IV** *or* **der** ~ Charles IV *or* the Fourth.

vierte(r, s) *adj* fourth. **der** ~ **Oktober** the fourth of October; **den 4. Oktober** October 4th, October the fourth; **am** ~**n Oktober** on the fourth of October; **der** ~ **Stock** the fourth (*Brit*) *or* fifth (*US*) floor; **der** ~ **Stand** the Fourth Estate; **im** ~**n Kapitel/Akt** in the fourth chapter/act, in chapter/act four; **er war** ~**r im Rennen** he was *or* came fourth in the race; **als** ~**r durchs Ziel gehen** to be fourth at the finish; **du bist der** ~, **der mich das fragt** you're the fourth person to ask me that; **jeder** ~ **muß ...** every fourth person/boy *etc* has to ...

viertletzte(r, s) *adj* fourth (from) last.

Vier-: ~**tonner, 4tonner** *m* -s, - = four-ton truck, four-tonner; **v**~**türig** *adj* four-door *attr*, with four doors; **v**~**türig sein** to have four doors; ~**uhrzug, 4-Uhr-Zug** *m* four o'clock (train); **v**~**undeinhalb** *num siehe* viereinhalb; ~**undsechzigstelnote** *f* hemidemisemiquaver (*Brit*), sixty-fourth note (*US*); ~**undsechzigstelpause** *f* hemidemisemiquaver/sixty-fourth note rest; **v**~**undzwanzig** *num* twenty-four.

Vierung *f* (*Archit*) crossing.

Vierungskuppel *f* (*Archit*) crossing cupola.

Viervierteltakt [-'fɪrtl-] *m* four-four *or* common time.

Vierwaldstättersee *m* Lake Lucerne.

vier-: ~**wertig** *adj* (*Chem*) quadrivalent, tetravalent; (*Ling*) four-place; ~**wöchentlich** *adj, adv* every four weeks; ~**wöchig** *adj* four-week *attr*, four weeks long.

vierzehn ['fɪrtseːn] *num* fourteen. ~ **Uhr 2 p.m.;** (*auf Fahrplan, Mil*) fourteen hundred hours, 14.00; ~ **Tage** two weeks, a fortnight *sing* (*Brit*); **die V**~ **Punkte** (*Hist*) the Fourteen Points.

Vierzehn-: ['fɪrtseːn-]: ~**ender** *m* (*Hunt*) fourteen-pointer; **v**~**tägig** *adj* two-week *attr*, lasting two weeks; **nach v**~**tägiger Dauer** after two weeks *or* a fortnight (*Brit*); **v**~**täglich** *adj, adv* fortnightly (*Brit*), every two weeks.

Vierzehntel ['fɪrtseːntl] *nt* -s, - fourteenth; *siehe* **Vierzigstel.**

vierzehnte(r, s) ['fɪrtseːntə(r, s)] *adj* fourteenth; *siehe* vierte(r, s).

Vier-: ~**zeiler** *m* -s, - four-line poem; (*Strophe*) four-line stanza, quatrain; **v**~**zeilig** *adj* four-line *attr*, of four lines; **v**~**zeilig sein** to have four lines.

vierzig [ˈfɪrtsɪç] *num* forty. **mit ~ (km/h) fahren** to drive at forty (kilometres an hour); **etwa ~ (Jahre alt)** about forty (years old); (*Mensch auch*) fortyish (*inf*); **mit ~ (Jahren), mit V~** at forty (years of age); **Mitte (der) V~** in one's mid-forties; **über ~** over forty; **der Mensch über V~** *or* ~ people *pl* over forty; **im Jahre ~** in forty; (~ *nach/vor Christi Geburt*) in (the year) forty (AD)/BC.

Vierzig [ˈfɪrtsɪç] *f* -, **-en** forty.

vierziger, 40er [ˈfɪrtsɪgɐ] *adj attr inv* **die ~ Jahre** the forties; **ein ~ Jahrgang** (*Mensch*) a person born in nineteen/eighteen forty; (*Wein*) a vintage forty.

Vierziger(in *f*) [ˈfɪrtsɪgɐ, -ərɪn] *m* **-s,** - (*Mensch*) forty-year-old; (*Wein*) wine of vintage forty; (*Aus, S Ger: Geburtstag*) fortieth (birthday). **die ~** *pl* (*Menschen*) people in their forties; **er ist Mitte der ~** he is in his mid-forties; **er ist in den ~n** he is in his forties; **in die ~ kommen** to be getting on for forty.

Vierzig- [ˈfɪrtsɪç-]: **v~fach 1** *adj* forty-fold; **2** *adv* forty times; *siehe* **vierfach; v~jährig** *adj attr* (*40 Jahre alt*) forty-year-old; (*40 Jahre dauernd*) forty-year; **ein ~jähriger** a forty-year-old; **v~mal** *adv* forty times; **~pfennigmarke, 40-Pfennig-Marke** *f* forty-pfennig stamp.

Vierzigstel [ˈfɪrtsɪçstl] *nt* **-s,** - fortieth. **ein ~ des Kuchens/der Summe** a fortieth (part) of the cake/the amount.

vierzigstel [ˈfɪrtsɪçstl] *adj inv* fortieth. **eine ~ Minute** a *or* one fortieth of a minute.

vierzigste(r, s) [ˈfɪrtsɪçstə(r, s)] *adj* fortieth.

Vierzigstundenwoche [fɪrtsɪç-] *f* forty-hour week.

Vier-: **~zimmerwohnung** *f* four-room flat (*Brit*) *or* apartment; **~zylindermotor** *m* four-cylinder engine; **v~zylindrig** *adj* four-cylinder *attr*.

Vietcong, Vietkong [viɛtˈkɔŋ] *m* -, -(s) Vietcong.

Vietnam [viɛtˈnam] *nt* -s Vietnam.

Vietnamese [viɛtnaˈmeːzə] *m* **-n,** **-n, Vietnamesin** *f* Vietnamese.

Vietnamisierung [viɛtnamiˈziːrʊŋ] *f* Vietnamization.

vietnamesisch [viɛtnaˈmeːzɪʃ] *adj* Vietnamese.

vif [viːf] *adj* (*old, dial*) bright.

Vigil [viˈgiːl] *f* -, **-ien** [-iən] vigil.

Vignette [vɪnˈjɛtə] *f* vignette.

Vikar [viˈkaːɐ] *m* curate; (*Sw Sch*) supply teacher.

Vikariat [vikaˈriaːt] *nt* curacy.

Viktorianisch [vɪktoˈriaːnɪʃ] *adj* Victorian.

Viktualien [vɪkˈtuaːliən] *pl* (*obs*) victuals *pl* (*old, form*).

Viktualienmarkt [vɪkˈtuaːliən-] *m* food market.

Villa [ˈvɪla] *f* -, **Villen** villa.

Villenviertel [ˈvɪlən-] *nt* exclusive residential area.

Vinaigrette [vinɛˈgrɛtə] *f* (*Cook*) vinaigrette (sauce).

Viola [ˈviːola] *f* - (*Mus*) viola. **(b)** (*Bot*) violet.

Viola da Gamba [ˈviːola da ˈgamba] *f* - - -, **Viole** - - viola da gamba.

Violett [vioˈlɛt] *nt* -s, - purple, violet; (*im Spektrum, Regenbogen*) violet.

violett [vioˈlɛt] *adj siehe* **n** purple, violet; violet.

Violine [vioˈliːnə] *f* violin; *siehe* **Geige.**

Violinist(in *f*) [violiˈnɪst(ɪn)] *m* violinist.

Violin- [vioˈliːn-]: **~konzert** *nt* violin concerto; (*Darbietung*) violin concert; **~schlüssel** *m* treble clef.

Violoncell *nt* -s, -e, **Violoncello** [violɔnˈtʃɛl(o)] *nt* violoncello.

Viper [ˈviːpɐ] *f* -, **-n** viper, adder.

Viren [ˈviːrən] *pl of* **Virus.**

Virginia¹ [vɪrˈdʒiːnia] *nt* -s Virginia.

Virginia² *f* -, **-s, Virginiazigarre** *f* [vɪrˈgiːnia-, (*Aus*) vɪrˈdʒiːnia-] Virginia cigar.

Virginiatabak [vɪrˈgiːnia-, vɪrˈdʒiːnia-] *m* Virginia tobacco.

viril [viˈriːl] *adj* virile.

Virilität [viriliˈtɛːt] *f* virility.

Virologe [viroˈloːgə] *m*, **Virologin** *f* virologist.

Virologie [viroloˈgiː] *f* virology.

virologisch [viroˈloːgɪʃ] *adj* virological.

virtuell [vɪrˈtuɛl] *adj* virtual.

virtuos [vɪrˈtuoːs] *adj* virtuoso *attr*. **~ spielen** to give a virtuoso performance, to play like a virtuoso.

Virtuose [vɪrˈtuoːzə] *m* **-n,** **-n, Virtuosin** *f* virtuoso.

Virtuosität [vɪrtuoziˈtɛːt] *f, no pl* virtuosity.

virulent [viruˈlɛnt] *adj* (*Med*) virulent.

Virulenz [viruˈlɛnts] *f* (*Med*) virulence, virulency.

Virus [ˈviːrʊs] *nt or m* -, **Viren** virus.

Virus- [ˈviːrʊs-]: **~infektion** *f* viral *or* virus infection; **~krankheit** *f* viral disease.

Visa [ˈviːza] *pl of* **Visum.**

Visage [viˈzaːʒə, (*Aus*) viˈzaːʒ] *f* -, **-n** (*pej*) face, physog (*dated inf*), (ugly) mug (*inf*); *siehe* **polieren.**

vis-à-vis [vizaˈviː] (*dated*) **1** *adv* opposite (*von* to). **2** *prep* +*dat* opposite (to).

Visavis [vizaˈviː] *nt* -, - (*dated*) person (sitting) opposite, vis-à-vis (*form*). **mein ~** the person opposite me.

Visen [ˈviːzən] *pl of* **Visum.**

Visier [viˈziːɐ] *nt* -s, -e **(a)** (*am Helm*) visor. **mit offenem ~ kämpfen** to fight with an open visor; (*fig*) to be open and above board (in one's dealings). **(b)** (*an Gewehren*) sight. **jdn/etw ins ~ bekommen** to get sb/sth in one's sights; **jdn/etw ins ~ fassen** to train one's sights on sb/sth.

visieren* [viˈziːrən] **1** *vi* **~ auf** (+*acc*) to take aim at. **2** *vt* **(a)** (*eichen*) *Fässer* to gauge. **(b)** *Paß* to endorse with a visa.

Vision [viˈzioːn] *f* vision.

visionär [vizioˈnɛːɐ] *adj* visionary.

Visionär [vizioˈnɛːɐ] *m* visionary.

Visitation [vizitaˈtsioːn] *f* (*form*) **(a)** (*Besuch*) visitation (*auch Eccl*), inspection. **(b)** (*Durchsuchung*) search, inspection.

Visite [viˈziːtə] *f* -, **-n** (*Med*) (*im Krankenhaus*) round; (*zu Hause*) visit, house call. **um 9 Uhr ist ~** the doctors do their rounds at 9 o'clock ; **~ machen** to do one's round; to do visits *or* house calls; (*dated inf*) to visit (*bei jdm* sb), to pay a visit (*bei* to); **zur ~ kommen** to come on one's round; to come on a visit *or* house call.

Visitenkarte [viˈziːtn-] *f* (*lit, fig*) visiting *or* calling (*US*) card.

visitieren* [viziˈtiːrən] *vt* **(a)** (*form*) *Amtsbezirk etc* to visit, to inspect. **(b)** (*old*) *Gepäck* to search, to inspect.

Visitkarte [viˈziːt-] *f* (*Aus*) *siehe* **Visitenkarte.**

viskos [vɪsˈkoːs], **viskös** [vɪsˈkøːs] *adj* viscous.

Viskose [vɪsˈkoːzə] *f* -, *no pl* viscose.

Viskosität [vɪskoziˈtɛːt] *f* viscosity.

visuell [viˈzuɛl] *adj* visual.

Visum [ˈviːzʊm] *nt* -s, **Visa** *or* **Visen** visa.

Visumzwang [ˈviːzʊm-] *m* obligation to hold a visa. **für San Serife besteht ~** it is necessary to obtain a visa for San Serife.

vital [viˈtaːl] *adj* vigorous, energetic; (*lebenswichtig*) vital.

Vitalität [vitaliˈtɛːt] *f* vitality, vigour.

Vitamin [vitaˈmiːn] *nt* -s, -e vitamin. **~ B** (*lit*) vitamin B; (*fig inf*) contacts *pl*; **wie willst du das machen? — mit ~ B!** (*inf*) how are you going to do it? — I have my ways.

Vitamin- [vitaˈmiːn-]: **v~arm** *adj* poor in vitamins; **v~arm leben/essen** to live on/have a vitamin-deficient diet; **eine v~arme Zeit** a time when there are/were few vitamins available; **~bedarf** *m* vitamin requirement; **v~-C-haltig** *adj* containing vitamin C; **v~-C-haltig sein** to contain vitamin C; **v~haltig, v~hältig** (*Aus*) *adj* containing vitamins; **v~haltig sein** to contain vitamins.

vitamin(is)ieren* [vitaminiˈziːrən, -ˈniːrən] *vt* to vitaminize, to add vitamins to.

Vitamin- [vitaˈmiːn-]: **~mangel** *m* vitamin deficiency; **~mangelkrankheit** *f* disease due to a vitamin deficiency; **v~reich** *adj* rich in vitamins; **~spritze** *f* vitamin injection; (*fig*) shot in the arm (*fig inf*); **~stoß** *m* (massive) dose of vitamins.

Vitrine [viˈtriːnə] *f* (*Schrank*) glass cabinet; (*Schaukasten*) showcase, display case.

Vitriol [vitriˈoːl] *nt* -s, -e vitriol.

Vivarium [viˈvaːriʊm] *nt* vivarium.

vivat [ˈviːvat] *interj* (*geh*) vivat (*form*).

Vivisektion [vivizɛkˈtsioːn] *f* vivisection.

vivisezieren* [viviˈtsiːrən] *vti* to vivisect.

Vize [ˈfiːtsə] *m* -s, - (*inf*) number two (*inf*), second-in-command; (~*meister*) runner-up.

Vize- [ˈfiːtsə-] *in cpds* vice-; **~kanzler** *m* vice-chancellor; **~könig** *m* viceroy; **~meister** *m* runner-up; **~präsident** *m* vice-president; **~rektor** *m* (*von Schule*) deputy headmaster *or* principal (*esp US*); (*von Universität*) deputy vice-chancellor *or* rector (*US*).

Vlies [fliːs] *nt* -es, -e fleece.

Vlieseline ® *f* interfacing.

V-Mann [ˈfau-] *m siehe* **Verbindungsmann.**

VN *pl abbr of* **Vereinte Nationen** UN *sing.*

Vogel *m* -s, ⸚ (*lit, fig*) bird. **ein seltener ~** (*lit, fig*) a rare bird; **ein seltsamer etc ~** (*inf*) a queer bird (*inf*) *or* customer (*inf*); **ein lustiger ~** (*inf*) a lively character (*inf*); **~ friß oder stirb** (*prov*) do or die! (*prov*); **den ~ abschießen** (*inf*) to surpass everyone (*iro*); **einen ~ haben** (*inf*) to be crazy (*inf*), to have a screw loose (*inf*); **jdm den ~ zeigen** (*inf*) to tap one's forehead to indicate to sb that he's not quite right in the head, ≈ to give sb the V sign (*Brit*) *or* the finger (*US*).

Vogel-: **~bauer** *nt* bird-cage; **~beere** *f* (*auch* **~beerbaum**) rowan-(tree), mountain ash; (*Frucht*) rowan-(berry).

Vögelchen, Vög(e)lein (*liter*) *nt* little bird. **gleich kommt's Vögelchen raus** (*inf*) watch the birdie (*inf*).

Vogel-: **~dreck** *m* bird droppings *pl*; **~ei** *nt* bird's egg; **~eier** *pl* (*von einem Vogel*) bird's eggs *pl*; (*verschiedene Arten*) birds' eggs *pl*; **~fänger** *m* bird-catcher, fowler; **~flug** *m* flight of birds; **v~frei** *adj* (*Hist*) outlawed; **für v~frei erklärt werden** to be outlawed *or* declared an outlaw/outlaws; **~futter** *nt* bird food; (*Samen*) birdseed; **~käfig** *m* bird-cage; (*auch* **~haus**) aviary; **~kirsche** *f* (*wilde Süßkirsche*) wild cherry; **~kunde** *f* ornithology; **~männchen** *nt* cock (bird), male bird.

vögeln *vti* (*vulg*) to screw (*sl*).

Vogel-: **~nest** *nt* bird's nest; **~perspektive, ~schau** *f* bird's-eye view; **(ein Bild von) Ulan Bator aus der ~perspektive** a bird's-eye view of Ulan Bator; **~scheuche** *f* (*lit, fig inf*) scarecrow; **~schutz** *m* protection of birds; **~steller** *m* -s, - bird-catcher, fowler; **~-Strauß-Politik** *f* head-in-the-sand *or* ostrich-like policy; **~-Strauß-Politik treiben** to bury one's head in the sand; **~warte** *f* ornithological station; **~weibchen** *nt* hen (bird), female bird; **~zug** *m* (*Wanderung*) bird migration.

Vogerlsalat *m* (*Aus*) *siehe* **Rapunzel.**

Vöglein *nt* (*liter*) little bird.

Vogt *m* -(e)s, ⸚e (*Hist*) (*Kirchen~*) church advocate; (*Reichs~*) protector; (*Land~*) landvogt, governor; (*von Burg, Gut*) steward, bailiff.

Vogtei *f siehe* **Vogt** office of church advocate; protectorate; governorship; (*Gebiet*) area administered by a/the church advocate; protectorate; province; (*Residenz*) church advocate's/protector's/landvogt's *or* governor's residence.

Vokabel [voˈkaːbl] *f* -, **-n** *or* (*Aus*) *nt* -s, - word. **~n** *pl* vocabulary *sing*, vocab *sing* (*Sch inf*).

Vokabelschatz [voˈkaːbl-] *m* vocabulary.

Vokabular [vokabuˈlaːɐ] *nt* -s, -e vocabulary.

Vokal [voˈkaːl] *m* -s, -e vowel.

vokal [voˈkaːl] *adj* (*Mus*) vocal.

Vokalisation [vokalizaˈtsioːn] *f* vocalization.

vokalisch [voˈkaːlɪʃ] *adj* (*Ling*) vocalic. **~e Anlaute/Auslaute** initial/final vowels.

Vokalismus [voka'lɪsmʊs] m (Ling) vocalism.
Vokalist(in f) [voka'lɪst(ɪn)] m (Mus geh) vocalist.
Vokalmusik [vo'ka:l-] f vocal music.
Vokativ ['vo:kati:f, voka'ti:f] m vocative.
vol. abbr of **Volumen.**
Vol.- % abbr of **Volumprozent.**
Volant [vo'lã:] m -s, -s (a) (Stoffbesatz) valance; (am Rock, Kleid) flounce. (b) auch nt (Aus, Sw, old: Lenkrad) steering wheel.
Volk nt -(e)s, ⁔er (a) no pl people pl; (Nation auch) nation; (Volksmasse auch) masses pl; (inf: Gruppe) crowd pl; (pej: Pack) rabble pl. alles ~ everybody; viel ~ lots of people pl, crowds pl; etw unters ~ bringen Nachricht to spread sth; Geld to spend sth; die sind ein lustiges ~ (inf) they are a lively lot (inf) or bunch (inf) or crowd; da verkehrt ein ~! there's a really strange crowd there!; siehe Mann, fahrend.
(b) (ethnische Gemeinschaft) people sing. die ⁔er Afrikas the peoples of Africa; ein ~ für sich sein to be a race apart.
(c) (Zool) colony.
Völkchen nt (a) (kleine Nation) small nation. (b) (inf: Gruppe) lot (inf), crowd. ein ~ für sich sein to be a race apart.
Völker-: ~ball m game for two teams where the object is to hit an opponent with a ball and thus put him out of the game; ~bund m (Hist) League of Nations; ~freundschaft f friendship among nations; ~kunde f ethnology; ~kundler(in f) m -s, - ethnologist; v~kundlich adj ethnological; ~mord m genocide; ~recht nt international law, law of nations; v~rechtlich 1 adj Vertrag, Entscheidung, Anerkennung under international law; Frage, Thema, Hinsicht, Standpunkt of international law; Anspruch, Haftung international; vom v~rechtlichen Standpunkt according to or under international law; v~rechtliche Anerkennung eines Staates recognition of a state; 2 adv regeln, entscheiden by international law; klären according to international law; bindend sein under international law; ~schaft f small group of people; (Stamm) tribe; ~schlacht f (Hist) Battle of the Nations; ~verständigung f international understanding; ~wanderung f (Hist) migration of the peoples; (hum) mass migration or exodus.
völkisch adj (NS) national.
volkreich adj populous.
Volks- in cpds popular; (auf ein Land bezogen) national; (Pol, esp DDR) people's; ~abstimmung f plebiscite; ~armee f (DDR) People's Army; ~armist m (DDR) soldier in the People's Army; ~ausgabe f popular edition; ~beauftragte(r) mf people's representative or delegate; ~befragung f public opinion poll; ~befreiungsarmee f people's liberation army; ~begehren nt petition for a referendum; ~belustigung f public entertainment; ~bibliothek f public library; ~bildung f national education; (Erwachsenenbildung) adult education; ~brauch m national custom; ~bücherei f public library; ~bühne f people's theatre; ~charakter m national character; ~demokratie f people's democracy; ~deutsche(r) mf ethnic German; ~dichter m poet of the people; ~dichtung f folk literature/poetry; v~eigen adj (DDR) nationally-owned; (in Namen) People's Own; ~eigentum nt (DDR) national property, property of the people; im ~eigentum nationally-owned, owned by the people; ~einkommen nt national income; ~empfinden nt national feeling; das gesunde ~empfinden popular sentiment; ~entscheid m referendum; ~erhebung f popular or national uprising; ~etymologie f folk etymology; ~feind m enemy of the people; v~feindlich adj hostile to the people; ~fest nt public festival; (Jahrmarkt) funfair; ~front f (Pol) popular front; ~geist m national spirit; ~gemeinschaft f (NS) national community; ~genosse m (NS) national comrade; ~gerichtshof m (NS) People's Court; ~gesundheit f public health; ~glaube(n) m popular belief; ~gruppe f ethnic group; (Minderheit) ethnic minority; ~held m popular hero; (Held des Landes) national hero; ~herrschaft f popular rule, rule of the people; ~hochschule f adult education centre; einen Kurs in der ~hochschule machen to do an adult education class; (am Abend auch) to do an evening class; etw in der ~hochschule lernen to learn sth in adult education classes/evening classes; an der ~hochschule unterrichten to teach in adult education; to give evening classes; ~justiz f popular justice; ~küche f soup kitchen; ~kunde f folklore; ~kundler(in f) m -s, - folklorist; v~kundlich adj folkloristic; ein v~kundliches Institut an institute of folklore; ~lauf m (Sport) open cross-country race; ~lied nt folk song; ~märchen nt folktale; ~meinung f public or popular opinion; ~menge f crowd, mob (pej); ~mund m vernacular; im ~mund nennt man das ... this is popularly called ..., in the vernacular this is called ...; ~musik f folk music; ~partei f people's party; ~poesie f folk poetry; ~polen nt (DDR) (People's Republic of) Poland; ~polizei f (DDR) People's Police; ~polizist m (DDR) member of the People's Police; ~rede f (rare: lit) public speech; (inf) (long) speech; du sollst keine ~reden halten! (inf) I/we don't want any speeches!; ~republik f people's republic; ~sage f folk legend, folktale; ~schicht f level of society, social stratum; ~schulabschluß m (dated) elementary school-leaving certificate; ~schule f (dated) ≈ elementary school (Hist), school providing basic primary and secondary education; ~schüler m (dated) pupil at elementary school (Hist); ~schullehrer m (dated) elementary school teacher (Hist); ~seele f soul of the people; die kochende ~seele the seething or angry populace; ~seuche f epidemic; ~souveränität f (Pol) sovereignty of the people; ~sprache f everyday language, vernacular; ~staat m (Pol) people's state; ~stamm m tribe; ~stimme f voice of the people; ~stück nt dialect folk play; ~sturm m (Hist) Volkssturm, German territorial army; ~tanz m folk dance; ~theater nt folk theatre; (Gattung auch) folk drama; ~tracht f traditional costume; (eines Landes) national costume; ~trauertag m national day of

mourning, ≈ Remembrance Day (Brit), Veterans' Day (US); ~tribun m (Hist) tribune (of the people); ~tum nt national traditions pl, folklore; ~tümelei f (inf) folksiness (inf); v~tümlich adj folk attr, folksy (inf); (traditionell, überliefert) traditional; (beliebt) popular; etw v~tümlich darstellen/ausdrücken to popularize sth/express oneself in plain language; ein v~tümlicher König a king with the common touch; ~tümlichkeit f siehe adj folk character, folksiness (inf); tradition; popularity; (von Darstellungs-, Ausdrucksweise) popular appeal; (von König) common touch; v~verbunden adj close to the people; ~verführer m demagogue; ~verhetzung f incitement (of the people); ~vermögen nt national wealth; ~versammlung f people's assembly; (Kundgebung) public gathering; ~vertreter m representative or delegate of the people; ~vertretung f representative body (of the people); ~wahl f direct election (s pl); ~wirt m economist; ~wirtschaft f national economy; (Fach) economics sing, political economy; ~- und Betriebswirtschaft economics and business studies; ~wirtschaftler m economist; ~wirtschaftslehre f economics sing, political economy; ~wohl nt good or welfare of the people, public weal; ~zählung f (national) census; ~zugehörigkeit f ethnic origin.
voll 1 adj (a) (gefüllt) full. ~er + gen full of; ~ (von or mit) etw full of sth; (bedeckt mit) covered with sth; ~ des Lobes full of praise; mit ~em Mund with one's mouth full; aus dem ~en leben to live a life of luxury, to live in the lap of luxury; aus dem ~en schöpfen to draw on unlimited resources.
(b) (ganz) full; Satz, Service, Erfolg complete; Woche, Jahr auch, Wahrheit whole. ein ~es Dutzend a full or whole dozen; ~e drei Jahre/Tage three whole years/days, fully three years/days; die Uhr schlägt nur alle ~en Stunden the clock only strikes the full hour; die Zahl ist ~ the numbers are complete; die ~e Summe bezahlen to pay the full sum or the sum in full; in ~er Fahrt/~em Galopp/~em Lauf at full speed/gallop/speed; in ~er Größe (Bild) life-size; (bei plötzlicher Erscheinung etc) large as life; sich zu ~er Größe aufrichten to draw oneself up to one's full height; etw in seinem ~en Umfang or in seiner ~en Tragweite erkennen to understand sth fully or with all its implications; ~e Gewißheit über etw (acc) haben to be completely or fully certain about sth; im ~en Tageslicht in full daylight; in ~er Uniform in full dress or uniform; den Mund ~ nehmen (fig) to exaggerate, to overdo it; jdn nicht für ~ nehmen not to take sb seriously; aus ~em Halse or ~er Kehle or Brust singen to sing at the top of one's voice; etw mit ~em Recht tun to be perfectly right to do sth; mit dem ~en Namen unterschreiben to sign one's full name, to sign one's name in full.
(c) ~ sein (inf) (satt) to be full (up); (betrunken) to be plastered (inf) or tight (inf); ~ wie ein Sack or eine Strandhaubitze or tausend Mann absolutely plastered (inf), roaring drunk (inf).
(d) (üppig) Gesicht, Busen etc full; Wangen chubby; Haar thick. ~er werden to fill out.
(e) Stimme, Ton full, rich; Farbton rich.
2 adv fully; (vollkommen auch) completely. ~ und ganz completely, wholly; die Straße ist ~ gesperrt/wieder ~ befahrbar the road is completely closed/completely free again; jdn ~ ansehen to look sb straight in the face; eine Rechnung ~ bezahlen to pay a bill in full; ~ hinter jdm/etw stehen to be or stand fully behind sb/sth; jdn etw ~ treffen (mit Stein, Bombe etc) to score a direct hit on sb/sth; (ins Gesicht) to hit sb full in the face; etw ~ ausnützen to take full advantage of sth; ~ zuschlagen (inf) to lam out (inf); ~ durcharbeiten (inf) to work solidly (throughout); ~ drinstecken (inf) (bei Arbeit) to be in the middle of it; (in unangenehmer Situation) to be right in it; ~ (Stoff) gegen etw fahren (inf) to run full tilt or slap-bang (inf) into sth; nicht ~ dasein (inf) to be not quite with it (inf); ~ dabeisein (inf) to be totally involved.
volladen vt sep irreg getrennt voll-laden to load up. **vollgeladen** fully-laden.
Voll|akademiker m honours graduate.
voll|auf adv fully, completely. ~ genug quite enough; das genügt ~ that's quite enough; ~ zu tun haben to have quite enough to do (mit with).
vollaufen vi sep irreg aux sein getrennt: voll-laufen to fill up. etw ~ lassen to fill sth (up); sich ~ lassen (inf) to get tanked up (inf).
Voll-: v~automatisch adj fully automatic; v~automatisiert adj fully automated; ~bad nt (proper) bath; ~bart m (full) beard; v~bekommen* vt sep irreg to (manage to) fill; v~berechtigt adj attr with full rights; Unterhändler fully authorized; Mitglied full; die Kinder sind in unserer Familie v~berechtigt the children enjoy the same rights as the adults in our family; v~beschäftigt adj Arbeiter employed full-time; (attr: sehr beschäftigt) fully occupied; v~beschäftigung f full employment; ~besitz m: im ~besitz + gen in full possession of; ~bier nt beer with 11-14% original wort.
Vollblut nt, no pl thoroughbred.
Vollblut- in cpds (lit: Tier) thoroughbred; (fig) full-blooded.
Voll-: ~blüter m -s, - thoroughbred; v~blütig adj thoroughbred; (fig) full-blooded; ~bremsung f emergency stop; eine ~bremsung machen to slam on the brakes (inf), to do an emergency stop; v~bringen¹ vt sep irreg (inf) siehe v~bekommen; v~bringen²* vt insep irreg (ausführen) to accomplish, to achieve; Wunder to work, to perform; es ist v~bracht (Bibl) it is done (Bibl); ~bringung f accomplishment, achievement; v~busig adj full-bosomed, bosomy (inf); ~busigkeit f full bosom.
Volldampf m (Naut) full steam. mit ~ at full steam or speed; (inf) flat out; mit ~ voraus full steam or speed ahead; (inf) full tilt.
Völlegefühl nt (unpleasant) feeling of fullness; satiety.

voll|enden* *insep* **1** *vt* (*abschließen*) to complete; (*liter*) *Leben* to bring to an end; (*vervollkommnen*) to make complete; *Geschmack* to round off.
   2 *vr* (*zum Abschluß kommen*) to come to an end; (*vollkommen werden*) to be completed; (*Liebe*) to be fulfilled.

voll|endet *adj* (*vollkommen*) completed; *Tugend, Schönheit* perfect; *Mensch* accomplished. **nach ~em 18. Lebensjahr** upon completion of one's 18th year; **~ Klavier spielen** to be an accomplished piano player; *siehe* **Tatsache**.

vollends *adv* (a) (*völlig*) completely, altogether. (b) (*besonders*) especially, particularly.

Voll|endung *f, no pl* completion; (*Vervollkommnung, Vollkommenheit*) perfection; (*von Liebe*) fulfilment.

voller *adj siehe* **voll**.

Völlerei *f* gluttony.

voll|essen *vr sep irreg* (*inf*) to gorge oneself.

Volley ['vɔli] *m* **-s, -s** volley.

Volleyball ['vɔli-] *m* volleyball.

Voll-: **v~fett** *adj* full fat; **~fettkäse** *m* full fat cheese; **v~fressen** *vr sep irreg* (*pej inf*) to stuff oneself (*inf*).

vollführen* *vt insep* to execute, to perform; *Lärm,* (*fig*) *Theater* to create.

Voll-: **v~füllen** *vt sep* to fill (up); **~gas** *nt, no pl* full speed or throttle; **~gas geben** to open it right up; (*mit Auto auch*) to put one's foot hard down; **mit ~gas fahren** to drive at full throttle; **mit ~gas** (*fig inf*) full tilt; **mit ~gas arbeiten** to work flat out; **~gefühl** *nt*: **im ~gefühl +gen** fully aware of; **~genuß** *m*: **im ~genuß +gen** in full enjoyment of; **v~gießen** *vt sep irreg* (*auffüllen*) to fill (up); **sie hat sich** (*dat*) **den Rock v~gegossen/mit Kaffee v~gegossen** (*inf*) she spilt it/coffee all over her skirt; **v~gültig** *adj attr Paß* fully valid; *Ersatz* completely satisfactory; *Beweis* conclusive; **~gummi** *nt or m* solid rubber; **~gummireifen** *m* solid rubber tyre; **~idiot** *m* (*inf*) complete idiot.

völlig **1** *adj* complete. **das ist mein ~er Ernst** I'm completely or absolutely serious. **2** *adv* completely. **es genügt ~** that's quite enough; **er hat ~ recht** he's absolutely right.

Voll-: **v~inhaltlich** *adj attr* full, complete; **v~jährig** *adj* of age; **v~jährig werden/sein** to come/be of age; **sie hat drei v~jährige Kinder** she has three children who are of age; **~jährige(r)** *mf decl as adj* major; **~jährigkeit** *f* majority *no art*; **bei ~jährigkeit** on attaining one's majority; **~jährigkeitsalter** *nt* age of majority; **~jährigkeitserklärung** *f* declaration of majority; **v~kaskoversichert** *adj* comprehensively insured; **v~kaskoversichert sein** to have fully comprehensive insurance; **~kasko(versicherung** *f*) *nt* fully comprehensive insurance; **v~klimatisiert** *adj* fully air-conditioned.

vollkommen **1** *adj* perfect; (*völlig*) complete, absolute. **sein Glück war ~** his happiness was complete. **2** *adv* completely.

Vollkommenheit *f, no pl siehe adj* perfection; completeness, absoluteness. **die ~ der Stille wurde durch nichts gestört** nothing disturbed the perfect or complete silence.

Voll-: **~kornbrot** *nt* coarse wholemeal bread; **~kraft** *f* (*geh*) **in der ~kraft seiner Jahre/seines Schaffens** in his prime; **v~machen** *sep* **1** *vt* (a) *Gefäß* to fill (up); *Zahl, Dutzend* to make up; *Sammlung, Set* to complete; **siehe Maß**[1]; (b) (*inf*) *Hosen, Windeln* to fill; **sich** (*dat*) **die Hosen v~machen** (*fig inf*) to wet oneself (*inf*); **2** *vr* (*inf*) to get messed up or dirty; (*in die Hosen etc machen*) to fill one's pants/nappy/diaper. **Vollmacht** *f* **-, -en** (legal) power or authority *no pl, no indef art*; (*Urkunde*) power of attorney. **jdm eine ~ erteilen or ausstellen** to give or grant sb power of attorney.

Vollmachtgeber *m* principal. **~ und Vollmachtnehmer** principal and agent.

Vollmachts|urkunde *f* power of attorney.

Voll-: **v~mast** *adv* full mast; **auf v~mast** at full mast; **~matrose** *m* able-bodied seaman; **~milch** *f* full-cream milk; **~milchschokolade** *f* full-cream milk chocolate; **~mond** *m* full moon; **heute ist v~mond** there's a full moon today; **~mondgesicht** *nt* (*inf*) moon-face; **~mondnacht** *f* night of a full moon; **v~mundig** *adj Wein* full-bodied; **~narkose** *f* general anaesthetic; **v~packen** *vt sep* (*lit, fig*) to pack full; **jdn** to load up; **~pension** *f* full board; **v~pfropfen** *vt sep* (*inf*) to cram full; **v~pumpen** *vt sep* to fill (up); **~rausch** *m* drunken stupor; **einen ~rausch haben** to be in a drunken stupor; **v~reif** *adj* fully ripe; **v~saugen** *vr sep reg or irreg* to become saturated; **v~schenken** *vt sep* to fill; **~schiff** *nt* full-rigged ship; **v~schlagen** *vr sep irreg* (*inf*) **sich** (*dat*) **den Bauch v~schlagen** to stuff oneself with food (*inf*); **v~schlank** *adj* plump, stout; **Mode für v~schlanke Damen** fashion for the fuller figure or for ladies with a fuller figure; **v~schmieren** *sep* **1** *vt* to mess up; **2** *vr* to mess oneself up; **v~schreiben** *vt sep irreg Heft, Seite* to fill (with writing); *Tafel* to cover (with writing); **~sinn** *m*: **im ~sinn des Wortes** in the fullest sense of the word; **~spur** *f* (*Rail*) standard gauge, standard-gauge track; **v~spurig** (*Rail*) **1** *adj* standard-gauge; **2** *adv* on standard-gauge track.

vollständig (*abbr* vollst.) **1** *adj* complete. *Sammlung, Satz auch* entire *attr*; *Adresse* full *attr*. **nicht ~** incomplete; **etw ~ machen** to complete sth; **etw ~ haben** to have sth complete. **2** *adv* completely, entirely.

Vollständigkeit *f, no pl* completeness. **der ~ halber** to complete the picture.

vollstopfen *vt sep* to cram full.

vollstreckbar *adj* enforceable, able to be carried out or executed. (*Jur*) **~e Urkunde** executory deed.

vollstrecken* *vt insep* to execute; *Todesurteil* to carry out; *Pfändung* to enforce. **~de Gewalt** executive (power); **ein Todesurteil an jdm ~** to execute sb.

Vollstrecker(in *f*) *m* **-s, -** executor; (*Frau auch*) executrix. **~ des Todesurteils** executioner.

Vollstreckung *f siehe vt* execution; carrying out; enforcement.

Vollstreckungs-: **~beamte(r)** *m* enforcement officer; **~befehl** *m* enforcement order, writ of execution; **~gericht** *nt* court of execution or enforcement; (*bei Konkursverfahren*) bankruptcy court.

Voll-: **v~synchronisiert** *adj* fully synchronized; **v~tanken** *vti sep* to fill up; **bitte v~tanken** fill her up, please; **v~tönend** *adj* resonant, sonorous; **~treffer** *m* (*lit, fig*) bull's eye; **v~trunken** *adj* completely or totally drunk; **in v~trunkenem Zustand Auto fahren** to drive when drunk or in a drunken state; **~trunkenheit** *f* total inebriation; **~versammlung** *f* general meeting; (*von Stadtrat etc*) full meeting or assembly; **~waise** *f* orphan; **v~wertig** *adj* full *attr*; *Stellung* equal; *Ersatz* (fully) adequate; **jdn als v~wertig behandeln/betrachten** to treat regard sb as an equal; **v~zählig** *adj usu pred Satz, Anzahl, Mannschaft* complete; (*ausnahmslos anwesend*) all present *pred*; **um v~zähliges Erscheinen wird gebeten** everyone is requested to attend; **sie sind v~zählig erschienen** everyone came; **v~zählig versammelt sein** to be assembled in full force or strength; **~zähligkeit** *f, no pl* full number; (*ausnahmslose Anwesenheit*) full attendance; **sich von der ~zähligkeit der Klasse/des Satzes überzeugen** to check that everyone is in class that the set is complete.

vollziehbar *adj Strafe, Urteil* enforceable, executable. **etw ist für jdn ~** sb is able to execute sth.

vollziehen* *insep irreg* **1** *vt* to carry out; *Befehl auch* to execute; *Strafe, Urteil auch* to execute, to enforce; *Opferung, Trauung* to perform; *Bruch* to make; (*form*) *Ehe* to consummate. **die Unterschrift ~** (*form*) to sign; **einen Gedankengang ~ können** to be capable of a train of thought; **die ~de Gewalt** the executive (power).
   2 *vr* to take place; *Trauung* to be performed; (*jds Schicksal*) to be fulfilled.

Vollziehung *f*, **Vollzug** *m, no pl* (a) *siehe vt* carrying out; execution; enforcement; performance; making; consummation. (b) *siehe vr* completion; performance; fulfilment. (c) (*Strafvollzug*) penal system.

Vollzugs-: **~anstalt** *f* (*form*) penal institution; **~beamte(r)** *m* (*form*) warder.

Volontariat [volɔntaˈriːt] *nt* (a) (*Zeit*) practical training. (b) (*Stelle*) post as a trainee.

Volontär(in *f*) [volɔnˈtɛːn, -ˈtɛːrɪn] *m* trainee.

volontieren* [volɔnˈtiːrən] *vi* to be training (*bei* with).

Volt [vɔlt] *nt* **-(e)s, -** volt.

Volte ['vɔltə] *f* **-, -n** (a) (*Fechten, Reiten*) volte. (b) (*Cards*) sleight of hand.

voltigieren* [vɔltiˈʒiːrən] *vi* to perform exercises on horseback; (*im Zirkus*) to do trick-riding.

Volt-: ['vɔlt-]: **~meter** *nt* voltmeter; **~zahl** *f* voltage.

Volumen [voˈluːmən] *nt* **-s, - or Volumina** (a) (*lit, fig: Inhalt*) volume. (b) (*obs: Schriftrolle, Band*) volume.

Volumgewicht [voˈluːm-] *nt* (*Phys*) volumetric weight.

voluminös [volumiˈnøːs] *adj* (*geh*) voluminous.

vom *contr of* **von dem**. **~ 10. September an** from the 10th September; **Bier ~ Faß** draught beer; **das kommt ~ Rauchen/Trinken** that comes from smoking/drinking; **ich kenne ihn nur ~ Sehen** I know him only by sight; **~ Kochen hat er keine Ahnung** he has no idea about cooking.

von *prep* **+dat** (a) (*einen Ausgangspunkt angebend, räumlich, zeitlich*) from. **der Wind kommt ~ Norden** the wind comes from the North; **nördlich ~ to the North of; ~ München nach Hamburg** from Munich to Hamburg; **~ Hamburg sein** (*inf*) to be from Hamburg; **~ weit her** from a long way away; **~ ... an from ...; ~ Jugend/vom 10 Lebensjahr an** from early on/since he/she etc was ten years old; **~ diesem Tag/Punkt an or ab** from this day/point on(wards); **~ heute ab or an** from today; **Waren ~ 5 Mark an or ab** goods from 5 marks; **~ ... aus** from ...; **~ dort aus** from there; **etw ~ sich aus wissen/tun** to know sth by oneself/do sth of one's own accord; **~ ... bis from ... to; ~ morgens bis abends** from morning till night; **Ihr Brief ~ vor 2 Wochen** your letter of two weeks ago; **~ ... zu** from ... to.

   (b) (*~ ... weg*) from. **etw ~ etw nehmen/abreißen** to take/tear sth off sth; **~ der Straßenbahn abspringen** to jump off the tram; **alles ~ sich werfen** to throw everything down or aside; **~ der Stelle weichen** to move from the spot.

   (c) *in Verbindung mit adj, vb siehe auch dort.* (*Ursache, Urheberschaft ausdrückend, im Passiv*) by. **das Gedicht ist ~ Schiller** the poem is by Schiller; **ein Kleid ~ Dior** a Dior dress; **ein Kind ~ jdm kriegen** to have a child by sb; **das Kind ist ~ ihm** the child is his; **~ etw müde tired from sth; ~ etw begeistert** enthusiastic about sth; **~ etw satt** full up with sth; **~ etw beeindruckt/überrascht** impressed/surprised by sth.

   (d) (*partitiv, anstelle von Genitiv*) of. **jeweils zwei ~ zehn** two out of every ten; **ein Riese ~ einem Mann** (*inf*) a giant of a man; **ein Prachtstück ~ einem Hund** (*inf*) a magnificent (specimen of a) dog; **dieser Dummkopf ~ Gärtner ...!** (*inf*) that idiot of a gardener ...!

   (e) *in Verbindung mit n, adj, vb siehe auch dort.* (*Beschaffenheit, Eigenschaft etc ausdrückend, bestehend aus*) of. **~ 50 m Länge** 50 m in length; **im Alter ~ 50 Jahren** at the age of 50; **Kinder ~ 10 Jahren** ten-year-old children; **~ Bedeutung sein** to be of significance; **~ Dauer sein** to be lasting; **das ist sehr freundlich ~ Ihnen** that's very kind of you; **frei ~ etw sein** to be free of sth; **jdn ~ etw erlösen** to save sb from sth.

   (f) (*in Titel*) of; (*bei deutschem Adelstitel*) von. **die Königin ~ England** the queen of England; **Otto ~ Bismarck** Otto von Bismarck; **~ und zu Falkenburg** von Falkenburg; **ein „~ (und zu)" sein** to have a handle to one's name; **sich „~" schreiben** (*lit*) to have a "von" before one's name; **da kannst du dich aber „~" schreiben** (*fig*) you can be really proud yourself (there).

(g) (*über*) about. **er erzählte vom Urlaub** he talked about his holiday; **Geschichten vom Weihnachtsmann/~ Feen** stories about Father Christmas/fairies.

(h) (*mit Fragepronomen*) from. **~ wo/wann/was** where/when/ what ... from, from where/when/what (*form*).

(i) (*inf: in aufgelösten Kontraktionen*) **~ dem halte ich gar nichts** I don't think much of him; **da weiß ich nichts ~** I don't know anything about it.

(j) (*inf*) **~ wegen** no way! (*inf*); **~ wegen der Karte/dem Buch** (*incorrect*) about the map/the book.

von|einander *adv* of each other *or* one another; from each other *or* one another. **etwas/nichts ~ haben** to see something/nothing of each other *or* one another; (*Zusammensein genießen*) to be able/not to be able to enjoy each other's company; (*ähnlich aussehen*) to look/not to look like each other; (*sich im Wesen ähnlich sein*) to have a lot/nothing in common; **sie konnten die Augen nicht ~ wenden** they couldn't take their eyes off *or* away from each other *or* one another; **sich ~ trennen** to part or separate (from each other *or* one another); **sie hatten ~ die Nase voll** (*inf*) they were fed up with each other *or* one another.

von|einandergehen *vi sep irreg aux sein* to part.

vonnöten *adj*: **~ sein** to be necessary.

vonstatten *adv*: **~ gehen** (*stattfinden*) to take place; **wie geht so etwas ~?** what is the procedure for that?; **es ging alles gut ~** everything went well.

Vopo ['fo:po] *m* -s, -s *abbr of* **Volkspolizist**.

vor 1 *prep* +*acc or dat* **(a)** +*dat* (*räumlich*) in front of; (*außerhalb von*) outside; (*~ Hintergrund*) against; (*in Gegenwart von*) in front of; (*in jds Achtung*) in the eyes of; (*bei Reihenfolge*) before; (*bei Rangordnung*) before, ahead of. **der See/die Stadt lag ~ uns** the lake/town lay before us; **~ jdm herfahren/hergehen** to drive/walk in front of *or* ahead of sb; **~ der Kirche rechts abbiegen** turn right before the church; **~ der Stadt** outside the town; **~ einer Kommission/allen Leuten** before *or* in front of a commission/everyone; **~ Gott sind alle Menschen gleich** all people are equal before God *or* in God's sight; **sich ~ jdm/etw verneigen** (*lit, fig*) to bow before *or* to sb/sth; **~ allen Dingen/allem** above all; **~ dem Fernseher sitzen** *or* **hocken** (*inf*) to sit in front of the TV.

(b) +*acc* (*Richtung angebend*) in front of; (*außerhalb von*) outside. **einen Schlag ~ den Oberkörper** a blow on the chest.

(c) +*dat* (*zeitlich*) before. **~ Christi Geburt** before Christ, BC; **zwanzig (Minuten) ~ drei** twenty (minutes) to three; **heute ~ acht Tagen** a week ago today; **das ist** *or* **liegt noch ~ uns** this is still to come; **ich war ~ ihm an der Reihe/da** I was in front of him/there before him; **~ einigen Tagen/langer Zeit/fünf Jahren** a few days/a long time/five years ago; **am Tage ~ der Prüfung** the day before the examination.

(d) +*acc* **~ sich hin summen/lachen/sprechen** *etc* to hum/laugh/talk *etc* to oneself; **~ sich hin schreiben/arbeiten** to write/work away; **~ sich hin wandern** to wander on.

(e) +*dat* **~ sich her** before one, in front of one; **er ließ die Schüler ~ sich her gehen** he let the pupils go in front (of him).

(f) +*dat* (*Ursache angebend*) with. **~ Hunger sterben** to die of hunger; **~ Kälte zittern** to tremble with *or* from cold; **~ Schmerz laut schreien** to cry out with *or* in pain; **~ lauter Arbeit** for *or* because of work; **alles strahlt ~ Sauberkeit** everything is shining clean.

(g) *in fester Verbindung mit n, vb, adj siehe auch dort.* **Schutz ~ jdm/etw suchen** to seek protection from sb/sth; **~ jdm/etw sicher sein** to be safe from sb/sth; **Achtung ~ jdm/etw haben** to have respect for sb/sth; **sich ~ jdm verstecken** to hide from sb; **wie ist das ~ sich gegangen?** how did it happen?

2 *adv* **(a) ~ und zurück** backwards and forwards; **alle kleinen Kinder ~!** all small children to the front!; **wer Karten will, ~!** come up and get your tickets!; **Borussia ~, noch ein Tor!** come on Borussia, let's have another!

(b) *siehe* **nach**.

vor|ab *adv* to begin *or* start with. **lassen Sie mich ~ erwähnen ...** first let me mention ...

Vor-: **~abdruck** *m* preprint; **~abend** *m* evening before; (*mit nachfolgendem Genitiv auch*) eve (*auch fig*); **das war am ~abend** that was the evening before; **am ~abend von Weihnachten** (on) the evening before Christmas, on Christmas Eve; **am ~abend der Hochzeit** (on) the evening before the wedding, on the eve of the wedding; **am ~abend der Revolution** (*fig*) on the eve of revolution; **~ahnung** *f* presentiment, premonition; **~alpen** *pl* foothills *pl* of the Alps.

voran *adv* **(a)** (*vorn, an der Spitze*) first. **ihm/ihr ~** in front of him/her; **der Festzug mit der Kapelle ~** the parade, led by the band; **mit dem Kopf ~ fallen** to fall head first.

(b) (*vorwärts*) forwards. **nur** *or* **immer ~** keep going; **immer langsam ~!** gently does it!

voran- *pref siehe auch* **voraus-**; **~bringen** *vt sep irreg* to make progress with; **~gehen** *vi sep irreg aux sein* **(a)** (*an der Spitze gehen*) to go first *or* in front; (*anführen auch*) to lead the way; (*fig: Einleitung etc*) to precede (*dat* sth); **jdm ~gehen** to go ahead of sb; **(b)** (*zeitlich vor jdm gehen*) to go on ahead; **sie war ihm ~gegangen** (*euph: gestorben*) she had passed on before him; **jdn ~gehen lassen** to let sb go first; **wie im ~gehenden berichtet** as reported (in the) above; *siehe* **Beispiel**; **(c)** (*zeitlich*) **einer Sache** (*dat*) **~gehen** to precede sth; **das V~gegangene** what has gone before; **(d)** *auch vi impers* (*Fortschritte machen*) to come on *or* along, to make progress *or* headway; **es will mit der Arbeit nicht so richtig ~gehen** the work's not coming on *or* along very well; **~gestellt** *adj* (*Gram*) preceding *attr*; **~gestellt sein** to precede; **~kommen** *vi sep irreg aux sein* to get on *or* along, to make progress *or* headway; **im Leben/beruflich ~kommen** to get on in life/in one's job; **nur langsam ~kommen** to make slow progress *or* little headway;

~machen *vi sep* (*inf*) to hurry up, to get a move on (*inf*).

Vor-: **~anmeldung** *f* appointment; (*von Telefongespräch*) booking; **ohne ~anmeldung** without an appointment/without booking; **er ist ohne ~anmeldung bei mir eingetroffen** he arrived at my house without warning; **~anschlag** *m* estimate.

voran-: **~schreiten** *vi sep irreg aux sein* (*geh*) (*lit*) to stride in front *or* ahead (*jdm of* sb); (*Zeit*) to march on; (*Fortschritte machen*) to progress; **~stellen** *vt sep* to put *or* place in front (*dat* of); (*fig*) to give precedence (*dat* over); **~treiben** *vt sep irreg* to drive forward *or* on; (*fig auch*) to hurry along.

Vor-: **~anzeige** *f* (*für Theaterstück*) advance notice; (*für Film*) trailer, preview (*US*); **~arbeit** *f* preparatory *or* preliminary work, groundwork; **gute ~arbeit leisten** to do good groundwork, to prepare the ground well; **v~arbeiten** *sep* **1** *vi* (*inf*) to (do) work in advance; **2** *vt* to work in advance; **3** *vr* to work one's way forward; **~arbeiter(in** *f*) *m* foreman; forewoman.

vorauf *adv* (*rare*) *siehe* **voran, voraus**.

voraus *adv* **(a)** (*voran*) in front (+*dat* of); (*Naut, fig*) ahead (+*dat* of). **er ist den anderen Schülern/seiner Zeit ~** he is ahead of the other pupils/his time. **(b)** (*vorher*) **im ~** in advance.

Voraus-: **~abteilung** *f* (*Mil*) advance party; **v~ahnen** *vt sep* to anticipate; **v~berechenbar** *adj* predictable; **v~berechnen*** *vt sep* to predict; *Wahlergebnis auch* to forecast; *Kosten* to estimate; **v~bestimmen*** *vt sep* to predict, to forecast; **~bezahlung** *f* payment in advance, advance payment; **v~blicken** *vi sep* to look ahead; **v~blickend 1** *adj* foresighted; **2** *adv* with regard to the future; **v~eilen** *vi sep aux sein* (*lit, fig*) to hurry on ahead, to rush (on) ahead (*dat* of); **einer Sache** (*dat*) **v~eilen** to be ahead of *or* in advance of sth; **v~fahren** *vi sep irreg aux sein* (*an der Spitze*) to drive/go in front (*dat* of); (*früher*) to drive/go on ahead; **v~gehen** *vi sep irreg aux sein** *siehe* **vorangehen** (a-c); **v~gesetzt 1** *ptp of* **v~setzen**; **2** *adj* **v~gesetzt, (daß)** ... provided (that) ...; **v~haben** *vt sep irreg* **jdm etw/viel v~haben** to have the advantage of sth/a great advantage over sb; **v~laufen** *vi sep irreg aux sein* (*an der Spitze*) to run in front (*dat* of); (*früher*) to run on ahead; **v~planen** *vti sep* to plan ahead; **v~reiten** *vi sep irreg aux sein* (*an der Spitze*) to ride in front (*dat* of); (*früher*) to ride on ahead; **~sage** *f* prediction; (*Wetter~*) forecast; **v~sagen** *vt sep* to predict (*jdm for* sb); (*prophezeien auch*) to prophesy; *Wahlergebnisse auch, Wetter* to forecast; **jdm die Zukunft v~sagen** to foretell sb's future; **das konnte ich noch nicht v~sagen, ob ich es schaffen würde** I couldn't say *or* tell then whether I would manage it; **~sagung** *f* *siehe* *vt* prediction; prophecy; forecast; **v~schauend** *adj, adv siehe* **v~blickend**; **v~schicken** *vt sep* to send on ahead *or* in advance (*dat* of); (*fig: vorher sagen*) to say in advance (*dat* of); **v~sehen** *vt sep irreg* to foresee; **ich habe es ja v~gesehen, daß ...** I knew that ...; **das war v~zusehen!** that was (only) to be expected!

voraussetzen *vt sep* to presuppose; (*als selbstverständlich, sicher annehmen*) *Interesse, Zustimmung, jds Liebe, Verständnis* to take for granted; (*erfordern*) *Qualifikation, Kenntnisse, Geduld etc* to require, to demand. **wenn wir einmal ~, daß ...** let us *or* if we assume that ...; **etw als selbstverständlich ~** to take sth for granted; **etw als bekannt ~** to assume that everyone knows sth.

Voraussetzung *f* prerequisite; (*Qualifikation*) qualification; (*Erfordernis*) requirement; (*Annahme*) assumption, premise. **unter der ~, daß ...** on condition that ...; **eine Mitarbeit hat zur ~, daß ...** a requirement of cooperation is that ...

Voraus-: **~sicht** *f* foresight; (*Erwartung*) anticipation; **aller ~sicht nach** in all probability; **in der ~sicht, daß ...** anticipating that ...; **in kluger** *or* **weiser ~sicht** with great foresight *or* forethought; **menschlicher ~sicht nach** as far as we can foresee; **v~sichtlich 1** *adj* expected; **2** *adv* probably; **er wird v~sichtlich gewinnen** he is expected to win; **v~sichtlich wird es keine Schwierigkeiten geben** we don't anticipate *or* expect any difficulties; **~zahlung** *f* payment in advance, advance payment.

Vorbau *m* porch; (*Balkon*) balcony; (*Min*) advancing working. **sie hat einen ganz schönen ~** (*hum: vollbusig*) she's well-stacked (*inf*).

vorbauen *sep* **1** *vt* (*anbauen*) to build on (in front). **Häuser bis an die Straße ~** to build houses right on the road; **ein weit vorgebauter Erker** a deep oriel window. **2** *vi* (*Vorkehrungen treffen*) to take precautions. **einer Sache** (*dat*) **~** to provide against sth; *siehe* **klug**.

Vorbedacht *m*: **mit/ohne ~** (*Überlegung*) with/without due care *or* consideration; (*Absicht*) intentionally/unintentionally; (*Jur*) with/without intent.

Vorbedeutung *f* portent, presage, prognostic. **eine schlimme ~ haben** to be a bad portent *or* presage *or* prognostic.

Vorbedingung *f* precondition.

Vorbehalt *m* -(e)s, -e reservation. **unter dem ~, daß ...** with the reservation that ...

vorbehalten* *vt sep irreg* **sich** (*dat*) **etw ~** to reserve sth (for oneself); *Recht* to reserve sth; **jdm etw ~** to leave sth (up) to sb; **diese Entscheidung ist** *or* **bleibt ihm ~** this decision is left (up) to him; **alle Rechte ~** all rights reserved; **Änderungen (sind) ~** subject to alterations; **Irrtümer ~** errors excepted.

vorbehaltlich, vorbehältlich *prep* +*gen* (*form*) subject to. **~ anderer Bestimmungen** unless otherwise provided (*form*); **~ Artikel 3** save as provided in paragraph 3 (*form*).

vorbehaltlos *adj* unconditional, unreserved. **~ zustimmen** to agree without reservations.

vorbei *adv* **(a)** (*räumlich*) past, by. **er möchte hier ~** he wants to go past *or* by; **~ an** (+*dat*) past; **~!** (*nicht getroffen*) missed! **(b)** (*zeitlich*) **~ sein** to be past; (*vergangen auch, beendet*) to be over *or* finished; (*Sorgen*) to be over; (*Schmerzen*) to be gone; **es ist schon 8 Uhr ~** it's already past *or* after *or* gone 8 o'clock; **damit ist es nun ~** that's all over now; **~ die schöne**

Zeit! gone are the days!; es war schon ~ mit ihm it was all up with him; aus und ~ over and done; ~ ist ~ what's past is past; (reden wir nicht mehr davon) let bygones be bygones.

vorbei- pref (vorüber) past; (zu Besuch) over; **~benehmen*** vr sep irreg (inf) siehe **danebenbenehmen**; **~bringen** vt sep irreg (inf) to drop off or by or in; **~drücken** vr sep (inf) (an jdm/etw sb/sth) to squeeze past; (fig) to slip past; **~dürfen** vi sep irreg (inf) to be allowed past; **dürfte ich bitte ~?** could I come or get past or by, please?; **~fahren** sep irreg 1 vi aux sein (an jdm/etw sb/sth) to go/drive/sail past, to pass; im V~fahren in passing; **bei jdm ~fahren** (inf) to drop or call in on sb, to stop or drop by sb's house (inf); 2 vt jdn an etw (dat) ~fahren to drive sb past sth; **ich kann dich ja schnell dort/bei ihnen ~fahren** (inf) I can run or drive you over there to their place; **~gehen** vi sep irreg aux sein (a) (lit, fig) (an jdm/etw sb/sth) to go past or by, to pass; **an etw** (dat) **~gehen** (fig: nicht beachten) to overlook sth; **bei jdm ~gehen** (inf) to drop or call in on sb, to stop or drop by sb's house (inf); **eine Gelegenheit ~gehen lassen** to let an opportunity pass or slip by; im V~gehen (lit, fig) in passing; (b) (vergehen) to pass; (Laune, Zorn auch) to blow over; (c) (danebengehen) to miss; (fig auch) to bypass; **er geht am Leben ~** life is passing him by; **an der Wirklichkeit ~gehen** (Bericht etc) to miss the truth; (Mensch) to be unrealistic; **~kommen** vi sep irreg aux sein (a) (an jdm/etw sb/sth) to pass, to go past; (an einem Hindernis) to get past or by; **an einer Sache/Aufgabe nicht ~kommen** to be unable to avoid a thing/task; **wir kommen nicht an der Tatsache ~, daß ...** there's no escaping the fact that ...; (b) bei jdm **~kommen** (inf) to drop or call in on sb, to stop or drop by sb's house (inf); **komm doch mal wieder ~!** (inf) drop or call in again sometime!, stop or drop by again sometime! (inf); **~können** vi sep irreg to be able to get past or by (an etw (dat) sth); **~lassen** vt sep irreg to let past (an jdm/etw sb/sth); **~laufen** vi sep irreg aux sein (an jdm/etw sb/sth) to run past; (inf: ~gehen) to go or walk past; (fig) to miss; V~marsch m march-past; **~marschieren*** vi sep aux sein to march past; **~müssen** vi sep irreg (an jdm/etw sb/sth) to have to go past, to have to pass; **bei jdm ~müssen** (inf) to have to call in at sb's; **~reden** vi sep an etw (dat) ~reden to talk round sth; (absichtlich) to skirt sth; **aneinander ~reden** to talk at cross purposes; **~schauen** vi sep (inf) siehe ~kommen (b); **~schießen** vi sep irreg (a) aux sein (an jdm/etw sb/sth) to shoot past or by; (an Kurve) to overshoot; (b) (am Ziel etc) to shoot wide (an + dat of), to miss (an etw (dat) sth); **~ziehen** sep irreg 1 vi aux sein (an jdm/etw sb/sth) to file past; (Truppen, Festzug etc) to march past; (Wolken, Rauch, Duft) to drift past or by; **an jdm or vor jds innerem Auge ~ziehen** to go through sb's mind; 2 vt to pull past (an jdm sb).

vorbelastet adj handicapped. **von den Eltern/vom Milieu her ~ sein** to be at a disadvantage because of one's parents/background; **dazu will ich mich nicht äußern, da bin ich ~** I don't want to comment on that, I'm biased; siehe **erblich**.

Vorbemerkung f introductory or preliminary remark; (kurzes Vorwort) (short) preface or foreword.

vorbereiten* sep 1 vt to prepare. **auf etw** (acc) **vorbereitet sein** to be prepared for sth; jdn (schonend) **auf etw** (acc) ~ to prepare sb for sth. 2 vr (Mensch) to prepare (oneself) (auf + acc for); (Ereignisse) to be in the offing (inf).

vorbereitend adj attr preparatory, preliminary.

Vorbereitung f preparation. **~en** (für or zu etw) **treffen** to make preparations (for sth).

Vorbereitungs- in cpds preparatory; **~dienst** m teaching practice; **~zeit** f preparation time.

Vor-: **~bericht** m preliminary report; **~besprechung** f preliminary meeting or discussion; **v~bestellen*** vt sep to order in advance; Platz, Tisch, Karten auch to book (in advance); to reserve; **~bestellung** f advance order; (von Platz, Tisch, Zimmer) (advance) booking; **bei ~bestellung** when ordering/booking in advance; **v~bestraft** adj previously convicted; **er ist schon einmal/dreimal v~bestraft** he (already) has a previous conviction/three previous convictions; **~bestrafte(r)** mf decl as adj man/woman etc with a previous conviction or a record (inf); **v~beten** sep 1 vi to lead the prayer/prayers; 2 vt jdm etw v~beten (lit) to lead sb in sth; (fig inf) to keep spelling sth out for sb (inf); **~beter** m prayer leader.

Vorbeugehaft f preventive custody.

vorbeugen sep 1 vi (einer Sache (dat) sth) to prevent; einer Möglichkeit, Fehlinterpretation, einem Fehler auch to preclude. ~ **ist besser als heilen** (Prov) prevention is better than cure (prov). 2 vt Kopf, Oberkörper to bend forward. 3 vr to lean or bend forward.

vorbeugend adj preventive.

Vorbeugung f prevention (gegen, von of). zur ~ (Med) as a prophylactic.

Vorbeugungs-: **~haft** f preventive custody; **~maßnahme** f preventive measure.

Vorbild nt model; (Beispiel) example. **das diente ihm als or war das ~ für seine Skulptur** his sculpture was modelled on this; **er/sein Verhalten kann uns zum ~ dienen** he/his behaviour is an example to us; **sich** (dat) **jdn zum ~ nehmen** to model oneself on sb; (sich ein Beispiel nehmen an) to take sb as an example; **sie ist ein ~ von Tugend** she's a model or paragon of virtue; **jdn/etw als ~/leuchtendes ~ hinstellen** to hold sb/sth up as an example/a shining example.

vorbildlich adj exemplary. **sich ~ benehmen** to be on one's best behaviour.

Vorbildlichkeit f exemplariness.

Vor-: **~bildung** f previous experience; (schulisch) educational background; **v~binden** vt sep irreg (inf) to put or tie on; jdm/sich etw v~binden to put or tie sth on sb/one; **v~blasen** sep irreg (Sch sl) 1 vi to whisper the answer; 2 vt jdm etw v~blasen to whisper sth to sb; **~bote** m (fig) harbinger, herald.

---

vorbringen vt sep irreg (a) (inf: nach vorn bringen) to take up or forward; (Mil) to take up to the front.

(b) (äußern) to say; Plan to propose; Meinung, Wunsch, Forderung to express, to state; Klage, Beschwerde to make, to lodge; Entschuldigung to make, to offer; Einwand to make, to raise; Argument, Beweis to produce, to bring forward; Grund to put forward. **können Sie dagegen etwas ~?** have you anything to say about it?; **was hast du zu deiner Entschuldigung vorzubringen?** what have you to say in your defence?; **er brachte vor, er hätte ...** (sagte) he said that he ...; (behauptete) he claimed or alleged that he ...

(c) (inf: hervorkommen) to get out (hinter + dat from behind). **die Katze war nicht hinter dem Ofen vorzubringen** the cat couldn't be got out from behind the stove.

Vor-: **~bühne** f apron; **v~christlich** adj pre-Christian; **das zweite v~christliche Jahrhundert** the second century before Christ; **~dach** nt canopy; **v~datieren*** vt sep to postdate; Ereignis to predate, to antedate, to foredate; **~datierung** f postdating; predating, antedating, foredating.

vordem adv (old) in days of yore (old, liter), in olden days.

Vorder-: **~achse** f front axle; **~ansicht** f front view; **v~asiatisch** adj Near Eastern; **~asien** nt Near East; **in ~asien** in the Near East; **~bein** nt foreleg; **~deck** nt foredeck.

Vordere(r) mf decl as adj person/man/woman etc in front.

vordere(r, s) adj front. **die ~ Seite des Hauses** the front of the house; **der V~ Orient** the Near East; siehe **vorderste(r, s)**.

Vorder-: **~front** f frontage; **~fuß** m forefoot; **~gaumenlaut** m palatal (sound); **~gebäude** nt front building; **~grund** m foreground; (fig auch) fore(front); **sich in den ~grund schieben** or **drängen** (fig auch) to push oneself to the fore(front); **im ~grund stehen** (fig) to be to the fore; **in den ~grund treten** to come to the fore; (Mensch auch) to step into the limelight; **v~gründig** adj (fig) (oberflächlich) superficial; (vorrangig) Probleme, Fragen central; **v~hand** adv for the time being, for the present; **~hand** f siehe **Vorhand**; **~haus** nt front-facing house; **~lader** m -s, - muzzle-loader; **v~lastig** adj Schiff, Flugzeug front-heavy; **~lauf** m (Hunt) foreleg; **~mann** m, pl **-männer** person in front; **sein ~mann** the person in front of him; **jdn auf ~mann bringen** (fig inf) to get sb to shape up; (gesundheitlich) to get sb fighting fit (inf); **etw auf ~mann bringen** (fig inf) Haushalt, Auto etc to get sth ship-shape; Kenntnisse, Wissen to brush sth up; Finanzen to get sth straightened out; (auf neuesten Stand bringen) Listen, Garderobe to bring sth up-to-date; **~pfote** f front paw; **~rad** nt front wheel; **~radantrieb** m front-wheel drive; **~schinken** m shoulder of ham; **~seite** f front; (von Münze) head, obverse; **~sitz** m front seat.

vorderste(r, s) adj superl of **vordere(r, s)** front(most). **der/die V~ in der Schlange** the first man/woman in the queue (Brit) or line (US).

Vorder-: **~steven** m (Naut) stem; **~teil** m or nt front; **~tür** f front door; **~zahn** m front tooth; **~zimmer** nt front room.

vordrängen vr sep to push to the front. **sich in einer Schlange ~** to jump a queue (Brit), to push to the front of a line (US).

vordringen vi sep irreg aux sein to advance; (Mil, in den Weltraum auch) to penetrate (in + acc into). **bis zu jdm/etw ~** to reach sb/sth, to get as far as sb/sth.

vordringlich adj urgent, pressing.

Vordruck m form.

vor|ehelich adj attr premarital.

vor|eilig adj rash. **~e Schlüsse ziehen** to jump to conclusions; **~ urteilen** to be rash in one's judgement.

Vor|eiligkeit f, no pl rashness.

vor|einander adv (räumlich) in front of or before one another or each other; (einander gegenüber) face to face. **wir haben keine Geheimnisse ~** we have no secrets from each other; **Angst ~ haben** to be afraid of each other; **sie schämten sich ~** they were embarrassed with each other.

vor|eingenommen adj prejudiced, biased.

Vor|eingenommenheit f, no pl prejudice, bias.

vor|enthalten* vt sep irreg jdm etw ~ to withhold sth from sb; Nachricht auch to keep sth from sb.

Vor|entscheidung f preliminary decision; (Sport: auch **~skampf, ~srunde**) preliminary round or heat.

vor|erst adv for the time being, for the moment or present.

vor|erwähnt adj attr (form) aforementioned, aforesaid.

Vorfahr m -en, -en forefather, ancestor.

vorfahren sep irreg 1 vi aux sein (a) to go or move forward, to move up; (in Auto auch) to drive forward.

(b) (ankommen) to drive up. **den Wagen ~ lassen** to have the car brought up, to send for or order the car.

(c) (früher fahren) to go on ahead. **in den Urlaub ~** to go on holiday ahead (of the others).

(d) (an der Spitze fahren) to drive in front.

2 vt (a) (weiter nach vorn fahren) to move up or forward.

(b) (vor den Eingang fahren) to drive up.

Vorfahrt f -, no pl right of way. **~ haben** to have (the) right of way; **die ~ beachten/nicht beachten** to observe/ignore the right of way; **„~ (be)achten"** "give way" (Brit), "yield" (US); (sich dat) **die ~ erzwingen** to insist on one's right of way; **jdm die ~ nehmen** to ignore sb's right of way.

Vorfahrts-: **v~berechtigt** adj having (the) right of way; **v~berechtigt sein** to have (the) right of way; **der/die ~berechtigte** the driver with (the) right of way; **~recht** nt right of way; **~regel** f rule on (the) right of way; **~schild** nt give way (Brit) or yield (US) sign; **~straße** f major road; **~zeichen** nt give way (Brit) or yield (US) sign.

Vorfall m (a) incident, occurrence. (b) (Med) prolapse.

vorfallen vi sep irreg aux sein (a) (sich ereignen) to occur, to happen. **was ist während meiner Abwesenheit vorgefallen?** what's been happening while I've been away? (b) (inf: nach vorn fallen) to fall forward.

vorfaseln *vt sep* jdm etw ~ *(pej inf)* to prattle on about sth to sb.

Vor-: ~**feier** *f* early celebration; **v~feiern** *vti sep* to celebrate early; ~**feld** *nt* (*Mil*) territory situated in front of the main battle-line; (*Aviat*) apron; (*fig*) run-up (+ *gen* to); **v~fertigen** *vt sep* to prefabricate; ~**film** *m* supporting film *or* programme; ~**finanzierung** *f* prefinancing; **v~finden** *vt sep irreg* to find, to discover; **v~flunkern** *vt sep* (*inf*) jdm etwas **v~flunkern** to tell sb a fib/fibs; ~**frage** *f* preliminary question; ~**freude** *f* anticipation; ~**frühling** *m* early spring, foretaste of spring.

vorfühlen *vi sep* (*fig*) to put *or* send out (a few) feelers. bei jdm ~ to sound sb out.

vorführen *vt sep* (a) Angeklagten to bring forward; Zeugen *auch* to produce. den Patienten einem Spezialisten ~ to have the patient seen by a specialist; den Angeklagten dem Richter ~ to bring the accused before the judge.
(b) (*zeigen*) *Film* to show; *Mode* to model; *Übung*, (*Vertreter*) Modell, Gerät to demonstrate (*dat* to); *Theaterstück auch*, Kunststücke to perform (*dat* to *or* in front of). den Zukünftigen der Familie ~ (*inf*) to present one's intended to the family.

Vorführer *m* projectionist.

Vorführraum *m* projection room.

Vorführung *f* presentation; (*von Angeklagten, Zeugen etc*) production *no pl*; (*von Filmen*) showing; (*von Mode*) modelling; (*von Geräten, Modellen, Übungen*) demonstration; (*von Theaterstück, Kunststücken*) performance.

Vorführwagen *m* demonstration model *or* car.

Vorgabe *f* handicap.

Vorgang *m* (a) (*Ereignis*) event, occurrence; (*Ablauf, Hergang*) series *or* course of events. jdm den genauen ~ eines Unfalls schildern to tell sb exactly what happened in an accident. (b) (*biologischer, chemischer, technischer Prozeß*) process. (c) (*form: Akten*) file, dossier.

Vorgänger(in *f*) *m s, -* predecessor, precursor (*form*).

Vorgarten *m* front garden.

vorgaukeln *vt sep* jdm etw ~ to lead sb to believe in sth; jdm ~, daß ... to lead sb to believe that ...; er hat ihr ein Leben im Luxus vorgegaukelt he led her to believe that he lived in luxury; er gaukelt ihr nur etwas vor he's just pulling the wool over her eyes (*inf*).

vorgeben *vt sep irreg* (a) (*vortäuschen*) to pretend; (*fälschlich beteuern*) to profess. sie gab Zeitmangel vor, um ... she pretended to be pressed for time in order to ... (b) (*Sport*) to give (a start of). (c) (*inf: nach vorn geben*) to pass forward.

Vorgebirge *nt* foothills *pl*.

vorgeblich *adj siehe* angeblich.

vorgeburtlich *adj attr* prenatal.

vorgefaßt *adj* Meinung preconceived.

Vorgefühl *nt* anticipation; (*böse Ahnung*) presentiment, foreboding. im ~ einer Katastrophe with a presentiment of disaster.

vorgehen *vi sep irreg aux sein* (a) (*handeln*) to act, to proceed. gerichtlich/energisch gegen jdn ~ to take legal proceedings *or* action/assertive action against sb.
(b) (*geschehen, vor sich gehen*) to go on, to happen.
(c) (*Uhr*) (*frühere Zeit anzeigen*) to be fast; (*zu schnell gehen*) to gain. meine Uhr geht (zwei Minuten) vor my watch is (two minutes) fast; meine Uhr geht pro Tag zwei Minuten vor my watch gains two minutes a day.
(d) (*nach vorn gehen*) to go forward *or* to the front; (*Mil*) to advance.
(e) (*als erster gehen*) to go first; (*früher gehen*) to go on ahead.
(f) (*den Vorrang haben*) to come first, to take precedence, to have priority.

Vorgehen *nt -s, no pl* action.

Vor-: **v~gelagert** *adj* offshore; **es ist dem Kap v~gelagert** it lies off the Cape; **v~genannt** *adj* (*form*) aforementioned, aforesaid; **v~gericht** *nt* hors d'œuvre, starter (*Brit*); **v~gerückt** *adj* Stunde late; Alter advanced; ~**geschichte** *f* (a) (*eines Falles*) past history; (b) (*Urgeschichte*) prehistory, prehistoric times *pl*; aus der ~geschichte from prehistoric times; **v~geschichtlich** *adj* prehistoric; ~**geschmack** *m* (*fig*) foretaste; **v~geschritten** *adj* advanced.

Vorgesetzte(r) *mf decl as adj* superior.

vorgestern *adv* the day before yesterday. von ~ (*fig*) antiquated; Methoden, Ansichten *auch*, Kleidung old-fashioned; ~ abend/morgen the evening/morning before last; ~ mittag midday the day before yesterday.

vorgestrig *adj attr* of the day before yesterday.

vorgreifen *vi sep irreg* to anticipate; (*verfrüht handeln*) to act prematurely. jdm ~ to forestall sb; einer Sache (*dat*) ~ to anticipate sth.

Vorgriff *m* anticipation (*auf* + *acc* of); (*in Erzählung*) leap ahead. verzeihen Sie mir den ~ auf (+ *acc*) ... excuse me for leaping ahead to ...

vorhaben *vt sep irreg* to intend; (*geplant haben*) to have planned. was haben Sie heute vor? what are your plans for today?, what do you intend doing today?; ich habe morgen nichts vor I've nothing planned *or* no plans for tomorrow; hast du heute abend schon etwas vor? have you already got something planned *or* are you already doing something this evening?; wenn du nichts Besseres vorhast ... if you've nothing better *or* else to do ...; etw mit jdm/etw ~ to intend doing sth with sb/sth; (*etw geplant haben*) to have sth planned for sb/sth; er hat einen Besuch bei Tante Emma vor he intends *or* plans to visit Aunt Emma; die ehrgeizigen Eltern haben viel mit dem Kind vor the ambitious parents have great plans for the child; du hast es ja gut vor! the ideas you have!; was hast du jetzt wieder vor? what are you up to now?

Vorhaben *nt* plan; *Absicht* intention.

Vorhalle *f* (*von Tempel*) portico; (*Diele*) entrance hall, vestibule; (*Foyer*) foyer; (*von Parlament*) lobby.

vorhalten *sep irreg* 1 *vt* (a) (*vorwerfen*) jdm etw ~ to reproach sb with *or* for sth.
(b) (*als Beispiel*) jdm jdn/etw ~ to hold sb/sth up to sb; man hält ihm den älteren Bruder als Vorbild vor his elder brother is held up to him as an example; jdm die Qualen der Hölle ~ to hold up the torments of hell before sb's eyes.
(c) (*vor den Körper halten*) to hold up; (*beim Niesen etc*) Hand, Taschentuch ~ to put in front of one's mouth. mit vorgehaltener Pistole at pistol point; sich (*dat*) ein Handtuch ~ to hold up a towel in front of oneself; *siehe* Spiegel.
2 *vi* (*anhalten*) to last.

Vorhaltung *f usu pl* reproach. jdm/sich (*wegen etw*) ~en machen to reproach sb/oneself (with *or* for sth).

Vorhand *f* (*Sport*) forehand; (*von Pferd*) forehand; (*Cards*) lead.

vorhanden *adj* (*verfügbar*) available; (*existierend*) in existence, existing. eine Dusche ist hier leider nicht ~ I'm afraid there isn't a shower here; davon ist genügend/nichts mehr ~ there's plenty/no more of that.

Vorhang *m -s,* **Vorhänge** curtain. die Schauspieler bekamen 10 Vorhänge the actors got *or* took 10 curtain calls *or* took 10 curtains.

Vorhängeschloß *nt* padlock.

Vorhang-: ~**stange** *f* (*zum Aufhängen*) curtain pole; (*zum Ziehen*) curtain rod; ~**stoff** *m* curtaining *no pl*, curtain(ing) material *or* fabric.

Vor-: ~**haus** *nt* (*Aus*) hall; ~**haut** *f* foreskin, prepuce (*spec*).

vorher *adv* before(hand); (*früher*) before. am Tage ~ the day before, the previous day; man weiß ~ nie, wie die Sache ausgeht one never knows beforehand *or* in advance how things will turn out; konntest du das nicht ~ sagen? couldn't you have said that earlier?

Vorher-: **v~bestimmen** *vt sep* to determine *or* ascertain in advance; Schicksal, Zukunft to predetermine; (*Gott*) to preordain; es war ihm **v~bestimmt** ... he was predestined ...; ~**bestimmung** *f siehe* **vt** determining *or* ascertaining in advance; predetermination; preordination; predestination; **v~gehen** *vi sep irreg aux sein* to go first *or* in front, to lead the way; (*fig*) to precede; **v~gehend** *adj* Tag, Ereignisse preceding, previous.

vorherig [foːɐˈheːrɪç, ˈfoːɐheːrɪç] *adj attr* prior, previous; (*ehemalig*) former.

Vorherrschaft *f* predominance, supremacy; (*Hegemonie*) hegemony.

vorherrschen *vi sep* to predominate, to prevail. Rot herrscht in diesem Winter vor red is predominant this winter.

vorherrschend *adj* predominant; (*weitverbreitet*) prevalent; Ansicht, Meinung *auch* prevailing.

Vorher-: ~**sage** *f* forecast; **v~sagen** *vt sep siehe* **voraussagen**; **v~sehen** *vt sep irreg* to foresee.

vorheucheln *vt sep* to feign, to pretend. jdm etw ~ to feign *or* pretend sth to sb; jdm ~, daß ... to pretend to sb that ...; er heuchelt dir doch bloß was vor! (*inf*) he's just putting on an act.

vorheulen *vt sep* (*inf*) jdm etwas ~ to give sb a sob-story (*inf*).

Vorhimmel *m* first heaven.

vorhin *adv* just now.

vorhinein *adv:* im ~ in advance.

Vor-: ~**hof** *m* forecourt; (*Anat: von Herz, Ohr*) vestibule; ~**hölle** *f* limbo; in der ~**hölle** in limbo; ~**hut** *f -, -en* (*Mil*) vanguard, advance guard.

vorig *adj attr* (*früher*) Besitzer, Wohnsitz previous; (*vergangen*) Jahr, Woche etc last. im ~en (in the) above, earlier; der/die/das ~e the above(-mentioned); die V~en (*Theat*) the same.

Vor-: ~**jahr** *nt* previous year, year before; **v~jährig** *adj* of the previous year *or* year before; **v~jammern** *vti sep* jdm (etwas) **v~jammern** to moan to sb (*von* about); ~**kammer** *f* (*Anat: von Herz*) vestibule; (*Tech*) precombustion chamber; ~**kämpfer(in** *f*) *m* (*für of*) pioneer, champion; **v~kauen** *vt sep* Nahrung to chew; jdm etw (*acc*) **v~kauen** (*fig inf*) to spoonfeed sth to sb (*inf*); ~**kaufsrecht** *nt* option of purchase *or* to buy.

Vorkehrung *f* precaution. ~en treffen to take precautions.

Vorkenntnis *f* previous knowledge *no pl*; (*Erfahrung*) previous experience *no pl*. sprachliche ~se previous knowledge of languages/the language.

vorknöpfen *vt sep* (*fig inf*) sich (*dat*) jdn ~ to take sb to task; den hat sich die Mafia vorgeknöpft the Mafia got him.

vorkommen *vi sep irreg aux sein* (a) *auch* vi *impers* (*sich ereignen*) to happen. so etwas ist mir noch nie vorgekommen such a thing has never happened to me before; daß mir das nicht noch einmal vorkommt! don't let it happen again!; das soll nicht wieder ~ it won't happen again; das kann schon mal ~ it can happen, it has been known to happen; (*das ist nicht ungewöhnlich*) that happens; so was soll ~! that's life!
(b) (*vorhanden sein, auftreten*) to occur; (*Pflanzen, Tiere*) to be found. in dem Aufsatz dürfen keine Fehler ~ there mustn't be any mistakes in the essay.
(c) (*erscheinen*) to seem. das kommt mir bekannt/merkwürdig vor that seems familiar/strange to me; sich (*dat*) überflüssig/dumm ~ to feel superfluous/silly; sich (*dat*) klug ~ to think one is clever; das kommt dir nur so vor it just seems that way *or* like that to you; wie kommst du mir eigentlich vor? (*inf*) who do you think you are?
(d) (*nach vorn kommen*) to come forward *or* to the front.
(e) (*herauskommen*) to come out.

Vorkommen *nt -s, -* (*no pl: das Auftreten*) occurrence, incidence; (*Min*) deposit.

Vorkommnis *nt* incident, event, occurrence.

Vorkriegs- *in cpds* pre-war; ~**zeit** *f* pre-war period.

vorladen *vt sep irreg* (*bei Gericht*) to summons; Zeugen *auch* to subpoena.

Vorladung f siehe vt summons; subpoena.

Vorlage f -, -n (a) no pl (das Vorlegen) (von Dokument) presentation, production; (von Scheck, Schuldschein) presentation; (von Beweismaterial) submission. **gegen** ~ **einer Sache** (gen) (up)on production or presentation of sth; **zahlbar bei** ~ payable on demand.

(b) (Muster) (zum Stricken, Nähen) pattern; (Liter) model. **etw von einer** ~ **abzeichnen/nach einer** ~ **machen** to copy sth; **hattest du dafür eine** ~? did you have a pattern for it?; did you copy it from something?

(c) (Entwurf) draft; (Parl: Gesetzes~) bill.

(d) (Ftbl) through-ball. **jdm eine** ~ **machen** to lay the ball on for sb; **das war eine tolle** ~ the ball was beautifully laid on.

(e) (Ski) vorlage, forward lean (position).

(f) siehe **Vorleger**.

Vorland nt (der Alpen etc) foothills pl; (vor Deich) foreshore.

vorlassen vt sep irreg (a) (inf) jdn ~ (nach vorn gehen lassen) to let sb go in front; (in der Schlange auch) to let sb go first; (vorbeigehen lassen) to let sb (go) past, to let sb pass; **ein Auto** ~ (einbiegen lassen) to let a car in; (überholen lassen) to let a car pass, to let a car (go) past.

(b) (Empfang gewähren) to allow in, to admit.

Vorlauf m (a) (Sport) qualifying or preliminary heat/round. **(b)** (Chem: bei Destillation) forerun. **(c)** (Tech: von Rad) offset. **(d)** (von Film, Band) leader.

vorlaufen vi sep irreg aux sein (inf) (vorauslaufen) to run on ahead or in front; (nach vorne laufen) to run to the front.

Vorläufer m forerunner (auch Ski), precursor.

vorläufig 1 adj temporary; (Regelung auch provisional; Urteil) preliminary; (Verfügung des Gerichts interim, provisional. **2** adv (einstweilig) temporarily; (fürs erste) for the time being, for the present, provisionally.

vorlaut adj cheeky, impertinent.

Vorleben nt past (life).

vorleben vt sep jdm etw ~ to set an example of sth to sb; **jdm eine Komödie** ~ to put on an act in front of sb.

Vorlege-: ~besteck nt serving cutlery, serving spoons pl; (Tranchierbesteck) carvers pl; ~gabel f serving fork; (von Tranchierbesteck) carving fork; ~löffel m serving or table spoon; ~messer nt carving knife.

vorlegen sep **1** vt (a) to present; (Entwurf, Doktorarbeit auch to submit; Paß to show, to produce; Beweismaterial to submit; Zeugnisse, Bewerbungsunterlagen to produce; Schulzeugnis to show; Schularbeit auch to hand in; (Pol) Entwurf to table (Brit), to introduce. **jdm etw zur Unterschrift** ~ to give or present sth to sb for signature or signing; **etw dem Parlament** ~ to lay sth before the house, to table sth (Brit); **jdm eine Frage** ~ to put a question to sb; **ein schnelles Tempo** ~ to go at a fast pace; **ein schnelleres Tempo** ~ to speed up, to quicken the pace.

(b) Speisen to serve; (hinlegen) Futter to put down (dat for). **jdm etw** ~ to serve sth to sb, to serve sb with sth.

(c) Riegel to put across, to shoot (across); Schloß, Kette to put on; (inf: davorlegen) to put in front.

(d) (Ftbl) **jdm den Ball** ~ to lay the ball on for sb.

2 vr to lean forward.

3 vi (Kellner) to serve.

Vorleger m -s, - mat; (Bett~ auch) (bedside) rug.

Vorlegeschloß nt siehe **Vorhängeschloß**.

vorlehnen vr sep to lean forward.

Vorleistung f (Econ) (Vorauszahlung) advance (payment); (finanzielle Aufwendung) outlay no pl (an +dat on); (vorausgehende Arbeit) preliminary work; (Pol) prior concession.

vorlesen vti sep irreg to read aloud or out. **jdm (etw)** ~ to read (sth) to sb.

Vorleser m reader.

Vorlesung f (Univ) lecture; (Vorlesungsreihe) course (of lectures), lectures pl. **über etw** (acc) ~en **halten** to give (a course of) lectures on sth; ~en **hören** to go to lectures.

Vorlesungs-: ~betrieb m lectures pl; ~verzeichnis nt lecture timetable.

vorletzte(r, s) adj last but one, penultimate. **im** ~n **Jahr** the year before last.

Vorliebe f predilection, special liking, preference. **etw mit** ~ **tun** to particularly like doing sth.

vorliebnehmen vi sep irreg **mit** jdm/etw ~ to make do with sb/sth, to put up with sb/sth.

vorliegen vr sep irreg **1** vi (zur Verfügung stehen: Beweise, Katalog, Erkenntnisse) to be available; (Urteil) to be known; (eingereicht, vorgelegt sein: Unterlagen, wissenschaftliche Arbeit) to be in, to have come in; (Pol (Gesetzesvorlage) to be before the house; (Haushalt) to be published, to be out; (vorhanden sein) (Irrtum, Schuld etc) to be; (Symptome) to be present; (Gründe) to be, to exist. **jdm** ~ (Unterlagen, Akten etc) to be with sb; **die Ergebnisse liegen der Kommission vor** the commission has the results; **das Beweismaterial liegt dem Gericht vor** the evidence is before the court; **mir liegt ein Brief vor** I have (here) a letter; **etw liegt gegen jdn vor** sth is against sb; (gegen Angeklagten) sb is charged with sth.

2 vi impers to be. **es liegen fünf Bewerbungen vor** there are or we have five applications; **es muß ein Irrtum** ~ there must be some mistake.

vorliegend adj attr Gründe existing; Akten, Unterlagen, (Typ) Auflage on hand; Frage at issue; Angelegenheit, Probleme in hand; Ergebnisse available. **im** ~en **Fall** in this or in the present case; **die uns** ~en **Ergebnisse** the results we have to hand.

vorlügen vt sep irreg **jdm etwas** ~ to lie to sb.

vorm. abbr of **vormittags**.

vormachen vt sep (a) **jdm etw** ~ (zeigen) to show sb how to do sth, to demonstrate sth to sb; (fig: als Beispiel dienen) to show sb sth.

(b) (fig) **jdm etwas** ~ (täuschen) to fool or kid (inf) sb; **ich**

lasse mir so leicht nichts ~ you/he etc can't fool or kid (inf) me so easily; **er läßt sich** (dat) **von niemandem etwas** ~ nobody can fool him, he's nobody's fool; **mach jdm doch nichts vor** don't try and fool or kid (inf) me; **sich** (dat) (selbst) **etwas** ~ to fool or kid (inf) oneself; siehe **Dunst**.

(c) (inf: davorlegen, -stellen etc) Kette, Schürze, Riegel to put on; Brett to put across.

Vormacht(stellung) f supremacy (gegenüber over). **eine** ~ **haben** to have supremacy.

Vormagen m (von Rind) rumen; (von Vogel) crop.

vormalig adj attr former.

vormals adv formerly.

Vormarsch m (Mil) advance. **im** ~ **sein** to be on the advance, to be advancing; (fig) to be gaining ground.

Vormärz m (Hist) period from 1815 to March revolution of 1848.

Vormast m foremast.

vormerken vt sep to note down, to make a note of; (bei Bestellung auch) to take an order for; Plätze to reserve, to book. **ich werde Sie für Mittwoch** ~ I'll put you or your name down for Wednesday; **können Sie für mich 5 Exemplare** ~? can you put me down for 5 copies?, can you reserve 5 copies for me?; **sich beim Friseur** ~ **lassen** to make an appointment at the hairdresser's; **sich für einen Kursus** ~ **lassen** to put one's name or oneself down for a course.

Vormittag m morning. **am** ~ in the morning.

vormittag adv **heute/gestern/morgen** ~ this/yesterday/tomorrow morning.

vormittägig adj morning.

vormittags adv in the morning; (jeden Morgen) in the morning(s).

Vormund m -(e)s, -e or **Vormünder** guardian. **ich brauche keinen** ~ (fig) I don't need anyone to tell me what to do.

Vormundschaft f guardianship, tutelage. **jdn unter** ~ **stellen** to place sb under the care of a guardian.

Vormundschaftsgericht nt court dealing with matters relating to guardianship.

vorn adv (a) in front. **von** ~ from the front; **nach** ~ (ganz nach ~) to the front; (weiter nach ~) forwards; **von weit** ~ from the very front; ~ **im Buch/in der Schlange/auf der Liste** at the front of the book/queue/at the top of the list; **sich** ~ **anstellen** to join the front of the queue (Brit) or line (US); ~ **im Bild** in the front of the picture; **nach** ~ **abgehen** (Theat) to exit at the front of the stage; **nach** ~ **laufen** to run to the front; ~ **bleiben** (lit) to stay in front; (fig) not to lag behind; **wenn es etwas umsonst gibt, ist er immer ganz** ~(e) when something's going free he's always (the) first on the scene.

(b) (am Anfang) **von** ~ from the beginning; **wie schon** ~ **erklärt** as explained above; **von** ~ **anfangen** to begin at or to start from the beginning; (von neuem) to start (all) over again, to start from scratch; **neues Leben** ~ to start afresh, to make a fresh start; **etw** ~ **anfügen** to add sth at the beginning; **das Auto kam von** ~ **auf ihn zugefahren** the car came at him head on.

(c) (am vorderen Ende) at the front; (Naut) fore. **von** ~ from the front; **jdn von** ~ **sehen** to see sb's face; ~ **im Auto/Bus** in the front of the car/bus; **der Blinker** ~ the front indicator; **nach** ~ to the front; **fallen, ziehen** forwards.

(d) (auf der Vorderseite) at the front. **das Buch ist** ~ **schmutzig** the front of the book is dirty; ~ **auf der Medaille** on the face of the medal; ~ **gelegenes Zimmer** a room facing the front; **ein Blick nach** ~ a look to the front.

(e) (weit entfernt) **das Auto da** ~ the car in front or ahead there; **sie waren ziemlich weit** ~ they were quite far ahead or quite a long way ahead; (Läufer auch) they were quite a long way (out) in front or quite a long way in the lead.

(f) **ich kann doch nicht** ~ **und hinten gleichzeitig sein** I can't be everywhere at once; **sich von** ~ e **bis** or **und hinten bedienen lassen** to be waited on hand and foot; **er betrügt sie von** ~ **bis hinten** he deceives her right, left and centre; siehe auch **hinten**.

Vornahme f -, -n (form) undertaking. **sie haben mit der** ~ **von Tests begonnen** they have begun to carry out tests; **die** ~ **von Änderungen am Text bleibt dem Autor überlassen** it is left to the author to undertake changes to the text.

Vorname m Christian name, first name.

vorne adv siehe **vorn**.

vornehm adj (a) (von hohem Rang) Familie, Kreise distinguished, high-ranking; (von adliger Herkunft) aristocratic, noble; (kultiviert) Herr, Dame distinguished, posh (inf); Manieren, Art, Benehmen genteel, refined; (edel) Gesinnung, Charakter, Handeln noble. **die** ~e **Gesellschaft** high society; **ihr seid mir eine** ~e **Gesellschaft** (iro) you're a fine lot! (inf); **die** ~e **Welt, die V**~en **in fashionable society, so was sagt/tut man nicht in** ~en **Kreisen** one doesn't say/do that in polite society; **ein** ~er **Besuch** a distinguished visitor; ~er **Anstrich** (fig) distinguished air; **es ist nicht** ~, **nach dem Preis zu fragen** it's simply not done to ask the price; ~ **heiraten** to marry into high society; ~ **tun** (pej inf) to act posh (inf).

(b) (elegant, luxuriös) Wohngegend fashionable, smart, posh (inf); Haus smart, posh (inf); Geschäft exclusive, posh (inf); Kleid, Äußeres elegant, stylish; Auto smart, posh (inf); Geschmack refined, exclusive.

(c) (dated) **die** ~ste **Pflicht/Aufgabe** the first or foremost duty/task.

vornehmen vt sep irreg (a) (ausführen) to carry out; Test, Untersuchung auch to do; Umfrage, Änderungen auch to make; Messungen to take.

(b) (in Angriff nehmen) (sich dat) **etw** ~ to get to work on sth.

(c) **sich** (dat) **etw** ~ (planen, vorhaben) to intend or mean to do sth; (Vorsatz fassen) to have resolved to do sth; **ich habe mir vorgenommen, das nächste Woche zu tun** I intend or mean to do that next week; **ich habe mir zuviel vorgenommen** I've taken on too much.

(d) *sich (dat)* jdn ~ *(inf)* to have a word with sb.

(e) *(früher drannehmen) Kunden, Patienten* to attend to *or* see first.

(f) *(inf: vorhalten) Schürze, Serviette* to put on; *Hand* to put in front of one's mouth; *(vorbeugen) Schultern* to hunch.

Vornehmheit *f, no pl siehe adj* **(a)** high rank; nobility; distinguished ways *pl*; refinement; nobility. **(b)** smartness, poshness *(inf)*; exclusiveness; elegance, stylishness; refinement.

vornehmlich **1** *adv (hauptsächlich, vor allem)* principally, especially, above all; *(vorzugsweise)* first and foremost. **2** *adj* principal, main, chief.

vorneigen *vtr sep* to lean forward.

vorn(e)weg *adv* ahead, in front, first; *(als erstes)* first. **er geht immer** ~ he always walks on ahead *or* in front; **mit dem Kopf** ~ head first; **gleich** ~ straight away; **mit dem Mund ist er immer** ~, **aber nicht mit seinen Taten** *(inf)* he's all talk (and) no action *(inf)*; **mit dem Mund** ~ **sein** *(inf)* to have a big mouth.

vornherein *adv*: **von** ~ from the start *or* outset.

Vorniere *f* pronephros *(spec)*.

vornotieren* *vt sep siehe* **vormerken**.

vorn-: ~**über** *adv* forwards; ~**über fallen** to fall (over) forwards; ~**weg** *adv siehe* **vorn(e)weg**.

Vor|ort *m (Vorstadt)* suburb.

Vor|ort-: ~**bahn** *f* suburban line; *(für Berufsverkehr)* commuter line; ~**verkehr** *m* suburban traffic; *(von öffentlichen Verkehrsmitteln)* suburban service; ~**zug** *m* suburban train; *(im Berufsverkehr)* commuter train.

Vor-: **v**~**österlich** *adj* immediately before Easter; ~**platz** *m* forecourt; ~**posten** *m (Mil)* outpost; ~**programm** *nt* supporting bill *or* programme; **im** ~**programm** on the supporting bill; **v**~**programmieren*** *vt sep* to preprogramme; *(fig auch)* to precondition; **v**~**programmiert** *adj Erfolg, Antwort* automatic; *Verhaltensweise* preprogrammed; *Weg* predetermined, preordained; ~**prüfung** *f* preliminary examination; **v**~**quellen** *sep irreg* **1** *vt Erbsen, Linsen etc* to soak; **2** *vi aux sein (Augen)* to bulge; *siehe* **hervorquellen**.

Vorrang *m* -**(e)s**, *no pl* **(a)** ~ **haben** to have priority, to take precedence; **den** ~ **vor etw** *(dat)* **haben** to take precedence over sth; **jdm/einer Sache den** ~ **geben** *or* **einräumen** to give sb/a matter priority; **jdm/einer Sache den** ~ **streitig machen** to challenge sb's/sth's pre-eminence.

(b) *(Aus: Vorfahrt)* right of way.

vorrangig **1** *adj* of prime importance, priority *attr*. **2** *adv* as a matter of priority. **eine Angelegenheit** ~ **erledigen/behandeln** to give a matter priority treatment.

Vorrangstellung *f* pre-eminence *no indef art*. **er hat in der Firma eine** ~ he has a position of prime importance in the firm.

Vorrat *m* -**(e)s**, ⸚**e** *(an +dat of)* stock, supply; *(von Waren)* stocks *pl*; *(an Lebensmitteln auch)* store, provisions *pl*; *(an Atomwaffen)* stockpile; *(Geld)* reserves *pl*; *(an Geschichten, Ideen)* stock. **heimlicher** ~ *(secret)* hoard; **etw auf** ~ **kaufen** to stock up with sth; **etw anlegen** *or* **anschaffen** *or* **ansammeln** to lay in a stock *or* stocks *pl*; **solange der** ~ **reicht** *(Comm)* while stocks last; **etw auf** ~ **haben** to have sth in reserve; *(Comm)* to have sth in stock.

vorrätig *adj* in stock; *(verfügbar)* available. **etw nicht mehr** ~ **haben** to be out (of stock) of sth.

Vorrats-: ~**kammer** *f* store cupboard; *(für Lebensmittel)* larder; ~**raum** *m* store room; *(in Geschäft)* stock room; ~**schrank** *m* store cupboard; *(für Lebensmittel)* larder.

Vorraum *m* anteroom; *(Büro)* outer office; *(von Gericht)* lobby; *(von Kino, Theater)* foyer.

vorrechnen *vt sep* **jdm etw** ~ to work out *or* reckon up *or* calculate sth for sb; **er rechnet mir dauernd vor, wieviel alles kostet** he's always pointing out to me how much everything costs; **jdm seine Fehler** ~ *(fig)* to enumerate sb's mistakes.

Vorrecht *nt* prerogative; *(Vergünstigung)* privilege.

Vorrede *f (Vorwort)* preface; *(Theat)* prologue; *(einleitende Rede)* introductory speech.

vorreden *vt sep (inf)* **jdm etwas** ~ to tell sb a tale; **jdm** ~, **daß** ... to kid sb that ... *(inf)*; **red mir doch nichts vor** don't give me that *(inf)*; **laß dir doch von ihm nichts** ~ don't let him kid you (on) *(inf)* *or* give you that *(inf)*.

Vorredner *m (vorheriger Redner)* previous speaker; *(einleitender Redner)* introductory speaker. **mein** ~ **hat gesagt** ... the previous speaker said ...

vorreiten *sep irreg* **1** *vt* **(a)** *aux sein (vorausreiten)* to ride on ahead.

(b) *(zur Demonstration)* to demonstrate *(a riding exercise)*. **2** *vt (demonstrieren) Übung* to demonstrate. **ein Pferd** ~ to put a horse through its paces; **jdm die Piaffe** ~ to show sb how to perform the piaffe, to demonstrate the piaffe to sb.

vorrennen *vi sep irreg aux sein (inf) (voraus)* to run *or* race (on) ahead; *(nach vorn)* to run forward.

vorrichten *vt sep* to prepare; *Zutaten, Gegenstände* to get ready.

Vorrichtung *f* device, gadget.

vorrücken *sep* **1** *vt* to move forward; *Schachfigur* to advance, to move on.

2 *vi aux sein* to move *or* go forward; *(Mil)* to advance; *(Sport, im Beruf etc)* to move up; *(Uhrzeiger)* to move on. **mit dem Stuhl** ~ to move one's chair forward; **in vorgerücktem Alter** in later life; **zu vorgerückter Stunde** at a late hour.

Vorrunde *f (Sport)* preliminary *or* qualifying round; *(von Saison)* first part (of the season).

vorsagen *sep* **1** *vt* **jdm etw** ~ *Gedicht* to recite sth to sb; *(Sch) Antwort, Lösung* to tell sb sth. **2** *vi (Sch)* **jdm** ~ to tell sb the answer.

Vorsaison *f* low season, early (part of the) season.

Vorsänger *m (Eccl)* precentor; *(in Chor)* choir leader.

Vorsatz *m* **(a)** (firm) intention. **mit** ~ *(Jur)* with intent; **den** ~ **haben, etw zu tun** to (firmly) intend to do sth; **den** ~ **fassen, etw zu tun** to make up one's mind to do sth, to resolve to do sth; **bei seinen Vorsätzen bleiben, seinen Vorsätzen treu bleiben** to keep to one's resolve *or* resolution; *siehe* **Weg**.

(b) *(von Buch) siehe* **Vorsatzblatt**.

Vorsatzblatt *nt (Typ)* endpaper.

vorsätzlich *adj* deliberate, intentional; *Lüge* deliberate; *(Jur)* wilful; *Mord* premeditated. **jdn** ~ **töten** to kill sb intentionally.

Vorsatzlinse *f (Phot)* ancillary lens.

Vorschaltgesetz *nt (Pol)* interim law *(preparing the way for a subsequent law)*.

Vorschau *f* preview; *(Film)* trailer; *(Wetter~)* forecast.

Vorschein *m*: **zum** ~ **bringen** *(lit: zeigen)* to produce; *Fleck* to show up; *(fig: deutlich machen)* to bring to light; **zum** ~ **kommen** *(lit: sichtbar werden)* to appear; *(fig: entdeckt werden)* to turn up, to come to light; *(Tatsachen)* to come to light, to come out.

vorschieben *sep irreg* **1** *vt* **(a)** *(davorschieben)* to push in front; *Riegel* to put across, to shoot (across); *(nach vorn schieben)* to push forward; *Kopf* to stick forward; *Unterlippe, Kinn* to stick out; *siehe* **Riegel**.

(b) *(Mil) Truppen* to move forward. **vorgeschobener Posten** advance guard, advance party.

(c) *(fig: vorschützen)* to put forward as a pretext *or* excuse.

(d) **jdn** ~ to put sb forward as a front man. **2** *vr (Wolken, Erdmassen)* to advance, to move forward; *(Menschen)* to push *or* press forward.

vorschießen *sep irreg* **1** *vt* **jdm Geld** ~ to advance sb money. **2** *vi aux sein* to shoot forward; *(Schlange, Läufer auch)* to dart forward.

Vorschiff *nt* forecastle, fo'c's'le.

Vorschlag *m* **(a)** suggestion, proposal; *(Rat)* recommendation, advice; *(Angebot)* offer, proposition; *(Pol: von Kandidaten)* proposal. **auf** ~ **von** *or* +*gen* **at** *or* **on the suggestion of; on the recommendation of; das ist ein** ~! that's an idea!; **wäre das nicht ein** ~? how's that for an idea?; *siehe* **Güte**.

(b) *(Mus)* appoggiatura.

(c) *(Typ)* sink.

(d) *(Sw: Gewinn)* profit.

vorschlagen *vt sep irreg* **(a)** to suggest, to propose. **jdn für ein Amt** ~ to propose *or* nominate sb for a post; **jdm** ~, **daß er etw tut** *or* to suggest that sb do(es) sth, to suggest to sb that he do(es) sth. **(b)** **den Takt** ~ to beat time.

Vorschlaghammer *m* sledge-hammer.

Vorschlußrunde *f (Sport)* semi-final(s).

vorschnell *adj siehe* **voreilig**.

vorschreiben *vt sep irreg* **(a)** *(befehlen)* to stipulate; *(gesetzlich, durch Bestimmungen, vertraglich auch)* to lay down; *(Med) Dosis* to prescribe. **jdm** ~, **wie/was** ... to dictate to sb how/what ...; **ich lasse mir nichts** ~ I won't be dictated to; **vorgeschriebene Lektüre** *(Sch, Univ)* prescribed texts.

(b) *(lit)* to write out *(dat for)*.

vorschreiten *vi sep irreg aux sein* to progress, to make progress. **im vorgeschrittenen Alter** at an advanced age; **zu vorgeschrittener Stunde** at a late hour.

Vorschrift *f* -, -**en** *(gesetzliche etc Bestimmung)* regulation, rule; *(Anweisung)* instruction, order, direction. **nach** ~ **des Arztes** according to doctor's orders *or* the doctor's instructions; ~**en für den Verkehr** traffic regulations; **jdm** ~**en machen** to give sb orders, to dictate to sb; **ich lasse mir (von dir) keine** ~**en machen lassen** I won't be dictated to (by you), I won't take orders (from you); **sich an die** ~**en halten** to observe the regulations; to follow the instructions; **Arbeit nach** ~ work to rule; **das ist** ~ that's the regulation.

vorschrifts-: ~**gemäß**, ~**mäßig** **1** *adj* regulation *attr*; *Signal, Parken, Verhalten* correct, proper *attr*; *(Med) Dosis* prescribed; **2** *adv (laut Anordnung)* as instructed *or* directed; according to (the) regulations; *(Med)* as directed; ~**gemäß** *or* ~**mäßig gekleidet sein** to be in regulation dress; ~**widrig** *adj*, *adv* contrary to (the) regulations; *(Med) Dosis* contrary to the prescription.

Vorschub *m*: **jdm** ~ **leisten** to encourage sb; **einer Sache** *(dat)* ~ **leisten** to encourage *or* foster sth.

Vorschul|alter *nt* pre-school age.

Vorschule *f* nursery school; *(Vorschuljahr)* pre-school years *pl*.

Vorschul|erziehung *f* pre-school education.

vorschulisch *adj* pre-school *attr*.

Vorschuß *m* advance. **jdm einen** ~ **leisten** to give sb an advance.

Vorschußlorbeeren *pl* premature praise *sing*.

vorschützen *vt sep* to plead as an excuse, to put forward as a pretext; *Krankheit auch* to feign; *Unwissenheit* to plead. **er schützte vor, daß** ... he pretended that ...; *siehe* **Müdigkeit**.

vorschwärmen *vti sep* **jdm von jdm/etw** ~ to go into raptures over sb/sth; **jdm** ~, **wie schön etw ist** to go into raptures over how beautiful sth is.

vorschwatzen *vt sep (inf)* **jdm etwas** ~ to tell sb a lot of rubbish *(inf)*; **schwatz mir doch nichts vor** don't give me that rubbish *(inf)*.

vorschweben *vi sep* **jdm schwebt etw vor** sb has sth in mind.

vorschwindeln *vt sep* **jdm etwas** ~ to lie to sb; **jdm** ~, **daß** ... to lie to sb that ...; **ich lasse mir doch von dir nichts** ~ I won't have any of your lies.

vorsehen *sep irreg* **1** *vt (planen)* to plan; *(zeitlich auch)* to schedule; *Gerät* to design; *(einplanen) Kosten, Anschaffungen* to provide *or* allow for; *Zeit* to allow; *Fall* to provide *or* cater for; *(im Gesetz, Vertrag)* to provide for. **etw für etw** ~ *(bestimmen)* to intend sth for sth; *Geld* to earmark *or* destine sth for sth; **jdn für etw** ~ *(beabsichtigen)* to have sb in mind for sth; **er ist für dieses Amt**

vorgesehen we have him in mind for this post; **was haben wir für heute vorgesehen?** what is on the agenda today?, what have we planned for today?; **der Plan sieht vor, daß das Projekt bis September abgeschlossen ist** the project is scheduled to be finished by September.

2 *vr* **(a)** (*sich in acht nehmen*) to be careful, to watch out, to take care. **sich vor jdm/etw ~** to beware of sb/sth, to be wary of sb/sth; *vor Hund auch* to mind sth.

(b) (*dated*) **sich mit etw ~** (*eindecken*) to lay in stocks of sth.

3 *vi* (*sichtbar sein*) to appear. **hinter/unter etw** (*dat*) **~** to peep out from behind/under sth.

Vorsehung *f, no pl* Providence. **die (göttliche) ~** (divine) Providence.

vorsetzen sep **1** *vt* **(a)** (*nach vorn*) to move forward; **Fuß** to put forward; **Schüler** to move (up) to the front.

(b) (*davorsetzen*) to put in front. **etw vor etw** (*acc*) **~** to put sth in front of sth or before sth.

(c) jdm etw ~ (*geben*) to give sb sth, to put sth in front of sb; (*anbieten*) to offer sb sth; (*fig inf*) **Lügen, Geschichte, Erklärung** to serve or dish sth up to sb.

(d) (*dated*) **jdn jdm/einer Sache ~** (*als Vorgesetzten*) to put sb in charge of sb/sth.

2 *vr* to (come/go and) sit in (the) front. **sich in die erste Reihe ~** to (come/go and) sit in the front row.

Vorsicht *f -, no pl* care; (*bei Gefahr*) caution; (*Überlegtheit*) circumspection, prudence; (*Behutsamkeit*) guardedness, wariness. **~ üben** to be careful; to exercise caution, to be cautious; to be circumspect or prudent; to be wary; **jdn zur ~ (er)mahnen** to advise sb to be careful/cautious/circumspect; **zur ~(er)mahnen** to advise sb to be careful/cautious/circumspect; **zur ~ raten** to advise caution; **~!** watch or look or mind out!; **~ bei der Benutzung eines Geräts** care or caution in using an appliance; „**~ bei Einfahrt des Zuges**“ "stand back when the train approaches the platform"; „**~ Bahnübergang/Gift/Kurve**" "Level crossing/Poison/Bend"; „**~ nicht stürzen/feuergefährlich/gefährliche Kreuzung**" "danger - steep drop/inflammable/crossroads"; „**~ zerbrechlich**" "fragile - with care"; „**~ Glas**" "glass – with care"; „**~ nicht knicken**" "do not bend"; „**~ Stufe**" "mind the step"; **mit ~** carefully; cautiously; prudently; guardedly, warily; **etw zur ~ tun** to do sth as a precaution, to do sth to be on the safe side; **was er sagt/dieser Artikel ist mit ~ zu genießen** (*hum inf*) you have to take what he says/this article with a pinch of salt (*inf*); **sie ist mit ~ zu genießen** (*inf*) she has to be handled with kid gloves; **dieser Wein ist mit ~ zu genießen** (*inf*) I should be a bit wary of this wine; **~ ist besser als Nachsicht** (*Prov*) better safe than sorry; **~ ist die Mutter der Porzellankiste** (*inf*) better safe than sorry.

vorsichtig *adj* careful; (*besonnen*) cautious; (*überlegt*) prudent; **Äußerung** *auch* guarded, wary; (*mißtrauisch*) wary; **Schätzung** cautious, conservative.

Vorsichtigkeit *f siehe adj* carefulness; caution, cautiousness; prudence; guardedness, wariness; wariness.

Vorsichts-: **v~halber** *adv* as a precaution, to be on the safe side; **~maßnahme**, **~maßregel** *f* precaution, precautionary measure; **~maßnahmen treffen** to take precautions or precautionary measures.

Vor-: **~signal** *nt* (*Rail*) warning signal; **~silbe** *f* prefix; **v~singen** sep irreg **1** *vti* **(a)** (*vor Zuhörern*) **jdm (etw) v~singen** to sing (sth) to sb; **ich singe nicht gern v~** I don't like singing to people or in front of people; **(b)** (*als erster singen*) to sing first; **2** *vi* (*zur Prüfung*) to have a singing test; (*esp Theat: vor Einstellung*) to audition; **v~sintflutlich** *adj* (*inf*) antiquated, prehistoric (*hum*), antediluvian.

Vorsitz *m* chairmanship; (*Amt eines Präsidenten*) presidency. **unter dem ~ von** under the chairmanship of; **den ~ haben or führen (bei etw)** to be chairman (of sth); (*bei Sitzung*) to chair sth; **den ~ übernehmen** to take the chair.

vorsitzen *vi sep irreg* **einer Versammlung/Diskussion ~** to chair a meeting/discussion.

Vorsitzende(r) *mf decl as adj* chairman; (*von Firma auch*) president; (*US*) (*von Verein*) president; (*von Partei, Gewerkschaft etc*) leader. **der ~** Mao Chairman Mao.

Vorsorge *f, no pl* (*Vorsichtsmaßnahme*) precaution; (*vorherplanende Fürsorge*) provision(s *pl*) *no def art.* **zur ~ als a** precaution; **~ tragen** to make provisions; **~ treffen** to take precautions; (*fürs Alter*) to make provisions.

vorsorgen *vi sep* to make provisions (*daß* so that). **für etw ~** to provide for sth, to make provisions for sth.

Vorsorge|untersuchung *f* (*Med*) medical check-up.

vorsorglich 1 *adj* precautionary; **Mensch** cautious. **2** *adv* as a precaution, to be on the safe side.

Vorspann *m* **-(e)s, -e (a)** (*Vordergespann*) extra team (of horses). **(b)** (*Vorlauf: von Film, Tonband*) leader; (*Film, TV: Titel und Namen*) opening credits *pl*; (*Press*) introductory or opening paragraph.

vorspannen *vt sep* **Pferde** to harness; (*Elec*) to bias. **jdn ~** (*fig*) to enlist sb's help, to rope sb in (*inf*).

Vorspannung *f* (*Elec*) bias (voltage).

Vorspeise *f* hors d'œuvre, starter.

vorspiegeln *vt sep* to feign, to sham; **Krankheit, Bedürftigkeit** *auch* to plead. **jdm ~(, daß ...)** to pretend to sb (that ...).

Vorspiegelung *f* pretence. **unter ~ der pretence of sth; **das ist nur (eine) ~ falscher Tatsachen** (*hum*) it's all sham; *siehe* **Tatsache**.

Vorspiel *nt* (*Einleitung*) prelude; (*Ouvertüre*) overture; (*Theat*) prologue; (*Sport*) preliminary match/game; (*bei Geschlechtsverkehr*) foreplay; (*von Musiker*) performance; (*bei Prüfung*) practical (exam); (*bei Einstellung*) audition. **das ist erst das ~** (*hum*) that is just for starters (*inf*).

Vorspiel|abend *m* (*music school*) concert.

vorspielen sep **1** *vt* **(a) jdm etw ~** (*Mus*) to play sth to or for sb; (*Theat*) to act sth to or for sb; (*fig*) to act out a sham of sth in front of sb; **jdm eine Szene ~** to play a scene to or for sb; **jdm eine Komödie ~** (*fig*) to play or act out a farce in front of sb; **jdm ~, daß ...** to pretend to sb that ...; **spiel mir doch nichts vor** don't try and put on an act, don't try and pretend to me.

(b) (*zuerst spielen*) to play first.

2 *vi* (*vor Zuhörern*) to play; (*Mus, Theat*) (*zur Prüfung*) to do one's practical (exam); (*bei Einstellung*) to audition. **jdm ~** (*Mus*) to play for sb; (*Theat*) to act (a role) for or in front of sb; **jdn ~ lassen** (*bei Einstellung*) to audition sb.

Vorsprache *f* (*form: Besuch*) visit (*bei, auf* +dat to).

vorsprechen sep irreg **1** *vt* to say first; (*vortragen*) to recite. **jdm etw ~** to pronounce sth for sb, to say sth for sb; **wiederholt, was ich euch vorspreche** repeat after me. **2** *vi* **(a)** (*form: jdn aufsuchen*) to call (*bei jdm* on sb). **bei** or **auf einem Amt ~** to call at an office. **(b)** (*Theat*) to audition. **jdn ~ lassen** to audition sb.

vorspringen *vi sep irreg aux sein* to jump or leap out; (*vorwärts*) to jump or leap forward; (*herausragen*) to jut out, to project; (*Nase*) to be prominent; (*Kinn*) to be prominent, to protrude. **vor etw** (*dat*) **~** to jump or leap (out) in front of sth.

vorspringend *adj* projecting; **Nase** prominent; **Kinn, Backenknochen** prominent, protruding.

Vorsprung *m* **(a)** (*Archit*) projection; (*Fels~*) ledge; (*von Küste*) promontory.

(b) (*Sport, fig: Abstand*) lead (*vor* +dat over); (*Vorgabe*) start. **jdm 2 Meter/10 Minuten ~ geben** to give sb a 2-metre/a 10-minute start, to give sb 2 metres'/10 minutes' start; **einen ~ vor jdm haben** to be ahead of sb; (*Sport auch*) to be leading sb, to be in the lead; **einen ~ vor jdm gewinnen** to gain a lead over sb, to get ahead of sb.

Vor-: **~stadt** *f* suburb; **~städter** *m* suburbanite, suburban; **v~städtisch** *adj* suburban.

Vorstand *m* **(a)** (*leitendes Gremium*) board; (*von Firma*) board (of directors); (*von Verein*) committee; (*von Partei*) executive; (*von Akademie*) board (of governors). **(b)** (*Leiter*) chairman, managing director. **(c)** (*Aus*) *siehe* **Vorsteher(in)**.

Vorstands-: **~mitglied** *nt siehe* **Vorstand (a)** member of the board; committee member; member of the executive; member of the board; **~sitzung** *f* (*von Firma*) board meeting; (*von Partei*) executive meeting; **~wahl** *f* (*in Firma*) elections *pl* to the board; (*in Partei*) elections *pl* to the executive.

vorstecken *vt sep* **(a)** to put forward; **Kopf** to stick out or forward. **(b)** (*anstecken*) to put on; **Brosche** auch to pin on.

Vorstecknadel *f* (*Brosche*) brooch; (*Krawattennadel*) tie-pin.

vorstehen *vi sep irreg aux haben or sein* **(a)** (*hervorragen*) to project, to jut out; **Zähne** to stick out, to protrude; **Backenknochen, Kinn** to be prominent, to protrude; **Nase** to be prominent. **~de Zähne** protruding teeth, buck-teeth.

(b) einer Sache ~ dem Haushalt to preside over sth; **einer Firma, einer Partei** to be the chairman of sth; **einer Schule** to be the head(master/mistress) (*Brit*) or principal (*US*) of sth; **einem Geschäft** to manage sth; **einer Abteilung** to be in charge of sth; **einem Amt** to hold sth.

(c) (*form*) **wie im ~den** as above; **die ~den Erläuterungen** the above explanations.

(d) (*Hunt: Hund*) to set, to point.

Vorsteher(in *f*) *m* **-s, -** (*Kloster~*) abbot/abbess; (*Büro~*) manager; (*Gefängnis~*) governor; (*Gemeinde~*) chairman of parish council; (*dated Sch*) head(master/mistress) (*Brit*), principal (*US*); (*Bahnhofs~*) station-master.

Vorsteherdrüse *f* prostate (gland).

Vorstehhund *m* pointer; (*langhaariger*) setter.

vorstellbar *adj* conceivable, imaginable. **das ist nicht ~** that is inconceivable or unimaginable.

vorstellen sep **1** *vt* **(a)** (*nach vorn*) **Tisch, Stuhl, Auto** to move forward; **Bein** to put out; **Uhr** to put forward or on (*um* by).

(b) (*inf: davorstellen*) **etw** (*vor etw acc*) **~** to put sth in front of sth; **Auto** auch to park sth in front of sth.

(c) (*darstellen*) to represent; (*bedeuten*) to mean, to signify. **was soll das ~?** (*inf*) what is that supposed to be?; **etwas ~** (*fig*) (*gut aussehen*) to look good; (*Ansehen haben*) to count for something.

(d) (*bekannt machen*) **jdn jdm ~** to introduce sb to sb.

(e) (*bekanntmachen, vorführen*) to present; **Folgen, Gefahren** to point out (*jdm* to sb). **jdm etw ~** to show sb sth.

2 *vr* **(a) sich** (*dat*) **etw ~** to imagine sth; **stell dir mal vor** just imagine; **das kann ich mir gut ~** I can imagine that well; **das muß man sich** (*dat*) **mal (bildlich or plastisch) ~** just imagine or picture it!; **sich** (*dat*) **etw unter etw** (*dat*) **~ Begriff, Wort** to understand sth by sth; **darunter kann ich mir nichts ~** it doesn't mean anything to me; **das Kleid ist genau, was ich mir vorgestellt hatte** the dress is just what I had in mind; **was haben Sie sich (als Gehalt) vorgestellt?** what (salary) did you have in mind?; **ich kann sie mir gut als Lehrerin ~** I can just imagine or see her as a teacher; **stell dir das nicht so einfach vor** don't think it's so easy; **so stelle ich mir einen gelungenen Urlaub vor** that's my idea of a successful holiday.

(b) (*sich nach vorn stellen*) to move or go forward; (*in Schlange*) to stand at the front.

(c) (*sich bekannt machen*) to introduce oneself (*jdm* to sb); (*bei Bewerbung*) to come/go for an interview; (*Antrittsbesuch machen*) to present oneself (*dat, bei* to). **hast du dich auch bei Meier vorgestellt?** have you had an interview with Meier too?

vorstellig *adj* **bei jdm ~ werden** to go to sb; (*wegen Beschwerde*) to complain to sb, to lodge a complaint with sb.

Vorstellung *f* **(a)** (*Gedanke*) idea; (*bildlich*) picture; (*Einbildung*) illusion; (*~skraft*) imagination. **in meiner ~ sah das größer aus** I imagined it bigger; **in meiner ~ ist Gott kein alter Mann** I don't picture God as an old man; **du hast falsche ~en**

you are wrong (in your ideas); **es übertrifft alle ~en** it's incredible or unbelievable; **das entspricht ganz meiner ~** that is just how I imagined or saw it; **sich** (dat) **eine ~ von etw machen** to form an idea or (Bild) picture of sth; **du machst dir keine ~, wie schwierig das ist** you have no idea how difficult that is.

   (b) (Theat etc) performance; (Film auch) showing.

   (c) (das Bekanntmachen) (zwischen Leuten) introduction; (bei Hofe) presentation (bei at); (Vorführung: von Geräten, neuem Artikel etc) presentation; (bei Bewerbung, Antrittsbesuch) interview (bei with).

   (d) (Einwand) objection, protest. **jdm wegen etw ~en machen** to remonstrate with sb about sth.

Vorstellungs-: ~**gespräch** nt interview; ~**kraft** f imagination; ~**vermögen** nt powers of imagination pl; ~**welt** f imagination.

Vorstopper m -s, - (Ftbl) centre-half.

Vorstoß m **(a)** (Vordringen) venture; (Mil) advance, push; (fig: Versuch) attempt. **(b)** (Tech: an Rädern) wheel rim; (Sew) edging; (Litze) braiding.

vorstoßen sep irreg **1** vt to push forward. **2** vi aux sein to venture; (Sport) to attack; (Mil) to advance. **ins All ~** (Rakete, Mensch) to venture into space.

Vorstrafe f previous conviction.

Vorstrafenregister nt criminal or police record; (Kartei) criminal or police records pl.

vorstrecken vt sep to stretch forward; **Arme** to stretch out; **Hand** to stretch or put out; **Krallen** to put out; (fig) **Geld** to advance (jdm sb).

Vorstufe f preliminary stage; (von Entwicklung) early stage.

vorstürmen vi sep aux sein to charge or rush forward (hinter +dat from behind).

Vortag m day before, eve. **am ~ der Konferenz** (on) the day before the conference, on the eve of the conference.

vortanzen sep **1** vt **jdm einen Tanz/die Schritte ~** to dance a dance/the steps for sb; (zur Demonstration) to demonstrate a dance/the steps for sb. **2** vi (zur Demonstration) to demonstrate a dance/step etc (jdm to sb); (als Prüfung) to dance (jdm in front of sb).

Vortänzer m leading dancer; (Anführer eines Tanzes) leader of the dance.

vortäuschen vt sep **Krankheit, Armut** to feign; **Schlag, Orgasmus** to fake. **sie hat mir eine glückliche Ehe vorgetäuscht** she pretended to me that her marriage was happy.

Vortäuschung f pretence, fake. **die ~ einer Krankheit/eines Schlags** feigning an illness/faking a blow; ~ **von Tatsachen** (Jur) misrepresentation of the facts; **unter ~ falscher Tatsachen** under false pretences; **das ist nur (eine) ~ falscher Tatsachen** (hum) that's all sham.

Vorteil m -s, -e advantage (auch Sport). **die Vor- und Nachteile** the pros and cons; **auf den eigenen ~ bedacht sein** to have an eye to one's own interests; **jdm gegenüber im ~ sein** to have an advantage over sb; **sich zu seinem ~ ändern** to change for the better; **ein ~ sein** to be an advantage, to be advantageous; **von ~ sein** to be advantageous; **das kann für dich nur von ~ sein** it can only be to your advantage; **ich habe dabei an deinen ~ gedacht** I was thinking of your interests; **im ~ sein** to have the advantage (jdm gegenüber over sb); **den ~ von etw haben** to benefit from sth; ~**e aus etw ziehen** to benefit from sth, to gain advantage from sth.

vorteilhaft adj advantageous; **Kleider** flattering; **Geschäft** lucrative, profitable. ~ **aussehen** to look one's best; **etw ~ verkaufen** (finanziell) to sell sth for a profit; **ein ~er Kauf** a good buy, a bargain; **der helle Teppich wirkt ~** the light carpet looks good.

Vortrag m -(e)s, **Vorträge** **(a)** (Vorlesung) lecture; (Bericht, Beschreibung) talk. **einen ~ halten** to give a lecture/talk; **halt keine Vorträge** (inf) don't give a whole lecture.

   (b) (Darbietung) performance; (eines Gedichtes) reading, recitation; (Mus: Solo~) recital.

   (c) (Art des Vortragens) performance.

   (d) (Fin) balance carried forward.

vortragen vt sep irreg **(a)** (lit) to carry forward.

   (b) (berichten) to report; (förmlich mitteilen) **Fall, Angelegenheit** to present; **Forderungen** to present, to convey; **Beschwerde** to lodge; **Meinung** to express, to convey; **Wunsch** to express; (einen Vortrag halten über) to give a lecture/talk on.

   (c) (vorsprechen) **Gedicht** to recite; **Rede** to give; (Mus) to perform, to play; **Lied** to sing, to perform.

   (d) (Fin) to carry forward.

Vortragende(r) mf decl as adj lecturer; (von Rede, Bericht) speaker; (von Musikstück, Lied etc) performer.

Vortrags-: ~**abend** m lecture evening; (mit Gedichten) poetry evening; (mit Musik) recital; ~**folge** f series of lectures; (einzelne Sendung) lecture in a series; ~**kunst** f skill as a performer; (von Redner) skill as a speaker; ~**reihe** f series of lectures.

vortrefflich adj excellent, splendid, superb.

Vortrefflichkeit f excellence.

vortreten vi sep irreg aux sein **(a)** (lit) to step forward, to come forward. **(b)** (hervorragen) to project, to jut out; (Augen) to protrude. ~**de Backenknochen** prominent cheek-bones.

Vortritt m, no pl precedence, priority; (Sw: Vorfahrt) right of way. **in etw** (dat) **den ~ haben** (fig) to have precedence in sth (vor +dat over); **jdm den ~ lassen** (lit) to let sb go first; (fig auch) to let sb go ahead.

vortrocknen vt to dry partially.

Vortrupp m advance guard, advance party.

vortun vt sep irreg (inf) **Schürze, Riegel, Kette etc** to put on. **die Hand ~** to put one's hand over one's mouth.

vorturnen sep **1** vt **jdm eine Übung ~** (vormachen) to demonstrate an exercise to sb; (öffentlich zeigen) to perform an exer-

cise in front of sb. **2** vi **jdm ~** (vormachen) to demonstrate to sb; (öffentlich) to perform in front of sb.

Vorturner m demonstrator (of gymnastic exercises); (fig sl) front man.

vorüber adv ~ **sein** (räumlich, Jugend) to be past; (zeitlich auch, Gewitter, Winter, Kummer) to be over; (Schmerz) to have gone.

vorüber- pref siehe auch **vorbei-**; ~**gehen** vi sep irreg aux sein **(a)** (räumlich) (an etw (dat) sth) to go past, to pass (by); **jdm/etw ~gehen** (fig: ignorieren) to ignore sb/sth; **(b)** (zeitlich) to pass; (Gewitter) to blow over; **eine Gelegenheit ~gehen lassen** to let an opportunity slip; **(c)** **an jdm ~gehen** (sich nicht bemerkbar machen) to pass sb by; **an jdm nicht ~gehen** (Erlebnis etc) to leave its/their mark on sb; ~**gehend** adj (flüchtig) momentary, passing attr; **Krankheit** short; (zeitweilig) temporary; **sich ~gehend aufhalten** to stay for a short time.

Vor-: ~**übung** f preliminary exercise; ~**untersuchung** f preliminary examination; (Jur) preliminary or initial investigation.

Vorurteil nt prejudice (gegenüber against). **das ist ein ~ it's** prejudice; ~**e haben** or **hegen, in ~en befangen sein** to be prejudiced.

Vorurteils-: **v~frei, v~los 1** adj unprejudiced; **Entscheidung, Verhalten** auch unbiased; **2** adv without prejudice; without bias; ~**losigkeit** f freedom from prejudice.

Vor-: ~**väter** pl forefathers, ancestors, forebears all pl; ~**vergangenheit** f (Gram) pluperfect; ~**verhandlung** f preliminary negotiations or talks pl; (Jur) preliminary hearing; ~**verkauf** m (Theat, Sport) advance booking; **sich** (dat) **Karten im ~verkauf besorgen** to buy tickets in advance; ~**verkaufskasse, ~verkaufsstelle** f advance booking office.

vorverlegen* vt sep **(a)** **Termin** to bring forward. **(b)** (Mil) **Front, Gefechtslinie** to push forward. **das Feuer ~** to increase the range.

Vor-: ~**verständnis** nt preconception; ~**verstärker** m preamplifier; ~**vertrag** m preliminary contract/treaty; **v~vorgestern** adv (inf) three days ago; **v~vorig** adj (inf) **v~vorige Woche/v~voriges Jahr** the week/year before last; **v~vorletzte(r, s)** adj last but two.

vorwagen vr sep (lit) to venture forward; (fig auch) to venture.

Vorwahl f **(a)** preliminary election; (US) primary. **(b)** (Telec) dialling or area (US) code.

vorwählen vt sep (Telec) to dial first.

Vorwahlnummer f dialling or area (US) code.

vorwalten vi sep to prevail.

Vorwand m -(e)s, **Vorwände** pretext, excuse. **unter dem ~, daß ...** under the pretext that ...

vorwärmen vt sep to pre-heat; **Teller** to heat.

Vorwarnung f (prior or advance) warning; (Mil: vor Angriff) early warning.

vorwärts adv forwards, forward. ~! (inf) let's go (inf); (Mil) forward march!; **weiter ~** further ahead or on; ~ **und rückwärts** backwards and forwards; **etw ~ und rückwärts kennen** (fig inf) to know sth backwards, to know sth inside out; **wir kamen nur langsam ~** we made slow progress; **Rolle/Salto ~** forward roll/somersault.

Vorwärts-: ~**bewegung** f forward movement; **v~bringen** vt sep irreg (fig) to advance; **jdn v~bringen** to help sb to get on; ~**gang** m forward gear; **v~gehen** sep irreg aux sein (fig) **1** vi to progress, to come on; (Gesundheit) to improve; **2** vi impers **es geht wieder v~** things are looking up; **mit etw geht es v~** sth is progressing or going well; **v~kommen** vi sep irreg aux sein (fig) to make progress, to get on (in, mit with); (beruflich, gesellschaftlich) to get on; **im Leben/Beruf v~kommen** to get on in life/one's job; ~**verteidigung** f (Mil) forward defence.

Vorwäsche f, **Vorwaschgang** m prewash.

vorweg adv (voraus, an der Spitze) at the front; (vorher) before(hand); (als erstes, von vornherein) at the outset.

Vorweg-: ~**leistung** f (Sw: Vorauszahlung) advance (payment); ~**nahme** f -, -n anticipation; **v~nehmen** vt sep irreg to anticipate; **um das Wichtigste v~zunehmen** to come to the most important point first.

Vorweihnachtszeit f pre-Christmas period.

vorweisen vt sep irreg to show, to produce; **Zeugnisse** to produce. **etw ~ können** (fig) to have or possess sth.

vorwerfen vt sep irreg **(a)** (fig) **jdm etw/Unpünktlichkeit ~** (anklagen) to reproach sb for sth/for being unpunctual; (beschuldigen) to accuse sb of sth/of being unpunctual; **jdm ~, daß er etw getan hat** to reproach sb for having done sth; **jdm ~, daß er etw nicht getan hat** to accuse sb of not having done sth; **das wirft er mir heute noch vor** he still holds it against me; **ich habe mir nichts vorzuwerfen** my conscience is clear; **sie haben einander nichts vorzuwerfen** the one is as bad as the other.

   (b) (lit) **Tieren/Gefangenen etw ~** to throw sth down for the animals/prisoners.

Vorwerk nt (von Gut) outlying estate; (von Burg) outwork.

vorwiegen vi sep irreg to predominate.

vorwiegend 1 adj attr predominant. **2** adv predominantly, mainly, chiefly.

Vorwissen nt previous knowledge; (Vorherwissen) foreknowledge. **ohne mein ~** without my previous knowledge.

Vorwitz m, no pl (Keckheit) cheek(iness); (Vorlautheit) forwardness, pertness; (dial: Neugier) inquisitiveness, curiosity.

vorwitzig adj (keck) cheeky; (vorlaut) forward, pert; (dial: neugierig) inquisitive, curious.

Vorwort nt -(e)s, -e **(a)** foreword; (esp von Autor) preface. **(b)** pl **-wörter** (Aus: Präposition) preposition.

Vorwurf m -(e)s, **Vorwürfe** **(a)** reproach; (Beschuldigung) accusation. **man machte ihm den ~ der Bestechlichkeit** he was accused of being open to bribery; **jdm/sich große Vorwürfe**

machen, daß ... to reproach sb/oneself for ...; **ich habe mir keine Vorwürfe zu machen** my conscience is clear; **jdm etw zum ~ machen** to reproach sb with sth.
  (b) (*Vorlage*) subject.

vorwurfsvoll *adj* reproachful.

vorzählen *vt sep* **jdm etw ~** to count sth out to sb; (*fig: auflisten*) to enumerate sth (to sb).

vorzaubern *vt sep* **jdm Kunststücke ~** to perform conjuring tricks for sb; **jdm etw ~** (*fig*) to conjure sth up for sb.

Vorzeichen *nt* (*Omen*) omen, sign; (*Med*) early symptom; (*Math*) sign; (*Mus*) (*Kreuz/b*) sharp/flat (sign); (*vor einzelner Note*) accidental; (*von Tonart*) key-signature. **positives/ negatives ~** (*Math*) plus/minus (sign); **mit umgekehrtem ~** (*fig*) the other way round; **unter dem gleichen ~** (*fig*) under the same circumstances; **dadurch haben die Verhandlungen ein negatives ~ erhalten** that put the negotiations under a cloud.

vorzeichnen *vt sep* **Linien etc** to sketch or draw (out). **jdm etw ~** (*zum Nachmalen*) to sketch or draw sth out for sb; (*fig*) to map or mark sth out for sb.

vorzeigen *vt sep* to show, to produce; **Zeugnisse** to produce. **jdm die Hände ~** to show sb one's hands.

Vorzeit *f* prehistoric times *pl*. **in der ~** in prehistoric times; (*vor langem*) in the dim and distant past; *siehe* **grau**.

vorzeiten *adv* (*liter*) in days gone by, in olden times.

vorzeitig *adj* early; **Geburt, Altern etc** premature.

Vorzeitigkeit *f* (*Gram*) anteriority.

vorzeitlich *adj* prehistoric; (*fig*) archaic.

vorziehen *vt sep irreg* **(a)** (*hervorziehen*) to pull out; (*nach vorne ziehen*) **Stuhl etc** to pull up; **Truppen** to move up; (*zuziehen*) **Vorhänge** to draw, to close. **etw hinter/unter etw** (*dat*) **~** to pull sth out from behind/under sth.
  (b) (*fig*) (*lieber mögen*) to prefer; (*bevorzugen*) **jdn** to favour. **etw einer anderen Sache ~** to prefer sth to sth else; **es ~, etw zu tun** to prefer to do sth; (*allgemein gesehen*) to prefer doing sth; **ich ziehe es vor, jetzt zu gehen** I'd or I would prefer to go now, I'd rather go now.
  (c) (*zuerst behandeln, abfertigen*) to give priority to.

Vorzimmer *nt* anteroom; (*Büro*) outer office; (*Aus: Diele*) hall.

Vorzimmer-: **~dame** *f* receptionist; **~wand** *f* (*Aus*) hall stand.

Vorzug¹ *m* **-(e)s, Vorzüge** **(a)** preference; (*Vorteil*) advantage; (*gute Eigenschaft*) merit, asset. **einer Sache** (*dat*) **den ~ geben** (*form*) to prefer sth, to give sth preference; (*Vorrang*

geben) to give sth precedence; **den ~ vor etw** (*dat*) **haben** to be preferable to sth; **den ~ haben, daß ...** to have the advantage that ...; **ich hatte nicht den ~, ihn kennenzulernen** (*geh*) I did not have the privilege of meeting him.
  (b) (*Aus Sch*) distinction.

Vorzug² *m* (*Rail*) train in front; (*früher fahrend*) train before; (*Entlastungszug*) relief train.

vorzüglich [(*esp Aus*) 'foːɐtsyːklɪç] **1** *adj* excellent, superb; **Qualität, Arbeit** *auch* exquisite; *siehe* **Hochachtung**. **2** *adv* excellently, superbly; (*vornehmlich*) especially, particularly. **der Wein schmeckt ~** the wine tastes excellent or superb.

Vorzüglichkeit *f, no pl* excellence.

Vorzugs-: **~aktien** *pl* (*St Ex*) preference shares *pl*; **~behandlung** *f* preferential treatment *no indef art*: **~milch** *f* milk with high fat content, ≈ gold-top milk (*Brit*); **~preis** *m* special discount price; **~schüler** *m* (*Aus*) star pupil; **v~weise** *adv* preferably, by preference; (*hauptsächlich*) mainly, chiefly; **etw v~weise trinken** to prefer to drink or drinking sth.

Vorzündung *f* (*Aut*) pre-ignition.

Voten ['voːt(ə)n], **Vota** (*geh*) *pl of* **Votum**.

votieren* [voˈtiːrən] *vi* (*geh*) to vote.

Votiv- [voˈtiːf]: **~bild** *nt* votive picture; **~kapelle** *f* votive chapel; **~tafel** *f* votive tablet.

Votum ['voːtʊm] *nt* **-s, Voten** or **Vota** (*geh*) vote.

Voyeur [voaˈjøːɐ] *m* voyeur.

VP [faʊˈpeː] *f* – *abbr of* **Volkspolizei**.

v.R.w. *abbr of* **von Rechts wegen**.

v.T. *abbr of* **vom Tausend**.

vulgär [vʊlˈɡɛːɐ] *adj* vulgar.

Vulgärausdruck [vʊlˈɡɛːɐ-] *m* vulgar expression, vulgarity.

Vulgarität [vʊlɡariˈtɛːt] *f* vulgarity.

Vulgärlatein [vʊlˈɡɛːɐ-] *nt* vulgar Latin.

Vulkan [vʊlˈkaːn] *m* **-(e)s, -e** volcano. **auf einem ~ leben** (*fig*) to be living on the edge of a volcano; *siehe* **Tanz**.

Vulkan-: [vʊlˈkaːn-]: **~ausbruch** *m* volcanic eruption; **~fiber** *f* vulcanized fibre.

Vulkanisation [vʊlkanizaˈtsi̯oːn] *f* (*Tech*) vulcanization.

vulkanisch [vʊlˈkaːnɪʃ] *adj* volcanic.

Vulkanisieranstalt [vʊlkaniˈtsiːr-] *f* vulcanization plant.

vulkanisieren* [vʊlkaniˈtsiːrən] *vt* to vulcanize.

v.u.Z. *abbr of* **vor unserer Zeitrechnung** BC.

V-Waffen ['faʊ-] *pl siehe* **Vergeltungswaffen**.

W

W, w [veː] *nt* -, - **W, w**.

W *abbr of* **Westen**.

Waage *f* -, **-n** **(a)** (*Gerät*) scales *pl*; (*Feder~, Apotheker~*) balance; (*für Lastwagen, Autos*) weighbridge. **eine ~ a pair of scales; sich** (*dat*) **die ~ halten** (*fig*) to balance one another or each other; **einer Sache** (*dat*) **die ~ halten** to balance sth (out); *siehe* **Zünglein**.
  (b) (*Astron, Astrol*) **die ~** Libra; **er ist (eine) ~** he's (a) Libra.
  (c) (*Sport: Stand~/Knie~*) horizontal single leg/knee stand.

Waagebalken *m* (balance or scale) beam.

Waag(e)-: **w~recht** *adj* horizontal, level; **Linie, Ebene** horizontal; **~rechte** *f* horizontal; **etw in die ~rechte bringen** to make sth horizontal or level; **in der ~rechten transportieren** to transport sth horizontally.

Waagschale *f* (scale) pan, scale. **(schwer) in die ~ fallen** (*fig*) to carry weight; **jedes Wort auf die ~ legen** to weigh every word (carefully); **jds Worte/etw auf die ~ legen** to take sb's words/sth literally; **seinen Einfluß/seine Autorität/sein ganzes Gewicht in die ~ werfen** (*fig*) to bring one's influence/one's authority/one's full weight to bear.

wabb(e)lig *adj* **Pudding, Gelee** wobbly; **Mensch** flabby.

wabbeln *vi* to wobble.

Wabe *f* -, **-n** honeycomb.

Waben-: **w~förmig** *adj* honeycombed; **~honig** *m* comb honey.

wabern *vi* (*geh*) to undulate; (*obs, dial: flackern*) to flicker.

wach *adj* awake *pred*; (*fig: aufgeweckt*) alert, wide-awake; **Nacht** sleepless, wakeful. **in ~em Zustand** in the waking state; **sich ~ halten** to keep or stay awake; **~ werden** to wake up; **~ liegen** to lie awake; **jdn ~ schütteln/küssen** to shake sb awake/to wake sb with a kiss.

Wach-: **~ablösung** *f* changing of the guard; (*fig: Regierungswechsel*) change of government; (*Mensch*) relief guard; **wann ist ~ablösung?** when is the changing of the guards?; **~bataillon** *nt* guard battalion, guards *pl*; **~boot** *nt* patrol boat; **~dienst** *m* look-out, guard (duty); (*Mil*) guard (duty); (*Naut*) watch; **~dienst haben/machen** to be on guard (duty); (*Naut*) to have the watch.

Wache *f* -, **-n** **(a)** *no pl* (*Wachdienst*) guard (duty). **auf ~ on guard (duty); (bei jdm) ~ halten** to keep guard or watch (over

sb); (*Kranken~*) to keep watch (at sb's bedside), to watch over sb; (*Toten~*) to watch over sb; **~ stehen** or **schieben** (*inf*) to be on guard (duty); (*Dieb, Schüler etc*) to keep a look-out.
  (b) (*Mil*) (*Wachposten*) guard, sentry; (*Gebäude*) guardhouse; (*Raum*) guard-room.
  (c) (*Naut: Personen, Dauer*) watch. **~ haben** to be on watch.
  (d) (*Polizei~*) (police) station.

wachen *vi* **(a)** (*wach sein*) to be awake; (*nicht schlafen können*) to lie awake. **(b)** (*Wache halten*) to keep watch. **bei jdm ~** to sit up with sb, to keep watch by sb's bedside; **das W~ am Krankenbett** sitting up with a/the patient or at a/the sickbed; **über etw** (*acc*) **~** to (keep) watch over sth; **über Verkehr** to supervise sth; **der Polizist wachte darüber, daß niemand ...** the policeman watched that no-one ...

Wach-: **w~habend** *adj attr* duty; **~habende(r)** *m decl as adj* (*Offizier*) duty officer; (*Naut*) watch; **w~halten** *vt sep irreg* (*fig*) **Interesse etc** to keep alive or up; **~heit** *f* (*fig*) alertness; (*die*) **~heit des Geistes** alertness of mind, an alert or wide-awake mind; **~hund** *m* (*lit, fig*) watchdog; (*lit auch*) guard-dog; **~leute** *pl of* **~mann**; **~lokal** *nt* guard-room; **~mann** *m, pl* **-leute** watchman; (*Aus*) policeman; **~mannschaft** *f* men or squad on guard; (*Naut*) watch; **~offizier** *m* (*Naut*) officer of the watch.

Wacholder *m* **-s, -** **(a)** (*Bot*) juniper (tree). **(b)** *siehe* **Wacholderschnaps**.

Wacholder-: **~beere** *f* juniper berry; **~branntwein** (*form*), **~schnaps** *m* spirit made from juniper berries, ≈ gin; **~strauch** *m siehe* **Wacholder (a)**.

Wach-: **~posten** *m siehe* **Wachtposten**; **w~rufen** *vt sep irreg* (*fig*) **Erinnerung etc** to call to mind, to evoke; **w~rütteln** *vt sep* (*fig*) to shake up, to (a)rouse; **Gewissen** to stir, to (a)rouse; **jdn aus seiner Apathie w~rütteln** to shake sb out of his apathy.

Wachs [vaks] *nt* **-es, -e** wax. **weich wie ~** as soft as butter; **meine Knie wurden weich wie ~** my knees turned to jelly; **~ in jds Händen sein** (*fig*) to be putty in sb's hands.

wachsam *adj* watchful, vigilant; (*vorsichtig*) on one's guard. **ein ~es Auge auf jdn/etw haben** to keep a watchful or sharp eye on sb/sth.

Wachsamkeit *f, no pl* watchfulness, vigilance; (*Vorsichtigkeit*) guardedness.

Wachs- ['vaks-]: ~**bild** nt waxen image; ~**bildnerei** f, no pl ceroplastics sing (spec), modelling in wax; w~**bleich** adj waxen; ~**bohne** f wax bean; ~**buntstift** m wax crayon.

Wachschiff nt patrol ship.

wachseln ['vaksln] vt (Aus) siehe **wachsen**².

wachsen¹ ['vaksn] pret **wuchs** [vu:ks], ptp **gewachsen** vi aux sein to grow; (Spannung, Begeisterung auch) to mount. in die Breite/Länge ~ to broaden (out)/to lengthen, to get or grow broader/longer; in die Höhe ~ to grow taller; (Kind) to shoot up (inf); sich (dat) einen Bart/die Haare ~ lassen to grow a beard/to let one's hair grow or to grow one's hair; Sauerkraut kann ich mit ~der Begeisterung essen I can eat sauerkraut till the cows come home (hum inf); gut gewachsen Baum well-grown; Mensch with or having a good figure; wie gewachsen with fat and gristle not removed; er wächst mit or an seiner Verantwortung (fig) he grows with his responsibility.

wachsen² ['vaksn] vt to wax.

wächsern ['vɛksən] adj (lit, fig) waxen.

Wachs- ['vaks-]: ~**farbe** f (a (Farbstift) wax crayon; mit ~**farbe(n) gemalt** drawn with or in wax crayons; (b) (Farbstoff) wax dye; ~**farbstift** m wax crayon; ~**figur** f wax figure; ~**figurenkabinett** nt waxworks pl; ~**kerze** f wax candle; ~**licht** nt night light; ~**malerei** f (a) no pl (Technik) encaustic painting; (b) (Bild) encaustic; ~**malstift** m, ~**malkreide** f wax crayon; ~**maske** f wax mask; ~**matrize** f stencil; ~**papier** nt waxed paper; ~**stift** m wax crayon; ~**stock** m wax taper.

Wachstube ['vax∫tu:bə] f guard-room; (von Polizei) duty room.

Wachstuch ['vaks-] nt oilcloth.

Wachstum ['vakstu:m] nt, no pl growth. im ~ zurückgeblieben stunted; eigenes ~ (des Winzers) from or grown in our own vineyards.

Wachstums-: w~**hemmend** adj growth-inhibiting; ~**hemmung** f inhibition of growth no pl; ~**hormon** nt growth hormone; ~**politik** f growth policy; ~**rate** f (Biol, Econ) growth rate; ~**schmerzen** pl growing pains pl; ~**störung** f disturbance of growth.

Wachs- ['vaks-]: w~**weich** adj (as) soft as butter; w~**weich werden** (Mensch) to melt; (Knie) to turn to jelly; ~**zieher(in** f) m -s, - chandler.

Wacht f -, -en (obs, liter) siehe **Wache**.

Wächte f -, -n siehe **Schneewächte**.

Wachtel f -, -n quail; (fig inf: Frau) silly goose (inf). alte ~ (inf) (unfreundlich) old hen (inf); (dumm) silly old goose (inf).

Wächter m -s, - guardian; (Nacht~) watchman; (Turm~) watch; (Museums~, Parkplatz~) attendant; (Hund) guard-dog, watchdog.

Wacht-: ~**meister** m (a) (old Mil) sergeant; (b) (Polizist) (police) constable (Brit), patrolman (US); **Herr** ~**meister** officer, constable (Brit); ~**posten** m sentry, guard; (Schüler, Dieb etc) look-out.

Wachtraum m daydream.

Wach(t)turm m watch-tower.

Wach-: ~- **und Schließgesellschaft** f security corps; ~**zimmer** nt (Aus) siehe ~**lokal**; ~**zustand** m im ~**zustand** in the waking state.

Wackelei f (inf) wobbling.

wack(e)lig adj wobbly; (Möbelstück auch) rickety; Zahn, Schraube auch loose; (fig) Firma, Unternehmen shaky. ~ auf den Beinen sein (inf) (Patient) to be wobbly on one's legs, to be shaky; (alter Mensch) to be doddery; ~ stehen (lit) to be unsteady or wobbly; (fig: Unternehmen, Schüler) to be shaky.

Wackelkontakt m loose connection.

wackeln vi to wobble; (zittern) to shake; (Zahn, Schraube) to be loose; (fig) (Thron) to totter; (Position) to be shaky. du hast gewackelt you wobbled/shook; (beim Fotografieren) you moved; mit den Ohren/Hüften/dem Kopf/Schwanz ~ to waggle one's ears/wiggle one's hips/wag one's head/its tail.
(b) aux sein (langsam, unsicher gehen) to totter; (kleines Kind) to toddle.

Wackelpeter m -s, - (inf) jelly.

wacker adj (a) (tapfer) brave, valiant. sich ~ halten (inf) to stand or hold one's ground; sich ~ schlagen (inf) to put up a brave fight; ~**er Streiter** (old, hum) doughty fighter (old). (b) (old: tüchtig) upright, honest.

Wackerstein m boulder.

wacklig adj siehe **wack(e)lig**.

Wade f -, -n calf.

Waden-: ~**bein** nt fibula; ~**krampf** m cramp in the/one's calf; ~**strumpf** m half stocking; ~**wickel** m (Med) compress around the leg.

Waffe f -, -n (lit, fig) weapon; (Schuß~) gun; (Mil: Waffengattung) arm. ~n (Mil) arms; ~n **tragen** to carry arms; zu den ~n **rufen** to call to arms; **unter** ~n (stehen) (to be) under arms; die ~n **strecken** (lit, fig) to lay down one's arms, to surrender; **seine** ~n **aus der Hand geben** (fig) to throw away one's weapons; **jdn mit seinen eigenen** ~n **schlagen** (fig) to beat sb at his own game or with his own weapons.

Waffel f -, -n waffle; (Keks, Eis~) wafer; (Eistüte) cornet.

Waffel-: ~**eisen** nt waffle iron; ~**stoff** m honeycomb cloth.

Waffen- in cpds arms; ~**arsenal** nt arsenal; (von Staat) stockpile; ~**besitz** m possession of firearms; ~**bruder** m (old) comrade in arms (old); ~**dienst** m (old) military service; w~**fähig** adj capable of bearing arms, able-bodied; ~**gang** m (old Mil) passage at arms, armed encounter; (Univ) round; ~**gattung** f (Mil) arm of the service; ~**gewalt** f force of arms; **mit** ~**gewalt** by force of arms; ~**handel** m arms trade or traffic; (illegal auch) gunrunning; **der** ~**handel ist ... arms trade or traffic/gunrunning is ...;** ~**hilfe** f military assistance; ~**kammer** f armoury (Brit), armory (US); ~**lager** nt (von Armee) ordnance depot; (von Terroristen) cache; ~**lieferung** f supply of arms; w~**los** adj unarmed; ~**rock** m (old) uniform;

~**ruhe** f ceasefire; ~**schein** m firearms or gun licence; ~**schmied** m (Hist) armourer; ~**schmuggel** m gunrunning, arms smuggling; ~-**SS** f (NS) Waffen-SS.

Waffenstillstand m armistice.

Waffenstillstands-: ~**abkommen** nt armistice agreement; ~**linie** f armistice line.

Waffen-: ~**system** nt weapon system; ~**tanz** m war dance (showing skill with weapons); ~**träger** m (Mensch) bearer of a weapon; (Fahrzeug) weapon carrier.

waffnen vr siehe **wappnen**.

wägbar adj (geh) ponderable. **ein nicht** ~**es Risiko an** imponderable risk.

Wage-: ~**hals** m daredevil; w~**halsig** adj siehe **waghalsig**.

Wägelchen nt dim of **Wagen**.

Wage-: ~**mut** m, no pl (geh) (heroic) daring or boldness; w~**mutig** adj daring, bold.

wagen 1 vt to venture; (riskieren) hohen Einsatz, sein Leben to risk; (sich getrauen) to dare. **es** ~, **etw zu tun** to venture to do sth; to risk doing sth; to dare (to) do sth; **wage nicht, mir zu widersprechen!** don't you dare (to) contradict me!; **ich wag's** I'll risk it, I'll take the risk or plunge; **wer wagt, gewinnt** (Prov), **wer nichts wagt, der nichts gewinnt** (Prov) nothing ventured, nothing gained (Prov); **siehe gewagt, Tänzchen, frisch.**
2 vr to dare. **sich** ~, **etw zu tun** to dare (to) do sth; **sich an etw** (acc) ~ to venture to do sth; **ich wage mich nicht daran** I dare not do it; **sich auf ein Gebiet** ~ to venture into an area; **bei dem schönen Wetter kann ich mich aus dem Haus/ins Wasser** ~ in this lovely weather I can venture out of doors/into the water; **er wagt sich nicht mehr aus dem Haus** he doesn't venture out (of the house) any more, he doesn't dare leave the house any more.

Wagen m -s, - or (S Ger, Aus) ¨ (a) (Personen~) car; (Liefer~) van; (Plan~) (covered) wag(g)on; (Zirkus~, Zigeuner~) caravan, wag(g)on; (von Pferden gezogen) wag(g)on, cart; (Kutsche) coach; (Puppen~, Kinder~) pram (Brit), baby carriage (US); (Hand~) (hand)cart; (Kofferkuli, Einkaufs~) trolley; (Schreibmaschinen~) carriage; (Straßenbahn~, Seilbahn~) car; (Eisenbahn~) coach (Brit), car, carriage (Brit); (Omnibus) bus. **jdm an den** ~ **fahren** (fig) to pick holes in sb; **sich nicht vor jds** ~ **spannen lassen** (fig) not to allow oneself to be used or made use of by sb; **siehe Rad.**
(b) (Astrol) **der Große/Kleine** ~ the Plough or (Big) Dipper/the Little Dipper.

wägen pret **wog** or **wägte**, ptp **gewogen** or **gewägt** vt (old, form) to weigh; (geh: bedenken auch) to ponder. **erst** ~, **dann wagen** (Prov) look before you leap (Prov).

Wagen-: ~**abteil** nt (Rail) compartment; ~**bauer** m coach builder; ~**burg** f barricade (of wag(g)ons); ~**deichsel** f shaft; ~**folge** f order of cars/coaches or carriages etc; ~**führer** m driver; ~**heber** m jack; ~**ladung** f (von Lastwagen) lorryload (Brit), truckload; (von Eisenbahn) wag(g)onload; ~**lenker** m (Hist) charioteer; ~**park** m fleet of cars/vans; ~**pflege** f care of the/one's car; ~**plane** f tarpaulin; ~**rad** nt cartwheel; (hum: Hut) picture hat; ~**rennen** nt (Hist) chariot racing; (einzelner Wettkampf) chariot race; ~**schlag** m (von Kutsche) carriage door; (von Auto) car door; ~**schmiere** f cart-grease; ~**typ** m type of car; ~**wäsche** f car wash; (das Waschen) car washing.

Wagestück nt daring deed, deed of daring.

Waggon [va'gõ:, va'gɔ] m -s, -s (goods) wag(g)on (Brit), freight car (US); (Ladung) wag(g)onload/carload.

waggonweise [va'gõ:-, va'gɔ-] adv by the wag(g)onload (Brit) or carload (US).

Wag-: ~**hals** m daredevil; w~**halsig** adj foolhardy, daredevil attr; ~**halsigkeit** f foolhardiness.

Wagner m -s, - (dial) coach builder.

Wagnerianer(in f) m -s, - Wagnerian.

Wagnis nt hazardous business; (Risiko) risk.

Wahl f -, -en (a) (Auswahl) choice. **die** ~ **fiel auf ihn/dieses Buch** he/this book was chosen; **aus freier** ~ of one's own free choice; **wir hatten keine (andere)** ~(, **als) we had no alternative** or choice (but); **es gab/blieb keine andere** ~(, **als) there was no alternative (but); jdm die** ~ **lassen** to leave (it up to) sb to choose; **jdm etw zur** ~ **stellen** to give sb the choice of sth; **3 Farben stehen zur** ~ there is a choice of 3 colours; **seine/eine** ~ **treffen** to make one's/a choice or selection; **du hast die** ~ **take your choice or pick; sie hat die** ~, **ob sie ... the choice is hers** or it's up to her whether she ...; **wer die** ~ **hat, hat die Qual** (Prov) he is/you are etc spoilt for choice; **siehe eng.**
(b) (Pol etc) election; (Abstimmung) vote; (geheim) ballot. **geheime/freie** ~ secret ballot/free elections; ~ **durch Handerheben** vote by (a) show of hands; **(die)** ~**en (the) elections;** ~ **eines Präsidenten** election of a president; **wann ist die** ~ **des Clubpräsidenten?** when is the election for president of the club?; **seine** ~ **in den Vorstand/zum Präsidenten** his election to the board/as president; **die** ~ **gewinnen** to win the election; **zur** ~ **gehen** to go to vote, to go to the polls; **jdn zur** ~ **aufstellen** or **vorschlagen** to propose sb or put sb up as a candidate (for election); **sich zur** ~ **stellen** to stand (as a candidate or at the/an election), to run (for parliament/president etc); **zur** ~ **gehen** to go to the polls; **zur** ~ **schreiten** to take a vote or (geheim) ballot; **die** ~ **annehmen** to accept the or one's election.
(c) (Qualität) quality. **erste** ~ top quality; Gemüse, Eier class or grade one; **zweite/dritte** ~ second/third quality; Gemüse, Eier class or grade two/three; **Waren/Eier/Fleisch erster** ~ top-quality goods/class- or grade-one eggs/prime meat; **Waren/Gemüse zweiter** ~ seconds pl/class- or grade-two vegetables; **der Teller war zweite** ~ the plate was a second.

Wahl-: ~**akt** m polling; ~**alter** nt voting age; ~**aufruf** m election announcement; ~**auftrag** m election brief; ~**ausgang** m outcome of an/the election, election results pl; ~**ausschuß** m election committee.

wählbar adj eligible (for office), able to stand at an/the election.

Wählbarkeit f, no pl eligibility (for office).
Wahl-: ~**benachrichtigung** f polling card; **w~berechtigt** adj entitled to vote; ~**berechtigte(r)** mf decl as adj person entitled to vote; ~**berechtigung** f (right to) vote; ~**beteiligung** f poll; **eine hohe** ~**beteiligung** a heavy poll, a high or good turnout (at an/the election); ~**bezirk** m ward.

wählen 1 vt (a) (von from, out of) to choose; (aus~ auch) to select, to pick. **seine Worte** ~ to choose one's words, to select or pick one's words carefully; siehe **gewählt**.
   (b) (Telec) Nummer to dial.
   (c) (durch Wahl ermitteln) Regierung, Sprecher etc to elect; (sich entscheiden für) Partei, Kandidaten to vote for. **jdn ins Parlament/in den Vorstand** ~ to elect or return sb to Parliament/to elect or vote sb onto the board; **jdn zum Präsidenten** ~ to elect sb president.
   2 vi (a) (auswählen) to choose.
   (b) (Telec) to dial.
   (c) (Wahlen abhalten) to hold elections; (Stimme abgeben) to vote. **wann wird gewählt?** when are the elections?; **man darf ab 18** ~ you can vote at 18; **durch Handerheben** ~ to vote by (a) show of hands; ~ **gehen** to go to the polls, to go to vote.

Wähler(in f) m -s, - (a) (Pol) elector, voter. **der** or **die** ~ the electorate sing or pl, the electors pl. (b) (Tech) selector.
Wahl|ergebnis nt election result; (Stimmenverteilung auch) election returns pl.
Wähler|initiative f pressure from the electorate.
wählerisch adj particular; Geschmack, Kunde discriminating. **sei nicht so** ~! don't be so choosy (inf) or fussy.
Wählerschaft f, no pl electorate sing or pl; (eines Wahlkreises) constituents pl.
Wähler-: ~**stimme** f vote; 10% **der** ~**stimmen** 10% of the vote(s) or poll; ~**verzeichnis** nt electoral roll or register.
Wahl-: ~**fach** nt (Sch) option, optional subject; ~**feldzug** m election(eering) campaign; ~**fieber** nt election fever; **w~frei** adj (Sch) optional; ~**freiheit** f (Pol) electoral freedom; (Sch) freedom of choice; ~**gang** m ballot; ~**geheimnis** nt secrecy of the ballot; ~**geschenk** nt pre-election promise; ~**gesetz** nt electoral law; ~**handlung** f poll; ~**heimat** f country of adoption or of (one's) choice; ~**helfer** m (im ~kampf) electoral or election assistant; (bei der Wahl) polling officer; ~**kabine** f polling booth; ~**kampf** m election(eering) campaign; **einen** ~**kampf führen** to conduct an election campaign; ~**kreis** m constituency; ~**leiter** m returning officer (Brit); ~**lokal** nt polling station; ~**lokomotive** f (inf) vote-puller; **w~los** 1 adj indiscriminate; 2 adv at random, haphazardly; (nicht wählerisch) indiscriminately; ~**mann** m, pl -männer delegate; ~**möglichkeit** f choice, option; ~**nacht** f election night; ~**ordnung** f election regulations pl; ~**periode** f lifetime of a/the parliament; ~**pflicht** f electoral duty; **seine** ~**pflicht erfüllen** to use one's vote; ~**pflichtfach** nt (Sch) (compulsory) optional subject; ~**propaganda** f election propaganda; ~**prüfung** f scrutiny; ~**recht** nt (a) (right to) vote; **allgemeines** ~**recht** universal franchise or suffrage; **das aktive** ~**recht** the right to vote; **das passive** ~**recht** eligibility (for political office); **mit 25 bekommt man das passive** ~**recht** at 25 one becomes eligible for political office; (b) (Gesetze) electoral law no def art; ~**rede** f election speech; ~**reform** f electoral reform.
Wählscheibe f dial.
Wahl-: ~**schein** m polling card; ~**sieg** m electoral or election victory; ~**slogan** m election slogan; ~**sonntag** m polling Sunday; ~**spruch** m (a) motto, watchword; (b) siehe ~**slogan**; ~**system** nt electoral system; ~**tag** m election or polling day; ~**urne** f ballot box; ~**verfahren** nt electoral procedure; ~**vergehen** nt electoral misdemeanour; ~**verhalten** nt behaviour at the polls; ~**versammlung** f election meeting; ~**versprechungen** pl election promises pl; ~**verwandtschaft** f (Chem) elective attraction; (fig) affinity (von between); „**die** ~**verwandtschaften**" (Liter) "The Elective Affinities"; ~**vorschlag** m election proposal; **w~weise** adv alternatively; **w~weise Kartoffeln oder Reis** (a) choice of potatoes or rice; **Sie können w~weise Wasserski fahren oder reiten** you have a choice between water-skiing and riding.
Wählzeichen nt (Telec) dialling tone.
Wahlzelle f polling booth.
Wahn m - (e)s, no pl (a) illusion, delusion. **in dem** ~ **leben, daß ...** to labour under the delusion that ... (b) (Manie) mania.
Wahnbild nt delusion, illusion.
wähnen (geh) 1 vt to imagine (wrongly), to believe (wrongly). **wir wähnten ihn glücklich** we (wrongly) imagined or believed him (to be) happy. 2 vr **sich sicher/von allen verlassen** ~ to imagine or believe oneself (to be) safe/abandoned by all.
Wahn|idee f delusion; (verrückte Idee) mad or crazy notion.
Wahnsinn m, no pl (a) (old Psych) insanity, lunacy, madness. **in** ~ **verfallen** to go mad or insane.
   (b) (Unvernunft) madness, insanity. **des** ~**s feste Beute sein** (inf) to be off one's rocker (sl); **das ist doch (heller)** ~, **so ein** ~! that's sheer madness or idiocy!; **Mensch,** ~ **or einfach** ~! (sl: prima) way or far out! (sl).
   (c) religiöser ~ religious mania.
wahnsinnig 1 adj (a) (old Psych) insane, mad.
   (b) (inf) (verrückt) mad, crazy; (attr: sehr groß, viel) terrible, awful, dreadful. **eine** ~**e Arbeit/ein** ~**es Geld** a crazy or incredible amount of work/money; **wie** ~ (inf) like mad; **das macht mich** ~ (inf) it's driving me mad or crazy or round the bend (inf); ~ **werden** to go mad or crazy or round the bend (inf); **ich werde** ~! it's mind-blowing! (sl).
   2 adv (inf) incredibly (inf). ~ **verliebt** madly in love; ~ **viele/viel** an incredible number/amount (inf).
Wahnsinnige(r) mf decl as adj madman/madwoman, lunatic.
Wahnsinnigwerden nt **zum** ~ enough to drive you round the bend (inf) or up the wall (inf).

Wahnsinns- in cpds (inf: verrückt) crazy; (sl: prima) fantastic (inf), incredible (inf); ~**arbeit** f **eine** ~**arbeit** a crazy or incredible amount of work (inf).
Wahn-: ~**vorstellung** f delusion; ~**witz** m, no pl utter or sheer foolishness; **w~witzig** 1 adj mad, crazy, lunatic attr; 2 adv terribly, awfully.
wahr adj Geschichte, Liebe, Glaube etc true; (echt) Kunst, Glück etc auch real, genuine; Freund, Freundschaft auch real; (attr: wirklich) real, veritable. **im** ~**sten Sinne des Wortes, in des Wortes** ~**ster Bedeutung** in the true sense of the word; **daran ist kein** ~**es Wort, davon ist kein Wort** ~ there's not a word of truth in it; **das ist etwas W~es daran** there's some truth in that; **da hast du ein** ~**es Wort gesprochen** (inf) that's very true, there's a lot of truth in that; **er hat** ~ **gesprochen** (liter) he has spoken the truth; **etw** ~ **machen** Pläne to make sth a reality; Versprechung, Drohung to carry out; ~ **werden** to come true; (Hoffnung, Pläne auch) to become a reality; **so** ~ **mir Gott helfe!** so help me God!; **so** ~ **ich lebe/hier stehe** as sure as I'm alive/standing here, as sure as eggs are eggs (inf); **das darf or kann doch nicht** ~ **sein!** (inf) it can't be true!; **das ist schon gar nicht mehr** ~ (inf) (verstärkend) it's not true! (inf); (schon lange her) that was ages ago; **das ist nicht der** ~**e Jakob** or Otto (inf), **das ist nicht das W~e** (inf) it's no great shakes (inf); **die Stelle ist nicht gerade der** ~**e Jakob** or Otto **or das W~e** (inf) it's not exactly the greatest job (on earth); **siehe nicht, einzig**.
wahren vt (a) (wahrnehmen) Interessen, Rechte to look after, to protect, to safeguard.
   (b) (erhalten) Autorität, Ruf, Würde to preserve, to keep; Geheimnis to keep; gute Manieren to adhere to, to observe. **die Form/den Anstand** ~ to adhere to correct form/to observe the proprieties; siehe **Schein¹, Gesicht¹**.
währen vi (geh) to last. **es währte nicht lange, da geschah ein Unglück** it was not long before misfortune struck; **was lange währt, wird (endlich) gut** (Prov) a happy outcome is worth waiting for; siehe **ehrlich**.
während 1 prep +gen or dat during. ~ **eines Zeitraums** over a period of time; ~ **der ganzen Nacht** all night long, all during the night, throughout the night. 2 conj while; (wohingegen auch) whereas.
während-: ~**dem** (inf), ~**des** (geh), ~**dessen** adv meanwhile, in the meantime.
Wahr-: **w~haben** vt sep irreg **etw nicht w~haben wollen** not to want to admit sth; **w~haft** 1 adj (ehrlich) truthful; (echt) Freund true, real; Enttäuschung real; (attr: wirklich) real, veritable; 2 adv really, truly; **w~haftig** 1 adj (geh) (aufrichtig) truthful; Gemüt honest; Worte etc true; **der w~haftige Gott** the true God; **w~haftiger Gott!** (inf) strewth! (inf); 2 adv really; (tatsächlich) actually; **w~haftigkeit** f, no pl (geh) truthfulness; (von Aussage auch) veracity.
Wahrheit f truth. **in** ~ in reality; **die** ~ **sagen** to tell the truth; **um die** ~ **zu sagen** to tell the truth; **jdm ein paar** ~**en sagen** to tell sb a few (home) truths; **das schlägt der** ~ **ins Gesicht** that's patently untrue; **er nimmt es mit der** ~ **nicht so genau** (inf) you have to take what he says with a pinch of salt; siehe **Ehre**.
Wahrheits-: ~**beweis** m (Jur) **den** ~**beweis bringen** or **antreten** to supply proof of the truth of a/one's statement; **w~getreu** adj Bericht truthful; Darstellung faithful; **ein w~getreues Bild** (fig) a factual or true picture; ~**liebe** f love of truth; **w~liebend** adj truth-loving; (ehrlich) truthful.
wahrlich adv really, indeed, verily (Bibl); (garantiert) certainly, definitely.
Wahr-: **w~nehmbar** adj perceptible, noticeable; **nicht w~nehmbar** imperceptible, not noticeable; **mit bloßem Auge w~nehmbar/nicht w~nehmbar** visible/invisible to the naked eye; **w~nehmen** vt sep irreg (a) (mit den Sinnen erfassen) to perceive; (bemerken) Vorgänge, Veränderungen etc to be aware of; (entdecken, erkennen) Geräusch, Licht auch to distinguish; Geruch to detect; (heraushören) Unterton, Stimmung to detect, to discern; **nichts mehr/alles um sich herum w~nehmen** to be no longer aware of anything/to be aware of everything around one; (b) (nutzen, vertreten) Frist, Termin to observe; Gelegenheit to take; Interessen, Angelegenheiten, Rechte to look after; ~**nehmung** f siehe vt (a) perception; awareness; detection; (b) observing; taking; looking after; ~**nehmungsvermögen** nt perceptive faculty; **w~sagen** sep or insep 1 vi to tell fortunes, to predict the future; **aus dem Kaffeesatz/aus den Teeblättern/aus den Karten w~sagen** to read coffee grounds/tea leaves/cards; **jdm w~sagen** to tell sb's fortune, to predict the future (to sb); **sich (dat) w~sagen lassen** to have one's fortune told; 2 vt (jdm) **die Zukunft w~sagen** to tell sb's fortune, to predict the future (to sb); **er hat mir w~gesagt, daß ... he predicted (to me) that ...; ~sager(in f)** m -s, - fortuneteller, soothsayer (old); ~**sagerei** f, no pl fortunetelling; **w~sagerisch** adj prophetic; ~**sagung** f prediction.
Wahrschau f: ~! (inf) watch out! (Naut) attention!
wahrscheinlich 1 adj probable, likely; (glaubhaft) plausible. **es liegt im Bereich des W~en** it is quite within the bounds of probability. 2 adv probably. **er kommt** ~ **erst später** he probably won't come till later, he won't come till later most likely.
Wahrscheinlichkeit f probability, likelihood no pl; (Glaubhaftigkeit) plausibility. **mit großer** ~, **aller** ~ **nach, in aller** ~ in all probability or likelihood.
Wahrscheinlichkeitsrechnung f probability calculus, theory of probabilities.
Wahrspruch m verdict.
Wahrung f, no pl (a) (Wahrnehmung) protection, safeguarding. (b) (Erhaltung) preservation; (von Geheimnis) keeping. ~ **der guten Manieren** adherence to or observance of good manners.
Währung f currency.
Währungs- in cpds currency, monetary; ~**ausgleich** m cur-

rency conversion compensation; ~**block** m monetary bloc; ~**einheit** f monetary unit; ~**fonds** m Monetary Fund; ~**krise** f monetary or currency crisis; ~**parität** f mint par of exchange; ~**reform** f monetary or currency reform; ~**reserve** f monetary or currency reserve; ~**schlange** f (currency) snake.

Wahrzeichen nt (von Stadt, Verein) emblem; (Gebäude, Turm etc) symbol.

Waid- in cpds siehe **Weid-**.

Waise f -, -n orphan.

Waisen-: ~**haus** nt orphanage; ~**kind** nt orphan; ~**knabe** m (liter) orphan (boy); **gegen dich ist er ein ~knabe** or ~**kind** (inf) he's no match for you, you would run rings round him (inf); ~**rente** f orphan's allowance.

Wal m -(e)s, -e whale.

Wald m -(e)s, ~er wood(s pl); (großer) forest; (no pl: ~land) woodland(s pl), wooded country. ~ **und Wiese/Feld** or **Flur** (liter) woods and meadows/fields; **ich glaub, ich steh im ~** (inf) I must be seeing/hearing things! (inf); **er sieht den ~ vor lauter Bäumen nicht** he can't see the wood for the trees (prov); **wie es in den ~ hineinschallt** or **wie man in den ~ hineinruft, so schallt es wieder heraus** (Prov) you get as much as you give.

Wald-: ~**ameise** f red ant; ~**arbeiter** m forestry worker; (Holzfäller) lumberjack, woodman; ~**bestand** m forest land; ~**blume** f woodland flower; ~**boden** m forest soil; ~**brand** m forest fire.

Wäldchen nt dim of **Wald** little wood.

Wald-: ~**einsamkeit** f solitude or seclusion of the forest, sylvan or silvan solitude (poet); ~**erdbeere** f wild strawberry.

Waldes- (liter): ~**dunkel** nt gloom of the forest; ~**rauschen** nt rustling or whispering of the woods/forest; ~**saum** m edge of the wood(s)/forest.

Wald-: ~**frevel** m offence against the forest laws; ~**geist** m sylvan (poet) or silvan (poet) or forest spirit; ~**heini** m (inf) nitwit (inf); ~**horn** nt (Mus) French horn.

waldig adj wooded, woody.

Wald-: ~**land** nt woodland(s pl); ~**landschaft** f woodland/forest landscape; ~**lauf** m cross-country running; (einzelner Lauf) cross-country run; ~**lehrpfad** m nature trail; ~**meister** m (Bot) woodruff.

Waldorf-: ~**salat** m (Cook) Waldorf salad; ~**schule** f Rudolf Steiner School.

Wald-: **w~reich** adj densely wooded; ~**reichtum** m abundance of woods/forests; ~**schneise** f lane, aisle; ~**schrat** m wood gnome; ~**tier** nt woodland/forest creature.

Wald- und Wiesen- in cpds (inf) common-or-garden (inf).

Waldung f (geh) woodland(s pl).

Wald-: ~**vogel** m woodland bird; ~**weg** m woodland/forest path; ~**wiese** f glade; ~**wirtschaft** f siehe **Forstwirtschaft**.

Wales [weilz] nt - Wales.

Wal-: ~**fang** m whaling; ~**fangboot** nt whaler, whaling boat; ~**fänger** m (Schiff, Mensch) whaler; ~**fisch** m (inf) whale; ~**fischspeck** m blubber; ~**fischtran** m siehe **Waltran**.

walgen, wälgern vt (dial) Teig to roll out.

Walhall(a) ['valhal, val'hal(a)] f -, no pl (Myth) Valhalla.

Waliser(in f) m -s, - Welshman; Welsh woman.

walisisch adj Welsh.

Walke f -, -n fulling machine.

walken vt Felle, Leder to drum, to tumble; Wollgewebe to full, to mill; Blech to flex. **jdn ~** (inf) to give sb a belting (inf).

Walker m -s, - fuller.

Walküre f -, -n (Myth, fig) Valkyrie.

Wall m -(e)s, ~e embankment; (Mil) rampart; (fig) bulwark, rampart.

Wallach m -(e)s, -e gelding.

wallen vi (a) (liter) (Meer) (brodeln) to surge, to seethe; (fließen) to flow; (Dämpfe, Nebel) to surge; (fig: Blut) to boil; (hum: Busen) to heave. (b) (obs) **aux sein** siehe **wallfahren**.

wallfahren vi insep reg aux sein to go on a pilgrimage.

Wallfahrer(in f) m -s, - pilgrim.

Wallfahrt f pilgrimage.

Wallfahrts-: ~**kirche** f pilgrimage church; ~**ort** m place of pilgrimage; ~**stätte** f place of pilgrimage; (Grab, Kirche etc auch) shrine.

Wallgraben m moat.

Wallis nt -, no pl Valais.

Walliser(in f) m -s, - inhabitant of the Valais.

Walliser Alpen pl die ~ ~ the Valais Alps pl.

walliserisch adj Valaisan.

Wallone m -n, -n, **Wallonin** f Walloon.

Wallung f -, -en (a) (geh) **das Meer war in ~** the sea was surging or swelling; **in ~ geraten** (See, Meer) to begin to surge or seethe; (vor Leidenschaft) to be in a turmoil; (vor Wut) to fly into a rage or passion; **sein Blut geriet in ~** his blood began to surge through his veins; **Poseidon brachte das Meer in ~** Poseidon made the sea surge or seethe; **jds Blut/jdn in ~ bringen** to make sb's blood surge through his/her veins.
(b) (Med) (hot) flush usu pl.

Walmdach nt (Archit) hipped roof.

Walnuß f walnut.

Walnußbaum m walnut (tree).

Walpurgisnacht f Walpurgis Night, Walpurgisnacht.

Walroß nt -sses, -sse walrus; (pej: Mensch) baby elephant (inf). **schnaufen wie ein ~** (pej) to puff like a grampus.

Walstatt f (obs) battlefield.

walten vi (geh) to prevail, to reign (in +dat over); (wirken) Mensch, Naturkräfte) to be at work. **über jdm/etw ~** to rule (over) sb/sth; **Vernunft ~ lassen** to let reason prevail; **Vorsicht/Milde/Gnade ~ lassen** to exercise caution/leniency/to show mercy; **das W~** der Naturgewalten/Gottes the workings of the forces of nature/of God; **es war eine Freude, ihr W~ im Hause zu sehen** it was a joy to watch her at work in the house;

jdn ~ lassen to let sb have a free rein, to let sb do as he pleases; **das walte Gott** or (inf) **Hugo** amen (to that)!; siehe **Amt**.

Waltran m sperm oil.

Walzblech nt sheet metal.

Walze f -, -n roller; (Schreibmaschinen~ auch) platen; (Drehorgel~) barrel; (von Spieluhr) cylinder, drum. **immer die gleiche** or **alte ~** (inf) always the same old stuff (inf); **auf die ~ gehen** (old inf) to go off on one's travels; **auf der ~ sein** (old inf) to be on the road or on the move.

walzen 1 vt to roll. **2** vi (a) **aux sein** or **haben** (dated: tanzen) to waltz. (b) **aux sein** (old inf: wandern) to tramp, to hike.

wälzen 1 vt (a) (rollen) to roll; (Cook) (in Ei, Mehl) to coat (in +dat with); (in Butter, Petersilie) to toss.
(b) (inf) Akten, Bücher to pore over; Probleme, Gedanken, Pläne to turn over in one's mind. **die Schuld/Verantwortung auf jdn ~** to shift or shove (inf) the blame/responsibility onto sb.
2 vr to roll; (vor Schmerzen) to writhe (vor +dat with); (schlaflos im Bett) to toss and turn; (fig: Menschenmenge, Wassermassen) to surge; (im Schlamm) to wallow.

Walzen-: **w~förmig** adj cylindrical; ~**straße** f siehe **Walzstraße**.

Walzer m -s, - waltz. **Wiener ~** Viennese waltz; **~ tanzen** to (dance the/a) waltz; **sich im ~ drehen** (liter) to waltz around and around.

Wälzer m -s, - (inf) heavy or weighty tome (hum).

Walzer-: ~**musik** f waltz music; ~**schritt** m waltz step; ~**takt** m waltz time.

Walz-: ~**straße** f rolling train; ~**werk** nt rolling mill.

Wamme f -, -n (a) (Hautfalte) dewlap. (b) (von Pelz) belly part. (c) (dial: Bauch) paunch.

Wampe f -, -n (dial) paunch.

Wams nt -es, ~er (old, dial: Jacke) jerkin; (unter Rüstung) gambeson; (dial: Weste) waistcoat (Brit), vest (US).

wand pret of **winden**[1].

Wand f -, ~e wall; (auch Anat); (nicht gemauerte Trenn~) partition (wall); (von Gefäß, Behälter, Schiff) side; (Fels~) (rock) face; (Wolken~) bank of clouds; (Biol) septum (spec); (fig) barrier, wall. **spanische ~** (folding) screen; **etw an die ~ werfen** or **schmeißen** or **schleudern** (inf) (lit) to throw sth against or at the wall; (fig: aus Wut, Verzweiflung) to throw sth out of the window; **~ an ~ wall to wall; in seinen vier ~en** (fig) within one's own four walls; **weiß wie die ~** as white as a sheet; **wenn die ~e reden könnten** if walls could speak; **man rennt bei denen gegen eine ~ with them you come up against a brick wall; mit dem Kopf gegen die ~ rennen** (fig) to bang one's head against a brick wall; **jdn an die ~ drücken** (fig) to push or drive sb to the wall; **jdn an die ~ spielen** (fig) to outdo or outshine sb; (Theat) to steal the show from sb, to upstage sb; **jdn an die ~ stellen** (fig) to shoot sb, to send sb before the firing squad; **er lachte/tobte** etc, **daß die ~e wackelten** (inf) or **zitterten** (inf) he raised the roof (with his laughter/ranting and raving etc) (inf); **die ~** or ~**e hochgehen** (inf) to go up the wall (inf); **das ist, um an den ~en hochzugehen** (inf), **es ist zum Die-~e-Hochgehen** (inf) it's enough to drive you up the wall (inf).

Wandale m -n, -n (Hist) Vandal; siehe **hausen**.

Wandalismus m siehe **Vandalismus**.

Wand-: ~**behang** m wall hanging; ~**bekleidung** f wall covering; (aus Holz) panelling; ~**bewurf** m plaster(ing); (Rauhputz) roughcast; ~**bord**, ~**brett** nt (wall) shelf.

Wandel m -s, no pl (a) change. **im ~ der Zeiten** throughout the ages or the changing times; **im ~ der Jahrhunderte** down the centuries. (b) (Lebens~) way or mode of life; siehe **Handel**[1].

Wandel-: ~**altar** m polyptych; ~**anleihe** f convertible loan; **w~bar** adj changeable; ~**barkeit** f, no pl changeability; ~**gang** m covered walk; ~**halle** f foyer; (im Parlament) lobby; (im Kurhaus) pump room.

wandeln[1] vtr (ändern) to change.

wandeln[2] vi aux sein (geh: gehen) to walk, to stroll. **ein ~des Wörterbuch** (hum) a walking dictionary; **er ist die ~de Güte** he is goodness or kindness itself or personified; siehe **Leiche**.

Wandelstern m (old) planet.

Wander-: ~**ameise** f army ant; ~**ausstellung** f travelling or touring exhibition; ~**bühne** f touring company; (Hist) strolling players pl; ~**bursche** m (obs) journeyman; ~**düne** f shifting or drifting (sand) dune.

Wanderer m -s, - hiker; (esp Angehöriger eines Wandervereins) rambler; (old: Reisender) traveller, wayfarer (old).

Wander-: ~**fahrt** f hiking trip; (old: Reise) journey; ~**falke** m peregrine (falcon); ~**freund(in** f) m hiker; ~**gewerbe** nt siehe **Reisegewerbe**; ~**heuschrecke** f migratory locust.

Wanderin f siehe **Wanderer**.

Wander-: ~**jahre** pl years of travel; ~**karte** f map of walks or trails; ~**kleidung** f hiking outfit; ~**leben** nt roving or wandering life; (fig) unsettled life; ~**leber** f floating liver; ~**lied** nt hiking song; ~**lust** f wanderlust; **w~lustig** adj filled with wanderlust, with a passion for travel.

wandern vi aux sein (a) (gehen) to wander, to roam; (old: reisen) to travel, to journey; (Wanderbühne, Zigeuner) to travel. **durchs Leben ~** (liter) to journey through life.
(b) (sich bewegen) to move, to travel; (Wolken, Gletscher) to drift; (Düne) to shift, to drift; (Med: Leber, Niere) to float; (Blick) to rove, to roam, to wander; (Gedanken) to roam, to wander, to stray; (weitergegeben werden) to be passed (on).
(c) (Vögel, Tiere, Völker) to migrate.
(d) (zur Freizeitgestaltung) to hike; (esp in Verein) to ramble.
(e) (inf: ins Bett, in den Papierkorb, ins Feuer) to go. **hinter Schloß und Riegel/ins Krankenhaus/ins Leihhaus ~** to be put behind bars/to end or land up in hospital/at the pawnbroker's.

Wander-: ~**niere** f floating kidney; ~**pokal** m challenge cup; ~**prediger** m itinerant preacher; ~**preis** m challenge trophy; ~**ratte** f brown rat.

Wanderschaft f, no pl travels pl. **auf (der)** ~ **sein** to be on one's travels; **auf** ~ **gehen** to go off on one's travels; **mein Bleistift ist auf** ~ **gegangen** (inf) my pencil seems to have walked off (inf).

Wander-: ~**schauspieler** m travelling actor; (Hist) strolling player; ~**schuhe** pl walking shoes pl.

Wandersmann m, pl **-leute** (liter) siehe **Wanderer**.

Wander-: ~**stab** m staff; **den** ~**stab ergreifen** (fig) to take to the road; ~**trieb** m (von Tier) migratory instinct; (Psych) urge to travel, dromomania (spec); (fig) wanderlust, passion for travel; ~**truppe** f touring company; (Hist) strolling players pl.

Wanderung f (a) (Ausflug) walk. **eine** ~ **machen** to go on a walk or hike or ramble. (b) (old: Reise, von Handwerksgesellen, fig liter: durchs Leben) journey. (c) (von Vögeln, Tieren, Völkern) migration; (Sociol: Wohnortwechsel) shift (in the population), population shift.

Wanderungsgewinn m (Sociol) increase in population (through population shifts).

Wander-: ~**verein** m rambling club; ~**vogel** m (Hist) member of the Wandervogel youth movement; (begeisterter Wanderer) hiker; (fig inf) bird of passage, rolling stone (inf); ~**weg** m walk, trail, (foot)path; ~**zirkus** m travelling circus.

Wandgemälde nt mural, wall-painting.

-wandig adj suf -walled.

Wand-: ~**kalender** m wall calendar; ~**karte** f wall map; ~**lampe** f wall lamp/light; ~**leuchter** m wall bracket, sconce.

Wandlung f (a) (Wechsel, Wandel) change; (völlige Um~) transformation. ~ **zum Guten** change for the better; **eine** ~ **durchmachen** to undergo a change. (b) (Eccl) transubstantiation; (Teil der Messe) consecration. (c) (Jur) cancellation of sale contract.

wandlungsfähig adj adaptable; Schauspieler etc versatile.

Wand-: ~**malerei** f mural painting; (Bild) mural, wall-painting; ~**pfeiler** m (Archit) pilaster.

Wandrer(in f) m, -, - siehe **Wanderer**.

Wand-: ~**schirm** m screen; ~**schrank** m wall cupboard; ~**tafel** f (black)board.

wandte pret of **wenden**.

Wand-: ~**teller** m wall plate; ~**teppich** m tapestry, wall hanging; ~**uhr** f wall clock; ~**verkleidung** f wall covering; (aus Holz) panelling; ~**zeitung** f wall news-sheet.

Wange f -, -n (a) (geh) cheek. ~ **an** ~ cheek to cheek. (b) (von Treppe) stringboard.

Wank m (Sw): **keinen** ~ **tun** not to lift a finger.

Wankelmotor m Wankel engine.

Wankelmut m, **Wankelmütigkeit** f fickleness, inconstancy.

wankelmütig adj fickle, inconstant.

wanken vi (a) (schwanken) (Mensch, Gebäude) to sway; (Knie) to shake, to wobble; (Boden) to rock; (fig: Thron, Regierung) to totter; (unsicher sein/werden) to waver, to falter; (schwanken) to vacillate. **nicht** ~ **und nicht weichen** not to move or budge an inch; **ihm wankt der Boden unter den Füßen** (fig) he is on shaky ground; **ins W**~ **geraten** (lit) to begin to sway/rock; (fig) to begin to totter/waver or falter/vacillate; **etw ins W**~ **bringen** (lit) to cause sth to sway/rock; (fig) Thron, Regierung to cause sth to totter; Glauben, Moral to shake sth; Moral to throw doubt upon sth; **jdn ins W**~ **bringen** to make sb falter or waver, to make sb unsure of himself; **jds Entschluß ins W**~ **bringen** to make sb waver in his decision.

(b) aux sein (gehen) to stagger; (alter Mensch) to totter.

wann interrog adv when. ~ **ist er angekommen?** when did he arrive?; ~ **kommt ihr?** when or (at) what time are you coming?; ~ **(auch) immer** whenever; **bis** ~ **ist das fertig?** when will that be ready (by)?; **bis** ~ **gilt der Ausweis?** until when is the pass valid?, when is the pass valid until?; **seit** ~ **bist/hast du ...?** (zeitlich) how long have you been/had ...?; (bezweifelnd, entrüstet etc) since when are you/do you have ...?; **von** ~ **an bist du in Deutschland?** from when will you be in Germany?; **von** ~ **bis** ~? when?, during what times?

Wanne f -, -n bath; (Bade~ auch) (bath)tub; (Öl~) reservoir; (im Auto) sump (Brit), oil pan (US).

wannen adv (obs) **von** ~ whence (liter).

Wannenbad nt bath.

Wanst m -(e)s, ⸚e (Zool: Pansen) rumen; (inf: dicker Bauch) paunch (inf), belly (inf). **sich** (dat) **den** ~ **vollschlagen** (inf) to stuff oneself (inf).

Want f -, -en (Naut) shroud.

Wanze f -, -n (Zool, inf: Abhörgerät) bug. **du freche** ~! (inf) you cheeky monkey! (inf); **frech wie eine** ~ (inf) (as) bold as brass, very cheeky.

Wanzen-: ~**bude** f, ~**loch** nt (inf) hole (inf), dump (inf).

Wappen nt -s, - coat of arms; (auf Münze) heads no art. **etw im** ~ **führen** to have or bear sth on one's coat of arms; (fig) to have sth as one's trademark.

Wappen-: ~**kunde** f heraldry; ~**schild** m or nt shield; ~**seite** f heads side; ~**tier** nt heraldic animal.

wappnen vr (fig) **sich (gegen etw)** ~ to prepare (oneself) (for sth); **gewappnet sein** to be prepared or forearmed.

war pret of **sein**[1].

warb pret of **werben**.

ward (old, liter) pret of **werden 1** (c) and 2.

Ware f -, -n product; (einzelne ~) article; (als Sammelbegriff) goods pl, merchandise. ~**n** pl goods pl; (zum Verkauf auch) merchandise sing, wares pl (esp old, hum); **gute** ~ **hält sich** (prov) good-quality goods last longer.

wäre pret subjunc of **sein**[1].

Waren-: ~**angebot** nt range of goods for sale; ~**aufzug** m goods hoist; ~**ausfuhr** f export of goods or merchandise; ~**austausch** m exchange or (bei Tauschgeschäft) barter of goods; ~**beleihung** f loan against goods; ~**bestand** m stocks pl of goods or merchandise; ~**einfuhr** f import of goods or merchandise; ~**export** m export of goods or merchandise; ~**haus** nt

(department) store, emporium (old); ~**import** m import of goods or merchandise; ~**lager** nt warehouse; (Bestand) stocks pl; ~**muster** nt, ~**probe** f trade sample; ~**sendung** f trade sample (sent by post); ~**test** m test of goods; ~**umsatz** m turnover of goods or merchandise; ~**zeichen** nt trade-mark.

warf pret of **werfen**.

warm adj comp ⸚**er**, superl ⸚**ste(r, s)** or adv **am** ⸚**sten** (lit, fig) warm; Wetter auch, Getränk, Speise, (auf Wasserhahn) hot; (sl: homosexuell) queer (pej inf). **mir ist** ~ I'm warm; **aus dem W**~**en in die Kälte kommen** to come out of the warm(th) into the cold; **das hält** ~ it keeps you warm; **das macht** ~ it warms you up; **das Essen** ~ **machen** to warm or heat up the food; **das Essen** ~ **stellen** to keep the food hot or warm; ~**e Miete** rent including heating; **nur einen** ~**en Händedruck bekommen** (fig inf) to get nothing for one's pains; **wie** ~**e Semmeln weggehen** (inf) to sell or go like hot cakes; ~ **sitzen** to sit in a warm place; **sich** ~ **anziehen** to dress up warmly; **jdn/etw** ⸚**stens empfehlen** to recommend sb/sth warmly; **weder** ~ **noch kalt sein** (fig) to be indifferent; ~ **werden** (fig inf) to thaw out (inf); **mit jdm** ~ **werden** (inf) to get close to sb; **mit etw** ~ **werden** mit Stelle to get used to sth; **mit Stadt** auch to get to know sth; siehe Bruder, laufen.

Warm-: ~**bier** nt mulled ale or beer; ~**blut** nt crossbreed; ~**blüter** m -s, - warm-blooded animal; **w**~**blütig** adj warm-blooded.

Wärme f -, (rare) -n (lit, fig) warmth; (von Wetter etc, Phys) heat; (Wetterlage) warm weather. **10 Grad** ~ 10 degrees above zero or above freezing; **an dem Gerät kann man verschiedene** ~**n einstellen** you can adjust the appliance to different heat settings; **ist das eine** ~! isn't it warm!; **komm in die** ~ come into the warm(th); **mit** ~ (fig) warmly.

Wärme-: ~**behandlung** f (Med) heat treatment; **w**~**beständig** adj heat-resistant; ~**einheit** f thermal unit, unit of heat; ~**energie** f thermal energy; ~**grad** m degree of heat; ~**lehre** f theory of heat; ~**leiter** m heat conductor; ~**messer** m -s, - thermometer.

wärmen 1 vt to warm; Essen, Kaffee etc to warm or heat up. **2** vi (Kleidung, Sonne) to be warm; (Ofen auch) to provide warmth. **Schnaps wärmt** schnapps warms you up. **3** vr to warm oneself (up), to warm up. **sich gegenseitig** ~ to keep each other warm.

Wärme(r) m decl as adj (sl) queer (inf), poof (sl), fag (US sl).

Wärme-: ~**regler** m thermostat; ~**speicher** m storer of heat; (Gerät) heat storer or accumulator; ~**strahlung** f thermal radiation, radiant heat; ~**technik** f heat technology; ~**verlust** m heat loss.

Wärmflasche f hot-water bottle. **eine** ~ **mit zwei Beinen** (hum inf) a human hot-water bottle (inf).

Warm-: ~**front** f (Met) warm front; **w**~**gemäßigt** adj (Geog) temperate; **w**~**halten** vt sep irreg sich (dat) **jdn w**~**halten** (fig inf) to keep in with sb (inf); ~**halteplatte** f hot plate; **w**~**herzig** adj warm-hearted; ~**herzigkeit** f warm-heartedness; **w**~**laufen** vi sep irreg aux sein to warm up; ~**luft** f warm air; ~**luftzufuhr** f inflow or influx of warm air; (von Heizung) warm air supply; ~**miete** f rent including heating.

Warmwasser-: ~**bereiter** m -s, - water heater; ~**heizung** f hot-water central heating; ~**leitung** f hot-water pipe; ~**speicher** m hot-water tank; ~**versorgung** f hot-water supply.

Warn-: ~**anlage** f warning system; ~**blinkanlage** f flashing warning lights pl; (an Auto) hazard warning lights pl; ~**blinkleuchte** f flashing warning light; ~**blinklicht** nt flashing warning light; (an Auto) hazard warning light; ~**dreieck** nt warning triangle.

warnen vti to warn (vor + dat of). **die Polizei warnt vor Schneeglätte** the police have issued a warning of snow and ice on the roads; **jdn (davor)** ~, **etw zu tun** to warn sb against doing sth, to warn sb not to do sth; **vor Taschendieben wird gewarnt!** beware of pickpockets!

Warn-: ~**kreuz** nt warning cross (before level crossing); ~**meldung** f warning (announcement); ~**ruf** m warning cry; ~**schild** nt warning sign; ~**schuß** m warning shot; ~**signal** nt warning signal; ~**streik** m token strike.

Warnung f warning. ~ **vor etw** warning about sth; **vor Gefahr** warning of sth.

Warn-: ~**vorrichtung** f warning system; ~**zeichen** nt warning sign; (hörbar) warning signal.

Warrant [auch ˈvɔrənt] m -s, -s warrant.

Warschau nt -s Warsaw.

Warschauer-Pakt-Staaten pl Warsaw Pact states pl.

Warte f -, -n observation point; (fig) standpoint, viewpoint. **von jds** ~ **(aus)** (fig) from sb's point of view or sb's standpoint; **von seiner hohen** ~ **aus** (fig iro) from his lofty standpoint (iro).

Warte-: ~**frist** f waiting period; (für Lieferung) delivery time; ~**halle** f waiting room; (im Flughafen) departure lounge; ~**liste** f waiting list.

warten[1] vi to wait (auf + acc for). **warte mal!** hold on, wait a minute; (überlegend) let me see; **na warte!** (inf) just you wait!; **warte, wenn ich das noch mal sehe!** just let me see that again; **bitte** ~ (Telec) hold the line please; (Zeichen) please wait; **du wirst** ~ **können** you'll have to wait; **da kannst du** ~, **bis du schwarz wirst** (inf), **da(rauf) kannst du lange** ~ (inf) you can wait till the cows come home; **auf Antwort/Einlaß** ~ to wait for an answer/to be let in; **mit dem Essen auf jdn** ~ to wait for sb (to come) before eating; **to wait with lunch/dinner etc for sb; mit dem Essen nicht auf jdn** ~ to eat without sb; **ich bin gespannt, was da auf mich wartet** I wonder what's waiting for me or what awaits me or what's in store for me there; **auf sie/darauf habe ich gerade noch gewartet!** (iro) she/that was all I needed!; **lange auf sich** ~ **lassen** to be a long time (in) coming; **nicht lange auf sich** ~ **lassen** to be not long in coming; **das lange W**~ **hatte ihn müde gemacht** the long wait had made him tired.

warten[2] vt (a) (liter: pflegen) Kinder etc to look after; Tiere to tend. **(b)** *Auto* to service; *Maschine auch* to maintain.

Wärter(in f) *m* -s, - attendant; (*Leuchtturm~*, *Tier~*) keeper; (*Kranken~*) nurse, orderly; (*Gefängnis~*) warder/wardress (*Brit*), guard.

Warte-: ~**raum** *m* waiting room; ~**saal** *m* waiting room; ~**zeit** f waiting period; (*an Grenze, im Verkehr*) wait; ~**zimmer** *nt* waiting room.

-wärts *adv suf* -wards.

Wartung f (*von Auto*) servicing; (*von Maschine auch*) maintenance.

wartungsfrei *adj* maintenance-free.

warum *interrog adv* why. ~ **nicht**? why not?; ~ **nicht gleich so!** that's better; **nach dem W~ fragen** to ask why; **das W~ und Weshalb** the whys and wherefores.

Warze f -, -n wart; (*Brust~*) nipple.

Warzen-: ~**hof** *m* (*Anat*) areola (*spec*); ~**schwein** *nt* warthog.

was 1 *interrog pron* **(a)** what; (*wieviel auch*) how much. ~ **kostet das**? how much is that?, what does *or* how much does that cost?; ~ **ist** *or* **gibt's**? what is it?, what's up?; ~ **ist, kommst du mit**? well, are you coming?; **sie kommt nicht —** ~? she's not coming — what?; ~ **hast du denn**?, ~ **ist denn los**? what's the matter?, what's wrong?; ~ **willst** *or* **hast du denn**? what are you talking about?; ~ **denn**? (*ungehalten*) what (is it)?; (*um Vorschlag bittend*) but what?; ~ **denn, bist du schon fertig**? what, are you finished already?; **das ist gut,** ~? (*inf*) that's good, isn't it *or* what (*dated*)?; ~ **haben wir gelacht!** (*inf*) how we laughed!; ~ **ist das doch schwierig** (*inf*) it's really difficult.

(b) (*inf: warum*) why, what ... for. ~ **lachst du denn so**? what are you laughing for?, why are you laughing?

(c) ~ **für ...** what sort *or* kind of ...; ~ **für ein Haus hat er**? what sort *or* kind of (a) house does he have?; ~ **für ein schönes Haus!** what a lovely house!; **und** ~ **für ein Haus!** and what a house!; ~ **für ein Wahnsinn!** what madness!

2 *rel pron* (*auf ganzen Satz bezogen*) which. **das,** ~ **...** that which ..., what ...; **ich weiß,** ~ **ich/er tun soll** I know what I should do *or* what to do/what he should do; ~ **auch (immer)** whatever; **das ist etwas,** ~ **ich nicht verstehe** that is something (which) I don't understand; **alles,** ~ **...** everything *or* all (that) ...; **das Beste/Schönste/wenige/einzige,** ~ **ich ...** the best/prettiest/little/only thing (that) I ...; **schreib/iß** *etc,* ~ **du kannst** (*inf*) write/eat *etc* what you can; **lauf,** ~ **du kannst!** (*inf*) run as fast as you can!; ~ **du immer hast!** you do go on!

3 (*inf*) *indef pron* abbr of **etwas** something; (*fragend, bedingend auch, verneint*) anything; (*unbestimmter Teil einer Menge*) some; any. **(na,) so** ~! well I never!; **so** ~ **von Blödheit** such stupidity; **kann ich dir** ~ **helfen**? (*inf*) can I give you a hand?; **ist (mit dir)** ~? is something the matter (with you)?; *siehe auch* **etwas, sehen.**

Was *nt* -, *no pl* **das** ~ **und nicht das Wo ist das Wichtigste** the most important thing is what is done, not where it is done.

Wasch-: ~**anlage** f (*für Autos*) car-wash; (*Scheiben~*) wipers *pl*; ~**anleitung** f washing instructions *pl*; ~**anstalt** f (*dated*) laundry; ~**anweisung** f washing instructions *pl*; ~**automat** *m* automatic washing machine; **w~bar** *adj* washable; ~**bär** *m* rac(c)oon; ~**becken** *nt* wash-basin; (*Schüssel*) wash-bowl; ~**benzin** *nt* benzine; ~**beutel** *m* sponge bag; ~**brett** *nt* washboard; ~**bütte** f wash-tub; ~**creme** f cream detergent.

Wäsche f -, *no pl* **(a)** washing; (*Schmutz~, bei Wäscherei*) laundry. **große/kleine** ~ **haben** (*in bezug auf Menge*) to have a large/small amount of washing (to do); (*in bezug auf Größe*) to wash the big/small things; **bei** *or* **in der** ~ in the wash; **in der** ~ **sein** to be in the wash; (*in der Wäscherei*) to be at the laundry; **etw in die** ~ **geben** to put sth in the wash; (*in die Wäscherei*) to send sth to the laundry; *siehe* **schmutzig.**

(b) (*Stoffwaren*) (*Bett~, Tisch~, Küchen~*) linen; (*Unter~*) underwear. **dumm aus der** ~ **gucken** (*inf*) to look stupid.

Wäschebeutel *m* dirty clothes bag; (*für Wäscherei*) laundry bag.

wasch|echt *adj Farbe* fast; *Stoff auch* colourfast; (*fig*) genuine, real, pukka (*inf*).

Wäsche-: ~**geschäft** *nt* draper's (shop); ~**klammer** f clothespeg; ~**knopf** *m* linen-covered button; ~**korb** *m* dirty clothes basket; ~**leine** f (clothes-)line; ~**mangel** f mangle.

waschen *pret* **wusch,** *ptp* **gewaschen 1** *vt* to wash; *Gold etc* to pan. (*Wäsche*) ~ to do the washing; **etw (acc) warm/kalt** ~ to wash sth in hot/cold water; **sich (dat) die Hände/Haare** *etc* ~ to wash one's hands/hair *etc*; **W~ und Legen** (*beim Friseur*) shampoo and set.

2 *vr* (*Mensch, Tier*) to wash (oneself/itself); (*Stoff*) to wash. **das hat sich gewaschen** (*inf*) that really made itself felt, that really had an effect; **eine Geldbuße/Ohrfeige/Klassenarbeit, die sich gewaschen hat** (*inf*) a really heavy fine/hard box on the ears/a real stinker of a test (*inf*).

Waschepuff *m* dirty clothes basket.

Wäscher *m* -s, - (*Gold~*) panner; (*Erz~*) washer. ~ **und Plätter** launderer.

Wäscherei f laundry.

Wäscherin f washerwoman; (*Berufsbezeichnung*) laundress.

Wäsche-: ~**rolle** f (*esp Aus*) mangle; ~**sack** *m* laundry bag; ~**schleuder** f spin-drier; ~**schrank** *m* linen cupboard; ~**ständer** *m* clothes-horse; ~**stärke** f starch; ~**tinte** f marking ink; ~**trockner** *m* (*Ständer*) clothes-horse; (*Trockenautomat*) drier; ~**zeichen** *nt* name tape.

Wasch-: ~**faß** *nt* wash-tub; ~**frau** f washerwoman; ~**gang** *m* stage of the washing programme; ~**gelegenheit** f washing facilities *pl*; ~**handschuh** *m* flannel mitt; ~**haus** *nt* wash-house, laundry; ~**kessel** *m* (wash-)boiler, copper; ~**küche** f washroom, laundry; (*inf: Nebel*) pea-souper (*inf*); (*beim Rauchen*) **eine** ~**küche machen** (*inf*) to make the cigarette tip wet; ~**lappen** *m* flannel; (*fürs Gesicht auch*) facecloth; (*inf: Feigling*) sissy (*inf*), softy (*inf*); **w~lappig** *adj* (*inf*) soft, sissy;

~**lauge** f suds *pl*; ~**leder** *nt* chamois leather; ~**maschine** f washing-machine; **w~maschinenfest** *adj* machine-washable; ~**mittel** *nt* detergent; ~**pulver** *nt* washing-powder; ~**raum** *m* wash-room; ~**rumpel** f -, -n (*Aus*) *siehe* ~**brett**; ~**salon** *m* laundry; (*zum Selbstwaschen*) launderette; ~**samt** *m* washable velvet; ~**schüssel** f wash-bowl, wash-basin; ~**seide** f washable silk; ~**tag** *m* wash-day; ~**tag haben** to have one's wash-day; ~**tisch** *m*, ~**toilette** f wash-stand; ~**trog** *m* washing trough.

Waschung f (*Rel, Med*) ablution.

Wasch-: ~**wasser** *nt* washing water; ~**weib** *nt* (*fig pej*) washerwoman; ~**zettel** *m* (*Typ*) blurb; ~**zeug** *nt* toilet *or* washing things *pl*; ~**zuber** *m* wash-tub; ~**zwang** *m* (*Psych*) obsession with washing oneself.

Waserl *nt* -s, -(n) (*Aus inf*) **armes** ~ poor thing.

Wasser *nt* -s, - (**a**) *no pl* water. **bei** ~ **und Brot** (*euph*) behind bars, in prison; **das ist** ~ **auf seine Mühle** (*fig*) this is all grist to his mill; **bis dahin fließt noch viel** ~ **den Bach** *or* **den Rhein** *or* **die Donau** *etc* **hinunter** a lot of water will have flowed under the bridge by then; ~ **in den Wein gießen** (*fig*) to pour cold water on sb's ideas/plans *etc*; **dort wird auch nur mit** ~ **gekocht** (*fig*) they're no different from anybody else (there); **ihr kann er nicht das** ~ **reichen** (*fig*) he can't hold a candle to her, he's not a patch on her; *siehe* **Blut, Rotz, abgraben, rein²**.

(b) *pl* ~ (*Flüssigkeit*) (*Abwasch~ etc*) water; (*medizinisch*) lotion; (*Parfüm*) cologne, scent; (*Mineral~*) mineral water; (*Schnaps*) schnapps; (*Tränen*) tears *pl*; (*Speichel*) saliva; (*Schweiß*) sweat; (*Urin*) water, urine; (*Med: in Benen etc*) fluid; (*Ab~*) sewage *no pl*. ~ **mit Geschmack** (*inf*) pop (*inf*); **das** ~ **läuft mir im Mund zusammen** my mouth is watering.

(c) ~**masse, im Gegensatz zu Land**) water. **die** ~ *pl* (*geh*) the waters *pl*; **etw unter** ~ **setzen** to flood sth; **unter** ~ **stehen** to be flooded, to be under water; ~ **treten** (*beim Schwimmen*) to tread water; (*Med*) to paddle (*in cold water as a therapy*); **zu** ~ on the water *or* (*Meer*) sea; (*auf dem* ~**weg**) by water/sea; **ein Boot zu** ~ **lassen** to launch a boat; **einen Ort zu** ~ **erreichen** to reach a place by water; **ins** ~ **fallen, zu** ~ **werden** (*fig*) to fall through; **nahe ans** ~ **gebaut haben** (*inf*) to be inclined to tears; **ins** ~ **gehen** (*euph*) to drown oneself; **sich über** ~ **halten** (*fig*) to keep one's head above water; **er ist mit allen** ~**n gewaschen** he is a shrewd customer, he knows all the tricks; *siehe* **Schlag, Hals¹**.

(d) (*Gezeiten*) tide. **das** ~ **kommt/läuft ab** the tide is coming in/going out; *siehe* **auflaufen.**

Wasser-: **w~abstoßend** *adj* water-repellent; **w~arm** *adj* arid; ~**armut** f aridity; ~**aufbereitung** f treatment of water; ~**bad** *nt* water bath; (*Cook*) double-boiler, bain-marie; **im** ~**bad** (*Cook*) in a double boiler *or* bain-marie; ~**ball** *m* (a) *no pl*: *Spiel*) water polo; (*Ball*) beach-ball; (*fürs* ~**ballspiel**) water-polo ball; ~**bau** *m, no pl* hydraulic engineering; ~**bett** *nt* water-bed; ~**blase** f (water) blister; ~**bombe** f (*Mil*) depth charge; (*inf*) water bomb; ~**bruch** *m* (*Med*) hydrocele; ~**burg** f castle built in water.

Wässerchen *nt* little stream *or* brook; (*Parfüm*) scent, perfume; (*kosmetisch*) lotion, potion. **ein** ~ **machen** (*baby-talk*) to do a wee-wee (*baby-talk*); **er sieht aus, als ob er kein** ~ **trüben könnte** he looks as if butter wouldn't melt in his mouth.

Wasser-: ~**dampf** *m* steam; **w~dicht** *adj* (*lit, fig*) watertight; *Uhr, Stoff etc* waterproof; ~**eimer** *m* bucket, pail; ~**enthärter** *m* water-softener; ~**erhitzer** *m* water-heater; ~**fahrzeug** *nt* water-craft; ~**fall** *m* waterfall; **wie ein** ~**fall reden** (*inf*) to talk nineteen to the dozen (*inf*); ~**farbe** f water-colour; **w~fest** *adj* waterproof; ~**floh** *m* water-flea; ~**flugzeug** *nt* seaplane; ~**frosch** *m* aquatic frog; ~**gas** *nt* water-gas; ~**gehalt** *m* water content; ~**geist** *m* water sprite; **w~gekühlt** *adj* water-cooled; ~**glas** *nt* (a) (*Trinkglas*) water glass, tumbler; *siehe* **Sturm**; (b) *no pl* (*Chem*) water-glass; ~**glätte** f slippery roads due to surface water; ~**graben** *m* (*Sport*) water-jump; (*um Burg*) moat; ~**hahn** *m* water tap, faucet (*US*); (*Haupthahn*) stopcock; **w~haltig** *adj* (*Chem*) aqueous; **w~haltig sein** to contain water; ~**härte** f hardness of water; ~**haushalt** *m* (*Biol etc*) water balance; ~**hose** f (*Met*) waterspout; ~**huhn** *nt* coot.

wässerig *adj* (*lit, fig*) watery; *Augen* pale-coloured; (*Chem*) aqueous. **jdm den Mund** ~ **machen** (*inf*) to make sb's mouth water.

Wasser-: ~**jungfer** f (*Zool*) dragonfly; ~**jungfrau** f (*Myth*) naiad; ~**kante** f *siehe* **Waterkant**; ~**kessel** *m* kettle; (*Tech*) boiler; ~**kissen** *nt* (*Med*) water cushion; ~**klosett** *nt* watercloset; ~**kopf** *m* water on the brain *no indef art*, hydrocephalus *no indef art* (*spec*); (*inf*) big head; ~**kraft** f water-power; ~**kraftwerk** *nt* hydroelectric power station; ~**kreislauf** *m* water cycle; ~**kresse** f watercress; ~**kühlung** f (*Aut*) water-cooling; **mit** ~**kühlung** water-cooled; ~**kühlung haben** to be water-cooled; ~**lassen** *nt* (*Med*) passing water, urination; ~**latte** f (*vulg*) early-morning erection *or* hard-on (*sl*); ~**lauf** *m* watercourse; ~**läufer** *m* (*Vogel*) shank, sandpiper; (*Insekt*) water-measurer *or* -skater; **dunkler** ~**läufer** spotted redshank; ~**leiche** f drowned body; ~**leitung** f (*Rohr*) water pipe; (*Anlagen*) plumbing *no pl*; (*inf: Hahn*) tap, faucet (*US*); ~**lilie** f water-lily; ~**linie** f (*Naut*) water-line; ~**loch** *nt* water-hole; **w~löslich** *adj* water-soluble, soluble in water; ~**mangel** *m* water shortage; ~**mann** *m, pl* -**männer** (a) (*Myth*) water sprite. (b) (*Astrol*) Aquarius *no art*, Water-carrier; ~**mann sein** to be (an) Aquarius; ~**melone** f water-melon; ~**messer** *m* -s, - water-meter; ~**mühle** f water-mill.

wassern *vi* (*Aviat*) to land on water *or* (*im Meer auch*) in the sea; (*Space*) to splash down.

wässern 1 *vt Heringe, Erbsen etc* to soak; (*Phot*) to rinse; (*bewässern*) *Pflanzen, Felder* to water. **2** *vi* to water. **mir** ~ **die Augen** my eyes are watering.

Wasser-: ~**nixe** f (*Myth*) water-nymph; ~**orgel** f hydraulic organ; ~**pfeife** f hookah, hubble-bubble; ~**pflanze** f aquatic

plant; ~pistole f water-pistol; ~pocken pl (Med) chickenpox
sing; ~polizei f siehe ~schutzpolizei; ~rad nt water-wheel;
~ratte f water-rat or -vole; (inf: Kind) water-baby; ~recht nt
laws pertaining to water and waterways; w~reich adj Gebiet
with plenty of water, abounding in water; Fluß containing a lot
of water; ~reservoir nt reservoir; ~rohr nt water-pipe;
~säule f water column; ~schaden m water damage; ~schaff nt
-(e)s, -e (Aus) water tub; ~scheide f watershed; w~scheu adj
scared of water; ~scheu f fear of water; (Psych) water phobia;
~schi m, nt siehe ~ski; ~schildkröte f turtle; ~schlange f (a)
(Zool) water-snake; (Myth) (sea)serpent; (b) (Astron) Hydra;
~schlauch m (a) (water) hose; (Behälter) skin; (b) (Bot)
bladderwort; ~schloß nt castle surrounded by water;
~schutzpolizei f (auf Flüssen, ~wegen) river police; (im
Hafen) harbour police; (auf der See) coastguard service; ~ski
1 m water-ski; 2 nt water-skiing; ~speier m -s, - gargoyle;
~spiegel m (Oberfläche) surface of the water; (~stand) water-
level; ~sport m der ~sport water sports pl; ~spülung f flush
Klosett mit ~spülung flush toilet, water-closet; ~stand m
water-level; niedriger/hoher ~stand low/high water;
~standsanzeiger m water-level indicator; ~standsmeldungen
pl water-level or (für Gezeiten) tide report; ~stein m siehe
Kesselstein; ~stiefel pl wellington boots pl.
Wasserstoff m hydrogen.
Wasserstoff-: w~blond adj attr Haar peroxide blonde; ein
w~blondes Mädchen a peroxide blonde (inf); ~bombe f hydrogen bomb, H-bomb; ~superoxid, ~superoxyd nt hydrogen
peroxide.
Wasser-: ~strahl m jet of water; ~straße f waterway; ~sucht f
dropsy; w~süchtig adj suffering from dropsy, dropsical;
~tank m water-tank; (für WC) cistern; ~tier nt aquatic animal;
~träger m water-carrier; ~treten nt (Sport) treading water;
(Med) paddling (in cold water as therapy); ~tropfen m water-
drop, drop of water; ~turm m water-tower; ~uhr f (~zähler)
water-meter; (Hist) water-clock.
Wasserung f sea/water landing; (Space) splashdown.
Wässerung f, no pl siehe wässern 1 soaking, steeping; rinsing,
washing; watering.
Wasser-: ~verbrauch m water consumption no def art;
~versorgung f water-supply; Maßnahmen zur ~versorgung
measures to ensure the supply of water; ~vogel m waterfowl;
~waage f spirit-level; ~weg m water-way; auf dem ~weg by
water or (Meer) sea; ~welle f water-wave; ~werfer m water-
cannon; ~werk nt waterworks sing or pl; ~wirtschaft f water-
supply (and distribution); ~zähler m water-meter; ~zeichen nt
watermark.
wäßrig adj siehe **wässerig**.
waten vi aux sein to wade.
Waterkant f -, no pl coast esp North Sea coast of Germany.
watschelig adj waddling attr. ~ laufen to waddle.
watscheln vi aux sein to waddle.
Watschen f -, - (Aus, S Ger inf) siehe **Ohrfeige**.
watschen vt (S Ger inf) jdm eine ~ (auf Backe) to slap sb's
face; (ans Ohr) to give sb a clip round the ear; eine gewatscht
kriegen to get a slap in the face/clip round the ear.
Watschenmann m, pl -männer (Aus) (lit) fairground dummy;
(fig) Aunt Sally (fig).
Watt¹ nt -s, - (Elec) watt.
Watt² nt -(e)s, -en (Geog) mud-flats pl.
Watte f -, -n cotton wool, cotton (US); (zur Polsterung) padding,
wadding. jdn in ~ packen (fig inf) to wrap sb in cotton wool; laß
dich doch in ~ packen! you're far too over-sensitive!
Wattebausch m cotton-wool ball.
Wattenmeer nt mud-flats pl.
Wattestäbchen nt cotton-(wool) swab.
wattieren* vt to pad; (füttern) to line with padding; (und
absteppen) Stoff, Steppdecke to quilt. wattierte Umschläge/
Jacken padded envelopes/quilted jackets.
Wattierung f siehe vt padding; lining; quilting; (die Füllung)
padding.
Watt-: ~meter nt wattmeter; ~sekunde f watt-second; ~stunde
f watt-hour; ~zahl f wattage.
Watvogel m wader.
wau wau interj bow-wow, woof-woof.
Wauwau m -s, -s (baby-talk) bow-wow (baby-talk).
WC [ve:'tse:] nt -s, -s WC.
Webe f -, -n (Aus) linen.
Webekante f siehe **Webkante**.
weben pret webte or (liter, fig) wob, ptp gewebt or (liter, fig)
gewoben vti (lit, fig) weave; Spinnennetz, Lügennetz to spin.
Weber(in f) m -s, - weaver.
Weberei f (a) no pl (das Weben) weaving. (b) (Betrieb)
weaving mill. (c) (Zeug) woven article. eine handgemachte ~ a
hand-woven article.
Weber-: ~kamm m weaver's reed; ~knecht m (Zool) daddy-
long-legs; ~knoten m reef knot.
Web-: ~fehler m weaving flaw; ~garn nt weaving yarn; ~kante
f selvage, selvedge; ~stuhl m loom; ~waren pl woven goods pl.
Wechsel ['vɛksl] m -s, - (a) (Änderung) change; (abwechselnd)
alternation; (Geld~) exchange; (der Jahreszeiten, Agr:
Frucht~) rotation. ein ~ der Wohnung/Schule etc a change of
address/school etc; der von Tag und Nacht the alternation of
day and night; im ~ der Zeiten through the ages; in buntem ~
in motley succession.
(b) (Sport) (Staffel~) (baton) change, change-over; (Ftbl etc)
substitution.
(c) (Fin) bill (of exchange); (inf: Geldzuwendung) allowance.
(d) (Hunt) trail used by game or wild animals.
Wechsel- ['vɛksl-]: ~bäder pl alternating hot and cold baths pl;
~balg m changeling (child); (inf) little monster (inf);
~beziehung f correlation, interrelation; in ~beziehung

miteinander or zueinander stehen to be correlated or interrelated; ~bürgschaft f guarantee (on a bill); ~fälle pl vicis-
situdes pl; ~fieber nt (old) malaria; ~geld nt change; ~gesang
m antiphonal singing; ~gespräch nt dialogue; ~getriebe nt
(Tech) variable gears pl; w~haft adj changeable; Schicksal,
Mensch auch fickle, capricious; ~jahre pl menopause sing,
change of life sing. in die ~jahre kommen/in den ~jahren sein
to start the menopause/be suffering from the menopause;
~kurs m rate of exchange.
wechseln ['vɛksln] 1 vt to change (in + acc into); (austauschen)
to exchange; (Ftbl etc) to substitute (gegen for). den Arzt ~ to
change doctors or one's doctor; den Tisch/die Schule/das Hemd
~ to change tables/schools/one's shirt; die Farbe ~ to change
colour; den Platz mit jdm ~ to exchange one's seat with sb;
Briefe ~ to correspond or be in correspondence (mit with); die
Wohnung ~ to move house; den Wohnsitz ~ to move to another
place; können Sie (mir) 10 Mark ~? can you change 10 marks
(for me)?; Wäsche zum W~ a change of underwear.
2 vi (a) to change; (Sport auch) to change over; (einander
ablösen) to alternate. ich kann Ihnen leider nicht ~ I'm sorry, I
don't have any change; wer oft wechselt, wird rasch Kleingeld
(prov) if you sleep around you make yourself cheap.
(b) (Hunt) to pass by. über die Straße etc ~ to cross the road
etc; über die Grenze ~ (Mensch) to cross the border.
wechselnd ['vɛkslnt] adj changing; (einander ablösend, ab~)
alternating; Launen, Stimmungen changeable; Winde variable; Bewölkung variable, intermittent. mit ~em Erfolg with
varying (degrees of) success; ~ bewölkt cloudy with sunny
intervals.
Wechsel ['vɛksl-]: ~nehmer m payee of a bill; ~protest m protest of a bill; ~rahmen m clip-on picture frame; ~recht nt law
relating to bills of exchange; ~schalter m (a) (Elec) change-
over switch; (b) (in Bank) counter for foreign currency
exchange; ~schuldner m payer of a bill; w~seitig adj reciprocal; (gegenseitig auch) mutual; ~seitigkeit f siehe adj
reciprocity; mutuality; ~spiel nt interplay; w~ständig adj
(Bot) alternate; ~strom m alternating current; ~stube f
(foreign currency) exchange office; ~tierchen nt amoeba;
w~voll adj varied; w~weise adv in turn, alternately;
~wirkung f interaction; in ~wirkung stehen to interact.
Wechsler ['vɛkslɐ] m -s, - (a) (Automat) change machine,
change dispenser. (b) (Mensch) money-changer.
Weck m -(e)s, -e (dial) (bread) roll; (Aus: Brot) loaf.
Weck-: ~apparat ® m preserving and bottling equipment;
~dienst m (Telec) alarm call; (Mil) reveille; den ~dienst übernehmen (inf) to be in charge of reveille; ~dienst machen to do
reveille.
Wecke f -, -n, **Wecken** m -s, - (dial) (bread) roll.
wecken vt to wake (up), to waken; (fig) to arouse; Bedarf to
create; Erinnerungen to bring back, to revive. sich ~ lassen to
have sb wake one up; (telephonisch) to get an alarm call.
Wecken nt -s, no pl waking-up time; (Mil) reveille. Ausgang bis
zum ~ overnight leave (until reveille).
Wecker m -s, - alarm clock. jdm auf den ~ fallen or gehen (inf)
to get on sb's nerves or wick (sl), to drive sb up the wall (inf).
Weck-: ~glas ® nt preserving or Kilner ® jar; ~radio nt radio-
alarm clock; ~ring ® m rubber ring (for preserving jars); ~ruf
m (Telec) alarm call; (Mil) reveille.
Wedel m -s, - fly whisk; (Fächer) fan; (Staub~ aus Federn)
feather duster; (zum Besprengen) sprinkler; (Zweig) twig;
(Eccl) ≈ palm leaf; (Bot: Blatt) frond; (Hunt) tail.
wedeln 1 vi (a) (mit dem Schwanz) ~ (Hund) to wag its tail; mit
etw ~ (winken) to wave sth; mit dem Fächer ~ to wave the fan.
(b) (Ski) to wedel. das W~ wedel(l)ing. 2 vt to waft.
weder conj ~ ... noch ... neither ... nor ...; er ist ~ gekommen,
noch hat er angerufen he neither came nor phoned up; ~ das
eine noch das andere (als Antwort) neither.
weg adv (fort) ~ sein (fortgegangen, abgefahren, verschwunden) to have or be gone; (nicht hier, entfernt) to be
away; von zu Hause ~ sein to be away from home; (erwachsene
Kinder) to have left home; über den Tisch/meinen Kopf ~
across the table/over my head; weit ~ von hier far (away) from
here; ~ (von hier)! get away from here!; let's get away from
here; ~ mit euch! away with you!, scram! (inf); nichts wie or
nur ~ von hier! let's scram (inf); ~ da! (get) out of the way!; ~
damit! (mit Schere etc) put it away!; immer ~ damit throw or
chuck it all out; ~ mit den alten Traditionen! away with these
old traditions!; Hände ~! hands off!; in einem ~ (inf) non-stop;
~ vom Fenster sein (sl) to be out of the game (sl); siehe weggehen
etc.
Weg m -(e)s, -e (a) (Pfad, Geh~, fig) path; (Wald~, Wander~
etc auch) track, trail; (Straße) road. am ~e by the wayside;
woher des ~(e)s? (old) where have you come from?, whence
comest thou? (obs); wohin des ~(e)s? (old) where are you going
to?, whither goest thou? (obs); des ~(e)s kommen (old) to come
walking/riding etc up; in einer Gegend ~ und Steg kennen to
know an area like the back of one's hand; jdm in den ~ treten,
jdm den ~ versperren or verstellen to block or bar sb's way;
jdm/einer Sache im ~ stehen (fig) to stand in the way of sb/sth;
jdm Hindernisse or Steine in den ~ legen (fig) to put obstruc-
tions in sb's way; jdm nicht über den ~ trauen (fig) not to trust
sb an inch; jdn aus dem ~ räumen (fig) to get rid of sb; etw aus
dem ~ räumen (fig) to remove sth; Mißverständnisse aus dem ~
räumen (fig) to clear sth up; neue ~e beschreiten (fig) to tread new paths; den ~ der
Sünde/Tugend gehen to follow the path of sin/virtue; die ~e
Gottes the ways of the Lord; den ~ des geringsten Widerstandes gehen to follow the line of least resistance; der ~ zur
Hölle ist mit guten Vorsätzen gepflastert (Prov) the road to
Hell is paved with good intentions; siehe irdisch.
(b) (lit, fig: Route) way; (Entfernung) distance; (Reise)
journey; (zu Fuß) walk; (fig: zum Erfolg auch, Bildungs~) road.

ich muß diesen ~ jeden Tag zweimal gehen/fahren I have to walk/drive this stretch twice a day; auf dem ~ nach London/zur Arbeit on the way to London/work; auf dem ~ zu jdm/nach einem Ort sein to be on the or one's way to sb's/a place; 6 km ~ 6 kms away; noch zwei Stunden/ein Stück ~ vor sich haben to still have two hours/some distance to travel; der lange ~ hat mich müde gemacht the long journey or (zu Fuß) walk has tired me out; jdn ein Stück ~(es) begleiten (geh) to accompany sb part of the way; mein erster ~ war zur Bank the first thing I did was go to the bank; jdm auf seinem letzten ~ begleiten (euph) to pay one's last respects to sb; seiner ~e gehen (geh) (lit) to go on one's way; (fig) to go one's own way; welchen ~ haben sie eingeschlagen? (lit) what road did they take?; einen neuen ~ einschlagen (fig) to follow a new avenue; (beruflich) to follow a new career; den falschen/richtigen ~ einschlagen (lit) to follow the wrong/right path or road or (fig) avenue; jdm etw mit auf den ~ geben (lit) to give sb sth to take with him/her etc; jdm einen guten Rat mit auf den ~ geben to give sb good advice to follow in life; jdm/einer Sache aus dem ~ gehen (lit) to get out of sb's way/the way of sth; (fig) to avoid sb/sth; jdm über den ~ laufen (fig) to run into sb; seinen ~ (im Leben/Beruf) machen (fig) to make one's way in life/one's career; seinen ~ nehmen (fig) to take its/their course; etw in die ~e leiten to arrange sth; jdm/sich den ~ verbauen (fig) to ruin sb's/one's chances or prospects (für etw); auf dem besten ~ sein, etw zu tun to be well on the way to doing sth; damit hat es noch gute ~e (fig geh) there is still a long way to go (as regards that); der gerade ~ ist der kürzeste or beste (Prov) honesty is the best policy.

(c) (Mittel, Art und Weise) way; (Methode) method. auf welchem ~ kommt man am schnellsten zu Geld? what's the fastest way of making or to make money?; auf welchem ~ sind Sie zu erreichen? how can I get in touch with you?; auf diesem ~e this way; auf diplomatischem ~e through diplomatic channels; auf gesetzlichem or legalen ~e legally, by legal means; auf künstlichem ~e artificially, by artificial means; siehe schriftlich.

(d) (inf: Besorgung) errand.

wegbekommen* vt sep irreg (a) (entfernen, loswerden) to get rid of (von from); Klebstoff, Fleck etc to remove (von from), to get off; (von bestimmtem Ort) jdn, Hund to get away (von from). (b) (inf: erhalten) to get; Grippe to catch.

Weg-: ~bereiter m precursor, forerunner; ~bereiter einer Sache (gen) or für etw sein to pave the way for sth; ~bereiter für jdn sein to prepare the way for sb; ~biegung f turn, bend.

weg-: ~blasen vt sep irreg to blow away; wie ~geblasen sein (fig) to have vanished; ~bleiben vi sep irreg aux sein to stay away; (nicht mehr kommen) to stop coming; (Satz, Wort etc) to be left out or omitted; (Vergünstigung etc) not to apply; mir blieb die Luft ~ (lit) I couldn't breathe; mir bleibt die Spucke or Luft ~! (inf) I'm absolutely speechless or flabbergasted!; sein W~bleiben his absence; ~bringen vt sep irreg to take away; (zur Reparatur) to take in; (inf: ~bekommen) to get rid of; ~denken vt sep irreg: sich (dat) etw ~denken to imagine or picture things/the place/one's life etc without sth; die Elektrizität ist aus unserem modernen Leben nicht mehr ~zudenken we cannot imagine life today without electricity; ~diskutieren* vt sep to explain away; dieses Problem läßt sich nicht ~diskutieren talking about it won't make the problem go away; ~dürfen vi sep irreg to be allowed to go or leave; (inf: ausgehen dürfen) to be allowed to go out.

Wegegeld nt (Hist) (road) toll.

weg|ekeln vt sep (inf) to drive away.

Wegelagerer m -s, - highwayman; (zu Fuß) footpad.

wegen prep +gen or (inf) +dat because of, on account of; (infolge auch) due to. jdn ~ einer Sache bestrafen/verurteilen/entlassen etc to punish/sentence/dismiss sb for sth; von ~! (inf) you've got to be kidding! (inf); (Verbot auch) no way! (inf), no chance! (inf); ... aber von ~! (inf) ... but not a bit of it! (inf); er ist krank — von ~ krank! (inf) he's ill — since when? (iro), what do you mean "ill"? (iro); ~ mir (inf) or meiner (obs) = meinetwegen; siehe Amt, Recht.

Wegerich m -s, -e (Bot) plantain.

wegessen vt sep irreg jdm den Kuchen etc ~ to eat sb's cake etc; er hat (mir) alles weggegessen he's eaten all my food.

wegfahren sep irreg 1 vi aux sein (abfahren) to leave; (Auto, Bus, Fahrer) to drive off or away; (im Boot) to sail away; (zum Einkaufen, als Ausflug) to go out; (verreisen) to go away. 2 vt Menschen, Gegenstände to take away; Fahrzeug to drive away; (umstellen) to move.

Wegfall m, no pl (Einstellung) discontinuation; (Aufhören) cessation (form); (Streichung) cancellation; (Unterbleiben) loss; (Auslassung) omission. in ~ kommen (form) to be discontinued; (Bestimmung) to cease to apply.

wegfallen vi sep irreg aux sein to be discontinued; (Bestimmung, Regelung) to cease to apply; (unterbleiben) to be lost; (überflüssig werden) to become no longer necessary; (ausgelassen werden) to be omitted. ~ lassen to discontinue; (auslassen) to omit; wir haben den Nachtisch ~ lassen we did without or dispensed with dessert.

weg-: ~fegen vt sep (lit, fig) to sweep away; (sl: besiegen) to wipe the floor with (inf); ~fischen vt sep (inf: essen) to snap up; er hat uns alle Forellen ~gefischt he's caught all our trout; ~fliegen vi sep irreg aux sein to fly away or off; (Hut) to fly off; (mit Flugzeug) to fly out; wann bist du denn in Frankfurt ~geflogen? when did you fly out of Frankfurt?; ~fressen vt sep (inf) siehe ~essen; ~führen sep 1 vt to lead away; 2 vi das führt zu weit (vom Thema) ~ that will lead or take us too far off the subject.

Weggabelung f fork (in the road), bifurcation (form).

Weggang m departure, leaving.

weggeben vt sep irreg (verschenken) to give away; (in Pflege

geben) to have looked after. eine kaputte Uhr ~ to take in a broken watch; seine Wäsche (zum Waschen) ~ to have one's washing done.

Weggefährte m (fig) companion.

weggehen vi sep irreg aux sein to go, to leave; (verreisen, umziehen etc) to go away; (ausgehen) to go out; (inf: Fleck) to come off; (inf: Ware) to sell. über etw (acc) ~ (inf) to ignore sth, to pass over sth; aus Heidelberg/aus dem Büro/von der Firma ~ to leave Heidelberg/the office/the firm; geh mir damit weg! (inf) don't give me that! (inf); geh mir mit dem weg! (inf) don't talk to me about him!

Weggenosse m (lit, fig) companion.

Weggli nt -s, - (Sw) (bread) roll.

weggucken sep 1 vi to look away. 2 vt es wird dir schon niemand was ~! (hum) we/they etc won't be seeing anything we/they etc haven't seen before (hum).

weghaben vt sep irreg (inf) (erledigt haben) to have got done; (bekommen, verstanden haben) to have got; (entfernt haben) Fleck etc to have got rid of (inf); (umstellen, umhängen) Tisch, Bild to have moved. jdn/etw ~wollen (inf) to want to get rid of sb/sth; der hat was weg (inf) he's really clever; darin hat er was weg (inf) he's pretty good at that; du hast deine Strafe/deinen Denkzettel weg you have had your punishment; einen ~ (sl) (verrückt sein) to be off one's head (inf), to have a screw loose (inf); (betrunken sein) to be tight (inf); siehe Fett, Ruhe, Teil.

weg-: ~helfen vi sep irreg jdm von irgendwo ~helfen to help sb get away from or out of (any) a place; jdm über etw (acc) ~helfen (fig) to help sb (to) get over sth; ~holen vt sep to take away; (abholen) to fetch; sich (dat) was/eine Krankheit ~holen (inf) to catch something/a disease; ~jagen vt sep to chase away, to drive away or off; Menschen auch to send packing (inf); (aus Land) to turn out.

wegkommen vi sep irreg aux sein (inf) (entfernt werden) to go; (abhanden kommen) to disappear; (weggehen können) to get away; (aus dem Haus) to get out. was ich nicht brauche, kommt weg what I don't want can go; das Buch ist mir weggekommen the book has disappeared, I've lost the book; mach, daß du wegkommst! make yourself scarce! (inf), hop it! (inf); gut/schlecht (bei etw) ~ to come off well/badly (with sth); über etw (acc) ~/nicht ~ to get over/be unable to get over sth; ich komme nicht darüber weg, daß ... (inf) I can't get over the fact that ...

Weg-: ~kreuz nt (a) (Kruzifix) wayside cross; (b) siehe ~kreuzung; ~kreuzung f crossroads.

wegkriegen vt sep (inf) siehe wegbekommen (a).

Weg-: ~krümmung f bend in the road; w~kundig adj eine w~kundige Person a person who knows/knew the area.

weg-: ~lassen vt sep irreg (auslassen) to leave out; (nicht benutzen) not to use; (inf: gehen lassen) to let go; ich lasse heute den Zucker im Kaffee ~ I won't have any sugar in my coffee today; ~laufen vi sep irreg aux sein to run away (vor +dat from); seine Frau ist ihm ~gelaufen his wife has run away (from him) or run off (and left him); das läuft (dir) nicht ~! (fig hum) that can wait; ~legen vt sep (in Schublade etc) to put away; (zur Seite, zum späteren Verbrauch) to put aside; ~leugnen vt sep to deny.

weglos adj (geh) pathless; roadless.

wegmachen sep 1 vt (inf) to get rid of. sie ließ sich (dat) das Kind ~ (sl) she got rid of the baby (inf). 2 vr (sl) to clear or shove off (inf). 3 vi aux sein or haben (dial, inf) to get away (aus from), to get out (aus of).

wegmüssen vi sep irreg to have to go; (weggehen müssen auch) to have to leave or be off (inf); (entfernt werden) to have to be removed. ich muß eine Zeitlang von/aus New York weg I must get away from/get out of New York for a while; du mußt da weg, du behinderst ja den ganzen Verkehr you'll have to move (from there), you're blocking all the traffic; die paar Reste müssen weg we/you etc can't leave those little bits; wenn wir die Wand streichen wollen, muß der Schrank weg if we're going to paint the wall, we'll have to move the cupboard or get the cupboard out of it (inf).

Wegnahme f -, no pl (rare) siehe wegnehmen taking; taking away; removal; absorption; blocking out; blocking.

wegnehmen vt sep irreg to take (auch Chess); (fortnehmen, entfernen, entziehen) to take away; Fleck, Rost to get rid of, to remove; (absorbieren) Strahlen, Licht, Lärm to absorb; (verdecken) Licht, Sonne to block out; Aussicht, Sicht to block; (beanspruchen) Zeit, Platz to take up. Gas ~ (Aut) to ease off the accelerator or gas (US); fünf Tage vom Urlaub ~ to take five days off the holiday; die Bässe ~ to turn down or reduce the bass; jdm seine Kinder/Frau ~ to take sb's children away from him/to steal sb's wife.

weg-: ~packen vt sep to pack or put away; (inf: essen) to put away (inf); ~praktizieren* vt sep (inf) to manage to get rid of or eliminate; ~putzen vt sep to wipe away or off; (inf: essen) to polish off; er putzt ganz schön was ~ (inf) he doesn't half eat a lot or stow a lot away (inf); ~raffen vt sep to snatch away; (liter: durch Tod) to carry off.

Wegrand m wayside, side of the path/road.

weg-: ~rasieren* vt sep to shave off; er hat mir den vorderen Kotflügel ~rasiert (fig inf) he took my front mudguard with him (hum); ~räumen vt sep to clear away; (in Schrank) to put away; ~reißen vt sep irreg to tear away (jdm from sb); Zweige to break off; (inf) Häuser etc to tear or pull down; der Fluß hat die Brücke ~gerissen the river swept away the bridge; ~rennen vi sep irreg aux sein (inf) to run away; ~retuschieren* vt sep to spot out; ~rücken vti sep (vi: aux sein) to move away; ~rufen vt sep irreg to call away; ~rutschen vi aux sein (aus der Hand etc) to slip away; (auf Eis etc) to slide away; mein Wagen ist mir ~gerutscht my car went into a skid.

wegsam adj (obs) passable.

weg-: ~schaffen vt sep (beseitigen, loswerden) to get rid of;

(*~räumen*) to clear away; (*~tragen*, *~fahren*) to remove, to cart away (*inf*); (*erledigen*) *Arbeit* to get done; ~schauen *vi sep siehe* ~sehen.

Wegscheide f parting of the ways (*liter*).

weg-: ~schenken *vt sep* (*inf*) to give away; ~scheren *vr sep* (*inf*) to clear out *or* shove off (*inf*); ~schicken *vt sep Brief etc* to send off *or* away; jdn to send away; (*um etwas zu holen etc*) to send off; ~schießen *vt sep irreg* jdm den Arm *etc* ~schießen to shoot sb's arm *etc* off; ~schlaffen *vi sep aux sein* (*sl*) to peg *or* poop out (*inf*); er schlaffte ihm immer wieder ~ it kept on going limp on him (*inf*); ~schleichen *vir sep irreg* (*vi: aux sein*) to creep *or* steal away; ~schleppen *sep* 1 *vt* to drag *or* lug (*inf*) *or* haul away *or* off; (*tragen*) to carry off; 2 *vr* to drag *or* haul oneself away; ~schließen *vt sep irreg* to lock away; ~schmeißen *vt sep irreg* (*inf*) to chuck away (*inf*); ~schnappen *vt sep* jdm eine ~schnappen to snatch sth (away) from sb; die andere Kundin hat mir das Kleid ~geschnappt the other customer snapped up the dress before I could; jdm die Freundin/den Job ~schnappen to pinch sb's girl-friend/job (*inf*).

Wegschnecke f slug (*of the genus Arionidae*).

weg-: ~schütten *vt sep* to tip away; ~schwemmen *vt sep* to wash away; ~sehen *vi sep irreg* to look away; über etw (*acc*) ~sehen (*lit*) to look over sth; (*fig inf*) to overlook sth, to turn a blind eye to sth.

wegsein (*Zusammenschreibung nur bei infin und ptp*) *vi sep irreg aux sein* (*inf*) to be out cold (*inf*); (*geistesabwesend*) to be not quite with it (*inf*); (*eingeschlafen*) to have dozed off; (*tot*) to be dead; (*begeistert*) to be really taken, to be bowled over (*von by*). über etw (*acc*) ~ to have got over sth; er ist schon lange darüber weg he got over it a long while ago.

wegsetzen *sep* 1 *vt* to move (away); (*wegstellen*) to put away.
2 *vr* to move away. sich über etw (*acc*) ~ (*inf*) to ignore sth, to pay no attention to sth.
3 *vi aux sein or haben* über etw (*acc*) ~ to leap *or* jump over sth, to clear sth.

weg-: ~sollen *vi sep irreg* (*inf*) das soll ~ that is to go; ich soll von London ~ I should leave London; warum soll ich/mein Auto da ~? why should I move/my car be moved?; ~spülen *vt sep* to wash away; (*in der Toilette*) to flush away; (*inf*) *Geschirr* to wash up; ~stecken *vt sep* to put away; einen ~stecken (*sl*) to have it (off) (*sl*); ~stehlen *vr sep irreg* to steal away; ~stellen *vt sep* to put away; (*abstellen*) to put down; ~sterben *vi sep irreg aux sein* (*inf*) to die off; jdm ~sterben to die on sb (*inf*); ~stoßen *vt sep irreg* to push *or* shove away; (*mit Fuß*) to kick away.

Weg-: ~strecke f (*rare*) stretch of road; schlechte ~strecke poor road surface; ~stunde f (*old*) hour.

weg-: ~tragen *vt sep irreg* to carry away *or* off; ~treiben *sep irreg* 1 *vt Boot etc* to carry away *or* off; (*vertreiben*) *Tier etc* to drive away *or* off; 2 *vi aux sein* to drift away; ~treten *vi sep irreg aux sein* (*rare*) to step away *or* aside; (*Mil*) to fall out; (*lassen Sie*) ~treten! (*Mil*) dismiss!; er ist (*geistig*) ~getreten (*inf*) (*geistesabwesend*) he's miles away (*inf*); (*schwachsinnig*) he's soft in the head (*inf*), he's not all there (*inf*); ~tun *vt sep irreg* to put away; (*sparen*) *Geld etc auch* to put by *or* aside; (*~werfen*) to throw away; (*verstecken*) to hide away; tu die Hände ~! take your hands off!

Wegwarte f (*Bot*) chicory.

weg-: ~waschen *vt sep irreg Fleck* to wash off; (*~spülen*) *Erde etc* to wash away; ~wehen *vti sep* (*vi: aux sein*) to blow away.

Weg-: w~weisend *adj* pioneering attr, revolutionary, pathbreaking (*US*); ~weiser m -s, - sign; (*an einem Pfosten*) signpost; (*fig: Buch etc*) guide.

Wegwerf- in cpds disposable, throw-away.

weg-: ~werfen *sep irreg* 1 *vt* to throw away; ~geworfenes Geld money down the drain; 2 *vr sich (an jdn) ~werfen* to waste oneself (on sb), to throw oneself away (on sb); ~werfend *adj* dismissive, disdainful; ~wischen *vt sep* to wipe off; (*fig*) to dismiss; ~wollen *vi sep irreg* (*verreisen*) to want to go away; (*~gehen: von Haus, Party etc*) to want to leave *or* go; (*hinausgehen*) to want to go out; ~wünschen *vt sep* jdn ~wünschen to wish sb would go away; eine Tatsache ~wünschen to wish a fact away; etwas Geschehenes ~wünschen to wish a thing had never happened; ~zählen *vt sep* (*Aus*) to take away, to subtract; ~zaubern *vt sep* to make disappear (*lit* by magic/fig as if by magic).

Wegzehrung f (*liter*) provisions for the journey pl; (*Eccl*) viaticum.

wegziehen *sep irreg* 1 *vt* to pull away (jdm from sb); *Vorhang* to draw back. 2 *vi aux sein* to move away; (*Vögel*) to migrate.

Wegzug m move (aus, von (away) from).

weh 1 *adj* (a) (*wund*) sore; (*geh: schmerzlich*) aching attr. sie verspürte ein ~es Gefühl (*geh*) her heart ached; mir ist so ~ zumute or ums Herz (*old, liter*) my heart is sore (*liter*), I am sore of heart (*old*).
(b) ~ tun (*lit, fig*) to hurt; mir tut der Rücken ~ my back hurts or is aching; mir tut mein verbrannter Finger ~ my finger hurts or is sore where I burnt it; jdm/sich ~ tun (*lit, fig*) to hurt oneself/sb; es tut mir ~, dir das sagen zu müssen it grieves me to have to tell you this; was tut dir denn nun schon wieder ~? what's the matter now?; wo tut es denn ~? (*fig inf*) what's your problem?, what's up? (*inf*); *siehe* ach.
2 *interj* (*geh, liter*) woe (*old*); (*bedauernd*) alas (*liter*), alack (*old*). o ~! oh dear!, oh, my goodness!; (*über jdn*) ~ schreien to lament (sb); ~ mir! woe is me! (*liter*); ~ mir, wenn ... woe betide me if ...

Weh nt -(e)s, -e (*old, liter*) woe; (*dumpfes Gefühl*) ache; (*Leid, Gram*) grief. ein tiefes ~ erfüllte ihn his heart ached.

wehe *interj* ~ (dir), wenn du das tust you'll be sorry or you'll regret it if you do that; darf ich das anfassen? — ~ (dir)! can I touch? — you dare! (*inf*) ~ dem, der ...! woe betide anyone who

...!; ~, ~, dreimal ~! no good will come of it!

Wehe f -, -n (a) (*Schnee~ etc*) drift. (b) (*Geburts~*) ~n pl (*lit*) (labour) pains pl, contractions pl; (*fig*) birth pangs; in den ~n liegen to be in labour; die ~n setzten ein labour or the contractions started, she went into labour.

wehen 1 *vi* (a) (*Wind*) to blow; (*Fahne*) to wave, to flutter; (*Haare*) to blow about. der Geist der Aufklärung wehte durch Deutschland (*geh*) the spirit of enlightenment was abroad or reigned in Germany; es weht ein warmer Wind there's a warm wind (blowing), a warm wind is blowing; *siehe* Fahne, frisch, Wind.
(b) *aux sein* (*Geruch, Klang*) to drift; (*Duft*) to waft.
2 *vt* to blow (*von off*); (*sanft*) to waft.

Weh-: ~gefühl nt (*geh*) ache; ein ~gefühl befiel ihn his heart ached; ~geschrei nt wailing, cries pl of woe (*liter*); in ~geschrei ausbrechen, ein ~geschrei anstimmen to start to wail, to give vent to one's woe (*liter*); ~klage f (*liter*) lament(ation); w~klagen *vi insep* (*liter*) to lament, to wail; über etw (*acc*) w~klagen to lament (over) or bewail sth; um jdn w~klagen to lament the loss of sb; ~laut m (*liter*) cry of pain; (*bei Kummer*) cry of woe; (*leise*) whimper; w~leidig *adj* oversensitive to pain; (*jammernd*) whining attr, snivelling attr; (*voller Selbstmitleid*) sorry for oneself, self-pitying; tu or sei nicht so w~leidig! don't be such a sissy!; stop feeling sorry for yourself; er ist ja so w~leidig he whines at the least little thing; he's always feeling sorry for himself; er ist w~leidiger als ich he makes more fuss about pain than I do; ~leidigkeit f(*also geh*) over-sensitivity to pain; whininess; self-pity; ~mut f -, no pl (*geh*) melancholy; (*Sehnsucht*) wistfulness; (*nach Vergangenem*) nostalgia; w~mütig, w~mutsvoll *adj siehe* n (*geh*) melancholy; wistful; nostalgic.

Wehr¹ f -, -en (a) (*Feuer~*) fire brigade or department (*US*).
(b) (*old*) (*Bollwerk*) defences pl; (*no pl: Widerstand*) defence. mit ~ und Waffen (*old*) in full panoply (*old*); sich zur ~ setzen to defend oneself.

Wehr² nt -(e)s, -e weir.

Wehr-: in cpds defence, defense (*US*); ~beauftragte(r) m decl as adj commissioner for the armed forces; ~bereich m military district; ~dienst m military service; jdn zum ~dienst einberufen to call sb up, to draft sb (*US*); w~(dienst)pflichtig *adj* liable for military service; ~(dienst)pflichtige(r) mf decl as adj person liable for military service; (*der schon eingezogen ist*) conscript, draftee (*US*); ~dienstverweigerer m conscientious objector.

wehren 1 *vt* (*obs*) *siehe* verwehren.
2 *vr* to defend oneself; (*sich aktiv widersetzen*) to (put up a) fight. sich gegen einen Plan etc ~ to fight (against) a plan etc; dagegen weiß ich mich zu ~ I know how to deal with that.
3 *vi* + dat (*geh*) to fight; (*Einhalt gebieten*) to check. wehret den Anfängen! these things must be nipped in the bud or stopped before they get out of hand.

Wehr-: ~erfassung f compilation of the call-up list for military service; ~ersatzbehörde f military recruitment board or agency; ~ersatzdienst m alternative national service; ~etat m defence budget; w~fähig *adj* fit for military service, ablebodied; ~gang m walk along the battlements; w~haft *adj* (*geh*) able to put up a fight; *Stadt etc* well-fortified; ~hoheit f military sovereignty; ~kirche f fortified church; w~los *adj* defenceless; (*fig: gegenüber Gemeinheiten etc*) helpless; jdm w~los ausgeliefert sein to be at sb's mercy; ~losigkeit f defencelessness; helplessness; ~macht f armed forces pl; (*Hist*) Wehrmacht; ~mann m, pl -männer (*Sw*) soldier; ~paß m service record (book); ~pflicht f (*allgemeine*) ~pflicht (universal) conscription, compulsory military service; w~pflichtig *adj siehe* w~(dienst)pflichtig; ~sold m (*military*) pay; ~stand m (*old, liter*) warriors pl (*liter*), soldiers pl; (*Philos*) guardian-auxiliaries pl; ~turm m fortified tower; ~übung f reserve duty training exercise; ~wesen nt (*form*) military system.

Wehweh nt -s, -s (*baby-talk*) hurt (place).

Wehwehchen nt (*inf*) (minor) complaint. seine tausend ~ all his little aches and pains.

Weib nt -(e)s, -er woman, female (*pej*), broad (*US sl*); (*old, Bibl: Ehefrau*) wife; (*pej inf: Mann*) old woman. ~ und Kind (*old*) wife and children; eine Frau zu seinem ~(e) nehmen (*old*) to take a woman to wife (*old*); sie ist ein tolles ~ (*inf*) she's quite a woman or quite a dame (*US inf*).

Weibchen nt (*Zool*) female; (*hum: Ehefrau*) little woman (*hum*); (*pej: nicht emanzipierte Frau*) dumb female.

Weiber-: ~art f (*old, pej*) woman's way; es ist ~art, ... it's a woman's way or the way of (a) woman ...; ~fastnacht f day during the carnival period when women assume control; ~feind m woman-hater, misogynist; ~geschichten pl sexploits pl (*hum*); (*Affären auch*) womanizing sing; ~geschwätz nt (*pej*) women's talk; ~haß m (*inf*) misogyny; ~held m (*pej*) lady-killer, womanizer; ~hengst m (*sl*) tail-chaser (*inf*); ~herrschaft f (*pej*) petticoat government (*inf*); ~knoten m (*inf*) granny knot; ~kram m (*pej*) women's stuff; ~scheu f (*inf*) fear of women; w~scheu *adj* (*inf*) woman-shy (*inf*); ~volk nt (*obs*) womenfolk pl; (*pej*) females pl (*pej*); ~wirtschaft f (*pej*) henhouse (*inf*).

weibisch *adj* effeminate.

Weiblein nt little woman. ein altes ~ a little old woman, an old dear (*inf*).

weiblich *adj* (*Zool, Bot, von Frauen*) female; (*Gram, Poet, fraulich, wie Frauen*) feminine.

Weiblichkeit f femininity; (*Frauen*) women pl. die holde ~ (*hum*) the fair sex.

Weibsbild nt (*old*) woman; (*junges* ~) wench (*old*); (*pej auch*) female.

Weibsen nt -s, - usu pl (*hum inf*) woman, female.

Weibsperson f (old) woman.
Weib(s)stück nt (pej) bitch (inf), cow (inf).
weibstoll ['vaips-] adj woman-mad.
weich adj soft (auch fig, Ling, Phot); Ei soft-boiled; Fleisch, Gemüse tender; (geschmeidig) Bewegungen smooth; Mensch (nachgiebig) soft; (mitleidig) soft-hearted. ~ landen to land softly; (auf ~em Untergrund) to have a soft landing; ~ werden (lit, fig) to soften; **die Knie wurden mir ~** my knees turned to jelly, I went weak at the knees; ~ **machen** to soften; **ein ~es Herz haben** to be soft-hearted, to have a soft heart; **eine ~e Birne or einen ~en Keks haben** (sl) to be soft in the head (inf).
Weich- in cpds soft; ~**bild** nt im ~**bild der Stadt** within the city/town precincts.
Weiche¹ f -, -n (a) no pl siehe **Weichheit**. (b) (Seite) side; (von Tier auch) flank.
Weiche² f -, -n (a) (Rail) points pl (Brit), switch (US). **die ~n stellen** (lit) to switch the points; (fig) to set the course. (b) (Ausweichstelle) passing place.
weichen¹ vti (vi: aux haben or sein) to soak.
weichen² pret **wich**, ptp **gewichen** (vi aux sein (a) (Mensch, Tier, Fahrzeug: weggehen, verlassen) to move; (Armee, Mensch, Tier: zurück~) to retreat (dat, vor + dat from); (Platz machen, fig: nachgeben) to give way (dat to). **(nicht) von jdm or jds Seite ~** (not) to leave sb's side; **er wich nicht or keinen Schritt vom Wege** he did not deviate an inch; **sie wich nicht von der Stelle** she refused to or wouldn't budge (an inch); **er wich nicht von seinem Standpunkt** he would not budge or be moved from his point of view; **alles or das Blut/die Farbe wich aus ihren Wangen** (liter) the blood/colour drained from her cheeks; **die Angst ist von ihr gewichen** her fear has left her or disappeared; **weiche böser Geist!** (liter) begone evil spirit! (liter).
  (b) (Gefühl, Druck, Schmerz) (nachlassen) to ease, to abate; (verschwinden) to go.
Weichensteller m -s, - pointsman (Brit), switchman (US); (fig) guiding spirit, moving force (+ gen behind).
weich-: ~**geklopft** adj attr Fleisch hammered tender; ~**gekocht** adj attr Ei soft-boiled; Fleisch, Gemüse boiled until tender; Nudeln cooked until soft.
Weichheit f, no pl siehe **weich** softness; softness; tenderness; smoothness; softness; soft-heartedness, kindness.
Weich-: **w~herzig** adj soft-hearted; ~**herzigkeit** f soft-heartedness; ~**holz** nt softwood; ~**käse** m soft cheese; **w~klopfen**, **w~kriegen** vt sep (fig inf) to soften up.
weichlich adj (lit) soft; (fig) weak; (weibisch) effeminate; (verhätschelt) soft. **ein Kind zu ~ erziehen** to mollycoddle a child.
Weichlichkeit f (fig) weakness; effeminacy; softness.
Weichling m (pej) weakling, softy (inf).
Weich-: **w~machen** vt sep (fig) to soften up; ~**macher** m (Chem) softener, softening agent; ~**mann** m, pl **-männer** (inf) softy (inf); **w~schalig** adj soft-shelled; Apfel soft-skinned.
Weichsel¹ ['vaiksl] f - Vistula.
Weichsel² ['vaiksl] f -, -n siehe **Weichsel(kirsch)baum**, **Weichselkirsche**.
Weichsel- ['vaiksl-]: ~**(kirsch)baum** m St Lucie cherry tree; ~**kirsche** f St Lucie cherry; ~**zopf** m matted hair.
Weich-: **w~spülen** vt sep to condition; Wäsche to use (fabric) conditioner or softener on; ~**spüler** m conditioner; (für Wäsche auch) (fabric) softener; ~**teile** pl soft parts pl; (sl: Geschlechtsteile) privates pl, private parts pl; ~**tier** nt mollusc; ~**zeichner** m (Phot) soft-focusing lens.
Weide¹ f -, -n (Bot) willow.
Weide² f -, -n (Agr) pasture; (Wiese) meadow. **auf die or zur ~ treiben** to put out to pasture or to graze or to grass; **auf der ~ sein** to be grazing, to be out at pasture.
Weide-: ~**land** nt (Agr) pasture(land), grazing land, pasturage; ~**monat** m (old) month of May.
weiden 1 vi to graze. 2 vt (to put out to) graze, to put out to pasture. **seine Blicke or Augen an etw** (dat) ~ to feast one's eyes on sth. 3 vr **sich an etw** (dat) ~ (fig) to revel in; (sadistisch auch) to gloat over.
Weiden-: ~**baum** m willow tree; ~**busch** m willow bush; ~**gerte** f willow rod or switch; (zum Korbflechten) osier, wicker; ~**kätzchen** nt (pussy) willow catkin; ~**korb** m wicker basket; ~**laubsänger** m (Orn) chiffchaff; ~**rost** m cattle grid.
Weide-: ~**platz** m pasture; ~**wirtschaft** f (Econ) pastural agriculture.
weidgerecht adj in accordance with hunting principles.
Weidicht nt -(e)s, -e (obs) willow thicket.
weidlich 1 adv (mit adj) pretty. **sich über etw** (acc) ~ **amüsieren** to be highly amused at sth; **jdn ~ auslachen** to have a good laugh at sb; **etw ~ ausnutzen** to make full use of sth; **jdn ~ ausschimpfen** to give sb a good scolding; **er hat sich ~ bemüht** he tried pretty hard. 2 adj (rare) siehe **weidmännisch**.
Weid-: ~**mann** m, pl **-männer** (liter) huntsman, hunter; **w~männisch** 1 adj huntsman's attr; **das ist nicht w~männisch** that's not done in hunting; 2 adv in a huntsman's manner; **ausgebildet** as a huntsman; ~**mannsdank** interj (Hunt) thank you (as answer to ~mannsheil); ~**mannsheil** interj (Hunt) good hunting; ~**werk** nt art of hunting; **w~wund** adj (Hunt) wounded in the belly; **wie ein w~wundes Reh/ein w~wunder Hirsch** (liter) like a wounded spaniel.
Weigand m -(e)s, -e (obs) warrior.
weigern 1 vr to refuse. 2 vt (old) **jdm etw** ~ to deny sb sth.
Weigerung f refusal.
Weigerungsfall m (form) **im ~** in case of refusal (form).
Weih m -(e)s, -e (Orn) siehe **Weihe**¹.
Weihbischof m suffragan bishop.
Weihe¹ f -, -n (Orn) harrier.
Weihe² f -, -n (a) (Eccl) consecration; (Priester~) ordination. **die niederen/höheren ~n** minor/major orders. (b) (Ein-

weihung) (eines Gebäudes) inauguration; (einer Brücke) (ceremonial) opening; (eines Denkmals) unveiling. **(c)** (Feierlichkeit) solemnity.
Weihe|akt m siehe **Weihe**² (a) consecration; ordination. **(b)** inauguration; opening ceremony; unveiling ceremony.
weihen 1 vt **(a)** (Eccl) Altar, Glocke, Kirche, Bischof to consecrate; Priester to ordain. **jdn zum Bischof/Priester ~** to consecrate sb bishop/ordain sb priest.
  (b) Gebäude to inaugurate; Brücke to open; Denkmal to unveil.
  (c) (widmen) **etw jdm/einer Sache ~** to dedicate sth to sb/sth; (Eccl auch), (sehr feierlich) to consecrate sth to sb/sth; **dem Tod(e)/Untergang geweiht** (liter) doomed (to die/fall).
  2 vr + dat (liter) to devote or dedicate oneself to.
Weiher m -s, - pond.
Weihe-: ~**stätte** f holy place; **w~voll** adj (liter) solemn.
Weih-: ~**gabe** f (Rel) (votive) offering, oblation (form); ~**gefäß** nt (Rel) votive vessel.
Weihnacht f -, no pl siehe **Weihnachten**.
Weihnachten nt -, - Christmas; (geschrieben or) Xmas (inf). **fröhliche or gesegnete or schöne or frohe(s) or ein fröhliches ~!** happy or merry Christmas!; **(an) ~** at Christmas; **(zu or an) ~ nach Hause fahren** to go home for Christmas; **weiße/grüne ~** (a) white Christmas/(a) Christmas without snow; **das ist ein Gefühl wie ~(, nur nicht so feierlich)** (iro inf) it's an odd feeling.
weihnachten vi impers (poet, iro) **es weihnachtet sehr** Christmas is very much in evidence; **in der Geschäftswelt weihnachtet es schon ab Oktober** Christmas starts in October for the business world.
weihnachtlich adj Christmassy (inf), festive.
Weihnachts- in cpds Christmas; ~**abend** m Christmas Eve; ~**bäckerei** f Christmas baking; ~**baum** m Christmas tree; ~**einkauf** m Christmas shopping; ~**einkäufe** Christmas shopping sing; ~**feier** f Christmas celebration(s pl); ~**(feier)tag** nt (erster) Christmas Day; (zweiter) Boxing Day; ~**fest** nt Christmas; ~**gans** f Christmas goose; **jdn ausnehmen wie eine ~gans** (sl) to fleece sb (inf), to take sb to the cleaners (sl); ~**geld** nt Christmas money; (~**gratifikation**) Christmas bonus; (für Briefträger etc) Christmas box; ~**geschenk** nt Christmas present or gift; ~**geschichte** f Christmas story; ~**gruß** m Christmas greeting; ~**insel** f Christmas Island; ~**kaktus** m (Bot) Christmas cactus; ~**karte** f Christmas card; ~**lied** nt (Christmas) carol; ~**mann** m, pl **-männer** Father Christmas, Santa Claus; (pej inf) clown (pej inf); ~**märchen** nt (Christmas) pantomime; ~**markt** m Christmas fair; ~**spiel** nt nativity play; ~**stern** m (a) (Bot) poinsettia; (b) (Rel) star of Bethlehem; ~**tag** m siehe ~**(feier)tag**; ~**teller** m plate of biscuits, chocolates etc; ~**tisch** m table for Christmas presents; ~**zeit** f Christmas (time), Yuletide (old, liter), Christmas season (esp Comm).
Weih-: ~**rauch** m incense; **jdm ~rauch streuen** (fig) to praise or laud sb to the skies; ~**rauchfaß** nt censer, thurible (form); ~**rauchschiffchen** nt incense boat; ~**wasser** nt holy water; ~**wasserbecken** nt stoup, holy-water font.
weil conj because.
weiland adv (obs, hum) formerly. **Botho von Schmettwitz, ~ Leutnant der Kürassiere** Botho von Schmettwitz, formerly or erstwhile or one-time lieutenant of the cuirassiers; **er hat eine Frisur, wie ~ Napoleon** he has a haircut like Napoleon's in former times.
Weilchen nt **ein ~** (a little) while, a bit.
Weile f -, no pl while. **wir können eine ~ Karten spielen** we could play cards for a while; **vor einer (ganzen) ~, eine (ganze) ~ her** quite a while ago; **damit hat es noch (gute) ~, das hat noch (gute) ~** there's no hurry.
weilen vi (geh) to be; (bleiben) to stay, to tarry (poet). **er weilt nicht mehr unter uns** he is no longer with or among us.
Weiler m -s, - hamlet.
Weimarer Republik f Weimar Republic.
Wein m -(e)s, -e wine; (no pl: ~**stöcke**) vines pl; (no pl: ~**trauben**) grapes pl. **in Frankreich wächst viel ~** there is a lot of wine-growing in France; **wilder ~** Virginia creeper; **jungen ~ in alte Schläuche füllen** (prov) to pour new wine into old bottles (prov); **jdm reinen or klaren ~ einschenken** to tell sb the truth, to come clean with sb (inf); **im ~ ist Wahrheit** (Prov) in vino veritas (Prov); **heimlich ~ trinken und öffentlich Wasser predigen** (geh) not to practise what one preaches; **voll des süßen ~es sein** (liter, hum) to be heavy with wine.
Wein- in cpds (auf Getränk bezogen) wine; (auf Pflanze bezogen) vine; ~**bau** m wine-growing, viniculture (form); ~**bauer** m wine-grower; ~**beere** f grape; (Rosine) raisin; ~**beißer** m -s, - (Aus: ~**kenner**) wine connoisseur; (Aus: Lebkuchenart) sugar-coated ginger biscuit; (~**prüfer**) wine taster; ~**berg** m vineyard; ~**bergschnecke** f snail; (auf Speisekarte) escargot; ~**brand** m brandy; ~**brennerei** f brandy distillery.
Weinchen nt dim of Wein (inf) **ein ~** (etwas Wein) a little wine; **das ist vielleicht ein ~!** that's a really beautiful wine!
weinen vti to cry; (aus Trauer, Kummer auch) to weep (um for, über + acc over, aus, vor + dat with). **etw naß ~** to make sth wet with one's tears; **sich** (dat) **die Augen rot or aus dem Kopf ~** to cry one's eyes or heart out; **sich in den Schlaf ~** to cry oneself to sleep; **sich müde ~** to tire oneself out crying; **es ist zum W~!**, **man könnte ~!** it's enough to make you weep!, it makes you want to weep or cry!; **es ist zum W~ mit dieser Frau** that woman is enough to make you want to weep or cry; **leise ~d** weeping or crying softly; (inf: kleinlaut) rather crestfallen or subdued; (inf: resigniert) resignedly; (iro inf: mir nichts, dir nichts) with a shrug of the shoulders.
Weinerei f (inf) crying, howling.
weinerlich adj whining, whiny (inf).
Wein-: ~**essig** m wine vinegar; ~**faß** nt wine cask; ~**garten** m

vineyard; **~gärtner** m wine-grower; **~gegend** f wine-growing area; **~geist** m spirits of wine (old), (ethyl) alcohol; **~gummi** nt or m winegum; **~gut** nt wine-growing estate; **~händler** m wine dealer; (für Großhandel auch) vintner; **~handlung** f wine shop (Brit) or store; **~hauer** m -s, - (esp Aus) wine-grower; **~haus** nt wine tavern, wine bar; (Geschäft) wine shop; **~heber** m -s, - wine cradle or basket.

weinig adj winy, vinous (form).

Wein-: **~jahr** nt ein gutes/schlechtes **~jahr** a good/bad year for wine; **~karte** f wine list; **~keller** m wine-cellar; (Lokal) wine bar or tavern; **~kelter** f wine press; **~kenner** m connoisseur of wine, wine connoisseur.

Weinkrampf m crying fit; (Med) uncontrollable fit of crying.

Wein-: **~küfer** m cellarman; **~kultur** f wine culture; (~bau) wine-growing, viniculture (form); **~lage** f vineyard location; **~land** nt wine-growing or -producing country; **~laub** nt vine leaves pl; **~laube** f vine arbour or bower; **~laune** f in einer **~laune** beschlossen sie ... after a few glasses of wine they decided ...; **~lese** f grape harvest, vintage; **~lokal** nt wine bar; **~monat, ~mond** (old) m grape-harvesting month; (Oktober) (month of) October; **~panscher** m wine-adulterator, wine-doctorer (inf); **~panscherei** f wine-adulterating, wine-doctoring (inf); **~probe** f wine-tasting; **~prüfer** m wine taster; **~rebe** f (grape)vine; **w~rot** adj wine-red, claret; **~säure** f (Chem) tartaric acid; **~schlauch** m wineskin; **w~selig** adj merry with wine; **~sorte** f sort or type of wine; **~stein** m tartar; **~stock** m vine; **~stube** f wine tavern or bar; **~traube** f grape; **~zierl** m -s, - (n) (Aus) wine-grower; **~zwang** m obligation to order wine; **in diesem Restaurant ist ~zwang** you have to order wine in this restaurant.

weise adj (geh) wise. **die ~e Frau** (old) the midwife; **ein ~s Schicksal hat es so gewollt, daß ...** fate had so ordained that.

Weise f -, -n (a) (Verfahren etc) way, manner, fashion. **auf diese ~** in this way; **auf geheimnisvolle etc ~** in a mysterious etc way or manner or fashion, mysteriously etc; **auf jede (erdenkliche) ~** in every conceivable way; **in gewisser/keiner or keinster (inf) ~** in a/no way; **in der ~, daß ...** in such a way that ...; **jeder nach seiner ~** each in his own way, each after his own fashion; siehe **Art**.

(b) (liter: Melodie) tune, melody.

-weise adv suf (an Substantiv) as a ...; (bei Maßangabe) by the ...; (an Adjektiv) -ly. **ausnahms~** as an exception; **meter~** by the metre; **bedauerlicher~** regrettably; **er hat mir netter~ ...** it was kind of him to ...

Weisel m -s, - queen bee.

weisen pret **wies**, ptp **gewiesen** (geh) 1 vt **jdm etw ~** (lit, fig) to show sb sth; **jdn aus dem Lande ~** to expel sb; **jdn aus dem Saal ~** to eject sb (from the hall); **jdn vom Feld or Platz ~** (Sport) to order sb off (the field); (als Strafe) to send sb off; **jdn von der Schule ~** to expel sb (from school); **etw (weit) von sich ~** (fig) to reject sth (emphatically); **jdn zur Ruhe/Ordnung ~** (form) to order sb to be quiet/to behave himself; siehe **Hand**.

2 vi to point (nach to(wards), auf + acc at); siehe **Finger**.

Weise(r) m decl as adj wise man; (Denker auch) sage. **die drei ~n aus dem Morgenland** the three Wise Men from the East.

Weiser m -s, - siehe **Weisel**.

Weisheit f (a) no pl wisdom. **das war der ~ letzter Schluß** that was all they've etc came up with; **das ist auch nicht der ~ letzter Schluß** that's not exactly the ideal solution; **er glaubt, er hat die ~ mit Löffeln gegessen or gefressen** he thinks he knows it all; **er hat die ~ nicht mit Löffeln gegessen or gefressen** he's not so bright; siehe **Ende**.

(b) (weiser Spruch) wise saying, pearl of wisdom (usu iro). **eine alte ~** a wise old saying; **behalte deine ~(en) für dich!** keep your pearls of wisdom to yourself!

Weisheitszahn m wisdom tooth.

weismachen vt sep **jdm etw ~** to make sb believe sth; **er wollte uns ~, daß ...** he would have us believe that ...; **wie konnten sie ihm ~, daß ...?** how could they fool him into believing that ...?; **das kannst du mir nicht ~!** you can't expect me to believe that; **das kannst du (einem) andern ~!** (go) tell that to the marines! (inf), pull the other one(, it's got bells on)! (hum inf).

weiß adj white. **ein ~es (Blatt) Papier** a blank or clean sheet of paper; **ein ~er Fleck (auf der Landkarte)** a blank area (on the map); **das W~e Haus** the White House; **das W~e Meer** the White Sea; **der W~e Nil** the White Nile; **W~er Sonntag** Low Sunday; **der ~e Sport** tennis; skiing; **der W~e Tod** death in the snow; **~ werden** to go or turn white; (Sachen auch) to whiten; **~ wie Kreide or die Wand** white as chalk or a sheet or a ghost; **das W~e des Eis or vom Ei/von drei Eiern** eggwhite/the white(s) of three eggs; **das W~e im Auge** the whites of one's/the eyes; **er gönnt mir das W~e im Auge nicht** (inf) he begrudges me the very air I breathe.

Weiß nt -(es), - white.

Weißafrika nt White Africa.

Weis-: **w~sagen** vt insep to prophesy, to foretell; **~sager(in** f) m -s, - (liter) seer, prophet; **~sagung** f prophecy.

Weiß-: **~bier** nt weissbier (light, fizzy beer made using top-fermentation yeast); **~binder** m (dial) (Böttcher) cooper; (Anstreicher) house-painter; **~blech** nt tinplate; **w~blond** adj ash-blond(e); **~bluten** nt: **jdn bis zum ~bluten ausbeuten** to bleed sb white; **bis zum ~bluten zahlen müssen** to be bled white; **~brot** nt white bread; (Laib) loaf of white bread, white loaf; **~buch** nt (Pol) white paper; **~buche** f (Bot) hornbeam; **~dorn** m (Bot) whitehorn.

Weiße f -, -n (a) (Weißheit) whiteness. (b) siehe **Berliner**[2].

weißeln vti (S Ger, Aus) whitewash.

weißen vt to whiten; (weiß tünchen) to whitewash.

Weiße(r) mf decl as adj white, white man/woman. **die ~n** the whites, white people pl.

Weiß-: **~fisch** m whitefish; **~fuchs** m white fox; **~gardist** m

(Hist) member of the White Guard; **w~glühend** adj white-hot, incandescent; **~glut** f white heat, incandescence; **jdn zur ~glut bringen, jdn bis zur ~glut reizen** to make sb see red (inf); **~gold** nt white gold; **w~haarig** adj white-haired.

Weißheit f whiteness.

Weiß-: **~herbst** m rosé; **~käse** m (dial) siehe **Quark**; **~kohl** m, **~kraut** nt (S Ger, Aus) white cabbage.

weißlich adj whitish.

Weiß-: **~metall** nt white metal; **~näherin** f (plain) seamstress; **~russe** m, **w~russisch** adj White Russian; **~rußland** nt White Russia; **~sucht** f albinism; **~tanne** f (Bot) silver fir; **~wal** m white whale; **~wandreifen** m (Aut) whitewall (tyre); **~waren** pl linen sing; **w~waschen** vtr sep irreg (fig, usu pej) **sich/jdn w~waschen** to whitewash one's/sb's reputation; **~wein** m white wine; **~wurst** f veal sausage; **~zeug** nt linen.

Weisung f directive, instruction, direction; (Jur) ruling. **auf ~** on instructions; **ich habe ~, keine Auskünfte zu geben** I have instructions not to give any details.

Weisungs-: **~befugnis** f authority to issue directives; **w~berechtigt** adj (Jur) authorized to issue directives; **w~gebunden** adj subject to directives; **w~gemäß** adj according to or as per instructions, as instructed or directed.

weit siehe auch **weiter** 1 adj (a) wide; (fig) Begriff, Horizont etc broad; Pupille dilated; Meer open; Gewissen elastic; Herz big. **~e Kreise** or **Teile (der Bevölkerung)** large sections or parts (of the population); **im ~eren Sinne** in the broader or wider sense; **das Herz wurde mir ~** (liter) my heart swelled (with emotion); **das ist ein ~es Feld** (fig) that is a big subject.

(b) (lang) Weg, Reise, Wurf etc long. **in ~en Abständen** widely spaced; (zeitlich) at long intervals; **man hat hier einen ~en Blick** or **eine ~e Sicht** you can see a long way from here; **in ~er Ferne** far in the distance, in the far distance; **das liegt (noch) in ~er Ferne** it's still a long way away; (zeitlich auch) it's still in the distant future.

(c) (groß) Unterschied great, big.

2 adv (a) far. **~er** further, farther; **am ~esten** (the) furthest, (the) farthest; **wie ~ ist Bremen?** how far is Bremen?; **Bremen ist 10 km ~** Bremen is 10 kms away or off; **es ist noch ~ bis Bremen** it's still a long way to Bremen, there's still a long way to go till Bremen; **3,60 m ~ springen** to jump 3m 60; **wie ~ bist du gesprungen?** how far did you jump?; (sehr) **~ springen/fahren** to jump/drive a (very) long way; **~ und breit** for miles around; **~ ab** or **weg (von)** far away (from); **~ am Anfang/Ende/Rand** right at the beginning/end/edge; **ziemlich ~ am Ende** fairly near the end; **hast du es noch ~ (nach Hause)?** have you got a long way or far to go (to get home)?; **von ~em** from a long way away or off, from afar (liter); **von ~ her** from a long way away.

(b) (breit) verzweigt, herumkommen, bekannt widely; offen, öffnen wide. **10 cm ~** 10 cm wide; **~ verbreitet** widespread.

(c) **~ entfernt** far away or off, a long way away or off; **~er entfernt** further or farther away or off; **ich bin ~ davon entfernt, das zu tun** I have no intention of doing that; **der Film ist ~ davon entfernt, fertig zu sein** the film is far from (being) finished; **~ entfernt or gefehlt!** far from it!

(d) (in Entwicklung) **~ fortgeschritten** far or well advanced; **der Junge/der Frühling/die Krankheit ist schon ziemlich ~** the boy/spring/the disease is already quite (far) advanced; **wie ~ bist du?** how far have you got?; **wie ~ ist das Essen?** how far have you/they got with the food?; **so ~, so gut** so far so good; **er wird es ~ bringen** he will go far; **er hat es ~ gebracht** he has come a long way, he has got on in the world; **es so ~ bringen, daß ...** to bring it about that ...; **sie hat es so ~ gebracht, daß man sie entließ** she drove them to the point of dismissing her; **jdn so ~ bringen, daß ...** to bring sb to the point where ...; **~ kommen** to get far.

(e) (zeitlich) **es ist noch ~ bis Ostern** there's still a long way to go till Easter, Easter is still a long way off; (bis) **~ in die Nacht** (till) well or far into the night; **~ zurückliegen** to be a long way back, to be far back in the past; **~ nach Mitternacht** well or long after midnight.

(f) (fig: erheblich) (mit adj, adv) far; (mit vb) by far. **das hat unsere Erwartungen ~ übertroffen** that far exceeded our expectations; **~ über 60** well over 60; **bei ~em besser etc** als far better etc than, better etc by far than; **bei ~em der beste** far and away or by far the best; **bei ~em nicht so gut etc (wie ...)** not nearly as good etc (as ...), nowhere near as good etc (as ...); **bei ~em nicht!** not by a long shot (inf) or chalk (inf) or way!

(g) (fig: andere Wendungen) **das ist nicht ~ her** (inf) that's not up to much (inf), that's nothing to write home about (inf); **damit/mit ihm ist es nicht ~ her** (inf) this/he isn't up to much (inf), this/he isn't much use; **~/~er vom Thema** well off the subject/further away from the subject; **das würde zu ~ führen** that would be taking things too far; **zu ~ gehen** to go too far; **das geht zu ~!** that's going too far; **das Geld reicht nicht ~** the money won't go far; **sein Einfluß reicht sehr ~** his influence is far-reaching; **etw zu ~ treiben** to carry sth too far.

Weit-: **w~ab** adv **w~ab von** far (away) from; **w~aus** adv (vor comp) far; (vor superl) (by) far, far and away; **w~ausholend** adj Geste etc expansive; (fig) Erzählung etc long-drawn-out, long-winded; **etw w~ausholend erzählen** to tell sth at great length; **w~bekannt** adj attr widely known; **~blick** m (fig) vision, far-sightedness; **w~blickend** adj (fig) far-sighted.

Weite[1] f -, -n (Entfernung, Ferne) distance; (Länge) length; (Größe) expanse; (Durchmesser, Breite) width. **in die ~ blicken** to look into the distance; **etw in der ~ ändern** to alter the width of sth; **in der ~ paßt das Hemd** the shirt fits as regards width; **etw in die ~ ziehen** to pull sth out; **Pullover** to stretch out.

Weite[2] nt -n, no pl distance. **ins ~ gehen** to go out into the dis-

tance; das ~ suchen/gewinnen (liter) to take to one's heels/to
reach freedom.
weiten 1 vt to widen; (durch Ziehen auch) to stretch. 2 vr to
widen, to broaden (auch fig); (Pupille, Gefäße) to dilate; (fig
liter: Herz) to swell.
weiter 1 comp of **weit**.
   2 adj (fig) further; (zusätzlich auch) additional; (andere)
other. ~e Auskünfte further information.
   3 adv (noch hinzu) further; (außerdem) furthermore; (sonst)
otherwise; (nachher) afterwards. nichts ~, ~ nichts (darüber
hinaus nichts) nothing further or more or else; ~ nichts? is that
all?; nichts ~ or ~ nichts als ... nothing more than ..., nothing
but ...; ich brauche ~ nichts that's all I need, I don't need anything else; ich brauche nichts ~ als ... all I need is ...; er wollte ~
nichts, als nach Hause gehen all he wanted was to go home;
wenn es ~ nichts ist, ... well, if that's all (it is), ...; außer uns war
~ niemand or niemand ~ da there was nobody else there
besides us; nicht ~, ~ nicht (eigentlich) not really; das stört ~
keinen that doesn't really bother anybody; das hat ~ nichts zu
sagen that doesn't really matter, that's neither here nor there;
das macht ~ nichts it's not that or really important; etw ~ tun
to continue to do or continue doing sth, to go or carry on doing
sth; immer ~ on and on; (Anweisung) keep on (going); er hat
sich immer ~ verbessert he kept on improving; (nur) immer
~! keep at it!; und ~? and then?; was geschah (dann) ~? what
happened then or next?; und so ~ and so on or forth, et cetera;
und so ~ und so fort and so on and so forth, et cetera et cetera;
kein Wort ~! not another word!; siehe **Weitere(s)**.
weiter- pref (~machen mit) to carry on or go on or continue
+prp, to continue to +infin; (nicht aufhören mit) to keep on or
go on +prp; (bei Bewegung, Beförderung, Reise etc) vb+ on.
Weiter- pref mit n further; (bei Bewegung, Beförderung, Reise
etc) continuation of.
Weiter-: w~arbeiten vi sep siehe **weiter-** to carry on etc
working, to work on; an einer Sache (dat) w~arbeiten to do
some more work on sth; w~befördern* vt sep to send on; jdn (in
Firma etc) to promote further; w~behandeln* vt sep siehe
weiter- to carry on etc treating; ~behandlung f further treatment; w~bestehen* vi sep irreg to continue to exist, to survive;
~bestehen nt continued existence; w~bewegen* sep 1 vt to
move further; 2 vr to move further; (w~hin) to carry on etc
moving; w~bilden sep 1 vt jdn w~bilden to give sb further
education, to educate sb further; 2 vr to continue one's education; ~bildung f continuation of one's education; (an
Hochschule) further education; das bringt uns auch nicht w~ that's not
much help (to us), that doesn't get us any further; w~denken
sep irreg 1 vt to think out (further); 2 vi to think it out; (an
Zukünftiges) to think ahead; w~empfehlen* vt sep irreg to
recommend (to one's friends etc); w~entwickeln* sep 1 vt to
develop; Idee to develop (further); 2 vr to develop (zu into);
~entwicklung f development; w~erzählen* vt sep siehe
weiter- to carry on etc telling; Geheimnis etc to repeat, to pass
on; das hat er der ganzen Klasse w~erzählt he told the whole
class.
Weitere(s) nt decl as adj further details pl. ich habe nichts ~s
zu sagen I have nothing further to say; das ~ the rest; alles ~
everything else, all the rest; des w~n in addition, furthermore;
bis auf w~s for the time being; (amtlich, auf Schildern etc)
until further notice; im w~n subsequently, afterwards; zum
w~n furthermore, in addition, on top of that; siehe **ohne**.
Weiter-: w~fahren sep irreg 1 vt siehe **weiter-** to carry on etc
driving, to keep on driving; 2 vi aux sein (a) (Fahrt fortsetzen)
to go on, to continue; (durchfahren) to drive on; (w~reisen) to
travel on; (b) (dial) siehe **fortfahren**. 2b; über der ~fahrt sahen wir ... before continuing our journey we saw ...; w~fliegen vi sep irreg aux sein
to fly on; die Maschine fliegt in 10 Minuten w~ the plane will
take off again in 10 minutes; ~flug m continuation of the/one's
flight; auf dem ~flug after we'd taken off again; Passagiere
zum ~flug nach ... passengers continuing their flight to ...;
w~führen sep 1 vt to continue; Gespräch auch to carry on
(with); 2 vi to continue, to lead on; das führt nicht w~ (fig) that
doesn't lead or get us anywhere; w~führend adj Schule secondary; ~gabe f passing on; (von Informationen, Erbfaktoren
auch) transmission; w~geben vt sep irreg to pass on; to
transmit; w~gehen vi sep irreg aux sein to go on; bitte
w~gehen! (Polizist etc) move along or on (there), please!; so
kann es nicht w~gehen (fig) things can't go on like this; wie soll
es nun w~gehen? what's going to happen now?; w~gehend adj,
adv (Aus) comp of **weitgehend**; w~helfen vi sep irreg to help
(along) (jdm sb); w~hin siehe **außerdem** furthermore, on top of
that; etw w~hin tun to carry on etc doing sth; w~kämpfen vi
sep to fight on; w~kommen vi sep irreg aux sein to get further;
(fig auch) to make progress or headway; nicht w~kommen
(fig) to be stuck or bogged down; wir kommen einfach nicht w~
we're just not getting anywhere; ~kommen nt advancement;
w~können vi sep irreg to be able to carry on or go on or continue; ich kann nicht w~ I can't go on; (bei Rätsel, Prüfung etc)
I'm stuck; w~laufen vi sep irreg aux sein to run/walk on; (Film)
to go on; (Betrieb, Produktion) to go on, to continue; (Gehalt) to
continue to be paid; (Motor) to keep on running; ich kann nicht
w~laufen I can't walk any further; den Motor w~laufen lassen
to leave the engine running; w~leben vi sep to live on, to continue to live; w~leiten vt sep to pass on (an +acc to);
(w~befördern, senden) to forward; w~machen vti sep to carry
on (etw with sth), to continue; w~machen! (Mil) carry on!;
~marsch m zum ~marsch bereit ready to march on; auf dem
~marsch waren sie ... as they marched on they were ...;
w~reichen vt sep to pass on; w~reichend adj further-
reaching; ~reise f continuation of the/one's journey; ich

wünsche Ihnen eine gute ~reise I hope the rest of the journey
goes well; auf der ~reise nach ... when I etc was travelling on to
...; w~rücken sep 1 vt to move further along; 2 vi aux sein to
move up, to move further along.
weiters adv (Aus) siehe **ferner**.
weiter-: ~sagen vt sep to repeat, to pass on; ~sagen! pass it on!;
nicht ~sagen! don't tell anyone!; ~schenken vt sep to give
away (to somebody else); ~schlafen vi sep irreg to sleep on, to
go on sleeping; (wieder einschlafen) to go back to sleep;
~schleppen sep 1 vt to haul or drag further; 2 vr to drag or haul
oneself on; ~senden sep irreg vti (Rad, TV) siehe **weiter-** to
carry on etc broadcasting; 2 vt (form) to forward; ~spinnen vt
sep irreg (fig) Gedanken etc to develop further; den Faden
einer Erzählung ~spinnen to tease out the threads of a story;
~tragend adj (Mil) longer-range attr; (fig) further-reaching.
Weiterungen pl (old, form) complications pl, difficulties pl.
unangenehme ~ zur Folge haben to have unpleasant consequences.
Weiter-: w~verarbeiten* vt sep to process; w~verbreiten* vt
1 vt to spread (further), to repeat, to propagate (form); 2 vr to
spread (further); w~verfolgen* vt sep siehe **weiter-** Entwicklung, Straße to carry on etc following; Verbrecher to continue
to pursue; Idee to pursue further; ~verkauf m resale; nicht
zum ~verkauf bestimmt not for resale; w~verkaufen* vti sep
to resell; w~vermieten* vt sep to sublet; ~versand m redis-
patch; w~wissen vi sep irreg nicht (mehr) w~wissen not to
know how to go on; (bei Rätsel, Prüfung) to be stuck; (verzweifelt sein) to be at one's wits' end; w~wollen vi sep irreg to
want to go on; der Esel wollte einfach nicht w~ the donkey
simply wouldn't go any further; w~wursteln vi sep (inf) to
muddle on; w~zahlen vti sep to continue paying or to pay.
weitestgehend 1 adj superl of **weitgehend**. 2 adv to the
greatest possible extent.
weit-: ~gehend comp ~gehender or (Aus) weitergehend,
superl weitestgehend or ~gehendst 1 adj Vollmachten etc far-
reaching, extensive, wide; Übereinstimmung etc a large
degree of; er hatte viel ~gehende Befürchtungen his fears
went a lot further than that; 2 adv to a great or large extent,
largely; ~gereist adj attr, comp weiter gereist, superl am
weitesten gereist widely travelled; ~gesteckt adj attr
ambitious; ~greifend adj attr far-reaching; ~her adv (auch
von ~her) from a long way away, from far away, from afar
(liter); ~hergeholt adj attr far-fetched; ~herzig adj understanding, charitable; ~hin adv over a long distance, for a long
way; (fig) bekannt, beliebt widely; unbekannt largely; (wert-
gehend) to a large or great extent; ~hinaus adv a long way.
weitläufig adj (a) Park, Gebäude spacious; (verzweigt)
rambling; Dorf covering a wide area, sprawling attr; (fig)
Erzählung lengthy, long-drawn-out, long-winded. etw ~
erzählen to tell sth at (great) length. (b) Verwandte distant.
Weitläufigkeit f siehe adj (a) spaciousness; rambling nature;
sprawling nature; length, long-windedness.
Weit-: w~maschig adj Netz coarse-meshed, wide-meshed,
broad-meshed; Gestricktes loosely knitted, loose-knit;
w~reichend adj, comp w~reichender or (Aus) weiter-
reichend, superl weitestreichend (fig) far-reaching; (Mil)
long-range attr; w~schauend adj (fig) far-sighted;
w~schweifig adj long-winded, circumlocutory, prolix (form);
~schweifigkeit f long-windedness, prolixity (form); ~sicht f
(fig) far-sightedness; w~sichtig adj (Med) long-sighted, far-
sighted (esp US); (fig) far-sighted; ~sichtigkeit f (Med) long-
sightedness, far-sightedness (esp US); w~springen vi sep
(infin only) (Sport) to do the long jump or broad jump (US);
~springen nt (Sport) long-jumping, broad-jumping (US);
~springer m (Sport) long-jumper, broad-jumper (US);
~sprung m (Sport) the long jump or broad jump (US);
w~tragend adj, comp w~tragender or (Aus) weitertragend,
superl weitesttragend (Mil) long-range attr; (fig) far-reaching,
far-ranging; w~um adv for miles around.
Weitung f (geh) widening.
Weit-: w~verbreitet adj attr widespread, common; Ansicht
auch widely held; Zeitung with a wide circulation;
w~verzweigt adj attr Straßensystem branching out in all
directions; Konzern with many branches; ~winkelobjektiv nt
wide-angle lens.
Weizen m -s, no pl wheat; siehe **Spreu**.
Weizen-: ~bier nt light, very fizzy beer made by using wheat,
malt and top-fermentation yeast; ~brot nt wheat(en) bread;
~keime pl (Cook) wheatgerm sing; ~keimöl nt (Cook)
wheatgerm oil; ~mehl nt wheat(en) flour; ~schrot m or nt
wheatmeal.
welch 1 interrog pron inv (a) (geh: in Ausrufen) what. ~ fried-
liches Bild! what a peaceful scene!; ~ unbeschreibliche
Wonne! what indescribable bliss!
   (b) (in indirekten Fragesätzen) ~ (ein) what.
   2 rel pron inv X, Y und Z, ~ letztere(r, s) ... (obs, form) X, Y
and Z, the last of which/whom ...
welche(r, s) 1 interrog pron (a) (adjektivisch) what; (bei Wahl
aus einer begrenzten Menge) which. ~r Mensch könnte
behaupten ...? what person could claim ...?; ~s Kleid soll ich
anziehen, das rote oder das grüne? which dress shall I wear, the
red one or the green one?
   (b) (substantivisch) which (one). ~r von den beiden? which
(one) of the two?; ~s sind die Symptome dieser Krankheit?
what are the symptoms of this illness?; es gibt viele schöne
Frauen, aber ~ könnte sich mit Isabella vergleichen? there are
many beautiful women, but which of them could compare with
Isabella?
   (c) (in Ausrufen) ~ Schande/Freude etc! what (a) dis-
grace/what joy etc!
   2 indef pron some; (in Fragen, konditional auch, verneint)

any. **es gibt ~, die glauben ...** there are some (people) who think ...; **ich habe keine Tinte/Äpfel, haben Sie ~?** I don't have any ink/apples, do you have some *or* any?

3 *rel pron* (*rare*) (*Mensch*) who; (*Sache*) which, that. **~(r, s)** *auch* **immer** whoever/whichever/whatever.

welcher|art 1 *interrog adj inv* (*geh*) (*attributiv*) what kind of; (*substantivisch*) of what kind. **sagen Sie mir, ~ Ihre Erfahrungen sind** tell me what sort of experiences you (have) had; **~ Ihre Erfahrungen auch sein mögen** whatever your experiences may have been like. **2** *interrog adv* in what way.

welchergestalt *interrog adv* (*rare*) in what manner, how.

welcherlei *interrog adj inv* (*geh*) what kind *or* sort of.

welches *pron siehe* **welche(r, s).**

Welfe *m* **-n, -n** (*Hist*) Guelph.

welfisch *adj* (*Hist*) Guelphic.

welk *adj Blume, Pflanze* wilted, faded; *Blatt* dead; (*fig*) *Schönheit* fading, wilting; *Haut, Gesicht* tired-looking; (*schlaff*) flaccid; *Hände* withered. **wie ein ~es Pflänzchen** (*inf*) like a wet rag (*inf*).

welken *vi aux* sein (*lit, fig*) to fade, to wilt; (*Haut, Gesicht*) to grow tired-looking; (*schlaff werden*) to sag.

Welkheit *f* wilted state; (*von Haut, Gesicht*) tired look.

Wellblech *nt* corrugated iron.

Welle *f* **-, -n** (a) wave (*auch fig, Phys, im Haar etc*); (*Rad: Frequenz*) wavelength. **sein Grab in den ~n finden** (*geh*) to go to a watery grave; **weiche ~** (*inf*) soft line; **mach keine ~n!** (*inf*) don't make such a fuss; (*hohe*) **~n schlagen** (*fig*) to create (quite) a stir.

(b) (*fig: Mode*) craze. **die Neue ~** (*Film*) the nouvelle vague, the New Wave.

(c) (*Tech*) shaft.

(d) (*Sport*) circle.

(e) (*dial: Bündel*) faggot.

wellen 1 *vt Haar* to wave; *Blech etc* to corrugate. **2** *vr* to be/become wavy. **gewelltes Haar** wavy hair.

Wellen-: **w~artig** *adj* wave-like; *Linie etc* wavy; **~bad** *nt* swimming-pool with artificially induced waves; **~bereich** *m* (*Phys, Telec*) frequency range; (*Rad*) waveband; **~berg** *m* mountainous *or* giant wave; **~brecher** *m* breakwater, groyne; **w~förmig 1** *adj* wave-like; *Linie* wavy; **2** *adv* in the form of waves; **~gang** *m, no pl* waves *pl*, swell; *starker* **~gang** heavy sea(s) *or* swell; *leichter* **~gang** light swell; **~kamm** *m* crest (of a wave); **~länge** *f* (*Phys, Telec*) wavelength; **sich auf jds ~länge** (*acc*) **einstellen** (*inf*) to get on sb's wavelength (*inf*); **auf der gleichen ~länge sein** *or* **liegen, die gleiche ~länge haben** (*inf*) to be on the same wavelength (*inf*); **~linie** *f* wavy line; **~mechanik** *f* (*Phys*) wave mechanics *sing*; **~reiten** *nt* (*Sport*) surfing; (*auf Fluß*) sport of balancing on a board attached by a rope to the riverbank; **~schlag** *m* breaking of the waves; (*sanft auch*) lapping of the waves; (*heftig auch*) pounding of the waves; **~sittich** *m* budgerigar, budgie (*inf*); **~tal** *nt* trough (of a wave).

Well-: **~fleisch** *nt* boiled pork; **~hornschnecke** *f* whelk.

wellig *adj Haar etc* wavy; *Oberfläche, Fahrbahn* uneven; *Hügelland* rolling, undulating.

Wellpappe *f* corrugated cardboard.

Welpe *m* **-n, -n** pup, whelp; (*von Wolf, Fuchs*) cub, whelp.

Wels *m* **-es, -e** catfish.

welsch *adj* (a) (*old*) Latin, Southern European; (*~sprachig*) Romance-speaking. **~e Nuß** (*old*) walnut; **~e Sitten und Gebräuche** dubious morals and practices. **(b)** (*Aus pej: italienisch*) Eyetie (*pej sl*). **die W~en** the Eyeties (*pej sl*). **(c)** (*Sw*) (Swiss-)French. **die ~e Schweiz** French Switzerland.

Welsch-: **~land** *nt* (*Sw*) French Switzerland; **~schweizer** *m* (*Sw*) French Swiss; **w~schweizerisch** *adj* (*Sw*) Swiss-French.

Welt *f* **-, -en** (*lit, fig*) world. **die ~ im Kleinen/Großen** the microcosm/macrocosm; **die (große) weite ~** the big wide world; **der höchste Berg der ~** the highest mountain in the world, the world's highest mountain; **die ~ von heute/morgen** the world of today/tomorrow, today's/tomorrow's world; **die ~ des Theaters/Kindes** the world of the theatre/child, the theatre/child's world; **die Alte/Neue/Freie/Dritte ~** the Old/New/Free/Third World; **die große** *or* **vornehme ~** high society; **alle ~, Gott und die ~** everybody, the whole world, the world and his wife (*hum*); **eine ~ brach für ihn zusammen** his whole world collapsed about him *or* his ears, the bottom fell out of his world; **das ist doch nicht die ~** it isn't as important as all that; **davon** *or* **deswegen geht die ~ nicht unter** (*inf*) it isn't the end of the world; **das kostet doch nicht die ~** it won't cost the earth; **uns/sie trennen ~en, zwischen uns/ihnen liegen ~en** (*fig*) we/they are worlds apart; **auf der ~** in the world; **davon gibt es noch mehr auf der ~** there are plenty of those around; **etw mit auf die ~ bringen** to be born with sth; **aus aller ~** from all over the world; **dieser Ort ist doch nicht aus der ~** this place isn't *that* cut off; **aus der ~ schaffen** to eliminate; **aus der ~ scheiden** (*geh*) to depart this life (*liter*); (*Selbstmord begehen*) to put an end to one's life; **in aller ~** all over the world; **in alle ~ zerstreut** scattered all over the world *or* globe; **warum/wer in aller ~ ...?** why/who on earth *or* in the world ...?; **so geht es nun mal in der ~** that's the way of the world, that's the way things go; **in einer anderen ~ leben** to live in a different world; **in seiner eigenen ~ leben** to live in a world of one's own; **um nichts in der ~, nicht um alles in der ~, um keinen Preis der ~** not for anything on earth, not for love (n)or money, not at any price; **fröhlich/finster in die ~ gucken** to look happy/gloomy; **ein Kind in die ~ setzen** to bring a child into the world; **ein Gerücht in die ~ setzen** to put about *or* spread a rumour; **ein Mann/eine Dame von ~** a man/woman of the world; **die beste Frau etc (von) der ~** the best woman *etc* in the world; **vor aller ~** publicly, in front of everybody, openly; **zur ~ bringen** to give birth to, to bring into the world; **auf die** *or* **zur ~ kommen** to come into the world, to be born; *siehe* **Brett, Ende.**

Welt- *in cpds* world; **w~abgewandt** *adj* withdrawn; **~all** *nt, no pl* universe, cosmos; **~alter** *nt* age, epoch; **w~anschaulich** *adj* ideological; **~anschauung** *f* philosophy of life; (*Philos, Pol*) world view, weltanschauung; **~ausstellung** *f* world exhibition, world's fair; **~bank** *f* World Bank; **w~bekannt** *adj* world-famous; **w~berühmt** *adj* world-famous; *Schriftsteller, Künstler etc auch* world-renowned; **~beste(r)** *mf* world's best; **w~beste(r, s)** *adj attr* world's best; **~bestleistung** *f* world's best performance, world best (*inf*); **w~bewegend** *adj* world-shaking, world-shattering; **~bild** *nt* conception of the world; (*jds Ansichten*) philosophy, view of life; **~blatt** *nt* (*Press*) international (news)paper; **~bürger** *m* citizen of the world, cosmopolitan; **~bürgertum** *nt* cosmopolitanism; **~chronik** *f* world chronicle; **~dame** *f* woman of the world.

Welten-: **~bummler** *m* globetrotter; **~raum** *m siehe* Weltraum.

weltentrückt *adj* remote, unworldly.

Weltergewicht *nt* (*Boxen*) welterweight.

Welt-: **w~erschütternd** *adj* world-shattering, world-shaking; **w~fern** *adj* unrealistic, naive; **~flucht** *f* flight from reality, escapism; **w~fremd** *adj* unworldly; **~fremdheit** *f* unworldliness; **~friede(n)** *m* world peace; **~friedenstag** *m* (*esp DDR*) World Peace Day; **~gefüge** *nt* universe, world system, scheme of things; **~geist** *m* (*Philos*) world spirit; **~geistliche(r)** *m* secular priest; **~geltung** *f* international standing, world-wide recognition; **~gericht** *nt* Last Judgement; **~gerichtshof** *m* International Court; **~geschichte** *f* world history; **in der ~geschichte herumfahren** (*inf*) to travel around all over the place; **w~geschichtlich** *adj* **~geschichtliche Kenntnisse** knowledge of world history; **ein w~geschichtliches Ereignis** an important event in the history of the world; **von w~geschichtlicher Bedeutung** of great significance in world history; **w~geschichtlich gesehen, aus w~geschichtlicher Sicht** looked at from the point of view of world history; **~gesundheitsorganisation** *f* World Health Organization; **~getriebe** *nt* (*liter*) (hustle and) bustle of the world; **w~gewandt** *adj* sophisticated, well-versed in the ways of the world; **~gewandtheit** *f* sophistication, experience in the ways of the world; **~handel** *m* world trade; **~herrschaft** *f* world domination; **~hilfssprache** *f* international auxiliary language; **~karte** *f* map of the world; **~kenntnis** *f* (*rare*) knowledge of the world; **w~kind** *nt* (*liter*) worldling (*liter*); **~kirchenrat** *m* World Council of Churches; **~klasse** *f* ein Hochspringer der **~klasse** a world-class high-jumper; **~klasse sein** to be world-class; (*inf*) to be great (*inf*) *or* fantastic (*inf*); **w~klug** *adj* worldly-wise; **~klugheit** *f* worldly wisdom, experience in the ways of the world; **~körper** *m* (*old*) *siehe* Himmelskörper; **~krieg** *m* world war; **der erste** *or* **Erste** (*abbr* I.)/**zweite** *or* **Zweite** (*abbr* II.) **~krieg** World War One/Two (*abbr* I/II), the First/Second World War; **~kugel** *f* globe; **~lauf** *m* way of the world; **w~lich** *adj* worldly, mundane; (*nicht kirchlich, geistlich*) secular; *Macht* temporal; **~literatur** *f* world literature; **~macht** *f* world power; **~mann** *m, pl* **-männer** man of the world; **w~männisch** *adj* urbane, sophisticated; **~marke** *f* name known all over the world; **~markt** *m* world market; **~marktpreis** *m* world (market) price; **~meer** *nt* ocean; **die sieben ~meere** the seven seas; **~meister** *m* world *or* world's (*US*) champion; **England/die englische Mannschaft ist ~meister** England/the English team are (the) world *or* world's (*US*) champions; **~meisterschaft** *f* world *or* world's (*US*) championship; (*Ftbl*) World Cup; **w~offen** *adj* liberal-minded, cosmopolitan; **~offenheit** *f* cosmopolitan attitudes *pl*; **~ordnung** *f* world order; **~politik** *f* world politics *pl*; **w~politisch** *adj* eine/die **w~politische Entwicklung** a development in/the development of world politics; **eine w~politische Entscheidung** a decision affecting world politics; **von w~politischer Bedeutung** of importance in world politics; **w~politisch gesehen, aus w~politischer Sicht** seen from the standpoint of world politics.

Weltraum *m* (outer) space.

Weltraum- *in cpds* space; **~fahrer** *m* space traveller; **~fahrt** *f* space travel; **~fahrzeug** *nt* spacecraft, spaceship; **~forschung** *f* space research; **~station** *f* space station.

Welt-: **~reich** *nt* empire; **~reise** *f* world tour, journey round the world; **eine ~reise machen** to go round the world; **das ist doch schließlich keine ~reise** (*inf*) it's not the other end of the world; **~reisende(r)** *mf* globetrotter; **~rekord** *m* world *or* world's (*US*) record; **~rekordinhaber(in** *f*), **~rekordler(in** *f*) *m* **-s, -** world *or* world's (*US*) record holder; **~religion** *f* world religion; **~revolution** *f* world revolution; **~ruf** *m* world(-wide) reputation; **~ruf haben** to have a world(-wide) reputation; **~ruhm** *m* world fame; **~schmerz** *m* world-weariness, weltschmerz (*liter*); **~sicherheitsrat** *m* (*Pol*) (United Nations) Security Council; **~sprache** *f* world language; **~stadt** *f* international *or* cosmopolitan city, metropolis; **w~städtisch** *adj* cosmopolitan; **~umsegler** *m* **-s, -** circumnavigator (of the globe); (*Sport*) round-the-world yachtsman; **w~umspannend** *adj* world-wide, global; **~untergang** *m* (*lit, fig*) end of the world; **~verbesserer** *m* starry-eyed idealist; **~weisheit** *f* (*liter*) worldly wisdom; **w~weit** *adj* world-wide, global; **~wirtschaft** *f* world economy; **~wirtschaftskrise** *f* world economic crisis; **~wunder** *nt* **die sieben ~wunder** the Seven Wonders of the World; **er starrte mich an wie ein ~wunder** (*fig*) he stared at me as if I were from another planet *or* as if I were some kind of freak.

wem *dat of* **wer 1** *interrog pron* who ... to, to whom. **mit/von etc ~ ...** who ... with/from *etc*, with/from *etc* whom; **von euch soll ich den Schlüssel geben?** which (one) of you should I give the key to?, to which (one) of you should I give the key?

2 *rel pron* (*derjenige, dem*) the person (who ...) to, the person to whom ...; (*jeder, dem*) anyone to whom ..., anyone ... to ~ ... *auch* (**immer**) whoever ... to, no matter who ... to.

3 *indef pron* (*inf: jemandem*) to/for somebody; (*mit prep, bestimmten Verben*) somebody; (*in Fragen, konditionalen Sätzen auch*) (to/for) anybody.

Wemfall *m* dative (case).

wen *acc of* **wer 1** *interrog pron* who, whom. **an ~ hast du geschrieben?** who did you write to?, to whom did you write?; **~ von den Schülern kennst du?** which (one) of these pupils do you know?

2 *rel pron* (*derjenige, den*) the person (who *or* whom); (*jeder, den*) anybody (who *or* whom). **~ ... auch immer** whoever ...

3 *indef pron* (*inf: jemanden*) (*inf*) somebody; (*in Fragen, konditionalen Sätzen auch*) anybody.

Wende[1] *f* **-, -n** turn; (*Veränderung*) change; (*Turnen: am Pferd*) face *or* front vault. **die ~ vom 19. zum 20. Jahrhundert** the transition from the 19th to the 20th century; **nach dem Tod seines Vaters nahm seine Entwicklung eine ~** after the death of his father his development changed direction *or* started to take a different direction.

Wende[2] *m* **-n, -n** Wend.

Wendehals *m* (*Orn*) wryneck.

Wendekreis *m* **(a)** tropic. **der nördliche ~** (*Geog*), **der ~ des Krebses** (*Astrol*) the Tropic of Cancer; **der südliche ~** (*Geog*), **der ~ des Steinbocks** (*Astrol*) the Tropic of Capricorn. **(b)** (*Aut*) turning circle.

Wendel *f* **-, -n** spiral, helix; (*in Glühbirne etc*) coil.

Wendel-: **~bohrer** *m* twist drill; **~rutsche** *f* spiral chute; **~treppe** *f* spiral staircase.

Wendemarke *f* (*Sport*) turning mark.

wenden *pret* **wendete** *or* (*liter*) **wandte**, *ptp* **gewendet** *or* (*liter*) **gewandt 1** *vt* **(a)** to turn (*auch Sew*); (*auf die andere Seite*) to turn (over); (*in die entgegengesetzte Richtung*) to turn (round); (*Cook*) to toss. **bitte ~!** please turn over; **seinen Blick nach Norden ~** (*geh*) to turn *or* bend one's eyes *or* to look to(wards) the north; **seinen Schritt gen Süden ~** (*liter*) to turn *or* bend one's steps southwards (*liter*); **sie wandte kein Auge von ihm** (*geh*) she did not take her eyes off him; **wie man es auch wendet ..., man kann die Sache *or* es drehen und ~, wie man will** ... (*fig*) whichever way you (care to) look at it ...

(b) (*aufbringen*) **Geld/Zeit an etw** (*acc*) **~** (*geh*) to spend money/time on sth; **viel Mühe/Sorgfalt *etc* an etw** (*acc*) **~** (*geh*) to devote a lot of effort/care *etc* to sth.

2 *vr* **(a)** to turn (round); (*Wetter, Glück*) to change, to turn. **sich nach links/zum Gehen/zur Tür ~** to turn to the left/to go/to the door; **sich ins Gegenteil ~** to become the opposite; **das Gespräch wendete sich** the conversation took another turn; **seine Liebe/Freude *etc* wendete sich ins Gegenteil** his love/joy turned to hate/despair; **sich von jdm ~** (*esp Bibl*) to turn from sb (*liter*); **sich zu jdm/etw ~** to turn to face sb/sth, to turn towards sb/sth; **sich zum Guten *or* Besseren/Schlimmeren ~** to take a turn for the better/worse; **sich zum besten ~** to turn out for the best; **sich zur Flucht ~** (*old, liter*) to take to flight.

(b) sich an jdn ~ (*um Auskunft*) to consult sb; (*um Hilfe*) to turn to sb; (*Buch, Fernsehserie etc*) to be directed at sb, to be (intended) for sb; **sich gegen jdn/etw ~** to come out against sb/sth, to oppose sb/sth.

3 *vi* to turn (*auch Sport*); (*umkehren*) to turn round.

Wende-: **~platz** *m* turning area *or* place; **~punkt** *m* turning point; (*Geometry*) point of inflection.

wendig *adj* agile, nimble; *Auto etc* manoeuvrable; (*fig*) *Mensch* agile.

Wendigkeit *f* *siehe adj* agility, nimbleness; manoeuvrability; agility.

Wendin *f* Wendish woman, Wend.

wendisch *adj* Wendish.

Wendung *f* **(a)** turn (*auch Mil*); (*Veränderung*) change. **eine interessante/unerwartete ~ nehmen** (*fig*) to take an interesting/unexpected turn; **eine ~ zum Besseren *or* Guten/Schlechten nehmen** to take a turn for the better/worse, to change for the better/worse; **einer Sache** (*dat*) **eine unerwartete/neue ~ geben** to give sth an unexpected/new turn; **das gab seinem Leben eine neue ~** that changed the direction of his life; **eine interessante *etc* ~ trat ein** there was an interesting *etc* turn of events.

(b) (*Rede~*) expression, phrase.

Wenfall *m* accusative (case).

wenig *siehe auch* **weniger, wenigste(r, s) 1** *adj, indef pron* **(a)** *sing* little; (*unverändert alleinstehend*) not much. **ich habe ~** I have only a little; (*nur*) **~ Geld** (only a) little money; **ich besitze nur ~** I only own a few things, I don't own much, I own little; **hast du Zeit? — ~!** I have you got time? — not much; **das ist ~** that isn't much; **so ~** so little; **du sagst so ~** you're not saying much; **darüber weiß ich ~** I don't know much about that, I know little about that; **mein ~es Geld** what little money I have; **das ~e, was er übrig hatte** the little he had left; **das ~e Geld muß ausreichen** we'll have to make do with this small amount of money; **um ein ~es jünger (als)** (*geh*) a little younger (than); **es fehlte (nur) ~, und er wäre überfahren worden** he was very nearly run over; **wir haben nicht ~ Mühe damit gehabt** we had more than a little *or* no little difficulty with that; **er gibt sich mit ~(em) zufrieden** (*verlangt nicht viel*) he is satisfied with a little; (*ist selten zufrieden*) he isn't satisfied with much; **sie hat zu ~ Geld *etc*** she doesn't have enough money *etc*; **ein Exemplar zu ~** haben to have one copy too few; **ich habe ihm £ 20 zu ~ geboten** I offered him £20 too little.

(b) **~e** *pl* (*ein paar*) a few; (*einschränkend: nicht viele*) few; **da wir nur ~e sind** as there are only a few of us, as we are only a few; **er ist ein Freund, wie es nur ~e gibt** there are few friends like him; **in ~en Tagen** in (just) a few days; **es sind nur noch ~e Stunden, bis ...** there are only a few hours to go until ...; **nicht ~e (waren da)** quite a few people (were there); **einige ~e Leute** a few people.

(c) (*auch adv*) **ein ~** a little; **ein ~ Salz/besser** a little salt/better.

2 *adv* little. **sie kommt (nur) ~ raus** she doesn't get out very often; **er hat sich nicht ~ geärgert** he was not a little annoyed; **das überraschte ihn nicht ~** he was more than a little surprised; **~ besser** little better; **~ bekannt** little-known *attr*, little known *pred*; **~ mehr** little more, not much more; **~ erfreulich** not very pleasant.

Wenig *nt*: **viele ~ machen ein Viel** (*Prov*) it all adds up, many a mickle makes a muckle (*Scot Prov*).

weniger *comp of* **wenig 1** *adj, indef pron* less; *pl* fewer. **~ werden** to get less and less; **mein Geld wird immer ~** my money is dwindling away; **er wird immer ~** (*inf*) he's getting thinner and thinner; **~ wäre mehr gewesen** it's quality not quantity that counts.

2 *adv* less. **ihr kommt es ~ auf die Liebe als (vielmehr) auf das Geld an** she's less interested in love than in money; **die Vorlesung war ~ lehrreich als belustigend** the lecture was not so much instructive as amusing; **das finde ich ~ schön!** that's not so nice!; **ich kann seinen Brief kaum lesen, noch viel ~ verstehen** I can hardly read his letter much less *or* let alone understand it; **je mehr ... desto *or* um so ~ ...** the more ... the less ...; **ich glaube ihm um so ~, weil ...** I believe him all the less because ...; **ich möchte nichts ~, als ihn (zu) beleidigen** the last thing I'd want to do is insult him.

3 *conj, prep + acc or gen* less. **sieben ~ drei ist vier** seven less three is four.

Wenigkeit *f* (*dated: Kleinigkeit*) little, small amount. **meine ~** (*hum inf*) yours truly (*inf*); **und meine ~ hat er vergessen** and he forgot little me (*hum inf*).

wenigstens *adv* at least.

wenigste(r, s) *superl of* **wenig** *adj, indef pron*, **am ~n** *adv* least; *pl* fewest. **er hat von uns allen das ~ *or* am ~n Geld** he has the least money of any of us; **sie hat von uns allen die ~n *or* am ~n Sorgen** she has the fewest worries of any of us; **von den vier Farben finde ich diese am ~n schön** of the four colours I think this one is the least attractive; **das konnte er am ~n vertragen** he could tolerate that least of all; **die ~n (Leute) glauben das** very few (people) believe that; **das ist (doch) das ~, was du tun könntest** that's the (very) least you could do; **das ist noch das ~!** (*inf*) that's the least of it!; **er kam, als sie es am ~n erwartete** he came when she least expected it; **das am ~n!** that least of all!; **zum ~n** (*form*) at least.

wenn *conj* **(a)** (*konditional, konzessiv bei Wünschen*) if. **~ er nicht gewesen wäre, hätte ich meine Stelle verloren** if it had not been *or* had it not been for him, I'd have lost my job; **selbst *or* und ~ even if**; **~ das Wörtchen ~ nicht wär'(, wär' mein Vater Millionär)** (*prov*) if ifs and ans were pots and pans (there'd be no need for tinkers) (*Prov*); **~ ... auch ... even though** *or* if ...; **~ ... gleich ...** (*geh*) although ..., even though ...; **~ er auch noch so dumm sein mag, ...** however stupid he may be, ...; **~ auch!** (*inf*) even so!, all the same!; **~ schon!** (*inf*) what of it?, so what? (*inf*); **~ es denn gar nicht anders geht** well, if there's no other way; **~ es schon sein muß** well, if that's the way it's got to be; **es ist nicht gut, ~ man mit vollem Magen schwimmt** it's not good to swim on a full stomach; **~ man bedenkt, daß ...** when you consider that ..., considering ...; **~ wir erst die neue Wohnung haben** once we get the new flat; **~ ich doch *or* nur *or* bloß ...** if only I ...; **~ er nur da wäre!** if only he were *or* was here!; **~ ich das wüßte!** if only I knew!; **es ist, als *or* wie** (*inf*) **~ ...** it's as if ...; **außer ~ except if, unless**; **~ du das schon machen willst, (dann) mache es wenigstens richtig** if you want to do it at least do it properly.

(b) (*zeitlich*) when. **jedesmal *or* immer ~ whenever**; **außer ~ except when, unless**.

Wenn *nt*: (*die pl or das*) **~ und Aber** (the) ifs and buts.

wenngleich *conj* (*geh*) although, even though; (*mit adj auch*) albeit (*form*).

wennschon *adv* (*inf*) (**na,**) **~!** what of it?, so what? (*inf*); **~, dennschon!** in for a penny, in for a pound!, if you're going to do something at all, you might as well do it properly!

Wenzel *m* **-s, -** (*Cards*) jack, knave (*form, dated*).

wer 1 *interrog pron* who. **~ von ...** which (one) of ...; **~ da?** (*Mil*) who goes there?

2 *rel pron* (*derjenige, der*) the person who; (*jeder, der*) anyone *or* anybody who; (*esp in Sprichwörtern*) he who. **~ ... auch** (*immer*) whoever ...

3 *indef pron* (*inf: jemand*) somebody, someone; (*in Fragen, konditionalen Sätzen auch*) anybody, anyone. **ist da ~?** is somebody *or* anybody there?; **~ sein** to be somebody (*inf*).

Werbe- *in cpds* advertising; **~abteilung** *f* publicity department; **~agentur** *f* advertising agency; **~aktion** *f* advertising campaign; **~antwort** *f* business reply card; **~büro** *nt siehe* **~agentur**; **~chef** *m* advertising *or* publicity manager; **~etat** *m* advertising budget; **~fachmann** *m* advertising man; **~feldzug** *m* advertising campaign; **~fernsehen** *nt* commercial television; (*Sendung*) TV advertisements *pl or* commercials *pl*; **~film** *m* advertising *or* promotional film; (*Spot*) (filmed) commercial; **~funk** *m* (programme of) radio commercials *pl*; **~gag** *m* publicity stunt *or* gimmick; **~gemeinschaft** *f* joint advertising arrangement; **~geschenk** *nt* gift (*from company*); (*zu Gekauftem*) free gift; **~kampagne** *f* publicity campaign; (*für Verbrauchsgüter*) advertising campaign; **w~kräftig** *adj* *Aufmachung etc* catchy; **ein w~kräftiger Slogan** an effective publicity slogan; **ein w~kräftiger Faktor** a good advertising point; **eine Blondine auf dem Umschlag wäre w~kräftiger** a blonde on the cover would be more effective (advertising); **~leiter** *m* advertising *or* publicity manager, head of advertising *or* promotions; **~mittel** *nt* means of advertising; **~muster** *nt* advertising sample.

werben *pret* **warb**, *ptp* **geworben 1** *vt* Mitglieder, Mitarbeiter to recruit; *Kunden, Abonnenten, Stimmen* to attract, to win; *Soldaten* to recruit, to enlist.

  2 *vi* to advertise. **für etw ~** to advertise sth, to promote sth; **für eine Partei ~** to try to get support for a party; **Plakate, die für den linken Kandidaten ~** placards supporting the left-wing candidate; **um etw ~** to solicit sth, to court sth; **um Unterstützung ~** to try to enlist support; **um junge Wähler/neue Leser ~** to try to attract or woo young voters/new readers; **um ein Mädchen ~** to court or woo (*old*) a girl; **er hat bei ihren Eltern um sie geworben** he asked her parents for permission to marry her.

Werbe|offizier *m* recruiting officer.

Werber *m* -s, - (*um Kunden, Wähler*) canvasser; (*um Mädchen*) suitor; (*für Mitglieder etc, Mil Hist*) recruiter, recruiting officer; (*inf: Werbefachmann*) advertising man, adman (*inf*).

werberisch 1 *adj* advertising *attr*, promotional. **2** *adv* publicity-wise.

Werbe-: **~schrift** *f* publicity leaflet; (*für Verbrauchsgüter*) advertising leaflet; **~schriften** promotional literature *sing*; **~slogan** *m* publicity slogan; (*für Verbrauchsgüter*) advertising slogan; **~spot** *m* commercial; **~spruch** *m siehe* **~slogan**; **~text** *m* advertising copy *no pl*; **zwei ~texte** two pieces of advertising copy; **~texte verfassen** to write (advertising) copy; **~texter** *m* (advertising) copywriter; **~träger** *m* carrier of advertising; **~trommel** *f*: **die ~trommel (für etw) rühren** (*inf*) to beat the big drum (for sth) (*inf*), to push sth (*inf*); **w~wirksam** *adj* effective (for advertising purposes); **der Skandal erwies sich als äußerst w~wirksam** the scandal proved to be excellent publicity or to have excellent publicity value; **~wirksamkeit** *f* publicity value.

werblich *adj* advertising *attr*, promotional. **~ gesehen** from an advertising point of view.

Werbung *f* (*esp Comm*) advertising; (*Werbeabteilung*) publicity department; (*Pol: Propaganda*) pre-election publicity; (*von Kunden, Stimmen*) winning, attracting; (*von Mitgliedern, Soldaten etc*) recruitment, recruiting; (*um Mädchen*) courting (*um of*). **~ für etw machen** to advertise sth.

Werbungskosten *pl* (*von Mensch*) professional outlay *sing* or expenses *pl*; (*von Firma*) business expenses *pl*.

Werdaruf *m* (*Mil*) call of "who goes there?", challenge.

Werdegang *m, no pl* development; (*beruflich*) career.

werden *pret* **wurde**, *ptp* **geworden** *aux sein* **1** *v aux* **(a)** (*zur Bildung des Futurs und Konjunktivs*) **ich werde/wir ~ es tun** I/we will or shall do it, I'll/we'll do it; **er wird/du wirst/ihr werdet es tun** he/you will do it, he'll/you'll do it; **ich werde das nicht tun** I shall not or shan't or will not or won't do that; **er wird das nicht tun** he will not or won't do that; **du wirst heute schön zu Hause bleiben!** you'll or you will stay at home today!; **es wird gleich regnen** it's going to rain; **wer wird denn gleich weinen!** you're not going to cry now, are you?; **wer wird denn gleich!** (*inf*) come on, now!; **er hat gesagt, er werde/würde kommen** he said he would or he'd come; **das würde ich gerne tun** I would or I'd gladly do that.

  (b) (*Ausdruck der Vermutung*) **sie wird wohl in der Küche sein** she will or she'll probably be in the kitchen; **er wird (wohl) ausgegangen sein** he will or he'll (probably) have gone out; **das wird etwa 20 Mark kosten** it will cost roughly 20 marks.

  (c) (*zur Bildung des Passivs*) *pret auch* **ward** (*old, liter*), *ptp* **worden geschlagen** ~ to be beaten; **er ist erschossen worden** he was shot/he has been shot; **das Haus wird (gerade) renoviert** the house is being redecorated (just now); **es wurde gesungen** there was singing; **hier wird nicht geraucht!** there's no smoking here; **in England wird links gefahren** in England people drive on the left; **mir wurde gesagt, daß ...** I was told ...

  2 *vi pret auch* **ward** (*old, liter*), *ptp* **geworden (a)** (*mit adj*) to become, to get; (*allmählich*) to grow. **verrückt/blind ~** to go crazy/blind; **rot/sauer/blaß/kalt ~** to turn or go red/sour/pale/cold; **es wird kalt/dunkel/spät** it's getting cold/dark/late; **mir wird kalt/warm** I'm getting cold/warm; **mir wird schlecht/wohl/besser** I feel bad/good/better; **anders ~** to change; **die Fotos sind gut geworden** the photos have turned or come out nicely; **es wird schon wieder (gut) ~** it'll turn out all right.

  (b) (*mit Gleichsetzungsnominativen, Pronomen*) to become; (*sich verwandeln in auch*) to turn into; (*sein werden*) to be going to be. **Lehrer ~** to become a teacher; **was willst du einmal ~?** what do you want to be when you grow up?; **ich will Lehrer ~** I want to be or become a teacher; **Erster ~** to come or be first; **er ist nichts (Rechtes)/etwas geworden** he hasn't got anywhere/he's got somewhere in life, he hasn't made anything/he has made something of himself; **das ist nichts geworden** it came to nothing; **das Eis wird Wasser** the ice is turning (in)to water; **das wird bestimmt ein guter Eintopf** the stew is going to turn out nicely; **was soll das ~?** — **das wird ein Pullover** what's that going to be? — it's going to be a pullover; **es wird sicher ein Junge** (~) it's bound to be a boy; **das wird ein guter Urlaub** (~) it's going to be a good holiday; **... es werde Licht! und es ward Licht** (*Bibl*) ... let there be light, and there was light (*Bibl*).

  (c) (*mit Zeitangaben*) **es wird bald ein Jahr, daß ...** it's almost a year since ...; **es wird Zeit, daß er kommt** it's time (that) he came or (that) he was coming; **es wird Nacht** it's getting dark, night is falling; **es wird Tag** it's getting light, day is dawning; **es wird Winter** winter is coming; **es wurde 10 Uhr, und ... 10 o'clock came, and ...; es wird jetzt 13 Uhr** in a moment it will be 1 o'clock; **er wird am 8. Mai 36** he is or will be 36 on the 8th of May; **er ist gerade 40 geworden** he has just turned 40.

  (d) (*mit prep*) **was ist aus ihm geworden?** what has become of him?; **aus ihm ist ein großer Komponist geworden** he has become a great composer; **aus ihm ist nichts (Rechtes)/etwas geworden** he hasn't got anywhere/has got somewhere in life; **daraus wird nichts** that won't come to anything, nothing will come of that; **daraus wird bestimmt nichts Gutes/kann nichts**

Gutes ~ no good will/can come of it; **was wird daraus (~)?** what will come of it?; **zu etw ~** to turn into sth, to become sth; **zu Staub ~** to turn to dust; *siehe nichts.*

  (e) (*andere Wendungen*) **alles Leben wird und vergeht** (*liter*) life comes into being and then passes away (*liter*); **was nicht ist, kann noch ~** (*prov inf*) my/your etc day will come; **was soll nun ~?** so what's going to happen now?, so what do we do now?; **es wird schon ~** (*inf*) it'll come out okay (*inf*) or all right in the end, everything'll turn out okay (*inf*) or all right; **es will einfach nicht ~** (*inf*) it's simply not working; **ich denke, ich werde nicht wieder!** (*sl*) I was flabbergasted (*inf*), I got the shock of my life; **er wird mal wie sein Vater** he's going to be like his father; **wie sind die Fotos geworden?** how did the photos turn or come out?; **wie soll der Pullover ~?** what's the pullover going to be like?; **ihm ist ein großes Glück geworden** (*old, liter*) he has been favoured with great fortune (*liter*).

Werden *nt* -s, *no pl* **(a)** (*Entstehung*) development. **im ~ sein** to be in the making; **die lebenden Sprachen sind immer im ~ begriffen** living languages are in a state of continual development. **(b)** (*Philos*) Becoming.

werdend *adj* nascent, emergent. **~e Mutter** expectant mother, mother-to-be.

Werfall *m* nominative (case).

werfen *pret* **warf**, *ptp* **geworfen 1** *vt* **(a)** to throw (*auch beim Ringkampf*) (*nach at*), to cast (*liter, Bibl*); *Tor, Korb* to score. **Bomben ~** (*von Flugzeug*) to drop bombs; **eine Münze ~** to toss a coin; **„nicht ~"** "handle with care"; **Bilder an die Wand ~** to project pictures onto the wall; **etw auf jdn/etw ~** to throw sth at sb/sth; **etw auf den Boden/das Dach ~** to throw sth to the ground, to throw sth on(to) the ground/roof; **die Sonne warf ihre Strahlen auf den See** the sun cast its rays on the lake; **die Tischlampe wirft ihr Licht auf ...** the table-lamp throws its light on ...; **die Laterne wirft ein helles Licht** the lantern gives off a bright light; **billige Waren auf den Markt ~** to dump cheap goods on the market; **jdn aus der Firma/dem Haus etc ~** to throw or kick sb out (of the firm/house etc); **jdn ins Gefängnis etc ~** to throw sb into prison etc; **alle Sorgen hinter or von sich ~** (*fig*) to cast aside all one's worries; **etw in den Briefkasten ~** to put sth in the letter box; **etw ins Gespräch/in die Debatte ~** to throw sth into the conversation/debate etc; **etw aufs Papier ~** (*geh*) to jot sth down; **sie hat ihn mit Steinen geworfen** (*incorrect*) she threw stones at him; **die Kleider von sich ~** to throw or cast off one's clothes; *siehe Blick, Licht etc.*

  (b) (*Junge kriegen*) to have, to throw (*spec*).

  2 *vi* **(a)** to throw. **mit etw (auf jdn/etw) ~** to throw sth (at sb/sth); **die Demonstranten, die auf Polizisten geworfen hatten** the demonstrators who had thrown things at the police; **mit Geld um sich ~** (*inf*) to throw or chuck (*inf*) one's money about; **mit Komplimenten um sich ~** to be free and easy or be lavish with one's compliments; **mit Fremdwörtern um sich ~** to bandy foreign words about.

  (b) (*Tier*) to have its young; (*Katze, Hund etc auch*) to have a litter, to litter; (*bei einzelnen Jungen*) to have a pup etc.

  3 *vr* to throw oneself (*auf +acc* (up)on, at); (*Holz*) to warp; (*Metall, Asphalt etc*) to buckle. **sich auf eine Aufgabe etc ~** to throw oneself into a task etc; **sich in die Kleider ~** to throw on one's clothes; *siehe Brust, Hals¹.*

Werfer *m* -s, - thrower; (*Cricket*) bowler; (*Baseball*) pitcher.

Werft *f* -, -en shipyard; (*für Flugzeuge*) hangar.

Werft|arbeiter *m* shipyard worker.

Werg *nt* -(e)s, *no pl* tow.

Wergeld *nt* (*Hist Jur*) wer(e)gild.

Werk *nt* -(e)s, -e **(a)** (*Arbeit, Tätigkeit*) work *no indef art*; (*geh: Tat*) deed, act; (*Schöpfung, Kunst~, Buch*) work; (*Gesamt~*) works *pl*. **Schweitzer hat in Afrika ein bedeutendes ~ vollbracht** Schweitzer has done (some) important work in Africa; **ein ~ wie das verdient unsere Förderung** work such as that deserves our support; **das ~ eines Augenblicks** the work of a moment; **das ist sein ~** this is his doing; **das ~ vieler Jahrzehnte** the work of many decades; **das ~ jahrelanger Arbeit/seines Fleißes** the product of many years of work/of his industry; **die ~e Gottes** the works of God; **gute ~e tun** to do good works; **ein gutes ~ (an jdm) tun** to do a good deed (for sb); **du tätest ein gutes ~, wenn ...** (*auch hum*) you'd be doing me/him etc a good turn if ..., you'd be doing your good deed for the day if ... (*hum*); **ein ~ der Nächstenliebe** an act of charity; **ans ~ gehen, sich ans ~ machen, zu ~e gehen** (*geh*) to set to or go to work; (*frisch*) **ans ~!** (*old, liter*) to work!; **am ~ sein** to be at work; **etw ins ~ setzen** (*geh*) to set sth in motion; **wir müssen vorsichtig zu ~e gehen** we must proceed cautiously.

  (b) (*Betrieb, Fabrik*) works *sing* or *pl*, factory, plant. **ab ~** (*Comm*) ex works.

  (c) (*Trieb~*) works *pl*, mechanism.

  (d) *usu pl* (*Festungswerke*) works *pl*.

Werk- *in cpds* works, factory; *siehe auch* **Werk(s)-**; **~arbeit** *f* piece of woodwork/metalwork etc, piece of handicraft; **~bank** *f* workbench.

Werkel *nt* -s, -(n) (*Aus*) hurdy-gurdy, street organ.

Werkelmann *m, pl* **-männer** (*Aus*) organ grinder.

werkeln *vi* (*dated inf*) to potter about or around. **daran ist noch einiges zu ~** it still needs a bit of fixing.

werken 1 *vi* to work, to be busy; (*handwerklich*) to do handicrafts. **W~** (*Sch*) handicrafts. **2** *vt* to make.

Werk-: **w~getreu** *adj* true or faithful to the original; **~halle** *f* factory building; **~kunstschule** *f* arts and crafts school; **~lehrer** *m* woodwork/metalwork etc teacher, handicrafts teacher; **~leute** *pl* (*old, liter*) craftsmen *pl*, artisans *pl*; **~meister** *m* foreman.

Werk(s)-: **~angehörige(r)** *mf* works or factory employee; **~arzt** *m* works or company doctor.

Werkschutz *m* works or factory security service.

Werks-: w~eigen *adj* company *attr*; w~eigen sein to be company-owned, to belong to the company; ~fahrer *m* company *or* factory driver; ~feuerwehr *f* works *or* factory fire service; ~gelände *nt* works *or* factory premises *pl*; ~kantine *f* works *or* factory canteen; ~kindergarten *m* company *or* factory crèche; ~küche *f* works kitchen; ~leiter *m* works *or* factory director *or* manager; ~leitung *f* works *or* factory management; ~spionage *f* industrial espionage.

Werkstatt, Werkstätte *f* workshop *(auch fig)*; *(für Autoreparaturen)* garage; *(von Künstler)* studio.

Werkstattwagen *m* breakdown truck, wrecker *(US)*.

Werkstoff *m* material.

Werkstoff-: ~prüfer *m* materials tester; ~prüfung *f* testing of materials.

Werk-: ~stück *nt (Tech)* workpiece; ~student *m* working student; ~student sein to work one's way through college.

Werk(s)-: ~verkehr *m* company transport; ~vertrag *m* contract of manufacture; ~wohnung *f* company flat *(Brit)* or apartment; ~zeitschrift *f* company *(news)* paper *or* newsletter.

Werktag *m* working day, workday.

werktäglich 1 *adj attr Kleidung etc* workaday. ~e Öffnung opening on workdays *or* working days. 2 *adv (werktags)* on workdays *or* working days.

werktags *adv* on workdays *or* working days.

werktätig *adj* working.

Werktätige(r) *mf decl as adj* working man/woman. die ~n the working people *pl*.

Werk-: ~tisch *m* work-table; ~treue *f* faithfulness to the original; ~unterricht *m* handicraft lessons *pl*, woodwork/metalwork *etc* instruction.

Werkzeug *nt (lit, fig)* tool.

Werkzeug-: ~kasten *m* toolbox; ~macher *m* toolmaker; ~maschine *f* machine tool; ~stahl *m (Tech)* tool steel.

Wermut *m* -(e)s, *no pl (a) (Bot)* wormwood. ein Tropfen ~ *(fig geh)* a drop of bitterness. **(b)** *(~wein)* vermouth.

Wermut-: ~bruder *m (inf)*, ~penner *m (sl)* wino *(sl)*.

Wermutstropfen *m (fig geh)* drop of bitterness.

Werst *f* -, -e *(Maß)* verst.

wert *adj (a) (old, form: Anrede)* dear. Ihr ~es Schreiben *(form)* your esteemed letter *(form)*; wie war doch gleich Ihr ~er Name? *(form)* what was the name, sir/madam?
(b) etw ~ sein to be worth sth; nichts ~ sein to be worthless *or* worth nothing; *(untauglich)* to be no good; sie war ihm offenbar nicht viel ~ she obviously didn't mean all that much to him; er ist £ 100.000 ~ *(Press sl)* he is worth £100,000; Glasgow ist eine Reise ~ Glasgow is worth a visit; einer Sache *(gen)* ~ sein *(geh)* to be worthy of sth; es ist der Mühe ~ it's worth the trouble *or* it; es ist nicht der Rede ~ it's not worth mentioning; er ist es nicht ~, daß man ihm vertraut he doesn't deserve to be trusted; er ist (es) nicht ~, daß wir ihn unterstützen he is not worthy of *or* he does not deserve our support; dieser Film ist es durchaus ~, daß man sich ihn ansieht this film is definitely worth seeing.
(c) *(nützlich)* useful. ein Auto ist viel ~ a car is very useful; das ist schon viel ~ *(erfreulich)* that's very encouraging.

Wert *m* -(e)s, -e value; *(esp menschlicher)* worth; *(von Banknoten, Briefmarken)* denomination; *(~sache)* article of value, valuable object. ~e *pl (von Test, Analyse)* results *pl*; einen ~ von DM 5 haben to be worth DM 5, to have a value of DM 5; im ~e von to the value of, worth; an ~ verlieren/zunehmen, im ~ sinken/steigen to decrease/increase in value, to depreciate/appreciate *(esp Econ)*; eine Sache unter/über *(ihrem wirklichen)* ~ verkaufen to sell sth for less/more than its true value; sie hat innere ~e she has certain inner qualities; er ist sich *(dat)* seines ~es sehr bewußt he is very conscious of his value *or* importance; ~ auf etw *(acc)* legen *(fig)* to set great store by sth, to attach importance to sth; ich lege ~ darauf, festzustellen, daß ... I think it important to establish that ...; das hat keinen ~ *(inf)* there's no point.

Wert-: ~angabe *f* declaration of value; ~arbeit *f* craftsmanship, workmanship; w~beständig *adj* stable in value; ~beständigkeit *f* stability of value; ~brief *m* registered letter *(containing sth of value)*.

werten *vti (einstufen)* to rate *(als* as); *Klassenarbeit etc* to grade; *(beurteilen)* to judge *(als* to be); *(Sport) (als gültig ~)* to allow; *(Punkte geben)* to give a score. ein Tor *etc* nicht ~ *(Ftbl etc)* to disallow a goal; der Punktrichter aus Polen wertete besonders hoch the Polish judge gave particularly high marks; je nachdem, wie gewertet wird according to how the scoring is done; ohne (es) ~ zu wollen ... without wanting to make any judgement (on it) ...

Wertgegenstand *m* object of value. ~e *pl* valuables *pl*.

-wertig *adj suf (a)* -valued. **(b)** *(Chem, Ling)* -valent.

Wertigkeit *f (Chem, Ling)* valency.

Wert-: w~los *adj* worthless, valueless; ~losigkeit *f* worthlessness; ~marke *f* ticket; *(zum Aufkleben)* stamp; ~maß *nt*, ~maßstab *m*, ~messer *m* -s, - standard, yardstick; ~minderung *f* reduction in value; w~neutral *adj* nonnormative, value-free; ~objekt *nt siehe* ~gegenstand; ~ordnung *f* system of values; ~paket *nt* registered parcel *(containing sth of value)*; ~papier *nt* security, bond; ~papiere *pl* stocks and shares *pl*; ~papierbörse *f* stock exchange; ~philosophie *f (analytische)* ~ axiology; *(allgemeine Ethik)* moral philosophy; ~sache *f siehe* ~gegenstand; w~schätzen *vt sep (liter)* to (hold in high) esteem; ~schätzung *f (liter)* esteem, high regard; ~schöpfung *f (Econ)* net product; ~schrift *f (Sw) siehe* ~papier; ~sendung *f* registered consignment; ~setzung *f* scale of values; *(das Festsetzen)* fixing of values; ~steigerung *f* increase in value; ~system *nt* system of values, value system.

Wertung *f (a)* evaluation, assessment; *(von Jury etc)* judging,

scoring; *(Punkte)* score. aus der ~ fallen to be disqualified. **(b)** *(das Werten)* siehe *vti* rating; grading; judging; allowing; scoring.

Wertungs- *(Sport etc)*: ~gericht *nt* jury; ~richter *m* judge.

Werturteil *nt* value judgement.

Wert|urteils-: w~frei *adj* free from value judgements; ~freiheit *f* non-normativity.

wertvoll *adj* valuable; *(moralisch)* Mensch worthy, estimable.

Wert-: ~vorstellung *f* moral concept; ~zeichen *nt (form)* postage stamp; ~zoll *m* ad valorem duty; ~zuwachssteuer *f* capital gains tax.

werweißen *vi insep (Sw)* to guess.

Werwolf *m* werewolf.

wes *pron (old)* 1 *gen of* wer whose. 2 *gen of* was of which.

Wesen *nt* -s, - *(a) no pl* nature; *(Wesentliches)* essence. am ~ unserer Beziehung hat sich nichts geändert the basic nature of our relationship remains unchanged; es liegt im ~ einer Sache ... it's in the nature of a thing ...; das gehört zum ~ der Demokratie it is of the essence of democracy.
(b) *no pl* sein ~ treiben *(geh) (Dieb etc)* to be at work; *(Schalk etc)* to be up to one's tricks; *(Gespenst)* to be abroad; viel ~s machen (um *or* von) to make a lot of fuss (about).
(c) *(Geschöpf)* being; *(tierisches ~ auch)* creature; *(Mensch)* person, creature. armes ~ poor thing *or* creature; das höchste ~ the Supreme Being; das kleine ~ the little thing; ein weibliches/männliches ~ a female/male.

wesen *vi (liter)* to be present.

Wesen-: w~haft *adj* intrinsic, essential; ~haftigkeit *f* intrinsicality; ~heit *f (Philos)* being; w~los *adj* insubstantial, unreal; ohne Menschen wäre jede Ethik w~los without people any ethic would be meaningless *or* would have no substance.

Wesens-: w~ähnlich *adj* similar in nature; ~art *f* nature, character; es ist griechische ~art, zu ... it's a Greek characteristic to ...; w~eigen *adj* intrinsic; w~fremd *adj (im Wesen verschieden)* different *or* dissimilar in nature; das Lügen ist ihm völlig w~fremd lying is completely foreign *or* alien to his nature; w~gemäß *adj* das ist ihm nicht w~gemäß it's not in accordance with his nature; w~gleich *adj* essentially alike, identical in character *or* nature; w~verwandt *adj* related in character; ~verwandtschaft *f* relatedness of character; ~zug *m* characteristic, trait.

wesentlich 1 *adj (den Kern der Sache betreffend, sehr wichtig)* essential; *(grundlegend)* fundamental; *(erheblich)* substantial, considerable, appreciable; *(wichtig)* important. das W~e the essential part *or* thing; *(von dem, was gesagt wurde)* the gist; im ~en in essence, basically, essentially; *(im großen)* in the main.
2 *adv (grundlegend)* fundamentally; *(erheblich)* considerably. es ist mir ~ lieber, wenn wir ... I would much rather we ...; sie hat sich nicht ~ verändert she hasn't changed much.

Wesfall *m* genitive case.

weshalb 1 *interrog adv* why. 2 *rel adv* which is why, for which reason. der Grund, ~ ... the reason why ...; das ist es ja, ~ ... that is why ...

Wesir *m* -s, -e vizi(e)r.

Wespe *f* -, -n wasp.

Wespen-: ~nest *nt* wasp's nest; in ein ~nest stechen *(fig)* to stir up a hornets' nest; das war ein Stich ins ~nest *(fig)* that stirred up a hornets' nest; ~stich *m* wasp sting; ~taille *f (fig)* wasp waist.

wessen *pron* 1 *gen of* wer *(a)* interrog whose.
(b) *rel, indef* ~ Handschrift das auch *(immer)* sein mag, ... no matter whose handwriting it may be, ...
2 *gen of* was *(liter) (a) interrog* ~ hat man dich angeklagt? of what have you been accused?
(b) *rel, indef* ~ man dich auch *(immer)* anklagt, ... whatever they *or* no matter what they accuse you of ...

wessentwegen *interrog adv (geh)* on whose/what account.

wessentwillen *interrog adv (geh)*: um ~ for whose sake.

West *m* -s, *no pl (a) (Naut, Met, liter)* west; siehe Nord. **(b)** *(liter: ~wind)* west wind.

West- in *cpds (in Ländernamen) (politisch)* West; *(geographisch auch)* the West of ..., Western; ~afrika *nt* West Africa; ~australien *nt* Western Australia; ~-Berlin, ~berlin *nt* West Berlin; w~deutsch *adj (Pol)* West German; *(Geog)* Western German; ~deutsche(r) *mf* West German; ~deutschland *nt (Pol)* West Germany, Western Germany; *(Geog)* the West of Germany.

Weste *f* -, -n waistcoat, vest *(US)*. eine reine *or* saubere *or* weiße ~ haben *(fig)* to have a clean slate.

Westen *m* -s, *no pl* west; *(von Land)* West. der ~ *(Pol)* the West; *(im Gegensatz zum Orient auch)* the Occident; siehe Norden.

Westentasche *f* waistcoat *or* vest *(US)* pocket. etw wie seine ~ kennen *(inf)* to know sth like the back of one's hand *(inf)*.

Westentaschenformat *nt (hum)* ein X im ~ a miniature X.

Western *m* -(s), - western.

West-: ~europa *nt* Western Europe; w~europäisch *adj* West(ern) European; w~europäische Zeit Greenwich Mean Time, Western European Time *(rare)*; die w~europäische Union the Western European Union.

Westfale *m* -n, -n Westphalian.

Westfalen *nt* -s Westphalia.

Westfälin *f* Westphalian (woman).

westfälisch *adj* Westphalian. der W~e Friede *(Hist)* The Treaty of Westphalia.

Westfriesische Inseln *pl* West Frisians *pl*, West Frisian Islands *pl*.

West-: ~germanen *pl (Hist)* West Germanic peoples *pl* or tribes *pl*; w~germanisch *adj (Hist, Ling)* West Germanic; ~goten *pl (Hist)* Visigoths *pl*, West Goths *pl*; ~gotenreich *nt (Hist)* kingdom of the Visigoths; w~gotisch *adj (Hist)* West Gothic,

Visigoth *attr*; w~griechisch *adj* Western Greek; ~indien *nt* the West Indies *pl*; w~indisch *adj* West Indian; die w~indischen Inseln the West Indies *pl*; ~küste *f* west coast.

Westler *m* -s, - (*DDR inf*) westerner; (*Hist*) westernist.

westlerisch *adj* (*DDR inf*) western; (*Hist*) westernist.

westlich 1 *adj* western; *Kurs, Wind, Richtung* westerly; (*Pol*) Western. der ~ste Ort the westernmost place. **2** *adv* (to the) west (*von of*). **3** *prep* +*gen* (to the) west of.

West-: ~mächte *pl* (*Pol*) die ~mächte the western powers *pl*; ~mark *f* (*inf*) West German mark; w~mitteldeutsch *adj* West Middle German; ~nordwest *m* (a) (*Naut, Met, liter*) west-north-west; (b) (*liter: Wind*) west-north-west wind; w~östlich *adj* west-to-east; in w~östlicher Richtung from west to east; ~politik *f* policy towards the west, western policy; ~preußen *nt* West Prussia; ~rom *nt* (*Hist*) Western Roman Empire; w~römisch *adj* (*Hist*) Western Roman; ~russen *pl* White Russians *pl*; ~schweiz *f* die ~schweiz Western Switzerland; ~sektor *m* western sector; ~südwest *m* (a) (*Naut, Met, liter*) west-south-west; (b) (*liter: Wind*) west-south-west wind; ~wall *m* (*Hist*) Siegfried Line; w~wärts *adv* westward(s), (to the) west; ~wind *m* west wind.

weswegen *interrog adv* why.

wett *adj pred* ~ sein to be quits.

Wett|annahme(stelle) *f* betting office.

Wettbewerb *m* competition. mit jdm in ~ stehen/treten to be in/enter into competition with sb, to be competing/to compete with sb; außer ~ teilnehmen *or* laufen to take part hors concours *or* as a non-competitor.

Wettbewerber *m* competitor.

Wettbewerbs-: ~bedingungen *pl* terms of a/the competition *pl*; ~beschränkung *f* restraint of trade; w~fähig *adj* competitive; ~teilnehmer *m* competitor; ~wirtschaft *f* competitive economy.

Wettbüro *nt* betting office.

Wette *f* -, -n bet (*auch Sport*); wager. eine ~ machen *or* abschließen/annehmen to make/take up *or* accept a bet; eine ~ auf ein Pferd abschließen to place a bet on a horse; darauf gehe ich jede ~ ein I'll bet you anything you like; was gilt die ~? what will you bet me?, what are you betting?; die ~ gilt! done!, you're on! (*inf*); um die ~ laufen/schwimmen to run/swim a race (with each other); mit jdm um die ~ laufen *or* rennen to race sb; sie arbeiten/singen/schreien um die ~ they're working as hard as they can/singing at the tops of their voices/having a screaming competition.

Wett|eifer *m* competitive zeal, competitiveness.

wett|eifern *vi insep* mit jdm um etw ~ to compete *or* contend *or* vie with sb for sth.

wetten *vti* to bet (*auch Sport*); to wager. (wollen wir) ~? (do you) want to bet?; ~, daß ich recht habe? (I) bet you I'm right!; so haben wir nicht gewettet! that's not part of the deal *or* bargain!; auf etw (*acc*) ~ to bet on sth; mit jdm ~ to bet with sb; (mit jdm) (darauf) ~, daß ... to bet (sb) that ...; (mit jdm) um 5 Mark/ eine Flasche Bier *etc* ~ to bet (sb) 5 marks/a bottle of beer *etc*; wir wetteten um einen Kasten Sekt we bet each other a case of champagne; ich habe mit ihm um 10 Mark auf/gegen den Sieg der Sozialisten gewettet I bet him 10 marks that the Socialists would win/wouldn't win *or* would lose; gegen etw ~ to bet against sth; da wette ich gegen (*inf*) *or* dagegen I bet you that isn't so/won't happen *etc*; ich wette 100 gegen 1 (darauf)(, daß ...) I'll bet *or* lay (you) 100 to 1 (that ...); ich wette meinen Kopf (darauf)(, daß ...) I'll bet you anything (you like) (that ...).

Wetter¹ *m* -s, - better.

Wetter² *nt* -s, - (a) weather *no indef art*. bei jedem ~ in all weathers; bei so einem ~ in weather like this/that, in such weather; das ist vielleicht ein ~! (*inf*) what weather!; was haben wir heute für ~? what's the weather like today?; wir haben herrliches ~ the weather's marvellous; ein ~ zum Eierlegen (*inf*) *or* Heldenzeugen (*inf*) fantastic weather (*inf*); übers *or* vom ~ sprechen to talk about the weather; (bei jdm) gut ~ machen (*inf*) to make up to sb; (jdn) um gutes ~ bitten (*inf*) to try to smooth things over (with sb); alle ~! (*inf*) my goodness!, by Jove! (*dated*).
(b) (*Un~*) storm.
(c) *usu pl* (*Min*) air. matte ~ *pl* chokedamp *sing*, blackdamp *sing*; giftige *or* böse ~ *pl* whitedamp *sing*; schlagende ~ *pl* firedamp *sing*.

Wetter-: ~amt *nt* weather *or* met(eorological) office; ~aussichten *pl* weather outlook *sing or* prospects *pl*; ~ballon *m* weather *or* meteorological balloon; ~beobachtung *f* meteorological observation; ~bericht *m* weather report; ~besserung *f* improvement in the weather; w~beständig *adj* weatherproof; w~bestimmend *adj* weather-determining; w~bestimmend sein to determine the weather.

Wetterchen *nt* (*inf*) das ist ja heute ein ~! the weather's really great *or* fantastic today! (*inf*).

Wetter-: ~dienst *m* weather *or* meteorological service; w~empfindlich *adj* sensitive to (changes in) the weather; ~fahne *f* weather vane; w~fest *adj* weatherproof; ~fleck *m* (*Aus*) weatherproof cape; ~front *f* front; w~frosch *m* (a) type of barometer using a frog; (b) (*hum inf*) weatherman (*inf*); w~fühlig *adj* sensitive to (changes in) the weather; ~führung *f* (*Min*) ventilation; w~geschützt *adj* sheltered; ~glas *nt* (*old*) weatherglass; ~gott *m* weather god; der ~gott (*hum*) the person up there who controls the weather (*hum*); ~hahn *m* weathercock; ~häuschen *nt* weather house *or* box; ~kanal *m* (*Min*) fan drift; ~karte *f* weather map *or* chart; ~krankheit *f* illness caused by the weather; ~kunde *f* meteorology; ~kundler *m* -s, - meteorologist; w~kundlich *adj* meteorological; ~lage *f* weather situation, state of the weather; ~lampe *f* (*Min*) safety lamp; ~leiden *nt* ailment *or* complaint caused by the weather; w~leuchten *insep* **1** *vi impers* es

w~leuchtet there's sheet lightning; (*fig*) there's a storm brewing; **2** *vi* (*fig*) am Horizont w~leuchtete bereits die Revolution the storm clouds of revolution were already gathering on the horizon; ~leuchten *nt* -s, *no pl* sheet lightning; (*fig*) storm clouds *pl*; ~meldung *f* weather *or* meteorological report.

wettern 1 *vi impers* es wettert it's thundering and lightening, there's a thunderstorm. **2** *vi* to curse and swear. gegen *or* auf etw (*acc*) ~ to rail against sth.

Wetter-: ~prognose *f* (*Aus*) weather forecast; ~prophet *m* (*hum*) weatherman (*inf*); ~regel *f* weather maxim *or* saying; ~satellit *m* weather satellite; ~schacht *m* (*Min*) ventilation shaft; ~schaden *m* weather damage; ~scheide *f* weather *or* meteorological divide; ~schiff *nt* weather ship; ~seite *f* windward side, side exposed to the weather; ~station *f* weather *or* meteorological station; ~störung *f* weather *or* meteorological disturbance; ~sturz *m* sudden fall in temperature and atmospheric pressure; ~umbruch (*esp Sw*), ~umschlag, ~umschwung *m* sudden change in the weather; ~verhältnisse *pl* weather conditions *pl*; ~verschlechterung *f* deterioration in *or* worsening of the weather; ~voraussage, ~vorhersage *f* weather forecast; ~warte *f* weather station; ~wechsel *m* change in the weather; w~wendisch *adj* (*fig*) changeable, moody; ~wolke *f* storm cloud.

Wetteufel *m getrennt* Wett-teufel (*inf*) betting bug (*inf*). ihn hat der ~ gepackt he's got the betting bug (*inf*).

Wett-: ~fahrt *f* race; ~kampf *m* competition; ~kämpfer *m* competitor; ~lauf *m* race; einen ~lauf machen to run a race; ein ~lauf mit der Zeit a race against time; w~laufen *vi* (*infin only*) to run a race/races; ~läufer *m* runner (in a/the race).

wettmachen *vt sep* to make up for; *Verlust etc* to make good; *Rückstand* to make up.

Wett-: w~rennen *vi* (*infin only*) to run a race; ~rennen *nt* (*lit, fig*) race; ein ~rennen machen to run a race; ~rudern *nt* boat race; ~rüsten *nt* arms race; ~schein *m* betting slip; ~schießen *nt* shooting competition *or* contest; ~schuld *f* betting debt; ~schwimmen *nt* swimming competition *or* contest; ~singen *nt* singing competition *or* contest; ~streit *m* competition (*auch fig*), contest; mit jdm im ~streit liegen to compete with sb; mit jdm in ~streit treten to enter into competition with sb; ~teufel *m siehe* Wetteufel.

Wetturnen *nt getrennt* Wett-turnen gymnastics competition.

Wettzettel *m* betting slip *or* ticket.

wetzen 1 *vt* to whet. **2** *vi aux sein* (*inf*) to scoot (*inf*).

Wetz-: ~stahl *m* steel; ~stein *m* whetstone.

WEU [ve:|e:'|u:] *abbr of* **Westeuropäische Union** WEU.

WEZ [ve:|e:'tset] *abbr of* **Westeuropäische Zeit** GMT.

WGB [ve:ge:'be:] *abbr of* **Weltgewerkschaftsbund** WFTU.

Whisky ['vɪski] *m* -s, -s whisky, whiskey (*US*); (*schottischer auch*) Scotch; (*irischer*) whiskey; (*amerikanischer Mais~ auch*) bourbon whisky (e)y); (*amerikanischer Roggen~ auch*) rye (whisk(e)y). ~ mit Eis/(mit) Soda whisky and ice *or* on the rocks/and soda.

Whist [vɪst] *nt* -(e)s, *no pl* whist.

wich *pret of* **weichen²**.

Wichs [vɪks] *m* -es, -e, (*Aus*) *f* -, -en in vollem *or* (*Aus*) voller ~ (*Univ*) in full dress, in full regalia; sich in ~ werfen (*Univ, fig*) to dress up.

Wichse ['vɪksə] *f* -, -n (a) (*dated: Schuh~*) shoe polish. schwarze ~ blacking (*dated*), black shoe polish. (b) *no pl* (*inf: Prügel*) ~ bekommen to get a hiding (*inf*); wenn du das machst, gibt's ~! if you do that you'll get a good hiding!

wichsen ['vɪksn] **1** *vt* (a) *auch vi* (*dated*) *Schuhe* to polish; (mit schwarzer Wichse) to black (*dated*); *Schnurrbart, Boden etc* to wax; *siehe* gewichst. (b) (*inf: prügeln*) jdn (ganz schön) ~ to give sb a (good) hiding (*inf*). **2** *vi* (*sl: onanieren*) to jerk *or* toss off (*sl*), to (have a) wank (*Brit vulg*).

Wichsleinwand ['vɪks-] *f* (*Aus*) *siehe* **Wachstuch**.

Wicht *m* -(e)s, -e (*Kobold*) goblin, wight (*obs*); (*kleiner Mensch*) titch (*inf*); (*Kind*) (little) creature; (*fig: verachtenswerter Mensch*) scoundrel. ein armer ~ a poor devil *or* wretch; (*Kind*) a poor little thing *or* creature.

Wichte *f* -, -n (*Phys*) density.

Wichtel *m* -s, - (a) (*auch* ~männchen) gnome; (*Kobold*) goblin, imp; (*Heinzelmännchen*) brownie. (b) (*bei Pfadfinderinnen*) brownie.

wichtig *adj* important. eine ~e Miene machen to put on an air of importance; sich ~ machen *or* tun to be full of one's own importance, to be self-important *or* pompous; er will sich nur ~ machen he just wants to get attention; sich mit etw ~ machen *or* tun to go on and on about sth; sich selbst/etw (zu) ~ nehmen to take oneself/sth (too) seriously; es mit etw ~ haben (*inf*) to take sth (very) seriously; du hast's aber ~! (*inf*) what's all the fuss about?; ~ tun (*inf*), sich (*dat*) ~ vorkommen to be full of oneself; alles W~e everything of importance; W~eres zu tun haben to have more important things *or* better things to do; nichts W~eres zu tun haben to have nothing better to do; das W~ste (die ~ste Sache) the most important thing; (die ~sten Einzelheiten) the most important details.

Wichtigkeit *f* importance. einer Sache (*dat*) große *etc* ~ beimessen *or* beilegen to place great *etc* importance on sth.

Wichtigmacher(in *f*) (*Aus*), **Wichtigtuer(in** *f*) [-tu:ɐ, -ərɪn] *m* -s, - (*pej*)pompous ass (*inf*), stuffed shirt (*inf*).

Wichtigtuerei [-tu:əˈrai] *f* (*pej*) pomposity, pompousness.

wichtigtuerisch [-tu:ərɪʃ] *adj* pompous.

Wicke *f* -, -n (*Bot*) vetch; (*Garten~*) sweet pea. in die ~n gehen (*fig inf*) to be lost *or* mislaid.

Wickel *m* -s, - (a) (*Med*) compress. (b) (*Rolle*) reel, spool; (*Locken~*) roller, curler. (c) (*inf*) jdn am *or* beim ~ packen *or* nehmen *or* kriegen/haben to grab/have sb by the scruff of the neck; (*fig*) to give sb a good talking to (*inf*); (*stärker*) to have sb's guts for garters (*inf*).

Wickel-: ~bluse f wrap-around blouse; ~gamasche f puttee; ~kind nt babe-in-arms; (fig auch) baby; ~kleid nt wrap-around dress; ~kommode f baby's changing unit.

wickeln 1 vt (a) (schlingen) to wind (um round); (Tech) Spule, Transformator etc auch to coil; Verband etc to bind; Haare, Locken to put in rollers or curlers; Zigarren to roll; (umschlagen) to wrap. sich (dat) eine Decke um die Beine ~ to wrap a blanket around one's legs; wenn du das denkst, bist du schief gewickelt! (fig inf) if you think that, you're very much mistaken; siehe Finger.
(b) (einwickeln) to wrap (in + acc in); (mit Verband) to dress, to bandage. einen Säugling ~ to put on a baby's nappy (Brit) or diaper (US); (frisch ~) to change a baby's nappy/diaper.
2 vr to wrap oneself (in + acc in). sich um etw ~ to wrap itself around sth; Schlange, Pflanze to wind itself around sth.

Wickel-: ~rock m wrap-around skirt; ~tisch m baby's changing table.

Widder m -s, - (Zool) ram; (Astrol) Aries; (Mil, Hist) battering ram. er/sie ist (ein) ~ (Astrol) he's/she's an Arian or(an) Aries; der ~ (Astron, Astrol) Aries, the Ram.

Widder-: ~frau f (Astrol, inf) (female) Arian, Aries (woman); ~mann m, pl -männer (Astrol, inf) (male) Arian, Aries (man).

wider prep + acc (geh) against; (entgegen auch) contrary to. ~ Erwarten contrary to expectations; ~ alles Erwarten against all or contrary to all expectations; siehe Für, löcken, Wille.

widerborstig adj contrary, perverse.

Widerborstigkeit f contrariness, perversity.

wider|einander adv (liter) siehe gegeneinander.

widerfahren* vi, vi impers insep irreg aux sein + dat (geh) to happen (jdm to sb); (Unglück etc) to befall (jdm sb) (liter). mir ist in meinem Leben schon viel Gutes ~ life has given me many good things.

Wider-: ~haken m barb; (an größerer Harpune) fluke; ~hall m echo, reverberation; (bei jdm) keinen ~hall finden (Interesse) to meet with no response (from sb); (Gegenliebe etc) not to be reciprocated (by sb); w~hallen vi sep or (rare) insep to echo or reverberate (von with); ~handlung f (Sw) siehe Zuwiderhandlung; ~klage f counterclaim; w~klingen vi sep irreg to resound or ring (von with).

widerlegbar adj refutable, disprovable. nicht ~ irrefutable.

widerlegen* vt insep Behauptung etc to refute, to disprove; jdn to prove wrong.

Widerlegung f refutation, disproving.

widerlich adj disgusting, revolting; Mensch repulsive; Kopfschmerzen nasty.

Widerlichkeit f (widerliche Sache) disgusting or revolting thing; (von Mensch) repulsiveness; (von Kopfschmerzen) nastiness. die ~ des Anblicks/seines Benehmens the disgusting or revolting sight/his disgusting or revolting behaviour.

Widerling m (pej inf) repulsive creep (inf).

widern vt, vt impers es/etw widert jdn sb finds it/sth disgusting or revolting; wenn ich schon daran denke, widert es mich, schon der Gedanke daran widert mich the very thought of it disgusts or revolts me.

Wider-: w~natürlich adj unnatural; (pervers auch) perverted; ~natürlichkeit f unnaturalness; perversion; ~part m (old, geh: Gegner) adversary, opponent; jdm ~part bieten or geben (geh) to oppose sb.

widerraten* vi insep irreg (old) jdm ~, etw zu tun to advise or counsel sb against doing sth.

Wider-: w~rechtlich adj unlawful, illegal; etw w~rechtlich betreten Gelände to trespass (up)on sth; Gebäude to enter sth unlawfully or illegally; sich (dat) etw w~rechtlich aneignen to misappropriate sth; ~rechtlichkeit f unlawfulness, illegality; ~rede f (a) siehe Gegenrede; (b) (Widerspruch) contradiction, argument; keine ~rede! no arguing!, don't argue!; er duldet keine ~rede he will not have any arguments about it; ohne ~rede without protest or demur.

Widerruf m siehe vb revocation, withdrawal, cancellation; retraction; withdrawal; cancellation, countermand; recantation. ~ leisten to recant; bis auf ~ until revoked or withdrawn or cancelled.

widerrufen* insep irreg 1 vt Erlaubnis, Anordnung etc to revoke (auch Jur), to withdraw, to cancel; Aussage, Geständnis, Behauptung to retract (auch Jur), to withdraw; Befehl to cancel, to countermand. 2 vi (bei Verleumdung etc) to withdraw; (esp bei ketzerischen Behauptungen) to recant.

widerruflich (form) 1 adj revocable, revokable. 2 adv until revoked or withdrawn.

Wider-: ~sacher(in f) m -s, - adversary, antagonist, opponent; der ~sacher (Teufel) the Adversary; w~schallen vi sep (old) siehe w~hallen; ~schein m (liter) reflection; w~setzen vr insep sich jdm/einer Sache w~setzen to oppose sb/sth; einem Polizisten, der Festnahme to resist sb/sth; einem Befehl, einer Aufforderung to refuse to comply with sth; w~setzlich adj contrary, obstreperous; Befehlsempfänger insubordinate; ~setzlichkeit f siehe adj contrariness, obstreperousness; insubordination; ~sinn m, no pl absurdity, illogicality; w~sinnig adj absurd, nonsensical; w~spenstig adj unruly, wilful; (störrisch) stubborn; (fig) unmanageable; Haar unruly, unmanageable; „der ~spenstigen Zähmung" "The Taming of the Shrew"; ~spenstigkeit f siehe adj unruliness, wilfulness, stubbornness; unmanageableness; w~spiegeln sep 1 vt (lit, fig) to reflect; Gegenstand auch to mirror; 2 vr (lit, fig) to be reflected/mirrored; ~spieg(e)lung f reflection; ~spiel nt das ~spiel der Kräfte the play of forces.

widersprechen* insep irreg 1 vi jdm/einer Sache ~ to contradict sb/sth; (nicht übereinstimmen mit) den Tatsachen etc auch to be inconsistent with sth; da muß ich aber ~ I've got to contradict you there; das widerspricht meinen Grundsätzen

---

that goes or is against my principles.
2 vr (einander) to contradict each other or one another; (nicht übereinstimmen: Aussagen etc auch) to be inconsistent, to conflict. sich (selbst) ~ to contradict oneself.

widersprechend adj (sich or einander) ~ contradictory, conflicting, inconsistent.

Widerspruch m (a) (Gegensätzlichkeit) contradiction (auch Philos); (Unvereinbarkeit auch) inconsistency. ein ~ in sich selbst a contradiction in terms; in or im ~ zu contrary to; in ~ zu or mit etw geraten to come into conflict with sth, to contradict sth; sich in ~ zu jdm/etw setzen to go against sb/sth; in or im ~ zu or mit etw stehen to conflict with sth, to stand in contradiction to sth, to be contrary to sth.
(b) (Widerrede) contradiction, dissent; (Protest) protest; (Ablehnung) opposition. kein ~! don't argue!; er duldet keinen ~ he won't have any argument; es erhob sich ~ there was opposition (gegen to), there were protests (gegen against); ~ erheben to protest; ~ erfahren, auf ~ stoßen to meet with opposition (bei from).

widersprüchlich adj contradictory; Erzählung, Theorie auch, Verhalten inconsistent.

Widersprüchlichkeit f siehe adj contradiction, contradictoriness; inconsistency.

Widerspruchs-: w~frei adj Theorie consistent; ~freiheit f consistency; ~geist m spirit of opposition; w~los 1 adj (unangefochten) Zustimmung, Annahme unopposed; (ohne Einwände) Zuhören, Befolgen von Anordnung without contradiction; (folgsam) Kind, Gehorchen unprotesting; (nicht widersprüchlich) Theorie, Mensch, Verhalten consistent; 2 adv siehe adj without opposition; without contradiction; without protest; consistently; w~voll adj full of contradictions; (voller Unvereinbarkeiten) full of inconsistencies.

Widerstand m -(e)s, -e resistance (auch Pol, Elec etc); (im 2. Weltkrieg) Resistance; (Ablehnung) opposition; (Elec: Bauelement) resistor. zum ~ aufrufen to call upon people to resist; es erhebt sich ~ there is resistance; jdm/einer Sache or gegen jdn/etw ~ leisten to resist sb/sth, to put up or offer (form) resistance to sb/sth; seine inneren ~e überwinden to overcome one's inhibitions; ~ gegen die Staatsgewalt obstructing an officer in the performance of his duties; siehe Weg.

Widerstands-: ~bewegung f resistance movement; (im 2. Weltkrieg) Resistance movement; w~fähig adj robust; Pflanze hardy; (Med, Tech etc) resistant (gegen to); ~fähigkeit f siehe adj robustness; hardiness; resistance (gegen to); ~kämpfer m member of the resistance; (im 2. Weltkrieg) member of the Resistance, Resistance fighter; ~kraft f (power of) resistance; w~los adj, adv without resistance; ~messer m -s, - (Elec) ohmmeter; ~nest nt (Mil) pocket of resistance.

widerstehen* vi insep irreg + dat (a) to resist; (standhalten) to withstand. einer Versuchung/einem Erdbeben ~ können to be able to resist a temptation/withstand an earthquake. (b) (anekeln) etw widersteht jdm sb loathes sth.

widerstreben* vi insep + dat jdm/einer Sache ~ (Mensch) to oppose sb/sth; etw widerstrebt einer Sache sth conflicts with sth; jds sittlichen Empfinden/jds Interessen etc ~ to go against sb's moral sense/sb's interests etc; das widerstrebt mir (das möchte ich nicht tun) I can't do things like that, I can't be like that; so eine Handlungsweise widerstrebt mir (lehne ich ab) I find such behaviour repugnant; es widerstrebt mir, so etwas zu tun (lehne ich ab) it goes against the grain to do anything like that; (möchte ich nicht) I am reluctant to do anything like that.

Widerstreben nt -s, no pl reluctance. nach anfänglichem ~ after some initial reluctance.

widerstrebend adj (gegensätzlich) Interessen conflicting; (widerwillig, zögernd) reluctant. mit ~en Gefühlen with (some) reluctance; eine unseren Plänen ~e Entwicklung a development conflicting with or in conflict with our plans.

Widerstreit m (geh) conflict. im or in ~ zu etw stehen to be in conflict with sth.

widerstreitend adj (geh) (einander) ~ conflicting.

widertönen vi sep to echo. seine Worte tönten ihr noch im Ohr wider his words were still ringing in her ears.

widerwärtig adj offensive; (ekelhaft auch) disgusting; Aufgabe, Arbeit, Verhalten objectionable. etw ist jdm ~ sb finds sth offensive/disgusting/objectionable; es ist mir ~, ihn enttäuschen zu müssen I really hate having to disappoint him.

Widerwärtigkeit f siehe adj offensiveness; disgusting nature; objectionable nature.

Widerwille m (Abscheu, Ekel) disgust (gegen for), revulsion; (Abneigung) distaste (gegen for), aversion (gegen to); (Widerstreben) reluctance. etw mit größtem ~n tun/trinken to do sth with the greatest reluctance/drink sth with intense distaste.

widerwillig adj reluctant, unwilling.

Widerworte pl answering back sing. ~ geben or machen to answer back; er tat es ohne ~ he did it without protest.

widmen 1 vt jdm etw ~ to dedicate sth to sb; (schenken, verwenden auf) to devote sth to sb.
2 vr + dat to devote oneself to; (sich kümmern um) den Gästen etc to attend to; einem Problem, einer Aufgabe to apply oneself to, to attend to. nun kann ich mich dir/dieser Aufgabe ganz ~ I can now give you/this task my undivided attention.

Widmung f (in Buch etc) dedication (an + acc to).

widrig adj adverse; Winde, Umstände auch unfavourable.

widrigenfalls adv (form) if this is not the case, otherwise; (Nebensatz einleitend) failing which.

Widrigkeit f siehe adj adversity; unfavourability.

wie 1 interrog adv (a) how. ~ anders ...? how else ...?; ~ schwer/oft etc? how heavy/often etc?; ~ viele? how many?; ~ das? how come?; ~ ist dir (zumute)? how do you feel?; aber frag (mich) nicht ~! but don't ask me how!; ~ wär's (mit uns beiden *etc*) (*inf*) how about it? (*inf*); **wie wär's mit einem Whisky?** (*inf*) how about a whisky?; ~ **wäre es, wenn du mir ein Bier bezahlen würdest?** how *or* how's (*inf*) about (you) buying me a beer?

(b) (*welcher Art*) ~ **war's bei der Party/in Italien?** what was it like at the party/in Italy?, what was the party/Italy like?, how was the party/Italy?; ~ **ist er** (*denn*)? what's he like?; ~ **war das Wetter?** what was the weather like?, how was the weather?; ~ **ist es eigentlich, wenn ...?** what's the situation if ...?, what happens if ...?; ~ **war das** (*noch mal genau*) **mit dem Unfall?** what (exactly) happened in the accident?; **und** ~ **ist es mit deinem Job?** and what about your job?; **Sie wissen ja,** ~ **das so ist** well, you know how it is.

(c) (*was*) ~ **heißt er/das?** what's he/it called?; ~ **nennt man das?** what is that called?; ~? what?; ~ **bitte?,** ~ **war das?** (*inf*), ~ **meinen** *or* **belieben?** (*inf*) sorry?, pardon?, come again? (*inf*); ~ **bitte?!** (*entrüstet*) I beg your pardon!

(d) (*in Ausrufen*) **how. und** ~!, **aber** ~! and how! (*inf*); ~ **groß er ist!** how big he is!, isn't he big!; ~ **schrecklich!** how terrible!; ~ **haben wir gelacht, als ...** how we laughed when ...

(e) (*nicht wahr*) **er. das macht dir Spaß,** ~? you like that, don't you?; **das macht dir keinen Spaß,** ~? you don't like that, do you?

2 adv (a) (*relativ*) **die Art,** ~ **sie geht** the way (in which) she walks; **in dem Maße,** ~ ... to the same extent that ...; **in dem Stil,** ~ **er jetzt Mode ist** in the style which *or* that is now fashionable; **es war ein Sonnenuntergang,** ~ **er noch nie einen gesehen hatte** it was a sunset the like of which he had never seen before.

(b) (*in Verbindung mit auch*) ~ **stark du auch sein magst** however strong you may be; ~ **auch immer du das machen wirst** however you *or* whatever way you are going to do it; ~ **sie auch alle heißen** whatever they're called.

3 conj (a) (*vergleichend*) (*wenn sich Vergleich auf adj, adv bezieht*) as; (*wenn sich Vergleich auf n bezieht, bei Apposition*) like. **so ...** ~ **as ...** as; **so lang** ~ **breit** the same length and width, as long as it *etc* is wide; **weiß** ~ **Schnee** (as) white as snow; **mutig** ~ **ein Löwe** as brave as a lion; **eine Nase** ~ **eine Kartoffel** a nose like a potato; **ein Mann** ~ **er** a man like him, a man such as he (*form*); **in einer Lage** ~ **diese(r)** in a situation like this *or* such as this; **er ist Lehrer,** ~ **sein Vater** es war he is a teacher like his father was (*inf*) *or* as was his father; **T** ~ **Theodor** "t" as in "Tommy"; (*bei Rundfunk etc*) **t** for Tommy; **er ist intelligent,** ~ **wir** he is intelligent like us; ~ **gewöhnlich/immer** as usual/always *or* ever; **der Käse sah** ~ **verschimmelt aus** the cheese looked (as if it were *or* was) mouldy; **ich fühlte mich** ~ **betrunken/im Traum** I felt (as if I were *or* was) drunk/as if I were *or* was *or* like I (*inf*) was dreaming; ~ **sie nun** (**ein**)**mal ist, mußte sie ...** the way she is she just had to ...; ~ **du weißt/man sagt** as you know/they say; ~ **noch nie** as never before.

(b) (*zum Beispiel*) ~ (**zum Beispiel** *or* **etwa**) such as (for example).

(c) (*incorrect: als*) **größer/schöner** ~ bigger/more beautiful than; **nichts** ~ **Ärger** *etc* nothing but trouble *etc*.

(d) (*und*) **as well as. Alte** ~ **Junge** old and young alike.

(e) (*inf*) ~ **wenn** as if *or* though.

(f) (*bei Verben der Gefühlsempfindung*) **er sah,** ~ **es geschah** he saw it happen; **sie spürte,** ~ **es kalt wurde** she felt it getting cold; **er hörte,** ~ **der Regen fiel** he heard the rain falling.

(g) (*zeitlich: als*) ~ **ich mich umdrehte, sah ich ...** as I turned round, I saw ..., turning round, I saw ...; ~ **ich mit der Schule fertig war, ...** (*inf*) when I was finished with school, ...

Wie *nt* **-s**, *no pl* **das** ~ **spielt dabei keine Rolle** how (it'll happen/it'll be done *etc*) is unimportant; **daß es geschehen muß, ist klar, nur das** ~ **ist noch ein Problem** it's clear that it has to happen, the only problem is how; **das** ~ **und Wann werden wir später besprechen** we'll talk about how and when later.

Wiedehopf *m* **-(e)s, -e** hoopoe.

wieder *adv* **(a)** again. ~ **nüchtern/glücklich** *etc* sober/happy *etc* again; **immer** ~, ~ **und** ~ again and again; ~ **mal,** (**ein**)**mal** ~ (once) again; **komm doch** ~ **mal vorbei** come and see me/us again; ~ **ist ein Jahr vorbei** another year has passed; ~ **was anderes** *or* **Neues** something else again, something quite different; **wie, schon** ~? what, again?; ~ **da** (back) (again); **da bin ich** ~! I'm back!, here I am again!; **das ist auch** ~ **wahr** that's true; **da sieht man mal** ~, **...** it just shows ...

(b) (*in Verbindung mit vb*) **again. das fällt mir schon** ~ **ein** I'll remember it again; **das Boot tauchte** ~ **auf** the boat resurfaced; **wenn die Wunde** ~ **aufbricht** if the wound reopens.

Wieder- *pref* **re**; (*bei Verben*) (*erneut, noch einmal*) again; (*zurück*) back; ~**abdruck** *m* reprint; ~**aufbau** *m* (*lit, fig*) reconstruction, rebuilding; **der** ~**aufbau nach dem Krieg/des Hauses** post-war reconstruction/the rebuilding of the house; **w~aufbauen** *vti sep, ptp* **w~aufgebaut** to reconstruct, to rebuild; **w~aufbereiten** *vt sep* to recycle; *Atommüll* to reprocess; **w~auferstehen*** *vi sep irreg aux sein* to rise from the dead, to be resurrected; ~**auferstehung** *f* resurrection; **w~aufforsten** *vti sep, ptp* **w~aufgeforstet** to reforest; **w~aufführen** *vt sep, ptp* **w~aufgeführt** *Theaterstück* to revive; *Film* to reshow, to rerun; *Musikwerk* to reperform; **w~aufladen** *vt sep irreg, ptp* **w~aufgeladen** to recharge; **w~aufleben** *vi sep, ptp* **w~aufgelebt** *aux sein* to revive; ~**aufleben** *nt* revival; (*von Nationalismus etc auch*) resurgence; **w~auflegen** *vt sep, ptp* **w~aufgelegt** to republish; ~**aufnahme** *f* **(a)** (*von Tätigkeit, Gespräch etc*) resumption; (*von Beziehungen auch*) re-establishment; (*von Gedanken, Idee*) readoption; (*von Thema*) reversion (*gen* to); **die** ~**aufnahme des Verfahrens** (*Jur*) the reopening of proceedings; **(b)** (*von verstoßenem Menschen*) taking back; (*im Verein etc*) readmittance, reacceptance; (*von Patienten*) readmission; ~**aufnahmeverfahren** *nt* (*Jur*) (*im Zivilrecht*) rehearing; (*im Strafrecht*) retrial; **w~aufnehmen** *vt sep irreg, ptp* **w~aufgenommen** (**a**) to resume; *Beziehungen auch* to re-

establish; *Gespräch auch, Gedanken, Idee, Hobby* to take up again; *Thema* to revert to; (*Jur*) *Verfahren* to reopen; **(b)** *verstoßenen Menschen* to take back; (*in Verein etc*) to readmit, to reaccept; *Patienten* to readmit; **w~aufrichten** *vt sep, ptp* **w~aufgerichtet** (*fig*) *jdn* to give new heart to; **w~aufrüsten** *vti sep, ptp* **w~aufgerüstet** to rearm; *jdn moralisch* **w~aufrüsten** to raise sb's morale; ~**aufrüstung** *f* rearmament; **jds moralische** ~**aufrüstung** the raising of sb's morale; **w~ausführen** *vt sep, ptp* **w~ausgeführt** to re-export; ~**beginn** *m* recommencement, restart; (*von Schule*) reopening; **w~bekommen*** *vt sep irreg* to get back; **das bekommst du w~, du gemeines Stück!** I'll get my own back, you bastard (*sl*)!; **w~beleben*** *vt sep* to revive, to resuscitate; (*fig*) *Brauch etc* to revive, to resurrect; ~**belebung** *f* resuscitation, revival; (*fig*) revival, resurrection; ~**belebungsversuch** *m* attempt at resuscitation; (*fig*) attempt at revival; ~**belebungsversuche bei jdm anstellen** to attempt to revive *or* resuscitate sb.

wiederbeschaffen* *vt sep* to replace; (*zurückbekommen*) to recover.

Wiederbeschaffung *f siehe vt* replacement; recovery.

Wiederbeschaffungs- (*Comm*): ~**kosten** *pl* replacement cost *sing*; ~**wert** *m* replacement value.

Wieder-: **w~bewaffnen*** *vr sep* to rearm; ~**bewaffnung** *f* rearmament; **w~bringen** *vt sep irreg* to bring back; **w~einbürgern** *vt sep, ptp* **w~eingebürgert** to renaturalize; ~**einbürgerung** *f* renaturalization; **w~einfinden** *vr sep irreg, ptp* **w~eingefunden** to turn up again; ~**einfuhr** *f* reimport(ation); **w~einführen** *vt sep, ptp* **w~eingeführt** to reintroduce; *Todesstrafe auch* to bring back; (*Comm*) *Waren* to reimport; ~**einführung** *f* reintroduction; **w~eingliedern** *vt sep, ptp* **w~eingegliedert** to reintegrate (*in + acc* into); **einen Straftäter in die Gesellschaft** **w~eingliedern** to rehabilitate a criminal offender; ~**eingliederung** *f* reintegration; **die** ~**eingliederung eines Straftäters in die Gesellschaft** the rehabilitation of a criminal offender; **w~einliefern** *vt sep, ptp* **w~eingeliefert** *Kranken* to readmit (*in + acc* to); *Häftling* to reimprison; *jdn ins Gefängnis* **w~einliefern** to reimprison sb, to return sb to prison; ~**einnahme** *f* (*Mil*) recapture, retaking; **w~einnehmen** *vt sep irreg, ptp* **w~eingenommen** (*Mil*) to retake, to recapture; **w~einsetzen** *sep, ptp* **w~eingesetzt 1** *vt* to reinstate (*in + acc* in); *jdn als König* **w~einsetzen** to restore sb to the throne; *jdn in seinen Besitz* **w~einsetzen** to restore sb's possessions to him; **2** *vi* (*Regen*) to start up again; (*Med: Fieber, Schmerzen, Wehen*) to recur; ~**einsetzung** *f* reinstatement; (*von König*) restoration; **w~einstellen** *vt sep, ptp* **w~eingestellt** to re-employ, to re-engage; (*nach ungerechtfertigter Entlassung*) to reinstate; ~**einstellung** *f siehe vt* re-employment, re-engagement; reinstatement; ~**einstellungsklausel** *f* reinstatement clause; ~**eintritt** *m* re-entry (*auch Space*) (*in + acc* into); **w~entdecken*** *vt sep* (*lit, fig*) to rediscover; ~**entdeckung** *f* rediscovery; **w~ergreifen*** *vt sep irreg* to recapture; ~**ergreifung** *f* recapture; **w~erhalten*** *vt sep irreg* to recover; **w~erkennen*** *vt sep irreg* to recognize; **das war nicht w~zuerkennen** it/he was unrecognizable; **w~erlangen*** *vt sep* to regain; *Eigentum* to recover; ~**erlangung** *f siehe vt* regaining; recovery; **w~ernennen*** *vt sep irreg* to reappoint (*zu etw* (as) sth); ~**ernennung** *f* reappointment (*zu* as); **w~eröffnen*** *vti sep* to reopen; ~**eröffnung** *f* reopening; **w~erscheinen*** *vi sep irreg aux sein* to reappear; (*Buch etc*) to be republished; **w~erstatten*** *vt sep Unkosten etc* to refund, to reimburse (*jdm etw* sb for sth); *Schulden, geliehenes Geld* to repay; ~**erstattung** *f siehe vt* refund(ing), reimbursement; repayment; **w~erstehen*** *vi sep irreg aux sein* to rise again; **w~erwachen*** *vi sep aux sein* to reawake(n); **w~erwecken*** *vt sep* to bring back to life, to revive (*auch fig*); ~**erweckung** *f* bringing back to life, revival (*auch fig*); **w~finden** *sep irreg* **1** *vt* to find again; (*fig*) *Selbstachtung, Mut etc* to regain; *die Sprache* **w~finden** to find one's tongue again; **2** *vr* (*nach Schock*) to recover; **sich irgendwo** **w~finden** to find oneself somewhere; **sich** *or* **einander** **w~finden** to find each other again.

Wiedergabe *f* **-, -n** (*a*) (*von Rede, Ereignis, Vorgang*) account, report; (*Beschreibung*) description; (*Wiederholung: von Äußerung etc*) repetition.

(b) (*Darbietung: von Stück etc*) rendering, rendition.

(c) (*Übersetzung*) translation.

(d) (*Darstellung*) representation.

(e) (*Reproduktion*) (*von Gemälde, Farben, akustisch*) reproduction. **bei der** ~ in reproduction.

(f) (*Rückgabe*) return; (*von Rechten, Freiheit etc*) restitution.

Wiedergabe-: ~**gerät** *nt* playback unit; ~**treue** *f* fidelity of sound reproduction; **hohe** ~**treue** high fidelity; ~**verstärker** *m* playback amplifier.

wiedergeben *vt sep irreg* **(a)** *Gegenstand, Geld* to give back; (*fig*) *Rechte, Mut etc auch* to restore. **jdm ein Buch** ~ to give a book back to sb, to give sb his/her book back; **jdm die Freiheit** ~ to restore sb's freedom, to give sb back his freedom.

(b) (*erzählen*) to give an account of; (*beschreiben*) to describe; (*wiederholen*) to repeat. **seine Worte sind nicht wiederzugeben** his words are unrepeatable.

(c) *Gedicht* to recite; *Theaterstück, Musik* to perform.

(d) (*übersetzen*) to translate.

(e) (*darstellen, porträtieren*) to represent.

(f) (*reproduzieren*) *Gemälde, Farbe, Ton* to reproduce.

(g) (*vermitteln*) *Bedeutung, Gefühl, Erlebnis* to convey.

Wieder-: **w~geboren** *adj* (*lit, fig*) reborn; **w~geboren werden** to be reborn; to be reincarnated; ~**geburt** *f* (*lit, fig*) rebirth; reincarnation; ~**genesung** *f* recovery; **w~gewinnen*** *vt sep irreg* (*lit, fig*) to regain; *jdn* to win back; *Land, Rohstoffe etc* to reclaim; *Geld, Selbstvertrauen* to recover; w~grüßen *vti sep* (jdn) w~grüßen to return sb's greeting; (*einen ausgerichteten Gruß erwidern*) to send sb one's regards in return; (*Mil*) to return the/sb's salute; w~gutmachen *vt sep, ptp* w~gutgemacht to make good; *Schaden* to compensate for; *Fehler* to rectify; *Beleidigung* to put right; (*sühnen*) to atone for; (*Pol*) to make reparations for; (*Jur*) to redress; das ist nie w~gutzumachen that can never be put right; ~gutmachung *f* compensation; (*Sühne*) atonement; (*Pol*) reparations *pl*; (*Jur*) redress; als ~gutmachung für mein Benehmen/den Schaden/den Fehler/die Beleidigung to make up for my behaviour/compensate for the damage/rectify the fault/put right the insult; w~haben *vt sep irreg (inf)* to have (got) back; etw w~haben wollen to want sth back; w~herrichten *vt sep, ptp* w~hergerichtet to repair; *Zimmer* to redecorate; w~herstellen *vt sep, ptp* w~hergestellt *Gebäude, Ordnung, Frieden, jds Gesundheit* to restore; *Beziehungen* to re-establish; *Patienten* to restore to health; von einer *Krankheit* w~hergestellt sein to have recovered from an illness; ~herstellung *f siehe* wiederherstellen; re-establishment; restoration of sb's health; ~herstellungskosten *pl* restoration costs *pl*.

wiederhol̄bar *adj* repeatable. leicht/schwer ~ easy/hard to repeat; das ist nicht ~ that can't be repeated.

wiederho̊len [1]* *insep* 1 *vti* to repeat; (*zum zweiten Mal, mehrmals*) *Forderung etc* to reiterate; (*zusammenfassend*) to recapitulate; *Lernstoff* to revise; (*Film*) *Szene auch* to retake; (*Sport*) *Elfmeter etc* to retake, to take again; *Spiel* to replay. wiederholt, was ich euch vorsage repeat after me; (*eine Klasse or ein Jahr*) ~ (*Sch*) to repeat a year.

2 *vr* (*Mensch*) to repeat oneself; (*Thema, Ereignis*) to recur, to be repeated; (*Dezimalstelle*) to recur. es wiederholt sich doch alles im Leben life has a habit of repeating itself.

wiederho̊len [2] *vt sep* to get back.

wiederholt *adj* repeated. zu ~en Malen repeatedly, on repeated occasions; zum ~en Male once again.

Wiederho̊lung *f* repetition; (*von Aufführung*) repeat performance; (*von Sendung*) repeat; (*in Zeitlupe*) replay; (*von Lernstoff*) revision; (*zum zweiten Mal, mehrmals: von Forderung etc*) reiteration; (*zusammenfassend*) recapitulation; (*von Filmszene*) retaking; (*Sport*) (*von Elfmeter*) retaking, retake; (*von Spiel*) replay. trotz zweimaliger ~ derselben Klasse in spite of repeating the year twice.

Wiederho̊lungs-: ~kurs *m* refresher course; ~spiel *nt* (*Sport*) replay; ~taste *f* repeat key; ~täter *m* (*bei erster Wiederholung*) second offender; (*bei ständiger Wiederholung*) persistent offender, recidivist (*Psych*); ~zahlwort *nt* (*Gram*) siehe Iterativum; ~zeichen *nt* (*Mus*) repeat (mark); ~zwang *m* (*Psych*) recidivism; (*Sprachfehler*) palilalia (*spec*).

Wieder-: ~sehen *nt* (auf) ~hören! (*am Telefon*) goodbye!; (*im Hörfunk*) goodbye for now!; um 10 Uhr gibt es ein ~hören mit Richard Tauber at 10 o'clock you can hear Richard Tauber once again; ~impfung *f* revaccination; ~inbesitznahme *f* (*form*) resumption of possession; ~inbetriebnahme *f* (*form*) putting into operation again; (*von U-Bahnlinie*) reopening; ~instandsetzung *f* (*form*) repair, repairs *pl* (+*gen* to); w~käuen *sep* 1 *vt* to ruminate, to chew again; (*fig inf*) to go over again and again; 2 *vi* to ruminate, to chew the cud; (*fig inf*) to harp on; ~käuer *m -s, -* ruminant.

Wiederkehr *f -, no pl* (*geh*) (*Rückkehr*) return; (*zweites, ständiges Vorkommen*) recurrence; (*esp langweilig*) repetition; (*von Datum, Ereignis*) anniversary. die ewige ~ the eternal recurrence.

wiederkehren *vi sep aux sein* (*zurückkehren*) to return; (*sich wiederholen, wieder vorkommen*) to recur, to be repeated.

wiederkehrend *adj* recurring. regelmäßig/oft ~ recurrent; ein jährlich ~es Fest an annual festival.

Wieder-: w~kennen *vt sep irreg (inf)* to recognize; w~kommen *vi sep irreg aux sein* (*lit, fig*) to come back, to return; komm doch mal w~! you must come again!; w~kriegen *vt sep (inf)* to get back; warte nur, das kriegst du (von mir) w~! just you wait, I'll get my own back (on you)!; ~kunft *f -, no pl* (*liter*) return; die ~kunft Christi the Second Coming; w~lieben *vt sep* to love back; ~schauen *nt* (auf) ~schauen! goodbye!, good day! (*form*); (auf) ~schauen sagen to say goodbye; w~schenken *vt sep jdm etw* w~schenken to give sth back to sb; er wurde dem Leben w~geschenkt he was restored to life; w~sehen *vt sep irreg* to see again; (*wieder zusammentreffen mit auch*) to meet again; wann sehen wir uns w~? when will we see each other or meet again?; ~sehen *nt -s, -* (*nach kürzerer Zeit*) (another) meeting; (*nach längerer Zeit*) reunion; ich freue mich auf das ~sehen mit meinen Freunden/mit der Heimat I'm looking forward to seeing my friends/being back home again; sie hofften auf ein baldiges ~sehen they hoped to see each other or meet again soon; irgendwo, irgendwann gibt es ein ~sehen we'll meet again, don't know where, don't know when; (auf) ~sehen! goodbye!; (auf) ~sehen sagen to say goodbye; ~sehen macht Freude! (*hum*) I hope that's not the last I see of it!, I wouldn't mind having it back again!; ~taufe *f* (*Rel*) rebaptism; ~täufer *m* (*Rel, Hist*) Anabaptist; w~tun *vt sep irreg* to do again.

wiederum *adv* (a) (*andrerseits*) on the other hand; (*allerdings*) though. das ist ~ richtig, daran habe ich nicht gedacht that's quite correct, I didn't think of that. (b) (*geh: nochmals*) again, anew (*liter*). (c) (*seinerseits etc*) in turn. er ~ wollte ... he, for his part, wanted ...

Wieder-: ~vereinigen* *sep* 1 *vt Menschen, Fraktionen* to reunite; *Kirche auch, Land* to reunify; 2 *vr* to reunite, to come together again; ~vereinigung *f* reunification; w~verheiraten* *vr sep* to remarry; ~verheiratung *f* remarriage; ~verkauf *m* resale; (*durch Einzelhandel*) retail; w~verkaufen* *vt sep* to resell; (*Einzelhändler*) to retail; ~verkäufer *m* reseller; (*Einzelhändler*) retailer; ~verkörpe-

rung *f* reincarnation; w~verpflichten* *vr sep* (*Mil*) to re-enlist; w~verwendbar *adj* reusable; w~verwenden* *vt sep* to reuse; ~verwendung *f* reuse; w~verwerten* *vt sep* to reutilize, to reuse; ~verwertung *f* reutilization, reuse; ~wahl *f* re-election; eine ~wahl ablehnen to decline to run for re-election; wenn es zu einer ~wahl der Partei kommt if the party is returned again; w~wählen *vt sep* to re-elect; w~zulassen *vt sep irreg, ptp* w~zugelassen *Auto* to relicense; ~zulassung *f* relicensing; w~zusammentreten *vi sep irreg, ptp* w~zusammengetreten *aux sein* to reconvene.

wiefern *adv siehe* inwiefern.

Wie̊ge *f -, -n* (*lit, fig, Tech*) cradle. seine ~ stand in Schwaben (*geh*) his birthplace was Swabia; es ist mir/ihm auch nicht an der ~ gesungen worden, daß ... no-one could have foreseen that ...; das ist ihm (schon or gleich) in die ~ gelegt worden he inherited it; damals lagst du noch in der ~ at that time you were still a babe-in-arms; von der ~ bis zur Bahre (*geh*) from the cradle to the grave.

Wie̊gemesser *nt* chopper, chopping knife.

wie̊gen [1] 1 *vt* (a) to rock; *Kopf* to shake (slowly); *Hüften*, (*Wind*) *Äste etc* to sway. ~de Bewegung swaying motion; einen ~den Gang haben to sway one's hips when one walks.

(b) (*zerkleinern*) to chop up.

2 *vr* (*Boot etc*) to rock (gently); (*Mensch, Äste etc*) to sway. sich im Tanz ~ to do an undulating dance; sich in trügerischen Hoffnungen ~ to nurture false hopes; *siehe* gewiegt.

wie̊gen [2] *pret* wog, *ptp* gewogen *vti* to weigh. ein knapp gewogenes Kilo something short of a kilo; wieviel wiegst du? what weight are you?, what do you weigh?; schwer ~ (*fig*) to carry a lot of weight; (*Irrtum*) to be serious; gewogen und zu leicht befunden (*Bibl, fig*) weighed and found wanting.

Wiegen-: ~druck *m* incunabulum; (*Verfahren*) early printing; ~fest *nt* (*geh*) birthday; ~kind *nt* (*liter*) infant, babe-in-arms; ~lied *nt* lullaby, cradle-song.

wie̊hern *vi* to neigh; (*leiser*) to whinny. (*vor Lachen*) ~ to bray with laughter; das ist ja zum W~ (*inf*) that's dead funny (*inf*).

Wien *nt -s* Vienna.

Wie̊ner *adj attr* Viennese. ~ Würstchen frankfurter, wiener (sausage) (*esp US*); ~ Schnitzel Wiener schnitzel.

Wie̊ner(in *f*) *m -s, -* Viennese.

wie̊nerisch *adj* Viennese. das W~e Viennese, the Viennese accent/dialect.

wie̊ner(l)n *vti* (*inf*) to speak Viennese.

wienern *vti* (*usu pej*) to polish, to shine (*vt only*).

wies *pret of* weisen.

Wie̊se *f -, -n* (*dial*) meadow; (*inf: Rasen*) grass, lawn. auf der grünen ~ (*fig*) in the open countryside.

wie̊sehr *conj* (*Aus*) ~ ... auch however much.

Wie̊sel *nt -s, -* weasel. schnell or flink wie ein ~ quick as a flash; laufen or rennen wie ein ~ to run like a hare.

wie̊selflink 1 *adj* quick, quicksilver *attr*. 2 *adv* quick as a flash.

wie̊seln *vi aux sein* to scurry, to scuttle.

Wie̊sen-: ~blume *f* meadow flower; ~grund *m* (*poet*) meadow, mead (*poet*); ~rain *m* (*liter*) meadow's edge; ~schaumkraut *nt* lady's smock.

Wiesn *f -, -* (*dial*) fair.

wie̊so *interrog adv* why; (*aus welchem Grund auch*) how come (*inf*). ~ gehst du nicht? how come you're not going? (*inf*), why aren't you going?; ~ nicht why not; ~ sagst du das? why do you say that?; ~ weißt du das? how do you know that?

wie̊viel *interrog adv* how much; (*bei Mehrzahl*) how many. (um) ~ größer how much bigger.

wie̊vielerlei *interrog adj inv* how many sorts or kinds of. ~ verschiedene (Whiskys etc)? how many different sorts or kinds (of whisky etc)?

wie̊vielmal *interrog adv* how many times.

Wie̊vielte(r) *m decl as adj* (*bei Datum*) den ~n haben wir or der ~ ist heute? what's the date today?; am ~n (*des Monats*) what date?, what day of the month?; der ~ ist Donnerstag? what's the date on Thursday?

wie̊vielte(r, s) *interrog adj* das ~ Kind ist das jetzt? how many children is that now?; das ~ Kind bist du? — das zweite which child are you? — the second; der ~ Band fehlt? which volume is missing?; den ~n Platz hat er im Wettkampf belegt? where did he come in the competition?; als ~r ging er durchs Ziel? what place did he come?; das ~ Mal or zum ~n Mal bist du schon in England? how often or how many times have you been to England?; am ~n September hast du Geburtstag? when or what date in September is your birthday?; das ~ Jahr bist du jetzt in Schottland? how many years have you lived in Scotland now?; ich habe morgen Geburtstag! — der ~ ist es denn? it's my birthday tomorrow! — how old will you be?

wie̊weit *conj siehe* inwieweit.

wie̊wohl *conj* (*old*) (a) *siehe* obwohl. (b) (*dafür aber auch*) and at the same time, as well as.

Wigwam *m or nt -s, -s* wigwam.

Wi̊kinger *m -s, -* Viking.

Wi̊kinger-: ~drache *m* (Viking) longboat or longship; ~sage *f* Viking saga; ~schiff *nt* longboat, Viking ship; ~zeit *f* age of the Vikings, Viking age.

wi̊kingisch *adj* Viking *attr*.

wild *adj* wild; *Stamm* savage; *Schönheit auch* rugged; *Kind auch, Haar* unruly; (*laut, ausgelassen*) boisterous; (*heftig*) *Kampf*, (*zornig*) *Blick* fierce, furious; (*ungesetzlich*) *Parken, Zelten etc* illegal; *Streik* wildcat *attr*, unofficial. ~es Fleisch proud flesh; die W~e Jagd or Fahrt or Horde, das W~e Heer the Wild Hunt; der W~e Jäger the Wild Huntsman; den ~en Mann spielen (*inf*) or machen (*inf*) to come the heavy (*inf*); der W~e Westen the Wild West; ~ leben to live in the wild; ~ wachsen to grow wild; ~ ins Gesicht hängende Haare wild, tousled hair hanging over one's face; ~ durcheinanderliegen

to be strewn all over the place; **dann ging alles ~ durch-einander** there was chaos then; **wie ~ rennen/arbeiten** *etc* to run/work *etc* like mad; **~ drauflosreden/drauflosschreiben** to talk nineteen to the dozen/to write furiously; **seid nicht so ~!** calm down a bit!; **jdn ~ machen** to make sb furious *or* mad (*inf*); (*esp vor Vergnügen etc*) to drive sb wild; **einen Hund ~ machen** to drive a dog wild; **~ werden to go wild** (*auch inf*); (*Kinder: ausgelassen werden*) to run wild; **der Bulle wurde ~** (*inf*) the bull was enraged; **ich könnte ~ werden** (*inf*) I could scream (*inf*); **~ auf jdn/etw sein** (*inf*) to be wild *or* crazy *or* mad about sb/sth (*inf*); **das ist nicht so *or* halb so ~** (*inf*) never mind; **~ entschlossen** (*inf*) really *or* dead (*inf*) determined; *siehe* **Ehe, Wein.**
Wild *nt* -(e)s, *no pl* (*Tiere, Fleisch*) game; (*Rot~*) deer; (*Fleisch von Rot~*) venison. **ein Stück ~** a head of game.
Wild-: **~bach** *m* torrent; **~bad** *nt* (thermal) spa; **~bahn** *f* hunting ground *or* preserve; **auf *or* in freier ~bahn** in the wild; **~bestand** *m* game population, stock of game; **~braten** *m* roast venison; **ein ~braten** a roast of venison; **~bret** *nt* -s, *no pl* game; (*von Rotwild*) venison; **~dieb** *m* poacher; **~diebstahl** *m* poaching; **~ente** *f* wild duck.
Wilde(r) *mf decl as adj* savage, wild man/woman; (*fig*) madman, maniac. **die ~n** the savages.
Wilderei *f* poaching.
Wilderer *m* -s, - poacher.
wildern *vi* (*Mensch*) to poach; (*Hund etc*) to kill game. **~der Hund** dog which kills game.
Wildern *nt* -s, *no pl* poaching; (*von Hund etc*) killing game.
Wild-: **~esel** *m* wild ass; **~fang** *m* (a) (*Hunt*) (*Falke*) passage *or* wild-caught hawk; (*Tier*) animal captured in the wild; (b) (*dated inf*) little rascal *or* devil, scamp; (*Mädchen*) tomboy; **~fleisch** *nt* game; (*von Rotwild*) venison; **~fraß** *m* damage caused by game; **w~fremd** *adj* (*inf*) completely strange; **w~fremde Leute** complete strangers; **ein ~fremder, ein w~fremder Mensch** a complete stranger; **~fütterung** *f* feeding of game animals; **~gans** *f* wild goose; **~gehege** *nt* game enclosure *or* preserve; **~geschmack** *m* gam(e)y taste.
Wildheit *f* wildness; (*von Stamm etc*) savagery; (*von Kind auch, von Haar*) unruliness; (*von Kampf, Blick*) fierceness; (*Leidenschaft*) wild passion.
Wild-: **~hüter** *m* gamekeeper; **~kaninchen** *nt* wild rabbit; **~katze** *f* wildcat; **w~lebend** *adj attr* wild, living in the wild; **~leder** *nt* suede; **w~ledern** *adj* suede.
Wildnis *f* (*lit, fig*) wilderness. **Tiere der ~** wild animals; **in der ~ leben/geboren werden** to live/be born in the wild.
Wild-: **~park** *m* game park; (*für Rotwild*) deer park; **~pret** *nt* -(e)s, *no pl siehe* **~bret**; **~reichtum** *m* abundance of game; **~reservat** *nt* game reserve; **w~romantisch** *adj* (*iro*) terribly romantic; **~sau** *f* wild sow; (*fig sl*) pig (*inf*); **~schaden** *m* damage caused by game; **~schütz(e)** *m* (*obs*) poacher; **~schutzgebiet** *nt* game preserve; **~schwein** *nt* wild boar *or* pig; **w~wachsend** *adj attr* wild(-growing); **~wasser** *nt* white water; **~wasserboot** *nt* fast-water canoe; **~wasserrennen** *nt* fast-water canoe race; **~wechsel** *m* path used by game *or* wild animals; (*bei Rotwild*) deer path; „**~wechsel**" "wild animals"; **~west** *no art* the wild west; **~westfilm** *m* western; **~westroman** *m* western; **~wuchs** *m* (*geh*) rank growth; (*fig*) proliferation.
Wilhelm [ˈvɪlhɛlm] *m* -s William. **falscher ~** (*inf*) toupee; **seinen (Friedrich) ~ unter etw** (*dat*) **setzen** (*inf*) to put one's signature *or* moniker (*inf*) to sth.
Wilhelminisch [vɪlhɛlˈmiːnɪʃ] *adj* (*Hist*) Wilhelminian (pertaining to the reign of William II of Germany 1888–1918).
will *1. pers present of* **wollen**[2].
Wille *m* -ns, *no pl* will; (*Absicht, Entschluß*) intention. **nach jds ~n** as sb wanted/wants; (*von Architekt etc*) as sb intended/intends; **wenn es nach ihrem ~n ginge** if she had her way; **etw mit ~n tun** to do sth on purpose *or* deliberately; **das geschah gegen *or* wider meinen ~n** (*unabsichtlich*) I didn't intend that to happen; **er mußte wider ~n gegen seinen ~n lachen** he couldn't help laughing; **jds ~n tun** to do sb's will; **es steht (nicht) in unserem ~n, das zu tun** (*geh*) it is (not) our intention to do that; **seinen ~n durchsetzen** to get one's (own) way; **auf seinem ~n bestehen** to insist on having one's way; **jdm seinen ~n lassen** to let sb have his own way; **er soll seinen ~n haben** let him have his (own) way; **seinen eigenen ~n haben** to be self-willed, to have a mind of one's own; **beim besten ~n nicht** not with all the will *or* with the best will in the world; **ich hätte das beim besten ~n nicht machen können** I couldn't have done that for the life of me; **es war kein *or* nicht böser ~** there was no ill-will intended; **etw aus freiem ~n tun** to do sth of one's own free will; **es war dein freier ~, das zu tun** it was your own decision to do that; **der gute ~ good will**; **guten ~ns sein** to be full of good intentions; **alle Menschen, die guten ~ns sind** all people of good will; **den guten ~n für die Tat nehmen** to take the thought for the deed; **den redlichen ~n haben, etw zu tun** to have a sincere desire to do sth; **jdm zu ~n sein** to comply with sb's wishes; (*Mädchen: sich hingeben*) to yield to sb, to let sb have his way with one; **sich** (*dat*) **jdn zu ~n machen** to bend sb to one's will, to force sb to do one's will; **Mädchen** to have one's way with sb; **wo ein ~ ist, ist auch ein Weg** (*Prov*) where there's a will there's a way (*Prov*); *siehe* **letzte(r, s).**
willen *prep siehe* **um** 2.
Willen-: **w~los** *adj* weak-willed, spineless; **völlig w~los sein** to have no will of one's own; **sich jdm w~los unterwerfen** to submit totally to sb; **jds w~loses Werkzeug sein** to be sb's mere tool; **~losigkeit** *f* weakness of will, spinelessness.
willens *adj* (*geh*) **~ sein** to be willing *or* prepared.
Willens-: **~akt** *m* act of will; **~anstrengung** *f* effort of will;

~äußerung *f* expression of will; **~bildung** *f* development of an informed opinion; **~freiheit** *f* freedom of will; **~kraft** *f* will-power, strength of mind; **~mensch** *m* (*inf*) very determined person; **w~schwach** *adj* weak-willed; **~schwäche** *f* weakness of will; **w~stark** *adj* strong-willed, determined; **~stärke** *f* will-power; **~vollstrecker** *m* (*Sw*) *siehe* **Testamentsvollstrecker.**
willentlich *adj* wilful, deliberate.
willfahren *pret* **willfahrte**, *ptp* **willfahrt** *vi* +*dat* (*old, liter*) to please, to satisfy, to obey (*jdm* sb). **jds Wunsch** (*dat*) **~** to comply with sb's wish.
willfährig *adj* (*old, liter*) submissive, compliant. **jdm ~ sein** to submit to sb.
Willfährigkeit *f* (*old, liter*) submissiveness, compliance.
willig *adj* willing.
willigen *vi* (*old, liter*) **in etw** (*acc*) **~** to agree to sth.
Willigkeit *f* willingness.
Willkomm *m* -s, -e (*old, liter*) (a) welcome. (b) (*auch* **~becher**) cup of welcome (*old*).
willkommen *adj* welcome. **du bist (mir) immer ~** you are always welcome; **jdn ~ heißen** to welcome *or* greet sb; **seid (herzlich) ~!** welcome, welcome!; **herzlich ~** welcome (*in* +*dat* to); **es ist mir ganz ~, daß ...** I quite welcome the fact that ...; **die Gelegenheit, das zu sagen/zu tun, ist mir ~** I welcome the opportunity of saying/doing this.
Willkommen *nt* -s, - welcome. **jdm ein ~ bieten** (*liter*) to bid sb welcome; **ein herzliches ~!** welcome indeed!
Willkommens-: **~gruß** *m* greeting, welcome; **~trunk** *m* welcoming drink, cup of welcome (*old*).
Willkür *f* -, *no pl* capriciousness; (*politisch*) despotism; (*bei Entscheidungen, Handlungen*) arbitrariness. **sie sind seiner ~ schutzlos preisgegeben** *or* **ausgeliefert** they are completely at his mercy; **das ist reinste ~** that is purely arbitrary *or* just a whim; **ein Akt der ~** an act of caprice/a despotic act/an arbitrary act.
Willkür-: **~akt** *m siehe* **Willkür** act of caprice; despotic act; arbitrary act; **~herrschaft** *f* tyranny, despotic rule.
willkürlich *adj* (a) arbitrary; **Herrscher** autocratic. **sie kann ~ Tränen produzieren** she can produce tears at will. (b) *Muskulatur* voluntary.
Willkürlichkeit *f siehe adj* (a) arbitrariness; autocracy. (b) voluntariness. (c) *siehe* **Willkürakt.**
Willkürmaßnahme *f* arbitrary measure.
wimmeln *vi* (a) *auch vi impers* (*in Mengen vorhanden sein*) **der See wimmelt von Fischen, in dem See wimmelt es von Fischen** the lake is teeming with fish; **hier wimmelt es von Mücken/Pilzen/Menschen/Fehlern** this place is swarming with midges/overrun with mushrooms/teeming with people/this is teeming with mistakes; **der Käse wimmelt von Maden** the cheese is crawling with maggots.
(b) *aux sein* (*sich bewegen*) to teem; (*Menschen, Mücken, Ameisen auch*) to swarm.
wimmen (*Sw*) **1** *vt* to harvest, to gather. **2** *vi* to harvest *or* gather (the) grapes.
Wimmer(in *f*) *m* -s, - (*Sw*) *siehe* **Winzer(in).**
Wimmerl *nt* -(s), -n (*Aus*) (a) (*Pickel*) spot, pimple. (b) (*Skiläufertasche*) pouch.
wimmern *vi* to whimper.
Wimmet *m or f* -, *no pl* (*esp Sw, Aus*) grape harvest.
Wimpel *m* -s, - pennant.
Wimper *f* -, -n (a) (eye)lash. **ohne mit der ~ zu zucken** (*fig*) without batting an eyelid. (b) (*Bot, Zool*) cilium.
Wimperntusche *f* mascara.
Wimpertierchen *nt* ciliate.
Wind *m* -(e)s, -e (a) wind. **bei *or* in ~ und Wetter** in all weathers; **~ und Wetter ausgesetzt sein** to be exposed to the elements; **laufen/sich verbreiten wie der ~** to run like the wind/to spread like wildfire; **der ~ dreht sich** the wind is changing direction; (*fig*) the climate is changing; **wissen/merken, woher der ~ weht *or* bläst** (*fig*) to know/notice the way the wind is blowing; **daher weht der ~!** (*fig*) so that's the way the wind is blowing; **seither weht *or* bläst ein anderer/frischer ~** (*fig*) things have changed since then; **ein neuer ~ weht durch das Land** (*fig*) the wind of change is blowing in the country; **frischen *or* neuen ~ in etw** (*acc*) **bringen** (*fig*) to breathe new life into sth; **mach dir nicht so einen ~** (*inf*) don't make such a to-do (*inf*); **viel ~ um etw machen** (*inf*) to make a lot of fuss *or* to-do (*inf*) about sth; **vor dem/gegen den ~ segeln** (*lit*) to sail with the wind (behind one)/into the wind; **mit dem ~ zu segeln verstehen** (*fig*) to know how to bend with the wind; **den Mantel *or* das Mäntelchen *or* die Fahne *or* das Fähnchen nach dem ~ hängen *or* drehen *or* richten** to trim one's sails to the wind, to swim with the tide; **jdm den ~ aus den Segeln nehmen** (*fig*) to take the wind out of sb's sails; **sich** (*dat*) **den ~ um die Nase *or* Ohren wehen lassen** to see a bit of the world; **etw in den ~ schlagen** *Warnungen, Rat* to turn a deaf ear to sth; *Vorsicht, Vernunft* to throw *or* cast sth to the winds; **in den ~ reden** to waste one's breath; **wer ~ sät, wird Sturm ernten** (*Prov*) sow the wind and reap the whirlwind (*prov*).
(b) (*Himmelsrichtung*) wind (direction). **in alle (vier) ~e** to the four winds.
(c) (*Med: Blähung*) wind. **einen ~ fahren *or* streichen lassen** to break wind.
(d) (*Hunt*) wind. **von jdm/etw ~ nehmen *or* bekommen** to take *or* get the wind of sb/sth; **jdn/etw im ~ haben** to have the wind of sb/sth; **von etw ~ bekommen/kriegen/haben** (*fig inf*) to get/have wind of sth.
wind *adj* (*S Ger, Sw*) **jdm wird es ~ und weh** (*übel*) sb feels really ill; (*traurig*) sb feels really sad; (*angst*) sb feels really afraid.
Wind-: **~beutel** *m* (a) cream puff; (b) (*inf: Mensch*) rake; **~beutelei** *f* (*inf*) irresponsibility, unreliability; **~bluse** *f*

windcheater; ~**bö(e)** f gust of wind; ~**büchse** f (inf) air rifle; ~**drift** f drift current.
Winde[1] f -, -n (Tech) winch, windlass.
Winde[2] f -, -n (Bot) bindweed, convulvulus.
Wind|ei nt (fig) non-starter.
Windel f -, -n nappy (Brit), diaper (US). **damals lagst du noch in den ~n** you were still in nappies/diapers then; **noch in den ~n stecken** or **liegen** (fig) to be still in its infancy.
windeln 1 vt **ein Baby** ~ to put a baby's nappy (Brit) or diaper (US) on; (neu ~) to change a baby or a baby's nappy/diaper. **2** vi to put on nappies/a nappy (Brit) or diapers/a diaper (US).
windelweich adj **jdn** ~ **schlagen** or **hauen** (inf) to beat sb black and blue, to beat the living daylights out of sb.
winden[1] pret **wand**, ptp **gewunden 1** vt to wind; Kranz to bind; (hoch~) Eimer, Last to winch. **jdm etw aus der Hand** ~ to wrest sth out of sb's hand.
  2 vr (Pflanze, Schlange) to wind (itself); (Bach) to wind, to meander; (Mensch) (durch Menge, Gestrüpp etc) to wind (one's way); (vor Schmerzen) to writhe (vor with, in); (vor Scham, Verlegenheit) to squirm (vor with, in); (fig: ausweichen) to try to wriggle out. **sich** ~ **wie ein (getretener) Wurm** to squirm.
winden[2] vti impers **es windet (sehr)** the wind is blowing (hard).
winden[3] vti (Hunt) siehe **wittern**.
Windes-: ~**eile** f **etw in** or **mit** ~**eile tun** to do sth in no time (at all); **sich in** or **mit** ~**eile verbreiten** to spread like wildfire; ~**flügel** pl (liter) **auf** ~**flügeln** like the wind.
Wind-: ~**fahne** f (Met) windvane; ~**fang** m draught-excluder; (Raum) porch; ~**fangtür** f porch door; **w~geschützt 1** adj sheltered (from the wind). **2** adv **in a sheltered place;** ~**geschwindigkeit** f wind speed; ~**hafer** m wild oat; ~**harfe** f wind harp; ~**hauch** m breath of wind; ~**hose** f vortex.
Windhuk nt -s Windhoek.
Windhund m **(a)** (Hund) greyhound; (Afghanischer ~) Afghan (hound). **(b)** (fig pej) rake.
windig adj windy; (fig) Bursche, Sache dubious, dodgy (inf).
windisch adj (Aus usu pej) Slovene.
Wind-: ~**jacke** f windcheater; ~**jammer** m -s, - (Naut) windjammer; ~**kanal** m wind-tunnel; (an Orgel) wind-trunk; ~**licht** nt lantern; ~**loch** nt (Aviat) air-pocket; ~**mühle** f windmill; **gegen** ~**mühlen (an)kämpfen** (fig) to tilt at windmills; ~**mühlenflügel** m windmill sail or vane; ~**pocken** pl chickenpox sing; ~**richtung** f wind direction; ~**röschen** nt anemone; ~**rose** f (Naut) compass card; (Met) wind rose; ~**sack** m (Aviat) windsock, airsock; (an Dudelsack etc) (pipe)bag.
Windsbraut f (old, liter) storm, tempest (liter), (Wirbelwind) whirlwind. **wie eine** or **die** ~ (fig geh) like a whirlwind.
Wind-: ~**schatten** m lee; (von Fahrzeugen) slipstream; ~**scheibe** f (Sw) siehe ~**schutzscheibe**; **w~schief** adj crooked; Dach auch askew pred; Haus crooked; ~**schirm** m windbreak; **w~schlüpf(r)ig, w~schnittig** adj streamlined; ~**schutzscheibe** f windscreen (Brit), windshield (US); ~**seite** f windward side; ~**skala** f wind scale; ~**spiel** nt greyhound; ~**stärke** f strength of the wind; (Met) wind-force; **w~still** adj still, windless; Platz, Ecke etc sheltered; **wenn es völlig w~still ist** when there is no wind at all; ~**stille** f calm; ~**stoß** m gust of wind.
Windung f (von Weg, Fluß etc) meander; (von Schlange) coil; (Anat: von Darm) convolution; (Tech: von Schraube) thread; (eine Umdrehung) revolution; (Elec: von Spule) coil.
Wingert m -s, -e (dial, Sw) siehe **Weinberg**.
Wink m -(e)s, -e (Zeichen) sign; (mit der Hand) wave (mit of); (mit dem Kopf) nod (mit of); (Hinweis, Tip) hint, tip. **er gab mir einen** ~, **daß ich still sein sollte** he gave me a sign to be quiet.
Winkel m -s, - **(a)** (Math) angle; siehe **tot**.
  (b) (Tech) square.
  (c) (Mil: Rangabzeichen) stripe.
  (d) (fig: Stelle, Ecke) corner; (Plätzchen: esp von Land, Wald etc) place, spot. **jdn/etw in allen (Ecken und)** ~**n suchen** to look high and low for sb/sth; **in einem verborgenen** ~ **seines Herzens** in a hidden corner of his heart.
Winkel-: ~**advokat** m (pej) incompetent lawyer; ~**eisen** nt angle iron; **w~förmig** adj angled; **w~förmig gebogen** bent at an angle; ~**funktion** f (Math) trigonometrical function; ~**halbierende** f -n, -n bisector of an/the angle.
wink(e)lig adj siehe **winklig**.
Winkel-: ~**maß** nt (a) (Astron) Norma, the Level; **(b)** (Winkel) square; ~**messer** m -s, - protractor; ~**zug** m (Trick) dodge, trick; (Ausflucht) evasion; **mach keine** ~**züge** stop evading the issue.
winken ptp **gewinkt** or (dial) **gewunken 1** vi to wave (jdm to sb). **jdm ..., etw zu tun** to signal sb to do sth; **sie winkte mit einem Fähnchen/den Armen** she waved a flag/her arms; **einem Taxi** ~ to hail a taxi; **jdm mit den Augen** ~ (liter) to wink at sb; **jdm winkt etw** (fig: steht in Aussicht) sb can expect sth; **bei der Verlosung** ~ **wertvolle Preise** valuable prizes are being offered in the draw; **dem Sieger winkt eine Reise nach Italien** the winner will receive (the attractive prize of) a trip to Italy; **ihm winkt das Glück** fortune or luck is smiling on him, luck is on his side.
  2 vt to wave; (esp Sport: anzeigen) to signal; Taxi, Kellner to call. **jdn zu sich** ~ to beckon sb over to one; **eine Nachricht** ~ to send a message by semaphore.
Winker m -s, - (Aut) indicator, trafficator.
Winker|alphabet nt semaphore alphabet.
winke-winke machen vi (baby-talk) to wave.
winklig adj Haus, Altstadt full of nooks and crannies; Gasse twisty, windy.
Winkzeichen nt signal; (Mot) hand signal; (mit Fahne) semaphore signal.
Winsch f -, -en (Naut) windlass, winch.
winseln vti to whimper; (pej: um Gnade etc) to grovel.
Winter m -s, - winter. **es ist/wird** ~ winter is here or has

come/is coming; **im/über den** ~ in (the)/over the winter; **über den** ~ **kommen** to get through the winter; **der nächste** ~ **kommt bestimmt** (inf) you never know how long the good times are going to last.
Winter- in cpds winter; ~**anfang** m beginning of winter; **vor/seit** ~**anfang** before/since the beginning of winter; ~**einbruch** m onset of winter; **w~fest** adj hardy; Saat winter attr; ~**frucht** f siehe ~**getreide**; ~**garten** m winter garden; ~**getreide** nt winter crop; ~**halbjahr** nt winter; **im** ~**halbjahr** from September to March; **im** ~**halbjahr 1976/77** in the winter of 1976/77; **w~hart** adj Pflanzen hardy; ~**kälte** f cold winter weather; **in der größten** ~**kälte** in the depths of winter; ~**kartoffeln** pl (old) potatoes pl; ~**kleid** nt winter dress; (Zool) winter coat; (liter: von Landschaft etc) winter covering (of snow); ~**kleider** pl winter clothes pl; ~**kleidung** f winter clothing; ~**landschaft** f winter landscape; **w~lich** adj wintry; Wetter auch, Kleidung, Beschäftigung winter attr; **w~lich gekleidet** dressed for winter; ~**monat** m winter month.
wintern vi impers (liter) **es winterte schon** winter was coming.
Winter-: ~**nacht** f winter night; ~**obst** nt winter fruit; ~**olympiade** f Winter Olympics pl; ~**pause** f winter break; ~**quartier** nt (Mil) winter quarters pl; ~**reifen** m winter tyre.
winters adv in winter, in the wintertime.
Winter-: ~**saat** f winter seed; ~**sachen** pl winter clothes pl; ~**schlaf** m (Zool) hibernation; (den) ~**schlaf halten** to hibernate; ~**schlußverkauf** m winter sale; ~**semester** nt winter semester; ~**sonnenwende** f winter solstice; ~**spiele** pl (Olympische) ~**spiele** Winter Olympic Games or Olympics pl; ~**sport** m winter sports pl; (Sportart) winter sport; **in den** ~**sport fahren** to go on a winter sports holiday.
Winters-: **w~über** adv in winter; ~**zeit** f (liter) wintertime.
Winter-: ~**tag** m winter('s) day; ~**wetter** nt winter weather; ~**zeit** f winter time; (Jahreszeit) wintertime.
Winzer(in f) m -s, - , wine-grower; (Weinleser) grape-picker.
Winzergenossenschaft f wine-growers' organization.
winzig adj tiny. **ein** ~**es bißchen** a tiny little bit; ~ **klein** minute, tiny little attr.
Winzigkeit f tininess.
Wipfel m -s, - treetop. **in den** ~**n der Bäume** in the treetops or tops of the trees.
Wippe f -, -n (zum Schaukeln) seesaw.
wippen vi (auf und ab) to bob up and down; (hin und her) to teeter; (Schwanz) to wag; (mit Wippe schaukeln) to seesaw. **mit dem Schwanz** ~ to wag its tail; **mit dem Fuß** ~ to jiggle one's foot; **in den Knien** ~ to give at the knees; ~**der Gang** bouncing gait.
wir pers pron gen **unser**, dat **uns**, acc **uns** we. ~ **alle/beide/drei** all/both or the two/the three of us; ~ **als Betroffene/Kollegen ...** as those affected/as colleagues, we ...; ~ **Armen/Kommunisten** we poor people/we Communists; ~ (selbst) **sind/waren es, die ...** we are/were the ones who ..., it is/was we (form) or us who ...; **nicht nur** ~ **sind der Ansicht** ... it's not only we who are of the opinion ...; **immer sollen** ~**'s gewesen sein** everyone always blames us; **wer war das? —** ~ **nicht** who was that? — it wasn't us; **wer kommt noch mit? —** ~**/**~ **nicht** who's coming along? — we are/not us; **wer ist da? —** ~ (sind's) who's there? — (it's) us; **trinken** ~ **erst mal einen** let's have a drink first; **da haben** ~ **wohl nicht aufgepaßt?** (iro) we weren't paying attention, were we?; ~, **Wilhelm, Kaiser von ...** we, William, Emperor of ...
wirb imper sing of **werben**.
Wirbel m -s, - **(a)** (lit, fig) whirl; (in Fluß etc) whirlpool, eddy; (von Wind auch) eddy; (Drehung beim Tanz etc) pirouette; (der Gefühle, Ereignisse) turmoil; (Aufsehen) to-do. **im** ~ **des Festes** in the whirl or hurly-burly of the party; (viel/großen) ~ **machen/verursachen** to make/cause (a lot of/a big) commotion.
  (b) (Haar~) crown; (nicht am Hinterkopf) cowlick; (auf Fingerkuppe, in Stein) whorl. **vom** ~ **bis zur Zehe** (dated) from head or top to toe.
  (c) (Trommel~) (drum) roll.
  (d) (Anat) vertebra.
  (e) (an Saiteninstrument) peg; (an Fenster) catch.
wirb(e)lig adj (temperamentvoll) vivacious, lively; (wirr) dizzy. **mir ist ganz** ~ (im Kopf) my head is spinning.
wirbellos adj (Zool) invertebrate. **die W~en** the invertebrates.
wirbeln 1 vi **(a)** aux sein (Mensch, Wasser etc) to whirl; (Laub, Staub, Rauch etc auch) to swirl. **(b) mir wirbelt der Kopf** (inf) my head is spinning or reeling. **(c)** (Trommeln etc) to roll. **2** vt jdn, Wasser to whirl; Staub, Laub etc auch to swirl.
Wirbel-: ~**säule** f (Anat) spinal column; ~**sturm** m whirlwind; ~**tier** nt vertebrate; ~**wind** m whirlwind; **wie der/ein** ~**wind** like a whirlwind.
wirblig adj siehe **wirb(e)lig**.
wird 3. pers sing present of **werden**.
wirf imper sing of **werfen**.
Wirform, Wir-Form f first person plural.
wirken[1] **1** vi **(a)** (geh: tätig sein) (Mensch) to work; (Einflüsse, Kräfte etc) to be at work. **ich werde dahin** ~, **daß man ihn befördert** I will work for his promotion.
  (b) (Wirkung haben) to have an effect; (erfolgreich sein) to work. **als Gegengift/Katalysator** ~ to work as an antidote/to act as a catalyst; **schalldämpfend/abführend** ~ to have a soundproofing/laxative effect; **das wirkt auf viele als Provokation** many people see that as a provocation; **die Frau wirkt abstoßend auf mich** I find this woman repulsive; **die Pillen** ~ **gut gegen Bauchschmerzen** the pills are good for stomachache; **eine stark** ~**de Droge** a strong drug.
  (c) (einwirken) **auf etw** (acc) ~ (esp Chem) to act on sth; **etw auf sich** (acc) ~ **lassen** to take sth in.
  (d) (erscheinen) to seem, to appear. **nervös/ruhig (auf jdn)** ~ to give (sb) the impression of being nervous/calm, to seem nervous/calm (to sb).

(e) *(zur Geltung kommen)* to be effective. neben diesen Gardinen wirkt das Muster nicht *(richtig)* the pattern loses its effect next to those curtains; ich finde, das Bild wirkt I think the picture has something; die Musik wirkt erst bei einer gewissen Lautstärke you only get the full effect of the music when it's played loud.

2 *vt (geh: tun) Gutes* to do; *Wunder* to work; *siehe* Wunder.

wirken² *vt* **(a)** *(liter) Teppiche, Stoffe* to weave. **(b)** *(spec) Maschinentextilien* to knit. Goldfäden durch etw ~ to work gold threads into sth.

wirken³ *vt (rare: kneten) Teig* to knead, to work.

Wirken *nt* **-s,** *no pl* work.

Wirker(in *f)* *m* **-s,** - knitter.

Wirkerei *f* **(a)** knitting. **(b)** *(Fabrik)* knitwear factory.

Wirkkraft *f* effect.

wirklich **1** *adj* **(a)** *(zur Wirklichkeit gehörig)* real; *(tatsächlich auch) Sachverhalt, Aussage, Meinung etc* actual. im ~en Leben in real life.

(b) *(echt)* real; *Freund auch* true.

2 *adv* really. ich wüßte gern, wie es ~ war I would like to know what really happened; das meinst du doch nicht ~ you don't really mean that; ich war das ~ nicht it really was not me; ~?/nein, ~? *(als Antwort)* really?/what, really?; er ist es ~ it really is him; ~ und wahrhaftig really and truly.

Wirklichkeit *f* reality. ~ werden to come true; die Literatur spiegelt die ~ wider literature reflects reality; in ~ in reality; in ~ heißt er anders his real name is different; *siehe* Boden.

Wirklichkeits-: w~fern *adj* unrealistic, impractical; ~ferne *f* impracticality; ~form *f (Gram)* indicative; w~fremd *adj* unrealistic; w~getreu, w~nah *adj* realistic; etw w~getreu *or* w~nah abbilden/erzählen to paint a realistic picture/give a realistic account of sth; ~sinn *m* realism.

Wirkmaschine *f* knitting machine.

wirksam *adj* effective. ~ bleiben to remain in effect; mit (dem)/am 1. Januar ~ werden *(form: Gesetz)* to take effect on *or* from January 1st.

Wirksamkeit *f* effectiveness.

Wirkstoff *m (esp Physiol)* active substance.

Wirkung *f* effect *(bei* on); *(von Tabletten etc)* effects *pl.* seine ~ tun to have an effect; *(Droge)* to take effect; ohne ~ bleiben to have no effect; an ~ verlieren to lose its effect; seine ~ verfehlen not to have the desired effect; zur ~ kommen *(Medikament)* to take effect; *(fig: zur Geltung)* to come into effect; mit ~ vom 1. Januar *(form)* with effect from January 1st.

Wirkungs-: ~bereich *m (eines Menschen)* domain; *(einer Tageszeitung)* area of influence; *(von Atombombe, Golfstrom)* affected area; der ~bereich des atlantischen Tiefs the area affected by the Atlantic depression; ~dauer *f* period *or* over which sth is effective; ~feld *nt* field *(of activity/interest etc)*; ~kreis *m* sphere of activity; w~los *adj* ineffective; ~losigkeit *f* ineffectiveness; ~stätte *f (geh)* domain; w~voll *adj* effective; ~weise *f (von Medikament)* action; die ~weise eines Kondensators the way a condenser works.

Wirkwaren *pl* knitwear *sing; (Strümpfe etc auch)* hosiery *sing.*

wirr *adj* confused; *Blick* crazed; *(unordentlich) Haare, Fäden* tangled; *Gedanken, Vorstellungen* weird; *(unrealistisch, verstiegen)* wild. er ist ~ im Kopf *(geistig gestört)* he is confused in his mind; *(konfus)* he is confused *or* muddled; *(benommen: esp von Lärm)* his head is reeling *or* swimming; mach mich nicht ~ don't confuse me; alles lag ~ durcheinander everything was in chaos; das Haar hängt ihm ~ ins Gesicht his hair is hanging all in tangles over his face; er ist ein ~er Kopf he has crazy ideas; sich ~ ausdrücken to express oneself in a confused way.

Wirren *pl* confusion *sing,* turmoil *sing.*

Wirrheit *f siehe adj* confusion; tangledness; weirdness; wildness. die ~ seines Blicks his crazed look.

Wirrkopf *m (pej)* muddle-head. das sind alles ~e they've all got crazy ideas.

Wirrnis *f,* **Wirrsal** *nt* **-(e)s,** **-e** *(liter)* confusion.

Wirrung *f (liter)* confusion.

Wirrwarr *m* **-s,** *no pl* confusion; *(von Stimmen)* hubbub; *(von Verkehr)* chaos *no indef art; (von Fäden, Haaren etc)* tangle.

Wirsing *m* **-s,** *no pl,* **Wirsingkohl** *m* savoy cabbage.

Wirt *m* **-(e)s,** **-e** *(Gastwirt, Untervermieter)* landlord; *(Biol, rare: Gastgeber)* host. den ~ machen to play the host, to do the honours; *siehe* Rechnung.

wirten *vi (Sw)* to be a/the landlord.

Wirtin *f* landlady; *(Gastgeberin)* hostess; *(Frau des Wirts)* landlord's wife.

wirtlich *adj (geh)* agreeable, congenial.

Wirtlichkeit *f (geh)* agreeableness, congeniality.

Wirtschaft *f* **(a)** *(Volks~)* economy; *(Handel, Geschäftsleben)* industry and commerce; *(Finanzwelt)* business world. freie ~ free market economy; er ist in der ~ tätig he works in industry; he's a businessman; ein Mann der ~ a man of industry and commerce; seitens der ~ können wir keine Unterstützung erwarten we can expect no support from the business world.

(b) *(Gast~)* = pub *(Brit),* public house *(Brit form),* saloon *(US).* ~! *(inf)* waiter!; Frau ~! *(hum inf)* waitress!

(c) *(dated: Haushalt)* household. jdm die ~ führen to keep house for sb; er gründete eine eigene ~ he set up house on his own.

(d) *(dated: landwirtschaftlicher Betrieb)* farm. in einer ~ arbeiten to work on a farm.

(e) *(inf: Zustände)* state of affairs. du hast vielleicht eine ~ in deinem Haus/auf deinem Schreibtisch a fine mess *or* state your house/desk is in; eine schöne/saubere ~ *(iro)* a fine state of affairs; jetzt werden wir hier erst mal reine ~ machen *(dial)* first of all we'll put this house in order.

(f) *(inf: Umstände)* trouble, bother. eine ~ haben/sich *(dat)* eine ~ machen to have/go to a lot of trouble *or* bother.

wirtschaften **1** *vi* **(a)** *(sparsam sein)* to economize. gut ~ können to be economical;. sparsam ~ to economize, to budget carefully; ins Blaue hinein ~ not to budget at all; *siehe* Tasche.

(b) *(den Haushalt führen)* to keep house.

(c) *(inf: sich betätigen)* to busy oneself; *(gemütlich)* to potter about; *(herumfummeln)* to rummage about.

2 *vt* jdn/etw zugrunde ~ to ruin sb/sth financially.

Wirtschafter(in *f)* *m* **-s,** - **(a)** *(Verwalter)* manager. **(b)** *(im Haushalt, Heim etc)* housekeeper. **(c)** *(dial:* Wirtschaftler) economist.

Wirtschaftler *m* **-s,** - **(a)** *(Wissenschaftler)* economist. **(b)** *(Mann der Wirtschaft)* businessman.

wirtschaftlich *adj* **(a)** *(die Wirtschaft betreffend)* economic. jdm geht es ~ gut/schlecht sb is in a good/bad financial *or* economic position. **(b)** *(sparsam)* economical; *Hausfrau* careful.

Wirtschaftlichkeit *f* economy; *(mit Genitiv)* economicalness.

Wirtschafts- *in cpds* economic; ~aufschwung *m* economic upswing *or* upturn; ~berater *m* business consultant; ~beziehungen *pl* business relations *pl;* ~block *m (Pol)* economic bloc; ~demokratie *f* industrial democracy; ~form *f* economic system; gemischte ~form mixed economy; ~führer *m* leading businessman/industrialist; ~führung *f* management; ~gebäude *nt* working quarters *pl;* ~geld *nt* housekeeping (money); ~gemeinschaft *f* economic community; ~geographie *f* economic geography; ~güter *pl* economic goods *pl;* ~gymnasium *nt* grammar school which places emphasis on economics, law, management studies etc; ~hilfe *f* economic aid; ~hochschule *f* business school; ~kapitän *m (inf)* captain of industry; ~kraft *f* economic power; ~krieg *m* economic war/warfare; ~kriminalität *f* fraudulent manipulation of trade and tax laws; ~krise *f* economic crisis; ~lage *f* economic situation; ~leben *nt* business life; er ist im ~leben zu Hause he is at home in the business world; Persönlichkeiten des ~lebens business personalities; ~lenkung *f* economic control; ~macht *f* economic power; ~minister *m* minister of trade and commerce; ~ministerium *nt* ministry of trade and commerce; ~ordnung *f* economic order *or* system; ~politik *f* economic policy; w~politisch *adj* political-economic; w~politisch ist es unmöglich ... in terms of economic policy it is impossible ...; ~prüfer *m* accountant; *(zum Überprüfen der Bücher)* auditor; ~psychologie *f* industrial psychology; ~raum *m* **(a)** *(Agr)* working area; **(b)** *(Econ)* economic area; ~recht *nt* commercial *or* business law; ~spionage *f* industrial espionage; ~system *nt* economic system; ~teil *m* business *or* financial section; ~theorie *f* economic theory; ~treibende(r) *mf decl as adj (Aus) siehe* Gewerbetreibende(r); ~union *f* economic union; ~verband *m* business *or* commercial association; ~wissenschaft *f* economics *sing;* ~wissenschaftler *m* economist; ~wunder *nt* economic miracle; ~zeitung *f* financial *or* business (news)paper; ~zweig *m* branch of industry.

Wirts-: ~haus *nt* = pub *(Brit),* saloon *(US); (esp auf dem Land)* inn; ~hausschlägerei *f* pub brawl; ~leute *pl* landlord and landlady; ~pflanze *f* host (plant); ~stube *f* lounge; ~tier *nt* host (animal).

Wisch *m* **-(e)s,** **-e** *(pej inf)* piece of paper; *(mit Gedrucktem, Dokument)* piece of bumph *(inf); (Zettel mit Notiz)* note.

wischen **1** *vti* to wipe; *(mit Lappen reinigen)* to wipe clean. mit einem Tuch über eine Schallplatte ~ to wipe a record with a cloth; jdm über den Ärmel ~ to wipe sb's sleeve; mit dem Ärmel über die feuchte Tinte ~ to get one's sleeve in the wet ink; sie wischte ihm/sich den Schweiß mit einem Handtuch von der Stirn she wiped the sweat from his/her brow with a towel; Schmutz in eine Wunde ~ to get dirt into a wound; Bedenken/Einwände (einfach) vom Tisch ~ *(fig)* to sweep aside thoughts/objections; sich *(dat)* den Mund ~ können *or* dürfen *(dated inf)* to be left with one's mouth watering.

2 *vi aux sein (sich schnell bewegen)* to whisk.

3 *vt (inf)* jdm eine ~ to clout sb one *(inf);* eine gewischt bekommen *(elektrischen Schlag)* to get a shock.

Wischer *m* **-s,** - *(Aut)* (windscreen) wiper.

Wischerblatt *nt (Aut)* wiper blade.

Wischiwaschi *nt* **-s,** *no pl (pej inf)* drivel *(inf).* was du sagst, ist ein ~ what you're saying is a load of drivel *(inf).*

Wisch-: ~lappen *m* cloth; *(für Fußboden)* floorcloth; *(dial: für Geschirr)* dishcloth; ~tuch *nt* cloth; *(dial: für Geschirr)* dishcloth; ~-Wasch-Automatik *f (Aut)* wash-wipe.

Wisent *m* **-s,** **-e** bison.

Wismut *nt or (Aus) m* **-(e)s** bismuth.

wispern *vti* to whisper; *(unverständlich auch)* to mumble.

Wißbegier(de) *f* thirst for knowledge.

wißbegierig *adj* Kind eager to learn.

wisse *imper sing of* wissen.

wissen *pret* **wußte,** *ptp* **gewußt** **1** *vti* **(a)** *(informiert sein)* to know *(von* about). ich weiß (es) (schon)/nicht I know/don't know; weißt du schon das Neuste? have you heard the latest?; das weiß alle Welt/jedes Kind (absolutely) everybody/any fool knows that; was ich alles ~ soll!, als ob ich das wüßte! how should I know?; ich weiß von ihr *or* über sie nur, daß sie ... I only know that she ...; von ihr weiß ich das Alter I know her age *or* how old she is; von jdm/etw nichts ~ wollen not to be interested in sb/sth; er weiß es nicht anders/besser he doesn't know any different/better; er weiß zu genießen/schönen Urlaub zu machen he knows how to enjoy himself/how to have a nice holiday; jdn/etw zu schätzen ~ to appreciate sb/sth; das mußt du (selbst) ~ it's your decision; das solltest du selber ~ you ought to know; das hättest du ja ~ müssen! you ought to have realized that; man kann nie ~ you never know; man weiß nie, wozu das (noch mal) gut ist you never know when it will come in handy; das ~ die Götter *(inf),* das weiß der Henker *(inf)* God only knows; **weiß Gott** (*inf*) God knows (*inf*); **sich für weiß Gott was halten** (*inf*) to think one is somebody really special; **sie hält sich für wer weiß wie klug** (*inf*) she doesn't half think she's clever (*inf*); **... oder was weiß ich** (*inf*) ... or something; **... und was weiß ich noch alles** (*inf*) ... and whatever (*inf*); **er ist wieder wer weiß wo** (*inf*) goodness knows where he's got to again (*inf*); **(ja) wenn ich das wüßte!** goodness knows!; **wenn ich nur wüßte ... if only I knew ...**; **nicht, daß ich wüßte** not to my knowledge, not as far as I know; **gewußt wie/wo!** *etc* sheer brilliance!; **weißt du das?** (do) you know what?; **weißt du, ... you know ...; ja, weißt du** well, you see; **daß du es (nur) gleich weißt** just so you know; **ich weiß sie in Sicherheit/glücklich** I know that she is safe/happy; **ich wüßte die Angelegenheit gerne bald erledigt** I wish the matter to be settled soon; **was ich/er nicht weiß, macht mich/ihn nicht heiß** (*Prov*) what the eye does not see the heart cannot grieve over (*Prov*).

(b) (*kennen*) to know. **ich weiß keinen größeren Genuß, als ...** I know (of) no greater delight than ...

(c) (*erfahren*) **jdn etw ~ lassen** to let sb know sth, to tell sb sth.

(d) (*sich erinnern*) to remember; (*sich vor Augen führen*) to realize. **ich weiß seine Adresse nicht mehr** I can't remember his address; **weißt du noch, wie schön es damals war?** do you remember how lovely things were then?; **weißt du noch, damals im Mai/in Stone?** do you remember that May/the times in Stone?; **du mußt ~, daß ...** you must realize that ...

2 *vi* **um etw** (*acc*) **~** (*geh*), **von etw ~** to know of *or* about sth; **ich/er weiß von nichts** I don't/he doesn't know anything about it; **... als ob er von nichts wüßte** ... as if he didn't know a thing.

Wissen *nt* **-s**, *no pl* knowledge. **meines ~s** to my knowledge; **ohne jds ~ tun** to do sth without sb's knowledge; **etw gegen** *or* **wider** (*geh*) (**sein**) **besseres ~ tun** to do sth against one's better judgement; **nach bestem ~ und Gewissen** to the best of one's knowledge and belief; **mit jds ~ und Willen** with sb's knowledge and consent; **~ ist Macht** knowledge is power.

wissend *adj* **Blick** *etc* knowing.

Wissende(r) *mf decl as adj* (*Eingeweihter*) initiate. **die ~n schwiegen** those who knew kept silent.

Wissenschaft *f* science.

Wissenschaftler(in *f*), **Wissenschafter(in** *f*) (*old, Sw, Aus form*) *m* **-s**, **-** scientist; (*Geistes~*) academic.

wissenschaftlich *adj* scientific; (*geistes~*) academic. **W~er Assistent** assistant lecturer; **W~er Rat** lecturer, assistant professor (*US*).

Wissenschaftlichkeit *f* scientific nature *or* character; (*in bezug auf Geisteswissenschaften*) academic nature *or* character. **der Arbeit mangelt es an ~** this thesis lacks a scientific approach.

Wissenschafts-: **~betrieb** *m* academic life; **~lehre** *f* epistemology.

Wissens-: **~drang** *m*, **~durst** *m* (*geh*) urge *or* thirst for knowledge; **~gebiet** *nt* field (of knowledge); **~schatz** *m* (*geh*) store of knowledge; **~stoff** *m* material; **das ist ~stoff der 3. Klasse** that's material learned in the 3rd form; **ein enormer ~stoff** an enormous amount of material; **w~wert** *adj* worth knowing; **Information** *auch* valuable; **das Buch enthält viel ~wertes** the book contains much valuable information.

wissentlich 1 *adj* deliberate, intentional. **2** *adv* knowingly, deliberately, intentionally.

wisset, wißt *imper pl of* **wissen**.

Witfrau *f* (*old*), **Witib** *f* **-**, **-e** (*obs*) widow.

Witmann *m* (*old*) widower.

wittern 1 *vi* (*Wild*) to sniff the air. **2** *vt* (*Wild*) to scent, to get wind of; (*Riese, Teufel*) to smell; (*fig: ahnen*) **Gefahr** *etc* to sense, to scent. **wenn er eine Klassenarbeit witterte ...** whenever he suspected that a test was in the offing ...

Witterung *f* **(a)** (*Wetter*) weather. **bei günstiger/guter ~** if the weather is good. **(b)** (*Hunt*) (*Geruch*) scent (*von* of); (*Geruchssinn*) sense of smell.

Witterungs-: **w~beständig** *adj* weather-proof; **~einflüsse** *pl* effects *pl* of the weather; **~lage** *f* weather; **~umschlag** *m* change in the weather; **~verhältnisse** *pl* weather conditions *pl*.

Wittib *f* **-**, **-e**, **Wittiber** *m* **-s**, **-** (*Aus*) *siehe* **Witwe, Witwer**.

Witwe *f* **-**, **-n** widow. **~ werden** to be widowed.

Witwen-: **~geld** *nt* widow's allowance; **~jahr** *nt* year of mourning; **~pension** *f* (civil service) widow's pension; **~rente** *f* widow's pension; **~schaft** *f* widowhood; **~schleier** *m* widow's veil; **~stand** *m* widowhood; **~tröster** *m* (*pej inf*) widow chaser (*inf*); **~verbrennung** *f* suttee.

Witwer *m* **-s**, **-** widower.

Witz *m* **-es**, **-e (a)** (*Geist*) wit.

(b) (*Äußerung*) joke (*über* | *acc* about). **einen ~ machen** *or* **reißen** (*inf*) to make *or* crack a joke; **mach keine ~e!** don't be funny; **ich mach' keine ~e** I'm not being funny; **das soll doch wohl ein ~ sein, das ist doch wohl ein ~** that must be a joke, **he/you** *etc* must be joking; **die Prüfung/der Preis war ein ~** (*inf*) the exam/price was a joke.

(c) der ~ an der Sache ist, daß ... the great thing about it is that ...; **das ist der ganze ~** that's the thing.

Witz-: **~blatt** *nt* joke book; **~blattfigur** *f* (*fig inf*) joke figure; **sich** (*dat*) **wie eine ~blattfigur vorkommen** to feel ridiculous; **~bold** *m* **-(e)s**, **-e** joker; (*unterhaltsamer Mensch*) comic; **du bist vielleicht ein ~bold!** (*iro*) you're a great one! (*iro*).

Witzelei *f* teasing *no pl*. **laß doch diese blöde ~** stop teasing.

witzeln *vi* to joke (*über* | *acc* about).

Witzfigur *f* (*lit*) joke character; (*fig inf*) figure of fun.

witzig *adj* funny.

Witzigkeit *f* humour.

witz-: **~los** *adj* (*inf: unsinnig*) pointless, futile; **~sprühend** *adj* witty, sparkling.

w.L. *abbr of* **westlicher Länge**.

Wladiwostok *nt* **-s** Vladivostok.

WNW *abbr of* **Westnordwest** WNW.

w.o. *abbr of* **wie oben**.

wo 1 *interrog, rel adv* where; (*irgendwo*) somewhere. **überall, ~** wherever; **~ könnte er anders** *or* **~ anders könnte er sein als in der Kneipe?** where else could he be but in the pub?; **~ immer ...** wherever ...; **das muß doch hier ~ sein** (*inf*) it must be here somewhere; **der Tag/eine Zeit ~ ...** (*inf*) the day/a time when ...; **der Mann, ~ mich geschlagen hat** (*incorrect*) the man what hit me (*incorrect*); **ach** *or* **i ~!** (*inf*) nonsense!

2 *conj* **~ nicht/möglich** if not/possible; **~ er doch wußte, daß ich nicht kommen konnte** when he knew I couldn't come; **~ du doch in die Stadt gehst, könntest du ...?** (*inf*) seeing that you're going into town, could you ...?; **~ ich gerade daran denke** (*inf*) while I'm thinking about it; **und das jetzt, ~ ich doch dazu keine Lust habe** (*inf*) and that now when I'm just not in the mood.

wo-: **~anders** *adv* somewhere else, elsewhere; **~andersher** *adv* from somewhere else *or* elsewhere; **~andershin** *adv* somewhere else, elsewhere.

wob *pret of* **weben**.

wobei *adv siehe auch* **bei (a)** *interrog* **~ ist das passiert?** how did that happen?; **~ hast du ihn erwischt?** what did you catch him at *or* doing?; **~ seid ihr gerade?** what are you doing just now?; (*im Buch*) where are you at just now?

(b) *rel* in which. **ich erzähle mal, was passiert ist, ~ ich allerdings das Unwichtige auslasse** I will tell you what happened but I will leave out all the unimportant details; **~ man sehr aufpassen muß, daß man nicht betrogen wird/keinen Sonnenstich bekommt** and you have to be very careful that you don't get cheated/don't get sunburnt; **~ mir gerade einfällt** which reminds me; **das Auto prallte gegen einen Baum, ~ der Fahrer schwer verletzt wurde** the car hit a tree severely injuring the driver.

Woche *f* **-**, **-n** week. **zweimal in der ~** twice a week; **in dieser ~** this week; **in die ~n kommen** (*old*) to be near one's time (*old*); **in den ~n liegen** *or* **sein** (*old*) to be lying in (*old*).

Wochen-: **~bericht** *m* weekly report; **~bett** *nt* **im ~bett liegen** to be lying in (*old*); **im ~bett sterben** to die in the weeks following childbirth; **~bettfieber** *nt* puerperal fever.

Wochen|end- *in cpds* weekend; **~ausgabe** *f* weekend edition; **~beilage** *f* weekend supplement.

Wochen|ende *nt* weekend. **schönes ~!** have a nice weekend; **langes** *or* **verlängertes ~** long weekend.

Wochen|endler(in *f*) *m* **-s**, **-** (*inf*) weekend tripper.

Wochen-: **~fluß** *m* (*Med*) lochia (*spec*); **~hilfe** *f* maternity benefit; **~kalender** *m* week-by-week calendar; **~karte** *f* weekly season ticket; **w~lang** *adj, adv* for weeks; **nach w~langem Warten** after waiting for weeks, after weeks of waiting; **~lohn** *m* weekly wage; **~markt** *m* weekly market; **~schau** *f* newsreel; **~schrift** *f* weekly (periodical); **~tag** *m* weekday (*including Saturday*); **was ist heute für ein ~tag?** what day (of the week) is it today?; **w~tags** *adv* on weekdays.

wöchentlich 1 *adj* weekly. **2** *adv* weekly; (*einmal pro Woche*) once a week. **zwei Vormittage ~ kommen** to come two mornings a week; **~ zweimal** twice a week; **sich ~ abwechseln** to take turns every week.

Wochen-: **~übersicht** *f* (*inf*) (*gedrängte*) **~übersicht** the week's leftovers *pl*; **w~weise** *adv* week by week; (*einmal pro Woche*) once a week; (*für eine Woche*) by the week; **~zeitschrift** *f* weekly (magazine *or* periodical); **~zeitung** *f* weekly (paper).

Wöchnerin *f* woman who has recently given birth, woman in childbed (*old*), puerpera (*spec*).

Wöchnerinnenstation *f* maternity ward.

Wodan *m* **-s** (*Myth*) *siehe* **Wotan**.

Wodka *m* **-s**, **-s** vodka.

wodurch *adv siehe auch* **durch (a)** *interrog* how. **(b)** *rel* which. **alles, ~ sie glücklich geworden war ...** everything which had made her happy ...

wofern *conj* (*old*) if.

wofür *adv siehe auch* **für (a)** *interrog* for what, what ... for; (*warum auch*) why. **(b)** *rel* for which, which ... for.

wog *pret of* **wägen, wiegen²**.

Woge *f* **-**, **-n** wave; (*fig auch*) surge. **wenn sich die Wogen geglättet haben** (*fig*) when things have calmed down.

wogegen *adv siehe auch* **gegen (a)** *interrog* against what, what ... against. **~ ist dieses Mittel?** what's this medicine for? **(b)** *rel* against which, which ... against.

wogen *vi* (*liter*) to surge (*auch fig*); (*Kornfeld*) to wave, to undulate; (*fig: Kampf*) to rage; (*Busen*) to heave.

Wogenschlag *m* pounding (of the waves).

woher *adv* (**a**) *interrog* where ... from. **~ weißt du das?** how do you (come to) know that?; **~ kommt es eigentlich, daß ...** how is it that ...?, how come ... (*inf*); **ach ~!** (*dial inf*) nonsense! **(b)** *rel* from which, where ... from.

wohin *adv* (**a**) *interrog* where. **~, bitte?**; **~ so eilig?** where are you off to so fast** *or* **rushing off to?; **~ damit?** where shall I/we put it?; **ich muß mal ~** (*euph inf*) I've got to go somewhere (*euph inf*). **(b)** *rel* where. **~ man auch schaut** wherever you look.

wohinein *adv siehe* **worein**.

wohingegen *conj* whereas, while.

wohinter *adv siehe auch* **hinter (a)** *interrog* what *or* where ... behind. **~ kann ich in Deckung gehen?** what can I take cover behind?, behind what can I take cover?

(b) *rel* behind which. **die Mauer, ~ er in Deckung ging** (*inf*) the wall behind which he took cover *or* which he took cover behind; **~ man sich auch versteckt** whatever you hide behind.

wohl 1 *adv* (**a**) *comp* **-er**, *superl* **-sten** (*angenehm zumute*) happy; (*gesund*) well. **sich ~/~er fühlen** to feel happy/happier; (*wie zu Hause*) to feel at home/more at home; (*gesundheitlich*) to feel well/better; **bei dem Gedanken ist mir nicht ~** I'm not very happy at the thought; **am ~sten wäre mir, wenn ...** I'd feel happier if ...; **jdm ist ~ ums Herz** sb feels light of heart; **~ oder übel** whether one likes it or not, willy-nilly; **~ dem, der ... happy the man who ...; ~ ihm, daß ...** it's a good thing for him that ...; **es sich (dat) ~ gehen/sein/ergehen lassen** to enjoy oneself.

(b) (gut) comp **besser**, superl **bestens** or am **besten** well. **nun ~!** now then!; **ich wünsche ~ gespeist/geruht zu haben** (dated) I do hope you have enjoyed your meal/had a pleasant sleep; **laßt es euch ~ schmecken!** I hope you like or enjoy it; siehe **bekommen**.

(c) (wahrscheinlich) probably, no doubt; (iro: bestimmt) surely. **er ist ~ schon zu Hause** he's probably at home by now, no doubt he's at home by now; **das ist ~ nicht gut möglich** I should think it's unlikely; **es ist ~ anzunehmen, daß** ... it is to be expected that ...; **ich werde ~ noch ein Bier trinken gehen** I think I'll go out for a beer; **du bist ~ verrückt** you must be crazy!; **das ist doch ~ nicht dein Ernst!** surely you're not serious!, you can't be serious!

(d) (vielleicht) perhaps, possibly; (etwa) about. **ob ~ noch jemand kommt?** I wonder if anybody else is coming?; **das kann man sich ~ vorstellen, nicht wahr?** you can just imagine something like that, can't you?; **das mag ~ sein** that may well be; **willst du das ~ lassen!** I wish you'd stop (doing) that.

(e) (durchaus) well. **das kann ~ mal vorkommen** that might well happen; **ich denke, ich verstehe dich sehr ~!** I think I understand you very or perfectly well; **doch, das glaube ich ~** I certainly do believe it; **sehr ~ (der Herr)!** (old) very good (sir); **~!** (doch) yes!; (S Ger, Sw: selbstverständlich) of course!

2 conj (zwar) **er hat es ~ versprochen, aber ...** he may have promised, but ...; **~, aber ...** that may well be, but ...

Wohl nt -(e)s, no pl welfare, well-being. **das öffentliche ~ und das ~ des Individuums** the public good or common weal and the welfare of the individual; **der Menschheit zum ~e** for the benefit of mankind; **das ~ und Weh(e)** the weal and woe; **zu eurem ~** for your benefit or good; **zum ~!** cheers!; **auf dein ~!** your health!; **auf jds ~ trinken** to drink sb's health.

Wohl-: **w~achtbar** adj worthy; **w~an** interj (old, poet) come or well now; **w~anständig** adj respectable; Benehmen proper, correct; **w~auf 1** adj pred well, in good health; **2** interj siehe **w~an**; **w~ausgewogen** adj, comp besser ausgewogen, superl bestausgewogen (well) balanced; **w~bedacht** adj, comp besser bedacht, superl bestbedacht well considered; **~befinden** nt well-being; **w~begründet** adj, comp besser begründet, superl bestbegründet well-founded; Maßnahme, Strafe well-justified; **w~behagen** nt feeling of well-being; **w~behalten** adj Mensch safe and sound; Gegenstand intact; **w~bekannt** adj, comp besser bekannt, superl bestbekannt well-known; **sie ist mir w~bekannt** I know her well; **w~beleibt** adj (hum) stout, portly; **w~beraten** adj, comp besser beraten, superl bestberaten well-advised; **w~bestallt** adj attr (form) well-established; **w~durchdacht** adj, comp besser durchdacht, superl bestdurchdacht well or carefully thought out; **~ergehen** nt -s, no pl welfare; **w~erprobt** adj, comp besser erprobt, superl besterprobt well-tested, well-tried; Mitarbeiter experienced; **w~erwogen** adj, comp besser erwogen, superl besterwogen well or carefully considered; **w~erworben** adj (dated form) **w~erworbene Rechte** vested rights pl; **w~erzogen** adj, comp besser erzogen, superl besterzogen (geh) well-bred; Kind well-mannered; **w~erzogen sein/sich w~erzogen benehmen** to be well-bred/well-mannered.

Wohlfahrt f -, no pl (a) (old geh: Wohlergehen) welfare. **(b)** (Fürsorge) welfare. **bei der ~ arbeiten** to do welfare work.

Wohlfahrts-: **~amt** nt (dated, inf) siehe **Sozialamt**; **~ausschuß** m (Hist) Committee of Public Safety; **~einrichtung** f social service; **~marke** f charity stamp; **~organisation** f charity, charitable institution or organization; **~pflege** f social or welfare work; **freie ~pflege** voluntary social or welfare work; **~rente** f benefit pension; **~staat** m welfare state; **~unterstützung** f (dated) siehe **Sozialhilfe**.

Wohl-: **w~feil** adj, comp w~feiler, superl w~feilste(r, s) (old, liter) inexpensive; **w~geboren** adj (obs) Eure or Euer **~geboren** Sir; Seiner **~geboren Herr XY XY Esq**; **~gefallen** nt -s, no pl satisfaction, pleasure. **sein ~gefallen an etw (dat) haben** to take pleasure in sth; **sich in ~gefallen auflösen** (hum) (Freundschaft, Argument) to peter out; (Plan, Problem) to vanish into thin air; (Auto, Kleidung) to fall apart; **w~gefällig** adj (gefallend) pleasing; (zufrieden, erfreut) well-pleased; Gott **w~gefällig** well-pleasing to God; **w~geformt** adj, comp besser geformt, superl bestgeformt well-shaped; Körperteil shapely; Satz well-formed; **~gefühl** nt feeling or sense of well-being; **w~gelitten** adj, comp w~gelittener, superl w~gelittenste(r, s) (geh) well-liked; **w~gemeint** adj, comp besser gemeint, superl bestgemeint well-meant, well-intentioned; **w~gemerkt** adv mark you, mind (you); **das waren w~gemerkt englische Pfund** that was English pounds, mark or mind you; **w~gemut** adj, comp w~gemuter, superl w~gemuteste(r, s) (old, liter) cheerful; **w~genährt** adj, comp w~genährter, superl w~genährteste(r, s) well-fed; **w~geneigt** adj, comp w~geneigter, superl w~geneigteste(r, s) (old) well-disposed (dat towards); **Ihr Ihnen w~geneigter XY** Yours truly, XY; **w~geordnet** adj, comp besser geordnet, superl bestgeordnet (geh) well-ordered; Leben auch well-regulated; **w~geraten** adj, comp w~geratener, superl w~geratenste(r, s) (geh) Kind fine; Werk successful; **~geruch** m (geh) pleasant smell; (von Garten, Blumen etc auch) fragrance; **~geschmack** m (geh) flavour, pleasant taste; **w~gesinnt** adj, comp w~gesinnter, superl w~gesinnteste(r, s) (geh) well-disposed (dat towards); Worte well-meaning; **w~gestalt** adj (geh) Gegenstand well-shaped; Körperteil, Frau shapely; Mann well-proportioned; **w~gestaltet** adj, comp w~gestalteter, superl

w~gestaltetste(r, s) well-shaped, well-proportioned; **w~getan** adj (old, liter) well done pred; **w~habend** adj, comp w~habender, superl w~habendste(r, s) well-to-do, prosperous; **~habenheit** f prosperity, affluence.

wohlig adj pleasant; (gemütlich) cosy; Ruhe blissful. **~ rekelte er sich in der Sonne** he stretched luxuriously in the sun.

Wohl-: **~klang** m (geh) melodious sound; **w~klingend** adj, comp w~klingender, superl w~klingendste(r, s) pleasant (-sounding), melodious; **~laut** m (geh) pleasant sound; **~leben** nt (geh) life of luxury; **w~meinend** adj, comp w~meinender, superl w~meinendste(r, s) well-meaning; **w~proportioniert** adj, comp besser proportioniert, superl bestproportioniert well-proportioned; **w~riechend** adj, comp w~riechender, superl w~riechendste(r, s) (geh) fragrant; **w~schmeckend** adj, comp w~schmeckender, superl w~schmeckendste(r, s) (geh) palatable; **~sein** nt: zum/auf Ihr **~sein!** your health!

Wohlstand m -(e)s, no pl affluence, prosperity, siehe **ausbrechen**.

Wohlstands-: **~bürger** m (pej) member of the affluent society; **~gesellschaft** f affluent society; **~kriminalität** f crimes typical of the affluent society; **~müll** m refuse of the affluent society.

Wohltat f (a) (Genuß) relief. **(b)** (Dienst, Gefallen) favour; (gute Tat) good deed. **jdm eine ~ erweisen** to do sb a favour or a good turn.

Wohltäter(in f) m benefactor; benefactress.

wohltätig adj (a) charitable. **(b)** (DDR) siehe **wohltuend**.

Wohltätigkeit f charity, charitableness.

Wohltätigkeits-: **~basar** m charity bazaar; **~konzert** nt charity concert; **~verein** m charitable organization, charity; **~zweck** m charitable cause, good cause.

Wohl-: **w~temperiert** adj, comp besser temperiert, superl besttemperiert Wein, Bad, Zimmer at the right temperature no comp; **das „~temperierte Klavier"** "The Well-Tempered Clavier"; **w~tuend** adj, comp w~tuender, superl w~tuendste(r, s) (most) agreeable; **w~tun** vi sep irreg (a) (angenehm sein) to do good (jdm sb), to be beneficial (jdm to sb); **das tut w~** that's good; **(b)** (old, liter: Gutes tun) to benefit (jdm sb); **w~überlegt** adj, comp besser überlegt, superl bestüberlegt well thought out; **etw w~überlegt machen** to do sth after careful consideration; **w~unterrichtet** adj attr well-informed; **w~verdient** adj Strafe well-deserved; Belohnung, Ruhe etc auch well-earned; **~verhalten** nt (usu iro) good conduct or behaviour; **w~versorgt** adj, comp besser versorgt, superl bestversorgt well-provided; **w~verstanden 1** adj attr (geh) well-understood; **2** adv mark or mind you; **w~weislich** adv very wisely; **ich habe das w~weislich nicht gemacht** I was careful not to do that; **w~wollen** vi sep irreg (geh) **jdm w~wollen** to wish sb well; **~wollen** nt -s, no pl goodwill; **selbst bei dem größten ~wollen** with the best will in the world; **jdn mit ~wollen betrachten** to regard sb benevolently; **sich (dat) jds ~wollen erwerben** to win sb's favour; **w~wollend** adj, comp w~wollender, superl w~wollendste(r, s) benevolent; **jdm w~wollend geneigt or gesonnen sein, jdm gegenüber w~wollend sein** to be kindly disposed towards sb; **jdm ein w~wollendes Ohr schenken** to lend sb a willing ear.

Wohn-: **~anhänger** m caravan; **~bau** m, pl -ten residential building; **~bevölkerung** f residential population; **~block** m, pl -s block of flats, apartment house (US); **~dichte** f (Sociol) occupant density; **~diele** f hall-cum-living-room; **~einheit** f accommodation unit.

wohnen vi (a) to live; (vorübergehend) to stay. **wo ~ Sie?** what's your address?, where do you live/are you staying?; **er wohnt (in der) Friedrichstraße 11** he lives at (number) 11 Friedrichstraße; **wir ~ sehr schön** we have a very nice flat/house etc; **wir ~ da sehr schön** it's very nice where we live; **hier wohnt es sich gut, hier läßt es sich gut ~** it's a nice place to live/stay; siehe **möblieren**.

(b) (fig liter) to dwell (liter), to live.

Wohn-: **~fläche** f living space; **20m² ~fläche** living room (,dining room and bedroom(s) totalling 20 sq m; **~gebäude** nt siehe **~bau**; **~gebiet** nt residential area; **~gegend** f residential area; **~geld** nt a rent rebate; **~gemeinschaft** f (Menschen) people sharing a/the flat (Brit) or apartment/house; **unsere ~gemeinschaft** the people I share a flat etc with; **in einer ~gemeinschaft leben** to share a flat etc; **w~haft** adj (form) resident; **~haus** nt residential building; **~heim** nt (esp für Arbeiter) hostel; (für Studenten) hall (of residence), dormitory (US); (für alte Menschen) home; **~komfort** m comfort of one's home; **ein Appartement mit sämtlichem ~komfort** an apartment with every modern convenience or all mod cons; **~komplex** m housing estate; **~küche** f kitchen-cum-living-room; **~kultur** f style of home décor; **keine ~kultur haben** to have no taste in home décor; **~lage** f residential area; **unsere ~lage ist schön/ungünstig** our house/apartment is nicely/awkwardly situated; **~landschaft** f landscaped interior; **w~lich** adj homely, cosy; **es sich (dat) w~lich machen** to make oneself comfortable; **~lichkeit** f homeliness, cosiness; **~objekt** nt (Aus form) accommodation unit; **~ort** m place of residence; **~partei** f (esp Aus) tenant; (mehrere Personen) tenants pl; **~raum** m living-room; (no pl: ~fläche) living space; **~-Schlafzimmer** nt bed-sitting-room; **~siedlung** f housing estate; **~silo** m (pej) concrete block; **~sitz** m domicile; **ohne festen ~sitz** of no fixed abode; **~stadt** f residential town; **~stube** f siehe **~zimmer**.

Wohnung f flat (Brit), apartment; (liter: von Tieren etc) habitation; (Wohneinheit) dwelling (form); (Unterkunft) lodging. **1.000 neue ~en** 1,000 new homes; **~ nehmen** (form) to take up residence; **freie ~ haben** to have free lodging.

Wohnungs-: **~amt** nt housing office; **~bau** m, no pl house building no def art; **~bauprogramm** nt housing programme; **~bedarf** m housing requirements pl; **~besetzer(in** f) m -s, -

squatter; ~inhaber m householder, occupant; (Eigentümer auch) owner-occupier; w~los adj (form) homeless; ~makler m estate agent, real estate agent (US); ~mangel m housing shortage; ~markt m housing market; ~nachweis m accommodation registry; ~not f serious housing shortage or lack of housing; ~suche f flat-hunting (Brit); auf ~suche sein to be looking for a flat (Brit) or apartment, to be flat-hunting (Brit); w~suchend adj after looking for accommodation; ~tausch m exchange of (flats/houses); ~tür f door (to the flat (Brit) or apartment); ~wechsel m change of address; ~wesen nt housing.

Wohn-: ~verhältnisse pl (von Familie) living conditions pl; (in Stadt) housing conditions pl; ~viertel nt residential area or district; ~wagen m caravan (Brit), trailer (US); ~zimmer nt living-room; ~zwecke pl residential purposes pl.

wölben 1 vt to curve; Blech etc to bend; Dach etc to vault.
2 vr to curve; (Asphalt) to bend or buckle; (Tapete) to bulge out; (Brust) to swell; (Stirn) to be domed; (Decke, Brücke) to arch. ein klarer Sternenhimmel wölbte sich über uns the clear sky formed a star-studded dome above us (liter).

Wölbung f curvature; (kuppelförmig) dome; (bogenförmig) arch; (von Körperteil) curve; (von Straße) camber; (von Tapete) bulge.

Wolf m -(e)s, ‐e (a) wolf. ein ~ im Schafspelz a wolf in sheep's clothing; mit den ‐en heulen (fig) to run with the pack.
(b) (Tech) shredder; (Fleisch~) mincer (Brit), grinder (US). jdn durch den ~ drehen (fig) to put sb through his paces; ich fühle mich wie durch den ~ gedreht I feel as if I've been on the rack.
(c) (Med) intertrigo no art (spec) (inflammation of the skin between the buttocks).

Wölfchen nt dim of **Wolf** wolf-cub.

Wölfin f she-wolf.

wölfisch adj wolfish.

Wölfling m (Pfadfinder) cub (scout).

Wolfram nt -s, no pl (Chem) tungsten; wolfram.

Wolfs-: ~hund m Alsatian (Brit), German shepherd (US); irischer ~hund Irish wolfhound; ~hunger m (fig inf) ravenous hunger; ich hatte einen ~hunger I was ravenous; ~mensch m (a) wolf child; er war ein ~mensch he had been reared by wolves; (b) (Werwolf) werewolf; ~milch f (Bot) spurge; ~rachen m (Med) cleft palate; ~rudel nt pack of wolves; ~spinne f wolf spider.

Wolga f - Volga.

Wölkchen nt dim of **Wolke**.

Wolke f -, -n (lit, fig) cloud; (in Edelstein) flaw. aus allen ~n fallen (fig) to be flabbergasted (inf); das ist 'ne ~ (inf) it's fantastic (inf); siehe schweben.

Wolken-: ~bank f cloudbank; ~bildung f cloud formation; es kann zu ~bildung kommen it may become cloudy or overcast; ~bruch m cloudburst; w~bruchartig adj torrential; ~decke f cloud cover; die Stadt liegt unter einer dichten ~decke the town lies under a heavy layer of cloud; ~himmel m cloudy or overcast sky; ~kratzer m skyscraper; ~kuckucksheim nt cloud-cuckoo-land; in einem ~kuckucksheim leben to live in cloud-cuckoo-land; ~landschaft f (liter) clouds pl; w~los adj cloudless; ~meer nt (liter) sea of clouds; ~schicht f layer of cloud, cloud layer; ~schleier m (liter) veil of cloud (liter); von einem ~schleier eingehüllt veiled in cloud; ~streifen m streak of cloud; w~verhangen adj overcast; ~wand f cloudbank; ~zug m passage of clouds.

wolkig adj cloudy.

Wolldecke f (woollen) blanket.

Wolle f -, -n wool. in der ~ gefärbt (fig) dyed-in-the-wool; jdn in die ~ bringen (fig inf) to get sb's back up (inf); mit jdm in die ~ kommen or geraten, sich mit jdm in die ~ kriegen (fig inf) to start squabbling with sb; sich mit jdm in der ~ haben (fig inf) to be at loggerheads with sb.

wollen¹ adj attr woollen.

wollen² 1. pers present will, pret wollte, ptp gewollt 1 vi (a) (Willen zeigen, haben) er kann schon, wenn er nur will he can (do it) if he really wants (to); man muß nur ~ you simply have to have the will; man muß sich nur sagen: ich will I will only have to say: I will do it; da ist nichts zu ~ there is nothing we/you can do (about it).
(b) (bereit, gewillt sein) wenn er will if he wants to; er will nicht so recht he doesn't seem all that willing, he seems rather unwilling; so Gott will God willing.
(c) (mögen) to want to, to like. geborgt oder, wenn du willst, gestohlen borrowed or, if you like, stolen; wenn man so will, wenn du so willst if you like, as it were; ganz wie du willst just as you like; wenn du willst, machen wir das so if you want to or if you like, we'll do it that way; wer nicht will, hat gehabt if you don't/he doesn't like it, you/he can lump it (inf); ob du willst oder nicht whether you like it or not.
(d) (an bestimmten Ort gehen etc) to want to go. ich will nach Hause/hier raus/weg I want to go home/to get out of here/to get away; er will unbedingt ins Kino he is set on going or determined to go to the cinema; wo willst du hin? where do you want to go?; zu wem ~ Sie? whom do you want to see?

2 vt (a) to want. er will doch nur dein Bestes he only wants the best for you; ~, daß jd etw tut to want sb to do sth; was wollten sie denn von dir? what did they want then?; was willst du (noch) mehr! what more do you want!; ich weiß nicht, was du willst, das ist doch ausgezeichnet I don't know what you're on about, it's excellent; er hat gar nichts zu ~ he has no say at all; ohne es zu ~ without wanting to; das wollte ich nicht (war unbeabsichtigt) I didn't mean to (do that); was ~ sie? what do they want?; siehe gewollt.
(b) etw lieber ~ to prefer sth; etw unbedingt ~ to want sth desperately.

(c) (bezwecken) etw mit etw ~ to want sth with sth, to want sth for sth; was willst du mit dem Messer? what are you doing with that knife?; was willst du mit der Frage? why are you asking that?; was ~ die Leute mit solchen Filmen? what do people hope to achieve with films like that?
(d) (brauchen) to want, to need.

3 modal aux vb ptp ~ (a) etw haben ~ to want (to have) sth; ich will so einen Fehler nie wieder machen I won't make a mistake like that again; er will immer alles besser wissen he thinks he knows it all; was will man da schon machen/sagen? what can you do/say?; wenn man darauf noch Rücksicht nehmen wollte if one were to take that into account too.
(b) (beabsichtigen) etw gerade tun ~ to be going to do sth; wolltest du gerade weggehen? were you just leaving?; ich wollte schon gehen/gerade aufhören, als ... I was just going to leave/just about to stop when ...
(c) (werden) das ~ wir doch erst mal sehen! we'll have to see about that!
(d) (Anschein haben) es sieht aus, als wollte es regnen it looks as if it's going to rain; es will nicht besser/wärmer werden it just won't get better/warmer; die Arbeit will mir nicht schmecken I don't seem to be able to get down to work; es will und will nicht aufhören it just goes on and on; er will und will sich nicht ändern he just will not change.
(e) (in bezug auf Behauptung) keiner wollte etwas gehört/gesehen haben nobody will admit to having heard/seen anything; keiner will es gewesen sein nobody will admit to it; der Zeuge will den Dieb beobachtet haben the witness claims to have seen the thief; und so jemand will Lehrer sein! and he calls himself a teacher.
(f) (in Wunsch, Aufforderung) ich wollte, ich wäre ... I wish I were ...; das wolle Gott verhüten heaven forbid; wollte Gott, du hättest recht I wish to God you were right; ~ wir uns nicht setzen? why don't we sit down?; wir ~ beten! let us pray; man wolle bitte ... would you kindly ...; wenn Sie bitte Platz nehmen ~ if you would care to sit down please; wenn er mir das doch ersparen wollte! if only he would spare me that!; na, ~ wir gehen? well, shall we go?; darauf ~ wir mal anstoßen! let's drink to that; wir ~ mal nicht übertreiben/in Ruhe überlegen let's not exaggerate/let's think about it calmly.
(g) komme, was da wolle come what may; sei er, wer er wolle whoever he may be.
(h) impers es will mir nicht einleuchten, warum I really can't see why; es will mir nicht scheinen, daß ... it seems to me that ...
(i) (müssen) das will alles genauestens überlegt sein/werden it all has to be most carefully considered; die Pflanzen ~ oft gegossen werden the plants have to be watered frequently.

Woll-: ~faser f wool fibre; ~fett nt wool-fat, lanolin; ~garn nt woollen yarn; ~gras nt (Bot) cotton grass.

wollig adj woolly.

Woll-: ~jacke f cardigan; ~kämmerei f (a) (Fabrik) wool-carding shop; (b) (Tätigkeit) wool-carding; ~knäuel nt ball of wool; ~sachen pl woollens pl; ~siegel nt Woolmark ®; ~spinnerei f (a) (Fabrik) woolmill; (b) (Tätigkeit) wool-spinning; ~stoff m woollen material; ~strumpf m woollen stocking.

Wollust f -, no pl (liter) (Sinnlichkeit) sensuality, voluptuousness; (Lüsternheit) lust, lewdness, lasciviousness. ~ empfinden to be in ecstasy; etw mit wahrer ~ tun (fig) to delight in doing sth.

wollüstig adj (geh) (sinnlich) sensual; Frau auch voluptuous; (lüstern) lascivious, lusty; (verzückt, ekstatisch) ecstatic. seine ~e Freude an etw (dat) haben (fig) to go into ecstasies over sth; jdn ~ anblicken to give sb a lascivious look; sich ~ im warmen Bad rekeln to luxuriate in a warm bath.

Wollüstling m (hum inf) sensualist.

Woll-: ~waren pl woollen goods pl, woollens pl; ~wäsche f washing woollens no art; (Artikel) woollens pl.

womit adv siehe auch mit (a) interrog with what, what ... with. ~ kann ich dienen? what can I do for you?
(b) rel with which; (auf ganzen Satz bezüglich) by which. ein Gerät, ~ man auch bohren kann an appliance you can drill with too; das ist es, ~ ich nicht einverstanden bin that's what I don't agree with; ~ ich nicht sagen will, daß ... by which I don't mean or which doesn't mean to say that ...; ~ man es auch versuchte ... whatever they tried to do it with ...

womöglich adv possibly; siehe wo.

wonach adv siehe auch nach (a) interrog after what, what ... after. ~ sehnst du dich? what do you long for?; ~ riecht das? what does it smell of?; ~ sollen wir uns richten? what should we go by?
(b) rel das Land, ~ du dich sehnst the land for which you are longing or (which) you are longing for; das war es, ~ ich mich erkundigen wollte that was what I wanted to ask about; die Nachricht, ~ er ... the news that he ...

Wonne f -, -n (geh) (Glückseligkeit) bliss no pl; (Vergnügen) joy, delight. mit ~ with great delight; (aber) mit ~! with great pleasure!; das ist ihre ganze ~ that's all her joy; in eitel ~ schwimmen to be lost in rapture; die ~n der Liebe/~(n) des Paradieses the joys or delights of love/delights of paradise; es ist eine wahre ~ it's a sheer delight.

Wonne-: ~gefühl nt blissful feeling; ~monat, ~mond (poet) m May; im ~monat Mai in the merry month of May; ~proppen m (hum inf) bundle of joy; ~schauer m thrill of joy; ~schrei m cry of delight; w~voll adj Gefühl blissful; Kind, Anblick delightful; Gesichtsausdruck delighted; ein w~volles Leben a life of bliss; w~voll lächeln to smile with delight.

wonnig adj delightful; Gefühl, Ruhe blissful.

wonniglich adj (poet) Gefühl, Stunden blissful; Kind, Anblick delightful.

woran adv siehe auch an (a) interrog ~ soll ich den Kleiderbügel hängen? what shall I hang the coat-hanger on?; ~ denkst du? what are you thinking about?; man weiß bei ihm nie, ~ man ist you never know where you are with him; ~ liegt das? what's the reason for it?; ~ ist er gestorben? what did he die of?

(b) rel (auf vorausgehenden Satz bezogen) by which. das, ~ ich mich gerne erinnere what I like to recall; die Wand, ~ sie immer die Plakate kleben the wall on which they are always sticking posters, the wall they're always sticking posters on; ..., ~ ich schon gedacht hatte ... which I'd already thought of; ~ ich merkte, daß ... which made me realize that ...; ~ er auch immer gestorben ist ... whatever he died of ...

worauf adv siehe auch **auf** (a) interrog (räumlich) on what, what ... on. ~ wartest du? what are you waiting for?; ~ sollte ich mich freuen? what do I have to look forward to?

(b) rel (zeitlich) whereupon. ~ du dich verlassen kannst of that you can be sure; das ist etwas, ~ ich mich freue that's something I'm looking forward to; das, ~ er sich vorbereitet hatte what he was prepared for; ~ er einen Wutanfall bekam whereupon he flew into a rage; ~ er sich auch beruft ... whatever his arguments are ...

woraufhin rel adv whereupon.

woraus adv siehe auch **aus** (a) interrog out of what, what ... out of. ~ ist der Pullover? what is the pullover made (out) of?; ~ schließt du das? from what do you deduce that?

(b) rel out of which, which ... out of. das Buch, ~ ich gestern vorgelesen habe the book I was reading from yesterday; ~ ich schließe/gelernt habe, daß ... from which I conclude/have learned that ...; ~ man das Öl auch gewinnt ... whatever oil is obtained from ...

worden ptp of **werden** 1 (c).

worein adv siehe auch **hinein** (a) interrog in what, what ... in. **(b)** rel in which, which ... in. das ist etwas, ~ ich mich nie fügen werde that's something I shall never submit to or put up with.

worfeln vti (Agr) to winnow.

worin adv siehe auch **in** (a) interrog in what, what ... in. ~ war das eingewickelt? what was it wrapped in?; ~ liegt der Unterschied/Vorteil? what is the difference/advantage?

(b) rel in which, which ... in, wherein (form). das ist etwas, ~ wir nicht übereinstimmen that's something we don't agree on; dann sagte er ..., ~ ich mit ihm übereinstimme then he said ..., which is where I agree with him; ~ du es auch einwickelst ... whatever you wrap it in ...

Wort nt -(e)s, -e (a) pl usu ¨-er (Vokabel) word. ein ~ mit sechs Buchstaben a word with six letters, a six-letter word; ~ für ~ word for word; siehe **wahr**.

(b) (Äußerung) word. nichts als ~ e nothing but words or talk; genug der ~ e! enough talk!; das ist ein ~! wonderful!; in ~ und Schrift in speech and writing; er beherrscht die Sprache in ~ und Schrift he has a command of the written and spoken language; in ~ und Tat in word and deed; in ~ en und Werken sündigen to sin in words and deeds; ~ en Taten folgen lassen to suit the action to the word(s); mit einem ~ in a word; mit anderen/wenigen ~ en in other/a few words; hast du/hat der Mensch (da noch) ~ e! it leaves you speechless; kein ~ mehr not another word; kein ~ von etw sagen/erwähnen/fallenlassen not to say one word or a thing about sth; kein ~ von etw wissen/verstehen not to know/understand a thing about sth; ich verstehe kein ~! I don't understand a word (of it); (hören) I can't hear a word (that's being said); er sagte or sprach kein einziges ~ he didn't say a single word; ein ~ mit jdm sprechen or reden to have a word with sb; mit dir habe ich noch ein ~ zu reden! I want a word with you!; ein ernstes ~ mit jdm reden to have a serious talk with sb; kein ~ miteinander/mit jdm sprechen or reden not to say a word to each other/to sb; sag doch ein ~! say something!; hättest du doch ein ~ gesagt if only you had said something; davon hat man mir kein ~ gesagt they didn't tell me anything about it; man kann sein eigenes ~ nicht (mehr) verstehen or hören you can't hear yourself speak; man muß ihn mit seinen eigenen ~ en schlagen you have to beat him at his own game; er brach in die ~ e aus: ... he burst out: ...; um nicht viel(e) ~ e zu machen to make it brief; ich konnte kein ~ anbringen I couldn't get a word in edgeways; ein ~ gab das andere one thing led to another; jdm das ~ or die ~ e im Mund (her)umdrehen to twist sb's words; du sprichst ein großes or wahres ~ gelassen aus how true, too true; die passenden/keine ~ e für etw finden to find the right/no words for sth; das rechte ~ zur rechten Zeit the right word at the right time; jdn mit schönen ~ en abspeisen to fob sb off; er hat nur schöne ~ e gemacht it was just talk; jdm schöne ~ e machen to soft-soap sb; auf ein ~! a word!; jdm aufs ~ glauben to believe sb implicitly; das glaub ich dir aufs ~ I can well believe it; ohne ein ~ (zu sagen) without (saying) a word; dein ~ in Gottes Ohr let us hope so; seine ~ e galten dir he meant you, he was talking about you; siehe **verlieren**.

(c) no pl (Rede, Recht zu sprechen) das ~ nehmen to speak; (bei Debatte auch) to take the floor; das große ~ haben or führen (inf) to shoot one's mouth off (inf); das ~ an jdn richten to address (oneself to) sb; jdm ins ~ fallen to interrupt sb; jdm das ~ abschneiden to cut sb short; zu ~ kommen to get a chance to speak; ums ~ bitten, sich zu ~ melden to ask to speak; er hat das ~ it's his turn to speak; (bei Debatte auch) he has the floor; jdm das ~ erteilen or geben to allow sb to speak; (in Debatte auch) to allow sb to take the floor; er hat mir das ~ verboten he forbade me to speak.

(d) (Ausspruch) saying; (Zitat) quotation; (Rel) Word. ein ~, das er immer im Munde führt one of his favourite sayings; ein ~ Goethes/aus der Bibel a quotation from Goethe/the Bible; das ~ zum Sonntag short religious broadcast on Saturday night, ≈ late call (Brit); nach dem ~ des Evangeliums according to the Gospel.

(e) (Text, Sprache) words pl. in ~ en in words; in ~ und Bild in words and pictures; etw in ~ e fassen to put sth into words;

das geschriebene/gedruckte/gesprochene ~ the written/printed/spoken word; das ~ als Kommunikationsmittel language as a means of communication.

(f) (Befehl, Entschluß) das ~ des Vaters ist ausschlaggebend the father's word is law; das ~ des Königs the king's command; jdm aufs ~ gehorchen or folgen to obey sb's every word; dabei habe ich auch (noch) ein ~ mitzureden or mitzusprechen I (still) have something to say about that too; das letzte ~ ist noch nicht gesprochen the final decision hasn't been taken yet.

(g) no pl (Versprechen) word. auf mein ~ I give (you) my word; jdn beim ~ nehmen to take sb at his word; ich gebe mein ~ darauf I give you my word on it; sein ~ halten to keep one's word.

Wort-: ~ akzent m word stress; ~ armut f lack of vocabulary; ~ art f (Gram) part of speech; ~ aufwand m verbosity; ~ auswahl f choice of words; ~ bedeutung f meaning of a/the word; ~ bildung f (Ling) morphology; ~ bruch m das wäre ein ~ bruch that would be breaking your/my etc promise; w~ brüchig adj false; w~ brüchig werden to break one's word.

Wörtchen nt dim of **Wort** little word. da habe ich wohl ein ~ mitzureden (inf) I think I have some say in that; mit ihm habe ich noch ein ~ zu reden (inf) I want a word with him.

Wörter-: ~ buch nt dictionary; ~ verzeichnis nt vocabulary; (von Spezialbegriffen) glossary.

Wort-: ~ familie f word family; ~ feld nt semantic field; ~ folge f (Gram) word order; ~ forschung f lexicology; (Etymologie) etymology; ~ führer m spokesman; ~ gebühr f (Telec) rate per word; ~ gefecht nt battle of words; ~ geklingel nt (pej) verbiage; ~ geographie f word geography; ~ geplänkel nt banter; w~ getreu adj, adv verbatim; w~ gewandt adj eloquent; ~ gottesdienst m spoken service; ~ gut nt vocabulary; w~ karg adj taciturn; ~ kargheit f taciturnity; ~ klauber m -s, - caviller, quibbler; ~ klauberei f cavilling, quibbling; ~ kunde f lexicology; (Vokabelsammlung) vocabulary; ~ laut m wording; im ~ laut verbatim; folgenden ~ laut haben to read as follows.

Wörtlein nt dim of **Wort**; siehe **Wörtchen**.

wörtlich adj Bedeutung literal; Übersetzung, Wiedergabe etc auch word-for-word; Rede direct. etw ~ wiedergeben/abschreiben to repeat/copy sth verbatim or word for word; etw ~ übersetzen to translate sth literally or word for word; das darf man nicht so ~ nehmen you mustn't take it literally; das hat er ~ gesagt those were his very or actual words.

Wort-: w~ los 1 adj silent; 2 adv without saying a word; ~ meldung f request to speak; wenn es keine weiteren ~ meldungen gibt if nobody else wishes to speak; ~ prägung f (auch ~ neubildung) neologism; ein Meister der ~ prägung a master at coining words; ~ rätsel nt word puzzle; w~ reich adj Rede, Erklärung etc verbose, wordy; Sprache rich in vocabulary or words; sich w~ reich entschuldigen to apologize profusely; ~ reichtum m siehe adj verbosity, wordiness; richness in vocabulary or words; ~ schatz m vocabulary; ~ schöpfung f neologism; ~ schwall m torrent of words; ~ sinn m meaning of a/the word; ~ spiel nt pun, play on words; ~ stamm m (Ling) root of a/the word); ~ stellung f (Gram) word order; ~ verdrehung f twisting of words; ~ wahl f choice of words; ~ wechsel m exchange (of words), verbal exchange; ~ witz m pun; w~ wörtlich 1 adj word-for-word; 2 adv word for word, quite literally.

worüber adv siehe auch **über** (a) interrog about what, what ... about; (örtlich) over what, what ... over.

(b) rel about which, which ... about; (örtlich) over which, which ... over; (auf vorausgehenden Satz bezogen) which. das Thema, ~ ich gerade einen Artikel gelesen habe the subject I have just read an article about; ~ sie sich auch unterhalten, sie ... whatever they talk about they ...

worum adv siehe auch **um** (a) interrog about what, what ... about. ~ handelt es sich? what's it about? **(b)** rel about which, which ... about. der Ast, ~ ich die Schnur gebunden hatte the branch I tied the rope (a)round; ~ die Diskussion auch geht, ... whatever the discussion is about ...

worunter adv siehe auch **unter** (a) interrog under what, what ... under. ich weiß nicht, ~ er leidet I don't know what he is suffering from. **(b)** rel under which, which ... under.

woselbst rel adv (obs) where.

Wotan m -s (Myth) Wotan.

wovon adv siehe auch **von** (a) interrog from what, what ... from. ~ hat er das abgeleitet? what did he derive that from?

(b) rel from which, which ... from; (auf vorausgehenden Satz bezogen) about which, which ... about. das ist ein Gebiet, ~ er viel versteht that is a subject he knows a lot about; ~ du dich auch ernährst, ... whatever you eat ...

wovor adv siehe auch **vor** (a) interrog (örtlich) before what, what ... before. ~ fürchtest du dich? what are you afraid of?

(b) rel before which, which ... before. das Ereignis, ~ ich schon immer gewarnt habe the event I have always warned you about; ~ du dich auch fürchtest, ... whatever you're afraid of ...

wozu adv siehe auch **zu** (a) interrog to what, what ... to; (warum) why. ~ soll ich das legen? where shall I put it?; ~ hast du dich entschlossen? what have you decided on?; ~ soll das gut sein? what's the point of that?; ~ denn das? what for?; ~ denn? why should I/you? etc.

(b) rel to which, which ... to. das, ~ ich am meisten neige what I'm most inclined to do; das Verfahren, ~ ich raten würde the procedure I would advise; ein Projekt, ~ man viel Zeit braucht a project which you need a lot of time for; ..., ~ ich mich jetzt auch entschlossen habe ... which I have now decided to do; sie haben geheiratet, ~ ich nichts weiter sagen möchte they have got married, and I shall say no more about that; ~ du dich auch entschließt, ... whatever you decide (on) ...

Wrack nt -s, -s or (rare) -e wreck; (fig) (physical) wreck.

Wrackboje, Wracktonne f (Naut) wreck buoy.

wrang pret of **wringen**.

Wrasen m -s, - (esp N Ger) vapour.

wringen, pret wrang, ptp gewrungen vti to wring.

Wruke f -, -n (dial) siehe **Steckrübe**.

WSW abbr of **Westsüdwest** WSW.

Wucher m -s, no pl profiteering; (bei Geldverleih) usury. **das ist doch ~!** that's daylight robbery!

Wucherer(in f) m -s, - profiteer; (Geldverleiher) usurer.

Wuchergeschäft nt profiteering no pl; usury no pl.

wucherisch adj profiteering; Geldverleih, Zinsen usurious; Bedingungen, Preis, Miete etc exorbitant, extortionate.

Wuchermiete f exorbitant or extortionate rent.

wuchern vi **(a)** aux sein or haben (Pflanzen) to grow rampant, to proliferate; (wildes Fleisch) to proliferate; (Bart, Haare) to grow profusely. **in die Höhe ~** to shoot up(wards). **(b)** (fig: sich verbreiten) to be rampant. **sein Haß wuchert im verborgenen** his hatred is quietly intensifying. **(c)** (Kaufmann etc) to profiteer; (Geldverleiher) to practise usury. **mit seinen Talenten ~** (fig) to make the most of one's talents.

wuchernd adj Pflanzen rampant, proliferous; Bart, wildes Fleisch proliferous.

Wucherpreis m exorbitant price. **~e bezahlen** to pay through the nose.

Wucherung f rank growth, proliferation; (Med) growth; (wildes Fleisch) proud flesh.

Wucherzins m exorbitant or usurious interest.

wuchs [vu:ks] pret of **wachsen**[1].

Wuchs [vu:ks] m -es, no pl (Wachstum) growth; (Gestalt, Form) stature; (von Mensch) build, stature.

Wucht f -, no pl **(a)** force; (von Angriff auch) brunt; (Stoßkraft auch) momentum; (fig auch) power. **mit aller ~** with all one's force or might; **mit voller ~** with full force. **(b)** (inf: Menge) load (inf). **eine ~ (Prügel)** a good hiding. **(c)** (inf) **er/das ist die or eine ~!** he's/that's smashing! (inf).

wuchten vti **(a)** to heave. **(b)** siehe **auswuchten**.

wuchtig adj massive, solid; Schlag heavy, powerful; Wein, (fig) heavy.

Wuchtigkeit f massiveness, solidness; power; heaviness.

Wühl|**arbeit** f (fig pej) subversive activities pl.

wühlen 1 vi **(a)** (nach for) to dig; (Maulwurf etc) to burrow; (Schwein, Vogel) to root. **in den Haaren ~** to run one's fingers through one's hair; **im Bett ~** to toss and turn; **im Schmutz ~** (fig) to wallow in the mire. **(b)** (suchen) to rummage, to root (nach etw for sth). **in den Schubladen ~** to rummage or root through the drawers. **(c)** (fig) to gnaw (in + dat at). **der Schmerz/Hunger wühlte ihm im Magen** the pain/hunger gnawed (away) at his stomach. **(d)** (inf: schwer arbeiten) to slog (inf). **(e)** (Untergrundarbeit leisten) to stir things up. 2 vt to dig, to burrow. **er wühlte seinen Kopf in die Kissen** he buried his face in the pillows. 3 vr **sich durch die Menge/das Gestrüpp/die Akten ~** to burrow one's way through the crowd/the undergrowth/the files.

Wühler m -s, - **(a)** (pej: Aufrührer) agitator, subversive. **(b)** (inf: schwer Arbeitender) slogger (inf). **(c)** (inf: unruhig Schlafender) wriggler.

Wühlerei f siehe vi **(a, b, d, e)** **(a)** digging; burrowing; rooting. **(b)** rummaging or rooting (about). **(c)** (inf: Arbeiten) slogging. **(d)** (Pol inf) agitation.

Wühl-: **~maus** f vole; (fig pej) subversive; **~tisch** m (inf) bargain counter.

Wulst m -es, ¨-e or f -, ¨-e bulge; (an Reifen) bead; (an Flasche, Glas) lip; (Archit) torus; (Her) wreath; (Naut) bulb. **ein ~ von Fett** a roll of fat; **die dicken ~e seiner Lippen** his thick lips.

wulstig adj bulging; Rand, Lippen thick.

Wulst-: **~lippen** pl thick lips pl; **~reifen** m bead tyre.

wummern vi (inf) **(a)** (dröhnen) to rumble; (pochen) to drum. **an or gegen die Tür ~** to hammer at the door. **(b)** aux sein (dröhnend fahren) to rumble along.

wund adj sore. **etw ~ kratzen/scheuern** to make sth sore by scratching/chafing it; **das Pferd/ich war vom Reiten ~ gescheuert** the horse/I was saddle-sore; **ein Tier ~ schießen** to wound an animal; **sich** (dat) **die Füße/Fersen ~ laufen** (lit) to get sore feet/heels from walking; (fig) to walk one's legs off; **sich** (dat) **die Finger ~ schreiben** (fig) to write one's fingers to the bone; **sich** (dat) **den Mund ~ reden** (fig) to talk till one is blue in the face; **ein ~er Punkt, eine ~e Stelle** a sore point; **ein ~es Herz** (liter) a wounded heart.

Wund-: **~arzt** m (old) surgeon; **~benzin** nt surgical spirit; **~brand** m gangrene.

Wunde f -, -n (lit, fig) wound. **alte ~n/eine alte ~ wieder aufreißen** (fig) to open up old sores; **an eine alte ~ rühren** (fig geh) to touch on a sore point; **in einer alten/jds alter ~ wühlen** (fig) to open an old sore; (bei jdm) **tiefe ~n schlagen** (fig) to scar sb; **den Finger auf die (brennende) ~ legen** (fig) to bring up a painful subject; **Salz in eine/jds ~ streuen** (fig) to turn the knife in the wound; **Balsam or Öl in eine/jds ~ gießen or träufeln** (fig geh) to comfort sb.

Wunder nt -s, - **(a)** (übernatürliches Ereignis, Rel) miracle; (wunderbare Erscheinung) wonder; (Leistung auch) marvel; (erstaunlicher Mensch) marvel. **~ tun or wirken** (Rel) to work miracles; **das grenzt an ein ~** it verges on the miraculous, it's almost a miracle; **durch ein ~** by a miracle; **nur durch ein ~ können sie noch gerettet werden** only a miracle can save them now; **die ~ der Natur/dieser Welt** the wonders of nature/this world; **ein architektonisches ~** an architectural miracle. **(b)** (überraschendes Ereignis) **~ tun or wirken** to do wonders; **es ist ein/kein ~, daß ...** it's a wonder/no wonder or small wonder that ...; **ist es ein ~, daß er dick ist?** is it any wonder that

he's fat?; **kein ~ no wonder; was ~, wenn ...** it's no wonder or surprise if ...; siehe **blau**.

wunder adv inv **meine Eltern denken ~ was passiert ist/~ was über mein Privatleben** my parents think goodness knows what has happened/goodness knows what about my private life; **das hat er sich ~ wie einfach vorgestellt** he imagined it would be ever so easy; **da macht man sich ~ wieviel Sorgen** you worry yourself sick; **er glaubt, ~ wer zu sein/~ was geleistet zu haben** he thinks he's marvellous/done something marvellous; **er meint, ~ wie schön das sei** he thinks it's fantastic; **er bildet sich ~ was ein** he thinks he's too wonderful for words.

wunderbar adj **(a)** (schön) wonderful, marvellous. **(b)** (übernatürlich, wie durch ein Wunder) miraculous.

wunderbarerweise adv miraculously.

Wunder-: **~ding** nt marvellous thing; **daß er überlebt hat, ist ein ~ding** that he survived is a miracle; **~doktor** m wonder doctor; (pej: Quacksalber) quack; **~droge** f (von Zauberer, Fee etc) miracle drug; (fig auch) wonder drug; **~geschichte** f (Geschichte von Wundern) miraculous tale; (wundersame Geschichte) wondrous tale or story; **~glaube** m belief in miracles; **w~gläubig** adj **w~gläubig sein** to believe in miracles; **ein w~gläubiger Mensch** a person who believes in miracles; **~heiler** m wonder doctor; (pej) faith-healer; **~horn** nt (liter, Myth) magic horn; **w~hübsch** adj wonderfully pretty, wondrously beautiful (liter); **~kerze** f sparkler; **~kind** nt child prodigy; **~knabe** m (usu iro) wonder boy or child; **~kur** f (iro) miracle cure; **~lampe** f magic lamp or lantern; **~land** nt wonderland; **w~lich** adj **(a)** (merkwürdig) strange, odd; **(b)** (w~sam) wondrous; **~lichkeit** f siehe adj **(a)** strangeness, oddness; **(b)** wondrousness; **~mittel** nt miracle cure; (von Fee etc) magic potion.

wundern 1 vt, vi impers to surprise. **es wundert mich or mich wundert, daß er noch nicht hier ist** I'm surprised or it surprises me that he is not here yet; **das wundert mich nicht** I'm not surprised, that doesn't surprise me; **das würde mich nicht ~** I shouldn't be surprised; **mich wundert gar nichts mehr** nothing surprises me any more. 2 vr to be surprised (über + acc at). **du wirst dich ~!** you'll be amazed!; **ich wunderte mich über seine schnelle Rückkehr** I was surprised at or about his quick return; **du wirst dich noch einmal ~!** you're in for a shock or surprise!; **da wirst du dich aber ~!** you're in for a surprise!; **ich muß mich doch sehr ~!** well, I am surprised (at you/him etc); **ich wundere mich über gar nichts mehr** nothing surprises me any more; **dann darfst/brauchst du dich nicht ~, wenn ...** then don't be surprised if ...

Wunder-: **w~nehmen** sep irreg 1 vi impers (geh) to be surprising; 2 vt impers to surprise; **w~sam** adj (liter) wondrous (liter); **w~schön** adj beautiful, lovely; (herrlich auch) wonderful; **einen w~schönen guten Morgen/Tag etc** a very good morning/day etc to you; **~tat** f miracle; **~täter** m miracle worker; **w~tätig** adj magic, miraculous; **Leben, Heilige** miracle-working; **w~tätig wirken** to perform miracles; **~tier** nt (hum) weird and wonderful animal (hum); **~tüte** f surprise packet; **w~voll** adj wonderful, marvellous; **~waffe** f wonder weapon; **~welt** f (im Märchen etc) magic world; (zauberhafte Umgebung) world of wonders; **die w~welt der Mineralien** the wonderful world of minerals; **~werk** nt miracle, marvel; **~zeichen** nt miraculous sign.

Wund-: **~fieber** nt traumatic fever; **w~gelegen** adj **ein w~gelegener Patient** a patient with bedsores; **eine w~gelegene Stelle** a bedsore; **w~gelegen sein** to have bedsores; **~heit** f soreness; **~infektion** f wound infection; **w~liegen** vr sep irreg to get bedsores; **~mal** nt **(a)** (Rel) stigma; **(b)** (liter) scar; **~pflaster** nt adhesive plaster; **~rand** m edge (of a/the wound); **~rose** f (Med) erysipelas (spec), St Anthony's fire; **~salbe** f ointment; **~sein** nt soreness; **~sekret** nt secretion of a/the wound; **~starrkrampf** m tetanus; **~versorgung** f dressing a/the wound/wounds; **~watte** f surgical wool.

Wunsch m -(e)s, ¨-e **(a)** wish; (sehnliches Verlangen) desire; (Bitte) request. **ein Pferd war schon immer mein ~** I've always wanted a horse; **nach ~** just as he/she etc wants/wanted; (wie geplant) according to plan, as planned; (nach Bedarf) as required; **auf or nach ~ der Eltern** as his/her etc parents wish/wished; **alles geht nach ~** everything is going smoothly; **ihm geht immer alles nach ~** things always turn out as he wants; **von dem ~ beseelt sein, ...** to be filled with the desire ...; **hier ist der ~ der Vater des Gedankens** (prov) the wish is father to the thought (prov); **ich habe einen ~ an dich** I've a request to make of you; **haben Sie (sonst) noch einen ~?** (beim Einkauf etc) is there anything else you would like or I can do for you?; **was haben Sie für einen ~?** what can I do for you?; **auf ~ by or on request; auf jds (besonderen/ausdrücklichen) ~ hin** at sb's (special/express) request; **auf allgemeinen/vielfachen ~ hin** by popular request or demand; **jdm jeden ~ von or an den Augen ablesen** to anticipate sb's every wish; siehe **fromm**. **(b)** usu pl (Glückwunsch) wish. **beste ~e zum Fest** the compliments of the season.

wünschbar adj (Sw) siehe **wünschenswert**.

Wunsch-: **~bild** nt ideal; **~denken** nt wishful thinking.

Wünschelrute f divining or dowsing rod.

Wünschelrutengänger(in f) m -s, - diviner, dowser.

wünschen 1 vt **(a)** sich (dat) etw ~ to want sth; (den Wunsch äußern) to ask for sth; (im stillen: bei Sternschnuppe etc) to wish for sth; **ich wünsche mir das Blaue vom Himmel** (inf), **ich wünsche mir, daß du ...** I would like you to ...; **... wie ich mir das gewünscht habe** ... as I wanted; **das habe ich mir von meinen Eltern zu Weihnachten gewünscht** I asked my parents to give me that for Christmas, I asked for that for Christmas from my parents; **ich wünsche mir einen Mantel von dir** I'd like a coat from you; **er wünscht sich** (dat), **daß es erfolgreich wird**

he so wants it to be *or* he hopes it will be successful; **er wünscht sich** (*dat*) **ein glückliches Leben für seine Kinder** he would like his children to have a happy life; **er wünscht sich** (*dat*) **diesen Mann als Lehrer/Vater/als** *or* **zum Freund** he wishes that this man was his teacher/father/friend; **was wünschst du dir?** what do you want?, what would you like?; (*im Märchen*) what is your wish?; **du darfst dir was** (**zum Essen**) ~ you can say what you'd like (to eat); **du darfst dir etwas** ~ (*Wunsch frei haben*) you can make a wish; (*im Märchen auch*) I'll give you a wish; **sie haben alles, was man sich** (*dat*) **nur** ~ **kann** they have everything you could possibly wish for; **man hätte es sich** (*dat*) **nicht besser** ~ **können** you couldn't have wished for anything better.

(**b**) **jdm etw** ~ to wish sb sth; **jdm einen guten Morgen** ~ to wish sb good morning; **wir** ~ **dir gute Besserung/eine gute Reise** we hope you get well soon/have a pleasant journey; **wir** ~ **gute Fahrt** we hope you have *or* we wish you a good journey; **jdm den Tod/die Pest an den Hals** ~ (*fig inf*) to wish sb would die/drop dead (*inf*); **das würde ich meinem schlimmsten Feind nicht** ~ (*prov*) I wouldn't wish that on my worst enemy.

(**c**) (*ersehnen, hoffen*) to wish. **jdn fort/weit weg** ~ to wish sb would go away/were far away; **es bleibt/wäre zu** ~, **daß ...** it is to be hoped that ...; **ich wünschte, ich hätte dich nie gesehen** I wish I'd never seen you.

(**d**) (*begehren, verlangen*) to want. **was** ~ **Sie?** (*Diener*) yes, Sir/Madam?; (*in Geschäft*) what can I do for you?, can I help you?; (*in Restaurant*) what would you like?; **wen** ~ **Sie zu sprechen?** to whom would you like to speak?; **ich wünsche, daß du das machst** I want you to do that; **es wird gewünscht, daß sich die Schüler ruhig verhalten** pupils are requested to remain quiet.

2 *vi* (*begehren*) to wish. **Sie** ~? what can I do for you?; (*in Restaurant*) what would you like?; **ganz wie Sie** ~ (just) as you wish *or* please *or* like; **zu** ~/**viel zu** ~ **übrig lassen** to leave something/a great deal to be desired.

3 *vr* **sich in eine andere Lage/weit weg** ~ to wish one were in a different situation/far away.

wünschenswert *adj* desirable.

Wunsch-: ~**form** *f* (*Gram*) optative (mood); **w~gemäß 1** *adj* requested; (*erwünscht*) desired; (*geplant*) planned; **2** *adv siehe adj* as requested; as desired; as planned; ~**kind** *nt* planned child; **unser Töchterchen war ein** ~**kind** our little daughter was planned; ~**kindpille** *f* (*DDR*) birth control pill; ~**konzert** *nt* (*Rad*) musical request programme; **w~los** *adj* **Mensch** content(ed); (*respektieren*) **Glück** perfect; **w~los glücklich** perfectly happy; ~**satz** *m* (*Gram*) optative clause; ~**sendung** *f* (*Rad*) request programme; ~**traum** *m* dream; (*Illusion*) illusion; **das ist doch bloß ein** ~**traum** that's just a pipe-dream; ~**zettel** *m* list of things one would like; **das steht schon lange auf meinem** ~**zettel** (*fig*) I've wanted that for a long time.

wupp (**dich**), **wupps** *interj* whoomph.

Wupp(dich) *m* **-s**, *no pl* (*inf*) **mit einem** ~ **in a flash**; **sich** (*dat*) **einen** ~ **geben** (*fig*) to give oneself a push.

wurde *pret of* **werden**.

Würde *f* **-**, **-n** *adj no pl* dignity. ~ **bewahren** to preserve one's dignity; **unter aller** ~ **sein** to be beneath contempt; **unter jds** ~ **sein** to be beneath sb *or* sb's dignity; **etw mit** ~ **tragen** to bear sth with dignity. (**b**) (*Auszeichnung*) honour; (*Titel*) title; (*Amt*) rank. ~ **bringt Bürde** (*prov*) the burdens of office.

würdelos *adj* undignified.

Würdelosigkeit *f* lack of dignity.

Würdenträger(in *f*) *m* **-s**, **-** dignitary.

würdevoll *adj siehe* **würdig (a)**.

würdig *adj* (**a**) (*würdevoll*) dignified. **sich** ~ **verhalten** to behave with dignity.

(**b**) (*wert*) worthy. **jds/einer Sache** ~/**nicht** ~ **sein** to be worthy/unworthy of sb/sth; **eine ihm** ~**e Verabschiedung** a farewell worthy of him; **sich jds/einer Sache** ~ **erweisen** *or* **zeigen** to prove oneself to be worthy of sb/sth; **jdn einer Sache** (*gen*) **für** ~ **halten** *or* **befinden** (*geh*) to find sb worthy of sth.

würdigen *vt* (**a**) to appreciate; (*lobend erwähnen*) to acknowledge; (*respektieren*) to respect. **etw gebührend** *or* **nach Gebühr/richtig** ~ to appreciate sth properly/fully; **etw zu** ~ **wissen** to appreciate sth.

(**b**) (*geh: für würdig befinden*) **jdn einer Sache** (*gen*) ~ to deem sb worthy of sth; **jdn eines/keines Blickes/Grußes** *etc* ~ to deign/not to deign to look at/greet *etc* sb.

Würdigkeit *f*, *no pl* (**a**) *siehe* **Würde**. (**b**) (*Wertsein*) merit.

Würdigung *f* (**a**) *siehe vt* appreciation; acknowledgement; respect. (**b**) (*lobende Worte, Artikel*) appreciation. (**c**) (*Ehrung*) honour. **die zahlreichen** ~**en der Gäste** the numerous tributes paid to the guests.

Wurf *m* **-(e)s**, **·e** (**a**) throw; (*beim Kegeln etc*) bowl; (*gezielter* ~, *beim Handball etc auch*) shot; (*beim Baseball*) pitch. **drei** ~ *or* **·e zwei Mark** three goes *or* throws for two marks.

(**b**) *no pl* (*das Werfen*) throwing. **beim** ~ when throwing; **zum** ~ **ansetzen/ausholen** to get ready to throw; **sich auf den** ~ **konzentrieren** to concentrate on throwing.

(**c**) (*fig: Erfolg*) success, hit (*inf*). **mit dem Film ist ihm ein großer** ~ **gelungen** this film is a great success *or* big hit (*inf*) for him; **einen großen/glücklichen** ~ **tun** (*Erfolg haben*) to be very successful *or* have great success; (*Glück haben*) to have a stroke of luck.

(**d**) (*Zool*) litter; (*das Gebären*) birth.

(**e**) (*Falten*~) fall. **einen eleganten** ~ **haben** to hang elegantly.

(**f**) (*Mil*) *siehe* **Abwurf**.

Wurf-: ~**arm** *m* (*Sport*) throwing arm; ~**bahn** *f* trajectory; ~**disziplin** *f* (*Sport*) throwing discipline *or* event.

Würfel *m* **-s**, **-** (**a**) (*auch Math*) cube. **etw in** ~ **schneiden** to cut sth into cubes. (**b**) (*Spiel*~) dice, die (*form*). **die** ~ **sind gefallen** the die is cast; ~ **spielen** to play at dice.

Würfel-: ~**becher** *m* shaker; ~**brett** *nt* dice board; ~**form** *f* cube shape; ~**form haben** to be cube-shaped; **w~förmig** *adj* cube-shaped, cubic (*esp Math*).

würf(e)lig *adj* cubic. **etw** ~ **schneiden** to cut sth into cubes.

würfeln 1 *vi* to throw, to have a throw; (*Würfel spielen*) to play at dice. **hast du schon gewürfelt?** have you had your throw *or* go?; **um etw** ~ to throw dice for sth. **2** *vt* (**a**) to throw. (**b**) (*in Würfel schneiden*) to cut into cubes.

Würfel-: ~**spiel** *nt* (*Partie*) game of dice; (*Spielart*) dice; **beim** ~**spiel** at dice; ~**spieler** *m* dice player; ~**zucker** *m* cube sugar.

Wurf-: ~**geschoß** *nt* projectile, missile; ~**hammer** *m* (*Sport*) hammer; ~**hand** *f* (*Sport*) throwing hand; ~**körper** *m* (*Phys*) projectile; ~**kraft** *f* (*Phys*) projectile force; (*Sport*) throwing strength; **w~kräftig** *adj* (*Sport*) strong-armed.

würflig *adj siehe* **würf(e)lig**.

Wurf-: ~**mal** *nt* (*Baseball*) pitcher's mound; ~**maschine** *f* (*Mil, Hist*) catapult; (*beim Tontaubenschießen*) trap; ~**messer** *nt* throwing knife; ~**parabel** *f* (*Phys*) trajectory (parabola); ~**pfeil** *m* dart; ~**ring** *m* quoit; ~**sendung** *f* circular; Reklame durch ~**sendungen** direct advertising; ~**speer**, ~**spieß** *m* javelin; ~**taube** *f* (*Sport*) clay pigeon; ~**taubenschießen** *nt* (*Sport*) clay pigeon shooting; ~**waffe** *f* missile; (*Speer*) throwing spear; ~**weite** *f* throwing range; (*von Geschütz*) mortar range; ~**winkel** *m* (*Sport*) throwing angle.

Würge-: ~**engel** *m siehe* **Würgengel**; ~**griff** *m* (*lit, fig*) stranglehold; ~**mal** *nt* strangulation mark.

würgen 1 *vt* **jdn** to strangle, to throttle; (*fig: Angst*) to choke. **2** *vi* (**a**) (*mühsam schlucken*) to choke; (*Schlange*) to gulp. **an etw** (*dat*) ~ (*lit*) to choke on sth; (*fig*) (*an Kritik*) to find sth hard to swallow; (*an Arbeit*) to struggle over sth. (**b**) (*beim Erbrechen*) to retch. **ein W~ im Hals spüren** to feel one is going to be sick.

3 *vt impers* **es würgte sie** (**im Hals** *etc*) she felt she was going to be sick; **mit Hängen und W~** by the skin of one's teeth.

Würgengel *m* Angel of Death.

Würger *m* **-s**, **-** (**a**) strangler; (*poet: der Tod*) death *no art*. (**b**) (*Orn*) shrike.

Würgschraube *f siehe* **Garotte**.

Wurm *m* **-(e)s**, **·er** (**a**) worm; (*Made*) maggot; (*poet: Schlange*) snake; (*Myth: Lind*~) dragon. **der** (**nagende**) ~ **des schlechten Gewissens** the (gnawing) pangs of a guilty conscience; **da ist** *or* **steckt** *or* **sitzt der** ~ **drin** (*fig inf*) there's something wrong somewhere; (*seltsam*) there's something odd about it; (*verdächtig*) there's something fishy about it (*inf*); *siehe* **winden**.

(**b**) *auch nt* (*inf: Kind*) (little) mite.

Würmchen *nt dim of* **Wurm** little worm; (*inf: Kind*) (poor) little mite *or* thing.

wurmen *vt*, *vt impers* (*inf*) to rankle with.

Wurm-: ~**fortsatz** *m* (*Anat*) vermiform appendix; ~**fraß** *m*, *no pl* worm damage.

wurmig *adj* wormeaten; (*madig*) *Obst* maggoty.

Wurm-: ~**krankheit** *f* worm disorder, helminthiasis (*spec*); ~**kur** *f* worming treatment; **die Katze braucht eine** ~**kur** the cat needs to be wormed; **eine** ~**kur machen** to have worm treatment; ~**loch** *nt* worm-hole; ~**mittel** *nt* vermicide, vermifuge; ~**stich** *m*, *no pl* worm-holes *pl*; **w~stichig** *adj* **Holz** full of worm-holes; (*madig auch*) *Obst* maggoty.

Wurscht *etc* (*inf*) *siehe* **Wurst** *etc*.

Wurst *f* **-**, **·e** (*wurstförmiges Gebilde auch*) roll; (*inf: Kot von Hund*) dog's mess (*inf*). **jetzt geht es um die** ~ (*fig inf*) the moment of truth has come (*inf*); **mit der** ~ **nach der Speckseite** *or* **dem Schinken werfen** (*fig inf*) to cast a sprat to catch a mackerel; **Mutti, ich habe eine lange** ~ **gemacht** (*inf*) Mummy, I've done a big one (*baby-talk*); **es ist jdm** ~ *or* **Wurscht** (*inf*) it's all the same to sb.

Wurst-: ~**aufschnitt** *m* assortment of sliced sausage; ~**blatt** *nt* (*pej inf*) *siehe* **Käseblatt**; ~**brot** *nt* open sausage sandwich; (*zusammengeklappt*) sausage sandwich; ~**brühe** *f* sausage stock.

Würstchen *nt* (**a**) *dim of* **Wurst** small sausage. **heiße** *or* **warme** ~ hot sausages; (*in Brötchen*) ≈ hot dogs; Frankfurter/Wiener ~ frankfurters/wiener-wursts. (**b**) (*pej: Mensch*) squirt (*inf*), nobody. **ein armes** ~ (*fig*) a poor soul.

Würstchen-: ~**bude** *f*, ~**stand** *m* sausage stand; hot-dog stand.

wurstlegal *adj* (*inf*) **das ist mir** ~ I couldn't care less (about that).

Wurstel *m* **-s**, **-** (*Aus*) *siehe* **Hanswurst**.

Würstel *nt* **-s**, **-** (*dial*) *siehe* **Würstchen**.

Wurstelei *f* (*inf*) muddle.

wursteln *vi* (*inf*) to muddle along. **sich durchs Leben/die Schule** ~ to muddle (one's way) through life/school.

wursten *vi* to make sausages.

Wurster *m* **-s**, **-** (*dial*) *siehe* **Fleischer**.

Wursterei *f* (*dial*) *siehe* **Fleischerei**.

Wurstfinger *pl* (*pej inf*) podgy fingers *pl*.

wurstig *adj* (*inf*) devil-may-care *attr*, couldn't-care-less *attr* (*inf*). **sei doch nicht so** ~! don't be such a wet blanket! (*inf*).

Wurstigkeit *f* (*inf*) devil-may-care *or* couldn't-care-less (*inf*) attitude.

Wurst-: ~**konserve** *f* tinned (*Brit*) *or* canned sausages; ~**maxe** *m* **-n**, **-n** (*inf*) ≈ man who sells sausages, hot-dog man (*inf*); ~**ring** *m* sausage ring; ~**salat** *m* sausage salad; ~**vergiftung** *f* sausage poisoning; ~**waren** *pl* sausages *pl*; ~**zipfel** *m* sausage-end.

Würze *f* **-**, **-n** (**a**) (*Gewürz*) seasoning, spice; (*Aroma*) aroma; (*fig: Reiz*) spice. **das gibt dem Leben die** ~ that adds spice to life; *siehe* **Kürze**. (**b**) (*von Bier*) wort.

Wurzel *f* **-**, **-n** (**a**) (*lit, fig*) root; (*Hand*~) wrist; (*Fuß*~) ankle. **etw mit der** ~ **ausreißen** to pull sth out by the root; **etw mit der** ~ **ausrotten** (*fig*) to eradicate sth; ~**n schlagen** (*lit*) to root; (*fig: sich einleben*) to put down roots; (*an einem Ort hängenbleiben*)

to grow roots; **die ~ Jesse** (*Bibl*) the stem of Jesse.
(b) (*Math*) root. **~n ziehen** to find the roots; **die ~ aus einer Größe ziehen** to find the root of a number; **(die) ~ aus 4 ist 2** the square root of 4 is 2; **die vierte ~ aus 16 ist 2** the fourth root of 16 is 2; **unter/außerhalb der ~ stehen** to be inside/outside the radical sign.
(c) (*N Ger*) siehe **Möhre.**
Wurzel-: **~ballen** *m* (*Hort*) bale of roots, root bale; **~behandlung** *f* (*von Zahn*) root treatment; **~bildung** *f* rooting; **~bürste** *f* (*coarse*) scrubbing brush.
Würzelchen *nt dim of* **Wurzel** little root, rootlet.
Wurzel-: **~entzündung** *f* (*an Zahn*) inflammation of the root/roots; **~exponent** *m* (*Math*) radical index; **~gemüse** *nt* root vegetables *pl*; **w~los** *adj Pflanze* without roots; (*fig auch*) rootless; **~mann** *m*, **~männchen** *nt* (*Alraune*) mandrake; (*Figur aus Wurzel*) small figure carved out of a root; (*Kräutersucher*) herb man.
wurzeln *vi* **(a)** (*lit, fig*) to be rooted. **in etw** (*dat*) **~** (*fig*) to be rooted in sth; (*verursacht sein*) to have its/their roots in sth. **(b)** (*rare: Wurzeln schlagen*) to (take) root.
Wurzel-: **~resektion** *f* (*Zahnmedizin*) root resection; **~silbe** *f* (*Ling*) root syllable; **~stock** *m* (*Bot*) rhizome; **~werk** *nt, no pl* **(a)** root system, roots *pl*; **(b)** (*Cook*) flavouring greens *pl*; **~zeichen** *nt* (*Math*) radical sign; **~ziehen** *nt -s, no pl* (*Math*) root extraction.
wurzen *vti* (*Aus inf*) to get everything one can (*jdn* out of sb).
würzen *vt* to season; (*fig*) to add spice to. **eine Geschichte mit etw ~** to season a story with sth.
Wurzerei *f* (*Aus inf*) robbery (*inf*).
würzig *adj Speise* tasty; (*scharf*) spicy; *Zigaretten, Tabak, Geruch etc* aromatic; *Luft* fragrant, tangy; *Wein, Bier* full-bodied.
Würz-: **~nelke** *f siehe* **Gewürznelke;** **~pilz** *m* flavouring mushroom; **~stoff** *m* flavouring.
wusch[1] *pret of* **waschen.**
wusch[2] *interj* (*Aus*) (*erstaunt*) whoops; (*schnell*) zoom.
Wuschelhaar *nt* (*inf*) mop of curly hair.
wusch(e)lig *adj* (*inf*) *Tier* shaggy; *Haare* fuzzy (*inf*).
Wuschelkopf *m* **(a)** (*Haare*) mop of curly hair, fuzz (*inf*). **(b)** (*Mensch*) fuzzy-head (*inf*).
wuselig *adj* (*dial*) (*lebhaft*) lively; (*unruhig*) fidgety; (*bewegt*) busy, bustling; *Ameisenhaufen* teeming. **das ~e Treiben** the hustle and bustle.
wuseln *vi* (*dial*) **(a)** (*belebt sein*) to be teeming. **(b)** *aux sein* (*sich schnell bewegen*) to scurry.
wußte *pret of* **wissen.**
Wust *m -(e)s, no pl* (*inf*) (*Durcheinander*) jumble; (*Menge*) pile; (*unordentlicher Haufen*) heap; (*Kram, Gerümpel*) junk (*inf*). **dieser ~ von Kleidern** this pile of clothes.
wüst *adj* (*öde*) desert *attr*, waste, desolate. **die Erde war ~ und leer** (*Bibl*) the earth was without form, and void (*Bibl*). **(b)** (*unordentlich*) wild, chaotic; *Aussehen, Haar* wild. **~ aussehen** to look a real mess.

(c) (*ausschweifend*) wild. **~ feiern** to have a wild party.
(d) (*rüde*) *Beschimpfung, Beleidigung etc* vile. **jdn ~ beschimpfen** to use vile language to sb.
(e) (*arg*) terrible, awful; *Übertreibung auch* wild.
Wüste *f -, -n* (*Geog*) desert; (*Ödland*) waste, wilderness (*liter*); (*fig*) waste(land), wilderness, desert. **die ~ Gobi** the Gobi Desert; **jdn in die ~ schicken** (*fig*) to send sb packing (*inf*).
wüsten *vi* (*inf*) **mit etw ~** to squander *or* waste sth; **mit seiner Gesundheit/seinen Kräften ~** to ruin one's health/strength.
Wüstenei *f* (*öde Gegend*) wasteland, desert. **(b)** (*fig: wildes Durcheinander*) chaos.
Wüsten-: **~fuchs** *m* desert fox; **~klima** *nt* desert climate; **~könig** *m* (*poet*) king of the desert (*poet*); **~landschaft** *f* desert landscape; **~sand** *m* desert sand; **~savanne** *f* savanna; **~schiff** *nt* (*poet*) ship of the desert (*poet*), camel; **~steppe** *f* steppe.
Wüstling *m* (*dated, iro*) lecher.
Wüstung *f* deserted settlement.
Wut *f -, no pl* **(a)** (*Zorn, Raserei*) rage, fury; (*fig: der Elemente*) fury. **(auf jdn/etw) eine ~ haben** to be furious (with sb/sth), to be mad (at sb/sth); **eine ~ im Bauch haben** (*inf*) to be seething, to be hopping mad (*inf*); **eine ~ haben/kriegen** *or* **bekommen** to be in/get into a rage; **in ~ geraten, von der ~ gepackt werden** to fly into a rage; **jdn in ~ bringen** *or* **versetzen** to infuriate sb.
(b) (*Verbissenheit*) frenzy. **mit einer wahren ~** as if possessed, like crazy (*inf*).
-wut *f* (*inf*) *in cpds* bug (*inf*).
Wut-: **~anfall** *m* fit of rage; (*esp von Kind*) tantrum; **~ausbruch** *m* outburst of rage *or* fury; (*esp von Kind*) tantrum.
wüten *vi* (*lit, fig*) (*toben*) to rage; (*zerstörerisch hausen*) to cause havoc; (*verbal*) to storm (*gegen* at); (*Menge*) to riot.
wütend *adj* furious, enraged; *Tier* enraged; *Menge* angry; *Kampf, Elemente* raging; (*fig*) *Schmerz, Haß etc* fierce. **~ raste der Stier auf ihn zu** the enraged bull raced towards him; **auf jdn/etw** (*acc*) **~ sein** to be mad at sb/sth; **über jdn/etw** (*acc*) **~ sein** to be furious about sb/sth.
wut-: **~entbrannt** *adj* furious, enraged; **~entbrannt hinausgehen** to leave in a fury *or* rage; **~erfüllt** *adj* filled *or* seething with rage, furious.
Wüterich *m* brute.
Wut-: **~geheul** *nt* howl of fury; **~geschrei** *nt* cries *pl* of rage.
-wütig *adj suf* (*inf*) bitten by the ... bug (*inf*).
wutsch *interj* whoosh.
wutschäumend *adj* foaming with rage.
wutschen *vi aux sein* (*inf*) to whoosh (*inf*); (*schnell verschwinden*) to whiz (*inf*), to zoom (*inf*).
Wut-: **w~schnaubend** *adj* snorting with rage; **~schrei** *m* yell of rage; **w~verzerrt** *adj* distorted with rage.
Wutz *f -, -en* (*pej dial*) pig (*inf*).
Wuzerl *nt -s, -(n)* (*Aus*) **(a)** (*Kind*) porker (*inf*). **(b)** (*Fussel*) piece of fluff.
wuzerldick *adj* (*Aus*) porky (*inf*).
Wwe. *abbr of* **Witwe.**
Wz *abbr of* **Warenzeichen.**

X, x [ɪks] *nt -, - X, x.* **Herr X** Mr X; **jdm ein X für ein U vormachen** to put one over on sb (*inf*); **er läßt sich kein X für ein U vormachen** he's not easily fooled.
x-Achse [ˈɪks-] *f* x-axis.
Xanthippe [ksanˈtɪpə] *f -, -n* (*fig inf*) shrew.
X-Beine [ˈɪks-] *pl* knock-knees *pl.* **~ haben** to be knock-kneed.
x-beinig [ˈɪks-] *adj* knock-kneed.
x-beliebig [ˈɪks-] *adj* any old (*inf*). **wir können uns an einem ~en Ort treffen** we can meet anywhere you like.
X-Chromosom [ˈɪks-] *nt* X-chromosome.
Xerographie [kseroɡraˈfiː] *f* Xerox (copy).
xerographieren* [kseroɡraˈfiːrən] *vti insep* to Xerox.

Xerokopie [kseroˈkoˈpiː] *f* Xerox (copy).
xerokopieren* [kserokopiˈrən] *vti insep* to Xerox.
x-fach [ˈɪks-] *adj* **die ~e Menge** (*Math*) n times the amount; **trotz ~er Ermahnungen** (*inf*) in spite of umpteen *or* n warnings (*inf*).
x-mal [ˈɪks-] *adv* (*inf*) n (number of) times (*inf*), umpteen times (*inf*).
x-malig [ˈɪks-] *adj* (*inf*) n number of (*inf*), umpteen (*inf*). **wenn ein ~er Weltmeister ...** when somebody who has been world champion n (number of) times *or* umpteen times ...
X-Strahlen [ˈɪks-] *pl* (*dated*) X-rays *pl.*
x-te [ˈɪkstə] *adj* (*Math*) nth; (*inf*) nth (*inf*), umpteenth (*inf*). **zum ~n Male, zum ~nmal** for the nth *or* umpteenth time (*inf*).
Xylophon [ksyloˈfoːn] *nt -s, -e* xylophone.

Y

Y, y ['ʏpsilɔn] *nt* -, - Y, y.
y-Achse ['ʏpsilɔn-] *f* y-axis.
Yacht [jaxt] *f* -, -en *siehe* **Jacht.**
Yankee ['jɛŋki] *m* -s, -s (*pej*) Yankee, yank.
Yard [jaːɐt] *nt* -s, -s yard.
Y-Chromosom ['ʏpsilɔn-] *nt* Y-chromosome.
Yen [jɛn] *m* -(s), -(s) yen.

Yeti ['jeːti] *m* -s, -s Yeti, Abominable Snowman.
Yoga ['joːga] *m or nt* -(s) *siehe* **Joga.**
Yogi ['joːgi] *m* -s, -s *siehe* **Jogi.**
Yoghurt ['joːgurt] *m or nt* -s, -s *siehe* **Joghurt.**
Ypsilon ['ʏpsilɔn] *nt* -(s), -s y; (*griechischer Buchstabe*)
upsilon.
Ysop ['iːzɔp] *m* -s, -e (*Bot*) hyssop.

Z

Z, z [tsɛt] *nt* -, - Z, z.
z.A. *abbr of* **zur Ansicht; zur Anstellung** on probation.
Zack *m* -s, *no pl* (*inf*) auf ~ bringen to knock into shape (*inf*); auf ~ sein to be on the ball (*inf*).
zack *interj* (*inf*) pow, zap (*inf*). ~, ~! chop-chop! (*inf*); **sei nicht so langsam, mach mal ein bißchen** ~, ~ don't be so slow, get a move on (*inf*); **bei uns muß alles** ~, ~ **gehen** we have to do everything chop-chop (*inf*); **die Leute waren so gut gedrillt, die ganze Sache lief** ~, ~ the people were drilled so well that the whole thing went off just like that (*inf*).
Zacke *f* -, -n, **Zacken** *m* -s, - point; (*von Gabel*) prong; (*von Kamm*) tooth; (*Berg*~) jagged peak; (*Auszackung*) indentation; (*von Fieberkurve etc*) peak; (*inf: Nase*) conk (*inf*), beak (*inf*).
zacken *vt* to serrate; *Kleid, Saum, Papier* to pink; *siehe* **gezackt.**
Zacken-: ~**linie** *f* jagged line; (*Zickzack*) zig-zag (line); ~**litze** *f* ric-rac braid.
zackig *adj* (a) (*gezackt*) jagged; *Stern* pointed. ~ **schreiben** to write a very angular hand.
  (b) (*inf*) *Soldat, Bursche* smart; *Tempo, Musik* brisk; *Team, Manager etc* dynamic, zippy (*inf*). **bring mir meine Hausschuhe, aber ein bißchen** ~! fetch me my slippers, and make it snappy (*inf*)!
zag *adj* (*liter*) *siehe* **zaghaft.**
zagen *vi* (*liter*) to be apprehensive, to hesitate; *siehe* **Zittern.**
zaghaft *adj* timid.
Zaghaftigkeit, Zagheit *f* timidity.
zäh *adj* tough; (*dickflüssig*) glutinous; (*schleppend*) *Verkehr etc* slow-moving; (*ausdauernd*) dogged, tenacious. **ein** ~**es Leben haben** (*lit: Mensch, Tier*) to have a tenacious hold on life; (*fig*) to die hard; **mit** ~**em Fleiß** doggedly, with dogged application.
Zäheit ['tsɛːhait] *f, no pl* toughness.
zähflüssig *adj* thick, viscous; *Verkehr, Verhandlung* slow-moving.
Zähflüssigkeit *f* thickness, viscosity. **die** ~ **des Verkehrs** the slow-moving traffic.
Zähigkeit *f* *siehe* **zäh** toughness; glutinousness; doggedness, tenacity. **die** ~ **der Verhandlungen** the fact that the negotiations were so slow-moving.
Zahl *f* -, -en (*Math, Gram*) number; (*Verkaufs*~, *Maßangabe, bei Geldmengen etc auch*) figure; (*Ziffer auch*) numeral, figure. ~**en nennen** to give figures; **wie waren die** ~**en im letzten Jahr?** what did the figures look like last year?; **sie hat ein gutes Gedächtnis für** ~**en** she has a good memory for figures or numbers; **eine fünfstellige** ~ a five-figure number; **der** ~ **nach** numerically; **gut mit** ~**en umgehen können** to be good with figures, to be numerate; **die** ~**en stimmen nicht** die figures don't add up or tally; **100 DM sind für ihn gar nichts, der rechnet mit großen** ~**en** 100 DM is nothing for him, he only works with big figures; ~ **oder Wappen** heads or tails; **100 an der** ~ (*old*) 100 in number; **in großer** ~ in large or great numbers; **die** ~ **ist voll** the numbers are complete; **in voller** ~ in full number; **der Aufsichtsrat war in voller** ~ **versammelt** there was a full turn-out for the meeting of the board; **ohne** ~ (*geh*) without number; **Leiden/Wonnen ohne** ~ (*poet*) countless tribulations/joys.
zahlbar *adj* payable (*an* +*acc* to). ~ **bei Lieferung** *or* **nach Erhalt** payable on or to be paid for on delivery or receipt.
zählbar *adj* countable.
Zahlbrett, Zahlbrett *nt* money tray.
zählebig *adj* hardy, tough; (*fig*) *Gerücht, Vorurteil* persistent.
zahlen 1 *vi* to pay. **Herr Ober, (bitte)** ~! waiter, the bill (*Brit*) *or* check (*US*) please; **dort zahlt man gut/schlecht** the pay there is

good/bad, they pay well/badly; wenn er nicht bald zahlt, dann ... if he doesn't pay up soon, then ...
  2 *vt* (*bezahlen*) to pay. **was habe ich (Ihnen) zu** ~ what do I owe you?; **einen hohen Preis** ~ (*lit, fig*) to pay a high price; **ich zahle dir ein Bier** I'll buy you a beer; **ich zahle dir den Flug/das Kino** I'll pay for your flight/for you (to go to the cinema); **laß mal, ich zahl's no no,** I'll pay or it's on me or it's my treat (*inf*).
zählen 1 *vi* (a) to count. **bis hundert** ~ to count (up) to a hundred; **seine Verbrechen** ~ **nach Hunderten** (*geh*) his crimes run into hundreds.
  (b) (*gehören*) **zu einer Gruppe/Menge** ~ to be one of a group/set; **er zählt zu den besten Schriftstellern unserer Zeit** he ranks as one of the best authors of our time; **dieses Gebiet zählt immer noch zu Österreich** this region still counts as part of Austria; **zu welcher Sprachengruppe zählt Gälisch?** to which language group does Gaelic belong?
  (c) (*sich verlassen*) **auf jdn/etw** ~ to count or rely on sb/sth.
  (d) (*gelten*) to count.
  2 *vt* to count. **jdn/etw zu einer Gruppe/Menge** ~ to regard sb/sth as one of a group/set, to number or count sb/sth among a group/set; **etw zu einem Gebiet** ~ to count or regard sth as part of a region; **seine Tage sind gezählt** his days are numbered; **sie zählt 27 Jahre** (*liter*) she is 27 years old; **Stanford zählt 12 000 Studenten** Stanford numbers or has 12,000 students; **bei diesem Spiel zählt der König 5 Punkte** in this game the King counts as 5 points.
Zahlen-: ~**akrobatik** *f* (*inf*) juggling with statistics or figures, statistical sleight of hand; ~**angabe** *f* figure; **ich kann keine genauen** ~**angaben machen** I can't give or quote any precise figures; ~**beispiel** *nt* numerical example; ~**folge** *f* order of numbers; ~**gedächtnis** *nt* memory for numbers; ~**lehre** *f* arithmetic; ~**lotterie** *f*, ~**lotto** *nt* *siehe* **Lotto;** **z**~**mäßig** *adj* numerical; **etw z**~**mäßig ausdrücken** to express sth in figures; ~**material** *nt* figures *pl*; ~**mystik** *f* number mysticism; (*Astrol*) numerology; ~**rätsel** *nt* number or numerical puzzle; ~**reihe** *f* sequence of numbers; ~**schloß** *nt* combination lock; ~**sinn** *m* head for figures; ~**symbolik** *f* number symbolism; ~**theorie** *f* (*Math*) theory of numbers, number theory; ~**toto** *m* *siehe* **Toto;** ~**verhältnis** *nt* (numerical) ratio; ~**wert** *m* numerical value; (*auf Meßgeräten*) (numerical) reading; **welche** ~**werte hat die Analyse ergeben?** what figures did the analysis give?; **die** ~**werte der beiden Versuche** the figures yielded by the two experiments.
Zahler *m* -s, - payer.
Zähler *m* -s, - (a) (*Math*) numerator. (b) (*Meßgerät*) meter.
Zähler-: ~**ablesung** *f* meter reading; ~**stand** *m* meter reading.
Zahl-: ~**grenze** *f* fare stage; ~**karte** *f* giro transfer form; ~**kellner** *m* waiter who presents the bill and collects payment.
zahllos *adj* countless, innumerable.
Zahlmaß *nt* numerical measure, unit of measurement.
Zahlmeister *m* (*Naut*) purser; (*Mil*) paymaster.
Zählmuster *nt* pattern.
zahlreich *adj* numerous. **wir hatten mit einer** ~**eren Beteiligung gerechnet** we had expected more participants; **die Veranstaltung war** ~ **besucht** the event was (very) well attended.
Zählrohr *nt* (*Phys*) Geiger counter.
Zahl-: ~**stelle** *f* payments office; ~**tag** *m* payday.
Zahlung *f* payment. **eine einmalige** ~ **leisten** to make a lump-sum payment; **in** ~ **nehmen** to take in part-exchange or as a trade-in; **in** ~ **geben** to trade in, to give in part-exchange; **gegen eine** ~ **von $ 500 erhalten Sie ...** on payment of $500 you will receive ...

Zählung f count; (*Volks~*) census.
Zahlungs-: ~**abkommen** nt payments agreement; ~**anweisung** f giro transfer order; ~**art** f method or mode of payment; ~**aufforderung** f request for payment; ~**aufschub** m extension (of credit), moratorium (*Jur*); ~**bedingungen** pl terms (of payment) pl; erleichterte ~**bedingungen** easy terms; ~**befehl** m order to pay; ~**bilanz** f balance of payments; ~**empfänger** m payee; ~**erleichterung** f more convenient method of payment; ~**erleichterungen** easy terms; z~**fähig** adj able to pay; *Firma* solvent; ~**fähigkeit** f ability to pay; solvency; ~**frist** f time or period allowed for payment; z~**kräftig** adj wealthy; ~**mittel** nt means sing of payment; (*Münzen, Banknoten*) currency; gesetzliches ~**mittel** legal tender; z~**pflichtig** adj obliged to pay; ~**schwierigkeiten** pl financial difficulties pl; ~**termin** m date for payment; z~**unfähig** adj unable to pay; *Firma* insolvent; ~**unfähigkeit** f inability to pay; insolvency; z~**unwillig** adj unwilling to pay; ~**verkehr** m payments pl, payment transactions pl; ~**verpflichtung** f obligation or liability to pay; ~**verzug** m default, arrears pl; ~**weise** f mode or method of payment; z~**willig** adj willing to pay; ~**ziel** nt (*Comm*) period allowed for payment.
Zählwerk nt counter.
Zahl-: ~**wort** nt numeral; ~**zeichen** nt numerical symbol.
zahm adj (*lit, fig*) tame. er ist schon ~er geworden (*inf*) he has calmed down a bit (*inf*), he's a bit tamer now (*inf*).
zähmbar adj tam(e)able.
zähmen vt to tame; (*fig*) *Leidenschaft, Bedürfnisse* to control.
Zahmheit f tameness.
Zähmung f taming.
Zahn m -(e)s, ⁻e (a) (*Anat, Zacke*) tooth; (*von Briefmarke*) perforation; (*Rad~ auch*) cog. künstliche or falsche ⁻e false teeth pl; ⁻e bekommen or kriegen (*inf*) to cut one's teeth; die ersten/zweiten ⁻e one's milk teeth/second set of teeth; die dritten ⁻e (*hum*) false teeth; diese Portion reicht or ist für den hohlen ~ (*inf*) that's hardly enough to satisfy a mouse (*inf*); der ~ der Zeit the ravages pl of time; ihm tut kein ~ mehr weh (*inf*) he's gone to join his ancestors; die ⁻e zeigen (*Tier*) to bare one's teeth; (*fig inf*) to show one's teeth; jdm einen ~ ziehen (*lit*) to pull a tooth out, to extract a tooth; (*fig*) to put an idea out of sb's head; ich muß mir einen ~ ziehen lassen I've got to have a tooth out or extracted; den ~ kannst du dir ruhig ziehen lassen! you can put that idea right out of your head!; jdm auf den ~ fühlen (*aushorchen*) to sound sb out; (*streng befragen*) to grill sb, to give sb a grilling; etw zwischen den ⁻en knurren to mutter sth between one's teeth; *siehe* bewaffnet, ausbeißen.
(b) (*sl: Geschwindigkeit*) einen ~ draufhaben to be going like the clappers (*inf*); mit einem unheimlichen ~ at an incredible lick (*inf*); *siehe* zulegen.
Zahn-: ~**arzt** m dentist; ~**arzthelferin** f dental nurse; z~**ärztlich** adj dental; sich in z~**ärztliche** Behandlung begeben (*form*) to have dental treatment; z~**ärztliche Helferin** (*form*) dental nurse; ~**behandlung** f dental treatment; ~**belag** m film on the teeth; ~**bett** nt socket (of a/the tooth); ~**bürste** f tooth brush; ~**creme** f toothpaste.
Zähne-: ~**fletschen** nt baring of teeth, snarling; z~**fletschend** adj attr, adv snarling; der Hund sprang z~**fletschend** an mir hoch the dog leapt up at me, snarling; ~**klappern** nt chattering of teeth; *siehe* Heulen; z~**klappernd** adj attr, adv with teeth chattering; ~**knirschen** nt grinding one's teeth; (*fig*) gnashing of teeth; z~**knirschend** adj attr, adv grinding one's teeth; (*fig*) gnashing one's teeth; er fand sich z~**knirschend** damit ab he agreed with (a) bad grace.
zahnen vi to teethe, to cut one's teeth/a tooth. das Z~ teething.
zähnen vt to tooth; *Briefmarken* to perforate.
Zahn-: ~**ersatz** m dentures pl, set of dentures; ~**fäule** f tooth decay, caries sing; ~**fleisch** nt gum(s pl); (nur noch) auf dem ~**fleisch** gehen or kriechen (*inf*) to be all-in (*inf*), to be on one's last legs (*inf*); ~**fleischbluten** nt bleeding of the gums; ~**füllung** f filling; ~**hals** m neck of a tooth; ~**heilkunde** f dentistry; ~**höhle** f pulp cavity; ~**klempner** m (*hum*) dentist; ~**klinik** f dental clinic or hospital; ~**kranz** m (*Tech*) gear rim; ~**krone** f crown; ~**laut** m (*Ling*) dental (consonant); z~**los** adj toothless; ~**losigkeit** f toothlessness; ~**lücke** f gap between one's teeth; ~**lücken bei Erwachsenen** adults with gappy teeth; ~**mark** nt dental pulp; ~**medizin** f dentistry; ~**pasta**, ~**paste** f toothpaste; ~**pflege** f dental hygiene; ~**prothese** f set of dentures; ~**pulver** nt tooth powder; ~**putzglas** nt toothbrush glass; ~**rad** nt cogwheel, gear (wheel); ~**radbahn** f rack-railway (*Brit*), rack-railroad (*US*); ~**radgetriebe** nt gear mechanism; ~**reihe** f row of teeth; ~**schein** m (*inf*) form for free dental treatment; ~**schlosser** m (*hum*) dentist; ~**schmelz** m (tooth) enamel; ~**schmerz** m usu pl toothache no pl; ~**spange** f brace; ~**stein** m tartar; ~**stocher** m -s, - toothpick; ~**stummel** m stump; ~**techniker** m dental technician.
Zähnung f (*Zähne, Gezahntsein*) teeth pl; (*von Briefmarken*) perforations pl; (*das Zähnen*) toothing; perforation.
Zahn-: ~**wal** m toothed whale; ~**wechsel** m second dentition (*form*); ~**weh** nt toothache; ~**wurzel** f root (of a/the tooth); ~**zement** m (dental) cement.
Zähre f -, -n (*old, poet*) tear.
Zaire [za'iːr] nt -s Zaire.
Zairer(in f) [za'iːrɐ, -ərɪn] m -s, - Zairean.
Zander m -s, - (*Zool*) pike-perch.
Zange f -, -n (*Flach~, Rund~*) (pair of) pliers pl; (*Beiß~*) (pair of) pincers pl; (*Greif~, Kohlen~, Zucker~*) (pair of) tongs pl; (*von Tier*) pincers pl; (*Med*) forceps pl; (*inf: Ringen*) double lock. jdn in die ~ nehmen (*Ringen*) to put a double lock on sb; (*Ftbl etc*) to sandwich sb; (*fig*) to put the screws on sb (*inf*); jetzt haben wir ihn in der ~ (*fig*) we've got him now; ihn/das möchte ich nicht mit der ~ anfassen (*inf*) I wouldn't touch him/it with a barge-pole (*Brit inf*) or a ten-foot pole (*US inf*).

Zangen-: ~**bewegung** f (*Mil*) pincer movement; z~**förmig** adj pincer-shaped; ~**geburt** f forceps delivery; ~**griff** m (*Ringen*) double lock.
Zank m -(e)s, no pl squabble, quarrel, row. zwischen ihnen gab es dauernd ~ they were continually squabbling or quarrelling or rowing; ~ und Streit trouble and strife.
Zank|apfel m (*fig*) bone of contention.
zanken 1 vi to scold. mit jdm ~ to scold sb, to tell sb off; (*ständig*) to nag sb. 2 vr to quarrel, to squabble, to row. wir haben uns gezankt we've had a row, we've quarrelled.
Zänker m -s, - quarreller, squabbler.
Zankerei f quarrelling, squabbling.
Zänkerin f (*rare*) shrew, quarrelsome woman.
zänkisch adj (*streitsüchtig*) quarrelsome; (*tadelsüchtig*) *Frau* nagging attr, shrewish.
Zanksucht f quarrelsomeness; (*Tadelsucht: von Frau*) nagging, shrewishness.
zanksüchtig adj siehe zänkisch.
Zäpfchen nt dim of **Zapfen** small plug etc; (*Gaumen~*) uvula; (*Suppositorium*) suppository. ~-R (*Ling*) uvular "r".
Zapfen m -s, - (*Spund*) bung, spigot; (*Pfropfen*) stopper, bung; (*Tannen~ etc, von Auge*) cone; (*Eis~*) icicle; (*Mech: von Welle, Lager etc*) journal; (*Holzverbindung*) tenon.
zapfen vt to tap, to draw. dort wird das Pils frisch gezapft they have draught Pilsener or Pilsener on draught or tap there.
Zapfenstreich m (*Mil*) tattoo, last post (*Brit*), taps sing (*US*). den ~ blasen to sound the tattoo; der Große ~ the Ceremonial Tattoo; um 12 Uhr ist ~ (*fig inf*) lights out is at 12 o'clock.
Zapfer m -s, - (*dial*) barman, tapster (*old*).
Zapf-: ~**hahn** m tap; ~**säule** f petrol pump (*Brit*), gas pump (*US*); ~**stelle** f tap; (*Elec*) (power) point; (*Tankstelle*) petrol (*Brit*) or gas (*US*) station.
Zaponlack ® m cellulose lacquer.
zapp(e)lig adj wriggly; (*unruhig*) fidgety.
zappeln vi to wriggle; (*Hampelmann*) to jiggle; (*unruhig sein*) to fidget. er zappelte mit Armen und Beinen he was all of a fidget, he couldn't sit still; jdn ~ lassen (*fig inf*) to keep sb in suspense; in der Schlinge ~ (*fig*) to be caught in the net.
Zappelphilipp m -s, -e or -s fidget(er).
zappenduster adj (*inf*) pitch-black, pitch-dark. wie sieht es denn mit euren Plänen aus? — ~ how are your plans working out? — grim; dann ist es ~ you'll/we'll etc be in trouble or (dead) shtook (*sl*).
zapplig adj siehe zapp(e)lig.
Zar m -en, -en Tsar, Czar.
Zarewitsch m -(e)s, -e tsarevitch.
Zarge f -, -n frame; (*von Geige etc*) rib; (*von Plattenspieler*) plinth.
Zarin f tsarina, czarina.
Zarismus m tsarism.
zaristisch adj tsarist no adv.
zart adj (*weich*) *Haut, Flaum, (leise) Töne, Stimme* soft; *Braten, Gemüse* tender; *Porzellan, Blüte, Gebäck, Farben, Teint*, (*schwächlich*) *Gesundheit, Kind* delicate; (*feinfühlig*) *Gemüt, Gefühle* sensitive, tender, delicate; (*sanft*) *Wind, Berührung* gentle, soft. mit jdm/etw ~ umgehen to treat or handle sb/sth gently; etw nur ~ andeuten to hint at sth only gently; nichts für ~e Ohren not for tender or sensitive ears; im ~en Alter von ... at the tender age of ...; das ~e Geschlecht the gentle sex; ~ besaitet sein to be very sensitive.
zart-: ~**besaitet** adj attr highly sensitive; ~**bitter** adj *Schokolade* plain; ~**blau** adj pale blue.
Zärtelei f mollycoddling.
Zart-: z~**fühlend** adj sensitive; ~**gefühl** nt delicacy of feeling, sensitivity; z~**gliedrig** adj dainty; z~**grün** adj pale green.
Zartheit f siehe adj softness; tenderness; delicacy, delicateness; sensitivity, tenderness, delicacy, delicateness; gentleness, softness.
zärtlich adj tender, affectionate, loving.
Zärtlichkeit f (a) no pl affection, tenderness. (b) (*Liebkosung*) caress. ~en (*Worte*) tender or loving words, words of love; jdm ~en ins Ohr flüstern to whisper sweet nothings in sb's ear.
Zaster m -s, no pl (*sl*) lolly (*inf*), loot (*inf*).
Zäsur f caesura; (*fig*) break.
Zauber m -s, - (*Magie*) magic; (~*bann*) (magic) spell; (*fig: Reiz*) magic, charm. den ~ lösen to break the spell; fauler ~ (*inf*) humbug no indef art; der ganze ~ (*inf*) the whole lot (*inf*); warum der ganze ~? (*inf: Getue*) why all the fuss?
Zauber-: ~**bann** m (magic) spell; unter einem ~**bann** stehen to be under a spell; ~**buch** nt book of spells; (*für ~kunststücke*) conjuring book.
Zauberei f (a) no pl (*das Zaubern*) magic. (b) (*Zauberkunststück*) conjuring trick.
Zauberer m -s, - magician; (*in Märchen etc auch*) sorcerer, wizard; (*Zauberkünstler auch*) conjurer.
Zauber-: ~**flöte** f magic flute; ~**formel** f magic formula.
Zauberin f (female) magician; (*in Märchen etc auch*) enchantress, sorceress; (*Zauberkünstlerin auch*) (female) conjurer.
zauberisch adj siehe zauberhaft.
Zauber-: ~**kraft** f magic power; ~**kunst** f magic, conjuring; ~**künstler** m conjurer, magician; ~**kunststück** nt conjuring trick; ~**landschaft** f fairytale scene; ~**macht** f magical powers pl; ~**mittel** nt magical cure; (*Trank*) magic potion, philtre.
zaubern 1 vi to do or perform magic; (*Kunststück vorführen*) to do conjuring tricks. ich kann doch nicht ~! (*inf*) I'm not a magician!, I can't perform miracles! 2 vt (a) etw aus etw ~ to conjure sth out of sth. (b) (*fig*) *Lösung, Essen* to produce as if by magic, to conjure up.
Zauber-: ~**nuß** f wych-hazel, witch-hazel; ~**priester** m sorcerer-priest; ~**reich** nt enchanted or magic realm; ~**schloß**

nt enchanted castle; ~spruch *m* (magic) spell; ~stab *m* (magic) wand; ~trank *m* magic potion, philtre; ~trick *m* conjuring trick; ~werk *nt* sorcery, wizardry; ~wesen *nt* magical being; ~wort *nt* magic word; ~wurzel *f* mandrake root.

Zauderer *m* -s, - vacillator, irresolute person.

zaudern *vi* to hesitate, to vacillate. etw ohne zu ~ tun to do sth without hesitating *or* any hesitation.

Zaum *m* -(e)s, **Zäume** bridle. einem Pferd den ~ anlegen to put a bridle on a horse; jdn/etw im ~(e) halten (*fig*) to keep a tight rein on sb/sth, to keep sb/sth in check; sich im ~(e) halten (*fig*) to control oneself, to keep oneself in check; seine Ungeduld/seinen Zorn im ~e halten (*fig*) to control *or* curb one's impatience/anger.

zäumen *vt* to bridle.

Zäumung *f* bridling.

Zaumzeug *nt* bridle.

Zaun *m* -(e)s, **Zäune** fence. einen Streit vom ~(e) brechen to pick a quarrel, to start a fight.

Zaun-: ~eidechse *f* sand lizard; ~gast *m sb who manages to get a free view of an event*; ~könig *m* (*Orn*) wren; ~pfahl *m* (fencing) post; jdm einen Wink mit dem ~pfahl geben to give *or* drop sb a broad hint; mit dem ~pfahl winken (*inf*) to drop a broad hint; ~rebe *f* climbing plant; ~winde *f* (*Bot*) great bindweed.

zausen 1 *vt* to ruffle; *Haare* to tousle. 2 *vi* in etw (*dat*) ~ (*Wind*) to ruffle sth.

z.B. [tsɛt'beː] *abbr of* **zum Beispiel** eg.

z.b.V. *abbr of* **zur besonderen Verwendung.**

ZDF [tsɛtdeː'ʔɛf] *nt -s abbr of* **Zweites Deutsches Fernsehen.**

Zebaoth *m*: der Herr ~ (*Bibl*) Jehovah.

Zebra *nt* -s, -s zebra.

Zebrastreifen *m* zebra crossing (*Brit*), pedestrian crossing *or* crosswalk (*US*).

Zebu *nt* -s, -s zebu.

Zechbruder *m* boozer (*inf*); (*Kumpan*) drinking-mate (*inf*), drinking-buddy (*inf*).

Zeche *f* -, -n (a) (*Rechnung*) bill (*Brit*), check (*US*). die (ganze) ~ (be)zahlen (*lit, fig*) to foot the bill; (den Wirt um) die ~ prellen to leave without paying the bill; eine (hohe) ~ machen to run up a (large) bill. (b) (*Bergwerk*) (coal-)mine, pit, colliery.

zechen *vi* to booze (*inf*); (*Zechgelage abhalten*) to carouse.

Zecher(in *f*) *m* -s, - boozer (*inf*); (*bei einem Zechgelage*) carouser, reveller.

Zecherei *f* booze-up (*inf*); (*Zechgelage*) carousal; (*das Zechen*) boozing; carousing.

Zechgelage *nt* carousal.

Zechinen *pl* (*inf*) pennies (*inf*), shekels (*sl*).

Zech-: ~kumpan *m* drinking-mate (*inf*), drinking-buddy (*inf*); ~preller *m* -s, - *person who leaves without paying the bill at a restaurant, bar etc*; ~prellerei *f* failure to pay the bill for drink *or* food consumed at a restaurant, bar etc; ~stein *m* (*Geol*) Zechstein (period), Upper Permian; ~tour *f* (*inf*) pub-crawl (*esp Brit inf*).

Zeck¹ *nt or m* -(e)s, -e (*dial: Fangspiel*) tag.

Zeck² *m* -(e)s, -en (*Aus*), **Zecke** *f* -, -n tick.

Zedent *m* (*Jur*) assignor.

Zeder *f* -, -n cedar.

zedern *adj* cedar.

Zedernöl *nt* cedarwood oil.

zedieren* *vt* (*Jur*) to cede, to assign, to transfer.

Zeh *m* -s, -en, **Zehe** *f* -, -n toe; (*Knoblauch~*) clove. auf (den) ~en gehen/schleichen to tiptoe, to walk/creep on tiptoe; sich auf die ~en stellen to stand on tiptoe; jdm auf die ~en treten (*fig inf*) to tread on sb's toes.

Zehen-: ~nagel *m* toenail; ~spitze *f* tip of the toe; auf (den) ~spitzen on tiptoe, on tippy-toes (*US inf*); auf (den) ~spitzen gehen to tiptoe, to walk on tiptoe; auf den ~spitzen tanzen to dance on one's toes.

zehn *num* ten. (ich wette) ~ zu *or* gegen eins (I bet) ten to one; *siehe auch* vier.

Zehn *f* -, -en ten; *siehe auch* Vier.

Zehn-: ~eck *nt* decagon; z~eckig *adj* ten-sided, decagonal.

Zehner *m* -s, - (a) (*Math*) ten; *siehe auch* Vierer. (b) (*inf*) (*Zehnpfennigstück*) ten-pfennig piece, ten; (*Zehnmarkschein*) tenner (*inf*).

Zehner-: ~bruch *m* decimal (fraction); ~packung *f* packet of ten; ~stelle *f* ten's (place); in der ~stelle stehen to be in the tens; ~system *nt* decimal system.

Zehn-: ~fingersystem *nt* touch-typing method; ~kampf *m* (*Sport*) decathlon; ~kämpfer *m* decathlete; z~mal *adv* ten times; *siehe auch* viermal; ~markschein *m* ten-mark note; ~meterbrett *nt* ten-metre board.

Zehnt *m* -en, -en, **Zehnte(r)** *m decl as adj* (*Hist*) tithe.

zehntausend *num* ten thousand. Z~e von Menschen tens of thousands of people; *siehe* obere(r, s).

Zehntel *nt* -s, - tenth.

zehntel *adj* tenth.

zehntens *adv* tenth(ly), in the tenth place.

Zehnte(r) *m siehe* Zehnt.

zehnte(r, s) *adj* tenth; *siehe auch* vierte(r, s).

zehren *vi* (a) von etw ~ (*lit*) to live off *or* on sth; (*fig*) to feed on sth. (b) an jdm/etw ~ an *Menschen, Kraft* to wear sb/sth out; *an Kraft auch* to sap sth; *an Nerven* to ruin sth; (*Anstrengung*) *am Herzen* to weaken sth; (*Kummer*) to gnaw at sth; *an Gesundheit* to undermine sth.

Zehrgeld *nt*, **Zehrpfennig** *m* (*old*) travelling monies *pl* (*old*).

Zehrung *f* -, no *pl* (*old*) provisions *pl*.

Zeichen *nt* -s, - sign; (*Sci, algebraisch, auf Landkarte*) symbol; (*Schrift~*) character; (*An~: von Krankheit, Winter, Beweis: von Friedfertigkeit*) sign, indication; (*Hinweis, Signal*) signal; (*Erkennungs~*) identification; (*Lese~*) bookmark, marker;

(*Vermerk*) mark; (*auf Briefköpfen*) reference; (*Satz~*) punctuation mark; (*Waren~*) trade mark. wenn nicht alle ~ trügen if I'm/we're *etc* not completely mistaken; es ist ein ~ unserer Zeit, daß ... it is a sign of the times that ...; die ~ erkennen to see the writing on the wall; die ~ der Zeit erkennen to recognize the mood of the times; es geschehen noch ~ und Wunder! (*hum*) wonders will never cease! (*hum*); als/zum ~ as a sign; ein ~ des Himmels a sign from heaven; als ~ von etw as a sign *or* indication of sth; zum ~, daß ... as a sign that ...; to show that ...; als ~ der Verehrung as a mark *or* token of respect; jdm ein ~ geben *or* machen to give sb a signal *or* sign, to signal to sb; etw zum ~ tun to do sth as a signal, to signal by doing sth; das ~ zum Aufbruch geben to give the signal to leave; unser/Ihr ~ (*form*) our/your reference; seines ~s (*old, hum*) by trade; er ist im ~ *or* unter dem ~ des Widders geboren he was born under the sign of Aries; unter dem ~ von etw stehen (*fig: Konferenz etc*) to take place against a background of sth; sie steht unter dem ~ des Widders her sign is Aries; das Jahr 1979 steht unter dem ~ des Kindes 1979 is the year of the child; 1969 stand unter dem ~ der ersten Mondlandung 1969 was the year of the first landing on the moon.

Zeichen-: ~block *m* drawing *or* sketch pad; ~brett *nt* drawing-board; ~dreieck *nt* set-square; ~erklärung *f* (*auf Fahrplänen etc*) key (to the symbols); (*auf Landkarte*) legend; ~feder *f* drawing-pen; z~haft *adj* symbolic; ~heft *nt* drawing-book; ~kohle *f* charcoal; ~kunst *f* (art of) drawing; ~lehrer *m* art teacher; ~papier *nt* drawing paper; ~saal *m* art-room; ~schutz *m* protection of registered trade marks; ~setzung *f* punctuation; ~sprache *f* sign language; ~stift *m* drawing pencil; ~stunde *f* art *or* drawing lesson; ~system *nt* notation; ~tisch *m* drawing table; ~trickfilm *m* (animated) cartoon; ~unterricht *m* art; (*Unterrichtsstunde*) drawing *or* art lesson; ~vorlage *f* original, model (*for a drawing or trade mark*).

zeichnen *vi* (a) to draw; (*form: unter~*) to sign. an dem Entwurf hat er lange gezeichnet he has spent a long time drawing the blueprint; gezeichnet: XY signed, XY; ich zeichne hochachtungsvoll (*form*) I remain yours faithfully.

2 *vt* (a) (*abzeichnen*) to draw; (*entwerfen*) *Plan, Grundriß* to draw up, to draft; (*fig: porträtieren*) to portray, to depict.

(b) (*kennzeichnen*) to mark. das Gefieder des Vogels ist hübsch gezeichnet the bird's plumage has attractive markings.

(c) (*Fin*) *Betrag* to subscribe; *Aktien* to subscribe (for); *Anleihe* to subscribe to.

Zeichner(in *f*) *m* -s, - artist. muß ein Maler auch immer ein guter ~ sein? must a painter always be a good draughtsman too?; *siehe* technisch. (b) (*Fin*) subscriber (*von* to).

zeichnerisch 1 *adj* Darstellung, Gestaltung graphic(al). sein ~es Können his drawing ability. 2 *adv* ~ begabt sein to have a talent for drawing; etw ~ erklären to explain sth with a drawing.

Zeichnung *f* (a) (*Darstellung*) drawing; (*Entwurf*) draft, drawing; (*fig: Schilderung*) portrayal, depiction. (b) (*Muster*) patterning; (*von Gefieder, Fell*) markings *pl*. (c) (*Fin*) subscription. eine Anleihe zur ~ auflegen to invite subscriptions for a loan.

Zeichnungs-: z~berechtigt *adj* authorized to sign; ~vollmacht *f* authority to sign.

Zeigefinger *m* index finger, forefinger.

zeigen 1 *vi* to point. nach Norden/rechts ~ to point north *or* to the north/to the right; auf jdn/etw ~ to point at sb/sth; (*hinweisen auch*) to point to sb/sth.

2 *vt* to show; (*Thermometer auch*) to be at *or* on, to indicate. jdm etw ~ to show sb sth *or* sth to sb; ich muß mir mal von jemandem ~ lassen, wie man das macht I'll have to get someone to show me how to do it; dem werd' ich's (aber) ~! (*inf*) I'll show him!; zeig mal, was du kannst! let's see what you can do!, show us what you can do!

3 *vr* to appear; (*Gefühle*) to show. sich mit jdm ~ to let oneself be seen with sb; in dem Kleid kann ich mich doch nicht ~ I can't be seen in a dress like that; er zeigt sich nicht gern in der Öffentlichkeit he doesn't like showing himself *or* being seen in public; sich ~ als ... to show *or* prove oneself to be ...; er zeigte sich befriedigt he was satisfied; er hat sich feige gezeigt he showed *or* proved himself (to be) a coward; es zeigt sich, daß ... it turns out that ...; es zeigt sich (doch) wieder einmal, daß ... it just goes to show; es wird sich ~, wer recht hat time will tell who is right, we shall see who's right; daran zeigt sich, daß ... that shows (that) ...; das zeigt sich jetzt it's beginning to show.

Zeiger *m* -s, - indicator, pointer; (*Uhr~*) hand. der große/kleine ~ the big/little hand.

Zeigerausschlag *m* pointer *or* indicator deflection.

Zeigestock *m* pointer.

zeihen *pret* **zieh**, *ptp* **geziehen** *vt* (*old*) jdn einer Sache (*gen*) ~ to accuse sb of sth.

Zeile *f* -, -n line; (*Häuser~, Baum~ etc auch*) row. davon habe ich keine ~ gelesen I haven't read a single word of it; zwischen den ~n lesen to read between the lines; vielen Dank für Deine ~n many thanks for your letter; jdm ein paar ~n schreiben to write sb a few lines; (*Brief schreiben auch*) to drop sb a line.

Zeilen-: ~abstand *m* line spacing; ~abtastung *f* (*TV*) line scan(ning); ~bauweise *f* ribbon development; ~fang *m* (*TV*) horizontal hold; ~honorar *nt* payment per line; ~honorar bekommen to be paid by the line; ~länge *f* length (of a/the line); ~norm *f* (*TV*) line standard; ~schalter *m* line spacer; ~setzmaschine *f* Linotype machine ®; z~weise *adv* in lines; (*nach Zeilen*) by the line; etw z~weise vorlesen to read sth out line by line.

-zeilig *adj suf* -line. es ist vier~ it has four lines.

Zeisig *m* -s, -e (*Orn*) siskin; *siehe* locker.

Zeit *f* -, -en (a) time; (*Epoche*) age. die gute alte ~ the good old days; das waren noch ~en! those were the days; die ~en sind

schlecht times are bad; die ~en haben sich geändert times have changed; die ~ Goethes the age of Goethe; die damalige ~ machte die Einführung neuer Methoden erforderlich the situation at the time required the introduction of new methods; wenn ~ und Umstände es erfordern if circumstances demand it, if the situation requires it; die jetzigen ~en erfordern, ... the present situation requires ...; für alle ~en for ever, for all time (liter); etw für alle ~en entscheiden to decide sth once and for all; in seiner/ihrer besten ~ at his/her/its peak; mit der ~ gehen to move with the times; vor der ~ alt werden to get old before one's time; vor jds (dat) ~ before sb's time; die ~ ist knapp bemessen time is short; die ~ wurde mir lang time hung heavy on my hands; eine lange ~ hersein or zurückliegen, daß ... to be a long time (ago or back) since ...; eine Stunde ~ haben to have an hour (to spare); wir haben noch zwei Stunden ~ bis ... we have another two hours before ...; Fräulein Glück, haben Sie vielleicht einen Augenblick ~? Miss Glück, do you have a moment?; sich (dat) für jdn/etw ~ nehmen to devote time to sb/sth; dafür muß ich mir mehr ~ nehmen I need more time for that; sich (dat) die ~ nehmen, etw zu tun to take the time to do sth; du hast dir aber reichlich ~ gelassen you certainly took your time; hier bin ich die längste ~ gewesen it's about time or high time I was going; keine ~ verlieren to lose no time; damit hat es noch ~ there's no rush or hurry, there's plenty of time; das hat ~ bis morgen that can wait until tomorrow; laß dir ~ take your time; ... aller ~en ... of all time, ... ever; auf bestimmte ~ for a certain length of time; auf unbestimmte ~ for an indefinite period; in letzter ~ recently; die ganze ~ über the whole time; mit der ~ gradually, in time; nach ~ bezahlt werden to be paid by the hour; die ~ heilt alle Wunden (Prov) time is a great healer (prov); auf ~ spielen (Sport) to play for time; es wird langsam ~, daß ... it's about time that ...; für dich wird es langsam ~, daß ... it's about time that you ...; seine ~ ist gekommen his time has come; hast du (die) genaue ~? do you have the exact time?; in der ~ von 10 bis 12 between 10 and 12 (o'clock); es ist an der ~, daß ... it is about time or high time (that) ...; Vertrag auf ~ fixed-term contract; Beamter auf ~ = non-permanent civil servant; Soldat auf ~ soldier serving for a set time; seit dieser ~ since then; zur ~ or zu ~en Königin Viktorias in Queen Victoria's times; zu der ~, als ... (at the time) when ...; zu der ~, als es noch einen Kaiser gab in the days when there was still an emperor; alles zu seiner ~ (Prov) all in good time; von ~ zu ~ from time to time; zur ~ at the moment.
   (b) (Ling) tense. in welcher ~ steht das Verb? what tense is the verb in?

zeit prep +gen ~ meines/seines Lebens in my/his lifetime.

-zeit f in cpds time.

Zeit-: ~abschnitt m period (of time); ~alter nt age; das goldene ~alter the golden age; in unserem ~alter nowadays, in this day and age; ~angabe f (Datum) date; (Uhrzeit) time (of day); die ~angabe kommt vor der Ortsangabe (Gram) time is given before place; seine ~angaben sind sehr ungenau his times are very imprecise; ~ansage f (Rad) time check; (Telec) speaking clock; ~arbeit f temporary work/job; ~aufnahme f (Phot) time exposure; ~aufwand m time (needed to complete a task); mit möglichst wenig ~aufwand taking as little time as possible; ~begriff m conception of time; ~bestimmung f (Gram) designation of the tense of a verb; ~bombe f time bomb; ~dokument nt contemporary document; ~druck m pressure of time; unter ~druck under pressure.

Zeiten-: ~folge f (Gram) sequence of tenses; ~wende f nach/vor der ~wende anno Domini/before Christ.

Zeit-: ~ersparnis f saving of time; ~form f (Gram) tense; ~frage f question of time; z~gebunden adj tied to or dependent on a particular time; Mode temporary; ~geist m Zeitgeist, spirit of the times; z~gemäß adj up-to-date; z~gemäß sein to be in keeping with the times; ~genosse m contemporary; ein seltsamer ~genosse (iro) an odd bod (inf), an oddball (esp US inf); z~genössisch adj contemporary; ~geschäft nt (Comm) siehe Termingeschäft; ~geschichte f contemporary history; ~gewinn m gain in time; sich um einen ~gewinn bemühen to try to gain time; z~gleich 1 adj Erscheinungen contemporaneous; Läufer with the same time; (Film) synchronized, in sync(h) (inf); 2 adv at the same time; z~gleich den ersten Platz belegen to tie for first place.

zeitig adj, adv early.

zeitigen vt (geh) Ergebnis, Wirkung to bring about; Erfolg auch to lead to. Früchte ~ to bear fruit.

Zeit-: ~karte f season ticket; (Wochenkarte) weekly ticket; ~karteninhaber m season-ticket holder; weekly ticket holder; ~kontrolle f time study; z~kritisch adj Aufsatz, Artikel full of comment on contemporary issues; seine z~kritischen Bemerkungen his thoughtful remarks on contemporary issues; seine z~kritische Haltung his awareness of contemporary issues; ~lang f eine ~lang a while, a time; wir sind eine ~lang dort geblieben we stayed there (for) a while or for a time; eine ~lang ist das ganz schön or time it's quite nice; z~lebens adv all one's life.

zeitlich 1 adj temporal; (vergänglich auch) transitory; (chronologisch) Reihenfolge chronological. in kurzem/großem ~em Abstand at short/long intervals (of time); das Z~e segnen (euph: Mensch) to depart this life; (Sache) to bite the dust (inf).
   2 adv timewise (inf), from the point of view of time; (chronologisch) chronologically. das kann sie ~ nicht einrichten she can't fit that in (timewise inf), she can't find (the) time for that; das paßt ihr ~ nicht the time isn't convenient for her; ~ zusammenfallen to coincide; die Uhren/Pläne ~ aufeinander abstimmen to synchronize one's watches/plans.

Zeitlichkeit f temporality, transitoriness.

Zeit-: ~limit nt time limit; ~lohn m hourly rate; ~lohn bekommen to be paid by the hour; z~los adj timeless; Stil auch which doesn't date; Kleidung auch classic; ~lupe f slow motion no art; etw in (der) ~lupe zeigen to show sth in slow motion; Wiederholung in (der) ~lupe slow-motion replay; ~lupenaufnahme f slow-motion shot; ~lupentempo nt slow speed; im ~lupentempo (lit) in slow motion; (fig) at a snail's pace; ~mangel m lack of time; aus ~mangel for lack of time; ~maschine f time machine; ~maß nt tempo; ~messer m -s, - timekeeper; ~messung f timekeeping (auch Sport), measurement of time; z~nah adj contemporary; Problem auch of our age; Gottesdienst, Übersetzung auch modern; Bücher, Unterricht relevant to present times; ~nähe f siehe adj contemporary nature; modernness; relevance to present times; ~nahme f -, -n (Sport) timekeeping no pl; ~nehmer m (Sport, Ind) timekeeper; ~not f shortage of time; in ~not sein to be pressed for or short of time; ~plan m schedule, timetable; ~punkt m (Termin) time; (Augenblick auch) moment; zu diesem ~punkt at that time; den ~punkt für etw festlegen to set a time for sth; ~raffer m -s, no pl time-lapse photography; einen Film im ~raffer zeigen to show a time-lapse film; z~raubend adj time-consuming; ~raum m period of time; in einem ~raum von ... over a period of ...; ~rechnung f calendar; nach christlicher/jüdischer ~rechnung according to the Christian/Jewish calendar; vor/nach unserer ~rechnung (abbr v.u.Z./n.u.Z.) (esp DDR) before Christ/anno Domini (abbr BC/AD); ~schrift f (Illustrierte) magazine; (wissenschaftlich) periodical, journal; ~schriftenkatalog m periodicals catalogue; ~sinn m sense of time; ~spanne f period of time; z~sparend adj timesaving; ~studie f (Ind) time (and motion) study; ~tafel f chronological table.

Zeitung f (news)paper. er hat bei der ~ gearbeitet he worked for a newspaper.

Zeitungs- in cpds newspaper; ~abonnement nt subscription to a newspaper; ~anzeige f newspaper advertisement; (Familienanzeige) announcement in the (news)paper; ~ausschnitt m newspaper cutting; ~austräger m newspaper carrier, = paperboy/girl; ~beilage f newspaper supplement; ~ente f (inf) canard, false newspaper report; ~frau f (inf) newspaper carrier; ~händler m newsagent, newsdealer (US); ~inserat nt newspaper advertisement; ~junge m paperboy; ~kiosk m newspaper kiosk; ~korrespondent m newspaper correspondent; ~lesen nt reading the (news)paper no art; er war gerade beim ~lesen he was just reading the paper/papers; ~leser m newspaper reader; ~papier nt newsprint; (als Altpapier) newspaper; ~redakteur m newspaper editor; ~roman m novel published in serial form in a newspaper; ~ständer m magazine or newspaper rack; ~verleger m newspaper publisher; ~wesen nt press, newspaper world; das ~wesen in Deutschland the German press; im ~wesen tätig sein to be in the newspaper business; (Journalist) to be in journalism; ~wissenschaft f journalism.

Zeit-: ~unterschied m time difference; ~vergeudung f waste of time; ~verlust m loss of time; das bedeutet mehrere Stunden ~verlust this will mean wasting several hours; ohne ~verlust without losing any time; ~verschwendung f waste of time; das wäre ~verschwendung that would be a waste of time; ~vertreib m way of passing the time; (Hobby) pastime; zum ~vertreib to pass the time, as a way of passing the time; z~weilig adj temporary; z~weise adv at times; und z~weise Regen with rain at times; ~wende f siehe Zeitenwende; ~wert m (Fin) current value; (Meßergebnis) time; ~wort nt verb; ~zeichen nt time signal; ~zünder m time fuse.

zelebrieren* vt to celebrate.

Zelebrität f (rare) celebrity.

Zell|atmung f cellular respiration.

Zelle f -, -n cell (auch Sci, Pol); (Kabine) cabin; (Telefon~) (phone) box (Brit) or booth; (bei Flugzeug) airframe.

Zell-: ~gewebe nt cell tissue; ~glas nt cellophane; ~kern m nucleus (of a/the cell); ~membran f cell membrane.

Zellophan nt -s, no pl cellophane.

Zell-: ~stoff m cellulose; ~stoffwindel f disposable nappy (Brit) or diaper (US); ~teilung f cell division.

zellular adj cellular.

Zelluloid [auch -'lɔyt] nt -s, no pl celluloid.

Zellulose f -, -n cellulose.

Zell-: ~verschmelzung f cell fusion; ~wand f cell wall; ~wolle f spun rayon.

Zelot (in f) m -en, -en (fig geh) zealot.

Zelt nt -(e)s, -e tent; (Bier~, Fest~ etc auch) marquee; (Indianer~) wigwam, te(e)pee; (Zirkus~) big top; (liter: des Himmels) canopy. seine ~e aufschlagen/abbrechen (fig) to settle down/to pack one's bags.

Zelt-: ~bahn f strip of canvas; ~dach nt tent-roof; (Dachform) pyramid roof.

zelten vi to camp. Z~ verboten no camping.

Zelter m -s, - (Hist: Pferd) palfrey.

Zelter (in f) m -s, - camper.

Zelt-: ~hering m tent peg; ~lager nt camp; wann fahrt ihr ins ~lager? when are you going to camp?; ~leben nt life under canvas; ~mast m tent pole; ~mission f evangelistic mission with a tent as its base; ~pflock m tent peg; ~plane f tarpaulin; ~platz m camp site; ~stange f tentpole.

Zement m -(e)s, -e cement.

zementieren* vt to cement; (verputzen) to cement over; Stahl to carburize (spec); (fig) to reinforce; Freundschaft to cement.

Zementierung f (fig) reinforcement; (von Freundschaft) cementing.

Zement(misch)maschine f cement mixer.

Zen nt -s, no pl Zen (Buddhism).

Zenit m -(e)s, no pl (lit, fig) zenith. die Sonne steht im ~ the sun is at its zenith; im ~ des Lebens stehen (liter) to be at one's peak.

Zenotaph m -s, -e cenotaph.

zensieren* vt (a) auch vi (benoten) to mark. einen Aufsatz mit einer Drei ~ to give an essay a three. (b) (Bücher etc) to censor.

Zensor m censor.

Zensur f (a) (no pl: Kontrolle) censorship no indef art; (Prüfstelle) censors pl; (esp bei Film) board of censors. eine ~ findet nicht statt there is no censorship, it is/they are not censored; durch die ~ gehen/einer ~ unterliegen to be censored.
(b) (Note) mark. der Plan erhielt von der Presse schlechte ~en the plan got the thumbs-down from the press (inf).
(c) ~en pl (Zeugnis) report sing; wenn es auf die ~en zugeht when report time approaches.

zensurieren* vt (Aus) to censor.

Zensus m -, - (Volkszählung) census.

Zentaur m -en, -en centaur.

Zenti-: ~grad m hundredth of a degree; ~gramm nt centigram(me); ~liter m or nt centilitre; ~meter m or nt centimetre; ~metermaß nt (metric) tape measure.

Zentner m -s, - (metric) hundredweight; (Aus, Sw) 100kg.

Zentner-: ~last f (fig) heavy burden; mir fiel eine ~last vom Herzen it was a great weight or load off my mind; z~schwer adj (fig) heavy; z~schwer auf jdm or jds Seele lasten to weigh sb down; z~weise adv by the hundredweight.

zentral adj (lit, fig) central.

Zentral- in cpds central; ~bank f central bank; ~bankrat m council of the German central bank.

Zentrale f -, -n (von Firma etc, Mil) head office; (für Taxis) headquarters sing or pl; (für Busse etc) depot; (Schalt~) central control (office); (Telefon~) exchange; (von Firma etc) switchboard.

Zentralheizung f central heating.

Zentralisation f centralization.

zentralisieren* vt to centralize.

Zentralisierung f centralization.

Zentralismus m centralism.

zentralistisch adj centralist.

Zentral-: ~komitee nt central committee; ~nervensystem nt central nervous system; ~verschluß m leaf shutter.

Zentren pl of Zentrum.

zentrieren* vt to centre.

zentrifugal adj centrifugal.

Zentrifugalkraft f centrifugal force.

Zentrifuge f -, -n centrifuge.

zentripetal adj centripetal.

Zentripetalkraft f centripetal force.

zentrisch adj concentric; Anziehung centric.

Zentrum nt -s, Zentren (lit, fig) centre (Brit), center (US); (Innenstadt) (town) centre; (von Großstadt) (city) centre. sie wohnt im ~ (der Stadt)/von Chicago she lives in the (town/city) centre/in the centre of Chicago, she lives downtown/in downtown Chicago (US); im ~ des Interesses stehen to be the centre of attention.

Zentrumspartei f (Hist) Centre party, German Catholic party representing the centre politically.

Zephir (esp Aus), **Zephyr** m -s, -e (liter) zephyr.

Zeppelin m -s, -e zeppelin.

Zepter nt -s, - sceptre. das ~ führen or schwingen (inf) to wield the sceptre; (esp Ehefrau) to rule the roost.

zerbeißen* vt irreg to chew; Knochen, Bonbon, Keks etc to crunch; (beschädigen) Pantoffel etc to chew to pieces; (auseinanderbeißen) Kette, Leine to chew through.

zerbersten* vi irreg aux sein to burst; (Glas) to shatter.

Zerberus m -, -se (a) no pl (Myth) Cerberus. (b) (fig hum) watchdog.

zerbeulen* vt to dent. zerbeult battered.

zerbomben* vt to flatten with bombs, to bomb to smithereens (inf); Gebäude auch to bomb out. zerbombt Stadt, Gebäude bombed out; zerbombt werden to be flattened by bombs.

zerbrechen* irreg 1 vt (lit) to break into pieces; Glas, Porzellan etc to smash, to shatter; Ketten (lit, fig) to break, to sever; (fig) Widerstand to break down; Lebenswille to destroy; siehe Kopf.
2 vi aux sein to break into pieces; (Glas, Porzellan etc) to smash, to shatter; (fig) to be destroyed (an + dat by); (Widerstand) to collapse (an + dat in the face of); er ist am Leben zerbrochen he has been broken or destroyed by life.

zerbrechlich adj fragile; Mensch auch frail. „Vorsicht ~!" "fragile, handle with care".

Zerbrechlichkeit f fragility; (von Mensch auch) frailness.

zerbröckeln* vti to crumble.

zerdätschen* vt (inf) to squash, to crush.

zerdeppern* vt (inf) to smash.

zerdrücken* vt to squash, to crush; Gemüse to mash; (zerknittern) to crush, to crease, to crumple; (inf) Träne to squeeze out.

Zeremonie [tseremo'niː, -mo'niːə] f ceremony.

Zeremoniell nt -s, -e ceremonial.

zeremoniell adj ceremonial.

Zeremonienmeister [-'moːniən-] m master of ceremonies.

zerfahren adj scatty; (unkonzentriert) distracted.

Zerfahrenheit f siehe adj scattiness; distraction.

Zerfall m -(e)s, no pl disintegration; (von Gebäude auch, von Atom) decay; (von Leiche, Holz etc) decomposition; (von Land, Kultur) decline, decay, fall; (von Gesundheit) decline.

zerfallen* 1 vi irreg aux sein (a) to disintegrate; (Gebäude auch) to decay, to fall into ruin; (Atomkern) to decay; (auseinanderfallen auch) to fall apart; (Leiche, Holz etc) to decompose; (Reich, Kultur, Moral) to decay, to decline; (Gesundheit) to decline. zu Staub ~ to crumble (in)to dust.
(b) (sich gliedern) to fall (in + acc into).
2 adj (a) Haus tumble-down; Gemäuer auch crumbling.

(b) (verfeindet) mit jdm ~ sein to have fallen out with sb; mit sich (dat) und der Welt/mit sich (dat) selbst ~ sein to be at odds with the world/oneself.

Zerfalls-: ~erscheinung f sign of decay; ~geschwindigkeit f rate of decay; ~produkt nt daughter product.

zerfetzen* vt to tear or rip to pieces or shreds; Brief etc to rip up, to tear up (into little pieces); (Geschoß) Arm etc to mangle, to tear to pieces; (fig) to pull or tear to pieces.

zerfetzt adj Hose ragged, tattered; Arm lacerated.

zerfleddern*, zerfledern* vt (inf) to tatter, to get tatty (inf).

zerfleischen* 1 vt to tear limb from limb, to tear to pieces. 2 vt (fig) er zerfleischt sich in (Selbst)vorwürfen he torments or tortures himself with self-reproaches; sich gegenseitig ~, einander ~ to tear each other apart.

zerfließen* vi irreg aux sein (Tinte, Makeup etc) to run; (Eis etc, fig: Reichtum etc) to melt away. in Tränen ~ to dissolve into tears; seine Hoffnungen zerflossen in nichts his hopes melted away; vor Mitleid ~ to be overcome with pity.

zerfranst adj frayed.

zerfressen* vt irreg to eat away; (Motten, Mäuse etc) to eat; (Säure, Rost auch) to corrode; (fig) to consume. die Säure hat ihr das Gesicht ~ the acid burnt into her face; (von Motten/Würmern) ~ sein to be moth-/worm-eaten.

zerfurchen* vt to furrow.

zergehen* vi irreg aux sein to dissolve; (schmelzen) to melt. auf der Zunge ~ (Gebäck etc) to melt in the mouth; (Fleisch) to fall apart; vor Mitleid ~ to be overcome with pity.

zergliedern* vt (Biol) to dissect; Satz to parse; (fig) to analyse.

Zergliederung f siehe vt dissection; parsing; analysis.

zerhacken* vt to chop up.

zerhauen* vt irreg to chop in two; (in viele Stücke) to chop up; Knoten (lit, fig) to cut; (inf: kaputtschlagen) to smash.

zerkauen* vt to chew; (Hund) Leine to chew up.

zerkleinern* vt to cut up; (zerhacken) to chop (up); (zerbrechen) to break up; (zermahlen) to crush.

zerklüftet adj rugged; Mandeln fissured. tief ~es Gestein rock with deep fissures, deeply fissured rock.

zerknautschen* vt (inf) to crease, to crumple.

zerknautscht adj (inf) Kleidung creased, crumpled; Gesicht (faltig) wizened. du siehst heute fürchterlich ~ aus you're looking somewhat the worse for wear today.

zerknirscht adj remorseful, overcome with remorse.

Zerknirschtheit, Zerknirschung f remorse.

zerknittern* vt to crease, to crumple.

zerknittert adj (a) Kleid, Stoff creased. (b) (inf) (schuldbewußt) overcome with remorse; (unausgeschlafen) washed-out (inf).

zerknüllen* vt to crumple up, to scrunch up (inf).

zerkochen* vti (vi: aux sein) to cook to a pulp; (zu lange kochen auch) to overcook.

zerkratzen* vt to scratch to pieces.

zerkrümeln* vt to crumble; Boden to loosen.

zerlassen* vt irreg to melt.

zerlaufen* vi irreg aux sein to melt.

zerlegbar adj able to be taken apart; Maschine, Gerüst auch able to be dismantled; (Gram) analysable; (Math) reducible. die Möbel waren leicht ~ the furniture could easily be taken apart or was easily taken apart.

zerlegen* vt (auseinandernehmen) to take apart or to pieces; Gerüst, Maschine auch to dismantle; Motor, Getriebe auch to strip down; Theorie, Argumente to break down; (Gram) to analyse; (Math) to reduce (in + acc to); (zerschneiden) to cut up; Geflügel, Wild to carve up; (Biol) to dissect. etw in seine Einzelteile ~ to take sth to pieces; to dismantle sth completely; to strip sth down; to break sth down into its (individual) constituents; Satz to parse sth; eine Zahl in ihre Faktoren ~ to factorize a number.

Zerlegung f, no pl siehe vt taking apart; dismantling; stripping down; breaking down; analysis; reduction; cutting up; carving up; dissection. die ~ einer Zahl in ihre Faktoren the factorization of a number.

zerlesen adj well-thumbed.

zerlumpt adj ragged, tattered no adv.

zermahlen* vt to grind; (in Mörser) to crush.

zermalmen* vt (lit, fig) to crush; (mit den Zähnen) to crunch, to grind.

zermanschen* vt (inf) to squash; (mit Gabel) to mash.

zermartern* vt sich (dat) den Kopf or das Hirn ~ to rack or cudgel one's brains.

zermatschen* vt (inf) siehe zermanschen.

zermürben* vt (a) (fig) jdn ~ to wear sb down; ~d wearing, trying. (b) (rare: brüchig machen) to make brittle.

Zermürbung f (eines Gegners etc) wearing down no pl, attrition.

Zermürbungs-: ~krieg m war of attrition; ~taktik f tactics of attrition pl.

zernagen* vt to chew to pieces; (Nagetiere) to gnaw to pieces.

zernieren* vt (obs) Festung to besiege.

Zero ['zeːro] f -, -s or nt -s, -s zero.

zerpflücken* vt (lit, fig) to pick to pieces.

zerplatzen* vi aux sein to burst; (Glas) to shatter.

zerquält adj tortured.

zerquetschen* vt to squash, to crush; (mit Gabel) Kartoffeln etc to mash; (inf) Träne to squeeze out.

Zerquetschte pl (inf) 10 Mark und ein paar ~ 10 marks something (or other), 10 marks odd; Hundert und ein paar ~ a hundred odd; elf Uhr und ein paar ~ eleven something (or other).

zerraufen* vt to ruffle. zerrauft dishevelled.

Zerrbild nt (lit: in Spiegel) distorted picture or image; (fig auch) caricature; (von Verhältnissen, System, Gesellschaft etc auch) travesty.

zerreden* vt to flog to death (inf).

zerreiben* vt irreg to crumble, to crush; (in Mörser etc) to grind; (fig) to crush.

zerreißbar adj tearable.

zerreißen* irreg 1 vt (aus Versehen) to tear; (in Stücke) to tear to pieces or shreds; Faden, Seil etc to break; (absichtlich) Brief etc to tear up; (zerfleischen) to tear apart or limb from limb; (plötzlich aufreißen, durchbrechen) Wolkendecke, Stille etc to rend (liter); (fig) Land to tear apart or in two; Bindungen to break. es zerreißt mir das Herz (liter) it is heart-rending or heartbreaking, it breaks my heart.
2 vi aux sein (Stoff) to tear; (Band, Seil etc) to break.
3 vr (fig) ich könnte mich vor Wut ~ I'm hopping (mad) (inf); ich kann mich doch nicht ~! I can't be in two places at once; sich ~, (um) etw zu tun to go to no end of trouble to do sth.

Zerreiß-: z~fest adj tear-resistant; ~probe f (lit) pull test; (fig) real test; eine ~probe für ihre Ehe etc a crucial test of their marriage etc; eine ~probe für meine Geduld a real test of my patience.

zerren 1 vt to drag; Sehne to pull, to strain. jdm/sich die Kleider vom Leib ~ to tear the clothes from sb's body/to tear one's clothes off; etw an die Öffentlichkeit ~ to drag sth into the public eye. 2 vi an etw (dat) ~ to tug or pull at sth; an den Nerven ~ to be nerve-racking.

zerrinnen* vi irreg aux sein to melt (away); (fig) (Träume, Pläne) to melt or fade away; (Geld, Vermögen) to disappear. jdm unter den Händen or zwischen den Fingern ~ (Geld) to run through sb's hands like water; die Zeit zerrinnt mir unter den Händen the time just goes without me knowing where.

zerrissen 1 ptp of zerreißen. 2 adj (fig) Volk, Partei strifetorn, disunited; Mensch (inwardly) torn.

Zerrissenheit f siehe adj disunity no pl; (inner) conflict.

Zerrspiegel m (lit) distorting mirror; (fig) travesty.

Zerrung f (das Zerren: von Sehne, Muskel) pulling. eine ~ a pulled ligament/muscle.

zerrupfen* vt to pick or pull to pieces.

zerrütten* vt to destroy, to ruin, to wreck; Ehe to break up, to destroy; Geist to destroy; Nerven to shatter. eine zerrüttete Ehe/Familie a broken marriage/home; sich in einem zerrütteten Zustand befinden to be in a very bad way.

Zerrüttung f destruction; (von Ehe) breakdown; (von Nerven) shattering, (Zustand) shattered state. der Staat/ihre Ehe befindet sich im Zustand der ~ the state is in a bad way/their marriage is breaking down.

Zerrüttungsprinzip nt principle of irretrievable breakdown.

zersägen* vt to saw up.

zerschellen* vi aux sein (Schiff, Flugzeug) to be dashed or smashed to pieces; (Vase etc) to smash (to pieces or smithereens). das zerschellte Schiff the wrecked ship.

zerschießen* vt irreg to shoot to pieces; (durchlöchern) to riddle with bullets. er hatte ein zerschossenes Bein his leg had been shot to pieces/was riddled with bullets.

zerschlagen* irreg 1 vt (a) (Mensch) to smash (to pieces or smithereens); (Stein etc auch) to shatter; (Hagel) Ernte, Wein to crush; (auseinanderschlagen) to break up.
(b) (fig) Angriff, Widerstand, Opposition to crush; Hoffnungen, Pläne to shatter; Spionagering, Vereinigung to break.
2 vr (nicht zustande kommen) to fall through; (Hoffnung, Aussichten) to be shattered.
3 adj pred washed out (inf); (nach Anstrengung, langer Reise etc) shattered (inf), worn out. ich wachte wie ~ auf I woke up feeling washed out.

Zerschlagenheit f exhaustion.

Zerschlagung f (fig) suppression; (von Hoffnungen, Plänen) shattering.

zerschleißen* pret zerschliß, ptp zerschlissen vti (usu ptp) to wear out. zerschlissene Kleider worn-out or threadbare clothes.

zerschmeißen* vt (inf) irreg to shatter, to smash (to pieces).

zerschmelzen* vi irreg aux sein (lit, fig) to melt. vor Rührung/Mitleid (dat) ~ (iro) to brim (over) with emotion/pity.

zerschmettern* 1 vt (lit, fig) to shatter; Feind to crush; (Sport) Gegner to smash. 2 vi aux sein to shatter.

zerschneiden* vt irreg to cut; (in zwei Teile) to cut in two; (in Stücke) to cut up; (verschneiden) Stoff to cut wrongly; (fig) Stille to pierce. jdm das Herz ~ to cut sb to the quick.

zerschnippeln* vt (inf) to snip to pieces.

zerschrammen* vt Haut, Möbel to scratch to pieces.

zersetzen* 1 vt to decompose; (Säure) to corrode; (fig) to undermine, to subvert. 2 vr to decompose; (durch Säure) to corrode; (fig) to become undermined or subverted.

zersetzend adj (fig) subversive.

Zersetzung f (Chem) decomposition; (durch Säure) corrosion; (fig: Untergrabung) undermining, subversion; (von Gesellschaft) decline (von in), decay.

Zersetzungs-: ~erscheinung f (fig) sign of decline or decay; ~produkt nt substance produced by decomposition; ~prozeß m siehe Zersetzung (process of) decomposition/corrosion/subversion; decline (von in), decay.

zersiedeln* vt to spoil (by development).

Zersied(e)lung f overdevelopment.

zersingen* vt irreg (pej, hum) to flog to death (inf).

zerspalten* vt to split; Gemeinschaft to split up.

zersplittern* 1 vt to shatter; Holz to splinter; (fig) Kräfte, Zeit to dissipate, to squander; Gruppe, Partei to fragment.
2 vi aux sein to shatter; (Holz, Knochen) to splinter; (fig) to split up.
3 vr to shatter; (Holz) to splinter; (fig) to dissipate or squander one's energies; (Gruppe, Partei) to fragment, to become fragmented. der Widerstand ist zu zersplittert the opposition is too fragmented.

Zersplitterung f siehe vb shattering; splintering; dissipation, squandering; fragmentation.

zersprengen* vt to burst; (fig) Volksmenge to disperse, to scatter.

zerspringen* vi irreg aux sein to shatter; (Saite) to break; (einen Sprung bekommen) to crack. in tausend Stücke ~ to shatter in(to) a thousand pieces; das Herz wollte ihr vor Freude/Ungeduld fast ~ (liter) her heart was bursting with joy/impatience.

zerstampfen* vt (zertreten) to stamp or trample on; (zerkleinern) to crush; (im Mörser) to grind, to pound; Kartoffeln etc to mash.

zerstäuben* vt to spray.

Zerstäuber m -s, - spray; (Parfüm~ auch) atomizer.

zerstechen* vt irreg (a) (Mücken) to bite (all over); (Bienen etc) to sting (all over). wir sind von den Mücken ganz zerstochen worden we've been bitten all over by the midges. (b) Material, Haut to puncture; Finger to prick.

zerstieben* vi irreg aux sein to scatter; (Wasser) to spray.

zerstörbar adj destructible. nicht ~ indestructible.

zerstören* 1 vt (lit, fig) to destroy; Gebäude, Ehe, Glück auch to wreck; (verwüsten auch) to ruin; (Rowdys) to vandalize; Gesundheit to wreck, to ruin. 2 vi to destroy; siehe Boden.

Zerstörer m -s, - (old Aviat) fighter; (Naut) destroyer.

Zerstörer(in f) m -s, - destroyer.

zerstörerisch adj destructive.

Zerstörung f (a) no pl siehe vt destruction; wrecking; ruining; vandalizing. (b) (von Krieg, Katastrophe etc) destruction no pl, devastation no pl.

Zerstörungs-: ~drang m destructive urge or impulse; ~lust f delight in destruction; ~trieb m destructive urge or impulse; ~werk nt work of destruction; ~wut f destructive mania.

zerstoßen* vt irreg (a) (zerkleinern) to crush; (im Mörser) to pound, to grind. (b) (durch Stoßen beschädigen) to damage; Leder, Schuh to scuff.

zerstreiten* vr irreg to quarrel, to fall out.

zerstreuen* 1 vt (a) to scatter (in + dat over); Volksmenge etc auch to disperse; Licht to diffuse; (fig) to dispel, to allay.
(b) jdn ~ to take sb's mind off things, to divert sb.
2 vr (a) (sich verteilen) to scatter; (Menge auch) to disperse; (fig) to be dispelled or allayed.
(b) (sich ablenken) to take one's mind off things; (sich amüsieren) to amuse oneself.

zerstreut adj (fig) Mensch absent-minded. sie ist heute sehr ~ her mind is elsewhere today.

Zerstreutheit f, no pl absent-mindedness.

Zerstreuung f (a) no pl siehe vt scattering; dispersal; diffusion; dispelling, allaying. (b) (Ablenkung) diversion. zur ~ as a diversion. (c) (Zerstreutheit) absent-mindedness.

zerstritten 1 ptp of zerstreiten. 2 adj estranged. mit jdm ~ sein to be on very bad terms with sb.

zerstückeln* vt (lit) to cut up; Leiche to dismember; Land to divide or carve up; (fig) Tag, Semester etc to break up.

Zerstückelung f, no pl siehe vt cutting up; dismemberment; dividing up; breaking up.

zertalt adj (Geog) dissected.

zerteilen* vt to split up; (in zwei Teile auch) to divide; (zerschneiden) to cut up; Wogen, Wolken to part. ich kann mich nicht ~! I can't be in two places at once.

zerteppern* vt (inf) siehe zerdeppern.

Zertifikat nt certificate.

zertrampeln* vt to trample on.

zertrennen* vt to sever, to cut through; (auftrennen) Nähte to undo; Kleid to undo the seams of.

zertreten* vt irreg to crush (underfoot); Rasen to ruin. jdn wie einen Wurm ~ to grind sb into the ground.

zertrümmern* vt to smash; Einrichtung to smash up; Gebäude auch, Hoffnungen, Ordnung to wreck, to destroy; (dated) Atom to split.

Zertrümmerung f, no pl siehe vt smashing; smashing up; wrecking, destruction; splitting.

Zervelatwurst [tsɛrvəˈlaːt-] f cervelat, German salami.

zervikal [tsɛrviˈkaːl] adj (spec) cervical.

zerwerfen* vr irreg (fig) to fall out (mit jdm with sb).

zerwühlen* vt to ruffle up, to tousle; Bett, Kopfkissen to rumple (up); (aufwühlen) Erdboden to churn up; (Wildschwein etc) to churn or root up.

Zerwürfnis nt row, disagreement.

zerzausen* vt to ruffle; Haar to tousle.

zerzaust adj windswept; Haare auch dishevelled, tousled.

zerzupfen* vt to pull to pieces; Blume auch to pull the petals off.

Zeter nt: ~ und Mord(io) schreien (lit) to scream blue murder (inf); (fig) to raise a hue and cry.

Zeter-: ~geschrei nt (inf) hullabaloo; (fig) hue and cry; z~mordio: z~mordio schreien to scream blue murder (inf).

zetern vi (pej) to clamour; (keifen) to scold or nag; (jammern) to moan.

Zett nt -s, no pl (sl) gaol, jail. jdn zu 10 Jahren ~ verurteilen to send sb down for 10 years (inf); er hat ~ gekriegt he got sent down (inf).

Zettel m -s, - piece of paper; (Notiz~) note; (Kartei~) card; (Anhänge~) label; (mit Angabe über Inhalt, Anschrift etc) chit (inf), ticket; (Bekanntmachung) notice; (Hand~) leaflet, handbill (esp US); (Formular) form; (Stimm~) ballot paper; (Bestell~) coupon; (Kassen~, Beleg) receipt. „~ ankleben verboten" "stick no bills".

Zettel-: ~kartei f card index; ~kasten m file-card box; (~kartei) card index; ~katalog m card index; ~verteiler m person who hands out leaflets; ~wirtschaft f (pej) eine ~wirtschaft haben to have bits of paper everywhere; du mit deiner ~wirtschaft you and all your bits of paper.

Zeug nt -(e)s, no pl (a) (inf) stuff no indef art, no pl; (Ausrüstung auch) gear (inf); (Kleidung) clothes pl, things pl (inf); (mehrere Gegenstände auch, Getier) things pl. altes ~ junk, trash; ... und solches ~ ... and such things.

(b) (inf: Unsinn) nonsense, rubbish. ein/dieses ~ a/this load of nonsense or rubbish; dummes or ungereimtes ~ reden to talk a lot of nonsense or drivel (inf) or twaddle (inf); rede kein dummes ~ don't talk nonsense; dummes ~ treiben to be stupid.

(c) (Fähigkeit, Können) das ~ zu etw haben to have (got) what it takes to be sth (inf); er hat nicht das ~ dazu he hasn't got what it takes (inf).

(d) (old) (Stoff) material; (Wäsche) linen. jdm etwas am ~ flicken (inf) to tell sb what to do; was das ~ hält (inf) for all one is worth; laufen like mad; fahren like the blazes (inf); lügen, was das ~ hält (inf) to lie one's head off (inf); sich für jdn ins ~ legen (inf) to stand up for sb; sich ins ~ legen to go flat out; (bei Arbeit auch) to work flat out.

Zeug|amt nt (obs Mil) arsenal.

Zeuge m -n, -n (Jur, fig) witness (gen to). ~ eines Unfalls/Gesprächs sein to be a witness to an accident/a conversation; sich als ~ zur Verfügung stellen to come forward as a witness; vor/ unter ~n in front of witnesses; Gott ist mein ~ as God is my witness; die ~n Jehovas Jehovah's witnesses.

zeugen¹ vt Kind to father; (Bibl) to beget; (fig geh) to generate, to give rise to.

zeugen² vi (a) (vor +dat to) (aussagen) to testify; (vor Gericht auch) to give evidence. für/gegen jdn ~ to testify or give evidence for/against sb; von etw ~ to show sth.

Zeugen-: ~aussage f testimony; ~bank f witness box, witness stand (US); er sitzt auf der ~bank he's in the witness box or witness stand (US); ~beeinflussung f subornation of a witness/witnesses; ~ladung f summoning of a witness/witnesses; ~stand m witness box, witness stand (US); in den ~stand treten to go into the witness box, to take the (witness) stand; ~vereidigung f swearing in of a witness/witnesses; ~vernehmung f examination of the witness(es).

Zeughaus nt (obs Mil) arsenal, armoury.

Zeugin f witness.

Zeugnis nt (a) (esp liter: Zeugenaussage) evidence. für/gegen jdn ~ ablegen to give evidence or to testify for/against sb; für jds Ehrlichkeit etc ~ ablegen to bear witness to sb's honesty etc; falsches ~ ablegen, falsch ~ reden (Bibl) to bear false witness.

(b) (fig: Beweis) evidence.

(c) (Schul~) report; (Note) mark, grade (esp US).

(d) (Bescheinigung) certificate; (von Arbeitgeber) testimonial, reference. gute ~se haben to have good qualifications; (von Arbeitgeber) to have good references; jdm ein ~ ausstellen to give sb a reference or testimonial; ich kann ihm nur das beste ~ ausstellen (fig) I cannot speak too highly of him.

Zeugnis-: ~abschrift f copy of one's report/certificate/ testimonial; ~heft nt (Sch) report book; ~konferenz f (Sch) staff meeting to decide on marks etc; ~papiere pl certificates pl; testimonials pl; ~verweigerungsrecht nt right of a witness to refuse to give evidence.

Zeugs nt -, no pl (pej inf) siehe Zeug (a, b).

Zeugung f siehe zeugen¹ fathering; begetting; generating.

Zeugungs-: ~akt m act of procreation; (fig) creative act; z~fähig adj fertile; ~fähigkeit, ~kraft (geh) f fertility; ~organ nt (spec) male reproductive organ; z~unfähig adj sterile; ~unfähigkeit f sterility.

Zeus m - (Myth) Zeus.

z.H(d). abbr of zu Händen att.

Zibebe f -, -n (S Ger, Aus) sultana.

Zichorie [tsɪˈçoːriə] f chicory.

Zichorienkaffee [tsɪˈçoːriən-] m coffee with chicory.

Zicke f -, -n (a) nanny goat. (b) (pej inf: Frau) cow (sl), bitch (sl); (prüde) prude; (albern) silly thing.

Zickel nt -s, -(n) siehe Zicklein.

Zicken pl (inf) nonsense no pl. mach bloß keine ~! no nonsense now!; ~ machen to make trouble.

zickig adj (albern) silly; (prüde) prudish.

Zicklein nt (junge Ziege) kid; (junges Reh) fawn.

Zickzack m -(e)s, -e zigzag. z~ or im ~ laufen to zigzag; ~ nähen to zigzag.

Zickzack-: z~förmig adj zigzag; z~förmig verlaufen to zigzag; ~kurs m zigzag course; (von Hase etc) zigzag path; im ~kurs fahren/laufen to zigzag; ~linie f zigzag; ~schere f pinking shears; ~stich m zigzag stitch.

Ziege f -, -n (a) goat; (weiblich auch) nanny-goat. (b) (pej inf: Frau) cow (sl), bitch (sl).

Ziegel m -s, - (Backstein) brick; (Dach~) tile. ein Dach mit ~n decken to tile a roof.

Ziegel-: ~bau m, pl -ten brick building; ~brenner m brickmaker; (von Dachziegeln) tilemaker; ~brennerei f siehe Ziegelei; ~dach nt tiled roof.

Ziegelei f brickworks sing or pl; (für Dachziegel) tile-making works sing or pl.

Ziegel-: z~rot adj brick-red; ~stein m brick.

Ziegen-: ~bart m (a) (an Hut) shaving brush (hum); (hum.: Bart) goatee (beard); (Bot) goat's-beard mushroom; ~bock m billy goat; ~fell nt goatskin; ~herde f herd of goats; ~hirt(e) m goatherd; ~käse m goat's milk cheese; ~leder nt kid (-leather), kidskin; ~milch f goat's milk; ~peter m -s, - mumps sing.

zieh pret of zeihen.

Zieh-: ~brücke f drawbridge; ~brunnen m well; ~eltern pl foster parents pl.

ziehen pret zog, ptp gezogen 1 vt (a) to pull; (heftig auch) to tug; (schleppen) to drag; (dehnen auch) to stretch; (vom Kopf)

Hut to raise; Handbremse to put on; Choke, Starter to pull out. der Hund zog die Tischdecke vom Tisch the dog pulled the cloth off the table; den Ring vom Finger ~ to pull one's ring off (one's finger); die Knie/Schultern in die Höhe ~ to raise one's knees/shoulders; das Flugzeug nach oben/unten ~ to put the plane into a climb/descent; etw durch etw ~ to pull sth through sth; jdn nach unten ~ to pull or (fig) drag sb down; jdn auf die Seite or beiseite ~ to take sb aside or to one side; die Stirn kraus or in Falten ~ to knit one's brow; Wein auf Flaschen ~ to bottle wine; (neue) Saiten auf ein Instrument ~ to (re)string an instrument; etw ins Komische ~ to ridicule sth; mußt du immer alles ins Ironische ~? must you always be so ironical?; unangenehme Folgen nach sich ~ to have unpleasant consequences.

(b) (heraus~) to pull out (aus of); Zahn auch to take out, to extract; Fäden to take out, to remove; Korken, Schwert, Revolver auch to draw; Los, Spielkarte, (fig) Schlüsse to draw; Vergleich to draw, to make; (Math) Wurzel to work out. die Pflanze zieht ihre Nahrung aus dem Boden the plant gets or draws its nourishment from the soil; Zigaretten (aus dem Automaten) ~ to get or buy cigarettes from the machine.

(c) (zeichnen) Kreis, Linie to draw.

(d) (verlegen, anlegen) Kabel, Leitung etc to lay; Graben, Furchen to dig; Grenze, Mauer to erect, to build. Perlen auf eine Schnur ~ to thread pearls.

(e) (herstellen) Draht, Kerzen to make; (züchten) Blumen to grow; Tiere to breed. sie haben die Kinder gut gezogen (inf) they brought the children up well.

(f) die Mütze tiefer ins Gesicht ~ to pull one's hat further down over one's face; den Mantel fest um sich ~ to pull one's coat tight around one; die Vorhänge vors Fenster ~ to pull the curtains; den Mantel übers Kleid ~ to put one's coat on over one's dress.

(g) in Verbindungen n siehe auch dort. die Aufmerksamkeit or die Blicke auf sich (acc) ~ to attract attention; jds Haß auf sich (acc) ~ to incur sb's hatred; jdn ins Gespräch/in die Unterhaltung ~ to bring sb into the conversation.

2 vi (a) (zerren) to pull. an etw (dat) ~ to pull (on or at) sth.

(b) aux sein (sich bewegen) to move, to go; (Soldaten, Volksmassen) to march; (durchstreifen) to wander, to roam; (Wolken, Rauch) to drift; (Gewitter) to move; (Vögel) to fly; (während des Vogelzugs) to migrate. durch die Welt/die Stadt ~ to wander through the world/town; in den Krieg/die Schlacht ~ to go to war/battle; heimwärts ~ to make one's way home; laß mich ~ (old, liter) let me go; die Jahre zogen ins Land (liter) the years passed; einen ~ lassen (sl) to let one off (sl), to fart (vulg).

(c) aux sein (um~) to move. nach Bayern/München ~ to move to Bavaria/Munich; zu jdm ~ to move in with sb.

(d) (Feuer, Ofen, Pfeife) to draw. an der Pfeife/Zigarette ~ to pull or puff on one's pipe/cigarette.

(e) aux sein (eindringen) to penetrate (in etw (acc) sth).

(f) (mit Spielfigur) to move; (Cards) to play; (abheben) to draw. mit dem Turm ~ to move the rook; wer zieht? whose move is it?

(g) (Cook) (Tee, Kaffee) to draw; (in Marinade) to marinade; (in Kochwasser) to simmer.

(h) (Auto) to pull.

(i) (inf: Eindruck machen) so was zieht beim Publikum/bei mir nicht the public/I don't like that sort of thing; der Film zieht immer noch the film is still popular; so was zieht immer that sort of thing always goes down well.

3 vi impers (a) es zieht there's a draught; wenn es dir zieht if you're in a draught, if you find it draughty; mir zieht's im Nacken there is or I can feel a draught round my neck; in diesem Haus zieht es aus allen Ritzen there are draughts everywhere in this house.

(b) (Schmerzen verursachen) mir zieht's im Rücken my back hurts.

4 vt impers mich zieht nichts in die Heimat there is nothing to draw me home; was zieht dich denn nach Hause? what is drawing you home?; es zog ihn in die weite Welt he felt drawn towards the big wide world.

5 vr (a) (sich erstrecken) to stretch; (zeitlich) to drag on (in + acc into). dieses Thema zieht sich durch das ganze Buch this theme runs throughout the whole book.

(b) (verlaufen) sich zickzackförmig durchs Land ~ to zigzag through the countryside; sich in Schlingen/Serpentinen durch etw ~ to twist or wind its way through sth.

(c) (sich dehnen) to stretch; (Klebstoff) to be tacky; (Käse) to form strings; (Holz) to warp; (Metall) to bend.

(d) sich an etw (dat) aus dem Schlamm/in die Höhe ~ to pull oneself out of the mud/up on sth; siehe Affäre, Patsche.

Ziehen nt -s, no pl (Schmerz) ache; (im Unterleib) dragging pain.

Zieh-: ~harmonika f concertina; (mit Tastatur) accordion; ~kind nt (old) foster-child; ~mutter f (old) foster-mother; ~tochter f foster-daughter.

Ziehung f draw.

Ziehvater m (old) foster-father.

Ziel nt -(e)s, -e (a) (Reise~) destination; (von Expedition auch) goal; (Absicht, Zweck) goal, aim, objective; (von Wünschen, Spott) object. mit dem ~ with the aim or intention; etw zum ~ haben to have sth as one's goal or aim; jdm/sich ein ~ stecken or setzen to set sb/oneself a goal; er hatte sich sein ~ zu hoch gesteckt he had set his sights too high; sich (dat) etw zum ~ setzen to set sth as one's goal etc; einer Sache (dat) ein ~ setzen to put a limit on sth; (eindämmen) to limit sth; zum ~ kommen or gelangen (fig) to reach or attain one's goal etc; am ~ sein to be at or to have reached one's destination; (fig) to have reached or achieved one's goal; dieser Weg führte (ihn) nicht zum ~

(fig) this avenue did not lead (him) to his goal.
 (b) (Sport) finish; (bei Pferderennen auch) finishing-post, winning-post; (bei Rennen auch) finishing-line. **durchs ~ gehen** to pass the winning- or finishing-post; **to cross the finishing line.**
 (c) (Mil, Schießsport, fig) target. **ins ~ treffen** to hit the target; **über das ~ hinausschießen** (fig) to overshoot the mark.
 (d) (Comm: Frist) credit period. **mit drei Monaten ~** with a three-month credit period.
Ziel-: ~**bahnhof** m destination; ~**band** nt finishing-tape; z~**bewußt** adj purposeful, decisive; ~**bewußtsein** nt purposefulness, decisiveness; **mangelndes** ~**bewußtsein** lack of purpose.
zielen vi **(a)** (Mensch) to aim (auf +acc, nach at); (Waffe, Schuß) to be aimed (auf +acc at).
 (b) (fig: Bemerkung, Tat) to be aimed or directed (auf +acc at). **ich weiß, worauf deine Bemerkungen ~** I know what you're driving at; **das zielt auf uns** that's aimed at or meant for us, that's for our benefit.
zielend adj (Gram) Zeitwort transitive.
Ziel-: ~**fernrohr** nt telescopic sight; ~**fluggerät** nt homing indicator; ~**foto** nt, ~**fotografie** f photograph of the finish; **Ermittlung des Siegers durch** ~**foto** photo-finish; ~**gerade** f home or finishing straight; ~**gerät** nt (Mil) bomb-sight; ~**gruppe** f target group; ~**hafen** m port of destination; ~**kauf** m (Comm) credit purchase; ~**konflikt** m conflict of aims; ~**kurve** f final bend; ~**linie** f (Sport) finishing-line; z~**los** adj aimless, purposeless; ~**losigkeit** f lack of purpose, purposelessness; ~**ort** m destination; ~**richter** m (Sport) finishing-line judge; ~**scheibe** f target; (von Spott auch) object; ~**setzung** f target, objective; z~**sicher** adj unerring; Handeln, Planen purposeful; z~**sicher auf jdn/etw zugehen** to go straight up to sb/sth; ~**sprache** f target language; ~**springen** nt accuracy-jumping; (Wettkampf) accuracy-jumping competition; z~**strebig** 1 adj Mensch, Handlungsweise determined, single-minded; 2 adv full of determination; ~**strebigkeit** f determination, single-mindedness; ~**vorstellung** f objective; ~**wasser** nt (hum inf) schnapps (drunk at a shooting match).
ziemen 1 vr, vr impers (geh) es ziemt sich nicht it is not proper or seemly; **das ziemt sich nicht (für dich)** it is not proper (for you). 2 vi (old) **jdm ~** to become sb.
Ziemer m -s, - **(a)** (Wildrücken) saddle. **(b)** (Peitsche) whip.
ziemlich 1 adj (old: geziemend) proper, fitting.
 (b) attr (beträchtlich) Anzahl, Strecke considerable, fair; Vermögen sizable; Genugtuung reasonable. **das ist eine ~e Frechheit** that's a real cheek; **eine ~e Zeit/Anstrengung/Arbeit** quite a time/an effort/a lot of work; **sie unterhielten sich mit ~er Lautstärke** they were talking quite loudly; **mit ~er Sicherheit** pretty (inf) or fairly certainly; sagen, behaupten with a reasonable or fair degree of certainty, with reasonable certainty.
 2 adv **(a)** (beträchtlich) quite, pretty (inf); sicher, genau reasonably. **sie hat sich ~ anstrengen müssen** she had to make quite an effort; **wir haben uns ~ beeilt** we've hurried quite a bit; **~ lange** quite a long time, a fair time; **~ viel** quite a lot.
 (b) (inf: beinahe) almost, nearly. **so ~ more or less; so ~ alles** just about everything, more or less everything; **so ~ dasselbe** pretty well (inf) or much the same; **~ fertig** almost or nearly ready/finished; **sie ist so ~ in meinem Alter** she is about the same age as me.
ziepen 1 vi to chirp, to tweet, to cheep. **2** vi impers (inf: weh tun) es ziept it hurts. **3** vt (inf: ziehen) to pull, to tweak. **jdn an den Haaren ~** to pull or tug sb's hair.
Zier f -, no pl (old, poet) siehe **Zierde**.
Zieraffe m (pej) dandy, fop (old).
Zierat m -(e)s, -e (geh) decoration.
Zierde f -, -n ornament, decoration; (Schmuckstück) adornment; (fig: Tugend) virtue. **zur ~** for decoration; **das alte Haus ist eine ~ der Stadt** the old house is one of the beauties of the town; **eine Eins im Betragen war die einzige ~ seines Zeugnisses** a one for behaviour was the only bright spot on his report; **eine ~ des männlichen/weiblichen Geschlechts** a fine specimen of the male sex/a flower of the female sex; **die ~ der Familie** (fig) a credit to the family.
zieren 1 vt to adorn; Speisen to garnish; Kuchen to decorate; (fig: auszeichnen) to grace. **deine Eifersucht ziert dich nicht gerade** your envy does not exactly do you credit.
 2 vr (sich bitten lassen) to make a fuss, to need a lot of pressing; (Mädchen) to act coyly; (sich gekünstelt benehmen) to be affected. **du brauchst dich nicht zu ~, es ist genügend da** there's no need to be polite, there's plenty there; **er zierte sich nicht lange und sagte ja** he didn't need much pressing before he agreed; **ohne sich zu ~** without having to be pressed; **zier dich nicht!** don't be shy or silly (inf); siehe **geziert**.
Ziererei f -, no pl siehe vr pretended hesitance; coyness; affectedness.
Zier-: ~**farn** m decorative fern; ~**fisch** m ornamental fish; ~**garten** m ornamental garden; ~**gewächs** nt ornamental plant; ~**gras** nt ornamental grass; ~**leiste** f border; (an Auto) trim; (an Möbelstück) edging; (an Wand) moulding.
zierlich adj dainty; Frau auch petite; Porzellanfigur etc delicate.
Zierlichkeit f siehe adj daintiness; petiteness; delicateness.
Zier-: ~**pflanze** f ornamental plant; ~**puppe** f (pej) fashion plate; ~**rat** m siehe **Zierat**; ~**schrift** f ornamental lettering; ~**stich** m embroidery stitch; ~**strauch** m ornamental shrub.
Ziesel m -s, - ground-squirrel, suslik.
Ziffer f -, -n **(a)** (abbr Ziff.) (Zahlzeichen) digit; (Zahl) figure, number. **römische/arabische ~n** roman/arabic numerals; **eine Zahl mit drei ~n** a three-figure number; **etw in ~n schreiben** to write sth in figures or numbers. **(b)** (eines Paragraphs) clause.

Zifferblatt nt (an Uhr) dial, (clock) face; (von Armbanduhr) (watch)face; (inf: Gesicht) face, phiz (sl).
zig adj (inf) umpteen (inf).
zig- pref (inf) umpteen (inf). ~**hundert** umpteen hundred (inf).
Zigarette f cigarette. **~ mit Filter** filter cigarette.
Zigaretten- in cpds cigarette; ~**automat** m cigarette machine; ~**dose** f cigarette box; ~**etui** nt cigarette case; ~**kippe** f cigarette end, fag-end (Brit inf); ~**länge** f **auf or für eine ~länge hinausgehen** to go out for a cigarette or smoke; **wir waren nur eine ~länge draußen** we were only out for five minutes or for a quick smoke; ~**papier** nt cigarette paper; ~**pause** f break for a cigarette or a smoke; ~**raucher** m cigarette smoker; ~**schachtel** f cigarette packet or (US) pack; ~**spitze** f cigarette-holder; ~**stummel** m cigarette end, fag-end (Brit inf).
Zigarillo m or nt -s, -s cigarillo.
Zigarre f -, -n **(a)** cigar. **(b)** (inf: Verweis) dressing-down. **jdm eine ~ verpassen** to give sb a dressing-down.
Zigarren- in cpds cigar; ~**abschneider** m -s, - cigar-cutter; ~**kiste** f cigar-box; ~**raucher** m cigar smoker; ~**spitze** f cigar-holder; ~**stummel** m cigar butt.
Zigeuner(in f) m -s, - gypsy, gipsy; (Rasse auch) Romany; (pej inf) vagabond; (Streuner) gypsy, gipsy.
zigeunerhaft, zigeunerisch adj gypsylike, gipsylike.
Zigeuner-: ~**lager** nt gypsy camp or encampment; ~**leben** nt gypsy life; (fig) vagabond or rootless life.
zigeunern* vi aux haben or (bei Richtungsangabe) sein (inf) to rove, to roam.
Zigeuner-: ~**primas** m leader of a gypsy band; ~**schnitzel** nt (Cook) cutlet served in a spicy sauce with green and red peppers; ~**sprache** f Romany, Romany or Gypsy language; ~**steak** nt (Cook) steak served in a spicy sauce with green and red peppers; ~**wagen** m gypsy caravan.
zigmal adv (inf) umpteen times (inf).
Zikade f cicada.
ziliar adj (Anat) ciliary.
Zille f -, -n barge.
Zimbal nt -s, -e or -s cymbals.
Zimbel f -, -n (Mus)) cymbal; (Hackbrett) cymbalon.
zimbrisch adj Cimbrian.
Zimmer nt -s, - room. **~ frei** vacancies.
Zimmer-: ~**antenne** f indoor aerial; ~**arbeit** f carpentry job, piece of carpentry; ~**arrest** m **Stubenarrest**; ~**blume** f house plant; ~**brand** m fire in a/the room; ~**decke** f ceiling.
Zimmerei f **(a)** (Handwerk) carpentry. **(b)** (Werkstatt) carpenter's shop.
Zimmereinrichtung f furniture.
Zimmerer m -s, - carpenter.
Zimmer-: ~**flucht** f suite of rooms; ~**geselle** m journeyman carpenter; ~**handwerk** nt carpentry, carpenter's trade; ~**herr** m (gentleman) lodger.
-zimm(e)rig adj suf -roomed, with ... rooms.
Zimmer-: ~**kellner** m room-waiter; ~**kellner bitte 5 wählen** dial 5 for room-service; ~**lautstärke** f low volume; ~**lehre** f apprenticeship in carpentry; ~**lehrling** m carpenter's apprentice, apprentice carpenter; ~**linde** f African hemp; ~**mädchen** nt chambermaid.
Zimmermann m, pl -leute carpenter. **jdm zeigen, wo der ~ das Loch gelassen hat** (inf) to show sb the door.
Zimmermanns-: ~**knoten**, ~**stek** m timber-hitch.
Zimmermeister m master carpenter.
zimmern 1 vt to make or build or construct from wood; (fig) Alibi to construct; Ausrede to make up. 2 vi to do woodwork or carpentry. **an etw** (dat) **~** (lit) to make sth from wood; (fig) to work on sth.
Zimmer-: ~**pflanze** f house plant; ~**suche** f room hunting, hunting for rooms/a room; **auf ~suche sein** to be looking for rooms/a room; ~**temperatur** f room temperature; ~**theater** nt small theatre; ~**vermittlung** f accommodation service.
Zimmet m -s, no pl (obs) cinnamon.
-zimmrig adj suf siehe **-zimm(e)rig**.
zimperlich adj (überempfindlich) nervous (gegen about); (beim Anblick von Blut etc) squeamish; (prüde) prissy; (wehleidig) soft. **sei doch nicht so ~** don't be so silly; **du behandelst ihn viel zu ~** you're much too soft with him; **da ist er gar nicht (so) ~** he doesn't have any qualms about that; **da darf man nicht so ~ sein** you can't afford to be soft.
Zimperlichkeit f siehe adj nervousness; squeamishness; prissiness; softness. **keine ~ zeigen** to be hard(-hearted).
Zimperliese f -, -n (pej inf) cissy (inf).
Zimt m -(e)s, -e **(a)** (Gewürz) cinnamon. **(b)** (fig inf: Kram) rubbish, garbage; (Unsinn auch) nonsense.
Zimt-: z~**farben**, z~**farbig** adj cinnamon-coloured; ~**stange** f stick of cinnamon; ~**stern** m (Cook) cinnamon-flavoured star-shaped biscuit; ~**zicke**, ~**ziege** f (inf) stupid cow (sl).
Zink¹ nt -(e)s, no pl zinc.
Zink² m -(e)s, -e(n) (Mus) cornet.
Zink-: ~**blech** nt sheet-zinc; ~**blende** f zinc-blende; ~**dach** nt zinc roof.
Zinke f -, -n (von Gabel) prong; (von Kamm, Rechen) tooth; (Holzzapfen) tenon.
Zinken m -s, - **(a)** (sl: Gaunerzeichen) secret mark. **(b)** (inf: Nase) hooter (inf). **(c)** siehe **Zinke**. **(d)** siehe **Zink²**.
zinken¹ vt **(a)** Karten to mark. **(b)** Holz etc to tenon.
zinken² adj zinc attr, made of zinc.
Zinkenist(in f) m cornet player.
Zink-: ~**farbe** f zinc(-based) paint; z~**haltig** adj containing zinc; z~**haltig sein** to contain zinc.
-zinkig adj suf siehe **Gabel** -pronged; Kamm, Rechen -toothed.
Zink-: ~**leim** m Unna's paste; ~**salbe** f zinc ointment; ~**weiß** nt Chinese white.

Zinn nt -(e)s, no pl (a) tin. (b) (Legierung) pewter. (c) (~produkte) pewter, pewterware.
Zinnbecher m pewter tankard.
Zinne f -, -n (Hist) merlon. ~n (von Burg) battlements; (von Stadt) towers; (von Gebirgsmassiv) peaks, pinnacles.
zinne(r)n adj pewter.
Zinn-: ~figur f pewter figure or statuette; ~geschirr nt pewterware; ~gießer m pewterer.
Zinnie [-iə] f zinnia.
Zinnkraut nt horsetail.
Zinnober m -s, no pl (a) (Farbe) vermilion, cinnabar. (b) (inf) (Getue) fuss, commotion; (Kram) stuff (inf); (Unsinn) nonsense no indef art, rubbish no indef art. **macht keinen (solchen)** ~ stop making such a fuss or commotion.
Zinnober-: ~rot nt vermilion; z~rot adj vermilion.
Zinn-: ~pest f tin disease; ~soldat m tin soldier; ~verbindung f tin compound.
Zins¹ m -es, -e (Hist: Abgabe) tax; (S Ger, Aus, Sw) (Pacht~, Miet~) rent; (Wasser~) water rates pl.
Zins² m -es, -en usu pl (Geld~) interest no pl. ~en bringen to earn interest; ~en tragen (lit) to earn interest; (fig) to pay dividends; **Darlehen zu 10% ~en** loan at 10% interest; **Kapital auf ~en legen** to invest capital at interest; **jdm etw mit ~en or mit ~ und Zinseszins heimzahlen** or **zurückgeben** (fig) to pay sb back for sth with interest.
Zins-: ~bauer m (Hist) tenant farmer; ~bogen m (Fin) interest sheet.
zinsen vi (Hist: Abgaben zahlen) to pay one's tax; (Sw: Pacht zahlen) to pay one's rent.
Zinsenkonto nt interest account.
Zinseszins m compound interest; siehe Zins².
Zinseszinsrechnung f calculation of compound interest.
Zins-: z~frei adj (a) (frei von Abgaben) tax-free; (S Ger, Aus, Sw) (pachtfrei, mietfrei) rent-free; Wasser rate-free; (b) Darlehen interest-free; ~fuß m interest rate, rate of interest; ~gefälle nt difference between interest levels; ~gut nt (Hist) tenant farm; ~herr m (Hist) landlord, lord of the manor; ~knechtschaft f (Hist) system of holding land in tenancy to a landlord; ~leute pl (Hist) tenant farmers pl; z~los adj interest free; ~pflicht f (Hist) obligation to pay tax; z~pflichtig adj (Hist) tax-paying; z~pflichtig sein to be obliged to pay tax; ~politik f interest policies pl; ~rechnung f calculation of interest; ~satz m interest rate, rate of interest; ~schein m siehe ~bogen; ~senkung f reduction in the interest rate; ~spanne f margin between interest rates paid by borrowers and to investors; ~verbilligung f reduction in the interest rate; ~wucher m usury.
Zionismus m Zionism.
Zionist(in f) m Zionist.
zionistisch adj Zionist.
Zipfel m -s, - (a) (von Tuch, Decke, Stoff) corner; (von Mütze) point; (von Hemd, Jacke) tail; (am Saum) dip (an + dat in); (von Wurst) end; (von Land) tip. **etw am or beim rechten ~ packen** (fig inf) to go about or tackle sth the right way; **jdn (gerade noch) am (letzten)** ~ **erwischen** (fig inf) to catch sb (just) at the last minute.
(b) (inf: Mensch) silly (inf).
zipf(e)lig adj (a) Saum uneven. (b) (inf: nervös) fidgety (inf).
Zipfelmütze f pointed cap or hat.
zipflig vi (Rock) to be uneven.
Zipperlein nt -s, no pl (old, hum) gout.
Zipp(verschluß) m (Aus) zip (fastener).
Zirbeldrüse f pineal body.
Zirbelkiefer f Swiss or stone pine.
zirka adv about, approximately; (bei Datumsangaben) circa, about.
Zirkel m -s, - (a) (Gerät) pair of compasses, compasses pl; (Stech~) pair of dividers, dividers pl. (b) (lit, fig: Kreis) circle. (c) (studentischer ~) monogram of a student organization.
Zirkel-: ~definition f circular definition; ~kasten m compasses case.
zirkeln vi (genau abmessen) to measure exactly. **wir haben gezirkelt und gemessen** we made all kinds of measurements.
Zirkelschluß m circular argument.
Zirkonium nt zirconium.
Zirkular nt -s, -e (old) circular.
Zirkulation f circulation.
Zirkulations-: ~pumpe f circulation pump; ~störung f circulation or circulatory problem.
zirkulieren* vi to circulate.
Zirkumflex m -es, -e (Ling) circumflex.
Zirkumpolarstern m circumpolar star.
zirkumvenieren* [tsɪrkumvɛˈniːrən] vt (rare) to circumvent.
Zirkus m -, -se (a) circus. **in den** ~ **gehen** to go to the circus. (b) (inf: Getue, Theater) fuss, to-do (inf).
Zirkus- in cpds circus; ~artist m circus performer or artiste; ~wagen m circus caravan; ~zelt nt big top.
Zirpe f -, -n cicada.
zirpen vi to chirp, to cheep.
Zirrhose [tsɪˈroːzə] f -, -n cirrhosis.
Zirrus m -, - or **Zirren, Zirruswolke** f cirrus (cloud).
zirzensisch adj circus attr.
zisalpin(isch) adj cisalpine.
zisch interj hiss; (Rakete, Schnellzug etc) whoosh.
zischeln vi to whisper.
zischen 1 vi (a) to hiss; (Limonade) to fizz; (Fett, Wasser) to sizzle. (b) aux sein (inf: ab~) to whizz.
2 vt (a) (~d sagen) to hiss. (b) (inf: trinken) **einen** ~ to have a quick one (inf). (c) (inf: ohrfeigen) **jdm eine** ~ to belt or clout sb one (inf); **eine gezischt bekommen** to get belted or clouted (inf).

Zischer m -s, - hisser.
Zischlaut m (Ling) sibilant.
ziselieren* vti to chase.
Ziselierer(in f) m -s, - engraver.
Zisterne f -, -n well.
Zisterzienser(in f) [tsɪstɛrˈtsiːɛnzɐ, -ərɪn] m -s, - Cistercian (monk/nun).
Zisterzienserlorden [-ˈtsiːɛnzər-] m Cistercian order.
Zitadelle f citadel.
Zitat nt -(e)s, -e quotation. **ein falsches** ~ a misquotation; ~ ... **Ende des ~s** quote ... unquote.
Zitaten-: ~lexikon nt dictionary of quotations; ~sammlung f collection of quotations; ~schatz m store of quotations; (Buch) treasury of quotations.
Zither f -, -n zither.
Zither-: ~spiel nt zither-playing; ~spieler m zither-player.
zitieren* vt (a) to quote; Beispiel auch to cite. (b) (vorladen, rufen) to summon (vor + acc before, an + acc, zu to).
Zitronat nt candied lemon peel.
Zitrone f -, -n lemon; (Getränk) lemon drink; (Baum) lemon tree. **jdn wie eine** ~ **auspressen** or **ausquetschen** to squeeze sb dry.
Zitronen-: ~falter m brimstone (butterfly); z~gelb adj lemon yellow; ~limonade f lemonade; ~melisse f (lemon) balm; ~presse f lemon squeezer; ~saft m lemon juice; ~säure f citric acid; ~schale f lemon peel; ~wasser nt fresh lemon squash.
Zitrusfrucht f citrus fruit.
Zitter-: ~aal m electric eel; ~gras nt quaking grass; ~greis m (inf) old dodderer (inf), doddering old man.
zitt(e)rig adj shaky.
zittern vi (a) (vor + dat with) to shake, to tremble; (vor Kälte auch) to shiver; (vor Angst auch) to quake; (Stimme auch) to quaver; (Lippen, Blätter, Gräser) to tremble, to quiver; (Pfeil) to quiver. **an allen Gliedern or am ganzen Körper** ~ to shake or tremble all over; **mir** ~ **die Knie** my knees are shaking or trembling.
(b) (erschüttert werden) to shake.
(c) (inf: Angst haben) to tremble or shake with fear. **vor jdm** ~ to be terrified of sb; **sie zittert jetzt schon vor der nächsten Englischarbeit** she's already trembling or terrified at the thought of the next English test.
Zittern nt -s, no pl siehe vi (a) shaking, trembling; shivering; quaking; quavering; trembling, quivering, quivering. **ein** ~ **ging durch seinen Körper** a shiver ran through his body; **mit** ~ **und Zagen** in fear and trembling; **da hilft kein** ~ **und Zagen** it's no use being afraid. (b) shaking. **ein** ~ a tremor.
Zitter-: ~pappel f aspen (tree); ~rochen m electric ray.
zittrig adj siehe zitt(e)rig.
Zitze f -, -n teat, dug; (sl: Brustwarze) tit (sl).
zivil [tsiˈviːl] adj (a) (nicht militärisch) civilian; Schaden non-military. **im** ~**en Leben** in civilian life, in civvy street (inf); ~er Ersatzdienst community service (as alternative to military service); ~er Bevölkerungsschutz civil defence.
(b) (inf: angemessen, anständig) civil, friendly; Bedingungen, Forderungen, Preise reasonable.
Zivil [tsiˈviːl] nt -s, no pl (a) (alter Uniform) civilian clothes pl, civvies pl (inf). **in** ~ Soldat in civilian clothes or civvies; (inf) Arzt etc in mufti (inf); Polizist in ~ plain-clothes policeman.
(b) (old: Bürgerstand) civilian populace no pl. **in den Tagen des** ~s in his/her etc days as a civilian.
Zivil-: ~beruf m civilian profession/trade; ~bevölkerung f civilian population; ~courage f courage (to stand up for one's beliefs); der Mann hat ~courage that man has the courage to stand up for his beliefs; ~dienst m community service (as alternative to military service); ~ehe f civil marriage.
Zivile(r) [tsiˈviːlə, tsiˈviːlɐ] mf decl as adj (inf) plainclothes policeman/policewoman.
Zivil-: ~flughafen m civil airport; ~gericht nt civil court; ~gesetzbuch nt (Sw) code of civil law.
Zivilisation [tsiviliˈzaˈtsioːn] f civilization (especially its technological aspects).
Zivilisations- [tsiviliˈzaˈtsioːnz-]: z~krank adj z~krank sein to suffer from an illness produced by a civilized society; ~krankheit f illness produced by a civilized society or caused by civilization.
zivilisatorisch [tsiviliˈzaˈtoːrɪʃ] 1 adj of civilization. 2 adv in terms of civilization.
zivilisierbar [tsiviliˈziːrbaːr] adj civilizable.
zivilisieren* [tsiviliˈziːrən] vt to civilize.
zivilisiert [tsiviliˈziːrt] adj civilized.
Zivilist [tsiviˈlɪst] m civilian.
Zivil-: ~kammer f civil division; ~kleidung f siehe Zivil (a); ~leben nt civilian life, civvy street (inf); ~liste f civil list; ~person f civilian; ~prozeß m civil action; ~prozeßordnung f (Jur) code of civil procedure; ~recht nt civil law; z~rechtlich adj civil law attr, of civil law; etw z~rechtlich klären to settle sth in a civil court; jdn z~rechtlich verfolgen/belangen to bring a civil action against sb; ~richter m civil court judge; ~sache f matter for a civil court; ~schutz m (Sw) civil defence; ~senat m (Jur) civil court of appeal; ~stand m civilian status; ~standsamt nt (Sw) registry office; ~trauung f civil marriage; ~verfahren nt civil proceedings pl.
ZK [tsɛtˈkaː] nt -s, -s abbr of Zentralkomitee.
Zmittag m -, - (Sw) lunch.
Zmorge m -, - (Sw) breakfast.
Znacht m -s, - (Sw) supper.
Znüni m -, - (Sw) morning break, = elevenses (Brit).
Zobel m -s, - (a) (Zool) sable. (b) (auch ~pelz) sable (fur).
zockeln vi aux sein (inf) siehe zuckeln.
Zofe f -, -n lady's maid; (von Königin) lady-in-waiting.
zog pret of ziehen.

zögern vi to hesitate. **er tat es ohne zu** ~ he did it without hesitating or hesitation; **er zögerte lange mit der Antwort** he hesitated (for) a long time before replying; **sie zögerte nicht lange mit ihrer Zustimmung** she lost little time in agreeing.

Zögern nt -s, no pl hesitation. **ohne** ~ without hesitation, unhesitatingly; **nach langem** ~ after hesitating a long time.

zögernd adj hesitant, hesitating.

Zögling m (old, hum) pupil.

Zölibat nt or m -(e)s, no pl celibacy; (Gelübde) vow of celibacy. **im** ~ **leben** to be celibate, to practise celibacy.

Zoll¹ m -(e)s, ⁼e - (old: Längenmaß) inch. **jeder** ~ **ein König,** ~ **für** ~ **ein König** every inch a king.

Zoll² m -(e)s, ⁼e (a) (Waren~) customs duty; (Brücken~, Straßen~) toll. **für etw** ~ **bezahlen** to pay (customs) duty on sth; **einem** ~ **unterliegen** to carry duty; **darauf liegt (ein)** ~, **darauf wird** ~ **erhoben** there is duty to pay on that. (b) (Stelle) **der** ~ customs pl.

Zollabfertigung f (a) (Vorgang) customs clearance. (b) (Dienststelle) customs post or checkpoint.

Zollager nt getrennt **Zoll-lager** bonded warehouse.

Zoll-: ~**amt** nt customs house or office; **z~amtlich** adj customs attr; **z~amtlich geöffnet** opened by the customs; ~**ausland** nt foreign country which one has to go through customs to enter; ~**beamte(r)** m customs officer or official; ~**behörde** f customs authorities pl, customs pl; ~**bestimmung** f usu pl customs regulation; **z~breit** adj one inch wide, inch-wide attr; ~**breit** m -, - inch; **keinen** ~**breit zurückweichen** not to give or yield an inch; ~**deklaration** f (form) customs declaration; **z~dick** adj one inch thick, inch-thick attr; ~**einnahmen** pl customs revenue sing; ~**einnehmer** m -s, - (old) siehe **Zöllner**.

zollen vt jdm **Anerkennung/Achtung/Bewunderung** ~ to acknowledge/respect/admire sb; **jdm Beifall** ~ to applaud sb, to give sb applause; **jdm Dank** ~ to extend or offer one's thanks to sb; **jdm seinen Tribut** ~ to pay tribute to sb.

Zoller m -s, - (Sw) customs officer or official.

Zoll-: ~**erklärung** f customs declaration; ~**fahndung** f customs investigation department; **z~frei** adj duty-free; **etw z~frei einführen** to import sth free of duty; siehe **Gedanke**; ~**gebiet** nt customs area or territory; ~**grenzbezirk** m customs and border district; ~**grenze** f customs border or frontier; ~**inhaltserklärung** f customs declaration; ~**kontrolle** f customs check; ~**lager** nt siehe **Zollager**.

Zöllner m -s, - (old, Bibl) tax collector; (inf: Zollbeamter) customs officer or official.

Zoll-: ~**niederlage** f siehe **Zollager**; ~**papiere** pl customs documents pl; **z~pflichtig** adj dutiable; ~**recht** nt (a) (Hist) right to levy tolls; (b) (Jur) customs law; ~**schranke** f customs barrier; ~**speicher** m bonded warehouse; ~**stock** m ruler, inch rule; ~**tarif** m customs tariff; ~**union** f customs union; ~**verein** m (Hist) Deutscher ~**verein** German Customs Union (of 1844).

Zone f -, -n zone; (von Fahrkarte) fare stage; (fig: von Mißtrauen etc) area. **blaue** ~ (in Straßenverkehr) restricted parking area; **die** ~ (dated inf) the Eastern Zone, East Germany.

Zonen-: ~**grenzbezirk** m border district (with East Germany); ~**grenze** f zonal border; **die** ~**grenze** (inf) the border (with East Germany); ~**randgebiet** nt border area (with East Germany); ~**tarif** m (Fahrgeld) fare for a journey within a fare stage; (Post, Telec) zonal charge; ~**zeit** f zonal time.

Zönobit m -en, -en coenobite.

Zönobium nt coenobium.

Zoo [tsoː] m -s, -s zoo. **gestern waren wir im** ~ we went to the zoo yesterday.

Zoologe [tsooˈloːgə] m -n, -n, **Zoologin** f zoologist.

Zoologie [tsooloˈgiː] f zoology.

zoologisch [tsooˈloːgɪʃ] adj zoological.

Zoom [zuːm] nt -s, -s zoom shot; (Objektiv) zoom lens.

zoomen ['zuːmən] 1 vt to zoom in on. 2 vi to zoom (in).

Zoom|objektiv ['zuːm-] nt zoom lens.

Zoon-politikon ['tsoːɔn-] nt -, no pl political animal.

Zoowärter m zoo keeper.

Zopf m -(e)s, ⁼e (a) (Haartracht) pigtail; (von Mädchen auch) plait. **das Haar in** ⁼e **flechten** to plait one's hair; **ein alter** ~ (, der abgeschnitten werden müßte) (fig) an antiquated custom (that should be done away with). (b) (Gebäck) plait, plaited loaf. (c) (Baumwipfel) tree-top.

Zopf-: ~**band** nt hair ribbon; ~**muster** nt cable stitch; ~**spange** f clip; ~**zeit** f mid-18th century period in which men wore a pigtail.

Zorn m -(e)s, no pl anger, rage, wrath (liter). **der** ~ **Gottes** the wrath of God; **jds** ~ **fürchten** to fear sb's anger or wrath; **jds** ~ **heraufbeschwören** to incur sb's wrath; **jdn in** ~ **bringen** to anger or enrage sb; **wenn ihn der** ~ **überkommt** when he becomes angry or loses his temper; **in** ~ **geraten** or **ausbrechen** to fly into a rage, to lose one's temper; **der** ~ **packte ihn** he became angry, he flew into a rage; **im** ~ **in a rage, in anger; in gerechtem** ~ in righteous anger; **einen** ~ **auf jdn haben** to be furious with sb.

Zorn-: ~**ader** f siehe **Zornesader**; ~**ausbruch** m siehe **Zornesausbruch**.

Zornes-: ~**ader** f **auf seiner Stirn schwoll eine** ~**ader** he was so angry you could see the veins standing out on his forehead; ~**ausbruch** m fit of anger or rage; ~**röte** f flush of anger; ~**tränen** pl tears pl of rage.

zornig adj angry, furious. **(leicht)** ~ **werden** to lose one's temper (easily); **auf jdn** ~ **sein** to be angry or furious with sb; **ein** ~**er junger Mann** (fig) an angry young man.

zornmutig adj (obs) irascible, ill-tempered.

zoroastrisch adj zoroastrian.

Zote f -, -n dirty joke.

zotig adj dirty, filthy, smutty.

Zotte f -, -n (a) (Anat) villus. (b) (Haarsträhne) rat's tail (inf).

Zottel f -, -n (inf) rat's tail (inf); (an Mütze) pom-pom.

Zottelhaar nt (inf) shaggy hair.

zottelig adj (inf) Haar shaggy.

zotteln vi aux sein (inf) to amble.

Zotteltrab m gentle trot.

zottig adj (a) Fell shaggy. (b) (Anat) villous, villose.

ZPO [tsetpeːˈʔoː] abbr of **Zivilprozeßordnung**.

z.T. abbr of **zum Teil**.

Ztr. abbr of **Zentner**.

zu 1 prep +dat (a) (örtlich: Bewegung, Ziel) to. ~**m Bahnhof/zu the station;** ~**r Stadt/Stadtmitte gehen** to go to town/the town centre; ~**m Bäcker/Arzt gehen** to go to the baker's/doctor's; **bis** ~ **as far as;** (bis) ~**m Bahnhof sind es 5 km** it's 5 kms to the station; **etw** ~ **sich stecken** to take sth; ~**m Theater gehen** to go on the stage or into the theatre; ~**m Militär** or ~ **den Soldaten gehen** to join the army, to join up.

(b) (örtlich: Richtung bezeichnend) ~**m Fenster herein/hinaus in** (at)/out of the window; ~**r Tür hinaus/herein** out of/in the door; ~**m Himmel weisen** to point heavenwards or up at the heavens; ~**r Decke sehen** to look (up) at the ceiling; ~ **jdm/etw hinaufsehen** to look up at sb/sth; ~ **jdm herüber/hinübersehen** to look across at sb; **sie wandte sich/sah** ~ **ihm hin** she turned to(wards) him/looked towards him; **das Zimmer liegt** ~**r Straße hin** the room looks out onto the street; ~**m Meer hin** towards the sea; ~**r Stadtmitte hin** towards the town/city centre.

(c) (örtlich: Lage) at; (bei Stadt) in. ~ **Frankfurt** (old) in Frankfurt; **der Dom** ~ **Köln** the cathedral in Cologne, Cologne cathedral; **der Reichstag** ~ **Worms** (Hist) the Diet of Worms; ~ **Hause** at home; ~ **seiner Linken saß ...** (geh) on his left sat ...; ~ **beiden Seiten (des Hauses)** on both sides (of the house); ~ **Lande** und ~ **Wasser** on land and sea; **jdm** ~**r Seite sitzen** (geh) to sit at sb's side; **sich** ~ **Tisch setzen** (geh) to sit down to dinner.

(d) (bei Namen) **der Graf** ~ **Ehrenstein** the Count of Ehrenstein; **Gasthof** ~**m goldenen Löwen** the Golden Lion (Inn).

(e) (Zusatz, Zusammengehörigkeit, Begleitung) with. **Wein** ~**m Essen trinken** to drink wine with one's meal; **der Deckel** ~ **diesem Topf** the lid for this pan; ~**r Gitarre singen** to sing to a/the guitar; **Lieder** ~**r Laute** songs accompanied by the lute; **die Melodie** ~ **dem Lied** the tune of the song; **Vorwort/Anmerkungen** ~ **etw** preface/notes to sth; ~ **dem kommt noch, daß ich ...** on top of that I ...; **etw** ~ **etw legen** to put sth with sth; **sich** ~ **jdm setzen** to sit down next to or beside sb; **setz dich doch** ~ **uns** (come and) sit with us; **etw** ~ **etw tragen** (Kleidung) to wear sth with sth.

(f) (zeitlich) at. ~ **früher/später Stunde** at an early/late hour; ~ **Mittag** (am Mittag) at midday or noon; (bis Mittag) by midday or noon; ~ **Ostern** at Easter; **letztes Jahr** ~ **Weihnachten** last Christmas; (bis) ~**m 15. April/Donnerstag/Abend** until 15th April/Thursday/(this) evening; (nicht später als) **by 15th April/Thursday/(this) evening;** ~**m Wochenende hat sich Besuch angesagt** we're having visitors at the weekend; **der Wechsel ist** ~**m 15. April fällig** the allowance is due on 15th April; ~**m 31. Mai kündigen** to give in one's notice for May 31st; siehe **Anfang, Schluß, Zeit**.

(g) (Bestimmung) for. **Stoff** ~ **einem Kleid** material for a dress; **die Tür** ~**m Keller** the door to the cellar; **Milch** ~**m Kaffee** milk for coffee.

(h) (Zweck) for. **Wasser** ~**m Waschen** water for washing; **Papier** ~**m Schreiben** paper to write on, writing paper; **ein Bett** ~**m Schlafen** a bed to sleep in; **der Knopf** ~**m Abstellen** the off-button; **die Luke** ~**m Einsteigen** the entrance-hatch; **das Zeichen** ~**m Aufbruch** the signal to leave; **etw** ~ **Antwort geben** to say sth in reply; ~**r Einführung ...** by way of (an) introduction ...; ~**r Einführung in den Problemkreis ...** as an introduction to the problems ...; ~ **seiner Entschuldigung/**~**r Erklärung** in apology/explanation, by way of apology/explanation; **er sagte das nur** ~ **ihrer Beruhigung** he said that just to set her mind at rest; ~ **nichts taugen,** ~ **nichts zu gebrauchen sein** to be no use at all, to be no earthly use (inf).

(i) (Anlaß) **etw** ~**m Geburt/**~ **Weihnachten bekommen** to get sth for one's birthday/for Christmas; **ein Geschenk** ~**m Hochzeitstag** a wedding anniversary present; ~ **Ihrem 60. Geburtstag** on the occasion of your 60th birthday (form); **jdm** ~ **etw gratulieren** to congratulate sb on sth; **jdn** ~**m Essen einladen** to invite sb for a meal; ~ **Ihrem schweren Verlust** on your sad loss; **Ausstellung** ~**m Jahrestag der Revolution** exhibition to mark the anniversary of the revolution; ~ **dieser Frage möchte ich folgendes sagen** I should like to say the following to this question, on this I would like to say the following; **was sagen Sie** ~ **diesen Preisen?** what do you say to these prices?; ~**m Thema Gleichberechtigung** on the subject of equal rights; **eine Rede** ~**m Schillerjahr** a speech (up)on the anniversary of Schiller's death/birth; **„Zum Realismusbegriff"** "On the Concept of Realism"; **jdn** ~ **etw vernehmen** to question or examine sb about sth.

(j) (Folge, Umstand) ~ **seinem Besten** for his own good; ~**m Glück** luckily; ~ **meiner Schande/Freude** etc to my shame/joy etc; ~/~**m Tode** to death; **es ist** ~**m Lachen** it's really funny; **es ist** ~**m Weinen** it's enough to make you (want to) weep.

(k) (Mittel, Art und Weise) ~ **Fuß/Pferd** on foot/horseback; ~ **Schiff** by ship or sea; ~ **deutsch in German; etw** ~ **einem hohen Preis verkaufen/versteigern** to sell sth at a high price/to bid up the price of sth.

(l) (in festen Verbindungen mit n siehe auch dort. ~**m Beispiel** for example; ~ **Hilfe! help!; jdm** ~ **Hilfe kommen** to come to sb's aid; ~ **jds Gedächtnis,** ~**m Gedächtnis von jdm** in memory of sb, in sb's memory; ~**m Lobe von jdm/etw** in praise of sb/sth; ~**r Strafe** as a punishment; ~**r Belohnung** as a reward; ~**r Warnung** as a warning; ~**r Beurteilung/Einsicht** for inspection; ~r **Probe/Ansicht** on trial *or* test/approval; ~r Unterschrift for signature *or* signing.

(m) (*Veränderung*) into. ~ **etw werden** to turn into sth; (*Mensch auch*) to become sth; **Leder ~ Handtaschen verarbeiten** to make handbags out of leather; **jdn/etw ~ etw machen** to make sb/sth (into) sth; **jdn ~m Manne machen** to make a man of sb; ~ **Asche verbrennen** to burn to ashes; **(wieder)** ~ **Staub werden** to (re)turn to dust; **etw ~ Pulver zermahlen** to grind sth (in)to powder; ~ **etw heranwachsen** to grow up into sth; **jdn ~m Major befördern** to promote sb to (the rank of) major.

(n) (*als*) as. **jdn ~m König wählen** to choose sb as king; **jdn ~ etw ernennen** to nominate sb sth; **er machte mich ~ seinem Stellvertreter** he made me his deputy; **jdn ~m Freund haben** to have sb as a friend; **er machte sie ~ seiner Frau, er nahm sie ~r Frau** he made her his wife, he took her as his wife; **sich** (*dat*) **jdn/etw ~m Vorbild nehmen** to take sb/sth as one's example, to model oneself on sb/sth; ~**m Künstler geboren sein** to be born to be an artist.

(o) (*Verhältnis, Beziehung*) **Liebe ~ jdm** love for sb; **aus Freundschaft ~ jdm** because of one's friendship with sb; **Vertrauen ~ jdm/etw** trust in sb/sth; **meine Beziehung ~ ihm** my relationship with him.

(p) im Vergleich ~ in comparison with, compared with; im Verhältnis ~ in relation to, in proportion to; **im Verhältnis drei ~ zwei** (*Math*) in the ratio (of) three to two; **drei ~ zwei** (*Sport*) three-two; **das Spiel steht 3 ~ 2** (*geschrieben* 3:2) the score is 3-2 (*gesprochen* three-two); **wir haben 4 ~ 3** (*geschrieben* 4:3) **gewonnen** we won 4-3 *or* by 4 goals/games *etc* to 3.

(q) (*bei Zahlenangaben*) ~ **Prozent** at two per cent; **wir verkaufen die Äpfel jetzt das Stück ~ 5 Pfennig** we're selling the apples now at *or* for 5 pfennigs each; **fünf (Stück) ~ 30 Pfennig** five for 30 pfennigs; ~ **zwei Dritteln (gefüllt)** two-thirds (full); ~**m halben Preis** at half price; **die Arbeit ist schon ~r Hälfte getan** the work is already half done; ~**m ersten Male** for the first time; ~**m ersten ...**, ~**m zweiten ...** (*Aufzählung*) first ..., second ...; ~**m ersten**, ~**m zweiten**, ~**m dritten** (*bei Auktionen*) for the first time, for the second time, for the third time; *siehe* **vier, bis**[2].

(r) (*mit Fragepronomen*) ~ **wem wollen/gehen/sprechen Sie?** who do you want/who are you going to see/who are you talking to?; ~ **was** (*inf*) (*Zweck*) for what; (*warum*) why.

(s) (*inf: getrenntes „dazu"*) **da komme ich nicht ~** I can't get round to it; *siehe* **da, dazu**.

2 adv (a) (*allzu*) too. ~ **sehr** too much; **sie liebte ihn ~ sehr, als daß sie ihn verraten hätte** she loved him too much to betray him; ~ **verliebt** too much *or* too deeply in love; **das war einfach ~ dumm!** (*inf*) it was so stupid!; **ich wäre ~ gern mitgekommen** I should have been only too pleased to come.

(b) (*geschlossen*) shut, closed. **auf, ~** (*an Hähnen etc*) on, off; **Tür ~!** (*inf*) shut the door; **die Geschäfte haben jetzt ~** the shops are shut *or* closed now.

(c) (*inf: los, weiter*) **dann mal ~!** right, off we go!; **du wolltest mir was vorsingen, dann mal ~** you wanted to sing me something? right then, go ahead; **immer** *or* **nur ~!** just keep on!; **ihr seid auf dem richtigen Wege, nur ~!** you're on the right track, just keep going; **schreie nur ~, es hilft doch nichts!** go on, scream then, but it won't do any good!; **mach ~!** hurry up!, get a move on!, come on!; **lauft schon ~, ich komme nach** you go on, I'll catch you up.

(d) (*zeitlich*) *siehe* **ab**.

(e) (*örtlich*) towards. **nach hinten ~** towards the back; **auf den Wald ~** towards the forest; **dem Ausgang ~** towards the exit.

3 conj (a) (*mit Infinitiv*) to. **etw ~ essen** sth to eat; **der Fußboden ist noch ~ fegen** the floor still has to be swept; **er hat ~ gehorchen** he has to do as he's told, he has to obey; **jdm befehlen** *or* **den Auftrag erteilen, etw ~ tun** to order sb to do sth; **das Material ist noch/nicht mehr ~ gebrauchen** the material is still/is no longer usable; **diese Rechnung ist bis Montag ~ bezahlen** this bill has to be paid by Monday; ~ **stehen kommen** to come to a stop; ~ **liegen kommen** to come to rest; **ich habe ~ arbeiten** I have to do some work, I have some work to do; **ohne es ~ wissen** without knowing it; **um besser sehen ~ können** in order to see better; **ich komme, um mich ~ verabschieden** I've come to say goodbye.

(b) (*mit Partizip*) **noch ~ bezahlende Rechnungen** outstanding bills; **nicht ~ unterschätzende Probleme** problems (that are) not to be underestimated; **nur winzige, leicht ~ übersehende Punkte** only very small points (that are) easily overlooked; **der ~ prüfende Kandidat, der ~ Prüfende** the candidate to be examined.

4 adj (*inf*) ~ **sein** (*Tür, Geschäft, Kiste etc*) to be shut; (*Kleid, Verschluß*) to be done up; **die ~(n)e Tür** (*strictly incorrect*) the shut door; *siehe* ~**sein**.

zu|aller-: ~**allerletzt** *adv* (*inf*) very last of all; ~**erst** *adv* first of all; ~**letzt** *adv* last of all.

zubauen *vt sep* **Lücke** to fill in; **Platz, Gelände** to build up; **Blick** to block with buildings/a building.

Zubehör *nt or m* -(e)s, (*rare*) -e equipment *no pl*; (*Zusatzgeräte, Auto*~) accessories *pl*; (~*teil*) attachments *pl*, accessories *pl*; (*zur Kleidung*) accessories *pl*. **Wohnung mit allem ~** fully furnished flat; **Küche mit allem ~** fully equipped kitchen.

Zubehör-: ~**handel** *m* accessories trade; ~**teil** *nt* accessory, attachment.

zubeißen *vi sep irreg* to bite; (*beim Zahnarzt*) to bite (one's teeth) together. **der Hund faßte mich am Bein und biß zu** the dog got hold of my leg and sank his teeth into me.

zubekommen* *vt sep irreg* (*inf*) **Kleidung** to get done up; **Koffer auch, Tür, Fenster** to get shut or closed.

zubenannt *adj* (*liter*) also called.

Zuber *m* -s, - (wash)tub.

---

zubereiten* *vt sep* **Essen** to prepare; **Arznei** *auch* to make up; **Cocktail** to mix.

Zubereitung *f* **(a)** *siehe vt* preparation; making up; mixing. **eine neue ~ für Blumenkohl** a new way of preparing cauliflower.

(b) (*Präparat*) preparation.

Zubettgehen *nt* **vor dem/beim/nach dem ~** before (going to) bed/on going to bed/after going to bed.

zubiegen *vt sep irreg* to bend shut.

zubilligen *vt sep* **jdm etw ~** to grant sb sth, to allow sb sth; **jdm mildernde Umstände ~** to recognize that there are mitigating circumstances for sb; **ich will ihm gerne ~, daß er sich bemüht hat** I'll certainly made an effort, I'll grant *or* allow him that.

zubinden *vt sep irreg* to tie up, to do up; **Schuhe** *auch* to lace up. **jdm die Augen ~** to blindfold sb.

zubleiben *vi sep irreg aux sein* (*inf*) to stay shut.

zublinzeln *vi sep* **jdm ~** to wink at sb.

zubringen *vt sep irreg* **(a)** (*verbringen*) to spend.

(b) (*herbeibringen*) **jdm etw ~** to take to. **jdm ~, daß ...** (*fig*) to inform sb that ...; **es ist mir zugebracht worden** (*fig*) it has been brought to my notice *or* attention, I have been informed.

(c) (*inf: zumachen können*) **Knöpfe, Reißverschluß, Kleidung** to get done up; **Kiste, Koffer** *auch*, **Tür, Fenster** to get shut *or* closed.

Zubringer *m* -s, - **(a)** (*Tech*) conveyor. **(b)** *siehe* **Zubringerstraße**. **(c)** (~*bus*) shuttle (bus); (*zum Flughafen*) airport bus; ~(*flugzeug*) feeder plane.

Zubringer-: ~**dienst** *m* shuttle service; ~**linie** *f* feeder route; ~**straße** *f* feeder road.

Zubrot *nt* (*dial: zusätzlicher Verdienst*) extra income. **ein kleines ~ verdienen** to earn *or* make a bit on the side (*inf*).

zubuttern *vt sep* (*inf*) (*zuschießen*) to contribute, to add on; (*zuzüglich bezahlen*) to pay out (on top); (*dazuverdienen*) to add on. **zu seinem Gehalt etwas ~** to boost *or* up (*inf*) one's salary a bit.

Zucht *f* -, -en **(a)** (*Disziplin*) discipline. ~ **und Ordnung** discipline; **jdn in strenge ~ nehmen** (*liter*) to take sb firmly in hand; **jdn in ~ halten** to keep a tight rein on sb; **was ist das für eine ~ hier?** (*inf*) what sort of behaviour is this?

(b) *no pl* (*Aufzucht, das Züchten*) (*von Tieren*) breeding; (*von Pflanzen*) growing, cultivation; (*von Bakterien, Perlen*) culture; (*von Bienen*) keeping. **Tiere zur ~ halten** to keep animals for breeding; **die ~ von Bienen/Pferden** beekeeping/horse breeding.

(c) (~*generation*) (*von Tieren*) breed, stock; (*von Pflanzen*) stock, variety; (*von Bakterien, Perlen*) culture.

Zucht-: ~**buch** *nt* studbook; ~**bulle** *m* breeding bull; ~**eber** *m* breeding boar.

züchten *vt* **Tiere** to breed; **Bienen** to keep; **Pflanzen** to grow, to cultivate; **Perlen, Bakterien** to cultivate; **Kristalle** to grow, to synthesize; (*fig*) **Haß** to breed.

Züchter(in *f*) *m* -s, - (*von Tieren*) breeder; (*von Pflanzen*) grower, cultivator; (*von Bienen*) keeper; (*von Perlen, Bakterien*) culturist.

Zuchthaus *nt* (*Gebäude*) prison (*for capital offenders*), penitentiary (*US*). **zu 7 Jahren ~ verurteilt werden** to be sentenced to 7 years' in prison *or* 7 years' imprisonment; **dafür bekommt man ~, darauf steht ~** you'll go to prison for that.

Zuchthäusler *m* -s, - (*inf*) convict, con (*sl*).

Zuchthausstrafe *f* prison sentence.

Zuchthengst *m* stud horse, breeding stallion.

züchtig *adj* (*liter*) (*keusch, anständig*) **Mädchen** modest, chaste; **Wangen** innocent; **Augen, Benehmen** modest; (*tugendhaft*) virtuous.

züchtigen *vt* (*geh*) to beat; (*stärker, Jur*) to flog; **Schüler** to use corporal punishment (*on form*), ≈ to cane.

Züchtigkeit *f* (*liter*) modesty, chasteness.

Züchtigung *f siehe vt* beating; flogging; caning. **körperliche ~** corporal punishment.

Züchtigungsrecht *nt* right to use corporal punishment.

Zucht-: ~**kristall** *m* synthetic crystal; **z~los** *adj* (*dated*) undisciplined; ~**losigkeit** *f*, *no pl* (*dated*) lack of discipline; ~**meister** *m* (*liter*) disciplinarian; ~**mittel** *nt* (*old*) disciplinary measure; ~**perle** *f* cultured pearl; ~**rute** *f* (*fig*) rod; **unter jds ~rute** (*dat*) **stehen** to be under sb's rod; ~**stier** *m siehe* ~**bulle**; ~**stute** *f* broodmare, breeding mare; ~**tier** *nt* breeding animal, animal for breeding.

Züchtung *f* **(a)** *siehe vt* breeding; keeping; growing; cultivation; culture; growing, synthesis. **(b)** (*Zuchtart*) (*Pflanzen*) strain, variety; (*Tiere*) breed.

Zucht-: ~**vieh** *nt* breeding cattle; ~**wahl** *f* selective breeding. **natürliche ~wahl** natural selection.

zuck *interj siehe* **ruck**.

Zuck *m* -s, *no pl* (*Körperbewegung*) sudden movement; (*mit Augenlidern*) flutter; (*beim Reißen*) jerk, tug, yank; (*beim Ziehen*) jerk, tug. **mit einem ~ war er/es verschwunden** he/it was gone in a flash.

zuckeln *vi aux sein* (*inf*) to jog. **er zuckelte müde hinter den anderen drein** he trotted wearily along behind the others.

Zuckeltrab *m* jog trot. **im ~** at a jog trot.

zucken 1 vi (a) (*nervös, krampfhaft*) to twitch; (*Augenlider auch*) to flutter; (*vor Schreck*) to start; (*vor Schmerzen*) to flinch; (*Fisch, verwundetes Tier*) to thrash about. **er zuckte ständig mit dem Mund** his mouth kept twitching; **mit den Schultern** *or* **Achseln ~** to shrug (one's shoulders); **es zuckte um ihre Mundwinkel** the corner of her mouth twitched; **ein Lächeln zuckte um ihren Mund** a smile played around her lips; **es zuckte mir in den Fingern, das zu tun** (*fig*) I was itching to do that; **es zuckte mir in der Hand** (*fig*) I was itching to hit him/her; *siehe* **Wimper**.

(b) (*aufleuchten*) (*Blitz*) to flash; (*Flammen*) to flare up. die ~den Flammen the flames flaring up.

(c) (*weh tun*) der Schmerz zuckte (mir) durch den ganzen Körper the pain shot right through my body *or* me; es zuckte mir im Knie (*inf*) I had a twinge in my knee.

2 *vt* die Achseln *or* Schultern ~ to shrug (one's shoulders).

zücken *vt* Degen, Schwert to draw; (*inf: hervorziehen*) Notizbuch, Bleistift, Brieftasche to pull *or* take out.

Zucker *m* -s, *no pl* **(a)** sugar. ein Stück ~ a lump of sugar, a sugar lump; du bist doch nicht aus *or* von ~! (*inf*) don't be such a softie! (*inf*); das ist ~! (*dated inf*) that's smashing! (*inf*).

(b) (*Med*) (*~gehalt*) sugar; (*Krankheit*) diabetes *sing*. ~ haben (*inf*) to be a diabetic; bei ~ muß Insulin gespritzt werden diabetics need insulin injections.

Zucker-: ~bäcker *m* (*old, S Ger, Aus*) confectioner; ~bäckerei *f* (*old, S Ger, Aus*) confectioner's (shop); ~bäckerstil *m* wedding-cake style; ~brot *nt* (*obs*) sweetmeat (*old*); mit ~brot und Peitsche (*prov*) with a stick and a carrot.

Zuckerchen, Zückerchen *nt* (*dial: Bonbon*) sweet (*Brit*), candy (*US*).

Zucker-: ~couleur *f* (*Cook*) caramel; ~dose *f* sugar basin *or* bowl; ~erbse *f* mange-tout (pea); ~früchte *pl* crystallized fruits *pl*; ~gehalt *m* sugar content; ~guß *m* icing, frosting (*esp US*); mit ~guß überziehen to ice, to frost; ein Kuchen mit ~guß an iced *or* a frosted cake; ~hut *m* sugarloaf; der ~hut in Rio the Sugar Loaf Mountain in Rio.

zuck(e)rig *adj* sugary.

Zucker-: ~kand(is) *m siehe* Kandis(zucker); z~krank *adj* diabetic; ~kranke(r) *mf decl as adj* diabetic; ~krankheit *f* diabetes *sing*.

Zuckerl *nt* -s, -(n) (*S Ger, Aus*) sweet (*Brit*), candy (*US*).

Zucker-: ~lecken *nt*: das ist kein ~lecken (*inf*) it's no picnic (*inf*); ~mäulchen *nt* (*dated inf*) sweet-tooth; ein ~mäulchen sein to have a sweet tooth; ~melone *f* muskmelon.

zuckern *vt* to sugar, to put sugar in. zu stark gezuckert sein to have too much sugar in it.

Zucker-: ~plantage *f* sugar plantation; ~plätzchen *nt* (*Bonbon*) sweet (*Brit*), candy (*US*); (*Keks*) sugar-coated biscuit (*Brit*) *or* cookie (*US*); ~puppe *f* (*dated inf*) sweetie (*inf*); (*als Anrede auch*) sugar (*inf*), sweetie-pie (*inf*); ~raffinade *f* refined sugar; ~raffinerie *f* sugar refinery; ~rohr *nt* sugar-cane; ~rübe *f* sugar beet; ~spiegel *m* (*Med*) (blood) sugar level; ~stange *f* stick of rock (*Brit*) *or* candy (*US*); ~streuer *m* sugar sprinkler; z~süß *adj* (*lit, fig*) sugar-sweet, as sweet as sugar; seinen Kaffee z~süß trinken to drink one's coffee really sweet; ~tüte *f siehe* Schultüte; ~wasser *nt* sugar(ed) water; ~watte *f* candy floss; ~werk *nt* sweets *pl* (*Brit*), candies *pl* (*US*); ~zange *f* sugar tongs *pl*; ~zeug *nt, no pl* (*pej*) sweet stuff.

zuckrig *adj siehe* zuck(e)rig.

Zuckung *f* (*nervöse* ~) twitch; (*stärker: krampfhaft*) convulsion; (*von Muskeln auch*) spasm; (*von Augenlidern auch*) flutter; (*von sterbendem Tier*) convulsive movement. die letzten ~en (*lit, fig*) the death throes.

Zudecke *f* (*dial*) cover (on bed).

zudecken *vt sep* to cover up; jdn, Beine *auch* to cover up; (*im Bett*) to tuck up *or* in; Gestorbenen, Grube, Fleck *auch* to cover up *or* over. jdn/sich (mit etw) ~ to cover sb/oneself up (with sth); to tuck sb/oneself up (in sth); zugedeckt werden (*Mil*) to come under heavy fire.

zudem *adv* (*geh*) moreover, furthermore, in addition.

zudenken *vt sep irreg* (*geh*) jdm etw ~ to intend *or* destine sth for sb; dieses Glück war uns aber offenbar nicht zugedacht but we were evidently not destined to be so lucky; das Schicksal hatte mir schwere Schläge zugedacht Fate had some cruel blows in store for me.

zudiktieren* *vt sep* (*inf*) Strafe to hand out.

Zudrang *m, no pl* (*rare*) *siehe* Andrang.

zudrehen *sep* 1 *vt* Wasserhahn *etc* to turn off; (*zuwenden*) to turn (*dat* to). 2 *vr* to turn (*dat* to).

zudringlich *adj* Mensch, Art pushing, pushy (*inf*); Nachbarn intrusive. ~ werden (*zu einer Frau*) to make advances (*zu* to), to act improperly (*zu* towards).

Zudringlichkeit *f* pushiness (*inf*); intrusiveness; (*einer Frau gegenüber*) advances *pl*.

zudrücken *vt sep* to press shut; Tür *auch* to push shut. jdm die Kehle ~ to throttle sb; einem Toten die Augen ~ to close a dead person's eyes; *siehe* Auge.

zueignen *vt sep* (*geh*) Buch, Gedicht to dedicate (*jdm* to sb).

Zueignung *f* (*geh*) (*von Gedicht, Buch*) dedication.

zueilen *vi sep aux sein* auf jdn ~ to rush *or* hurry towards sb *or* (*bis zu jdm*) up to sb; auf etw (*acc*) ~ to hurry *or* rush towards/up to sth.

zueinander *adv* (*gegenseitig*) to each other, to one another; Vertrauen in each other, in one another; (*zusammen*) together. ~ passen to go together; (*Menschen*) to suit each other *or* one another, to be suited; Braun und Grün passen gut ~ brown and green go together well *or* go well together.

zueinander-: ~finden *vi sep irreg* to find common ground; (*sich versöhnen*) to be reconciled; ~gesellen* *vr sep* (*geh*) to join each other; (*fig*) to be combined; ~stehen *vi sep irreg* (*geh*) *siehe* zusammenhalten.

zuerkennen* *vt sep irreg* Preis to award (*jdm* to sb); Würde, Auszeichnung, Orden *auch* to confer, to bestow (*jdm* on sb); Sieg *auch*, Recht to grant, to accord (*jdm etw* sb sth); (*vor Gericht*) Entschädigung, Rente *etc* to award (*jdm etw* sb sth); Strafe to impose, to inflict (*jdm* (up)on sb). das Gemälde wurde dem höchsten Bieter zuerkannt the painting went to the highest bidder; ihm wurde der Preis zuerkannt he was awarded the prize.

Zuerkennung *f siehe vt* awarding; conferring, bestowing; granting, accordance; awarding; imposition.

zuerst *adv* **(a)** (*als erster*) first. ich kam ~ an I was (the) first to arrive, I arrived first; wollen wir ~ essen? shall we eat first?; ~ an die Reihe kommen to be first; ~ bin ich Geschäftsmann, dann Privatmann I am first and foremost a businessman, and only then a private individual; das muß ich morgen früh ~ machen I must do that first thing tomorrow (morning) *or* first thing in the morning; *siehe* kommen (p).

(b) (*zum ersten Mal*) first, for the first time.

(c) (*anfangs*) at first. er sprach ~ gar nicht at first he didn't speak at all; ~ muß man ... to begin *or* start with you have to ...; first (of all) you have to ...

zuerteilen* *vt sep siehe* zuerkennen.

zufächeln *vt sep* (*geh*) to fan. sich/jdm Kühlung ~ to fan oneself/sb.

zufahren *vi sep irreg aux sein* **(a)** auf jdn ~ to drive/ride towards sb; (*direkt*) to drive/ride up to sb; auf etw (*acc*) ~ to drive/ride towards sth, to head for sth; er kam genau auf mich zugefahren he drove/rode straight at *or* for me.

(b) (*weiterfahren, losfahren*) fahren Sie doch zu! go on then!, get a move on then! (*inf*).

(c) (*Tür*) (*plötzlich schließen*) to slide shut.

Zufahrt *f* approach (road); (*Einfahrt*) entrance; (*zu einem Haus*) drive(way). „keine ~ zum Krankenhaus" "no access to hospital".

Zufahrtsstraße *f* access road; (*zur Autobahn*) approach road.

Zufall *m* chance, accident; (*Zusammentreffen*) coincidence. das ist ~ it's pure chance; durch ~ (quite) by chance *or* accident; ich habe durch ~ gesehen, wie er das Geld in die Tasche gesteckt hat I happened to see him putting the money in his pocket; per ~ (*inf*) by a (pure) fluke; per ~ trafen wir uns im Bus we happened to meet on the bus; ein merkwürdiger ~ a remarkable *or* strange coincidence; es war reiner *or* purer ~, daß ... it was pure chance that ...; es ist kein ~, daß ... it's no accident that ...; es war ein glücklicher ~, daß ... it was lucky that ..., it was a stroke *or* bit of luck that ...; welch ein ~! what a coincidence!; etw dem ~ überlassen to leave sth to chance; etw dem ~ verdanken to owe sth to chance; es hängt vom ~ ab, ob ... it's a matter of chance whether ...

zufallen *vi sep irreg aux sein* **(a)** (*sich schließen*) (*Fenster etc*) to close, to shut. die Tür fiel laut zu the door slammed *or* banged shut; ihm fielen beinahe die Augen zu he could hardly *or* scarcely keep his eyes open.

(b) jdm ~ (*zuteil werden: Erbe*) to pass to *or* devolve upon (*Jur*) sb; (*Preis etc*) to go to sb, to be awarded to sb; (*Aufgabe, Rolle*) to fall to *or* upon sb.

(c) (*zukommen*) diesem Treffen fällt große Bedeutung zu this meeting is of the utmost importance.

zufällig 1 *adj* chance *attr*; Ergebnis *auch* accidental; Zusammentreffen *auch* coincidental, accidental. das war rein ~ it was pure chance *or* purely by chance; es ist nicht ~, daß er ... it's no accident that he ...; das kann doch nicht ~ gewesen sein that can't have happened by chance; „Ähnlichkeiten mit lebenden Personen sind rein ~" "any similarities with persons living or dead are purely coincidental".

2 *adv* by chance; (*bei Zusammentreffen von Ereignissen auch*) coincidentally. er ging ~ vorüber he happened to be passing; ich traf ihn ~ im Bus I happened to meet him *or* I bumped *or* ran into him on the bus; das habe ich ganz ~ gesehen I just happened to see it, I saw it quite by chance *or* accident; wir haben gestern darüber gesprochen, und heute habe ich ~ einen Artikel darüber gefunden we were talking about it yesterday, and quite coincidentally I found an article on it; wenn Sie das ~ wissen sollten if you (should) happen to know; ~ auf ein Zitat stoßen to chance upon *or* happen to find a quotation.

(b) (*in Fragen*) by any chance. kannst du mir ~ 10 Mark leihen? can you lend me 10 marks by any chance?

zufälligerweise *adv* *siehe* zufällig 2.

Zufälligkeit *f* **(a)** *siehe adj* chance nature; accidental nature; coincidence. **(b)** (*Statistik*) chance; (*Philos auch*) contingency.

Zufalls- *in cpds* chance; ~auswahl *f* random selection; ~bekanntschaft *f* chance acquaintance; ~glaube *m* fortuitism; ~treffer *m* fluke; einen ~treffer machen to make a lucky choice; ~tor *nt* (*Sport*) lucky *or* fluke (*inf*) goal.

zufassen *vi sep* **(a)** (*zugreifen*) to take hold of it/them; (*Hund*) to make a grab; (*fig: schnell handeln*) to seize *or* grab an/the opportunity. **(b)** (*helfen*) to lend a hand, to muck in (*inf*).

zufliegen *vi sep irreg aux sein* **(a)** auf etw (*acc*) ~ to fly towards *or* (*direkt*) into sth; auf etw (*acc*) zugeflogen kommen to come flying towards sth.

(b) +*dat* to fly to. der Vogel ist uns zugeflogen the bird flew into our house/flat *etc*; „grüner Wellensittich zugeflogen" "green budgerigar found"; alle Herzen flogen ihr zu she won the heart(s) of everyone; ihm fliegt alles nur so zu (*fig*) everything comes so easily to him.

(c) (*inf: Fenster, Tür*) to bang *or* slam shut.

zufließen *vi sep irreg aux sein* +*dat* to flow to(wards); (*Süßwasser etc, fig: Geld*) to flow into. das Wasser wird nie warm, weil immer kaltes zufließt the water never gets warm because cold water is constantly flowing into it; jdm Geld ~ lassen to pour money into sb's coffers.

Zuflucht *f* refuge (*auch fig*), shelter (*vor* +*dat* from). du bist meine letzte ~ (*fig*) you are my last hope *or* resort; zu etw ~ nehmen (*fig*) to resort to sth; zu Lügen ~ nehmen to take refuge in lying; er findet ~ in seiner Musik (*liter*) he finds refuge in his music.

Zufluchts|ort *m*, **Zufluchtsstätte** *f* place of refuge (*fig auch*) sanctuary.

Zufluß *m* **(a)** *no pl* (*l:t, fig: Zufließen*) influx, inflow; (*Mech: Zufuhr*) supply. ~ kalter Meeresluft a stream of cold air from the sea. **(b)** (*Nebenfluß*) affluent, tributary; (*zu Binnensee*) inlet.

zuflüstern vti sep jdm (etw) ~ to whisper (sth) to sb; (*Theat*) to prompt sb (with sth).

zufolge prep +dat or gen (form) (gemäß) according to; (*auf Grund*) as a consequence or result of. dem Bericht ~ , ~ des Berichtes according to the report.

zufrieden adj contented, content. ein ~es Gesicht machen to look pleased; ~ lächeln to smile contentedly; mit jdm/etw ~ sein to be satisfied or happy with sb/sth; wie geht es? — man ist ~ (inf) how are things? — can't complain, mustn't grumble (inf); er ist nie ~ he's never content or satisfied; er ist mit nichts ~ nothing pleases him, there's no pleasing him (inf); es ~ sein (old) to be well.

Zufrieden-: z~geben vr sep irreg sich mit etw z~geben to be content or satisfied with sth; gib dich endlich z~! can't you be content with what you have?; ~heit f contentedness; (*Befriedigtsein*) satisfaction; zu meiner ~heit to my satisfaction; zur allgemeinen ~heit to everyone's satisfaction; z~lassen vt sep irreg to leave alone or in peace; laß mich damit z~! (inf) shut up about it! (inf); z~stellen vt sep to satisfy; Wünsche, Ehrgeiz auch to gratify; Kunden etc auch to give satisfaction to; schwer z~zustellen sein to be hard or difficult to please; eine z~stellende Note a satisfactory mark; eine wenig z~stellende Antwort a less than satisfactory answer.

zufrieren vi sep irreg aux sein to freeze (over).

zufügen vt sep (a) Kummer, Leid to cause; Verlust auch to inflict. jdm Schaden ~ to harm sb; jdm etw ~ to cause sb sth; to inflict sth on sb; jdm eine Verletzung (mit einem Messer etc) ~ to injure sb (with a knife etc); was du nur willst, daß man dir tu, das füg auch keinem andern zu (*Prov*) do as you would be done by (*Prov*). (b) siehe hinzufügen.

Zufuhr f -, -en (Versorgung) supply (in +acc, nach to); (*Mil: Nachschub, von Stadt*) supplies pl; (*Met: von Luftstrom*) influx. die ~ von Lebensmitteln the supply of provisions, supplies of provisions; jdm die ~ abschneiden to cut off sb's supplies, to cut off supplies to sb.

zuführen sep 1 vt +dat etw (a) (versorgen mit, beliefern) to supply. jdm etw ~ to supply sb with sth; einem Gerät Elektrizität ~ to supply an appliance with electricity; dem Heer Lebensmittel ~ to supply the army with provisions, to provision the army; etw seiner Bestimmung (dat) ~ to put sth to its intended use. (b) (*bringen, zur Verfügung stellen*) to bring. einem Geschäft Kunden ~ to bring customers to a business; er führte ihm junge Mädchen zu he supplied him with young girls; dem Magen Nahrung ~ to supply food to the stomach; jdn der gerechten Strafe ~ to give sb the punishment he/she deserves; jdn dem Verderben ~ to lead sb on the road to ruin. 2 vi sep auf etw (acc) ~ (lit, fig) to lead to.

Zuführung f (a) no pl (Versorgen, Beliefern) supplying; (*Versorgung*) supply. (b) (*Zuführungsleitung*) feed-pipe.

Zufußgehen nt, no pl walking no art.

Zug¹ m -(e)s, ⁻e (a) no pl (Ziehen) (an +dat on, at) pull, tug; (~kraft, Spannung) tension.
(b) no pl (Fortziehen: von Zugvögeln, Menschen) migration; (*der Wolken*) drifting. im ~ (im Verlauf) in the course (gen of); einen ~ durch die Kneipen machen to do the rounds of the pubs/bars; im besten ~ sein to be going great guns (inf); das ist der or liegt im ~ der Zeit it's a sign of the times, that's the way things are today; dem ~ seines Herzens folgen to follow the dictates of one's heart.
(c) (Luft~) draught (Brit), draft (US); (Atem~) breath; (an Zigarette, Pfeife) pull, puff, drag; (Schluck) gulp, mouthful, swig (inf). ~ in die Sache bringen (inf) to give things a bit of go (inf) or drive; einen ~ machen (an Zigarette etc) to take a pull etc; das Glas in einem ~ leeren to empty the glass with one gulp or in one go, to down the glass in one (inf); da ist kein ~ drin (fig inf) there's no go in it (inf); etw in vollen ~en genießen to enjoy sth to the full; er genoß sein Leben in vollen ~en he enjoyed life to the full; in den letzten ~en liegen (inf) to be at one's last gasp (inf) or on one's last legs; er hat einen guten ~ (inf) he can really put it away (inf).
(d) (beim Schwimmen) stroke; (beim Rudern) pull (mit at); (Feder~) stroke (of the pen); (bei Brettspiel) move. einen ~ machen beim Schwimmen to do a stroke; ~ um ~ (fig) step by step, stage by stage; (nicht) zum ~e kommen (inf) (not) to get a look-in (inf); du bist am ~ (bei Brettspiel, fig) it's your move or turn; etw in großen ~en darstellen/umreißen to outline sth, to describe/outline sth in broad or general terms.
(e) (~vorrichtung) (Klingel~) bell-pull; (Schnur am Anorak) draw-string; (bei Feuerwaffen) groove; (Orgel~) stop.
(f) (Gruppe) (von Fischen) shoal; (Gespann von Ochsen etc) team; (von Vögeln) flock, flight; (von Menschen) procession; (Mil) platoon; (Abteilung) section.
(g) (Feld~) expedition, campaign; (Fisch~) catch, haul.

Zug² m -(e)s, ⁻e (Eisenbahn~) train; (Last~) truck and trailer. mit dem ~ fahren to go/travel by train; jdn zum ~ bringen to take sb to the station or train, to see sb off at the station; im falschen ~ sitzen (fig inf) to be on the wrong track, to be barking up the wrong tree (inf); siehe abfahren.

Zug³ m -(e)s, ⁻e (Gesichts~) feature; (Charakter~ auch) characteristic, trait; (sadistisch, brutal etc) streak; (Anflug) touch. das ist ein/kein schöner ~ von ihm that's one of the nice things about him/that's not one of his nicer characteristics; das war kein schöner ~ von dir that wasn't nice of you; die Sache hat einen ~ ins Lächerliche (fig) the affair has something (of the) ridiculous about it or verges on the ridiculous; er hat einen ~ ins Humorlose/Maßlose (fig) he tends or is inclined to be lacking in humour/to be immoderate.

Zugabe f extra, bonus; (Comm: Werbegeschenk etc) free gift; (Mus, Theat) encore. ~! ~! encore! encore!, more! more!

Zug-: ~abstand m interval between trains; ~abteil nt railway or train compartment.

Zugang m (a) (Eingang, Einfahrt) entrance; (auf Schild auch) way in; (Zutritt) admittance, access; (fig) access. ~ zu einem Tresor/Informationen etc haben to have access to a safe/information etc; das Tal gab freien ~ zum Meer the valley gave direct access to the sea; er hat/findet keinen ~ zur Musik/Kunst etc music/art etc doesn't mean anything to him; „kein ~" "no admittance or entry".
(b) (von Patienten) admission; (von Schülern) intake; (von Soldaten) recruitment; (von Waren) receipt; (von Büchern) acquisition; (von Abonnements) new subscription. in dieser Schule haben wir die meisten Zugänge im Herbst our largest intake at school is in autumn.

zugange adj pred (esp N Ger) ~ sein (beschäftigt) to be busy; (aufgestanden) to be up and about; (euph: in Nebenzimmer etc) to be carrying on (inf).

zugänglich adj (dat, für to) (erreichbar) Gelände, Ort accessible; (verfügbar auch) Bücher, Dokumente available; öffentliche Einrichtungen open; (fig: umgänglich auch) Mensch, Vorgesetzter approachable. eine private Sammlung der Allgemeinheit ~ machen to open a private collection to the public; der Allgemeinheit ~ open to the public; sein Charakter ist mir nur wenig ~ his character is more or less a closed book to me; er ist nur schwer ~, er ist ein schwer ~er Mensch (fig) he's not very approachable; für etw leicht/nicht ~ sein to respond/not to respond to sth; für Komplimente, Annäherungsversuche, guten Rat etc auch to be/not to be amenable to sth.

Zugänglichkeit f (Erreichbarkeit) accessibility; (Verfügbarkeit) availability; (Umgänglichkeit) approachability. die leichte ~ dieser Dokumente the availability of these documents; ihre ~ für Komplimente/Ironie her responsiveness or amenability to compliments/her responsiveness to irony.

Zug-: ~begleiter m (Rail) ~ sein (beschäftigt) a guard (Brit), conductor (US); (b) (~fahrplan) train time-table; ~begleitpersonal nt (Rail) train crew; ~brücke f drawbridge.

zugeben vt sep irreg (a) (zusätzlich geben) to give as an extra or bonus; (bei Verkauf auch) to throw in (inf). jdm etw ~ to give sb sth extra or as a bonus, to throw sth in for sb (inf).
(b) (hinzufügen: Cook) to add; (Mus, Theat) to do or perform as an encore.
(c) (zugestehen, einräumen) to admit, to acknowledge; (eingestehen) to admit (to), to own up to. er gab zu, es getan zu haben he admitted (to) having done it, he confessed or owned up to having done it; jdm gegenüber etw ~ to confess sth to sb; zugegeben admittedly, granted; gib's zu! admit it!

zugedacht 1 ptp of zudenken. 2 adj jdm ~ sein to be intended or destined or earmarked for sb; (Geschenk) to be intended or meant for sb.

zugegebenermaßen adv admittedly.

zugegen adv (geh) ~ sein to be present; (bei Versammlung, Konferenz etc auch) to be in attendance (form).

zugehen sep irreg aux sein 1 vi (a) (Tür, Deckel) to shut, to close. der Koffer geht nicht zu the case won't shut or close.
(b) auf jdn/etw ~ to approach sb/sth, to go towards sb/sth; direkt auf jdn/etw ~ to go straight or right up to sb/sth; geradewegs auf etw (acc) ~ (fig) to get straight or right down to sth; es geht nun dem Winter or auf den Winter zu winter is drawing in or near; er geht schon auf die Siebzig zu he's getting on for or nearing or approaching seventy; dem Ende ~ to draw to a close, to near its end; (Vorräte) to be running out.
(c) +dat (Nachricht, Brief etc) to reach. der Brief ist uns noch nicht zugegangen the letter hasn't reached us yet, we haven't received the letter yet; mir ist gestern ein Brief zugegangen I received a letter yesterday; die Nachricht, die ich Ihnen gestern habe ~ lassen the news I sent you yesterday; der Polizei sind schon mehrere Hinweise zugegangen the police have already received several clues.
(d) (inf: weiter-, losgehen) to get a move on (inf).
2 vi impers (a) dort geht es ... zu things are ... there; es ging sehr lustig/fröhlich etc zu (inf) we/they etc had a great time (inf); du kannst dir nicht vorstellen, wie es dort zugeht you can't imagine what a carry-on it is there (inf); hier geht's ja zu wie in einem Affenhaus! it's like a bear-garden here!
(b) (geschehen) to happen. hier geht es nicht mit rechten Dingen zu there's something odd going on here; so geht es nun einmal zu in der Welt that's the way of the world; es müßte mit dem Teufel ~, wenn ... it'll be very bad luck if ...

Zugeherin, Zugehfrau, Zugehhilfe f (S Ger, Aus) char(-woman) (Brit), cleaning woman.

Zugehör nt -(e)s, no pl (Sw) siehe Zubehör.

zugehören* vi sep irreg +dat (liter) to belong to.

zugehörig adj attr (a) (geh) (dazugehörend) accompanying; (verbunden) affiliated (dat to).
(b) (old: gehörend) belonging to. die einst dem britischen Weltreich ~e Insel the island that once belonged to the British Empire.

Zugehörigkeit f (a) (zu Land, Glauben) affiliation; (Mitgliedschaft) membership (zu of). (b) (Zugehörigkeitsgefühl) sense of belonging.

zugeknöpft 1 ptp of zuknöpfen. 2 adj (fig inf) Mensch close, reserved.

Zugeknöpftheit f (fig inf) closeness, reserve.

Zügel m -s, - rein (auch fig). einem Pferd in die ~ fallen to seize a horse by the reins, to seize a horse's reins; die ~ anziehen (lit) to draw in the reins; (fig) to keep a tighter rein (bei on); die ~ fest in der Hand haben/behalten (fig) to have/keep things firmly in hand or under control; die ~ locker lassen (lit) to slacken one's hold on the reins; (fig) to give free rein (bei to); die ~ an sich (acc) reißen (fig) to seize the reins; seiner Wut/seinen Gefühlen etc die ~ schießen lassen (fig) to give full vent or free rein to one's rage/feelings etc; die ~ verlieren (fig) to lose control (über +acc of); jds Übermut/seinen Begierden

~ anlegen (*liter*) to curb sb's over-exuberance/to curb *or* bridle one's desires; *siehe* anlegen, schleifen[1].

zugelassen 1 *ptp of* zulassen.

  2 *adj* authorized; *Heilpraktiker* licensed, registered; *Kfz* licensed. amtlich/staatlich ~ sein to be authorized/to be state-registered; er ist an allen/für alle Gerichte ~ he is authorized to practise in any court; eine nicht ~e Partei an illegal party; als Kassenarzt ~ sein ≈ to be registered as a GP; als Heilpraktiker ~ sein to be a licensed *or* registered non-medical practitioner; für Personenbeförderung nicht ~ not licensed to carry passengers.

Zügel-: ~hand *f* hand holding the reins; z~los *adj* (*fig*) unbridled *no adv*, unrestrained; ~losigkeit *f* (*fig*) lack of restraint, unrestraint; (*in sexueller Hinsicht*) promiscuity; (*esp Pol*) anarchy.

zügeln 1 *vt Pferd* to rein in; (*fig*) to curb, to check. **2** *vr* to restrain oneself. **3** *vi aux sein* (*Sw: umziehen*) to move (house).

Zügelung *f* (*a*) *siehe vt* reining in; curbing, checking. (*b*) *siehe vr* self-restraint.

zugenäht 1 *ptp of* zunähen. **2** *adj*: verflixt *or* verflucht und ~! (*inf*) damn and blast! (*inf*).

Zügenglöcklein *nt* (*S Ger, Aus*) *siehe* Sterbeglocke.

Zugereiste(r) *mf decl as adj* (*S Ger*) newcomer.

zugesellen* *sep* 1 *vt* (*rare*) to give as a companion. **2** *vr* sich jdm ~ (*Mensch*) to join sb; seinem Bankrott gesellten sich dann noch familiäre Probleme zu on top of his bankruptcy he had family problems.

zugestandenermaßen *adv* admittedly, granted. er ist ~ ein sympathischer Mann he is admittedly a nice man, granted he is a nice man.

Zugeständnis *nt* concession (*dat, an* +*acc* to). er war zu keinem ~ bereit he would make no concession(s).

zugestehen* *vt sep irreg* (*einräumen*) *Recht, Erlaß etc* to concede, to grant; (*zugeben*) to admit, to acknowledge. jdm etw ~ (*einräumen*) to grant sb sth; man gestand ihm zu, daß ... it was admitted *or* acknowledged that ...; man gestand ihm zu, nicht aus Habgier gehandelt zu haben it was acknowledged that he had not acted out of greed; zugestanden, Sie haben recht you're right, I grant you (that), I admit you're right.

zugetan *adj* jdm/einer Sache ~ sein to be fond of sb/sth; der dem Alkohol sehr ~e Major X Major X who was very fond of alcohol; der Hund war seinem Herrn sehr ~ the dog was very attached *or* devoted to his master.

Zugewanderte(r) *mf decl as adj* (*Admin*) newcomer.

zugewandt 2 *ptp of* zuwenden. **2** *adj* facing, overlooking. der Zukunft (*dat*) ~ sein turned toward(s) the future.

Zugewinn *m* (*Jur*) increase in value of a married couple's property during the years of joint ownership through marriage.

Zugewinngemeinschaft *f* (*Jur*) joint ownership of property by a married couple.

Zugezogene(r) *mf decl as adj* newcomer.

Zug-: z~fest *adj* (*Mech*) tension-proof; *Stahl* high-tensile; ~festigkeit *f* (*Mech*) tensile strength; ~folge *f* (*Rail*) succession of trains; z~frei *adj Raum* draught-free (*Brit*), draft-free (*US*); ~führer *m* (*a*) (*Rail*) chief guard (*Brit*) *or* conductor (*US*); (*b*) (*Aus Mil*) platoon leader; ~funk *m* (*Rail*) train radio.

zugießen *vt sep irreg* (*a*) (*hin-*) to add. darf ich Ihnen noch (etwas Kaffee) ~? may I pour you a little more (coffee)?; er goß sich (*dat*) ständig wieder zu he kept topping up his glass/cup. (*b*) (*mit Beton etc*) to fill (in).

zugig *adj* draughty (*Brit*), drafty (*US*).

zügig *adj* swift, speedy; *Tempo, Bedienung auch* brisk, rapid, smart; *Handschrift* smooth.

zugipsen *vt sep Loch* to plaster up, to fill (in).

Zug-: ~kraft *f* (*Mech*) tractive power; (*fig*) attraction, appeal; z~kräftig *adj* (*fig*) *Werbetext, Titel, Plakat* catchy, eye-catching; *Schauspieler* crowd-pulling *attr*, of wide appeal.

zugleich *adv* (*zur gleichen Zeit*) at the same time; (*ebenso auch*) both. er ist ~ Gitarrist und Komponist he is both a guitarist and a composer; die älteste und ~ modernste Stadt des Landes the country's oldest and at the same time most modern town.

Zug-: ~loch *nt* (*bei Ofen*) airhole, air vent; ~luft *f* draught (*Brit*), draft (*US*); zuviel ~luft bekommen to be in too much of a draught; ~maschine *f* towing vehicle; (*von Sattelschlepper*) traction engine, tractor; ~nummer *f* (*a*) (*Rail*) train number; (*b*) (*fig*) crowd puller, drawing card (*US*); ~ochse *m* draught (*Brit*) *or* draft (*US*) ox; ~personal *nt* (*Rail*) train personnel; ~pferd *nt* carthorse, draught (*Brit*) *or* draft (*US*) horse; (*fig*) crowd puller; ~pflaster *nt* (*Med*) poultice; ~regler *m* (*bei Ofen*) damper, draught (*Brit*) *or* draft (*US*) regulator.

zugreifen *vi sep irreg* (*a*) (*schnell nehmen*) to grab it/them; (*fig*) to act fast *or* quickly, to get in quickly (*inf*); (*bei Tisch*) to help oneself. greifen Sie bitte zu! please help yourself! (*b*) (*fig: einschreiten*) to step in quickly, to act fast *or* quickly. (*c*) (*schwer arbeiten*) to put one's back into it *or* one's work, to get down to it *or* to work.

Zugriff *m* (*a*) durch raschen ~ by stepping in *or* acting quickly, by acting fast; sich dem ~ der Polizei/Gerichte entziehen to evade justice. (*b*) (*Computers*) access.

Zugriffszeit *f* access time.

zugrunde *adv* (*a*) ~ gehen to perish; jdn/etw ~ richten to destroy sb/sth; (*finanziell*) to ruin sb/sth; er wird daran nicht ~ gehen he'll survive; (*finanziell*) it won't ruin him. (*b*) einer Sache (*dat*) ~ liegen to form the basis of sth, to underlie sth; diesem Lied liegt ein Gedicht von Heine ~ this song is based on a poem by Heine; etw einer Sache (*dat*) ~ legen to take sth as a basis for sth, to base sth on sth; und welche Überlegungen haben Sie diesen Ihren Behauptungen ~ gelegt? and on what considerations do you base these claims of yours?

Zugrunde-: ~legung *f, no pl* unter/bei ~legung dieser Daten

taking these data as a basis; z~liegend *adj attr* underlying.

Zugs- *in cpds* (*Aus*) *siehe* Zug-.

Zug-: ~salbe *f* (*Med*) poultice; ~tier *nt* draught animal.

zugucken *vi sep siehe* zusehen.

Zugunglück *nt* train accident.

zugunsten *prep* +*gen* (*bei Voranstellung*) *or dat* (*bei Nachstellung*) in favour of. ~ von in favour of; ~ seines Bruders, seinem Bruder ~ in favour of his brother.

zugute *adv* jdm etw ~ halten to grant sb sth; (*Verständnis haben*) to make allowances for sth; Sie waren monatelang krank, das haben wir Ihnen ~ gehalten you were ill for some months and we've made allowances for that; einer Sache/jdm ~ kommen to come in useful for sth/to sb, to be of benefit to sth/sb; (*Geld, Erlös*) to benefit sth/sb; das ist seiner Gesundheit ~ gekommen his health benefited by *or* from it; jdm etw ~ kommen lassen to let sb have sth; sich (*dat*) auf etw (*acc*) etwas ~ halten *or* tun (*geh*) to pride *or* preen oneself on sth.

Zug-: ~verband *m* (*Med*) *siehe* Streckverband; ~verbindung *f* train connection; ~verkehr *m* (*Rail*) rail *or* train services *pl*; starker ~verkehr heavy rail traffic; ~vieh *nt, no pl* draught (*Brit*) *or* draft (*US*) cattle; ~vogel *m* migratory bird; (*fig*) bird of passage; ~wagen *m* towing vehicle; ~wind *m siehe* ~luft; ~zwang *m* (*Chess*) zugzwang; (*fig*) tight spot; jdn in ~zwang bringen to put sb in zugzwang/on the spot; in ~zwang geraten to get into zugzwang/to be put on the spot; unter ~zwang stehen to be in zugzwang/in a tight spot; die Gegenseite steht jetzt unter ~zwang the other side is now forced to move.

zuhaben *sep irreg* (*inf*) 1 *vi* (*Geschäft, Museum, Behörde etc*) to be closed *or* shut. **2** *vt irreg Geschäft, Tür etc* to keep closed *or* shut; *Kleid, Mantel etc* to have done up. jetzt habe ich den Koffer endlich zu I've finally got the case shut.

zuhaken *vt sep* to hook up.

zuhalten *sep irreg* 1 *vt* to hold closed *or* shut *or* to. sich (*dat*) die Nase ~ to hold one's nose; sich (*dat*) die Augen/Ohren/den Mund ~ to put one's hands over one's eyes/ears/mouth, to cover one's eyes/ears/mouth with one's hands; er hielt ihr beide Augen zu he put his hands over her eyes.

  2 *vi* auf etw (*acc*) ~ to head *or* make straight for.

Zuhälter(in *f*) *m* -s, - pimp, procurer.

Zuhälterei *f* procuring, pimping.

zuhälterisch *adj* pimp-like.

Zuhälter-: ~typ *m* (*pej*) mit so einem ~typ with someone who looks like a pimp; ~unwesen *nt* (*pej*) procuring.

zuhanden *adv* (*form: Sw, Aus*) (*a*) (*auch old*) to hand. es ist mir ~ gekommen it came to hand, it came into my hands. (*b*) for the attention of. ~ (*von*) Herrn Braun *or* des Herrn Braun (*rare*) for the attention of Mr Braun, attention Mr Braun.

zuhängen *vt sep* to cover up *or* over. etw mit einem Tuch ~ to cover sth (up *or* over) with a cloth, to hang a cloth over sth.

zuhauen *sep irreg* 1 *vt* (*a*) *Baumstamm* to hew; *Stein* to trim, to pare. (*b*) (*inf*) *Tür etc* to slam *or* bang (shut). **2** *vi* (*inf: mit Axt*) to strike; (*mit Fäusten, Schwert*) to strike out. hau zu! let him *etc* have it! (*b*) (*inf: Tür, Fenster*) to slam *or* bang (shut).

zuhauf *adv* (*old*) in throngs, in droves. ~ liegen/legen to lie/put in a heap *or* pile, to be piled up/to pile up.

zuhause *adv, zu Hause siehe* Haus.

Zuhause *nt* -s, *no pl* home.

Zuhausegebliebene(r) *mf decl as adj* he/she/those who stay/stayed at home.

zuheilen *vi sep aux sein* to heal up *or* over.

Zuhilfenahme *f*: unter ~ von *or* +*gen* with the aid *or* help of.

zuhinterst *adv* right at the back, at the very back.

zuhöchst *adv* (*a*) (*ganz oben*) right at the top, at the very top. (*b*) (*sehr*) highly, extremely.

zuhören *vi sep* to listen (*dat* to); (*lauschen, abhören auch*) to listen in (*dat on or* to), to eavesdrop (*dat on*). hör mal zu! (*drohend*) now (just) listen (to me)!; gut ~ können to be a good listener; hör mir mal genau zu! now listen carefully to me.

Zuhörer *m* listener. die ~ (*das Publikum*) the audience *sing*; (*Radio~ auch*) the listeners.

Zuhörerschaft *f* (*a*) audience. (*b*) (*Rad*) *siehe* Hörerschaft.

zuinnerst *adv* deeply. tief ~ in his/her *etc* heart of hearts, deep down.

zujubeln *vi sep* jdm ~ to cheer sb.

zukaufen *vt sep* etw ~ to buy more (of) sth; Einzelstücke ~ to buy extra separate parts.

zukehren *vt sep* (*zuwenden*) to turn. jdm das Gesicht ~ to turn to face sb, to turn one's face to *or* towards sb; jdm den Rücken ~ (*lit, fig*) to turn one's back on sb.

zuklappen *vti sep* (*vi aux sein*) to snap shut; (*Tür, Fenster*) to click shut.

zukleben *vt sep Loch etc* to stick over *or* up; *Briefumschlag* to stick down; *Brief* to seal (up); (*mit Klebstoff, Klebeband*) to stick up.

zuklinken *sep* 1 *vt Tür* to latch. **2** *vi aux sein* die Tür klinkte zu the latch fell shut.

zuknallen *vti sep* (*vi aux sein*) (*inf*) to slam *or* bang (shut).

zukneifen *vti sep irreg* to pinch hard; *Augen* to screw up; *Mund* to shut tight(ly).

zuknöpfen *vt sep* to button (up). sich (*dat*) die Jacke/Hose ~ to button (up) one's jacket/trousers; *siehe* zugeknöpft.

zuknoten *vt sep* to knot up.

zukommen *vi sep irreg aux sein* (*a*) auf jdn/etw ~ to come towards *or* (*direkt*) up to sb/sth; das Gewitter kam genau auf uns zu the storm was heading straight for us *or* coming right at us; die Aufgabe, die nun auf uns zukommt the task which is now in store for us, the task which now awaits before *or* confronts us; die Dinge/alles auf sich (*acc*) ~ lassen to take things as they come/to let everything take its course.

  (*b*) jdm etw ~ lassen *Brief etc* to send sb sth; (*schenken auch*) *Hilfe* to give sb sth.

(c) +*dat* (*geziemen, gebühren*) to befit, to become. **ein solches Verhalten kommt dir nicht zu** such behaviour doesn't become *or* befit you *or* ill becomes you; **es kommt Ihnen nicht zu, darüber zu entscheiden** it isn't up to you to decide this; **dieser Titel kommt ihm nicht zu** he has no right to this title; **diesem Treffen kommt große Bedeutung zu** this meeting is of (the) utmost importance.

zukorken *vt sep* to cork (up).

zukriegen *vt sep* (*inf*) *siehe* **zubekommen**.

Zukunft *f* -, *no pl* (a) **die ~** the future; **in ~** in future; **in ferner/naher ~** in the remote *or* distant/near future; **das hat keine ~** it has no future, there's no future in it; **unsere gemeinsame ~** our future together; **in die ~ blicken** *or* **sehen** to look *or* see into the future; **wir müssen abwarten, was die ~ bringt** we must wait and see what the future holds *or* has in store; **das gilt für alle ~** that applies without exception from now on; **das bleibt der ~** (*dat*) **überlassen** *or* **vorbehalten** that remains to be seen; **viel Glück für Ihre ~!** best wishes for the future!

(b) (*Gram*) future (tense).

zukünftig **1** *adj* future. **der ~e Präsident/Bischof** the president/bishop elect *or* designate; **meine Z~e** (*inf*)/**mein Z~er** (*inf*) my future wife/husband, my wife-/husband-to-be, my intended (*hum*). **2** *adv* in future, from now on.

Zukunfts-: **~aussichten** *pl* future prospects *pl*; **~forscher** *m* futurologist; **~forschung** *f* futurology; **~glaube** *m* belief in the future; **z~gläubig** *adj* believing in the future; **~musik** *f* (*fig inf*) pie in the sky (*inf*), Zukunftsmusik; **~pläne** *pl* plans *pl* for the future; **z~reich** *adj* (*geh*) *siehe* **z~trächtig**; **~roman** *m* (*naturwissenschaftlich*) science fiction novel; (*gesellschaftspolitisch*) utopian novel; **z~trächtig** *adj* with a promising future; **z~weisend** *adj* forward-looking.

zulächeln *vi sep* **jdm ~** to smile at sb.

zulachen *vi sep* **jdm ~** to give sb a friendly laugh.

zuladen *vti sep irreg* to load more on/in.

Zuladung *f* (*bei Kfz*) useful load; (*Naut*) deadweight.

Zulage *f* (a) (*Geld~*) extra *or* additional pay *no indef art*; (*Sonder~ auch*) bonus (payment); (*Gefahren~*) danger-money *no indef art*. **eine ~ von 100 Mark** an extra 100 marks pay; a bonus (payment) of 100 marks; 100 marks danger-money. (b) (*Gehaltserhöhung*) rise (*Brit*), raise (*US*); (*regelmäßig*) increment.

zulande *adv* **bei uns/euch ~** back home, where we/you come from *or* live, in our/your country.

zulangen *vi sep* (a) (*inf*) (*Dieb, beim Essen*) to help oneself (*auch fig*). (b) (*dial: reichen*) to do (*inf*). **haben Sie genug Geld?** **— es langt zu** have you enough money? **—** it'll do; **das Geld langt zu** the money will do, there's enough money; **es langt nicht zu** there's not enough.

zulänglich *adj* (*geh*) adequate.

Zulänglichkeit *f* (*geh*) adequacy.

zulassen *vt sep irreg* (a) (*Zugang gewähren*) to admit.

(b) (*amtlich*) to authorize; *Arzt* to register; *Heilpraktiker* to register, to license; *Kraftfahrzeug* to license; *Rechtsanwalt* to call (to the bar), to admit (as a barrister *or* to the bar); *Prüfling* to admit.

(c) (*dulden, gestatten*) to allow, to permit. **das läßt nur den Schluß zu, daß ...** that leaves *or* allows only one conclusion: that ...; **eine Ausnahme ~** (*Vorschriften*) to allow (of) *or* admit (of) *or* permit an exception; (*Mensch*) to allow *or* permit an exception; **sein Verhalten läßt keine andere Erklärung zu(, als daß)** there is no other explanation for his behaviour (but that); **ich lasse nicht zu, daß mein Bruder benachteiligt wird** I shan't allow *or* permit my brother to be discriminated against; **das läßt mein Pflichtbewußtsein nicht zu** my sense of duty won't allow *or* permit *or* countenance that.

(d) (*geschlossen lassen*) to leave *or* keep shut *or* closed.

zulässig *adj* permissible, permitted, allowed; (*amtlich auch*) authorized. **~e Abweichung** (*Tech*) tolerance, permissible variation; **~es Gesamtgewicht** (*Mot*) maximum laden weight; **~e Höchstgeschwindigkeit** (upper) speed limit; **~e Höchstbelastung** weight limit; **es ist nicht ~, hier zu parken** parking is prohibited *or* not permitted here.

Zulassung *f* (a) *no pl* (*Gewährung von Zugang*) admittance, admission.

(b) *no pl* (*amtlich*) authorization; (*von Kfz*) licensing; (*als Rechtsanwalt*) call to the bar; (*von Prüfling*) admittance (*form*); (*als praktizierender Arzt*) registration. **Antrag auf ~ zu einer Prüfung** application to enter an examination; **seine ~ als Rechtsanwalt bekommen** to be called to the bar.

(c) (*Dokument*) papers *pl*; (*von Kfz auch*) vehicle registration document; (*Lizenz*) licence.

Zulassungs-: **~beschränkung** *f* (*esp Univ*) restriction on admissions; **~sperre** *f* (*esp Univ*) bar on admissions; **~stelle** *f* registration office; **~stopp** *m* (*esp Univ*) block on admissions.

Zulauf *m, no pl* **großen ~ haben** (*Geschäft, Restaurant*) to be very popular; (*Arzt etc auch*) to be much sought after *or* in great demand; **die Aufführung hat sehr großen ~** gehabt the performance drew large crowds.

zulaufen *vi sep irreg aux sein* (a) **auf jdn/etw ~** *or* **zugelaufen kommen** to run towards sb/sth, to come running towards sb/sth; (*direkt*) to run up to sb/sth, to come running up to sb/sth.

(b) *siehe* **spitz**.

(c) (*Wasser etc*) to run in, to add. **laß noch etwas kaltes Wasser ~** run in *or* add some more cold water.

(d) (*inf: sich beeilen*) to hurry (up). **lauf zu!** hurry up!

(e) (*Hund etc*) **jdm ~** to stray into sb's house/place; **eine zugelaufene Katze** a stray (cat).

zulegen *sep* **1** *vt* (a) (*dazulegen*) to put on. **legen Sie noch zwei Scheiben zu, bitte** please put on another two slices.

(b) *Geld* to add; (*bei Verlustgeschäft*) to lose. **der Chef hat mir 50 DM im Monat zugelegt** the boss has given me DM 50 a

month extra, the boss has given me an extra DM 50 a month; **die fehlenden 20 DM legte meine Mutter zu** my mother made up the remaining DM 20.

(c) **etwas Tempo** *or* **einen Zahn** (*sl*) **~** (*inf*) to get a move on (*inf*), to step on it (*inf*); (*sich anstrengen*) to get one's finger out (*sl*).

(d) (*inf: an Gewicht*) to put on. **er hat schon wieder 5 kg zugelegt** he's put on another 5 kg.

2 *vi* (*inf*) (a) (*an Gewicht*) to put on weight.

(b) (*sich mehr anstrengen*) (*inf*) to pull one's finger out (*sl*); (*Sport*) to step up the pace (*inf*).

3 *vr* **sich** (*dat*) **etw ~** (*inf*) to get oneself sth; **er hat sich** (*dat*) **eine teure Pfeife zugelegt** he has treated himself to an expensive pipe; **er hat sich eine Braut/Freundin zugelegt** (*hum*) he has got himself *or* has acquired a fiancée/girlfriend.

zuleide *adv* **etw jdm ~** tun to do sb harm, to harm sb; **was hat er dir ~ getan?** what (harm) has he done to you?; **wer hat dir etwas ~ getan?** who has harmed you?; *siehe* **Fliege**.

zuleiten *vt sep Wasser, Strom* to supply; *Schreiben, Waren* to send on, to forward.

Zuleitung *f* (*Tech*) supply.

zuletzt *adv* (a) (*schließlich, endlich, zum Schluß*) in the end. **~ kam sie doch** she came in the end; **~ kam auch Gaston** in the end *or* finally Gaston came too; **wir blieben bis ~** we stayed to the very *or* bitter end; **ganz ~** right at the last moment, at the very last moment.

(b) (*als letzte(r, s*), *an letzter Stelle, zum letzten Mal*) last. **ich kam ~** I came last, I was last to come; **wann haben Sie ihn ~ gesehen?** when did you last see him?; **ganz ~** last of all; **nicht ~ dank/wegen** not least thanks to/because of.

zuliebe *adv* **etw jdm ~** tun to do sth for sb's sake *or* for sb; **das geschah nur ihr ~** it was done just for her.

Zulieferbetrieb, Zulieferer *m* (*Econ*) supplier.

Zulieferlindustrie *f* (*Econ*) supply industry.

zulöten *vt sep* to solder.

Zulu[1] ['tsu:lu] *mf* -(s), -(s) Zulu.

Zulu[2] ['tsu:lu] *nt* -(s) (*Sprache*) Zulu.

zum *contr of* **zu dem** (a) (*räumlich*) **geht es hier ~ Bahnhof?** is this the way to the station?; **Z~ Löwen** The Lion Inn.

(b) (*mit Infinitiv*) **~ Schwimmen/Essen gehen** to go swimming/to go and eat.

(c) (*Folge*) **es ist ~ Verrücktwerden/Weinen** it's enough to drive you mad/make you weep.

(d) (*Zweck*) **dies Gerät ist ~ Messen des Blutdrucks** this apparatus is for measuring (the) blood pressure.

(e) *in Verbindung mit vb siehe auch dort.* **~ Spießbürger/Verräter werden** to become bourgeois/a traitor.

zumachen *sep* **1** *vt* (*schließen*) to shut, to close; *Flasche* to close; *Brief* to seal; (*inf: auflösen*) *Laden etc* to close (down). **2** *vi* (*inf*) (a) (*den Laden ~*) to close (down), to shut up shop; (*fig*) to pack *or* jack it in (*inf*), to call it a day. (b) (*sich beeilen*) to get a move on (*inf*), to step on it (*inf*).

zumal 1 *conj* **~** (*da*) (*besonders or* particularly *as or* since. **2** *adv* (a) (*besonders*) especially, particularly. (b) (*obs: zugleich*) at the same time.

zumauern *vt sep* to brick up, to wall up.

zumeist *adv* mostly, in the main, for the most part.

zumessen *vt sep irreg* (*geh*) to measure out (*jdm* for sb), to apportion (*jdm* to sb); *Essen* to dish out (*jdm* to sb); *Zeit* to allocate (*dat* for); *Schuld* to attribute (*jdm* to sb). **ihm wurde eine hohe Strafe zugemessen** he was dealt a stiff punishment; **dem darf man keine große Bedeutung ~** one can't attach too much importance to that.

zumindest *adv* at least. **er hätte mich ~ anrufen können** he could at least have phoned me, he could have phoned me at least, at least he could have phoned me.

zumutbar *adj* reasonable. **jdm** *or* **für jdn ~ sein** to be reasonable for sb; **es ist ihm (durchaus) ~, daß er das tut** he can reasonably be expected to do that.

Zumutbarkeit *f* reasonableness.

zumute *adv* **wie ist Ihnen ~?** how do you feel?; **mir ist traurig/seltsam** *etc* **~** I feel sad/strange *etc*; **mir ist lächerlich/gar nicht lächerlich ~** I'm in a silly mood/I'm not in a laughing mood; **ihm war recht wohl ~** he felt wonderful *or* good; **mir war dabei gar nicht wohl ~** I didn't feel right about it, I felt uneasy about it; **ihm war bänglich ~** (*old*) he was sore afraid (*old*).

zumuten *vt sep* **jdm etw ~** to expect *or* ask sth of sb; **Sie wollen mir doch wohl nicht ~, diesen Unsinn zu lesen** you surely don't expect me *or* aren't asking me to read this nonsense; **das können Sie niemandem ~** you can't ask *or* expect that of anyone; **Sie muten mir doch wohl nicht zu, das zu glauben!** you surely don't expect me to *or* aren't asking me to believe that; **sich** (*dat*) **zuviel ~** to take on too much, to overdo things, to overtax oneself; **seinem Körper zuviel ~** to overtax oneself.

Zumutung *f* unreasonable demand; (*Unverschämtheit*) cheek, nerve (*inf*). **das ist eine ~!** that's a bit much!

zunächst 1 *adv* (a) (*zuerst*) first (of all). **~ einmal** first of all. (b) (*vorläufig*) for the time being, for the moment. **2** *prep* +*dat* (*rare*) (*neben*) next to.

zunageln *vt sep Fenster etc* to nail up; (*mit Brettern, Pappe etc*) to board up; *Sarg, Kiste etc* to nail down.

zunähen *vt sep* to sew up.

Zunahme *f* -, -n (*gen, an* + *dat* in) increase; (*Anstieg auch*) rise.

Zuname *m* surname, last name.

Zündlanlaß- (*Aut*): **~schalter** *m* ignition switch; **~schloß** *nt* ignition lock.

Zündblättchen *nt siehe* **Zündplättchen**.

zündeln *vi* to play (about) with fire. **mit Streichhölzern ~** to play (about) with matches.

zünden 1 *vi* to catch light *or* fire, to ignite; (*Pulver*) to ignite; (*Streichholz*) to light; (*Motor*) to fire; (*Sprengkörper*) to go off;

(fig) to kindle enthusiasm. dieses Streichholz zündet nicht this match won't light; hat es endlich bei dir gezündet? *(inf)* has the penny finally dropped?, have you finally cottoned on? *(inf)*.

2 *vt* to ignite, to set alight; *Rakete* to fire; *Sprengkörper* to set off, to detonate; *Feuerwerkskörper* to let off.

zündend *adj (fig)* stirring, rousing; *Vorschlag* exciting.

Zunder *m* -s, - tinder; *(Schicht auf Metall)* scale (oxide); *(inf: Prügel)* good hiding *(inf)*, thrashing. wie ~ brennen to burn like tinder; ~ kriegen/jdm ~ geben *(inf)* to get/to give sb a good hiding *(inf)* or thrashing.

Zünder *m* -s, - (a) igniter; *(für Sprengstoff, Bombe, Torpedo etc)* fuse; *(für Mine)* detonator. (b) *(Aus, inf: Zündholz)* match.

Zunderschwamm *m (Bot)* touchwood.

Zünd-: ~flamme *f* pilot light; ~folge *f (Tech)* ignition sequence, firing order; ~funke *m (Aut)* ignition spark; ~holz *nt* match(stick); ein ~holz anreißen to strike a match; ~hütchen *nt* percussion cap; ~kabel *nt (Aut)* plug lead; ~kapsel *f* detonator; ~kerze *f (Aut)* spark(ing) plug; ~plättchen *nt (für Spielzeugpistole)* cap; ~schloß *nt (Aut)* ignition lock; ~schlüssel *m (Aut)* ignition key; ~schnur *f* fuse; ~spule *f* ignition or spark coil; ~stoff *m* inflammable or flammable *(esp US)* matter; *(Sprengstoff)* explosives *pl*, explosive material; *(fig)* inflammatory or explosive stuff.

Zündung *f* ignition; *(Zündvorrichtung bei Sprengkörpern)* detonator, detonating device. die ~ ist nicht richtig eingestellt *(Aut)* the timing is out or wrongly set; die ~ einstellen *(Aut)* to adjust the timing.

Zünd-: ~versteller *m (Aut)* ignition timing mechanism; ~verteiler *m (Aut)* distributor; ~vorrichtung *f* igniting device, detonator; ~warensteuer *f* tax on matches; ~willigkeit *f (Tech)* ignition quality, combustibility; ~zeitpunkt *m* moment of ignition.

zunehmen *vi sep irreg* **1** *vi (an Zahl etc, beim Stricken)* to increase; *(anwachsen auch)* to grow; *(Tage)* to draw out; *(an Weisheit, Erfahrung etc)* to gain *(an + dat* in); *(Mensch: an Gewicht)* to put on or gain weight; *(Mond)* to wax. im Z~ sein to be on the increase; *(Mond)* to be waxing; der Wind nimmt (an Stärke) zu the wind is increasing or getting up.

2 *vt (Mensch: an Gewicht)* to gain, to put on. ich habe 2 kg/viel zugenommen I've gained or put on 2 kg/a lot of weight.

zunehmend **1** *adj* increasing, growing; *Mond* crescent. mit ~en Jahren glaubte er ... as he advanced in years he believed ...; bei or mit ~em Alter with advancing age; wir haben ~en Mond there is a crescent moon; in ~em Maße to an increasing degree.

2 *adv* increasingly. ~ an Einfluß gewinnen to gain increasing influence.

zuneigen *sep + dat* **1** *vi* to be inclined towards. ich neige der Ansicht zu, daß ... I am inclined to think that ...; jdm zugeneigt sein *(geh)* to be well disposed towards sb.

2 *vr* to lean towards; *(fig: Glück etc)* to favour. sich dem Ende ~ *(geh)* *(Tag etc)* to be drawing to a close; *(knapp werden: Vorräte etc)* to be running out.

Zuneigung *f* affection. eine starke ~ zu jdm empfinden to feel strong affection towards sb; ~ zu jdm fassen to take a liking to sb, to grow fond of sb.

Zunft *f* -, ⁀e *(Hist)* guild; *(hum inf)* brotherhood. die ~ der Bäcker/Fleischer *etc* the bakers'/butchers' *etc* guild; ihr seid mir ja eine saubere ~! *(iro inf)* you're a great bunch! *(inf)*.

Zunft-: ~brief *m (Hist)* guild charter; ~genosse *m* guildsman *(fig pej)* crony *(pej)*.

zünftig *adj* (a) *(Hist)* belonging to a guild. (b) *(fachmännisch)* Arbeit *etc* expert, professional; *Kleidung* professional (-looking); *(inf: ordentlich, regelrecht)* proper; *(inf: gut, prima)* great. eine ~e Ohrfeige a hefty box on the ears.

Zunft- *(Hist)*: ~meister *m* master of a/the guild, guild master; ~wesen *nt* guild system, system of guilds; ~zwang *m* compulsory membership of a guild.

Zunge *f* -, -n tongue; *(Mus: von Fagott, Akkordeon)* reed; *(von Waage)* pointer; *(geh: Sprache)* tongue; *(Zool: See~)* sole. mit der ~ anstoßen to lisp; das brennt auf der ~ that burns the tongue; jdm die ~ herausstrecken to put or stick one's tongue out at sb; die ~ herausstrecken *(beim Arzt)* to put out one's tongue; eine böse or giftige/scharfe or spitze/lose ~ haben to have an evil/a sharp/a loose tongue; lose/böse ~n behaupten, ... rumour/malicious gossip has it ...; eine feine ~ haben to be a gourmet, to have a discriminating palate; sich *(dat)* die ~ abbrechen *(fig)* to tie one's tongue in knots; eher b=oder *etc* sich *(dat)* die ~ ab, als ... he'd do anything rather than ...; das Wort liegt or schwebt mir auf der ~, ich habe das Wort auf der ~ the word is on the tip of my tongue; es lag mir auf der ~ zu sagen, daß ... it was on the tip of my tongue to say that ...; der Wein löste ihm die ~ the wine loosened his tongue; mir hängt die ~ zum Hals heraus *(inf)* my tongue is hanging out; ein Lyriker polnischer *(gen)* ~ a poet of the Polish tongue; alle Länder arabischer *(gen)* ~ all Arabic-speaking countries.

züngeln *vi (Schlange)* to dart its tongue in and out; *(Flamme)* to lick.

Zungen-: ~bein *nt* tongue-bone, hyoid bone; ~belag *m* coating of the tongue; ~brecher *m* tongue-twister; ~fertig *adj (geh)* eloquent, fluent; *(pej)* glib; ~fertigkeit *f siehe adj* eloquence, fluency; glibness; ~kuß *m* French kiss; ~laut *m (Ling)* lingual (sound); ~pfeife *f (Mus)* reed pipe; ~-R *nt (Ling)* trilled or rolled "r"; ~rücken *m* back of the tongue; ~schlag *m (durch Alkohol)* slur; *(Mus)* tonguing; ein falscher ~schlag an unfortunate turn of phrase; zwei Töne mit ~schlag spielen to tongue two notes; ~spitze *f* tip of the tongue; ~wurst *f (Cook)* tongue sausage; ~wurzel *f* root of the tongue.

Zünglein *nt dim of* Zunge tongue; *(rare: der Waage)* pointer. das ~ an der Waage sein *(fig)* to tip the scales; *(Pol)* to hold the balance of power.

zunichte *adv* ~ machen/werden *(geh)* to wreck, to ruin/to be

wrecked, to be ruined; *Hoffnungen auch* to shatter, to destroy/to be shattered, to be destroyed.

zunicken *vi sep* jdm ~ to nod to or at sb; jdm freundlich/aufmunternd ~ to give sb a friendly/encouraging nod.

zunutze *adv* sich *(dat)* etw ~ machen *(verwenden)* to make use of, to utilize; *(ausnutzen)* to capitalize on, to take advantage of.

zuoberst *adv* on or at the (very) top, right on or at the top; *siehe* unterste(r, s).

zuordnen *vt sep + dat* to assign to. ein Tier einer Gattung ~ to assign an animal to a species; jdn/etw jdm ~ to assign sb/sth to sb; diesen Dichter ordnet man der Romantik zu this poet is classified as a Romantic(ist); wie sind diese Begriffe einander zugeordnet? how are these concepts related (to each other)?

Zuordnung *f siehe vt* assignment; classification, relation.

zupacken *vi sep (inf)* (a) *(zugreifen)* to make a grab for it *etc*. (b) *(bei der Arbeit)* to knuckle down (to it), to get down to it. (c) *(helfen)* mit ~ to give me/them *etc* a hand.

zupaß, zupasse *adv* jdm ~ kommen *(Mensch, Hilfe)* to come at the right time; dieser Holzblock kommt mir ~ this block of wood is just what I needed.

zupfen *vti* to pick; *Saite auch* to pluck; *Unkraut* to pull (up); *(auseinanderziehen)* Fäden, Maschen to pull, to stretch. jdn am Ärmel *etc* ~ to tug at sb's sleeve *etc*; sich *(dat or acc)* am Bart/Ohr *etc* ~ to pull at one's beard/ear *etc*; zupf dich an deiner eigenen Nase! *(dial)* put your own house in order!

Zupf-: ~geige *f (dated)* guitar; ~instrument *nt (Mus)* plucked string instrument.

zupfropfen *vt sep* to cork, to stopper.

zupressen *vt sep* Tür *etc* to press shut. ein Loch/Leck (mit der Hand *etc)* ~ to press one's hand *etc* over a hole/leak.

zuprosten *vi sep* jdm ~ to raise one's glass to sb, to drink sb's health.

zur *contr of* zu der. ~ Schule gehen to go to school; jdn ~ Tür bringen to see sb to the door; ~ See fahren to go to sea; Gasthof „Z~ Post" The Post Inn; ~ Zeit at the moment; ~ Weihnachtszeit at Christmastime; ~ Orientierung for orientation; ~ Abschreckung as a deterrent.

zuraten *vi sep irreg* jdm ~, etw zu tun to advise sb to do sth; er hat mich gefragt, ob er ins Ausland gehen soll, und ich habe ihm zugeraten he asked me whether he should go abroad and I said he should; ich will weder ~ noch abraten I won't advise you one way or the other; auf sein Z~ *(hin)* on his advice.

zuraunen *vt sep (liter)* jdm etw ~ to whisper sth to sb.

Zürcher(in *f) m* -s, - native of Zurich.

zürcherisch *adj* of Zurich.

zurechnen *vt sep* (a) *(inf: dazurechnen)* to add to. (b) *(fig: zuordnen)* *(dat* with) to class, to include; *Kunstwerk etc (dat* to) to attribute, to ascribe.

Zurechnung *f* (a) unter ~ aller Kosten inclusive of all charges. (b) *(Zuordnung)* assignment (to), inclusion (with).

Zurechnungs-: z~fähig *adj* of sound mind; *(esp Jur, fig inf)* compos mentis *pred*; ~fähigkeit *f* soundness of mind; verminderte ~fähigkeit diminished responsibility; ich muß doch schon manchmal an seiner ~fähigkeit zweifeln! *(inf)* I sometimes wonder if he's quite compos mentis *(inf)*.

zurecht-: ~basteln *vt sep* sich *(dat)* etw ~basteln *(auch fig, iro)* to construct sth; ~biegen *vt sep irreg* to bend into shape; *(fig)* to twist; er hat alles wieder ~gebogen *(inf)* he has straightened or smoothed everything out again; ~feilen *vt sep* to file into shape; ~finden *vr sep irreg* to find one's way *(in + dat* around); sich in der Welt nicht mehr ~finden not to be able to cope with the world any longer; ich finde mich in dieser Tabelle nicht ~ I can't make head nor tail of this table; sich mit etw ~finden to get the hang of sth *(inf)*; *(durch Gewöhnung)* to get used to sth; ~hämmern *vt sep* to hammer into shape; ~kommen *vi sep irreg aux sein* (a) *(rechtzeitig kommen)* to come in time; ich bin gerade noch zum Zug ~gekommen I just made it to the train in time; (b) *(fig)* to get on; *(schaffen, bewältigen)* to cope; *(genug haben)* to have enough; kommen Sie ohne das ~? *(inf)* can you manage without it?; er kam nie ~ im Leben he was never able to cope with life; (c) *(finanziell)* to manage; mit 20 Mark am Tag kann man gut ~kommen you can manage easily on 20 marks a day; ~legen *vt sep irreg* to lay or get out ready; sich *(dat)* etw ~legen to lay or get sth out ready; *(fig)* to work sth out; sich *(dat)* alle Argumente ~legen to marshal all one's arguments; das hast du dir (bloß) ~gelegt! *(gedeutet)* that's just your interpretation; *(erfunden)* you just made that up!; ~machen *vt sep (inf)* (a) Zimmer, Essen etc to prepare, to get ready; Bett to make up; (b) *(anziehen)* to dress; *(schminken)* to make up; sich ~machen to get dressed or ready; to put on one's make-up; auf etw *(acc)* ~gemacht sein *(inf)* to be done up as sth *(inf)*; ~rücken *vt sep* Brille, Hut etc to adjust; Stühle etc to straighten (up), to put straight; *(fig)* to straighten out, to put straight; siehe Kopf; ~schneiden *vt sep irreg* to cut to shape; Haar, Nagel, Hecke to trim, to cut; etw so ~schneiden, wie man es haben will to cut sth to the required shape; ~schustern *vt sep (inf)* to knock together; ~setzen *sep* **1** *vt* sich *(dat)* den Hut/die Brille ~setzen to adjust or straighten one's hat/glass; siehe Kopf; **2** *vr* to settle oneself; ~stellen *sep* **1** *vt* to set out ready; **2** *vr* to pose, to arrange oneself; ~stutzen *vt sep* to trim, to cut; Hecke auch to clip; *(fig)* to lick into shape; ~weisen *vt sep irreg (form)* to rebuke; Schüler etc to reprimand; Z~weisung *f siehe vt* rebuke; reprimand; ~zimmern *vt sep* to knock together; *(fig)* to construct.

zureden *vi sep* jdm ~ *(ermutigen)* to encourage sb; *(überreden)* to persuade sb; wenn du ihm gut zuredest, hilft er dir if you talk to him nicely, he'll help you; sie hat ihrem Vater so lange zugeredet, bis er ihr das Auto kaufte she kept on at her father till he bought her the car; auf mein Z~ *(hin)* with my encouragement; *(Überreden)* with my persuasion; freundliches Z~ friendly persuasion.

zureichen sep 1 vt jdm etw ~ to hand or pass sth to sb. 2 vi to be enough or sufficient. ein ~der Grund a sufficient or adequate reason; der Satz vom ~den Grunde (Philos) the law of sufficient reason.

zureiten sep irreg 1 vt Pferd to break in. 2 vi aux sein (weiterreiten) to ride on; (schneller) to ride faster. ~ auf jdn/etw ~ or zugeritten kommen to ride toward(s) or (direkt) up to sb/sth.

Zureiter(in f) m -s, - roughrider; (für Wildpferde auch) broncobuster (US).

Zürich nt -s Zurich.

Züricher(in f) m -s, - siehe **Zürcher(in).**

züricherisch adj siehe **zürcherisch.**

Zürichsee m Lake Zurich.

zurichten vt sep (a) Essen etc to prepare; Stein, Holz to square; Leder, Pelz, Stoff to finish, to dress; (Typ) to justify. (b) (beschädigen, verunstalten) to make a mess of; (verletzen) to injure. jdn übel ~ to knock sb about, to beat sb up.

Zurichter(in f) m -s, - (Typ) justifier; (von Stoffen, Pelzen) dresser, finisher.

Zurichtung f (Typ) justifying, justification; (von Geweben, Pelzen) dressing, finishing.

zuriegeln vt sep to bolt (shut).

zürnen vi (geh) jdm ~ to be angry with sb; dem Schicksal ~ to rage against fate.

zurollen vti sep (vi aux sein) to roll. auf jdn/etw ~ or zugerollt kommen to roll toward(s) or (direkt) up to sb/sth.

zurren vt (Naut) to lash; Deckladung, Beiboot etc to lash down.

Zurschaustellung f display, exhibition.

zurück adv back; (mit Zahlungen) behind; (fig: zurückgeblieben) (von Kind) backward. in Mathematik (sehr) ~ sein (fig) to be (really) behind in maths; fünf Punkte ~ (Sport) five points behind; ~ nach etc back to etc; ~! get back!; ~ an Absender return to sender; seit wann ist Trevor ~? since when has Trevor been back?; ich bin in zehn Minuten wieder ~ I will be back (again) in 10 minutes; ein paar Jahre ~ a few years back or ago; hinter jdm ~ sein (fig) to lie behind sb; es gibt kein Z~ (mehr) there's no going back.

Zurück-: z~begeben* vr irreg (geh) to return, to go back; z~begleiten* vt sep jdn z~begleiten to accompany sb back; z~behalten* vt sep irreg to keep (back); er hat Schäden/einen Schock z~behalten he suffered lasting damage/lasting shock; ~behaltungsrecht nt (Jur) right of retention; z~bekommen* vt sep irreg (a) to get back; (b) (inf: heimgezahlt bekommen) das wirst du (von mir) z~bekommen! I'll get my own back on you for that!; z~beordern* vt sep to recall, to order back; z~berufen* vt sep irreg to recall; z~beugen sep 1 vt to bend back; 2 vr to lean or bend back; z~bewegen* vtr sep to move back(wards); (drehend) to turn backwards; z~bilden vr sep (Geschwür) to recede; (Muskel) to become wasted, to atrophy; (Biol) to regress.

zurückbleiben vi sep irreg aux sein (a) (an einem Ort) to stay or remain behind; (weiter hinten gehen) to stay (back) behind. (b) (übrigbleiben) Rest, Rückstand) to be left; (als Folge von Krankheit etc: Schaden, Behinderung) to remain. er blieb als Waise/Witwer zurück he was left an orphan/a widower. (c) (nicht Schritt halten, auch fig: mit Arbeitsleistung etc) to fall behind; (Uhr) to lose; (in Entwicklung) to be retarded or backward; (Sport) to be behind. 20 Meter ~ to be 20 metres behind; ihre Leistung blieb hinter meinen Erwartungen zurück her performance did not come up to my expectations; siehe **zurückgeblieben.**

zurück-: ~blenden vi sep (lit, fig) to flash back (auf +acc to); ~blicken vi sep to look back (auf +acc at); (fig) to look back (auf +acc on); ~bringen vt sep irreg (wieder herbringen) to bring back (lit, fig); (wieder wegbringen) to take back; jdn ins Leben ~bringen to bring sb back to life, to revive sb; ~datieren* vt sep to backdate; ~denken vi sep irreg to think back (an +acc to); so weit ich ~denken kann as far as I can recall or remember; wenn man so ~denkt when I think back; ~drängen vt sep to force or push back; (Mil) to drive back, to repel; (fig: eindämmen) to repress, to restrain; ~drehen vt sep to turn back; Uhr to put back; die Uhr or Zeit ~drehen to turn or put back the clock; ~dürfen vi sep irreg (inf) to be allowed back; ~eilen vi sep aux sein (geh) to hurry back; ~erbitten* vt sep irreg (geh) etw ~erbitten to ask for the return of sth; ~erhalten* vt sep irreg to have returned; ~erinnern* vr sep to remember, to recall (an +acc sth); sich bis zu seinem 5. Lebensjahr/bis 1945 ~erinnern können to be able to remember being 5 years old/as far back as 1945; ~erobern* vt sep (Mil) to recapture, to retake; to reconquer; (fig) Freund etc to win back; ~erstatten* vt sep siehe rückerstatten; ~erwarten* vt sep jdn ~erwarten to expect sb back; ~fahren sep irreg 1 vi aux sein (a) to go back, to return; (als Fahrer auch) to drive back; (b) (~weichen) to start back; 2 vt to drive back.

zurückfallen vi sep irreg aux sein to fall back; (Sport) to drop back; (fig: Umsätze etc) to fall, to drop (back); (fig: an Besitzer) to revert (an +acc to); (in Leistungen) to fall behind; (Schande, Vorwurf etc) to reflect (auf +acc on). sich auf einen Stuhl ~ lassen to drop back onto a chair; er fällt immer wieder in den alten Fehler zurück he always lapses back into his old mistake; das würde bloß auf deine armen Eltern ~ that would only reflect (badly) on your poor parents.

zurück-: ~finden vi sep irreg to find the or one's way back; findest du allein ~? can you find your own way back?; er fand zu sich selbst/zu Gott/zum Sozialismus ~ he found himself again/he found his way back to God/to Socialism; ~fliegen vti sep irreg (vi aux sein) to fly back; ~fließen vi sep irreg aux sein (lit, fig) to flow back; ~fluten vi sep aux sein (Wellen) to flow back; to stream back; ~fordern vt sep etw ~fordern to ask for sth back; (stärker) to demand sth back; ~fragen sep 1 vt etw ~fragen to ask sth back or in return; 2 vi to ask something

or a question back; (wegen einer Auskunft) to check back; ~führbar adj traceable (auf +acc to); auf eine Formel ~führbar reducible to a formula.

zurückführen sep 1 vt (a) (zurückbringen) to lead back. (b) (ableiten aus) to put down to. etw auf seine Ursache ~ to put sth down to its cause; etw auf eine Formel/Regel ~ to reduce sth to a formula/rule; das ist darauf zurückzuführen, daß ... that can be put down to the fact that ... (c) (bis zum Ursprung zurückverfolgen) to trace back. 2 vi to lead back. es führt kein Weg zurück there's no way back; (fig) there's no going back.

zurückgeben vt sep irreg to give back, to return; Wechselgeld to give back; Ball, Kompliment, Beleidigung to return; (erwidern) to retort, to rejoin. er gab mir/der Bibliothek das Buch zurück he gave the book back or returned the book to me/returned the book to the library; das Geld kannst du dir von der Firma ~ lassen you can ask the firm to give you the money back; dieser Erfolg gab ihm seine Zuversicht wieder zurück this success gave him back or restored his confidence; jdm sein Wort ~ to release sb from his/her etc word; (sich entloben) to break off one's engagement.

zurückgeblieben 1 ptp of **zurückbleiben.** 2 adj geistig/körperlich ~ mentally/physically retarded.

zurückgehen vi sep irreg aux sein (a) to go back, to return (nach, in +acc to); (fig: in der Geschichte etc) to go back (auf +acc, in +acc to); (seinen Ursprung haben) to go back to (auf +acc to). er ging zwei Schritte zurück he stepped back two paces, he took two steps back; Waren/Essen etc ~ lassen to send back goods/food etc; der Brief ging ungeöffnet zurück the letter was returned unopened. (b) (zurückweichen) to retreat, to fall back; (fig: abnehmen) (Hochwasser, Schwellung, Vorräte, Preise etc) to go down; (Geschäft, Umsatz) to fall off; (Seuche, Schmerz, Sturm) to die down. im Preis ~ to fall or drop in price.

Zurück-: z~geleiten* vt sep (geh) to escort or conduct back; z~gesetzt 1 ptp of z~setzen; 2 adj neglected; (dial) Waren reduced, marked down; im Preis z~gesetzt reduced in price; z~gezogen 1 ptp of z~ziehen; 2 adj Mensch withdrawn, retiring; Lebensweise secluded; 3 adv in seclusion; er lebt sehr z~gezogen he lives a very secluded life; ~gezogenheit f seclusion; z~greifen vi sep irreg (fig) to fall back (auf +acc upon); (zeitlich) to go back (auf +acc to); da müßte ich weit z~greifen I would have to go back a long way; z~haben vt sep irreg (inf) to have (got Brit) back; ich will mein Geld z~haben I want my money back; hast du das Buch schon z~? have you got (Brit) or gotten (US) the book back yet?

zurückhalten sep irreg 1 vt (daran hindern, sich zu entfernen) to hold back; (nicht durchlassen, aufhalten) jdn to hold up, to detain; (nicht freigeben) Manuskript, Film, Informationen to withhold; (dämmen) Gefühle, Ärger etc to restrain, to suppress; (unterdrücken) Tränen, Orgasmus to keep or hold back. jdn von etw (dat) ~ to keep sb from sth. 2 vr (sich beherrschen) to contain or restrain oneself, to control oneself; (reserviert sein) to be retiring or withdrawn; (im Hintergrund bleiben) to keep in the background; (bei Verhandlung, Demonstration etc) to keep a low profile. ich mußte mich schwer ~ I had to take a firm grip on myself; Sie müssen sich beim Essen sehr ~ you must cut down a lot on what you eat. 3 vi mit etw ~ (verheimlichen) to hold sth back.

zurückhaltend adj (beherrscht, kühl) restrained; (reserviert) reserved; (vorsichtig) cautious, guarded; Börse dull. sich ~ über etw (acc) äußern to be restrained in one's comments about sth; das Publikum reagierte ~ the audience's response was restrained. (b) (nicht großzügig) sparing. mit Tadel or Kritik nicht ~ sein to be unsparing in one's criticism.

Zurück-: ~haltung f siehe adj (a) (restraint; reserve; caution; dullness; sich (dat) ~haltung auferlegen to exercise restraint; z~holen vt sep to fetch back; Geld to get back; jdn z~holen (fig) to ask sb to come back; z~jagen sep 1 vt to chase back; 2 vi aux sein to chase or dash back; z~kämmen vt sep to comb back; z~kaufen vt sep to buy back, to repurchase; z~kehren vi sep aux sein to return or come back (von, aus from); to return or go back (nach, zu to); z~kommen vi sep irreg aux sein (lit, fig) to come back, to return; (Bezug nehmen) to refer (auf +acc to); der Brief kam z~ the letter was returned or came back; ich werde später auf deinen Vorschlag/dieses Angebot z~kommen I'll come back to your suggestion/this offer later; z~können vi sep irreg (inf) to be able to go back; ich kann nicht mehr z~ (fig) there's no going back!; z~kriegen vt sep (inf) siehe z~bekommen; z~lassen vt sep irreg (a) (hinterlassen) to leave; (liegenlassen) to leave behind; (fig: übertreffen) to leave behind, to outstrip; (Leichtathletik) to leave behind, to outdistance; (b) (inf: z~kehren lassen) to allow back, to allow to come/go back or to return; ~lassung f: unter ~lassung all seiner Habseligkeiten etc leaving behind all one's possessions etc; z~laufen vi sep irreg aux sein to run back; (z~gehen) to walk or go back.

zurücklegen sep 1 vt (a) (an seinen Platz) to put back. (b) Kopf to lay or lean back. (c) (aufbewahren, reservieren) to put aside or to one side; (sparen) to put away, to lay aside. jdm etw ~ to keep sth for sb. (d) Strecke to cover, to do. er hat schon ein ganzes Stück auf seinem Weg zum Diplomaten zurückgelegt he has already gone a long way towards becoming a diplomat. 2 vr to lie back.

Zurück-: z~lehnen vtr sep to lean back; z~leiten vt sep to lead back; Postsendung to return; Wasser etc to feed back, to run back; z~liegen vi sep irreg (örtlich) to be behind; der Unfall liegt etwa eine Woche z~ the accident was about a week ago, it is about a week since the accident; das liegt schon so weit z~,

daß ... that is so long ago now that ...; **es liegt zwanzig Jahre z~,
daß** ... it is twenty years since ...; **z~melden** *vtr sep* to report
back; **z~müssen** *vi sep irreg* (*inf*) to have to go back; **~nahme** *f* -,
-n withdrawal (*auch Jur, Mil*); (*von Entscheidung*) reversal;
(*von Aussage auch*) retraction; **wir bitten um ~nahme dieser
Sendung** we ask you to accept the return of this consignment.

zurücknehmen *vt sep irreg* to take back; (*Mil*) to withdraw;
Verordnung etc to revoke; *Entscheidung* to reverse; *Angebot* to
withdraw; *Auftrag, Bestellung* to cancel; (*Sport*) *Spieler* to
bring *or* call back; *Schachzug* to go back on. **sein Wort/Verspre-
chen ~** to go back on *or* break one's word/promise; **ich nehme
alles zurück und behaupte das Gegenteil** I take it all back.

zurück-: **~pfeifen** *vt sep irreg Hund etc* to whistle back; *jdn*
~pfeifen (*fig inf*) to bring sb back into line; **~prallen** *vi sep aux
sein* to rebound, to bounce back; (*Geschoß*) to ricochet;
(*Strahlen, Hitze*) to be reflected; **vor Schreck ~prallen** to
bounce/ricochet/be reflected off sth; **vor Schreck ~prallen** to
recoil in horror; **~rechnen** *vti sep* to count back; **~reichen** *sep*
1 *vt Gegenstand* to hand *or* pass back; 2 *vi Erinnerung, Tradition etc* to go back (*in* +*acc* to); **~reisen** *vi sep aux sein* to travel
back, to return; **~reißen** *vt sep irreg* to pull back; **~rollen** *vti
sep* (*vi: aux sein*) to roll back; **~rufen** *vti sep irreg* to call back;
(*am Telefon auch*) to ring back; (*aus Urlaub, Botschafter,
fehlerhafte Autos*) to recall; **jdn ins Leben ~rufen** to bring sb
back to life; **jdm etw in die Erinnerung/ins Gedächtnis ~rufen**
to conjure sth up for sb; **sich** (*dat*) **etw in die Erinnerung/ins
Gedächtnis ~rufen** to recall sth, to call sth to mind; **~schallen**
vi sep to re-echo, to resound; **~schalten** *vi sep* to change back;
~schaudern *vi sep aux sein* to shrink back *or* recoil (*vor* +*dat*
from); **~schauen** *vi sep* (*lit, fig*) to look back (*auf* +*acc* (*lit*) at,
(*fig*) on); **~scheuchen** *vt sep* to chase back; **~scheuen** *vi sep aux
sein* to shy away (*vor* +*dat* from); **vor nichts ~scheuen** to stop
at nothing; **~schicken** *vt sep* to send back; **jdm etw ~schicken**
to send sth back to sb, to send sb sth back; **~schieben** *vt sep
irreg* to push back.

zurückschlagen *sep irreg* 1 *vt* (**a**) to knock away; (*mit
Schläger*) *Ball* to return, to hit back; *Feind, Angriff etc* to beat
back, to beat off, to repulse.
   (**b**) (*umschlagen*) *Gardinen* to pull back; *Decke* to fold back;
Kragen to turn down; *Schleier* to lift; *Buchseiten* to leaf back.
   2 *vi* (*lit, fig*) to hit back; (*Mil, fig*) to retaliate, to strike back;
(*Flamme*) to flare back; (*Pendel*) to swing back.

zurück-: **~schnappen** *vi sep aux sein* to spring back, to snap
back; **~schnellen** *vi sep aux sein* to spring back; **~schrauben** *vt
sep* to screw back; (*fig inf*) *Erwartungen* to lower; **seine
Ansprüche ~schrauben** to lower one's sights; **~schrecken** *vi
sep irreg aux sein or haben* to shrink back, to start back, to
recoil; (*fig*) to shy away (*vor* +*dat* from); **vor nichts
~schrecken** to stop at nothing; **~sehen** *vi sep irreg* to look back;
auf etw (*acc*) **~sehen** (*fig*) to look back on sth; **~sehnen** *sep* 1 *vr*
to long to return (*nach* to); **sich nach der guten alten Zeit
~sehnen** to long for the good old days; 2 *vt* (*liter*) *jdn*
~sehnen to long for the return of sb/sth; **sie sehnte ihn/die
Jugendzeit ~** she yearned for him/the days of her youth to
return; **~senden** *vt sep irreg* to send back, to return.

zurücksetzen *sep* 1 *vt* (**a**) (*nach hinten*) to move back; *Auto* to
reverse, to back.
   (**b**) (*an früheren Platz*) to put back.
   (**c**) (*dial*) *Preis, Waren* to reduce, to mark down.
   (**d**) (*fig: benachteiligen*) to neglect; *siehe* **zurückgesetzt**.
   2 *vr* to sit back. **er setzte sich zwei Reihen zurück** he went to
sit *or* he sat two rows back.
   3 *vi* (*mit Fahrzeug*) to reverse, to back.

Zurück-: **~setzung** *f* (*fig: Benachteiligung*) neglect; **von
~setzung der Mädchen kann keine Rede sein** there's no question of the girls being neglected; **z~sinken** *vi sep irreg aux sein*
(*lit, fig*) to sink back (*in* +*acc* into); **z~spielen** *vt* (*Sport*) to
play back; (*Ftbl auch*) to pass back; 2 *vi* to play the ball *etc*
back; (*Ftbl auch*) to pass back; **~springen** *vi sep irreg aux sein*
to leap *or* jump back; (*fig: Häuserfront*) to be set back;
z~stecken *sep* 1 *vt* to put back; 2 *vi* (**a**) (*weniger Ansprüche
stellen*) to lower one's expectations; (*weniger ausgeben*) to cut
back; (**b**) (*nachgeben, einlenken*) to backtrack.

zurückstehen *vi sep irreg* (**a**) (*Haus etc*) to stand back.
   (**b**) (*an Leistung etc*) to be behind (*hinter jdm* sb).
   (**c**) (*verzichten*) to miss out; (*ausgelassen werden*) to be left
out.
   (**d**) (*hintangesetzt werden*) to take second place. **hinter etw**
(*dat*) **~** to take second place to sth; **sie muß immer hinter ihm ~**
she always comes off worse than he does.

zurückstellen *vt sep* (**a**) (*an seinen Platz, Uhr*) to put back;
(*nach hinten*) to move back.
   (**b**) *Waren* to put aside *or* by.
   (**c**) (*Aus: zurücksenden*) to send back, to return.
   (**d**) (*fig*) *Schüler* to keep down; (*Mil: vom Wehrdienst*) to
defer. **jdn vom Wehrdienst ~** to defer sb's military service.
   (**e**) (*fig: verschieben*) to defer; *Pläne auch* to shelve;
Bedenken etc to put aside; *Sport, Privatleben, Hobbys etc* to
spend less time on. **persönliche Interessen hinter etw** (*dat*) **~**
to put one's personal interests after sth, to subordinate one's
personal interests to sth; **persönliche Interessen ~** to put one's
own interests last.

Zurück-: **~stellung** *f* (**a**) (*Aus:* **~sendung**) return; (**b**)
(*Aufschub, Mil*) deferment; (**c**) (*Hintanstellung*) unter
~stellung seiner eigenen Interessen putting his own interests
last *or* aside; **z~stoßen** *sep irreg* 1 *vt* (**a**) (*wegstoßen*) to push
back; (*fig*) to reject; (**b**) (*fig: abstoßen*) to put off; 2 *vti* (*Aut:*
z~setzen) to reverse, to back; **z~strahlen** *sep* 1 *vt* to reflect; 2
vi to be reflected; (*Mensch: lächeln*) to beam back;
z~streichen *vt sep irreg Haar* to smooth back; **sich** (*dat*) **das
Haar z~streichen** to smooth one's hair back; **z~streifen** *vt sep*

Ärmel etc to pull up; **z~strömen** *vi sep aux sein* to flow back;
(*Menschen*) to stream back; **z~stufen** *vt sep* to downgrade;
z~taumeln *vi sep aux sein* to reel back; **z~telegraphieren** *vti
sep* to telegraph back; **z~tragen** *vt sep irreg* (**a**) to carry *or* take
back; (**b**) (*inf*) *siehe* **z~bringen**; **z~treiben** *vt sep irreg* to drive
back; (*Mil auch*) to repel, to repulse.

zurücktreten *sep irreg* 1 *vi aux sein* (**a**) (*zurückgehen*) to step
back; (*Mil: ins Glied auch*) to fall back; (*fig: Fluß, Hochwasser
etc*) to go down, to subside. **bitte ~! stand back, please!; einen
Schritt ~** to take a step back.
   (**b**) (*Regierung*) to resign; (*von einem Amt*) to step down.
   (**c**) (*von einem Vertrag etc*) to withdraw (*von* from), to back
out (*von* of). **von einem Anspruch/einem Recht ~** to renounce a
claim/a right.
   (**d**) (*fig: geringer werden*) to decline, to diminish; (*Wald*) to
recede; (*an Wichtigkeit verlieren*) to fade (in importance); (*im
Hintergrund bleiben*) to come second (*hinter jdm/etw* behind
sb/sth).
   2 *vti* (*mit Fuß*) to kick back.

Zurück-: **z~tun** *vt sep irreg* (*inf*) to put back; **z~übersetzen*** *vt
sep* to translate back; **z~verfolgen*** *vt sep* (*fig*) to trace back, to
retrace; **z~verlangen*** *sep* 1 *vt* to demand back; 2 *vi nach etw*
z~verlangen (*geh*) to yearn for the return of sth; **z~verlegen***
vt sep (**a**) (*zeitlich*) to set back; (**b**) (*Mil*) *Front etc* to move back,
to withdraw; (**c**) *Wohn-, Firmensitz* to move back;
z~versetzen* *sep* 1 *vt* (**a**) (*in seinen alten Zustand*) to restore
(*in* +*acc* to); (*in eine andere Zeit*) to take back (*in* +*acc* to); **wir
fühlten uns ins 18. Jahrhundert z~versetzt** we felt as if we had
been taken back *or* transported to the 18th century; (**b**) *Beamte
etc* to transfer back; *Schüler* to move down (*in* +*acc* into); 2 *vr*
to think oneself back (*in* +*acc* to); **z~verwandeln*** *vtr sep* to
turn *or* change back (*in* +*acc, zu* to); **z~verweisen*** *vt sep irreg*
(*auch Jur*) to refer back; *jdn auch* to direct back; (*Parl*)
Gesetzentwurf to recommit; **z~weichen** *vi sep irreg aux sein*
(*vor* +*dat* from) (*erschrocken*) to shrink back; (*ehrfürchtig*) to
stand back; (*nachgeben*) to retreat; (*vor Verantwortung, Hindernis*) to shy away; (*Mil*) to withdraw, to fall back; (*Hochwasser*) to recede, to subside; **z~weisen** *vt sep irreg* to reject;
Geschenk, Angebot etc auch to refuse; *Gäste, Bittsteller* to
turn away; *Angriff* to repel, to repulse; (*Jur*) *Klage, Berufung
auch* to dismiss; (*an der Grenze*) to turn back; **~weisung** *f siehe
vt* rejection; refusal; turning away; repulsion; dismissal;
turning back; **er protestierte gegen seine ~weisung an der
Grenze** he protested against being turned away at the border;
z~wenden *vtr sep irreg* to turn back; **z~werfen** *vt sep irreg
Ball, Kopf* to throw back; *Feind* to repulse, to repel; *Strahlen,
Schall* to reflect; (*fig: wirtschaftlich, gesundheitlich*) to set
back (*um* by); **z~wirken** *vi sep* to react (*auf* +*acc* upon);
z~wollen *vi sep* (*inf*) to want to go back; **z~wünschen** *vt sep
sich* (*dat*) *jdn/etw* **z~wünschen** to wish sb/sth back, to wish that
sb/sth were back; **z~zahlen** *vt sep* to repay, to pay back;
Schulden auch to pay off; *Spesen etc* to refund; **das werde ich
ihm noch z~zahlen!** (*fig*) I'll pay him back for that!

zurückziehen *sep irreg* 1 *vt* to pull *or* draw back; *Hand, Fuß* to
pull *or* draw away *or* back; *Truppen* to pull back; (*rückgängig
machen*) *Antrag, Bemerkung, Klage etc* to withdraw.
   2 *vr* to retire, to withdraw; (*sich zur Ruhe begeben*) to retire;
(*Mil*) to withdraw, to retreat; (*vom Geschäft, von der Politik
etc*) to retire (*von, aus* from). **sich von jdm ~** to withdraw from
sb; **sich von der Welt/in sich** (*acc*) **~** to retire from the
world/into oneself; *siehe* **zurückgezogen**.
   3 *vi aux sein* to move back; (*Truppen*) to march back; (*Vögel*)
to fly back.

Zurück-: **~ziehung** *f* withdrawal, retraction; **z~zucken** *vi sep
aux sein* to recoil, to start back; (*Hand, Fuß*) to jerk back.

Zuruf *m* shout, call; (*aufmunternd*) cheer. **durch ~ abstimmen
or wählen** to vote by acclamation; **~e shouts**; (*Zwischenrufe*)
heckling.

zurufen *vti sep irreg jdm etw ~* to shout sth to *or* at sb; (*feierlich*) to call sth out to sb; **jdm anfeuernd ~** to cheer sb.

zurüsten *sep* 1 *vt* to set up, to get ready, to prepare. 2 *vi* to get
everything set up *or* ready.

Zurüstung *f* setting-up, preparation.

zurzeit *adv* (*Aus, Sw*) at present, at the moment; *siehe* Zeit.

Zusage *f* -, **-n** (**a**) (*Zustimmung*) assent, consent. (**b**)
(*Verpflichtung*) undertaking, commitment. (**c**) (*Annahme*)
acceptance; (*Bestätigung*) confirmation. (**d**) (*Versprechen*)
promise, pledge. **ich kann Ihnen keine ~n machen** I can't make
you any promises.

zusagen *sep* 1 *vt* (**a**) (*versprechen*) to promise; (*bestätigen*) to
confirm. **er hat sein Kommen fest zugesagt** he has promised
firmly that he will come.
   (**b**) **jdm etw auf den Kopf ~** (*inf*) to tell sb sth outright; **ich
kann ihm auf den Kopf ~, wenn er mich belügt** I can tell by his
face when he's lying; **eine ~de Antwort** a favourable reply.
   2 *vi* (**a**) (*annehmen*) (*jdm*) **~** to accept.
   (**b**) (*gefallen*) *jdm* **~** to appeal to sb; **das will mir gar nicht ~** I
don't like it one little bit.

zusammen *adv* together. **alle/alles ~** all together; **wir haben
das Buch ~ geschrieben** we have written the book together *or*
between us; **wir hatten ~ 100 Mark zum Ausgeben** between us
we had 100 marks to spend; **wir bestellten uns ~ eine Portion**
we ordered one portion between us; **~ mit together** *or* along
with; **mit jdm ~ sein** to be together with sb; (*euph*) to be with
sb; **das macht ~ 50 Mark** that comes to *or* makes 50 marks all
together *or* in all; **er zahlt mehr als wir alle ~** he pays more than
all of us *or* the rest of us put together.

Zusammen-: **~arbeit** *f* co-operation; (*mit dem Feind*)
collaboration; **in ~arbeit mit** in co-operation with; **z~arbeiten**
vi sep to co-operate, to work together; (*mit dem Feind*) to
collaborate; **z~backen** *vi sep aux sein* (*inf*) *siehe* **z~kleben**.

zusammenballen sep 1 vt Schnee, Lehm to make into a ball; Papier to screw up into a ball. **2** vr (sich ansammeln) to accumulate; (Menge) to mass (together); (Mil) to be concentrated or massed. **das Unheil ballte sich über seinem Haupt zusammen** (liter) disaster loomed over him; **zusammengeballt leben** to live crammed together.

Zusammen-: ~**ballung** f accumulation; ~**bau** m, no pl assembly; z~**bauen** vt sep to assemble, to put together; **etw wieder z~bauen** to reassemble sth; z~**beißen** vt sep irreg **die Zähne z~beißen** (lit) to clench one's teeth; (fig) to grit one's teeth; z~**bekommen*** vt sep irreg siehe z~**kriegen;** z~**betteln** vt sep sich (dat) **etw z~betteln** to raise the money for sth; Geld **to get sth together;** z~**binden** vt sep irreg to tie or bind together; z~**bleiben** vi sep irreg aux sein to stay together; z~**borgen** vt sep sich (dat) **Geld z~borgen** to raise money; **sich** (dat) **etw z~borgen** to borrow sth; z~**brauen** vt sep 1 vt (inf) to concoct, to brew (up); **2** vr (Gewitter, Unheil etc) to be brewing.

zusammenbrechen vi sep irreg aux sein (Gebäude) to cave in; (Brücke auch) to give way; (Wirtschaft) to collapse; (Widerstand) to crumble; (zum Stillstand kommen) (Verkehr etc) to come to a standstill or halt; (Verhandlungen, Telefonverbindung, Mil: Angriff) to break down; (Elec: Spannung) to fail; (Mensch) to break down; (vor Erschöpfung) to collapse.

zusammenbringen vt sep irreg **(a)** (sammeln) to bring together, to collect; Geld to raise.
(b) (inf: zustande bringen) to manage; Gedanken to collect; Worte, Sätze to put together; (ins Gedächtnis zurückrufen) to remember; (zusammenkriegen, -bauen) to get together.
(c) (in Kontakt bringen) Stoffe to bring into contact with each other; (bekannt machen) Menschen to bring together. **wieder** ~ (versöhnen) to reconcile, to bring back together; **die beiden Katzen darfst du nicht** ~ you must not let the two cats get near each other.

Zusammenbruch m (von Beziehungen, Kommunikation) breakdown; (fig) collapse; (Nerven~) breakdown.

zusammendrängen sep 1 vt Menschen to crowd or herd together; (fig) Ereignisse, Fakten to condense.
2 vr (Menschen) to crowd (together); (Mil: Truppen) to be concentrated or massed. **die ganze Handlung des Stücks drängt sich im letzten Akt zusammen** all the action of the play is concentrated into the last act.

Zusammen-: z~**drücken** sep 1 vt to press together; (verdichten) to compress; 2 vr to be compressed; z~**fahren** sep irreg 1 vi aux sein **(a)** (z~stoßen) to collide; **(b)** (erschrecken) to start; (vor Schmerz) to flinch; **2** vt (inf) (a) (überfahren) to run over; **(b)** Fahrzeug to crash, to wreck; ~**fall** m (von Ereignissen) coincidence.

zusammenfallen vi sep irreg aux sein **(a)** (einstürzen) to collapse; (Hoffnungen) to be shattered. **in sich** (acc) ~ (lit, fig) to collapse; (Hoffnungen) to be shattered; (Lügengebäude auch) to fall apart. **(b)** (niedriger werden, sich senken) to go down. **die Glut war** (in sich) **zusammengefallen** the fire had died down. **(c)** (durch Krankheit etc) to wither away. **er sah ganz zusammengefallen aus** he looked very decrepit. **(d)** (Ereignisse) to coincide.

zusammenfalten vt sep to fold up.

zusammenfassen sep 1 vt **(a)** to combine (zu in); (vereinigen) to unite; (Math) to sum; (Mil) Truppen to concentrate. **(b)** Bericht etc to summarize. **2** vi (das Fazit ziehen) to summarize, to sum up. **ein** ~**der Bericht** a summary, a résumé; **jdm etw in** ~**der Form vortragen** to give sb a summary of sth; ~**d kann man sagen, ...** to sum up or in summary, one can say ...; **wenn ich kurz** ~ **darf** just to sum up.

Zusammen-: ~**fassung** f **(a)** siehe vt **(a)** combination; union; summing; concentration; **(b)** (Überblick) summary, synopsis, résumé; (von Abhandlung) abstract; z~**fegen** vt sep to sweep together; z~**finden** vr sep irreg to meet; (sich versammeln) to congregate; z~**flicken** vt sep to patch together; (inf) Verletzten to patch up (inf); (fig) Aufsatz etc to throw together; z~**fließen** vi sep irreg aux sein to flow together, to meet; (Farben) to run together; ~**fluß** m confluence; z~**fügen** sep 1 vt to join together; (Tech) to fit together; **etw zu etw z~fügen** to join/fit sth together to make sth; **2** vr to fit together; **sich gut z~fügen** (fig) to turn out well; z~**führen** vt sep to bring together; Familie to reunite; z~**geben** vt sep irreg (dial) Zutaten to mix together; z~**gehen** vi sep irreg aux sein **(a)** (sich vereinen) to unite; (Linien etc) to meet; **(b)** (einlaufen: Wäsche) to shrink; **(c)** (inf: sich verbinden lassen) to go together; z~**gehören*** vi sep (Menschen, Städte, Firmen etc) to belong together; (Gegenstände) to go together, to match; (als Paar) to form a pair; (Themen etc) to go together; z~**gehörig** adj Kleidungsstücke etc matching; (verwandt) related, connected; z~**gehörig sein** to match; to be related or connected; ~**gehörigkeit** f (Einheit) unity, identity; ~**gehörigkeitsgefühl** nt (in Gemeinschaft) communal spirit; (esp Pol) feeling of solidarity; (in Mannschaft) team spirit; (in Familie) sense of a common bond; z~**geraten*** vi sep irreg aux sein **(a)** mit jdm z~**geraten** to get together with sb; **(b)** (fig) siehe aneinandergeraten.

zusammengesetzt 1 ptp of **zusammensetzen.** **2** adj **aus etw** ~ **sein** to consist of sth, to be composed of sth; ~**es Wort/Verb** compound (word)/verb; ~**e Zahl** compound or complex number; ~**er Satz** complex sentence.

Zusammen-: z~**gewürfelt** adj oddly assorted, motley; Mannschaft scratch attr; **ein bunt z~gewürfelter Haufen** a motley crowd; z~**gießen** vt sep irreg to pour together; z~**haben** vt sep irreg (inf) **etw z~haben** to have got sth together; Geld auch to have raised sth; ~**halt** m, no pl (Tech) (cohesive) strength; (einer Erzählung) coherence, cohesion; (fig: in einer Gruppe) cohesion; (esp Pol) solidarity; (fig: einer Mannschaft) team spirit.

zusammenhalten sep irreg 1 vt **(a)** to hold together; (inf) Geld etc to hold on to. **seine fünf Sinne** ~ to keep one's wits about one. **(b)** (nebeneinanderhalten) to hold side by side. **2** vi to hold together; (fig: Freunde, Gruppe etc) to stick or stay together; siehe Pech.

Zusammenhang m (Beziehung) connection (von, zwischen +dat between); (Wechselbeziehung) correlation (von, zwischen +dat between); (Verflechtung) interrelation (von, zwischen +dat between); (von Ideen auch, von Geschichte) coherence; (im Text) context. **etw mit etw in** ~ **bringen** to connect sth with sth; **im or in** ~ **mit etw stehen** to be connected with sth; **etw aus dem** ~ **reißen** to take sth out of its context; **nicht im** ~ **mit etw stehen** to have no connection with sth; **ich habe seinen Namen im** ~ **mit dieser Sache gehört** I've heard his name mentioned in connection with this.

zusammenhängen sep 1 vt Kleider in Schrank etc to hang (up) together. **2** vi irreg to be joined (together); (fig) to be connected. ~**d** Rede, Erzählung coherent; **das hängt damit zusammen, daß ...** that is connected with the fact that ...

Zusammenhang(s)-: z~**los** 1 adj incoherent, disjointed; (weitschweifig auch) rambling; **2** adv incoherently; Sachen z~**los anordnen** to arrange things haphazardly; ~**losigkeit** f incoherence, disjointedness.

Zusammen-: z~**harken** vt sep to rake together; z~**hauen** vt sep irreg (inf) **(a)** (zerstören) to smash to pieces; **jdn z~hauen** to beat sb up (inf); **(b)** (fig: pfuschen) to knock together; Geschriebenes to scribble (down); z~**heften** vt sep (mit Heftklammern) to staple together; (Sew) to tack together; z~**heilen** vi sep aux sein (Wunde) to heal (up); (Knochen) to knit (together); z~**holen** vt sep Sachen to gather together; Menschen to bring together; z~**kauern** vr sep (vor Kälte) to huddle together; (vor Angst) to cower; z~**kaufen** vt sep to buy (up); z~**kehren** vt sep to sweep together; z~**ketten** vt sep to chain together; (fig) to bind together; z~**kitten** vt sep to cement together; (fig) Freundschaft etc to patch up; **etw notdürftig z~kitten** to patch sth up; ~**klang** m (Mus, fig geh) harmony, accord; z~**klappbar** adj folding; Stuhl, Tisch auch collapsible.

zusammenklappen sep 1 vt Messer, Stuhl etc to fold up; Schirm to shut. **die Hacken** ~ to click one's heels. **2** vi aux sein **(a)** (Stuhl etc) to collapse. **(b)** (fig inf) to flake out (inf); (nach vorne) to double up.

Zusammen-: z~**klauben** vt sep to gather (together), to collect; z~**klauen** vt sep sich (dat) **etw z~klauen** to collect sth (by stealing); z~**kleben** vti sep (vi: aux haben or sein) to stick together; z~**kleistern** vt sep (inf) **(a)** to paste together; **(b)** (fig) to patch up or together; z~**klingen** vi sep irreg to sound together; (fig: Farben etc) to harmonize; z~**klumpen** vir sep (vi: aux sein) to clot (together); z~**kneifen** vt sep irreg Lippen etc to press together; Augen to screw up; z~**gekniffen** Augen screwed-up; Mund pinched; z~**knoten** vt sep to knot or tie together; z~**knüllen** vt sep to screw or crumple up; z~**knüpfen** vt sep siehe z~**knoten.**

zusammenkommen vi sep irreg aux sein to meet (together), to come together; (Umstände) to combine; (fig: sich einigen) to agree, to come to an agreement; (fig: sich ansammeln) (Schulden etc) to mount up, to accumulate; (Geld bei einer Sammlung) to be collected. **er kommt viel mit Menschen zusammen** he meets a lot of people; **wir kommen zweimal jährlich zusammen** we meet or we get together twice a year; **heute kommt wieder mal alles zusammen** (inf) it's all happening at once today.

Zusammen-: z~**koppeln** vt sep Anhänger, Wagen to couple together; (Space) to dock; z~**krachen** vi sep aux sein (inf) **(a)** (einstürzen) to crash down; (fig: Börse, Wirtschaft) to crash; **(b)** (z~stoßen: Fahrzeuge) to crash (into each other); z~**krampfen** vr (Hände) to clench; (Muskel) to tense up; **da krampfte sich mein Herz z**~ my heart nearly stopped; z~**kratzen** vt sep to scrape or scratch together; (fig inf) Geld etc to scrape together; z~**kriegen** vt sep (inf) to get together; Wortlaut etc to remember; Geld, Spenden to collect; ~**kunft** f -, -**künfte** meeting; (von mehreren auch) gathering; (zwanglos) get-together; z~**läppern** vr sep (inf) to add or mount up; z~**lassen** vt sep irreg to leave together.

zusammenlaufen vi sep irreg aux sein **(a)** (an eine Stelle laufen) to gather; (Flüssigkeit) to collect. **(b)** (Flüsse etc) to flow together, to meet; (Farben) to run together; (Math) to intersect, to meet; (Straßen) to converge; (fig: Fäden etc) to meet. **(c)** (Stoff) to shrink. **(d)** (Milch) to curdle, to coagulate.

zusammenleben sep 1 vi to live together. **2** vr to learn to live with each other.

Zusammenleben nt living together no art; (von Ländern etc) co-existence. **das** ~ **der Menschen** the social life of man; **mein** ~ **mit ihm war ...** living with him was ...; **das menschliche** ~ social existence; **eheliches** ~ married life; **außereheliches** ~ cohabitation.

zusammenlegen sep 1 vt **(a)** (falten) to fold (up). **(b)** (stapeln) to pile or heap together. **(c)** (vereinigen) to combine, to merge; Aktien to amalgamate, to consolidate; Grundstücke to join; Termine, Veranstaltungen to hold together or at the same time; (zentralisieren) to centralize. **sie legten ihr Geld zusammen** they pooled their money, they clubbed together. **2** vi (Geld gemeinsam aufbringen) to club together, to pool one's money. **für ein Geschenk** ~ to club together for a present.

Zusammen-: ~**legung** f (Vereinigung) amalgamation, merging; (von Aktien) amalgamation, consolidation; (von Grundstücken) joining; (Zentralisierung) centralization; z~**leihen** vt sep irreg sich (dat) **etw z~leihen** to borrow sth; z~**leimen** vt sep to glue together; z~**lesen** vt sep irreg to gather (together); z~**löten** vt sep to solder together; z~**lügen** vr sep irreg (inf) to make up, to concoct; **was der (sich) wieder z~lügt!** the stories he makes up!; z~**nageln** vt sep to nail together;

z~**nähen** vt sep to sew or stitch together.

zus**ammennehmen** sep 1 vt to gather up or together; Mut to summon up, to muster up; Gedanken to collect. alles zusammengenommen all together, all in all; wenn wir alle Ereignisse ~ if we consider everything that happened.

  2 vr (sich zusammenreißen) to pull oneself together, to get a grip on oneself; (sich beherrschen) to control oneself, to take a grip on oneself.

Zusammen-: z~**packen** sep 1 vt to pack up together; pack (deine Sachen) z~! get packed!; 2 vi siehe einpacken 2; z~**passen** vi sep (Menschen) to suit each other, to be suited to each other; (Farben, Stile) to go together; gut/überhaupt nicht z~**passen** to go well together/not to go together at all; z~**pferchen** vt sep to herd together; (fig) to pack together; z~**phantasieren*** vt sep (sich dat) etw z~**phantasieren** to dream sth up; (inf: lügen) to make sth up; ~**prall** m collision; (fig) clash; z~**prallen** vi sep aux sein to collide; (fig) to clash; z~**pressen** vt sep to press or squeeze together; (verdichten) to compress; z~**raffen** sep 1 vt (a) to bundle together; Röcke to gather up; (b) (fig) Mut to summon up, to muster (up); (c) (fig pej: anhäufen) to amass, to pile up; 2 vr to pull oneself together; z~**rasseln** vi sep aux sein (inf) to collide; (fig) to have a row or set-to (inf); z~**raufen** vr sep to get it all together (sl), to achieve a viable working relationship; z~**rechnen** vt sep to add or total up; alles z~**gerechnet** all together; (fig) all in all.

zus**ammenreimen** sep 1 vt (inf) sich (dat) den Rest ~ to put two and two together; das kann ich mir nicht ~ I can't make head or tail of this, I can't figure it out at all; das kann ich mir jetzt ~, warum ... I can see now why ... 2 vr to make sense. wie reimt sich das zusammen? it doesn't make sense.

Zusammen-: z~**reißen** sep irreg 1 vr to pull oneself together; 2 vt die Hacken z~**reißen** to click one's heels; z~**rollen** sep 1 vt to roll up; 2 vr to curl up; (Igel) to roll or curl (itself) up (into a ball); (Schlange) to coil up; z~**rotten** vr sep (pej Jugendliche) to gang up (gegen against); (in aufrührerischer Absicht) to form a mob; ~**rottung** f (a) siehe vr ganging up; banding together; (in aufrührerischer Absicht) forming of a mob; (b) (Gruppe) (esp von Jugendlichen) gang; (in aufrührerischer Absicht) mob; (Jur) riotous assembly; z~**rücken** sep 1 vt Möbel etc to move closer together; (schreiben) Wörter etc to close up; 2 vi aux sein to move up closer, to move closer together; z~**rufen** vt sep irreg to call together; z~**rutschen** vi sep aux sein siehe z~**rücken** 2; z~**sacken** vi sep aux sein siehe z~**sinken**; in sich z~**sacken** (lit) to collapse; (fig) (bei Nachricht etc) to seem to crumble. (Schwung verlieren) to have lost all interest; z~**scharen** vr sep to gather; (Menschen auch) to congregate; ~**schau** f overall view; erst in der ~**schau** ... only when you view everything as a whole ...; z~**scheißen** vt sep irreg (sl) jdn z~**scheißen** to give sb a bollocking (sl); z~**schießen** sep irreg 1 vt to shoot up, to riddle with bullets, to shoot to pieces; (mit Artillerie) to pound to pieces; 2 vi aux sein (Farben) to come together; (Kristalle) to shoot.

zus**ammenschlagen** sep irreg 1 vt (a) (aneinanderschlagen) to knock or bang or strike together; Becken to clash; Hacken to click; Hände to clap. (b) (falten) to fold up. (c) (verprügeln) to beat up; (zerschlagen) Einrichtung to smash up, to wreck. 2 vi aux sein über jdm/etw ~ (Wellen etc) to close over sb/sth; (stärker) to engulf sb/sth; (fig: Unheil etc) to descend upon sb/sth, to engulf sb/sth.

Zusammen-: z~**schließen** vr sep irreg to join together, to combine; (Comm) to amalgamate, to merge; sich gegen jdn z~**schließen** to band together against sb; ~**schluß** m siehe vr joining together, combining; amalgamation, merger; (von politischen Gruppen) amalgamation; z~**schmelzen** sep irreg 1 vt (verschmelzen) to fuse; 2 vi aux sein (a) (verschmelzen) to fuse, to melt together; (b) (zerschmelzen) to melt (away); (Widerstand) to melt away; (Anzahl, Vermögen) to dwindle; z~**schnüren** vt sep to tie up; dieser traurige Anblick schnürte mir das Herz z~ this pitiful sight made my heart bleed; z~**schrecken** vi sep irreg aux sein to start.

zus**ammenschreiben** vt sep irreg (a) Wörter (orthographisch) to write together; (im Schriftbild) to join up. (b) (pej: verfassen) to scribble down. was für ein Mist zusammenschreibt what a load of rubbish he writes. (c) (inf: durch Schreiben verdienen) sich (dat) ein Vermögen ~ to make a fortune with one's writing.

Zusammen-: z~**schrumpfen** vi sep aux sein to shrivel up; (fig) to dwindle (auf + acc tb); z~**schustern** vt sep to throw together; z~**schweißen** vt sep (lit, fig) to weld together; ~**sein** nt being together no art; (von Gruppe) get-together.

zus**ammensetzen** sep 1 vt (a) Schüler etc to put or seat together.

  2 vr (a) to sit together; (um etwas zu besprechen, zu trinken etc) to get together. sich mit jdm (am Tisch) ~ to join sb (at their table); sich gemütlich ~ to have a cosy get-together; sich auf ein Glas Wein ~ to get together over a glass of wine.

  (b) sich ~ aus to consist of, to be composed or made up of.

Zusammen-: ~**setzspiel** nt puzzle; (Puzzle) jigsaw (puzzle); ~**setzung** f (a) putting together; (von Gerät auch) assembly; (Struktur) composition, make-up; (Mischung) mixture, combination (aus of); (Gram) compound; das Team in dieser ~**setzung** the team, in this line-up; z~**sinken** vi sep irreg aux sein (in sich) z~**sinken** to slump; (Gebäude) to cave in; z~**gesunken** (vor Kummer etc) bowed; z~**sparen** vt sep to save up; ~**spiel** nt (Mus) ensemble playing; (Theat) ensemble acting; (Sport) teamwork; (fig auch) co-operation, teamwork; (von Kräften etc) interaction; z~**stauchen** vt sep (inf) to give a dressing-down (inf); z~**stecken** sep 1 vt Einzelteile to fit together; (mit Nadeln etc) to pin together; die Köpfe

z~**stecken** (inf) to put their/our etc heads together; (flüstern) to whisper to each other; 2 vi (inf) to be together; **immer** z~**stecken** to be inseparable, to be as thick as thieves (pej inf); z~**stehen** vi sep irreg to stand together or side by side; (Gegenstände) to be together or side by side; (fig) to stand by each other.

zus**ammenstellen** vt sep to put together; (nach einem Muster, System) to arrange; Bericht, Programm auch, (sammeln) Daten to compile; Liste, Fahrplan to draw up; Rede to draft; Sammlung auch, Gruppe to assemble; (Sport) Mannschaft to pick. etw nach Gruppen etc z~ to arrange sth in groups etc.

Zusammenstellung f (a) siehe vt putting together; arranging; compiling; drawing up; drafting; assembling; picking. (b) (nach Muster, System) arrangement; (von Daten, Programm) compilation; (Liste) list; (Zusammensetzung) composition; (Übersicht) survey; (Gruppierung) assembly, group; (von Farben) combination.

Zusammen-: z~**stimmen** vi sep (farblich) to match; (musikalisch) to harmonize; (übereinstimmen) to agree, to tally (mit with); z~**stoppeln** vt sep (inf) to throw together; sich (dat) eine Rede etc z~**stoppeln** to throw a speech etc together; ~**stoß** m collision, crash; (Mil, fig: Streit) clash.

zus**ammenstoßen** sep irreg 1 vi aux sein (z~prallen) to collide; (Mil, fig: sich streiten) to clash; (sich treffen) to meet; (gemeinsame Grenze haben) to adjoin. mit jdm ~ to collide with sb, to bump into sb; (fig) to clash with sb; sie stießen mit den Köpfen zusammen they banged or bumped their heads together; mit der Polizei ~ to clash with the police.

  2 vt to knock together. er stieß sie mit den Köpfen zusammen he banged or knocked their heads together.

Zusammen-: z~**streichen** vt sep irreg to cut (down) (auf + acc to); z~**strömen** vi sep aux sein (Flüsse) to flow into one another, to flow together; (Menschen) to flock or swarm together; z~**stückeln** vt sep to patch together; z~**stürzen** vi sep aux sein (a) (einstürzen) to collapse, to tumble down; (b) (z~laufen) to rush to gather round; z~**suchen** vt sep to collect; sich (dat) etw z~**suchen** to find sth; z~**tragen** vt sep irreg (lit, fig) to collect; z~**treffen** vi sep irreg aux sein (Menschen) to meet; (Ereignisse) to coincide; mit jdm z~**treffen** to meet sb; ~**treffen** nt meeting; (von zufälliger) encounter; (zeitlich) coincidence; z~**treten** sep irreg 1 vt (zertrampeln) to trample or crush underfoot; 2 vi aux sein (Verein etc) to meet; (Parlament auch) to assemble; (Gericht) to sit; ~**tritt** m siehe vi meeting; assembly; session; z~**trommeln** vt sep (inf) to round up (inf); z~**tun** sep irreg 1 vt (inf) to put together; (vermischen) to mix; 2 vr to get together; z~**wachsen** vi sep irreg aux sein to grow together; (zuheilen: Wunde) to heal (up), to close; (Knochen) to knit; (fig) to grow close; z~**gewachsen sein** (Knochen) to be joined or fused; z~**werfen** vt sep irreg (a) to throw together; (fig) (durcheinanderbringen) to mix or jumble up; (in einen Topf werfen) to lump together; (b) (umwerfen) to throw down; z~**wirken** vi sep to combine, to act in combination; z~**zählen** vt sep to add up; alles z~**gezählt macht es 50 Mark** that makes 50 marks altogether or all told or in all.

zus**ammenziehen** sep irreg 1 vt (a) to draw or pull together; (verengen) to narrow; Augenbrauen to knit. ein Loch in einem Strumpf ~ to mend a hole in a stocking (by pulling the sides together and sewing it up); der saure Geschmack zog ihm den Mund zusammen he screwed up his mouth at the bitter taste; das zieht einem das Herz zusammen it really pulls at the heartstrings; da zieht es einem ja alles zusammen! (inf) that really makes you want to curl up! (inf); ~**de Mittel** (Med) astringents.

  (b) (fig) Truppen, Polizei to assemble.

  (c) (kürzen) Wörter etc to contract, to shorten; (Math) Zahlen to add together; mathematischen Ausdruck to reduce.

  2 vr (esp Biol, Sci) to contract; (enger werden) to narrow; (Wunde) to close (up); (Gewitter, Unheil) to be brewing.

  3 vi aux sein to move in together. mit jdm ~ to move in (together) with sb.

zus**ammenzucken** vi sep aux sein to start.

Zusatz m addition; (Bemerkung) additional remark; (zu Gesetz, Vertrag etc) rider; (zu Testament) codicil; (Gram) appositive expression; (Verb~) separable element; (Beimischung auch) admixture, additive. durch/nach ~ von etw by/after adding sth, with or by/after the addition of sth.

Zusatz- in cpds additional, supplementary; ~**abkommen** nt supplementary agreement; ~**antrag** m (Parl etc) amendment; ~**artikel** m additional or supplementary article; ~**bestimmung** f supplementary provision; ~**gerät** nt attachment.

zus**ätzlich** 1 adj additional; (weiter auch) added attr, further attr; (ergänzend auch) supplementary. 2 adv in addition.

Zusatz-: ~**mittel** nt, ~**stoff** m additive; ~**versicherung** f additional or supplementary insurance; ~**zahl** f additional number, seventh number in Lotto.

zus**chanden** adv (geh) ~ **machen** (fig) to ruin, to wreck; ein Auto ~ **fahren** to wreck a car; ein Pferd ~ **reiten** to ruin a horse; ~ **werden** (fig) to be wrecked or ruined.

zus**chanzen** vt sep (inf) jdm etw ~ to make sure sb gets sth.

zus**charren** vt sep to cover over or up.

zus**chauen** vi sep siehe zusehen.

Zuschauer m -s, - spectator (auch Sport); (TV) viewer; (Theat) member of the audience; (Beistehender) onlooker; die ~ pl the spectators pl; (esp Ftbl auch) the crowd sing; (TV) the (television) audience sing, the viewers; (Theat) the audience sing; einer der ~ (Theat) one of the audience, a member of the audience; wieviele ~ waren da? (Sport) how many spectators were there?; (esp Ftbl auch) how large was the crowd?

Zuschauer-: ~**befragung** f (TV) (television) audience survey; ~**kulisse** f (Sport) crowd; ~**rang** m (Sport) stand; ~**raum** m auditorium; ~**tribüne** f (esp Sport) stand; ~**umfrage** f (TV) *siehe* ~**befragung**; ~**zahl** *f* attendance figure; (*Sport auch*) gate.

zuschaufeln *vt sep* to fill up.

zuschicken *vt sep* jdm etw ~ to send sth to sb *or* sb sth; (*mit der Post auch*) to mail sth to sb; **sich** (*dat*) **etw** ~ **lassen** to send for sth; **etw zugeschickt bekommen** to receive sth (by post), to get sth sent to one.

zuschieben *vt sep irreg* (**a**) **jdm etw** ~ to push sth over to sb; (*heimlich*) to slip sb sth; (*fig: zuschanzen*) to make sure sb gets sth; **jdm die Verantwortung/Schuld** ~ to put the responsibility/blame on sb; *siehe* **schwarz**. (**b**) (*schließen*) *Tür, Fenster* to slide shut; *Schublade* to push shut.

zuschießen *sep irreg* 1 *vt* (**a**) **jdm den Ball** ~ to kick the ball (over) to sb; **jdm wütende Blicke** ~ to dart angry glances at sb, to look daggers at sb.
(**b**) *Geld etc* to contribute. **Geld für etw** ~ to put money towards sth; **jdm 100 Mark** ~ to give sb 100 marks towards it/sth.
2 *vi aux sein* (*inf*) **auf jdn** ~ *or* **zugeschossen kommen** to rush *or* shoot up to sb.

Zuschlag *m* (**a**) (*Erhöhung*) extra charge, surcharge (*esp Comm, Econ*); (*Rail*) supplement, supplementary charge. **für diese Züge muß man** ~ **bezahlen** you have to pay a supplement *or* a supplementary charge on these trains.
(**b**) (*Tech*) addition.
(**c**) (*bei Versteigerung*) acceptance of a bid; (*Auftragserteilung*) acceptance of a/the tender. **mit dem** ~ **des Versteigerers** ... when the auctioneer concluded the bidding; **jdm den** ~ **erteilen** (*form*) *or* **geben** to knock down the lot *or* item to sb; (*nach Ausschreibung*) to award the contract to sb; **er erhielt den** ~ the lot went to him; (*nach Ausschreibung*) he obtained *or* was awarded the contract.

zuschlagen *sep irreg* 1 *vt* (**a**) *Tür, Fenster* to slam (shut), to bang shut. **die Tür hinter sich** (*dat*) ~ to slam the door behind one.
(**b**) (*Sport: zuspielen*) **jdm den Ball** ~ to hit the ball to sb; (*Ftbl inf*) to kick the ball to sb.
(**c**) (*rare: zufügen*) to add (on) (*dat, zu* to).
(**d**) (*bei Versteigerung*) **jdm etw** ~ to knock sth down to sb; **einer Firma einen Vertrag** ~ to award a contract to a firm.
(**e**) *Gebiet* to annex (*dat* to).
2 *vi* (**a**) (*kräftig schlagen*) to strike (*auch fig*); (*losschlagen*) to hit out. **schlag zu!** hit me/him/it etc!; **das Schicksal hat entsetzlich zugeschlagen** (*geh*) fate has struck a terrible blow.
(**b**) *Sport* (*Tür*) to slam (shut), to bang shut.

Zuschlag(s)- (*Rail*: z~**frei** *adj* *Zug* not subject to a supplement; ~**karte** *f* (*Rail*) supplementary ticket (*for trains on which a supplement is payable*); z~**pflichtig** *adj* *Zug* subject to a supplement.

zuschließen *sep irreg* 1 *vt* to lock; *Laden* to lock up. 2 *vi* to lock up.

zuschmeißen *vt sep irreg* (*inf*) (**a**) *Tür etc* to slam (shut), to bang shut. (**b**) **jdm etw** ~ (*inf*) to bung *or* chuck sth over to sb (*inf*).

zuschmieren *vt sep* (*inf*) to smear over; *Löcher* to fill in.

zuschnallen *vt sep* to fasten, to buckle; *Koffer* to strap up.

zuschnappen *vi sep* (**a**) (*zubeißen*) *der Hund* **schnappte zu** the dog snapped at me/him etc. (**b**) *aux sein* (*Schloß*) to snap *or* click shut.

zuschneiden *vt sep irreg* to cut to size; (*Sew*) to cut out. **auf etw** (*acc*) **zugeschnitten sein** (*fig*) to be geared to sth; **auf jdn/etw genau zugeschnitten sein** (*lit, fig*) to be tailor-made for sb/sth.

Zuschneider *m* cutter.

zuschneien *vi sep aux sein* to snow in *or* up.

Zuschnitt *m* (**a**) *no pl* (*Zuschneiden*) cutting. (**b**) (*Form*) cut; (*fig*) calibre.

zuschnüren *vt sep* to tie up; *Schuhe, Mieder* to lace up. **die Angst/innere Bewegung etc schnürte ihm die Kehle zu** he was choked with fear/emotion etc; **der Hals** *or* **die Kehle** (*geh*) **war ihm wie zugeschnürt** (*fig*) he felt choked (with emotion/grief etc); **jdm das Herz** ~ to make sb's heart bleed.

zuschrauben *vt sep* *Hahn etc* to screw shut; *Deckel etc* to screw on. **eine Flasche** ~ to screw on the top of a bottle.

zuschreiben *vt sep irreg* (**a**) (*inf: hin*~) to add.
(**b**) (*übertragen*) to transfer, to sign over (*dat* to).
(**c**) (*fig*) to ascribe, to attribute (*dat* to). **das hast du dir selbst zuzuschreiben** you've only got yourself to blame; **das ist nur seiner Dummheit/ihrem Geiz zuzuschreiben** that can only be put down to his stupidity/her meanness.

zuschreiten *vi sep irreg aux sein* (*geh*) **tüchtig** ~ to walk briskly; **auf jdn/etw** ~ to stride *or* walk towards *or* (*bis zu*) up to sb/sth.

Zuschrift *f* letter; (*auf Anzeige*) reply; (*amtlich auch*) communication.

zuschulden *adv*: **sich** (*dat*) **etwas** ~ **kommen lassen** to do something wrong; **solange man sich nichts** ~ **kommen läßt** as long as you don't do anything wrong.

Zuschuß *m* subsidy, grant; (*nicht amtlich*) something towards it, contribution; (*esp regelmäßig von Eltern*) allowance. **einen** ~ **zu einer Sache gewähren** *or* **geben** to give a subsidy for sth; **to make a contribution towards sth; mit einem kleinen** ~ **von meinen Eltern kann ich** ... if my parents give me something towards it I can ...

Zuschuß-: ~**betrieb** *m* loss-making concern; ~**geschäft** *nt* loss-making deal; (*inf:* ~**unternehmen**) loss-making business.

zuschustern *vt sep* (*inf*) **jdm etw** ~ to make sure sb gets sth.

zuschütten *vt sep* to fill in *or* up; (*hin*~) to add.

zusehen *vi sep irreg* (**a**) to watch; (*unbeteiligter Zuschauer sein*) to look on; (*etw dulden*) to sit back *or* stand by (and watch). **jdm/einer Sache** ~ to watch sb/sth; **bei etw** ~ to watch sth; (*etw dulden*) to sit back *or* stand by and watch sth; **jdn bei**

der Arbeit ~ to watch sb working; **er sah zu, wie ich das machte** he watched me doing it; **ich kann doch nicht** ~, **wie er** ... (*dulden*) I can't sit back *or* stand by and watch him ...; **ich habe nur zugesehen** I was only a spectator *or* an onlooker; **durch bloßes Z**~ just by watching; **bei näherem Z**~ when you watch/I watched *etc* more closely.
(**b**) (*dafür sorgen*) ~, **daß** ... to see to it that ..., to make sure (that) ...; **sieh mal zu!** (*inf*) see what you can do.

zusehends *adv* visibly; (*merklich auch*) noticeably, appreciably; (*rasch*) rapidly. ~ **im Verfall begriffen sein** to be in rapid decline.

Zuseher(in *f*) *m* -s, - (*Aus TV*) viewer.

zusein *vi sep irreg aux sein* (*Zusammenschreibung nur bei infin und ptp*) (*inf*) to be shut *or* closed; (*sl: betrunken sein*) to have had a skinful (*inf*).

zusenden *vt sep irreg* to send, to forward; *Geld auch* to remit (*form*).

zusetzen *sep* 1 *vt* (*hinzufügen*) to add; (*inf: verlieren*) *Geld* to shell out (*inf*), to pay out. **er setzt immer (Geld) zu** (*inf*) he's always having to shell out (*inf*) *or* pay out; **er hat nichts mehr zuzusetzen** (*inf*) he has nothing in reserve.
2 *vi* **jdm** ~ (*unter Druck setzen*) to lean on sb (*inf*); *dem Gegner, Feind* to harass sb, to press sb hard; (*drängen*) to badger *or* pester sb; (*schwer treffen*) to hit sb hard, to affect sb (badly); (*Kälte, Krankheit etc*) to take a lot out of sb.

zusichern *vt sep* **jdm etw** ~ to assure sb of sth, to promise sb sth; **mir wurde zugesichert, daß** ... I was assured *or* promised that ...

Zusicherung *f* assurance, promise.

Zuspätkommende(r) *mf dec as adj* latecomer.

zusperren *vt sep* (*S Ger, Aus, Sw*) (*zuschließen*) to lock; *Haus, Laden* to lock up; (*verriegeln*) to bolt.

Zuspiel *nt* (*Sport*) passing.

zuspielen *vt sep Ball* to pass (*dat* to). **jdm etw** ~ (*fig*) to pass sth on to sb; (*der Presse*) to leak sth to sb.

zuspitzen *sep* 1 *vt Stock etc* to sharpen. **zugespitzt** sharpened; *Turm, Schuhe etc* pointed; (*fig*) exaggerated. 2 *vr* to be pointed; (*fig: Lage, Konflikt*) to intensify. **die Lage spitzt sich immer mehr zu** the situation is worsening.

Zuspitzung *f* (*von Stock etc*) sharpening; (*von Turm, Schuhen etc*) pointing; (*fig: von Lage, Konflikt*) worsening.

zusprechen *sep irreg* 1 *vt* (*Jur*), *Preis, Gewinn etc* to award; *Kind* to award *or* grant custody of. **das Kind wurde dem Vater zugesprochen** the father was granted custody (of the child); **jdm Mut/Trost** ~ (*fig*) to encourage/comfort sb.
2 *vi* (**a**) **jdm** (**gut/besänftigend**) ~ to talk *or* speak (nicely/gently) to sb.
(**b**) **dem Essen/Wein etc tüchtig** *or* **kräftig** ~ to tuck into the food/wine etc.

zuspringen *vi sep irreg aux sein* (*Schloß, Tür*) to spring *or* snap shut. (**b**) **auf jdn** ~ *or* **zugesprungen kommen** to spring *or* leap towards sb; (*Ball*) to bounce towards sb.

Zuspruch *m, no pl* (**a**) (*Worte*) words *pl*; (*Aufmunterung*) (words *pl* of) encouragement; (*Rat*) advice; (*tröstlich*) (words *pl* of) comfort.
(**b**) (*Anklang*) (**großen**) ~ **finden** *or* **haben, sich großen** ~**s erfreuen** to be (very) popular; (*Stück, Film*) to meet with general acclaim; (*Anwalt, Arzt*) to be (very) much in demand.

Zustand *m* state; (*von Haus, Ware, Auto, Med*) condition; (*Lage*) state of affairs, situation. **Zustände** *pl* conditions; (*von Mensch*) fits; **in gutem/schlechtem** ~ in good/poor condition; (*Mensch auch*) in good/bad shape; (*Haus*) in good/bad repair; **in ungepflegtem/baufälligem** ~ in a state of neglect/disrepair; **in angetrunkenem** ~ under the influence of alcohol; **Wasser in flüssigem** ~ water in its fluid state; **eine Frau in ihrem** ~ ... a woman in her condition ...; **er war wirklich in einem üblen** ~ he really was in a bad way; (*seelisch*) he really was in a state; **Zustände bekommen** *or* **kriegen** (*inf*) to have a fit (*inf*), to hit the roof (*inf*); **das ist doch kein** ~ that's not right; **das sind ja schöne** *or* **nette Zustände!** (*iro*) that's a fine state of affairs! (*iro*); **das sind ja Zustände!** (*inf*) it's terrible; **das sind doch keine Zustände!** (*inf*) it's just dreadful *or* terrible!

zustande *adv* (**a**) ~ **bringen** to manage; *Arbeit* to get done; *Ereignis, Frieden etc* to bring about, to achieve; **es** ~ **bringen, daß jd etw tut** to (manage to) get sb to do sth; **ein Gespräch** ~ **bringen** (*am Fernsprecher*) to (manage to) put a call through (*nach* to). (**b**) ~ **kommen** (*erreicht werden*) to be achieved; (*geschehen*) to come about; (*stattfinden*) to take place; (*Plan etc*) to materialize; (*Gewagtes, Schwieriges*) to come off.

Zustandekommen *nt siehe* **zustande(b)**, *gebrauche Verbalkonstruktion*.

zuständig *adj* (*verantwortlich*) responsible; (*entsprechend*) *Amt etc* appropriate, relevant; (*Kompetenz habend*) competent (*form, Jur*). **dafür ist er** ~ that's his responsibility; **der dafür** ~**e Beamte** the official responsible for *or* in charge of such matters; ~ **sein** (*Jur*) to have jurisdiction; **in erster Instanz** ~ **sein** (*Jur*) to have original jurisdiction; **nach einer Stadt** ~ **sein** (*Aus form*) (*wohnhaft sein*) to be domiciled in a town; (*Wohnrecht haben*) to have the right of domicile in a town.

Zuständigkeit *f* (**a**) (*Kompetenz*) competence; (*Jur auch*) jurisdiction; (*Verantwortlichkeit*) responsibility. (**b**) *siehe* **Zuständigkeitsbereich**.

Zuständigkeits-: ~**bereich** *m* area of responsibility; (*Jur*) jurisdiction, competence; **das fällt/fällt nicht in unseren** ~**bereich** that is/isn't our responsibility; (*Jur*) that is within/outside our jurisdiction (*Jur*); z~**halber** *adv* (*Admin, form*) for reasons of competence.

zustatten *adv* **jdm** ~ **kommen** (*geh*) to come in useful for sb.

zustecken *vt sep* (**a**) *Kleid etc* to pin up *or* together. (**b**) **jdm etw** ~ to slip sb sth.

zustehen vi sep irreg etw steht jdm zu sb is entitled to sth; darüber steht mir kein Urteil zu it's not for me or up to me to judge that; es steht ihr nicht zu, das zu tun it's not for her or up to her to do that.

zusteigen vi sep irreg aux sein to get on, to board; to join or board the train/flight/ship. noch jemand zugestiegen? (in Bus) any more fares, please?; (in Zug) tickets please!

Zustell-: ~bereich m postal district; ~dienst m delivery service.

zustellen vt sep (a) Brief to deliver; (Jur) to serve (jdm etw sb with sth). (b) Tür etc to block.

Zusteller(in f) m -s, - deliverer; (Jur) server; (Briefträger) postman; (Zustellfirma) delivery agent.

Zustellgebühr f delivery charge.

Zustellung f delivery; (Jur) service (of a writ).

Zustellungs|urkunde f (Jur) writ of summons.

zusteuern sep 1 vi aux sein auf etw (acc) ~, einer Sache (dat) ~ (geh) (lit, fig) to head for sth; (beim Gespräch) to steer towards sth. 2 vt (beitragen) to contribute (zu to).

zustimmen vi sep (einer Sache dat) ~ to agree (to sth); (einwilligen) to consent (to sth); (billigen) to approve (of sth); jdm (in einem Punkt) ~ to agree with sb (on a point); einer Politik ~ to endorse a policy; dem kann man nur ~ I/we etc quite agree with you/him etc; er nickte ~d he nodded in agreement; eine ~de Antwort an affirmative answer.

Zustimmung f (Einverständnis) agreement, assent; (Einwilligung) consent; (Beifall) approval. seine ~ geben/verweigern or versagen (geh) to give/refuse one's consent or assent; allgemeine ~ finden to meet with general approval; das fand meine ~ I agreed with it completely.

zustopfen vt sep to stop up, to plug; (mit Faden) to darn.

zustöpseln vt sep to plug (up); Flasche to stopper; (mit Korken) to cork.

zustoßen sep irreg 1 vt Tür etc to push shut.
2 vi (a) to plunge a/the knife/sword etc in; (Stier, Schlange) to strike. stoß zu! go on, stab him/her etc!; der Mörder hatte (mit dem Messer) dreimal zugestoßen the murderer had stabbed him/her etc three times.
(b) (passieren) aux sein jdm ~ to happen to sb; wenn mir einmal etwas zustößt ... (euph) if anything should happen to me ...; ihm muß etwas zugestoßen sein he must have had an accident, something must have happened to him.

zustreben vi sep aux sein ~ auf (+acc) to make or head for; (fig) to strive for.

Zustrom m, no pl (fig: Menschenmenge) (hineinströmend) influx; (herbeiströmend) stream of visitors etc); (Andrang) crowd, throng; (Met) inflow. großen ~ haben to be very popular, to have crowds of people coming to it/them etc.

zuströmen vi sep aux sein +dat (Fluß) to flow toward(s); (fig) (Menschen) to stream toward(s); (Aufträge etc) to pour in to. die Glückwünsche strömten uns förmlich zu the good wishes literally poured in, we were inundated with good wishes.

zustürzen vi sep aux sein auf jdn/etw ~ or zugestürzt kommen to rush up to sb/sth.

zutage adj etw ~ fördern to unearth sth (auch hum); (aus Wasser) to bring sth up; etw ~ bringen (fig) to bring sth to light, to reveal sth; (offen) ~ liegen to be clear or evident; ~ kommen or treten (lit, fig) to come to light, to be revealed.

Zutaten pl (Cook) ingredients pl; (fig) accessories pl, extras pl.

zuteil adv (geh) jdm wird etw ~ sb is granted sth, sth is granted to sb; mir wurde die Ehre ~, zu ... I was given or had the honour of ...; jdm etw/große Ehren ~ werden lassen to give sb sth/bestow great honours upon sb; da ward ihm großes Glück ~ (old) he was favoured with great fortune.

zuteilen vt sep (jdm to sb) (als Anteil) Wohnung, Aktien to allocate; Rolle, Aufgabe auch to allot; Arbeitskraft to assign. etw zugeteilt bekommen to be allocated sth; Aufgabe etc auch to be assigned sth; Lebensmittel to be apportioned sth.

Zuteilung f siehe vt allocation; allotment; assignment; apportionment. Fleisch gab es nur auf ~ meat was only available on rations.

zutiefst adv deeply. er war ~ betrübt he was greatly saddened.

zutragen sep irreg 1 vt to carry (jdm to sb); (fig: weitersagen) to report (jdm to sb). 2 vr (liter) to take place.

Zuträger m informer.

zuträglich adj good (dat for), beneficial (dat to); (förderlich auch) conducive (dat to). ein der Gesundheit ~es Klima a salubrious climate, a climate conducive to good health.

Zuträglichkeit f (geh) beneficial effect; (von Klima auch) salubrity (liter, form).

zutrauen vt sep jdm etw ~ (Aufgabe, Tat) to believe or think sb (is) capable of (doing) sth; sich (dat) ~, etw zu tun to think one can do sth or is capable of doing sth; seiner Gesundheit (dat) zuviel ~ to overtax one's health; sich (dat) zuviel ~ to overrate one's own abilities; (sich übernehmen) to take on too much; sich (dat) nichts ~ to have no confidence in oneself; der traut sich was zu! (inf) he's pretty confident, isn't he?; den Mut/die Intelligenz (dazu) traue ich ihr nicht zu I don't credit her with or I don't believe she has the courage/intelligence to do it; das hätte ich ihm nie zugetraut! I would never have thought him capable of it!; (bewundernd auch) I never thought he had it in him!; jdm viel/wenig ~ to think/not to think a lot of sb, to have/not to have a high opinion of sb; ich traue ihnen viel or einiges/alles zu (Negatives) I wouldn't put much/anything past them; das ist ihm zuzutrauen! (iro) I can well believe it (of him)!; (esp als Antwort auf Frage) I wouldn't put it past him!

Zutrauen nt -s, no pl confidence (zu in). zu jdm ~ fassen to begin to trust sb.

zutraulich adj Kind trusting; Tier friendly.

Zutraulichkeit f siehe adj trusting nature; friendliness.

zutreffen vi sep irreg (gelten) to apply (auf +acc, für to);

(richtig sein) to be accurate or correct; (wahr sein) to be true, to be the case. es trifft nicht immer zu, daß ... it doesn't always follow that ...; seine Beschreibung traf überhaupt nicht zu his description was completely inaccurate; das trifft zu that is so.

zutreffend adj (richtig) accurate; (auf etw ~) applicable. Z~es bitte unterstreichen underline where applicable or appropriate.

zutreffendenfalls adv (form) if applicable or appropriate.

zutrinken vi sep irreg jdm ~ to drink to sb; (mit Trinkspruch) to toast sb.

Zutritt m, no pl (Einlaß) admission, admittance, entry; (Zugang) access. kein ~, ~ verboten no admittance or entry; freien ~ zu einer Veranstaltung haben to be admitted to an event free of charge; ~ bekommen or erhalten, sich ~ verschaffen to gain admission or admittance (zu to); jdm ~ gewähren (geh) to admit sb; jdm den ~ verwehren or verweigern to refuse sb admission or admittance.

zutun vt sep irreg (a) ich habe die ganze Nacht kein Auge zugetan I didn't sleep a wink all night; die Augen für immer ~ (euph) to pass away. (b) (inf: hinzufügen) to add (dat to).

Zutun nt, no pl assistance, help. es geschah ohne mein ~ I did not have a hand in the matter.

zu|ungunsten prep (vor n) +gen, (nach n) +dat to the disadvantage of.

zu|unterst adv right at the bottom.

zuverlässig adj reliable; (verläßlich) Mensch auch dependable; (vertrauenswürdig auch) trustworthy. aus ~er Quelle from a reliable source; etw ~ wissen to know sth for sure or for certain.

Zuverlässigkeit f siehe adj reliability; dependability; trustworthiness.

Zuversicht f, no pl confidence; (religiös) faith, trust. die feste ~ haben, daß ... to be quite confident that ..., to have every confidence that ...; in der festen ~, daß ... confident that ...

zuversichtlich adj confident.

Zuversichtlichkeit f confidence.

zuviel adj, adv too much; (inf: zu viele) too many. viel ~ much or far too much; besser ~ als zuwenig better too much than too little; wenn's dir ~ wird, sag Bescheid say if it gets too much for you; ihm ist alles ~ (inf) it's all too much for him; da krieg' ich ~ (inf) I blow my top (inf); einer/zwei etc ~ one/two etc too many; einen/ein paar ~ trinken (inf) to drink or have a (inf) one/a few too many; was ~ ist, ist ~ that's just too much, there's a limit to everything; ein Z~ an etw (dat) an excess of sth.

zuvor adv before; (zuerst) beforehand. im Jahr ~ the year before, in the previous year; am Tage ~ the day before, the previous day.

zuvorderst adv right at the front.

zuvörderst adv (old) first and foremost.

zuvorkommen vi sep irreg aux sein +dat to anticipate; (verhindern) einer Gefahr, unangenehmen Fragen etc to forestall. jemand ist uns zuvorgekommen somebody beat us to it.

zuvorkommend adj courteous; (gefällig) obliging; (hilfsbereit) helpful.

Zuvorkommenheit f, no pl siehe adj courtesy, courteousness; obligingness; helpfulness.

Zuwachs ['tsu:vaks] m -es, Zuwächse (a) no pl (Wachstum) growth (an +dat of). (b) (Höhe, Menge des Wachstums) increase (an +dat in). ~ bekommen (inf: ein Baby) to have an addition to the family; ein Kleid auf ~ kaufen (inf) to buy a dress big enough to last.

zuwachsen ['tsu:vaksn] vi sep irreg aux sein (a) (Öffnung, Loch) to grow over; (Garten etc, hum Gesicht) to become overgrown; (Aussicht) to become blocked (by trees etc). (b) (Wunde) to heal (over); (esp Econ, Gewinn etc) to accrue (jdm to sb). ihm wächst alles zu (fig) everything comes easy to him.

Zuwachs- ['tsu:vaks-]: ~quote, ~rate f rate of increase.

Zuwanderer m immigrant.

zuwandern vi sep aux sein to immigrate.

Zuwanderung f immigration.

zuwarten vi sep to wait.

zuwege adv etw ~ bringen to manage sth; (erreichen) to achieve or accomplish sth; mit etw ~ kommen to (be able to) cope with sth; mit jdm ~ kommen to get on with sb all right; es ~ bringen, daß jd etw tut to (manage to) get sb to do sth; gut/schlecht ~ sein (inf) to be in good/bad or poor health; er ist ganz schön ~ (dial) he's a bit on the heavy side (inf).

zuwehen sep 1 vt (a) (zutreiben) to waft (dat towards, over to). jdm (kalte etc) Luft ~ to fan sb (with cold etc air).
(b) (zudecken) to block (up). mit Schnee zugeweht werden to become snowed up.
2 vi aux sein auf jdn/etw ~ to blow towards sb/sth; (sachte) to waft towards sb/sth.

zuweilen adv (geh) (every) now and then, occasionally, from time to time.

zuweisen vt sep irreg to assign, to allocate (jdm etw sth to sb).

Zuweisung f allocation, assignment.

zuwenden sep irreg 1 vt (a) (lit, fig) to turn (dat to, towards); (fig: völlig widmen) to devote (dat to). jdm das Gesicht ~ to turn to face sb, to turn one's face towards sb; jdm seine ganze Liebe ~ to bestow all one's affections on sb; die dem Park zugewandten Fenster the windows facing the park.
(b) jdm Geld etc ~ to give sb money etc.
2 vr sep jdm/einer Sache ~ to turn to (face) sb/sth; (fig) to turn to sb/sth; (sich widmen, liebevoll) to devote oneself to sb/sth; wann wird das Glück sich uns wieder ~? when will luck smile on us again?

Zuwendung f (a) (fig: das Sichzuwenden) turning (zu to); (Liebe) care. (b) (Geldsumme) sum (of money); (Beitrag) financial contribution; (Schenkung) donation.

zuwenig adj too little, not enough; (inf: zu wenige) too few, not enough. **du schläfst ~** you don't get enough sleep; **einer/zwei** etc **~** one/two etc too few; **ein Z~ an etw a** lack of sth.

zuwerfen vt sep irreg **(a)** (schließen) Tür to slam (shut). **(b)** (auffüllen) Graben to fill up. **(c)** (hinwerfen) **jdm etw ~** to throw sth to sb; **jdm einen Blick ~** to cast a glance at sb; **jdm einen bösen** or **giftigen/feurigen** etc **Blick ~** to look daggers at sb/to flash a fiery etc glance at sb; **jdm Blicke ~** to make eyes at sb; **jdm eine Kußhand ~** to blow sb a kiss.

zuwider adj **(a) er/das ist mir ~** I find him/that unpleasant; (stärker) I detest or loathe him/that; (ekelerregend) I find him/that revolting; **er ist mir ~ geworden** I have come to dislike him; I have come to detest or loathe him.
(b) (liter: entgegen) **dem Gesetz ~** contrary to or against the law; **etw einem Befehl ~ tun** to do sth in defiance of an order.
(c) (old: ungünstig) **unseren Plänen** etc **~** unfavourable to our plans etc; **das Glück war ihm ~** luck was against him.

Zuwider-: z~handeln vi sep +dat (geh) to go against; **einem Verbot, Befehl** auch to defy; **dem Gesetz z~** to contravene, to violate; **einem Prinzip** auch to violate; **~handelnde(r)** mf decl as adj (form) offender, transgressor, violator (esp US); **~handlung** f (form) contravention, violation; **z~laufen** vi sep irreg aux sein +dat to run counter to, to go directly against.

zuwinken vi sep **jdm ~** to wave to sb; (Zeichen geben) to signal to sb.

zuzahlen sep **1** vt **10 Mark ~** to pay another 10 marks. **2** vi to pay extra.

zuzählen vt sep (inf) (addieren) to add; (einbeziehen) to include (zu in).

zuzeiten adv (old) at times.

zuziehen sep irreg **1** vt **(a)** Vorhang to draw; Tür to pull shut; Knoten, Schlinge to pull tight, to tighten; Arzt etc to call in, to consult. **einen weiteren Fachmann ~** to get a second opinion.
(b) sich (dat) **jds Zorn/Haß** etc **~** to incur sb's anger/hatred etc; sich (dat) **eine Krankheit ~** (form) to contract an illness; sich (dat) **eine Verletzung ~** (form) to sustain an injury.
2 vr (Schlinge etc) to tighten, to pull tight. **es hat sich zugezogen** (Wetter) it has clouded over.
3 vi aux sein to move in, to move into the area. **er ist kürzlich aus Berlin zugezogen** he has recently moved here from Berlin; **auf die Stadt** etc **~** to move towards the town etc.

Zuzug m (Zustrom) influx; (von Familie etc) arrival (nach in), move (nach to).

zuzüglich prep +gen plus.

zuzwinkern vi sep **jdm ~** to wink at sb, to give sb a wink.

Zvieri ['tsfiːri] m or nt -s, no pl (Sw) afternoon snack.

zw. abbr of **zwischen**.

zwang pret of **zwingen**.

Zwang m -(e)s, ⁀e (Notwendigkeit) compulsion; (Gewalt) force; (Verpflichtung) obligation; (hemmender ~) constraint. **einem inneren ~ folgen** to follow an inner compulsion; **das ist ~ that is** compulsory; **der ~ der Ereignisse** the pressure of events; **der ~ der Pflicht** the obligation to do one's duty; **gesellschaftliche ~e** social constraints; **unter ~** (dat) **stehen/handeln** to be/act under duress; **etw aus ~ tun** to do sth under duress, to be forced to do sth; **etw ohne ~ tun** to do sth without being forced to; **auf jdn ~ ausüben** to exert pressure on sb; **sich** (dat) **~ antun** to force oneself to be something one isn't; (sich zurückhalten) to restrain oneself (etw nicht zu tun from doing sth); **tu dir keinen ~ an** don't feel you have to be polite; (iro) don't force yourself; **darf ich rauchen? — ja, tu dir keinen ~ an** may I smoke? — feel free; **seinen Gefühlen ~ antun** to force oneself to ignore one's true feelings; **sie tut ihren Gefühlen keinen ~ an** she doesn't hide her feelings; **dem Gesetz ~ antun** to stretch the law; **der ~ des Gesetzes/der Verhältnisse/Konvention** the force of the law/of circumstances/of convention; **allen ~ ablegen** to dispense with all formalities; **er brauchte sich** (dat) **keinen ~ aufzuerlegen** he didn't need to make a big effort; **das kannst du ohne ~ tun** feel free to do that.

zwängen vt to force; mehrere Sachen (in Koffer etc) to cram. **sich in/durch etw** (acc) **~** to squeeze into/through sth.

Zwang-: z~haft adj (Psych) compulsive; **z~los** adj (ohne Förmlichkeit) informal; (locker, unbekümmert) casual, free and easy; (frei) free; **in z~loser Folge, z~los** at irregular intervals; **da geht es recht z~los zu** (im Hotel, Club) things are very informal there; (bei der Arbeit auch) things are very relaxed there; **~losigkeit** f siehe adj informality; casualness, freeness.

Zwangs-: ~abgabe f (Econ) compulsory levy or charge; **~ablieferung** f compulsory delivery; **~abtretung** f compulsory cession; **~anleihe** f compulsory or forced loan; **~beitreibung** f siehe **~vollstreckung**; **z~bewirtschaftet** adj controlled; **Wohnraum** rent-controlled; **~bewirtschaftung** f (economic) control; (von Wohnraum) rent control; **die ~bewirtschaftung aufheben** to decontrol the economy/rents; **~einweisung** f compulsory hospitalization; **~enteignung** f compulsory expropriation; **~ernährung** f force feeding; **~erscheinung** f (Psych) compulsion; **~handlung** f (Psych) compulsive act; **~hypothek** f compulsory mortgage to enforce payment of debt(s); **~jacke** f (lit, fig) straitjacket; **jdn in eine ~jacke stecken** to put sb in a straitjacket, to straitjacket sb; **~kurs** m (Fin) compulsory rate; **~lage** f predicament, dilemma; **z~läufig** adj inevitable, unavoidable; **das mußte ja z~läufig so kommen** that had to happen, it was inevitable that that would happen; **~läufigkeit** f inevitability, unavoidability; **z~mäßig** adj (form) compulsory; **~maßnahme** f compulsory measure; (Pol) sanction; **~mittel** nt means of coercion; (Pol) sanction; **~neurose** f obsessional neurosis; **~neurotiker** m obsessional neurotic; **~pensionierung** f compulsory retirement; **~räumung** f compulsory evacuation; **~regime** nt despotic or tyrannical regime; **z~umsiedeln** vt, ptp **z~umgesiedelt**, infin, ptp only to displace (by force); **~verkauf** m (en)forced sale; **z~verpflichtet** adj

---

drafted (zu into); **~verschickung** f deportation; **~versicherung** f siehe **Pflichtversicherung**; **z~versteigern*** vt infin, ptp only to put (sth) up for compulsory auction; **~versteigerung** f compulsory auction; **~vollstreckung** f execution; **~vorführung** f (Jur) enforced appearance in court; **~vorstellung** f (Psych) obsession, obsessive idea; **z~weise 1** adv compulsorily; **2** adj compulsory; **~wirtschaft** f Government or State control.

zwanzig num twenty; siehe auch **vierzig, vier**.

Zwanzig f -, -en twenty; siehe auch **Vierzig, Vier**.

Zwanziger m -s, - (Mann) twenty-year-old; (zwischen 20 und 30) man in his twenties; (inf: Geldschein) twenty mark etc note; siehe auch **Vierziger(in)**.

Zwanzigerpackung f packet or pack (US) of twenty.

Zwanzigmarkschein m twenty mark note.

zwanzigste(r, s) adj twentieth; siehe auch **vierzigste(r, s)**.

zwar adv **(a)** (wohl) **er war ~ Zeuge des Unfalls, kann sich aber nicht mehr so genau erinnern** he did witness the accident or it's true he witnessed the accident but he can't remember much about it any more; **sie ist ~ sehr schön/krank, aber ...** it's true she's very beautiful/ill but ..., she may be very beautiful/ill but ...; **ich weiß ~, daß es schädlich ist, aber ...** I do know it's harmful but ...
(b) (erklärend, betont) **und ~ in fact, actually; er ist tatsächlich gekommen, und ~ um 4 Uhr** he really did come, at 4 o'clock actually or in fact; **er hat mir das anders erklärt, und ~** so ... he explained it differently to me, (like this) ...; **ich mache das, und ~ so, wie ich es für richtig halte** I'll do it and I'll do it just as I see fit; **und ~ einschließlich ...** inclusive of ...; **die Schulen, und ~ vor allem die Volksschulen** the schools, (and more) especially the primary schools; **das hat er gemacht, und ~ so gründlich, daß ...** he did it and (he did it) so thoroughly that ...; **er haßt ihn, und ~ so sehr, daß ...** he hates him so much that ...; **ich werde ihm schreiben, und ~ noch heute** I'll write to him and I'll do it today or this very day.

Zweck m -(e)s, -e **(a)** (Ziel, Verwendung) purpose. **einem ~ dienen** to serve a purpose; **einem guten ~ dienen** to be for or in a good cause; **Spenden für wohltätige ~e** donations to charity; **seinen ~ erfüllen** to serve its/one's purpose; **seinem ~ entsprechen** to serve its purpose; **das entspricht nicht meinen ~en** that won't serve my purpose.
(b) (Sinn) point. **was soll das für einen ~ haben?** what's the point of that?; **das hat keinen ~** there is no point in it, it's pointless; **es hat keinen ~, darüber zu reden** there is no point (in) talking about it, it's pointless talking about it; **es hat ja doch alles keinen ~ mehr** there is no point (in) or it's pointless going on any more; **das ist ja der ~ der Übung** that's the point of the exercise, that's what it's all about (inf).
(c) (Absicht) aim. **zum ~ der Völkerverständigung** (in order) to promote understanding between nations; **zu welchem ~?** for what purpose?, to what end?; **zu diesem ~** to this end, with this aim in view; **einen ~ verfolgen** to have a specific aim.

Zweck-: ~bau m, pl -ten functional building; **z~bedingt** adj determined by its function; **~bindung** f predetermination for a specific purpose; **z~dienlich** adj (z~entsprechend) appropriate; (nützlich) useful; **z~dienliche Hinweise** (any) relevant information; **es wäre z~dienlich, das zu tun** it would be expedient to do that.

Zwecke f -, -n tack; (Schuh~) nail; (Reiß~) drawing-pin (Brit), thumbtack (US).

zwecken vt to tack; (mit Reißzwecken) to pin.

Zweck-: z~entfremden* vt insep to use sth in a way in which it wasn't intended to be used; **etw als etw z~entfremden** to use sth as sth; **~entfremdung** f misuse; **z~entsprechend** adj appropriate; **etw z~entsprechend benutzen** to use sth properly or correctly, to put sth to its proper or correct use; **z~frei** adj Forschung etc pure; **z~gebunden** adj for a specific purpose, appropriated (spec) no adv; **z~gemäß** adv siehe **z~entsprechend**; **z~los** adj pointless, useless, futile, of no use; **es ist z~los, hier zu bleiben** it's pointless etc staying here, there's no point (in) staying here; **~losigkeit** f, no pl pointlessness, uselessness, futility; **z~mäßig** adj (nützlich) useful; (wirksam) effective; (ratsam) advisable, expedient (form) (z~entsprechend) Arbeitskleider etc suitable; **~mäßigkeit** f siehe adj usefulness, effectiveness, efficacy; advisability, expediency (form); suitability; **~mäßigkeitserwägung** f consideration of expediency; **~optimismus** m calculated optimism; **~pessimismus** m calculated pessimism; **~propaganda** f calculated propaganda.

zwecks prep +gen (form) for the purpose of. **~ Wiederverwendung** for re-use.

Zweck-: ~satz m (Gram) final clause; **~sparen** nt target saving; **~steuer** f regulatory tax; **z~voll** adj siehe **z~mäßig**; **z~widrig** adj inappropriate.

zween num (obs) twain (obs).

zwei num two. **wir ~** (beiden inf) the two of us, we two, us two (inf); **das ist so sicher wie ~ mal ~ vier ist** (inf) you can bet on that (inf); **dazu gehören ~** (inf) it takes two; **da kann man ~ draus machen** (fig inf) it's quite incredible; **~ Gesichter haben** (fig) to be two-faced; siehe **vier, Dritte(r)**.

Zwei f -, -en two; siehe auch **Vier**.

Zwei- in cpds siehe auch **Vier-; ~achser** m -s, - two-axle vehicle; **z~achsig** adj two-axled; **~akter** m -s, - (Theat) two-act play or piece; **z~armig** adj (Physiol) with two arms; (Tech) with two branches; **z~atomig** adj (Phys) diatomic; **~beiner** m -s, - (hum inf) human being; **die ~beiner** human beings, the bipeds (hum); **z~beinig** adj two-legged, biped(al) (spec); **~bettzimmer** nt twin room; **~bund** m (Hist) dual alliance; **~decker** m -s, - (Aviat) biplane; **z~deutig** adj ambiguous, equivocal; (schlüpfrig) suggestive; **z~deutige Reden führen** to use a lot of doubles entendres; **~deutigkeit** f **(a)** siehe adj ambiguity, equivocalness; suggestiveness; risqué nature; **(b)** (*Bemerkung*) ambiguous *or* equivocal remark, double entendre; (*Witz*) risqué joke; z~**dimensional** *adj* two-dimensional; ~**drittelmehrheit** *f* (*Parl*) two-thirds majority; **der Streikbeschluß wurde mit** ~**drittelmehrheit gefaßt** the decision to strike was taken with a two-thirds majority; z~**eiig** *adj* **Zwillinge** non-identical, fraternal (*spec*).

Zweier *m* -**s**, - two; (*Sch dial*) good; (*Zweipfennigstück*) two pfennig piece; *siehe auch* **Vierer**.

Zweier- (*Sport*): ~**bob** *m* two-man bob; ~**kajak** *m or nt* (*Kanu*) double kayak; (*Disziplin*) kayak pairs; ~**kanadier** *m* Canadian pair; (*Disziplin*) Canadian pairs.

zweierlei *adj inv* **(a)** *attr* **Brot, Käse, Wein** two kinds *or* sorts of; **Möglichkeiten, Größen, Fälle** two different. **auf** ~ **Art** in two different ways; ~ **Handschuhe/Strümpfe** *etc* odd gloves/socks *etc*; ~ **Meinung sein** to be of (two) different opinions; *siehe* **Maß**.
   (b) (*substantivisch*) two different things; (*2 Sorten*) two different kinds.

Zweierreihe *f* two rows *pl*. ~**n** rows of twos; **in** ~**n marschieren** to march two abreast *or* in twos.

zweifach *adj* double; (*zweimal*) twice. **in** ~**er Ausfertigung** in duplicate; ~ **gesichert** doubly secure; **ein Tuch** ~ **legen** to lay a cloth double.

Zwei-: ~**familienhaus** *nt* two family house; ~**farbendruck** *m* (*Typ*) two-colour print; (*Verfahren*) two-colour printing; z~**farbig** *adj* two-colour, two-tone; **etw** z~**farbig anstreichen** to paint sth in two (different) colours.

Zweifel *m* -**s**, - doubt. **außer** ~ beyond doubt; **im** ~ in doubt; **ohne** ~ without doubt, doubtless; **über allen** ~ **erhaben** beyond all (shadow of a) doubt; **da kann es gar keinen** ~ **geben** there can be no doubt about it; **es besteht kein** ~, **daß** ... there is no doubt that ...; ~ **an etw** (*dat*) **haben** to have one's doubts about sth; **da habe ich meine** ~ I have my doubts, I'm doubtful; **etw in** ~ **ziehen** to call sth into question, to challenge sth; **ich bin mir im** ~, **ob ich das tun soll** I'm in two minds *or* I'm doubtful whether I should do that; **ich weiß es nicht mehr ganz genau, ich bin mir im** ~ I don't know exactly any more, I'm unsure *or* uncertain.

zweifelhaft *adj* doubtful; (*verdächtig auch*) dubious. **von** ~**em Wert** of doubtful *or* debatable value; **es ist** ~, **ob** ... it is doubtful *or* questionable *or* debatable whether ...

zweifellos 1 *adv* without (a) doubt, undoubtedly, unquestionably; (*als Antwort*) undoubtedly. **er hat** ~ **recht** he is undoubtedly *or* unquestionably right, without (a) doubt he is right. **2** *adj* **Sieger** *etc* undisputed.

zweifeln *vi* to doubt. **an etw/jdm** ~ to doubt sth/sb; (*skeptisch sein auch*) to be sceptical about sth/sb; **daran ist nicht zu** ~ there's no doubt about it; **ich zweifle nicht, daß** ... I do not doubt *or* I have no doubt that ...; **ich zweifle noch, wie ich mich entscheiden soll** I am still in two minds about it.

Zweifels-: ~**fall** *m* doubtful *or* borderline case; **im** ~**fall** in case of doubt, when in doubt; (*inf: gegebenenfalls*) if need be, if necessary; z~**frei 1** *adj* unequivocal; **2** *adv* beyond (all) doubt; z~**ohne** *adv* undoubtedly, without (a) doubt.

Zweifler(in *f*) *m* -**s**, - sceptic.

zweiflerisch *adj* sceptical.

Zwei-: z~**flüg(e)lig** *adj* **Tür, Tor** double; *Insekt* two-winged, dipterous (*spec*); ~**flügler** *m* -**s**, - (*Zool*) dipteran (*spec*); ~**frontenkrieg** *m* war/warfare on two fronts.

Zweig *m* -(**e**)**s**, -**e** **(a)** (*Ast*) branch, bough (*liter*); (*dünner, kleiner*) twig. **(b)** (*fig*) (*von Wissenschaft, Familie etc, Rail*) branch; (*Abteilung*) department; *siehe* **grün**.

Zwei-: z~**geschlechtig** *adj* (*Biol*) hermaphroditic; ~**geschlechtigkeit** *f* (*Biol*) hermaphroditism; ~**gespann** *nt* carriage and pair; (*fig inf*) duo, two-man band (*hum inf*); z~**gestrichen** *adj* (*Mus*) **das** z~**gestrichene C/A** the C (an octave) above middle C/the A an octave above middle C.

Zweig-: ~**geschäft** *nt* branch; ~**gesellschaft** *f* subsidiary (company).

zwei-: ~**gleisig** *adj* double tracked, double-track *attr*; ~**gleisig fahren** (*lit*) to be double-tracked; (*fig inf*) to have two strings to one's bow; ~**gleisig argumentieren** to argue along two different lines; ~**gliedrig** *adj* (*fig*) bipartite; (*Admin*) **System** two-tier; (*Math*) binominal.

Zweig-: ~**linie** *f* branch line; ~**niederlassung** *f* subsidiary; ~**postamt** *nt* sub post office; ~**stelle** *f* branch (office); ~**stellenleiter** *m* (branch) manager; ~**werk**[1] *nt* (*Fabrik*) branch; ~**werk**[2] *nt* (*von Baum, Gesträuch*) branches *pl*.

Zwei-: ~**händer** *m* -**s**, - (**a**) (*Schwert*) two-handed sword; **(b)** (*Zool*) two-handed *or* bimanous (*spec*) animal; z~**händig** *adj* with two hands, two-handed; (*Mus*) for two hands; z~**häusig** *adj* (*Bot*) dioecian; ~**heit** *f*, no *pl* (*Philos, Liter etc*) duality; z~**henk(e)lig** *adj* two-handled, double-handled; z~**höck(e)rig** *adj* **Kamel** two-humped.

zweihundert *num* two hundred.

Zweihundert-: ~**jahrfeier** *f* bicentenary, bicentennial; z~**jährig** *adj* **Dauer** two-hundred-year *attr*; **Tradition, Geschichte** two-hundred-year-old *attr*; **nach über** z~**jähriger Knechtschaft** after more than two hundred years of servitude.

zweijährig *adj* **(a)** *attr* **Kind** *etc* two-year-old *attr*, two years old; (*Dauer*) two-year *attr*, of two years. **mit** ~**er Verspätung** two years late. **(b)** (*Bot*) **Pflanze** biennial.

zweijährlich 1 *adj* two-yearly *attr*, biennial, every two years. **2** *adv* biennially, every two years; every other year.

Zwei-: ~**kammersystem** *nt* (*Pol*) two-chamber system; ~**kampf** *m* single combat; (*Duell*) duel; **jdn zum** ~**kampf** (**heraus**)**fordern** to challenge sb to a duel; ~**keimblätt(e)rige** *pl* (*Bot*) dicotyledons *pl*.

Zweiklang-: ~**horn** *nt*, ~**hupe** *f* two-tone horn.

Zwei-: z~**köpfig** *adj* two-headed; ~**kreisbremse** *f* dual-circuit brake.

zweimal *adv* twice. ~ **jährlich** *or* **im Jahr/täglich** *or* **am Tag** twice yearly *or* a year/twice daily *or* a day; **sich** (*dat*) **etw** ~ **überlegen** to think twice about sth; **das lasse ich mir nicht** ~ **sagen** I don't have to be told twice; **das mache ich bestimmt nicht** ~ I certainly shan't do that/it again.

zweimalig *adj attr* twice repeated. **nach** ~**er Aufforderung** after being told twice; **nach** ~**er Wiederholung konnte er den Text auswendig** after twice repeating the text he knew it (off) by heart.

Zwei-: ~**mannboot** *nt* two-man boat; ~**markstück** *nt* two-mark piece; ~**master** *m* -**s**, - two-master; z~**monatig** *adj attr* **(a)** (*Dauer*) two-month *attr*, of two months; **(b)** **Säugling** *etc* two-month-old *attr*, two months old; z~**monatlich 1** *adj* every two months, bimonthly (*esp Comm, Admin*); **2** *adv* every two months, bimonthly (*esp Comm, Admin*), every other month; ~**monatsschrift** *f* bimonthly; z~**motorig** *adj* twin-engined; ~**parteiensystem** *nt* two-party system; ~**pfennigstück** *nt* two-pfennig piece; ~**phasenstrom** *m* two-phase current; z~**polig** *adj* (*Elec*) double-pole, bipolar; ~**punkt-Sicherheitsgurt** *m* diagonal (safety *or* seat) belt; ~**rad** *nt* (*form*) two-wheeled vehicle, two-wheeler; (*Fahrrad*) (bi)cycle; (*für Kinder*) two-wheeler, bicycle; z~**räd(e)rig** *adj* two-wheeled; ~**reiher** *m* -**s**, - double-breasted suit *etc*; z~**reihig 1** *adj* double-row *attr*, in two rows; **Anzug** double-breasted; **2** *adv* in two rows; ~**samkeit** *f* (*liter, hum*) togetherness; z~**schläfig**, z~**schläf(e)rig** *adj* double; z~**schneidig** *adj* two-edged, double-edged (*auch fig*); **das ist ein** z~**schneidiges Schwert** (*fig*) it cuts both ways; z~**seitig 1** *adj* **Vertrag** *etc* bilateral, bipartite; *Kleidungsstück* reversible; **2** *adv* on two sides; **ein** z~**seitig tragbarer Anorak** a reversible anorak; z~**silbig** *adj* disyllabic; **ein** z~**silbiges Wort** a disyllable (*spec*), a disyllabic word; ~**sitzer** *m* -**s**, - (*Aviat*) two-seater; z~**sitzig** *adj* two-seater *attr*; z~**spaltig** *adj* double-columned, in two columns; **der Artikel ist** z~**spaltig** (**abgedruckt**) the article is printed in two columns; ~**spänner** *m* -**s**, - carriage and pair; z~**spännig** *adj* drawn by two horses; z~**spännig fahren** to drive (in) a carriage and pair; ~**spitz** *m* two-cornered hat; z~**sprachig** *adj* **Mensch, Wörterbuch** bilingual; *Land auch* two-language *attr*; *Dokument* in two languages; ~**sprachigkeit** *f* bilingualism; z~**spurig** *adj* double-tracked, double-track *attr*; *Autobahn* two-laned, two-lane *attr*; **ein Band** z~**spurig bespielen** to record a tape on both/two tracks; ~**spur(tonband)gerät** *nt* twin-track (tape) recorder; z~**stellig** *adj* **Zahl** two-digit *attr*, with two digits; z~**stelliger Dezimalbruch** number with two decimal places; z~**stimmig** *adj* (*Mus*) for two voices, two-part *attr*; z~**stimmig singen** to sing in two parts; z~**stöckig** *adj* two-storey *attr*, two-storeyed; **ein** z~**stöckiges Bett** bunk bed; z~**stöckig bauen** to build houses/offices *etc* with two storeys; *siehe auch* **doppelstöckig**; z~**strahlig** *adj* **Flugzeug** twin-jet *attr*; ~**stromland** *nt* **das** ~**stromland** Mesopotamia; ~**stufenscheibenwischer** *m* (*Aut*) two-speed windscreen wiper; z~**stufig** *adj* two-stage; **System** *auch* two-tier; *Plan auch* two-phase; *Scheibenwischer, Schaltgetriebe* two-speed; z~**stündig** *adj* two-hour *attr*, of two hours; z~**stündlich** *adj*, *adv* every two hours, two-hourly.

zweit *adv*: **zu** ~ (*in Paaren*) in twos; **wir gingen zu** ~ **spazieren** the two of us went for a walk; **ich gehe lieber zu** ~ **ins Kino** I prefer going to the cinema with somebody *or* in a twosome; **das Leben zu** ~ **ist billiger** two people can live more cheaply than one; **das Leben zu** ~ living with someone; *siehe auch* **viert**.

Zwei-: z~**tägig** *adj* two-day *attr*, of two days; ~**takter** *m* -**s**, - (*inf*) two-stroke (*inf*); ~**taktergemisch** *nt* two-stroke mixture; ~**taktmotor** *m* two-stroke engine.

zweitälteste(r, s) *adj* second eldest *or* oldest. **unser** Z~**r** our second (child *or* son).

Zwei-: z~**tausend** *num* two thousand; **das Jahr** z~**tausend** the year two thousand; ~**tausendjahrfeier** *f* bimillenary.

Zweit-: ~**ausfertigung** *f* (*form*) copy, duplicate; **es liegt nur in** ~**ausfertigung vor** we/I have only a copy *or* duplicate; ~**auto** *nt* second car; z~**beste(r, s)** *adj* second best; **er ist der** Z~**beste** he is the second best; ~**druck** *m* reprint.

Zwei-: z~**teilen** *vt sep, infin, ptp only* to divide (into two); z~**teilig** *adj* **Roman** two-part *attr*, in two parts; *Plan* two-stage; *Kleidungsstück* two-piece; *Formular etc* two-part *attr*, in two sections; ~**teilung** *f* division; (*Math: von Winkel*) bisection.

Zweitempfänger *m* (*Rad, TV*) second set.

zweitens *adv* secondly; (*bei Aufzählungen auch*) second.

zweite(r, s) *adj* second. ~ **Klasse** (*Rail etc*) second class; ~**r Klasse fahren** to travel second(-class); **Bürger** ~**r Klasse** second-class citizen(s); **jeden** ~**n Tag** every other *or* second day; **jeder** ~ (*lit, inf: sehr viele*) every other; **zum** ~**n secondly**; **ein** ~**r Caruso** another Caruso; **in** ~**r Linie** secondly; *siehe* **Garnitur, Hand, Ich, Wahl** *etc*; *siehe auch* **erste(r, s), vierte(r, s)**.

Zweite(r) *mf decl as adj* second; (*Sport etc*) runner-up. **wie kein** z~**r** as no-one else can, like nobody else.

Zweit-: ~**erkrankung** *f* secondary illness/disease; ~**frisur** *f* wig; z~**geboren** *adj attr* second-born; ~**gerät** *nt* (*Rad, TV*) second set; z~**größte(r, s)** *adj* second biggest/largest; **Stadt** *auch* second; z~**höchste(r, s)** *adj* second highest/tallest; (*fig: im Rang*) second most senior; z~**klassig** *adj* (*fig*) second-class, second-rate (*esp pej*); z~**letzte(r, s)** *adj* last but one *attr*, pred; (*in Reihenfolge auch*) penultimate; z~**rangig** *adj* siehe z~**klassig**; ~**schrift** *f* copy; ~**stimme** *f* second vote.

Zwei-: (*Aut*): ~**türer** *m* -**s**, - two-door; z~**türig** *adj* two-door.

Zweit-: ~**wagen** *m* second car; ~**wohnung** *f* second home.

Zweiunddreißigstel *nt*, **Zweiunddreißigstelnote** *f* (*Mus*) demisemiquaver (*Brit*), thirty-second note (*US*).

Zweiunddreißigstelpause *f* (*Mus*) demisemiquaver rest (*Brit*), thirty-second note rest (*US*).

Zwei-: ~vierteltakt m (Mus) two-four time; z~wertig adj (Chem) bivalent, divalent; (Ling) two-place; z~wöchentlich adj, adv twice a week, twice weekly; z~wöchig adj two-week attr, of two weeks; z~zackig adj two-pronged; ~zeiler m -s, - (Liter) couplet; z~zeilig adj two-lined; (Typ) Abstand double-spaced; z~zeilig schreiben to double-space; ~zimmerwohnung f two-room(ed) flat (Brit) or apartment; ~züger m (Chess) -s, - two-mover; ~zylinder m two-cylinder; ~zylindermotor m two-cylinder engine; z~zylindrig adj two-cylinder attr.

Zwerchfell nt (Anat) diaphragm. **jdm das ~ massieren** (hum inf) to make sb split his/her sides (laughing) (inf).

Zwerchfell-: z~erschütternd adj side-splitting (inf); ~massage f (hum inf) es war die reinste ~massage it was an absolute scream (inf) or hoot (inf).

Zwerg(in f) m -(e)s, -e dwarf; (Garten~) gnome; (fig: Knirps) midget; (pej: unbedeutender Mensch) squirt (inf).

zwergenhaft adj dwarfish; (fig) diminutive, minute; (pej: minderwertig) insignificant.

Zwerg-: ~huhn nt bantam; ~pinscher m pet terrier; ~pudel m toy poodle; ~schule f (Sch inf) village school; ~staat m miniature state; ~stamm m, ~volk nt pygmy tribe; ~wuchs m stunted growth, dwarfism; z~wüchsig adj attr dwarfish.

Zwetschge f -, -n plum.

Zwetschgen-: ~datschi m -s, -s (S Ger) (type of) plum cake; ~knödel m (S Ger) plum dumpling; ~schnaps m, ~wasser nt plum brandy.

Zwetschke f -, -n (Aus) (a) siehe Zwetschge. (b) seine/die sieben ~n (ein)packen (inf) to pack one's bags (and go).

Zwickel m -s, - (Sew) gusset; (am Segel) gore; (Archit) spandrel.

zwicken 1 vt (inf, Aus) (kneifen) to pinch; (leicht schmerzen) to hurt; (esp S Ger: ärgern) to bother. **2** vi to pinch; (leicht schmerzen) to hurt.

Zwicker m -s, - pince-nez.

Zwickmühle f (beim Mühlespiel) double mill. **in der ~ sitzen** (fig) to be in a catch-22 situation (inf), to be in a dilemma.

Zwieback m -(e)s, -e or ¨e rusk.

Zwiebel f -, -n onion; (Blumen~) bulb; (hum inf: Uhr) watch; (Haarknoten) tight bun.

Zwiebel-: ~fisch m (Typ) literal (character typed in wrong face); z~förmig adj bulbiform; ~haube, ~kuppel f (Archit) imperial roof; ~kuchen m onion tart; ~muster nt onion pattern.

zwiebeln vt (inf) jdn ~ to drive or push sb hard; (schikanieren) to harass sb; **er hat uns so lange gezwiebelt, bis wir das Gedicht konnten** he kept (on) at us until we knew the poem.

Zwiebel-: ~ring m onion ring; ~schale f onion-skin; ~suppe f onion soup; ~turm m onion tower.

Zwie-: z~fach, z~fältig adj (old) siehe zweifach; ~gespräch nt dialogue; ein ~gespräch mit sich selbst an internal dialogue; (laut) a soliloquy; ~laut m (Ling) siehe Diphthong; ~licht nt, no pl twilight; (abends auch) dusk; (morgens) half-light; ins ~licht geraten sein (fig) to appear in an unfavourable light; z~lichtig adj (fig) shady.

Zwiesel m -s, - or f -, -n (Bot) fork, bifurcation.

Zwie-: ~spalt m (pl rare) (der Natur, der Gefühle etc) conflict; (zwischen Menschen, Parteien etc) rift, gulf; **ich bin im ~spalt mit mir, ob ich ...** I'm in conflict with myself whether to ...; in ~spalt mit jdm geraten to come into conflict with sb; in einen fürchterlichen ~spalt geraten to get into a terrible conflict; z~spältig adj Gefühle mixed, conflicting attr; mein Eindruck war z~spältig my impressions were very mixed; ein z~spältiger Mensch a man/woman of contradictions; ~spältigkeit f duality; (Wankelmut) contradictory nature; ~sprache f dialogue; ~sprache mit jdm/etw halten to commune with sb/sth; ~tracht f -, no pl discord; ~tracht säen to sow (the seeds of) discord.

Zwille f -, -n (N Ger) catapult (Brit), slingshot (US).

Zwil(li)ch m -s, -e (Tex) siehe Drillich.

Zwilling m -s, -e twin; (Gewehr) double-barrelled gun; (Chem: Doppelkristall) twin crystal. **die ~e** (Astrol) Gemini, the Twins; (Astron) Gemini; **~ sein** (Astrol) to be (a) Gemini.

Zwillings-: ~bruder m twin brother; ~formel f (Ling) dual expression, set phrase with two elements; ~geburt f twin birth; ~paar nt twins pl; ~reifen m (Aut) double or twin tyres; ~schwester f twin sister.

Zwingburg f (Hist, fig) stronghold, fortress.

Zwinge f -, -n (Tech) (screw) clamp; (am Stock) tip, ferrule; (an Schirm) tip; (an Werkzeuggriff) ferrule.

zwingen pret zwang, ptp gezwungen **1** vt **(a)** to force, to compel. **jdn ~, etw zu tun** to force or compel sb to do sth; (Mensch auch) to make sb do sth; **jdn zu etw ~** to force sb to do sth; **sie ist dazu gezwungen worden** she was forced or compelled or made to do it; **ich lasse mich nicht (dazu) ~** I shan't be forced (to do it) or into it; **I don't/shan't respond to force; jdn an den Verhandlungstisch/in die Kneipe** (hum) **~** to force sb to the bargaining table/into the pub (Brit) or bar; **jdn zum Handeln ~** to force sb into action or to act; **jdn zum Gehorsam ~** to force or compel sb to obey, to make sb obey; **die Regierung wurde zum Rücktritt gezwungen** the government was forced or compelled to step down; **man kann niemanden zu seinem Glück ~** you can't force people; siehe gezwungen.

(b) (inf: bewältigen) Essen, Arbeit to manage; siehe Knie.

2 vr to force oneself. **sich ~, etw zu tun** to force oneself to do sth, to make oneself do sth; **sich zur Ruhe ~** to force oneself to be calm.

3 vi (von Handeln/Umdenken) ~ to force or compel us/them etc to act/re-think; **diese Tatsachen ~ zu der Annahme, daß ...** these facts force or compel one to assume that ...

zwingend adj Notwendigkeit urgent; (logisch notwendig)

necessary; Schluß, Beweis, Argumente conclusive; Argument cogent; Gründe compelling. **daß B aus A resultiert, ist nicht ~** it isn't necessarily so or the case that B results from A; **etwas ~ darlegen** to present sth conclusively.

Zwinger m -s, - (Käfig) cage; (Bären~) bear-pit; (Hunde~) kennels pl; (von Burg) (outer) ward.

Zwing-: ~herr m (Hist, fig) oppressor, tyrant; ~herrschaft f (Hist, fig) oppression, tyranny.

Zwinglianer(in f) m -s, - (Hist, Rel) Zwinglian.

zwinkern vi to blink; (um jdm etw zu bedeuten) to wink; (lustig) to twinkle. **mit den Augen ~** to blink (one's eyes)/wink/twinkle.

Zwirbelbart m handlebar moustache.

zwirbeln vt Bart to twirl; Schnur to twist.

Zwirn m -s, -e (strong) thread, yarn. **ihm ist der ~ ausgegangen** (dial sl) he's run out of cash (inf); siehe Himmel.

zwirnen vti to twist. **dieses Handtuch ist gezwirnt** this towel is made of strong thread.

Zwirnerei f mill.

Zwirnsfaden m thread. **an einem ~ hängen** (inf) to hang by a thread; **über einen ~ stolpern** (inf) to be caught out by a trifle; **dünn wie ein ~** (as) thin as a rake.

zwischen prep + dat or (mit Bewegungsverben) + acc between; (in bezug auf mehrere auch) among. **mitten ~** right in the middle or midst of; **die Liebe ~ den beiden** the love between the two of them; **die Kirche stand ~ Bäumen** the church stood among(st) trees; siehe Stuhl, Tür, Zeile etc.

Zwischen-: ~akt m (Theat) interval, intermission; **im ~akt** during the interval or intermission; ~akt(s)musik f interlude; ~ansage f (Rad etc) announcement (interrupting a programme); (Kurznachricht) newsflash; ~applaus m (Theat) spontaneous applause (during the performance); ~aufenthalt m stopover; ~bemerkung f interjection; (Unterbrechung) interruption; **wenn Sie mir eine kurze ~bemerkung erlauben** if I may just interrupt; ~bericht m interim report; ~bescheid m provisional notification no indef art; z~betrieblich adj (DDR) intercompany attr, between companies; ~bilanz f (Comm) interim balance; (fig) provisional appraisal; **eine ~bilanz/~bilanzen ziehen** (fig) to take stock provisionally; z~blenden vt sep to blend in; (Film, Rad etc) to insert; (nachträglich) Musik etc to dub on; ~blutung f (Med) breakthrough or intermenstrual (spec) bleeding; ~boden m siehe ~decke; ~buchhandel m intermediate book trade; ~deck nt (Naut) 'tween deck; **im ~deck** 'tween decks, between the decks; ~decke f false ceiling; ~ding nt cross (between the two), hybrid; **was er schreibt, ist ein ~ding zwischen Lyrik und Prosa** his writing is a cross between or is halfway between poetry and prose; z~drin adv (dial) (a) siehe z~durch; (b) siehe dazwischen; z~durch adv (a) (zeitlich) in between times; (inzwischen) (in the) meantime; (nebenbei) on the side; **er macht z~durch mal Pausen** he keeps stopping for a break in between times; **das mache ich so z~durch** I'll do that on the side; **Schokolade für z~durch** chocolate for between meals; **(b)** (örtlich) in between; ~eiszeit f (Geol) interglacial period; ~ergebnis nt interim result; (von Untersuchung auch) interim findings; (Sport) latest score; ~fall m incident; **ohne ~fall** without incident, smoothly; **es kam zu schweren ~fällen** there were serious incidents, there were clashes; ~frage f question; ~frequenz f (Rad) intermediate frequency; ~fruchtbau m (Agr) intercropping; ~futter nt (Sew) interlining; ~gang m (Cook) siehe ~gericht; ~gas nt, no pl (Aut) ~gas geben to double-declutch; ~gericht nt (Cook) entrée; ~geschoß nt mezzanine (floor); ~glied nt (lit, fig) link; ~größe f in-between size; ~halt m (Sw) siehe ~aufenthalt; ~handel m intermediate trade; ~händler m middleman; z~hinein adv (Sw) siehe z~durch; ~hirn nt (Anat) interbrain, diencephalon (spec); ~hoch nt (Met) ridge of high pressure; ~kiefer(knochen) m (Anat) intermaxillary (bone); z~landen vi sep (Aviat) to stop over or off; ~landung f (Aviat) stopover; **ohne ~landung** without a stopover; ~lauf m (Sport) intermediate heat; ~lösung f temporary or interim or provisional solution; ~mahlzeit f snack (between meals); z~menschlich adj attr interhuman; ~musik f interlude; ~produkt nt intermediate product; ~prüfung f intermediate examination; ~raum m gap, space; (Wort-, Zeilenabstand) space; (zeitlich) interval; **ein ~raum von 5 m, 5 m ~raum** a gap/space of 5m, a 5m gap/space; ~ring m (Phot) adapter; ~ruf m interruption; ~rufe heckling; **einen Redner durch ~rufe stören** to heckle a speaker; ~rufer(in f) m -s, - heckler; ~runde f (esp Sport) intermediate round; ~satz m (Gram) inserted or parenthetic clause, parenthesis; z~schalten vt sep (Elec) to insert; (fig) to interpose, to put in between; ~schalter m (Elec) interruptor; ~schaltung f (Elec) insertion; (fig) interposition; z~schieben vt sep irreg Termin etc to fit or squeeze in; ~sohle f midsole; ~spiel nt (Mus) intermezzo; (Theat, fig) interlude; ~spurt m (Sport) short burst (of speed); **einen ~spurt einlegen** to put in a burst of speed; z~staatlich adj attr international; (zwischen Bundesstaaten) interstate; ~stadium nt intermediate stage; ~station f (intermediate) stop; **in London machten wir ~station** we stopped off in London; ~stecker m (Elec) adaptor (plug); ~stellung f intermediate position; ~stock m, ~stockwerk nt mezzanine (floor); ~stück nt connection, connecting piece; ~stufe f (fig) siehe ~stadium; ~stunde f (Sch) hour's break, break of an hour; ~summe f subtotal; ~text m inserted text; ~titel m (Film etc) title link; ~ton m (Farbe) shade; ~töne (fig) nuances; ~träger(in f) m informer, telltale; ~urteil nt (Jur) interlocutory decree; ~vorhang m (Theat) drop scene; ~wand f dividing wall; (Stellwand) partition; ~wirt m (Biol) intermediate host; ~zähler m (Elec) intermediate meter; ~zeit f (a) (Zeitraum) interval; **in der ~zeit** (in the) meantime, in the interim; **(b)** (Sport) intermediate time; z~zeitlich adv (rare) in between; (inzwischen) (in the) meantime; ~zeugnis nt (Sch)

interim report; ~zins m (Fin) interim interest.
Zwist m -es, (rare) -e (geh) discord, discordance; (Fehde, Streit) dispute, strife no indef art. den alten ~ begraben to bury the hatchet; mit jdm über etw (acc) in ~ (acc) geraten to become involved in a dispute with sb about or over sth.
Zwistigkeit f usu pl dispute.
zwitschern vti to twitter, to chir(ru)p; (Lerche) to warble. ~d sprechen to twitter; bei dir zwitschert's wohl! (inf) you must be batty (inf) or barmy (Brit inf); Z~ twittering, chir(ru)ping; warbling; einen ~ (inf) to have a drink.
Zwitter m -s, - hermaphrodite; (fig) cross (aus between).
Zwitter-: ~bildung f hermaphroditism; ~blüte f (Bot) hermaphrodite; ~ding nt (fig) hybrid, cross-breed; ~form f (Biol) hermaphroditic stage; (fig) hybrid form; z~haft adj hermaphroditic; er kam sich (dat) z~haft vor he felt neither one thing nor the other.
zwitt(e)rig adj hermaphroditic; (Bot auch) androgynous.
Zwitter-: ~tum nt hermaphroditism; (Bot auch) androgyny; ~wesen nt siehe Zwitter.
zwo num (Telec, inf) two.
zwölf num twelve. die ~ Apostel the twelve apostles; die Z~ Nächte the Twelve Days of Christmas; ~ Uhr mittags/nachts (12 o'clock) noon or midday/midnight; fünf Minuten vor ~ (fig) at the eleventh hour; davon gehen ~ aufs Dutzend they're ten a penny (inf); siehe auch vier.
Zwölf- in cpds siehe auch Vier-; ~eck nt (Math) dodecagon; z~eckig adj dodecagonal; ~ender m -s, - (Hunt) royal; (dated Mil sl) soldier who has served twelve years; z~fach adj twelvefold; siehe auch vierfach; ~fingerdarm m duodenum; ein Geschwür am ~fingerdarm a duodenal ulcer; ~flach nt -(e)s, -e, ~flächner m -s, - (Math) dodecahedron; ~kampf m (Sport) twelve-exercise event; ~meilenzone f twelve-mile zone.
zwölftens adv twelfth(ly), in twelfth place.
zwölfte(r, s) adj twelfth; siehe auch vierte(r, s).
Zwölftöner m -s, - (Mus) twelve-tone composer.
Zwölfton-: ~musik f twelve-tone music; ~reihe f twelve-tone row or series.
zwote(r, s) adj (Telec, inf) siehe zweite(r, s).

Zyan [tsyaːn] nt -s, no pl (Chem) cyanogen.
Zyanid [tsyaˈniːt] nt -s, -e cyanide.
Zyankali [tsyaːnˈkaːli] nt -s, no pl (Chem) potassium cyanide.
Zygote f -, -n (Biol) zygote.
Zykladen pl (Geog) Cyclades pl.
Zyklame f -, -n (Aus), **Zyklamen** nt -s, - (spec) cyclamen.
zyklisch 1 adj cyclic(al). 2 adv cyclically.
Zyklon¹ m -s, -e cyclone.
Zyklon² nt -s, no pl (Chem) cyanide-based poison, cyanide.
Zyklone f -, -n (Met) depression, low(-pressure area).
Zyklop m -en, -en (Myth) Cyclops.
Zyklopenmauer f (Archeol) cyclopean wall.
zyklopisch adj (Myth) Cyclopean; (liter: gewaltig) gigantic.
Zyklotron [ˈtsyˈklotroːn, ˈtsyk-] nt -s, -e (Phys) cyclotron.
Zyklus [ˈtsyːklus] m -, **Zyklen** [ˈtsyːklon] cycle.
Zykluszeit [ˈtsyːklus-] f (Datenverarbeitung) store cycle time.
Zylinder m -s, - (a) (Math, Tech) cylinder; (Lampen~) chimney. (b) (Hut) top-hat, topper (inf).
Zylinder-: ~block m (Aut) engine or cylinder block; ~dichtungsring m (Aut) cylinder ring; z~förmig adj siehe zylindrisch; ~hut m siehe Zylinder (b); ~kopf m (Aut) cylinder head; ~kopfdichtung f cylinder head gasket; ~mantel m (Tech) cylinder jacket; ~schloß nt cylinder lock.
-zylindrig adj suf -cylinder.
zylindrisch adj cylindrical.
Zymbal [ˈtsʏmbal] nt -s, -e (Mus) cymbal.
Zyniker(in f) [ˈtsyːnikɐ, -ərɪn] m -s, - cynic.
zynisch [ˈtsyːnɪʃ] adj cynical.
Zynismus m cynicism.
Zypern [ˈtsyːpɛn] nt -s Cyprus.
Zypresse f (Bot) cypress.
Zypr(i)er(in f) [ˈtsyːprɛ, -ərɪn, ˈtsyːpriɐ, -iərɪn] m -s, - (rare), **Zypriot(in** f) m -en, -en Cypriot.
zypriotisch, zyprisch [ˈtsyːprɪʃ] adj Cyprian, Cypriot.
Zyste [ˈtsʏstə] f -, -n cyst.
Zytologie f (Biol) cytology.
Zytoplasma nt (Biol) cytoplasm.
z.Z(t). abbr of zur Zeit.

A, a [eɪ] n A, a nt; (Sch: as a mark) eins, sehr gut; (Mus) A, a nt. from A to Z von A bis Z; **to get from A to B** von A nach B kommen; **A-1** (dated inf) Ia (inf), eins a (inf); **A sharp/flat** (Mus) Ais, ais nt/As, as nt; see also **major, minor, natural.**

a [eɪ, ə] indef art, before vowel **an** (a) ein(e). **so large ~ country** so ein großes or ein so großes Land; **~ Mr X/~ certain young man** ein Herr X/ein gewisser junger Mann.

  (b) (in negative constructions) **not ~** kein(e); **not ~ single man/woman/child** kein einziger or nicht ein einziger Mann/ keine einzige or nicht eine einzige Frau/kein einziges or nicht ein einziges Kind; **he didn't want ~ present** er wollte kein Geschenk.

  (c) (with profession, nationality etc) **he's ~ doctor/French-man** er ist Arzt/Franzose; **he's ~ famous doctor/Frenchman** er ist ein berühmter Arzt/Franzose; **as ~ young girl** als junges Mädchen; **~ Washington would have ...** ein Washington hätte ...

  (d) (with quantities) ein(e). **~ few** ein paar, einige; **~ dozen** ein Dutzend nt; **~ handful** eine Handvoll; **~ great many** viele; **~ lot of** eine Menge.

  (e) (the same) **to be of ~n age/~ size** gleich alt/groß sein, in einem Alter sein/eine Größe haben; see **kind.**

  (f) (per) pro. **£4 ~ head** £ 4 pro Person or Kopf (inf); **50p ~ kilo** 50 Pence das or pro Kilo; **twice ~ month** zweimal im or pro Monat; **50 km ~n hour** 50 Stundenkilometer, 50 Kilometer pro Stunde.

  (g) **in ~ good/bad mood** gut/schlecht gelaunt; **in ~ hurry** in Eile; **to come/to have come to ~n end** zu Ende gehen/sein; **in ~ loud voice** mit lauter Stimme, laut; **to have ~ headache/ temperature/fear** Kopfschmerzen/erhöhte Temperatur/Angst haben.

A abbr of (a) **answer** Antw. (b) (Brit Film) von der Filmkontrolle als nicht ganz jugendfrei gekennzeichneter Film. **~ certificate** Filmkennzeichnung, die Eltern vor dem nicht ganz jugendfreien Inhalt eines Films warnt.

a- pref (a) (privative) ~moral/~typical amoralisch/atypisch. (b) (old, dial) **they came ~running** sie kamen angerannt; **the bells were ~ringing** die Glocken läuteten.

AA abbr of (a) **Automobile Association** Britischer Automobilclub. (b) **Alcoholics Anonymous.** (c) (Brit Film) ≈ für Jugendliche ab 14 freigegebener Film.

aardvark ['ɑːdvɑːk] n Erdferkel nt.

Aaron's beard ['eərnz'bɪəd] n Harthen nt.

AB abbr of (a) (Naut) **able-bodied seaman.** (b) (US Univ) see **BA.**

aback [ə'bæk] adv: **to be taken ~** erstaunt sein; (upset) betroffen sein.

abacus ['æbəkəs] n, pl **abaci** ['æbəsiː] Abakus m.

abaft [ə'bɑːft] (Naut) 1 adv achtern. **to go ~** achtern gehen. 2 prep achtern von.

abalone [æbə'ləunɪ] n Seeohr nt.

abandon [ə'bændən] 1 vt (a) (leave, forsake) verlassen; woman also sitzenlassen; baby aussetzen; car also (einfach) stehenlassen. **they ~ed the city to the enemy** sie flohen und überließen dem Feind die Stadt; **to ~ ship** das Schiff verlassen.

  (b) (give up) project, hope, attempt aufgeben. **to ~ play** das Spiel abbrechen.

  (c) (fig) **to ~ oneself to sth** sich einer Sache (dat) hingeben. 2 n, no pl Hingabe, Selbstvergessenheit f. **with ~** mit ganzer Seele, mit Leib und Seele.

abandoned [ə'bændənd] adj (a) (dissolute) verkommen. (b) (unrestrained) dancing selbstvergessen, hingebungsvoll, hemmungslos (pej); joy unbändig.

abandonment [ə'bændənmənt] n (a) (forsaking, desertion) Verlassen nt. (b) (giving-up) Aufgabe f. (c) (abandon) Hingabe, Selbstvergessenheit f, Hemmungslosigkeit (pej) f.

abase [ə'beɪs] vt person erniedrigen; morals verderben. **to ~ oneself** sich (selbst) erniedrigen; **to ~ oneself so far as to do sth** sich dazu erniedrigen, etw zu tun.

abasement [ə'beɪsmənt] n Erniedrigung f; (of concept of love etc) Abwertung f; (lowering of standards) Verfall, Niedergang m. **~ of morality** Verfall der Moral.

abashed [ə'bæʃd] adj beschämt. **to feel ~** sich schämen.

abate [ə'beɪt] 1 vi nachlassen; (storm, eagerness, interest, noise also) abflauen; (pain, fever also) abklingen; (flood) zurückgehen. 2 vt (form) noise, sb's interest, enthusiasm dämpfen; anger beschwichtigen; rent, tax, fever senken; pain lindern.

abatement [ə'beɪtmənt] n (a) see vi Nachlassen nt; Abflauen nt; Abklingen nt; Rückgang m. (b) (form: reducing) see vt Dämpfung f; Beschwichtigung f; Senkung f; Linderung f. the

noise ~ society die Gesellschaft zur Bekämpfung von Lärm.

abattoir ['æbətwɑːᵣ] n Schlachthof m.

abbess ['æbɪs] n Äbtissin f.

abbey ['æbɪ] n Abtei f; (church in ~) Klosterkirche f.

abbot ['æbət] n Abt m.

abbreviate [ə'briːvɪeɪt] vt word, title abkürzen (to mit); book, speech verkürzen. **an ~d skirt** (hum inf) ein kurzes Röckchen.

abbreviation [ə,briːvɪ'eɪʃən] n (of word, title) Abkürzung f; (of book, speech) Verkürzung f.

ABC¹ ['eɪbiː'siː] n (lit, fig) Abc nt. **it's as easy as ~** das ist doch kinderleicht.

ABC² abbr of **American Broadcasting Company** Amerikanische Rundfunkgesellschaft.

abdicate ['æbdɪkeɪt] 1 vt verzichten auf (+acc). 2 vi (monarch) abdanken, abdizieren (dated geh); (pope) zurücktreten.

abdication [,æbdɪ'keɪʃən] n (of monarch) Abdankung, Abdikation (dated geh) f; (of pope) Verzicht m. **his ~ of the throne** sein Verzicht auf den Thron.

abdomen ['æbdəmən] n (Med) æb'dəumen] n Abdomen nt (form); (of man, mammals also) Unterleib m; (of insects also) Hinterleib m.

abdominal [æb'dɒmɪnl] adj see n abdominal (form); Unterleibs-; Hinterleibs-. **~ segments** Abdominalsegmente pl; **~ wall** Bauchdecke f.

abduct [æb'dʌkt] vt entführen.

abduction [æb'dʌkʃən] n Entführung f.

abductor [æb'dʌktəᵣ] n Entführer(in f) m.

abeam [ə'biːm] adv (Naut) querab.

abed [ə'bed] adv (old) im Bett. **to be ~** (im Bette) ruhen (geh).

Aberdeen Angus ['æbədiːn'æŋgəs] n Aberdeen Angus nt (Fett-Mastrind).

Aberdonian [,æbə'dəunjən] 1 n Aberdeener(in f) m. 2 adj Aberdeener inv.

aberrant [ə'berənt] adj anomal.

aberration [,æbə'reɪʃən] n Anomalie f; (Astron, Opt) Aberration f; (in statistics, from course) Abweichung f; (mistake) Irrtum m; (moral) Verirrung f. **in a moment of (mental) ~** (inf) in einem Augenblick geistiger Verwirrung; **I must have had an ~** (inf) da war ich wohl (geistig) weggetreten (inf); **the housing scheme/this translation is something of an ~** (inf) die Wohnsiedlung/diese Übersetzung ist (ja) eine Krankheit (inf).

abet [ə'bet] 1 vt crime, criminal begünstigen, Vorschub leisten (+dat); (fig) unterstützen. 2 vi see **aid 2.**

abetter, abettor [ə'betəᵣ] n Helfershelfer(in f) m.

abeyance [ə'beɪəns] n, no pl **to be in ~** (law, rule, issue) ruhen; (custom, office) nicht mehr ausgeübt werden; **to fall into ~** außer Gebrauch kommen, nicht mehr wirksam sein; **to hold sth in ~** etw ruhenlassen.

abhor [əb'hɔːᵣ] vt verabscheuen.

abhorrence [əb'hɒrəns] n Abscheu f (of vor +dat). **to hold sb/sth in ~** Abscheu vor jdm/etw haben.

abhorrent [əb'hɒrənt] adj abscheulich. **the very idea is ~ to me** schon der Gedanke daran ist mir zuwider; **the notion is ~ to the rational mind** der Verstand widersetzt sich einer solchen Idee; **it is ~ to me to have to ...** es widerstrebt mir, ... zu müssen.

abidance [ə'baɪdəns] n (form) **~ by the rules/laws** die Einhaltung der Regeln/Gesetze.

abide [ə'baɪd] 1 vt (usu neg, interrog: tolerate) ausstehen; (endure) aushalten. **I cannot ~ living here** ich kann es nicht aushalten, hier zu leben. (b) (liter: wait for) harren (+gen) (liter). 2 vi (old: remain, live) weilen (geh).

♦**abide by** vi +prep obj rule, law, decision, promise, results sich halten an (+acc); consequences tragen. **I ~ ~ what I said** ich bleibe bei dem, was ich gesagt habe.

abiding [ə'baɪdɪŋ] adj (liter: lasting) unvergänglich; desire also bleibend.

ability [ə'bɪlɪtɪ] n Fähigkeit f. **~ to pay/hear** Zahlungs-/ Hörfähigkeit f; **to the best of my ~** nach (besten) Kräften; (with mental activities) so gut ich es kann; **a pianist/man of great ~** ein ausgesprochen fähiger or begabter Pianist/ein sehr fähiger Mann; **a man of many abilities** ein sehr vielseitiger Mensch; **his ~ in German** seine Fähigkeiten im Deutschen; **he has great ~** er ist ausgesprochen fähig.

abject ['æbdʒekt] adj (a) (wretched) state, liar, thief elend, erbärmlich; poverty bitter. (b) (servile) submission, apology demütig; person, gesture also unterwürfig.

abjection [æb'dʒekʃn] n see **abjectness.**

abjectly ['æbdʒektlɪ] adv see adj erbärmlich; demütig; unterwürfig.

abjectness ['æbdʒektnɪs] n see adj Erbärmlichkeit f; Demut f;

Unterwürfigkeit f. such was the ~ of their poverty ... so bitter war ihre Armut ...

abjuration [ˌæbdʒʊəˈreɪʃn] n Abschwören nt.

abjure [əbˈdʒʊəʳ] vt abschwören (+dat).

ablative [ˈæblətɪv] 1 n Ablativ m. ~ absolute Ablativus absolutus. 2 adj ending, case Ablativ-; noun im Ablativ.

ablaut [ˈæblaʊt] n Ablaut m.

ablaze [əˈbleɪz] adv, adj pred in Flammen. to be ~ in Flammen stehen; to set sth ~ etw in Brand stecken; the paraffin really set the fire ~ das Paraffin ließ das Feuer wirklich auflodern; his face was ~ with joy/anger sein Gesicht glühte vor Freude/brannte vor Ärger; to be ~ with light/colour hell erleuchtet sein/in leuchtenden Farben erstrahlen.

able [ˈeɪbl] adj (a) (skilled, talented) person fähig, kompetent; piece of work, exam paper, speech gekonnt.
(b) to be ~ to do sth etw tun können; if you're not ~ to understand that wenn Sie nicht fähig sind, das zu verstehen; I'm afraid I am not ~ to give you that information ich bin leider nicht in der Lage, Ihnen diese Informationen zu geben, ich kann Ihnen leider diese Informationen nicht geben; you are better ~ to do it than he Sie sind eher dazu in der Lage als er; yes, if I'm ~ ja, wenn es mir möglich ist.

-able [-əbl] adj suf -bar, -lich.

able-bodied [ˌeɪblˈbɒdɪd] adj (gesund und) kräftig; (Mil) tauglich.

able(-bodied) seaman n Vollmatrose m.

ablution [əˈbluːʃn] n Waschung f. ~s pl (lavatory) sanitäre Einrichtungen pl; to perform one's ~s (esp hum) seine Waschungen vornehmen; (go to lavatory) seine Notdurft verrichten.

ably [ˈeɪblɪ] adv gekonnt, fähig.

ABM abbr of **anti-ballistic missile.**

abnegate [ˈæbnɪgeɪt] vt entsagen (+dat).

abnegation [ˌæbnɪˈgeɪʃn] n Verzicht m (of auf +acc), Entsagung f. self-~ Selbstverleugnung f.

abnormal [æbˈnɔːml] adj anormal; (deviant, Med) abnorm. ~ psychology Psychologie f des Abnormen.

abnormality [ˌæbnɔːˈmælɪtɪ] n Anormale(s) nt; (deviancy, Med) Abnormität f.

abnormally [æbˈnɔːməlɪ] adv see adj.

Abo [ˈæbəʊ] n (Austral inf) (australischer) Ureinwohner.

aboard [əˈbɔːd] 1 adv (on plane, ship) an Bord; (on train) im Zug; (on bus) im Bus. all ~! alle an Bord!; (on train, bus) alles einsteigen!; to go ~ an Bord gehen; they were no sooner ~ than the train/bus moved off sie waren kaum eingestiegen, als der Zug/Bus auch schon abfuhr.
2 prep ~ the ship/train/bus an Bord des Schiffes/im Zug/Bus.

abode [əˈbəʊd] 1 pret, ptp of abide. 2 n (liter: dwelling place) Behausung f, Aufenthalt m (liter); (Jur: also place of ~) Wohnsitz m. a humble ~ (iro) eine bescheidene Hütte (iro); of no fixed ~ ohne festen Wohnsitz.

abolish [əˈbɒlɪʃ] vt abschaffen; law also aufheben.

abolishment [əˈbɒlɪʃmənt], **abolition** [ˌæbəʊˈlɪʃən] n Abschaffung f; (of slavery also) Abolition f (form); (of law also) Aufhebung f.

abolitionist [ˌæbəʊˈlɪʃənɪst] n Abolitionist m (form).

A-bomb [ˈeɪbɒm] n Atombombe f.

abominable [əˈbɒmɪnəbl] adj gräßlich, abscheulich; spelling gräßlich, entsetzlich. A~ Snowman Schneemensch m.

abominably [əˈbɒmɪnəblɪ] adv gräßlich, abscheulich. ~ rude furchtbar unhöflich.

abominate [əˈbɒmɪneɪt] vt verabscheuen.

abomination [əˌbɒmɪˈneɪʃən] n (a) no pl Verabscheuung f. to be held in ~ by sb von jdm verabscheut werden. (b) (loathsome act) Abscheulichkeit f; (loathsome thing) Scheußlichkeit f.

aboriginal [ˌæbəˈrɪdʒənl] 1 adj der (australischen) Ureinwohner, australid; tribe also australisch. 2 n see aborigine.

aborigine [ˌæbəˈrɪdʒɪnɪ] n Ureinwohner(in f) m (Australiens), Australide m, Australidin f.

abort [əˈbɔːt] 1 vi (Med) (mother) eine Fehlgeburt haben, abortieren (form); (foetus) abgehen; (perform abortion) die Schwangerschaft abbrechen, einen Abort herbeiführen (form); (fig: go wrong) scheitern.
2 vt (Med) foetus (durch Abort) entfernen, abtreiben (pej); (Space) mission abbrechen.
3 n (Space) Abort m (form).

abortion [əˈbɔːʃən] n Schwangerschaftsabbruch m, Abtreibung f (pej); (miscarriage) Fehlgeburt f, Abort m (form); (fig: plan, project etc) Fehlschlag, Reinfall (inf) m; (pej: person) Mißgeburt f (pej). to get or have an ~ abtreiben lassen, eine Abtreibung vornehmen lassen.

abortionist [əˈbɔːʃənɪst] n Abtreibungshelfer(in f) m; (doctor also) Abtreibungsarzt m/-ärztin f; see back-street.

abortive [əˈbɔːtɪv] adj (a) (unsuccessful) attempt, plan gescheitert, fehlgeschlagen. to be ~ scheitern, fehlschlagen. (b) (Med) drug abortiv (form), abtreibend.

abound [əˈbaʊnd] vi (exist in great numbers) im Überfluß vorhanden sein; (persons) sehr zahlreich sein; (have in great numbers) reich sein (in an +dat)/wimmeln (with von). students/rabbits/berries ~ in ... es wimmelt von Studenten/Kaninchen/Beeren in ...

about [əˈbaʊt] 1 adv (a) herum, umher; (present) in der Nähe. to run/walk ~ herum- or umherrennen/-gehen; I looked all ~ ich sah ringsumher; with flowers all ~ mit Blumen ringsumher or überall; the castle walls are half a mile ~ die Mauer (rings) um das Schloß ist eine halbe Meile lang; to leave things (lying) ~ Sachen herumliegen lassen; to be (up and) ~ again wieder auf den Beinen sein; we were ~ early wir waren früh auf den Beinen; there's a thief/a lot of measles/plenty of money ~ ein Dieb geht um/die Masern gehen um/es ist Geld in Mengen vor-

handen; there was nobody ~ who could help es war niemand in der Nähe or um den Weg, der hätte helfen können; at night when there's nobody ~ nachts, wenn niemand unterwegs ist; wait till there is nobody ~ before ... warte, bis niemand um den Weg ist, bevor ...; where is he/it? — he's/it's ~ somewhere wo ist er/es? — (er/es ist) irgendwo in der Nähe; it's the other way ~ es ist gerade umgekehrt; day and day ~ (täglich) abwechselnd; see out, turn, up.

(b) to be ~ to im Begriff sein zu; (esp US inf: intending) vorhaben, zu ...; I was ~ to go out ich wollte gerade ausgehen; it's ~ to rain es regnet gleich or demnächst; he's ~/almost ~ to start school er kommt demnächst in die Schule; we are ~ to run out of petrol uns geht demnächst das Benzin aus, uns geht gleich das Benzin aus; are you ~ to tell me ...? willst du mir etwa erzählen ...?

(c) (approximately) ungefähr, (so) um ... (herum). he's ~ 40 er ist ungefähr 40 or (so) um (die) 40 (herum); ~ 2 o'clock ungefähr or so um 2 Uhr; he is ~ the same, doctor sein Zustand hat sich kaum geändert, Herr Doktor; that's ~ it das ist so ziemlich alles, das wär's (so ziemlich) (inf); that's ~ right das stimmt (so) ungefähr; I've had ~ enough (of this nonsense) jetzt reicht es mir aber allmählich (mit diesem Unsinn) (inf); I'm ~ fed up with him ich hab's allmählich satt mit ihm (inf); he was ~ dead from exhaustion er war halb tot vor Erschöpfung; see just, round, time.

2 prep (a) um (... herum); (in) in (+dat) (... herum). the fields ~ the house die Felder ums Haus (herum); scattered ~ the room im ganzen or über das ganze Zimmer verstreut; somewhere ~ here irgendwo hier herum; all ~ the house im ganzen Haus (herum); to sit/do jobs ~ the house im Haus herumsitzen/sich im Haus (herum) nützlich machen; he looked ~ him er schaute sich um; I have no money ~ me ich habe kein Geld bei mir; he had a mysterious air ~ him er hatte etwas Geheimnisvolles an sich; there's something ~ him/~ the way he speaks er/seine Art zu reden hat so etwas an sich; while you're ~ it wenn du gerade or schon dabei bist; you've been a long time ~ it du hast lange dazu gebraucht; and be quick ~ it! und beeil dich damit!, aber ein bißchen dalli! (inf).

(b) (concerning) über (+acc). tell me all ~ it erzähl doch mal; he knows ~ it er weiß darüber Bescheid, er weiß davon; what's it all ~? worum or um was (inf) handelt es sich or geht es (eigentlich)?; he knows what it's all ~ er weiß Bescheid; he's promised to do something ~ it er hat versprochen, (in der Sache) etwas zu unternehmen; they fell out ~ money sie haben sich wegen Geld zerstritten; how or what ~ me? und ich, was ist mit mir? (inf); how or what ~ it/going to the pictures? wie wär's damit/mit (dem) Kino?; what ~ that book? have you brought it back? was ist mit dem Buch? hast du es zurückgebracht?; (yes,) what ~ it/him? ja or na und(, was ist damit/mit ihm)?; he doesn't know what he's ~ er weiß nicht, was er (eigentlich) tut.

about-face [əˌbaʊtˈfeɪs], **about-turn** [əˌbaʊtˈtɜːn] 1 n (Mil)Kehrtwendung f; (fig also) Wendung f um hundertachtzig Grad. to do an ~ kehrtmachen; (fig) sich um hundertachtzig Grad drehen. 2 vi (Mil) eine Kehrtwendung ausführen or machen. 3 interj about face or turn! (und) kehrt!

above [əˈbʌv] 1 adv (a) (overhead) oben; (in heaven also) in der Höhe; (in a higher position) darüber. from ~ von oben; (from heaven also) aus der Höhe; look straight ~ schau genau nach oben; the flat ~ die Wohnung oben or (~ that one) darüber.
(b) (in text) oben.
2 prep über (+dat); (with motion) über (+acc); (upstream of) oberhalb (+gen). ~ all vor allem, vor allen Dingen; I couldn't hear ~ the din ich konnte bei dem Lärm nichts hören; he valued money ~ his family er schätzte Geld mehr als seine Familie; to be ~ sb/sth über jdm/etw stehen; ~ criticism/praise über jede Kritik/jedes Lob erhaben; he's ~ that sort of thing er ist über so etwas erhaben; he's not ~ a bit of blackmail er ist sich (dat) nicht zu gut für eine kleine Erpressung; it's ~ my head or me das ist mir zu hoch; to be/get ~ oneself (inf) größenwahnsinnig werden (inf).
3 adj attr the ~ persons/figures die obengenannten or -erwähnten Personen/Zahlen; the ~ paragraph der vorher- or vorangehende or obige Abschnitt.
4 n: the ~ (statement etc) Obiges nt (form); (person) der/die Obengenannte/die Obengenannten pl.

above: ~ board adj pred korrekt; open and ~ board offen und ehrlich; ~-mentioned adj obenerwähnt; ~-named adj obengenannt.

abracadabra [ˌæbrəkəˈdæbrə] n Abrakadabra nt.

abrade [əˈbreɪd] vt (form) skin aufschürfen, abschürfen; (Geol) abtragen.

Abraham [ˈeɪbrəhæm] n Abraham m. in ~'s bosom in Abrahams Schoß.

abrasion [əˈbreɪʒən] n (Med) (Haut)abschürfung f; (Geol) Abtragung f; (by the sea also) Abrasion f (form).

abrasive [əˈbreɪsɪv] 1 adj (a) cleanser Scheuer-, scharf; surface rauh. ~ paper Schmirgel- or Schleifpapier nt. (b) (fig) personality, person aggressiv; tongue, voice scharf. 2 n (cleanser) Scheuermittel nt; (~ substance) Schleifmittel nt.

abrasiveness [əˈbreɪsɪvnɪs] n see adj (a) Schärfe f; Rauheit f. (b) Aggressivität f; Schärfe f.

abreact [ˌæbrɪˈækt] vt (Psych) abreagieren.

abreaction [ˌæbrɪˈækʃən] n (Psych) Abreaktion f.

abreast [əˈbrest] adv Seite an Seite; (Naut also) Bug an Bug. to march four ~ im Viererglied or zu viert nebeneinander marschieren; twelve horses came in, four ~ jeweils zu viert nebeneinander kamen zwölf Pferde herein; ~ of sb/sth neben jdm/etw, auf gleicher Höhe mit jdm/etw; to come ~ (of sb/sth) mit jdm/etw gleichziehen, auf gleiche Höhe mit jdm/etw kommen; **to keep ~ of the times/news/events** *etc* mit seiner Zeit/den Nachrichten/den Ereignissen *etc* auf dem laufenden bleiben.

abridge [ə'brɪdʒ] *vt book* kürzen.

abridgement [ə'brɪdʒmənt] *n* (*act*) Kürzen *nt*; (*abridged work*) gekürzte Ausgabe.

abroad [ə'brɔːd] *adv* (a) im Ausland. **to go/be sent ~** ins Ausland gehen/geschickt werden; **from ~** aus dem Ausland.
(b) (*esp liter: out of doors*) draußen. **to venture ~** sich nach draußen *or* ins Freie wagen; **he was ~ very early** er war schon sehr früh unterwegs.
(c) **there is a rumour ~ that ...** ein Gerücht geht um *or* kursiert, daß ...; **to get ~** an die Öffentlichkeit dringen; *see* **publish**.
(d) (*liter: far and wide*) *scatter* weit.

abrogate ['æbrəʊgeɪt] *vt law, treaty* außer Kraft setzen; *responsibility* ablehnen.

abrogation [,æbrəʊ'geɪʃən] *n see vt* Außerkraftsetzung, Ungültigkeitserklärung *f*; Ablehnung *f*.

abrupt [ə'brʌpt] *adj* abrupt; *descent, drop* unvermittelt, jäh; *bend* plötzlich; *manner, reply* schroff, brüsk.

abruptly [ə'brʌptlɪ] *adv see adj* abrupt; unvermittelt, jäh; plötzlich; schroff, brüsk.

abruptness [ə'brʌptnɪs] *n* abrupte Art; (*of person*) schroffe *or* brüske Art; (*of descent, drop, bend*) Plötzlichkeit, Jäheit *f*; (*of style, writing also*) Abgerissenheit *f*; (*of reply*) Schroffheit *f*.

abscess ['æbsɪs] *n* Abszeß *m*.

abscond [əb'skɒnd] *vi* sich (heimlich) davonmachen, türmen (*inf*); (*schoolboys also*) durchbrennen.

abseil ['æpsaɪl] **1** *vi* (*Mountaineering: also ~ down*) sich abseilen. **2** *n* Abstieg *m* (am Seil).

absence ['æbsəns] *n* (a) Abwesenheit *f*; (*from school, work etc also*) Fehlen *nt*; (*from meetings etc also*) Nichterscheinen *nt* (*from* bei). **in the ~ of the chairman** in Abwesenheit des Vorsitzenden; **sentenced in one's ~** in Abwesenheit verurteilt; **it's not fair to criticize him in his ~** es ist nicht fair, ihn in seiner Abwesenheit zu kritisieren; **her many ~s on business** ihre häufige Abwesenheit aus geschäftlichen Gründen; **~ makes the heart grow fonder** (*Prov*) die Liebe wächst mit der Entfernung (*Prov*).
(b) (*lack*) Fehlen *nt*. **~ of enthusiasm** Mangel *m* an Enthusiasmus; **in the ~ of further evidence/qualified staff** in Ermangelung weiterer Beweise/von Fachkräften.
(c) (*person absent*) **he counted the ~s** er stellte die Zahl der Abwesenden fest; **how many ~s do we have today?** wie viele fehlen heute *or* sind heute nicht da *or* anwesend?; **there's only one ~** es fehlt nur einer, nur einer ist nicht da *or* anwesend.
(d) **~ of mind** Geistesabwesenheit *f*.

absent ['æbsənt] **1** *adj* (a) (*not present*) *person* abwesend, nicht da. **to be ~ from school/work** in der Schule/am Arbeitsplatz fehlen; **~!** (*Sch*) fehlt!; **why were you ~ from class?** warum warst du nicht in der Stunde?, warum hast du gefehlt?; **to be ~ or go ~ without leave** (*Mil*) sich unerlaubt von der Truppe entfernen; **to ~ friends!** auf unsere abwesenden Freunde!
(b) (*~-minded*) *expression, look* (geistes)abwesend. **in an ~ moment** in einem Augenblick geistiger Abwesenheit.
(c) (*lacking*) **to be ~** fehlen; **nothing was further ~ from my mind** nichts lag mir ferner.
2 [æb'sent] *vr* **to ~ oneself (from)** (*not go, not appear*) fernbleiben (+*dat*, von); (*leave temporarily*) sich zurückziehen *or* absentieren (*raum, geh*).

absentee [,æbsən'tiː] *n* Abwesende(r) *mf*. **there were a lot of ~s** es fehlten viele; (*pej*) es haben viele krank gefeiert.

absentee ballot *n* (*esp US*) ≃ Briefwahl *f*.

absenteeism [,æbsən'tiːɪzəm] *n* häufige Abwesenheit; (*of workers also*) Nichterscheinen *nt* am Arbeitsplatz; (*pej*) Krankfeiern *nt*; (*Sch*) Schwänzen *nt*. **the rate of ~ among workers** die Abwesenheitsquote bei Arbeitern.

absentee: **~ landlord** *n* nicht ortsansässiger Haus-/Grundbesitzer; **~ voter** *n* (*esp US*) ≃ Briefwähler(in *f*) *m*.

absently ['æbsəntlɪ] *adv* (geistes)abwesend.

absent-minded [,æbsənt'maɪndɪd] *adj* (*lost in thought*) geistesabwesend; (*habitually forgetful*) zerstreut.

absent-mindedly [,æbsənt'maɪndɪdlɪ] *adv behave* zerstreut; *look* (geistes)abwesend. **he ~ forgot it** in seiner Zerstreutheit hat er es vergessen.

absent-mindedness [,æbsənt'maɪndɪdnɪs] *n see adj* Geistesabwesenheit *f*; Zerstreutheit *f*.

absinth(e) ['æbsɪnθ] *n* Absinth *m*.

absolute ['æbsəluːt] *adj* absolut; *power, liberty, support also, command* uneingeschränkt; *monarch also* unumschränkt; *lie, idiot* ausgemacht. **the ~** das Absolute; **~ majority** absolute Mehrheit; **~ pitch** absolute Tonhöhe; (*of person*) absolutes Gehör; **~ zero** absoluter Nullpunkt.

absolutely ['æbsəluːtlɪ] *adv* absolut; *prove* eindeutig; *agree, trust also, true* vollkommen, völlig; *deny, refuse also* strikt; *forbidden also* streng; *stupid also* völlig; *necessary also* unbedingt. **~!** durchaus; (*I agree*) genau!; **do you/don't you agree?** — **~** sind Sie einverstanden? — vollkommen/sind Sie nicht einverstanden? — doch, vollkommen; **do you ~ insist?** muß das unbedingt *or* durchaus sein?; **he ~ refused to do that** er wollte das absolut *or* durchaus nicht tun; **it's ~ amazing** es ist wirklich erstaunlich; **you look ~ stunning/awful** du siehst wirklich großartig/schrecklich aus; **you're ~ right** Sie haben völlig recht.

absolution [,æbsə'luːʃən] *n* (*Eccl*) Absolution, Lossprechung *f*. **to say the ~** die Absolution erteilen.

absolutism ['æbsəluːtɪzəm] *n* Absolutismus *m*.

absolve [əb'zɒlv] *vt person* (*from sins*) lossprechen (*from* von); (*from blame*) freisprechen (*from* von); (*from vow, oath etc*) entbinden (*from* von, gen).

---

absorb [əb'sɔːb] *vt* absorbieren, aufnehmen; *liquid also* aufsaugen; *knowledge, news also* in sich (*acc*) aufnehmen; *vibration* auffangen, absorbieren; *shock* dämpfen; *light, sound* absorbieren, schlucken; *people, firm also* integrieren (*into* in +*acc*); *costs etc* tragen; *one's time* in Anspruch nehmen. **she ~s things quickly** sie hat eine rasche Auffassungsgabe; **to be/get ~ed in a book** *etc* in ein Buch *etc* vertieft *or* versunken sein/sich in ein Buch *etc* vertiefen; **she was completely ~ed in her family/job** sie ging völlig in ihrer Familie/Arbeit auf.

absorbency [əb'sɔːbənsɪ] *n* Saug- *or* Absorptionsfähigkeit *f*.

absorbent [əb'sɔːbənt] *adj* saugfähig, absorbierend.

absorbent cotton *n* (*US*) Watte *f*.

absorbing [əb'sɔːbɪŋ] *adj* fesselnd.

absorption [əb'sɔːpʃən] *n see vt* Absorption, Aufnahme *f*; Aufsaugung *f*; Aufnahme *f*; Auffangen *nt*; Dämpfung *f*; Integration *f*. **her total ~ in her family/studies/book** ihr vollkommenes Aufgehen in ihrer Familie/ihrem Studium/ihre völlige Versunkenheit in dem Buch; **to watch with ~** gefesselt *or* gebannt beobachten.

abstain [əb'steɪn] *vi* (a) sich enthalten (*from gen*). **to ~ from alcohol/drinking** sich des Alkohols/Trinkens enthalten (*geh*); **to ~ from comment** sich eines Kommentars enthalten (*geh*). (b) (*in voting*) sich der Stimme enthalten.

abstainer [əb'steɪnər] *n* (a) (*from alcohol*) Abstinenzler(in *f*) *m*. (b) *see* **abstention (b)**.

abstemious [əb'stiːmɪəs] *adj person, life* enthaltsam; *meal, diet* bescheiden.

abstemiousness [əb'stiːmɪəsnɪs] *n see adj* Enthaltsamkeit *f*; Bescheidenheit *f*.

abstention [əb'stenʃən] *n* (a) *no pl* Enthaltung *f*; (*from alcohol also*) Abstinenz *f*. (b) (*in voting*) (Stimm)enthaltung *f*. **were you one of the ~s?** waren Sie einer von denen, die sich der Stimme enthalten haben?

abstinence ['æbstɪnəns] *n* Abstinenz, Enthaltung *f* (*from von*); (*self-restraint*) Enthaltsamkeit *f*. **total ~** völlige Abstinenz; **day of ~** Abstinenztag, Fasttag *m*.

abstract[1] ['æbstrækt] **1** *adj* (*all senses*) abstrakt. **in the ~** abstrakt; **~ noun** Abstraktum *nt*, abstraktes Substantiv. **2** *n* (*kurze*) Zusammenfassung *f*; (*as title*) Übersicht *f* (*of gen*, über +*acc*).

abstract[2] [æb'strækt] *vt* abstrahieren; *information* entnehmen (*from aus*); *metal etc* trennen; (*inf: steal*) entwenden.

abstracted [æb'stræktɪd] *adj* abwesend, entrückt (*geh*).

abstraction [æb'strækʃən] *n* Abstraktion *f*; (*abstract term also*) Abstraktum *nt*; (*mental separation also*) Abstrahieren *nt*; (*extraction: of information etc*) Entnahme *f*; (*absent-mindedness*) Entrücktheit *f* (*geh*). **to argue in ~s** in abstrakten Begriffen *or* Abstraktionen argumentieren.

abstractness ['æbstræktnɪs] *n* Abstraktheit *f*.

abstruse [æb'struːs] *adj* abstrus.

abstruseness [æb'struːsnɪs] *n* abstruse Unklarheit.

absurd [əb'sɜːd] *adj* absurd. **don't be ~!** sei nicht albern; **if you think that, you're just being ~** du bist ja nicht recht bei Trost, wenn du das glaubst; **what an ~ waste of time!** so eine blödsinnige Zeitverschwendung!; **the management is being ~ again** das Management spielt mal wieder verrückt (*inf*); **theatre of the ~** absurdes Theater.

absurdity [əb'sɜːdɪtɪ] *n* Absurde(s) *nt no pl* (*of an +dat*); (*thing etc also*) Absurdität *f*.

absurdly [əb'sɜːdlɪ] *adv behave, react* absurd; *fast*, (*inf*) *rich, expensive etc* unsinnig. **he talked/suggested very ~ ...** er redete großen Unsinn/er machte absurderweise den Vorschlag ...

abundance [ə'bʌndəns] *n* (*großer*) Reichtum (*of an +dat*); (*of hair, vegetation, details, illustrations, information, ideas, colours also, proof*) Fülle *f* (*of von, gen*). **in ~** in Hülle und Fülle; **a country with an ~ of oil/raw materials** ein Land mit reichen Ölvorkommen/großem Reichtum an Rohstoffen; **with his ~ of energy** mit seiner ungeheuren Energie; **such an ~ of open space** so unermeßlich viel freies Land.

abundant [ə'bʌndənt] *adj* reich; *growth, hair* üppig; *time, proof* reichlich; *energy, self-confidence etc* ungeheuer. **to be ~ in sth** reich an etw (*dat*) sein; **apples are in ~ supply in autumn** im Herbst gibt es reichlich Äpfel *or* gibt es Äpfel in Hülle und Fülle.

abundantly [ə'bʌndəntlɪ] *adv* reichlich; *grow* in Hülle und Fülle, üppig. **to make it ~ clear that ...** mehr als deutlich zu verstehen geben, daß ...; **it was ~ clear (to me) that ...** es war (mir) mehr als klar, daß ...; **that is ~ obvious** das ist mehr als offensichtlich.

abuse [ə'bjuːs] **1** *n* (a) *no pl* (*insults*) Beschimpfungen *pl*. **a term of ~** ein Schimpfwort *nt*; **to shout ~ at sb** jdm Beschimpfungen an den Kopf werfen; **to heap ~ on sb** jdn mit Beschimpfungen überschütten; *see* **shower, stream**.
(b) (*misuse*) Mißbrauch *m*; (*unjust practice*) Mißstand *m*. **~ of confidence/authority** Vertrauens-/Amtsmißbrauch *m*; **the system is open to ~** das System läßt sich leicht mißbrauchen.
2 [ə'bjuːz] *vt* (a) (*revile*) beschimpfen, schmähen (*geh*). (b) (*misuse*) mißbrauchen; *one's health* Raubbau treiben mit.

abusive [ə'bjuːsɪv] *adj* beleidigend. **~ language** Beschimpfungen, Beleidigungen *pl*; **to be ~ (to sb)** (jdm gegenüber) beleidigend *or* ausfallend sein; **he muttered something ~** er murmelte etwas Beleidigendes; **to become/get ~ (with sb)** (jdm gegenüber) beleidigend *or* ausfallend werden.

abusiveness [ə'bjuːsɪvnɪs] *n* (*of person*) ausfallende Art. **language of such ~** eine derart ausfallende Ausdrucksweise; **a critic should not descend to mere ~** ein Kritiker sollte sich nicht in reinen Ausfälligkeiten ergehen.

abut [ə'bʌt] *vi* stoßen (*on/to* an +*acc*); (*land also*) grenzen (*on/to* an +*acc*); (*two houses, fields etc*) aneinanderstoßen/-grenzen.

abutment [ə'bʌtmənt] *n (Archit)* Flügel- *or* Wangenmauer *f.*

abutter [ə'bʌtə^r] *n (US)* Anlieger *m*; *(to one's own land)* (Grenz)nachbar(in *f*) *m.*

abutting [ə'bʌtɪŋ] *adj* (daran) anstoßend *attr*; *(fields also)* (daran) angrenzend *attr.* the two ~ houses die zwei aneinanderstoßenden Häuser.

abysmal [ə'bɪzməl] *adj (fig)* entsetzlich; *performance, work, taste etc* miserabel.

abysmally [ə'bɪzməlɪ] *adv* entsetzlich; *perform, work etc also* miserabel. our team did ~ in the competition unsere Mannschaft schnitt bei dem Wettkampf entsetzlich (schlecht) *or* miserabel ab.

abyss [ə'bɪs] *n (lit, fig)* Abgrund *m.* the ~ of space die Weite des Alls.

Abyssinia [,æbɪ'sɪnɪə] *n* Abessinien *nt.*

Abyssinian [,æbɪ'sɪnɪən] 1 *adj attr* abessinisch. 2 *n* Abessinier(in *f*) *m.*

A/C *abbr of* **account.**

AC *abbr of* **alternating current; aircraftman.**

acacia [ə'keɪʃə] *n (also ~ tree)* Akazie *f.*

academic [,ækə'demɪk] 1 *adj* **(a)** akademisch; *publisher, reputation* wissenschaftlich.
(b) *(intellectual)* approach, quality, interest wissenschaftlich; *interests* geistig; *person, appearance* intellektuell; *style, book also* akademisch.
(c) *(theoretical)* akademisch. out of ~ interest aus rein akademischem Interesse; since the decision has already been made the discussion is purely ~ dạ die Entscheidung schon getroffen wurde, ist das eine (rein) akademische Diskussion.
2 *n* Akademiker(in *f*) *m*; *(Univ)* Universitätslehrkraft *f.*

academically [,ækə'demɪkəlɪ] *adv* **(a)** wissenschaftlich. to be ~ inclined/minded geistige Interessen haben/wissenschaftlich denken; ~ respectable wissenschaftlich akzeptabel; ~ gifted intellektuell begabt.
(b) she is not doing well ~ sie ist in der Schule nicht gut/mit ihrem Studium nicht sehr erfolgreich; she's good at handicraft but is not doing so well ~ im Werken ist sie gut, aber in den wissenschaftlichen Fächern hapert es.

academicals [,ækə'demɪkəlz] *npl* akademische Tracht.

academician [ə,kædə'mɪʃən] *n* Akademiemitglied *nt.*

academy [ə'kædəmɪ] *n* Akademie *f. naval/military ~* Marine/Militärakademie *f*; ~ **for young ladies** ≈ höhere Töchterschule.

acanthus [ə'kænθəs] *n (plant)* Bärenklau *f*, Akanthus *m (also Archit).*

acc *abbr of* **account; accommodation** Übern.

accede [æk'siːd] *vi* **(a)** to ~ to the throne den Thron besteigen; to ~ to the Premiership/office of President die Nachfolge als Premierminister/Präsident antreten. **(b)** *(agree)* zustimmen *(to dat)*; *(yield)* einwilligen *(to in +acc).* **(c)** to ~ to a treaty einem Pakt beitreten.

accelerate [æk'seləreɪt] 1 *vt* beschleunigen; *speed also* erhöhen.
2 *vi* beschleunigen; *(driver also)* Gas geben; *(work-rate, speed, change)* sich beschleunigen, zunehmen; *(growth, inflation etc)* zunehmen. he ~d away er gab Gas und fuhr davon; he ~d out of the bend er hat in der Kurve beschleunigt *or* Gas gegeben; to ~ away *(runner etc)* lossspurten; *(car etc)* losfahren.

acceleration [æk,selə'reɪʃən] *n* Beschleunigung *f*; *(of speed also)* Erhöhung *f.* to have good/poor ~ eine gute/schlechte Beschleunigung haben, gut/schlecht beschleunigen.

acceleration ratio *n* Beschleunigungswert *m.*

accelerator [æk'seləreɪtə^r] *n* **(a)** *(also ~ pedal)* Gaspedal, Gas *(inf) nt.* to step on the ~ aufs Gas treten *or* drücken *(inf).* **(b)** *(Phys)* Beschleuniger *m.*

accent ['æksənt] 1 *n (all senses)* Akzent *m*; *(stress also)* Betonung *f*; *(mark on letter also)* Akzentzeichen *nt*; *(pl liter: tones)* Töne *pl*, Tonfall *m.* to speak (a language) without/with an ~ (eine Sprache) akzentfrei *or* ohne/mit Akzent sprechen; in ~s of some surprise *(liter)* in ziemlich überraschtem Ton(fall); to put the ~ on sth *(fig)* den Akzent auf etw *(acc)* legen; to shift the ~ from sth to sth den Akzent von etw auf etw *(acc)* verlagern; the ~ is on bright colours der Akzent *or* die Betonung liegt auf leuchtenden Farben.
2 [æk'sent] *vt* betonen.

accentuate [æk'sentjʊeɪt] *vt* betonen; *(in speaking, Mus)* akzentuieren; *(Ling: give accent to)* mit einem Akzent versehen. to ~ the need for sth die Notwendigkeit einer Sache *(gen)* betonen *or* hervorheben.

accentuation [æk,sentjʊ'eɪʃən] *n* Betonung *f*; *(in speaking, Mus)* Akzentuierung *f.* his ~ of the need to ... seine Betonung der Notwendigkeit zu ...

accept [ək'sept] 1 *vt* **(a)** *offer, gift* annehmen; *suggestion, work also, report, findings* akzeptieren; *responsibility* übernehmen; *person* akzeptieren; *(believe)* story glauben; *excuse* akzeptieren, gelten lassen. a photograph of the President ~ing the award ein Bild von dem Präsidenten, wie er die Auszeichnung entgegennimmt; we will not ~ anything but the best wir werden nur das Allerbeste akzeptieren *or* annehmen; to ~ sb into society jdn in die Gesellschaft aufnehmen.
(b) *(recognize)* need einsehen, anerkennen; *person, duty* akzeptieren, anerkennen. it is generally ~ed that ... es ist allgemein anerkannt, daß ...; we must ~ the fact that ... wir müssen uns damit abfinden, daß ...; we ~ that it is so es ist nun (ein)mal so, und wir müssen uns damit abfinden; I ~ that it might take a little longer ich sehe ein, daß es etwas länger dauern könnte; while I ~ that you have a fairly reasonable excuse, nevertheless ... ich sehe zwar ein, daß Sie eine recht überzeugende Entschuldigung haben, doch ...; the government ~ed that the

treaty would on occasions have to be infringed die Regierung akzeptierte, daß der Vertrag gelegentlich verletzt werden würde; to ~ that sth is one's responsibility/duty etw als seine Verantwortung/Pflicht akzeptieren.
(c) *(allow, put up with)* behaviour, fate, conditions hinnehmen. we'll just have to ~ things as they are wir müssen die Dinge eben so (hin)nehmen, wie sie sind.
(d) *(Comm)* cheque, orders annehmen; *delivery also* abnehmen.
2 *vi* annehmen; *(with offers also)* akzeptieren; *(with invitations also)* zusagen.

acceptability [ək,septə'bɪlətɪ] *n see adj* Annehmbarkeit, Akzeptierbarkeit *f*; Zulässigkeit *f*; Passendheit *f.* **social ~** *(of person)* gesellschaftliche Akzeptabilität; *(of behaviour)* gesellschaftliche Zulässigkeit.

acceptable [ək'septəbl] *adj* annehmbar *(to für)*, akzeptabel *(to für)*; *behaviour* zulässig; *(suitable)* gift passend. **tea is always ~** Tee ist immer gut *or* willkommen; that would be most ~ das wäre sehr *or* höchst willkommen; any job would be ~ to him ihm wäre jede Stelle recht, er würde jede Stelle (an)nehmen; nothing less than the best is ~ nur das Beste kann angenommen werden.

acceptance [ək'septəns] *n see vt* **(a)** Annahme *f*; Akzeptierung *f*; Übernahme *f*; *(believing)* Glauben *nt*; Akzeptierung *f*; *(receiving: of award)* Entgegennahme *f.* **his ~ into the family** seine Aufnahme in der *or* die Familie; to find *or* win *or* gain ~ *(theories, people)* anerkannt werden, Anerkennung finden; to find *or* win *or* gain ~ for one's ideas Anerkennung *f* für seine Ideen finden; to meet with general ~ allgemeine Anerkennung finden.
(b) Anerkennung *f.*
(c) Hinnahme *f.*
(d) Annahme *f*; Abnahme *f.*

acceptance house *n (Fin)* Akzept- *or* Wechselbank *f.*

acceptation [,æksep'teɪʃən] *n (old, form: of word)* Bedeutung *f.*

accepted [ək'septɪd] *adj truth, fact* (allgemein) anerkannt. **it's the ~ thing** es ist üblich *or* der Brauch; to do sth because it is the ~ thing etw tun, weil es (eben) so üblich ist.

access ['ækses] 1 *n* **(a)** Zugang *m (to zu)*; *(to room, private grounds etc also)* Zutritt *m (to zu).* to be easy of ~ leicht zugänglich sein; to give sb ~ jdm Zugang gewähren *(to sb/sth zu jdm/etw)*; jdm Zutritt gewähren *(to sth zu etw)*; to refuse sb ~ jdm den Zugang verwehren *(to sb/sth zu jdm/etw)*; jdm den Zutritt verwehren *(to sth zu etw)*; he refused to give us ~ to the Duke er weigerte sich, uns zum Herzog vorzulassen; this door gives ~ to the garden diese Tür führt in den Garten; this location offers easy ~ to shops and transport facilities von hier sind Läden und Verkehrsmittel leicht zu erreichen; to have/gain ~ to sb/sth Zugang zu jdm/etw haben/sich *(dat)* Zugang zu jdm/etw verschaffen; the thieves gained ~ through the window die Diebe gelangten durch das Fenster hinein; ~ road Zufahrt(sstraße) *f*; "~ only" „nur für Anlieger", „Anlieger frei"; right of ~ to one's children/a house Besuchsrecht für seine Kinder/Wegerecht zu einem Haus.
(b) *(liter: attack, fit)* Anfall *m.* **in an ~ of rage** etc in einem Zornesausbruch etc.
(c) *(Computers)* Zugriff *m.*
2 *vt (Computers)* file, data Zugriff haben auf *(+acc).*

accessary [æk'sesərɪ] *n see* **accessory (b).**

accessibility [æk,sesɪ'bɪlɪtɪ] *n (of place, information)* Zugänglichkeit *f.*

accessible [æk'sesəbl] *adj information, person* zugänglich *(to dat)*; *place also* (leicht) zu erreichen *(to für).* to be ~ to reason/bribery vernünftigen Argumenten/Bestechungen zugänglich sein.

accession [æk'seʃən] *n* **(a)** *(to an office)* Antritt *m (to gen)*; *(also ~ to the throne)* Thronbesteigung *f*; *(to estate, power)* Übernahme *f (to gen).* **since his ~ to power** seit seiner Machtübernahme.
(b) *(consent: to treaty, demand)* Zustimmung *(to zu)*, Annahme *(to gen) f.*
(c) *(addition)* *(to property)* Zukauf *m*; *(to library also)* (Neu)anschaffung *f.* a sudden ~ of strength eine plötzliche Anwandlung von Kraft.

accessory [æk'sesərɪ] *n* **(a)** Extra *nt*; *(in fashion)* Accessoire *nt.* **accessories** *pl* Zubehör *nt*; toilet accessories Toilettenartikel *pl.*
(b) *(Jur)* Helfershelfer(in *f*) *m*; *(actively involved)* Mitschuldige(r) *mf (to an +dat).* to be an ~ after/before the fact sich der Begünstigung/Beihilfe schuldig machen; this made him an ~ to the crime dadurch wurde er an dem Verbrechen mitschuldig.

accidence ['æksɪdəns] *n (Gram)* Formenlehre *f.*

accident ['æksɪdənt] *n (Mot, in home, at work)* Unfall *m*; *(Rail, Aviat, disaster)* Unglück *nt*; *(mishap)* Mißgeschick *nt*; *(chance occurrence)* Zufall *m*; *(inf: unplanned child)* (Verkehrs)unfall *m (inf).* ~ insurance Unfallversicherung *f*; she has had an ~ sie hat einen Unfall gehabt *or* (caused it) gebaut *(inf)*; *(by car, train etc also)* sie ist verunglückt; *(in kitchen etc)* ihr ist etwas *or* ein Mißgeschick *or* ein Malheur passiert; little Jimmy has had an ~ *(euph)* bei dem kleinen Jimmy hat es ein Unglück gegeben *(inf)*; by ~ *(by chance)* durch Zufall, zufällig; *(unintentionally)* aus Versehen; who by some ~ of birth possessed riches der zufälligerweise reich geboren wurde; ~s will happen *(prov)* so was kann vorkommen, so was kommt in den besten Familien vor *(inf)*; it was an ~ es war ein Versehen; it was pure ~ that ... es war reiner Zufall, daß ...; it's no ~ that ... es ist kein Zufall, daß ...; *(not surprisingly)* es kommt nicht von ungefähr, daß ...

accidental [,æksɪ'dentl] 1 *adj* **(a)** *(unplanned)* meeting, benefit zufällig, Zufalls-; *(unintentional)* blow, shooting versehentlich.

one of the ~ effects of this scheme will be ... eine der Wirkungen, die dieser Plan mit sich bringt, wird ... sein.
  (b) (resulting from accident) injury, death durch Unfall. **2** n (Mus) (sign) Versetzungszeichen nt, Akzidentale f (form); (note) erhöhter/erniedrigter Ton.

accidentally [ˌæksɪˈdentəlɪ] adv (by chance) zufällig; (unintentionally) versehentlich.

accident-prone adj vom Pech verfolgt. **she is very** ~ sie ist vom Pech verfolgt, sie ist ein richtiger Pechvogel.

acclaim [əˈkleɪm] **1** vt **(a)** (applaud) feiern (as als); (critics) anerkennen. **(b)** (proclaim) **to** ~ **sb king/winner** jdn zum König/als Sieger ausrufen. **2** n Beifall m; (of critics) Anerkennung f.

acclamation [ˌæklæˈmeɪʃən] n Beifall m, no pl; (of audience etc also) Beifallskundgebung, Beifallsbezeigung f; (of critics also) Anerkennung f. **by** ~ durch Akklamation.

acclimate [əˈklaɪmət] vt (US) see **acclimatize**.

acclimatization [əˌklaɪmətaɪˈzeɪʃən], (US) **acclimation** [ˌæklaɪˈmeɪʃən] n Akklimatisierung, Akklimatisation f (to an +acc); (to new surroundings etc also) Gewöhnung f (to an +acc).

acclimatize [əˈklaɪmətaɪz], (US) **acclimate** [əˈklaɪmət] **1** vt gewöhnen (to an +acc). **to become** ~**d** sich akklimatisieren; (person also) sich eingewöhnen. **2** vi (also vr ~ **oneself**) sich akklimatisieren (to an +acc, to a country etc in einem Land etc).

acclivity [əˈklɪvɪtɪ] n (form) Hang m.

accolade [ˈækəʊleɪd] n (award) Auszeichnung f; (praise) Lob nt, no pl; (Hist, Mus) Akkolade f.

accommodate [əˈkɒmədeɪt] **1** vt **(a)** (provide lodging for) unterbringen.
  (b) (hold, have room for) Platz haben für. **the car can** ~ **five people** das Auto bietet fünf Personen Platz or hat Platz für fünf Personen; **the housing** ~**s several components** das Gehäuse enthält verschiedene Baugruppen.
  (c) (be able to cope with: theory, plan, forecasts) Rechnung f tragen (+dat).
  (d) (form: oblige) dienen (+dat); wishes entgegenkommen (+dat). **I think we might be able to** ~ **you** ich glaube, wir können Ihnen dienen.
  2 vi (eye) sich einstellen (to auf +acc).
  3 vr **to** ~ **oneself to** sich mit etw or sich einer Sache (dat) anpassen.

accommodating [əˈkɒmədeɪtɪŋ] adj entgegenkommend.

accommodation [əˌkɒməˈdeɪʃən] n **(a)** (US also ~**s** pl: lodging) Unterkunft f; (room also) Zimmer nt; (flat also) Wohnung f; (holiday ~ also) Quartier nt. "~" „Fremdenzimmer"; **hotel** ~ **is scarce** Hotelzimmer sind knapp; ~ **wanted** Zimmer/Wohnung gesucht; **they found** ~ **in a youth hostel** sie fanden in einer Jugendherberge Unterkunft, sie kamen in einer Jugendherberge unter.
  (b) (space: US also ~**s**) Platz m. **seating/library** ~ Sitz-/Bibliotheksplätze pl; **there is** ~ **for twenty passengers in the plane** das Flugzeug bietet zwanzig Passagieren Platz or hat für zwanzig Passagiere Platz; **I didn't book sleeping** ~ ich habe kein Bett/keine Betten bestellt; ~ **in the hospital is inadequate** die Unterbringungsmöglichkeiten im Krankenhaus sind unzureichend.
  (c) (form: agreement) **to reach an** ~ eine Übereinkunft or ein Übereinkommen erzielen.
  (d) (of eye) Einstellung f (to auf +acc).

accommodation: ~ **address** n Briefkastenadresse f; ~ **bill** n Gefälligkeitswechsel m; ~ **bureau** n Wohnungsvermittlung f; (Univ) Zimmervermittlung f; ~ **ladder** n (Naut) Fallreep nt; ~ **train** n (US) Personenzug, Bummelzug (inf) m.

accompaniment [əˈkʌmpənɪmənt] n Begleitung f (also Mus). **to the** ~ **of sth** zu der Begleitung von etw; **with piano** ~ mit Klavierbegleitung.

accompanist [əˈkʌmpənɪst] n Begleiter(in f) m.

accompany [əˈkʌmpənɪ] **1** vt begleiten (also Mus). **pork is often accompanied by apple sauce** Schweinefleisch wird oft mit Apfelmus (als Beilage) serviert. **2** vr **to** ~ **oneself** (Mus) sich selbst begleiten.

accomplice [əˈkʌmplɪs] n Komplize m, Komplizin f, Mittäter(in f) m. **to be an** ~ **to a crime** Komplize bei einem Verbrechen or Mittäter eines Verbrechens sein.

accomplish [əˈkʌmplɪʃ] vt schaffen. **he** ~**ed a great deal in his short career** er hat in der kurzen Zeit seines Wirkens Großes geleistet; **that didn't** ~ **anything** damit war nichts erreicht.

accomplished [əˈkʌmplɪʃt] adj **(a)** (skilled) player, carpenter fähig; performance vollendet; young lady vielseitig. **to be** ~ **in the art of ...** die Kunst ... (gen) beherrschen. **(b)** fact vollendet.

accomplishment [əˈkʌmplɪʃmənt] n **(a)** no pl (completion) Bewältigung f. **(b)** (skill) Fertigkeit f; (achievement) Leistung f. **social** ~**s** gesellschaftliche Gewandtheit.

accord [əˈkɔːd] **1** n (agreement) Übereinstimmung, Einigkeit f; (esp US Pol) Abkommen nt. **I'm not in** ~ **with him/his views** ich stimme mit ihm/seinen Ansichten nicht überein; **of one's/its own** ~ von selbst; (of persons also) aus freien Stücken; **with one** ~ geschlossen; sing, cheer, say etc wie aus einem Mund(e); **to be in** ~ **with sth** mit etw in Einklang stehen; **the Helsinki** ~ das Abkommen or der Vertrag von Helsinki.
  2 vt (sb sth jdm etw) gewähren; praise erteilen; courtesy erweisen; honorary title verleihen; welcome bieten.
  3 vi sich or einander entsprechen. **to** ~ **with sth** einer Sache (dat) entsprechen.

accordance [əˈkɔːdəns] n **in** ~ **with** entsprechend (+dat), gemäß (+dat).

accordingly [əˈkɔːdɪŋlɪ] adv (correspondingly) (dem)entsprechend; (so, therefore also) folglich.

according to [əˈkɔːdɪŋˈtuː] prep (as stated or shown by) zufolge

(+dat), nach; person, book, letter also laut; (in agreement with, in proportion to) entsprechend (+dat), nach. ~ **the map** der Karte nach or zufolge; ~ **Peter** laut Peter, Peter zufolge; **we did it** ~ **the rules** wir haben uns an die Regeln gehalten.

accordion [əˈkɔːdɪən] n Akkordeon nt, Ziehharmonika f.

accordionist [əˈkɔːdɪənɪst] n Akkordeonspieler(in f), Akkordeonist(in f) m.

accost [əˈkɒst] vt ansprechen, anpöbeln (pej).

account [əˈkaʊnt] **1** n **(a)** Darstellung f; (written also) Aufzeichnung f; (report also) Bericht m. **to keep an** ~ **of one's expenses/experiences** über seine Ausgaben Buch führen/seine Erlebnisse schriftlich festhalten; **by all** ~**s** nach allem, was man hört; **by your own** ~ nach Ihrer eigenen Darstellung; **to give an** ~ **of sth** über etw (acc) Bericht erstatten; **to give an** ~ **of oneself** Rede und Antwort stehen; **to give a good/bad** ~ **of oneself** sich in einem guten/schlechten Licht zeigen; **to call or hold sb to** ~ jdn zur Rechenschaft ziehen; **to be held to** ~ **for sth** über etw (acc) Rechenschaft ablegen müssen.
  (b) (consideration) **to take** ~ **of sb/sth, to take sb/sth into** ~ jdn/etw in Betracht ziehen; **to take no** ~ **of sb/sth, to leave sb/sth out of** ~ jdn/etw außer Betracht lassen; **on no** ~, **not on any** ~ auf (gar) keinen Fall; **on this/that** ~ deshalb, deswegen; **on** ~ **of him/his mother/the weather** seinetwegen/wegen seiner Mutter/wegen des Wetters; **on my/his/their** ~ meinet-/seinet-/ihretwegen; **on one's own** ~ für sich (selbst).
  (c) (benefit) Nutzen m. **to turn or put sth to (good)** ~ (guten) Gebrauch von etw machen, etw (gut) nützen; money also etw gut anlegen.
  (d) (importance) of no/small/great etc ~ ohne/von geringer/großer Bedeutung.
  (e) (Fin, Comm) (at bank, shop) Konto nt (with bei); (client) Kunde m; (bill) Rechnung f. **to win sb's** ~ jdn als Kunden gewinnen; **to buy sth on** ~ etw auf (Kunden)kredit kaufen; **please put it down to or charge it to my** ~ stellen Sie es mir bitte in Rechnung; **£50 on** ~ £ 50 als Anzahlung; ~**(s) department** (of shop) Kreditbüro nt; **to settle or square** ~**s or one's** ~ **with sb** (fig) mit jdm abrechnen; **the duel squared all** ~**s between them** das Duell bereinigte alles zwischen ihnen.
  (f) ~**s** pl (of company, club) (Geschäfts)bücher pl; (of household) Einnahmen und Ausgaben pl; **to keep the** ~**s** die Bücher führen, die Buchführung machen; ~**(s) book** Geschäftsbuch nt.
  2 vt (form: consider) erachten als. **to be** ~**ed innocent** als unschuldig gelten; **to** ~ **oneself lucky** sich glücklich preisen or schätzen.

♦**account for** vi +prep obj **(a)** (explain) erklären; (give account of) actions, expenditure Rechenschaft ablegen über (+acc); (illness) dahinraffen; chances zunichte machen. **how do you** ~ **it?** wie erklären Sie sich (dat) das?; **he wasn't able to** ~ ~ **the missing money** er konnte den Verbleib des fehlenden Geldes nicht erklären; **all the children were/money was** ~**ed** ~ der Verbleib aller Kinder/des (ganzen) Geldes war bekannt, man wußte, wo die Kinder alle waren/wo das Geld (geblieben) war; **there's no** ~**ing** ~ **taste** über Geschmack läßt sich (nicht) streiten; **John** ~**ed** ~ **most of the sandwiches** die meisten Brote hat John vertilgt.
  (b) (be the source of) der Grund sein für. **this area** ~**s** ~ **most of the country's mineral wealth** aus dieser Gegend stammen die meisten Bodenschätze des Landes; **this area alone** ~**s** ~ **some 25% of the population** diese Gegend allein macht etwa 25% der Bevölkerung aus or stellt etwa 25% der Bevölkerung.
  (c) (be the cause of defeat, destruction etc) zur Strecke bringen. **Proctor** ~ ~ **five Australian batsmen** Proctor hat fünf australische Schlagmänner ausgeschlagen.

accountability [əˌkaʊntəˈbɪlətɪ] n Verantwortlichkeit f (to sb jdm gegenüber).

accountable [əˈkaʊntəbl] adj verantwortlich (to sb jdm). **to hold sb** ~ **(for sth)** jdn (für etw) verantwortlich machen.

accountancy [əˈkaʊntənsɪ] n Buchführung, Buchhaltung f; (tax ~) Steuerberatung f.

accountant [əˈkaʊntənt] n Buchhalter(in f) m; (external financial adviser) Wirtschaftsprüfer(in f) m; (auditor) Rechnungsprüfer(in f) m; (tax ~) Steuerberater(in f) m.

accoutrements [əˈkuːtrəmənts], (US also) **accouterments** [əˈkuːtərmənts] npl Ausrüstung f. **the** ~ **of knighthood/the trade** die Ritterrüstung/das Handwerkszeug.

accredit [əˈkredɪt] vt **(a)** ambassador, representative akkreditieren (form); beglaubigen. **to be** ~**ed to an embassy** bei einer Botschaft akkreditiert sein/werden.
  (b) (approve officially) zulassen, genehmigen; herd staatlich überwachen; (US) educational institution anerkennen; (establish) belief, custom anerkennen. ~**ed herd** staatlich überwachter Viehbestand.
  (c) (ascribe, attribute) zuschreiben (to sb jdm).

accretion [əˈkriːʃən] n (process) Anlagerung f; (sth accumulated) Ablagerung f.

accrual [əˈkruːəl] n see vi **(a)** Ansammlung f; Auflaufen nt; Hinzukommen nt.

accrue [əˈkruː] vi **(a)** (accumulate) sich ansammeln, zusammenkommen (to für); (Fin: interest) auflaufen; (be added to) hinzukommen (to zu). **(b) to** ~ **to sb** (honour, costs etc) jdm erwachsen (geh) (from aus).

accumulate [əˈkjuːmjʊleɪt] **1** vt ansammeln, anhäufen, akkumulieren (form); evidence sammeln; (Fin) interest akkumulieren or zusammenkommen lassen. **2** vi sich ansammeln or akkumulieren (form); (possessions, wealth also) sich anhäufen; (evidence) sich häufen.

accumulation [əˌkjuːmjʊˈleɪʃən] n see vi Ansammlung, Akkumulation f (form); Anhäufung f; Häufung f.

accumulative [əˈkjuːmjʊlətɪv] adj see **cumulative**.

accumulator [əˈkjuːmjʊleɪtə^r] n Akkumulator m.

accuracy ['ækjʊrəsɪ] n Genauigkeit f.
accurate ['ækjʊrɪt] adj worker, observation, translation, copy, instrument genau, akkurat (rare). **the clock is** ~ die Uhr geht genau; **his aim/shot was** ~ er hat genau gezielt/getroffen; **her work is slow but** ~ sie arbeitet langsam, aber genau; **to be strictly** ~ um ganz genau zu sein.
accurately ['ækjʊrɪtlɪ] adv genau.
accursed, accurst [ə'kɜ:st] adj (a) (old, liter: under a curse) unter einem Fluch or bösen Zauber pred. (b) (inf: hateful) verwünscht.
accusation [,ækjʊ'zeɪʃən] n Beschuldigung, Anschuldigung f; (Jur) Anklage f; (reproach) Vorwurf m. **he denied her** ~ **of dishonesty** er wehrte sich gegen ihren Vorwurf, daß er unehrlich sei; **a look of** ~ ein anklagender Blick.
accusative [ə'kju:zətɪv] **1** n Akkusativ m. **2** adj ending Akkusativ-. ~ **case** Akkusativ m.
accusatorial [ə,kju:zə'tɔ:rɪəl] adj (Jur) Anklage-.
accuse [ə'kju:z] vt (a) (Jur) anklagen (of wegen, gen). **he is or stands** ~**d of murder/theft** er ist des Mordes/Diebstahls angeklagt, er steht unter Anklage des Mordes/Diebstahls (form); **it is the function of the prosecution to** ~ **the defendant of a crime** die Aufgabe der Staatsanwaltschaft ist es, die Anklage gegen den Angeklagten zu führen.
(b) sb beschuldigen, bezichtigen. **to** ~ **sb of doing sth** jdn beschuldigen or bezichtigen, etw getan zu haben; **are you accusing me? I didn't take it!** ich bin unschuldig, ich habe es nicht genommen; **are you accusing me of lying/not having checked the brakes?** willst du (damit) vielleicht sagen, daß ich lüge/die Bremsen nicht nachgesehen habe?; **to** ~ **sb of being untidy** jdm vorwerfen, unordentlich zu sein; **who are you accusing, the police or society?** wem machen Sie einen Vorwurf or wen klagen Sie an, die Polizei oder die Gesellschaft?; **I** ~ **the government of neglect** ich mache der Regierung Nachlässigkeit zum Vorwurf; **a generation stands** ~**d of hypocrisy** eine Generation wird der Scheinheiligkeit beschuldigt or angeklagt or geziehen (geh); **we all stand** ~**d** uns alle trifft eine Schuld.
accused [ə'kju:zd] n **the** ~ der/die Angeklagte/die Angeklagten pl.
accuser [ə'kju:zə'] n Ankläger m.
accusing [ə'kju:zɪŋ] adj anklagend. **he had an** ~ **look on his face** sein Blick klagte an.
accusingly [ə'kju:zɪŋlɪ] adv see adj.
accustom [ə'kʌstəm] vt **to** ~ **sb/oneself to sth/to doing sth** jdn/sich an etw (acc) gewöhnen/daran gewöhnen, etw zu tun; **to be** ~**ed to doing sth** an etw (acc) gewöhnt sein/gewöhnt sein, etw zu tun; **it is not what I am** ~**ed to** ich bin so etwas nicht gewöhnt; **to become** or **get** ~**ed to sth/to doing sth** sich an etw (acc) gewöhnen/sich daran gewöhnen, etw zu tun.
accustomed [ə'kʌstəmd] adj attr (usual) gewohnt.
AC/DC adj (a) abbr of alternating current/direct current Allstrom(-). (b) ac/dc (sl) bi (sl).
ace [eɪs] **1** n (a) (Cards) As nt. **the** ~ **of clubs** das Kreuzas; **to have an** ~ **up one's sleeve** noch einen Trumpf in der Hand haben; **he was/came within an** ~ **of success or of succeeding/of winning** es wäre ihm um ein Haar gelungen/er hätte um ein Haar gesiegt.
(b) (inf: expert) As nt (in +dat). **tennis** ~ Tennisas nt.
(c) (Tennis: serve) As nt. **to serve an** ~ ein As spielen.
2 adj attr swimmer, pilot, reporter Star-.
acerbity [ə'sɜ:bɪtɪ] n Schärfe f.
acetate ['æsɪteɪt] n Acetat nt.
acetic [ə'si:tɪk] adj essigsauer. ~ **acid** Essigsäure f.
acetone ['æsɪtəʊn] n Aceton nt.
acetylene [ə'setɪli:n] n Acetylen nt.
ache [eɪk] **1** n (dumpfer) Schmerz m. **I have an** ~ **in my side** ich habe Schmerzen in der Seite; **her body was a mass of** ~**s and pains** es tat ihr am ganzen Körper weh; **a few little** ~**s and pains** ein paar Wehwehchen (inf); **with an** ~ **in one's heart** (fig) mit wehem Herzen (liter).
2 vi (a) weh tun, schmerzen. **my head/stomach** ~**s** mir tut der Kopf/Magen weh; **it makes my head/eyes** ~ davon bekomme ich Kopfschmerzen/tun mir die Augen weh; **I'm aching all over** mir tut alles weh; **it makes my heart** ~ **to see him** (fig) es tut mir in der Seele weh, wenn ich ihn sehe; **my heart** ~**s for you** mir bricht fast das Herz (also iro).
(b) (fig: yearn) **to** ~ **for sb/sth** sich nach jdm/etw sehnen; **to** ~ **to do sth** sich danach sehnen, etw zu tun; **I** ~**d to help him** es drängte mich, ihm zu helfen.
achieve [ə'tʃi:v] **1** vt erreichen, schaffen; success erzielen; victory erringen; rank also, title erlangen. **she** ~**d a great deal** (did a lot of work) sie hat eine Menge geleistet; (was quite successful) sie hat viel erreicht; **he will never** ~ **anything** er wird es nie zu etwas bringen.
2 vi (Psych, Sociol) leisten. **the achieving society** die Leistungsgesellschaft.
achievement [ə'tʃi:vmənt] n (a) (act) see vt Erreichen nt; Erzielen nt; Erringen nt; Erlangen nt.
(b) (thing achieved) (of individual) Leistung f; (of society, civilization, technology) Errungenschaft f. **that's quite an** ~! das ist schon eine Leistung! (also iro); **for his many** ~**s** für seine zahlreichen Verdienste; ~ **quotient/test** Leistungsquotient m/-test m.
Achilles [ə'kɪli:z] n Achill(es) m. ~ **' heel** (fig) Achillesferse f; ~ **' tendon** Achillessehne f.
aching ['eɪkɪŋ] adj attr bones, head schmerzend; (fig) heart wund, weh (liter).
acid ['æsɪd] **1** adj (sour, Chem) sauer; (fig) ätzend, beißend. ~ **drop** saurer or saures Drops; ~ **test** (fig) Feuerprobe f. **2** n (a) (Chem) Säure f. (b) (sl: LSD) Acid nt (sl).

acidhead ['æsɪd,hed] n (sl) Säurekopf m (sl).
acidic [ə'sɪdɪk] adj sauer.
acidity [ə'sɪdɪtɪ] n Säure f; (Chem also) Säuregehalt m; (of stomach) Magensäure f.
acidly ['æsɪdlɪ] adv (fig) ätzend, beißend.
ack-ack ['æk'æk] n (fire) Flakfeuer nt; (gun) Flak f.
acknowledge [ək'nɒlɪdʒ] vt anerkennen; quotation angeben; (admit) truth, fault, defeat etc eingestehen, zugeben; (note receipt of) letter etc bestätigen; present den Empfang bestätigen von; (respond to) greetings, cheers etc erwidern. **to** ~ **oneself beaten** sich geschlagen geben; **to** ~ **receipt of sth** den Empfang von etw bestätigen; **to** ~ **sb's presence** jds Anwesenheit zur Kenntnis nehmen.
acknowledged [ək'nɒlɪdʒd] adj attr anerkannt.
acknowledgement [ək'nɒlɪdʒmənt] n see vt Anerkennung f; Angabe f; Eingeständnis nt; Bestätigung f; Empfangsbestätigung f; Erwiderung f. **he waved in** ~ er winkte zurück; **in** ~ **of** in Anerkennung (+gen); **to make** ~ **of sth** (form) seinen Dank für etw zum Ausdruck bringen; **to quote without** ~ ohne Quellenangabe zitieren; **I received no** ~ ich erhielt keine Antwort; **as an** ~ **of my gratitude/your kindness** zum Zeichen meiner Dankbarkeit/zum Dank für Ihre Freundlichkeit; ~**s are due to ...** ich habe/wir haben ... zu danken; (in book) mein/unser Dank gilt ...
acme ['ækmɪ] n Höhepunkt, Gipfel m; (of task, elegance etc) Inbegriff m. **at the** ~ **of his powers** auf dem Gipfel seiner (Schaffens)kraft.
acne ['æknɪ] n Akne f.
acolyte ['ækəʊlaɪt] n (Eccl) (Catholic) Akoluth m; (Protestant: server) Meßdiener, Ministrant m; (fig) Gefolgsmann m.
aconite ['ækənaɪt] n (Bot) Eisenhut m, Aconitum nt; (drug) Aconitin nt.
acorn ['eɪkɔ:n] n Eichel f.
acoustic [ə'ku:stɪk] adj akustisch; (soundproof) tiles, panel Dämm-.
acoustically [ə'ku:stɪkəlɪ] adv akustisch.
acoustics [ə'ku:stɪks] n (a) sing (subject) Akustik f. (b) pl (of room etc) Akustik f.
acquaint [ə'kweɪnt] vt (a) (make familiar) bekannt machen. **to be** ~**ed/thoroughly** ~**ed with sth** mit etw bekannt/vertraut sein; **to be** ~**ed with grief** mit Leid vertraut sein; **he's** ~**ed/well** ~**ed with the situation** die Situation ist ihm bekannt/er ist mit der Situation vertraut; **to become** ~**ed with sth** etw kennenlernen; **facts, truth** etw erfahren; **to** ~ **oneself or make oneself** ~**ed with sth** sich mit etw vertraut machen.
(b) (with person) **to be** ~**ed with sb** mit jdm bekannt sein; **we're not** ~**ed** wir kennen einander or uns nicht; **to become** or **get** ~**ed** sich (näher) kennenlernen; **I'll leave you two to get** ~**ed** ich laß euch erst einmal allein, damit ihr euch kennenlernen or beschnuppern (inf) könnt.
acquaintance [ə'kweɪntəns] n (a) (person) Bekannte(r) mf. **we're just** ~**s** wir kennen uns bloß flüchtig; **a wide circle of** ~**s** ein großer Bekanntenkreis.
(b) (with person) Bekanntschaft f; (with subject etc) Kenntnis f (with gen); (intimate, with sorrow etc) Vertrautheit f. **to make sb's** ~, **to make the** ~ **of sb** jds Bekanntschaft or die Bekanntschaft jds machen; **I have some** ~ **with Italian wines** ich kenne mich mit italienischen Weinen einigermaßen aus; **he/it improves on** ~ er gewinnt bei näherer Bekanntschaft/man kommt mit der Zeit auf den Geschmack (davon); see nodding.
acquiesce [,ækwɪ'es] vi einwilligen (in in +acc); (submissively) sich fügen (in dat).
acquiescence [,ækwɪ'esns] n see vi Einwilligung f (in in +acc); Fügung f (in in +acc). **with an air of** ~ mit zustimmender Miene.
acquiescent [,ækwɪ'esnt] adj fügsam; smile ergeben; attitude zustimmend. **he was perfectly** ~ **when ...** er war vollkommen einverstanden, als ...
acquire [ə'kwaɪə'] vt erwerben; (by dubious means) sich (dat) aneignen; habit annehmen. **I see he has** ~**d a secretary/wife** wie ich sehe, hat er sich eine Sekretärin/Frau angeschafft (inf); **he** ~**d a fine tan** er hat eine gute Farbe bekommen; **where did you** ~ **that?** woher hast du das?; **they have** ~**d a reputation for quality** sie haben sich (dat) einen Namen für Qualität gemacht or erworben; **to** ~ **a taste/liking for sth** Geschmack/Gefallen an etw (dat) finden; **once you've** ~**d a taste for it** wenn du erst mal auf den Geschmack gekommen bist; **caviar is an** ~**d taste** Kaviar ist (nur) für Kenner; ~**d** (Psych) erworben; ~**d characteristics** (Biol) erworbene Eigenschaften pl.
acquirement [ə'kwaɪəmənt] n (a) (act) see acquisition (a). (b) (skill etc acquired) Fertigkeit f.
acquisition [,ækwɪ'zɪʃən] n (a) (act) Erwerb m; (by dubious means) Aneignung f; (of habit) Annahme f. (b) (thing acquired) Anschaffung f; (hum: secretary, girlfriend etc) Errungenschaft f. **he's a useful** ~ **to the department** er ist ein Gewinn für die Abteilung.
acquisitive [ə'kwɪzɪtɪv] adj auf Erwerb aus, habgierig (pej), raffgierig (pej). **the** ~ **society** die Erwerbsgesellschaft; **magpies are** ~ **birds** Elstern sind Vögel mit ausgeprägtem Sammeltrieb.
acquisitiveness [ə'kwɪzɪtɪvnɪs] n Habgier f (pej).
acquit [ə'kwɪt] **1** vt freisprechen. **to** ~**ted of a crime/on a charge** von einem Verbrechen/einer Anklage freigesprochen werden.
2 vr (conduct oneself) sich verhalten; (perform) seine Sache machen. **he** ~**ted himself well** er hat seine Sache gut gemacht; (stood up well) er hat sich gut aus der Affäre gezogen.
acquittal [ə'kwɪtl] n Freispruch m. **an** ~ **on the charge** ein Freispruch von der Anklage.

acre ['eɪkə'] n ≃ Morgen m. ~s (old, liter: land) Fluren pl (old, liter); ~s (and ~s) of garden/open land hektarweise Garten/meilenweise freies Land.

acreage ['eɪkərɪdʒ] n Land nt; (Agr) Anbaufläche f. what ~ do they have? wieviel Land or wie viele Morgen (Agr) haben sie?

acrid ['ækrɪd] adj taste bitter; (of wine) sauer; comment, smoke beißend.

Acrilan ® ['ækrɪlæn] n Acryl nt.

acrimonious [ˌækrɪ'məʊnɪəs] adj discussion, argument erbittert; person, words bissig.

acrimoniously [ˌækrɪ'məʊnɪəslɪ] adv see adj.

acrimony ['ækrɪmənɪ] n see acrimonious erbitterte Schärfe; Bissigkeit f.

acrobat ['ækrəbæt] n Akrobat(in f) m.

acrobatic [ˌækrəʊ'bætɪk] adj akrobatisch.

acrobatics [ˌækrəʊ'bætɪks] npl Akrobatik f. **mental ~** (fig) Gedankenakrobatik f, geistige Klimmzüge pl (inf).

acronym ['ækrənɪm] n Akronym nt.

acropolis [ə'krɒpəlɪs] n Akropolis f.

across [ə'krɒs] **1** adv (a) (direction) (to the other side) hinüber; (from the other side) herüber; (crosswise) (quer)durch. **shall I go ~ first?** soll ich zuerst hinüber(gehen/-schwimmen etc)?; **to throw/row ~/help sb ~** hinüberwerfen/hinüberrudern/jdm hinüberhelfen; herüberwerfen/herüberrudern/jdm herüberhelfen; **to cut sth ~** etw (quer) durchschneiden; **he was already ~** er war schon drüben; **~ from your house** gegenüber von eurem Haus, eurem Haus gegenüber; **the stripes go ~** es ist quer gestreift; **draw a line ~** machen Sie einen Strich; (diagonal) machen Sie einen Strich querdurch.
(b) (measurement) breit; (of round object) im Durchmesser.
(c) (in crosswords) waagerecht.
2 prep (a) (direction) über (+acc); (diagonally ~) quer durch (+acc). **to run ~ the road** über die Straße laufen; **to wade ~ a river** durch einen Fluß waten; **a tree fell ~ the path** ein Baum fiel quer über den Weg; **~ country** querfeldein; (over long distance) quer durch das Land; **to draw a line ~ the page** einen Strich machen; (diagonal) einen Strich quer durch die Seite machen; **the stripes go ~ the material** der Stoff ist quer gestreift.
(b) (position) über (+dat). **a tree lay ~ the path** ein Baum lag quer über dem Weg; **he was sprawled ~ the bed** er lag quer auf dem Bett; **with his arms (folded) ~ his chest** die Arme vor der Brust verschränkt; **with his hand ~ his heart** mit der Hand auf dem Herzen; **from ~ the sea** von jenseits des Meeres (geh), von der anderen Seite des Meeres; **he lives ~ the street from us** er wohnt uns gegenüber; **you could hear him (from) ~ the hall** man konnte ihn von der anderen Seite der Halle hören; see vbs.

across-the-board [ə'krɒsðə'bɔːd] adj attr allgemein; see also board.

acrostic [ə'krɒstɪk] n Akrostichon nt.

acrylic [ə'krɪlɪk] **1** n Acryl nt. **2** adj Acryl-; dress aus Acryl.

act [ækt] **1** n (a) (deed, thing done) Tat f; (official, ceremonial) Akt m. **my first ~ was to phone him** meine erste Tat or mein erstes war, ihn anzurufen; **an ~ of mercy/judgement** ein Gnadenakt m/eine (wohl)überlegte Tat; **an ~ of God** höhere Gewalt no pl; **an ~ of folly/madness** reine Dummheit/reiner Wahnsinn, ein Akt m der Dummheit/des Wahnsinns; **a small/great ~ of kindness** eine Freundlichkeit/ein Akt der Freundlichkeit; **A~s, the A~s of the Apostles** (Bibl) die Apostelgeschichte; see faith.
(b) (process of doing) **to be in the ~ of doing** (gerade) dabei sein, etw zu tun; **to catch sb in the ~** jdn auf frischer Tat or (sexually) in flagranti ertappen; **to catch/watch sb in the ~ of doing sth** jdn dabei ertappen/beobachten, wie er etw tut.
(c) (Parl) Gesetz nt. **under an ~ of Parliament passed in 1976** this is illegal nach einem 1976 vom Parlament verabschiedeten Gesetz ist das verboten; **it would take an ~ of Parliament to get him to do that** (fig) es wäre schon ein Wunder nötig, ihn dazu zu bringen.
(d) (Theat) (of play, opera) Akt m; (turn) Nummer f. **a one-~ play/opera** ein Einakter m/eine Oper in einem Akt; **to get into or in on the ~** (fig inf) mit von der Partie sein; **how did he get in on the ~?** (inf) wie kommt es, daß er da mitmischt? (inf).
(e) (fig: pretence) Theater nt, Schau f (inf). **it's all an ~** das ist alles nur Theater or Schau (inf); **to put on an ~** Theater spielen.
2 vt part spielen; play also aufführen. **to ~ the fool/injured innocent** herumalbern/die gekränkte Unschuld spielen.
3 vi (a) (Theat) (perform) spielen; (to be an actor) schauspielern, Theater spielen; (fig) Theater spielen, schauspielern, markieren. **to ~ on TV/on the radio** fürs Fernsehen/in Hörspielen auftreten or spielen; **who's ~ing in it?** wer spielt darin?; **he learned to ~** er erlernte die Schauspielkunst or Schauspielerei; **he should learn to ~** er sollte erst mal richtig schauspielern lernen; **... but she can't ~** ... aber sie kann nicht spielen or ist keine Schauspielerin; **he's only ~ing** er tut (doch) nur so, er markiert or spielt (doch) nur; **to ~ stupid/innocent etc** sich dumm/unschuldig etc stellen, den Dummen/Unschuldigen spielen.
(b) (function) (brakes etc) funktionieren; (drug) wirken. **to ~ as ...** wirken als ...; (have function) fungieren als ...; (person) das Amt des/der ... übernehmen, fungieren als ...; **~ing in my capacity as chairman** in meiner Eigenschaft als Vorsitzender; **it ~s as a deterrent** das wirkt abschreckend; **to ~ for sb** jdn vertreten.
(c) (behave) sich verhalten. **~ like a man!** sei ein Mann!; she **~ed as if or as though she was hurt/surprised etc** sie tat so, als ob sie verletzt/überrascht etc wäre; **he ~s as though or like he owns the place** (inf) er tut so, als ob der Laden ihm gehört (inf).
(d) (take action) handeln. **he ~ed to stop it** er unternahm etwas or Schritte, um dem ein Ende zu machen; the police

couldn't ~ die Polizei konnte nichts unternehmen.
♦**act on** or **upon** vi +prep obj (a) (affect) wirken auf (+acc). **~ing ~ an impulse** einer plötzlichen Eingebung gehorchend or folgend; **the yeast ~s ~ the sugar** to produce alcohol die Hefe wirkt auf den Zucker ein und führt zur Alkoholbildung.
(b) (take action on) warning, report, evidence handeln auf (+acc) ... hin; suggestion, advice folgen (+dat). **~ing ~ information received, the police** ... die Polizei handelte aufgrund der ihr zugegangenen Information und ...; **did you ~ the letter?** haben Sie auf den Brief hin etwas unternommen?
♦**act out** vt sep fantasies, problems etc durchspielen. the drama/affair was **~ed ~ at** ... das Drama/die Affäre spielte sich in ... ab.
♦**act up** vi (inf) jdm Ärger machen; (person also) Theater machen (inf); (to attract attention) sich aufspielen; (machine also) verrückt spielen (inf).
♦**act upon** vi +prep obj see act on.

actable ['æktəbl] adj play spielbar. **it is very ~** es läßt sich gut spielen or aufführen.

acting ['æktɪŋ] **1** adj (a) stellvertretend attr, in Stellvertretung pred.
(b) attr (Theat) schauspielerisch.
2 n (Theat) (performance) Darstellung f; (activity) Spielen nt; (profession) Schauspielerei f. **what was the/his ~ like?** wie waren die Schauspieler/wie hat er gespielt? **I didn't like his ~** ich mochte seine Art zu spielen nicht; **he's done some ~** er hat schon Theater gespielt; (professionally also) er hat schon etwas Schauspielerfahrung.

actinic [æk'tɪnɪk] adj aktinisch.

action ['ækʃən] n (a) no pl (activity) Handeln nt; (of play, novel etc) Handlung f. **now is the time for ~** die Zeit zum Handeln ist gekommen; **a man of ~** ein Mann der Tat; **to take ~** etwas or Schritte unternehmen; **have you taken any ~ on his letter?** haben Sie auf seinen Brief hin irgend etwas or irgendwelche Schritte unternommen?; course of ~ Vorgehen nt; **"~"** (on office tray) „zur Bearbeitung"; **no further ~** keine weiteren Maßnahmen; (label on file etc) abgeschlossen; **the ~ of the play/novel takes place** ... das Stück/der Roman spielt ...; **~!** (Film) Achtung, Aufnahme!
(b) (deed) Tat f. **his first ~ was to phone me** als erstes rief er mich an, seine erste Tat war, mich anzurufen; **to suit the ~ to the word** dem Wort die Tat folgen lassen, sein Wort in die Tat umsetzen; **~s speak louder than words** (Prov) die Tat wirkt mächtiger als das Wort (prov).
(c) (motion, operation) in/out of ~ in/nicht in Aktion; (machine) in/außer Betrieb; (operational) einsatzfähig/nicht einsatzfähig; **to go into ~** in Aktion treten; **to put a plan into ~** einen Plan in die Tat umsetzen; **to put out of ~** außer Gefecht setzen; **he's been out of ~ since he broke his leg** er ist nicht mehr in Aktion gewesen or war nicht mehr einsatzfähig, seit er sich das Bein gebrochen hat; **he needs prodding into ~** man muß ihm immer erst einen Stoß geben.
(d) (exciting events) Action f (sl). **there's no ~ in this film** in dem Film passiert nichts, dem Film fehlt (die) Action (sl); **a novel full of ~** ein handlungsreicher Roman; **let's have some ~!** (inf) machen wir mal was los! (inf); **to go where the ~ is** (inf) hingehen, wo was los ist (inf); **that's where the ~ is** (inf) da ist was los (inf); **where's the ~, man?** (sl) he, wo ist hier was los? (inf); **he was out looking for ~** (inf) er wollte was erleben (inf) or was losmachen (sl).
(e) (Mil) (fighting) Aktionen pl; (battle) Kampf m, Gefecht nt. **enemy ~** feindliche Handlungen or Aktionen pl; **killed in ~** gefallen; **he saw ~ in the desert** er war in der Wüste im Einsatz; **the first time they went into ~** bei ihrem ersten Einsatz; **they never once went into ~** sie kamen nie zum Einsatz.
(f) (way of operating) (of machine) Arbeitsweise f; (of piano etc) Mechanik f; (of watch, gun) Mechanismus m; (way of moving) (of athlete etc) Bewegung f; (of horse) Aktion f. **the piano/typewriter has a stiff ~** das Klavier/die Schreibmaschine hat einen harten Anschlag; **to move/hit with an easy/a smooth ~** (Sport) sich ganz locker und leicht bewegen/ganz weich schlagen.
(g) (esp Chem, Phys: effect) Wirkung f (on auf +acc).
(h) (Jur) Klage f. **to bring an ~ (against sb)** eine Klage (gegen jdn) anstrengen.
(i) (Fin sl) **a piece of the ~** ein Stück aus dem Kuchen (sl).

actionable ['ækʃnəbl] adj verfolgbar; statement klagbar.

action: **~ group** n Bürger-/Studenten-/Elterninitiative etc f; **~-packed** adj film, book aktions- or handlungsgeladen; **~ painting** n Aktion f; **~ replay** n Wiederholung f; **~ stations** npl Stellung f; **~ stations!** Stellung!; (fig) an die Plätze!

activate ['æktɪveɪt] vt mechanism (person) betätigen; (heat) auslösen; (switch, lever) in Gang setzen; alarm auslösen; bomb zünden; (Chem, Phys) aktivieren; (US Mil) mobilisieren.

active ['æktɪv] **1** adj aktiv (also Gram); mind, social life rege; volcano also tätig; hostility also offen; dislike offen, unverhohlen; file im Gebrauch; (radio~) radioaktiv. **to be ~ in politics** politisch aktiv or tätig sein; **they should be more ~ in improving their safety standards** sie sollten sich der Verbesserung der Sicherheitsvorschriften etwas tatkräftiger vorantreiben; **to be under ~ consideration** ernsthaft erwogen werden; **on ~ service** (Mil) im Einsatz; **to see ~ service** (Mil) im Einsatz sein; **to be on the ~ list** (Mil) zur ständigen Verfügung stehen.
2 n (Gram) Aktiv nt.

actively ['æktɪvlɪ] adv aktiv; dislike offen, unverhohlen.

activism ['æktɪvɪzm] n Aktivismus m.

activist ['æktɪvɪst] n Aktivist(in f) m.

activity [æk'tɪvɪtɪ] n (a) no pl Aktivität f; (in classroom, station, on beach etc also) reges Leben; (in market, town, office) Geschäftigkeit f, geschäftiges Treiben; (mental) Betätigung f.

a scene of great ~ ein Bild geschäftigen Treibens; **a new sphere of** ~ ein neues Betätigungsfeld, ein neuer Wirkungskreis.

(b) *(pastime)* Betätigung *f*. **classroom activities** schulische Tätigkeiten *pl*; **the church organizes many activities** die Kirche organisiert viele Veranstaltungen; **business/social activities** geschäftliche/gesellschaftliche Unternehmungen *pl*; **criminal activities** kriminelle Tätigkeiten *or* Aktivitäten *pl*; **a programme of activities** ein Veranstaltungsprogramm *nt*.

(c) *(radio~)* Radioaktivität *f*.

activity holiday *n* Aktivurlaub *m*.

actor ['æktə^r] *n (lit, fig)* Schauspieler *m*.

actress ['æktrɪs] *n (lit, fig)* Schauspielerin *f*.

actual ['æktjʊəl] *adj* eigentlich; *reason, price also, result* tatsächlich; *case, example* konkret. **in** ~ **fact** tatsächlich; **what were his** ~ **words?** *(what did he really say)* was hat er eigentlich gesagt?; *(what were his exact words)* was genau hat er gesagt?; **this is the** ~ **house** das ist hier das Haus; **there is no** ~ **contract** es besteht kein eigentlicher Vertrag; **your** ~ ... *(inf)* ein echter/eine echte/ein echtes ...; der/die/das echte ...

actuality [ˌæktjʊˈælɪtɪ] *n (reality)* Wirklichkeit, Realität *f*; *(realism)* Aktualität *f*. **the actualities of the situation** die tatsächlichen Gegebenheiten.

actualize ['æktjʊəlaɪz] *vt* verwirklichen.

actually ['æktjʊəlɪ] *adv* **(a)** *(used as a filler) usually not translated.* ~ **I haven't started yet** ich habe noch (gar) nicht damit angefangen; ~ **we were just talking about you** wir haben eben von Ihnen geredet; ~ **his name is Smith** er heißt (übrigens) Smith; **I'm going too** ~ ich gehe (übrigens) auch; ~ **what we could do is to ...** (wissen Sie,) wir könnten doch ...

(b) *(to tell the truth, in actual fact)* eigentlich; *(by the way)* übrigens. **as you said before – and** ~ **you were quite right** wie Sie schon sagten – und eigentlich hatten Sie völlig recht; ~ **you were quite right, it was a bad idea** Sie hatten übrigens völlig recht, es war eine schlechte Idee; **I don't** ~ **feel like going there** ich habe eigentlich keine Lust, da hinzugehen; **do you want that/know him?** — ~ **I do/don't** möchten Sie das/kennen Sie ihn? — ja, durchaus *or* schon/nein, eigentlich nicht; **you don't want that/know him, do you?** — ~ **I do** Sie möchten das/kennen ihn (doch) nicht, oder? — doch, eigentlich schon; **do you know her?** ~ **I'm her husband** kennen Sie sie? — ja, ich bin nämlich ihr Mann; **I thought I could give you a lift but I won't be going** ~ ich dachte, ich könnte Sie mitnehmen, aber ich gehe nun doch nicht; **I bet you haven't done that!** — ~ **I have** Sie haben das bestimmt nicht gemacht! — doch; **I'm going soon, tomorrow** ~ ich gehe bald, nämlich morgen; **it won't be easy, it'll be very difficult** ~ es wird nicht leicht, ja es wird sogar sehr schwierig sein; **you're never home** — ~ **I was home last night** du bist nie zu Hause — doch, gestern abend war ich da.

(c) *(truly, in reality, showing surprise)* tatsächlich. **if you** ~ **own a flat** wenn Sie tatsächlich eine Wohnung besitzen; **don't tell me you're** ~ **going now!** sag bloß, du gehst jetzt tatsächlich *or* wirklich!; **oh, you're** ~ **in/dressed/ready!** oh, du bist sogar da/angezogen/fertig!; ... **but** ~ **I could do it** ... aber ich konnte es doch; **I haven't** ~ **started/done it/met him** yet ich habe noch nicht angefangen/es noch nicht gemacht/ihn noch nicht kennengelernt; **not** ~ ..., **but** ... zwar nicht ..., aber ...; **I wasn't** ~ **there, but/so** ... ich war zwar selbst nicht dabei, aber .../ich war selbst nicht dabei, deshalb ...; **did he** ~ **say that?** hat er das tatsächlich *or* wirklich gesagt?; **what did he** ~ **say?** *(what did he really say)* was hat er eigentlich gesagt?; *(what were his exact words)* was genau hat er gesagt?, was hat er tatsächlich gesagt?; **what do you** ~ **want?** was möchten Sie eigentlich?; **does that** ~ **exist/happen?** gibt es das denn überhaupt *or* tatsächlich/kommt das denn überhaupt *or* tatsächlich vor?; **as for** ~ **working** ... was die Arbeit selbst betrifft ...; **as for** ~ **doing it** wenn es dann daran geht, es auch zu tun; **it's the first time that I've** ~ **seen him/that I've** ~ **been home in time for the news** das ist das erste Mal, daß ich ihn mal gesehen habe/daß ich mal rechtzeitig für die Nachrichten zu Hause bin; **without** ~ **knowing him/his books** ohne ihn/seine Bücher überhaupt zu kennen.

(d) **it's** ~ **taking place this very moment** das findet genau in diesem Augenblick statt; **it was** ~ **taking place when he** ... es fand genau zu der Zeit statt, als er ...

actuarial [ˌæktjʊˈeərɪəl] *adj (Insur)* versicherungsmathematisch, versicherungsstatistisch.

actuary ['æktjʊərɪ] *n (Insur)* Aktuar *m*.

actuate ['æktjʊeɪt] *vt (lit)* auslösen; *(fig)* treiben.

acuity [əˈkjuːɪtɪ] *n* Schärfsinn *m*, Klugheit *f*; *(of mind)* Schärfe *f*.

acumen ['ækjʊmen] *n* Scharfsinn *m*. **to show (great)** ~ großen Scharfsinn beweisen; **business/political** ~ Geschäftssinn *m*/politische Klugheit.

acupuncture ['ækjʊˌpʌŋktʃə^r] *n* Akupunktur *f*.

acute [əˈkjuːt] **1** *adj* **(a)** *(intense, serious, Med) pain, shortage, appendicitis* akut. **(b)** *(keen) eyesight* scharf; *hearing also,* sense of smell fein. **(c)** *(shrewd)* scharf; *person* scharfsinnig; *child* aufgeweckt. **(d)** *(Math)* angle spitz. **(e)** *(Ling)* ~ **accent** Akut *m*. **2** *n (Ling)* Akut *m*.

acutely [əˈkjuːtlɪ] *adv* **(a)** *(intensely)* äußerst; *feel* intensiv; *embarrassed, sensitive, uncomfortable* äußerst; *aware* schmerzlich. **(b)** *(shrewdly)* scharfsinnig; *criticize, observe* scharf.

acuteness [əˈkjuːtnɪs] *n see adj* **(a)** Intensität *f*. **due to the** ~ **of the drought** da die Trockenheit so akut ist/wurde. **(b)** Schärfe *f*. Feinheit *f*. **(c)** Schärfe *f*; Scharfsinn *m*; Aufgewecktheit *f*.

AD *abbr of* **Anno Domini** A.D., a.D.

ad [æd] *n abbr of* **advertisement** Anzeige *f*, Inserat *nt*. **small** ~**s** Kleinanzeigen *pl*.

adage ['ædɪdʒ] *n* Sprichwort *nt*.

adagio [əˈdɑːdʒɪəʊ] **1** *adv* adagio. **2** *n* Adagio *nt*.

Adam ['ædəm] *n* Adam *m*. ~**'s apple** Adamsapfel *m*; **I don't know him from** ~ *(inf)* ich habe keine Ahnung, wer er ist *(inf)*.

adamant ['ædəmənt] *adj* hart; *refusal also* hartnäckig. **an** ~ **no** ein unerbittliches Nein; **to be** ~ unnachgiebig sein, darauf bestehen; **since you're** ~ da Sie darauf bestehen; **he was** ~ **about going** er bestand hartnäckig darauf zu gehen; **he was** ~ **in his refusal** er weigerte sich hartnäckig.

adamantine [ˌædəˈmæntaɪn] *adj (liter)* *(lit)* diamanten *(liter)*; *(fig)* hartnäckig.

adapt [əˈdæpt] **1** *vt* anpassen *(to dat)*; *machine* umstellen *(to, for auf +acc)*; *vehicle, building* umbauen *(to, for für)*; *text, book* adaptieren, bearbeiten *(for für)*. ~**ed to your requirements** nach Ihren Wünschen abgeändert; ~**ed for Arctic conditions** arktischen Verhältnissen angepaßt; ~**ed for children/television** für Kinder/für das Fernsehen adaptiert *or* bearbeitet; **it is perfectly** ~**ed to its environment** es ist seiner Umgebung vollkommen angepaßt; ~**ed from the Spanish** aus dem Spanischen übertragen und bearbeitet.

2 *vi* sich anpassen *(to dat)*; *(Sci also)* sich adaptieren *(to an +acc)*.

adaptability [əˌdæptəˈbɪlɪtɪ] *n see adj* Anpassungsfähigkeit *f*; Vielseitigkeit *f*; Flexibilität *f*; Eignung *f* zur Adaption.

adaptable [əˈdæptəbl] *adj* plant, animal, person anpassungsfähig; *vehicle, hairstyle* vielseitig; *schedule* flexibel; *book* zur Adaption *or* Bearbeitung geeignet. **to be** ~ **to sth** *(person, animal, plant)* sich an etw *(acc)* anpassen können; *(vehicle)* sich in etw *(dat)* verwenden lassen.

adaptation [ˌædæpˈteɪʃən] *n* **(a)** *(process)* Adaptation *f (to an +acc)*; *(of person, plant, animal also)* Anpassung *f (to an +acc)*; *(of machine)* Umstellung *f (to auf +acc)*; *(of vehicle, building)* Umbau *m*; *(of text also)* Bearbeitung *f*. **the** ~ **of space technology to medical ends** die Nutzung der Raumfahrttechnik für medizinische Zwecke.

(b) *(of book, play etc)* Adaption, Bearbeitung *f*.

adapter, adaptor [əˈdæptə^r] *n* **(a)** *(of book etc)* Bearbeiter(in *f*) *m*. **(b)** *(for connecting pipes etc)* Verbindungs- *or* Zwischenstück *nt*; *(to convert machine etc)* Adapter *m*. **(c)** *(Elec)* Adapter *m*; *(for several plugs)* Doppel-/Dreifachstecker, Mehrfachstecker *m*; *(on appliance)* Zwischenstecker *m*.

ADC *abbr of* **aide-de-camp**.

add [æd] **1** *vt* **(a)** *(Math)* addieren; *(~ on)* one number also hinzu- *or* dazuzählen *(to zu)*; *(~ up)* several numbers also zusammenzählen. **to** ~ **8 and/to 5** 8 und 5 zusammenzählen *or* addieren/8 zu 5 hinzuzählen.

(b) hinzufügen *(to zu)*; *ingredients, money also* dazugeben, dazutun *(to zu)*; *name also* dazusetzen *(to auf +acc)*; *(say in addition also)* dazusagen; *(build on)* anbauen. ~**ed to which ...** hinzu kommt, daß ...; **it** ~**s nothing to our knowledge** unser Wissen wird dadurch nicht erweitert; **transport/VAT** ~ **10% to the cost** es kommen 10% Transportkosten hinzu/zu den Kosten kommen noch 10% Mehrwertsteuer; **they** ~ **10% for service** sie rechnen *or* schlagen 10% für Bedienung dazu; ~**ed together the books weigh several tons** zusammengenommen wiegen die Bücher mehrere Tonnen; **if we** ~ **all the money together we can get them a really nice gift** wenn wir das ganze Geld zusammenlegen, können wir ihnen ein wirklich hübsches Geschenk besorgen; *see* **insult**.

2 *vi* **(a)** *(Math)* zusammenzählen, addieren. **she just can't** ~ sie kann einfach nicht rechnen.

(b) **to** ~ **to sth** zu etw beitragen; **to** ~ **to one's income** sein Einkommen aufbessern; **it will** ~ **to the time the job takes** es wird die Arbeitszeit verlängern; **the house had been** ~**ed to** an das Haus war (etwas) angebaut worden.

♦ **add on** *vt sep* number, amount dazurechnen; *two weeks* mehr rechnen; *room* anbauen; *storey* aufstocken; *(append)* comments etc anfügen.

♦ **add up 1** *vt sep* zusammenzählen *or* -rechnen.

2 *vi* **(a)** *(figures etc)* stimmen; *(fig: make sense)* sich reimen. **it's beginning to** ~ jetzt wird so manches klar.

(b) **to** ~ ~ **to** *(column, figures)* ergeben; *(expenses also)* sich belaufen auf *(+acc)*; **that all** ~**s** ~ **to a rather unusual state of affairs** alles in allem ergibt das eine recht ungewöhnliche Situation; **it doesn't** ~ ~ **to much** *(fig)* das ist nicht berühmt *(inf)*.

added ['ædɪd] *adj attr* zusätzlich.

addend ['ædend] *n (US)* Summand *m*.

addendum [əˈdendəm] *n, pl* **addenda** [əˈdendə] Nachtrag *m*.

adder ['ædə^r] *n* Viper, Natter *f*.

addict ['ædɪkt] *n (lit, fig)* Süchtige(r) *mf*. **he's a television/heroin/real** ~ er ist fernseh-/heroinsüchtig/richtig süchtig; **to become an** ~ süchtig werden.

addicted [əˈdɪktɪd] *adj* süchtig. **to be/become** ~ **to heroin/drugs/drink** heroin-/rauschgift-/trunksüchtig sein/werden; **he's** ~ **to smoking** er ist nikotinsüchtig; **he is** ~ **to sport/films** Sport ist/Filme sind bei ihm zur Sucht geworden; **you might get** ~ **to it** das kann zur Sucht werden; *(Med)* davon kann man süchtig werden.

addiction [əˈdɪkʃən] *n* Sucht *f (to nach)*; *(no pl: state of dependence also)* Süchtigkeit *f*. ~ **to drugs/alcohol/pleasure/sport** Rauschgift-/Trunk-/Vergnügungssucht/übermäßige Sportbegeisterung; **to become an** ~ zur Sucht werden; **his** ~ **to driving fast cars** seine Sucht, schnelle Autos zu fahren.

addictive [əˈdɪktɪv] *adj* **to be** ~ *(lit)* süchtig machen; *(fig)* zu einer Sucht werden können; **these drugs/watching TV can become** ~ diese Drogen können/Fernsehen kann zur Sucht werden.

adding machine *n* Addiermaschine *f*.

Addis Ababa [ˌædɪsˈæbəbə] *n* Addis Abeba *nt*.

addition [əˈdɪʃən] *n* **(a)** *(Math)* Addition *f*; *(act also)* Zusammenzählen *nt*. ~ **sign** Pluszeichen *nt*.

(b) (*adding*) Zusatz *m*. the ~ of one more person would make the team too large eine zusätzliche *or* weitere Person würde das Team zu groß machen; the ~ of one more country to the EEC/of a native speaker to the language department die Erweiterung der EG um ein weiteres Land/der Sprachabteilung um einen Muttersprachler.

(c) (*thing added*) Zusatz *m* (*to* zu); (*to list*) Ergänzung *f* (*to* zu); (*to building*) Anbau *m* (*to an* +*acc*); (*to income*) Aufbesserung *f* (*to gen*); (*to bill*) Zuschlag (*to* zu), Aufschlag (*to auf* +*acc*) *m*. they are expecting an ~ to their family (*inf*) sie erwarten (Familien)zuwachs (*inf*).

(d) in ~ außerdem, obendrein; in ~ (to this) he said ... und außerdem sagte er ...; in ~ to sth zusätzlich zu etw; she's studying for her exams in ~ to her other pursuits zusätzlich zu ihren anderen Tätigkeiten bereitet sie sich auch noch auf ihr Examen vor; in ~ to being unjustified his demand was also ... seine Forderung war nicht nur ungerechtfertigt, sondern außerdem noch ...

additional [əˈdɪʃənl] *adj* zusätzlich. ~ charge Aufpreis *m*; any ~ expenditure beyond this limit alle weiteren Ausgaben über diese Grenze hinaus; any ~ suggestions will have to be raised at the next meeting irgendwelche weiteren Vorschläge müssen bei der nächsten Sitzung vorgebracht werden; the author has inserted an ~ chapter der Autor hat ein weiteres Kapitel eingefügt.

additionally [əˈdɪʃənlɪ] *adv* außerdem; *say* ergänzend. ~ there is ... außerdem ist da noch ..., dazu kommt noch ...; ~ difficult/complicated (nur) noch schwieriger/komplizierter.

additive [ˈædɪtɪv] *n* Zusatz *m*.

addle [ˈædl] 1 *vt* **(a)** verdummen. **(b)** egg faul werden lassen, verderben lassen. 2 *vi* (*egg*) verderben, faul werden.

addled [ˈædld] *adj* **(a)** brain, person benebelt; (*permanently*) verdummt. **(b)** egg verdorben, faul.

addle-headed [ˈædlˈhedɪd], **addle-pated** [ˈædlˈpeɪtɪd] *adj* (*inf*) trottelig (*inf*), dußlig (*inf*).

address [əˈdres] 1 *n* **(a)** (*of person, on letter etc*) Adresse, Anschrift *f*. home ~ Privatadresse *f*; (*when travelling*) Heimatanschrift *f*; what's your ~? wo wohnen Sie?; I've come to the wrong ~ ich bin hier falsch *or* an der falschen Adresse; at this ~ unter dieser Adresse; who else lives at this ~? wer wohnt noch in dem Haus?; "not known at this ~" „Adressat unbekannt".

(b) (*speech*) Ansprache *f*. the A~ (*Parl*) die Adresse (*die Erwiderung auf die Thronrede*).

(c) (*bearing, way of behaving*) Auftreten *nt*; (*way of speaking*) Art *f* zu reden.

(d) (*form: skill, tact*) Gewandtheit *f*.

(e) form of ~ (*Form f der*) Anrede *f*.

(f) to pay one's ~es to a lady (*liter*) einer Dame die Cour machen (*liter*).

(g) (*Computers*) Adresse *f*.

2 *vt* **(a)** letter, parcel adressieren (*to an* +*acc*). **(b)** (*direct*) complaints richten (*to an* +*acc*); speech, remarks also adressieren (*to an* +*acc*).

(c) (*speak to*) meeting sprechen zu; jury sich wenden an (+*acc*); person anreden. don't ~ me as "Colonel" nennen Sie mich nicht „Colonel"; how should one ~ an earl? wie redet man einen Grafen an?

3 *vr* **(a)** to ~ oneself to sb (*speak to*) jdn ansprechen; (*apply to*) sich an jdn wenden.

(b) (*form*) to ~ oneself to a task sich einer Aufgabe widmen.

address book *n* Adreßbuch *nt*.

addressee [ˌædreˈsiː] *n* Empfänger(in *f*), Adressat(in *f*) *m*.

addresser, addressor [əˈdresəʳ] *n* (*form*) Absender(in *f*) *m*.

address label *n* Klebeadresse *f*.

addressograph [əˈdresəʊɡrɑːf] *n* Adressiermaschine, Adrema ® *f*.

adduce [əˈdjuːs] *vt* (*form*) anführen; proof erbringen.

adduction [æˈdʌkʃən] *n* (*form*) see *vt* Anführung *f*; Erbringung *f*.

Aden [ˈeɪdn] *n* Aden *nt*. Gulf of ~ Golf *m* von Aden.

adenoidal [ˈædɪnɔɪdl] *adj* adenoid; voice, adolescent näselnd. ~ infection Infektion *f* der Rachenmandeln.

adenoids [ˈædɪnɔɪdz] *npl* Rachenmandeln, Polypen (*inf*) *pl*.

adept [ˈædept] 1 *n* (*form*) Meister(in *f*) *m*, Experte *m*, Expertin *f* (*in, at* +*dat*). 2 *adj* geschickt (*in, at* +*dat*). to be ~ at sewing/hanging wallpaper geschickt *or* ein Meister *or* Experte im Nähen/Tapezieren sein.

adequacy [ˈædɪkwəsɪ] *n* Adäquatheit, Angemessenheit *f*. we doubt the ~ of his explanation/theory/this heating system wir bezweifeln, daß seine Erklärung/Theorie/diese Heizung angemessen *or* adäquat *or* ausreichend ist; he's beginning to doubt his ~ as a father/for the job er zweifelt langsam an seiner Eignung als Vater/für diese Stelle.

adequate [ˈædɪkwɪt] *adj* adäquat; (*sufficient also*) supply, heating system ausreichend; time genügend *inv*; (*good enough also*) zulänglich; excuse angemessen. to be ~ (*sufficient*) (aus)reichen, genug sein; (*good enough*) zulänglich *or* adäquat sein; this is just not ~ das ist einfach unzureichend *or* (*not good enough also*) nicht gut genug; more than ~ mehr als genug; (*heating*) mehr als ausreichend.

adequately [ˈædɪkwɪtlɪ] *adv* see adj.

adhere [ədˈhɪəʳ] *vi* (*to an* +*dat*) (*stick*) haften; (*more firmly*) kleben.

♦ **adhere to** *vi* +*prep obj* (*support, be faithful*) bleiben bei; to plan, belief, determination also festhalten an (+*dat*); to rule sich halten an (+*acc*).

adherence [ədˈhɪərəns] *n* Festhalten *nt* (*to an* +*dat*); (*to rule*) Befolgung *f* (*to gen*).

adherent [ədˈhɪərənt] *n* Anhänger(in *f*) *m*.

adhesion [ədˈhiːʒən] *n* **(a)** (*of particles etc*) Adhäsion, Haftfähigkeit *f*; (*more firmly: of glue*) Klebefestigkeit *f*. powers of ~ Adhäsionskraft *f*; (*of glue*) Klebekraft *f*. **(b)** see adherence.

adhesive [ədˈhiːzɪv] 1 *n* Klebstoff *m*. 2 *adj* haftend; (*more firmly*) klebend. to be highly/not very ~ sehr/nicht gut haften/kleben; ~ plaster Heftpflaster *nt*; ~ tape Klebstreifen *m*; ~ strength/powers Adhäsionskraft *f*; (*of glue*) Klebekraft *f*.

ad hoc [ˌædˈhɒk] *adj, adv* ad hoc *inv*.

adieu [əˈdjuː] (*old, liter*) 1 *n* Adieu, Lebewohl *nt* (*old*). to make one's ~s adieu sagen (*old*), Abschied nehmen. 2 *interj* adieu (*old*). to bid sb ~ jdm adieu *or* Lebewohl sagen (*old*).

ad infinitum [ˌædɪnfɪˈnaɪtəm] *adv* ad infinitum (*geh*), für immer.

adipose [ˈædɪpəʊs] *adj* (*form*) adipös (*form*), Fett-. ~ tissue Fettgewebe *nt*; (*hum*) Fettpölsterchen *pl*.

adjacent [əˈdʒeɪsənt] *adj* angrenzend; room also, angles Neben-. to be ~ to sth an etw (*acc*) angrenzen, neben etw (*dat*) liegen; in the ~ room to ours in dem Zimmer, das neben unserem liegt *or* das an unseres angrenzt.

adjectival *adj*, ~ly *adv* [ˌædʒekˈtaɪvəl, -l] adjektivisch.

adjective [ˈædʒektɪv] *n* Adjektiv, Eigenschaftswort *nt*.

adjoin [əˈdʒɔɪn] 1 *vt* grenzen an (+*acc*). 2 *vi* nebeneinander liegen, aneinander grenzen.

adjoining [əˈdʒɔɪnɪŋ] *adj* room Neben-, Nachbar-; (*esp Archit etc*) anstoßend; field Nachbar-, angrenzend; (*of two things*) nebeneinanderliegend. in the ~ office im Büro daneben *or* nebenan.

adjourn [əˈdʒɜːn] 1 *vt* **(a)** vertagen (*until* auf +*acc*). he ~ed the meeting for three hours er unterbrach die Konferenz für drei Stunden.

(b) (*US: end*) beenden.

2 *vi* **(a)** sich vertagen (*until* auf +*acc*). to ~ for lunch/one hour zur Mittagspause/für eine Stunde unterbrechen.

(b) (*go to another place*) sich begeben. to ~ to the sitting room sich ins Wohnzimmer begeben.

adjournment [əˈdʒɜːnmənt] *n* (*to another day*) Vertagung *f* (*until* auf +*acc*); (*within a day*) Unterbrechung *f*.

adjudge [əˈdʒʌdʒ] *vt* **(a)** (*Jur*) the court ~d that ... das Gericht entschied *or* befand, daß ...; to ~ sb guilty/insane jdn für schuldig/unzurechnungsfähig erklären *or* befinden; the estate was ~d to the second son der Besitz wurde dem zweiten Sohn zugesprochen.

(b) (*award*) prize zuerkennen, zusprechen (*to sb* jdm). he was ~d the winner er wurde zum Sieger *or* Gewinner erklärt.

(c) (*form: consider*) erachten für *or* als (*geh*).

adjudicate [əˈdʒuːdɪkeɪt] 1 *vt* **(a)** (*judge*) claim entscheiden; competition Preisrichter sein bei.

(b) (*Jur: declare*) to ~ sb bankrupt jdn für bankrott erklären.

2 *vi* entscheiden, urteilen (*on, in* bei); (*in dispute*) Schiedsrichter sein (*on* bei, *in* +*dat*); (*in competition, dog-show etc*) als Preisrichter fungieren.

adjudication [əˌdʒuːdɪˈkeɪʃən] *n* Entscheidung, Beurteilung *f*; (*result also*) Urteil *nt*. ~ of bankruptcy Bankrotterklärung *f*.

adjudicator [əˈdʒuːdɪkeɪtəʳ] *n* (*in competition, dog-show etc*) Preisrichter(in *f*) *m*; (*in dispute*) Schiedsrichter(in *f*) *m*.

adjunct [ˈædʒʌŋkt] *n* Anhängsel *nt*. correct grammar is not merely an ~ of good prose style grammatikalische Fehlerlosigkeit ist mehr als nur eine Nebenerscheinung guten Prosastils; a dictionary is an indispensable ~ to language learning ein Wörterbuch ist unerläßlich fürs Sprachenlernen

adjuration [ˌædʒʊəˈreɪʃən] *n* (*liter*) Beschwörung *f*.

adjure [əˈdʒʊəʳ] *vt* (*liter*) beschwören.

adjust [əˈdʒʌst] 1 *vt* **(a)** (*set*) machine, engine, carburettor, brakes, height, speed, flow etc einstellen; knob, lever (richtig) stellen; (*alter*) height, speed verstellen; length of clothes ändern; (*correct, re-adjust*) nachstellen; height, speed, flow regulieren; formula, plan, production, exchange rates, terms (entsprechend) ändern; salaries angleichen (*to an* +*acc*); hat, tie zurechtrücken. you can ~ the record-player to three different speeds Sie können den Plattenspieler auf drei verschiedene Geschwindigkeiten (ein)stellen; you can ~ the speed of the record-player die Geschwindigkeit des Plattenspielers läßt sich verstellen; to ~ the lever upwards/downwards den Hebel nach oben/unten stellen; you have to ~ this knob to regulate the ventilation Sie müssen an diesem Knopf drehen, um die Ventilation zu regulieren, die Ventilation läßt sich an diesem Knopf regulieren; he ~ed the knobs on the TV set er hat die Knöpfe am Fernsehapparat richtig gestellt; do not ~ your set ändern Sie nichts an der Einstellung Ihres Geräts; to ~ sth to new requirements/conditions etc etw auf neue Erfordernisse/Umstände etc abstimmen, etw neuen Erfordernissen/Umständen etc anpassen; because of increased demand production will have to be appropriately ~ed die Produktion muß auf die verstärkte Nachfrage abgestimmt werden *or* der verstärkten Nachfrage angepaßt werden; the terms have been ~ed slightly in your favour die Bedingungen sind zu Ihren Gunsten leicht abgeändert worden; the layout can be ~ed to meet different needs die Anordnung läßt sich je nach Bedarf ändern; we ~ed all salaries upwards/downwards wir haben alle Gehälter nach oben/unten angeglichen; would you please ~ your dress, sir (*euph*) ich glaube, Sie haben vergessen, etwas *or* Ihre Hose zuzumachen; if you could ~ the price slightly (*hum*) wenn wir uns vielleicht noch über den Preis unterhalten könnten.

(b) to ~ oneself to sth (*to new country, circumstances etc*) sich einer Sache (*dat*) anpassen; (*to new requirements, demands etc*) sich auf etw (*acc*) einstellen.

(c) (*settle*) *differences* beilegen, schlichten; (*Insur*) *claim* regulieren.
2 *vi* **(a)** (*to new country, circumstances etc*) sich anpassen (*to dat*); (*to new requirements, demands etc*) sich einstellen (*to auf +acc*).
(b) (*machine etc*) sich einstellen lassen. **the chair ~s to various heights** der Stuhl läßt sich in der Höhe verstellen.

adjustability [ə,dʒʌstə'bilɪtɪ] *n* see *adj* Verstellbarkeit *f*; Veränderlichkeit, Variabilität *f*; Regulierbarkeit *f*; Beweglichkeit, Flexibilität *f*; Anpassungsfähigkeit *f*.

adjustable [ə'dʒʌstəbl] *adj tool, height, angle* verstellbar; *shape* veränderlich, variabel; *height also, speed, temperature* regulierbar; *tax, deadline, rate of production/repayment* beweglich, flexibel; *person, animal, plant* anpassungsfähig. **partitions make the shape of the office ~** durch Trennwände läßt sich die Form des Büros verändern.

adjustable-pitch [ə'dʒʌstəbl'pɪtʃ] *adj* **~ propeller** Verstell-Luftschraube *f*.

adjuster [ə'dʒʌstəʳ] *n* (*Insur*) (Schadens)sachverständige(r) *mf*.

adjustment [ə'dʒʌstmənt] *n* **(a)** (*setting*) (*of machine, engine, carburettor, brakes, height, speed, flow etc*) Einstellung *f*; (*of knob, lever*) (richtige) Stellung; (*alteration*) (*of height, speed*) Verstellung *f*; (*of length of clothes*) Änderung *f*; (*correction, readjustment*) Nachstellung *f*; (*of height, speed, flow*) Regulierung *f*; (*of formula, plan, production, exchange rate, terms*) (entsprechende) Änderung; (*of hat, tie*) Zurechtrücken *nt*. **if you could make a slight ~ to my salary** (*hum inf*) wenn Sie eine leichte Korrektur meines Gehalts vornehmen könnten (*hum*); **a certain ~ of our traditional outlook** eine gewisse Änderung unserer traditionellen Haltung; **to make ~s** Änderungen vornehmen; **to make ~s to the manuscript/play/one's plans** Änderungen am Manuskript/Stück vornehmen/seine Pläne ändern; **brakes require regular ~** Bremsen müssen regelmäßig nachgestellt werden; **the text needs a lot of ~** am Text muß noch viel geändert werden.
(b) (*socially etc*) Anpassung *f*.
(c) (*settlement*) Beilegung, Schlichtung *f*; (*Insur*) Regulierung *f*.

adjutant ['ædʒətənt] *n* **(a)** (*Mil*) Adjutant *m*. **(b)** (*Orn: also ~ bird*) Indischer Marabu.

ad-lib [æd'lɪb] **1** *adv* aus dem Stegreif. **2** *n* Improvisation *f*. **3** *adj* improvisiert, Stegreif-. **4** *vti* improvisieren.

Adm *abbr of* **admiral** Adm.

adman ['ædmæn] *n* (*inf*) Werbefachmann, Reklamemensch (*inf*) *m*. **admen** Werbeleute *pl*.

admass ['ædmæs] *n* durch Werbung leicht beeinflußbares Publikum.

admin ['ædmɪn] *abbr of* **administration** Verw.

administer [əd'mɪnɪstəʳ] **1** *vt* **(a)** *institution, funds* verwalten; *business, affairs* führen; (*run*) *company, department* die Verwaltungsangelegenheiten regeln von. **the civil service ~s the country** die Beamtenschaft verwaltet das Land.
(b) (*dispense*) *relief, alms* gewähren; *law* ausführen, vollstrecken; *punishment* verhängen (*to über +acc*). **to ~ justice** Recht sprechen; **to ~ a severe blow to sb** (*fig*) jdm einen schweren Schlag versetzen.
(c) (*cause to take*) *to sb* jdm *medicine, drugs* verabreichen; *sacraments* spenden; *last rites* geben. **to ~ an oath to sb** jdm einen Eid abnehmen.
2 *vi* **(a)** (*act as administrator*) die Verwaltungsangelegenheiten regeln.
(b) (*form*) **to ~ to the sick/sb's needs** *etc* sich der Kranken/sich jds annehmen (*geh*).

administrate [əd'mɪnɪstreɪt] see **administer 1, 2 (a)**.

administration [əd,mɪnɪs'treɪʃən] *n* **(a)** *no pl* Verwaltung *f*; (*of an election, a project etc*) Organisation *f*. **to spend a lot of time on ~** viel Zeit auf Verwaltungsangelegenheiten *or* -sachen verwenden.
(b) (*government*) Regierung *f*. **the Schmidt ~** die Regierung Schmidt.
(c) *no pl* (*of remedy*) Verabreichung *f*; (*of sacrament*) Spenden *nt*. **the ~ of an oath** die Vereidigung; **the ~ of justice** die Rechtsprechung.

administrative [əd'mɪnɪstrətɪv] *adj* administrativ. **~ body** Verwaltungsbehörde *f*.

administrator [əd'mɪnɪstreɪtəʳ] *n* Verwalter *m*; (*Jur*) Verwaltungsbeamte(r), Administrator *m*.

admirable *adj*, **~bly** *adv* ['ædmərəbl, -ɪ] (*praiseworthy, laudable*) bewundernswert, erstaunlich; (*excellent*) vortrefflich, ausgezeichnet.

admiral ['ædmərəl] *n* Admiral *m*. **A~ of the Fleet** (*Brit*) Großadmiral *m*; see **red ~**.

Admiralty ['ædmərəltɪ] *n* (*Brit*) Admiralität *f*; (*department, building*) britisches Marineministerium. **First Lord of the ~** britischer Marineminister.

admiration [,ædmə'reɪʃən] *n* **(a)** Bewunderung *f*. **(b)** (*person, object*) **to be the ~ of all/of the world** von allen/von aller Welt bewundert werden.

admire [əd'maɪəʳ] *vt* bewundern.

admirer [əd'maɪərəʳ] *n* Bewund(e)rer(in *f*), Verehrer(in *f*) *m*; (*dated, hum: suitor*) Verehrer *m* (*hum*).

admiring *adj*, **~ly** *adv* [əd'maɪərɪŋ, -lɪ] bewundernd.

admissibility [əd,mɪsə'bɪlɪtɪ] *n* Zulässigkeit *f*.

admissible [əd'mɪsəbl] *adj* zulässig.

admission [əd'mɪʃən] *n* **(a)** (*entry*) Zutritt *m*; (*to club also, university*) Zulassung *f*; (*price*) Eintritt *m*. **no ~ to minors** Zutritt für Minderjährige verboten; **to gain ~ to a building** Zutritt zu einem Ort erhalten; (*thieves etc*) sich (*dat*) Zutritt zu einem Ort verschaffen; **he had gained ~ to a whole new world** er hatte

Zugang zu einer ganz neuen Welt gefunden; **a visa is necessary for ~ to the country** für die Einreise ist ein Visum nötig; **unrestricted ~ to a country** unbegrenzte Einreiseerlaubnis; **at last he was granted ~ to the society/to society** endlich wurde er zur Gesellschaft zugelassen/in die Gesellschaft aufgenommen.
(b) (*Jur: of evidence etc*) Zulassung *f*.
(c) (*confession*) Eingeständnis *nt*. **on ~ or by his own ~** nach eigenem Eingeständnis; **that would be an ~ of failure** das hieße, sein Versagen eingestehen.

admit [əd'mɪt] *vt* **(a)** (*let in*) hinein-/hereinlassen; (*permit to join*) zulassen (*to zu*), aufnehmen (*to in +acc*). **children not ~ted** kein Zutritt für Kinder; **he was not ~ted to the cinema/to college** er wurde nicht ins Kino hineingelassen/zur Universität zugelassen *or* in der Universität aufgenommen; **to be ~ted to the Bar** bei Gericht zugelassen werden; **this ticket ~s two** die Karte ist für zwei (Personen).
(b) (*have space for: halls, harbours etc*) Platz bieten für.
(c) (*acknowledge*) zugeben. **do you ~ stealing his hat?** geben Sie zu, seinen Hut gestohlen zu haben?; **he ~ted himself beaten** er gab sich geschlagen; **it is generally ~ted that ...** es wird allgemein zugegeben, daß ...; **to ~ the truth of sth** zugeben, daß etw wahr ist.
◆**admit of** *vi +prep obj* (*form*) zulassen (*+acc*).
◆**admit to** *vi +prep obj* eingestehen. **I have to ~ ~ a certain feeling of admiration** ich muß gestehen, daß mir das Bewunderung abnötigt.

admittance [əd'mɪtəns] *n* (*to building*) Zutritt (*to zu*), Einlaß (*to in +acc*) *m*; (*to club*) Zulassung (*to zu*), Aufnahme (*to in +acc*) *f*. **I gained ~ to the hall** mir wurde der Zutritt zum Saal gestattet; **I was denied ~** mir wurde der Zutritt verwehrt *or* verweigert; **no ~ except on business** Zutritt für Unbefugte verboten.

admittedly [əd'mɪtɪdlɪ] *adv* zugegebenermaßen. **~ this is true** zugegeben, das stimmt.

admixture [əd'mɪkstʃəʳ] *n* (*thing added*) Zusatz *m*, Beigabe *f*.

admonish [əd'mɒnɪʃ] *vt* **(a)** (*reprove*) ermahnen (*for wegen*).
(b) (*warn*) (er)mahnen; (*exhort*) ermahnen.

admonishment [əd'mɒnɪʃmənt], **admonition** [,ædməʊ'nɪʃən] *n* **(a)** (*rebuke*) Ermahnung *f*. **(b)** (*warning*) (Er)mahnung *f*; (*exhortation*) Ermahnung *f*.

admonitory [əd'mɒnɪtərɪ] *adj* ermahnend.

ad nauseam [æd'nɔːsɪæm] *adv* bis zum Überdruß, bis zum Geht-nicht-mehr (*inf*). **and so on ~** undsoweiter, undsoweiter.

ado [ə'duː] *n* Aufheben, Trara (*inf*) *nt*. **much ~ about nothing** viel Lärm um nichts; **without more or further ~** ohne weiteres.

adobe [ə'dəʊbɪ] *n* (*brick*) (ungebrannter) Lehmziegel, Adobe *m*; (*house*) Haus *nt* aus Adobeziegeln. **~ wall** Mauer *f* aus Adobeziegeln.

adolescence [,ædəʊ'lesns] *n* Jugend *f*; (*puberty*) Pubertät, Adoleszenz (*form*) *f*. **the problems of ~** Pubertätsprobleme *pl*; **in his late ~** in seiner späteren Jugend.

adolescent [,ædəʊ'lesnt] **1** *n* Jugendliche(r) *mf*. **he's still an ~** er ist noch im Heranwachsen/in der Pubertät.
2 *adj* Jugend-; (*in puberty*) Pubertäts-, pubertär; (*immature*) unreif. **he is so ~** er ist *or* steckt noch in der Pubertät; **~ phase** Pubertätsphase *f*; **~ spots** Pubertätspickel *pl*; **~ love** jugendliche Liebe.

Adonis [ə'dəʊnɪs] *n* (*Myth, fig*) Adonis *m*.

adopt [ə'dɒpt] *vt* **(a)** *child* adoptieren, an Kindes Statt annehmen (*form*); *child in a different country, family, city also* die Patenschaft übernehmen für. **the waif was ~ed into the family** der/die Waise wurde in die Familie aufgenommen; **the London court ~ed the young musician as its own** der Londoner Hof nahm den jungen Musiker als einen der ihren auf; **your cat has ~ed me** (*inf*) deine Katze hat sich mir angeschlossen.
(b) *idea, suggestion, attitude, method* übernehmen; *mannerisms* annehmen; *career* einschlagen, sich (*dat*) wählen.
(c) (*Pol*) *motion* annehmen; *candidate* nehmen.

adopted [ə'dɒptɪd] *adj son, daughter* Adoptiv-, adoptiert; *country* Wahl-.

adoption [ə'dɒpʃən] *n* **(a)** (*of child*) Adoption *f*, Annahme *f* an Kindes Statt (*form*); (*of city, of child in other country*) Übernahme *f* der Patenschaft; (*into the family*) Aufnahme *f*. **parents/Japanese by ~** Adoptiveltern *pl*/Japaner(in *f*) *m* durch Adoption.
(b) (*of method, idea*) Übernahme *f*; (*of mannerisms*) Annahme *f*; (*of career*) Wahl *f*. **his country of ~** die Heimat seiner Wahl; **this custom is Japanese only by ~** dieser Brauch ist von den Japanern nur übernommen worden.
(c) (*of motion, law, candidate*) Annahme *f*.

adoptive [ə'dɒptɪv] *adj parent, child* Adoptiv-. **~ country** Wahlheimat *f*.

adorable [ə'dɔːrəbl] *adj* bezaubernd, hinreißend. **you are ~** du bist ja so lieb.

adorably [ə'dɔːrəblɪ] *adv* bezaubernd, hinreißend.

adoration [,ædə'reɪʃən] *n see vt* **(a)** Anbetung *f*. **(b)** grenzenlose Liebe (*of für*). **(c)** Liebe *f* (*of für*).

adore [ə'dɔːʳ] *vt* **(a)** *God* anbeten. **(b)** (*love very much*) *family, wife* über alles lieben. **(c)** (*inf: like very much*) *French, whisky etc* (über alles) lieben; *Mozart also* schwärmen für. **like it? I ~ it** ob es mir gefällt? ich finde es hinreißend.

adoring [ə'dɔːrɪŋ] *adj* bewundernd. **his ~ fans** seine bewundernden *or* ihn anbetenden Fans.

adoringly [ə'dɔːrɪŋlɪ] *adv* bewundernd, voller Verehrung.

adorn [ə'dɔːn] *vt* schmücken, zieren (*geh*); *oneself* schmücken.

adornment [ə'dɔːnmənt] *n* **(a)** Schmuck *m no pl*; (*act*) Schmücken *nt*; (*on dress, cake, design*) Verzierung *f* (*also act*); (*on manuscript*) Ornament *nt*; (*in prose style*) Ausschmückung *f*.

adrenal [ə'driːnl] *adj* Adrenal-, Nebennieren-. **~ glands** Nebennieren *pl*.

adrenalin(e) [ə'drenəlɪn] n Adrenalin nt. **I could feel the ~ rising** ich fühlte, wie mein Blutdruck stieg; **to build up sb's ~** jdn in Stimmung bringen; **you burn up a lot of ~** Sie verbrauchen eine Menge Energie; **it's impossible to relax now the ~'s going** es ist unmöglich abzuschalten, wenn man so aufgedreht or high (sl) ist.

Adriatic (Sea) [ˌeɪdrɪ'ætɪk('siː)] n Adria f, Adriatisches Meer.

adrift [ə'drɪft] adv, adj pred (a) (Naut) treibend. **to be ~** treiben; **to go ~** sich losmachen or loslösen; **to set** or **cut a boat ~** ein Boot losmachen.
   (b) (fig) **to come ~** (wire, hair etc) sich lösen; (plans) fehlschlagen; (theory) zusammenbrechen. **we are ~ on the sea of life** wir treiben dahin auf dem Meer des Lebens; **hindered through the city, lost and ~** (ziellos und) verloren irrte er in der Stadt umher; **you're all ~** (inf) da liegst du völlig verkehrt or falsch; **after a month's philosophy I felt all ~** nach einem Monat Philosophie war ich vollkommen durcheinander; **to cast** or **turn sb ~** jdn auf die Straße setzen.

adroit [ə'drɔɪt] adj lawyer, reply, reasoning gewandt, geschickt; mind scharf. **to be ~ at sth/doing sth** gewandt or geschickt in etw (dat) sein/gewandt or geschickt darin sein, etw zu tun.

adroitly [ə'drɔɪtlɪ] adv gewandt, geschickt.

adroitness [ə'drɔɪtnɪs] n see adj Gewandtheit, Geschicklichkeit f; Schärfe f.

adsorb [æd'sɔːb] vt adsorbieren.

adsorption [æd'sɔːpʃən] n Adsorption f.

adulation [ˌædjuː'leɪʃən] n Verherrlichung f.

adult ['ædʌlt] **1** n Erwachsene(r) mf. **~s only** nur für Erwachsene. **2** adj (a) person erwachsen; animal ausgewachsen. **(b)** (for adults) book, film für Erwachsene; (mature) decision reif. **~ classes** Kurse pl für Erwachsene; **~ education** Erwachsenenbildung f.

adulterate [ə'dʌltəreɪt] vt (a) wine, whisky etc panschen; food abwandeln. **some ~d Scottish version of Italian cooking** ein schottischer Abklatsch italienischer Küche. **(b)** (fig) text, original version vergewaltigen.

adulteration [əˌdʌltə'reɪʃən] n (a) (of wine) Panschen nt; (of food) Abwandlung f. **(b)** (fig) Vergewaltigung f.

adulterer [ə'dʌltərər] n Ehebrecher m.

adulteress [ə'dʌltərɪs] n Ehebrecherin f.

adulterous [ə'dʌltərəs] adj ehebrecherisch.

adultery [ə'dʌltərɪ] n Ehebruch m. **to commit ~** Ehebruch begehen; **because of his ~ with three actresses** weil er mit drei Schauspielerinnen Ehebruch begangen hatte.

adulthood ['ædʌlthʊd] n Erwachsenenalter nt. **to reach ~** erwachsen werden.

adumbrate ['ædʌmbreɪt] vt (liter) (a) (outline) theory umreißen, skizzieren. **(b)** (foreshadow) coming event ankündigen.

adumbration [ˌædʌm'breɪʃən] n (liter) (a) (of theory) Umriß m, Skizzierung f. **(b)** (of event) Ankündigung f, Anzeichen nt.

advance [əd'vɑːns] **1** n (a) (progress) Fortschritt m.
   (b) (movement forward) (of old age) Voranschreiten nt; (of science) Weiterentwicklung f; (of ideas) Vordringen nt, Vormarsch m; (of sea) Vordringen nt. **with the ~ of old age** mit fortschreitendem Alter.
   (c) (Mil) Vormarsch m, Vorrücken nt.
   (d) (money) Vorschuß m (on auf +acc).
   (e) (amorous, fig) **~s** pl Annäherungsversuche pl.
   (f) in ~ im voraus; (temporal also) vorher; **to send sb on in ~** jdn vorausschicken; **£10 in ~** £ 10 als Vorschuß; **thanking you in ~** mit bestem Dank im voraus; **to arrive in ~ of the others** vor den anderen ankommen; **to be (well) in ~ of sb/one's time** jdm/seiner Zeit (weit) vorausssein; **let us know in ~, if ...** lassen Sie uns vorher or im voraus wissen, ob ...

2 vt (a) (move forward) date, time vorverlegen. **the dancer slowly ~s one foot** die Tänzerin setzt langsam einen Fuß vor.
   (b) (Mil) troops vorrücken lassen.
   (c) (further) work, project vor- or weiterbringen, weiterhelfen sein für; cause, interests fördern; knowledge vergrößern; (accelerate) growth vorantreiben; (promote) employee etc befördern.
   (d) (put forward) reason, suggestion, opinion, idea, plan vorbringen.
   (e) (pay beforehand) (sb jdm) (als) Vorschuß geben, vorschießen (inf); (lend) als Kredit geben.
   (f) (raise) prices anheben.

3 vi (a) (Mil) vorrücken.
   (b) (move forward) vorankommen. **to ~ towards sb/sth auf** jdn/etw zugehen/-kommen; **to ~ upon sb** drohend auf jdn zukommen; **as the sea ~s over the rocks** während die See über die Felsen vordringt; **old age ~s** das Alter schreitet voran; **old age is advancing on all of us** das Alter macht sich bei uns allen bemerkbar; **the forces of evil are advancing against us** die Mächte des Bösen nahen sich uns drohend.
   (c) (fig: progress) Fortschritte machen. **we've ~d a long way since those days** wir sind seither ein gutes Stück voran- or weitergekommen; **the work is advancing well** die Arbeit macht gute Fortschritte pl; **is civilization advancing towards some level of perfection?** geht die Zivilisation in irgendeiner Weise der Perfektion entgegen?; **as mankind ~s in knowledge** während die Menschheit an Wissen gewinnt.
   (d) (prices) anziehen; (costs) hochgehen, ansteigen.

advance: **~ booking** n Reservierung f; (Theat) Vorverkauf m; **~ booking opens on ...** der Vorverkauf beginnt am ...; **have you an ~ booking at?** (Theat) haben Sie (die Karten) vorbestellt?; (in hotel) haben Sie reserviert or reservieren lassen?; **~ booking office** n (Theat) Vorverkauf(sstelle) f m; **~ copy** n Vorausexemplar nt, Vorabdruck m.

advanced [əd'vɑːnst] adj student, level, age fortgeschritten; studies, mathematics etc höher; technology also, ideas fortschrittlich; version, model anspruchsvoll, weiterentwickelt; level of civilization hoch; position, observation post etc vorgeschoben. **~ work** anspruchsvolle Arbeit; **~ in years** in fortgeschrittenem Alter; **she is more/less ~ in years than ...** sie hat mehr/weniger Jahre auf dem Rücken als ... (inf); **the summer was well ~** der Sommer war schon weit vorangeschritten; see A level.

advance: **~ guard** n Vorhut f; **~ man** n (US Pol) Wahlhelfer m.

advancement [əd'vɑːnsmənt] n (a) (furtherance) Förderung f.
   (b) (promotion in rank) Vorwärtskommen nt, Aufstieg m.

advance: **~ notice** or **warning** n frühzeitiger Bescheid; (of sth bad) Vorwarnung f; **to give/receive ~ notice** frühzeitig Bescheid/eine Vorwarnung geben/erhalten; **~ party** n (Mil, fig) Vorhut f; **~ payment** n Vorauszahlung f.

advantage [əd'vɑːntɪdʒ] **1** n (a) Vorteil m. **to have an ~ (over sb)** (jdm gegenüber) im Vorteil sein; **to have the ~ of sb** jdm überlegen sein; **you have the ~ of me** (form) ich kenne leider Ihren werten Namen nicht (form); **he had the ~ of youth/greater experience** er hatte den Vorzug der Jugend/er war durch seine größere Erfahrung im Vorteil; **that gives you an ~ over me** damit sind Sie mir gegenüber im Vorteil, das verschafft Ihnen mir gegenüber einen Vorteil; **to get the ~ of sb (by doing sth)** sich (dat) (durch etw) jdm gegenüber einen Vorteil verschaffen; **don't let him get the ~ of us** er darf uns gegenüber keine Vorteile bekommen; **to have the ~ of numbers** zahlenmäßig überlegen sein.
   (b) (use, profit) Vorteil m. **to take ~ of sb/sth** jdn ausnutzen/etw ausnutzen or sich (dat) zunutze machen; **to take ~ of sb** (euph) jdn mißbrauchen; **he took ~ of her while she was drunk** er machte sich (dat) ihre Trunkenheit zunutze; **to turn sth to (good) ~** Nutzen aus etw ziehen; **he turned it to his own ~** er machte es sich (dat) zunutze; **of what ~ is that to us?** welchen Nutzen haben wir davon?; **I find it to my ~ to ..., it is to my ~ to ...** es ist vorteilhaft für mich ..., es ist für mich von Vorteil ...; **to use sth to the best ~** das Beste aus etw machen; **the dress shows her off to ~** das Kleid ist vorteilhaft für sie.
   (c) (Tennis) Vorteil m.

2 vt (old, liter) zum Vorteil or Nutzen gereichen (+dat) (geh).

advantageous [ˌædvən'teɪdʒəs] adj von Vorteil, vorteilhaft. **to be ~ to sb** für jdn von Vorteil sein.

advantageously [ˌædvən'teɪdʒəslɪ] adv vorteilhaft. **it worked out ~ for us** es wirkte sich zu unserem Vorteil or vorteilhaft für uns aus.

advent ['ædvənt] n (a) (of age, era) Beginn, Anbruch m; (of jet plane etc) Aufkommen nt. **(b)** (Eccl) **A~** Advent m.

adventitious [ˌædven'tɪʃəs] adj (form) zufällig.

adventure [əd'ventʃər] **1** n (a) Abenteuer, Erlebnis nt. **an ~ into the unknown** ein Vorstoß ins Unbekannte. **(b)** no pl love/spirit of ~ Abenteuerlust f; **to look for ~** (das) Abenteuer suchen; **a life of ~** ein abenteuerliches Leben. **2** vi see venture. **3** attr story, film, holiday Abenteuer-. **~ playground** Abenteuerspielplatz m.

adventurer [əd'ventʃərər] n Abenteurer(in f) m; (pej also) Windhund m.

adventuresome [əd'ventʃəsəm] adj see adventurous.

adventuress [əd'ventʃərɪs] n (pej) Abenteurerin f.

adventurous [əd'ventʃərəs] adj (a) person abenteuerlustig, journey abenteuerlich. **(b)** (bold) gewagt.

adventurousness [əd'ventʃərəsnɪs] n see adj (a) Abenteuerlust f; Abenteuerlichkeit f. **(b)** Gewagte(s) nt. **the ~ of his style** sein gewagter Stil.

adverb ['ædvɜːb] n Adverb, Umstandswort nt.

adverbial adj, **~ly** adv [əd'vɜːbɪəl, -ɪ] adverbial.

adversary ['ædvəsərɪ] n Widersacher(in f) m; (in contest) Gegner(in f) m.

adverse ['ædvɜːs] adj ungünstig; criticism, comment also, reaction negativ, ablehnend; wind, conditions also widrig; effect also nachteilig.

adversely [əd'vɜːslɪ] adv comment, criticize, react negativ; affect also nachteilig. **if they decide ~ for our interests** falls sie sich zu unseren Ungunsten or entgegen unseren Interessen entscheiden sollten.

adversity [əd'vɜːsɪtɪ] n (a) no pl Not f. **a period of ~** eine Zeit der Not; **in ~** im Unglück, in der Not. **(b)** (misfortune) Widrigkeit f (geh). **the adversities of war** die Härten des Krieges.

advert[1] [əd'vɜːt] vi (form) hinweisen, aufmerksam machen (to auf +acc).

advert[2] ['ædvɜːt] n (Brit inf) abbr of advertisement Anzeige, Annonce f, Inserat nt; (on TV, radio) Werbespot m.

advertise ['ædvətaɪz] **1** vt (a) (publicize) Werbung or Reklame machen für, werben für. **I've seen that soap ~d on television** ich habe die Werbung or Reklame für diese Seife im Fernsehen gesehen; **as ~d on television** wie durch das Fernsehen bekannt.
   (b) (in paper etc) flat, table etc inserieren, annoncieren; job, post also ausschreiben. **to ~ sth in a shop window/on local radio** etw durch eine Schaufensteranzeige/im Regionalsender anbieten; **I saw it ~d in a shop window** ich habe die Anzeige dafür in einem Schaufenster gesehen.
   (c) (make conspicuous) fact publik machen; ignorance also offen zeigen.

2 vi (a) (Comm) Werbung or Reklame machen, werben.
   (b) (in paper) inserieren, annoncieren (for für). **to ~ for sb/sth** jdn/etw (per Anzeige) suchen; **to ~ for sth on local radio/in a shop window** etw per Regionalsender/durch Anzeige im Schaufenster suchen.

advertisement [əd'vɜːtɪsmənt] n (a) (Comm) Werbung, Reklame f no pl; (in paper also) Anzeige f. **the TV ~s** die Werbung or Reklame im Fernsehen; **70% of the magazine is ~s** die

Zeitschrift besteht zu 70% aus Anzeigen *or* Werbung *or* Reklame; **he is not a good ~ for his school** er ist nicht gerade ein Aushängeschild für seine Schule.
  (b) *(announcement)* Anzeige *f*; *(in paper also)* Annonce *f*, Inserat *nt*. **to put an ~ in the paper (for sb/sth)** eine Anzeige (für jdn/etw) in die Zeitung setzen, (für jdn/etw) in der Zeitung inserieren; **~ column** Anzeigenspalte *f*.

advertiser [ˈædvətaɪzə^r] *n (in paper)* Inserent(in *f*) *m*. **this company never was a very big ~** diese Firma hat nie viel Werbung *or* Reklame gemacht.

advertising [ˈædvətaɪzɪŋ] *n* Werbung, Reklame *f*. **he is in ~** er ist in der Werbung (tätig).

advertising *in cpds* Werbe-; **~ agency** *n* Werbeagentur *f or* -büro *nt*; **~ campaign** *n* Werbekampagne *f or* -feldzug *m*; **~ rates** *npl* Inseratkosten *pl*; *(for TV, radio)* Einschaltpreise *pl* für Werbespots; **~ space** *n* Platz *m* für Anzeigen.

advice [ədˈvaɪs] *n* **(a)** *no pl* Rat *m no pl*. **a piece of *or* some ~** ein Rat(schlag) *m*; **let me give you a piece of *or* some ~** ich will Ihnen einen guten Rat geben; **you're a fine one to give ~** du hast gut raten, ausgerechnet du willst hier Ratschläge geben; **his ~ was always useful** er gab immer guten Rat auf gute Ratschläge; **that's good ~** das ist ein guter Rat; **I didn't ask for your ~** ich habe dich nicht um (deinen) Rat gebeten *or* gefragt; **to take sb's ~** jds Rat (be)folgen; **take my ~** höre auf mich; **to seek (sb's) ~** (jdn) um Rat fragen; *(from doctor, lawyer etc)* Rat (bei jdm) einholen; **to take medical/legal ~** einen Arzt/Rechtsanwalt zu Rate ziehen; **my ~ to him would be ...** ich würde ihm raten ...; **it's not ~ we need** wir brauchen keine guten Ratschläge.
  (b) *(Comm: notification)* Mitteilung, Benachrichtigung *f*, Bescheid *m*. **~ note** Benachrichtigung *f*, Benachrichtigungsschreiben *nt*.

advisability [ədˌvaɪzəˈbɪlɪtɪ] *n* Ratsamkeit *f*. **he questioned the ~ of going on strike** er bezweifelte, ob es ratsam wäre zu streiken.

advisable [ədˈvaɪzəbl] *adj* ratsam, empfehlenswert.

advisably [ədˈvaɪzəblɪ] *adv* zu Recht.

advise [ədˈvaɪz] **1** *vt* **(a)** *(give advice to)* person raten *(+dat)*; *(professionally)* beraten. **to ~ discretion/caution** zur Diskretion/Vorsicht raten, Diskretion/Vorsicht empfehlen; **I wouldn't ~ it** ich würde es nicht raten *or* empfehlen; **I would ~ you to do it/not to do it** ich würde dir zuraten/abraten; **to ~ sb against sth/doing sth** jdm von etw abraten/jdm abraten, etw zu tun; **what would you ~ me to do?** was *or* wozu würden Sie mir raten?
  (b) *(Comm: inform)* unterrichten, verständigen. **to ~ sb of sth** jdn von etw in Kenntnis setzen; **our agent keeps us ~d of developments** unser Vertreter unterrichtet uns ständig über neue Entwicklungen.
  2 *vi* **(a)** raten. **I shall do as you ~** ich werde tun, was Sie mir raten; **his function is merely to ~** er hat nur beratende Funktion.
  (b) *(US)* **to ~ with sb** sich mit jdm beraten.

advisedly [ədˈvaɪzɪdlɪ] *adv* richtig. **and I use the word ~** ich verwende bewußt dieses Wort.

advisedness [ədˈvaɪzɪdnɪs] *n* Klugheit, Ratsamkeit *f*.

advisement [ədˈvaɪzmənt] *n (US)* **to keep sth under ~** etw im Auge behalten; **to take sth under ~** etw ins Auge fassen.

adviser [ədˈvaɪzə^r] *n* Ratgeber(in *f*) *m*; *(professional)* Berater(in *f*) *m*. **legal ~** Rechtsberater(in *f*) *m*; **spiritual ~** geistlicher Berater.

advisory [ədˈvaɪzərɪ] *adj* beratend. **to act in a purely ~ capacity** rein beratende Funktion haben.

advocacy [ˈædvəkəsɪ] *n* Eintreten *nt (of* für*)*, Fürsprache *f (of* für*)*; *(of plan)* Befürwortung *f*. **the skills of legal ~** juristische Wortgewandtheit.

advocate [ˈædvəkɪt] **1** *n* **(a)** *(upholder: of cause etc)* Verfechter, Befürworter *m*.
  (b) *(esp Scot: Jur)* (Rechts)anwalt *m*/-anwältin *f*, Advokat(in *f*) *m* (old, dial).
  2 [ˈædvəkeɪt] *vt* eintreten für; plan etc befürworten. **those who ~ extending the licensing laws** die, die eine Verlängerung der Öffnungszeiten befürworten; **what course of action would you ~?** welche Maßnahmen würden Sie empfehlen?

advocator [ˈædvəkeɪtə^r] *n see* **advocate 1.**

adz(e) [ædz] *n* Dechsel *f*.

Aegean [iːˈdʒiːən] *adj* ägäisch; islands in der Ägäis. **the ~ (Sea)** die Ägäis, das Ägäische Meer.

aegis [ˈiːdʒɪs] *n* Ägide *f (geh)*. **under the ~ of** unter der Ägide *(geh) or* Schirmherrschaft von.

aegrotat [ˈaɪɡrəʊˌtæt] *n* Examen, an dem der Prüfling aus Krankheitsgründen nicht teilnimmt, und das bei Vorlage eines ärztlichen Attestes für bestanden erklärt wird.

Aeneas [ɪˈniːəs] *n* Äneas *m*.

Aeneid [ɪˈniːɪd] *n* Äneide *f*.

Aeolian [iːˈəʊlɪən] *adj* äolisch.

aeon [ˈiːən] *n* Äon *m (geh)*, Ewigkeit *f*. **through ~s of time** äonenlang *(geh)*.

aerate [ˈɛəreɪt] *vt* liquid mit Kohlensäure anreichern; **blood** Sauerstoff zuführen *(+dat)*; soil auflockern. **~d water** kohlensaures Wasser.

aerial [ˈɛərɪəl] **1** *n (esp Brit)* Antenne *f*. **~ input** *(TV)* Antennenanschluß *m*. **2** *adj* Luft-.

aerial: ~ barrage *n (air to ground)* Bombardement *nt*; *(ground to air)* Flakfeuer *nt*; **~ cableway** *n* Seilbahn *f*; **~ camera** *n* Luftbildkamera *f*;

aerialist [ˈɛərɪəlɪst] *n (US) (on trapeze)* Trapezkünstler(in *f*) *m*; *(on highwire)* Seiltänzer(in *f*) *m*.

aerial: ~ ladder *n* Drehleiter *f*; **~ map** *n* Luftbildkarte *f*; **~ navigation** *n* Luftfahrt *f*; **~ photograph** *n* Luftbild *nt*, Luftauf-

nahme *f*; **~ photography** *n* Luftaufnahmen *pl*; **~ railway** *n* Schwebebahn *f*; **~ reconnaissance** *n* Luftaufklärung *f*; **~ view** *n* Luftbild *nt*, Luftansicht *f*; **to obtain an ~ view of the site** um das Gelände von der Luft aus zu betrachten; **~ warfare** *n* Luftkrieg *m*.

aero- [ˈɛərəʊ] *pref* aero- *(form)*, Luft-.

aerobatic [ˌɛərəʊˈbætɪk] *adj* display, skills kunstfliegerisch, Kunstflug-.

aerobatics [ˌɛərəʊˈbætɪks] *npl* Kunstfliegen *nt*, Aerobatik *f (form)*.

aerodrome [ˈɛərədrəʊm] *n (Brit)* Flugplatz *m*, Aerodrom *nt (old)*.

aerodynamic [ˌɛərəʊdaɪˈnæmɪk] *adj* aerodynamisch.

aerodynamics [ˌɛərəʊdaɪˈnæmɪks] *n* **(a)** *sing (subject)* Aerodynamik *f*. **(b)** *pl (of plane etc)* Aerodynamik *f*.

aero-engine [ˈɛərəʊˌendʒɪn] *n* Flugzeugmotor *m*.

aerofoil [ˈɛərəʊfɔɪl] *n* Tragflügel *m*; *(on racing cars)* Spoiler *m*.

aeromodelling [ˈɛərəʊˌmɒdlɪŋ] *n* Modellflugzeugbau *m*.

aeronaut [ˈɛərənɔːt] *n* Aeronaut(in *f*), Luftschiffer *m (old)*.

aeronautic(al) [ˌɛərəˈnɔːtɪk(əl)] *adj* aeronautisch, Luftfahrt-. **~ engineering** Flugzeugbau *m*.

aeronautics [ˌɛərəˈnɔːtɪks] *n sing* Luftfahrt, Aeronautik *f*.

aeroplane [ˈɛərəpleɪn] *n (Brit)* Flugzeug *nt*.

aerosol [ˈɛərəsɒl] *n (can)* Spraydose *f*; *(mixture)* Aerosol *nt*. **~ paint** Spray- *or* Sprühfarbe *f*; **~ spray** Aerosolspray *nt*.

aerospace [ˈɛərəspeɪs] *n* äußere Erdatmosphäre.

aerospace *in cpds* Raumfahrt-; **~ industry** *n* Raumfahrtindustrie *f*; **~ research** *n* Raumforschung *f*.

Aertex ® [ˈɛərteks] *n* Baumwolltrikotstoff mit Lochmuster.

Aeschylus [ˈiːskələs] *n* Aischylos, Äschylus *m*.

Aesop [ˈiːsɒp] *n* Äsop *m*. **~'s fables** die Äsopischen Fabeln.

aesthete, (US) esthete [ˈiːsθiːt] *n* Ästhet(in *f*) *m*.

aesthetic(al), (US) esthetic(al) [iːsˈθetɪk(əl)] *adj* ästhetisch. **an ~ discussion/argument** eine Diskussion über Ästhetik/ein Argument der Ästhetik.

aesthetically, (US) esthetically [iːsˈθetɪkəlɪ] *adv* in ästhetischer Hinsicht. **~ decorated** ästhetisch schön dekoriert; **~ pleasing** ästhetisch schön.

aestheticism, (US) estheticism [iːsˈθetɪsɪzəm] *n* Ästhetizismus *m*.

aesthetics, (US) esthetics [iːsˈθetɪks] *n sing* Ästhetik *f*.

aestival, (US) estival [iːˈstaɪvəl] *adj (form)* sommerlich, Sommer-.

aestivate, (US) estivate [ˈiːstɪveɪt] *vi (form) (animals)* Sommerschlaf halten; *(person)* den Sommer verbringen.

aetiological, (US) etiological [ˌiːtɪəˈlɒdʒɪkəl] *adj (Med, fig)* ätiologisch.

aetiology, (US) etiology [ˌiːtɪˈɒlədʒɪ] *n (Med, fig)* Ätiologie *f*.

afar [əˈfɑː^r] *adv (liter)* weit. **from ~** aus der Ferne, von weit her.

affability [ˌæfəˈbɪlɪtɪ] *n* Umgänglichkeit, Freundlichkeit *f*.

affable *adj*, **~ly** *adv* [ˈæfəbl, -ɪ] umgänglich, freundlich.

affair [əˈfɛə^r] *n* **(a)** *(event, concern, matter, business)* Sache, Angelegenheit *f*. **it was an odd ~ altogether, that investigation** die Untersuchung war schon eine seltsame Sache *or* Angelegenheit; **a scandalous ~** ein Skandal *m*; **a novel entitled "The ~ of the golden glove"** ein Roman mit dem Titel „Der goldene Handschuh" *or* „Die Affäre mit dem goldenen Handschuh"; **the Watergate/Profumo ~** die Watergate-/Profumo-Affäre; **the state of ~s with the economy** die Lage der Wirtschaft; **in the present state of ~s** bei *or* in der gegenwärtigen Lage *or* Situation, beim gegenwärtigen Stand der Dinge; **a state of ~s I don't approve of** ein Zustand, den ich nicht billige; **what's the state of ~s with your forthcoming marriage?** wie steht's eigentlich mit deiner geplanten Hochzeit?; **there's a fine state of ~s!** das sind ja schöne Zustände!; **your private ~s don't concern me** deine Privatangelegenheiten sind mir egal; **financial ~s have never interested me** Finanzfragen haben mich nie interessiert; **I never interfere with his business ~s** ich mische mich nicht in seine geschäftlichen Angelegenheiten ein; **man of ~s** *(liter, form)* Geschäftsmann *m*; **~s of state** Staatsangelegenheiten *pl*; **~s of the heart** Herzensangelegenheiten *pl*; **it's not your ~ what I do in the evenings** was ich abends tue, geht dich nichts an; **that's my/his ~!** das ist meine/seine Sache!; *see also* current, foreign ~s.
  (b) *(love ~)* Verhältnis *nt*, Affäre *f (dated)*. **to have an ~ with sb** ein Verhältnis mit jdm haben.
  (c) *(duel)* **~ of honour** Ehrenhandel *m*.
  (d) *(inf: object, thing)* Ding *nt*. **what's this funny aerial ~?** was soll dieses komische Antennendings? *(inf)*; **the committee was an odd ~** das Kommitee war eine seltsame Sache.

affect² [əˈfekt] *vt* **(a)** *(have effect on)* sich auswirken auf *(+acc)*; decision, sb's life also beeinflussen; *(detrimentally)* health, nerves, condition, material also angreifen; health, person schaden *(+dat)*.
  (b) *(concern)* betreffen.
  (c) *(emotionally, move)* berühren, treffen. **he was obviously ~ed by the news** er war von der Nachricht offensichtlich sehr betroffen, die Nachricht hatte ihn sichtlich mitgenommen; **he was so emotionally ~ed that ...** er war so betroffen, daß ...
  (d) *(diseases: attack)* befallen.

affect² *vt* **(a)** *(feign)* ignorance, indifference vortäuschen, vorgeben. **(b)** *(liter: like to use etc)* clothes, colours eine Vorliebe *or* Schwäche haben für; accent sich befleißigen *(+gen) (geh)*.

affectation [ˌæfekˈteɪʃən] *n* **(a)** *(pretence)* Vortäuschung, Vorgabe *f*. **(b)** *(artificiality)* Affektiertheit *f no pl*. **her ~s annoy me** ihr affektiertes Benehmen ärgert mich; **an ~** eine affektierte Angewohnheit.

affected [əˈfektɪd] *adj* person, clothes affektiert; behaviour, style, accent also gekünstelt; behaviour also geziert.

affectedly [əˈfektɪdlɪ] *adv see* adj.

affecting [əˈfektɪŋ] *adj* rührend.

affection [əˈfekʃən] *n* **(a)** (*fondness*) Zuneigung *f no pl* (*for, towards* zu). **to win sb's ~s** (*dated, hum*) jds Zuneigung gewinnen; **I have** *or* **feel a great ~ for her** ich mag sie sehr gerne; **don't you even feel any ~ for her at all?** fühlst du denn gar nichts für sie?; **you could show a little more ~ towards me** du könntest mir gegenüber etwas mehr Gefühl zeigen; **children who lacked ~** Kinder, denen die Liebe fehlte; **everybody needs a little ~** jeder braucht ein bißchen Liebe; **he has a special place in her ~s** er nimmt einen besonderen Platz in ihrem Herzen ein; **displays of ~** Zärtlichkeiten in der Öffentlichkeit.
(b) (*form: Med*) Erkrankung, Affektion (*form*) *f.*

affectionate [əˈfekʃənɪt] *adj* liebevoll, zärtlich. **your ~ daughter** Deine liebende Tochter; **to feel ~ towards sb** jdm sehr zugetan sein, jdn sehr gern haben.

affectionately [əˈfekʃənɪtlɪ] *adv* liebevoll, zärtlich. **yours ~, Wendy** (*letter-ending*) in Liebe, Deine Wendy.

affective [əˈfektɪv] *adj* (*Psych*) affektiv.

affidavit [ˌæfɪˈdeɪvɪt] *n* (*Jur*) eidesstattliche Versicherung; (*to guarantee support of immigrant*) Affidavit *nt*. **to swear an ~** (*to the effect that*) eine eidesstattliche Versicherung abgeben (, daß).

affiliate [əˈfɪlɪeɪt] **1** *vt* angliedern (*to dat*). **the two banks are ~d** die zwei Banken sind aneinander angeschlossen; **~d** angeschlossen, Schwester-. **2** *vi* sich angliedern (*with an +acc*). **3** *n* Schwestergesellschaft *f*; (*union*) angegliederte Gewerkschaft.

affiliation [əˌfɪlɪˈeɪʃən] *n* **(a)** Angliederung *f* (*to, with an +acc*); (*state*) Verbund *m*. **what are his political ~s?** was ist seine politische Zugehörigkeit? **(b)** (*Brit Jur*) **~ order** Verurteilung *f* zur Leistung des Regelunterhalts; **~ proceedings** gerichtliche Feststellung der Vaterschaft, Vaterschaftsklage *f.*

affinity [əˈfɪnɪtɪ] *n* **(a)** (*liking*) Neigung *f* (*for* zu); (*for person*) Verbundenheit *f* (*for, to* mit). **(b)** (*resemblance, connection*) Verwandtschaft, Affinität (*form*) *f*. **(c)** (*Chem*) Affinität *f.*

affirm [əˈfɜːm] **1** *vt* **(a)** versichern; (*very forcefully*) beteuern. **he ~ed his innocence** er versicherte, daß er unschuldig sei; er beteuerte seine Unschuld. **(b)** (*ratify*) bestätigen. **2** *vi* (*Jur*) eidesstattlich *or* an Eidesstatt versichern *or* erklären.

affirmation [ˌæfəˈmeɪʃən] *n* **(a)** *see vt* **(a)** Versicherung *f*; Beteuerung *f*. **(b)** (*Jur*) eidesstattliche Versicherung *or* Erklärung.

affirmative [əˈfɜːmətɪv] **1** *n* (*Gram*) Bejahung *f*; (*sentence*) bejahender *or* positiver Satz. **the reply was in the ~** die Antwort war bejahend *or* „ja"; **to answer in the ~** bejahend *or* mit „ja" antworten; **put these sentences into the ~** drücken Sie diese Sätze bejahend aus.
2 *adj* bejahend, positiv; (*Gram*) affirmativ (*form*), bejahend. **the answer is ~** die Antwort ist bejahend *or* „ja".
3 *interj* richtig.

affirmatively [əˈfɜːmətɪvlɪ] *adv* bejahend, positiv.

affix¹ [əˈfɪks] *vt* anbringen (*to* auf +*dat*); **seal** setzen (*to* auf +*acc*); **signature** setzen (*to* unter +*acc*).

affix² [ˈæfɪks] *n* (*Gram*) Affix *nt.*

afflatus [əˈfleɪtəs] *n* Inspiration *f.*

afflict [əˈflɪkt] *vt* plagen, zusetzen (+*dat*); (*emotionally, mentally also*) belasten; (*troubles, inflation, injuries*) heimsuchen. **to be ~ed by a disease** an einer Krankheit leiden; **~ed with gout** von (der) Gicht geplagt; **to be ~ed with a tiresome child** mit einem anstrengenden Kind gestraft *or* geschlagen sein; **to be ~ed by doubts** von Zweifeln gequält werden; **all the troubles which ~ the nation** all die Schwierigkeiten, die das Land heimsuchen; **the ~ed** die Leidenden *pl.*

affliction [əˈflɪkʃən] *n* **(a)** (*distress*) Not, Bedrängnis *f*; (*pain*) Leiden, Schmerzen *pl.*
(b) (*cause of suffering*) (*blindness etc*) Gebrechen *nt*; (*illness*) Beschwerde *f*; (*worry*) Sorge *f*. **the ~s of old age** Altersbeschwerden *pl*; **a delinquent son was not the least of his ~s** er war nicht zuletzt mit einem kriminellen Sohn geschlagen; **the government is itself the greatest ~ the nation has** die Regierung ist selbst die größte Last für das Volk.

affluence [ˈæflʊəns] *n* Reichtum, Wohlstand *m*. **to live in ~** im Wohlstand leben; **to rise to ~** zu großem Wohlstand kommen.

affluent¹ [ˈæflʊənt] *adj* reich, wohlhabend. **the ~ society** die Wohlstandsgesellschaft; **you ~ so-and-so!** du reicher Sack! (*inf*), du Großkapitalist!

affluent² *n* (*Geog form*) Nebenfluß *m.*

afford [əˈfɔːd] *vt* **(a)** sich (*dat*) leisten. **I can't ~ to buy both of them** ich kann es mir nicht leisten, beide zu kaufen; **he can't ~ to make a mistake** er kann es sich nicht leisten, einen Fehler zu machen; **you can't ~ to miss the chance** Sie können es sich nicht leisten, die Gelegenheit zu verpassen; **I can't ~ the time (to do it)** ich habe einfach nicht die Zeit (, das zu tun), ich kann es mir zeitlich nicht leisten (, das zu tun); **an offer you can't ~ to miss** ein Angebot, das Sie sich (*dat*) nicht entgehen lassen können; **can you ~ to go?** — **I can't ~ not to!** können Sie gehen? — ich kann wohl nicht anders.
(b) (*liter: provide*) (*sb sth* jdm etw) gewähren, bieten; **shade** *also* spenden; **pleasure** bereiten.

afforest [æˈfɒrɪst] *vt* aufforsten.

afforestation [æˌfɒrɪˈsteɪʃən] *n* Aufforstung *f.*

affranchise [æˈfræntʃaɪz] *vt* befreien.

affray [əˈfreɪ] *n* (*esp Jur*) Schlägerei *f.*

affright [əˈfraɪt] *vt* (*old, liter*) erschrecken.

affront [əˈfrʌnt] **1** *vt* beleidigen. **2** *n* Beleidigung *f* (*to sb* jds, *to sth* für etw), Affront *m* (*to* gegen). **such poverty is an ~ to our national pride** solche Armut verletzt unseren Nationalstolz.

Afghan [ˈæfgæn] **1** *n* **(a)** Afghane *m*, Afghanin *f*. **(b)** (*language*) Afghanisch *nt*. **(c)** (*also ~ hound*) Afghane *m*, afghanischer Windhund. **(d)** **a~** (*coat*) Afghan *m*. **2** *adj* afghanisch.

Afghanistan [æfˈgænɪstæn] *n* Afghanistan *nt.*

---

aficionado [əˌfɪʃjəˈnɑːdəʊ] *n, pl* **-s** Liebhaber(in *f*) *m.*

afield [əˈfiːld] *adv* **countries further ~** weiter entfernte Länder; **too/very far ~** zu/sehr weit weg *or* entfernt; **to venture further ~** (*lit, fig*) sich etwas weiter (vor)wagen; **to explore farther ~** die weitere Umgebung erforschen; **to go farther ~ for help** (*fig*) in der weiteren Umgebung Hilfe suchen; **his studies took him farther ~ into new areas of knowledge** seine Forschungen führten ihn immer weiter in neue Wissensbereiche.

afire [əˈfaɪər] *adj pred, adv* in Brand. **to set sth ~** etw in Brand stecken, etw anzünden; (*fig*) etw entzünden; **~ with anger** wutentbrannt, flammend vor Zorn (*geh*); **this set his imagination ~** das entzündete seine Phantasie.

aflame [əˈfleɪm] *adj pred, adv* in Flammen. **to set sth ~** etw in Brand stecken, etw anzünden; **to be ~** in Flammen stehen; **to be ~ with colour** in roter Glut leuchten; **~ with anger/passion** flammend *or* glühend vor Zorn/Leidenschaft.

afloat [əˈfləʊt] *adj pred, adv* **(a)** (*Naut*) **to be ~** schwimmen; **to stay ~** sich über Wasser halten; (*thing*) schwimmen, nicht untergehen; **to set a ship ~** ein Schiff flottmachen; **at last we were ~ again** endlich waren wir wieder flott; **cargo ~** schwimmende Ladung; **the largest navy ~** die größte Flotte auf See; **service ~** Dienst *m* auf See; **to serve ~** auf See dienen.
(b) (*awash*) überschwemmt, unter Wasser. **to be ~** unter Wasser stehen, überschwemmt sein.
(c) (*fig*) **to get a business ~** ein Geschäft auf die Beine stellen; **those who stayed ~ during the slump** die, die sich auch während der Krise über Wasser gehalten haben.
(d) (*fig: rumour etc*) **there is a rumour ~ that ...** es geht das Gerücht um, daß ...

aflutter [əˈflʌtər] *adj pred, adv* aufgeregt. **to be ~ with anticipation** vor Erwartung zittern; **her heart was/nerves were all ~** ihr Herz flatterte/sie war fürchterlich aufgeregt.

afoot [əˈfʊt] *adj pred, adv* **there is something ~** da ist etwas im Gange; **what's ~?** was geht hier vor?

afore [əˈfɔːr] **1** (*obs, dial*) **1** *conj* bevor. **2** *adv* zuvor.

aforementioned [əˌfɔːˈmenʃənd], **aforesaid** [əˌfɔːˈsed] *adj attr* (*form*) obengenannt, obenerwähnt.

aforethought [əˈfɔːθɔːt] *adj see* malice.

a fortiori [ˌeɪfɔːtɪˈɔːraɪ] *adv* aufgrund des Vorhergehenden.

afoul [əˈfaʊl] *adj pred, adv* **lines, ropes** verheddert, verwirrt. **to run ~ of the law** mit dem Gesetz in Konflikt geraten.

afraid [əˈfreɪd] *adj pred* **(a)** (*frightened*) **to be ~ (of sb/sth)** (vor jdm/etw) Angst haben, sich (vor jdm/etw) fürchten; **don't be ~!** keine Angst!; **it's quite safe, there's nothing to be ~ of** es ist ganz sicher, Sie brauchen keine Angst zu haben; **go and talk to him then, there's nothing to be ~ of** geh und sprich mit ihm, da ist doch nichts dabei; **I am ~ of hurting him** *or* **that I might hurt him** ich fürchte, ihm weh zu tun *or* ich könnte ihm weh tun; **I am ~ he will** *or* **might hurt me, I am ~ lest he (might) hurt me** (*liter*) ich fürchte, er könnte mir weh tun; **to make sb ~** jdm Angst machen *or* einjagen, jdn ängstigen; **I am ~ to leave her alone** ich habe Angst davor, sie allein zu lassen; **I was ~ of not being precise enough** ich fürchtete, daß ich mich nicht genau genug ausdrückte; **I was ~ of waking the children** ich wollte die Kinder nicht wecken; **to be ~ of work** arbeitsscheu sein; **he's not ~ of hard work** er scheut schwere Arbeit nicht, er hat keine Angst vor schwerer Arbeit; **he's not ~ to say what he thinks** er scheut sich nicht, zu sagen, was er denkt; **that's what I was ~ of, I was ~ that would happen** das habe ich befürchtet; **go on, do it, what are you ~ of?** tu's doch, wovor hast du denn Angst?; **I was ~ you'd ask that** ich habe diese Frage befürchtet.
(b) (*expressing polite regret*) **I'm ~ I can't** I can't leider kann ich es nicht machen; **there's nothing I can do, I'm ~** ich kann da leider gar nichts machen; **I'm ~ to say that ...** ich muß Ihnen leider sagen, daß ...; **I'm ~ you'll have to wait** Sie müssen leider warten; **he said he's ~ you'll have to wait** er sagte, Sie müßten leider warten; **I am ~ I shall not be able to come** leider kann ich nicht kommen; **are you going?** — **I'm ~ not/I'm ~ so** gehst du? — leider nicht/ja, leider; **well, I'm ~ you're wrong** so leid es mir tut, aber Sie haben unrecht; **can I go now?** — **no, I'm ~ you can't** kann ich jetzt gehen? — nein, tut mir leid, noch nicht.

afresh [əˈfreʃ] *adv* noch einmal von vorn *or* neuem.

Africa [ˈæfrɪkə] *n* Afrika *nt.*

African [ˈæfrɪkən] **1** *n* Afrikaner(in *f*) *m*. **2** *adj* afrikanisch. **~ violet** Usambara-Veilchen *nt.*

Afrika(a)ner [ˌæfrɪˈkɑːnər] *n* Afrika(a)nder(in *f*) *m.*

Afrikaans [ˌæfrɪˈkɑːns] *n* Afrikaans *nt.*

Afro [ˈæfrəʊ] **1** *pref* afro-. **2** *n* (*hairstyle*) Afro-Frisur *f*, Afro-Look *m.*

Afro-: **~-American** **1** *adj* afro-amerikanisch; **2** *n* Afro-Amerikaner(in *f*) *m*; **~-Asian** **1** *adj* afro-asiatisch; **2** *n* Asiat(in *f*) *m* in Afrika.

aft [ɑːft] (*Naut*) **1** *adv* sit achtern; **go nach achtern. 2** *adj* Achter-, achter.

after¹ [ˈɑːftər] *adj attr* (*Naut*) Achter-.

after² **1** *prep* **(a)** (*time*) nach (+*dat*). **~ dinner** nach dem Essen; **~ that** danach; **the day ~ tomorrow** übermorgen; **the week ~ next** die übernächste Woche; **I'll be back the week ~ next** ich bin übernächste Woche wieder da; **it was ~ two o'clock** es war nach zwei.
(b) (*order*) nach (+*dat*), hinter (+*dat*); (*in priorities etc*) nach (+*dat*). **the noun comes ~ the verb** das Substantiv steht nach *or* hinter dem Verb; **I would put Keats ~ Shelley** für mich rangiert Keats unter Shelley; **~ you** nach Ihnen; **~ you with the salt** (*in queue etc*) ich war nach ihm dran; **~ you with the salt** kann ich das Salz nach dir haben?
(c) (*place*) hinter (+*dat*). **to run ~ sb** hinter jdm herlaufen *or* -rennen; **he shut the door ~ him** er machte die Tür hinter ihm zu; **to shout ~ sb** hinter jdm herrufen *or* -schreien; **to shout sth ~ sb** jdm etw nachrufen.

(d) (*as a result of*) nach (+*dat*). ~ what has happened nach allem, was geschehen ist; ~ this you might believe me jetzt wirst du mir vielleicht endlich glauben.

(e) (*in spite of*) to do sth ~ all etw schließlich doch tun; ~ all our efforts! und das, nachdem *or* wo (*inf*) wir uns soviel Mühe gegeben haben!; ~ all I've done for you! und das nach allem, was ich für dich getan habe!; ~ all, he is your brother er ist immerhin *or* schließlich dein Bruder; ~ ~ I had warned him ... und das, nachdem ich ihn gewarnt hatte.

(f) (*succession*) nach (+*dat*). you tell me lie ~ lie du erzählst mir eine Lüge nach der anderen, du belügst mich am laufenden Band; it's just one complaint ~ the other es kommen Beschwerden über Beschwerden *or* am laufenden Band Beschwerden; one ~ the other eine(r, s) nach dem/dem anderen; one ~ the other she rejected all the offers sie schlug ein Angebot nach dem anderen aus *or* Angebot um Angebot aus; day ~ day Tag für *or* um Tag; we marched on mile ~ mile wir marschierten Meile um *or* für Meile weiter; before us lay ~ mile of barren desert vor uns erstreckte sich meilenweit trostlose Wüste.

(g) (*manner: according to*) nach (+*dat*). ~ El Greco in der Art von *or* nach El Greco; she takes ~ her mother sie schlägt ihrer Mutter nach; *see* name.

(h) (*pursuit, inquiry*) to be ~ sb/sth hinter jdm/etw hersein; she asked *or* inquired ~ you sie hat sich nach dir erkundigt; what are you ~? was willst du?; (*looking for*) was suchst du?; he's just ~ a free meal/a bit of excitement er ist nur auf ein kostenloses Essen/ein bißchen Abwechslung aus; *see vbs.*

2 *adv* (*time, order*) danach; (*place, pursuit*) hinterher. for years/weeks ~ noch Jahre/Wochen *or* jahrelang/wochenlang danach; the year/week ~ das Jahr/die Woche danach *or* darauf; I'll be back sometime the year ~ ich komme irgendwann im Jahr danach *or* im darauffolgenden Jahr wieder; soon ~? kurz danach *or* darauf; what comes ~? was kommt danach *or* nachher?; the car drove off with the dog running ~ das Auto fuhr los, und der Hund rannte hinterher.

3 *conj* nachdem. ~ he had closed the door he began to speak nachdem er die Tür geschlossen hatte, begann er zu sprechen; what will you do ~ he's gone? was machst du, wenn er weg ist?; ~ finishing it I will/I went ... wenn ich das fertig habe, werde ich .../als ich das fertig hatte, ging ich ...; ~ arriving they went ... nachdem sie angekommen waren, gingen sie ...

4 *adj* in ~ years in späteren Jahren.

5 *n* ~s *pl* (*Brit inf*) Nachtisch *m*; what's for ~s? was gibt's hinterher *or* als *or* zum Nachtisch?

after: ~birth *n* Nachgeburt *f*; ~burner *n* Nachbrenner *m*; ~burning *n* Nachverbrennung *f*; ~-care *n* (*of convalescent*) Nachbehandlung *f*; (*of ex-prisoner*) Resozialisierungshilfe *f*; ~deck *n* Achterdeck *nt*; ~-dinner *adj speech, speaker* Tisch-; *walk, rest etc* Verdauungs-; ~-effect *n* (*of illness, Psych*) Nachwirkung *f*; (*of events etc also*) Folge *f*; ~glow *n* (*of sun*) Abendrot, Abendleuchten *nt*; (*fig*) angenehme Erinnerung; ~-image *n* (*Psych*) Nachempfindung *f*, Nachbild *nt*; ~-life *n* Leben *nt* nach dem Tode; ~-lunch *adj* to have an ~-lunch nap ein Mittagsschläfchen halten; ~math *n* Nachwirkungen *pl*; in the ~math of sth nach etw; the country was still in the ~math of war das Land litt immer noch an den Folgen *or* Auswirkungen des Krieges; ~most *adj* (*Naut*) Achter-, Heck-.

afternoon ['ɑ:ftə'nu:n] **1** *n* Nachmittag *m*. in the ~, ~s (*esp US*) am Nachmittag, nachmittags; at three o'clock in the ~ (um) drei Uhr nachmittags; on Sunday ~ (am) Sonntag nachmittag; on Sunday ~s Sonntag *or* sonntags nachmittags, am Sonntagnachmittag; on the ~ of December 2nd am Nachmittag des 2. Dezember, am 2. Dezember nachmittags; this/tomorrow/yesterday ~ heute/morgen/gestern nachmittag; good ~! Guten Tag!; ~! Tag! (*inf*).

2 *adj attr* Nachmittags-. ~ tea Tee *m*.

after: ~-pains *npl* Nachwehen *pl*; ~-sales service *n* Kundendienst *m*; ~-shave (lotion) *n* After-shave, Rasierwasser *nt*; ~thought *n* nachträgliche *or* zusätzliche Idee; if you have any ~thoughts about ... wenn Ihnen noch irgend etwas zu ... einfällt; he added as an ~thought fügte er hinzu, schickte er nach; I just mentioned that as an ~thought das fiel mir noch dazu *or* nachträglich ein; the window was added as an ~thought das Fenster kam erst später dazu.

afterwards ['ɑ:ftəwədz] *adv* nachher; (*after that, after some event etc*) danach. ~ things were never the same again danach war alles anders; and ~ we could go to a disco und anschließend *or* nachher *or* danach gehen wir in eine Disko; can I have mine now? — no, ~ kann ich meins jetzt haben? — nein, nachher; this ~ was added ~ das kam nachträglich dazu.

afterworld ['ɑ:ftə,wɜ:ld] *n* Jenseits *nt*.

again [ə'gen] *adv* (a) wieder. ~ and ~, time and ~ immer wieder; to do sth ~ etw noch (ein)mal tun; not to do sth ~ etw nicht wieder tun; I'll ring ~ tomorrow ich rufe morgen noch einmal an; never *or* not ever ~ nie wieder; if that happens ~ wenn das noch einmal passiert; all over ~ noch (ein)mal von vorn; what's his name ~? wie heißt er noch gleich?; to begin ~ von neuem *or* noch einmal anfangen; ~!, not ~! schon wieder!; not mince ~! schon wieder Hackfleisch!; it's me ~ (*arriving*) da bin ich wieder; (*phoning*) ich bin's noch (ein)mal; (*my fault*) wieder mal ich; not you ~! du schon wieder!?; he was soon well ~ er war bald wieder gesund; and these are different ~ und diese sind wieder anders; here we are ~! da wären wir wieder! (*finding another example etc*) oh, schon wieder!; ~ we find that ... und wieder einmal *or* wiederum stellen wir fest, daß ...

(b) (*in quantity*) as ~ doppelt so ...; as much ~ doppelt soviel, noch (ein)mal soviel; he is as old ~ as Mary er ist doppelt so alt wie Mary.

(c) (*on the other hand*) wiederum; (*besides, moreover*)

außerdem. but then ~, it may not be true vielleicht ist es auch gar nicht wahr.

against [ə'genst] *prep* (a) (*opposition, protest*) gegen (+*acc*). he's ~ her going er ist dagegen, daß sie geht; everybody's ~ me! alle sind gegen mich!; to have something ~ sb/sth etwas gegen jdn/etw haben; ~ that you have to consider ... Sie müssen aber auch bedenken ...; ~ my will, I decided ... wider Willen habe ich beschlossen ...; ~ their wish entgegen ihrem Wunsch; to fight ~ sb gegen *or* wider (*liter*) jdn kämpfen.

(b) (*indicating impact, support, proximity*) an (+*acc*), gegen (+*acc*). to hit one's head against the mantelpiece mit dem Kopf gegen *or* an das Kaminsims stoßen; push all the chairs right back ~ the wall stellen Sie alle Stühle direkt an die Wand.

(c) (*in the opposite direction to*) gegen (+*acc*).

(d) (*in front of, in juxtaposition to*) gegen (+*acc*). ~ the light gegen das Licht; by the juxtaposition of dark colours ~ light ... durch die Gegenüberstellung von dunklen und hellen Farben ...

(e) (*in preparation for*) sb's arrival, departure, one's old age für (+*acc*); misfortune, bad weather etc im Hinblick auf (+*acc*). ~ the possibility of a bad winter für den Fall, daß es einen schlechten Winter gibt.

(f) (*compared with*) (as) ~ gegenüber (+*dat*); she had three prizes (as) ~ his six sie hatte drei Preise, er hingegen sechs; the advantages of flying (as) ~ going by boat die Vorteile von Flugreisen gegenüber Schiffsreisen.

(g) (*Fin: in return for*) gegen. the visa will be issued ~ payment of ... das Visum wird gegen Zahlung von ... ausgestellt; to draw money ~ security gegen Sicherheit(sleistung) *or* Deckung Geld abheben.

Agamemnon [,ægə'memnɒn] *n* Agamemnon *m*.

agape [ə'geɪp] *adj pred person* mit (vor Staunen) offenem Mund, baß erstaunt (*geh*).

agaric ['ægərɪk] *n* Blätterpilz *m*.

agate ['ægət] *n* Achat *m*.

agave [ə'geɪvɪ] *n* Agave *f*.

age [eɪdʒ] **1** *n* (a) (*of person, star, building etc*) Alter *nt*. what is her ~, what ~ is she? wie alt ist sie?; he is ten years of ~ zehn Jahre alt; trees of such great ~ Bäume von so hohem Alter; ~ doesn't matter das Alter spielt keine Rolle; at the ~ of 15 im Alter von 15 Jahren, mit 15 Jahren; at your ~ in deinem Alter; when I was your ~ als ich in deinem Alter war, als ich so alt war wie du; when you're my ~ wenn du erst in mein Alter kommst, wenn du erst mal so alt bist wie ich; I have a daughter your ~ ich habe eine Tochter in Ihrem Alter; but he's twice your ~ aber er ist ja doppelt so alt wie du; 16, such a lovely ~ to be! 16, ein wunderbares Alter!; we're of an ~ wir sind gleichaltrig; he is now of an ~ to understand these things er ist jetzt alt genug, um das zu verstehen; over ~ zu alt; she doesn't look her ~ man sieht ihr ihr Alter nicht an, sie sieht jünger aus, als sie ist; be *or* act your ~! sei nicht kindisch!

(b) (*length of life*) (*of star, neutron etc*) Lebensdauer *f*; (*of human, animal, object also*) Lebenserwartung *f*. the ~ of a star can be millions of years ein Stern kann viele Millionen Jahre existieren.

(c) (*Jur*) to be of ~ volljährig *or* mündig sein; to come of ~ volljährig *or* mündig werden, die Volljährigkeit erlangen; under ~ minderjährig, unmündig; ~ of consent Ehemündigkeitsalter *nt*; intercourse with girls under the ~ of consent Unzucht *f* mit Minderjährigen.

(d) (*old*) Alter *nt*. his back was bent with ~ sein Rücken war vom Alter gebeugt; ~ before beauty (*hum*) Alter vor Schönheit.

(e) (*period, epoch*) Zeit(alter *nt*) *f*. the atomic ~ das Atomzeitalter; the ~ of technology das technologische Zeitalter; in this ~ of inflation in dieser inflationären Zeit; the Stone ~ die Steinzeit; the Edwardian ~ die Zeit *or* Ära Edwards VII; the ~ of Socrates das Zeitalter Sokrates; down the ~s durch alle Zeiten; what will future ~s think of us? was werden kommende Generationen von uns halten?

(f) (*inf: long time*) ~s, an ~ eine Ewigkeit, Ewigkeiten *pl*, ewig (lang) (all *inf*); I haven't seen him for ~s *or* for an ~ ich habe ihn eine Ewigkeit *or* Ewigkeiten *or* ewig (lang) nicht gesehen (*inf*); it's been ~s since we met wir haben uns ja eine Ewigkeit *etc* nicht mehr gesehen (*inf*); to take ~s eine Ewigkeit dauern (*inf*); (*person*) ewig brauchen (*inf*).

2 *vi* alt werden, altern; (*wine, cheese*) reifen. you have ~d du bist alt geworden; she seems to have ~d ten years sie scheint um zehn Jahre gealtert zu sein, sie scheint zehn Jahre älter geworden zu sein.

3 *vt* (a) (*dress, hairstyle etc*) alt machen; (*worry, experience etc*) alt werden lassen, altern lassen.

(b) *wine, cheese* lagern, reifen lassen.

aged [eɪdʒd] **1** *adj* (a) im Alter von, ... Jahre alt, -jährig. a boy ~ ten ein zehnjähriger Junge. (b) ['eɪdʒɪd] *person* bejahrt, betagt; *animal, car, building etc* alt, betagt (*hum*). **2** ['eɪdʒɪd] *npl* the ~ die alten Menschen, die Alten *pl*.

age: ~ difference *or* gap *n* Altersunterschied *m*; ~-group *n* Altersgruppe *f*; the forty to fifty ~-group die (Alters)gruppe der Vierzig- bis Fünfzigjährigen.

age(e)ing ['eɪdʒɪŋ] **1** *adj person* alternd *attr*; *animal, thing* älter werdend *attr*. **2** *n* Altern *nt*.

age: ~less *adj* zeitlos; she seems to be one of those ~less people sie scheint zu den Menschen zu gehören, die nie alt werden; ~ limit *n* Altersgrenze *f*; ~-long *adj* sehr lange, ewig (*inf*).

agency ['eɪdʒənsɪ] *n* (a) (*Comm*) (*news, theatrical, advertising* ~) Agentur *f*; (*subsidiary of a company*) Geschäftsstelle *f*; typing/tourist ~ Schreib-/Reisebüro *nt*; this garage is *or* has the Citroën ~ dies ist eine Citroën-Vertragswerkstätte, diese Werkstatt ist eine *or* hat die Citroën-Vertretung.

(b) (*instrumentality*) through *or* by the ~ of friends durch die

Vermittlung *or* mit Hilfe von Freunden, durch Freunde; **through the** ~ **of water** mit Hilfe vonWasser, durchWasser; **to put sth down to the** ~ **of Providence** etw der Vorsehung zuschreiben.

agenda [ə'dʒendə] *n* Tagesordnung *f.* **a full** ~ (*lit*) eine umfangreiche Tagesordnung; (*fig*) ein volles Programm; **on the** ~ auf dem Programm.

agent ['eɪdʒənt] *n* (a) (*Comm*) (*person*) Vertreter(in *f*) *m*; (*organization*) Vertretung *f.* **who is the** ~ **for this car in Scotland?** wer hat die schottische Vertretung für dieses Auto?
(b) (*literary, press* ~ *etc*) Agent(in *f*) *m*; (*Pol*) Wahlkampfleiter(in *f*) *m.* **business** ~ Agent(in *f*) *m*; **see my** ~ **about the contract** wegen des Vertrages müssen Sie mit meinem Agenten verhandeln.
(c) (*secret* ~*, FBI etc*) Agent(in *f*) *m.* ~ **extraordinary** Spezialagent(in *f*) *m.*
(d) (*person having power to act*) **man must be regarded as a moral** ~ der Mensch muß als moralisch verantwortlich handelndes Wesen angesehen werden; **determinism states that we are not free** ~**s** der Determinismus behauptet, daß wir nicht frei entscheiden können; **you're a free** ~ **, do what you want** du bist dein eigener Herr, tu was du willst.
(e) (*means by which sth is achieved*) Mittel *nt.* **she became the unwitting** ~ **of his wicked plot** unwissentlich wurde sie zum Werkzeug für seinen niederträchtigen Plan; **bees are** ~**s of pollination play a very important role in nature** durch ihre Funktion bei der Bestäubung spielen Bienen eine wichtige Rolle in der Natur.
(f) (*Chem*) **cleansing** ~ Reinigungsmittel *nt*; **special protective** ~ Spezialschutzmittel *nt.*

agent provocateur ['æʒɑ̃:ɡprɔˌvɒkə'tɜ:ʳ] *n, pl* **-s** ~ Agent provocateur *m*, Lockspitzel *m.*

age-old ['eɪdʒəʊld] *adj* uralt.

agglomerate [ə'ɡlɒməreɪt] **1** *vti* agglomerieren. **2** [ə'ɡlɒmərət] *adj* agglomeriert. **3** [ə'ɡlɒmərət] *n* Agglomerat *nt.*

agglomeration [əˌɡlɒmə'reɪʃən] *n* Anhäufung *f*, Konglomerat *nt*; (*Sci*) Agglomeration *f.*

agglutinate [ə'ɡlu:tɪneɪt] **1** *vi* agglutinieren (*also Ling*), verklumpen, verkleben. **2** [ə'ɡlu:tɪnət] *adj* agglutiniert (*also Ling*), verklumpt, verklebt.

agglutinating [ə'ɡlu:tɪneɪtɪŋ] *adj* (*Ling*) agglutinierend.

agglutination [əˌɡlu:tɪ'neɪʃən] *n* Agglutination (*also Ling*), Verklumpung, Verklebung *f.*

agglutinative [ə'ɡlu:tɪnətɪv] *adj* agglutinierend.

aggrandize [ə'ɡrændaɪz] *vt one's power, empire* vergrößern, ausdehnen, erweitern; *person, one's family* befördern. **to** ~ **oneself** sich befördern; (*be self-important*) sich wichtig machen.

aggrandizement [ə'ɡrændɪzmənt] *n see vt* Vergrößerung, Ausdehnung, Erweiterung *f*; Beförderung *f.*

aggravate ['æɡrəveɪt] *vt* (a) verschlimmern. (b) (*annoy*) aufregen; (*deliberately*) reizen. **don't get** ~**d** regen Sie sich nicht auf.

aggravating ['æɡrəveɪtɪŋ] *adj* ärgerlich, enervierend (*geh*); *noise, child* lästig, enervierend (*geh*). **how** ~ **for you** wie ärgerlich für Sie!

aggravation [ˌæɡrə'veɪʃən] *n* (a) (*worsening*) Verschlimmerung *f.* (b) (*annoyance*) Ärger *m.* **her constant** ~ **made him ...** sie reizte ihn so, daß er ...

aggregate ['æɡrɪɡɪt] **1** *n* (a) Gesamtmenge, Summe, Gesamtheit *f.* **considered in the** ~ insgesamt betrachtet. (b) (*Build*) Zuschlagstoffe *pl*; (*Geol*) Gemenge *nt.* **2** *adj* gesamt, Gesamt-. ~ **value** Gesamtwert *m.* **3** ['æɡrɪɡeɪt] *vt* (a) (*gather together*) anhäufen, ansammeln. (b) (*amount to*) sich belaufen auf (+*acc*). **4** ['æɡrɪɡeɪt] *vi* sich anhäufen, sich ansammeln.

aggression [ə'ɡreʃən] *n* (a) (*attack*) Aggression *f*, Angriff *m.* **an act of** ~ ein Angriff *m*, eine aggressive Handlung. (b) *no pl* Aggression *f*; (*aggressiveness*) Aggressivität *f.* **to get rid of one's** ~**s** seine Aggressionen loswerden.

aggressive [ə'ɡresɪv] *adj* (a) aggressiv; (*physically also*) angriffslustig; (*Sport*) *play also* hart; *lover* draufgängerisch, ungestüm. (b) *salesman, businessman etc* dynamisch, aufdringlich (*pej*).

aggressively [ə'ɡresɪvlɪ] *adv see adj* (a) Aggressivität *f*; Härte *f*; Draufgängertum, Ungestüm *nt.* (b) Dynamik, Aufdringlichkeit (*pej*) *f.*

aggressiveness [ə'ɡresɪvnɪs] *n see adj* (a) Aggressivität *f*; Härte *f*; Draufgängertum, Ungestüm *nt.* (b) Dynamik, Aufdringlichkeit (*pej*) *f.*

aggressor [ə'ɡresəʳ] *n* Angreifer(in *f*), Aggressor(in *f*) *m.*

aggrieved [ə'ɡri:vd] *adj* betrübt (*at, by* über + *acc*); (*offended*) verletzt (*at, by* durch); *voice, look also* gekränkt. **the** ~ (**party**) (*Jur*) der Beschwerte, die beschwerte Partei.

aggro ['æɡrəʊ] *n* (*Brit sl*) Stunk *m* (*inf*); (*aggressive feeling*) Scheißstimmung *f* (*sl*).

aghast [ə'ɡɑ:st] *adj pred* entgeistert (*at* über + *acc*).

agile ['ædʒaɪl] *adj person, thinker* beweglich, wendig; *person also* agil; *body also, movements* gelenkig, geschmeidig; *animal* flink, behende; *debater* geschickt, gewandt, wendig. **he has an** ~ **mind** er ist geistig sehr wendig *or* beweglich *or* flexibel.

agilely ['ædʒaɪllɪ] *adv move, jump etc* geschickt, behende; *argue* geschickt, gewandt; *think* flink, beweglich.

agility [ə'dʒɪlɪtɪ] *n see adj* Beweglichkeit, Wendigkeit *f*; Agilität *f*; Gelenkigkeit, Geschmeidigkeit *f*; Flinkheit, Behendigkeit *f*; Geschick *nt*, Gewandtheit, Wendigkeit *f.*

aging *adj, n see* **age(ing)**.

agitate ['ædʒɪteɪt] **1** *vt* (a) (*lit*) *liquid* aufrühren; *surface of water* aufwühlen; *washing* hin- und herbewegen. **don't let him** ~ **you** laß dich von ihm nicht aufregen. **2** *vi* agitieren. **to** ~ **for sth** sich für etw stark machen.

agitated *adj,* ~**ly** *adv* ['ædʒɪteɪtɪd, -lɪ] aufgeregt, erregt.

agitation [ˌædʒɪ'teɪʃən] *n* (a) *see vt* (a) Aufwühlen *nt*; Hin- und Herbewegung *f.* (b) (*anxiety, worry*) Erregung *f*, Aufruhr *m*; (*on stock market*) Bewegung *f.* (c) (*incitement*) Agitation *f.*

agitator ['ædʒɪteɪtəʳ] *n* (a) (*person*) Agitator(in *f*) *m.* (b) (*device*) Rührwerk *nt*, Rührapparat *m.*

agleam [ə'ɡli:m] *adj pred* erleuchtet. **the whole town was** ~ **with lights** die ganze Stadt war hell erleuchtet; **his eyes were** ~ **with mischief** seine Augen blitzten *or* funkelten schelmisch.

aglitter [ə'ɡlɪtəʳ] *adj pred* **to be** ~ funkeln, glitzern.

aglow [ə'ɡləʊ] *adj pred* **to be** ~ (*sky, fire, face*) glühen; **the sun set the mountains/sky** ~ die Sonne ließ die Berge/den Himmel erglühen *or* brachte die Berge/den Himmel zum Glühen; **to be** ~ **with happiness/health** vor Glück strahlen/vor Gesundheit strotzen.

agnail ['æɡneɪl] *n* Niednagel *m.*

agnostic [æɡ'nɒstɪk] **1** *adj* agnostisch. **2** *n* Agnostiker(in *f*) *m.*

agnosticism [æɡ'nɒstɪsɪzəm] *n* Agnostizismus *m.*

ago [ə'ɡəʊ] *adv* vor. **years/a week/a little while** ~ vor Jahren/einer Woche/kurzem; **that was years/a week** ~ das ist schon Jahre/eine Woche her; **ah, that's a long long time** ~ o, lang, lang ist's her; **he was here less than a minute** ~ er war erst vor einer Minute hier; **how long** ~ **is it since you last saw him?** wie lange haben Sie ihn schon nicht mehr gesehen?, wann haben Sie ihn das letzte Mal gesehen?; **how long** ~ **did it happen?** wie lange ist das her?; **he left 10 minutes** ~ er ist vor 10 Minuten gegangen; **long, long** ~ vor langer, langer Zeit; **how long** ~? wie lange ist das her?; **that was long** ~ das ist schon lange her; **as long** ~ **as 1950** schon 1950; **no longer** ~ **than yesterday** erst gestern (noch).

agog [ə'ɡɒɡ] *adj pred* gespannt. **the children sat there** ~ **with excitement** die Kinder sperrten Augen und Ohren auf; **the whole village was** ~ (**with curiosity**) das ganze Dorf platzte fast vor Neugierde; ~ **for news** wild nach Neuigkeiten; **we're all** ~ **to hear your news** wir warten gespannt auf deine Nachrichten; **to set sb** ~ jdn auf die Folter spannen.

agonize ['æɡənaɪz] *vi* sich (*dat*) den Kopf zermartern (*over* über + *acc*). **after weeks of agonizing he finally made a decision** nach wochenlangem Ringen traf er endlich eine Entscheidung.

agonized ['æɡənaɪzd] *adj* gequält.

agonizing ['æɡənaɪzɪŋ] *adj* qualvoll, quälend; *cry, experience* qualvoll.

agonizingly ['æɡənaɪzɪŋlɪ] *adv* qualvoll. ~ **slow** aufreizend langsam.

agony ['æɡənɪ] *n* (a) Qual *f*; (*mental also*) Leid *nt.* **that's** ~ das ist eine Qual; **it's** ~ **doing that** es ist eine Qual, das zu tun; **to be in** ~ Schmerzen *or* Qualen leiden; **in an** ~ **of indecision/suspense** *etc* in qualvoller Unentschlossenheit/Ungewißheit *etc*; **to go through** *or* **suffer agonies** Qualen ausstehen. (b) (*death* ~) Todeskampf *m*, Agonie *f*; (*of Christ*) Todesangst *f.* **put him out of his** ~ (*lit*) mach seiner Qual ein Ende; (*fig*) nun spann ihn doch nicht länger auf die Folter.

agony column *n* (*Brit inf*) Kummerkasten *m.*

agony columnist *n* (*Brit inf*) Kummerkastenonkel *m*/-tante *f* (*inf*).

agoraphobia [ˌæɡərə'fəʊbjə] *n* Platzangst, Agoraphobie (*form*) *f.*

agrarian [ə'ɡreərɪən] *adj* Agrar-.

agree [ə'ɡri:] *pret, ptp* ~**d 1** *vt* (a) *price, date etc* vereinbaren, abmachen.
(b) (*consent*) **to** ~ **to do sth** sich einverstanden *or* bereit erklären, etw zu tun.
(c) (*admit*) zugeben. **I** ~ (**that**) **I was wrong** ich gebe zu, daß ich mich geirrt habe.
(d) (*come to or be in agreement about*) zustimmen (+*dat*). **we all** ~ **that ...** wir sind alle der Meinung, daß ...; **it was** ~**d that ...** man kam überein, daß ...; **man einigte sich darauf** *or* **es wurde beschlossen, daß ...; we** ~**d to do it** wir haben beschlossen, das zu tun; **to** ~ **to differ** sich (*dat*) verschiedene Meinungen zugestehen; **is that** ~**d then, gentlemen?** sind alle einverstanden?; *see also* **agreed.**
2 *vi* (a) (*hold same opinion*) (*two or more people*) sich einig sein, übereinstimmen, einer Meinung sein; (*one person*) der gleichen Meinung sein. **to** ~ **with sb** jdm zustimmen; **I** ~! er Meinung bin ich auch; **we all** ~**, it's a silly suggestion** wir sind uns alle einig, das ist ein alberner Vorschlag; **I couldn't** ~ **more/less** ich bin völlig/überhaupt nicht dieser Meinung, ich stimme dem völlig/überhaupt nicht zu; **it's too late now, don't you** ~? finden *or* meinen Sie nicht auch, daß es jetzt zu spät ist?; **wouldn't you** ~**, it's an impossible hope?** finden *or* meinen Sie nicht auch, daß das eine völlig unberechtigte Hoffnung ist?
(b) **to** ~ **with a theory/the figures** *etc* (*accept*) eine Theorie/die Zahlen akzeptieren *or* für richtig halten.
(c) (*come to an agreement*) sich einigen, Einigkeit erzielen (*about* über + *acc*).
(d) (*people: get on together*) sich vertragen, miteinander auskommen.
(e) (*statements, accounts, figures etc: tally*) übereinstimmen.
(f) **to** ~ **with sth** (*approve of*) etw befürworten, mit etw einverstanden sein; **I don't** ~ **with children drinking wine** ich bin dagegen *or* ich befürworte es nicht *or* ich bin nicht damit einverstanden, daß Kinder Wein trinken.
(g) (*food, climate etc*) **sth** ~**s with sb** jdm bekommt etw; **whisky doesn't** ~ **with me** ich vertrage Whisky nicht, Whisky bekommt mir nicht.
(h) (*Gram*) übereinstimmen.

♦**agree on** *vi* +*prep obj solution* sich einigen auf (+*acc*), Einigkeit erzielen über (+*acc*); *price, policy also* vereinbaren. **a** price/policy/solution has been ~d ~ man hat sich auf einen Preis/eine Linie/eine Lösung geeinigt; we ~d ~ the need to save wir waren uns darüber einig, daß gespart werden muß.

♦**agree to** vi +prep obj zustimmen (+dat); marriage also einwilligen in (+acc), seine Einwilligung geben zu; conditions, terms also annehmen, akzeptieren; increase, payment also sich einverstanden erklären mit. **I cannot ~ ~ your marrying her** ich kann einer Ehe nicht zustimmen.

agreeable [əˈgriːəbl] adj **(a)** (pleasant) angenehm; decor, behaviour nett. **(b)** pred (willing to agree) einverstanden. **are you ~ to that?** sind Sie damit einverstanden?

agreeably [əˈgriːəbli] adv angenehm; decorated nett. **she behaved ~ for once** sie benahm sich ausnahmsweise nett.

agreed [əˈgriːd] adj **(a)** pred (in agreement) einig. **to be ~ on sth/doing sth** sich über etw einig sein/sich darüber einig sein, etw zu tun; **are we all ~?** sind wir uns da einig?; (on course of action) sind alle einverstanden?

(b) (arranged) vereinbart; price also festgesetzt; time also verabredet, abgesprochen. **it's all ~** es ist alles abgesprochen; **~?** einverstanden?; **~!** (regarding price etc) abgemacht, in Ordnung; (I agree) stimmt, genau.

agreement [əˈgriːmənt] n **(a)** (understanding, arrangement) Abmachung, Übereinkunft f; (treaty, contract) Abkommen nt, Vertrag m. **to break the terms of an ~** einen Vertrag brechen, die Vertragsbestimmungen verletzen; **to enter into an ~ (with sb)** (mit jdm) einen Vertrag eingehen or (ab)schließen; **to reach an ~ (with sb)** (mit jdm) zu einer Einigung kommen, (mit jdm) Übereinstimmung erzielen; **there's a tacit ~ in the office that** ... im Büro besteht die stillschweigende Übereinkunft, daß ...; **we have an ~ whereby if I'm home first** ... wir haben abgemacht, daß, wenn ich zuerst nach Hause komme, ...; see **gentleman**.

(b) (sharing of opinion) Einigkeit f. **unanimous ~** Einmütigkeit f; **by mutual ~** in gegenseitigem Einverständnis or Einvernehmen; **to be in ~ with sb** mit jdm einer Meinung sein; **to be in ~ with/about sth** mit etw einverstanden/über etw (acc) einig sein; **for once we were both in ~ on that point** ausnahmsweise waren wir uns in diesem Punkt einig or waren wir in diesem Punkt einer Meinung; **to find oneself in ~ with sb** mit jdm übereinstimmen or einiggehen.

(c) (consent) Einwilligung, Zustimmung f (to zu).
(d) (between figures, accounts etc) Übereinstimmung f.
(e) (Gram) Übereinstimmung f.

agricultural [ˌægrɪˈkʌltʃərəl] adj produce, expert, tool etc landwirtschaftlich; ministry, association, science etc Landwirtschafts-. **~ worker** Landarbeiter(in f) m; **~ nation** Agrarstaat m, Agrarland nt; **the ~ country in the north** das landwirtschaftliche Gebiet im Norden; **~ college** Landwirtschaftsschule f; **~ show** landwirtschaftliche Leistungsschau f.

agricultur(al)ist [ˌægrɪˈkʌltʃər(əl)ɪst] n Landwirtschaftsexperte m/-expertin f; (farmer) Landwirt(in f) m.

agriculturally [ˌægrɪˈkʌltʃərəli] adv landwirtschaftlich.

agriculture [ˈægrɪkʌltʃəʳ] n Landwirtschaft f.

agronomist [əˈgrɒnəmɪst] n Agronom(in f) m.

agronomy [əˈgrɒnəmi] n Agronomie f.

aground [əˈgraʊnd] **1** adj pred ship gestrandet, aufgelaufen, auf Grund gelaufen. **2** adv **to go** or **run ~** auflaufen, auf Grund laufen, stranden.

ague [ˈeɪgjuː] n Schüttelfrost m no art.

ah [ɑː] interj ah; (pain) au, autsch; (pity) o, ach.

aha [ɑːˈhɑː] interj aha.

ahead [əˈhed] adv **(a)** there's some thick cloud ~ vor uns or da vorne ist eine große Wolke; **the mountains lay ~** vor uns/ihnen etc lagen die Berge; **the German runner was/drew ~** der deutsche Läufer lag vorn/zog nach vorne; **he is ~ by about two minutes** er hat etwa zwei Minuten Vorsprung; **keep straight ~** immer geradeaus; **full speed ~** (Naut) volle Kraft voraus; **we sent him on ~** wir schickten ihn voraus; **in the months ~** in den bevorstehenden Monaten; **I can see problems ~** ich sehe Probleme auf mich/uns etc zukommen; **we've a busy time ~** vor uns liegt eine Menge Arbeit; **to plan ~** vorausplanen; see **vbs**.

(b) **~ of sb/sth** vor jdm/etw; **walk ~ of me** geh voran; **the leader is two laps ~ of the others** der Führende hat zwei Runden Vorsprung or liegt zwei Runden vor den anderen; **we arrived ten minutes ~ of time** wir kamen zehn Minuten vorher an; **to be/get ~ of schedule** schneller als geplant vorankommen; **the dollar is still ~ of the mark** der Dollar führt immer noch vor der Mark; **to be ~ of one's time** (fig) seiner Zeit voraus sein.

ahem [əˈhəm] interj hm.

ahoy [əˈhɔɪ] interj (Naut) ahoi. **ship ~!** Schiff ahoi!

aid [eɪd] **1** n **(a)** no pl (help) Hilfe f. **(foreign) ~** Entwicklungshilfe f; **with the ~ of his uncle/a screwdriver** mit Hilfe seines Onkels/eines Schraubenziehers; **to come to sb's ~** jdm zu Hilfe kommen; **a sale in ~ of the blind** ein Verkauf zugunsten der Blinden; **what's all this wiring in ~ of?** (inf) wozu sind all diese Drähte da or gut?; **what's all this in ~ of?** (inf) wozu soll das gut sein?

(b) (useful person, thing) Hilfe f (to für); (piece of equipment, audio-visual ~ etc) Hilfsmittel nt; (hearing ~) Hörgerät nt; (teaching ~) Lehrmittel nt.

(c) (esp US) see **aide**.

2 vt unterstützen, helfen (+dat). **to ~ one another** sich gegenseitig helfen or unterstützen; **to ~ sb's recovery** jds Heilung fördern; **to ~ and abet sb** (Jur) jdm Beihilfe leisten; **(after crime)** jdm begünstigen; **he was accused of ~ing and abetting** ihm wurde Beihilfe/Begünstigung vorgeworfen.

aide [eɪd] n Helfer(in f) m; (adviser) (persönlicher) Berater.

aide-de-camp [ˈeɪddəkɒŋ] n, pl **aides-de-camp (a)** (Mil) Adjutant m. **(b)** see **aide**.

aide-memoire [ˈeɪdmemˈwɑː] n Gedächtnisstütze f; (official memorandum) Aide-memoire nt.

aiding and abetting [ˈeɪdɪʌndəˈbetɪŋ] n (Jur) Beihilfe f; (after crime) Begünstigung f.

aigrette [ˈeɪgret] n Reiherfeder f, Reiherbusch m (old).

ail [eɪl] **1** vt (old) plagen. **what's ~ing you?** (inf) was hast du?, was ist mit dir? **2** vi (inf) kränklich sein, kränkeln.

aileron [ˈeɪlərɒn] n (Aviat) Querruder nt.

ailing [ˈeɪlɪŋ] adj (lit) kränklich, kränkelnd; (fig) industry, economy etc krankend, krank.

ailment [ˈeɪlmənt] n Gebrechen, Leiden nt. **minor ~s** leichte Beschwerden pl; **inflation, a national ~** die Inflation, eine nationale Krankheit; **all his little ~s** all seine Wehwehchen.

aim [eɪm] **1** n **(a)** Zielen nt. **to take ~** zielen (at auf +acc); **to miss one's ~** sein Ziel verfehlen; **as a result of his poor ~** weil er so schlecht gezielt hat; **his ~ was bad/good** etc er zielte schlecht/gut etc.

(b) (purpose) Ziel nt, Absicht f. **with the ~ of doing sth** mit dem Ziel or der Absicht, etw zu tun; **what is your ~ in life?** was ist Ihr Lebensziel?; **to achieve one's ~** sein Ziel erreichen; **what is your ~ in saying/doing that?** warum sagen Sie das?/was wollen Sie damit bezwecken?; **our actions were directed at the same ~** wir verfolgten dasselbe Ziel.

2 vt **(a)** (direct) guided missile, camera richten (at auf +acc); stone etc zielen mit (at auf +acc). **to teach sb how to ~ a gun** jdm zeigen, wie man zielt; **to ~ a pistol at sb/sth** eine Pistole auf jdn/etw richten, mit einer Pistole auf jdn/etw zielen, die Pistole auf jdn anlegen; **he ~ed his pistol at my heart** er zielte auf mein Herz; **the guns were ~ed directly at the city walls** die Kanonen waren direkt auf die Stadtmauer gerichtet; **you didn't ~ the camera properly** du hast die Kamera nicht richtig gehalten; **he ~ed his camera at me** er hat die Kamera auf mich gerichtet.

(b) (fig) remark, insult, criticism richten (at gegen). **this book/programme is ~ed at the general public** dieses Buch/Programm wendet sich an die Öffentlichkeit; **to be ~ed at sth** (cuts, measure, new law etc) auf etw (acc) abgezielt sein; **I think that was ~ed at me** ich glaube, das war auf mich gemünzt or gegen mich gerichtet.

3 vi **(a)** (with gun, punch etc) zielen (at, for auf +acc).

(b) (try, strive for) **to ~ high** sich (dat) hohe Ziele setzen or stecken; **isn't that ~ing a bit high?** wollen Sie nicht etwas hoch hinaus?; **to ~ at** or **for sth** etw anstreben, auf etw (acc) abzielen; **with this TV programme we're ~ing at a much wider audience** mit diesem Fernsehprogramm wollen wir einen größeren Teilnehmerkreis ansprechen; **we ~ to please** bei uns ist der Kunde König; **he always ~s for perfection** er strebt immer nach Perfektion; **he ~s at only spending £10 per week** er hat sich zum Ziel gesetzt, mit £ 10 pro Woche auszukommen.

(c) (inf: intend) **to ~ to do sth** vorhaben, etw zu tun, etw tun wollen.

aimless adj, **~ly** adv [ˈeɪmlɪs, -lɪ] ziellos; talk, act planlos.

aimlessness [ˈeɪmlɪsnɪs] n see adj Ziellosigkeit f; Planlosigkeit f.

ain't [eɪnt] (incorrect) = **am not; is not; are not; has not.**

air [eəʳ] **1** n **(a)** Luft f. **a change of ~** eine Luftveränderung; **war in the ~** Luftkrieg m; **perfumes drifting in on the ~** vom Windhauch hereingetragene Düfte; **to go out for a breath of (fresh) ~** frische Luft schöpfen (gehen); **to take the ~** (old) frische Luft schöpfen; **to take to the ~** sich in die Lüfte schwingen (geh); **by ~** per or mit dem Flugzeug; **to transport sth by ~** etw auf dem Luftweg transportieren; **to go by ~** (person) fliegen, mit dem Flugzeug reisen; (goods) per Flugzeug or auf dem Luftwege transportiert werden.

(b) (fig phrases) **there's something in the ~** es liegt etwas in der Luft; **there's a rumour in the ~ that** ... es geht ein Gerücht um, daß ...; **it's still all up in the ~** (inf) es hängt noch alles in der Luft, es ist noch alles offen; **all her plans were up in the ~** (inf) all ihre Pläne hingen in der Luft; **to give sb the ~** (US inf) jdn abblitzen or abfahren lassen (inf); **to clear the ~** die Atmosphäre reinigen; **he went up in the ~ when he heard that** (inf) (in anger) als er das hörte, ist er in die Luft or an die Decke gegangen; (in excitement) als er das hörte, hat er einen Luftsprung gemacht; **to be up in the ~ about sth** (inf) wegen etw aus dem Häuschen sein (inf); **to be walking** or **treading on ~** wie auf Wolken gehen; see **castle**, **thin**.

(c) (Rad, TV) **to be on the ~** (programme) gesendet werden; (station) senden; **you're on the ~** Sie sind auf Sendung; **he's on the ~ every day** er ist jeden Tag im Radio zu hören; **the programme goes** or **is put on the ~ every week** das Programm wird jede Woche gesendet; **we come on the ~ at 6 o'clock** unsere Sendezeit beginnt um 6 Uhr; **to go off the ~** (broadcaster) die Sendung beenden; (station) das Programm beenden.

(d) (demeanour, manner) Auftreten nt; (facial expression) Miene f; (of building, town etc) Atmosphäre f. **with an ~ of** bewilderment mit bestürzter Miene; **an unpleasant ~ of** selfsatisfaction ein unangenehm selbstzufriedenes Gehabe; **there is a certain military ~ about him** er hat etwas Militärisches an sich; **there was** or **she had an ~ of mystery about her** sie hatte etwas Geheimnisvolles an sich; **it gives** or **lends her an ~ of** affluence das gibt ihr einen wohlhabenden Anstrich; **with a proud ~** mit stolzer Haltung; **she has a certain ~ about her** sie hat so etwas an sich, sie hat so ein gewisses Etwas.

(e) **~s** pl Getue, Gehabe nt; **to put on ~s, to give oneself ~s** sich zieren, vornehm tun; **~s and graces** Allüren pl; **to put on** or **assume ~s and graces** den Vornehmen/die Vornehme herauskehren.

(f) (liter, Naut: breeze) leichte Brise, Lüftchen nt (liter).

(g) (Mus) Weise f (old); (tune also) Melodie f.

2 vt **(a)** clothes, bed, room (aus)lüften.
(b) anger, grievance Luft machen (+dat); opinion darlegen. **3** vi (clothes etc) (after washing) nachtrocknen; (after storage) (aus)lüften. **to put clothes out to** ~ Kleidung zum Lüften raushängen.

air in cpds Luft-; ~ **base** n Luftwaffenstützpunkt m; ~-**bed** n Luftmatratze f; ~**borne** adj troops Luftlande-; **to be** ~**borne** sich in der Luft befinden; ~ **brake** n (on truck) Druckluftbremse f; (Aviat) Brems- or Landeklappe f; ~**brick** n Entlüftungsziegel m; ~-**bridge** n Luftbrücke f; ~ **bubble** n Luftblase f; ~**bus** n Airbus m; A~ **Chief Marshal** n (Brit) General m; A~ **Commodore** n (Brit) Brigadegeneral m; ~-**conditioned** adj klimatisiert; ~-**conditioning** n (plant) Klimaanlage f; (process) Klimatisierung f; ~-**conditioning plant** n Klimaanlage f; ~-**cooled** adj engine luftgekühlt; ~ **corridor** n Luftkorridor m; ~ **cover** n Luftunterstützung f; ~**craft** n, pl ~**craft** Flugzeug nt, Maschine f; **various types of** ~**craft** verschiedene Luftfahrzeuge pl; ~**craft carrier** n Flugzeugträger m; ~**craft(s)man** n Gefreite(r) m; ~**crew** n Flugpersonal nt; ~-**cushion** n Luftkissen nt; ~ **display** n Flugschau f; ~**drome** n (US) Flugplatz m, Aerodrom nt (old); ~**drop** 1 n Fallschirmabwurf m; 2 vt mit Fallschirmen abwerfen; ~-**duct** n Luftkanal m.

Airedale ['ɛərdeɪl] n Airedale-Terrier m.

airer ['ɛərəʳ] n Trockenständer m.

air: ~**field** n Flugplatz m; ~**flow** n Luftstrom m; (in air-conditioning) Luftzufuhr f; ~**foil** n (US) Tragflügel m; (on racing cars) Spoiler m; ~ **force** n Luftwaffe f; ~ **force pilot** n Luftwaffenpilot m; ~**frame** n (Aviat) Flugwerk nt, Zelle f; ~-**freight** 1 n Luftfracht f; (charge) Luftfrachtgebühr f; **to send sth by** ~-**freight** etw als Luftfracht verschicken; 2 vt per Luftfracht senden; ~**gun** n Luftgewehr nt; ~**hole** n Luftloch nt; ~ **hostess** n Stewardeß f.

airily ['ɛərɪlɪ] adv (casually) say, reply etc leichthin, lässig; (vaguely) vage; (flippantly) blasiert, erhaben.

airiness ['ɛərɪnɪs] n see adj **(a, b)** **(a)** she liked the ~ of the rooms ihr gefiel, daß die Zimmer so luftig waren. **(b)** Lässigkeit, Nonchalance f; Vagheit f; Versponnenheit f; Blasiertheit, Erhabenheit f.

airing ['ɛərɪŋ] n (a) (of linen, room etc) (Aus- or Durch)lüften nt. **to give sth a good** ~ etw gut durch- or auslüften lassen. **(b) to go for an** ~ (hum inf) sich durchlüften (hum inf); **to give an idea an** ~ (fig inf) eine Idee darlegen.

airing cupboard n (Brit) (Wäsche)trockenschrank m.

air: ~ **intake** n Lufteinlaß or -eintritt m; (for engine) Luftansaugstutzen m; (quantity) Luftmenge f; ~**lane** n Flugroute f; ~**less** adj (lit) space luftleer; (stuffy) room stickig; (with no wind) day windstill; ~ **letter** n Luftpostbrief m; ~**lift** 1 n Luftbrücke f; 2 vt **to** ~**lift sth into a place** etw über eine Luftbrücke herein-/hineinbringen; ~**line** n (a) Fluggesellschaft, Luftverkehrsgesellschaft, Fluglinie f. **(b)** (diver's tube) Luftschlauch m; ~**liner** n Verkehrsflugzeug nt; ~**lock** n (in spacecraft etc) Luftschleuse f; (in pipe) Luftsack m.

airmail ['ɛəmeɪl] 1 n Luftpost f. **to send sth (by)** ~ etw per or mit Luftpost schicken. 2 vt letter, parcel mit or per Luftpost schicken.

airmail: ~ **edition** n (of newspaper) Luftpostausgabe f; ~ **letter** n Luftpostbrief m; ~ **stamp** or **sticker** n Luftpostaufkleber m.

air: ~**man** n (flier) Flieger m; (US: in ~ force) Gefreite(r) m; A~ **Marshal** n (Brit) Generalleutnant m; ~ **mass** n Luftmasse f; ~ **mattress** n Luftmatratze f; ~ **passenger** n Fluggast m; ~**plane** n (US) Flugzeug nt; ~ **pocket** n Luftloch m; ~**port** n Flughafen m; ~ **pressure** n Luftdruck m; ~ **pump** n Luftpumpe f.

air raid n Luftangriff m.

air-raid: ~ **shelter** n Luftschutzkeller m; ~ **warden** n Luftschutzwart m; ~ **warning** n Fliegeralarm m.

air: ~ **rifle** n Luftgewehr nt; ~ **route** n Flugroute f; ~**screw** n Luftschraube f; ~-**sea rescue** n Rettung f durch Seenotflugzeuge; ~-**sea rescue service** n Seenotrettungsdienst m; ~**shaft** n (Min) Wetterschacht m; ~**ship** n Luftschiff nt; ~ **show** n Luftfahrtausstellung f; ~**sick** adj luftkrank; ~**sickness** n Luftkrankheit f; ~ **sleeve** or **sock** n Windsack m; ~**space** n Luftraum m; ~**speed** n Eigen- or Fluggeschwindigkeit f; ~**stream** n (of vehicle) Luftsog m; (Met) Luftstrom m; ~**strip** n Start- und Landebahn f; ~ **supremacy** n Luftüberlegenheit f; ~**terminal** n (Air) Terminal m; ~**tight** adj (lit) luftdicht; (fig) argument, case hieb- und stichfest; ~ **time** n (Rad, TV) Sendezeit f; ~-**to-** ~ adj (Mil) Luft-Luft-; ~-**to-ground**, ~-**to-surface** adj (Mil) Luft-Boden-; ~-**traffic controller** n Fluglotse m; ~ **vent** n Ventilator m; (shaft) Belüftungsschacht m; A~ **Vice Marshal** n (Brit) Generalmajor m; ~**way** n (route) Flugroute f; (airline company) Fluggesellschaft, Luftverkehrsgesellschaft f; ~**woman** n Fliegerin f; ~**worthiness** n Flugtüchtigkeit f; ~**worthy** adj flugtüchtig.

airy ['ɛərɪ] adj (+er) **(a)** room luftig; **(b)** (casual) manner, gesture lässig, nonchalant; (vague) promise vage; theory versponnen; (superior, flippant) blasiert, erhaben. **(c)** (liter: immaterial) phantom körperlos.

airy-fairy ['ɛərɪ'fɛərɪ] adj (inf) versponnen; excuse windig; talk also larifari inv (inf). **you seem rather** ~ **about your plans** deine Pläne scheinen ziemlich unausgegoren; **he just muddles through in this** ~ **way** er wurstelt sich so aufs Geratewohl durch (inf).

aisle [aɪl] n Gang m; (in church) Seitenschiff nt; (central ~) Mittelgang m. **to lead a girl up the** ~ ein Mädchen zum Altar führen; **he had them rolling in the** ~**s** er brachte sie soweit, daß sie sich vor Lachen kugelten (inf) or wälzten (inf).

aitch [eɪtʃ] n h, H nt. **to drop one's** ~**es** den Buchstaben „h" nicht aussprechen; (be lower class) ≈ „mir" und „mich" verwechseln.

ajar [ə'dʒɑːʳ] adj, adv angelehnt, einen Spalt offen stehend.

akela [ɑː'keɪlə] n Wölflingsführer m.

akimbo [ə'kɪmbəʊ] adv: **with arms** ~ die Arme in die Hüften gestemmt.

akin [ə'kɪn] adj pred ähnlich (to dat), verwandt (to mit).

à la [ɑːlɑː] prep à la.

alabaster ['æləbɑːstəʳ] 1 n Alabaster m. 2 adj (lit) alabastern, Alabaster-; (fig liter) skin, neck Alabaster-, wie Alabaster.

à la carte [ɑːlɑː'kɑːt] 1 adv eat à la carte, nach der (Speise)karte. 2 adj menu à la carte.

alack [ə'læk] interj (obs) wehe. ~ **the day** wehe dem Tag, verflucht sei der Tag.

alacrity [ə'lækrɪtɪ] n (willingness) Bereitwilligkeit f; (eagerness) Eifer m, Eilfertigkeit f. **to accept with** ~ ohne zu zögern annehmen.

à la mode [ɑːlɑː'məʊd] adj (US) mit Eis.

alarm [ə'lɑːm] 1 n **(a)** no pl (fear) Sorge, Besorgnis, Beunruhigung f. **to be in a state of** ~ (worried) besorgt or beunruhigt sein; (frightened) erschreckt sein; **to cause a good deal of** ~ große Unruhe auslösen; **to cause sb** ~ jdn beunruhigen. **(b)** (warning) Alarm m. **to raise** or **give/sound the** ~ Alarm geben or (fig) schlagen. **(c)** (device) Alarmanlage f; ~ (clock) Wecker m. **2** vt **(a)** (worry) beunruhigen; (frighten) erschrecken. **don't be** ~**ed** erschrecken Sie nicht; **the news** ~**ed the whole country** die Nachricht alarmierte das ganze Land or versetzte das ganze Land in Aufregung. **(b)** (warn of danger) warnen; fire brigade etc alarmieren.

alarm in cpds Alarm-; ~ **bell** n Alarmglocke f; ~ **call** n (Telec) Weckruf m; ~ **clock** n Wecker m.

alarming [ə'lɑːmɪŋ] adj (worrying) beunruhigend; (frightening) erschreckend; news alarmierend.

alarmingly [ə'lɑːmɪŋlɪ] adv erschreckend.

alarmist [ə'lɑːmɪst] 1 n Unheilsprophet m, Kassandra f (geh). 2 adj speech Unheil prophezeiend attr.

alarum [ə'lærəm] n (old) see **alarm**.

alas [ə'læs] interj leider. ~, **he didn't come** leider kam er nicht.

Alaska [ə'læskə] n Alaska nt.

Alaskan [ə'læskən] 1 n Einwohner(in f) m von Alaska. 2 adj Alaska-; customs, winter in Alaska; fish, produce aus Alaska.

alb [ælb] n (Eccl) Alba f.

Albania [æl'beɪnɪə] n Albanien nt.

Albanian [æl'beɪnɪən] 1 adj albanisch. 2 n **(a)** Albaner(in f) m. **(b)** (language) Albanisch nt.

albatross ['ælbətrɒs] n Albatros m.

albeit [ɔːl'biːɪt] conj (liter) obgleich, wenn auch, wenngleich (geh).

albinism ['ælbɪnɪzəm] n Albinismus m.

albino [æl'biːnəʊ] 1 n Albino m. 2 adj Albino-.

Albion ['ælbɪən] n (poet) Albion nt.

album ['ælbəm] n Album nt.

albumen ['ælbjʊmɪn] n Albumin nt.

albuminous [æl'bjuːmɪnəs] adj albuminös.

alchemist ['ælkɪmɪst] n Alchemist m.

alchemy ['ælkɪmɪ] n Alchemie, Alchimie f.

alcohol ['ælkəhɒl] n Alkohol m.

alcoholic [ˌælkə'hɒlɪk] 1 adj drink alkoholisch; person alkoholsüchtig, trunksüchtig. 2 n (person) Alkoholiker(in f) m, Trinker(in f) m. **to be an** ~ Alkoholiker(in) or Trinker(in) sein; **A~s Anonymous** Anonyme Alkoholiker.

alcoholism ['ælkəhɒlɪzəm] n Alkoholismus m, Trunksucht f.

alcove ['ælkəʊv] n Alkoven m, Nische f; (in wall) Nische f.

alder ['ɔːldəʳ] n Erle f.

alderman ['ɔːldəmən] n, pl -**men** [-mən] Alderman m (Ratsherr).

ale [eɪl] n (old) Ale nt; see **real**.

aleck ['ælɪk] n see **smart** ~.

alehouse ['eɪlhaʊs] n (old) Wirtshaus nt, Schenke f.

alert [ə'lɜːt] 1 adj aufmerksam; (as character trait) aufgeweckt; mind scharf, hell; dog wachsam. **to be** ~ **to** etw (dat) auf der Hut sein. 2 vt warnen (to vor +dat); troops in Gefechtsbereitschaft versetzen; fire brigade etc alarmieren. 3 n Alarm m. **to give the** ~ (Mil) Gefechtsbereitschaft befehlen; (in the fire brigade etc) den Alarm auslösen; (fig) warnen; **to put on the** ~ in Gefechts-/Alarmbereitschaft versetzen; **to be on (the)** ~ einsatzbereit sein; (be on lookout) auf der Hut sein (for vor +dat).

alertness [ə'lɜːtnɪs] n see adj Aufmerksamkeit f; Aufgewecktheit f; Schärfe f; Wachsamkeit f.

Aleutian Islands [ə'luːʃən] npl Aleuten pl.

A level ['eɪˌlevl] n (Brit) Abschluß m der Sekundarstufe 2. **to take one's** ~**s** ≈ das Abitur machen; **3** ~**s** das Abitur in drei Fächern.

Alexander [ˌælɪg'zɑːndəʳ] n Alexander m. ~ **the Great** Alexander der Große.

alexandrine [ˌælɪg'zændraɪn] 1 n Alexandriner m. 2 adj alexandrinisch.

alfalfa [æl'fælfə] n Luzerne, Alfalfa f.

alfresco [æl'freskəʊ] adj, adv im Freien. **an** ~ **lunch** ein Mittagessen im Freien.

alga ['ælgə] n, pl -**e** ['ælgiː] Alge f.

algebra ['ældʒɪbrə] n Algebra f.

algebraic [ˌældʒɪ'breɪɪk] adj algebraisch.

Algeria [æl'dʒɪərɪə] n Algerien nt.

Algerian [æl'dʒɪərɪən] 1 n Algerier(in f) m. 2 adj algerisch.

Algiers [æl'dʒɪəz] n Algier nt.

alias ['eɪlɪəs] 1 adv alias. 2 n Deckname m.

alibi ['ælɪbaɪ] 1 n Alibi nt. 2 vt ein Alibi liefern für.

alien ['eɪlɪən] 1 n (esp Pol) Ausländer(in f) m; (Sci-Fi) außerirdisches Wesen. 2 adj **(a)** (foreign) ausländisch; (Sci-Fi) außerirdisch. **(b)** (*different*) fremd. **to be ~ to sb/sb's nature/sth** jdm/jds Wesen/einer Sache fremd sein.

alienate ['eɪlɪəneɪt] *vt* **(a)** *people* befremden; *affections* zerstören, sich (*dat*) verscherzen. **to ~ oneself from sb/sth** sich jdm/einer Sache entfremden; **Brecht set out to ~ his audience** Brecht wollte, daß sich die Zuschauer distanzieren. **(b)** (*Jur*) *property, money* übertragen.

alienation [‚eɪlɪə'neɪʃən] *n* **(a)** Entfremdung *f* (*from* von); (*Theat*) Distanzierung *f*. **~ effect** Verfremdungseffekt *m*; **~ of affections** (*Jur*) Entfremdung *f*. **(b)** (*Jur: property*) Übertragung *f*. **(c)** (*Psych*) Alienation *f*.

alight[1] [ə'laɪt] *vi* **(a)** (*from: person*) aussteigen (*from* aus); (*from horse*) absitzen (*from* von). **(b)** (*bird*) sich niederlassen (*on* auf +*dat*); (*form: aircraft etc*) niedergehen, landen (*on* auf +*dat*). **his eyes ~ed on the gold ring** sein Blick fiel auf den goldenen Ring. **(c)** (*form*) **to ~ on a fact/an idea** *etc* auf ein Faktum/eine Idee *etc* stoßen.

alight[2] *adj pred* **to be ~** (*fire*) brennen; (*building also*) in Flammen stehen; **to keep the fire ~** das Feuer in Gang halten; **to set sth ~** etw in Brand setzen *or* stecken; **her face was ~ with pleasure** ihr Gesicht *or* sie glühte vor Freude.

align [ə'laɪn] **1** *vt* **(a)** *wheels of car, gun sights etc* ausrichten; (*bring into line also*) in eine Linie bringen. **(b)** (*Fin, Pol*) *currencies, policies* aufeinander ausrichten. **to ~ sth with sth** etw auf etw (*acc*) ausrichten; **to ~ oneself with a party** (*follow policy of*) sich nach einer Partei ausrichten; (*join forces with*) sich einer Partei anschließen; **they have ~ed themselves against him/it** sie haben sich gegen ihn/dagegen zusammengeschlossen; *see* **non-aligned**. **2** *vi* **(a)** (*lit*) ausgerichtet sein (*with* nach); (*come into line*) in einer Linie bilden. **(b)** (*side*) *see vt* (*b*).

alignment [ə'laɪnmənt] *n* **(a)** *see vt* (*a*) Ausrichtung *f*. **to be out of ~** nicht richtig ausgerichtet sein (*with* nach). **(b)** (*of currencies, policies etc*) Ausrichtung (*with* auf + *acc*), Orientierung (*with* nach) *f*. **to be out of ~ with one another** nicht übereinstimmen, sich nicht aneinander orientieren; **to bring sb back into ~ with the party** jdn zwingen, wieder auf die Parteilinie einzuschwenken; **his unexpected ~ with the Socialists** seine unerwartete Parteinahme für die Sozialisten; **he argued for a new ~ of the governing parties** er war für eine Neuordnung der Regierungsparteien; **the new ~ of world powers** die Neugruppierung der Weltmächte.

alike [ə'laɪk] *adj pred, adv* gleich. **they're/they look very ~** sie sind/sehen sich (*dat*) sehr ähnlich; **they all look ~ to me** für mich sehen sie alle gleich aus; **you men are all ~!** ihr Männer seid doch alle gleich!; **it's all ~ to me** mir ist das gleich *or* einerlei; **they always think ~** sie sind immer einer Meinung; **winter and summer ~** Sommer wie Winter, sommers wie winters.

alimentary [‚ælɪ'mentərɪ] *adj* (*Anat*) Verdauungs-. **~ canal** Verdauungskanal *m*.

alimony ['ælɪmənɪ] *n* Unterhaltszahlung *f*. **to pay ~** Unterhalt zahlen.

alive [ə'laɪv] *adj* **(a)** *pred* (*living*) lebendig, lebend *attr*. **dead or ~ tot** oder lebendig; **to be ~** leben; **the greatest musician ~** der größte lebende Musiker; **while ~ he was always ...** zu seinen Lebzeiten war er immer ...; **it's good to be ~** das Leben ist schön; **no man ~** niemand auf der ganzen Welt; **the wickedest man ~** der schlechteste Mensch auf der ganzen Welt; **to stay or keep ~** am Leben bleiben; **to keep sb/sth ~** (*lit, fig*) jdn am Leben erhalten/etw am Leben *or* lebendig erhalten; **to do sth as well as anyone ~** etw so gut wie jeder andere können; **to be ~ and kicking** (*hum inf*) *or* **~ and well** gesund und munter sein; **he's very much ~** er ist ausgesprochen lebendig.

(b) (*lively*) lebendig. **to keep one's mind ~** geistig rege bleiben; **to come ~** (*liven up*) lebendig werden; (*prick up ears etc*) wach werden.

(c) *pred* (*aware*) **to be ~ to sth** sich (*dat*) einer Sache (*gen*) bewußt sein; **to be ~ to certain possibilities/sb's interests** gewisse Möglichkeiten/jds Interessen im Auge haben.

(d) **~ with** (*full of*) erfüllt von; **to be ~ with tourists/fish/insects** *etc* von Touristen/Fischen/Insekten *etc* wimmeln.

alkali ['ælkəlaɪ] *n, pl* **-(e)s** Base, Lauge *f*; (*metal, Agr*) Alkali *nt*.

alkaline ['ælkəlaɪn] *adj* basisch, alkalisch. **~ solution** Lauge *f*.

alkalinity [‚ælkə'lɪnɪtɪ] *n* Alkalität *f*.

alkaloid ['ælkəlɔɪd] *n* Alkaloid *nt*.

all [ɔːl] **1** *adj* **(a)** (*with pl n*) alle *no art*; (*every single one also*) sämtliche *no art*; (*with sing n*) ganze(r, s), alle(r, s) *no art*; (*preceding poss art also*) all. **~ the books/people** alle Bücher/Leute, die ganzen Bücher/Leute; **she brought ~ the children** sie brachte alle *or* sämtliche Kinder mit; **~ the tobacco/milk/fruit** der ganze Tabak/die ganze Milch/das ganze Obst, all der *or* aller Tabak/all die *or* alle Milch/all das *or* alles Obst; **~ my strength/books/friends** all meine Kraft/all/(e) meine Bücher/Freunde, meine ganze Kraft/ganzen Bücher/Freunde; **~ my life** mein ganzes Leben (lang); **~ Spain** ganz Spanien; **we ~ sat down** wir setzten uns alle; **~ you boys can come with me** ihr Jungen könnt alle mit mir kommen; **I invited them ~** ich habe sie alle eingeladen; **they ~ came** sie sind alle gekommen; **~ the time** die ganze Zeit; **~ day (long)** den ganzen Tag (lang); **to dislike ~ sport** jeglichen Sport ablehnen; **I don't understand ~ that** ich verstehe das alles nicht; **what's ~ that water?** wo kommt das ganze *or* all das Wasser her?; **what's ~ this/that about?** was soll das Ganze?; **what's ~ this/that mess?** was ist das denn für eine Unordnung?; (*annoyed*) was soll denn das!; **what's ~ this this mess?** was ist das denn für eine Unordnung?; **what's ~ this I hear about you leaving?** was höre ich da! Sie wollen gehen?; **he took/spent it ~** er hat alles genommen/ausgegeben; **the money was ~ there** alles Geld *or* das ganze Geld war da; **~ kinds or sorts or manner of people** alle möglichen Leute; **to be ~ things**

to ~ men sich mit jedem gut stellen; **it is beyond ~ doubt/question** es steht außer Zweifel/Frage; **in ~ respects** in jeder Hinsicht; **why me of ~ people?** warum ausgerechnet ich?; **of ~ the idiots/stupid things!** so ein Idiot/so was Dummes!

(b) (*utmost*) **with ~ possible speed** so schnell wie möglich; **with ~ due care/speed** mit angemessener Sorgfalt/in angemessenem Tempo; **they will take ~ possible care of it** sie werden sich so gut wie möglich darum kümmern.

(c) (*US inf*) **you ~** ihr (alle).

(d) **for ~ his wealth** trotz (all) seines Reichtums; **for ~ that** trotz allem, trotzdem; **for ~ I know she could be ill** was weiß ich, vielleicht ist sie krank; **is he in Paris? — for ~ I know he could be** ist er in Paris? — schon möglich, was weiß ich!

2 *pron* **(a)** (*everything*) alles; (*everybody*) alle *pl*. **~ who knew him** alle, die ihn kannten; **~ of them/of it** (sie) alle/alles; **~ of Paris/of the house** ganz Paris/das ganze Haus; **that is ~ I can tell you** mehr kann ich Ihnen nicht sagen; **he was ~ to her** er bedeutete ihr alles; **it was ~ I could do not to laugh** ich mußte an mich halten, um nicht zu lachen; **and I don't know what ~** (*dial inf*) und was weiß ich noch alles; **~ of 5 kms/£5** ganze 5 km/£ 5; **he ate the orange, peel and ~** er hat die ganze Orange gegessen, samt der Schale; **what with the snow and ~** (*inf*) mit dem ganzen Schnee und so (*inf*); **the whole family came, children and ~** (*inf*) die Familie kam mit Kind und Kegel; **the score was/the teams were two ~** es stand zwei beide; **~ found** insgesamt, alles in allem.

(b) **at ~ überhaupt; nothing at ~** überhaupt *or* gar nichts; **did/didn't you say anything at ~?** haben Sie überhaupt etwas gesagt/gar *or* überhaupt nichts gesagt?; **it's not bad at ~** das ist gar nicht schlecht.

(c) **in ~ insgesamt; ten people in ~** *or* **~ told** insgesamt zehn Personen; **~ in ~** alles in allem.

(d) (*with superl*) **happiest/earliest/clearest** *etc* **of ~ am** glücklichsten/frühsten/klarsten etc; **that would be best of ~** das wäre am besten; **I like him best of ~** von allen mag ich ihn am liebsten; **most of ~** am meisten; **most of ~ I'd like to be ...** am liebsten wäre ich ...; **the best car of ~** das allerbeste Auto.

3 *adv* **(a)** (*quite, entirely*) ganz. **~ dressed ~ in white, ~ dressed in white** ganz in Weiß (gekleidet); **~ woman** ganz Frau; **~ dirty/excited** *etc* ganz schmutzig/aufgeregt *etc*; **~ wool** reine Wolle; **an ~ wool carpet** ein reinwollener Teppich, ein Teppich aus reiner Wolle; **it was red ~ over** es war ganz rot; **~ up the side of the building** auf der ganzen Seite des Gebäudes; **~ along the road** die ganze Straße entlang; **I feared that ~ along** das habe ich schon die ganze Zeit befürchtet; **there were chairs ~ round the room** rundum im Zimmer standen Stühle; **he ordered whiskies/drinks ~ round** er hat für alle Whisky/Getränke bestellt; **~ the same** trotzdem, trotz allem; **it's ~ the same** *or* **~ one to me** das ist mir (ganz) egal *or* einerlei; **~ at once** auf einmal; (*suddenly also*) ganz plötzlich; **they spoke ~ at once/~ together** sie sprachen alle auf einmal/alle gleichzeitig; **~ too soon** viel zu schnell, viel zu früh; **what's the film ~ about?** wovon handelt der Film überhaupt?; **I'll tell you ~ about it** ich erzähl dir alles; **it was ~ about a little girl** es handelte von einem kleinen Mädchen; **that's ~ very fine** *or* **well** das ist alles ganz schön und gut; **it's not as bad as ~ that** so schlimm ist es nun auch wieder nicht; **it isn't ~ that** expensive! so teuer ist es nun wieder auch nicht; **if at ~ possible** wenn irgend möglich; **I'm not at ~ sure/angry** *etc*, **I'm not sure/angry** *etc* **at ~** ich bin mir ganz und gar nicht sicher, ich bin gar nicht ganz sicher/ich bin ganz und gar nicht wütend *etc*; **I don't know at ~** ich weiß es überhaupt nicht; **I'm ~ for it!** ich bin ganz dafür; **to be** *or* **feel ~ in** (*inf*) total erledigt sein (*inf*); **he's ~/not ~ there** (*inf*) er ist voll/nicht ganz da (*inf*).

(b) **~ but fast; he ~ but died** er wäre fast gestorben; **he ~ but lost it** er hätte es fast verloren.

(c) (*with comp*) **~ the hotter/prettier/happier** *etc* noch heißer/hübscher/glücklicher etc; **~ the funnier because ...** um so lustiger, weil ...; **I feel ~ the better for my holiday** jetzt, wo ich Urlaub gemacht habe, geht's mir viel besser; **~ the more so since ...** besonders weil ...; **~ the better to see you with** damit ich dich besser sehen kann.

4 *n* **one's ~** alles; **he staked his ~ on this race/venture** er setzte alles auf dieses Rennen/Unternehmen; **I am absolutely sure of this, I would stake my ~ on it** ich bin ganz sicher, dafür kann ich meine Hand ins Feuer legen; **the horses were giving their ~** die Pferde gaben ihr Letztes.

Allah ['ælə] *n* Allah *m*.

all-: **~-American** *adj team, player* amerikanische(r, s) National-; **an ~-American boy** ein richtiger amerikanischer Junge; **~-around** *adj* (*US*) *see* **~-round**.

allay [ə'leɪ] *vt* verringern; *doubt, fears, suspicion* (weitgehend) zerstreuen.

all-: **~-clear** *n* Entwarnung *f*; **to give/sound the ~-clear** Entwarnung geben, entwarnen; **~-day** *adj* ganztägig; **it was an ~-day meeting** die Sitzung dauerte den ganzen Tag.

allegation [‚ælɪ'geɪʃən] *n* Behauptung *f*.

allege [ə'ledʒ] *vt* behaupten. **the remarks ~d to have been made by him** die Bemerkungen, die er gemacht haben soll *or* angeblich gemacht hat; **he is ~d to have said that ...** er soll angeblich gesagt haben, daß ...

alleged *adj*, **~ly** *adv* [ə'ledʒd, ə'ledʒɪdlɪ] angeblich.

allegiance [ə'liːdʒəns] *n* Treue *f* (*to* dat). **oath of ~** Fahnen- *or* Treueeid *m*.

allegoric(al) [‚ælɪ'gɒrɪk(əl)] *adj*, **allegorically** [‚ælɪ'gɒrɪkəlɪ] *adv* allegorisch.

allegory ['ælɪgərɪ] *n* Allegorie *f*.

allegro [ə'legrəʊ] **1** *adj, adv* Allegro. **2** *n* Allegro *nt*.

all-electric [‚ɔːlɪ'lektrɪk] *adj* **an ~ house** ein Haus, in dem alles elektrisch ist; **we're ~** bei uns ist alles elektrisch.

alleluia [ˌælɪˈluːjə] **1** *interj* (h)alleluja. **2** *n* (H)alleluja *nt*.
all-embracing [ˌɔːlɪmˈbreɪsɪŋ] *adj* (all)umfassend.
allergen [ˈæləˌdʒən] *n* (*Med*) Allergen *nt*.
allergic [əˈlɜːdʒɪk] *adj* (*lit, fig*) allergisch (*to* gegen).
allergy [ˈælədʒɪ] *n* Allergie *f* (*to* gegen). **he seems to have an** ~ **to work** (*hum*) er scheint gegen Arbeit allergisch zu sein.
alleviate [əˈliːvɪeɪt] *vt* lindern.
alleviation [əˌliːvɪˈeɪʃən] *n* Linderung *f*.
alley [ˈælɪ] *n* (a) (*between buildings*) (enge) Gasse; (*between gardens*) Weg, Pfad *m*; (*in garden*) Laubengang *m*; (*in supermarket*) Gang *m*. (b) (*bowling* ~, *skittle* ~) Bahn *f*.
alley: ~ **cat** *n* streunende Katze; **to fight like** ~ **cats** sich in den Haaren liegen; **to yell like** ~ **cats** kreischen; **she's got the morals of an** ~ **cat** (*inf*) sie treibt's mit jedem; ~**way** *n* Durchgang *m*.
All: ~ **Fools' Day** *n der* erste April; ~ **Hallows' (Day)** *n see* ~ **Saints' Day**.
alliance [əˈlaɪəns] *n* Verbindung *f*; (*institutions also, of states*) Bündnis *nt*; (*in historical contexts*) Allianz *f*. **partners in an** ~ Bündnispartner *pl*.
allied [ˈælaɪd] *adj* (a) verbunden; (*for attack, defence etc*) verbündet, alliiert. (b) (*Biol, fig*) verwandt.
Allied [ˈælaɪd] *adj* the ~ **forces** die Alliierten; **an** ~ **attack** eine Offensive der Alliierten.
alligator [ˈælɪgeɪtəʳ] *n* Alligator *m*. ~**(-skin) bag** Alligatorledertasche *f*.
all: ~**-important** *adj* außerordentlich wichtig; **the** ~**-important question** die Frage, auf die es ankommt; ~**-in** *adj* (a) (*inclusive*) Inklusiv-; (b) (*Sport*) ~**-in wrestling** Freistilringen *nt*; *see also* **all 3 (a)**.
alliterate [əˈlɪtəreɪt] *vi* einen Stabreim bilden, alliterieren.
alliteration [əˌlɪtəˈreɪʃən] *n* Alliteration *f*, Stabreim *m*.
alliterative [əˈlɪtərətɪv] *adj* Stabreim-, stabend, alliterierend.
all: ~**-merciful** *adj* God allbarmherzig, allgütig; ~**-night** *adj attr* café (die ganze Nacht) durchgehend geöffnet; **an** ~**-night party** eine Party, die die ganze Nacht durchgeht; **we had an** ~**-night party** wir haben die ganze Nacht durchgemacht; **it was an** ~**-night journey** wir/sie *etc* sind die ganze Nacht durchgefahren; **we have an** ~**-night opening** wir haben (die ganze Nacht) durchgehend geöffnet; ~**-night opening is allowed in some countries** in manchen Ländern sind 24stündige Öffnungszeiten erlaubt; **we have an** ~**-night service** wir haben einen durchgehenden Nachtdienst; **there is an** ~**-night bus service** die Busse verkehren die ganze Nacht über.
allocate [ˈæləʊkeɪt] *vt* (*allot*) zuteilen, zuweisen (*to sb* jdm); (*apportion*) verteilen (*to* auf +*acc*); *tasks* vergeben (*to* an +*acc*). **to** ~ **money to** *or* **for a project** Geld für ein Projekt bestimmen.
allocation [ˌæləʊˈkeɪʃən] *n see vt* Zuteilung, Zuweisung *f*; Verteilung *f*; (*sum allocated*) Zuwendung *f*.
allot [əˈlɒt] *vt* zuteilen, zuweisen (*to sb/sth* jdm/etw); *time* vorsehen (*to* für); *money* bestimmen (*to* für).
allotment [əˈlɒtmənt] *n* (a) ~ *of* Zuteilung, Zuweisung *f*; Vorsehen *nt*; Bestimmung *f*; (*amount of money allotted*) Zuwendung *f*. (b) (*Brit: plot of ground*) Schrebergarten *m*.
all: ~**-out 1** *adj strike* total; *attack* massiv; *effort, attempt* äußerste(r, s); *support* uneingeschränkt; **2** *adv* mit aller Kraft; **to go** ~**-out** sein Letztes *or* Äußerstes geben; **to go** ~**-out to do sth** alles daransetzen, etw zu tun; **to go** ~**-out for victory** alles daransetzen, (um) zu siegen; ~**-over** *adj* ganzflächig.
allow [əˈlaʊ] **1** *vt* (a) (*permit*) *sth* erlauben, gestatten; *behaviour etc also* zulassen. **to** ~ **sb sth/to do sth** jdm etw erlauben *or* gestatten/jdm erlauben *or* gestatten, etw zu tun; **to be** ~**ed to do sth** etw tun dürfen; **smoking is not** ~**ed** Rauchen ist nicht gestattet; **"no dogs** ~**ed"** „Hunde müssen draußen bleiben"; **we were** ~**ed one drink** uns wurde ein Drink erlaubt *or* gestattet; **we're not** ~**ed much freedom** wir haben nicht viel Freiheit; **will you be** ~**ed to?** darfst du denn?; **will you** ~ **him to?** erlauben Sie es ihm?, lassen Sie ihn denn? (*inf*); **to** ~ **oneself sth** sich (*dat*) etw erlauben; (*treat oneself*) sich (*dat*) etw gönnen; **to** ~ **oneself to be persuaded/convinced/waited on** *etc* sich überreden/überzeugen/bedienen *etc* lassen; ~ **me!** gestatten Sie (*form*); ~ **me to help you** gestatten Sie, daß ich Ihnen helfe (*form*); **to** ~ **sth to happen** etw zulassen, zulassen, daß etw geschieht; **to** ~ **sb in/out/past** *etc* jdn hinein-/hinaus-/vorbeilassen; **to be** ~**ed in/out/past** hinein-/hinaus-/vorbeidürfen; **they only** ~**ed a few cars through** sie ließen nur einige Autos durch.
(b) (*recognize, accept*) *claim, appeal* anerkennen; *goal also* geben.
(c) (*allocate, grant*) *discount* geben; *space* lassen; *time* einplanen, einberechnen; *money* geben, zugestehen; (*in tax, Jur*) zugestehen. **to** ~ (*yourself*) **an hour to cross the city** rechnen Sie mit einer Stunde, um durch die Stadt zu kommen; **he** ~**ed me two hours for that** er gab mir zwei Stunden dafür; ~ **5 cms extra** geben Sie 5 cm zu.
(d) (*concede*) annehmen. ~**ing** *or* **if we** ~ **that** ... angenommen, (daß) ...
2 *vi* **if time** ~**s** falls es zeitlich möglich ist.
♦**allow for** *vi* +*prep obj* berücksichtigen; *factor, cost, shrinkage, error also* einrechnen, einkalkulieren. ~**ing** ~ **the circumstances** unter Berücksichtigung der gegebenen Umstände; **after** ~**ing** ~ nach Berücksichtigung (+*gen*).
♦**allow of** *vi* +*prep obj* zulassen.
allowable [əˈlaʊəbl] *adj* zulässig; (*Fin: in tax*) absetzbar, abzugsfähig. ~ **expenses** (*Fin*) abzugsfähige Kosten.
allowance [əˈlaʊəns] *n* (a) finanzielle Unterstützung, (*paid by state*) Beihilfe *f*; (*father to son*) Unterhaltsgeld *nt*; (*as compensation: for unsociable hours, overseas* ~ *etc*) Zulage *f*; (*on business trip*) Spesen *pl*; (*spending money*) Taschengeld *nt*.

clothing ~ Kleidungsgeld *nt*; *petrol* ~ Benzingeld *nt*; *travelling* ~ Fahrkostenzuschuß *m*; **his father still gives him an** ~ sein Vater unterstützt ihn noch immer finanziell; **he gives his wife a dress** ~ er gibt seiner Frau einen Zuschuß zu den Kleidungskosten; **he made her an** ~ **of £50 a month** er stellte ihr monatlich £ 50 zur Verfügung.
(b) (*Fin: tax* ~) Freibetrag *m*.
(c) (*Fin, Comm: discount*) (Preis)nachlaß *m* (*on* für); (*quantity allowed: for shrinkage etc*) Zugabe *f*.
(d) (*admission, acceptance: of goal, claim, appeal*) Anerkennung *f*.
(e) Zugeständnisse *pl*. **to make** ~**(s) for sth** etw berücksichtigen; **you have to make** ~**s** Sie müssen (gewisse) Zugeständnisse machen.
allowedly [əˈlaʊɪdlɪ] *adv* gewiß, zugegeben.
alloy [ˈælɔɪ] **1** *n* Legierung *f*. **2** *vt* legieren; (*fig liter*) (ver)mischen. **pleasure** ~**ed with suffering** von Leid getrübte Freude.
all: ~**-powerful** *adj* allmächtig; ~**-purpose** *adj* Allzweck-.
all right [ˈɔːlˈraɪt] **1** *adj pred* (a) (*satisfactory*) in Ordnung, okay (*inf*). **it's** ~ (*not too bad*) es geht; (*working properly*) es ist in Ordnung; **that's** *or* **it's** ~ (*after thanks*) schon gut, gern geschehen; (*after apology*) schon gut, das macht nichts; **it's** ~, **you don't have to** schon gut, du mußt nicht unbedingt; **to taste/look/smell** ~ ganz gut schmecken/aussehen/riechen; **is it** ~ **for me to leave early?** kann ich früher gehen?; **it's** ~ **by me** ich habe nichts dagegen, von mir aus gern; **it's** ~ **for you** du hast's gut; **it's** ~ **for you (to talk)** du hast gut reden; **it's** ~ **for him to laugh** er hat gut lachen; **I made it** ~ **with him** ich habe das (mit ihm) wieder eingerenkt; **I saw him** ~ (*inf*) (*for petrol, money etc*) ich hab ihn (dafür) entschädigt; **it'll be** ~ **on the night** es wird schon klappen, wenn es darauf ankommt; **I don't like it particularly but I suppose it's** ~ besonders gut finde ich es nicht, aber es geht; **he's** ~ (*inf: is a good guy*) der ist in Ordnung (*inf*).
(b) (*safe, unharmed*) *person, machine, mechanical object* in Ordnung, okay (*inf*); *object, building, tree etc* heil, ganz, okay (*inf*). **are you** ~? (*healthy*) geht es Ihnen gut?; (*unharmed*) ist Ihnen etwas passiert?; **are you feeling** ~? fehlt Ihnen was?; (*iro*) sag mal, fehlt dir was?; **he's** ~ **again** es geht ihm wieder gut, er ist wieder in Ordnung (*inf*); **are you** ~ **(in there)?** ist alles in Ordnung (da drin)?; **that bomb damaged half the street but our house was** ~ die Bombe hat die halbe Straße zerstört, aber unserem Haus ist nichts passiert; **can we come out? is it** ~? können wir rauskommen? ist es sicher?; **is it** ~ **for us to come out now?** können wir jetzt rauskommen?; **it's** ~ **now, Mummy's here** jetzt ist alles wieder gut, Mutti ist ja da; **it's** ~, **don't worry** keine Angst, machen Sie sich keine Sorgen; **we're** ~ **for the rest of our lives** wir haben für den Rest des Lebens ausgesorgt.
2 *adv* (a) (*satisfactorily*) ganz gut, ganz ordentlich; (*safely*) gut. **did I do it** ~? habe ich es recht gemacht?; **did you get home** ~? bist du gut nach Hause gekommen?; **did you get/find it** ~? haben Sie es denn bekommen/gefunden?
(b) (*certainly*) schon. **he'll come** ~ er wird schon kommen; **that's the boy** ~ das ist der Junge; **he's a clever man** ~ er ist schon intelligent; **oh yes, we heard you** ~ o ja, und ob wir dich gehört haben.
3 *interj* gut, schön, okay (*inf*); (*in agreement also*) in Ordnung. **may I leave early?** — ~ kann ich früher gehen? — ja; ~ **that's enough!** okay *or* komm, jetzt reicht's (aber)!; ~, ~! **I'm coming** schon gut, schon gut, ich komme ja!
all: ~**-round** *adj athlete* Allround-; *student* vielseitig begabt; *improvement* in jeder Beziehung *or* Hinsicht; ~**-rounder** *n* Allroundmann *m*; (*Sport*) Allroundsportler(in *f*) *m*; A~ **Saints' Day** *n* Allerheiligen *nt*; A~ **Souls' Day** *n* Allerseelen *nt*; ~**spice** *n* Piment *m or nt*; ~**-star** *adj* Star-; ~**-time** *adj* aller Zeiten; **an** ~**-time record** der Rekord aller Zeiten; **an** ~**-time high/low** der höchste/niedrigste Stand aller Zeiten; ~**-time great** Unvergeßliche(r), Unvergessene(r) *mf*; **to be an** ~**-time favourite** seit eh und je beliebt sein.
allude to [əˈluːd] *vi* +*prep obj* anspielen auf (+*acc*).
allure [əˈljʊəʳ] **1** *vt* locken, anlocken. **2** *n* Reiz *m*.
allurement [əˈljʊərmənt] *n* Anziehungskraft *f*, Reiz *m*.
alluring [əˈljʊərɪŋ] *adj* verführerisch.
alluringly [əˈljʊərɪŋlɪ] *adv see adj*.
allusion [əˈluːʒən] *n* Anspielung *f* (*to* auf +*acc*).
allusive [əˈluːsɪv] *adj* voller Anspielungen. ~ **comments** Anspielungen *pl*.
allusively [əˈluːsɪvlɪ] *adv* indirekt. **to mention sth** ~ auf etw (*acc*) anspielen.
alluvial [əˈluːvɪəl] *adj* angeschwemmt.
alluvium [əˈluːvɪəm] *n* Anschwemmung *f*.
all-weather [ˈɔːlˈweðəʳ] *adj* Allwetter-.
ally [ˈælaɪ] **1** *n* Verbündete(r) *mf*, Bundesgenosse *m*; (*Hist*) Alliierte(r) *m*. **2** [əˈlaɪ] *vt* verbinden (*with, to* mit); (*for attack, defence etc*) verbünden, alliieren (*with, to* mit). **to** ~ **oneself with** *or* **to sb** sich mit jdm zusammentun/verbünden *or* alliieren; **to be allied by interests/marriage** durch Interessen/Heirat verbunden sein.
alma mater [ˈælməˈmeɪtəʳ] *n* Alma Mater *f*.
almanac [ˈɔːlmənæk] *n* Almanach *m*; *see* **nautical**.
almighty [ɔːlˈmaɪtɪ] **1** *adj* (a) *god, person* allmächtig; *power* unumschränkt. A~ **God, God A~** (*Eccl*) der Allmächtige; (*address in prayer*) allmächtiger Gott; **God A~!** (*inf*) Allmächtiger! (*inf*), allmächtiger Gott! (*inf*).
(b) (*inf*) *fool, idiot* mordsmäßig (*inf*); *blow* mächtig (*inf*). **to make an** ~ **fool of oneself** sich mordsmäßig blamieren (*inf*).
2 *n* the A~ der Allmächtige.
almond [ˈɑːmənd] *n* Mandel *f*; (*tree*) Mandelbaum *m*.
almond *in cpds* Mandel-; ~**-eyed** *adj* mandeläugig; ~ **oil** *n*

Mandelöl *nt*; ~ **paste** *n* Marzipanmasse *f*; ~**-shaped** *adj* mandelförmig.

almoner ['ɑːmənəʳ] *n* **(a)** *(dated Brit: in hospital)* Krankenhausfürsorger(in *f*) *m*. **(b)** *(old: distributor of alms)* Almosenpfleger *m*.

almost ['ɔːlməʊst] *adv* fast, beinahe. he ~ fell er wäre fast gefallen.

alms [ɑːmz] *npl* Almosen *pl*.

alms: ~ **box** *n* Almosenstock *m*; ~ **house** *n* Armenhaus *nt*.

aloe ['æləʊ] *n* (*Bot, Med*) Aloe *f*.

aloft [ə'lɒft] *adv* (*into the air*) empor; (*in the air*) hoch droben; (*Naut*) oben in der Takelung. to go ~ (*Naut*) in die Takelung hinaufklettern.

alone [ə'ləʊn] 1 *adj pred* allein(e). we're not ~ in thinking that wir stehen mit dieser Meinung nicht allein; there is one man who, ~ in the world, knows ... es gibt einen, der als einziger auf der Welt weiß ...; *see* leave, let³.

  2 *adv* allein(e). to live on bread ~ von Brot allein leben; it's mine ~ das gehört mir (ganz) allein(e); that charm which is hers ~ der ihr ganz eigene Charme; the hotel ~ cost £35 das Hotel allein kostete (schon) £ 35, schon das Hotel kostete £ 35; to stand ~ (*fig*) einzig dastehen.

along [ə'lɒŋ] 1 *prep* (*direction*) entlang (+*acc*), lang (+*acc*) (*inf*); (*position*) entlang (+*dat*). he walked ~ the river er ging den/(an) dem Fluß entlang; somewhere ~ the way irgendwo unterwegs *or* auf dem Weg; (*fig*) irgendwann einmal; somewhere ~ here/there irgendwo hier/dort (herum); (*in this/that direction*) irgendwo in dieser Richtung/der Richtung; the Red Lion? isn't that somewhere ~ your way? der Rote Löwe? ist der nicht irgendwo in Ihrer Nähe *or* Gegend?; *see* all.

  2 *adv* **(a)** (*onwards*) weiter-, vorwärts-. to move ~ weitergehen; he was just strolling ~ er ist bloß so dahingeschlendert; run ~ nun lauf!; he'll be ~ soon er muß gleich da sein; I'll be ~ about eight ich komme ungefähr um acht; are you coming now? — yes, I'll be ~ kommst du? — ja, (ich komme) gleich; *see* vbs. **(b)** (*together*) ~ with zusammen mit; to come/sing ~ with sb mit jdm mitkommen/mitsingen; take an umbrella ~ nimm einen Schirm mit.

alongside [ə'lɒŋ'saɪd] 1 *prep* neben (+*dat*). he parked ~ the kerb er parkte am Bordstein; we were moored ~ the pier/the other boats wir lagen am Pier vor Anker/lagen Bord an Bord mit den anderen Schiffen; the houses ~ the river die Häuser am Fluß entlang; he works ~ me (*with*) er ist ein Kollege von mir; (*next to*) er arbeitet neben mir.

  2 *adv* daneben. is the launch still ~? liegt die Barkasse immer noch längsseits?; a police car drew up ~ ein Polizeiauto fuhr neben mich/ihn *etc* heran; she was driving ~ sie fuhr nebenher; they brought their dinghy ~ sie brachten ihr Dingi heran.

aloof [ə'luːf] 1 *adv* (*lit, fig*) abseits. to remain ~ sich abseits halten; buyers held ~ (*Comm*) die Käufer verhielten sich zurückhaltend. 2 *adj* unnahbar.

aloofness [ə'luːfnɪs] *n* Unnahbarkeit *f*.

aloud [ə'laʊd] *adv* laut.

alp [ælp] *n* Berg *m* in den Alpen.

alpaca [æl'pækə] 1 *n* Alpaka *nt*. 2 *attr* Alpaka-.

alpenhorn ['ælpɪn,hɔːn] *n* Alphorn *nt*.

alpenstock ['ælpɪnstɒk] *n* Bergstock *m*.

alpha ['ælfə] *n* **(a)** (*letter*) Alpha *nt*. **(b)** (*Brit: Sch, Univ*) Eins *f*. ~ plus Eins (plus *hum*); (*Sch also*) Eins (mit Stern *hum*).

alphabet ['ælfəbet] *n* Alphabet *nt*. does he know the *or* his ~? kann er schon das Abc?

alphabetic(al) [,ælfə'betɪk(əl)] *adj* alphabetisch. in ~ order in alphabetischer Reihenfolge.

alphabetically [,ælfə'betɪkəlɪ] *adv* alphabetisch, nach dem Alphabet.

alphabetization [,ælfəbətaɪ'zeɪʃən] *n* Alphabetisierung *f*.

alphabetize ['ælfəbətaɪz] *vt* alphabetisieren, alphabetisch ordnen.

alpha: ~ **particle** *n* Alphateilchen *nt*; ~ **ray** *n* Alphastrahl *m*.

alpine ['ælpaɪn] *adj* **(a)** A~ alpin, Alpen-; *dialects* der Alpen. **(b)** (*general*) alpin; *flowers* Alpen-, Gebirgs-; (*Geol*) alpinisch; *scenery* Gebirgs-; *hut* Berg-; *club* Alpen-.

alpinism ['ælpɪnɪzəm] *n* Alpinistik *f*, Alpinismus *m*.

alpinist ['ælpɪnɪst] *n* Alpinist(in *f*) *m*.

Alps [ælps] *npl* Alpen *pl*.

already [ɔːl'redɪ] *adv* schon. I've ~ seen it, I've seen it ~ ich habe es schon gesehen.

alright ['ɔːl,raɪt] *adj, adv see* all right.

Alsace ['ælsæs] *n* Elsaß *nt*.

Alsace-Lorraine ['ælsæslə'reɪn] *n* Elsaß-Lothringen *nt*.

alsatian [æl'seɪʃən] *n* (*Brit: also* ~ **dog**) Schäferhund *m*.

Alsatian [æl'seɪʃən] 1 *adj* elsässisch. the ~ people die Elsässer *pl*. 2 *n* (*dialect*) Elsässisch *nt*.

also ['ɔːlsəʊ] *adv* **(a)** auch. her ~ cousin ~ came *or* came ~ ihre Kusine kam auch; he has ~ been there er ist auch (schon) dort gewesen; not only ... but ~ nicht nur ... sondern auch; ~ present were ... außerdem waren anwesend ... **(b)** (*moreover*) außerdem, ferner. ~, I must explain that ... außerdem muß ich erklären, daß ...

also-ran [,ɔːlsəʊ'ræn] *n* to be among the ~s, to be an ~ (*Sport, fig*) unter „ferner liefen" kommen.

altar ['ɒltəʳ] *n* Altar *m*. to lead sb to the ~ jdn zum Altar führen; she was left standing at the ~ sie wurde in letzter Minute sitzengelassen (*inf*); to be sacrificed on the ~ of pride *etc* auf dem Altar des Stolzes *etc* geopfert werden.

altar: ~ **boy** *n* Ministrant *m*; ~ **cloth** *n* Altartuch *nt*, Altardecke *f*; ~**piece** *n* Altarbild *nt*; ~ **rail(s)** *n(pl)* Kommunionbank *f*.

alter ['ɒltəʳ] 1 *vt* **(a)** ändern; (*modify also*) abändern. to ~ sth completely etw vollkommen verändern; that ~s things das

ändert die Sache; it does not ~ the fact that ... das ändert nichts an der Tatsache, daß ... **(b)** (*US: castrate, spay*) kastrieren.

  2 *vi* sich (ver)ändern. to ~ for the better/worse sich zu seinem Vorteil/Nachteil (ver)ändern; (*things, situation*) sich zum Besseren/Schlechteren wenden.

alterable ['ɒltərəbl] *adj* veränderbar. to be ~ sich ändern lassen.

alteration [,ɒltə'reɪʃən] *n* Änderung *f*; (*modification also*) Abänderung *f*; (*of appearance*) Veränderung *f*. a complete ~ eine vollständige Veränderung; to make ~s in sth Änderungen an etw (*dat*) vornehmen; (this timetable is) subject to ~ Änderungen (im Fahrplan sind) vorbehalten; closed for ~s wegen Umbau geschlossen.

altercation [,ɒltə'keɪʃən] *n* Auseinandersetzung *f*.

alter ego ['æltər'iːgəʊ] *n* Alter ego *nt*.

alternate [ɒl'tɜːnɪt] 1 *adj* **(a)** I go there on ~ days ich gehe jeden zweiten Tag *or* alle zwei Tage hin; they do their shopping on ~ days (*every other day*) sie machen ihre Einkäufe jeden zweiten Tag; (*taking turns*) sie wechseln sich täglich mit dem Einkaufen ab; Petra and Alexa come here on ~ days Petra und Alexa kommen abwechseln an verschiedenen Tagen; to go through ~ periods of happiness and despair abwechselnd Zeiten des Glücks und der Verzweiflung durchmachen; they put down ~ layers of brick and mortar sie schichteten (immer) abwechselnd Ziegel und Mörtel aufeinander. **(b)** (*alternative*) Alternativ-. ~ route Ausweichstrecke *f*.

  2 *n* (*US*) Vertreter(in *f*) *m*; (*Sport*) Ersatzspieler(in *f*) *m*.

  3 [ˈɔːltɜːneɪt] *vt* abwechseln lassen; *crops* im Wechsel anbauen. to ~ one thing with another zwischen einer Sache und einer anderen (ab)wechseln; the chairs were ~d with benches Stühle und Bänke waren abwechselnd aufgestellt; she ~d the two jobs sie verrichtete die beiden Arbeiten immer abwechselnd.

  4 [ˈɔːltəneɪt] *vi* (sich) abwechseln; (*Elec*) alternieren. to ~ between one thing and another zwischen einer Sache und einer anderen (ab)wechseln; the two singers ~d in the part die beiden Sänger sangen die Partie abwechselnd.

alternately [ɒl'tɜːnɪtlɪ] *adv* **(a)** (*in turn*) im Wechsel, wechselweise, (immer) abwechselnd. **(b)** *see* alternatively.

alternating ['ɒltɜːneɪtɪŋ] *adj* wechselnd. a pattern with ~ stripes of red and white ein Muster mit abwechselnd roten und weißen Streifen; ~ current Wechselstrom *m*.

alternation [,ɒltɜː'neɪʃən] *n* Wechsel *m*. the ~ of crops der Fruchtwechsel.

alternative [ɒl'tɜːnətɪv] 1 *adj* Alternativ-; *route* Ausweich-. the only ~ way/possibility die einzige Alternative; ~ theatre Antitheater *nt*; ~ society Alternativgesellschaft *f*; for him, other than London, the only possible ~ place to live is ... außer London kommt für ihn als Wohnort nur ... in Frage, ... ist für ihn als Wohnort die einzige Alternative zu London.

  2 *n* Alternative *f*. I had no ~ (but ...) ich hatte keine andere Wahl *or* keine Alternative (als ...).

alternatively [ɒl'tɜːnətɪvlɪ] *adv* als Alternative, als andere Möglichkeit. or ~, he could come with us oder aber, er kommt mit uns mit; a prison sentence of three months or ~ a fine of £500 eine Gefängnisstrafe von drei Monaten *or* wahlweise eine Geldstrafe von £ 500.

alternator ['ɒltɜːneɪtəʳ] *n* (*Elec*) Wechselstromgenerator *m*; (*Aut*) Lichtmaschine *f*.

althorn ['ælthɔːn] *n* B-Horn *nt*.

although [ɔːl'ðəʊ] *conj* obwohl, obgleich. the house, ~ small ... wenn das Haus auch klein ist, obwohl *or* obgleich das Haus klein ist.

altimeter ['æltɪmiːtəʳ] *n* Höhenmesser *m*.

altitude ['æltɪtjuːd] *n* Höhe *f*. what is our ~? in welcher Höhe befinden wir uns?; we are flying at an ~ of ... wir fliegen in einer Höhe von ...; at this ~ in dieser Höhe.

alto ['æltəʊ] 1 *n* **(a)** (*voice*) Alt *m*, Altstimme *f*; (*person*) Alt *m*. **(b)** (*also* ~ **saxophone**) Altsaxophon *nt*. 2 *adj* Alt-. an ~ voice eine Altstimme. 3 *adv* to sing ~ Alt singen.

alto clef *n* Altschlüssel, C-Schlüssel *m*.

altogether [,ɔːltə'geðəʳ] 1 *adv* **(a)** (*including everything*) im ganzen, insgesamt. taken ~, *or* ~ it was very pleasant alles in allem war es sehr nett, es war im ganzen sehr nett.

  (b) (*wholly*) vollkommen, ganz und gar. he wasn't ~ wrong/pleased/surprised er hatte nicht ganz unrecht/war nicht übermäßig *or* besonders zufrieden/überrascht; it was ~ a waste of time es war vollkommene Zeitverschwendung.

  2 *n* in the ~ (*hum inf*) hüllenlos, im Adams-/Evaskostüm; the King is in the ~ der König hat ja gar nichts an.

alto part *n* Altpartie *f*.

alto sax(ophone) *n* Altsaxophon *nt*.

altruism ['æltrʊɪzəm] *n* Altruismus *m*.

altruist ['æltrʊɪst] *n* Altruist(in *f*) *m*.

altruistic *adj*, ~**ally** *adv* [æltrʊ'ɪstɪk, -əlɪ] altruistisch.

alum ['æləm] *n* Alaun *m*.

aluminium [,æljʊ'mɪnɪəm], (*US*) **aluminum** [ə'luːmɪnəm] *n* Aluminium *nt*. ~ foil Alu(minium)folie *f*.

alumna [ə'lʌmnə] *n, pl* -e [ə'lʌmniː] (*US*) ehemalige Schülerin/ Studentin, Ehemalige *f*.

alumnus [ə'lʌmnəs] *n, pl* alumni [ə'lʌmnaɪ] (*US*) ehemaliger Schüler/Student, Ehemalige(r) *m*.

alveolar [æl'vɪələʳ] 1 *adj* alveolar, Alveolar-. 2 *n* (*Phon*) Alveolar *m*.

always ['ɔːlweɪz] *adv* **(a)** immer; (*constantly, repeatedly also*) ständig. he is ~ forgetting er vergißt das immer *or* ständig; you can't ~ expect to be forgiven du kannst nicht immer (wieder) erwarten, daß man dir vergibt.

  (b) we could ~ go by train/sell the house wir könnten doch auch den Zug nehmen/könnten ja auch das Haus verkaufen; there's ~ the possibility that ... es besteht immer noch die Möglichkeit, daß ...; there's ~ that to fall back on wir können ja immer noch darauf zurückgreifen; you can ~ come later Sie können ja auch noch später kommen.

am [æm] *1st pers sing present of* **be**.

amalgam [əˈmælgəm] *n* Amalgam *nt*; *(fig also)* Gemisch *nt*, Mischung *f*.

amalgamate [əˈmælgəmeɪt] **1** *vt companies, unions* fusionieren, verschmelzen; *departments* zusammenlegen; *metals* amalgamieren. **2** *vi (companies etc)* fusionieren; *(metals)* amalgamieren.

amalgamation [ə,mælgəˈmeɪʃən] *n (of companies etc)* Fusion *f*; *(of metals)* Amalgamation *f*.

amanuensis [ə,mænjuˈensɪs] *n, pl* **amanuenses** [ə,mænjuˈensiːz] Sekretär *m*; *(Hist)* Amanuensis *m*.

amaryllis [,æməˈrɪlɪs] *n* Amaryllis *f*.

amass [əˈmæs] *vt* anhäufen; *money also* scheffeln; *fortune, material, evidence also* zusammentragen.

amateur [ˈæmətəʳ] **1** *n* **(a)** Amateur *m*. **(b)** *(pej)* Dilettant(in *f*) *m*. **2** *adj* **(a)** *attr* Amateur-; *photographer also, painter, painting* Hobby-; *dramatics, work also* Laien-. **(b)** *(pej) see* **amateurish**.

amateurish [ˈæmətərɪʃ] *adj (pej)* dilettantisch; *performance, work also* laienhaft.

amateurishly [ˈæmətərɪʃlɪ] *adv (pej)* dilettantisch.

amateurishness [ˈæmətərɪʃnɪs] *n (pej)* Dilettantismus *m*; *(of performance, work)* Laienhaftigkeit *f*.

amateurism [ˈæmətərɪzəm] *n* **(a)** Amateursport *m*. **(b)** *(pej)* Dilettantentum *nt*, Dilettantismus *m*.

amatory [ˈæmətərɪ] *adj poem, letter* Liebes-; *adventure also* amourös; *glance, look, remark, feelings* verliebt.

amaze [əˈmeɪz] **1** *vt* erstaunen, in Erstaunen (ver)setzen. I was ~d to learn that ... ich war erstaunt zu hören, daß ..., mit Erstaunen hörte ich, daß ...; to be ~d at sth über etw *(acc)* erstaunt *or* verblüfft sein, sich über etw *(acc)* wundern; you don't know that, you ~ me! Sie wissen das nicht, das wundert mich aber; no, really? you ~ me *(iro)* nein wirklich? da bin ich aber erstaunt *or* Sie setzen mich in Erstaunen; it ~s me to think that only two years ago ... es ist erstaunlich, wenn ich denke, daß erst vor zwei Jahren ...; it ~s me that *or* how he doesn't fall ich finde es erstaunlich, daß er nicht fällt.

2 *vi* his virtuosity never fails to ~ seine Virtuosität versetzt einen immer wieder in Erstaunen, man muß sich immer wieder über seine Virtuosität wundern.

amazement [əˈmeɪzmənt] *n* Erstaunen *nt*, Verwunderung *f*. much to my ~ zu meinem großen Erstaunen.

amazing [əˈmeɪzɪŋ] *adj* erstaunlich. he's the most ~ lawyer/idiot I've ever met er ist der erstaunlichste Rechtsanwalt/der größte Trottel, den ich je gesehen habe; darling, you're ~, such a super meal from two tins wie machst du das bloß, mein Schatz, ein so tolles Essen aus zwei Büchsen!

amazingly [əˈmeɪzɪŋlɪ] *adv* erstaunlich; *simple, obvious also* verblüffend. ~, he got it right first time erstaunlicherweise hat er es gleich beim ersten Male richtig gemacht.

Amazon [ˈæməzən] *n* Amazonas *m*; *(Myth, fig)* Amazone *f*.

ambassador [æmˈbæsədəʳ] *n* Botschafter *m*; *(fig)* Repräsentant, Vertreter *m*. ~ extraordinary, ~-at-large *(esp US)* Sonderbotschafter(in *f*) *m*, Sonderbeauftragte(r) *mf*; *see* **roving**.

ambassadorial [æm,bæsəˈdɔːrɪəl] *adj* Botschafter-; *rank, dignity* eines Botschafters.

ambassadress [æmˈbæsɪdrɪs] *n (female ambassador)* Botschafterin *f*; *(ambassador's wife)* Frau *f* des Botschafters.

amber [ˈæmbəʳ] **1** *n* **(a)** *(substance)* Bernstein *m*; *(colour)* Bernsteingelb *nt*; *(in traffic lights)* Gelb *nt*. **2** *adj (made of ~)* Bernstein-, aus Bernstein; *(~-coloured)* bernsteinfarben; *traffic light* gelb.

ambergris [ˈæmbəgriːs] *n* Amber *m*, Ambra *f*.

ambidextrous [,æmbɪˈdekstrəs] *adj* ambidexter *(form)*, mit beiden Händen gleich geschickt, beidhändig.

ambidextrousness [,æmbɪˈdekstrəsnɪs] *n* Ambidextrie *(form)*, Beidhändigkeit *f*.

ambience [ˈæmbɪəns] *n* Atmosphäre *f*, Ambiente *nt (geh)*.

ambient [ˈæmbɪənt] *adj (liter) air* umgebend.

ambiguity [,æmbɪˈgjuːɪtɪ] *n see* **ambiguous** Zwei- *or* Doppeldeutigkeit *f*; Zweideutigkeit *f*; Mehr- *or* Vieldeutigkeit *f*.

ambiguous *adj*, **~ly** *adv* [æmˈbɪgjuəs, -lɪ] zwei- *or* doppeldeutig; *joke, comment etc* zweideutig; *(with many possible meanings)* mehr- *or* vieldeutig.

ambiguousness [æmˈbɪgjuəsnɪs] *n* Zwei- *or* Doppeldeutigkeit *f*; *(with many possible meanings)* Mehr- *or* Vieldeutigkeit *f*.

ambit [ˈæmbɪt] *n* Bereich *m*.

ambition [æmˈbɪʃən] *n* **(a)** *(desire)* Ambition *f*. she has ~s in that direction/for her son sie hat Ambitionen in dieser Richtung/ehrgeizige Pläne für ihren Sohn; my one *or* big ~ in life is ... meine große Ambition ist es, ...; it is my ~ to become Prime Minister/to travel to the moon es ist mein Ehrgeiz *or* Ziel *or* meine Ambition, Premierminister zu werden/auf den Mond zu reisen; it was never my ~ to take over your job es war nie mein Bestreben *or* meine Absicht, Ihre Stelle zu übernehmen.

(b) *(ambitious nature)* Ehrgeiz *m*.

ambitious [æmˈbɪʃəs] *adj* **(a)** *person* ehrgeizig, ambitioniert *(geh)*, ambitiös *(pej)*. he is ~ to ... er setzt seinen ganzen Ehrgeiz daran, zu ...; she is ~ for her husband sie hat ehrgeizige Pläne für ihren Mann; to be ~ of fame *(liter)* nach Ruhm streben.

(b) ehrgeizig, ambitiös *(pej)*; *idea, undertaking also* kühn.

ambitiously [æmˈbɪʃəslɪ] *adv* voll(er) Ehrgeiz, ehrgeizig. rather ~, we set out to prove the following wir hatten uns das

ehrgeizige Ziel gesteckt, das Folgende zu beweisen.

ambitiousness [æmˈbɪʃəsnɪs] *n see adj* **(a)** Ehrgeiz *m*. **(b)** Ehrgeiz *m*; Kühnheit *f*.

ambivalence [æmˈbɪvələns] *n* Ambivalenz *f*.

ambivalent [æmˈbɪvələnt] *adj* ambivalent.

amble [ˈæmbl] **1** *vi (person)* schlendern; *(horse)* im Paßgang gehen. **2** *n* Schlendern *nt*; *(of horse)* Paßgang *m*. he went for an ~ along the riverside er machte einen gemütlichen Spaziergang am Fluß entlang.

ambrosia [æmˈbrəʊzɪə] *n (Myth, fig)* Ambrosia *f*.

ambulance [ˈæmbjuləns] *n* Krankenwagen *m*, Krankenauto *nt*, Ambulanz *f*.

ambulance: ~-chaser *n (US sl)* Rechtsanwalt, der Unfallopfer als Klienten zu gewinnen sucht; ~ driver *n* Krankenwagenfahrer(in *f*) *m*; ~man *n* Sanitäter *m*; ~ service *n* Rettungs- *or* Ambulanzdienst *m*; *(system)* Rettungswesen *nt*.

ambulant [ˈæmbjulənt] *adj* ~ patients gehfähige Patienten.

ambush [ˈæmbuʃ] **1** *n (place)* Hinterhalt *m*; *(troops etc)* im Hinterhalt liegende Truppe/Guerillas etc; *(attack)* Überfall *m* (aus dem Hinterhalt). to lay an ~ (for sb) (jdm) einen Hinterhalt legen; to lie *or* wait in ~ (Mil, fig) im Hinterhalt liegen; to lie *or* wait in ~ for sb (Mil, fig) jdm im Hinterhalt auflauern; to fall into an ~ in einen Hinterhalt geraten.

2 *vt* (aus dem Hinterhalt) überfallen.

ameba *n (US) see* **amoeba**.

ameliorate [əˈmiːlɪəreɪt] *(form)* **1** *vt* verbessern. **2** *vi* sich verbessern, besser werden.

amelioration [ə,miːlɪəˈreɪʃən] *n (form)* Verbesserung *f*.

amen [,ɑːˈmen] **1** *interj* amen. ~ to that! *(fig inf)* ja, wahrlich *or* fürwahr! *(hum)*. **2** *n* Amen *nt*. we'll all say ~ to that *(fig inf)* wir befürworten das alle, wir sind alle dafür.

amenability [ə,miːnəˈbɪlɪtɪ] *n (responsiveness: of people)* Zugänglichkeit *f*. the ~ of these data to the theory die Möglichkeit, diese Daten in die Theorie einzuordnen.

amenable [əˈmiːnəbl] *adj* **(a)** *(responsive)* zugänglich *(to dat)*. he is ~ to reasonable suggestions er ist vernünftigen Vorschlägen zugänglich; it is not ~ to this theory/method of classification es läßt sich in diese Theorie/dieses Klassifikationssystem nicht einordnen.

(b) *(Jur: answerable)* verantwortlich. ~ to the law dem Gesetz verantwortlich.

amend [əˈmend] *vt* **(a)** *law, bill, constitution, text* ändern, amendieren *(form)*, ein Amendement einbringen zu *(form)*; *(by addition)* ergänzen. I'd better ~ that to "most people" ich werde das lieber in „die meisten Leute" (ab)ändern.

(b) *(improve)* habits, behaviour bessern.

(c) *see* **emend**.

amendment [əˈmendmənt] *n* **(a)** *(to bill, in text)* Änderung *f (to gen)*, Amendement *nt (form)* *(to gen)*; *(addition)* Amendement *nt (form)* *(to gen)*, Zusatz *m (to zu)*. the First/Second etc A~ *(US Pol)* das Erste/Zweite etc Amendement, Zusatz 1/2 etc. **(b)** *(in behaviour)* Besserung *f*.

amends [əˈmendz] *npl* to make ~ (for sth) etw wiedergutmachen; to make ~ to sb for sth jdn für etw entschädigen; I'll try to make ~ ich werde versuchen, das wiedergutzumachen.

amenity [əˈmiːnɪtɪ] *n* **(a)** *(aid to pleasant living)* **(public)** ~ öffentliche Einrichtung; the lack of amenities in many parts of the city der Mangel an Einkaufs-, Unterhaltungs- und Transportmöglichkeiten in vielen Teilen der Stadt; close to all amenities in günstiger (Einkaufs- und Verkehrs)lage; this house has every ~ dieses Haus bietet jeden Komfort; a high/low ~ district eine Gegend mit hoher/geringer Wohnqualität.

(b) *(pleasantness: of place)* angenehme Lage. the ~ of the climate/surroundings das angenehme Klima/die angenehme Umgebung.

America [əˈmerɪkə] *n* Amerika *nt*. the ~s Amerika *nt*, der amerikanische Kontinent.

American [əˈmerɪkən] **1** *adj* amerikanisch. ~ English amerikanisches Englisch; ~ Indian Indianer(in *f*) *m*; ~ plan Vollpension *f*. **2** *n* **(a)** Amerikaner(in *f*) *m*. **(b)** *(language)* Amerikanisch *nt*.

americanism [əˈmerɪkənɪzəm] *n* **(a)** *(Ling)* Amerikanismus *m*. **(b)** *(quality)* Amerikanertum *nt*.

americanization [ə,merɪkənaɪˈzeɪʃən] *n* Amerikanisierung *f*.

americanize [əˈmerɪkənaɪz] **1** *vt* amerikanisieren. **2** *vi* sich amerikanisieren.

amethyst [ˈæmɪθɪst] **1** *n* Amethyst *m*; *(colour)* Amethystblau *nt*. **2** *adj jewellery* Amethyst-; *(~-coloured)* amethystfarben.

amiability [,eɪmɪəˈbɪlɪtɪ] *n* Liebenswürdigkeit *f*.

amiable [ˈeɪmɪəbl] *adj* liebenswürdig.

amiably [ˈeɪmɪəblɪ] *adv* liebenswürdig. he very ~ offered to help er hat sich liebenswürdigerweise angeboten zu helfen.

amicable [ˈæmɪkəbl] *adj* person, manner freundlich; *relations* freundschaftlich; *discussion* friedlich; *(Jur)* settlement gütlich.

amicably [ˈæmɪkəblɪ] *adv* freundlich; *discuss* friedlich, in aller Freundschaft; *(Jur)* settle gütlich. they got on quite ~ sie kamen ganz gut miteinander aus.

amidships [əˈmɪdʃɪps] *adv (Naut)* mittschiffs.

amid(st) [əˈmɪd(st)] *prep* inmitten *(+gen)*.

amino acid [əˈmiːnəʊˈæsɪd] *n* Aminosäure *f*.

amiss [əˈmɪs] **1** *adj pred* there's something ~ da stimmt irgend etwas nicht; what's ~ with you? *(liter)* was fehlt Ihnen (denn)?

2 *adv* to take sth ~ (jdm) etw übelnehmen; to speak ~ of sb schlecht über jdn sprechen; to say something ~ etwas Falsches *or* Verkehrtes sagen; a drink would not come *or* go ~ etwas zu trinken wäre gar nicht verkehrt; nothing comes ~ to him ihm kommt alles recht.

amity [ˈæmɪtɪ] *n* Freundschaftlichkeit *f*.

ammeter ['æmɪtə^r] n Amperemeter nt.
ammo ['æməʊ] n (inf) Munition, Mun (sl) f.
ammonia [ə'məʊnɪə] n Ammoniak nt.
ammunition [,æmjʊ'nɪʃən] n (lit, fig) Munition f.
ammunition: ~ **belt** n Patronengurt m; ~ **dump** n Munitionslager nt.
amnesia [æm'niːzɪə] n Amnesie f (form), Gedächtnisschwund m.
amnesty ['æmnɪstɪ] n Amnestie f. **during** or **under the** ~ unter der Amnestie; **a general** ~ eine Generalamnestie; **A**~ **International** Amnesty International no art.
amoeba, (US) **ameba** [ə'miːbə] n Amöbe f.
amoebic, (US) **amebic** [ə'miːbɪk] adj amöbisch. ~ **dysentery** Amöbenruhr f.
amok [ə'mɒk] adv see **amuck.**
among(st) [ə'mʌŋ(st)] prep unter (+acc or dat). ~ **other things** unter anderem; ~ **the crowd** unter die/der Menge; **they shared it out** ~ **themselves** sie teilten es unter sich or untereinander auf; **he's** ~ **our best players** er gehört zu unseren besten Spielern; **Manchester is** ~ **the largest of our cities** Manchester gehört zu unseren größten Städten; **to count sb** ~ **one's friends** jdn zu seinen Freunden zählen; **this habit is widespread** ~ **the French** diese Sitte ist bei den Franzosen weitverbreitet; **there were ferns** ~ **the trees** zwischen den Bäumen wuchs Farnkraut; **to hide** ~ **the bushes** sich in den Büschen verstecken.
amoral [æ'mɒrəl] adj amoralisch.
amorous ['æmərəs] adj amorös; look also verliebt. **to make** ~ **advances** Annäherungsversuche pl machen.
amorously ['æmərəslɪ] adv verliebt, voller Verliebtheit.
amorphous [ə'mɔːfəs] adj amorph, strukturlos, formlos; style, ideas, play, novel strukturlos, ungegliedert; (Geol) amorph.
amorphousness [ə'mɔːfəsnɪs] n Strukturlosigkeit f.
amortization [ə,mɔːtaɪ'zeɪʃən] n Amortisation f.
amortize [ə'mɔːtaɪz] vt debt amortisieren, tilgen.
amount [ə'maʊnt] **1** vi **(a)** (total) sich belaufen (to auf +acc).
  (b) (be equivalent) gleichkommen (to +dat). **it** ~ **s to the same thing** das läuft or kommt (doch) aufs gleiche hinaus or raus (inf); **he will never** ~ **to much** aus ihm wird nie etwas or viel werden, der wird es nie zu etwas or zu viel bringen; **their promises don't** ~ **to very much** ihre Versprechungen sind recht nichtssagend; **so what this** ~**s to is that** ... worauf es also hinausläuft, daß ...
  2 n (a) (of money) Betrag m. **total** ~ Gesamtsumme f, Endbetrag m; **debts to the** ~ **of £20** Schulden in Höhe von £ 20; **I was shocked at the** ~ **of the bill** ich war über die Höhe der Rechnung erschrocken; **in 12 equal** ~**s** in 12 gleichen Teilen, in 12 gleichen Beträgen; **an unlimited/a large/a small** ~ **of money** eine unbeschränkte or unbegrenzte/große/geringe Summe (Geldes); **a modest** ~ **of money** ein bescheidener Betrag; **any/quite an** ~ **of money** beliebig viel/ziemlich viel Geld, ein ziemlicher Betrag; **large** ~**s of money** Unsummen pl (Geldes); **it's not the** ~ **of the donation that counts** nicht die Höhe der Spende ist maßgeblich.
  (b) (quantity) Menge f; (of luck, intelligence, skill etc) Maß nt (of an +dat). **an enormous/a modest** ~ **of work/time** sehr viel/verhältnismäßig wenig Arbeit/Zeit; **any/quite an** ~ **of time/food** beliebig viel/ziemlich viel Zeit/Essen, eine ziemliche Menge Essen; **no** ~ **of talking would persuade him** kein Reden würde ihn überzeugen; **no** ~ **of paint can hide the rust** keine noch so dicke Farbschicht kann den Rost verdecken; **if we increase the** ~ **of the current/loan/noise factor** wenn wir den Strom/die Anleihe or die Höhe der Anleihe/den Lärmfaktor erhöhen.
amour [ə'mʊə^r] n (dated, liter) Liebschaft f; (person) Liebe f.
amour-propre [,æmʊə'prɒprə] n Eigenliebe f.
amp(ère) ['æmp(εə^r)] n Ampere nt.
ampersand ['æmpəsænd] n Et-Zeichen nt.
amphetamine [æm'fetəmiːn] n Amphetamin nt.
amphibian [æm'fɪbɪən] n (animal, plant) Amphibie f; (vehicle) Amphibienfahrzeug nt; (aircraft) Amphibienflugzeug, Wasser-Land-Flugzeug nt. ~ **tank** Amphibienpanzer m.
amphibious [æm'fɪbɪəs] adj animal, plant, (Mil) amphibisch; vehicle, aircraft Amphibien-.
amphitheatre, (US) **amphitheater** ['æmfɪθɪətə^r] n **(a)** Amphitheater nt; (lecture-hall) Hörsaal m (Halbrund mit ansteigenden Sitzreihen). **(b)** (Geog) Halbkessel m. **a natural** ~ ein natürliches Amphitheater.
amphora ['æmfərə] n, pl -s or -e ['æmfəriː] (form) Amphora, Amphore f.
ample ['æmpl] adj (+er) **(a)** (plentiful) reichlich. **that will be** ~ das ist reichlich; **more than** ~ überreichlich; **the house is** ~ **for his family** das Haus bietet reichlich Platz für seine Familie or bietet seiner Familie reichlich Platz.
  (b) (large) figure, proportions üppig; boot of car etc geräumig; garden weitläufig, ausgedehnt.
amplification [,æmplɪfɪ'keɪʃən] n weitere Ausführungen pl, Erläuterungen pl; (Rad) Verstärkung f. **in** ~ **of this** ... dies weiter ausführend ...
amplifier ['æmplɪfaɪə^r] n (Rad) Verstärker m.
amplify ['æmplɪfaɪ] **1** vt **(a)** (Rad) verstärken.
  (b) (expand) statement, idea näher or ausführlicher erläutern, ausführen; argument ausführen.
  (c) (inf: exaggerate) übertreiben.
  2 vi **would you care to** ~ **a little?** würden Sie das bitte näher or ausführlicher erläutern?, würden Sie bitte auf diesen Punkt näher eingehen?; **to** ~ **on sth** etw näher erläutern, einen Punkt ausführen.
amplitude ['æmplɪtjuːd] n (of knowledge) Weite, Breite f; (of bosom) Üppigkeit, Fülle f; (Phys) Amplitude f.
amply ['æmplɪ] adv reichlich; proportioned figure üppig;

proportioned rooms geräumig, großzügig.
ampoule, (US) **ampull(e)** ['æmpuːl] n Ampulle f.
ampulla [æm'pʊlə] n, pl -e [æm'pʊliː] (Hist, Eccl) Ampulla f.
amputate ['æmpjʊteɪt] vti amputieren.
amputation [,æmpjʊ'teɪʃən] n Amputation f.
amputee [,æmpjʊ'tiː] n Amputierte(r) mf.
amuck, amok [ə'mʌk] adv: **to run** ~ (lit, fig) Amok laufen.
amulet ['æmjʊlɪt] n Amulett nt.
amuse [ə'mjuːz] **1** vt (a) (cause mirth) amüsieren, belustigen. **I was** ~**d to hear** ... es hat mich amüsiert or belustigt zu hören ...; **we are not** ~**d** das ist nicht spaßig (dated), das ist durchaus nicht zum Lachen or nicht komisch; **he was anything but** ~**d to find the door locked** er fand es keineswegs or durchaus nicht komisch, daß die Tür verschlossen war; **the teacher shouldn't appear to be** ~**d by the pupils' mistakes** der Lehrer sollte es sich nicht anmerken lassen, daß ihn die Fehler der Schüler amüsieren; **you** ~ **me, how can anyone** ... daß ich nicht lache or da muß ich ja (mal) lachen, wie kann man nur ...
  (b) (entertain) unterhalten. **let the children do it if it** ~**s them** laß die Kinder doch, wenn es ihnen Spaß macht; **give him his toys, that'll keep him** ~**d** gib ihm sein Spielzeug, dann ist er friedlich; **I have no problem keeping myself** ~**d now I'm retired** ich habe keinerlei Schwierigkeiten, mir die Zeit zu vertreiben, jetzt wo ich im Ruhestand bin.
  2 vr **the children can** ~ **themselves for a while** die Kinder können sich eine Zeitlang selbst beschäftigen; **could you** ~ **yourself with the magazines in the meantime?** könntest du dir derweil ein bißchen die Zeitschriften ansehen or dich derweil mit den Zeitschriften beschäftigen?; **to** ~ **oneself (by) doing sth** etw zu seinem Vergnügen or aus Spaß tun; **how do you** ~ **yourself now you're retired?** wie vertreiben Sie sich (dat) die Zeit, wo Sie jetzt im Ruhestand sind?; **he** ~**s himself with cross-word puzzles** er löst zum Zeitvertreib Kreuzworträtsel; **he's just amusing himself with her** er amüsiert sich nur mit ihr.
amusement [ə'mjuːzmənt] n **(a)** (enjoyment, fun) Vergnügen nt; (state of being entertained) Belustigung f, Amüsement nt. **the toys were a great source of** ~ das Spielzeug bereitete großen Spaß; **he gets no** ~ **out of life** er kann dem Leben kein Vergnügen abgewinnen; **what do you do for** ~? was machst du als Freizeitbeschäftigung?; (retired people) was machen Sie zu Ihrer Unterhaltung or als Zeitvertreib?; **what do you do for** ~ **in a town like this!** was kann man denn schon in so einer Stadt zu seiner Unterhaltung machen or tun!; **I see no cause for** ~ ich sehe keinen Grund zur Heiterkeit; **to do sth for one's own** ~ etw zu seinem Vergnügen or Amüsement tun; **to my great** ~/**to everyone's** ~ zu meiner großen/zur allgemeinen Belustigung.
  (b) (entertainment: of guests) Belustigung, Unterhaltung f.
  (c) ~**s** pl (place of entertainment) Vergnügungsstätte f usu pl; (at fair) Attraktionen pl; (stand, booth) Buden pl; (at the seaside) Spielautomaten und Spiegelkabinett etc; **what sort of** ~**s do you have around here?** was für Vergnügungs- und Unterhaltungsmöglichkeiten gibt es hier?
amusement: ~ **arcade** n Spielhalle f; ~ **park** n Vergnügungspark, Lunapark (dated) m.
amusing [ə'mjuːzɪŋ] adj **(a)** amüsant. **how** ~ wie lustig or witzig!, das ist aber lustig or witzig!; **I've just had an** ~ **thought** mir ist gerade etwas Lustiges or Amüsantes eingefallen; **I don't find that very** ~ das finde ich nicht gerade or gar nicht lustig or zum Lachen.
  (b) (inf) hat, little dress etc charmant, apart. **an** ~ **little wine** ein nettes Weinchen (hum).
amusingly [ə'mjuːzɪŋlɪ] adv amüsant. **he was so** ~ **indignant** er war so entrüstet, daß es (schon wieder) komisch or lustig or amüsant war.
an [æn, ən, n] **1** indef art see **a. 2** conj (obs: if) so (old).
Anabaptism [,ænə'bæptɪzəm] n Anabaptismus m.
Anabaptist [,ænə'bæptɪst] n Anabaptist, Wiedertäufer(in f) m.
anabolic steroid [,ænə'bɒlɪk'stɪərɔɪd] n Anabolikum nt.
anachronism [ə'nækrənɪzəm] n Anachronismus m.
anachronistic [ə,nækrə'nɪstɪk] adj anachronistisch; (not fitting modern times) nicht zeitgemäß, unzeitgemäß.
anaconda [,ænə'kɒndə] n Anakonda f.
anaemia, (US) **anemia** [ə'niːmɪə] n Anämie, Blutarmut f.
anaemic, (US) **anemic** [ə'niːmɪk] adj **(a)** anämisch, blutarm. **(b)** (fig) anämisch, saft- und kraftlos; colour, appearance also bleichsüchtig.
anaesthesia, (US) **anesthesia** [,ænɪs'θiːzɪə] n Betäubung f.
anaesthetic, (US) **anesthetic** [,ænɪs'θetɪk] **1** n Narkose, Anästhesie f; (substance) Narkosemittel, Anästhetikum (spec) nt. **general** ~ Vollnarkose f; **local** ~ örtliche Betäubung, Lokalanästhesie (spec) f; **the nurse gave him a local** ~ die Schwester gab ihm eine Spritze zur örtlichen Betäubung; **the patient is still under the** ~ der Patient ist noch in der Narkose; **when he comes out of the** ~ wenn er aus der Narkose aufwacht. **2** adj effect betäubend, anästhetisch; drug Betäubungs-.
anaesthetist, (US) **anesthetist** [æ'niːsθɪtɪst] n Anästhesist(in f) m, Narkose(fach)arzt m/-(fach)ärztin f.
anaesthetize, (US) **anesthetize** [æ'niːsθɪtaɪz] vt (Med) betäuben; (generally also) narkotisieren.
anagram ['ænəgræm] n Anagramm nt.
anal ['eɪnəl] adj anal, Anal-, After-. (Med). ~ **eroticism** Analerotik f.
analgesia [ænæl'dʒiːzɪə] n Schmerzlosigkeit, Analgesie (spec) f.
analgesic [ænæl'dʒiːsɪk] **1** n schmerzstillendes Mittel, Schmerzmittel, Analgetikum (spec) nt. **2** adj schmerzstillend.
analog computer ['ænəlɒgkəm'pjuːtə^r] n Analogrechner m.
analogic(al) ['ænə'lɒdʒɪk(əl)] adj, **analogically** [,ænə'lɒdʒɪkəlɪ] adv analog.
analogous adj, ~**ly** adv [ə'næləgəs, -lɪ] analog (to, with zu).

analogue ['ænəlɒg] n Gegenstück nt, Parallele f.

analogy [ə'nælədʒɪ] n Analogie f. **to argue from** or **by** ~ analog argumentieren, Analogieschlüsse/einen Analogieschluß ziehen; **arguing from** ~ **one could claim that ...** analog könnte man behaupten ...; **to draw an** ~ eine Analogie herstellen, einen analogen Vergleich ziehen; **on the** ~ **of** analog zu, nach dem Muster (+gen); **it's an argument by** ~ es ist ein Analogiebeweis, es ist eine analoge Argumentation.

analyse, (US) **analyze** ['ænəlaɪz] vt (a) analysieren; (Chem also) untersuchen; (in literary criticism also) kritisch untersuchen; (Gram) sentence also (zer)gliedern. **to** ~ **the situation** (fig) die Situation analysieren or (to others) erläutern; **to** ~ **sth into its parts** etw in seine Bestandteile zerlegen.
(b) (psycho~) psychoanalytisch behandeln, analysieren (inf). **stop analysing me!** hör auf, mich zu analysieren!

analysis [ə'næləsɪs] n, pl **analyses** [ə'næləsiːz] (a) see vt Analyse f; (Zer)gliederung f. **what's your** ~ **of the situation?** wie beurteilen Sie die Situation?; **in the last** or **final** ~ letzten Endes; **on (closer)** ~ bei genauerer Untersuchung. (b) (psycho~) Psychoanalyse f, Analyse (inf) f.

analyst ['ænəlɪst] n Analytiker m; (Chem) Chemiker(in f) m. **food** ~ Lebensmittelchemiker(in f) m; **the police sent specimens off to the** ~ die Polizei schickte Proben zur Untersuchung or Analyse or ins Labor; **he gave it to the** ~ **in the lab** er ließ im Labor eine Analyse davon machen.

analytic [ˌænə'lɪtɪk] adj (Philos) analytisch.

analytical [ˌænə'lɪtɪkəl] adj analytisch. **you should try to be more** ~ Sie sollten versuchen, etwas analytischer vorzugehen; **he hasn't got a very** ~ **mind** er kann nicht analytisch denken.

analytically [ˌænə'lɪtɪkəlɪ] adv analytisch.

analyze ['ænəlaɪz] vt see **analyse**.

anapaest, (US) **anapest** ['ænəpiːst] n (Poet) Anapäst m.

anarchic(al) [æ'nɑːkɪk(əl)] adj anarchisch.

anarchism ['ænəkɪzəm] n Anarchismus m.

anarchist ['ænəkɪst] n Anarchist(in f) m.

anarchist(ic) [ˌænə'kɪst(ɪk)] adj anarchistisch.

anarchy ['ænəkɪ] n Anarchie f.

anathema [ə'næθɪmə] n (Eccl) Anathema (form) nt, Kirchenbann m; (fig: no art) ein Greuel m. **voting Labour was** ~ **to them** der Gedanke, Labour zu wählen, war ihnen ein Greuel.

anathematize [ə'næθɪmətaɪz] vt (Eccl) mit dem Bann belegen.

anatomical [ˌænə'tɒmɪkəl] adj anatomisch.

anatomist [ə'nætəmɪst] n Anatom m.

anatomy [ə'nætəmɪ] n Anatomie f; (structure also) Körperbau m; (fig) Struktur f und Aufbau m. **on a certain part/certain parts of her** ~ (euph) an einer gewissen Stelle/an gewissen Stellen or Körperteilen (euph).

ancestor ['ænsɪstə'] n Vorfahr, Ahne m; (progenitor) Stammvater m. ~ **worship** Ahnenkult m.

ancestral [æn'sestrəl] adj Ahnen-, seiner/ihrer Vorfahren. ~ **home** Stammsitz m.

ancestress ['ænsɪstrɪs] n Vorfahrin, Ahne f; (progenitor) Ahnfrau, Stammutter f.

ancestry ['ænsɪstrɪ] n (descent) Abstammung, Herkunft f; (ancestors) Ahnenreihe, Familie f. **to trace one's** ~ seine Abstammung zurückverfolgen; **of noble** ~ vornehmer Abstammung or Herkunft.

anchor ['æŋkə'] **1** n (Naut) Anker m; (fig: hope, love, person etc) Zuflucht f, Rettungsanker m. **to cast** or **drop** ~ Anker werfen, vor Anker gehen; **to weigh** ~ den Anker lichten; **to be** or **lie** or **ride at** ~ vor Anker liegen; **to come to** ~ vor Anker gehen; **the stone served as an** ~ **for the tent** der Stein diente dazu, das Zelt zu beschweren or am Boden festzuhalten.
2 vt (Naut, fig) verankern. **we** ~**ed the tablecloth with stones** to stop it blowing away wir beschwerten das Tischtuch mit Steinen, damit es nicht weggeweht wurde.
3 vi (Naut) ankern, vor Anker gehen.

anchorage ['æŋkərɪdʒ] n (Naut) (a) Ankerplatz m. (b) (also ~ dues) Anker- or Liegegebühren pl.

anchor buoy n Ankerboje f.

anchorite ['æŋkəraɪt] n Einsiedler, Eremit m.

anchorman ['æŋkə'mæn] n (TV etc) Koordinator(in f) m; (last person in relay race etc) Letzte(r) mf; (in tug-of-war) hinterster Mann; (fig) eiserne Stütze f, Eckpfeiler m.

anchovy ['æntʃəvɪ] n Sardelle, An(s)chovis f. ~ **paste** Sardellen- or An(s)chovispaste f.

ancient ['eɪnʃənt] **1** adj (a) alt. **in** ~ **times** im Altertum; (Greek, Roman also) in der Antike; ~ **Rome** das alte Rom; **the** ~ **Romans** die alten Römer; ~ **monument** (Brit) historisches Denkmal, historische Stätte; ~ **history** (lit) Alte Geschichte; (fig) graue Vorzeit; **that's** ~ **history** (fig) das ist schon längst Geschichte; **he's well-known in the field of** ~ **history** er ist ein sehr bekannter Altertumsforscher.
(b) (inf) person, clothes etc uralt.
2 n **the** ~**s** die Völker or Menschen des Altertums or im Altertum; (writers) die Schriftsteller des Altertums.

ancillary [æn'sɪlərɪ] adj (subordinate) roads, (Univ) subject Neben-; (auxiliary) service, troops Hilfs-. ~ **course** (Univ) Begleitkurs m; ~ **industry** Zulieferindustrie, Zubringerindustrie f.

and [ænd, ənd, nd, ən] conj (a) und. **nice** ~ **early/warm** schön früh/warm; **when I'm good** ~ **ready** wenn es mir paßt, wenn ich soweit bin; **you** ~ **you alone** du, nur du allein; **try** ~ **come** versuch zu kommen; **wait** ~ **see!** abwarte!, wart's ab!; **don't go** ~ **spoil it!** nun verdirb nicht alles!; **come** ~ **get it!** komm und hol's!; **one more** ~ **I'm finished** noch eins, und ich bin fertig; **there are dictionaries** ~ **dictionaries** es gibt Wörterbücher und Wörterbücher, es gibt so'ne Wörterbücher und solche (inf); ~/**or** und/oder; ~ **so on,** ~ **so forth,** ~ **so on** ~ **so forth** und so weiter, und so fort, und so weiter und so fort.

(b) (in repetition, continuation) und; (between comps also) immer. **better** ~ **better** immer besser; **for hours** ~ **hours/days** ~ **days/weeks** ~ **weeks** stundenlang, Stunde um Stunde (geh)/tagelang/wochenlang; **for miles** ~ **miles** meilenweit; I **rang** ~ **rang** ich klingelte und klingelte, ich klingelte immer wieder; **I tried** ~ **tried** ich habe es immer wieder versucht; ~ **he pulled** ~ **he pulled** und er zog und zog.
(c) (with numbers) **three hundred** ~ **ten** dreihundertzehn; (when the number is said more slowly) dreihundertundzehn; **one** ~ **a half** anderthalb, eineinhalb; **two** ~ **twenty** (old, form) zweiundzwanzig.

Andean ['ændɪən] adj Anden-.

Andes ['ændiːz] npl Anden pl.

andiron ['ændaɪrən] n Kaminbock m.

Andrew ['ændruː] n Andreas m.

androgynous [æn'drɒdʒɪnəs] adj zweigeschlechtig, zwittrig.

anecdotal [ˌænɪk'dəʊtəl] adj anekdotenhaft, anekdotisch.

anecdote ['ænɪkdəʊt] n Anekdote f.

anemia [ə'niːmɪə] n (US) see **anaemia**.

anemic [ə'niːmɪk] adj (US) see **anaemic**.

anemometer [ˌænɪ'mɒmɪtə'] n Windmesser m.

anemone [ə'nemənɪ] n (Bot) Anemone f, Buschwindröschen nt; (sea ~) Seeanemone f.

aneroid barometer ['ænərɔɪdbə'rɒmɪtə'] n Aneroidbarometer nt.

anesthesia n (US), **anesthetic** adj, n (US), **anesthetize** vt (US) etc see **anaesthesia** etc.

anew [ə'njuː] adv (a) (again) aufs neue. **let's start** ~ fangen wir wieder von vorn or von neuem an. (b) (in a new way) auf eine neue Art und Weise.

angel ['eɪndʒəl] n (lit, fig) Engel m; (US inf: backer) finanzkräftiger Hintermann.

angel cake n = Biskuitkuchen m.

Angeleno [ændʒə'liːnəʊ] n Einwohner(in f) m von Los Angeles.

angel: ~ **face** interj (hum inf) mein Engel; ~ **fish** n (shark) Meerengel, Engelhai m; (tropical fish) Großer Segelflosser.

angelic [æn'dʒelɪk] adj (a) (of an angel) Engels-; hosts himmlisch; salutation Englisch. (b) (like an angel) engelhaft, engelgleich (liter).

angelica [æn'dʒelɪkə] n (Bot) Angelika, Brustwurz f; (Cook) kandierte Angelika.

angelically [æn'dʒelɪkəlɪ] adv wie ein Engel, engelgleich.

angelus ['ændʒɪləs] n Angelusläuten nt; (prayer) Angelus nt.

anger ['æŋgə'] **1** n Ärger m; (wrath: of gods etc) Zorn m. **a fit of** ~ ein Wutanfall m, ein Zorn(es)ausbruch m; **red with** ~ rot vor Wut; **public** ~ öffentliche Entrüstung; **to speak/act in** ~ im Zorn sprechen/handeln; **words spoken in** ~ was man in seiner Wut or im Zorn sagt; **to be filled with** ~ (liter) zornig or zornerfüllt (liter) sein; **to provoke sb's** ~ jdn reizen; **to rouse sb to** ~ (liter) jdn in Wut or Rage bringen; **to make one's** ~ **felt** seinem Ärger or Unmut Luft machen; **in great** ~ in großem Zorn.
2 vt (stressing action) ärgern; (stressing result) verärgern; gods erzürnen (liter). **what** ~**s me is ...** was mich ärgert, ist ...; **to be easily** ~**ed** sich schnell or leicht ärgern; (quick to take offence) schnell verärgert sein.

angina [æn'dʒaɪnə] n Angina, Halsentzündung f. ~ **pectoris** Angina pectoris f.

angle¹ ['æŋgl] **1** n (a) Winkel m. **at an** ~ **of 40°** in einem Winkel von 40°; **at an** ~ schräg; **at an** ~ **to the street** schräg or im Winkel zur Straße; **he was wearing his hat at an** ~ er hatte seinen Hut schief aufgesetzt; ~ **of climb** (Aviat) Steigwinkel m; ~ **of elevation** (Math) Steigungswinkel m; ~ **of incidence** (Opt) Einfallswinkel m.
(b) (projecting corner) Ecke f; (angular recess) Winkel m. **the building/her figure was all** ~**s** das Gebäude bestand bloß aus Ecken/sie hatte eine sehr eckige Figur.
(c) (position) Winkel m. **if you take the photograph from this** ~ wenn du die Aufnahme aus or von diesem (Blick)winkel machst.
(d) (on problem etc: aspect) Seite f.
(e) (point of view) Standpunkt m, Position f; (when used with adj also) Warte f. **a journalist** usually has an ~ **on a story** ein Journalist schreibt seine Berichte gewöhnlich von einer gewissen Warte aus; **an inside** ~ **on the story** die Geschichte vom Standpunkt eines Insiders or eines Direktbeteiligten.
2 vt lamp etc (aus)richten, einstellen; (Sport) shot im Winkel schießen/schlagen; (fig) information, report färben. **the question was** ~**d at getting one particular answer** es war eine Suggestivfrage.

angle² vi (Fishing) angeln.
♦**angle for** vi +prep obj (a) (lit) trout angeln. (b) (fig) compliments fischen nach. **to** ~ ~ **sth** auf etw (acc) aus sein; **to** ~ ~ **sb's attention** jds Aufmerksamkeit auf sich (acc) zu lenken versuchen.

angle: ~ **bracket** n Winkelband nt, Winkelkonsole f; ~ **iron** n Winkeleisen nt; ~ **parking** n Schrägparken nt.

angler ['æŋglə'] n Angler(in f) m.

Angles ['æŋglz] npl (Hist) Angeln pl.

Anglican ['æŋglɪkən] **1** n Anglikaner(in f) m. **2** adj anglikanisch.

Anglicanism ['æŋglɪkənɪzəm] n Anglikanismus m.

anglicism ['æŋglɪsɪzəm] n Anglizismus m.

anglicist ['æŋglɪsɪst] n Anglist(in f) m.

anglicize ['æŋglɪsaɪz] vt anglisieren.

angling ['æŋglɪŋ] n Angeln nt.

Anglo- ['æŋgləʊ] pref Anglo-; (between two countries) Englisch-; ~**-German** adj deutsch-englisch; ~**-Catholic 1** n Anglo-katholik(in f) m; **2** adj hochkirchlich, anglokatholisch; ~**-Indian 1** n (of British origin) in Indien lebende(r) Engländer(in

f) m; (Eurasian) Anglo-Inder(in *f) m;* 2 *adj* anglo-indisch; *relations* englisch-indisch.

anglomania [,æŋgləʊ'meɪnɪə] *n* Anglomanie *f*.

anglophile ['æŋgləʊfaɪl] 1 *n* Anglophile(r) *mf (form)*, Englandfreund *m*. 2 *adj* anglophil *(form)*, englandfreundlich.

anglophobe ['æŋgləʊfəʊb] *n* Anglophobe(r) *mf (form)*, Englandhasser, Englandfeind *m*.

anglophobia [,æŋgləʊ'fəʊbɪə] *n* Anglophobie *f (form)*, Englandhaß *m*.

anglophobic [,æŋgləʊ'fəʊbɪk] *adj* anglophob *(form)*, antienglisch, englandfeindlich.

Anglo-Saxon ['æŋgləʊ'sæksən] 1 *n* **(a)** *(person, Hist)* Angelsachse *m*, Angelsächsin *f*. **(b)** *(language)* Angelsächsisch *nt*. 2 *adj* angelsächsisch.

Angola [æŋ'gəʊlə] *n* Angola *nt*.

Angolan [æŋ'gəʊlən] 1 *n* Angolaner(in *f) m*. 2 *adj* angolanisch.

angora [æŋ'gɔːrə] 1 *adj* Angora-. 2 *n* Angora(wolle *f) nt; (Tex)* Angoragewebe *nt; (~ rabbit, ~ cat, ~ goat)* Angora *nt*.

angostura [,æŋgə'stjʊərə] *n (bark)* Angosturarinde *f; (also ® ~ bitters)* Angosturabitter *m*.

angrily ['æŋgrɪlɪ] *adv* wütend.

angry ['æŋgrɪ] *adj (+er)* **(a)** zornig, ungehalten *(geh); letter, look also, animal* wütend. **to be ~** wütend *or* böse *or* verärgert sein; **to be ~ with** *or* **at sb** jdm *or* auf jdn *or* mit jdm böse sein, über jdn verärgert sein; **to be ~ at** *or* **about sth über** etw *(acc)* böse *or* ungehalten *or* verärgert sein; **to get ~ (with** *or* **at sb/about sth)** (mit jdm/über etw *acc)* böse werden; **you're not ~, are you?** du bist (mir) doch nicht böse(, oder)?; **to be ~ with oneself** sich über sich *(acc)* selbst ärgern, sich *(dat)* selbst böse sein, über sich *(acc)* selbst verärgert sein; **to make sb ~** *(stressing action)* jdn ärgern; *(stressing result)* jdn verärgern; **it makes me so ~** es ärgert mich furchtbar, es macht mich so wütend *or* böse; **~ young man** Rebell, Angry young man *m (geh)*.
(b) *(fig) sea* aufgewühlt; *sky, clouds* bedrohlich, finster. **the sky was an ~ purple** der Himmel war bedrohlich violett. **(c)** *(inflamed) wound* entzündet, böse. **an ~ red** hochrot.

Angst [æŋst] *n* (Existenz)angst *f*.

anguish ['æŋgwɪʃ] *n* Qual, Pein *(old) f*. **to be in ~** Qualen leiden; **the look of ~ on the faces of the waiting wives** der angsterfüllte Blick in den Gesichtern der wartenden Frauen; **he wrung his hands in ~** er rang die Hände in Verzweiflung; **those who suffer the ~ of indecision** wer die Qual der Entschlußlosigkeit erleidet; **you can imagine her ~** du kannst dir die Qualen vorstellen, die sie ausgestanden hat; **writhing in ~ on the ground** sich in Qualen auf dem Boden windend; **her children/the news/the decision caused her great ~** ihre Kinder bereiteten ihr großen Kummer *or* großes Leid/die Nachricht bereitete ihr großen Schmerz/die Entscheidung bereitete ihr große Qual(en).

anguished ['æŋgwɪʃt] *adj* qualvoll.

angular ['æŋgjʊlə'] *adj* **(a)** *shape* eckig; *face, features, prose* kantig. **(b)** *(bony)* knochig. **(c)** *(awkward)* linkisch, steif.

angularity [,æŋgjʊ'lærɪtɪ] *n see adj* **(a)** Eckigkeit *f*; Kantigkeit *f*. **(b)** Knochigkeit *f*.

aniline ['ænɪliːn] *n* Anilin *nt*. **~ dye** Anilinfarbstoff *m*.

animadversion [,ænɪmæd'vɜːʃən] *n (form)* kritische Äußerung.

animal ['ænɪməl] 1 *n* Tier *nt; (as opposed to insects etc)* Vierbeiner *m; (brutal person also)* Bestie *f*. **man is a social ~** der Mensch ist ein soziales Wesen; **a political ~** ein politisches Wesen, ein Zoon politikon *(geh) nt*; **there's no such ~** *(fig)* so was gibt es nicht! *(inf);* **what sort of ~ is that?** *(fig)* was soll denn das sein?; **the ~ in him** das Tier(ische) *or* Animalische in ihm; **he's nothing but a little ~** er ist nicht besser als ein Tier. 2 *adj attr story, picture* Tier-; *products, cruelty, lust* tierisch. **~ behaviour** *(lit)* das Verhalten der Tiere, tierhaftes Verhalten; *(fig: brutal)* tierisches Verhalten; **~ desire** animalischer Trieb; **~ kingdom** Tierreich *nt*, Tierwelt *f;* **~ lover** Tierfreund *m;* **~ magnetism** rein körperliche Anziehungskraft; **~ needs** *(fig)* animalische Bedürfnisse *pl;* **~ spirits** Vitalität *f*.

animalcule [,ænɪ'mælkjuːl] *n* mikroskopisch kleines Tierchen.

animal husbandry *n* Viehwirtschaft *f*.

animality [,ænɪ'mælɪtɪ] *n* Tierhaftigkeit *f*. **the ~ of their actions/habits** das Tierische ihrer Handlungen/Gewohnheiten.

animate ['ænɪmɪt] 1 *adj* belebt; *creation, creatures* lebend. 2 ['ænɪmeɪt] *vt (lit: God)* mit Leben erfüllen; *(fig) (enliven)* beleben; *(move to action)* anregen, animieren; *(Film)* animieren. **Disney was the first to ~ cartoons** Disney machte als erster Zeichentrickfilme.

animated ['ænɪmeɪtɪd] *adj* **(a)** *(lively)* lebhaft, rege; *discussion, talk also* angeregt. **(b)** *(Film)* **~ cartoon** Zeichentrickfilm *m*.

animatedly ['ænɪmeɪtɪdlɪ] *adv* rege; *talk also* angeregt.

animation [,ænɪ'meɪʃən] *n* Lebhaftigkeit *f; (Film)* Animation *f*. **she loved the ~ of** Parisian life sie liebte das Getriebe des Pariser Lebens.

animator ['ænɪmeɪtə'] *n* Animator(in *f) m*.

animism ['ænɪmɪzəm] *n* Animismus *m*.

animosity [,ænɪ'mɒsɪtɪ] *n* Animosität *(geh)*, Feindseligkeit *f (towards)* gegenüber, gegen, *(between)* zwischen *+ dat)*.

animus ['ænɪməs] *n, no pl* Feindseligkeit *f*.

anise ['ænɪs] *n* Anis *m*.

aniseed ['ænɪsiːd] *n (seed)* Anis(samen) *m; (flavouring)* Anis *m; (liqueur)* Anislikör *m*. **~ ball** Anisbonbon *m or nt*.

ankle ['æŋkl] *n* Knöchel *m*.

ankle: **~bone** *n* Sprungbein *nt;* **~-deep** 1 *adj* knöcheltief; 2 *adv* **he was ~-deep in water** er stand bis an die Knöchel im Wasser; **the field was ~-deep in mud** auf dem Feld stand der Schlamm knöcheltief; **~ sock** *n* Söckchen *nt;* **~ strap** *n* Schuhriemchen *nt*.

anklet ['æŋklɪt] *n* **(a)** Fußring *m*, Fußspange *f*. **(b)** *(US: sock)* Söckchen *nt*.

annalist ['ænəlɪst] *n* Chronist, Geschichtsschreiber *m*.

annals ['ænəlz] *npl* Annalen *pl; (of society etc)* Bericht *m*. **in all the ~ of recorded history** in der gesamten bisherigen Geschichte.

anneal [ə'niːl] *vt glass* kühlen; *metal* ausglühen; *earthenware* brennen; *(fig)* stählen.

annex [ə'neks] 1 *vt* annektieren. 2 ['æneks] *n* **(a)** *(to document etc)* Anhang, Nachtrag *m*. **(b)** *(building)* Nebengebäude *nt*, Annex *m; (extension)* Anbau *m*.

annexation [,ænek'seɪʃən] *n* Annexion *f*.

annexe ['æneks] *n see* **annex** 2 **(b)**.

annihilate [ə'naɪəleɪt] *vt* vernichten; *army also* aufreiben, auslöschen *(geh); (fig) hope* zerschlagen; *theory* vernichten, zerschlagen; *(inf) person, team* fertigmachen *(inf)*. **I felt completely ~d when he pointed out how wrong I was** ich war völlig am Boden zerstört *(inf)*, als er mir klarmachte, wie sehr ich im Unrecht war.

annihilation [ə,naɪə'leɪʃən] *n* Vernichtung, Auslöschung *(geh) f; (fig: of theory)* Vernichtung, Zerschlagung *f*. **our team's ~ die vollständige Niederlage unserer Mannschaft; her ~ of her opponents** die Art, wie sie *or* in der sie ihre Gegner fertigmachte *(inf)*.

anniversary [,ænɪ'vɜːsərɪ] *n* Jahrestag *m; (wedding ~)* Hochzeitstag *m*. **~ celebrations** Feiern *pl* anläßlich eines Jahrestages/Hochzeitstages; **~ dinner/gift** (Fest)essen *nt*/Geschenk *nt* zum Jahrestag/Hochzeitstag; **the ~ of his death** sein Todestag *m*.

anno Domini ['ænəʊ'dɒmɪnaɪ] *n* **(a)** *(abbr AD)* anno *or* Anno Domini. **in 53 ~** Anno Domini 53. **(b)** *(inf: age)* Alter *nt*.

annotate ['ænəʊteɪt] *vt* mit Anmerkungen versehen, kommentieren. **~d text** kommentierter Text.

annotation [,ænəʊ'teɪʃən] *n (no pl: commentary, act)* Kommentar *m; (comment)* Anmerkung *f*.

announce [ə'naʊns] *vt (lit, fig: person)* bekanntgeben, verkünden; *arrival, departure, radio programme* ansagen; *(over intercom)* durchsagen; *(signal)* anzeigen; *(formally) birth, marriage etc* anzeigen; *coming of spring etc* ankündigen. **to ~ sb** jdn melden; **the arrival of flight BA 742 has just been ~d** soeben ist die Ankunft des Fluges BA 742 gemeldet worden.

announcement [ə'naʊnsmənt] *n (public declaration)* Bekanntgabe, Bekanntmachung *f; (of impending event, speaker)* Ankündigung *f; (over intercom etc)* Durchsage *f; (giving information: on radio etc)* Ansage *f; (written: of birth, marriage etc)* Anzeige *f*. **after they had made the ~** nach der Bekanntgabe *etc*.

announcer [ə'naʊnsə'] *n (Rad, TV)* Ansager(in *f)*, Radio-/Fernsehsprecher(in *f) m*.

annoy [ə'nɔɪ] *vt (make angry, irritate)* ärgern; *(get worked up: noise, questions etc)* aufregen; *(pester)* belästigen. **to be ~ed that ...** ärgerlich *or* verärgert sein, weil ...; **to be ~ed with sb/about sth** sich über jdn/etw ärgern, (mit) jdm/über etw *(acc)* böse sein; **to get ~ed** sich ärgern, sich aufregen, böse werden; **don't get ~ed** reg dich nicht auf, nur keine Aufregung; **it's nothing to get ~ed about** deswegen braucht man sich nicht aufzuregen; **don't let it ~ you** ärgere dich nicht darüber.

annoyance [ə'nɔɪəns] *n* **(a)** *no pl (irritation)* Ärger, Verdruß *(geh) m*. **to cause (great) ~** (großes) Ärgernis erregen; **smoking can cause ~ to others** Rauchen kann eine Belästigung für andere sein; **to his ~** zu seinem Ärger *or* Verdruß. **(b)** *(nuisance)* Plage, Belästigung *f*, Ärgernis *nt*.

annoying [ə'nɔɪɪŋ] *adj* ärgerlich; *habit* lästig. **the ~ thing (about it) is that ...** das Ärgerliche (daran *or* bei der Sache) ist, daß ...; **it's so ~!** das kann einen ärgern, das ist derart ärgerlich; **he has an ~ way of speaking slowly** er hat eine Art, langsam zu sprechen, die einen ärgern *or* aufregen kann.

annoyingly [ə'nɔɪɪŋlɪ] *adv* aufreizend. **the bus didn't turn up, rather ~** ärgerlicherweise kam der Bus nicht.

annual ['ænjʊəl] 1 *n* **(a)** *(Bot)* einjährige Pflanze. **(b)** *(book)* Jahresalbum *nt*. 2 *adj (happening once a year)* jährlich; *(of or for the year) salary etc* Jahres-. **~ ring** Jahresring *m*.

annually ['ænjʊəlɪ] *adv* jährlich. **once ~** einmal im Jahr, einmal jährlich.

annuity [ə'njuːɪtɪ] *n (Leib)*rente *f*. **to invest money in an ~** Geld in einer Rentenversicherung anlegen; **to buy an ~** eine Rentenversicherung abschließen.

annul [ə'nʌl] *vt* annullieren; *law, decree, judgement also* aufheben; *contract, marriage also* auflösen, für ungültig erklären; *will also* für ungültig erklären.

annulment [ə'nʌlmənt] *n see vt* Annullierung *f;* Aufhebung *f;* Auflösung *f;* Ungültigkeitserklärung *f*.

Annunciation [ə,nʌnsɪ'eɪʃən] *n (Bibl)* Mariä Verkündigung *f*. **the feast of the ~** das Fest Maria *or* Mariä Verkündigung.

anode ['ænəʊd] *n* Anode *f*.

anodize ['ænədaɪz] *vt* anodisch behandeln, anodisieren.

anodyne ['ænədaɪn] 1 *n (Med)* schmerzstillendes Mittel, Schmerzmittel *nt; (fig)* Wohltat *f*. 2 *adj (Med)* schmerzstillend; *(fig)* wohltuend, beruhigend.

anoint [ə'nɔɪnt] *vt* salben. **to ~ sb king** jdn zum König salben.

anomalous [ə'nɒmələs] *adj* anomal, regelwidrig, ungewöhnlich; *(Gram)* verb unregelmäßig.

anomaly [ə'nɒməlɪ] *n* Anomalie *f; (in law etc)* Besonderheit *f*.

anon[1] [ə'nɒn] *adv (old)* alsbald *(dial, old)*, bald. **ever and ~** *(old)* dann und wann; **see you ~** *(hum)* bis demnächst.

anon[2] [ə'nɒn] *adj abbr of* **anonymous** *(at end of text)* "A~" Anonymus *(liter)*, Verfasser unbekannt.

anonymity [,ænə'nɪmɪtɪ] *n* Anonymität *f*.

anonymous *adj,* **~ly** *adv* [ə'nɒnɪməs, -lɪ] anonym.

anorak ['ænəræk] *n* Anorak *m*.

anorexia (nervosa) [ænə'reksɪə(nɜ:'vəʊsə)] n Appetitlosigkeit, Magersucht, Anorexie (spec) f.

another [ə'nʌðə^r] 1 adj (a) (additional) noch eine(r, s). ~ one noch eine(r, s); take ~ ten nehmen Sie noch (weitere) zehn; I won't give you ~ chance ich werde dir nicht noch eine or keine weitere Chance geben; I don't want ~ drink! ich möchte nichts mehr trinken; in ~ 20 years he ... noch 20 Jahre, und er ...; without ~ word ohne ein weiteres Wort; and (there's) ~ thing und noch eins, und (da ist) noch (et)was (anderes).

(b) (similar, fig: second) ein zweiter, eine zweite, ein zweites. there is not ~ such man so einen Mann gibt es nicht noch einmal or gibt es nur einmal; ~ Shakespeare ein zweiter Shakespeare; there will never be ~ you für mich wird es nie jemand geben wie dich or du.

(c) (different) ein anderer, eine andere, ein anderes. that's quite ~ matter das ist etwas ganz anderes; ~ time ein andermal; but maybe there won't be ~ time aber vielleicht gibt es keine andere Gelegenheit or gibt es das nicht noch einmal.

2 pron ein anderer, eine andere, ein anderes. have ~! nehmen Sie (doch) noch einen!; he has found ~ (dated, liter) er hat eine andere gefunden; many ~ manch anderer; such ~ noch so einer; taking one with ~ alles zusammengenommen, im großen (und) ganzen; tell me ~! (inf) Sie können mir sonst was erzählen (inf), das können Sie mir nicht weismachen; what with one thing and ~ bei all dem Trubel; is this ~ of your brilliant ideas! ist das wieder so eine deiner Glanzideen!; she's ~ of his girlfriends sie ist (auch) eine seiner Freundinnen; yes, I'm ~ of his fans ja, ich bin auch einer seiner Fans.

answer ['ɑːnsə^r] 1 n (a) (to auf +acc) Antwort, Entgegnung (geh), Erwiderung (geh) f; (in exam) Antwort f. to give no ~ Antwort/keine Antwort bekommen; there was no ~ (to telephone, doorbell) es hat sich niemand gemeldet; the ~ to our prayers ein Geschenk des Himmels; the ~ to a maiden's prayer (hum) ein Traummann m (inf), der ideale Mann; there's no ~ to that (inf) was soll man da groß machen/sagen! (inf); Germany's ~ to Concorde Deutschlands Antwort auf die Concorde; they had no ~ to this new striker (Ftbl) sie hatten dem neuen Stürmer nichts or niemanden entgegenzusetzen; in ~ to your letter/my question in Beantwortung Ihres Briefes (form)/auf meine Frage hin; I could find no ~ ich wußte keine Antwort darauf; she's always got an ~ sie hat immer eine Antwort parat.

(b) (solution) Lösung f (to gen). his ~ to any difficulty is to ignore it seine Reaktion auf jedwede Schwierigkeit ist: einfach nicht wahrhaben wollen; there's no easy ~ es gibt dafür keine Patentlösung; there's only one ~ for depression ... es gibt nur ein Mittel gegen Depression ...; this one ~ for all ailments is ... sein Allheilmittel für alle or bei allen Beschwerden ist ...

(c) (Jur) Einlassung (form), Stellungnahme f. the defendant's ~ to the charge was ... laut Einlassung des Beklagten ...(form); what is your ~ to the charge? was haben Sie dazu zu sagen?

2 vt (a) answorten auf (+acc), erwidern auf (+acc) (geh); person answorten (+dat); exam questions beantworten, antworten auf (+acc); objections, criticism also beantworten. will you ~ that? (phone, door) gehst du ran/hin?; to ~ the telephone/bell or door das Telefon abnehmen, rangehen (inf)/die Tür öffnen or aufmachen, hingehen (inf); who ~ed the phone? wer war dran (inf) or am Apparat?; shall I ~ it? (phone) soll ich rangehen?; (door) soll ich hingehen?; to ~ the call of nature (also hum)/of duty dem Ruf der Natur/der Pflicht folgen; 5,000 men ~ed the call for volunteers 5.000 Männer meldeten sich auf den Freiwilligenaufruf hin; the fire brigade ~ed the alarm call die Feuerwehr rückte auf den Alarm hin aus; ..., he ~ed ..., antwortete er; ~ me this sagen or beanworten Sie mir eins; ~ me! answorte (mir)!, antworten Sie! I didn't ~ a word ich habe nichts or kein Wort erwidert; to anyone who claims ... I would ~ this jemandem, der ... behauptet, würde ich folgendes erwidern or entgegen.

(b) (fulfil) description entsprechen (+dat); hope, expectation also erfüllen; prayer (God) erhören; need befriedigen. people who ~ that description Leute, auf die diese Beschreibung paßt or zutrifft; this ~ed our prayers das war (wie) ein Geschenk des Himmels; it ~s the/our purpose es erfüllt seinen Zweck/es erfüllt für uns seinen Zweck.

(c) (Jur) charge sich verantworten wegen (+gen).

3 vi (a) (also react) antworten. if the phone rings, don't ~ wenn das Telefon läutet, geh nicht ran or nimm nicht ab.

(b) (suffice) geeignet or brauchbar sein, taugen.

♦**answer back** 1 vi widersprechen; (children also) patzige or freche Antworten geben. don't ~ ~! keine Widerrede!; it's not fair to criticize him because he can't ~ ~ es ist unfair, ihn zu kritisieren, weil er sich nicht verteidigen kann.

2 vt sep to ~ sb ~ jdm widersprechen; (children also) jdm patzige or freche Antworten geben.

♦**answer for** vi +prep obj (a) (be responsible for) verantwortlich sein für; (person also) verantworten; mistakes also einstehen für. he has a lot to ~ ~ er hat eine Menge auf dem Gewissen; I won't ~ ~ the consequences ich will für die Folgen nicht verantwortlich gemacht werden.

(b) (guarantee) sich verbürgen für; (speak for also) sprechen für. to ~ ~ the truth of sth für die Wahrheit von etw einstehen.

♦**answer to** vi +prep obj (a) (be accountable to) to ~ ~ sb for sth jdm für etw or wegen einer Sache (gen) Rechenschaft schuldig sein; if anything goes wrong you'll have me to ~ ~ wenn etwas nicht klappt, dann stehen Sie mir dafür ein or gerade or dann müssen Sie sich vor mir dafür verantworten.

(b) to ~ ~ a description einer Beschreibung entsprechen.

(c) to ~ ~ the name of ... auf den Namen ... hören.

(d) to ~ ~ the wheel/helm/controls auf das Steuer/das Ruder/die Steuerung ansprechen.

answerable ['ɑːnsərəbl] adj (a) question beantwortbar, zu beantworten pred; charge, argument widerlegbar.

(b) (responsible) verantwortlich. to be ~ to sb (for sth) jdm gegenüber für etw verantwortlich sein; to be held ~ verantwortlich gemacht werden; parents are ~ for their children's behaviour Eltern haften für ihre Kinder.

answerer ['ɑːnsərə^r] n Antwortende(r) mf.

answering service ['ɑːnsərɪŋ'sɜːvɪs] n (automatischer) Anrufbeantworter.

answer paper n (in exam) Lösung f, Antwortbogen m.

ant [ænt] n Ameise f. to have ~s in one's pants (inf) Pfeffer or Hummeln im Hintern haben (sl), kein Sitzfleisch haben.

antacid ['ænt'æsɪd] n säurebindendes Mittel.

antagonism [æn'tægənɪzəm] n (between people, theories etc) Antagonismus m; (towards sb, ideas, a suggestion, change etc) Feindseligkeit, Feindlichkeit f (to(wards) gegenüber). to arouse sb's ~ jdn gegen sich aufbringen.

antagonist [æn'tægənɪst] n Kontrahent, Gegner, Antagonist m; (esp Pol) Gegenspieler m.

antagonistic [æn,tægə'nɪstɪk] adj reaction, attitude feindselig; force gegnerisch, feindlich; interests widerstreitend, antagonistisch. to be ~ to or towards sb/sth jdm/gegen etw feindselig gesinnt sein.

antagonize [æn'tægənaɪz] vt person gegen sich aufbringen or stimmen; (annoy) verärgern.

antarctic [ænt'ɑːktɪk] 1 adj antarktisch, der Antarktis. A~ Circle südlicher Polarkreis; A~ Ocean Südpolarmeer nt. 2 n: the A~ die Antarktis.

Antarctica [ænt'ɑːktɪkə] n die Antarktis.

ante ['æntɪ] 1 n (Cards) Einsatz m. to up the ~ (fig inf) den Einsatz erhöhen. 2 vt (also ~ up) einsetzen. 3 vi setzen, seinen Einsatz machen. his father ~d up as usual (fig inf) sein Vater blechte wie gewöhnlich (inf).

ante- pref vor-.

anteater ['ænt,iːtə^r] n Ameisenbär, Ameisenfresser m.

antecedent [,æntɪ'siːdənt] 1 adj früher. the crisis and its ~ events die Krise und die ihr vorangehenden or vorausgehenden Ereignisse; to be ~ to sth einer Sache (dat) voran- or vorausgehen.

2 n (a) ~s (of person) (past history) Vorleben nt; (ancestry) Abstammung f; (of event) Vorgeschichte f.

(b) (Gram) Bezugswort nt.

ante-: ~chamber n Vorzimmer nt; ~date vt document, cheque vordatieren (to auf +acc); event vorausgehen (+dat) (by um); ~diluvian adj (lit, fig inf) vorsintflutlich.

antelope ['æntɪləʊp] n Antilope f.

ante meridiem [,æntɪmə'rɪdɪəm] adv (abbr am) vormittags.

antenatal ['æntɪ'neɪtl] adj vor der Geburt, pränatal (form). ~ care/exercises Schwangerschaftsfürsorge f/-übungen pl; ~ clinic Sprechstunde f/Station f für Schwangere or für werdende Mütter.

antenna [æn'tenə] n (a) pl -e [æn'teniː] (Zool) Fühler m. (b) pl -e or -s (Rad, TV) Antenne f.

antepenultimate ['æntɪpɪ'nʌltɪmɪt] adj drittletzte(r, s), vorvorletzte(r, s).

anterior [æn'tɪərɪə^r] adj (a) (prior) früher (to als). to be ~ to vorangehen (+dat), vorausgehen (+dat). (b) (Anat etc) vordere(r, s). ~ brain Vorderhirn nt.

anteroom ['æntɪruːm] n Vorzimmer nt.

anthem ['ænθəm] n Hymne f; (by choir) Chorgesang m.

anther ['ænθə^r] n (Bot) Staubbeutel m, Anthere f (spec).

anthill ['ænt,hɪl] n Ameisenhaufen m.

anthology [æn'θɒlədʒɪ] n Anthologie f.

anthracite ['ænθrəsaɪt] n Anthrazit m.

anthrax ['ænθræks] n (Med, Vet) Anthrax (form), Milzbrand m.

anthropocentric [,ænθrəpəʊ'sentrɪk] adj anthropozentrisch.

anthropoid ['ænθrəʊpɔɪd] 1 n Anthropoid m (spec); (ape) Menschenaffe m. 2 adj anthropoid (spec). ~ ape Menschenaffe m.

anthropological [,ænθrəpə'lɒdʒɪkəl] adj anthropologisch.

anthropologist [,ænθrə'pɒlədʒɪst] n Anthropologe m, Anthropologin f.

anthropology [,ænθrə'pɒlədʒɪ] n Anthropologie f.

anthropomorphic [,ænθrəʊpə'mɔːfɪk] adj anthropomorphisch.

anthropomorphism [,ænθrəʊpə'mɔːfɪzəm] n Anthropomorphismus m.

anti ['æntɪ] (inf) 1 adj pred in Opposition (inf). are you in favour? — no, I'm ~ bist du dafür? — nein, ich bin dagegen. 2 prep gegen (+acc). ~ everything grundsätzlich gegen alles.

anti- in cpds anti-, gegen-; ~aircraft adj gun, rocket Flugabwehr-; ~aircraft defence Luftverteidigung f; ~aircraft gun/fire Flak(geschütz nt) f/Flakfeuer nt; ~ballistic adj: ~ballistic missile Anti-Raketen-Rakete f; ~biotic 1 n Antibiotikum nt; 2 adj antibiotisch; ~body n Antikörper m.

antic ['æntɪk] n see antics.

Antichrist ['æntɪkraɪst] n Antichrist m.

anticipate [æn'tɪsɪpeɪt] 1 vt (a) (expect) erwarten. as ~d wie vorausgesehen or erwartet.

(b) (see in advance) vorausberechnen, vorhersehen; (see in advance and cater for) objection, need etc zuvorkommen (+dat). he always has to ~ what his opponent will do next er muß immer vorhersehen können or vorausahnen, was sein Gegner als nächstes tun wird; don't ~ what I'm going to say nimm nicht vorweg, was ich noch sagen wollte.

(c) (do before sb else) zuvorkommen (+dat). in his discovery he was ~d by others bei seiner Entdeckung sind ihm andere zuvorgekommen; a phrase which ~s a later theme eine Melodie, die auf ein späteres Thema vor(aus)greift.

(d) (do, use, act on prematurely) income im voraus ausgeben; inheritance im voraus in Anspruch nehmen.

2 vi (manager, driver, chess-player etc) vorauskalkulieren.
anticipation [æn,tɪsɪ'peɪʃən] n (a) (expectation) Erwartung f. thanking you in ~ herzlichen Dank im voraus; to wait in ~ gespannt warten; we took our umbrellas in ~ of rain wir nahmen unsere Schirme mit, weil wir mit Regen rechneten.
(b) (seeing in advance) Vorausberechnung f. impressed by the hotel's ~ of our wishes beeindruckt, wie man im Hotel unseren Wünschen zuvorkommt/zuvorkam; his uncanny ~ of every objection die verblüffende Art, in der or wie er jedem Einwand zuvorkam; the driver showed good ~ der Fahrer zeigte or bewies, daß er gut vorauskalkuliert hatte.
(c) (of discovery, discoverer) Vorwegnahme f. this phrase is an ~ of a later theme diese Melodie ist im Vorgriff auf ein späteres Thema.
anticipatory [æn'tɪsɪ,peɪtərɪ] adj vorwegnehmend.
anti: ~clerical adj antiklerikal, kirchenfeindlich; ~climactic adj enttäuschend; ~climax n Enttäuschung f; (no pl: Liter) Antiklimax f; ~clockwise 1 adj movement, direction Links-; 2 adv nach links, gegen den Uhrzeigersinn or die Uhrzeigerrichtung; ~coagulant 1 n Antikoagulans nt (spec); 2 adj antikoagulierend (spec), blutgerinnungshemmend; ~corrosive adj paint Korrosionsschutz-.
antics ['æntɪks] npl Eskapaden pl; (tricks) Possen, lustige Streiche pl; (irritating behaviour) Mätzchen pl (inf).
anti: ~cyclone n Antizyklone f, Hoch(druckgebiet) nt; ~dazzle adj blendfrei; ~depressant 1 n Antidepressivum nt; 2 adj antidepressiv; ~dote n (Med, fig) Gegenmittel, Antidot (form) nt (against, to, for gegen); ~freeze n Frostschutz m.
antigen ['æntɪdʒən] n Antigen nt.
anti: ~hero n Antiheld m; ~histamine n Antihistamin(ikum) nt; ~knock 1 adj Antiklopf-; 2 n Antiklopfmittel nt; ~log(arithm) n Antilogarithmus, Numerus m; ~macassar n (Sessel-/Sofa)schoner m; ~malarial 1 adj gegen Malaria; 2 n Malariamittel nt; ~matter n Antimaterie f; ~missile adj Raketenabwehr-.
antimony ['æntɪmənɪ] n Antimon nt.
antipasto [,æntɪ'pæstəʊ] n italienische Vorspeise.
antipathetic [,æntɪpə'θetɪk] adj to be ~ to sb/sth eine Antipathie or Abneigung gegen jdn/etw haben; sb/sth is ~ to sb (arouses antipathy in) jd/etw ist jdm unsympathisch.
antipathy [æn'tɪpəθɪ] n Antipathie, Abneigung f (towards gegen, between zwischen +dat).
anti: ~-personnel adj gegen Menschen gerichtet; ~-personnel bomb/mine Splitterbombe f/Schützenmine f; ~perspirant n Antitranspirant nt.
antiphony [æn'tɪfənɪ] n (Eccl, Mus) Antiphon f.
antipodean [æn,tɪpə'diːən], (US) **antipodal** [æn'tɪpədəl] adj antipodisch, (Brit) australisch und neuseeländisch.
antipodes [æn'tɪpədiːz] npl (diametral) entgegengesetzte Teile der Erde. A~ (Brit) Australien und Neuseeland; (Geog) Antipoden-Inseln pl.
antipope ['æntɪpəʊp] n Gegenpapst m.
antiquarian [,æntɪ'kweərɪən] 1 adj books antiquarisch; coins also alt; studies des Altertums, der Antike. ~ bookshop Antiquariat nt; he has ~ interests.er interessiert sich für Antiquitäten. 2 n see antiquary.
antiquary ['æntɪkwərɪ] n (collector) Antiquitätensammler(in f) m; (seller) Antiquitätenhändler(in f) m.
antiquated ['æntɪkweɪtɪd] adj antiquiert; machines, ideas also überholt; institutions also veraltet.
antique [æn'tiːk] 1 adj antik. 2 n Antiquität f.
antique: ~ dealer n Antiquitätenhändler(in f) m; ~ shop n Antiquitätengeschäft nt or -laden m.
antiquity [æn'tɪkwɪtɪ] n (a) (ancient times) das Altertum, (Roman, Greek ~) die Antike. (b) (great age) großes Alter. (c) antiquities pl (old things) Altertümer pl.
antirrhinum [,æntɪ'raɪnəm] n Löwenmaul nt.
anti: ~-rust adj Rostschutz-; ~scorbutic adj antiskorbutisch; ~-Semite n Antisemit(in f) m; ~-Semitic adj antisemitisch; ~-Semitism n Antisemitismus m; ~septic 1 n Antiseptikum nt; 2 adj (lit, fig) antiseptisch; ~-skid adj rutschsicher; ~slavery adj attr Antisklaverei-; speech gegen die Sklaverei; politician, groups Abolitions-; ~social adj unsozial; (Psych, Sociol) asozial; to be in an ~social mood nicht in Gesellschaftslaune sein; ~static adj antistatisch; ~tank adj gun, fire Panzerabwehr-; ~tank ditch/obstacle Panzersperre f.
antithesis [æn'tɪθɪsɪs] n, pl **antitheses** [æn'tɪθɪsiːz] (direct opposite) genaues Gegenteil (to, of gen); (of idea, in rhetoric) Antithese f (to, of zu) (form); (contrast) Gegensatz m (between zwischen +dat).
antithetic(al) [,æntɪ'θetɪk(əl)] adj (contrasting) gegensätzlich; ideas also, phrases antithetisch (form); idea entgegengesetzt.
anti: ~toxin n Gegengift, Antitoxin nt; ~trade (wind) n Antipassat(wind) m; ~trust adj (US) Antitrust-; ~vivisectionism n Ablehnung f der Vivisektion; ~vivisectionist 1 n Gegner(in f) m der Vivisektion; 2 adj his ~vivisectionist views seine ablehnende Haltung der Vivisektion gegenüber.
antler ['æntlə'] n Geweihstange f. (set or pair of) ~s Geweih nt.
antonym ['æntənɪm] n Antonym, Gegenwort (geh) nt.
Antwerp ['æntwɜːp] n Antwerpen nt.
anus ['eɪnəs] n After, Anus (spec) m.
anvil ['ænvɪl] n Amboß m (also Anat).
anxiety [æŋg'zaɪətɪ] n (a) Sorge f. to feel ~ sich (dat) Sorgen machen (about um, at wegen); no cause for ~ kein Grund zur Sorge or Besorgnis; it's a great ~ to her es ist ihr eine große Sorge; to cause sb ~ jdm Sorgen machen; ~ neurosis (Psych) Angstneurose f.
(b) (keen desire) Verlangen nt.
anxious ['æŋkʃəs] adj (a) (worried) besorgt; person (as character trait), thoughts ängstlich. to be ~ about sb/sth sich

(dat) um jdn/etw Sorgen machen, um jdn/etw besorgt sein.
(b) (worrying) moment, minutes der Angst, bang (geh). it's been an ~ time for us all es war für uns alle eine Zeit banger Sorge; he had an ~ time waiting for ... es war für ihn eine Zeit voll bangen Wartens auf (+acc) ...
(c) (strongly desirous) to be ~ for sth auf etw (acc) aussein; we are ~ for all the assistance we can get uns geht es darum, jede nur mögliche Hilfe zu bekommen; to be ~ to do sth bestrebt sein or darauf aussein, etw zu tun; they were ~ to start/for his return sie warteten sehr darauf abzufahren/auf seine Rückkehr; I am ~ that he should do it or for him to do it mir liegt viel daran, daß er es tut.
anxiously ['æŋkʃəslɪ] adv (a) besorgt. (b) (keenly) begierig.
anxiousness ['æŋkʃəsnɪs] n, no pl see anxiety.
any ['enɪ] 1 adj (a) (in interrog, conditional, neg sentences) not translated; (emph: ~ at all) (with sing n) irgendein(e); (with pl n) irgendwelche; (with uncountable n) etwas. not ~ kein/keine; not any ... at all überhaupt kein/keine ...; if I had ~ plan/ideas/money wenn ich einen Plan/Ideen/Geld hätte; if I had any plan/ideas/money (at all) wenn ich irgendeinen Plan/irgendwelche Ideen/(auch nur) etwas Geld hätte; if you think it'll do ~ good/any good (at all) wenn du glaubst, daß es etwas/irgend etwas nützt; if it's ~ help (at all) wenn das (irgendwie) hilft; it won't do ~ good es wird nichts nützen; it wasn't ~ good or use (at all) es nützte (überhaupt or gar) nichts; you mustn't do that on ~ account das darfst du auf gar keinen Fall tun; without ~ difficulty (at all) ohne jede Schwierigkeit; hardly ~ difference/any difference at all kaum ein Unterschied/beinahe überhaupt kein Unterschied.
(b) (no matter which) jede(r, s) (beliebige); (with pl or uncountable n) alle. ~ one will do es ist jede(r, s) recht; ~ excuse will do jede Entschuldigung ist recht; you can have ~ book/books you can find du kannst jedes Buch/alle Bücher haben, das/die du finden kannst; take ~ two points wähle zwei beliebige Punkte; ~ one you like was du willst; ~ one of us would have done the same jeder von uns hätte dasselbe getan; you can't just/can come at ~ time du kannst nicht einfach zu jeder beliebigen Zeit kommen/du kannst jederzeit kommen; ~ fool could do that das kann jedes Kind; ~ old ... (inf) jede(r, s) x-beliebige ... (inf); see old.
2 pron (a) (in interrog, conditional, neg sentences) (replacing sing n) ein(e), welche(r, s); (replacing pl n) einige, welche; (replacing uncountable n) etwas, welche. I want to meet psychologists/a psychologist, do you know ~? ich würde gerne Psychologen/einen Psychologen kennenlernen, kennen Sie welche/einen?; I need some butter/stamps, do you have ~? ich brauche Butter/Briefmarken, haben Sie welche?; have you seen ~ of my ties? haben Sie eine von meinen Krawatten gesehen?; haven't you ~ (at all)? haben Sie (denn) (gar or überhaupt) keine/keine/keines?; he wasn't having ~ (of it/that) (inf) er wollte nichts davon hören; the profits, if ~ die eventuellen Gewinne; I'd like some tea/tomatoes if you have ~ ich hätte gerne Tee, wenn Sie welchen haben/Tomaten, wenn Sie welche haben; if ~ of you can sing wenn (irgend) jemand or (irgend)einer/-eine von euch singen kann; show me the work you've done, if ~ zeig mir deine Arbeit, wenn es (überhaupt) etwas zu zeigen gibt; few, if ~, will come wenn überhaupt, werden nur wenige kommen.
(b) (no matter which) alle. ~ who do come ... alle, die kommen ...; ~ I have ... alle, die ich habe ...
3 adv (a) colder, bigger etc noch. not ~ colder/bigger etc nicht kälter/größer etc; it won't get ~ colder es wird nicht mehr kälter; we can't go ~ further wir können nicht mehr weitergehen; should he grow ~ bigger he'll ... wenn er noch mehr wächst, wird er ...; are you feeling ~ better? geht es dir etwas besser?; he wasn't ~ too pleased er war nicht allzu begeistert; do you want ~ more soup? willst du noch etwas Suppe?; don't you want ~ more tea? willst du keinen Tee mehr?; ~ more offers? noch weitere Angebote?; I don't want ~ more (at all) ich möchte (überhaupt or gar) nichts mehr; do/don't you want ~ more? möchten Sie noch etwas/möchten Sie (denn) nichts mehr?
(b) (esp US inf: at all) überhaupt. you can't improve it ~ du kannst es überhaupt nicht mehr verbessern; it didn't help them ~ es hat ihnen gar or überhaupt nichts genützt.
anybody ['enɪ,bɒdɪ] 1 pron (a) (irgend) jemand, (irgend)eine(r). not ... ~ niemand, keine(r); is ~ there? ist (irgend) jemand da?; (does) ~ want my book? will jemand or einer mein Buch?; I can't see ~ ich kann niemand or keinen sehen; don't tell ~ erzähl das niemand(em) or keinem.
(b) (no matter who) jede(r). ~ will tell you the same jeder wird dir dasselbe sagen; ~ with any sense jeder halbwegs vernünftige Mensch; it's ~'s game/race das Spiel/Rennen kann von jedem gewonnen werden; ~ but he, ~ else jeder außer ihm, jeder andere; is there ~ else I can talk to? gibt es sonst jemand(en), mit dem ich sprechen kann?; I don't want to see ~ else ich möchte niemand anderen sehen.
2 n (person of importance) jemand, wer (inf). she'll never be ~ sie wird nie wer sein (inf); he's not just ~ er ist nicht einfach irgendwer or irgend jemand; everybody who is ~ was there alles, was Rang und Namen hat, war dort; she wasn't ~ before he married her sie war niemand, bevor er sie geheiratet hat.
anyhow ['enɪhaʊ] adv (a) (at any rate) jedenfalls; (regardless) trotzdem. ~, that's what I think das ist jedenfalls meine Meinung; ~, I went to see him (also) jedenfalls, ich habe ihn besucht; ~, you're here now jetzt bist du jedenfalls da; he agrees ~, so it doesn't matter er ist sowieso einverstanden, es spielt also keine Rolle; it's no trouble, I'm going there ~ es ist keine Mühe, ich gehe sowieso hin; I told him not to, but he did it ~ ich habe es ihm verboten, aber er hat es trotzdem gemacht;

who cares, ~? überhaupt, wen kümmert es denn schon?; ~! gut!, na ja!
(b) (*carelessly*) irgendwie; (*at random also*) aufs Geratewohl. **the papers were scattered ~ on his desk** die Papiere lagen bunt durcheinander auf seinem Schreibtisch; **things are all ~** alles ist durcheinander.
anyone ['enɪwʌn] *pron, n see* **anybody.**
anyplace ['enɪpleɪs] *adv* (*US inf*) *see* **anywhere.**
anything ['enɪθɪŋ] **1** *pron* **(a)** (irgend) etwas. **not ~** nichts; (*emph*) gar *or* überhaupt nichts; **is it/isn't it worth ~?** ist es etwas/gar nichts wert?; **have/haven't you ~ to say?** hast du etwas/(gar) nichts zu sagen?; **did/didn't he say ~ else?** hat er (sonst) noch etwas/sonst (gar) nichts gesagt?; **did/didn't they give you ~ at all?** haben sie euch überhaupt etwas/überhaupt nichts gegeben?; **are you doing ~ tonight?** hast du heute abend schon etwas vor?; **is there ~ more tiring than ...?** gibt es etwas Ermüdenderes als ...?; **hardly ~** kaum etwas.
(b) (*no matter what*) alles. **~ you like** (alles,) was du willst; **they eat ~** sie essen alles; **not just ~** nicht bloß irgend etwas; **I wouldn't do it for ~** ich würde es um keinen Preis tun; **~ else is impossible** alles andere ist unmöglich; **this is ~ but pleasant** das ist alles andere als angenehm; **~ but that!** alles, nur das nicht!; **~ but!** von wegen!; *see* **if, go, like**[1] **2.**
2 *adv* (*inf*) **it isn't ~ like him** das sieht ihm überhaupt nicht ähnlich *or* gleich; **if it looked ~ like him ...** wenn es ihm gleichsehen würde ...; **it didn't cost ~ like £ 100** es kostete bei weitem keine £ 100; **if it costs ~ like as much as before ...** wenn es auch nur annähernd so viel kostet wie früher ...; **~/not ~ like as wet as ...** auch nur annähernd/nicht annähernd so naß wie ...
anyway ['enɪweɪ], (*US dial*) **anyways** *adv see* **anyhow (a);** *see also* **way.**
anywhere ['enɪweər] *adv* **(a)** be, stay, live irgendwo; go, travel irgendwohin. **not ~** nirgends/nirgendwohin; **too late to go ~** zu spät, um (noch) irgendwohin zu gehen; **we never go ~** wir gehen nie (irgend)wohin; **I haven't found ~ to live/to put my books yet** ich habe noch nichts gefunden, wo ich wohnen/meine Bücher unterbringen kann; **he'll never get ~** er wird es zu nichts bringen; **I wasn't getting ~** ich kam (einfach) nicht weiter; **there's no such thing ~ in the world** so etwas gibt es (überhaupt) nirgends auf der Welt.
(b) (*no matter where*) be, stay, live überall; go, travel überallhin. **they could be ~** sie könnten überall sein; **~ you like** wo/wohin du willst; **ready to go ~** bereit, überallhin zu gehen.
aorist ['eəɒrɪst] *n* Aorist *m*.
aorta [eɪˈɔːtə] *n* Aorta *f*.
apace [əˈpeɪs] *adv* geschwind (*geh*).
Apache [əˈpætʃɪ] **1** *n* **(a)** Apache *m*, Apachin *f*. **(b)** (*language*) Apache *nt*. **2** *adj* Apachen-, der Apachen.
apart [əˈpɑːt] *adv* **(a)** auseinander. **to stand with one's feet ~/to sit with one's legs ~** mit gespreizten Beinen dastehen/dasitzen; **I can't tell them ~** ich kann sie nicht auseinanderhalten; **to live ~** getrennt leben; **they're still far** *or* **miles ~** (*fig*) ihre Meinungen klaffen *or* gehen immer noch weit auseinander; **to come** *or* **fall ~** entzweigehen, auseinanderfallen; **it came ~ in my hands** es fiel mir in der Hand auseinander; **to take sth ~** etw auseinandernehmen.
(b) (*to one side*) zur Seite, beiseite; (*on one side*) abseits (*from gen*). **to take sb ~** jdn beiseite nehmen; **he stood ~ from the group** er stand abseits von der Gruppe; **to set sth ~** etw beiseite legen/stellen; **to hold oneself ~** sich abseits halten; **a class/thing ~** eine Klasse/Sache für sich.
(c) (*excepted*) abgesehen von, bis auf (+*acc*). **these problems ~** abgesehen von *or* außer diesen Problemen; **~ from that** there's nothing else wrong with it abgesehen davon *or* bis auf das ist alles in Ordnung; **~ from that, the gearbox is also faulty** darüber hinaus *or* außerdem ist (auch) das Getriebe schadhaft; **~ from suggesting a couple of alterations he was quite happy with the plan** abgesehen von einigen Änderungen *or* bis auf einige Änderungen, die er vorzuschlagen hatte, war er ganz zufrieden mit dem Plan.
apartheid [əˈpɑːteɪt] *n* Apartheid *f*.
apartment [əˈpɑːtmənt] *n* **(a)** (*Brit: room*) Raum *m*. **(b)** ~s *pl* (*Brit: suite of rooms*) Appartement *nt*. **(c)** (*esp US: flat*) Wohnung *f*. **~ house** Wohnblock *m*, Appartementhaus *nt*.
apathetic [ˌæpəˈθetɪk] *adj* apathisch, teilnahmslos. **they are completely ~ about politics/their future** sie sind in politischen Dingen vollkommen apathisch/sie sind vollkommen apathisch, was ihre Zukunft angeht.
apathetically [ˌæpəˈθetɪkəlɪ] *adv see adj.*
apathy ['æpəθɪ] *n* Apathie, Teilnahmslosigkeit *f*.
ape [eɪp] **1** *n* (*lit, fig*) Affe *m*. **2** *vt* nachäffen (*pej*), nachmachen.
aperient [əˈpɪərɪənt] **1** *n* Abführmittel *nt*. **2** *adj* abführend.
apéritif [əˌperɪˈtiːf], **aperitive** [əˈperɪtɪv] *n* Aperitif *m*.
aperture ['æpətʃʊər] *n* Öffnung *f*; (*Phot*) Blende *f*.
apex ['eɪpeks] *n, pl* **-es** *or* **apices** Spitze *f*; (*fig*) Höhepunkt *m*.
aphasia [əˈfeɪzɪə] *n* Aphasie *f*.
aphasic [əˈfeɪzɪk] **1** *adj* aphasisch. **2** *n* Aphasiker(in *f*) *m*.
aphid ['eɪfɪd] *n* Blattlaus *f*.
aphorism ['æfərɪzəm] *n* Aphorismus *m*.
aphoristic [ˌæfəˈrɪstɪk] *adj* aphoristisch.
aphrodisiac [ˌæfrəʊˈdɪzɪæk] **1** *n* Aphrodisiakum *nt*. **2** *adj* aphrodisisch.
apian ['eɪpɪən] *adj* Bienen-.
apiarist ['eɪpɪəˌrɪst] *n* Bienenzüchter, Imker *m*.
apiary ['eɪpɪərɪ] *n* Bienenhaus *nt*.
apices ['eɪpɪsiːz] *pl of* **apex.**
apiculture ['eɪpɪˌkʌltʃər] *n* (*form*) Bienenzucht, Imkerei *f*.
apiece [əˈpiːs] *adv* pro Stück; (*per person*) pro Person. **I gave them two ~** ich gabe ihnen je zwei; **they had two cakes ~** sie hatten jeder zwei Kuchen.

aplomb [əˈplɒm] *n* Gelassenheit *f*.
Apocalypse [əˈpɒkəlɪps] *n* Apokalypse *f*.
apocalyptic [əˌpɒkəˈlɪptɪk] *adj* apokalyptisch.
Apocrypha [əˈpɒkrɪfə] *n*: **the ~** die Apokryphen *pl*.
apocryphal [əˈpɒkrɪfəl] *adj* apokryph; (*of unknown authorship*) anonym.
apogee ['æpəʊdʒiː] *n* (*Astron*) Apogäum *nt*, Erdferne *f*; (*fig: apex*) Höhepunkt *m*.
apolitical [ˌeɪpəˈlɪtɪkəl] *adj* apolitisch.
Apollo [əˈpɒləʊ] *n* (*Myth*) Apollo *m*; (*fig also*) Apoll *m*.
apologetic [əˌpɒləˈdʒetɪk] *adj* (*making an apology*) gesture, look entschuldigend *attr*; (*sorry, regretful*) bedauernd *attr*. **a very ~ Mr Smith rang back** Herr Smith rief zurück und entschuldigte sich sehr; **he gave her an ~ smile when he trod on her foot** er warf ihr ein entschuldigendes Lächeln zu, als er ihr auf den Fuß trat; **I'm afraid you didn't win, he said with an ~ look** es tut mir leid, aber Sie haben nicht gewonnen, sagte er mit bedauernder Miene; **he was most ~ (about it)** er entschuldigte sich vielmals (dafür); **his tone/expression was very ~** sein Ton war sehr bedauernd/seine Miene drückte deutlich sein Bedauern aus.
apologetically [əˌpɒləˈdʒetɪkəlɪ] *adv see adj.*
apologia [ˌæpəˈləʊdʒɪə] *n* Rechtfertigung, Apologie (*also Philos*) *f*.
apologist [əˈpɒlədʒɪst] *n* Apologet *m*.
apologize [əˈpɒlədʒaɪz] *vi* sich entschuldigen (*to* bei). **to ~ for sb/sth** sich für jdn/etw entschuldigen.
apology [əˈpɒlədʒɪ] *n* **(a)** (*expression of regret*) Entschuldigung *f*. **to make** *or* **offer sb an ~** jdn um Verzeihung bitten; **to make one's apologies** sich entschuldigen; **Mr Jones sends his apologies** Herr Jones läßt sich entschuldigen; **I owe you an ~** ich muß dich um Verzeihung bitten; **are there any apologies?** läßt sich jemand entschuldigen?; **I make no ~ for it, we must ...** wir müssen ..., ohne mich dafür zu entschuldigen; **I make no ~ for the fact that ...** ich entschuldige mich nicht dafür, daß ... **(b)** (*defence*) Rechtfertigung, Apologie *f*. **(c)** (*poor substitute*) trauriges *or* armseliges Exemplar (*for gen*). **an ~ for a breakfast/a car** ein armseliges Frühstück/Vehikel.
apoplectic [ˌæpəˈplektɪk] *adj* (*Med*) apoplektisch; *person also* zu Schlaganfällen neigend; (*inf*) disbeliefe. **~ fit** *or* **attack** (*Med*) Schlaganfall *m*; **he just about had an ~ fit** (*fig*) ihn hat fast der Schlag gerührt; **he was ~ with rage** (*inf*) er platzte fast vor Wut (*inf*).
apoplexy ['æpəpleksɪ] *n* Apoplexie *f* (*spec*), Schlaganfall *m*.
apostasy [əˈpɒstəsɪ] *n* Abfall *m*; (*Rel also*) Apostasie *f* (*form*).
apostate [əˈpɒstɪt] **1** *n* Renegat, Abtrünnige(r) *m*; (*Rel also*) Apostat *m*. **an ~ from the party** ein Parteirenegat *m*. **2** *adj* abtrünnig, abgefallen.
apostatize [əˈpɒstətaɪz] *vi* (*from church, faith, party*) abfallen, sich lossagen (*from* von); (*from one's principles also*) untreu werden (*from dat*).
a posteriori ['eɪpɒsˌterɪˈɔːraɪ] *adv* a posteriori.
apostle [əˈpɒsl] *n* (*lit, fig*) Apostel *m*. **the A~s' Creed** das Apostolische Glaubensbekenntnis.
apostolic [ˌæpəˈstɒlɪk] *adj* apostolisch. **~ succession** apostolische Nachfolge; **the A~ See** der Apostolische Stuhl.
apostrophe [əˈpɒstrəfɪ] *n* **(a)** (*Gram*) Apostroph *m*. **(b)** (*Liter*) Apostrophe *f*.
apostrophize [əˈpɒstrəfaɪz] **1** *vt* apostrophieren (*form*). **2** *vi* sich in feierlichen Reden ergehen.
apothecary [əˈpɒθɪkərɪ] *n* (*old*) Apotheker(in *f*) *m*. **apothecaries' weights and measures** Apothekergewichte und -maße.
apotheosis [əˌpɒθɪˈəʊsɪs] *n* Apotheose *f* (*liter*) (*into* zu).
appal, (*US also*) **appall** [əˈpɔːl] *vt* entsetzen. **to be ~led (at** *or* **by sth)** (über etw *acc*) entsetzt sein.
appalling *adj*, **~ly** *adv* [əˈpɔːlɪŋ, -lɪ] entsetzlich.
apparatus [ˌæpəˈreɪtəs] *n* (*pl* Apparat *m*; (*equipment also*) Ausrüstung *f*; (*in gym*) Geräte *pl*. **a piece of ~** ein Gerät *nt*; **the ~ of government** der Regierungsapparat.
apparel [əˈpærəl] **1** *n, no pl* (*liter, US Comm*) Gewand *nt* (*old, liter*), Kleidung *f*. **2** *vt usu pass* (*old*) gewanden (*old*).
apparent [əˈpærənt] *adj* **(a)** (*clear, obvious*) offensichtlich, offenbar. **to be ~ to sb** jdm klar sein, für jdn offensichtlich sein; **it must be ~ to everyone** es muß jedem klar sein; **to become ~** sich (deutlich) zeigen. **(b)** (*seeming*) scheinbar. **more ~ than real** mehr Schein als Wirklichkeit.
apparently [əˈpærəntlɪ] *adv* anscheinend.
apparition [ˌæpəˈrɪʃən] *n* **(a)** (*ghost, hum: person*) Erscheinung *f*. **(b)** (*appearance*) Erscheinen *nt*.
appeal [əˈpiːl] **1** *n* **(a)** (*request: for help, money etc*) Aufruf, Appell *m*, (*dringende*) Bitte (*for* um); (*for mercy*) Gesuch *nt* (*for* um). **~ for funds** Spendenappell *or* -aufruf *m* *or* -aktion *f*; **to make an ~ to sb (to do sth)/to sb for sth** an jdn appellieren, etw zu tun)/jdn um etw bitten; (*charity, organization etc*) einen Appell *or* Aufruf an jdn richten/jdn zu etw aufrufen; **to make an ~ for mercy** (*officially*) ein Gnadengesuch einreichen.
(b) (*supplication*) Flehen *nt*. **with a look of ~** mit flehendem *or* flehentlichem Blick.
(c) (*against decision*) Einspruch *m*; (*Jur: against sentence*) Berufung, Appellation (*old*) *f*; (*actual trial*) Revision *f*, Revisionsverfahren *nt*. **he lost his ~** er verlor in der Berufung; **to lodge an ~** Einspruch erheben; (*Jur*) Berufung einlegen (*with* bei); **right of ~** Einspruchsrecht *nt*; (*Jur*) Berufungsrecht, Appellationsrecht (*old*) *nt*; **on ~** auf Grund der Berufung, bei der Revisionsverhandlung; **Court of A~** Berufungsgericht, Appellationsgericht (*old*) *nt*; **A~ judge** Richter *m* am Berufungsgericht *etc*.
(d) (*for decision, support*) Appell, Aufruf *m*. **the captain made an ~ against the light** der Mannschaftskapitän erhob Einspruch *or* Beschwerde wegen der Lichtverhältnisse.

(e) *(power of attraction)* Reiz *m* (to für), Anziehungskraft *f* (to auf +*acc*). **his music has a wide ~** seine Musik spricht viele Leute *or* weite Kreise an *or* findet großen Anklang; **skiing has lost its ~ (for me)** Skifahren hat seinen Reiz (für mich) verloren; **I just don't understand the ~ of it** ich verstehe nicht, was daran so reizvoll sein soll.

2 *vi* **(a)** *(make request)* (dringend) bitten, ersuchen *(geh)*. **to ~ to sb for sth** jdn um etw bitten *or* ersuchen *(geh)*; **to ~ to the public to do sth** die Öffentlichkeit (dazu) aufrufen, etw zu tun.

(b) *(against decision: to authority etc)* Einspruch erheben (to bei); *(Jur)* Berufung einlegen (to bei). **he was given leave to ~** *(Jur)* es wurde ihm anheimgestellt, Berufung einzulegen.

(c) *(apply: for support, decision)* sich wenden, appellieren (to an +*acc*); *(to sb's feelings etc)* appellieren (to an +*acc*); *(Sport)* Einspruch erheben (to bei), Beschwerde einlegen. **to ~ to sb's better nature** an jds besseres Ich appellieren.

(d) *(be attractive)* reizen (to sb jdn), zusagen (to sb jdm); *(plan, candidate, idea)* zusagen (to sb jdm); *(book, magazine)* ansprechen (to sb jdn). **it simply doesn't ~** es findet einfach keinen Anklang; **how does that ~?** wie gefällt dir/Ihnen das?; **the plan ~ed to me/him** der Plan gefiel mir *or* sagte mir zu/gefiel ihm *or* fand Anklang bei ihm; **the story ~ed to his sense of humour** die Geschichte sprach seinen Sinn für Humor an.

3 *vt* **to ~ a case/verdict** *(Jur)* mit einem Fall/gegen ein Urteil in die Berufung gehen; **to ~ a decision** Einspruch gegen eine Entscheidung einlegen *or* erheben.

appealing [ə'piːlɪŋ] *adj* **(a)** *(attractive)* attraktiv; *person, character also* ansprechend, gewinnend; *smile, eyes also* reizvoll; *kitten, child* süß, niedlich; *cottage, house also* reizvoll, reizend. **(b)** *(supplicating)* *look, voice* flehend.

appealingly [ə'piːlɪŋlɪ] *adv* **(a)** *(in supplication)* bittend; *look, speak* flehentlich, inbrünstig *(geh)*. **(b)** *(attractively)* reizvoll.

appear [ə'pɪəʳ] *vi* **(a)** erscheinen, auftauchen; *(person, sun also)* sich zeigen. **to ~ from behind/through sth** hinter etw *(dat)* hervorkommen *or* auftauchen/sich zwischen *or* durch etw hindurch zeigen; **as will presently ~** *(fig)* wie sich gleich zeigen wird.

(b) *(arrive)* erscheinen, auftauchen.

(c) *(in public)* *(Jur)* erscheinen; *(personality, ghost also)* sich zeigen; *(Theat)* auftreten. **to ~ in public** sich in der Öffentlichkeit zeigen; **to ~ in court** vor Gericht erscheinen; *(lawyer)* bei einer Gerichtsverhandlung (dabei)sein; **to ~ for sb** jdn vertreten; **to ~ before the court as defendant/as a witness** als Angeklagter vor Gericht erscheinen/als Zeuge vor Gericht auftreten.

(d) *(be published)* erscheinen. **to ~ in print** gedruckt werden/sein.

(e) *(seem)* scheinen. **he ~ed to (be) tired/drunk** er wirkte müde/betrunken, er schien müde/betrunken zu sein; **it ~s that ... es hat den Anschein, daß ..., anscheinend ...; so it ~s, so it would ~** so will es scheinen, so hat es den Anschein; **it ~s not** anscheinend nicht, es sieht nicht so aus; **there ~s** *or* **there would ~ to be a mistake** anscheinend liegt (da) ein Irrtum vor, da scheint ein Irrtum vorzuliegen; **how does it ~ to you?** wie verwelchen Eindruck haben Sie?, wie wirkt das auf Sie?; **it ~s to me that ...** mir scheint, daß ...; **it ~s from his statement that ... aus seiner Bemerkung geht hervor** *or* **ergibt sich, daß ...**

appearance [ə'pɪərəns] *n* **(a)** Erscheinen *nt*; *(unexpected)* Auftauchen *nt no pl*; *(Theat)* Auftritt *m*. **many successful court ~s** viele erfolgreiche Auftritte vor Gericht; **to put in** *or* **make an ~** sich sehen lassen; **to make one's ~** sich zeigen; *(Theat)* seinen Auftritt haben; **cast in order of ~** Darsteller in der Reihenfolge ihres Auftritts *or* Auftretens.

(b) *(look, aspect)* Aussehen *nt*; *(of person also)* Äußere(s) *nt*, äußere Erscheinung. **~s** *(outward signs)* der äußere (An)schein; **good ~ essential** gepflegtes Äußeres *or* gepflegte Erscheinung wichtig; **in ~** dem Aussehen nach, vom Äußeren her; **at first ~** auf den ersten Blick; **he/it has the ~ of being ...** er/es erweckt den Anschein, ... zu sein; **for ~s' sake, for the sake of ~s** um den Schein zu wahren, um des Schein(e)s willen; *(as good manners)* der Form halber; **to keep up** *or* **save ~s** den Anschein geben, ... zu sein; **~s are often deceptive** der Schein trügt oft; **~s were against him** der Schein sprach gegen ihn; **to all ~s** allem Anschein nach; *see* **judge**.

appease [ə'piːz] *vt (calm) person, anger* beschwichtigen, besänftigen; *(Pol)* (durch Zugeständnisse) beschwichtigen; *(satisfy) hunger, thirst* stillen; *(curiosity)* stillen, befriedigen.

appeasement [ə'piːzmənt] *n see vt* Beschwichtigung, Besänftigung *f*; Beschwichtigung *f* (durch Zugeständnisse); Stillung, Befriedigung *f*.

appellant [ə'pelənt] *n (Jur)* Berufungskläger, Appellant *(old) m*.

appellation [ˌæpe'leɪʃən] *n* Bezeichnung, Benennung *f*.

append [ə'pend] *vt notes etc* anhängen (to an +*acc*), hinzufügen; *seal* drücken (to auf +*acc*); *signature* setzen (to unter +*acc*). **the seal/signature ~ed to this document** das Siegel/die Unterschrift, mit dem/der das Dokument versehen ist.

appendage [ə'pendɪdʒ] *n (limb)* Gliedmaße *f*; *(fig)* Anhängsel *nt*. **the British forces and their ~s** die britischen Truppen und das dazugehörige Personal *or (families)* und ihr Anhang.

appendectomy [ˌæpen'dektəmɪ], **appendicectomy** [ˌæpendɪ'sektəmɪ] *n* Blinddarmoperation, Appendektomie *(spec) f*.

appendices [ə'pendɪsiːz] *pl of* **appendix**.

appendicitis [əˌpendɪ'saɪtɪs] *n (eine)* Blinddarmentzündung, Appendizitis *(spec) f*.

appendix [ə'pendɪks] *n, pl* **appendices** *or* **-es (a)** *(Anat)* Blinddarm, Appendix *(spec) m*. **to have one's ~ out** sich *(dat)* den

Blinddarm herausnehmen lassen. **(b)** Anhang, Appendix *m*.

appertain [ˌæpə'teɪn] *vi (form) (belong)* gehören (to zu), eignen (+*dat*) *(geh)*; *(relate)* betreffen (to sb/sth jdn/etw). **this does not ~ to the argument** das gehört nicht zur Sache.

appetite ['æpɪtaɪt] *n (for food etc)* Appetit *m*, (Eß)lust *f*; *(fig: desire)* Verlangen, Bedürfnis *nt*, Lust *f*; *(sexual ~)* Lust, Begierde *f*. **to have an/no ~ for sth** Appetit *or* Lust/keinen Appetit *or* keine Lust auf etw *(acc)* haben; *(fig)* Verlangen *or* Bedürfnis/kein Verlangen *or* Bedürfnis nach etw haben; **to have a good/bad ~** einen guten *or* gesunden/schlechten Appetit haben; **I hope you've got an ~** ich hoffe, ihr habt Appetit!; **he ate with a good ~** er aß mit gutem *or* kräftigem Appetit; **to take away** *or* **spoil one's ~** sich *(dat)* den Appetit verderben.

appetizer ['æpɪtaɪzəʳ] *n (food)* Appetitanreger *m*; *(hors d'oeuvres also)* Vorspeise *f*, Appetithappen *m*; *(drink)* appetitanregendes Getränk.

appetizing ['æpɪtaɪzɪŋ] *adj* appetitlich *(also fig)*; *food also* appetitanregend, lecker; *smell* lecker; *description* verlockend.

appetizingly ['æpɪtaɪzɪŋlɪ] *adv see adj*.

Appian ['æpɪən] *adj* Appisch.

applaud [ə'plɔːd] **1** *vt (lit, fig)* applaudieren, Beifall spenden *or* klatschen (+*dat*); *(fig) efforts, courage* loben; *decision* gutheißen, begrüßen. **the play was vigorously ~ed** das Stück erhielt stürmischen Beifall *or* wurde lebhaft beklatscht.

2 *vi* applaudieren, klatschen, Beifall spenden.

applause [ə'plɔːz] *n, no pl* Applaus, Beifall *(also fig) m*, Klatschen *nt*. **to be greeted with ~** mit Applaus *or* Beifall *(also fig)* begrüßt werden; **to win sb's ~** bei jdm Beifall finden.

apple ['æpl] *n* Apfel *m*. **an ~ a day keeps the doctor away** *(Prov)* eßt Obst, und ihr bleibt gesund; **to be the ~ of sb's eye** jds Liebling sein.

apple *in cpds* Apfel-; **~cart** *n (fig)*: **to upset the ~cart** alles über den Haufen werfen *(inf)*; **~ dumpling** *n* ≃ Apfel *m* im Schlafrock; **~-green** *adj* apfelgrün; **~jack** *n (US)* Apfelschnaps *m*; **~-pie** *n* ≃ gedeckter Apfelkuchen, Apfelpastete *f*; **~-pie bed** *Bett nt, bei dem Laken und Decken aus Scherz so gefaltet sind, daß man sich nicht ausstrecken kann*; **in ~-pie order** *(inf)* pikobello *(inf)*; **~ sauce** *n* **(a)** *(Cook)* Apfelmus *nt*; **(b)** *(US inf: nonsense)* Schmus *m (inf)*; **~-tree** *n* Apfelbaum *m*; **~ turnover** *n* Apfeltasche *f*.

appliance [ə'plaɪəns] *n* **(a)** Vorrichtung *f*; *(household ~)* Gerät *nt*; *(fire-engine)* Feuerwehrwagen *m*. **(b)** *(rare) see* **application (b)**.

applicability [ˌæplɪkə'bɪlɪtɪ] *n* Anwendbarkeit *f (to auf +acc)*.

applicable [ə'plɪkəbl] *adj* anwendbar (to auf +*acc*); *(on forms)* zutreffend (to für). **delete as ~** Nichtzutreffendes streichen; **only fill in the parts of the form ~ to you** nur die Teile des Formulars ausfüllen, die auf *or* für Sie zutreffen *or* zutreffend sind; **that is/isn't ~ to you** das trifft auf Sie nicht zu, das gilt nicht für Sie; **not ~** *(on forms)* entfällt, nicht zutreffend.

applicant ['æplɪkənt] *n (for job)* Bewerber(in *f) m (for* um, für); *(for grant, loan etc)* Antragsteller(in *f) (for* für, auf +*acc*); *(for patent)* Anmelder(in *f) m (for* gen).

application [ˌæplɪ'keɪʃən] *n* **(a)** *(for job etc)* Bewerbung *f (for* um, für); *(for grant, loan etc)* Antrag *m (for* auf +*acc*), Gesuch *nt (for* für); *(for patent)* Anmeldung *f (for* gen). **available on ~** auf Anforderung *or* (written) Antrag erhältlich; **~ form** Bewerbung(sformular *nt) f*, Antrag(sformular *nt) m*; Anmeldeformular *nt*; **to make ~ to sb for sth** *(form)* bei jdm etw anfordern; *(written)* einen Antrag auf etw *(acc)* an jdn richten.

(b) *(act of applying)* see **apply 1** Auftragen *nt*; Anlegen, Applizieren *nt*, Applikation *f (form)*; Anwenden *nt*, Anwendung *f*; Verwendung *f*, Gebrauch *m*; Betätigung *f*; Verwertung *f*; Zuwendung *f*, (Aus)richten *nt*; Verhängen *nt*, Verhängung *f*. **the ~ of a dressing to a head wound** das Anlegen eines Kopfverbandes; **"for external ~ only"** *(Med)* „nur zur äußerlichen Anwendung".

(c) *(form, esp Med)* Mittel *nt*; *(ointment also)* Salbe *f*.

(d) *(diligence, effort)* Fleiß, Eifer *m*.

(e) *see* **applicability**.

applicator ['æplɪkeɪtəʳ] *n* Aufträger *m*.

applied [ə'plaɪd] *adj attr maths, linguistics etc* angewandt.

appliqué [æ'pliːkeɪ] *(Sew)* **1** *n* Applikationen *pl*. **to do ~** applizieren. **2** *vt* applizieren. **3** *adj attr* ~ **work** Stickerei *f*.

apply [ə'plaɪ] **1** *vt paint, ointment, lotion etc* auftragen (to auf +*acc*), applizieren *(spec)*; *dressing, plaster* anlegen, applizieren *(spec)*; *force, pressure, theory, rules, knowledge, skills* anwenden (to +*acc*); *knowledge, skills, funds* verwenden (to für), gebrauchen (to für); *brakes* betätigen; *results, findings* verwerten (to für); *one's attention, efforts* zuwenden (to *dat*), richten (to auf +*acc*); *embargo, sanctions* verhängen (to über +*acc*). **to ~ oneself/one's mind** *or* **intelligence (to sth)** sich/seinen Kopf *(inf)* (bei etw) anstrengen; **that term can be applied to many things** dieser Begriff kann auf viele Dinge angewendet werden *or* trifft auf viele Dinge zu.

2 *vi* **(a)** sich bewerben *(for* um, für). **to ~ to sb for sth** sich an jdn wegen etw wenden; *(for job, grant also)* sich bei jdm für *or* um etw bewerben; *(for loan, grant also)* bei jdm etw beantragen; **no-one applied for the reward** keiner hat sich für die Belohnung gemeldet; **~ at the office/next door/within** Anfragen im Büro/nebenan/im Laden; **she has applied for university** sie hat sich um einen Studienplatz beworben.

(b) *(be applicable)* gelten (to für); *(warning, threat also)* betreffen (to acc); *(regulation also)* zutreffen (to auf +*acc*, für), betreffen (to acc); *(description)* zutreffen (to auf +*acc*, für).

appoint [ə'pɔɪnt] *vt* **(a)** *(to a job)* einstellen; *(to a post)* ernennen. **to ~ sb to an office** jdn in ein Amt berufen; **to ~ sb sth** jdn zu etw ernennen *or* bestellen *(geh) or* als etw *(acc)* berufen; **to ~**

sb to do sth jdn dazu bestimmen, etw zu tun; **they ~ed him to the vacant post** sie gaben ihm die (freie) Stelle; (*professorship*) sie haben ihn auf den Lehrstuhl berufen.

(b) (*designate, ordain*) bestimmen; (*agree*) festlegen *or* -setzen, verabreden, ausmachen. **at the ~ed time** *or* **the time ~ed** zur festgelegten *or* -gesetzten *or* verabredeten Zeit; **his ~ed task** die ihm übertragene Aufgabe; **the date ~ed for that meeting** (*form*) der angesetzte Tagungstermin (*form*).

-appointed [-ə'pɔɪntɪd] *adj suf* **well-/poorly-~** gut/dürftig ausgestattet.

appointee [əpɔɪn'tiː] *n* Ernannte(r) *mf*. **he was a Wilson/ political ~** er war von Wilson/aus politischen Gründen ernannt worden; **the ~ to the ambassadorship** der neubestellte Botschafter.

appointment [ə'pɔɪntmənt] *n* **(a)** (*pre-arranged meeting*) Verabredung *f*; (*business ~, with doctor, lawyer etc*) Termin *m* (*with* bei). **to make** *or* **fix an ~ with sb** mit jdm eine Verabredung treffen; **einen Termin mit jdm vereinbaren; I made an ~ to see the doctor** ich habe mich beim Arzt angemeldet *or* mir beim Arzt einen Termin geben lassen; **do you have an ~?** sind Sie angemeldet?; **by ~** auf Verabredung; (*on business, to see doctor, lawyer etc*) mit (Vor)anmeldung, nach Vereinbarung; **~(s) book** Terminkalender *m*.

(b) (*act of appointing*) *see vt (a)* Einstellung *f*; Ernennung *f*; Berufung *f* (*to zu*); Bestellung *f*. **this office is not filled by ~ but by election** für dieses Amt wird man nicht bestellt *or* berufen, sondern gewählt; **"by ~ (to Her Majesty)"** (*on goods*) „königlicher Hoflieferant".

(c) (*post*) Stelle *f*. **~s (vacant)** Stellenangebote *pl*; **~s bureau** Stellenvermittlung *f*.

(d) **~s** *pl* (*furniture etc*) Ausstattung, Einrichtung *f*.

apportion [ə'pɔːʃən] *vt money, food, land* aufteilen; *duties* zuteilen. **to ~ sth to sb** jdm etw zuteilen; **to ~ sth among** *or* **between several people** etw zwischen mehreren Leuten aufteilen, etw unter mehrere Leute (gleichmäßig) verteilen; **the blame must be ~ed equally** die Schuld muß allen in gleicher Weise *or* zu gleichen Teilen angelastet werden.

apposite ['æpəzɪt] *adj comment, phrase* treffend, passend; *question* angebracht.

apposition [ˌæpə'zɪʃən] *n* Apposition, Beifügung *f*. **A is in ~ to B, A and B are in ~** A ist eine Apposition zu B, A und B sind Gleichsetzungsnomina.

appraisal [ə'preɪzəl] *n see vt* Abschätzung *f*; Beurteilung *f*. **to make an ~ of the situation** die Lage abschätzen; **his false/accurate ~** seine falsche/genaue Einschätzung.

appraise [ə'preɪz] *vt* (*estimate*) *value, damage* (ab)schätzen; (*weigh up*) *character, ability* (richtig) einschätzen, beurteilen; *situation* abschätzen; *poem etc* beurteilen. **an appraising look** ein prüfender Blick; **he ~d the situation accurately/falsely** er hat die Lage genau/falsch eingeschätzt.

appreciable [ə'priːʃəbl] *adj* beträchtlich, deutlich; *difference, change also* nennenswert, merklich.

appreciably [ə'priːʃəblɪ] *adv see adj*.

appreciate [ə'priːʃɪeɪt] 1 *vt* **(a)** (*be aware of*) *dangers, problems, value etc* sich (*dat*) bewußt sein (+*gen*); (*understand*) *sb's wishes, reluctance etc also* Verständnis haben für. **I ~ that you cannot come** ich habe Verständnis dafür, daß ihr nicht kommen könnt.

(b) (*value, be grateful for*) zu schätzen wissen. **nobody ~s me!** niemand weiß mich zu schätzen!; **thank you, I ~ it** vielen Dank, sehr nett von Ihnen; **my liver would ~ a rest** meine Leber könnte eine kleine Erholung gebrauchen; **I would really ~ that** das wäre mir wirklich sehr lieb; **I would ~ it if you could do this by tomorrow** können Sie das bitte bis morgen erledigen?; **I would ~ it if you could be a little quieter** könnten Sie nicht vielleicht etwas leiser sein?; **the boss would really ~ it if you would pay up** der Chef hätte nichts dagegen, wenn du bezahlst.

(c) (*enjoy*) *art, music, poetry* schätzen.

2 *vi* (*Fin*) **to ~ (in value)** im Wert steigen, an Wert gewinnen.

appreciation [əˌpriːʃɪ'eɪʃən] *n* **(a)** (*awareness: of problems, dangers, advantages, value*) Erkennen *nt*.

(b) (*esteem, respect*) Anerkennung *f*; (*of abilities, efforts also*) Würdigung *f*; (*of person also*) Wertschätzung *f*. **in ~ of sth** in Anerkennung von etw, zum Dank für etw; **to show** *or* **acknowledge one's ~** seine Dankbarkeit (be)zeigen; **to smile one's ~** zum Dank lächeln.

(c) (*enjoyment, understanding*) Verständnis *nt*; (*of art*) Sinn *m* (*of für*). **to show (great) ~ of Mozart/art** großes Mozart-/Kunstverständnis zeigen; **to write an ~ of sb/sth** einen Bericht über jdn/etw schreiben.

(d) (*comprehension*) Verständnis *nt*.

(e) (*increase*) (Wert)steigerung *f* (*in* bei).

appreciative [ə'priːʃɪətɪv] *adj* anerkennend; *audience also* dankbar; (*prepared to accept*) bereitwillig; (*grateful*) dankbar. **to be ~ of sth** etw zu schätzen wissen; (*of music, art etc*) Sinn für etw haben.

appreciatively [ə'priːʃɪətɪvlɪ] *adv* anerkennend; (*gratefully*) dankbar.

apprehend [ˌæprɪ'hend] *vt* **(a)** (*arrest*) festnehmen; *escape also* aufgreifen. **(b)** (*old, form: understand*) verstehen. **(c)** (*form: anticipate*) befürchten.

apprehension [ˌæprɪ'henʃən] *n* **(a)** (*fear*) Besorgnis, Befürchtung *f*. **a feeling of ~** eine dunkle Ahnung *or* Befürchtung; **she knew a moment of ~** sie war einen Moment lang beklommen *or* voller Befürchtung; **to feel ~ for sth** sich (*dat*) Gedanken *or* Sorgen um etw machen. **(b)** (*arrest*) Festnahme *f*. **(c)** (*old, form: understanding*) Erkennen *nt*.

apprehensive [ˌæprɪ'hensɪv] *adj* ängstlich. **to be ~ of sth/that ...** etw befürchten/fürchten, daß ...; **he was ~ about the future** er schaute mit ängstlicher Sorge *or* verzagt in die Zukunft; **to be**

~ for sb/sb's safety sich (*dat*) Sorgen um jdn/jds Sicherheit machen.

apprehensively [ˌæprɪ'hensɪvlɪ] *adv see adj*.

apprentice [ə'prentɪs] 1 *n* Lehrling, Lehrjunge (*dated*), Auszubildende(r) (*form*) *m*. **to be an ~** Lehrling sein, in der Lehre sein; **~ plumber/electrician** Klempner-/Elektrikerlehrling *m*; **~ jockey** angehender Jockey.

2 *vt* **in die Lehre geben** *or* **schicken** (*to zu*, bei). **to be ~d to sb** bei jdm in die Lehre gehen *or* in der Lehre sein.

apprenticeship [ə'prentɪʃɪp] *n* Lehre, Lehrzeit *f*. **to serve one's ~** seine Lehre *or* Lehrzeit absolvieren *or* machen.

apprise [ə'praɪz] *vt* (*form*) in Kenntnis setzen (*geh*), Kenntnis geben (+*dat*) (*geh*). **I am ~d that ...** man hat mich davon in Kenntnis gesetzt *or* mir davon Kenntnis gegeben, daß ... (*geh*).

appro ['æprəʊ] *n abbr of* **approval: on ~** (*Comm*) (*to try out*) zur Probe; (*to look at*) zur Ansicht.

approach [ə'prəʊtʃ] 1 *vi* (*physically*) sich nähern, näherkommen; (*date, summer etc*) nahen.

2 *vt* **(a)** (*come near*) sich nähern (+*dat*); *person, building also* zukommen auf (+*acc*); (*Aviat*) anfliegen; (*in figures, temperature, time also*) zugehen auf (+*acc*); (*in quality, stature*) herankommen an (+*acc*); (*fig*) heranreichen an (+*acc*). **to ~ thirty/adolescence/manhood** auf die Dreißig zugehen/ins Pubertätsalter/Mannesalter kommen; **the train is now ~ing platform 3** der Zug hat Einfahrt auf Gleis 3.

(b) (*make an ~ to*) *person, committee, organization* herantreten an (+*acc*) (*about* wegen), angehen (*about* um), ansprechen (*about* wegen, auf +*acc* hin). **I haven't ~ed him yet** ich habe ihn daraufhin noch nicht angesprochen, ich bin damit noch nicht an ihn herangetreten; **he is easy/difficult to ~** er ist leicht/nicht leicht ansprechbar.

(c) (*tackle*) *question, problem, task* angehen, herangehen an (+*acc*), anpacken.

3 *n* **(a)** (*drawing near*) (Heran)nahen *nt*; (*of troops, in time also*) Heranrücken *nt*; (*of night*) Einbruch *m*; (*Aviat*) Anflug *m* (*to an* +*acc*). **at the ~ of Easter** als das Osterfest nahte/wenn das Osterfest naht.

(b) (*to person, committee, organization*) Herantreten *nt*. **to make ~es/an ~ to sb** (*with request*) an jdn herantreten; (*man to woman*) Annäherungsversuche machen.

(c) (*way of tackling, attitude*) Ansatz *m* (*to zu*). **an easy ~ to maths/teaching** ein einfacher Weg, Mathematik zu lernen/eine einfache Lehrmethode; **his ~ to the problem** seine Art *or* Methode, an das Problem heranzugehen, sein Problemansatz *m*; **you've got the wrong ~** du machst das verkehrt; **try a different ~** versuch's doch mal anders; **new ~es in psychology** neue Ansätze in der Psychologie.

(d) (*approximation*) Annäherung *f* (*to an* +*acc*). **this work is his nearest ~ to greatness** mit diesem Werk erreicht er fast dichterische Größe; **we achieved some ~ to a festive atmosphere** wir haben eine annähernd festliche Stimmung erreicht.

(e) (*access*) Zugang, Weg *m*; (*road also*) Zufahrt(sstraße) *f*.

approachable [ə'prəʊtʃəbl] *adj* **(a)** *person* umgänglich, leicht zugänglich. **he's still ~/not ~ today** man kann immer noch mit ihm reden/er ist heute nicht ansprechbar.

(b) *place* zugänglich. **it's ~ from above** man kommt von oben (heran).

approaching [ə'prəʊtʃɪŋ] *adj attr* näherkommend; *date, occasion* herannahend, bevorstehend.

approach: ~ lights *npl* (*Aviat*) Lichter *pl or* Befeuerung *f* der Anflugschneise; **~ road** *n* (*to city etc*) Zufahrtsstraße *f*; (*to motorway*) (Autobahn)zubringer *m*; (*slip-road*) Auf- *or* Einfahrt *f*; **~ shot** *n* (*Golf*) Schlag *m* zwischen Abschlag und Grün.

approbation [ˌæprə'beɪʃən] *n* Zustimmung *f*; (*of decision also*) Billigung *f*; (*from critics*) Beifall *m*.

appropriate¹ [ə'prəʊprɪɪt] *adj* **(a)** (*suitable, fitting*) passend, geeignet (*for, to* für); angebracht (*for, to* für); (*to a situation, occasion*) angemessen (*to* dat); *name, remark also* treffend. **it was ~ that he came at that moment** es traf sich gut, daß er da gerade kam; **clothing ~ for** *or* **to the weather conditions** wettergemäße Kleidung; **a style ~ to one's subject** ein dem Thema entsprechender *or* angemessener Stil.

(b) (*relevant*) entsprechend; *body, authority also* zuständig. **where ~** wo es angebracht ist/war, an gegebener Stelle; **put a tick where ~** Zutreffendes bitte ankreuzen; **delete as ~** Nichtzutreffendes streichen.

appropriate² [ə'prəʊprɪeɪt] *vt* **(a)** (*assume possession or control of*) beschlagnahmen; (*take for oneself*) sich (*dat*) aneignen, mit Beschlag belegen; *sb's ideas* sich (*dat*) zu eigen machen. **(b)** (*allocate*) *funds* zuteilen, zuweisen.

appropriately [ə'prəʊprɪtlɪ] *adv* treffend; *dressed* passend (*for, to* für), entsprechend (*for, to* dat); (*to fit particular needs*) designed, equipped entsprechend (*for, to* dat), zweckmäßig (*for, to* für). **~ enough the letter arrived at that very moment** passenderweise kam der Brief genau in dem Augenblick; **rather ~ she was called Goldilocks** der Name Goldköpfchen paßte sehr gut zu ihr.

appropriateness [ə'prəʊprɪtnɪs] *n* (*suitability, fittingness*) Eignung *f*; (*of dress, remark, name, for a particular occasion*) Angemessenheit *f*.

appropriation [əˌprəʊprɪ'eɪʃən] *n see vt* **(a)** Beschlagnahme, Beschlagnahmung *f*; Aneignung *f*. **(b)** Zuteilung, Zuweisung *f*. **to make an ~ for sth** Mittel für etw zuteilen *or* zuweisen.

approval [ə'pruːvəl] *n* **(a)** Beifall *m*, Anerkennung *f*; (*consent*) Zustimmung (*of* zu), Billigung *f*, Einverständnis *nt* (*of* mit). **to meet with sb's ~** jds Zustimmung *or* Beifall finden; **to seek sb's ~ for sth** jds Zustimmung zu etw suchen; **to have sb's ~** jds Zustimmung haben; **to show one's ~ of sth** zeigen, daß man einer Sache (*dat*) zustimmt *or* etw billigt; **submitted for the Queen's ~** der Königin zur Genehmigung vorgelegt.

(b) (Comm) on ~ auf Probe; (to look at) zur Ansicht.

approve [ə'pruːv] **1** vt (consent to) decision billigen, gutheißen; minutes, motion annehmen; project genehmigen; (recommend) hotel, campsite etc empfehlen. **an ~d campsite** ein empfohlener Campingplatz.

2 vi to ~ **of sb/sth** von jdm/etw etwas halten, etw billigen or gutheißen; **I don't** ~ **of him/it** ich halte nichts von ihm/davon; **do you** ~ **of him/that?** hältst du etwas von ihm/davon?; **I don't** ~ **of children smoking** ich billige nicht or kann es nicht gutheißen, daß Kinder rauchen; **she doesn't** ~ sie mißbilligt das; **how's this shirt, do you** ~? gefällt dir dies Hemd?

approved school [ə'pruːvd'skuːl] n (Brit) Erziehungsheim nt.

approving [ə'pruːvɪŋ] adj (satisfied, pleased) anerkennend, beifällig; (consenting) zustimmend.

approvingly [ə'pruːvɪŋlɪ] adv see adj.

approximate [ə'prɒksɪmɪt] **1** adj ungefähr. **these figures are only** ~ dies sind nur ungefähre Werte; **three hours is the** ~ **time needed** man braucht ungefähr drei Stunden.

2 [ə'prɒksəmeɪt] vti to ~ **(to)** sth einer Sache (dat) in etwa entsprechen; **they** ~ **(to one another)** sie entsprechen einander in etwa.

approximately [ə'prɒksɪmətlɪ] adv ungefähr, etwa, circa; correct in etwa, annähernd.

approximation [ə,prɒksɪ'meɪʃən] n Annäherung f (of, to an +acc); (figure, sum etc) (An)näherungswert m. **his story was an** ~ **of** or **to the truth** seine Geschichte entsprach in etwa or ungefähr der Wahrheit.

appurtenances [ə'pɜːtɪnənsɪz] npl (equipment) Zubehör nt; (accessories) Attribute pl; (Jur: rights etc) Rechte pl. **with all the** ~ **of affluence** mit allen Attributen des Wohlstands.

après-ski [,æpreɪ'skiː] **1** n Après-Ski. **2** adj attr Après-Ski-.

apricot ['eɪprɪkɒt] **1** n Aprikose f. **2** adj (also ~-coloured) aprikosenfarben. **3** attr Aprikosen-.

April ['eɪprəl] n April m. ~ **shower** Aprilschauer m; ~ **fool!** = April, April!; ~ **Fool's Day** der Erste April; **to make an** ~ **fool of sb** jdn in den April schicken; see also September.

a priori [eɪpraɪ'ɔːraɪ] **1** adv a priori. **2** adj apriorisch.

apron ['eɪprən] n Schürze f; (of workman also) Schurz m; (Aviat) Vorfeld nt; (Theat) Vorbühne f.

apron: ~ **stage** n Bühne f mit Vorbühne; ~-**strings** npl Schürzenbänder pl; **to be tied to one's mother's** ~-**strings** seiner Mutter (dat) am Schürzenzipfel hängen (inf).

apropos [,æprə'pəʊ] **1** prep (also ~ **of**) apropos (+nom). ~ **of nothing** ganz nebenbei. **2** adj pred remark passend, treffend.

apse [æps] n Apsis f.

apt [æpt] adj (+er) **(a)** (suitable, fitting) passend; description, comparison, remark also treffend.

(b) (able, intelligent) begabt (at für).

(c) (liable, likely) **to be** ~ **to do sth** leicht etw tun, dazu neigen, etw zu tun; **he is always** ~ **to be late** er kommt gern (inf) zu spät, er neigt dazu, stets zu spät zu kommen; **it is** ~ **to rain in Glasgow** es regnet oft in Glasgow; **we are** ~ **to forget that** ... wir vergessen leicht or gern (inf), daß ...; **I was** ~ **to believe him until** ... ich war geneigt, ihm zu glauben, bis ...

aptitude ['æptɪtjuːd] n Begabung f. **she has a great** ~ **for saying the wrong thing** (hum) sie hat ein besonderes Talent dafür, (immer gerade) das Falsche zu sagen; ~ **test** Eignungsprüfung f.

aptly ['æptlɪ] adv passend. **it did not fit** ~ **into the context** es paßte nicht richtig in den Zusammenhang.

aptness ['æptnɪs] n see adj **I doubted the** ~ **of the comparison** ich bezweifelte, daß das ein passender Vergleich war; **the** ~ **of the name was obvious** der Name war offensichtlich passend. **(b)** Begabung f. **(c)** Neigung f.

aqualung ['ækwəlʌŋ] n Tauchgerät nt.

aquamarine [,ækwəmə'riːn] **1** n Aquamarin m; (colour) Aquamarin nt. **2** adj aquamarin.

aquaplane ['ækwəpleɪn] **1** n Monoski m. **2** vi **(a)** Wasserski laufen. **(b)** (car etc) (auf nasser Straße) ins Rutschen geraten. **aquaplaning** Aquaplaning nt.

aquarium [ə'kwɛərɪəm] n Aquarium nt.

Aquarius [ə'kwɛərɪəs] n Wassermann m.

aquatic [ə'kwætɪk] adj sports, pastimes Wasser-, im Wasser; plants, animals, organisms etc aquatisch (form).

aquatint ['ækwətɪnt] n Aquatinta f.

aqueduct ['ækwɪdʌkt] n Aquädukt m or nt.

aqueous ['eɪkwɪəs] adj (form) Wasser-; rocks wasserhaltig. ~ **humour** (Med) Kammerwasser nt, Humor aquosus m (spec).

aquiline ['ækwɪlaɪn] adj nose Adler-, gebogen; profile mit Adlernase, dinarisch (geh).

Aquinas [ə'kwaɪnəs] n Thomas von Aquin.

Arab ['ærəb] **1** n Araber m (also horse), Araberin f. **the** ~s die Araber. **2** adj attr arabisch; policies, ideas also der Araber; horse Araber-.

arabesque [,ærə'besk] n Arabeske f.

Arabia [ə'reɪbɪə] n Arabien nt.

Arabian [ə'reɪbɪən] adj arabisch. **tales of the** ~ **Nights** Märchen aus Tausendundeiner Nacht.

Arabic ['ærəbɪk] **1** n Arabisch nt. **2** adj arabisch. ~ **numerals** arabische Ziffern or Zahlen; ~ **studies** Arabistik f.

arable ['ærəbl] adj land bebaubar; (being used) Acker-.

arachnid [ə'ræknɪd] n Spinnentier nt.

Aragon ['ærəgən] n Aragon, Aragonien nt.

arbiter ['ɑːbɪtəʳ] n **(a)** (of fate etc) Herr, Gebieter m (of über +acc). **to be the** ~ **of Herr sein über** (+acc); **they are the** ~s **of fashion** sie haben die Mode bestimmt. **(b)** see **arbitrator**.

arbitrarily ['ɑːbɪtrərəlɪ] adv see adj.

arbitrariness ['ɑːbɪtrərɪnɪs] n Willkürlichkeit f.

arbitrary ['ɑːbɪtrərɪ] adj willkürlich, arbiträr (geh).

arbitrate ['ɑːbɪtreɪt] **1** vt dispute schlichten. **2** vi **(a)** vermit-

teln. **(b)** (go to arbitration) vor eine Schlichtungskommission gehen.

arbitration [,ɑːbɪ'treɪʃən] n Schlichtung f. **to submit a dispute to** ~ einen Streit vor ein Schiedsgericht or (esp Ind) eine Schlichtungskommission bringen; **to go to** ~ vor eine Schlichtungskommission gehen; (dispute) vor eine Schlichtungskommission gebracht werden.

arbitrator ['ɑːbɪtreɪtəʳ] n Vermittler m; (esp Ind) Schlichter m.

arbor n (US) see **arbour**.

arboreal [ɑː'bɔːrɪəl] adj Baum-; habitat auf Bäumen.

arboretum [,ɑːbə'riːtəm] n Arboretum nt (form), Baumschule f.

arbour, (US) **arbor** ['ɑːbəʳ] n Laube f.

arbutus [ɑː'bjuːtəs] n Arbutus m.

arc [ɑːk] n Bogen m.

arcade [ɑː'keɪd] n (Archit) Arkade f; (shopping ~) Passage f.

Arcadia [ɑː'keɪdɪə] n Arkadien nt.

Arcadian [ɑː'keɪdɪən] adj (lit, fig) arkadisch.

arcane [ɑː'keɪn] adj obskur.

arch¹ [ɑːtʃ] **1** n **(a)** Bogen m. ~ **of the heavens** Himmelsbogen m, Himmelsgewölbe nt.

(b) (Anat: of foot) Gewölbe nt (spec). **high/fallen** ~es hoher Spann/Senkfuß m.

2 vi sich wölben; (arrow etc) einen Bogen machen or beschreiben.

3 vt back krümmen; (cat also) krumm machen; eyebrows hochziehen. **the cat** ~ed **his back** (to be fierce) die Katze machte einen Buckel.

arch² adj (wicked, mischievous) neckisch, schelmisch.

arch³ adj attr Erz-. ~ **traitor** Hochverräter m.

archaeological, (US) **archeological** [,ɑːkɪə'lɒdʒɪkəl] adj archäologisch.

archaeologist, (US) **archeologist** [,ɑːkɪ'ɒlədʒɪst] n Archäologe m, Archäologin f.

archaeology, (US) **archeology** [,ɑːkɪ'ɒlədʒɪ] n Archäologie f.

archaic [ɑː'keɪɪk] adj word etc veraltet, archaisch (spec); (inf) vorsintflutlich. **my car is getting rather** ~ mein Auto wird allmählich museumsreif.

archaism ['ɑːkeɪɪzəm] n veralteter Ausdruck, Archaismus m.

arch: ~**angel** ['ɑːk,eɪndʒəl] n Erzengel m; ~**bishop** n Erzbischof m; ~**bishopric** n (district) Erzbistum nt, Erzdiözese f; (office) Amt nt des Erzbischofs; ~**deacon** n Archidiakon, Erzdiakon m; ~**diocese** n Erzdiözese f, Erzbistum nt; ~**ducal** adj erzherzoglich; ~**duchess** n Erzherzogin f; ~**duchy** n Erzherzogtum nt; ~**duke** n Erzherzog m.

arched [ɑːtʃt] adj gewölbt; window (Rund)bogen-. **the** ~ **curve of the temple roof** die Wölbung des Tempeldachs.

archeological etc (US) see **archaeological** etc.

archer ['ɑːtʃəʳ] n Bogenschütze m; (Astron, Astrol) Schütze m.

archery ['ɑːtʃərɪ] n Bogenschießen nt. **an** ~ **competition** ein Wettkampf im Bogenschießen.

archetypal ['ɑːkɪtaɪpəl] adj archetypisch (geh); (typical) typisch. **he is the** ~ **millionaire** er ist ein Millionär, wie er im Buche steht; **an** ~ **Scot** ein Urschotte (inf).

archetype ['ɑːkɪtaɪp] n Archetyp(us) m (form); (original, epitome also) Urbild nt, Urtyp m.

arch-fiend [ɑːtʃ'fiːnd] n **the** ~ der Erzfeind.

archiepiscopal [,ɑːkɪ'pɪskəpəl] adj erzbischöflich.

Archimedes [,ɑːkɪ'miːdɪːz] n Archimedes m.

archipelago [,ɑːkɪ'pelɪgəʊ] n, pl -**(e)s** Archipel m. **the A**~ (agos); (sea) die Ägäis.

architect ['ɑːkɪtekt] n (lit, fig) Architekt(in f) m. ~-**designed** von (einem) Architekten entworfen; **he was/everybody is the** ~ **of his own fate** er hat sein Schicksal selbst verursacht/jeder ist seines (eigenen) Glückes Schmied (prov).

architectural adj, ~**ly** adv [,ɑːkɪ'tektʃərəl, -lɪ] architektonisch.

architecture ['ɑːkɪtektʃəʳ] n Architektur f; (of building also) Baustil m.

archives ['ɑːkaɪvz] npl Archiv nt.

archivist ['ɑːkɪvɪst] n Archivar(in f) m.

archly ['ɑːtʃlɪ] adv neckisch, schelmisch.

archness ['ɑːtʃnɪs] n neckische or schelmische Art.

archpriest ['ɑːtʃ'priːst] n (lit, fig) Hohepriester m.

archway ['ɑːtʃweɪ] n Torbogen m.

arc: ~**lamp**, ~**light** n Bogenlampe f, Bogenlicht nt.

arctic ['ɑːktɪk] **1** adj (lit, fig) arktisch. **A**~ **Circle** nördlicher Polarkreis; **A**~ **Ocean** Nordpolarmeer nt. **2** n (also **the A**~) die Arktis. **(b)** (US: shoe) gefütterter, wasserundurchlässiger Überschuh.

arc welding n (Licht)bogenschweißung f.

ardent ['ɑːdənt] adj leidenschaftlich; supporter, admirer also begeistert; admirer, love also glühend; desire, longing also brennend, glühend; request, imprecations inständig.

ardently ['ɑːdəntlɪ] adv leidenschaftlich; love heiß; desire, admire glühend.

ardour, (US) **ardor** ['ɑːdəʳ] n (of person) Begeisterung, Leidenschaft f; (of voice also) Überschwang m; (of feelings also) Heftigkeit f; (of passions) Glut f (liter), Feuer nt; (of poems, letters) Leidenschaftlichkeit f. **the** ~s **of youth** die Leidenschaft der Jugend.

arduous ['ɑːdjʊəs] adj beschwerlich, mühsam; course, work anstrengend; task mühsvoll.

arduousness ['ɑːdjʊəsnɪs] n see adj Beschwerlichkeit f; Mühseligkeit f. **because of the** ~ **of the work** weil die Arbeit so anstrengend war/ist.

are¹ [ɑːʳ] n Ar nt.

are² 2nd pers sing, 1st, 2nd, 3rd pers pl present of **be**.

area ['ɛərɪə] n **(a)** (measure) Fläche f. **20 sq metres in** ~ eine Fläche von 20 Quadratmetern.

(b) *(region, district)* Gebiet nt; *(neighbourhood, vicinity)* Gegend f; *(separated off, piece of ground etc)* Areal, Gelände nt; *(on plan, diagram etc)* Bereich m; *(slum ~, residential ~, commercial ~ also)* Viertel nt. this is not a very nice ~ to live in dies ist keine besonders gute Wohngegend; in the ~ in der Nähe; do you live in the ~? wohnen Sie hier in der Gegend?; protected/prohibited/industrial ~ Schutz-/Sperr-/Industriegebiet nt; drying/packaging/despatch ~ Trocken-/Pack-/Verteilerzone f; dining/sleeping ~ Eß-/Schlafbereich or -platz m; no smoking/relaxation/recreation ~ Nichtraucher-/Erholungs-/Freizeitzone f; we use this corner as a discussion ~ wir benutzen diese Ecke für Diskussionen; the goal ~ der Torraum; this ~ is for directors' cars dieser Platz ist für Direktorenwagen vorgesehen; you must keep out of this ~ dies Gebiet darf nicht betreten werden; this ~ must be kept clear diesen Platz frei halten; the public were told to keep well away from the ~ die Öffentlichkeit wurde aufgefordert, das Gebiet unbedingt zu meiden; a mountainous ~/mountainous ~s eine bergige Gegend/Bergland nt; a wooded ~ ein Waldstück nt; *(larger)* ein Waldgebiet nt; desert ~s Wüstengebiete pl; the infected ~s of the lungs die befallenen Teile or *(smaller)* Stellen der Lunge; the patchy ~s on the wall die fleckigen Stellen an der Wand; the additional message ~ on an airletter der Raum für zusätzliche Mitteilungen auf einem Luftpostleichtbrief; in the ~ of the station in der Bahnhofsgegend; the thief is believed to be still in the ~ man nimmt an, daß sich der Dieb noch in der Umgebung aufhält; in the London ~ im Raum London, im Londoner Raum; the sterling ~ die Sterlingzone; ~ bombing Flächenbombardierungen pl; ~ code *(US Telec)* (Gebiets)vorwahl(nummer) f; postal ~ Zustellbezirk *(form)*, Postbezirk m; ~ command Gebiets- or Abschnittskommandantur f; ~ office Bezirksbüro nt.

(c) *(fig)* Bereich m. ~s of uncertainty/agreement Bereiche, in denen Unklarheit/Übereinstimmung besteht; his ~ of responsibility sein Verantwortungsbereich m; ~ of interest/study Interessen-/Studiengebiet nt; a sum in the ~ of £100 eine Summe um die hundert Pfund.

(d) *(Brit: basement courtyard)* Vorplatz m.

areaway ['ɛərɪəˌweɪ] n *(US)* **(a)** Vorplatz m. **(b)** *(passage)* Durchgang m, Passage f.

arena [ə'riːnə] n *(lit, fig)* Arena f. ~ of war Kriegsschauplatz m; to enter the ~ *(fig)* die Arena betreten, auf den Plan treten.

aren't [ɑːnt] = are not; am not; see be.

argent ['ɑːdʒənt] *(obs, poet, Her)* 1 n Silber nt. 2 adj silbern.

Argentina [ɑːdʒən'tiːnə] n Argentinien nt.

Argentine ['ɑːdʒəntaɪn] n: the ~ Argentinien nt.

Argentinian [ɑːdʒən'tɪnɪən] 1 n *(person)* Argentinier(in f) m. 2 adj argentinisch.

argon ['ɑːgon] n Argon nt.

Argonaut ['ɑːgənɔːt] n Argonaut m.

argot ['ɑːgəʊ] n Argot nt or m; *(criminal also)* Rotwelsch nt.

arguable ['ɑːgjʊəbl] adj **(a)** *(capable of being maintained)* vertretbar. it is ~ that ... es läßt sich der Standpunkt vertreten, daß ..., man kann behaupten, daß ... **(b)** *(open to discussion)* it is ~ whether ... es ist (noch) die Frage, ob ...

arguably ['ɑːgjʊəblɪ] adv wohl. this is ~ his best book dies dürfte (wohl) sein bestes Buch sein.

argue ['ɑːgjuː] 1 vi **(a)** *(dispute)* streiten; *(quarrel)* sich streiten; *(about trivial things)* sich zanken. he is always arguing er widerspricht ständig, er muß immer streiten; he can't stand women who ~ zankende or streitsüchtige Frauen kann er nicht ausstehen; there's no arguing with him mit ihm kann man nicht reden; don't ~ (with me)! keine Widerrede!; don't ~ with your mother! du sollst deiner Mutter nicht widersprechen!; I don't want to ~, if you don't want to ... ich will mich nicht streiten, wenn Sie nicht wollen ...; there is no point in arguing da erübrigt sich jede (weitere) Diskussion; you can't ~ with a line of tanks mit Panzern kann man nicht diskutieren; a 25% increase, you can't ~ with that *(inf)* eine 25%ige Erhöhung, da kann man nichts sagen *(inf)* or noch meckern *(sl)*; he wasn't used to employees arguing Angestellte, die ihre Meinung sagten, war er nicht gewöhnt.

(b) *(present reasons)* he ~s that ... er vertritt den Standpunkt, daß ..., er behauptet, daß ...; I'm not arguing that ... ich will nicht behaupten, daß ...; to ~ for or in favour of sth für etw sprechen; *(in book)* sich für etw aussprechen; to ~ against sth gegen etw sprechen; *(in book)* sich gegen etw aussprechen; to ~ from a position of ... von einem or dem Standpunkt (+gen) aus argumentieren; this ~s in his favour das spricht zu seinen Gunsten; to ~s well for him es spricht für ihn; just one thing ~s against him/it nur eins spricht gegen ihn/dagegen.

2 vt **(a)** *(debate)* case, matter diskutieren, erörtern; *(Jur)* vertreten. a well ~d case ein gut begründeter or dargelegter Fall; to ~ a case for reform die Sache der Reform vertreten; to ~ one's way out of sth sich aus etw herausreden.

(b) *(maintain)* behaupten.

(c) *(persuade)* to ~s sb out of/into sth jdm etw aus-/einreden.

(d) *(indicate)* erkennen lassen, verraten.

♦**argue away** 1 vi diskutieren. 2 vt sep facts wegdiskutieren.
♦**argue out** vt sep problem, issue ausdiskutieren. to ~ sth ~ with sb etw mit jdm durchsprechen.

argument ['ɑːgjʊmənt] n **(a)** *(discussion)* Diskussion f. to spend hours in ~ about how to do sth stundenlang darüber diskutieren, wie man etw macht; for the sake of ~ rein theoretisch; he just said that for the sake of ~ das hat er nur gesagt, um etwas (dagegen) zu sagen; it is beyond ~ das ist unbestreitbar; he is open to ~ er läßt mit sich reden; this is open to ~ darüber läßt sich streiten.

(b) *(quarrel)* Auseinandersetzung f. to have an ~ sich streiten; *(over sth trivial)* sich zanken.

(c) *(reason)* Beweis(grund) m, Argument nt; *(line of reasoning)* Argumentation, Beweisführung f. first state your theory, then list the ~s for and against stellen Sie erst Ihre These auf, und nennen Sie dann die Gründe und Gegengründe; one of the best ~s I have heard in favour of private education eines der besten Argumente zugunsten der Privatschule, die ich gehört habe; there's an even stronger ~ than that es gibt ein noch stärkeres Argument; that's not a rational ~, it's just a dogmatic assertion das ist kein rationales Argument, das ist bloß eine dogmatische Behauptung.

(d) *(theme: of play, book etc)* Aussage, These *(esp Philos)* f; *(claim)* These f.

(e) *(statement of proof)* Beweis m. the two main types of ~ die beiden wichtigsten Beweisarten; Professor Ayer's ~ is that ... Professor Ayers These lautet, daß ...; the Ontological/Teleological ~ der ontologische/teleologische Gottesbeweis; all the various ~s for the existence of a god all die verschiedenen Gottesbeweise; I can reach the same conclusion using a different (type of) ~ ich kann auch mit einer anderen Beweisführung zum selben Ergebnis kommen; I don't think that's a valid ~ ich glaube, das ist kein gültiger Beweis/Gegenbeweis; that's an interesting ~ das ist eine interessante These.

(f) *(Math)* Argument nt.

argumentation [ˌɑːgjʊmən'teɪʃən] n Argumentation, Beweisführung f; *(discussion)* Diskussion f. an ingenious piece of ~ eine geniale Beweisführung.

argumentative [ˌɑːgjʊ'mentətɪv] adj person streitsüchtig.

argy-bargy ['ɑːdʒɪ'bɑːdʒɪ] *(inf)* 1 n Hin und Her nt *(inf)*, Hickhack m or nt *(inf)*. 2 vi hin und her reden, endlos debattieren.

aria ['ɑːrɪə] n Arie f.

Arian ['ɛərɪən] n, adj see Aryan.

ARIBA [ə'riːbə] abbr of Associate of the Royal British Institute of Architects.

arid ['ærɪd] adj *(lit)* countryside, soil dürr; climate trocken, arid *(spec)*; *(fig)* subject trocken, nüchtern; existence freudlos, öd.

aridity [ə'rɪdɪtɪ] n see adj Dürre f; Trockenheit, Aridität *(spec)* f; *(fig)* Trockenheit, Nüchternheit f; Freudlosigkeit, Öde f.

Aries ['ɛəriːz] n *(Astrol)* Widder m. she is an ~ sie ist Widder(frau).

aright [ə'raɪt] adv recht, wohl *(old)*. if I understand you ~ wenn ich Sie recht verstehe.

arise [ə'raɪz] pret arose [ə'rəʊz], ptp arisen [ə'rɪzn] vi **(a)** *(occur)* sich ergeben, entstehen; *(misunderstanding, argument also)* aufkommen; *(problem)* aufkommen, sich ergeben; *(clouds of dust)* entstehen, sich bilden; *(protest, cry)* sich erheben; *(question, wind)* aufkommen, sich erheben *(geh)*; *(question)* sich stellen. should the need ~ falls sich die Notwendigkeit ergibt.

(b) *(result)* to ~ out of or from sth sich aus etw ergeben.

(c) *(old, liter: get up)* sich erheben *(liter)*. ~ Sir Humphrey! erhebt Euch, Sir Humphrey!

aristocracy [ˌærɪs'tɒkrəsɪ] n *(system, state)* Aristokratie f; *(class also)* Adel m. ~ of wealth Geldadel m, Geldaristokratie f.

aristocrat ['ærɪstəkræt] n Aristokrat(in f) m, Adlige(r) mf. he is too much of an ~ to ... *(fig)* er ist sich *(dat)* zu fein, um ... zu ...; the ~ of the dog/cat family der edelste Vertreter der Hunde-/Katzenfamilie.

aristocratic [ˌærɪstə'krætɪk] adj *(lit, fig)* aristokratisch, adlig; *(fig also)* vornehm.

Aristotelian [ˌærɪstə'tiːlɪən] 1 adj aristotelisch. 2 n Aristoteliker m.

Aristotle ['ærɪstɒtl] n Aristoteles m.

arithmetic [ə'rɪθmətɪk] n Rechnen nt; *(calculation)* Rechnung f. could you check my ~? kannst du mal gucken, ob ich richtig gerechnet habe?; your ~ is wrong du hast dich verrechnet; ~ book Rechenfibel f or -buch nt; *(exercise book)* Rechenheft nt.

arithmetical [ˌærɪθ'metɪkəl] adj Rechen-, rechnerisch. ~ genius Rechenkünstler(in f) m; the basic ~ skills Grundwissen nt im Rechnen; ~ progression arithmetische Reihe.

arithmetician [əˌrɪθmə'tɪʃən] n Rechner(in f) m.

arithmetic mean n arithmetisches Mittel.

ark [ɑːk] n **(a)** Arche f. Noah's ~ die Arche Noah; it looks as though it's come out of the ~ *(inf)* das sieht aus wie von Anno Tobak *(inf)*. **(b)** A~ of the Covenant Bundeslade f.

arm¹ [ɑːm] n **(a)** *(Anat)* Arm m. in one's ~s im Arm; under one's ~ unter dem or unterm Arm; he had a bandage on his ~ er hatte einen Verband am Arm or um den Arm; to give one's ~ to sb jdm den Arm geben or reichen *(geh)*; with his ~s full of books den Arm or die Arme voller Bücher; to have sb/sth on one's ~ jdn/etw am Arm haben; to take sb in one's ~s jdn in die Arme nehmen or schließen *(geh)*; to hold sb in one's ~s jdn umarmen, jdn in den or seinen Armen halten *(geh)*; to put or throw one's ~s round sb jdn umarmen, die Arme um jdn schlingen *(geh)*; to put an ~ round sb's shoulders jdm den Arm um die Schulter legen; ~ in ~ Arm in Arm; *(~s linked)* eingehakt, untergehakt; at ~'s length auf Armeslänge; to keep sb at ~'s length *(fig)* jdn auf Distanz halten; to receive or welcome sb/sth with open ~s jdn mit offenen Armen empfangen/etw mit Kußhand nehmen *(inf)*; within ~'s reach in Reichweite; the long ~ of the law der lange Arm des Gesetzes; a list as long as your ~ eine ellenlange Liste; a criminal with a record as long as your ~ ein Verbrecher mit einer langen Latte von Vorstrafen *(inf)*.

(b) *(sleeve)* Arm, Ärmel m.

(c) *(of river)* (Fluß)arm m; *(of sea)* Meeresarm m; *(of armchair)* (Arm)lehne f; *(of record player)* Tonarm m; *(of balance etc)* Balken m; *(of railway signal)* (Signal)arm m; *(Naut: yard~)* Rahnock f.

(d) *(branch)* Zweig m; *(Mil)* Truppengattung f.

arm² 1 n *(Mil, Her)* see arms.

2 vt person, nation, ship etc bewaffnen. **to ~ sth with sth** etw mit etw ausrüsten; **to ~ oneself with sth** (lit, fig) sich mit etw bewaffnen; (fig: non-aggressively) sich mit etw wappnen; **he came ~ed with an excuse** er hatte eine Ausrede parat; **~ed only with her beauty, she ...** ihre Schönheit war die einzige Waffe, mit der sie ...

3 vi aufrüsten. **to ~ for war** zum Krieg rüsten.

armada [ɑːˈmɑːdə] n Armada f. **the A~** die Armada; (battle) die Armadaschlacht.

armadillo [ˌɑːməˈdɪləʊ] n Gürteltier nt.

Armageddon [ˌɑːməˈgedn] n (Bibl) Armageddon nt; (fig also) weltweite or globale Katastrophe.

armament [ˈɑːməmənt] n **(a)** ~s pl (weapons) Ausrüstung f. **(b)** (preparation) Aufrüstung f no pl. **much of the national budget is devoted to ~** ein großer Teil des Staatshaushalts geht in die Rüstung.

armature [ˈɑːmətjʊəʳ] n (Elec) Anker m.

armband [ˈɑːmbænd] n Armbinde f.

armchair [ˌɑːmˈtʃɛəʳ] **1** n Sessel, Lehnstuhl m. **2** adj ~ philosopher/philosophy Stubengelehrte(r) m/Stubengelehrsamkeit f; ~ politician Stammtischpolitiker m; ~ strategist Stammtisch- or Salonstratege m; **he is an ~ traveller** er reist nur mit dem Finger auf der Landkarte (inf).

-armed [-ɑːmd] adj suf -armig.

armed [ɑːmd] adj bewaffnet.

armed: ~ **forces** or **services** pl Streitkräfte pl; ~ **neutrality** n bewaffnete Neutralität f; ~ **robbery** n bewaffneter Raubüberfall.

Armenia [ɑːˈmiːnɪə] n Armenien nt.

Armenian [ɑːˈmiːnɪən] **1** adj armenisch. **2** n **(a)** (person) Armenier(in f) m. **(b)** (language) Armenisch nt.

arm: ~**ful** n Armvoll m no pl, Ladung f (inf); **she's quite an ~ful!** (inf) sie ist eine ganz schöne Handvoll (inf) or Portion (inf); ~**hole** n Armloch nt.

armistice [ˈɑːmɪstɪs] n Waffenstillstand m. **A~ Day** (Brit) 11.11., Tag des Waffenstillstands (1918).

arm: ~**let** n **(a)** see ~**band**; **(b)** (liter: of sea) kleiner Meeresarm; ~**lock** n Armschlüssel m; (of police etc) Polizeigriff m.

armor etc (US) see **armour** etc.

armorial [ɑːˈmɔːrɪəl] **1** adj Wappen-. **2** n Wappenbuch nt.

armour, (US) **armor** [ˈɑːməʳ] **1** n **(a)** Rüstung f; (of animal) Panzer m. **suit of ~** Rüstung f; (fig) Panzer m, Rüstung f; **to wear ~** eine Rüstung tragen. **(b)** (no pl: steel plates) Panzerplatte(n pl) f. **(c)** (vehicles) Panzerfahrzeuge pl; (forces) Panzertruppen pl. **2** vt panzern; (fig) wappnen. ~**ed division,** **cruiser** Panzer-; ~**ed car** Panzerwagen m.

armour-clad, (US) **armor-clad** [ˈɑːməˈklæd] adj (Mil, Naut) gepanzert.

armourer, (US) **armorer** [ˈɑːmərəʳ] n **(a)** (maker) Waffenschmied m. **(b)** (keeper) Waffenmeister, Feldzeugmeister (old) m.

armour: ~**-piercing** adj panzerbrechend; ~**-plated** adj gepanzert; ~**-plating** n Panzerung f; **a sheet of ~-plating** eine Panzerplatte.

armoury, (US) **armory** [ˈɑːmərɪ] n **(a)** Arsenal, Waffenlager nt. **(b)** (US: factory) Munitionsfabrik f.

arm: ~**pit** n Achselhöhle f; (of garments) Achsel f; ~**rest** n Armlehne f.

arms [ɑːmz] npl **(a)** (weapons) Waffen pl. **to ~!** zu den Waffen!; **to carry ~** Waffen tragen; **to be under ~** unter Waffen stehen; **to take up ~** (against sb/sth) (gegen jdn/etw) zu den Waffen greifen; (fig) gegen jdn/etw zum Angriff übergehen; **to be up in ~** (about sth) (fig inf), (über etw acc) empört sein; ~ **race** Wettrüsten nt, Rüstungswettlauf m. **(b)** (Her) Wappen nt.

arm-twisting [ˈɑːmˈtwɪstɪŋ] n (inf) Überredungskunst f. **with a bit of ~ ...** wenn man etwas nachhilft ...; **it took a lot of/didn't take much ~ to get him to agree** er ließ sich schnell/schnell breitschlagen (inf).

army [ˈɑːmɪ] **1** n **(a)** Armee f, Heer nt. ~ **of occupation** Besatzungsarmee f; **to be in the ~** beim Militär sein; (BRD) bei der Bundeswehr sein; (DDR) bei der NVA sein; (Aus) beim Bundesheer sein; **to join the ~** zum Militär gehen.
(b) (fig) Heer nt.
(c) (division) Armee(korps nt) f.
2 attr Militär-; doctor also Stabs-; discipline militärisch; life, slang Soldaten-. ~ **issue** Armee-; ~ **list** (Brit) Rangliste f; ~ **officer** Offizier m in der Armee; **an ~ type** (inf) einer vom Barras (inf) or Bund (BRD inf).

aroma [əˈrəʊmə] n Duft m, Aroma nt.

aromatic [ˌærəʊˈmætɪk] adj aromatisch, wohlriechend.

arose [əˈrəʊz] pret of **arise**.

around [əˈraʊnd] **1** adv herum, rum (inf). **a house with gardens all ~** ein von Gärten umgebenes Haus, ein Haus mit Gärten ringsherum; **I looked all ~** ich sah mich nach allen Seiten um; **books lying all ~** überall herumliegende Bücher; **they appeared from all ~** sie kamen aus allen Richtungen or von überallher; **slowly, he turned ~** er drehte sich langsam um; **for miles ~** meilenweit im Umkreis; **to stroll/travel ~** herumschlendern/-reisen; **is he ~?** ist er da?; **if you want me I'll be ~** ich bin da, falls du mich brauchst; **he must be ~ somewhere** er muß hier irgendwo sein or stecken (inf); **I didn't know you were ~** ich wußte nicht, daß du hier bist; **he's been ~!** der kennt sich aus!; **it's been ~ for ages** das ist schon uralt; **he's been ~ for ages** (inf) der ist schon ewig hier (inf); **see you ~!** (inf) also, bis demnächst!, bis bald!; **where have you been? — ~** wo warst du? — weg!

2 prep **(a)** (right round) (movement, position) um (+acc); (in a circle) um (+acc) ... herum.
(b) (in, through) **to wander ~ the city** durch die Stadt spazieren; **to travel ~ Scotland** durch Schottland reisen; **to talk**

~ **a subject** um ein Thema herumreden; **to be** or **stay ~ the house** zu Hause bleiben; **I left it ~ your office somewhere** ich habe es irgendwo in deinem Büro gelassen; **the paper/church must be ~ here somewhere** die Zeitung muß hier irgendwo (he)rumliegen/die Kirche muß hier irgendwo sein.
(c) (approximately) (with date) um (+acc); (with time of day) gegen (+acc); (with weight, price) etwa, um die (inf); see also **round**.

arouse [əˈraʊz] vt **(a)** (lit liter) aufwecken, erwecken (liter). **(b)** (fig: excite) erregen; interest, suspicion etc also erwecken. **to ~ sb from his slumbers** (fig) jdn aus dem Schlaf wachrütteln; **to ~ sb to action** jdn zum Handeln anspornen.

arpeggio [ɑːˈpedʒɪəʊ] n Arpeggio nt.

arr abbr of **arrives** Ank.

arrack [ˈærək] n Arrak m.

arraign [əˈreɪn] vt (Jur) person Anklage erheben gegen; (liter: denounce) rügen. **to be ~ed on a charge** wegen etw angeklagt werden.

arraignment [əˈreɪnmənt] n (Jur) Anklageerhebung f.

arrange [əˈreɪndʒ] vt **(a)** (order) ordnen; furniture, objects aufstellen, hinstellen; items in a collection, books in library etc anordnen; flowers arrangieren; room einrichten; (fig) thoughts ordnen. **to ~ one's affairs** seine Angelegenheiten regeln or ordnen; **I don't want you arranging my life for me** ich will nicht, daß du mein Leben planst.
(b) (fix, see to) vereinbaren, ausmachen; details regeln; party arrangieren. **to ~ a mortgage for sb** jdm eine Hypothek beschaffen; **I'll ~ for you to meet him** ich arrangiere für Sie ein Treffen mit ihm; **I have ~d for a car to pick you up** ich habe Ihnen einen Wagen besorgt, der Sie mitnimmt; **can you ~ an interview with the President for me?** können Sie mir ein Interview mit dem Präsidenten besorgen?; **there aren't enough glasses — I'll ~ that** es sind nicht genug Gläser da — das mache or reg(e)le (inf) ich; **his manager wants to ~ another fight next month** sein Manager will nächsten Monat noch einen Kampf ansetzen; **to ~ a sale/marriage** einen Verkauf/die Ehe vereinbaren; **I'll ~ the drinks, you get the food** ich besorge die Getränke, und du kümmerst dich um das Essen; **if you could ~ to be ill that morning/there at five** wenn du es so einrichten kannst, daß du an dem Morgen krank/um fünf Uhr da bist; **I think I could ~ that** ich glaube, das läßt sich machen or einrichten; **that's easily ~d** das läßt sich leicht einrichten or arrangieren (inf); **how can we ~ it so it looks like an accident?** wie können wir es machen or drehen (inf), daß es wie ein Unfall aussieht?; **the murder was ~d to look like an accident** es wurde so gemacht, daß der Mord nach einem Unfall aussah; **they'd obviously ~d things between themselves before the meeting started** sie hatten die Dinge offenbar vor Beginn des Treffens untereinander abgesprochen.
(c) (settle, decide on) vereinbaren, abmachen. **nothing definite has been ~d yet** es ist noch nichts Verbindliches vereinbart worden; **a meeting has been ~d for next month** nächsten Monat ist ein Treffen angesetzt; **good, that's ~d then** gut, das ist abgemacht!; **I don't like having things ~d for me** ich habe es nicht gern, wenn man Dinge für mich entscheidet; **but you ~d to meet me!** aber du wolltest dich doch mit mir treffen!
(d) (Mus) bearbeiten, arrangieren.

arrangement [əˈreɪndʒmənt] n **(a)** Anordnung f; (of room) Einrichtung f; (inf: contrivance) Gerät nt (inf). **a floral ~** ein Blumenarrangement nt; **the very unusual ~ of her hair** ihre sehr ungewöhnliche Haartracht.
(b) (agreement) Vereinbarung f; (to meet) Verabredung f; (esp shifty) Arrangement nt. **by ~** laut or nach Vereinbarung or Absprache; **by ~ with** mit freundlicher Genehmigung (+gen); **salary by ~** Gehalt nach Vereinbarung; **a special ~** eine Sonderregelung; **to have an ~ with sb** eine Regelung mit jdm getroffen haben; **he has an ~ with his wife ...** er hat mit seiner Frau ein Arrangement ...; **I've got a nice little ~ going** ich habe da so eine Abmachung or Absprache getroffen; **to make an ~ with sb** eine Vereinbarung or Absprache mit jdm treffen; **to come to an ~** eine Regelung finden; **to come to an ~ with sb** eine Regelung mit jdm treffen.
(c) (usu pl: plans) Pläne pl; (preparations) Vorbereitungen pl. **to make ~s for sb/sth** für jdn/etw Vorbereitungen treffen; **to make ~s for sth to be done** veranlassen, daß etw getan wird; **to make one's own ~s** selber zusehen(, wie ...), es selber arrangieren(, daß ...); **how are the ~s coming along for the sales conference?** gehen die Vorbereitungen für die Verkaufskonferenz voran?; **who's in charge of transport ~s?** wer regelt die Transportfrage?; **the new fire drill ~s** die neuen Feuerschutzmaßnahmen; **seating ~s** Sitzordnung f; **"funeral ~s"** „Ausführung von Bestattungen"; **who will look after the funeral ~s?** wer kümmert sich um die Beerdigung?
(d) (Mus) Bearbeitung f; (light music) Arrangement nt.

arranger [əˈreɪndʒəʳ] n (Mus) Arrangeur m.

arrant [ˈærənt] adj Erz-. ~ **coward** Erzfeigling m; ~ **nonsense** barer Unsinn.

arras [ˈærəs] n (old) (Arazzo)wandteppich m.

array [əˈreɪ] **1** vt **(a)** (line up) aufstellen; (Mil: troops) in Aufstellung bringen.
(b) (dress) person schmücken (geh), herausputzen (hum).
2 n **(a)** (Mil: arrangement) Aufstellung f. **in ~** in Aufstellung; **in battle ~** in Kampfaufstellung, in Schlachtordnung.
(b) (collection) Ansammlung f, Aufgebot nt (hum); (of objects) stattliche or ansehnliche Reihe f.
(c) (liter) Schmuck m (geh); (dress) Staat m. **the trees in all their spring ~** die Bäume im Frühlingskleid (poet).

arrears [əˈrɪəz] npl Rückstände pl. **to be in ~ with sth** im Rückstand mit etw sein; **to get** or **fall into ~** in Rückstand kommen.

arrest [əˈrest] **1** vt **(a)** (apprehend) festnehmen; (with warrant) verhaften; *ship* aufbringen. **I am ~ing you** ich muß Sie festnehmen/verhaften; **to ~ sb's attention** (*fig*) jds Aufmerksamkeit erregen *or* erheischen (*liter*).

(b) (*check*) hemmen; *sth unwanted* (Ein)halt gebieten (+*dat*) (*geh*). **~ed development** Entwicklungshemmung *f*.

2 *n* (*of suspect*) Festnahme *f*; (*with warrant*) Verhaftung *f*; (*of ship*) Aufbringen *nt*. **to be under ~** festgenommen/verhaftet sein; **you are under ~** Sie sind festgenommen/verhaftet; **to put sb under ~** jdn festnehmen/verhaften; **to make an ~** jdn festnehmen/verhaften; **they hope to make an ~ soon** man hofft, daß es bald zu einer Festnahme/Verhaftung kommt.

arresting [əˈrestɪŋ] *adj* **(a)** (*striking*) atemberaubend; *features* markant. **(b) the ~ officer** der festnehmende Beamte.

arrival [əˈraɪvəl] *n* **(a)** (*coming*) Ankunft *f no pl*; (*of person also*) Kommen, Eintreffen *nt no pl*; (*of train also, of goods, news*) Eintreffen *nt no pl*. **our eventual ~ at a decision ...** daß wir endlich zu einer Entscheidung kamen ...; **on ~** bei Ankunft; **~ time, time of ~** Ankunftszeit *f*; **~ lounge** Ankunftshalle *f*; **~s and departures** (*Rail*) Ankunft/Abfahrt *f*; (*Aviat*) Ankunft *f*/Abflug *m*.

(b) (*person*) Ankömmling *m*. **new ~** Neuankömmling *m*; (*at school also*) Neue(r) *mf*; (*in hotel, boarding house*) neuangekommener Gast; (*in firm, office*) neuer Mitarbeiter, neue Mitarbeiterin. **a new ~ on the pop scene** ein neues Gesicht auf der Popszene; **when our firm was still a new ~ in the publishing world** als unsere Firma noch ein Neuling im Verlagswesen war; **the new ~ is a little girl** der neue Erdenbürger ist ein kleines Mädchen; **he was the latest ~** er kam als letzter.

arrive [əˈraɪv] *vi* **(a)** (*come*) ankommen, eintreffen (*geh*); (*be born*) ankommen. **to ~ home** nach Hause kommen; (*stressing after journey etc*) zu Hause ankommen; **I'll wait for him to ~ before ...** ich warte, bis er kommt, bevor ...; **to ~ at a town/the airport** in einer Stadt/am Flughafen ankommen *or* eintreffen (*geh*); **the train will ~ at platform 10** der Zug läuft auf Gleis 10 ein; **the great day ~d** der große Tag kam; **a new era has ~d!** ein neues Zeitalter ist angebrochen!; **the time has ~d here yet** das Fernsehen ist noch nicht bis hier durchgedrungen; **to ~ at a decision** zu einer Entscheidung kommen *or* gelangen; **to ~ at the age of ...** das Alter von ... Jahren erreichen; **to ~ at an answer/a conclusion/result** zu einer Antwort/einem Schluß/Ergebnis kommen; **to ~ at a price** auf einen Preis kommen; (*agree on*) sich auf einen Preis einigen.

(b) (*inf: succeed*) **then you know you've really ~d** dann weiß man, daß man es geschafft hat.

arriviste [ˌæriːˈviːst] *n* Emporkömmling, Parvenü (*geh*) *m*.

arrogance [ˈærəgəns] *n* Arroganz, Überheblichkeit *f*.

arrogant *adj*, **~ly** *adv* [ˈærəgənt, -lɪ] arrogant, überheblich.

arrogate [ˈærəʊgeɪt] *vt* **to ~ sth to oneself** etw für sich in Anspruch nehmen; *title* sich (*dat*) etw anmaßen.

arrow [ˈærəʊ] **1** *n* (*weapon, sign*) Pfeil *m*. **2** *vt way, direction* durch Pfeile/einen Pfeil markieren.

♦ **arrow in** *vt sep* (*in text*) durch Pfeil einzeichnen.

arrow: **~ bracket** *n* spitze Klammer; **~head** *n* Pfeilspitze *f*; **~root** *n* (*plant*) Pfeilwurz *f*; (*flour*) Arrowroot *m*.

arse [ɑːs] *n* **(a)** (*vulg*) Arsch *m* (*sl*). **move** *or* **shift your ~!** sei nicht so lahmarschig! (*sl*); **get your ~ in gear!** setz mal deinen Arsch in Bewegung! (*sl*); **tell him to get his ~ into my office** (*esp US*) sag ihm, er soll mal in meinem Büro antanzen (*inf*); **get your ~ out of here!** (*esp US*) verpiß dich hier! (*sl*).

(b) (*sl: fool: also silly ~*) Armleuchter *m* (*inf*).

♦ **arse about** *or* **around** *vi* (*sl*) rumblödeln (*inf*).

arse: **~hole** *n* (*vulg*) Arschloch *nt* (*vulg*); **~licker** *n* (*vulg*) Arschlecker *m* (*vulg*).

arsenal [ˈɑːsɪnl] *n* (*Mil*) (*store*) Arsenal, Zeughaus (*old*) *nt*; (*factory*) Waffen-/Munitionsfabrik *f*; (*fig*) Waffenlager *nt*.

arsenic [ˈɑːsnɪk] *n* Arsen, Arsenik *nt*. **~ poisoning** Arsenvergiftung *f*.

arson [ˈɑːsn] *n* Brandstiftung *f*.

arsonist [ˈɑːsənɪst] *n* Brandstifter(in *f*) *m*.

art¹ [ɑːt] **1** *n* **(a)** (*painting etc*) Kunst *f*. **the ~s** die schönen Künste; **~ for ~'s sake** Kunst um der Kunst willen, Kunst als Selbstzweck; (*slogan*) L'art pour l'art; *see* **work**.

(b) (*skill*) Kunst *f*; (*physical technique also*) Geschick *nt*. **there's an ~ to driving this car/doing this sort of work** es gehört ein gewisses Geschick dazu, mit diesem Auto zu fahren/zu dieser Arbeit gehört ein gewisses Geschick; **there's an ~ to it** das ist eine Kunst; **the ~ of war/government** die Kriegs-/Staatskunst; **the ~ of conversation/translation** die Kunst der Unterhaltung/Übersetzung; **~s and crafts** Kunsthandwerk, Kunstgewerbe *nt*.

(c) (*human endeavour*) Künstlichkeit *f*. **unspoiled by ~** unverbildet; **are they the products of ~ or nature?** sind sie natürlich oder von Menschenhand geschaffen?; **her beauty owes more to ~ than nature** sie verdankt ihre Schönheit mehr der Kunst als der Natur.

(d) **~s** (*Univ*) Geisteswissenschaften *pl*; **A~s Faculty, Faculty of A~s** Philosophische Fakultät; **~s degree** Abschlußexamen *nt* der philosophischen Fakultät; **~s subject** geisteswissenschaftliches Fach; *see* **bachelor, liberal**.

(e) (*usu pl: trick*) List *f*, Kunstgriff *m*.

2 *adj attr* Kunst-.

art² (*old*) 2nd pers sing present of **be**.

art college *n see* **art school**.

Art Deco [ˈɑːtˈdekəʊ] *n* Art Déco *no art*.

artefact (*Brit*), **artifact** [ˈɑːtɪfækt] *n* Artefakt *nt*. **are these human ~s?** sind das Schöpfungen von Menschenhand?

arterial [ɑːˈtɪərɪəl] *adj* **(a)** (*Anat*) arteriell. **(b) ~ road** (*Aut*) Fernverkehrsstraße *f*; **~ line** (*Rail*) Hauptstrecke *f*.

arteriosclerosis [ɑːˈtɪərɪəʊsklɪˈrəʊsɪs] *n* (*Med*) Arteriosklerose, Arterienverkalkung *f*.

artery [ˈɑːtərɪ] *n* **(a)** (*Anat*) Arterie *f*, Schlag- *or* Pulsader *f*. **(b)** (*also traffic ~*) Verkehrsader *f*.

Artesian well [ɑːˈtiːzɪənˈwel] *n* artesischer Brunnen.

art form *n* (*Kunst*)gattung *or* -form *f*.

artful [ˈɑːtfʊl] *adj person, trick* raffiniert, schlau. **~ dodger** Schlawiner *m* (*inf*).

artfully [ˈɑːtfəlɪ] *adv* raffiniert.

artfulness [ˈɑːtfʊlnɪs] *n* Raffinesse *f*.

art gallery *n* Kunstgalerie *f*.

arthritic [ɑːˈθrɪtɪk] *adj* arthritisch. **she is ~** sie hat Arthritis.

arthritis [ɑːˈθraɪtɪs] *n* Arthritis, Gelenkentzündung *f*.

arthropod [ˈɑːθrəpɒd] *n* Gliederfüßer *m*. **the ~s** die Arthropoden *pl*.

Arthur [ˈɑːθəʳ] *n* Art(h)ur *m*. **King ~** König Artus.

Arthurian [ɑːˈθjʊərɪən] *adj* Artus-.

artic [ɑːˈtɪk] *n* (*Brit sl*) (Sattel)schlepper *m*.

artichoke [ˈɑːtɪtʃəʊk] *n* Artischocke *f*; *see* **Jerusalem**.

article [ˈɑːtɪkl] **1** *n* **(a)** (*item*) Gegenstand *m*; (*in list*) Posten *m*; (*Comm*) Ware *f*, Artikel *m*. **~ of value** Wertgegenstand *m*; **~ of furniture** Möbelstück *nt*; **~s of clothing** Kleidungsstücke *pl*; **toilet ~s** Toilettenartikel *pl*; *see* **genuine**.

(b) (*in newspaper etc*) Artikel, Beitrag *m*; (*encyclopedia entry*) Eintrag *m*.

(c) (*of constitution*) Artikel *m*; (*of treaty, contract*) Paragraph *m*. **~s of association** Gesellschaftsvertrag *m*; **~s of apprenticeship** Lehrvertrag *m*; **~ of faith** Glaubensartikel *m*; (*fig*) Kredo *nt*; **~s of war** (*Hist*) Kriegsartikel *pl*.

(d) (*Gram*) Artikel *m*, Geschlechtswort *nt*. **definite/indefinite ~** bestimmter/unbestimmter Artikel.

(e) (*of articled clerk*) **to be under ~s** (Rechts)referendar sein; **to take one's ~s** seine Referendarprüfung machen.

2 *vt apprentice* in die Lehre geben (*to* bei). **to be ~d to sb** bei jdm eine Lehre machen, bei jdm in die Lehre gehen; **~d clerk** (*Brit Jur*) Rechtsreferendar(in *f*) *m*.

articulate [ɑːˈtɪkjʊlɪt] **1** *adj* **(a)** *sentence, book* klar. **to be ~** sich gut *or* klar ausdrücken können; *clear and ~* klar und deutlich; **that is amazingly ~ for a five-year old** das ist erstaunlich gut ausgedrückt für einen Fünfjährigen.

(b) (*Anat*) gegliedert; *limb* Glieder-.

2 [ɑːˈtɪkjʊleɪt] *vt* **(a)** (*pronounce*) artikulieren.

(b) (*state*) *reasons, views* darlegen.

(c) (*Anat*) **to be ~d** zusammenhängen (*to, with* mit); **~d lorry** *or* **truck** Sattelschlepper *m*; **~d bus** Gelenk(omni)bus, Großraumbus *m*.

3 [ɑːˈtɪkjʊleɪt] *vi* artikulieren.

articulately [ɑːˈtɪkjʊltlɪ] *adv pronounce* artikuliert; *write, express oneself* klar, flüssig. **an ~ presented argument** eine klar verständlich vorgetragene These.

articulateness [ɑːˈtɪkjʊlɪtnɪs] *n* Fähigkeit *f*, sich gut auszudrücken.

articulation [ɑːˌtɪkjʊˈleɪʃən] *n* **(a)** Artikulation *f*. **(b)** (*Anat*) Gelenkverbindung *f*.

articulatory [ɑːˈtɪkjʊləˌtərɪ] *adj* (*Phon*) Artikulations-.

artifact *n see* **artefact**.

artifice [ˈɑːtɪfɪs] *n* **(a)** (*guile*) List *f no pl*. **(b)** (*stratagem*) (Kriegs)list *f*.

artificial [ˌɑːtɪˈfɪʃəl] *adj* **(a)** (*synthetic*) künstlich. **~ manure** Kunstdünger *m*; **~ hair** Kunsthaar *nt*; **~ limb** Prothese *f*, Kunstglied *nt*.

(b) (*fig*) (*not genuine*) künstlich; (*pej: not sincere*) *smile, manner* gekünstelt, unecht. **you're so ~** du bist nicht echt; **if you say it that way it sounds ~** wenn du es so sagst, klingt das unecht; **roses can be so ~** Rosen können so etwas Künstliches *or* Artifizielles (*geh*) haben.

artificial: **~ horizon** *n* künstlicher Horizont; **~ insemination** *n* künstliche Besamung.

artificiality [ˌɑːtɪfɪʃɪˈælɪtɪ] *n* **(a)** Künstlichkeit *f*. **(b)** (*insincerity, unnaturalness*) Gekünsteltheit *f*.

artificially [ˌɑːtɪˈfɪʃəlɪ] *adv* künstlich; (*insincerely*) gekünstelt.

artificial: **~ respiration** *n* künstliche Beatmung *f*; **~ silk** *n* Kunstseide *f*.

artillery [ɑːˈtɪlərɪ] *n* (*weapons, troops*) Artillerie *f*.

artilleryman [ɑːˈtɪlərɪmən] *n, pl* **-men** [-mən] Artillerist *m*.

artisan [ˈɑːtɪzæn] *n* Handwerker *m*.

artist [ˈɑːtɪst] *n* Künstler(in *f*) *m*; (*fig also*) Könner *m*. **an ~ in words** ein Wortkünstler *m*.

artiste [ɑːˈtiːst] *n* Künstler(in *f*) *m*; (*circus ~*) Artist(in *f*) *m*. **~'s entrance** Bühneneingang *m*.

artistic [ɑːˈtɪstɪk] *adj* künstlerisch; (*tasteful*) *arrangements* kunstvoll; (*appreciative of art*) *person* kunstverständig *or* -sinnig (*geh*). **the café has an ~ clientele** in dem Café verkehren Künstler; **~ temperament** Künstlertemperament *nt*; **an ~ life** ein Künstlerleben *nt*; **to look ~** wie ein Künstler aussehen; **she's very ~** sie ist künstlerisch veranlagt *or* begabt/sehr kunstverständig.

artistically [ɑːˈtɪstɪkəlɪ] *adv* künstlerisch; (*tastefully*) kunstvoll.

artistry [ˈɑːtɪstrɪ] *n* (*lit, fig*) Kunst *f*.

artless [ˈɑːtlɪs] *adj* unschuldig.

artlessly [ˈɑːtlɪslɪ] *adv* unschuldig. **she asked ~ whether ...** sie fragte voller Unschuld, ob ...

artlessness [ˈɑːtlɪsnɪs] *n* Unschuld *f*.

art lover *n* Kunstliebhaber(in *f*) *or* -freund *m*.

Art Nouveau [ˈɑːnuːˈvəʊ] *n* Jugendstil *m*.

art: **~ paper** *n* Kunstdruckpapier *nt*; **~ school** *n* Kunstakademie *or* -hochschule *f*; **~work** *n* (*in book*) Bildmaterial *nt*.

arty [ˈɑːtɪ] *adj* (+ *er*) (*inf*) Künstler-; *type also, tie, clothes* verrückt (*inf*); *person* auf Künstler machend (*pej*); *decoration,* *style* auf Kunst gemacht (*inf*); *film, novel* geschmäcklerisch. he was more of an ~ type than his brother er war mehr ein Künstlertyp als sein Bruder; she's in publishing/the theatre — oh yes, I knew it was something ~ sie arbeitet im Verlag/ Theater — ach ja, ich wußte doch, daß es etwas Geistiges/Künstlerisches war.

arty-crafty ['ɑːtɪ'krɑːftɪ], (*US*) **artsy-craftsy**['ɑːtsɪ'krɑːftsɪ] *adj* (*inf*) (a) see arty. (b) *object* kunstgewerblerisch.

arty-farty ['ɑːtɪ'fɑːtɪ] *adj* (*hum inf*) see arty.

Aryan ['ɛərɪən] 1 *n* Arier(in *f*) *m*. 2 *adj* arisch.

as [æz, əz] 1 *conj* (a) (*when, while*) als; (*two parallel actions*) während, als, indem (*geh*). he got deafer ~ he got older mit zunehmendem Alter nahm seine Schwerhörigkeit zu; ~ a child he would ... als Kind hat er immer ...

(b) (*since*) da.

(c) (*although*) rich ~ he is I won't marry him obwohl er reich ist, werde ich ihn nicht heiraten; stupid ~ he is, he ... so dumm er auch sein mag, ... er; big ~ he is I'll ... so groß, wie er ist, ich ...; much ~ I admire her, ... so sehr ich sie auch bewundere, ...; be that ~ it may wie dem auch sei *or* sein mag, sei dem, wie ihm wolle; try ~ he might so sehr er sich auch bemüht/bemühte.

(d) (*manner*) wie. do ~ you like machen Sie, was Sie wollen; leave it ~ it is laß das so; I did it ~ he did ich habe es wie er gemacht; the first door ~ you go upstairs/ ~ you go in die erste Tür oben/, wenn Sie hereinkommen; knowing him ~ I do so wie ich ihn kenne; ~ you yourself said ... wie Sie selbst gesagt haben ...; he drinks enough ~ it is er trinkt sowieso schon genug; it is bad enough ~ it is es ist schon schlimm genug; ~ it is, I'm heavily in debt ich bin schon tief verschuldet; ~ it were sozusagen, gleichsam; ~ you were! (*Mil*) weitermachen!; (*fig*) lassen Sie uns nicht stören; (*in dictation, speaking*) streichen Sie das; my husband ~ was (*inf*) mein verflossener *or* (*late*) verstorbener Mann.

(e) (*phrases*) ~ if *or* though als ob, wie wenn; he rose ~ if to go er erhob sich, als wollte er gehen; it isn't ~ if he didn't see me schließlich hat er mich ja gesehen; ~ for him/you (und) was ihn/dich anbetrifft *or* angeht; ~ from *or* of the 5th/now vom Fünften an/von jetzt an, ab dem Fünften/jetzt; so ~ to (*in order to*) um zu +*infin*; (*in such a way*) so, daß; be so good ~ to ... (*form*) hätten Sie die Freundlichkeit *or* Güte, ... zu ... (*form*); he's not so silly ~ to do that er ist nicht so dumm, das zu tun, so dumm ist er nicht.

2 *adv* ~ ... ~ so ... wie; not ~ ... ~ nicht so ... wie; twice ~ old doppelt so alt; just ~ nice genauso nett; late ~ usual! wie immer, zu spät!; is it ~ difficult ~ that? ist das denn so schwierig?; if he eats ~ quickly ~ that wenn er so schnell ißt; it is not ~ *or* so good ~ all that so gut ist es auch wieder nicht; you hate it ~ much ~ I do du magst das doch genausowenig wie ich; ~ recently ~ yesterday erst gestern; she is very clever, ~ is her brother sie ist sehr intelligent, genau(so) wie ihr Bruder; she was ~ nice ~ could be (*inf*) sie war so freundlich wie nur was (*inf*); ~ many/much ~ I could so viele/soviel ich (nur) konnte; there were ~ many ~ 100 es waren mindestens *or* bestimmt 100 da; not everyone is ~ tolerant nicht jeder ist so tolerant; this one is ~ good diese(r, s) ist genauso gut; ~ often happens, he was ... wie so oft, war er ...

3 *rel pron* (a) (*with same, such*) der/die/das; *pl* die. the same man ~ was here yesterday derselbe Mann, der gestern hier war; *see* such.

(b) (*dial*) der/die/das; *pl* die. those ~ knew him die ihn kannten.

4 *prep* (a) (*in the capacity of*) als. to treat sb ~ a child jdn als Kind *or* wie ein Kind behandeln; he appeared ~ three different characters er trat in drei verschiedenen Rollen auf.

(b) (*esp: such as*) wie, zum Beispiel. animals such ~ cats and dogs Tiere wie (zum Beispiel) Katzen und Hunde.

asbestos [æz'bestəs] *n* Asbest *m*.

asbestosis [ˌæzbes'təʊsɪs] *n* (*Med*) Asbestose, Asbeststaublunge *f*.

ascend [ə'send] 1 *vi* (*rise*) aufsteigen; (*Christ*) auffahren; (*slope upwards*) ansteigen (*to* auf +*acc*). in ~ing order in aufsteigender Reihenfolge. 2 *vt* stairs hinaufsteigen; *mountain, heights of knowlege* erklimmen (*geh*); *throne* besteigen. to ~ the scale (*Mus*) die Tonleiter aufwärts singen.

ascendancy, ascendency [ə'sendənsɪ] *n* Vormachtstellung *f*. to gain/have (the) ~ over sb die Vorherrschaft über jdn gewinnen/haben; to gain (the) ~ over one's fears/interviewer die Oberhand über seine Ängste/jdn, der einen befragt, gewinnen.

ascendant, ascendent [ə'sendənt] *n* to be in the ~ (*Astrol, fig*) im Aufgang sein; (*Astrol also*) aszendieren (*spec*); his star is in the ~ (*fig*) sein Stern ist im Aufgehen.

ascender [ə'sendər] *n* (*Typ*) Oberlänge *f*.

ascension [ə'senʃən] *n* the ~ (*Christi*) Himmelfahrt *f*; ~ Day Himmelfahrt(stag *m*) *nt*.

ascent [ə'sent] *n* Aufstieg *m*. the ~ of Ben Nevis der Aufstieg auf den Ben Nevis; it was his first ~ in an aeroplane er ist das erstemal in einem Flugzeug geflogen.

ascertain [ˌæsə'teɪn] *vt* ermitteln, feststellen.

ascertainable [ˌæsə'teɪnəbl] *adj* feststellbar. ~ quantities nachweisbare Mengen.

ascetic [ə'setɪk] 1 *adj* asketisch. 2 *n* Asket *m*. she's something of an ~ sie lebt ziemlich asketisch.

asceticism [ə'setɪsɪzəm] *n* Askese *f*. a life of ~ ein Leben in Askese.

ascorbic acid [ə'skɔːbɪkˈæsɪd] *n* Askorbinsäure *f*.

ascribable [ə'skraɪbəbl] *adj* to be ~ to sth einer Sache (*dat*) zuzuschreiben sein.

ascribe [ə'skraɪb] *vt* zuschreiben (*sth to sb* jdm etw); *importance, weight* beimessen (*to sth* einer Sache *dat*).

ascription [ə'skrɪpʃən] *n* Zuschreibung *f*. difficulties arising from the ~ of emotions to animals Schwierigkeiten, die sich ergeben, wenn man Tieren Gefühle zuschreibt.

asdic ['æzdɪk] *n* Echo(tiefen)lot *nt*.

aseptic [eɪ'septɪk] *adj* aseptisch, keimfrei; (*fig*) *atmosphere* steril, klinisch.

asexual [eɪ'seksjʊəl] *adj* ungeschlechtlich, geschlechtslos; *person* asexuell; *reproduction* ungeschlechtlich.

ash¹ [æʃ] *n* (*also* ~ tree) Esche *f*.

ash² *n* (a) Asche *f*. ~es Asche *f*; to reduce sth to ~es etw total *or* völlig niederbrennen; (*in war etc*) etw in Schutt und Asche legen; to rise from the ~es (*fig*) aus den Trümmern wieder auferstehen; ~es to ~es Erde zu Erde; *see* sackcloth.

(b) ~es *pl* (*of the dead*) Asche *f*.

(c) (*Cricket*) the A~es Testmatch zwischen Australien und England.

ashamed [ə'ʃeɪmd] *adj* beschämt. to be *or* feel ~ (*of sb/sth*) sich schämen (für jdn/etw, jds/einer Sache *geh*); it's nothing to be ~ of deswegen braucht man sich nicht zu genieren *or* schämen; I felt ~ for him ich habe mich für ihn geschämt; he is ~ to do it es ist ihm peinlich, das zu tun, er schämt sich, das zu tun; ... I'm ~ to say ..., muß ich leider zugeben; you ought to be ~ (of yourself) du solltest dich (was) schämen!, schäm dich!; you may well look ~ schäm dich ruhig!

ash: ~ bin *n* Asch(en)eimer *m*, Aschentonne *f*; ~ blonde *adj* aschblond; ~ can *n* (*US*) *see* ~ bin.

ashen ['æʃn] *adj* *colour* aschgrau, aschfarbig; *face* aschfahl (*geh*), kreidebleich.

ashen-faced [ˌæʃn'feɪst] *adj* kreidebleich.

ashlar ['æʃlər] *n* Quaderstein *m*.

ashore [ə'ʃɔːr] *adv* an Land. to run ~ stranden, auf den Strand auflaufen; to put ~ an Land gehen.

ash: ~pan *n* Aschenkasten *m*; ~tray *n* Aschenbecher *m*; A~ Wednesday *n* Aschermittwoch *m*.

ashy ['æʃɪ] *adj* (a) *see* ashen. (b) (*covered with ashes*) mit Asche bedeckt.

Asia ['eɪʃə] *n* Asien *nt*. ~ Minor Kleinasien *nt*.

Asian ['eɪʃn], **Asiatic** [ˌeɪʃɪ'ætɪk] 1 *adj* asiatisch. **Asian flu** asiatische Grippe. 2 *n* Asiat(in *f*) *m*.

aside [ə'saɪd] 1 *adv* (a) (*with verbal element*) zur Seite, beiseite. to push/lead sb ~ jdn zur Seite *or* beiseite schieben/nehmen; to keep sth ~ for sb für jdn etw beiseite legen; to turn ~ sich zur Seite drehen, sich abwenden (*esp fig*).

(b) (*Theat etc*) beiseite.

(c) (*esp US*) ~ from außer; ~ from demanding an extra 10% ... außer einer Zusatzforderung von 10% ...; ~ from being chairman of this committee he is ... außer Vorsitzender dieses Ausschusses ist er auch ...; this criticism, ~ from being wrong, is ... diese Kritik ist nicht nur falsch, sondern ...

2 *n* (*Theat*) Aparte *nt* (*rare*). to say sth in an ~ etw beiseite sprechen; there are too many ~s to the audience es wird zuviel zum Publikum gesprochen.

asinine ['æsɪnaɪn] *adj* idiotisch. what an ~ thing to do! wie kann man bloß so ein Esel sein!

ask [ɑːsk] 1 *vt* (a) (*inquire*) fragen; *question* stellen. to ~ sb the way/the time/his opinion jdn nach dem Weg/der Uhrzeit/seiner Meinung fragen; to ~ if ... (nach)fragen, ob ...; he ~ed me where I'd been er fragte mich, wo ich gewesen sei *or* wäre (*inf*) *or* bin (*inf*); if you ~ me wenn du mich fragst; don't ~ me! (*inf*), ~ me another! (*inf*) frag mich nicht, was weiß ich! (*inf*); I ~ you! (*inf*) ich muß schon sagen!

(b) (*invite*) einladen; (*in dancing*) auffordern. to ~ sb for *or* to lunch jdn zum (Mittag)essen einladen.

(c) (*request*) bitten (*sb for sth* jdn um etw); (*require, demand*) verlangen (*sb for sth* von jdm etw). to ~ sb to do sth jdn darum bitten, etw zu tun; are you ~ing me to believe that? und das soll ich glauben; all I ~ is ... ich will ja nur ...; you don't ~ for much, do you? (*iro*) mehr *or* sonst *or* weiter nichts? (*iro*); could I ~ your advice? darf ich Sie um Rat bitten?; he ~ed to be excused er bat, ihn zu entschuldigen, er entschuldigte sich; that's ~ing the impossible das ist ein Ding der Unmöglichkeit; he ~s too much of me er verlangt zuviel von mir; that's ~ing too much (of your staff) das ist zuviel verlangt (von Ihren Angestellten); it's not ~ing much das ist nicht (zu)viel verlangt.

(d) (*Comm*) *price* verlangen, fordern. ~ing price Verkaufspreis *m*; (*for car, house etc also*) Verhandlungsbasis *f*; what's your ~ing price? was verlangen Sie (dafür)?

2 *vi* (a) (*inquire*) fragen. to ~ about sb/sth sich nach jdm/etw erkundigen; ~ away! frag nur!; I only ~ed ich habe doch nur gefragt; and what does that mean, may I ~? und was soll das bedeuten, wenn ich mal fragen darf?; well may you ~ das fragt man sich mit Recht.

(b) (*request*) bitten (*for sth* um etw). you just have to ~ du mußt nur was sagen (*inf*), du brauchst nur zu fragen; I'm not ~ing for sympathy ich will kein Mitleid; there's no harm in ~ing Fragen kostet nichts!; it's yours for the ~ing du kannst es haben; you are ~ing for trouble du willst wohl Ärger haben; you ... you're ~ing for trouble wenn du ..., dann kriegst du Ärger; that's ~ing for trouble das kann ja nicht gutgehen; you ~ed for it (*inf*) du hast es ja so gewollt; he's ~ing for it (*inf*) er will es ja so, er will es ja nicht anders; to ~ for Mr X Herrn X verlangen; she was ~ing for you (*Scot*) sie hat sich nach dir erkundigt; to ~ for sth back etw wiederhaben wollen.

♦**ask after** *vi* +*prep obj* sich erkundigen nach. tell her I was ~ing ~ her grüß sie schön von mir.

♦**ask around** 1 *vi* herumfragen. 2 *vt sep* (*invite*) einladen.

♦**ask back** *vt sep* (a) (*invite*) zu sich einladen. he ~ed us ~ for a drink er lud uns sich auf einen Drink ein. (b) they never ~ed me ~ again sie haben mich nie wieder eingeladen. (c) let me ~ you something ~ lassen Sie mich eine Gegenfrage stellen.

♦**ask in** *vt sep* (*to house*) hereinbitten. she ~ed her boyfriend ~ sie hat ihren Freund mit reingenommen.

♦**ask out** *vt sep* einladen.

♦**ask up** *vt sep* heraufbitten; *boyfriend* mit raufnehmen.

askance [ə'skɑːns] *adv* to look ~ at sb jdn entsetzt ansehen; to look ~ at a suggestion/sb's methods *etc* über einen Vorschlag/jds Methoden *etc* die Nase rümpfen.

askew [ə'skjuː] *adv* schief.

aslant [ə'slɑːnt] (*liter*) **1** *adv* quer, schräg. **2** *prep* quer *or* schräg über.

asleep [ə'sliːp] *adj pred* **(a)** (*sleeping*) schlafend. to be (fast *or* sound) ~ (fest) schlafen; he was sitting there, ~ er saß da und schlief; to fall ~ einschlafen (*also euph*); to lie ~ schlafen; he is not dead, only ~ er ist nicht tot, er schläft nur *or* liegt nur im Schlaf (*geh*). **(b)** (*inf: numb*) eingeschlafen.

ASLEF ['æzlef] (*Brit*) *abbr of* **Associated Society of Locomotive Engineers and Firemen.**

asocial [eɪ'səʊʃəl] *adj* ungesellig.

asp [æsp] *n* (*Zool*) Natter *f*.

asparagus [əs'pærəgəs] *n, no pl* Spargel *m*. ~ tips Spargelspitzen *pl*; ~ **fern** Spargelkraut *nt*, Asparagus *m*.

aspect ['æspekt] *n* **(a)** (*liter: appearance*) Anblick *m*, Erscheinung *f*; (*face also*) Antlitz *nt*; (*of thing*) Aussehen *nt*. **(b)** (*of question, subject etc*) Aspekt *m*, Seite *f*. under the ~ of town planning aus stadtplanerischer Sicht; the political ~ of his novel der politische Aspekt des Romans, das Politische an dem Roman; what about the security/heating ~? was ist mit der Sicherheit/Heizung?, und die Sicherheits-/Heizungsfrage? (*inf*). **(c)** (*of building*) to have a southerly ~ Südlage haben. **(d)** (*Gram*) Aspekt *m*.

aspectual [æ'spektjuəl] *adj* (*Gram*) im Aspekt.

aspen ['æspən] *n* (*Bot*) Espe, Zitterpappel *f*. to tremble like an ~ (*liter*) zittern wie Espenlaub.

aspergillum [ˌæspə'dʒɪləm] *n* Weih(wasser)wedel *m*.

asperity [æs'perɪtɪ] *n* Schroffheit, Schärfe *f no pl*. the asperities of the winter (*liter*) der rauhe Winter (*geh*).

aspersion [əs'pɜːʃən] *n*: to cast ~s upon sb/sth abfällige Bemerkungen über jdn/etw machen; without wishing to cast any ~s ohne mich abfällig äußern zu wollen.

asphalt ['æsfælt] **1** *n* Asphalt *m*. **2** *vt* asphaltieren. **3** *adj attr* Asphalt-, asphaltiert. ~ **jungle** Asphaltdschungel *m*.

asphodel ['æsfədel] *n* Asphodelus, Affodill *m*.

asphyxia [æs'fɪksɪə] *n* Erstickung, Asphyxie (*spec*) *f*.

asphyxiate [æs'fɪksɪeɪt] *vti* ersticken. to be ~d ersticken.

asphyxiation [æsˌfɪksɪ'eɪʃən] *n* Erstickung *f*.

aspic ['æspɪk] *n* (*Cook*) Aspik *m or nt*, Gelee *nt*.

aspidistra [ˌæspɪ'dɪstrə] *n* Aspidistra *f*.

aspirant ['æspɪrənt] *n* Anwärter(in *f*) *m* (*to, for* auf +*acc*); (*for job*) Kandidat(in *f*) (für), Aspirant(in *f*) (*hum*) *m*; (*for sb's hand in marriage*) Bewerber *m* (um). ~ **to the throne** Thronanwärter(in *f*) *m*.

aspirate ['æspɪrət] **1** *n* Aspirata *f* (*spec*), Hauchlaut *m*. **2** *vt* ['æspɪreɪt] aspirieren, behauchen.

aspiration [ˌæspə'reɪʃən] *n* **(a)** (*hohes*) Ziel, Aspiration *f* (*geh*). his ~ towards Lady Sarah's hand (*liter*) seine Hoffnung auf Lady Sarahs Hand. **(b)** (*Phon*) Aspiration, Behauchung *f*.

aspire [ə'spaɪər] *vi* to ~ to sth nach etw streben, etw erstreben; to ~ to do sth danach streben, etw zu tun.

aspirin ['æsprɪn] *n* Kopfschmerztablette *f*.

aspiring [ə'spaɪərɪŋ] *adj* aufstrebend.

ass¹ [æs] *n* (*lit, fig inf*) Esel *m*. silly ~! blöder Esel!; don't be an ~! sei kein Esel!, sei nicht blöd!; to make a ~ of oneself sich lächerlich machen, sich blamieren.

ass² *n* (*US vulg*) see **arse**.

assagai *see* **assegai**.

assail [ə'seɪl] *vt* (*lit, fig*) angreifen; (*fig: with questions etc*) überschütten, bombardieren. a harsh sound ~ed my ears ein scharfes Geräusch drang an mein Ohr; to be ~ed by doubts von Zweifeln befallen sein *or* geplagt werden.

assailant [ə'seɪlənt] *n* Angreifer(in *f*) *m*.

assassin [ə'sæsɪn] *n* Attentäter(in *f*), Mörder(in *f*) *m*.

assassinate [ə'sæsɪneɪt] *vt* ein Attentat *or* einen Mordanschlag verüben auf (+*acc*). JFK was ~d in Dallas JFK fiel in Dallas einem Attentat *or* Mordanschlag zum Opfer, JFK wurde in Dallas ermordet; they ~d him sie haben ihn ermordet.

assassination [əˌsæsɪ'neɪʃən] *n* (geglücktes) Attentat, (geglückter) Mordanschlag (*of auf* +*acc*). ~ **attempt** Attentat *nt*; to plan an ~ ein Attentat planen; before/after the ~ vor dem Attentat/nach dem (geglückten) Attentat.

assault [ə'sɔːlt] **1** *n* **(a)** (*Mil*) Sturm(angriff) *m* (*on auf* +*acc*); (*fig*) Angriff *m* (*on gegen*). to make an ~ on sth einen (Sturm)angriff gegen etw führen; to take sth by ~ etw im Sturm nehmen, etw erstürmen. **(b)** (*Jur*) Körperverletzung *f*; indecent/sexual ~ Notzucht *f*. **2** *vt* **(a)** (*Jur: attack*) tätlich werden gegen; (*sexually*) herfallen über (+*acc*); (*rape*) sich vergehen an (+*dat*). to ~ sb with a stick jdn mit einem Stock angreifen. **(b)** (*Mil*) angreifen.

assault: ~ **course** *n* Übungsgelände *nt*; ~ **craft** *n* Sturmlandefahrzeug *nt*; ~ **troops** *npl* Sturmtruppen *pl*.

assay [ə'seɪ] **1** *n* Prüfung *f*. ~ **mark** Prüfzeichen *nt*. **2** *vt* **(a)** *mineral, ore,* (*fig*) *value, sb's worth* prüfen. **(b)** (*liter*) (*try*) sich versuchen an (+*dat*); (*put to the test*) *troops* prüfen.

assegai ['æsəgaɪ] *n* Assagai *m*.

assemblage [ə'semblɪdʒ] *n* **(a)** (*assembling*) Zusammensetzen *nt*, Zusammenbau *m*; (*of car, machine also*) Montage *f*. **(b)** (*collection*) (*of things*) Sammlung *f*; (*of facts*) Anhäufung *f*; (*of people*) Versammlung *f*.

assemble [ə'sembl] **1** *vt* zusammensetzen, zusammenbauen;

car, machine *etc also* montieren; *facts* zusammentragen; *Parliament* einberufen, versammeln; *people* zusammenrufen; *team* zusammenstellen. **2** *vi* sich versammeln. we are ~d here today to ... wir haben uns *or* sind heute versammelt, um ...

assembly [ə'semblɪ] *n* **(a)** (*gathering of people, Parl*) Versammlung *f*. what an ~ greeted the Queen! welch eine Menge hatte sich zur Begrüßung der Königin versammelt!; to meet in open ~ sich öffentlich versammeln, in öffentlicher Versammlung zusammenkommen. **(b)** (*Sch*) Morgenandacht *f*; tägliche Versammlung. **(c)** (*putting together*) Zusammensetzen *nt*, Zusammenbau *m*; (*of machine, cars also*) Montage *f*; (*of facts*) Zusammentragen *nt*. **(d)** (*thing assembled*) Konstruktion *f*.

assembly: ~ **hall** *n* (*Sch*) Aula *f*; ~ **line** *n* Montageband *nt*; ~ **plant** *n* Montagewerk *nt*; ~ **point** *n* Sammelplatz *m*; ~ **shop** *n* Montagehalle *f*; ~ **worker** *n* Montagearbeiter(in *f*) *m*.

assent [ə'sent] **1** *n* Zustimmung *f*. to give one's ~ to sth seine Zustimmung zu etw geben; by common ~ mit allgemeiner Zustimmung; royal ~ königliche Genehmigung. **2** *vi* zustimmen. to ~ to sth einer Sache (*dat*) zustimmen.

assert [ə'sɜːt] *vt* **(a)** (*declare*) behaupten; *one's innocence* beteuern. **(b)** (*insist on*) to ~ one's authority seine Autorität geltend machen; to ~ one's rights sein Recht behaupten; to ~ oneself sich behaupten *or* durchsetzen (*over gegenüber*); if you ~ yourself too much you will lose their support wenn Sie zu bestimmt auftreten, verlieren Sie ihre Unterstützung.

assertion [ə'sɜːʃən] *n* **(a)** (*statement*) Behauptung *f*; (*of innocence*) Beteuerung *f*. to make ~s/an ~ Behauptungen/eine Behauptung aufstellen. **(b)** *no pl* (*insistence*) Behauptung *f*.

assertive *adj*, ~**ly** *adv* [ə'sɜːtɪv, -lɪ] bestimmt.

assertiveness [ə'sɜːtɪvnɪs] *n* Bestimmtheit *f*.

assess [ə'ses] *vt* **(a)** *person, chances, abilities* einschätzen; *problem, situation, prospects also* beurteilen; *proposal, advantages also* abwägen. **(b)** *property* schätzen, taxieren; *person (for tax purposes)* veranlagen (*at mit*). to ~ sth at its true worth einer Sache (*dat*) den richtigen Wert beimessen. **(c)** *fine, tax* festsetzen, bemessen (*at auf* +*acc*); *damages* schätzen (*at auf* +*acc*).

assessment [ə'sesmənt] *n see vt* **(a)** Einschätzung *f*; Beurteilung *f*; Abwägen *nt*. in my ~ meines Erachtens; what's your ~ of the situation wie sehen *or* beurteilen Sie die Lage? **(b)** Schätzung, Taxierung *f*; Veranlagung *f*. **(c)** Festsetzung, Bemessung *f*; Schätzung *f*.

assessor [ə'sesər] *n* Schätzer, Taxator (*form*) *m*; (*Univ*) Prüfer(in *f*) *m*.

asset ['æset] *n* **(a)** *usu pl* Vermögenswert *m*; (*on balance sheet*) Aktivposten *m*. ~**s** Vermögen *nt*; (*on balance sheet*) Aktiva *pl*; personal ~**s** persönlicher Besitz; ~ **stripping** Aufkauf von finanziell gefährdeten Firmen und anschließender Verkauf ihrer Vermögenswerte. **(b)** (*fig*) it would be an ~ ... es wäre von Vorteil ...; he is one of our great ~**s** er ist einer unserer besten Leute; this player, the club's newest ~ dieser Spieler, die neueste Errungenschaft des Clubs; good health is a real ~ Gesundheit ist ein großes Kapital; his appearance is not an ~ to him aus seinem Aussehen kann er kein Kapital schlagen; he's hardly an ~ to the company er ist nicht gerade ein großes Kapital für die Firma.

asseverate [ə'sevəreɪt] *vt* (*form*) beteuern.

asseveration [əˌsevə'reɪʃən] *n* (*form*) Beteuerung *f*.

assiduity [ˌæsɪ'djuːɪtɪ] *n* gewissenhafter Eifer.

assiduous *adj*, ~**ly** *adv* [ə'sɪdjuəs, -lɪ] gewissenhaft.

assiduousness [ə'sɪdjuəsnɪs] *n* Gewissenhaftigkeit *f*.

assign [ə'saɪn] **1** *vt* **(a)** (*allot*) zuweisen, zuteilen (*to sb* jdm); *task etc also* übertragen (*to sb* jdm); (*to a purpose*) *room* bestimmen (*to* für); (*to a word*) *meaning* zuordnen (*to dat*); (*fix*) *date, time* bestimmen, festsetzen; (*attribute*) *cause, novel, play, music* zuschreiben (*to dat*). at the time ~ed zur festgesetzten Zeit; which class have you been ~ed? welche Klasse wurde Ihnen zugewiesen? **(b)** (*appoint*) berufen; (*to a mission, case, task etc*) betrauen (*to mit*), beauftragen (*to mit*). she was ~ed to this school sie wurde an diese Schule berufen; he was ~ed to the post of ambassador er wurde zum Botschafter berufen; I was ~ed to speak to the boss ich wurde damit beauftragt *or* betraut, mit dem Chef zu sprechen. **(c)** (*Jur*) übertragen, übereignen (*to sb* jdm). **2** *n* (*Jur*) (*also* ~**ee**) Abtretungsempfänger *m*.

assignation [ˌæsɪg'neɪʃən] *n* **(a)** Stelldichein, Rendezvous *nt*. **(b)** *see* **assignment (b-d).**

assignment [ə'saɪnmənt] *n* **(a)** (*task*) Aufgabe *f*; (*mission also*) Auftrag *m*, Mission *f*. **(b)** (*appointment*) Berufung *f*; (*to a mission, case, task etc*) Betrauung, Beauftragung *f* (*to mit*). his ~ to the post of ambassador/to this school seine Berufung zum Botschafter/an diese Schule. **(c)** (*allotment*) *see vt* **(a)** Zuweisung, Zuteilung *f*; Übertragung *f*; Bestimmung *f*; Zuordnung *f* (*to zu*). **(d)** (*Jur*) Übertragung, Übereignung *f*.

assimilate [ə'sɪmɪleɪt] *vt food, knowledge* aufnehmen; (*fig: into society etc also*) integrieren. newcomers are easily ~d Neuankömmlinge können leicht integriert werden.

assimilation [əˌsɪmɪ'leɪʃən] *n see vt* Aufnahme *f*; Integration *f*. his powers of mental ~ seine geistige Aufnahmefähigkeit.

assist [ə'sɪst] **1** *vt* helfen (+*dat*); (*act as an assistant to*) assistieren (+*dat*); *growth, progress, development* fördern, begünstigen. to ~ sb with sth jdm bei etw helfen *or* behilflich sein; to ~ sb in doing *or* to do sth jdm helfen, etw zu tun; ... who was ~ing the surgeon ..., der dem Chirurgen assistierte; in a wind-

~ed time of 10.01 seconds mit Rückenwind in einer Zeit von 10,01 Sekunden; **a man is ~ing the police (with their enquiries)** (euph) ein Mann wird von der Polizei vernommen.
2 vi **(a)** (help) helfen. **to ~ with sth** bei etw helfen; **to ~ in doing sth** helfen, etw zu tun.
(b) (be present in order to help, doctor) assistieren (at bei); (in church) ministrieren.
assistance [ə'sɪstəns] n Hilfe f. **to give ~ to sb** (come to aid of) jdm Hilfe leisten; **my secretary will give you every ~** meine Sekretärin wird Ihnen in jeder Hinsicht behilflich sein; **to come to sb's ~** jdm zu Hilfe kommen; **to be of ~ (to sb)** jdm helfen or behilflich sein; **can I be of any ~?** kann ich irgendwie helfen or behilflich sein?
assistant [ə'sɪstənt] **1** n Assistent(in f) m; (shop ~) Verkäufer(in f) m. **are you in charge here?** — **no, I am just an ~** sind Sie hier der Chef? — nein, ich bin bloß Mitarbeiter.
2 adj attr manager etc stellvertretend. **~ master/mistress** Lehrer(in f) m (ohne besondere zusätzliche Verantwortung); **~ priest** Hilfspriester m; **~ professor** (US) Assistenz-Professor(in f) m.
assizes [ə'saɪzɪz] npl (Brit dated) Gerichtstage, Assisen (old) pl. **at the county ~** während der Bezirksgerichtstage.
assn abbr of **association**.
associate [ə'səʊʃɪt] **1** n **(a)** (colleague) Kollege m, Kollegin f; (Comm: partner) Partner, Kompagnon, Teilhaber(in f) m; (accomplice) Komplize m, Komplizin f.
(b) (of a society) außerordentliches or assoziiertes Mitglied.
2 [ə'səʊʃɪeɪt] vt in Verbindung bringen, assoziieren (also Psych). **to ~ oneself with sb/sth** sich jdm/einer Sache anschließen, sich mit jdm/einer Sache assoziieren; **to be ~d with sb/sth** mit jdm/einer Sache in Verbindung gebracht or assoziiert werden; **it is ~d in their minds with ...** sie denken dabei gleich an (+acc) ...; **I don't ~ him with sport** ich assoziiere ihn nicht mit Sport, ich denke bei ihm nicht an Sport; **the A~d Union of ...** der Gewerkschaftsverband der ...
3 [ə'səʊʃɪeɪt] vi **to ~ with** verkehren mit.
associate: **~ member** n außerordentliches or assoziiertes Mitglied; **~ partner** n (Geschäfts)partner(in f) m; **~ professor** n (US) außerordentlicher Professor.
association [ə,səʊsɪ'eɪʃən] n **(a)** no pl (associating: with people) Verkehr, Umgang m; (co-operation) Zusammenarbeit f. **he has benefited from his ~ with us** er hat von seiner Beziehung zu uns profitiert; **he has had a long ~ with the party** er hat seit langem Verbindung mit der Partei.
(b) (organization) Verband m.
(c) (connexion in the mind) Assoziation f (with an +acc) (also Psych). **~ of ideas** Gedankenassoziation f; **to have unpleasant ~s for sb** unangenehme Assoziationen bei jdm hervorrufen; **I always think of that in ~ with ...** daran denke ich immer im Zusammenhang mit ...; **free ~** (Psych) freie Assoziation.
association football n (Brit) Fußball m, Soccer nt.
associative [ə'səʊʃɪətɪv] adj assoziativ.
assonance ['æsənəns] n Assonanz f.
assort [ə'sɔːt] vi (form) **(a)** (agree, match) passen (with zu). **(b)** (consort) Umgang pflegen (with mit).
assorted [ə'sɔːtɪd] adj **(a)** (mixed) gemischt. **(b)** (matched) zusammengestellt; see **ill-assorted**.
assortment [ə'sɔːtmənt] n Mischung f; (of goods also) Auswahl f (of an +dat), Sortiment nt (of von); (of ideas) Sammlung f. **this shop has a good ~** dieser Laden hat eine große Auswahl; **a whole ~ of boyfriends** ein ganzes Sortiment von Freunden.
asst abbr of **assistant**.
assuage [ə'sweɪdʒ] vt hunger, thirst, desire stillen, befriedigen; anger, fears etc beschwichtigen; pain, grief lindern.
assume [ə'sjuːm] vt **(a)** (take for granted, suppose) annehmen; (presuppose) voraussetzen. **let us ~ that you are right** nehmen wir an or gehen wir davon aus, Sie hätten recht; **assuming this to be true ...** angenommen or vorausgesetzt, (daß) das stimmt ...; **assuming (that) ...** angenommen, (daß) ...; **Professor X ~s as his basic premise that ...** Professor X geht von der Grundvoraussetzung aus, daß ...
(b) power, control übernehmen; (forcefully) ergreifen.
(c) (take on) name, title annehmen; sich (dat) zulegen; (guise, shape, attitude) annehmen. **to ~ a look of innocence/surprise** eine unschuldige/überraschte Miene aufsetzen; **the problem has ~d a new importance** das Problem hat neue Bedeutung gewonnen; **the sky ~d a reddish glow** (liter) der Himmel nahm rötliche Glut an (poet).
assumed [ə'sjuːmd] adj **(a)** name angenommen; (for secrecy etc also) Deck-. **(b)** (pretended) surprise, humility gespielt, vorgetäuscht. **in the ~ guise of a beggar** als Bettler verkleidet.
assumption [ə'sʌmpʃən] n **(a)** Annahme f; (presupposition) Voraussetzung f. **to go on the ~ that ...** von der Voraussetzung ausgehen, daß ...; **the basic ~s of this theory are ...** diese Theorie geht grundsätzlich davon aus, daß ...
(b) (of power, role etc) Übernahme f; (of office also) Aufnahme f; (forcefully) Ergreifen nt.
(c) (of guise, false name etc) Annahme f; (insincere: of look of innocence etc) Vortäuschung f, Aufsetzen nt. **with an ~ of innocence** mit unschuldiger Miene.
(d) (Eccl) **the A~** Mariä Himmelfahrt f.
assurance [ə'ʃʊərəns] n **(a)** Versicherung f; (promise also) Zusicherung f. **he gave me his ~ that it would be done** er versicherte mir, daß es getan (werden) würde; **do I have your ~ that ...?** garantieren Sie mir das ...?; **you have my ~ that ...** Sie können versichert sein, daß ... **(b)** (self-confidence) Sicherheit f. **(c)** (confidence) Zuversicht f; (in) Vertrauen nt (in in +acc). **in the ~ that ...** (liter) im Vertrauen darauf, daß ..., in der Zuversicht, daß ... **(d)** (esp Brit: life ~) Versicherung f.
assure [ə'ʃʊər] vt **(a)** (say with confidence) versichern (+dat). (promise) zusichern (+dat). **to ~ sb of sth** (of love,

willingness etc) jdn einer Sache (gen) versichern; (of service, support, help) jdm etw zusichern; **to ~ sb that ...** jdm versichern/zusichern, daß ...; **... I ~ you ...** versichere ich Ihnen.
(b) (make certain of) success, happiness, future sichern. **he is ~d of a warm welcome wherever he goes** er kann sich überall eines herzlichen Empfanges sicher sein.
(c) (esp Brit: insure) life versichern. **she ~d her life for £10,000** sie schloß eine Lebensversicherung über £10.000 ab.
assured [ə'ʃʊəd] **1** n (esp Brit) Versicherte(r) mf. **2** adj sicher; income, future also gesichert; (self-confident) sicher. **to rest ~ that ...** sicher sein, daß ...; **to rest ~ of sth** einer Sache (gen) sicher sein.
assuredly [ə'ʃʊərɪdlɪ] adv mit Sicherheit. **yes, most ~** ganz sicher.
Assyria [ə'sɪrɪə] n Assyrien nt.
Assyrian [ə'sɪrɪən] **1** adj assyrisch. **2** n **(a)** Assyrer(in f) m. **(b)** (language) Assyrisch nt.
aster ['æstər] n Aster f.
asterisk ['æstərɪsk] **1** n Sternchen nt. **2** vt mit Sternchen versehen.
astern [ə'stɜːn] (Naut) **1** adv achtern; (towards the stern) nach achtern; (backwards) achteraus. **2** prep **~ (of) the ship/of us** achteraus.
asteroid ['æstərɔɪd] n Asteroid m.
asthma ['æsmə] n Asthma nt.
asthmatic [æs'mætɪk] **1** n Asthmatiker(in f) m. **2** adj asthmatisch.
asthmatically [æs'mætɪkəlɪ] adv asthmatisch.
astigmatic [,æstɪg'mætɪk] adj astigmatisch.
astigmatism [æs'tɪgmətɪzəm] n Astigmatismus m.
astir [ə'stɜːr] adj pred **(a)** (in motion, excited) voller or in Aufregung. **(b)** (old, liter: up and about) auf den Beinen, auf.
ASTMS abbr of **Association of Scientific Technical and Management Staffs**.
astonish [ə'stɒnɪʃ] vt erstaunen, überraschen. **you ~ me!** (iro) das wundert mich aber! (iro), was du nicht sagst! (iro); **to be ~ed** erstaunt or überrascht sein; **I am ~ed or it ~es me that ...** ich bin erstaunt or es wundert mich, daß ...; **I am ~ed to learn that ...** ich höre mit Erstaunen or Befremden (geh), daß ...
astonishing [ə'stɒnɪʃɪŋ] adj erstaunlich.
astonishingly [ə'stɒnɪʃɪŋlɪ] adv erstaunlich. **~ (enough)** erstaunlicherweise.
astonishment [ə'stɒnɪʃmənt] n Erstaunen nt, Überraschung f (at über +acc). **look of ~** erstaunter or überraschter Blick; **she looked at me in (complete) ~** sie sah mich (ganz) erstaunt or überrascht an; **speechless with ~** sprachlos vor Überraschung; **to my ~** zu meinem Erstaunen or Befremden (geh).
astound [ə'staʊnd] vt sehr erstaunen, in Erstaunen (ver)setzen. **to be ~ed (at)** höchst erstaunt sein (über +acc).
astounding [ə'staʊndɪŋ] adj erstaunlich.
astrakhan [,æstrə'kæn] n Astrachan m. **2** attr Astrachan-.
astral ['æstrəl] adj Sternen-; (in theosophy) Astral-.
astray [ə'streɪ] adj verloren. **to go ~** (person) (lit) vom Weg abkommen; (fig: morally) vom rechten Weg abkommen, auf Abwege geraten; (letter, object) verlorengehen; (go wrong: in argument etc) irregehen; **to lead sb ~** (fig) jdn vom rechten Weg abbringen; (mislead) jdn irreführen.
astride [ə'straɪd] **1** prep rittlings auf. **2** adv rittlings; **ride im Herrensitz**.
astringency [əs'trɪndʒənsɪ] n (fig) Ätzende(s) nt.
astringent [əs'trɪndʒənt] **1** adj adstringierend; (fig) remark, humour ätzend, beißend. **2** n Adstringens nt.
astro- ['æstrəʊ] pref Astro-.
astrolabe ['æstrəleɪb] n Astrolab(ium) nt.
astrologer [əs'trɒlədʒər] n Astrologe m, Astrologin f.
astrological [,æstrə'lɒdʒɪkəl] adj astrologisch; sign also Tierkreis-.
astrology [əs'trɒlədʒɪ] n Astrologie f.
astronaut ['æstrənɔːt] n Astronaut(in f) m.
astronautics [,æstrə'nɔːtɪks] n sing Raumfahrt, Astronautik f.
astronomer [əs'trɒnəmər] n Astronom(in f) m.
astronomical [,æstrə'nɒmɪkəl] adj (lit, fig also astronomic) astronomisch. **~ year** Sternjahr nt.
astronomically [,æstrə'nɒmɪkəlɪ] adv (lit, fig) astronomisch.
astronomy [əs'trɒnəmɪ] n Astronomie f.
astrophysics [,æstrəʊ'fɪzɪks] n sing Astrophysik f.
astute [ə'stjuːt] adj schlau; remark also scharfsinnig; businessman also clever (inf); (shrewd) raffiniert, ausgebufft (inf); child aufgeweckt; mind scharf. **he's very ~ for one so old** er ist für sein Alter geistig sehr rege.
astutely [ə'stjuːtlɪ] adv see adj.
astuteness [əs'tjuːtnɪs] n see adj Schlauheit f; Scharfsinnigkeit f; Cleverneß f (inf); Aufgewecktheit f; Schärfe f.
asunder [ə'sʌndər] adv (liter) (apart) auseinander; (in pieces) entzwei, in Stücke. **to cleave/split ~** spalten; **her heart was rent ~** ihr brach das Herz; **... let no man put ~ ...**, soll der Mensch nicht trennen or scheiden.
asylum [ə'saɪləm] n **(a)** Asyl nt. **to ask for (political) ~** um (politisches) Asyl bitten. **(b)** (lunatic ~) (Irren)anstalt f.
asymmetric(al) [,eɪsɪ'metrɪk(əl)] adj asymmetrisch.
asymmetry [æ'sɪmɪtrɪ] n Asymmetrie f.
at [æt] prep **(a)** (position) an (+dat), bei (+dat); (with place) in (+dat). **~ the window/corner/top** am or beim Fenster/an der Ecke/Spitze; **~ university/school/a hotel/the zoo** an or auf der Universität/in der Schule/im Hotel/im Zoo; **~ my brother's** bei meinem Bruder; **~ a party** auf or bei einer Party; **to arrive ~ the station** am Bahnhof ankommen; **he/the rain came in ~ the window** er ist durch das Fenster hereingekommen/es hat durchs Fenster hineingeregnet.
(b) (direction) **to aim/shoot/point etc ~ sb/sth** auf jdn/etw zielen/schießen/zeigen etc; **to look/growl/swear etc ~ sb/sth** jdn/etw ansehen/anknurren/beschimpfen etc; **~ him!** auf ihn!

(c) (*time, frequency, order*) ~ ten o'clock um zehn Uhr; ~ night/dawn bei Nacht/beim *or* im Morgengrauen; ~ Christmas/Easter *etc* zu Weihnachten/Ostern *etc*; ~ your age/16 (years of age) in deinem Alter/mit 16 (Jahren); three ~ a time drei auf einmal; ~ the start/end of sth am Anfang/am Ende einer Sache (*gen*).

(d) (*activity*) ~ play/work beim Spiel/bei der Arbeit; good/bad/an expert ~ sth gut/schlecht/ein Experte in etw (*dat*); his employees/creditors are ~ him seine Angestellten/Gläubiger setzen ihm zu; while we are ~ it (*inf*) wenn wir schon mal dabei sind; the couple in the next room were ~ it all night (*inf*) die beiden im Zimmer nebenan haben es die ganze Nacht getrieben (*inf*); the brakes are ~ it again (*inf*) die Bremsen mucken schon wieder (*inf*); he doesn't know what he's ~ (*inf*) der weiß ja nicht, was er tut (*inf*); *see vbs*.

(e) (*state, condition*) to be ~ an advantage im Vorteil sein; ~ a loss/profit mit Verlust/Gewinn; I'd leave it ~ that ich würde es dabei belassen; see best, worst, that[1].

(f) (*as a result of, upon*) auf (+*acc*) ... (hin). ~ his request auf seine Bitte (hin); ~ her death bei ihrem Tod; ~ that/this he left the room daraufhin verließ er das Zimmer.

(g) (*cause: with*) angry, annoyed, delighted *etc* über (+*acc*).

(h) (*rate, value, degree*) ~ full speed/50 km/h mit voller Geschwindigkeit/50 km/h; ~ 50p a pound für *or* zu 50 Pence pro *or* das Pfund; ~ 5% interest zu 5% Zinsen; ~ a high/low price zu einem hohen/niedrigen Preis; when the temperature/thermometer is ~ 90° wenn die Temperatur bei *or* auf 90° ist/das Thermometer auf 90° steht; with prices ~ this level bei solchen Preisen; *see* all, cost, rate[1].

atavism ['ætəvɪzəm] *n* Atavismus *m*.
atavistic [ˌætə'vɪstɪk] *adj* atavistisch.
ataxia [ə'tæksɪə] *n* Ataxie *f*.
ataxic [ə'tæksɪk] *adj* ataktisch.
ate [et, (*US*) eit] *pret of* eat.
atheism ['eiθɪɪzəm] *n* Atheismus *m*.
atheist ['eiθɪɪst] 1 *n* Atheist *m*. 2 *adj attr* atheistisch.
atheistic [ˌeiθɪ'ɪstɪk] *adj* atheistisch.
Athenian [ə'θiːnɪən] 1 *n* Athener(in *f*) *m*. 2 *adj* athenisch; (*esp modern*) Athener.
Athens ['æθɪnz] *n* Athen *nt*.
athirst [ə'θɜːst] *adj* (*fig liter*) to be ~ for sth nach etw (*dat*) dürsten (*liter*); they are ~ for ... es dürstet sie nach ... (*liter*).
athlete ['æθliːt] *n* Athlet(in *f*) *m*; (*specialist in track and field events*) Leichtathlet(in *f*) *m*. he is a natural ~ er ist der geborene Sportler; ~'s foot Fußpilz *m*.
athletic [æθ'letɪk] *adj* sportlich; (*referring to athletics, build*) athletisch.
athletically [æθ'letɪkəlɪ] *adv* sportlich; *built* athletisch.
athleticism [æθ'letɪsɪzəm] *n* Athletentum *nt*.
athletics [æθ'letɪks] *n sing or pl* Leichtathletik *f*. ~ meeting Leichtathletikwettkampf *m*; sexual ~ Sexualakrobatik *f*.
at-home ['æt'həum] *n* Empfang *m* bei sich (*dat*) zu Hause.
athwart [ə'θwɔːt] 1 *adv* quer; (*Naut*) dwars. 2 *prep* quer über; (*Naut*) dwars, quer.
Atlantic [ət'læntɪk] 1 *n* (*also* ~ Ocean) Atlantik *m*, Atlantischer Ozean. 2 *adj attr* atlantisch. ~ crossing Atlantiküberquerung *f*; ~ Charter Atlantik-Charta *f*; ~ liner Ozeandampfer *m*; ~ wall Atlantikwall *m*.
atlas ['ætləs] *n* Atlas *m*.
atmosphere ['ætməsfɪər] *n* (*lit, fig*) Atmosphäre *f*; (*fig: of novel also*) Stimmung *f*.
atmospheric [ˌætməs'ferɪk] *adj* atmosphärisch; (*full of atmosphere*) *description* stimmungsvoll.
atmospherics [ˌætməs'ferɪks] *npl* (*Rad*) atmosphärische Störungen *pl*.
atoll ['ætɒl] *n* Atoll *nt*.
atom ['ætəm] *n* (a) Atom *nt*. (b) (*fig*) to smash sth to ~s etw völlig zertrümmern; not an ~ of truth kein Körnchen Wahrheit.
atom bomb *n* Atombombe *f*.
atomic [ə'tɒmɪk] *adj* atomar.
atomic *in cpds* Atom-; ~ age *n* Atomzeitalter *nt*; ~ bomb *n* Atombombe *f*; ~ clock *n* Atomuhr *f*; ~ energy *n* Atomenergie *f*; ~ energy authority (*Brit*) *or* (*US*) commission *n* Atomkommission *f*; ~ number *n* Ordnungszahl *f*; ~ power *n* Atomkraft *f*; (*propulsion*) Atomantrieb *m*; ~ powered *adj* atomgetrieben, Atom-; ~ structure *n* Atombau *m*; ~ weight *n* Atomgewicht *nt*.
atomism ['ætəmɪzəm] *n* (*Philos*) Atomismus *m*.
atomistic [ˌætə'mɪstɪk] *adj* (*Philos*) atomistisch.
atomize ['ætəmaɪz] *vt liquid* zerstäuben.
atomizer ['ætəmaɪzər] *n* Zerstäuber *m*.
atonal [æ'təunl] *adj* atonal.
atone [ə'təun] *vi* to ~ for sth (für) etw sühnen *or* büßen.
atonement [ə'təunmənt] *n* Sühne, Buße *f*. to make ~ for sth für etw Sühne *or* Buße tun; in ~ for sth als Sühne *or* Buße für etw; the A~ (*Eccl*) das Sühneopfer (Christi).
atop [ə'tɒp] *prep* (*liter*) (oben) auf (+*dat*).
atrocious *adj*, ~ly *adv* [ə'trəuʃəs, -lɪ] *adj* grauenhaft.
atrocity [ə'trɒsɪtɪ] *n* Grausamkeit *f*; (*act also*) Greueltat *f*.
atrophy ['ætrəfɪ] 1 *n* Atrophie *f* (*geh*), Schwund *m*. 2 *vt* schwinden lassen. 3 *vi* verkümmern, schwinden.
Att, Atty *abbr of* **Attorney** (*US*).
attach [ə'tætʃ] 1 *vt* (a) (*join*) festmachen, befestigen (*to an* +*dat*); *document to a letter etc* an- *or* beiheften. please find ~ed ... beigeheftet ...; to ~ oneself to sb/a group sich jdm/einer Gruppe anschließen, sich an jdn/eine Gruppe anschließen; is he/she ~ed? ist er/sie schon vergeben?
(b) to be ~ed to sb/sth (*be fond of*) an jdm/etw hängen.
(c) (*attribute*) *value, importance* beimessen, zuschreiben (*to dat*).
(d) (*Mil etc*) *troops, personnel* angliedern, zuteilen (*to dat*).

he/this office is ~ed to us er ist uns (*dat*) zugeteilt/diese Stelle ist uns (*dat*) angegliedert.
(e) (a) (*Mil etc*) *troops, personnel* angegliedert.
2 *vi no blame* ~es *or can* ~ to him ihm haftet keine Schuld an, ihn trifft keine Schuld; *salary/responsibility* ~ing *or* ~ed to this post Gehalt, das mit diesem Posten verbunden ist/Verantwortung, die dieser Posten mit sich bringt; great importance ~es to this dem haftet größte Bedeutung an.
attachable [ə'tætʃəbl] *adj* to be ~ sich befestigen lassen.
attaché [ə'tæʃeɪ] *n* Attaché *m*.
attaché case *n* Aktenkoffer *m*.
attachment [ə'tætʃmənt] *n* (a) (*act of attaching*) *see vt* (a) Festmachen, Befestigen *nt*; An- *or* Beiheften *nt*.
(b) (*accessory*) Zusatzteil, Zubehörteil *nt*.
(c) (*fig: affection*) Zuneigung *f* (*to* zu).
(d) (*Mil etc: temporary transfer*) Zuordnung, Angliederung *f*. to be on ~ to sth einer Sache (*dat*) angegliedert *or* zugeteilt sein.
attack [ə'tæk] 1 *n* (a) (*Mil, Sport, fig*) Angriff *m* (*on auf* +*acc*). there have been two ~s on his life es wurden bereits zwei Anschläge auf sein Leben gemacht *or* verübt; to be under ~ angegriffen werden; (*fig also*) unter Beschuß stehen; to go over to the ~ zum Angriff übergehen; to return to the ~ wieder zum Angriff übergehen; to launch/make an ~ zum Angriff ansetzen/einen Angriff vortragen *or* machen (*on auf* +*acc*); (*on sb's character*) angreifen (*on acc*); ~ is the best form of defence Angriff ist die beste Verteidigung; to leave oneself open to ~ Angriffsflächen bieten; she played the sonata with ~ sie nahm die Sonate kraftvoll *or* mit Schwung in Angriff.
(b) (*Med etc*) Anfall *m*. an ~ of fever/hay fever ein Fieberanfall/ein Anfall von Heuschnupfen; to have an ~ of nerves plötzlich Nerven bekommen.
2 *vt* (a) (*Mil, Sport, fig*) angreifen; (*from ambush, in robbery etc*) überfallen. to be ~ed by doubts Zweifel befielen ihn.
(b) (*tackle*) *task, problem, sonata* in Angriff nehmen.
(c) (*Med: illness*) befallen.
3 *vi* angreifen. an ~ing side (*Sport*) eine angriffsfreudige *or* offensive Mannschaft; he was ready to ~ er war zum Angriff bereit.
attacker [ə'tækər] *n* Angreifer *m*.
attain [ə'teɪn] 1 *vt* *aim, rank, age, perfection* erreichen; *knowledge* erlangen; *happiness, prosperity, power* gelangen zu. he has ~ed his hopes seine Hoffnungen haben sich erfüllt.
2 *vi* to ~ to sth *to perfection* etw erreichen; *to prosperity, power* zu etw gelangen; to ~ to man's estate (*form*) das Mannesalter erreichen (*form*).
attainable [ə'teɪnəbl] *adj* erreichbar, zu erreichen; *knowledge, happiness, power* zu erlangen.
attainder [ə'teɪndər] *n see* bill[3] (h).
attainment [ə'teɪnmənt] *n* (a) (*act of attaining*) Erreichung *f*, Erreichen *nt*; (*of knowledge, happiness, prosperity, power*) Erlangen *nt*. difficult/easy *etc* of ~ (*form*) schwierig/leicht zu erreichen *or* erlangen.
(b) (*usu pl: accomplishment*) Fertigkeit *f*. a low/high standard of ~ ein niedriger/hoher Leistungsstandard.
attempt [ə'tempt] 1 *vt* versuchen; *smile, conversation* den Versuch machen *or* unternehmen zu; *task, job* sich versuchen an (+*dat*). to ~ to do sth versuchen, etw zu tun; ~ed murder Mordversuch *m*.
2 *n* Versuch *m*; (*on sb's life*) (Mord)anschlag *m* (*on auf* +*acc*). an ~ on Mount Everest/the record ein Versuch, Mount Everest zu bezwingen/einen Rekord zu brechen; an ~ at a joke/at doing sth ein Versuch, einen Witz zu machen/etw zu tun; to make an ~ on sb's life einen Anschlag auf jdn *or* jds Leben verüben; to make an ~ at doing sth versuchen, etw zu tun; he made no ~ to help us er unternahm keinen Versuch, uns zu helfen; at the first ~ auf Anhieb, beim ersten Versuch; in the ~ dabei.
attend [ə'tend] 1 *vt* (a) *classes, church, meeting etc* besuchen; *wedding, funeral* anwesend *or* zugegen sein bei, beiwohnen (+*dat*) (*geh*). the wedding was well ~ed/was ~ed by fifty people die Hochzeit war gut besucht/fünfzig Leute waren bei der Hochzeit anwesend *or* wohnten der Hochzeit bei (*geh*).
(b) (*accompany*) begleiten; (*wait on*) *queen etc* bedienen, aufwarten (+*dat*). which doctor is ~ing you? von welchem Arzt werden Sie behandelt?, wer ist Ihr behandelnder Arzt?; a method ~ed by great risks eine Methode, die mit großen Risiken verbunden ist *or* von großen Risiken begleitet ist.
2 *vi* (a) (*be present*) anwesend sein. are you going to ~? gehen Sie hin?; to ~ at a birth bei einer Geburt helfen *or* assistieren; to ~ upon sb jdm aufwarten (*old*).
(b) (*pay attention*) aufpassen.
♦ **attend** to *vi* +*prep obj* (*see to*) sich kümmern um; (*pay attention to*) *work etc* Aufmerksamkeit schenken *or* widmen (+*dat*); (*listen to*) *teacher, sb's remark* zuhören (+*dat*); (*heed*) *advice, warning* hören auf (+*acc*), Beachtung schenken (+*dat*); (*serve*) *customers etc* bedienen. are you being ~ed ~? werden Sie schon bedient?; that's being ~ed ~ das wird (bereits) erledigt.
attendance [ə'tendəns] *n* (a) to be in ~ at sth bei etw anwesend sein; to be in ~ on sb jdm aufwarten, jdn bedienen; to be in ~ on a patient einen Patienten behandeln; she came in with her maids in ~ sie kam von ihren Hofdamen begleitet herein; the police are in ~ (*form*) die Polizei ist vor Ort (*form*).
(b) (*being present*) Anwesenheit *f* (*at* bei). ~ officer Beamter, der sich um Fälle häufigen unentschuldigten Fehlens in der Schule kümmert; ~ record (*school register etc*) Anwesenheitsliste *f*; he doesn't have a very good ~ record er fehlt oft; regular ~ at school regelmäßiger Schulbesuch.
(c) (*number of people present*) Teilnehmerzahl *f*. record ~ eine Rekordteilnehmerzahl, eine Rekordzahl von Teilnehmern *pl*.
attendant [ə'tendənt] 1 *n* (*in retinue*) Begleiter(in *f*) *m*; (*in public toilets*) Toilettenwart *m*, Toilettenfrau *f*; (*in swimming baths*) Bademeister(in *f*) *m*; (*in art galleries, museums*)

Aufseher(in f), Wärter(in f) m; (medical ~) Krankenpfleger(in f) m; (of royalty) Kammerherr m/-frau f. her ~s ihr Gefolge nt.

2 adj **(a)** problems etc (da)zugehörig, damit verbunden; circumstances, factors Begleit-. old age and its ~ ills Alter und die damit verbundenen Beschwerden; to be ~ (up)on sth mit etw zusammenhängen, etw begleiten.

(b) (form: serving) to be ~ on sb (lady-in-waiting etc) jdm aufwarten; there were two ~ nurses es waren zwei Krankenschwestern anwesend.

attention [ə'tenʃən] n **(a)** no pl (consideration, observation, notice) Aufmerksamkeit f. to call ~ to sth die Aufmerksamkeit auf etw (acc) lenken, auf etw (acc) aufmerksam machen; to call or draw sb's ~ to sth, to call sth to sb's ~ jds Aufmerksamkeit auf etw (acc) lenken, jdn auf etw (acc) aufmerksam machen; to attract sb's ~ jds Aufmerksamkeit erregen, jdn auf sich (acc) aufmerksam machen; to turn one's ~ to sb/sth jdm/einer Sache seine Aufmerksamkeit zuwenden, seine Aufmerksamkeit auf jdn/etw richten; to pay ~/no ~ to sb/sth jdn/etw beachten/nicht beachten; to pay ~ to the teacher dem Lehrer zuhören; to hold sb's ~ jdn fesseln; can I have your ~ for a moment? dürfte ich Sie einen Augenblick um (Ihre) Aufmerksamkeit bitten?; ~! Achtung!; your ~, please ich bitte um Aufmerksamkeit; (official announcement) Achtung, Achtung!; I was all ~ ich war ganz Ohr; it has come to my ~ that ... ich bin darauf aufmerksam geworden, daß ...; it has been brought to my ~ that ... es ist mir zu Ohren gekommen, daß ...

(b) ~s pl (kindnesses) Aufmerksamkeiten pl; to pay one's ~s to sb (dated: court) jdm den Hof machen.

(c) (Mil) to stand to or at ~, to come to ~ stillstehen; ~! stillgestanden!

(d) (Comm) ~ Miss Smith, for the ~ of Miss Smith zu Händen von Frau Smith; your letter will receive our earliest ~ Ihr Brief wird baldmöglichst or umgehend bearbeitet; for your ~ zur gefälligen Beachtung.

attentive [ə'tentɪv] adj aufmerksam. to be ~ to sb/sth sich jdm gegenüber aufmerksam verhalten/einer Sache (dat) Beachtung schenken; to be ~ to sb's interests/advice sich um jds Interessen kümmern/jds Rat (acc) beachten.

attentively [ə'tentɪvlɪ] adv aufmerksam.

attentiveness [ə'tentɪvnɪs] n Aufmerksamkeit f.

attenuate [ə'tenjueɪt] **1** vt (weaken) abschwächen; statement also abmildern; gas verdünnen; (make thinner) dünn machen. attenuating circumstances mildernde Umstände.

2 vi (get weaker) schwächer or abgeschwächt werden; (gas) sich verdünnen; (get thinner) dünner werden.

3 adj (Bot) ~ leaf lanzettförmiges Blatt.

attenuation [ə,tenju'eɪʃən] n see vt Abschwächen nt, Abschwächung f; Abmildern nt, Abmilderung f; Verdünnen nt, Verdünnung f; (making thinner) Verdünnung f.

attest [ə'test] vt **(a)** (certify, testify to) sb's innocence, authenticity bestätigen, bescheinigen; signature also beglaubigen; (on oath) beschwören. ~ed herd (Brit) tuberkulosefreier Bestand. **(b)** (be proof of) beweisen, bezeugen.

♦**attest to** vi +prep obj bezeugen.

attestation [,ætes'teɪʃən] n adj **(a)** (certifying) Bestätigung f; (of signature also) Beglaubigung f; (document) Bescheinigung f. **(b)** (proof: of ability etc) Beweis m.

attestor [ə'testə'] n Beglaubiger m.

attic [ætɪk] n Dachboden, Speicher m; (lived-in) Mansarde f. ~ room Dachstube, Dachkammer f; Mansardenzimmer, Dachzimmer nt; in the ~ auf dem (Dach)boden or Speicher.

Attic [ætɪk] adj attisch.

Attica [ætɪkə] n Attika nt.

Attila [ætɪlə] n Atilla m. ~ the Hun Attila, der Hunnenkönig.

attire [ə'taɪə'] **1** vt kleiden (in in +acc). **2** n, no pl Kleidung f. ceremonial ~ Festtracht f, volles Ornat.

attitude [ætɪtju:d] n **(a)** (way of thinking) Einstellung f (to, towards zu); (way of acting, manner) Haltung f (to, towards gegenüber). ~ of mind Geisteshaltung f; I don't like your ~ ich bin mit dieser Einstellung überhaupt nicht einverstanden; (manner) ich bin mit Ihrem Benehmen überhaupt nicht einverstanden; well, if that's your ~ ja, wenn du so denkst ... **(b)** (way of standing) Haltung f. to strike an ~/a defensive ~ eine Pose einnehmen/in Verteidigungsstellung gehen. **(c)** (in ballet) Attitüde f. **(d)** (Aviat, Space) Lage f.

attitudinize [,ætɪ'tju:dɪnaɪz] vi so tun, als ob, posieren (geh).

attn prep z. Hd(n) von.

attorney [ə'tɜ:nɪ] n **(a)** (Comm, Jur: representative) Bevollmächtigte(r) mf, Stellvertreter m. letter of ~ (schriftliche) Vollmacht; see power. **(b)** (US: lawyer) (Rechts)anwalt m. **(c)** ~ general (US) (public prosecutor) of state government) ≈ Generalstaatsanwalt m; (of federal government) ≈ Generalbundesanwalt m; (Brit) ≈ Justizminister m.

attract [ə'trækt] vt **(a)** (Phys: magnet etc) anziehen. **(b)** (fig: appeal to) (person) anziehen; (idea, music, place etc) ansprechen. she feels ~ed to him/to the idea sie fühlt sich von ihm angezogen or von der Idee reizt sie; I am not ~ed to her/by it sie zieht mich nicht an/es reizt mich nicht. **(c)** (fig: win, gain) interest, attention etc auf sich (acc) ziehen or lenken; new members, investors etc anziehen, anlocken. to ~ publicity/notoriety (öffentliches) Aufsehen erregen.

attraction [ə'trækʃən] n **(a)** (Phys, fig) Anziehungskraft f. to lose one's/its ~ seinen Reiz verlieren; I still feel a certain ~ towards him ich fühle mich noch immer von ihm angezogen; to have an ~ for sb Anziehungskraft or einen Reiz auf jdn ausüben; what are the ~s of this subject? was ist an diesem Fach reizvoll?; he couldn't resist the ~ of the city er konnte den Reizen der Stadt nicht widerstehen. **(b)** (attractive thing) Attraktion f.

attractive [ə'træktɪv] adj **(a)** attraktiv; personality, smile

anziehend; house, view, furnishings, picture, dress, location reizvoll; story, music nett, ansprechend; price, idea, offer also verlockend, reizvoll. **(b)** (Phys) Anziehungs-.

attractively [ə'træktɪvlɪ] adv attraktiv; smile anziehend; dress, furnish, paint reizvoll. ~ priced zum attraktiven or verlockenden Preis (at von).

attractiveness [ə'træktɪvnɪs] n Attraktivität f; (of house, furnishing, view etc) Reiz m. the ~ of her appearance ihr reizvolles or ansprechendes or anziehendes Äußeres; the ~ of the melody die ansprechende Melodie.

attributable [ə'trɪbjutəbl] adj to be ~ to sb/sth jdm/einer Sache zuzuschreiben sein.

attribute [ə'trɪbju:t] **1** vt to ~ sth to sb play, remark etc jdm etw zuschreiben; (credit sb with sth) intelligence, feelings etc also jdm etw beimessen; to ~ sth to sth success, accident etc etw auf etw (acc) zurückführen, einer Sache (dat) etw zuschreiben; (attach) importance etc einer Sache (dat) etw beimessen; to ~ sb/sth with sth jdm/einer Sache etw beimessen.

2 [ætrɪbju:t] n **(a)** (quality) Merkmal, Attribut nt. **(b)** (esp Liter, Art: symbol) Attribut nt. **(c)** (Gram) Attribut nt.

attribution [,ætrɪ'bju:ʃən] n **(a)** no pl the ~ of this play to Shakespeare (die Tatsache), daß man Shakespeare dieses Schauspiel zuschreibt; the ~ of the accident to mechanical failure (die Tatsache), daß man den Unfall auf mechanisches Versagen zurückführt. **(b)** (attribute) Attribut nt, Eigenschaft f.

attributive [ə'trɪbjutɪv] (Gram) **1** adj attributiv, Attributiv-. **2** n Attributiv nt.

attrition [ə'trɪʃən] n (lit, form) Abrieb m, Zerreibung f; (fig) Zermürbung f; (Rel) unvollkommene Reue, Attrition f (spec). war of ~ (Mil) Zermürbungskrieg m.

attune [ə'tju:n] vt (fig) abstimmen (to auf +acc). to ~ oneself to sth sich auf etw (acc) einstellen; to become ~d to sth sich an etw (acc) gewöhnen; the two of them are so well ~d to each other that ... die beiden sind so gut aufeinander eingespielt, daß ...

Atty Gen abbr of **Attorney General.**

atwitter [ə'twɪtə'] adj pred (fig) in heller Aufregung.

atypical [,eɪ'tɪpɪkəl] adj atypisch.

aubergine ['əʊbəʒi:n] **1** n Aubergine f; (colour) Aubergine nt. **2** adj aubergine(farben).

auburn ['ɔ:bən] adj hair rotbraun, rostrot.

auction ['ɔ:kʃən] **1** n Auktion, Versteigerung f. to sell sth by ~ etw versteigern; to put sth up for ~ etw zum Versteigern or zur Versteigerung anbieten; ~ bridge (Cards) Auktionsbridge nt. **2** vt (also ~ off) versteigern.

auctioneer [,ɔ:kʃə'nɪə'] n Auktionator m.

auction: ~ room n Auktionshalle f, Auktionssaal m; ~ rooms npl Auktionshalle f; ~ sale n Auktion, Versteigerung f.

audacious [ɔ:'deɪʃəs] adj, ~ly adv ['deɪʃəs, -lɪ] **(a)** (impudent) dreist, unverfroren. **(b)** (bold) kühn, wagemutig, verwegen.

audacity [ɔ:'dæsɪtɪ], **audaciousness** [ɔ:'deɪʃəsnɪs] n **(a)** (impudence) Dreistigkeit, Unverfrorenheit f. to have the ~ to do sth die Dreistigkeit or Unverfrorenheit besitzen, etw zu tun. **(b)** (boldness) Kühnheit, Verwegenheit f; (of person also) Wagemut m.

audibility [,ɔ:dɪ'bɪlɪtɪ] n Hörbarkeit, Vernehmbarkeit f.

audible ['ɔ:dɪbl] adj hörbar, (deutlich) vernehmbar. she was hardly ~ man konnte sie kaum hören.

audibly ['ɔ:dɪblɪ] adv hörbar, vernehmlich.

audience ['ɔ:dɪəns] n **(a)** Publikum nt no pl; (Theat, TV also) Zuschauer pl; (of speaker also) Zuhörer pl; (of writer, book also) Leserkreis m, Leserschaft f; (Rad, Mus also) Zuhörerschaft f. to have a large ~ ein großes Publikum haben or ansprechen (also Rad, TV etc); I prefer London ~s ich ziehe das Publikum in London vor. **(b)** (formal interview) Audienz f.

audio ['ɔ:dɪəʊ] adj attr Audio-.

audio-frequency [,ɔ:dɪəʊ'fri:kwənsɪ] n Hörfrequenz f.

audiometer [,ɔ:dɪ'ɒmɪtə'] n Audiometer nt, Gehörmesser m.

audio: ~ typist n Phonotypistin f; ~-visual adj audiovisuell.

audit ['ɔ:dɪt] **1** n Bücherrevision, Buchprüfung f. **2** vt **(a)** accounts prüfen. **(b)** (US Univ) belegen, ohne einen Schein zu machen, Gasthörer sein bei.

audition [ɔ:'dɪʃən] **1** n (Theat) Vorsprechprobe f; (of musician) Probespiel nt; (of singer) Vorsingen nt. she was asked for ~ sie wurde zum Vorsprechen/Probespiel/Vorsingen eingeladen. **2** vt vorsprechen/vorspielen/vorsingen lassen. **3** vi vorsprechen; vorspielen; vorsingen.

auditor ['ɔ:dɪtə'] n **(a)** (listener) Zuhörer(in f) m. **(b)** (Comm) Rechnungsprüfer, Buchprüfer m. **(c)** (US Univ) Gasthörer m.

auditorium [,ɔ:dɪ'tɔ:rɪəm] n Auditorium nt; (in theatre, cinema also) Zuschauerraum m; (in concert hall also) Zuhörersaal m.

auditory ['ɔ:dɪtərɪ] adj ability Hör-; nerve, centre Gehör-.

au fait [,əʊ'feɪ] adj vertraut.

Aug abbr of **August** Aug.

Augean stables [ɔ:'dʒi:ən'steɪblz] npl Augiasstall m. to clean out the ~ (Myth, fig) den Augiasstall ausmisten.

auger ['ɔ:gə'] n Handbohrer, Stangenbohrer m; (Agr) Schnecke f.

aught [ɔ:t] n (old, liter) irgend etwas. he might have moved for ~ I know was weiß ich, vielleicht ist er umgezogen; for ~ I care das ist mir einerlei.

augment [ɔ:g'ment] **1** vt vermehren; income also vergrößern. **2** vi zunehmen; (income etc also) sich vergrößern.

augmentation [,ɔ:gmən'teɪʃən] n see vti Vermehrung f; Vergrößerung f; Zunahme f; (Mus) Augmentation f.

augmented [ɔ:g'mentɪd] adj (Mus) fourth, fifth übermäßig.

au gratin [,əʊ'grætæŋ] adv überbacken, au gratin. **cauliflower**

~ überbackener Blumenkohl, Blumenkohl *m* au gratin.
augur ['ɔːgə'] **1** *n* (*person*) Augur *m*. **2** *vi* to ~ well/ill etwas Gutes/nichts Gutes verheißen. **3** *vt* verheißen. it ~s no good das verheißt nichts Gutes.
augury ['ɔːgjʊrɪ] *n* (*sign*) Anzeichen, Omen *nt*.
august [ɔː'gʌst] *adj* illuster; *occasion, spectacle* erhaben.
August ['ɔːgəst] *n* August *m*; *see* **September.**
Augustan [ɔː'gʌstən] **1** *adj* Augusteisch. **2** *n* Schriftsteller *m* im Augusteischen Zeitalter.
Augustine [ɔː'gʌstɪn] *n* Augustinus *m*.
Augustinian [ˌɔːgəs'tɪnɪən] **1** *adj* Augustiner-. **2** *n* Augustiner *m*.
auk [ɔːk] *n* (*Zool*) Alk *m*. great ~ Toralk *m*; little ~ Krabbentaucher *m*.
auld [ɔːld] *adj* (+*er*) (*Scot*) alt. **A~ Lang Syne** (*song*) Nehmt Abschied, Brüder; **for ~ lang syne** um der alten Zeiten willen.
aunt [ɑːnt] *n* Tante *f*.
auntie, aunty ['ɑːntɪ] *n* (*inf*) Tante *f*. ~! Tantchen!; **A~** (*Brit hum*) die BBC, britische Rundfunk- und Fernsehanstalt.
Aunt Sally [ˌɑːnt'sælɪ] *n* (*Brit*) (*lit*) Schießbudenfigur *f*; (*stall*) Schieß- *or* Wurfbude *f*; (*fig*) Zielscheibe *f*.
au pair ['əʊ'pɛə] **1** *n, pl - -s* (*also* ~ **girl**) Au-pair(-Mädchen) *nt*. **2** *adv* au pair.
aura ['ɔːrə] *n* Aura *f* (*geh*), Fluidum *nt* (*geh*). **he has an ~ of saintliness about him** ihn umgibt eine Aura der Heiligkeit (*geh*), er steht im Nimbus der Heiligkeit; **she has a mysterious ~ about her** eine geheimnisvolle Aura (*geh*) *or* ein geheimnisvoller Nimbus umgibt sie; **an ~ of prosperity/culture** ein Flair von Wohlstand/Kultur (*geh*); **he has an ~ of calm** er strömt *or* strahlt Ruhe aus; **the castle has an ~ of evil** vom Schloß strömt etwas Böses aus; **it gives the hotel an ~ of respectability** es verleiht dem Hotel einen Anstrich von Achtbarkeit.
aural ['ɔːrəl] *adj* Gehör-, aural (*spec*); *examination* Hör-.
aureole ['ɔːrɪˌəʊl] *n* (*Astron*) Korona *f*; (*because of haze*) Hof *m*, Aureole *f*; (*Art*) Aureole *f*.
auricle ['ɔːrɪkl] *n* (*Anat*) Ohrmuschel, Auricula (*spec*); (*of heart*) Vorhof *m*, Atrium *nt* (*spec*).
auricular [ɔː'rɪkjʊlə'] *adj* (*Anat*) (*of ear*) aurikular (*spec*), Ohren-, Gehör-. ~ **nerve** Hörnerv *m*; ~ **confession** Ohrenbeichte *f*, geheime Beichte. **(b)** (*of heart*) aurikular (*spec*), Aurikular- (*spec*). ~ **flutter** (Herz)vorhofflattern *nt*.
aurochs ['ɔːrɒks] *n* Auerochse, Ur *m*.
aurora [ɔː'rɔːrə] *n* (*Astron*) Polarlicht *nt*. ~ **australis/borealis** südliches/nördliches Polarlicht, Süd-/Nordlicht *nt*.
auscultate ['ɔːskəlteɪt] *vt* abhören, auskultieren (*spec*).
auscultation [ˌɔːskəl'teɪʃən] *n* Abhören *nt*.
auspices ['ɔːspɪsɪz] *npl* **(a)** (*sponsorship*) Schirmherrschaft *f*. **under the ~ of** unter der Schirmherrschaft (+*gen*), unter den Auspizien (+*gen*) (*geh*). **(b)** (*auguries*) Vorzeichen, Auspizien (*geh*) *pl*. **under favourable ~** unter günstigen Vorzeichen *or* Auspizien (*geh*).
auspicious [ɔːs'pɪʃəs] *adj* günstig; *start* vielverheißend, vielversprechend. **an ~ occasion** ein feierlicher Anlaß.
auspiciously [ɔːs'pɪʃəslɪ] *adv* verheißungsvoll, vielversprechend.
Aussie ['ɒzɪ] (*inf*) **1** *n* **(a)** (*person*) Australier(in *f*) *m*. **(b)** (*Austral*) (*country*) Australien *nt*; (*dialect*) australisches Englisch. **2** *adj* australisch.
austere [ɒs'tɪə'] *adj* streng; *way of life also* asketisch, entsagend; *style also* schmucklos; *room* schmucklos, karg.
austerely [ɒs'tɪəlɪ] *adv* streng; *furnish* karg, schmucklos; *live* asketisch, entsagend.
austerity [ɒs'terɪtɪ] *n* **(a)** (*severity*) Strenge *f*; (*simplicity*) strenge Einfachheit, Schmucklosigkeit *f*; (*of landscape*) Härte *f*. **(b)** (*hardship, shortage*) Entbehrung *f*. **after the ~ of the war years** nach den Entbehrungen der Kriegsjahre; **a life of ~** ein Leben der Entsagung; ~ **budget** Sparhaushalt *m*; ~ **measures** Sparmaßnahmen, Austerity-Maßnahmen *pl*.
Australasia [ˌɔːstrə'leɪsɪə] *n* Australien und Ozeanien *nt*.
Australasian [ˌɔːstrə'leɪsjən] **1** *n* Ozeanier(in *f*) *m*. **2** *adj* ozeanisch, südwestpazifisch, Südwestpazifik-.
Australia [ɒs'treɪlɪə] *n* Australien *nt*.
Australian [ɒs'treɪlɪən] **1** *n* Australier(in *f*) *m*; (*accent*) australisches Englisch. **2** *adj* australisch.
Austria ['ɒstrɪə] *n* Österreich *nt*.
Austria-Hungary ['ɒstrɪə'hʌŋgərɪ] *n* Österreich-Ungarn *nt*.
Austrian ['ɒstrɪən] **1** *n* Österreicher(in *f*) *m*; (*dialect*) Österreichisch *nt*. **2** *adj* österreichisch.
Austro- ['ɒstrəʊ] *pref* Austro-. ~-**Hungarian** österreichisch-ungarisch.
aut *abbr of* **automatic.**
autarchy ['ɔːtɑːkɪ] *n* **(a)** Selbstregierung *f*. **(b)** *see* **autarky.**
autarky ['ɔːtɑːkɪ] *n* Autarkie *f*.
authentic [ɔː'θentɪk] *adj signature, manuscript, portrait* authentisch; *accent, antique, tears* echt; *claim to title etc* berechtigt.
authenticate [ɔː'θentɪkeɪt] *vt* bestätigen, authentifizieren (*geh*); *signature, document* beglaubigen; *manuscript, work of art* für echt befinden *or* erklären; *claim* bestätigen. it was ~d as being ... es wurde bestätigt, daß es ... war.
authentication [ɔːˌθentɪ'keɪʃən] *n see vt* Bestätigung, Authentifizierung (*geh*) *f*; Beglaubigung *f*; Echtheitserklärung *f*; Bestätigung *f*.
authenticity [ˌɔːθen'tɪsɪtɪ] *n* Echtheit, Authentizität (*geh*) *f*; (*of claim to title etc*) Berechtigung *f*.
author ['ɔːθə'] *n* (*profession*) Autor(in *f*), Schriftsteller(in *f*) *m*; (*of report, pamphlet*) Verfasser(in *f*) *m*; (*fig*) Urheber(in *f*) *m*; (*of plan*) Initiator(in *f*) *m*; (*of invention*) Vater *m*. **the ~ of the book** der Autor (des Buches); ~'s **copy** Autorenexemplar *nt*.
authoress ['ɔːθərɪs] *n* Schriftstellerin *f*.
authoritarian [ˌɔːθɒrɪ'tɛərɪən] **1** *adj* autoritär. **2** *n* autoritärer

Mensch/Vater/Politiker *etc*. to be an ~ autoritär sein.
authoritarianism [ˌɔːθɒrɪ'tɛərɪənɪzəm] *n* Autoritarismus *m*.
authoritative [ɔː'θɒrɪtətɪv] *adj* **(a)** (*commanding*) bestimmt, entschieden; *manner also* respekteinflößend. **to sound** ~ Respekt einflößen, bestimmt auftreten.
(b) (*reliable*) verläßlich, zuverlässig; (*definitive*) maßgeblich, maßgebend. **I won't accept his opinion as** ~ seine Meinung ist für mich nicht maßgeblich *or* maßgebend.
authoritatively [ɔː'θɒrɪtətɪvlɪ] *adv* (*with authority*) bestimmt, mit Autorität; (*definitively*) maßgeblich *or* maßgebend; (*reliably*) zuverlässig.
authority [ɔː'θɒrɪtɪ] *n* **(a)** (*power*) Autorität *f*; (*right, entitlement*) Befugnis *f*; (*specifically delegated power*) Vollmacht *f*; (*Mil*) Befehlsgewalt *f*. **people who are in** ~ Menschen, die Autorität haben; **the person in** ~ der Zuständige *or* Verantwortliche; **who's in** ~ **here?** wer ist hier der Verantwortliche?; **I'm in** ~ **here!** hier bestimme ich!; **parental** ~ Autorität der Eltern; (*Jur*) elterliche Gewalt; **to be in** *or* **have** ~ **over sb** Weisungsbefugnis gegenüber jdm haben (*form*); (*describing hierarchy*) jdm übergeordnet sein; **those who are placed in** ~ **over us** diejenigen, denen Autorität wir unterstehen; **the Queen and those in** ~ **under her** die Königin und die ihr untergebenen Verantwortlichen; **to place sb in** ~ **over sb** jdm die Verantwortung für jdn übertragen; **to be under the** ~ **of sb** unter jds Aufsicht (*dat*) stehen; (*in hierarchy*) jdm unterstehen; (*Mil*) jds Befehlsgewalt (*dat*) unterstehen; **on one's own** ~ auf eigene Verantwortung; **you'll have to ask a teacher for the** ~ **to take the key** du brauchst die Erlaubnis *or* Genehmigung des Lehrers, wenn du den Schlüssel haben willst; **under** *or* **by what** ~ **do you claim the right to ...?** mit welcher Berechtigung verlangen Sie, daß ...?; **to have no** ~ **to do sth** nicht befugt *or* berechtigt sein, etw zu tun; **to have no** ~ **to do sth** nicht befugt *or* berechtigt sein, etw zu tun; **to have exceeding his area of** ~ er hat seinen Kompetenzbereich *or* seine Befugnisse überschritten; **to give sb the** ~ **to do sth** jdn ermächtigen (*form*) *or* jdm die Vollmacht erteilen, etw zu tun; **he had my** ~ **to do it** ich habe es ihm gestattet *or* erlaubt; **to have full** ~ **to act** volle Handlungsvollmacht haben; **to do sth on sb's** ~ etw in jds Auftrag (*dat*) tun; **who gave you the** ~ **to do that?** wer hat Sie dazu berechtigt?; **who gave you the** ~ **to treat people like that?** mit welchem Recht glaubst du, Leute so behandeln zu können?
(b) (*also pl: ruling body*) Behörde *f*, Amt *nt*; (*body of people*) Verwaltung *f*; (*power of ruler*) (Staats)gewalt, Obrigkeit *f*. **the university authorities** die Universitätsverwaltung; **the water** ~ die Wasserbehörde; **the local** ~ *or* **authorities** die Gemeindeverwaltung; **the Prussian respect for** ~ das preußische Obrigkeitsdenken, der preußische Respekt gegenüber der Obrigkeit; **the concept of** ~ **in a state** der Autoritätsgedanke im Staat; **they appealed to the supreme** ~ **of the House of Lords** sie wandten sich an die höchste Autorität *or* Instanz, das Oberhaus; **this will have to be decided by a higher** ~ das muß an höherer Stelle entschieden werden; **to represent** ~ die Staatsgewalt verkörpern; **the father represents** ~ der Vater verkörpert die Autorität; **you must have respect for** ~ du mußt Achtung gegenüber Respektspersonen haben.
(c) (*weight, influence*) Autorität *f*. **to have** *or* **carry (great)** ~ viel gelten (*with* bei); (*person also*) (große *or* viel) Autorität haben (*with* bei); **to speak/write with** ~ mit Sachkunde *or* mit der Autorität des Sachkundigen sprechen/schreiben; **I/he can speak with** ~ **on this matter** darüber kann ich mich/kann er sich kompetent äußern; **to give an order with** ~ einen Befehl mit der nötigen Autorität geben; **to appeal to the** ~ **of precedent** auf einen Präzedenzfall zurückgreifen.
(d) (*expert*) Autorität *f*, Fachmann *m*. **I'm no** ~ **but ...** ich bin kein Fachmann, aber ...; **he is an** ~ **on art** er ist eine Autorität *or* ein Fachmann auf dem Gebiet der Kunst.
(e) (*definitive book etc*) (anerkannte) Autorität *f*; (*source*) Quelle *f*. **to have sth on good** ~ etw aus zuverlässiger Quelle wissen; **on the best** ~ aus bester Quelle; **the best** ~ **on philosophical terminology** die zuverlässigste Quelle für philosophische Terminologie; **what is his** ~ **for that assertion?** worauf stützt er diese Behauptung?; **on whose** ~ **do you have that?** aus welcher Quelle haben Sie das?
authorization [ˌɔːθəraɪ'zeɪʃən] *n* Genehmigung *f*; (*delegation of authority*) Bevollmächtigung, Autorisation (*geh*) *f*; (*right*) Recht *nt*. **Parliament can't be dissolved without** ~ **from the Queen** das Parlament kann nicht ohne die Zustimmung *or* Ermächtigung der Königin aufgelöst werden.
authorize ['ɔːθəraɪz] *vt* **(a)** (*empower*) berechtigen, ermächtigen, autorisieren (*geh*); (*delegate authority*) bevollmächtigen. **to be ~d to do sth** (*have right*) berechtigt sein *or* das Recht haben, etw zu tun; **he was specially ~d to ...** er hatte eine Sondervollmacht, zu ...; **this licence ~s you to drive ...** dieser Führerschein berechtigt Sie zum Fahren von ...
(b) (*permit*) genehmigen; *money, claim etc* also bewilligen; *translation, biography etc* autorisieren. **the A~d Version** *engl. Bibelfassung von 1611*; **to be/become ~d by custom** zum Gewohnheitsrecht geworden sein/werden.
authorship ['ɔːθəʃɪp] *n* **(a)** Autorschaft, Verfasserschaft *f*. **of unknown** ~ eines unbekannten Autors *or* Verfassers; **he admitted** ~ **of the article** er bekannte, den Artikel verfaßt *or* geschrieben zu haben; **there are disagreements as to the** ~ **of the play** der Autor des Stückes ist umstritten.
(b) (*occupation*) Schriftstellerberuf *m*.
autism ['ɔːtɪzəm] *n* Autismus *m*.
autistic [ɔː'tɪstɪk] *adj* autistisch.
auto ['ɔːtəʊ] *n* (*US*) Auto *nt*, PKW *m*.
auto- ['ɔːtəʊ] *pref* auto-, Auto-.
autobiographical ['ɔːtəʊˌbaɪəʊ'græfɪkəl] *adj* autobiographisch.

autobiography [ˌɔːtəʊbaɪˈɒgrəfɪ] n Autobiographie f.

autocade [ˈɔːtəʊkeɪd] n (US) Wagenkolonne f or -konvoi m.

autochanger [ˈɔːtəʊˌtʃeɪndʒəʳ] n (automatischer) Plattenwechsler.

autocracy [ɔːˈtɒkrəsɪ] n Autokratie f.

autocrat [ˈɔːtəʊkræt] n Autokrat(in f) m.

autocratic [ˌɔːtəʊˈkrætɪk] adj autokratisch.

autocross [ˈɔːtəʊkrɒs] n Auto-Cross nt.

autocue [ˈɔːtəʊkjuː] n (Brit TV) Neger m.

auto-da-fé [ˈɔːtəʊdɑːˈfeɪ] n, pl autos-da-fé Autodafé nt.

auto-eroticism [ˌɔːtəʊˈrɒtɪˌsɪzəm] n Autoerotik f.

autograph [ˈɔːtəgrɑːf] 1 n (signature) Autogramm nt; (manuscript) Originalmanuskript nt. ~ album or book Autogrammalbum or -buch nt; ~ copy/letter handgeschriebenes Manuskript/handgeschriebener Brief.

2 vt signieren. he ~ed my album er hat mir ein Autogramm fürs Album gegeben.

automat [ˈɔːtəmæt] n (US) Automatenrestaurant nt.

automata [ɔːˈtɒmətə] pl of automaton.

automate [ˈɔːtəmeɪt] vt automatisieren.

automatic [ˌɔːtəˈmætɪk] 1 adj (lit, fig) automatisch; weapon also Maschinen-. ~ choke Startautomatik f; ~ gearbox Getriebeautomatik f; the ~ model das Modell mit Automatik; ~ pilot Autopilot m; the refund is not ~ Rückerstattung erfolgt nicht automatisch; he has the ~ right ... er hat automatisch das Recht ...; the film star's ~ smile das Routinelächeln des Filmstars; you shouldn't need telling, it should be ~ das sollte man dir nicht erst sagen müssen, das solltest du automatisch tun.

2 n (car) Automatikwagen m; (gun) automatische Waffe, Maschinenwaffe f; (washing machine) Waschautomat m.

automatically [ˌɔːtəˈmætɪkəlɪ] adv automatisch.

automation [ˌɔːtəˈmeɪʃən] n Automatisierung f.

automaton [ɔːˈtɒmətən] n, pl -s or automata [-ətə] (robot) Roboter m; (fig also) Automat f.

automobile [ˈɔːtəməbiːl] n Auto(mobil) nt, Kraftwagen m (form).

automotive [ˌɔːtəˈməʊtɪv] adj vehicle selbstfahrend, mit Selbstantrieb; engineering, mechanic Kfz-. ~ power Selbstantrieb m.

autonomous [ɔːˈtɒnəməs] adj autonom.

autonomy [ɔːˈtɒnəmɪ] n Autonomie f.

autopilot [ˌɔːtəʊˈpaɪlət] n Autopilot m.

autopsy [ˈɔːtɒpsɪ] n Autopsie, Leichenöffnung f.

autosuggestion [ˈɔːtəʊsəˈdʒestʃən] n Autosuggestion f.

autumn [ˈɔːtəm] (esp Brit) 1 n (lit, fig) Herbst m. in (the) ~ im Herbst; two ~s ago im Herbst vor zwei Jahren. 2 adj attr Herbst-, herbstlich. ~ leaves bunte (Herbst)blätter pl; ~ crocus Herbstzeitlose f.

autumnal [ɔːˈtʌmnəl] adj herbstlich, Herbst-. ~ equinox Herbst-Tagundnachtgleiche f.

auxiliary [ɔːgˈzɪlɪərɪ] 1 adj Hilfs-; (emergency also) Not-; (additional) engine, generator etc Zusatz-. ~ note (Mus) Nebennote f; ~ nurse Schwesternhelferin f.

2 n (a) (Mil: esp pl) Soldat m der Hilfstruppe. auxiliaries pl Hilfstruppe(n pl) f.

(b) (general: assistant) Hilfskraft f, Helfer(in f) m. teaching/nursing ~ (Aus)hilfslehrer(in f) m/Schwesternhelferin f.

(c) (~ verb) Hilfsverb or -zeitwort nt.

AV abbr of Authorized Version (of Bible).

av abbr of average Durchschn.

Av, Ave abbr of avenue.

avail¹ abbr of available.

avail² [əˈveɪl] 1 vr to ~ oneself of sth von etw Gebrauch machen; to ~ oneself of the opportunity of doing sth die Gelegenheit, etw zu tun, wahrnehmen or nutzen, Gelegenheit nehmen, etw zu tun (geh).

2 vi (form) helfen. nothing could ~ against their superior strength gegen ihre Überlegenheit war nichts auszurichten.

3 n of no ~ erfolglos, ohne Erfolg, vergeblich; of little ~ wenig erfolgreich, mit wenig or geringem Erfolg; his advice was/his pleas were of no/little ~ seine Ratschläge/Bitten haben nicht(s)/wenig gefruchtet; to no ~ vergebens, vergeblich; of what ~ is it to ...? (liter) was nützt es, zu ...?; and to what ~? (liter) und zu welchem Behuf? (old).

availability [əˌveɪləˈbɪlɪtɪ] n see adj Erhältlichkeit f; Lieferbarkeit f; Vorrätigkeit f; Verfügbarkeit f; (presence: of secretarial staff, mineral ore etc) Vorhandensein nt. the market price is determined by ~ der Marktpreis richtet sich nach dem vorhandenen Angebot; because of the greater ~ of their product ... weil ihr Produkt leichter erhältlich/lieferbar ist ...; we'd like to sell you one, but it's a question of ~ wir würden Ihnen gern eines verkaufen, das hängt aber davon ab, ob es erhältlich/lieferbar ist; greater ~ of jobs größeres Stellenangebot; because of the limited ~ of seats weil nur eine begrenzte Anzahl an Plätzen zur Verfügung steht; to increase the ~ of culture to the masses breiteren Bevölkerungsschichten den Zugang zu Kultur erleichtern; his ~ for discussion is, I'm afraid, determined by ... ob er Zeit für eine Besprechung hat, hängt leider von ... ab; the Swedish au-pair gained a reputation for "~" das schwedische Au-pair-Mädchen hatte bald den Ruf, „leicht zu haben" zu sein.

available [əˈveɪləbl] adj (a) object erhältlich; (Comm) (from supplier also) lieferbar; (in stock) vorrätig; (free) time, post frei; theatre seats etc frei, zu haben pred; (at one's disposal) worker, means, resources etc verfügbar, zur Verfügung stehend. to be ~ (at one's disposal) zur Verfügung stehen; (person: not otherwise occupied) frei or abkömmlich (form) sein; (can be reached) erreichbar sein; (for discussion) zu sprechen sein; to make sth ~ to sb jdm etw zur Verfügung stellen; (accessible) culture, knowledge, information jdm etw

zugänglich machen; to make oneself ~ to sb sich jdm zur Verfügung stellen; could you make yourself ~ for discussion between 2 and 3? könnten Sie sich zwischen 2 und 3 für eine Besprechung freihalten or zur Verfügung halten?; the best dictionary ~, the best ~ dictionary das beste Wörterbuch, das es gibt; offer ~ only while stocks last (das Angebot gilt) nur, solange der Vorrat reicht; to try every ~ means (to achieve sth) nichts unversucht lassen(, um etw zu erreichen); reference books/consultants are ~ Nachschlagewerke/Berater stehen einem/Ihnen etc zur Verfügung; all ~ staff were asked to help out das abkömmliche or verfügbare or zur Verfügung stehende Personal wurde gebeten auszuhelfen; are you ~ for tennis/a discussion tonight? können Sie heute abend Tennis spielen/an einer Diskussion teilnehmen?; when will you be ~ to start in the new job? wann können Sie die Stelle antreten?; I'm not ~ until October ich bin vor Oktober nicht frei; a professor should always be ~ to his students ein Professor sollte stets für seine Studenten da sein or seinen Studenten stets zur Verfügung stehen; he's ~ for consultation on Mondays er hat montags Sprechzeit; you shouldn't make yourself so ~ to him du solltest es ihm nicht so leicht machen; she's what is known as "~" es ist bekannt, daß sie „leicht zu haben" ist.

(b) (form) ticket gültig.

avalanche [ˈævəlɑːnʃ] n (lit, fig) Lawine f.

avant-garde [ˈævɑ̃ˈgɑːd] 1 n Avantgarde f. 2 adj avantgardistisch.

avarice [ˈævərɪs] n Habgier, Habsucht f.

avaricious [ˌævəˈrɪʃəs] adj habgierig, habsüchtig.

avariciously [ˌævəˈrɪʃəslɪ] adv (hab)gierig.

avdp abbr of avoirdupois.

Ave (Maria) [ˈɑːveɪ(məˈriːə)] n Ave(-Maria) nt.

avenge [əˈvendʒ] vt rächen. to ~ oneself on sb (for sth) sich an jdm (für etw) rächen; an avenging angel ein Racheengel m.

avenger [əˈvendʒəʳ] n Rächer(in f) m.

avenue [ˈævənjuː] n (a) (tree-lined) Allee f; (broad street) Boulevard m. (b) (fig) (method) Weg m. ~s of approach Verfahrensweisen; an ~ of approach to the problem ein Weg, das Problem anzugehen; ~ of escape Ausweg m; to explore every ~ alle sich bietenden Wege prüfen.

aver [əˈvɜːʳ] vt (form) mit Nachdruck betonen; love, innocence beteuern.

average [ˈævərɪdʒ] 1 n (Durch)schnitt m; (Math also) Mittelwert m. to do an ~ of 50 miles a day/3% a week durchschnittlich or im (Durch)schnitt 50 Meilen pro Tag fahren/3% pro Woche erledigen; what's your ~ over the last six months? was haben Sie im letzten halben Jahr durchschnittlich geleistet/verdient etc?; on ~ durchschnittlich, im (Durch)schnitt; (normally) normalerweise; if you take the ~ (Math) wenn Sie den (Durch)schnitt or Mittelwert nehmen; (general) wenn Sie den durchschnittlichen Fall nehmen; above/below ~ überdurchschnittlich, über dem Durchschnitt/unterdurchschnittlich, unter dem Durchschnitt; the law of ~s das Gesetz der Serie; by the law of ~s aller Wahrscheinlichkeit nach.

2 adj durchschnittlich; (ordinary) Durchschnitts-; (not good or bad) mittelmäßig. above/below ~ über-/unterdurchschnittlich; the ~ man, Mr A~ der Durchschnittsbürger; the ~ Scot der Durchschnittsschotte; he's a man of ~ height er ist von mittlerer Größe.

3 vt (a) (find the ~ of) den Durchschnitt ermitteln von.

(b) (do etc on ~) auf einen Schnitt von ... kommen. we ~d 80 km/h wir kamen auf einen Schnitt von 80 km/h, wir sind durchschnittlich 80 km/h gefahren; the factory ~s 500 cars a week die Fabrik produziert durchschnittlich or im (Durch)schnitt 500 Autos pro Woche.

(c)(~ out at) sales are averaging 10,000 copies per day der Absatz beläuft sich auf or beträgt durchschnittlich or im (Durch)schnitt 10.000 Exemplare pro Tag.

♦**average out 1** vt sep we have to ~ ~ our weekly output over a six-month period wir müssen unsere durchschnittliche Arbeitsleistung pro Woche über einen Zeitraum von sechs Monaten ermitteln; the accountant ~d ~ the firm's profits over the last five years der Buchhalter ermittelte den Durchschnittsgewinn der Firma in den letzten fünf Jahren; it'll ~ itself ~ es wird sich ausgleichen.

2 vi durchschnittlich ausmachen (at acc); (balance out) sich ausgleichen. how does it ~ ~ on a weekly basis? wieviel ist das durchschnittlich or im Schnitt pro Woche?

averse [əˈvɜːs] adj pred abgeneigt. I am not ~ to a glass of wine einem Glas Wein bin ich nicht abgeneigt; I am rather ~ to doing that es ist mir ziemlich zuwider, das zu tun; I feel ~ to doing it es widerstrebt mir, das zu tun.

aversion [əˈvɜːʃən] n (a) (strong dislike) Abneigung, Aversion (geh, Psych) f (to gegen). he has an ~ to getting wet er hat eine Abscheu davor, naß zu werden; ~ therapy (Psych) Aversionstherapie f. (b) (object of ~) Greuel m. smoking is his pet ~ Rauchen ist ihm ein besonderer Greuel.

avert [əˈvɜːt] vt (a) (turn away) eyes, gaze abwenden, abkehren (geh). to ~ one's mind or thoughts from sth seine Gedanken von etw abwenden. (b) (prevent) verhindern, abwenden; suspicion ablenken; blow etc abwehren; accident verhindern, verhüten.

aviary [ˈeɪvɪərɪ] n Vogelhaus, Aviarium (geh) nt, Voliere f (geh).

aviation [ˌeɪvɪˈeɪʃən] n die Luftfahrt. the art of ~ die Kunst des Fliegens.

aviator [ˈeɪvɪeɪtəʳ] n Flieger(in f) m.

aviculture [ˈeɪvɪˌkʌltʃəʳ] n (form) Vogelzucht f.

avid [ˈævɪd] adj (a) (desirous) gierig (for nach); (for fame, praise also) süchtig (for nach). ~ for fame ruhmsüchtig; to be ~ for success erfolgssüchtig sein, nach Erfolg gieren (pej).

(b) (keen) begeistert, passioniert; supporter also eifrig; interest lebhaft, stark. he is an ~ follower of this series er verfolgt diese Serie mit lebhaftem Interesse; as an ~ reader of your column als eifriger Leser Ihrer Spalte; I am an ~ reader ich lese leidenschaftlich gern.

avidity [ə'vɪdɪtɪ] *n*, *no pl* (*liter*) *see adj* (**a**) Begierde *f* (*for* nach); (*pej*) Gier *f* (*for* nach). **with** ~ begierig; gierig. (**b**) Begeisterung *f*; Eifer *m*.

avidly ['ævɪdlɪ] *adv see adj* (**a**) begierig; (*pej*) gierig. (**b**) eifrig; read leidenschaftlich gern.

avocado [ˌævə'kɑːdəʊ] *n*, *pl* -**s** (*also* ~ **pear**) Avocado(birne), Avocado(birne) *f*; (*tree*) Avocato- *or* Avocadobaum *m*.

avocation [ˌævəʊ'keɪʃən] *n* (*form*) (*calling*) Berufung *f*.

avoid [ə'vɔɪd] *vt* vermeiden; *damage, accident also* verhüten; *person, danger* meiden, aus dem Weg gehen (+*dat*); *obstacle* ausweichen (+*dat*); *difficulty, duty, truth* umgehen. **we've managed to** ~ **the danger** wir konnten der Gefahr entgehen; **in order to** ~ **being seen** um nicht gesehen zu werden; **he'd do anything to** ~ **the washing-up/going there** er würde alles tun, um nur nicht abwaschen zu müssen/dort hingehen zu müssen; **I'm not going if I can possibly** ~ **it** wenn es sich irgendwie vermeiden läßt, gehe ich nicht; ... **you can hardly** ~ **visiting them** ... dann kommst du wohl kaum darum herum *or* kannst du es wohl schlecht vermeiden, sie zu besuchen; **I can't** ~ **leaving now** ich muß jetzt unbedingt gehen; **to** ~ **sb's eye** jds Blick (*dat*) ausweichen, es vermeiden, jdn anzusehen; **to** ~ **notice** unbemerkt bleiben; *see* plague.

avoidable [ə'vɔɪdəbl] *adj* vermeidbar. **if it's (at all)** ~ wenn es sich (irgend) vermeiden läßt.

avoidance [ə'vɔɪdəns] *n* Vermeidung *f*. **he advised us on the** ~ **of death duties** er hat uns beraten, wie wir die Erbschaftssteuer umgehen können; **the** ~ **of death duties** die Umgehung der Erbschaftssteuer; **his persistent** ~ **of the truth** sein ständiges Umgehen der Wahrheit; **thanks only to her steady** ~ **of bad company** nur weil sie konsequent schlechte Gesellschaft mied.

avoirdupois [ˌævwɑːdjuːˈpwɑː] *n* Avoirdupois *nt*; (*hum: excess weight*) Fülligkeit, Üppigkeit *f*. **she's been putting on the** ~ **a bit** sie ist ziemlich in die Breite gegangen.

avow [ə'vaʊ] *vt* (*liter*) erklären; *belief, faith* bekennen. **to** ~ **one's love (to sb)** (jdm) seine Liebe erklären *or* gestehen, sich (jdm) erklären; **he** ~**ed himself to be a royalist** er bekannte (offen), Royalist zu sein; **he** ~**ed himself her willing slave** er erklärte sich als ihr williger Sklave.

avowal [ə'vaʊəl] *n* Erklärung *f*; (*of faith*) Bekenntnis *nt*; (*of love also*) Geständnis *nt*; (*of belief, interest*) Bekundung *f*. **he is on his own** ~ **a** ... er ist erklärtermaßen ...

avowed [ə'vaʊd] *adj* erklärt.

avowedly [ə'vaʊɪdlɪ] *adv* erklärtermaßen.

avuncular [ə'vʌŋkjʊlə*r*] *adj* onkelhaft; *figure* Onkel-.

aw *abbr of* **atomic weight**.

await [ə'weɪt] *vt* (**a**) (*wait for*) erwarten; *future events, decision etc* entgegensehen (+*dat*). **the long** ~**ed day** der langersehnte Tag; **parcels** ~**ing despatch** zum Versand bestimmte Pakete; **we** ~ **your reply with interest** wir sehen Ihrer Antwort mit Interesse entgegen. (**b**) (*be in store for*) erwarten.

awake [ə'weɪk] *pret* **awoke**, *ptp* **awoken** *or* **awaked** [ə'weɪkt] 1 *vi* (*lit, fig*) erwachen. **to** ~ **from sleep/one's dreams** aus dem Schlaf/seinen Träumen erwachen; **to** ~ **to sth** (*fig: realize*) sich (*dat*) einer Sache (*gen*) bewußt werden; (*become interested*) beginnen, sich für etw zu interessieren; **to** ~ **to the joys of sth** (*plötzlich*) Vergnügen an etw (*dat*) finden; **he/his interest was slow to** ~ (*fig*) es brauchte lange, bis es bei ihm zündete (*inf*), er ist erst spät richtig aufgewacht/sein Interesse ist erst spät erwacht.

2 *vt* wecken; (*fig*) *suspicion, interest etc also* erwecken. **to** ~ **sb to sth** (*make realize*) jdm etw bewußt machen; (*make interested*) jds Interesse für etw wecken.

3 *adj pred* (*lit, fig*) wach; (*alert also*) aufmerksam. **to be/lie/ stay** ~ wach sein/liegen/bleiben; **to keep sb** ~ jdn wachhalten; **wide** ~ (*lit, fig*) hellwach; **to be** ~ **to sth** (*fig*) sich (*dat*) einer Sache (*gen*) bewußt sein.

awaken [ə'weɪkən] *vti see* **awake**.

awakening [ə'weɪknɪŋ] 1 *n* (*lit, fig*) Erwachen *nt*. **a rude** ~ (*lit, fig*) ein böses Erwachen. 2 *adj* (*fig*) erwachend.

award [ə'wɔːd] 1 *vt* *prize, penalty, free kick etc* zusprechen (*to sb* jdm), zuerkennen (*to sb* jdm); (*present*) *prize, degree, medal etc* verleihen (*to sb* jdm). **to be** ~**ed damages** Schadenersatz zugesprochen bekommen; **to** ~ **sb first prize** jdm den ersten Preis zuerkennen. 2 *n* (**a**) (*prize*) Preis *m*; (*for bravery etc*) Auszeichnung *f*; (*Jur*) Zuerkennung *f*, Zuspruch *m*. **to make an** ~ **(to sb)** einen Preis (an jdn) vergeben. (**b**) (*Univ*) Stipendium *nt*.

aware [ə'weə*r*] *adj esp pred* bewußt. **to be/become** ~ **of sb/sth** sich (*dat*) jds/einer Sache bewußt sein/werden; (*notice also*) jdn bemerken/etw merken; **I was not** ~ (**of the fact**) **that** ... es war mir nicht klar *or* bewußt, daß ...; **you will be** ~ **of the importance of this** es muß Ihnen bewußt sein, wie wichtig das ist; **are you** ~ **that** ...? ist dir eigentlich klar, daß ...? **not that I am** ~ (**of**) nicht daß ich wüßte; **as far as I am** ~ soviel ich weiß; **we try to remain** ~ **of what is going on in other companies/the world** wir versuchen, uns auf dem laufenden darüber zu halten, was in anderen Firmen/auf der Welt vor sich geht; **to make sb** ~ **of sth** jdm etw bewußt machen *or* zum Bewußtsein bringen; **to make sb more** ~/~ **of sth** jds Bewußtsein wecken/jdm etw bewußt machen; **for a three-year-old he's very** ~ für einen Dreijährigen ist er sehr aufgeweckt; **he's very** ~ **of language** er ist sehr sprachbewußt.

awareness [ə'weənɪs] *n* Bewußtsein *nt*. **he showed no** ~ **of the urgency of the problem** er schien sich der Dringlichkeit des Problems nicht bewußt zu sein; **her tremendous** ~ **of the shades of meaning in the language/of other people's feelings** ihr außerordentlich waches Gespür für die Bedeutungsnuancen der Sprache/für die Empfindungen anderer;

drugs which increase one's ~ **of the outer world** bewußtseinserweiternde Drogen *pl*.

awash [ə'wɒʃ] *adj pred decks, rocks etc* überspült; *cellar* unter Wasser.

away [ə'weɪ] *adv* 1 (**a**) (*to or at a distance*) weg. **three miles** ~ (**from here**) drei Meilen (entfernt) von hier; **lunch seemed a long time** ~ es schien noch lange bis zum Mittagessen zu sein; ~ **in the distance/past** weit in der Ferne/vor sehr langer Zeit; **they're** ~ **behind/out in front/off course** sie sind weit zurück/voraus/ab vom Kurs.

(**b**) (*motion*) ~! (*old, liter*) fort!, hinweg! (*old, liter*); ~ **with the old philosophy, in with the new!** fort mit der alten Philosophie, her mit der neuen!; **come, let us** ~! (*liter*) kommt, laßt uns fort von hier (*old*); ~ **with him!** fort mit ihm!; **but he was** ~ **before I could say a word** aber er war fort *or* weg, bevor ich den Mund auftun konnte; **to look** ~ wegsehen; ~ **we go!** los (geht's)!; **they're** ~! (*horses, runners etc*) sie sind gestartet; **they're** ~ **first time** gleich der erste Start hat geklappt.

(**c**) (*absent*) fort, weg. **he's** ~ **from work (with a cold)** er fehlt (wegen einer Erkältung); **he's** ~ **in London** er ist in London; **when I have to be** ~ wenn ich nicht da sein kann.

(**d**) (*Sport*) **to play** ~ auswärts spielen; **they're** ~ **to Arsenal** sie haben ein Auswärtsspiel bei Arsenal.

(**e**) (*out of existence, possession etc*) **to put/give** ~ weglegen/weggeben; **to boil/gamble/die** ~ verkochen/verspielen/verhallen; **we talked the evening** ~ wir haben den Abend verplaudert.

(**f**) (*continuously*) unablässig. **to work/knit etc** ~ unablässig arbeiten/stricken *etc*.

(**g**) (*forthwith*) **ask** ~! frag nur!, schieß los (*inf*); **pull/heave** ~! und los(, zieht/hebt an)!; **right** *or* **straight** ~ sofort.

(**h**) (*inf*) **he's** ~ **again** (*talking, giggling, drunk etc*) es geht wieder los; **he's** ~ **with the idea that** ... er hat den Fimmel, daß ...; ~ **with you!** ach wo!

2 *adj attr* (*Sport*) **team** auswärtig, Gast-; **match**, **win** Auswärts-.

3 *n* (*in Ftbl pools*: ~ **win**) Auswärtssieg *m*.

awe [ɔː] 1 *n* Ehrfurcht *f*, ehrfürchtige Scheu. **to be** *or* **stand in** ~ **of sb** Ehrfurcht vor jdm haben; (*feel fear*) große Furcht vor jdm haben; **to hold sb in** ~ Ehrfurcht *or* großen Respekt vor jdm haben; **to strike sb with** ~, **to strike** ~ **into sb's heart** jdm Ehrfurcht einflößen; (*make fearful*) jdm Furcht einflößen; **the sight filled me with** ~ der Anblick erfüllte mich mit ehrfurchtsvoller Scheu.

2 *vt* Ehrfurcht *or* ehrfürchtige Scheu einflößen (+*dat*). ~**d by the beauty/silence** von der Schönheit/der Stille ergriffen; **in an** ~**d voice** mit ehrfürchtiger Stimme.

awe-inspiring ['ɔːɪn,spaɪərɪŋ], **awesome** ['ɔːsəm] *adj* ehrfurchtgebietend.

awe-stricken ['ɔːˌstrɪkən], **awe-struck** ['ɔːstrʌk] *adj* von Ehrfurcht ergriffen; *voice, expression also* ehrfurchtsvoll; (*frightened*) von Schrecken ergriffen. **I was quite** ~ **by its beauty** ich war von seiner Schönheit ergriffen.

awful ['ɔːfəl] 1 *adj* (*a*) (*inf*) schrecklich, furchtbar. **how** ~! das ist wirklich schlimm!; **you are** ~! du bist wirklich schrecklich!; **the film was just too** ~ **for words** der Film war unbeschreiblich schlecht; **it's not an** ~ **lot better** das ist nicht arg viel besser. (**b**) (*old: awe-inspiring*) ehrfurchtgebietend.

2 *adv* (*strictly incorrect*) *see* **awfully**. **he was crying something** ~ er weinte ganz schrecklich *or* furchtbar.

awfully ['ɔːflɪ] *adv* (*inf*) furchtbar (*inf*), schrecklich (*inf*). **thanks** ~ vielen, vielen Dank! (*inf*); **I'm afraid I'm** ~ **late** tut mir leid, daß ich so schrecklich spät komme (*inf*); **it's not** ~ **important** es ist nicht so schrecklich *or* furchtbar wichtig (*inf*); **she is rather** ~ ~ (*Brit hum*) sie ist furchtbar vornehm (*inf*).

awfulness ['ɔːfulnɪs] *n* (*of situation*) Schrecklichkeit, Furchtbarkeit *f*; (*of person*) abscheuliche Art, Abscheulichkeit *f*. **we were shocked by the** ~ **of it all** wir waren von der Schrecklichkeit *or* Furchtbarkeit des Ganzen überwältigt.

awhile [ə'waɪl] *adv* (*liter*) eine Weile. **not yet** ~! noch eine ganze Weile nicht!

awkward ['ɔːkwəd] *adj* (**a**) (*difficult*) schwierig; *time, moment, angle, shape* ungünstig. **4 o'clock is a bit** ~ (**for me**) 4 Uhr ist ein bißchen ungünstig *or* schlecht (*inf*) (für mich).

(**b**) (*embarrassing*) peinlich.

(**c**) (*embarrassed*) verlegen; (*shamefaced*) betreten; *silence* betreten. **the** ~ **age** das schwierige Alter; **to feel** ~ **in sb's company** sich in jds Gesellschaft (*dat*) nicht wohl fühlen; **I felt** ~ **when I had to** ... es war mir peinlich, als ich ... mußte.

(**d**) (*clumsy*) *person, movement, style* unbeholfen.

awkwardly ['ɔːkwədlɪ] *adv see adj* (**a**) schwierig; ungünstig. (**b**) peinlich. (**c**) verlegen; betreten. (**d**) unbeholfen. **he wriggled** ~ **in his chair** er rutschte verlegen auf seinem Stuhl hin und her.

awkwardness ['ɔːkwədnɪs] *n see adj* (**a**) Schwierigkeit *f*; Ungünstigkeit *f*. (**b**) Peinlichkeit *f*. (**c**) Verlegenheit *f*; Betretenheit *f*. (**d**) Unbeholfenheit *f*.

awl [ɔːl] *n* Ahle *f*, Pfriem *m*.

awning ['ɔːnɪŋ] *n* (*on window, of shop*) Markise *f*; (*on boat*) Sonnensegel *nt*; (*of wagon*) Plane *f*; (*caravan* ~) Vordach *nt*.

awoke [ə'wəʊk] *pret of* **awake**.

awoken [ə'wəʊkən] *ptp of* **awake**.

AWOL (*Mil*) *abbr of* **absent without leave**.

awry [ə'raɪ] *adj pred, adv* (*askew*) schief. **the picture/hat is** ~ das Bild hängt/der Hut sitzt schief; **to go** ~ (*plans etc*) schiefgehen.

axe, (*US*) **ax** [æks] 1 *n* Axt *f*, Beil *nt*; (*fig*) (radikale) Kürzung. **to wield the** ~ **on sth** (*fig*) mit dem Rotstift an etw (*acc*) gehen, etw radikal kürzen; **the** ~ **has fallen on the project** das Projekt ist dem Rotstift zum Opfer gefallen; **to have an/no** ~ **to grind** (*fig*) ein/kein persönliches Interesse haben.

2 *vt plans, projects, jobs* streichen; *person* entlassen.
axiom ['æksɪəm] *n* Axiom *nt*.
axiomatic [,æksɪəʊ'mætɪk] *adj* axiomatisch. **we can take it as ~ that ...** wir können von dem Grundsatz ausgehen, daß ...
axis ['æksɪs] *n, pl* **axes** ['æksi:z] Achse *f*. the A~ (powers) (*Hist*) die Achse, die Achsenmächte *pl*.
axle ['æksl] *n* Achse *f*.
axle: ~ **bearing** *n* Achslager *nt*; ~ **box** *n* Achsgehäuse *nt*; ~ **grease** *n* Achs(en)fett *nt*; ~ **housing** *n* Achsgehäuse *nt*; ~ **pin** *n* Achs(en)nagel *m*; ~ **tree** *n* Achswelle *f*.

ay(e) [aɪ] **1** *interj* (*esp Scot, dial*) ja. aye, aye, Sir (*Naut*) jawohl, Herr Kapitänleutnant/Admiral *etc*. **2** *n* (*esp Parl*) Jastimme *f*, Ja *nt*. the ~s diejenigen, die dafür sind, die dafür; the ~s have it die Mehrheit ist dafür.
aye [eɪ] *adv* (*old, Scot*) immer.
azalea [ə'zeɪlɪə] *n* Azalee *f*.
azimuth ['æzɪməθ] *n* (*Astron*) Azimut *nt or m*.
Aztec ['æztek] **1** *n* Azteke *m*, Aztekin *f*. **2** *adj* aztekisch.
azure ['æʒə'] **1** *n* Azur(blau *nt*) *m*. **2** *adj sky* azurblau; *eyes also* tiefblau. ~ **blue** azurblau.

B

B, b [bi:] *n* (a) B, b *nt*. (b) (*Mus*) H, h *nt*. ~ **flat/sharp** B, b *nt*/His, his *nt*; *see also* **major, minor, natural**.
B *adj* (*on pencil*) B.
b *abbr of* **born** geb.
BA *abbr of* **Bachelor of Arts**.
baa [bɑ:] **1** *n* Mähen *nt no pl*. ~! mäh!; ~**lamb** (*baby-talk*) Bählamm, Mähschäfchen *nt* (*baby-talk*). **2** *vi* mähen, mäh machen (*baby-talk*).
babble ['bæbl] **1** *n* (a) Gemurmel *nt*; (*of baby, excited person etc*) Geplapper *nt*. ~ (*of voices*) Stimmengewirr *nt*.
   (b) (*of stream*) Murmeln (*liter*), Plätschern *nt no pl*.
   2 *vi* (a) (*person*) plappern, quasseln (*inf*); (*baby*) plappern, lallen. **don't ~, speak slowly** nicht so schnell, rede langsam; the other actress tended to ~ die andere Schauspielerin neigte dazu, ihren Text herunterzurasseln.
   (b) (*stream*) murmeln (*liter*), plätschern.
◆**babble away** *or vi* quatschen (*inf*) (*about* über +*acc*), quasseln (*inf*) (*about* von). she ~d ~ excitedly sie quasselte *or* plapperte aufgeregt drauflos (*inf*).
◆**babble out** *vt sep* brabbeln; *secret* ausplaudern.
babbler ['bæblə'] *n* Plaudertasche *f* (*inf*). **don't tell him, he's a ~** sag ihm nichts, er quatscht (*inf*).
babbling ['bæblɪŋ] *adj brook* murmelnd (*liter*), plätschernd.
babe [beɪb] *n* (a) (*liter*) Kindlein *nt* (*liter*). ~ **in arms** Säugling *m*.
   (b) (*esp US inf*) Baby *nt* (*inf*), Puppe *f* (*inf*). **hey Susie/Mike ~!** he du, Susie!/Mike!; *see also* **baby (e)**.
babel ['beɪbəl] *n* (a) the Tower of B~ (*story*) der Turmbau zu Babel *or* Babylon; (*edifice*) der Babylonische Turm. (b) (*confusion*) Durcheinander *nt*; (*several languages also*) babylonisches Sprachengewirr.
baboon [bə'bu:n] *n* Pavian *m*.
babuschka [bə'bu:ʃkə] *n* Kopftuch *nt*.
baby ['beɪbɪ] **1** *n* (a) Kind, Baby *nt*; (*in weeks after birth also*) Säugling *m*; (*of animal*) Junge(s) *nt*. **to have a ~** ein Kind *or* Baby bekommen; **she's going to have a ~** sie bekommt ein Kind *or* Baby; **I've known him since he was a ~** ich kenne ihn von klein auf *or* von Kindesbeinen an; **the ~ of the family** der/die Kleinste *or* Jüngste, das Nesthäkchen; (*boy also*) der Benjamin; **don't be such a ~!** sei nicht so ein Baby! (*inf*), stell dich nicht so an! (*inf*); **to be left holding the ~** der Dumme sein (*inf*), die Sache ausbaden müssen (*inf*); **the bank cancelled the loan and I was left holding a very expensive ~** als die Bank das Darlehen rückgängig machte, hatte ich eine teure Suppe auszulöffeln; **to throw out the ~ with the bathwater** das Kind mit dem Bade ausschütten; **that encyclopedia is his first ~** (*inf*) das Lexikon ist sein Erstling (*hum*) *or* erstes Kind.
   (b) (*small object of its type*) Pikkolo *m* (*hum*).
   (c) (*sl: thing for which one is responsible*) **that's a costing problem, that's Harrison's ~** das ist eine Kostenfrage, das ist Harrisons Problem; **I think this problem's your ~** das ist wohl dein Bier (*inf*).
   (d) (*inf: girlfriend, boyfriend*) Schatz *m*, Schätzchen *nt*.
   (e) (*esp US inf: as address*) Schätzchen *nt* (*inf*); (*man to man*) mein Freund, mein Junge. **that's my ~** jawohl, so ist's prima (*inf*); **that's great, ~** Mensch, das ist dufte (*inf*); **Mike/Susie ~, listen du, Mike/Susie, hör mal her!
   2 *vt* (*inf*) wie eine Säugling behandeln.
baby *in cpds* (a) (*for baby*) Baby-, Säuglings-. (b) (*little*) Klein-.
   (c) (*of animal*) ~ **crocodile/giraffe** Krokodil-/Giraffenjunge(s) *nt*.
baby: ~ **boy** *n* Sohn *m*, kleiner Junge; ~ **car** *n* Kleinwagen *m*, Autochen *nt* (*hum*); ~ **carriage** *n* (*US*) Kinderwagen *m*; ~ **clothes** *npl* Kindersachen *pl*, Babywäsche *f*; ~**doll face** *n* Puppengesicht *nt*; ~**doll pyjamas** *npl* Babydoll *nt*; ~ **elephant** *n* Elefantenjunge(s) *or* -baby *nt*; ~ **face** *n* Kindergesicht *nt*; (*of adult male*) Milchgesicht *nt*; ~ **girl** *n* Töchterchen *nt*; ~ **grand** (*piano*) *n* Stutzflügel *m*.
bab·hood ['beɪbɪhʊd] *n* frühe Kindheit, Säuglingsalter *nt*.
babyish ['beɪbɪɪʃ] *adj* kindisch.
baby linen *n* Babywäsche *f no pl*.
Babylon ['bæbɪlən] *n* Babylon *nt*.

Babylonian [,bæbɪ'ləʊnɪən] **1** *adj* babylonisch. **2** *n* Babylonier(in *f*) *m*.
baby: ~**-minder** *n* Tagesmutter *f*, Kinderpfleger(in *f*) *m*; ~ **scales** *npl* Baby- *or* Säuglingswaage *f*; ~**-sit** *pret, ptp* ~**-sat** *vi* babysitten, einhüten (*dial*); **she ~-sits for them** sie geht bei ihnen babysitten *or* einhüten (*dial*); ~**-sitter** *n* Babysitter(in *f*) *m*; ~**-sitting** *n* Babysitten, Babysitting, (Ein)hüten (*dial*) *nt*; ~**-snatcher** *n* (a) Kindesentführer(in *f*) *m*; (b) (*fig inf*) **what a ~-snatcher** der könnte ja ihr Vater sein/sie könnte ja seine Mutter sein!; ~**-snatching** *n* (a) Kindesentführung *f*; (b) (*fig inf*) **not her, that's ~-snatching** sie nicht, ich vergreife mich doch nicht an kleinen Kindern!; ~**-stroller** *n* (*US*) Sportwagen *m*.
baccara(t) ['bækərɑ:] *n* Bakkarat *nt*.
bacchanalia [,bækə'neɪlɪə] *n* (*Hist, fig*) Bacchanal *nt* (*geh*).
bacchanalian [,bækə'neɪlɪən] *adj* bacchantisch (*geh*).
Bacchus ['bækəs] *n* Bacchus *m*.
baccy ['bækɪ] *n* (*inf*) Tabak, Knaster (*inf*) *m*.
bachelor ['bætʃələ'] *n* (a) Junggeselle *m*. **still a ~** immer noch Junggeselle. (b) (*Univ*) B~ of Arts/Science Bakkalaureus *m* der philosophischen Fakultät/der Naturwissenschaften.
bachelordom ['bætʃələdəm] *n see* **bachelorhood**.
bachelor: ~ **flat** *n* Junggesellenwohnung *f*; ~ **girl** *n* Junggesellin *f*.
bachelorhood ['bætʃələhʊd] *n* Junggesellentum *nt*.
bacillary [bə'sɪlərɪ] *adj* (*Med*) Bazillen-, bazillär; *form* stäbchenförmig.
bacillus [bə'sɪləs] *n, pl* **bacilli** [bə'sɪlaɪ] Bazillus *m*.
back [bæk] **1** *n* (a) (*of person, animal, book*) Rücken *m*; (*of chair also*) (Rücken)lehne *f*. **with one's ~ to the engine** mit dem Rücken in Fahrtrichtung, rückwärts; **to be on one's ~** (*be ill*) auf der Nase liegen (*inf*), krank sein; **to wear one's hair down one's ~** überschulterlange Haare haben; **to break one's ~** (*fig*) sich abrackern, sich abmühen; **we've broken the ~ of the job** wir sind mit der Arbeit überm Berg (*inf*); **behind sb's ~** (*fig*) hinter jds Rücken (*dat*); **to put one's ~ into sth** (*fig*) sich bei etw anstrengen, bei etw Einsatz zeigen; **to put or get sb's ~ up** (*fig*) gegen sich aufbringen; **to turn one's ~ on sb** (*lit*) jdm den Rücken zuwenden; (*fig*) sich von jdm abwenden; **when I needed him he turned his ~ on me** als ich ihn brauchte, ließ er mich im Stich; **he's at the ~ of all the trouble** er steckt hinter dem ganzen Ärger; **get these people off my ~** (*inf*) schaff mir diese Leute vom Hals! (*inf*); **to get off my ~!** (*inf*) laß mich endlich in Ruhe!; **he's got the boss on his ~ all the time** er hat dauernd seinen Chef auf dem Hals; **to have a broad ~** (*fig*) einen breiten Rücken haben; **to have one's ~ to the wall** (*fig*) in die Enge getrieben sein/werden; **I was pleased to see the ~ of them** (*inf*) ich war froh, sie endlich los zu sehen (*inf*).
   (b) (*as opposed to front*) Rück- *or* Hinterseite *f*; (*of hand, dress*) Rücken *m*; (*of house, page, coin, cheque*) Rückseite *f*; (*of material*) linke Seite. **I know London like the ~ of my hand** ich kenne London wie meine Westentasche; **the index is at the ~ of the book** das Verzeichnis ist hinten im Buch; **he drove into the ~ of me** er ist mir hinten reingefahren (*inf*); **on the ~ of his hand** auf dem Handrücken; **the ~ of one's head** der Hinterkopf; **at/on the ~ of the bus** hinten im/am Bus; **in the ~ (of a car)** hinten (im Auto); **one consideration was at the ~ of my mind** ich hatte dabei eine Überlegung im Hinterkopf; **there's one other worry at the ~ of my mind** da ist noch etwas, das mich beschäftigt; **the ~ of the cupboard is empty** hinten im Schrank ist nichts; **at the very ~ of the classroom** ganz hinten ·im Klassenzimmer; **at the ~ of the stage** im Hintergrund der Bühne; **at the ~ of the garage** (*inside*) hinten in der Garage; (*outside*) hinter der Garage; **at the ~ of beyond** am Ende der Welt, j.w.d. (*hum*); **in ~** (*US*) hinten.
   (c) (*Ftbl*) Verteidiger *m*; (*Rugby*) Hinterspieler *m*.
   2 *adj wheel, yard* Hinter-; *rent* ausstehend, rückständig.
   3 *adv* (a) (*to the rear*) (*stand*) ~! zurück(treten)!, (treten Sie) zurück!; ~ **and forth** hin und her.
   (b) (*in return*) zurück. **to pay sth ~** etw zurückzahlen.
   (c) (*returning*) zurück. **to come/go ~** zurückkommen/-gehen;

to fly to London and ~ nach London und zurück fliegen; **there and** ~ hin und zurück.

(d) *(again)* wieder. **he went** ~ **several times** er fuhr noch öfters wieder hin; **I'll never go** ~ da gehe ich nie wieder hin.

(e) *(ago: in time phrases)* **a week** ~ vor einer Woche; **as far** ~ **as the 18th century** *(dating back)* bis ins 18. Jahrhundert zurück; *(point in time)* schon im 18. Jahrhundert; **far** ~ **in the past** vor langer, langer Zeit, vor Urzeiten.

4 *prep (US)* ~ **of** hinter.

5 *vt* **(a)** *(support)* unterstützen. **I will** ~ **you whatever you do** egal, was du tust, ich stehe hinter dir; **if the bank won't** ~ **us** wenn die Bank nicht mitmacht; **to** ~ **a bill** *(Fin)* einen Wechsel indossieren.

(b) *(Betting)* setzen *or* wetten auf (+*acc*). **the horse was heavily** ~**ed** auf das Pferd wurden viele Wetten abgeschlossen.

(c) *(cause to move)* car zurückfahren *or* -setzen; cart zurückfahren; horse rückwärts gehen lassen. **he** ~**ed his car into the tree/garage** er fuhr rückwärts gegen den Baum/in die Garage; **to** ~ **water** *(Naut)* rückwärts rudern.

(d) *(Mus)* singer begleiten.

(e) *(put sth behind)* picture mit einem Rücken versehen, unterlegen; *(stick on)* aufziehen.

6 *vi* **(a)** *(move backwards)* *(car, train)* zurücksetzen *or* -fahren. **the car** ~**ed into the garage** das Auto fuhr rückwärts in die Garage; **she** ~**ed into me** sie fuhr rückwärts in mein Auto.

(b) *(Naut: wind)* drehen.

♦**back away** *vi* zurückweichen *(from* vor +*dat)*.

♦**back down** *vi (fig)* nachgeben, klein beigeben.

♦**back off** *vi (vehicle)* zurücksetzen.

♦**back on to** *vi* +*prep obj* hinten angrenzen an (+*acc*).

♦**back out 1** *vi* **(a)** *(car etc)* rückwärts herausfahren *or* -setzen. **(b)** *(fig: of contract, deal etc)* aussteigen *(of, from* aus) *(inf)*. **2** *vt sep* vehicle rückwärts herausfahren *or* -setzen.

♦**back up 1** *vi (car etc)* zurückstoßen. **to** ~ **to sth** rückwärts an etw *(acc)* heranfahren.

2 *vt sep* **(a)** *(support)* unterstützen; *(confirm)* story bestätigen; *(in discussion etc also)* Schützenhilfe leisten (+*dat*), den Rücken stärken (+*dat*); knowledge fundieren; claim, theory untermauern. **he** ~**ed** ~ **the boy's story that ... er** bestätigte den Bericht des Jungen, wonach ...; **he can** ~ **me** ~ **in this** er kann das bestätigen.

(b) car etc zurückfahren.

back: ~**ache** *n* Rückenschmerzen *pl*; ~ **bench** *n (esp Brit)* Abgeordnetensitz *m*; ~ **benches** das Plenum; ~**bencher** *n (esp Brit)* Abgeordnete(r) *m (auf den hinteren Reihen im britischen Parlament)*; ~**biting** *n* Lästern *nt*; ~ **boiler** *n* Warmwasserboiler *m (hinter der Heizung angebracht)*; ~**bone** *n (lit, fig)* Rückgrat *nt*; ~**-breaking** *adj* erschöpfend, ermüdend; ~**chat** *n, no pl (inf)* Widerrede *f*; **none of your** ~**chat**! keine Widerrede!; ~**cloth** *n* Prospekt, Hintergrund *m*; ~**comb** *vt* hair toupieren; ~ **copy** *n* alte Ausgabe *or* Nummer; ~**date** *vt* (zu)rückdatieren; **salary increase** ~**dated to May** Gehaltserhöhung rückwirkend ab Mai; ~ **door** *n (lit)* Hintertür *f*; *(fig)* Hintertürchen *nt*; **if you use the** ~**door method** wenn Sie das durchs Hintertürchen machen; ~**drop** *n* Prospekt, Hintergrund *(auch fig) m*.

backed [bækt] *adj* **low-/high-**~ mit niedriger/hoher Rückenlehne; **a low-**~ **dress** ein Kleid mit tiefem Rückenausschnitt; **straight-**~ **chair** mit gerader Rückenlehne; person mit geradem Rücken.

back end *n (rear)* hinteres Ende. **at the** ~ **of the year** gegen Ende des Jahres, in den letzten Monaten des Jahres; **she looks like the** ~ **of a bus** *(sl)* sie ist potthäßlich *(inf)*.

backer ['bækə^r] *n* **(a)** *(supporter)* **his** ~**s** (diejenigen,) die ihn unterstützen.

(b) *(Betting)* Wettende(r) *mf*.

(c) *(Comm)* Geldgeber *m*.

back: ~ **file** *n* alte Akte; ~**fire 1** *n* **(a)** *(Aut)* Fehlzündung *f*; **(b)** *(US)* Gegenfeuer *nt*; **2** *vi* **(a)** *(Aut)* fehlzünden; **(b)** *(inf: plan etc)* ins Auge gehen *(inf)*; **it** ~**fired on us** der Schuß ging nach hinten los *(inf)*; ~ **formation** *n (Ling)* Rückbildung, Backformation *f*; ~**gammon** *n* Backgammon, Tricktrack *nt*; ~ **garden** *n* Garten *m (hintern Haus)*.

background ['bækgraund] **1** *n* **(a)** *(of painting etc, fig)* Hintergrund *m*. **to stay in the** ~ im Hintergrund bleiben, sich im Hintergrund halten; **to keep sb in the** ~ jdn nicht in den Vordergrund treten lassen; **against a** ~ **of poverty and disease** vor dem Hintergrund von Armut und Krankheit.

(b) *(of person)* *(educational etc)* Werdegang *m*; *(social)* Verhältnisse *pl*; *(family* ~*)* Herkunft *f no pl*. **he comes from a** ~ **of poverty** er kommt aus ärmlichen Verhältnissen; **comprehensive schools take children from all** ~**s** Gesamtschulen nehmen Kinder aus allen Schichten auf; **given the right sort of** ~ wenn man (nur) aus den richtigen Kreisen kommt; **what do we know about the main character's** ~? was wissen wir über das Vorleben *or* den Werdegang der Hauptperson?; **what's your educational** ~? was für eine Ausbildung haben Sie?

(c) *(of case, event, problem etc)* Zusammenhänge, Hintergründe *pl*, Hintergrund *m*. **he briefly filled in the** ~ **to the present crisis** er erläuterte kurz die Zusammenhänge *or* Hintergründe der gegenwärtigen Krise.

2 *adj* reading vertiefend. ~ **music** Backgroundmusik, Musikuntermalung *f*; ~ **noises** *pl* Geräuschkulisse *f*, Geräusch *nt* im Hintergrund; ~ **information** Hintergrundinformationen *pl*; **what's the** ~ **information on this**? welche Hintergründe *or* Zusammenhänge bestehen hierfür?

back: ~**hand 1** *n (Sport)* Rückhand, Backhand *f no pl*; *(one stroke)* Rückhandschlag *m*; **2** *adj* stroke, shot Rückhand-; **3** *adv* mit der Rückhand; ~**handed** *adj* compliment zweifelhaft; shot Rückhand-; writing nach links geneigt; ~**hander** *n (Sport)*

Rückhandschlag *m*; **(b)** *(inf: bribe)* Schmiergeld *nt*; **to give sb a** ~**hander** jdn schmieren *(inf)*.

backing ['bækɪŋ] *n* **(a)** *(support)* Unterstützung *f*. **(b)** *(Mus)* Begleitung *f*. ~ **group** Begleitband, Begleitung *f*. **(c)** *(for picture frame, for strengthening)* Rücken(verstärkung *f) m*; *(for carpet, wallpaper etc)* Rücken(beschichtung *f) m*.

back: ~**lash** *n* **(a)** *(Tech)* *(jarring reaction)* Gegenschlag *m*; *(play)* zuviel Spiel; **(b)** *(fig)* Gegenreaktion *f*; ~**less** *adj* dress rückenfrei; ~**log** *n* Rückstände *pl*; **I have a** ~**log of work** ich bin mit der Arbeit im Rückstand; **look at this** ~**log of typing** sehen Sie sich diesen Berg unerledigter Schreibarbeiten an; ~**marker** *n (Sport)* Nachzügler *m*, Schlußlicht *nt*; **the** ~**markers** die Nachhut; ~ **number** *n (of paper)* alte Ausgabe *or* Nummer; *(fig)* *(person)* altmodischer Mensch; *(thing)* veraltetes Ding; **that/he is a** ~ **number** das ist überholt/er ist altmodisch; ~**pack** *n* Rucksack *m*; **to go** ~**packing** auf (Berg)tour gehen; ~ **pay** *n* Nachzahlung *f*; ~**pedal** *vi (lit)* rückwärts treten; *(fig inf)* langsam treten *(inf)*, bremsen *(inf)* *(on* bei); ~**pedal brake** *n* Rücktrittbremse *f*; ~ **projection** *n (Film)* Rückprojektion *f*; ~ **rest** *n* Rückenstütze *f*; ~ **room** *n* Hinterzimmer *nt*; ~**-room boy** *n (inf)* Experte *m* im Hintergrund; ~ **seat** *n* Rücksitz *m*; **to take a** ~ **seat** *(fig)* sich zurückhalten *or* raushalten *(inf)*; ~**seat driver** *n* Beifahrer, der dem Fahrer dazwischenredet; **she is a terrible** ~**seat driver** sie redet beim Fahren immer rein *(inf)*; ~**shift** *n* Spätschicht *f*; ~**side** *n (inf)* Hintern *m*, Hinterteil *nt*; ~ **sight** *n (on rifle)* Visier *nt*, Kimme *f*; ~**slapping** *n (inf)* Schulterklopfen *nt*; ~**slide** *vi (fig)* rückfällig werden; *(Eccl)* abtrünnig werden; ~**slider** *n* Rückfällige(r) *mf*; Abtrünnige(r) *mf*; ~**space** *vi (Typing)* zurücksetzen; ~**spacer** *n (Typing)* Rücktaste *f*; ~**stage** *adv, adj* hinter den Kulissen; *(in dressing-room area)* in die/der Garderobe; ~**stage people** Leute hinter den Kulissen; ~**stairs** *n* sing Hintertreppe *f*; ~**stitch** *n* Steppstich *m*; ~ **straight** *n (Sport)* Gegengerade *f*; ~ **street** *n* Seitenstraßchen *nt*; **he comes from the** ~ **streets of Liverpool** er kommt aus dem ärmeren Teil von Liverpool; ~**street abortion** *n* illegale Abtreibung; ~**street abortions** Engelmacherei *f (inf)*; **she had a** ~**street abortion** sie war bei einem Engelmacher *(inf)*; ~**street abortionist** *n* Engelmacher(in *f) m (inf)*; ~**stroke** *n (Swimming)* Rückenschwimmen *nt*; **can you do the** ~**stroke**? können Sie rückenschwimmen?; ~**talk** *n* Widerrede, Frechheit *f*; ~ **to** ~ *adv* Rücken an Rücken; *(things)* mit den Rückseiten aneinander; ~ **to front** *adv* verkehrt herum; **read** von hinten nach vorne; ~ **tooth** *n* Backenzahn *m*; ~**track** *vi (over ground)* denselben Weg zurückgehen *or* zurückverfolgen; *(on policy etc)* einen Rückzieher machen *(on sth* bei etw); ~**up 1** *n* Unterstützung *f*; **2** *adj* troops Unterstützungs-, Hilfs-; train, plane Entlastungs-; ~ **vowel** *n (Phon)* hinterer Vokal, Rachenvokal *m*.

backward ['bækwəd] **1** *adj* **(a)** ~ **and forward movement** Vor- und Zurückbewegung *f*; ~ **flow of information** Rückenfluß *m* von Daten; **a** ~ **glance** ein Blick zurück.

(b) *(fig)* **a** ~ **step/move** ein Schritt *m* zurück/eine (Zu)rückentwicklung.

(c) *(retarded)* child zurückgeblieben; region, country rückständig.

2 *adv* see **backwards**.

backwardness ['bækwədnɪs] *n (mental)* Zurückgebliebenheit *f*; *(of region)* Rückständigkeit *f*.

backwards ['bækwədz] *adv* **(a)** rückwärts. **to fall** ~ nach hinten fallen; **to walk** ~ **and forwards** hin und her gehen; **to say the alphabet** ~ das Alphabet rückwärts *or* von hinten aufsagen; **to stroke a cat** ~ eine Katze gegen den Strich streicheln; **to lean** *or* **bend over** ~ **to do sth** *(inf)* sich fast umbringen *or* sich *(dat)* ein Bein ausreißen, um etw zu tun *(inf)*; **I know it** ~ das kenne ich in- und auswendig.

(b) *(towards the past)* zurück. **to look** ~ zurückblicken.

back: ~**wash** *n (Naut)* Rückströmung *f*; *(fig)* Nachwirkung *f usu pl*; **those caught up in the** ~**wash of the scandal** diejenigen, die in den Skandal mit hineingezogen wurden; ~**water** *n (lit)* Stauwasser *nt*, totes Wasser; *(fig)* rückständiges Nest; **this town is a cultural** ~**water** kulturell (gesehen) ist diese Stadt tiefste Provinz; ~**woods** *npl* unerschlossene (Wald)gebiete *pl*; ~**woodsman** *n* Waldsiedler *m*; *(US inf)* Hinterwäldler *m*; ~**yard** *n* Hinterhof *m*; **they found one in their own** ~**yard** *(fig)* sie haben einen vor der eigenen Haustür gefunden.

bacon ['beɪkən] *n* Frühstücks- *or* Schinkenspeck *m*. ~ **and eggs** Eier mit Speck; **to save sb's** ~ *(inf)* jds Rettung sein; **to bring home the** ~ *(inf: earn a living)* die Brötchen verdienen *(inf)*.

bacteria [bæk'tɪərɪə] *pl* of **bacterium**.

bacterial [bæk'tɪərɪəl] *adj* Bakterien-, bakteriell.

bacteriological [bæk,tɪərɪə'lɒdʒɪkəl] *adj* bakteriologisch.

bacteriologist [bæk,tɪərɪ'ɒlədʒɪst] *n* Bakteriologe *m*, Bakteriologin *f*.

bacteriology [bæk,tɪərɪ'ɒlədʒɪ] *n* Bakteriologie *f*.

bacterium [bæk'tɪərɪəm] *n, pl* **bacteria** [bæk'tɪərɪə] Bakterie *f*, Bakterium *nt (old)*.

bad [bæd] **1** *adj, comp* **worse**, *superl* **worst** **(a)** schlecht; news *also* schlimm; smell, habit *also* übel; insurance risk hoch; word unanständig, schlimm; *(immoral, wicked also)* böse; *(naughty, misbehaved)* unartig, ungezogen; dog böse. **it was a** ~ **thing to do** das hättest du nicht tun sollen; **he went through a** ~ **time** er hat eine schlimme Zeit durchgemacht; **you** ~ **boy!** du ungezogener Junge!; **du Lümmel!** *(also iro)*; **he's been a** ~ **boy** er war unartig *or* böse; **I didn't mean that word in a** ~ **sense** ich habe mir bei dem Wort nichts Böses gedacht; **it's a** ~ **business** das ist eine üble Sache; **things are going from a** ~ **to worse** es wird immer schlimmer; **to go** ~ schlecht werden, verderben; **to be** ~ **for sb/sth** schlecht *or* nicht gut für jdn/etw sein; **he's** ~ **at tennis** er spielt schlecht Tennis; **he's** ~ **at sport** im Sport ist er schlecht *or* nicht gut, er ist unsportlich; **I'm very** ~ **at telling lies** ich kann schlecht *or* nicht gut lügen; **he speaks** ~ **English**

er spricht schlecht(es) Englisch; **to be ~ to sb** jdn schlecht behandeln; **there's nothing ~ about living together** es ist doch nicht schlimm *or* es ist doch nichts dabei, wenn man zusammenlebt; **this is a ~ town for violence** in dieser Stadt ist es wirklich schlimm mit der Gewalttätigkeit; **this is a ~ district for wheat** dies ist eine schlechte *or* keine gute Gegend für Weizen; **it would not be a ~ thing** *or* **plan** das wäre nicht schlecht *or* keine schlechte Idee; **(that's) too ~!** (*indignant*) so was!; (~ *luck*) Pech!; **it's too ~ of you** das ist wirklich nicht nett *or* kein schöner Zug von dir; **too ~ you couldn't make it** (es ist) wirklich schade, daß Sie nicht kommen konnten.
    (b) (*serious*) *wound, sprain* schlimm; *accident, mistake, cold also* schwer; *headache also, deterioration* stark. **he's got it ~** (*inf*) ihn hat's schwer erwischt (*inf*); **to have it ~ for sb** (*inf*) in jdn schwer *or* unheimlich verknallt sein (*inf*).
    (c) (*unfavourable*) *time, day* ungünstig, schlecht. **Thursday's ~, can you make it Friday?** Donnerstag ist ungünstig *or* schlecht, geht's nicht Freitag?
    (d) (*in poor health, sick*) *stomach* krank; *leg, knee, hand* schlimm; *tooth* (*generally*) schlecht; (*now*) schlimm. **he/the economy is in a ~ way** es geht ihm schlecht/es steht schlecht um die *or* mit der Wirtschaft; **I've got a ~ head** ich habe einen dicken Kopf (*inf*); **to feel ~** sich nicht wohl fühlen; **I feel ~** mir geht es *or* ist nicht gut; **to be taken ~** (*inf*) plötzlich krank werden; **how is he? — he's not so ~** wie geht es ihm? — nicht schlecht; **I didn't know she was so ~** ich wußte nicht, daß es ihr so schlecht geht *or* daß sie so schlimm dran ist (*inf*).
    (e) (*regretful*) **I feel really ~ about not having told him** es tut mir wirklich leid *or* ich habe ein schlechtes Gewissen, daß ich ihm das nicht gesagt habe; **don't feel ~ about it** machen Sie sich (*dat*) keine Gedanken *or* Sorgen (darüber).
    (f) *debt* uneinbringlich; *voting slip, coin* ungültig; *cheque* ungültig; (*uncovered*) ungedeckt; (*damaged*) *copies etc* beschädigt.
    2 *n, no pl* **(a) to take the good with the ~** (auch) die schlechten Seiten in Kauf nehmen; **there is good and ~** in everything/everybody alles/jeder hat seine guten und schlechten Seiten.
    (b) he's gone to the ~ er ist auf die schiefe Bahn geraten.
baddie ['bædɪ] *n* (*inf*) Schurke, Bösewicht *m*.
baddish ['bædɪʃ] *adj* (*inf*) ziemlich schlecht.
bad(e) [beɪd] *pret of* **bid**.
badge [bædʒ] *n* **(a)** Abzeichen *nt*; (*made of metal: women's lib, joke* ~*, on car etc*) Plakette *f*. ~ **of office** Dienstmarke *f*. **(b)** (*fig: symbol*) Merkmal *nt*.
badger ['bædʒəʳ] **1** *n* Dachs *m*. **2** *vt* zusetzen (+*dat*), bearbeiten (*inf*), keine Ruhe lassen (+*dat*). **don't ~ me** laß mich in Ruhe *or* Frieden; **to ~ sb for sth** jdm mit etw in den Ohren liegen.
badlands ['bædləndz] *npl* Ödland *nt*.
badly ['bædlɪ] *adv* **(a)** schlecht. **the party went ~** die Party war ein Reinfall *or* ist schlecht gelaufen (*inf*).
    (b) *wounded, mistaken* schwer. ~ **beaten** (*Sport*) vernichtend geschlagen; *person* schwer *or* schlimm verprügelt; **the ~ disabled** die Schwerstbeschädigten.
    (c) (*very much*) äußerst, sehr; **in debt, overdrawn** hoch. **to want sth ~** etw unbedingt wollen; **I need it ~** ich brauche es dringend; **he ~ needs** *or* **wants a haircut** er muß dringend zum Friseur.
bad-mannered [,bæd'mænəd] *adj* ungezogen, unhöflich.
badminton ['bædmɪntən] *n* Badminton, Federball *nt*.
badness ['bædnɪs] *n, no pl* **(a)** Schlechtheit *f*; (*moral*) Schlechtigkeit *f*; (*naughtiness*) Unartigkeit, Ungezogenheit *f*. **(b)** (*seriousness*) Schwere *f*; (*of mistake also*) Ernst *m*; (*of headache*) Stärke *f*.
bad-tempered [,bæd'tempəd] *adj* schlechtgelaunt *attr*, übellaunig. **to be ~** schlechte Laune haben; (*as characteristic*) ein übellauniger Mensch sein.
baffle ['bæfl] **1** *vt* **(a)** (*confound, amaze*) verblüffen; (*cause incomprehension*) vor ein Rätsel stellen. **a ~d look** ein verdutzter Blick; **the case has ~d the police** die Polizei steht vor einem Rätsel; **it really ~s me how ...** es ist mir wirklich ein Rätsel, wie ...; **a case that ~d all the experts** ein Fall, der den Experten Rätsel aufgab; **this one's got me ~d** ich stehe vor einem Rätsel.
    (b) (*Tech*) *sound* dämpfen.
    2 *n* (*also* ~**-plate**) (*Aut*) Umlenkblech *nt*.
baffling ['bæflɪŋ] *adj case* rätselhaft; *complexity* verwirrend; *mystery* unergründlich. **I find it ~ how ...** es ist mir ein Rätsel, wie ...
bag [bæg] **1** *n* **(a)** Tasche *f*; (*with drawstrings, pouch*) Beutel *m*; (*for school*) Schultasche *f*; (*made of paper, plastic*) Tüte *f*; (*sack*) Sack *m*; (*suitcase*) Reisetasche *f*. ~**s** (Reise)gepäck *nt*; **with ~ and baggage** mit Sack und Pack; **to be a ~ of bones** (*fig inf*) nur Haut und Knochen sein (*inf*); **the whole ~ of tricks** (*inf*) die ganze Trickkiste (*inf*).
    (b) (*Hunt*) **the ~** die (Jagd)beute; **to get a good ~** (eine) fette Beute machen *or* heimbringen; **it's in the ~** (*fig inf*) das habe ich etc schon in der Tasche (*inf*), das ist gelaufen (*inf*).
    (c) ~**s under the eyes** (*black*) Ringe *pl* unter den Augen; (*of skin*) (hervortretende) Tränensäcke *pl*.
    (d) ~**s** *pl* (*Oxford* ~**s**) weite Hose; (*dated inf: trousers*) Buxe *f* (*dated inf*).
    (e) (*inf: a lot*) ~**s of** jede Menge (*inf*).
    (f) (*pej sl: woman*) (**old**) ~ (alte) Ziege (*pej sl*), Weibsstück *nt* (*pej*); **ugly old ~** Schreckschraube *f* (*inf*).
    2 *vt* **(a)** in Tüten/Säcke verpacken.
    (b) (*Hunt*) erlegen, erbeuten.
    (c) (*Brit sl: get*) (sich *dat*) schnappen (*inf*). ~**s I have first go!** will anfangen!; **I ~s that ice-cream!** will das Eis!
    3 *vi* (*garment*) sich (aus)beulen.
bagatelle [,bægə'tel] *n* **(a)** (*liter: trifle*) Bagatelle, Nichtigkeit (*geh*) *f*. **(b)** (*game*) Tivoli *nt*.

bagful ['bægfʊl] *n* **a ~ of groceries** eine Tasche voll Lebensmittel; **20 ~s of wheat** 20 Sack Weizen.
baggage ['bægɪdʒ] *n* **(a)** (*luggage*) (Reise)gepäck *nt*. **(b)** (*Mil*) Gepäck *nt*. **(c)** (*pej inf: woman*) Stück *nt* (*inf*).
baggage (*esp US*): ~ **car** *n* Gepäckwagen *m*; ~ **check** *n* Gepäckkontrolle *f*; ~ **master** *n* Beamte(r) *m* am Gepäckschalter; ~ **room** *n* Gepäckaufbewahrung *f*; ~ **wagon** *n* Gepäckwagen *m*.
bagging ['bægɪŋ] *n* (*material*) Sack- *or* Packleinen *nt*.
baggy ['bægɪ] *adj* (+*er*) (*ill-fitting*) zu weit; *dress* sackartig; *skin* schlaff (hängend); (*out of shape*) *trousers, suit* ausgebeult; *jumper* ausgeleiert. ~ **trousers are fashionable again** weite (Flatter)hosen sind wieder modern.
Baghdad [,bæg'dæd] *n* Bagdad *nt*.
bagpiper ['bægpaɪpəʳ] *n* Dudelsackpfeifer *or* -bläser *m*.
bagpipe(s *pl*) ['bægpaɪp(s)] *n* Dudelsack *m*.
bags [bægz] *npl see* **bag 1 (d, e)**.
bag-snatcher ['bæg,snætʃəʳ] *n* Handtaschenräuber *m*.
Bahamas [bə'hɑːməz] *npl*: **the ~** die Bahamas, die Bahamainseln *pl*.
bail[1] [beɪl] *n* (*Jur*) Kaution, Sicherheitsleistung (*form*) *f*. **to go** *or* **stand** *or* **put in ~ for sb** für jdn (die) Kaution stellen *or* leisten; **to grant/refuse ~** die Freilassung gegen Kaution bewilligen/verweigern; **he was refused ~** sein Antrag auf Freilassung gegen Kaution wurde abgelehnt; **to be (out) on ~** gegen Kaution freigelassen sein; **to let sb out on ~** jdn gegen Kaution freilassen.
♦ **bail out** *vt sep* **(a)** (*Jur*) gegen Kaution *or* Sicherheitsleistung freibekommen, die Kaution stellen für. **(b)** (*fig*) aus der Patsche helfen (+*dat*) (*inf*). **(c)** *boat see* **bale out**.
bail[2] *n* **(a)** (*Cricket*) Querholz *nt*. **(b)** (*in stable*) Trennstange *f*.
bail[3] *vti see* **bale**[2].
Bailey bridge ['beɪlɪ'brɪdʒ] *n* Behelfsbrücke *f*.
bailiff ['beɪlɪf] *n* **(a)** (*Jur*) (*sheriff's*) ~ Amtsdiener *m*; (*for property*) Gerichtsvollzieher *m*; (*in court*) Gerichtsdiener *m*. **(b)** (*on estate*) (Guts)verwalter, Landvogt (*obs*) *m*.
bairn [bɛən] *n* (*Scot*) Kind *nt*.
bait [beɪt] **1** *n* (*lit, fig*) Köder *m*. **to take** *or* **swallow** *or* **rise to the ~** (*lit, fig*) anbeißen; (*fig: be trapped*) sich ködern lassen. **2** *vt* **(a)** *hook, trap* mit einem Köder versehen, beködern. **(b)** (*torment*) *animal* (mit Hunden) hetzen; *person* quälen.
baize [beɪz] *n* Fries, Flaus *m*. **green ~** Billardtuch *nt*.
bake [beɪk] **1** *vt* **(a)** (*Cook*) backen. ~**d apples** *pl* Bratäpfel *pl*; ~**d potatoes** *pl* gebackene Pellkartoffeln *pl*.
    (b) *pottery, bricks* brennen; (*sun*) *earth* ausdörren.
    2 *vi* **(a)** backen; (*cake*) im (Back)ofen sein.
    (b) (*pottery etc*) gebrannt werden, im (Brenn)ofen sein.
    (c) (*inf*) **we are baking in this heat** wir kommen ja um in dieser Hitze; **I'm baking** ich komme um vor Hitze; **it's baking (hot) today** es ist eine Affenhitze heute (*inf*); **I just want to lie in the sun and ~** ich möchte mich in der Sonne braten lassen.
bakehouse ['beɪkhaʊs] *n* Backhaus *nt*.
bakelite ® ['beɪkəlaɪt] *n* Bakelit *nt*.
baker ['beɪkəʳ] *n* Bäcker(in *f*) *m*; ~**'s man** *or* **boy** Bäckerjunge *m*; ~**'s (shop)** Bäckerei *f*, Bäckerladen *m*; ~**'s dozen** 13 (Stück).
bakery ['beɪkərɪ] *n* Bäckerei *f*.
baking ['beɪkɪŋ] *n* **(a)** (*act*) (*Cook*) Backen *nt*; (*of earthenware*) Brennen *nt*. **it's our own ~** das ist selbstgebacken. **(b)** (*batch: of bread, of bricks etc*) Ofenladung *f*, Schub *m*.
baking: ~ **day** *n* Backtag *m*; ~ **dish** *n* Backform *f*; ~ **powder** *n* Backpulver *nt*; ~ **sheet** *n* Back- *or* Plätzchenblech *nt*; ~ **soda** *n* Backpulver *nt*; ~ **tin** *n* Backform *f*; ~ **tray** *n* Kuchenblech *nt*.
baksheesh ['bækʃiːʃ] *n* Bakschisch *nt*.
Balaclava [,bælə'klɑːvə] *n* (*also* ~ **helmet**) Kapuzenmütze *f*.
balalaika [,bælə'laɪkə] *n* Balalaika *f*.
balance ['bæləns] **1** *n* **(a)** (*apparatus*) Waage *f*. **to be** *or* **hang in the ~** (*fig*) in der Schwebe sein; **his life hung in the ~** sein Leben hing an einem dünnen *or* seidenen Faden; **to put sth in the ~** (*risk*) etw in die Waagschale werfen.
    (b) (*counterpoise*) Gegengewicht *nt* (*to* zu); (*fig also*) Ausgleich *m* (*to* für).
    (c) (*lit, fig: equilibrium*) Gleichgewicht *nt*. **sense of ~** Gleichgewichtssinn *m*; **to keep one's ~** das Gleichgewicht (be)halten; **to lose one's ~** aus dem Gleichgewicht kommen, das Gleichgewicht verlieren; **to recover one's ~** wieder ins Gleichgewicht kommen, das Gleichgewicht wiedererlangen; **off ~** aus dem Gleichgewicht; **to throw sb off (his) ~** jdn aus dem Gleichgewicht bringen; **the right ~ of personalities in the team** eine ausgewogene Mischung verschiedener Charaktere in der Mannschaft; **the ~ of probabilities is such that ...** wenn man die Möglichkeiten gegeneinander abwägt, dann ...; **the ~ of power** das Gleichgewicht der Mächte; **to strike the right ~ between old and new/import and export** den goldenen Mittelweg zwischen Alt und Neu finden/das richtige Verhältnis von Import zu Export finden; **on ~** (*fig*) alles in allem.
    (d) (*Art*) Ausgewogenheit *f*. **he has no sense of ~** er hat kein Gefühl für Ausgewogenheit *or* Harmonie.
    (e) (*preponderant weight*) Hauptgewicht *nt*. **the ~ of advantage lies with you** der Hauptvorteil ist auf Ihrer Seite.
    (f) (*Comm, Fin: state of account*) Saldo *m*; (*with bank also*) Konto(be)stand *m*; (*of company*) Bilanz *f*. ~ **in hand** (*Comm*) Kassen(be)stand *m*; ~ **carried forward** Saldovortrag *or* -übertrag *m*; ~ **due** (*banking*) Debetsaldo *m*, Soll *nt*; (*Comm*) Rechnungsbetrag *m*; ~ **in your favour** Saldoguthaben, Haben *nt*; **to pay off the ~** (*banking*) den Saldo begleichen; (*Comm*) den Rest bezahlen; **my father has promised to make up the ~** mein Vater hat versprochen, die Differenz zu (be)zahlen; ~ **of payments/trade** Zahlungs-/Handelsbilanz *f*.
    (g) (*fig: remainder*) Rest *m*.
    2 *vt* **(a)** (*keep level, in equilibrium*) im Gleichgewicht halten; (*bring into equilibrium*) ins Gleichgewicht bringen, ausbalan-

cieren. to ~ oneself on one foot auf einem Fuß balancieren; the seal ~s a ball on its nose der Seehund balanciert einen Ball auf der Nase.

(b) *(weigh in the mind) two arguments, two solutions* (gegeneinander) abwägen. to ~ sth against sth etw einer Sache *(dat)* gegenüberstellen.

(c) *(equal, make up for)* ausgleichen.

(d) *(Comm, Fin) account (add up)* saldieren, abschließen; *(make equal)* ausgleichen; *(pay off)* begleichen; *budget* ausgleichen. to ~ the books die Bilanz ziehen *or* machen.

(e) *(Aut) wheel* auswuchten.

3 *vi* (a) *(be in equilibrium)* Gleichgewicht halten; *(scales)* sich ausbalancieren; *(painting)* ausgewogen sein. he ~d on one foot or balancierte auf einem Bein; with a ball balancing on its nose mit einem Ball, den er auf der Nase balancierte.

(b) *(Comm, Fin: of accounts)* ausgeglichen sein. the books don't ~ die Abrechnung stimmt nicht; to make the books ~ die Abrechnung ausgleichen.

♦ **balance out** 1 *vt sep* aufwiegen, ausgleichen. they ~ each other ~ sie wiegen sich auf, sie halten sich die Waage; *(personalities)* sie gleichen sich aus. 2 *vi* sich ausgleichen.

balanced ['bælənst] *adj personality* ausgeglichen; *diet also, painting, photography, mixture* ausgewogen.

balance: ~ sheet *n* (Fin) Bilanz *f*; *(document)* Bilanzaufstellung *f*; ~ wheel *n (in watch)* Unruh *f*.

balancing: ~ act *n (lit, fig)* Balanceakt *m*; ~ trick *n* Balancekunststück *nt*.

balcony ['bælkənɪ] *n* (a) Balkon *m*. (b) *(Theat)* Galerie *f*.

bald [bɔːld] *adj (+er)* (a) *person* kahl, glatzköpfig; *bird* federlos; *tree* kahl. he is ~ er hat eine Glatze; to go ~ eine Glatze bekommen, kahl werden; he is going ~ at the temples or hat Geheimratsecken; ~ patch kahle Stelle.

(b) *style, statement* knapp.

bald eagle *n* weißköpfiger Seeadler.

balderdash ['bɔːldədæʃ] *n (dated inf)* Kokolores *m (dated inf)*.

bald-headed ['bɔːld,hedɪd] *adj* kahl- *or* glatzköpfig.

balding ['bɔːldɪŋ] 1 *adj* his ~ head sein schütter werdendes Haar; a ~ gentleman ein Herr mit schütterem Haar; he is ~ er bekommt langsam eine Glatze. 2 *n* Haarausfall *m*.

baldly ['bɔːldlɪ] *adv (fig) (bluntly)* unverblümt, unumwunden; *(roughly)* grob, knapp. to state the facts quite ~ die Dinge beim Namen nennen.

baldness ['bɔːldnɪs] *n* (a) Kahlheit *f*. (b) *(of style, statement)* Knappheit *f*.

baldy ['bɔːldɪ] *n (inf)* Glatzkopf *m*.

bale[1] [beɪl] 1 *n (of hay etc)* Bündel *nt; (out of combine harvester, of cotton)* Ballen *m; (of paper etc)* Pack *m*. 2 *vt* bündeln; zu Ballen verarbeiten.

bale[2] *vti (Naut)* schöpfen.

♦ **bale out** 1 *vi* (a) *(Aviat)* abspringen, aussteigen *(inf) (of* aus).

(b) *(Naut)* schöpfen. 2 *vt sep (Naut) water* schöpfen; *ship* ausschöpfen, leer schöpfen.

Balearic [,bælɪ'ærɪk] *adj*: the ~ Islands die Balearen *pl*.

baleful ['beɪlfʊl] *adj* (a) *(evil)* böse; *look (of bull etc)* stier. (b) *(sad)* traurig.

balefully ['beɪlfəlɪ] *adv see adj*.

balk, baulk [bɔːk] 1 *n* (a) *(beam)* Balken *m*. (b) *(obstacle)* Hindernis *nt*, Hemmschuh *m (to* für). 2 *vt person* hemmen; *plan* vereiteln. 3 *vi (person)* zurückschrecken *(at vor + dat); (horse)* scheuen, bocken *(at* bei).

Balkan ['bɔːlkən] 1 *adj* Balkan-. the ~ Mountains der Balkan. 2 *n*: the ~s der Balkan, die Balkanländer *pl*.

ball[1] [bɔːl] 1 *n* (a) Ball *m; (sphere)* Kugel *f; (of wool, string)* Knäuel *m*. the cat lay curled up in a ~ die Katze hatte sich zusammengerollt; ~ and chain Fußfessel *f* (mit Gewicht).

(b) *(Sport)* Ball *m; (Billiards, Croquet)* Kugel *f*.

(c) *(delivery of a ~)* Ball *m; (Tennis, Golf also)* Schlag *m; (Ftbl, Hockey also)* Schuß *m; (Cricket)* Wurf *m*. the backs were giving their strikers a lot of good ~(s) die Verteidiger spielten den Stürmern gute Bälle zu; no ~ *(Cricket)* falsch ausgeführter Wurf.

(d) *(game)* Ball *m; (US: baseball)* Baseball *nt*. to play ~ Ball/Baseball spielen.

(e) *(fig phrases)* to keep the ~ rolling das Gespräch in Gang halten; to start *or* set the ~ rolling den Stein ins Rollen bringen; to have the ~ at one's feet seine große Chance haben; the ~ is with you *or* in your court Sie sind am Ball *(inf)*; to be on the ~ *(inf)* am Ball sein *(inf)*, auf Zack *or* Draht sein *(inf); see* play.

(f) *(old: for gun)* Kugel *f; see* cannon ball.

(g) *(Anat)* ~ of the foot/thumb Fuß-/Handballen *m*.

(h) *(Cook: of meat, fish)* Klößchen *nt*, Klops *m*.

(i) *(sl: testicle)* Ei *nt usu pl (sl); pl also* Sack *m (sl)*. ~s! *(nonsense)* red keinen Scheiß *(sl)*; ~s to him/the regulations der kann mich am Arsch lecken *(vulg)*/ich scheiß' doch auf die Bestimmungen *(vulg)*.

2 *vti (US sl)* bumsen *(inf)*.

ball[2] *n* (a) *(dance)* Ball *m*. (b) *(inf: good time)* Spaß *m*. to have a ~ sich prima amüsieren *(inf)*.

ballad ['bæləd] *n (Mus, Liter)* Ballade *f*.

ball-and-socket joint *n* Kugelgelenk *nt*.

ballast ['bæləst] 1 *n* (a) *(Naut, Aviat, fig)* Ballast *m*. to take in/discharge ~ Ballast aufnehmen/abwerfen. (b) *(stone, clinker)* Schotter *m; (Rail)* Bettung(sschotter *m) f*. 2 *vt (Naut, Aviat)* mit Ballast beladen.

ball: ~-bearing *n* Kugellager *nt; (ball)* Kugellagerkugel *f*; ~-boy *n (Tennis)* Balljunge *m*; ~-cock *n* Schwimmerhahn *m*; ~-control *n* Ballführung *f*.

ballerina [,bælə'riːnə] *n* Ballerina, Ballerine *f; (principal)* Primaballerina *f*.

ballet ['bæleɪ] *n* Ballett *nt*.

ballet: ~-dancer *n* Ballettänzer(in *f) m*, Balleteuse *f*; ~ pump,

---

~shoe *n* Ballettschuh *m*; ~ skirt *n* Ballettröckchen *nt*.

ball game *n* Ballspiel *nt*. it's a whole new/different ~ *(fig inf)* das ist 'ne ganz andere Chose *(inf)*.

ballistic [bə'lɪstɪk] *adj* ballistisch. ~ missile Raketengeschoß *nt*.

ballistics [bə'lɪstɪks] *n sing* Ballistik *f*. ~ expert Schußwaffenfachmann *m*.

balloon [bə'luːn] 1 *n* (a) *(Aviat)* (Frei)ballon *m; (toy)* (Luft)-ballon *m; (Met)* (Wetter)ballon *m*. the ~ went up *(fig inf)* da ist die Bombe geplatzt *(inf)*. (b) *(in cartoons)* Sprechblase *f*. (c) *(Chem: also* ~ flask) *(Rund)*kolben *m*. 2 *vi* (a) to go ~ing auf Ballonfahrt gehen. (b) *(swell out)* sich blähen.

balloon glass *n* Kognakglas *nt or* -schwenker *m*.

balloonist [bə'luːnɪst] *n* Ballonfahrer(in *f) m*.

balloon-tyre [bə'luːn,taɪə[r]] *n* Ballonreifen *m*.

ballot ['bælət] 1 *n* (a) *(method of voting)* geheime Abstimmung; *(election)* Geheimwahl *f*. voting is by ~ die Wahl/Abstimmung ist geheim; to decide sth by ~ über etw *(acc)* (geheim) abstimmen.

(b) *(vote)* Abstimmung *f; (election)* Wahl *f*. first/second ~ erster/zweiter Wahlgang; to take *or* hold a ~ abstimmen; eine Wahl abhalten, wählen; they demanded a ~ sie verlangten eine (geheime) Wahl.

(c) *(numbers)* abgegebene Stimmen. a large ~ eine hohe Wahlbeteiligung.

2 *vi* abstimmen; *(elect)* eine (geheime) Wahl abhalten.

3 *vt members* abstimmen lassen.

ballot: ~-box *n* Wahlurne *f*; ~-paper *n* Stimm- *or* Wahlzettel *m*.

ball: ~-park *n (US)* Baseballstadion *nt*; ~-point (pen) *n* Kugelschreiber *m*; ~-room *n* Ball- *or* Tanzsaal *m*; ~-room dancing *n* klassische Tänze, Gesellschaftstänze *pl*.

balls-up ['bɔːlzʌp], *(esp US)* **ball up** ['bɔːlʌp] *n (sl)* Durcheinander *nt*. he made a complete ~ of the job er hat bei der Arbeit totale Scheiße gebaut *(sl)*; the meeting was a complete ~ die Konferenz ist in die Hose gegangen *(sl)*; what a ~ of a repair! so'ne Scheißreparatur! *(sl)*.

balls up, *(esp US)* **ball up** *vt sep (sl)* verhunzen *(inf)*.

ballyhoo [,bælɪ'huː] *(inf)* 1 *n* Trara *(inf)*, Tamtam *(inf) nt*. to make a lot of ~ about sth ein großes Trara *or* Tamtam um etw machen *(inf)*. 2 *vt (US)* marktschreierisch anpreisen.

balm [bɑːm] *n* (a) *(lit,fig)* Balsam *m*. (b) *(Bot)* Melisse *f*.

balmy ['bɑːmɪ] *adj (+er) (fragrant)* balsamisch *(geh)*, wohlriechend; *(mild)* sanft, lind *(geh)*. ~ breezes sanfte Brisen, linde Lüfte *(geh)*.

baloney [bə'ləʊnɪ] *n* (a) *(sl)* Stuß *(sl)*, Quatsch *(inf) m*. she gave me some ~ about having had a flat tyre sie faselte was von einem Platten *(inf)*. (b) *(US: sausage)* Mortadella *f*.

balsa ['bɔːlsə] *n (also* ~ wood) Balsa(holz) *nt*.

balsam ['bɔːlsəm] *n* (a) Balsam *m*. ~ fir Balsamtanne *f*. (b) *(Bot)* Springkraut *nt*.

Baltic ['bɔːltɪk] *adj* Ostsee-; *language, (of* ~ States) baltisch. ~ Sea Ostsee *f*; the ~ States *(Hist)* die baltischen Staaten, das Baltikum.

baluster ['bæləstə[r]] *n* Baluster *m*, Balustersäule *f*.

balustrade [,bælə'streɪd] *n* Balustrade *f*.

bamboo [bæm'buː] 1 *n* Bambus *m*. 2 *attr* Bambus-. ~ shoots *pl* Bambussprossen; the B~ Curtain *(Pol)* der Bambusvorhang.

bamboozle [bæm'buːzl] *vt (inf) (baffle)* verblüffen, baff machen *(inf); (trick)* hereinlegen *(inf)*, tricksen *(inf)*. he was ~d into signing the contract sie haben ihn so getrickst, daß er den Vertrag unterschrieben hat *(inf)*.

ban [bæn] 1 *n* Verbot *nt; (Eccl)* (Kirchen)bann *m*. to put a ~ on sth etw verbieten, etw mit einem Verbot belegen *(form)*; a ~ on smoking Rauchverbot *nt*.

2 *vt (prohibit)* verbieten; *(Eccl)* auf den Index setzen; *footballer etc* sperren. to ~ sb from doing sth jdm verbieten *or* untersagen, etw zu tun; he is ~ned from this pub er hat hier Lokalverbot; she was ~ned from driving ihr wurde Fahrverbot erteilt.

banal [bə'nɑːl] *adj* banal.

banality [bə'nælɪtɪ] *n* Banalität *f*.

banana [bə'nɑːnə] *n* Banane *f*.

banana *in cpds* Bananen-; ~ republic *n* Bananenrepublik *f*.

bananas [bə'nɑːnəz] *adj pred (sl: crazy)* bekloppt *(inf)*, bescheuert *(sl)*, beknackt *(sl)*. this is driving me ~ dabei dreh' ich durch *(inf)*; he's ~ about her er steht unheimlich auf sie *(sl)*; the whole place went ~ der ganze Saal drehte durch *(inf)*.

banana: ~ skin *n* Bananenschale *f*; ~ tree *n* Bananenstaude *f*.

band[1] [bænd] *n* (a) *(of cloth, iron)* Band *nt; (on barrel)* Faßband *nt*, Reifen *m; (over book jacket)* (Einband)streifen *m; (of leather)* Band *nt*, Riemen *m; (waist* ~) Bund *m; (on cigar)* Banderole, Bauchbinde *f; (ring: on bird, US: wedding* ~) Ring *m; (on machine)* Riemen *m*.

(b) *(stripe)* Streifen *m*.

(c) *(Eccl, Univ: collar)* ~s *pl* Beffchen *pl*.

(d) *(Rad)* Band *nt; see* frequency ~, waveband.

2 *vt bird* beringen.

band[2] *n* (a) *(group)* Schar *f; (of robbers etc)* Bande *f; (of workers)* Trupp *m*, Kolonne *f*. (b) *(Mus)* Band *f; (dance* ~) *(Tanz)*orchester *nt; (in circus, brass* ~, *Mil etc)* (Musik)kapelle *f*.

♦ **band together** *vi* sich zusammenschließen.

bandage ['bændɪdʒ] 1 *n* Verband *m; (strip of cloth)* Binde *f*. 2 *vt (also* ~ up) *cut* verbinden; *broken limb* bandagieren. with his heavily ~d wrist mit einem dick verbundenen Handgelenk.

bandan(n)a [bæn'dænə] *n* großes Schnupftuch; *(round neck)* Halstuch *nt*.

B & B [,biːənd'biː] *n abbr of* bed and breakfast *(as sign)* Ü & Fr.

bandbox ['bændbɒks] *n* Hutschachtel *f*.

banderol(e) ['bændərəʊl] *n (Naut)* Wimpel *m*, Fähnlein *nt; (Her)* Fähnchen *nt; (Archit)* Inschriftenband *nt*.

bandit ['bændɪt] n Bandit, Räuber m.
banditry ['bændɪtrɪ] n Banditentum or -unwesen nt.
band: ~ leader n Bandleader m; ~master n Kapellmeister m.
bandolier [,bændə'lɪəʳ] n Schulterpatronengurt m.
band saw n Bandsäge f.
bandsman ['bændzmən] n, pl -men [-mən] Musiker, Musikant (old) m. military ~ Mitglied nt eines Musikkorps.
band: ~stand n Musikpavillon m or -podium nt; ~wagon n (US) Musikwagen m, (Fest)wagen der Musikkapelle; **to jump or climb on the** ~wagon (fig inf) sich dranhängen, auf den fahrenden Zug aufspringen; ~width n (Rad) Bandbreite f.
bandy¹ ['bændɪ] adj krumm. ~ legs (of people) O-Beine.
bandy² vt jokes sich (dat) erzählen; (old) ball hin- und herspielen. **to** ~ **blows with sb** (old) Hiebe mit jdm austauschen (old); **to** ~ **words (with sb)** sich (mit jdm) herumstreiten (old).
♦ **bandy about or around** vt sep story, secret herumerzählen, herumtragen; ideas verbreiten; words, technical expressions um sich werfen mit; sb's name immer wieder nennen. **the press have been** ~**ing his name/these words** ~ **a lot** die Presse hat seinen Namen/diese Wörter stark strapaziert; **he doesn't like having his name bandied** ~ **in connection with it** er mag es nicht, daß sein Name dauernd im Zusammenhang damit erwähnt wird; **I'd rather you didn't** ~ **my nickname** ~ **the office** es wäre mir lieber, wenn Sie meinen Spitznamen nicht im Büro herumposaunen würden (inf).
bandy-legged [,bændɪ'legd] adj mit krummen Beinen; person krummbeinig, O-beinig.
bane [beɪn] n (a) (cause of distress) Fluch m. **he's the** ~ **of my life** er ist noch mal mein Ende (inf), mit ihm bin ich geschlagen. (b) (old: poison) Gift nt.
baneful ['beɪnfʊl] adj verhängnisvoll.
bang¹ [bæŋ] **1** n (a) (noise) Knall m; (of sth falling) Plumps m. **there was a** ~ **outside** draußen hat es geknallt; **to go off with a** ~ mit lautem Knall losgehen; (inf: be a success) eine Wucht sein (inf). (b) (violent blow) Schlag m. **he gave himself a** ~ **on the shins** er hat sich (dat) die Schienbeine angeschlagen. (c) (sl: sex) Fick m (vulg). **to have a** ~ **with sb** mit jdm bumsen (inf). **2** adv (a) **to go** ~ knallen; (gun also, balloon) peng machen (inf); (balloon) zerplatzen. (b) (inf: exactly, directly etc) voll (inf), genau. **his answer was** ~ **on** seine Antwort war genau richtig; **is that right?** — ~ **on** stimmt das? — haargenau; **she came** ~ **on time** sie war auf die Sekunde pünktlich; **they came** ~ **up against fierce opposition** sie stießen auf heftige Gegenwehr; **the whole** ~ **shoot** das ganze Zeug (inf); (people) die ganze Bande (inf). **3** interj peng; (of hammer) klopf. ~ **went a £10 note** (inf) peng, weg war ein 10-Pfund-Schein (inf). **4** vt (a) (thump) schlagen, knallen (inf). **he** ~**ed his fist on the table** er schlug or haute mit der Faust auf den Tisch; **I'll** ~ **your heads together if you don't shut up!** (inf) wenn ihr nicht ruhig seid, knallt's (inf); **I felt like** ~**ing their heads together** (inf) ich hätte ihnen am liebsten ein paar links und rechts geknallt (inf). (b) (shut noisily) door zuschlagen, zuknallen (inf). **you have to** ~ **the door to close it** Sie müssen die Tür richtig zuschlagen. (c) (hit, knock) head, shin sich (dat) anschlagen (on an + dat). **to** ~ **one's head etc on sth** sich (dat) den Kopf etc an etw (dat) anschlagen, mit dem Kopf etc gegen etw knallen (inf). **5** vi (a) (door: shut) zuschlagen, zuknallen (inf); (fireworks, gun) knallen; (engine) krachen; (hammer) klopfen. **the door was** ~**ing in the wind** die Tür schlug im Wind. (b) **to** ~ **on or at sth** gegen or an etw (acc) schlagen. (c) (sl) bumsen (inf).
♦ **bang about 1** vi Krach machen; (heavy noise) herumpoltern. **2** vt sep Krach machen mit; chairs also herumstoßen.
♦ **bang away** vi (a) (guns) knallen; (persons: keep firing) wild (drauflos)feuern (at auf + acc), wild (drauflos)ballern (inf) (at auf + acc); (workman etc) herumklopfen or -hämmern (at an + dat). **to** ~ ~ **at the typewriter** auf der Schreibmaschine herumhauen or -hämmern (inf). (b) (inf: work industriously) **to** ~ ~ **(at sth)** sich hinter etw (acc) klemmen (inf). (c) (sl: have sexual intercourse) bumsen (inf).
♦ **bang down** vt sep (hin)knallen (inf); nail einschlagen; (flatten) flachschlagen; lid zuschlagen, zuknallen (inf). **to** ~ ~ **the receiver** den Hörer aufknallen (inf).
♦ **bang in** vt sep nail einschlagen.
♦ **bang into** vt + prep obj (a) (collide with) knallen (inf) or prallen (inf) gegen (+ acc). (b) (inf: meet) zufällig treffen.
♦ **bang out** vt sep (a) nail, brick heraiusschlagen, heraushauen (inf). (b) **to** ~ ~ **a tune on the piano/a letter on the typewriter** eine Melodie auf dem Klavier hämmern (inf)/einen Brief auf der Schreibmaschine herunterhauen (inf).
bang² n (fringe) Pony m, Ponyfransen pl. ~s Ponyfrisur f.
banger ['bæŋəʳ] n (a) (inf: sausage) Wurst f. (b) (inf: old car) Klapperkiste f (inf). (c) (Brit: firework) Knallkörper m.
Bangladesh [,bæŋglə'deʃ] n Bangladesc(h)h nt.
bangle ['bæŋgl] n Armreif(en) m; (for ankle) Fußreif or -ring m.
bang-up ['bæŋʌp] adj (US sl) bombig (inf), prima (inf).
banish ['bænɪʃ] vt person verbannen; cares, fear also vertreiben.
banishment ['bænɪʃmənt] n Verbannung f.
banister, bannister ['bænɪstəʳ] n (also ~s) Geländer nt.
banjo ['bændʒəʊ] n, pl -es, (US) -s Banjo nt.
bank¹ [bæŋk] **1** n (a) (of earth, sand) Wall, Damm m; (Rail) (Bahn)damm m; (slope) Böschung f, Abhang m; (on racetrack) Kurvenüberhöhung f. ~ **of snow** Schneeverwehung f. (b) (of river, lake) Ufer nt. **we sat on the** ~**s of a river/lake** wir saßen an einem Fluß/See or Fluß-/Seeufer. (c) (in sea, river) (Sand)bank f.

(d) (of clouds) Wand, Bank f. (e) (Aviat) Querlage f. **to go into a** ~ in den Kurvenflug gehen. **2** vt (a) road überhöhen. (b) river mit einer Böschung versehen, einfassen. (c) plane in die Querlage bringen. **3** vi (Aviat) den Kurvenflug einleiten, in die Querlage gehen.
♦ **bank up 1** vt sep earth etc aufhäufen, aufschütten; (support) mit einer Böschung stützen; fire mit Kohlestaub ab- or bedecken (damit es langsam brennt). **2** vi (snow etc) sich anhäufen; (clouds also) sich zusammenballen.
bank² **1** n (a) Bank f. (b) (Gambling) Bank f. **to keep or be the** ~ die Bank halten or haben. (c) (Med) Bank f. (d) (fig) Vorrat m (of an + dat). **2** vt money zur Bank bringen, einzahlen. **3** vi **where do you** ~? bei welcher Bank haben Sie Ihr Konto?; **I** ~ **with Lloyds** ich habe ein Konto or ich bin bei Lloyds.
♦ **bank (up)on** vi + prep obj sich verlassen auf (+ acc), rechnen mit; sb, sb's help also zählen or bauen auf (+ acc). **you mustn't** ~ ~ **it** darauf würde ich mich nicht verlassen; **I was** ~**ing** ~ **your coming** ich hatte fest damit gerechnet, daß du kommst.
bank³ n (a) (Naut: rower's bench) Ruderbank f. (b) (row of objects, oars) Reihe f; (on organ, typewriter) (Tasten)reihe f.
bank: ~ account n Bankkonto nt; ~book n Sparbuch nt; ~ clerk n Bankangestellte(r) mf.
banker ['bæŋkəʳ] n (Fin) Bankier, Bankfachmann, Banker (inf) m; (gambling) Bankhalter m.
banker's: ~ card n Scheckkarte f; ~ order n Bankauftrag m; **by** ~ order durch Bankauftrag.
bank holiday n (Brit) öffentlicher Feiertag; (US) Bankfeiertag m.
banking¹ ['bæŋkɪŋ] n (a) (on road, racetrack) Überhöhung f. (b) (Aviat) Kurvenflug m.
banking² ['bæŋkɪŋ] n (a) Bankwesen nt. **the world of** ~ die Bankwelt; **he wants to go into** ~ er will ins Bankfach or Bankgewerbe gehen; **who looks after your** ~? wer kümmert sich um Ihre Bankangelegenheiten? **2** attr matter, systems Bank-. **the** ~ **side of the business** die Bankangelegenheiten der Firma.
banking: ~ hours npl (Bank)öffnungszeiten pl; ~ house n Bankhaus nt.
bank: ~note n Banknote f, Geldschein m; ~ rate n Diskontsatz m.
bankrupt ['bæŋkrʌpt] **1** n (a) Gemein- or Konkursschuldner m (Jur), Bankrotteur m. ~**'s certificate** Eröffnungsbeschluß m; ~**'s estate** Konkursmasse f. (b) (fig) **to be a moral/political** ~ moralisch/politisch bankrott sein. **2** adj (a) (Jur) bankrott. **to go** ~ Bankrott machen, in Konkurs gehen; **to be** ~ bankrott or pleite (inf) sein. (b) (fig) morally, politically bankrott. **they are totally** ~ **of ideas** sie haben keinerlei Ideen. **3** vt person zugrunde richten, ruinieren; firm also in den Konkurs treiben.
bankruptcy ['bæŋkrəptsɪ] n (a) (Jur) Bankrott, Konkurs m; (instance) Konkurs m. **the possibility of** ~ die Möglichkeit eines or des Bankrotts or Konkurses. (b) (fig) Bankrott m.
bankruptcy: **B**~ **Court** n Konkursgericht nt; ~ **proceedings** npl Konkursverfahren nt.
bank statement n Kontoauszug m.
banner ['bænəʳ] n Banner (also fig) nt; (in processions) Transparent, Spruchband nt. ~ **headlines** Schlagzeilen pl.
bannister ['bænɪstəʳ] n see **banister**.
banns [bænz] npl (Eccl) Aufgebot nt. **to read the** ~ das Aufgebot verlesen; **where are you having your** ~ **called?** wo haben Sie das Aufgebot bestellt?
banquet ['bæŋkwɪt] **1** n (lavish feast) Festessen nt; (ceremonial dinner also) Bankett nt. **2** vt üppig or festlich bewirten (on mit); (ceremoniously) ein Bankett abhalten für. **3** vi speisen, tafeln (geh). **to** ~ **on sth** etw speisen.
banquet(ing)-hall ['bæŋkwɪt(ɪŋ)'hɔːl] n Festsaal, Bankettsaal m.
banshee [bæn'ʃiː] n (Ir Myth) Banshee, Todesfee f. **to howl like a** ~ gespenstisch heulen.
bantam ['bæntəm] n Bantamhuhn nt.
bantamweight ['bæntəm,weɪt] n Bantamgewicht nt.
banter ['bæntəʳ] **1** n Geplänkel nt. **enough of this foolish** ~ lassen wir das alberne Gerede! **2** vt (old) verulken, necken.
bantering ['bæntərɪŋ] adj (joking) scherzhaft; (teasing) neckend, flachsig (dial).
Bantu [,bæn'tuː] **1** n (language) Bantu nt; (pl: tribes) Bantu pl; (person) Bantu mf, Bantuneger(in f) m. **2** adj Bantu-.
banyan (tree) ['bænjən,(trī):] n bengalische Feige, Banyan m.
BAOR abbr of **British Army of the Rhine**.
bap (bun) ['bæp(bʌn)] n (Brit) weiches Brötchen.
baptism ['bæptɪzəm] n Taufe f. ~ **of fire** (fig) Feuertaufe f.
baptismal [bæp'tɪzməl] adj Tauf-.
Baptist ['bæptɪst] n Baptist(in f) m. **the** ~ **Church** (people) die Baptistengemeinde; (teaching) der Baptismus; see **John**.
baptize [bæp'taɪz] vt taufen.
bar¹ [baːʳ] **1** n (a) (of metal, wood) Stange f; (of toffee etc) Riegel m; (of electric fire) Element nt. ~ **of gold/silver** Gold-/Silberbarren m; **a** ~ **of chocolate, a chocolate** ~ (esp US) (slab) eine Tafel Schokolade; (Mars ® etc) ein Schokoladenriegel m; **a** ~ **of soap** ein Stück nt Seife. (b) (of window, grate, cage) (Gitter)stab m; (of door) Stange f. **the window has** ~s das Fenster ist vergittert; **behind** ~s hinter Gittern, hinter schwedischen Gardinen; **to put sb behind** ~s jdn hinter Gitter or hinter Schloß und Riegel bringen. (c) (Sport) (horizontal) Reck nt; (for high jump etc) Latte f; (one of parallel ~s) Holm m. ~s (parallel) Barren m; (wall) ~s Sprossenwand f; **to exercise on the** ~s am Barren turnen. (d) (Ballet) Stange f. **at the** ~ an der Stange.

(e) (*in river, harbour*) Barre *f*.

(f) (*fig: obstacle*) Hindernis (*to* für), Hemmnis (*to* für) *nt*. to be *or* present a ~ to sth einer Sache (*dat*) im Wege stehen.

(g) (*of light, colour*) Streifen *m*; (*of light also*) Strahl *m*.

(h) (*Jur*) the B~ die Anwaltschaft; **to be a member of the B~** Anwalt vor Gericht sein; **to be called** *or* **admitted** (*US*) **to the B~** als Anwalt (vor Gericht) *or* Verteidiger zugelassen werden; **to read for the B~** Jura studieren.

(i) (*for prisoners*) Anklagebank *f*. **to stand at the ~** auf der Anklagebank sitzen; **prisoner at the ~** „Angeklagter!"

(j) (*fig*) **at the ~ of public opinion** vor dem Forum der Öffentlichkeit.

(k) (*for drinks*) Lokal *nt*; (*esp expensive*) Bar *f*; (*part of pub*) Gaststube, Schankstube (*dated*), Schwemme (*inf*) *f*; (*counter*) Theke *f*, Tresen *m*; (*at railway station*) Ausschank *m*.

(l) (*Comm: counter*) Tresen *m*, (Verkaufs)tisch *m*.

(m) (*Mus*) Takt *m*; (~ **line** *also*) Taktstrich *m*.

(n) (*on medal*) DSO and ~ zweimal verliehener DSO.

(o) (*Her*) Balken *m*. ~ **sinister** Bastardfaden *m*.

(p) (*Met*) Bar *nt*.

2 *vt* **(a)** (*obstruct*) **road** blockieren, versperren. **to ~ sb's way** jdm den Weg versperren *or* verstellen; **to ~ the way to progress** dem Fortschritt im Wege stehen.

(b) (*fasten*) **window, door** versperren. **to ~ the door against sb** jdm die Tür versperren.

(c) (*exclude, prohibit*) **person, possibility** auschließen; **action, thing** untersagen, verbieten. **to ~ sb from a competition** jdn von (der Teilnahme an) einem Wettbewerb ausschließen; **to ~ sb from a career** jdm eine Karriere unmöglich machen; **they've been ~red** (**from the club**) sie haben Clubverbot; **minors are ~red from this club** Minderjährige haben keinen Zutritt zu diesem Club.

bar², **barring** *prep* barring accidents falls nichts passiert; **bar none** ohne Ausnahme, ausnahmslos; **bar one** außer einem; ~ **these few mistakes it is a good essay** abgesehen von diesen paar Fehlern ist der Aufsatz gut.

barb [baːb] **1** *n* **(a)** (*of fish-hook, arrow*) Widerhaken *m*; (*of barbed wire*) Stachel *m*, Spitze *f*; (*of feather*) Fahne *f*; (*Bot, Zool*) Bart *m*, bartbewachsene Stelle. **(b)** (*fig: of wit etc*) Spitze *f*; (*liter: of remorse*) Stachel *m*. **2** *vt* (*lit*) mit Widerhaken versehen.

Barbados [baːˈbeɪdɒs] *n* Barbados *nt*.

barbarian [baːˈbɛərɪən] **1** *n* (*Hist, fig*) Barbar(in *f*) *m*. **2** *adj* (*Hist, fig*) barbarisch.

barbaric [baːˈbærɪk] *adj* barbarisch; (*Hist also*) Barbaren-; **guard etc** grausam, roh; (*fig inf*) **conditions** grauenhaft.

barbarically [baːˈbærɪkəlɪ] *adv* barbarisch.

barbarism [ˈbaːbərɪzəm] *n* **(a)** (*Hist*) Barbarei *f*; (*fig also*) Unkultur *f*. **(b)** (*Ling*) Barbarismus *m*.

barbarity [baːˈbærɪtɪ] *n* Barbarei *f*; (*fig*) Primitivität *f*; (*cruelty: of guard etc*) Grausamkeit, Roheit *f*. **the barbarities of modern warfare** die Barbarei *or* die Greuel *pl* des modernen Krieges.

barbarous [ˈbaːbərəs] *adj* (*Hist, fig*) barbarisch; (*cruel*) grausam; **guard etc** roh; **accent** also grausam.

barbarously [ˈbaːbərəslɪ] *adv see adj* barbarisch, wie ein Barbar/die Barbaren; grausam; grauenhaft (*inf*).

Barbary [ˈbaːbərɪ] *n* Berberei *f*.

Barbary *in cpds* Berber-; ~ **ape** *n* Berberaffe *m*; ~ **coast** *n* Barbareskenküste *f*; ~ **states** *npl* Barbareskenstaaten *pl*.

barbecue [ˈbaːbɪkjuː] **1** *n* **(a)** (*Cook: grid*) Grill *m*. **(b)** (*occasion*) Grillparty *f*, Barbecue *nt*. **(c)** (*meat*) Grillfleisch *nt*/-wurst *f etc*. **2** *vt* **steak etc** grillen, auf dem Rost braten; **animal** am Spieß braten.

barbed [baːbd] *adj* **(a)** **arrow** mit Widerhaken. **(b)** (*fig*) **wit** beißend; **remark** also spitz, bissig.

barbed: ~ **wire** *n* Stacheldraht *m*; ~**-wire fence** *n* Stacheldrahtzaun *m*.

barbel [ˈbaːbəl] *n* (*fish*) Barbe *f*; (*filament on fish*) Bartel, Bartfaden *m*.

barbell [ˈbaːbel] *n* Hantel *f*.

barber [ˈbaːbəʳ] *n* (*Herren*)friseur, Barbier (*old*) *m*. **the ~'s** der Friseur(laden), das (Herren)friseurgeschäft; **at/to the ~'s** beim/zum Friseur; ~**'s pole** Ladenzeichen *nt* der Friseure: Stange mit rot-weißer Spirale.

barbershop [ˌbaːbəˈʃɒp] (*US*) **1** *n* (Herren)friseurgeschäft *nt* *or* -laden *m*. **2** *adj* ~ **quartet** Barbershop-Quartett *nt*.

barbican [ˈbaːbɪkən] *n* Außen- *or* Vorwerk *nt*; (*tower*) Wachtturm *m*.

bar billiards *n sing*: in Lokalen gespielte Form des Billard.

barbitone [ˈbaːbɪtəʊn] *n* (*Med*) barbiturathaltiges Mittel.

barbiturate [baːˈbɪtjʊrɪt] *n* Schlafmittel, Barbiturat *nt*. ~ **poisoning** Schlafmittelvergiftung, Barbiturvergiftung *f*.

bar chart *n* Balkendiagramm *nt*.

bard [baːd] *n* **(a)** (*minstrel*) (*esp Celtic*) Barde *m*; (*in Ancient Greece*) (Helden)sänger *m*. **(b)** (*old Liter, hum: poet*) Barde *m*. **the B~ of Avon** Shakespeare.

bardic [ˈbaːdɪk] *adj* **poetry etc** bardisch.

bare [bɛəʳ] **1** *adj* (*+er*) **(a)** (*naked, uncovered*) **skin, boards, floor** nackt, bloß; **summit, tree, countryside** kahl, nackt; **room, garden** leer; **sword** blank; **wire** blank; **style** nüchtern. **he stood there ~ to the waist** er stand mit nacktem Oberkörper da; ~ **patch** kahle Stelle; **to sleep on ~ boards** auf blanken Brettern schlafen; **to lay ~ one's heart** sein Innerstes bloßlegen; **the ~ facts** die nackten Tatsachen; **the ~ fact that he ...** allein die Tatsache, daß er ...; **with his ~ hands** mit bloßen Händen; **to fight with ~ hands** *or* **fists** mit bloßen Fäusten kämpfen; **a ~ statement of the facts** eine reine Tatsachenfeststellung.

(b) (*scanty, mere*) knapp. **a ~ majority** eine knappe Mehrheit; **a ~ thank you** kaum ein Dankeschön; **a ~ subsistence wage** gerade das Existenzminimum; **a ~ ten centimetres** knappe *or* kaum zehn Zentimeter; **he shuddered at the ~**

idea es schauderte ihn beim bloßen Gedanken (daran); **with just the ~st hint of garlic** nur mit einer winzigen Spur Knoblauch.

2 *vt* **breast, leg** entblößen; (*at doctor's*) freimachen; **teeth** also blecken; (*in anger*) fletschen; **end of a wire** freilegen. **she ~d her teeth in a forced smile** sie grinste gezwungen; **to ~ one's head** den Hut *etc* ziehen, das Haupt entblößen (*liter*); **to ~ one's heart to sb** jdm sein Herz ausschütten.

bare: ~**back** *adv, adj* ohne Sattel; ~**faced** *adj* (*fig: shameless*) **liar** unverfroren, unverschämt, schamlos; **it is ~faced robbery** das ist der reine Wucher (*inf*); ~**foot** *adv* barfuß; ~**footed** 1 *adj* barfüßig, barfuß *pred*; **2** *adv* barfuß; ~**headed** 1 *adj* barhäuptig (*geh*), ohne Kopfbedeckung; **2** *adv* ohne Kopfbedeckung, barhaupt (*geh*); ~**legged** *adj* mit bloßen Beinen.

barely [ˈbɛəlɪ] *adv* **(a)** (*scarcely*) kaum; (*with figures also*) knapp. **we ~ know him** wir kennen ihn kaum; ~ **had he started when ...** er hatte kaum angefangen, als ... **(b)** *furnished* dürftig, spärlich.

bareness [ˈbɛənɪs] *n* Nacktheit *f*; (*of person also*) Blöße *f*; (*of trees, countryside*) Kahlheit *f*; (*of room, garden*) Leere *f*; (*of style*) Nüchternheit *f*.

Barents Sea [ˈbærənts'siː] *n* Barentssee *f*.

bargain [ˈbaːgɪn] **1** *n* **(a)** (*transaction*) Handel *m*, Geschäft *nt*. **to make** *or* **strike a ~** sich einigen; **they are not prepared to make a ~** sie wollen nicht mit sich handeln lassen; **I'll make a ~ with you, if you ...** ich mache Ihnen ein Angebot, wenn Sie ...; **it's a ~!** abgemacht!, einverstanden!; **you drive a hard ~** Sie stellen ja harte Forderungen!; **to offer sb a good ~** jdm ein gutes Angebot machen; **then it started raining into the ~** dann hat es (obendrein) auch noch angefangen zu regnen; **and she was rich into the ~** und außerdem war sie reich; **to get the worst/best of the ~** den schlechteren/besseren Teil erwischen.

(b) (*cheap offer*) günstiges Angebot, Sonderangebot *nt*; (*thing bought*) Gelegenheitskauf *m*. **this jacket is a good ~** diese Jacke ist wirklich günstig; **what a ~!** das ist aber günstig!

2 *vi* handeln (*for* um); (*in negotiations*) verhandeln. **the traders are not prepared to ~** die Ladenbesitzer lassen nicht mit sich handeln.

♦ **bargain away** *vt sep* **rights, advantage etc** sich (*dat*) abhandeln lassen; (*in Verhandlungen*) verspielen; **freedom, independence** also veräußern.

♦ **bargain for** *vi* +*prep obj* (*inf: expect*) rechnen mit, erwarten. **I hadn't ~ed ~ that** damit hatte ich nicht gerechnet; **I got more than I ~ed ~** ich habe vielleicht mein blaues Wunder erlebt! (*inf*); (*in argument also*) ich habe vielleicht eins draufbekommen! (*inf*).

♦ **bargain on** *vi* +*prep obj* zählen auf (+*acc*), sich verlassen auf (+*acc*).

bargain: ~ **basement** *n* Untergeschoß *nt* eines Kaufhauses mit Sonderangeboten; ~ **buy** *n* Preisschlager *m* (*inf*); **that's a real ~ buy** das ist wirklich günstig; ~ **counter** *n* Sonder(angebots)tisch *m*.

bargainer [ˈbaːgɪnəʳ] *n* **to be a good/poor ~** handeln/nicht handeln können; (*in negotiations*) gut/nicht gut verhandeln können; **as a ~ he ...** beim Handeln/bei Verhandlungen ... er.

bargain: ~**-hunter** *n* the ~**-hunters** Leute *pl* auf der Jagd nach Sonderangeboten; ~ **hunting** *n* Jagd *f* nach Sonderangeboten; **to go ~ hunting** auf Jagd nach Sonderangeboten gehen.

bargaining [ˈbaːgɪnɪŋ] *n* Handeln *nt*; (*negotiating*) Verhandeln *nt*. ~ **position** Verhandlungsposition *f*.

bargain: ~ **offer** *n* Sonderangebot *nt*, günstiges Angebot; ~ **price** *n* Sonderpreis *m*; **at a ~ price** zum Sonderpreis; ~ **rates** *npl* Sonderpreise *pl*; ~ **sale** *n* Ausverkauf *m*.

barge [baːdʒ] **1** *n* **(a)** (*for freight*) Last- *or* Frachtkahn *m*; (*unpowered*) Schleppkahn *m*; (*lighter*) Leichter *m*; (*ship's boat*) Barkasse *f*; (*houseboat*) Hausboot *nt*. **the Royal/state ~** die königliche Barkasse/die Staatsbarkasse; (*unpowered*) das königliche Boot/das Staatsboot.

(b) (*shove*) Stoß, Rempler (*inf*) *m*.

2 *vt* **(a)** **he ~d me out of the way** er hat mich weggestoßen; **he ~d his way into the room/through the crowd** er ist (ins Zimmer) hereingeplatzt (*inf*)/er hat sich durch die Menge geboxt (*inf*).

(b) (*Sport*) rempeln. **he ~d him off the ball** er hat ihm vom Ball weggestoßen.

3 *vi* **(a)** **to ~ into/out of a room** (in ein Zimmer) herein-/hineinplatzen (*inf*)/aus einem Zimmer heraus-/hinausstürmen; **he ~d through the crowd** er drängte *or* boxte (*inf*) sich durch die Menge; **will you boys stop barging!** hört auf zu drängeln, Jungs!

(b) (*Sport*) rempeln.

♦ **barge about** *or* **around** *vi* (*inf*) herumtrampeln (*inf*), herumpoltern (*inf*).

♦ **barge in** *vi* (*inf*) **(a)** hinein-/hereinplatzen (*inf*) *or* -stürzen. **(b)** (*interrupt*) dazwischenplatzen (*inf*) (*on* bei); (*interfere also*) sich einmischen (*on* in +*acc*).

♦ **barge into** *vi* +*prep obj* **(a)** (*knock against*) **person** (hinein)rennen in (+*acc*); (*shove*) (an)rempeln; **thing** rennen gegen (*inf*). **(b)** (*inf*) **room, party, conversation** (hinein-/herein)platzen in (+*acc*) (*inf*).

bargee [baːˈdʒiː] *n* Lastschiffer *m*; (*master*) Kahnführer *m*.

barge pole *n* Bootsstange *f*. **I wouldn't touch it/him with a (ten-foot) ~** (*Brit inf*) so etwas/so jemandem lasse ich die Finger (*inf*); (*because disgusting, unpleasant*) das/den würde ich noch nicht mal mit der Kneifzange anfassen (*inf*).

baritone [ˈbærɪtəʊn] **1** *n* (*voice, singer*) Bariton *m*. **2** *adj* **voice, part** Bariton-.

barium [ˈbɛərɪəm] *n* Barium *nt*. ~ **meal** Bariumbrei, Kontrastbrei *m*.

bark¹ [baːk] **1** *n* (*of tree*) Rinde, Borke *f*. **to strip the ~ off a tree** einen Baumstamm schälen. **2** *vt* (*rub off skin*) aufschürfen;

(*knock against*) anstoßen, anschlagen. **to ~ one's shin against the table** sich (*dat*) das Schienbein am Tisch anschlagen.

bark² 1 n (*of dog, seal, gun, cough*) Bellen *nt*. **his ~ is worse than his bite** (*Prov*) Hunde, die bellen, beißen nicht (*Prov*); **next! came the sudden ~ from the surgery** der Nächste! bellte es plötzlich aus dem Behandlungszimmer.

2 *vi* (*all senses*) bellen. **to ~ at sb** jdn anbellen; (*person also*) jdn anfahren; **to be ~ing up the wrong tree** (*fig inf*) auf dem Holzweg sein (*inf*).

♦ **bark out** *vt sep* orders bellen.

bark³, barque n (a) (*poet*) Barke f (*liter*). (b) (*Naut*) Bark f.

barkeep(er) ['bɑːkiːp(əʳ)] n (*US*) Barbesitzer(in f), Gastwirt m; (*bartender*) Barkeeper, Barmann m.

barker ['bɑːkəʳ] n (*outside shop, club*) Anreißer m (*inf*); (*at fair*) Marktschreier m (*inf*).

barley ['bɑːlɪ] n Gerste f. **pearl ~** (Gersten- or Perl)graupen pl.

barley: **~corn** n Gerstenkorn *nt*; *see* John; **~ sugar** n Gersten- or Malzzucker m; (*sweet*) hartes Zuckerbonbon; **~ water** n *Art* Gerstenextrakt; **lemon/orange ~ water** konzentriertes Zitronen-/Orangegetränk; **~ wine** n (*Brit*) *Art* Starkbier nt.

bar line n (*Mus*) Taktstrich m.

barm [bɑːm] n (*Bier*)hefe, Bärme f.

bar: **~maid** n Bardame f; **~man** n Barkeeper, Barmann m.

bar mitzvah [bɑːˈmɪtsvə] n (*ceremony*) Bar Mizwa nt; (*boy*) Junge, der Bar Mizwa feiert.

barmy ['bɑːmɪ] adj (*Brit sl*) bekloppt (*inf*), plemplem pred (*inf*); idea etc blödsinnig (*inf*).

barn [bɑːn] n (a) Scheune, Scheuer f; (*in field*) Schober m (S Ger, Aus). **a great ~ of a house** eine große Scheune (*inf*). (b) (*US: for streetcars, trucks*) Depot nt, Hof m.

barnacle ['bɑːnəkl] n (a) (*shellfish*) (Rankenfuß)krebs, Rankenfüßer m. (b) (*fig: person*) Klette f (*inf*).

barnacle goose n Nonnengans f.

barn-dance ['bɑːndɑːns] n Bauerntanz m.

barney ['bɑːnɪ] n (*sl: noisy quarrel*) Krach m (*inf*); (*punch-up*) Schlägerei, Keilerei (*inf*) f.

barn: **~ owl** n Schleiereule f; **~storm** vi (*esp US*) (*Theat*) in der Provinz spielen; (*Pol*) in der Provinz Wahlreden halten; **~stormer** n (*US Pol*) Wahlredner(in f) m in der Provinz; (*Theat*) Wanderschauspieler(in f) m; **~yard** n (*Bauern*)hof m; **~yard fowl(s)** npl (*Haus*)geflügel nt.

barograph ['bærəʊɡrɑːf] n Barograph m.

barometer [bəˈrɒmɪtəʳ] n (*lit, fig*) Barometer nt.

barometric [,bærəʊˈmetrɪk] adj barometrisch, Barometer-. **~ pressure** Atmosphären- or Luftdruck m.

baron ['bærən] n (a) Baron m. (b) (*fig*) Baron, Magnat m. **industrial/oil ~** Industriebaron/Ölmagnat m; **Press ~** Pressebaron m. (c) (*of beef*) doppeltes Lendenstück.

baroness ['bærənɪs] n Baronin f; (*unmarried*) Baronesse f.

baronet ['bærənɪt] n Baronet m.

baronetcy ['bærənɪtsɪ] n (*rank*) Baronetstand m; (*title*) Baronetswürde f.

baronial [bəˈrəʊnɪəl] adj (*lit*) Barons-; (*fig*) fürstlich, feudal.

barony ['bærənɪ] n Baronie f.

baroque [bəˈrɒk] 1 adj barock, Barock-. 2 n (*style*) Barock m or nt. **the ~ period** das or der Barock, die Barockzeit.

barouche [bəˈruːʃ] n Landauer m.

barque [bɑːk] n *see* bark³.

barrack¹ ['bærək] vt soldiers kasernieren.

barrack² 1 vt actor etc auspfeifen; auszischen. 2 vi pfeifen; zischen.

barracking¹ ['bærəkɪŋ] n (*Mil*) Kasernierung f.

barracking² n Pfeifen nt; Zischen nt; Buhrufe pl. **to get a ~** ausgepfiffen/ausgezischt werden.

barrack-room ['bærəkruːm] adj attr rauh, roh. **~ language** Landersprache f; **~ lawyer** (*pej*) Paragraphenreiter m (*inf*).

barracks ['bærəks] 1 npl (*often with sing vb*) (*Mil*) Kaserne f; (*fig pej also*) Mietskaserne f. **to live in ~** in der Kaserne wohnen; **houses like ~** Häuser wie Kasernen; **these appalling ~ of houses** diese entsetzlichen Mietskasernen.

2 attr **~ life** Kasernenleben nt; **~ square** Kasernenhof m.

barracuda [,bærəˈkjuːdə] n Barrakuda, Pfeilhecht m.

barrage ['bærɑːʒ] n (a) (*across river*) Wehr nt; (*larger*) Staustufe f. (b) (*Mil*) Sperrfeuer nt. **under this ~ of stones** ... unter diesem Steinhagel ...; **they kept up a ~ of stones** sie bedeckten die Polizei/uns etc mit einem Steinhagel. (c) (*fig: of words, questions etc*) Hagel m. **he was attacked with a ~ of questions** er wurde mit Fragen beschossen.

barrage balloon n Sperrballon m.

barre [bɑːʳ] n (*Ballet*) Stange f. **at the ~** an der Stange.

barred [bɑːd] adj (a) suf **five-~** gate Weidengatter nt (mit fünf Querbalken). (b) **~ window** Gitterfenster nt.

barrel ['bærəl] 1 n (a) Faß nt; (*for oil, tar, rainwater etc*) Tonne f; (*measure: of oil*) Barrel nt. **they've got us over a ~** (*inf*) sie haben uns in der Zange (*inf*); *see* biscuit, scrape.

(b) (*of handgun*) Lauf m; (*of cannon etc*) Rohr nt. **to give sb both ~s** auf jdn aus beiden Läufen feuern; **I found myself looking down the ~ of a gun** ich hatte plötzlich eine Kanone or ein Schießeisen vor der Nase (*sl*); *see* lock².

(c) (*of fountain pen*) Tank m.

2 vt wine etc (*in Fässer*) (ab)füllen; herring (*in Fässer*) einlegen. **~led beer** Faßbier nt.

♦ **barrel along** vi (*inf*) entlangbrausen (*inf*).

barrel: **~-chested** adj breitbrüstig, mit gewölbter Brust; **to be ~-chested** einen gewölbten Brustkasten haben; **~ful** n Faß nt; (*of oil*) Barrel nt; **two ~fuls of beer/herrings** zwei Faß Bier/Fässer Heringe; **~house** (*US*) 1 n Kneipe f; (*jazz*) Kneipenjazz m; 2 adj **~house blues** alte, in Kneipen gespielte Form des Blues; **~ organ** n Drehorgel f, Leierkasten m; **~-shaped** adj faß- or tonnenförmig; **~-shaped man/woman** Faß nt (*inf*)/Tonne f (*inf*); **~ vault** n Tonnengewölbe nt.

barren ['bærən] 1 adj (a) unfruchtbar; land also karg.

(b) (*fig*) years unfruchtbar, unproduktiv; discussion also fruchtlos; atmosphere also steril; style, subject, study trocken; topic unergiebig. **to be ~ of interest/success** völlig uninteressant/erfolglos sein; **the house looks ~ without any furniture** das Haus wirkt ohne Möbel leer.

2 n (*esp US*) **~s** pl Ödland nt.

barrenness ['bærənnɪs] n see adj (a) Unfruchtbarkeit f; Kargheit f. (b) Unfruchtbarkeit, Unproduktivität f; Fruchtlosigkeit f; Sterilität f; Trockenheit f; Unergiebigkeit f.

barrette [bəˈret] n (*US*) (Haar)spange f.

barricade [,bærɪˈkeɪd] 1 n Barrikade f. 2 vt verbarrikadieren.

♦ **barricade in** vt sep verbarrikadieren.

♦ **barricade off** vt sep (mit Barrikaden) absperren.

barrier ['bærɪəʳ] n (a) (*natural*) Barriere f; (*man-made, erected also*) Sperre f; (*railing etc*) Schranke f; (*crash ~*) (Leit)planke f. **ticket ~** Sperre f.

(b) (*fig*) (*obstacle*) Hindernis nt, Barriere f (*to für*); (*of class, background, education, between people*) Schranke, Barriere f. **trade ~s** Handelsschranken pl; **~ of language** Sprachbarriere f; **a ~ to success/progress** etc ein Hindernis für den Erfolg/Fortschritt etc; **because of the ~ of her shyness** auf Grund ihrer Schüchternheit, die ein Hemmnis ist/war etc.

barrier cream n (*Haut*)schutzcreme f.

barring ['bɑːrɪŋ] prep see bar².

barrister ['bærɪstəʳ] n (*Brit*) Rechtsanwalt m/-anwältin f (bei Gericht), Barrister m.

barrow¹ ['bærəʊ] n Karre(n m) f; (*wheel~*) Schubkarre(n m) f; (*Rail: luggage*) Gepäckkarre(n m) f; (*costermonger's*) (hand-gezogner) Obst-/Gemüse-/Fischkarren etc m.

barrow² n (*Archeol*) Hügelgrab nt.

barrow boy n Straßenhändler m (mit Karren).

bartender ['bɑːtendəʳ] n (*US*) Barkeeper m. **~! hallo!**

barter ['bɑːtəʳ] 1 vt tauschen (*for gegen*). 2 vi tauschen; (*as general practice also*) Tauschhandel treiben. **to ~ for sth** um etw handeln; **to ~ for peace** über einen Frieden verhandeln. 3 n (*Tausch*)handel m.

♦ **barter away** vt sep one's rights verspielen. **to ~ sth ~ for sth** etw für etw verschachern.

barter: **~ economy** n Tauschwirtschaft f; **~ society** n Tauschgesellschaft f.

basal ['beɪsl] adj (a) (*lit, fig*) Grund-, fundamental. (b) (*Med*) **~ metabolism** Grundumsatz m.

basalt ['bæsɔːlt] n Basalt m.

bascule ['bæskjuːl] n Brückenklappe f. **~ bridge** Klappbrücke f.

base¹ [beɪs] 1 n (a) (*lowest part*) Basis f; (*that on which sth stands also*) Unterlage f; (*Archit: of column also*) Fuß m; (*support for statue etc*) Sockel m; (*of lamp, tree, mountain*) Fuß m; (*undercoat also*) Grundierung f. **at the ~ (of)** unten (an +dat).

(b) (*main ingredient*) Basis f, Haupt- or Grundbestandteil m.

(c) (*of theory*) Basis f; (*starting point also*) Ausgangspunkt m; (*foundation also*) Grundlage f.

(d) (*Mil etc, fig: for holidays, climbing etc*) Standort, Stützpunkt m. **to return to ~** zur Basis or zum Stützpunkt zurückkehren; **~ of operations** Operationsbasis f.

(e) (*Chem*) Lauge, Base f.

(f) (*Math*) Basis, Grundzahl f.

(g) (*Geometry*) Basis f; (*of plane figure also*) Grundlinie f; (*of solid also*) Grundfläche f.

(h) (*Gram*) Wortstamm m, Wortwurzel f.

(i) (*Baseball*) Mal nt, Base f. **at or on second ~** auf Mal or Base 2, auf dem zweiten Mal or der zweiten Base.

2 vt (a) stellen. **to be ~d on** ruhen auf (+dat); (*statue*) stehen auf (+dat); **the supports are firmly ~d in concrete** die Stützen sind fest in Beton eingelassen; **you need something to ~ it on** Sie brauchen dafür eine feste or stabile Unterlage; **the scaffolding is not very solidly ~d** das Gerüst steht nicht sehr fest.

(b) (*fig*) opinion, theory gründen, basieren (*on auf +acc*); hopes also setzen (*on auf +acc*); relationship also bauen (*on auf +acc*). **to be ~d on sb/sth** auf jdm/etw basieren; (*hopes, theory also*) sich auf jdn/etw stützen; **to ~ one's technique/morality on sb/sth** in seiner Technik/seinem Moralverständnis von jdm/etw ausgehen; **he tried to ~ his life on this theory** er versuchte, nach dieser Theorie zu leben.

(c) (*Mil*) stationieren. **the company/my job is ~d in London** die Firma hat ihren Sitz in London/ich arbeite in London; **I am ~d in Glasgow but cover all Scotland** mein Büro ist in Glasgow, aber ich bereise ganz Schottland.

base² adj (+er) (a) motive, character niedrig; person, thoughts, action, lie, slander gemein, niederträchtig. (b) (*inferior*) task, level niedrig; coin falsch, unecht; metal unedel. (c) (*obs*) birth (*low*) niedrig (*old*); (*illegitimate*) unehelich.

baseball ['beɪsbɔːl] n Baseball m or nt.

base: **~board** n (*US*) Fußleiste, Lambrie (S Ger) f; **~ camp** n Basislager, Versorgungslager nt.

-based [beɪst] adj suf **London-~** mit Sitz in London; **to be computer-~** auf Computerbasis arbeiten.

base hit n (*Baseball*) Treffer, durch den der Schlagmann sicher das Mal erreichen kann.

baseless ['beɪslɪs] adj accusations etc ohne Grundlage, aus der Luft gegriffen; fears, suspicion also unbegründet, grundlos.

base line n (*Baseball*) Verbindungslinie f zwischen zwei Malen; (*Surv*) Basis, Grundlinie f; (*of a diagram, Tennis*) Grundlinie f; (*Art*) Schnittlinie f von Grundebene und Bildebene.

basely ['beɪslɪ] adv gemein, niederträchtig; act also niedrig.

baseman ['beɪsmən] n, pl **-men** [-mən] (*Baseball*) Spieler m an einem Mal.

basement ['beɪsmənt] n (a) (*in building*) Untergeschoß nt; (*in house also*) Keller m, Kellergeschoß nt. **~ flat** Kellerwohnung f. (b) (*Archit: foundations*) Fundament nt.

baseness ['beɪsnɪs] n see adj (a) Niedrigkeit f; Gemeinheit,

Niederträchtigkeit *f.* **(b)** Niedrigkeit *f*; Falschheit *f.* **(c)** Niedrigkeit *f (old)*; Unehelichkeit *f.*

base wallah [ˌbeɪsˈwɒlə] *n (Mil sl)* Etappenhengst *m (Mil sl).*

bash [bæʃ] *(inf)* **1** *n* **(a)** Schlag *m.* **to give sb a ~ on the nose** jdm (eine) auf die Nase hauen *(inf)*; **he gave himself a ~ on the shin** er hat sich *(dat)* das Schienbein angeschlagen; **the bumper has had a ~** die Stoßstange hat 'ne Delle abgekriegt *(inf).*
(b) I'll have a ~ (at it) ich probier's mal *(inf)*; **have a ~** probier mal! *(inf).*
2 *vt person* (ver)hauen *(inf)*, verprügeln *(inf)*; *ball* knallen *(inf)*, dreschen *(inf)*; *car, wing* eindellen *(inf).* **to ~ one's head/shin (against or on sth)** sich *(dat)* den Kopf/das Schienbein an etw *dat* anschlagen; **I ~ed my shin against the table** ich bin mit dem Schienbein gegen den Tisch geknallt *(inf)*; **to ~ sb on/round the head with sth** jdm etw auf den Kopf hauen *(inf)*/jdm etw um die Ohren schlagen *(inf)*; **they ~ed him on the nose/head** sie hauten ihm eins auf die Nase/auf *or* über den Schädel *(inf).*

♦ **bash about** *vt sep (inf) person* durchprügeln *(inf)*, verdreschen *(inf)*; *objects* demolieren *(inf)*. **he/his luggage got rather ~ed** ~ **in the accident** er/sein Gepäck ist bei dem Unfall ziemlich lädiert worden *(inf).*

♦ **bash down** *vt sep (inf) door* einschlagen.

♦ **bash in** *vt sep (inf) door* einschlagen; *hat, car* eindellen *(inf).* **to ~ sb's head** ~ jdm den Schädel einschlagen *(inf).*

♦ **bash up** *vt sep (Brit inf) person* vermöbeln *(inf)*, verkloppen *(inf)*; *car* demolieren *(inf)*, kaputtfahren *(inf).*

bashful ['bæʃfʊl] *adj* schüchtern; *(on particular occasion)* verlegen. **give us a song! ah, he's ~** sing was! och, er geniert sich!

bashfully ['bæʃfəlɪ] *adv see adj* schüchtern; verlegen.

bashfulness ['bæʃfʊlnɪs] *n see adj* Schüchternheit *f*; Verlegenheit *f.*

bashing ['bæʃɪŋ] *n (inf)* Prügel *pl*, Dresche *f (inf).* **he/his luggage got a nasty ~** er/sein Gepäck hat ganz schön was abgekriegt *(inf).*

basic ['beɪsɪk] **1** *adj* **(a)** *(fundamental)* Grund-; *problem also, reason, issue* Haupt-; *points, issues* wesentlich; *(rudimentary) knowledge, necessities, equipment also* elementar; *character, intention, purpose also* eigentlich; *incompatibility, misconception, indifference, problem* grundsätzlich. **there's no ~ difference** es besteht kein grundlegender Unterschied; **he has a ~ mistrust of women** er mißtraut Frauen grundsätzlich; **a certain ~ innocence** eine gewisse elementare Unschuld; **he is, in a very ~ sense, ...** er ist, im wahrsten Sinne des Wortes, ...; **the thing to remember is ...** woran man vor allem denken muß, ist ...; **must you be so ~!** müssen Sie sich denn so direkt ausdrücken?; **his knowledge/the furniture is rather ~** er hat nur ziemlich elementare Kenntnisse/die Möbel sind ziemlich primitiv; **the pub is rather ~** es ist eine recht einfache Kneipe; **you should know that, that's ~** das müßten Sie aber wissen, das ist doch elementar; **this is ~ to the whole subject** das liegt dem Fach zu Grunde; **~ salary/working hours** Grundgehalt *nt*/-arbeitszeit *f*; **the four ~ operations** *(Math)* die vier Grundrechenarten; **~ English** englischer Grundwortschatz, Basic English *nt*; **~ vocabulary** Grundwortschatz *m.*
(b) *(original)* zu Grunde liegend; *theory also, assumption* ursprünglich.
(c) *(essential)* notwendig. **knowledge of French is/good boots are absolutely ~** Französischkenntnisse/gute Stiefel sind unbedingt nötig *or* sind eine Voraussetzung.
(d) *(Chem)* basisch. **~ slag** Thomasschlacke *f.*
2 *npl* **the ~s** das Wesentliche; **to get down to (the) ~s** zum Kern der Sache *or* zum Wesentlichen kommen.

basically ['beɪsɪkəlɪ] *adv* im Grunde; *(mainly)* im wesentlichen, hauptsächlich. **is that correct? — ~ yes** stimmt das? — im Prinzip, ja, im Grunde schon; **it's ~ finished** es ist praktisch *or* im Grunde fertig; **that's ~ it** das wär's im wesentlichen.

basil ['bæzl] *n (Bot)* Basilikum, Basilienkraut *nt.*

basilica [bə'zɪlɪkə] *n* Basilika *f.*

basilisk ['bæzɪlɪsk] *n (Myth, Zool)* Basilisk *m.*

basin [beɪsn] *n* **(a)** *(vessel)* Schüssel *f*; *(wash~)* (Wasch)becken *nt*; *(of fountain)* Becken *nt.* **(b)** *(Geog)* Becken *nt*; *(harbour ~)* Hafenbecken *nt*; *(yacht~)* Jachthafen *m*; *(hollow between mountains also)* Kessel *m.*

basinful ['beɪsnfʊl] *n* Schüssel(voll) *f.*

basis ['beɪsɪs] *n* **(a)** *(of food, mixture etc)* Basis, Grundlage *f.*
(b) *(fig: foundation)* Basis *f*; *(for assumption)* Grund *m.* **we're working on the ~ that ...** wir gehen von der Annahme aus, daß ...; **to be on a firm ~** *(business)* auf festen Füßen stehen; *(theory)* auf einer soliden Basis ruhen; **to put sth on a firmer ~** einer Sache *(dat)* eine solidere Basis geben, etw auf eine solidere Basis stellen; **on the ~ of this evidence** aufgrund dieses Beweismaterials; **to approach a problem on a scientific ~** an ein Problem wissenschaftlich herangehen.

bask [bɑːsk] *vi (in sun)* sich aalen *(in in + dat)*; *(in sb's favour etc)* sich sonnen *(in in + dat).*

basket ['bɑːskɪt] *n* **(a)** Korb *m*; *(for rolls, fruit etc)* Körbchen *nt.* **a ~ of eggs** ein Korb *or* Körbchen (voll) Eier. **(b)** *(Basketball)* Korb *m.* **(c)** *(euph sl: bastard)* Idiot, Blödmann *m (inf).*

basket: ~**ball** *n* Basketball *m*; ~ **chair** *n* Korbsessel *m*; ~ **maker** *n* Korbmacher(in *f*), Korbflechter(in *f*) *m.*

basketry ['bɑːskɪtrɪ] *n* Korbflechterei *f.*

basket: ~**weave** *n* Leinenbindung *f*; ~**work** *n* Korbflechterei *f*; *(articles)* Korbarbeiten *pl*; **a ~work chair** ein Korbstuhl *m.*

basking shark ['bɑːskɪŋˌʃɑːk] *n* Riesenhai *m.*

Basle [bɑːl] *n* Basel *nt.*

Basque [bæsk] **1** *n* **(a)** *(person)* Baske *m*, Baskin *f.* **(b)** *(language)* Baskisch *nt.* **2** *adj* baskisch.

bas-relief [ˈbæsrɪˌliːf] *n* Flachrelief *nt.*

bass¹ [beɪs] *(Mus)* **1** *n* Baß *m.* **2** *adj* Baß-. ~ **clef** Baßschlüssel *m*; ~ **drum** große Trommel; ~ **viol** Gambe *f.*

bass² [bæs] *n, pl* **-(es)** *(fish)* Barsch *m.*

basset hound ['bæsɪthaʊnd] *n* Basset *m.*

bassinet [ˌbæsɪ'net] *n* Babykorb *m*; *(old: pram)* Kinderwagen *m.*

bassoon [bə'suːn] *n* Fagott *nt.*

bassoonist [bə'suːnɪst] *n* Fagottbläser(in *f*), Fagottist(in *f*) *m.*

basso profundo [ˌbæsəʊprə'fʊndəʊ] *n* tiefer Baß.

basswood ['bæswʊd] *n (Schwarz)*linde *f.*

bastard ['bɑːstəd] **1** *n* **(a)** *(lit)* uneheliches Kind, Bastard *m (old)*; *(fig: hybrid)* Bastard *m*, Kreuzung *f.*
(b) *(sl: person)* Scheißkerl *m (sl).* **stupid ~** Arschloch *nt (sl)*; **poor ~** armes Schwein *(sl)*, armer Hund *(inf).*
(c) *(sl: difficult job etc)* **this question is really a ~** diese Frage ist wirklich hundsgemein *(inf)*; **a ~ of a word/job etc** ein Scheißwort/eine Scheißarbeit *etc (sl).*
2 *adj* **(a)** *(lit)* *child* unehelich.
(b) *(fig: hybrid)* *dog, plant* Bastard-; *language* Misch-.
(c) *(Tech)* ~ **file** Bastardfeile *f.*
(d) *(Typ)* ~ **title** Schmutztitel *m.*

bastardize ['bɑːstədaɪz] *vt (fig)* verfälschen.

bastardy ['bɑːstədɪ] *n (form)* Unehelichkeit *f.*

baste¹ [beɪst] *vt (Sew)* heften.

baste² *vt (Cook)* (mit Fett) beträufeln *or* begießen.

bastinado [ˌbæstɪ'nɑːdəʊ] **1** *n* Bastonade *f*, Stockschläge *pl* auf die Fußsohlen. **2** *vt* eine Bastonade verabreichen (+*dat).*

basting¹ ['beɪstɪŋ] *n (Sew) (act)* Heften *nt*; *(stitches)* Heftnaht *f.* **to take out the ~** die Heftfäden herausziehen.

basting² *n (inf) (beating)* Prügel *pl.* **to give sb a ~** *(team, critics)* jdn fertigmachen *(inf).*

bastion ['bæstɪən] *n (lit, fig)* Bastion *f*; *(person)* Stütze, Säule *f.*

bat¹ [bæt] *n (Zool)* Fledermaus *f.* **to have ~s in the belfry** *(inf)* eine Meise *or* einen Sparren haben *(inf)*; **he fled like a ~ out of hell** er lief *or* rannte, wie wenn der Teufel hinter ihm her wäre; **(as) blind as a ~** stockblind *(inf).*

bat² *(Sport)* **1** *n* **(a)** *(Baseball, Cricket)* Schlagholz *nt*, Keule *f*; *(Table-tennis)* Schläger *m.* **to go to ~ for sb** *(fig)* sich für jdn einsetzen; **off one's own ~** *(fig)* auf eigene Faust *(inf)*; **right off the ~** *(US)* prompt.
(b) *(batsman)* **he is a good ~** er schlägt gut.
(c) *(inf: blow)* Schlag *m.*
2 *vt (Baseball, Cricket)* schlagen.

bat³ *vt* **not to ~ an eyelid** nicht mal mit der Wimper zucken.

bat⁴ *n* **(a)** *(Brit sl: speed)* **at a fair old ~** mit 'nem ganz schönen Zahn drauf *(sl).* **(b)** *(US sl: binge)* Sauftour *f (sl).* **to go on a ~** auf Sauftour gehen *(sl).*

batch [bætʃ] *n (of people)* Schwung *(inf) m*; *(of loaves)* Schub *m*; *(of prisoners, recruits also)* Trupp *m*; *(of things dispatched also)* Sendung, Ladung *f*; *(of letters, books, work also)* Stoß, Stapel *m*; *(of dough, concrete etc)* Ladung *f.*

bated ['beɪtɪd] *adj:* **with ~ breath** mit angehaltenem Atem.

bath [bɑːθ] **1** *n* **(a)** Bad *nt.* **to have *or* take a ~** baden, ein Bad nehmen *(geh)*; **to give sb a ~** jdn baden; **I was just in my *or* the ~** ich war *or* saß gerade im Bad *or* in der Wanne *(inf)*; **a room with ~** ein Zimmer mit Bad; *see* **bloodbath, Turkish** *etc.*
(b) *(bath-tub)* (Bade)wanne *f.* **to empty the ~** das Badewasser ablassen; *see* **eyebath, footbath** *etc.*
(c) *(swimming)* ~**s** *pl*, *swimming* ~ (Schwimm)bad *m*; **(public)** ~**s** *pl* Badeanstalt *f*, öffentliches Bad; *(Hist)* Bäder, Badeanlagen *pl.*
(d) *(Tech, Chem, Phot)* Bad *nt*; *(container)* Behälter *m.*
(e) *(Brit)* **the Order of the B~** der Orden vom Bade.
2 *vt (Brit)* baden.
3 *vi (Brit)* (sich) baden.

bath: **B~ bun** *n* Hefebrötchen *m* mit Zitronat und Orangeat; ~**chair** *n* Kranken- *or* Rollstuhl *m*; ~**cube** *n* Würfel *m* Badesalz.

bathe [beɪð] **1** *vt* **(a)** *person, feet, eyes, wound etc* baden; *(with cottonwool etc)* waschen. **to ~ one's eyes** ein Augenbad machen; ~**d in tears** tränenüberströmt; **to be ~ in light/sweat** in Licht/Schweiß gebadet sein, schweißgebadet sein.
(b) *(US) see* **bath 2.**
2 *vi* baden.
3 *n* Bad *nt.* **to have *or* take a ~** baden.

bather ['beɪðəʳ] *n* Badende(r) *mf.*

bathhouse ['bɑːθhaʊs] *n (old)* Bad(e)haus *nt (old).*

bathing ['beɪðɪŋ] *n* Baden *nt.*

bathing: ~**beauty** *n* Badeschönheit *f*; ~-**cap** *n* Bademütze, Badekappe *f*; ~-**costume** *n* Badeanzug *m*; ~-**hut** *n* Badehäuschen *nt*; ~ **machine** *n* transportable Umkleidekabine; ~-**suit** *n (dated) see* ~-**costume**; ~-**trunks** *npl* Badehose *f.*

bathmat ['bɑːθmæt] *n* Badematte *f or* -vorleger *m.*

bathos ['beɪθɒs] *n (anticlimax)* Abfall *or* Umschlag *m* ins Lächerliche; *(sentimentality)* falsches Pathos.

bathrobe ['bɑːθrəʊb] *n* Bademantel *m.*

bathroom ['bɑːθruːm] *n* Bad(ezimmer) *nt*; *(euph: lavatory)* Toilette *f.*

bathroom: ~ **cabinet** *n* Toiletten- *or* Badezimmerschrank *m*; ~ **fittings** *npl* Badezimmerausstattung *f*; ~ **scales** *npl* Personenwaage *f.*

bath: ~**salts** *npl* Badesalz *nt*; ~**towel** *n* Badetuch *nt*; ~**tub** *n* Badewanne *f.*

bathysphere ['bæθɪsfɪəʳ] *n* Tauchkugel, Bathysphäre *f.*

batik ['bætɪk] *n* Batik *f*; *(cloth)* Batikdruck *m.*

batiste [bæ'tiːst] *n* Batist *m.*

batman ['bætmən] *n, pl* -**men** [-mən] *(Mil)* Putzer *m.*

baton ['bætən] *n* **(a)** *(Mus)* Taktstock, Stab *m*; *(Mil)* (Kommando)stab *m.* **under the ~ of** *(Mus)* unter der Stabführung von.
(b) *(of policeman)* Schlagstock *m*; *(for directing traffic)* Stab *m.* ~ **charge** Schlagstockeinsatz *m*; **to make a ~ charge** Schlagstöcke einsetzen. **(c)** *(in relay race)* Staffelholz *nt*, Stab *m.*

bats [bæts] *adj pred (inf)* bekloppt *(inf).* **you must be ~** du spinnst wohl! *(inf).*

batsman ['bætsmən] *n, pl* -**men** [-mən] *(Sport)* Schlagmann *m.*

battalion [bə'tælɪən] n (Mil, fig) Bataillon nt.
batten ['bætn] **1** n (a) Leiste, Latte f; (for roofing) Dachlatte f; (for flooring) (Trag)latte f. (b) (Naut) (for sail) Segellatte f; (for hatch) Schalklatte f. **2** vt (a) roof, floor mit Latten versehen. (b) (Naut) sail mit Latten verstärken; hatch (ver)schalken.
♦**batten down** vt sep to ∼ **the hatches** die Luken schalken (spec) or dicht machen; (fig) (close doors, windows) alles dicht machen; (prepare oneself) sich auf etwas gefaßt machen.
♦**batten on** vi +prep obj schmarotzen bei.
♦**batten onto** vi +prep obj idea sich (dat) aneignen.
batter[1] ['bætə[r]] n (Cook) (for frying) (Ausback)teig m; (for pancakes, waffles etc) Teig m.
batter[2] n (Sport) Schlagmann m.
batter[3] **1** vt (a) einschlagen auf (+acc); (strike repeatedly) wife, baby schlagen, (ver)prügeln; (with ∼ing ram) berennen. he ∼ed him about the head with an iron bar er schlug mit einer Eisenstange auf seinen Kopf ein; the ship/house was ∼ed by the waves/wind die Wellen krachten unentwegt gegen das Schiff/der Wind rüttelte unentwegt am Haus.
(b) (damage) böse or übel zurichten; car also, metal zer- or verbeulen. the town was badly ∼ed during the war die Stadt wurde während des Krieges schwer zerbombt.
(c) (inf) opponent eins or eine draufgeben (+dat) (inf). to get ∼ed eins or eine draufbekommen (inf).
2 vi schlagen, trommeln (inf). to ∼ at/against the door an/gegen die Tür hämmern (inf) or trommeln (inf).
♦**batter about** vt sep sb schlagen, verprügeln; sth grob umgehen mit, ramponieren (inf).
♦**batter down** vt sep wall zertrümmern; door also einschlagen; resistance zerschlagen.
♦**batter in** vt sep door einschlagen; (with ram) einrennen; skull einschlagen.
battered ['bætəd] adj böse or übel zugerichtet, lädiert (inf); wife, baby mißhandelt; hat, car, teapot also verbeult; city zerbombt; house, furniture mitgenommen, ramponiert (inf); nerves zerrüttet. ∼ **baby syndrome** Phänomen nt der Kindesmißhandlung.
battering ['bætərɪŋ] n (lit) Schläge, Prügel pl; (of baby, wife) Mißhandlung f. he/it got or took a real ∼ er/es hat ganz schön was abgekriegt (inf), es hat schwer gelitten; to give sb/sth a ∼ jdn verprügeln/etw ramponieren (inf) or demolieren (inf); he'll give his opponent a ∼ er wird es seinem Gegner geben (inf).
battering ram n Rammbock, Sturmbock m.
battery ['bætərɪ] n (all senses) Batterie f; (fig: of arguments etc) Reihe f; see assault.
battery: ∼-**charger** n Ladesatz m; ∼ **farming** n (Hühneretc)batterien pl; ∼ **fire** n (Mil) Geschützfeuer nt; ∼ **hen** n (Agr) Batteriehenne f; ∼ **set** n (radio) Batteriegerät nt.
battle ['bætl] **1** n (lit) Schlacht f; (fig) Kampf m. to give/offer/refuse ∼ sich zum Kampf or zur Schlacht stellen/bereit erklären/den Kampf or die Schlacht verweigern; to fight a ∼ eine Schlacht schlagen (also fig), einen Kampf führen; I don't need you to fight my ∼s for me ich kann mich schon alleine durchsetzen; to do ∼ for sb/sth sich für jdn schlagen, sich für jdn/etw einsetzen; killed in ∼ (im Kampf) gefallen; ∼ of words/wits Wortgefecht nt/geistiger Wettstreit; to have a ∼ of wits sich geistig messen; we are fighting the same ∼ wir ziehen am selben Strang; that's half the ∼ damit ist schon viel gewonnen.
2 vi schlagen; (fig also) kämpfen, streiten. to ∼ for breath um Atem ringen; to ∼ through a book etc sich durch ein Buch etc (durch)kämpfen.
3 vt (fig) to ∼ one's way through difficulties/a book sich (durch Schwierigkeiten) durchschlagen/sich durch ein Buch (durch)kämpfen.
♦**battle on** vi (fig) weiterkämpfen.
battle: ∼-**axe** n (weapon) Streitaxt f; (inf: woman) Drachen m (inf); ∼ **cruiser** n Schlachtkreuzer m; ∼ **cry** n Schlachtruf m.
battledore ['bætldɔː[r]] n (Federball)schläger m. ∼ **and shuttlecock** Federball nt.
battle: ∼ **dress** m Kampfanzug m; ∼**field**, ∼**ground** n Schlachtfeld nt.
battlements ['bætlmənts] npl Zinnen pl.
battle: ∼ **order** n Schlachtordnung f; ∼ **royal** n (fig: quarrel) heftige Auseinandersetzung; ∼-**scarred** adj person, country vom Krieg gezeichnet; furniture schwer mitgenommen, ramponiert (inf); ∼ **ship** n Kriegs- or Schlachtschiff nt; ∼-**song** n Kampf- or Kriegslied nt; ∼ **zone** n Kriegs- or Kampfgebiet nt.
batty ['bætɪ] adj (+er) (inf) verrückt; person also plemplem pred (inf). to go ∼ überschnappen (inf).
bauble ['bɔːbl] n Flitter m no pl. ∼s Flitterzeug nt; jester's ∼ Narrenzepter nt.
baulk [bɔːk] n see balk.
bauxite ['bɔːksaɪt] n Bauxit m.
Bavaria [bə'veərɪə] n Bayern nt.
Bavarian [bə'veərɪən] **1** n (a) (person) Bayer(in f) m. (b) (dialect) Bairisch nt. **2** adj bay(e)risch; dialect also bairisch.
bawd [bɔːd] n (brothel-keeper) Bordellwirtin, Puffmutter (inf) f.
bawdiness ['bɔːdɪnɪs] n Derbheit f.
bawdy ['bɔːdɪ] adj (+er) derb. ∼ **talk** derbes Gerede.
bawl [bɔːl] **1** vi (a) (shout) brüllen, schreien; (sing) grölen (inf). to ∼ for help um Hilfe schreien. (b) (inf: weep) plärren (inf), heulen (inf). **2** vt order brüllen, schreien; song grölen (inf).
♦**bawl out** vt sep (a) order brüllen; song schmettern, grölen (pej inf). (b) (inf: scold) ausschimpfen.
bawling-out [ˌbɔːlɪŋ'aʊt] n (inf) Schimpfkanonade f (inf). to give sb a ∼ jdn zur Schnecke machen (inf).
bay[1] [beɪ] n Bucht f; (of sea also) Bai f. the Hudson B∼ die Hudsonbai.
bay[2] n (Bot) Lorbeer(baum) m.
bay[3] n (a) (Archit) Erker m. (b) (loading ∼) Ladeplatz m;

(parking ∼) Parkbucht f; (Rail) Abstellgleis nt. (c) (Aviat: bomb ∼) Bombenschacht m. (d) (sick ∼) (Kranken)revier nt.
bay[4] **1** n (of dogs) Bellen nt no pl; (Hunt) Melden nt no pl. to bring to/be at ∼ (Hunt) stellen/gestellt sein; (fig) in die Enge treiben/getrieben sein; to have sb at ∼ (fig) jdn in der Zange haben (inf); to keep or hold sb/sth at ∼ jdn/etw in Schach halten.
2 vi bellen; (Hunt also) melden. to ∼ at the moon den Mond anbellen or anheulen.
bay[5] **1** adj horse (kastanien)braun. **2** n Braune(r) m. red ∼ (horse) rötlicher Brauner.
bayleaf ['beɪliːf] n Lorbeerblatt nt.
bayonet ['beɪənɪt] **1** n Bajonett, Seitengewehr nt. with ∼s fixed/at the ready mit aufgepflanztem/gefälltem Bajonetten. **2** vt mit dem Bajonett or Seitengewehr aufspießen.
bayonet fitting n (Elec) Bajonettfassung f.
bay: ∼ **rum** n Pimentöl nt; ∼ **tree** n Lorbeerbaum m; ∼ **window** n Erkerfenster nt.
bazaar [bə'zɑː[r]] n Basar m.
bazooka [bə'zuːkə] n Bazooka, Panzerfaust f, Panzerschreck m.
BB 1 n (Brit) abbr of **Boys' Brigade. 2** adj (on pencil) 2B.
BBC abbr of **British Broadcasting Corporation** BBC f or m.
BC[1] abbr of **before Christ** v. Chr., a. Chr.
BC[2] abbr of **British Columbia.**
BCG abbr of **Bacille Calmette Guérin** BCG.
BD abbr of **Bachelor of Divinity.**
be [biː] present **am, is, are,** pret **was, were,** ptp **been 1** copulative vb (a) (with adj, n) sein. he is a soldier/a German er ist Soldat/Deutscher; he wants to ∼ a doctor er möchte Arzt werden; who is that? — it's me/that's Mary wer ist das? — ich bin's/das ist Mary; to ∼ critical/disparaging sich kritisch/verächtlich äußern, kritisch sein; if I were you wenn ich Sie or an Ihrer Stelle wäre; ∼ sensible! sei vernünftig.
(b) (health) how are you? wie geht's?; I'm better now es geht mir jetzt besser; she's none too well es geht ihr gar nicht gut.
(c) (physical, mental state) to ∼ hungry/thirsty Hunger/Durst haben, hungrig/durstig sein (geh); I am hot/cold/frozen ich schwitze/friere/bin halb erfroren, mir ist heiß/kalt/eiskalt; to ∼ ashamed/worried sich schämen/sich (dat) Sorgen machen, besorgt sein; to ∼ right/wrong recht/nicht recht haben; they were horrified sie waren entsetzt.
(d) (age) sein. he'll ∼ three er wird drei (Jahre alt).
(e) (cost) kosten. how much is that? wieviel or was kostet das?; (altogether also) wieviel or was macht das?
(f) (Math) sein. two times two is or are four zwei mal zwei ist or sind or gibt vier.
(g) (with poss) gehören (+dat). that book is your brother's/his das Buch gehört Ihrem Bruder/ihm, das ist das Buch Ihres Bruders/das ist sein Buch.
(h) (in exclamations) was he pleased to hear it! er war vielleicht froh, das zu hören!; but wasn't she glad when ... hat sie sich vielleicht gefreut, als ...
2 v aux (a) (+prp: continuous tenses) what are you doing? was tun Sie?; she is always complaining sie beklagt sich dauernd; they're coming tomorrow sie kommen morgen; you will ∼ hearing from us Sie werden von uns hören; will you ∼ seeing her tomorrow? sehen or treffen Sie sie morgen?; I've just been packing my case ich war gerade beim Kofferpacken, ich war gerade dabei, den Koffer zu packen; I was packing my case when ... ich war gerade beim Kofferpacken, als ...; I have been waiting for you for half an hour ich warte schon seit einer halben Stunde auf Sie.
(b) (+ptp: passive) werden. he was run over er ist überfahren worden, er wurde überfahren; the box had been opened die Schachtel war geöffnet worden; it is/was ∼ing repaired es wird/wurde gerade repariert; the car is to ∼ sold das Auto soll verkauft werden; they are shortly to ∼ married sie werden bald heiraten; they were to have been married last week sie hätten letzte Woche heiraten sollen, in fact she was to ∼/was to have been dismissed but ... sie sollte eigentlich entlassen werden, aber .../sie hätte eigentlich entlassen werden sollen, aber ...
(c) he is to ∼ pitied/not to ∼ envied er ist zu bedauern/nicht zu beneiden; not to ∼ confused with nicht zu verwechseln mit; he was not to ∼ persuaded er war nicht zu überreden, er ließ sich nicht überreden; I will not ∼/am not to ∼ intimidated ich lasse mich nicht einschüchtern.
(d) (intention, obligation, command) sollen. I am to look after my mother ich soll mich um meine Mutter kümmern; he is not to open it er soll es nicht öffnen; I wasn't to tell you his name ich sollte or durfte Ihnen nicht sagen, wie er heißt; (but I did) ich hätte Ihnen eigentlich nicht sagen sollen or dürfen, wie er heißt.
(e) (∼ destined) sollen. she was never to return sie sollte nie zurückkehren.
(f) (suppositions, wishes) if it were or was to snow falls or wenn es schneien sollte; and were I or if I were to tell him? und wenn ich es ihm sagen würde?; would I were able to (liter) ich wünschte, ich könnte (es) (geh); I would ∼ surprised if ... ich wäre überrascht, wenn ...
(g) (in tag questions, short answers) he's always late, isn't he? — yes he is er kommt doch immer zu spät, nicht? — ja, das stimmt; he's never late, is he? — yes he is er kommt nie zu spät, oder? — o, doch; you are not ill, are you? — yes I am/no I'm not Sie sind doch nicht (etwa) krank? — doch!/nein; it's all done, is it? — yes it is/no it isn't es ist also alles erledigt? — ja/nein.
3 vi (a) sein; (remain) bleiben. to ∼ or not to ∼ Sein oder Nichtsein; the powers that ∼ die zuständigen Stellen; let me/him ∼ laß mich/ihn (in Ruhe); ∼ that as it may wie dem auch sei; he is there at the moment but he won't ∼ much longer im Augenblick ist er dort, aber nicht mehr lange; we've been here a long time wir sind schon lange hier.

(b) *(be situated)* sein; *(town, country, forest etc also)* liegen; *(car, tower, crate, bottle, chair also)* stehen; *(ashtray, papers, carpet also)* liegen.

(c) *(visit, call)* **I've been to Paris** ich war schon in Paris; **the postman has already been** der Briefträger war schon da; **he has been and gone** er war da und ist wieder gegangen.

(d) now you've been and (gone and) done it *(inf)* jetzt hast du aber was angerichtet! *(inf)*; **I've just been and (gone and) broken it!** jetzt hab' ich's tatsächlich kaputtgemacht *(inf)*.

(e) *(used to present, point out)* **here is a book/are two books** hier ist ein Buch/sind zwei Bücher; **over there are two churches** da drüben sind or stehen zwei Kirchen; **here/there you are** *(you've arrived)* da sind Sie ja; *(take this)* hier/da, bitte; *(here/there it is)* hier/da ist es/sind sie doch; **there he was sitting at the table** da saß er nun am Tisch.

4 *vb impers* **(a)** sein. **it is dark/morning** es ist dunkel/Morgen; **tomorrow is Friday the 14th of June** morgen ist Freitag/der 14. Juni, morgen haben wir Freitag/den 14. Juni; **it is 5 km to the nearest town** es sind 5 km bis zur nächsten Stadt.

(b) *(emphatic)* **it was us** or **we** *(form)* **who found it** das haben wir gefunden, wir haben das gefunden, wir waren diejenigen, die das gefunden haben.

(c) *(wishes, suppositions, probability)* **were it not that I am a teacher, I would** ... wenn ich ja kein Lehrer wäre, dann würde ich ...; **were it not for my friendship with him** wenn ich ja nicht mit ihm befreundet wäre; **were it not for him, if it weren't** or **wasn't for him** wenn er nicht wäre; **had it not been** or **if it hadn't been for him** wenn er nicht gewesen wäre; **and even if it were** not so und selbst wenn das or dem nicht so wäre.

beach [biːtʃ] **1** *n* Strand *m*. **on the ~** am Strand. **2** *vt boat* auf Strand setzen.

beach: **~ball** *n* Wasserball *m*; **~ buggy** *n* Strandbuggy *m*; **~comber** *n* Strandgutsammler *m*; *(living rough)* am Strand lebender Einsiedler; **~head** *n* (Mil) Landkopf *m*; **~ hut** *n* Strandhäuschen *nt*; **~ umbrella** *n* Sonnenschirm *m*; **~wear** *n* Badesachen *pl*, Badezeug *nt* (inf); *(Fashion)* Strandmode *f*.

beacon ['biːkən] *n (fire, light)* Leuchtfeuer *nt*; *(radio ~)* Funkfeuer *nt*; *(one of a series of lights, radio ~s)* Bake *f*.

bead [biːd] *n* **(a)** Perle *f*. **(string of) ~s** Perlenschnur *f*; *(necklace)* Perlenkette *f*; **to tell** or **say one's ~s** den Rosenkranz beten. **(b)** *(drop: of dew, sweat)* Perle *f*, Tropfen *m*. **(c)** *(of gun)* Korn *nt*. **to draw a ~ on sb** auf jdn zielen.

beading ['biːdɪŋ] *n* Perlstab *m*, Perlschnur *f*.

beadle ['biːdl] *n (old Eccl)* Kirchendiener *m*; *(Univ)* Angestellter, der bei Prozessionen den Amtsstab trägt.

beady ['biːdɪ] *adj* **~ eye** waches Äuglein; **I've got my ~ eye on you** *(inf)* ich beobachte Sie genau!; **cast your ~ eyes over this** *(hum inf)* wirf mal einen Blick darauf.

beagle ['biːgl] *n* Beagle *m* *(englischer Spürhund)*.

beak [biːk] *n* **(a)** *(of bird, turtle)* Schnabel *m*. **(b)** *(inf: of person)* Zinken, Rüssel *m* (inf). **(c)** *(Brit inf: judge etc)* Kadi *m* (inf); *(Brit Sch sl)* (Di)rex *m* (sl).

beaker ['biːkə^r] *n* Becher *m*; *(Chem etc)* Becherglas *nt*.

be-all and end-all ['biːɔːlənd'endɔːl] *n* **the ~** das A und O; **it's not the ~** das ist auch nicht alles.

beam [biːm] **1** *n* **(a)** *(Build, of scales)* Balken *m*. **(b)** *(Naut)* *(side)* Seite *f*; *(width)* Breite *f*. **on the ~** querschiffs; **on the port ~** backbords; **the ~ of a ship** die Schiffsbreite; **to be broad in the ~** *(ship)* sehr breit sein; *(person)* breit gebaut sein.

(c) *(of light etc)* Strahl *m*. **to drive/be on full** or **high** or **main ~** mit Fernlicht fahren/Fernlicht eingestellt haben.

(d) *(radio ~)* Leitstrahl *m*. **to be on/off ~** auf Kurs sein/vom Kurs abgekommen sein; *(fig)* *(person)* richtig liegen *(inf)*/danebenliegen *(inf)*; *(figures)* stimmen/nicht stimmen; **you're/your guess is way off ~** Sie haben total danebengehauen *(inf)*/danebengeraten *(inf)*.

(e) *(smile)* Strahlen *nt*. **a ~ of delight** ein freudiges Strahlen.

2 *vi* **(a)** strahlen. **to ~ down** *(sun)* niederstrahlen.

(b) *(fig: person, face)* strahlen. **her face was ~ing with joy** sie strahlte übers ganze Gesicht.

3 *vt* *(Rad, TV)* *message, programme* ausstrahlen, senden *(to in* or *an +acc)*.

beam-ends ['biːmendz] *npl:* **to be on one's ~** *(Naut)* stark Schlagseite haben; *(fig)* aus dem letzten Loch pfeifen *(inf)*.

beaming ['biːmɪŋ] *adj sun* strahlend; *smile, face* (freude)strahlend.

bean [biːn] *n* **(a)** Bohne *f*. **he hasn't a ~** *(Brit inf)* er hat keinen roten or lumpigen Heller *(inf)*; **hallo, old ~!** *(dated Brit inf)* hallo, altes Haus! *(dated inf)*. **(b)** *(fig)* **to be full of ~s** *(inf)* putzmunter sein *(inf)*.

bean: **~bag** *n* mit Bohnen gefülltes Säckchen, das zum Spielen verwendet wird; **~feast** *n* *(inf)* Schmaus *m* (inf).

beano ['biːnəʊ] *n (dated inf)* Schmaus *m* (inf).

bean: **~pole** *n* *(lit, fig)* Bohnenstange *f*; **~sprout** *n* Sojabohnensprosse *f*; **~stalk** *n* Bohnenstengel *m*.

bear¹ [bɛə^r] *pret* **bore**, *ptp* **borne 1** *vt* **(a)** *(carry)* *burden, arms* tragen; *gift, message* mit sich tragen, mit sich führen. **to ~ away/back** mitnehmen/mit (sich) zurücknehmen; *(through the air)* fort- or wegtragen/zurücktragen; **the music was borne/borne away on the wind** *(liter)* die Musik wurde vom Wind weiter-/weggetragen; **he was borne along by the crowd** die Menge trug ihn mit (sich).

(b) *(show)* *inscription, signature* tragen; *mark, traces also, likeness, relation* aufweisen, zeigen; *see* **witness**.

(c) *(be known by)* *name, title* tragen, führen.

(d) *(have in heart* or *mind)* *love* empfinden, in sich *(dat)* tragen; *hatred, grudge also* hegen *(geh)*. **the love/hatred he bore her** die Liebe, die er für sie empfand/der Haß, den er gegen sie hegte *(geh)* or empfand; *see* **mind**.

(e) *(lit, fig: support, sustain)* *weight, expense, responsibility*

tragen. **to ~ examination/comparison** einer Prüfung/einem Vergleich standhalten; **it doesn't ~ thinking about** man darf gar nicht daran denken; **his language doesn't ~ repeating** seine Ausdrucksweise läßt sich nicht wiederholen.

(f) *(endure, tolerate)* ertragen; *(with neg also)* ausstehen, leiden; *pain, smell, noise etc also* vertragen; *criticism, joking, smell, noise etc also* vertragen. **she can't ~ flying/doing nothing/being laughed at** sie kann einfach nicht fliegen/untätig sein/sie kann es nicht vertragen, wenn man über sie lacht; **could you ~ to stay a little longer?** können Sie es noch ein bißchen länger hier aushalten?; **a pain that cannot be borne** ein nicht auszuhaltender Schmerz.

(g) *(produce, yield)* *fruit etc* tragen; *see* **interest**.

(h) *(give birth to)* gebären; *see* **born**.

2 *vi* **(a)** *(move)* **to ~ right/left/north** sich rechts/links/nach Norden halten; **to ~ away** or **off** *(Naut)* abdrehen.

(b) *(fruit-tree etc)* tragen.

(c) to bring one's energies/powers of persuasion to ~ seine Energie/Überzeugungskraft aufwenden *(on für)*; **to bring one's mind to ~** on sth seinen Verstand or Geist für etw anstrengen; **to bring pressure to ~ on sb/sth** Druck auf jdn/etw ausüben.

3 *vr* sich halten. **he bore himself with dignity** er hat Würde gezeigt.

♦ **bear down 1** *vi* **(a)** sich nahen *(geh)*; *(hawk etc)* herabstoßen. **to ~ ~ on sb/sth** *(driver etc)* auf jdn/etw zuhalten. **(b)** *(woman in labour)* drücken. **2** *vt sep* niederdrücken. **he was borne ~ by poverty** seine Armut lastete schwer auf ihm; **to be borne ~ by the weight of** ... von der Last *(+gen)* gebeugt sein.

♦ **bear in (up)on** *vt +prep obj:* **to be borne ~ ~ sb** jdm zu(m) Bewußtsein kommen.

♦ **bear on** *vi +prep obj see* **bear (up)on**.

♦ **bear out** *vt sep* bestätigen. **to ~ sb ~ in sth** jdn in etw bestätigen; **you will ~ me ~ that ...** Sie werden bestätigen, daß ...

♦ **bear up** *vi* sich halten. **he bore ~ well under the death of his father** er trug den Tod seines Vaters mit Fassung; **~ ~!** Kopf hoch!; **how are you?** — **~ ~!** wie geht's? — man lebt!

♦ **bear (up)on** *vi +prep obj* **(a)** *(relate to)* betreffen. **does this ~ ~ what you were saying?** hat das einen Bezug zu dem, was Sie sagten? **(b)** **to ~ hard/severely ~ sb** sich hart auf jdn auswirken.

♦ **bear with** *vi +prep obj* tolerieren. **if you would just ~ ~ me for a couple of minutes** wenn Sie sich vielleicht zwei Minuten gedulden wollen.

bear² 1 *n* **(a)** Bär *m*; *(fig: person)* Brummbär *m* (inf). **he is like a ~ with a sore head** er ist ein richtiger Brummbär *(inf)*. **(b)** *(Astron)* **the Great/Little B ~** der Große/Kleine Bär or Wagen. **(c)** *(St Ex)* Baissespekulant, Baissier *m*. **2** *vi* *(St Ex)* auf Baisse spekulieren.

bearable ['bɛərəbl] *adj* erträglich, zum Aushalten.

bear: **~-baiting** *n* Bärenhatz *f*; **~-cub** *n* Bärenjunge(s) *nt*.

beard [bɪəd] *n* **(a)** Bart *m*; *(full-face)* Vollbart *m*. **a man with a ~** ein Mann mit Bart; **a week's (growth of) ~** ein eine Woche alter Bart; **small pointed ~** Spitzbart *m*.

(b) *(of goat, bird)* Bart *m*; *(of fish also)* Barthaare *pl*; *(of grain)* Grannen *pl*.

2 *vt* *(confront)* ansprechen. **to ~ sb about sth** jdn auf etw *(acc)* hin ansprechen; **to ~ the lion in his den** *(fig)* sich in die Höhle des Löwen wagen.

bearded ['bɪədɪd] *adj man, animal* bärtig. **the ~ woman** or **lady** die Dame mit dem Bart.

beardless ['bɪədlɪs] *adj* bartlos. **~ youth** Milchbart *m* (pej inf), Milchgesicht *nt* (pej inf).

bearer ['bɛərə^r] *n* **(a)** *(carrier)* Träger(in *f*) *m*; *(of news, letter, cheque, banknote)* Überbringer *m*; *(of name, title also, of passport, bond, cheque)* Inhaber(in *f*) *m*. **~ bond** Inhaberschuldverschreibung *f*.

(b) *(tree etc)* **a good ~** ein Baum/Busch *etc*, der gut trägt.

bear: **~ garden** *n* Tollhaus *nt*; **~ hug** *n* ungestüme Umarmung; *(Wrestling)* Klammer, Umklammerung *f*.

bearing ['bɛərɪŋ] *n* **(a)** *(posture)* Haltung *f*; *(behaviour)* Verhalten, Auftreten, Gebaren *nt*.

(b) *(relevance, influence)* Auswirkung *f* *(on auf +acc)*; *(connection)* Bezug *m* *(on zu)*. **to have some/no ~ on sth** von Belang/belanglos für etw sein; *(be/not be connected with)* einen gewissen/keinen Bezug zu etw haben.

(c) *(endurance)* **to be beyond (all) ~** unerträglich or nicht zum Aushalten sein.

(d) *(direction)* **to take/get a ~ on sth** sich an etw *(dat)* orientieren; **to take a compass ~** den Kompaßkurs feststellen; **to get one's ~s** sich zurechtfinden, sich orientieren; **to lose one's ~s** die Orientierung verlieren.

(e) *(Tech)* Lager *nt*.

bear: **~ market** *n* (St Ex) Baissemarkt *m*; **~pit** *n* Bärengehege *nt*; **~skin** *n* (Mil) Bärenfellmütze *f*.

beast [biːst] *n* **(a)** Tier *nt*; *see* **burden, prey**.

(b) *(inf)* *(person)* Biest, Ekel *nt*. **don't be a ~!** sei nicht so eklig! *(inf)*; **that ~ of a brother-in-law** dieser fiese Schwager *(inf)*; **this (problem) is a ~, it's a ~** *(of a problem)* das (Problem) hat's in sich *(inf)*; **have you finished it yet?** — **no, it's a ~** sind Sie fertig damit? — nein, es ist verflixt schwierig *(inf)*.

beastliness ['biːstlɪnɪs] *n* *(inf)* *see adj* Scheußlichkeit, Garstigkeit *f*; Gemeinheit, Ekligkeit *(inf)* *f*.

beastly ['biːstlɪ] *(inf)* **1** *adj* scheußlich, garstig *(inf)*; *person, conduct also* gemein, eklig *(inf)*. **what ~ weather** so ein Hundewetter; **it's a ~ business** das ist eine üble Angelegenheit; **what a ~ shame!** *(dated)* so ein Jammer!

2 *adv* *(dated)* scheußlich. **it's ~ difficult** es ist verteufelt schwierig *(inf)*.

beat [biːt] *(vb: pret* **~**, *ptp* **~en) 1** *n* **(a)** *(of heart, pulse, drum)* *(single ~)* Schlag *m*; *(repeated beating)* Schlagen *nt*. **the ~ of**

her heart grew weaker ihr Herzschlag wurde schwächer; to the ~ of the drum zum Schlag der Trommeln.

(b) (of policeman, sentry) Runde f, Rundgang m; (district) Revier nt. **to be on** or **to patrol one's** ~ seine Runde machen.

(c) (Mus, Poet) Takt m; (of metronome, baton) Taktschlag m. **to have a strong** ~ einen ausgeprägten Rhythmus haben.

(d) (~music) (Beat(musik f) m.

(e) (Hunt) Treibjagd f.

2 vt **(a)** (hit) schlagen; person, animal also (ver)prügeln, hauen (inf); carpet klopfen; (search) countryside, woods absuchen, abkämmen. **the crocodile** ~ **the ground with its tail** das Krokodil schlug mit dem Schwanz auf den Boden; **to** ~ **a/one's way through** sth einen/sich (dat) einen Weg durch etw bahnen; **to** ~ **a path to sb's door** (fig) jdm die Bude einrennen (inf); **to** ~ **a/the drum** trommeln, die Trommel schlagen; **to** ~ **the air um** sich schlagen, herumfuchteln; **to** ~ **one's breast** sich (dat) an die Brust schlagen; (ape) sich (dat) gegen die Brust trommeln; ~ **it!** (fig inf) hau ab! (inf), verschwinde!

(b) (hammer) metal hämmern; (shape also) treiben. **to** ~ **sth flat** etw flach- or platthämmern.

(c) (defeat) schlagen; record brechen; inflation in den Griff bekommen. **to** ~ **sb** at chess/tennis jdn im Schach/Tennis schlagen; **his shot/forehand** ~ **me** ich war dem Schuß/Vorhandschlag nicht gewachsen; **you can't** ~ **these prices** diese Preise sind nicht zu übertreffen; **you can't** ~ **central heating/real wool** es geht doch nichts über Zentralheizung/reine Wolle; **he** ~s **the rest of them any day** er steckt sie alle (jederzeit) in die Tasche (inf); **coffee** ~s **tea any day** Kaffee ist allemal besser als Tee; **that** ~s **everything** das ist doch wirklich der Gipfel or die Höhe, das schlägt dem Faß den Boden aus (all inf); (is very good) darüber geht nichts; **that** ~s **me** (inf) das ist mir ein Rätsel (inf); **well can you** ~ **it!** (inf) ist das denn zu fassen? (inf); **that problem** ~s **me** (inf) das Problem geht über meinen Verstand.

(d) (be before) budget, crowds zuvorkommen (+dat). **to** ~ **sb to the top of a hill** vor jdm oben auf dem Berg sein or ankommen; **I'll** ~ **you down to the beach** ich bin vor dir am Strand; **to** ~ **sb home** vor jdm zu Hause sein; **to** ~ **the deadline** vor Ablauf der Frist fertig sein; **to** ~ **sb to the draw** schneller ziehen als jd; **to** ~ **sb to it** jdm zuvorkommen.

(e) (move up and down regularly) schlagen. **the bird** ~s **its wings** der Vogel schlägt mit den Flügeln.

(f) (Mus) **to** ~ **time (to the music)** den Takt schlagen.

(g) cream, eggs schlagen.

3 vi **(a)** (heart, pulse, drum) schlagen. **to** ~ **on the door (with one's fists)** (mit den Fäusten) gegen die Tür hämmern or schlagen; **with** ~**ing heart** mit pochendem or klopfendem Herzen; **her heart was** ~**ing with joy** ihr Herz schlug vor Freude höher; see **bush¹**.

(b) (wind, waves) schlagen; (rain also) trommeln; (sun) brennen.

(c) (cream) sich schlagen lassen.

4 adj **(a)** (inf: exhausted) **to be (dead)** ~ total kaputt or geschafft or erledigt sein (inf).

(b) (inf: defeated) **to be** ~(**en**) aufgeben müssen (inf), sich geschlagen geben müssen; **I'm** ~ ich gebe mich geschlagen; **he doesn't know when he's** ~(**en**) er gibt nicht auf (inf); **we've got him** ~ wir haben ihn schachmatt gesetzt; **this problem's got me** ~ mit dem Problem komme ich nicht klar (inf).

♦**beat back** vt sep flames, enemy zurückschlagen.

♦**beat down 1** vi (rain) herunterprasseln; (sun) herunterbrennen. **2** vt sep **(a)** (reduce) prices herunterhandeln; opposition kleinkriegen (inf). **I managed to** ~ **him/the price** ~ ich konnte den Preis herunterhandeln; **I** ~ **him** ~ **to £2 for the chair** ich habe den Stuhl auf £ 2 heruntergehandelt. **(b)** (flatten) door einrennen; wheat, crop niederwerfen.

♦**beat in** vt sep door einschlagen. **to** ~ **sb's brains** ~ (inf) jdm den Schädel einschlagen (inf).

♦**beat off** vt sep attack, attacker abwehren.

♦**beat out** vt sep fire ausschlagen; metal, dent, wing aushämmern; tune, rhythm schlagen; (on drum) trommeln; plan ausarbeiten, ausklamüsern (inf), austüfteln (inf). **to** ~ **sb's brains** ~ (inf: kill) jdm den Schädel einschlagen (inf).

♦**beat up** vt sep **(a)** person zusammenschlagen. **(b)** (Cook) eggs, cream schlagen.

beaten ['biːtn] **1** ptp of **beat**. **2** adj **(a)** metal gehämmert. **(b)** earth festgetreten; path also ausgetreten. **a well-**~ **path** ein Trampelpfad m; **to be off the** ~ **track** (fig) abgelegen sein. **(c)** (defeated) **a** ~ **man** ein geschlagener Mann.

beater ['biːtəʳ] n **(a)** (carpet ~) Klopfer m; (egg ~) Rührbesen m. **(b)** (Hunt) Treiber(in f) m.

beat in cpds Beat-; ~ **generation** n Beatgeneration f; ~ **group** n Beatgruppe or -band f.

beatific [ˌbiːəˈtɪfɪk] adj glückselig; vision himmlisch.

beatification [biːˌætɪfɪˈkeɪʃən] n Seligsprechung f.

beatify [biːˈætɪfaɪ] vt seligsprechen, beatifizieren (spec).

beating ['biːtɪŋ] n **(a)** (series of blows) Schläge, Prügel pl. **to give sb a** ~ jdn verprügeln; (as punishment also) jdm eine Tracht Prügel verabreichen (inf); **to get a** ~ verprügelt werden; (as punishment also) Schläge or Prügel bekommen, eine Tracht Prügel beziehen (inf). **(b)** (of drums, heart, wings) Schlagen nt. **(c)** (defeat) Niederlage f. **to take a** ~ eine Schlappe einstecken (inf); **to take a** ~ (at the hands of sb) (von jdm) nach allen Regeln der Kunst geschlagen werden. **(d)** **to take some** ~ nicht leicht zu übertreffen sein; (idea, insolence etc) seinesgleichen suchen. **(e)** (Hunt) Treiben nt.

beating-up [ˌbiːtɪŋˈʌp] n Abreibung f (inf). **to give sb a** ~ jdn zusammenschlagen; **to get a** ~ zusammengeschlagen werden.

beatitude [biːˈætɪtjuːd] n Glückseligkeit f. **the B**~s (Bibl) die Seligpreisungen pl.

beatnik ['biːtnɪk] n Beatnik m.

beat poetry n Beatlyrik f.

beat-up ['biːtʌp] adj (inf) zerbeult, ramponiert (inf).

beau [bəʊ] n (old) **(a)** (dandy) Beau m (dated). **(b)** (suitor) Galan m (dated), Kavalier m.

Beaufort scale ['bəʊfə'skeɪl] n Beaufortskala f.

beaut [bjuːt] n (esp Austral sl) (thing) Prachtexemplar nt. **to be a (real)** ~ einsame Klasse sein (sl).

beauteous ['bjuːtɪəs] adj (poet) wunderschön, prachtvoll.

beautician [bjuːˈtɪʃən] n Kosmetiker(in f) m.

beautiful ['bjuːtɪfʊl] adj schön; weather, morning also, idea, meal herrlich, wunderbar; (good) swimmer, swimming, organization, piece of work hervorragend, wunderbar. **that's a** ~ **specimen** das ist ein Prachtexemplar; **the** ~ **people** die Schickeria; ~! prima! (inf), toll! (inf). **2** n **(a)** **the** ~ das Schöne. **(b)** (inf) hello, ~ hallo, schönes Kind.

beautifully ['bjuːtɪfəlɪ] adv schön; warm, prepared, shine, simple herrlich, wunderbar; (well) sew, cook, sing, swim hervorragend, sehr gut, prima (inf). **that will do** ~ das ist ganz ausgezeichnet.

beautify ['bjuːtɪfaɪ] vt verschönern. **to** ~ **oneself** (hum) sich schönmachen (hum).

beauty ['bjuːtɪ] n **(a)** Schönheit f. ~ **is only skin-deep** (prov) der äußere Schein kann trügen; (referring to women also) ein schönes Gesicht hat schon manchen getäuscht (prov); ~ **is in the eye of the beholder** (Prov) schön ist, was (einem) gefällt. **(b)** (beautiful person) Schönheit f. **B**~ **and the Beast** die Schöne und das Tier. **(c)** (good example) Prachtexemplar nt. **isn't it a** ~! ist das nicht ein Prachtstück or Prachtexemplar? **(d)** (pleasing feature) **the** ~ **of it is that** ... das Schöne or Schönste daran ist, daß ...; **that's the** ~ **of it** das ist das Schöne daran; **one of the beauties of this job is** ... ist eine der schöne Seiten dieser Arbeit ist ...

beauty in cpds Schönheits-; ~ **competition** or **contest** n Schönheitswettbewerb m; ~ **parlour** n Schönheits- or Kosmetiksalon m; ~ **queen** n Schönheitskönigin f; ~ **sleep** n (hum) Schlaf m; ~ **specialist** n Kosmetiker(in f) m; ~ **spot** n **(a)** Schönheitsfleck m; (patch also) Schönheitspflästerchen nt; **(b)** (place) schönes or hübsches Fleckchen (Erde), schöner or hübscher Fleck; ~ **treatment** n kosmetische Behandlung.

beaver¹ ['biːvəʳ] n **(a)** Biber m. **to work like a** ~ wie ein Wilder/eine Wilde arbeiten; **be eager**. **(b)** (fur) Biber(pelz) m. **(c)** (hat) Biber- or Kastorhut m.

♦**beaver away** vi (inf) schuften (inf) (at an +dat).

beaver² n (of helmet) Kinnreff nt.

becalm [bɪˈkɑːm] vt (Naut) **to be** ~**ed** in eine Flaute geraten; **the ship lay** or **was** ~**ed for three weeks** das Schiff war or befand sich drei Wochen lang in einer Flaute.

became [bɪˈkeɪm] pret of **become**.

because [bɪˈkɒz] **1** conj weil; (since also) da. **it was the more surprising** ~ **we were not expecting it** es war um so überraschender, als wir es nicht erwarteten; **if I did it, it was** ~ **it had to be done** ich habe es nur getan, weil es getan werden mußte; ~ **if I am not wrong, he/I** ... weil er/ich, wenn ich mich nicht täusche, ...; **why did you do it?** — ~ (inf) warum or weshalb hast du das getan? — darum or deshalb.

2 prep ~ **of** wegen (+gen or (inf) dat); **I only did it** ~ **of you** ich habe es nur deinetwegen/Ihretwegen getan.

beck [bek] n **to be (completely) at sb's** ~ **and call** jdm voll und ganz zur Verfügung stehen; **I'm not at your** ~ **and call** du kannst doch nicht so einfach über mich verfügen; **his wife is completely at his** ~ **and call** seine Frau muß nach seiner Pfeife tanzen; **to have sb at one's** ~ **and call** jdn zur ständigen Verfügung haben, ganz über jdn verfügen können.

beckon ['bekən] vti winken. **he** ~**ed (to) her to follow (him)** er gab ihr ein Zeichen or winkte ihr, ihm zu folgen; **he** ~**ed me in/back/over** er winkte mich herein/zurück/herüber.

become [bɪˈkʌm] pret **became**, ptp ~ **1** vi **(a)** (grow to be) werden. **to** ~ **old/fat/tired** alt/dick/müde werden; **it has** ~ **a rule/habit/duty/custom/nuisance** es ist jetzt Vorschrift/es ist zur Gewohnheit geworden/es ist Pflicht/üblich/lästig geworden; **he's becoming a problem** er wird zum Problem; **to** ~ **accustomed to** sb/sth sich an jdn/etw gewöhnen; **to** ~ **interested in** sb/sth sich für jdn/etw zu interessieren. **(b)** (acquire position of) werden. **to** ~ **king/a doctor** König/Arzt werden. **(c)** **what has** ~ **of him?** was ist aus ihm geworden?; **what's to** ~ **of him?** was soll aus ihm werden?; **I don't know what will** ~ **of him** ich weiß nicht, was aus ihm noch werden soll.

2 vt **(a)** (suit) stehen (+dat). **(b)** (befit) sich schicken für, sich ziemen für (geh).

becoming [bɪˈkʌmɪŋ] adj **(a)** (suitable, fitting) schicklich. **it's not** ~ (for a lady) **to sit like that** es schickt sich (für eine Dame) nicht, so zu sitzen. **(b)** (flattering) vorteilhaft, kleidsam.

B Ed abbr of **Bachelor of Education**.

bed [bed] **1** n **(a)** Bett nt. **to go to** ~ zu or ins Bett gehen; **to put** or **get sb to** ~ jdn ins or zu Bett bringen; **to get into** ~ sich ins Bett legen; **he couldn't get her into** ~ with him er hat sie nicht ins Bett gekriegt (inf); **to go to** or **jump into** (inf) ~ **with sb** mit jdm ins Bett gehen or steigen (inf); **he must have got out of** ~ **on the wrong side** (inf) er ist wohl mit dem linken Fuß zuerst aufgestanden; **to be in** ~ im Bett sein; (through illness also) das Bett hüten müssen; **a** ~ **of nails** ein Nagelbrett nt; **life isn't always a** ~ **of roses** (prov) man ist im Leben nicht immer auf Rosen gebettet; **his life is not exactly a** ~ **of roses** er ist nicht gerade auf Rosen gebettet; **as you make your** ~ **so you must lie on it** (Prov) wie man sich bettet, so liegt man (Prov); **a** ~ **for the night** eine Übernachtungsmöglichkeit; **can I have a** ~ **for the night?** kann ich hier/bei euch etc übernachten?; **to put a**

newspaper to ~ (*Press*) eine Zeitung in Druck *or* zum Druck geben; **the paper has gone to ~** (*Press*) die Zeitung ist im Druck.
 (**b**) (*of ore*) Lager *nt*; (*of coal also*) Flöz *nt*; (*of building, road etc*) Unterbau *m*. **a ~ of clay** Lehmboden *m*.
 (**c**) (*base: of engine, lathe, machine*) Bett *nt*.
 (**d**) (*bottom*) (*sea ~*) Grund, Boden *m*; (*river ~*) Bett *nt*.
 (**e**) (*oyster ~, coral ~*) Bank *f*.
 (**f**) (*flower ~, vegetable ~*) Beet *nt*.
 2 *vt* (**a**) *plant* setzen, pflanzen.
 (**b**) (*old, hum: have sex with*) beschlafen (*old, hum*).
♦ **bed down 1** *vi* sein Lager aufschlagen. **~ for the night** sein Nachtlager aufschlagen. **2** *vt sep* (**a**) *person* das Bett machen (+*dat*); *child* schlafen legen. **the soldiers were ~ed ~ in the shed** die Soldaten hatten ihr (Nacht)quartier im Schuppen. (**b**) *animals* einstreuen (+*dat*).
♦ **bed in 1** *vt sep foundations* einlassen (*in +dat*); *machine* betten; *brakes* einfahren. **2** *vi* (*brakes*) eingefahren werden.
bed and breakfast *n* Zimmer *nt* mit Frühstück; (*also ~ place*) Frühstückspension *f*. "**~**" "Fremdenzimmer".
bedaub [bɪˈdɔːb] *vt* beschmieren; *face* anmalen, anschmieren.
bedazzle [bɪˈdæzl] *vt* blenden.
bed *in cpds* Bett-; **~-bath** *n* (Kranken)wäsche *f* im Bett; **to give sb a ~-bath** jdn im Bett waschen; **~-chamber** *n* (*old*) Schlafgemach *nt* (*old*); **~-clothes** *npl* Bettzeug *nt*; **to turn down the ~-clothes** das Bett aufdecken; **~-cover** *n* Bettdecke *f*.
bedding [ˈbedɪŋ] *n* (**a**) Bettzeug *nt*. (**b**) (*for horses*) Streu *f*.
bedding plant *n* Setzling *m*.
bedeck [bɪˈdek] *vt* schmücken.
bedevil [bɪˈdevl] *vt* komplizieren, erschweren. **~led by misfortune/bad luck** vom Schicksal/Pech verfolgt; **~led by injuries** von Verletzungen heimgesucht; **the tour/machine seemed to be ~led** die Tour/Maschine schien wie verhext.
bed: **~fellow** *n* **to be** *or* **make strange ~fellows** (*fig*) eine eigenartige Kombination *or* ein merkwürdiges Gespann sein; **~-head** *n* Kopfteil *m* des Bettes; **~-jacket** *n* Bettjäckchen *nt*.
bedlam [ˈbedləm] *n* (*fig: uproar*) Chaos *nt*. **the class was a regular ~** in der Klasse ging es zu wie im Irrenhaus.
bed-linen [ˈbedlɪnɪn] *n* Bettwäsche *f*.
Bedouin [ˈbeduɪn] **1** *n* Beduine *m*; Beduinin *f*. **2** *adj* beduinisch.
bed: **~-pan** *n* Bettpfanne *for* -schüssel *f*; **~post** *n* Bettpfosten *m*.
bedraggled [bɪˈdrægld] *adj* (*wet*) trief- *or* tropfnaß; (*dirty*) verdreckt; (*untidy*) *person, appearance* ungepflegt, schlampig.
bed-ridden [ˈbedrɪdn] *adj* bettlägerig.
bedrock [ˈbedrɒk] *n* (**a**) (*Geol*) Grundgebirge *or* -gestein *nt*. (**b**) (*fig*) **to get down to** *or* **to reach ~** zum Kern der Sache kommen.
bedroom [ˈbedruːm] *n* Schlafzimmer *nt*.
bedroom *in cpds* Schlafzimmer-; **~ slipper** *n* Hausschuh *m*.
Beds *abbr of* **Bedfordshire**.
beds *abbr of* **bedrooms** Zi.
bedside [ˈbedsaɪd] *n* **to be/sit at sb's ~** an jds Bett (*dat*) sein/sitzen.
bedside: **~ lamp** *n* Nachttischlampe *f*; **~ manner** *n* Art *f* mit Kranken umzugehen; **he has a good/bad ~ manner** er kann gut/nicht gut mit den Kranken umgehen; **~ rug** *n* Bettvorleger *m*; **~ table** *n* Nachttisch *m*.
bed: **~-sit(ter)** (*inf*), **~-sitting room** *n* (*Brit*) (**a**) (*rented*) möbliertes Zimmer; (**b**) Wohnschlafzimmer *nt*; (*for teenager etc*) Jugendzimmer *nt*; **~sock** *n* Bettschuh *m*; **~sore** *n* aufgelegene *or* wundgelegene Stelle; **to get ~sores** sich wund- *or* aufliegen; **~spread** *n* Tagesdecke *f*; **~stead** *n* Bettgestell *nt*; **~straw** *n* (*Bot*) Labkraut *nt*; **~time** *n* Schlafenszeit *f*; **it's ~time** es ist Schlafenszeit; **his ~time is 10 o'clock** er geht um 10 Uhr schlafen; **it's past your ~time** du müßtest schon lange im Bett sein; **~time story** *n* Gutenachtgeschichte *f*; **~-wetter** *n* Bettnässer(in *m*) *m*; **~-wetting** *n* Bettnässen *nt*.
bee [biː] *n* (**a**) Biene *f*. **like ~s round a honeypot** wie die Motten ums Licht; **to have a ~ in one's bonnet** (*inf*) einen Fimmel *or* Tick haben (*inf*); **to have a ~ in his bonnet about cleanliness** er hat einen Sauberkeitsfimmel (*inf*) *or* -tick (*inf*); **it's something of a ~ in his bonnet** das ist so ein Fimmel *or* Tick von ihm (*inf*).
 (**b**) (*sewing ~*) Kränzchen *nt*; (*competition*) Wettbewerb *m*.
beech [biːtʃ] *n* (**a**) (*tree*) Buche *f*. (**b**) (*wood*) Buche(nholz *nt*) *f*.
beech: **~ mast** *n* Bucheckern *pl*; **~nut** *n* Buchecker *f*; **~ tree** *n* Buche *f*; **~wood** *n* (**a**) (*material*) Buchenholz *nt*; (**b**) (*trees*) Buchenwald *m*.
beef [biːf] **1** *n* (**a**) (*meat*) Rindfleisch *nt*. **roast ~** Roastbeef *nt*.
 (**b**) (*inf*) (*flesh*) Speck *m* (*pej*); (*muscles*) Muskeln *pl*. **there's too much ~ on him** er ist zu massig; **to have plenty of ~** jede Menge Bizeps haben (*inf*); **you'd better get rid of some of this ~** du mußt ein bißchen abspecken (*inf*).
 2 *vi* (*inf: complain*) meckern (*inf*) (*about über +acc*). **what are you ~ing about?** was hast du zu meckern? (*inf*).
beef: **~burger** *n* Hamburger *m*; **~cake** *n*, *no pl* (*inf: male photos*) Männerfleisch *nt* (*hum*), Muskelprotze *pl*; **~ cattle** *npl* Schlachtvieh *pl*; **~eater** *n* (a) Beefeater *m*; (**b**) (*US inf*) Engländer(in *f*) *m*; **~ sausage** *n* Rindswürstchen *nt*; **~steak** *n* Beefsteak *nt*; **~ tea** *n* Kraft- *or* Fleischbrühe *f*.
beefy [ˈbiːfɪ] *adj* (+*er*) fleischig.
bee: **~hive** *n* (**a**) Bienenstock *m*; (*dome-shaped*) Bienenkorb *m*; (**b**) (*hairstyle*) toupierte Hochfrisur; **2** *adj* **~hive hairdo** toupierte Hochfrisur; **~keeper** *n* Bienenzüchter(in *f*), Imker(in *f*) *m*; **~-line** *n* **to make a ~-line for sb/sth** schnurstracks auf jdn/etw zugehen; **he made a ~-line for the food** er stürzte sich sofort auf das Essen.
been [biːn] *ptp of* **be**.
beep [biːp] (*inf*) **1** *n* Tut(tut) *nt* (*inf*). **2** *vt* **to ~ one's horn** hupen (*inf*). **3** *i* tuten (*inf*). **~!** tut, tut (*inf*).
beer [bɪəʳ] *n* Bier *nt*. **two ~s, please** zwei Bier, bitte; **life is not all ~ and skittles** das Leben ist nicht nur eitel Sonnenschein.

beer *in cpds* Bier-; **~-bottle** *n* Bierflasche *f*; **~ glass** *n* Bierglas *nt*; **~mat** *n* Bierfilz, Bierdeckel *m*; **~ money** *n* (*inf*) Geld *nt* für Getränke; **~-pull** *n* Zapfhahn *m*.
beery [ˈbɪərɪ] *adj* Bier-; *person* mit einer Bierfahne (*inf*); (*tipsy*) bierselig; *face* biergerötet. **to have ~ breath, to smell ~** eine Bierfahne haben (*inf*), nach Bier riechen.
beeswax [ˈbiːzwæks] *n* Bienenwachs *nt*.
beet [biːt] *n* Rübe, Bete (*form*) *f*.
beetle[1] [ˈbiːtl] *n* Käfer *m*.
♦ **beetle along** *vi* (*inf*) entlangpesen (*inf*); (*on foot also*) entlanghasten (*inf*).
♦ **beetle off** *vi* (*inf*) abschwirren (*inf*).
beetle[2] *n* (*tool*) Stampfer *m*; (*for paving, pile-driving also*) Ramme *f*.
beetle: **~-browed** *adj* mit buschigen, zusammengewachsenen Augenbrauen; **~ brows** *npl* buschige, zusammengewachsene Augenbrauen *pl*; **~-crushers** *npl* (*inf*) Elbkähne (*inf*), Kindersärge (*inf*) *pl*.
beetling [ˈbiːtlɪŋ] *adj cliffs* überhängend; *brows* buschig und zusammengewachsen.
beet: **~root** *n* rote Bete *or* Rübe; **~ sugar** *n* Rübenzucker *m*.
befall [bɪˈfɔːl] *pret* **befell** [bɪˈfel], *ptp* **befallen** [bɪˈfɔːlən] (*old, liter*) **1** *vi* sich begeben (*old*), sich zutragen. **2** *vt* widerfahren (+*dat*) (*geh*).
befit [bɪˈfɪt] *vt* (*form*) *sb* anstehen (+*dat*) (*geh*), sich ziemen für (*geh*); *occasion* angemessen sein (+*dat*), entsprechen (+*dat*). **it ill ~s him to speak thus** es steht ihm schlecht an *or* ziemt sich nicht für ihn, so zu reden (*geh*).
befitting [bɪˈfɪtɪŋ] *adj* gebührend, geziemend (*dated*). **~ for a lady** einer Dame geziemend (*dated*), für eine Dame schicklich.
befog [bɪˈfɒg] *vt* (*fig*) *issue* vernebeln; *person, mind* verwirren; (*alcohol, blow*) benebeln. **to be ~ged** (*person*) benebelt sein; (*issue*) verwirrt sein.
before [bɪˈfɔːʳ] **1** *prep* (**a**) (*earlier than*) vor (+*dat*). **the year ~** last/this vorletztes/letztes Jahr, das vorletzte/letzte Jahr; **the day ~ yesterday** vorgestern; **the day/time ~ that** der Tag/die Zeit davor; **I cannot do it ~ next week** vor nächster Woche kann ich es nicht machen; **~ Christ** (*abbr* BC) vor Christi Geburt (*abbr* v. Chr.); **I got/was here ~ you** ich war vor dir da; **that was ~ my time** das war vor meiner Zeit; **he died ~ his time** er ist früh gestorben; **to be ~ sb/sth** vor jdm/etw liegen; **~ then** vorher; **~ now** früher, eher, vorher; **you should have done it ~ now** das hättest du schon (eher) gemacht haben sollen; **~ long** bald; **~ everything** else zuallererst.
 (**b**) (*in order, rank*) vor (+*dat*). **to come ~ sb/sth** vor jdm/etw kommen; **I believe in honour ~ everything** die Ehre geht mir über alles, für mich ist die Ehre das Wichtigste; **ladies ~ gentlemen** Damen haben den Vortritt.
 (**c**) (*in position*) vor (+*dat*); (*with movement*) vor (+*acc*). **~ my (very) eyes** vor meinen Augen; **the question ~ us** (*with which we are confronted*) die Frage, vor der wir stehen; (*with which we are dealing*) die uns vorliegende Frage; **the task ~ us** (*with which we are confronted*) die Aufgabe, vor der wir stehen; (*which lies ahead of us*) die uns bevorstehende Aufgabe; **to sail ~ the wind** (*Naut*) vor dem Wind segeln.
 (**d**) (*in the presence of*) vor (+*dat*). **he said it ~ us all** er sagte das vor uns allen; **~ God/a lawyer** vor Gott/einem Anwalt; **to appear ~ a court/judge** vor Gericht/einem Richter erscheinen.
 (**e**) (*rather than*) **death ~ surrender** eher *or* lieber tot als sich ergeben; **he would die ~ betraying his country** er würde eher sterben als sein Land verraten.
 2 *adv* (**a**) (*in time*) (*~ that*) davor; (*at an earlier time, ~ now*) vorher. **have you been to Scotland ~?** waren Sie schon einmal in Schottland?; **I have seen/read etc this ~** ich habe das schon einmal gesehen/gelesen *etc*; **never ~** noch nie; **it has never happened ~** das ist noch nie passiert; (*on the evening/day ~* am Abend/Tag davor *or* zuvor *or* vorher; (*in the month/year ~* im Monat/Jahr davor; **two hours ~** zwei Stunden vorher; **two days ~** zwei Tage davor *or* zuvor; **to continue as ~** (*person*) (so) wie vorher weitermachen; **things/life continued as ~** alles war wie gehabt/das Leben ging seinen gewohnten Gang.
 (**b**) (*ahead*) **to march on ~** vorausmarschieren.
 (**c**) (*indicating order*) davor. **that chapter and the one ~** dieses Kapitel und das davor.
 3 *conj* (**a**) (*in time*) bevor. **~ doing sth** bevor man etw tut; **you can't go ~ this is done** du kannst erst gehen, wenn das gemacht ist; **it will be six weeks ~ the boat comes again** das Boot wird erst in sechs Wochen wieder kommen; **it will be a long time ~ he comes back** es wird lange dauern, bis er zurückkommt.
 (**b**) (*rather than*) **he will die ~ he surrenders** eher will er sterben als sich geschlagen geben.
beforehand [bɪˈfɔːhænd] *adv* im voraus. **you must tell me ~** Sie müssen mir vorher Bescheid sagen.
befoul [bɪˈfaʊl] *vt* (*liter: lit, fig*) besudeln; *atmosphere* verpesten.
befriend [bɪˈfrend] *vt* (*help*) sich annehmen (+*gen*); (*be friend to*) Umgang pflegen mit.
befuddle [bɪˈfʌdl] *vt* (**a**) (*make tipsy*) benebeln. (**b**) (*confuse*) durcheinanderbringen. **he is completely ~d** er ist völlig durcheinander (*inf*) *or* verwirrt *or* konfus; **I became ~d** ich war verwirrt.
beg [beg] **1** *vt* (**a**) *money, alms* betteln um.
 (**b**) (*crave, ask for*) *forgiveness, mercy, a favour* bitten um. **to ~ sth of sb** jdn um etw bitten; **he ~ged to be allowed to ...** er bat darum, ... zu dürfen; **the children ~ged me to let them go to the circus** die Kinder bettelten, ich solle sie in den Zirkus gehen lassen; **to ~ leave to do sth** um Erlaubnis bitten, etw zu tun dürfen; **I ~ leave to be dismissed** (*form*) gestatten Sie, daß ich mich entferne? (*form*); **I ~ to inform you ...** (*form*) ich erlaube mir, Sie davon in Kenntnis zu setzen ...; **I ~ to differ** ich erlaube mir, anderer Meinung zu sein; *see* **pardon**.

(c) (*entreat*) sb anflehen, inständig bitten. **I ~ you!** ich flehe dich an!
(d) to ~ the question an der eigentlichen Frage vorbeigehen.
2 *vi* **(a)** (*beggar*) betteln; (*dog*) Männchen machen.
(b) (*for help, time etc*) bitten (*for* um).
(c) (*entreat*) **to ~ of sb to do sth** jdn anflehen *or* inständig bitten, etw zu tun; **I ~ of you** ich bitte Sie.
(d) to go ~ging (*inf*) noch zu haben sein; (*to be unwanted*) keine Abnehmer finden.

began [bɪˈgæn] *pret of* **begin**.
beget [bɪˈget] *pret* **begot** *or* (*obs*) **begat** [bɪˈgæt], *ptp* **begotten** *or* **begot** *vt* **(a)** (*obs, Bibl*) zeugen; *see* **begotten. (b)** (*fig*) difficulties etc zeugen (*geh*).
beggar [ˈbegəʳ] **1** *n* **(a)** Bettler(in *f*) *m.* **~s can't be choosers** (*prov*) wer arm dran ist, kann nicht wählerisch sein; **oh well, ~s can't be choosers!** na ja, in der Not frißt der Teufel Fliegen (*prov*).
(b) (*inf*) Kerl *m* (*inf*). **poor ~!** armer Tropf *or* Kerl! (*inf*), armes Schwein! (*sl*); **a lucky ~** ein Glückspilz *m*; **a funny little ~** ein drolliges Kerlchen; (*girl*) ein drolliger Fratz.
2 *vt* **(a)** an den Bettelstab bringen.
(b) (*fig*) **to ~ description** jeder Beschreibung (*gen*) spotten.
beggarly [ˈbegəlɪ] *adj* kümmerlich.
beggar: **~man** *n* (*old*) Bettler, Bettelmann (*old*) *m*; **~-my-** *or* **-your-neighbour** *n* (*Cards*) Kartenspiel *nt*, *bei dem der gewinnt, der zum Schluß alle Karten hat*; **~ woman** *n* (*old*) Bettlerin, Bettelfrau (*old*) *f*.
beggary [ˈbegərɪ] *n* Bettelarmut *f*; (*beggars*) Bettler *pl*, Bettelvolk *nt*. **to have been reduced to ~** bettelarm sein.
begin [bɪˈgɪn] *pret* **began**, *ptp* **begun 1** *vt* **(a)** (*start*) beginnen, anfangen; *conversation also* anknüpfen; *song also* anstimmen; *bottle* anbrechen, anfangen; *book, letter, new cheque book, new page* anfangen; *rehearsals, work* anfangen mit; *task* in Angriff nehmen, sich machen an (+*acc*). **to ~ to do sth** *or* **doing sth** anfangen *or* beginnen, etw zu tun; **to ~ working** *or* **to work on sth** mit der Arbeit an etw (*dat*) anfangen *or* beginnen, anfangen *or* beginnen, an etw (*dat*) zu arbeiten; **to ~ an attack** zum Angriff schreiten; **when did you ~ (learning** *or* **to learn) English?** wann haben Sie angefangen, Englisch zu lernen?; **she ~s the job next week** sie fängt nächste Woche (bei der Stelle) an; **he began his speech by saying that ...** er leitete seine Rede damit *or* mit den Worten ein, daß ...; **to ~ school** eingeschult werden, in die Schule kommen; **to ~ life as a ... als ...** anfangen *or* beginnen; **she began to feel tired** sie wurde allmählich *or* langsam müde; **she's ~ning to understand** sie fängt langsam an zu verstehen, sie versteht so langsam; **his mother began to fear the worst** seine Mutter befürchtete schon das Schlimmste; **I'd begun to think you weren't coming** ich habe schon gedacht, du kommst nicht mehr; **that doesn't even ~ to compare with ...** das läßt sich nicht mal annähernd mit ... vergleichen; **they didn't even ~ to solve the problem** sie haben das Problem nicht mal annähernd gelöst; **I couldn't even ~ to count the mistakes** ich konnte die Fehler überhaupt nicht zählen; **I can't ~ to think what would have happened** es ist nicht auszudenken *or* ich darf überhaupt nicht daran denken, was passiert wäre. **I can't ~ to thank you for what you've done** ich kann Ihnen gar nicht genug dafür danken, was Sie getan haben; **I can't ~ to imagine what it'll be like** ich kann mir überhaupt nicht vorstellen, wie das sein wird.
(b) (*initiate, originate*) anfangen; *fashion, custom, policy* einführen; *society, firm, movement* gründen; (*cause*) war auslösen. **he/that began the rumour** er hat das Gerücht in die Welt gesetzt/dadurch entstand das Gerücht.
(c) (*start to speak*) anfangen, beginnen. **it's late, he began** es ist spät, begann *or* fing *or* hub (*old*) er an.
2 *vi* **(a)** (*start*) anfangen, beginnen; (*new play etc*) anlaufen. **to ~ by doing sth** etw zuerst (einmal) tun; **he began by saying that ...** er sagte eingangs *or* einleitend, daß ...; **where the hair ~s** am Haaransatz; **before October ~s** vor Anfang Oktober; **to ~ in business/teaching** ins Geschäftsleben eintreten/zu unterrichten anfangen *or* beginnen; **~ning from Monday** ab Montag, von Montag an; **~ning from page 10** von Seite 10 an; **say your names ~ning from the back** nennen Sie Ihre Namen von hinten nach vorn; **it all/the trouble began when ...** es fing alles/der Ärger fing damit an, daß ...; **to ~ with sb/sth** mit jdm/etw anfangen; **~ with me** fangen Sie bei *or* mit mir an; **he began with the intention of writing a thesis** anfänglich wollte er eine Doktorarbeit schreiben; **to ~ with there were only three** anfänglich waren es nur drei; **this is wrong to ~ with** das ist schon einmal falsch; **to ~ with, this is wrong, and ...** erstens einmal ist das falsch, dann ...; **to ~ on sth** mit etw anfangen *or* beginnen; **to ~ on a new venture/project** ein neues Unternehmen/Projekt in Angriff nehmen; **to ~ on a new bottle** eine neue Flasche anbrechen *or* anfangen.
(b) (*come into being*) beginnen, anfangen; (*custom*) entstehen; (*river*) entspringen. **since the world began** seit (An)beginn *or* Anfang der Welt; **when did this movement ~?** seit wann gibt es diese Bewegung?
beginner [bɪˈgɪnəʳ] *n* Anfänger(in *f*) *m*. **~'s luck** Anfängerglück *nt.*
beginning [bɪˈgɪnɪŋ] *n* **(a)** (*act of starting*) Anfang *m*. **to make a ~** einen Anfang machen.
(b) (*place, of book etc*) Anfang *m*; (*temporal also*) Beginn *m*; (*of river*) Ursprung *m*. **at the ~** anfänglich, zuerst; **at the ~ of sth** am Anfang *or* (*temporal also*) zu Beginn einer Sache (*gen*); **in the ~** (*time*) the world over der Anbeginn *or* Anfang der Welt; **in the ~** (*Bibl*) am Anfang; **from the ~** von Anfang an; **from the ~ of the week/poem** seit Anfang *or* Beginn der Woche/vom Anfang des Gedichtes an; **read the paragraph from the ~** lesen Sie den Paragraphen von (ganz) vorne; **from ~ to end** von vorn bis hinten; (*temporal*) von Anfang bis Ende; **to start again at** *or* **from the ~** noch einmal von vorn anfangen; **to begin at the ~** ganz vorn anfangen; **the ~ of negotiations** der Beginn der Verhandlungen, der Verhandlungsbeginn.
(c) (*origin*) Anfang *m*; (*of custom, movement*) Entstehen *nt* **no pl. the shooting was the ~ of the rebellion** die Schießerei bedeutete den Beginn *or* Anfang der Rebellion; **it was the ~ of the end for him** das war der Anfang vom Ende für ihn; **Nazism had its ~s in Germany** der Nazismus hatte seine Anfänge *or* seinen Ursprung in Deutschland; **the ~s of science** die Anfangsgründe der Naturwissenschaft.
begone [bɪˈgɒn] *vi imper and infin only* (*old*) **~!** fort (mit dir/ Ihnen); (*esp Rel*) weiche; **they bade him ~** sie befahlen ihm, sich fortzuscheren.
begonia [bɪˈgəʊnɪə] *n* Begonie *f*.
begot [bɪˈgɒt] *pret, ptp of* **beget.**
begotten [bɪˈgɒtn] *ptp of* **beget. the only ~ son** der eingeborene Sohn.
begrime [bɪˈgraɪm] *vt* beschmutzen.
begrudge [bɪˈgrʌdʒ] *vt* **(a)** (*be reluctant*) **to ~ doing sth** etw widerwillig tun.
(b) (*envy*) mißgönnen (*sb sth* jdm etw). **no one ~s you your good fortune** wir gönnen dir ja dein Glück; **he ~s him the air he breathes** er gönnt ihm das Salz in der Suppe nicht.
(c) (*give unwillingly*) nicht gönnen (*sb sth* jdm etw). **I wouldn't ~ you the money** ich würde dir das Geld ja gönnen; **I shan't ~ you £5** du sollst die £ 5 haben.
begrudging *adj*, **~ly** *adv* [bɪˈgrʌdʒɪŋ, -lɪ] widerwillig.
beguile [bɪˈgaɪl] *vt* **(a)** (*deceive*) betören (*geh*). **to ~ sb into doing sth** jdn dazu verführen, etw zu tun. **(b)** (*charm*) *person* betören; (*liter*) *time* sich (*dat*) angenehm vertreiben.
beguiling [bɪˈgaɪlɪŋ] *adj* betörend, verführerisch.
begun [bɪˈgʌn] *ptp of* **begin.**
behalf [bɪˈhɑːf] *n* **on** *or* (*US also*) **in ~ of** für, im Interesse von; (*as spokesman*) im Namen von; (*as authorized representative*) im Auftrag von; **I'm not asking on my own ~** ich bitte nicht für mich selbst *or* in meinem eigenen Interesse darum.
behave [bɪˈheɪv] **1** *vi* sich verhalten; (*people also*) sich benehmen; (*children also*) sich betragen, sich benehmen; (*be good*) sich benehmen. **to ~ well/badly** sich gut/schlecht benehmen; **what a way to ~!** was für ein Benehmen!; **to ~ shamefully/badly/well towards sb** jdn schändlich/schlecht/gut behandeln; **to ~ like an honest man** wie ein ehrlicher Mensch handeln; **to ~ very wisely** sich sehr klug verhalten; **~! benimm dich!; can't you make your son/dog ~?** kannst du deinem Sohn/ Hund keine Manieren beibringen?; **he knows how to ~ at a cocktail party** er weiß sich bei Cocktailpartys zu benehmen; **the car ~s well/badly at high speeds** das Auto zeigt bei hoher Geschwindigkeit ein gutes/schlechtes Fahrverhalten; **how is your car behaving these days?** wie fährt dein Auto zur Zeit?
2 *vr* **to ~ oneself** sich benehmen; **~ yourself!** benimm dich!; **can't you make your son/dog ~ himself/itself?** kannst du deinem Sohn/Hund keine Manieren beibringen?
behaviour, (*US*) **behavior** [bɪˈheɪvjəʳ] *n* **(a)** (*manner, bearing*) Benehmen *nt*; (*esp of children also*) Betragen *nt*. **to be on one's best ~** sich von seiner besten Seite zeigen, sein bestes Benehmen an den Tag legen.
(b) (*towards others*) Verhalten *nt* (*to(wards*) gegenüber).
(c) (*of car, machine*) Verhalten *nt*.
behavioural, (*US*) **behavioral** [bɪˈheɪvjərəl] *adj* Verhaltens-. **~ science/scientist** Verhaltensforschung *f*/-forscher *m*.
behaviourism, (*US*) **behaviorism** [bɪˈheɪvjərɪzəm] *n* Behaviorismus *m*.
behaviourist, (*US*) **behaviorist** [bɪˈheɪvjərɪst] **1** *n* Behaviorist *m.* **2** *adj* behavioristisch.
behead [bɪˈhed] *vt* enthaupten, köpfen.
beheld [bɪˈheld] *prep, ptp of* **behold.**
behest [bɪˈhest] *n* (*liter*) Geheiß *nt* (*liter*). **at his ~/the ~ of his uncle** auf sein Geheiß (*liter*)/auf Geheiß seines Onkels (*liter*).
behind [bɪˈhaɪnd] **1** *prep* **(a)** (*in or at the rear of*) (*stationary*) hinter (+*dat*); (*with motion*) hinter (+*acc*). **come out from ~ the door** komm hinter der Tür (her)vor; **he came up ~ me** er trat von hinten an mich heran; **walk close ~ me** gehen Sie dicht hinter mir; **put it ~ the books** stellen Sie es hinter die Bücher; **he has the Communists ~ him** er hat die Kommunisten hinter sich (*dat*); **an idea eine Idee unterstützen; what is ~ this/this incident?** was steckt dahinter/steckt hinter diesem Vorfall?; **self-interest was** *or* **lay ~ her offer** hinter ihrem Angebot verbarg sich *or* steckte Eigennutz.
(b) (*more backward than*) **to be ~ sb** hinter jdm zurücksein.
(c) (*in time*) **to be ~ time** (*train etc*) Verspätung haben; (*with work etc*) im Rückstand sein; **to be ~ schedule** im Verzug sein; **to be three hours ~ time** drei Stunden Verspätung haben; **to be ~ the times** (*fig*) hinter seiner Zeit zurück(geblieben) sein; **you must put the past ~ you** Sie müssen Vergangenes vergangen sein lassen, Sie müssen die Vergangenheit begraben; **their youth is far ~ them** ihre Jugend liegt weit zurück.
2 *adv* **(a)** (*in or at rear*) hinten; (*~ this, sb etc*) dahinter. **the runner was (lying) a long way ~** der Läufer lag weit hinten *or* zurück; **from ~** von hinten; **to look ~** zurückblicken; **to stand ~** (*be standing*) dahinter stehen; (*position oneself*) sich dahinter stellen; *see vbs.*
(b) (*late*) **to be ~ with one's studies/payments** mit seinen Studien/Zahlungen im Rückstand sein; **we are three days ~ with the schedule** wir sind drei Tage im Rückstand *or* Verzug.
3 *n* (*inf*) Hinterteil *nt* (*inf*), Hintern *m* (*inf*).
behindhand [bɪˈhaɪndhænd] *adv, adj* **(a)** (*late*) **to be ~** Verspätung haben. **(b)** (*in arrears*) **to be ~ with sth** mit etw im Rückstand *or* Verzug sein.
behold [bɪˈhəʊld] *pret, ptp* **beheld** *vt* (*liter*) sehen, erblicken (*liter*). **~!** und siehe (da); (*Rel*) siehe; **~ thy servant** siehe deinen Diener.

beholden [bɪ'həʊldən] adj (liter): to be ~ to sb for sth jdm für etw verpflichtet sein (geh).

behove, (US) **behoove** [bɪ'həʊv] vt impers (form) sich geziemen (geh) (sb to do sth für jdn, etw zu tun).

beige [beɪʒ] 1 adj beige. 2 n Beige nt.

being [bi:ɪŋ] n (a) (existence) Dasein, Leben nt. to come into ~ entstehen; (club etc also) ins Leben gerufen werden; to bring into ~ ins Leben rufen, (er)schaffen; then in ~ damals bestehend. (b) (that which exists) (Lebe)wesen, Geschöpf nt. (c) (essence) Wesen nt.

bejewelled, (US) **bejeweled** [bɪ'dʒu:əld] adj mit Edelsteinen geschmückt. ~ with sequins mit Pailletten besetzt; ~ with dew/stars (poet) mit glitzernden Tautropfen besät/~sternenbesät (poet).

belabour, (US) **belabor** [bɪ'leɪbəʳ] vt (a) einschlagen auf (+acc). (b) (fig: with insults etc) überhäufen; (with questions) beschießen, bearbeiten.

belated adj, **~ly** adv [bɪ'leɪtɪd, -lɪ] verspätet.

belay [bɪ'leɪ] (Naut) 1 vt belegen, festmachen; (Mountaineering) sichern. 2 interj ~ there aufhören.

belaying pin [bɪ'leɪɪŋpɪn] n (Naut) Belegklampe f; (Mountaineering) (Kletter)haken m.

belch [beltʃ] 1 vi (person) rülpsen, aufstoßen; (volcano) Lava speien or ausstoßen; (smoke, fire) herausquellen. 2 vt (also ~ forth or out) smoke, flames (aus)speien, ausstoßen. 3 n (a) Rülpser m (inf). (b) (of smoke etc) Stoß m.

beleaguer [bɪ'li:gəʳ] vt belagern; (fig) umgeben.

belfry [belfrɪ] n Glockenstube f; see bell[1].

Belgian [beldʒən] 1 n Belgier(in f) m. 2 adj belgisch.

Belgium [beldʒəm] n Belgien nt.

belie [bɪ'laɪ] vt (a) (prove false) words, proverb Lügen strafen, widerlegen. (b) (give false impression of) hinwegtäuschen über (+acc). (c) (fail to justify) hopes enttäuschen.

belief [bɪ'li:f] n (a) Glaube m (in an +acc). it is beyond ~ es ist unglaublich or nicht zu glauben; a statement unworthy of your ~ (form) eine Aussage, der Sie keinen Glauben schenken sollten. (b) (Rel: faith) Glaube m; (doctrine) (Glaubens)lehre f. (c) (convinced opinion) Überzeugung f, Glaube m no pl. what are the ~s of the average citizen today? woran glaubt der heutige Durchschnittsbürger?; in the ~ that ... im Glauben, daß ...; acting in this ~ in gutem Glauben, im guten Glauben; it is my ~ that ... ich bin der Überzeugung, daß ...; it is some of my ~s that ... es ist meine Überzeugung, daß ...; yes, that is my ~ ich glaube schon; it is the best of my ~ meines Wissens. (d) no pl (trust) Glaube m (in an +acc). to have ~ in glauben an (+acc).

believable [bɪ'li:vəbl] adj glaubhaft, glaubwürdig. hardly ~ wenig glaubhaft.

believe [bɪ'li:v] 1 vt (a) sth glauben; sb glauben (+dat). I don't ~ you das glaube ich (Ihnen) nicht; don't ~ him, he's a liar glauben Sie ihm doch nicht, er lügt; don't you ~ it wer's glaubt, wird selig (inf); it's true, please ~ me es stimmt, bitte glauben Sie mir das; ~ me, I mean it glauben Sie mir, es ist mir ernst; ~ you me! (inf) das können Sie mir glauben!; ~ it or not ob Sie's glauben oder nicht; would you ~ it! (inf) ist das (denn) die Möglichkeit (inf); I would never have ~d it of him das hätte ich ihm nie zugetraut, das hätte ich nie von ihm geglaubt; he could hardly ~ his eyes/ears er traute seinen Augen/Ohren nicht; if he is to be ~d wenn man ihm glauben darf or Glauben schenken kann. (b) (think) glauben. he is ~d to be ill es heißt, daß er krank ist; I ~ so/not ich glaube schon/nicht; see make-believe. 2 vi (have a religious faith) an Gott glauben. you must ~! Sie müssen glauben!

♦**believe in** vi +prep obj (a) God, ghosts glauben an (+acc). (b) (have trust in) promises glauben an (+acc); method also Vertrauen haben zu. the boss/his mother still ~s ~ him der Chef/seine Mutter glaubt immer noch an ihn; please trust me, ~ ~ me bitte haben Sie Vertrauen zu mir; he doesn't ~ ~ medicine/doctors er hält nicht viel von Medikamenten/Ärzten. (c) (support idea of) to ~ ~ sth (prinzipiell) für etw sein; he ~s ~ getting up early/giving people a second chance er ist überzeugter Frühaufsteher/er gibt prinzipiell jedem noch einmal eine Chance; I don't ~ ~ compromises ich halte nichts von Kompromissen, ich bin gegen Kompromisse.

believer [bɪ'li:vəʳ] n (a) (Rel) Gläubige(r) mf. (b) to be a (firm) ~ in sth (grundsätzlich) für etw sein; I'm a ~ in doing things properly ich bin grundsätzlich der Meinung, daß man, was man macht, richtig machen sollte; he's a (firm)/not much of a ~ in getting up early er ist überzeugter Frühaufsteher/er hält nicht viel vom Frühaufstehen.

Belisha beacon [bɪ'li:ʃə'bi:kən] n gelbes Blinklicht an Zebrastreifen.

belittle [bɪ'lɪtl] vt herabsetzen, heruntermachen (inf); achievement also schmälern. to ~ oneself sich schlechter machen, als man ist.

belittlement [bɪ'lɪtlmənt] n see vt Herabsetzung f; Schmälerung f.

bell[1] [bel] 1 n (a) Glocke f; (small: on toys, pet's collar etc) Glöckchen nt, Schelle f; (school~, door~, of cycle) Klingel, Glocke (dated) f; (hand~ also) Schelle f (of typewriter, Telec) Klingel f. as sound as a ~ kerngesund. (b) (sound of) Läuten nt; (of door~, school~, telephone) Klingeln nt; (in athletics) Glocke f zur letzten Runde. there's the ~ es klingelt or läutet; was that the ~? hat es gerade geklingelt or geläutet?; the teacher came in on the ~ der Lehrer kam mit dem Klingeln or Läuten herein; he's coming up to the ~ er geht nun in die letzte Runde; it was 3.02 at the ~ zu Beginn der letzten Runde hatte es eine Zeit von 3.02. (c) (Naut) Schiffsglocke f; (ringing) Läuten nt (der Schiffsglocke); (for time also) Glasen nt (spec). it is eight ~s es ist acht Glas (spec); to ring one ~ einmal glasen (spec). (d) (of flower) Glocke f, Kelch m; (of trumpet) Stürze f; (of loudspeaker) (Schall)trichter m.

bell[2] n (of stag) Röhren nt. 2 vi röhren.

belladonna [,belə'dɒnə] n (Bot) Tollkirsche, Belladonna f; (Med) Belladonin nt.

bell: ~-bottomed trousers, ~-bottoms npl ausgestellte Hosen; ~-boy n (esp US) Page, Hoteljunge m.

belle [bel] n Schöne, Schönheit f. the ~ of the ball die Ballkönigin.

bell: ~ heather n Glockenheide f; ~ hop n (US) see ~-boy.

bellicose ['belɪkəʊs] adj nation, mood kriegerisch, kriegslustig; (pugnacious) kampflustig, streitsüchtig.

bellicosity [,belɪ'kɒsɪtɪ] n see adj Kriegslust f; Kampf(es)lust, Streitsüchtigkeit f.

belligerence, belligerency [bɪ'lɪdʒərəns, -sɪ] n see adj (a) Kriegslust, Kampf(es)lust f; Streitlust, Kampf(es)lust f; Aggressivität f.

belligerent [bɪ'lɪdʒərənt] 1 adj (a) nation kriegslustig, kampflustig, kriegerisch; person, attitude streitlustig, kampflustig; speech aggressiv. (b) (waging war) kriegführend, streitend. ~ power Streitmacht f. 2 n (nation) kriegführendes Land; (person) Streitende(r) mf.

bell-jar ['beldʒɑːʳ] n (Glas)glocke f.

bellow ['beləʊ] 1 vi (animal, person) brüllen; (singing also) grölen (inf). to ~ at sb jdn anbrüllen. 2 vt (also ~ out) brüllen; song also grölen (inf). 3 n Brüllen nt.

bellows ['beləʊz] npl Blasebalg m. a pair of ~ ein Blasebalg.

bell: ~-pull n Klingelzug m; ~-push n Klingel f; ~-ringer n Glöckner m; ~-ringing n Glockenläuten nt; ~-rope n (in church) Glockenstrang m; (in house) Klingelzug m; ~-shaped adj glockenförmig, kelchförmig; ~-tent n Rundzelt nt; ~-wether n Leithammel m.

belly ['belɪ] n (general) Bauch m; (of violin etc) Decke f.

♦**belly out** 1 vt sep sails blähen, schwellen lassen. 2 vi (sails) sich blähen, schwellen.

belly: ~-ache 1 n (inf) Bauchweh nt (inf), Bauchschmerzen pl; 2 vi (inf: complain) murren (about über +acc); ~-aching n (inf) Murren, Gemurre nt; ~ button n (inf) Bauchnabel m; ~ dance n Bauchtanz m; ~ dancer n Bauchtänzerin f; ~-flop n; to do a ~ flop einen Bauchplatscher machen (inf).

bellyful ['belɪfʊl] n (a) (sl: more than enough) I've had a ~ of him/writing these letters ich habe die Nase voll von ihm/davon, immer diese Briefe zu schreiben (inf). (b) (inf: of food) after a good ~ of beans nachdem ich mir/er sich etc den Bauch mit Bohnen vollgeschlagen hatte (inf).

belly: ~-land vi (inf) bauchlanden; ~-landing n Bauchlandung f; ~ laugh n dröhnendes Lachen; he gave a great ~ laugh er lachte lauthals los.

belong [bɪ'lɒŋ] vi (a) (be the property of) gehören (to sb jdm). who does it ~ to? wem gehört es?; the parks ~ to everybody die Parkanlagen sind für alle da. (b) (be part of) gehören (to zu); (to town: person) gehören (to nach), sich zuhause fühlen (to in +dat). to ~ together zusammengehören; the lid ~s to this box der Deckel gehört zu dieser Schachtel; to ~ to a club einem Club angehören; why don't you ~? warum sind Sie nicht Mitglied?; attributes which ~ to people Attribute, die sich auf Personen beziehen; concepts that ~ to physics Begriffe, die in die Physik gehören. (c) (be in right place) gehören. I don't ~ here ich gehöre nicht hierher, ich bin hier fehl am Platze; to feel that one doesn't ~ das Gefühl haben, daß man fehl am Platze ist or daß man nicht dazugehört; you don't ~ here, so scram Sie haben hier nichts zu suchen, also verschwinden Sie; the vase ~s on the mantelpiece die Vase gehört auf den Sims; animals don't ~ in cages Tiere gehören nicht in Käfige; where does this one ~? wo gehört das hin?; that doesn't ~ to my area of responsibility das gehört nicht in meinen Verantwortungsbereich; it ~s under the heading of ... das gehört or fällt in die Rubrik der ... (d) this case ~s to the Appeal Court dieser Fall gehört vor das Appellationsgericht; that doesn't ~ to this department das gehört nicht in diese Abteilung.

belongings [bɪ'lɒŋɪŋz] npl Sachen pl, Besitz m, Habe f (geh). personal ~ persönliches Eigentum, persönlicher Besitz; all his ~ sein ganzes Hab und Gut.

beloved [bɪ'lʌvɪd] 1 adj geliebt; memory ~ lieb, teuer. 2 n Geliebte(r) mf. dearly ~ (Rel) liebe Brüder und Schwestern im Herrn.

below [bɪ'ləʊ] 1 prep (a) (under) unterhalb (+gen); (with line, level etc also) unter (+dat or with motion +acc). on it and ~ it darauf und darunter; her skirt comes well ~ her knees ihr Rock geht bis weit unters Knie; Naples is ~ Rome (on the map) Neapel liegt unterhalb Roms; the ship/sun disappeared ~ the horizon das Schiff/die Sonne verschwand hintern Horizont; to be ~ sb (in rank) (rangmäßig) unter jdm stehen. (b) (downstream from) unterhalb (+gen), nach. (c) (unworthy of) or is that ~ you? oder ist das unter Ihrer Würde?

2 adv (a) (lower down) unten. the cows in the valley ~ die Kühe drunten im Tal; they live one floor ~ sie wohnen ein Stockwerk tiefer; the tenants/flat ~ die Mieter/die Wohnung darunter; (below us) die Mieter/Wohnung unter uns; write the name here with the address ~ schreiben Sie den Namen hierher und die Adresse darunter; in the class ~ in der Klasse darunter; (below me) in der Klasse unter mir; what's the next rank ~? was ist der nächstniedere Rang? (b) (Naut) unter Deck. to go ~ unter Deck gehen.

(c) (*in documents*) (weiter) unten. see ~ siehe unten.
(d) 15 degrees ~ 15 Grad unter Null, 15 Grad minus.
(e) (*on earth*) here ~ hier unten; **and on earth** ~ (*Bibl*) und unten auf der Erde; **down** ~ (*in hell*) dort drunten.

Belshazzar [bel'ʃæzəʳ] *n* Belsazar *m*. **~'s Feast** Belsazars Gastmahl.

belt [belt] **1** *n* **(a)** (*on clothes*) Gürtel *m*; (*for holding, carrying etc, seat*~) Gurt *m*; (*Mil etc: on uniform*) Koppel, Gehenk *nt*; (*Mil: for cartridges*) Patronengurt *m*; (*shoulder-gun*~) (Gewehr)riemen *m*. **a blow below the** ~ (*lit, fig*) ein Schlag *m* unterhalb der Gürtellinie, ein Tiefschlag *m*; **to hit below the** ~ (*lit, fig*) (*person*) jdm einen Schlag unter die Gürtellinie or einen Tiefschlag versetzen; **that was below the** ~ das war ein Schlag unter die Gürtellinie; **to be a Black B**~ den Schwarzen Gürtel haben; **to get the** ~ (mit dem Lederriemen) eine auf die Finger bekommen; **to tighten one's** ~ (*fig*) (sich *dat*) den Riemen enger schnallen; **under one's** ~ (*fig inf*) auf dem Rücken (*inf*).
(b) (*Tech*) (Treib)riemen *m*; (*conveyor* ~) Band *nt*. ~ **drive** Riemenantrieb *m*.
(c) (*tract of land*) Gürtel *m*. ~ **of trees** Waldstreifen *m*; (*around house etc*) Baumgürtel *m*; **industrial** ~ Industriegürtel *m*; see commuter.
(d) (*inf: hit*) Schlag *m*. **to give sb/the ball a** ~ jdm eine knallen (*inf*)/den Ball knallen (*inf*).
(e) (*US: ringroad*) Umgehungsstraße *f*.
(f) (*US sl: drink*) Schluck *m* aus der Pulle (*inf*).
2 *vt* **(a)** (*fasten*) den Gürtel zumachen (*sth gen*). **he** ~**ed his raincoat** er machte den Gürtel seines Regenmantels zu.
(b) (*Sch etc: thrash*) (mit dem Lederriemen) schlagen (*inf*).
(c) (*inf: hit*) knallen (*inf*). **she** ~**ed him one in the eye** sie verpaßte or haute or knallte ihm eins aufs Auge (*inf*).
3 *vi* (*inf: rush*) rasen (*inf*). **to** ~ **out** hinaus-/herausrasen (*inf*); **to** ~ **across** hinüber-/herüberrasen (*inf*); **we were really** ~**ing along** wir sind wirklich gerast (*inf*); **he** ~**ed off down the street** er raste davon die Straße hinunter (*inf*); **this novel really** ~**s along** dieser Roman ist wirklich tempogeladen (*inf*).
♦ **belt on** *vt sep* sword umschnallen, sich umgürten mit (*geh*); raincoat anziehen.
♦ **belt out** *vt sep* (*inf*) tune schmettern (*inf*); *rhythm* voll herausbringen (*inf*); (*on piano*) hämmern (*inf*).
♦ **belt up 1** *vt sep* jacket den Gürtel (+*gen*) zumachen. **2** *vi* **(a)** (*inf*) die Klappe (*inf*) or Schnauze (*sl*) halten; (*stop making noise*) mit dem Krach aufhören (*inf*). **(b)** (*hum: put seat-belt on*) sich anschnallen.

belting ['beltɪŋ] *n* (*inf*) Dresche *f* (*inf*). **to give sb a good** ~ jdn ganz schön verdreschen (*inf*).

bemoan [bɪ'məʊn] *vt* beklagen.

bemused [bɪ'mjuːzd] *adj* (*puzzled*) verwirrt; (*preoccupied*) look abwesend.

bench [bentʃ] **1** *n* **(a)** (*seat*) Bank *f*. **laughter from the government** ~**es** Gelächter von der Regierungsbank.
(b) (*Jur: office of a judge*) Richteramt *nt*; (*judges generally*) Richter *pl*; (*court*) Gericht *nt*. **member of the** ~ Richter *m*; **to be raised to the** ~ zum Richter bestellt werden; **to be on the** ~ (*permanent office*) Richter sein; (*when in court*) der Richter sein, auf dem Richterstuhl sitzen (*geh*).
(c) (*work* ~) Werkbank *f*; (*in lab*) Experimentiertisch *m*.
2 *vt* (*US Sport*) auf die Strafbank schicken; (*keep as substitute*) auf die Reservebank setzen.

bench mark *n* (*Surv*) Höhenfestpunkt *m*; (*fig*) Maßstab *m*.

bend [bend] (*vb: pret, ptp* bent) **1** *n* **(a)** (*in river, tube, etc*) Krümmung, Biegung *f*; (*90°*) Knie *nt*; (*in road also*) Kurve *f*. **there is a** ~ **in the road** die Straße macht (da) eine Kurve; ~**s for 3 miles** 3 Meilen kurvenreiche Strecke; **don't park on the** ~ parken Sie nicht in der Kurve; **to go/be round the** ~ (*inf*) durchdrehen (*inf*), verrückt werden/sein (*inf*); **to drive sb round the** ~ (*inf*) jdn verrückt or wahnsinnig machen (*inf*).
(b) (*knot*) Stek *m*.
(c) (*Her*) ~ **sinister** Schräglinksbalken *m*.
2 *vt* **(a)** (*curve, make angular*) biegen; *rod, rail, pipe also* krümmen; *bow* spannen; *arm, knee also* beugen; *leg, arm also* anwinkeln; (*forwards*) back also beugen, krümmen; head beugen, neigen. **he can** ~ **an iron bar with his teeth** er kann mit den Zähnen eine Eisenstange verbiegen; **to** ~ **sth at right angles** etw rechtwinklig abbiegen or abknicken; **to** ~ **sth out of shape** etw verbiegen; **the bumper got bent in the crash** die Stoßstange hat sich bei dem Zusammenstoß verbogen; **on** ~**ed knees** auf Knien (*fig also*) kniefällig; **to go down on** ~**ed knees** auf die Knie fallen; (*fig also*) einen Kniefall machen.
(b) (*fig*) rules frei auslegen. **to** ~ **the law** das Gesetz beugen; **to** ~ **sb to one's will** sich (*dat*) jdn gefügig machen.
(c) (*direct*) one's steps, efforts lenken, richten.
(d) (*Naut*) sail befestigen.
3 *vi* **(a)** sich biegen; (*pipe, rail also*) sich krümmen; (*forwards also*) (*tree, corn etc*) sich neigen; (*person*) sich beugen. **this metal** ~**s easily** (*a bad thing*) dieses Metall verbiegt sich leicht; (*a good thing*) dieses Metall läßt sich leicht biegen; **my arm won't** ~ ich kann den Arm nicht biegen; ~**ing strain,** ~ **stress** Biegespannung *f*.
(b) (*river*) eine Biegung machen; (*at right angles*) ein Knie machen; (*road also*) eine Kurve machen. **the road/river** ~**s sharply/gradually** die Straße/der Fluß macht eine scharfe/leichte Kurve/Biegung; **the road/river** ~**s to the left** die Straße/der Fluß macht hier eine Linkskurve/-biegung.
(c) (*fig: submit*) sich beugen, sich fügen (*to dat*).
♦ **bend back 1** *vi* sich zurückbiegen; (*over backwards*) sich nach hinten biegen; (*road, river*) in einer Schleife zurückkommen. **2** *vt sep* zurückbiegen.
♦ **bend down 1** *vi* (*person*) sich bücken; (*branch, tree*) sich neigen, sich nach unten biegen. **she bent** ~ **to look at the baby**

sie beugte sich hinunter, um das Baby anzusehen. **2** *vt sep edges* nach unten biegen.
♦ **bend over 1** *vi* (*person*) sich bücken. **to** ~ ~ **to look at sth** sich nach vorn beugen, um etw anzusehen. **2** *vt sep* umbiegen.

bender ['bendəʳ] *n* (*inf*) Kneiptur *f* (*hum inf*). **to go out on a** ~ einen heben gehen (*inf*).

bends [bendz] *n* **the** ~ Taucherkrankheit *f*.

beneath [bɪ'niːθ] **1** *prep* **(a)** unter (+*dat or with motion* +*acc*); (*with line, level etc also*) unterhalb (+*gen*). **to marry** ~ **one** unter seinem Stand heiraten; *see also* below 1 ~. **(b)** (*unworthy of*) **it is** ~ **him** das ist unter seiner Würde. **2** *adv* unten; *see also* below 2 ~.

Benedictine [,benɪ'dɪktɪn] **1** *n* **(a)** (*Eccl*) Benediktiner(in *f*) *m*. **(b)** (*liqueur*) Benediktiner *m*. **2** *adj* Benediktiner-.

benediction [,benɪ'dɪkʃən] *n* **(a)** (*blessing*) Segen *m*; (*act of blessing*) Segnung *f*. **(b)** (*consecration*) Einsegnung *f*.

benefaction [,benɪ'fækʃən] *n* **(a)** (*good deed*) Wohltat *f*, gute Tat. **(b)** (*gift*) Spende *f*.

benefactor ['benɪfæktəʳ] *n* Wohltäter *m*; (*giver of money also*) Gönner *m*.

benefactress ['benɪfæktrɪs] *n* Wohltäterin *f*; Gönnerin *f*.

benefice ['benɪfɪs] *n* Pfründe *f*, kirchliches Benefizium (*spec*).

beneficence [bɪ'nefɪsəns] *n* (*liter*) Wohltätigkeit, Mildtätigkeit *f*.

beneficent [bɪ'nefɪsənt] *adj* (*liter*) wohltätig, mildtätig.

beneficial [,benɪ'fɪʃəl] *adj* **(a)** gut (*to für*); *climate also* zuträglich (*geh*) (*to dat*); *influence also* vorteilhaft; *advice, lesson* nützlich (*to für*). **the change will be** ~ **to you** die Veränderung wird Ihnen guttun; **if the drug is not** ~ ... wenn das Medikament nicht hilft ...; **it would be** ~ **to lower taxes** (*for the public*) es wäre gut, die Steuern zu senken; (*for our election chances*) es wäre von Vorteil or günstig, die Steuern zu senken.
(b) (*Jur*) ~ **owner** Nutznießer(in *f*) *m*.

beneficiary [,benɪ'fɪʃərɪ] *n* **(a)** Nutznießer(in *f*) *m*; (*of will, insurance etc*) Begünstigte(r) *mf*. **(b)** (*Eccl*) Pfründner *m*.

benefit ['benɪfɪt] **1** *n* **(a)** (*advantage*) Vorteil *m*; (*profit*) Nutzen, Gewinn *m*. **to derive** or **get** ~ **from sth** aus etw Nutzen ziehen; **for the** ~ **of his family/the poor** zum Wohl or für das Wohl seiner Familie/der Armen; **for the** ~ **of your health** Ihrer Gesundheit zuliebe, um Ihrer Gesundheit willen; **for your** ~ Ihretwegen, um Ihretwillen (*geh*); **this money is for the** ~ **of the blind** dieses Geld kommt den Blinden zugute; **it is for his** ~ **that this was done** das ist seinetwegen geschehen; **to give sb the** ~ **of the doubt** im Zweifelsfall zu jds Gunsten entscheiden; **we should give him the** ~ **of the doubt** wir sollten das zu seinen Gunsten auslegen.
(b) (*allowance*) Unterstützung *f*; (*sickness* ~) Krankengeld *nt*; (*family* ~) Kindergeld *nt*; (*social security* ~) Sozialhilfe *f*; (*maternity* ~) Wochengeld *nt*; (*insurance* ~) Versicherungsleistung *f*. **old age** ~ Altersrente *f*; *see* fringe ~**s**.
(c) (*special performance*) Benefizveranstaltung *f*; (*Theat also*) Benefiz(vorstellung *f*) *nt*; (*Sport also*) Benefizspiel *nt*. **it's his** ~ es ist eine Benefizvorstellung für ihn.
(d) ~ **without** ~ **of clergy** ohne kirchlichen Segen.
2 *vt* guttun (+*dat*), nützen (+*dat*), zugute kommen (+*dat*); (*healthwise*) guttun (+*dat*).
3 *vi* profitieren (*from, by* von); (*from experience also*) Nutzen ziehen (*from* aus). **who will** ~ **from that?** wem wird das nützen?; **but how do we** ~? aber was nützt das uns?, aber wie profitieren wir davon?; **he would** ~ **from a holiday** Ferien würden ihm guttun; **I think you'll** ~ **from the experience** ich glaube, diese Erfahrung wird Ihnen nützlich sein or von Nutzen sein; **a case from which many have** ~**ted** eine Behandlung, die schon manchem geholfen hat.

benefit: ~ **match** *n* Benefizspiel *nt*; ~ **performance** *n* Benefizveranstaltung *f*.

Benelux ['benɪlʌks] *n* Benelux-Wirtschaftsunion *f*. ~ **countries** Beneluxstaaten or -länder *pl*.

benevolence [bɪ'nevələns] *n* *see adj* **(a)** Wohlwollen *nt*; Gutmütigkeit *f*; Güte *f*; Milde *f*.

benevolent [bɪ'nevələnt] *adj* **(a)** wohlwollend; *pat, smile, twinkle* gutmütig; (*as character trait*) emperor, judge mild. **B**~ **Despotism** der Aufgeklärte Absolutismus. **(b)** (*charitable*) ~ **institution** Wohltätigkeitseinrichtung *f*; ~ **society** Wohltätigkeitsverein *m*.

benevolently [bɪ'nevələntlɪ] *adv see adj* **(a)**.

Bengal [beŋ'gɔːl] *n* Bengalen *nt*. ~ **light** or **match** bengalisches Feuer or Hölzchen; ~ **tiger** bengalischer Tiger, Königstiger *m*.

Bengalese [beŋgə'liːz] **1** *n* Bengale *m*, Bengalin *f*. **2** *adj* bengalisch.

Bengali [beŋ'gɔːlɪ] **1** *n* (*language*) Bengali *nt*; (*person*) Bengale *m*, Bengalin *f*. **2** *adj* bengalisch.

benighted [bɪ'naɪtɪd] *adj* **(a)** (*fig*) person unbedarft; country gottverlassen; *policy etc* hirnrissig. **(b)** (*lit*) von der Dunkelheit or Nacht überfallen or überrascht.

benign [bɪ'naɪn], **benignant** (*rare*) [bɪ'nɪgnənt] *adj* **(a)** smile, planet, influence günstig; climate mild. **(b)** (*Med*) tumour gutartig.

benignity [bə'nɪgnɪtɪ] *n see adj* **(a)** Güte *f*; Günstigkeit *f*; Milde *f*. **(b)** Gutartigkeit *f*.

bent [bent] **1** *pret, ptp of* bend.
2 *adj* **(a)** metal etc gebogen; (*out of shape*) verbogen.
(b) (*Brit sl: dishonest*) person korrupt; affair unsauber (*inf*). **he's** ~ er ist ein krummer Hund (*inf*).
(c) (*sl: homosexual*) andersrum pred (*inf*).
(d) **to be** ~ **on sth/doing sth** etw unbedingt or partout wollen/tun wollen; **he seemed** ~ **on self-destruction** er schien von einem Selbstzerstörungstrieb besessen zu sein.
3 *n* (*aptitude*) Neigung *f* (*for zu*); (*type of mind, character*) Schlag *m*. **to follow one's** ~ seiner Neigung folgen; **people with** or **of a musical** ~ Menschen mit einer musikalischen Veran-

lagung; **people of his ~** Leute seines Schlags.

benumb [bɪ'nʌm] *vt* **(a)** *limb* gefühllos machen; *person* betäuben; (*with cold also*) erstarren lassen. **he was/his fingers were ~ed with cold** er war starr vor Kälte/seine Finger waren starr *or* taub vor Kälte. **(b)** (*fig*) *mind* betäuben; (*panic, experience etc*) lähmen. **~ed by alcohol** vom Alkohol benommen.

Benzedrine ® ['benzɪdriːn] *n* Benzedrin *nt*.

benzene ['benziːn] *n* Benzol *nt*.

benzine ['benziːn] *n* Leichtbenzin *nt*.

bequeath [bɪ'kwiːð] *vt* **(a)** (*in will*) vermachen, hinterlassen (*to sb* jdm). **(b)** (*fig*) *tradition* hinterlassen, vererben (*to sb* jdm).

bequest [bɪ'kwest] *n* (*act of bequeathing*) Vermachen *nt* (*to an* +*acc*); (*legacy*) Nachlaß *m*.

berate [bɪ'reɪt] *vt* (*liter*) schelten, auszanken.

Berber ['bɜːbəʳ] **1** *n* **(a)** Berber *m*, Berberfrau *f*. **(b)** (*language*) die Berbersprache. **2** *adj* berberisch.

bereave [bɪ'riːv] *vt* **(a)** *pret, ptp* **bereft** (*liter*) (*deprive*) berauben (*geh*) (*of gen*).
(b) *pret, ptp* **~d** (*cause loss by death: illness*) (*sb of sb* jdm jdn) rauben (*geh*), nehmen. **an accident ~d him of his son** er hat seinen Sohn durch einen Unfall verloren; **he was ~d of his son** sein Sohn ist ihm genommen worden (*geh*).

bereaved [bɪ'riːvd] *adj* leidtragend, vom Verlust betroffen. **the ~ die** Hinterbliebenen.

bereavement [bɪ'riːvmənt] *n* **(a)** (*death in family*) Trauerfall *m*. **owing to a/his recent ~** wegen *or* auf Grund eines Trauerfalls/dieses für ihn so schmerzlichen Verlusts; **to sympathize with sb in his ~** jds Leid teilen. **(b)** (*feeling of loss*) schmerzlicher Verlust. **to feel a sense of ~ at sth** etw als schmerzlichen Verlust empfinden.

bereft [bɪ'reft] **1** *ptp of* **bereave**. **2** *adj* **to be ~ of sth** einer Sache (*gen*) bar sein (*geh*); **his life was ~ of happiness** seinem Leben fehlte jegliches Glück; **he is ~ of reason** es mangelt ihm vollkommen an Vernunft.

berg [bɜːg] *n see* **iceberg**.

beribboned [bɪ'rɪbənd] *adj* mit Bändern geschmückt, bebändert; *general* mit Ordensbändern geschmückt.

beri-beri ['berɪ'berɪ] *n* Beriberi *f*.

Bering ['berɪŋ]: **~ Sea** *n* Beringmeer *nt*; **~ Straits** *npl* Beringstraße *f*.

berk [bɜːk] *n* (*Brit sl*) Dussel *m* (*inf*).

Berks [bɑːks] *abbr of* **Berkshire**.

Berlin [bɜː'lɪn] *n* Berlin *nt*. **the ~ wall** die Mauer.

Bermuda [bɜː'mjuːdə] *n* Bermuda *nt* (*form rare*). **the ~s** die Bermudas, die Bermudainseln *pl*; **to go to ~** auf die Bermudas fahren; **~ shorts** Bermudashorts *pl*.

Bernard ['bɜːnəd] *n* Bernhard *m*.

Berne [bɜːn] *n* Bern *nt*.

Bernese [bɜː'niːz] *adj* Berner; *village* im Berner Oberland.

berry ['berɪ] *n* **(a)** (*fruit*) Beere *f*. **as brown as a ~** schwarz wie ein Neger (*inf*). **(b)** (*Bot*) Beerenfrucht *f*.

berrying ['berɪɪŋ] *n* Beerensammeln *nt*. **to go ~** Beeren sammeln gehen.

berserk [bə'sɜːk] *adj* wild. **to go ~** wild werden; (*audience*) aus dem Häuschen geraten (*inf*), zu toben anfangen; (*go mad*) überschnappen (*inf*), verrückt werden.

berth [bɜːθ] **1** *n* **(a)** (*on ship*) Koje *f*; (*on train*) Bett *nt*.
(b) (*Naut: place for ship*) Liegeplatz *m*.
(c) (*Naut: sea-room*) Raum *m*. **to give a wide ~ to a ship** Abstand zu einem Schiff halten; **to give sb/sth a wide ~** (*fig*) einen (weiten) Bogen um jdn/etw machen.
2 *vi* anlegen.
3 *vt* **to ~ a ship** mit einem Schiff (am Kai) anlegen; (*assign ~ to*) einem Schiff einen Liegeplatz zuweisen; **where is she ~ed?** wo liegt es?; wo hat es angelegt?

beryl ['berɪl] *n* Beryll *m*.

beseech [bɪ'siːtʃ] *pret, ptp* **~ed** *or* (*liter*) **besought** *vt person* anflehen, beschwören; *forgiveness* flehen um, erflehen (*geh*).

beseeching *adj*, **~ly** *adv* [bɪ'siːtʃɪŋ, -lɪ] flehentlich (*geh*), flehend.

beset [bɪ'set] *pret, ptp* **~** *vt* (*difficulties, dangers*) (von allen Seiten) bedrängen; (*doubts*) befallen; (*temptations, trials*) heimsuchen. **to be ~ with difficulties/danger** (*problem, journey etc*) reich an *or* voller Schwierigkeiten/Gefahren sein; (*person*) von Schwierigkeiten heimgesucht werden/von Gefahren bedrängt werden; **~ by doubts** von Zweifeln befallen.

besetting [bɪ'setɪŋ] *adj* **his ~ sin** eine ständige Untugend von ihm; **his one ~ worry/idea etc** die Sorge/Vorstellung etc, die ihn nicht losläßt.

beside [bɪ'saɪd] *prep* **(a)** (*at the side of*) neben (+*dat or with motion* +*acc*); (*at the edge of*) *road, river* an (+*dat or with motion* +*acc*). **~ the road** am Straßenrand.
(b) (*compared with*) neben (+*dat*). **if you put it ~ the original** wenn man es neben dem Original sieht.
(c) (*irrelevant to*) **to be ~ the question** *or* **point** damit nichts zu tun haben.
(d) **to be ~ oneself** (*with anger*) außer sich sein (*with vor*); (*with joy also*) sich nicht mehr zu lassen wissen (*with vor*).

besides [bɪ'saɪdz] **1** *adv* **(a)** (*in addition*) außerdem, obendrein. **he wrote a novel and several short stories ~** er hat einen Roman und außerdem noch mehrere Kurzgeschichten geschrieben; **many more ~** noch viele mehr; **have you got any others ~?** haben Sie noch andere *or* noch welche?
(b) (*anyway, moreover*) außerdem.
2 *prep* **(a)** (*in addition to*) außer. **others ~ ourselves** außer uns noch andere; **there were three of us ~ Mary** Mary nicht mitgerechnet, waren wir zu dritt; **~ which he was unwell** überdies *or* außerdem fühlte er sich nicht wohl.
(b) (*except*) außer, abgesehen von.

besiege [bɪ'siːdʒ] *vt* **(a)** (*Mil*) *town* belagern. **(b)** (*fig*) belagern; (*with information, offers*) überschütten, überhäufen;

(*pester: with letters, questions*) bestürmen, bedrängen.

besieger [bɪ'siːdʒəʳ] *n* (*Mil*) Belagerer *m*.

besmirch [bɪ'smɜːtʃ] *vt* (*lit, fig*) beschmutzen, besudeln.

besom ['biːzəm] *n* (Reisig)besen *m*.

besotted [bɪ'sɒtɪd] *adj* **(a)** (*drunk*) berauscht (*with* von). **(b)** (*infatuated*) völlig vernarrt (*with* in +*acc*); (*with idea*) berauscht (*with* von).

besought [bɪ'sɔːt] (*liter*) *pret, ptp of* **beseech**.

bespake [bɪ'speɪk] (*old*) *pret of* **bespeak**.

bespangle [bɪ'spæŋgl] *vt* besetzen. **~d costume** mit Pailletten besetztes Kostüm; **the sky ~d with ...** (*liter*) der mit ... übersäte Himmel.

bespatter [bɪ'spætəʳ] *vt* bespritzen.

bespeak [bɪ'spiːk] *pret* **bespoke** *or* (*old*) **bespake**, *ptp* **bespoken** *or* **bespoke** *vt* **(a)** (*indicate*) verraten, erkennen lassen. **(b)** (*old: reserve*) reservieren lassen, bestellen.

bespectacled [bɪ'spektɪkld] *adj* bebrillt.

bespoke [bɪ'spəʊk] **1** *prep, ptp of* **bespeak**. **2** *adj goods* nach Maß; *garment also* Maß-. **a ~ tailor** ein Maßschneider *m*.

bespoken [bɪ'spəʊkən] *ptp of* **bespeak**.

besprinkle [bɪ'sprɪŋkl] *vt* (*with liquid*) besprengen, bespritzen; (*with powder*) bestäuben.

Bess [bes] *n dim of* **Elizabeth**. **good Queen ~** Elisabeth I.

Bessemer ['besɪməʳ] *in cpds* Bessemer-; **~ converter** Bessemerbirne *f*.

best [best] **1** *adj, superl of* **good** beste(r, s) *attr*; (*most favourable*) *route, price also* günstigste(r, s) *attr*. **to be ~ am** besten/günstigsten sein; **to be ~ of all am** allerbesten/allergünstigsten sein; **that was the ~ thing about her/that could happen** das war das Beste an ihr/, was geschehen konnte; **that would be ~ or the ~ thing for everybody** das wäre für alle das beste; **the ~ thing to do is or it's ~ to wait** das beste ist zu warten; **the ~ years of one's life** die besten Jahre des Lebens; **may the ~ man win!** dem Besten der Sieg!; **to put one's ~ foot forward** (*lit*) seinen schnellsten Gang anschlagen; (*fig*) sein Bestes geben *or* tun; **the ~ part of the year/my money** fast das ganze Jahr/fast all mein Geld; **she spends the ~ part of the year in Italy** den größten Teil des Jahres verbringt sie in Italien.
2 *adv, superl of* **well (a)** am besten; *like* am liebsten *or* meisten; *enjoy* am meisten. **the ~ fitting dress** das am besten passende Kleid; **the ~ known title** der bekannteste Titel; **he was ~ known for ...** er war vor allem bekannt für ...; **~ of all am** allerbesten/-liebsten/-meisten; **I helped him as ~ I could** ich half ihm, so gut ich konnte; **I thought it ~ to go** ich hielt es für das beste, zu gehen; **do as you think ~** tun Sie, was Sie für richtig halten; **you know ~** Sie müssen es (am besten) wissen.
(b) (*better*) **you had ~ go now** am besten gehen Sie jetzt.
3 *n* **(a)** (*person, thing*) **the ~** der/die/das beste; **the ~ of the bunch** (*inf*) (noch) der/die/das Beste; **his last book was his ~** sein letztes Buch war sein bestes; **with the ~ of intentions** mit den besten Absichten; **even the ~ of us can make mistakes** selbst die Besten von uns sind gegen Fehler nicht gefeit; **he can sing with the ~ of them** er kann sich im Singen mit den Besten messen.
(b) (*clothes*) beste Sachen, Sonntagskleider (*inf*) *pl*. **to be in one's (Sunday) ~ in** Schale sein (*inf*), im Sonntagsstaat sein.
(c) (*to do one's level*) **~ sein Bestes** *or* möglichstes tun; **that's the ~ you can expect** Sie können nichts Besseres erwarten; **do the ~ you can!** machen Sie es so gut Sie können!; **it's not perfect but it's the ~ I can do** es ist nicht perfekt, aber mehr kann ich nicht tun; **what a lame excuse, is that the ~ you can do?** so eine lahme Ausrede, fällt Ihnen nichts Besseres ein?; **to get or have the ~ of sb** jdn unterkriegen; **to get the ~ out of sb/sth** das Beste aus jdm/etw herausholen; **to get the ~ of the bargain** *or* **of it** am besten dabei wegkommen; **to play the ~ of three/five** nur so lange spielen, bis eine Partei zweimal/dreimal gewonnen hat; **to make the ~ of it/a bad job** das Beste daraus machen; **to make the ~ of one's opportunities** seine Chancen voll nützen; **the ~ of it is that ...** das beste daran ist, daß ...; **we've had the ~ of the day** der Tag ist so gut wie vorbei; (*the weather's getting worse*) das schöne Wetter wäre für heute vorbei; **it's all for the ~** es ist nur zum Guten; **I meant it for the ~** ich habe es doch nur gut gemeint; **to do sth for the ~** etw in bester Absicht tun; **to the ~ of my ability** so gut ich kann/ konnte; **to the ~ of my knowledge** meines Wissens; **to the ~ of my recollection** *or* **memory** soviel ich mich erinnern kann; **to look one's ~** besonders gut aussehen; **to be at one's ~** (*on form*) in Hochform sein; **he is at his ~ at about 8 in the evening** so gegen 8 abends ist seine beste Zeit; **roses are at their ~ just now** jetzt ist die beste Zeit für Rosen; **that is Goethe at his ~** das ist Goethe, wie er besser nicht sein könnte; **it's not enough (even) at the ~ of times** das ist schon normalerweise nicht genug; **at ~ bestenfalls**; **to wish sb all the ~ jdm** alles Gute wünschen; **all the ~ (to you)** alles Gute!
4 *vt* schlagen.

best-dressed ['best'drest] *adj* bestgekleidet *attr*.

bestial ['bestɪəl] *adj acts, cruelty* bestialisch, tierisch; *person, look, appearance* (*cruel*) brutal; (*carnal*) tierisch.

bestiality [,bestɪ'ælɪtɪ] *n* **(a)** *see adj* Bestialität *f*, Tierische(s) *nt*; Brutalität *f*; Tierische(s) *nt*. **(b)** (*act*) Greueltat *f*. **(c)** (*buggery*) Sodomie *f*.

bestiary ['bestɪərɪ] *n* Bestiaire, Bestiarium *nt*.

bestir [bɪ'stɜːʳ] *vr* (*hum, liter*) sich regen, sich rühren. **to ~ one-self to do sth** sich dazu aufraffen, etw zu tun.

best man *n* Trauzeuge *m* (des Bräutigams).

bestow [bɪ'stəʊ] *vt* **(a)** (*on or upon sb* jdm) (*grant, give*) *gift, attention* schenken; *favour, friendship, kiss also* gewähren (*geh*); *honour* erweisen, zuteil werden lassen (*geh*); *title, medal* verleihen. **(b)** (*old: place*) verstauen, unterbringen.

bestowal [bɪ'stəʊəl] *n see vt* **(a)** Schenken *nt*; Gewähren *nt*; Erweisung *f*; Verleihung *f* (*up)on an* +*acc*).

bestraddle [bɪ'strædl] vt see **bestride**.

bestride [bɪ'straɪd] pret **bestrode** [bɪ'strəud] or **bestrid** [bɪ'strɪd], ptp **bestridden** [bɪ'strɪdn] vt (sit astride) rittlings sitzen auf (+dat); (stand astride) (mit gespreizten Beinen) stehen über (+dat); (mount) sich schwingen auf (+acc). to ~ the world like a Colossus die Welt beherrschen.

best: ~-seller n Verkaufs- or Kassenschlager m; (book) Bestseller m; (author) Erfolgsautor(in f) m; ~-selling adj absatzstark, der/die/das am besten geht; author Erfolgs-; a ~-selling novel ein Bestseller m; this month's ~-selling books die Bestsellerliste dieses Monats.

bet [bet] (vb: pret, ptp ~) 1 n Wette f (on auf +acc); (money etc staked) Wetteinsatz m. to make or have a ~ with sb mit jdm wetten, mit jdm eine Wette eingehen; I have a ~ (on) with him that ... ich habe mit ihm gewettet, daß ...; it's a safe/bad ~ das ist ein sicherer/schlechter Tip; it's a safe ~ he'll be in the pub er ist bestimmt or garantiert in der Kneipe; he's a bad ~ for the job er ist nichts für diese Arbeit (inf).
2 vt (a) wetten, setzen (against gegen, on auf +acc). I ~ him £5 ich habe mit ihm (um) £ 5 gewettet; to ~ ten to one zehn gegen eins wetten.
(b) (inf) wetten. I ~ he'll come! wetten, daß er kommt! (inf); I'll ~ you anything (you like) ich gehe mit dir jede Wette (darauf) ein; (I'll) ~ you won't do it wetten, daß du das nicht tust (inf); ~ you! wetten! (inf); you can ~ your boots or your bottom dollar that ... Sie können Gift darauf nehmen, daß ... (inf); ~ you I can! (inf) wetten, daß ich das kann! (inf).
3 vi wetten. to ~ on a horse/horses auf ein Pferd/Pferde setzen or wetten, Pferdewetten abschließen; you ~! (inf) und ob! (inf); (do you want to) ~? (wollen wir) wetten?

beta ['biːtə] n Beta nt; (Brit Sch) gut. ~ ray Betastrahl m.

betake [bɪ'teɪk] pret **betook**, ptp **betaken** [bɪ'teɪkn] vr (old, hum) sich begeben.

betcha ['betʃə] interj (sl) wetten(, daß) (inf).

betel [bɪ'tɑl] n Betel m. ~ nut Betelnuß f.

bête noire [beɪt'nwɑːʳ] n to be a ~ to sb jdm ein Greuel sein.

bethink [bɪ'θɪŋk] pret, ptp **bethought** vr (liter, obs) to ~ oneself of sth/that ... etw bedenken/bedenken, daß ...

Bethlehem ['beθlɪhem] n Bethlehem nt.

bethought [bɪ'θɔːt] pret, ptp of **bethink**.

betide [bɪ'taɪd] vti geschehen (sb jdm). whatever (may) ~ immer auch geschehen mag (geh); see **woe**.

betimes [bɪ'taɪmz] adv (old, liter) beizeiten (geh).

betoken [bɪ'təukən] vt (old) bedeuten, hindeuten auf (+acc).

betook [bɪ'tuk] pret of **betake**.

betray [bɪ'treɪ] vt verraten (also Pol) (to dat or (Pol) an +acc); trust enttäuschen, brechen; plans also preisgeben; (be disloyal to also) im Stich lassen; (be unfaithful to) untreu werden (+dat). to ~ oneself sich verraten; his accent verriet or ließ ihn als or zum Ausländer erkennen; his accent ~ed him as a foreigner sein Akzent verriet, daß er ein Ausländer war.

betrayal [bɪ'treɪəl] n (act) Verrat m (of gen); (instance) Verrat m (of an +dat); (of trust) Enttäuschung f; (of friends also) Untreue f (of gegenüber); (of plans also) Preisgabe f. the ~ of Christ der Verrat an Christus; a ~ of trust ein Vertrauensbruch m.

betrayer [bɪ'treɪəʳ] n Verräter(in f) m (of gen or (Pol) an +dat).

betroth [bɪ'trəuð] vt (obs, liter) angeloben (obs, liter) (to sb jdm), versprechen (liter) (to sb jdm), verloben (to sb mit jdm).

betrothal [bɪ'trəuðəl] n (obs, liter, hum) Verlobung f.

betrothed [bɪ'trəuðd] n (obs, liter, hum) Anverlobte(r) mf (obs).

better¹ ['betəʳ] n Wetter(in f) m.

better² 1 adj, comp of **good** besser; route, way also günstiger. he's ~ (recovered) es geht ihm wieder besser; he's much ~ es geht ihm viel besser; the patient/ his foot is getting ~ dem Patienten/seinem Fuß geht es schon viel besser; I hope you get ~ soon hoffentlich sind Sie bald wieder gesund; ~ and ~ immer besser; that's ~! (approval) so ist es besser!; (relief etc) so!; to be ~ than one's word wenn ich, nein man versprochen hat; it couldn't be ~ es könnte gar nicht besser sein; I am none the ~ for it das hilft mir auch nicht; she is no ~ than she should be ist auch keine Heilige; the ~ part of an hour/my money/our holidays fast eine Stunde/fast mein ganzes Geld/fast die ganzen Ferien; it/you would be ~ to go early es wäre besser, früh zu gehen/Sie gehen besser früh; to go one ~ einen Schritt weiter gehen; (in offer) höher gehen; this hat has seen ~ days dieser Hut hat auch schon bessere Tage gesehen (inf).
2 adv, comp of **well** (a) besser; like lieber, mehr; enjoy mehr. they are ~ off than we are sie sind besser dran als wir; you would do ~ or be ~ advised to go early Sie sollten lieber früh gehen, Sie wären gut beraten, wenn Sie früh gingen (geh); to think ~ of it es sich (dat) noch einmal überlegen; I didn't think any ~ of him for that deswegen hielt ich auch nicht mehr von ihm; see **know**, **late**.
(b) I had ~ go ich gehe jetzt wohl besser; you'd ~ do what he says tun Sie lieber, was er sagt; I'd ~ answer that letter soon ich beantworte den Brief lieber or besser bald; I won't touch it Mummy — you'd ~ not! ich fasse es nicht an, Mutti — das will ich dir auch geraten haben.
3 n (a) one's ~s Leute, die über einem stehen; (socially also) Höhergestellte; that's no way to talk to your ~s man muß immer wissen, wen man vor sich (dat) hat; respect for one's ~s Achtung Respektspersonen gegenüber.
(b) (person, object) the ~ der/die/das Bessere.
(c) it's a change for the ~ es ist eine Wendung zum Guten; to think (all) the ~ of sb (um so) mehr von jdm halten; all the ~, so much the ~ um so besser; it would be all the ~ for a drop of paint ein bißchen Farbe würde Wunder wirken; it's done now for ~ or worse so oder so, es ist geschehen; for ~, for worse (in marriage ceremony) in Freud und Leid; to get the ~ of sb (person) jdn unterkriegen (inf); (illness) jdn erwischen

(inf); (problem etc) jdm schwer zu schaffen machen.
4 vt (improve on) verbessern; (surpass) übertreffen.
5 vr (increase one's knowledge) sich weiterbilden; (in social scale) sich verbessern.

better half n (inf) bessere Hälfte (inf).

betterment ['betəmənt] n (a) Verbesserung f; (educational) Weiterbildung f. (b) (Jur) Wertsteigerung f; (of land) Melioration f.

betting ['betɪŋ] n Wetten nt. the ~ was brisk das Wettgeschäft war rege; what is the ~ on his horse? wie stehen die Wetten auf sein Pferd?

betting: ~ man n (regelmäßiger) Wetter; I'm not a ~ man ich wette eigentlich nicht; if I were a ~ man I'd say ... wenn ich ja wetten würde, würde ich sagen ...; ~ news n Wettnachrichten pl; ~ shop n Annahmestelle f für Wetten; ~ slip n Wettschein m.

Betty ['betɪ] n dim of **Elizabeth**.

between [bɪ'twiːn] 1 prep (a) zwischen (+dat); (with movement) zwischen (+acc). I was sitting ~ them ich saß zwischen ihnen; sit down ~ those two boys setzen Sie sich zwischen diese beiden Jungen; in ~ zwischen (+dat/acc); ~ now and next week we must ... wir müssen in der Woche ...; there's nothing ~ them (they're equal) sie sind gleich gut; (no feelings, relationship) zwischen ihnen ist nichts.
(b) (amongst) unter (+dat/acc). divide the sweets ~ the two children/the children teilen Sie die Süßigkeiten zwischen den beiden Kinder auf/verteilen Sie die Süßigkeiten unter die Kinder; we shared an apple ~ us wir teilten uns (dat) einen Apfel; ~ ourselves or ~ you and me he is not very clever unter uns (dat) (gesagt), er ist nicht besonders gescheit; that's just ~ ourselves das bleibt aber unter uns; let's keep that piece of information ~ ourselves diese Information sollte unter uns (dat) bleiben.
(c) (jointly, showing combined effort) ~ us/them zusammen; we have a car ~ the two/three of us wir haben zu zweit/dritt ein Auto, wir zwei/drei haben zusammen ein Auto; ~ the two/three of us we have enough zusammen haben wir (zwei/drei) genug; we got the letter written ~ us wir haben den Brief zusammen or gemeinsam or mit vereinten Kräften geschrieben.
(d) (what with, showing combined effect) neben (+dat). ~ housework and study I have no time for that neben or zwischen Haushalt und Studium bleibt mir keine Zeit dazu.
2 adv (place) dazwischen; (time also) zwischendurch. in ~ dazwischen; the space/time ~ der Zwischenraum/die Zwischenzeit, der Raum/die Zeit dazwischen.

between: ~-time, ~-whiles adv in der Zwischenzeit.

betwixt [bɪ'twɪkst] 1 prep (obs, liter, dial) see **between**. 2 adv: ~ and between zwischendrin.

bevel ['bevl] 1 n (surface) Schräge, Schrägfläche, Abschrägung f; (also ~ edge) abgeschrägte Kante, Schrägkante f; (tool: also ~ square) Schrägmaß nt, Stellwinkel m.
2 vt abschrägen, schräg abflachen. ~led edge Schrägkante f, abgeschrägte Kante; ~led mirror Spiegel m mit schrägeschliffenen Kanten.

bevel gear n Kegelradgetriebe nt.

beverage ['bevərɪdʒ] n Getränk nt.

bevy ['bevɪ] n (of birds) Schwarm m; (of girls also) Schar f.

bewail [bɪ'weɪl] vt (deplore) beklagen; (lament also) bejammern; sb's death also betrauern.

beware [bɪ'weəʳ] vti imper and infin only to ~ (of) sb/sth sich vor jdm/etw hüten, sich vor jdm/etw in acht nehmen; to ~ (of) doing sth sich davor hüten, etw zu tun; ~ of falling passen Sie auf or sehen Sie sich vor, daß Sie nicht fallen; ~ of being deceived, ~ lest you are deceived (old) geben Sie acht or sehen Sie sich vor, daß Sie nicht betrogen werden; ~ (of) how you speak geben Sie acht or sehen Sie sich vor, was Sie sagen; ~! (old, liter) gib acht!; "~ of the dog" „Vorsicht, bissiger Hund"; "~ of pickpockets" „vor Taschendieben wird gewarnt".

bewigged [bɪ'wɪgd] adj mit Perücke, perückentragend attr.

bewilder [bɪ'wɪldəʳ] vt (confuse) verwirren, irremachen; (baffle) verblüffen, verwundern.

bewildered [bɪ'wɪldəd] adj see vt verwirrt, durcheinander pred (inf); verblüfft, perplex (inf), verwundert.

bewildering [bɪ'wɪldərɪŋ] adj see vt verwirrend; verblüffend.

bewilderment [bɪ'wɪldəmənt] n see vt Verwirrung f; Verblüffung f, Erstaunen nt. in ~ verwundert; his ~ was obvious er war offensichtlich verwirrt/verblüfft.

bewitch [bɪ'wɪtʃ] vt verhexen, verzaubern; (fig) bezaubern.

bewitching adj, ~ly adv [bɪ'wɪtʃɪŋ, -lɪ] bezaubernd, hinreißend.

beyond [bɪ'jɒnd] 1 prep (a) (in space) (on the other side of) über (+dat), jenseits (+gen) (geh); (further than) über (+acc), hinaus, weiter als. ~ the Alps jenseits der Alpen; I saw peak ~ snow-capped peak ich sah schneebedeckte Gipfel bis weit in die Ferne; ~ the convent walls außerhalb der Klostermauern.
(b) (in time) ~ 6 o'clock/next week/the 17th century nach 6 Uhr/nächster Woche/dem 17. Jahrhundert; until ~ 6 o'clock/next week/the 17th century bis nach 6 Uhr/bis über nächste Woche/das 17. Jahrhundert hinaus; ~ the middle of June/the week über Mitte Juni/der Woche hinaus; it's ~ your bedtime es ist längst Zeit, daß du ins Bett kommst.
(c) (surpassing, exceeding) a task ~ her abilities eine Aufgabe, die über ihre Fähigkeiten geht, it's ~ your authority das liegt außerhalb Ihrer Befugnis; that is ~ human understanding das geht über menschliches Verständnis, das übersteigt menschliches Verständnis; that's almost ~ belief das ist fast unglaublich or nicht zu glauben; ~ repair nicht mehr zu reparieren; it was ~ her to pass the exam sie schaffte es nicht, das Examen zu bestehen; that's ~ me (I don't understand) das geht über meinen Verstand, das kapiere ich nicht (inf); see **compare**, **grave¹**, **help** etc.
(d) (with neg, interrog) außer. have you any money ~ what

you have in the bank? haben Sie außer dem, was Sie auf der Bank haben, noch Geld?; ~ this/that sonst; I've got nothing to suggest ~ this sonst habe ich keine Vorschläge.

2 adv (on the other side of) jenseits davon (geh); (after that) danach; (further than that) darüber hinaus, weiter. India and the lands ~ Indien und die Gegenden jenseits davon; …a river, and ~ is a small field … ein Fluß, und danach kommt ein kleines Feld; the world ~ das Jenseits.

3 n the great B~ das Jenseits; (space) der weite Raum.

BF (euph) abbr of **bloody fool**.

B/F, b/f abbr of **brought forward** Übertrag.

BFPO abbr of **British Forces Post Office**.

bi- [baɪ] pref bi, Bi-.

Biafra [bɪˈæfrə] n Biafra nt.

Biafran [bɪˈæfrən] **1** n Einwohner(in f) m Biafras. **2** adj Biafra-.

biannual adj, **~ly** adv [baɪˈænjʊəl, -ɪ] zweimal jährlich; (half-yearly) halbjährlich.

bias [ˈbaɪəs] (vb: pret, ptp **~(s)ed**) **1** n **(a)** (inclination) (of course, newspaper etc) (einseitige) Ausrichtung f (towards auf +acc); (of person) Vorliebe f (towards für). **to have a ~ against** sth (course, newspaper etc) gegen etw eingestellt sein; (person) eine Abneigung gegen etw haben; **to have a left-wing/right-wing ~ or a ~ to the left/right** nach links/rechts ausgerichtet sein, einen Links-/Rechtsdrall haben (inf); **to be without ~** unvoreingenommen sein, ohne Vorurteile sein. **(b)** (Sew) on the ~ schräg zum Fadenlauf; ~ **binding** Schrägband nt or -streifen m. **(c)** (Sport) (shape of bowl) Überhang m.

2 vt report, article etc (einseitig) färben; (towards sth) ausrichten (towards auf +acc); person beeinflussen. he ~ed his article in favour of a purely historical approach to the problem er gab in seinem Artikel den historischen Lösung des Problems den Vorzug; **to ~ sb towards/against sth** jdn für/gegen etw einnehmen.

bias(s)ed [ˈbaɪəst] adj voreingenommen, befangen. … but then I'm … aber ich bin natürlich voreingenommen or befangen.

biathlon [baɪˈæθlɒn] n Biathlon nt.

bib [bɪb] n **(a)** (for baby) Latz m, Lätzchen nt. **(b)** (on garment) Latz m. **(c)** (inf) in one's best ~ and tucker in Schale (inf); she put on her best ~ and tucker sie warf sich in Schale (inf).

Bible [ˈbaɪbl] n Bibel f; (fig also) Evangelium nt.

Bible-: ~ **basher** n (inf) Jesusjünger(in f) m (sl); ~ **class** n Bibelstunde f; ~ **story** n biblische Geschichte; ~ **thumper** n (inf) Halleluja-Billy m (sl).

biblical [ˈbɪblɪkəl] adj biblisch, Bibel-.

bibliographer [ˌbɪblɪˈɒgrəfəʳ] n Bibliograph m.

bibliographic(al) [ˌbɪblɪəʊˈgræfɪk(əl)] adj bibliographisch.

bibliography [ˌbɪblɪˈɒgrəfɪ] n (list) Bibliographie f; (science also) Bücherkunde f.

bibliomania [ˌbɪblɪəʊˈmeɪnɪə] n Bibliomanie f.

bibliophile [ˈbɪblɪəʊfaɪl] n Bibliophile(r) mf, Büchernarr m.

bibulous [ˈbɪbjʊləs] adj (form) person trunksüchtig.

bicameral [baɪˈkæmərəl] adj (Pol) Zweikammer-.

bicarbonate of soda [baɪˌkɑːbənɪtəvˈsəʊdə] n (Cook) Natron nt; (Chem) doppelt kohlensaures Natrium.

bi-: ~**centenary** or (US) ~**centennial 1** n zweihundertjähriges Jubiläum, Zweihundertjahrfeier f (of gen); the ~**centenary of** Beethoven's birth/death Beethovens zweihundertster Geburts-/Todestag; **2** adj Zweihundertjahr-, zweihundertjährig; celebrations Zweihundertjahr-.

bicephalous [baɪˈsefələs] adj (spec) dizephal (spec), bikephalisch (spec).

biceps [ˈbaɪseps] n Bizeps m.

bichromate [baɪˈkrəʊmɪt] n Bichromat nt.

bicker [ˈbɪkəʳ] vi (quarrel) sich zanken, aneinandergeraten. they are always ~ing sie liegen sich dauernd in den Haaren.

bickering [ˈbɪkərɪŋ] n Gezänk nt.

bicuspid [baɪˈkʌspɪd] **1** adj mit zwei Spitzen, zweihöckrig, bikuspidal (spec). **2** n (Anat) vorderer Backenzahn.

bicycle [ˈbaɪsɪkl] **1** n Fahrrad nt. **to ride a ~** Fahrrad fahren, radfahren. **2** vi mit dem (Fahr)rad fahren.

bicycle in cpds see **cycle** in cpds.

bid [bɪd] **1** vt pret, ptp ~ **(a)** (at auction) bieten (for auf +acc). **(b)** pret, ptp ~ (Cards) reizen, bieten. **(c)** pret bade or bad, ptp ~ den (say) to ~ sb good-morning jdm einen guten Morgen wünschen; **to ~ farewell to sb, to ~ sb farewell** von jdm Abschied nehmen, jdm Lebewohl sagen (geh); **to ~ sb welcome** jdn willkommen heißen. **(d)** pret bade or bad, ptp ~ den. **to ~ sb to do sth** (old, liter) jdn etw tun heißen (old); **do what I ~** you tu, was ich dich heiße (old).

2 vi **(a)** pret, ptp ~ (at auction) bieten. **(b)** pret, ptp ~ (Cards) bieten, reizen. **(c)** pret bad, ptp ~ den. **to ~ fair to …** versprechen zu …; everything ~s fair to be successful es sieht alles recht erfolgversprechend aus.

3 n **(a)** (at auction) Gebot nt (for auf +acc); (Comm) Angebot nt (for für). **(b)** (Cards) Bieten, Reizen nt. **to raise the ~** höher bieten or reizen, überrufen; **to make no ~** passen; no ~! passe! **(c)** (attempt) Versuch m. **to make a ~ for power** nach der Macht greifen; **to make a ~ for fame/freedom** versuchen, Ruhm/die Freiheit zu erlangen; **his ~ for fame/freedom failed** sein Versuch, Ruhm/die Freiheit zu erlangen, scheiterte; **the ~ for the rescue ~ fails** Rettungsversuch erfolglos; **the ~ for the summit** der Griff nach dem Gipfel.

biddable [ˈbɪdəbl] adj (liter) fügsam, willfährig (geh).

bidden [ˈbɪdn] ptp of **bid**.

bidder [ˈbɪdəʳ] n Bietende(r) mf, Steigerer m. **to sell to the highest ~** an den Höchst- or Meistbietenden verkaufen; there were no ~s niemand hat geboten or ein Gebot gemacht.

bidding [ˈbɪdɪŋ] n **(a)** (at auction) Steigern, Bieten nt. how high did the ~ go? wie hoch wurde gesteigert?; **to raise the ~** den Preis in die Höhe treiben; the ~ is closed es werden keine Gebote mehr angenommen, keine Gebote mehr. **(b)** (Cards) Bieten, Reizen nt. **(c)** (order) Geheiß (old), Gebot nt. **at whose ~?** auf wessen Geheiß? (old); **the slave does his master's ~** der Sklave tut, was sein Herr ihn heißt (old) or ihm befiehlt; **he needed no second ~** man mußte es ihm nicht zweimal sagen.

biddy [ˈbɪdɪ] n (inf) (hen) Huhn nt, Henne f; (old lady) Muttchen (inf), Tantchen (inf) nt.

bide [baɪd] vt **to ~ one's time** den rechten Augenblick abwarten or abpassen; **to ~ awhile** (old) verweilen (geh).

bidet [ˈbiːdeɪ] n Bidet nt.

biennial [baɪˈenɪəl] **1** adj (every two years) zweijährlich; (rare: lasting two years) zweijährig. **2** n (Bot) zweijährige Pflanze.

biennially [baɪˈenɪəlɪ] adv zweijährlich, alle zwei Jahre; (Bot) bienn.

bier [bɪəʳ] n Bahre f.

biff [bɪf] **1** n (inf) Stoß, Puff (inf) m. **a ~ on the nose** eins auf die Nase (inf); **my car got a bit of a ~** mein Auto hat ein bißchen was abgekriegt (inf). **2** interj bums. **3** vt (inf) car eine Beule fahren in (+acc); door anschlagen; lamp post bumsen an (+acc) or gegen (inf). **he ~ed the car against a lamp post/the door against the wall** er ist mit dem Auto gegen einen Laternenpfahl gebumst (inf)/er hat die Tür gegen die Wand geschlagen; **to ~ sb on the nose** jdm eins auf die Nase geben (inf).

bifocal [baɪˈfəʊkəl] **1** adj Bifokal-. **2** n ~**s** pl Bifokalbrille f.

bifurcate [ˈbaɪfɜːkeɪt] **1** vi (form) sich gabeln. **2** adj gegabelt.

bifurcation [ˌbaɪfɜːˈkeɪʃən] n Gabelung f.

big [bɪg] **1** adj (+er) **(a)** (in size, amount) groß; lie also faustdick (inf). **a ~ man** ein großer, schwerer Mann; **she's a ~ girl** (inf) sie hat einen ganz schönen Vorbau (inf); **5 ~ ones** (sl) 5 Riesen (sl); ~ **with child/young** hochschwanger/trächtig. **(b)** (of age) groß. **my ~ brother** mein großer Bruder; **you're ~ enough to know better** du bist groß or alt genug und solltest es besser wissen. **(c)** (important) groß, wichtig. the B~ **Four/Five** die Großen Vier/Fünf; **to look ~** (inf) ein bedeutendes Gesicht machen. **(d)** (conceited) ~ **talk** Angeberei (inf), Großspurigkeit f; ~ **talker** Angeber (inf), Maulheld (sl) m, eingebildeter Schwätzer; **he is too ~ for his boots** (inf) der ist ja größenwahnsinnig; **to have a ~ head** (inf) eingebildet sein. **(e)** (generous, iro) großzügig, nobel (inf); (forgiving) großmütig, nobel (inf); heart groß. **few people have a heart as ~ as his** es sind nur wenige so großzügig/großmütig wie er; **that's really ~ of you** (iro) wirklich nobel von dir (iro). **(f)** (fig phrases) **to earn ~ money** das große Geld verdienen (inf); **to have ~ ideas** große Pläne haben, Rosinen im Kopf haben (pej inf); **to have a ~ mouth** (inf) eine große Klappe haben (inf); **to do things in a ~ way** alles im großen (Stil) tun or betreiben; **to live in a ~ way** auf großem Fuß or in großem Stil leben; **what's the ~ idea?** (inf) was soll denn das? (inf); ~ **deal!** (iro inf) na und? (inf); (that's not much etc) das ist ja ergreifend! (iro); **what's the ~ hurry?** warum denn so eilig? **2** adv **to talk ~** groß daherreden (inf), große Töne spucken (sl); **to act ~** sich aufspielen, großtun; **to think ~** im großen (Maßstab) planen; **to go over or down ~** (inf) ganz groß ankommen (inf), große Anklang finden (with bei).

bigamist [ˈbɪgəmɪst] n Bigamist m.

bigamous [ˈbɪgəməs] adj bigamistisch.

bigamy [ˈbɪgəmɪ] n Bigamie f.

big-: ~ **bang theory** n Urknalltheorie f; B~ **Ben** n Big Ben m; B~ **Bertha** n die Dicke Berta; ~**-boned** adj breit- or grobknochig; B~ **Brother** n der Große Bruder; ~ **bug** n (inf) hohes Tier (inf); ~ **business** n (a) (high finance) Großkapital nt, Hochfinanz f; to be ~ business das große Geschäft sein; (b) (baby-talk) großes Geschäft (baby-talk); ~ **dipper** n (a) (Brit: at fair) Achterbahn, Berg-und-Talbahn f; (b) (US Astron) B~ **Dipper** Großer Bär or Wagen; ~ **end** n (Tech) Pleuelfuß, Schubstangenkopf m; ~ **game** n (Hunt) Großwild nt; ~**head** n (inf: person) Angeber m (inf), eingebildeter Fatzke (sl); ~**-headed** adj (inf) eingebildet, angeberisch (inf); ~**-hearted** adj großherzig, großmütig; (forgiving) weitherzig.

bight [baɪt] n (Geog) Bucht f.

big-: ~**mouth** n (inf) Großmaul nt (sl), Angeber m (inf); (blabbermouth) Schwätzer m (pej), Klatschbase f (inf); ~ **name** n (inf: person) Größe f (in gen); **all the ~ names were there** alles, was Rang und Namen hat, war da; ~ **noise** n (inf) hohes Tier (inf).

bigot [ˈbɪgət] n Eiferer m; (Rel also) bigotter Mensch.

bigoted [ˈbɪgətɪd] adj, ~**ly** adv [ˈbɪgətɪd, -lɪ] eifernd; (Rel) bigott.

bigotry [ˈbɪgətrɪ] n eifernde Borniertheit; (Rel) Bigotterie f.

big-: ~ **shot** n hohes Tier (inf); **he thinks he is a ~ shot in his new Jag** (inf) er hält sich mit seinem neuen Jaguar für den Größten (inf); ~**-time 1** adj (inf) one of the ~**-time boys** eine ganz große Nummer (inf); a ~**-time politician/industrialist/entertainer** eine große Nummer (inf) in der Politik/in der Industrie/im Schaugeschäft; **2** n (inf) **to make or hit the ~-time** groß einsteigen (inf); **once he'd had a taste of the ~-time** nachdem er einmal ganz oben or groß gewesen war; ~ **toe** n große Zehe; ~ **top** n (circus) Zirkus m; (main tent) Hauptzelt nt; ~ **wheel** n (a) (US inf) see ~ shot; (b) (Brit: at fair) Riesenrad nt; ~**wig** n (inf) hohes Tier (inf); the local ~**wigs** die Honoratioren des Ortes.

bike [baɪk] (inf) **1** n (Fahr)rad nt; (motor ~) Motorrad nt, Maschine (inf) f. **2** vi radeln (inf).

bike in cpds see **cycle** in cpds.

bikini [bɪˈkiːnɪ] n Bikini m.

bi-: ~**labial 1** n Bilabial m; **2** adj bilabial; ~**lateral** adj, ~**laterally** adv bilateral.

bilberry ['bɪlbərɪ] n Heidelbeere, Blaubeere f.
bile [baɪl] n **(a)** (Med) Galle f. ~ **stone** Gallenstein m. **(b)** (fig: anger) Übellaunigkeit f. **a man full of** ~ ein Griesgram m.
bilge [bɪldʒ] n **(a)** (Naut) Bilge f. **(b)** (also ~ **water**) Leckwasser nt. **(c)** (of cask) (Faß)bauch m. **(d)** (Brit inf: nonsense) Quatsch (inf), Mumpitz (dated inf) m. **to talk** ~ Unsinn verzapfen (inf).
(e) (Sch sl: biology) Bio no art.
bilharzia [bɪl'hɑːzɪə] n Bilharziose f.
bi-: ~**linear** adj bilinear; ~**lingual** adj, ~**lingually** adv zweisprachig; ~**lingualism** n Zweisprachigkeit f.
bilious ['bɪlɪəs] adj **(a)** (Med) Gallen-. ~ **attack** Gallenkolik f. **(b)** (irritable) reizbar. **he is very** ~ ihm läuft immer gleich die Galle über (inf). **(c)** (sickly) colour widerlich. **you're looking a bit** ~ Sie sind ein bißchen grün um die Nase (inf).
biliousness ['bɪlɪəsnɪs] n see adj Gallenkrankheit f, Gallenleiden nt; Reizbarkeit f; Widerlichkeit f.
bilk [bɪlk] vt creditor prellen (of um); debt nicht bezahlen.
bill[1] [bɪl] n **(a)** (of bird, turtle) Schnabel m. **(b)** (Geog) Landzunge f. **2** vi (bird) schnäbeln. **to** ~ **and coo** (birds) schnäbeln und gurren; (fig: people) (miteinander) turteln.
bill[2] n (tool) see **billhook**.
bill[3] **1** n **(a)** (esp Brit: statement of charges) Rechnung f. **could we have the** ~ **please** zahlen bitte!, wir möchten bitte zahlen.
(b) (US: banknote) Banknote f, Schein m. **five-dollar** ~ Fünfdollarschein m or -note f.
(c) (poster) Plakat nt; (on notice board) Anschlag m; (public announcement) Aushang m; (of house for sale) (Verkaufs)schild nt. **"stick no** ~**s"** „Plakate ankleben verboten".
(d) (Theat: programme) Programm nt. **to head** or **top the** ~, **to be top of the** ~ Star m des Abends/der Saison sein; (act) die Hauptattraktion sein.
(e) ~ **of fare** Speisekarte f.
(f) (Parl) (Gesetzes)entwurf m, (Gesetzes)vorlage f. **the** ~ **was passed** das Gesetz wurde verabschiedet.
(g) (esp Comm, Fin: certificate, statement) ~ **of health** (Naut) Gesundheitsattest nt; **to give sb a clean** ~ **of health** (lit, fig) jdm (gute) Gesundheit bescheinigen; ~ **of lading** (Naut) Seefrachtbrief m, Ladeschein m; ~ **of exchange** Wechsel m, Tratte f; ~ **of sale** Verkaufsurkunde f; **to fit** or **fill the** ~ (fig) der/die/das richtige sein, passen; B~ **of Rights** (Brit) Bill f of Rights; (US) Zusatzklauseln 1–10 zu den Grundrechten.
(h) (Jur) ~ **of attainder** (Brit Hist) Anklage und Urteil gegen politische Persönlichkeiten in Form eines Gesetzes; (US) unmittelbare Bestrafung einer Person durch den Gesetzgeber; ~ **of indictment** Anklageschrift f.
2 vt **(a)** customers eine Rechnung ausstellen (+dat). **we won't** ~ **you for that, sir** (give free) wir werden Ihnen das nicht berechnen or in Rechnung stellen (form).
(b) play, actor ankündigen. **he's** ~**ed at the King's Theatre** er soll im King's Theatre auftreten.
Bill [bɪl] n dim of **William**.
billboard ['bɪlbɔːd] n Reklametafel f.
billet ['bɪlɪt] **1** n **(a)** (Mil) (document) Quartierschein m; (accommodation) Quartier nt, Unterkunft f.
(b) (fig inf) **to have a soft** or **cushy** ~ einen schlauen Posten haben.
2 vt (Mil) soldier einquartieren (on sb bei jdm). **troops were** ~**ed on** or **in our town** in unserer Stadt wurden/waren Truppen einquartiert.
billet-doux [bɪleɪ'duː] n Liebesbrief m, Billetdoux nt (old).
billeting ['bɪlɪtɪŋ] n (Mil) Einquartierung f. ~ **officer** Quartiermeister m.
bill: ~**fold** n (US) Brieftasche f; ~**head** n (heading) Rechnungskopf m; (sheet) Rechnungsformular nt; ~**hook** n Hippe f.
billiard ['bɪljəd] adj attr Billard-. ~ **ball** Billardkugel f; ~ **cue** Queue m, Billardstock m.
billiards ['bɪljədz] n Billard nt. **to have a game of** ~ Billard spielen.
billion ['bɪljən] n **(a)** (Brit) Billion f. **(b)** (US) Milliarde f.
billionaire ['bɪljəneə'] n (US) Milliardär(in f) m.
billionth ['bɪljənθ] **1** adj (Brit) billionste(r, s); (US) milliardste(r, s). **2** n (Brit) Billionstel nt; (US) Milliardstel nt.
billow ['bɪləʊ] **1** n **(a)** (liter: of sea) Woge f (geh). **(b)** (fig: of dress etc) Bauschen nt no pl; (of sail) Blähen nt no pl; (of smoke) Schwaden m. **2** vi **(a)** (liter: sea) wogen (geh). **(b)** (fig: sail) sich blähen; (dress etc) sich bauschen.
♦**billow out** vi (sail etc) sich blähen; (dress etc) sich bauschen.
billowy ['bɪləʊɪ] adj **(a)** (liter) sea wogend (geh). **(b)** sails, curtains etc gebläht; smoke in Schwaden ziehend.
bill: ~**poster**, ~**sticker** n Plakat(an)kleber m.
Billy ['bɪlɪ] n dim of **William**.
billy(-can) ['bɪlɪ(kæn)] n Kochgeschirr nt.
billy(-goat) ['bɪlɪ(gəʊt)] n Ziegenbock m.
billy-(h)o ['bɪlɪhəʊ] n (inf) **like** ~ wie verrückt (inf).
bi-: ~**metallic** adj **(a)** rod, bar Bimetall-; **(b)** (Fin) ~**metallic currency** Doppelwährung f; ~**metallic nation** Land mit Doppelwährung; ~**metallism** n Doppelwährung f; ~**monthly 1** adj **(a)** (every two months) vierzehntäglich; **(b)** (twice a month) zweimonatlich; **2** adv **(a)** zweimal monatlich or im Monat; **(b)** alle zwei Monate, jeden zweiten Monat.
bin [bɪn] n **(a)** (esp Brit) (for bread) Brotkasten m; (for coal) (Kohlen)kasten m; (rubbish~) Mülleimer m; (dust~) Mülltonne f; (litter-~) Abfallbehälter m. **(b)** (for grain) Tonne f.
binary ['baɪnərɪ] adj binär; (Mus) form zweiteilig. ~ **fission** Zellteilung f; ~ **number** (Math) Dualzahl f, binäre Zahl; ~ **system** (Math) Dualsystem, binäres System; ~ **star**/~ **star system** (Astron) Doppelsternm/Doppelsternsystem.
bind [baɪnd] pret, ptp **bound 1** vt **(a)** (make fast, tie together) binden (to an +acc); person fesseln; (fig) verbinden (to mit). **bound hand and foot** an Händen und Füßen gefesselt or gebunden; **the emotions which** ~ **her to him** ihre emotionale Bindung an ihn.
(b) (tie round) wound, arm etc verbinden; bandage wickeln; binden; artery abbinden; (for beauty) waist einschnüren; feet einbinden or -schnüren; hair binden.
(c) (secure edge of) material, hem einfassen.
(d) book binden.
(e) (oblige: by contract, promise) **to** ~ **sb to sth/to do sth** jdn an etw (acc) binden, jdn zu etw verpflichten/jdn verpflichten, etw zu tun; **to** ~ **sb as an apprentice** jdn in die Lehre geben (to zu); see **bound**[1].
(f) (Med) bowels verstopfen.
(g) (make cohere, Cook) binden.
2 vi **(a)** (cohere: cement etc) binden. **stop the soil** ~**ing by adding some compost** lockern Sie den Boden mit Kompost; **the clay soil tended to** ~ der Lehmboden war ziemlich schwer or klebte ziemlich; **the grass should help the soil** ~ das Gras sollte den Boden festigen.
(b) (Med: food) stopfen.
(c) (stick: brake, sliding part etc) blockieren.
3 n (inf: nuisance) **to be (a bit of) a** ~ recht lästig sein.
♦**bind on** vt sep anbinden (+prep obj, -to an +acc); (+prep obj: on top of) binden auf (+acc).
♦**bind over** vt (Jur) **to** ~ **sb** ~ **(to keep the peace)** jdn verwarnen; **he was bound** ~ **for six months** er bekam eine sechsmonatige Bewährungsfrist.
♦**bind together** vt sep (lit) zusammenbinden; (fig) verbinden.
♦**bind up** vt sep **(a)** wound verbinden; hair hochbinden. **(b)** prisoner fesseln. **(c)** (fig) verknüpfen, verbinden. **to be bound** ~ **(with one another)** verbunden or verknüpft sein.
binder ['baɪndə'] n **(a)** (Agr) (machine) (Mäh)binder, Bindemäher m; (person) (Garben)binder(in f) m. **(b)** (Typ) (person) Buchbinder(in f) m; (machine) Bindemaschine f. **(c)** (for papers) Hefter m; (for magazines also) Mappe f.
bindery ['baɪndərɪ] n Buchbinderei f.
binding ['baɪndɪŋ] **1** n **(a)** (of book) Einband m; (act) Binden nt. **(b)** (Sew) Band nt. **(c)** (on skis) Bindung f. **2** adj **(a)** agreement, promise bindend, verbindlich (on für). **(b)** (Tech) bindend, Binde-. **(c)** (Med) food etc stopfend.
bindweed ['baɪndwiːd] n Winde f.
binge [bɪndʒ] n (inf) Gelage, Sauf /Freßgelage (sl) nt. **to go on a** ~ auf Sauftour (sl) gehen/eine Freßtour (sl) machen.
bingo ['bɪŋgəʊ] n Bingo nt.
binnacle ['bɪnəkl] n Kompaßhaus nt.
binoculars [bɪ'nɒkjʊləz] npl Fernglas nt. **a pair of** ~ ein Fernglas nt.
bi-: ~**nominal 1** adj (Math) binomisch; **2** n Binom nt; ~**nuclear** adj binuklear, zweikernig.
bio- [baɪəʊ-]: ~**chemical** adj biochemisch; ~**chemist** n Biochemiker(in f) m; ~**chemistry** n Biochemie f; ~**degradable** adj biologisch abbaubar; ~**genesis** n Biogenese f.
biographer [baɪ'ɒgrəfə'] n Biograph(in f) m.
biographic(al) [ˌbaɪəʊ'græfɪk(əl)] adj biographisch.
biography [baɪ'ɒgrəfɪ] n Biographie, Lebensbeschreibung f.
biological [ˌbaɪə'lɒdʒɪkəl] adj biologisch.
biologist [baɪ'ɒlədʒɪst] n Biologe m, Biologin f.
biology [baɪ'ɒlədʒɪ] n Biologie f.
biometrics [ˌbaɪə'metrɪks], **biometry** [baɪ'ɒmətrɪ] n Biometrie f.
biophysics [ˌbaɪəʊ'fɪzɪks] n Biophysik f.
biopsy ['baɪɒpsɪ] n Biopsie f.
bio-: ~**sphere** n Biosphäre f; ~**synthesis** n Biosynthese f.
bipartisan [ˌbaɪpɑːtɪ'zæn] adj Zweiparteien-.
bi-: ~**partite** adj zweiteilig; (affecting two parties) zweiseitig; ~**ped 1** n Zweifüßer m; (hum: human) Zweibeiner m; **2** adj zweifüßig; ~**plane** n Doppeldecker m; ~**polar** adj zwei- or doppelpolig.
birch [bɜːtʃ] **1** n **(a)** Birke f. **(b)** (for whipping) Rute f. **2** attr Birken-. **3** vt (mit Ruten) schlagen.
birching ['bɜːtʃɪŋ] n (act) Prügeln nt; (Jur) Prügelstrafe f. **to get a** ~ mit der Rute geschlagen werden.
bird [bɜːd] n **(a)** Vogel m. ~ **of paradise/passage** Paradies-/Zugvogel m; **the** ~ **has flown** (fig) der Vogel ist ausgeflogen; **a little** ~ **told me** (inf) das sagt mir mein kleiner Finger; **strictly for the** ~**s** (sl) das ist geschenkt (inf); **a** ~ **in the hand is worth two in the bush** (Prov) der Spatz in der Hand ist besser als die Taube auf dem Dach (Prov); **to tell sb about the** ~**s and the bees** jdm erzählen, wo die kleinen Kinder herkommen; see **feather**, **kill**.
(b) (Cook) Vogel m (hum inf).
(c) (Brit inf: girl) Biene f (inf).
(d) (inf: person) Vogel m (inf). **he's a cunning old** ~ er ist ein alter Fuchs.
(e) (inf) **to give sb the** ~ jdn auspfeifen; **to get the** ~ ausgepfiffen werden.
bird: ~ **bath** n Vogelbad nt; ~ **brain** n (inf) **to be a** ~ **brain** ein Spatzenhirn haben (inf); ~**-cage** n Vogelbauer nt or -käfig m; ~ **call** n Vogelruf m; ~ **dog** (US) **1** n (lit, fig) Spürhund m; **2** vt (inf) beschatten (inf); ~ **fancier** n Vogelzüchter m.
birdie ['bɜːdɪ] n **(a)** (inf) Vögelchen nt. **watch the** ~ gleich kommt's Vögelchen raus! **(b)** (Golf) Birdie nt.
bird: ~**-like** adj vogelartig; ~**-lime** n Vogelleim m; ~ **sanctuary** n Vogelschutzgebiet nt; ~ **seed** n Vogelfutter nt.
bird's: ~**-eye view** n Vogelperspektive f. **to get a** ~**-eye view of the town** die Stadt aus der Vogelperspektive sehen; ~ **foot** n Vogelfuß m; ~ **nest** n Vogelnest nt; ~**-nest** vi **to go** ~**-nesting** Vogelnester ausnehmen; ~ **nest soup** n Schwalben- or Vogelnestersuppe f.
bird watcher n Vogelbeobachter(in f) m.
biretta [bɪ'retə] n Birett nt.
Biro ® ['baɪərəʊ] n (Brit) Kugelschreiber, Kuli (inf) m.

birth [bɜ:θ] n **(a)** Geburt f. **the town/country of his** ~ seine Geburtsstadt/sein Geburtsland nt; **deaf from** or **since** ~ von Geburt an taub; **within a few minutes of** ~ einige Minuten nach der Geburt; **the rights which are ours by** ~ unsere angeborenen Rechte; **to give** ~ **to** gebären; (woman also) entbunden werden von; **to give** ~ entbinden; (animal) jungen; **she's going to give** ~! sie bekommt ihr Kind! **(b)** (parentage) Abstammung, Herkunft f. **Scottish by** ~ Schotte von Geburt, gebürtiger Schotte; **of good/low** or **humble** ~ aus gutem Hause or guter Familie/von niedriger Geburt. **(c)** (fig) Geburt f; (of movement, fashion etc) Aufkommen nt; (of nation, party, company also) Gründung f, Entstehen nt; (of new era) Anbruch m, Geburt f (geh); (of star) Entstehung f. **to give** ~ **to sth** etw schaffen/aufkommen lassen/gründen/anbrechen lassen.

birth: ~ **certificate** n Geburtsurkunde f; ~ **control** n Geburtenkontrolle or -regelung f; ~**-control clinic** n Familienberatungsstelle f.

birthday ['bɜ:θdeɪ] n Geburtstag m. **what did you get for your** ~? was hast du zum Geburtstag bekommen?; **on my** ~ an meinem Geburtstag; **see happy**.

birthday: ~ **cake** n Geburtstagskuchen m or -torte f; ~ **card** n Geburtstagskarte f; ~ **celebrations** npl Geburtstagsfeierlichkeiten pl; ~ **honours** npl Titel- und Ordensverleihungen pl am offiziellen Geburtstag des britischen Monarchen; ~ **party** n Geburtstagsfeier f; (with dancing etc) Geburtstagsparty f; (for child) Kindergeburtstag m; ~ **present** n Geburtstagsgeschenk nt; ~ **suit** n (inf) Adams-/Evaskostüm nt (inf); **the little boy in his** ~ **suit** der kleine Nackedei; **in one's** ~ **suit** im Adams-/Evaskostüm (inf).

birth: ~**mark** n Muttermal nt; ~**place** n Geburtsort m; ~**rate** n Geburtenrate or -ziffer f; ~**right** n **(a)** Geburtsrecht nt; **(b)** (right of firstborn) Erstgeburtsrecht nt; ~**stone** n Monatsstein m; ~ **trauma** n Geburtstrauma nt.

Biscay ['bɪskeɪ] n die Biskaya or Biscaya. **the Bay of** ~ der Golf von Biskaya or Biscaya.

biscuit ['bɪskɪt] **1** n **(a)** (Brit) Keks m; (dog ~) Hundekuchen m. **that takes/you take the** ~! (inf) das übertrifft alles or (negatively) schlägt dem Faß den Boden aus; ~ **barrel** Keksdose f. **(b)** (US) Brötchen nt. **(c)** (porcelain): ~**-ware** Biskuitporzellan nt. **(d)** (colour) Beige nt. **2** adj (colour) beige.

biscuity ['bɪskətɪ] adj texture keksartig; colour beige.

bisect [baɪ'sekt] **1** vt in zwei Teile or (equal parts) Hälften teilen; (Math) halbieren. **2** vi sich teilen.

bisection [baɪ'sekʃən] n (Math) Halbierung f.

bisector [baɪ'sektər] n (Math) Halbierende f.

bisexual [,baɪ'seksjuəl] **1** adj bisexuell; (Biol) zwittrig, doppelgeschlechtig. **2** n (person) Bisexuelle(r) mf.

bisexuality [,baɪ,seksju'ælɪtɪ] n Bisexualität f; (Biol) Zwittrigkeit, Doppelgeschlechtigkeit f.

bishop ['bɪʃəp] n **(a)** (Eccl) Bischof m. **thank you,** ~ vielen Dank, Herr Bischof. **(b)** (Chess) Läufer m.

bishopric ['bɪʃəprɪk] n (diocese) Bistum nt; (function) Bischofsamt nt.

bismuth ['bɪzməθ] n Wismut nt.

bison ['baɪsn] n (American) Bison m; (European) Wisent m.

bisque [bɪsk] n **(a)** (pottery) Biskuitporzellan nt. **(b)** (soup) Fischcremesuppe f.

bissextile [bɪ'sekstaɪl] (form) **1** n Schaltjahr nt. **2** adj Schalt-.

bistro ['bi:strəʊ] n Bistro nt.

bit[1] [bɪt] n **(a)** (for horse) Gebiß(stange f) nt. **to take the** ~ **between one's teeth** (fig) sich ins Zeug legen; **see champ**[1]. **(b)** (of drill) (Bohr)einsatz, Bohrer (inf) m; (of plane) (Hobel)messer nt. **(c)** (of key) (Schlüssel)bart m.

bit[2] n **(a)** (piece) Stück nt; (smaller) Stückchen; (of glass also) Scherbe f; (section: of book, film, symphony) Teil m; (part or place in book, drama, text, symphony etc) Stelle f. **a few** ~**s of furniture** ein paar Möbelstücke; **this island is a little** ~ **of America** diese Insel ist ein Stück(chen) Amerika; **I gave my** ~ **to my sister** ich habe meiner Schwester meinen Teil gegeben; **this is the** ~ **I hate,** he said, taking out his wallet das tue ich gar nicht gern, sagte er und zückte seine Brieftasche; **a** ~ (not much, small amount) ein bißchen, etwas; **would you like a** ~ **of ice cream?** möchten Sie etwas or ein bißchen Eis?; **there's a** ~ **of truth in what he says** daran ist etwas Wahres; **a** ~ **of advice/luck/news** ein Rat m/ein Glück nt/eine Neuigkeit; **we had a** ~ **of trouble/excitement** wir hatten ein wenig Ärger/Aufregung; **I only read a** ~ **of the novel** ich habe nur ein bißchen or Stückchen von dem Roman gelesen; **don't you feel the slightest** ~ **of remorse?** hast du denn nicht die geringsten Gewissensbisse?; **it might be a** ~ **of help** das könnte eine kleine Hilfe sein; **it did me a** ~ **of good** das hat mir geholfen; **it wasn't a** ~ **of help/use** das war überhaupt keine Hilfe/hat überhaupt nichts genützt; **the drug hasn't done him a** ~ **of good** das Medikament hat ihm überhaupt nicht geholfen; **quite a** ~ **of** einiges; **there's quite a** ~ **of work/bread left** es ist noch eine ganze Menge Arbeit/Brot da; **I've experienced quite a** ~ **in my life** ich habe in meinem Leben schon (so) einiges erlebt; **in** ~**s and pieces** (broken) in tausend Stücken; (lit, fig: come apart) in die Brüche gegangen; **to do the work in** ~**s and pieces** die Arbeit stückchenweise machen; **the** ~**s and pieces** die einzelnen Teile; (broken ~s) die Scherben pl; **bring all your** ~**s and pieces** bring deine Siebensachen; **to pick up the** ~**s and pieces** (fig) retten, was zu retten ist; **to come** or **fall to** ~**s** kaputtgehen, aus dem Leim gehen; **to pull** or **tear sth to** ~**s** (lit) etw in (tausend) Stücke reißen; (fig) keinen guten Faden an etw (dat) lassen; **to go to** ~**s** (fig inf) durchdrehen (inf). **(b)** (with time) **a** ~ ein Weilchen nt; **he's gone out for a** ~ er ist ein Weilchen or mal kurz weggegangen.

(c) (with cost) **a** ~ eine ganze Menge; **it cost quite a** ~ das hat ganz schön (viel) gekostet (inf). **(d)** **to do one's** ~ sein(en) Teil tun; (fair share also) das Seine tun; **look, you're not doing your** ~ hör mal zu, du setzt dich nicht genügend ein. **(e)** **a** ~ **of** a crack/bruise etc (ein kleiner Riß/Fleck etc; **he's a** ~ **of a rogue/musician/expert/connoisseur** er ist ein zsemlicher Schlingel/er ist gar kein schlechter Musiker/er versteht einiges davon/er ist ein Kenner; **you're a** ~ **of an idiot, aren't you?** du bist ganz schön dumm; **he's got a** ~ **of a nerve!** der hat vielleicht Nerven!; **it's a** ~ **of a nuisance** das ist schon etwas ärgerlich; **now that's a** ~ **of an improvement** das ist schon besser. **(f)** **by** ~ Stück für Stück; (gradually) nach und nach; **he's every** ~ **a soldier/Frenchman** er ist durch und durch Soldat/Franzose; **not a** ~ **of it!** keineswegs; **as good as ... es/er ist genauso gut, wie ...; **not a** ~ **of it** keineswegs, keine Spur (inf). **(g)** **when it comes to the** ~ wenn es drauf ankommt. **(h)** (coin) (Brit) Stück nt, Münze f. **2/4/6** ~**s** (US) 25/50/75 Cents. **(i)** (Brit sl) Weib nt (sl). **cheeky little** ~ freches Stück (sl). **2** adv **a** ~ ein bißchen, etwas; **were you angry?** — **a** ~ haben Sie sich geärgert? — ja, schon etwas or ein bißchen; **wasn't she a little** ~ **surprised?** war sie nicht etwas erstaunt?; **I'm not a (little)** ~ **surprised** das wundert mich überhaupt nicht or kein bißchen (inf) or keineswegs; **he wasn't a** ~ **the wiser for it** danach war er auch nicht viel klüger or schlauer; **quite a** ~ ziemlich viel; **that's quite a** ~ **better** das ist schon besser; **he's improved quite a** ~ er hat sich ziemlich or um einiges gebessert.

bit[3] pret of **bite**.

bitch [bɪtʃ] **1** n **(a)** (of dog) Hündin f; (of canines generally) Weibchen nt; (of fox) Füchsin f; (of wolf) Wölfin f. **terrier** ~ weiblicher Terrier. **(b)** (inf: woman) Miststück nt (sl); (spiteful) Hexe f. **silly** ~ doofe Ziege (inf); **don't be a** ~ sei nicht so gemein or gehässig; **she's a mean** ~ sie ist ein gemeines Stück (sl). **(c)** (sl: complaint) **he has to have his little** ~ er muß natürlich meckern (inf); **what's your** ~ **this time?** was hast du diesmal zu meckern? (inf). **2** vi (sl: complain) meckern (inf) (about über +acc).

♦**bitch up** vt sep (sl) versauen (sl).

bitchiness ['bɪtʃɪnɪs] n Gehässigkeit, Gemeinheit f; (of remark also) Bissigkeit f.

bitchy ['bɪtʃɪ] adj (+er) (inf) woman gehässig, gemein; remark also bissig. **that was a** ~ **thing to do/say** das war gehässig or gemein; **she started getting** ~ **about her** sie fing an, bissige or gehässige Bemerkungen über sie zu machen.

bite [baɪt] (vb: pret **bit**, ptp **bitten**) **1** n **(a)** Biß m. **in two** ~**s** mit zwei Bissen; **he took a** ~ **(out) of the apple** er biß in den Apfel. **(b)** (wound etc) (dog, snake, flea ~ etc) Biß m; (insect ~) Stich m; (love ~) (Knutsch)fleck m (inf). **(c)** (Fishing) **I think I've got a** ~ ich glaube, es hat einer angebissen. **(d)** (of food) Happen m. **there's not a** ~ **to eat** es ist überhaupt nichts zu essen da; **come and have a** ~ komm und iß 'ne Kleinigkeit; **do you fancy a** ~ **(to eat)?** möchten Sie etwas essen? **(e)** **there's a** ~ **in the air** es ist beißend kalt; **the** ~ **of the wind** der beißend-kalte Wind. **(f)** (of file, saw) **the file has lost its** ~ die Feile ist stumpf geworden; **these screws don't have enough** ~ diese Schrauben greifen or fassen nicht richtig. **(g)** (of sauce etc) Schärfe f. **2** vt **(a)** (person, dog) beißen; (insect) stechen. **to** ~ **one's nails** Nägel kauen; **to** ~ **one's tongue/lips** sich (dat) auf die Zunge/Lippen beißen; **the trapeze artist** ~**s the rope between her teeth** die Trapezkünstlerin hält das Seil mit den Zähnen fest; **don't worry, he won't** ~ **you** (fig inf) keine Angst, er wird dich schon nicht beißen (inf); **to** ~ **the dust** (inf) daran glauben müssen (inf); **he had been bitten by the urge to ...** der Drang, zu ..., hatte ihn erfaßt or gepackt; **once bitten twice shy** (Prov) (ein) gebranntes Kind scheut das Feuer (Prov); **what's biting you?** (fig inf) was ist mit dir los? (inf), was hast du denn? **(b)** (cold, frost, wind) schneiden in (+dat). **(c)** (file, saw) schneiden in (+acc); (acid) ätzen. **(d)** (inf: swindle) **I've been bitten** ich bin reingelegt worden (inf). **3** vi **(a)** (dog etc) beißen; (insects) stechen. **(b)** (fish, fig inf) anbeißen. **(c)** (cold, frost, wind) beißen, schneiden. **(d)** (wheels) fassen, greifen; (saw, anchor) fassen; (screw) greifen.

♦**bite into** vi +prep obj (person) (hinein)beißen in (+acc); (teeth) (tief) eindringen in (+acc); (acid, saw) sich hineinfressen in (+acc); (screw, drill) sich hineinbohren in (+acc).

♦**bite off** vt sep abbeißen. **he won't** ~ **your head** ~ er wird dir schon nicht den Kopf abreißen; **to** ~ ~ **more than one can chew** (prov) sich (dat) zuviel zumuten.

♦**bite on** vi +prep obj beißen auf (+acc). **give the baby something to** ~ ~ gib dem Kind etwas zum Beißen.

♦**bite through** vt insep durchbeißen.

biter ['baɪtər] n **the** ~ **bitten!** mit den eigenen Waffen geschlagen!; (in deception also) der betrogene Betrüger!

biting ['baɪtɪŋ] adj beißend; cold, wind also schneidend.

bit part n kleine Nebenrolle.

bit-part player n Schauspieler(in f) m in kleinen Nebenrollen.

bitten ['bɪtn] ptp of **bite**.

bitter ['bɪtər] **1** adj (+er) **(a)** taste bitter. ~ **lemon** Bitter Lemon nt; **it was a** ~ **pill to swallow** es war eine bittere Pille. **(b)** cold, winter bitter; weather, wind bitterkalt attr, eisig. **it's** ~ **today** es ist heute bitter kalt.

(c) *enemy, struggle, opposition* erbittert.
(d) *disappointment, hatred, reproach, remorse, tears* bitter; *criticism* scharf, heftig. **to the ~ end** bis zum bitteren Ende.
(e) *(embittered)* bitter; *person also* verbittert. **to be or feel ~ at sth** über etw (*acc*) bitter or verbittert sein.
2 *adv*: **~ cold** bitterkalt *attr*, bitter kalt *pred*.
3 *n* (a) *(Brit: beer)* halbdunkles obergäriges Bier.
(b) **~s** *npl* Magenbitter *m*; **gin and ~s** Gin mit Bitterlikör.
bitterly ['bitəli] *adv* (a) *reproach, disappointed* bitter; *complain also, weep* bitterlich; *oppose* erbittert; *criticize* scharf; *jealous* sehr. (b) *cold* bitter. (c) *(showing embitteredness)* verbittert; *criticize* erbittert.
bittern ['bitən]*n* Rohrdommel *f*.
bitterness ['bitənis] *n see adj* (a) Bitterkeit *f*. (b) Bitterkeit *f*; bittere Kälte. (c) Erbittertheit *f*. (d) Bitterkeit *f*; Schärfe, Heftigkeit *f*. **such was the ~ of his disappointment/jealousy** er war so bitter enttäuscht/derart eifersüchtig. (e) Bitterkeit *f*; Verbitterung *f*.
bitter-sweet ['bitə,swi:t] **1** *adj* *(lit, fig)* bittersüß. **2** *n* *(Bot)* Kletternder Baumwürger; *(nightshade)* Bittersüßer Nachtschatten.
bitty ['biti] *adj* (*+er*) *(Brit inf: scrappy)* zusammengestoppelt *(pej inf)* or *-gestückelt (inf)*.
bitumen ['bitjumin] *n* Bitumen *nt*.
bituminous [bi'tju:minəs] *adj* bituminös. **~ coal** Stein- or Fettkohle *f*.
bivalent ['bai'veilənt] *adj* bivalent, zweiwertig.
bivalve ['baivælv] *(Zool)* **1** *n* zweischalige Muschel. **2** *adj* zweischalig.
bivouac ['bivuæk] *(vb: pret, ptp ~ked)* **1** *n* Biwak *nt*. **2** *vi* biwakieren.
bi-weekly ['bai'wi:kli] **1** *adj* (a) *(twice a week)* **~ meetings/editions** Konferenzen/Ausgaben, die zweimal wöchentlich or in der Woche stattfinden/erscheinen.
(b) *(fortnightly)* zweiwöchentlich, vierzehntäglich.
2 *adv* (a) *(twice a week)* zweimal wöchentlich, zweimal in der Woche.
(b) *(fortnightly)* alle vierzehn Tage, vierzehntäglich.
biz [biz] *(inf)* *abbr of* **business**.
bizarre [bi'za:ʳ] *adj* bizarr.
BL *abbr of* **Bachelor of Law**.
blab [blæb] **1** *vi* quatschen *(inf)*; *(talk fast, tell secret)* plappern; *(criminal)* singen *(sl)*. **2** *vt (also ~ out)* *secret* ausplaudern.
blabbermouth ['blæbə,mauθ] *n (inf)* Klatschmaul *nt* *(inf)*.
black [blæk] **1** *adj* (*+er*) (a) schwarz. **~ man/woman** Schwarze(r) *mf*; **a ~ eye** ein blaues Auge; **to give sb a ~ eye** jdm ein blaues Auge schlagen or verpassen *(inf)*; **~ and blue** grün und blau; **~ and white photography/film** Schwarzweißfotografie *f*/-film *m*; **to swear that ~ is white** schwören, daß zwei mal zwei fünf ist; **the situation isn't so ~ and white as** that die Situation ist nicht so eindeutig schwarz-weiß; **a western makes things ~ and white** ein Western stellt alles in Schwarzweißmalerei dar; **he pretends that things are much more ~ and white than they really are** er stellt die Dinge viel zu sehr schwarz-weiß dar.
(b) *(dirty)* schwarz.
(c) *(wicked)* *thought, plan, deed* schwarz. **he's not so ~ as he's painted** *(prov)* er ist nicht so schlecht wie sein Ruf.
(d) *future, prospects, mood* düster, finster. **he painted their conduct in the ~est colours** er malte ihr Betragen in den schwärzesten Farben; **things are looking ~ for our project** es sieht für unser Vorhaben ziemlich schwarz or düster aus; **maybe things aren't as ~ as they seem** vielleicht ist alles gar nicht so schlimm, wie es aussieht; **in ~ despair** in tiefster Verzweiflung.
(e) *(fig: angry)* *looks* böse. **he looked as ~ as thunder** er machte ein bitterböses Gesicht; **his face went ~** er wurde rot vor Zorn.
(f) *(during strike)* **to declare a cargo etc ~** eine Ladung *etc* für bestreikt erklären; **~ goods** bestreikte Waren.
2 *n* (a) *(colour)* Schwarz *nt*. **he is dressed in ~** er trägt Schwarz; **to wear ~** for sb für jdn Trauer tragen; **it's written down in ~ and white** es steht schwarz auf weiß geschrieben; **a ~ and white** *(Art)* eine Schwarzweißzeichnung; **a film which oversimplifies and presents everything in ~ and white** ein Film, der durch seine Schwarzweißmalerei alles vereinfacht darstellt.
(b) *(negro)* Schwarze(r) *mf*.
(c) *(of night)* Schwärze *f*.
(d) *(Chess etc)* Schwarz *nt*; *(Billiards)* schwarzer Ball; *(Roulette)* Schwarz, Noir *nt*.
(e) **in the ~** *(Fin)* in den schwarzen Zahlen.
3 *vt* (a) schwärzen. **to ~ one's face** sich *(dat)* das Gesicht schwarz machen; **to ~ sb's eye** jdm ein blaues Auge schlagen or verpassen *(inf)*.
(b) *shoes* wichsen.
(c) *(trade union)* bestreiken; *goods* boykottieren.
♦**black out 1** *vi* das Bewußtsein verlieren, ohnmächtig werden. **2** *vt sep* (a) *building, stage* verdunkeln. (b) *(not broadcast)* **the technicians have ~ed ~ tonight's programmes** durch einen Streik des technischen Personals kann das heutige Abendprogramm nicht ausgestrahlt werden. (c) *(with ink, paint)* schwärzen.
♦**black up** *vt (Theat inf)* sich schwarz anmalen.
blackamoor ['blækəmuəʳ] *n (obs)* Mohr *m (obs)*.
black: **~ball** *vt (vote against)* stimmen gegen; *(inf: exclude)* ausschließen; **~ beetle** *n* Küchenschabe *f*; **~berry** *n* Brombeere *f*; **to go ~berrying** Brombeeren pflücken gehen, in die Brombeeren gehen *(inf)*; **~bird** *n* Amsel *f*; **~board** *n* Tafel *f*; **to write sth on the ~board** etw an die Tafel schreiben; **~ book** *n*: **to be in sb's ~ books** bei jdm schlecht angeschrieben sein

(inf); **little ~ book** Notizbuch *nt* *(mit Adressen der Mädchenbekanntschaften)*; **~ box** *n (Aviat)* Flugschreiber *m*; **~ bread** *n* Schwarzbrot *nt*; **~cap** *n (bird)* Mönchsgrasmücke *f*; *(US: berry)* Barett *nt*; **~ cap** *n* schwarze Kappe *(des Richters bei Todesurteilen)*; **~ comedy** *n* schwarze Komödie; **B~ Country** *n* Industriegebiet *nt* in den englischen Midlands; **~currant** *n* schwarze Johannisbeere; **B~ Death** *n (Hist)* Schwarzer Tod.
blacken ['blækən] **1** *vt* (a) schwarz machen; **one's face** schwarz anmalen. **the walls were ~ed by the fire** die Wände waren vom Feuer geschwärzt. (b) *(fig)* *character* verunglimpfen. **to ~ sb's name or reputation** jdn schlechtmachen. **2** *vi* schwarz werden.
black: **~-eyed** *adj* schwarzäugig; **B~ Forest** *n* Schwarzwald *m*; **~ friar** *n* Dominikaner *m*; Benediktiner *m*; **~ grouse** *n* Birkhuhn *nt*.
blackguard ['blæga:d] *n (old)* Bösewicht, (Spitz)bube *m (old)*.
blackguardly ['blæga:dli] *adj* *deed, person* niederträchtig.
black: **~head** *n* Mitesser *m*; **~-hearted** *adj* böse; **~ hole** *n (Astron)* schwarzes Loch; **B~ Hole of Calcutta** *n (cramped)* Affenstall *m*; *(dirty, dark)* scheußliches Verlies; **~ humour** *n* schwarzer Humor; **~ ice** *n* Glatteis *nt*.
blacking ['blækiŋ] *n* (a) *(for shoes)* schwarze (Schuh)wichse; *(for stoves)* Ofenschwärze *f*. (b) *(by trade union)* Bestreikung *f*; *(of goods)* Boykottierung *f*.
blackish ['blækiʃ] *adj* schwärzlich.
black: **~jack** **1** *n* (a) *(flag)* schwarze (Piraten)flagge; (b) *(Hist: drinking vessel)* (lederner) Becher; (c) *(US: weapon)* Totschläger *m*; (d) *(Cards: pontoon)* Siebzehn und Vier *nt*; **2** *vt (US: hit)* prügeln; **~ lead** *n* Graphit *m*; *(for stoves)* Schwärze *f*; **~-lead** *vt stove* schwärzen; **~ leg** *(Brit: Ind)* **1** *n* Streikbrecher *m*; **2** *vi* Streikbrecher sein, sich als Streikbrecher betätigen; **3** *vt* **one's fellow workers** sich unsolidarisch verhalten gegen; **~ list** *n* schwarze Liste; **~-list** *vt auf die schwarze Liste setzen.
blackly ['blækli] *adv (gloomily)* düster, finster.
black: **~ magic** *n* Schwarze Kunst or Magie *f*; **~mail 1** *n* Erpressung *f*; **2** *vt* erpressen; **to ~mail sb into doing sth** jdn durch Erpressung dazu zwingen, etw zu tun; **he had ~mailed £500 out of her** er hatte £ 500 von ihr erpreßt; **~mailer** *n* Erpresser(in *f*) *m*; **B~ Maria** *n* grüne Minna *(inf)*; **~ mark** *n* Tadel *m*; *(in school register also)* Eintrag *m*; **that's a ~ mark for him** das ist ein Minuspunkt für ihn; **~ market 1** *n* schwarzer Markt, Schwarzmarkt *m*; **2** *adj attr* Schwarzmarkt-; **~ marketeer** *n* Schwarzhändler *m*; **~ mass** *n* Schwarze Messe; **B~ Muslim** *n* Black Moslem *m*.
blackness ['blæknis] *n* Schwärze *f*. **the ~ of his mood** seine düstere Laune.
black: **~out** *n* (a) *(Med)* Ohnmacht(sanfall *m*) *f no pl*; **I must have had a ~out** ich muß wohl in Ohnmacht gefallen sein; **he had a ~out** ihm wurde schwarz vor Augen; (b) *(light failure)* Stromausfall *m*; *(Theat)* Blackout *nt*; *(during war)* Verdunkelung *f*; *(TV)* Ausfall *m*; (c) *(news ~out)* (Nachrichten)sperre *f*; **B~ Panther** *n* Black Panther *m*; **B~ Power** *n* Black Power *f*; **~ pudding** *n* = Blutwurst *f*; **B~ Rod** *n* Zeremonienmeister *m des britischen Oberhauses*; **B~ Sea** *n* Schwarzes Meer; **~ sheep** *n (fig)* schwarzes Schaf; **B~shirt** *n* Schwarzhemd *nt*; **~smith** *n* (Grob- or Huf)schmied *m*; **at/to the ~smith's** beim/zum Schmied; **~ spot** *n (also accident ~spot)* Gefahrenstelle *f*; **~thorn** *n (Bot)* Schwarzdorn *m*; **~ tie 1** *n (on invitation)* Abendanzug *m*; **2** *adj* *dinner, function* mit Smokingzwang; **is it ~ tie?** ist da Smokingzwang?; **~top** *n (US) (substance)* schwarzer Straßenbelag; *(road)* geteerte Straße; *(paved with asphalt)* Asphaltstraße *f*; **~ velvet** *n* Sekt *m* mit Starkbier; **~ widow** *n* Schwarze Witwe *f*.
bladder ['blædəʳ] *n* (a) *(Anat, Bot)* Blase *f*. **with all that beer in your ~** mit dem vielen Bier im Bauch. (b) *(Ftbl)* Blase *f*.
bladderwrack ['blædəræk] *n* Blasentang *m*.
blade [bleid] *n* (a) *(of knife, tool, weapon, razor)* Klinge *f*; *(of pencil sharpener)* Messerchen *nt*; *(of guillotine)* Beil *nt*.
(b) *(of tongue)* vorderer Zungenrücken; *(of oar, spade, saw, windscreen wiper)* Blatt *nt*; *(of plough)* Schar *f*; *(of turbine, paddle wheel)* Schaufel *f*; *(of propeller)* Blatt *nt*, Flügel *m*.
(c) *(of leaf)* Blatt *nt*, Spreite *f (spec)*; *(of grass, corn)* Halm *m*, Spreite *f (spec)*. **wheat in the ~** Weizen auf dem Halm.
(d) *(liter: sword)* Klinge *f (liter)*.
(e) *(old: dashing fellow)* schmucker Bursch *(old)*.
(f) *(Anat) see* **shoulder ~**.
-bladed ['bleidid] *adj suf* **a twin~ propeller** ein Zweiblattpropeller *m*; **a two~ knife** ein Messer *nt* mit zwei Klingen.
blaeberry ['bleibəri] *n (Scot, N Engl) see* **bilberry**.
blah [bla:] *(inf)* **1** *n (dated: nonsense)* Blabla *(inf)*, Geschwafel *(inf)* *nt*. **2** *interj* **~, ~, ~** blabla *(inf)*.
blame [bleim] **1** *vt* (a) *(hold responsible)* die Schuld geben (*+dat*), beschuldigen. **to ~ sb for sth/sth on sb** jdm die Schuld an etw *(dat)* geben or zuschreiben *(geh)*, die Schuld an etw *(dat)* auf jdn schieben; **to ~ sth on sth** die Schuld an etw *(dat)* auf etw *(acc)* schieben, einer Sache *(dat)* die Schuld an etw *(dat)* geben; **you only have yourself to ~** das hast du dir selbst zuzuschreiben, du bist ganz allein (dran) schuld; **I'm to ~ for this** daran bin ich schuld; **whom/what are we to ~ or who/what is to ~ for this accident?** wer/was ist schuld an diesem Unfall?; **I ~ him for leaving the door open** er ist schuld, daß die Tür aufblieb; **to ~ oneself for sth** sich *(dat)* etw selbst zuzuschreiben haben, selbst an etw *(dat)* schuld sein; *(feel responsible)* sich für etw verantwortlich fühlen, sich selbst bezichtigen; **he ~s himself for starting the fire** er gibt sich selbst die Schuld daran, daß das Feuer ausgebrochen ist.
(b) *(reproach)* Vorwürfe machen *(sb for jdm für or wegen)*. **you can't go on blaming yourself for something that wasn't your fault** du kannst dir doch nicht dauernd (selbst) Vorwürfe für etwas machen, was gar nicht deine Schuld war; **nobody is blaming you** es macht Ihnen ja niemand einen Vorwurf.

(c) he decided to turn down the offer — well, I can't say I ~ him er entschloß sich, das Angebot abzulehnen — das kann ich aber auch gut verstehen, das kann man ihm wahrhaftig nicht verdenken; **so I told her to get lost** — **(I)** don't ~ you da habe ich ihr gesagt, sie soll zum Teufel gehen — da hattest du ganz recht; **so I told him what I really thought, do you** ~ **me?** da habe ich ihm gründlich meine Meinung gesagt, und doch wohl auch zu Recht, oder?

2 n **(a)** (responsibility) Schuld f. **to put the** ~ **for sth on sb** jdm die Schuld an etw (dat) geben; **to take the** ~ die Schuld auf sich (acc) nehmen; (for sb's mistakes also) den Kopf hinhalten; **why do I always have to take the** ~? warum muß denn immer ich an allem schuld sein?; **parents must take the** ~ **for their children's failings** Eltern haben die Verantwortung für die Fehler ihrer Kinder zu tragen; **we share the** ~ wir haben beide/alle schuld; **the** ~ **lies with him** er hat or ist schuld (daran). **(b)** (censure) Tadel m. **without** ~ ohne Schuld; (irreproachable) life etc untadelig.

blameless ['bleimlis] adj schuldlos; life untadelig.
blamelessly ['bleimlisli] adv unschuldig.
blameworthy ['bleimwɜ:ðɪ] adj schuldig; neglect tadelnswert. **he is to be held** ~ er hat sich schuldig gemacht; **he cannot be considered** ~ ihn trifft keine Schuld.

blanch [blɑ:ntʃ] **1** vt (Hort) bleichen; (illness) face bleich machen; (fear) erbleichen lassen; (Cook) vegetables blanchieren; almonds brühen. **2** vi (with vor +dat) (person) blaß werden; (with fear also) bleich werden, erbleichen (geh).
blancmange [blə'mɒnʒ] n Pudding m.
bland [blænd] adj (+er) **(a)** (suave) expression, look, manner verbindlich; face ausdruckslos-höflich, glatt (pej); person verbindlich; (trying to avoid trouble) konziliant. **(b)** (mild) air, weather mild; taste also nüchtern, fade (pej). **(c)** (harmless, lacking distinction) nichtssagend.
blandish ['blændɪʃ] vt schönreden (+dat).
blandishment ['blændɪʃmənt] n Schmeichelei f.
blandly ['blændlɪ] adv see adj.
blandness ['blændnɪs] n see adj **(a)** Verbindlichkeit f; ausdruckslose Höflichkeit; Konzilianz f. **(b)** Milde f; Fadheit f. **(c)** nichtssagende Art.

blank [blæŋk] **1** adj (+er) **(a)** piece of paper, page, wall leer; silence, darkness tief; coin ungeprägt. ~ **cheque** Blankoscheck m; (fig) Freibrief f; **to give sb a** ~ **cheque** (fig) jdm Carte blanche geben (geh), jdm freie Hand geben; **a** ~ **space** eine Lücke, ein freier Platz; (on form) ein freies Feld; **there is a** ~ **space after each question** nach jeder Frage ist eine Lücke (gelassen) or ein Platz frei gelassen; ~ **form** Formular(blatt) nt, Vordruck m; **please leave** ~ (on form) bitte frei lassen or nicht ausfüllen.
(b) (empty) life etc unausgefüllt, leer. **these** ~ **and characterless house fronts** diese nackten, charakterlosen Fassaden.
(c) (expressionless) face, look ausdruckslos; (stupid) verständnislos; (puzzled) verdutzt, verblüfft. **he looked at me with** ~ **stupidity** er sah mich völlig verständnislos an; **to look** ~ (expressionless) eine ausdruckslose Miene aufsetzen; (stupid) verständnislos dreinschauen; (puzzled) ein verdutztes Gesicht machen; **he just looked** ~ or **gave me a** ~ **look** er guckte mich nur groß an (inf); **my mind went** ~ ich hatte Mattscheibe (inf) or ein Brett vor dem Kopf (inf); **sorry, I've gone** ~ (inf) tut mir leid, aber ich habe totale Mattscheibe (inf).
(d) ~ **(cartridge)** Platzpatrone f.
(e) ~ **verse** Blankvers m.
2 n **(a)** (in document) freier Raum, leere Stelle; (~ document) Vordruck m, Formular nt; (gap) Lücke f.
(b) (void) Leere f. **my mind was/went a complete** ~ ich hatte totale Mattscheibe (inf).
(c) (in lottery) Niete f. **to draw a** ~ (fig) kein Glück haben.
(d) (in a target) Scheibenmittelpunkt m.
(e) (cartridge) Platzpatrone f.
(f) (domino) Blank nt.
(g) (coin) Schrötling m (spec); (key) Rohling m.
blanket ['blæŋkɪt] **1** n (lit, fig) Decke f. **a** ~ **of snow/fog** eine Schnee-/Nebeldecke; **born on the wrong side of the** ~ (hum inf) unehelich (geboren) sein. **2** adj attr statement pauschal; insurance etc umfassend. **3** vt **(a)** (snow, smoke) zudecken. **fog** ~**ed the town** Nebel hüllte die Stadt ein. **(b)** (Naut) ship den Wind abhalten von.
blanket: ~ **bath** n Waschen nt im Bett; **to give sb a** ~ **bath** jdn im Bett waschen; ~ **stitch** n Languettenstich m.
blankly ['blæŋklɪ] adv see adj **(c)** ausdruckslos; verständnislos; verdutzt, verblüfft. **she just looked at me** ~ sie sah mich nur groß an (inf).
blankness ['blæŋknɪs] n (emptiness) Leere f; (of expression) Ausdruckslosigkeit f; (not understanding) Verständnislosigkeit f; (puzzlement) Verdutztheit, Verblüffung f.
blare [blɛəʳ] **1** n Plärren, Geplärr nt; (of car horn etc) lautes Hupen; (of trumpets etc) Schmettern nt.
2 vi see n plärren; laut hupen; schmettern. **the orchestra tends to** ~ **a bit** das Orchester wird gern etwas laut; **the music/his voice** ~**d through the hall** die Musik/seine Stimme schallte durch den Saal.
3 vt be quiet! he ~**d** Ruhe!, brüllte er.
♦ **blare out 1** vi (loud voice, music) schallen; (trumpets) schmettern; (radio, music also) plärren; (car horn) laut hupen; (person) brüllen. **2** vt sep (trumpets) tune schmettern; (radio) music plärren; (person) order, warning etc brüllen.
blarney ['blɑ:nɪ] n Schmeichelei f, Schmus m (inf). **he has kissed the** ~ **stone** der kann einen beschwatzen (inf). **2** vt sb schmeicheln (+dat). **he could** ~ **his way out of trouble** er könnte sich aus allem herausreden. **3** vi schmeicheln.
blaspheme [blæs'fi:m] **1** vt lästern, schmähen (geh). **2** vi Gott lästern. **to** ~ **against sb/sth** (lit, fig) jdn/etw schmähen (geh).

blasphemer [blæs'fi:məʳ] n Gotteslästerer m.
blasphemous ['blæsfɪməs] adj (lit, fig) blasphemisch; words also lästerlich, frevelhaft.
blasphemously ['blæsfɪməslɪ] adv blasphemisch; speak also lästerlich, frevlerisch.
blasphemy ['blæsfɪmɪ] n Blasphemie f; (Rel also) (Gottes-)lästerung f; (words also) Schmähung f (geh).
blast [blɑ:st] **1** n **(a)** (of wind) Windstoß m; (of hot air) Schwall m. **a** ~ **of wind** ein Windstoß; **an icy** ~ ein eisiger Wind.
(b) (sound: of trumpets) Geschmetter, Schmettern nt; (of foghorn) Tuten nt. **the ship gave a long** ~ **on its foghorn** das Schiff ließ sein Nebelhorn ertönen; **to blow a** ~ **on the bugle** auf dem Horn blasen.
(c) (noise, explosion) Explosion f; (shock wave) Druckwelle f. **to get the full** ~ **of sb's anger** jds Wut in voller Wucht abkriegen.
(d) (in quarrying etc) Sprengladung f.
(e) (of furnace) (Blas)wind m. **(to go) at full** ~ (lit, fig) auf Hochtouren (laufen); **with the radio turned up (at) full** ~ mit dem Radio voll aufgedreht.
2 vt **(a)** (lightning) schlagen in (+acc); (with powder) sprengen.
(b) (send) rocket schießen.
(c) (blight) plant vernichten, zerstören; reputation also, future ruinieren.
3 vi (in quarry) sprengen.
4 interj (inf) ~ **(it)!** verdammt! (inf), so ein Mist! (inf); ~ **what he wants!** das ist doch wurscht, was der will! (inf); ~ **him for coming so late** Herrgott, daß er aber auch so spät kommen muß! (inf); ~ **that work, I'm going out tonight/I'd rather go out** die Arbeit kann mich mal (inf), ich geh' heut abend weg/diese verdammte Arbeit (inf), ich würde viel lieber weggehen; ~ **this car!** dieses verdammte Auto! (inf).
♦ **blast off** vi (rocket, astronaut) abheben, starten.
blasted ['blɑ:stɪd] **1** adj (a) öde. **(b)** (inf) verdammt (inf), Mist-(inf). **he was talking all the** ~ **time** verdammt, er hat die ganze Zeit geredet (inf). **2** adv (inf) verdammt (inf).
blast furnace n Hochofen m.
blasting ['blɑ:stɪŋ] n (Tech) Sprengen nt. "**danger** ~ **in progress**" „Achtung! Sprengarbeiten!"
blast-off ['blɑ:stɒf] n Abschuß m.
blatancy ['bleɪtənsɪ] n see blatant Offensichtlichkeit f; Eklatanz f; Kraßheit f; Unverfrorenheit f. **the** ~ **of their disregard for ...** ihre unverhohlene or offene Mißachtung der ...
blatant ['bleɪtənt] adj (very obvious) offensichtlich; injustice, lie, error, lack also eklatant; error also kraß; liar, social climber unverfroren; disregard offen, unverhohlen. **there's no need (for you) to be quite so** ~ **about it** (in talking) Sie brauchen das nicht so herumzuposaunen (inf); (in doing sth) Sie brauchen das nicht so deutlich zu tun.
blatantly ['bleɪtntlɪ] adv offensichtlich; (openly) offen; (without respect) unverfroren. **you don't have to make it quite so** ~ **obvious** Sie brauchen es nicht so überdeutlich zu zeigen; **she** ~ **ignored it** sie hat das schlicht und einfach ignoriert.
blather ['blæðəʳ] n, vi see blether.
blaze¹ [bleɪz] **1** n **(a)** (fire) Feuer nt; (of building etc also) Brand m. "~ **at factory**" „Brand in Fabrik"; **six people died in the** ~ sechs Menschen kamen in den Flammen um.
(b) (of guns etc) Feuer, Funkeln nt. **a** ~ **of lights/colour** ein Lichtermeer nt/Meer nt von Farben; **a sudden** ~ **of light from the watchtower** ein plötzlicher Lichtstrahl vom Wachturm; **he went out in a** ~ **of glory** er trat mit Glanz und Gloria ab.
(c) (of fire, sun) Glut f; (fig: of rage) Anfall m.
(d) (inf) **go to** ~**s** scher dich zum Teufel! (inf); **it can go to** ~**s** das kann mir gestohlen bleiben (inf); **what/how the** ~**s ...?** was/wie zum Teufel ...? (inf); **like** ~**s** wie verrückt (inf).
2 vi **(a)** (sun) brennen; (fire also) lodern. **to** ~ **with anger** vor Zorn glühen. **(b)** (guns) feuern. **with all guns blazing** aus allen Rohren feuernd.
♦ **blaze abroad** vt sep (liter) verbreiten (throughout in +dat).
♦ **blaze away** vi **(a)** (soldiers, guns) drauflos feuern (at auf +acc). **(b)** (fire etc) lodern.
♦ **blaze down** vi (sun) niederbrennen (on auf +acc).
♦ **blaze up** vi aufflammen, auflodern.
blaze² **1** n (of horse etc) Blesse f; (on tree) Anreißung f. **2** vt tree anreißen. **to** ~ **a trail** (lit) einen Weg markieren; (fig) den Weg bahnen.
blazer ['bleɪzəʳ] n Blazer m (also Sch), Klubjacke f.
blazing ['bleɪzɪŋ] adj (a) building etc brennend; fire, torch lodernd; sun, light grell; sun (hot) brennend. **(b)** (fig) eyes funkelnd (with vor +dat); red knall-, leuchtend. **he is** ~ (inf) er kocht vor Wut (inf), er ist fuchsteufelswild (inf).
blazon ['bleɪzn] **1** n (Her) Wappen nt. **2** vt (liter: also ~ **abroad**) news verbreiten (throughout in +dat).
bldg abbr of **building**.
bleach [bli:tʃ] **1** n **(a)** Bleichmittel nt. **(b)** (act) Bleichen nt. **to give sth a** ~ etw bleichen. **2** vt linen, bones, hair bleichen. **3** vi (bones) (ver)bleichen.
♦ **bleach out** vt sep ausbleichen.
bleachers ['bli:tʃəz] n pl (US) unüberdachte Zuschauertribüne.
bleaching ['bli:tʃɪŋ] n Bleichen nt. **they need a good** ~ sie müßten richtig gebleicht werden; ~ **agent** Bleichmittel nt; ~ **powder** Bleichkalk m.
bleak [bli:k] adj (+er) **(a)** öde, trostlos. **(b)** weather, wind rauh, kalt. **(c)** (fig) trostlos; existence also freudlos; prospects also trüb. **things look rather** ~ **for him** es sieht ziemlich trostlos für ihn aus.
bleakly ['bli:klɪ] adv see adj **(a)** öde, trostlos. **(b)** rauh, kalt.
bleakness ['bli:knɪs] n see adj **(a)** Öde, Trostlosigkeit f. **(b)** Rauheit, Kälte f. **(c)** Trostlosigkeit f; Freudlosigkeit f; Trübheit f.

bleary ['blɪərɪ] adj (+er) (a) eyes trübe; (after sleep) verschlafen. (b) (blurred) verschwommen.
bleary-eyed ['blɪərɪ,aɪd] adj (after sleep) verschlafen. ~ after proof reading mit ganz trüben Augen nach dem Korrekturlesen.
bleat [bliːt] 1 vi (a) (sheep, calf) blöken; (goat) meckern.
(b) (fig inf: complain, moan) meckern (inf).
2 n (a) (of sheep, calf) Blöken, Geblök nt; (of goat) Meckern nt. (b) (inf: moan) Meckern (inf), Gemecker (inf) nt. they'll have to have their little ~ about ... sie müssen natürlich ein bißchen über (+acc) ... meckern (inf).
bleed [bliːd] pret, ptp bled [bled] 1 vi (a) bluten. to ~ to death verbluten; my heart ~s for you (iro) ich fang' gleich an zu weinen; our hearts ~ for the oppressed (liter) wir leiden mit den Unterdrückten (geh).
(b) (plant) bluten, schwitzen; (wall) schwitzen.
2 vt (a) person zur Ader lassen.
(b) (fig inf) schröpfen (inf) (for um), bluten lassen (inf). to ~ sb white jdn total ausnehmen (inf).
(c) (Aut) brakes lüften.
♦**bleed away** vi (lit, fig) ausströmen, verströmen (geh).
bleeder ['bliːdəʳ] n (a) (Med inf) Bluter m. (b) (Brit sl) (person) Arschloch nt (vulg); (thing) Scheißding nt (sl). you're a cheeky little ~ du bist ein frecher Hund (inf).
bleeding ['bliːdɪŋ] 1 n (a) (loss of blood) Blutung f. internal ~ innere Blutungen pl.
(b) (taking blood) Aderlaß m.
(c) (of plant) Blutung f, Schwitzen nt.
(d) (of brakes) Lüftung f.
2 adj (a) wound blutend; (fig) heart gebrochen. he is a ~ heart sein Herz ist gebrochen, ihm blutet das Herz (geh).
(b) (Brit sl) verdammt (inf), Scheiß- (sl); (in positive sense) miracle etc verdammt (inf). get your ~ hands off me nimm deine Dreckpfoten weg (inf); just a ~ minute nu mal sachte (inf).
3 adv (Brit sl) verdammt (inf). that's ~ marvellous das ist sauber! (inf); who does he/she think he/she ~ well is? für was hält sich der Kerl/die Kuh eigentlich? (sl); not ~ likely da ist nichts drin (sl), glaube kaum (inf).
bleep [bliːp] 1 n (Rad, TV) Piepton m. 2 vi (transmitter) piepen. 3 vt (in hospital) doctor rufen.
bleeper ['bliːpəʳ] n Funkrufempfänger m.
blemish ['blemɪʃ] 1 n (lit, fig) Makel m. without (a) ~ makellos, ohne Makel. 2 vt object beschädigen; work, beauty beeinträchtigen; reputation, honour beflecken. slightly ~ed pottery leicht fehlerhafte Keramik.
blench [blentʃ] vi bleich werden, erbleichen (geh).
blend [blend] 1 n Mischung f. a ~ of tea eine Teemischung.
2 vt teas, colours etc (ver)mischen; cultures vermischen, miteinander verbinden. to ~ a building (in) with its surroundings ein Gebäude seiner Umgebung anpassen.
(b) (Cook) (stir) einrühren; (in blender) liquids mixen; semisolids pürieren.
3 vi a (mix together) (teas, whiskies) sich vermischen, sich mischen lassen; (voices, colours) verschmelzen. sea and sky seemed to ~ together Meer und Himmel schienen ineinander überzugehen or miteinander zu verschmelzen.
(b) (also ~ in: go together, harmonize) harmonieren (with mit), passen (with zu).
♦**blend in** 1 vt sep flavouring einrühren; colour, tea daruntermischen; building anpassen (with dat). 2 vi see blend 3 (b).
blended ['blendɪd] adj ~ whisky Blended m.
blender ['blendəʳ] n Mixer m, Mixgerät nt.
bless [bles] vt a (God, priest) segnen. ~ you, my son Gott segne dich, mein Sohn; did you buy that for me, ~ you (inf) hast du das für mich gekauft? das ist aber lieb von dir! (inf); ~ you, darling, you're an angel (inf) du bist wirklich lieb, du bist ein Engel (inf); ~ your little cotton socks (inf) du bist ja ein Schatz (inf); ~ you! (to sneezer) Gesundheit!; ~ me! (inf), ~ my soul! (inf) du mein Güte! (inf); he's lost it again, ~ him (iro) prima, er hat es wieder mal verloren! (iro); I'll be ~ed or blest if I'm going to do that! (inf) das fällt mir ja nicht im Traum ein! (inf); well, I'll be ~ed! (inf) so was!
(b) to ~ sb with sth jdm mit etw segnen; to be ~ed with gesegnet sein mit.
(c) (Eccl: adore) preisen.
blessed ['blesɪd] 1 adj (a) (Rel) heilig. B~ Virgin Heilige Jungfrau (Maria); the B~ X der selige X; ~ be God! gepriesen sei Gott!; of ~ memory seligen Angedenkens.
(b) (fortunate) selig. ~ are the pure in heart (Bibl) selig sind, die reinen Herzens sind.
(c) (liter: giving joy) willkommen.
(d) (euph inf: cursed) verflixt (inf). I couldn't remember a ~ thing ich konnte mich an rein gar nichts mehr erinnern (inf); the whole ~ day den lieben langen Tag (inf); every ~ evening aber auch jeden Abend.
2 adv verflixt (inf). he's too ~ lazy er ist einfach zu faul.
3 n the ~, the Blest die Seligen pl.
blessing ['blesɪŋ] n (Rel, fig) Segen m. he can count his ~s da kann er von Glück sagen; you can count your ~s you didn't get caught du kannst von Glück sagen, daß du nicht geschnappt worden bist; the ~s of civilization die Segnungen der Zivilisation; what a ~ that ... welch ein Segen or Glück, daß ...; it was a ~ in disguise es war schließlich doch ein Segen.
blest [blest] 1 adj (liter) see blessed 1 (b, c). 2 n see blessed 2.
blether ['bleðəʳ] (inf) 1 vi quatschen (inf), schwätzen (S Ger inf). 2 n (Scot) (a) to have a good ~ einen ordentlichen Schwatz halten (inf). (b) (person) Quasselstrippe f (inf).
blethering ['bleðərɪŋ] n (inf) Gequatsche nt (inf).
blew [bluː] pret of blow².

blight [blaɪt] 1 n (a) (on plants) Braunfäule f.
(b) (fig) to be a ~ on or upon sb's life/happiness jdm das Leben/jds Glück vergällen; these slums are a ~ upon the city diese Slums sind ein Schandfleck für die Stadt; this poverty which is a ~ upon our nation die Armut, mit der unser Volk geschlagen ist.
2 vt (a) plants zerstören.
(b) (fig) hopes vereiteln; sb's career, future also, life verderben. to ~ sb's life jdm das Leben verderben.
blighter ['blaɪtəʳ] n (Brit inf) Kerl m (inf); (boy) ungezogener Bengel; (girl) Luder nt (inf). a poor ~ ein armer Hund (inf); you ~ du Idiot! (inf); what a lucky ~! so ein Glückspilz!; this question/window's a real ~ diese Frage ist sauschwer (inf)/das Fenster ist ein Mistding (inf).
Blighty ['blaɪtɪ] n (Brit Mil sl) (leave) Heimaturlaub m; (England) die Heimat. he's going back to ~ er geht nach Hause; a ~ one (wound) ein Heimatschuß m.
blimey ['blaɪmɪ] interj (Brit sl) verflucht (inf), Mensch (inf).
blimp [blɪmp] n (a) (Brit inf) (Colonel) B~ Stockkonservativer m, alter Oberst (inf). (b) (Aviat) Kleinluftschiff nt. (c) (Film) Blimp m, Schallschutzgehäuse nt.
blind [blaɪnd] 1 adj (+er) (a) blind. a ~ man/woman ein Blinder/eine Blinde; ~ in one eye auf einem Auge blind.
(b) (fig) (to faults, beauty, charm etc) blind (to für, gegen). to be ~ to the possibilities die Möglichkeiten nicht sehen; to turn a ~ eye to sth bei etw ein Auge zudrücken; she remained ~ to the fact that ... sie sah einfach nicht, daß ...
(c) (fig: lacking judgement) obedience, passion blind; fury, panic also hell. in a ~ fury in heller Wut; ~ with passion/rage blind vor Leidenschaft/Wut; he came home in a ~ stupor er kam sinnlos betrunken nach Hause; ~ forces blinde Kräfte.
(d) (vision obscured) corner unübersichtlich; see ~ spot.
(e) (inf) it's not a ~ bit of use trying to persuade him es hat überhaupt keinen Zweck, ihn überreden zu wollen; he hasn't done a ~ bit of work er hat keinen Strich or Schlag getan (inf); but he didn't take a ~ bit of notice aber er hat sich nicht die Spur darum gekümmert (inf).
(f) (false) door, window blind.
(g) (without exit) passage ohne Ausgang, blind endend attr.
2 vt (a) blenden. the explosion ~ed him er ist durch die Explosion blind geworden; he was ~ed in the war er ist kriegsblind; the war-~ed die Kriegsblinden pl.
(b) (sun, light) blenden.
(c) (fig) (love, hate etc) blind machen (to für, gegen); (wealth, beauty) blenden. to ~ sb with science jdn mit Fachjargon beeindrucken (wollen).
3 n (a) the ~ die Blinden pl; it's the ~ leading the ~ (fig) das hieße, einen Lahmen einen Blinden führen lassen.
(b) (window shade) (cloth) Rollo, Rouleau nt; (slats) Jalousie f; (outside) Rolladen m.
(c) (cover) Tarnung f. to be a ~ zur Tarnung dienen.
(d) (fig sl: booze-up) Sauferei f (inf).
(e) (US: hide) Versteck nt.
4 adv (a) (Aviat) fly blind.
(b) ~ drunk (inf) sinnlos betrunken.
blind: ~ alley n (lit, fig) Sackgasse f; to be up a ~ alley (fig) in einer Sackgasse stecken; ~ date n Rendezvous nt mit einem/einer Unbekannten; (person) unbekannter (Rendezvous)partner; unbekannte (Rendezvous)partnerin.
blinder ['blaɪndəʳ] n (a) (US: blinker) Scheuklappe f. (b) (sl: drinking spree) Kneipkur f (inf).
blind flying n (Aviat) Blindflug m.
blindfold ['blaɪndfəʊld] 1 vt die Augen verbinden (+dat). 2 n Augenbinde f. 3 adj mit verbundenen Augen. I could do it ~ (inf) das mach' ich mit links (inf).
blinding ['blaɪndɪŋ] adj light blendend; truth ins Auge stechend. in the ~ light of day im grellen Tageslicht; as ~ tears filled her eyes von Tränen geblendet.
blindingly ['blaɪndɪŋlɪ] adv it is ~ obvious das sieht doch ein Blinder (inf).
blind landing n (Aviat) Blindlandung f.
blindly ['blaɪndlɪ] adv (lit, fig) blind (lings).
blind man's buff n Blindekuh f, Blindekuhspiel nt.
blindness ['blaɪndnɪs] n (lit, fig) Blindheit f (to gegenüber).
blind: ~ side n (Sport) ungedeckte Seite; ~ spot n (Med) blinder Fleck; (Aut, Aviat) toter Winkel; (Rad) tote Zone; trigonometry was his ~ spot Trigonometrie war sein schwacher Punkt; ~ staggers n sing Taumelsucht f; ~worm n Blindschleiche f.
blink [blɪŋk] 1 n Blinzeln nt. to be on the ~ (inf) kaputt sein (inf). 2 vi blinzeln, zwinkern. (b) (light) blinken. 3 vt to ~ one's eyes mit den Augen zwinkern.
♦**blink at** vi +prep obj (ignore) hinwegsehen über (+acc).
♦**blink away** vt sep tears wegblinzeln (inf).
blinker ['blɪŋkəʳ] n (a) (light) Blinker m. (b) ~s pl Scheuklappen pl.
blinkered ['blɪŋkəd] adj (fig) stirnig. they are all so ~ sie laufen alle mit Scheuklappen herum.
blinking ['blɪŋkɪŋ] 1 adj (Brit inf) verflixt (inf), blöd (inf). what a ~ cheek! so eine bodenlose Frechheit! (inf); it's about ~ time too! das wird aber auch Zeit! (inf). 2 adv verflixt (inf). 3 n (a) (of eyes) Blinzeln, Zwinkern nt. (b) (of light) Blinken nt.
blip [blɪp] n leuchtender Punkt (auf dem Radarschirm).
bliss [blɪs] n Glück nt; (Rel) (Glück)seligkeit f. a feeling of ~ ein Gefühl der Wonne; this is ~! das ist herrlich or eine Wohltat!; a beach, a drink, the sun, ah sheer ~ Strand, Sonne, ein Drink - ah, das wahre Paradies; ah ~, she sighed herrlich, seufzte sie; a life of marital/academic ~ ein glückliches Eheleben/Leben an der Universität; ignorance is ~ (prov) Unwissenheit ist ein Geschenk des Himmels.
blissful ['blɪsfʊl] adj time herrlich, paradiesisch; respite also wohltuend; feeling also wonnig; happiness höchste(s), state,

look, smile (glück)selig; *moments* selig. **in ~ ignorance of the facts** (iro) in herrlicher Ahnungslosigkeit; **in ~ ignorance of the fact that ...** (iro) in keinster Weise ahnend, daß ...

blissfully ['blɪsfəlɪ] *adv stretch* wohlig; *peaceful* paradiesisch, herrlich; *smile* selig. **~ happy** überglücklich; **to be ~ ignorant/unaware** so herrlich ahnungslos/arglos sein; **he remained ~ ignorant of what was going on** er ahnte in keinster Weise, was eigentlich vor sich ging.

blister ['blɪstə'] **1** *n* (*on skin, paint*) Blase *f*; (*Aviat: for gun*) Bordwaffenstand *m*. **2** *vi* (*skin*) Blasen bekommen; (*paintwork, metal*) Blasen werfen. **3** *vt skin, paint* Blasen hervorrufen auf (+*dat*). **to be ~ed** Blasen haben.

blistering ['blɪstərɪŋ] *adj heat, sun* glühend; *pace* mörderisch.

blister pack *n* Sichtpackung *f*.

blithe [blaɪð] *adj* (+*er*) fröhlich, munter.

blithely ['blaɪðlɪ] *adv* (**a**) *see adj.* (**b**) *ignore, carry on* munter. **he ~ ignored the problem** er setzte sich ungeniert über das Problem hinweg.

blithering ['blɪðərɪŋ] *adj* (*inf*) **a ~ idiot** ein Trottel *m* (*inf*); **don't be such a ~ idiot** du bist ja total bescheuert (*sl*).

B Litt *abbr of* **B**achelor of **Lett**ers.

blitz [blɪts] **1** *n* (**a**) Blitzkrieg *m*; (*aerial*) Luftangriff *m*. **the B~** deutscher Luftangriff auf britische Städte 1940-41. (**b**) (*fig inf*) Blitzaktion *f*. **he had a ~ on his room** er machte gründlich in seinem Zimmer sauber. **2** *vt* heftig bombardieren.

blitzed [blɪtst] *adj area* zerbombt.

blizzard ['blɪzəd] *n* Schneesturm, Blizzard *m*.

bloated ['bləʊtɪd] *adj* (**a**) aufgedunsen. **I feel absolutely ~** (*inf*) ich bin fürchterlich voll (*inf*). (**b**) (*fig: with pride, self-importance*) aufgeblasen (*with* vor +*dat*).

bloater ['bləʊtə'] *n* Räucherhering *m*.

blob [blɒb] *n* (*of water, honey, wax*) Tropfen *m*; (*of ink*) Klecks *m*; (*of paint*) Tupfer *m*; (*of ice-cream, mashed potatoes*) Klacks *m*. **until he was just a ~ on the horizon** bis er nur noch ein Punkt am Horizont war.

bloc [blɒk] *n* (**a**) (*Pol*) Block *m*. **b) en ~** en bloc.

block [blɒk] **1** *n* (**a**) Block, Klotz *m*; (*executioner's ~*) Richtblock *m*; (*engine ~*) Motorblock *m*. **~s** (*toys*) (Bau)klötze *pl*; **huge ugly ~s** of concrete riesige, häßliche Betonklötze; **to be sent to** *or* **to go to the ~** dem Henker überantwortet werden/vor den Henker treten. (**b**) (*building*) Block *m*. **~ of flats** Wohnblock *m*; **to take a stroll round the ~** einen Spaziergang um den Block machen; **she lived in the next ~/three ~s from us** (*esp US*) sie wohnte im nächsten Block/drei Blocks *or* Straßen weiter. (**c**) (*division of seats*) Block *m*. (**d**) (*obstruction*) (*in pipe, Med*) Verstopfung *f*; (*mental*) geistige Sperre (*about* in bezug auf +*acc*), Mattscheibe *f* (*inf*). **I've a complete ~ about it** da habe ich total Mattscheibe (*inf*). (**e**) (*Typ*) Druckstock *m*. (**f**) (*of tickets, shares*) Block *m*. (**g**) (*inf: head*) **to knock sb's ~ off** jdm eins überziehen (*inf*). (**h**) (*also writing ~*) Block *m*. (**i**) (*usu pl: also starting ~*) Startblock *m*. (**j**) (*in ballet shoe*) Spitzenverstärkung *f*; (*ballet shoe*) spitzenverstärkter Ballettschuh. **2** *vt* (**a**) (*obstruct*) *road, harbour, wheel* blockieren; *plans also* im Wege stehen (+*dat*); *traffic also, progress* aufhalten; *pipe* verstopfen; (*Ftbl*) *one's opponent* blocken; *ball* stoppen. **to ~ sb's way/view** jdm den Weg/die Sicht versperren. (**b**) *credit* sperren. **3** *vi* (*Sport*) blocken.

♦**block in** *vt sep* (**a**) (*Art*) andeuten. (**b**) (*hem in*) einkeilen.

♦**block off** *vt sep street* absperren; *fireplace* abdecken.

♦**block out** *vt sep* (**a**) (*obscure*) *light* nicht durchlassen; *sun also* verdecken. **the trees are ~ing ~ all the light** die Bäume nehmen uns das ganze Licht. (**b**) (*sketch roughly*) andeuten. (**c**) (*obliterate*) *part of picture, photograph* wegretuschieren.

♦**block up** *vt sep* (**a**) (*obstruct*) *gangway* blockieren, versperren; *pipe* verstopfen. **my nose is all ~ed ~** meine Nase ist völlig verstopft. (**b**) (*close, fill in*) *window, entrance* verschließen; *hole* zustopfen.

blockade [blɒ'keɪd] **1** *n* (**a**) (*Mil*) Blockade *f*. **under ~** im Blockadezustand; **to break** *or* **run the ~** die Blockade brechen; **~ runner** Blockadebrecher *m*. (**b**) (*barrier, obstruction*) Sperre, Barrikade *f*. **2** *vt* blockieren, sperren.

blockage ['blɒkɪdʒ] *n* Verstopfung *f*; (*in windpipe etc*) Blockade *f*; (*act*) Blockierung *f*.

block: **~ and tackle** *n* Flaschenzug *m*; **~ booking** *n* (*travel booking*) Gruppenbuchung *f*; (*Theat*) Gruppenbestellung *f*; **~buster** *n* (a) (*inf*) Knüller *m* (*inf*); (b) (*Mil*) große Bombe; **~ capitals** *npl* Blockschrift *f*; **~head** *n* (*inf*) Dummkopf *m*; **~house** *n* Blockhaus *nt*; **~ish** *adj* (*inf*) dumm, doof (*inf*); **~ letters** *npl* Blockschrift *f*; **~ vote** *n* Stimmenblock *m*.

bloke [bləʊk] *n* (*Brit inf*) Kerl (*inf*), Typ (*inf*) *m*.

blond [blɒnd] *adj man, hair, beard* blond.

blonde [blɒnd] **1** *adj blond*; *skin* hell. **2** *n* (*woman*) Blondine *f*.

blood [blʌd] **1** *n* (**a**) Blut *nt*. **to give ~** Blut spenden; **it makes my ~ boil** das macht mich rasend; **his ~ is up** er ist wütend; **she's after** *or* **out for his ~** sie will ihm an den Kragen (*inf*); **his ~ ran cold** es lief ihm eiskalt über den Rücken; **this firm needs new ~** diese Firma braucht frisches Blut; **it is like trying to get ~ from a stone** (*prov*) das ist verlorene Liebesmüh; **bad ~** böses Blut; **there is bad ~ between them** sie haben ein gestörtes Verhältnis. (**b**) (*fig*) (*lineage*) Blut, Geblüt (*geh*) *nt*, Abstammung *f*. **a prince of the ~** ein Prinz von edlem Geblüt (*geh*); **it's in his ~** das liegt ihm im Blut; **~ is thicker than water** (*prov*) Blut ist dicker als Wasser (*prov*). (**c**) (*old: dandy*) Geck (*old*), Stutzer (*dated*) *m*. **2** *attr* (*pure-bred*) reinrassig.

3 *vt hounds* an Blut gewöhnen.

blood *in cpds* Blut-; **~ and thunder** *n* Mord und Totschlag *m*; **~-and-thunder novel** *n* Reißer *m*; **~ bank** *n* Blutbank *f*; **~bath** *n* Blutbad *nt*; **~ blister** *n* Blutblase *f*; **~ brother** *n* Blutsbruder *m*; **~ clot** *n* Blutgerinnsel *nt*; **~ count** *n* (*Med*) Blutbild *nt*; **~-curdling** *adj* grauenerregend; **they heard a ~-curdling cry** sie hörten einen Schrei, der ihnen das Blut in den Adern erstarren ließ (*geh*); **~ donor** *n* Blutspender (*in f*) *m*; **~ feud** *n* Blutfehde *f*; **~ group** *n* Blutgruppe *f*; **~ heat** *n* Körpertemperatur *f*; **~hound** *n* (a) (*Zool*) Bluthund *m*; (b) (*fig: detective*) Schnüffler (*inf*), Detektiv *m*.

bloodiness ['blʌdɪnɪs] *n* (**a**) (*of sight, war etc*) Blutigkeit *f*. **the ~ of his face/coat** das Blut in seinem Gesicht/auf seinem Anzug. (**b**) (*inf: horribleness*) Gräßlichkeit, Abscheulichkeit *f*.

bloodless ['blʌdlɪs] *adj* (*rare: without blood*) blutlos; (*without bloodshed*) *victory, coup* unblutig; (*pallid*) blutleer, bleich.

bloodlessly ['blʌdlɪslɪ] *adv* unblutig.

bloodlessness ['blʌdlɪsnɪs] *n see adj* Blutlosigkeit *f*; Unblutigkeit *f*; Blutleere, Bleichheit *f*.

blood: **~-letting** *n* Aderlaß *m*; **~ lust** *n* Blutrünstigkeit *f*; **~mobile** *n* (*US*) Blutspendewagen *m*; **~ money** *n* Mordgeld *nt*; **~ orange** *n* Blutorange *f*; **~-poisoning** *n* Blutvergiftung *f*; **~ pressure** *n* Blutdruck *m*; **to have (high) ~ pressure** hohen Blutdruck haben; **~ pudding** *n* = Blutwurst *f*; **~-red** *adj* blutrot; **~ relation** *n* Blutsverwandte(r) *mf*; **~ shed** *n* Blutvergießen *nt*; **~shot** *adj* blutunterlaufen; **~ sports** *npl* Jagdsport, Hahnenkampf *m etc*; **~stain** *n* Blutfleck *m*; **~stained** *adj* blutig, blutbefleckt; **~ stock** *n* reinrassige Zucht; **~stone** *n* Blutjaspis, Heliotrop *m*; **~stream** *n* Blut *nt*, Blutkreislauf *m*; **~sucker** *n* (*Zool, fig*) Blutsauger *m*; **~ test** *n* Blutprobe *f*; **~thirstiness** *n see adj* Blutrünstigkeit *f*; Blutgier *f*, Blutdurst *m* (*geh*); **~thirsty** *adj tale* blutrünstig; *person, animal, disposition also* blutgierig, blutdürstig (*geh*); **~ transfusion** *n* Bluttransfusion *f*; **~ transfusion** *n* Blutübertragung, (Blut)transfusion *f*; **~ vessel** *n* Blutgefäß *nt*; **he almost burst a ~ vessel** (*lit*) ihm wäre beinahe eine Ader geplatzt; (*fig inf*) ihn traf fast der Schlag.

bloody ['blʌdɪ] **1** *adj* (+*er*) (**a**) (*lit*) *nose, bandage, battle* blutig. (**b**) (*Brit sl: damned*) verdammt (*inf*), Scheiß- (*sl*); (*in positive sense*) *genius, wonder* echt (*inf*), verdammt (*inf*). **it was a ~ nuisance/waste of time** Mann *or* Mensch, das war vielleicht ein Quatsch (*inf*) *or* Scheiß (*sl*)/das war reine Zeitverschwendung; **it was there all the ~ time** Mann (*inf*) *or* Mensch (*inf*) *or* Scheiße (*sl*), das war schon die ganze Zeit da; **I haven't got any ~ time** verdammt noch mal, ich hab' keine Zeit (*inf*); **he hasn't got a ~ hope** Mensch *or* Mann, der hat doch überhaupt keine Chance (*inf*); **~ hell!** verdammt! (*inf*), Scheiße! (*sl*); (*in indignation*) verdammt noch mal! (*inf*); (*in amazement*) Menschenskind! (*inf*), meine Fresse! (*sl*); **he is a ~ marvel** er ist echt *or* verdammt gut (*inf*); **just a ~ minute** nu mal sachte! (*inf*). (**c**) (*inf: awful*) greulich (*inf*); *person, behaviour* abscheulich. **2** *adv* (*Brit sl*) verdammt (*inf*), saumäßig (*sl*); *hot, cold, stupid* sau- (*sl*); (*in positive sense*) *good, brilliant* echt (*inf*), verdammt (*inf*). **that's ~ useless/no ~ good** Mensch, das taugt doch überhaupt nichts (*inf*)/das ist Scheiße (*sl*); **not ~ likely** da ist überhaupt nichts drin (*inf*); **he can ~ well do it himself** das soll er schön alleine machen, verdammt noch mal! (*inf*); **who does he ~ well think he is?** Mensch *or* verdammt noch mal, für wen hält der sich eigentlich? (*inf*).

3 *vt* blutig machen.

Bloody Mary *n* Cocktail *m* aus Tomatensaft und Wodka.

bloody-minded ['blʌdɪ'maɪndɪd] *adj* (*Brit inf*) stur (*inf*).

bloom [blu:m] **1** *n* (**a**) Blüte *f*. **to be in** (*full*) **~** in (voller) Blüte stehen; **to come/burst into ~** aufblühen/plötzlich erblühen. (**b**) (*fig*) **in the ~ of youth** in der Blüte der Jugend; **she has lost the ~ of youth/her ~** sie hat den Schmelz der Jugend (*geh*)/ihre Frische verloren; **in the first ~ of love** in der ersten Begeisterung ihrer Liebe. (**c**) (*on fruit*) satter Schimmer; (*on peaches*) Flaum *m*. **2** *vi* (*lit fig*) blühen.

bloomer ['blu:mə'] *n* (*inf*) grober Fehler. **to make a ~** einen Bock schießen (*inf*).

bloomers ['blu:məz] *npl* Pumphose *f*.

blooming ['blu:mɪŋ] **1** *prp of* **bloom**. **2** *adj* (*inf*) verflixt (*inf*). **it was there all the ~ time** verflixt, das war schon die ganze Zeit da! (*inf*). **3** *adv* verflixt (*inf*).

blossom ['blɒsəm] **1** *n* Blüte *f*. **in ~** in Blüte. **2** *vi* (**a**) blühen. (**b**) (*fig*) (*relationship*) blühen; (*person, trade etc also*) aufblühen. **to ~ into sth** sich zu etw aufblühen; (*person also*) zu etw erblühen (*geh*); (*relationship*) zu etw wachsen.

♦**blossom out** *vi* (*fig*) aufblühen (*into* zu).

blot [blɒt] **1** *n* (**a**) (*of ink*) (Tinten)klecks *m*. (**b**) (*fig: on honour, reputation*) Fleck *m* (*on* auf +*dat*). **a ~ on his character** ein Fleck auf seiner weißen Weste; **a ~ on the landscape** ein Schandfleck in der Landschaft. **2** *vt* (**a**) (*make ink spots on*) beklecksen. **to ~ one's copybook** (*fig*) sich unmöglich machen; (*with sb*) es sich (*dat*) verderben. (**b**) (*dry*) *ink, page* ablöschen; *skin, face etc* abtupfen.

♦**blot out** *vt sep* (**a**) (*lit*) *words* unleserlich machen, verschmieren. (**b**) (*fig*) (*hide from view*) *landscape* verdecken; (*obliterate*) *memories* auslöschen.

blotch [blɒtʃ] **1** *n* (*on skin*) Fleck *m*; (*of ink, colour*) Klecks *m*. **2** *vt* *paper, written work* beklecksen, Flecken machen auf (+*acc*); *skin* fleckig werden lassen.

blotchy ['blɒtʃɪ] *adj* (+*er*) *skin* fleckig; *drawing, paint* klecksig. **~ splashes of colour** Farbkleckse *pl*; **a rather ~ drawing** ein richtiges Klecksbild.

blotter ['blɒtə'] *n* (**a**) (Tinten)löscher *m*. (**b**) (*US*) (*record book*) Kladde *f*; (*police*) Polizeiregister *nt*.

blotting ['blɒtɪŋ-]: **~ pad** *n* Schreibunterlage *f*; **~ paper** *n* Löschpapier *nt*.

blotto ['blɒtəʊ] *adj pred* (*sl: drunk*) sternhagelvoll (*inf*).

blouse [blauz] n (a) Bluse f. (b) (US Mil) (Feld)bluse f.
bloused [blauzd] adj blusig, wie eine Bluse.
blow¹ [bləu] n (lit, fig) Schlag m; (fig: sudden misfortune also) Schicksalsschlag m (for, to für). **to come to ~s** handgreiflich werden; **it came to ~s** es gab Handgreiflichkeiten; **at a (single) or one ~** (fig) mit einem Schlag (inf); **to give sb/sth a ~** jdn/etw schlagen; **to deal sb/sth a ~** (lit, fig) jdm/einer Sache einen Schlag versetzen; **to strike a ~ for sth** (fig) einer Sache (dat) einen großen Dienst erweisen; **without striking a ~** ohne jede Gewalt; **he returned ~ for ~** er gab Schlag um Schlag zurück.
blow² (vb: pret **blew**, ptp **~n**) 1 vi (a) (wind) wehen, blasen. **there was a draught ~ing from the window** es zog vom Fenster her; **the wind was ~ing hard** es wehte ein starker Wind; see hot.
(b) (person) blasen, pusten (on auf +acc). **to ~ on one's soup** auf die Suppe pusten.
(c) (move with the wind) fliegen; (leaves, hat, papers also) geweht werden. **the door blew open/shut** die Tür flog auf/zu.
(d) (make sound: bugle horn) blasen; (whistle) pfeifen. **then the whistle blew** (Sport) da kam der Pfiff.
(e) (pant) pusten (inf), schnaufen (inf); (animal) schnaufen.
(f) (whale) spritzen. **there she ~s!** Wal in Sicht!
(g) (fuse, light bulb) durchbrennen; (gasket) platzen.
(h) (inf: leave) abhauen (inf).
2 vt (a) (move by ~ing) (breeze) wehen; (strong wind, draught) blasen; (gale etc) treiben; (person) blasen, pusten (inf). **the wind blew the ship off course** der Wind trieb das Schiff vom Kurs ab; **to ~ sb a kiss** jdm eine Kußhand zuwerfen.
(b) (drive air into) fire anblasen; eggs ausblasen. **to ~ one's nose** sich (dat) die Nase putzen.
(c) (make by ~ing) glass blasen; bubbles machen.
(d) trumpet blasen; (Hunt, Mil) horn blasen in (+acc). **the referee blew his whistle** der Schiedsrichter pfiff; **to ~ one's own trumpet** (fig) sein eigenes Lob singen.
(e) (burn out, ~ up) safe, bridge etc sprengen; valve, gasket platzen lassen; transistor zerstören. **be careful not to ~ the fuse** passen Sie auf, daß die Sicherung nicht durchbrennt; **I've ~n a fuse/light bulb** mir ist eine Sicherung/Birne durchgebrannt; **to be ~n to pieces** (bridge, car) in die Luft gesprengt werden; (person) zerfetzt werden.
(f) (sl: spend extravagantly) money verpulvern (inf).
(g) (inf: reveal) secret verraten; see gaff².
(h) (inf: damn) **~!** Mist! (inf); **~ this rain!** dieser mistige Regen! (inf); **~ the expense/what he likes!** das ist doch wurscht, was es kostet/was er will (inf); **well, I'm ~ed** Mensch(enskind)! (inf); **I'll be ~ed if I do it** ich denke nicht im Traum dran(, das zu tun) (inf); **... and ~ me if he still didn't forget** und er hat es doch glatt trotzdem vergessen (inf).
(i) (inf) **to ~ one's chances of doing sth** sich (dat) verscherzen, etw zu tun.
(j) (sl) see mind 1.
3 n (a) (expulsion of breath) Blasen, Pusten (inf) nt. **to give a ~** blasen, pusten (inf); (when ~ing nose) sich schneuzen.
(b) (breath of air) **to go for a ~** sich durchlüften lassen.
♦ **blow away** 1 vi (hat, paper etc) wegfliegen. 2 vt sep wegblasen; (breeze also) wegwehen.
♦ **blow down** 1 vi (tree etc) umfallen, umgeweht werden. 2 vt sep (lit) umwehen. **~ me ~!** (inf) Mensch(enskind)! (inf).
♦ **blow in** 1 vi (a) (lit) (be blown down: window etc) eingedrückt werden; (be ~n ~ side: dust etc) hinein-/hereinfliegen, hinein-/hereingeweht or -geblasen werden; (wind) hereinwehen, hereinblasen. **there was a draught ~ing ~** es zog herein.
(b) (inf: arrive unexpectedly) hereinschneien (inf) (+prep obj, -to in +acc).
2 vt sep window, door etc eindrücken; dust etc hinein-/hereinblasen or -wehen (+prep obj, -to in +acc).
♦ **blow off** 1 vi wegfliegen. 2 vt sep wegblasen; (+prep obj) blasen von; (breeze also) wegwehen; (+prep obj) wehen von; (storm etc also) wegtreiben (+prep obj von). 3 vt insep (fig) steam ablassen (inf).
♦ **blow out** 1 vi (a) (candle etc) ausgehen.
(b) (Aut: tyre) platzen; (Elec: fuse) durchbrennen.
(c) (gas, oil) ausbrechen; (oilwell) einen Ausbruch haben.
2 vt sep (a) candle ausblasen, löschen.
(b) (fill with air) one's cheeks aufblasen.
(c) **to ~ one's brains ~** sich (dat) eine Kugel durch den Kopf jagen.
3 vr (wind, storm) sich legen; (fig: passion) verpuffen (inf).
♦ **blow over** 1 vi (a) (tree etc) umfallen. (b) (lit, fig: storm, dispute) sich legen. 2 vt sep tree etc umstürzen.
♦ **blow up** 1 vi (a) (be exploded) in die Luft fliegen; (bomb) explodieren.
(b) (lit, fig: gale, crisis, row) ausbrechen.
(c) (fig inf: person) explodieren (inf).
2 vt sep (a) mine, bridge, person in die Luft jagen, hochjagen.
(b) tyre, balloon aufblasen. **he was all ~n ~ with pride** er platzte fast vor Stolz.
(c) photo vergrößern.
(d) (fig: magnify, exaggerate) event aufbauschen (into zu).
blow: **~-by-~** adj account detailliert; **~-dry** 1 n **to have a ~-dry** sich fönen lassen; 2 vt fönen.
blower ['bləuər] n (a) (device) Gebläse nt. (b) (glass~) Glasbläser m. (c) (Brit inf: telephone) Telefon nt. **to be on the ~** an der Strippe hängen (inf); **to get on the ~ to sb** jdn anrufen.
blow: **~fly** n Schmeißfliege f; **~gun** n (weapon) Blasrohr nt; **~hole** n (a) (of whale) Atemloch nt; (b) (Min) Abzugsloch nt; **~job** n (vulg) **to do a ~-job on sb** jdm einen blasen (vulg); **~lamp** n Lötlampe f.
blown [bləun] 1 ptp of blow². 2 adj flower voll aufgeblüht.
blow: **~-out** n (a) (inf: meal) Schlemmerei f; **to go for a ~-out** tüchtig schlemmen gehen (inf); **to have a ~-out** schlemmen (inf); (b) (burst tyre) **he had a ~-out** ihm ist ein Reifen geplatzt.

in the case of a ~-out wenn ein Reifen platzt; (c) (Elec) there's been a ~-out die Sicherung ist durchgebrannt; (d) (Min) Ausbruch m; (on oil-rig) Ölausbruch m; **~ pipe** n (a) (weapon) Blasrohr nt; (b) (Tech) Gebläsebrenner m, Lötrohr nt; (c) (for glassmaking) Glasbläserpfeife f; **~ torch** n Lötlampe f; **~-up** n (a) (inf: outburst of temper) Wutausbruch m; (b) (inf: row) Krach m; **they've had a ~-up** sie hatten Krach; (c) (Phot) Vergrößerung f.
blowy ['bləui] adj (+er) windig.
blowzy ['blauzi] adj (+er) woman schlampig.
blubber ['blʌbər] 1 n (a) Walfischspeck m; (inf: on person) Wabbelspeck m (inf). (b) (inf: weep) **to have a ~** flennen (inf), heulen (inf). 2 vti (inf) flennen (inf), heulen (inf).
♦ **blubber out** vt sep (inf) flennen (inf), heulen (inf).
blubberer ['blʌbərər] n (inf) Heulsuse f (inf).
blubbery ['blʌbəri] adj (a) wabb(el)ig (inf). (b) (inf: weepy) verheult (inf).
bludgeon ['blʌdʒən] 1 n Knüppel m, Keule f. 2 vt (a) verprügeln. **to ~ sb to death** jdn zu Tode prügeln. (b) (fig) bearbeiten (inf). **he ~ed me into doing it** er hat mich so lange bearbeitet, bis ich es getan habe (inf); **I don't want to ~ you** ich möchte dich nicht dazu zwingen.
blue [blu:] 1 adj (+er) (a) blau. **~ with cold** blau vor Kälte; **until you're ~ in the face** (inf) bis zur Vergasung (inf), bis zum Gehtnichtmehr (inf); **once in a ~ moon** alle Jubeljahre (einmal).
(b) (inf: miserable) melancholisch, trübsinnig. **to feel/look ~** den Moralischen haben (inf)/traurig aussehen.
(c) (inf: obscene) language derb, nicht salonfähig; joke schlüpfrig; film Porno-, Sex-. **the air was ~ (with oaths)** da habe ich/hat er etc vielleicht geflucht (inf).
(d) (Pol) konservativ.
2 n (a) Blau nt.
(b) (Univ Sport) Student von Oxford oder Cambridge, der bei Wettkämpfen seine Universität vertritt (oder vertreten hat); (colours) blaue Mütze, als Symbol dafür, daß man seine Universität in Wettkämpfen vertreten hat.
(c) (liter: sky) Himmel m. **out of the ~** (fig inf) aus heiterem Himmel (inf).
(d) (Pol) Konservative(r) mf.
(e) (inf) **the ~s** pl (depression) der Moralische (inf); **to have (a fit of) the ~s** den Moralischen haben (inf).
(f) (Mus) **the ~s** pl der Blues; **a ~s** sing ein Blues.
3 vt (inf: spend) auf den Kopf hauen (inf) (on für).
blue: **~ baby** n Baby nt mit angeborenem Herzfehler; B**~beard** n Ritter Blaubart m; **~bell** n Sternhyazinthe f; (Scot: harebell) Glockenblume f; **~berry** n Blau- or Heidelbeere f; **~bird** n Rotkehlhüttensänger m; **~ blood** n blaues Blut; **~-blooded** adj blaublütig; **~ book** n (a) (Brit Parl) Blaubuch nt; (b) (US = Who's Who nt; **~bottle** n Schmeißfliege f; **~ cheese** n Blauschimmelkäse m; **~-collar** adj **~-collar worker/union/jobs** Arbeiter m/Arbeitergewerkschaft f/Stellen pl für Arbeiter; **~-eyed** adj blauäugig; **sb's ~-eyed boy** (fig) jds Liebling(sjunge) m; **~jacket** n (dated inf) Matrose m; **to join the ~jackets** zu den blauen Jungs gehen (dated); **~ jeans** npl Blue jeans pl.
blueness ['blu:nis] n (a) (lit) Bläue f. (b) see adj (c) Derbheit f; Schlüpfrigkeit f; Sexgeladenheit f (inf).
blue: B**~ Nile** n Blauer Nil; **~-pencil** vt (edit, revise) mit dem Rotstift gehen an (+acc), korrigieren; (delete) ausstreichen; B**~ Peter** n (Naut) Blauer Peter; **~print** n Blaupause f; (fig) Plan, Entwurf m; **do I have to draw you a ~print?** (inf) muß ich dir erst 'ne Zeichnung machen? (inf); **~ ribband** n Blaues Band; **~ stocking** n (fig) Blaustrumpf m; **~tit** n Blaumeise f; **~ whale** n Blauwal m.
bluff¹ [blʌf] 1 n (headland) Kliff nt; (inland) Felsvorsprung m. 2 adj rauh aber herzlich (inf); honesty, answer aufrichtig.
bluff² 1 vti bluffen. 2 n Bluff m. **to call sb's ~** es darauf ankommen lassen.
♦ **bluff out** vt sep **to ~ sth ~** sich rausreden (inf); **to ~ one's way ~ of sth** sich aus etw rausreden (inf).
bluffer ['blʌfər] n Bluffer m.
bluish ['blu:iʃ] adj bläulich.
blunder ['blʌndər] 1 n (dummer) Fehler, Schnitzer m (inf); (socially also) Fauxpas m. **to make a ~** einen Bock schießen (inf); (socially) einen Fauxpas begehen.
2 vi (a) einen Bock schießen (inf), Mist bauen (sl); (socially) sich danebenbenehmen.
(b) (move clumsily) tappen (into gegen). **to ~ in/out** hinein-/herein-/hinaus-/heraustappen; **to ~ into a trap** (lit, fig) in eine Falle tappen; **he ~ed through the poem** er kämpfte sich mühsam durch das Gedicht.
blunderbuss ['blʌndəbʌs] n Donnerbüchse f.
blunderer ['blʌndərər] n Schussel m (inf); (socially) Elefant m (inf).
blundering ['blʌndəriŋ] 1 adj (a) person (making mistakes) schusselig (inf); (socially) ohne jedes Feingefühl. **~ idiot** Erztrottel m (inf). (b) (clumsy) tolpatschig; reading holp(e)rig. 2 n Schußligkeit f (inf); gesellschaftliche Schnitzer pl.
blunt [blʌnt] 1 adj (a) knife stumpf. **with a ~ instrument** mit einem stumpfen Gegenstand.
(b) (outspoken) person geradeheraus pred, sich deutlich ausdrückend attr; speech unverblümt; fact nackt, unbeschönigt. **he's rather a ~ sort of person** er drückt sich ziemlich unverblümt or deutlich aus; **to be ~ about sth** sich unverblümt zu etw äußern; **he was very ~ about it** er hat sich sehr deutlich ausgedrückt; **to be ~ about this** lassen Sie mich das ganz ohne Umschweife or knallhart (inf) sagen.
2 vt knife etc stumpf machen; (fig) palate, sense abstumpfen. **his wits had been ~ed** er war geistig abgestumpft.
bluntly ['blʌntli] adv speak freiheraus, geradeheraus. **he told us quite ~ what he thought** er sagte uns ganz unverblümt seine Meinung.

bluntness ['blʌntnɪs] n (a) (of blade, needle) Stumpfheit f. (b) (outspokenness) Unverblümtheit f.

blur [blɜːʳ] 1 n verschwommener Fleck. **the ~ of their faces** ihre verschwommenen Gesichter; **the trees became just a ~** er etc konnte die Bäume nur noch verschwommen erkennen.

2 vt (a) inscription verwischen; writing also verschleiern; view verschleiern; outline, photograph unscharf or verschwommen machen; sound verzerren. **to be/become ~red** undeutlich sein/werden; (image etc also) verschwommen sein/verschwimmen; **her eyes were ~red with tears** ihre Augen schwammen in Tränen, ihr Blick war von Tränen verschleiert (geh); **the tape is ~red here** an dieser Stelle ist die Aufnahme verzerrt.

(b) (fig) senses, mind, judgement trüben; memory also, meaning verwischen; intention in den Hintergrund drängen. **the meaning of the message had become ~red** die Bedeutung der Nachricht war unklar geworden.

blurb [blɜːb] n Material nt, Informationen pl; (on book cover) Klappentext, Waschzettel m.

blurt (out) [blɜːt(ˈaʊt)] vt sep herausplatzen mit (inf).

blush [blʌʃ] 1 vi (a) rot werden, erröten (with vor +dat).

(b) (fig: be ashamed) sich schämen (for für). **I ~ to say so** es ist mir peinlich, das zu sagen.

2 n Erröten nt no pl. **with a ~/a slight ~** errötend/mit leichtem Erröten; **without a ~** ohne rot zu werden; **spare my ~es!** bring mich nicht in Verlegenheit; **to put sb to the ~** (dated) jdn in Verlegenheit bringen; **the first ~ of dawn** (fig) der zarte Schimmer der Morgenröte; **at first ~** auf den ersten Blick.

blushing ['blʌʃɪŋ] adj errötend. **the ~ bride** die sittsame Braut.

bluster ['blʌstəʳ] 1 vi (a) (wind) tosen, toben. (b) (fig: person) ein großes Geschrei machen; (angrily also) toben. 2 vt **to ~ one's way out of it/sth** es/etw lautstark abstreiten. 3 n see vi (a) Tosen, Toben nt. (b) großes Geschrei; Toben nt.

blustery ['blʌstərɪ] adj wind, day stürmisch.

BM abbr of (a) British Museum. (b) Bachelor of Medicine.

BMA abbr of British Medical Association.

B Mus abbr of Bachelor of Music.

BO (inf) abbr of body odour Körpergeruch m.

boa ['bəʊə] n Boa f. **~ constrictor** Boa constrictor f.

boar [bɔːʳ] n (male pig) Eber m; (wild) Keiler m. **~'s head** Schweinskopf m.

board [bɔːd] 1 n (a) Brett nt; (black~) Tafel f; (notice~) Schwarzes Brett; (sign~) Schild nt; (floor~) Diele(nbrett nt) f. **the ~s** (Theat) die Bretter.

(b) (provision of meals) Kost, Verpflegung f. **~ and lodging** Kost und Logis; **full/half ~** Voll-/Halbpension f.

(c) (group of officials) Ausschuß m; (~of inquiry, examiners also) Kommission f; (with advisory function, ~ of trustees) Beirat m; (permanent official institution: gas ~, harbour ~ etc) Behörde f; (of company: also ~ of directors) Vorstand m; (including shareholders, advisers) Aufsichtsrat m. **B~ of Trade** (Brit) Handelsministerium nt; (US) Handelskammer f.

(d) (Naut, Aviat) on ~ an Bord; **to go on ~** an Bord gehen; on ~ **the ship/plane** an Bord des Schiffes/Flugzeugs; on ~ **the bus** im Bus; **he held a party on ~ his yacht** er veranstaltete eine Party auf seiner Jacht.

(e) (cardboard) Pappe f; (Typ) Deckel m.

(f) (~ of interviewers) Gremium nt (zur Auswahl von Bewerbern); (interview) Vorstellungsgespräch nt (vor einem Gremium). **to be on a ~** einem Gremium zur Auswahl von Bewerbern angehören; **to go on a ~** (as interviewer) eine Gremiumssitzung zur Bewerberauswahl haben; (as candidate) sich einem Gremium vorstellen.

(g) (US St Ex) Notierung f; (inf: stock exchange) Börse f.

(h) (fig phrases) **across the ~** allgemein, generell; criticize, agree, reject pauschal; **an increase of £10 per week across the ~** eine allgemeine or generelle Lohnerhöhung von £ 10 pro Woche; **to go by the ~** (work, plans, ideas) unter den Tisch fallen; (dreams, hopes) zunichte werden; (principles) über Bord geworfen werden; (business) zugrunde gehen; **that's all gone by the ~** daraus ist nichts geworden; see **sweep, above ~**.

2 vt (a) (cover with ~s) mit Brettern verkleiden.

(b) ship, plane besteigen, an Bord gehen/kommen; train, bus einsteigen in (+acc); (Naut: in attack) entern.

3 vi (a) in Pension sein (with bei).

(b) (Sch) Internatsschüler(in f) m sein.

(c) (Aviat) die Maschine besteigen. **flight ZA173 now ~ing through gate 13** Aufruf für Passagiere des Fluges ZA173, sich zum Flugsteig 13 zu begeben.

♦ **board in** or **up** vt sep door, window mit Brettern vernageln.

♦ **board out** 1 vt sep person in Pension schicken (with bei). 2 vi in Pension wohnen (with bei).

boarder ['bɔːdəʳ] n (a) Pensionsgast m. **to take in ~s** Leute in Pension nehmen. (b) (Sch) Internatsschüler(in f) m; (weekly ~) während der Woche im Internat wohnender Schüler; (dated: day ~) Tagesschüler, der in der Schule zu Mittag ißt. (c) (Naut) Mitglied nt eines Enterkommandos.

boarding ['bɔːdɪŋ-]: **~ card** n Bordkarte f; **~ house** n (a) Pension f; (b) (Sch) Wohngebäude nt eines Internats; **~ party** n (Naut) Enterkommando nt; **~ school** n Internat nt.

board: **~room** n Sitzungssaal m; **~room politics** npl Firmenklüngel n m (inf); **~ school** n (Brit Hist) staatliche Schule; **~walk** n (US) Holzsteg m; (on beach) hölzerne Uferpromenade.

boast [bəʊst] 1 n (a) Prahlerei f. (b) (source of pride) Stolz m. **it is their ~ that ...** sie rühmen sich, daß ... 2 vi prahlen (about, of mit, to sb jdm gegenüber). **without ~ing, without wishing to ~** ohne zu prahlen. 3 vt (a) (possess) sich rühmen (+gen) (geh); (town, country also) stolz sein eigen nennen. (b) (say boastfully) prahlen.

boaster ['bəʊstəʳ] n Aufschneider(in f) m, Prahlhans m (inf).

boastful ['bəʊstfʊl] adj, **~ly** ['bəʊstfəlɪ] adv prahlerisch.

boastfulness ['bəʊstfʊlnɪs] n Prahlerei f.

boasting ['bəʊstɪŋ] n Prahlerei f (about, of mit).

boat [bəʊt] n (a) (small vessel) Boot nt; (wooden: on lake, river etc also) Kahn m; (sea-going, passenger ~) Schiff nt; (pleasure steamer etc) Dampfer m. **by ~** mit dem Schiff; **to miss the ~** (fig inf) den Anschluß verpassen; **we're all in the same ~** (fig inf) wir sitzen alle in einem or im gleichen Boot.

(b) (gravy ~) Sauciere f.

boat: **~-builder** n Bootsbauer m; **~-building** n Bootsbau m; **~-deck** n Bootsdeck nt.

boater ['bəʊtəʳ] n (a) (hat) steifer Strohhut, Kreissäge f (inf). (b) (person boating) Bootsfahrer(in f), Kahnfahrer(in f) m.

boat: **~ful** n Schiffs-/Bootsladung f; **~ hire** n Bootsverleih m; (company) Bootsverleiher m; **~hook** n Bootshaken m; **~house** n Bootshaus nt or -schuppen m.

boating ['bəʊtɪŋ] n Bootfahren nt. **to go ~** Bootsfahrten/eine Bootsfahrt machen.

boating in cpds Boots-; **~ holiday** n Bootsferien pl; **~ trip** n Bootsfahrt f.

boat: **~load** n Bootsladung f; **~man** n (handling boat) Segler m; Ruderer m; Paddler m; (working with boats) Bootsbauer m; (hirer) Bootsverleiher m; **~ race** n Regatta f; **~-shaped** adj kahnförmig.

boatswain, bosun, bo's'n ['bəʊsn] n Bootsmann m. **~'s mate** Bootsmanngehilfe m.

boat: **~ train** n Zugfähre f; **~yard** n Bootshandlung f; (as dry dock) Liegeplatz m.

Bob [bɒb] n dim of Robert ... **and ~'s your uncle!** (inf) ... und fertig ist der Lack! (inf).

bob[1] [bɒb] 1 vi (a) sich auf und ab bewegen; (rabbit) hoppeln; (bird's tail) wippen; (boxer) tänzeln. **to ~ (up and down) in** or **on the water** auf dem Wasser schaukeln; (cork, piece of wood etc) sich im Wasser auf und ab bewegen; **he ~bed out of sight** er duckte sich.

(b) (curtsey) knicksen (to sb vor jdm).

2 vt (a) (move jerkily) head nicken mit; (bird) tail wippen mit. (b) curtsey machen. **to ~ a greeting** zum Gruß kurz nicken. 3 n (a) (curtsey) Knicks(chen nt) m. (b) (of head) Nicken nt no pl; (of bird's tail) Wippen nt no pl.

♦ **bob down** 1 vi sich ducken. 2 vt sep **one's head** ducken.

♦ **bob up** 1 vi (lit, fig) auftauchen. 2 vt sep **he ~bed his head ~** sein Kopf schnellte hoch.

bob[2] n, pl ~ (Brit inf) Schilling m. **that must have cost a ~ or two** das muß schon ein paar Mark gekostet haben (inf).

bob[3] 1 n (a) (haircut) Bubikopf m. (b) (horse's tail) gestutzter Schwanz. (c) (weight: on pendulum, plumbline) Gewicht nt. (d) (Fishing: float) Schwimmer m. 2 vt **to have one's hair ~bed** sich (dat) einen Bubikopf schneiden lassen.

bob[4] n (sleigh) Bob m; (runner) Kufe f. **two-/four-man ~** Zweier-/Viererbob m.

bobbin ['bɒbɪn] n Spule f; (cotton reel) Rolle f.

bobble ['bɒbl] n Bommel f, Pompon m.

Bobby ['bɒbɪ] n dim of Robert. **b~** (dated Brit inf) Bobby, Schupo (dated) m.

bobby: **~ pin** n Haarklemme f; **~ socks** npl (US) kurze Söckchen pl; **~soxer** n (US inf) Teenager m, junges Mädchen.

bob: **~cap** n Pudelmütze f; **~cat** n (US) Luchs m; **~sled, ~sleigh** 1 n Bob m; 2 vi Bob fahren; **~tail** n gestutzter Schwanz; **~tail cap** or **hat** n Bommelmütze f; **~tailed** adj horse, dog mit gestutztem Schwanz.

Boche [bɒʃ] n (pej inf) Boche m.

bod [bɒd] n (Brit inf) Mensch m. **odd ~** komischer Kerl.

bode [bəʊd] 1 vi: **to ~ well/ill** ein gutes/schlechtes Zeichen sein. 2 vt bedeuten, ahnen lassen. **that ~s no good** das bedeutet nichts Gutes, das läßt Böses ahnen.

bodge [bɒdʒ] n, vt see **botch**.

bodice ['bɒdɪs] n (a) Mieder nt; (of dress also) Oberteil nt. (b) (vest) Leibchen nt.

-bodied ['bɒdɪd] adj suf -gebaut, von ... Körperbau.

bodiless ['bɒdɪlɪs] adj körperlos.

bodily ['bɒdɪlɪ] 1 adj (physical) körperlich. **~ illness** Krankheit f des Körpers; **~ needs/wants** leibliche Bedürfnisse pl; **~ harm** Körperverletzung f. 2 adv (a) (forcibly) gewaltsam. (b) (in person) leibhaftig. (c) (all together) geschlossen; (in one piece) ganz.

bodkin ['bɒdkɪn] n (a) (Sew) Durchziehnadel f. (b) (Hist: hairpin) lange Haarnadel; (obs: dagger) Dolch m.

body ['bɒdɪ] n (a) (of man, animal) Körper m; (of human also) Leib m (geh). **the ~ of Christ** der Leib des Herrn; **just enough to keep ~ and soul together** gerade genug, um Leib und Seele zusammenzuhalten.

(b) (corpse) Leiche f, Leichnam m (geh); see **dead**.

(c) (main part of structure) (of plane, ship) Rumpf, Körper m; (of string instrument) Korpus, Schallkörper m; (of church, speech, army: also main ~) Haupteil m. **the main ~ of his readers/the students** das Gros seiner Leser/der Studenten; **in the ~ of the House** (Brit Parl) im Plenum.

(d) (coachwork of car) Karosserie f.

(e) (group of people) Gruppe f. **the student ~** die Studentenschaft; **a ~ of troops** ein Truppenverband m; **a great ~ of followers/readers** eine große Anhängerschaft/Leserschaft; **the great ~ of readers who buy his books** die große Anzahl von Lesern, die seine Bücher kaufen; **a large ~ of people** eine große Menschenmenge; **in a ~** geschlossen; **taken in a ~** geschlossen or als Ganzes betrachtet.

(f) (organization) Organ nt; (committee) Gremium nt; (corporation) Körperschaft f; see **corporate, politic**.

(g) (collection, quantity) **a ~ of facts/evidence/data etc** Tatsachen-/Beweis-/Datenmaterial nt etc; **a ~ of laws/legislation** ein Gesetzeskomplex m; **a large ~ of water** eine große Wassermasse.

(h) (*inf: person*) Mensch *m*.
(i) (*Math, Phys, Chem*) Körper *m*.
(j) (*substance, thickness*) (*of wine*) Körper *m*; (*of soup*) Substanz *f*; (*of paper, cloth*) Festigkeit, Stärke *f*. **the material hasn't enough** ~ der Stoff ist nicht fest *or* stark genug; **this soup hasn't enough** ~ diese Suppe ist zu dünn.
body: ~ **blow** *n* Körperschlag *m*; (*fig*) Schlag *m* ins Kontor (*to, for* für); ~**builder** *n* **(a)** (*food*) Kraftnahrung *f*; **(b)** (*apparatus*) Heimtrainer *m*; **(c)** (*person*) Bodybuilder *m*; ~**building** 1 *n* Bodybuilding *nt*; 2 *adj exercise* muskelkräftigend; *food* stärkend, kräftigend; ~**check** *n* Bodycheck *m*; ~**guard** *n* (*one person*) Leibwächter *m*; (*group*) Leibwache *f*; ~ **scissors** *n sing* (*Wrestling*) über den Körper angelegte Schere; ~**slam** *n* (*Wrestling*) Wurf *m*; ~**snatcher** *n* Leichenräuber *m*; ~**stocking** *n* Bodystocking *m*; ~**work** *n* (*Aut*) Karosserie *f*.
Boer ['bəʊəʳ] 1 *n* Bure *m*, Burin *f*. 2 *adj* burisch. **the** ~ **War** der Burenkrieg.
B of E *abbr of* **Bank of England**.
boffin ['bɒfɪn] *n* (*Brit inf*) Eierkopf (*inf*), Egghead (*inf*) *m*.
bog [bɒg] *n* **(a)** Sumpf *m*; (*peat* ~) (Torf)moor *nt*. **(b)** (*Brit inf: toilet*) Lokus *m* (*inf*), Klo *nt* (*inf*).
♦ **bog down** *vt sep* to be ~**ged** ~ (*lit*) steckenbleiben; (*fig*) steckengeblieben sein, sich festgefahren haben; (*in details*) sich verzettelt haben; **to get** ~**ged** ~ (*lit*) steckenbleiben; (*fig also*) sich festfahren; (*in details*) sich verzetteln.
bogey¹, **bogy** ['bəʊgɪ] *n*, *pl* **bogeys**, **bogies (a)** (*spectre, goblin*) Kobold, Butzemann *m*. ~ **man** Butzemann *m*, Schwarzer Mann. **(b)** (*fig: bugbear*) Popanz *m*, Schreckgespenst *nt*. **(c)** (*baby-talk*) Popel *m* (*inf*).
bogey² *n* (*Golf*) Bogey *nt*.
boggle ['bɒgl] *vi* (*inf*) glotzen (*inf*), völlig sprachlos sein. **he** ~**d at the sight** als er das sah, war er völlig sprachlos; **the mind or imagination** ~**s** das hältse ja im Kopf nicht aus (*sl*).
boggy ['bɒgɪ] *adj* (+*er*) *ground* sumpfig, morastig.
bogie ['bəʊgɪ] *n* (*Rail*) Drehgestell *nt*; (*trolley*) Draisine *f*.
bogus ['bəʊgəs] *adj doctor, lawyer* falsch; *money, pearls also* gefälscht; *company, transaction* Schwindel-; *claim* erfunden.
bogy ['bəʊgɪ] *n see* **bogey¹**.
Bohemia [bəʊ'hiːmɪə] *n* (*Geog*) Böhmen *nt*; (*fig*) Boheme *f*.
Bohemian [bəʊ'hiːmɪən] 1 *n* **(a)** Böhme *m*, Böhmin *f*. **(b)** (*fig*) b~ Bohemien *m*. 2 *adj* **(a)** böhmisch. **(b)** (*fig*) b~ *lifestyle* unkonventionell, unbürgerlich; *circles, quarter* Künstler-.
bohemianism [bəʊ'hiːmɪənɪzəm] *n* unkonventionelle *or* unbürgerliche Lebensweise.
boil¹ [bɔɪl] *n* (*Med*) Furunkel *m*.
boil² 1 *vi* **(a)** kochen; (*water also, Phys*) sieden. **the kettle was** ~**ing** das Wasser im Kessel kochte; ~**ing oil** siedendes Öl; **allow to** ~ **gently** (*Cook*) langsam kochen; **to let the kettle** ~ **dry** das Wasser im Kessel verkochen lassen.
(b) (*fig: sea, river*) brodeln, tosen.
(c) (*fig inf: be angry*) kochen, schäumen (*with* vor +*dat*).
(d) (*fig inf: be hot*) ~**ing hot water** kochendheißes Wasser; **it was** ~**ing (hot) in the office** es war im Büro eine Affenhitze (*inf*); **I was** ~**ing (hot)** mir war fürchterlich heiß; **you'll** ~ **in that thick sweater** in dem dicken Pullover schwitzt du ja tot (*inf*).
2 *vt* kochen. ~**ed shirt** (*inf*) weißes Hemd; ~**ed/hard** ~**ed egg** weichgekochtes *or* weiches/hartgekochtes Ei; ~**ed potatoes** Salzkartoffeln *pl*.
3 *n* **to bring sth to the** ~ etw aufkochen lassen; **to keep sth on the** ~ etw kochen *or* sieden lassen; **to keep sb on the** ~ (*fig inf*) jdn hinhalten; **to be on/come to/go off the** ~ kochen/zu kochen anfangen, zum Sieden kommen/zu kochen aufhören.
♦ **boil away** *vi* **(a)** (*go on boiling*) weiterkochen. **(b)** (*evaporate completely*) verdampfen.
♦ **boil down** 1 *vt sep* einkochen. 2 *vi* **(a)** (*jam etc*) dickflüssig werden. (*fig*) **to** ~ ~ **to** sth auf etw (*acc*) hinauslaufen; **what it** ~**s** ~ **to is that ...** das läuft darauf hinaus, daß ...
♦ **boil over** *vi* **(a)** (*lit*) überkochen. **(b)** (*fig: situation, quarrel*) den Siedepunkt erreichen. **he just** ~**ed** ~ ihm platzte der Kragen (*inf*).
♦ **boil up** *vi* **(a)** (*lit*) aufkochen. **(b)** **he could feel the anger** ~**ing** ~ **in him** er fühlte, wie die Wut in ihm aufstieg.
boiler ['bɔɪləʳ] *n* **(a)** (*domestic*) Boiler, Warmwasserbereiter *m*; (*in ship, engine*) (Dampf)kessel *m*; (*old: for washing*) Waschkessel *m*. **(b)** (*chicken*) Suppenhuhn *nt*.
boiler: ~ **house** *n* Kesselhaus *nt*; ~**maker** *n* Kesselschmied *m*; ~**making** *n* Kesselbau *m*; ~**man** *n* Heizer *m*; ~ **room** *n* Kesselraum *m*; ~**suit** *n* Overall, blauer Anton (*inf*), Blaumann (*inf*) *m*.
boiling ['bɔɪlɪŋ-]: ~ **fowl** *n* Suppenhuhn *nt*; ~ **point** *n* (*lit, fig*) Siedepunkt *m*; **at** ~ **point** (*lit, fig*) auf dem Siedepunkt; **to reach** ~ **point** (*lit, fig*) den Siedepunkt erreichen; (*feelings also, person*) auf dem Siedepunkt angelangen.
boisterous ['bɔɪstərəs] *adj* **(a)** (*exuberant, noisy*) *person* ausgelassen; *game, party, dance also* wild. **(b)** (*rough*) *wind* tosend; *sea also* aufgewühlt.
boisterously ['bɔɪstərəslɪ] *adv see adj*.
bold [bəʊld] *adj* (+*er*) **(a)** (*valiant*) kühn (*geh*); (*brave*) mutig; *deed, plan also* verwegen.
(b) (*impudent, forward*) unverfroren, dreist. **to be** *or* **make so** ~ **as to ...** sich erlauben *or* erkühnen (*geh*), zu ...; **might I be so** ~ **as to ...?** wenn ich es mir erlauben darf, zu ...?; **might I make so** ~ **as to help myself?** darf ich so frei sein und mich bedienen?; **to make** ~ **with sth** sich (*dat*) die Freiheit herausnehmen, sich bei etw einfach zu bedienen.
(c) (*striking*) *colours, pattern, stripes* kräftig; *checks also* grob; *strokes also* kühn (*geh*); *handwriting* kraftvoll, kühn (*geh*); *style* kraftvoll, ausdrucksvoll. **to bring out in** ~ **relief** stark hervortreten lassen.
(d) (*Typ*) fett; (*secondary* ~) halbfett. ~ **type** Fettdruck *m*; **to set sth in** ~ (**type**) etw fett/halbfett drucken.

boldness ['bəʊldnɪs] *n see adj* **(a)** Kühnheit (*geh*) *f*; Mut *m*; Verwegenheit *f*. **(b)** Unverfrorenheit, Dreistigkeit *f*. **(c)** Kräftigkeit *f*; Grobheit *f*; Kühnheit (*geh*) *f*; Kühnheit (*geh*) *f* Ausdruckskraft *f*.
bole [bəʊl] *n* Baumstamm *m*.
bolero [bə'lɛərəʊ] *n* (*all senses*) Bolero *m*.
Bolivia [bə'lɪvɪə] *n* Bolivien *nt*.
Bolivian [bə'lɪvɪən] 1 *n* Bolivianer(in *f*), Bolivier(in *f*) *m*. 2 *adj* bolivianisch.
boll [bəʊl] *n* Samenkapsel *f*. ~ **weevil** Baumwollkapselkäfer *m*.
bollard ['bɒləd] *n* (*on quay, road*) Poller *m*.
bollocking ['bɒləkɪŋ] *n* (*Brit sl*) Schimpfkanonade *f* (*inf*). **to give sb a** ~ jdn zur Sau machen (*sl*).
bollocks ['bɒləks] *npl* (*vulg*) **(a)** Eier *pl* (*sl*). **(b)** (*nonsense*) **(that's)** ~! Quatsch mit Soße! (*sl*); **he was talking** ~ der hat einen Scheiß geredet (*sl*).
boloney [bə'ləʊnɪ] *n see* **baloney**.
Bolshevik ['bɒlʃəvɪk] 1 *n* Bolschewik *m*. 2 *adj* bolschewistisch.
Bolshevism ['bɒlʃəvɪzəm] *n* Bolschewismus *m*.
Bolshevist ['bɒlʃəvɪst] *n*, *adj see* **Bolshevik**.
bolshie, **bolshy** ['bɒlʃɪ] (*inf*) 1 *n* Bolschewik *m*. 2 *adj* (+*er*) **(a)** (*fig*) (*uncooperative*) stur; (*aggressive*) pampig (*inf*), rotzig (*sl*). **(b)** (*pej*) bolschewistisch.
bolster ['bəʊlstəʳ] 1 *n* (*on bed*) Nackenrolle *f*. 2 *vt* (*also* ~ **up**) (*fig*) *person* Mut machen (+*dat*); *status* aufbessern; *currency* stützen. **to** ~ **up sb's morale** jdm Mut machen.
bolt [bəʊlt] 1 *n* **(a)** (*on door etc*) Riegel *m*.
(b) (*Tech*) Schraube *f* (ohne Spitze), Bolzen *m*.
(c) (*of lightning*) Blitzstrahl *m*. **it came/was like a** ~ **from out of the blue** (*fig*) das schlug ein/war wie ein Blitz aus heiterem Himmel.
(d) (*of cloth*) Ballen *m*.
(e) (*of crossbow*) Bolzen *m*; *see* **shoot**.
(f) (*of rifle*) Kammer *f*.
(g) (*sudden dash*) Satz *m* (*inf*). **his** ~ **for freedom** sein Fluchtversuch *m*; **he made a** ~ **for the door** er machte einen Satz zur Tür; **to make a** ~ **for it** losrennen.
2 *adv:* ~ **upright** kerzengerade.
3 *vi* **(a)** (*horse*) durchgehen; (*person*) Reißaus nehmen (*inf*).
(b) (*move quickly*) sausen, rasen, pesen (*inf*).
4 *vt* **(a)** *door, window* zu- *or* verriegeln.
(b) (*Tech*) *beams, machine parts* verschrauben (*to* mit), mit Schraubenbolzen befestigen (*to an* +*dat*). **to** ~ **together** verschrauben.
(c) (*also* ~ **down**) *one's food* hinunterschlingen.
♦ **bolt in** 1 *vi* (*rush in*) herein-/hineinplatzen *or* -stürzen. 2 *vt sep* (*lock in*) einsperren.
♦ **bolt on** *vt sep* (*Tech*) festschrauben (*prep obj, -to an* +*dat*).
♦ **bolt out** 1 *vi* (*rush out*) hinaus-/herausstürzen. 2 *vt sep* (*lock out*) aussperren.
bolthole ['bəʊlthəʊl] *n* Schlupfloch *nt*.
bolus ['bəʊləs] *n*, *pl* -**es** (*Med*) große Pille.
bomb [bɒm] 1 *n* **(a)** Bombe *f*.
(b) (*inf*) **his party went like a** ~ seine Party war ein Bombenerfolg (*inf*); **the car goes like a** ~ das ist die reinste Rakete von Wagen (*inf*); **the car cost a** ~ das Auto hat ein Bombengeld gekostet (*inf*); **to go down a** ~ Riesenanklang finden (*with bei*) (*inf*); **to do a** ~ (*US: fail*) durchfallen (*inf*).
2 *vt town* bombardieren.
3 *vi* **(a)** (*inf: go fast*) fegen (*inf*), zischen (*inf*).
(b) (*US inf: fail*) durchfallen (*inf*).
♦ **bomb out** *vt sep* ausbomben.
bombard [bɒm'bɑːd] *vt* (*Mil, fig*) bombardieren (*with* mit) (*Phys*) beschießen.
bombardier [ˌbɒmbə'dɪəʳ] *n* (*Mil*) Artillerieunteroffizier *m* (*Aviat*) Bombenschütze *m*.
bombardment [bɒm'bɑːdmənt] *n* (*Mil*) Bombardierung *f* (*also fig*), Bombardement *nt*; (*Phys*) Beschießen *nt*.
bombast ['bɒmbæst] *n* Schwulst, Bombast *m*.
bombastic *adj*, ~**ally** *adv* [bɒm'bæstɪk, -əlɪ] schwülstig, bombastisch.
Bombay [bɒm'beɪ] *n* Bombay *nt*. ~ **duck** kleiner getrockneter Fisch als Beigabe zur indischen Reistafel.
bomb: ~ **bay** *n* Bombenschacht *m*; ~ **crater** *n* Bombentrichter *m*; ~ **disposal** *n* Bombenräumung *f*; ~ **disposal squad** *or* **unit** *n* Bombenräumtrupp *m or* -kommando *nt*.
bombed [bɒmd] *adj* (*sl*) (*drunk*) knülle (*sl*); (*on drugs*) high (*sl*).
bomber ['bɒməʳ] *n* **(a)** (*aircraft*) Bomber *m*, Bombenflugzeug *nt*. **(b)** (*person*) (*Aviat*) Bombenschütze *m*; (*terrorist*) Bombenattentäter(in *f*) *m*.
bomber: ~ **command** *n* Bombenverband *m or* -geschwader *nt*; ~ **jacket** *n* Blouson *m or nt*; ~ **pilot** *n* Bomberpilot *m*.
bombing ['bɒmɪŋ] 1 *n* Bombenangriff *m* (*of* auf +*acc*); (*of target also*) Bombardierung *f* 2 *adj raid, mission* Bomben-.
bomb: ~**proof** *adj* bombensicher; ~**shell** *n* (*a*) (*Mil*) Bombe *f*; **(b)** (*fig*) Bombe *f*, plötzliche Überraschung; **this news was a** ~**shell** die Nachricht schlug wie eine Bombe ein; **the director revealed his latest** ~**shell** die neueste Idee des Direktors schlug wie eine Bombe ein; **a blonde** ~**shell** ein blonder Superbomber (*inf*); ~ **shelter** *n* Luftschutzkeller *m*; (*specially built*) (Luftschutz)bunker *m*; ~ **sight** *n* Fliegerbombenzielgerät *nt*; ~ **site** *n* Trümmergrundstück *nt*.
bona fide [ˌbəʊnə'faɪdɪ] *adj bona fide; traveller, word, antique* echt. **it's a** ~ **offer** es ist ein Bona-fide-Angebot *or* ein Angebot auf Treu und Glauben.
bona fides [ˌbəʊnə'faɪdɪz] *n* Echtheit *f*.
bonanza [bə'nænzə] 1 *n* **(a)** (*US Min*) reiche Erzader. **(b)** (*fig*) Goldgrube *f*. **the oil** ~ *or* **der Ölboom**. 2 *adj attr year* Boom-.
bonce [bɒns] *n* (*Brit sl: head*) Birne *f* (*sl*). **curly** ~ Krauskopf *m* (*inf*).
bond [bɒnd] 1 *n* **(a)** (*agreement*) Übereinkommen *nt*. **to enter**

into a ~ with sb ein Übereinkommen mit jdm treffen.
(b) (*fig: link*) Band *nt* (*geh*), Bindung *f*.
(c) ~s *pl* (*lit: chains*) Fesseln, Bande (*liter*) *pl*; (*fig: ties*) Bande *pl* (*geh*); (*burdensome*) Fesseln *pl*; **marriage** ~s das Band/die Fesseln der Ehe.
(d) (*Comm, Fin*) Obligation *f*, Pfandbrief *m*; (*Brit, US*) festverzinsliches Wertpapier, Bond *m*. **government** ~ Staatsanleihe *f* or -papiere *pl*.
(e) (*Comm: custody of goods*) Zollverschluß *m*. **to put sth into** ~ etw unter Zollverschluß geben; **goods in** ~ Zollgut *nt*.
(f) (*adhesion between surfaces*) Haftfestigkeit, Haftwirkung *f*. **nothing can break the** ~ **between the two surfaces** die beiden Flächen haften *or* kleben fest und unlösbar aneinander.
(g) (*Build*) Verband *m*.
(h) (*Chem*) Bindung *f*.
2 *vt* **(a)** (*Comm*) goods unter Zollverschluß legen *or* nehmen.
(b) (*Build*) bricks im Verband verlegen.
3 *vi* (*glue*) binden; (*bricks*) einen Verband bilden.

bondage ['bɒndɪdʒ] *n* **(a)** (*lit*) Sklaverei *f*; (*in Middle Ages*) Leibeigenschaft *f*. **in** ~ **to sb** in Sklaverei/Leibeigenschaft bei jdm, jdm hörig.
(b) (*fig liter*) vollständige Unterjochung. **we are held in** ~ **by our desires/economic system** wir sind Gefangene unserer Begierden/unseres Wirtschaftssystems; **she was held in** ~ **by her mother** sie lebte unter der Knute ihrer Mutter; **her stronger will kept him in** ~ ihr stärkerer Wille hielt ihn vollständig unterjocht.
(c) (*sexual*) Fesseln *nt*.

bonded ['bɒndɪd] *adj* goods unter Zollverschluß. ~ **warehouse** Zollager, Zolldepot *nt*.

bond: ~ **holder** *n* Pfandbrief- *or* Obligationsinhaber(in *f*) *m*; ~**man**, ~**sman** *n* Sklave *m*; (*medieval*) Leibeigene(r) *mf*.

bone [bəʊn] **1** *n* **(a)** Knochen *m*; (*of fish*) Gräte *f*. ~s *pl* (*of the dead*) Gebeine *pl*; **ham off the** ~ Schinken *m* vom Knochen; **meat on the** ~ Fleisch *m* am Knochen; **chilled to the** ~ völlig durchgefroren; ~ **of contention** Zankapfel *m*; **to have a** ~ **to pick with sb** (*inf*) mit jdm ein Hühnchen zu rupfen haben (*inf*); **I'll make no** ~s **about it, you're/this is ...** (*inf*) du bist/das ist, offen gestanden *or* ehrlich gesagt, ...; **he made no** ~s **about saying what he thought** (*inf*) er hat seine Meinung nicht hinterm Berg gehalten, er hat aus seinem Herzen keine Mördergrube gemacht (*prov*); **I can feel it in my** ~s **das spüre** *or* **habe ich in den Knochen; my old** ~s (*inf*) meine alten Knochen (*inf*).
(b) (*substance*) Knochen *m*.
(c) (*of corset*) (Fischbein)stange *f*; (*smaller*) (Fischbein)stäbchen *nt*.
(d) (*Mus*) ~s *pl* Klangstäbe *pl*.
(e) (*dice*) ~s *pl* (*inf*) Würfel, Knöchel (*old*) *pl*.
2 *adj attr* (*made of* ~) Bein-, beinern.
3 *vt* die Knochen lösen aus, ausbeinen (*dial*); *fish* entgräten.
♦**bone up on** *vi +prep obj* (*esp US inf*) *subject* pauken (*inf*).
bone china *n* Knochen-Porzellan *nt*.
boned [bəʊnd] *adj meat* ohne Knochen; *fish* entgrätet.
-boned *adj suf* -knochig.
bone: ~-**dry** *adj* (*inf*) knochentrocken; *earth also* staubtrocken; ~**head** *n* (*inf*) Dummkopf, Armleuchter (*inf*) *m*; ~**headed** *adj* (*inf*) blöd(e) (*inf*), doof (*inf*); ~-**idle** *adj* (*inf*) stinkfaul (*inf*); ~**less** *adj meat* ohne Knochen; *fish* ohne Gräten; ~ **meal** *n* Knochenmehl *nt*.
boner ['bəʊnəʳ] *n* (*US sl*) Schnitzer, Hammer (*inf*) *m*.
boneshaker ['bəʊnʃeɪkəʳ] *n* **(a)** (*inf*) Klapperkiste (*inf*), Mühle (*inf*) *f*. **(b)** (*old: cycle*) Fahrrad *nt* ohne Gummireifen.
bonfire ['bɒnfaɪəʳ] *n* (*for burning rubbish*) Feuer *nt*; (*as beacon*) Leucht- *or* Signalfeuer *nt*; (*Guy Fawkes*) Guy-Fawkes-Feuer *nt*; (*for celebration*) Freudenfeuer *nt*.
bongo ['bɒŋgəʊ] *n* Bongo *nt or f*.
bonhomie ['bɒnɒmiː] *n* Bonhomie (*geh*), Jovialität *f*.
boniness ['bəʊnɪnɪs] *n* Knochigkeit *f*.
bonkers ['bɒŋkəz] *adj* (*Brit sl*) meschugge (*inf*). **to be** ~ spinnen (*inf*); **to go** ~ überschnappen (*inf*).
bon mot ['bɒn'məʊ] *n* Bonmot *nt* (*geh*).
bonnet ['bɒnɪt] *n* **(a)** (*woman's*) Haube *f*; (*baby's*) Häubchen *nt*; (*esp Scot: man's*) Mütze *f*. **(b)** (*Brit Aut*) Motor- *or* Kühlerhaube *f*. **(c)** (*of chimney*) Schornsteinkappe *f*.
bonnie, bonny ['bɒnɪ] *adj* (*esp Scot*) schön; *lassie also* hübsch; *baby* prächtig.
bonus ['bəʊnəs] *n* **(a)** Prämie *f*; (*output, production also*) Zulage *f*; (*cost-of-living* ~) Zuschlag *m*; (*Christmas* ~) Gratifikation *f*. **(b)** (*Fin: on shares*) Extradividende, Sonderausschüttung *f*. **(c)** (*inf: sth extra*) Zugabe *f*.
bony ['bəʊnɪ] *adj* (+*er*) (*of bone*) knöchern; (*like bone*) knochenartig; *person, knee, hips* knochig; *fish* grätig, mit viel Gräten; *meat* mit viel Knochen.
bonze [bɒnz] *n* Bonze *m*.
bonzer ['bɒnzəʳ] *adj* (*Austral inf*) klasse (*inf*).
boo [buː] **1** *interj* buh. **he wouldn't say** ~ **to a goose** (*inf*) er ist ein schüchternes Pflänzchen. **2** *vt actor, play, speaker, referee* auspfeifen, ausbuhen. **to be** ~**ed off the stage** ausgepfiffen *or* ausgebuht werden. **3** *vi* buhen. **4** *n* Buhruf *m*.
boob [buːb] **1** *n* **(a)** (*Brit inf: mistake*) Schnitzer *m*. **a common** ~ ein häufig gemachter Fehler.
(b) (*inf: woman's breast*) Brust *f*. **look at those** ~s **die hat vielleicht Holz vor der Hütte** (*sl*); **big** ~s **große Dinger** *pl* (*sl*). **2** *vi* (*Brit inf*) einen Schnitzer machen; (*fail*) Mist bauen (*sl*). **somebody** ~**ed, I didn't get the letter** da hat jemand was verbockt (*inf*), ich habe den Brief überhaupt nicht gekriegt.
booby ['buːbɪ] *n* (*inf*) **(a)** (*fool*) Trottel *m*. **(b)** see **boob 1 (b)**.
booby: ~ **hatch** *n* (*US sl*) Klapsmühle *f* (*sl*); ~ **prize** *n* Scherzpreis *m* für den schlechtesten Teilnehmer; ~ **trap 1** *n* **(a)** (*als Schabernack versteckt angebrachte*) Falle *f*; **(b)** (*Mil etc*)

versteckte Bombe; **don't open that box, it's a** ~ **trap** machen Sie die Schachtel nicht auf, da ist eine Bombe drin; **2** *vt* the suitcase was ~-**trapped** in dem Koffer war eine Bombe versteckt, der Koffer war gesalzen (*sl*).
boogie-woogie ['buːgɪ'wuːgɪ] *n* Boogie-Woogie *m*.
boo-hoo ['buː'huː] *interj* (*to indicate crying*) huh-huh; (*to mock crying*) schluchz-schluchz.
booing ['buːɪŋ] *n* Buhrufen *nt*.
book [bʊk] **1** *n* **(a)** Buch *nt*; (*exercise* ~) Heft *nt*; (*division: in Bible, poem etc*) Buch *nt*. **the (good) B~** das Buch der Bücher; **the B~ of Genesis** die Genesis, das 1. Buch Moses; **to bring sb to** ~ jdn zur Rechenschaft ziehen; **to throw the** ~ **at sb** (*inf*) jdn nach allen Regeln der Kunst fertigmachen (*inf*); **to go by** *or* **stick to the** ~ sich an die Vorschriften halten; **according to** *or* **by the** ~ nach dem Buchstaben; **he does everything according to** *or* **by the** ~ er hält sich bei allem strikt an die Vorschriften; **to be in sb's good/bad** ~s bei jdm gut/schlecht angeschrieben sein (*inf*); **I can read him like a** ~ ich kann in ihm lesen wie in einem Buch; **it's a closed** ~ **to me** das ist ein Buch mit sieben Siegeln für mich; **he/my life is an open** ~ er/mein Leben ist ein offenes Buch; **that's one for the** ~ (*inf*) das muß man sich im Kalender (rot) anstreichen; **he knows/used every trick in the** ~ (*inf*) er ist/war mit allen Wassern gewaschen (*inf*); **that counts as cheating in my** ~ (*inf*) für mich ist das Betrug; **I'm in the** ~ (*Telec*) ich stehe im Telefonbuch.
(b) (*of tickets*) Heft *nt*; (*thicker*) Block *m*. ~ **of stamps/matches** Briefmarken-/Streichholzheftchen *nt*.
(c) (*Comm, Fin*) ~s *pl* Bücher *pl*; **to keep the** ~s **of a firm** die Bücher einer Firma führen; **to do** *or* **look after the** ~s **for sb** jdm die Bücher führen; **I've been doing the** ~s ich habe die Abrechnung gemacht.
(d) (*of club, society*) (Mitglieder)verzeichnis *nt*, Mitgliedsliste *f*. **to be on the** ~s **of an organization** im Mitgliederverzeichnis *or* auf der Mitgliedsliste einer Organisation stehen.
(e) (*Gambling*) Wettbuch *nt*. **to make** *or* **keep a** ~ (*Horseracing*) Buch machen; (*generally*) Wetten abschließen.
(f) (*libretto: of opera etc*) Textbuch *nt*.
(g) (*Comm*) ~ **of samples** Musterbuch *nt*.
2 *vt* **(a)** bestellen; *seat, room also* buchen, reservieren lassen; *artiste* engagieren, verpflichten; *cabaret act* nehmen; (*privately*) sorgen für. **this performance/flight/hotel is fully** ~**ed** diese Vorstellung ist ausverkauft/dieser Flug ist ausgebucht/das Hotel ist voll belegt; **can I** ~ **a time to see him?** kann ich einen Termin bei ihm bekommen?; **to** ~ **sb through to Hull** (*Rail*) jdn bis Hull durchbuchen.
(b) (*Fin, Comm*) *order* aufnehmen. **to** ~ **goods to sb's account** jdm Waren in Rechnung stellen.
(c) (*inf*) *driver etc* aufschreiben (*inf*), einen Strafzettel verpassen (+*dat*) (*inf*); *football player* verwarnen. **to be** ~**ed for speeding** wegen zu schnellen Fahrens aufgeschrieben werden.
3 *vi see vt* **(a)** bestellen; buchen. **to** ~ **through to Hull** bis Hull durchlösen.
♦**book in 1** *vi* (*in hotel etc*) sich eintragen. **we** ~**ed** ~ **at the Hilton** wir sind im Hilton abgestiegen. **2** *vt sep* **(a)** (*register*) eintragen. **(b)** (*make reservation for*) **to** ~ **sb** ~ **to a hotel** jdm ein Hotelzimmer reservieren lassen; **we're** ~**ed** ~ **at the Hilton** unsere Zimmer sind im Hilton bestellt *or* reserviert.
♦**book up 1** *vi* buchen. **2** *vt sep* (*usu pass*) reservieren lassen. **to be (fully)** ~**ed** ~ (*ganz*) ausgebucht sein; (*evening performance, theatre*) (bis auf den letzten Platz) ausverkauft sein.
bookable ['bʊkəbl] *adj* im Vorverkauf erhältlich.
book: ~**binder** *n* Buchbinder *m*; ~**binding** *n* Buchbinderei *f*; ~**case** *n* Bücherregal *nt*; (*with doors*) Bücherschrank *m*; ~ **club** *n* Buchgemeinschaft *f*; ~**end** *n* Bücherstütze *f*.
bookie ['bʊkɪ] *n* (*inf*) Buchmacher *m*.
booking ['bʊkɪŋ] *n* Buchung, Bestellung, Reservierung *f*; (*of artiste, performer*) Engagement *nt*, Verpflichtung *f*. **to make a** ~ buchen; **to cancel a** ~ den Tisch/die Karte *etc* abbestellen; **die Reise/den Flug** *etc* stornieren; **to change one's** ~ umbuchen; **have you got a** ~ **in the name of Higgins?** ist bei Ihnen etwas auf den Namen Higgins gebucht?
booking: ~ **clerk** *n* Fahrkartenverkäufer(in *f*) *m*; (*official also*) Schalterbeamte(r) *m*, Schalterbeamtin *f*; ~ **office** *n* (*Rail*) Fahrkartenschalter *m*; (*Theat*) Vorverkaufsstelle *or* -kasse *f*.
bookish ['bʊkɪʃ] *adj* gelehrt (*pej, hum*); (*given to reading*) lesewütig; (*not wordly*) lebensfremd; *language, expression* buchsprachlich; (*pej*) trocken, papieren. **a** ~ **word** ein Wort *m* der Schriftsprache; **he is a very** ~ **person** er hat eine Nase dauernd in einem Buch; (*not worldly*) er ist ein richtiger Stubengelehrter (*pej*); ~ **woman** Blaustrumpf *m* (*pej*); **she married a** ~ **sort of person** sie hat einen vertrockneten Gelehrtentyp geheiratet; ~ **style** Buchstil *m* (*pej*) papierener Stil.
book: ~ **jacket** *n* Schutzumschlag *m*, Buchhülle *f*; ~-**keeper** *n* Buchhalter(in *f*) *m*; ~-**keeping** *n*, ~-**führung** *f*; ~ **knowledge** *or* **learning** *n* Buchgelehrsamkeit, Bücherweisheit *f*.
booklet ['bʊklɪt] *n* Broschüre *f*.
book: ~ **lover** *n* Bücherfreund *m*; ~**maker** *n* Buchmacher *m*; ~**mark** *n* Buch- *or* Lesezeichen *nt*; ~**mobile** *n* (*US*) Fahrbücherei *f*; ~**plate** *n* Exlibris *nt*; ~ **post** *n* Büchersendung *f*; **to send sth by** ~ **post** etw als Büchersendung schicken; ~ **post** is ... Büchersendungen sind ...; ~**rest** *n* Lesepult *nt*; ~**seller** *n* Buchhändler, Sortimenter *m*; ~**shelf** *n* Bücherbord *or* -brett *nt*; ~**shelves** *npl* (~*case*) Bücherregal *nt*; ~**shop** (*Brit*), ~**store** (*US*) *n* Buchhandlung *f or* -laden *nt*; ~**stall** *n* Bücherstand *m*; ~-**token** *n* Buchgutschein *m*; ~ **trade** *n* Buchhandel *m*; ~**worm** *n* (*fig*) Bücherwurm *m*.
boom¹ [buːm] *n* **(a)** (*barrier, across river etc*) Sperre *f*; (*at factory gate etc*) Schranke *f*. **(b)** (*Naut*) Baum *m*. **(c)** (*Tech: also derrick* ~) Ladebaum *m*; (*jib of crane*) Ausleger *m*. **(d)** (*for microphone*) Galgen *m*.

boom² 1 n (of sea, waves, wind) Brausen nt; (of thunder) Hallen nt; (of guns) Donnern nt; (of organ, voice) Dröhnen nt. 2 vi (a) (sea, wind) brausen; (thunder) hallen. (b) (organ, person, voice: also ~ out) dröhnen; (guns) donnern. 3 interj bum.

♦**boom out** 1 vi see **boom²** 2 (b). 2 vt sep (person) order brüllen. to ~ ~ a command to sb jdm mit Donnerstimme einen Befehl zubrüllen; **the bass ~s ~ the chorus** der Baß singt den Refrain mit dröhnender Stimme.

boom³ 1 vi (trade, sales) einen Aufschwung nehmen, boomen (inf); (prices) anziehen, in die Höhe schnellen. **business/he is ~ing** das Geschäft blüht or floriert/er floriert.
   2 n (of business, fig) Boom, Aufschwung m; (period of economic growth) Hochkonjunktur f; (of prices) Preissteigerung f. **to undergo or have a sudden ~** einen plötzlichen Aufschwung nehmen or erfahren.

boomerang ['buːməræŋ] 1 n (lit, fig) Bumerang m. **to have a ~ effect** einen Bumerangeffekt haben. 2 vi (fig inf: words, actions) wie ein Bumerang zurückkommen (on zu).

booming ['buːmɪŋ] adj sound dröhnend; surf brausend.

boom: ~ **microphone** n Mikrophon nt am Galgen; ~**-slump cycle** n Konjunktur-Zyklus m; ~ **town** n Goldgräberstadt f.

boon¹ [buːn] n (a) (blessing, advantage) Segen m. **it's such a ~** es ist ein wahrer Segen. (b) (obs: favour, wish) Gunst, Gnade f.

boon² adj: ~ **companion** (old, liter) lustiger Gesell (old).

boondockers ['buːndɒkəz] npl (US inf: heavy boots) (schwere) Stiefel pl.

boondocks ['buːndɒks] npl (US inf: backwoods) Wildnis f. **in the ~** irgendwo j.w.d. (inf).

boondoggle ['buːndɒgl] (US inf) 1 vi auf Staatskosten Zeit und Geld verplempern (inf). 2 n Zeitverschwendung f or Kleinkrämerei f auf Staatskosten.

boondoggler ['buːndɒglə'] n (US inf) staatlich angestellte Niete, kleinkarierte Beamtenseele, beamteter Kleinkrämer.

boor [buə'] n Rüpel, Flegel m.

boorish adj, ~**ly** adv ['buərɪʃ, -lɪ] rüpelhaft, flegelhaft.

boorishness ['buərɪʃnɪs] n Rüpelhaftigkeit, Flegelhaftigkeit f.

boost [buːst] 1 n Auftrieb m no pl; (Elec, Aut) Verstärkung f; (rocket) Zusatzantrieb m. **to give sb/sth a ~** jdm/einer Sache Auftrieb geben, jdn aufmöbeln (inf)/etw ankurbeln or in Schwung bringen; (by advertising) für jdn/etw die Werbetrommel rühren; **to give my bank account a ~** um meinem Bankkonto eine Finanzspritze zu verabreichen; **this device gives the heart/electric charge/motor a ~** dieser Apparat verstärkt den Herzschlag/die elektrische Ladung/die Motorleistung; **to give a ~ to sb's morale/confidence** jdm Auftrieb geben or Mut machen/jds Selbstvertrauen stärken.
   2 vt production, output, sales, economy ankurbeln; electric charge, engine, heart beat etc verstärken; confidence, sb's ego stärken; morale heben.

booster ['buːstə'] n (a) (Elec) Puffersatz m; (Rad) Zusatzverstärker m; (TV) Zusatzgleichrichter m; (Aut) (supercharger) Kompressor m; (for heating) Gebläse nt; (~ rocket) Booster m; (for launching) Booster m, Startrakete f; (Aviat) Hilfstriebwerk nt; (Space) Booster m, Zusatztriebwerk nt. **to act as a ~** zur Verstärkung dienen.
   (b) (Med: also ~ **shot**) Wiederholungsimpfung f. ~ **dose** zusätzliche Dosis.

boot¹ [buːt] 1 n (a) Stiefel m. **the ~ is on the other foot** (fig) es ist genau umgekehrt; (the other side is responsible) die Verantwortung/Schuld liegt ganz im Gegenteil, bei den anderen; **to give sb the (order of the hum) ~** (inf) jdn rausschmeißen (inf), jdn an die Luft setzen (inf); **to get the ~** (inf) rausgeschmissen werden (inf); **it's the ~ for him** (inf) der fliegt (inf); **to die with one's ~s on** (inf) über der Arbeit or in den Sielen sterben; **to put the ~ in** (sl) kräftig zutreten.
   (b) (Brit: of car etc) Kofferraum m.
   (c) (inf: kick) **to give sb/sth a ~** jdm/einer Sache einen Tritt geben or versetzen.
   (d) (Brit pej sl: woman) Schreckschraube f (inf).
   2 vt (inf: kick) einen (Fuß)tritt geben (+dat); ball kicken.

♦**boot out** vt sep (inf: lit, fig) rausschmeißen (inf).

boot² adv (hum, form): **to ~** obendrein, noch dazu.

bootblack ['buːtblæk] n Schuhputzer m.

bootee [buː'tiː] n (baby's) gestrickter Babyschuh.

booth [buːð] n (at fair) (Markt)bude f or -stand m; (at show) (Messe)stand m. (b) (telephone ~) (offene) Zelle f; (polling ~, in cinema, language laboratory) Kabine f; (in restaurant) Nische f, Séparée nt (geh).

boot: ~**jack** n Stiefelknecht m; ~**lace** n Schnürsenkel m; **to pull oneself up by one's own ~laces** (inf) sich am eigenen Haar herausziehen; ~**leg** n vt (US) (make) schwarz brennen (inf); (sell) schwarz verkaufen; (transport) schmuggeln; 2 adj whisky etc schwarz gebrannt; ~**legger** n (US) Bootlegger m; (producer also) Schwarzbrenner m; (seller also) Schwarzhändler m (mit Alkohol); (purveyor also) (Alkohol)schmuggler m.

bootless ['buːtlɪs] adj (liter) nutzlos, eitel (liter).

boot: ~**licker** n (pej inf) Speichellecker m (pej inf); ~**maker** n Schuhmacher m; ~ **polish** n Schuhcreme f.

boots [buːts] n sing (Brit) Hausbursche or -diener m.

bootstraps ['buːtstræps] npl see **bootlace**.

booty ['buːtɪ] n (lit, fig) Beute f.

booze [buːz] (inf) 1 n (alcoholic drink) Alkohol m; (spirits also) Schnaps m; (drinking bout) Sauftour f (inf). **keep off the ~** laß das Saufen sein (inf); **bring some ~** bring was zu schlucken mit (inf); **he's gone on the ~ again** er säuft wieder (inf).
   2 vi saufen (inf). **all this boozing** diese Sauferei (inf); **boozing party** Besäufnis nt (inf); **to go out boozing** saufen gehen (inf).

boozed(-up) ['buːzd(ʌp)] adj (inf) blau (inf), alkoholisiert (inf).

boozer ['buːzə'] n (a) (pej inf: drinker) Säufer(in f) (pej inf), Schluckspecht (inf) m. (b) (Brit sl: pub) Kneipe f (inf).

booze-up ['buːzʌp] n (inf) Besäufnis nt (inf).

boozy ['buːzɪ] adj (+er) (inf) look, face versoffen (inf). **a ~ person** ein Schluckspecht m (inf); (stronger) ein versoffenes Loch (sl); **to have ~ breath** eine Fahne haben (inf); ~ **party** Sauferei f (inf); ~ **lunch** Essen nt mit reichlich zu trinken.

bop [bɒp] 1 n (a) (Mus) Bebop m. (b) (inf: dance) Schwof m (inf). (c) (inf: blow) Knuff (inf), Puff (inf) m. **to give sb a ~ on the nose** jdm eins auf die Nase geben. 2 vi (inf: dance) schwofen (inf). 3 vt (inf) **to ~ sb on the head** jdm eins auf den Kopf geben.

boracic [bə'ræsɪk] adj (Chem) Bor-, borhaltig.

borage ['bɒrɪdʒ] n Borretsch m.

borax ['bɔːræks] n Borax m.

border ['bɔːdə'] 1 n (a) (edge, side: woods, field) Rand m. (b) (boundary, frontier) Grenze f. **on the French ~** an der französischen Grenze; **on the ~s of France** an der französischen Grenze; **on the ~s of France and Switzerland** an der Grenze zwischen Frankreich und der Schweiz, an der französisch-schweizerischen Grenze; **the B~s** (Brit Geog) das Grenzgebiet zwischen England und Schottland; **north/south of the ~** (Brit) in/nach Schottland/England; ~ **dispute** Grenzstreitigkeit f; **fighting** Grenzzwischenfall m.
   (c) (in garden) Rabatte f; see **herbaceous.**
   (d) (edging: on dress) Bordüre f; (of carpet) Einfassung f; (of picture) Umrahmung f. **black ~** (on notepaper) schwarzer Rand, Trauerrand m.
   2 vt (a) (line edges of) road, path säumen; garden, estate etc begrenzen; (on all sides) umschließen.
   (b) (land etc: lie on edge of) grenzen an (+acc).

♦**border on or upon** vi +prep obj (lit, fig) grenzen an (+acc). **it was ~ing ~ being rude** das grenzte an Unhöflichkeit.

borderer ['bɔːdərə'] n Grenzbewohner, Grenzer (inf) m; (Brit) Bewohner m des Grenzgebiets zwischen England und Schottland.

border: ~ **guard** n Grenzsoldat m; ~ **incident** n Grenzzwischenfall m.

bordering ['bɔːdərɪŋ] adj country angrenzend.

border: ~**land** n (lit) Grenzgebiet nt; (fig) Grenzbereich m; ~**line** 1 n (a) (between states, districts) Grenze, Grenzlinie f. (b) (fig: between categories, classes etc) Grenze f; **to be on the ~line** an der Grenze liegen, ein Grenzfall sein; **his marks were on the ~line between a pass and a fail** er stand mit seinen Noten auf der Kippe; 2 adj (fig) **a ~line case** ein Grenzfall m; **it was a ~line pass/fail** er etc ist ganz knapp durchgekommen/durchgefallen; **he/it is ~line** er/es ist ein Grenzfall; **it's too ~line** das liegt zu sehr an der Grenze; ~ **raid** n Grenzüberfall m; ~ **state** n Grenzstaat m; ~ **town** n Grenzstadt f.

bore¹ [bɔː'] 1 vt hole, well, tunnel bohren; rock durchbohren. 2 vi bohren (for nach). 3 n (hole) Bohrloch nt; (of tube, pipe) lichte Weite, Durchmesser m; (of shotgun, cannon) Kaliber nt. **a 12 ~ shotgun** eine Flinte vom Kaliber 12.

bore² 1 n (a) (person) Langweiler m. **what a ~ he is!** das ist ein Langweiler!, der kann einen langweilen or anöden (inf); **the club/office** ~ der Langweiler vom Dienst.
   (b) (thing, profession, situation etc) **to be a ~** langweilig sein.
   (c) (nuisance) **don't be a ~** nun sei doch nicht so (schwierig!); **he's a ~, he never wants ...** er ist eine Plage, er will nie ...; **this car is such a ~** das Auto ist wirklich eine Plage; **it's such a ~ having to go** es ist wirklich zu dumm or lästig, daß ich etc gehen muß; **oh what a ~!** das ist aber auch zu dumm or lästig!
   2 vt langweilen. **to ~ sb stiff or to death or to tears, to ~ the pants off sb** (inf) jdn zu Tode langweilen; **to be/get ~d** sich langweilen; **I'm ~d** mir ist es langweilig, ich langweile mich; **he is/gets ~d with her/his job** sie/seine Arbeit langweilt ihn; **he was ~d with reading/life** er war des Lesens/Lebens überdrüssig (geh), er hatte das Lesen/Leben über.

bore³ pret of **bear¹**.

bore⁴ n (tidal wave) Flutwelle f.

boredom ['bɔːdəm] n Lang(e)weile f; (boringness) Stumpfsinn m, Langweiligkeit f. **with a look of utter ~ on his face** mit einem völlig gelangweilten Gesichtsausdruck.

bore-hole ['bɔːhəʊl] n Bohrloch nt.

borer ['bɔːrə'] n (Tech) Bohrer m; (insect) Bohrkäfer m.

boric ['bɔːrɪk] adj (Chem) Bor-.

boring¹ ['bɔːrɪŋ] 1 n (Tech) (act) Bohren nt; (hole) Bohrloch nt. 2 adj ~ **machine** Bohrmaschine f.

boring² adj langweilig.

born [bɔːn] ptp of **bear¹** 1 (h). **to be ~** geboren werden; (fig) entstehen; (idea) geboren werden; **I was ~ in 1948** ich bin or wurde 1948 geboren; **when were you ~?** wann sind Sie geboren?; **to be ~ again** wiedergeboren werden; **every baby ~ into the world** jedes Kind, das auf die Welt kommt; **he was ~ to a life of hardship** (inf) in ein schweres Leben/eine reiche Familie hineingeboren; **to be ~ lucky/deaf** unter einem glücklichen Stern/taub geboren sein; **he was just ~ to be Prime Minister** er war zum Ministerpräsidenten geboren; **I wasn't ~ yesterday** (inf) ich bin nicht von gestern (inf); **there's one ~ every minute!** (fig inf) die Dummen werden nicht alle!; **the characteristics which are ~ in us** die uns angeborenen Eigenschaften; **he was ~ of poor parents** er war das Kind armer Eltern; **simple ideas which are ~ of complex reasoning** einfache Ideen, die aus komplizierten Gedankengängen hervorgehen; **with that confidence ~ of experience** mit dem aus Erfahrung hervorgegangenen Selbstvertrauen.
   2 adj suf (a) (native of) **he is Chicago-~** er ist ein gebürtiger or geborener Chicagoer; **his foreign-/French-~ wife** seine Frau, die Ausländerin/gebürtige Französin ist.
   (b) (of certain parentage) **high-/low-~** von vornehmer/niedriger Geburt.
   3 adj geboren. **he is a ~ poet/teacher** er ist der geborene Dichter/Lehrer; **an Englishman ~ and bred** ein echter or waschechter (inf) Engländer; **in all my ~ days** (inf) mein Lebtag (dated), in meinem ganzen Leben.

borne [bɔːn] ptp of bear[1].

borough [ˈbʌrə] n (a) (also municipal ~) Bezirk m, Stadtgemeinde f. (b) (Parl) städtischer Wahlbezirk.

borrow [ˈbɒrəʊ] 1 vt (a) (sich dat) borgen, sich (dat) leihen (from von); £500 (from bank), car sich (dat) leihen (from von); library book ausleihen; word entlehnen (from von); (fig) idea, methodology borgen (inf), übernehmen (from von). to ~ money from the bank/another country Kredit bei der Bank/eine Anleihe bei einem anderen Land aufnehmen; ~ed word Lehnwort nt; he is living on ~ed time seine Uhr ist abgelaufen.
 (b) (Math: in subtraction) borgen (inf).
 2 vi borgen; (from bank) Kredit aufnehmen. ~ing country kreditnehmendes Land.

borrower [ˈbɒrəʊəʳ] n Entleiher(in f) m; (of capital, loan etc) Kreditnehmer(in f) m. he's a terrible ~ er borgt ständig.

borrowing [ˈbɒrəʊɪŋ] n see vt Borgen, Leihen nt; Leihen nt; Ausleihen nt; Entlehnung f; Übernahme f. ~ of money from the bank Kreditaufnahme or (short-term) Geldaufnahme f bei der Bank; ~s (Fin) aufgenommene Schulden pl; (of country also) Anleihen pl.

borstal [ˈbɔːstl] n (Brit Jur) Jugendheim nt, Besserungsanstalt f.

borzoi [ˈbɔːzɔɪ] n Barsoi m.

bosh [bɒʃ] n (dated inf) Quatsch (inf), Quark (dated inf) m.

bo's'n [ˈbəʊsn] n see boatswain.

bosom [ˈbuzəm] 1 n (a) (lit, fig: of person) Busen m. to lay bare one's ~ to sb (fig liter) jdm sein Herz erschließen (liter), jdm sein Innerstes offenbaren (liter). (b) (of dress) Brustteil m. (c) (fig) in the ~ of his family im Schoß der Familie; deep in the ~ of the earth/sea (liter) tief im Schoße der Erde (liter)/in den Tiefen des Meeres (liter). 2 adj attr friend etc Busen-.

bosomy [ˈbuzəmɪ] adj (inf) vollbusig.

Bosp(h)orus [ˈbɒsfərəs, bɒspərəs] n: the ~ der Bosporus.

boss[1] [bɒs] n Chef, Boß (inf) m. industrial/union ~es Industrie-/Gewerkschaftsbosse pl (inf); his wife is the ~ seine Frau hat das Sagen, bei ihm zu Hause bestimmt die Frau; OK, you're the ~ in Ordnung, du hast zu bestimmen.
 ◆**boss about** or **around** vt sep (inf) rumkommandieren (inf).

boss[2] n (knob on shield) Buckel m; (Archit) Bosse f.

bossa nova [ˌbɒsəˈnəʊvə] n Bossa Nova m.

boss-eyed [ˈbɒsaɪd] adj (inf) schielend attr. to be ~ schielen, einen Knick in der Optik haben (inf).

bossiness [ˈbɒsɪnɪs] n Herrschsucht f, herrische Art.

boss man n (sl) Boß m (inf).

bossy [ˈbɒsɪ] adj (+er) herrisch. don't you get ~ with me! kommandier mich nicht so rum (inf); she tends to be rather ~ sie kommandiert einen gern rum (inf).

Boston (crab) [ˈbɒstən(kræb)] n (Wrestling) Beinschraube f.

bosun [ˈbəʊsn] n see boatswain.

BOT (Brit) abbr of Board of Trade.

botanical [bəˈtænɪkəl] adj botanisch, Pflanzen-. ~ gardens botanischer Garten.

botanist [ˈbɒtənɪst] n Botaniker(in f) m.

botany [ˈbɒtənɪ] n Botanik, Pflanzenkunde f.

botch [bɒtʃ] (inf) 1 vt (also ~ up) verpfuschen, vermurksen (inf); plans etc vermasseln (inf). 2 n Murks (inf), Pfusch (inf) m. to make a ~ of sth etw verpfuschen/vermasseln (inf).

botcher [ˈbɒtʃəʳ] n (inf) Murkser (inf), Pfuscher (inf) m.

botch-up [ˈbɒtʃʌp] (inf) 1 n see botch 2. 2 adj attr job vermurkst (inf), verpfuscht.

botchy [ˈbɒtʃɪ] adj (inf) verpfuscht, vermurkst (inf).

both [bəʊθ] 1 adj beide. ~ (the) boys beide Jungen; see way.
 2 pron beide; (two different things) beides. ~ of them were there, they were ~ there sie waren (alle) beide da; two pencils/a pencil and a picture - he took ~ zwei Bleistifte/ein Bleistift und ein Bild - er hat beide/beides genommen; ~ of these answers/you are wrong beide Antworten sind falsch/ihr habt (alle) beide unrecht; some in ~ of you kommt beide herein; I meant ~ of you ich habe euch beide gemeint.
 3 adv ~ ... and ... sowohl ..., als auch ...; ~ you and I wir beide; John and I ~ came John und ich sind beide gekommen; she was ~ laughing and crying sie lachte und weinte zugleich or gleichzeitig; I'm ~ pleased and not pleased ich freue mich und auch wieder nicht; is it black or white? — ~ ist es schwarz oder weiß? — beides; you and me ~ (esp US inf) wir zwei beide (inf).

bother [ˈbɒðəʳ] 1 vt (a) (annoy, trouble: person, noise) belästigen; (sb's behaviour, tight garment, hat, long hair) ärgern, stören; (cause disturbance to: light, noise, sb's presence, mistakes etc) stören; (give trouble: back, teeth etc) zu schaffen machen (+dat); (worry) Sorgen machen (+dat); (matter, problem, question) beschäftigen, keine Ruhe lassen (+dat). I'm sorry to ~ you but ... es tut mir leid, daß ich Sie damit belästigen muß, aber ...; well I'm sorry I ~ed you entschuldigen Sie, daß ich (überhaupt) gefragt habe; don't ~ your head about that zerbrechen Sie sich (dat) darüber nicht den Kopf; don't ~ yourself about that machen Sie sich (dat) darüber mal keine Gedanken or Sorgen; I wouldn't let it ~ me darüber würde ich mir keine Sorgen or Gedanken machen; I shouldn't let it ~ you machen Sie sich mal keine Sorgen; don't ~ me! laß mich in Frieden; he was always ~ing me to lend him money er hat mich dauernd um Geld angegangen; could I ~ you for a light? dürfte ich Sie vielleicht um Feuer bitten?; one thing is still ~ing him eins stört ihn noch; what's ~ing you? was haben Sie denn?; is something ~ing you? haben Sie etwas?; see hot.
 (b) I/he can't be ~ed ich habe/er hat keine Lust; I can't be ~ed with people like him/opera für solche Leute/für Opern habe ich nichts übrig; I can't be ~ed with doing that ich habe einfach keine Lust, das zu machen; he can't be ~ed with matters like that mit solchen Kleinigkeiten gibt er sich nicht ab; do you want to stay or go? — I'm not ~ed willst du bleiben oder gehen? — das ist mir egal; I'm not ~ed about him/the money seinetwegen/wegen des Geldes mache ich mir keine Gedanken.
 2 vti (take trouble to do) don't ~ to do it again/to ask das brauchen Sie nicht nochmals zu tun/Sie brauchen nicht zu fragen; don't ~! nicht nötig!; I won't ~ to ask you again! dich werde ich bestimmt nicht mehr fragen!; she didn't even ~ to ask/check sie hat gar nicht erst nachgesehen; please don't ~ to get up bitte, bleiben Sie doch sitzen; you needn't ~ to come Sie brauchen wirklich nicht (zu) kommen; really you needn't have ~ed! das wäre aber wirklich nicht nötig gewesen!
 3 vi (take trouble) sich kümmern (about um); (get worried) sich (dat) Sorgen machen (about um). don't ~ about me! machen Sie sich meinetwegen keine Sorgen; (sarcastic) ist ja egal, was ich will; to ~ with sb sich mit jdm abgeben; he/it is not worth ~ing about über ihn/darüber brauchen wir gar nicht zu reden, er/das ist nicht der Mühe wert; I'm not going to ~ with that das lasse ich; I didn't ~ about lunch ich habe das Mittagessen ausgelassen.
 4 n (a) (nuisance) Plage f. it's such a ~ das ist wirklich lästig or eine Plage; I've forgotten it, what a ~ ich habe es vergessen, wie ärgerlich or so was Ärgerliches; he/the car can be a bit of a ~ er/das Auto kann einem wirklich Schwierigkeiten machen; I know it's an awful ~ for you but ... ich weiß, daß Ihnen das fürchterliche Umstände macht, aber ...
 (b) (trouble, contretemps etc) Ärger m; (difficulties) Schwierigkeiten pl. she's in a spot of ~ sie hat Schwierigkeiten; we had a spot or bit of ~ with the car wir hatten Ärger mit dem Auto; I didn't have any ~ getting the visa es war kein Problem, das Visum zu bekommen; I'll do it tonight, no ~ (inf) kein Problem, das mache ich heute abend; that's all right, it's no ~ bitte schön, das tue ich doch gern; it wasn't any ~ (don't mention it) das ist gern geschehen; (not difficult) das war ganz einfach; the children were no ~ at all wir hatten mit den Kindern überhaupt keine Probleme; to go to a lot of ~ to do sth sich (dat) mit etw viel Mühe geben; please don't put yourself to any ~ on my account machen Sie meinetwegen keine Umstände.
 5 interj Mist (inf). ~ that man! zum Kuckuck mit ihm! (inf); oh ~ this lock! das ist ein doofes Schloß! (inf).

botheration [ˌbɒðəˈreɪʃən] interj verflixt und zugenäht (inf).

bothersome [ˈbɒðəsəm] adj lästig; child unleidlich. the cooker has been rather ~ lately mit dem Herd hatte ich etc in letzter Zeit viel Ärger.

bothy, bothie [ˈbɒθɪ] n (Scot) Schutzhütte f.

Botswana [ˌbɒtˈswɑːnə] n Botsuana, Botswana nt.

bottle [ˈbɒtl] 1 n (a) Flasche f. a ~ of wine eine Flasche Wein.
 (b) (Brit sl) Mumm (in den Knochen) m (inf).
 (c) (fig inf: drink) Flasche f (inf). to be on/off the ~ trinken/nicht mehr trinken; to take to the ~ zur Flasche greifen; he's too fond of the ~ er trinkt zu gern; see hit.
 2 vt in Flaschen abfüllen. ~d in ... abgefüllt in ...
 ◆**bottle up** vt sep emotion in sich (dat) aufstauen, in sich (acc) hineinfressen (inf). there's a lot of hate ~d inside her es ist viel aufgestaute Haß in ihr.

bottled [ˈbɒtld] adj wine in Flaschen (abgefüllt); gas in Flaschen; beer Flaschen-; fruit eingemacht.

bottle-: ~-fed adj he is ~-fed er wird aus der Flasche ernährt; a ~-fed baby ein Flaschenkind nt; ~-feed vt aus der Flasche ernähren; ~ green 1 adj flaschengrün; 2 n Flaschengrün nt; ~neck n (lit, fig) Engpaß m; ~ opener n Flaschenöffner m; ~ party n Bottle-Party f; ~ rack n Flaschengestell nt; ~-washer n Flaschenreiniger m.

bottling [ˈbɒtlɪŋ] n Abfüllen nt; (of fruit) Einmachen nt. ~ plant Abfüllanlage f.

bottom [ˈbɒtəm] 1 n (a) (lowest part) (of receptacle, box, glass) Boden m; (of mountain, pillar, spire) Fuß m; (of well, canyon) Grund m; (of page, screen, wall) unteres Ende; (of list, road) Ende nt; (of trousers) unteres Beinteil; (of dress) Saum m. trousers with wide/narrow ~s unten ausgestellte/enge Hosen; the ~ of the league das Tabellenende, der Tabellenschluß; which end is the ~? wo ist unten?; the ~ of the tree/page/list/wall etc is ... der Baum/die Seite/Liste/Wand etc ist unten ...; at the ~ of the page/list/league/hill/wall/tree etc unten auf der Seite/Liste/am Berg/an der Wand/am Baum etc; at the ~ of the canyon unten in der Schlucht; at the ~ of the mountain/cliff am Fuß des Berges/Felsens; to be (at the) ~ of the class der/die Letzte in der Klasse sein; he's near the ~ in English in Englisch gehört er zu den Schlechtesten; at the ~ of the garden hinten im Garten; at the ~ of the table/road am unteren Ende des Tisches/am Ende der Straße; ~(s) up! hoch die Tassen (inf); from the ~ of my heart aus tiefstem Herzen; he took a card from the ~ of the pack er nahm eine Karte unten aus dem Stapel; your books would have to be right at the ~! deine Bücher müssen natürlich ganz unten sein!; at ~ (fig) im Grunde; to knock the ~ out of an argument ein Argument gründlich widerlegen; the ~ fell out of his world (inf) für ihn brach alles zusammen; the ~ fell out of the market die Marktlage hat einen Tiefstand erreicht, die Preise sind ins Bodenlose gesunken (inf).
 (b) (underneath, underside) Unterseite f, untere Seite f. on the ~ of the tin/ashtray unten an der Dose/am Aschenbecher.
 (c) (of sea, lake, river) Grund, Boden m. on the ~ of the sea auf dem Meeresboden or -grund (geh); to send a ship to the ~ ein Schiff versenken; the wreck lying on the ~ das auf dem Grund or Meeresboden liegende Wrack; the ship went to the ~ das Schiff sank auf den Grund.
 (d) (of chair) Sitz m, Sitzfläche f.
 (e) (of person) Hintern (inf), Po (inf) m; (of trousers etc) Hosenboden m.
 (f) (fig: causally) to be at the ~ of sth (person) hinter etw (dat) stecken; (thing) einer Sache (dat) zugrunde liegen; to get to the ~ of sth einer Sache (dat) auf den Grund kommen, hinter etw (acc) kommen; let's get to the ~ of the matter wir

wollen der Sache auf den Grund gehen.

(g) (*Naut: of ship*) Boden *m*. **the ship floated** ~ **up** das Schiff trieb kieloben.

(h) (*Brit Aut: gear*) erster Gang. **in** ~ im ersten Gang.

(i) (*US: low land*) ~s Ebene *f*.

2 *adj attr* (*lower*) untere(r, s); (*lowest*) unterste(r, s); *price* niedrigste(r, s); (*Fin*) Tiefst-; *pupil* schlechteste(r, s). ~ **half** (*of box*) untere Hälfte; (*of list, class*) zweite Hälfte.

♦**bottom out** *vi* (*market, prices, graph*) den tiefsten Stand erreichen (*at bei*).

bottom: ~ **drawer** *n* (*Brit*) **to put sth away in one's** ~ **drawer** etw für die Aussteuer beiseite legen; ~ **gear** *n* (*Brit Aut*) erster Gang; **we're still in** ~ **gear** (*inf*) wir sind immer noch nicht richtig auf Touren gekommen (*inf*); ~**less** *adj* (*lit*) bodenlos; (*fig*) *despair* tiefste(r, s); **a** ~**less pit** (*fig*) ein Faß ohne Boden; ~**most** *adj* allerunterste(r, s).

botulism ['bɒtjʊlɪzəm] *n* Nahrungsmittelvergiftung *f*, Botulismus *m*.

bouclé [buːˈkleɪ] *n* Bouclé *nt*.

boudoir ['buːdwaːʳ] *n* Boudoir *nt* (*old*).

bouffant ['buːfɔ̃ːŋ] *adj hairstyle* aufgetürmt.

bougainvillea [ˌbuːgənˈvɪlɪə] *n* Bougainvillea *f*.

bough [baʊ] *n* Ast *m*.

bought [bɔːt] *pret, ptp of* **buy**.

bouillon ['buːjɔ̃ːŋ] *n* Bouillon *f*, klare Fleischbrühe.

boulder ['bəʊldəʳ] *n* Felsblock, Felsbrocken *m*.

boulder clay *n* (*Geol*) Geschiebelehm *m*.

boulevard ['buːləvaːʳ] *n* Boulevard *m*.

bounce [baʊns] **1** *vi* (*ball etc*) springen; (*Sport: ball*) aufspringen; (*chins, breasts etc*) wackeln. **rubber** ~**s** Gummi federt; **the child** ~**d up and down on the bed** das Kind hüpfte auf dem Bett herum; **the car** ~**d along the bumpy road** das Auto holperte die schlechte Straße entlang; **he came bouncing into the room** er kam munter ins Zimmer; **he** ~**d up out of his chair** er sprang von seinem Stuhl hoch.

(b) (*inf: cheque*) platzen (*inf*).

2 *vt* **(a)** aufprallen lassen, prellen (*Sport*). **he** ~**d the ball against the wall** er warf den Ball gegen die Wand; **he** ~**d the baby on his knee** er ließ das Kind auf den Knien reiten.

(b) (*sl: throw out*) rausschmeißen (*inf*).

3 *n* **(a)** (*of ball: rebound*) Aufprall *m*. **to hit a ball on the** ~ den Ball beim Aufprall nehmen; **count the number of** ~**s** zählen Sie, wie oft der Ball etc aufspringt.

(b) *no pl* (*of ball*) Sprungkraft *f*; (*of hair also, rubber*) Elastizität *f*; (*inf: of person*) Schwung *m* (*inf*).

♦**bounce back 1** *vt sep* Ball zurückprallen lassen. **2** *vi* abprallen, zurückprallen; (*fig inf: person*) sich nicht unterkriegen lassen (*inf*); (*to boyfriend*) zurückkommen.

♦**bounce off 1** *vt always separate* **to** ~ **sth** ~ **sth** etw von etw abprallen lassen; *radio waves etc* an etw an etw (*dat*) reflektieren; **to** ~ **an idea** ~ **sb** (*fig inf*) eine Idee an jdm testen (*inf*). **2** *vi* abprallen; (*radio waves*) reflektieren.

bouncer ['baʊnsəʳ] *n* (*inf*) Rausschmeißer *m* (*inf*).

bouncing ['baʊnsɪŋ] *adj* ~ **baby** strammer Säugling.

bouncy ['baʊnsɪ] *adj* (~ *er*) *ball* gut springend; *mattress, step* federnd; *springs, hair* elastisch; *ride* holpernd. **(b)** (*fig inf: exuberant*) vergnügt und munter, quietschvergnügt (*inf*).

bound[1] [baʊnd] **1** *n usu pl* (*lit, fig*) Grenze *f*. **to keep within** ~**s** innerhalb der Grenzen bleiben; **to keep within the** ~**s of propriety** den Anstand wahren, im Rahmen bleiben; **within the** ~**s of probability** im Bereich des Wahrscheinlichen; **there are no** ~**s to his ambition** sein Ehrgeiz kennt keine Grenzen; **the pub/this part of town is out of** ~**s** das Betreten des Lokals ist verboten/dieser Stadtteil ist Sperrzone.

2 *vt usu pass country* begrenzen; *area also* abgrenzen.

bound[2] **1** *n* Sprung, Satz *m*; *see* **leap**.

2 *vi* springen; (*rabbit*) hoppeln. **to** ~ **in/away/back herein-/weg-/zurückspringen**; **the dog came** ~**ing up** der Hund kam angesprungen; **the ball** ~**ed back** der Ball prallte zurück.

bound[3] [baʊnd] **1** *pret, ptp of* **bind**. **2** *adj* **(a)** gebunden. ~ **hand and foot** an Händen und Füßen gebunden.

(b) *book* gebunden. **paper-**~, ~ **in paper** broschiert; ~ **in boards** kartoniert.

(c) ~ **variable** (*Math*) abhängige Variable; ~ **form** (*Ling*) gebundene Form.

(d) (*sure*) **to be** ~ **to do sth** etw bestimmt tun; **but then of course he's** ~ **to say that** das muß er ja sagen; **it's** ~ **to happen** das muß so kommen.

(e) (*obliged*) *person* verpflichtet; (*by contract, word, promise*) gebunden. **but I'm** ~ **to say ...** (*inf*) aber ich muß schon sagen ...; **if you say X then you're** ~ **to say that ...** wenn Sie X behaupten, müssen Sie zwangsläufig sagen, daß ...; **I'm not** ~ **to agree** ich muß nicht zwangsläufig zustimmen; *see* **honour**.

bound[4] *adj pred* **to be** ~ **for London** (*heading for*) auf dem Weg nach London sein, nach London unterwegs sein; (*ship also*) nach London bestimmt sein; (*about to start*) (*ship, plane, lorry etc*) nach London gehen; (*person*) nach London reisen wollen; **the plane/all passengers** ~ **for London will ...** das Flugzeug/alle Passagiere nach London wird/werden ...; **two hitchhikers** ~ **for Scotland** zwei Tramper auf dem Weg nach Schottland; **where are you** ~ **for?** wohin geht die Reise?, wohin wollen Sie?; **we were northward-/California-** ~ wir waren nach Norden/Kalifornien unterwegs; *see* **homeward**.

boundary ['baʊndərɪ] *n* Grenze *f*; (*Cricket*) Spielfeldgrenze *f*. **to hit/score a** ~ den Ball über die Spielfeldgrenze schlagen/4 oder 6 Punkte für einen Schlag über die Spielfeldgrenze erzielen.

boundary: ~ **line** *n* Grenzlinie *f*; (*Sport*) Spielfeldgrenze *f*; ~ **rider** *n* (*Austral*) Arbeiter, der die Grenzen des Weidelandes abreitet; ~ **stone** *n* Grenzstein *m*.

bounden ['baʊndən] *adj:* ~ **duty** (*old, liter*) Pflicht und Schuldigkeit *f* (*geh*).

bounder ['baʊndəʳ] *n* (*dated Brit inf*) Lump *m* (*dated inf*).

boundless ['baʊndlɪs] *adj* (*lit, fig*) grenzenlos.

bounteous ['baʊntɪəs], **bountiful** ['baʊntɪfʊl] *adj* großzügig; *sovereign, god* gütig; *harvest, gifts* (über)reich.

bounteousness ['baʊntɪəsnɪs], **bountifulness** ['baʊntɪfʊlnɪs] *n see adj* Großzügigkeit *f*; Güte *f*; reiche Fülle (*geh*).

bounty ['baʊntɪ] *n* **(a)** (*generosity*) Freigebigkeit *f*; (*of nature*) reiche Fülle (*geh*). **(b)** (*gift*) großzügige or reiche Gabe (*geh*). **(c)** (*reward money*) Kopfgeld *nt*. ~ **hunter** Kopfgeldjäger *m*.

bouquet ['bʊkeɪ] *n* **(a)** Strauß *m*, Bukett *nt* (*geh*). ~ **garni** (*Cook*) Kräutermischung *f*. **(b)** *wine* Bukett *nt*, Blume *f*.

Bourbon ['bʊəbən] *n* **(a)** (*Hist*) Bourbone *m*, Bourbonin *f*. **(b)** (*also* b~ *whisky*) Bourbon *m*.

bourgeois ['bʊəʒwɑː] **1** *n* Bürger(in *f*), Bourgeois (*esp Sociol*) *m*; (*pej*) Spießbürger(in *f*), Spießer *m*. **2** *adj* bürgerlich; (*pej*) spießbürgerlich, spießig.

bourgeoisie [ˌbʊəʒwɑːˈziː] *n* Bürgertum *nt*, Bourgeoisie *f*.

bout [baʊt] *n* **(a)** (*of flu etc*) Anfall *m*; (*of negotiations*) Runde *f*. **a** ~ **of fever/rheumatism** ein Fieber-/Rheumaanfall *m*; **a drinking** ~ eine Zecherei; **I did another final** ~ **of revision before the exam** ich habe vor dem Examen noch einmal alles wiederholt.

(b) (*Boxing, Wrestling, Fencing*) Kampf *m*. **to have a** ~ **with sb** einen Kampf mit jdm austragen.

boutique [buːˈtiːk] *n* Boutique *f*.

bovine ['bəʊvaɪn] **1** *adj* (*lit*) Rinder-; *appearance* rinderartig; (*fig*) stupide, einfältig. **2** *n* Rind *nt*.

bovver ['bɒvəʳ] *n* (*Brit sl*) Schlägerei *f* (*inf*). ~ **boots** Rockerstiefel *pl*; ~ **boys** (*youths*) Rocker *pl*; (*heavy gang*) Rollkommando *nt* (*inf*).

bow[1] [bəʊ] **1** *n* **(a)** (*for shooting arrows*) Bogen *m*. **a** ~ **and arrow** Pfeil und Bogen *pl*. **(b)** (*Mus*) Bogen *m*. **up** ~/**down** ~ **stroke** Auf-/Abstrich *m*. **(c)** (*knot: of ribbon etc*) Schleife *f*. **2** *vi* (*Mus*) den Bogen führen. **3** *vt* (*Mus*) streichen.

bow[2] [baʊ] **1** *n* (*with head, body*) Verbeugung *f*; (*by young boy*) Diener *m*. **to make one's** ~ **to sb** sich vor jdm verbeugen or verneigen (*geh*), jdm seine Reverenz erweisen (*form*).

2 *vi* **(a)** sich verbeugen, sich verneigen (*geh*) (*to sb* vor jdm); (*young boy*) einen Diener machen. **to** ~ **and scrape** katzbuckeln (*pej*), liebedienern (*pej*).

(b) (*bend: branches etc*) sich biegen or beugen.

(c) (*fig: defer, submit*) sich beugen (*before* vor + *dat, under* unter + *dat, to dat*). **I** ~ **to your greater knowledge** ich beuge mich deinem besseren Wissen; **to** ~ **to the majority/inevitable** sich der Mehrheit beugen/sich in das Unvermeidliche fügen.

3 *vt* **(a)** **to** ~ **one's head** den Kopf senken; (*in prayer*) sich verneigen; **to be** ~**ed in prayer** den Kopf im Gebet gesenkt halten.

(b) (*bend*) *branches* beugen. **old age had not** ~**ed his head/him** er war vom Alter ungebeugt (*geh*).

♦**bow down** *vi* (*lit*) sich beugen or neigen. **to** ~ ~ **to** or **before sb** (*fig*) sich jdm beugen.

♦**bow out 1** *vi* (*fig*) sich verabschieden. **2** *vt sep* unter Verbeugungen hinausgeleiten.

bow[3] [baʊ] *n*, ~**s** *npl* Bug *m*. **in the** ~**s** im Bug; **on the port/starboard** ~ backbord(s)/steuerbord(s) voraus.

bowdlerize ['baʊdləraɪz] *vt book* von anstößigen Stellen säubern, reinigen. **a** ~**d version** eine zensierte Ausgabe.

bowel ['baʊəl] *n usu pl* **(a)** (*Anat*) (*of person*) Eingeweide *nt usu pl*, Gedärm *nt usu pl*; (*of animal also*) Innereien *pl*. **a** ~ **movement** Stuhl(gang) *m*; **to move/control one's** ~**s** Stuhl(gang) haben/seine Darmentleerung kontrollieren; **he had something wrong with his** ~**s** mit seiner Verdauung stimmte etwas nicht.

(b) (*fig*) **the** ~**s of the earth/ship** etc das Erdinnere/Schiffsinnere etc, das Innere der Erde/der Schiffsbauch.

bower ['baʊəʳ] *n* Laube *f*.

bowing ['bəʊɪŋ] *n* (*Mus*) Bogenführung *f*.

bowl[1] [bəʊl] *n* **(a)** Schüssel *f*; (*smaller, shallow also, finger-*~) Schale *f*; (*for sugar etc*) Schälchen *nt*; (*for animals, prisoners also*) Napf *m*; (*punch* ~) Bowle *f*; (*wash-* also) Becken *nt*. **a** ~ **of milk** eine Schale/ein Napf Milch.

(b) (*of pipe*) Kopf *m*; (*of spoon*) Schöpfteil *m*; (*of lavatory*) Becken *nt*; (*of lamp*) Schale *f*; (*of wineglass*) Kelch *m*; (*of retort*) Bauch *m*.

(c) (*Geog*) Becken *nt*.

(d) (*US: stadium*) Stadion *nt*.

bowl[2] **1** *n* (*Sport: ball*) Kugel *f*; *see also* **bowls**.

2 *vi* **(a)** (*Bowls*) Bowling/Boccia/Boule spielen; (*tenpin*) bowlen, Bowling spielen; (*skittles*) kegeln. **(b)** (*Cricket*) (mit gestrecktem Arm) werfen. **(c)** (*travel: car, cycle etc*) brausen (*inf*). **he came** ~**ing down the street** er kam auf der Straße angerauscht (*inf*).

3 *vt* **(a)** (*roll*) *ball* rollen; *hoop also* treiben. **(b)** (*Cricket: ball*) werfen; *batsman* ausschlagen.

♦**bowl along** *vi* dahergerauscht kommen/dahinrauschen (*prep obj* auf + *dat*).

♦**bowl out** *vt sep* (*Cricket*) ausschlagen.

♦**bowl over** *vt sep* **(a)** (*lit*) (*with ball etc*) umwerfen; (*in car etc*) umfahren, über den Haufen fahren (*inf*). **(b)** (*fig*) umwerfen, umhauen (*inf*). **to be** ~**ed** ~ sprachlos or platt (*inf*) sein; **he was** ~**ed** ~ **by the news/her/the idea** die Nachricht/sie/die Idee hat ihn (einfach) überwältigt or umgehauen (*inf*).

bow: ~**-legged** *adj* O-beinig; ~**legs** *npl* O-Beine *pl*.

bowler[1] ['bəʊləʳ] *n* (*Sport*) **(a)** Bowlingspieler(in *f*) *m*; (*of bowls also*) Boccia-/Boulespieler(in *f*) *m*. **(b)** (*Cricket*) Werfer *m*.

bowler[2] *n* (*Brit*) (*also* ~ *hat*) Melone *f*.

bowline ['bəʊlɪn] *n* Palstek, Pfahlstek *m*; (*rope*) Bulin(e) *f*.

bowling ['bəʊlɪŋ] *n* **(a)** (*Cricket*) Werfen *nt*. **renowned for his fast** ~ für seine schnellen Bälle berühmt. **(b)** (*tenpin* ~) Bowling *nt*; (*skittles*) Kegeln *nt*. **to go** ~ bowlen/kegeln gehen.

bowling: ~ **alley** n Bowlingbahn f; ~ **green** n Spiel- or Rasenfläche f für Bowling/Boccia/Boule.

bowls [bəʊlz] n Bowling nt; (Italian, German) Boccia nt; (French) Boule nt.

bowman ['bəʊmən] n, pl -**men** [-mən] Bogenschütze m.

bows npl see bow³.

bowsprit ['bəʊsprɪt] n Bugspriet nt or m.

Bow Street runner [bəʊ-] n (Brit Hist) Büttel m (der offiziellen Detektei in der Londoner Bow Street).

bow: ~**string** n (Mus) (Bogen)bezug m; (in archery) (Bogen-) sehne f; ~ **tie** n Fliege f; ~ **window** n Erkerfenster nt.

bow-wow ['baʊ'waʊ] (baby-talk) **1** interj wauwau (baby-talk). **2** ['baʊwaʊ] n (dog) Wauwau m (baby-talk).

box¹ [bɒks] **1** vti (Sport) boxen. **2** vt to ~ sb's ears or sb on the ears jdn ohrfeigen, jdm eine Ohrfeige geben. **3** n a ~ **on the ear** or **round the ears** eine Ohrfeige, eine Backpfeife (inf).

box² n (Bot) Buchsbaum m.

box³ 1 n (a) (made of wood or strong cardboard) Kiste f; (cardboard ~) Karton m; (made of light cardboard, ~ of matches) Schachtel f; (snuff~, cigarette ~ etc, biscuit tin) Dose f; (of crackers, chocolates etc) Packung, Schachtel f; (jewellery ~) Schatulle f, Kasten m; (tool ~) (Werkzeug)kasten m; (ballot ~) Urne f; (money ~) (with lid and lock) Kassette f; (for saving) Sparbüchse or -dose f; (collection ~) (Sammel-) büchse f; (in church) Opferbüchse f; (fixed to wall etc) Opferstock m; (Brit old: trunk) (Schrank)koffer m.
  (b) (two-dimensional) (umrandetes) Feld; (Baseball) Box f; (in road junction) gelb schraffierter Kreuzungsbereich. draw a ~ round it umranden Sie es; do not enter the ~ (unless the exit is clear) (bei Stau) nicht in die Kreuzung einfahren.
  (c) (area of seating etc) (Theat) Loge f; (jury ~) Geschworenenbank f; (witness ~) Zeugenstand m; (press ~) Pressekabine f; (outside) Pressetribüne f; (in court) Pressebank f.
  (d) (Tech: housing) Gehäuse nt. gear ~ Getriebe nt.
  (e) (building) (sentry ~) Schilderhaus nt; (signal ~) Häuschen nt; (hunting ~) (Jagd)hütte f.
  (f) (horse ~) Box f.
  (g) (Brit: pillar ~) (Brief)kasten m.
  (h) (Brit: phone ~) Zelle f.
  (i) (Brit inf: TV) Glotze f (inf), Glotzkasten m (inf). what's on the ~? was gibt's im Fernsehen?; I was watching the ~ ich habe in die Röhre geguckt (inf) or geglotzt (sl).
  (j) (Brit: gift of money) Geldgeschenk nt.
  (k) (on stagecoach) (Kutsch)bock m.
  2 vt (a) (in eine(r) Schachtel etc) verpacken.
  (b) to ~ **the compass** (Naut) alle Kompaßpunkte der Reihe nach aufzählen.

♦ **box in** vt sep (a) competitor, player in die Zange nehmen; parked car einklemmen; (fig) einengen, keinen or zuwenig Spielraum lassen (+dat). (b) bath etc verkleiden; (with wood also) verschalen.

♦ **box off** vt sep abteilen, abtrennen.

♦ **box up** vt sep einsperren.

box: ~ **bed** n Klappbett nt; ~ **calf** n Boxkalf nt; ~ **camera** n Box f; ~ **car** n (US Rail) (geschlossener) Güterwagen.

boxer ['bɒksə'] n (a) (Sport) Boxer m. (b) (dog) Boxer m.

box: ~ **girder** n Kastenträger m; ~ **hedge** n streng geschnittene Hecke.

boxing ['bɒksɪŋ] n Boxen nt.

boxing in cpds Box-; **B~ Day** n (Brit) zweiter Weihnachts(feier)tag; ~ **match** n Boxkampf m; ~ **ring** n Boxring m.

box: ~ **junction** n (Mot) gelbschraffierte Kreuzung(, in die bei Stau nicht eingefahren werden darf); ~ **kite** n Kastendrachen m; ~ **number** n Chiffre f; (at post office) Postfach nt; ~ **office 1** n Kasse, Theater-/Kinokasse f; **to be good** ~ **office** ein Kassenschlager sein; **2** attr ~ **office success/hit/attraction** Kassenschlager m; ~ **pleat** n Kellerfalte f; ~**room** n (Brit) Abstellraum m; ~ **spanner** n Steckschlüssel m; ~ **wood** n Buchsbaum(holz nt) m.

boy [bɔɪ] n (a) (male child) Junge, Bub (dial) m. bad or naughty ~! du frecher Bengel; (to animal) böser Hund! etc; sit, ~! (to dog) sitz!; the Jones ~ der Junge von Jones; ~s will be ~s Jungen sind nun mal so; a school for ~s eine Jungenschule; good morning, ~s guten Morgen(, Jungs)!; see old ~.
  (b) (inf: fellow) Knabe m (inf). the old ~ (boss) der Alte (inf); (father) mein etc alter Herr.
  (c) (friend) the ~s meine/seine Kumpels; our ~s (team) unsere Jungs; jobs for the ~s Vetternwirtschaft f.
  (d) (native servant, lift~) Boy m; (messenger ~, ship ~) Junge m; (butcher's etc ~) (Lauf)junge m; (page ~) (Hotel)boy m; (stable ~) Stalljunge or (older) -bursche m.
  (e) oh ~! (inf) Junge, Junge! (inf).

boycott ['bɔɪkɒt] **1** n Boykott m. to put a ~ on sth den Boykott über etw (acc) verhängen. **2** vt boykottieren.

boy: ~**friend** n Freund m; ~**hood** n Kindheit f; (as teenager) Jugend(zeit) f.

boyish ['bɔɪɪʃ] adj jungenhaft; (of woman) figure, appearance knabenhaft.

Boys' Brigade n Jugendorganisation, ≈ Junge Pioniere pl (DDR).

boy: ~ **scout** n Pfadfinder m; **B~ Scouts** n sing Pfadfinder pl.

bozo ['bəʊzəʊ] n (US) (primitiver) Kerl (inf).

BR abbr of British Rail.

bra [brɑː] n abbr of brassière BH m.

brace¹ [breɪs] n, pl - (pair: of pheasants etc) Paar nt.

brace² 1 n (a) (Build) Strebe f.
  (b) (tool) (wheel ~) Radschlüssel m; (to hold bit) Bohrwinde f. ~ **and bit** Bohrer m (mit Einsatz).
  (c) (on teeth) Klammer, Spange f; (Med) Stützapparat m.
  (d) (Typ) geschweifte Klammer, Akkolade f.

2 vt (a) (ab)stützen; (horizontally) verstreben; (in vice etc) verklammern.
  (b) (climate etc: invigorate) stärken, kräftigen.
  3 vr sich bereit halten; (fig) sich wappnen (geh), sich bereit machen. to ~ **oneself for sth** sich auf etw (acc) gefaßt machen; ~ **yourself, I've got bad news for you** mach dich auf eine schlechte Nachricht gefaßt.

bracelet ['breɪslɪt] n (a) Armband nt; (bangle) Armreif(en) m; (ankle ~) Fußreif(en) m. (b) ~**s** pl (inf: handcuffs) Handschellen pl.

bracer ['breɪsə'] n (a) (inf: drink) kleine Stärkung, Schnäpschen nt. (b) (Sport) Armschutz m.

braces ['breɪsɪz] npl (Brit) Hosenträger pl. **a pair of** ~ (ein Paar) Hosenträger.

bracing ['breɪsɪŋ] adj belebend, anregend; climate Reiz-.

bracken ['brækən] n Adlerfarn m.

bracket ['brækɪt] **1** n (a) (angle ~) Winkelträger m; (for shelf) (Regal)träger m; (Archit) Konsole f; (of stone) Kragstein m.
  (b) (gas ~) Anschluß m; (for electric light) (Wand)arm m.
  (c) (Typ, Mus) Klammer f. in ~s in Klammern.
  (d) (group) Gruppe, Klasse f. the lower income ~ die untere Einkommensgruppe; tax ~ Steuerklasse f.
  2 vt (a) (put in ~s) einklammern.
  (b) (also ~ **together**) (join by ~s) mit einer Klammer verbinden; (Mus also) mit einer Akkolade verbinden; (fig: group together) zusammenfassen.

brackish ['brækɪʃ] adj water brackig.

bract [brækt] n Tragblatt nt.

brad [bræd] n Stift m.

bradawl ['brædɔːl] n Ahle f, Pfriem m.

brae [breɪ] n (Scot) Berg m.

brag [bræg] **1** vi prahlen, angeben (about, of mit). **2** vt prahlen. to ~ **that** prahlen, daß, damit angeben, daß. **3** n (a) (boast) Prahlerei, Angeberei f. (b) (inf) see braggart.

braggart ['brægət] n Prahler, Angeber m.

braid [breɪd] **1** n (a) (of hair) Flechte f (geh), Zopf m. (b) (trimming) Borte f; (self-coloured) Litze f. (c) (Mil) Tressen pl. gold ~ Goldtressen pl. (d) (to tie hair) (Haar)band nt. **2** vt (a) (plait) hair, straw etc flechten. (b) (trim) mit einer Borte besetzen. (c) (tie up with braid) hair binden.

braille [breɪl] **1** n Blinden- or Brailleschrift f. **2** adj Blindenschrift-. ~ **library** Blindenbücherei f; ~ **books** Bücher in Blindenschrift.

brain [breɪn] **1** n (a) (Anat, of machine) Gehirn nt. he's got sex/ cars on the ~ (inf) er hat nur Sex/Autos im Kopf; I've got that tune on the ~ (inf) das Lied geht or will mir nicht aus dem Kopf.
  (b) ~**s** pl (Anat) Gehirn nt; (Cook) Hirn nt.
  (c) (mind) Verstand m. ~**s** pl (intelligence) Intelligenz f, Grips m (inf), Köpfchen nt (inf); to have a good ~ einen klaren or guten Verstand haben; he has ~**s** er ist intelligent, er hat Grips (inf) or Köpfchen (inf); he's the ~**s** of the family er ist das Familiengenie (hum), er ist der Schlauste in der Familie; you're the one with the ~**s** du bist doch der Schlaue or Intelligente hier; use your ~**s** streng mal deinen Kopf or Grips (inf) an; he didn't have the ~**s** to ... er ist nicht einmal darauf gekommen, zu ...
  2 vt den Schädel einschlagen (sb jdm).

brain: ~**child** n Erfindung f; (idea) Geistesprodukt nt; ~ **drain** n Abwanderung f von Wissenschaftlern, Brain-Drain m; ~ **fever** n Hirnhautentzündung f; ~**less** adj plan, idea hirnlos, dumm; person also unbedarft; ~**storm** n (a) (Brit) to have a ~**storm** geistig weggetreten sein (inf); (b) (US: ~**wave**) Geistesblitz m; ~**storming** n gemeinsame Problembewältigung, Brainstorming nt.

brains trust n (discussion) Podiumsdiskussion f; (panel) Gruppe f von Sachverständigen or Experten.

brain: ~ **teaser** n Denksportaufgabe, Knobelei (hum) f; ~ **trust** n (US) Brain Trust, Expertenausschuß m; ~ **tumour** n Gehirntumor m; ~**wash** vt einer Gehirnwäsche (dat) unterziehen; to ~**wash sb into believing/accepting** etc that ... jdm (ständig) einreden, daß ...; ~**washing** n Gehirnwäsche f; ~**wave** n (Brit) Geistesblitz m; ~**work** n Kopfarbeit f.

brainy ['breɪnɪ] adj (+ er) (inf) gescheit, helle pred (inf).

braise [breɪz] vt (Cook) schmoren.

brake¹ [breɪk] n (thicket) Unterholz nt.

brake² n (Bot) Adler)farn m.

brake³ n (shooting ~) Kombi(wagen) m.

brake⁴ 1 n (Tech) Bremse f. to put the ~**s** on (lit, fig) bremsen; to put the ~**s** on sth (fig) etw bremsen; to act as a ~ (lit) als Bremse wirken (on auf +acc); (fig) dämpfend wirken (on auf +acc), bremsen (on acc). **2** vi bremsen.

brake in cpds Brems-; ~ **block** n Bremsbacke f; ~ **drum** n Bremstrommel f; ~ **horsepower** n Bremsleistung f; ~**light** n Bremslicht nt; ~ **lining** n Bremsbelag m; ~ **man** n (US Rail) Bremser m; ~ **shoe** n Bremsbacke f; ~ **van** n Bremswagen m.

braking ['breɪkɪŋ] n Bremsen nt.

braking: ~ **distance** n Bremsweg m; ~ **power** n Bremskraft f.

bramble ['bræmbl] n (a) (thorny shoot) dorniger Zweig, Dornenzweig m. (b) (blackberry) Brombeere f; (bush also) Brombeerstrauch m. ~ **jam** Brombeermarmelade f.

bran [bræn] n Kleie f.

branch [brɑːntʃ] **1** n (a) (Bot) Zweig m; (growing straight from trunk) Ast m.
  (b) (of river, pipe, duct) Arm m; (of road) Abzweigung f; (of family, race, language) Zweig m; (of railway) Abzweigung f; (of antler) Sprosse f, Ende nt.
  (c) (in river, road, railway, pipe, duct) Gabelung f.
  (d) (Comm) Filiale f; (of company, bank also) Geschäftsstelle f. main ~ Haupt(geschäfts)stelle f; (of store) Hauptgeschäft nt; (of bank) Hauptgeschäftsstelle, Zentrale f; ~ **manager** Filialleiter m/Geschäftsstellenleiter m.

(e) *(field: of subject etc)* Zweig *m.*
2 *vi (divide: river, road etc)* sich gabeln; *(in more than two)* sich verzweigen.
♦**branch off** *vi (road)* abzweigen; *(driver)* abbiegen.
♦**branch out** *vi (fig: person, company)* sein Geschäft erweitern *or* ausdehnen *(into* auf +*acc)*. **the firm is ~ing ~ into cosmetics** die Firma erweitert ihren (Geschäfts)bereich jetzt auf Kosmetika; **to ~ ~ on one's own** sich selbständig machen.
branch: ~ **line** *n (Rail)* Zweiglinie, Nebenlinie *f;* ~ **office** *n* Filiale *f.*
brand [brænd] **1** *n* **(a)** *(make)* Marke *f.* **(b)** *(mark) (on cattle)* Brandzeichen *nt; (on criminal, prisoner, fig)* Brandmal *m.* **(c)** *see* **branding iron.** **(d)** *(obs, poet: sword)* Klinge *f (liter).*
2 *vt* **(a)** *(Comm) goods* mit seinem Warenzeichen versehen. ~**ed goods** Markenartikel *pl.* **(b)** *cattle, property* mit einem Brandzeichen kennzeichnen. **(c)** *(stigmatize) person* brandmarken.
branding iron ['brændɪŋˌaɪən] *n* Brandeisen *nt.*
brandish ['brændɪʃ] *vt* schwingen, fuchteln mit *(inf).*
brand: ~ **name** *n* Markenname *m;* ~**-new** *adj* nagelneu, brandneu *(inf).*
brandy ['brændɪ] *n* Weinbrand, Brandy *m.*
brandy: ~ **butter** *n* Weinbrandbutter *f;* ~**snap** *n* Gebäckröllchen *nt aus dünnem, mit Ingwer gewürztem Teig.*
brash [bræʃ] *adj (+er)* naßforsch, dreist; *(tasteless colour etc)* laut, aufdringlich.
brasier *n see* **brazier.**
brass [brɑːs] **1** *n* **(a)** Messing *nt.*
(b) **the** ~ *(Mus)* die Blechbläser *pl,* das Blech *(inf).*
(c) *(thing made of* ~*) (plaque)* Messingtafel *or* -schild *nt;* *(in church: on tomb)* Grabplatte *f* aus Messing; *(no pl:* ~ *articles)* Messing *nt.* **to do or clean the** ~*(es)* das Messing putzen.
(d) *(inf)* **the top** ~ die hohen Tiere *(inf).*
(e) *(sl: impudence)* Frechheit *f.*
(f) *(sl: money)* Moos *nt (sl),* Kies *m (sl).*
2 *adj (made of* ~*)* Messing-, messingen *(rare); (Mus)* Blech-.
~ **player** Blechbläser *m;* ~ **section** Blech(bläser *pl) nt;* **I don't care or give a ~ farthing** *(inf)* es ist mir wurscht(egal) *(inf);* **real** ~ **monkey weather, eh?** *(hum sl)* arschkalt, was? *(sl);* **to get down to ~ tacks** *(inf)* zur Sache kommen; **to have a ~ neck** Nerven haben *(inf).*
brass: ~ **band** *n* Blaskapelle *f;* ~ **foundry** *n* Messinggießerei *f;* ~ **hat** *n (Brit Mil sl)* hohes Tier *(inf).*
brassière ['bræsɪəʳ] *n (dated, form)* Büstenhalter *m.*
brass: ~ **plaque** *or* **plate** *n* Messingschild *nt;* *(in church)* Messinggedenktafel *f;* ~ **rubbing** *n (activity)* Durchpausen *or* -zeichnen *nt (des Bildes auf einer Messinggrabtafel); (result)* Pauszeichnung *f (des Bildes auf einer Messinggrabtafel).*
brassy ['brɑːsɪ] *adj (+er)* **(a)** *metal* messingartig; *hair, blonde* messingfarben; *sound* blechern. **(b)** *(inf: impudent)* frech, dreist.
brat [bræt] *n (pej inf)* Balg *m or nt (inf),* Gör *nt (inf); (esp girl)* Göre *f (inf).* **all these** ~**s** *(boys and girls)* diese Gören.
bravado [brəˈvɑːdəʊ] *n (showy bravery)* Draufgängertum *nt,* Wagemut *m; (hiding fear)* gespielte Tapferkeit. **this is just** *literary* ~ das ist nur ein literarisches Bravourstückchen.
brave [breɪv] **1** *adj (+er)* **(a)** *person, act* mutig, unerschrocken *(geh); (showing courage, suffering pain)* tapfer; *attack* mutig; *smile* tapfer. **be ~!** nur Mut!; *(more seriously)* sei tapfer! **(b)** *(obs, liter: fine)* schmuck *(dated),* ansehnlich. ~ **new world** schöne neue Welt.
2 *n (Indian)* Krieger *m.*
3 *vt* **die Stirn** bieten (+*dat*); *weather, elements* trotzen (+*dat*); *death* tapfer ins Auge sehen (+*dat*).
♦**brave out** *vt sep* **to ~ it ~ es** *or* **das durchstehen.**
bravely ['breɪvlɪ] *adv see adj.*
braveness ['breɪvnɪs], **bravery** ['breɪvərɪ] *n see adj* Mut *m;* Tapferkeit *f.*
bravo [brɑːˈvəʊ] **1** *interj* bravo! **2** *n, pl* **-es** Bravoruf *m.*
bravura [brəˈvʊərə] *n* Bravour *f; (Mus)* Bravourstück *nt.*
brawl [brɔːl] **1** *vi* sich schlagen. **2** *n* Schlägerei *f.*
brawn [brɔːn] *n* **(a)** *(Cook)* Preßkopf *m,* Sülze *f.* **(b)** Muskeln *pl,* Muskelkraft *f.* **to have plenty of ~** starke Muskeln haben, ein Muskelpaket *or* Muskelprotz sein *(inf);* **he's all ~ and no brains** *(er hat)* Muskeln, aber kein Gehirn.
brawny ['brɔːnɪ] *adj (+er)* muskulös, kräftig.
bray [breɪ] **1** *n (of ass)* (Esels)schrei *m; (inf: laugh)* Wiehern, Gewieher *nt.* **2** *vi (ass)* schreien; *(inf: person)* wiehern.
brazen ['breɪzn] *adj* **(a)** *(impudent)* unverschämt, dreist; *lie* schamlos. **(b)** *(obs: of brass)* messingen *(rare).*
♦**brazen out** *vt sep* **to ~ it ~ es** mit eiserner Stirn leugnen.
brazen-faced ['breɪzn,feɪst] *adj* schamlos, unverschämt.
brazenly ['breɪznlɪ] *adv see adj* unverschämt, dreist; schamlos.
brazenness ['breɪznnɪs] *n see adj* Unverschämtheit, Dreistigkeit *f;* Schamlosigkeit *f.*
brazier ['breɪzɪəʳ] *n* (Kohlen)feuer *nt (im Freien); (container)* Kohlenbecken *nt.*
brazil [brəˈzɪl] *n (also* ~ **nut)** Paranuß *f.*
Brazil [brəˈzɪl] *n* Brasilien *nt.*
Brazilian [brəˈzɪlɪən] **1** *n* Brasilianer(in *f) m.* **2** *adj* brasilianisch.
breach [briːtʃ] **1** *n* **(a)** *(lit)* Verletzung *f (of gen),* Verstoß *m (of gegen); (of law)* Übertretung *f (of gen),* Verstoß *m.* **a ~ of confidence/contract/faith** ein Vertrauens-/Vertrags-/Vertrauensbruch *m;* ~ **of the peace** *(Jur)* öffentliche Ruhestörung; ~ **of privilege** Privilegienmißbrauch *m;* ~ **of promise** *(Jur)* Bruch *m* des Eheversprechens.
(b) *(estrangement: in friendship etc)* Bruch *m.*
(c) *(gap) (in wall etc)* Bresche, Lücke *f; (in security)* Lücke *f.* **to make a ~ in the enemy's lines** *(Mil)* eine Bresche in die feindlichen Linien schlagen; **to step into/throw oneself into the**

the ~ *(fig)* in die Bresche springen.
2 *vt wall* eine Bresche schlagen (in +*acc); defences, security* durchbrechen.
bread [bred] **1** *n* **(a)** Brot *nt.* **a piece of ~ and butter** ein Butterbrot *nt;* **we just had ~ and butter** wir aßen nur Brot mit Butter; **he was put on (dry)** ~ **and water** er saß bei Wasser und (trocken) Brot; **he knows which side his ~ is buttered (on)** er weiß, wo was zu holen ist.
(b) *(food, livelihood)* **daily** ~ tägliches Brot; **to earn one's daily** ~ *(sich dat)* sein Brot verdienen; **writing is his ~ and butter** Schreiben ist sein Broterwerb, er verdient sich seinen Lebensunterhalt mit Schreiben; **to take the** ~ **out of sb's mouth** *(fig)* jdn seiner Existenzgrundlage *(gen)* berauben; **to break** ~ **with sb** *(old)* sein Brot mit jdm teilen, das Brot mit jdm brechen *(old).*
(c) *(sl: money)* Moos *nt (inf),* Kies *m (inf),* Flöhe *pl (sl).*
2 *vt* panieren.
bread: ~**-and-butter letter** *or* **note** *n* Bedankemichbrief *m;* ~-**and-butter pudding** *n* Brotauflauf *m;* ~ **basket** *n (a)* Brotkorb *m;* **(b)** *(sl)* Bauch *m;* ~**bin** *n* Brotkasten *m,* ~**board** *n* Brot(schneide)brett *nt;* ~**crumb** *n* Brotkrume *f or* -krümel *m;* ~**crumbs** *npl (Cook)* Paniermehl *nt;* **in** ~**crumbs** paniert; ~**fruit** *n* Brotfrucht *f;* ~**knife** *n* Brotmesser *nt;* ~**line** *n* Schlange *f vor einer Nahrungsmittelausgabestelle;* **to be on the** ~**line** *(fig)* nur das Allernotwendigste zum Leben haben; ~ **sauce** *n* Brottunke *f.*
breadth [bretθ] *n see* **broad 1 (a, d)** Breite *f;* Großzügigkeit *f; (of ideas, of theory)* (Band)breite *f.* **a hundred metres in** ~ hundert Meter breit; **his** ~ **of outlook** *(open-mindedness)* seine große Aufgeschlossenheit; *(variety of interests)* seine große Vielseitigkeit; **the** ~ **of his comprehension/theory** sein umfassendes Verständnis/seine umfassende Theorie.
breadthways ['bretθweɪz], **breadthwise** ['bretθwaɪz] *adv* in der Breite, der Breite nach.
breadwinner ['bredwɪnəʳ] *n* Ernährer, Geldverdiener *m.*
break [breɪk] *(vb: pret* **broke,** *ptp* **broken)** **1** *n* **(a)** *(fracture) (in bone, pipe etc)* Bruch *m; (in pottery, vase etc)* Sprung *m; (Gram, Typ: word break)* (Silben)trennung *f.* **... he said with a ~ in his voice ...** sagte er mit stockender Stimme; ~ **in the circuit** *(Elec)* Stromkreisunterbrechung *f.*
(b) *(gap) (in wall, clouds)* Lücke *f; (in rock)* Spalte *f,* Riß *m; (in line)* Lücke *f; (in drawn line)* Unterbrechung *f.* **row upon row of houses without a ~** Häuserzeile auf Häuserzeile, ohne Lücke *or* lückenlos; **where we had made a ~ in the wall** wo wir die Mauer durchbrochen hatten.
(c) *(pause, rest: in conversation, tea* ~, *Brit Sch etc)* Pause *f; (in journey also)* Unterbrechung *f.* **without a ~** ohne Unterbrechung *or* Pause, ununterbrochen; **to take** *or* **have a ~** *(eine)* Pause machen; **at** ~ *(Sch)* in der Pause.
(d) *(end of relations)* Bruch *m.*
(e) *(change) (in contest etc)* Wende *f,* Umschwung *m; (holiday, change of activity etc)* Abwechslung *f.* **just to give you a ~** nur zur Abwechslung, damit du mal was anderes siehst/hörst/machst; ~ **in the weather** Witterungsumschlag, Wetterumschwung *m.*
(f) **at ~ of day** bei Tagesanbruch.
(g) *(inf: escape)* Ausbruch *m.* **they made a ~ for it** sie versuchten zu entkommen.
(h) *(inf: luck, opportunity)* **to have a good/bad ~** Glück *or* Schwein *(inf)* nt/Pech *nt* haben; **we had a few lucky ~s** wir haben ein paarmal Glück *or* Schwein *(inf)* gehabt; **give me a ~!** gib mir eine Chance!
(i) *(Billiards)* Ballfolge, Serie *f.*
2 *vt* **(a)** *(fracture, snap) bone* sich *(dat)* brechen; *stick* zerbrechen; *rope* zerreißen; *(smash)* kaputtmachen, kaputtmachen; *glass, cup also* zerbrechen; *window also* einschlagen; *egg* aufbrechen. **to ~ sth from etw** von etw abbrechen; **to ~ one's leg** sich *(dat)* das Bein brechen; *see* **heart.**
(b) *(put out of working order) toy, chair* kaputtmachen.
(c) *(violate) promise, treaty, vow* brechen; *traffic laws, rule, commandment* verletzen; *appointment* nicht einhalten. **to ~ bail** der Haftverschonung brechen.
(d) *(interrupt) journey, current, silence, thread of story, fast* unterbrechen; *spell, curse* brechen; *(relieve) monotony, routine, pattern also* auflockern. **to ~ a holiday** short seinen Urlaub abbrechen.
(e) *(go through, penetrate) skin* ritzen; *surface, shell* durchbrechen.
(f) *(go beyond, surpass) sound barrier* durchbrechen; *record* brechen, schlagen. **his skin is grazed but not broken** die Haut ist zwar abgeschürft, aber nicht aufgeplatzt; **to ~ surface** *(submarine)* auftauchen.
(g) *(open up) path* schlagen, sich *(dat)* bahnen; *see* **ground.**
(h) **to ~ a habit** mit einer Gewohnheit brechen, sich *(dat)* etw abgewöhnen; **he couldn't ~ the habit of smoking** er konnte sich das Rauchen nicht abgewöhnen; **to ~ sb/oneself of a habit** jdm/sich etw abgewöhnen.
(i) *(tame, discipline) horse* zureiten; *spirit, person* brechen; *wilful child* fügsam machen.
(j) *(destroy) sb* kleinkriegen *(inf),* mürbe machen; *sb's health* ruinieren, kaputtmachen *(inf); resistance, strike* brechen; *alibi* entkräften; *code* entziffern; *(Sport) serve* durchbrechen. **his spirit was broken by her death** ihr Tod hatte ihn seelisch gebrochen; **to ~ sb** *(financially)* jdn ruinieren, jdn bankrott machen; *(with grief)* jdn seelisch brechen; **to ~ the bank** *(Gambling)* die Bank sprengen; **37p, well that won't exactly ~ the bank** 37 Pence, na, davon gehe ich/gehen wir noch nicht bankrott; **his service was broken** *(Tennis)* er hat das Aufschlagspiel abgegeben.
(k) *(soften, weaken) fall* dämpfen, abfangen. **the wall ~s the force of the wind** der Wind bricht sich an der Mauer.

(l) (get out of, escape from) jail, one's bonds ausbrechen aus. **to ~ step** (Mil) aus dem Schritt fallen; see **camp, cover, rank**.
(m) (disclose) news mitteilen. **how can I ~ it to her?** wie soll ich es ihr sagen?
(n) (start spending) five-dollar bill anbrechen; (give change for) kleinmachen.

3 vi **(a)** (snap, be fractured) (twig, bone) brechen; (rope) zerreißen; (smash: window, cup) kaputtgehen; (cup, glass etc also) zerbrechen. **~ing strain or strength** Belastbarkeit f.
(b) (stop working etc: toy, watch, chair) kaputtgehen; (toy, chair etc also) zerbrechen.
(c) (become detached) **to ~ from sth** von etw abbrechen.
(d) (pause) (eine) Pause machen, unterbrechen.
(e) (wave) sich brechen.
(f) (day, dawn) anbrechen; (suddenly: storm) losbrechen.
(g) (change: weather, luck) umschlagen.
(h) (disperse) (clouds) aufreißen; (crowd) sich teilen.
(i) (give way) (health) leiden, zerstört werden, Schaden nehmen; (stamina) gebrochen werden; (under interrogation etc) zusammenbrechen. **his courage/spirit broke** sein Mut verließ ihn, ihn verließ der Mut.
(j) (voice) (with emotion) brechen. **his voice is beginning to ~** (boy) er kommt in den Stimmbruch.
(k) (become known: story, news, scandal) bekanntwerden, an den Tag or ans Licht kommen. **the news broke on Wall Street yesterday** gestern platzte diese Nachricht in Wall Street.
(l) (end relations) brechen.
(m) (let go: Boxing etc) sich trennen. **~! break!**
(n) (~ away, escape) (from jail) ausbrechen (from aus). **to ~ even** seine (Un)kosten decken; see **loose**.
(o) (ball) **to ~ to the right/left** nach rechts/links wegspringen.
(p) (Billiards) anstoßen.

♦**break away 1** vi **(a)** (chair leg, handle etc) abbrechen (from von); (railway coaches, boats) sich losreißen (from von).
(b) (dash away) weglaufen (from von); (prisoner) sich losreißen (from von); (Ftbl) sich absetzen. **he broke ~ from the rest of the field** er hängte das ganze Feld ab.
(c) (cut ties) sich trennen or lossagen (from von); (US Sport: start too soon) fehlstarten, zu früh starten. **to ~ ~ from a group** sich von einer Gruppe trennen; **he wanted to ~ ~ from the everyday routine** er wollte aus der täglichen Routine ausbrechen; **to ~ ~ from an idea** sich von einer Vorstellung lösen.
2 vt sep abbrechen (from von).

♦**break down 1** vi **(a)** (vehicle) eine Panne haben; (machine) versagen; (binding machine etc) stehenbleiben.
(b) (fail) (negotiations, plan) scheitern; (communications) zum Erliegen kommen; (law and order) zusammenbrechen; (marriage) scheitern, in die Brüche gehen.
(c) (give way) (argument, resistance, person: start crying, have a breakdown) zusammenbrechen. **his health has broken ~** ihm geht es gesundheitlich schlecht.
(d) (be analysed) (expenditure) sich aufschlüsseln or -gliedern; (theory) sich unter- or aufgliedern (lassen); (Chem: substance) sich zerlegen (lassen); (change its composition: substance) sich aufspalten (into in +acc).
2 vt sep **(a)** (smash down) door einrennen; wall niederreißen.
(b) (overcome) opposition brechen; hostility, reserve, shyness, suspicion überwinden.
(c) (reduce to constituent parts) expenditure aufschlüsseln, aufgliedern; theory, argument auf- or untergliedern; substance aufspalten; (change composition of) substance umsetzen.

♦**break forth** vi (liter) (light, water) hervorbrechen; (smile) sich ausbreiten; (storm) losbrechen.

♦**break in 1** vi **(a)** (interrupt) unterbrechen (on sb/sth jdn/etw.).
(b) (enter illegally) einbrechen. **2** vt sep **(a)** door einbrechen.
(b) (tame, train) horse zureiten; new employee einarbeiten.
(c) shoes einlaufen.

♦**break into** vi +prep obj **(a)** house einbrechen in (+acc); safe, car aufbrechen. **his house/car has been broken ~** bei ihm ist eingebrochen worden/sein Auto ist aufgebrochen worden.
(b) (use part of) savings, £5 note, rations anbrechen.
(c) (begin suddenly) **to ~ ~ song/a run/a trot** zu singen/laufen/traben anfangen, in Laufschritt/Trab (ver)fallen; **to ~ ~ a laugh/loud cheers** in Lachen/lauten Beifall ausbrechen.

♦**break off 1** vi **(a)** abbrechen (from von).
(b) (stop) abbrechen, aufhören; (stop speaking) abbrechen; (temporarily) unterbrechen. **to ~ ~ from work** die Arbeit abbrechen, mit der Arbeit aufhören; **we ~ ~ at 5 o'clock** wir hören um 5 Uhr auf.
2 vt sep **(a)** twig, piece of rock, chocolate etc abbrechen.
(b) (end, interrupt) negotiations, relations abbrechen; engagement lösen. **she's broken it ~** sie hat sich entlobt.

♦**break open 1** vi aufspringen. **2** vt sep aufbrechen.

♦**break out** vi **(a)** (epidemic, fire, war) ausbrechen.
(b) **to ~ ~ in a rash/in(to) spots** einen Ausschlag/Pickel bekommen; **he broke ~ in a sweat/a cold sweat** er kam ins Schwitzen, ihm brach der Schweiß/Angstschweiß aus.
(c) (escape) ausbrechen (from, of aus).
(d) (speak suddenly) herausplatzen, losplatzen.

♦**break through 1** vi (Mil, sun) durchbrechen. **2** vi +prep obj defences, barrier, crowd durchbrechen. **to ~ ~ sb's reserve** jdn aus der Reserve locken.

♦**break up 1** vi **(a)** (road) aufbrechen; (ice also) bersten; (ship in storm) zerbersten; (on rocks) zerschellen.
(b) (clouds) sich lichten; (crowd, group) auseinanderlaufen; (meeting, partnership) sich auflösen; (marriage, relationship) in die Brüche gehen; (party) zum Ende kommen; (Pol: party) sich auflösen, auseinandergehen; (friends, partners) sich trennen; (sentence, theory) sich aufspalten, zerfallen; (empire) auseinanderfallen. **when did the party ~ ~ last night?** wie lange ging die Party gestern abend?
(c) (Brit Sch) (school, pupils) aufhören. **when do you ~ ~?** wann hört bei euch die Schule auf, wann gibt es Ferien?
2 vt sep **(a)** ground, road aufbrechen; oil slick auflösen; ship auseinanderbrechen lassen; (in breaker's yard) abwracken.
(b) estate, country aufteilen; room also, paragraph, sentence unterteilen; empire auflösen; lines, expanse of colour unterbrechen; (make more interesting) auflockern.
(c) (bring to an end, disperse) marriage, home zerstören; meeting (police etc) auflösen; (trouble-makers) sprengen; crowd (police) zerstreuen, auseinandertreiben. **he broke ~ the fight** er trennte die Kämpfer; **~ it ~!** auseinander!

breakable ['breɪkəbl] **1** adj zerbrechlich. **2** n ~s pl zerbrechliche Ware.

breakage ['breɪkɪdʒ] n **(a)** (in chain, link) Bruch m. **(b)** (of glass, china) Bruch m. **to pay for ~s** für zerbrochene Ware or Bruch bezahlen; **were there any ~s?** hat es Bruch gegeben?, ist irgend etwas kaputtgegangen or zu Bruch gegangen?

breakaway ['breɪkə,weɪ] **1** n **(a)** (Pol) Abfall m; (of state also) Loslösung f. **(b)** (Sport) Aus- or Durchbruch m. **(c)** (US Sport: false start) Fehlstart m. **2** adj group abgefallen.

breakdown ['breɪkdaʊn] n **(a)** (of machine) Betriebsschaden m; (of vehicle) Panne f, Motorschaden m.
(b) (of communications, system) Zusammenbruch m.
(c) (Med: physical, mental) Zusammenbruch m.
(d) (of figures, expenditure etc) Aufschlüsselung f; (of thesis, theory etc) Auf- or Untergliederung f.
(e) (Chem) Aufspaltung f; (change in composition) Umsetzung f.

breakdown: **~ service** n Pannendienst, Reparatur- und Schleppdienst m; **~ truck** or **van** n Abschleppwagen m.

breaker ['breɪkəʳ] n **(a)** (wave) Brecher m. **(b)** **~'s (yard): to send a ship to the ~'s (yard)** ein Schiff abwracken.

break-even point ['breɪk'iːvən,pɔɪnt] n Kostendeckung f.

breakfast ['brekfəst] **1** n **(a)** Frühstück nt. **to have ~** frühstücken, Frühstück essen; **for ~** zum Frühstück. **(b)** wedding **~** Hochzeitsessen nt. **2** vi frühstücken. **he ~ed on bacon and eggs** er frühstückte Eier mit Speck.

breakfast in cpds Frühstücks-; **~ cereal** npl Cornflakes, Getreideflocken pl; **~ set** n Frühstücksservice nt; **~-time** n Frühstückszeit f.

break-in ['breɪkɪn] n Einbruch m. **we've had a ~** bei uns ist eingebrochen worden.

breaking ['breɪkɪŋ] n ~ and entering (Jur) Einbruch m.

breaking point n **(a)** (Tech) Festigkeitsgrenze f. **(b)** (fig) she has reached or is at **~** sie ist nervlich völlig am Ende (ihrer Kräfte.)

break: **~neck** adj at **~neck speed** mit halsbrecherischer Geschwindigkeit; **~-out** n Ausbruch m; **~through** n (Mil, fig) Durchbruch m; **~-up** n **(a)** (lit) (of ship) Zerbersten nt; (on rocks) Zerschellen nt; (of ice) Bersten nt; **(b)** (fig) (of friendship) Bruch m; (of marriage) Zerrüttung f; (of empire) Zerfall m; (of political party) Zersplitterung f; (of partnership, meeting) Auflösung f; (by trouble-makers) Sprengung f; **~water** n Wellenbrecher m.

bream [briːm] n Brasse f, Brachsen m.

breast [brest] **1** n **(a)** (chest) Brust f; (Cook: of chicken, lamb) Brust(stück nt) f.
(b) (of woman) Brust f. **a child/baby at the ~** ein Kind/Säugling an der Brust.
(c) (fig liter) Brust f, Busen m (liter).
2 vt **(a)** **to ~ the waves/the storm** gegen die Wellen/den Sturm ankämpfen.
(b) **to ~ the tape** (Sport) durchs Ziel gehen.

breastbone ['brestbəʊn] n Brustbein nt; (of bird) Brustknochen m.

-breasted [-'brestɪd] adj suf woman -brüstig. **a double-/single-~ jacket** ein Einreiher m/Zweireiher m.

breast: **~fed** adj to be **~fed** gestillt werden; **~fed child** Brustkind nt; **~feed** vti stillen; **~feeding** n Stillen nt; **~plate** n (on armour) Brustharnisch m; (of high priest) Brustplatte f or -gehänge nt; **~ pocket** n Brusttasche f; **~ stroke** n Brustschwimmen nt; **to swim** or **do the ~ stroke** brustschwimmen; **~work** n (Mil) Brustwehr f.

breath [breθ] n **(a)** Atem m. **to take a deep ~** einmal tief Luft holen; (before diving, singing etc) einmal tief einatmen; **bad ~** Mundgeruch m; **to have bad ~** aus dem Munde riechen, Mundgeruch haben; **with one's dying ~** mit dem letzten Atemzug; **to draw one's last ~** (liter) seinen letzten Atemzug tun; **out of** or **short of ~** außer Atem, atemlos; **to stop for ~** sich verschnaufen, eine Pause zum Luftholen machen; **in the same ~** im selben Atemzug; **to say sth all in one ~** etw in einem Atemzug sagen; **to take sb's ~ away** jdm den Atem verschlagen; **to say sth under one's ~** etw vor sich (acc) hin murmeln; **save your ~** spar dir die Spucke (inf); **you're wasting your ~** du redest umsonst; **to go out for a ~ of (fresh) air** an die frische Luft gehen, frische Luft schnappen gehen; **she brought a ~ of fresh air to the ward** (fig) sie brachte etwas Schwung in die Station; **you're like a ~ of fresh air** du bist so erfrischend.
(b) (slight stirring) ~ of wind Lüftchen nt; **there wasn't a ~ of air** es regte sich or wehte kein Lüftchen.
(c) (fig: whisper) Hauch m, Sterbenswörtchen nt.

breathalyze ['breθəlaɪz] vt (Brit) blasen lassen. **he refused to be ~d** er weigerte sich, (ins Röhrchen) zu blasen.

breathalyzer ['breθəlaɪzəʳ] n (Brit) Alcotest ® m (für die Atemalkoholbestimmung). **to give sb a ~** jdn ins Röhrchen blasen lassen; **to blow into the ~** ins Röhrchen blasen.

breathe [briːð] **1** vi atmen; (inf: rest) verschnaufen, Luft holen or schöpfen; (liter: live) leben. **now we can ~ again** jetzt

können wir wieder frei atmen; (*have more space*) jetzt haben wir wieder Luft; I don't want him breathing down my neck all the time (*inf*) ich will ihn nicht die ganze Zeit auf dem Hals haben (*inf*).
  2 *vt* **(a)** *air* einatmen. **to ~ one's last (breath)** seinen letzten Atemzug tun; **to ~ the air of one's own country again** wieder auf heimatlichem Boden sein *or* stehen.
  (b) (*exhale*) atmen, (*into* in +*acc*). **he ~d alcohol/garlic all over me** er hatte eine solche Fahne, er verströmte einen solchen Alkohol-/Knoblauchgeruch; **to ~ fire** Feuer spucken; **he ~d new life into the firm** er brachte neues Leben in die Firma.
  (c) (*utter*) *prayer* flüstern, hauchen. **to ~ a sigh of relief** erleichtert aufatmen; **don't ~ a word of it!** sag kein Sterbenswörtchen darüber!
♦ **breathe in** *vi, vt sep* einatmen.
♦ **breathe out** *vi, vt sep* ausatmen.
breather ['briːðəʳ] *n* (*short rest*) Atempause, Verschnaufpause *f*. **to give sb a ~** jdn verschnaufen lassen; **to take** *or* **have a ~** sich verschnaufen.
breathing ['briːðɪŋ] *n* (*respiration*) Atmung *f*. **the child's peaceful ~** die ruhigen Atemzüge des Kindes.
breathing: **~ apparatus** *n* Sauerstoffgerät *nt*; **~ space** *n* (*fig*) Atempause, Ruhepause *f*.
breathless ['breθlɪs] *adj* atemlos; (*with exertion also*) außer Atem; **he said in a ~ voice** sagte er, nach Luft ringend; **he is rather ~** (*through illness*) er leidet an Atemnot; **it left me ~** (*lit, fig*) es verschlug mir den Atem.
breathlessly ['breθlɪslɪ] *adv see adj* atemlos; außer Atem.
breathlessness ['breθlɪsnɪs] *n* (*due to exertion*) Atemlosigkeit *f*; (*due to illness*) Kurzatmigkeit *f*.
breathtaking ['breθteɪkɪŋ] *adj* atemberaubend.
breathy ['breθɪ] *adj* (+*er*) rauchig; (*through shyness*) hauchig.
bred [bred] *pret, ptp of* **breed**.
-bred *adj suf* -erzogen.
breech[1] [briːtʃ] *n* (*of gun*) Verschluß *m*. **~-loader** (*Mil*) Hinterlader *m*.
breech[2] *adj attr* (*Med*) *birth, delivery* Steiß-. **~ presentation** Steißlage *f*; **to be a ~ baby** eine Steißlage sein.
breeches ['brɪtʃɪz] *npl* Kniehose *f*; (*riding ~*) Reithose *f*; (*for hiking*) (Knie)bundhose *f*.
breeches buoy *n* Hosenboje *f*.
breed [briːd] (*vb: pret, ptp* **bred**) **1** *n* (*lit, fig*) (*species*) Art, Sorte *f*. **they produced a new ~** sie haben eine neue Züchtung hervorgebracht; **a ~ apart** (*fig*) eine besondere *or* spezielle Sorte *or* Gattung.
  2 *vt* **(a)** (*raise, rear*) *animals, flowers* züchten; *see* **born**.
  (b) (*fig: give rise to*) erzeugen. **dirt ~s disease** Schmutz verursacht Krankheit, Schmutz zieht Krankheit nach sich.
  3 *vi* (*animals*) Junge haben; (*birds*) brüten; (*pej, hum: people*) sich vermehren. **rabbits ~ quickly** Kaninchen vermehren sich schnell.
breeder ['briːdəʳ] *n* **(a)** (*person*) Züchter *m*. **(b)** (*Phys: also* **~ reactor**) Brutreaktor, Brüter *m*.
breeding ['briːdɪŋ] *n* **(a)** (*reproduction*) Fortpflanzung und Aufzucht *f* der Jungen. **(b)** (*rearing*) Zucht *f*. **(c)** (*upbringing, good manners: also* **good ~**) gute Erziehung, Kinderstube *f*.
breeding: **~ place** *n* (*lit, fig*) Brutstätte *f*; **~ season** *n* (*of birds*) Brutzeit *f*; (*of animal*) Zeit *f* der Fortpflanzung und Aufzucht der Jungen.
breeze [briːz] **1** *n* Brise *f*. **2** *vi* **to ~ in/out** fröhlich angetrabt kommen *or* hereinschneien/vergnügt abziehen (*of* aus); **he ~d into the room** er kam fröhlich ins Zimmer geschneit.
breezeblock ['briːzblɒk] *n* (*Build*) Ytong ® *m*.
breezily ['briːzɪlɪ] *adv* (*fig*) forsch-fröhlich.
breeziness ['briːzɪnɪs] *n* (*fig*) Forschheit *f*.
breezy ['briːzɪ] *adj* (+*er*) **(a)** *weather, day* windig; *corner, spot also* luftig. **(b)** *manner* forsch-fröhlich.
Bren gun ['brenɡʌn] *n* (*Mil*) leichtes Maschinengewehr. **~ carrier, Bren carrier** kleines leichtes Panzerfahrzeug.
brer, br'er ['breəʳ] *n* (*old*) Gevatter *m* (*old*).
brethren ['breðrɪn] *npl* (*obs, Eccl*) Brüder *pl*.
Breton ['bretən] **1** *adj* bretonisch. **2** *n* **(a)** Bretone *m*, Bretonin *f*. **(b)** (*language*) Bretonisch *nt*.
breve [briːv] *n* (*Mus*) Brevis *f*.
breviary ['briːvɪərɪ] *n* Brevier *nt*.
brevity ['brevɪtɪ] *n* **(a)** (*shortness*) Kürze *f*. **(b)** (*conciseness*) Kürze, Bündigkeit, Knappheit *f*. **~ is the soul of wit** (*Prov*) in der Kürze liegt die Würze (*Prov*).
brew [bruː] **1** *n* **(a)** (*beer*) Bräu *nt*. **(b)** (*of tea*) Tee *m*, Gebräu *nt* (*iro*); (*of herbs*) Kräutermischung *f*. **witch's ~** Zaubertrank *m*.
  2 *vt* **(a)** *beer, ale* brauen; *tea* aufbrühen, aufgießen, kochen. **(b)** (*fig*) *scheme, mischief, plot* ausbrüten, aushecken. **to ~ a plot** ein Komplott schmieden.
  3 *vi* **(a)** (*beer*) gären; (*tea*) ziehen. **(b)** (*make beer*) brauen. **(c)** (*fig*) **there's trouble/mischief/a storm** *etc* **~ing (up)** da braut sich ein Konflikt/Unheil/ein Sturm zusammen; **there's something ~ing** da braut sich etwas zusammen.
♦ **brew up** *vi* **(a)** (*inf: make tea*) sich (*dat*) einen Tee machen. **(b)** (*fig*) *see* **brew 3 (c)**.
brewer ['bruːəʳ] *n* Brauer *m*. **~'s yeast** Bierhefe *f*.
brewery ['bruːərɪ] *n* Brauerei *f*.
brew-up ['bruːʌp] *n* (*inf*) **to have a ~** Tee kochen.
briar ['braɪəʳ] *n* **(a)** (*also* **~wood**) Bruyère(holz) *nt*; (*also* **~ pipe**) Bruyère(pfeife) *f*. **(b)** *see* **brier (a)**.
bribable ['braɪbəbl] *adj* bestechlich.
bribe [braɪb] **1** *n* Bestechung *f*; (*money also*) Bestechungsgeld *nt*. **as a ~** als Bestechung; **to take a ~** sich bestechen lassen, Bestechungsgeld nehmen; **to offer sb a ~** jdn bestechen wollen, jdm Bestechungsgeld anbieten. **2** *vt* bestechen. **to ~ sb**

to do sth jdn bestechen, damit er etw tut.
bribery ['braɪbərɪ] *n* Bestechung *f*. **open to ~** bestechlich.
bric-à-brac ['brɪkəbræk] *n* Nippes *m*, Nippsachen *pl*.
brick [brɪk] *n* **(a)** (*Build*) Ziegel- *or* Backstein *m*. **you can't make ~s without straw** (*Prov*) wo nichts ist, kann auch nichts werden; **he came** *or* **was down on me like a ton of ~s** (*inf*) er hat mich unheimlich fertiggemacht (*inf*); **to drop a ~** (*fig inf*) ins Fettnäpfchen treten; **to drop sb/sth like a hot ~** (*inf*) jdn/etw wie eine heiße Kartoffel fallenlassen.
  (b) (*toy*) (Bau)klotz *m*. **box of (building) ~s** Baukasten *m*.
  (c) (*of ice-cream*) Block *m*.
  (d) (*dated inf*) feiner Kerl (*inf*). **be a ~!** sei ein Kumpel!
♦ **brick in** *or* **up** *vt sep* *door, window* zumauern.
brick *in cpds* Backstein-; **~bat** *n* (*missile*) Backsteinbrocken *m*; (*fig*) Beschimpfung *f*.
brickie ['brɪkɪ] *n* (*Brit inf*) Maurer *m*.
brick: **~-kiln** *n* Ziegelofen *m*; **~layer** *n* Maurer *m*; **~laying** *n* Maurerarbeit *f*; (*trade*) Maurerhandwerk *nt*; **~ red** *adj* ziegelrot; **~ wall** *n* (*fig inf*) **I might as well be talking to a ~ wall** ich könnte genausogut gegen eine Wand reden; **it's like beating** *or* **banging one's head against a ~ wall** es ist, wie wenn man mit dem Kopf gegen die Wand rennt; **to come up against a ~ wall** plötzlich vor einer Mauer stehen; **~work** *n* Backsteinmauerwerk *nt*; **~works** *npl*, **~yard** *n* Ziegelei *f*.
bridal ['braɪdl] *adj* Braut-; *procession also, feast* Hochzeits-. **~ party** Angehörige und Freunde *pl* der Braut; **~ vow** Eheversprechen *nt* der Braut.
bride [braɪd] *n* Braut *f*. **the ~ and (bride)groom** Braut und Bräutigam, das Hochzeitspaar; **~ of Christ** Braut Christi.
bridegroom ['braɪdɡruːm] *n* Bräutigam *m*.
bridesmaid ['braɪdzmeɪd] *n* Brautjungfer *f*.
bridge[1] [brɪdʒ] **1** *n* **(a)** (*lit, fig*) Brücke *f*.
  (b) (*Naut*) (Kommando)brücke *f*.
  (c) (*of nose*) Sattel *m*; (*of spectacles, violin*) Steg *m*.
  (d) (*Dentistry*) Brücke *f*.
  (e) (*Billiards*) Steg *m*.
  2 *vt river, railway* eine Brücke schlagen *or* bauen über (+*acc*); (*fig*) überbrücken. **to ~ the gap** (*fig*) die Zeit überbrücken; (*between people*) die Kluft überbrücken.
bridge[2] *n* (*Cards*) Bridge *nt*.
bridge: **~-building** *n* Brückenbau *m*; **~head** *n* Brückenkopf *m*; **to establish a ~head** einen Brückenkopf errichten; **~house** *n* Brückenhaus *nt*; **~ roll** *n* längliches Brötchen.
bridging loan ['brɪdʒɪŋləʊn] *n* Überbrückungskredit *m*.
bridle ['braɪdl] **1** *n* (*of horse*) Zaum *m*. **2** *vt* **(a)** *horse* aufzäumen. **(b)** (*fig*) *one's tongue, emotions* im Zaume halten. **3** *vi* sich entrüstet wehren (*at* gegen).
bridlepath ['braɪdl.pɑːθ] *n* Reitweg *m*.
brief [briːf] **1** *adj* (+*er*) kurz; (*curt also*) *manner* kurz angebunden. **in ~** in kurz; **to be ~** um es kurz zu machen; **you give me a ~ idea** ... könnten Sie mir kurz erzählen ...
  2 *n* **(a)** (*Jur*) Auftrag *m* (*an einen Anwalt*); (*document*) Unterlagen *pl* zu dem/einem Fall; (*instructions*) Instruktionen *pl*. **to take a ~** (*Jur*) einen Fall *or* Auftrag annehmen; **to hold a ~ for sb** (*Jur*) jds Sache vor Gericht vertreten; **I hold no ~ for him** (*fig*) ich will nicht für ihn plädieren, ich will mich nicht für ihn einsetzen.
  (b) (*instructions*) Auftrag *m*.
  3 *vt* **(a)** (*Jur*) *lawyer* instruieren; (*employ*) beauftragen. **(b)** (*give instructions, information to*) instruieren (*on* über +*acc*). **the pilots were ~ed on what they had to do** die Piloten wurden instruiert, was sie tun sollten.
briefcase ['briːfkeɪs] *n* (Akten)tasche, (Akten)mappe *f*.
briefing ['briːfɪŋ] *n* (*instructions*) Instruktionen *pl*, Anweisungen *pl*; (*also* **~ session**) Einsatzbesprechung *f*.
briefly ['briːflɪ] *adv* kurz.
briefness ['briːfnɪs] *n* Kürze *f*.
briefs [briːfs] *npl* Slip *m*. **a pair of ~** ein Slip.
brier ['braɪəʳ] *n* **(a)** (*wild rose*) wilde Rose; (*bramble runner*) Ranke *f*; (*thorny bush*) Dornbusch *m*. **(b)** *see* **briar (a)**.
brig [brɪɡ] *n* **(a)** (*ship*) Brigg *f*. **(b)** (*US: cell*) Arrestzelle *f* (*auf einem Schiff*); (*US Mil sl*) Bunker *m* (*sl*).
brigade [brɪˈɡeɪd] *n* (*Mil*) Brigade *f*.
brigadier [.brɪɡəˈdɪəʳ] *n* (*Brit*) Brigadegeneral *m*.
brigadier (general) *n* (*Brit Hist, US*) Brigadegeneral *m*.
brigand ['brɪɡənd] *n* (*old*) Räuber, Bandit *m*.
bright [braɪt] *adj* (+*er*) **(a)** hell; *colour* leuchtend; *sunshine, star also, eyes, gem* strahlend; *day, weather* heiter; *reflection* stark; *metal* glänzend. **~ red** knallrot; **it was really ~** *or* **a ~ day** outside es war wirklich sehr hell draußen; **~ with lights** hell erleuchtet; **~ intervals** *or* **periods** (*Met*) Aufheiterungen *pl*; **the outlook is ~er** (*Met*) die Aussichten sind etwas freundlicher; (*fig*) es sieht etwas besser aus; **the ~ lights** (*inf*) der Glanz der Großstadt.
  (b) (*cheerful*) *person, smile* fröhlich, heiter. **I wasn't feeling too ~** es ging mir nicht besonders gut; **her face was ~ with joy** (*liter*) sie strahlte vor Freude; **~ and early** in aller Frühe; *see* **side**.
  (c) (*intelligent*) *person* intelligent, schlau; *child* aufgeweckt; *idea* glänzend; (*iro*) intelligent. **I'm not very ~ this morning** ich habe heute morgen Mattscheibe (*inf*); **I forgot to tell him — that's ~** (*inf*) ich habe vergessen, ihm das zu sagen — toll! (*inf*).
  (d) (*hopeful, favourable*) *future* glänzend; *prospects also* freundlich. **things aren't looking too ~** es sieht nicht gerade rosig aus.
brighten (up) ['braɪtn(ʌp)] **1** *vt* (*sep*) **(a)** (*make cheerful*) *spirits, person* aufmuntern, aufheitern; *room, atmosphere* aufhellen, aufheitern; *conversation* beleben; *prospects, situation* verbessern.
  (b) (*make bright*) *colour, hair* aufhellen; *metal* aufpolieren.
  2 *vi* **(a)** (*weather, sky*) sich aufklären *or* aufheitern.

(b) (person) fröhlicher werden; (face) sich aufhellen or aufheitern; (eyes) aufleuchten; (prospects) sich verbessern, freundlicher werden; (future) freundlicher aussehen.

bright-eyed ['braɪtaɪd] adj mit strahlenden Augen.

brightly ['braɪtlɪ] adv **(a)** hell; reflected stark. **(b)** fröhlich, heiter. **(c)** intelligent, schlau. he very ~ left it at home (iro) er hat es intelligenterweise zu Hause gelassen.

brightness ['braɪtnɪs] n see adj **(a)** Helligkeit f; Leuchten nt; Strahlen nt; Heiterkeit f; Stärke f; Glanz m. **(b)** Fröhlichkeit, Heiterkeit f. **(c)** Intelligenz, Schlauheit f; Aufgewecktheit f. **(d)** Freundlichkeit f. the ~ of the future die glänzende Zukunft.

Bright's disease ['braɪtsdɪ,ziːz] n Brightsche Krankheit.

brill [brɪl] n Glattbutt m.

brilliance ['brɪljəns], **brilliancy** ['brɪljənsɪ] (rare) n **(a)** heller Glanz, Strahlen nt; (of colour) Strahlen nt. **(b)** (fig) see adj **(b)** Großartigkeit f; Brillanz f. a man of such ~ ein Mann von so hervorragender Intelligenz.

brilliant ['brɪljənt] adj **(a)** sunshine, light, eyes, colour strahlend. **(b)** (fig) großartig (also iro); scientist, artist, wit, achievement also glänzend, brillant; student hervorragend. she is a ~ woman sie ist eine sehr intelligente Frau.

brilliantine [,brɪljən'tiːn] n Brillantine, Haarpomade f.

brilliantly ['brɪljəntlɪ] adv **(a)** shine hell; sunny strahlend. **(b)** (very well, superbly) großartig; talented glänzend; play, perform brillant; funny, witty, simple herrlich. a ~ original idea eine Idee von glänzender Originalität.

brim [brɪm] **1** n (of cup) Rand m; (of hat also) Krempe f. full to the ~ randvoll. **2** vi strotzen (with von or vor +dat). her eyes were ~ming with tears ihre Augen schwammen in Tränen.

♦brim over vi (lit, fig) überfließen (with vor +dat).

brimful ['brɪm'fʊl] adj (lit) randvoll; (fig) voll (of, with von). he is ~ of energy er sprüht vor Energie.

-brimmed [brɪmd] adj suf hat -krempig.

brimstone ['brɪmstəʊn] n (sulphur) Schwefel m.

brindled ['brɪndld] adj gestreift.

brine [braɪn] n **(a)** (salt water) Sole f; (for pickling) Lake f. **(b)** (sea water) Salzwasser nt; (liter: sea) See f.

bring [brɪŋ] pret, ptp **brought** vt **(a)** bringen; (also: ~ with one) mitbringen. did you ~ the car/your guitar etc? haben Sie den Wagen/die Gitarre etc mitgebracht?; to ~ sb across/inside etc jdn herüber-/hereinbringen etc.
(b) (result in, be accompanied by) snow, rain, luck bringen. to ~ a blush/tears to sb's cheeks/eyes jdm die Röte ins Gesicht/die Tränen in die Augen treiben.
(c) (+infin: persuade) I cannot ~ myself to speak to him ich kann es nicht über mich bringen, mit ihm zu sprechen; to ~ sb to do sth jdn dazu bringen or bewegen, etw zu tun.
(d) (esp Jur: present for trial, discussion) case, matter bringen (before vor +acc). the trial will be brought next week der Prozeß findet nächste Woche statt; see action, charge.
(e) (sell for, earn) price, income (ein)bringen.
(f) in phrases see also relevant nouns to ~ sth to a close or end etw zu Ende bringen; to ~ sth low jdn auf Null bringen (inf); to ~ sth to sb's knowledge/attention jdm etw zur Kenntnis bringen/jdn auf etw (acc) aufmerksam machen; to ~ to perfection perfektionieren, vervollkommnen.

♦bring about vt sep **(a)** (cause) herbeiführen, verursachen. **(b)** (Naut) wenden. he brought us ~ er wendete.

♦bring along vt sep **(a)** mitbringen. **(b)** see bring on (b).

♦bring around vt sep see bring round (a, d).

♦bring away vt sep person wegbringen; memories, impression mitnehmen.

♦bring back vt sep **(a)** (lit) person, object zurückbringen. **(b)** (restore) custom, hanging wieder einführen; government wiederwählen. a rest will ~ him ~ to normal ein wenig Ruhe wird ihn wiederherstellen; to ~ sb ~ to life/health jdn wieder lebendig/gesund machen; to ~ a government ~ to power eine Regierung wieder an die Macht bringen. **(c)** (recall) memories zurückbringen, wecken; events erinnern an (+acc).

♦bring down vt sep **(a)** (out of air) (shoot down) bird, plane herunterholen; (land) plane, kite herunterbringen. to ~ sb's wrath ~ (up)on one sich (dat) jds Zorn zuziehen; you'll ~ the boss ~ on us da werden wir es mit dem Chef zu tun bekommen. **(b)** opponent, footballer zu Fall bringen; (by shooting) animal zur Strecke bringen; person niederschießen; see house. **(c)** government etc zu Fall bringen. **(d)** (reduce) temperature, prices, cost of living senken; swelling reduzieren, zurückgehen lassen.

♦bring forth vt sep (old, liter) **(a)** fruit hervorbringen (geh); child, young zur Welt bringen (geh). **(b)** (fig) ideas hervorbringen; suggestions vorbringen; criticisms, protests auslösen.

♦bring forward vt sep **(a)** (lit) person, chair nach vorne bringen. **(b)** (fig: present) witness vorführen; evidence, argument, proposal vorbringen, unterbreiten. **(c)** (advance time of) meeting vorverlegen; clock vorstellen. **(d)** (Comm) figure, amount übertragen. amount brought ~ Übertrag m.

♦bring in vt sep **(a)** (lit) person, object hereinbringen (prep obj, -to in +acc); harvest einbringen, bergen (esp DDR); sails einziehen. to ~ ~ the New Year das Neue Jahr begrüßen. **(b)** (fig: introduce) fashion, custom einführen; (Parl) bill einbringen. to ~ sth ~(to) fashion etw in Mode bringen. **(c)** (involve, call in) police, consultant etc einschalten (on bei). don't ~ him ~to it laß ihn aus der Sache raus; she's bound to ~ Freud ~ sie wird bestimmt Freud mit hereinbringen; why ~ Freud/that ~? was hat Freud/das damit zu tun? **(d)** (Fin) income, money, interest (ein)bringen (-to sb jdm); (Comm) business bringen. **(e)** (Jur: jury) verdict fällen. to ~ ~ a verdict of guilty einen Schuldspruch fällen.

♦bring into vt always separate to ~ ~ action/blossom/view zum Einsatz bringen/blühen lassen/sichtbar werden lassen.

♦bring off vt sep **(a)** people from wreck retten, wegbringen (prep obj von). **(b)** (succeed with) plan zustande or zuwege bringen. to ~ ~ a coup ein Ding drehen (inf); he brought it ~! er hat es geschafft! (inf). **(c)** (sl: bring to orgasm) befriedigen.

♦bring on vt sep **(a)** (cause) illness, quarrel herbeiführen, verursachen; attack also auslösen.
(b) (help develop) pupil, young athlete weiterbringen; crops, flowers heraufbringen.
(c) (Theat) person auftreten lassen; thing auf die Bühne bringen; (Sport) player einsetzen. to ~ sb ~ the scene (fig) jdn auf die Szene rufen.
(d) to ~ sth (up)~ oneself etw selbst verursachen; you brought it (up)~ yourself das hast du dir selbst zuzuschreiben.

♦bring out vt sep **(a)** (lit) (heraus)bringen (of aus); (of pocket) herausholen (of aus).
(b) (draw out) person die Hemmungen nehmen (+dat). can't you ~ him ~ a bit? können Sie nichts tun, damit er ein bißchen aus sich herausgeht?
(c) (elicit) greed, bravery zum Vorschein bringen; best qualities also herausbringen. to ~ ~ the best/worst in sb das Beste/Schlimmste in jdm zum Vorschein bringen.
(d) (also ~ ~ on strike) workers auf die Straße schicken.
(e) (make blossom) flowers herausbringen.
(f) (to society) debutante in die Gesellschaft einführen.
(g) (bring on the market) new product, book herausbringen.
(h) (emphasize, show up) herausbringen, hervorheben.
(i) (utter) few words herausbringen; cry ausstoßen.
(j) to ~ sb ~ in spots/a rash bei jdm Pickel/einen Ausschlag verursachen.

♦bring over vt sep **(a)** (lit) herüberbringen. **(b)** (fig) (to ideas) überzeugen (to von); (to other side) bringen (to auf +acc).

♦bring round vt sep **(a)** (to one's house etc) vorbeibringen. **(b)** (steer) discussion, conversation bringen (to auf +acc). **(c)** unconscious person wieder zu Bewußtsein bringen. **(d)** (convert) herumkriegen (inf).

♦bring through vt always separate patient, business durchbringen. to ~ sb ~ a crisis/an illness jdn durch eine Krise bringen/jdm helfen, eine Krankheit zu überstehen.

♦bring to vt always separate **(a)** (Naut) stoppen. **(b)** unconscious person wieder zu Bewußtsein bringen. **(c)** to ~ sb ~ himself/herself jdn wieder zu sich bringen.

♦bring together vt sep zusammenbringen.

♦bring under 1 vt always separate (subdue) unterwerfen. **2** vt +prep obj (categorize) bringen unter (+dat). this can be brought ~ four main headings dies läßt sich in vier Kategorien gliedern; see control.

♦bring up vt sep **(a)** (to a higher place) heraufbringen; (to the front) her-/hinbringen.
(b) (raise, increase) amount, reserves erhöhen (to auf +acc); level, standards also bringen. to ~ sb ~ to a certain standard jdn auf ein gewisses Niveau bringen.
(c) (rear) child, animal groß- or aufziehen; (educate) erziehen. a well/badly brought ~ child ein gut/schlecht erzogenes Kind; to ~ sb ~ to do sth jdn dazu erziehen, etw zu tun; he was brought ~ to believe that ... man hatte ihm beigebracht, daß ...
(d) (vomit up) brechen; (esp baby, patient) spucken (inf).
(e) (mention) fact, problem zur Sprache bringen, erwähnen. do you have to ~ that ~? müssen Sie davon anfangen?
(f) (Jur) to ~ sb ~ (before a judge) jdn (einem Richter) vorführen.
(g) (Mil) battalion heranbringen; see rear.
(h) to ~ sb ~ short jdn innehalten lassen.
(i) to ~ sb ~ against sth jdn mit etw konfrontieren.

♦bring upon vt sep +prep obj see bring on (d).

bring-and-buy (sale) ['brɪŋənd'baɪ(,seɪl)] n (Brit) Basar m, wo mitgebrachte Sachen angeboten und verkauft werden.

brink [brɪŋk] n (lit, fig) Rand m. on the ~ of sth/doing sth (lit, fig) am Rande von etw/nahe daran, etw zu tun.

brinkmanship ['brɪŋkmənʃɪp] n (inf) Spiel nt mit dem Feuer.

briny ['braɪnɪ] **1** adj salzhaltig, salzig. **2** n (inf) See f.

Bri-nylon® [,braɪ'naɪlən] n (Brit) britische Kunstfaser.

briquet(te) [brɪ'ket] n Brikett nt.

brisk [brɪsk] adj (+er) person, way of speaking resch; sales assistant, service flott, flink; walk, pace flott. to go for a ~ walk einen ordentlichen Spaziergang machen. **(b)** (fig) trade, betting, bidding lebhaft, rege. business etc was ~ das Geschäft etc ging lebhaft or war rege; the market made a ~ start der Markt begann lebhaft. **(c)** wind, weather frisch.

brisket ['brɪskɪt] n (Cook) Bruststück nt.

briskly ['brɪsklɪ] adv see adj **(a)** forsch; flott, flink; flott. **(b)** lebhaft, rege.

briskness ['brɪsknɪs] n see adj **(a)** Forschheit f; Flottheit, Flinkheit f; Flottheit f. **(b)** Lebhaftigkeit f. **(c)** Frische f.

brisling ['brɪzlɪŋ] n Brisling m, Sprotte f.

bristle ['brɪsl] **1** n (of brush, boar etc) Borste f; (of beard) Stoppel f.
2 vi **(a)** (animal's hair) sich sträuben. the dog ~d dem Hund sträubte sich das Fell.
(b) (fig: person) zornig werden. to ~ with anger vor Wut schnauben.
(c) (fig) to be bristling with people/mistakes von or vor Leuten/Fehlern wimmeln; bristling with difficulties mit Schwierigkeiten gespickt; the dress was bristling with pins das Kleid steckte voller Nadeln; the soldiers ~d with weapons die Soldaten waren bis an die Zähne bewaffnet.

bristly ['brɪslɪ] adj (+er) animal borstig; chin Stoppel-, stoppelig; hair, beard borstig.

Bristol fashion ['brɪstəl,fæʃn] *adj see* **shipshape**.
bristols ['brɪstəlz] *npl* (*Brit sl*) Titten *pl* (*sl*).
Brit [brɪt] *n* (*inf*) Engländer, Tommy (*inf*) *m*.
Britain ['brɪtən] *n* Großbritannien, Britannien (*Press*) *nt*; (*in ancient history*) Britannien *nt*.
Britannia [brɪ'tænɪə] *n* (*poet: country*) Britannien *nt*; (*personification*) Britannia *f*.
Britannic [brɪ'tænɪk] *adj*: Her/His ~ Majesty Ihre/Seine Britannische Majestät.
briticism ['brɪtɪsɪzəm] *n* Britizismus *m*.
briticize ['brɪtɪsaɪz] *vt* anglisieren, britifizieren.
British ['brɪtɪʃ] **1** *adj* britisch. **I'm** ~ ich bin Brite/Britin; **the** ~ **Isles** die Britischen Inseln; ~ **Empire** Britisches Weltreich; **and the best of** ~ **(luck)!** (*inf*) na, dann mal viel Glück! **2** *n* **the** ~ *pl* die Briten *pl*.
Britisher ['brɪtɪʃəʳ] *n* (*US*) Brite *m*, Britin *f*.
Briton ['brɪtən] *n* Brite *m*, Britin *f*.
Brittany ['brɪtənɪ] *n* die Bretagne.
brittle ['brɪtl] *adj* spröde, zerbrechlich; *old paper* bröcklig; *biscuits* mürbe. ~ **bones** schwache Knochen. **(b)** (*fig*) *nerves* schwach; *person* empfindlich; *voice, laugh* schrill. **to have a** ~ **temper** aufbrausend sein.
brittleness ['brɪtlnɪs] *n see adj* **(a)** Sprödigkeit, Zerbrechlichkeit *f*; Bröckligkeit *f*; Mürbheit *f*. **(b)** Schwäche *f*; Empfindlichkeit *f*; Schrillheit *f*.
broach [brəʊtʃ] *vt* **(a)** *barrel* anstechen, anzapfen. **(b)** *subject, topic* anschneiden.
broad [brɔːd] **1** *adj* (*+er*) **(a)** (*wide*) breit. **to grow** ~**er** breiter werden; (*road, river also*) sich verbreitern; **to make** ~**er** verbreitern; **it's as** ~ **as it is long** (*fig*) es ist Jacke wie Hose (*inf*).
    (b) (*widely applicable*) *theory* umfassend; (*general*) allgemein.
    (c) (*not detailed*) *distinction, idea, outline* grob; *instructions* vage; *sense* weit. **as a very** ~ **rule** als Faustregel.
    (d) (*liberal*) *mind, attitude, ideas* großzügig, tolerant. **a man of** ~ **sympathies** ein aufgeschlossener Geist.
    (e) *wink, hint* deutlich; (*indelicate*) *humour* derb.
    (f) (*strongly marked*) *accent* stark; (*with long vowel sounds also*) breit. **he speaks** ~ **Scots** er spricht breit(est)es Schottisch *or* starken schottischen Dialekt.
  2 *n* **(a)** (*widest part*) **the** ~ **of the back** die Schultergegend. **(b)** **the** (*Norfolk*) **B**~**s** *pl* die Norfolk Broads. **(c)** (*esp US sl: woman*) Frau *f*; (*younger*) Mieze *f* (*sl*).
broad bean *n* dicke Bohne, Saubohne *f*.
broadcast ['brɔːdkɑːst] (*vb: pret, ptp* ~) **1** *n* (*Rad, TV*) Sendung *f*; (*of match etc*) Übertragung *f*. ~**s** Programm *nt*, Sendungen *pl*.
  2 *vt u* (*Rad, TV*) senden, ausstrahlen; *football match, event* übertragen.
    (b) (*fig*) *news, rumour etc* verbreiten.
    (c) (*Agr*) *seed* aussäen.
  3 *vi* (*Rad, TV: station*) senden; (*person*) im Rundfunk/Fernsehen sprechen. **we're not** ~**ing tonight** heute abend strahlen wir kein Programm aus.
broadcaster ['brɔːdkɑːstəʳ] *n* (*Rad, TV*) (*announcer*) Rundfunk-/Fernsehsprecher(in *f*) *m*; (*personality*) Mitarbeiter(in *f*) *m* beim Rundfunk. **he's not a very good** ~ er ist nicht besonders gut im Fernsehen/Rundfunk; **a famous** ~ eine vom Rundfunk/Fernsehen bekannte Persönlichkeit.
broadcasting ['brɔːdkɑːstɪŋ] *n* (*Rad, TV*) Sendung *f*; (*of event*) Übertragung *f*. **end of** ~ Ende des Programms; **to work in** ~ beim Rundfunk/Fernsehen arbeiten; **the early days of** ~ die Anfänge des Rundfunks/Fernsehens. **2** *attr* (*Rad*) Rundfunk-; (*TV*) Fernseh-. ~ **station** (*Rad*) Rundfunkstation *f*; (*TV*) Fernsehstation *f*.
broadcloth ['brɔːdklɒθ] *n* merzerisierter Baumwollstoff.
broaden (out) ['brɔːdn(aʊt)] **1** *vt* (*sep*) *road etc* verbreitern; (*fig*) *person, attitudes* aufgeschlossen machen. **to** ~ **one's mind/one's horizons** (*fig*) seinen Horizont erweitern. **2** *vi* breiter werden, sich verbreitern; (*fig*) (*person, attitudes*) aufgeschlossen werden; (*horizon*) sich erweitern.
broad: ~ **gauge** *n* Breitspur *f*; ~ **jump** *n* (*US Sport*) Weitsprung *m*; ~**loom** *adj carpet* überbreit.
broadly ['brɔːdlɪ] *adv* **(a)** (*in general terms*) allgemein, in großen Zügen; *outline, describe* grob. ~ **speaking** ganz allgemein gesprochen. **(b)** (*greatly, widely*) *differ* beträchtlich; *applicable* allgemein. **(c)** *grin, smile, laugh* breit; *hint, wink* deutlich. **(d)** *see adj* (*f*) *speak a dialect* stark; breit.
broad: ~**-minded** *adj* großzügig, tolerant; ~**-mindedness** *n* Großzügigkeit, Toleranz *f*; ~**ness** *n see* **breadth**; ~**sheet** *n* Flugblatt *nt*; ~**-shouldered** *adj* breitschult(e)rig; ~**side** (*Naut*) **1** *n* Breitseite *f*; (*fig also*) Attacke *f*; **to fire a** ~**side** eine Breitseite abgeben *or* abfeuern; **he let him have a** ~**side** (*fig*) er attackierte ihn heftig; **2** *adv* ~**side on** mit der Breitseite (*to* nach); ~**sword** *n* breites Schwert.
brocade [brəʊ'keɪd] **1** *n* Brokat *m*. **2** *attr* Brokat-, brokaten.
brocaded [brəʊ'keɪdɪd] *adj* (*wie Brokat*) verziert *or* bestickt.
broccoli ['brɒkəlɪ] *n* Brokkoli *pl*, Spargelkohl *m*.
brochure ['brəʊʃʊəʳ] *n* Broschüre *f*, Prospekt *m*.
brogue[1] [brəʊg] *n* (*shoe*) = Haferlschuh (*Aus*), Budapester *m*.
brogue[2] *n* (*Irish accent*) irischer Akzent.
broil [brɔɪl] *vti* (*Cook*) grillen.
broiler ['brɔɪləʳ] *n* **(a)** (*chicken*) Brathähnchen *nt*, (*Gold*)broiler *m* (*DDR*). **(b)** (*grill*) Grill *m*.
broke [brəʊk] **1** *pret of* **break**. **2** *adj pred* (*inf*) abgebrannt (*inf*), pleite (*inf*). **to go for** ~ (*inf*) den Bankrott riskieren.
broken ['brəʊkən] **1** *ptp of* **break**.
  2 *adj* **(a)** kaputt (*inf*); *twig* geknickt; *bone* gebrochen; *rope also* gerissen; (*smashed*) *cup, glass etc also* zerbrochen.
    (b) (*fig*) *voice* brüchig; *chord* gebrochen; *heart, spirit, man* gebrochen; *health, marriage* zerrüttet. **surely his voice has** ~

by now er muß den Stimmbruch schon hinter sich (*dat*) haben; **from a** ~ **home** aus zerrütteten Familienverhältnissen.
    (c) *promise* gebrochen; *appointment* nicht (ein)gehalten.
    (d) *road, surface, ground* uneben; *coastline* zerklüftet; *water, sea* aufgewühlt, bewegt; *set* unvollständig.
    (e) (*interrupted*) *journey* unterbrochen; *line also* gestrichelt; *sleep* also gestört.
    (f) *English, German etc* gebrochen.
broken: ~**-down** *adj machine, car* kaputt (*inf*); *horse* ausgemergelt; ~**-hearted** *adj* untröstlich; ~ **white** *n* gebrochenes Weiß; ~**-winded** *adj* kurzatmig, dämpfig (*spec*).
broker ['brəʊkəʳ] *n* (*St Ex, Fin, real estate*) Makler *m*. **yachting** ~ Bootshändler *m*.
brokerage ['brəʊkərɪdʒ] *n* **(a)** (*commission*) Maklergebühr *f*; (*of insurance broker also*) Maklerlohn *m*. **(b)** (*trade*) Maklergeschäft *nt*.
broking ['brəʊkɪŋ] *n* Geschäft *nt* eines Maklers. **there was some rather dubious** ~ **involved** es wurden dabei einige recht zweifelhafte Maklergeschäfte getätigt.
brolly ['brɒlɪ] *n* (*Brit inf*) (Regen)schirm *m*.
bromide ['brəʊmaɪd] *n* **(a)** (*Chem*) Bromid *nt*; (*Med inf*) Beruhigungsmittel *nt*. ~ **paper** (*Phot*) Bromsilberpapier *nt*. **(b)** (*fig: platitude*) Platitüde *f*, Allgemeinplatz *m*.
bronchia ['brɒŋkɪə] *npl* Bronchien *pl*.
bronchial ['brɒŋkɪəl] *adj* bronchial. ~ **tubes** Bronchien *pl*.
bronchitis [brɒŋ'kaɪtɪs] *n* Bronchitis *f*.
bronchus ['brɒŋkəs] *n, pl* **bronchi** ['brɒŋkiː] Bronchus *m*.
bronco ['brɒŋkəʊ] *n* wildes oder halbwildes Pferd in den USA.
broncobuster ['brɒŋkəʊˌbʌstəʳ] *n* (*inf*) Zureiter *m* wilder *oder* halbwilder Pferde.
brontosaurus [ˌbrɒntə'sɔːrəs] *n* Brontosaurus *m*.
bronze [brɒnz] **1** *n* (*all senses*) Bronze *f*. **2** *vi* (*person*) braun werden, bräunen. **3** *vt* **(a)** *metal* bronzieren. **(b)** *face, skin* bräunen. **4** *adj* Bronze-.
Bronze: ~ **Age** *n* Bronzezeit *f*; ~ **Age man** *n* der Mensch der Bronzezeit.
bronzed [brɒnzd] *adj skin, face, person* braun, (sonnen)gebräunt.
brooch [brəʊtʃ] *n* Brosche *f*.
brood [bruːd] **1** *n* (*lit, fig*) Brut *f*. **2** *vi* **(a)** (*bird*) brüten. **(b)** (*fig: person*) grübeln; (*despondently also*) brüten.
♦**brood over** *or* **(up)on** *vi +prep obj* nachgrübeln über (*+acc*); (*despondently also*) brüten über (*+dat*).
brood mare *n* Zuchtstute *f*.
broody ['bruːdɪ] *adj* **(a)** *hen* brütig. **the hen is** ~ die Henne gluckt; **to be feeling** ~ (*hum inf*) den Wunsch nach einem Kind haben. **(b)** *person* grüblerisch; (*sad, moody*) schwerblütig.
brook[1] [brʊk] *n* Bach *m*.
brook[2] *vt* (*liter: tolerate*) dulden. **to** ~ **no delay** keinen Aufschub dulden.
brooklet ['brʊklɪt] *n* Bächlein *nt*.
broom [bruːm] *n* **(a)** Besen *m*. **a new** ~ **sweeps clean** (*Prov*) neue Besen kehren gut (*Prov*). **(b)** (*Bot*) Ginster *m*.
broom: ~ **cupboard** *n* Besenschrank *m*; ~**stick** *n* Besenstiel *m*; **a witch on her** ~**stick** eine Hexe auf ihrem Besen.
Bros *npl* (*Comm*) *abbr of* **Brothers** Gebr.
broth [brɒθ] *n* Fleischbrühe *f*; (*thickened soup*) Suppe *f*.
brothel ['brɒθl] *n* Bordell *nt*, Puff *m* (*inf*).
brothel: ~**-creepers** *npl* (*hum*) Leisetreter *pl* (*hum*); ~**-keeper** *n* Bordellwirt(in *f*) *m*.
brother ['brʌðəʳ] *n, pl* **-s** *or* (*obs, Eccl*) **brethren (a)** (*also Eccl*) Bruder *m*. **they are** ~ **and sister** sie sind Geschwister, sie sind Bruder und Schwester; **my/his** ~**s and sisters** meine/seine Geschwister; **the Clarke** ~**s** die Brüder Clarke; (*Comm*) die Gebrüder Clarke; (*pop group*) die Clarke Brothers; **oh** ~**!** (*esp US inf*) Junge, Junge! (*inf*).
    (b) (*in trade unions*) Kollege *m*.
    (c) (*fellow man, DDR Pol*) Bruder *m*. **his** ~ **officers** seine Offizierskameraden; **our** ~ **men, our** ~**s** unsere Mitmenschen *or* Brüder (*geh, Eccl*).
brother: ~**hood** *n* **(a)** brüderliches Einvernehmen, Brüderlichkeit *f*; sense of ~**hood** (*lit*) Brudersinn *m*; (*fig*) Gefühl *nt* der Brüderlichkeit; **(b)** (*organization*) Bruderschaft *f*; ~**hood of man** Gemeinschaft *f* der Menschen; ~**-in-arms** *n* Waffenbruder *m*; ~**-in-law** *n, pl* ~**s-in-law** Schwager *m*.
brotherliness ['brʌðəlɪnɪs] *n* Brüderlichkeit *f*.
brotherly ['brʌðəlɪ] *adj* brüderlich.
brougham ['bruːəm] *n* Brougham *m*.
brought [brɔːt] *pret, ptp of* **bring**.
brow [braʊ] *n* **(a)** (*eyebrow*) Braue *f*. **(b)** (*forehead*) Stirn *f*. **(c)** (*of hill*) (Berg)kuppe *f*.
browbeat ['braʊbiːt] *pret* ~, *ptp* ~**en** *vt* unter (moralischen) Druck setzen. **to** ~ **sb into doing sth** jdn so unter Druck setzen, daß er etw tut; **I can't** ~ **you into accepting it** ich kann euch natürlich nicht (dazu) zwingen, es anzunehmen; **I won't be** ~**en** ich lasse mich nicht tyrannisieren *or* unter Druck setzen.
brown [braʊn] **1** *adj* (*+er*) braun; (*Cook*) *roast etc also* braun gebraten. **2** *n* Braun *nt*. **3** *vt* (*sun*) *skin, person* bräunen; (*Cook*) (an)bräunen; *meat also* anbraten. **4** *vi* braun werden.
♦**brown off** *vt* **to be** ~**ed** ~ **with sb/sth** (*esp Brit inf*) jdn/etw satt haben (*inf*); **I was pretty** ~**ed** ~ **at the time** ich war es damals ziemlich satt; **you're looking a bit** ~**ed** ~ du siehst so aus, als hättest du alles ziemlich satt.
brown: ~ **ale** *n* Malzbier *nt*; ~ **bear** *n* Braunbär *m*; ~ **bread** *n* Grau- *or* Mischbrot *nt*; (*from wholemeal*) Vollkornbrot *nt*; (*darker*) Schwarzbrot *nt*.
brownie ['braʊnɪ] *n* **(a)** (*fairy*) Heinzelmännchen *nt*. **(b)** **B**~ (*in Guide Movement*) Wichtel *m*.
browning ['braʊnɪŋ] *n* (*Cook*) (*act*) Anbraten *nt*; (*substance*) Bratensoße(npulver *nt*) *f*.
brownish ['braʊnɪʃ] *adj* bräunlich.

brown: ~ **owl** n (a) (Orn) Waldkauz m; (b) B~ **Owl** (in Brownies) die Weise Eule; ~ **paper** n Packpapier nt; ~ **rice** n geschälter Reis; B~**shirt** n Braunhemd nt; ~**stone** n (US) (material) rötlichbrauner Sandstein; (house) (rotes) Sandsteinhaus nt; ~ **study** n to be in a ~ **study** (liter) geistesabwesend sein, in Gedanken verloren sein; ~ **sugar** n brauner Zucker.

browse [brauz] **1** vi (a) to ~ **among the books** in den Büchern schmökern; to ~ **through a book** in einem Buch schmökern; to ~ (**around**) sich umsehen.
   (b) (cattle) weiden; (deer) äsen.
  2 n to have a ~ (**around**) sich umsehen; to have a ~ **through the books** in den Büchern schmökern; to have a ~ **around the book-shops** sich in den Buchläden umsehen.

Bruges [bruːʒ] n Brügge nt.

bruin [ˈbruːɪn] n (Meister) Petz m.

bruise [bruːz] **1** n (on person) blauer Fleck, Bluterguß (esp Med) m; (on fruit) Druckstelle f.
  2 vt (person) einen blauen Fleck/blaue Flecke(n) schlagen (+dat) or beibringen (+dat); (fruit) beschädigen; (fig) (person, spirit, feelings) verletzen. to ~ **oneself/one's elbow** sich stoßen, sich (dat) einen blauen Fleck holen/sich (dat) einen blauen Fleck am Ellbogen holen; **the fruit is ~d** das Obst hat Druckstellen; **I feel ~d all over** mir tut's am ganzen Körper weh.
  3 vi (person, part of body) einen blauen Fleck/blaue Flecke(n) bekommen; (fruit) eine Druckstelle/Druckstellen bekommen; (fig: person, feelings) verletzt werden. **he ~s easily** er bekommt leicht blaue Flecken; (fig) er ist sehr empfindlich.

bruiser [ˈbruːzəʳ] n (inf) Rabauke, Räuber (hum) m.

brunch [brʌntʃ] n Frühstück und Mittagessen nt in einem.

brunette [bruːˈnet] **1** n Brünette f. **2** adj brünett.

brunt [brʌnt] n: to bear the (main) ~ of the attack/work/costs die volle Wucht des Angriffs/die Hauptlast der Arbeit/Kosten tragen; to bear the ~ das meiste abkriegen; the (main) ~ of the attack fell on us wir waren der vollen Wucht des Angriffs ausgesetzt.

brush [brʌʃ] **1** n (a) Bürste f; (artist's ~, paint ~, shaving ~, pastry ~) Pinsel m; (hearth ~) Besen m; (with dustpan) Handbesen or -feger m; (flue ~) Stoßbesen m; (flue ~ with weight) Sonne f. **to be as daft as a ~** (inf) total meschugge sein (inf).
  (b) (action) to give sth a ~ etw bürsten; jacket, shoes etw abbürsten; your jacket/hair/teeth could do with a ~ du solltest deine Jacke/dein Haar/deine Zähne mal wieder bürsten.
  (c) (light touch) leichte, flüchtige Berührung, Streifen nt. I felt the ~ of the cobwebs against my face ich spürte, wie Spinnweben mein Gesicht streiften.
  (d) (of fox) Lunte f.
  (e) (undergrowth) Unterholz nt.
  (f) (Mil: skirmish) Zusammenstoß m, Scharmützel nt; (quarrel, incident) Zusammenstoß m. to have a ~ with sb jdm aneinandergeraten.
  (g) (Elec or commutator) Bürste f.
  2 vt (a) bürsten; (with hand) wischen. to ~ **one's teeth/hair** sich (dat) die Zähne putzen/sich (dat) das Haar bürsten.
  (b) (sweep) dirt fegen, kehren; (with hand, cloth) wischen.
  (c) (touch lightly) streifen.
  (d) fabric bürsten, aufrauhen.

♦**brush against** vi +prep obj streifen.

♦**brush aside** vt sep obstacle, person (einfach) zur Seite schieben; objections (einfach) abtun; ideas verwerfen.

♦**brush away** vt sep (with brush) abbürsten; (with hand, cloth) ab- or wegwischen; insects verscheuchen.

♦**brush down** vt sep abbürsten; horse striegeln.

♦**brush off 1** vt sep (a) mud, snow abbürsten; insect verscheuchen. (b) (inf: reject) person abblitzen lassen (inf); suggestion, criticism zurückweisen. **2** vi (mud etc) sich abbürsten or (with hand, cloth) abwischen lassen.

♦**brush past** vi streifen (prep obj acc). as he ~ed ~ als er mich/ihn etc streifte.

♦**brush up** vt sep (a) crumbs, dirt auffegen, aufkehren. to ~ sth ~ into a pile etw zusammenfegen or -kehren.
  (b) wool, nap aufrauhen, rauhen (form).
  (c) (fig: also ~ ~ on) subject, one's German auffrischen.

brushed nylon [ˌbrʌʃtˈnaɪlən] n Nylon-Velours m.

brush: ~**off** n (inf) Abfuhr f; to give sb the ~**off** jdn abblitzen lassen (inf), jdm einen Korb geben (inf); to get the ~**off** abblitzen (inf), einen Korb kriegen (inf); ~**stroke** n Pinselstrich m; (way of painting) Pinselführung f. ~**up** n (inf) I must give my Italian a ~**up** ich muß meine Italienischkenntnisse auffrischen; ~**wood** n (a) (undergrowth) Unterholz nt; (b) (cut twigs) Reisig nt; ~**work** n (Art) Pinselführung f.

brusque [bruːsk] adj (+er) person, tone, manner brüsk, schroff.

brusquely [ˈbruːsklɪ] adv behave brüsk, schroff; speak brüsk, in schroffem Ton.

brusqueness [ˈbruːsknɪs] n Schroffheit f.

Brussels [ˈbrʌslz] n Brüssel nt.

Brussels: ~ **lace** n Brüsseler Spitze(n pl) f; ~ **sprouts** npl Rosenkohl m.

brutal [ˈbruːtl] adj brutal.

brutality [bruːˈtælɪtɪ] n Brutalität f.

brutalize [ˈbruːtəlaɪz] vt brutalisieren, verrohen lassen.

brutally [ˈbruːtəlɪ] adv brutal. I'll be ~ **frank** ich werde schonungslos offen sein.

brute [bruːt] **1** n (a) Tier, Vieh (pej) nt.
  (b) (person) brutaler Kerl; (savage) Bestie f. **drink brings out the ~ in him** Alkohol bringt das Tier in ihm zum Vorschein.
  (c) (inf: thing) it's a ~ of a problem es ist ein höllisches Problem (inf); this nail's a real ~ (to get out) dieser Nagel geht höllisch schwer raus (inf).
  2 adj attr strength roh; passion tierisch, viehisch (pej). by ~ force mit roher Gewalt.

brutish [ˈbruːtɪʃ] adj person, behaviour viehisch, brutal.

BSc abbr of **Bachelor of Science.**

BSc Econ abbr of **Bachelor of Economic Science.**

BST abbr of **British Summer Time; British Standard Time.**

Bt. abbr of **baronet.**

bubble [ˈbʌbl] **1** n Blase f; (on plane etc) (Glas)kuppel f. to blow ~s Blasen machen; the ~ has burst (fig) alles ist wie eine Seifenblase zerplatzt.
  2 vi (a) (liquid) sprudeln; (heated area) strudeln; (wine) perlen; (gas) Blasen/Bläschen machen or bilden.
  (b) (make bubbling noise) blubbern (inf); (cooking liquid, geyser etc) brodeln; (stream) plätschern.

♦**bubble out** vi (liquid) herausprudeln.

♦**bubble over** vi (lit) überschäumen; (fig) übersprudeln (with vor +dat).

♦**bubble up** vi (liquid) aufsprudeln; (gas) in Blasen/Bläschen hochsteigen.

bubble: ~**-and-squeak** n (Brit) zusammen gebratene Fleischreste und Gemüse; ~ **bath** n Schaumbad nt; ~ **car** n (Brit) (opening at the top) Kabinenroller m; (opening at the front) Isetta ® f; ~ **chamber** n Blasenkammer f; ~ **gum** n Bubble-Gum m.

bubbly [ˈbʌblɪ] **1** adj (+er) (lit) sprudelnd; (fig inf) personality temperamentvoll, lebendig; mood übersprudelnd. **2** n (inf) Schampus m (inf).

bubonic plague [bjuːˈbɒnɪkpleɪg] n Beulenpest f.

buccaneer [ˌbʌkəˈnɪəʳ] n Seeräuber, Freibeuter m; (ship) Seeräuber- or Piratenschiff nt.

buck [bʌk] **1** n (a) (male of deer) Bock m; (rabbit, hare) Rammler m. ~ **rabbit** Rammler m.
  (b) (old, hum: dandy) Stutzer, Geck (old) m.
  (c) (US inf: dollar) Dollar m. **20** ~**s** 20 Dollar.
  (d) to pass the ~ (difficulty, unpleasant task) den Schwarzen Peter weitergeben; (responsibility also) die Verantwortung abschieben; to pass the ~ to sb jdm den Schwarzen Peter zuschieben; jdm die Verantwortung aufhalsen; the ~ stops here der Schwarze Peter bleibt bei mir/uns etc hängen.
  (e) (leap by horse) Bocken nt.
  (f) (in gymnastics) Bock m.
  2 vi (a) (horse) bocken.
  (b) (resist, object) sich sträuben (at gegen).

♦**buck for** vi +prep obj (US inf) to ~ ~ **promotion** mit aller Gewalt or auf Teufel komm raus (inf) befördert werden wollen.

♦**buck off** vt sep rider abwerfen.

♦**buck up** (inf) **1** vi (a) (hurry up) sich ranhalten (inf), rasch or fix machen (inf). ~ ~! halt dich ran! (inf).
  (b) (cheer up) aufleben. ~ ~! Kopf hoch!
  2 vt sep (a) (make hurry) Dampf machen (+dat) (inf).
  (b) (make cheerful) aufmuntern.
  (c) to ~ one's ideas ~ sich zusammenreißen (inf).

buckboard [ˈbʌkbɔːd] n (US) (einfache, offene) Kutsche f.

bucket [ˈbʌkɪt] n (also of dredger, grain elevator) Eimer m; (of excavator) Schaufel f, Löffel m; (of water wheel) Schaufel f. a ~ of water ein Eimer m Wasser; to weep or cry ~s (of tears) (inf) wie ein Schloßhund heulen (inf); see kick, drop.
  2 vi (inf) it's ~ing!, the rain is ~ing (down)! es gießt or schüttet wie aus or mit Kübeln (inf).

♦**bucket about** vt sep usu pass (inf) durchrütteln.

♦**bucket along** vi (dated inf) mit einem Affenzahn dahin-/entlangkutschen (inf) or- karriolen (inf).

♦**bucket down** vi (inf) see bucket 2.

bucketful [ˈbʌkɪtfʊl] n Eimer m.

bucket: ~ **seat** n Schalensitz m; ~ **shop** n (Fin) unreelle Maklerfirma, Schwindelmakler m.

buckeye [ˈbʌkaɪ] n (US) Roßkastanie f; (seed) Kastanie f.

buckle [ˈbʌkl] **1** n (a) (on belt, shoe) Schnalle, Spange f.
  (b) (in metal etc) Beule f; (concave also) Delle f. there's a nasty ~ in this girder/wheel dieser Träger ist übel eingebeult or (twisted) verbogen/dieses Rad ist übel verbogen.
  2 vt (a) belt, shoes zuschnallen.
  (b) wheel, girder etc verbiegen; (dent) verbeulen.
  3 vi (a) (belt, shoe) mit einer Schnalle or Spange geschlossen werden, geschnallt werden.
  (b) (wheel, metal) sich verbiegen.

♦**buckle down** vi (inf) sich dahinterklemmen (inf), sich dranmachen (inf). to ~ ~ to a task sich hinter eine Aufgabe klemmen (inf), sich an eine Aufgabe machen.

♦**buckle on** vt sep armour anlegen; sword, belt umschnallen.

♦**buckle to** vi sich am Riemen reißen (inf).

buckram [ˈbʌkrəm] **1** n Buckram f. **2** adj attr Buckram-.

Bucks [bʌks] abbr of **Buckinghamshire.**

buckshee [ˌbʌkˈʃiː] adj (Brit inf) gratis, umsonst.

buck: ~**shot** n grober Schrot, Rehposten (spec) m; ~**skin** n (a) Wildleder nt, Buckskin m; (b) ~**skins** pl Lederhose(n pl) f; ~**tooth** n vorstehender Zahn; ~**toothed** adj mit vorstehenden Zähnen; ~**wheat** n Buchweizen m.

bucolic [bjuːˈkɒlɪk] adj (liter) bukolisch (liter).

bud[1] [bʌd] **1** n (a) Knospe f. to be in ~ knospen, Knospen treiben.
  (b) (Anat) see taste. **2** vi (plant, flower) knospen, Knospen treiben; (tree also) ausschlagen; (horns) wachsen.

bud[2] interj (US inf) see buddy.

Buddha [ˈbʊdə] n Buddha m.

Buddhism [ˈbʊdɪzəm] n Buddhismus m.

Buddhist [ˈbʊdɪst] **1** n Buddhist(in f) m. **2** adj buddhistisch.

budding [ˈbʌdɪŋ] adj knospend; (fig) poet etc angehend.

buddy [ˈbʌdɪ] n (US inf) Kumpel m. hey, ~! he, Kumpel, hör mal!; (threatening) hör mal zu, Kumpel or Freundchen (inf).

buddy-buddy [ˈbʌdɪbʌdɪ] adj (US inf) to be ~ with sb mit jdm dick befreundet sein (inf); to try to get ~ with sb sich bei jdm anbiedern.

budge [bʌdʒ] **1** vi (a) (move) sich rühren, sich bewegen. ~ up or over! mach Platz!, rück mal ein Stückchen!

(b) (fig: give way) nachgeben, weichen. **I will not** ~ **an inch** ich werde keinen Fingerbreit nachgeben or weichen; **he is not going to** ~ er gibt nicht nach, der bleibt stur (inf). **2** vt **(a)** (move) (von der Stelle) bewegen. **(b)** (force to give way) zum Nachgeben bewegen. **we can't** ~ **him** er läßt sich durch nichts erweichen.

budgerigar ['bʌdʒərɪgaːʳ] n Wellensittich m.

budget ['bʌdʒɪt] **1** n Etat m, Budget nt; (Parl also) Haushalt(s-plan) m. **2** vi haushalten, wirtschaften. **responsible for** ~ing für das Budget or den Etat or (Parl also) den Haushalt verantwortlich.
♦**budget for** vi +prep obj (im Etat) einplanen.

budget account n Kundenkonto nt.

budgetary ['bʌdʒɪtrɪ] adj Etat-, Budget-, Haushalts-.

budget: ~ **day** n = Haushaltsdebatte f; ~ **speech** n Etatrede f.

budgie ['bʌdʒɪ] n (inf) abbr of **budgerigar** Wellensittich m.

buff[1] [bʌf] **1** n **(a)** (leather) (kräftiges, weiches) Leder. **(b)** in **the** ~ nackt, im Adams-/Evaskostüm (hum). **(c)** (polishing disc) Schwabbelscheibe (spec), Polierscheibe f; (cylinder) Schwabbelwalze f (spec). **(d)** (colour) Gelbbraun nt. **2** adj **(a)** ledern, Leder-. **(b)** gelbbraun. **3** vt metal polieren.

buff[2] n (inf) (movie/theatre etc ~) Fan m (inf).

buffalo ['bʌfələʊ] n, pl ~es, collective pl ~ Büffel m.

buffalo grass n (US) Büffelgras nt.

buffer[1] ['bʌfəʳ] n (lit, fig) Puffer m; (Rail: at terminus) Prell-bock m.

buffer[2] n (Brit inf) Heini m (inf).

buffer: ~ **solution** n (Chem) Puffer(lösung f) m; ~ **state** n (Pol) Pufferstaat m.

buffet[1] ['bʌfɪt] **1** n (blow) Schlag m. **2** vt hin und her werfen. ~ed **by the wind** vom Wind gerüttelt; ~ing **wind** böiger Wind.

buffet[2] ['bʊfeɪ] n Büffet nt; (Brit Rail) Speisewagen m; (meal) Stehimbiß m; (cold ~) kaltes Büffett.

buffet car n (Brit Rail) Speisewagen m.

buffeting ['bʌfɪtɪŋ] n heftiges Schaukeln; (Aviat) Rütteln nt. **to get** or **take a** ~ hin und her geworfen or (Aviat) gerüttelt werden.

buffet ['bʊfeɪ-]: ~ **lunch/meal/supper** n Stehimbiß m.

buffoon [bə'fuːn] n Clown m; (stupid) Blödmann m (pej inf); (child also) Kasper m (inf). **to act** or **play the** ~ den Clown or Hanswurst spielen.

buffoonery [bə'fuːnərɪ] n Clownerie f.

bug [bʌg] **1** n **(a)** (Wanze f; (inf: any insect) Käfer m. ~s pl Ungeziefer nt.
  (b) (bugging device) Wanze f.
  (c) (inf: germ, virus) Bazillus f. **I might get your** ~ du könn-test mich anstecken; **he picked up a** ~ **while on holiday** er hat sich (dat) im Urlaub eine Krankheit geholt; **there must be a** ~ **about** das geht zur Zeit um.
  (d) (inf: obsession) now **he's got the** ~ jetzt hat's ihn gepackt (inf); **she's got the travel** ~ die Reiselust hat sie gepackt; **I went sailing once and caught the** ~ ich bin einmal segeln gegangen, und da hat's mich gepackt (inf).
  (e) (inf: snag, defect) Fehler m. ~s Mucken pl (inf).
2 vt **(a)** room, building verwanzen (inf), Wanzen pl instal-lieren in (+dat) or einbauen in (+acc) (inf); conversation, tele-phone lines abhören. **this room is** ~ged hier sind Wanzen (inf), das Zimmer ist verwanzt (inf).
  (b) (inf) (worry) stören; (annoy) nerven (sl), den Nerv töten (+dat) (inf). **don't let it** ~ **you** mach dir nichts draus (inf).

bugaboo ['bʌgəbuː] n Schreckgespenst nt.

bug: ~**bear** n Schreckgespenst nt; ~**-eyed** adj mit vorstehenden or vorquellenden Augen.

bugger ['bʌgəʳ] **1** n (sl) Scheißkerl m (sl), Arschloch nt (vulg); (when not contemptible) Kerl m (inf); (thing) Scheißding nt (sl). **this nail's a** ~, **it won't come out** dieser Scheißnagel geht einfach nicht raus (sl); **you lucky** ~! du hast vielleicht ein Schwein! (sl); **to play silly** ~s (inf) Scheiß machen (sl).
2 interj (sl) Scheiße (sl). ~ **this car/pen!** dieses Scheißauto (sl)/dieser Scheißfüller (sl); ~ **him** dieser Scheißkerl (sl); (he can get lost) der kann mich mal (sl); ~ **me!** (surprise) (du) meine Fresse! (sl); (annoyance) so'n Scheiß! (sl).
3 vt **(a)** (lit) anal verkehren mit.
  (b) (Brit sl) versauen (sl). **I couldn't be** ~ed es ist/war mir scheißegal (sl); **well, I'll be** ~ed! ich glaub', ich krieg' die Tür nicht zu! (sl).
♦**bugger about** or **around** (Brit sl) **1** vi (laze about etc) rumgammeln (sl); (be ineffective) blöd rummachen (sl). **stop** ~ing ~ **and get on with it** nun mach mal Nägel mit Köpfen (inf); **he's not serious about her, he's just** ~ing ~ ihm ist es nicht ernst, er treibt nur sein Spielchen (inf); **to** ~ ~ **with sth** an etw (dat) rumpfuschen (inf). **2** vt sep verarschen (sl).
♦**bugger off** vi (Brit sl) abhauen (inf), Leine ziehen (sl).
♦**bugger up** vt sep (Brit sl) versauen (sl). **I'm sorry if I've** ~ed **you** ~ tut mir leid, daß ich dich in eine solche Scheißlage ge-bracht habe (sl).

bugger all [,bʌgər'ɔːl] n (Brit sl: nothing) rein gar nichts.

buggery ['bʌgərɪ] n Analverkehr m; (with animals) Sodomie f.

bugging ['bʌgɪŋ] n Abhören nt. **the use of** ~ der Gebrauch von Abhörgeräten; **elaborate** ~ raffiniertes Abhörsystem.

bugging device n Abhörgerät nt, Wanze f (inf).

buggy ['bʌgɪ] n (with horse) Buggy m, leichter Einspänner. ~ **baby** ~ (Brit) Sportwagen m; (US) Kinderwagen m; **beach** ~ Buggy m; **moon** ~ Mondauto nt.

bugle ['bjuːgl] n Bügelhorn nt. ~ **call** Hornsignal nt.

bugler ['bjuːgləʳ] n Hornist m.

build [bɪld] (vb: pret, ptp **built**) **1** n Körperbau m. **2** vt **(a)** (generally) bauen. **the house is being built** das Haus ist im Bau or befindet sich im Bau. **(b)** (fig) new nation, relationship, career, system etc aufbauen; a better future schaffen. **3** vi bauen. **to** ~ **on a piece of land** auf einem Grundstück bauen;

(cover with houses etc) ein Grundstück bebauen.
♦**build in** vt sep (lit, fig) wardrobe, proviso etc einbauen; (fig) extra time einplanen; see **built-in**.
♦**build on 1** vt sep anbauen. **to** ~ ~**to sth** etw an etw (acc) anbauen. **2** vi +prep obj bauen auf (+acc).
♦**build up 1** vi **(a)** entstehen; (anticyclone, atmosphere also) sich aufbauen; (increase) zunehmen; (Tech: pressure) sich erhöhen. **the music** ~s **to a huge crescendo** die Musik steigert sich zu einem gewaltigen Crescendo.
  (b) (traffic) sich verdichten; (queue, line of cars) sich bilden.
  (c) **the parts** ~ ~ **into a complete** ... die Teile bilden zusammen ein vollständiges ...
2 vt sep **(a)** aufbauen (into zu); finances aufbessern. **to** ~ ~ **a reputation** sich (dat) einen Namen machen.
  (b) (increase) ego, muscles, forces aufbauen; production, pressure steigern, erhöhen; forces (mass) zusammenziehen; health kräftigen; sb's confidence stärken. **porridge** ~s **you** ~ von Porridge wirst du groß und stark; **growing children need lots of vitamins to** ~ **them** ~ Kinder im Wachstumsalter brauchen viele Vitamine als Aufbaustoffe; **to** ~ ~ **sb's hopes** jdm Hoffnung(en) machen.
  (c) (cover with houses) area, land (ganz) bebauen.
  (d) (publicize) person aufbauen. **he wasn't as good as he had been built** ~ **to be** er war nicht so gut, wie die Werbung erwarten ließ.

builder ['bɪldəʳ] n (worker) Bauarbeiter(in f) m; (of ships) Schiffsbauer m; (contractor) Bauunternehmer m; (future owner) Bauherr m; (fig: of state) Baumeister (geh), Erbauer m. **John Higgins, B~s** Bauunternehmen John Higgins; ~'s **labourer** Bauarbeiter m; ~'s **merchant** Baustoff- or Baumaterialhändler m.

building ['bɪldɪŋ] n **(a)** Gebäude nt; (usually big or in some way special also) Bau m. **it's the next** ~ **but one** das ist zwei Häuser weiter; **the** ~s **in the old town** die Häuser or Gebäude in der Altstadt. **(b)** (act of constructing) Bau m, Bauen nt; (of new nation etc) Aufbau m. **the** ~ **of the church took seven years** der Bau der Kirche hat sieben Jahre gedauert.

building: ~ **contractor** n Bauunternehmer m; ~ **contractors** npl Bauunternehmen nt; ~ **materials** npl Baumaterial nt, Bau-stoffe pl; ~ **site** n Baustelle f; ~ **society** n Bausparkasse f; ~ **trade** n Baugewerbe nt.

build-up ['bɪldʌp] n **(a)** (inf) Werbung f. **publicity** ~ Werbekampagne f; **they gave the play a good** ~ sie haben das Stück ganz groß herausgebracht (inf); **the chairman gave the speaker a tremendous** ~ der Vorsitzende hat den Redner ganz groß angekündigt. **(b)** (of pressure) Steigerung f; (Tech also) Verdichtung f. ~ **of troops** Truppenmassierung pl; **a traffic** ~, **a** ~ **of traffic** eine Verkehrsverdichtung.

built [bɪlt] pret, ptp of **build**.

built: ~**-in** adj (a) cupboard etc eingebaut, Einbau-; ~**-in obsolescence** geplanter Verschleiß; **(b)** (fig: instinctive) instinktmäßig; ~**-up** adj shoulders gepolstert; ~**-up area** bebautes Gebiet; (Mot) geschlossene Ortschaft; ~**-up shoes** Schuhe pl mit überhoher Sohle; (Med) orthopädische Schuhe pl.

bulb [bʌlb] n **(a)** Zwiebel f; (of garlic) Knolle f. **(b)** (Elec) (Glüh)birne f. **(c)** (of thermometer etc) Kolben m.

bulbous ['bʌlbəs] adj plant knollig, Knollen-; (bulb-shaped) growth etc knotig, Knoten-. ~ **nose** Knollennase f.

Bulgaria [bʌl'gɛərɪə] n Bulgarien nt.

Bulgarian [bʌl'gɛərɪən] **1** adj bulgarisch. **2** n **(a)** Bulgare m, Bulgarin f. **(b)** (language) Bulgarisch nt.

bulge [bʌldʒ] **1** n **(a)** (in surface) Wölbung f; (irregular) Unebenheit f, Buckel m (inf); (in jug, glass etc also) Bauch m; (in plaster, metal: accidental) Beule f; (in line) Bogen m; (in tyre) Wulst m. **the Battle of the B~** die Ardennenoffensive; **what's that** ~ **in your pocket?** was steht denn in deiner Tasche so vor?
  (b) (in birth rate etc) Zunahme f, Anschwellen nt (in gen). **the post-war** ~ der Babyboom der Nachkriegsjahre.
2 vi **(a)** (also ~ out) (swell) (an)schwellen; (metal, sides of box) sich wölben; (plaster) uneben sein; (stick out) vorstehen. **his eyes were bulging out of his head** (lit) die Augen traten ihm aus dem Kopf; (fig) er bekam Stielaugen (inf).
  (b) (pocket, sack) prall gefüllt sein; gestopft voll sein (inf) (with mit); (cheek) voll sein (with mit). **his notebooks were absolutely bulging with ideas** seine Notizbücher waren ber-stend or zum Bersten voll mit Ideen.

bulge baby n Kind nt der starken Nachkriegsjahrgänge.

bulging ['bʌldʒɪŋ] adj stomach prall, vorstehend; pockets, suit-case prall gefüllt, gestopft voll (inf). ~ **eyes** Glotzaugen pl.

bulk [bʌlk] **1** n **(a)** (size) Größe f; (of task) Ausmaß nt; (large shape) (of thing) massige Form; (of person, animal) massige Gestalt. **of great** ~ massig.
  (b) (also great ~) größter Teil; (of debt, loan also) Hauptteil m; (of work, mineral deposits also) Großteil m; (of people, votes also) Gros nt; (of property, legacy etc also) Masse f.
  (c) (Comm) **in** ~ im großen, en gros.
2 vi: **to** ~ **large** eine wichtige Rolle spielen.

bulk buying [,bʌlk'baɪɪŋ] n Mengen- or Großeinkauf m.

bulkhead ['bʌlkhed] n Schott nt; (in tunnel) Spundwand f.

bulkiness ['bʌlkɪnɪs] n see adj **(a)** Sperrigkeit f; Dicke f; Unförmigkeit f; Umständlichkeit f. **(b)** Massigkeit, Wuchtig-keit f.

bulky ['bʌlkɪ] adj (+er) **(a)** object sperrig; book dick; sweater, space-suit unförmig; system umständlich. ~ **goods** Sperrgut nt. **(b)** person massig, wuchtig.

bull[1] [bʊl] **1** n (a) Stier m; (for breeding) Bulle m. **to take** or **seize the** ~ **by the horns** (fig) den Stier bei den Hörnern packen; **like a** ~ **in a china shop** (inf) wie ein Elefant im Porzellanladen (inf); **with a neck like a** ~ stiernackig.

(b) (*male of elephant, whale etc*) Bulle *m*. **a** ~ **elephant** ein Elefantenbulle *m*; ~ **caif** Bullenkalb *nt*.
(c) (*St Ex*) Haussier, Haussespekulant(in *f*) *m*.
(d) (*Brit Mil sl*) Drill *m* und Routine *f*.
(e) (*inf: nonsense*) Unsinn, Quatsch (*inf*) *m*.
2 *vi* (*St Ex*) auf Hausse spekulieren.
3 *vt* (*St Ex*) stocks, shares hochtreiben. **to** ~ **the market** die Kurse hochtreiben.
bull² *n* (*Eccl*) Bulle *f*.
bulldog ['buldɔg] *n* **(a)** Bulldogge *f*. **he has the tenacity of a** ~ **er** hat eine zähe Ausdauer. **(b)** (*Brit Univ*) Helfer *m* des Proctors.
bulldog: ~ **breed** *n* **he is one of the** ~ **breed** er ist ein zäher Mensch; ~ **clip** *n* Papierklammer *f*.
bulldoze ['buldəuz] *vt* **(a)** (*fig: force*) **to** ~ **sb into doing sth** jdn zwingen, etw zu tun, jdn so unter Druck setzen, daß er *etc* etw tut; **to** ~ **a measure through** eine Maßnahme im Parlament durchpeitschen; **she** ~**d her way through the crowd** sie boxte sich durch die Menge.
(b) **to** ~ **a track through** ... mit Bulldozern einen Weg durch ... bahnen; **they** ~**d the rubble out of the way** sie räumten den Schutt mit Bulldozern weg.
bulldozer ['buldəuzə'] **1** *n* Planierraupe *f*, Bulldozer *m*. **2** *adj attr* (*fig*) tactics *etc* Holzhammer- (*inf*).
bull-dyke ['buldaık] *n* (*sl*) kesser Vater (*sl*).
bullet ['bulɪt] *n* Kugel *f*.
bullet: ~-**headed** *adj* rundköpfig; ~ **hole** *n* Einschuß(loch *nt*) *m*.
bulletin ['bulɪtɪn] *n* **(a)** Bulletin *nt*, amtliche Bekanntmachung. health ~ Krankenbericht *m*, Bulletin *nt*; ~ **board** (*US*) Schwarzes Brett; **a** ~ **to the press** ein Pressekommuniqué *nt*. **(b)** (*of club, society*) Bulletin *nt*.
bullet: ~**proof** **1** *adj* kugelsicher; **2** *vt* kugelsicher machen; ~ **wound** *n* Schußwunde *f* oder -verletzung *f*.
bull: ~**fight** *n* Stierkampf *m*; ~**fighter** *n* Stierkämpfer *m*; ~**fighting** *n* Stierkampf *m*; ~**fighting is** ... Stierkämpfe sind ..., der Stierkampf ist ...; ~**finch** *n* Dompfaff, Gimpel *m*; ~**frog** *n* Ochsenfrosch *m*.
bullion ['buljən] *n*, *no pl* Gold-/Silberbarren *pl*.
bull-necked ['bulnekt] *adj* stiernackig.
bullock ['bulək] *n* Ochse *m*.
bull: ~**ring** *n* Stierkampfarena *f*; ~'s **eye** *n* **(a)** (*of target*) Scheibenmittelpunkt *m* oder -zentrum *nt*; (*hit*) Schuß *m* ins Schwarze oder Zentrum; (*in darts*) Bull's eye *nt*; (*in archery*) Mouche *f*; **to get a** oder **hit the** ~'s **eye** (*lit, fig*) ins Schwarze treffen; ~'s **eye!** (*lit, fig*) genau getroffen!, ein Schuß ins Schwarze!; **(b)** (*sweet*) hartes Pfefferminzbonbon; ~**shit** (*vulg*) **1** *n* (*lit*) Kuhscheiße *f* (*vulg*); (*fig*) Bockmist (*sl*), Scheiß (*sl*) *m*; **2** *interj* Quatsch mit Soße (*sl*); ~**shit, of course you can red** keinen Scheiß, klar kannst du das (*sl*); **3** *vi* Scheiß erzählen (*sl*); **4** *vt* **he** ~**shitted his way out of trouble** er hat sich ganz großkotzig aus der Affäre gezogen (*sl*); ~**shitter** *n* (*vulg*) Quatschkopf *m* (*inf*); ~**terrier** *n* Bullterrier *m*.
bully¹ ['bulɪ] **1** *n* **(a)** Tyrann *m*; (*esp Sch*) Rabauke *m*. **you great big** ~ du Rüpel; **to be a bit of a** ~ den starken Mann markieren (*inf*); **don't be a** ~ **with your little sister** schikaniere oder tyrannisiere deine kleine Schwester nicht.
(b) (*Hockey*) Bully *nt*.
2 *vt* tyrannisieren, schikanieren; husband, staff *also* kujonieren; (*using violence*) drangsalieren, traktieren; (*into doing sth*) unter Druck setzen. **to** ~ **sb into doing sth** jdn so unter Druck setzen, daß er *etc* etw tut.
♦ **bully about** oder **around** *vt sep* herumkommandieren, tyrannisieren.
♦ **bully off** *vi* (*Hockey*) das Bully machen.
bully² *interj* (*dated*) prima (*inf*), hervorragend. ~ **for you!** (*dated, iro*) gratuliere!
bully: ~ **beef** *n* (*Mil inf*) Corned beef *nt*; ~ **boy** *n* (*inf*) Schlägertyp *m* (*inf*).
bullying ['bulɪŋ] **1** *adj* person, manner tyrannisch; boss, wife *also* herrisch. **2** *n* *vt* Tyrannisieren, Schikanieren *nt*; Kujonieren *nt*; Drangsalieren, Traktieren *nt*; Anwendung *f* von Druck (*of* auf +*acc*).
bully-off ['bulɪ'ɔf] *n* (*Hockey*) Bully *nt*.
bulrush ['bulrʌʃ] *n* Rohrkolben *m*. **in the** ~**es** im Schilfrohr.
bulwark ['bulwək] *n* **(a)** (*lit, fig*) Bollwerk *nt*. **(b)** (*Naut*) Schanzkleid *nt*.
bum¹ [bʌm] *n* (*esp Brit inf*) Hintern (*inf*), Popo (*inf*) *m*.
bum² (*sl*) **1** *n* **(a)** (*good-for-nothing*) Rumtreiber *m* (*inf*); (*young*) Gammler *m*; (*down-and-out, tramp*) Penner, Pennbruder *m* (*sl*).
(b) (*despicable person*) Saukerl *m* (*sl*).
(c) to be on the ~ schnorren (*inf*); **he's always on the** ~ **for cigarettes** er schnorrt immer Zigaretten (*inf*).
2 *adj* (*bad*) beschissen (*sl*); trick hundsgemein (*inf*).
3 *vt* **(a)** money, food schnorren (*inf*) (*off sb* bei jdm). **could I** ~ **a lift into town?** kannst du mich in die Stadt mitnehmen?; **could I** ~ **a fag?** kann ich 'ne Kippe abstauben (*sl*) oder schnorren (*inf*)?
(b) he ~**med his way round Europe** er ist durch Europa gegammelt (*sl*) oder gezogen (*inf*).
4 *vi* (*scrounge*) schnorren (*inf*) (*off sb* bei jdm).
♦ **bum about** oder **around** *vi* (*sl*) rumgammeln (*sl*); (+*prep obj*) ziehen durch (*inf*).
bumbershoot ['bʌmbəʃuːt] *n* (*US inf*) Musspritze *f* (*hum inf*).
bumble-bee ['bʌmblbiː] *n* Hummel *f*.
bumbledom ['bʌmbldəm] *n* (*inf*) kleinlicher Bürokratismus.
♦ **bumble through** ['bʌmbl'θruː] *vi* sich durchwursteln (*inf*) oder -mogeln (*inf*) (+*prep obj* durch).
bumboat ['bʌmbəut] *n* Proviantboot *nt*.
bumf, bumph [bʌmf] *n* (*inf*) **(a)** (*forms*) Papierkram *m* (*inf*). **(b)** (*toilet paper*) Klopapier *nt* (*inf*).
bump [bʌmp] **1** *n* **(a)** (*blow, noise, jolt*) Bums *m* (*inf*); (*of sth falling also*) Plumps *m* (*inf*). **to get a** ~ **on the head** sich (*dat*)

---

den Kopf anschlagen; **I accidentally gave her a** ~ **on the chin** ich habe sie aus Versehen ans Kinn geboxt oder gestoßen; **the car has had a few** ~**s** mit dem Auto hat es ein paarmal gebumst (*inf*); **each** ~ **was agony as the ambulance** ... jede Erschütterung war eine Qual, als der Krankenwagen ...; ~ **and grind** (*inf*) erotische Zuckungen *pl*; (*sex*) Bumserei *f* (*inf*).
(b) (*on any surface*) Unebenheit *f*, Hubbel *m* (*inf*); (*on head, knee etc*) Beule *f*; (*on car*) Delle *f*.
(c) (*Aviat: rising air current*) Bö *f*.
2 *vt* **(a)** stoßen; car wing etc, one's own car eine Delle fahren in (+*acc*); another car auffahren auf (+*acc*). **to** ~ **one's head/knee** sich (*dat*) den Kopf/das Knie anstoßen oder anschlagen (*on against* an +*dat*); **her father sat** ~**ing her up and down on his knee** ihr Vater ließ sie auf den Knien reiten.
(b) (*Sch sl*) hochwerfen.
3 *vi* (*move joltingly*) holpern. **he fell and went** ~**ing down the stairs** er stürzte und fiel polternd die Treppe hinunter.
4 *adv* **to go** ~ bumsen (*inf*); **things that go** ~ **in the night** Geräusche im Dunkeln oder in der Nacht.
♦ **bump about** *vi* herumpoltern.
♦ **bump into** *vi* +*prep obj* **(a)** (*knock into*) stoßen oder bumsen (*inf*) gegen; (*driver, car*) fahren gegen; another car fahren auf (+*acc*).
(b) (*inf: meet*) über den Weg laufen (+*dat*).
♦ **bump off** *vt sep* (*inf*) abmurksen (*inf*), kaltmachen (*inf*).
♦ **bump up** *vt sep* (*inf*) (*to auf* +*acc*) prices raufgehen mit (*inf*); total erhöhen; salary aufbessern.
bumper ['bʌmpə'] **1** *n* (*of car*) Stoßstange *f*. **2** *adj* ~ **crop** Rekordernte *f*; **a special** ~ **edition** eine Riesen-Sonderausgabe; ~ **offer** großes Sonderangebot.
bumper car *n* Boxauto *nt* (*dial*), Autoskooter *m*.
bumph *n* *see* bumf.
bumpiness ['bʌmpɪnɪs] *n* *see adj* Unebenheit, Hubbeligkeit (*inf*) *f*; Holp(e)rigkeit *f*; Böigkeit *f*.
bumpkin ['bʌmpkɪn] *n* (*also country* ~) (*man*) (Bauern)tölpel *m*; (*woman*) Trampel *f* vom Land.
bumptious ['bʌmpʃəs] *adj* aufgeblasen, wichtigtuerisch.
bumptiousness ['bʌmpʃəsnɪs] *n* Aufgeblasenheit, Wichtigtuerei *f*.
bumpy ['bʌmpɪ] *adj* (+*er*) surface uneben, hubbelig (*inf*); road, drive holp(e)rig; flight böig, unruhig. **we had a very** ~ **drive** auf der Fahrt wurden wir tüchtig durchgerüttelt.
bum's rush *n*: **to give sb the** ~ (*sl*) jdn rausschmeißen (*sl*).
bun [bʌn] *n* **(a)** (*bread*) süßes Brötchen; (*iced* ~ etc) süßes Stückchen oder Teilchen; (*N Engl: small cake*) Biskuittörtchen *nt*. **to have a** ~ **in the oven** (*sl*) ein Kind kriegen (*inf*). **(b)** (*hair*) Knoten *m*. **she wears her hair in a** ~ sie trägt einen Knoten.
bunch [bʌntʃ] **1** *n* **(a)** (*of flowers*) Strauß *m*; (*of bananas*) Büschel *nt*; (*of radishes, asparagus*) Bund *nt*; (*of hair*) (Ratten)schwanz *m*, Zöpfchen *nt*. **a** ~ **of roses/flowers** ein Strauß *m* Rosen/ein Blumenstrauß *m*; ~ **of grapes** Weintraube *f*; ~ **of keys** Schlüsselbund *m*; **to wear one's hair in** ~**es** (Ratten)schwänze *pl* oder Zöpfchen *pl* haben; **the pick** oder **best of the** ~ die Allerbesten; (*things*) das Beste vom Besten; **to take the pick of the** ~ sich (*dat*) die Allerbesten/das Beste aussuchen.
(b) (*inf: of people*) Haufen *m* (*inf*). **a small** ~ **of tourists** ein Häufchen *nt* oder eine kleine Gruppe Touristen; **a** ~ **of fives** (*sl: fist*) 'ne Faust ins Gesicht (*sl*).
2 *vi* (*dress*) sich bauschen.
(b) *see* ~ **together 2,** ~ **up 2**.
♦ **bunch together 1** *vt sep* zusammenfassen; (*at random*) zusammenwürfeln. **the girls/prisoners were sitting all** ~**ed** ~ die Mädchen/Gefangenen saßen alle auf einem Haufen.
2 *vi* (*people*) Grüppchen oder eine Haufen bilden; (*atoms*) Cluster bilden. **they** ~**ed** ~ **for warmth** sie kauerten sich aneinander, um sich zu wärmen; **don't** ~ ~, **spread out!** bleibt nicht alle auf einem Haufen, verteilt euch!
♦ **bunch up 1** *vt sep* **(a)** dress, skirt bauschen. **(b)** (*put together*) objects auf einen Haufen legen. **2** *vi* (*people*) Grüppchen oder Haufen bilden. **don't** ~ ~ **so much, space out!** nicht alle auf einem Haufen, verteilt euch! **(b)** (*material*) sich bauschen.
bundle ['bʌndl] **1** *n* **(a)** Bündel *nt*. **to tie sth in a** ~ etw bündeln.
(b) (*fig*) **he is a** ~ **of nerves** er ist ein Nervenbündel; **that child is a** ~ **of mischief** das Kind hat nichts als Unfug im Kopf; **her little** ~ **of joy** (*inf*) ihr kleiner Wonneproppen (*inf*); **a** ~ **of fun** (*inf*) das reinste Vergnügen.
2 *vt* **(a)** bündeln; *see* ~ **up**.
(b) (*put, send hastily*) things stopfen; people verfrachten, schaffen; (*into vehicle*) packen (*inf*), schieben (*inf*).
♦ **bundle off** *vt sep* person schaffen. **he was** ~**d** ~ **to Australia** er wurde nach Australien verfrachtet.
♦ **bundle up** *vt sep* **(a)** (*tie into bundles*) bündeln; (*collect hastily*) zusammenraffen. ~**d** ~ **in his overcoat** in seinen Mantel eingehüllt oder gemummelt (*inf*).
bun fight *n* (*dated inf*) Festivität *pl* (*dated*).
bung [bʌŋ] **1** *n* (*of cask*) Spund(zapfen) *m*. **2** *vt* **(a)** cask spunden, verstopfen. **(b)** (*Brit inf: throw*) schmeißen (*inf*).
♦ **bung in** *vt sep* (*Brit inf: include*) dazutun.
♦ **bung out** *vt sep* (*Brit inf*) rausschmeißen (*inf*).
♦ **bung up** *vt sep* (*inf*) pipe verstopfen. **I'm all** ~**ed** ~ meine Nase ist verstopft.
bungalow ['bʌŋgələu] *n* Bungalow *m*.
bung-ho [bʌŋ'həu] *interj* (*inf*) famos (*dated inf*).
bunghole ['bʌŋhəul] *n* Spundloch *nt*.
bungle ['bʌŋgl] **1** *vt* verpfuschen, vermasseln (*inf*). **it was a** ~**d job** die Sache war zusammengepfuscht oder verpfuscht.
2 *vi* **I see you've** ~**d again, Higgins** wie ich sehe, haben Sie wieder einmal alles verpfuscht oder vermasselt (*inf*), Higgins.
3 *n* verpfuschte Sache, Stümperei *f*.
bungler ['bʌŋglə'] *n* Nichtskönner, Stümper *m*.
bungling ['bʌŋglɪŋ] **1** *adj* person unfähig, trottelhaft, dusselig

(*inf*); *attempt* stümperhaft. **some ~ idiot has ... irgendein Trottel hat ... (*inf*). 2** *n* Stümperei, Dusseligkeit (*inf*) *f*.
bunion ['bʌnjən] *n* Ballen *m*, X-Großzehe *f*.
bunk¹ [bʌŋk] *n*: **to do a ~ (*inf*) türmen (*inf*).
bunk² *n* (*inf*) Quatsch *m* (*inf*).
bunk³ *n* (*in ship*) Koje *f*; (*in train, dormitory*) Bett *nt*.
♦ **bunk down** *vi* (*inf*) kampieren (*inf*).
bunk-beds [bʌŋk'bedz] *npl* Etagenbett *nt*.
bunker ['bʌŋkə^r] **1** *n* (*Naut, Golf, Mil*) Bunker *m*. **2** *vt* he was ~ed (*Golf*) er hatte den Ball in den Bunker geschlagen.
bunkhouse ['bʌŋkhaʊs] *n* Schlafbaracke *f*.
bunkum ['bʌŋkəm] *n* (*inf*) Blödsinn, Quatsch (*inf*) *m*.
bunny ['bʌnɪ] *n* (*also* ~ **rabbit**) Hase *m*, Häschen *nt*.
bunny girl *n* Häschen *nt*.
Bunsen (burner) ['bʌnsn('bɜ:nə^r)] *n* Bunsenbrenner *m*.
bunting¹ [bʌntɪŋ] *n* (*Orn*) Ammer *f*; *see* **corn ~, reed ~**.
bunting² *n* (*material*) Fahnentuch *nt*; (*flags*) bunte Fähnchen *pl*, Wimpel *pl*.
buoy [bɔɪ] **1** *n* Boje *f*. **to put down a ~ eine Boje verankern. 2** *vt* **waterway** mit Bojen markieren *or* kennzeichnen.
♦ **buoy up** *vt sep* (**a**) (*lit*) über Wasser halten. (**b**) (*fig*) *person* Auftrieb geben (+*dat*); *sb's hopes* beleben. ~**ed ~ by new hope** von neuer Hoffnung beseelt. (**c**) (*Fin*) *market, prices* Auftrieb geben (+*dat*).
buoyancy ['bɔɪənsɪ] *n* (**a**) (*of ship, object*) Schwimmfähigkeit *f*; (*of liquid*) Auftrieb *m*. ~ **chamber** (*Naut*) Trimmtank *m*; ~ **tank** Luftkammer *f*. (**b**) (*fig: cheerfulness*) Schwung, Elan *m*. (**c**) (*Fin: of market, prices*) Festigkeit *f*; (*resilience*) Erholungsfähigkeit *f*.
buoyant ['bɔɪənt] *adj* (**a**) *ship, object* schwimmend; *liquid* tragend. **fresh water is not so ~ as salt water** Süßwasser trägt nicht so gut wie Salzwasser. (**b**) (*fig*) *person, mood* heiter; (*energetic*) *step* federnd, elastisch. (**c**) (*Fin*) *market, prices* fest; (*resilient*) erholungsfähig; *trading* rege.
buoyantly ['bɔɪəntlɪ] *adv see adj*.
bur, burr [bɜ:^r] *n* (*Bot, fig inf*) Klette *f*. **chestnut ~** Kastanienschale *f*.
Burberry ® ['bɜ:bərɪ] *n* teurer Gabardinemantel.
burble ['bɜ:bl] **1** *vi* (**a**) (*stream*) plätschern, gurgeln. (**b**) (*fig: person*) plappern; (*baby*) gurgeln. **what's he burbling (on) about?** (*inf*) worüber quasselt er eigentlich? (*inf*). **2** *n* (*of stream*) Plätschern, Gurgeln *nt*; (*on tape etc*) Gemurmel *nt*.
burbot ['bɜ:bət] *n* Quappe *f*.
burden¹ ['bɜ:dn] **1** *n* (**a**) (*lit*) Last *f*. **it puts too much of a ~ on him/the engine** das überlastet ihn/den Motor; **beast of ~** Lasttier *nt*.
  (**b**) (*fig*) Belastung *f* (*on, to* für). **he has such a ~ of responsibility** er hat eine schwere Last an Verantwortung zu tragen; **the guilt was a constant ~ on his mind** das Gefühl der Schuld belastete ihn sehr; ~ **of taxation** Steuerlast *f*; **the ~ of years/debts** die Last der Jahre/die Schuldenlast; **I don't want to be a ~ on you** ich möchte Ihnen nicht zur Last fallen; **the ~ of proof lies with him** er muß den Beweis dafür erbringen *or* liefern; (*Jur*) er trägt die Beweislast.
  (**c**) (*Naut*) Tragfähigkeit, Tragkraft *f*.
  2 *vt* belasten.
burden² *n* (**a**) (*of song*) Refrain, Kehrreim *m*. (**b**) (*of speech, essay etc*) Grundgedanke *m*.
burdensome ['bɜ:dnsəm] *adj load* schwer; *condition* lästig; *task* mühsam, beschwerlich. **she finds the children ~** sie empfindet die Kinder als eine Belastung; **to be ~** eine Belastung darstellen.
burdock ['bɜ:dɒk] *n* Klette *f*.
bureau [bjʊə'rəʊ] *n* (**a**) (*Brit: desk*) Sekretär *m*. (**b**) (*US: chest of drawers*) Kommode *f*. (**c**) (*office*) Büro *nt*. (**d**) (*government department*) Amt *nt*, Behörde *f*. **federal ~** Bundesamt *nt*.
bureaucracy [bjʊə'rɒkrəsɪ] *n* Bürokratie *f*.
bureaucrat ['bjʊərəʊkræt] *n* Bürokrat *m*.
bureaucratic *adj*, ~**ally** *adv* [,bjʊərəʊ'krætɪk, -əlɪ] bürokratisch.
burgeon ['bɜ:dʒən] *vi* (*liter: also* ~ **forth**) (*flower*) knospen (*liter*); (*plant*) sprießen (*liter*); (*fig*) hervorsprießen (*geh*). **when young love first ~s** wenn die junge Liebe erblüht (*liter*).
burger ['bɜ:gə^r] *n* (*esp US inf*) Hamburger *m*.
burgess ['bɜ:dʒɪs] *n* (**a**) (*freier*) Bürger, (*freie*) Bürgerin. (**b**) (*Hist*) Abgeordnete(r) *mf*. (**c**) (*US*) *Abgeordneter m der Volksvertretung der Kolonien Maryland oder Virginia*.
burgh ['bʌrə] *n* (*Scot*) freie Stadt.
burgher ['bɜ:gə^r] *n* (*old*) Bürger(in *f*) *m*.
burglar ['bɜ:glə^r] *n* Einbrecher(in *f*) *m*. ~ **alarm** Alarmanlage *f*.
burglarize ['bɜ:gləraɪz] *vt* (*US*) einbrechen in (+*acc*). **the place/he was ~d** in dem Gebäude/bei ihm wurde eingebrochen.
burglarproof ['bɜ:gləpru:f] *adj* einbruchsicher.
burglary ['bɜ:glərɪ] *n* Einbruch *m*; (*offence*) (Einbruchs)diebstahl *m*.
burgle ['bɜ:gl] *vt* einbrechen in (+*acc*). **the place/he was ~d** in dem Gebäude/bei ihm wurde eingebrochen.
Burgundian [bɜ:'gʌndɪən] **1** *adj* burgundisch. **2** *n* Burgunder(in *f*) *m*.
Burgundy ['bɜ:gəndɪ] *n* (**a**) (*Geog*) Burgund *nt*. (**b**) (*wine*) Burgunder *m*.
burial ['berɪəl] *n* Beerdigung, Bestattung *f*; (~ *ceremony also*) Begräbnis *nt*; (*in cemetery also*) Beisetzung *f* (*form*). **Christian ~** christliches Begräbnis; ~ **at sea** Bestattung *f* zur See.
burial: ~ **ground** *n* Begräbnisstätte *f*; ~ **mound** *n* Grabhügel *m*; ~ **place** *n* Grabstätte *f*; ~ **service** *n* Trauerfeier *f*.
burin ['bjʊərɪn] *n* (*Art*) Stichel *m*.
burlap ['bɜ:læp] *n* Sackleinen *nt*.
burlesque [bɜ:'lesk] **1** *n* (**a**) (*parody*) Parodie *f*; (*Theat*) Burleske *f*; (*Liter*) Persiflage *f*.
  (**b**) (*US Theat*) Varieté *nt*; (*show*) Varietévorstellung *f*.

(**a**) *see n* parodistisch; burlesk; persiflierend.
  (**b**) (*US Theat*) *comedian, actor* Varieté-. ~ **show** Varietévorstellung *f*.
3 *vt* parodieren; *book, author, style* persiflieren.
burly ['bɜ:lɪ] *adj* (+*er*) kräftig, stramm.
Burma ['bɜ:mə] *n* Birma, Burma *nt*.
Burmese [bɜ:'mi:z] **1** *adj* birmanisch, burmesisch. **2** *n* (**a**) Birmane, Burmese *m*, Birmanin, Burmesin *f*. (**b**) (*language*) Birmanisch, Burmesisch *nt*.
burn¹ [bɜ:n] *n* (*Scot*) Bach *m*.
burn² (*vb: pret, ptp* ~**ed** *or* ~**t**) **1** *n* (**a**) (*on skin*) Brandwunde *f*; (*on material*) verbrannte Stelle, Brandfleck *m*. **severe ~s** schwere Verbrennungen *pl*; **second degree ~s** Verbrennungen zweiten Grades; **cigarette ~** Brandfleck *m or* (*hole*) Brandloch *nt or* (*on skin*) Brandwunde *f* von einer Zigarette.
  (**b**) (*Space: of rocket*) Zündung *f*.
  2 *vt* (**a**) verbrennen; *incense* abbrennen; *village, building* niederbrennen. **he ~t me with his cigarette** er hat mich mit der Zigarette gebrannt; **to ~ oneself** sich verbrennen; **to be ~t to death** (*at stake*) verbrannt werden; (*in accident*) verbrennen; **to be ~t alive** bei lebendigem Leibe verbrannt werden *or* (*in accident*) verbrennen; **to ~ a hole in sth** ein Loch in etw (*acc*) brennen; **to ~ one's fingers** (*lit, fig*) sich (*dat*) die Finger verbrennen; **he's got money to ~** (*fig*) er hat Geld wie Heu; **to ~ one's boats** *or* **bridges** (*fig*) alle Brücken hinter sich (*dat*) abbrechen; **to ~ the midnight oil** (*fig*) bis tief in die Nacht arbeiten.
  (**b**) *meat, sauce, toast, cakes* verbrennen lassen; (*slightly*) anbrennen lassen; (*sun*) *person, skin* verbrennen.
  (**c**) (*acid*) ätzen. **the curry ~t his throat/lips** das Currygericht brannte ihm im Hals/auf den Lippen.
  (**d**) (*use as fuel: ship etc*) befeuert werden mit; (*use up*) *petrol, electricity* verbrauchen.
  3 *vi* (**a**) (*wood, fire etc*) brennen. **you will ~ in hell** du wirst in der Hölle schmoren; **to ~ to death** verbrennen; *see* **~¹**.
  (**b**) (*meat, pastry etc*) verbrennen; (*slightly*) anbrennen. **she/her skin ~s easily** sie bekommt leicht einen Sonnenbrand.
  (**c**) (*ointment, curry, sun*) brennen; (*acid*) ätzen. **the acid ~ed into the metal** die Säure fraß sich ins Metall.
  (**d**) (*feel hot: wound, eyes, skin*) brennen. **his face was ~ing** (*with heat/shame*) sein Gesicht glühte *or* war rot (vor Hitze/Scham); **it's so hot, I'm ~ing** es ist so heiß, ich komm bald um vor Hitze.
  (**e**) **to be ~ing to do sth** darauf brennen, etw zu tun; **he was ~ing to get his revenge** er brannte auf Rache; **he was ~ing with anger/passion** er war wutentbrannt/er glühte in Leidenschaft (*geh*); **to ~ (with love/desire) for sb** (*liter*) vor glühender Liebe/glühendem Verlangen nach jdm verzehrt werden (*liter*).
  (**f**) (*Space: rockets*) zünden.
♦ **burn away 1** *vi* (**a**) (*go on burning*) vor sich hin brennen. (**b**) (*wick, candle, oil*) herunterbrennen; (*part of roof etc*) abbrennen. **2** *vt sep* abbrennen; (*Med*) wegbrennen.
♦ **burn down 1** *vi* (**a**) (*house etc*) ab- *or* niederbrennen. (**b**) (*fire, candle, wick*) herunterbrennen. **2** *vt sep* ab- *or* niederbrennen.
♦ **burn off** *vt sep paint etc* abbrennen.
♦ **burn out 1** *vi* (*fire, candle*) ausbrennen, ausgehen; (*fuse, dynamo etc*) durchbrennen; (*rocket*) den Treibstoff verbraucht haben.
  2 *vr* (**a**) (*candle, lamp*) herunterbrennen; (*fire*) ab- *or* ausbrennen.
  (**b**) (*fig inf*) **to ~ oneself ~** sich kaputtmachen (*inf*), sich völlig verausgaben; **by the thirteenth round he had ~t himself ~** in der dreizehnten Runde war er kaputt (*inf*) *or* erledigt.
  3 *vt sep a enemy troops etc* ausräuchern. **they were ~t ~ of house and home** ihr Haus und Hof war abgebrannt.
  (**b**) *usu pass* ~**t ~** *lorries/houses* ausgebrannte Lastwagen/Häuser; **he/his talent is ~t ~** (*inf*) mit ihm/seinem Talent ist's vorbei (*inf*), er hat sich völlig verausgabt; **he looked ~t ~** (*inf*) er sah völlig kaputt (*inf*) *or* verbraucht aus.
♦ **burn up 1** *vi* (**a**) (*fire etc*) auflodern.
  (**b**) (*rocket etc in atmosphere*) verglühen.
  (**c**) +*prep obj* (*Brit sl*) **to ~ ~ the road** die Straße entlangbrausen (*inf*).
  2 *vt sep* (**a**) *rubbish* verbrennen; *fuel, energy* verbrauchen; *excess fat also* abbauen.
  (**b**) **he was ~ed ~ with envy** er verzehrte sich vor Neid (*geh*).
  (**c**) (*US inf: make angry*) zur Weißglut bringen (*inf*).
burner ['bɜ:nə^r] *n* (*of gas cooker, lamp*) Brenner *m*.
burning ['bɜ:nɪŋ] **1** *adj* (**a**) *candle, town* brennend; *coals also*, (*fig*) *face* glühend. **I still have this ~ sensation in my mouth/on my skin** mein Mund/meine Haut brennt immer noch; **the ~ bush** (*Bibl*) der brennende Dornbusch. (**b**) (*fig*) *thirst* brennend; *desire also, fever, hate, passion* glühend; *question, topic* brennend. **2** *n* **there is a smell of ~, I can smell ~** es riecht verbrannt *or* (*Cook also*) angebrannt.
burning glass *n* Brennglas *nt*.
burnish ['bɜ:nɪʃ] *vt metal* polieren.
burnt [bɜ:nt] *adj* verbrannt. ~ **offering** (*Rel*) Brandopfer *nt*; (*hum: food*) angebranntes Essen; **there's a ~ smell** es riecht verbrannt *or* brenzlig *or* (*Cook also*) angebrannt; **the coffee has a slightly ~ taste** der Kaffee schmeckt wie frisch geröstet.
burn-up ['bɜ:nʌp] *n* (*Brit inf*) Rennfahrt *f* (*inf*). **to go for a ~** ein Rennfährtchen machen (*inf*); **to have a ~** volle Pulle fahren (*inf*), voll aufdrehen (*inf*).
burp [bɜ:p] **1** *vi* rülpsen (*inf*); (*baby*) aufstoßen. **2** *vt baby* aufstoßen lassen. **3** *n* Rülpser *m* (*inf*).
burp gun *n* (*inf*) MG *nt* (*inf*).
burr¹ [bɜ:^r] *n see* **bur**.
burr² *n* (*Ling*) breiige Aussprache (*von R*). **to speak with a ~** breiig sprechen.

burrow ['bʌrəʊ] **1** *n* (*of rabbit etc*) Bau *m*.
2 *vi* (*rabbits, dogs etc*) graben, buddeln (*inf*); (*make a ~*) einen Bau graben. **they had ~ed under the fence** sie hatten sich (*dat*) ein Loch *or* (*below ground*) einen Gang unterm Zaun gegraben *or* gebuddelt (*inf*).
3 *vt* *hole* graben, buddeln (*inf*). **to ~ one's way underground** sich (*dat*) einen unterirdischen Gang graben *or* buddeln (*inf*).
bursar ['bɜːsə^r] *n* Schatzmeister, Finanzverwalter *m*.
bursary ['bɜːsərɪ] *n* (a) (*grant*) Stipendium *nt*. (b) (*office*) Schatzamt *nt*; (*Univ*) Quästur *f*.
burst [bɜːst] (*vb: pret, ptp ~*) **1** *n* (a) (*of shell etc*) Explosion *f*.
(b) (*in pipe etc*) Bruch *m*.
(c) (*of anger, enthusiasm, activity etc*) Ausbruch, Anfall *m*; (*of flames*) (plötzliches) Auflodern, Hochschießen *nt*. *~ of* **laughter** Lachsalve *f*; *~ of* **eloquence** Wortschwall *m*; *~ of* **applause** Beifallssturm *m*; *~ of* **speed** Spurt *m*; (*of cars etc*) Riesenbeschleunigung *f* (*inf*); **a ~ of automatic gunfire** eine Maschinengewehrsalve; **give them another ~** verpaß ihnen noch eine Salve.
2 *vi* (a) platzen. **to ~ open** (*box, door etc*) aufspringen; (*buds, wound*) aufbrechen; (*abscess, wound*) aufplatzen.
(b) (*be full to overflowing: sack etc*) **to fill sth to ~ing point** etw bis zum Platzen *or* Bersten füllen; **to be full to ~ing** zum Platzen *or* Bersten voll; **to be ~ing with health** vor Gesundheit strotzen; **to be ~ing with a desire to do sth** vor Begierde brennen, etw zu tun; **to be ~ing with pride** vor Stolz platzen; **if I eat any more, I'll ~** (*inf*) wenn ich noch mehr esse, platze ich (*inf*); **he was ~ing to tell us** (*inf*) er brannte darauf, uns das zu sagen; *see* **seam**.
(c) (*start, go suddenly*) **to ~ into tears/flames** in Tränen ausbrechen/in Flammen aufgehen; **he ~ past me/into the room** er schoß an mir vorbei/er platzte ins Zimmer; **we ~ through the enemy lines** wir durchbrachen die feindlichen Linien; **the sun ~ through the clouds** die Sonne brach durch die Wolken; **sunlight ~ into the room** Sonnenlicht fiel plötzlich ins Zimmer; **the oil ~ from the well** das Öl brach aus dem Brunnen; **to ~ into view** plötzlich in Sicht kommen; **to ~ into a gallop/into song/into bloom** losgaloppieren/lossingen/plötzlich aufblühen.
3 *vt* *balloon, bubble, tyre* zum Platzen bringen, platzen lassen; (*person*) kaputt machen (*inf*); *boiler, pipe, dyke* sprengen. **the river has ~ its banks** der Fluß ist über die Ufer getreten; **to ~ one's sides with laughter** vor Lachen platzen; *see* **blood vessel**.
♦**burst forth** *vi* (*liter*) (*blood, sun*) hervorbrechen; (*blossoms*) ausbrechen.
♦**burst in** *vi* hinein-/hereinstürzen; (*on conversation*) dazwischenplatzen (*on bei*). **he ~ ~ on us** er platzte bei uns herein.
♦**burst out** *vi* (a) (*emotions*) hervorbrechen, herausbrechen; (*lava*) ausbrechen. **she's ~ing ~ of that dress** sie sprengt das Kleid fast.
(b) **to ~ ~ of a room** aus einem Zimmer stürzen *or* stürmen.
(c) (*in speech*) losplatzen. **he ~ ~ in a violent speech** er zog plötzlich vom Leder.
(d) **to ~ ~ laughing/crying** in Gelächter/Tränen ausbrechen, loslachen/losheulen.
burthen ['bɜːðən] *n*, *vt* (*old, liter*) *see* **burden**[1].
burton ['bɜːtn] *n* (*Brit sl*) **to have gone for a ~** im Eimer sein (*sl*), futsch sein (*sl*).
bury ['berɪ] *vt* (a) *person, animal, possessions, differences* begraben; (*with ceremony also*) beerdigen, bestatten (*geh*); (*hide in earth*) *treasure, bones* vergraben; (*put in earth*) *end of post, roots* eingraben. **where is he buried?** wo liegt *or* ist er begraben?; (*in cemetery also*) wo liegt er?; **to ~ sb at sea** jdn auf See bestatten (*geh*), jdm ein Seemannsgrab geben; **he is dead and buried** er ist schon lange tot; **that's all dead and buried** (*fig*) das ist schon lange passé (*inf*); **she has buried three husbands** (*fig*) sie hat schon drei Männer begraben (*inf*); **buried by an avalanche** von einer Lawine verschüttet *or* begraben; **to ~ one's head in the sand** (*fig*) den Kopf in den Sand stecken.
(b) (*conceal*) *one's face* verbergen. **to ~ one's face in one's hands** das Gesicht in den Händen vergraben; **to ~ oneself under the blankets/(away) in the country** sich unter den Dekken/auf dem Land vergraben; **a village buried in the heart of the country** ein im Landesinnern versteckt gelegenes Dorf.
(c) (*put, plunge*) *hands, fingers* vergraben (*in* in +*dat*); *claws, teeth* schlagen (*in* in +*acc*); *dagger* stoßen (*in* in +*acc*).
(d) (*engross: usu in ptp*) **to ~ oneself in one's books** sich in seine Bücher vergraben; **buried in thought/in one's work** gedankenversunken, in Gedanken/in seine Arbeit versunken.
bus [bʌs] **1** *n*, *pl* **-es** *or* (*US*) **-ses** (a) Bus *m*. **by ~** mit dem Bus; *see* **miss**[1]. (b) (*inf: car, plane*) Kiste *f*. **2** *vi* (*inf*) mit dem Bus fahren. **3** *vt* (*esp US*) mit dem Bus befördern *or* fahren.
busboy ['bʌsbɔɪ] *n* (*US*) Bedienungshilfe *f*.
busby ['bʌzbɪ] *n* hohe Pelzmütze.
bus: *~* **conductor** *n* (*Omni*)busschaffner *m*; *~* **conductress** *n* (*Omni*)busschaffnerin *f*; *~* **depot** *n* (*Omni*)busdepot *nt*; *~* **driver** *n* (*Omni*)busfahrer (*in f*) *m*; *~* **garage** *n* (*Omni*)bushalle *f*.
bush[1] [buʃ] *n* (a) (*shrub*) Busch, Strauch *m*; (*thicket: also ~es*) Gebüsch *nt*. **to beat about the ~** (*fig*) wie die Katze um den heißen Brei herumschleichen.
(b) (*in Africa, Australia*) Busch *m*; (*Austral: the country*) freies *or* offenes Land.
(c) (*fig*) *~* **of hair** Haarschopf *m*; *~* **of a beard** buschiger Bart.
♦**bush out** *vi* (*hair, tail*) buschig sein.
bush[2] *n* (*Tech*) Buchse *f*.
bushbaby ['buʃ,beɪbɪ] *n* Buschbaby *nt*.
bushed [buʃt] *adj* (*sl: exhausted*) groggy (*sl*).
bushel ['buʃl] *n* Scheffel *m*. **to hide one's light under a ~** (*prov*) sein Licht unter den Scheffel stellen (*prov*).

bush fire *n* Buschfeuer *nt*.
bushiness ['buʃɪnɪs] *n* Buschigkeit *f*.
bushing ['buʃɪŋ] *n* (*US*) *see* **bush**[2].
bush: *~* **league** *n* (*US*) Provinzliga *f*; *~* **leaguer** *n* (*US*) Provinzspieler *m*; (*fig*) Dilettant *m*; *~* **man** *n* (*Austral*) jd, der im Busch lebt und arbeitet; B*~*man *n* (*S Africa*) Buschmann *m*; *~* **ranger** *n* (a) (*Austral*) Bandit, Strauchdieb (*dated*) *m*; (b) (*US, Canada*) jd, der in der Wildnis lebt; *~* **telegraph** *n* (*inf*) Urwaldtelephon *nt*; **I heard it on the ~ telegraph** (*fig inf*) ich habe da so was läuten gehört (*inf*), das ist mir zu Ohren gekommen; *~***whack 1** *vi* in den Wäldern hausen; **2** *vt* (*ambush*) aus dem Hinterhalt überfallen; *~***whacker** *n* (*frontiersman*) jd, der in den Wäldern haust; (*bandit*) Bandit *m*; (*guerilla*) Guerilla(kämpfer) *m*.
bushy ['buʃɪ] *adj* (+*er*) buschig.
busily ['bɪzɪlɪ] *adv* (*actively, eagerly*) eifrig.
business ['bɪznɪs] *n* (a) *no pl* (*commerce*) Geschäft *nt*; (*line of ~*) Branche *f*. **to be in ~** Geschäftsmann sein; **I am in ~ with him** ich habe geschäftlich mit ihm zu tun; **to go into ~** Geschäftsmann werden; **to go into ~ with sb** mit jdm ein Geschäft gründen; **to be in the plastics/insurance ~** mit Plastik/Versicherungen zu tun haben, in der Plastikbranche/im Versicherungsgewerbe sein; **to set up in ~** ein Geschäft gründen; **to set up in ~ as a butcher/lawyer** *etc* sich als Fleischer/Rechtsanwalt *etc* niederlassen; **to go out of ~** zumachen; **to do ~ with sb** Geschäfte *pl* mit jdm machen; *~* **is ~** Geschäft ist Geschäft; **how's ~?** wie gehen die Geschäfte?; **to look for ~** sich nach Aufträgen umsehen; **I must be about my ~** (*form*) ich muß (jetzt) meinen Geschäften nachgehen; **to go to Paris on ~** geschäftlich nach Paris fahren; **he is here/away on ~** er ist geschäftlich hier/unterwegs; **to know one's ~** seine Sache verstehen; **to get down to ~** zur Sache kommen; **to combine ~ with pleasure** das Angenehme mit dem Nützlichen verbinden.
(b) (*fig inf*) **now we're in ~** jetzt kann's losgehen (*inf*); **to mean ~** es ernst meinen.
(c) (*commercial enterprise*) Geschäft *nt*, Betrieb *m*.
(d) (*concern*) Sache, Angelegenheit *f*; (*task, duty also*) Aufgabe *f*. **that's my ~ and none of yours** das ist meine Sache *or* Angelegenheit, das geht dich gar nichts an (*inf*); **that's no ~ of mine/yours, that's none of my/your ~** das geht mich/dich nichts an; **to make it one's ~ to do sth** es sich (*dat*) zur Aufgabe machen, etw zu tun; **you should make it your ~ to see that all the products ...** Sie sollten sich darum kümmern, daß alle Produkte ...; **you've no ~ doing that** du hast kein Recht, das zu tun; **to send sb about his ~** jdn in seine Schranken weisen; *see* **mind**.
(e) (*difficult job*) Problem *nt*.
(f) (*inf: affair*) Sache *f*. **I am tired of this protest ~** ich hab' genug von dieser Protestiererei (*inf*); *see* **funny**.
(g) (*Theat*) dargestellte Handlung.
(h) (*inf: defecation: of dog, child*) Geschäft *nt* (*inf*). **to do one's ~** sein Geschäft machen *or* verrichten (*inf*).
business: *~* **address** *n* Geschäftsadresse *f*; *~* **college** *n* Wirtschaftshochschule *f*; *~* **end** *n* (*inf*) (*of knife, chisel etc*) scharfes Ende; (*of rifle etc*) Lauf *m*; *~* **expenses** *npl* Geschäftsspesen *pl*; *~* **hours** *npl* Geschäftsstunden *pl*, Geschäftszeit *f*.
businesslike ['bɪznɪslaɪk] *adj* *person, firm* (*good at doing business*) geschäftstüchtig; *person, manner* geschäftsmäßig; *manner, transaction* geschäftlich; (*efficient*) *person, prose* kühl und sachlich, nüchtern.
business: *~***man** *n* Geschäftsmann *m*; *~* **sense** *n* Geschäftssinn *m*; *~* **studies** *npl* Wirtschaftslehre *f*; *~* **suit** *n* Straßenanzug *m*; *~* **trip** *n* Geschäftsreise *f*; *~***woman** *n* Geschäftsfrau *f*.
busing *n* *see* **bussing**.
busk [bʌsk] *vi* als Straßenmusikant vor Kinos und Theatern spielen.
busker ['bʌskə^r] *n* Straßenmusikant *m*.
bus: *~***load** *n* **a ~load of children** eine Busladung Kinder; **by the ~load** (*inf*), **in ~loads** (*inf*) busweise (*inf*); *~***man** *n*: **a ~man's holiday** (*fig*) praktisch eine Fortsetzung der Arbeit im Urlaub; *~* **service** *n* Busverbindung *f*; (*network*) Busverbindungen *pl*; *~* **shelter** *n* Wartehäuschen *nt*.
bussing ['bʌsɪŋ] *n* (*esp US*) Busbeförderung *f* von Schulkindern in andere Bezirke, um Rassentrennung zu verhindern.
bus: *~* **station** *n* Busbahnhof *m*; *~* **stop** *n* Bushaltestelle *f*.
bust[1] [bʌst] *n* Büste *f*; (*Anat also*) Busen *m*. *~* **measurement** Brustumfang *m*, Oberweite *f*.
bust[2] (*vb: pret, ptp ~*) (*inf*) **1** *adj* (a) (*broken*) kaputt (*inf*).
(b) (*bankrupt*) pleite (*inf*).
2 *adv* (*bankrupt*) **to go ~** pleite gehen *or* machen (*inf*).
3 *n* (*US: bankruptcy*) Pleite *f* (*inf*).
4 *vt* (a) (*break*) kaputtmachen (*inf*). **the case ~ its sides** der Koffer ist an den Seiten kaputtgegangen (*inf*); **they ~ed their way in** sie haben sich die Tür/das Fenster eingeschlagen; (*to a meeting*) sie haben sich hineingedrängt; **to ~ sth open** etw aufbrechen; **to ~ a gut** (*sl*) *or* **one's arse** (*vulg*) machen (*inf*); **he just about ~ a gut** (*sl*) *or* **his arse** (*vulg*) **doing it** er hat sich (*dat*) dabei fast einen abgebrochen (*sl*).
(b) (*US: catch, convict*) hinter Schloß und Riegel bringen; *drugs, ring, syndicate* auffliegen lassen (*inf*).
(c) (*US Mil: demote*) degradieren (*to* zu).
5 *vi* (*break*) kaputtgehen (*inf*).
♦**bust out** *vi* **1** ausbrechen. **2** *vt sep* herausholen (*inf*).
♦**bust up** *vt sep* (*inf*) *box, marriage* kaputtmachen (*inf*); *meeting* auffliegen lassen (*inf*); (*by starting fights*) stören. **I hate to ~ ~ the party** tut mir leid, daß ich die traute Runde stören muß.
bustard ['bʌstəd] *n* Trappe *f*.
buster ['bʌstə^r] *n* (*esp US inf: as address*) Meister *m* (*inf*); (*threatening*) Freundchen *nt* (*inf*).
bus ticket *n* Busfahrschein *m*.

bustle¹ ['bʌsl] **1** n Betrieb m (of in +dat); (of fair, streets also) geschäftiges or reges Treiben (of auf or in +dat).

2 vi to ~ about geschäftig hin und her eilen or sausen (inf); to ~ in/out geschäftig hinein-/herein-/hinaus-/herauseilen or -sausen (inf); **the marketplace was ~ing with activity** auf dem Markt herrschte großer Betrieb or ein reges Treiben.

bustle² n (Fashion) Turnüre f.

bustling ['bʌslɪŋ] adj person geschäftig; place, scene belebt, voller Leben.

bust-up ['bʌstʌp] n (inf) Krach m (inf). **they had a ~** sie haben Krach gehabt (inf); (split up) sie haben sich verkracht (inf).

busty ['bʌstɪ] adj (+er) (inf) woman vollbusig.

busy ['bɪzɪ] **1** adj (+er) **(a)** (occupied) person beschäftigt. **a very ~ man** ein vielbeschäftigter Mann; **are you ~?** haben Sie gerade Zeit?; (in business) haben Sie viel zu tun?; **not now, I'm ~** jetzt nicht, ich bin gerade beschäftigt; **the boss is always ~** der Chef hat immer viel zu tun; (never available) der Chef hat nie Zeit; **I'll come back when you're less ~** ich komme wieder, wenn Sie mehr Zeit haben; **to keep sb/oneself ~** jdn/sich selbst beschäftigen; **I was ~ studying when you called/all evening** ich war gerade beim Lernen, als Sie kamen/ich war den ganzen Abend mit Lernen beschäftigt; **she's always too ~ thinking about herself** sie ist immer zu sehr mit sich selbst beschäftigt; **they were ~ plotting against him** sie haben eifrig Pläne gegen ihn geschmiedet; **let's get ~** an die Arbeit!

(b) (active) life, time bewegt; place, street, town belebt; (with traffic) verkehrsreich; street (with traffic) stark befahren. **it's been a ~ day/week** heute oder diese Woche war viel los; **have you had a ~ day, dear?** hast du heute viel zu tun gehabt?; **he leads a very ~ life** bei ihm ist immer etwas los; **the shop was ~ all day** im Geschäft war den ganzen Tag viel los.

(c) (esp US) telephone line besetzt.

(d) (officious) person, manner (über)eifrig.

(e) pattern, design, print unruhig.

2 vr to ~ oneself doing sth sich damit beschäftigen, etw zu tun; to ~ oneself with sth sich mit etw beschäftigen.

busybody ['bɪzɪbɒdɪ] n Mitmensch, der sich in alles einmischt, Gschaftlhuber m (S Ger). **don't be such a ~** misch dich nicht überall ein.

but [bʌt] **1** conj **(a)** aber. **~ you must know that ...** Sie müssen aber wissen, daß ...; aber Sie müssen wissen, daß ...; **~ he didn't know that aber er hat das nicht gewußt**, er hat das aber nicht gewußt; **~ he didn't know that aber er hat das nicht gewußt**; **they all went ~ I didn't** sie sind alle gegangen, nur ich nicht.

(b) not X ~ Y nicht X sondern Y.

(c) (subordinating) ohne daß. **never a week passes ~ she is ill** keine Woche vergeht, ohne daß sie krank ist; **I would have helped ~ that I was ill** (old, liter) ich hätte geholfen, wäre ich nicht krank gewesen (old).

(d) ~ then he couldn't have known that aber er hat das ja gar nicht wissen können; ~ then you must be my brother! dann müssen Sie ja mein Bruder sein!; ~ then do you mean to say ... wollen Sie dann etwa sagen ...; ~ then since he wasn't here aber da er ja nicht hier war; ~ then it is well paid aber dafür wird es gut bezahlt.

2 adv she's ~ a child sie ist doch noch ein Kind; I cannot (help) ~ think that ... ich kann nicht umhin, zu denken, daß ...; one cannot ~ admire him/suspect that ... man kann ihn nur bewundern/nur annehmen, daß ...; you can ~ try du kannst es immerhin versuchen; I had no alternative ~ to leave mir blieb keine andere Wahl, als zu gehen; she left ~ a few minutes ago sie ist erst vor ein paar Minuten gegangen.

3 prep no one ~ me could do it niemand außer mir or nur ich konnte es tun; who ~ Fred would ...? wer außer Fred würde ...?; anything ~ that! (alles,) nur das nicht!; it was anything ~ simple das war alles andere als einfach; he/it was nothing ~ trouble er/das hat nichts als or nur Schwierigkeiten gemacht; the last house ~ one/two/three das vorletzte/vorvorletzte/drittletzte Haus; the first ~ one der/die/das zweite; the next street ~ one/two/three die übernächste/überübernächste Straße/vier Straßen weiter; ~ for you I would be dead ohne Sie wäre ich tot, wenn Sie nicht gewesen wären, wäre ich tot.

4 n no ~s about it kein Aber nt.

but and ben n (Scot) Hütte f bestehend aus Küche und kleiner Schlafkammer.

butane ['bju:teɪn] n Butan nt.

butch [butʃ] adj (inf) clothes, hairstyle, manner maskulin.

butcher ['butʃə'] **1** n **(a)** Fleischer, Metzger (dial), Schlachter (N Ger) m. ~'s (shop) Fleischerei, Metzgerei (dial), Schlachterei (N Ger) f; **at the ~'s** beim Fleischer etc; ~'s boy Fleischerjunge etc m; ~'s wife Fleischersfrau etc f.

(b) (fig: murderer) Schlächter m.

(c) ~'s (Brit sl: look) give us a ~ laß mal gucken (inf); take or have a ~ (at that) guck mal (das an) (inf); do you want a ~? willst du mal gucken? (inf).

2 vt animals schlachten; people abschlachten, niedermetzeln; (fig) play, piece of music, language vergewaltigen. his ~ed body seine schrecklich zugerichtete Leiche.

butchery ['butʃərɪ] n (slaughter) Gemetzel nt, Metzelei f. the ~ of millions das Abschlachten or Niedermetzeln von Millionen; stop the fight, this is ~! brechen Sie den Kampf ab, das ist ja das reinste Gemetzel!

butler ['bʌtlə'] n Butler m.

butt¹ [bʌt] n (for wine) großes Faß; (for rainwater) Tonne f.

butt² n (also ~ end) dickes Ende; (of rifle) (Gewehr)kolben m; (of cigar, cigarette) Stummel m. the ~ end of the conversation der letzte Rest der Unterhaltung.

butt³ n (US sl: cigarette) Kippe f (inf).

butt⁴ n (a) (target) Schießscheibe f.

(b) usu pl (on shooting range) (behind targets) Kugelfang m; (in front of targets) Schutzwall m; (range itself) Schießstand m.

(c) (fig: person) Zielscheibe f. she's always the ~ of his jokes sie ist immer (die) Zielscheibe seines Spottes.

butt⁵ **1** n (Kopf)stoß m. to give sb a ~ see vt. **2** vt mit dem Kopf stoßen; (goat also) mit den Hörnern stoßen.

♦ butt at vi +prep obj (goat) mit den Hörnern stoßen gegen.

♦ butt in vi sich einmischen (on in +acc), dazwischenfunken or -platzen (inf).

♦ butt into vi +prep obj sich einmischen in (+acc), dazwischenfunken or dazwischenplatzen bei (inf).

butt⁶ n (US sl: backside) Arsch m (sl). get up off your ~ setz mal deinen Arsch in Bewegung (sl).

butter ['bʌtə'] **1** n Butter f. she looks as if ~ wouldn't melt in her mouth sie sieht aus, als ob sie kein Wässerchen trüben könnte.

2 vt bread etc mit Butter bestreichen, buttern.

♦ butter up vt sep jdm schöntun (+dat), um den Bart gehen (+dat) (inf).

butter: ~ **bean** n Mondbohne f; ~**cup** n Butterblume f, Hahnenfuß m; ~**dish** n Butterdose f; ~**-fingers** n sing (inf) Schussel m (inf); **I've got butter-fingers!** du Schussel! (inf).

butterfly ['bʌtəflaɪ] n **(a)** Schmetterling m. I've got/I get butterflies (in my stomach) mir ist/wird ganz flau im Magen (inf), mir ist/wird ganz mulmig zumute (inf).

(b) (Swimming) Delphinschwimmen nt, Schmetterlingsstil, Butterfly m. can you do the ~? können Sie delphinschwimmen or Butterfly or den Schmetterlingsstil?

butterfly: ~ **kiss** n Schmetterlingskuß m; ~ **net** n Schmetterlingsnetz nt; ~ **nut** n Flügelmutter f; ~ **stroke** n Delphinstil, Schmetterlingsstil, Butterfly m; I can do the ~ stroke ich kann delphinschwimmen.

butter: ~ **icing** n ≈ Buttercreme f; ~ **knife** n Buttermesser nt; ~**milk** n Buttermilch f; ~ **scotch** n ≈ Karamellbonbon m.

buttery ['bʌtərɪ] n Vorratskammer f; (Univ) Cafeteria f.

buttock ['bʌtək] n (Hinter)backe, Gesäßhälfte (form) f. ~s pl Gesäß nt, Hintern m (inf).

button ['bʌtn] **1** n **(a)** Knopf m. not worth a ~ (inf) keinen Pfifferling wert (inf); **his answer was/he arrived right on the ~** (inf) seine Antwort hat voll ins Schwarze getroffen (inf)/er kam auf den Glockenschlag (inf).

(b) (mushroom) junger Champignon.

(c) ~s sing (inf: pageboy) (Hotel)page m.

2 vt garment zuknöpfen. ~ your lip (inf) halt den Mund (inf).

3 vi (garment) geknöpft werden.

♦ button up vt sep zuknöpfen. to have a deal all ~ed ein Geschäft unter Dach und Fach haben.

button: ~**-down** adj collar mit angeknöpften Enden; ~**hole 1** n **(a)** (in garment) Knopfloch nt; ~**hole stitch** Knopflochstich nt.

(b) (flower) Blume f im Knopfloch; to sell ~holes Blumen fürs Knopfloch verkaufen; **2** vt (fig) zu fassen bekommen, sich (dat) schnappen (inf); ~**hook** n (for boots) Stiefelknöpfer m; ~ **mushroom** n junger Champignon.

buttress ['bʌtrɪs] **1** n (Archit) Strebepfeiler m; (fig) Pfeiler m. **2** vt (Archit) wall (durch Strebepfeiler) stützen; (fig) stützen.

butty ['bʌtɪ] n (N Engl inf) Stulle f (dial).

buxom ['bʌksəm] adj drall.

buy [baɪ] (vb: pret, ptp bought) **1** vt **(a)** kaufen; (Rail) ticket also lösen. there are some things that money can't ~ es gibt Dinge, die man nicht kaufen kann; **all that money can ~** alles, was man mit Geld kaufen kann; **to ~ and sell goods** Waren an- und verkaufen.

(b) (fig) victory, fame sich (dat) erkaufen; time gewinnen. the victory was dearly bought der Sieg war teuer erkauft.

(c) to ~ sth (inf: accept) etw akzeptieren; (believe) jdm etw abnehmen (inf) or abkaufen (inf). I'll ~ that das ist o.k. (inf); (believe) ja, das glaube ich.

(d) (sl: be killed) he bought it den hat's erwischt (sl).

2 vi kaufen.

3 n (inf) Kauf m. to be a good ~ ein guter Kauf sein; (clothes also, food) preiswert sein.

♦ buy back vt sep zurückkaufen.

♦ buy in 1 vt sep (acquire supply of) goods einkaufen. **2** vi +prep obj to ~ to a business sich in ein Geschäft einkaufen.

♦ buy off vt sep (inf: bribe) kaufen (inf).

♦ buy out vt sep shareholders etc auszahlen; firm aufkaufen. **(b)** (from army) los- or freikaufen (of von).

♦ buy over vt sep (get on one's side) für sich gewinnen.

♦ buy up vt sep aufkaufen.

buyer ['baɪə'] n Käufer m; (agent) Einkäufer m. ~'s market Käufermarkt m.

buzz [bʌz] **1** vi **(a)** (insect) summen, brummen; (smaller or agitated insects) schwirren; (device) summen. did you ~, sir? haben Sie nach mir verlangt?; Miss Jones, I've been ~ing for 10 minutes Fräulein Jones, ich versuche schon seit 10 Minuten, Sie zu erreichen.

(b) my ears are ~ing mir dröhnen die Ohren; my head is ~ing mir schwirrt der Kopf; (from noise) mir dröhnt der Kopf.

(c) the town is ~ing in der Stadt ist was los or herrscht reges Leben; the city was ~ing with excitement die Stadt war in heller Aufregung; the news set the town ~ing die Nachricht versetzte die Stadt in helle Aufregung.

2 vt **(a)** (call) secretary (mit dem Summer) rufen.

(b) (US inf: telephone) anrufen.

(c) (plane) plane, building nicht vorbeifliegen or vorbeizischen (inf) an (+dat). we were ~ed Flugzeuge flogen dicht an uns heran.

3 n **(a)** see vi **(a)** Summen, Brummen nt; Schwirren nt; Summen nt.

(b) (of conversation) Stimmengewirr, Gemurmel nt. ~ of approval beifälliges Gemurmel.

(c) (inf: telephone call) Anruf m. to give sb a ~ jdn anrufen; (signal) secretary etc jdn (mit dem Summer) rufen.

♦ buzz about or around vi (inf) herumschwirren.

♦**buzz off** *vi* (*Brit inf*) abzischen (*inf*).
buzzard ['bʌzəd] *n* Bussard *m*.
buzz bomb *n* Fernrakete *f*.
buzzer ['bʌzəʳ] *n* Summer *m*.
by [baɪ] **1** *prep* **(a)** (*close to*) bei, an (+*dat*); (*with movement*) an (+*acc*); (*next to*) neben (+*dat*); (*with movement*) neben (+*acc*). ~ **the** window/fire/river/church am *or* beim Fenster/Feuer/Fluß/an *or* bei der Kirche; **a holiday** ~ **the sea** Ferien *pl* an der See; **come and sit** ~ **me** komm, setz dich neben mich; **she sat** ~ **me** sie saß neben mir; **to keep sth** ~ **one** etw bei sich haben.
(b) (*via*) über (+*acc*).
(c) (*past*) **to go/rush** *etc* ~ **sb/sth** an jdm/etw vorbeigehen/-eilen *etc*.
(d) (*time: during*) ~ **day/night** bei Tag/Nacht.
(e) (*time: not later than*) bis. **can you do it** ~ **tomorrow?** kannst du es bis morgen machen?; ~ **tomorrow I'll be in France** morgen werde ich in Frankreich sein; ~ **the time I got there, he had gone** bis ich dorthin kam, war er gegangen; **but** ~ **that time** *or* ~ **then I had understood/it will be too late/he will have forgotten** aber inzwischen hatte ich gemerkt .../aber dann ist es schon zu spät/aber bis dann *or* dahin hat er es schon vergessen; ~ **now** inzwischen.
(f) (*indicating amount*) ~ **the** metre/kilo/hour/month meter-/kilo-/stunden-/monatsweise; **one** ~ **one** einer nach dem anderen; **they came in two** ~ **two** sie kamen paarweise *or* (*with children also*) zwei und zwei herein; **letters came in** ~ **the hundred** Hunderte von Briefen kamen.
(g) (*indicating agent, cause*) von. **killed** ~ **a bullet** durch eine *or* von einer Kugel getötet; **indicated** ~ **an asterisk** durch Sternchen gekennzeichnet; **a painting** ~ **Picasso** ein Bild von Picasso; **surrounded** ~ umgeben von.
(h) (*indicating method, means, manner: see also nouns*) ~ **bus/car/bicycle** mit dem *or* per Bus/Auto/Fahrrad; ~ **land and** (~) **sea** zu Land und zu Wasser; **to pay** ~ **cheque** mit Scheck bezahlen; **made** ~ **hand/machine** handgearbeitet/maschinell hergestellt; ~ **daylight/moonlight** bei Tag(eslicht)/im Mondschein; **to know sb** ~ **name/sight** jdn dem Namen nach/vom Sehen her kennen; **to be known** ~ **the name of ...** unter dem Namen ... bekannt sein; **to lead** ~ **the hand** an der Hand führen; **to grab sb** ~ **the collar** jdn am Kragen packen; **he had a daughter** ~ **his first wife** von seiner ersten Frau hatte er eine Tochter; ~ **myself/himself** *etc* allein.
(i) ~ **saving hard he managed to ...** durch eisernes Sparen *or* dadurch, daß er eisern sparte, gelang es ihm ...; ~ **turning this knob** durch Drehen dieses Knopfes, indem Sie diesen Knopf drehen, wenn Sie an diesem Knopf drehen; ~ **saying that I didn't mean ...** ich habe damit nicht gemeint; **animals which move** ~ **wriggling** Tiere, die sich schlängelnd fortbewegen; **he could walk** ~ **supporting himself on ...** gestützt auf ... könnte er gehen.
(j) (*according to: see also nouns*) nach. **to judge** ~ **appearances** nach dem Äußern urteilen; ~ **my watch it is nine o'clock** nach meiner Uhr ist es neun; **if you go** ~ **the rule** wenn du dich

an die Regel hältst; ~ **the terms of Article I** gemäß *or* nach (den Bestimmungen von) Artikel I; **to call sb/sth** ~ **his/its proper name** jdn/etw beim richtigen Namen nennen; **if it's OK** ~ **you/him** *etc* wenn es Ihnen/ihm *etc* recht ist; **it's all right** ~ **me** von mir aus gern *or* schon.
(k) (*measuring difference*) um. **broader** ~ **a meter** um einen Meter breiter; **it missed me** ~ **inches** es verfehlte mich um Zentimeter.
(l) (*Math, Measure*) **to divide/multiply** ~ dividieren durch/multiplizieren mit; **a room 20 metres** ~ **30** ein Zimmer 20 auf *or* mal 30 Meter.
(m) (*points of compass*) **South** ~ **South West** Südsüdwest.
(n) (*in oaths*) **I swear** ~ **Almighty God** ich schwöre beim allmächtigen Gott; ~ **heaven, I'll get you for this** das sollst *or* wirst du mir, bei Gott, büßen!
(o) ~ **the right!** (*Mil*) rechts, links ...!
(p) ~ **the way** *or* **by(e)** übrigens.
2 *adv* **(a)** (*near: see close*). ~
(b) (*past*) **to pass/wander/rush** *etc* ~ vorbei- *or* vorüberkommen/-wandern/-eilen *etc*.
(c) (*in reserve*) **to put** *or* **lay** ~ beiseite legen.
(d) (*phrases*) ~ **and** ~ irgendwann; (*with past tense*) nach einiger Zeit; ~ **and large** im großen und ganzen.
by(e) [baɪ] *n* **(a)** (*Cricket*) Lauf bei Bällen, die nicht vom Schlagmann geschlagen worden sind. **(b)** (*Sport*) **to get a bye into the second round** spielfrei in die zweite Runde kommen.
bye [baɪ] *interj* (*inf*) tschüs. ~ **for now!** bis bald!
bye-bye ['baɪbaɪ] **1** *interj* (*inf*) Wiedersehen (*inf*). **that's** ~ **£200** (da sind) £ 200 futsch! (*inf*). **2** *n* **to go (to)** ~**s** (*baby-talk*) in die Heia gehen (*baby-talk*).
by(e)-election [baɪɪˈlekʃən] *n* Nachwahl *f*.
bygone ['baɪgɒn] **1** *adj* längst vergangen. **2** *n* **to let** ~**s be** ~**s** die Vergangenheit ruhen lassen.
by: ~**law** *n* (*also* **bye-law**) Verordnung *f*; ~**name** *n* Inbegriff *m* (*for von*); **X is a** ~**name for tractors** X ist *der* Name für Traktoren.
bypass ['baɪpɑːs] **1** *n* (*road*) Umgehungsstraße *f*; (*Tech: pipe etc*) Bypass *m*.
2 *vt* **town, village** umgehen; (*Tech*) **fluid, gas** umleiten; (*fig*) **person** übergehen; **intermediate stage** *also* überspringen; **difficulties** umgehen.
bypass surgery *n* Bypass-Chirurgie *f*. **to have** ~ sich einer Bypass-Operation unterziehen.
by: ~**play** *n* (*Theat*) Nebenhandlung *f*; ~**product** *n* (*lit, fig*) Nebenprodukt *nt*.
byre ['baɪəʳ] *n* (Kuh)stall *m*.
by: ~**road** *n* Neben- *or* Seitenstraße *f*; ~**stander** *n* Umstehende(r) *mf*, Zuschauer *m*; **innocent** ~**stander** unbeteiligter Zuschauer; ~**way** *n* Seitenweg *m*; *see* **highway**; ~**word** *n* **to be/become a** ~**word for sth** gleichbedeutend mit etw sein/werden.
Byzantine [baɪˈzæntaɪn] **1** *adj* byzantinisch. **2** *n* Byzantiner(in *f*) *m*.
Byzantium [baɪˈzæntɪəm] *n* Byzanz *nt*.

C

C, c [siː] C, c *nt*. **C sharp/flat** Cis, cis *nt*/Ces, ces *nt*; *see also* **major, minor, natural**.
C *abbr of* **centigrade** C.
c *abbr of* **(a) cent** c, ct. **(b) circa** ca.
CA *abbr of* **chartered accountant.**
cab [kæb] *n* **(a)** (*horsedrawn*) Droschke *f*; (*taxi*) Taxi *nt*, Taxe (*inf*), Droschke (*form*) *f*. ~ **driver** Taxifahrer(in *f*) *m*; ~ **rank**, ~ **stand** Taxistand, Droschkenplatz (*form*) *m*. **(b)** (*of railway engine, lorry, crane*) Führerhaus *nt*.
cabal [kəˈbæl] *n* **(a)** (*intrigue*) Intrige *f*, Komplott *nt*, Kabale *f* (*old liter*). **(b)** (*group*) Clique, Kamarilla (*geh*) *f*.
cabaret ['kæbəreɪ] *n* **(a)** Varieté *nt*; (*satire*) Kabarett *nt*.
cabbage ['kæbɪdʒ] *n* **(a)** Kohl *m*, Kraut *nt* (*esp S Ger*). **a head of** ~ ein Kopf *m* Kohl, ein Kohlkopf *m*. **(b)** (*inf: person*) geistiger Krüppel (*inf*). **to become a** ~ verblöden (*inf*); (*sick person*) dahinvegetieren.
cabbage: ~ **lettuce** *n* Kopfsalat *m*; ~ **rose** *n* Zentifolie *f*; ~ **white (butterfly)** *n* Kohlweißling *m*.
cab(b)alistic [ˌkæbəˈlɪstɪk] *adj* kabbalistisch.
cabby ['kæbɪ] *n* (*inf: of taxi*) Taxifahrer *m*; (*of horsedrawn vehicle*) Kutscher *m*.
caber ['keɪbəʳ] *n* (*Scot*) Pfahl, Stamm *m*; *see* **toss**.
cabin ['kæbɪn] *n* **(a)** (*hut*) Hütte *f*. **(b)** (*Naut*) Kabine, Kajüte *f*; (*stateroom*) Kabine *f*. **(c)** (*of lorries, buses etc*) Führerhaus *nt*. **(d)** (*Aviat*) (*for passengers*) Passagierraum *m*; (*for pilot*) Cockpit *nt*, (Flug)kanzel *f*.
cabin: ~ **boy** *n* Schiffsjunge *m*; (*steward*) Kabinensteward *m*; ~

class *n* zweite Klasse; ~ **cruiser** *n* Kajütboot *nt*.
cabinet ['kæbɪnɪt] *n* **(a)** Schränkchen *nt*; (*for display*) Vitrine *f*; (*for TV, record-player*) Schrank *m*, Truhe *f*; (*loudspeaker* ~) Box *f*. **(b)** (*Parl*) Kabinett *nt*, Regierungsmannschaft *f* (*inf*).
cabinet: ~**maker** *n* (Möbel)tischler, (Möbel)schreiner *m*; ~**making** *n* Tischlern *nt*, Tischlerei *f*; ~ **meeting** *n* Kabinettssitzung *f*; ~ **minister** *n* Mitglied *nt* des Kabinetts, Minister *m*; ~**reshuffle** *n* Kabinettsumbildung *f*; ~**-size** *adj* (*Phot*) im Kabinettformat.
cabin: ~ **luggage** *n* Kabinengepäck *nt*; ~ **trunk** *n* Schrank- *or* Überseekoffer *m*.
cable ['keɪbl] **1** *n* **(a)** (*of wire*) Tau *nt*; (*of wire*) Kabel *nt*, Trosse *f* (*Naut*). **(b)** (*Elec*) Kabel *nt*, Leitung *f*. **(c)** (~*gram*) Telegramm *nt*; (*from abroad*) (Übersee)telegramm, Kabel *nt*. **by** ~ per Telegramm/Kabel.
2 *vt* **information** telegrafisch durchgeben; (*overseas*) kabeln. **to** ~ **sb** jdm telegraphieren/kabeln.
3 *vi* telegraphieren, ein Telegramm/Kabel schicken.
cable: ~**-car** *n* (*hanging*) Drahtseilbahn *f*; (*streetcar*) (*gezogene*) Straßenbahn *f*; (*funicular*) Standseilbahn *f*; ~**gram** *n* *see* **cable 1 (c)**; ~ **laying** *n* Kabelverlegung *f*, Kabellegen *nt*; ~ **length** *n* (*Naut*) Kabellänge *f*; ~ **railway** *n* Bergbahn *f*; ~ **stitch** *n* (*Knitting*) Zopfmuster *nt*.
caboodle [kəˈbuːdl] *n* (*inf*): **the whole (kit and)** ~ das ganze Zeug(s) (*inf*), der ganze Kram (*inf*).
caboose [kəˈbuːs] *n* **(a)** (*Naut*) Kombüse *f*. **(b)** (*US Rail*) Dienstwagen *m*.

cabriole ['kæbrɪəʊl] n (of table etc) geschwungenes or geschweiftes Bein.
cabriolet [,kæbrɪəʊ'leɪ] n Kabriolett nt.
cacao [kə'kɑːəʊ] n (tree, bean) Kakao m.
cache [kæʃ] 1 n Versteck, geheimes (Waffen-/Proviant)lager nt. 2 vt verstecken.
cachet ['kæʃeɪ] n Gütesiegel, Gütezeichen nt.
cachou ['kæʃuː] n Cachou(bonbon) m or nt.
cack-handed [kæk'hændəd] adj (Brit inf) tolpatschig (inf).
cackle ['kækl] 1 n (of hens) Gackern nt; (laughter) (mekerndes) Lachen; (inf) (chatter) Geblödel nt (inf). 2 vi (hens) gackern; (inf) (talk) schwatzen; (laugh) meckernd lachen.
cacophonous [kæ'kɒfənəs] adj mißtönend, kakophon (geh).
cacophony [kæ'kɒfənɪ] n Kakophonie f (geh), Mißklang m.
cactus ['kæktəs] n Kaktus m.
cad [kæd] n (dated) Schurke (old), Schuft m.
cadaver [kə'deɪvəʳ] n Kadaver m; (of humans) Leiche f.
cadaverous [kə'dævərəs] adj (corpse-like) Kadaver-, Leichen-; (gaunt) ausgezehrt, ausgemergelt; (pale) leichenblaß.
caddie ['kædɪ] 1 n (Golf) Schlägerträger, Caddie m. 2 vi Caddie sein or spielen (inf).
caddis fly ['kædɪsflaɪ] n Köcherfliege, Frühlingsfliege f.
caddish ['kædɪʃ] adj (dated) schurkisch (old), niederträchtig.
caddy ['kædɪ] n (tea ~) Behälter m, Büchse f; see caddie.
cadence ['keɪdəns] n (Mus) Kadenz f; (of voice) Tonfall m, Melodie f; (rhythm) Rhythmus m, Melodie f. the ~s of his speech seine Sprachmelodie.
cadenza [sɪ'denzə] n (Mus) Kadenz f.
cadet [kə'det] n (a) (Mil etc) Kadett m. ~ corps Kadettenkorps nt. (b) (old) jüngerer Sohn/Bruder.
cadge [kædʒ] 1 vt (er)betteln, abstauben (inf), schnorren (inf) (from sb bei or von jdm). could I ~ a lift with you? könnten Sie mich vielleicht (ein Stück) mitnehmen? 2 vi schnorren (inf).
cadger ['kædʒəʳ] n Schnorrer (inf), Abstauber (inf) m.
cadmium ['kædmɪəm] n Kadmium, Cadmium nt.
cadre ['kɑːdrɪ] n (Mil, fig) Kader m.
caecum, (US) cecum ['siːkəm] n (Anat) Blinddarm m.
Caesar ['siːzəʳ] n Cäsar, Caesar m.
Caesarean, Caesarian [siː'zeərɪən] adj cäsarisch, Cäsaren-; (of Caesar) Cäsarisch. ~ (section) (Med) Kaiserschnitt m.
caesura [sɪ'zjʊərə] n Zäsur f.
café ['kæfeɪ] n Café nt.
cafeteria [,kæfɪ'tɪərɪə] n Cafeteria f.
caff [kæf] n (Brit sl) Café nt.
caffein(e) ['kæfiːn] n Koffein nt.
caftan ['kæftæn] n Kaftan m.
cage [keɪdʒ] 1 n (a) (Mus m; (small bird~) Bauer nt or m. ~ bird Käfigvogel m. (b) (of lift) Aufzug m; (Min) Förderkorb m. 2 vt (also ~ up) in einen Käfig sperren, einsperren.
cagey ['keɪdʒɪ] adj (inf) vorsichtig; behaviour, answer also zugeknöpft (inf); (evasive) ausweichend. what are you being so ~ about? warum tust du so geheimnisvoll?; she was very ~ about her age sie hat aus ihrem Alter ein großes Geheimnis gemacht; he was very ~ about his plans er hat mit seinen Absichten hinterm Berg gehalten.
cagily ['keɪdʒɪlɪ] adv see cagey.
caginess ['keɪdʒɪnɪs] n (inf) Vorsicht, Zugeknöpftheit (inf) f; (evasiveness) ausweichende Art.
cagoule [kə'guːl] n K-Vay ® m, Windhemd nt.
cahoots [kə'huːts] n (inf): to be in ~ with sb jdm unter einer Decke stecken.
caiman ['keɪmən] n Kaiman m.
Cain [keɪn] n Kain m. to raise ~ (inf) (be noisy) Radau machen (inf), lärmen; (protest) Krach schlagen (inf).
cairn [kɛən] n (a) Steinpyramide f, Steinhügel m. (b) (also ~ terrier) Cairn-Terrier m.
Cairo ['kaɪərəʊ] n Kairo nt.
caisson ['keɪsən] n (a) (Mil) Munitionskiste f; (wagon) Munitionswagen m. (b) (Tech: underwater ~) Senkkasten, Caisson m.
cajole [kə'dʒəʊl] vt gut zureden (+dat), beschwatzen (inf). to ~ sb into doing sth jdn dazu bringen or jdn beschwatzen (inf), etw zu tun; to ~ sb out of doing sth jdm etw ausreden; he would not be ~d er ließ sich nicht beschwatzen (inf).
cajolery [kə'dʒəʊlərɪ] n Überredung f, Beschwatzen nt (inf).
cake [keɪk] 1 n (a) (Kuchen m; (gateau) Torte f; (bun, individual ~) Gebäckstück, Teilchen (dial) nt. ~s and pastries Gebäck nt; a piece of ~ (fig inf) ein Kinderspiel nt, ein Klacks m (inf); he/that takes the ~ (inf) das ist das Schärfste (sl); (negatively also) das schlägt dem Faß den Boden aus; to sell like hot ~s weggehen wie warme Semmeln (inf); you can't have your ~ and eat it (prov) beides auf einmal geht nicht; he wants to have his ~ and eat it (prov) er will das eine, ohne das andere zu lassen.
(b) (of soap) Stück nt, Riegel m; (of chocolate) Tafel f. 2 vt dick einschmieren. my shoes are ~d with mud meine Schuhe sind völlig verdreckt or dreckverkrustet. 3 vi festtrocknen, eine Kruste bilden.
cake: ~ shop n Konditorei f; ~ tin n (for baking) Kuchenform f; (for storage) Kuchenbüchse f.
calabash ['kæləbæʃ] n Kalebasse f. ~ tree Kalebassenbaum m.
calamine ['kæləmaɪn] n Galmei m. ~ lotion Galmeilotion f.
calamitous [kə'læmɪtəs] adj katastrophal.
calamity [kə'læmɪtɪ] n Katastrophe f. C~ Jane Pechmarie f.
calcification [,kælsɪfɪ'keɪʃən] n Kalkablagerung f; (Med) Verkalkung f.
calcify ['kælsɪfaɪ] 1 vt Kalk m ablagern auf/in (+dat), verkalken lassen. 2 vi verkalken.
calcination [,kælsɪ'neɪʃən] n Kalzination f.
calcine ['kælsaɪn] 1 vt kalzinieren. 2 vi kalziniert werden.
calcium ['kælsɪəm] n Kalzium, Calcium nt. ~ carbonate

Kalziumkarbonat nt, kohlensaurer Kalk.
calculable ['kælkjʊləbl] adj berechenbar, kalkulierbar.
calculate ['kælkjʊleɪt] 1 vt (a) (mathematically, scientifically) berechnen; costs also ermitteln.
(b) (fig: estimate critically) kalkulieren, schätzen.
(c) to be ~d to do sth (be intended) auf etw (acc) abzielen; (have the effect) zu etw angetan sein.
(d) (US inf: suppose) schätzen, annehmen, meinen.
2 vi (Math) rechnen. calculating machine Rechenmaschine f.
♦**calculate on** vi +prep obj rechnen mit. I had ~d to ~ finishing by this week ich hatte damit gerechnet, diese Woche fertig zu werden.
calculated ['kælkjʊleɪtɪd] adj (deliberate) berechnet. ~ insult ein bewußter Affront; a ~ risk ein kalkuliertes Risiko.
calculating adj, ~ly adv ['kælkjʊleɪtɪŋ, -lɪ] berechnend.
calculation [,kælkjʊ'leɪʃən] n Berechnung, Kalkulation f; (critical estimation) Schätzung f. to do a ~ die Sache schnell überschlagen; you're out in your ~s du hast dich verrechnet; by my ~s he will arrive on Sunday nach meiner Schätzung müßte er Sonntag ankommen.
calculator ['kælkjʊleɪtəʳ] n (a) (person) Kalkulator, Rechnungsbeamte(r) m. (b) (machine) Rechner m. (c) (table of figures) Rechentabelle f.
calculus ['kælkjʊləs] n (a) (Math) Infinitesimalrechnung, Differential- und Integralrechnung f. (b) (Med) Stein m.
Calcutta [kæl'kʌtə] n Kalkutta nt.
Caledonia [,kælə'dəʊnɪə] n Kaledonien nt.
Caledonian [,kælə'dəʊnɪən] adj kaledonisch.
calefactory [kælə'fæktərɪ] adj (form) Wärme-.
calendar ['kæləndəʳ] n (a) Kalender m. ~ month Kalendermonat m. (b) (schedule) Terminkalender m; (Jur) Prozeßregister nt. Church ~ Kirchenkalender m, Kalendarium nt.
calender ['kæləndəʳ] 1 n Kalander m. 2 vt kalandern.
calf¹ [kɑːf] n, pl calves (a) Kalb nt. a cow in or with ~ eine trächtige Kuh. (b) (young elephant, seal etc) Junge(s), -junge(s) nt. (c) (leather) Kalb(s)leder nt.
calf² n, pl calves (Anat) Wade f.
calf: ~ love n (juvendliche) Schwärmerei; ~skin n Kalb(s)leder nt.
caliber n (US) see calibre.
calibrate ['kælɪbreɪt] vt gun kalibrieren; meter, instrument also eichen.
calibration [,kælɪ'breɪʃən] n see vt Kalibrieren nt; Eichen nt; (mark) Kalibrierung f; Eichung f.
calibre, (US) caliber ['kælɪbəʳ] n (lit) Kaliber nt; (fig also) Format nt. a man of his ~ ein Mann seines Kalibers, ein Mann von seinem Format.
calico ['kælɪkəʊ] n Kattun m.
California [kælɪ'fɔːnɪə] n (abbr Cal(if)) Kalifornien nt.
Californian [kælɪ'fɔːnɪən] adj kalifornisch.
calipers ['kælɪpəz] npl (US) see callipers.
caliph ['keɪlɪf] n Kalif m.
calisthenics [,kælɪs'θenɪks] n (US) see callisthenics; shoe also mit Nägeln beschlagen. 2 n Stollen m; (on shoe also) Nagel m.
calk¹ ['kɔːk] 1 vt mit Stollen versehen; shoe also mit Nägeln beschlagen. 2 n Stollen m; (on shoe also) Nagel m.
calk² vt drawing, design durchpausen.
calk³ vt see caulk.
call [kɔːl] 1 n (a) (shout, cry) Ruf m; (of bugle) Signal nt. to give sb a ~ jdn (herbei)rufen; (inform sb) jdm Bescheid sagen; (wake sb) jdn wecken; they came at my ~ sie kamen auf meinen Ruf hin, als ich rief, kamen sie; within ~ in Rufweite f; a ~ for help (lit, fig) ein Hilferuf m.
(b) (telephone ~) Gespräch nt, Anruf m. I'll give you a ~ ich rufe Sie an; to take a ~ ein Gespräch entgegennehmen; will you take the ~? nehmen Sie das Gespräch an?
(c) (fig: summons) (for flight, meal) Aufruf m; (of religion) Berufung f; (Theat: to actors) Aufruf m; (fig: lure) Ruf m, Verlockung f. to be on ~ Bereitschaftsdienst haben; the doctor had a ~ at midnight der Arzt wurde um Mitternacht zu einem Patienten gerufen; that's your ~! (Theat) Ihr Auftritt!; the ~ of conscience/nature die Stimme des Gewissens/der Natur; to attend to a ~ of nature (euph) mal kurz verschwinden gehen (inf); the C~ or ~ came when he was 17 mit 17 Jahren spürte er die Berufung; the ~ of duty der Ruf der Pflicht; with him the ~ of duty was particularly strong er hatte ein besonders stark ausgeprägtes Pflichtgefühl; to make a ~ for unity zur Einigkeit aufrufen.
(d) (visit) Besuch m. to make or pay a ~ on sb jdn besuchen, jdm einen Besuch abstatten (form); I have several ~s to make ich muß noch einige Besuche machen; port of ~ Anlaufhafen m; (fig) Station f; to pay a ~ (euph) mal verschwinden (inf).
(e) (demand, claim) Inanspruchnahme, Beanspruchung f; (Comm) Nachfrage f (for nach). to have many ~s on one's purse/time finanziell/zeitlich sehr in Anspruch genommen sein; the sudden rain made for heavy ~s on the emergency services die plötzlichen Regenfälle bedeuteten eine starke Belastung der Notdienste.
(f) at or on ~ (Fin) auf Abruf.
(g) (need, occasion) Anlaß, Grund m, Veranlassung f. there is no ~ for you to worry es besteht kein Grund zur Sorge, Sie brauchen sich (dat) keine Sorgen zu machen.
(h) (Cards) Ansage f. to make a ~ of three diamonds drei Karo ansagen; whose ~ is it? wer sagt an?
(i) (Tennis) Entscheidung f.
2 vt (a) (shout out) rufen. the landlord ~ed time der Wirt rief „Feierabend"; to ~ spades (Cards) Pik reizen; the ball was ~ed out der Ball wurde für „aus" erklärt; see halt.
(b) (name, consider) nennen. to be ~ed heißen; what's he ~ed? wie heißt er?; what do you ~ your cat? wie nennst du deine Katze?, wie heißt deine Katze?; what's this ~ed in German? wie heißt das auf Deutsch?; let's ~ it a day machen

wir Schluß or Feierabend für heute; ~ it £5 sagen wir £ 5.
   (c) *(summon) person, doctor* rufen; *meeting* einberufen; *strike* ausrufen; *(Jur) witness* aufrufen; *(subpoena)* vorladen; *(waken)* wecken. **he was ~ed to his maker** *(liter)* er ist in die Ewigkeit abberufen worden; **to ~ sth into being** etw ins Leben rufen; *see* **mind, question, bluff²**.
   (d) *(telephone)* anrufen; *(contact by radio)* rufen.
   (e) *(Fin) bond* aufrufen; *loan* abrufen.
  3 *vi* (a) *(shout: person, animal)* rufen. **to ~ for help** um Hilfe rufen; **to ~ to sb** jdm zurufen.
   (b) *(visit)* vorbeigehen/-kommen. **she ~ed to see her mother** sie machte einen Besuch bei ihrer Mutter; **the gasman ~ed about the meter** der Gasmann war wegen des Zählers da; **he was out when I ~ed** er war nicht da, als ich ihn besuchen wollte.
   (c) *(Telec)* anrufen; *(by radio)* rufen. **who's ~ing, please?** wer spricht da bitte?; **London ~ing!** *(Rad)* hier ist London; **thanks for ~ing** vielen Dank für den Anruf.
♦ **call aside** *vt sep person* beiseite rufen.
♦ **call at** *vi +prep obj (person)* vorbeigehen bei; *(Naut)* anlaufen in *(+dat)*; *(Rail)* halten in. **a train for Lisbon ~ing ~ ...** ein Zug nach Lissabon über ...
♦ **call away** *vt sep weg- or* abrufen. **I was ~ed ~ on business** ich wurde geschäftlich abgerufen; **he was ~ed ~ from the meeting** er wurde aus der Sitzung gerufen.
♦ **call back** *vti sep* zurückrufen.
♦ **call down** *vt sep* (a) *(invoke)* **to ~ ~ curses on sb's head** jdn verfluchen. (b) **to ~ sb ~** *(lit)* jdn herunterrufen; *(US: reprimand)* jdn ausschimpfen, jdn herunterputzen *(inf)*.
♦ **call for** *vi +prep obj* (a) *(send for) person* rufen; *food, drink* kommen lassen; *(ask for)* verlangen (nach).
   (b) *(need) courage, endurance* verlangen, erfordern. **that ~s ~ a drink/celebration!** darauf muß ich/müssen wir einen trinken!, das muß begossen/gefeiert werden!
   (c) *(collect) person, goods* abholen; *(come to see)* fragen nach. **"to be ~ed ~"** *(goods sent by rail)* „bahnlagernd"; *(by post)* „postlagernd"; *(in shop)* „wird abgeholt".
♦ **call forth** *vt insep protests* hervorrufen; *abilities etc* wachrufen, wecken.
♦ **call in 1** *vt sep* (a) *doctor* zu Rate ziehen. (b) *(withdraw) faulty goods etc* aus dem Verkehr ziehen; *currency also* aufrufen *(form)*; *hire-boats* zurück- or aufrufen; *books* an- or zurückfordern. **2** *vi* vorbeigehen or -schauen *(at, on* sb).
♦ **call off** *vt sep* (a) *(cancel) appointment, holiday* absagen; *deal* rückgängig machen; *strike* absagen, abblasen *(inf)*; *(end)* abbrechen; *engagement* lösen. **let's ~ the whole thing ~** blasen wir die ganze Sache ab *(inf)*. (b) *dog* zurückrufen. **2** *vi* absagen.
♦ **call on** *vi +prep obj* (a) *(visit)* besuchen. (b) *see* **call upon**.
♦ **call out 1** *vi* rufen, schreien. **2** *vt sep* (a) *names* aufrufen; *(announce)* ansagen. (b) *doctor* rufen; *troops, fire brigade* alarmieren. (c) *(order to strike)* zum Streik aufrufen.
♦ **call out for** *vi +prep obj food, drink* verlangen; *help* rufen um.
♦ **call round** *vi (inf)* vorbeikommen.
♦ **call up 1** *vt sep* (a) *(Mil) reservist* einberufen; *reinforcements* mobilisieren. **~ed ~ to go to Vietnam** nach Vietnam einberufen. (b) *(Telec)* anrufen. (c) *(fig)* (herauf)beschwören; *images, thoughts also* erwecken; *memories also* wachrufen. **to ~ ~ the Devil** den Teufel beschwören. **2** *vi (Telec)* anrufen.
♦ **call upon** *vi +prep obj* (a) *(ask)* **to ~ ~ sb to do sth** jdn bitten or auffordern, etw zu tun; **I now ~ ~ the vicar to say a few words** ich möchte nun den Herrn Pfarrer um ein paar Worte bitten. (b) *(invoke)* **to ~ ~ sb's generosity** an jds Großzügigkeit *(acc)* appellieren; **to ~ ~ God** Gott anrufen.

call: **~box** *n* Telefonzelle *f*, öffentlicher Fernsprecher *m*; **~boy** *n (Theat)* Inspizientengehilfe *m (der die Schauspieler zu ihrem Auftritt ruft)*.
caller [ˈkɔːlə^r] *n* (a) *(visitor)* Besuch(er) *m*. (b) *(Telec)* Anrufer *m*. **hold the line please ~!** bitte bleiben Sie am Apparat!
callgirl [ˈkɔːlgɜːl] *n* Callgirl *nt*.
calligraphic [ˌkælɪˈgræfɪk] *adj* kalligraphisch, Schönschreib-.
calligraphy [kəˈlɪgrəfɪ] *n* Kaligraphie, Schönschreibkunst *f*.
calling [ˈkɔːlɪŋ] *n* Berufung *f*. **~ card** Visitenkarte *f*; **to leave one's ~ card** *(euph: cats or dogs)* seine Visitenkarte hinterlassen *(hum)*.
calliper or *(US)* **caliper brake** [ˈkælɪpəˌbreɪk] *n* Felgenbremse *f*.
callipers, *(US)* **calipers** [ˈkælɪpəz] *npl* Tastzirkel *m*.
callisthenics, *(US)* **calisthenics** [ˌkælɪsˈθeniks] *n* Gymnastik, Kallisthenie *(dated) f*.
call money *n (Fin)* täglich kündbares Geld.
callous [ˈkæləs] *adj* (a) *(cruel)* gefühllos, herzlos. (b) *(Med)* schwielig, kallös.
callously [ˈkæləslɪ] *adv* herzlos.
callousness [ˈkæləsnɪs] *n* Gefühllosigkeit, Herzlosigkeit *f*.
callow [ˈkæləʊ] *adj* unreif, unausgegoren. **a ~ youth** ein grüner Junge *(inf)*.
call-up: **~ sign** *n (Rad)* Sendezeichen *nt*; **~-up** *n* Einberufung *f*; **~-up papers** *npl* Einberufungsbescheid *m*.
callus [ˈkæləs] *n (Med)* Schwiele *f*; *(of bone)* Kallus *m*, Knochenschwiele *f*; *(Bot)* Wundholz *nt*, Kallus *m*.
calm [kɑːm] **1** *adj (+er)* ruhig; *weather also* windstill. **keep ~!** bleib ruhig!; **the weather grew ~ again after the storm** nach dem Sturm beruhigte sich das Wetter wieder.
  2 *n* (a) *(lit)* Ruhe, Stille *f*; *(at sea)* Flaute *f*; *(of wind)* Windstille *f*. **a dead ~** absolute Stille, Totenstille *f*; **there was ~ after the hurricane** nach dem Orkan trat Stille ein or herrschte Stille; **the ~ before the storm** *(lit, fig)* die Ruhe vor dem Sturm.
   (b) *(composure)* Ruhe, Gelassenheit *f*.
  3 *vt* beruhigen.
♦ **calm down 1** *vt sep* beruhigen, beschwichtigen. **2** *vi* sich beruhigen; *(wind)* abflauen. **~ ~!** beruhigen Sie sich!

calming [ˈkɑːmɪŋ] *adj* beruhigend.
calmly [ˈkɑːmlɪ] *adv speak, act* ruhig, gelassen. **he spoke ~** er redete mit ruhiger Stimme; **she ~ told me that she'd crashed the car** sie erzählte mir seelenruhig, daß sie das Auto kaputtgefahren hatte.
calmness [ˈkɑːmnɪs] *n (of person)* Ruhe, Gelassenheit *f*; *(of wind, sea)* Stille *f*.
Calor gas ® [ˈkæləgæs] *n* Butangas *nt*.
caloric [ˈkælərɪk] *adj* kalorisch, Wärme-.
calorie [ˈkælərɪ] *n* Kalorie *f*.
calorie *in cpds* Kalorien-, kalorien-; **~-conscious** *adj* kalorienbewußt.
calorific [ˌkæləˈrɪfɪk] *adj* wärmeerzeugend. **~ value** Heizwert *m*.
calumniate [kəˈlʌmnɪeɪt] *vt (liter)* schmähen *(geh)*, verunglimpfen.
calumny [ˈkæləmnɪ] *n (liter)* Schmähung *(geh)*, Verunglimpfung *f*.
Calvary [ˈkælvərɪ] *n* (a) Golgatha *nt*, Kalvarienberg *m*. (b) **c~** Bildstock *m*, Marterl *nt (S Ger, Aus)*.
calve [kɑːv] *vi* kalben.
calves [kɑːvz] *pl of* **calf¹, calf²**.
Calvin [ˈkælvɪn] *n* Calvin *m*.
Calvinism [ˈkælvɪnɪzəm] *n* Kalvinismus *m*.
Calvinist [ˈkælvɪnɪst] **1** *n* Kalvinist(in *f) m*. **2** *adj* kalvinistisch.
Calvinistic [ˌkælvɪˈnɪstɪk] *adj* kalvinistisch.
calypso [kəˈlɪpsəʊ] *n* Calypso *m*.
calyx [ˈkeɪlɪks] *n, pl* **calyces** [ˈkeɪlɪsiːz] or **-es** [ˈkeɪlɪksəz] Blütenkelch *m*.
cam [kæm] *n* Nocken *m*.
camaraderie [ˌkæməˈrɑːdərɪ] *n* Kameradschaft *f*.
camber [ˈkæmbə^r] **1** *n (of road, ship, aircraft wing)* Wölbung *f*; *(of road also)* Überhöhung *f*; *(of wheels)* Radsturz *m*. **2** *vt road, deck* wölben. **a ~ed wheel** ein Rad *nt* mit Sturz.
Cambodia [kæmˈbəʊdɪə] *n* Kambodscha *nt*.
Cambodian [kæmˈbəʊdɪən] **1** *adj* kambodschanisch. **2** *n* (a) Kambodschaner(in *f) m*. (b) *(language)* Kambodschanisch *nt*.
cambric [ˈkeɪmbrɪk] *n (Tex)* Kambrik, Cambrai *m*, Kammertuch *nt*.
came [keɪm] *pret of* **come**.
camel [ˈkæməl] *n* Kamel *nt*.
camel *in cpds (colour) coat* kamelhaarfarben; **~ driver** *n* Kameltreiber *m*; **~-hair**, *(US)* **~'s-hair 1** *n* Kamelhaar *nt*; **2** *attr coat, paintbrush* Kamelhaar-.
camellia [kəˈmiːlɪə] *n* Kamelie *f*.
cameo [ˈkæmɪəʊ] *n* (a) *(jewellery)* Kamee *f*. (b) *(Liter)* Miniatur *f*. **~ part** Miniaturrolle *f*.
camera¹ [ˈkæmərə] *n* Kamera *f*; *(for stills also)* Photoapparat *m*.
camera² *n (Jur)*: **in ~** unter Ausschluß der Öffentlichkeit; *(fig)* hinter verschlossenen Türen, in geschlossener Gesellschaft.
cameraman [ˈkæmərəmæn] *n, pl* **-men** [-mən] Kameramann *m*.
camera obscura [ˈkæmərəɒbˈskjʊərə] *n (Opt)* Camera obscura, Lochkamera *f*.
camera-shy [ˈkæmərəˈʃaɪ] *adj* kamerascheu.
Cameroons [ˌkæməˈruːnz] *npl* **the ~** Kamerun *nt*.
cami-knickers [ˈkæmɪˌnɪkəz] *npl* Spitzenhemdhöschen *nt*.
camisole [ˈkæmɪsəʊl] *n* Mieder, Leibchen *nt*.
camomile [ˈkæməʊmaɪl] *n* Kamille *f*. **~ tea** Kamillentee *f*.
camouflage [ˈkæməflɑːʒ] **1** *n (Mil, fig)* Tarnung *f*; *(fig also)* Camouflage *f (geh)*. **for ~** zur Tarnung.
  2 *vt (Mil, fig)* tarnen. **she smiled but it didn't ~ her despair** ihr Lächeln konnte nicht über ihre Verzweiflung hinwegtäuschen.
camouflage *in cpds* Tarn-; **~ nets** *npl* Tarnnetze *pl*.
camp¹ [kæmp] **1** *n* (a) Lager *nt*; *(Mil) (Feld)lager nt*. **to be in ~** im Lager leben or sein; *(Mil)* im Felde leben; **to pitch ~** Zelte or ein Lager aufschlagen; **to strike or break ~** die Zelte abbauen, das Lager or die Zelte abbrechen.
   (b) *(fig)* Lager *nt*. **to have a foot in both ~s** mit beiden Seiten zu tun haben; **the socialist ~** das sozialistische Lager.
  2 *vi* zelten, kampieren; *(Mil)* lagern. **to go ~ing** zelten (gehen).
♦ **camp out** *vi* zelten.
camp² *adj (theatrical, stagey)* übertrieben, extrem *(inf)*; *performance* manieriert, geschmäcklerisch; *person's appearance* aufgedonnert, aufgemotzt *(inf)*; *(effeminate)* tuntenhaft *(inf)*; *(homosexual)* schwul *(inf)*.
♦ **camp up** *vt sep* **to ~ sth ~** *(vamp up)* etw aufmöbeln *(inf)*, etw aufmotzen *(inf)*; *(overact)* etw überziehen, in or bei etw zu dick auftragen; **to ~ it ~** *(overact, exaggerate)* es zu weit treiben; *(Theat)* es übertreiben, zu dick auftragen; *(act homosexually)* sich tuntenhaft *(inf)* or wie eine Schwuchtel *(sl)* benehmen.
campaign [kæmˈpeɪn] **1** *n* (a) *(Mil)* Feldzug *m*, Kampagne *f (old)*. **Hitler's Russian ~** Hitlers Rußlandfeldzug *m*.
   (b) *(fig)* Kampagne, Aktion *f*; *(election ~)* Feldzug *m*, Kampagne *f*.
  2 *vi* (a) *(Mil)* kämpfen, Krieg führen. **~ing in Ruritania** im Einsatz in Ruritanien.
   (b) *(fig, for, against* gegen) sich einsetzen, sich stark machen *(inf)*, agitieren; *(outdoors also)* auf die Straße gehen; *(politician, candidate)* im Wahlkampf stehen, den Wahlkampf führen; *(supporters)* Wahlwerbung treiben. **we were out on the streets ~ing** wir waren auf der Straße im Einsatz.
campaigner [kæmˈpeɪnə^r] *n* (a) *(Mil)* Krieger *m*. **old ~** alter Kämpe.
   (b) Befürworter(in *f) m (for gen)*; Gegner(in *f) m (against gen)*; *(for politician)* Wahlwerber(in *f) m*.
camp: **~bed** *n* Campingliege *f*; **~ chair** *n* Campingstuhl *m*.
camper [ˈkæmpə^r] *n* Zeltler(in *f) m*; *(Camper)* Wohnmobil *nt*.
camp: **~ fire** *n* Lagerfeuer *nt*; **~ follower** *n* (a) Marketender(in *f) m*; (b) *(fig)* Anhänger(in *f)*, Mitläufer(in *f) (pej) m*; **~ground** *n (US)* Campingplatz, Zeltplatz *m*.

camphor ['kæmfə'] n Kampfer m.
camphorated ['kæmfəreɪtɪd] adj mit Kampfer präpariert. ~ oil Kampferöl nt.
camping ['kæmpɪŋ] n Zelten, Camping nt. no ~ Zelten verboten!
camping in cpds Camping-; ~ **ground** n Zeltplatz m; ~ **site** n (also **camp site**) Campingplatz, Zeltplatz m.
camp stool n Campinghocker m.
campus ['kæmpəs] n Campus m, Universitätsgelände nt.
campy ['kæmpɪ] adj (sl) see **camp²**.
camshaft ['kæmʃɑːft] n Nockenwelle f.
can¹ [kæn] pret **could** modal aux vb, defective parts supplied by **to be able to** (a) (be able to) können. ~ **you come tomorrow?** kannst du morgen kommen?; **I** ~'t or ~**not go to the theatre tomorrow** ich kann morgen nicht ins Theater (gehen); **I'll do it if I** ~ wenn ich kann(, tue ich es); **he'll help you all he** ~ er wird sein möglichstes tun, er wird tun, was in seinen Kräften steht; **as soon as it** ~ **be arranged** sobald es sich machen läßt; **could you tell me** ... können or könnten Sie mir sagen, ...; ~ **you speak German?** können or sprechen Sie Deutsch?; **we** ~ **but hope that, we** ~ **only hope that** ... wir können nur hoffen, daß ...; **they could not (help) but condemn it** sie konnten nicht anders, als das zu verurteilen.
 (b) (may) dürfen, können. ~ **I come too?** kann ich mitkommen?; ~ **or could I take some more?** darf ich mir noch etwas or noch einmal nehmen?; ~ **you go now** Sie können jetzt gehen; ~ **I help you?** darf or kann ich Ihnen helfen?; **could I possibly go with you?** könnte or dürfte ich vielleicht mitkommen?; **I'd like to go,** ~ **I?** — no, you ~'t ich würde gerne gehen, darf ich? — nein, du darfst nicht; ~ **I use your car?** — no, you ~'t kann or darf ich dein Auto nehmen? — nein.
 (c) (expressing surprise etc) können. **how** ~/could **you say such a thing!** wie können/konnten Sie nur or bloß so etwas sagen!; **where** ~ **it be?** wo kann das bloß sein?; **where** ~ **they have gone?** wo können sie denn nur hingegangen sein?; **you** ~'t **be serious** das kann doch wohl nicht dein Ernst sein.
 (d) (expressing possibility) können. **it could be that he's got lost** vielleicht hat er sich verlaufen, (es ist) möglich, daß er sich verlaufen hat; **could he have got lost?** ob er sich wohl or vielleicht verlaufen hat?; **he could be on the next train** er könnte im nächsten Zug sein; **and it could have been such a good party!** und es hätte so eine so gute Party sein können!; **to think he could have become a doctor** wenn man bedenkt, daß er hätte Arzt werden können.
 (e) (with verbs of perception) können. ~ **you hear me?** hören Sie mich?, können Sie mich hören?
 (f) (be capable of occasionally) können. **she** ~ **be very nice when she wants to** wenn sie will, kann sie sehr nett sein.
 (g) (indicating suggestion) können. **you could try telephoning him** Sie könnten ihn ja mal anrufen; **you could have been a little more polite** Sie hätten etwas höflicher sein können; **you could have told me** das hätten Sie mir auch sagen können.
 (h) (feel inclined to) können. **I could hit him** ich könnte ihm ins Gesicht schlagen; **I could have murdered her** ich hätte sie umbringen können.
 (i) **we could do with some new furniture** wir könnten neue Möbel gebrauchen; **I could do with a drink now** ich könnte jetzt etwas zu trinken vertragen; **this room could do with a coat of paint** das Zimmer könnte mal wieder gestrichen werden; **he looks as though he could do with a wash/haircut** ich glaube, er müßte sich mal waschen/er müßte sich (dat) mal wieder die Haare schneiden lassen.
can² 1 n (a) (container) Kanister m; (milk~) Kanne f; (esp US: garbage ~) (Müll)eimer m. **in the** ~ (Film) im Kasten; **the contract's in the** ~ (inf) wir haben den Vertrag in der Tasche (inf); **to carry the** ~ (fig inf) die Sache ausbaden (inf).
 (b) (tin) Dose f; (of food also) Büchse f. **a** ~ **of beer** eine Dose Bier; **a beer** ~ eine Bierdose; **a** ~ **of paint** eine Dose Farbe; (with handle) ein Eimer Farbe.
 (c) (US sl: prison) Knast m (sl).
 (d) (US sl: lavatory) Klo (inf), Scheißhaus (sl) nt. 2 vt (a) foodstuffs einmachen, eindosen; see **canned**.
 (b) (inf) ~ **it!** Klappe! (inf).
can in cpds Büchsen-, Dosen-.
Canaan ['keɪnən] n Kanaan nt.
Canaanite ['keɪnənaɪt] n Kanaaniter(in f) m.
Canada ['kænədə] n Kanada nt.
Canadian [kə'neɪdɪən] 1 adj kanadisch. 2 n Kanadier(in f) m.
canal [kə'næl] n (a) Kanal m. ~ **barge** Schleppkahn m. (b) (Anat) Gang, Kanal m.
canalization [ˌkænəlaɪ'zeɪʃən] n (lit) Kanalisation f; (fig) Kanalisierung f.
canalize ['kænəlaɪz] vt (lit, fig) kanalisieren.
canapé ['kænəpeɪ] n Cocktail- or Appetithappen m.
canard [kæ'nɑːd] n (Zeitungs)ente f.
Canaries [kə'neərɪz] npl see **Canary Isles**.
canary [kə'neərɪ] n (a) Kanarienvogel m. (b) (old: wine) Kanarienwein m (old). (c) (US sl: female singer) Sängerin f.
canary in cpds (colour: also ~ yellow) kanariengelb.
Canary Isles [kə'neərɪ'aɪlz] npl Kanarische Inseln pl.
canasta [kə'næstə] n Canasta nt.
cancan ['kænkæn] n Cancan m.
cancel ['kænsəl] 1 vt (a) (call off) absagen; holiday, journey absagen, rückgängig machen; (officially) stornieren; plans aufgeben, fallenlassen; train, bus streichen, ausfallen lassen. **the last train has been** ~**led** der letzte Zug fällt aus.
 (b) (revoke, annul) rückgängig machen; command, invitation also zurücknehmen; contract also (auf)lösen; debt streichen; order for goods stornieren; magazine subscription kündigen; decree aufheben; (Aut) indicator ausschalten. **no,** ~ **that** (in dictation etc) nein, streichen Sie das.
 (c) stamp, ticket, cheque entwerten, ungültig machen.
 (d) (Math) kürzen. **this X** ~**s that one** dieses X hebt das X auf. 2 vi (a) (revoke commercial order, contract) stornieren; (call off appointment, holiday) absagen.
 (b) (Math) sich kürzen lassen, sich aufheben.
♦**cancel out** 1 vt sep (Math) aufheben; (fig) zunichte machen. **to** ~ **each other** ~ (Math) sich aufheben, sich kürzen lassen; (fig) einander aufheben, sich gegenseitig aufheben. 2 vi (Math) sich aufheben, sich wegkürzen lassen (inf).
cancellation [ˌkænsə'leɪʃən] n see vt (a) Absage f; Stornierung f; Aufgabe f; Streichung f, Ausfall m. (b) Rückgängigmachung f; Zurücknahme f; Auflösung f; Streichung f; Stornierung f; Kündigung f; Aufhebung f. (c) Entwertung f. (d) (Math) Kürzung f.
cancer ['kænsə'] n (Med) Krebs m, Karzinom nt; (fig) Krebsgeschwür nt. ~ **of the throat** Kehlkopfkrebs m; ~ **research** Krebsforschung f; **C~** (Astrol) der Krebs.
cancerous ['kænsərəs] adj krebsartig. ~ **growth** (lit, fig) krebsartige Wucherung.
cancer stick n (sl: cigarette) Sargnagel m (sl).
candelabra [ˌkændɪ'lɑːbrə] n Kandelaber, Leuchter m.
candid ['kændɪd] adj offen, ehrlich. **he was quite** ~ **about it** er war ganz offen, er sprach ganz offen darüber; **in my** ~ **opinion he** ... ich bin offen gesagt der Meinung, daß er ...
candidacy ['kændɪdəsɪ] n Kandidatur f.
candidate ['kændɪdeɪt] n (Pol) Kandidat(in f) m; (exam ~ also) Prüfling m. **to stand as** (a) ~ kandidieren.
candidature ['kændɪdətʃə'] n (Brit) see **candidacy**.
candidly ['kændɪdlɪ] adv offen, ehrlich. **quite** ~, ... offen gestanden, ...; **to speak** ~ offen or ehrlich sein.
candidness ['kændɪdnɪs] n Offenheit, Ehrlichkeit f.
candied ['kændɪd] adj (Cook) kandiert, gezuckert. ~ **peel** (of lemon) Zitronat nt; (of orange) Orangeat nt; **his** ~ **words** seine schmeichelhaften or süßen Worte.
candle ['kændl] n Kerze f. **to burn the** ~ **at both ends** mit seinen Kräften Raubbau treiben; **he can't hold a** ~ **to his brother** er kann seinem Bruder nicht das Wasser reichen; **the game is not worth the** ~ das ist nicht der Mühe wert.
candle in cpds Kerzen-; ~ **grease** n Kerzenwachs nt; ~**light** n Kerzenlicht nt, Kerzenschein m; **by** ~**light** im Kerzenschein, bei Kerzenlicht; **a** ~**light dinner** ein Essen nt bei Kerzenlicht.
Candlemas ['kændlməs] n Mariä Lichtmeß nt.
candle: ~ **power** n (Elec) Lichtstärke f; **a 20-**~ **power lamp** eine Lampe von 20 Kerzen, eine 20kerzige Lampe; ~**stick** n Kerzenhalter m; ~**wick** 1 n (a) Kerzendocht m; (b) (Tex) Frottierplüschmuster nt; 2 attr bedspread im Frottierplüschmuster.
candour, (US) candor ['kændə'] n Offenheit, Ehrlichkeit f.
candy ['kændɪ] n (US) (sweet) Bonbon m or nt; (sweets) Süßigkeiten pl, Bonbons pl; (bar of chocolate) (Tafel) Schokolade f; (individual chocolate) Praline f. 2 vt sugar kristallisieren lassen; fruit etc kandieren.
candy: ~**floss** n (Brit) Zuckerwatte f; ~ **store** n (US) Süßwarenhandlung f, Bonbonladen m (inf); ~**-striped** adj dunt gestreift (auf weißem Hintergrund).
cane [keɪn] 1 n (a) (stem of bamboo, sugar etc) Rohr nt; (of raspberry) Zweig m; (for supporting plants) Stock m. **a chair made of** ~ ein Rohrstuhl m.
 (b) (walking stick) (Spazier)stock m; (instrument of punishment) (Rohr)stock m. **to use the** ~ den Rohrstock benutzen; **to get the** ~ Prügel bekommen; (on hand) eine auf die Finger bekommen, eine Tatze bekommen (S Ger).
 2 vt schoolboy mit dem Stock schlagen.
cane in cpds Rohr-; ~ **brake** n (US) Röhricht, Rohrdickicht nt; ~ **chair** n Rohrstuhl m; ~ **sugar** n Rohrzucker m.
canine ['keɪnaɪn] 1 n (a) (animal) Hund m. (b) (also ~ **tooth**) Eckzahn m. 2 adj Hunde-.
caning ['keɪnɪŋ] n (beating with cane) Schläge pl mit dem Stock, Prügeln nt (inf). **to give sb a** ~ jdm eine Tracht Prügel verabreichen; **to get a** ~ (Sport) haushoch geschlagen werden; (new play etc) verrissen werden.
canister ['kænɪstə'] n Behälter m; (for tea, coffee etc also) Dose f. ~ **shot** (Mil) Kartätsche f.
canker ['kæŋkə'] n (Med) Mund- or Lippengeschwür nt; (Vet) Hufkrebs m, Strahlfäule f; (Bot) Brand m; (fig) (Krebs)geschwür nt.
cankerous ['kæŋkərəs] adj (Med) entzündet; (Vet, Bot) brandig; (fig) krebsartig.
cannabis ['kænəbɪs] n Cannabis m. ~ **resin** Cannabisharz nt.
canned [kænd] adj (a) (US: food, beer) Dosen-. (b) (inf) ~ **music** Musikberieselung f (inf); ~ **heat** Brennspiritus m. (c) (sl: drunk) blau (inf), voll (sl).
cannery ['kænərɪ] n (US) Konservenfabrik f.
cannibal ['kænɪbəl] n (person) Kannibale, Menschenfresser m. **these are** ~**s** diese Fische fressen sich gegenseitig. 2 adj kannibalisch; animals sich gegenseitig auffressend.
cannibalism ['kænɪbəlɪzəm] n (of people) Kannibalismus m, Menschenfresserei f.
cannibalize ['kænɪbəlaɪz] vt old car etc ausschlachten.
canning ['kænɪŋ] n Konservenabfüllung f; (preserving) Konservierung f. **the** ~ **of meat** die Herstellung von Fleischkonserven.
cannon ['kænən] n (a) (Mil) Kanone f. (b) (Brit: Billiards) Karambolage f. 2 vi (Brit: Billiards) karambolieren.
♦**cannon into** vi+prep obj prallen gegen, zusammenprallen mit.
cannonade [ˌkænə'neɪd] n Kanonade f.
cannon: ~**ball** n Kanonenkugel f; ~ **fodder** n Kanonenfutter nt.
cannot ['kænɒt] = **can not**.
canny ['kænɪ] adj (+er) (Scot) (cautious) vorsichtig; (shrewd also) schlau; (careful with money also) sparsam.
canoe [kə'nuː] 1 n Kanu nt. **to paddle one's own** ~ (fig) auf

eigenen Füßen or Beinen stehen. **2** vi Kanu fahren, paddeln.
canoeing [kə'nuːɪŋ] n Kanusport m, Kanufahren nt.
canoeist [kə'nuːɪst] n Kanufahrer(in f) m, Kanute m, Kanutin f.
canon[1] ['kænən] n (all senses) Kanon m. ~ **law** (Eccl) Kanon m, kanonisches Recht.
canon[2] n (priest) Kanoniker, Kanonikus m.
cañon n (US) see canyon.
canonical [kə'nɒnɪkəl] adj (a) (Eccl) kanonisch. ~ **dress** Priestergewand nt. (b) (fig: accepted) anerkannt, rechtmäßig.
canonization [ˌkænənaɪ'zeɪʃən] n (Eccl) Heiligsprechung, Kanonisation, Kanonisierung f.
canonize ['kænənaɪz] vt (Eccl) heiligsprechen, kanonisieren.
canoodle [kə'nuːdl] vi (inf) rumschmusen (inf).
can opener n Dosen- or Büchsenöffner m.
canopy ['kænəpɪ] n (a) (awning) Markise, Überdachung f; (over entrance) Vordach nt, Pergola f; (of bed, throne) Baldachin m; (of aircraft) Kanzeldach nt; (of parachute) Fallschirmkappe f. (b) (fig liter: of sky, foliage) Baldachin m (liter). the ~ of the heavens das Himmelszelt (liter).
canst [kænst] (obs) 2nd pers sing of can[1].
cant[1] [kænt] n (a) (hypocrisy) Heuchelei f, scheinheiliges or leeres Gerede. that's just so many ~ **phrases!** das sind doch alles nur (leere) Phrasen! (b) (jargon) Jargon m, Kauderwelsch nt; (of thieves, gipsies) Rotwelsch nt.
cant[2] **1** n (tilt) Schräge f. **2** vt schräg stellen, kanten. the wind ~ed the boat der Wind brachte das Boot zum Kippen. **3** vi schräg or schief sein, sich neigen; (boat) kippen.
can't [kɑːnt] contr of can not.
Cantab ['kæntæb] abbr of **Cantabrigiensis** von der Universität Cambridge.
cantaloup(e) ['kæntəluːp] n Honigmelone, Buttermelone f.
cantankerous [kæn'tæŋkərəs] adj mürrisch, knurrig.
cantata [kæn'tɑːtə] n Kantate f.
canteen [kæn'tiːn] n (a) (restaurant) Kantine f. (b) (Mil) (flask) Feldflasche f; (mess tin) Kochgeschirr nt. (c) (of cutlery) Bestecksten m.
canter ['kæntə'] **1** n Handgalopp, Kanter m. to ride at a ~ langsamen Galopp reiten; to go for a ~ einen Ausritt machen. **2** vi langsam galoppieren.
canticle ['kæntɪkl] n (Eccl) Lobgesang m; (song) Volksweise f. C~s Hohelied nt, Hohes Lied.
cantilever ['kæntɪliːvə'] n Ausleger m; (support also) Freiträger m.
cantilever in cpds Ausleger-; ~ **bridge** n Auslegerbrücke f.
canto ['kæntəu] n (Liter) Canto, Gesang m.
canton ['kæntɒn] n Kanton m.
Cantonese [ˌkæntə'niːz] **1** adj kantonesisch. **2** n (a) Kantonese m, Kantonesin f. (b) (language) Kantonesisch nt.
cantonment [kən'tuːnmənt] n Truppenunterkunft f, Kantonnement nt (old).
cantor ['kæntɔː'] n Kantor m.
canvas ['kænvəs] n Leinwand f; (for sails) Segeltuch nt; (set of sails) Segel pl; (for tent) Zeltbahn f; (Art) (material) Leinwand f; (painting) Gemälde nt. under ~ (in a tent) im Zelt; (Naut) mit gehißtem Segel; ~ **chair** Liegestuhl, Klappstuhl m; ~ **shoes** Segeltuchschuhe pl.
canvass ['kænvəs] **1** vt (a) (Pol) district Wahlwerbung machen in (+dat); person für seine Partei zu gewinnen suchen. to ~ **the local electorate** in seinem Wahlkreis Stimmen werben or auf Stimmenfang gehen (inf).
(b) customers, citizens etc ansprechen, werben; issue unter die Leute bringen; district bereisen; (sound out) opinions erforschen.
2 vi (a) (Pol) um Stimmen werben (for sb für jdn).
(b) (Comm) werben, eine Werbekampagne durchführen, Klinken putzen (inf). to ~ **for an applicant** (for job) einen Bewerber anpreisen, für einen Bewerber Stimmung machen.
3 n (Pol, Comm) Aktion, Kampagne f.
canvasser ['kænvəsə'] n (a) (Pol) Wahlhelfer m. (b) (Comm) Vertreter, Klinkenputzer (inf) m.
canvassing ['kænvəsɪŋ] n (a) (Pol) Durchführung f des Wahlkampfs, Wahlwerbung f. (b) (Comm) Von-Haus-zu-Haus-Gehen, Klinkenputzen (inf) nt; (sounding-out: of opinions) Meinungsforschung f. ~ **for applicants is not allowed** es ist nicht gestattet, einen Bewerber anzupreisen or für einen Bewerber Stimmung zu machen.
canyon, (US) **cañon** ['kænjən] n Cañon m.
cap[1] [kæp] **1** n (a) (hat) Mütze f; (soldier's ~ also) Käppi nt; (nurse's ~) Haube f; (Jur, Univ) Barett nt; (for swimming) Bademütze or -kappe f; (of jester) Kappe f; (of cardinal) Hut m; (skull-~) Käppchen nt. ~ **in hand** kleinlaut; if the ~ **fits** (, wear it) (prov) wem die Jacke paßt, der soll sie sich anziehen; to set one's ~ **at sb** es auf jdn abgesehen haben, sich (dat) jdn zu angeln versuchen (inf); ~ **and bells** Schellenkappe f; **in ~ and gown** mit Doktorhut und Talar; he's got his ~ **for England, he's an English ~** (Sport) er ist/war in der englischen Nationalmannschaft; see thinking, feather etc.
(b) (lid, cover: of bottle) Verschluß, Deckel m; (of fountain pen) (Verschluß)kappe f; (of valve) Kappe f; (Mil: of shell, fuse) Kapsel f; (Aut: petrol ~, radiator ~) Verschluß m.
(c) (contraceptive) Pessar nt.
(d) (of mushroom) Hut m.
(e) (explosive) Platzpatrone f; (for toy gun) Zündplättchen nt.
(f) (of shoe) Kappe f.
2 vt (a) (put ~ on) bottle etc verschließen, zumachen; (fig: cover top of) peaks bedecken.
(b) (Sport) he was ~ped four times for England er wurde viermal für die englische Nationalmannschaft aufgestellt.
(c) (do or say better) überbieten. and then to ~ it all ... und, um dem Ganzen die Krone aufzusetzen, ...

(d) (Scot Univ) einen akademischen Grad verleihen (+dat).
cap[2] n (Typ, inf) großer Buchstabe. in ~s in Großbuchstaben.
capability [ˌkeɪpə'bɪlɪtɪ] n (a) (potential ability) Fähigkeit f; (no pl: capableness also) Kompetenz f. (b) (Mil) Potential nt.
capable ['keɪpəbl] adj (a) (skilful, competent) fähig, kompetent; mother gut.
(b) to be ~ **of doing sth** etw tun können; (person: have physical, mental ability also) fähig sein, etw zu tun; to be ~ **of sth** etw können; zu etw fähig sein; it's ~ **of exploding any minute** es kann jede Minute explodieren; it's ~ **of speeds of up to ...** es erreicht Geschwindigkeiten bis zu ...; he's ~ **of better** er kann Besseres leisten, er ist zu Besserem fähig; the poem is ~ **of several interpretations** das Gedicht läßt mehrere Interpretationsmöglichkeiten zu; ~ **of improvement** verbesserungsfähig; he's quite ~ **of changing his mind at the last minute** er ist imstande or er bringt es fertig und ändert seine Meinung in der letzten Minute; thank you but I'm quite ~ **of doing that myself** danke, ich bin durchaus imstande or fähig, das allein zu machen, danke, ich kann das durchaus allein.
capably ['keɪpəblɪ] adv kompetent, geschickt.
capacious [kə'peɪʃəs] adj geräumig; dress weit.
capacitor [kə'pæsɪtə'] n Kondensator m.
capacity [kə'pæsɪtɪ] n (a) (cubic content etc) Fassungsvermögen nt, (Raum)inhalt m; (maximum output) Kapazität f; (maximum weight) Höchstlast f; (Aut: engine ~) Hubraum m. **filled to ~** randvoll; (hall) bis auf den letzten Platz besetzt; **seating ~ of** 400 400 Sitzplätze; to work to ~ voll ausgelastet sein; **working at full ~** voll ausgelastet; the Stones played to ~ **audiences** die „Stones" spielten vor ausverkauften Sälen.
(b) (ability) Fähigkeit f. he had lost all ~ **for happiness** er hatte die Fähigkeit, Glück zu empfinden, völlig verloren; his ~ **for learning** seine Lern- or Aufnahmefähigkeit; he has a great ~ **for work** er kann sehr gut arbeiten; **this work is within/beyond his ~** er ist zu dieser Arbeit fähig/nicht fähig.
(c) (role, position) Eigenschaft, Funktion f. in my ~ **as a doctor** (in meiner Eigenschaft) als Arzt; the mayor, **speaking in his official ~, said** ... er sagte in seiner Eigenschaft als Bürgermeister ...; they refused to **employ him in any ~ whatsoever** sie lehnten es ab, ihn in irgendeiner Form zu beschäftigen.
(d) (legal power) Befugnis f.
caparison [kə'pærɪsn] (liter) **1** n Schabracke f (old). **2** vt mit einer Schabracke bedecken (old).
cape[1] [keɪp] n Cape nt, Umhang m, Pelerine f (old).
cape[2] n (Geog) Kap nt.
Cape: ~ **buffalo** n Kaffernbüffel m; ~ **coloured** adj farbig, gemischtrassig; ~ **Horn/of Good Hope** n Kap nt Hoorn/der guten Hoffnung.
caper[1] ['keɪpə'] **1** vi herumtollen. **2** n (a) (skip) Luft- or Freudensprung m. (b) (prank) Eskapade, Kapriole f. (c) (sl: crime) Ding nt (sl).
caper[2] n (Bot, Cook) Kaper f; (shrub) Kapernstrauch m.
capercaille, capercailzie [ˌkæpə'keɪlɪ] n Auerhahn m.
Cape: ~ **Town** n Kapstadt nt; ~ **Verde Islands** npl Kapverdische Inseln, Kapverden pl.
capful ['kæpful] n one ~ **to one litre of water** eine Verschlußkappe auf einen Liter Wasser.
capillary [kə'pɪlərɪ] **1** adj kapillar, Kapillar-. ~ **attraction** or **action** Kapillarwirkung f. **2** n Kapillare f, Kapillargefäß nt.
capital ['kæpɪtl] **1** n (a) (also ~ **city**) Hauptstadt, Kapitale (geh) f.
(b) (also ~ **letter**) Großbuchstabe m. **large/small ~s** Groß-/Kleinbuchstaben, Versalien (spec) pl/Kapitälchen pl (spec); **please write in ~s** bitte in Blockschrift schreiben!
(c) no pl (Fin) Kapital nt. to make ~ **out of sth** (fig) aus etw Kapital schlagen; ~ **and labour** Kapital und Arbeit.
(d) (Archit) Kapitell nt.
2 adj (a) letter Groß-. **love with a ~ L** die große Liebe; a car **with a ~ C** ein richtiges Auto; **unity with a ~ U** hundertprozentige Einheit.
(b) (dated inf) prächtig (dated), famos (dated).
capital in cpds Kapital-; ~ **expenditure** n Kapitalaufwendungen pl; ~ **gains** npl Kapitalgewinn m; ~ **gains tax** n Kapitalertragssteuer f; ~ **goods** npl Produktionsmittel or -güter pl.
capitalism ['kæpɪtəlɪzəm] n Kapitalismus m.
capitalist ['kæpɪtəlɪst] **1** n Kapitalist(in f) m. **2** adj kapitalistisch.
capitalistic [ˌkæpɪtə'lɪstɪk] adj kapitalistisch.
capitalization [ˌkæpɪtəlaɪ'zeɪʃən] n (Fin) Kapitalisierung, Kapitalisation f; (Typ) Großschreibung f.
capitalize ['kæpɪtəlaɪz] vt (a) (Fin) kapitalisieren. (b) (Typ) word groß schreiben.
♦**capitalize on** vi+prep (fig) Kapital schlagen aus.
capital: ~ **offence** n Kapitalverbrechen nt; ~ **punishment** n Todesstrafe f; ~ **sum** n Kapitalbetrag m, Kapital nt.
capitation [ˌkæpɪ'teɪʃən] n Kopfsteuer f.
Capitol ['kæpɪtl] n Kapitol nt.
capitulate [kə'pɪtjuleɪt] vi kapitulieren (also Mil) (to vor +dat), aufgeben (to gegenüber).
capitulation [kə,pɪtju'leɪʃən] n Kapitulation f.
capo ['kæpəu] n Kapodaster m.
capon ['keɪpən] n Kapaun m.
caprice [kə'priːs] n (a) Laune(nhaftigkeit), Kaprice (geh) f. (b) (Mus) Capriccio nt.
capricious [kə'prɪʃəs] adj launisch, kapriziös (geh), unberechenbar.
capriciously [kə'prɪʃəslɪ] adv act, behave launenhaft; decide, do sth einer Laune gehorchend (geh).
capriciousness [kə'prɪʃəsnɪs] n Launenhaftigkeit, Unberechenbarkeit f.
Capricorn ['kæprɪkɔːn] n Steinbock m.

capsicum ['kæpsɪkəm] *n* (*Bot: plant, fruit*) Pfefferschote *f*, Peperoni *pl*.

capsize [kæp'saɪz] **1** *vi* kentern. **2** *vt* zum Kentern bringen.

capstan ['kæpstən] *n* Poller *m*.

capsular ['kæpsjʊlə'] *adj* Kapsel-.

capsule ['kæpsjuːl] *n* Kapsel *f*.

captain ['kæptɪn] (*abbr* **Capt**) **1** *n* (*Mil*) Hauptmann *m*; (*Naut, Aviat, Sport*) Kapitän *m*; (*US: in restaurant*) Oberkellner *m*. **yes**, ~! jawohl, Herr Hauptmann/Kapitän!; ~ **of industry** Industriekapitän *m*.
2 *vt* (*Sport*) *team* anführen; (*Naut*) *ship* befehligen. **he** ~**ed the team for years** er war jahrelang Kapitän der Mannschaft.

captaincy ['kæptənsɪ] *n* Befehligung *f*, Befehl *m*; (*Sport*) Führung *f*. **to get one's** ~ **sein Kapitänspatent** *nt* **erhalten; under his** ~ mit ihm als Kapitän.

caption ['kæpʃən] **1** *n* Überschrift *f*; (*under cartoon*) Bildunterschrift *f*; (*Film: subtitle*) Untertitel *m*. **2** *vt* betiteln, mit einer Überschrift *or* einem Titel *etc* versehen.

captious ['kæpʃəs] *adj person* überkritisch, pedantisch; *remark* spitzfindig.

captivate ['kæptɪveɪt] *vt* faszinieren, entzücken.

captivating ['kæptɪveɪtɪŋ] *adj* bezaubernd; *personality* einnehmend.

captive ['kæptɪv] **1** *n* Gefangene(r) *mf*. **to take sb** ~ jdn gefangennehmen; **to hold sb** ~ jdn gefangenhalten; (*fig*) jdn fesseln, jdn gefangennehmen. **2** *adj person* gefangen; a ~ **audience** ein unfreiwilliges Publikum; ~ **balloon** Fesselballon *m*; **in a** ~ **state** in Gefangenschaft *f*.

captivity [kæp'tɪvɪtɪ] *n* Gefangenschaft *f*.

captor ['kæptə'] *n* derjenige, der jdn gefangennimmt. **his** ~**s treated him kindly** er wurde nach seiner Gefangennahme gut behandelt; **his** ~**s were Ruritanian** er wurde von Ruritaniern gefangengenommen; **his** ~**s later freed him** man ließ ihn später wieder frei.

capture ['kæptʃə'] **1** *vt* (**a**) *town* einnehmen, erobern; *treasure* erobern; *person* gefangennehmen; *animal* (ein)fangen; *ship* kapern, aufbringen (*spec*). **they** ~**d the town from the enemy** sie eroberten die vom Feind beherrschte Stadt.
(**b**) (*fig*) *votes* erringen, auf sich (*acc*) vereinigen; *prizes* erringen; (*painter etc*) *atmosphere* einfangen; *attention, sb's interest* erregen.
2 *n* Eroberung *f*; (*thing captured also*) Fang *m*; (*of escapee*) Gefangennahme *f* (*animal*) Einfangen *nt*.

capuchin ['kæpjutʃɪn] *n* (**a**) (*hooded cloak*) Kapuzencape *nt*. (**b**) (*Zool*) Kapuziner(affe) *m*. (**c**) (*Eccl*) C~ Kapuziner-(mönch) *m*.

car [kɑː'] *n* (**a**) Auto *nt*, Wagen *m*. **by** ~ mit dem Auto *or* Wagen. (**b**) (*esp US: Rail, tram*~) Wagen *m*. (*of airship, balloon, cable*~) Gondel *f*; (*US: of elevator*) Fahrkorb *m*.

carafe [kə'ræf] *n* Karaffe *f*.

caramel ['kærəməl] *n* (*substance*) Karamel *m*; (*sweet*) Karamelle *f*.

caramel *in cpds* Karamel-; ~-**coloured** *adj* hellbraun; ~-**flavoured** *adj* mit Karamelgeschmack.

carapace ['kærəpeɪs] *n* Schale *f*; (*of tortoise etc*) (Rücken)-panzer *m*.

carat ['kærət] *n* Karat *nt*. **nine** ~ **gold** neunkarätiges Gold.

caravan ['kærəvæn] *n* (**a**) (*Brit: Aut*) Wohnwagen, Caravan *m*. (**b**) (*gipsy* ~) Zigeunerwagen *m*. (**c**) (*desert* ~) Karawane *f*.

caravan holiday *n* Ferien *pl* im Wohnwagen.

caravanning ['kærəvænɪŋ] *n* Caravaning *nt*, Urlaub *m* im Wohnwagen. **to go** ~ Urlaub im Wohnwagen machen.

caravanserai [ˌkærə'vænsəˌraɪ] *n* Karawanserei *f*.

caravan site *n* Campingplatz *m* für Wohnwagen.

caravel ['kærə'vel] *n* Karavelle *f*.

caraway ['kærəweɪ] *n* Kümmel *m*. ~ **seeds** Kümmel(körner *pl*) *m*.

carbide ['kɑːbaɪd] *n* Karbid *nt*.

carbine ['kɑːbaɪn] *n* Karabiner *m*.

carbohydrate ['kɑːbəʊ'haɪdreɪt] *n* Kohle(n)hydrat *nt*.

carbolic [kɑː'bɒlɪk] *adj* (**a**) Karbol-. ~ **acid** Karbolsäure *f*. (**b**) (*also* ~ **soap**) Karbolseife *f*.

carbon ['kɑːbən] *n* (*Chem*) Kohlenstoff *m*; (*Elec*) Kohle *f*.

carbonaceous [ˌkɑːbə'neɪʃəs] *adj* Kohlenstoff-, kohlenstoffhaltig.

carbonate ['kɑːbənɪt] *n* Karbonat *nt*.

carbonated ['kɑːbəˌneɪtəd] *adj* mit Kohlensäure (versetzt).

carbon: ~ **copy** *n* Durchschlag *m*; **to be a** ~ **copy of sth** das genaue Ebenbild einer Sache (*gen*) sein; **she's a** ~ **copy of her sister** sie sieht ihrer Schwester zum Verwechseln ähnlich; ~ **dating** *n* Radiokarbonmethode, Kohlenstoffdatierung *f*; ~ **dioxide** *n* Kohlendioxyd *nt*.

carbonic [kɑː'bɒnɪk] *adj* Kohlen-. ~ **acid** Kohlensäure *f*.

carboniferous [ˌkɑːbə'nɪfərəs] *adj* (*Geol*) kohlehaltig.

carbonization [ˌkɑːbənaɪ'zeɪʃən] *n* Karbonisation, Verkohlung *f*.

carbonize ['kɑːbənaɪz] *vt* karbonisieren, verkohlen (lassen).

carbon: ~ **monoxide** *n* Kohlenmonoxyd *nt*; ~ **paper** *n* Kohlepapier *nt*.

carboy ['kɑːbɔɪ] *n* Korbflasche *f*.

carbuncle ['kɑːˌbʌŋkl] *n* (**a**) (*Med*) Karbunkel *m*. (**b**) (*jewel*) Karfunkel(stein) *m*.

carburettor, (*US*) **carburetor** [ˌkɑːbə'retə'] *n* Vergaser *m*.

carcass ['kɑːkəs] *n* (**a**) (*corpse*) Leiche *f*; (*of animal*) Kadaver *m*, (Tier)leiche *f*; (*at butcher's*) Rumpf *m*. **move your fat** ~ (*inf*) geh mal mit deinem fetten Kadaver hier weg! (*sl*). (**b**) (*of ship, house*) Skelett *nt*; (*remains*) Überbleibsel *pl*, Trümmer *pl*.

carcinogen [kɑː'sɪnədʒen] *n* Krebserreger *m*.

carcinogenic [ˌkɑːsɪnə'dʒenɪk] *adj* karzinogen, krebserregend.

carcinoma [ˌkɑːsɪ'nəʊmə] *n* Karzinom *nt*.

car *in cpds* Auto-; ~ **coat** *n* Dreivierteljacke *f*; ~ **crash** *n* (Auto)unfall *m*.

card¹ [kɑːd] *n* (**a**) *no pl* (~**board**) Pappe *f*.
(**b**) (*greetings, visiting* ~ *etc*) Karte *f*.
(**c**) ~**s** *pl* (*employment* ~**s**) Papiere *pl*; **he asked for his** ~**s** (*inf*) er wollte sich (*dat*) seine Papiere geben lassen (*inf*).
(**d**) (*Sport: programme*) Programm *nt*.
(**e**) (*playing* ~) (Spiel)karte *f*. **to play** ~**s** Karten spielen; **to lose money at** ~**s** Geld beim Kartenspiel verlieren; **pack of** ~**s** Karten *pl*, Kartenspiel, Kartenpaket *nt*; **game of** ~**s** Kartenspiel *nt*; **house of** ~**s** (*lit, fig*) Kartenhaus *nt*.
(**f**) (*fig uses*) **put one's** ~**s on the table** seine Karten aufdecken *or* (offen) auf den Tisch legen; **to play one's** ~**s right/badly** geschickt/ungeschickt taktieren, taktisch geschickt/unklug vorgehen; **to hold all the** ~**s** alle Trümpfe in der Hand haben; **to play one's last/best** ~ seinen letzten/höchsten Trumpf ausspielen; **it's on the** ~**s** das ist zu erwarten.
(**g**) (*dated inf: person*) ulkiger Vogel (*inf*).

card² (*Tex*) **1** *n* Wollkamm *m*, Krempel, Karde *f*. **2** *vt wool, cotton* kämmen, krempeln, karden.

cardamom ['kɑːdəməm] *n* Kardamom *m or nt*.

card: ~**board 1** *n* Karton *m*, Pappe *f*; **2** *attr* Papp-; (*fig*) *character* stereotyp, klischeehaft, schablonenhaft; ~**board box** *n* (Papp)karton *m*, Pappschachtel *f*; **a** ~-**carrying member** ein eingetragenes Mitglied; ~ **catalogue** *or* **file** *n* Zettelkatalog *m*; (*in library*) Katalog(karten *pl*) *m*; ~ **game** *n* Kartenspiel *nt*.

cardiac ['kɑːdɪæk] *adj* Herz-. ~ **arrest** Herzstillstand *m*.

cardigan ['kɑːdɪgən] *n* Strickjacke *f*.

cardinal ['kɑːdɪnl] **1** *n* (**a**) (*Eccl*) Kardinal *m*. (**b**) *see* ~ **number**. **2** *adj* (*chief*) Haupt-; (*utmost*) äußerste(r, s) *attr*.

cardinal: ~ **number** *n* Kardinalzahl *f*; ~ **points** *npl* Himmelsrichtungen *pl*; ~ **red** *n* Purpurrot *nt*; ~ **sin** *n* Todsünde *f*; ~ **virtue** *n* Kardinaltugend *f*.

card index *n* Kartei *f*; (*in library*) Katalog *m*.

cardio ['kɑːdɪəʊ] *pref* Kardio-. ~**gram** Kardiogramm *nt*.

cardiologist [ˌkɑːdɪ'ɒlɪdʒɪst] *n* Kardiologe *m*, Kardiologin *f*.

cardiology [ˌkɑːdɪ'ɒlədʒɪ] *n* Kardiologie *f*.

card: ~ **punch** *n* Lochkartenmaschine *f*; ~ **reader** *n* Lesemaschine *f*; ~ **sharp(er)** *n* Falschspieler, Zinker (*inf*) *m*; ~ **table** *n* Spieltisch *m*; ~ **trick** *n* Kartenkunststück *nt*; ~ **vote** *n* (*Brit*) = Abstimmung *f* durch Wahlmänner.

CARE [kɛə'] *abbr of* **Cooperative for American Relief Everywhere.** ~ **packet** Carepaket *nt*.

care [kɛə'] **1** *n* (**a**) (*worry, anxiety*) Sorge *f* (*of* um). **free from** ~**(s)** ohne Sorgen, frei von Sorge; **he hasn't a** ~ **in the world** er hat keinerlei Sorgen; **the** ~**s of the world** die Sorgen der Alltags; **the** ~**s of state** die Staatsgeschäfte *pl*.
(**b**) (*carefulness, attentiveness*) Sorgfalt *f*. **driving without due** ~ **and attention** fahrlässiges Verhalten im Straßenverkehr; **to drive with due** ~ **and attention** sich umsichtig im Straßenverkehr verhalten; **"fragile, with** ~**"**, **"handle with** ~**"** „Vorsicht, zerbrechlich"; **to take** ~ aufpassen, achtgeben, vorsichtig sein; **take** ~ **he doesn't cheat you** sehen Sie sich vor *or* nehmen Sie sich in acht, daß er Sie nicht betrügt; **bye-bye, take** ~ tschüß, mach's gut; **it got broken despite all the** ~ **we took** es ist trotz aller Vorsicht *or* trotz sorgsamster Behandlung kaputtgegangen; **to take** ~ **to do sth/not to do sth** sich bemühen *or* sich (*dat*) Mühe geben, etw zu tun/etw nicht zu tun; **I'll take** ~ **not to trust him again** ich werde mich hüten, ihm noch einmal zu trauen; **to take** ~ **over** *or* **with sth/in doing sth** etw sorgfältig tun; **you should take more** ~ **with** *or* **over the details** Sie sollten sich sorgfältiger mit den Einzelheiten befassen; **have a** ~ (*old: be careful*) gib acht *or* Obacht! (*old*); (*inf: be considerate*) nun mach mal einen Punkt! (*inf*).
(**c**) (*of teeth, skin, car, furniture etc*) Pflege *f*. **to take** ~ **of sth** auf etw (*acc*) aufpassen; *of one's appearance, hair, car, furniture etc* pflegen; (*not treat roughly*) *car, furniture, health* schonen; **to take** ~ **of oneself** sich um sich selbst kümmern; (*as regards health*) sich schonen, auf sich (*acc*) aufpassen; (*as regards appearance*) etwas für sich tun, sich pflegen.
(**d**) (*of old people, children*) Versorgung, Fürsorge *f*. **medical** ~ **in this area is rather poor** die ärztliche Versorgung in diesem Gebiet ist ziemlich schlecht; **he needs medical** ~ er muß ärztlich behandelt werden; **he is in the** ~ **of Dr Smith** er ist bei Dr. Smith in Behandlung; **to take** ~ **of sb** sich um jdn kümmern; *of patients* jdn versorgen; *of one's family* für jdn sorgen; **they took good** ~ **of her** while she was in hospital sie wurde im Krankenhaus gut versorgt.
(**e**) (*protection, supervision*) Obhut *f*. ~ **of** (*abbr* **c/o**) bei; **in** *or* **under sb's** ~ in jds (*dat*) Obhut; **to take a child into** ~ ein Kind in Pflege nehmen; **to be taken into** ~ in Pflege gegeben werden; **the children/valuables in my** ~ die mir anvertrauten Kinder/Wertsachen; **to take** ~ **of sth** *of valuables etc* auf etw (*acc*) aufpassen; *of plants, animals etc* sich um etw kümmern; (*over longer period*) etw versorgen.
(**f**) **to take** ~ **of sb/sth** (*see to*) sich um jdn/etw kümmern; *of arrangements, affairs etc also* etw erledigen; **that takes** ~ **of him/it** er/das wäre abgehakt (*inf*), das wäre erledigt; **let me take** ~ **of that** lassen Sie mich das mal machen, überlassen Sie das mir; **that can take** ~ **of itself** das wird sich schon irgendwie geben; **let the housework take** ~ **of itself for a moment** nun laß doch mal einen Augenblick die Hausarbeit (sein).
(**g**) (*caringness, concern*) (*of person*) Anteilnahme, Fürsorglichkeit *f*; (*of state, council*) Interesse *nt* am Mitmenschen. **if the city planners showed more** ~ wenn die Städteplaner etwas mehr Menschenfreundlichkeit zeigen würden *or* den Bedürfnissen des Menschen mehr Rechnung tragen würden; **if only she showed a little** ~ wenn sie nur nicht so gleichgültig wäre; **the party has a genuine** ~ **for senior citizens** der Partei liegt das Wohl der älteren Mitbürger am Herzen.

2 *vi* (*be concerned*) sich kümmern (*about* um). **we ~ about our image** wir kümmern uns um unser Image, wir sorgen für unser Image; **a company that ~s about its staff** eine Firma, die sich um ihr Personal kümmert *or* für ihr Personal sorgt; **money is all he ~s about** er interessiert sich nur fürs Geld, ihm liegt nur etwas am Geld; **that's all he ~s about** alles andere ist ihm egal; **he ~s deeply about her/this** sie/das liegt ihm sehr am Herzen; **he doesn't ~ about her** sie ist ihm gleichgültig; **I know you don't ~ about me/such things** ich weiß, daß ich dir gleichgültig bin/daß dir so etwas gleichgültig *or* egal ist; **I didn't know you ~d** (*hum*) ich wußte gar nicht, daß ich dir was bedeute; **the party that ~s** die Partei, die sich um ihr Wohl kümmert, die Partei mit Herz; **I wish you'd ~ a bit more** ich wünschte, das wäre dir nicht alles egal *or* gleichgültig; **but Karin darling, you know I ~** aber Karin, mein Schatz, du weißt doch, daß du mir nicht gleichgültig bist; **I don't ~** das ist mir egal *or* gleich-gültig; **as if I ~d** als ob mir das etwas ausmachen würde; **for all I ~** meinetwegen, von mir aus; **who ~s?** na und?, und wenn schon?; **he just doesn't ~** das ist ihm so egal, das kümmert ihn nicht.

3 *vt* (**a**) (*mind, be concerned*) **I don't ~ what people say** es ist mir egal *or* es kümmert mich nicht, was die Leute sagen; **don't you ~ that half the world is starving?** berührt es Sie überhaupt nicht, daß die halbe Welt hungert?; **what do I ~?** was geht mich das an?; **I don't ~ a rap or jot** (*inf*) das ist mir schnurz(egal) (*inf*); **I couldn't ~ less what people say** es ist mir doch völlig egal *or* gleich(gültig), was die Leute sagen; **you don't ~ what happens to me — but I do ~** dir ist es ja egal, was mir passiert — nein, das ist mir überhaupt nicht egal; **I didn't think you ~d what I do** ich habe nicht gedacht, daß dich das kümmert, was ich mache, ich habe gedacht, das ist dir egal, was ich mache.

(**b**) (*like*) **to ~ to do sth** etw gerne tun mögen *or* wollen; **would you ~ to take off your coat?** würden Sie gerne Ihren Mantel ablegen?, wollen *or* möchten Sie vielleicht (Ihren Mantel) ablegen?; **can I help you? — if you ~ to** kann ich Ihnen helfen? — wenn Sie so freundlich wären; **I wouldn't ~ to meet him/try** ich würde keinen gesteigerten Wert darauf legen, ihn kennenzuler-nen/das zu probieren; **I don't ~ to believe him** ich bin nicht gewillt, ihm zu glauben; **but I don't ~ to** ich will aber nicht.

♦ **care for** *vi* +*prep obj* (**a**) (*look after*) sich kümmern um; **invalid also** versorgen; **hands, furniture etc** pflegen. **well ~d-~ person** gut versorgt; **hands, garden, hair, house** gepflegt; **the children are being ~d ~ by their grandmother** die Großmutter kümmert sich um die Kinder.

(**b**) (*like*) **I don't ~ ~ that suggestion/picture/him** dieser Vor-schlag/das Bild/er sagt mir nicht zu; **I don't ~ ~ your tone of voice** wie reden Sie denn mit mir?; **would you ~ ~ a cup of tea?** hätten Sie gerne eine Tasse Tee?; **~ ~ a drink?** wie wär's mit einem Drink?, etwas zu trinken?; **~ ~ another?** noch einen?; **I never have much ~d ~ his films** ich habe mir noch nie viel aus seinen Filmen gemacht; **yes, sir, what would you ~ ~?** was hätte der Herr gern?; **what sort of hotel would madam ~ ~?** an welche Art von Hotel hatten gnädige Frau gedacht?; **but you know I do ~ ~** you aber du weißt doch, daß du mir viel bedeutest *or* daß du mir nicht egal *or* gleichgültig bist.

career [kə'rɪəʳ] **1** *n* Karriere *f*; (*profession, job*) Beruf *m*; (*working life*) Laufbahn *f*; (*life, development, progress*) Wer-degang *m*. **~s officer** Berufsberater(in *f*) *m*; **~s guidance** Berufsberatung *f*; **journalism is his new ~** er hat jetzt die Lauf-bahn des Journalisten eingeschlagen; **to make a ~ for oneself** Karriere machen.

2 *attr* Karriere-; **soldier, diplomat** Berufs-. **~ girl** *or* **woman** Karrierefrau *f*.

3 *vi* rasen. **to ~ along** rasen.

careerist [kə'rɪərɪst] *n* Karrierist(in *f*) *m*, Karrieremacher *m*.

carefree ['kɛəfriː] *adj* sorglos, unbekümmert; **song** heiter.

careful ['kɛəful] *adj* sorgfältig; (*cautious, circumspect*) sorgsam, vorsichtig; (*with money etc*) sparsam. **~!** Vorsicht!, passen Sie auf!; **to be ~** aufpassen (*of* auf +*acc*); **be ~ with** *or* **of the glasses** sei mit den Gläsern vorsichtig; **be ~ what you do** sieh dich vor, nimm dich in acht; **be ~ (that) they don't hear you** gib acht *or* sei vorsichtig, damit *or* daß sie dich nicht hören; **be ~ not to drop it** paß auf, daß du das nicht fallen läßt; **he is very ~ with his money** er hält sein Geld gut zusammen.

carefully ['kɛəfulɪ] *adv see adj*.

carefulness ['kɛəfulnɪs] *n see adj* Sorgfalt *f*; Sorgsamkeit, Vor-sicht *f*; Sparsamkeit *f*.

careless ['kɛəlɪs] *adj* (**a**) (*negligent, heedless*) **person, worker, work** nachlässig; **driver** unvorsichtig; **driving** leichtsinnig; **remark** gedankenlos. **~ mistake** Flüchtigkeitsfehler *m*; **to be ~ of one's health** nicht auf seine Gesundheit achten; **to be ~ of sb's feelings** nicht an jds (*acc*) Gefühle denken.

(**b**) (*carefree*) sorglos, unbekümmert.

(**c**) **dress, elegance** lässig.

carelessly ['kɛəlɪslɪ] *adv see adj*.

carelessness ['kɛəlɪsnɪs] *n see adj* (**a**) Nachlässigkeit *f*; Unvorsicht(igkeit) *f*, Leichtsinn *m*; Gedankenlosigkeit *f*.

(**b**) Sorglosigkeit, Unbekümmertheit *f*.

(**c**) Lässigkeit *f*.

caress [kə'res] **1** *n* Liebkosung, Zärtlichkeit *f usu pl*; Streicheln *nt no pl*. **2** *vt* streicheln, liebkosen.

caressing [kə'resɪŋ] *adj* zärtlich, sanft, streichelnd.

caret ['kærət] *n* (*Typ*) Einschaltungszeichen *nt*.

care: **~taker** *n* Hausmeister *m*; **~taker government** *n* ge-schäftsführende Regierung *f*; **~worn** *adj* von Sorgen gezeichnet.

car: **~ fare** *n* (*US*) Fahrpreis *m*; **~-ferry** *n* Autofähre *f*.

cargo ['kɑːgəʊ] *n* (Schiffs)fracht *or* -ladung *f*, Kargo *m* (*spec*). **~ boat** Frachter, Frachtdampfer *m*, Frachtschiff *nt*.

carhop ['kɑːhɒp] *n* (*US*) Bedienung *f* in einem Drive-in-Restaurant.

Caribbean [,kærɪ'biːən, (*US*) kæ'rɪbiːən] **1** *adj* karibisch. **~ Sea** Karibisches Meer. **2** *n* Karibik *f*.

caribou ['kærɪbuː] *n* Karibu *m*.

caricature ['kærɪkətjʊəʳ] **1** *n* Karikatur *f*. **2** *vt* karikieren.

caricaturist [,kærɪkə'tjʊərɪst] *n* Karikaturist(in *f*) *m*.

caries ['kɛəriːz] *n* Karies *f*.

carillon [kə'rɪljən] *n* Glockenspiel *nt*.

caring ['kɛərɪŋ] *adj* **person, attitude** warmherzig, mitfühlend, einfühlsam; **parent, husband** liebevoll; **teacher** engagiert; **government, society** sozial, mitmenschlich. **a child needs a ~ environment** ein Kind braucht Zuwendung *or* braucht eine Umgebung, die es mit sich umgeht.

Carmelite ['kɑːməlaɪt] *n* Karmelit(in *f*), Karmeliter(in *f*) *m*.

carmine ['kɑːmaɪn] **1** *adj* karm(es)inrot. **2** *n* Karmesin- *or* Kar-min(rot) *nt*.

carnage ['kɑːnɪdʒ] *n* Blutbad, Gemetzel *nt*. **a scene of ~** ein blutiges Schauspiel; **fields covered with the ~ of battle** mit Toten *or* Leichen übersäte Schlachtfelder *pl*.

carnal ['kɑːnl] *adj* fleischlich, körperlich. **~ desires** sinnliche Begierden; **~ lusts** Fleischeslust *f* (*liter*); **to have ~ knowledge of sb** mit jdm (Geschlechts)verkehr haben.

carnation [kɑː'neɪʃən] *n* Nelke *f*.

carnival ['kɑːnɪvəl] **1** *n* Volksfest *nt*; (*village ~ etc*) Schützen-fest *nt*; (*based on religion*) Karneval *m*. **2** *attr* Fest-; Karne-vals-. **~ procession** Fest-/Karnevalszug *m*.

carnivore ['kɑːnɪvɔːʳ] *n*, *pl* **carnivora** [kɑː'nɪvərə] (*animal*) Fleischfresser *m*; (*plant*) fleischfressende Pflanze.

carnivorous [kɑː'nɪvərəs] *adj* fleischfressend, karnivor.

carob ['kærəb] *n* Johannisbrotbaum *m*; (*fruit*) Johannisbrot *nt*.

carol ['kærəl] **1** *n* Lied *nt*. **Christmas ~** Weihnachtslied *nt*. **2** *vi* (*old, liter*) (fröhlich) singen, jubilieren (*old, liter*); (*bird*) tirilieren (*old, liter*).

carol: **~ singers** *npl* ≈ Sternsinger *pl*; **~ singing** *n* Weihnachtssingen *nt*.

carom ['kærəm] (*US*) **1** *n* Karambolage *f*. **2** *vi* (*Billiards*) karam-bolieren; (*rebound*) abprallen.

carotid (artery) [kə'rɒtɪd('ɑːtərɪ)] *n* Halsschlagader, Karotide (*spec*) *f*.

carousal [kə'raʊzəl] *n* (*old*) (Zech)gelage *nt*, Schmaus *m*.

carouse [kə'raʊz] *vi* (*old*) zechen, Gelage feiern.

carousel [,kæru'sel] *n see* **car(r)ousel**.

carp¹ [kɑːp] *n* (*fish*) Karpfen *m*.

carp² *vi* etwas auszusetzen haben, nörgeln. **to ~ at sb/sth** an jdm/etw etwas auszusetzen haben, an jdm herummeckern (*inf*)/über etw (*acc*) meckern (*inf*).

carpal bone ['kɑːpl'bəʊn] *n* Handwurzelknochen *m*.

car: **~ park** *n* (*open-air*) Parkplatz *m*; (*covered*) Parkhaus *nt*; **~ parking** *n* **~ parking facilities are available** Parkplatz *or* Parkmöglichkeit(en) vorhanden.

Carpathians [kɑː'peɪθɪənz] *npl* (*Geog*) Karpaten *pl*.

carpel ['kɑːpl] *n* Fruchtblatt *nt*.

carpenter ['kɑːpɪntəʳ] *n* Zimmermann *m*; (*for furniture*) Tischler *m*.

carpentry ['kɑːpɪntrɪ] *n* Zimmerhandwerk *nt*, (Bau)tischlerei *f*; (*as hobby*) Tischlern *nt*. **a piece of ~** eine Tischlerarbeit.

carpet ['kɑːpɪt] **1** *n* (*lit, fig*) Teppich *m*; (*fitted ~*) Teppichboden *m*. **the subject which is on the ~** das Thema, das zur Zeit dis-kutiert wird; **to have sb on the ~** (*inf*) jdn zur Minna machen (*inf*).

2 *vt* (**a**) **floor** (mit Teppichen/Teppichboden) auslegen. **the wood ~ed in** *or* **with moss** der moosbedeckte Waldboden.

(**b**) (*inf: reprimand*) zur Minna machen (*inf*).

carpet: **~ bag** *n* Reisetasche *f*; **~bagger** *n* (*US*) (*inf*) politischer Abenteurer; (*Hist*) politischer Ämterjäger, der mit nichts als einer Reisetasche nach dem Sezessionskrieg in die besetzten Südstaaten kam; **~-beater** *n* Teppich- *or* Ausklopfer *m*.

carpeting ['kɑːpɪtɪŋ] *n* Teppiche *pl*.

carpet: **~ slippers** *npl* Pantoffeln, Hausschuhe *pl*; **~ sweeper** *n* Teppichkehrer *m*, Teppichkehrmaschine *f*.

carping ['kɑːpɪŋ] **1** *adj* **a ~ old woman** eine alte Meckerziege (*inf*); **she grew weary of his ~ criticism** sie wurde sein stän-diges Nörgeln leid. **2** *n* Nörgelei(en *pl*) *f*, Gemecker *nt* (*inf*).

carport ['kɑːpɔːt] *n* Einstellplatz *m*.

carrel ['kærəl] *n* Arbeitsnische *f*, Arbeitsplatz *m* (*in Bibliothek*).

carriage ['kærɪdʒ] *n* (**a**) (*horse-drawn vehicle*) Kutsche *f*; (*esp US: baby ~*) Kinderwagen *m*. **~ and pair** Zweispänner *m*.

(**b**) (*Brit Rail*) Wagen *m*.

(**c**) (*Comm: conveyance*) Beförderung *f*; (*cost of ~* also) Beförderungskosten *pl*. **~ forward** per Frachtnachnahme; **~ free** gebührenfrei, frachtfrei; **~ paid** Gebühr bezahlt.

(**d**) (*Typ*) Wagen *m*; (*Mil: gun-~*) Lafette *f*.

(**e**) (*of person: bearing*) Haltung *f*.

carriageway ['kærɪdʒweɪ] *n* (*Brit*) Fahrbahn *f*.

car ride *n* Autofahrt *f*, Fahrt *f* mit dem Auto.

carrier ['kærɪəʳ] *n* (**a**) (*goods haulier*) Spediteur, Transportunternehmer *m*.

(**b**) (*of disease*) Überträger *m*.

(**c**) (*aircraft ~*) Flugzeugträger *m*; (*troop ~*) Transportflug-zeug *nt*/-schiff *nt*.

(**d**) (*Chem*) Träger(substanz *f*) *m*; (*catalyst*) Katalysator *m*.

(**e**) (*luggage rack*) Gepäckträger *m*.

(**f**) (*Brit also: ~ bag*) Tragetasche, Tragetüte *f*.

(**g**) (*also: ~ pigeon*) Brieftaube *f*. **by ~ pigeon** mit der Taubenpost.

carrion ['kærɪən] *n* Aas *nt*. **~ crow** Rabenkrähe *f*.

carrot ['kærət] *n* Mohrrübe, Karotte, Möhre *f*; (*fig*) Köder *m*. **to dangle a ~ before sb** *or* **in front of sb** jdm einen Köder unter die Nase halten; **the stick and the ~** Zuckerbrot und Peitsche.

carroty ['kærətɪ] *adj* **hair** kupferrot.

car(r)ousel [,kæru'sel] *n* Karussell *nt*.

carry ['kærɪ] **1** *vt* (**a**) tragen; **message** (über)bringen.

(b) (*vehicle: convey*) befördern; *goods also* transportieren. **this coach carries 30 people** dieser Bus kann 30 Personen befördern; **a boat ~ing missiles to Cuba** ein Schiff mit Raketen für Kuba; **the boat was carried along by the wind** der Wind trieb das Boot dahin; **the sea carried the boat westward** das Boot wurde nach Westen abgetrieben, die Strömung trieb das Boot westwärts; **the wind carried the sound to him** der Wind trug die Laute zu ihm hin *or* an sein Ohr.

(c) (*have on person*) *documents, money* bei sich haben *or* führen (*form*); *gun, sword* tragen. **to ~ sth about** *or* **around with one** etw mit sich herumtragen; **to ~ money on one** Geld bei sich haben; **to ~ the facts in one's head** die Fakten im Kopf haben; (*remember*) die Fakten (im Kopf) behalten; **the ship was ~ing too much sail** das Schiff hatte zu viele Segel gesetzt.

(d) (*fig*) **his voice carries conviction** seine Stimme klingt überzeugend; **he carried his audience with him** er riß das Publikum mit, er begeisterte das Publikum; **to ~ interest** (*Fin*) Zinsen tragen *or* abwerfen; **the loan carries 5% interest** das Darlehen wird mit 5% verzinst; **this job carries extra pay/a lot of responsibility** dieser Posten bringt eine höhere Bezahlung/ viel Verantwortung mit sich; **the offence carries a penalty of £5** auf dies Vergehen *or* darauf steht eine Geldstrafe von £ 5; **to ~ a mortgage** mit einer Hypothek belastet sein.

(e) (*bridge etc: support*) tragen, stützen. **he carries his drink well** er kann viel vertragen; **he can't ~ the responsibility** er ist der Verantwortung nicht gewachsen.

(f) (*Comm*) *goods, stock* führen, (*auf Lager*) haben.

(g) (*Tech: pipe*) *water, oil, electricity* führen; (*wire*) *sound* (weiter)leiten, übertragen.

(h) (*extend*) führen, (ver)legen. **they carried the pipes under the street** sie verlegten die Rohre unter der Straße; **to ~ sth too far** (*fig*) etw zu weit treiben; **they carried the war into the enemy's territory** sie trugen den Krieg in feindliches Gebiet; **this theme is carried through the whole book** dies Thema zieht sich durch das ganze Buch.

(i) (*win*) einnehmen, erobern. **to ~ the day** siegreich sein, den Sieg davontragen; **to ~ all** *or* **everything before one** freie Bahn haben; (*hum: woman*) viel Holz vor der Tür haben (*inf*); **the motion was carried unanimously** der Antrag wurde einstimmig angenommen; **he carried his point** er ist mit diesem Punkt durchgekommen; **he carried all seven states** er hat die Wahl in allen sieben Ländern gewonnen.

(j) **he carries himself well/like a soldier** er hat eine gute/sol-datische Haltung; **he carries himself with dignity** er tritt würdig auf; **she carries her head very erect** sie trägt den Kopf sehr aufrecht.

(k) (*Press*) **story** bringen.

(l) (*be pregnant with*) erwarten, schwanger gehen mit (*geh*). **to be ~ing a child** schwanger sein, ein Kind erwarten.

(m) (*Math*) **... and ~ 2** ... übertrage *or* behalte 2, ... und 2 im Sinn (*inf*).

2 *vi* **(a)** (*voice, sound*) tragen. **the sound of the alphorn carried for miles** der Klang des Alphorns war meilenweit zu hören.

(b) (*ball, arrow*) fliegen.

♦**carry away** *vt sep* **(a)** (*lit*) (hin)wegtragen; (*torrent, flood*) (hin)wegspülen; (*whirlwind, tornado*) hinwegfegen.

(b) (*fig*) **to get carried ~** es übertreiben, sich nicht mehr bremsen können (*inf*); **don't get carried ~!** übertreib's nicht!, brems dich (*inf*); **to get carried ~ by sth** bei etw in Fahrt kommen, sich an etw (*dat*) hochziehen (*sl*); **to be carried ~ by one's feelings** sich (in seine Gefühle) hineinsteigern; **don't get carried ~ by your success** daß dir dein Erfolg nicht in den Kopf steigt!; **she got carried ~ by the atmosphere of excitement** sie wurde von der Aufregung mitgerissen *or* angesteckt.

♦**carry back** *vt sep* (*fig*) *person* zurückversetzen (*to* in +*acc*).

♦**carry forward** *vt sep* (*Fin*) vortragen.

♦**carry off** *vt sep* **(a)** (*seize, carry away*) wegtragen. **(b)** (*win*) *prizes, medals* gewinnen, mit nach Hause nehmen (*inf*). **(c) to ~ it ~** es hinkriegen (*inf*). **(d)** (*kill*) (hin)wegraffen (*geh*).

♦**carry on 1** *vi* **(a)** (*continue*) weitermachen; (*life*) weitergehen. **here's £5/some work to be ~ing ~ with** hier sind erst einmal 5 Pfund/hier ist etwas Arbeit fürs nächste.

(b) (*inf*) (*talk*) reden und reden; (*make a scene*) ein Theater machen (*inf*). **to ~ ~ about sth** sich über etw (*acc*) auslassen; **they just kept ~ing ~ about sth** sie haben so lange weitergebohrt, bis jemand etwas gemacht hat; **she does tend to ~ ~** sie redet und redet.

(c) (*have an affair*) es haben (*inf*) (*with sb* mit jdm).

2 *vt sep* **(a)** (*continue*) *tradition, family business* fortführen.

(b) (*conduct*) *conversation, correspondence, business* führen; *profession, trade* ausüben.

♦**carry out** *vt sep* **(a)** (*lit*) herausträgen. **(b)** (*fig*) *order, rules, job* ausführen; *promises, obligations* erfüllen; *plan, reform, search, experiment* durchführen; *search also* veranstalten; *threats* wahrmachen.

♦**carry over** *vt sep* **(a)** (*Fin*) vortragen. **(b)** (*to next meeting etc*) vertagen.

♦**carry through** *vt sep* **(a)** (*carry out*) zu Ende führen. **(b)** (*sustain*) überstehen lassen.

♦**carry up** *vt sep* hinauftragen, hochtragen.

carry: **~-all** *n* (*US*) (Einkaufs-/Reise)tasche *f*; **~-cot** *n* Säuglingstragetasche *f*.

carryings-on ['kærɪɪŋz'ɒn] *npl* (*inf*) übles Treiben (*inf*). **all these ~ next door** was die da nebenan alles so treiben (*inf*), was sich da nebenan alles so abspielt.

carry: **~-on** *n* (*inf*) Theater *nt* (*inf*); **~-out** (*US, Scot*) **1** *n* **(a)** (*restaurant*) Imbißstube *f*/Restaurant *nt* für Außer-Haus-Verkauf; (*bar*) Schalter *m* für Außer-Haus-Verkauf, Gassenschenke *f* (*S Ger*); **(b)** (*meal, drink*) Speisen *pl*/Getränke *pl* zum Mitnehmen; **let's get a ~-out** wir können uns ja etwas (zu

essen/trinken) holen *or* mitnehmen; **~-outs aren't allowed in the grounds** ins Stadion dürfen keine Getränke mitgebracht werden; **2** *adj attr* Außer-Haus-; **the ~-out menu is quite different** für Gerichte zum Mitnehmen gibt es eine ganz andere Speisekarte; **~-over** *n* Überbleibsel *nt*; (*Fin*) Saldovortrag, Übertrag *m*; (*Math*) Rest *m*.

car: **~sick** *adj* **I used to get ~sick** früher wurde mir beim Autofahren immer übel *or* schlecht; **~sickness** *n* Übelkeit *f* beim Autofahren.

cart [ka:t] **1** *n* Wagen, Karren *m*. **to put the ~ before the horse** (*prov*) das Pferd beim Schwanz aufzäumen (*prov*); **to be in the ~** (*inf*) in der Klemme *or* Tinte sitzen (*inf*); **to land sb in the ~** (*inf*) jdm etwas einbrocken (*inf*), jdn in etwas *or* eine Sache hineinreiten (*inf*). **2** *vt* (*fig inf*) mit sich schleppen.

♦**cart away** *or* **off** *vt sep* abtransportieren, wegbringen.

cartage ['ka:tɪdʒ] *n* (*act, cost*) Transport *m*.

carte blanche ['ka:t'blɑ̃ʃ] *n, no pl* Blankovollmacht *f*. **to give sb ~** jdm Carte Blanche (*geh*) *or* (eine) Blankovollmacht geben.

cartel [ka:'tel] *n* Kartell *nt*.

carter ['ka:tə'] *n* Fuhrmann *m*.

Cartesian [ka:'ti:zɪən] **1** *adj* kartesianisch, kartesisch. **2** *n* Kartesianer *m*.

Carthage ['ka:θɪdʒ] *n* Karthago *nt*.

Carthaginian [,ka:θə'dʒɪnɪən] **1** *adj* karthagisch. **2** *n* Karthager(in *f*) *m*.

carthorse ['ka:thɔ:s] *n* Zugpferd *nt*.

cartilage ['ka:tɪlɪdʒ] *n* Knorpel *m*.

cartload ['ka:tləʊd] *n* Wagenladung *f*.

cartographer [ka:'tɒgrəfə'] *n* Kartograph(in *f*) *m*.

cartographic(al) [,ka:təʊ'græfɪk(əl)] *adj* kartographisch.

cartography [ka:'tɒgrəfɪ] *n* Kartographie *f*.

cartomancy ['ka:tə,mænsɪ] *n* Kartenlegen *nt*, Kartomantie *f* (*spec*).

carton ['ka:tən] *n* (Papp)karton *m*; (*of cigarettes*) Stange *f*; (*of milk*) Tüte *f*.

cartoon [ka:'tu:n] *n* **(a)** (*in newspaper etc*) Karikatur *f*; (*strip ~*) Zeichengeschichte *f*, Comics *pl*. **(b)** (*Film, TV*) (Zeichen)trickfilm *m*. **Mickey Mouse ~** Mickymausfilm *m*. **(c)** (*Art: sketch*) Karton *m*.

cartoonist [,ka:'tu:nɪst] *n* **(a)** (*in newspaper etc*) Karikaturist(in *f*) *m*. **(b)** (*Film, TV*) Trickzeichner(in *f*) *m*.

cartouche ['ka:tu:ʃ] *n* Kartusche *f*.

cartridge ['ka:trɪdʒ] *n* (*for rifle, pen*) Patrone *f*; (*Phot, for tape recorder*) Kassette *f*; (*for record player*) Tonabnehmer *m*.

cartridge *in cpds* Patronen-; **~ belt** *n* Patronengurt *or* -gürtel *m*; **~ case** *n* Patronenhülse *f*; **~ clip** *n* Magazin *nt*; **~ paper** *n* Zeichenpapier *nt*.

cart: **~-track** *n* Feldweg *m*; **~-wheel** *n* (*lit*) Wagenrad *nt*; (*Sport*) Rad *nt*; **to turn** *or* **do ~wheels** radschlagen.

carve [ka:v] **1** *vt* **(a)** (*Art: cut*) *wood* schnitzen; *stone etc* (be)hauen. **~d out of** *or* **in wood/marble** aus Holz geschnitzt/aus Marmor gehauen; **to ~ sth on a stone** etw in einen Stein einmeißeln; **to ~ one's initials on a tree** seine Initialen in einen Baum einritzen *or* schnitzen; **a frieze ~d with flowers** ein geschnitzter *or* (*in stone*) gemeißelter Blumenfries; **the sculptor was still carving the face** der Bildhauer schnitzte *or* (*in stone*) meißelte noch das Gesicht; **he ~d a notch on the piece of wood** er schnitzte *or* machte eine Kerbe in das Holz.

(b) (*Cook*) aufschneiden, zerteilen, tranchieren.

(c) (*fig*) **to ~ one's way through the crowd/jungle** sich (*dat*) seinen Weg durch die Menge/den Dschungel bahnen.

2 *vi* (*Cook*) tranchieren.

♦**carve out** *vt sep* **(a)** (*in wood*) schnitzen; (*in stone*) meißeln. **(b)** (*fig*) *piece of land* abtrennen, loslösen. **(c) to ~ ~ a career for oneself** sich (*dat*) eine Karriere aufbauen.

♦**carve up** *vt sep* **(a)** *meat*, (*inf: surgeon*) aufschneiden; *body* zerstückeln. **(b)** (*fig*) *country* aufteilen, zerstückeln; *area of town etc* zerreißen, auseinanderreißen. **(c)** (*inf: with knife*) *person* (mit dem Messer) böse zurichten (*inf*). **to ~ ~ sb's face** jdm das Gesicht zerfetzen. **(d)** (*sl: driver*) schneiden.

carver ['ka:və'] *n* (*knife*) Tranchiermesser *nt*. **a set of ~s** ein Tranchierbesteck *nt*.

carve-up ['ka:vʌp] *n* (*inf*) (*of inheritance*) Verteilung *f*; (*of estate, country*) Zerstückelung *f*.

carving ['ka:vɪŋ] *n* (*Art*) (*thing carved*) Skulptur *f*; (*in wood also*) (Holz)schnitzerei *f*; (*relief*) Relief *nt*; (*in wood*) Holzschnitt *m*. **~ knife** Tranchiermesser *nt*.

carwash ['ka:wɒʃ] *n* (*place*) Autowaschanlage, Waschstraße *f*; (*wash*) Autowäsche *f*.

caryatid [,kærɪ'ætɪd] *n* Karyatide *f*.

casanova [,kæsə'nəʊvə] *n* (*hum*) Casanova *m* (*inf*).

cascade [kæs'keɪd] **1** *n* Kaskade *f*; (*fig*) (*of lace etc*) (Spitzen)besatz *m*; (*of sparks*) Regen *m*. **a ~ of green sparks** ein grüner Funkenregen. **2** *vi* (*also ~ down*) (*onto* auf +*acc*) (in Kaskaden) herabfallen; (*sparks*) herabsprühen, herabregnen; (*hair*) wallend herabfallen; (*boxes etc*) herunterpurzeln (*inf*).

case¹ [keɪs] *n* **(a)** (*situation*) Fall *m*. **if that's the ~** wenn das der Fall ist, wenn das zutrifft *or* stimmt; **is that the ~ with you?** ist das bei Ihnen der Fall?, trifft das auf Sie zu?; **if it is the ~ that you're right** ... sollten Sie wirklich *or* tatsächlich recht haben ...; **im Fall(e), daß Sie tatsächlich recht haben** ...; **as is generally the ~** wie das normalerweise der Fall ist; **such being the ~** da das der Fall ist, da dem so ist (*geh*); **if it is a ~ of his not being informed** wenn er nicht benachrichtigt worden ist; **as the ~ may be** je nachdem.

(b) (*instance, police ~, Med etc*) Fall *m*. **in most ~s** meist(ens), in den meisten Fällen; **a typical ~ (of)** ein typischer Fall (von); **it's a clear ~ of lying** das ist eindeutig gelogen; **in ~** falls; (*just*) **in ~** für alle Fälle; **in ~ of emergency** im Notfall *m*, bei Gefahr *f*; **in any ~** sowieso; **in this/that ~** in dem Fall; **in no**

~ unter keinen Umständen, auf keinen Fall; **five ~s of smallpox/pneumonia** fünf Pockenfälle/Fälle von Lungenentzündung f.

(c) (Jur) Fall m. **to win one's ~** seinen Prozeß gewinnen; the **~ for the defence/prosecution** die Verteidigung/Anklage; **what's the ~ for the prosecution?** worauf stützt sich die Anklage?; **could we hear the ~ for the defence?** das Wort hat die Verteidigung; **the Keeler ~** der Fall Keeler; **in the ~ Higgins v Schwarz** in der Sache Higgins gegen Schwarz; **to make out a good ~ for sth** überzeugende Argumente für etw liefern; the **~ for/against the abolition of capital punishment** die Argumente für/gegen die Abschaffung der Todesstrafe; **you haven't got a ~** das Belastungsmaterial reicht nicht für ein Verfahren; (fig) **Sie haben keine Handhabe**; **to have a good ~** (Jur) gute Chancen haben, durchzukommen; **you/they have a good ~** es ist durchaus gerechtfertigt, was Sie/sie sagen; **there's a very good ~ for adopting this method** es spricht sehr viel dafür, diese Methode zu übernehmen; **they do not have a very good ~** sie haben nicht viel Chancen, damit durchzukommen; **to put one's ~** seinen Fall darlegen; **to put the ~ for sth** etw vertreten; **there's a strong ~ for legalizing pot** es spricht viel für die Legalisierung von Hasch; **there's a good ~ for voting Labour** es gibt viele Gründe, Labour zu wählen; **the court decided that there was no ~ against him** das Gericht entschied, daß nichts gegen ihn vorlag; **that is my ~** das war es, was ich sagen wollte; **a ~ of conscience** eine Gewissensfrage or -entscheidung.

(d) (Gram) Fall, Kasus m. **in the genitive ~** im Genitiv.

(e) (inf: person) Witzbold m, Type f (inf). **he's a ~** das ist vielleicht 'ne Type (inf); **a hard ~** ein schwieriger Fall.

case² 1 n **(a)** (suit~) Koffer m; (crate, packing ~) Kiste f; (display ~) Vitrine f, Schau- or Glaskasten m. **~s of oranges** Apfelsinenkisten pl.

(b) (box) Schachtel f; (for jewels) Schatulle f, Kästchen nt; (for spectacles) Etui, Futteral nt; (seed~) Hülse, Hülle f; (for umbrella) Hülle f; (pillow~) Bezug m; (for musical instrument) Kasten m; (of watch) Gehäuse nt.

(c) (Typ) (Setz)kasten m; (of book) Schuber m. **upper/lower ~** groß/klein geschrieben.

2 vt (sl) bank, house inspizieren. **to ~ the joint** sich (dat) den Laden ansehen (sl).

case in cpds **~book** n (Med) (Kranken)fälle pl; (in social work, Jur) Fallsammlung f; **~-bound** adj (Typ) mit Pappeinband; **~ending** n (Gram) Endung f; **~-harden** vt metal verstählen, vereisenen; **~-hardened** adj (fig) abgebrüht (inf); **~ history** n (Med) Krankengeschichte f; (Sociol, Psych) Vorgeschichte f; **~-load** n to have a heavy/light **~-load** viele/wenig Fälle haben.

casement ['keɪsmənt] n (window) Flügelfenster nt; (frame) Fensterflügel m.

case: ~work n (Sociol) ≈ Sozialarbeit f; **~worker** n (Sociol) ≈ Sozialarbeiter(in f) m.

cash [kæʃ] 1 n **(a)** Bargeld nt; (change also) Kleingeld nt. **~ in hand** Barbestand, Kassenbestand m; **to pay (in) ~** bar bezahlen; **ready ~** verfügbares Geld; **how much do you have in ready ~?** wieviel Geld haben Sie verfügbar?

(b) (immediate payment) Barzahlung f; (not credit) Sofortzahlung f. **~ down** Barzahlung f; Sofortzahlung f; **£25 ~ down and the rest over ...** £ 25 sofort (zu bezahlen), und der Rest über ...; **to pay ~ (down)** (in) bar/sofort bezahlen; **~ with order** zahlbar bei Bestellung; **~ on delivery** per Nachnahme.

(c) (money) Geld nt. **to be short of ~** knapp bei Kasse sein (inf); **I'm out of ~** ich bin blank (inf), ich habe kein Geld.

2 vt cheque einlösen.

cash in 1 vt sep einlösen. 2 vi **to ~ ~ on sth** aus etw Kapital schlagen, sich (dat) etw zunutze machen; **we want to stop others ~ing ~** (on the act) (inf) wir wollen verhindern, daß andere aus der Sache Kapital schlagen.

cash up vi (Brit) Kasse machen.

cash: ~-and-carry 1 adj Cash-and-carry-; 2 n (for retailers) Cash and Carry, Abholmarkt m; (for public) Verbrauchermarkt m; **~ book** n Kassenbuch nt; **~ box** n (Geld)kassette f; **~ crop** n zum Verkauf bestimmte Ernte; **~ desk** n Kasse f, Kassentisch m; **~ discount** n Rabatt m bei Sofortzahlung; **~ dispenser** n Nachtschalter (einer Bank), Bankomat m.

cashew [kæ'ʃuː] n (tree) Nierenbaum m; (nut) Cashewnuß f.

cash-flow ['kæʃfləʊ] n Bruttoertragsziffer f. **~ position** Bruttoertragslage f.

cashier¹ [kæ'ʃɪəʳ] n Kassierer(in f) m.

cashier² vt (Mil) (unehrenhaft) entlassen, kassieren (old).

cashless ['kæʃləs] adj bargeldlos.

cashmere [kæʃ'mɪəʳ] n Kaschmir m. **~ wool** Kaschmirwolle f.

cash: ~ offer n Bar(zahlungs)angebot nt; **~ office** n Kasse f, Kassenbüro nt; **~ payment** n Barzahlung f; **~ price** n Bar(zahlungs)preis m; **~ register** n Registrierkasse f.

casing ['keɪsɪŋ] n (Tech) Gehäuse nt; (of cylinder, tyre) Mantel m; (of sausage) Haut f, Darm m.

casino [kə'siːnəʊ] n (Spiel)kasino nt, Spielbank f.

cask [kɑːsk] n Faß nt.

casket ['kɑːskɪt] n Schatulle f; (for cremated ashes) Urne f; (US: coffin) Sarg m, Totenschrein m (geh).

Caspian Sea ['kæspɪən'siː] n Kaspisches Meer, Kaspisee m.

Cassandra [kə'sændrə] n (Myth) Kassandra f. **despite all the C~s** (fig) allen Kassandrarufen or Unkenrufen zum Trotz.

cassava [kə'sɑːvə] n Maniok m.

casserole ['kæsərəʊl] n (Cook) Schmortopf m, Kasserolle f. **a lamb ~**, **a ~ of lamb** eine Lammkasserolle f. 2 vt schmoren.

cassette [kæ'set] n Kassette f. **~ deck** Kassettendeck nt; **~ recorder** Kassettenrecorder m.

cassock ['kæsək] n Talar m, Soutane f.

cast [kɑːst] (vb: pret, ptp ~) 1 n **(a)** (of dice, net, line) Wurf m. **(b)** (mould) (Guß)form f; (object moulded) Abdruck m; (in metal) (Ab)guß m.

(c) (plaster ~) Gipsverband m.

(d) (Theat) Besetzung f. **~ (in order of appearance)** Mitwirkende pl (in der Reihenfolge ihres Auftritts); **the ~ includes several famous actors** das Stück ist mit mehreren berühmten Schauspielern besetzt; **who's in the ~?** wer spielt mit?

(e) the **~ of sb's features** jds Gesichtsschnitt m; **~ of mind** Gesinnung f; **he's a man of quite a different ~** er ist aus anderem Holz geschnitzt, er ist ein Mensch von ganz anderem Zuschnitt.

(f) (tinge) Schimmer m.

(g) (of worm) aufgeworfene Erde; (of bird) Gewölle nt.

(h) (Med: squint) schielender Blick. **to have a ~ in one eye** auf einem Auge schielen.

2 vt **(a)** (lit liter, fig: throw) werfen; anchor, net, fishing lines auswerfen; horoscope erstellen. **to ~ one's vote** seine Stimme abgeben; **a picture of the bishop ~ing his vote** ein Bild des Bischofs bei der Stimmabgabe; **to ~ lots (aus)losen**; **to ~ in one's lot with sb** sich auf jds (acc) Seite stellen; **to ~ one's eyes over sth** einen Blick auf etw (acc) werfen; **to ~ the blame on sb** jdm die Schuld geben, die Schuld auf jdn abwälzen; **to ~ a shadow** (lit, fig) einen Schatten werfen (on auf +acc).

(b) (shed) **to ~ its skin** sich häuten; **to ~ a shoe** ein Hufeisen nt verlieren; **to ~ its feathers** (form) sich mausern; **to ~ its leaves** (form) die Blätter abwerfen; **to ~ its young** (form) (Junge) werfen.

(c) (Tech, Art) gießen; see mould¹.

(d) (Theat) parts, play besetzen; parts also verteilen. **he was well/badly ~** die Rolle paßte gut/schlecht zu ihm; **he was ~ for the part of Hamlet** er sollte den Hamlet spielen; **I don't know why they ~ him as the villain** ich weiß nicht, warum sie ihm die Rolle des Schurken gegeben or zugeteilt haben.

3 vi **(a)** (Fishing) die Angel auswerfen.

(b) (Theat) die Rollen verteilen, die Besetzung vornehmen.

cast about or **around for** vi +prep obj zu finden versuchen; for new job etc also sich umsehen nach. **he was ~ing ~ (in his mind) ~ something to say** er suchte nach Worten; (for answer/excuse) er suchte nach einer Antwort/Ausrede.

cast aside vt sep cares, prejudices, inhibitions, habits ablegen; old clothes etc ausrangieren; person fallenlassen.

cast away vt sep wegwerfen. **to be ~ ~** (Naut) gestrandet sein; **he was ~ ~ on a desert island** er wurde auf eine einsame Insel verschlagen.

cast back 1 vi (fig) **to ~ ~ (in one's mind)** im Geiste zurückdenken (to an +acc). 2 vt sep **to ~ one's thoughts or mind ~** seine Gedanken zurückschweifen lassen (to in +acc).

cast down vt sep eyes niederschlagen; (liter: throw down) weapons hinwerfen. **to be ~ ~** (fig) niedergeschlagen sein.

cast off 1 vt sep **(a)** (get rid of) abwerfen; friends fallenlassen. **she ~ ~ three boyfriends in one week** in einer Woche hat sie drei Freunden den Laufpaß gegeben. **(b)** stitches abketten. **(c)** (Naut) losmachen. 2 vi **(a)** (Naut) losmachen. **(b)** (in knitting) abketteln.

cast on vti (Knitting) anschlagen.

cast out vt sep (liter) vertreiben; demons austreiben.

cast up vt sep **(a)** **to ~ one's eyes ~ (to the heavens)** seine Augen (zum Himmel) emporrichten.

(b) (wash up) flotsam, sailors anspülen. **they were ~ ~ on a desert island** sie wurden auf einer einsamen Insel an Land gespült; **the wreckage was ~ ~ on the shore** die Wrackteile wurden ans Ufer gespült; **~ ~ on the shores of life** im Leben gestrandet.

(c) (refer to) sb's misdemeanours etc aufbringen. **to ~ sth ~ (at sb)** jdm etw vorhalten.

castanets [ˌkæstə'nets] npl Kastagnetten pl.

castaway ['kɑːstəweɪ] n (lit, fig) Schiffbrüchige(r), Gestrandete(r) mf.

caste [kɑːst] 1 n Kaste f. **to lose ~** an Rang verlieren, absteigen; **he lost ~ with or among his friends** er verlor in den Augen seiner Freunde or bei seinen Freunden an Ansehen.

2 adj attr mark, system Kasten-. **a high/low ~ family** eine Familie, die einer hohen/niedrigen Kaste angehört.

castellan ['kæstələn] n Schloßvogt, Kastellan m.

castellated ['kæstəleɪtɪd] adj mit (Türmen und) Zinnen.

caster ['kɑːstəʳ] n see castor.

castigate ['kæstɪɡeɪt] vt person (old: physically) züchtigen; (verbally) geißeln.

castigation [ˌkæstɪ'ɡeɪʃən] n see vt Züchtigung f; Geißelung f.

Castile [kæ'stiːl] n Kastilien nt.

casting ['kɑːstɪŋ] n **(a)** (Fishing) Auswerfen nt; (Tech, Art: act, object) (Ab)guß m; (in plaster) Abdruck, Abguß m. **(b)** (Theat) Rollenverteilung, Besetzung f.

casting vote n ausschlaggebende Stimme. **he used his ~** seine Stimme gab den Ausschlag.

cast iron 1 n Gußeisen nt. 2 adj (~-iron) **(a)** (lit) gußeisern; **(b)** (fig) will, constitution eisern; case, alibi hieb- und stichfest.

castle ['kɑːsl] 1 n **(a)** Schloß nt; (medieval fortress) Burg f. **to build ~s in the air** or **in Spain** Luftschlösser bauen. **(b)** (Chess) Turm m. 2 vi (Chess) rochieren.

castling ['kɑːslɪŋ] n (Chess) Rochade f.

cast: ~-off 1 adj clothes abgelegt attr; 2 npl **~-offs** (inf) abgelegte Kleider; **she's one of his ~-offs** (fig inf) sie ist eine seiner ausrangierten Freundinnen (inf).

castor ['kɑːstəʳ] n **(a)** (Brit: for sugar, salt etc) Streuer m. **(b)** (wheel) Rolle f, Rad nt.

castor: ~ oil n Rizinus(öl), Kastoröl nt; **~ sugar** n (Brit) Sandzucker m.

castrate ['kæstreɪt] vt kastrieren; (fig) text verstümmeln.

castrati [kæs'trɑːtiː] pl of castrato.

castration [kæs'treɪʃən] n Kastration f.

castrato [kæs'trɑːtəʊ] n, pl castrati Kastrat m.

casual ['kæʒjʊl] 1 adj **(a)** (not planned) zufällig; acquaintance, glance flüchtig. **we were in the area, so we paid them a ~ visit** wir waren gerade in der Gegend und haben sie bei der Gelegenheit besucht; **~ sex** Gelegenheitssex *m*; freie Liebe.

(b) *(offhand, careless)* lässig; *attitude* gleichgültig; *remark* beiläufig; *(lacking emotion)* gleichgültig. **it was just a ~ remark** das war nicht so ernst gemeint, das habe ich/hat er *etc* nur so gesagt; **he was very ~ about it** das hat ihn kaltgelassen *or* nicht tangiert *(inf)*; **you shouldn't be so ~ about it** du solltest das nicht so leicht *or* auf die leichte Schulter nehmen; **he tried to sound ~** er tat so, als ob ihm das nichts ausmachen würde; **he had a rather ~ manner for a policeman** für einen Polizisten war er ziemlich salopp *or* lässig.

(c) *(informal)* zwanglos; *discussion, chat also* ungezwungen; *clothes* leger. **a ~ shirt** ein Freizeithemd *nt*; **~ wear** Freizeitkleidung *f*; **he was wearing ~ clothes** er war leger gekleidet.

(d) *(irregular) work, worker, labourer* Gelegenheits-.

2 *n* **(a)** ~**s** *pl (shoes)* Slipper *pl.*

(b) *(~ worker)* Gelegenheitsarbeiter(in *f*) *m.* ~**s** Aushilfen *pl.*

casually ['kæʒjʊlɪ] *adv (without planning)* zufällig; *(without emotion)* ungerührt; *(incidentally, in an offhand manner)* beiläufig; *(without seriousness)* lässig; *(informally)* zwanglos; *dressed* leger.

casualness ['kæʒjʊlnɪs] *n (informality)* Zwanglosigkeit *f*; *(carelessness)* Lässigkeit *f*; *(lack of emotion)* Ungerührtheit, Schnodderigkeit *(inf) f*; *(offhand nature: of remark)* Beiläufigkeit *f.* **the ~ of his dress** seine legere Kleidung.

casualty ['kæʒjʊltɪ] *n* **(a)** *(lit, fig)* Opfer *nt*; *(injured also)* Verletzte(r) *mf*; *(killed also)* Tote(r) *mf.* **were there many casualties?** gab es viele Opfer?; *(Mil)* gab es hohe Verluste? **(b)** *(also ~ ward)* Unfallstation *f.*

casualty: ~ list *n* Verlustliste *f*; **~ ward** *n* Unfallstation *f.*

casuist ['kæʒjʊɪst] *n* Kasuist *m.*

casuistry ['kæʒjʊɪstrɪ] *n* Kasuistik *f.*

cat [kæt] *n* **(a)** Katze *f*; *(tiger etc)* (Raub)katze *f.* **the (big) ~s** die großen Katzen; **to let the ~ out of the bag** die Katze aus dem Sack lassen; **to wait for the ~ to jump, to wait to see which way the ~ jumps** (abwarten, um zu) sehen, wie der Hase läuft; **they fight like ~ and dog** die sind *or* die vertragen sich wie Hund und Katze; **to lead a ~-and dog life** *(inf)* wie Hund und Katze leben; **to play a ~-and-mouse game with sb** mit jdm Katz und Maus spielen; **there isn't room to swing a ~ (in)** *(inf)* man kann sich nicht rühren(, so eng ist es); **a ~ may look at a king** *(prov)* es wird doch noch erlaubt sein zu gucken!; **it's enough to make a ~ ~ laugh** da lachen ja die Hühner! *(inf)*; **to be like a ~ on hot bricks** wie auf glühenden Kohlen sitzen; **that's put the ~ among the pigeons** da hast du *etc* aber was (Schönes) angerichtet!; **he thinks he's the ~'s whiskers** *(inf)* er hält sich für wer weiß was; **when the ~'s away the mice will play** *(Prov)* wenn die Katze aus dem Haus ist, tanzen die Mäuse *(Prov)*; *see* **bell¹.**

(b) *(inf: woman)* Katze *f.*

(c) *(whip)* (neunschwänzige) Katze *f.*

(d) *(dated US sl)* Typ *m (inf).*

(e) *(inf: caterpillar tractor)* Raupe *f.*

catabolism [kə'tæbəlɪzm] *n* Abbaustoffwechsel, Katabolismus *(spec) m.*

cataclysm ['kætəklɪzm] *n* Verheerung *f*; *(fig)* Umwälzung *f.*

cataclysmic [,kætə'klɪzmɪk] *adj* verheerend; *(fig)* umwälzend.

catacombs ['kætəku:mz] *npl* Katakomben *pl.*

catafalque ['kætəfælk] *n* Katafalk *m.*

catalepsy ['kætəlepsɪ] *n* Katalepsie, Starrsucht *f.*

cataleptic [,kætə'leptɪk] *adj* kataleptisch.

catalogue, *(US)* **catalog** ['kætəlɒg] **1** *n* Katalog *m.* **2** *vt* katalogisieren.

catalysis [kə'tæləsɪs] *n* Katalyse *f.*

catalyst ['kætəlɪst] *n (lit, fig)* Katalysator *m.*

catalytic [,kætə'lɪtɪk] *adj (lit, fig)* katalytisch.

catamaran [,kætəmə'ræn] *n* Katamaran *m.*

catapult ['kætəpʌlt] **1** *n (slingshot)* Schleuder *f*; *(Mil, Aviat)* Katapult *nt or m.* **~ launching** *(Aviat)* Katapultstart *m.* **2** *vt* schleudern, katapultieren; *(Aviat)* katapultieren. **3** *vi* geschleudert *or* katapultiert werden.

cataract ['kætərækt] *n* **(a)** *(rapids)* Katarakt *m.* **(b)** *(Med)* grauer Star.

catarrh [kə'tɑːʳ] *n* Katarrh *m.*

catarrhal [kə'tɑːrəl] *adj* katarrhalisch.

catastrophe [kə'tæstrəfɪ] *n* Katastrophe *f.* **to end in ~** verhängnisvoll *or* in einer Katastrophe enden; **to be heading for ~** auf eine Katastrophe zusteuern; **to be the final ~ for sb** jdm schließlich zum Verhängnis werden.

catastrophic [,kætə'strɒfɪk] *adj* katastrophal; *event, decision, course also* verhängnisvoll.

catastrophically [,kætə'strɒfɪkəlɪ] *adv see adj.*

catatonia [,kætə'təʊnɪə] *n* Katatonie *f.*

cat: ~bird *n (US)* amerikanische Spottdrossel; **~ burglar** *n* Fassadenkletterer *m*; **~call** *(Theat)* **1** *n* **~calls** Pfiffe und Buhrufe *pl*; **2** *vi* pfeifen.

catch [kætʃ] *(vb: pret, ptp* **caught)** **1** *n* **(a)** *(of ball etc)* **to make a (good) ~** *(gut)* fangen; **good ~!** gut gefangen!; **it was a difficult ~** das war schwer zu fangen; **he missed an easy ~** er hat einen leichten Ball nicht gefangen.

(b) *(Fishing, Hunt)* Fang *m*; *(of trawler etc also)* Fischzug *m.* **he didn't get a ~** er hat nichts gefangen; **he's a good ~** *(fig inf)* er ist eine gute Partie; *(for marriage also)* er ist eine gute Partie.

(c) *(children's game)* Fangen *nt.*

(d) *(trick, snag)* Haken *m.* **where's the ~?** wo liegt *or* ist (da) der Haken?; **there's a ~ in it somewhere!** die Sache hat irgendwo einen Haken, da ist irgendwo ein Haken dabei; **~-22** ausweglose Falle, Sackgasse *f*; **a ~-22 situation** *(inf)* eine Zwickmühle; **~ question** Fangfrage *f.*

(e) *(device for fastening)* Verschluß(vorrichtung *f*) *m*; *(hook)* Haken *m*; *(latch)* Riegel *m.*

(f) *(break in voice)* Stocken *nt.* **with a ~ in one's voice** mit stockender Stimme.

(g) *(Mus)* Kanon *m* für Singstimmen mit heiter-komischem Text.

(h) *(fragment)* Bruchstück *nt.*

2 *vt* **(a)** *object* fangen; *batsman* durch Abfangen des Balls ausscheiden lassen.

(b) *fish, mice* fangen; *thief, offender* fassen, schnappen *(inf)*, erwischen *(inf)*; *escaped animal* (ein)fangen; *(inf: manage to see)* erwischen *(inf).* **to ~ sb by the arm** jdn am Arm fassen; **to ~ sight/a glimpse of sb/sth** jdn/etw erblicken *or* zu sehen kriegen *(inf)*; **to ~ sb's attention/eye** jdn auf sich *(acc)* aufmerksam machen.

(c) *(take by surprise)* erwischen, ertappen. **to ~ sb at sth** jdn bei etw erwischen; **I caught him flirting with my wife** ich habe ihn (dabei) erwischt, wie er mit meiner Frau flirtete; **you won't ~ me signing any contract** *(inf)* ich unterschreibe doch keinen Vertrag; **you won't ~ me in that restaurant** *(inf)* in das Restaurant gehe ich garantiert *or* bestimmt nicht; **(you won't) ~ me doing that again!** *(inf)* das mache ich bestimmt nicht wieder!; **you won't ~ me falling for that trick again** *(inf)* auf den Trick falle ich nicht noch einmal herein; **aha, caught you hab' ich dich doch erwischt** *(inf)*; *(with question)* ha ha, reingefallen *(inf)*; **caught in the act** auf frischer Tat ertappt; *(sexually)* in flagranti erwischt; **we were caught in a storm** wir wurden von einem Unwetter überrascht; **to ~ sb on the wrong foot** *or* **off balance** *(fig)* jdn überrumpeln.

(d) *(be in time for) train, bus* erreichen, kriegen *(inf).* **can I still ~ the post?** kommt der Brief noch mit?; **if you want to ~ the 4 o'clock post** ... wenn das mit der Vieruhrleerung mitsoll ...

(e) *(become entangled)* hängenbleiben mit. **a nail caught her dress** ihr Kleid blieb an einem Nagel hängen; **I caught my finger in the car door** ich habe mir den Finger in der Wagentür eingeklemmt; **he caught his foot in the grating** er ist mit dem Fuß im Gitter hängengeblieben.

(f) *(with stitches)* mit ein paar Stichen befestigen. **to ~ a dress (in) at the waist** ein Kleid an der Taille fassen.

(g) *(understand, hear)* mitkriegen *(inf).*

(h) **to ~ an illness** sich *(dat)* eine Krankheit zuziehen *or* holen *(inf)*; **he's always ~ing cold(s)** er erkältet sich leicht; **you'll ~ your death (of cold)!** du holst dir den Tod! *(inf).*

(i) *(portray) mood, atmosphere etc* einfangen.

(j) **to ~ one's breath** *(after exercise etc)* Luft holen, verschnaufen; **to ~ sb a blow** jdm einen Schlag versetzen; **the blow/ball caught him on the arm** der Schlag/Ball traf ihn am Arm; **she caught him one on the nose** *(inf)* sie haute ihm auf die Nase; **you'll ~ it!** *(inf)* es setzt was! *(inf)*, du kannst (aber) was erleben! *(inf)*; **he caught it all right!** *(inf)* *(physically)* der hat vielleicht eine Abreibung bekommen! *(inf)*; *(verbally)* der hat aber was zu hören bekommen! *(inf).*

3 *vi* **(a)** *(with ball)* fangen.

(b) *(fire)* in Gang kommen, brennen; *(wood etc)* Feuer fangen, brennen; *(Cook)* anbrennen.

(c) *(get stuck)* klemmen, sich verklemmen; *(get entangled)* hängenbleiben, sich verfangen. **her dress caught in the door** sie blieb mit ihrem Kleid in der Tür hängen.

♦**catch at** *vi* +*prep obj (grab for)* greifen nach; *opportunity* ergreifen.

♦**catch on** *vi (inf)* **(a)** *(become popular)* ankommen; *(fashion also)* sich durchsetzen; *(book etc also)* einschlagen. **(b)** *(understand)* kapieren *(inf).*

♦**catch out** *vt sep (fig)* überführen; *(with trick question etc)* hereinlegen; *(Sport)* abfangen. **I caught you ~ there!** du bist durchschaut; *(with trick question)* jetzt bist du aber reingefallen *(inf)*; **to ~ sb ~ in a lie** jdn beim Lügen ertappen.

♦**catch up 1** *vi* aufholen. **to ~ ~ on one's sleep** Schlaf nachholen; **to ~ ~ on** *or* **with one's work** Arbeit nachholen; **to ~ ~ with sb** *(running, in work etc)* jdn einholen; **hurry, they're ~ing ~!** beeil dich, sie holen auf!; **you've got a lot of ~ing ~ to do** du mußt noch eine Menge nachholen.

2 *vt sep* **(a)** **to ~ sb ~** *(walking, working etc)* jdn einholen.

(b) *(snatch up)* (vom Boden) hochheben; *hair* hochstecken. **she caught ~ her skirts** sie raffte *or* schürzte ihre Röcke.

(c) **to get caught ~ in sth** *(entangled)* sich in etw *(dat)* verheddern *or* verfangen; *in traffic* in etw *(acc)* kommen; *in discussion* in etw *(acc)* verwickelt werden.

catch: ~all *n (US) (drawer etc)* Schublade *f* für Krimskrams *(inf)*; *(phrase, clause etc)* allgemeine Bezeichnung/Klausel/allgemeiner Rahmen *etc*; **~-as-catch-can** *n (Sport)* Catch-as-catch-can *nt*; **~crop** *n* Zwischenfrucht *f.*

catcher ['kætʃəʳ] *n* Fänger *m.* **he's a good ~** er ist gut im Fangen, er fängt gut.

catching ['kætʃɪŋ] *adj (Med, fig)* ansteckend.

catchment ['kætʃmənt] *n:* **~ area** Einzugsgebiet *nt*, Einzugsbereich *m*; **~ basin** Einzugsgebiet *nt.*

catch: ~penny *adj* publikumswirksam, zugkräftig; **~ phrase** *n* Schlagwort *nt*, Slogan *m.*

catchup ['kætʃəp] *n (US) see* **ketchup.**

catch: ~ weight *adj (Sport)* ohne Gewichtsklasse; **~ word** *n* Schlagwort *nt.*

catchy ['kætʃɪ] *adj (+er) tune* eingängig.

catechism ['kætɪkɪzəm] *n (instruction)* Katechese *f*; *(fig)* Verhör *nt*; *(book)* Katechismus *m.*

catechize ['kætɪkaɪz] *vt* katechisieren.

categorical [,kætɪ'gɒrɪkəl] *adj statement, denial* kategorisch. **he was quite ~ about it** er hat das mit Bestimmtheit gesagt; **~ imperative** kategorischer Imperativ.

categorically [,kætɪ'gɒrɪkəlɪ] *adv* kategorisch; *say* mit Bestimmtheit.

categorization [,kætɪgəraɪ'zeɪʃən] *n* Kategorisierung, Klassifizierung *f.*

categorize ['kætɪgəraɪz] vt kategorisieren, klassifizieren.
category ['kætɪgorɪ] n Kategorie, Klasse f.
cater ['keɪtəʳ] vi (provide food) die Speisen und Getränke liefern. who's ~ing at the wedding? wer richtet die Hochzeit aus?

♦**cater for** vi +prep obj (a) (serve) mit Speisen und Getränken versorgen; coach party etc (mit Speisen und Getränken) bedienen. weddings and functions ~ed ~ wir richten Hochzeiten und andere Veranstaltungen aus; that café ~s mainly ~ students das Café ist hauptsächlich auf Studenten eingestellt.
(b) ausgerichtet or eingestellt sein auf (+acc); (also cater to) needs, tastes gerecht werden (+dat), etwas zu bieten haben (+dat). to ~ ~ all tastes jedem Geschmack gerecht werden, für jeden (Geschmack) etwas zu bieten haben; a region which ~s more ~ old people eine Gegend, die mehr für alte Menschen tut or die alten Menschen mehr zu bieten hat; this magazine ~s ~ all ages diese Zeitschrift hat jeder Altersgruppe etwas zu bieten; a town which ~s ~ children eine kinderfreundliche Stadt; a dictionary which ~s ~ the user ein benutzerfreundliches Wörterbuch.
(c) (expect, be prepared for) I hadn't ~ed ~ that darauf bin/war ich nicht eingestellt.
cater-cornered ['keɪtə'kɔːnəd] adj (US) diagonal.
caterer ['keɪtərəʳ] n Lieferfirma f für Speisen und Getränke; (for parties etc) Lieferfirma, die Partys etc ausrichtet, Stadtküche f; (owner, manager) Gastronom(in f) m.
catering ['keɪtərɪŋ] n Versorgung f mit Speisen und Getränken (for gen); (trade) Gastronomie f. who's doing the ~? welche Firma richtet die Veranstaltung aus?; ~ trade (Hotel- und) Gaststättengewerbe nt.
caterpillar ['kætəpɪləʳ] n (Zool) Raupe f; (Tech) Raupe(nkette), Gleiskette f; (vehicle) Raupenfahrzeug nt.
caterpillar: (Tech) ~-track n Raupenkette, Gleiskette f; ~ tractor n Raupenfahrzeug, Gleiskettenfahrzeug nt.
caterwaul ['kætəwɔːl] vi jaulen.
caterwauling ['kætəwɔːlɪŋ] n Gejaule nt.
catharsis [kə'θɑːsɪs] n (a) (Med) Darmreinigung, Darmentleerung f. (b) (Liter, Philos) Katharsis, Läuterung f.
cathartic [kə'θɑːtɪk] 1 adj (a) (Med) abführend. (b) (Liter, Philos) kathartisch. 2 n (Med) Abführmittel nt.
cathedral [kə'θiːdrəl] n Dom m; (esp in England, France, Spain) Kathedrale f. ~ town/city Domstadt f.
Catherine ['kæθərɪn] n Katharina f. c~ wheel Feuerrad nt.
catheter ['kæθɪtəʳ] n Katheter m.
cathode ['kæθəʊd] n Kathode f.
cathode: ~ ray n Kathodenstrahl m; ~-ray tube n Kathodenstrahlröhre f.
catholic ['kæθəlɪk] adj (varied, all-embracing) vielseitig. he's a man of very ~ tastes er ist (ein) sehr vielseitig interessiert(er Mensch).
Catholic 1 adj (Eccl) katholisch. the ~ Church die katholische Kirche. 2 n Katholik(in f) m.
Catholicism [kə'θɒlɪsɪzəm] n Katholizismus m.
cat: ~kin n (Bot) Kätzchen nt; ~lick n (inf) Katzenwäsche f; ~like adj katzenhaft, katzengleich; ~mint n Katzenminze f; ~nap 1 n to have a ~nap ein Nickerchen nt machen (inf); 2 vi dösen; ~nip n (US) see ~mint; ~-o'-nine-tails n neunschwänzige Katze; ~'s cradle n Abnehmspiel, Fadenspiel nt; ~'s eye n Katzenauge nt, rückstrahlender Nagel m; ~'s paw n Handlanger m; ~suit n einteiliger Hosenanzug.
catsup ['kætsəp] n (US) see ketchup.
cattail ['kæt,teɪl] n (US) Rohrkolben, Kanonenputzer (inf) m.
cattle ['kætl] npl Rind(vieh) nt. 500 head of ~ 500 Rinder, 500 Stück Vieh; "~ crossing" „Vorsicht Viehtrieb!"
cattle: ~ breeding n Rinderzucht f; ~ grid n Weidenrost m, Viehtor nt; ~ man n Rinderzüchter m; ~ rustler n Viehdieb m; ~ show n Rinder(zucht) schau f; ~ truck n (Aut) Viehanhänger m; (Rail) Viehwagen m.
catty ['kætɪ] adj (+er) gehässig, boshaft.
catwalk ['kætwɔːk] n Steg m, Brücke f; (for models) Laufsteg m.
Caucasian [kɔː'keɪzɪən] 1 adj kaukasisch. 2 n Kaukasier(in f) m.
Caucasus ['kɔːkəsəs] n Kaukasus m.
caucus ['kɔːkəs] n (committee) Gremium nt, Ausschuß m; (US: meeting) Sitzung f.
caudal ['kɔːdl] adj Schwanz-, kaudal (spec). the ~ vertebrae/fin die Schwanzwirbel/Schwanzflosse.
caught [kɔːt] pret, ptp of catch.
caul [kɔːl] n Glückshaube f.
cauldron ['kɔːldrən] n großer Kessel; (witch's ~) (Hexen)kessel m.
cauliflower ['kɒlɪflaʊəʳ] n Blumenkohl m. ~ ear Boxerohr nt.
caulk [kɔːk] vt seams, joints abdichten; (on ship) kalfatern.
caulking ['kɔːkɪŋ] n Material nt zum Abdichten; (Naut) Teer m.
causal ['kɔːzəl] adj kausal, ursächlich. ~ relationship Kausalzusammenhang m.
causality [kɔː'zælɪtɪ] n Kausalität f.
causally ['kɔːzəlɪ] adv kausal, ursächlich. these are two ~ connected events zwischen den beiden Ereignissen besteht ein Kausalzusammenhang.
causation [kɔː'zeɪʃən] n Kausalität f; (of particular event) Ursache f. the law of ~ das Kausalgesetz or -prinzip.
causative ['kɔːzətɪv] 1 adj factor verursachend; (Gram) kausativ. 2 n (Gram) Kausativ nt.
cause [kɔːz] 1 n (a) (reason) Ursache f (of für). ~ and effect Ursache und Wirkung; what was the ~ of the fire? wodurch ist das Feuer entstanden?
(b) (reason) Grund, Anlaß m. she has no ~ to be angry sie hat keinen Grund, sich zu ärgern; the ~ of his failure der Grund für sein Versagen; with/without (good) ~ mit (triftigem)/ohne (triftigen) Grund; there's no ~ for alarm es besteht kein Grund

or Anlaß zur Aufregung; you have every ~ to be worried du hast allen Anlaß zur Sorge; you have good ~ for complaint Sie haben allen Grund zur Klage, Sie beklagen sich zu Recht.
(c) (purpose, ideal) Sache f. to make common ~ with sb mit jdm gemeinsame Sache machen; to work for or in a good ~ sich für eine gute Sache einsetzen; he died for the ~ of peace er starb für den Frieden or für die Sache des Friedens; in the ~ of justice für die (Sache der) Gerechtigkeit, im Namen der Gerechtigkeit; it's all in a good ~ es ist für eine gute Sache.
(d) (Jur: action) Fall m, Sache f. ~ célèbre Cause célèbre f.
2 vt verursachen. to ~ grief to sb jdm Kummer machen; to ~ sb to do sth (form) jdn veranlassen, etw zu tun (form).
causeway ['kɔːzweɪ] n Damm m.
caustic ['kɔːstɪk] adj (Chem) ätzend, kaustisch; (fig) ätzend; remark bissig. he was very ~ about the project er äußerte sich sehr bissig über das Projekt; ~ soda Ätznatron nt.
caustically ['kɔːstɪklɪ] adv in ätzendem or bissigem Ton.
cauterization [,kɔːtəraɪ'zeɪʃən] n (Med) Kaustik, Kauterisation f.
cauterize ['kɔːtəraɪz] vt (Med) kauterisieren.
caution ['kɔːʃən] 1 n (a) (circumspection) Vorsicht, Umsicht f, Bedacht m. "~!" „Vorsicht!"; to act with ~ umsichtig or mit Bedacht vorgehen, Vorsicht walten lassen.
(b) (warning) Warnung f; (official) Verwarnung f.
(c) (inf) to be a real ~ zum Piepen sein (inf).
2 vt (warn) to ~ sb jdn warnen (against vor +dat); (officially) jdn verwarnen; to ~ sb against doing sth jdn davor warnen, etw zu tun.
cautionary ['kɔːʃənərɪ] adj belehrend; sign Warn-. a ~ tale eine Geschichte mit Moral.
cautious ['kɔːʃəs] adj vorsichtig. to play a ~ game Vorsicht walten lassen.
cautiously ['kɔːʃəslɪ] adv see adj.
cautiousness ['kɔːʃəsnɪs] n Vorsicht f.
cavalcade [,kævəl'keɪd] n Kavalkade f.
cavalier [,kævə'lɪəʳ] 1 n (horseman, knight) Kavalier m. C~ (Hist) Kavalier m. 2 adj (a) (Hist) C~: the C~ resistance der Widerstand der Kavaliere. (b) (offhand) person, nature unbekümmert-keck; disregard, overruling unbekümmert, ungeniert, kaltlächelnd. ... he said in his ~ tone ... sagte er leichthin; treat it seriously, don't be so ~ nehmen Sie das ernst, und gehen Sie nicht so leichthin darüber hinweg.
cavalierly [,kævə'lɪəlɪ] adv mit einer unbekümmerten Keckheit, kaltlächelnd; say leichthin.
cavalry ['kævəlrɪ] n Kavallerie, Reiterei f.
cavalry: ~man n Kavallerist m; ~ officer n Kavallerieoffizier m.
cave[1] ['keɪv] n: to keep ~ (dated Brit Sch sl) Schmiere stehen (inf).
cave[2] [keɪv] 1 n Höhle f. 2 vi to go caving auf Höhlenexpedition(en) gehen; he did a lot of caving in his youth in seiner Jugend hat er viel Höhlenforschung betrieben.
♦**cave in** vi (a) einstürzen. (b) (inf: surrender, yield) nachgeben, kapitulieren.
caveat ['kæviæt] n Vorbehalt m. to enter or file a ~ (Jur) Einspruch einlegen.
cave: ~-dweller n Höhlenbewohner m; ~-in n Einsturz m; (place) Einsturzstelle f; ~man n Höhlenmensch m; (fig) Tier nt (inf), Urmensch m; ~man instincts Urinstinkte pl; ~ painting n Höhlenmalerei f.
cavern ['kævən] n Höhle f.
cavernous ['kævənəs] adj (a) cellar, pit, darkness tief; hole gähnend; eyes tiefliegend; cheeks eingefallen, hohl; voice hohl(tönend); yawn herzhaft, breit. (b) mountain etc höhlenreich, voller Höhlen.
caviar(e) ['kævɪɑːʳ] n Kaviar m.
cavil ['kævɪl] vi kritteln. to ~ at sth an etw (dat) herumkritteln.
cavity ['kævɪtɪ] n Hohlraum m, Höhlung f; (in tooth) Loch nt. nasal/chest ~ (Anat) Nasen-/Brusthöhle f; ~ wall Hohlwand f; ~ wall insulation Schaumisolierung f.
cavort [kə'vɔːt] vi tollen, toben. to ~ along or about herumtollen or -toben.
cavy ['keɪvɪ] n Meerschweinchen nt.
caw [kɔː] 1 vi krächzen. 2 n (heiserer) Schrei.
cawing ['kɔːɪŋ] n Krächzen, Gekrächz(e) nt.
cay [keɪ] n (kleine) Insel, Koralleninsel f.
cayenne pepper ['keɪen'pepəʳ] n Cayennepfeffer m.
CB abbr of Citizens' Band.
CBC abbr of Canadian Broadcasting Company.
CBE (Brit) abbr of Commander of the Order of the British Empire.
CBI (Brit) abbr of Confederation of British Industry ≈ BDI.
CBS abbr of Columbia Broadcasting System CBS.
cc abbr of cubic centimetre cc, cm^3.
CC (Brit) abbr of (a) County Council. (b) Cricket Club.
cease [siːs] 1 vi enden, aufhören; (noise, shouting etc) verstummen. we shall not ~ from our endeavours (liter) wir werden in unserem Streben nicht nachlassen (geh); without ceasing ohne Pause, unaufhörlich; to ~ from doing sth (form) von etw ablassen (geh).
2 vt beenden; fire, payments, production einstellen. to ~ doing sth aufhören, etw zu tun; to ~ to exist aufhören zu bestehen; ~ fire! Feuer halt!
3 n without ~ (liter) unaufhörlich, ohne Unterlaß (liter).
ceasefire [siːs'faɪəʳ] n Feuerpause or -einstellung f; (longer) Waffenruhe f, Einstellung f der Kampfhandlungen. to give or sound the ~ den Befehl zur Feuereinstellung geben.
ceaseless ['siːslɪs] adj endlos, unaufhörlich; (relentless) vigilance unablässig.
ceaselessly ['siːslɪslɪ] adv see adj.

cecum ['si:kəm] *n see* **caecum.**

cedar ['si:dəʳ] *n* (a) *(tree)* Zeder *f.* (b) *(also ~wood)* Zedernholz *nt.* ~ **of Lebanon** Libanonzeder *f.*

cede [si:d] *vt territory* abtreten *(to an +acc).* **to ~ a point in an** **argument** in einem Punkt *or* in einer Sache nachgeben.

cedilla [sɪ'dɪlə] *n* Cedille *f.*

ceiling ['si:lɪŋ] *n* (a) *(Zimmer)*decke *f; see* **hit 2 (l).** (b) *(Aviat)* *(cloud~)* Wolkenhöhe *f; (aircraft's ~)* Gipfelhöhe *f.* (c) *(fig: upper limit)* ober(st)e Grenze, Höchstgrenze *f.* **price ~** oberste Preisgrenze; **to put a ~ on sth** etw nach oben begrenzen.

celandine ['seləndaɪn] *n* (a) *(greater ~)* Schöllkraut *nt.* (b) *(lesser ~)* Scharbockskraut *nt.*

celebrant ['selɪbrənt] *n (Eccl)* Zelebrant *m.*

celebrate ['selɪbreɪt] 1 *vt* (a) feiern; *event, birthday also* begehen. (b) *(extol)* sb's *name, deeds* feiern, preisen *(geh).* (c) *mass, ritual* zelebrieren; *communion* feiern. 2 *vi* feiern.

celebrated ['selɪbreɪtɪd] *adj* gefeiert *(for* wegen*)*, berühmt *(for* für*).*

celebration [,selɪ'breɪʃən] *n* (a) *(party, festival)* Feier *f; (commemoration, jubilee also)* Gedenkfeier *f; (act of cel-ebrating)* Feiern *nt.* **during the centenary ~s** während der Hundertjahrfeier(n); **in ~ of** zur Feier *(+gen).* (b) *(praise)* Verherrlichung *f.* (c) *(of mass, ritual)* Zelebration *f; (of communion)* Feier *f.*

celebrity [sɪ'lebrɪtɪ] *n* Berühmtheit *f; (person also)* berühmte Persönlichkeit.

celeriac [sə'lerɪæk] *n (Knollen)*sellerie *f.*

celerity [sɪ'lerɪtɪ] *n (form)* Geschwindigkeit *f.*

celery ['selərɪ] *n* Stangensellerie *m or f.* **three stalks of ~** drei Stangen Sellerie; ~ **hearts** Sellerieherzen *pl.*

celesta [sɪ'lestə], **celeste** [sɪ'lest] *n (Mus)* Celesta *f.*

celestial [sɪ'lestɪəl] *adj (heavenly)* himmlisch; *(Astron)* Himmels-.

celibacy ['selɪbəsɪ] *n* Zölibat *nt or m; (fig)* Enthaltsamkeit *f.*

celibate ['selɪbɪt] 1 *adj (Rel)* keusch, zölibatär *(spec); (fig)* enthaltsam. 2 **n to be a ~** im Zölibat leben.

cell [sel] *n (all meanings)* Zelle *f.* ~ **wall** Zellwand *f.*

cellar ['seləʳ] *n* Keller *m.* **he keeps an excellent ~** er hat einen ausgezeichneten Weinkeller.

cellarage ['selərɪdʒ] *n (cellar space)* Kellerfläche *f; (storage cost)* Lagerkosten *pl.*

cellist ['tʃelɪst] *n* Cellist(in *f)* *m.*

cello, 'cello ['tʃeləu] *n* Cello *nt.*

cellophane ® ['seləfeɪn] *n* Cellophan ® *nt.*

cellular ['seljʊləʳ] *adj* (a) zellular, Zellular-, Zell-. (b) *(of tex-tiles)* aus porösem Material.

celluloid ['seljʊlɔɪd] *n* Zelluloid *nt.* ~ **heroes** Zelluloidhelden *pl;* **on the ~** auf der Leinwand.

cellulose ['seljʊləus] 1 *n* Zellulose *f,* Zellstoff *m.* 2 *adj* Zellulose-.

Celsius ['selsɪəs] *adj* Celsius. **30 degrees ~** 30°C *(spoken:* 30 Grad Celsius*).*

Celt [kelt, selt] *n* Kelte *m,* Keltin *f.*

Celtic ['keltɪk, 'seltɪk] 1 *adj* keltisch. 2 *n (language)* Keltisch *nt.*

cement [sə'ment] 1 *n* (a) *(Build)* Zement *m; (inf: concrete)* Beton *m.* ~ **mixer** Betonmischmaschine *f.* (b) *(glue)* Leim, Klebstoff *m; (for holes etc, fig)* Kitt *m.* (c) *(of tooth)* (Zahn)zement *m.* 2 *vt (Build)* zementieren; *(glue)* leimen; kitten; *(fig)* festigen, zementieren.

cemetery ['semɪtrɪ] *n* Friedhof *m.*

cenotaph ['senəta:f] *n* Mahnmal, Ehrenmal *nt,* Kenotaph *m.*

censer ['sensəʳ] *n (Eccl)* Rauchfaß, Räuchergefäß *nt.*

censor ['sensəʳ] 1 *n* Zensor *m.* 2 *vt* zensieren; *(remove) chapter* herausnehmen.

censorious [sen'sɔ:rɪəs] *adj remark, glance* strafend. **he was very ~ of the new policy** er kritisierte die neue Politik scharf.

censorship ['sensəʃɪp] *n* Zensur *f.* ~ **of the press** Pressezensur *f.*

censure ['senʃəʳ] 1 *vt* tadeln. **they ~d him for being lazy** sie tadelten ihn wegen seiner Faulheit. 2 *n* Tadel *m.* **vote of ~** Tadelsantrag *m.*

census ['sensəs] *n* Zensus *m,* Volkszählung *f; (Bibl)* Schätzung *f; (traffic ~)* Verkehrszählung *f.* **to take a ~ (of the population)** eine Volkszählung durchführen.

cent [sent] *n* Cent *m.* **I haven't a ~** *(US)* ich habe keinen Pfennig.

centaur ['sentɔ:ʳ] *n* Zentaur *m.*

centenarian [,sentɪ'neərɪən] 1 *adj* hundertjährig. 2 *n* Hundert-jährige(r) *mf,* Zentenar *m (geh).*

centenary [sen'ti:nərɪ] *n (anniversary)* hundertster Jahrestag; *(birthday)* hundertster Geburtstag; *(100 years)* Jahrhundert *nt.* **she has just passed her ~** sie ist gerade hundert Jahre alt geworden; ~ **celebrations** Hundertjahrfeier *f.*

centennial [sen'tenɪəl] 1 *adj* hundertjährig, hundertjährlich. 2 *n (esp US)* Hundertjahr- *or* Zentenarfeier *(geh) f.*

center *n (US) see* **centre.**

centesimal [sen'tesɪməl] *adj* zentesimal, hundertteilig. **a ~ part** ein Hundertstel.

centigrade ['sentɪgreɪd] *adj* Celsius-. **one degree ~** ein Grad Celsius.

centigramme, (US) centigram ['sentɪgræm] *n* Zentigramm *nt.*

centilitre, (US) centiliter ['sentɪ,li:təʳ] *n* Zentiliter *m or nt.*

centimetre, (US) centimeter ['sentɪ,mi:təʳ] *n* Zentimeter *m or nt.*

centipede ['sentɪpi:d] *n* Tausendfüßler, Hundertfüßer *(form) m.*

central ['sentrəl] 1 *adj* (a) zentral, Zentral-; *(main, chief)* Haupt-. ~ **station** Hauptbahnhof *m;* ~ **government** Zentral-regierung *f;* **the ~ area of the city** das Innenstadtgebiet; **our**

---

house is very ~ unser Haus liegt sehr zentral.

(b) *(fig)* wesentlich; *importance, figure* zentral. **to be ~ to sth** das Wesentliche an etw *(dat)* sein; **he plays a ~ part in ...** er spielt eine zentrale *or* wesentliche Rolle bei ...

2 *n (US: exchange, operator)* (Telefon)zentrale *f,* Fernamt *nt.*

central: C~ America *n* Mittelamerika *nt;* **C~ American** 1 *adj* mittelamerikanisch; 2 *n* Mittelamerikaner(in *f) m;* **C~ Europe** *n* Mitteleuropa *nt;* **C~ European** 1 *adj* mitteleuropäisch; 2 *n* Mitteleuropäer(in *f) m;* ~ **heating** *n* Zentralheizung *f.*

centralization [,sentrəlaɪ'zeɪʃən] *n* Zentralisierung *f.*

centralize ['sentrəlaɪz] *vt* zentralisieren.

centrally ['sentrəlɪ] *adv* zentral.

central: ~ **nervous system** *n* Zentralnervensystem *nt;* ~ **reservation** *n* Mittelstreifen *m;* Grünstreifen *m.*

centre, (US) center ['sentəʳ] 1 *n* (a) *(chief place)* Zentrum *nt.* **business ~** Geschäftszentrum *nt.*

(b) *(middle)* Mitte *f; (of circle)* Mittelpunkt *m; (town ~)* Stadtmitte *f; (city ~)* Zentrum *nt,* City *f.* ~ **of gravity** Schwer-punkt *m;* ~ **of attraction** Hauptanziehungspunkt *m,* Haupt-attraktion *f; (person)* Mittelpunkt *m der* Aufmerksamkeit; **she always wants to be the ~ of attraction** sie will immer im Mittel-punkt stehen; **left of ~** *(Pol)* links der Mitte; **the ~ of the field** *(Sport)* das Mittelfeld; **a politician of the ~** ein Politiker der Mitte; **let's go into the ~** komm, wir gehen in die Stadt!

(c) *(community ~, sports ~, shopping ~)* Zentrum, Center *nt.*

(d) *(Rugby)* mittlerer Dreiviertelspieler; *(Basketball, Net-ball)* Center *m.*

2 *vt* (a) *(put in the middle)* zentrieren.

(b) *(concentrate)* konzentrieren.

(c) *(Sport) ball* zur Mitte (ab)spielen.

♦**centre up** *vt sep* zentrieren.

♦**centre (up)on** *vi +prep obj (thoughts, problem, talk etc)* kreisen um, sich drehen um.

centre: ~**-bit** *n (Tech)* Zentrumbohrer *m;* ~**-board** *n (Naut)* (Kiel)schwert *nt;* ~**-fold** *n* Ausklapper *m;* ~**-forward** *n (Sport)* Mittelstürmer *m;* ~**-half** *n (Sport)* Stopper *m;* ~**-piece** *n* Tafelaufsatz *m;* ~**-three-quarter** *n (Rugby)* mittlerer Dreiviertelspieler.

centrifugal [,sentrɪ'fju:gəl] *adj* zentrifugal. ~ **force** Zentrifugal- *or* Fliehkraft *f.*

centrifuge ['sentrɪfju:ʒ] *n (Tech)* Zentrifuge, Schleuder *f.*

centripetal [,sentrɪ'pi:tl] *adj* zentripetal. ~ **force** Zentripetal-kraft *f.*

centuries-old ['sentjʊrɪz'əʊld] *adj* jahrhundertealt.

centurion [sen'tjʊərɪən] *n* Zenturio *m.*

century ['sentjʊrɪ] *n* (a) Jahrhundert *nt.* **in the twentieth ~** im zwanzigsten *(geschrieben:* 20.) Jahrhundert. (b) *(Cricket)* Hundert *f.*

cephalic [sɪ'fælɪk] *adj (form)* Kopf-, Schädel-.

ceramic [sɪ'ræmɪk] 1 *adj* keramisch. 2 *n* Keramik *f.*

ceramics [sɪ'ræmɪks] *n* (a) *sing (art)* Keramik *f.* (b) *pl (arti-cles)* Keramik(en *pl) f,* Keramikwaren *pl.*

cereal ['sɪərɪəl] *n* (a) *(crop)* Getreide *nt.* ~ **crop** Getreideernte *f;* **the growing of ~s** der Getreideanbau; **maize, rye and other ~s** Mais, Roggen und andere Getreidearten. (b) *(food)* Getreide-flocken *pl.* **a new ~** ein neues Getreideprodukt.

cerebellum [,serɪ'beləm] *n* Kleinhirn, Zerebellum *(spec) nt.*

cerebral ['serɪbrəl] *adj (Physiol)* zerebral; *(intellectual)* geistig; *person* durchgeistigt, vergeistigt.

cerebration [,serɪ'breɪʃən] *n (usu hum)* Reflexion *f.*

cerebrum ['serəbrəm] *n* Großhirn, Zerebrum *(spec) nt.*

ceremonial [,serɪ'məʊnɪəl] 1 *adj* zeremoniell. 2 *n* Zeremoniell *nt.*

ceremonially [,serɪ'məʊnɪəlɪ] *adv* feierlich, zeremoniell.

ceremonious [,serɪ'məʊnɪəs] *adj* förmlich, zeremoniös *(geh).*

ceremoniously [,serɪ'məʊnɪəslɪ] *adv* mit großem Zeremoniell.

ceremony ['serɪmənɪ] *n* (a) *(event etc)* Zeremonie, Feier(lich-keiten *pl) f.* (b) *(formality)* Förmlichkeit(en *pl) f.* **to stand on ~** förmlich sein.

cerise [sə'ri:z] 1 *adj* kirschrot, cerise *pred.* 2 *n* Kirschrot *nt.*

cert¹ [sɜ:t] *abbr of* **certificate.**

cert² *n (sl)* **a (dead) ~** eine todsichere Sache *(inf);* **it's a dead ~** **he'll be coming** er kommt todsicher *(inf);* **this horse is a dead ~** **for the 2.30** dieses Pferd ist ein todsicherer Tip für das Rennen um 14³⁰ *(inf).*

certain ['sɜ:tən] *adj* (a) *(positive, convinced)* sicher; *(inevit-able, guaranteed)* bestimmt, gewiß. **are you ~ of or about that?** sind Sie sich *(dat)* dessen sicher?; **is he ~?** weiß er das genau?; **can we be ~ of his support?** können wir mit seiner Unterstüt-zung rechnen?; **there's no ~ cure for this disease/for inflation** für *or* gegen diese Krankheit/gegen die Inflation gibt es kein sicheres Mittel; **for ~** ganz sicher, ganz genau; **I don't know for ~,** **but I think** ... ich bin mir nicht ganz sicher, aber ich glaube ...; **I can't say for ~** ich kann das nicht genau *or* mit Sicherheit sagen; **he is ~ to come** er wird ganz bestimmt *or* gewiß kommen; **we are ~ to succeed** wir werden ganz bestimmt Erfolg haben; **to make ~ of sth** *(check)* sich einer Sache *(gen)* vergewissern, etw nachprüfen; *(ensure)* für etw sorgen; **to make ~ of a seat** sich *(dat)* einen Platz sichern; **will you please make ~?** vergewissern Sie sich bitte noch einmal; **be ~ to tell** **him** vergessen Sie bitte nicht, ihm das zu sagen; **that was ~ to happen** das mußte ja so kommen.

(b) *(attr: not named or specified)* gewiß; *reason, conditions* bestimmt. **a ~ gentleman** ein gewisser Herr; **to a ~ extent** in gewisser Hinsicht, zu einem bestimmten Grade.

certainly ['sɜ:tənlɪ] *adv (admittedly)* sicher(lich); *(positively,* *without doubt)* bestimmt, gewiß *(geh).* ~ **not!** ganz bestimmt nicht, auf keinen Fall!; **I ~ will not!** ich denke nicht daran!; ~! sicher, gewiß! *(geh).*

certainty ['sɜ:təntɪ] *n* (a) *(sure fact)* Gewißheit *f.* **to know for a** ~ **that** ... mit Sicherheit wissen, daß ...; **he was faced with the ~**

of defeat er sah seiner sicheren Niederlage entgegen; **his suc-cess is a ~** er wird mit Sicherheit Erfolg haben, sein Erfolg ist **gewiß**; **the ultimate ~ of death** die letztliche Gewißheit des Todes; **will it happen?** — yes, **it's a ~** wird das passieren? — ja, mit Sicherheit; **it's a ~ that ...** es ist absolut sicher, daß ...
 (b) *no pl (conviction)* Gewißheit, Sicherheit *f*.

Cert Ed (*Brit*) *abbr of* **Certificate of Education.**
certifiable [ˌsɜːtɪˈfaɪəbl] *adj* (a) *fact, claim* nachweisbar. (b) (*Psych*) unzurechnungsfähig; (*inf: mad*) nicht zurech-nungsfähig.
certificate [səˈtɪfɪkɪt] *n* Bescheinigung *f*, Nachweis *m*; (*of qualifications*) Zeugnis *nt*, Urkunde *f*; (*of health*) Zeugnis *nt*; (*marriage ~*) Trauschein *m*; (*of baptism*) Taufschein *m*; (*share ~*) Zertifikat *nt*; (*Film*) Freigabe *f*.
certify [ˈsɜːtɪfaɪ] **1** *vt* (a) bescheinigen, bestätigen; (*Jur*) be-glaubigen. **this is to ~ that ...** hiermit wird bescheinigt *or* be-stätigt, daß ...; **certified as a true copy** beglaubigte Abschrift; **certified cheque** gedeckter Scheck; **certified mail** (*US*) Einschreiben *nt*; **certified milk** (*US*) Vorzugsmilch *f*; **certified public accountant** (*US*) geprüfter Buchhalter.
 (b) (*Psych*) für unzurechnungsfähig erklären; (*put in asylum*) in eine Anstalt einweisen. **the doctor certified him insane** der Arzt erklärte ihn für geistig nicht zurech-nungsfähig; **he should be certified** (*inf*) der ist doch nicht ganz zurechnungsfähig (*inf*).
 2 *vi* **to ~ to sb/sth** sich für jdn/etw verbürgen.
certitude [ˈsɜːtɪtjuːd] *n* Gewißheit, Sicherheit *f*.
cervical [ˈsɜːvɪkəl] *adj* zervikal (*spec*). **~ cancer** Gebärmut-terhalskrebs *m*; **~ smear** Abstrich *m*.
cervix [ˈsɜːvɪks] *n* (*of uterus*) Gebärmutterhals *m*.
cessation [seˈseɪʃən] *n* Ende *nt*; (*of hostilities*) Einstellung *f*. **the ~ of the heartbeat** Herzstillstand *m*.
cession [ˈseʃən] *n* Abtretung *f*. **~ of lands/territories** Gebietsab-tretung(en *pl*) *f*.
cesspit [ˈsespɪt] *n* see **cesspool** (a).
cesspool [ˈsespuːl] *n* (a) Senk- *or* Jauchegrube, Latrine *f*. (b) (*fig*) Sumpf *m*. **a ~ of vice** ein Sündenpfuhl *m*.
CET *abbr of* **Central European Time** MEZ.
cetacean [sɪˈteɪʃən] **1** *n* Wal *m*, Zetazee *f* (*spec*). **2** *adj* Wal(fisch)-, Zetazeen- (*spec*).
Ceylon [sɪˈlɒn] *n* Ceylon *nt*.
Ceylonese [ˌsɪləˈniːz] **1** *adj* ceylonesisch. **2** *n* Ceylonese *m*, Ceylonesin *f*.
cf *abbr of* **confer** vgl.
c/f *abbr of* **carry forward.**
ch, chap *abbr of* **chapter** Kap.
cha-cha [ˈtʃɑːtʃɑː] **1** *n* Cha-Cha-Cha *m*. **2** *vi* Cha-Cha-Cha tanzen.
chafe [tʃeɪf] **1** *vt* (a) (*rub, abrade*) (auf)scheuern, wund-scheuern. **his shirt ~d his neck** sein (Hemd)kragen scheuerte (ihn); **the rope was ~d** das Seil war durchgescheuert.
 (b) (*fig*) aufregen, nervös machen.
 2 *vi* (a) (*rub*) sich auf- *or* wundscheuern; (*cause soreness*) scheuern. **her skin ~s easily** ihre Haut wird leicht wund; **the rope was chafing against the railings** das Seil scheuerte an der Reling.
 (b) (*fig*) sich ärgern, wütend werden (*at, against* über +*acc*).
 3 *n* wundgescheuerte Stelle.
chaff¹ [tʃɑːf] *n* (a) (*husks of grain*) Spreu *f*; see **wheat.** (b) (*straw*) Häcksel *m or nt*.
chaff² **1** *n* (*banter: also ~ing*) Scherze *pl*, Flachserei *f* (*inf*). **2** *vt* aufziehen (*about* mit).
chaffinch [ˈtʃæfɪntʃ] *n* Buchfink *m*.
chagrin [ˈʃæɡrɪn] **1** *n* Ärger, Verdruß (*geh*) *m*. **2** *vt* ärgern, ver-drießen (*geh*). **he was much ~ed by the news** die Nachricht bekümmerte *or* verdroß (*geh*) ihn sehr.
chain [tʃeɪn] **1** *n* (a) Kette *f*. **~s** (*lit, fig: fetters*) Ketten, Fesseln *pl*; (*Aut*) (Schnee)ketten *pl*; **~ of office** Amtskette *f*; **to keep a dog on a ~** einen Hund an der Kette halten; **in ~s** in Ketten.
 (b) (*of mountains*) (Berg)kette, (Gebirgs)kette *f*; (*of atoms etc*) Kette *f*. **~ of shops** Ladenkette *f*; **to make a ~** eine Kette bilden; **~ of ideas** Gedankenkette *f*; **~ of events** Kette von Ereignissen.
 (c) (*measure of length*) Meßkette *f*.
 2 *vt* (*lit, fig*) anketten, festketten; *dog* an die Kette legen, anketten. **to ~ sb/sth to sth** jdn/etw an etw (*acc*) ketten.
♦**chain up** *vt sep prisoner* in Ketten legen; *dog* an die Kette legen, anketten.
chain *in cpds* Ketten-; **~ drive** *n* Kettenantrieb *m*, Kettenge-triebe *f*; **~ gang** *n* Truppe *f* aneinandergeketteter Sträflinge, Sträflingskolonne *f*; **~ letter** *n* Kettenbrief *m*; **~ lightning** *n* Linienblitz *m*; **~ mail** *n* Kettenhemd *nt*; **~ reac-tion** *n* Kettenreaktion *f*; **~ saw** *n* Kettensäge *f*; **~ smoke** *vi* eine (Zigarette) nach der anderen rauchen, kettenrauchen *infin only*; **~ smoker** *n* Kettenraucher(in *f*) *m*; **~ stitch** *n* (*Sew*) Kettenstich *m*; **~ store** *n* Kettenladen *m*.
chair [tʃeər] **1** *n* (a) (*seat*) Stuhl *m*; (*arm~*) Sessel *m*; (*sedan ~*) Sänfte *f*. **please take a ~** bitte nehmen Sie Platz!
 (b) (*in committees etc*) Vorsitz *m*. **to be in the ~** den Vorsitz führen; **to address the ~** sich an den Vorsitzenden/die Vorsitzende wenden; **all questions through the ~, please** bitte alle Fragen (direkt) an den Vorsitzenden richten!
 (c) (*professorship*) Lehrstuhl *m* (*of* für).
 (d) (*electric ~*) (elektrischer) Stuhl.
 2 *vt* (a) *meeting* den Vorsitz führen bei.
 (b) (*Brit: carry in triumph*) auf den Schultern (davon)tragen.
chair: **~lift** *n* Sessellift *m*; **~man** *n* Vorsitzende(r) *mf*; **Mr/Madam C~man** Herr Vorsitzender/Frau Vorsitzende; **~manship** *n* Vorsitz *m*; **under the ~manship of** unter (dem) Vorsitz von; **~person** *n* Vorsitzende(r) *mf*; **~woman** *n* Vorsit-zende *f*.

chaise [ʃeɪz] *n* (*Hist*) Einspänner *m*.
chaise longue [ˌʃeɪzˈlɔːŋ] *n* Chaiselongue *f*.
chalet [ˈʃæleɪ] *n* Chalet *nt*; (*in motel etc*) Apartment *nt*.
chalice [ˈtʃælɪs] *n* (*poet, Eccl*) Kelch *m*.
chalk [tʃɔːk] **1** *n* (a) Kreide *f*; (*limestone also*) Kalkstein *m*. **~ pit** Kalk(stein)bruch *m*; **not by a long ~** (*Brit inf*) bei weitem nicht, noch nicht einmal annähernd; **they're as different as ~ and cheese** sie sind (so verschieden) wie Tag und Nacht.
 2 *vt message etc* mit Kreide schreiben; *luggage etc* mit Kreide kennzeichnen; *billiard cue* mit Kreide einreiben.
♦**chalk out** *vt sep* (*lit*) mit Kreide zeichnen *or* malen; (*fig*) *plan* umreißen.
♦**chalk up** *vt sep* (a) (*lit*) (mit Kreide) aufschreiben, notieren. (b) (*fig: gain, win*) *success, victory* verbuchen; *medal* ein-heimsen. (c) (*fig: mark up as credit*) anschreiben (*inf*).
chalkiness [ˈtʃɔːkɪnɪs] *n* Kalkigkeit *f*; (*chalky content*) Kalk-haltigkeit *f*.
chalky [ˈtʃɔːkɪ] *adj* (+*er*) (*containing chalk*) kalkhaltig, kalkig; (*like chalk*) kalkartig; (*covered with chalk*) voller Kalk.
challenge [ˈtʃælɪndʒ] **1** *n* (a) (*to duel, match etc*) Herausfor-derung *f* (*to an* +*acc*); (*fig: demands*) Anforderung(en *pl*) *f*. **to issue a ~ to sb** jdn herausfordern; **this job is a ~** bei dieser Arbeit ist man gefordert; **I see this task as a ~** ich sehe diese Aufgabe als Herausforderung; **the ~ of modern life** die Anfor-derungen des heutigen Lebens; **those who rose to the ~** diejenigen, die sich der Herausforderung stellten; **the office job held no ~ for him** die Bürotätigkeit stellte keine Ansprüche an ihn; **the ~ of new ideas/the unknown** der Reiz neuer Ideen/des Unbekannten.
 (b) (*bid: for leadership etc*) Griff *m* (*for* nach). **a direct ~ on his authority** eine direkte Infragestellung seiner Autorität.
 (c) (*Mil: of sentry*) Anruf, Werdaruf *m*.
 (d) (*Jur: of witness*) Ablehnung *f*.
 2 *vt* (a) *person, champion* (*to duel, race etc*) herausfordern; *world record etc* überbieten wollen. **to ~ sb to a duel** jdn zum Duell fordern; **to ~ sb to a match** jdn zu einem Kampf *or* einer Begegnung *etc* herausfordern.
 (b) (*fig: make demands on*) fordern.
 (c) (*fig*) *remarks, sb's authority* in Frage stellen, anfechten.
 (d) (*sentry*) anrufen.
 (e) (*Jur*) *witnesses* ablehnen; *evidence, verdict* anfechten.
challenger [ˈtʃælɪndʒər] *n* (*to duel, match etc*) Herausforderer *m*. **a ~ of traditional beliefs** einer, der überkommene Glaubenssätze in Frage stellt.
challenging [ˈtʃælɪndʒɪŋ] *adj* (*provocative*) herausfordernd; (*thought-provoking*) reizvoll; (*demanding*) anspruchsvoll, for-dernd. **a ~ idea** eine reizvolle Vorstellung; **I don't find this work very ~** diese Arbeit fordert mich nicht.
chamber [ˈtʃeɪmbər] *n* (a) (*old*) (*room*) Gemach *nt* (*old*), Raum *m*; (*bedroom*) Schlafgemach (*old*), Kabinett (*old*) *nt*. **~ of hor-rors** Schreckenskammer *f*, Schreckenskabinett *nt*. (b) (*Brit*) **~s** (*of solicitor*) Kanzlei *f*; (*of judge*) Dienst- *or* Amtszimmer *nt*. (c) **C~ of Commerce** Handelskammer *f*; **the Upper/Lower C~** (*Parl*) die Erste/Zweite Kammer. (d) (*Anat*) (Herz)kammer *f*. (e) (*of revolver*) Kammer *f*.
chamberlain [ˈtʃeɪmbəlɪn] *n* Kammerherr *m*.
chamber: **~maid** *n* Zimmermädchen *nt*, Kammerzofe *f* (*old*); **~ music** *n* Kammermusik *f*; **~ pot** *n* Nachttopf *m*.
chambray [ˈtʃæmbreɪ] *n* (*US*) see **cambric**.
chameleon [kəˈmiːlɪən] *n* (*Zool, fig*) Chamäleon *nt*.
chamfer [ˈtʃæmfər] **1** *n* Fase, Schrägkante *f*. **2** *vt* abfasen, abschrägen.
chamois [ˈʃæmwɑː] *n* (a) (*leather*) Gamsleder *nt*. **a ~ (leather)** ein Ledertuch *nt*, ein Fensterleder *nt*. (b) (*Zool*) Gemse *f*.
champ¹ [tʃæmp] *vt* (*animals*) geräuschvoll mahlen *or* kauen; (*people*) mampfen (*inf*). **to ~ at the bit** (*lit*) an der Gebißstange kauen; (*fig*) vor Ungeduld fiebern.
champ² *n* (*inf*) Meister, Champion *m*. listen, **~ to** hör zu, Meister.
champagne [ʃæmˈpeɪn] **1** *n* Sekt, Schaumwein *m*; (*French ~*) Champagner *m*. **2** *adj* (*also* **~-coloured**) champagner(farben).
champion [ˈtʃæmpjən] **1** *n* (a) (*Sport*) Meister, Champion *m*. **~s** (*team*) Meister *m*; **world ~** Weltmeister *m*; **boxing ~** Box-champion *m*; **heavyweight ~ of the world** Weltmeister *m* im Schwergewicht.
 (b) (*of a cause*) Verfechter *m*.
 2 *adj* (a) (*prize-winning*) siegreich; *dog, bull, show animal* preisgekrönt. **~ boxer** erfolgreicher Boxer; **~ horse** (*racing*) Turfsieger *m*; (*show-jumping*) siegreiches Turnierpferd.
 (b) (*N Engl inf*) klasse *inv* (*inf*), prima *inv* (*inf*).
 3 *vt person, action, cause* eintreten für, sich engagieren für.
championship [ˈtʃæmpjənʃɪp] *n* (a) (*Sport*) Meisterschaft *f*. **he defended his ~** er verteidigte den Titel. (b) **~s** *pl* (*event*) Mei-sterschaftskämpfe *pl*. (c) (*support*) Eintreten, Engagement *nt* (*of* für).
chance [tʃɑːns] **1** *n* (a) (*coincidence*) Zufall *m*; (*luck, fortune*) Glück *nt*. **by ~** durch Zufall, zufällig; **a game of ~** ein Glücks-spiel *nt*; **would you by any ~ be able to help?** könnten Sie mir wohl *or* vielleicht behilflich sein?; **to leave things to ~** die Dinge dem Zufall überlassen; **to trust to ~** auf sein Glück ver-trauen.
 (b) (*possibility*) Aussicht(en *pl*), Chance(n *pl*) *f*; (*probability, likelihood*) Möglichkeit *f*. **the ~s are that ...** aller Wahrscheinlichkeit nach ..., wahrscheinlich ...; **the ~s are against that happening** vieles spricht dagegen *or* die Wahrscheinlichkeit ist gering, daß das eintritt; **what are his ~s of him agreeing?** wie sind die Aussichten *or* wie stehen die Chancen, daß er zustimmt?; **is there any ~ of us meeting again?** könnten wir uns vielleicht wiedersehen?; **what are the ~s of his coming?** wie groß ist die Wahrscheinlichkeit, daß er kommt?; **is there any ~ he might be lost?** besteht die Möglichkeit, daß er sich verirrt hat?; **on the ~ of your returning** für den Fall, daß du

or falls du zurückkommst *or* zurückkommen solltest; **he has not much/a good ~ of winning** er hat wenig/gute Aussicht zu gewinnen, er hat nicht sehr gute/gute Siegeschancen; **to be in with a ~** eine Chance haben; **he doesn't stand** *or* **hasn't got a ~** er hat keine(rlei) Chance(n); **no ~!** (*inf*) nee! (*inf*), ist nicht drin (*inf*); **will you lend me £50 — sorry, no ~** leihst du mir £ 50? — bedaure, nichts zu machen *or* ist nicht drin (*inf*).

(c) (*opportunity*) Chance *f.* **the ~ of a lifetime** eine einmalige Chance; **you won't get another ~ of going there** *or* **to go there** die Gelegenheit, dahin zu fahren, bietet sich (dir) nicht noch einmal; **you won't get another ~** das ist eine einmalige Gelegenheit; **I had the ~ to go** *or* **of going** ich hatte (die) Gelegenheit, dahin zu gehen; **now's your ~!** das ist deine Chance!; **this is my big ~** das ist *die* Chance für mich; **to have an eye to the main ~** (*pej*) nur auf seinen Vorteil bedacht sein; **he never had a ~**, he was bound to lose er hatte von vornherein keine Chance, er mußte ja verlieren; **he never had a ~ in life** er hat im Leben nie eine Chance gehabt; **give me a ~!** nun mach aber mal langsam (*inf*); **to give sb a ~** jdm eine Chance geben; **you never gave me a ~ to explain** du hast mir ja nie die Chance gegeben, das zu erklären.

(d) (*risk*) Risiko *nt.* **to take a/one's ~** ein Risiko eingehen, es darauf ankommen lassen; **he's not taking any ~s** er geht kein Risiko ein.

2 *attr* zufällig. **~ meeting** zufällige Begegnung.

3 *vi* **it ~d that ...** es traf *or* fügte (*geh*) sich, daß ...

4 *vt* (a) **to ~ to do sth** zufällig etw tun.

(b) **I'll ~ it!** (*inf*) ich versuch's mal (*inf*); **to ~ one's arm** (*inf*) (et)was riskieren; **to ~ one's luck** (*have a try*) sein Glück versuchen; (*risk*) das Glück herausfordern; **I'll just have to ~ that happening** das muß ich eben riskieren.

♦ **chance (up)on** *vi +prep obj* *person* zufällig begegnen (*+dat*), zufällig treffen; *thing* zufällig stoßen auf (*+acc*).

chancel ['tʃɑːnsəl] *n* Chor, Altarraum *m.*

chancellery ['tʃɑːnsələrɪ] *n* (*offices*) Kanzleramt *nt*; (*position*) Kanzlerschaft *f.*

chancellor ['tʃɑːnsələ^r] *n* (*Jur, Pol, Univ*) Kanzler *m.* **C~ (of the Exchequer)** (*Brit*) Schatzkanzler, Finanzminister *m.*

chancellorship ['tʃɑːnsələʃɪp] *n* Kanzlerschaft *f.*

chancery ['tʃɑːnsərɪ] *n*: **ward in ~** Mündel *nt* in Amtsvormundschaft.

chancre ['ʃæŋkə^r] *n* Schanker *m.*

chancy ['tʃɑːnsɪ] *adj* (*+er*) (*inf: risky*) riskant.

chandelier [ˌʃændə'lɪə^r] *n* Kronleuchter *m.*

chandler ['tʃɑːndlə^r] *n* (*for candles*) Kerzenmacher *m*; (*shop*) Kerzenladen *m.* **ship's ~** Schiffsausrüster *m.*

change [tʃeɪndʒ] **1** *n* (a) Veränderung *f*; (*modification also*) Änderung *f* (*to gen*). **a ~ for the better/worse** ein Fortschritt *m*, eine Verbesserung/ein Rückschritt *m*, eine Verschlechterung; **~ of address** Adressen- *or* Anschriftenänderung *f*; **a ~ in the weather** eine Wetterveränderung; **a ~ of air** eine Luftveränderung; **a ~ is as good as a rest** (*prov*) Abwechslung wirkt *or* tut Wunder; **no ~** unverändert; **I need a ~ of scene** ich brauche Tapetenwechsel; **to make ~s** (to sth) (an etw *dat*) (Ver)änderungen vornehmen; **to make a ~/a considerable ~ in sth** etw ändern/bedeutend verändern; **the ~ of life** der Wechseljahre; **he needs a ~ of clothes** er müßte sich mal wieder umziehen; **I didn't have a ~ of clothes with me** ich hatte nichts zum Wechseln mit; **we need a ~ of horses** wir müssen die Pferde wechseln; **a ~ of job** ein Stellenwechsel *m.*

(b) (*variety*) Abwechslung *f.* (**just**) **for a ~** zur Abwechslung (mal); **that makes a ~** das ist mal was anderes; (*iro*) das ist ja was ganz Neues!; **it'll make a nice ~** das wäre eine nette Abwechslung; **see ring.**

(c) *no pl* (*changing*) Veränderung *f.* **those who are against ~** diejenigen, die gegen jegliche Veränderung sind; **the constant ~ will only confuse people** der ständige Wechsel verwirrt die Leute nur.

(d) (*of one thing for another*) Wechsel *m.* **a ~ of government** ein Regierungswechsel, ein Wechsel in der Regierung; **a wheel ~** ein Radwechsel.

(e) *no pl* (*money*) Wechselgeld *nt*; (*small ~*) Kleingeld *nt.* **can you give me ~ for a pound?** können Sie mir ein Pfund wechseln?; **I haven't got any ~** ich habe kein Kleingeld; **I haven't got ~ for £5** ich kann auf £ 5 nicht rausgeben *or* £ 5 nicht wechseln; **you won't get much ~ out of £5** von £ 5 wird wohl nicht viel übrigbleiben; **keep the ~** der Rest ist für Sie; **you won't get much ~ out of him** (*fig*) aus ihm wirst du nicht viel rauskriegen.

(f) (*St Ex*) **C~** Börse *f.*

2 *vt* (a) (*by substitution*) wechseln; *address, name* ändern. **to ~ trains/buses** *etc* umsteigen; **to ~ one's clothes** sich umziehen; **to ~ a wheel/the oil** einen Rad-/Ölwechsel vornehmen, ein Rad/das Öl wechseln; **to ~ a baby's nappy** *or* **a baby** (bei einem Baby) die Windeln wechseln, ein Baby wickeln; **to ~ the sheets** *or* **the bed** die Bettwäsche wechseln, das Bett neu beziehen; **to ~ one's seat** den Platz wechseln, sich woanders hinsetzen; **to ~ hands** den Besitzer wechseln; **would you ~ the record?** kannst du (mal) eine andere Platte auflegen?; (*turn it over*) kannst du mal die andere Seite auflegen?; **to ~ places with sb** mit jdm den Platz tauschen; **she ~d places with him/Mrs Brown** er/Frau Brown und sie tauschten die Plätze; **I wouldn't ~ places with him for the world** ich möchte *or* würde um nichts in der Welt mit ihm tauschen; **to ~ horses in midstream** plötzlich einen anderen Kurs einschlagen.

(b) (*alter*) (ver)ändern; *person, ideas* ändern; (*transform*) verwandeln. **to ~ sb/sth into sth** jdn/etw in etw (*acc*) verwandeln; **you won't be able to ~ her** du kannst sie nicht ändern; **he ~d her from a factory girl into a top model** er hat aus dem Fabrikmädchen ein Spitzenmodell gemacht; **a chameleon can ~ its colour** das Chamäleon kann seine Farbe wechseln.

(c) (*exchange: in shop etc*) umtauschen. **she ~d the dress for**

one of a different colour sie tauschte das Kleid gegen ein andersfarbiges um; **he ~d his Rolls Royce for a Mini** er vertauschte seinen Rolls Royce mit einem Mini; **see guard.**

(d) *money* (*into smaller money*) wechseln; (*into other currency*) (um)tauschen.

(e) (*Aut*) **to ~ gear** schalten.

3 *vi* (a) sich ändern; (*town, person also*) sich verändern. **you've ~d!** du hast dich aber verändert!; **he will never ~** er wird sich nie ändern, der ändert sich nie!; **to ~ from sth into sth else** sich aus etw in etw (*acc*) anderes verwandeln.

(b) (**~ clothes**) sich umziehen. **she ~d into an old skirt** sie zog sich einen alten Rock an; **I'll just ~ out of these old clothes** ich muß mir noch die alten Sachen ausziehen.

(c) (**~ trains** *etc*) umsteigen. **you ~ at Edinburgh** in Edinburgh müssen Sie umsteigen; **all ~!** Endstation!, alle aussteigen!

(d) (**~ gear**) schalten; (*traffic lights*) umspringen (*to auf +acc*).

(e) (*from one thing to another*) (*seasons*) wechseln. **to ~ to a different system** auf ein anderes System umstellen, zu einem anderen System übergehen; **I ~d to philosophy from maths** ich habe von Philosophie zu Mathematik gewechselt, ich bin von Philosophie auf Mathematik umgestiegen (*inf*); **do you want to ~ with me?** (*places*) möchten Sie mit mir tauschen?

♦ **change down** *vi* (*Aut*) einen niedrigeren Gang einlegen, in einen niedrigeren Gang schalten, (he)runterschalten.

♦ **change over** *vi* (a) (*change to sth different*) sich umstellen auf (*+acc*). **we have just ~d ~ from gas to electricity** hier *or* bei uns ist gerade von Gas auf Strom umgestellt worden; **the mechanism ~s ~ automatically** der Mechanismus schaltet automatisch um *or* schaltet (sich) selbsttätig um.

(b) (*exchange places, activities etc*) wechseln; (*Sport also*) die Seiten wechseln. **do you mind if I ~ ~?** (*TV*) hast du was dagegen, wenn ich umschalte?

2 *vt sep* austauschen.

♦ **change round 1** *vi see* **change over 1** (b). **2** *vt sep room* umräumen; *furniture* umstellen; *tyres* austauschen, auswechseln.

♦ **change up** *vi* (*Aut*) einen höheren Gang einlegen, in einen höheren Gang schalten, höherschalten (*inf*). **to ~ ~ into top in** den höchsten Gang schalten.

changeability [ˌtʃeɪndʒə'bɪlɪtɪ] *n* Unbeständigkeit, Veränderlichkeit *f.*

changeable ['tʃeɪndʒəbl] *adj person, character* unbeständig; *weather* veränderlich, wechselhaft; *mood, winds* wechselnd.

changeless ['tʃeɪndʒlɪs] *adj* unveränderlich.

changeling ['tʃeɪndʒlɪŋ] *n* (*child*) Wechselbalg *m.*

changeover ['tʃeɪndʒəʊvə^r] *n* Umstellung *f* (*from von, to auf +acc*); (*of governments*) Regierungswechsel *m*; (*of baton in relay race*) (Stab)wechsel *m*; (*of teams changing ends*) Seitenwechsel *m.*

changing ['tʃeɪndʒɪŋ] **1** *adj* sich verändernd, wechselnd. **the fast-~ face of Munich** das sich rapide wandelnde Gesicht *or* Stadtbild Münchens. **2** *n* **the ~ of the Guard** die Wachablösung.

changing-room ['tʃeɪndʒɪŋ'ruːm] *n* (*in store*) Ankleideraum *m*, Kabine *f*; (*Sport*) Umkleideraum *m*, Umkleidekabine *f.*

channel ['tʃænl] **1** *n* (a) (*watercourse*) (Fluß)bett *nt*; (*strait*) Kanal *m*; (*deepest part of river etc*) Fahrrinne *f.* **the (English) C~** der Ärmelkanal; **C~ Islands** Normannische Inseln, Kanalinseln *pl.*

(b) (*fig, usu pl*) (*of bureaucracy etc*) Dienstweg *m*; (*of information etc*) Kanal *m*; (*of thought, interest etc*) Bahn *f.* **if you go through the right ~s** wenn Sie sich an die richtigen Stellen wenden; **to go through the official ~s** den Dienstweg gehen; **you'll have to go through ~s** (*US*) Sie werden den Dienstweg einhalten müssen; **through the usual ~s** auf dem üblichen Wege.

(c) (*groove*) Furche, Rinne *f.*

(d) (*TV, Rad*) Kanal *m*, Programm *nt.*

2 *vt* (a) (*dig out, furrow*) way, course sich (*dat*) bahnen.

(b) (*direct*) *water, river* (hindurch)leiten (*through durch*).

(c) (*fig*) *efforts, interest* lenken (*into auf +acc*); *energy also* kanalisieren; *crowd also* dirigieren.

♦ **channel off** *vt sep* (*lit*) ableiten; (*fig*) abzweigen.

chant [tʃɑːnt] **1** *n* (*Eccl, Mus*) Gesang, Cantus *m*; (*monotonous song*) Sprechgesang, Singsang *m*; (*of football fans*) Sprechchor *m.* **tribal ~s** Stammesgesänge *pl.* **2** *vt* im (Sprech)chor rufen; (*Eccl*) singen. **3** *vi* Sprechchöre anstimmen; (*Eccl*) singen.

chanterelle ['tʃæntərel] *n* Pfifferling *m.*

chanticleer ['tʃæntɪkliːə^r] *n* (*old*) Hahn *m.*

chaos ['keɪɒs] *n* Chaos, Durcheinander *nt.* **complete ~** ein totales Durcheinander.

chaotic *adj*, **~ally** *adv* [keɪ'ɒtɪk-əlɪ] chaotisch.

chap[1] [tʃæp] **1** *n* (*Med: of skin*) **he's got ~s on his hands** seine Hände sind aufgesprungen *or* rauh. **2** *vi* (*skin*) aufspringen. **3** *vt* spröde machen. **~ped lips** aufgesprungene *or* rauhe Lippen.

chap[2] *n* (*Brit inf: man*) Kerl (*inf*), Typ (*inf*) *m.* **old ~** alter Junge (*inf*) *or* Knabe (*inf*); **poor little ~** armer Kleiner!, armes Kerlchen!; **now look here you ~s** hört mal zu, Jungs (*inf*).

chap[3] *abbr of* **chapter** Kap.

chapel ['tʃæpəl] *n* (a) Kapelle *f*; (*Sch, Univ: service*) Andacht *f.* **~ of rest** Kapelle *f* in einem Bestattungsunternehmen, wo Tote aufgebahrt werden. (b) (*non-conformist church*) Sektenkirche *f.* (c) (*Press: of union*) Betriebsgruppe *f* innerhalb der Gewerkschaft der Drucker und Journalisten.

chaperon(e) ['ʃæpərəʊn] **1** *n* (a) (*for propriety*) Anstandsdame *f*, Anstandswauwau *m* (*hum inf*). (b) (*escort*) Begleiter(in *f*) *m.* (c) (*esp US: supervisor*) Aufsichts- *or* Begleitperson *f.* **2** *vt* (a) (*for propriety*) begleiten, Anstandsdame spielen bei. (b) (*escort*) begleiten. (c) (*US*) beaufsichtigen.

chaplain ['tʃæplɪn] *n* Kaplan *m.*

chaplaincy ['tʃæplənsɪ] n Amt nt or Stelle f eines Kaplans; (building) Dienstraüme pl eines Kaplans.
chaplet ['tʃæplɪt] n (of flowers etc) Kranz m.
chappy ['tʃæpɪ] n (inf) Kerlchen nt (inf).
chaps [tʃæps] npl lederne Reithosen, Cowboyhosen pl.
chapter ['tʃæptəʳ] n (a) (of book) Kapitel nt. **to give ~ and verse (for sth)** (fig) etw genau belegen. **(b)** (fig) Kapitel nt. **a ~ of accidents** eine Serie von Unfällen. **(c)** (Eccl) Kapitel nt. **~ house** Kapitel(saal m) nt. **(d)** (esp US: branch) Ortsgruppe f.
char¹ [tʃɑːʳ] vt (burn black) verkohlen.
char² (Brit inf) **1** n (charwoman) Putzfrau f. **2** vi putzen. **to ~ for sb** bei jdm putzen.
char³ n (fish) Saibling m.
char⁴ n (Brit inf: tea) Tee, Tschai (inf) m.
charabanc, char-à-banc ['ʃærəbæŋ] n (old) offener Omnibus für Ausflugsfahrten.
character ['kærɪktəʳ] n (a) (nature) Charakter m; (of people) Wesen nt no pl, Wesensart f. **there's quite a difference in ~ between them** sie sind wesensmäßig sehr verschieden; **to be in ~ for sb** typisch für jdn sein; **it is out of ~ for him to behave like that** solches Benehmen ist untypisch für ihn; **it's completely out of ~ for him to do that** es ist eigentlich gar nicht seine Art, so etwas zu tun; **to be of good/bad ~** ein guter/schlechter Mensch sein; **we've changed the ~ of the exam** wir haben die Form or den Charakter der Prüfung geändert.
(b) no pl (strength of ~) Charakter m. **a man of ~** ein Mann von Charakter; **she's got no ~** sie hat keinen Charakter.
(c) no pl (individuality) (of towns etc) Charakter m; (of person) Persönlichkeit f. **she has no ~** sie hat keine Persönlichkeit; **her face is full of ~** sie hat ein Charaktergesicht.
(d) (in novel) (Roman)figur, (Roman)gestalt f; (Theat) Gestalt f.
(e) (person in public life) Persönlichkeit, Gestalt f; (original person) Original nt; (inf: person) Typ m (inf), Type f (inf).
(f) (reference) Zeugnis nt.
(g) (Typ) Buchstabe m, Letter f (spec); (Chinese etc) Schriftzeichen nt. **to type 100 ~s per minute** 100 Anschläge pro Minute machen; **Gothic ~s** gotische Schrift.
character in cpds (Theat) Charakter-; **~ actor** n Charakterdarsteller m; **~ assassination** n Rufmord m.
characteristic [‚kærɪktə'rɪstɪk] **1** adj charakteristisch, typisch (of für). **2** n (typisches) Merkmal, Charakteristikum nt; (Math) Charakteristik, Kennziffer f. **one of the main ~s of his style is ...** besonders charakteristisch für seinen Stil ist ..., eines der Hauptmerkmale seines Stils ist ...; **he has all the ~s of the true aristocrat** er hat alle Züge des echten Aristokraten.
characteristically [‚kærɪktə'rɪstɪkəlɪ] adv typisch.
characterization [‚kærɪktərar'zeɪʃən] n (in a novel etc) Personenbeschreibung f; (of one character) Charakterisierung f.
characterize ['kærɪktəraɪz] vt (a) (be characteristic of) kennzeichnen, charakterisieren. **(b)** (describe) beschreiben.
characterless ['kærɪktəlɪs] adj person nichtssagend, farblos; room nichtssagend, nichts Besonderes pred; wine fade.
character: ~ part n Charakterrolle f; **~ reference** n Referenz f; **~ sketch** n Charakterstudie f.
charade [ʃə'rɑːd] n Scharade f; (fig) Farce f, Affentheater nt (inf).
charcoal ['tʃɑːkəʊl] n Holzkohle f; (drawing) Kohlezeichnung f; (pencil) Kohle(stift m) f.
charcoal: ~ burner n (person) Köhler, Kohlenbrenner (rare) m; (stove) Holzkohlenofen m; **~ drawing** n Kohlezeichnung f; **~-grey** adj schwarzgrau.
charge [tʃɑːdʒ] **1** n (a) (Jur: accusation) Anklage f (of wegen). **convicted on all three ~s** in allen drei Anklagepunkten für schuldig befunden; **to bring a ~ against sb** gegen jdn Anklage erheben, jdn unter Anklage stellen; **to press ~s (against sb)** (gegen jdn) Anzeige erstatten; **what is the ~?** wessen werde ich/wird er etc beschuldigt?; **to be on a murder ~** unter Mordanklage stehen; **he was arrested on a ~ of murder** er wurde wegen or unter Mordverdacht festgenommen; **to give sb in ~** (form) jdn in polizeilichen Gewahrsam bringen (form), jdn der Polizei (dat) übersteilen (form); **it was laid to his ~** (form) es wurde ihm angelastet or zur Last gelegt; **to be on a ~** (soldier) eine Disziplinarstrafe verbüßen; **to put a soldier on a ~** über einen Soldaten eine Disziplinarstrafe verhängen, einen Soldaten verknacken (sl); **you're on a ~, Smith!** das gibt eine Disziplinarstrafe, Smith!
(b) (attack: of soldiers, bull etc) Angriff m; (trumpet-call) Signal nt. **to sound the ~** zum Angriff blasen.
(c) (fee) Gebühr f. **what's the/your ~?** was kostet das?/was verlangen Sie?; **to make a ~ (of £5) for sth** (£ 5 für) etw berechnen or in Rechnung stellen; **he made no ~ for mending my watch** er hat mir für die Reparatur der Uhr nichts berechnet; **there's an extra ~ for the delivery** die Lieferung wird zusätzlich berechnet; **his ~s are quite reasonable** seine Preise sind ganz vernünftig; **free of ~** kostenlos, gratis; **delivered free of ~** Lieferung frei Haus.
(d) (explosive ~) (Spreng)ladung f; (in firearm, Elec, Phys) Ladung f. **to put a battery on ~** eine Batterie aufladen; **to be on ~** aufgeladen werden.
(e) (position of responsibility) Verantwortung f (of für). **to be in ~** verantwortlich sein, die Verantwortung haben; **who is in ~ here?** wer ist hier der Verantwortliche?; **look, I'm in ~ here** hören Sie mal zu, hier bestimme ich!; **to be in ~ of sth** für etw die Verantwortung haben; of department etw leiten; **to put sb in ~ of sth** jdm die Verantwortung für etw übertragen; of department jdm die Leitung von etw übertragen; **while in ~ of a car** (form) am Steuer eines Kraftfahrzeuges; **the man in ~** der Verantwortliche, die verantwortliche Person; **the children were placed in their aunt's ~** die Kinder wurden der Obhut der Tante anvertraut; **the patients in or under her ~** die ihr anvertrauten Patienten; **to take ~ of sth** etw übernehmen; **to take ~ das Kommando übernehmen**; **he took ~ of the situation** er nahm die Sache in die Hand; **will you take ~ of the children while I'm out?** kannst du mir die Kinder während meiner Abwesenheit anvertrauen?
(f) (ward) (child) Schützling m; (of authorities) Mündel nt; (patient) Patient(in f) m.
(g) (financial burden) **to be a ~ on sb** jdm zur Last fallen.
2 vt (a) (with gen) (Jur) anklagen; (fig) beschuldigen.
(b) (attack) stürmen; troops angreifen; (bull etc) losgehen auf (+acc); (Sport) goalkeeper, player angehen. **the forwards ~d the defence** die Stürmer griffen die Deckung an; **to ~ sb off the ball** jdn vom Ball abdrängen.
(c) (ask in payment) berechnen. **I won't ~ you for that** das kostet Sie nichts, ich berechne Ihnen nichts.
(d) (record as debt) in Rechnung stellen. **~ it to the company** stellen Sie das der Firma in Rechnung, das geht auf die Firma (inf); **please ~ all these purchases to my account** bitte setzen Sie diese Einkäufe auf meine Rechnung.
(e) firearm laden; (Phys, Elec) battery (auf)laden.
(f) (form: command) **to ~ sb to do sth** jdn beauftragen or anweisen (form), etw zu tun.
(g) (form: give as responsibility) **to ~ sb with sth** jdm mit etw beauftragen.
3 vi (a) (attack) stürmen; (at people) angreifen (at sb jdn); (bull) losgehen (at sb auf jdn). **~! vorwärts!**
(b) (inf: rush) rennen. **he ~d into a brick wall** er rannte gegen eine Mauer; **he ~d into the room/upstairs** er stürmte ins Zimmer/die Treppe hoch.
♦charge up vt sep (a) (credit) in Rechnung stellen (to sb jdm). **I'll ~ the expenses** ~ das geht auf Geschäftskosten. **(b)** (Elec) aufladen.
chargeable ['tʃɑːdʒəbl] adj (a) (Jur) **to be ~ with sth** für etw angeklagt werden können. **(b) to be ~ to sb** auf jds Kosten (acc) gehen; **are these expenses ~?** geht das auf Geschäftskosten?
charge account n Kunden(kredit)konto nt.
charged ['tʃɑːdʒd] adj (lit, fig) geladen; (Elec also) aufgeladen. **~ with emotion** emotionsgeladen.
chargé d'affaires ['ʃɑː‚ʒeɪdæ'feəʳ] n Chargé d'affaires m.
charge hand n Vorarbeiter(in f) m.
charger ['tʃɑːdʒəʳ] n (a) (battery ~) Ladegerät nt. **(b)** (horse) Roß nt. **(c)** (old: dish) Platte f.
charily ['tʃeərɪlɪ] adv vorsichtig.
chariness ['tʃeərɪnɪs] n Vorsicht f.
chariot ['tʃærɪət] n Wagen, Streitwagen (liter) m.
charioteer [‚tʃærɪə'tɪəʳ] n Wagenlenker, Rosselenker (liter) m.
charisma [kæ'rɪzmə] n Charisma nt.
charismatic [‚kærɪz'mætɪk] adj charismatisch.
charitable ['tʃærɪtəbl] adj menschenfreundlich, gütig; (dispensing charity) trust, organization Wohltätigkeits-, karitativ; (financially generous, tolerant) großzügig; thought, remark etc freundlich. **a ~ deed** eine gute Tat; **he wasn't very ~ about his boss** er äußerte sich nicht gerade schmeichelhaft über seinen Chef; **I'm feeling ~ today, here's £5** ich habe heute meinen sozialen Tag, hier hast du £ 5.
charitably ['tʃærɪtəblɪ] adv großzügig; think, say etc freundlich.
charity ['tʃærɪtɪ] n (a) (Christian virtue) tätige Nächstenliebe, Barmherzigkeit f.
(b) (tolerance, kindness) Menschenfreundlichkeit f. **for ~'s sake, out of ~** aus reiner Menschenfreundlichkeit; **~ begins at home** (Prov) man muß zuerst an seine eigene Familie/sein eigenes Land etc denken.
(c) (alms) **to live on ~** von Almosen leben.
(d) (charitable society) Wohltätigkeitsverein m, karitative Organisation; (charitable purposes) Wohlfahrt f. **to work for ~** für die Wohlfahrt arbeiten; **a collection for ~** eine Sammlung für wohltätige or karitative Zwecke.
charity in cpds Wohltätigkeits-.
charlady ['tʃɑː‚leɪdɪ] n (Brit) Putz- or Reinemachefrau f.
charlatan ['ʃɑːlətən] n Scharlatan m.
Charlemagne ['ʃɑːləmeɪn] n Karl der Große.
Charles [tʃɑːlz] n Karl m.
charleston ['tʃɑːlstən] n Charleston m.
charley horse ['tʃɑːlɪhɔːs] n (US inf) steifes Bein.
Charlie ['tʃɑːlɪ] n (a) dim of **Charles**. **(b)** c~ (inf: fool) Heini (inf), Blödmann (sl) m; **I felt a real ~** ich kam mir richtig blöd vor (inf); **I must have looked a proper c~** ich muß ziemlich dumm aus der Wäsche geguckt haben (inf).
Charlotte ['ʃɑːlət] n (a) Charlotte f. **(b)** (Cook) c~ Charlotte f; **c~ russe** Charlotte Malakoff.
charm [tʃɑːm] **1** n (a) (attractiveness) Charme m no pl; (of person also) Anziehungskraft f; (of cottage, village, countryside) Reiz m. **feminine ~s** (weibliche) Reize pl; **he fell victim to her ~s** er erlag ihrem Charme; **to turn on the ~** seinen (ganzen) Charme spielen lassen.
(b) (spell) Bann m. **it worked like a ~** das hat hervorragend geklappt.
(c) (amulet) Talisman m; (trinket) Anhänger m.
2 vt (a) (attract, please) bezaubern. **he could ~ the birds out of the trees** (prov) er könnte mit seinem Charme alles erreichen.
(b) (cast spell on) bannen; snakes beschwören. **to lead a ~ed life** einen Schutzengel haben.
♦charm away vt sep fears, worries etc zerstreuen.
charm bracelet n Armband nt mit Anhängern.
charmer ['tʃɑːməʳ] n **to be/look a real ~** wirklich charmant sein/zum Verlieben aussehen.
charming ['tʃɑːmɪŋ] adj reizend, charmant. **~!** (iro) wie reizend! (iro), na, das ist ja reizend! (iro).

charmingly ['tʃɑːmɪŋlɪ] *adv* reizend. **she behaved/welcomed us quite** ~ sie war/begrüßte uns äußerst charmant.

charnel-house ['tʃɑːnlhaus] *n* (*old*) Leichenhalle *f*; (*for bones*) Beinhaus *nt*.

chart [tʃɑːt] **1** *n* (**a**) Tabelle *f*; (*graph, diagram*) Schaubild, Diagramm *nt*; (*map, weather* ~) Karte *f*. **on a** ~ in einer Tabelle/einem Diagramm; **to keep a** ~ **of sth** etw in eine Tabelle eintragen/in einem Diagramm festhalten.
  (**b**) ~s *pl* (*top twenty*) Hitliste *f*.
  2 *vt* (*make a map of*) kartographisch erfassen; (*record progress of*) auswerten; (*keep a* ~ *of*) aufzeichnen, erfassen; (*plan*) festlegen.

charter ['tʃɑːtə'] **1** *n* (**a**) Charta *f*; (*town* ~, *Univ also*) Gründungsurkunde *f*; (*of a society*) Satzung *f*; (*permission to become established*) Charter *f or m*, Freibrief *m*. (**b**) (*Naut, Aviat: hire*) **on** ~ gechartert; **the plane is available for** ~ das Flugzeug kann gechartert werden. **2** *vt plane, bus etc* chartern. ~**ed accountant** Bilanzbuchhalter *m*.

charter *in cpds* Charter-; ~ **flight** *n* Charterflug *m*; ~ **party** *n* Chartergesellschaft *f*; ~ **plane** *n* Charterflugzeug *nt*.

charwoman ['tʃɑːˌwʊmən] *n* (*Brit*) see **charlady**.

chary ['tʃɛərɪ] *adj* (+*er*) (*cautious*) vorsichtig; (*sparing*) zurückhaltend (*of* mit). **I'd be** ~ **of taking lifts from strangers if I were you** an deiner Stelle würde ich nicht so ohne weiteres mit Fremden mitfahren; **he is** ~ **of giving praise** er ist mit Lob zurückhaltend.

Charybdis [kəˈrɪbdɪs] *n* Charybdis *f*.

Chas *abbr of* **Charles**.

chase¹ [tʃeɪs] **1** *n* Verfolgungsjagd *f*; (*Hunt*) Jagd *f*. **a car** ~ eine Verfolgungsjagd im Auto; **to give** ~ die Verfolgung aufnehmen; **to give** ~ **to sb** jds Verfolgung aufnehmen.
  2 *vt* jagen; (*follow*) verfolgen; *member of opposite sex* hinterherlaufen (+*dat*), nachlaufen (+*dat*). **go and** ~ **yourself!** (*sl*) scher dich zum Teufel! (*inf*); **he's been chasing that girl for months** er ist schon seit Monaten hinter der Frau her; **this letter has been chasing you all over London** dieser Brief ist dir schon durch ganz London gefolgt; *see* **shadow 1** (**a**).
  3 *vi* **to** ~ **after sb** hinter jdm herrennen (*inf*); (*in vehicle*) hinter jdm herrasen (*inf*); **to** ~ **around** herumrasen (*inf*); **he** ~**d out of the room** er rannte aus dem Zimmer.
♦**chase away** *or* **off 1** *vi* losrasen (*inf*); (*on foot also*) losrennen. **2** *vt sep* wegjagen; (*fig*) *sorrow etc* vertreiben.
♦**chase up** *vt sep person* rankriegen (*inf*); *information etc* ranschaffen (*inf*).

chase² *vt* (*Tech*) *silver, metal* ziselieren.

chaser ['tʃeɪsə'] *n* (**a**) (*pursuer*) Verfolger *m*. (**b**) (*drink*) **have a** ~ **whisky** ~ trinken Sie einen Whisky dazu; **I'll have a beer as a** ~ ich trinke ein Bier zum Nachspülen.

chasm ['kæzəm] *n* (*Geol*) Spalte, Kluft (*also fig*) *f*. **a yawning** ~ ein gähnender Abgrund; **the future lay before him, a great black** ~ die Zukunft tat sich wie ein riesiger dunkler Abgrund vor ihm auf.

chassis ['ʃæsɪ] *n* Chassis *nt*; (*Aut also*) Fahrgestell *nt*.

chaste [tʃeɪst] *adj* (+*er*) (*pure, virtuous*) keusch; (*simple, unadvanced*) *style, elegance* schlicht.

chastely ['tʃeɪstlɪ] *adv see adj*.

chasten ['tʃeɪsn] *vt* nachdenklich stimmen, zur Einsicht bringen; *pride, stubborn nature* zügeln. ~**ed by ... durch ... zur** Einsicht gelangt.

chasteness ['tʃeɪstnɪs] *n see adj* Keuschheit *f*; Schlichtheit *f*.

chastening ['tʃeɪsnɪŋ] *adj thought, experience* ernüchternd.

chastise [tʃæsˈtaɪz] *vt* züchtigen (*geh*); (*scold*) schelten.

chastisement ['tʃæstɪzmənt] *n see vt* Züchtigung *f* (*geh*); Schelte *f*.

chastity ['tʃæstɪtɪ] *n* (*sexual purity*) Keuschheit *f*; (*virginity also*) Unberührtheit, Reinheit *f*. ~ **belt** Keuschheitsgürtel *m*.

chasuble ['tʃæzjʊbl] *n* Meßgewand *nt*, Kasel *f*.

chat [tʃæt] **1** *n* Unterhaltung *f*; (*about unimportant things also*) Plauderei *f*, Schwatz *m* (*inf*). **could we have a** ~ **about it?** können wir uns mal darüber unterhalten?; **she dropped in for a** ~ sie kam zu einem Schwätzchen rein (*inf*). **2** *vi* plaudern; (*2 people also*) sich unterhalten.
♦**chat up** *vt sep* (*inf*) *person* einreden auf (+*acc*); *prospective girl-/boyfriend* sich heranmachen an (+*acc*), anquatschen (*inf*).

chatelaine ['ʃætəleɪn] *n* (**a**) (*of castle*) (*housekeeper*) Schloßverwalterin *f*; (*owner*) Schloßherrin *f*. (**b**) (*old*) *Gürtel, an dem ein Schlüsselbund getragen wird*.

chat show *n* (*Brit*) Talkshow *f*.

chattels ['tʃætlz] *npl* (*Jur*) bewegliches Vermögen, bewegliche Habe. **all his** (**goods and** ~) ~ seine gesamte Habe.

chatter ['tʃætə'] **1** *n* (*of person*) Geschwätz, Geplapper *nt*; (*of birds*) Schwatzen *nt*; (*of monkeys*) Geschnatter *nt*; (*of teeth*) Klappern *nt*; (*of typewriter*) Geklapper, Klappern *nt*; (*of guns*) Knattern, Geknatter *nt*.
  2 *vi see n* schwatzen, schwätzen (*esp S Ger*), plappern; schwatzen; schnattern; klappern; knattern.

chatterbox ['tʃætəbɒks] *n* Quasselstrippe *f* (*inf*).

chatty ['tʃætɪ] *adj* (+*er*) *person* geschwätzig, schwatzhaft. **written in a** ~ **style** im Plauderton geschrieben.

chauffeur ['ʃəʊfə'] *n* Chauffeur, Fahrer *m*. ~**-driven** mit Fahrer *or* Chauffeur; **to be** ~**-driven** einen Fahrer haben.

chauffeuse [ʃəʊˈfɜːz] *n* Fahrerin *f*.

chauvinism ['ʃəʊvɪnɪzəm] *n* Chauvinismus *m*.

chauvinist ['ʃəʊvɪnɪst] *n* (*jingoist*) Chauvinist(in *f*) *m*; (*male* ~) männlicher Chauvinist. (**male**) ~ **pig** (*typischer*) Pascha (*inf*), Chauvi *m* (*sl*).

chauvinistic [ˌʃəʊvɪˈnɪstɪk] *adj* chauvinistisch.

cheap [tʃiːp] **1** *adj* (+*er*) (**a**) *also adv* (*inexpensive*) billig. **to hold sth** ~ etw geringachten; **it's** ~ **at the price** es ist spottbillig; **I got it** ~ ich habe es billig gekriegt.
  (**b**) (*poor quality*) billig, minderwertig. **everything they sell is** ~ **and nasty** sie verkaufen nur Ramsch.
  (**c**) (*fig*) (*mean, shallow, sexually* ~) *joke, flattery, thrill, girl* billig; *person, behaviour, appearance* ordinär. **to feel** ~ sich (*dat*) schäbig vorkommen; **how can you be so** ~! wie kannst du nur so gemein sein!; **to make oneself** ~ sich entwürdigen; (*by loose living*) sich wegwerfen.
  2 on the ~ auf die billige (*inf*); **to buy sth on the** ~ (*inf*) etw für einen Pappenstiel (*inf*) *or* einen Apfel und ein Ei (*inf*) kaufen; **to make sth on the** ~ (*inf*) etw ganz billig produzieren.

cheapen ['tʃiːpən] **1** *vt* (*lit*) verbilligen, herabsetzen; (*fig*) herabsetzen, schlecht machen. **to** ~ **oneself** sich entwürdigen. **2** *vi* billiger werden, sich verbilligen.

cheapjack ['tʃiːpdʒæk] *adj* Ramsch- (*pej*).

cheaply ['tʃiːplɪ] *adv see adj*.

cheapness ['tʃiːpnɪs] *n see adj* (**a**) billiger Preis. (**b**) Billigkeit, Minderwertigkeit *f*. (**c**) Billigkeit *f*; ordinäre Art.

cheapskate ['tʃiːpskeɪt] *n* (*inf*) Knicker (*inf*), Knauser (*inf*) *m*.

cheat [tʃiːt] **1** *vt* betrügen; *authorities also* täuschen. **to** ~ **sb of sth** jdn um etw betrügen.
  2 *vi* betrügen; (*in exam, game etc*) mogeln (*inf*), schummeln (*Sch sl*); (*in card games also*) falschspielen, mogeln (*inf*).
  3 *n* (**a**) (*person*) Betrüger(in *f*) *m*; (*in exam, game etc*) Mogler(in *f*) (*inf*), Schummler(in *f*) (*Sch sl*) *m*; (*in card games also*) Falschspieler(in *f*), Mogler(in *f*) (*inf*) *m*.
  (**b**) (*dishonest trick*) Betrug *m*, Täuschung *f*.
♦**cheat on** *vi* +*prep obj* betrügen.

cheating ['tʃiːtɪŋ] **1** *n see* **cheat 2** Betrügen *nt*, Betrug *m*; Mogeln (*inf*), Schummeln (*Sch sl*) *nt*; Falschspielen, Mogeln (*inf*) *nt*. **2** *adj* betrügerisch.

check [tʃek] **1** *n* (**a**) (*examination*) Überprüfung, Kontrolle *f*. **to give sth a** ~ etw überprüfen *or* nachsehen; **to make a** ~ **on sb/sth** jdn/etw überprüfen, bei jdm/etw eine Kontrolle durchführen; **a random** ~ eine Stichprobe; **to keep a** ~ **on sb/sth** jdn/etw überwachen *or* kontrollieren.
  (**b**) (*restraint*) Hemmnis *nt*, Erschwernis *f*; (*Mil: to army*) Hindernis *nt*, Sperre *f*. **an efficient** ~ **on population growth** ein wirksames Mittel zur Eindämmung des Bevölkerungswachstums; **to hold** *or* **keep sb in** ~ jdn in Schach halten; **to hold** *or* **keep one's temper in** ~ sich beherrschen; (**a system of**) ~ **and balances** ein Sicherungssystem *nt*; **to act as a** ~ (**up)on sth** etw unter Kontrolle (*dat*) halten.
  (**c**) (*pattern*) Karo(muster) *nt*; (*square*) Karo *nt*.
  (**d**) (*Chess*) Schach *nt*. **to be in** ~ im Schach stehen; **to put sb in** ~ jdm Schach bieten.
  (**e**) (*US*) (*cheque*) Scheck *m*; (*bill*) Rechnung *f*. ~ **please** bitte (be)zahlen.
  (**f**) (*US*) (*room*) (*Rail*) Gepäckaufbewahrung *f*; (*Theat*) Garderobe *f*; (*ticket*) Gepäck)schein *m*; (Garderoben)marke *f*.
  (**g**) (*US: tick*) Haken *m*.
  2 *vt* (**a**) (*examine*) überprüfen, checken (*inf*); (*in book also*) nachschlagen; *tickets also* kontrollieren.
  (**b**) (*act as control on*) kontrollieren; (*stop*) *enemy, advance* aufhalten; *anger* unterdrücken, beherrschen. **I was going to say it, but I just managed to** ~ **myself in time** ich wollte es sagen, aber ich konnte mich gerade noch beherrschen.
  (**c**) (*Chess*) Schach bieten (+*dat*).
  (**d**) (*US*) *coat etc* abgeben; (*Rail*) *luggage* (*register*) aufgeben; (*deposit*) abgeben, zur Aufbewahrung geben.
  (**e**) (*US: tick*) abhaken.
  3 *vi* (**a**) (*make sure*) nachfragen (*with* bei); (*have a look*) nachsehen, nachgucken. **I was just** ~**ing** ich wollte nur nachprüfen.
  (**b**) (*stop, pause*) stocken; (*horse*) scheuen.
♦**check back** *vi* (*look back in records*) zurückgehen (*in zu sth*); (*re-contact*) rückfragen (*with* bei).
♦**check in 1** *vi* (*at airport*) sich bei der Abfertigung melden, einchecken; (*at hotel*) sich anmelden. **what time do you have to** ~ ~? wann mußt du am Flughafen sein?
  2 *vt sep* (*at airport*) *luggage* abfertigen lassen; (*at hotel*) *person* anmelden. **he isn't** ~**ed** ~ **at this hotel** er wohnt nicht in diesem Hotel; **they** ~**ed me** ~ **at a first-class hotel** ich wurde in einem erstklassigen Hotel untergebracht.
♦**check off** *vt sep* (*esp US*) abhaken.
♦**check out 1** *vi* sich abmelden; (*leave hotel*) abreisen; (*sign out*) sich austragen; (*clock out*) stempeln, stechen. **2** *vt sep* (**a**) *figures, facts, persons* überprüfen. ~ **it** ~ **with the boss** klären Sie das mit dem Chef ab. (**b**) (*hotel, airline etc*) abfertigen.
♦**check over** *vt sep* überprüfen.
♦**check through** *vt sep* (**a**) *account, proofs* durchsehen, durchgehen. (**b**) **they** ~**ed my bags** ~ **to Berlin** mein Gepäck wurde nach Berlin durchabgefertigt *or* durchgecheckt.
♦**check up** *vi* überprüfen.
♦**check up on** *vi* +*prep obj* überprüfen; *person also* Nachforschungen anstellen über (+*acc*); (*keep a check on*) *sb* kontrollieren.

checkbook ['tʃekbʊk] *n* (*US*) Scheckbuch *nt*.

checked [tʃekt] *adj* kariert. ~ **pattern** Karomuster *nt*.

checkerboard ['tʃekəbɔːd] *n* (*US*) Damebrett *nt*; (*chessboard*) Schachbrett *nt*.

checkered *adj* (*US*) see **chequered**.

checkers ['tʃekəz] *n* (*US*) Damespiel *nt*. **to play** ~ Dame spielen.

check-in (desk) ['tʃekɪnˈdesk] *n* Abfertigung *f*, Abfertigungsschalter *m*; (*US: in hotel*) Rezeption, Anmeldung *f*.

checking ['tʃekɪŋ] *n* Überprüfung, Kontrolle *f*. **it needs more** ~ es muß gründlicher überprüft werden; ~ **account** (*US*) Girokonto *nt*.

check: ~ **list** *n* Prüf- *or* Checkliste *f*; ~**mate 1** *n* Schachmatt *nt*; ~**mate!** (*Chess*) matt! (*fig*) aus!; **he found himself in** ~**mate** (*lit, fig*) er war matt gesetzt; **2** *vt* matt setzen; ~**out** *n* (*in supermarket*) Kasse *f*; ~**point** *n* Kontrollpunkt *m*; **C~point Charlie** *n*

Checkpoint Charlie *m*, Ausländerübergang *m* Friedrichstraße; **~room** *n* (*US*) (*Theat*) Garderobe *f*; (*Rail*) Gepäckaufbewahrung *f*; **~up** *n* (*Med*) Untersuchung *f*, Check-up *m*; **to have a ~-up to go for a ~-up** einen Check-up machen lassen.

cheddar ['tʃedə'] *n* Cheddar(käse) *m*.

cheek [tʃiːk] **1** *n* (**a**) Backe, Wange (*liter*) *f*. **to be ~ by jowl (with sb)** Tuchfühlung mit jdm haben, auf Tuchfühlung (mit jdm) sein; **to dance ~ to ~** Wange an Wange tanzen; **~ bone** Wangenknochen *m*, Jochbein *nt* (*spec*); **~ pouch** Futtertasche *f*; **to turn the other ~** die andere Wange hinhalten.
(**b**) (*buttock*) Backe *f*.
(**c**) (*impudence*) Frechheit, Unverschämtheit, Dreistigkeit *f*. **to have the ~ to do sth** die Frechheit *or* Stirn haben, etw zu tun, sich erdreisten, etw zu tun; **they gave him a lot of ~** sie waren sehr frech zu ihm; **enough of your ~!** jetzt reicht's aber!; **what (a) ~!** (was für *or* so eine) Frechheit *or* Unverschämtheit!; **well, of all the ~!**, **the ~ of it!** das ist doch die Höhe!, so eine Frechheit *or* Unverschämtheit!
2 *vt* **to ~ sb** frech sein zu jdm *or* gegen jdm.

-cheeked ['tʃiːkd] *adj suf* -backig. **rosy-~** rotbackig.

cheekily ['tʃiːkɪlɪ] *adv* frech, vorwitzig, dreist.

cheekiness ['tʃiːkɪnɪs] *n* Frechheit, Dreistigkeit *f*, Vorwitz *m* (*geh*); (*of person also*) freche Art.

cheeky ['tʃiːkɪ] *adj* (+*er*) frech, vorwitzig, dreist; *remark, person, smile also* schnippisch; *hat, dress* keß, flott; *driving* schneidig, schnittig, frech. **it's a bit ~ asking for another pay rise so soon** es ist etwas unverschämt, schon wieder eine Gehaltserhöhung zu verlangen; **~ girl** freche Göre.

cheep [tʃiːp] **1** *n* Piep, Piepser *m*. **2** *vi* piepsen.

cheer [tʃiə'] **1** *n* (**a**) Hurra- *or* Beifallsruf *m*; (*cheering*) Hurrageschrei *nt*, Jubel *m*. **to give three ~s for sb** jdn dreimal hochleben lassen, ein dreifaches Hoch auf jdn ausbringen; **three ~s for Mike!** ein dreifaches Hurra für Mike!; **~s!** (*Brit inf*) (*your health*) tschüs! (*inf*); (*thank you*) danke schön!; **~ leader** Anführer *m*.
(**b**) (*comfort*) Aufmunterung, Ermutigung *f*. **the news gave us some ~** die Nachricht munterte uns auf; **words of ~** aufmunternde Worte, Zuspruch *m*.
(**c**) (*old*) **be of good ~** seid guten Mutes *or* wohlgemut (*old*).
(**d**) (*old: food etc*) **good ~** Tafelfreude(n *pl*) *f* (*old*).
2 *vt* (**a**) *person* zujubeln (+*dat*); *thing, event* bejubeln.
(**b**) (*gladden*) aufmuntern, aufheitern, froh machen.
3 *vi* jubeln, hurra rufen.

♦**cheer on** *vt sep* anspornen, anfeuern.

♦**cheer up 1** *vt sep* aufmuntern, aufheitern; *room, place* aufheitern. **he needed a bit of ~ing** er brauchte etwas Aufmunterung *or* Aufheiterung; **tell him that, that'll ~ him ~** sag ihm das, dann freut er sich.
2 *vi* (*person*) vergnügter *or* fröhlicher werden, bessere Laune bekommen; (*things*) besser werden. **~ ~!** laß den Kopf nicht hängen!, nun lach doch mal!; **~ ~, it's not that bad** Kopf hoch *or* nur Mut, so schlimm ist es auch wieder nicht.

cheerful ['tʃiəful] *adj* fröhlich, vergnügt; *person also* gutgelaunt *attr*, heiter (*geh*); *place, appearance, colour etc* heiter; *prospect, news* erfreulich; (*iro*) heiter; *tune* fröhlich; *fire* lustig. **you're a ~ customer, aren't you?** (*iro*) du bist (mir) vielleicht ein schöner Miesmacher (*inf*); **that's ~!** (*iro*) das ist ja heiter!

cheerfully ['tʃiəfulɪ] *adv* fröhlich, vergnügt; *decorated* lustig, heiter. **the fire was burning ~** das Feuer brannte lustig.

cheerfulness ['tʃiəfulnɪs] *n see adj* Fröhlichkeit *f*; gute Laune, Vergnügtheit *f*, Frohsinn *m* (*geh*); Heiterkeit *f*; Erfreulichkeit *f*; fröhlicher Charakter. **I love the ~ of a log fire** ich mag es gern, wenn das offene Feuer so lustig brennt.

cheerily ['tʃiərɪlɪ] *adv* fröhlich, vergnügt.

cheering ['tʃiərɪŋ] **1** *n* Jubel *m*, Jubeln, Hurrageschrei *nt*; (**~ on**) anfeuernde Zurufe *pl*. **2** *adj* (**a**) *news, prospect* beglückend. (**b**) *crowds* jubelnd.

cheerio ['tʃiərɪ'əu] *interj* (*esp Brit inf*) (**a**) (*goodbye*) Wiedersehen (*inf*), Servus (*S Ger, Aus*); (*to friends*) tschüs (*inf*). (**b**) (*your health*) prost.

cheerless ['tʃiəlɪs] *adj* freudlos, trüb; *person* trübselig, trübsinnig; *prospect* trübe, düster, traurig; *scenery* grau.

cheers [tʃiəz] *interj see* **cheer 1** (**a**).

cheery ['tʃiərɪ] *adj* (+*er*) fröhlich, heiter (*geh*); *tune, colour also* lustig.

cheese [tʃiːz] *n* Käse *m*. **hard ~!** (*dated inf*) Künstlerpech! (*inf*); **say ~!** (*Phot*) bitte recht freundlich, sag „cheese".

cheese *in cpds* Käse-; **~board** *n* Käsebrett *nt*; (*course*) Käseplatte *f*; **~burger** *n* Cheeseburger *m*; **~cake** *n* (*Cook*) Käsekuchen *m*; (*sl*) (nacktes) Fleisch (*inf*); **~cloth** *n* Käseleinen *nt*, indische Baumwolle *f*.

cheesed-off [tʃiːzd'ɒf] *adj* (*Brit sl*) angeödet (*sl*). **I'm ~ with this job/her** diese Arbeit/sie ödet mich an (*sl*) *or* stinkt mir (*sl*).

cheese: **~paring 1** *n* Pfennigfuchserei (*inf*), Knauserei *f*; **2** *adj* knauserig, knickerig (*inf*); **~ straw** *n* kleine Käsestange.

cheesy ['tʃiːzɪ] *adj* (+*er*) (**a**) *adj* käsig; **to taste ~** nach Käse schmecken; **a ~ taste** ein Käsegeschmack; **a ~ smile** Pepsodentlächeln *nt* (*inf*). (**b**) (*US sl: shoddy*) mies (*inf*).

cheetah ['tʃiːtə] *n* Gepard *m*.

chef [ʃef] *n* Küchenchef *m*; (*as profession*) Koch *m*; (*head ~*) Chefkoch *m*. **my compliments to the ~** ein Lob der Küche.

chemical ['kemɪkəl] **1** *adj* chemisch. **~ engineering** Chemotechnik *f*; **~ warfare** chemische Krieg(s)führung. **2** *n* Chemikalie *f*.

chemically ['kemɪkəlɪ] *adv* chemisch.

chemise [ʃə'miːz] *n* Unterkleid *nt*.

chemist ['kemɪst] *n* (**a**) (*expert in chemistry*) Chemiker(in *f*) *m*. (**b**) (*Brit: in shop*) Drogist(in *f*) *m*; (*dispensing*) Apotheker(in *f*) *m*. **~'s shop** Drogerie *f*, Apotheke *f*.

chemistry ['kemɪstrɪ] *n* (**a**) Chemie *f*; (*chemical make-up*)

chemische Zusammensetzung (*fig*). **~ set** Chemiebaukasten *m*.
(**b**) (*fig*) Verträglichkeit *f*. **the good/bad ~ between them** ihre gute Verträglichkeit/ihre Unverträglichkeit; **the ~ between us was perfect** wir haben uns sofort vertragen, es hat sofort zwischen uns gefunkt (*inf*); **the ~ of physical attraction/of love** das Kräftespiel der körperlichen Anziehung in der Liebe.

chenille [ʃə'niːl] *n* Chenille *f*.

cheque, (*US*) **check** [tʃek] *n* Scheck *m*. **a ~ for £10** ein Scheck über £ 10; **to pay by ~** mit (einem) Scheck bezahlen; **~book** Scheckbuch *nt*; **~ card** Scheckkarte *f*.

chequered, (*US*) **checkered** ['tʃekəd] *adj* (*lit*) kariert; (*dappled*) gefleckt, gesprenkelt; (*fig*) *career, history* bewegt.

cherish ['tʃerɪʃ] *vt* (**a**) *person* liebevoll sorgen für. **to love and to ~** zu lieben und zu ehren.
(**b**) *feelings, hope* hegen; *idea, illusion* sich hingeben (+*dat*). **I shall always ~ that memory/present** die Erinnerung (daran)/das Geschenk wird mir immer lieb und teuer sein; **to ~ sb's memory** jds Andenken in Ehren halten, jdm ein treues Andenken bewahren.

Cherokee (Indian) ['tʃerəuki:('ɪndɪən)] *n* Tscherokese *m*, Tscherokesin *f*.

cheroot [ʃə'ruːt] *n* Stumpen *m*.

cherry ['tʃerɪ] **1** *n* Kirsche *f*; (*colour*) Kirschrot *nt*. **wild ~** Vogelkirsche *f*. **2** *adj* (*colour*) kirschrot; (*Cook*) Kirsch-.

cherry *in cpds* Kirsch-; **~ brandy** *n* Cherry Brandy *m*; **~ orchard** *n* Kirschgarten *m*; **~ red** *adj* kirschrot.

cherub ['tʃerəb] *n* **(a)** *pl* **-im** (*Eccl*) Cherub *m*. **(b)** *pl* **-s** (*Art*) Putte *f*, Putto *m* (*form*); (*baby*) Engelchen *nt*.

chervil ['tʃɜːvɪl] *n* Kerbel *m*.

chess [tʃes] *n* Schach(spiel) *nt*. **~ board** Schachbrett *nt*; **~man**, **~ piece** Schachfigur *f*.

chest¹ [tʃest] *n* (*for tea, tools etc*) Kiste *f*; (*piece of furniture, for clothes, money etc*) Truhe *f*. **~ of drawers** Kommode *f*.

chest² *n* (*Anat*) Brust *f*, Brustkorb *m* (*esp Med*). **the boxer's broad ~** der breite Brustkasten des Boxers; **to measure sb's ~** jds Brustweite *or* Brustumfang messen; **to get sth off one's ~** (*fig inf*) sich (*dat*) etw von der Seele reden, etw loswerden; **to have a weak ~** schwach auf der Brust sein (*inf*); **a cold on the ~** Bronchialkatarrh *m*; **~ specialist** Facharzt *m* für Lungenkrankheiten, Lungenfacharzt *m*.

-chested ['tʃestɪd] *adj suf* -brüstig.

chesterfield ['tʃestəfiːld] *n* Chesterfieldsofa *nt*.

chestnut ['tʃesnʌt] **1** *n* (**a**) (*nut, tree*) Kastanie *f*. (**b**) (*colour*) Kastanienbraun *nt*. (**c**) (*horse*) Fuchs *m*. (**d**) (*inf: old joke*) alte *or* olle Kamelle (*inf*). **2** *adj* (*colour*) *hair* kastanienbraun, rötlichbraun. **a ~ horse** ein Fuchs *m*.

chesty ['tʃestɪ] *adj* (+*er*) (*inf*) *person* erkältet, grippig (*inf*); *cough* rauh, schnarrend. **I'm a bit ~ this morning** ich hab's heute etwas auf der Brust (*inf*).

cheval glass [ʃə'vælgla:s] *n* Standspiegel *m* (zum Kippen).

chevron ['ʃevrən] *n* Winkel *m*.

chew [tʃuː] **1** *n* Kauen *nt*. **to have a good ~ on sth** auf *or* an etw (*dat*) gründlich herumkauen.
2 *vt* kauen. **this meat takes a lot of ~ing** an *or* bei diesem Fleisch muß man viel (herum)kauen; **that dog's been ~ing the carpet again** der Hund hat schon wieder am Teppich gekaut; **don't ~ your fingernails** kaue nicht an deinen Nägeln; **she always ~s her nails** sie kaut Nägel; *see* **cud**.

♦**chew away 1** *vi* lange herumkauen an *or* auf (+*dat*). **the rats have been ~ing ~ at the woodwork** die Ratten haben am Holz herumgenagt. **2** *vt sep* wegfressen.

♦**chew off** *or* **out** *vt sep* (*US inf*) zur Schnecke machen (*inf*).

♦**chew on** *vi* +*prep obj* (**a**) (*lit*) (herum)kauen auf (+*dat*). (**b**) (*also* **chew over**) (*inf*) *facts, problem* sich (*dat*) durch den Kopf gehen lassen.

♦**chew up** *vt sep* (**a**) (*lit*) aufessen, fertigessen; (*animal*) auffressen; *pencil etc* zerkauen; *ground, road surface* zerstören; *paper* zerfressen, zermalmen. (**b**) (*sl: tell off*) fertigmachen (*inf*), runterputzen (*inf*).

chewing gum ['tʃuːɪŋgʌm] *n* Kaugummi *m or nt*.

chewy ['tʃuːwɪ] *adj meat* zäh; *pasta* kernig; *sweets* weich.

chiaroscuro [kɪˌɑːrəs'kuərəu] *n* Chiaroscuro, Helldunkel *nt*.

chic [ʃiːk] **1** *adj* (+*er*) schick, elegant. **2** *n* Chic, Schick *m*.

chicane [ʃɪ'keɪn] *n* (*Sport*) Schikane *f*.

chicanery [ʃɪ'keɪnərɪ] *n* (*trickery*) Machenschaften *pl*; (*legal*) Winkelzüge *pl*.

chichi ['tʃiːtʃiː] *adj* (*inf*) todschick (*iro inf*), auf schön gemacht (*inf*); *dress etc* verspielt, niedlich. **he's gone all ~** er macht auf schön (*inf*).

chick [tʃɪk] *n* (**a**) (*of chicken*) Küken *nt*; (*young bird*) Junge(s) *nt*. (**b**) (*inf: child*) Kleine(s) *nt*. (**c**) (*sl: girl*) Mieze *f* (*sl*). **she's some ~** sie ist nicht ohne (*inf*).

chicken ['tʃɪkɪn] **1** *n* (**a**) Huhn *nt*; (*for roasting, frying*) Hähnchen *nt*. **she's no ~** (*inf*) sie ist nicht mehr die Jüngste; **~ liver** Hühner- *or* Geflügelleber *f*; **don't count your ~s before they're hatched** (*Prov*) man soll das Fell des Bären nicht verkaufen, ehe man ihn erlegt hat (*Prov*).
(**b**) (*inf: coward*) feiges Huhn (*inf*), Feigling *m*. **2** *adj* (*inf*) feig. **he's ~** er ist ein Feigling *or* ein feiges Huhn (*inf*); **he's too ~ to do it** er ist zu feig(e).

♦**chicken out** *vi* (*inf*) kneifen (*inf*).

chicken *in cpds* Hühner-; **~ farmer** *n* Hühnerzüchter *m*; **~feed** *n* (**a**) (*lit*) Hühnerfutter *nt*; (**b**) (*inf: insignificant sum*) ein paar Pfennige; **they expect us to work for ~feed** sie erwarten, daß wir für'n Appel und'n Ei arbeiten (*inf*); **~-hearted** *adj* feige, hasenherzig (*old, liter*); **~pox** *n* Windpocken *pl*; **~-run** *n* Hühnerhof, Auslauf *m*; **~ wire** *n* Hühnerdraht *m*.

chick: **~pea** *n* Kichererbse *f*; **~weed** *n* Sternmiere *f*.

chicle ['tʃɪkl] *n* Chiclegummi *m*.

chicory ['tʃɪkərɪ] *n* Chicorée *f or m*; (*in coffee*) Zichorie *f*.

chide [tʃaɪd] *pret* **chid** [tʃɪd] (*old*) *or* **~d** ['tʃaɪdɪd], *ptp* **chidden** ['tʃɪdn] (*old*) *or* ~**d** *vt* schelten, zurechtweisen, rügen.

chief [tʃiːf] **1** *n*, *pl* **-s** (*a*) (*of department or organization*) Leiter, Chef (*inf*) *m*; (*of family, clan*) Oberhaupt *nt*; (*of tribe*) Häuptling *m*; (*of gang*) Anführer *m*; (*inf: boss*) Boss (*inf*), Chef *m*. ~ **of police** Polizeipräsident *or* -chef *m*; ~ **of staff** (*Mil*) Stabschef *m*; ~ **of state** Staatschef *m*.
(**b**) (*Her*) Schildhaupt *nt*.
(**c**) **in** ~ hauptsächlich.
2 *adj* (**a**) (*most important*) Haupt-, wichtigste(r, s), bedeutendste(r, s). **the** ~ **thing** das Wichtigste, die Hauptsache; ~ **reason** Hauptgrund *m*.
(**b**) (*most senior*) Haupt-, Ober-, erste(r). ~ **clerk** Bürochef *m*; ~ **constable** (*Brit*) Polizeipräsident *or* -chef *m*; ~ **justice** (*Brit*) ≈ Oberrichter *m*; (*US*) Oberster Bundesrichter.

chiefly ['tʃiːflɪ] *adv* hauptsächlich, in erster Linie, vor allem.

chieftain ['tʃiːftən] *n* (*of tribe*) Häuptling *m*; (*of clan*) Oberhaupt *nt*, Älteste(r) *m*; (*of robber band*) Hauptmann *m*. **the** ~ **village** ~ der Dorfälteste.

chiffon ['ʃɪfɒn] **1** *n* Chiffon *m*. **2** *adj* Chiffon-.

chignon ['ʃiːnjɔ̃ː] *n* Nackenknoten, Chignon *m*.

chihuahua [tʃɪ'wauwɑː] *n* Chihuahua *m*.

chilblain ['tʃɪlbleɪn] *n* Frostbeule *f*.

child [tʃaɪld] *n*, *pl* **children** (*lit, fig*) Kind *nt*. **when I was a** ~ **in** *or* zu meiner Kindheit; **she was with** ~ (*old, liter*) sie trug ein Kind unter ihrem Herzen (*old, liter*); **the** ~ **of his imagination** das Produkt seiner Phantasie.

child *in cpds* Kinder-; ~**-bearing 1** *n* Mutterschaft *f*, Kinderkriegen *nt* (*inf*); **ten years of** ~**-bearing exhausted her** zehn Jahre mit kleinen Kindern erschöpften sie; **2** *adj of* ~**-bearing age** im gebärfähigen Alter; **good** ~**-bearing hips** gebärfreudiges Becken; ~**birth** *n* Geburt *f*, Gebären *nt*; **to die in** ~**birth** bei der Geburt sterben; ~ **care** *n* Kinderpflege *f*; (*social work dept*) Jugendfürsorge *f*; ~ **guidance** *n* Erziehungsberatung *f*; (*social work agency*) Erziehungsberatungsstelle *f*; ~**hood** *n* Kindheit *f*; **to be in one's second** ~**hood** seine zweite Kindheit erleben.

childish *adj*, ~**ly** *adv* ['tʃaɪldɪʃ, -lɪ] (*pej*) kindisch.

childishness ['tʃaɪldɪʃnɪs] *n* (*pej*) kindisches Gehabe.

child: ~ **labour** *n* Kinderarbeit *f*; ~**less** *adj* kinderlos; ~**like** *adj* kindlich; ~**minder** *n* Tagesmutter *f*.

children ['tʃɪldrən] *pl of* **child**.

child: ~ **prodigy** *n* Wunderkind *nt*; ~**'s play** *n* ein Kinderspiel *nt*; ~ **welfare** *n* Jugendfürsorge *f*; **C**~ **Welfare Centre** Kinderabteilung *f* im Gesundheitsamt.

Chile ['tʃɪlɪ] *n* Chile *nt*.

Chilean ['tʃɪlɪən] **1** *adj* chilenisch. **2** *n* Chilene *m*, Chilenin *f*.

chill [tʃɪl] **1** *n* (**a**) Frische *f*. **there's quite a** ~ **in the air** es ist ziemlich frisch; **the sun took the** ~ **off the water** die Sonne hat das Wasser ein bißchen erwärmt; **you should take the** ~ **off the wine** Sie sollten den Wein nicht so eiskalt servieren.
(**b**) (*Med*) fieberhafte Erkältung; (*shiver*) Schauder *m*, Frösteln *nt*. **a** ~ **of fear/horror** ein Angst-/Schreckensschauder *m*; **to catch a** ~ sich verkühlen.
(**c**) (*fig*) **a distinct** ~ **in East/West relations** eine deutliche Abkühlung der Ost-West-Beziehungen; **his presence cast a** ~ **over the meeting** durch seine Anwesenheit wurde das Treffen sehr kühl *or* frostig.
2 *adj* (*lit*) kühl, frisch; (*fig liter*) **reception** kühl, frostig.
3 *vt* (**a**) (*lit*) **wine, meat** kühlen. **I was** ~**ed to the bone** *or* **marrow** die Kälte ging mir bis auf die Knochen.
(**b**) (*fig*) **blood** gefrieren lassen; **enthusiasm etc** abkühlen.

chil(l)i ['tʃɪlɪ] *n* Peperoni *pl*; (*spice, meal*) Chili *m*.

chill(i)ness ['tʃɪl(ɪ)nɪs] *n* (*lit*) Kühle, Frische *f*; (*fig*) Kühle, Frostigkeit *f*.

chilling ['tʃɪlɪŋ] *adj look* frostig, eisig; **prospect, thought** äußerst unerquicklich, beunruhigend.

chilly ['tʃɪlɪ] *adj* (+*er*) **weather** kühl, frisch; **manner, look, smile etc** kühl, frostig. **to feel** ~ frösteln, frieren; **I feel** ~ mich fröstelt's, mir ist kühl.

chime [tʃaɪm] **1** *n* Glockenspiel, Geläut *nt*; (*of door-bell*) Läuten *nt no pl*. **2** *vt* schlagen. **3** *vi* läuten.
♦ **chime in** *vi* (*inf*) sich einschalten.
♦ **chime in with** *vi* +*prep obj* (*plans*) in Einklang stehen mit.

chimera [kaɪ'mɪərə] *n* Chimäre *f*; (*fig*) Schimäre *f*.

chimerical [kaɪ'merɪkəl] *adj* schimärisch.

chimney ['tʃɪmnɪ] *n* Schornstein *m*; (*on factory also*) Schlot *m*; (*open fire-place*) Kamin *m*; (*of lamp*) Zylinder *m*; (*of stove*) Rauchfang *m*; (*Mountaineering*) Kamin *m*.

chimney: ~**breast** *n* Kaminvorsprung *m*; ~**piece** *n* Kaminsims *m*; ~**pot** *n* Schornsteinkopf *m*; ~**stack** *n* Schornstein *m*; ~**sweep** *n* Schornsteinfeger *m*.

chimp [tʃɪmp] (*inf*), **chimpanzee** [,tʃɪmpæn'ziː] *n* Schimpanse *m*.

China ['tʃaɪnə] *n* China *nt*.

china ['tʃaɪnə] **1** *n* Porzellan *nt*. **2** *adj* Porzellan-.

china: ~ **clay** *n* Kaolin *m*; **C**~**man** *n* Chinese *m*; (*US pej*) Schlitzauge *nt*; **C**~**town** *n* Chinesenviertel *nt*; ~**ware** *n* Porzellanware(n *pl*) *f*.

chinchilla [tʃɪn'tʃɪlə] *n* Chinchilla *f*; (*fur*) Chinchilla(pelz) *m*.

Chinese [tʃaɪ'niːz] **1** *n* (**a**) (*person*) Chinese *m*, Chinesin *f*. (**b**) (*language, fig: gibberish*) Chinesisch *nt*. **2** *adj* chinesisch. ~ **lantern** Lampion *m*; ~ **puzzle** ≈ ein Gegenstand zum Zusammensetzen als Geduldsspiel; ~ **white** Chinesischweiß *nt*.

chink¹ [tʃɪŋk] **1** *n* Riß *m*, Ritze *f*; (*in door*) Spalt *m*. **a** ~ **of light** ein dünner Lichtstreifen *or* -strahl; **the** ~ **in sb's armour** (*fig*) jds

schwacher Punkt. **2** *vt* (*US*) stopfen.

chink² [tʃɪŋk] **1** *n* (*sound*) Klirren *nt*; (*of coins*) Klimpern *nt*. **2** *vt* klirren mit; **coins** klimpern mit. **3** *vi* klirren; (*coins*) klimpern.

Chink [tʃɪŋk] *n* (*pej*) Schlitzauge *nt*, Chinese *m*, Chinesin *f*.

chin: ~**less** *adj* **to be** ~**less** (*lit*) ein fliehendes Kinn haben; (*fig*) willensschwach sein; ~**less wonder** *n* (*hum*) leicht vertrottelter Vertreter der Oberschicht; ~ **rest** *n* Kinnstütze *f*; ~ **strap** *n* Kinnriemen *m*.

chintz [tʃɪnts] **1** *n* Chintz *m*. **2** *attr* **curtains** Chintz-.

chintzy ['tʃɪntsɪ] *adj* (+*er*) schmuck.

chinwag ['tʃɪnwæg] *n* (*Brit inf*) Schwatz *m* (*inf*).

chip [tʃɪp] **1** *n* (**a**) Splitter *m*; (*of glass also*) Scherbe *f*; (*of wood*) Span *m*. **he's a** ~ **off the old block** er ist ganz der Vater; **to have a** ~ **on one's shoulder** einen Komplex haben (*about wegen*); **sb with a** ~ **on his shoulder** jd, der sich ständig angegriffen fühlt.
(**b**) (*potato* ~) Pomme frite *m or nt usu pl*; (*US: crisp*) Chip *m usu pl*. ~ **basket** Frittiersieb *nt*; ~**pan** Fritteuse *f*.
(**c**) (*in crockery, furniture etc*) abgeschlagene *or* abgestoßene Ecke *or* Stelle *f*. **this cup has a** ~ diese Tasse ist angeschlagen.
(**d**) (*in poker etc*) Chip *m*, Spielmarke *f*. **to cash in one's** ~**s** (*euph*) den Löffel abgeben *or* wegwerfen (*sl euph*); **he's had his** ~**s** (*inf*) (d)er hat ausgespielt (*inf*); **to be in the** ~**s** (*US inf*) Kleingeld haben (*inf*), flüssig sein (*inf*); **when the** ~**s are down** wenn es drauf ankommt, wenn es Spitze auf Knopf steht (*inf*).
(**e**) **to give the ball a** ~ (*Golf, Tennis*) den Ball chippen.
(**f**) (*micro*~) Chip *nt*.
2 *vt* (**a**) **cup, stone** anschlagen; **varnish, paint** abstoßen; **wood** beschädigen; (~ *off*) wegschlagen, abstoßen. **to be badly** ~**ped** stark angeschlagen sein.
(**b**) (*Brit Cook*) ~**ped potatoes** Pommes frites *pl*.
(**c**) (*Sport*) **ball** chippen.
3 *vi* (*cup, china etc*) angeschlagen werden, Macken/eine Macke bekommen (*inf*); (*paint, varnish*) absplittern; (*stone*) splittern. **this pottery** ~**s easily** diese Keramik ist schnell angeschlagen.
♦ **chip away 1** *vt sep* weghauen. **the woodpecker** ~**ped** ~ **the bark** der Specht hackte die Rinde ab. **2** *vi* **the sculptor** ~**ped** ~ **until ...** der Bildhauer meißelte am Stein herum, bis ...
♦ **chip in** *vi* (*inf*) (**a**) (*interrupt*) sich einschalten. (**b**) (*contribute*) **he** ~**ped** ~ **with £3** er steuerte £3 bei; **would you like to** ~~? würdest du gerne etwas beisteuern?
♦ **chip off 1** *vt sep* **paint etc** wegschlagen; **piece of china** abstoßen, abschlagen. **2** *vi* (*paint etc*) absplittern.

chipboard ['tʃɪpbɔːd] *n* Spanholz *nt*. **piece of** ~ Spanplatte *f*.

chipmunk ['tʃɪpmʌŋk] *n* Backenhörnchen *nt*.

chipolata [tʃɪpə'lɑːtə] *n* (*Brit*) Cocktailwürstchen *nt*.

chippings ['tʃɪpɪŋz] *npl* Splitter *pl*; (*of wood*) Späne *pl*; (*road* ~) Schotter *m*.

chip shot *n* (*Golf*) Chip(shot) *m*; (*Tennis*) Chip *m*.

chiromancer ['kaɪərəmænsə'] *n* Chiromant(in *f*) *m*.

chiromancy ['kaɪərəmænsɪ] *n* Chiromantie *f*.

chiropodist [kɪ'rɒpədɪst] *n* Fußpfleger(in *f*) *m*.

chiropody [kɪ'rɒpədɪ] *n* Fußpflege *f*.

chiropractic ['kaɪərəpræktɪk] *n* Chiropraktik *f*.

chirp [tʃɜːp] **1** *vi* (*birds*) zwitschern; (*crickets*) zirpen.
2 *n* (*of birds*) Piepser *m*; (~*ing*) Piepsen, Zwitschern *nt no pl*; (*of crickets*) Zirpen *nt no pl*. **I don't want to hear another** ~ **from you** ich möchte keine Muckser mehr von dir hören (*inf*).

chirpy ['tʃɜːpɪ] *adj* (+*er*) (*inf*) munter.

chirrup ['tʃɪrəp] *see* **chirp**.

chisel ['tʃɪzl] **1** *n* Meißel *m*; (*for wood*) Beitel *m*. **2** *vt* meißeln; (*in wood*) stemmen. **her finely** ~**led features** ihr fein geschnittenes Gesicht.

chit¹ [tʃɪt] *n* junges Ding. **she's a mere** ~ **of a girl** sie ist ja noch ein halbes Kind.

chit² *n* (*also* ~ **of paper**) Zettel *m*.

chitchat ['tʃɪttʃæt] *n* (*inf*) Geschwätz, Gerede *nt*.

chivalric ['ʃɪvəlrɪk] *adj* ritterlich.

chivalrous *adj*, ~**ly** *adv* ['ʃɪvəlrəs, -lɪ] ritterlich.

chivalry ['ʃɪvəlrɪ] *n* Ritterlichkeit *f*; (*medieval concept*) Rittertum *nt*. ~ **is not dead** es gibt noch Kavaliere.

chives [tʃaɪvz] *n* Schnittlauch *m*.

chivvy ['tʃɪvɪ] *vt* (*Brit inf*) (*also* ~ **along** *or* **up**) antreiben. **to** ~ **sb into doing sth** jdn dazu antreiben, etw zu tun.

chlorate ['klɔːreɪt] *n* Chlorat *nt*.

chloric ['klɔːrɪk] *adj* chlorig, chlorhaltig. ~ **acid** Chlorsäure *f*.

chloride ['klɔːraɪd] *n* Chlorid *nt*. ~ **of lime** Chlorkalk *m*.

chlorinate ['klɔːrɪneɪt] *vt* **water** chloren.

chlorination [klɔːrɪ'neɪʃən] *n* (*of water*) Chloren *nt*.

chlorine ['klɔːriːn] *n* Chlor *nt*.

chloroform ['klɔrəfɔːm] **1** *n* Chloroform *nt*. **2** *vt* mit Chloroform betäuben, eine Chloroformnarkose geben (+*dat*).

chlorophyll ['klɔrəfɪl] *n* Chlorophyll *nt*.

choc-ice ['tʃɒkaɪs] *n* Eismohrle *nt* (*Eiscreme mit Schokoladenüberzug*).

chock [tʃɒk] **1** *n* Bremskeil, Bremsklotz *m*; (*Naut: under boat*) Bock *m*; (*Naut: for cables*) Lippe, Lippklampe *f*. ~**s away** Bremsklötze weg. **2** *vt* **wheel** blockieren; **boat** aufbocken.

chock-a-block ['tʃɒkəblɒk], **chock-full** ['tʃɒkfʊl] *adj* (*inf*) knüppelvoll (*inf*), gerammelt voll (*inf*).

chocolate ['tʃɒklɪt] **1** *n* (**a**) Schokolade *f*. (*hot or drinking*) ~ Schokolade *f*, Kakao *m*; **a** ~ eine Praline; **flavoured with** ~ mit Schokoladengeschmack. (**b**) (*colour*) Schokoladenbraun *nt*. **2** *adj* Schokoladen-; (*also* ~**-coloured**) schokoladenbraun.

choice [tʃɔɪs] **1** *n* (**a**) (*act of, possibility of choosing*) Wahl *f*. **it's your** ~ du hast die Wahl; **to make a** ~ eine Wahl treffen; **to take one's** ~ sich (*dat*) etwas aussuchen; **I didn't do it from** ~ ich habe es mir nicht ausgesucht; **he had no** ~ **but to obey** er hatte keine (andere) Wahl *or* es blieb ihm nichts anderes übrig, als zu gehorchen; **for** ~ **I would ...** wenn ich die Wahl hätte, würde ich ...; **the prize is a holiday of your own** ~ zu gewinnen ist eine Urlaubsreise an einen Ort Ihrer Wahl.

  (b) *(person, thing chosen)* Wahl *f*. **it was your** ~ du wolltest es ja so.

  (c) *(variety to choose from)* Auswahl *f (of an +dat,* von).

  2 adj (a) *(Comm)* **goods, fruit, wine** Qualitäts-, erstklassig. ~ **fruit** Obst erster Wahl; ~**st** allerfeinste(r, s), auserlesen.

  (b) **language** *(elegant)* gewählt; *(euph: strong)* sauber *(euph)*.

choir ['kwaɪə^r] *n* (a) Chor *m*. (b) *(Archit)* Chor(raum) *m*.

choir in *cpds* Chor-; ~**boy** *n* Chor- or Sängerknabe *m*; ~ **loft** *n* Chorempore *f*; ~ **master** *n* Chorleiter *m*; ~ **school** *n* Konvikt *nt* für Sängerknaben; ~ **stall** *n* Chorstuhl *m*; ~ **stalls** *npl* Chorgestühl *nt*.

choke [tʃəʊk] **1** *vt* (a) *person* ersticken, *(throttle)* (er)würgen, erdrosseln. **don't eat so fast, you'll** ~ **yourself** iß nicht so schnell, sonst erstickst du daran; **to** ~ **the life out of sb/sth** *(lit, fig)* jdm/einer Sache den Garaus machen; **in a voice** ~**d with sobs** mit tränenerstickter Stimme.

  (b) *(fig)* **pipe, tube, street** verstopfen; **fire, plants** ersticken.

  2 *vi* ersticken *(on an +dat)*. **he was choking with laughter/anger** er erstickte fast or halb vor Lachen/Wut.

  3 *n (Aut)* Choke, Starterzug *m*. **give it a bit of** ~ zieh den Choke etwas heraus.

◆**choke back** *vt sep* **feelings, tears, reply** unterdrücken.

◆**choke down** *vt sep* hinunterschlucken.

◆**choke off** *vt sep* **(a)** *supplies* drosseln. **(b)** *(sl)* **person** *(interrupt)* das Wort abschneiden *(+dat)*; *(put off)* abwimmeln *(inf)*.

  (c) *(sl: make fed up)* **I'm** ~**d** ~ mir stinkt's! *(sl)*.

◆**choke up** *vt sep* **(a)** *(block)* **pipe, drain etc** verstopfen.

  (b) *(usu pass)* **voice** ersticken. **you sound a bit** ~**d** ~ du klingst etwas verschnupft.

  (c) **to get/be** ~**d** ~ *(sl)* ganz fuchtig *(inf)* werden/sein *(about über* ~ *acc,* wegen).

chokedamp ['tʃəʊkdæmp] *n* Ferch *m*, böse or giftige Wetter *pl*.

choker ['tʃəʊkə^r] *n (collar)* Vatermörder *m*; *(necklace)* enger Halsreif; *(of velvet etc)* Kropfband *nt*.

choler ['kɒlə^r] *n (old)* (bile) (gelbe) Galle; *(bad temper)* Zorn *m*.

cholera ['kɒlərə] *n* Cholera *f*.

choleric ['kɒlərɪk] *adj* cholerisch, leicht aufbrausend.

cholesterol [kə'lestərəl] *n* Cholesterin *nt*.

chomp [tʃɒmp] *vt* laut mahlen; *(person)* mampfen *(inf)*.

choo-choo ['tʃuːtʃuː] *n (Brit baby-talk: train)* Puff-Puff *f (baby-talk)*.

choose [tʃuːz] *pret* **chose**, *ptp* **chosen 1** *vt* (a) *(select)* (aus)wählen, sich *(dat)* aussuchen. **to** ~ **a team** eine Mannschaft auswählen or zusammenstellen; **they chose him as their leader** *or* **to be their leader** sie wählten ihn zu ihrem Anführer; **in a few well-chosen words** in wenigen wohlgesetzten Worten.

  (b) *(decide, elect)* **to** ~ **to do sth** es vorziehen, etw zu tun; **I cannot** ~ **but obey** ich habe keine andere Wahl, als zu gehorchen; **may I come earlier?** — **if you** ~ **to** darfst du früher kommen? — wenn Sie wollen.

  2 *vi* **(a) to** ~ *(between or among/from)* wählen or eine Wahl treffen *(zwischen +dat/aus or unter +dat)*; **there is nothing to** ~ **between them** sie sind gleich gut; **there aren't many to** ~ **from** die Auswahl ist nicht sehr groß.

  (b) *(decide, elect)* **as/if you** ~ wie/wenn Sie wollen.

choos(e)y ['tʃuːzɪ] *adj (+er)* wählerisch.

chop¹ [tʃɒp] **1** *n* (a) *(blow)* Schlag *m*.

  (b) *(Cook)* Kotelett *nt*.

  (c) *(Sport)* harter (Kurz)schlag; *(Karate)* Karateschlag *m*.

  (d) *(of waves)* Klatschen, Schlagen *nt*.

  (e) *(sl)* **to get the** ~ *(be axed)* unter die Sense kommen *(sl)*, dem Rotstift zum Opfer fallen; *(be fired)* rausgeschmissen werden *(inf)*; **to give sb the** ~ jdn rausschmeißen *(inf)*.

  2 *vt* hacken; **meat, vegetables etc** kleinschneiden. **to** ~ **one's way through the undergrowth** sich *(dat)* einen Weg durchs Dickicht schlagen.

  (b) *(Sport)* **ball** (ab)stoppen; *(Wrestling etc)* **opponent** einen Schlag versetzen *(+dat)*.

◆**chop at** *vi +prep obj* hacken or schlagen nach; *(with axe)* einhacken auf *(+acc)*.

◆**chop back** *vt sep* zurück- or wegschneiden.

◆**chop down** *vt sep* **tree** fällen.

◆**chop off** *vt sep* abhacken, abschlagen, abhauen. **to** ~ ~ **the ends of one's words** abgehackt sprechen.

◆**chop up** *vt sep* zerhacken, zerkleinern; *(fig)* **country** aufteilen; **company** aufspalten.

chop² *vi* (a) *(Naut: wind)* drehen, umspringen. (b) *(fig)* **to** ~ **and change** ständig seine Meinung ändern.

chop-chop ['tʃɒp'tʃɒp] *(inf)* adv, interj hopp, hopp *(inf)*.

chophouse ['tʃɒphaʊs] *n* Steakhaus *nt*.

chopper ['tʃɒpə^r] *n* (a) *(axe)* Hackbeil *nt*. (b) *(inf: helicopter)* Hubschrauber *m*.

choppers ['tʃɒpəz] *npl (sl: teeth)* Beißerchen *pl (inf)*.

chopping ['tʃɒpɪŋ]: ~ **block** *n* Hackklotz *m*; *(for wood, executions etc)* Block *m* or Hackbrett *nt*.

choppy ['tʃɒpɪ] *adj (+er)* **sea** kabbelig; **wind** böig, wechselhaft.

chops [tʃɒps] *npl (of dog)* Lefzen *pl*; *(inf: of person)* Visage *f (sl)*.

chop: ~**stick** *n* Stäbchen *nt*; ~**suey** *n* Chop-Suey *nt*.

choral ['kɔːrəl] *adj* Chor-. ~ **society** Gesangverein, Chor *m*.

chorale [kɒ'rɑːl] *n* Choral *m*.

chord [kɔːd] *n* (a) *(Mus)* Akkord *m*. **to strike the right/a sympathetic** ~ *(fig)* den richtigen Ton treffen/auf Verständnis stoßen, *(b)* *(Geometry)* Sehne *f*. *(c)* *(Anat)* Band *nt*.

chordal ['kɔːdl] *adj (Mus)* Akkord-.

chore [tʃɔː^r] *n* lästige Pflicht; ~**s** *pl* Hausarbeit *f*; **to do the** ~**s** den Haushalt machen, die Hausarbeit erledigen.

choreographer [ˌkɒrɪ'ɒɡrəfə^r] *n* Choreograph(in *f*) *m*.

choreographic [ˌkɒrɪəʊ'ɡræfɪk] *adj* choreographisch.

choreography [ˌkɒrɪ'ɒɡrəfɪ] *n* Choreographie *f*.

chorister ['kɒrɪstə^r] *n* (Kirchen)chormitglied *nt*; *(boy)* Chorknabe *m*.

chortle ['tʃɔːtl] **1** *vi* gluckern, glucksen. **he was chortling over the newspaper/the article** er lachte in sich hinein *or* vor sich hin, als er die Zeitung/den Artikel las. **2** *n* Gluckser *m*.

chorus ['kɔːrəs] **1** *n* (a) *(refrain)* Refrain *m*.

  (b) *(Mus or of opera)* Opernchor *m*; *(dancers)* Tanzgruppe *f*. **she's in the** ~ sie singt im Chor/sie ist bei der Tanzgruppe; **in** ~ im Chor; **the teacher was greeted with a** ~ **of good morning, sir** als der Lehrer hereinkam, rief die Klasse im Chor: guten Morgen!

  2 *vi* im Chor singen/sprechen/rufen.

chorus: ~ **girl** *n* (Revue)tänzerin *f* or -girl *nt*; ~ **line** *n* Revue *f*.

chose [tʃəʊz] *pret of* **choose**.

chosen ['tʃəʊzn] **1** *ptp of* **choose**. **2** *adj* **the** ~ **people** das auserwählte Volk; **the** ~ **few** die wenigen Auserwählten.

choux pastry ['ʃuː'peɪstrɪ] *n* Brandteig *m*.

chow [tʃaʊ] *n (sl: food)* Futterage *f (inf)*, Proviant *m*.

chow(chow) ['tʃaʊ(tʃaʊ)] *n (dog)* Chow-Chow *m*.

chowder ['tʃaʊdə^r] *n (US)* sämige Fischsuppe.

Christ [kraɪst] **1** *n* Christus *m*. **2** *interj (sl)* Herrgott *(inf)*.

christen ['krɪsn] *vt* (a) taufen. **to** ~ **sb after sb** jdn nach jdm (be)nennen. (b) *(inf: use for first time)* einweihen.

Christendom ['krɪsndəm] *n (old)* Christenheit *f*.

christening ['krɪsnɪŋ] *n* Taufe *f*.

Christian ['krɪstɪən] **1** *n* Christ *m*. **2** *adj (lit, fig)* christlich.

Christianity [ˌkrɪstɪ'ænɪtɪ] *n* (a) *(faith, religion)* Christentum *nt*, christlicher Glaube; *(body of Christians)* Christenheit *f*.

  (b) *(being a Christian)* Christlichkeit, Frömmigkeit *f*. **his** ~ **did not prevent him from doing it** sein christlicher Glaube hinderte ihn nicht daran(, das zu tun).

  (c) *(Christian character)* christliche Haltung or Gesinnung.

Christianize ['krɪstɪənaɪz] *vt* christianisieren, zum Christentum bekehren.

Christian: ~ **name** *n* Vor- or Rufname *m*; ~ **Science** *n* Christian Science *f*; ~ **Scientist** *n* Anhänger(in *f*) *m* der Christian Science.

Christlike ['kraɪstlaɪk] *adj* Christus-gleich.

Christmas ['krɪsməs] *n* Weihnachten *nt*. **are you going home for** ~? fährst du (über) Weihnachten nach Hause?; **what did you get for** ~? was hast du zu Weihnachten bekommen?; **merry** *or* **happy** ~! frohe or fröhliche Weihnachten!

Christmas: ~ **box** *n (Brit)* Trinkgeld *nt* zu Weihnachten, ≈ Neujahrsgeld *nt*; ~ **cake** *n* Früchtekuchen *mit Zuckerguß zu* Weihnachten; ~ **card** *n* Weihnachtskarte *f*; ~ **carol** *n* Weihnachtslied *nt*; ~ **Day** *n* der erste Weihnachtstag *m*; **on** ~ **Day** an Weihnachten, am ersten (Weihnachts)feiertag; ~ **Eve** *n* Heiligabend *m*; **on** ~ **Eve** Heiligabend; ~ **Island** *n* Weihnachtsinsel *f*; ~ **present** *n* Weihnachtsgeschenk *nt*; ~ **pudding** *n* Plumpudding *m*; ~ **rose** *n* Christrose *f*; ~ **stocking** *n* Strumpf, *in den Weihnachtsgeschenke gelegt werden*; ~ **time** *n* Weihnachtszeit *f*; **at** ~ **time** zur or in der Weihnachtszeit; ~ **tree** *n* Weihnachtsbaum, Christbaum *(esp S Ger)* *m*.

chromatic [krə'mætɪk] *adj (Art, Mus)* chromatisch.

chrome [krəʊm] *n* Chrom *m*; ~ **steel** Chromstahl *m*; ~ **yellow** Chromgelb *nt*.

chromium ['krəʊmɪəm] *n* Chrom *nt*.

chromium: ~ **plate** *n* Chromschicht *f*; ~ **plated** *adj* verchromt; ~ **plating** *n* Verchromung *f*.

chromosome ['krəʊməsəʊm] *n* Chromosom *nt*.

chronic ['krɒnɪk] *adj* (a) *(Med, fig)* **disease, invalid, liar etc** chronisch. (b) *(inf: terrible)* schlecht, miserabel *(inf)*.

chronicle ['krɒnɪkl] **1** *n* Chronik *f*. **C**~**s** *(Bibl)* Bücher *pl* der Chronik. **2** *vt* aufzeichnen; **historic events** also eine Chronik *(+gen)* verfassen.

chronicler ['krɒnɪklə^r] *n* Chronist *m*.

chronological *adj*, ~**ly** *adv* [ˌkrɒnə'lɒdʒɪkəl, -ɪ] chronologisch. ~**ly arranged** in chronologischer Reihenfolge.

chronology [krə'nɒlədʒɪ] *n* zeitliche Abfolge, Chronologie *(form) f*; *(list of dates)* Zeittafel *f*.

chronometer [krə'nɒmɪtə^r] *n* Chronometer *m*.

chrysalis ['krɪsəlɪs] *n, pl* -**es** *(Biol)* Puppe *f*; *(covering)* Kokon *m*.

chrysanthemum [krɪ'sænθəməm], **chrysanth** [krɪ'sænθ] *(inf)* *n* Chrysantheme *f*.

chub [tʃʌb] *n, pl* - Döbel, Aitel *m*.

chubby ['tʃʌbɪ] *adj (+er)* pummelig, rundlich. ~ **cheeks** Pausbacken *pl*; ~**cheeked** pausbackig.

chuck¹ [tʃʌk] **1** *vt (inf)* (a) *(throw)* schmeißen *(inf)*.

  (b) *(sl)* **girlfriend, boyfriend** Schluß machen mit *(inf)*. ~ **it!** *(stop it)* Schluß jetzt!

  (c) **to** ~ **sb under the chin** jdm einen Kinnstüber versetzen.

  2 *n* (a) *(sl: dismissal)* Rausschmiß *m (inf)*. **to give sb the** ~ jdn rausschmeißen *(inf)*, jdn an die Luft setzen *(inf)*; **he got the** ~ er ist rausgeflogen *(inf)*, den haben sie an die Luft gesetzt *(inf)*.

  (b) **to give sb a** ~ **under the chin** see vt (c).

◆**chuck about** *vt sep (inf)* rumschmeißen (mit) *(inf)*.

◆**chuck away** *vt sep (inf)* **money** *(throw out)* wegschmeißen *(inf)*; *(waste)* **money** aus dem Fenster schmeißen *(inf)*.

◆**chuck in** *vt sep (inf)* **job** hinschmeißen *(inf)*, an den Nagel hängen *(inf)*. **to** ~ **it (all)** ~ den Laden hinschmeißen *(inf)*.

◆**chuck out** *vt sep (inf)* **unwanted people** rausschmeißen *(inf)*; **useless articles** also wegschmeißen *(inf)*. **to be** ~**ed** ~ rausfliegen *(of aus) (inf)*.

◆**chuck up** *vt sep (inf)* **job** hinschmeißen *(inf)*.

chuck² *n (Tech)* Spannfutter *nt*.

chuck³ *n (US sl: food)* Essen *nt*. ~ **wagon** Proviantwagen *m* mit fahrbarer Küche.

chucker-out ['tʃʌkər'aʊt] *n (inf)* Rausschmeißer *m (inf)*.

chuckle ['tʃʌkl] **1** *n* leises Lachen, Kichern *nt no pl*. **to have a good** ~ **about sth** sich *(dat)* eins lachen über etw *(acc) (inf)*. **2**

vi leise in sich (*acc*) hineinlachen, sich (*dat*) eins lachen (*inf*). to ~ away vor sich hin lachen *or* kichern.

chuffed [tʃʌft] *adj* (*Brit sl*) vergnügt und zufrieden; (*flattered*) gebauchpinselt (*inf*) (*about* wegen). **I was dead ~ about it** ich freute mich darüber wie ein Schneekönig (*inf*); **to be/look ~ with oneself** auf sich (*acc*) selbst stolz sein/sehr zufrieden aussehen.

chug [tʃʌg] **1** *n* Tuckern *nt*. **2** *vi* tuckern.
♦**chug along** *vi* entlangtuckern; (*fig inf*) gut vorankommen.

chukka, chukker [ˈtʃʌkəʳ] *n* (*Polo*) Chukka, Chukker *nt*.

chum [tʃʌm] *n* (*inf*) Kamerad, Kumpel (*inf*), Spezi (*S Ger*) *m*.
♦**chum up** *vi* sich anfreunden.

chummy [ˈtʃʌmɪ] *adj* (+*er*) (*inf*) kameradschaftlich. **to be ~ with sb** mit jdm sehr dicke sein (*inf*); **to get ~ with sb** sich mit jdm anfreunden.

chump [tʃʌmp] *n* **(a)** (*inf*) Trottel *m*, dummes Stück, Hornochse *m* (*inf*). **(b) he's off his ~** (*Brit inf*) der hat 'ne Meise (*inf*).

chump chop *n* Kotelett *nt*.

chunk [tʃʌŋk] *n* großes Stück, (*of meat*) Batzen *m*; (*of stone*) Brocken *m*.

chunky [ˈtʃʌŋkɪ] *adj* (+*er*) (*inf*) *legs, arms* stämmig; *person also* untersetzt, gedrungen; *knitwear* dick, klobig.

church [tʃɜːtʃ] *n* Kirche *f*; (*service*) die Kirche. **to go to ~** in die Kirche gehen; **the C~ Fathers** die Kirchenväter; **the C~ of England** die Anglikanische Kirche; **he has gone into** *or* **entered the C~** er ist Geistlicher geworden.

church *in cpds* Kirchen-; **~-goer** *n* Kirchgänger(in *f*) *m*; **~-going** *adj* **a ~-going family** eine Familie, die regelmäßig in die Kirche geht; **~man** *n* (*clergyman*) Geistliche(r), Seelsorger *m*; (**~goer**) Kirchgänger *m*; **~ mouse** *n*: **as poor as a ~ mouse** arm wie eine Kirchenmaus; **~ service** *n* Gottesdienst *m*; **~warden** *n* Gemeindevorsteher *m*.

churchy [ˈtʃɜːtʃɪ] *adj* (+*er*) (*inf*) *person* kirchlich.

churchyard [ˈtʃɜːtʃjɑːd] *n* Friedhof, Kirchhof (*old, dial*) *m*.

churlish *adj*, **~ly** *adv* [ˈtʃɜːlɪʃ, -lɪ] ungehobelt.

churlishness [ˈtʃɜːlɪʃnɪs] *n* ungehobeltes Benehmen.

churn [tʃɜːn] **1** *n* (*for butter*) Butterfaß *nt*; (*Brit: milk-~*) Milchkanne *f*. **2** *vt* **(a) to ~ butter** buttern, Sahne buttern. **(b)** (*agitate*) *sea, mud etc* aufwühlen. **3** *vi* (*water, mud*) wirbeln, strudeln; (*wheels, rage etc*) wühlen; (*propeller*) wirbeln, sich wild drehen. **the ~ing sea** die stampfende See.
♦**churn away** *vi* wild drehen; (*engine*) stampfen.
♦**churn out** *vt sep* am laufenden Band produzieren.
♦**churn up** *vt sep* aufwühlen.

chute [ʃuːt] *n* **(a)** Rutsche *f*; (*garbage ~*) Müllschlucker *m*. **(b)** (*rapid in river*) Stromschnelle *f*. **(c)** (*inf: parachute*) Fallschirm *m*. **(d)** (*in playground*) Rutschbahn, Rutsche *f*.

chutney [ˈtʃʌtnɪ] *n* Chutney *m*.

chutzpah [ˈtʃʌtspɑː] *n* Chuzpe *f*.

CIA *abbr of* **Central Intelligence Agency** CIA.

ciborium [sɪˈbɔːrɪəm] *n* Ziborium *nt*.

cicada [sɪˈkɑːdə] *n* Zikade *f*.

cicatrix [ˈsɪkətrɪks] *n*, *pl* **cicatrices** [sɪkəˈtraɪsiːz] wildes Fleisch, Granulationsgewebe *nt* (*spec*); (*scar*) Narbe *f*.

cicerone [tʃɪtʃəˈrəʊnɪ] *n* Cicerone *m*.

CID (*Brit*) *abbr of* **Criminal Investigation Department**.

cider [ˈsaɪdəʳ] *n* Apfelwein *m*. **hard ~** (*US*) (*voll vergorener*) Apfelwein; **sweet ~** süßer (*teilweise vergorener*) Apfelwein, Rauscher *m* (*dial*); **rough ~** Apfelwein *m* (*mit größerem Alkoholgehalt*).

cider: ~ apple *n* Mostapfel *m*; **~ press** *n* Apfelpresse *f*.

cigar [sɪˈgɑːʳ] *n* Zigarre *f*.

cigar: ~ box *n* Zigarrenkiste *f*; **~ cutter** *n* Zigarrenabschneider *m*.

cigarette [sɪgəˈret] *n* Zigarette *f*.

cigarette: ~ box *n* Zigarettenschachtel *f*; **~ case** *n* Zigarettenetui *nt*; **~ end** *n* Zigarettenstummel *m*; **~ holder** *n* Zigarettenspitze *f*; **~ lighter** *n* Feuerzeug *nt*; **~ paper** *n* Zigarettenpapier *nt*.

cigarillo [sɪgəˈrɪləʊ] *n* Zigarillo *m or nt*.

cigar-shaped [sɪˈgɑːʃeɪpt] *adj* zigarrenförmig.

ciggy [ˈsɪgɪ] *n* (*inf*) Glimmstengel *m* (*inf*), Kippe *f* (*inf*).

C-in-C *abbr of* **Commander in Chief**.

cinch [sɪntʃ] **1** *n* **(a)** (*US: saddle girth*) Sattelgurt *m*. **(b)** (*sl*) **it's a ~** (*easy*) das ist ein Kinderspiel *or* ein Klacks (*inf*); (*esp US: certain*) es ist todsicher (*inf*). **2** *vt* (*US*) **(a) to ~ a horse** den Sattelgurt anziehen. **(b)** (*sl*) *deal* regeln (*sl*).

cinder [ˈsɪndəʳ] *n* **~s** *pl* Asche *f*; (*lumpy*) Schlacke *f*; (*still burning*) glühendes Kohlestück. **burnt to a ~** (*fig*) verkohlt.

Cinderella [sɪndəˈrelə] *n* Aschenputtel *nt*.

cinder track *n* Aschenbahn *f*.

cineaste [ˈsɪnɪæst] *n* Cineast(in *f*), Kinoliebhaber(in *f*) *m*.

cine-camera [sɪnɪˈkæmərə] *n* (*Brit*) (*Schmal*)filmkamera *f*.

cine-film [ˈsɪnɪfɪlm] *n* (*Brit*) Schmalfilm *m*.

cinema [ˈsɪnəmə] *n* (*esp Brit*) Kino *nt*; (*films collectively also*) Film *m*. **at/to the ~** im/ins Kino.

cinemagoer [ˈsɪnəməgəʊəʳ] *n* (*esp Brit*) Kinogänger(in *f*) *m*.

Cinemascope ® [ˈsɪnəməskəʊp] *n* Cinemascope *nt*.

cinematic [sɪnəˈmætɪk] *adj* filmisch. **~ art** Filmkunst *f*.

cinematograph [sɪnəˈmætəgrɑːf] *n* (*dated*) Kinematograph *m* (*dated*).

cine-projector [sɪnɪprəˈdʒektəʳ] *n* (*Brit*) Filmprojektor *m*.

cinerama ® [sɪnəˈrɑːmə] *n* Cinerama *nt*.

cinerary [ˈsɪnərərɪ] *adj* Aschen-.

cinnabar [ˈsɪnəbɑːʳ] *n* Zinnober *m*.

cinnamon [ˈsɪnəmən] **1** *n* Zimt *m*. **2** *adj attr* **(a)** *cake, biscuit* Zimt-. **(b)** (*colour*) zimtfarben.

CIO (*US*) *abbr of* **Congress of Industrial Organizations**.

cipher [ˈsaɪfəʳ] **1** *n* **(a)** (*Arabic numeral*) Ziffer, Zahl *f*. **(b)** (*zero*) Null *f*. **(c)** (*nonentity*) Niemand *m no pl*.

(d) (*code*) Chiffre *f*, Code *m*. **~ clerk** (De)chiffreur *m*; **~ officer** (*army*) Fernmeldeoffizier *m*; (*secret service etc*) (De)chiffreur *m*; **in ~** chiffriert. **(e)** (*monogram*) Monogramm, Namenszeichen *nt*. **2** *vt* (*encode*) verschlüsseln, chiffrieren.

circ *abbr of* **circa** ca.

circa [ˈsɜːkə] *prep* zirka, circa.

circle [ˈsɜːkl] **1** *n* **(a)** Kreis *m*. **to stand in a ~** im Kreis stehen; **to go round in ever decreasing ~s** (*lit*) Spiralen drehen; (*fig*) sich unablässig im Kreis drehen; **to turn full ~** (*lit*) sich ganz herumdrehen, eine Volldrehung machen; **we're just going round in ~s** (*fig*) wir bewegen uns nur im Kreise; **to come full ~** (*fig*) zum Ausgangspunkt zurückkehren; **things have come full ~** der Kreis hat sich geschlossen; **when the seasons have come full ~** wenn sich der Kreis der Jahreszeiten schließt. **(b)** (*of hills etc*) Ring *m*, Kette *f*; (*round the eyes*) Ring *m* (*round* unter +*dat*); (*in gymnastics*) Welle *f*. **a Celtic stone ~** ein keltischer Steinkreis; **the ~ of the seasons** der Zyklus *or* Kreislauf der Jahreszeiten. **(c)** (*Brit: Theat*) Rang *m*; see **dress**, **upper**. **(d)** (*group of persons*) Kreis, Zirkel (*geh*) *m*. **a close ~ of friends** ein enger Freundeskreis; **in political ~s** in politischen Kreisen; **the family ~** der engste Familienkreis; **the whole family ~** die ganze Familie; **he's moving in different ~s now** er verkehrt jetzt in anderen Kreisen. **2** *vt* **(a)** (*surround*) umgeben. **(b)** (*move around*) kreisen um. **the enemy ~d the town** der Feind kreiste die Stadt ein. **(c)** (*draw a ~ round*) einen Kreis *or* Kringel machen um. **he ~d** (*off*) **several of the addresses** er machte einen Kreis um mehrere der Anschriften; **~d in red** rot umkringelt. **3** *vi* (*fly in a ~*) kreisen.
♦**circle around** *vi* (*people*) umhergehen *or* -wandern; (*birds*) Kreise ziehen; (*vehicles*) kreisen, Runden drehen; (*ships*) kreisen. **the wolves/Indians ~d**, **~ing** die Wölfe/Indianer kreisten lauernd um uns/sie/das Lager *etc*.

circlet [ˈsɜːklɪt] *n* Reif *m*.

circuit [ˈsɜːkɪt] **1** *n* **(a)** (*journey around etc*) Rundgang *m*/-fahrt *f*/-reise *f* (*of* um). **to make a ~ of sth** um etw herumgehen/-fahren, einen Rundgang/eine Rundfahrt um etw machen; **when the earth has completed its ~ of the sun** wenn die Erde ihre Bahn um die Sonne vollendet hat; **three ~s of the race-track** drei Runden auf der Rennbahn; **they made a wide ~ to avoid the enemy** sie machten einen großen Bogen um den Feind; **the diagram shows the ~ the oil takes** das Diagramm zeigt die Zirkulation des Öls. **(b)** (*of judges etc*) Gerichtsbezirk *m*. **to go on ~** den (Gerichts)bezirk bereisen; **he is on the eastern ~** er bereist *or* hat den östlichen (Gerichts)bezirk. **(c)** (*Theat*) Theaterring *m or* -kette *f*. **to travel the ~** die Theater (der Reihe nach) bereisen. **(d)** (*Elec*) Stromkreis *m*; (*apparatus*) Schaltung *f*. **(e)** (*Sport: track*) Rennbahn *f*. **(f)** **the professional golf/tennis ~** die Golf-/Tennisturnierrunde (der Berufsspieler). **2** *vt track, course* eine Runde drehen um.

circuit: ~ breaker *n* Stromkreisunterbrecher *m*; **~ court** *n* Bezirksgericht, *das an verschiedenen Orten eines Gerichtsbezirks Sitzungen abhält*; **~ diagram** *n* Schaltplan *m*; **~ judge** *n* Richter *m* an einem Bezirksgericht.

circuitous [sɜːˈkjuːɪtəs] *adj* umständlich. **~ path** Schlängelpfad *m*.

circuitously [sɜːˈkjuːɪtəslɪ] *adv* umständlich. **the road winds ~** die Straße schlängelt sich.

circuitousness [sɜːˈkjuːɪtəsnɪs] *n* Umständlichkeit *f*; (*of route*) Gewundenheit *f*.

circuitry [ˈsɜːkɪtrɪ] *n* Schaltkreise *pl*.

circuit training *n* Circuittraining *nt*.

circuity [sɜːˈkjuːɪtɪ] *n see* **circuitousness**.

circular [ˈsɜːkjʊləʳ] **1** *adj object* kreisförmig, rund. **~ saw** Kreissäge *f*; **~ motion** Kreisbewegung *f*; **~ tour** Rundfahrt *f*/-reise *f*; **a ~ tour of the island** eine Inselrundfahrt *f*; **~ argument** Zirkelschluß *m*; **~ letter** Rundschreiben *nt*, Rundbrief *m*. **2** *n* (*in firm*) Rundschreiben *nt*, Rundbrief *m*; (*single copy*) Umlauf *m*; (*printed advertisement*) Wurfsendung *f*.

circularize [ˈsɜːkjʊləraɪz] *vt person* durch Rundschreiben informieren; *letter, memo* zirkulieren lassen.

circulate [ˈsɜːkjʊleɪt] **1** *vi* (*water, blood, money*) fließen, zirkulieren; (*traffic*) fließen; (*news, rumour*) kursieren, in Umlauf sein; (*news*) sich verbreiten. **(b)** (*person: at party*) die Runde machen. **to keep the guests circulating** dafür sorgen, daß die Gäste keine Grüppchen bilden. **2** *vt news, rumour* verbreiten, in Umlauf bringen; *memo etc* zirkulieren lassen; *water* pumpen.

circulating [ˈsɜːkjʊleɪtɪŋ]: **~ capital** *n* flüssiges Kapital, Umlaufkapital *nt*; **~ library** *n* Fahrbücherei *f*; **~ medium** *n* (*Fin*) Zahlungs- *or* Umlaufsmittel *nt*.

circulation [sɜːkjʊˈleɪʃən] *n* **(a)** (*Med*) (*act of circulating*) Kreislauf *m*, Zirkulation *f*; (*of traffic*) Ablauf, Fluß *m*; (*of money also*) Umlauf *m*; (*of news, rumour*) Kursieren *nt*, Verbreitung *f*. **to have poor ~** Kreislaufstörungen haben; **to put notes into ~** Banknoten in Umlauf bringen; **when did these notes come into ~?** wann wurden diese Banknoten in Umlauf gebracht *or* gesetzt?; **this coin was withdrawn from ~ taken out of ~** diese Münze wurde aus dem Verkehr gezogen; **new words which come into ~** Wörter, die neu in Umlauf kommen; **he's back in ~** now (*inf*) er mischt wieder mit (*inf*); **the ideas then in ~** die Ideen, die damals im Schwang(e) waren. **(b)** (*of newspaper etc*) Auflage(nziffer) *f*. **for private ~** zum privaten Gebrauch.

circulatory [ˌsɜːkjʊˈleɪtərɪ] adj Kreislauf-. ~ **system** Blutkreislauf m.

circum- [ˈsɜːkəm-] pref um-, um ... herum.

circumcise [ˈsɜːkəmsaɪz] vt beschneiden.

circumcision [ˌsɜːkəmˈsɪʒən] n Beschneidung f. **the C~** (Eccl) der Tag der Beschneidung des Herrn.

circumference [səˈkʌmfərəns] n Umfang m. **the tree is 10 ft in** ~ der Baum hat einen Umfang von 10 Fuß.

circumflex [ˈsɜːkəmfleks] n Zirkumflex m.

circumlocution [ˌsɜːkəmləˈkjuːʃən] n Weitschweifigkeit f; (evasiveness) Umschreibung f, Drumherumreden nt (inf).

circumlocutory [ˌsɜːkəmləˈkjuːtərɪ] adj weitschweifig; expression umschreibend.

circumnavigate [ˌsɜːkəmˈnævɪgeɪt] vt the globe umfahren; (in yacht also) umsegeln; cape, island also umschiffen.

circumnavigation [ˈsɜːkəmˌnævɪˈgeɪʃən] n Fahrt f (of um); (in yacht also) Umseglung f. ~ **of the globe** Fahrt um die Welt; Weltumseglung f.

circumnavigator [ˌsɜːkəmˈnævɪgeɪtər] n ~ **of the globe** Weltumsegler(in f) m.

circumscribe [ˈsɜːkəmskraɪb] vt (a) (Math) einen Kreis umbeschreiben (+dat). (b) (restrict) eingrenzen.

circumscription [ˌsɜːkəmˈskrɪpʃən] n (a) (restriction) Eingrenzung f. (b) (on coin) Umschrift f.

circumspect adj, ~**ly** adv [ˈsɜːkəmspekt, -lɪ] umsichtig.

circumspection [ˌsɜːkəmˈspekʃən] n Umsicht f.

circumstance [ˈsɜːkəmstəns] n (a) Umstand m. **in** or **under the** ~s unter diesen Umständen; **in** or **under no** ~s unter gar keinen Umständen, auf keinen Fall; **in certain** ~s unter Umständen, eventuell; **what were the** ~s **surrounding the case?** wie waren die näheren Umstände des Falls?

   (b) ~s pl (financial condition) finanzielle Verhältnisse, Umstände (form) pl. **in easy** ~s in gesicherten Verhältnissen, gut situiert; **in poor** ~s in ärmlichen Verhältnissen.

   (c) see pomp.

circumstantial [ˌsɜːkəmˈstænʃəl] adj (a) (detailed) report, statement ausführlich, detailliert. (b) (Jur) ~ **evidence** Indizienbeweis m. (c) (secondary) nebensächlich, von untergeordneter Bedeutung.

circumstantiate [ˌsɜːkəmˈstænʃɪeɪt] vt (form) belegen, beweisen.

circumvent [ˌsɜːkəmˈvent] vt umgehen.

circumvention [ˌsɜːkəmˈvenʃən] n Umgehung f.

circus [ˈsɜːkəs] n Zirkus m; (in place names) Platz m.

cirrhosis [sɪˈrəʊsɪs] n Zirrhose f.

cirrus [ˈsɪrəs] n, pl **cirri** [ˈsɪraɪ] Zirruswolke f.

cisalpine [sɪˈzælpaɪn] adj zisalpin.

cissy [ˈsɪsɪ] n see **sissy**.

Cistercian [sɪsˈtɜːʃən] **1** n Zisterzienser m. **2** adj Zisterzienser-.

cistern [ˈsɪstən] n Zisterne f; (of WC) Spülkasten m.

citadel [ˈsɪtədl] n Zitadelle f.

citation [saɪˈteɪʃən] n (a) (quote) Zitat nt; (act of quoting) Zitieren nt. (b) (Mil) Belobigung f, lobende Erwähnung. (c) (Jur) Vorladung f (vor Gericht).

cite [saɪt] vt (a) (quote) anführen, zitieren. (b) (Mil) belobigen, lobend erwähnen (for wegen). (c) (Jur) vorladen. **he was ~d to appear** er wurde vorgeladen; **or erhielt eine Vorladung; he was ~d as the co-respondent** (mentioned) er wurde als der Dritte in der Scheidungssache genannt.

citizen [ˈsɪtɪzn] n (a) Bürger(in f) m. (b) (of a state) (Staats)bürger(in f) m. **French** ~ französischer Staatsbürger, Franzose m, Französin f; ~ **of the world** Weltbürger m.

citizenry [ˈsɪtɪznrɪ] n (liter) Bürgerschaft f.

citizen's arrest n Festnahme f durch eine Zivilperson.

citizenship [ˈsɪtɪznʃɪp] n Staatsbürgerschaft f.

citrate [ˈsɪtreɪt] n Zitrat nt.

citric [ˈsɪtrɪk] adj Zitrus-. ~ **acid** Zitronensäure f.

citron [ˈsɪtrən] n (fruit) Zitrone f; (tree) Zitronenbaum m.

citrus [ˈsɪtrəs] n Zitrusgewächs nt. ~ **fruits** Zitrusfrüchte pl.

city [ˈsɪtɪ] n (a) Stadt, Großstadt f. **towns and cities** Städte und Großstädte; **the** ~ **of Glasgow** die Stadt Glasgow. (b) (in London) **the C~** die City, das Banken- und Börsenviertel.

city: ~ **boy** n Großstadtkind nt, Großstadtjunge m; ~ **bred** adj in der (Groß)stadt aufgewachsen; ~ **centre** n Stadtmitte f, Stadtzentrum nt, Innenstadt f, City f; ~ **desk** n (Brit) Finanzund Wirtschaftsabteilung f (einer Redaktion); (US) Abteilung f für Lokalnachrichten; ~ **editor** n (Brit) Wirtschaftsredakteur m; (US) Lokalredakteur m; ~ **father** n Stadtverordnete(r) m; **the** ~ **fathers** die Stadtväter pl; ~ **hall** n Rathaus nt; ~ **life** n (Groß)stadtleben nt; ~ **manager** n (US) Oberstadtdirektor m; ~ **page** n (Brit) Wirtschaftsseite f; ~**scape** n (Groß)stadtlandschaft f; ~ **slicker** n (pej inf) feiner Pinkel aus der (Groß)stadt (pej inf); (dishonest) schlitzohriger Großstädter (pej inf); ~ **state** n Stadtstaat m; ~ **type** n (Groß)stadtmensch m.

civet [ˈsɪvɪt] n (substance) Zibet m; (cat) Zibetkatze f.

civic [ˈsɪvɪk] adj rights, virtues bürgerlich, Bürger-; guard, authorities Stadt-, städtisch. ~ **centre** (Brit) Verwaltungszentrum nt einer Stadt.

civics [ˈsɪvɪks] n sing Staatsbürgerkunde f.

civvies [ˈsɪvɪz] npl (sl) see **civvies**.

civil [ˈsɪvl] adj (a) (of society) bürgerlich; duties staatsbürgerlich, Bürger-. (b) (polite) höflich; (in behaviour also) aufmerksam, zuvorkommend. **cigar?** — **very** ~ **of you** Zigarre? — sehr zuvorkommend (von Ihnen). (c) (Jur) zivilrechtlich.

civil: ~ **defence** n Ziviler Bevölkerungsschutz; ~ **defence worker** Beauftragte(r) m f des Zivilen Bevölkerungsschutzes; ~ **disobedience** n ziviler Ungehorsam; ~ **disobedience campaign** Kampagne f für zivilen Ungehorsam; ~ **engineer** n Hoch- und Tiefbauingenieur m; ~ **engineering** n Hoch- und Tiefbau m.

civilian [sɪˈvɪlɪən] **1** n Zivilist m. **2** adj zivil, Zivil-. **in** ~ **clothes** in Zivil; ~ **casualties** Verluste unter der Zivilbevölkerung.

civility [sɪˈvɪlɪtɪ] n Höflichkeit f.

civilization [ˌsɪvɪlaɪˈzeɪʃən] n (a) (civilized world) Zivilisation f. **all** ~ die ganze zivilisierte Welt; ~**!**, **the explorer exclaimed** Menschen!, rief der Forscher aus. (b) (state: of Greeks etc) Kultur f. (c) (act) Zivilisierung f.

civilize [ˈsɪvɪlaɪz] vt zivilisieren; person also Kultur beibringen (+dat).

civilized [ˈsɪvɪlaɪzd] adj (a) zivilisiert. **all** ~ **nations** alle Kulturnationen. (b) working hours, conditions, hour zivil; (cultured) lifestyle, age etc kultiviert. **a more** ~ **place to live** in ein etwas zivilerer Ort zum Leben; **brandy after dinner, very** ~ Weinbrand nach dem Essen, sehr gepflegt.

civil: ~ **law** n Zivilrecht nt, Bürgerliches Recht; ~ **liberty** n Grundrecht nt der freien Entfaltung der Persönlichkeit; ~ **list** n Zivilliste f.

civilly [ˈsɪvɪlɪ] adv (politely) höflich, zuvorkommend.

civil: ~ **marriage** n standesamtliche Trauung, Ziviltrauung f; ~ **rights** 1 npl (staats)bürgerliche Rechte pl; 2 attr march, campaign, demonstration Bürgerrechts-; ~ **servant** n = Staatsbeamte(r) mf; ~ **service** n = Staatsdienst m (ohne Richter und Lehrer); (~ servants collectively) Beamtenschaft f; ~ **war** n Bürgerkrieg m.

civvies [ˈsɪvɪz] npl (sl) Zivil nt. **he put his** ~ **on** er schmiß sich in Zivil (inf).

civvy street [ˈsɪvɪˈstriːt] n (Brit sl) Zivilleben nt. **on** ~ im Zivilleben.

clack [klæk] **1** n Klappern, Geklapper nt. **2** vi klappern.

clad [klæd] **1** (old) pret, ptp of **clothe**. **2** adj (liter) gekleidet. **3** adj suf fur-/silk-~ in Pelze/Seide gekleidet; iron-/steel-~ mit Eisen/Stahl verkleidet; ivy-~ efeubewachsen.

claim [kleɪm] **1** vt (a) (demand as one's own or due) Anspruch erheben auf (+acc); social security, benefits, sum of money (apply for) beantragen; (draw) beanspruchen; lost property abholen. **he** ~**ed diplomatic immunity** er berief sich auf seine diplomatische Immunität; **he** ~**ed the right to decide** er beanspruchte das Recht zu entscheiden; **to** ~ **sth as one's own** etw für sich beanspruchen, Anspruch auf etw (acc) erheben; **both armies** ~**ed the victory** beide Armeen nahmen den Sieg für sich in Anspruch; **territories** ~**ed by the Arabs** von den Arabern beanspruchte Gebiete; **does anyone** ~ **this wallet?** gehört diese Brieftasche jemandem?

   (b) (profess, assert) behaupten. **he** ~**s to have seen you** er behauptet, Sie gesehen zu haben, **er will Sie gesehen haben; the club can** ~ **a membership of** ... der Verein kann ... Mitglieder vorweisen; **the advantages** ~**ed for this technique** die Vorzüge, die man dieser Methode zuschreibt.

   (c) one's attention, interest in Anspruch nehmen.

   2 vi (Insur) Anspruch geltend machen; (for damage done by people) Schadenersatz verlangen.

   (b) (for expenses etc) to ~ **for sth** sich (dat) etw zurückgeben or -zahlen lassen; **you can** ~ **for your travelling expenses** Sie können sich (dat) Ihre Reisekosten zurückerstatten lassen.

   3 n (a) (demand) Anspruch m; (pay~, Ind) Forderung f. **his** ~ **to the throne/title/property** etc sein Anspruch auf den Thron/Titel/das Grundstück etc; **I have many** ~**s on my time** meine Zeit ist or ich bin sehr in Anspruch genommen; **you have no** ~ **on me** du hast keine Ansprüche an mich (zu stellen); **children have first** ~ **on their parents** die Kinder müssen an erster Stelle stehen, die Kinder müssen vorgehen; **to make** ~**s on sb's friendship** an jds Freundschaft (acc) appellieren; **to lay** ~ **to sth** Anspruch auf etw (acc) erheben; **to put in a** ~ **(for sth)** etw beantragen; (Insur) Ansprüche geltend machen; **they put in a** ~ **for extra pay** sie forderten einen Zuschlag; **we want the** ~ **back-dated** wir wollen das Geld rückwirkend; **he put in an expenses** ~ **for £100** er reichte Spesen in Höhe von £ 100 ein; **the** ~**s were all paid** (Insur) der Schaden wurde voll ersetzt.

   (b) (assertion) Behauptung f. **to make a** ~ eine Behauptung aufstellen; **have you heard his** ~**?** haben Sie gehört, was er behauptet?; **the exaggerated** ~**s made for the new washing powder** die übertriebenen Eigenschaften, die man diesem neuen Waschpulver zuschreibt; **the book makes no** ~ **to be original** das Buch erhebt keinen Anspruch auf Originalität; **I make no** ~ **to be a genius** ich behaupte nicht or erhebe nicht den Anspruch, ein Genie zu sein.

   (c) (Min) Claim m (Anteil an einem Goldfeld etc); see **stake**.

♦**claim back** vt sep zurückfordern. **to** ~ **sth** ~ (as expenses) sich (dat) etw zurückzahlen or -geben or -erstatten lassen.

claimant [ˈkleɪmənt] n (for social security etc) Antragsteller(in f) m; (for inheritance etc) Anspruchsteller(in f) m (to auf +acc); (Jur) Kläger(in f) m. **a** ~ **to a title/throne** ein Titel-/Thronanwärter m, eine Titel-/Thronanwärterin.

claim form n Antragsformular nt.

clairvoyance [kleəˈvɔɪəns] n Hellsehen nt, Hellseherei f. **thanks to the** ~ **of the management** dank der Hellsichtigkeit der Firmenleitung.

clairvoyant [kleəˈvɔɪənt] **1** n Hellseher(in f) m. **2** adj hellseherisch. **I'm not** ~ ich bin (doch) kein Hellseher!

clam [klæm] n Venusmuschel f. **he shut up like a** ~ aus ihm war kein Wort mehr herauszubekommen.

♦**clam up** vi (inf) keinen Piep (mehr) sagen (inf). **he** ~**med** ~ **on** me ich habe kein Wort mehr aus ihm herausgekriegt (inf).

clambake [ˈklæmbeɪk] n (US) Muschelessen nt am Strand; (inf: party) Fête f (inf).

clamber [ˈklæmbər] **1** vi klettern, kraxeln (esp S Ger). **to** ~ **up a hill** auf einen Berg klettern, einen Berg hinaufklettern; **the baby** ~**ed all over the sofa** das Baby krabbelte auf dem Sofa herum; **to** ~ **over a wall** über eine Mauer klettern. **2** n Kletterei, Kraxelei (esp S Ger) f.

clamminess [ˈklæmɪnɪs] n Feuchtigkeit f, Klammheit f.

clammy ['klæmɪ] adj (+er) feucht, klamm. **a ~ handshake** ein feuchter Händedruck.

clamor n (US) see **clamour**.

clamorous ['klæmərəs] adj (liter) (a) mob lärmend. (b) demands lautstark.

clamour, (US) clamor ['klæmər] **1** n (a) (noise) Lärm m, Lärmen nt. **the ~ of the battle** der Kampf- or Schlachtenlärm, das Getöse der Schlacht.
(b) (demand) lautstark erhobene Forderung (for nach). **a ~ against sth** ein Aufschrei m gegen etw; **continuous ~ against the EEC** ständiges Geschrei gegen die EWG.
2 vi **to ~ for/against sth** nach etw schreien/sich gegen etw empören; **the paper ~ed against the government** die Zeitung wetterte gegen die Regierung; **the men were ~ing to go home** die Männer forderten lautstark die Heimkehr.

clamp[1] [klæmp] **1** n Schraubzwinge f; (Med, Elec) Klemme f. **2** vt (ein)spannen.

♦**clamp down 1** vt sep (lit) festmachen. **2** vi (fig inf) (on expenses etc) gewaltig bremsen (inf); (police, government) rigoros durchgreifen.

♦**clamp down on** vi +prep obj (inf) person an die Kandare nehmen; expenditure, activities einen Riegel vorschieben (+dat). **the government ~ed on ~ ~ private radio stations** die Regierung holte zum Schlag gegen private Rundfunksender aus; **they ~ed ~. ~ the news as soon as it was released** sofort nach Bekanntgabe wurde die Nachricht unterdrückt.

clamp[2] n (Brit: of potatoes) Miete f.

clamp-down ['klæmpdaʊn] n (inf) Schlag m (inf) (on gegen). **he ordered the ~ on the porn merchants** er hat dafür gesorgt, daß es den Pornohändlern an den Kragen ging; **the ~ has made tax-evasion almost impossible** das harte Durchgreifen hat Steuerhinterziehung fast unmöglich gemacht.

clan [klæn] n (lit, fig) Clan m.

clandestine [klæn'destɪn] adj geheim; meeting, society Geheim-; rendezvous heimlich.

clang [klæŋ] **1** n Klappern nt; (of hammer) Hallen, Dröhnen nt; (of swords) Klirren nt. **2** vi klappern; (hammer) hallen, dröhnen; (swords) klirren. **3** vt mit etw klappern; cymbal schlagen; bell läuten.

clanger ['klæŋər] n (Brit inf) Fauxpas, Schnitzer (inf) m. **to drop a ~** ins Fettnäpfchen treten (inf).

clangor ['klæŋgər] n (US) see **clangour**.

clangorous ['klæŋgərəs] adj (liter) hallend.

clangour ['klæŋgər] n Hallen nt; (irritating) Getöse nt.

clank [klæŋk] **1** n Klirren nt. **2** vt klirren mit. **3** vi klirren.

clannish ['klænɪʃ] adj group klüngelhaft, verfilzt (inf); person cliquenbewußt. **the office became unbearably ~** im Büro entwickelte sich eine unerträgliche Cliquenwirtschaft.

clansman ['klænzmən] n, pl -men [-mən] Clanmitglied nt. **all the McTaggart ~s** alle Mitglieder des Clans McTaggart.

clap[1] [klæp] n (sl) Tripper m. **to pick up a dose of the ~** sich (dat) was or den Tripper (weg)holen (sl).

clap[2] **1** n Klatschen nt no pl; (no pl: applause) (Beifall)klatschen nt. **a ~ of thunder** ein Donnerschlag m; **give him a ~!** klatscht ihm Beifall!, alle(s) klatschen!; **the audience gave him a big ~ on the back** das Publikum klatschte (ihm) begeistert Beifall; **a ~ on the back** ein Schlag m auf die Schulter.
2 vt (a) (applaud) Beifall klatschen (+dat).
(b) **to ~ one's hands** in die Hände klatschen; **to ~ sb on the back** jdm auf die Schulter klopfen.
(c) (put quickly) **he ~ped his hand over my mouth** er hielt mir den Mund zu; **to ~ sb into prison** jdn ins Gefängnis stecken; **to ~ eyes on sb/sth** (inf) jdn/etw zu sehen kriegen (inf).
3 vi (Beifall) klatschen.

♦**clap on** vt sep handcuffs anlegen (prep obj dat). **to ~ ~ one's hat** sich (dat) den Hut aufstülpen; **to ~ ~ sail** (Naut) Beisegel setzen; **to ~ ~ the brakes** (Aut) auf die Bremse latschen (inf).

♦**clap to** vti always separate door zuklappen.

clapboard ['klæpbɔːd] n Schindel f.

clapped-out ['klæptaʊt] adj (sl) **a ~ old car** ein klappriges Auto, eine alte Klapperkiste (inf); **I feel really ~** ich bin total geschafft (sl).

clapper ['klæpər] n (of bell) (Glocken)klöppel m. **to go/drive/work like the ~s** (Brit sl) einen Affenzahn draufhaben (sl).

clapping ['klæpɪŋ] n (Beifall)klatschen nt, Beifall m.

claptrap ['klæptræp] n (inf) Geschwafel nt (inf).

claque [klæk] n (Theat) Claque f, Claqueure pl.

claret ['klærət] **1** n (a) (wine) roter Bordeauxwein, Weinrot nt. **2** adj weinrot.

clarification [ˌklærɪfɪ'keɪʃən] n (a) Klarstellung f. **the whole issue needs a lot more ~** die Sache bedarf noch der Klärung; **I'd like a little ~ on this point** ich hätte diesen Punkt gerne näher erläutert; **in or as ~** zur Klarstellung. (b) (of wine) Klärungsprozeß m.

clarificatory [klærɪfɪ'keɪtərɪ] adj erklärend.

clarify ['klærɪfaɪ] **1** vt (a) klären, klarstellen; text erklären. **the matter has now clarified itself** die Sache hat sich jetzt geklärt; **could you ~ that statement?** könnten Sie diese Äußerung näher erläutern? (b) sugar, fat raffinieren; wine klären. **2** vi (wine) sich klären.

clarinet [ˌklærɪ'net] n Klarinette f.

clarinettist [ˌklærɪ'netɪst] n Klarinettist(in f) m.

clarion ['klærɪən] n (liter) Fanfare f. **a ~ call for liberty/to duty** ein Ruf nach Freiheit/zur Pflicht.

clarity ['klærɪtɪ] n Klarheit f.

clash [klæʃ] **1** vi (a) (armies, demonstrators) zusammenstoßen. **the chairman ~ed with the committee at the last meeting** der Vorsitzende hatte auf der letzten Sitzung eine Auseinandersetzung mit dem Komitee; **unions ~ with government** Konflikt zwischen Gewerkschaften und Regierung.

(b) (colours) nicht harmonieren, sich beißen; (interests) kollidieren, aufeinanderprallen; (programmes, films) sich überschneiden. **our personalities or we ~ too much** wir passen einfach nicht zusammen; **try to appoint staff whose personalities don't ~** (excessively) vermeiden Sie es, Mitarbeiter einzustellen, die überhaupt nicht miteinander harmonieren.
(c) (cymbals etc: also ~ together) aneinanderschlagen; (swords) klirrend aneinanderschlagen.
2 vt cymbals, swords schlagen.
3 n (a) (of armies, demonstrators etc) Zusammenstoß m.
(b) (of personalities) grundsätzliche Verschiedenheit, Unvereinbarkeit f. **we want to avoid a ~ of personalities in the office** wir wollen keine Leute im Büro, die absolut nicht miteinander harmonieren; **it's such a ~ of personalities** sie sind charakterlich grundverschieden; **I don't like that ~ of red and turquoise** mir gefällt diese Zusammenstellung von Rot und Türkis nicht; **what a (horrible) ~!** was für eine (schreckliche) Zusammenstellung!; **a ~ of interests** eine Interessenkollision.
(c) (of swords) Aufeinanderprallen nt; (between people, parties) Konflikt m. **there's bound to be a ~ between the chairman and the vice-chairman** zwischen dem Vorsitzenden und seinem Stellvertreter muß es ja zu einem Zusammenstoß kommen.

clasp [klɑːsp] **1** n (a) (on brooch, purse etc) (Schnapp)verschluß m.
(b) (with one's arms) Umklammerung f; (with hand) Griff m. **he had a firm ~ on the rope** er klammerte sich am Seil fest.
(c) (Mil: of medals) Ansteckabzeichen nt, Metallspange f auf dem Ordensband.
2 vt (a) (er)greifen. **to ~ sb's hand** jds Hand ergreifen; **to ~ one's hands (together)** die Hände falten; **with his hands ~ed in prayer** mit zum Gebet gefalteten Händen; **with his hands ~ed behind his back** mit auf dem Rücken verschränkten Händen; **to ~ sb in one's arms** jdn in die Arme nehmen or schließen; **they lay ~ed in each other's arms** sie lagen sich in den Armen; **to ~ sb to one's heart** jdn ans Herz drücken.
(b) (to fasten with a ~) befestigen, zuschnappen lassen. **she ~ed the bracelet round her wrist** sie legte ihr Armband an.

clasp knife n Taschenmesser nt.

class [klɑːs] **1** n (a) (group, division) Klasse f. **what ~ are you travelling?** in welcher Klasse reisen Sie?; **he's not in the same ~ as his brother** sein Bruder ist eine Klasse besser; **they're just not in the same ~** man kann sie einfach nicht vergleichen; **in a ~ by himself/itself** weitaus der/das Beste.
(b) (social rank) gesellschaftliche Stellung, Stand m (dated), Klasse f (Sociol). **the ruling ~** die herrschende Klasse, die Herrschenden pl; **considerations of ~** Standeserwägungen (dated), Klassengesichtspunkte pl; **it was ~ not ability that determined who ...** (die gesellschaftliche) Herkunft und nicht die Fähigkeiten bestimmten, wer ...; **what ~ does he come from?** aus welchem Stand (dated) or aus welcher Schicht or aus welcher Klasse kommt er?; **they're so concerned with a person's ~** sie legen schrecklich viel Wert auf gute Herkunft; **are you ashamed of your ~?** schämst du dich deines Standes (dated) or deiner Herkunft?; **~ and educational background** Klassenzugehörigkeit und Erziehung; **a society riddled with prejudice and ~** eine von Vorurteilen und Standesdünkel beherrschte Gesellschaft; **we were talking about ~** wir sprachen über die gesellschaftlichen Klassen.
(c) (Sch, Univ) Klasse f. **I don't like her ~es** ihr Unterricht gefällt mir nicht; **you should prepare each ~ in advance** du solltest dich auf jede (Unterrichts)stunde vorbereiten; **to give or take a Latin ~** Latein unterrichten or geben; (Univ) eine Lateinvorlesung halten; ein Lateinseminar etc abhalten; **the French ~** (lesson) die Französischstunde; (people) die Französischklasse; **an evening ~** ein Abendkurs m; **eating in ~** Essen während des Unterrichts; **the ~ of 1970** (US) Jahrgang m 1970, die Schul-/Universitätsabgänger etc des Jahres 1970.
(d) (Bot, Zool) Klasse f.
(e) (Brit Univ: of degree) Prädikat nt. **a first-~ degree** ein Prädikatsexamen nt; **second-/third-~ degree** ≈ Prädikat Gut/Befriedigend.
(f) (inf: quality, tone) Stil m. **to have ~** Stil haben, etwas hermachen (inf); (person) Format haben; **that gives the place a bit of ~** das macht (doch) (et)was her (inf); **I see we've got a bit of ~ in tonight, two guys in dinner jackets** heute abend haben wir ja vornehme or exklusive Gäste, zwei Typen im Smoking; **she's a real piece of ~** sie ist was Besseres (inf).
2 adj (sl) erstklassig, exklusiv.
3 vt einordnen, klassifizieren. **he was ~ed with the servants** er wurde genauso eingestuft wie die Diener.
4 vi eingestuft werden, sich einordnen lassen.

class: ~ conscious adj standesbewußt, klassenbewußt; **~ consciousness** n Standesbewußtsein, Klassenbewußtsein nt; **~ distinction** n gesellschaftlicher Unterschied, Klassenunterschied m; **there is too much ~ distinction** die gesellschaftlichen Unterschiede/Klassenunterschiede sind zu groß; **~ feeling** n (antagonism) Klassenantagonismus m (Sociol); (solidarity) Solidarität f, Klassenbewußtsein nt.

classic ['klæsɪk] **1** adj (lit, fig) klassisch. **it was ~!** (inf) das war geradezu klassisch! **2** n Klassiker m.

classical ['klæsɪkəl] adj klassisch; (in the style of ~ architecture) klassizistisch; education humanistisch; method, solution also altbewährt. **the ~ world** die antike Welt; **a ~ scholar** ein Altphilologe m.

classicism ['klæsɪsɪzəm] n Klassik f; (style of classic architecture) Klassizismus m.

classicist ['klæsɪsɪst] n Altphilologe m/-philologin f.

classics ['klæsɪks] n sing (Univ) Altphilologie f.

classifiable ['klæsɪfaɪəbl] adj klassifizierbar.

classification [ˌklæsɪfɪ'keɪʃən] n Klassifizierung, Einordnung f.

classified ['klæsɪfaɪd] adj in Klassen or Gruppen eingeteilt. ~ ad(vertisement) Kleinanzeige f; ~ information (Mil) Verschlußsache f; (Pol) Geheimsache f.

classify ['klæsɪfaɪ] vt (a) klassifizieren, (nach Klassen, Gruppen) einteilen. (b) information für geheim erklären.

classiness ['klæsɪnɪs] n (inf) Exklusivität f.

class: ~less adj society klassenlos; ~ list n (Brit Univ) Benotungsliste f; ~mate n Klassenkamerad(in f), Mitschüler(in f) m; ~ridden adj society von Klassengegensätzen beherrscht; ~room n Klassenzimmer nt; ~ society n Klassengesellschaft f; ~ struggle n Klassenkampf m; ~ war(fare) n Klassenkrieg m.

classy ['klɑːsɪ] adj (+er) (inf) nobel (inf), exklusiv. ~ hotel eine Nobelherberge (inf); a ~ woman eine Klassefrau (inf).

clatter ['klætəʳ] 1 n Klappern, Geklapper nt; (of hooves also) Trappeln, Getrappel nt. her workbox fell with a ~ to the ground mit lautem Klappern fiel der Nähkasten zu Boden.
2 vi klappern; (hooves also) trappeln. the box of tools went ~ing down the stairs der Werkzeugkasten polterte die Treppe hinunter; the cart ~ed over the cobbles der Wagen polterte or rumpelte über das Pflaster.
3 vt klappern mit.

clause [klɔːz] n (a) (Gram) Satz m. (b) (Jur etc) Klausel f.

claustrophobia [ˌklɔːstrə'fəubɪə] n Klaustrophobie, Platzangst (inf) f.

claustrophobic [ˌklɔːstrə'fəubɪk] adj klaustrophob(isch) (Psych). it's so ~ in here hier kriegt man Platzangst (inf); I get this ~ feeling ich kriege Platzangst (inf); a room of ~ proportions ein Zimmer, in dem man Platzangst kriegt (inf).

clave [kleɪv] ptp of cleave².

clavichord ['klævɪkɔːd] n Klavichord nt.

clavicle ['klævɪkl] n Schlüsselbein nt.

claw [klɔː] 1 n Kralle f; (of lions, birds of prey also, of excavator) Klaue f; (of lobster etc) Schere, Zange f; (of hammer) Nagelklaue f. to show one's ~s die Krallen zeigen; to get one's ~s into sb (inf) (dauernd) auf jdm herumhacken; once a woman like that has got her ~s into a man ... wenn eine Frau wie die erst einmal einen Mann in den Klauen hat, ...
2 vt kratzen. badly ~ed schlimm zerkratzt; the rabbit had been ~ed to shreds by the eagle der Adler hatte das Kaninchen zerfetzt or in Stücke gerissen; the prisoners ~ed a tunnel through the earth die Gefangenen gruben mit bloßen Händen einen Tunnel unter der Erde; the mole ~s its way through the soil der Maulwurf wühlt sich durch das Erdreich; two women, like cats, ~ing each other zwei Frauen, die wie Hyänen aufeinander losgingen; he ~ed back the sheets er riß die Laken weg.
3 vi to ~ at sth sich an etw (acc) krallen; he ~ed desperately for the handle er krallte verzweifelt nach der Klinke.
♦ **claw back** vt sep (taxman) sich (dat) zurückholen.
♦ **claw out** vt separable. to ~ sth ~ of sth etw mit der Tatze or (excavator) mit der Klaue aus etw herausholen.

claw: ~ hammer n Tischlerhammer m; ~ mark n Kratzer m.

clay [kleɪ] n Lehm m. potter's ~ Ton m.

clayey ['kleɪɪ] adj lehmig; soil also Lehm-.

claymore ['kleɪmɔːʳ] n zweischneidiges Langschwert.

clay: ~ pigeon n Tontaube f; ~ pigeon shooting n Tontaubenschießen nt; ~ pipe n Tonpfeife f.

clean [kliːn] 1 adj (+er) (a) (not dirty, also bomb) sauber. to wash/wipe/brush sth ~ etw abwaschen/-reiben/-bürsten; she has very ~ habits, she's a very ~ person sie ist sehr sauber.
(b) (new, not used) sheets, paper sauber, neu. I want to see a nice ~ plate ich will einen schön leer gegessenen Teller sehen; the vultures picked the carcass/bone ~ die Geier nagten den Kadaver bis aufs Skelett ab/nagten den Knochen ganz ab; to make a ~ start ganz von vorne anfangen; (in life) ein neues Leben anfangen.
(c) (free from blemish) joke stubenrein; film anständig; (Typ) proof sauber. keep television ~ das Fernsehen muß sauber or anständig bleiben; he's ~, no guns (inf) alles in Ordnung, nicht bewaffnet; see record.
(d) (well-shaped) lines klar.
(e) (regular, even) cut, break sauber, glatt.
(f) (Sport) fight, match sauber, fair; boxer fair.
(g) (acceptable to religion) rein.
(h) to make a ~ breast of sth etw gestehen, sich (dat) etw von der Seele reden; see sweep.
2 adv glatt. I ~ forgot das habe ich glatt(weg) vergessen (inf); he got ~ away er verschwand spurlos; he got ~ away from the rest of the field er ließ das übrige Feld weit hinter sich; the ball/he went ~ through the window der Ball flog glatt/er flog achtkantig durch das Fenster; to cut ~ through sth etw ganz durchschneiden/durchschlagen etc; to come ~ (inf) auspacken (inf); we're ~ out (of matches) es sind keine (Streichhölzer) mehr da.
3 vt saubermachen; (with cloth also) abwischen; carpets also reinigen; (remove stains etc) säubern; clothes also säubern (form); (dry-) reinigen; nails, paint-brush, furniture also, dentures, old buildings reinigen; window, shoes putzen, reinigen (form); fish, wound säubern; chicken ausnehmen; vegetables putzen; apple, grapes etc säubern (form); (wash) (ab)waschen; (wipe) abwischen; cup, plate etc säubern (form); (wash) spülen; (wipe) aus-/abwischen; car waschen, putzen. the cat is ~ing itself die Katze putzt sich; to ~ one's hands (wash) sich (dat) die Hände waschen or (wipe) abwischen or (scrape, with grease remover) säubern; to ~ one's teeth sich (dat) die Zähne putzen or (with toothpick) saubermachen, säubern; to ~ one's face (wash) sich (dat) das Gesicht waschen or (wipe) abwischen; ~ the dirt off your face wisch dir den Schmutz vom Gesicht!; he ~ed the butter off his beard er wischte sich (dat) die Butter aus dem Bart; ~ your shoes

before you come inside putz dir die Schuhe ab, bevor du reinkommst!; to ~ a room ein Zimmer saubermachen, in einem Zimmer putzen; clothes which are easy to ~ pflegeleichte Kleider pl.
4 vi reinigen. this paint ~s easily diese Farbe läßt sich leicht reinigen; brand X ~s better die Marke X reinigt gründlicher.
5 n see vt to give sth a ~ etw saubermachen/reinigen/putzen etc; your face/this house/the suit needs a good ~ du könntest dein Gesicht mal richtig waschen/das Haus/dieser Anzug müßte mal richtig gereinigt werden.
♦ **clean down** vt sep car, lorry waschen; walls abwaschen.
♦ **clean off** 1 vt sep (wash) abwaschen; (rinse) abspülen; (wipe) abwischen; (scrape, rub) abreiben; dirt, barnacles, rust entfernen, abmachen (inf). 2 vi sich abwaschen etc lassen.
♦ **clean out** vt sep (a) (lit) gründlich saubermachen; (with water also) ausspülen; stables also ausmisten; carburettor reinigen; stomach auspumpen or -räumen.
(b) (inf: to leave penniless) person ausnehmen (wie eine Weihnachtsgans) (inf); bank ausräumen (inf); (gambling) sprengen. to be ~ed ~ abgebrannt sein (inf).
(c) (inf: take all stock) to ~ sb ~ of sth jdm alles wegkaufen.
♦ **clean up** 1 vt sep (a) saubermachen; old building, old painting reinigen. to ~ oneself ~ sich saubermachen; who's going to ~ ~ this mess? wer soll dieses Durcheinander aufräumen?
(b) (fig) the new mayor ~ed ~ the city der neue Bürgermeister hat für Sauberkeit in der Stadt gesorgt; to ~ ~ television den Bildschirm (von Gewalt, Sex etc) säubern.
(c) (sl: make money) einstecken (inf), absahnen (sl).
2 vi (lit) aufräumen.
(b) (sl) abkassieren (inf), absahnen (sl). he certainly ~ed ~ on that sale bei dem Verkauf hat er kräftig abgesahnt (sl).

clean-cut ['kliːnkʌt] adj klar, klar umrissen. the ~ lines of his new suit der klare or einfache Schnitt seines neuen Anzuges; ~ features klare Gesichtszüge pl.

cleaner ['kliːnəʳ] n (a) (person) Reinemachefrau f; Gebäudereiniger m (form). a firm of office ~s eine Büroreinigungsfirma; the ~s come once a week das Reinigungspersonal kommt einmal pro Woche.
(b) (shop) ~'s Reinigung f; to take sb to the ~'s (inf) jdn übers Ohr hauen (inf), jdn reinlegen (inf).
(c) (thing) Reiniger m; see vacuum ~.
(d) (substance) Reiniger m, Reinigungsmittel nt.

cleaning ['kliːnɪŋ] n the ladies who do the ~ die Frauen, die (hier) saubermachen; ~ lady Reinemachefrau f.

clean-limbed ['kliːn'lɪmd] adj gutgebaut attr, gut gebaut pred.

cleanliness ['klenlɪnɪs] n Reinlichkeit f. ~ is next to godliness (Prov) Sauberkeit ist alles!

clean-living ['kliːn'lɪvɪŋ] adj anständig, sauber.

cleanly¹ ['kliːnlɪ] adv sauber. the bone broke ~ es war ein glatter Knochenbruch.

cleanly² ['klenlɪ] adj (+er) sauber; person reinlich.

cleanness ['kliːnnɪs] n (a) Sauberkeit f.
(b) (of joke) Anständigkeit, Stubenreinheit f; (of film) Anständigkeit f; (Typ: of proof) Sauberkeit f. the exemplary ~ of his record seine äußerst gute Führung.
(c) (of outline) Klarheit f.
(d) (of break etc) Sauberkeit, Glätte f. thanks to the ~ of the break weil es ein sauberer Bruch war.

clean-out ['kliːnaut] n to give sth a ~ etw saubermachen.

cleanse [klenz] vt (lit) reinigen; (spiritually) läutern (of von).

cleanser ['klenzəʳ] n (detergent) Reiniger m, Reinigungsmittel nt; (for skin) Reinigungscreme f; Reinigungsmilch f.

clean-shaven ['kliːn'ʃeɪvn] adj glattrasiert.

cleansing ['klenzɪŋ] adj agent Reinigungs-. ~ department Stadtreinigung f.

clean-up ['kliːnʌp] n (a) (of person) give yourself a good ~ before you come down to dinner wasch dich erst einmal, bevor du zum Essen kommst; to give sth a ~ etw saubermachen. (b) (by police) Säuberung f. (c) (sl: profit) Schnitt m (sl).

clear [klɪəʳ] 1 adj (+er) (a) water, soup, sky, head, weather etc klar; complexion rein; conscience rein, gut attr; photograph scharf. on a ~ day bei klarem Wetter.
(b) (of sounds) klar.
(c) (to one's understanding, distinct, obvious) klar. to be ~ to sb jdm klar sein; it's still not ~ to me why es ist immer noch nicht klar, warum, ich bin immer noch im unklaren (darüber), warum; a ~ case of murder ein klarer or eindeutiger Fall von Mord; to have a ~ advantage eindeutig or klar im Vorteil sein; you weren't very ~ du hast dich nicht sehr klar ausgedrückt; to make oneself or one's meaning ~ sich klar ausdrücken; is that ~? alles klar?; you'll do what you're told, is that ~? du tust, was dir gesagt wird, ist das klar?; do I make myself ~? habe ich mich klar (genug) ausgedrückt?; to make it ~ to sb that ... es jdm (unmißverständlich) klarmachen, daß ...; to make sth ~ to sb (explain) jdm etw klarmachen; I wish to make it ~ that ... ich möchte einmal ganz klar sagen, daß ...; let's get this ~, I'm the boss eins wollen wir mal klarstellen – ich bin hier der Chef; as ~ as day sonnenklar; as ~ as mud (inf) klar wie Kloßbrühe (inf).
(d) to be ~ on sth über etw (acc) im klaren sein; I'm not ~ on the implications ich bin mir nicht sicher, was das impliziert.
(e) (lit, fig: free of obstacles, danger etc) road, way frei. I want to keep the weekend ~ ich möchte mir das Wochenende freihalten; is it ~? (of road) ist jetzt frei?; leave a ~ space between each line laß etwas Platz zwischen den Zeilen; there's not a single ~ space on his desk auf seinem Schreibtisch ist überhaupt kein Platz; there's a small patch of ~ ground between the houses zwischen den Häusern ist ein kleines Stück Land frei; all ~! (alles) frei!; is it all ~ now? ist alles in Ordnung?, ist die Luft rein?; to be ~ of sth (freed from) von etw

befreit sein; **at last we were/got ~ of the prison walls** endlich hatten wir die Gefängnismauern hinter uns; **I'll come when I get ~ of all this work** ich komme, wenn ich diese ganze Arbeit erledigt or hinter mir habe; **you're ~,** said the customs officer alles in Ordnung, sagte der Zollbeamte; **the plane climbed until it was ~ of the clouds** das Flugzeug stieg auf, bis es aus den Wolken heraus war; **the lion got ~ of the net** der Löwe konnte sich aus dem Netz befreien; **he's ~ of all suspicion** er ist frei von jedem Verdacht; **the car was ~ of the town** das Auto hatte die Stadt hinter sich gelassen; **~ of debts** schuldenfrei; **the screw should be 2 mm ~ of the wire** zwischen Schraube und Draht müssen 2 mm Zwischenraum sein; **the bottom of the door should be about 3 mm ~ of the floor** zwischen Tür und Fußboden müssen etwa 3 mm Luft sein; **hold the blow-lamp about 6 cm ~ of the paint** die Lötlampe in etwa 6 cm Abstand zum Lack halten; **park at least 20 cm ~ of the pavement** parken Sie wenigstens 20 cm vom Bürgersteig entfernt; **OK, keep going, you're ~ of the wall** in Ordnung, fahr, bis zur Mauer ist noch ein ganzes Stück Platz; **hold his head well ~ of the water** den Kopf gut über Wasser halten; **the mortars landed well ~ of us** die Mörser schlugen ein ganzes Stück neben uns ein.

(f) a ~ profit ein Reingewinn m; **three ~ days** drei volle Tage; **a ~ majority** eine klare Mehrheit; **to have a ~ lead** klar führen.

2 n **(a)** (of message) **in ~** in/im Klartext.

(b) to be in the ~ nichts zu verbergen haben; **we're not in the ~ yet** (not out of debt, difficulties) wir sind noch nicht aus allem heraus; **this puts Harry in the ~** damit ist Harry entlastet or von jedem Verdacht frei.

3 adv **(a)** see **loud**.

(b) he got ~ away er verschwand spurlos; **he kicked the ball ~ across the field** er schoß den Ball quer über das Spielfeld.

(c) ~ of (Naut) **to steer ~ of sth** um etw herumsteuern; **to steer** or **keep ~ of sb/sth/a place** jdm aus dem Wege gehen/etw meiden/um etw einen großen Bogen machen; **keep ~ of the whisky for a while** du solltest mal eine Zeitlang die Finger vom Whisky lassen; **he always tries to keep ~ of trouble** er geht Unannehmlichkeiten möglichst aus dem Wege; **you'd better keep ~ of that pub** um die Kneipe würde ich lieber einen großen Bogen machen; **keep ~ of Slobodia until the revolution's over** fahr nicht nach Slobodia, solange die Revolution nicht vorüber ist; **if you can't stop gambling you'd better keep ~ of the horse races** wenn du das Wetten nicht lassen kannst, würde ich an deiner Stelle nicht zum Pferderennen gehen; **I prefer to keep ~ of town during the rush hour** während der Hauptverkehrszeit meide ich die Stadt nach Möglichkeit; **the public was asked to keep ~ of the area** die Öffentlichkeit wurde aufgefordert, dem Gebiet fernzubleiben; **exit, keep ~** Ausfahrt freihalten!; **dangerous chemicals, keep ~** Vorsicht, giftige Chemikalien!; **keep ~ of the testing area** Versuchsgebiet nicht betreten!; **personnel not wearing protective clothing must keep well ~ of the dump** Angestellte ohne Schutzkleidung dürfen sich nicht in unmittelbarer Nähe der Deponie aufhalten; **to stand ~** zurücktreten; zurückbleiben; **stand ~ of the doors!** bitte von den Türen zurücktreten!; **he kicked the ball ~** er klärte; **the helicopter lifted him ~ der** Hubschrauber brachte ihn außer Gefahr; **he leapt ~ of the burning car** er rettete sich durch einen Sprung aus dem brennenden Auto.

4 vt **(a)** (remove obstacles etc from) pipe reinigen; blockage beseitigen; land, road, railway line, snow räumen; one's conscience erleichtern. **to ~ the table** den Tisch abräumen; **to ~ the decks (for action)** (lit) das Schiff gefechtsklar machen; (fig) alles startklar machen; **to ~ a space for sth** für etw Platz schaffen; **to ~ sth of sth** etw von etw räumen; **he ~ed all the rubbish off his desk** er räumte den ganzen Kram von seinem Schreibtisch; **to ~ the way for sb/sth** den Weg für jdn/etw freimachen; **to ~ the streets of ice** das Eis auf den Straßen beseitigen; **~ the way!** Platz machen!, Platz da!; **to ~ a way through the crowd** sich (dat) einen Weg durch die Menge bahnen; **to ~ a room** (of people) ein Zimmer räumen; (of things) ein Zimmer ausräumen; **her singing ~ed the room** in no time ihr Gesang ließ die Leute fluchtartig den Raum verlassen; **to ~ the court** den Gerichtssaal räumen lassen; **to ~ the ground for further talks** den Boden für weitere Gespräche bereiten.

(b) letterbox leeren.

(c) (free from guilt etc, Jur: find innocent) person freisprechen; one's/sb's name reinwaschen. **that ~s him** das beweist seine Unschuld; **he will easily ~ himself** er wird seine Unschuld leicht beweisen können.

(d) (get past or over) he **~ed the bar easily** er übersprang die Latte mit Leichtigkeit; **the horse ~ed the gate by 10 cm/easily** das Pferd übersprang das Gatter mit 10 cm Zwischenraum/das Pferd nahm das Gatter mit Leichtigkeit; **the door should ~ the floor by 3 mm** zwischen Tür und Fußboden müssen 3 mm Luft sein; **raise the car till the wheel ~s the ground** das Auto anheben, bis das Rad den Boden nicht mehr berührt; **the ship's keel only just ~ed the reef** der Kiel des Schiffes kam an dem Riff nur um Haaresbreite vorbei.

(e) (Med) blood reinigen; bowels (ent)leeren. **to ~ one's head** (wieder) einen klaren Kopf bekommen.

(f) (Ftbl etc) **to ~ the ball** klären.

(g) (make profit of) machen, rausholen (inf). **I didn't even ~ my expenses** ich habe nicht einmal meine Ausgaben wieder hereinbekommen.

(h) debt begleichen, zurückzahlen.

(i) stock etc räumen.

(j) (pass, OK) abfertigen; ship klarieren; expenses, appointment bestätigen; goods zollamtlich abfertigen. **to ~ a cheque** bestätigen, daß ein Scheck gedeckt ist; (enquire) nachfragen, ob der Scheck gedeckt ist; **you'll have to ~ that with manage-**

ment Sie müssen das mit der Firmenleitung regeln or abklären; **he's been ~ed by security** er ist von den Sicherheitsbehörden für unbedenklich erklärt worden; **to ~ a plane for take-off** einem Flugzeug die Starterlaubnis erteilen, ein Flugzeug zum Start freigeben.

5 vi (weather) aufklaren, schön werden; (mist, smoke) sich legen, sich auflösen; (crystal ball) sich klären.

♦**clear away 1** vt sep wegräumen; dirty dishes also abräumen. **2** vi **(a)** (mist etc) sich auflösen, sich legen. **(b)** (to ~ ~ the table) den Tisch abräumen.

♦**clear off 1** vt sep debts begleichen, zurückzahlen; (Comm) stock räumen; mortgage abzahlen, abtragen; arrears of work aufarbeiten. **2** vi (inf) abhauen (inf), verschwinden (inf).

♦**clear out 1** vt sep cupboard, room ausräumen; unwanted objects also entfernen. **he ~ed everyone ~ of the room** er schickte alle aus dem Zimmer. **2** vi (inf) **(a)** verschwinden (inf). **(b)** (leave home etc) sich absetzen (inf).

♦**clear up 1** vt sep **(a)** point, matter klären; mystery, crime aufklären, aufdecken; doubts beseitigen. **(b)** (tidy) aufräumen; litter wegräumen. **2** vi **(a)** (weather) (sich) aufklaren; (rain) aufhören. **(b)** (tidy up) aufräumen.

clearance ['klɪərəns] n **(a)** (act of clearing) Entfernen nt, Beseitigung f. slum **~s** Slumsanierungen or -beseitigungen pl.

(b) (free space) Spielraum m; (headroom) lichte Höhe.

(c) (Ftbl etc) **a good ~ by the defender** saved a nasty situation der Verteidiger klärte gekonnt und rettete die Lage.

(d) (of cheque) Bestätigung f der Deckung.

(e) (by customs) Abfertigung f; (by security) Unbedenklichkeitserklärung f; (document) Unbedenklichkeitsbescheinigung f. **get your security ~ first** Sie müssen erst noch von den Sicherheitsorganen für unbedenklich erklärt werden; **the despatch was sent to the Foreign Office for ~** der Bericht wurde zur Überprüfung ans Außenministerium geschickt; **to land** Landeerlaubnis f; **~ for take-off** Startfreigabe f.

(f) (Naut) Klarierung f. **~ outwards** Ausklarierung f; **~ inwards** Einklarierung f.

clearance: ~ certificate n (Naut) Verzollungspapiere pl; **~ sale** n (Comm) Räumungsverkauf m.

clear-cut ['klɪə'kʌt] adj decision klar; features scharf.

clearing ['klɪərɪŋ] n (in forest) Lichtung f.

clearing: ~ bank n (Brit) Clearingbank f; **~ house** n Clearingstelle f.

clearly ['klɪəlɪ] adv **(a)** (distinctly) klar. **~ visible** klar or gut zu sehen; **to stand out ~ from the rest** sich deutlich vom übrigen hervorheben or abheben.

(b) (obviously) eindeutig. **is that so? — ~** ist das der Fall? — natürlich or selbstverständlich; **~ we cannot allow ...** wir können keinesfalls zulassen, ...; **this ~ can't be true** das muß eindeutig falsch sein, das kann auf keinen Fall stimmen.

clearness ['klɪənɪs] n (a) see **clear 1 (a)** Klarheit f; Reinheit f; Schärfe f. **(b)** see **clear 1 (b, c)** Klarheit f.

clear: ~-sighted adj (fig) klar- or scharfsichtig; **~-sightedness** n (fig) Klar- or Scharfsicht f; **~way** n (Brit) Straße f mit Halteverbot, Schnellstraße f.

cleat [kliːt] n (on shoes) Stoßplatte f; (made of metal) Absatzeisen nt; (on gangplank etc) Querleiste f; (for rope) Klampe f.

cleavage ['kliːvɪdʒ] n (a) (split) Spalte, Kluft (geh) f; (fig) Spaltung, Kluft f. **(b)** (of woman's breasts) Dekolleté nt.

cleave¹ [kliːv] pret **clove** or **cleft** or **~d**, ptp **cleft** or **cloven 1** vt spalten; **to ~ in two** in zwei Teile spalten; **to ~ a way through** sth sich (dat) einen Weg durch etw bahnen. **2** vi **(a)** to **~ through the waves** die Wellen durchschneiden. **(b)** (Biol) sich spalten.

cleave² vi pret **~d** or **clave**, ptp **cleaved** (adhere) festhalten (to an +dat), beharren (to auf +dat). **through all the difficulties they ~d fast to each other** (liter) durch alle Schwierigkeiten hindurch hielten sie fest zusammen.

cleaver ['kliːvəʳ] n Hackbeil nt.

clef [klef] n (Noten)schlüssel m.

cleft [kleft] **1** pret, ptp of **cleave¹**. **2** adj gespalten. **~ palate** Gaumenspalte f, Wolfsrachen m; **to be in a ~ stick** in der Klemme sitzen (inf). **3** n Spalte, Kluft (geh) f; (fig) Spaltung, Kluft f.

clematis ['klemətɪs] n Waldrebe, Klematis f.

clemency ['klemənsɪ] n (of person) Milde, Nachsicht(igkeit) f (towards sb jdm gegenüber); (of weather) Milde, Freundlichkeit f. **the prisoner was shown ~** dem Gefangenen wurde eine milde Behandlung zuteil.

clement ['klemənt] adj person, attitude mild, nachsichtig (towards sb jdm gegenüber); weather mild, freundlich.

clementine ['kleməntaɪn] n (fruit) Klementine f.

clench [klentʃ] vt **(a)** fist ballen; teeth zusammenbeißen; (grasp firmly) packen. **to ~ sth between one's teeth** etw zwischen die Zähne klemmen; **to ~ sth in one's hands** etw mit den Händen umklammern; **~ed-fist salute** Arbeiterkampfgruß m. **(b)** see **clinch 1 (a)**.

Cleopatra [ˌkliːəˈpætrə] n Kleopatra f.

clerestory ['klɪəstɔːrɪ] n (Archit) Lichtgaden m.

clergy ['klɜːdʒɪ] npl Klerus m, Geistlichkeit f, die Geistlichen pl. **to join the ~** Geistlicher werden.

clergyman ['klɜːdʒɪmən] n, pl **-men** [-mən] Geistlicher, Pfarrer m.

cleric ['klerɪk] n Geistlicher m.

clerical ['klerɪkəl] adj **(a)** (Eccl) geistlich. **~ collar** Stehkragen m (des Geistlichen), Priesterkragen m.

(b) ~ work/job Schreib- or Büroarbeit f; **~ worker** Schreib- or Bürokraft f; **~ staff** Schreibkräfte pl, Büropersonal nt; **~ error** Versehen nt; she **also had ~ duties** sie hatte auch Büroarbeiten zu verrichten; **~ inaccuracies** Versehen nt, Nachlässigkeit f; **work of a ~ nature** Schreibarbeit f; **the ~ branch of the civil service** = die mittlere Beamtenlaufbahn.

clericalism ['klerıkəlızəm]ˉ n Klerikalismus m.

clerihew ['klerıhju:] n Clerihew nt, witziger Vierzeiler.

clerk [klɑ:k, (US) klɜ:rk] n **(a)** (Büro)angestellte(r) mf. **(b)** (secretary) Schriftführer(in f) m. C~ **of the Court** (Jur) Protokollführer(in f) m; ~ **of works** (Brit) Bauleiter(in f) m. **(c)** (US: shop assistant) Verkäufer(in f) m. **(d)** (US: in hotel) Hotelsekretär(in f) m.

clever ['klevəʳ] adj **(a)** (mentally bright) schlau; animal also klug. **to be ~ at French** gut in Französich sein; **how ~ of you to remember my birthday!** wie aufmerksam von dir, daß du an meinen Geburtstag gedacht hast!
   (b) (ingenious, skilful, witty) klug; person, move in chess also geschickt; idea also schlau; device, machine raffiniert, geschickt. **to be ~ at sth** Geschick zu etw haben, in etw (dat) geschickt sein; **he's ~ at making things out of bits and pieces** er hat Geschick darin, aus allem möglichen (Krims)kram etwas zu machen; **to be ~ with one's hands** geschickte Hände haben; ~ **Dick** (inf) Schlaumeier (inf), Schlaukopf (inf) m.
   (c) (cunning, smart) schlau, clever (inf).

clever-clever ['klevə'klevəʳ] adj (inf) ausgeklügelt; person oberschlau (inf).

cleverly ['klevəlı] adv geschickt; (wittily) schlau, klug. **he very ~ remembered** it schlau wie er war, hat er es nicht vergessen.

cleverness ['klevənıs] n see adj **(a)** Schlauheit f; Klugheit f. **(b)** Klugheit f; Geschicktheit f; Schlauheit f; Raffiniertheit, Geschicktheit f. **(c)** Schläue, Cleverness f.

clew [klu:] 1 n **(a)** (thread) Knäuel nt. **(b)** (Naut: of sail) Schothorn nt; (of hammock) Schlaufe f. **(c)** = **clue.** 2 vt **(a)** thread aufwickeln. **(b)** (Naut) **to ~ (up)** aufgeien.

cliché ['kli:ʃeı] n Klischee nt. **~-ridden** voller Klischees.

clichéd ['kli:ʃeıd] adj klischeehaft.

click [klık] 1 n Klicken nt; (of joints) Knacken nt; (of light-switch) Knipsen nt; (of fingers) Knipsen, Schnipsen nt; (of latch, key in lock) Schnappen nt; (of tongue, Phon) Schnalzen nt. **he turned with a sharp ~ of his heels** er drehte sich um und klappte zackig die Hacken zusammen.
   2 vi **(a)** see n klicken; knacken; knipsen; knipsen, schnipsen; schnalzen; (high heels) klappern.
   (b) (inf: be understood) funken (inf). **suddenly it all ~ed (into place)** plötzlich hatte es gefunkt (inf); **what he was saying suddenly ~ed** plötzlich hatte es gefunkt, und ich/er etc verstand, was er meinte (inf).
   (c) (inf: get on well) funken (inf). **they ~ed right from the moment they first met** zwischen ihnen hatte es vom ersten Augenblick an gefunkt (inf); **some people you ~ with straight away** mit manchen Leuten versteht man sich auf Anhieb.
   3 vt heels zusammenklappen; fingers schnipsen mit; tongue schnalzen mit. **to ~ a door shut** eine Tür zuklinken; **to ~ sth into place** etw einschnappen lassen.

client ['klaıənt] n **(a)** Kunde m, Kundin f; (of solicitor) Klient(in f) m; (of barrister) Mandant(in f) m. **(b)** (US: receiving welfare) Bezieher m. ~ **state** Schützling, Satellitenstaat m.

clientele [,kli:ã:n'tel] n Kundschaft, Klientel f. **the regular ~** die Stammkundschaft.

cliff [klıf] n Klippe f; (along coast also) Kliff nt; (inland also) Felsen m. **the ~s of Cornwall/Dover** die Kliffküste Cornwalls/die Felsen von Dover.

cliff: ~-**dweller** n vorgeschichtlicher Höhlenbewohner im Colorado-Cañon; ~**hanger** n Superthriller m (inf); ~-**hanging** adj conclusion spannungsgeladen.

cliffy ['klıfı] adj coast Kliff-.

climacteric [klaı'mæktərık] n (Med) Klimakterium nt; (fig) (Lebens)wende f, Wendepunkt m (im Leben).

climactic [klaı'mæktık] adj **the conclusion was ~ in the extreme** der Schluß war ein absoluter Höhepunkt; **a ~ scene** ein Höhepunkt.

climate ['klaımıt] n (lit, fig) Klima nt. **the two countries have very different ~s** die beiden Länder haben (ein) sehr unterschiedliches Klima; **America has many different ~s** Amerika hat viele verschiedene Klimazonen or Klimate (spec); **to move to a warmer ~** in eine wärmere Gegend or in eine Gegend mit wärmerem Klima ziehen; **the ~ of popular opinion** die Stimmung in der Öffentlichkeit, das öffentliche Klima.

climatic [klaı'mætık] adj klimatisch, Klima-.

climatology [,klaımə'tɒlədʒı] n Klimatologie, Klimakunde f.

climax ['klaımæks] n (all senses) Höhepunkt m; (sexual also) Orgasmus m. **this brought matters to a ~** damit erreichte die Angelegenheit ihren Höhepunkt.

climb [klaım] 1 vt **(a)** (also ~ **up**) klettern auf (+acc); wall also, hill steigen auf (+acc); mountains also besteigen; ladder, steps hoch- or hinaufsteigen; pole, cliffs hochklettern. **my car can't ~ that hill** mein Auto schafft den Berg nicht or kommt den Berg nicht hoch; **to ~ a rope** an einem Seil hochklettern.
   (b) (also ~ **over**) wall etc steigen or klettern über (+acc).
   2 vi klettern; (into train, car etc) steigen; (road) ansteigen; (aircraft) (auf)steigen; (sun) steigen; (prices) steigen, klettern (inf). **when the sun had ~ed to its highest point** also die Sonne am höchsten stand; **he ~ed to the top of his profession** er hat den Gipfel seiner beruflichen Laufbahn erklommen.
   3 n **(a)** (climbing) **we're going out for a ~** wir machen eine Kletter- or Bergtour; **that was some ~!** das war eine Kletterei!; **Ben Lomond is an easy ~** Ben Lomond ist leicht zu besteigen; **I've never done that ~** den habe ich noch nicht bestiegen or gemacht (inf).
   (b) (of aircraft) Steigflug m. **the plane went into a steep ~** das Flugzeug zog steil nach oben.

♦**climb down** 1 vi **(a)** (lit) (person) (from tree, wall) herunterklettern; (from horse, mountain) absteigen; (from ladder) heruntersteigen; (road) abfallen. **(b)** (admit error) nachgeben. **it'll be a pleasure to make him ~ ~** es wird ein Vergnügen sein, ihn von seinem hohen Roß herunterzuholen.

2 vi +prep obj tree, wall herunterklettern von; ladder heruntersteigen; mountain etc absteigen.

♦**climb in** vi einsteigen; (with difficulty also) hineinklettern.

♦**climb up** 1 vi see climb 2. 2 vi +prep obj ladder etc hinaufsteigen; tree, wall hochklettern.

climbable ['klaıməbl] adj besteigbar.

climb-down ['klaımdaun] n (fig) Abstieg m. **it was quite a ~ for the boss to have to admit that he was wrong** der Chef mußte ziemlich zurückstecken und zugeben, daß er unrecht hatte.

climber ['klaıməʳ] n **(a)** (mountaineer) Bergsteiger(in f) m; (rock ~) Kletterer(in f) m. **(b)** (socially) Aufsteiger m. **(c)** (plant) Kletterpflanze f.

climbing ['klaımıŋ] 1 adj **(a)** club Berg(steiger)-; Kletter-. ~ **frame** Klettergerüst nt; **we are going on a ~ holiday** wir gehen im Urlaub zum Bergsteigen/Klettern; ~-**irons** Steigeisen pl; ~ **speed** (Aviat) Steiggeschwindigkeit f.
   (b) plant Kletter-.
   2 n Bergsteigen nt; (rock ~) Klettern nt. **we did a lot of ~** wir sind viel geklettert.

clime [klaım] n (old, liter) Himmelsstrich (old, liter), Landstrich (geh) m. **in these ~s** in diesen Breiten; **he moved to warmer ~s** er zog in wärmere Breiten.

clinch [klıntʃ] 1 vt **(a)** (Tech: also clench) nail krumm schlagen.
   (b) argument zum Abschluß bringen. **to ~ the deal** der Handel perfekt machen, den Handel besiegeln; **that ~es it** damit ist der Fall erledigt.
   2 vi (Boxing) in den Clinch gehen, clinchen.
   3 n **(a)** (Boxing) Clinch m.
   (b) (inf: embrace) **in a ~** im Clinch (inf).

clincher ['klıntʃəʳ] n (inf) ausschlaggebendes Argument. **that was the ~** das gab den Ausschlag.

cling[1] [klıŋ] pret, ptp **clung** vi (hold on tightly) sich festklammern (to an +dat), sich klammern (to an +acc); (to opinion also) festhalten (to an +dat); (remain close) sich halten (to an +acc); (clothes, paint) sich anschmiegen (to dat); (smell) haften (to an +dat), sich setzen (to in +acc). ~ **on tight!** halt dich gut fest!; **the car clung to the road** das Auto lag sicher auf der Straße; **to ~ together** or **to one another** sich aneinanderklammern; (lovers) sich umschlingen, sich umschlungen halten; **in spite of all the difficulties they've clung together** trotz aller Schwierigkeiten haben sie zusammengehalten; **she clung around her father's neck** sie hing ihrem Vater am Hals; **the boat clung to the shoreline** das Schiff hielt sich dicht an die Küste; **women who ~** Frauen, die sich an einen klammern.

cling[2] n Klingen nt; (of cash register) Klingeln nt. 2 vi klingen; (cash register) klingeln.

clinging ['klıŋıŋ] adj garment sich anschmiegend; smell lange haftend, hartnäckig. **she's the ~ sort** sie ist wie eine Klette (inf); ~ **vine** (inf) Klette f (inf).

cling(stone) peach ['klıŋ(stəun)'pi:tʃ] n Klingstone m (nichtsteinlösende Pfirsichsorte).

clinic ['klınık] n **(a)** Klinik f. **(b)** (medical course) klinischer Unterricht, Klinik f.

clinical ['klınıkəl] adj **(a)** (Med) klinisch. ~ **thermometer** Fieberthermometer nt. **(b)** (fig) (sterile) room, atmosphere steril, kalt; (detached, dispassionate) klinisch, nüchtern; sb's appearance streng.

clink[1] [klıŋk] 1 vt klirren lassen; (jingle) klimpern mit. **she ~ed a coin against the window** sie schlug mit einer Münze gegen die Scheibe, daß es klirrte; **to ~ glasses with sb** mit jdm anstoßen.
   2 vi klirren; (jingle) klimpern. **the thermometer ~ed against the glass** das Thermometer stieß klirrend an das Glas.
   3 n, no pl Klirren nt; Klimpern nt. **the ~ of glasses as they drank to his health** das Klingen der Gläser, als auf sein Wohl getrunken wurde.

clink[2] n (sl: prison) Knast m (sl). **in ~** im Knast.

clinker ['klıŋkəʳ] n **(a)** (from fire) Schlacke f. **a ~** ein Stück Schlacke. **(b)** (brick) Klinker m.

clinker-built ['klıŋkəbılt] adj (Naut) klinkergebaut.

clip[1] [klıp] 1 n **(a)** (for holding things) Klammer f.
   (b) (jewel) Klips m.
   (c) (of gun) Ladestreifen m.
   2 vt **to ~ on** anklemmen; (papers also) anheften; **to ~ sth onto sth** etw an etw (acc) anklemmen/-heften; **to ~ two things together** zwei Dinge zusammenklemmen/-heften.
   3 vi **to ~ on** angeklemmt werden; **to ~ onto sth** an etw (acc) angeklemmt werden; **to ~ together** zusammengeklemmt werden.

clip[2] 1 vt **(a)** scheren; dog also trimmen; hedge also, fingernails schneiden; wings stutzen. **to ~ sb's wings** (fig) jdm einen Dämpfer aufsetzen; **they'll find that the young baby will ~ their wings a bit** sie werden merken, daß das Kleinkind sie recht unbeweglich macht.
   (b) (also ~ **out**) article from newspaper ausschneiden; (also ~ **off**) hair, curl abschneiden. **the bullet ~ped a few inches off the top of the wall** die Kugel schlug ein paar Zentimeter oben aus der Mauer.
   (c) (Brit) ticket lochen, knipsen, entwerten.
   (d) **to ~ (the ends of) one's words** abgehackt sprechen.
   (e) (hit) treffen; (graze: car, bullet) streifen. **he ~ped him round the ear** er gab ihm eine Ohrfeige; **he ~ped his opponent on the jaw** er traf seinen Gegner am Unterkiefer; **the left jab just ~ped him on the chin** der linke Gerade streifte sein Kinn.
   2 n **(a)** see vt **(a)** Scheren nt; Trimmen nt; Schneiden nt; Stutzen nt. **to give the sheep/hedge a ~** die Schafe scheren/die Hecke scheren or (be)schneiden; **to give one's fingernails a ~** sich (dat) die Fingernägel schneiden.
   (b) (sound) Klappern nt.
   (c) (hit) Schlag m. **he gave him a ~ round the ears** er haute ihm um die Ohren (inf).

(d) (inf: high speed) at a fair ~ mit einem unheimlichen Zahn (sl); he made off at a fair ~ er legte ganz schön los (inf).
(e) (from film) Ausschnitt m.

clip: ~board n Klemmbrett nt, Manuskripthalter m; ~ clop n Klipp-Klapp nt; ~ joint n (sl) Nepplokal nt (inf), Neppschuppen m (sl); ~-on adj brooch mit Klips; tie zum An- or Vorstecken; ~-on earrings Clips pl.

clipped ['klɪpt] adj accent abgehackt. ~ form Kurzform f.

clipper ['klɪpə^r] n (Naut) Klipper m; (Aviat) Clipper m.

clippers ['klɪpəz] npl (also pair of ~) Schere f; (for hedge also) Heckenschere f; (for hair) Haarschneidemaschine f; (for fingernails) Zwicker m, Nagelzange f.

clippie ['klɪpɪ] n (Brit inf) Schaffnerin f.

clipping ['klɪpɪŋ] n (newspaper ~) Ausschnitt m. nail ~s abgeschnittene Nägel.

clique [kliːk] n Clique f, Klüngel m (inf).

cliquish ['kliːkɪʃ] adj cliquenhaft, klüngelhaft (inf).

cliquishness ['kliːkɪʃnɪs] n Cliquenwirtschaft f, Klüngel m (inf).

clitoris ['klɪtərɪs] n Klitoris f, Kitzler m.

cloak [kləʊk] 1 n (lit) Umhang m; (fig) (disguise) Deckmantel m; (veil: of secrecy etc) Schleier m. under the ~ of darkness im Schutz der Dunkelheit. 2 vt (fig) verhüllen. fog ~ed the town die Stadt war in Nebel gehüllt.

cloak: ~-and-dagger adj mysteriös, geheimnisumwittert; ~-and-dagger play Kriminalstück nt; a ~-and-dagger operation eine Nacht-und-Nebel-Aktion; there's something of a ~-and-dagger atmosphere about it die Sache ist reichlich mysteriös; ~room n (a) (for coats) Garderobe f; (b) (Brit euph) Waschraum m (euph).

clobber ['klɒbə^r] (sl) 1 n (Brit: clothes, belongings) Klamotten pl (sl). 2 vt (a) (hit, defeat) to get ~ed eins übergebraten kriegen (sl); to ~ sb one jdm ein paar vor den Latz knallen (sl). **(b)** (charge a lot) schröpfen. the taxman really ~ed me das Finanzamt hat mir ganz schön was abgeknöpft (inf).

clobbering ['klɒbərɪŋ] n (sl) (beating, defeat) Tracht f Prügel (inf), Dresche f (inf). to get a ~ Dresche (inf) or eine Tracht Prügel (inf) beziehen; (from the taxman) ganz schön geschröpft werden or was abgeknöpft kriegen (inf).

cloche [klɒʃ] n (a) (hat) Topfhut m. (b) (for plants) Folien-/Glasschutz m. ~ tunnel Folientunnel m.

clock [klɒk] 1 n (a) Uhr f. round the ~ rund um die Uhr; against the ~ (Sport) nach or auf Zeit; to work against the ~ gegen die Uhr arbeiten; to put the ~ back/forward or on (lit) die Uhr zurückstellen/vorstellen; to put or set or turn the ~ back (fig) die Zeit zurückdrehen.
(b) (inf: speedometer, milometer) Tacho m (inf); (of taxi) Uhr f. it's got 100 on the ~ es hat einen Tachostand von 100.
2 vt (a) (Sport) he ~ed four minutes for the mile er lief die Meile in vier Minuten; he's ~ed the fastest time this year er ist die schnellste Zeit dieses Jahres gelaufen/gefahren.
(b) (Brit inf: hit) he ~ed him one er hat ihm eine runtergehauen (inf).

♦**clock in** (Sport) he ~ed ~ at 3 minutes 56 seconds seine Zeit war 3 min 56 sec.

♦**clock in** or **on** 1 vi (den Arbeitsbeginn) stempeln or stechen. 2 vt sep to ~ sb ~ für jdn stempeln or stechen.

♦**clock off** or **out** 1 vi (das Arbeitsende) stempeln or stechen. 2 vt sep to ~ sb ~ für jdn stempeln or stechen.

♦**clock up** vt sep (a) (athlete, competitor) time laufen; fahren; schwimmen etc. (b) speed, distance fahren. (c) (inf) success verbuchen. that's another successful deal to ~ ~ to Jim noch ein erfolgreiches Geschäft, das Jim für sich verbuchen kann; to ~ ~ overtime Überstunden machen.

clock in cpds Uhr(en)-; ~ face n Zifferblatt nt; ~ golf n Uhrengolf nt; ~ maker n Uhrmacher(in f) m; ~-radio n Radiouhr f; ~ tower n Uhrenturm m; ~-watcher n she's a terrible ~-watcher sie sieht or guckt dauernd auf die Uhr; ~-watching n Auf-die-Uhr-Schauen nt; ~wise adj, adv im Uhrzeigersinn; in a ~wise direction im Uhrzeigersinn; ~work 1 n (of clock) Uhrwerk nt; (of toy) Aufziehmechanismus m; driven by ~work, ~work driven zum Aufziehen; like ~work wie am Schnürchen; 2 attr (a) train, car aufziehbar, zum Aufziehen; (b) with ~work precision/regularity mit der Präzision/Regelmäßigkeit eines Uhrwerks; he arrives every day at 9.30 with ~work regularity er kommt jeden Tag pünktlich auf die Minute um 9³⁰.

clod [klɒd] n (a) (of earth) Klumpen m. (b) (fig: person; also ~pole) Trottel m. this silly great ~ dieser Obertrottel (inf).

clodhopper ['klɒd,hɒpə^r] n (a) (person) Trampel nt (inf), Tolpatsch m. (b) (shoe) Quadratlatschen m (inf).

clog [klɒg] 1 n (shoe) Holzschuh m. ~s (modern) Clogs pl; ~ dance Holzschuhtanz m.
2 vt (also ~ up) pipe, drain etc verstopfen; mechanism, wheels blockieren. emotionally ~ged (fig) emotional blockiert; don't ~ your argument with inessential points verlieren Sie sich nicht in Nebensächlichkeiten.
3 vi (also ~ up) (pipe etc) verstopfen; (mechanism etc) blockiert werden.

cloggy ['klɒgɪ] adj (inf) klumpig.

cloister ['klɔɪstə^r] 1 n (a) (covered walk) Kreuzgang m. (b) (monastery) Kloster nt. 2 vr to ~ oneself (away) sich von der Welt abkapseln; he ~ed himself away with his books er hat sich mit seinen Büchern zurückgezogen.

cloistered ['klɔɪstəd] adj (a) (fig) weltabgeschieden; way of thinking weltfremd or -fern (liter). to lead a ~ life (isolated) in klösterlicher Abgeschiedenheit leben; (sheltered) ein streng or klösterlich behütetes Leben führen.
(b) (Archit) a ~ courtyard ein Klosterhof m mit Kreuzgang.

clone [kləʊn] 1 n Klon m. 2 vt klonen.

clonk [klɒŋk] (inf) 1 vt hauen. 2 n (blow) Schlag m; (sound) Plumps m.

close[1] [kləʊs] 1 adj (+er) (a) (near) nahe (to gen), in der Nähe (to gen, von). is Glasgow ~ to Edinburgh? liegt Glasgow in der Nähe von Edinburgh?; the buildings which are ~ to the station die Gebäude in der Nähe des Bahnhofs or in Bahnhofsnähe; ~ proximity in unmittelbarer Nähe (to gen); in such ~ proximity (to one another) so dicht zusammen; you're very ~ (in guessing etc) du bist dicht dran; ~ combat Nahkampf m; at ~ quarters aus unmittelbarer Nähe; he chose the ~st cake er nahm den Kuchen, der am nächsten lag; we use this pub because it's ~/the ~st wir gehen in dieses Lokal, weil es in der Nähe/am nächsten ist.
(b) (in time) nahe (bevorstehend). nobody realized how ~ a nuclear war was es war niemandem klar, wie nahe ein Atomkrieg bevorstand.
(c) (fig) friend, co-operation, connection etc eng; relative nahe; resemblance groß, stark. they were very ~ (to each other) sie waren or standen sich or einander (geh) sehr nahe.
(d) (not spread out) handwriting, print eng; texture, weave dicht, fest; grain dicht, fein; ranks dicht, geschlossen; (fig) argument lückenlos, stichhaltig; reasoning, (Sport) game geschlossen. ~ harmony singers Vokalgruppe f, die im Barbershop-Stil singt; they played a very ~ game sie spielten mit kurzen Pässen or geschlossen.
(e) (exact, painstaking) examination, study eingehend, genau; translation originalgetreu; watch streng, scharf; arrest scharf. now pay ~ attention to me jetzt hör mir gut zu; you have to pay very ~ attention to the traffic signs du mußt genau auf die Verkehrszeichen achten; to keep a ~ lookout for sb/sth scharf nach jdm/etw Ausschau halten.
(f) (stuffy) schwül; (inside) stickig.
(g) (almost equal) fight, result knapp. a ~(-fought) match ein (ganz) knappes Spiel; a ~ finish ein Kopf-an-Kopf-Rennen nt; a ~ election ein Kopf-an-Kopf-Rennen nt, eine Wahl mit knappem Ausgang; it was a ~ thing or call das war knapp!
(h) ~ on nahezu; ~ on sixty/midnight an die sechzig/kurz vor Mitternacht.
2 adv (+er) nahe; (spatially also) dicht. ~ by in der Nähe; ~ by us in unserer Nähe; stay ~ to me bleib dicht bei mir; ~ to the water/ground nahe or dicht am Wasser/Boden; ~ to or by the bridge nahe (bei) der Brücke; he followed ~ behind me er ging dicht hinter mir; don't stand too ~ to the fire stell dich nicht zu nahe or dicht ans Feuer; ~ against the wall dicht or nahe an der/die Mauer; to be ~ to tears den Tränen nahe sein; ~ together dicht or nahe zusammen; my exams were so ~ together meine Prüfungen lagen so kurz hintereinander; the ~r the exams came the more nervous he got je näher die Prüfung rückte, desto nervöser wurde er; that brought the two brothers ~r together das brachte die beiden Brüder einander näher; please stand ~r together bitte rücken Sie näher or dichter zusammen; this pattern comes ~/~st to the sort of thing we wanted dieses Muster kommt dem, was wir uns vorgestellt haben, nahe/am nächsten; what does it look like from ~ in/up? wie sieht es von nahem aus?; if you get too ~ up ... wenn du zu nahe herangehst ...
3 n (in street names) Hof m; (of cathedral etc) Domhof m; (Scot: outside passage) offener Hausflur.

close[2] [kləʊz] 1 vt (a) (shut) eyes, door, shop, window, curtains also zumachen; (permanently) business, shop, branch etc also schließen; factory stillegen; (block) pipe, opening etc verschließen; road sperren. "~d" „geschlossen"; sorry, we're ~d tut uns leid, wir haben geschlossen or zu; you shouldn't ~ your mind to new ideas du solltest dich neuen Ideen nicht verschließen; to ~ one's eyes/ears to sth sich einer Sache gegenüber blind/taub stellen; to ~ ranks (Mil) die Reihen schließen.
(b) (bring to an end) church service, meeting schließen, beenden; affair, discussion also abschließen; bank account etc auflösen. the matter is ~d der Fall ist abgeschlossen.
(c) (Elec) circuit schließen.
2 vi (a) (shut, come together) sich schließen; (door, window, box, lid, eyes, wound also) zugehen; (can be shut) schließen, zugehen; (shop, factory) schließen, zumachen; (factory: permanently) stillgelegt werden. his eyes ~d die Augen fielen ihm zu; (in death) seine Augen schlossen sich.
(b) (come to an end) schließen; (tourist season) aufhören, enden, zu Ende gehen; (Theat: play) auslaufen.
(c) (approach) sich nähern, näherkommen; (boxers etc) aufeinander losgehen. the battleship ~d to 100 metres das Kriegsschiff kam bis auf 100 Meter heran.
(d) (Comm: accept offer) abschließen, zu einem Abschluß kommen.
(e) (St Ex) schließen. the shares ~d at £5 die Aktien erreichten eine Schlußnotierung von £ 5.
3 n End *e* nt, Schluß m. to come to a ~ enden, aufhören, zu Ende gehen; to draw to a ~ sich dem Ende nähern, dem Ende zugehen; to draw or bring sth to a ~ etw beenden; at/towards the ~ of (the) day am/gegen Ende des Tages; at the ~ (of business) bei Geschäfts- or (St Ex) Börsenschluß.

♦**close about** or **around** vi +prep obj umschließen, sich schließen um. the waters ~d ~ the drowning man die Wellen schlugen über dem Ertrinkenden zusammen.

♦**close down** 1 vi (a) (business, shop etc) schließen, zumachen (inf); (factory: permanently) stillgelegt werden.
(b) (Rad, TV) das Programm beenden. television programmes ~ ~ at about 12 Sendeschluß (ist) gegen 24 Uhr; we're now closing ~ for the night (und) damit ist unser heutiges Programm beendet.
2 vt sep shop etc schließen; factory (permanently) stillegen.

♦**close in** 1 vi (evening, winter) anbrechen; (night, darkness) hereinbrechen; (days) kürzer werden; (enemy etc) bedrohlich nahekommen. the troops ~d ~ around the enemy die Truppen

zogen sich um den Feind zusammen; **to ~ ~ on sb** (*gang, individual etc*) jdm auf den Leib rücken; **the walls were slowly closing ~ on him** die Wände kamen langsam auf ihn zu; **the police are closing ~ on him** die Polizei zieht das Netz um ihn zu; (*physically*) die Polizisten umzingeln ihn.
2 *vt sep* umgeben, umfrieden (*geh*).

♦**close off** *vt sep* abriegeln, (ab)sperren; (*separate off*) *area of office etc* abteilen, abtrennen.

♦**close on** *vi* +*prep obj* einholen.

♦**close round** *vi* +*prep obj see* **close about**.

♦**close up 1** *vi* (a) (*line of people*) aufschließen, zusammenrücken; (*Mil*) aufschließen; (*wound*) (sich) schließen. (b) (*lock up*) ab- or zuschließen, ab- or zusperren. **2** *vt sep* (a) *house, shop* zumachen; *house also* verschließen; *shop also* ab- or zuschließen, ab- or zusperren. (b) (*block up*) zumachen.

♦**close with** *vi* +*prep obj* (a) *enemy* zum Nahkampf übergehen mit; *boxer etc* ringen or kämpfen mit. (b) (*strike bargain with*) handelseinig sein or werden mit; (*accept*) *offer* eingehen auf.

close-cropped [ ] *adj hair* kurzgeschnitten.

closed [kləʊzd]: **~ circuit** *n* geschlossener Stromkreis; **~-circuit television** *n* interne Fernsehanlage; (*for supervision*) Fernsehüberwachungsanlage *f*.

close-down ['kləʊzdaʊn] *n* (a) (*of shop, business etc*) (Geschäfts)schließung *f*; (*of factory*) Stillegung *f*. (b) (*Rad, TV*) Sendeschluß *m*.

closed [kləʊzd]: **~ scholarship** *n* an eine bestimmte Schule gebundenes Stipendium; **~ season** *n* Schonzeit *f*; **~ session** *n* (*Jur*) Sitzung *f* unter Ausschluß der Öffentlichkeit; **~ shop** *n* Closed Shop *m*; **we have a ~ shop** wir haben Gewerkschaftszwang.

close [kləʊs]: **~-fisted** *adj* geizig, knauserig (*inf*); **~-fitting** *adj* enganliegend, eng sitzend; **~-grained** *adj* fein gemasert; **~-knit** *adj, comp* **~r-knit** *community* eng or fest zusammengewachsen.

closely ['kləʊslɪ] *adv* (a) eng, dicht; *work, connect* eng; *woven* fest; *related* nah(e), eng; *follow* (*in time*) dicht. **he was ~ followed by a policeman** ein Polizist ging dicht hinter ihm; **she held the baby ~** sie drückte das Baby (fest) an sich; **~ reasoned** schlüssig dargestellt or -gelegt; **the match was ~ contested** der Spielausgang war hart umkämpft.
(b) (*attentively*) *watch, listen etc* genau; *study also* eingehend; *guard* scharf, streng.

close-mouthed [ˌkləʊs'maʊðd] *adj* verschwiegen.

closeness ['kləʊsnɪs] *n* (a) (*nearness, in time*) Nähe *f*. **she could feel his ~ to her** sie konnte seine Nähe fühlen.
(b) (*fig*) (*of friendship*) Innigkeit *f*. **thanks to the ~ of their cooperation ...** dank ihrer engen Zusammenarbeit ...; **the ~ of their relationship/resemblance caused problems** ihre so enge Beziehung/ihre große Ähnlichkeit verursachte Probleme.
(c) (*density*) (*fig: of argument, reasoning*) Schlüssigkeit *f*; (*Sport: of game*) Geschlossenheit *f*. **the ~ of the print/lines/weave etc** die große Druck-/Zeilen-/(Ge)webedichte; **the ~ of the grain** die feine Maserung.
(d) (*exactness, painstakingness*) (*of examination, interrogation*) Genauigkeit *f*; (*of watch*) Strenge *f*; (*of translation*) Textnähe or -treue *f*.
(e) (*of air, atmosphere*) **the ~ (of the air)** die Schwüle; (*indoors*) die stickige Luft.
(f) (*even match*) (*of finish*) knapper Ausgang.

close-set ['kləʊset] *adj, comp* **closer-set** *eyes* eng zusammenstehend; *print* eng.

closet ['klɒzɪt] (*vb: pret, ptp* **~ed** ['klɒzɪtɪd]) **1** *n* (a) Wandschrank *m*. (b) (*dated: water-~*) Klosett *nt*. (c) (*old: small room*) Kabinett, Nebenzimmer *nt*. **2** *vt* **to be ~ed** hinter verschlossenen Türen sitzen (*with sb* mit jdm).

close-up ['kləʊsʌp] **1** *n* Nahaufnahme *f*. **in ~** in Nahaufnahme; (*of face*) in Großaufnahme. **2** *attr shot, view* Nah-.

closing ['kləʊzɪŋ] **1** *n* (a) Schließung *f*; (*of factory: permanently*) Stillegung *f*; *see* **early ~**.
(b) (*St Ex*) **at the ~ of business** beim Börsenschluß.
2 *adj* (a) *remarks, words etc* abschließend, Schluß-.
(b) **~ time** Geschäfts- or Ladenschluß *m*; (*Brit*) (*in pub*) Polizei- or Sperrstunde *f*; **when is ~ time?** wann schließt die Bank/das Geschäft/der Laden/das Lokal etc?; **some pubs have an earlier ~ time** einige Lokale schließen schon früher.
(c) (*St Ex*) **~ prices** Schlußkurse, Schlußnotierungen *pl*.

closure ['kləʊʒəʳ] *n* (a) (*act of closing*) Schließung *f*; (*of road*) Sperrung *f*; (*of wound, incision*) Schließen *nt*; (*of shop also*) Schließung *f*; (*of factory, mine etc also*) Stillegung *f*.
(b) (*Parl*) Schluß *m* der Debatte. **to move the ~** den Schluß der Debatte beantragen; **to apply the ~ to a debate** das Ende einer Debatte erklären.

clot [klɒt] **1** *n* (a) (*of blood*) (Blut)gerinnsel *nt*; (*of milk*) (Sahne)klumpen *m*. (b) (*inf: person*) Trottel *m*. **2** *vt blood* zum Gerinnen bringen. **3** *vi* (*blood*) gerinnen; (*milk*) dick werden.

cloth [klɒθ] *n* (a) Tuch *nt*, Stoff *m*; (*as book-cover*) Leinen *nt*. **a nice piece of ~** ein schöner Stoff, ein gutes Tuch; **made of fine ~** aus feinem Tuch; **~ of gold** goldenes Tuch.
(b) (*dish~, tea~ etc*) Tuch *nt*; (*for cleaning also*) Lappen *m*; (*table~*) Tischdecke *f*, Tischtuch *nt*.
(c) *no pl* (*Eccl*) **a gentleman of the ~** ein geistlicher Herr; **the ~** der geistliche Stand, die Geistlichkeit.

cloth: **~-bound** *adj book* in Leinen (gebunden); **~ cap** *n* Schlägermütze *f*.

clothe [kləʊð] *pret, ptp* **clad** (*old*) or **~d** *vt* (a) (*usu pass: dress*) anziehen, kleiden. **she appeared ~d in white** (*liter*) sie erschien (ganz) in Weiß. (b) (*provide clothes for*) anziehen. (c) (*fig liter*) kleiden (*liter*). **~d in glory** mit Ruhm bedeckt; **the hills ~d in mist** die nebelverhangenen Hügel.

clothes [kləʊðz] *npl* (a) (*garments*) Kleider *pl*; (*clothing, outfit also*) Kleidung *f no pl*. **his mother still washes his ~** seine

Mutter macht ihm immer noch die Wäsche; **with one's ~ on/off** angezogen, (voll) bekleidet/ausgezogen, unbekleidet (*geh*); **you can't swim properly with your ~ on** mit or in Kleidern kann man nicht richtig schwimmen; **to put on/take off one's ~** sich an-/ausziehen; *see* **plain ~**.
(b) (*bed~*) Bettzeug *nt*.

clothes: **~ basket** *n* Wäschekorb *m*; **~ brush** *n* Kleiderbürste *f*; **~ hanger** *n* Kleiderbügel *m*; **~ horse** *n* Wäscheständer *m*; **~ line** *n* Wäscheleine *f*; **~ moth** *n* Kleidermotte *f*; **~ peg**, (*US*) **~ pin** *n* Wäscheklammer *f*; **~ pole** or **prop** *n* Wäschestütze *f*; **~ shop** *n* Bekleidungsgeschäft *nt*.

clothier ['kləʊðɪəʳ] *n* (*seller of clothes*) (*for men*) Herrenausstatter *m*; (*for women*) Modegeschäft *nt* or -salon *m*.

clothing ['kləʊðɪŋ] *n* Kleidung *f*.

clotted [klɒtɪd] *adj hair* **~ with mud** mit Schlamm verklebtes Haar; **~ cream** Sahne *f* (*aus erhitzter Milch*).

clottish ['klɒtɪʃ] *adj* (*inf*) trottelig. **a ~ thing to do** eine Eselei.

cloud [klaʊd] **1** *n* (a) Wolke *f*. **low ~(s)** verzögerten take-off tiefhängende Wolken verzögerten den Start; **to have one's head in the ~s** in höheren Regionen schweben; (*momentarily*) geistesabwesend sein; **to be up in the ~s** (*inf*) überglücklich sein; **to be on ~ nine** (*inf*) im siebten Himmel sein or schweben (*inf*); **there wasn't a ~ in the sky** (*fig*) alles war eitel Freude und Sonnenschein; **every ~ has a silver lining** (*Prov*) kein Unglück ist so groß, es hat sein Glück im Schoß (*Prov*).
(b) (*of smoke, dust etc*) Wolke *f*; (*of insects*) Schwarm, Haufen *m*; (*of gas, smoke from fire*) Schwaden *m*. **~ of dust/smoke** Staub-/Rauchwolke *f*; **a ~ of controversy/confusion surrounded the whole matter** die ganze Angelegenheit wurde von Kontroversen überschattet/nebulöses Durcheinander herrschte in der ganzen Angelegenheit; **the ~ of suspicion hanging over him suddenly dispersed** der Verdacht, der über ihm schwebte, verflog plötzlich; **will the ~ of international disapproval ever lift from his head?** wird sich der weltweite Unmut, der sich über ihm zusammengeballt hat, jemals verflüchtigen?; **he's been under a ~ for weeks** (*under suspicion*) seit Wochen haftet ein Verdacht an ihm; (*in disgrace*) die Geschichte hängt ihm schon wochenlang nach; **the ~s are gathering** es braut sich etwas zusammen.
(c) (*in liquid, marble*) Wolke *f*. **her cold breath formed ~s/a ~ on the mirror** durch ihren kalten Atem beschlug der Spiegel.
2 *vt* (a) (*lit*) *sky, view* verhängen (*geh*); *mirror* trüben. **a ~ed sky** ein bewölkter Himmel.
(b) (*fig*) (*cast gloom on*) *prospect, sb's enjoyment* trüben; *face, expression* umwölken (*geh*); (*mar, spoil*) *friendship, sb's future* überschatten; (*make less clear*) *mind, judgement, awareness* trüben; *nature of problem* verschleiern. **to ~ the issue** (*complicate*) es unnötig kompliziert machen; (*hide deliberately*) die Angelegenheit verschleiern.
3 *vi see* **~ over**.

♦**cloud over** *vi* (*sky*) sich bewölken, sich bedecken; (*mirror etc*) sich beschlagen, anlaufen. **his face ~ed** seine Stirn umwölkte sich (*geh*).

♦**cloud up 1** *vi* (*mirror etc*) beschlagen. **it's ~ing ~** (*weather*) es bezieht sich. **2** *vt sep* **the steam ~ed ~ the windows** die Fenster beschlugen (vom Dampf).

cloud: **~ bank** *n* Wolkenwand *f*; **~burst** *n* Wolkenbruch *m*; **~-capped** *adj* (*liter*) **the ~-capped mountains/peaks** die wolkenverhangenen Berge/Gipfel; **~ chamber** *n* Nebelkammer *f*; **~-cuckoo-land** *n* Wolkenkuckucksheim *nt*.

cloudiness ['klaʊdɪnɪs] *n* (*of sky*) Bewölkung *f*; (*of liquid, diamond, glass, plastic etc*) Trübung *f*.

cloudless ['klaʊdlɪs] *adj sky* wolkenlos.

cloudy ['klaʊdɪ] *adj* (+*er*) (a) *sky* wolkig, bewölkt, bedeckt; *weather* grau. **we had only three ~ days** wir hatten nur drei Tage, an denen es bewölkt war; **it's getting ~** es bewölkt sich; **the weather will be ~** es ist mit Bewölkung zu rechnen.
(b) *liquid, diamond, glass etc* trüb.

clout [klaʊt] **1** *n* (a) (*inf: blow*) Schlag *m*. **to give sb/sth a ~** jdm eine runterhauen (*inf*)/auf etw (*acc*) schlagen or hauen (*inf*); **to give sb a ~ round the ears/on the arm** jdm eine runterhauen (*inf*), jdm eine Ohrfeige geben/jdm eins or eine auf den Arm schlagen or hauen (*inf*); **to give oneself a ~ on the knee, to give one's knee a ~** sich (*dat*) aufs Knie hauen (*inf*); (*against door etc*) sich (*dat*) das Knie (an)stoßen or anschlagen.
(b) (*political, industrial*) Schlagkraft *f*.
2 *vt* (*inf*) schlagen, hauen (*inf*). **to ~ sb one** jdm eine runterhauen (*inf*) or eine verpassen (*inf*).

clove[1] [kləʊv] *n* (a) Gewürznelke *f*. **oil of ~s** Nelkenöl *nt*. (b) **~ of garlic** Knoblauchzehe *f*.

clove[2] *pret of* **cleave**[1].

clove hitch *n* Webeleinstek *m*.

cloven ['kləʊvn] *ptp of* **cleave**[1].

cloven hoof *n* Huf *m* der Paarhufer or -zeher; (*of devil*) Pferdefuß *m*. **pigs have ~ hooves** Schweine sind Paarzeher.

clover ['kləʊvəʳ] *n* Klee *m*. **to be/live in ~** wie Gott in Frankreich leben; **~ leaf** (*Bot, Mot*) Kleeblatt *nt*.

clown [klaʊn] **1** *n* (*in circus etc*) Clown *m*; (*inf: foolish person also*) Kasper, Hanswurst *m*; (*pej*) Idiot, Trottel *m*. **to act the ~** den Clown or Hanswurst spielen, herumkaspern (*inf*). **2** *vi* (*also* **~ about** or **around**) herumblödeln (*inf*) or -kaspern (*inf*).

cloy [klɔɪ] *vi* (*lit, fig*) zu süßlich sein/werden; (*pleasures*) an Reiz verlieren.

cloying ['klɔɪɪŋ] *adj* (*lit*) übersüß, widerwärtig süß. **these ~ pleasures** diese Freuden, deren man so schnell überdrüssig wird.

club [klʌb] **1** *n* (a) (*weapon*) Knüppel, Prügel *m*, Keule *f*; (*golf ~*) Golfschläger *m*; (*Indian ~*) Keule *f*.
(b) (*Cards*) **~s** *pl* Kreuz *nt*; **the ace/nine of ~s** (das) Kreuz-As/(die) Kreuz-Neun.
(c) (*society*) Klub, Verein *m*; (*tennis ~, golf ~, gentleman's*

~, night~) Club m; (Ftbl) Verein m. **to be in the** ~ (inf) in anderen Umständen sein (inf), ein Kind kriegen (inf); **to get or put sb in the** ~ (inf) jdm ein Kind machen (sl); **join the** ~**!** (inf) gratuliere! du auch!

2 vt einknüppeln auf (+acc), knüppeln.

♦ **club together** vi zusammenlegen.

♦ **clubbable** ['klʌbəbl] adj geeignet, in einen Klub aufgenommen zu werden; (sociable) gesellschaftsfähig.

club: ~ **foot** n Klumpfuß m; ~-**footed** adj klumpfüßig; ~**house** n Klubhaus nt; ~**land** n Klubviertel m, vornehmer Stadtteil, in dem sich besonders viele Klubs befinden; ~**man** n he isn't much of a ~man er interessiert sich nicht besonders für Klubs; as a ~man himself ... als einer, der sich in or mit Klubs auskennt ...; ~ **room** n Klubraum nt; ~ **sandwich** n (US) Club-Sandwich nt.

cluck [klʌk] 1 vi gackern; (hen: to chicks) glucken. 2 n Gackern nt; Glucken nt.

clue [kluː] n Anhaltspunkt, Hinweis m; (in police search also: object) Spur f; (in crosswords) Frage f. **to find a/the** ~ **to sth** den Schlüssel zu etw finden; **I'll give you a** ~ ich gebe dir einen Tip; **I haven't a** ~**!** (ich hab') keine Ahnung!

♦ **clue up** vt sep (inf) person informieren. **to get** ~**d** ~ **on or about sth** sich mit etw vertraut machen; **to be** ~**d** ~ **on or about sth** über etw (acc) im Bilde sein; (about subject) mit etw vertraut sein.

clueless ['kluːlɪs] adj (inf) ahnungslos, unbedarft (inf); expression, look ratlos.

cluelessly ['kluːlɪslɪ] adv (inf) see adj.

clump [klʌmp] 1 n (a) (of trees, flowers etc) Gruppe f; (of earth) Klumpen m. **a** ~ **of shrubs** ein Gebüsch nt. (b) (inf: blow) Schlag, Hieb m. 2 vt (inf: hit) schlagen, hauen (inf). 3 vi trampeln; (with adv of place) stapfen. **to** ~ **about** herumtrampeln; (in snow, mud etc) herumstapfen.

clumsily ['klʌmzɪlɪ] adv (a) ungeschickt; (in an ungainly way) schwerfällig; act ungeschickt. (b) (inelegantly) written, translated etc schwerfällig, unbeholfen. (c) (awkwardly, tactlessly) ungeschickt, unbeholfen; compliment also plump.

clumsiness ['klʌmzɪnɪs] n (a) Ungeschicklichkeit, Schwerfälligkeit f. (b) (of tool, shape) Unförmigkeit f; (of prose, translation etc) Schwerfälligkeit, Unbeholfenheit f. (c) (awkwardness of apology, excuse etc) Unbeholfenheit f.

clumsy ['klʌmzɪ] adj (+er) (a) ungeschickt; (all thumbs also) tolpatschig; (ungainly) schwerfällig.
(b) (unwieldy) plump; tool also wuchtig, klobig; shape also unförmig, klobig; (inelegant) prose, translation etc schwerfällig, unbeholfen; (careless) mistake dumm.
(c) (awkward, tactless) plump, ungeschickt.

clung [klʌŋ] pret, ptp of **cling**[1].

cluster ['klʌstə[r]] 1 n (of trees, flowers, houses) Gruppe f, Haufen m; (of curls, bananas) Büschel nt; (of bees, people, grapes) Traube f; (of islands) Gruppe f; (of diamonds) Büschel nt; (Phon) Häufung f. **the flowers grow in a** ~ **at the top of the stem** die Blumen sitzen or wachsen doldenförmig am Stengel; (of roses etc) mehrere Blüten wachsen am gleichen Stiel.
2 vi (people) sich drängen or scharen. **they all** ~**ed round to see what he was doing** alle drängten or scharten sich um ihn, um zu sehen, was er tat or um ihn zuzusehen.

clutch[1] [klʌtʃ] 1 n (a) (grip) Griff m. **he had a firm** ~ **on the rope** er hielt das Seil fest umklammert; **he made a sudden** ~ **at the rope** er griff plötzlich nach dem Seil.
(b) (Aut) Kupplung f. **to let in/out the** ~ ein-/auskuppeln; ~ **pedal** Kupplungspedal nt.
(c) (fig) **to fall into sb's** ~**es** jdm in die Hände fallen, jdm ins Netz gehen; **to be in sb's** ~**es** in jds Gewalt (dat) sein; **to have sb in one's** ~**es** jdn im Netz or in den Klauen haben; **he escaped her** ~**es** er entkam ihren Klauen.
2 vt (grab) umklammern, packen; (hold tightly) umklammern halten. **to** ~ **sth in one's hand** etw umklammern.

♦ **clutch at** vi +prep obj (lit) schnappen nach (+dat), greifen; (hold tightly) umklammert halten; (fig) sich klammern an (+acc); see straw.

clutch[2] n (of chickens) Brut f; (of eggs) Gelege nt.

clutch bag n Klemmtasche f.

clutter ['klʌtə[r]] 1 n (confusion) Durcheinander nt; (disorderly articles) Kram m (inf). **his desk was in a** ~ auf seinem Schreibtisch war ein fürchterliches Durcheinander; **his essay was a** ~ **of unrelated details** sein Aufsatz war ein Sammelsurium or Wirrwarr von zusammenhangslosen Einzelheiten.
2 vt (also ~ **up**) zu voll machen (inf/stellen; painting, photograph überladen; mind vollstopfen. **to be** ~**ed with sth** (mind, room, drawer etc) mit etw vollgestopft sein; (floor, desk etc) mit etw übersät sein; (painting etc) mit etw überladen sein; **the floor/his desk was absolutely** ~**ed** auf dem Fußboden lag alles verstreut/sein Schreibtisch war ganz voll; **he has a** ~**ed mind** in seinem Kopf geht alles drunter und drüber.

cm abbr of **centimetre** cm.

Cmdr abbr of **Commander**.

CNAA abbr of **Council for National Academic Awards**.

CND abbr of **Campaign for Nuclear Disarmament**.

Co abbr of (a) **company** KG f. (b) **county**.

CO abbr of **Commanding Officer**.

c/o abbr of (a) **care of** z.Hd., c/o. (b) **carried over** Übertr.

co- [kəʊ-] pref Mit-, mit-.

coach [kəʊtʃ] 1 n (a) (horsedrawn) Kutsche f; (state ~) (Staats)karosse f. ~ **and four** Vierspänner m.
(b) (Rail) (Eisenbahn)wagen, Waggon m.
(c) (motor ~) (Reise)bus m. **by** ~ mit dem Bus; ~ **travel/journeys** Busreisen pl; ~ **driver** Busfahrer m.
(d) (tutor) Nachhilfelehrer(in f) m; (Sport) Trainer m.
2 vt (a) (Sport) trainieren.
(b) pupil **to** ~ **sb for an exam** jdn aufs Examen vorbereiten;

he had been ~**ed in what to say** man hatte mit ihm eingeübt, was er sagen sollte.

coach: ~ **box** n (Kutsch)bock m; ~**builder** n (Brit) Karosseriebauer m; ~**-house** n (old) Remise f.

coaching ['kəʊtʃɪŋ] n (Sport) Trainerstunden pl; (Tennis) Training nt; (tutoring) Nachhilfe f.

coach: ~**man** n Kutscher m; ~**work** n (Brit) Karosserie f.

coagulate [kəʊˈægjʊleɪt] 1 vi (blood) gerinnen, koagulieren (spec); (junket, milk) dick werden; (jelly) fest werden; (paint, varnish) zähflüssig werden, eindicken. 2 vt blood gerinnen lassen; junket, milk dick werden lassen; jelly fest werden lassen; paint, varnish zähflüssig werden or eindicken lassen.

coagulation [kəʊˌægjʊˈleɪʃən] n see vb Gerinnen nt, Gerinnung, Koagulation (spec) f; Dickwerden nt; Festwerden nt; Eindicken nt.

coal [kəʊl] n Kohle f. **we still burn** ~ wir heizen noch mit Kohle; **to carry** ~**s to Newcastle** (Prov) Eulen nach Athen tragen (Prov); **to haul sb over the** ~**s** jdm eine Standpauke halten, jdm die Leviten lesen; **to heap** ~**s of fire on sb's head** glühende Kohlen auf jds Haupt (dat) sammeln.

coal in cpds Kohlen-; ~-**bin**, ~-**bunker** n Kohlenkasten m; ~ **black** adj kohlrabenschwarz; ~-**cellar** n Kohlenkeller m; ~**dust** n Kohlenstaub, (Kohlen)grus m.

coalesce [ˌkəʊəˈles] vi (Phys, Chem) sich verbinden, eine Verbindung eingehen; (fig) sich vereinigen, zusammengehen; (views, opinions etc) sich verquicken (geh).

coalescence [ˌkəʊəˈlesəns] n see vi Verbindung f; Vereinigung f; Verquickung f (geh).

coal: ~-**face** n Streb m; **men who work at or on the** ~-**face** Männer, die im Streb or vor Ort arbeiten; ~**field** n Kohlenrevier, Kohlengebiet nt; ~ **fire** n Kamin m; **a** ~ **fire heats better** ein Kohlefeuer wärmt besser; ~-**hole** n Kohlenbunker m.

coalition [ˌkəʊəˈlɪʃən] n Koalition f. ~ **government** Koalitionsregierung f.

coal: ~**man** n Kohlenmann m; ~-**merchant** n Kohlenhändler m; ~-**mine** n Grube, Zeche f, Kohlenbergwerk nt; ~-**miner** n Bergmann, Kumpel (inf) m; ~-**mining** n Kohle(n)bergbau m; ~-**mining area** n Kohlenrevier nt; **the** ~-**mining industry** der Kohle(n)bergbau; ~-**pit** n see ~-**mine**; ~ **scuttle** n Kohleneimer, Kohlenkasten m; ~**shed** n Kohlenschuppen m; ~ **tar** n Kohlenteer m; ~ **tar soap** n Teerseife f; ~ **yard** n Kohlenhof m.

coarse [kɔːs] adj (+er) (a) (in texture, not delicate) grob; sand, sugar also grobkörnig; features also derb. ~-**grained** grobfaserig; ~-**grained fibre** grobe Faser; ~-**grained paper** ungeleimtes Papier, Zeitungspapier nt.
(b) (uncouth) gewöhnlich; person, manners also grob, ungehobelt, ungeschliffen; laugh also rauh, derb; joke also derb, unanständig.
(c) (common) food derb, einfach. ~ **red wine** einfacher (Land)rotwein; ~ **fish** Süßwasserfisch m (mit Ausnahme aller Lachs- und Forellenarten).

coarsely ['kɔːslɪ] adv see adj (a, b).

coarsen ['kɔːsn] 1 vt person derber machen; skin gerben. 2 vi (person) derber werden; (skin) gröber werden.

coarseness ['kɔːsnɪs] n (a) (of texture) Grobheit f.
(b) (fig) see adj (b, c) Gewöhnlichkeit f; Grobheit, Ungeschliffenheit f; Derbheit f; Unanständigkeit f; Einfachheit f. **the** ~ **of the soldier's laugh** das rauhe Lachen des Soldaten; **the** ~ **of his accent** seine gewöhnliche Aussprache.

coast [kəʊst] 1 n Küste f, Gestade nt (poet). **at/on the** ~ an der Küste/am Meer; **we live on the** ~ wir fahren an die Küste or ans Meer; **the** ~ **is clear** (fig) die Luft ist rein.
2 vi (a) (car, cyclist) (in neutral) (im Leerlauf) fahren; (cruise effortlessly) dahinrollen; (athlete) locker laufen; (US: on sled) hinunterrodeln.
(b) (fig) **to be** ~**ing along** mühelos or spielend vorankommen; **he was just** ~**ing up to the exam** er steuerte ohne große Mühe aufs Examen zu.

coastal ['kəʊstəl] adj Küsten-. ~ **traffic** Küstenschiffahrt f.

coaster ['kəʊstə[r]] n (a) (Naut) Küstenmotorschiff, Kümo (abbr) nt. (b) (drip mat) Untersetzer m. (c) (US) (sled) (Rodel)schlitten m; (roller-~) Achterbahn, Berg- und Talbahn f. (d) (US) ~ **brake** Rücktrittbremse f.

coast: ~**guard** n Küstenwache f; **the** ~**guards** die Küstenwacht; ~**guard boat/station** Küstenwachtboot nt/-posten m; ~**line** n Küste f.

coat [kəʊt] 1 n (a) (outdoor wear) Mantel m; (doctor's ~ etc also) (Arzt)kittel m; (jacket of suit etc) Jacke f; (for men also) Jackett nt. ~ **and skirt** Kostüm nt.
(b) (Her) ~ **of arms** Wappen nt.
(c) ~ **of mail** Panzerhemd nt; (of chainmail) Kettenhemd nt.
(d) (of animal) Fell nt.
(e) (of paint, tar etc) (application) Anstrich m; (actual layer) Schicht f. **a thick** ~ **of fur on his tongue** ein dicker pelziger Belag auf seiner Zunge; **give it a second** ~ streich es noch einmal.
2 vt (with paint etc) streichen; (with chocolate, icing etc) überziehen. **to be** ~**ed with rust/dust/mud** mit einer Rost-/Staub-/Schmutzschicht überzogen sein, eine Rost-/Staub-/Schmutzschicht haben; **my hands were** ~**ed with grease/flour** meine Hände waren voller Schmiere/Mehl; **his tongue was** ~**ed** seine Zunge war belegt; ~**ed paper** gestrichenes Papier; **the chassis was** ~**ed with an anti-rust preparation** das Chassis war mit einem Rostschutzmittel beschichtet or (sprayed) gespritzt.

coat-hanger ['kəʊtˌhæŋə[r]] n Kleiderbügel m.

coating ['kəʊtɪŋ] n Überzug m, Schicht f; (of paint) Anstrich m.

coat: ~**less** adj ohne Mantel; ~**tails** npl Rockschöße pl.

co-author ['kəʊˌɔːθə[r]] n Mitautor, Mitverfasser m. **they were** ~**s of the book** sie haben das Buch gemeinsam geschrieben.

coax [kəʊks] vt überreden. to ~ sb into doing sth jdn beschwatzen (inf) or dazu bringen, etw zu tun; he ~ed the engine into life er brachte den Motor mit List und Tücke in Gang; you have to ~ the fire with a little paraffin du mußt dem Feuer mit einem Schuß Petroleum nachhelfen; to ~ sth out of sb jdm etw entlocken.

coaxing [ˈkəʊksɪŋ] 1 n gutes Zureden, Zuspruch m. with a little ~ the engine/fire started mit etwas List und Tücke kam der Motor/das Feuer in Gang. 2 adj einschmeichelnd.

coaxingly [ˈkəʊksɪŋlɪ] adv to speak/ask ~ mit einschmeichelnder Stimme reden/fragen; however ~ she spoke to him ... so sehr sich auch versuchte, ihn zu überreden ...

cob [kɒb] n (a) (horse) kleines, gedrungenes Pferd. (b) (swan) (männlicher) Schwan. (c) (also ~-nut) (große) Haselnuß. (d) (corn) (Mais)kolben m; (bread) rundes Brot. corn on the ~ Maiskolben m; a ~ of coal ein Stück Eier- or Nußkohle.

cobalt [ˈkəʊbɒlt] n Kobalt nt. ~ blue kobaltblau.

cobber [ˈkɒbəʳ] n (Austral inf) Kumpel m (inf).

cobble [ˈkɒbl] 1 n (also ~stone) Kopfstein m. 2 vt (a) shoe flicken. (b) a ~d street eine Straße mit Kopfsteinpflaster; the street was ~d die Straße hatte Kopfsteinpflaster.
♦ **cobble together** vt sep (inf) essay etc zusammenschustern.

cobbler [ˈkɒbləʳ] n (a) Schuster, Flickschuster m. (b) (esp US: fruit pie) Obst mit Teig überbacken; (drink) Cobbler m.

cobblers [ˈkɒbləz] npl (Brit sl: rubbish) Scheiße f (sl), Mist m (inf). (what a load of old) ~! was für'n Haufen Mist! (inf).

cobblestone [ˈkɒblstəʊn] n see cobble 1.

cobra [ˈkəʊbrə] n Kobra f.

cobweb [ˈkɒbweb] n (single thread, threads) Spinn(en)webe f; (network) Spinnennetz nt. a brisk walk will blow away the ~s (fig) ein ordentlicher Spaziergang, und man hat wieder einen klaren Kopf.

cocaine [kəˈkeɪn] n Kokain nt.

coccyx [ˈkɒksɪks] n Steißbein nt.

cochineal [ˈkɒtʃiniːl] n (insect, colouring) Koschenille f.

cock [kɒk] 1 n (a) (rooster) Hahn m; (weather~) Wetterhahn m. (the) ~ of the walk or roost der Größte (inf).
(b) (male bird) Männchen nt. turkey ~ Truthahn, Puter m.
(c) (tap) (Wasser)hahn m. fuel ~ Treibstoffhahn m.
(d) (of rifle) Hahn m.
(e) (of hat) schiefer Sitz.
(f) (Brit inf: mate) Kumpel m (inf).
(g) (vulg: penis) Schwanz m (vulg).
2 vt (a) to ~ the gun den Hahn spannen.
(b) ears spitzen. the parrot ~ed its head on one side der Papagei legte seinen Kopf schief or auf die Seite; to ~ a snook at sb (lit) jdm eine lange Nase machen; (fig) zeigen, daß man auf jdn pfeift; he ~ed his hat at a jaunty angle er setzte seinen Hut keck auf; ~ed hat (with two points) Zweispitz m; (with three points) Dreispitz m; to knock sb into a ~ed hat (inf) (lit beat up) aus jdm Kleinholz machen; (fig) jdn total an die Wand spielen; this painting knocks all the others into a ~ed hat (inf) dieses Gemälde stellt alle anderen in den Schatten.
♦ **cock up** vt sep (a) ears spitzen. (b) (Brit sl: mess up) versauen (sl).

cockade [kɒˈkeɪd] n Kokarde f.

cock: ~-a-doodle-doo n Kikeriki nt; ~-a-hoop adj ganz aus dem Häuschen, außer sich vor Freude; ~-a-leekie (soup) n Lauchsuppe f mit Huhn; ~-and-bull adj: ~-and-bull story or tale Lügengeschichte f.

cockatoo [ˌkɒkəˈtuː] n Kakadu m.

cockatrice [ˈkɒkətrɪs] n Basilisk m.

cockchafer [ˈkɒktʃeɪfəʳ] n Maikäfer m.

cockcrow [ˈkɒkrəʊ] n (old: dawn) Hahnenschrei m. at ~ beim ersten Hahnenschrei.

cocker [ˈkɒkəʳ] n (also ~ spaniel) Cocker(spaniel) m.

cockerel [ˈkɒkərəl] n junger Hahn.

cock: ~-eyed adj (inf) (a) (crooked) schief; (b) (absurd) idea verrückt, widersinnig; ~fight n Hahnenkampf m; ~horse n (old) Steckenpferd nt.

cockiness [ˈkɒkɪnɪs] n (inf) Großspurigkeit f.

cockle [ˈkɒkl] n (a) (shellfish: also ~shell) Herzmuschel f. (b) (boat) kleines Boot, Nußschale f. (c) it warmed the ~s of my heart es wurde mir warm ums Herz.

cockney [ˈkɒknɪ] 1 n (a) (dialect) Cockney nt. (b) (person) Cockney m. 2 adj Cockney-.

cockpit [ˈkɒkpɪt] n (a) (Aviat, of racing car) Cockpit nt; (Naut: on yacht) Plicht f, Cockpit m. (b) (for cockfighting) Hahnenkampfplatz m.

cockroach [ˈkɒkrəʊtʃ] n Küchenschabe f, Kakerlak m.

cockscomb [ˈkɒkskəʊm] n (a) (Orn, Bot) Hahnenkamm m. (b) see coxcomb.

cock: ~ sparrow n (männlicher) Spatz; ~sure adj (ganz) sicher, fest überzeugt; don't you be so ~sure sei dir deiner Sache (gen) nicht zu sicher; to be ~sure of oneself von sich (dat) selber or selbst sehr überzeugt sein.

cocktail [ˈkɒkteɪl] n (a) Cocktail m. we're invited for ~s wir sind zum Cocktail eingeladen. (b) fruit ~ Obstsalat m.

cocktail in cpds Cocktail-; ~ bar n Cocktail-Bar f; ~ cabinet n Hausbar f.

cock-up [ˈkɒkʌp] n (Brit sl) to be a ~ in die Hose gehen (sl); to make a ~ of sth bei or mit etw Scheiße bauen (sl).

cocky [ˈkɒkɪ] adj (+er) (inf) anmaßend, großspurig. he was so ~ before the exams er tat so großspurig vorm Examen.

cocoa [ˈkəʊkəʊ] n Kakao m. ~ bean Kakaobohne f.

coconut [ˈkəʊkənʌt] 1 n Kokosnuß f. 2 attr Kokos-. ~ ice Kokosnußriegel m; ~ matting Kokosmatte f; ~ palm, ~ tree Kokospalme f; ~ shy Wurfbude f.

cocoon [kəˈkuːn] 1 n Kokon m; (fig) (of scarves, blankets etc) Hülle f. the old warships were put in ~s die alten Kriegsschiffe wurden mit Planen abgedeckt.

2 vt einhüllen; ship etc abdecken. she looks well ~ed against the wind/winter sie ist warm eingemummt.

COD abbr of cash (Brit) or collect (US) on delivery.

cod [kɒd] n Kabeljau m; (in Baltic) Dorsch m.

coda [ˈkəʊdə] n Koda f.

coddle [ˈkɒdl] vt (a) child, invalid umhegen, verhätscheln. (b) (Cook) eggs im Backofen pochieren.

code [kəʊd] 1 n (a) (cipher) Kode, Code m, Chiffre f. in ~ verschlüsselt, chiffriert; to put into ~ verschlüsseln, chiffrieren; ~-name Deckname m; ~-number Kennziffer f.
(b) (Jur) Gesetzbuch nt, Kodex m.
(c) (rules, principles) Kodex m. ~ of honour/behaviour Ehren-/Sittenkodex m.
(d) post or zip (US) ~ Postleitzahl f.
(e) (for computer) Code m.
(f) (Ling, Sociol) Code, Kode m.
2 vt verschlüsseln, chiffrieren; (for computer) kodieren.

codeine [ˈkəʊdiːn] n Kodein nt.

codex [ˈkəʊdeks] n, pl codices Kodex m.

codfish [ˈkɒdfɪʃ] n see cod.

codger [ˈkɒdʒəʳ] n (inf) komischer (alter) Kauz.

codices [ˈkəʊdɪsiːz] pl of codex.

codicil [ˈkəʊdɪsɪl] n Kodizill nt.

codify [ˈkəʊdɪfaɪ] vt laws kodifizieren.

coding [ˈkəʊdɪŋ] n Chiffrieren nt. a new system of ~ ein neues Chiffriersystem; I don't understand the ~ ich verstehe den Kode nicht.

cod: ~-liver-oil n Lebertran m; ~piece n Hosenbeutel m.

co-driver [ˈkəʊdraɪvəʳ] n Beifahrer m.

codswallop [ˈkɒdzwɒləp] n (Brit inf) Stuß m (dated inf).

co-ed, coed [ˈkəʊˈed] 1 n (inf) (Brit: school) gemischte Schule, Koedukationsschule f; (US: girl student) Schülerin or Studentin f einer gemischten Schule. 2 adj school gemischt, Koedukations-. to go ~ Koedukation einführen.

coedition [ˌkəʊɪˈdɪʃən] n gemeinsame Ausgabe.

co-editor [ˈkəʊˈedɪtəʳ] n Mitherausgeber m.

coeducation [ˌkəʊˌedjʊˈkeɪʃən] n Koedukation f.

coeducational [ˌkəʊˌedjʊˈkeɪʃənl] adj teaching koedukativ; school Koedukations-.

coefficient [ˌkəʊɪˈfɪʃənt] n (Math, Phys) Koeffizient m.

coerce [kəʊˈɜːs] vt zwingen. to ~ sb into doing sth jdn dazu zwingen or nötigen (geh), etw zu tun; if he won't agree he'll have to be ~d wenn er nicht einwilligt, (dann) muß Zwang angewendet werden.

coercion [kəʊˈɜːʃən] n Zwang m; (Jur) Nötigung f.

coercive [kəʊˈɜːsɪv] adj Zwangs-.

coeval [kəʊˈiːvəl] (form) 1 adj der gleichen Periode or Zeit (with wie); manuscripts, music, paintings, authors etc also zeitgenössisch attr. the two composers were approximately ~ die beiden Komponisten waren ungefähre Zeitgenossen. 2 n Zeitgenosse m.

coexist [ˌkəʊɪgˈzɪst] vi koexistieren (Pol, Sociol, geh), nebeneinander bestehen. to ~ with or alongside sb/sth neben or mit jdm/etw bestehen or existieren.

coexistence [ˌkəʊɪgˈzɪstəns] n Koexistenz f.

coexistent [ˌkəʊɪgˈzɪstənt] adj koexistent (geh), nebeneinander bestehend. other creatures which were ~ with it andere Tiere, die zur gleichen Zeit or gleichzeitig lebten or existierten; the two states can now peacefully ~ die beiden Staaten leben jetzt friedlich nebeneinander or in friedlicher Koexistenz.

coextensive [ˌkəʊɪkˈstensɪv] adj (in time) zur gleichen Zeit; (in area) flächengleich; (in length) längengleich; (fig) (concepts) bedeutungs- or inhaltsgleich. to be ~ with sth mit etw zusammenfallen; (spatially) mit etw decken.

C of E abbr of Church of England.

coffee [ˈkɒfɪ] n Kaffee m. two ~s, please zwei Kaffee, bitte.

coffee in cpds Kaffee-; ~ bar n Café nt; ~ break n Kaffeepause f; ~ grinder n Kaffeemühle f; ~ house n (also Hist) Kaffeehaus nt; ~ percolator n Kaffeemaschine f; ~ pot n Kaffeekanne f; ~ table n Couchtisch m; ~-table book Bildband m.

coffer [ˈkɒfəʳ] n (a) Truhe f. (b) (fig) the ~s die Schatulle, das Geldsäckel; (of state) das Staatssäckel. (c) (Archit) Kassette f.

cofferdam [ˈkɒfədæm] n Caisson m.

coffin [ˈkɒfɪn] n Sarg m.

cog [kɒg] n (Tech) Zahn m; (~wheel) Zahnrad nt. he's only a ~ in the machine (fig) er ist nur ein Rädchen im Getriebe; each employee is a vital ~ in the company jeder einzelne Angestellte ist ein wichtiger Teil in der Firma.

cogency [ˈkəʊdʒənsɪ] n Stichhaltigkeit f.

cogent [ˈkəʊdʒənt] adj stichhaltig; argument, reason also zwingend; reasoning also überzeugend.

cogently [ˈkəʊdʒəntlɪ] adv stichhaltig.

cogitate [ˈkɒdʒɪteɪt] 1 vi (about, (up)on über +acc) nachdenken, nachsinnen, grübeln. 2 vt nachdenken, nachsinnen über (+acc); (devise) ersinnen.

cogitation [ˌkɒdʒɪˈteɪʃən] n Nachdenken, Nachsinnen nt, Überlegung f. these are my ~s on the subject dies sind meine Überlegungen or Gedanken zu dem Thema.

cognac [ˈkɒnjæk] n Kognak m; (French) Cognac m.

cognate [ˈkɒgneɪt] 1 adj verwandt; (Ling) urverwandt. 2 n (Ling) urverwandtes Wort; urverwandte Sprache. "night" is a ~ of "Nacht" „night" ist mit „Nacht" verwandt.

cognition [kɒgˈnɪʃən] n Erkenntnis f; (visual) Wahrnehmung f.

cognitive [ˈkɒgnɪtɪv] adj powers, faculties kognitiv.

cognizance [ˈkɒgnɪzəns] n (form) (a) (conscious knowledge, awareness) Kenntnis f; (range of perception) Erkenntnisbereich m. to take ~ of sth etw zur Kenntnis nehmen.
(b) (jurisdiction) Zuständigkeit, Befugnis f; (Jur) Gerichtsbarkeit f. he gave ~ of the matter to his deputy er übertrug seinem Stellvertreter alle Befugnis(se) in dieser or für diese Angelegenheit.

cognizant ['kɒgnɪzənt] adj (form) (a) (aware, conscious) to be ~ of sth sich (dat) einer Sache (gen) bewußt sein. (b) (having jurisdiction) zuständig.

cognoscente [ˌkɒgnəʊ'ʃenti] n, pl **cognoscenti** [ˌkɒgnəʊ'ʃenti:] Kenner m.

cog: ~ railway n (US) Zahnradbahn f; ~wheel n Zahnrad nt.

cohabit [kəʊ'hæbɪt] vi (esp Jur) in eheähnlicher Gemeinschaft leben, zusammenleben.

cohabitation [ˌkəʊhæbɪ'teɪʃən] n eheähnliche Gemeinschaft.

coheir ['kəʊ'eə'] n Miterbe m (to gen). to share ~s to the fortune sie waren gemeinsame Erben des Vermögens.

coheiress ['kəʊ'eərɪs] n Miterbin f (to gen).

cohere [kəʊ'hɪə'] vi (a) (lit) zusammenhängen. (b) (fig) (community) ein Ganzes or eine Einheit bilden; (essay, symphony etc) in sich geschlossen sein; (argument, reasoning, style) kohärent or zusammenhängend sein.

coherence [kəʊ'hɪərəns] n (a) (lit) Kohärenz f. (b) (of community) Zusammenhalt m; (of essay, symphony etc) Geschlossenheit f; (of argument, reasoning, style) Kohärenz f. his address lacked ~ seiner Rede (dat) fehlte der Zusammenhang; he wrote/spoke with ~ on the subject was er zu diesem Thema schrieb/sagte, war in sich geschlossen. (c) (fig: comprehensibility) after five whiskies he lacked ~ nach fünf Whiskys gab er nur noch unzusammenhängendes Zeug von sich.

coherent [kəʊ'hɪərənt] adj (a) (comprehensible) zusammenhängend. (b) (cohesive) logic, reasoning etc kohärent, schlüssig; case schlüssig.

coherently [kəʊ'hɪərəntlɪ] adv (a) (comprehensibly) zusammenhängend. (b) (cohesively) kohärent, schlüssig.

cohesion [kəʊ'hi:ʒən] n (Sci) Kohäsion f; (fig also) Zusammenhang m; (of group) Zusammenhalt m.

cohesive [kəʊ'hi:sɪv] adj (Sci) Binde-, Kohäsiv-; (fig) geschlossen.

cohesively [kəʊ'hi:sɪvlɪ] adv (Sci) kohäsiv; (fig) write, argue im Zusammenhang.

cohort ['kəʊhɔ:t] n Kohorte f, Trupp m.

coif [kɔɪf] n (Hist, Eccl) Haube f; (skullcap) Kappe f.

coiffure [kwɒ'fjʊə'] n Haartracht, Coiffure (geh) f.

coil [kɔɪl] 1 n (a) (of rope, wire etc) Rolle f; (in light-bulb) Glühdraht m; (on loop) Windung f; (of smoke) Kringel m; (of hair) Kranz m. ~ spring Sprungfeder f; she wore her hair in ~s (round head) sie hatte eine Gretchenfrisur; (round ears) sie trug ihr Haar in Schnecken; the sinewy ~s of the snake die kraftvoll gespannte Spirale des Schlangenkörpers. (b) (Elec) Spule f. (c) (contraceptive) Spirale f. 2 vt aufwickeln, aufrollen; wire aufspulen, aufwickeln. to ~ sth round sth etw um etw wickeln; the python ~ed itself around the rabbit/(up) in the basket die Pythonschlange umschlang das Kaninchen/rollte sich im Korb zusammen. 3 vi sich ringeln; (smoke also) sich kringeln; (river) sich schlängeln or winden.

coin [kɔɪn] 1 n (a) Münze f. ~-box (telephone) Münzfernsprecher m; (box) Geldkasten m; (on telephone, meter) Münzzähler m; ~-operated Münz-. (b) (no pl) Münzen pl. in the ~ of the realm in der Landeswährung; I'll pay you back in your own ~ (fig) das werde ich dir in gleicher Münze heimzahlen; the other side of the ~ (fig) die Kehrseite der Medaille. 2 vt (lit, fig) money, phrase prägen. he's ~ing money (fig inf) er scheffelt Geld (inf); ..., to ~ a phrase ..., um mich mal so auszudrücken.

coinage ['kɔɪnɪdʒ] n (a) (act) Prägen nt, Prägung f; (coins) Münzen pl, Hartgeld nt no pl; (system) Währung f. (b) (fig) Prägung, Neuschöpfung f.

coincide [kəʊɪn'saɪd] vi (in time, place) zusammenfallen; (in area) sich decken; (agree) übereinstimmen. the two concerts ~ die beiden Konzerte finden zur gleichen Zeit statt.

coincidence [kəʊ'ɪnsɪdəns] n (a) Zufall m, Fügung f (geh). what a ~! welch ein Zufall!; it is no ~ that ... es ist kein Zufall, daß ..., es ist nicht von ungefähr, daß ... (b) (occurring or coming together) (in time) Zusammentreffen nt; (in place) Zusammenfall m; (agreement) Übereinstimmung f.

coincident [kəʊ'ɪnsɪdənt] adj (in time) zusammentreffend; (in place) zusammenfallend; (agreeing) übereinstimmend. to be ~ zusammentreffen/zusammenfallen/übereinstimmen.

coincidental adj, ~ly adv [kəʊ,ɪnsɪ'dentl, -təlɪ] zufällig.

coir [kɔɪə'] n Kokosfaser f, Coir nt or f.

coition [kəʊ'ɪʃən], **coitus** ['kɔɪtəs] n (form) Koitus, Akt m. coitus interruptus Coitus interruptus m.

coke¹ [kəʊk] n Koks m.

coke² n (sl: cocaine) Koks m.

Coke ® [kəʊk] n (inf) (Coca-)Cola f, Coke nt.

col¹ [kɒl] n Sattel, Paß m.

col² abbr of **column** Sp.

Col abbr of **Colonel**.

colander ['kʌləndə'] n Seiher m, Sieb nt.

cold [kəʊld] 1 adj (+er) (a) kalt. ~ meats Aufschnitt m; I am ~ mir ist kalt, ich friere; my hands are ~/are getting ~ ich habe/kriege kalte Hände; don't get ~ paß auf, daß du nicht frierst!; if you get ~ wenn es dir zu kalt wird, wenn du frierst. (b) (fig) (unfriendly) kalt; answer, welcome, reception betont kühl; personality kühl, unnahbar; (dispassionate, not sensual) kühl. to be ~ to sb jdn kühl behandeln; that leaves me ~ das läßt mich kalt. (c) (inf: unconscious) bewußtlos; (knocked out) k.o. to be out ~ bewußtlos/k.o. sein. (d) (inf: in guessing game etc) kalt. you're still ~ (inf) immer noch kalt. (e) (Hunt) scent kalt.

(f) (phrases) in ~ blood kaltblütig; ~ comfort ein schwacher Trost; to get/have ~ feet (fig inf) kalte Füße kriegen (inf); to give sb the ~ shoulder (inf) jdm die kalte Schulter zeigen; to be in a ~ sweat vor Angst schwitzen; that brought him out in a ~ sweat dabei brach ihm der kalte Schweiß or der Angstschweiß aus; to throw ~ water on sb's plans/hopes (inf) jdm eine kalte Dusche geben/jds Hoffnungen (dat) einen Dämpfer aufsetzen.

2 adv to come to sth ~ unvorbereitet an eine Sache herangehen; to learn/know sth ~ (US) etw gut lernen/können; he stopped ~ when ... (US) er hielt unvermittelt an, als ...; she quit her job ~ sie hat glatt or eiskalt gekündigt (inf); he was turned down ~ sie wurde glatt abgelehnt.

3 n (a) Kälte f. to feel the ~ kälteempfindlich sein; don't go out in this ~! geh nicht raus bei dieser Kälte!; to be left out in the ~ (fig) ausgeschlossen werden, links liegengelassen werden; to feel left out in the ~ sich ausgeschlossen fühlen. (b) (Med) Erkältung f; (runny nose) Schnupfen m. a heavy or bad ~ eine schwere Erkältung; to have a ~ erkältet sein; (einen) Schnupfen haben; to get or catch a ~ sich erkälten, sich (dat) eine Erkältung holen; to catch ~ sich erkälten; ~ in the head/on the chest Schnupfen m/Bronchialkatarrh m.

cold: ~-blooded adj (Zool, fig) ~-blooded animal Kaltblüter m; ~ chisel n Kaltmeißel m; ~ cream n Cold Cream f or nt, halbfette Feuchtigkeitscreme; ~ cuts npl Aufschnitt m; ~ frame n (Hort) Frühbeet nt; ~-hearted adj kaltherzig.

coldly ['kəʊldlɪ] adv (lit, fig) kalt; answer, welcome, receive betont kühl. she ~ snubbed him sie ließ ihn eiskalt abblitzen (inf); they ~ planned the murder der Mord wurde von ihnen kaltblütig geplant.

coldness ['kəʊldnɪs] n (lit, fig) Kälte f; (of answer, reception, welcome) betonte Kühle. the unexpected ~ of the weather die unerwartete Kälte; the ~ with which they planned the murder die Kaltblütigkeit, mit der sie den Mord planten.

cold: ~ room n Kühlraum m; ~-shoulder vt (inf) links liegenlassen (inf); ~ sore n (Med) Bläschenausschlag m; ~ storage n Kühllagerung f; to put sth into ~ storage (lit) food etw kühl lagern; (fig) idea, plan etw auf Eis legen; ~ store n Kühlhaus nt; ~ turkey (sl) 1 adj a ~ turkey cure sofortiger Totalentzug; 2 adv to come off drugs ~ turkey eine radikale Entziehung(skur) machen; ~ war n kalter Krieg; ~ warrior n kalter Krieger.

coleslaw ['kəʊlslɔ:] n Krautsalat m.

colic ['kɒlɪk] n Kolik f.

coliseum [ˌkɒlɪ'si:əm] n Kolosseum nt.

collaborate [kə'læbəreɪt] vi (a) zusammenarbeiten. they asked him to ~ sie baten ihn mitzuarbeiten, sie baten um seine Mitarbeit; to ~ with sb on or in sth mit jdm bei etw zusammenarbeiten. (b) (with enemy) kollaborieren. he was suspected of collaborating er wurde der Kollaboration verdächtigt.

collaboration [kə,læbə'reɪʃən] n (a) Zusammenarbeit f; (of one party) Mitarbeit f. helpful ~ Mithilfe f. (b) (with enemy) Kollaboration f.

collaborator [kə'læbəreɪtə'] n (a) Mitarbeiter(in f) m. (b) (with enemy) Kollaborateur(in f) m.

collage [kɒ'lɑ:ʒ] n Collage f.

collapse [kə'læps] 1 vi (a) (person) zusammenbrechen; (mentally, have heart attack also) einen Kollaps erleiden or haben. his health ~d er hatte einen Kollaps; they all ~d with laughter sie konnten sich alle vor Lachen nicht mehr halten. (b) (fall down, cave in) zusammenbrechen; (building, wall, roof also) einstürzen; (lungs) zusammenfallen, kollabieren. (c) (fig: fail) zusammenbrechen; (negotiations also) scheitern; (civilization) zugrunde gehen; (prices) stürzen, purzeln (inf); (government) zu Fall kommen, stürzen; (plans) scheitern, zu Fall kommen; (hopes) sich zerschlagen. his whole world ~d about him eine ganze Welt stürzte über ihm zusammen; their whole society ~d ihre ganze Gesellschaftsordnung brach zusammen. (d) (fold) (table, umbrella, bicycle etc) sich zusammenklappen lassen; (telescope, walking-stick) sich zusammenschieben lassen; (life raft) sich zusammenlegen or -falten lassen. a collapsing bicycle/chair ein Klappfahrrad nt/-stuhl m. 2 vt table, umbrella, bicycle etc zusammenklappen; telescope, walking-stick zusammenschieben; life-raft zusammenlegen or -falten. 3 n (a) (of person) Zusammenbruch m; (nervous breakdown also, heart attack) Kollaps m. (b) see vi (b) Zusammenbruch m; Einsturz m; Kollaps m. (c) (failure) see vi (c) Zusammenbruch m; Scheitern nt; Untergang m; Sturz m; Sturz m; Scheitern nt; Zerschlagung f.

collapsible [kə'læpsəbl] adj see vi (d) zusammenklappbar, Klapp-; zusammenschiebbar; zusammenlegbar, zusammenfaltbar, Falt-.

collar ['kɒlə'] 1 n (a) Kragen m. he got hold of him by the ~ er packte ihn am Kragen; ~-bone Schlüsselbein nt; ~ stud Kragenknopf m. (b) (for dogs) Halsband nt; (for horses) Kum(me)t nt. (c) (chain and insignia) Hals- or Ordenskette f. (d) (Mech: on pipe etc) Bund m. 2 vt (capture) fassen; (latch onto) abfangen, schnappen (inf).

collate [kɒ'leɪt] vt (a) vergleichen, kollationieren. (b) (Typ) kollationieren, zusammentragen.

collateral [kɒ'lætərəl] 1 adj (a) (connected but secondary) evidence, questions etc zusätzlich, Zusatz-; events Begleit-. (b) (parallel, side by side) mountain ranges, states etc nebeneinanderliegend; (fig) aims etc Hand in Hand gehend. (c) descent, branch of family seitlich, kollateral (spec). (d) (Fin) security zusätzlich. 2 n (Fin) (zusätzliche) Sicherheit.

collation [kɒ'leɪʃən] n (a) (collating) Vergleich m, Kollationieren nt; (Typ) Kollationieren, Zusammentragen nt. (b) (form: meal) Imbiß m.

colleague ['kɒliːg] n Kollege m, Kollegin f. my ~s at work meine Arbeitskollegen.

collect[1] ['kɒlekt] n (Eccl) Kirchen- or Tagesgebet nt.

collect[2] [kə'lekt] 1 vt (a) (accumulate) ansammeln; (furniture) dust etc anziehen; empty glasses, exam papers, tickets etc einsammeln; litter aufsammeln; belongings zusammenpacken or -sammeln; (assemble) sammeln; one's thoughts also ordnen; facts, information also zusammentragen; volunteers zusammenbringen. she ~ed a lot of praise/a lot of teasing/five points for that das hat ihr viel Lob/viel Hänselei/fünf Punkte eingebracht or eingetragen; to ~ interest Zinsen bringen; the train ~s electricity from the overhead cables der Zug entnimmt den Strom der Oberleitung (dat).
(b) (pick up, fetch) goods, things, persons abholen (from bei).
(c) stamps, coins sammeln.
(d) taxes einziehen; money, jumble for charity sammeln; rent, fares kassieren; debts eintreiben.
2 vi (a) (gather) sich ansammeln; (dust) sich absetzen.
(b) (~ money) kassieren; (for charity) sammeln.
(c) (Comm: call for goods) abholen.
3 adj (US) ~ call R-Gespräch; ~ cable vom Empfänger bezahltes Telegramm.
4 adv (US) to pay ~ bei Empfang bezahlen; to call ~ ein R-Gespräch führen; to pay ~ on delivery bei Lieferung bezahlen; (through post) per Nachnahme bezahlen.

♦**collect together** vt sep zusammenbringen; information zusammentragen; team of people auf- or zusammenstellen. the officer ~ed his men ~ der Offizier rief seine Leute zusammen.

♦**collect up** vt sep einsammeln; litter aufsammeln; belongings zusammenpacken or -sammeln.

collected [kə'lektɪd] adj (a) the ~ works of Oscar Wilde Oscar Wildes gesammelte Werke. (b) (calm) ruhig, gelassen.

collectedly [kə'lektɪdlɪ] adv ruhig, gelassen.

collection [kə'lekʃən] n (a) (group of people, objects) Ansammlung f; (of stamps, coins etc) Sammlung f. they're an odd ~ of people das ist ein seltsamer Verein (inf).
(b) (collecting) (of facts, information) Zusammentragen nt; (of goods, person) Abholung f; (of mail) Abholung f; (from letterbox) Leerung f; (of stamps, coins) Sammeln nt; (of money, jumble for charity) Sammlung f; (in church) Kollekte f; (of rent, fares) Kassieren nt; (of taxes) Einziehen nt; (of debts) Eintreiben nt. the police organized the ~ of all firearms die Polizei ließ alle Schußwaffen einsammeln; to make or hold a ~ for sb/sth für jdn/etw eine Sammlung durchführen.
(c) (Fashion) Kollektion f.

collective [kə'lektɪv] 1 adj (a) kollektiv, Kollektiv-; responsibility, agreement, action also gemeinsam. ~ bargaining Tarifverhandlungen pl; ~ ticket Sammelfahrschein m; ~ farm landwirtschaftliche Produktionsgenossenschaft.
(b) (accumulated) wisdom, discoveries, experience gesamt attr. the ~ unconscious das kollektive Unbewußte.
(c) (Gram) ~ noun Kollektivum nt, Sammelbegriff m.
2 n Kollektiv nt; (farm also) Produktionsgenossenschaft f.

collectively [kə'lektɪvlɪ] adv gemeinsam, zusammen; (in socialist context also) kollektiv.

collectivism [kə'lektɪvɪzəm] n Kollektivismus m.

collectivist [kə'lektɪvɪst] 1 n Kollektivist m. 2 adj kollektivistisch.

collectivize [kə'lektɪvaɪz] vt kollektivieren.

collector [kə'lektə^r] n (a) (of taxes) Einnehmer(in f) m; (of rent, cash) Kassierer(in f) m; (of jumble etc) Abholer(in f) m; (ticket ~) Bahnbediensteter, der die abgefahrenen Fahrkarten einsammelt. (b) (of stamps, coins etc) Sammler(in f) m. ~'s item, piece, price Sammler-, Liebhaber-. (c) current ~ Stromabnehmer m.

colleen ['kɒliːn] n (Ir) junges Mädchen, Mädel nt.

college ['kɒlɪdʒ] n (a) (part of university) College nt; Institut nt. to go to ~ (university) studieren; to start ~ sein Studium beginnen; we met at ~ wir haben uns im Studium kennengelernt. (b) (of music, agriculture, technology etc) Fachhochschule f. ~ of Art Kunstakademie f. (c) (body) ~ of Cardinals Kardinalskollegium nt; ~ of Physicians/Surgeons Ärztebund m, Ärztekammer f.

collegiate [kə'liːdʒɪɪt] adj College-. ~ life das Collegeleben, das Leben auf dem College; Oxford is a ~ university Oxford ist eine auf dem College-System aufgebaute Universität.

collide [kə'laɪd] vi (lit) zusammenstoßen or -prallen; (Naut) kollidieren. they ~d head-on sie stießen frontal zusammen; to ~ with sb/sth mit jdm zusammenstoßen/gegen etw prallen. (b) (fig) (person) eine heftige Auseinandersetzung haben (with mit); (interest, demands) kollidieren.

collie ['kɒlɪ] n Collie m.

collier ['kɒlɪə^r] n (a) Bergmann, Kumpel (inf) m. (b) (coal-ship) Kohlenschiff nt.

colliery ['kɒlɪərɪ] n Grube, Zeche f.

collimate ['kɒlɪmeɪt] vt kollimieren.

collision [kə'lɪʒən] n (lit) Zusammenstoß, Zusammenprall m; (fig) Zusammenstoß, Konflikt m, Kollision f; (Naut) Kollision f. on a ~ course (lit, fig) auf Kollisionskurs; to be in ~ with sth mit etw zusammenstoßen; to come into ~ with sth (lit, fig) mit etw zusammenstoßen; (Naut) mit etw kollidieren; your activities are likely to bring you into ~ with the law dein Treiben kann dich leicht mit dem Gesetz in Konflikt bringen.

collocate ['kɒləkeɪt] vt (Gram) nebeneinanderstellen. to be ~d nebeneinanderstehen.

collocation [ˌkɒlə'keɪʃən] n (Gram) Kollokation f.

colloquial [kə'ləʊkwɪəl] adj umgangssprachlich.

colloquialism [kə'ləʊkwɪəlɪzəm] n umgangssprachlicher Ausdruck.

colloquially [kə'ləʊkwɪəlɪ] adv umgangssprachlich.

colloquium [kə'ləʊkwɪəm] n Kolloquium nt.

colloquy ['kɒləkwɪ] n (form) Gespräch nt; (Liter) Dialog m. in ~ im Gespräch.

collusion [kə'luːʒən] n (geheime) Absprache. they're acting in ~ sie haben sich abgesprochen; there's been some ~ between those two pupils diese beiden Schüler haben zusammengearbeitet.

collywobbles ['kɒlɪˌwɒblz] npl (inf) the ~ (upset stomach) Bauchgrimmen nt (inf); (nerves) ein flaues Gefühl im Magen.

Cologne [kə'ləʊn] 1 n Köln nt. 2 adj Kölner, kölnisch.

cologne [kə'ləʊn] n Kölnischwasser, Eau de Cologne nt.

colon[1] ['kəʊlən] n (Anat) Dickdarm m.

colon[2] n (Gram) Doppelpunkt m; (old, Typ) Kolon nt.

colonel ['kɜːnl] n Oberst m; (as address) Herr Oberst.

colonial [kə'ləʊnɪəl] 1 adj Kolonial-, kolonial. ~ architecture Kolonialstil m; ~ type Typ m des Herrenmenschen (iro). 2 n Bewohner(in f) m einer Kolonie/der Kolonien.

colonialism [kə'ləʊnɪəlɪzəm] n Kolonialismus m.

colonialist [kə'ləʊnɪəlɪst] 1 adj kolonialistisch. 2 n Kolonialist(in f) m.

colonist ['kɒlənɪst] n Kolonist(in f), Siedler(in f) m.

colonization [ˌkɒlənaɪ'zeɪʃən] n Kolonisation f.

colonize ['kɒlənaɪz] vt kolonisieren.

colonnade [ˌkɒlə'neɪd] n Kolonnade f, Säulengang m.

colony ['kɒlənɪ] n Kolonie f.

colophon ['kɒləfən] n Kolophon m, Signet nt.

color etc (US) see colour etc.

Colorado beetle [ˌkɒlə'rɑːdəʊ'biːtl] n Kartoffelkäfer m.

coloration [ˌkʌlə'reɪʃən] n Färbung f.

coloratura [ˌkɒlərə'tʊərə] n Koloratur f.

color guard n (US) see colour party.

colossal [kə'lɒsl] adj riesig, ungeheuer, gewaltig; prices, fool, cheek, mistake ungeheuer; car, man, park, lake, city riesig; prices, damage, building also kolossal.

colosseum [ˌkɒlɪ'sɪəm] n Kolosseum nt.

colossi [kə'lɒsaɪ] pl of colossus.

Colossians [kə'lɒʃəns] n (Epistle to the) ~ Kolosserbrief m.

colossus [kə'lɒsəs] n, pl colossi or -es (statue) Koloß m; (person also) Riese m. this ~ of the world of music dieser Gigant or Titan der Musik.

colour, (US) **color** ['kʌlə^r] 1 n (a) (lit, fig) Farbe f. what ~ is it? welche Farbe hat es?; red/yellow in ~ rot/gelb; a good sense of ~ ein guter Farbensinn; let's see the ~ of your money first (inf) zeig erst mal dein Geld her (inf); the ~ of a note (Mus) die Klangfarbe eines Tons; see glowing.
(b) (complexion) (Gesichts)farbe f. to change ~ die Farbe wechseln; to get one's ~ back wieder Farbe bekommen; to bring the ~ back to sb's cheeks jdm wieder Farbe geben; to have a high ~ eine gesunde Gesichtsfarbe haben; (look feverish) rot im Gesicht sein.
(c) (racial) Hautfarbe f. I don't care what ~ he is seine Hautfarbe interessiert mich nicht.
(d) ~s pl (paints) Farben pl; a box of ~s ein Mal- or Tuschkasten m.
(e) (fig: bias) (of newspaper, report) Färbung f.
(f) (of place, period etc) Atmosphäre f. to add ~ to a story einer Geschichte (dat) Farbe geben; the pageantry and ~ of Elizabethan England der Prunk und die Farbenpracht des Elisabethanischen England; local ~ Lokalkolorit nt.
(g) (appearance of truth) to give or lend ~ to a tale eine Geschichte ausschmücken.
(h) ~s pl (symbols of membership) Farben pl.
(i) (flag) ~s Fahne f; the regimental ~s die Regimentsfahne; to serve with the ~s (old) der Fahne dienen (dated)/den bunten Rock anziehen (old); to nail one's ~s to the mast (fig) Farbe bekennen; to sail under false ~s (fig) unter falscher Flagge segeln; to show one's true ~s (fig) sein wahres Gesicht zeigen; to stick to one's ~s (fig) seiner Überzeugung (dat) treu bleiben.
(j) (Sport) ~s (Sport)abzeichen nt.
2 vt (a) (lit) anmalen; (Art) kolorieren; (dye) färben. to ~ (in) a picture ein Bild anmalen/kolorieren.
(b) (fig) beeinflussen; (bias deliberately) färben.
3 vi (a) (leaves) sich (ver)färben.
(b) (person: also ~ up) rot werden, erröten.

♦**colour in** vt sep anmalen; (Art) kolorieren.

colour in cpds Farb-; (racial) Rassen-; (Mil) Fahnen-; ~-bar n Rassenschranke f; (in country also) Rassenschranken pl; to operate a ~-bar Rassentrennung praktizieren; ~-blind adj farbenblind; ~-blindness n Farbenblindheit f.

coloured, (US) **colored** ['kʌləd] 1 adj (a) bunt; fabric, walls also farbig. (b) (fig) (biased) gefärbt; (exaggerated) ausgeschmückt. (c) person, race farbig; (of mixed blood) gemischtrassig. 2 n Farbige(r) mf; (of mixed blood) Mischling m.

-coloured, (US) **-colored** adj suf yellow-/red-~ gelb/rot; straw-/dark-~ strohfarben/dunkel.

colourfast, (US) **colorfast** ['kʌləfɑːst] adj farbecht.

colourful, (US) **colorful** ['kʌləfʊl] adj (a) (lit) bunt; spectacle farbenfroh or -prächtig. (b) (fig) style of writing, account etc farbig, anschaulich; life, historical period (bunt)bewegt; personality (bunt)schillernd.

colourfully, (US) **colorfully** ['kʌləfəlɪ] adv see adj.

colourfulness, (US) **colorfulness** ['kʌləfʊlnɪs] n see adj (a) (lit) Buntheit f; Farbenpracht f. (b) (fig) Farbigkeit, Anschaulichkeit f; Bewegtheit f. the ~ of his character sein schillernder Charakter.

colour illustration n farbige Illustration.

colouring, (US) **coloring** ['kʌlərɪŋ] n (a) (complexion) Gesichtsfarbe f, Teint m. (b) (substance) Farbstoff m. (c) (painting) Malen nt. ~ book Malbuch nt; ~ set Mal- or Tuschkasten m; (box of crayons) Schachtel f Buntstifte. (d) (coloration) Farben pl. (e) (fig: of news, facts etc) Färbung f.

colourist, (US) **colorist** ['kʌlərɪst] n Farbkünstler(in f) m.

colourless, (US) **colorless** ['kʌləlɪs] adj (lit, fig) farblos; existence also grau.

colourlessly, (US) **colorlessly** ['kʌləlɪslɪ] adv see adj.

colourlessness, (US) **colorlessness** ['kʌləlɪsnɪs] n Farblosigkeit f.

colour: ~ **party** n Fahnenträgerkommando nt; ~ **photograph** n Farbfoto nt, Farbfotografie f; ~ **postcard** n bunte Ansichtskarte f; ~ **scheme** n Farbzusammenstellung f; ~ **television** n Farbfernsehen nt; (set) Farbfernseher m; ~**wash** n Farbtünche f.

colt [kəʊlt] n Fohlen nt; (dated fig: youth) junger Dachs (inf).

Co Ltd abbr of company limited GmbH f.

columbine ['kɒləmbaɪn] n (Bot) Akelei f.

Columbus [kə'lʌmbəs] n Kolumbus m.

column ['kɒləm] n (a) (Archit, of smoke, water etc) Säule f. ~ of mercury Quecksilbersäule f. (b) (of figures, names) Kolonne f; (division of page) Spalte, Kolumne (spec) f; (article in newspaper) Kolumne f. (c) (of vehicles, soldiers etc) Kolonne f.

columnist ['kɒləmnɪst] n Kolumnist(in f) m.

coma ['kəʊmə] n Koma nt. to be in a/to go or fall into a ~ im Koma liegen/ins Koma fallen.

comatose ['kəʊmətəʊs] adj komatös.

comb [kəʊm] 1 n (a) (also Tech, of fowl) Kamm m. (b) (act) to give one's hair a ~ sich kämmen; your hair could do with a ~ du könntest dich (auch) mal wieder kämmen. (c) (honey~) Wabe f. 2 vt (a) hair, wool kämmen; horse striegeln. to ~ one's hair sich (dat) die Haare kämmen, sich kämmen. (b) (search) durchkämmen; newspapers durchforsten.

♦**comb out** vt sep (a) hair auskämmen. (b) mistakes ausmerzen; useless stuff aussortieren.

♦**comb through** vi +prep obj hair kämmen; files, book etc durchgehen; shops durchstöbern.

combat ['kɒmbæt] 1 n Kampf m. ready for ~ kampfbereit, einsatzbereit. 2 vt (lit, fig) bekämpfen. 3 vi kämpfen.

combatant ['kɒmbətənt] n (lit, fig) Kombattant m.

combat: ~ **dress** n Kampfanzug m; ~ **fatigue** n Kriegsmüdigkeit f.

combative ['kɒmbətɪv] adj (pugnacious) kämpferisch; (competitive) aggressiv.

combat: ~ **troops** npl Kampftruppen pl; ~ **zone** n Kampfgebiet nt or -zone f.

combination [ˌkɒmbɪ'neɪʃən] n (a) Kombination f; (combining: of organizations, people etc) Vereinigung f, Zusammenschluß m; (of events) Verkettung f. in ~ zusammen, gemeinsam; an unusual colour ~ eine ungewöhnliche Farbzusammenstellung; pink is a ~ of red and white Rosa ist eine Mischung aus Rot und Weiß; they're a strange ~, that couple die beiden sind ein seltsames Paar; those two boys together are a nasty ~ diese beiden Jungen zusammen sind ein übles Duo.
(b) ~s pl (undergarment) Kombination, Hemdhose f.
(c) (motorcycle ~) Motorrad mit Beiwagen.
(d) (for lock) Kombination f. ~ **lock** Kombinationsschloß nt.

combine [kəm'baɪn] 1 vt kombinieren, verbinden. couldn't we ~ the two suggestions? lassen sich die beiden Vorschläge nicht kombinieren or miteinander verbinden?; your plan ~s the merits of the other two Ihr Plan vereinigt die Vorzüge der beiden anderen; he ~d generosity with discretion er verband Großzügigkeit mit Diskretion.
2 vi sich zusammenschließen; (Chem) sich verbinden. everything ~d against him alles hat sich gegen ihn verschworen.
3 ['kɒmbaɪn] n (a) Firmengruppe f, Konzern m; (in socialist countries) Kombinat nt.
(b) (also ~ harvester) Mähdrescher m.

combined [kəm'baɪnd] adj gemeinsam; talents, efforts vereint; forces vereinigt. ~ with in Kombination mit; (esp clothes, furniture) kombiniert mit; a ~ clock and wireless/radio and tape recorder eine Radiouhr/Radio und Tonband in einem.

combining form [kəm'baɪnɪŋfɔːm] n Affix m, Wortbildungselement nt.

combustibility [kəmˌbʌstɪ'bɪlɪtɪ] n Brennbarkeit f.

combustible [kəm'bʌstɪbl] 1 adj brennbar. 2 n brennbarer Stoff.

combustion [kəm'bʌstʃən] n Verbrennung f. ~ **chamber** Verbrennungsraum m.

come [kʌm] pret came, ptp ~ 1 vi (a) kommen. ~! (form: ~ in) herein!; ~ and get it! (das) Essen ist fertig!, Essen fassen! (esp Mil); to ~ and go kommen und gehen; (vehicle) hin- und herfahren; the picture/sound ~s and goes das Bild/der Ton geht immerzu weg; ~ and see me soon besuchen Sie mich bald einmal; he has ~ a long way er kommt von weit her, er hat einen weiten Weg hinter sich; (fig) er ist weit gekommen; the project has ~ a long way das Projekt ist schon ziemlich weit; he came running/hurrying/laughing into the room er kam ins Zimmer gerannt/er eilte ins Zimmer/er kam lachend ins Zimmer; coming! ich komme (gleich)!; ich komme ja schon!; ~ !, ~ now! (fig) komm, (komm), na, na!; to ~ home nach Hause kommen; Christmas is coming bald ist Weihnachten.
(b) (arrive) kommen; (reach, extend) reichen (to an/in/bis etc +acc). they came to a town/castle sie kamen in eine Stadt/zu einem Schloß; it came into my head that ... ich habe mir gedacht, daß ...; to ~ before a judge vor den Richter kommen.
(c) (have its place) kommen. May ~s before June Mai kommt vor Juni; the adjective must ~ before the noun das Adjektiv muß vor dem Substantiv stehen; where does your name ~ in the list? an welcher Stelle auf der Liste steht Ihr Name?; that must ~ first das muß an erster Stelle kommen.
(d) (happen) geschehen. ~ what may ganz gleich, was geschieht, komme, was (da) mag (geh); you could see it coming das konnte man ja kommen sehen, das war ja zu erwarten; she had had it coming to her (inf) das mußte ja so kommen; you've

got it coming to you (inf) mach dich auf was gefaßt!; recovery came slowly nur allmählich trat eine Besserung ein.
(e) how ~? (inf) wieso?, weshalb?, warum?; how ~ (inf) you are so late?, how do you ~ to be so late? wieso etc kommst du so spät?
(f) (be, become) werden. his dreams came true seine Träume wurden wahr; the handle has ~ loose der Griff hat sich gelockert; it ~s less expensive to shop in town es ist or kommt billiger, wenn man in der Stadt einkauft; everything came all right in the end zuletzt or am Ende wurde doch noch alles gut.
(g) (Comm: be available) erhältlich sein. milk now ~s in plastic bottles es gibt jetzt Milch in Plastikflaschen.
(h) (+infin: be finally in a position to) I have ~ to believe him inzwischen or mittlerweile glaube ich ihm; I'm sure you will ~ to agree with me ich bin sicher, daß du mir schließlich zustimmst; (now I) ~ to think of it wenn ich es mir recht überlege.
(i) the years/weeks etc to ~ die kommenden or nächsten Jahre/Wochen; in days/time to ~ in Zukunft/in künftigen Zeiten; the life (of the world) to ~ das ewige Leben.
(j) (inf uses) ... ~ next week nächste Woche ...; I've known him for three years ~ January im Januar kenne ich ihn drei Jahre; how long have you been away? — a week ~ Monday wie lange bist du schon weg? — (am) Montag acht Tage ~ (inf) or eine Woche; a week ~ Monday I'll be ... Montag in acht Tagen (inf) or in einer Woche bin ich ...; ~ again? wie bitte?; she is as vain as they ~ sie ist so eingebildet wie nur was (inf).
(k) (inf: have orgasm) kommen (inf).
2 vt (sl: act as if one were) spielen. don't ~ the innocent with me spielen Sie hier bloß nicht den Unschuldigen!, kommen Sie mir bloß nicht auf die unschuldige Tour (inf)!; he tried to ~ the innocent with me er hat versucht, den Unschuldigen zu markieren (inf), er hat es auf die unschuldige Tour versucht (inf); don't ~ that game or that (with me)! kommen Sie mir bloß nicht mit der Tour! (inf), die Masche zieht bei mir nicht! (inf); that's coming it a bit strong! das ist reichlich übertrieben.
3 n (sl: semen) Soße f (sl).

♦**come about** vi (a) impers (happen) passieren. how does it ~ that you are here? wie kommt es, daß du hier bist?; this is why it came ~ das ist so gekommen; this is how it came ~ ... das kam so ... (b) (Naut) (wind) drehen; (ship) beidrehen.

♦**come across** 1 vi (a) (cross) herüberkommen. (b) (be understood) verstanden werden; (message, speech) ankommen. (c) (make an impression) wirken. he wants to ~ like a tough guy er mimt gerne den starken Mann (inf). (d) (inf) (do what is wanted) mitmachen (inf). 2 vi +prep obj (find or meet by chance) treffen auf (+acc). if you ~ my watch ... wenn du zufällig meine Uhr siehst.

♦**come across with** vi +prep obj (inf) information rausrücken mit (inf); money rausrücken (inf).

♦**come after** vi +prep obj (a) (follow in sequence, be of less importance than) kommen nach. the noun ~s ~ the verb das Substantiv steht nach or hinter dem Verb. (b) (pursue) herkommen hinter (+dat). (c) also vi (follow later) nachkommen.

♦**come along** vi (a) (hurry up, make an effort etc: also come on) kommen.
(b) (attend, accompany) mitkommen. ~ with me kommen Sie mal (bitte) mit.
(c) (develop: also come on) to be coming ~ sich machen, vorangehen; (person) sich machen; how is your broken arm? — it's coming ~ nicely was macht dein gebrochener Arm? — dem geht's ganz gut or prima; the bulbs are coming ~ nicely die Blumenzwiebeln wachsen gut; the new apprentice is coming ~ nicely der neue Lehrling macht sich gut; my play isn't coming ~ at all well mein Stück macht überhaupt keine Fortschritte.
(d) (arrive, turn up) kommen, auftauchen; (chance etc) sich ergeben.

♦**come apart** vi (fall to pieces) kaputtgehen, auseinanderfallen; (be able to be taken apart) zerlegbar sein.

♦**come at** vi +prep obj (attack) sb losgehen auf (+acc); (approach) runway anfliegen; problem angehen.

♦**come away** vi (a) (leave) (weg)gehen. ~ with me for a few days fahr doch ein paar Tage mit mir weg!; ~ ~ from there! komm da weg!; ~ ~ in! (Scot) kommen Sie doch rein! (b) (become detached) abgehen.

♦**come back** vi (a) (return) zurückkommen; (drive back) zurückfahren. to ~ ~ to what I was saying um noch einmal auf das zurückzukommen, was ich vorhin gesagt habe; we always ~ ~ to the same difficulty wir stoßen immer wieder auf dieselbe Schwierigkeit; can I ~ ~ to you on that one? kann ich später darauf zurückkommen?; the colour is coming ~ to her cheeks langsam bekommt sie wieder Farbe; will his memory ever ~ ~? wird er je das Gedächtnis wiedererlangen?
(b) (return to one's memory) his face is coming ~ to me langsam erinnere ich mich wieder an sein Gesicht; ah yes, it's all coming ~ ach ja, jetzt fällt mir alles wieder ein; your German will very quickly ~ ~ du wirst ganz schnell wieder ins Deutsche reinkommen (inf).
(c) (become popular again) wieder in Mode kommen.
(d) (make a comeback) they thought Sinatra would never ~ ~ man glaubte, Sinatra würde niemals ein Comeback machen; he came ~ strongly into the game er spielte mächtig auf.
(e) (reply) reagieren. she came ~ at him with a fierce accusation sie entgegnete ihm mit einer heftigen Anschuldigung.

♦**come between** vi +prep obj people, lovers treten zwischen (+acc). I never let anything ~ ~ me and my evening pint ich lasse mich durch nichts von meinem abendlichen Bier(chen) abhalten; he tried to ~ ~ the two men fighting er versuchte, die beiden Kampfhähne zu trennen.

♦**come by** 1 vi +prep obj (obtain) kriegen; illness, bruise sich (dat) holen; idea kommen auf (+acc). 2 vi (visit) vorbeikommen.

♦**come close to** *vi +prep obj see* come near to.

♦**come down** *vi* **(a)** *(from ladder, stairs)* herunterkommen; *(aircraft also)* landen; *(from mountain also)* absteigen; *(snow, rain)* fallen. ~ ~ **from there at once!** komm da sofort runter!; **we came ~ to 6,000 metres** wir gingen auf 6.000 m runter.
(b) *(be demolished: building etc)* abgerissen werden; *(fall down)* (he)runterfallen.
(c) *(drop: prices)* sinken, runtergehen *(inf)*; *(seller)* runtergehen *(to auf +acc)*.
(d) *(be a question of)* ankommen *(to auf +acc)*. **it all ~s ~ to something very simple** das ist letzten Endes ganz einfach.
(e) *(lose social rank)* sinken, absteigen. **you've ~ ~ in the world a bit** du bist aber ganz schön tief gesunken; **she had ~ ~ to begging** es war schon so weit mit ihr (gekommen) *or* sie war schon so tief gesunken, daß sie betteln ging.
(f) *(reach)* reichen *(to bis auf +acc, zu)*. **her hair ~s ~ to her shoulders** die Haare gehen *or* fallen ihr bis auf die Schultern; **the dress ~s ~ to her knees** das Kleid geht ihr bis zum Knie.
(g) *(be transmitted: tradition, story etc)* überliefert werden.
(h) *(from university)* **when did you ~ ~?** wann bist du von der Uni runter *(inf)*, wann haben Sie die Universität verlassen?; *(for vac)* seit wann habt ihr Semesterferien?

♦**come down on** *vi +prep obj* **(a)** *(punish, rebuke)* rannehmen *(inf)*, zusammenstauchen *(inf)*; *see* brick. **(b)** *(decide in favour of)* setzen auf *(+acc)*. **he came ~ ~ ~ the side of expansion** er setzte auf Expansion; **you've got to ~ ~ ~ one side or the other** du mußt dich so oder so entscheiden.

♦**come down with** *vi +prep obj illness* kriegen.

♦**come for** *vi +prep obj* kommen wegen.

♦**come forward** *vi* **(a)** sich melden. **(b) to ~ ~ with help/money** Hilfe/Geld anbieten; **to ~ ~ with a good suggestion** mit einem guten Vorschlag kommen.

♦**come from** *vi +prep obj* kommen aus; *(suggestion)* kommen *or* stammen von. **where does he/it ~ ~?** wo kommt er/das her?

♦**come in** *vi* **(a)** *(he)*reinkommen; *(person also)* eintreten. **~ ~!** herein!; **to ~ ~ out of the cold** aus der Kälte kommen.
(b) *(arrive)* ankommen, eintreffen; *(train also)* einfahren; *(ship also)* einlaufen.
(c) *(tide)* kommen.
(d) *(report, information etc)* hereinkommen. **a report has just ~ ~ of ...** uns ist gerade eine Meldung über ... zugegangen.
(e) *(become seasonable)* **when do strawberries ~ ~?** wann ist die Zeit für Erdbeeren?, wann gibt es (frische) Erdbeeren?
(f) *(fashions, vogue)* aufkommen, in Mode kommen.
(g) *(in a race)* **he came ~ fourth** er wurde vierter, er belegte den vierten Platz; **where did he ~ ~?** wievielter ist er denn geworden?, welchen Platz hat er belegt?
(h) *(Pol: be elected to power)* **the socialists came ~ at the last election** bei den letzten Wahlen kamen die Sozialisten ans Ruder *or* an die Regierung.
(i) *(be received as income)* **he has £5,000 coming ~ every year** er kriegt *(inf)* or hat £ 5.000 im Jahr.
(j) *(have a part to play)* **where do I ~ ~?** welche Rolle spiele ich dabei?; **... but where does your brother ~ ~?** ... aber was hat dein Bruder mit der ganzen Sache zu tun?; **that will ~ ~ handy** *(inf)* or **useful** das kann ich/man noch gut gebrauchen.
(k) *(Telec)* **~ ~, Panda 5** Panda 5, melden!

♦**come in for** *vi +prep obj attention, admiration* erregen; *criticism etc also* hinnehmen *or* einstecken müssen.

♦**come in on** *vi +prep obj venture, scheme etc* mitmachen bei, sich beteiligen an *(+dat)*.

♦**come into** *vi +prep obj* **(a)** *legacy etc (inherit)* erben. **to ~ ~ one's own** zeigen, was in einem steckt.
(b) *(be involved)* **I don't see where I ~ ~ all this** ich verstehe nicht, was ich mit der ganzen Sache zu tun habe; **this is a donation, publicity doesn't ~ ~ ~ it** es handelt sich hier um eine Spende, Publicity ist dabei nicht im Spiel.
(c) *(in fixed collocations)* **to ~ ~ being** *or* **existence** entstehen; **to ~ ~ blossom/bud** zu blühen/knospen beginnen; **to ~ ~ sb's possession** in jds Besitz gelangen; *see* force, use[1] *etc.*

♦**come near to** *vi +prep obj* **to ~ ~ doing sth** nahe daran *or* drauf und dran sein, etw zu tun; **he came ~ ~ (committing) suicide** er war *or* stand kurz vor dem Selbstmord.

♦**come of** *vi +prep obj* **(a)** *(result from)* **nothing came ~** es ist nichts daraus geworden, es führte zu nichts; **that's what ~s ~ disobeying!** das kommt davon, wenn man nicht hören will!
(b) *(be descended from)* kommen *or* stammen aus.
(c) **to ~ ~ age** *(lit)* volljährig werden; *(fig)* aus den Kinderschuhen herauswachsen.

♦**come off** 1 *vi* **(a)** *(person: off bicycle etc)* runterfallen.
(b) *(button, handle, paint etc)* abgehen; *(be removable also)* sich abnehmen lassen.
(c) *(stains, marks)* weg- *or* rausgehen.
(d) *(take place)* stattfinden. **her wedding didn't ~ ~ after all** aus ihrer Hochzeit ist nun doch nichts geworden.
(e) *(plans etc)* klappen *(inf)*; *(attempts, experiments etc also)* glücken, gelingen.
(f) *(acquit oneself)* abschneiden. **he came ~ well in comparison to his brother** im Vergleich zu seinem Bruder ist er gut weggekommen; **he always came ~ badly in fights** bei Schlägereien zog er immer den kürzeren; **several companies are likely to ~ ~ badly with the new tax laws** mehrere Firmen kommen in der neuen Steuergesetzgebung schlecht weg.
(g) *(sl: have orgasm)* kommen *(inf)*. **eventually he came ~** endlich kam es ihm *(sl)*.
2 *vi +prep obj* **(a)** *bicycle, horse etc* fallen von.
(b) *(button, paint, stain)* abgehen von.
(c) *case, assignment etc* abgehen. **to ~ ~ the gold standard** *(Fin)* vom Goldstandard abgehen.
(d) *(be removed from price of)* runtergehen von *(inf)*.
(e) *(inf)* **~ ~ it!** nun mach mal halblang! *(inf)*.

♦**come on** 1 *vi* **(a)** *(follow)* nachkommen.
(b) *see* come along **(a)** ~ ~! komm!; ~ **on!** komm doch!, komm schon!
(c) *(continue to advance)* zukommen *(towards auf +acc)*.
(d) *(progress, develop)* *see* come along **(c)**.
(e) *(start)* *(night)* hereinbrechen; *(storm)* ausbrechen, einsetzen. **it came ~ to rain, the rain came ~** es begann zu regnen, es fing an zu regnen; **I feel a cold coming ~** ich habe das Gefühl, ich kriege eine Erkältung; **winter etc is coming ~** es wird Winter etc, der Winter etc naht *(liter)*.
(f) *(Jur: case)* verhandelt werden.
(g) *(Sport: player)* ins Spiel kommen; *(Theat)* *(actor)* auftreten, auf die Bühne kommen; *(play)* gegeben werden.
(h) *(inf)* **she's coming ~ seventeen** sie wird siebzehn.
(i) *(sl: make impression, behave)* **he tries to ~ ~ like a tough guy** er versucht, den starken Mann zu mimen *(inf)*; **he came ~ with this bit about knowing the director** er gab damit an, den Direktor zu kennen; **to ~ ~ strong** groß auftreten *(inf)*.
2 *vi +prep obj* = come (up)on.

♦**come out** *vi* **(a)** *(he)*rauskommen. **to ~ ~ of a room/meeting etc** aus einem Zimmer/einer Versammlung *etc* kommen; **can you ~ ~ tonight?** kannst du heute abend weg?; **do you want to ~ ~ with me?** gehst du mit mir weg?; **he asked her to ~ ~ for a meal/drive** er lud sie zum Essen/einer Spazierfahrt ein.
(b) *(be published, marketed)* *(book, magazine)* erscheinen, herauskommen; *(new product)* auf den Markt kommen; *(film)* (in den Kinos) anlaufen; *(become known)* *(exam results)* herauskommen, bekannt werden; *(news)* bekannt werden.
(c) *(Ind)* **to ~ ~ (on strike)** in den Streik treten, streiken.
(d) *(Phot: film, photograph)* **the photo of the hills hasn't ~ ~ very well** das Foto von den Bergen ist nicht sehr gut geworden; **let's hope the photos ~ ~** hoffentlich sind die Bilder was geworden *(inf)* or gut geworden; **you always ~ ~ well** *on or* **in photos** du bist sehr fotogen; **all the details have ~ ~ clearly** alle Einzelheiten kommen klar (he)raus.
(e) *(show itself)* *(meaning, truth)* herauskommen, sich zeigen. **his kindness/arrogance ~s ~ in everything he says** bei allem, was er sagt, spürt man seine Freundlichkeit/bei allem, was er sagt, kommt seine Arroganz durch.
(f) *(splinter, stains, dye etc)* (he)rausgehen.
(g) *(Math: of problems, divisions etc)* aufgehen.
(h) *(total, average)* betragen. **the total ~ ~ at £500** das Ganze beläuft sich auf *(acc)* or macht *(inf)* £ 500.
(i) *(in exams etc)* **he came ~ third in French** er wurde drittbester in Französich; **she came ~ of the interview well** sie hat bei dem Vorstellungsgespräch einen guten Eindruck gemacht.
(j) *(stars, sun, flowers)* (he)rauskommen.
(k) *(truth, meaning etc)* (he)rauskommen. **no sooner had the words ~ ~ than ...** kaum waren die Worte heraus, als ....
(l) *(go into society: girl)* debütieren.
(m) *(be released: prisoner)* (he)rauskommen.
(n) *(be covered with)* **his face came ~ in pimples** er bekam lauter Pickel im Gesicht; **he came ~ in a rash** er bekam einen Ausschlag; **he came ~ in a sweat** ihm brach der Schweiß aus.
(o) to ~ ~ against/in favour of *or* **for sth** sich gegen/für etw aussprechen, etw ablehnen/befürworten.
(p) to ~ ~ of sth badly/well bei etw schlecht/nicht schlecht wegkommen; **to ~ ~ on top** sich durchsetzen, Sieger bleiben.

♦**come out with** *vi +prep obj truth, facts* rausrücken mit *(inf)*; *remarks, nonsense* loslassen *(inf)*.

♦**come over** 1 *vi* **(a)** *(lit)* herüberkommen. **he came ~ to England** er kam nach England.
(b) *(change one's opinions, allegiance)* **he came ~ to our side** er trat auf unsere Seite über; **he came ~ to our way of thinking** er machte sich unsere Denkungsart zu eigen.
(c) *(inf: become suddenly)* werden. **I came ~ (all) queer** *or* **funny** mir wurde ganz komisch *(inf)* or ganz merkwürdig; **she came ~ faint/giddy** sie wurde ohnmächtig/ihr wurde schwindelig; **it came ~ cloudy** es bewölkte sich.
(d) *(be understood)* *see* come across 1 **(b)**.
(e) *(make an impression)* *see* come across 1 **(c)**.
2 *vi +prep obj* *(feelings)* überkommen. **I don't know what came ~ her to speak like that!** ich weiß nicht, was über sie gekommen ist, so zu reden!; **what's ~ ~ you?** was ist denn (auf einmal) mit dir los?, was ist in dich gefahren?

♦**come round** *vi* **(a)** **the road was blocked and we had to ~ ~ by the farm** die Straße war blockiert, so daß wir einen Umweg über den Bauernhof machen mußten.
(b) *(call round)* vorbeikommen *or* -schauen.
(c) *(recur)* **your birthday will soon ~ ~ again** du hast ja bald wieder Geburtstag; **Christmas has ~ ~ again** nun ist wieder Weihnachten.
(d) *(change one's opinions)* es sich *(dat)* anders überlegen. **eventually he came ~ ~ to our way of thinking** schließlich machte er (dat) unsere Denkungsart zu eigen.
(e) *(regain consciousness)* wieder zu sich *(dat)* kommen.
(f) to ~ ~ to doing sth *(get round)* dazu kommen, etw zu tun.
(g) *(throw off bad mood)* wieder vernünftig werden *(inf)*.
(h) *(Naut: boat)* wenden.

♦**come through** 1 *vi* **(a)** *message, phone-call, order* durchkommen. **your expenses/papers haven't ~ ~ yet** *(be cleared)* wir haben Ihre Ausgaben noch nicht durchgekriegt/Ihre Papiere sind noch nicht fertig.
(b) *(survive)* durchkommen.
2 *vi +prep obj* *(survive)* *illness, danger* überstehen, überleben. **he came ~ the war without a scratch** er überstand den Krieg ohne eine Schramme.

♦**come to** 1 *vi* **(a)** *(regain consciousness: also* ~ ~ **oneself)** wieder zu sich kommen.
(b) *(Naut)* beidrehen.
2 *vi +prep obj* **(a)** **he/that will never ~ ~ much** aus ihm/

daraus wird nie etwas werden; **that won't ~ ~ much** daraus wird nicht viel werden; **that didn't ~ ~ anything** daraus ist nichts geworden.

(b) (*impers*) **when it ~s ~ mathematics, no one can beat him** wenn es um Mathematik geht, kann ihm keiner etwas vormachen; **when it ~s ~ choosing, he ...** wenn er die Wahl hat *or* vor die Wahl gestellt wird, ...; **if it ~s ~ that we're sunk** wenn es dazu kommt, sind wir verloren; **~ ~ that** *or* **if it ~s ~ that, he's just as good** was das betrifft *or* an(be)langt, ist er genauso gut; **let's hope it never ~s ~ a court case** wollen wir hoffen, daß es nie zum Prozeß kommt; **it ~s ~ the same thing** das kommt *or* läuft auf dasselbe hinaus.

(c) (*price, bill*) **how much does it ~ ~?** wieviel macht das?; **it ~s ~ much less/more than I thought** es kommt viel billiger/teurer, als ich dachte.

(d) (*touch on*) *point, subject etc* kommen auf (+*acc*); (*tackle*) *problem, job etc* herangehen an (+*acc*).

(e) (*in certain collocations*) **to ~ ~ ~ a decision** zu einer Entscheidung kommen; **it's coming ~/we've ~ ~ something when ...** es will schon etwas heißen, wenn ...; *see* **attention, blow¹, light** *etc.*

♦**come together** *vi* zusammenkommen, sich treffen. **he and his wife have ~ ~ again** er ist wieder mit seiner Frau zusammen; **it's all coming ~ for him** (*sl*) es regelt sich jetzt alles für ihn (*inf*).

♦**come under** *vi +prep obj* **(a)** (*be subject to*) **to ~ ~ sb's influence/domination** unter jds Einfluß/Herrschaft geraten; **this shop has ~ ~ new management** dieser Laden hat einen neuen Besitzer/Pächter; **this ~s ~ another department** das ist Sache einer anderen Abteilung.

(b) (*be classified*) *category, heading* kommen unter (+*acc*).

♦**come up** *vi* **(a)** (*lit*) hochkommen; (*upstairs*) hoch- *or* raufkommen; (*diver, submarine*) nach oben kommen; (*sun, moon*) aufgehen. **do you ~ ~ to town often?** kommen Sie oft in die Stadt?; **he came ~ ~ (to Oxford) last year** (*Univ*) er ist voriges Jahr nach Oxford gekommen; **you've ~ ~ in the world** du bist ja richtig vornehm geworden!; **he came ~ to me with a smile** er kam lächelnd auf mich zu.

(b) (*supplies, troops etc*) herangeschafft werden.

(c) (*Jur*) (*case*) verhandelt werden, drankommen (*inf*); (*accused*) vor Gericht kommen.

(d) (*plants*) herauskommen.

(e) (*matter for discussion*) aufkommen, angeschnitten werden; (*name*) erwähnt werden.

(f) (*number in lottery etc*) gewinnen. **to ~ ~ for sale/auction** *etc* zum Verkauf/zur Auktion *etc* kommen.

(g) (*post, job*) frei werden. **if any vacancies ~ ~** wenn es eine freie Stelle gibt.

(h) (*be vomited*) wieder hochkommen.

(i) (*shine, show colour*) herauskommen.

♦**come up against** *vi +prep obj* stoßen auf (+*acc*); *opposing team* treffen auf (+*acc*). **his plan was doing well until he came ~ ~ the directors** sein Vorhaben machte gute Fortschritte, bis er an die Geschäftsleitung geriet; **the new teacher keeps coming ~ ~ the headmaster** der neue Lehrer gerät ständig mit dem Direktor aneinander.

♦**come (up)on** *vi +prep obj* **(a)** (*lit*) (*attack by surprise*) überfallen; (*fig*) (*disaster*) hereinbrechen über (+*acc*). **and the fear of the Lord came upon them** (*Bibl*) und die Furcht des Herrn kam über sie (*Bibl*). **(b)** (*find*) stoßen auf (+*acc*).

♦**come up to** *vi +prep obj* **(a)** (*reach up to*) gehen *or* reichen bis zu *or* an (+*acc*). **the water came ~ ~ his knees** das Wasser ging *or* reichte ihm bis an die Knie *or* bis zu den Knien.

(b) (*equal*) *hopes* erfüllen; *expectations* entsprechen (+*dat*).

(c) (*inf: approach*) **she's coming ~ ~ twenty** sie wird bald zwanzig; **we're coming ~ ~ 150 km/h** wir haben gleich 150 km/h drauf (*inf*); **it's just coming ~ ~ 10** es ist gleich 10.

♦**come up with** *vi +prep obj answer* haben; *idea, solution also* kommen auf (+*acc*); *plan* sich (*dat*) ausdenken, entwickeln; *suggestion* machen, bringen. **I can't ~ ~ ~ any answers either** ich habe auch keine Antwort; **let me know if you ~ ~ ~ anything** sagen Sie mir Bescheid, falls Ihnen etwas einfällt.

come-at-able [kʌm'ætəbl] *adj* (*inf*) leicht erreichbar.

comeback ['kʌmbæk] *n* **(a)** (*Theat etc, fig*) Comeback *nt*. **to make** *or* **stage a ~** ein Comeback versuchen/machen.

(b) (*inf: redress*) Anspruch *m* auf Schadenersatz; (*reaction*) Reaktion *f*. **we've got no ~ in this situation** wir können da nichts machen.

comedian [kə'miːdɪən] *n* Komiker *m*; (*fig also*) Witzbold *m*.

comedienne [kə,miːdɪ'en] *n* Komikerin *f*; (*actress*) Komödiendarstellerin, Komödin (*geh*) *f*.

comedown ['kʌmdaʊn] *n* (*inf*) Abstieg *m*.

comedy ['kʌmɪdɪ] *n* **(a)** (*Theat*) Komödie *f*, Lustspiel *nt*. **~ programme** Unterhaltungsprogramm *nt*; **~ writer** Lustspielautor *or* (*classical*) -dichter *m*; **"C~ of Errors"** „Komödie der Irrungen"; **the entire transaction was just one ~ of errors** (*fig*) die ganze Angelegenheit war eine einzige Kette von komischen Verwicklungen; **low/high ~** Klamauk *m*/echte *or* gekonnte Komödie; **to act (in) ~** Komödiendarsteller(in *f*) *m* sein.

(b) (*fig*) Komödie *f*, Theater *nt* (*inf*).

come-hither [kʌm'hɪðəʳ] *adj* (*inf*) **she gave him a ~ look** sie warf ihm einladende *or* aufmunternde Blicke zu.

comeliness ['kʌmlɪnɪs] *n* (*liter*) Wohlgestalt *f* (*liter*).

comely ['kʌmlɪ] *adj* (+*er*) (*liter*) wohlgestaltet (*geh*).

come-on ['kʌmɒn] *n* (*sl: lure, enticement*) Köder *m* (*fig*). **to give sb the ~** (*woman*) jdn anmachen (*sl*).

comer ['kʌməʳ] *n* **this competition is open to all ~s** an diesem Wettbewerb kann sich jeder beteiligen; **"open to all ~s"** „Teilnahme für jedermann".

comestible [kə'mestɪbl] **1** *n usu pl* Nahrungsmittel *pl*. **2** *adj* eßbar. **~ goods** Nahrungsmittel *pl*.

comet ['kɒmɪt] *n* Komet *m*.

come-uppance [,kʌm'ʌpəns] *n* (*inf*): **to get one's ~** die Quittung kriegen (*inf*).

comfit ['kʌmfɪt] *n* (*old*) Konfekt, Zuckerwerk (*old*) *nt*.

comfort ['kʌmfət] **1** *n* **(a)** Komfort *m*, Bequemlichkeit *f*. **relax in the ~ of a leather armchair** entspannen Sie sich in unseren behaglichen Ledersesseln; **he likes his ~s** er liebt seinen Komfort *or* seine Bequemlichkeit; **to live in ~** komfortabel leben; **a flat with every modern ~** eine Wohnung mit allem Komfort.

(b) (*consolation*) Beruhigung *f*, Trost *m*. **to take ~ from the fact that ...** sich mit dem Bewußtsein dessen damit trösten, daß ...; **your presence is/you are a great ~ to me** es beruhigt mich sehr, daß Sie da sind; **it is a ~ to know that ...** es ist tröstlich *or* beruhigend zu wissen, daß ...; **it is no ~ to know that ...** es ist nicht sehr tröstlich *or* es ist nicht gerade ein Trost zu wissen, daß ...; **some ~ you are!** (*iro*) das ist ja ein schöner Trost! (*iro*), **du bist gut!** (*iro*); **small ~** schwacher Trost; **a pipe is a great ~** Pfeiferauchen hat etwas sehr Beruhigendes; **your poems brought a little ~ to my life** Ihre Gedichte haben ein wenig Trost in mein Leben gebracht.

(c) (*US*) **~ station** Bedürfnisanstalt *f*, öffentliche Toilette.

2 *vt* (*console*) trösten. **the child needed a lot of ~ing** es dauerte eine ganze Weile, bis das Kind sich trösten ließ; **he stayed with the injured man to ~ him** er blieb bei dem Verletzten, um ihm Beistand zu leisten; **the hot soup ~ed him a little** nach der heißen Suppe fühlte er sich etwas wohler.

comfortable ['kʌmfətəbl] *adj* **(a)** *armchair, bed, shoes, life* bequem; *room, hotel etc* komfortabel; *temperature* angenehm. **to make sb/oneself ~** es jdm/sich bequem machen; (*make at home*) es jdm/sich gemütlich machen; **the sick man had a ~ night** der Kranke hatte *or* verbrachte eine ruhige Nacht; **the patient/his condition is ~** der Patient/er ist wohlauf; **are you ~?**, **asked the nurse** liegen/sitzen *etc* Sie bequem?, fragte die Schwester; **are you too hot? — no, I'm just ~** ist es Ihnen zu heiß? — nein, es ist angenehm so.

(b) (*fig*) *income, pension* ausreichend; *life* geruhsam, angenehm; *majority, lead* sicher; *figure* mollig. **his landlady was the ~, motherly type** seine Wirtin war der mütterliche Typ, bei dem man sich wohl fühlt; **he's very ~ to be with** bei ihm fühlt man sich sehr wohl; **she had quite a ~ feeling about it** sie hatte ein gutes Gefühl dabei; **I'm not very ~ about it** mir ist nicht ganz wohl bei der Sache, ich habe kein besonders gutes Gefühl dabei; **I'm not too ~ about giving her the job** mir ist nicht ganz wohl bei dem Gedanken, ihr die Stelle zu geben.

comfortably ['kʌmfətəblɪ] *adv* **(a)** *lie, sit, dress etc* bequem; *furnished, upholstered* komfortabel.

(b) (*fig*) *win, lead* sicher; *live* geruhsam, angenehm; *afford* gut und gern; *claim, say* ruhig. **they are ~ off** es geht ihnen gut; **he was ~ aware that he was the favourite** er fühlte sich wohl in dem Bewußtsein, (der) Favorit zu sein; **he was ~ certain of winning** er wiegte sich in der Gewißheit, daß er gewinnen würde.

comforter ['kʌmfətəʳ] *n* **(a)** (*person*) Tröster(in *f*) *m*. **my wife was my ~ in times of stress** in schweren Zeiten war meine Frau mein Beistand. **(b)** (*dated: scarf*) Wollschal *m*. **(c)** (*dummy, teat*) Schnuller *m*. **(d)** (*US: quilt*) Deckbett *nt*.

comforting ['kʌmfətɪŋ] *adj* tröstlich, beruhigend. **a ~ cup of tea** eine Tasse Tee zur Beruhigung.

comfortless ['kʌmfətlɪs] *adj* **(a)** *chair etc* unbequem; *room, hotel* ohne Komfort. **(b)** (*fig*) *person* ungemütlich; *life* unbequem; *thought, prospect* unerfreulich, unangenehm.

comfy ['kʌmfɪ] *adj* (+*er*) (*inf*) *chair* bequem; *hotel, flat, room* gemütlich. **are you ~?** sitzt/liegst du bequem?; **make yourself ~** machen Sie es sich (*dat*) bequem *or* gemütlich (*inf*).

comic ['kɒmɪk] **1** *adj* komisch. **~ actor** Komödiendarsteller, Komöde (*geh*) *m*; **~ opera** komische Oper; **~ relief** befreiende Komik; **~ strip** Comic strip *m*; **~ verse** humoristische Gedichte *pl*. **2** *n* **(a)** (*person*) Komiker(in *f*) *m*. **(b)** (*magazine*) Comic-Heft(chen) *nt*. **(c)** (*US*) **~s** Comics *pl*.

comical *adj*, **~ly** *adv* ['kɒmɪkəl, -ɪ] komisch, ulkig.

coming ['kʌmɪŋ] **1** *n* Kommen *nt*. **you can sense the ~ of spring** man spürt *or* spürt das Herannahen des Frühlings; **the first/second ~ (of the Lord)** die Ankunft/Wiederkunft des Herrn; **the ~ of a new manager caused a lot of excitement** die Ankunft eines neuen Geschäftsführers verursachte viel Aufregung; **~ and going/~s and goings** Kommen und Gehen *nt*; **~-out** gesellschaftliches Debüt, (offizielle) Einführung in die Gesellschaft; **~-out party** Debütantinnenparty *f*; **~ of age** Erreichung *f* der Volljährigkeit.

2 *adj* (*lit, fig*) kommend; *year, week also* nächst. **a ~ politician** einer der kommenden Männer in der Politik; **it's the ~ thing** (*inf*) das ist zur Zeit groß im Kommen (*inf*).

comma ['kɒmə] *n* Komma *nt*, Beistrich *m* (*form*).

command [kə'mɑːnd] **1** *vt* **(a)** (*order*) befehlen, den Befehl geben (*sb* jdm). **he ~ed that the prisoners be released** er befahl, die Gefangenen freizulassen.

(b) (*be in control of*) *army, ship* befehligen, kommandieren.

(c) (*be in a position to use*) *money, resources, vocabulary* verfügen über (+*acc*), gebieten über (+*acc*) (*geh*). **to ~ sb's services** jds Dienste *or* Hilfe in Anspruch nehmen.

(d) **to ~ sb's admiration/respect** jdm Bewunderung/Respekt abnötigen, jds Bewunderung/Respekt erheischen (*geh*); *antiques* **~ a high price** Antiquitäten stehen hoch im Preis.

(e) (*overlook*) *harbour, valley* überragen; *view* bieten (*of* über +*acc*).

2 *vi* **(a)** (*order*) befehlen.

(b) (*Mil, Naut: to be in ~*) das Kommando führen.

3 *n* **(a)** (*order*) Befehl *m*. **at/by the ~ of** auf Befehl +*gen*; **the word of ~** auf Kommando; **on ~** auf Befehl *or* Kommando.

(b) (*Mil: power, authority*) Kommando *nt*, Befehlsgewalt *f*. **to**

be in ~ das Kommando *or* den (Ober)befehl haben (*of* über +*acc*); **to take** ~ das Kommando übernehmen (*of gen*); **the new colonel arrived to take** ~ **of his regiment** der neue Oberst kam, um sein Regiment zu übernehmen; **during/under his** ~ unter seinem Kommando; **the battalion is under the** ~ *of* ... das Bataillon steht unter dem Kommando von ... *or* wird befehligt von ...; **to be second in** ~ zweiter Befehlshaber sein.
  (c) (*Mil*) (*troops*) Kommando *nt*; (*district*) Befehlsbereich *m*; (~ *post*) Posten *m*.
  (d) (*fig: possession, mastery*) Beherrschung *f*. ~ **of the seas** Seeherrschaft *f*; **the gymnast's remarkable** ~ **over his body** die bemerkenswerte Körperbeherrschung des Turners; **he has a** ~ **of three foreign languages** er beherrscht drei Fremdsprachen; **his** ~ **of English is excellent** er beherrscht das Englische ausgezeichnet; **to have sb/sth at one's** ~ über jdn/etw verfügen *or* gebieten (*geh*); **I am at your** ~ ich stehe zu Ihrer Verfügung.
commandant [ˌkɒmənˈdænt] *n* (*Mil*) Kommandant *m*.
commandeer [ˌkɒmənˈdɪəʳ] *vt* (*Mil*) *men* einziehen; (*from another battalion, fig*) abbeordern, abkommandieren; *stores, ship, car etc* (*lit, fig*) beschlagnahmen, requirieren.
commander [kəˈmɑːndəʳ] *n* **(a)** Führer *m*; (*Mil, Aviat*) Befehlshaber, Kommandant *m*; (*Naut*) Fregattenkapitän *m*. ~/~**s-in-chief** Oberbefehlshaber *m/pl*. **(b)** (*of order of chivalry*) Komtur *m*.
commanding [kəˈmɑːndɪŋ] *adj* **(a)** *position* Befehls-. ~ **officer** (*Mil*) befehlshabender Offizier. **(b)** *personality, voice, tone* gebieterisch; *voice, tone also* Kommando- (*pej*). **(c)** (*of place*) beherrschend. ~ **heights** Kommandohöhen *pl*.
commandment [kəˈmɑːndmənt] *n* (*esp Bibl*) Gebot *nt*. **to break a** ~ gegen ein Gebot verstoßen.
command module *n* (*Space*) Kommandokapsel *f*.
commando [kəˈmɑːndəʊ] *n, pl* -**s** (*Mil*) (*soldier*) Angehöriger *m* eines Kommando(trupp)s; (*unit*) Kommando(trupp *m*) *nt*.
command: ~ **performance** *n* (*Theat*) königliche Gala-vorstellung; ~ **post** *n* (*Mil*) Kommandoposten *m*.
commemorate [kəˈmeməreɪt] *vt* gedenken (+*gen*). **a festival to** ~ **the event** eine Feier zum Gedenken an das Ereignis.
commemoration [kəˌmeməˈreɪʃən] *n* Gedenken *nt*. **in** ~ **of** zum Gedenken an (+*acc*).
commemorative [kəˈmemərətɪv] *adj* Gedenk-. ~ **plaque** Gedenktafel *f*.
commence [kəˈmens] *vti* (*form*) beginnen.
commencement [kəˈmensmənt] *n* **(a)** (*form*) Beginn *m*. **(b)** (*Univ: Cambridge, Dublin, US*) Abschlußfeier *f* (*zur Verleihung der Diplome etc*).
commend [kəˈmend] **1** *vt* **(a)** (*praise*) loben; (*recommend*) empfehlen. **(b)** (*entrust*), (*Bibl*) *spirit, soul* befehlen (*to dat*). ~ **me to Mr Smith** (*form*) empfehlen Sie mich Herrn Smith (*form*). **2** *vr* sich empfehlen (*to dat*).
commendable [kəˈmendəbl] *adj* lobenswert, löblich.
commendably [kəˈmendəblɪ] *adv* lobenswerterweise.
commendation [ˌkɒmenˈdeɪʃən] *n* (*no pl: praise*) Lob *nt*; (*award*) Auszeichnung *f*; (*official recognition*) Belobigung *f*.
commendatory [kəˈmendətrɪ] *adj* anerkennend.
commensurate [kəˈmenʃərɪt] *adj* entsprechend (*with dat*). **to be** ~ **with sth** einer Sache (*dat*) entsprechen; **they made salaries** ~ **with those in comparable professions** die Gehälter wurden denen in vergleichbaren Berufen angeglichen.
commensurately [kəˈmenʃərətlɪ] *adv* entsprechend, angemessen.
comment [ˈkɒment] **1** *n* (*remark*) Bemerkung *f* (*on, about* über +*acc*, zu); (*official*) Kommentar *m* (*on* zu); (*no pl: talk, gossip*) Gerede *nt*; (*textual or margin note etc*) Anmerkung *f*. **no** ~ kein Kommentar!; **to make a** ~ eine Bemerkung machen/einen Kommentar abgeben (*on* zu). **need I** ~? Kommentar überflüssig! **3** *vt* bemerken, äußern.
commentary [ˈkɒməntərɪ] *n* Kommentar *m* (*on* zu). **he used to do the commentaries for football matches** früher war er Reporter bei Fußballspielen; **I don't need a constant** ~ **from you** ich brauche deine ständigen Kommentare nicht.
commentate [ˈkɒmenteɪt] *vi* (*Rad, TV*) Reporter(in) sein (*on* bei).
commentator [ˈkɒmenteɪtəʳ] *n* **(a)** (*Rad, TV*) Reporter(in *f*) *m*. **(b)** (*on texts etc*) Interpret(in *f*) *m*; (*of Bible*) Exeget(in *f*) *m*.
commerce [ˈkɒmɜːs] *n* **(a)** (*Comm*) Handel *m*; (*between countries also*) Handelsverkehr *m*. **in the world of** ~ im Geschäftsleben; **he is in** ~ er ist ein Geschäftsmann. **(b)** (*form: dealings*) Verkehr *m*.
commercial [kəˈmɜːʃəl] **1** *adj* Handels-; *custom also, ethics, training* kaufmännisch; *language, premises, vehicle* Geschäfts-; *production, radio, project, success, attitude etc* kommerziell. **fish fingers and similar** ~ **products** Fischstäbchen und ähnliche fabrikmäßig hergestellte Erzeugnisse; **the** ~ **world** die Geschäftswelt; **to think in** ~ **terms** kaufmännisch denken; **it makes good** ~ **sense** das läßt sich kaufmännisch durchaus vertreten.
  2 *n* (*Rad, TV*) Werbespot *m*. **during the** ~**s während der** (Fernseh)werbung.
commercial: ~ **art** *n* Werbegraphik *f*; ~ **artist** *n* Werbegraphiker(in *f*) *m*; ~ **college** *n* Fachschule *f* für kaufmännische Berufe.
commercialese [kəmɜːʃəˈliːz] *n* Wirtschaftssprache *f*.
commercialism [kəˈmɜːʃəlɪzəm] *n* Kommerzialisierung *f*; (*connected with art, literature also*) Kommerz *m*.
commercialization [kəˌmɜːʃəlaɪˈzeɪʃən] *n* Kommerzialisierung *f*.
commercialize [kəˈmɜːʃəlaɪz] *vt* kommerzialisieren.
commercially [kəˈmɜːʃəlɪ] *adv* geschäftlich; *manufacture, succeed* kommerziell. **to be** ~ **minded** kaufmännisch veranlagt *or* kommerziell eingestellt (*usu pej*) sein.

commercial: ~ **television** *n* kommerzielles Fernsehen, Werbefernsehen *nt*; ~ **traveller** *n* Handelsvertreter(in *f*) *m*.
commie [ˈkɒmɪ] (*pej inf*) **1** *n* Rote(r) (*pej inf*), Bolschewik (*often pej*) *m*. **2** *adj* rot (*pej inf*), Bolschewiken- (*often pej*).
commingle [kɒˈmɪŋgl] *vi* (*liter*) sich vermischen; (*colours*) ineinander verschwimmen.
commiserate [kəˈmɪzəreɪt] *vi* mitfühlen (*with* mit). **we** ~ **with you in the loss of your husband** wir nehmen Anteil am Tode Ihres Gatten.
commiseration [kəˌmɪzəˈreɪʃən] *n* Mitgefühl *n no pl*, (An)teilnahme *f no pl*. **my** ~**s** herzliches Beileid (*on* zu).
commissar [ˈkɒmɪsɑːʳ] *n* Kommissar *m*.
commissariat [ˌkɒmɪˈsɛərɪət] *n* **(a)** (*Mil*) Intendantur *f*. **(b)** (*in USSR etc*) Kommissariat *nt*.
commissary [ˈkɒmɪsərɪ] *n* **(a)** (*Mil*) Intendant *m*. **(b)** (*delegate*) Beauftragte(r) *mf*. **(c)** (*US Comm*) Laden *m* in Lagern/auf Baustellen *etc*.
commission [kəˈmɪʃən] **1** *n* **(a)** (*committing*) Begehen *nt* (*form*).
  (b) (*for building, painting etc*) Auftrag *m*.
  (c) (*Comm*) Provision *f*. **on** ~, **on a** ~ **basis** auf Provision(sbasis); ~ **agent** Kommissionär(in *f*) *m*.
  (d) (*Mil*) Patent *nt*.
  (e) (*special committee*) Kommission *f*, Ausschuß *m*. ~ **of enquiry** Untersuchungskommission *f or* -ausschuß *m*.
  (f) (*Naut, fig: use*) **to put in(to)** ~ in Dienst stellen; **to take out of** ~ aus dem Verkehr ziehen; **in/out of** ~ in/außer Betrieb.
  (g) (*form: task, errand*) Erledigung *f*. **I have a** ~ **for my uncle** ich habe etwas für meinen Onkel zu erledigen; **I was given a** ~ **to recruit new members** ich wurde (damit) beauftragt, neue Mitglieder zu werben.
  (h) **the** (EEC) **C**~ die EG-Kommission.
  2 *vt* **(a)** *person* beauftragen; *book, painting* in Auftrag geben. **to** ~ **sb to do sth** jdn damit beauftragen, etw zu tun. **(b)** (*Mil*) *sb* zum Offizier ernennen; *officer* ernennen. ~**ed officer** Offizier *m*. **(c)** (*Naut*) *ship* in Dienst stellen.
commissionaire [kəˌmɪʃəˈnɛəʳ] *n* Portier *m*.
commissioner [kəˈmɪʃənəʳ] *n* **(a)** (*member of commission*) Ausschußmitglied *nt*. **(b)** (*of police*) Polizeipräsident *m*. **(c)** (*Jur*) ~ **of** *or* **for oaths** Notar(in *f*) *m*.
commit [kəˈmɪt] **1** *vt* **(a)** (*perpetrate*) begehen. **the crimes they** ~**ted against humanity** ihre Verbrechen gegen die Menschlichkeit.
  (b) **to** ~ **sb (to prison/to a home)** jdn ins Gefängnis/in Heim einweisen; **to have sb** ~**ted (to an asylum)** jdn in eine Anstalt einweisen lassen; **to** ~ **sb for trial** jdn einem Gericht überstellen; **to** ~ **one's soul to God** seine Seele Gott befehlen; **to** ~ **sb/sth to sb's care** jdn/etw jds Obhut (*dat*) anvertrauen; **to** ~ **to writing** *or* **to paper** zu Papier bringen; **to** ~ **to the flames** den Flammen übergeben *or* überantworten; *see* memory.
  (c) (*involve, obligate*) festlegen (*to* auf +*acc*). **to** ~ **troops to a battle** Truppen in ein Gefecht schicken; **to** ~ **resources/manpower to a project** Mittel/Arbeitskräfte für ein Projekt einsetzen; **that doesn't** ~ **you to buying the book** das verpflichtet Sie nicht zum Kauf des Buches; **I don't want to be** ~**ted ich** möchte mich nicht festlegen.
  (d) (*Parl*) *bill* an den (zuständigen) Ausschuß überweisen.
  2 *vr* sich festlegen (*to* auf +*acc*). **to** ~ **oneself on an issue** sich in einer Frage festlegen; **you have to** ~ **yourself totally to the cause** man muß sich voll und ganz für die Sache einsetzen *or* engagieren; **the government has** ~**ted itself to (undertake) far-reaching reforms** die Regierung hat sich zu weitreichenden Reformen bekannt *or* verpflichtet; **he has** ~**ted himself to improving conditions** er hat sich zur Verbesserung der Bedingungen verpflichtet; ... **without** ~**ting myself to the whole contract** ... ohne damit an den ganzen Vertrag gebunden zu sein.
commitment [kəˈmɪtmənt] *n* **(a)** (*act*) *see* committal (a).
  (b) (*obligation*) Verpflichtung *f*; (*dedication*) Engagement *nt*. **his family/teaching** ~**s** seine familiären Verpflichtungen *pl*/seine Lehrverpflichtungen *pl*; **there's no** ~ **(to buy)** es besteht kein(erlei) Kaufzwang; **the trainer demands one hundred per cent** ~ **from his team** der Trainer verlangt von seiner Mannschaft hundertprozentigen Einsatz; **his** ~ **to his job is total** er geht völlig in seiner Arbeit auf; **political/military** ~ politisches/militärisches Engagement.
  (c) (*Parl: of bill*) Überweisung *f* an den (zuständigen) Ausschuß.
committal [kəˈmɪtl] *n* **(a)** (*to prison, asylum etc*) Einweisung *f*. **his** ~ **for trial** seine Überstellung ans Gericht; ~ **proceedings** gerichtliche Voruntersuchung.
  (b) (*of crime etc*) Begehen *nt* (*form*).
  (c) ~ **to memory** Auswendiglernen *nt*; (*of single fact*) Sich-Einprägen *nt*.
  (d) (*Parl*) *see* commitment (c).
committed [kəˈmɪtɪd] *adj* (*dedicated*) engagiert. **he is so** ~ **to his work that he has no time for his family** er geht so in seiner Arbeit auf, daß er keine Zeit für die Familie hat; **all his life he has been** ~ **to this cause** er hat sein Leben lang für diese Sache eingesetzt.
committee [kəˈmɪtɪ] *n* Ausschuß *m* (*also Parl*), Komitee *nt*. **to be** *or* **sit on a** ~ in einem Ausschuß *or* Komitee sein *or* sitzen; **C**~ **of 100** (*Brit*) Komitee der Hundert; ~ **meeting** Ausschußsitzung *f*; ~ **member** Ausschußmitglied *nt*; **the bill didn't reach the** ~ **stage** der Gesetzentwurf ist gar nicht erst an den (zuständigen) Ausschuß gelangt; **the** ~ **stage lasted weeks** der Gesetzentwurf wurde mehrere Wochen im Ausschuß verhandelt.
commode [kəˈməʊd] *n* **(a)** (*chest of drawers*) Kommode *f*. **(b)** (*night-*~) (Nacht)stuhl *m*.
commodious [kəˈməʊdɪəs] *adj* geräumig.
commodity [kəˈmɒdɪtɪ] *n* Ware *f*; (*agricultural*) Erzeugnis *nt*.

basic *or* staple commodities (*natural*) Grundstoffe *pl*; (*St Ex*) Rohstoffe *pl*; (*manufactured*) Bedarfsgüter *pl*; (*foodstuffs*) Grundnahrungsmittel *pl*; ~ market Rohstoffmarkt *m*; electricity is a ~ which every country needs Strom ist ein (Versorgungs)gut, das jedes Land braucht.

commodore ['kɒmədɔːʳ] *n* (*Naut*) Flottillenadmiral *m* (*BRD*); (*senior captain*) Kommodore *m*; (*of yacht club*) Präsident *m*.

common ['kɒmən] **1** *adj* (+*er*) **(a)** (*shared by many*) gemeinsam; *property also* Gemein-, gemeinschaftlich. ~ land Allmende *f*; ~ prostitute Straßendirne *f*; it is ~ knowledge that ... es is allgemein bekannt, daß ...; it is to the ~ advantage that ... es ist von allgemeinem Nutzen, daß ...; very little/no ~ ground kaum eine/keine gemeinsame Basis.
(b) (*frequently seen or heard etc*) häufig; *word also* weitverbreitet *attr*, weit verbreitet *pred*, allgemein; *animal, bird* häufig *pred*, häufig anzutreffend *attr*; *belief, custom*, (*over large area*) *animal, bird* (weit)verbreitet *attr*, weit verbreitet *pred*; (*customary, usual*) normal. it's quite a ~ occurrence/sight das geschieht/das sieht man ziemlich häufig; it's ~ for visitors to feel ill here Besucher fühlen sich hier häufig krank; nowadays it's quite ~ for the man to do the housework es ist heutzutage ganz normal, daß der Mann die Hausarbeit macht.
(c) (*ordinary*) gewöhnlich. the ~ man der Normalbürger; the ~ people die einfachen Leute, das gemeine Volk (*pej*); a ~ soldier ein einfacher *or* gemeiner (*dated*) Soldat; the ~ run of mankind die (breite) Masse; the ~ touch das Volkstümliche; the Book of C~ Prayer (*Eccl*) die Agende; it's only ~ decency to apologize es ist nur recht und billig *or* es gehört sich einfach, daß man sich entschuldigt.
(d) (*vulgar, low-class*) gewöhnlich. to be as ~ as muck (*inf*) schrecklich gewöhnlich *or* ordinär sein.
2 *n* **(a)** (*land*) Anger *m*, Gemeindewiese *f*.
(b) out of the ~ ausgefallen; nothing out of the ~ nichts Besonderes.
(c) to have sth in ~ etw miteinander gemein haben; to have a lot/nothing in ~ viel/nichts miteinander gemein haben, keine Gemeinsamkeiten haben; we do at least have that in ~ wenigstens das haben wir gemein; in ~ with many other people/towns/countries (ebenso *or* genauso) wie viele andere (Leute)/Städte/Länder ...; I, in ~ with ... ich, ebenso wie ...
commonalty ['kɒmənltɪ] *n* (*form*) the ~ die Bürgerlichen *pl*.
common: ~ denominator *n* (*Math, fig*) gemeinsamer Nenner; ~ divisor *n* gemeinsamer Teiler; ~ entrance (examination) *n* Aufnahmeprüfung *f* (*für eine britische Public School*).
commoner ['kɒmənəʳ] *n* **(a)** Bürgerliche(r) *mf*. **(b)** (*Brit Univ*) Student, der kein Universitätsstipendium erhält.
common: ~ factor *n* gemeinsamer Teiler; ~ fraction *n* gemeiner Bruch; ~ gender *n* (*Gram*) doppeltes Geschlecht; ~ law *n* **1** Gewohnheitsrecht *nt*; **2** *adj* she is his ~-law wife sie lebt mit ihm in eheähnlicher Gemeinschaft; the law regarded her as his ~-law wife vor dem Gesetz galt ihre Verbindung als eheähnliche Gemeinschaft.
commonly ['kɒmənlɪ] *adv* **(a)** (*often*) häufig; (*widely*) gemeinhin, weithin. a ~ held belief eine weitverbreitete Ansicht. **(b)** (*vulgarly*) gewöhnlich, ordinär.
common: C~ Market *n* Gemeinsamer Markt; C~ Marketeer *n* Befürworter *m* des Gemeinsamen Marktes; ~ multiple *n* gemeinsame(s) Vielfache(s); the lowest *or* least ~ multiple das kleinste gemeinsame Vielfache.
commonness ['kɒmənnɪs] *n* **(a)** *see adj* **(b)** Häufigkeit *f*; weite Verbreitung, Geläufigkeit *f*; Allgemeinheit *f*. **(b)** (*vulgarity*) Gewöhnlichkeit *f*; (*of person also*) ordinäre Art.
common: ~ noun *n* Gattungsbegriff *m*; ~-or-garden *adj* Feld-, Wald- und Wiesen- (*inf*); *topic, novel etc* ganz gewöhnlich; ~place **1** *adj* alltäglich; (*banal*) *remark* banal; **2** *n* Gemeinplatz *m*; a ~place (*frequent sight or event*) etwas Alltägliches; ~room *n* Aufenthalts- *or* Tagesraum *m*; (*for teachers*) Lehrerzimmer *nt*; (*Univ*) Dozentenzimmer *nt*.
commons ['kɒmənz] *npl* **(a)** the C~ (*Parl*) das Unterhaus; *see* house. **(b)** on short ~ auf Kurzration gesetzt.
common: ~ sense *n* gesunder Menschenverstand; ~sense *adj* vernünftig; *attitude also* gesund; it's the ~sense thing to do das ist das Vernünftigste; ~ time *n* Viervierteltakt *m*; ~weal *n* (*form*) Gemeinwohl *nt*; ~wealth *n* **(a)** Staat *m*, Gemeinwesen *nt*; (*US*) Bezeichnung für die US-Bundesstaaten Kentucky, Massachusetts, Pennsylvania und Virginia; the C~wealth of Australia der Australische Bund; the (British) C~wealth, the C~wealth of Nations das Commonwealth; **(b)** (*Hist*) the C~wealth die englische Republik unter Cromwell.
commotion [kə'məʊʃən] *n* Aufregung *f* usw no indef art; (*noise*) Lärm, Spektakel *m*. to cause a ~ Aufregung verursachen, Aufsehen erregen; to make a ~ Theater machen (*inf*); *noise* Krach machen, einen Spektakel veranstalten.
communal ['kɒmjuːnl] *adj* **(a)** (*of a community*) Gemeinde-. ~ life Gemeinschaftsleben *nt*.
(b) (*owned, used in common*) gemeinsam; *bathroom, kitchen also* Gemeinschafts-.
communally ['kɒmjuːnəlɪ] *adv* gemeinsam. to be ~ owned Gemein- *or* Gemeinschaftseigentum sein.
communard ['kɒmjuːnɑːd] *n* Kommunarde *m*, Kommunardin *f*.
commune¹ [kə'mjuːn] *vi* **(a)** Zwiesprache halten. to ~ with the spirits mit den Geistern verkehren. **(b)** (*esp US Eccl*) (*Catholic*) kommunizieren, die Kommunion empfangen; (*Protestant*) das Abendmahl empfangen.
commune² ['kɒmjuːn] *n* Kommune *f*; (*administrative division also*) Gemeinde *f*.
communicable [kə'mjuːnɪkəbl] *adj* **(a)** *disease* übertragbar.
(b) *ideas, knowledge* kommunizierbar, vermittelbar.
communicant [kə'mjuːnɪkənt] *n* (*Eccl*) Kommunikant(in *f*) *m*.
communicate [kə'mjuːnɪkeɪt] **1** *vt* *news etc* übermitteln;

ideas, feelings vermitteln; illness übertragen (to auf +acc).
2 *vi* **(a)** (*be in communication*) in Verbindung *or* Kontakt stehen. the ship was unable to ~ with the shore das Schiff konnte keine Verbindung zum Festland herstellen.
(b) (*convey or exchange thoughts*) sich verständigen, kommunizieren. the inability of modern man to ~ die Unfähigkeit des heutigen Menschen zur Kommunikation.
(c) (*rooms*) verbunden sein. communicating rooms Zimmer *pl* mit einer Verbindungstür.
(d) (*Eccl*) (*Catholic*) kommunizieren; (*Protestant*) das Abendmahl empfangen.
communication [kəˌmjuːnɪ'keɪʃən] *n* **(a)** (*communicating*) Verständigung, Kommunikation *f*; (*of ideas, information*) Vermittlung *f*; (*of disease*) Übertragung *f*; (*contact*) Verbindung *f*. system/means of ~ Kommunikationssystem *nt*/-mittel *nt*; to be in ~ with sb mit jdm in Verbindung stehen (*about* wegen); to get into ~ with sb about/on sth sich mit jdm wegen etw in Verbindung setzen.
(b) (*exchanging of ideas*) Verständigung, Kommunikation *f*.
(c) (*letter, message*) Mitteilung *f*.
(d) ~s (*roads, railways, telegraph lines etc*) Kommunikationswege *pl*, Kommunikationsnetz *nt*; all ~s with the mainland have been cut off sämtliche Verbindungen zum Festland sind unterbrochen; they're trying to restore ~s man versucht, die Verbindung wiederherzustellen.
(e) (*between rooms etc*) Verbindung *f*.
communication: ~ cord *n* (*Brit Rail*) = Notbremse *f*; ~ satellite *n* Nachrichtensatellit *m*; ~ studies *npl* Kommunikationswissenschaften *pl*; ~ trench *n* Verbindungsgraben *m*.
communicative [kə'mjuːnɪkətɪv] *adj* mitteilsam, gesprächig.
communion [kə'mjuːnɪən] *n* **(a)** (*intercourse, exchange of feelings etc*) Zwiesprache *f*; (*with spirits*) Verkehr *m*. a sense of ~ with nature ein Gefühl der Verbundenheit mit der Natur.
(b) (*religious group*) Gemeinde *f*; (*denomination*) Religionsgemeinschaft *f*. the ~ of saints/the faithful die Gemeinschaft der Heiligen/Gläubigen.
(c) (*Eccl: also* C~) (*Protestant*) Abendmahl *nt*; (*Catholic*) Kommunion *f*. to receive *or* take ~ die Kommunion/das Abendmahl empfangen; to make one's Easter ~ Ostern zum Abendmahl gehen.
communion: ~ rail *n* Kommunionbank *f*; ~ service *n* Abendmahlsgottesdienst *m*.
communiqué [kə'mjuːnɪkeɪ] *n* Kommuniqué *nt*, (amtliche) Verlautbarung.
communism ['kɒmjunɪzəm] *n* Kommunismus *m*.
communist ['kɒmjunɪst] **1** *n* Kommunist(in *f*) *m*. **2** *adj* kommunistisch. C~ Manifesto Kommunistisches Manifest; C~ Party Kommunistische Partei.
communistic [ˌkɒmjuˈnɪstɪk] *adj* pro-kommunistisch; (*esp US:* *communist*) kommunistisch.
community [kə'mjuːnɪtɪ] *n* **(a)** (*social, cultural etc group*) Gemeinde *f*; (*ethnic also*) Bevölkerungsgruppe *f*. the ~ at large das ganze Volk; the great ~ of nations die große Völkergemeinschaft; a sense of ~ (ein) Gemeinschaftsgefühl *nt*.
(b) (*the public*) Allgemeinheit *f*.
(c) (*Eccl: of monks, nuns*) (Ordens)gemeinschaft *f*.
(d) (*holding in common*) the ~ of love/goods die Liebes-/Gütergemeinschaft; they have no ~ of interests sie haben keine gemeinsamen Interessen.
community: ~ centre *n* Gemeindezentrum *nt*; ~ chest *n* (*US*) Wohltätigkeits- *or* Hilfsfonds *m*; ~ college *n* (*US*) Gemeinde-College *nt*; ~ relations *npl* das Verhältnis zwischen den Bevölkerungsgruppen; ~ singing *n* gemeinsames Singen.
communize ['kɒmjunaɪz] *vt* kommunistisch machen.
commutable [kə'mjuːtəbl] *adj* (*Jur*) umwandelbar.
commutation [ˌkɒmjuˈteɪʃən] *n* a (*Jur*) Umwandlung *f*. **(b)** ~ ticket (*US*) Zeitnetzkarte *f*.
commutator ['kɒmjuteɪtəʳ] *n* (*Elec*) Kommutator *m*.
commute [kə'mjuːt] **1** *vt* (*all senses*) umwandeln. **2** *vi* (*be commuter*) pendeln.
commuter [kə'mjuːtəʳ] *n* Pendler(in *f*) *m*. ~ train Pendlerzug *m*; the ~ belt das Einzugsgebiet, der Einzugsbereich; a ~ belt ein städtischer Einzugsbereich.
comp [kɒmp] *n* (*Typ inf*) Setzer(in *f*) *m*.
compact¹ [kəm'pækt] **1** *adj* (+*er*) kompakt; *style of writing, prose also* gedrängt; *soil, snow* fest. the print is too ~ der Druck ist zu eng, es ist zu eng bedruckt. **2** *vt* **(a)** *snow, soil* festtreten/-walzen/-fahren *etc*. **(b)** (*fig liter*) to be ~ed of ... sich aus ... zusammensetzen.
compact² ['kɒmpækt] *n* **(a)** (*powder* ~) Puderdose *f*. **(b)** (*US: car*) Kompaktauto *nt* or -wagen *m*.
compact³ ['kɒmpækt] *n* (*form: agreement*) Vereinbarung, Übereinkunft *f*.
compactly [kəm'pæktlɪ] *adv* kompakt; *expressed* gedrängt; *printed* eng.
compactness [kəm'pæktnɪs] *n* Kompaktheit *f*; (*of style also*) Gedrängtheit *f*; (*of print*) Dichte, Enge *f*.
companion [kəm'pænjən] **1** *n* **(a)** (*person with one*) Begleiter(in *f*) *m*. ~s in arms Kampfgefährten, Waffenbrüder (geh) *pl*; my ~s on the journey meine Reisegefährten *pl*; travelling/holiday/drinking ~ Reisebegleiter(in *f*) *m*/Urlaubsgefährte *m*, -gefährtin *f*/Zechgenosse *m*, -genossin *f*.
(b) (*friend*) Freund(in *f*), Kamerad(in *f*) *m*. his elder brother is not much of a ~ for him sein älterer Bruder ist ihm kein richtiger Freund; a faithful ~ for fifty years ein treuer Gefährte in fünfzig Jahren.
(c) (*one of pair of objects*) Pendant *nt*.
(d) (*lady* ~) Betreuerin *f*.
(e) (*handbook*) "the Gardener's C~" „der (Ratgeber für den) Gartenfreund"; "~ guide to Rome" „Reisebegleiter durch Rom".

(f) (*of order of knighthood*) Ritter *m*.
2 *attr* passend; *volume* Begleit-. **they have just brought out a**
~ set of Dickens in derselben Reihe ist jetzt eine Dickens-
Ausgabe erschienen.
companionable [kəm'pænjənəbl] *adj* freundlich.
companionably [kəm'pænjənəblı] *adv* vertraut; *smile also*
freundlich.
companion: ~**ship** *n* Gesellschaft *f*; ~**way** *n* (*Naut*) Niedergang *m*.
company ['kʌmpənı] **1** *n* **(a)** Gesellschaft *f*. **to keep sb ~** jdm
Gesellschaft leisten; **I enjoy ~** ich bin gern in Gesellschaft, ich
habe gern Gesellschaft; **female ~** Damengesellschaft *f*; **he**
arrived with female ~ er kam in Damenbegleitung; **he's good**
~ seine Gesellschaft ist angenehm; **just for ~** nur, um
Gesellschaft zu haben; **he came along just for ~** (*to provide ~*)
er kam bloß, um mir/uns Gesellschaft zu leisten; **he doesn't**
know how to behave in ~ er weiß nicht, wie man sich in
Gesellschaft benimmt; **I/he in ~ with ...** ich/er, genauso wie ...;
she is no or not fit ~ for your sister sie ist nicht der richtige
Umgang für deine Schwester; **a man is known by the ~** he
keeps (*prov*) sage mir, mit wem du umgehst, so sage ich dir,
wer du bist (*prov*); **she keeps a cat, it's ~ for her** sie hält sich
eine Katze, da hat sie (wenigstens) Gesellschaft; **you'll be in**
good ~ if ... wenn du ..., bist du in guter Gesellschaft.
(b) (*guests*) Besuch *m*.
(c) (*Comm*) Firma, Gesellschaft *f*. **Smith & C~, Smith & Co.**
Smith & Co.; **shipping ~** Schiffahrtsgesellschaft, Reederei *f*;
publishing ~ Verlagshaus *nt*, Verlag *m*; **a printing/clothes ~**
ein Druckerei-/Textilbetrieb *m*; **that's paid for by the ~** das
bezahlt die Firma.
(d) (*Theat*) (Schauspiel)truppe *f*.
(e) (*Naut*) ship's ~ Besatzung *f*.
(f) (*Mil*) Kompanie *f*. **~ commander** Kompaniechef *m*.
2 *attr* Firmen-. **~ car** Firmenwagen *m*.
comparable ['kɒmpərəbl] *adj* vergleichbar (*with*, *to* mit).
comparably ['kɒmpərəblı] *adv* gleichermaßen.
comparative [kəm'pærətıv] **1** *adj* **(a)** *religion, philology etc*
vergleichend. **~ literature** vergleichende Literaturwissenschaft, Komparatistik *f*; **the ~ form** (*Gram*) der Komparativ, die erste Steigerungsstufe.
(b) (*relative*) relativ. **to live in ~ luxury** relativ luxuriös
leben.
2 *n* (*Gram*) Komparativ *m*.
comparatively [kəm'pærətıvlı] *adv* **(a)** vergleichend. **(b)**
(*relatively*) verhältnismäßig, relativ.
compare [kəm'peəʳ] **1** *vt* vergleichen (*with*, *to* mit). **~d with** im
Vergleich zu, verglichen mit; **they cannot be ~d** man kann sie
nicht vergleichen, sie lassen sich nicht vergleichen; **his car is**
not to be or can't be ~d with my new one sein Wagen ist
überhaupt kein Vergleich zu meinem neuen Auto; **to ~ notes**
Eindrücke/Erfahrungen austauschen.
2 *vi* sich vergleichen lassen (*with* mit). **it ~s badly/well** es
schneidet vergleichsweise schlecht/gut ab; **it doesn't ~ very**
well at all es schneidet im Vergleich überhaupt nicht gut ab;
how do the two cars ~ for speed/quality? wie sieht ein
Geschwindigkeits-/Qualitätsvergleich bei beiden Wagen aus?;
the old car can't ~ for speed with the new one in puncto
Geschwindigkeit läßt sich der alte Wagen nicht mit dem neuen
vergleichen.
3 *n*: **beyond or without or past ~** unvergleichlich; **beautiful**
beyond ~ unvergleichlich schön.
comparison [kəm'pærɪsn] *n* **(a)** Vergleich *m* (*to* mit). **in ~ with**
im Vergleich zu; **to make or draw a ~** einen Vergleich
anstellen; **to bear ~** einem Vergleich standhalten, einen Vergleich aushalten; **there's no ~** das ist gar kein Vergleich.
(b) (*Gram*) Steigerung *f*. **degree of ~** Steigerungsstufe *f*.
compartment [kəm'pɑːtmənt] *n* (*in fridge, desk etc*) Fach *nt*;
(*Rail*) Abteil *nt*; (*Naut*) Schott(e *f*) *nt*; (*fig*) (Schub)fach *nt*.
compartmentalize [ˌkɒmpɑːt'mentəlaɪz] *vt* aufsplittern.
compass ['kʌmpəs] **1** *n* **(a)** Kompaß *m*. **by the ~** nach dem
Kompaß. **(b)** ~**es** *pl*, **pair of ~es** Zirkel *m*. **(c)** (*fig: extent*)
Rahmen *m*; (*of human mind, experience*) Bereich *m*; (*Mus: of*
voice) Umfang *m*. **2** *vt see* **encompass**. ~**ed about with**
enemies (*form*) von Feinden umzingelt.
compass: ~ **bearing** *n* Kompaßpeilung *f*; ~ **card** *n* Kompaß-
scheibe, Windrose *f*; ~ **course** *n* Navigationskurs *m*.
compassion [kəm'pæʃən] *n* Mitgefühl, Mitleid *nt* (*for* mit); (*esp*
Bibl) Erbarmen *nt* (*on, for* mit).
compassionate [kəm'pæʃənıt] *adj* mitfühlend, voller
Mitgefühl *or* Mitleid. **on ~ grounds** aus familiären Gründen; ~
leave Beurlaubung *f* wegen einer dringenden Familienange-
legenheit.
compatibility [kəm,pætə'bılıtı] *n* Vereinbarkeit, Kompatibilität (*geh*) *f*; (*Med*) Verträglichkeit, Kompatibilität
(*spec*) *f*. **their ~/lack of ~ was** obvious to everyone es war für
jeden offensichtlich, daß die beiden gut/schlecht zueinander
paßten.
compatible [kəm'pætıbl] *adj* vereinbar, kompatibel (*geh*);
(*Med*) verträglich, kompatibel (*spec*); *people* zueinander passend; *colours, furniture* passend. **to be ~** (*people*) zueinander
passen; (*colours, furniture*) zusammenpassen; (*plan*) vereinbar sein; **a salary ~ with the dangers of the job** ein Gehalt,
das den Gefahren des Berufs entspricht; **curtains which are ~**
with the existing colour scheme Vorhänge, die (im Ton) zu den
übrigen Farben passen.
compatibly [kəm'pætıblı] *adv* **to be ~ matched** gut zueinander
passen; **to be ~ married** in der Ehe gut zueinander passen; ~
high salaries Gehälter in vergleichbarer Höhe.
compatriot [kəm'pætrıət] *n* Landsmann *m*, Landsmännin *f*.
compel [kəm'pel] *vt* zwingen. **I feel ~led to tell you ...** ich
sehe mich (dazu) gezwungen *or* veranlaßt, Ihnen mitzuteilen, ...

(b) *admiration, respect* abnötigen (*from sb* jdm); *obedience*
erzwingen (*from sb* von jdm).
compelling [kəm'pelıŋ] *adj* zwingend; *performance, person-*
ality, eyes bezwingend.
compellingly [kəm'pelıŋlı] *adv see adj*. **he presented his case**
~ er legte seinen Fall mit zwingender Logik dar.
compendious [kəm'pendıəs] *adj book, notes etc* in Form einer
Übersicht.
compendium [kəm'pendıəm] *n* Handbuch, Kompendium *nt*.
compensate ['kɒmpənseıt] **1** *vt* (*recompense*) entschädigen;
(*Mech*) ausgleichen. **2** *vi* (*Psych*) kompensieren.
♦ **compensate for** *vi* + *prep obj* (*in money, material goods etc*)
ersetzen; (*make up for, offset*) wieder wettmachen *or*
ausgleichen; (*Psych*) kompensieren. **he was awarded £500 to ~**
~ the damage er erhielt £ 500 Schadensersatz *or* -ausgleich.
compensation [,kɒmpən'seıʃən] *n* (*damages*) Entschädigung
f; (*fig*) Ausgleich *m*; (*Psych*) Kompensation *f*. **he had the ~ of**
knowing that ... er hatte die Genugtuung zu wissen, daß ...; **in ~**
als Entschädigung/Ausgleich/Kompensation.
compensatory [kəm'pensətərı] *adj* kompensierend,
ausgleichend; *education*, (*Psych*) kompensatorisch.
compère ['kɒmpeəʳ] (*Brit*) **1** *n* Conférencier *m*. **2** *vt* **to ~ a show**
bei einer Show der Conférencier sein.
compete [kəm'piːt] *vi* **(a)** konkurrieren. **to ~ with each other**
sich (gegenseitig) Konkurrenz machen; **to ~ for sth** um etw
kämpfen *or* (*esp Comm*) konkurrieren; **able to ~ industrially**
industriell konkurrenzfähig; **his poetry can't ~ with Eliot's**
seine Gedichte können sich nicht mit denen Eliots messen; **he**
can't ~ (any more) er kann nicht mehr mithalten.
(b) (*Sport*) teilnehmen. **to ~ for the championship** um die
Meisterschaft kämpfen; **to ~ with/against sb** gegen jdn
kämpfen *or* antreten.
competence ['kɒmpıtəns], **competency** ['kɒmpıtənsı] *n* **(a)**
Fähigkeit *f*; (*of lawyer, scientist etc also, Ling*) Kompetenz *f*. **to**
do sth with surprising ~ etw mit erstaunlichem Geschick tun;
his ~ in handling money/dealing with awkward clients sein
Geschick im Umgang mit Geld/schwierigen Kunden; **he didn't**
have the necessary ~ to deal with that problem er war dem
Problem nicht gewachsen; **what level of ~ has the class**
reached in Spanish? auf welchem Stand ist die Klasse in
Spanisch?
(b) (*form: income*) Einkommen *nt*.
(c) (*Jur*) Zuständigkeit *f*.
competent ['kɒmpıtənt] *adj* **(a)** fähig, befähigt (*in* zu); (*in a*
particular field) kompetent; (*adequate*) *knowledge, under-*
standing angemessen, adäquat. **his English is quite ~** sein
Englisch ist recht gut.
(b) (*Jur*) zuständig; *evidence, witness* zulässig.
(c) (*form: relevant*) **to be ~/not ~** (*business, question*) von/
ohne *or* nicht von Belang sein.
competently ['kɒmpıtəntlı] *adv* geschickt, kompetent.
competition [,kɒmpı'tıʃən] *n* **(a)** *no pl* Konkurrenz *f* (*for* um).
unfair ~ unlauterer Wettbewerb; **a spirit of ~** Wettbewerbs-
or Konkurrenzdenken *nt*; **to be in ~ with sb** mit jdm wetteifern
or (*esp Comm*) konkurrieren; **to choose by ~** einem
Auswahlverfahren unterziehen, durch Auswahl ermitteln.
(b) (*contest*) Wettbewerb *m*; (*in newspapers etc*)
Preisausschreiben *nt*. **beauty/swimming ~** Schönheitskonkur-
renz *f* *or* -wettbewerb *m*/Schwimmwettbewerb *m*.
competitive [kəm'petıtıv] *adj* **(a)** *person, attitude* vom
Konkurrenzdenken geprägt; *sport* (Welt)kampf-. ~ **spirit**
Wettbewerbs- *or* Konkurrenzgeist *m*; (*of team*) Kampfgeist *m*;
he's a very ~ sort of person er genießt Wett-
bewerbssituationen; (*in job etc*) er ist ein sehr ehrgeiziger
Mensch; **the recruitment procedure is not ~** die Stellenver-
gabe erfolgt nicht auf Grund eines Auswahlverfahrens; **a ~**
examination eine Auswahlprüfung.
(b) (*Comm*) *business, prices, salaries* wettbewerbs- *or*
konkurrenzfähig. **a highly ~ market** ein Markt mit starker
Konkurrenz; **retailing is highly ~** der Einzelhandel ist stark
wettbewerbsbetont *or* -orientiert; **a ~ industry such as ...** ein
Industriezweig mit starkem Wettbewerb wie ...
competitor [kəm'petıtəʳ] *n* **(a)** (*Sport, in contest*) Teil-
nehmer(in *f*) *m*; (*for job*) Mitbewerber(in *f*) *m*. **to be a ~** teilnehmen; **to be sb's ~** jds Gegner sein. **(b)** (*Comm*) Konkur-
rent(in *f*) *m*. **our ~s** unsere Konkurrenz *or* Konkurrenten.
compilation [,kɒmpı'leıʃən] *n see vt* Zusammenstellung *f*;
Sammlung *f*.
compile [kəm'paıl] *vt* zusammenstellen, erstellen (*form*); *ma-*
terial sammeln, zusammentragen; *dictionary* verfassen.
compiler [kəm'paıləʳ] *n* (*of dictionary*) Verfasser(in *f*) *m*. **who's**
the ~ of this list/catalogue? *etc* wer hat diese Liste/diesen
Katalog zusammengestellt?
complacence [kəm'pleısns], **complacency** [kəm'pleısnsı]
n Selbstzufriedenheit, Selbstgefälligkeit *f*.
complacent [kəm'pleısnt] *adj* selbstzufrieden *or* -gefällig.
don't get ~ just because ... jetzt werde bloß nicht selbstgefällig
or überheblich, nur weil ...
complacently [kəm'pleısntlı] *adv* selbstzufrieden *or*
-gefällig. **those who ~ accept their parents' beliefs** diejenigen,
die die Ansichten ihrer Eltern unkritisch *or* unreflektiert übernehmen.
complain [kəm'pleın] *vi* sich beklagen, klagen (*about* über
+*acc*); (*to make a formal complaint*) sich beschweren, Beschwerde einlegen (*form*) (*about* über +*acc*, *to* bei ...). **you can't ~**
sich darüber beklagen/beschweren, daß ...; **(I) can't ~** (*inf*) ich
kann nicht klagen (*inf*); **stop ~ing!** beklag dich nicht dauernd!;
to ~ of sth über etw (*acc*) klagen; **she's always ~ing** sie muß
sich immer beklagen, sie hat immer etwas zu klagen; **to ~ of**
not having enough time/being ignored über Zeitmangel klagen/
darüber klagen, daß man sich nicht beachtet wird.

complainant [kəmˈpleɪnənt] n Beschwerdeführer(in f) m; (in court) Kläger(in f) m.

complaint [kəmˈpleɪnt] n (a) Klage f; (formal ~) Beschwerde f (to bei). I have no cause for ~ ich kann mich nicht beklagen; I wouldn't have any ~(s) if ... ich würde mich nicht beklagen, wenn ...; to lodge or lay a ~ against sb with the police jdn bei der Polizei anzeigen, gegen jdn Anzeige erstatten.
(b) (illness) Beschwerden pl. a very rare ~ eine sehr seltene Krankheit, ein sehr seltenes Leiden.

complaisance [kəmˈpleɪzəns] n (liter) Gefälligkeit f.

complaisant adj, ~ly adv [kəmˈpleɪzənt, -lɪ] gefällig, entgegenkommend; smile wohlwollend.

complement [ˈkɒmplɪmənt] 1 n (a) Ergänzung f (to gen); (to perfect sth) Vervollkommnung f (to gen); (colour) Komplementärfarbe f (to zu).
(b) (full number) volle Stärke; (crew of ship) Besatzung f. the battalion didn't have its full ~ of soldiers das Bataillon hatte seine Sollstärke nicht; we've got our full ~ in the office now unser Büro ist jetzt komplett or voll besetzt.
(c) (Gram) Ergänzung f.
(d) (Math: angle) Ergänzungswinkel m.
2 [ˈkɒmplɪment] vt (a) ergänzen; (make perfect) vervollkommnen, abrunden; (colour) herausbringen. to ~ each other sich ergänzen; (colours) aufeinander abgestimmt sein.
(b) (Gram) die Ergänzung bilden zu.
(c) (Math) zu 90° ergänzen.

complementary [ˌkɒmplɪˈmentərɪ] adj colour Komplementär-; angle Ergänzungs-. a ~ pair ein zusammengehöriges Paar; two ~ characters zwei einander ergänzende Charaktere; they are ~ to each other sie ergänzen sich or einander; they have ~ interests ihre Interessen ergänzen sich.

complete [kəmˈpliːt] 1 adj (a) (entire, whole) ganz attr; set also, wardrobe, deck of cards vollständig, komplett; (having the required numbers) vollzählig; edition Gesamt-. my happiness/disappointment was ~ mein Glück/meine Enttäuschung war perfekt or vollkommen; my life is now ~ mein Leben ist erfüllt; our victory was ~ unser Sieg war vollkommen; with that my happiness is made ~ damit ist mein Glück vollkommen; the ~ works of Shakespeare die gesammelten Werke Shakespeares; a very ~ account ein sehr umfassender or detaillierter Bericht; are we ~? sind wir vollzählig?; he invited the ~ staff er lud die ganze or gesamte Belegschaft ein.
(b) attr (total, absolute) völlig; failure, beginner, disaster, flop also, victory total; surprise, shambles also komplett; satisfaction also, approval voll. we were ~ strangers wir waren uns or einander völlig fremd.
(c) (finished) fertig. his novel is not yet ~ sein Roman ist noch nicht abgeschlossen; my life's work is now ~ mein Lebenswerk ist nun vollbracht.
(d) ~ with komplett mit; he came ~ with rucksack and boots er erschien komplett ausgerüstet mit Rucksack und Stiefeln.
(e) sportsman, gardener etc perfekt.
2 vt (a) (make whole) collection, set vervollständigen, komplettieren; team vollzählig machen; education, meal abrunden. to ~ our numbers damit wir vollzählig sind; that ~s my collection damit ist meine Sammlung vollständig.
(b) (fig) happiness vollkommen machen. and to ~ their misery ... und zu allem Unglück ...
(c) (finish) beenden, abschließen, zum Abschluß or zu Ende bringen; building, work fertigstellen; prison sentence verbüßen. ~ this phrase ergänzen Sie diesen Ausspruch; it's not ~d yet es ist noch nicht fertig; when you've ~d your repayments wenn Sie es ganz abzezahlt haben.
(d) form, questionnaire ausfüllen.

completely [kəmˈpliːtlɪ] adv völlig, vollkommen. he's ~ wrong er irrt sich gewaltig, er hat völlig unrecht; he's not ~ normal er ist nicht ganz normal.

completeness [kəmˈpliːtnɪs] n Vollständigkeit f. the design has a sense of ~ about it das Design erscheint vollendet or vollkommen; a work which demonstrates the ~ of his talent ein Werk, das sein vollendetes Talent beweist.

completion [kəmˈpliːʃən] n (a) (finishing) Fertigstellung f; (of work also) Beendigung f; (of project, course, education) Abschluß m; (of prison sentence) Verbüßung f. near ~ kurz vor dem Abschluß; to bring sth to ~ etw zum Abschluß bringen; we need more people for the ~ of the work wir brauchen noch mehr Leute, um die Arbeit zum Abschluß zu bringen; you get a certificate on ~ of the course am Ende or nach Abschluß des Kurses erhalten Sie eine Urkunde; on ~ of the contract/sale bei Vertrags-/Kaufabschluß.
(b) (making whole) Vervollständigung f; (of education, meal) Abrundung f; (of happiness etc) Vervollkommnung f.
(c) (filling in: of form etc) Ausfüllen nt.

complex [ˈkɒmpleks] 1 adj (a) komplex; person, mind, issue, question, problem, poem also vielschichtig; theory, task, system also, machine, pattern differenziert, kompliziert; situation also, paragraph verwickelt, kompliziert.
(b) (Gram) a ~ sentence ein Satzgefüge nt.
2 n (a) Komplex m. industrial ~ Industriekomplex m.
(b) (Psych) Komplex m. he has a ~ about his big ears er hat Komplexe or einen Komplex wegen seiner großen Ohren; don't get a ~ about it deswegen brauchst du keine Komplexe zu bekommen.

complexion [kəmˈplekʃən] n Teint m; (skin colour) Gesichtsfarbe f.
(b) (fig: aspect) Anstrich, Aspekt m. to put a new/different/sinister etc ~ on sth etw in einem neuen/anderen/düsteren etc Licht erscheinen lassen; of a different political/religious ~ mit anderen politischen/religiösen Anschauungen.

complexity [kəmˈpleksɪtɪ] n see adj (a) Komplexität f;

Vielschichtigkeit f; Differenziertheit, Kompliziertheit f; Kompliziertheit f.

compliance [kəmˈplaɪəns] n Einverständnis nt; (with rules etc) Einhalten nt (with gen); (submissiveness) Willfährigkeit (geh), Fügsamkeit f. in ~ with the law/our wishes etc dem Gesetz/unseren Wünschen etc gemäß.

compliant [kəmˈplaɪənt] adj entgegenkommend, gefällig; (submissive) nachgiebig, willfährig (geh).

complicate [ˈkɒmplɪkeɪt] vt komplizieren.

complicated [ˈkɒmplɪkeɪtɪd] adj kompliziert.

complication [ˌkɒmplɪˈkeɪʃən] n Komplikation f; (condition) Kompliziertheit f. his life had reached such a level of ~ sein Leben war so kompliziert or verwickelt geworden.

complicity [kəmˈplɪsɪtɪ] n Mittäterschaft f (in bei).

compliment [ˈkɒmplɪmənt] 1 n (a) Kompliment nt (on zu, wegen). to pay sb a ~ jdm ein Kompliment machen; that's quite a ~, coming from you wenn Sie das sagen, heißt das schon etwas or ist das wahrhaftig ein Kompliment; (give) my ~s to the chef mein Lob or Kompliment dem Koch/der Köchin.
(b) (form) ~s pl Grüße pl; give him my ~s empfehlen Sie mich ihm (dated form); to pay one's ~s to sb (on arrival) jdn begrüßen; (visit) jdm einen Höflichkeitsbesuch abstatten (form); the ~s of the season frohes Fest; "with the ~s of Mr X/the management" „mit den besten Empfehlungen von Herrn X/der Geschäftsleitung"; "with the ~s of the publishers" „zur gefälligen Kenntnisnahme, der Verlag"; ~s slip (Comm) Beilegzettel m mit Firmenaufdruck, Empfehlungszettel m.
2 [ˈkɒmplɪment] vt ein Kompliment/Komplimente machen (+dat) (on wegen, zu).

complimentary [ˌkɒmplɪˈmentərɪ] adj (a) (praising) schmeichelhaft. ~ close Schlußformel f. (b) (gratis) seat, ticket Frei-. ~ copy Freiexemplar nt; (of magazine) Werbenummer f.

compline [ˈkɒmplɪn] n (Eccl) Komplet f.

comply [kəmˈplaɪ] vi (person) einwilligen; (object, system etc) die Bedingungen erfüllen, den Bedingungen entsprechen. to ~ with sth einer Sache (dat) entsprechen; (system) in Einklang mit etw stehen; to ~ with a clause in a contract eine Vertragsbedingung erfüllen; to ~ with a request/a wish/instructions einer Bitte/einem Wunsch/den Anordnungen nachkommen (form) or entsprechen (form); to ~ with sb's wishes sich jds Wünschen (dat) fügen; to ~ with a time limit/the rules eine Frist einhalten/sich an die Regeln halten.

component [kəmˈpəʊnənt] 1 n Teil nt, Bestandteil m; (Chem, Phys) Komponente f. 2 adj a ~ part ein (Bestand)teil m; the ~ parts die Bestand- or Einzelteile pl; the ~ parts of a machine/sentence die einzelnen Maschinen-/Satzteile pl.

comport [kəmˈpɔːt] (form) 1 vr sich verhalten. 2 vi to ~ with sich vereinbaren lassen mit.

comportment [kəmˈpɔːtmənt] n Verhalten nt. to study ~ Anstandsunterricht nehmen.

compose [kəmˈpəʊz] vt (a) music komponieren; letter abfassen, aufsetzen; poem verfassen.
(b) (constitute, make up) bilden. to be ~d of sich zusammensetzen aus; water is ~d of ... Wasser besteht aus ...; a shyness ~d of both fear and pride eine Zurückhaltung, die eine Mischung aus Furcht und Stolz ist.
(c) to ~ oneself sich sammeln; to ~ one's features sich wieder in die Gewalt bekommen; to ~ one's thoughts Ordnung in seine Gedanken bringen.
(d) (Typ) setzen.

composed adj, ~ly adv [kəmˈpəʊzd, -zədlɪ] beherrscht, gelassen.

composer [kəmˈpəʊzəʳ] n (a) (Mus) Komponist(in f) m. (b) (of letter, poem etc) Verfasser(in f) m.

composite [ˈkɒmpəzɪt] 1 adj (a) zusammengesetzt. ~ photograph Photomontage f; ~ structure gegliederter Aufbau. (b) (Bot) Korbblütler-; flower zur Familie der Korbblütler gehörig. (c) (Math) number teilbar. 2 n (Bot) Korbblütler m.

composition [ˌkɒmpəˈzɪʃən] n (a) (act of composing) (of music) Komponieren nt; (of letter) Abfassen, Aufsetzen nt; (of poem) Verfassen nt. music/verse of his own ~ selbstkomponierte Musik/selbstverfaßte Verse.
(b) (arrangement, Mus, Art) Komposition f; (Mus: theory of ~ also) Kompositionslehre f.
(c) (Sch: essay) Aufsatz m.
(d) (constitution, make-up) Zusammensetzung f; (of sentence) Aufbau m, Konstruktion f; (of word) Zusammensetzung f. to change/decide on the ~ of sth die Zusammenstellung einer Sache (gen) ändern/etw zusammenstellen; this medicine/manure is a ~ of ... dieses Medikament/dieser Dünger setzt sich aus ... zusammen; there is a touch of madness in his ~ (old, liter) in ihm findet sich die Anlage zum Wahnsinn.
(e) (artificial substance) Kunststoff m.
(f) (Typ) Setzen nt. ~ by hand Handsatz m, manueller Satz.
(g) (Jur) Vergleich m.

composition in cpds Kunst-; ~ rubber n synthetischer Kautschuk; ~ sole n Kunststoffsohle f.

compositor [kəmˈpɒzɪtəʳ] n (Typ) (Schrift)setzer(in f) m.

compos mentis [ˈkɒmpəsˈmentɪs] adj I'm never really ~ first thing in the morning frühmorgens ist mein Verstand noch nicht so klar or bin ich noch nicht voll da (inf); he's quite ~ er ist voll zurechnungsfähig; he's not quite ~ er ist nicht voll zurechnungsfähig, er ist nicht ganz bei Trost (inf).

compost [ˈkɒmpɒst] n Kompost m. ~ heap Komposthaufen m.

composure [kəmˈpəʊʒəʳ] n Beherrschung, Fassung f. to lose/regain one's ~ aus der Fassung geraten or die Beherrschung verlieren/sich wieder fassen or seine Selbstbeherrschung wiederfinden.

compote [ˈkɒmpəʊt] n Kompott nt.

compound¹ ['kɒmpaʊnd] **1** n (*Chem*) Verbindung f; (*Gram*) Kompositum nt, zusammengesetztes Wort.
2 adj **(a)** (*Chem*) ~ **substance** Verbindung f.
(b) (*Math*) ~ **fraction** Doppelbruch m; ~ **interest** Zinseszins m; ~ **number** zusammengesetzte Zahl.
(c) (*Med*) ~ **fracture** offener or komplizierter Bruch.
(d) (*Gram*) tense, word zusammengesetzt. ~ **sentence** Satzgefüge nt; (*of two or more main clauses*) Satzreihe, Parataxe f.
(e) (*Zool*) ~ **eye** Facetten- or Netzauge nt.
3 [kəm'paʊnd] vt **(a)** (*rare: combine*) verbinden; (*Chem*) mischen. **to be ~ed of ...** (*liter*) sich zusammensetzen aus ...; **a strange character somehow ~ed of quite opposite qualities** (*liter*) ein eigenartiger Mensch, der in sich völlig gegensätzliche Eigenschaften vereinigt (*geh*).
(b) (*Jur*) debt begleichen, tilgen; *quarrel* beilegen. **to ~ a crime** ein Verbrechen wegen erhaltener Entschädigung nicht verfolgen.
(c) (*make worse*) verschlimmern; *problem* verstärken, vergrößern. **this only ~s our difficulties** das erschwert unsere Lage or Situation noch zusätzlich.
4 [kəm'paʊnd] vi einen Vergleich schließen; (*with creditors*) sich vergleichen. **to ~ with sb for sth** sich mit jdm auf etw (*acc*) einigen.

compound² ['kɒmpaʊnd] n (*enclosed area*) Lager nt; (*in prison*) Gefängnishof m; (*living quarters*) Siedlung f; (*in zoo*) Gehege nt.

comprehend [,kɒmprɪ'hend] vt **(a)** (*understand*) begreifen, verstehen. **(b)** (*include*) enthalten, umfassen, einschließen. **the states ~ed within this empire** die Staaten, die das Reich in sich schließt.
comprehensibility [,kɒmprɪ,hensɪ'bɪlɪtɪ] n Verständlichkeit f.
comprehensible [,kɒmprɪ'hensəbl] adj verständlich. **such behaviour is just not ~** ein solches Verhalten ist einfach unbegreiflich or unverständlich.
comprehension [,kɒmprɪ'henʃən] n **(a)** (*understanding*) Verständnis nt; (*ability to understand*) Begriffsvermögen nt. **that is beyond my ~** das übersteigt mein Begriffsvermögen; (*behaviour*) das ist mir unbegreiflich.
(b) (*inclusion*) Aufnahme f.
(c) (*school exercise*) Fragen pl zum Textverständnis.
comprehensive [,kɒmprɪ'hensɪv] **1** adj umfassend, ausführlich; *measures, knowledge* umfassend. ~ **school** (*Brit*) Gesamtschule f; **to go ~** (*Sch*) (eine) Gesamtschule werden; ~ **policy** (*Insur*) Vollkasko(versicherung f) nt; **are you ~?** (*Insur*) sind Sie vollkaskoversichert?, haben Sie Vollkasko? (*inf*).
2 n Gesamtschule f.
comprehensively [,kɒmprɪ'hensɪvlɪ] adv umfassend, ausführlich. **he argued well and ~** seine Argumentation war gekonnt und umfassend.
comprehensiveness [,kɒmprɪ'hensɪvnɪs] n Ausführlichkeit f. **the ~ of his report** sein umfassender Bericht.
compress¹ [kəm'pres] **1** vt komprimieren (*into* auf +*acc*); *air etc* also verdichten; *materials* zusammenpressen (*into* zu). **water can't be ~ed** Wasser läßt sich nicht komprimieren; **the story line is too ~ed** die Geschichte ist zu komprimiert or gedrängt erzählt.
2 vi sich verdichten, sich komprimieren lassen.
compress² ['kɒmpres] n Kompresse f, feuchter Umschlag.
compressed air [kəm'prest'ɛər] n Druck- or Preßluft f.
compression [kəm'preʃən] n Verdichtung, Kompression f; (*of information etc*) Komprimieren nt. ~ **ratio** Verdichtungs- or Kompressionsverhältnis nt; **the gas is in a state of very high ~** das Gas ist stark verdichtet or komprimiert.
compressor [kəm'presər] n Kompressor, Verdichter m.
comprise [kəm'praɪz] vt bestehen aus, umfassen.
compromise ['kɒmprəmaɪz] **1** n Kompromiß m. **to come to or reach or make a ~** zu einem Kompromiß kommen or gelangen, einen Kompromiß schließen; **one has to make ~s** man muß auch mal Kompromisse schließen.
2 adj attr Kompromiß-. ~ **decision** Kompromiß(lösung f) m; ~ **solution** Kompromißlösung f.
3 vi Kompromisse schließen (*about* in +*dat*). **we agreed to ~** wir einigten uns auf einen Kompromiß.
4 vt **(a)** kompromittieren. **to ~ oneself** sich kompromittieren; **to ~ one's reputation** seinem guten Ruf schaden.
(b) (*imperil*) gefährden.
compromising ['kɒmprəmaɪzɪŋ] adj kompromittierend.
comptometer ® [kɒmp'tɒmɪtər] n Rechenmaschine f. ~ **operator** Rechenmaschinenbediener(in f) m.
comptroller [kən'trəʊlər] n (*form*) Rechnungsprüfer, Bücherrevisor m. **C~ of the Queen's Household** Beamter des Rechnungshofes, der die königlichen Finanzen überprüft.
compulsion [kəm'pʌlʃən] n Zwang, Druck m; (*Psych*) innerer Zwang. **under ~** unter Druck or Zwang; **you are under no ~** Sie sind nicht gezwungen, niemand zwingt Sie.
compulsive [kəm'pʌlsɪv] adj zwanghaft, Zwangs-; *neurosis* Zwangs-; *behaviour* zwanghaft. **the ~ buying of ...** das krankhafte Zwang, ... zu kaufen; ~ **buying as a form of disease** Kaufzwang, eine Art Krankheit; **he has a ~ desire to ...** er steht unter dem Zwang, zu ...; **he is a ~ eater** er hat die Eßsucht, er leidet an einem Eßzwang; **he is a ~ liar** er hat einen krankhaften Trieb zu lügen; **he's a ~ smoker** das Rauchen ist bei ihm zur Sucht geworden; **she's a ~ talker** sie muß unbedingt reden; **this ~ TV-watching ruins every conversation** diese ständige Fernseherei zerstört jede Unterhaltung!
compulsively [kəm'pʌlsɪvlɪ] adv see adj **to act ~** unter einem (inneren) Zwang handeln.
compulsorily [kəm'pʌlsərɪlɪ] adv zwangsweise.
compulsory [kəm'pʌlsərɪ] adj obligatorisch; *liquidation, measures* Zwangs-; *subject, member* Pflicht-. **that is ~** das ist Pflicht or obligatorisch; **education is ~** es besteht (allgemeine)

Schulpflicht; ~ **purchase** Enteignung f; ~ **purchase order** Enteignungsbeschluß m; **to put a ~ purchase order on a place** die Enteignung eines Grundstückes verfügen; ~ **retirement** Zwangspensionierung f; ~ **service** (*US*) Wehrpflicht f.
compunction [kəm'pʌŋkʃən] n (*liter*) Schuldgefühle, Gewissensbisse pl. **with no ~/without the slightest ~** ohne sich schuldig/im geringsten schuldig zu fühlen.
computation [,kɒmpjʊ'teɪʃən] n Berechnung, Kalkulation f. **addition is a form of ~** die Addition ist eine Rechenart.
compute [kəm'pjuːt] vt berechnen (*at* auf +*acc*), errechnen, ausrechnen.
computer [kəm'pjuːtər] n Computer m; (*for calculating also*) Elektronenrechner m; (*digital ~ also*) (digitale) Rechenanlage; (*data processing also*) Datenverarbeitungsanlage f.
computer- in cpds Computer-; ~ **age** n Computerzeitalter nt.
computerization [kəm,pjuːtəraɪ'zeɪʃən] n (*of information etc*) Computerisierung f. **the ~ of the factory** die Umstellung der Fabrik auf Computer.
computerize [kəm'pjuːtəraɪz] vt information computerisieren; *company, accounting methods* auf Computer or EDV umstellen.
computer: ~-**operated** adj computergesteuert; ~ **program** n Programm nt; ~ **programmer** n Programmierer(in f) m; ~ **type-setting** n Computersatz m.
comrade ['kɒmrɪd] n Kamerad m; (*Pol*) Genosse m, Genossin f. ~-**in-arms** Waffenbruder (*old*), Kriegskamerad m.
comradely ['kɒmrɪdlɪ] adj kameradschaftlich.
comradeship ['kɒmrɪdʃɪp] n Kameradschaft(lichkeit) f. **the spirit of ~** der Kameradschaftsgeist.
con¹ [kɒn] vt (*rare: learn*) sich (*dat*) einprägen.
con² adv, n see pro³.
con³ vt (*Naut*) steuern, lenken.
con⁴ (*inf*) **1** n Schwindel, Beschiß (*sl*) m. **it's a ~!** das ist alles Schwindel or Beschiß (*sl*).
2 vt hereinlegen (*inf*), bescheißen (*sl*), filmen (*sl*). **he ~ned her out of all her money** er hat sie um ihr ganzes Geld gebracht; **to ~ sb into doing sth** jdn durch einen faulen Trick dazu bringen, daß er etw tut (*inf*); **don't let him ~ you into believing it** laß dir das bloß nicht von ihm aufbinden (*inf*) or einreden.
concatenation [kɒn,kætɪ'neɪʃən] n Verkettung f.
concave ['kɒn'keɪv] adj konkav; *mirror* Konkav-, Hohl-.
concavity [kɒn'kævɪtɪ] n Konkavität f.
concavo-convex [kɒn,keɪvəʊkɒn'veks] adj konkav-konvex.
conceal [kən'siːl] vt (*hide*) object, emotions, thoughts verbergen; (*keep secret*) verheimlichen (*sth from sb* jdm etw). **why did they ~ this information from us?** warum hat man uns diese Informationen vorenthalten?; **to ~ the fact that ...** (*die Tatsache*) verheimlichen, daß ...; **the chameleon was completely ~ed against its background** das Chamäleon war nicht mehr von seiner Umgebung zu unterscheiden.
concealed [kən'siːld] adj verborgen; *lighting, wiring, turning, entrance* verdeckt; *camera* versteckt, Geheim-.
concealment [kən'siːlmənt] n (*of facts*) Verheimlichung f; (*of evidence*) Unterschlagung f; (*of criminal*) Gewährung f von Unterschlupf (*of an* +*acc*). **to come out of ~** aus dem Versteck auftauchen; **to stay in ~** sich versteckt halten.
concede [kən'siːd] **1** vt **(a)** (*yield, give up*) privilege aufgeben; *lands* abtreten (*to an* +*acc*). **to ~ a privilege/right to sb** jdm ein Privileg/Recht abtreten, ein Privileg/Recht an jdn abtreten; **to ~ victory to sb** vor jdm kapitulieren; **to ~ a match** (*give up*) aufgeben, sich geschlagen geben; (*lose*) ein Match abgeben; **to ~ a penalty** einen Elfmeter verursachen; **to ~ a point to sb** jdm in einem Punkt recht geben; (*Sport*) einen Punkt an jdn abgeben.
(b) (*admit, grant*) zugeben, einräumen (*form*); *privilege* einräumen (*to sb* jdm); *right* zubilligen, zugestehen (*to sb* jdm). **it's generally ~d that ...** es ist allgemein anerkannt, daß ...; **to ~ defeat** sich geschlagen geben.
2 vi nachgeben, kapitulieren.
conceit [kən'siːt] n **(a)** (*pride*) Einbildung f. **he's full of ~** er ist schrecklich eingebildet; **of all the ~!** diese Einbildung! **(b) he is wise in his own ~** (*liter*) er dünkt sich weise (*liter*). **(c)** (*Liter*) Konzetto nt.
conceited [kən'siːtɪd] adj eingebildet.
conceitedly [kən'siːtɪdlɪ] adv see adj. **he ~ claimed ...** eingebildet wie er ist, hat er behauptet ...
conceitedness [kən'siːtɪdnɪs] n Eingebildetheit, Einbildung f.
conceivable [kən'siːvəbl] adj denkbar, vorstellbar. **it is hardly ~ that ...** es ist kaum denkbar, daß ..., man kann sich (*dat*) kaum vorstellen, daß ...; **it's not ~ that she would have gone without us** ich kann mir nicht vorstellen, daß sie ohne uns gegangen ist.
conceivably [kən'siːvəblɪ] adv she may ~ be right es ist durchaus denkbar, daß sie recht hat; **will it happen? — ~** wird das geschehen? — das ist durchaus denkbar.
conceive [kən'siːv] **1** vt **(a)** child empfangen.
(b) (*imagine*) sich (*dat*) denken or vorstellen; *idea, plan* haben; *novel* die Idee haben zu. **when we first ~d the idea of this film ...** als uns die Idee zu diesem Film kam, ...; **it was originally ~d as quite a different sort of book** ursprünglich war das Buch ganz anders geplant or konzipiert (*geh*); **the novel was ~d when ...** die Idee zu dem Buch kam mir/uns etc or entstand, als ...; **it was ~d in a Paris café** die Idee (dazu) wurde in einem Pariser Café geboren; **the way he ~s his role** seine Vorstellung or Auffassung von seiner Rolle; **she ~s it to be her duty** sie erachtet (*geh*) or betrachtet es als ihre Pflicht; **I can't ~ why** ich verstehe or begreife nicht, warum.
(c) **to ~ a dislike for sb/sth** eine Abneigung gegen jdn/etw entwickeln; **to ~ a liking for sb/sth** Zuneigung für jdn empfinden/seine Vorliebe für etw entdecken.
2 vi (*woman*) empfangen.
♦**conceive of** vi +prep obj sich (*dat*) vorstellen. **who first ~d**

~ **the idea?** wer hatte die Idee zuerst?, wem kam die Idee zuerst?; **he absolutely refuses to** ~ ~ **cheating** Betrug käme ihm überhaupt nicht in den Sinn.

concentrate ['kɒnsəntreɪt] **1** vt **(a)** konzentrieren (on auf +acc). **to** ~ **all one's energies on sth** sich (voll und) ganz auf etw (acc) konzentrieren; **to** ~ **one's mind on sth** seine Gedanken or sich auf etw (acc) konzentrieren; **it's amazing how he's** ~d **so much material into one novel** es ist erstaunlich, wieviel Material er in einem Roman zusammengedrängt hat.

(b) (Mil) troops konzentrieren.

(c) (Chem) konzentrieren.

2 vi **(a)** (give one's attention) sich konzentrieren. **to** ~ **on doing sth** sich darauf konzentrieren, etw zu tun.

(b) (people) sich sammeln; (troops also) sich konzentrieren. **a crowd had begun to** ~ **around the station** um den Bahnhof hatte sich ein Menschenauflauf gebildet.

3 adj (Chem) konzentriert.

4 n (Chem) Konzentrat nt.

concentration [ˌkɒnsən'treɪʃən] n **(a)** Konzentration f. **powers of** ~ Konzentrationsfähigkeit f. **(b)** (gathering) Ansammlung f.

(c) (Chem) Konzentration f.

concentration camp n Konzentrationslager, KZ nt.

concentric [kən'sentrɪk] adj circles konzentrisch.

concept ['kɒnsept] n Begriff m; (conception) Vorstellung f. **the** ~ **of evil** der Begriff des Bösen; **our** ~ **of the world** unser Weltbild; **his** ~ **of marriage** seine Vorstellungen von der Ehe; **the** ~ **of the play was good** das Stück war gut konzipiert (geh) or war in der Anlage or vom Konzept her gut.

conception [kən'sepʃən] n **(a)** (forming ideas) Vorstellung f. **the writer's powers of** ~ die Vorstellungskraft or das Vorstellungsvermögen des Schriftstellers.

(b) (idea) Vorstellung f; (way sth is conceived) Konzeption f. **what's your** ~ **of the ideal life?** was ist Ihrer Vorstellung nach ein ideales Leben?; **the Buddhist** ~ **of life/nature/morality** die buddhistische Auffassung von Leben/Vorstellung von der Natur/Moralvorstellung; **this statue represents the classical** ~ **of beauty** diese Statue stellt das klassische Schönheitsideal dar; **they have a totally different** ~ **of justice** sie haben eine völlig unterschiedliche Auffassung or Vorstellung von Gerechtigkeit; **in their** ~ **they are ...** sie sind von der Konzeption her ...; **this poem in its original** ~ **was shorter in the** anfänglichen Konzeption war dieses Gedicht kürzer; **he has no** ~ **of how difficult it is** er macht sich (dat) keinen Begriff davon or er hat keine Vorstellung, wie schwer das ist.

(c) (of child) die Empfängnis, die Konzeption (form).

conceptual [kən'septjʊəl] adj thinking begrifflich. **is this a** ~ **possibility?** ist ein solcher Begriff überhaupt denkbar?

conceptualism [kən'septjʊəlɪzəm] n Konzeptualismus m.

conceptualization [kənˌseptjʊəlaɪ'zeɪʃən] n Begriffsbildung f. **the** ~ **of experience** die begriffliche Erfassung der Erfahrung.

conceptualize [kən'septjʊəlaɪz] **1** vt in Begriffe fassen. **2** vi begrifflich denken.

conceptually [kən'septjʊəlɪ] adv begrifflich. **X is** ~ **impossible X** ist begrifflich undenkbar; **it only exists** ~ das existiert nur in der Vorstellung.

concern [kən'sɜːn] **1** n **(a)** (relation, connection) **do you have any** ~ **with banking?** haben Sie etwas mit dem Bankwesen zu tun?; **to have no** ~ **with sth** mit etw nichts zu tun haben.

(b) (business, affair) Angelegenheit (on pl) f; (matter of interest and importance to a person) Anliegen nt. **the day-to-day** ~**s of government** die täglichen Regierungsgeschäfte; **it's no** ~ **of his** das geht ihn nichts an; **what** ~ **is it of yours?** was geht Sie das an?; **my** ~ **is with his works**, not his life **mir geht es um sein Werk**, nicht um seine Biographie.

(c) (Comm) Konzern m; see going.

(d) (share) Beteiligung f. **he has a** ~ **in the business** er ist an dem Geschäft beteiligt; **what is your** ~ **in it?** wie hoch sind Sie beteiligt?, wie hoch ist Ihre Beteiligung?

(e) (anxiety) Sorge, Besorgnis f. **a look of** ~ ein besorgter or sorgenvoller Blick; **the situation in the Middle East is causing** ~ die Lage im Nahen Osten ist besorgniserregend; **there's some/no cause for** ~ es besteht Grund/kein Grund zur Sorge; **he showed great** ~ **for your safety** er war or zeigte sich (geh) sehr um Ihre Sicherheit besorgt; **don't you feel any** ~ **for the starving millions?** berührt Sie die Tatsache, daß Millionen am Verhungern sind, überhaupt nicht?

(f) (importance) Bedeutung f. **a matter of economic** ~ eine Angelegenheit von wirtschaftlicher Bedeutung; **issues of national** ~ Fragen von nationalem Interesse.

2 vt (be about) handeln von. **it** ~**s the following issue** es geht um die folgende Frage; **the last chapter is** ~ed **with ...** das letzte Kapitel behandelt ...

(b) (be the business of, involve) angehen, betreffen; (affect) betreffen. **that doesn't** ~ **you** das betrifft Sie nicht; (as snub) das geht Sie nichts an; **to whom it may** ~ (on letter) an den betreffenden Sachbearbeiter; (on certificate) Bestätigung f; (on reference) Zeugnis nt; **the countries** ~ed **with oil-production** die Länder, die mit der Ölproduktion zu tun haben; **where money/honour is** ~ed wenn es um Geld/die Ehre geht; **as far as the money is** ~ed was das Geld betrifft or angeht; **is it important? — not as far as I'm** ~ed ist es denn wichtig? — as mich betrifft, nicht; **as far as he is** ~ed **it's just another job, but** ... für ihn ist es nur ein anderer Job, aber ...; **as far as I'm** ~ed **you can do what you like** von mir aus kannst du tun und lassen, was du willst; **where we are** ~ed wo es um uns geht; (in so far as **we are affected**) wo wir betroffen sind; **the department** ~ed (relevant) die zuständige Abteilung; (involved) die betreffende Abteilung; **who are the people** ~ed **in this report?** wer sind die Leute, um die es in diesem Bericht geht?; **the persons** ~ed die Betroffenen, die betroffenen Personen; **my brother is the most**

closely ~ed **mein Bruder ist am meisten davon betroffen; the men** ~ed **in the robbery** die in den Überfall verwickelten Männer; **he's** ~ed **in some complicated court case** er ist in irgendeinen komplizierten Fall verwickelt.

(c) (interest) **he is only** ~ed **with facts** ihn interessieren nur die Fakten; (is only dealing with) ihm geht es nur um die Fakten; **I'm not** ~ed **now** or **I don't want to** ~ **myself now with the economic aspect of the problem** mir geht es jetzt nicht um den ökonomischen Aspekt des Problems.

(d) (have at heart) **we should be** ~ed **more with** or **about quality** Qualität sollte uns ein größeres Anliegen sein; **a mother is naturally** ~ed **about** or **will naturally** ~ **herself about the well-being of her children** das Wohl ihrer Kinder ist einer Mutter natürlich ein Anliegen; **he's not at all** ~ed **with** or **about her well-being** ihr Wohl kümmert ihn überhaupt nicht; **there's no need for you to** ~ **yourself about that** darum brauchen Sie sich nicht zu kümmern.

(e) (worry: usu pass) **to be** ~ed **about sth** sich (dat) um etw Sorgen machen, um etw besorgt sein; **I was very** ~ed **to hear about your illness** ich habe mir Sorgen gemacht, als ich von Ihrer Krankheit hörte; **he was** ~ed **at the news** die Nachricht beunruhigte ihn; **don't** ~ **yourself** machen Sie sich keine Sorgen; **I was very** ~ed **about** or **for your safety** ich war sehr um Ihre Sicherheit besorgt; **I am** ~ed **to hear that ...** es beunruhigt mich, daß ...; **a** ~ed **look** ein besorgter Blick.

concerning [kən'sɜːnɪŋ] prep bezüglich, hinsichtlich, betreffs (form) (all + gen). ~ **your request ...** apropos Ihrer Anfrage ...; **was ihre Anfrage betrifft ...;** ~ **what?** worüber?

concert¹ ['kɒnsət] n **(a)** (Mus) Konzert nt. **were you at the** ~? waren Sie in dem Konzert? **(b)** (of voices etc) **in** ~ im Chor, gemeinsam. **(c)** (fig) **in** ~ gemeinsam; **to work in** ~ **with sb** mit jdm zusammenarbeiten.

concert² [kən'sɜːt] vt efforts vereinen.

concerted [kən'sɜːtɪd] adj efforts, action, attack gemeinsam, konzertiert (esp Pol). ~ **through their** or ~ **efforts ...** mit vereinten Kräften ...; **to take** ~ **action** gemeinsam vorgehen; **to make a** ~ **attack** gemeinsam or geballt angreifen.

concert: ~**goer** n Konzertbesucher(in f) or -gänger(in f) m; ~ **grand** n Konzertflügel m; ~ **hall** n Konzerthalle f or -saal m.

concertina [ˌkɒnsə'tiːnə] **1** n Konzertina f. **2** vi sich wie eine Ziehharmonika zusammenschieben.

concertmaster ['kɒnsətmɑːstəʳ] n (US) Konzertmeister m.

concerto [kən'tʃɛːtəʊ] n Konzert, Concerto nt.

concert: ~ **performer** n konzertierender Künstler, konzertierende Künstlerin; ~ **pianist** n Pianist(in f) m; ~ **pitch** n Kammerton m; ~ **tour** n Konzerttournee f.

concession [kən'seʃən] n Zugeständnis, Konzession f (to an + acc); (Comm) Konzession f. **to make a** ~ **to sb** jdm Konzessionen or Zugeständnisse machen.

concessionaire [kənˌseʃə'neəʳ] n (Comm) Konzessionär m.

concessionary [kən'seʃənərɪ] adj (Comm) Konzessions-.

concessive [kən'sesɪv] adj (Gram) konzessiv, Konzessiv-.

conch [kɒntʃ] n große, spiralige Meeresschnecke; (used as trumpet) Trompetenschnecke f, Tritonshorn nt (also Myth).

conchy ['kɒntʃɪ] n (pej sl) Kriegsdienstverweigerer, Drückeberger (pej inf) m.

concierge ['kɒnsɪɛəʒ] n Portier m, Portiersfrau f.

conciliate [kən'sɪlɪeɪt] vt **(a)** (placate) besänftigen; (win the goodwill of) person versöhnlich stimmen. **(b)** (reconcile) opposing views auf einen Nenner bringen, in Einklang bringen.

conciliation [kənˌsɪlɪ'eɪʃən] n see vt **(a)** Besänftigung f; Versöhnung f. ~ **board** (in industry) Schlichtungskommission f.

conciliatory [kən'sɪlɪətərɪ] adj versöhnlich; (placatory) beschwichtigend, besänftigend.

concise [kən'saɪs] adj präzis(e), exakt. ~ **dictionary** Handwörterbuch nt.

concisely [kən'saɪslɪ] adv präzis(e), exakt.

conciseness [kən'saɪsnɪs], **concision** [kən'sɪʒən] n Präzision, Exaktheit f.

conclave ['kɒnkleɪv] n **(a)** Klausur f. **in** ~ in Klausur; **to meet in** ~ eine Klausurtagung abhalten. **(b)** (Eccl) Konklave nt.

conclude [kən'kluːd] **1** vt **(a)** (end) meeting, letter, speech beenden, schließen; meal abschließen, beenden. **this, gentlemen,** ~**s our business** damit, meine Herren, sind wir mit unserer Besprechung am Ende; **and now, to** ~ **tonight's programmes** zum Abschluß unseres heutigen Abendprogramms.

(b) (arrange) treaty, transaction, deal abschließen.

(c) (infer) schließen, folgern (from aus). **what did you** ~? was haben Sie daraus geschlossen or gefolgert?

(d) (decide, come to conclusion) zu dem Schluß kommen. **what have you** ~d **about his suggestion?** zu welchem Schluß sind Sie in bezug auf seinen Vorschlag gekommen?

2 vi (meetings, events) enden; (letter, speech etc also) schließen. **the chapter** ~**s on a note of optimism** das Kapitel endet mit einem optimistischen Ausblick; **to** ~ **I must say ...** abschließend wäre noch zu bemerken or bliebe noch zu sagen, ...

concluding [kən'kluːdɪŋ] adj remarks, words abschließend, Schluß-. ~ **bars/lines** Schlußtakte/-zeilen pl; **the** ~ **years of ...** die letzten Jahre von ...

conclusion [kən'kluːʒən] n **(a)** (end) Abschluß m; (of essay, novel etc) Schluß m. **in** ~ zum (Ab)schluß, abschließend.

(b) (settling: of treaty etc) Abschluß m, Zustandekommen nt.

(c) Schluß(folgerung f) m. **what** ~ **do you draw** or **reach from all this?** welchen Schluß or welche Schlußfolgerung ziehen Sie daraus or aus alldem?; **let me know your** ~**s** lassen Sie mich wissen, zu welchem Schluß Sie gekommen sind; **a rash** ~ ein voreiliger Schluß; **one is forced to the** ~ **that ...** man kommt unweigerlich zu dem Schluß, daß ...; **you don't have to agree with my** ~ Sie müssen nicht mit meiner Schlußfolgerung

einverstanden sein; *see* **foregone, jump.**
(d) (*Logic*) Folgerung *f*.
conclusive [kən'kluːsɪv] *adj* (*convincing*) schlüssig, überzeugend; (*decisive, final*) endgültig; (*Jur*) *evidence* einschlägig; *proof* schlüssig, eindeutig.
conclusively [kən'kluːsɪvlɪ] *adv see adj* schlüssig, überzeugend; endgültig; *prove* eindeutig, unwiderleglich. **this ~ settles this issue** damit ist die Sache endgültig beigelegt.
concoct [kən'kɒkt] *vt* (a) (*Cook etc*) zusammenstellen, (zu)bereiten; (*hum*) kreieren, zurechtzaubern. (b) (*fig*) *scheme, plan also* ausbrüten *or* -hecken; *excuse also* sich (*dat*) ausdenken; *new dress, hat* zaubern.
concoction [kən'kɒkʃən] *n* (a) (*food*) Kreation, Zusammenstellung *f*; (*drink*) Gebräu *nt*. **one of her little ~s** eines ihrer Spezialrezepte.
(b) (*excuse*) Münchhausiade *f*; (*story etc*) Erdichtung *f*; (*fashion*) Zauberei, Spielerei *f*. **the plot is an amazing ~ of bizarre events** der Plot ist eine erstaunliche Verkettung der merkwürdigsten Ereignisse.
concomitant [kən'kɒmɪtənt] **1** *adj* Begleit-. **2** *n* Begleiterscheinung *f*.
concord ['kɒŋkɔːd] *n* (*harmony*) Eintracht *f*; (*about decision etc*) Einvernehmen *nt*, Übereinstimmung *f*.
concordance [kən'kɔːdəns] *n* (a) (*agreement*) Übereinstimmung *f*. **in ~ with your specifications** (*form*) Ihren Angaben *or* Anweisungen gemäß. (b) (*Bibl, Liter*) Konkordanz *f*.
concordant [kən'kɔːdənt] *adj* (*form*) übereinstimmend. **a design ~ with his wishes** ein Entwurf, der seinen Wünschen entsprach/entspricht; **to be ~ with** entsprechen (+*dat*).
concordat [kən'kɔːdæt] *n* Konkordat *nt*.
concourse ['kɒŋkɔːs] *n* (a) (*liter: of people*) Menschenmenge *f*, Menschenauflauf *m*; (*of two rivers*) Zusammenfluß *m*; (*fig: of circumstances*) Zusammentreffen *nt*. **a fortuitous ~ of atoms** eine willkürliche Verbindung von Atomen.
(b) (*place*) Eingangshalle *f*; (*US: in park*) freier Platz. **station ~** Bahnhofshalle *f*.
concrete[1] ['kɒŋkriːt] *adj object, evidence, example* konkret. **a chair is a ~ object** ein Stuhl ist gegenständlich *or* etwas Gegenständliches; **~ noun** Konkretum *nt*; **~ music** konkrete Musik *f*; **~ poetry** Bilderlyrik *f*; **could you put your argument in a more ~ form?** könnten Sie Ihre Behauptung noch etwas konkretisieren?, könnten Sie etwas konkreter werden?
concrete[2] **1** *n* (*Build*) Beton *m*. **~ mixer** Betonmischmaschine *f*. **2** *adj* Beton-. **3** *vt wall, floor* betonieren.
concretely [kən'kriːtlɪ] *adv* konkret. **to express sth ~/more ~** etw konkretisieren/etw konkreter ausdrücken.
concretion [kən'kriːʃən] *n* (*coalescence*) Verschmelzung *f*; (*Geol also*) Konkretion *f*; (*Med*) Konkrement *nt*.
concubine ['kɒŋkjubaɪn] *n* (a) (*old*) Konkubine, Mätresse *f*. (b) (*in polygamy*) Konkubine, Nebenfrau *f*.
concupiscence [kən'kjuːpɪsəns] *n* Lüsternheit *f*.
concupiscent [kən'kjuːpɪsənt] *adj* lüstern.
concur [kən'kɜːʳ] *vi* (a) (*agree*) übereinstimmen; (*with a suggestion etc*) beipflichten (*with dat*); (*Math*) zusammenlaufen. **John and I ~red** John und ich waren einer Meinung; **I ~ with that** ich pflichte dem bei.
(b) (*happen together*) zusammentreffen, auf einmal eintreten. **everything ~red to bring about a successful result** alles trug zu einem erfolgreichen Ergebnis bei; **everything ~red perfectly to make the festival a success** es traf *or* ergab sich alles so günstig, daß das Festival ein Erfolg wurde.
concurrence [kən'kʌrəns] *n* (a) (*accordance*) Übereinstimmung *f*; (*agreement, permission*) Einverständnis *nt*, Zustimmung *f*. (b) (*of events*) Zusammentreffen *nt*. (c) (*Math*) Schnittpunkt *m*. **at the ~ of the two lines** im Schnittpunkt der beiden Geraden.
concurrent [kən'kʌrənt] *adj* (a) (*occurring at the same time*) gleichzeitig. **the ~ showing of the film and the play** die Tatsache, daß der Film und das Theaterstück gleichzeitig gezeigt wurden; **to be ~ with** mit etw zusammentreffen, zur gleichen Zeit wie etw stattfinden.
(b) (*acting together*) vereint, gemeinsam, gemeinschaftlich.
(c) (*in agreement*) übereinstimmend; *opinions, interpretation, statement also* gleichlautend. **to be ~ with sth** mit etw übereinstimmen.
(d) (*Math*) zusammenlaufend; (*intersecting*) sich schneidend.
concurrently [kən'kʌrəntlɪ] *adv* gleichzeitig. **the two sentences to run ~** (*Jur*) unter gleichzeitigem Vollzug beider Freiheitsstrafen.
concuss [kən'kʌs] *vt* (*usu pass*) **to be ~ed** eine Gehirnerschütterung haben.
concussion [kən'kʌʃən] *n* Gehirnerschütterung *f*.
condemn [kən'dem] *vt* (a) (*censure*) verurteilen.
(b) (*Jur*) verurteilen. **to ~ sb to death/10 years' imprisonment** jdn zum Tode/zu 10 Jahren Gefängnis verurteilen; **the ~ed man** der zum Tode Verurteilte; **the ~ed cell** die Todeszelle.
(c) (*fig*) verdammen, verurteilen (*to* zu).
(d) (*declare unfit*) *building, slums* für abbruchreif erklären; *ship* für nicht mehr seetüchtig erklären. **these houses are/should be ~ed** diese Häuser stehen auf der Abrißliste/sollten abgerissen werden; **the fruit was ~ed as unfit for consumption** das Obst wurde für den Verzehr ungeeignet erklärt.
(e) (*US Jur*) beschlagnahmen; *land* enteignen.
condemnation [,kɒndem'neɪʃən] *n* (a) Verurteilung *f*; (*fig also*) Verdammung *f*. **the state of these houses is a ~ of society** der Zustand dieser Häuser stellt der Gesellschaft ein Armutszeugnis aus; **what a ~ was that** ein Armutszeugnis.
(b) (*of slums, ship*) Kondemnation *f* (*spec*). **the new council was responsible for the immediate ~ of some of the old city**

slums die neue Stadtverwaltung war dafür verantwortlich, daß einige der alten Slums sofort auf die Abrißliste kamen.
(c) (*US Jur*) Beschlagnahme *f*; (*of land*) Enteignung *f*.
condemnatory [kɒndem'neɪtərɪ] *adj* aburteilend; *frown* mißbilligend; *criticism also* verurteilend, verdammend; *conclusion also* vernichtend.
condensation [,kɒnden'seɪʃən] *n* (a) (*of vapour*) Kondensation, Verflüssigung *f*; (*on window panes, walls etc*) Schwitzwasserbildung *f*; (*liquid formed*) Kondensat *nt*; (*on window panes, walls etc*) Schwitzwasser *nt*. **the windows/walls are covered with ~** die Fenster/Wände sind beschlagen.
(b) (*short form*) Kurzfassung *f*; (*act*) Kondensierung, Zusammenfassung *f*.
condense [kən'dens] **1** *vt* (a) kondensieren. **~d milk** Kondensmilch, Büchsen- *or* Dosenmilch *f*. (b) (*Phys*) *gas* kondensieren; (*compress*) verdichten; *rays* bündeln. (c) (*shorten*) zusammenfassen. **in a very ~d form** in sehr gedrängter Form. **2** *vi* (*gas*) kondensieren, sich niederschlagen.
condenser [kən'densəʳ] *n* (*Elec, Phys*) Kondensator *m*; (*Opt*) Kondensor *m*, Sammellinse *f*.
condescend [,kɒndɪ'send] *vi* (a) (*stoop*) sich herab- *or* herabeilassen. **to ~ to do sth** sich herab- *or* herablassen, etw zu tun, geruhen (*geh, iro*) *or* so gnädig sein, etw zu tun.
(b) (*be ~ing towards*) herablassend behandeln (*to sb* jdn). **he doesn't like being ~ed to** er läßt sich nicht gerne von oben herab behandeln.
condescending *adj*, **~ly** *adv* [,kɒndɪ'sendɪŋ, -lɪ] (*pej*) herablassend, von oben herab.
condescension [,kɒndɪ'senʃən] *n* (*pej*) Herablassung *f*; (*attitude also*) herablassende Haltung.
condiment ['kɒndɪmənt] *n* Würze *f*. **would you pass the ~s?** würden Sie mir bitte Pfeffer und Salz reichen?
condition [kən'dɪʃən] **1** *n* (a) (*determining factor*) Bedingung *f* (*also Jur, Comm*); (*prerequisite*) Voraussetzung *f*. **~s of sale** Verkaufsbedingungen *pl*; **on ~ that ...** unter der Bedingung *or* Voraussetzung, daß ..., vorausgesetzt, daß ...; **on this ~** unter folgender Bedingung *or* Voraussetzung; **on what ~?** zu welchen Bedingungen?, unter welchen Voraussetzungen?; **on no ~** auf keinen Fall; **to make ~s** Bedingungen stellen; **he made it a ~ that ...** er machte es zur Bedingung, daß ...
(b) **~s** *pl* (*circumstances*) Verhältnisse, Zustände (*pej*) *pl*; **working ~s** Arbeitsbedingungen *pl*; **living ~s** Wohnverhältnisse *pl*; **weather ~s** die Wetterlage; **in** *or* **under (the) present ~s** bei den derzeitigen Verhältnissen.
(c) *no pl* (*state*) Zustand *m*. **he is in good/bad ~** er ist in guter/schlechter Verfassung; **it is in good/bad ~** es ist in gutem/schlechtem Zustand; **not in your ~!** nicht in deinem Zustand!; **he/the car is in no ~ to make a journey** er ist nicht reisefähig/so wie das Auto ist, kann man damit keine Reise machen; **you're in no ~ to drive** du bist nicht mehr fahrtüchtig; **to be in/out of ~** in guter/keine Kondition sein; **to keep in/get into ~** in Form bleiben/kommen; (*Sport also*) seine Kondition beibehalten/sich (*dat*) eine gute Kondition antrainieren; **in an interesting ~** (*hum inf*) in anderen Umständen; **to change one's ~** (*old*) sich verehelichen (*dated*).
(d) (*Med*) Beschwerden *pl*. **heart/thyroid ~** Herz-/Schilddrüsenleiden *nt*; **he has a heart ~** er hat ein schlechtes Herz, er hat's auf den *or* am Herzen (*inf*).
(e) (*old: rank*) Stand *m*, Schicht *f*. **in every ~ of life** aus allen Ständen.
2 *vt* (a) (*esp pass: determine*) bedingen, bestimmen. **to be ~ed by** bedingt sein durch, abhängen von.
(b) (*bring into good ~*) *hair, athlete, animal* in Form bringen. **~ing powder** Aufbaumittel *nt*.
(c) (*Psych etc: train*) konditionieren; (*accustom*) gewöhnen. **they have become ~ed into believing it** sie sind so konditioniert, daß sie es glauben; **~ed reflex** bedingter Reflex.
conditional [kən'dɪʃənl] **1** *adj* (a) mit Vorbehalt, bedingt, vorbehaltlich; (*Comm, Jur*) *sale* mit Auflagen. **a ~ yes** ein Ja mit Vorbehalt; **to be ~ (up)on sth** von etw abhängen.
(b) (*Gram*) Konditional-, Konditional-, Bedingungs-. **the ~ mood/tense** das Konditional.
2 *n* (*Gram*) Konditional *nt*, Konditionalis *m*.
conditionally [kən'dɪʃnəlɪ] *adv* unter *or* mit Vorbehalt.
conditioner [kən'dɪʃənəʳ] *n* (*for hair*) Haarschnellkur *f*.
condo ['kɒndəʊ] *n* (*US inf see* **condominium b**.
condole [kən'dəʊl] *vi* **to ~ with sb** (*on or upon sth*) jdm (zu etw) sein Mitgefühl aussprechen; (*on death also*) jdm (zu etw) kondolieren.
condolence [kən'dəʊləns] *n* Beileid *nt* *no pl*, Anteilnahme, Kondolenz (*form*) *f no pl*. **letter of ~** Kondolenzbrief *m*; **please accept my ~s on the death of your mother** (meine) aufrichtige Anteilnahme zum Tode ihrer Mutter.
condom ['kɒndəm] *n* Kondom *nt or m*.
condominium ['kɒndə'mɪnɪəm] *n* (a) (*Pol*) Kondominium *nt*; (*rule also*) Kondominat *nt*. (b) (*US*) (*apartment house*) ≈ Haus *nt* mit Eigentumswohnungen, Eigentumsblock *m*; (*single apartment*) ≈ Eigentumswohnung *f*.
condone [kən'dəʊn] *vt* (*overlook*) (stillschweigend) hinwegsehen über (+*acc*); (*tacitly approve*) (stillschweigend) dulden.
condor ['kɒndɔːʳ] *n* Kondor *m*.
conduce [kən'djuːs] *vi* **to ~ to** (*form*) förderlich sein (+*dat*), beitragen zu.
conducive [kən'djuːsɪv] *adj* förderlich, dienlich (*to dat*).
conduct ['kɒndʌkt] **1** *n* (a) (*behaviour*) Verhalten, Benehmen *nt* (*towards* gegenüber); (*of children also*) Betragen *nt*; (*of prisoner*) Führung *f*. **the rules of ~** die Verhaltensregeln; **~ sheet** (*Mil*) militärische Beurteilung.
(b) (*management*) Führung *f*; (*of conference, commission of inquiry*) Leitung *f*; (*of investigation*) Durchführung *f*. **his ~ of**

the war/inquiry seine Kriegsführung/die Art, wie er die Untersuchung durchführte.

2 [kən'dʌkt] *vt* **(a)** *(guide)* führen; *(ceremoniously)* geleiten *(geh)*. ~ed tour (of) *(of country)* Gesellschaftsreise *f* (durch); *(of building)* Führung *f* (durch).

(b) *(direct, manage)* war, campaign, correspondence, conversation führen; meeting, business also leiten; investigation durchführen; private affairs handhaben. he ~ed his own defence er übernahm seine eigene Verteidigung.

(c) *(Mus)* dirigieren.

(d) *(Phys, Physiol)* leiten; lightning ableiten, erden.

3 [kən'dʌkt] *vi* **(a)** *(Mus)* dirigieren.

(b) *(Phys)* leiten.

4 [kən'dʌkt] *vr* sich verhalten, sich benehmen; *(prisoner)* sich führen. her husband ~ed himself abominably ihr Mann führte sich unmöglich auf.

conduction [kən'dʌkʃən] *n* *(Phys, Physiol)* Leitung *f* (along durch *or* Physiol) entlang).

conductive [kən'dʌktɪv] *adj* leitfähig, leitend.

conductivity [ˌkɒndʌk'tɪvɪtɪ] *n* *(Phys, Physiol)* Leitfähigkeit *f*.

conductor [kən'dʌktəʳ] *n* **(a)** *(Mus)* Dirigent(in *f*) *m*; *(of choir also)* Leiter(in *f*) *m*. **(b)** *(bus, tram ~)* Schaffner *m*; *(US Rail: guard)* Zugführer *m*. **(c)** *(Phys)* Leiter *m*; *(lightning ~)* Blitzableiter *m*. ~ rail (Fahr)leitung(sschiene) *f*.

conductress [kən'dʌktrɪs] *n* *(on bus etc)* Schaffnerin *f*.

conduit ['kɒndɪt] *n* Leitungsrohr *nt*; *(Elec)* Rohrkabel *nt*.

cone [kəʊn] *n* **(a)** Kegel *m*; *(Geol: of volcano)* (Berg)kegel *m*; *(storm ~)* Windsack *m*; *(traffic ~)* Pylon(e *f*) *m* *(form)*, Leitkegel *m*; *(Space: nose ~)* Nase *f*. a ~ of light ein Lichtkegel *m*. **(b)** *(Bot)* Zapfen *m*. **(c)** *(ice-cream ~)* (Eis)tüte *f*.

♦**cone off** *vt sep* mit Pylonen absperren.

cone-shaped ['kəʊn'ʃeɪpt] *adj* kegelförmig.

coney *n see* **cony.**

confab ['kɒnfæb] *n (inf)* kleine Besprechung. we'd better have a quick ~ wir bekakeln das am besten mal schnell *(inf)*.

confection [kən'fekʃən] *n* **(a)** *(sweets)* Konfekt *nt*, Zucker- *or* Naschwerk *nt* *(old)*. **(b)** *(Comm: item of ladies' clothing)* modischer Artikel. a charming little ~ from Dior eine bezaubernde kleine Kreation von Dior.

confectioner [kən'fekʃənəʳ] *n* *(maker)* Konditor, Zuckerbäcker *(old)* *m*; *(seller also)* Süßwarenverkäufer *m*. ~'s (shop) Süßwarenladen *m*; ~'s sugar (US) Puderzucker *m*.

confectionery [kən'fekʃənərɪ] *n* **(a)** Konditorwaren, Süßwaren *pl*; *(chocolates)* Konfekt *nt*. **(b)** *(shop)* Süßwarengeschäft *nt*.

confederacy [kən'fedərəsɪ] *n* *(Pol)* *(confederation)* Bündnis *nt*; *(of nations)* Staatenbund *m*, Konföderation *f*. the C~ *(US Hist)* die Konföderierten (Staaten) von Amerika.

confederate [kən'fedərɪt] **1** *adj* verbündet, konföderiert; nations also verbündet. the C~ States *(US Hist)* die Konföderierten Staaten von Amerika.

2 *n* *(Pol: ally)* Verbündete(r), Bündnispartner, Bundesgenosse *m*; *(pej: accomplice)* Komplize *m* *(pej)*. the C~s *(US Hist)* die Konföderierten *pl*.

confederation [kən,fedə'reɪʃən] *n* **(a)** *(Pol)* *(alliance)* Bündnis *nt*, Bund *m*; *(system of government)* Staatenbund *m*, Konföderation *f*. the Swiss C~ die Schweizer Eidgenossenschaft. **(b)** *(association)* Bund *m*. C~ of British Industry Bund *m* britischer Industrieller.

confer [kən'fɜːʳ] **1** *vt* *(on, upon sb* jdm) title, degree verleihen; power also übertragen. **2** *vi* sich beraten, sich besprechen, konferieren *(geh)*.

conference ['kɒnfərəns] *n* **(a)** Konferenz *f*; *(more informal)* Besprechung *f*. to be in a ~ (with) eine Besprechung *or* Unterredung haben (mit); to get round the ~ table sich an den Konferenztisch setzen; to get sb to the ~ table jdn an den Konferenztisch bringen; I'm sorry, he's in ~ tut mir leid, er ist in *or* bei einer Konferenz/Besprechung.

(b) *(convention)* Konferenz, Tagung *f*.

conferment [kən'fɜːmənt], **conferral** [kən'fɜːrəl] *n* *(of title, degree)* Verleihung *f*.

confess [kən'fes] **1** *vt* **(a)** *(acknowledge)* gestehen, zugeben; ignorance, mistake also bekennen, beichten *(hum inf)*.

(b) *(Eccl)* sins bekennen; *(to priest)* beichten; *(priest)* penitent die Beichte abnehmen (+dat).

2 *vi* **(a)** gestehen *(to sth* etw gestehen, sich zu etw bekennen; if you did it, you might as well ~ wenn du es warst, warum gestehst du es (dann) nicht?

(b) *(Eccl)* beichten. to ~ to sb/to sth jdm/etw *(acc)* beichten.

confessed [kən'fest] *adj* *(admitted)* plan zugegeben, erklärt, eingestanden; *(having confessed)* criminal geständig; *(self-~)* revolutionary erklärt; alcoholic, criminal eigenen Eingeständnisses, nach eigenen Angaben.

confessedly [kən'fesɪdlɪ] *adv* zugegebenermaßen; *(self-~ also)* nach eigenen Worten.

confession [kən'feʃən] *n* **(a)** Eingeständnis *nt*; *(of guilt, crime etc)* Geständnis *nt*. on his own ~ laut eigener Aussage; to make a full ~ of sth to sb *(Jur)* jdm ein volles Geständnis einer Sache *(gen)* *or* in einer Sache *(dat)* ablegen; I have a ~ to make ich muß dir etwas beichten *(inf)*, ich möchte *(Jur)* ich möchte ein Geständnis ablegen; "~s of a ..." „Bekenntnisse eines/einer ..."; *(film title)* „...-report" *m*; ~ magazine Zeitschrift *f* mit Geschichten, die das Leben schrieb.

(b) *(Eccl)* *(of sins)* Beichte *f*, (Schuld- *or* Sünden)bekenntnis *nt*. general ~/~ of faith allgemeines Sündenbekenntnis/Glaubensbekenntnis *nt*; to make one's ~ seine Sünden bekennen; to hear ~ (die) Beichte hören.

(c) *(faith)* (Glaubens)bekenntnis *nt*, Konfession *f*. what ~ are you? welche Konfession *or* Glaubenszugehörigkeit haben Sie?

confessional [kən'feʃənl] *n* Beichtstuhl *m*. the secrecy of the ~ das Beichtgeheimnis.

confessor [kən'fesəʳ] *n* **(a)** *(Eccl)* Beichtvater *m*. **(b)** Edward the C~ Edward der Bekenner.

confetti [kən'fetiː] *n*, no pl Konfetti *nt*.

confidant [ˌkɒnfɪ'dænt] *n* Vertraute(r) *m*.

confidante [ˌkɒnfɪ'dænt] *n* Vertraute *f*.

confide [kən'faɪd] *vt* anvertrauen *(to sb* jdm).

♦**confide in** *vi* **(a)** *(tell secrets to)* sich anvertrauen (+dat). to ~ ~ sb about sth jdm etw anvertrauen. **(b)** *(old: trust)* sein Vertrauen setzen in (+acc), bauen auf (+acc).

confidence ['kɒnfɪdəns] *n* **(a)** *(trust)* Vertrauen *nt*; *(in sb's abilities also)* Zutrauen *nt* *(in* zu); *(confident expectation)* Zuversicht *f*. to have (every/no) ~ in sb/sth *(volles/kein)* Vertrauen zu jdm/etw haben *or* in jdn/etw setzen; they have no ~ in his ability/the future sie haben kein Vertrauen *or* Zutrauen zu seinen Fähigkeiten/kein Vertrauen in die Zukunft; I have every ~ that ... ich bin ganz zuversichtlich, daß ...; to put one's ~ in sb/sth auf jdn/etw bauen, sich auf jdn/etw verlassen; I don't share your ~ that things will improve ich teile Ihre Zuversicht nicht, daß sich die Dinge bessern werden; I wish I had your ~ ich wünschte, ich hätte deine Zuversicht(lichkeit); we look with ~ ... wir schauen zuversichtlich ...; can you leave your car here with ~? kann man hier sein Auto beruhigt abstellen?; he talked with ~ on the subject er äußerte sich sehr kompetent zu dem Thema; I can't talk with any ~ about ... ich kann nichts Bestimmtes *or* Maßgebliches über (–acc) ... sagen; in the full ~ that ... im festen Vertrauen darauf, daß ...; issue of ~ *(Parl)* Vertrauensfrage *f*; to give/ask for a vote of ~ *(Parl)* das Vertrauen aussprechen/die Vertrauensfrage stellen; motion/vote of no ~ Mißtrauensantrag *m*/-votum *nt*.

(b) *(self-~)* (Selbst)vertrauen *nt*, Selbstsicherheit *f*.

(c) *(confidential relationship)* Vertrauen *nt*. in (strict) ~ *(streng)* vertraulich; to take sb into one's ~ jdn ins Vertrauen ziehen; to be in *or* enjoy sb's ~ jds Vertrauen besitzen *or* genießen.

(d) *(information confided)* vertrauliche Mitteilung.

confidence: ~ trick, ~trickster *n see con* trick, con-man.

confident ['kɒnfɪdənt] *adj* **(a)** *(sure)* überzeugt, zuversichtlich *(of gen)*; look etc zuversichtlich. to be ~ of success *or* succeeding vom Erfolg überzeugt sein, zuversichtlich *or* überzeugt sein, daß man gewinnt; it will happen — are you ~? es wird geschehen — sind Sie davon überzeugt *or* dessen sicher?; to be ~ in sb/sth Vertrauen zu jdm/etw haben, einer/seiner Sache vertrauen; ~ in her love ihrer Liebe gewiß *(geh)*.

(b) *(self-assured)* (selbst)sicher.

confidential [ˌkɒnfɪ'denʃəl] *adj* **(a)** information, whisper vertraulich. **(b)** *(enjoying sb's confidence)* ~ secretary Privatsekretär(in *f*) *m*; ~ agent Sonderbeauftragte(r) *mf* mit geheimer Mission. **(c)** *(inclined to confide)* vertrauensselig.

confidentiality [ˌkɒnfɪ,denʃɪ'ælɪtɪ] *n* Vertraulichkeit *f*.

confidentially [ˌkɒnfɪ'denʃəlɪ] *adv* vertraulich, im Vertrauen.

confidently ['kɒnfɪdəntlɪ] *adv* **(a)** zuversichtlich; look forward also vertrauensvoll. **(b)** *(self-~)* selbstsicher; *(with conviction)* mit Überzeugung.

confiding *adj*, **~ly** *adv* [kən'faɪdɪŋ, -lɪ] vertrauensvoll.

configuration [kən,fɪgjʊ'reɪʃən] *n* Konfiguration *f* *(form)*; *(Geog)* Form, Gestalt *f*; *(Sci)* Struktur *f*, Aufbau *m*; *(Astron)* Anordnung *f*, Aspekt *m* *(spec)*.

confine [kən'faɪn] **1** *vt* **(a)** *(keep in)* person, animal (ein)sperren; flood eindämmen. ~d to bed/the house ans Bett/ans Haus gefesselt; to be ~d to barracks/one's room/one's house Kasernen-/Stubenarrest haben/unter Hausarrest stehen; with her body ~d in a corset in ein Korsett gezwängt.

(b) *(limit)* remarks beschränken *(to auf* +acc). to ~ oneself to doing sth sich darauf beschränken, etw zu tun; the privilege/damage was ~d to ... das Privileg war/der Schaden ... beschränkte *or* erstreckte sich nur auf (+acc) .../der Schaden beschränkte *or* erstreckte sich nur auf (+acc) ...; he finds life here too confining er findet das Leben hier zu beengend *or* eingeengt; lions are ~d to Africa Löwen gibt es nur in Afrika.

(c) *(dated pass: in childbirth)* to be ~d niederkommen *(old)*.

2 ~s ['kɒnfaɪnz] *npl* *(of space, thing etc)* Grenzen *pl*.

confined [kən'faɪnd] *adj* space beschränkt, begrenzt; atmosphere beengend.

confinement [kən'faɪnmənt] *n* **(a)** *(imprisonment)* *(act)* Einsperren *nt*; *(in hospital)* Einweisung *f*; *(of animals)* Gefangenhalten *nt*; *(state)* Eingesperrtsein *nt*; *(in jail)* Haft *f*; *(of animals)* Gefangenschaft *f*; *(Mil)* Arrest *m* *(also hum)*. ~ to barracks/one's room Kasernen-/Stubenarrest *m*; to put sb in ~ jdn einsperren; to keep sb in close ~ jdn in strengem Gewahrsam halten.

(b) *(restriction)* Beschränkung *f* *(to auf* +acc).

(c) *(dated: childbirth)* Entbindung, Niederkunft *(old)* *f*.

confirm [kən'fɜːm] *vt* **(a)** *(verify)* bestätigen. to be ~ed in one's opinion *(liter)* sich in seiner Ansicht bestätigt sehen *(geh)*. **(b)** *(strengthen)* bestärken; one's resolve also bekräftigen. **(c)** *(Eccl)* konfirmieren; Roman Catholic firmen.

confirmation [ˌkɒnfə'meɪʃən] *n* **(a)** Bestätigung *f*. a letter in ~ (of) ein Brief *m* zur *or* als Bestätigung (+gen). **(b)** *(Eccl)* Konfirmation *f*; *(of Roman Catholics)* Firmung *f*. ~ classes Konfirmandenstunde *f or* -unterricht *m*; Firmunterricht *m*.

confirmatory [kən'fɜːmeɪtərɪ] *adj* bestätigend.

confirmed [kən'fɜːmd] *adj* erklärt; bachelor eingefleischt.

confiscate ['kɒnfɪskeɪt] *vt* beschlagnahmen, konfiszieren. to ~ sth from sb jdm etw abnehmen.

confiscation [ˌkɒnfɪs'keɪʃən] *n* Beschlagnahme, Konfiszierung *f*.

confiscatory [ˌkɒnfɪs'keɪtərɪ] *adj* they have ~ powers sie sind zur Beschlagnahme befugt.

conflagration [ˌkɒnflə'greɪʃən] *n* *(of forest, towns)* Feuersbrunst *f*; *(of building)* Großbrand *m*.

conflate [kən'fleɪt] *vt* zusammenfassen.

conflation [kənˈfleɪʃən] n Zusammenfassung f.

conflict [ˈkɒnflɪkt] **1** n Konflikt m; (of moral issues, ideas also) Widerstreit, Zwiespalt m; (between two accounts etc) Widerspruch m; (fighting) Zusammenstoß m. **to be in ~ with** sb/sth mit jdm/etw im Konflikt liegen; im Widerspruch zu jdm/etw stehen; **the ego is always in ~ with the id** das Ich ist immer im Widerstreit mit dem Es; **to come into ~ with** sb/sth mit jdm/etw in Konflikt geraten; **open/armed ~** offener Konflikt/bewaffneter Zusammenstoß; **border ~** Grenzkonflikt m; **~ of interests/opinions** Interessen-/Meinungskonflikt m.

2 [kənˈflɪkt] vi im Widerspruch stehen (with zu), widersprechen (with dat). **their opinions on the subject ~** in diesem Punkt stehen ihre Ansichten im Widerspruch zueinander.

conflicting [kənˈflɪktɪŋ] adj widersprüchlich.

confluence [ˈkɒnfluəns] n (of rivers) Zusammenfluß m.

conform [kənˈfɔːm] vi (a) (things: comply with) entsprechen (to dat); (people: socially) sich anpassen (to an +acc); (things, people: to rules etc) sich richten (to nach); (agree) übereinstimmen, konform gehen (with mit).

(b) (Brit Eccl) sich (der englischen Staatskirche dat) unterwerfen.

conformance [kənˈfɔːməns] n see **conformity**.

conformist [kənˈfɔːmɪst] **1** n Konformist m (also Brit Eccl). **2** adj konformistisch.

conformity [kənˈfɔːmɪtɪ] n (a) (uniformity) Konformismus m.

(b) (compliance) Übereinstimmung f; (of manners) Konformismus m; (socially) Anpassung f (with an +acc). **the outward ~ of his social manner and way of life** sein äußerer Konformismus in Benehmen und Lebensweise; **in ~ with sth** einer Sache (dat) entsprechend or gemäß; **to be in ~ with sth** einer Sache (dat) entsprechen; **to bring sth into ~ with sth** etw mit etw in Einklang or Übereinstimmung bringen.

confound [kənˈfaʊnd] vt (a) (amaze) verblüffen.

(b) (throw into confusion) verwirren, durcheinanderbringen. **that merely ~s the issue** das macht die Sache nur verworrener.

(c) (liter: mistake for sth else) verwechseln.

(d) (inf) ~ **it!** vermaledeit (dated) or verflixt (inf) noch mal!; ~ **him!** der vermaledeite (dated) or verflixte (inf) Kerl!

confounded [kənˈfaʊndɪd] adj (inf) vermaledeit (dated inf), verflixt (inf); **cheek** also verflucht (inf); **noise** also Heiden- (inf); **nuisance** elend (inf).

confoundedly [kənˈfaʊndɪdlɪ] adv (dated inf) verflucht (inf).

confront [kənˈfrʌnt] vt (a) (face) danger, enemy, the boss gegenübertreten (+dat); (fig) problems, issue also begegnen (+dat); (stand or be ~ing) wall of ice etc gegenüberstehen (+dat); (problems, decisions) sich stellen (+dat). **he found a lion ~ing him** er fand sich einem Löwen gegenüber(stehen).

(b) (bring face to face with) konfrontieren. **to ~ sb with** sb/sth jdn jdm gegenüberstellen, jdn mit jdm/etw konfrontieren; **to be ~ed with sth** mit etw konfrontiert sein, vor etw (dat) stehen; (when) ~**ed with** angesichts (+gen).

confrontation [ˌkɒnfrənˈteɪʃən] n Konfrontation f (also Pol); (defiant also) Auseinandersetzung f; (with witnesses, evidence etc) Gegenüberstellung f.

Confucian [kənˈfjuːʃən] **1** adj konfuzianisch. **2** n Konfuzianer(in f) m.

Confucianism [kənˈfjuːʃənɪzm] n Konfuzianismus m.

Confucius [kənˈfjuːʃəs] n Konfuzius, Konfutse m.

confuse [kənˈfjuːz] vt (a) (bewilder, perplex, muddle) people konfus machen, verwirren, durcheinanderbringen; (make unclear) situation verworren machen. **sorry, am I confusing you?** Entschuldigung, bringe ich Sie durcheinander or verwirrt Sie das?; **don't ~ the issue!** bring (jetzt) nicht alles durcheinander!

(b) (mix up) people verwechseln; matters, issues also durcheinanderbringen. **to ~ two problems** zwei Probleme durcheinanderbringen or miteinander verwechseln.

confused [kənˈfjuːzd] adj (a) (muddled) wirr, konfus; person also verwirrt; (through old age, after anaesthetic etc) wirr im Kopf; idea, report, situation also verworren; sound, jumble wirr. **(b)** (embarrassed) verwirrt, verlegen, betreten.

confusedly [kənˈfjuːzɪdlɪ] adv verwirrt; (in disorder also) wirr; (embarrassedly also) verlegen, betreten.

confusing [kənˈfjuːzɪŋ] adj verwirrend.

confusion [kənˈfjuːʒən] n (a) (disorder) Durcheinander nt, Wirrwarr m, Unordnung f; (jumble) Wirrwarr m. **to be in ~ in** Unordnung sein, durcheinander sein; **scenes of ~** allgemeines or wildes Durcheinander; **to retire in ~** (Mil) einen ungeordneten Rückzug antreten; **to throw everything into ~** alles durcheinanderbringen; **in the ~ of the battle/robbery** im Durcheinander der Schlacht/während des Raubüberfalls; **to run about in ~** wild durcheinanderlaufen.

(b) (perplexity) Verwirrung f, Verwirrtheit f; (mental ~: after drugs, blow on head etc) Verwirrtheit f; (through old age etc) Wirrheit f. **in the ~ of the moment** im Eifer des Gefechts.

(c) (embarrassment) Verlegenheit f; (at being found out) Betroffenheit f. **to be covered in ~** vor Verlegenheit erröten; **he was sitting there covered in ~** er saß da, schamrot vor Verlegenheit.

(d) (mixing up) Verwechslung f.

confutation [ˌkɒnfjuːˈteɪʃən] n Widerlegung f.

confute [kənˈfjuːt] vt widerlegen.

conga [ˈkɒŋgə] n Conga m.

congeal [kənˈdʒiːl] **1** vi erstarren, starr werden; (glue, mud) hart or fest werden; (blood) gerinnen; (with fear) erstarren. **2** vt erstarren lassen (also fig); glue, mud hart werden lassen; blood gerinnen lassen.

congelation [ˌkɒndʒəˈleɪʃən] n see vi Erstarren nt; Festwerden nt; Gerinnen nt.

congenial [kənˈdʒiːnɪəl] adj (a) (pleasant) ansprechend; person also sympathisch; place, job also, atmosphere angenehm.

(b) (liter: of like nature) kongenial (liter), geistesverwandt.

congenital [kənˈdʒenɪtl] adj deficiency, disease angeboren, kongenital (spec). ~ **defect** Geburtsfehler m; ~ **idiot** (inf) Erzdepp m (inf).

conger [ˈkɒŋgəʳ] n (also ~ eel) Meeraal m.

congeries [kənˈdʒɪriːz] n sing (liter) Konglomerat nt, Ansammlung, Anhäufung f.

congested [kənˈdʒestɪd] adj überfüllt; (with traffic) verstopft; (with people also) voll; pavement übervoll; (highly populated) über(be)völkert. **his lungs are** ~ in seiner Lunge hat sich Blut angestaut or ist es zu einem Blutstau gekommen.

congestion [kənˈdʒestʃən] n (traffic, pedestrians) Stau m, Stockung f; (in corridors etc) Gedränge nt; (overpopulation) Übervölkerung f; (Med) Blutstau, Blutandrang m. **the ~ in the city centre is getting so bad** ... die Verstopfung in der Innenstadt nimmt derartige Ausmaße an ...

conglomerate [kənˈglɒmərɪt] **1** adj nation zusammengewürfelt; language Misch-. ~ **rock** (Geol) Konglomeratgestein nt. **2** n (also Geol, Comm) Konglomerat nt. **3** [kənˈglɒməreɪt] vi sich zusammenballen, sich vereinigen, verschmelzen.

conglomeration [kənˌglɒməˈreɪʃən] n Ansammlung f, Haufen m; (of ideas) Gemisch nt.

Congo [ˈkɒŋgəʊ] n Kongo m.

Congolese [ˌkɒŋgəʊˈliːz] **1** adj kongolesisch. **2** n Kongolese m, Kongolesin f.

congrats [kənˈgræts] interj (dated inf) gratuliere.

congratulate [kənˈgrætjuleɪt] vt gratulieren (+dat) (also on birthday, engagement etc), beglückwünschen (on zu). **you are to be ~d on not having succumbed** man kann Ihnen nur gratulieren, daß Sie nicht nachgegeben haben.

congratulation [kənˌgrætjuˈleɪʃən] n Gratulation f; Glückwunsch m. **there was a tone of ~ in his voice** seine Stimme hatte einen anerkennenden Ton.

congratulations [kənˌgrætjuˈleɪʃənz] **1** npl Glückwunsch m, Glückwünsche pl. **to offer/send one's ~** gratulieren, jdn beglückwünschen/jdm gratulieren, jdm seine Glückwünsche senden.

2 interj (ich) gratuliere; (iro) gratuliere! ~ **(on your success)!** herzlichen Glückwunsch or herzliche Glückwünsche (zu deinem Erfolg)!

congratulatory [kənˈgrætjulətərɪ] adj card, telegram Glückwunsch-; look, tone anerkennend. **I wrote him a ~ letter on** ... ich gratulierte ihm brieflich zu ...

congregate [ˈkɒŋgrɪgeɪt] vi sich sammeln; (on a particular occasion) sich versammeln. **to be ~d in** ... sich sammeln in (+dat) ...; sich versammeln in (+dat) ...

congregation [ˌkɒŋgrɪˈgeɪʃən] n (a) Versammlung f; (not planned) Ansammlung f; (people in cities etc) Zusammenballung f. **(b)** (Eccl) Gemeinde f; (of cardinals) Kongregation f.

congregational [ˌkɒŋgrɪˈgeɪʃənl] adj (a) C~ kongregationalistisch. **(b)** (of a congregation) Gemeinde-.

Congregationalism [ˌkɒŋgrɪˈgeɪʃənəlɪzəm] n Kongregationalismus m.

Congregationalist [ˌkɒŋgrɪˈgeɪʃənəlɪst] n Kongregationalist(in f) m.

congress [ˈkɒŋgres] n (a) (meeting) Kongreß m, Tagung f; (of political party) Parteitag m. **(b)** C~ (US etc Pol) der Kongreß.

congressional [kɒŋˈgreʃənl] adj delegate, meeting Kongreß-. C~ **District** Kongreßwahlbezirk m; C~ **Record** Veröffentlichung f der Kongreßdebatten.

Congressman [ˈkɒŋgresmən] n, pl -men [-mən] Kongreßabgeordnete(r) m.

Congresswoman [ˈkɒŋgres,wʊmən] n, pl -women [-,wɪmɪn] Kongreßabgeordnete f.

congruence [ˈkɒŋgruəns] n Kongruenz, Übereinstimmung f; (Geometry) Deckungsgleichheit, Kongruenz f.

congruent [ˈkɒŋgruənt] adj (a) see **congruous**. **(b)** (Math) number kongruent; (Geometry also) deckungsgleich.

congruity [kɒŋˈgruːɪtɪ] n Übereinstimmung, Kongruenz (geh) f.

congruous [ˈkɒŋgruəs] adj (a) (corresponding) sich deckend, übereinstimmend. **to be ~ with** sich mit etw decken. **(b)** (appropriate, proper) vereinbar. **this is hardly ~ with his new position as** ... es ist kaum mit seiner neuen Stellung als ... vereinbar.

conic [ˈkɒnɪk] adj (a) (Math) Kegel-, konisch. ~ **section** Kegelschnitt m. **(b)** (also ~al) kegelförmig, Kegel-, konisch. ~ **projection** (Geog) Kegelprojektion or -abbildung f.

conifer [ˈkɒnɪfəʳ] n Nadelbaum m, Konifere f (spec). ~s Nadelhölzer pl.

coniferous [kəˈnɪfərəs] adj tree, forest Nadel-.

conjectural [kənˈdʒektʃərəl] adj auf Vermutungen or Mutmaßungen beruhend. **a conclusion which must remain ~** ein Schluß, der Vermutung or Mutmaßung bleiben muß; **what he claims as fact is entirely ~** was er als Tatsache hinstellt, ist reine Vermutung or nichts weiter als eine Vermutung; **the book's conclusion is purely ~** das Buch endet mit reinen Vermutungen.

conjecture [kənˈdʒektʃəʳ] **1** vt vermuten, mutmaßen (geh).

2 vi Vermutungen or Mutmaßungen anstellen, mutmaßen (geh). **it was just as scientists had ~d** es verhielt sich geradeso, wie es die Wissenschaftler gemutmaßt or vermutet hatten.

3 n Vermutung, Mutmaßung (geh) f. **what will come next is a matter of or for ~** was folgt, das kann man nur vermuten or das bleibt unserer Vermutung überlassen.

conjoin [kənˈdʒɔɪn] vt (form) verbinden.

conjoint adj, ~**ly** adv [kənˈdʒɔɪnt, -lɪ] gemeinsam.

conjugal [ˈkɒndʒugəl] adj rights, bliss, duties ehelich; state Ehe-. ~ **affection** Gattenliebe f.

conjugate [ˈkɒndʒugeɪt] **1** vt (Gram) konjugieren, beugen. **2** vi (Gram) sich konjugieren lassen; (Biol) konjugieren.

conjugation [ˌkɒndʒuˈgeɪʃən] n (Gram, Biol) Konjugation f.

conjunction [kən'dʒʌŋkʃən] n **(a)** (Gram) Konjunktion f, Bindewort nt.
(b) (association) Verbindung f; (co-occurrence: of events) Zusammentreffen nt. in ~ zusammen; in ~ with the new evidence in Verbindung mit dem neuen Beweismaterial; **the programme was broadcast/produced in** ~ **with the NBC** die Sendung wurde vom NBC übernommen/das Programm wurde in Zusammenarbeit mit NBC aufgezeichnet.
(c) (Astron) Konjunktion f.

conjunctive [kən'dʒʌŋktɪv] adj (Gram, Anat) Binde-, verbindend. ~ **word** Bindewort nt.

conjunctivitis [kən,dʒʌŋktɪ'vaɪtɪs] n (Med) Bindehautentzündung, Konjunktivitis (spec) f.

conjuncture [kən'dʒʌŋktʃə^r] n Zusammentreffen nt.

conjure¹ [kən'dʒuə^r] vt (liter: appeal to) beschwören.

conjure² [kʌndʒə^r] vti zaubern. **a name to** ~ **with** ein Name, der Wunder wirkt or der eine Ausstrahlung hat.
♦**conjure away** vi sep (lit, fig) wegzaubern.
♦**conjure up** vt sep ghosts, spirits beschwören; (fig) memories etc heraufbeschwören; (provide, produce) hervorzaubern; **meal** zusammenzaubern.

conjurer [kʌndʒərə^r] n Zauberer m, Zauberin f, Zauberkünstler(in f) m.

conjuring [kʌndʒərɪŋ] n Zaubern nt; (performance) Zauberei f. ~ **set** Zauberkasten m; ~ **trick** Zaubertrick m, (Zauber)kunststück nt.

conjuror [kʌndʒərə^r] n see **conjurer**.

conk [kɒŋk] (inf) **1** n (esp Brit: nose) Zinken m (inf). **2** vt (hit) hauen (inf).
♦**conk out** vi (inf) es aufstecken (inf), den Geist aufgeben; (person) (faint) umkippen (inf); (die) ins Gras beißen (sl).

conker [kɒŋkə^r] n (Brit inf) (Roß)kastanie f. **to play** ~**s** ein Wettspiel mit Kastanien machen.

con-man [kɒnmæn] n, pl **-men** [-men] (inf) Schwindler, Bauernfänger (inf) m; (pretending to have social status) Hochstapler m; (promising marriage) Heiratsschwindler m.

connect [kə'nekt] **1** vt **(a)** (join) verbinden (to, with mit); (Elec etc: also ~ **up**) appliances, subscribers anschließen (to an +acc). **I'll** ~ **you** (Telec) ich verbinde (Sie); **to be** ~**ed** (two things) miteinander verbunden sein; (several things) untereinander verbunden sein; **to** ~ **to earth** erden; ~**ed by telephone** telephonisch verbunden; see **parallel**.
(b) (fig: associate) in Verbindung or Zusammenhang bringen. **I always** ~ **Paris with springtime** ich verbinde Paris immer mit Frühling; **these things are** ~**ed in my mind** diese Dinge gehören für mich zusammen; **I'd never** ~**ed them in my mind** ich hatte sie nie zueinander in Beziehung gesetzt.
(c) (esp pass: link) ideas, theories etc verbinden. **to be** ~**ed with** eine Beziehung haben zu, in einer Beziehung or in Verbindung stehen zu; (be related to) verwandt sein mit; **he's** ~**ed with the BBC/university** er hat mit dem BBC/der Universität zu tun; **to be** ~**ed by marriage** verschwägert sein; **to be** ~**ed** (ideas etc) in Beziehung zueinander stehen; (firms) miteinander zu tun haben; **loosely** ~**ed ideas** lose verknüpfte Ideen.
2 vi **(a)** (join) (two rooms) eine Verbindung haben (to, with zu); (two parts, wires etc) Kontakt haben.
(b) (Rail, Aviat etc) Anschluß haben (with an +acc).
(c) (inf: hit) (fist etc) landen (inf) (with auf +dat); (golf-club etc) treffen (with acc). **he really** ~**ed** er hat voll getroffen.
♦**connect up** vt sep (Elec etc) anschließen (to, with an +acc).

connecting rod [kə'nektɪŋ,rɒd] n Pleuel- or Kurbelstange f.

connection [kə'nekʃən] n **(a)** Verbindung f (to, with zu, mit); (telephone line also, wire) Leitung f; (to mains) Anschluß m (to an +acc); (connecting part) Verbindung(sstück nt) f. **parallel/series** ~ Parallel-/Reihenschaltung f.
(b) (fig: link) Zusammenhang m, Beziehung f (with zu). **in this** ~ in diesem Zusammenhang; **in** ~ **with** in Zusammenhang mit.
(c) (relationship, business ~) Beziehung, Verbindung f (with zu); (family ~) familiäre Beziehung; (old, form: relative) (entfernter) Verwandter, (entfernte) Verwandte. **to have** ~**s** Beziehungen haben; **to break off/form a** ~ (with sb) die Beziehung or Verbindung (zu jdm) abbrechen/(mit jdm) in Verbindung or Beziehung treten; **there is some family** ~ **between them** sie sind weitläufig miteinander verwandt.
(d) (Rail etc) Anschluß m. **the train makes a** ~ **with the bus** der Zug hat Anschluß an den Bus.

connective [kə'nektɪv] **1** n (Gram) Bindewort nt. **2** adj verbindend. ~ **tissue** Bindegewebe nt.

connexion [kə'nekʃən] n see **connection**.

conning tower [kɒnɪŋtauə^r] n Kommandoturm m.

connivance [kə'naɪvəns] n (tacit consent) stillschweigendes Einverständnis; (dishonest dealing) Schiebung f. **his** ~ **at the wrong-doing** seine Mitwisserschaft bei dem Vergehen; **to do sth in** ~ **with sb** etw mit jds Wissen tun; **to be in** ~ **with sb** mit jdm gemeinsame Sache machen.

connive [kə'naɪv] vi **(a)** (conspire) sich verschwören, gemeinsame Sache machen. **he's a conniving little wretch** (inf) er ist ein hinterhältiger Tropf (inf). **(b)** (deliberately overlook) **to** ~ **at sth** etw stillschweigend dulden; **to** ~ **at a crime** einem Verbrechen Vorschub leisten.

connoisseur [,kɒnə'sɜ:^r] n Kenner, Connaisseur (geh) m. ~ **of wines/women** Wein-/Frauenkenner m.

connotation [,kɒnəu'teɪʃən] n Assoziation, Konnotation (spec) f. **the** ~**s of this word** die mit diesem Wort verbundenen Assoziationen, die Konnotationen dieses Wortes (spec).

connote [kɒ'nəut] vt suggerieren.

connubial [kə'nju:bɪəl] adj ehelich, Ehe-.

conquer [kɒŋkə^r] vt **(a)** (lit) country, the world erobern; enemy, people, nation besiegen. **(b)** (fig) difficulties, feelings, habits, disease bezwingen, besiegen; people, sb's heart erobern; mountain bezwingen.

conquering [kɒŋkərɪŋ] adj hero siegreich.

conqueror [kɒŋkərə^r] n (of country, heart) Eroberer m; (of enemy, difficulties, feelings, disease) Sieger (of über +acc), Besieger m; (of difficulties, feelings, mountains) Bezwinger m. **William the C~** Wilhelm der Eroberer.

conquest [kɒŋkwest] n Eroberung f; (of enemy etc, disease) Sieg m (of über +acc), Bezwingung f; (inf: person) Eroberung f.

Cons abbr of **Conservative**.

consanguinity [,kɒnsæŋ'gwɪnɪtɪ] n Blutsverwandtschaft f.

conscience [kɒnʃəns] n Gewissen nt. **to have a clear/easy/bad/guilty** ~ ein reines/gutes/schlechtes/böses Gewissen haben (about wegen); **doesn't it give you a guilty** ~ **telling lies?** haben Sie keine Gewissensbisse or kein schlechtes Gewissen, wenn Sie lügen?; **with an easy** ~ mit ruhigem Gewissen, ruhigen Gewissens (geh); **he has no** ~ **about lying** er macht sich (dat) kein Gewissen daraus zu lügen; **it/he will be on your** ~ **all your life** Sie werden das/ihn Ihr Leben lang auf dem Gewissen haben; **it's still on my** ~ (I still haven't done it) es steht mir noch bevor; **my** ~ **won't let me do it** das kann ich mit meinem Gewissen nicht vereinbaren; **in (all)** ~ allen Ernstes; **I can't in all** ~ **...** ich kann unmöglich ...; **let your** ~ **be your guide!** hör auf dein Gewissen; **it's between you and your** ~ das mußt du mit dir selbst or mit deinem Gewissen abmachen.

conscience: ~ **clause** n (Jur) ≈ Gewissensklausel f; ~ **money** n his donation looks like ~ **money** mit der Spende will er wohl sein Gewissen beruhigen; ~**-stricken** adj schuldbewußt.

conscientious [,kɒnʃɪ'enʃəs] adj (diligent) gewissenhaft; (conscious of one's duty) pflichtbewußt. ~ **objector** Kriegsdienstverweigerer m (aus Gewissensgründen); **he had** ~ **objections** er war aus Gewissensgründen dagegen.

conscientiousness [,kɒnʃɪ'enʃəsnɪs] n Gewissenhaftigkeit f; (sense of duty) Pflichtbewußtsein, Pflichtgefühl nt.

conscious [kɒnʃəs] adj **(a)** (Med) bei Bewußtsein. **(b)** (aware) bewußt (also Psych). **the** ~ **mind** das Bewußtsein; **to be/become** ~ **of sth** sich (dat) einer Sache (gen) bewußt sein/werden; **I was/became** ~ **that** es war/wurde mir bewußt, daß. **(c)** (deliberate) grace, effort etc bewußt; humour also absichtlich.

-conscious adj suf -bewußt. **weight-** ~ gewichtsbewußt.

consciously [kɒnʃəslɪ] adv bewußt; (deliberately also) absichtlich.

consciousness [kɒnʃəsnɪs] n **(a)** (Med) Bewußtsein nt. **to lose/regain** ~ das Bewußtsein verlieren/wiedererlangen, bewußtlos werden/wieder zu sich kommen.
(b) (awareness) Bewußtsein, Wissen nt. ~ **of her superior rank** das Wissen um ihre höhere Stellung.
(c) (conscious mind) Bewußtsein nt.

-consciousness n suf -bewußtheit f.

conscript [kən'skrɪpt] **1** vt einziehen, einberufen; army ausheben. **2** [kɒnskrɪpt] n Wehrpflichtige(r) m.

conscription [kən'skrɪpʃən] n Wehrpflicht f; (act of conscripting) Einberufung f; (of army) Aushebung f.

consecrate [kɒnsɪkreɪt] vt (lit, fig) weihen.

consecration [,kɒnsɪ'kreɪʃən] n Weihe f; (in Mass) Wandlung f.

consecutive [kən'sekjutɪv] adj **(a)** aufeinanderfolgend; numbers fortlaufend. **on four** ~ **days** vier Tage hintereinander; **this is the third** ~ **morning he's been late** er ist jetzt dreimal hintereinander morgens zu spät gekommen. **(b)** (Gram) clause Konsekutiv-, Folge-.

consecutively [kən'sekjutɪvlɪ] adv nacheinander, hintereinander; numbered fortlaufend.

consensus [kən'sensəs] n Übereinstimmung f; (accord also) Einigkeit f. **the** ~ **is that ...** man ist allgemein der Meinung, daß ...; **there's a** ~ **of opinion in favour of ...** die allgemeine Meinheit ist für ...; **cabinet decisions are based on** ~ Entscheidungen des Kabinetts beruhen auf einem Mehrheitsbeschluß; **there was no** ~ **(among them)** sie waren sich nicht einig, es gab keinen Konsens unter ihnen (form); ~ **politics** Politik f des Konsensus or Miteinander.

consent [kən'sent] **1** vi zustimmen (to dat), einwilligen (to in +acc). **to** ~ **to do sth** sich bereit erklären, etw zu tun; **to** ~ **to sb doing sth** einwilligen or damit einverstanden sein, daß jd etw tut; **homosexuality between** ~**ing adults** nicht qualifizierte Unzucht unter erwachsenen Männern.
2 n Zustimmung (to zu), Einwilligung (to in +acc) f. **it/he is by common or general** ~ **...** man hält es/ihn allgemein für ...; **to be chosen by general** ~ einstimmig gewählt werden; **by mutual** ~ in gegenseitigem Einverständnis; see **age 1 (c)**.

consequence [kɒnsɪkwəns] n **(a)** (result, effect) Folge f; (of actions also) Konsequenz f. **in** ~ folglich; **in** ~ **of** infolge (+gen); **in** ~ **of which** infolgedessen; **and the** ~ **is that we have** ... und folglich haben wir ...; **as a** ~ **of X** ... X hatte ... zur Folge; **with the** ~ **that he** ... was zur Folge hatte or mit dem Erfolg, daß er ...; **to take the** ~**s** die Folgen or Konsequenzen tragen.
(b) (importance) Wichtigkeit, Bedeutung f; (of decision, measure also) Tragweite f. **a person of** ~ eine bedeutende or wichtige Persönlichkeit; **did he have anything of** ~ **to say?** hatte er irgend etwas Wichtiges zu sagen?; **he's (a man) of no** ~ er hat nichts zu sagen; **it's of no** ~/**no** ~ **to me** das spielt keine Rolle/das ist mir einerlei, das tangiert mich nicht (inf); **of what** ~ **is that to you?** was tangiert Sie das? (inf).
(c) ~**s** sing (game) Schreibspiel, bei dem auf gefaltetem Papier ein nicht bekannter Vorsatz ergänzt wird.

consequent [kɒnsɪkwənt] adj attr daraus folgend, sich daraus ergebend; (temporal) darauffolgend. **to be** ~ **upon sth** (form, liter) sich aus etw ergeben.

consequential [,kɒnsɪ'kwenʃəl] adj **(a)** see **consequent**. **(b)** (self-important) wichtigtuerisch; smile, tone also überheblich. **(c)** (logically consistent) folgerichtig.

consequentially [ˌkɒnsɪ'kwenʃəlɪ] *adv* (*as a result*) daraufhin.
consequently ['kɒnsɪkwəntlɪ] *adv* folglich.
conservancy [kən'sɜːvənsɪ] *n* (**a**) (*Brit: board*) Schutzbehörde *f*; (*for ports, rivers etc*) Wasserschutzamt *nt*; (*for forests*) Forstamt *nt*. (**b**) (*official conservation*) Erhaltung *f*, Schutz *m*.
conservation [ˌkɒnsə'veɪʃən] *n* (**a**) (*preservation*) Erhaltung *f*, Schutz *m*. ~ **area** (*in the country*) Naturschutzgebiet *nt*; (*in town*) unter Denkmalschutz stehendes Gebiet. (**b**) (*Phys*) Erhaltung *f*.
conservationist [ˌkɒnsə'veɪʃənɪst] *n* Umweltschützer(in *f*) *m*; (*as regards old buildings etc*) Denkmalpfleger *m*.
conservatism [kən'sɜːvətɪzəm] *n* Konservatismus *m*.
conservative [kən'sɜːvətɪv] 1 *adj* (**a**) *person, outlook, clothing, style* konservativ; (*cautious, moderate*) vorsichtig. at a ~ **estimate** bei vorsichtiger Schätzung. (**b**) (*Pol*) konservativ. the C~ **Party** (*Brit*) die Konservative Partei. 2 *n* (*Pol:* C~) Konservative(r) *mf*. I'm a ~ in such **matters** in solchen Dingen bin ich konservativ.
conservatively [kən'sɜːvətɪvlɪ] *adv* konservativ; *estimate, invest* vorsichtig.
conservatoire [kən'sɜːvətwɑːʳ] *n* Konservatorium *nt*.
conservatory [kən'sɜːvətrɪ] *n* (**a**) (*Hort*) Wintergarten *m*. (**b**) (*esp US: Mus etc*) Konservatorium *nt*.
conserve [kən'sɜːv] *vt* erhalten, bewahren, konservieren; *building* erhalten; *one's strength* schonen; *strength, energy* (auf)sparen.
conserves [kən'sɜːvz] *npl* Eingemachte(s) *nt*.
consider [kən'sɪdəʳ] *vt* (**a**) (*reflect upon*) *plan, idea, offer* sich (*dat*) überlegen, nachdenken über (+*acc*); *possibilities* sich (*dat*) überlegen. I'll ~ **the matter** ich werde mir die Sache überlegen *or* durch den Kopf gehen lassen.
(**b**) (*have in mind*) in Erwägung ziehen. we're ~**ing a few changes** wir ziehen ein paar Änderungen in Erwägung; I'm ~**ing going abroad** ich spiele mit dem Gedanken, ins Ausland zu gehen, ich erwäge einen Auslandsaufenthalt (*geh*); he is **being** ~**ed for the job** er wird für die Stelle in Erwägung *or* Betracht gezogen.
(**c**) (*entertain*) in Betracht ziehen. he **refused even to** ~ **the possibility** er verwarf die Möglichkeit sofort, er weigerte sich, die Möglichkeit überhaupt in Betracht zu ziehen; I **won't even** ~ **the idea of** ... der Gedanke, zu ..., kommt für mich überhaupt nicht in Betracht; I **won't even** ~ **it!** ich denke nicht daran!; **would you** ~ **£500?** hielten Sie £ 500 für angemessen?; I'm **sure he would never** ~ **doing anything criminal** ich bin überzeugt, es käme ihm nie in den Sinn, etwas Kriminelles zu tun.
(**d**) (*think of*) denken an (+*acc*). ~ **George** denken Sie an George; ~ **my position** überlegen Sie sich meine Lage; ~ **this case, for example** nehmen Sie zum Beispiel diesen Fall; ~ **how he must have felt** überlegen Sie sich, wie ihm zumute gewesen sein muß; ~ **how much you owe him** denken Sie daran *or* bedenken Sie, wieviel Sie ihm schulden; **have you** ~**ed going by train?** haben Sie daran gedacht, mit dem Zug zu fahren?
(**e**) (*take into account*) denken an (+*acc*); *cost, difficulties, dangers also, facts* bedenken, berücksichtigen; *person, feelings also* Rücksicht nehmen auf (+*acc*). **when one** ~**s that** ... wenn man bedenkt, daß ...; **all things** ~**ed** alles in allem.
(**f**) (*regard as, deem*) betrachten als; *person* halten für. to ~ **sb to be** *or* **as** ... jdn als ... betrachten, jdn für ... halten; to ~ **oneself lucky/honoured** sich glücklich schätzen/geehrt fühlen; ~ **it (as) done!** schon so gut wie geschehen!; (**you can**) ~ **yourself sacked** betrachten Sie sich als entlassen; I ~ **it an honour** *or* **that it is an honour** ich betrachte es als besondere Ehre.
(**g**) (*look at*) (eingehend) betrachten.
considerable [kən'sɪdərəbl] *adj* beträchtlich, erheblich; *sum of money, achievement also* ansehnlich; *loss also, interest, income* groß; (*used admiringly*) *number, size, achievement, effort etc* beachtlich. to a ~ **extent** *or* **degree** weitgehend.
considerably [kən'sɪdərəblɪ] *adv* (*in comparisons*) *changed, older, better, grown* beträchtlich, um einiges; (*very*) *upset, impressed* höchst.
considerate [kən'sɪdərɪt] *adj* rücksichtsvoll (*to(wards)* gegenüber); (*kind*) aufmerksam.
considerately [kən'sɪdərɪtlɪ] *adv see adj.*
consideration [kənˌsɪdə'reɪʃən] *n* (**a**) *no pl* (*careful thought*) Überlegung *f*. I'll **give it my** ~ ich werde es mir überlegen; **please give my suggestion your careful** ~ würden Sie meinem Vorschlag bitte Ihre Aufmerksamkeit schenken? (*form*), würden Sie sich meinen Vorschlag bitte überlegen?
(**b**) *no pl* (*regard, account*) to **take sth into** ~ etw bedenken, etw berücksichtigen; *factors also* etw in Erwägung ziehen; **taking everything into** ~ alles in allem; to **leave sth out of** ~ etw außer acht lassen; **your request/the matter is under** ~ Ihr Gesuch/die Sache wird zur Zeit geprüft (*form*), wir gehen der Sache zur Zeit nach; **in** ~ **of** (*in view also*) mit Rücksicht auf (+*acc*), in Anbetracht (+*gen*); (*in return for*) als Dank für.
(**c**) *no pl* (*thoughtfulness*) Rücksicht *f* (*for* auf +*acc*). to **show sb** ~, to **show** *or* **have** ~ **for sb's feelings** Rücksicht auf jdn *or* jds Gefühle nehmen; **his lack of** ~ (**for others**) seine Rücksichtslosigkeit (anderen gegenüber).
(**d**) (*sth taken into account*) Erwägung *f*, Gesichtspunkt, Faktor *m*. **on no** ~ auf keinen Fall; **money is no** ~/**a minor** ~/**his first** ~ Geld spielt keine Rolle/eine unbedeutendere Rolle/bei ihm die größte Rolle; **it's a** ~ das wäre zu überlegen.
(**e**) (*reward, payment*) Entgelt *nt*, Gegenleistung *f*, kleine Anerkennung (*hum*). **for a** ~ gegen Entgelt, für eine Gegenleistung *or* kleine Anerkennung (*hum*).
considered [kən'sɪdɪd] *adj* *opinion* ernsthaft.
considering [kən'sɪdərɪŋ] 1 *prep* für (+*acc*), wenn man ... (*acc*) bedenkt.
2 *conj* wenn man bedenkt. ~ (**that**) **he's been ill** ... wenn man bedenkt, daß er krank war ..., dafür, daß er krank war ...

---

3 *adv* eigentlich. it's **not too bad** ~ es ist eigentlich gar nicht so schlecht; **yes it is,** ~ ach ja, eigentlich schon.
consign [kən'saɪn] *vt* (**a**) (*Comm*) (*send*) versenden, verschicken; (*address*) adressieren (*to* an +*acc*). the **goods are** ~**ed to** ... die Waren sind für ... bestimmt.
(**b**) (*commit*) übergeben (*to dat*); (*entrust also*) anvertrauen. it **was** ~**ed to the rubbish heap** es landete auf dem Abfallhaufen; to ~ **a child to sb's care** ein Kind in jds Obhut (*acc*) geben.
consignee [ˌkɒnsaɪ'niː] *n* Empfänger *m*.
consigner [kən'saɪnəʳ] *n see* consignor.
consignment [kən'saɪnmənt] *n* (*Comm*) (**a**) (*of goods*) Versendung, Verschickung *f*. **goods for** ~ **abroad** ins Ausland gehende Ware; **on** ~ in Kommission; (*overseas*) in Konsignation; ~ **note** Frachtbrief *m*. (**b**) (*goods*) Sendung *f*; (*bigger*) Ladung *f*.
consignor [kən'saɪnəʳ] *n* (*Comm*) Versender *m*.
consist [kən'sɪst] *vi* (**a**) (*be composed*) to ~ **of** bestehen aus. (**b**) (*have as its essence*) to ~ **in sth in etw** (*dat*) bestehen; his **happiness** ~**s in helping others** sein Glück besteht darin, anderen zu helfen.
consistency [kən'sɪstənsɪ] *n* (**a**) *no pl see adj* (*a*) Konsequenz *f*; Übereinstimmung, Vereinbarkeit *f*; Logik, Folgerichtigkeit *f*; Stetigkeit *f*. **his statements lack** ~ seine Aussagen widersprechen sich *or* sind nicht miteinander vereinbar.
(**b**) *no pl see adj* (*b*) Beständigkeit *f*; Stetigkeit *f*; Einheitlichkeit *f*.
(**c**) (*of substance*) Konsistenz *f*; (*of liquids also*) Dicke *f*; (*of glue, dough, rubber etc also*) Festigkeit(sgrad *m*) *f*. **beat it to a thick** ~/**to the** ~ **of cream** zu einer festen Masse/sahnig schlagen; **the steak had the** ~ **of leather** das Steak war zäh wie Leder.
consistent [kən'sɪstənt] *adj* (**a**) konsequent; *statements* übereinstimmend, miteinander vereinbar; (*logical*) *argument* logisch, folgerichtig; (*constant*) *failure* ständig, stetig.
(**b**) (*uniform*) *quality* beständig; *performance, results* gleichbleibend, stetig; *method, style* einheitlich.
(**c**) (*in agreement*) to **be** ~ **with sth** einer Sache (*dat*) entsprechen; **what you're saying now is not** ~ **with what you said before** was Sie jetzt sagen, widerspricht dem *or* läßt sich mit dem nicht vereinbaren, was Sie davor gesagt haben.
consistently [kən'sɪstəntlɪ] *adv* (**a**) *argue* konsequent; (*constantly*) *fail* ständig. (**b**) (*uniformly*) einheitlich, durchweg. (**c**) (*in agreement*) entsprechend (*with dat*).
consolation [ˌkɒnsə'leɪʃən] *n* Trost *m no pl*; (*act*) Tröstung *f*. it **is some** ~ **to know that** ... es ist tröstlich *or* ein Trost zu wissen, daß ...; **that's a big** ~! (*iro*) das ist ein schwacher Trost!; **old age has its** ~**s** das Alter hat auch seine guten Seiten; **a few words of** ~ ein paar tröstende Worte; ~ **prize** Trostpreis *m*.
consolatory [kən'sɒlətərɪ] *adj* tröstlich, tröstend.
console[1] [kən'səʊl] *vt* trösten. to ~ **sb for sth** jdn über etw (*acc*) hinwegtrösten.
console[2] ['kɒnsəʊl] *n* (**a**) (*control panel*) (Kontroll)pult *nt*; (*of organ*) Spieltisch *m*. (**b**) (*cabinet*) Schrank *m*, Truhe *f*. **our TV is a** ~ (**model**) wir haben eine Fernsehtruhe. (**c**) (*ornamental bracket*) Konsole *f*. ~ **table** Konsoltischchen *nt*.
consolidate [kən'sɒlɪdeɪt] *vt* (**a**) (*confirm*) festigen. (**b**) (*combine*) zusammenlegen, vereinigen; *companies* zusammenschließen; *funds, debts* konsolidieren. C~**d Fund** (*Brit*) konsolidierter Staatsfond, unablösbare Anleihe.
consolidation [kənˌsɒlɪ'deɪʃən] *n see vt* (**a**) Festigung *f*. (**b**) Zusammenlegung, Vereinigung *f*; Zusammenschluß *m*; Konsolidierung *f*.
consoling [kən'səʊlɪŋ] *adj* tröstlich, tröstend.
consols ['kɒnsɒlz] *npl* (*Brit Fin*) Konsols, konsolidierte Staatsanleihen *pl*.
consommé [kɒn'sɒmeɪ] *n* Kraftbrühe, Konsommee (*old*) *f*.
consonance ['kɒnsənəns] *n* (*Mus*) Konsonanz *f*; (*Poet*) Konsonantengleichklang *m*; (*fig*) (*of agreement, ideas*) Einklang *m*, Harmonie *f*; (*consistency*) Übereinstimmung *f*.
consonant ['kɒnsənənt] 1 *n* (*Phon*) Konsonant, Mitlaut *m*. ~ **shift** Lautverschiebung *f*. 2 *adj* (*Mus*) konsonant (*with* zu). to **be** ~ **with sth** (*fig*) mit etw in Einklang zu bringen sein.
consonantal [ˌkɒnsə'næntl] *adj* konsonantisch.
consort ['kɒnsɔːt] 1 *n* (*form: spouse*) Gemahl(in *f*) *m* (*form*), Gatte *m* (*form*), Gattin *f* (*form*). 2 [kən'sɔːt] *vi* (*form*) (**a**) verkehren (*with* mit). (**b**) (*be consistent*) passen (*with* zu), sich vereinbaren lassen (*with* mit).
consortium [kən'sɔːtɪəm] *n* Konsortium *nt*.
conspicuous [kən'spɪkjʊəs] *adj* *person, clothes, behaviour* auffällig, auffallend; (*easily visible*) *road signs* deutlich sichtbar, auffällig; (*obvious*) *lack of sympathy etc* deutlich, offensichtlich, auffallend; (*outstanding*) *bravery* bemerkenswert, hervorragend. to **be/make oneself** ~ auffallen; **why don't you put it in a more** ~ **position?** warum stellen Sie es nicht irgendwohin, wo es eher auffällt?; to **be/not to be** ~ **for sth** sich/sich nicht gerade durch etw auszeichnen; he **was** ~ **by his absence** er glänzte durch Abwesenheit; he **showed a** ~ **lack of tact** er fiel durch sein mangelndes Taktgefühl (unangenehm) auf; ~ **consumption** Prestigekäufe *pl*.
conspicuously [kən'spɪkjʊəslɪ] *adv see adj* auffällig, auffallend; *deutlich sichtbar, auffällig; deutlich, offensichtlich, auffallend; bemerkenswert. he's **not** ~ **intelligent** (*iro*) er fällt nicht gerade durch Intelligenz auf.
conspicuousness [kən'spɪkjʊəsnɪs] *n see adj* Auffälligkeit *f*; deutliche Sichtbarkeit, Auffälligkeit *f*; Deutlichkeit *f*.
conspiracy [kən'spɪrəsɪ] *n* Verschwörung *f*, Komplott *nt*, Konspiration *f* (*form*); (*Jur*) (strafbare) Verabredung. ~ **to defraud/murder** Verabredung zum Betrug/Mordkomplott; a ~ **of silence** ein verabredetes Schweigen; he **thinks they're all in** a ~ **against him** er meint, alle hätten sich gegen ihn verschworen.

conspirator [kən'spɪrətə'] n Verschwörer m.

conspiratorial [kən,spɪrə'tɔːrɪəl] adj verschwörerisch.

conspire [kən'spaɪə'] vi (a) (people) sich verschwören, sich zusammentun, konspirieren (form) (against gegen). to ~ (together) to do sth sich verabreden or heimlich planen, etw zu tun. (b) (events) zusammenkommen, sich verschwören (geh); (fate etc) sich verschwören (against gegen).

constable ['kʌnstəbl] n (Brit: police ~) Polizist, Gendarm (dial) m; (in address) Herr Wachtmeister.

constabulary [kən'stæbjʊlərɪ] n (Brit) Polizei f no pl.

constancy ['kɒnstənsɪ] n (a) (of support, supporter) Beständigkeit, Konstanz (liter) f; (of feelings) Unveränderlichkeit, Unwandelbarkeit f; (of friend, lover) Treue f; (also ~ of purpose) Ausdauer f. (b) (of temperature etc) Beständigkeit f.

constant ['kɒnstənt] 1 adj (a) (continuous) quarrels, interruptions, noise dauernd, ständig, konstant (geh). we have ~ hot water wir haben ständig heißes Wasser.
(b) (unchanging) temperature gleichmäßig, gleichbleibend, konstant. x remains ~ while y ... x bleibt konstant, während y ...; the price is not ~ der Preis bleibt nicht gleich or konstant.
(c) (steadfast) affection, devotion unwandelbar, beständig; friend, supporter, lover treu.
2 n (Math, Phys, fig) Konstante f, konstante Größe.

constantly ['kɒnstəntlɪ] adv (an)dauernd, ständig.

constellation [,kɒnstə'leɪʃən] n Sternbild nt, Konstellation f (also fig).

consternation [,kɒnstə'neɪʃən] n (dismay) Bestürzung f; (concern, worry) Sorge f; (fear and confusion) Aufruhr m. to my great ~ zu meiner großen Bestürzung; to cause ~ (state of £, sb's behaviour) Grund zur Sorge geben; (news) Bestürzung auslösen; the mouse caused ~ among the ladies die Maus versetzte die Damen in Aufruhr; with a look of ~ on his face mit bestürzter Miene; our ~ about what might happen unsere Sorge darüber, was geschehen könnte; the news filled me with ~ ich war bestürzt, als ich das hörte.

constipate ['kɒnstɪpeɪt] vt Verstopfung hervorrufen bei, verstopfen.

constipated ['kɒnstɪpeɪtɪd] adj bowels verstopft. he is ~ er hat Verstopfung, er ist verstopft (inf); it'll make you ~ davon bekommst du Verstopfung, das stopft.

constipation [,kɒnstɪ'peɪʃən] n, no pl Verstopfung f.

constituency [kən'stɪtjʊənsɪ] n (Pol) Wahlkreis m.

constituent [kən'stɪtjʊənt] 1 adj (a) (Pol) assembly konstituierend. (b) attr part, element einzeln. ~ part or element (of machine, matter) Bestandteil m. 2 n (a) (Pol) Wähler(in f) m. (b) (part, element) Bestandteil m. (c) (Ling) Satzteil m.

constitute ['kɒnstɪtjuːt] vt (a) (make up) bilden, ausmachen. society is so ~d that ... die Gesellschaft ist so aufgebaut, daß ...
(b) (amount to) darstellen. that ~s a lie das ist eine glatte Lüge.
(c) (set up, give legal authority to) committee, court einrichten, konstituieren (form).
(d) (form: appoint) ernennen or bestimmen zu. he ~d himself our judge er warf sich zu unserem Richter auf.

constitution [,kɒnstɪ'tjuːʃən] n (a) (Pol) Verfassung f; (of club etc) Satzung f.
(b) (of person) Konstitution, Gesundheit f. to have a strong/weak ~ eine starke/schwache Konstitution haben.
(c) (way sth is made) Aufbau m; (what sth is made of) Zusammensetzung f.
(d) (setting up: of committee etc) Einrichtung f.

constitutional [,kɒnstɪ'tjuːʃənl] 1 adj (a) (Pol) reform, crisis, theory Verfassungs-; monarchy konstitutionell; government, action verfassungsmäßig. ~ law Verfassungsrecht nt; it's not ~ das ist verfassungswidrig.
(b) (Med) konstitutionell (spec), körperlich bedingt; (fig) dislike etc naturgegeben or -bedingt.
2 n (hum inf) Spaziergang m.

constitutionally [,kɒnstɪ'tjuːʃənəlɪ] adv (Pol) verfassungsmäßig; (as the constitution says also) nach der Verfassung; (in accordance with the constitution) verfassungsgemäß; (Med) körperlich; (fig) von Natur aus.

constrain [kən'streɪn] vt zwingen; one's temper zügeln. to find oneself/feel ~ed to ... sich gezwungen sehen/fühlen, zu ...

constrained [kən'streɪnd] adj (forced) gezwungen.

constraint [kən'streɪnt] n (a) (compulsion) Zwang m. to act under ~ unter Zwang handeln.
(b) (restriction) Beschränkung, Einschränkung f. to place ~s on sth einer Sache (dat) Zwänge auferlegen.
(c) (in manner etc) Gezwungenheit f; (embarrassment) Befangenheit f. it wouldn't hurt you to show a little ~ es würde nicht schaden, wenn Sie etwas Zurückhaltung üben würden.

constrict [kən'strɪkt] vt (a) (compress) einzwängen, einengen; muscle zusammenziehen; vein verengen. (b) (hamper, limit) movements behindern, beschränken, einschränken (also fig); (rules, traditions etc) einengen, beengen; outlook, view etc beschränken, begrenzen.

constriction [kən'strɪkʃən] n (a) (of muscles) Zusammenziehen nt. he felt a ~ in his chest er hatte ein Gefühl der Enge in der Brust. (b) see vt (b) Behinderung f; (limiting) Einengung, Beengung f; Beschränkung f.

constrictor [kən'strɪktə'] n (a) (muscle) Schließmuskel, Konstriktor (spec) m. (b) (snake) Boa (constrictor) f.

construct [kən'strʌkt] vt (a) bauen; bridge, machine also, geometrical figure konstruieren; sentence bilden, konstruieren; novel, play etc aufbauen; theory entwickeln, konstruieren. 2 n Gedankengebäude nt.

construction [kən'strʌkʃən] n (a) (of building, road) Bau m; (of bridge, machine also, of geometrical figures) Konstruktion f; (of novel, play etc) Aufbau m; (of theory) Entwicklung, Konstruktion f. in course of or under ~ in or im Bau.

(b) (way sth is constructed) Struktur f; (of building) Bauweise f; (of machine, bridge) Konstruktion f; (of novel, play etc) Aufbau m.
(c) (sth constructed) Bau m, Bauwerk nt; (bridge, machine) Konstruktion f. primitive ~s primitive Bauten.
(d) (interpretation) Deutung f. to put a wrong/bad ~ on sth etw falsch auffassen or auslegen/etw schlecht aufnehmen; I don't know what ~ to put on it ich weiß nicht, wie ich das auffassen soll.
(e) (Gram) Konstruktion f. sentence ~ Satzbau m.

construction in cpds Bau-.

constructional [kən'strʌkʃənl] adj baulich; technique, tool Bau-; fault, toy Konstruktions-.

construction industry n Bauindustrie f.

constructive [kən'strʌktɪv] adj konstruktiv.

constructively [kən'strʌktɪvlɪ] adv konstruktiv; critical auf konstruktive Art. he suggested, not very ~, that ... er machte den nicht gerade konstruktiven Vorschlag, zu ...

construe [kən'struː] 1 vt (a) (Gram) words analysieren; sentence also zerlegen. in English it is ~d as an adjective im Englischen wird das als Adjektiv betrachtet. (b) (interpret) auslegen, auffassen. 2 vi (Gram: sentence) sich zerlegen or aufgliedern or analysieren lassen.

consubstantiation [,kɒnsəb,stænʃɪ'eɪʃən] n (Eccl) Konsubstantiation f.

consuetude [,kɒnswɪ'tjuːd] n (form) normative Kraft des Faktischen (form).

consul ['kɒnsəl] n Konsul m.

consular ['kɒnsjʊlə'] adj konsularisch.

consulate ['kɒnsjʊlɪt] n Konsulat nt.

consul general n, pl -s - Generalkonsul m.

consulship ['kɒnsəlʃɪp] n Konsulat nt.

consult [kən'sʌlt] 1 vt (a) sich besprechen mit, konsultieren; lawyer, doctor etc konsultieren, zu Rate ziehen; dictionary nachschlagen in (+dat), konsultieren (geh); map nachsehen auf (+dat); oracle befragen; horoscope nachlesen; clock sehen auf (+acc). he might have ~ed me das hätte er auch mit mir besprechen können, er hätte mich auch konsultieren können; you don't have to ~ me about every little detail Sie brauchen mich nicht wegen jeder Kleinigkeit zu fragen; he did it without ~ing anyone er hat das getan, ohne jemanden zu fragen.
(b) (form: consider) bedenken.
2 vi (confer) sich beraten, beratschlagen. to ~ together (over sth) (etw) gemeinsam beraten; to ~ with sb sich mit jdm beraten.

consultancy [kən'sʌltənsɪ] n (act) Beratung f; (business) Beratungsbüro nt.

consultant [kən'sʌltənt] 1 n (Brit Med) Facharzt m am Krankenhaus; (other professions) Berater m. 2 adj attr beratend.

consultation [,kɒnsəl'teɪʃən] n Beratung, Besprechung, Konsultation (form) f; (of doctor, lawyer) Konsultation f (of gen), Beratung f (of mit). in ~ with in gemeinsamer Beratung mit; to have a ~ with one's doctor/lawyer seinen Arzt/Rechtsanwalt konsultieren; to hold a ~ (with sb) sich (mit jdm) beraten, eine Besprechung (mit jdm) abhalten.

consultative [kən'sʌltətɪv] adj document beratend, konsultativ (form). in a ~ capacity in beratender Funktion.

consulting [kən'sʌltɪŋ] adj engineer, architect, psychiatrist beratend. ~ hours/room (Brit) Sprechstunde f/-zimmer nt.

consume [kən'sjuːm] vt (a) food, drink zu sich nehmen, konsumieren (form); food also verzehren (geh), auffessen, vertilgen (hum inf); (Econ) konsumieren.
(b) (destroy) (fire) vernichten; (use up) fuel, money verbrauchen; money, energy aufbrauchen, verzehren (geh); time in Anspruch nehmen. he was ~d with desire/jealousy/rage etc wurde von Begierde/Eifersucht verzehrt (geh)/die Wut fraß ihn nahezu auf.

consumer [kən'sjuːmə'] n Verbraucher, Konsument (form) m.

consumer in cpds Verbraucher-; ~ durables npl Gebrauchsgüter, langlebige Konsumgüter pl; ~ goods npl Verbrauchsgüter, Konsumgüter pl; ~ protection n Verbraucherschutz m; ~ research n Verbraucherbefragung f; ~ resistance n Kaufunlust f; ~s' advice centre n Verbraucherzentrale f; ~ society n Konsumgesellschaft f.

consuming [kən'sjuːmɪŋ] adj ambition, interest glühend, brennend; desire, passion also verzehrend (geh).

consummate [kən'sʌmɪt] 1 adj artistry, skill, folly vollendet, vollkommen; rogue ausgemacht; politician unübertrefflich. with ~ ease mit spielender Leichtigkeit. 2 ['kɒnsəmeɪt] vt marriage vollziehen.

consummation [,kɒnsə'meɪʃən] n (a) (of marriage) Vollzug m. (b) (fig) (peak) Höhepunkt m; (fulfilment) Erfüllung f.

consumption [kən'sʌmpʃən] n (a) (of food, fuel etc) Konsum m; (of non-edible products) Verbrauch m; (of food also) Verzehr m (geh). this letter is for private ~ only (inf) der Brief ist nur für den privaten Gebrauch; not fit for human ~ zum Verzehr ungeeignet; world ~ of oil Weltölverbrauch m; his daily ~ of three litres of beer sein täglicher Konsum von drei Liter Bier.
(b) (Med old) Auszehrung (old), Schwindsucht f.

consumptive [kən'sʌmptɪv] (old) 1 n Schwindsüchtige(r) mf. 2 adj schwindsüchtig.

contact ['kɒntækt] 1 n (a) Kontakt m; (touching also) Berührung f; (communication also) Verbindung f. to be in ~ with sb/sth (be touching) jdn/etw berühren; (in communication) mit jdm/etw in Verbindung or Kontakt stehen; to come into ~ with sb/sth (lit, fig) mit jdm/etw in Berührung kommen; with disease carrier also mit jdm in Kontakt kommen; he has no ~ with his family or hat keinen Kontakt zu seiner Familie; his first ~ with death seine erste Berührung mit dem Tod; on ~ with air/water wenn es mit Luft/Wasser in Berührung kommt;

I'll get in ~ ich werde mich melden (inf), ich werde von mir hören lassen; **I'll get in(to)** ~ **with** you ich werde mit Ihnen in Verbindung setzen; **how can we get in(to)** ~ **with him?** wie können wir ihn erreichen?; **to make** ~ (two things) sich berühren; (wires, wheels etc) in Berührung or Kontakt (miteinander) kommen; (two people) (get in touch) sich miteinander in Verbindung setzen; (by radio etc) eine Verbindung herstellen; (psychologically) Kontakt bekommen; **he could make** ~ **by radio** er konnte sich durch Funk in Verbindung setzen; **as soon as the glue makes** ~ **(with the surface)** sobald der Klebstoff mit der Fläche in Berührung or Kontakt kommt; **to make** ~ **with sb/sth** (touch) jdn/etw berühren, mit jdm/etw in Berührung kommen; (wire, wheels etc also) mit jdm/etw in Kontakt kommen; (get in touch with) sich mit jdm/etw in Verbindung setzen; (psychologically) Kontakt zu jdm/etw bekommen; **I finally made** ~ **with him** at his office ich habe ihn schließlich in seinem Büro erreicht; **to lose** ~ **(with sb/sth)** den Kontakt or die Verbindung (zu jdm/etw) verlieren; **point of** ~ (Math, fig) Berührungspunkt m.

(b) (Elec) (act) Kontakt m; (equipment) Kontakt- or Schaltstück nt. **to make/break** ~ den Kontakt herstellen/unterbrechen.

(c) (person) Kontaktperson f (also Med), Verbindungsmann m; (in espionage) Verbindungsmann, V-Mann m. ~**s** pl Kontakte, Verbindungen pl; **to make** ~**s** Kontakte herstellen; **he's made a useful** ~ er hat einen nützlichen Kontakt hergestellt, er hat eine nützliche Verbindung aufgetan.

2 vt person, agent, lawyer sich in Verbindung setzen mit; (for help) police sich wenden an (+acc). **I've been trying to** ~ **you for hours** ich versuche schon seit Stunden, Sie zu erreichen; **he doesn't want to be** ~**ed unless it's urgent** er möchte, daß man sich nur in dringenden Fällen mit ihm in Verbindung setzt.

contact: ~-**breaker** n Unterbrecher m; ~ **flight** n Sichtflug m; ~ **lens** n Kontaktlinse f; ~ **man** n Kontakt- or Mittelsmann m; ~ **print** n (Phot) Kontaktabzug m.

contagion [kən'teɪdʒən] n (contact) Ansteckung f; (disease) Ansteckungskrankheit f; (epidemic) Seuche f (also fig); (fig: spreading influence) schädlicher Einfluß. **some of the spectators got excited, the** ~ **spread, and** ... einige der Zuschauer ereiferten sich, das griff um sich, und ...

contagious [kən'teɪdʒəs] adj (Med, fig) ansteckend; disease also direkt übertragbar. **he's not** ~ (Med) seine Krankheit ist nicht ansteckend; (hum) er ist nicht giftig (inf).

contain [kən'teɪn] vt **(a)** (hold within itself) enthalten. **the envelope** ~**ed money** im Umschlag befand sich Geld, der Umschlag enthielt Geld.

(b) (have capacity for: box, bottle, room) fassen.

(c) (control) emotions, oneself beherrschen; tears zurückhalten; laughter unterdrücken; disease, inflation, sb's power in Grenzen halten; epidemic, flood aufhalten, unter Kontrolle bringen; enemy, (Sport) in Schach halten; attack abwehren. **he could hardly** ~ **himself** er konnte kaum an sich (acc) halten.

(d) (Math) angle einschließen.

container [kən'teɪnər] **1** n **(a)** Behälter m; (bottle, jar etc also) Gefäß nt. **(b)** (Comm: for transport) Container m. **2** adj attr Container-.

containerization [kən,teɪnəraɪ'zeɪʃən] n (of goods) Verpackung f in Container; (of ports) Umstellung f auf Container.

containerize [kən'teɪnəraɪz] vt freight in Container verpacken; port auf Container umstellen.

containment [kən'teɪnmənt] n (Mil) In-Schach-Halten nt; (of attack) Abwehr f. **their efforts at** ~ (of the rebels) ihre Bemühungen, die Rebellen in Schach zu halten.

contaminate [kən'tæmɪneɪt] vt verunreinigen, verschmutzen; (poison) vergiften; (radioactivity) verseuchen, kontaminieren (spec); (fig) mind verderben. **the oranges were** ~**d by poison** in den Orangen befanden sich Giftstoffe.

contamination [kən,tæmɪ'neɪʃən] n, no pl see vt Verunreinigung, Verschmutzung f; Vergiftung f; Verseuchung, Kontaminierung (spec) f; (substance) Giftstoffe pl; (fig) schädlicher Einfluß (of auf +acc); (fig: contaminated state) Verdorbenheit f.

contd abbr of **continued** Forts, Fortsetzung f.

contemplate ['kɒntempleɪt] vt **(a)** (look at) betrachten. **(b)** (think about, reflect upon) nachdenken über (+acc); (consider) changes, a purchase, action, accepting an offer in Erwägung ziehen, erwägen (geh); a holiday denken an (+acc). **he** ~**d the future with some misgivings** er sah der Zukunft mit einem unguten Gefühl entgegen; **he would never** ~ **violence** der Gedanke an Gewalttätigkeit würde ihm nie kommen; **it's too awful to** ~ schon der Gedanke (daran) ist zu entsetzlich. **(c)** (expect) voraussehen. **(d)** (intend) ~ **doing sth** daran denken, etw zu tun.

contemplation [,kɒntem'pleɪʃən] n, no pl **(a)** (act of looking) Betrachtung f. **(b)** (act of thinking) Nachdenken nt (of über +acc); (deep thought) Besinnung, Betrachtung, Kontemplation (esp Rel) f. **a life of** ~ ein beschauliches or kontemplatives (esp Rel) Leben; **a life of inner** ~ ein Leben der inneren Einkehr; **deep in** ~ in Gedanken versunken. **(c)** (expectation) Erwartung f. **in** ~ **of their visit** in Erwartung ihres Besuches.

contemplative [kən'templətɪv] adj look nachdenklich; mood also besinnlich; life, religious order beschaulich, kontemplativ.

contemplatively [kən'templətɪvlɪ] adv nachdenklich; sit also in Gedanken.

contemporaneous [kən,tempə'reɪnɪəs] adj gleichzeitig stattfindend attr. **an author's/a manuscript** ~ **with** ... ein Autor/Manuskript aus derselben Zeit or Epoche wie ...; **events** ~ **with the rebellion** Ereignisse zur Zeit des Aufstandes.

contemporary [kən'tempərərɪ] **1** adj **(a)** (of the same time)

events gleichzeitig; records, literature, writer zeitgenössisch, kontemporär (form), aus der(selben) Zeit or Epoche; (of the same age) manuscript gleich alt. **records** ~ **with the invasion** Aufzeichnungen aus der Zeit der Invasion.

(b) (of the present time) life heutig; art, design zeitgenössisch, modern.

2 n Altersgenosse m/-genossin f; (in history) Zeitgenosse m/-genossin f; (at university) Kommilitone m, Kommilitonin f.

contempt [kən'tempt] n **(a)** Verachtung f; (disregard also) Geringachtung, Geringschätzung f (for von). **to have** or **hold in/bring into** ~ verachten/in Verruf bringen; **to fall into** ~ (an) Ansehen einbüßen or verlieren; (lose popularity) (an) Popularität einbüßen; **in** ~ **of danger/public opinion** die Gefahr/öffentliche Meinung außer acht lassend, ohne Ansehen der Gefahr/öffentlichen Meinung; **beneath** ~ unter aller Kritik.

(b) (Jur: also ~ **of court**) Mißachtung f (der Würde) des Gerichts, Ungebühr f vor Gericht; (through non-appearance) Ungebühr f durch vorsätzliches Ausbleiben; (by press) Beeinflussung f der Rechtspflege. **to be in** ~ (of court) das Gericht or die Würde des Gerichts mißachten.

contemptible [kən'temptəbl] adj verachtenswert, verächtlich.

contemptuous [kən'temptjʊəs] adj manner, gesture, look geringschätzig, verächtlich. **to be** ~ **of sb/sth** jdn/etw verachten; **she was quite** ~ **of my offer** sie reagierte ziemlich verächtlich auf mein Angebot.

contemptuously [kən'temptjʊəslɪ] adv see adj.

contend [kən'tend] **1** vi kämpfen. **to** ~ **(with sb) for sth** (mit jdm) um etw kämpfen; (in business) (mit jdm) um etw konkurrieren; **then you'll have me to** ~ **with** dann bekommst du es mit mir zu tun; **but I've got two directors to** ~ **with** aber ich habe es mit zwei Direktoren zu tun. **(b)** (cope) **to** ~ **with sb/sth** mit jdm/etw fertigwerden. **2** vt behaupten.

contender [kən'tendər] n Kandidat(in f), Anwärter(in f) m (for auf +acc); (for job also) Bewerber(in f) m (for um); (Sport) Wettkämpfer(in f) m (for um).

contending [kən'tendɪŋ] adj emotions widerstreitend. **the** ~ **parties** (Sport) die Wettstreiter pl, die Wettkampfteilnehmer pl; (in lawsuit) die streitenden Parteien pl.

content¹ [kən'tent] **1** adj pred zufrieden (with mit). **to be/feel** ~ zufrieden sein; **she's quite** ~ **to stay at home** sie bleibt ganz gern zu Hause.

2 n Zufriedenheit f. **a grunt of** ~ ein zufriedenes Grunzen; see **heart (b)**.

3 vt person zufriedenstellen. **there's no** ~**ing him** er ist mit nichts zufrieden; **to** ~ **oneself with** sich zufriedengeben or begnügen or abfinden mit; **to** ~ **oneself with doing sth** sich damit zufriedengeben or begnügen or abfinden, etw zu tun.

content² ['kɒntent] n **(a)** ~**s** pl (of room, one's pocket, book etc) Inhalt m; (table of) ~**s** Inhaltsverzeichnis nt. **(b)** no pl (substance, component) Gehalt m; (of speech, book etc also) Inhalt m. **gold/vitamin** ~ Gold-/Vitamingehalt m.

contented adj, ~**ly** adv [kən'tentɪd, -lɪ] zufrieden.

contentedness [kən'tentɪdnɪs] n see **contentment**.

contention [kən'tenʃən] n **(a)** (dispute) Streit m. ~**s** Streitigkeiten pl; **the matter in** ~ die strittige Angelegenheit; **that is no longer in** ~ das steht nicht mehr zur Debatte; **to lead to** ~ between ... zu Streitigkeiten zwischen ... führen; see **bone**. **(b)** (argument) Behauptung f. **it is my** ~ **that** ... ich behaupte, daß ...

contentious [kən'tenʃəs] adj subject, issue strittig, umstritten; person streitlustig, streitsüchtig.

contentment [kən'tentmənt] n Zufriedenheit f.

contest ['kɒntest] **1** n (for um) Kampf m; (competition also) Wettkampf, Wettstreit (geh) m; (beauty ~ etc) Wettbewerb m. **boxing** ~ Boxkampf m; **election** ~ Wahlkampf m; **it's no** ~ das ist ein ungleicher Kampf; **it was a real** ~ **of skill** es kam dabei wirklich aufs Können an.

2 [kən'test] vt **(a)** (fight over) kämpfen um; (fight against, oppose) kämpfen gegen; (Parl) election teilnehmen an (+dat). **to** ~ **a seat** (Parl) um einen Wahlkreis kämpfen; **the seat was not** ~**ed** es gab keinen Kampf um den Wahlkreis. **(b)** (dispute) statement bestreiten, angreifen; measure angreifen; (Jur) will, right, legal action anfechten. **a** ~**ed measure** eine umstrittene Maßnahme; **to** ~ **sb's right to do sth** jdm das Recht streitig machen or jds Recht anfechten, etw zu tun.

3 [kən'test] vi kämpfen (for um).

contestant [kən'testənt] n (Wettbewerbs)teilnehmer(in f) m; (Parl, in quiz) Kandidat(in f) m; (Sport) Wettkampf)teilnehmer(in f) m; (Mil) Kämpfende(r) m. **the** ~**s in the election** die Wahlkandidaten.

context ['kɒntekst] n Zusammenhang, Kontext (geh) m. **(taken) out of** ~ aus dem Zusammenhang or Kontext (geh) gerissen; **in the wider European** ~ im weiteren europäischen Zusammenhang or Kontext (geh) or Rahmen; **in this** ~ in diesem Zusammenhang; **in an office** ~ im Rahmen eines Büros.

contextual [kən'tekstjʊəl] adj kontextuell (form); meaning aus dem Zusammenhang or Kontext (geh) ersichtlich.

contextualize [kən'tekstjʊəlaɪz] vt in einen Zusammenhang or Kontext (geh) setzen.

contiguity [,kɒntɪ'gjuːɪtɪ] n (unmittelbare) Nachbarschaft.

contiguous [kən'tɪgjʊəs] adj (form) aneinandergrenzend, sich berührend; (in time) (unmittelbar) aufeinanderfolgend. **the estates are** ~ die Grundstücke grenzen aneinander.

continence ['kɒntɪnəns] n **(a)** (Med) Kontinenz f (spec), Fähigkeit f, Stuhl und/oder Urin zurückzuhalten. **(b)** (abstinence) Enthaltsamkeit f.

continent¹ ['kɒntɪnənt] adj (self-controlled) mäßig, beherrscht, maßvoll; (sexually) (sexuell) enthaltsam. **the old lady was not** ~ (Med) die alte Dame konnte ihre Darmtätigkeit/Blasentätigkeit nicht mehr kontrollieren.

continent² n (Geog) Kontinent, Erdteil m; (mainland) Festland nt. the C~ in (Brit) Kontinentaleuropa nt; on the C~ in Europa, auf dem Kontinent.

continental [ˌkɒntɪˈnentl] 1 adj (a) (Geog) kontinental. (b) (Brit: European) europäisch; holidays in Europa. 2 n (Festlands)europäer(in f) m.

continental: ~ breakfast n kleines Frühstück; ~ drift n (Geog) Kontinentaldrift f; ~ quilt n Steppdecke f; ~ shelf n (Geog) Kontinentalschelf, Kontinentalsockel m.

contingency [kənˈtɪndʒənsɪ] n (a) möglicher Fall, Eventualität f. in this ~, should this ~ arise in diesem Fall, für diesen Fall, sollte dieser Fall eintreten; ~ fund Eventualfonds m; to provide for all contingencies alle Möglichkeiten einplanen, alle Eventualitäten berücksichtigen; a ~ plan ein Ausweichplan m.
(b) (Philos) Kontingenz f.

contingent [kənˈtɪndʒənt] 1 adj (a) ~ upon (form) abhängig von; to be ~ upon abhängen von. (b) (Philos) kontingent. 2 n Kontingent nt; (section) Gruppe f; (Mil) Trupp m.

continual [kənˈtɪnjʊəl] adj (frequent) dauernd, ständig; (unceasing) ununterbrochen, pausenlos.

continually [kənˈtɪnjʊəlɪ] adv see adj (an)dauernd, ständig; ununterbrochen, pausenlos.

continuance [kənˈtɪnjʊəns] n (a) (duration) Dauer f. (b) see continuation (a).

continuation [kənˌtɪnjʊˈeɪʃən] n (a) Fortsetzung, Fortführung f. the ~ of the human race der Weiterbestand or Fortbestand der menschlichen Rasse; the Government's ~ in office das Verbleiben der Regierung im Amt.
(b) (retention: of arrangement etc) Beibehaltung f.
(c) (resumption) Fortsetzung, Wiederaufnahme f.
(d) (sth continued) Fortsetzung, Weiterführung f.

continue [kənˈtɪnjuː] 1 vt (a) (carry on) fortfahren mit; policy, tradition, struggle fortsetzen, fortführen, weiterführen; activity, piece of work, meal fortsetzen, weitermachen mit. to ~ doing or to do sth etw weiter tun, fortfahren, etw zu tun; to ~ to fight/sing/read/eat, to ~ fighting/singing/reading/eating weiterkämpfen/-singen/-lesen/-essen; the patient ~s to improve das Befinden des Patienten bessert sich ständig.
(b) (resume) fortsetzen; conversation, work, journey also wiederaufnehmen. to be ~d Fortsetzung folgt; ~d on p 10 weiter or Fortsetzung auf Seite 10.
(c) (prolong) line verlängern, weiterführen.
2 vi (go on) (person) weitermachen; (crisis, speech) fortdauern, (an)dauern; (influence) fortdauern, andauern; (weather) anhalten; (road, forest etc) weitergehen, sich fortsetzen; (concert etc) weitergehen. to ~ on one's way weiterfahren; (on foot) weitergehen; he ~d after a short pause or redete/schrieb/las etc nach einer kurzen Pause weiter; to ~ with one's work seine Arbeit fortsetzen, mit seiner Arbeit weitermachen; please ~ bitte machen Sie weiter; (in talking) fahren Sie fort; to ~ to be obstinate/cheerful weiterhin starrköpfig/fröhlich bleiben; he ~s to be optimistic er ist nach wie vor optimistisch; to ~ at university/with a company/as sb's secretary auf der Universität/bei einer Firma/als Sekretärin bleiben; to ~ in office im Amt verbleiben; his influence ~d after his death sein Einfluß überdauerte seinen Tod.

continuing [kənˈtɪnjuːɪŋ] adj ständig, fortgesetzt; process stetig, kontinuierlich (geh).

continuity [ˌkɒntɪˈnjuːɪtɪ] n (a) Kontinuität f. the story lacks ~ der Geschichte fehlt der rote Faden. (b) (Film) Anschluß m; (Rad) (verbindende) Ansagen pl. ~ girl Scriptgirl nt.

continuo [kənˈtɪnjʊəʊ] n Continuo nt. to play the ~ Continuo spielen.

continuous [kənˈtɪnjʊəs] adj dauernd, ständig, kontinuierlich (geh); line durchgezogen, ununterbrochen; rise, movement etc stetig, stet attr (geh), gleichmäßig; (Math) function stetig. ~ performance (Film) durchgehende Vorstellung; ~ tense (Gram) Verlaufsform f; present/past ~ (Gram) Verlaufsform f Präsens/Imperfekt.

continuously [kənˈtɪnjʊəslɪ] adv see adj dauernd, ständig, kontinuierlich (geh); ununterbrochen; stetig, gleichmäßig.

continuum [kənˈtɪnjʊəm] n Kontinuum nt.

contort [kənˈtɔːt] vt (a) one's features verziehen (into zu); limbs verrenken, verdrehen; metal, wood verziehen. a face ~ed by pain ein schmerzverzerrtes Gesicht; a ~ed smile ein verkrampftes Lächeln.
(b) (fig) words verdrehen; report also verzerren.

contortion [kənˈtɔːʃən] n (esp of acrobat) Verrenkung f. (of features) Verzerrung f. mental ~s geistige Verrenkungen pl or Klimmzüge pl; he went through all sorts of ~s to avoid telling the truth er hat sich gedreht und gewendet, um nicht die Wahrheit sagen zu müssen.

contortionist [kənˈtɔːʃənɪst] n Schlangenmensch m.

contour [ˈkɒntʊəʳ] 1 n (a) (outline) Kontur f, Umriß m.
(b) (shape) ~s pl Konturen pl; the ~s of her body ihre Konturen.
(c) (Geog) see ~ line.
2 vt road der Gegend anpassen; land hügelig anlegen; map mit Höhenlinien versehen. the road was ~ed around the hill die Straße wurde/war der Landschaft angepaßt und um den Hügel herumgeführt.

contour: ~ line n (Geog) Höhenlinie f; ~ map n Höhenlinienkarte f.

contra- [ˈkɒntrə-] pref Gegen-, Kontra-; (Mus: pitched lower) Kontra-.

contraband [ˈkɒntrəbænd] 1 n, no pl (goods) Konterbande, Schmuggelware f; (form: smuggling) Schleichhandel m, Schmuggeln m. ~ of war Kriegskonterbande f. 2 adj Schmuggel-. ~ goods Konterbande, Schmuggelware f.

contraception [ˌkɒntrəˈsepʃən] n Empfängnisverhütung, Kontrazeption (form) f.

contraceptive [ˌkɒntrəˈseptɪv] 1 n empfängnisverhütendes or kontrazeptives (form) Mittel; (sheath) Verhütungsmittel, Präventivmittel (form) nt. 2 adj empfängnisverhütend, kontrazeptiv (form); pill Antibaby-; advice über Empfängnisverhütung or Kontrazeption (form).

contraclockwise [ˈkɒntrəˈklɒkwaɪz] adj, adv (US) see anticlockwise.

contract¹ [ˈkɒntrækt] 1 n (a) (agreement) Vertrag, Kontrakt (old) m; (document also) Vertragsdokument nt; (Comm) (order) Auftrag m; (delivery ~) Liefervertrag m. to enter into or make a ~ (with sb) (mit jdm) einen Vertrag eingehen or (ab)schließen; to be under ~ unter Vertrag stehen (to bei, mit); to be bound by ~ vertraglich gebunden sein (to an + acc); to put work out to ~ Arbeiten außer Haus machen lassen; terms of ~ Vertragsbedingungen pl -bestimmungen pl.
(b) (Bridge) Kontrakt m. ~ bridge Kontrakt-Bridge nt.
2 adj price, date vertraglich festgelegt or vereinbart.
3 [kənˈtrækt] vt (a) (acquire) debts machen, ansammeln; illness erkranken an (+dat); vices, habit sich (dat) zulegen, entwickeln, annehmen; passion entwickeln.
(b) (enter into) marriage, alliance schließen, eingehen.
4 [kənˈtrækt] vi (a) (Comm) to ~ to do sth sich vertraglich verpflichten, etw zu tun.
(b) (form: make an arrangement) sich verbünden.

♦**contract in** vi sich anschließen (-to dat); (into insurance scheme) beitreten (-to dat).

♦**contract out** 1 vi sich (dat) austreten, aussteigen (inf) (of aus); (not join) sich nicht anschließen (of dat); (of insurance scheme) nicht beitreten (of dat). 2 vi sep (Comm) work außer Haus machen lassen (to von), vergeben (to an + acc).

contract² [kənˈtrækt] 1 vt (a) zusammenziehen; muscles also kontrahieren (spec); brow in Falten legen, hochziehen; pupil verengen. (b) (Ling) zusammenziehen, kontrahieren (spec) (into zu). 2 vi (muscle, metal etc) sich zusammenziehen; (pupil also) sich verengen; (fig: influence, business) (zusammen)schrumpfen.

contraction [kənˈtrækʃən] n (a) (shrinking) (of metal) Zusammenziehen nt, Zusammenziehung f; (of muscles also) Kontraktion f (spec); (of pupils) Verengung f; (fig) Schrumpfung f.
(b) (Ling) Kontraktion f.
(c) (in childbirth) Wehe f.
(d) (form: acquisition) (of debts) Ansammlung f; (of habit) Entwicklung, Annahme f. his ~ of polio seine Erkrankung an Kinderlähmung.

contractor [kənˈtræktəʳ] n (individual) Auftragnehmer m, beauftragter Elektriker/Monteur etc; (company also) beauftragte Firma; (building ~) Bauunternehmer m; (company) Bauunternehmen nt. that is done by outside ~s damit ist ein Elektriker/Monteur/Spediteur etc (einer anderen Firma) beauftragt; the ~s have nearly finished the building die (von uns) beauftragten Elektriker/Spengler/Heizungsmonteure etc haben das Gebäude fast fertiggestellt.

contractual [kənˈtræktʃʊəl] adj vertraglich.

contradict [ˌkɒntrəˈdɪkt] vt (person) widersprechen (+dat); (event, action, statement also) im Widerspruch stehen zu. to ~ oneself sich (dat) widersprechen; he ~ed every word I said er widersprach mir bei jedem Wort.

contradiction [ˌkɒntrəˈdɪkʃən] n Widerspruch m (of zu); (contradictory) Widersprechen nt. full of ~s voller Widersprüchlichkeiten; to give a flat ~ einfach or rundheraus widersprechen (+dat); he dislikes any ~ of his views er duldet keinen Widerspruch.

contradictory [ˌkɒntrəˈdɪktərɪ] adj person widersprüchlich; statements also (sich) widersprechend, widerspruchsvoll. to be ~ to sth einer Sache (dat) widersprechen, zu etw im Widerspruch stehen; it is not ~ to say ... es ist kein Widerspruch, zu behaupten ...; he was in a ~ mood er war voller Widerspruchsgeist.

contradistinction [ˌkɒntrədɪsˈtɪŋkʃən] n (form): in ~ to im Gegensatz or Unterschied zu.

contra-flow [ˈkɒntrəˈfləʊ] adj (Mot) Gegenverkehrs-.

contralto [kənˈtræltəʊ] 1 n (voice) Alt m; (singer also) Altist(in f) m. 2 adj voice Alt-. the ~ part die Altstimme, der Alt.

contraption [kənˈtræpʃən] n (inf) Apparat m (inf); (gadget also) kluges Dings (inf); (vehicle also) Vehikel nt (inf), Kiste f (inf).

contrapuntal [ˌkɒntrəˈpʌntl] adj kontrapunktisch.

contrarily [kənˈtrɛərɪlɪ] adv (perversely) widerborstig; (of horse etc) widerspenstig.

contrariness [kənˈtrɛərɪnɪs] n see contrary² Widerborstigkeit f; Widerspruchsgeist m, Widerspenstigkeit f.

contrary¹ [ˈkɒntrərɪ] 1 adj (opposite) entgegengesetzt; effect, answer also gegenteilig; (conflicting) views, statements also gegensätzlich, gegenteilig; (adverse) winds, tides widrig. in a ~ direction in entgegengesetzter Richtung; sth is ~ to sth etw steht im Gegensatz zu etw, etw ist einer Sache (dat) entgegengesetzt; it is ~ to our agreement es entspricht nicht unseren Abmachungen; ~ to nature wider die Natur; ~ to our hopes/intentions wider all unsere Hoffnungen/Absichten, entgegen unseren Hoffnungen/Absichten; ~ to what I expected entgegen meinen Erwartungen.
2 n Gegenteil nt. on the ~ im Gegenteil; ~ of what I expected das Gegenteil von dem, was ich erwartet hatte; my intention was quite the ~ ich hatte genau das Gegenteil beabsichtigt; unless you hear to the ~ sofern Sie nichts Gegenteiliges hören.

contrary² [kənˈtrɛərɪ] adj widerborstig, widerspenstig; person also voll Widerspruchsgeist; horse widerspenstig.

contrast [ˈkɒntrɑːst] 1 n (a) (contrasting) Gegenüberstellung f. a ~ of the two reveals that ... bei einer Gegenüberstellung der beiden zeigt sich, daß ...

(b) Gegensatz m (with, to zu); (visual, striking difference of opposites) Kontrast m (with, to zu). by or in ~ im Gegensatz dazu; to be in ~ with or to sth im Gegensatz/in Kontrast zu etw stehen; **the red makes a good ~** das Rot stellt einen guten Kontrast dar; **she's quite a ~ to her sister** es besteht ein ziemlicher Gegensatz or Unterschied zwischen ihr und ihrer Schwester; **the ~ between the state of the £ now and last year** der Unterschied zwischen dem jetzigen Stand des Pfundes und seinem Wert im letzten Jahr; **and now, by way of ~** und nun etwas ganz anderes; **what a ~!** welch ein Gegensatz!
(c) (Art, Phot, TV) Kontrast m.
2 [kən'trɑːst] vt einen Vergleich anstellen (with zwischen +dat), gegenüberstellen (with dat).
3 [kən'trɑːst] vi im Gegensatz or in Kontrast stehen (with zu), kontrastieren (with mit); (colours also) sich abheben (with von), abstechen (with von). to ~ unfavourably with sth bei einem Vergleich mit or im Vergleich zu etw schlecht abschneiden; **his promises and his actions ~** sharply seine Versprechungen und seine Handlungsweise stehen in scharfem Kontrast or Gegensatz zueinander; **blue and yellow ~ nicely** Blau und Gelb ergeben einen hübschen Kontrast.
contrasting [kən'trɑːstɪŋ] adj opinions, lifestyle etc gegensätzlich, kontrastierend (form); colours kontrastierend, Kontrast-.
contrastive [kən'trɑːstɪv] adj gegenüberstellend; (Ling) kontrastiv.
contravene [,kɒntrə'viːn] vt law, custom etc (action, behaviour) verstoßen gegen, verletzen; (person also) zuwiderhandeln (+dat).
contravention [,kɒntrə'venʃən] n Verstoß m (of gegen), Verletzung f (of gen); (of law also) Übertretung f (of gen). to be in ~ of ... gegen ... verstoßen; **to act in ~ of sth** einer Sache (dat) zuwiderhandeln.
contretemps ['kɒntrə,tɒŋ] n, no pl Zwischenfall m; (unexpected setback) kleines Mißgeschick.
contribute [kən'trɪbjuːt] **1** vt beitragen (to zu); food, money, supplies beisteuern (to zu); (to charity) spenden (to für); time, talent zur Verfügung stellen (to dat); press article also, information liefern (to für), beisteuern (to dat). **to ~ one's share** sein(en) Teil dazu beitragen.
2 vi beitragen (to zu); (to pension fund etc) einen Beitrag leisten (to zu); (to present) beisteuern (to zu); (to charity) spenden (to für); (to newspaper, conference, society etc) einen Beitrag leisten (to zu); (regularly: to a magazine etc) mitwirken (to an +dat). **do you want me to ~?** möchten Sie, daß ich etwas dazu beisteuere or (to charity) etwas spende?
contribution [,kɒntrɪ'bjuːʃən] n Beitrag m (to zu); (donation also) Spende f (to für). **to make a ~ to sth** einen Beitrag zu etw leisten; **the beer is my ~** das Bier stelle ich; **I appreciate the ~ of so much of your time/effort** ich weiß es zu schätzen, daß Sie Ihre Zeit so großzügig zur Verfügung gestellt/solche Anstrengungen unternommen haben.
contributor [kən'trɪbjʊtə'] n (to magazine etc) Mitarbeiter(in f) m (to an +dat); (of goods, money) Spender(in f) m. **to be a ~ to a newspaper/an appeal** für eine Zeitung schreiben/auf einen Appell hin etwas spenden; **all the ~s to his present** alle, die etwas zu dem Geschenk für ihn beigesteuert haben.
contributory [kən'trɪbjʊtərɪ] adj (a) **it's certainly a ~ factor/cause** es ist sicherlich ein Faktor, der dazu beiträgt or der mit eine Rolle spielt; **to be a ~ cause of a disease** ein Faktor sein, der zu einer Krankheit beiträgt; ~ **negligence** (Jur) Mitverschulden nt. (b) ~ **pension scheme** beitragspflichtig.
con trick n (inf) Schwindel m.
contrite adj, ~**ly** adv ['kɒntraɪt, -lɪ] reuig, zerknirscht.
contrition [kən'trɪʃən] n Reue f. ~ act of ~ (Eccl) Buße f.
contrivance [kən'traɪvəns] n (a) (device) Vorrichtung f; (mechanical) Gerät nt, Apparat m.
(b) (devising, scheming) Planung f; (invention) Erfindung f; (inventiveness) Findigkeit, Erfindungsgabe f. **a plan/device of his ~** ein seinem Kopf entstammender Plan/ein von ihm erfundenes Gerät.
(c) (plan, scheme) List f.
contrive [kən'traɪv] vt (a) (devise) plan, scheme entwickeln, entwerfen, ersinnen; (make) fabrizieren. **to ~ a means of doing sth** einen Weg finden, etw zu tun.
(b) (manage, arrange) bewerkstelligen, zuwege bringen; meeting also arrangieren. **to ~ to do sth** es fertigbringen (also iro) or zuwege bringen, etw zu tun; **can you ~ to be here at three o'clock?** können Sie es so einrichten, daß Sie um drei Uhr hier sind?; **he always ~s to get his own way** er versteht (es) immer, seinen Kopf durchzusetzen.
contrived [kən'traɪvd] adj gestellt, arrangiert; style gekünstelt, gestellt, künstlich.
control [kən'trəʊl] **1** n **(a)** no pl (management, supervision) Aufsicht f (of über +acc); (of money, fortune) Verwaltung f (of gen); (of situation, emotion, language) Beherrschung f (of gen); (self-~) (Selbst)beherrschung f; (physical ~) (Körper)beherrschung f (of gen); (authority, power) Gewalt, Macht f (over über +acc); (over territory) Gewalt f (over über +acc); (regulation) (of prices, disease, inflation) Kontrolle f (of gen); (of traffic) Regelung f (of gen); (of pollution) Einschränkung f (of gen). **to be in ~ of sth**, **to have ~ of sb/sth** business, office etw leiten, etw unter sich (dat) haben; children jdn beaufsichtigen; money etw verwalten; **I'm in ~ here** hier die Leitung; **to be in ~ of sb/sth**, **to have sth under ~** etw in der Hand haben; children, class also jdn/etw unter Kontrolle haben; situation also Herr einer Sache (gen) sein, etw beherrschen; car, inflation, disease, pollution etw unter Kontrolle haben; **to be in ~ of oneself/one's emotions** sich in der Hand or in der Gewalt haben/Herr über seine Gefühle sein, Herr seiner Gefühle sein; **to have some/no ~ over sb** Einfluß/keinen Einfluß auf jdn haben; **she has no ~ over how the**

money is spent/what her children do sie hat keinen Einfluß darauf, wie das Geld ausgegeben wird/was ihre Kinder machen; **to have some/no ~ over sth** etw in der Hand/nicht in der Hand haben; **over money** Kontrolle/keine Kontrolle über etw (acc) haben; **over environment** Einfluß/keinen Einfluß auf etw (acc) haben; **over sb** (of sth) etw nicht mehr in der Hand haben, (über etw acc) die Gewalt or Herrschaft verlieren; **of business** die Kontrolle (über etw acc) verlieren; **of car** die Herrschaft (über etw acc) verlieren; **to lose ~ of oneself** die Beherrschung verlieren; **to lose ~ of the situation** nicht mehr Herr der Lage sein; **to be/get out of ~** child, class) außer Rand und Band sein/geraten; (situation) außer Kontrolle sein/geraten; (car) nicht mehr zu halten sein; (inflation, prices, disease, pollution) sich jeglicher Kontrolle (dat) entziehen/nicht mehr zu halten or zu bremsen (inf) sein; (fire) nicht unter Kontrolle sein/außer Kontrolle geraten; **the car spun out of ~** der Wagen begann sich ganz unkontrollierbar zu drehen; **under state ~** unter staatlicher Kontrolle or Aufsicht; **to bring or get sth under ~** etw unter Kontrolle bringen; situation Herr einer Sache (gen) werden; car etw in seine Gewalt bringen; **to be under ~** unter Kontrolle sein; (children, class) sich benehmen; (car) (wieder) lenkbar sein; **everything or the situation is under ~** wir/sie etc haben die Sache im Griff (inf); **the situation was beyond their ~** die Sache war ihnen völlig aus der Hand geglitten, sie hatten die Sache nicht mehr in der Hand; **he was beyond parental ~** er war seinen Eltern über den Kopf gewachsen; **circumstances beyond our ~** nicht in unserer Hand liegende Umstände; **his ~ of the ball** seine Ballführung.
(b) (check) Kontrolle f (on gen, über +acc). **wages/price ~s** Lohn-/Preiskontrolle f.
(c) (~ room) die Zentrale; (Aviat) der Kontrollturm.
(d) (knob, switch) Regler m; (of vehicle, machine) Schalter m. **to be at the ~s** (of spaceship, airliner) am Kontrollpult sitzen; (of small plane, car) die Steuerung haben; **to take over the ~s** die Steuerung übernehmen.
(e) (Sci) (person) Kontrollperson f; (animal) Kontrolltier nt; (group) Kontrollgruppe f. ~ **experiment** Kontrollversuch m.
(f) (Spiritualism) Geist m einer Persönlichkeit, dessen Äußerungen das Medium wiedergibt.
2 vt **(a)** (direct, manage) kontrollieren; business führen, leiten, unter sich (dat) haben; sea beherrschen; organization in der Hand haben; animal, child, class fertigwerden mit; car steuern, lenken; traffic regeln; emotions, movements beherrschen, unter Kontrolle halten; hair bändigen. **to ~ oneself/one's temper** sich beherrschen; ~ **yourself!** nimm dich zusammen!; **please try to ~ your children/dog** bitte sehen Sie zu, daß sich Ihre Kinder benehmen/sich Ihr Hund benimmt.
(b) (regulate, check) prices, rents, growth etc kontrollieren; temperature, speed regulieren; disease unter Kontrolle bringen; population eindämmen, im Rahmen halten.
control column n Steuersäule f (form), Steuerknüppel m.
controllable [kən'trəʊləbl] adj kontrollierbar, zu kontrollieren pred; child, animal lenkbar.
controlled [kən'trəʊld] adj emotion, movement, voice beherrscht; passion gezügelt; conditions, rent kontrolliert; prices gebunden; temperature geregelt.
controller [kən'trəʊlə'] n **(a)** (director) (Rad) Intendant m; (Aviat) (Flug)lotse m. **(b)** (financial head) Leiter m des Finanzwesens.
controlling [kən'trəʊlɪŋ] adj attr factor beherrschend; body Aufsichts-. ~ **interest** Mehrheitsanteil m.
control: ~ **panel** n Schalttafel, Schaltblende f; (on aircraft, TV) Bedienungsfeld nt; (on computer) Steuer- or Bedienungs- or Betriebspult nt; (on car) Armaturenbrett nt; ~ **point** n Kontrollpunkt m, Kontrollstelle f; ~ **rod** n Regelstab m; ~ **room** n Kontrollraum m; (Naut also) Kommandoraum m; (Mil) (Operations)zentrale f; (of police) Zentrale f; ~ **stick** n see ~ **column**; ~ **tower** n (Aviat) Kontrollturm m; ~ **unit** n (Computers) Steuer- or Leitwerk nt.
controversial [,kɒntrə'vɜːʃəl] adj (causing controversy) speech etc kontrovers; (debatable) matter, decision also umstritten, strittig. **it is still ~ whether ...** es ist immer noch umstritten, ob ...; **he is deliberately ~** er gibt sich bewußt kontrovers.
controversy ['kɒntrəvɜːsɪ, kən'trɒvəsɪ] n Kontroversen pl, Streit m. **there was a lot of ~ about it** es gab deswegen große Kontroversen or Differenzen; **to give rise to ~** Anlaß zu Kontroversen geben; **statements/facts that are beyond ~** völlig unumstrittene Behauptungen/Tatsachen.
controvert ['kɒntrəvɜːt] vt (form) anfechten, bestreiten.
contumacious adj, ~**ly** adv [,kɒntjʊ'meɪʃəs, -lɪ] verstockt; (insubordinate) den Gehorsam verweigernd.
contumacy ['kɒntjʊməsɪ] n see adj Verstocktheit f; Gehorsamsverweigerung f.
contumely ['kɒntjʊmɪlɪ] n (no pl: abuse) Schmähen nt (geh); (insult) Schmähung f (geh).
contuse [kən'tjuːz] vt (form) quetschen, prellen.
contusion [kən'tjuːʒən] n Quetschung, Kontusion (spec) f.
conundrum [kə'nʌndrəm] n (lit, fig) Rätsel nt.
conurbation [,kɒnɜː'beɪʃən] n Ballungsgebiet nt or -raum m or -zentrum nt, Conurbation f (spec).
convalesce [,kɒnvə'les] vi genesen (from, after von), rekonvaleszieren (rare, form) (from, after nach). **while convalescing** während der Genesung(szeit).
convalescence [,kɒnvə'lesəns] n Genesung, Rekonvaleszenz (form) f; (period) Genesung(szeit) f.
convalescent [,kɒnvə'lesənt] **1** n Rekonvaleszent(in f) m (form), Genesende(r) mf. **2** adj genesend. **to be ~** auf dem Wege der Besserung sein. ~ **home** Genesungsheim nt.
convection [kən'vekʃən] n Konvektion f.
convector [kən'vektə'] n (also ~ **heater**) Heizlüfter m.

convene [kən'vi:n] **1** vt meeting einberufen; group of people zusammenrufen, versammeln. **2** vi zusammenkommen, sich versammeln; (parliament, court) zusammentreten.

convener [kən'vi:nəʳ] n Person, die Versammlungen einberuft.

convenience [kən'vi:nɪəns] n (a) no pl (usefulness, advantageousness) Annehmlichkeit f; (functionalness) Zweckmäßigkeit f. for the sake of ~ aus praktischen Gründen; ~ foods Fertiggerichte pl.

(b) no pl to consider the ~ of the inhabitants/driver etc daran denken, was für die Bewohner/den Fahrer etc praktisch und bequem ist, die Zweckmäßigkeit für die Bewohner/den Fahrer etc in Betracht ziehen; for your ~ zum gefälligen Gebrauch; these chairs are for the ~ of customers diese Stühle sind für unsere Kunden gedacht; I'm not changing it for or to suit his ~ ich werde es seinetwegen or nur um es ihm recht zu machen nicht ändern; he did not find that date to his ~ der Termin war ihm nicht angenehm or recht, der Termin paßte ihm nicht or kam ihm nicht gelegen; at your own ~ zu einem Ihnen angenehmen Zeitpunkt, wann es Ihnen paßt; at your earliest ~ (Comm) möglichst bald, baldmöglichst (form).

(c) (convenient thing, amenity) Annehmlichkeit f. a house with every ~/with all modern ~s ein Haus mit allem/allem modernen Komfort; the ~s included a laundry room etc in der Ausstattung mit inbegriffen waren ein Wäscheraum usw.

(d) (Brit form: public ~) (öffentliche) Toilette, Bedürfnisanstalt f (dated, form).

convenient [kən'vi:nɪənt] adj (useful, functional) zweckmäßig, praktisch; area, house (for shops etc) günstig gelegen; time günstig, passend. at a more ~ time zu einem passenderen or günstigeren Zeitpunkt; if it is ~ wenn es Ihnen (so) paßt; if it is ~ to or for you wenn es Ihnen (so) paßt, wenn es Ihnen keine Umstände macht; a place/time ~ for all of us ein Ort, der/eine Zeit, die uns allen paßt or für uns alle günstig ist; is tomorrow ~ (to or for you)? paßt (es) Ihnen morgen?, geht es morgen?; well, then, you'd better make it ~ nun, dann machen Sie es eben passend (inf), dann sehen Sie eben zu, daß es paßt; he sat down on a ~ chair er setzte sich auf einen Stuhl, der gerade dastand; the trams are very ~ (nearby) die Straßenbahnhaltestellen liegen sehr günstig; (useful) die Straßenbahn ist sehr praktisch; a ~ place to stop eine geeignete or günstige Stelle zum Anhalten; is there a ~ train? gibt es einen geeigneten or passenden Zug?; her resignation was most ~ (for him) ihr Rücktritt kam ihm äußerst gelegen; how ~! sehr günstig!

conveniently [kən'vi:nɪəntlɪ] adv günstigerweise; situated günstig, vorteilhaft; (usefully) designed praktisch, zweckmäßig. he very ~ arrived home early er kam früh nach Hause, was äußerst günstig war; if you could ~ do it then wenn es Ihnen paßte; it ~ started to rain wie bestellt, fing es an zu regnen; the house is ~ close to the shops das Haus liegt in praktischer Nähe der Läden.

convent ['kɒnvənt] n (Frauen)kloster nt. to enter a ~ ins Kloster gehen; ~ school Klosterschule f.

convention [kən'venʃən] n (a) Brauch m, Sitte f; (social rule) Konvention f. ~ requires or demands that ... die Sitte or der Brauch will es so, daß ...; it's a ~ that ... es ist so üblich or Sitte or Brauch, daß ...; it's a ~ of our society es ist in unserer Gesellschaft so üblich; (point of etiquette) es ist eine gesellschaftliche Konvention; to disregard ~(s) sich nicht an die herkömmlichen Bräuche or Konventionen halten.

(b) (agreement) Abkommen nt.

(c) (conference) Tagung, Konferenz f; (Pol) Konvent m.

conventional [kən'venʃənl] adj dress, attitudes, warfare, weapons konventionell; person, behaviour also konventionsgebunden; philosophy, beliefs, theory, manner, technique herkömmlich; theatre, music, style traditionell; symbol, mealtimes normalerweise üblich. it is ~ to do sth es ist normalerweise üblich, etw zu tun.

conventionality [kən,venʃə'nælɪtɪ] n see adj Konventionalität f; Konventionsgebundenheit f; Herkömmlichkeit f; traditionelle Art.

conventionally [kən'venʃnəlɪ] adv see adj konventionell; konventionsgebunden; herkömmlicherweise; traditionell; normalerweise, üblicherweise. ~ one would be expected to ... herkömmlicherweise würde erwartet, daß man ...

converge [kən'vɜ:dʒ] vi (road, lines) zusammenlaufen (at in or an +dat); (river also) zusammenströmen (at in or an +dat); (Math, Phys) konvergieren (at in +dat); (fig: views etc) sich aneinander annähern, konvergieren (geh). to ~ on sth/sb/sth/New York sb über all her zu jdm/etw/nach New York strömen.

convergence [kən'vɜ:dʒəns] n see vi Zusammenlaufen nt; Zusammenströmen nt; Konvergenz f; Annäherung f. point of ~ Schnittpunkt m; (of rays) Brennpunkt m; (of rivers) Zusammenfluß m.

convergent [kən'vɜ:dʒənt] adj, **converging** [kən'vɜ:dʒɪŋ] adj see vi zusammenlaufend; zusammenströmend; konvergent (form), konvergierend; sich (aneinander) annähernd.

conversant [kən'vɜ:sənt] adj pred vertraut.

conversation [,kɒnvə'seɪʃən] n Gespräch nt, Unterhaltung f; (Sch) Konversation f. to make ~ sich unterhalten, (small talk) Konversation machen; to get into/be in ~ with sb mit jdm ins Gespräch kommen/im Gespräch sein; deep in ~ ins Gespräch vertieft; to have a ~/several ~s with sb (about sth) sich mit jdm/oft mit jdm (über etw acc) unterhalten; he has no ~ mit ihm kann man sich nicht unterhalten; his ~ is so amusing er ist ein unterhaltsamer Gesprächspartner; a subject of ~ ein Gesprächsthema nt; words used only in ~ Wörter, die nur in der gesprochenen Sprache gebraucht werden; we only mentioned it in ~ wir haben das nur gesprächsweise erwähnt; ~ piece Gesprächsgegenstand, Gesprächszünder m; the art of ~ die Kunst der gepflegten Konversation or Unterhaltung or des (guten) Gespräch(e)s.

conversational [,kɒnvə'seɪʃənl] adj tone, style Unterhaltungs-, Plauder-, leger. ~ German gesprochenes Deutsch; his tone was quiet and ~ er sagte es in ruhigem Gesprächston; that gave him a ~ opening das ermöglichte es ihm, sich in die Unterhaltung einzuschalten or (to get talking) eine Unterhaltung anzufangen.

conversationalist [,kɒnvə'seɪʃnəlɪst] n guter Unterhalter or Gesprächspartner, gute Unterhalterin or Gesprächspartnerin. not much of a ~ nicht gerade ein Konversationsgenie.

conversationally [,kɒnvə'seɪʃnəlɪ] adv write im Plauderton. he's somewhat lacking ~ er ist kein besonders guter Unterhalter.

converse[1] [kən'vɜ:s] vi (form) sich unterhalten, konversieren (old). he ~s fluently in Greek er kann sich fließend auf Griechisch unterhalten.

converse[2] ['kɒnvɜ:s] **1** adj umgekehrt; (Logic also) konvers (spec); opinions etc gegenteilig. **2** n (opposite) Gegenteil nt; (Logic: proposition) Umkehrung f, Konverse (spec) f. the ~ is true das Gegenteil trifft zu; quite the ~ ganz im Gegenteil.

conversely [kɒn'vɜ:slɪ] adv umgekehrt.

conversion [kən'vɜ:ʃən] n (a) Konversion f (into in +acc); (Fin, Sci also) Umwandlung f (into in +acc); (Rugby) Verwandlung f; (of measures) Umrechnung f (into in +acc); (of Dormobile etc) Umrüstung f, Umbau m; (model) Spezialausführung f; (of building) Umbau m (into zu); (of appliances) Umstellung f (to auf +acc). the attic flat is a ~ die Wohnung ist ein ausgebauter Dachstock; ~ table Umrechnungstabelle f.

(b) (Rel, fig) Bekehrung, Konversion f (to zu).

convert ['kɒnvɜ:t] **1** n (lit, fig) Bekehrte(r) mf; (to another denomination) Konvertit m. to become a ~ to sth (lit, fig) sich zu etw bekehren.

2 [kən'vɜ:t] vt (a) konvertieren (into in +acc); (Fin, Sci also) umwandeln (into in +acc); (Rugby) verwandeln; measures umrechnen (into in +acc); Dormobile etc umrüsten, umbauen (into zu); attic ausbauen (into zu); building umbauen (into zu); appliance umstellen (to auf +acc). a sofa that can be ~ed into a bed ein Sofa, das sich in ein Bett verwandeln läßt; most of the town has now been ~ed to natural gas der größte Teil der Stadt ist jetzt auf Erdgas umgestellt.

(b) (Rel, fig) bekehren (to zu); (to another denomination) konvertieren.

3 [kən'vɜ:t] vi sich verwandeln lassen (into in +acc).

converter [kən'vɜ:təʳ] n (Elec) Konverter m; (for AC/DC) Stromgleichrichter m.

convertibility [kən,vɜ:tə'bɪlɪtɪ] n (of currency) Konvertierbarkeit, Konvertibilität f; (of appliances) Umstellbarkeit f.

convertible [kən'vɜ:təbl] **1** adj verwandelbar; currency konvertibel, konvertierbar; car mit aufklappbarem Verdeck; appliances umstellbar. a ~ sofa ein Sofa, das sich in ein Bett verwandeln läßt. **2** n (car) Kabriolett nt.

convex [kɒn'veks] adj lens, mirror konvex, Konvex-.

convexity [kɒn'veksɪtɪ] n Konvexität f.

convey [kən'veɪ] vt (a) befördern; goods spedieren; water leiten.

(b) (make known or felt) opinion, idea vermitteln; (make understood) meaning klarmachen; (transmit) message, order, best wishes übermitteln, überbringen. what does this poem/music ~ to you? was sagt Ihnen dieses Gedicht/diese Musik?; words cannot ~ what I feel was ich empfinde, läßt sich nicht mit Worten ausdrücken; words which ~ a lot more than their mere dictionary definition Wörter, die sehr viel mehr ausdrücken, als in einem Wörterbuch definiert werden kann; the name ~s nothing to me der Name sagt mir nichts; try to ~ to him that he should ... versuchen Sie doch, ihm klarzumachen, daß er ... sollte.

(c) (Jur) property übertragen (to auf +acc).

conveyance [kən'veɪəns] n (a) (transport) Beförderung f; (of goods also) Spedition f. ~ of goods Güterverkehr m; means of ~ Beförderungsmittel nt. (b) (old, form: vehicle) Gefährt nt. public ~ öffentliches Verkehrsmittel. (c) (Eigentums)übertragung f (to auf +acc); (document) Übertragungsurkunde f.

conveyancing [kən'veɪənsɪŋ] n (Jur) (Eigentums)übertragung f.

conveyor [kən'veɪəʳ] n (of message etc) Überbringer(in f) m; (Tech) Förderer m. ~ belt Fließband nt; (for transport, supply) Förderband nt.

convict ['kɒnvɪkt] **1** n Sträfling m, Zuchthäusler(in f) m.

2 [kən'vɪkt] vt (a) (Jur) person verurteilen (of wegen), für schuldig erklären (of gen). a ~ed criminal ein verurteilter Verbrecher; to get sb ~ed jds Verurteilung (acc) bewirken.

(b) (actions etc: betray) überführen. to stand ~ed by one's own actions durch sein Handeln überführt werden.

3 [kən'vɪkt] vi jdn verurteilen. the jury refused to ~ die Geschworenen lehnten es ab, einen Schuldspruch zu fällen.

conviction [kən'vɪkʃən] n (a) (Jur) Verurteilung f. five previous ~s fünf Vorstrafen; to get a ~ (police, prosecution) einen Schuldspruch erreichen.

(b) (belief, act of convincing) Überzeugung f. to be open to ~ sich gern eines Besseren belehren lassen; to carry ~ überzeugend klingen; his speech lacked ~ seine Rede klang wenig überzeugend; he's a socialist by ~ er ist ein überzeugter Sozialist; he did it in the ~ that ... er tat es in der Überzeugung, daß ...; a man of strong ~s ein Mann, der feste Anschauungen vertritt; his fundamental political/moral ~s seine politische/moralische Gesinnung; see courage.

convince [kən'vɪns] vt überzeugen. I'm trying to ~ him that ... ich versuche, ihn davon zu überzeugen, daß ...

convinced [kən'vɪnst] adj überzeugt.

convincing adj, **~ly** adv [kən'vɪnsɪŋ, -lɪ] überzeugend.

convivial [kən'vɪvɪəl] adj heiter und unbeschwert; person also fröhlich; (sociable) gesellig.

conviviality [kən,vɪvɪ'ælɪtɪ] *n see adj* unbeschwerte Heiterkeit; Fröhlichkeit *f*; Geselligkeit *f*.

convocation [,kɒnvə'keɪʃən] *n* (*form*) (*calling together*) Einberufung *f*; (*meeting, Eccl*) Versammlung *f*.

convoke [kən'vəʊk] *vt meeting* einberufen; (*Parl also*) zusammentreten lassen.

convolute ['kɒnvəluːt] *adj shell* spiralig aufgewunden; *petal, leaf* eingerollt.

convoluted ['kɒnvəluːtɪd] *adj* (a) (*involved*) verwickelt; *plot also* verschlungen; *style* gewunden. (b) (*coiled*) gewunden; *shell* spiralig aufgewunden.

convolution [,kɒnvə'luːʃən] *n usu pl* Windung *f*; (*of plot*) Verschlungenheit *f no pl*; (*of style*) Gewundenheit *f no pl*.

convolvulus [kən'vɒlvjʊləs] *n* Winde *f*.

convoy ['kɒnvɔɪ] **1** *n* (a) (*escort*) Konvoi *m*, Geleit *nt*. **under ~** mit Geleitschutz, unter Konvoi; **one of our ~ was torpedoed** eines unserer Geleitboote *or* Begleitboote wurde torpediert; **to be on ~ duty** als Geleitschutz abgeordnet sein. (b) (*vehicles under escort, fig*) Konvoi *m*; (*ships also*) Verband *m*. **in ~** im Konvoi/Verband.
2 *vt* Geleitschutz geben (+*dat*), begleiten. **the ships were ~ed across** die Schiffe wurden unter Konvoi hinübergebracht.

convulse [kən'vʌls] *vt* (*earthquake, war etc*) *land* erschüttern; (*fig also*) schütteln; *sb's body, muscles* krampfhaft zusammenziehen. **to be ~d with laughter/pain** sich vor Lachen schütteln/Schmerzen krümmen; **a face ~d with rage/agony** ein vor Wut/Qual verzerrtes Gesicht; **a joke which ~d the audience** ein Witz *m*, bei dem sich das Publikum vor Lachen bog.

convulsion [kən'vʌlʃən] *n* (a) (*Med*) Schüttelkrampf *m no pl*, Konvulsion *f* (*spec*); (*caused by crying*) Weinkrampf *m no pl*.
(b) (*caused by social upheaval etc*) Erschütterung *f*.
(c) (*inf: of laughter*) **to go into/be in ~s** sich biegen *or* schütteln vor Lachen; **he had the audience in ~s** er rief beim Publikum wahre Lachstürme hervor.

convulsive [kən'vʌlsɪv] *adj* konvulsiv(isch) (*spec*), Krampf-; *movement also* krampfhaft. **~ laughter** Lachkrämpfe *pl*.

convulsively [kən'vʌlsɪvlɪ] *adv* krampfartig. **she laughed ~** sie schüttelte sich vor Lachen.

cony, coney ['kəʊnɪ] *n* (a) (*US*) Kaninchen *nt*. (b) (*also ~ skin*) Kaninchenfell *nt*.

coo [kuː] **1** *vi* (*pigeon, fig*) gurren. **2** *vt* gurren, girren. **3** *n* Gurren, Girren *nt*. **4** *interj* (*Brit inf*) ui.

cooee ['kuːiː] **1** *interj* huhu. **2** *vi* huhu rufen.

cook [kʊk] **1** *n* Koch *m*, Köchin *f*. **he is a good ~/good plain ~** sie kocht gut/sie kocht gute Hausmannskost; **too many ~s spoil the broth** (*Prov*) viele Köche verderben den Brei (*Prov*); **to be chief ~ and bottlewasher** (*inf*) Küchendienst machen.
2 *vt* (a) *food, meal* machen, zubereiten; (*in water, milk etc*) kochen; (*fry, roast*) braten; *pie, pancake also* backen. **how are you going to ~ the duck?** wie willst du die Ente zubereiten?; **a ~ed meal/breakfast/supper** eine warme Mahlzeit/ein warmes Abendessen/ein Frühstück *nt* mit warmen Gerichten; **to ~ sb's goose** (*fig*) jdm die Suppe versalzen.
(b) (*inf: falsify*) *accounts* frisieren (*inf*).
3 *vi* (*person, food*) kochen; (*fry, roast*) braten; (*pie*) backen. **it will ~ quickly** das ist schnell gekocht; **the pie ~s in half an hour** die Pastete ist in einer halben Stunde fertig; **what's ~ing?** (*fig inf*) was ist los?

♦**cook up** *vt sep* (*fig inf*) *story, excuse* sich (*dat*) einfallen lassen, zurechtbasteln (*inf*). **~ed ~ story** Lügenmärchen *nt*.

cookbook ['kʊkbʊk] *n* Kochbuch *nt*.

cooker ['kʊkə'] *n* (a) (*Brit: stove*) Herd *m*. (b) (*apple*) Kochapfel *m*.

cookery ['kʊkərɪ] *n* Kochen *nt* (*also Sch*), Kochkunst *f*. **French/native ~** französische/einheimische Küche; **~ book** Kochbuch *nt*; **~ classes** Kochkurs *m*; Kochkurse *pl*.

cookhouse ['kʊkhaʊs] *n* (*Naut*) Kombüse *f*; (*Mil*) Feldküche *f*.

cookie, cooky ['kʊkɪ] *n* (a) (*US: biscuit*) Keks *m*, Plätzchen *nt*. **that's the way the ~ crumbles** (*inf, also Brit*) das ist nun mal (im Leben), das ist der Lauf der Welt *or* der Dinge.
(b) (*inf: smart person*) Typ *m*. **he's a pretty sharp/tough ~** er ist ein richtiger Schlauberger/ziemlich zäher Typ.

cooking ['kʊkɪŋ] *n* Kochen *nt*; (*food*) Essen *nt*. **plain ~** einfaches Essen, Hausmannskost *f*; **French ~** die französische Küche, französisches Essen; **her ~ is atrocious** sie kocht miserabel.

cooking *in cpds* Koch-; **~ apple** *n* Kochapfel *m*; **~ chocolate** *n* Blockschokolade *f*; **~ foil** *n* Backfolie *f*.

cookout ['kʊkaʊt] *n* (*US*) Kochen *nt* am Lagerfeuer; (*on charcoal brazier*) Grillparty *f*.

cooky *n see* **cookie**.

cool [kuːl] **1** *adj* (+*er*) (a) *water, weather, drink* kühl; *clothes* luftig, leicht. **I've let my coffee get a bit ~** ich habe meinen Kaffee ein bißchen kalt werden lassen; **serve ~** kalt *or* (*gut*) gekühlt servieren; **it's nice to slip into something ~** es ist angenehm, in etwas Kühles *or* Leichtes schlüpfen zu können; **"keep in a ~ place"** „kühl aufbewahren".
(b) (*calm, unperturbed*) *person, manner* besonnen; *voice* kühl. **to keep ~, to keep a ~** einen kühlen Kopf behalten; **keep ~!** reg dich nicht auf!, (nur) ruhig Blut!; **as ~ as you please** mit kühler Gelassenheit, in aller Seelenruhe.
(c) (*audacious*) kaltblütig, unverfroren (*pej*), kaltschnäuzig (*inf*). **as ~ as you please** mit größter Unverfrorenheit (*pej*), seelenruhig; **he was very ~ of him** da hat er sich ein starkes Stück geleistet.
(d) (*unenthusiastic, unfriendly*) *greeting, reception, look* kühl. **to be ~ to(wards) sb** sich jdm gegenüber kühl verhalten; **play it ~!** immer mit der Ruhe!; **she decided to play it ~** sie entschied sich, ganz auf kühl zu machen.
(e) (*inf: with numbers etc*) glatt (*inf*). **he earns a ~ ten thousand a year** er verdient glatte zehntausend im Jahr (*inf*).

(f) (*sl: great, smart*) *idea, disco, pub, dress etc* stark (*sl*), cool (*sl*). **~** jazz Cool Jazz *m*.
2 *n* (a) (*lit, fig*) Kühle *f*. **in the ~ of the evening** in der Abendkühle; **to keep sth in the ~** etw kühl aufbewahren; **go/stay in the ~** geh ins Kühle/bleib im Kühlen.
(b) (*inf*) **keep your ~!** reg dich nicht auf!, immer mit der Ruhe!; **to lose one's ~** durchdrehen (*inf*); **he doesn't have the ~ to be a TV announcer** er hat nicht die Nerven für einen Fernsehansager.
3 *vt* (a) kühlen; (**~ down**) abkühlen; *wine also* kaltstellen.
(b) (*sl*) **~ it!** (*don't get excited*) reg dich ab! (*inf*), mach mal langsam (*inf*); (*don't cause trouble*) mach keinen Ärger! (*inf*); **tell those guys to ~ it** sag den Typen, sie sollen keinen Ärger machen (*inf*); **I think we should ~ it** ich glaube wir sollten etwas langsamer treten (*inf*).
4 *vi* (*lit, fig*) abkühlen; (*air also*) sich abkühlen; (*anger*) verrauchen, sich legen; (*enthusiasm, interest*) nachlassen. **he has definitely ~ed towards her** er ist ihr gegenüber deutlich kühler geworden.

♦**cool down 1** *vi* (a) (*lit, fig: person*) abkühlen; (*weather also*) sich abkühlen.
(b) (*feelings etc*) sich abkühlen; (*anger also*) verrauchen; (*critical situation*) sich beruhigen. **look, just ~ ~ will you!** komm, reg dich (bloß wieder) ab! (*inf*); **to let things ~ ~** die Sache etwas ruhen lassen.
2 *vt sep* (a) *food, drink* abkühlen; (*let ~ ~*) abkühlen lassen. **to ~ oneself ~** sich abkühlen.
(b) *situation* beruhigen. **put him in a cell for an hour, that'll ~ him ~** steck ihn eine Stunde lang in eine Zelle, dann wird er sich schon wieder beruhigen.

♦**cool off** *vi* (a) (*liquid, food*) abkühlen; (*person*) sich abkühlen.
(b) (*fig*) (sich) abkühlen; (*enthusiasm, interest*) nachlassen; (*become less angry*) sich abreagieren *or* beruhigen; (*become less friendly*) kühler werden (*about or towards* sb jdm gegenüber). **their friendship has ~ed ~** ihre Freundschaft hat sich abgekühlt *or* ist abgekühlt.

coolant ['kuːlənt] *n* Kühlmittel *nt*.

cool: **~ bag** *n* Kühltasche *f*; **~ box** *n* Kühlbox *f*.

cooler ['kuːlə'] *n* (a) (*for milk etc*) Kühlapparat *m*; (*for wine*) Kühler *m*. (b) (*sl: solitary*) Bau *m* (*inf*).

cool-headed [kuːl'hedɪd] *adj* kühl (und besonnen).

coolie ['kuːlɪ] *n* Kuli *m*.

cooling ['kuːlɪŋ] *adj drink, shower* kühlend; *effect* (ab)kühlend; *affection* abnehmend; *enthusiasm, interest* nachlassend.

cooling-off ['kuːlɪŋ'ɒf] *n* (*in relationship etc*) Abkühlung *f*. **there's been a distinct ~** (*of interest*) about this project das Interesse an diesem Projekt hat merklich nachgelassen. **2** *adj* **~ period** gesetzlich festgelegter Zeitraum für Schlichtungsverhandlungen (bei Arbeitskämpfen).

cooling tower *n* Kühlturm *m*.

coolly ['kuːlɪ] *adv* (a) (*calmly*) ruhig, gefaßt, besonnen. (b) (*unenthusiastically, in an unfriendly way*) kühl. (c) (*audaciously*) kaltblütig, unverfroren (*pej*), kaltschnäuzig (*inf*).

coolness ['kuːlnɪs] *n see adj* (a) Kühle *f*; Luftigkeit, Leichtigkeit *f*. (b) Besonnenheit *f*; Kühle *f*. (c) Kaltblütigkeit, Unverfrorenheit (*pej*), Kaltschnäuzigkeit (*inf*) *f*. (d) Kühle *f*.

coomb [kuːm] *n* Tal(mulde *f*) *nt*.

coon [kuːn] *n* (*Zool*) Waschbär *m*. (b) (*pej*) Nigger *m* (*pej*).

coop [kuːp] *n* (*also hen ~*) Hühnerstall *m*. **to fly the ~** (*fig inf*) sich aus dem Staub machen (*inf*).

♦**coop up** *vt sep person* einsperren; **several people** zusammenpferchen (*inf*).

co-op ['kəʊɒp] *n* Genossenschaft *f*; (*shop*) Coop, Konsum *m*.

cooper ['kuːpə'] *n* Böttcher, Küfer (*dial*) *m*.

cooperate [kəʊ'ɒpəreɪt] *vi* kooperieren, zusammenarbeiten; (*go along with, not be awkward*) mitmachen. **to ~ towards a common end** auf ein gemeinsames Ziel hinarbeiten; **even the weather ~d in making it a day to remember** auch das Wetter trug dazu bei, es zu einem denkwürdigen Tag zu machen; **if the weather ~s** wenn das Wetter mitmacht.

cooperation [kəʊ,ɒpə'reɪʃən] *n* Kooperation, Zusammenarbeit *f*; (*help*) Mitarbeit, Kooperation *f*. **we produced this model in ~ with …** wir haben dieses Modell in Gemeinschaftsarbeit *or* Kooperation *or* gemeinsam mit … produziert; **to further ~ between EEC countries** um die Kooperation *or* Zusammenarbeit zwischen EWG-Ländern zu fördern; **with the ~ of all members then …** wenn alle Mitglieder mitmachen, dann …

cooperative [kəʊ'ɒpərətɪv] **1** *adj* (a) (*prepared to comply*) kooperativ; (*prepared to help*) hilfsbereit. **the agency/management was most ~** die Agentur/Geschäftsleitung war sehr hilfsbereit; **if any member does not have a ~ attitude** wenn ein Mitglied nicht bereit ist mitzumachen.
(b) *firm* auf Genossenschaftsbasis. **~ society** Genossenschaft, Kooperative *f*; **~ farm** Bauernhof *m* auf Genossenschaftsbasis; **~ bank** (*US*) Genossenschaftsbank *f*.
2 *n* Genossenschaft, Kooperative *f*; (*also ~ farm*) Bauernhof *m* auf Genossenschaftsbasis.

cooperatively [kəʊ'ɒpərətɪvlɪ] *adv see adj* (a) kooperativ; hilfsbereit.

coopt [kəʊ'ɒpt] *vt* selbst (hinzu)wählen, kooptieren (*spec*). **he was ~ed onto the committee** er wurde vom Komitee selbst dazugewählt.

coordinate [kəʊ'ɔːdnɪt] **1** *adj* gleichwertig; (*in rank*) gleichrangig; (*Gram*) nebengeordnet (*with* zu). **~ geometry** analytische Geometrie.
2 *n* (*Math etc*) Koordinate *f*; (*equal*) etwas Gleichwertiges. **~s** (*clothes*) Kleidung *f* zum Kombinieren.
3 [kəʊ'ɔːdɪneɪt] *vt* (a) *movements, muscles, pieces of work* koordinieren; (*two people, firms*) *operations etc also* aufeinander abstimmen; *thoughts also* ordnen. **to ~ one thing with another** eine Sache auf eine andere abstimmen.

(b) (*Gram*) nebenordnen, koordinieren. **co-ordinating conjunction** nebenordnende *or* koordinierende Konjunktion.

coordination [kǝʊˌɔːdɪˈneɪʃǝn] *n* Koordination, Koordinierung *f*.

coordinator [kǝʊˈɔːdɪneɪtǝʳ] *n* Koordinator *m*; (*Gram*) koordinierende *or* nebenordnende Konjunktion.

coot [kuːt] *n* Wasserhuhn *nt*. **bald as a ~** völlig kahl; **to be as bald as a ~** eine Platte haben (*inf*); **daft as a ~** (*inf*) doof (*inf*); (*mad*) leicht übergeschnappt (*inf*).

cootie [ˈkuːtɪ] *n* (*US inf*) Laus *f*.

cop [kɒp] 1 *n* (a) (*inf: policeman*) Polizist(in *f*), Bulle (*pej inf*), Polyp (*pej sl*) *m*. **to play ~s and robbers** Räuber und Gendarm spielen.
    (b) (*Brit sl: arrest*) **it's a fair ~** jetzt hat's mich erwischt (*inf*).
    (c) (*Brit sl*) **it's no great ~** das ist nichts Besonderes.
  2 *vt* (*sl: catch*) sb schnappen (*inf*), erwischen (*inf*); clout, thump fangen (*inf*). **you'll ~ it when your dad gets home** warte nur, bis dein Vater nach Haus kommt!; **he ~ped one right on the nose** er fing eine genau auf der Nase (*inf*); **when they found out he didn't have a licence he really ~ped it** als sie herausfanden, daß er keinen Führerschein hatte, war er dran (*inf*); **hey, ~ a load of this!** he, hör dir das mal an! (*inf*).
  ♦**cop out** *vi* (*sl*) aussteigen (*sl*) (*of* aus).

cop *in cpds* (*sl*) Polizei-, Bullen- (*pej inf*).

copartner [ˈkǝʊˈpɑːtnǝʳ] *n* Teilhaber(in *f*), Partner *m*.

copartnership [ˈkǝʊˈpɑːtnǝʃɪp] *n* Teilhaberschaft, Partnerschaft *f*.

cope[1] [kǝʊp] *n* (a) (*Eccl*) Pluviale *nt*. (b) (*Archit*) see **coping**.

cope[2] *vi* zurechtkommen; (*with work*) es schaffen. **to ~ with** difficulties, problems, children, difficult person fertigwerden mit, zurechtkommen mit; **how do you ~ all by yourself?** wie werden Sie so allein fertig?, wie kommen Sie so allein zurecht?; **I can't ~ with all this work** ich bin mit all der Arbeit überfordert; **don't worry, we'll ~ somehow** keine Angst, wir werden es irgendwie schaffen; **she can't ~ with the stairs any more** sie schafft die Treppe nicht mehr.

Copenhagen [ˌkǝʊpnˈheɪgǝn] *n* Kopenhagen *nt*.

Copernican [kǝˈpɜːnɪkǝn] *adj* kopernikanisch.

Copernicus [kǝˈpɜːnɪkǝs] *n* Kopernikus *m*.

copestone [ˈkǝʊpstǝʊn] *n* (a) (*Archit*) Abdeckplatte *f*. (b) (*fig*) (*of career etc*) Krönung *f*; (*of theory*) Schlußstein *m*.

copier [ˈkɒpɪǝʳ] *n* (*copyist*) Kopist(in *f*) *m*; (*imitator also*) Nachmacher *m*; (*of writer, painter etc*) Imitator(in *f*) *m*; (*machine*) Kopiergerät *nt*, Kopierer *m* (*inf*).

co-pilot [ˈkǝʊˈpaɪlǝt] *n* Kopilot *m*.

coping [ˈkǝʊpɪŋ] *n* Mauerkrone *f*.

coping: **~ saw** *n* Laubsäge *f*; **~ stone** *n* see **copestone**.

copious [ˈkǝʊpɪǝs] *adj* supply groß, reichlich; information, details, illustrations zahlreich; writer fruchtbar. **amidst ~ tears** unter einer Flut von Tränen.

copiously [ˈkǝʊpɪǝslɪ] *adv* reichlich. **she wept ~** sie vergoß Ströme von Tränen.

copiousness [ˈkǝʊpɪǝsnɪs] *n* see adj Größe, Reichlichkeit *f*; Fülle *f*, Reichtum *m*; Fruchtbarkeit *f*.

cop-out [ˈkɒpaʊt] *n* (*sl*) Rückzieher *m* (*inf*).

copper[1] [ˈkɒpǝʳ] *n* (a) (*metal*) Kupfer *nt*. (b) (*colour*) Kupferrot *nt*. (c) (*esp Brit inf: coin*) Pfennig *m*. **~s** Kleingeld *nt*. 2 (*inf: policeman*) Polizist(in *f*), Bulle (*pej inf*), Polyp (*pej sl*) *m*. (e) (*for boiling clothes etc*) Kupferkessel, Waschkessel *m*.

copper: **~ beech** *n* Rotbuche *f*; **~-bottomed** *adj* mit Kupferboden *m* (*Fin, fig*) gesund; **~-coloured** *adj* kupferfarben; **~ mine** *n* Kupfermine *f*; **~nob** *n* (*inf*) Rotkopf *m* (*inf*); **~plate** 1 *vt* verkupfern; 2 *n* (a) (*plate for engraving*) Kupferplatte *f*; (*engraving*) Kupferstich *m*; (b) (*handwriting*) lateinische (*Ausgangs*)schrift; 3 *adj* **~plate engraving** Kupferstich *m*; (*process also*) Kupferstechen *nt*; **~plate (hand)writing** lateinische (*Ausgangs*)schrift; **in your best ~plate writing** in deiner besten Sonntagsschrift; **he does this real ~plate handwriting** er schreibt wie gestochen; **~-plating** *n* Verkupferung *f*; **~smith** *n* Kupferschmied *m*.

coppery [ˈkɒpǝrɪ] *adj* kupfern, kupferrot.

coppice [ˈkɒpɪs] *n* see **copse**.

copra [ˈkɒprǝ] *n* Kopra *f*.

coprophilia [ˌkɒprǝˈfɪlɪǝ] *n* Koprophilie *f*.

copse [kɒps] *n* Wäldchen *nt*.

cop-shop [ˈkɒpʃɒp] *n* (*sl*) Revier *nt*.

copter [ˈkɒptǝʳ] *n* (*inf*) Hubschrauber *m*.

Coptic [ˈkɒptɪk] *adj* koptisch.

copula [ˈkɒpjʊlǝ] *n* Kopula *f*, Satzband *nt*.

copulate [ˈkɒpjʊleɪt] *vi* kopulieren.

copulation [ˌkɒpjʊˈleɪʃǝn] *n* Kopulation *f*.

copulative [ˈkɒpjʊlǝtɪv] (*Gram*) 1 *n* Kopula *f*. 2 *adj* kopulativ. **~ conjunction** koordinierende Konjunktion.

copy [ˈkɒpɪ] 1 *n* (a) Kopie *f*; (*of document etc*) (*extra version also*) Zweitschrift *f*; (*separately written or typed also*) Abschrift *f*; (*typed carbon also*) Durchschlag *m*; (*handwritten carbon also*) Durchschrift *f*; (*Phot*) Abzug *m*. **to take or make a ~ of sth** eine Kopie/Zweitschrift *etc* von etw machen; **to write out a fair ~** etw ins reine schreiben, eine Reinschrift herstellen; see **rough**.
    (b) (*of book etc*) Exemplar *nt*. **have you got a ~ of today's "Times"?** hast du die „Times" von heute?
    (c) (*Press etc*) (*subject matter*) Stoff *m*; (*material to be printed*) Artikel *m*; (*Typ*) (Manu)skript *nt*. **that's always good ~** das zieht immer; **this murder story will make good ~** aus diesem Mord kann man etwas machen.
    (d) (*in advertising*) Werbetext *m*. **who did the ~ for this campaign?** wer hat den Text/die Texte für diese Werbekampagne gemacht?; **he writes good ~** er schreibt gute Werbetexte.
  2 *vi* (a) (*imitate*) nachahmen.
    (b) (*Sch etc*) abschreiben.

---

3 *vt* (a) (*make a ~ of*) see *n* kopieren; eine Zweitschrift/Abschrift anfertigen von; einen Durchschlag/eine Durchschrift machen von; abziehen; (*write out again*) abschreiben.
    (b) (*imitate*) nachmachen; gestures, accent, person also nachahmen. **they always ~ Ford** sie machen Ford immer alles nach.
    (c) (*Sch etc*) sb else's work abschreiben; (*painting*) abmalen. **to ~ Brecht** (von) Brecht abschreiben.

copy: **~book** 1 *n* Schönschreibheft *nt*; see **blot**; 2 *adj attr* mustergültig, wie es/er/sie im Lehrbuch steht; a **~book landing** eine Bilderbuchlandung; **~ boy** *n* (*Press*) Laufjunge *m*; **~cat** *n* (*inf*) Nachahmer(in *f*) *m*; (*with written work*) Abschreiber(in *f*) *m*; **she's a terrible ~cat** sie macht immer alles nach; sie schreibt immer ab; **~cat!** Nachmachen gilt nicht! (*inf*); **~ desk** *n* (*Press*) Redaktionstisch *m*; **~ editor** *n* (*Press*) Redakteur(in *f*) *m*; (*publishing also*) Lektor(in *f*) *m*; Manuskriptbearbeiter(in *f*) *m*.

copyist [ˈkɒpɪɪst] *n* Kopist(in *f*) *m*.

copyreader [ˈkɒpɪriːdǝʳ] *n* (*US*) see **copy editor**.

copyright [ˈkɒpɪraɪt] 1 *n* Copyright, Urheberrecht *nt*. **out of ~** urheberrechtlich nicht mehr geschützt. 2 *adj* urheberrechtlich geschützt. 3 *vt book* urheberrechtlich schützen; (*author*) urheberrechtlich schützen lassen.

copy: **~ typist** *n* Schreibkraft *f*; **~writer** *n* Werbetexter(in *f*) *m*.

coquetry [ˈkɒkɪtrɪ] *n* Koketterie *f*.

coquette [kǝˈket] *n* kokettes Mädchen, kokette Frau.

coquettish [kǝˈketɪʃ] *adj* kokett, keß.

cor [kɔːʳ] *interj* (*Brit sl*) Mensch (*inf*), Mann (*sl*).

coracle [ˈkɒrǝkl] *n* kleines ovales Ruderboot aus mit Leder bezogenem Flechtwerk.

coral [ˈkɒrǝl] *n* (a) Koralle *f*. (b) (*colour*) Korallenrot *nt*.

coral *in cpds* Korallen-; **~-coloured** *adj* korallenfarbig; **~ island** *n* Koralleninsel *f*; **~ necklace** *n* Korallenkette *f*; **~ reef** *n* Korallenriff *nt*; **C~ Sea** *n* Korallenmeer *nt*; **~ snake** *n* Korallennatter *f*.

cor anglais [ˈkɔːŋgleɪ] *n* (*esp Brit*) Englischhorn *nt*.

corbel [ˈkɔːbǝl] *n* Kragstein *m*, Konsole *f*.

cord [kɔːd] 1 *n* (a) Schnur *f*; (*for clothes*) Kordel *f*; (*US Elec*) Schnur *f*. (b) **~s** *pl* (*also a pair of ~s*) Kordhosen *pl*. (c) (*Tex*) see **corduroy**. (d) (*Anat*) see spinal, umbilical, vocal. 2 *attr* Kord-. **~ jacket** Kordjacke *f*; **~ trousers** Kordhosen *pl*.

cordage [ˈkɔːdɪdʒ] *n, no pl* Tauwerk *nt*.

corded [ˈkɔːdɪd] *adj* (*ribbed*) gerippt.

cordial [ˈkɔːdɪǝl] 1 *adj* freundlich, höflich; (*liter: intense*) dislike heftig. 2 *n* (*soft drink*) Fruchtsaftkonzentrat *nt*; (*alcoholic*) Fruchtlikör *m*.

cordiality [ˌkɔːdɪˈælɪtɪ] *n* Freundlichkeit, Höflichkeit *f*.

cordially [ˈkɔːdɪǝlɪ] *adv* freundlich, höflich. **we ~ dislike each other** wir begegnen einander mit kühler Höflichkeit; (*liter: intensely*) wir verabscheuen einander von (ganzem) Herzen; **~ yours** mit freundlichen Grüßen.

cordite [ˈkɔːdaɪt] *n* Cordit *nt*.

cordon [ˈkɔːdn] 1 *n* (a) (*Mil*) Kordon *m*, Postenkette *f*. **to put or fling a ~ round sth** einen Kordon um etw ziehen, etw (hermetisch) abriegeln. (b) (*ribbon of an Order*) Kordon *m*, (Ordens)band *nt*. (c) (*Hort*) Kordon, Schnurbaum *m*. 2 *vt* see **~ off**.
♦**cordon off** *vt* sep area, building absperren, abriegeln.

cordon bleu [ˌkɔːdɒnˈblɜː] 1 *n* (*Cook*) (*award*) Meisterkochdiplom *nt*; (*chef, cook*) Meisterkoch *m*, Meisterköchin *f*. 2 *adj* cook vorzüglich. **she's taking a ~ cookery course** sie macht einen Kochkurs für die feine Küche (mit).

corduroy [ˈkɔːdǝrɔɪ] *n* Kordsamt *m*. **~s** Kord(samt)hosen *pl*.

corduroy *in cpds* Kord(samt)-; **~ road** *n* Knüppeldamm *m*.

core [kɔːʳ] 1 *n* (*lit, fig*) Kern *m*; (*of apple, pear*) Kernhaus *nt*, Butzen *m* (*dial*); (*of rock*) Innere(s) *nt*; (*of nuclear reactor*) Core *nt*. **rotten/English to the ~** (*fig*) durch und durch schlecht/englisch; **to get to the ~ of the matter** (*fig*) zum Kern der Sache kommen.
  2 *vt* fruit entkernen; apple, pear das Kernhaus (+gen) entfernen *or* ausschneiden.

corelate *vti* see **correlate**.

co-religionist [ˈkǝʊrɪˈlɪdʒǝnɪst] *n* Glaubensgenosse *m*/-genossin *f*.

corer [ˈkɔːrǝʳ] *n* (*Cook*) Apfelstecher *m*.

co-respondent [ˈkǝʊrɪsˈpɒndǝnt] *n* (*Jur*) Mitbeklagte(r) *or* Dritte(r) *mf* (*im Scheidungsprozeß*), Scheidungsgrund *m* (*hum*).

core time *n* Kernzeit *f*.

Corfu [kɔːˈfuː] *n* Korfu *nt*.

corgi [ˈkɔːgɪ] *n* Corgi *m*.

coriander [ˌkɒrɪˈændǝʳ] *n* Koriander *m*.

Corinth [ˈkɒrɪnθ] *n* Korinth *nt*.

Corinthian [kǝˈrɪnθɪǝn] 1 *adj* korinthisch. 2 *n* Korinther(in *f*) *m*. **~s** +sing vb (*Eccl*) Korinther *pl*.

Coriolanus [ˌkɒrɪǝˈleɪnǝs] *n* Coriolan *m*.

cork [kɔːk] 1 *n* (a) no pl (*substance*) Kork *m*. (b) (*stopper*) Korken *m*. (c) (*Fishing: also ~ float*) Schwimmer *m*. 2 *vt* (*also ~ up*) bottle, wine zu- *or* verkorken. 3 *adj* Kork-, korken (*rare*).

corkage [ˈkɔːkɪdʒ] *n* Korkengeld *nt*.

corked [kɔːkt] *adj* **the wine is ~** der Wein schmeckt nach Kork.

corker [ˈkɔːkǝʳ] *n* (*dated sl*) a **~** einsame Klasse (*sl*).

cork *in cpds* Kork-; **~ flooring** *n* Kork(fuß)boden *m*.

corking [ˈkɔːkɪŋ] *adj* (*dated Brit sl*) Klasse- (*sl*).

cork: **~screw** *n* Korkenzieher *m*; **~screw curls** *npl* Korkenzieherlocken *pl*; **~ shoes** *npl* Schuhe *pl* mit Korksohlen; **~ tile** *n* Korkfliese *f*; **~-tipped** *adj* cigarette mit Korkfilter; **~ tree** *n* Korkbaum *m*.

corky [ˈkɔːkɪ] *adj* Kork-, korkartig; taste Kork-, korkig.

corm [kɔːm] *n* Knolle *f*.

cormorant [ˈkɔːmǝrǝnt] *n* Kormoran *m*.

corn[1] [kɔːn] *n* (a) no pl (*cereal*) Getreide, Korn *nt*. (b) (*seed of*

~) Korn nt. (c) no pl sweet~ (esp US: maize) Mais m; see cob.
corn² n Hühnerauge nt. ~ plaster Hühneraugenpflaster nt; to tread on sb's ~s (fig) jdm auf die Hühneraugen treten.
corn³ n (inf) (sentiment etc) Kitsch m, sentimentales Zeug; (trite humour) olle Kamellen pl (inf).
corn: C~ Belt n (Geog) Getreidegürtel m; ~ bread n (US) Maisbrot nt; ~bunting n (Orn) Grauammer f; ~ chandler n Kornhändler m; ~cob n Maiskolben m; ~-coloured adj strohfarben, strohgelb; ~crake n (Orn) Wachtelkönig m; ~crib n (US) Maisspeicher m; ~ dodger n (US) Maisfladen m.
cornea ['kɔːnɪə] n Hornhaut, Cornea (spec) f.
corned beef ['kɔːnd'biːf] n Corned beef nt.
corner ['kɔːnə'] 1 n (a) (generally, Boxing) Ecke f; (of sheet also) Zipfel m; (of mouth, eye) Winkel m; (sharp bend in road) Kurve f; (fig: awkward situation) Klemme f (inf). at or on the ~ an der Ecke; the teacher made him stand in the ~ der Lehrer stellte ihn in die Ecke; it's just round the ~ es ist gleich um die Ecke; to turn the ~ (lit) um die Ecke biegen; we've turned the ~ now (fig) wir sind jetzt über den Berg; the pages are curling up at the ~s die Seiten haben Eselsohren; out of the ~ of one's eye aus dem Augenwinkel (heraus); he always has a cigarette hanging out of the ~ of his mouth er hat immer eine Zigarette im Mundwinkel (hängen); to cut ~s (lit) Kurven schneiden; (fig) das Verfahren abkürzen; to drive sb into a ~ (fig) jdn in die Enge treiben; all four ~s of the world alle vier Winde; he has travelled to all four ~s of the world er hat die ganze Welt bereist; in every ~ of Europe/the globe/the house in allen (Ecken und) Winkeln Europas/der Erde/des Hauses; an attractive ~ of Britain eine reizvolle Gegend Großbritanniens.
(b) (out-of-the-way place) Winkel m. have you got an odd ~ somewhere where I could store my books? hast du irgendwo ein Eckchen or Plätzchen, wo ich meine Bücher lagern könnte?
(c) (Comm: monopoly) Monopol nt. to make/have a ~ in sth das Monopol für or auf etw (acc) erwerben/haben.
(d) (Ftbl) Ecke f, Eckball, Corner (Aus) m. to take a ~ eine Ecke ausführen.
2 vt (a) (lit, fig: trap) in die Enge treiben.
(b) (Comm) the market monopolisieren.
3 vi (take a ~) (person) Kurven/die Kurve nehmen. this car ~s well dieses Auto hat eine gute Kurvenlage; the car tends to skid when ~ing das Auto kommt in der Kurve leicht ins Schleudern.
corner in cpds Eck-; ~ cabinet n Eckschrank m; ~ chair n Eckstuhl m.
-cornered ['kɔːnəd] adj suf -eckig. three-~ dreieckig.
corner: ~ flag n (Sport) Eckfahne f; ~ kick n (Ftbl) Eckstoß m; ~ post n (Ftbl) Eckfahne f; ~ seat n (Rail) Eckplatz m; ~ shop n Laden m an der Ecke; ~stone n (lit, fig) Grundstein, Eckstein m; ~ table n Tisch m in der Ecke, Ecktisch m; ~ways, ~wise adv über Eck, diagonal.
cornet ['kɔːnɪt] n (a) (Mus) Kornett nt. (b) (ice-cream ~) (Eis)tüte f.
corn: C~ Exchange n Getreidebörse f; ~-fed adj mit Getreide gefüttert; ~field n (Brit) Korn- or Weizenfeld nt; (US) Maisfeld nt; ~flakes npl Corn-flakes® pl; ~flour n (Brit) Stärkemehl nt; ~flower 1 n (a) Kornblume f; (b) (colour) Kornblumenblau nt; 2 adj (also ~flower blue) kornblumenblau.
cornice ['kɔːnɪs] n (Archit: of wall, column) (Ge)sims nt; (fig: of snow) Wächte f.
Cornish ['kɔːnɪʃ] 1 adj kornisch, aus Cornwall. ~ pasty (Brit) Gebäckstück nt aus Blätterteig mit Fleischfüllung. 2 n (dialect) Kornisch nt.
Cornishman ['kɔːnɪʃmən] n, pl -men [-mən] Bewohner m Cornwalls.
corn: ~meal n (US) Maismehl nt; ~ oil n (Mais)keimöl nt; ~ pone n (US) see ~ bread; ~ poppy n Klatschmohn m, Mohnblume f; ~ shock n (Getreide)garbe f; ~starch n (US) Stärkemehl nt; ~ syrup n (US) (Mais)sirup m.
cornucopia [kɔːnjʊˈkəʊpɪə] n (Myth, horn-shaped container) Füllhorn nt; (fig: abundance) Fülle f.
corn whisky n (US) Maiswhisky m.
corny ['kɔːnɪ] adj (+er) (inf) joke blöd (inf); (sentimental) kitschig. what a ~ old joke! der Witz hat (so) einen Bart (inf).
corolla [kəˈrɒlə] n (Bot) Blumenkrone, Korolla (spec) f.
corollary [kəˈrɒlərɪ] 1 n (logische) Folge, Korollar nt (also Math). this would prove, as a ~, the existence of life after death damit würde dann gleichzeitig auch bewiesen, daß es ein Leben nach dem Tode gibt. 2 adj Begleit-.
corona [kəˈrəʊnə] n (Astron: of sun, moon etc) Hof m; (part of sun's atmosphere) Korona f; (of tooth) Krone f; (Bot) Nebenkrone f; (cigar) Corona f.
coronary ['kɒrənərɪ] 1 adj (Med) Koronar- (spec). ~ artery Kranzarterie f; ~ failure Herzversagen nt (inf), Koronarinsuffizienz f; ~ thrombosis Herzinfarkt m. 2 n Herzinfarkt m.
coronation [kɒrəˈneɪʃən] n Krönung f.
coronation in cpds Krönungs-; ~ robes npl Krönungsgewänder pl.
coroner ['kɒrənə'] n Beamter, der Todesfälle untersucht, die nicht eindeutig eine natürliche Ursache haben. ~'s inquest Untersuchung f nicht eindeutiger natürlicher Todesfälle; ~'s jury Untersuchungskommission f bei nicht eindeutig natürlichen Todesfällen.
coronet ['kɒrənɪt] n Krone f; (jewellery) Krönchen nt.
corporal¹ ['kɔːpərəl] n (abbr corp) (Mil) Stabsunteroffizier m.
corporal² adj körperlich; pleasures, needs leiblich. ~ punishment Prügel- or Körperstrafe f.
corporate ['kɔːpərɪt] adj (a) (of a group) gemeinsam, korporativ. ~ action/decision geschlossenes or gemeinsames Vorgehen/gemeinsame Entscheidung; to work for the ~ good für das Gemeinwohl arbeiten; to take out ~ membership of another society als geschlossene Gruppe Mitglied

eines anderen Vereins werden.
(b) (of a corporation) korporativ; (of a company) Firmen-; (Jur) Korporations-. I'm not a ~ man ich bin ein Mensch, der sich in großen Firmen nicht wohl fühlt; the ~ life of an organization das Leben in einer großen Vereinigung; an organization can only sue in its ~ name (Jur) eine Organisation kann nur als Körperschaft Klage erheben; body ~ Körperschaft f.
corporately ['kɔːpərɪtlɪ] adv see adj (a) gemeinsam. (b) körperschaftlich.
corporation [kɔːpəˈreɪʃən] n (a) (municipal ~) Gemeinde, Stadt f. the Mayor and C~ der Bürgermeister und die Stadt.
(b) (Brit Comm: incorporated company) Handelsgesellschaft f; (US Comm: limited liability company) Gesellschaft f mit beschränkter Haftung. private/public ~ (Comm) Privatunternehmen nt/staatliches Unternehmen.
(c) (Brit hum: large belly) Schmerbauch m.
corporation: ~ bus n Stadtbus m, städtischer Omnibus; ~ property n gemeindeeigener Besitz; ~ tax n Körperschaftssteuer f; ~ tram n städtische Straßenbahn; ~ transport n städtisches Verkehrsmittel.
corporeal [kɔːˈpɔːrɪəl] adj körperlich.
corps [kɔː'] n, pl - (Mil) Korps nt. ~ de ballet Corps de ballet nt; ~ diplomatique diplomatisches Korps; see diplomatic ~.
corpse [kɔːps] n Leiche f, Leichnam m (geh).
corpulence ['kɔːpjʊləns] n Korpulenz f.
corpulent ['kɔːpjʊlənt] adj korpulent.
corpus ['kɔːpəs] n (a) (collection) Korpus m; (of opinions) Paket nt. (b) (main body) Großteil m. the main ~ of his work der Hauptteil seiner Arbeit. (c) (Fin) Stammkapital nt.
Corpus Christi ['kɔːpəsˈkrɪstɪ] n (Eccl) Fronleichnam m.
corpuscle ['kɔːpʌsl] n Korpuskel nt (spec). blood ~ Blutkörperchen nt.
corpuscular [kɔːˈpʌskjuːlə'] adj Korpuskular- (spec).
corpus delicti ['kɔːpəsdɪˈlɪktaɪ] n (Jur) Corpus delicti nt; (corpse) Leiche f.
corral [kɒˈrɑːl] 1 n Korral m. 2 vt cattle in den Korral treiben.
correct [kəˈrekt] 1 adj (a) (right) richtig; answer, pronunciation also korrekt; time also genau. am I ~ in thinking that ...? gehe ich recht in der Annahme, daß ...?
(b) (proper, suitable, perfectly mannered) korrekt. it's the ~ thing to do das gehört sich so.
2 vt (a) korrigieren; person, pronunciation, error etc also berichtigen, verbessern; bad habit sich/jdm abgewöhnen. to ~ proofs Korrektur lesen; ~ me if I'm wrong Sie können mich gern berichtigen; I stand ~ed ich nehme alles zurück.
(b) (old) (by punishment, scolding) maßregeln; (by corporal punishment) züchtigen.
correction [kəˈrekʃən] n see vt (a) Korrektion, Korrektur f; Berichtigung, Verbesserung f; Abgewöhnung f. ~ of proofs Korrekturlesen nt; I am open to ~ ich lasse mich gerne berichtigen; to do one's ~s (Sch) die Verbesserung machen.
(b) (old) Maßregelung f; Züchtigung f. house of ~ Besserungsanstalt f.
correctitude [kəˈrektɪtjuːd] n see correctness (b).
corrective [kəˈrektɪv] 1 adj korrigierend. to take ~ action korrigierend eingreifen; to have ~ surgery sich einem korrigierenden Eingriff unterziehen. 2 n (Pharm) Korrektiv nt.
correctly [kəˈrektlɪ] adv (a) (accurately) richtig; answer, pronounce also korrekt. he had ~ assumed that ... er hatte richtigerweise angenommen, daß ... (b) (in proper way) behave, speak, dress korrekt.
correctness [kəˈrektnɪs] n (a) (accuracy) Richtigkeit f. (b) (of behaviour etc) Korrektheit f.
correlate ['kɒrɪleɪt] 1 vt two things zueinander in Beziehung setzen, korrelieren (geh). to ~ sth with sth etw mit etw in Beziehung setzen, etw mit etw korrelieren (geh).
2 vi (two things) sich entsprechen. to ~ with sth mit etw in Beziehung stehen.
correlation [kɒrɪˈleɪʃən] n (interdependence) wechselseitige Abhängigkeit, Wechselbeziehung f; (close relationship) enger or direkter Zusammenhang; (Math, Statistics) Korrelation f.
correlative [kɒˈrelətɪv] 1 n Korrelat nt. 2 adj (directly related) entsprechend; (interdependent) in Wechselbeziehung stehend, einander wechselseitig bedingend; (Gram) korrelativ.
correspond [kɒrɪsˈpɒnd] vi (a) (be equivalent) entsprechen (to, with dat); (two or more: to one another) sich entsprechen; (be in accordance also) sich decken (with mit). your version doesn't ~ Ihre Version deckt sich nicht damit.
(b) (exchange letters) korrespondieren (with mit).
correspondence [kɒrɪsˈpɒndəns] n (a) (agreement, equivalence) Übereinstimmung f (between zwischen, with mit).
(b) (letter-writing) Korrespondenz f; (letters also) Briefe pl; (in newspaper) Leserzuschriften or -briefe pl. to be in ~ with sb mit jdm in Korrespondenz stehen (form), mit jdm korrespondieren (private) mit jdm in Briefwechsel stehen, mit jdm korrespondieren (geh).
correspondence: ~ card n Briefkarte f; ~ column n (Press) Leserbriefspalte f; ~ course n Fernkurs m; ~ school n Fernlehrinstitut nt.
correspondent [kɒrɪsˈpɒndənt] 1 n (letter-writer) Briefschreiber(in f) m. to be a good/bad ~ ein eifriger Briefschreiber sein/schreibfaul sein; according to my ~ wie man mir geschrieben hat. (b) (Press) Korrespondent(in f) m.
(c) (Comm) Entsprechung f, Gegenstück n. 2 adj see corresponding.
corresponding [kɒrɪsˈpɒndɪŋ] adj entsprechend.
correspondingly [kɒrɪsˈpɒndɪŋlɪ] adv (dem)entsprechend.
corridor ['kɒrɪdɔː'] n Korridor m; (in building also) Gang m; (in train, bus) Gang m. in the ~s of power an den Schalthebeln der Macht; ~ train D-Zug m.

corrie ['kɒrɪ] n (Geol) Kar m.
corrigendum [kɒrɪ'dʒendəm] n, pl **corrigenda** [kɒrɪ'dʒendə] Corrigendum nt (geh).
corroborate [kə'rɒbəreɪt] vt bestätigen; theory also bekräftigen, erhärten, untermauern.
corroboration [kə,rɒbə'reɪʃən] n see vt Bestätigung f; Bekräftigung, Erhärtung, Untermauerung f. in ~ of zur Untermauerung or Unterstützung (+gen); lack of ~ (Jur) mangels unterstützenden Beweismaterials; (from witnesses) mangels bestätigender Zeugenaussagen.
corroborative [kə'rɒbərətɪv] adj see vt bestätigend; bekräftigend, erhärtend, untermauernd all attr. to be ~ of sth etw bestätigen/untermauern; for want of ~ evidence mangels unterstützenden Beweismaterials; (from witnesses) mangels bestätigender Zeugenaussagen.
corrode [kə'rəud] 1 vt metal zerfressen; (fig) zerstören. 2 vi (metal) korrodieren.
corrosion [kə'rəuʒən] n Korrosion f; (fig) Zerstörung f.
corrosive [kə'rəuzɪv] 1 adj korrosiv; (fig) zerstörend. 2 n Korrosion verursachendes Mittel.
corrugated ['kɒrəgeɪtɪd] adj gewellt. ~ **cardboard** dicke Wellpappe; ~ **iron** Wellblech nt; ~ **paper** Wellpappe f.
corrugation [,kɒrə'geɪʃən] n Welle f.
corrupt [kə'rʌpt] 1 adj verdorben, verworfen, schlecht; (open to bribery) korrupt, bestechlich; text, language verderbt, korrumpiert.
 2 vt (morally) verderben; (ethically) korrumpieren; (form: bribe) bestechen, korrumpieren. to become ~ed (text, language) verderbt or korrumpiert werden.
corruptible [kə'rʌptəbl] adj korrumpierbar; (bribable also) bestechlich.
corruption [kə'rʌpʃən] n (a) (act) (of person) Korruption f; (by bribery also) Bestechung f.
 (b) (corrupt nature) Verdorbenheit, Verderbtheit f; (by bribery) Bestechlichkeit f; (of morals) Verfall m; (of language, text) Verderbtheit, Korrumpierung f.
 (c) (form: decay of bodies etc) Zersetzung, Fäulnis f.
corsage [kɔː'sɑːʒ] n (a) (bodice) Mieder nt. (b) (flowers) Ansteckblume f.
corsair ['kɔːseəʳ] n (ship) Piratenschiff nt, Korsar m; (pirate) Pirat, Korsar m.
corselet [kɔːsə'let] n (a) (corset) Korselett nt. (b) see **corslet**.
corset ['kɔːsɪt] n (also ~s) Korsett nt; (to give wasp waist) Schnürmieder nt. surgical ~ Stützkorsett nt.
corseted ['kɔːsɪtɪd] adj geschnürt.
corsetry ['kɔːsɪtrɪ] n Miederwarenherstellung f; (corsets) Miederwaren pl. ~ **department** Miederwarenabteilung f.
Corsica ['kɔːsɪkə] n Korsika nt.
Corsican ['kɔːsɪkən] 1 adj korsisch. ~ **holiday** Urlaub auf Korsika. 2 n (a) Korse m, Korsin f. (b) (language) Korsisch nt.
corslet ['kɔːslɪt], **corselet** n Brust- (und Rücken)panzer m.
cortège [kɔː'teɪʒ] n (retinue) Gefolge nt; (procession) Prozession f; (funeral ~) Leichenzug m.
cortex ['kɔːteks] n, pl **cortices** (Anat) (of brain) Hirnrinde f; (of kidney) Nierenrinde f; (Bot) Kortex m.
cortical ['kɔːtɪkl] adj (Anat, Bot) kortikal.
cortices ['kɔːtɪsiːz] pl of **cortex**.
cortisone ['kɔːtɪzəun] n Kortison nt.
corundum [kə'rʌndəm] n (Geol) Korund m.
coruscate ['kɒrəskeɪt] vi funkeln. **coruscating** wit/humour (fig) sprühender Geist/Witz.
corvette [kɔː'vet] n (Naut) Korvette f.
cos¹ [kɒs] abbr of **cosine** cos.
cos² n (also ~ **lettuce**) Romagna-Salat, römischer Salat m.
cos³ conj (inf) = **because**.
cosec ['kəusek] abbr of **cosecant** cosec.
cosecant ['kəusekænt] n Kosekans m.
cosh [kɒʃ] 1 vt auf den Schädel schlagen, eins über den Schädel ziehen (+dat) (inf). 2 n (instrument) Totschläger m; (blow) Schlag m (auf den Kopf).
cosignatory ['kəu'sɪgnətərɪ] n Mitunterzeichner(in f) m.
cosine ['kəusaɪn] n Kosinus m.
cosiness, (US) **coziness** ['kəuzɪnɪs] n Gemütlichkeit, Behaglichkeit f; (warmth) mollige Wärme; (of chat) Freundschaftlichkeit, Traulichkeit (dated) f.
cosmetic [kɒz'metɪk] 1 adj kosmetisch. ~ **surgery** kosmetische Chirurgie; she's had ~ surgery sie hat eine Schönheitsoperation gehabt. 2 n Kosmetikum, Schönheitspflegemittel nt.
cosmetician [kɒzmə'tɪʃən] n Kosmetiker(in f) m.
cosmic ['kɒzmɪk] adj kosmisch. ~ **dust** Weltraumnebel m.
cosmogony [kɒz'mɒgənɪ] n Kosmogonie f.
cosmography [kɒz'mɒgrəfɪ] n Kosmographie f.
cosmology [kɒz'mɒlədʒɪ] n Kosmologie f.
cosmonaut ['kɒzmənɔːt] n Kosmonaut(in f) m.
cosmopolitan [,kɒzmə'pɒlɪtən] 1 adj kosmopolitisch, international. 2 n Kosmopolit, Weltbürger m.
cosmos ['kɒzmɒs] n (a) Kosmos m. (b) (Bot) Kosmee f.
cossack ['kɒsæk] 1 n Kosak(in f) m. 2 adj Kosaken-. ~ **hat** Kosakenmütze f.
cosset ['kɒsɪt] vt verwöhnen.
cost [kɒst] (vb: pret, ptp ~) 1 vt (a) (lit, fig) kosten. how much does it ~? wieviel kostet es?; how much will it ~ to have it repaired? wieviel kostet die Reparatur?; it ~ (him) a lot of money das hat (ihn) viel Geld gekostet; driving without a seat belt ~ him dear Fahren ohne Sicherheitsgurt kam ihn teuer zu stehen; it ~ him a great effort/a lot of time es kostete ihn viel Mühe/viel Zeit; that mistake could ~ you your life der Fehler könnte dich das Leben kosten; ~ what it may koste es, was es wolle; politeness doesn't ~ (you) anything es kostet (dich) nichts, höflich zu sein; it'll ~ you (inf) das kostet dich was (inf).

 (b) (Comm: put a price on) pret, ptp ~ed articles for sale auspreisen (at zu); piece of work veranschlagen (at mit).
 2 n (a) Kosten pl (of für). to bear the ~ of sth die Kosten für etw tragen, für die Kosten für etw aufkommen; the ~ of electricity/petrol these days die Strom-/Benzinpreise heutzutage; to buy sth at great ~ etw zu einem hohen Kosten kaufen; at little ~ to oneself ohne viele eigene Kosten; to buy sth ~ etw zum Selbstkostenpreis kaufen.
 (b) (fig) Preis m. at all ~s um jeden Preis; whatever the ~ kostet es, was es wolle; at the ~ of one's health/job/marriage etc auf Kosten seiner Gesundheit/Stelle/Ehe etc; at great/little personal ~ unter großen/geringen eigenen Kosten; he found out to his ~ that ... er machte die bittere Erfahrung, daß ...
 (c) (Jur) ~s pl Kosten pl; to be ordered to pay ~s zur Übernahme der Kosten verurteilt werden.
Costa Brava ['kɒstə'brɑːvə] n Costa Brava f.
cost: ~ **accountant** n Kostenbuchhalter(in f) m; ~ **accounting** n Kalkulation f; (department) Kostenbuchhaltung f, betriebliches Rechnungswesen.
Costa del Sol ['kɒstədel'sɒl] n Costa del Sol f.
co-star ['kəustɑːʳ] 1 n (Film, Theat) einer der Hauptdarsteller. Burton and Taylor were ~s Burton und Taylor spielten die Hauptrollen. 2 vt the film ~s R. Burton der Film zeigt R. Burton in einer der Hauptrollen. 3 vi als Hauptdarsteller auftreten.
Costa Rica ['kɒstə'riːkə] n Costa Rica nt.
Costa Rican ['kɒstə'riːkən] 1 adj costaricanisch. 2 n Costaricaner(in f) m.
cost: ~ **clerk** n Angestellte(r) mf in der Kostenbuchhaltung; ~-**effective** adj rentabel.
coster(monger) ['kɒstə(,mʌŋgəʳ)] n (Brit) Straßenhändler m.
costing ['kɒstɪŋ] n Kalkulation f. ~ **department** Kostenbuchhaltung f, betriebliches Rechnungswesen.
costive ['kɒstɪv] adj (form) (constipated) verstopft; (constipating) verstopfend.
costliness ['kɒstlɪnɪs] n Kostspieligkeit f; (in business, industry) hoher Kostenaufwand. the ~ of buying a new car die mit dem Kauf eines neuen Wagens verbundenen hohen Kosten.
costly ['kɒstlɪ] adj teuer, kostspielig; tastes, habits teuer. ~ in terms of time/labour zeitaufwendig/arbeitsintensiv.
cost: ~ **of living** n Lebenshaltungskosten pl; ~-**of-living bonus** n Lebenshaltungskostenzuschlag m; ~-**of-living index** n Lebenshaltungskostenindex m; ~ **price** n Selbstkostenpreis m.
costume ['kɒstjuːm] n Kostüm nt; (bathing ~) Badeanzug m. national ~ Nationaltracht f.
costume: ~ **ball** n Kostümfest nt; ~ **jewellery** n Modeschmuck m; ~ **piece**, ~ **play** n Schauspiel nt in historischen Kostümen; ~ **ring** n Modeschmuckring m.
costumier [kɒs'tjuːmɪəʳ], (US) **costumer** [kɒs'tjuːməʳ] n (a) (theatrical ~) Kostümverleih m. (b) (form: dressmaker) Schneider(in f) m.
cosy, (US) **cozy** ['kəuzɪ] 1 adj (+er) room, atmosphere gemütlich, behaglich; (warm) mollig warm; (fig) chat gemütlich, traulich (dated). to feel ~ (person) sich wohl und behaglich fühlen; (room etc) einen behaglichen or gemütlichen Eindruck machen; I'm very ~ here ich fühle mich hier sehr wohl, ich finde es hier sehr gemütlich; a ~ little tête-à-tête (fig) ein trautes Tête-à-Tête; warm and ~ mollig warm.
 2 n (tea ~, egg ~) Wärmer m.
cot [kɒt] n (esp Brit: child's bed) Kinderbett nt; (US: camp bed) Feldbett nt. ~ **death** bis jetzt unerklärtes Säuglingssterben.
cote [kəut] n (dove~) Taubenschlag m; (sheep~) Schafstall m.
coterie ['kəutərɪ] n Clique f; (literary ~) Zirkel m.
cotill(i)on [kə'tɪljən] n Kotillon m.
cotta ['kɒtə] n (Eccl) Chorhemd nt.
cottage ['kɒtɪdʒ] n Cottage, Häuschen nt; (US: in institution) Wohneinheit f.
cottage: ~ **cheese** n Hüttenkäse m; ~ **hospital** n (Brit) kleines Krankenhaus für leichtere Fälle; ~ **industry** n Manufaktur, Heimindustrie f; ~ **loaf** n (Brit) eine Art rundes, hohes Weißbrot; ~ **pie** n Hackfleisch mit Kartoffelbrei überbacken.
cottager ['kɒtɪdʒəʳ] n (Brit) Cottage-Bewohner(in f) m.
cotter (pin) ['kɒtə(,pɪn)] n Splint m.
cotton ['kɒtn] 1 n Baumwolle f; (plant) Baumwollstrauch m; (fibre) Baumwollfaser f; (fabric) Baumwollstoff m; (sewing thread) Baumwoll)garn nt. absorbent ~ (US) Watte f. 2 adj Baumwoll-, baumwollen; clothes, fabric also aus Baumwolle.
♦**cotton on** vi (inf) es kapieren (inf), es schnallen (sl). has he ~ed ~ yet? hat er es endlich kapiert (inf) or geschnallt? (sl).
♦**cotton to** vi +prep obj (inf) plan, suggestion gut finden.
cotton in cpds Baumwoll-; ~ **batting** n (US) Gaze f; ~ **cake** n Futtermittel nt; ~ **candy** n (US) Zuckerwatte f; ~ **gin** n Entkörnungsmaschine f (für Baumwolle); ~ **grass** n Wollgras nt; ~ **mill** n Baumwollspinnerei f; ~-**picker** n (person) Baumwollpflücker(in f) m; (machine) Baumwoll-Pflückmaschine f; ~-**picking** adj (US inf) verdammt (inf), verflucht (inf); ~ **plant** n Baumwollstaude f or -strauch m; ~ **print** n (fabric) bedruckter Baumwollstoff; ~**seed** n Baumwollsamen m; ~**seed cake** n see ~ **cake**; ~**seed oil** n Baumwollsamenöl nt; ~**tail** n (US) Kaninchen, Karnickel nt; ~**wood** n Pyramidenpappel f; ~**wool** n (Brit) Watte f; to bring a child up in ~**wool** (fig) ein Kind wohlbehütet aufwachsen lassen; to wrap sb in ~**wool** (fig) jdn in Watte packen; my legs feel like ~**wool** meine Beine sind wie Butter.
cotyledon [,kɒtɪ'liːdən] n Keimblatt nt.
couch [kautʃ] 1 n (sofa) Sofa nt; (studio ~) Schlafcouch f; (doctor's ~) Liege f; (psychiatrist's ~) Couch f; (poet: bed) Lager nt.
 2 vt (a) (put in words) request, reply formulieren, abfassen.
 (b) (lower) spear, lance anlegen.
 3 vi (liter: lion, cat etc) lauern, auf der Lauer liegen.
couchant ['kuːʃənt] adj (Her) liegend.

couchette [kuːʃet] n (Rail) Liegewagen(platz) m.

couchgrass [kautʃgraːs] n Quecke f.

cougar [kuːgəʳ] n Puma, Kuguar m.

cough [kɒf] **1** n Husten m. **to give a warning ~** sich warnend räuspern; **to clear one's throat with a loud ~** sich laut or vernehmlich räuspern; **a smoker's ~** Raucherhusten m. **2** vi husten. **3** vt blood husten.

♦ **cough out** vt sep aushusten, ausspucken.

♦ **cough up 1** vt sep (lit) aushusten. **2** vt insep (fig inf) money rausrücken (inf), ausspucken (sl), rüberkommen mit (sl). **3** vi (fig inf) rausrücken (inf), ausspucken (sl), rüberkommen (sl).

cough: ~ **drop** n Hustenpastille f; ~ **mixture** n Hustensaft m or -mittel nt; ~ **sweet** n Hustenbonbon nt.

could [kud] pret of **can¹**.

couldn't [ˈkudnt] contr of **could** or **could not**.

council [ˈkaunsl] **1** n (a) (body of representatives) Rat m; (meeting) Sitzung, Beratung f. **city/town ~** Stadtrat m; **to be on the ~** im Rat sitzen, Ratsmitglied sein; **to hold ~** Beratungen abhalten, Rat halten (old); ~ **of war** Kriegsrat m.
2 attr estate (of the sozialen Wohnungsbaus. ~ **house/housing** (Brit) Sozialwohnung f/sozialer Wohnungsbau; ~ **chamber** Sitzungssaal m des Rats; ~ **meeting** Ratssitzung f.

councillor, (US) **councilor** [ˈkaunsələʳ] n Ratsmitglied nt; (town) Stadtrat m/-rätin f. ~ **Smith** Herr Stadtrat/Frau Stadträtin Schmidt.

counsel [ˈkaunsəl] **1** n (a) (form: advice) Rat(schlag) m. **to hold ~ with sb/take ~ of sb over or about sth** mit jdm etw beraten or beratschlagen/jds Rat zu etw befolgen; **he held ~ with his partner about the wisdom of selling out** er beratschlagte mit seinem Partner, ob es ratsam sei zu verkaufen; **to keep one's own ~** seine Meinung für sich behalten, mit seiner Meinung zurückhalten; ~ **of perfection** schlaue Ratschläge.
(b) pl - (Jur) Rechtsanwalt m. ~ **for the defence/prosecution** Verteidiger(in f) m/Vertreter(in f) m der Anklage, ≈ Staatsanwalt m/-anwältin f; ~ **on both sides** Verteidigung and Anklage.
2 vt (form) person beraten; course of action empfehlen, raten zu. **to ~ sb to do sth** jdm raten or empfehlen, etw zu tun.

counsellor, (US) **counselor** [ˈkaunsələʳ] n (a) (adviser) Berater(in f) m. **(b)** (US, Ir: lawyer) Rechtsanwalt m/-anwältin f.

count¹ [kaunt] **1** n (a) (of votes) Zählung f; (Sport) Auszählen nt; (of votes) (Stimmen)zählung, (Stimmen)auszählung f. **I'll have a ~** ich zähle es mal (ab); **she lost ~ when she was interrupted** sie kam mit dem Zählen durcheinander, als sie unterbrochen wurde; **I've lost all ~ of her boyfriends** ich habe die Übersicht über ihre Freunde vollkommen verloren; **to keep ~ (of sth)** (etw) mitzählen; (keep track) die Übersicht über etw (acc) behalten; **she couldn't keep ~ of them** sie verlor die Übersicht; **at the last ~ there were twenty members** bei der letzten Zählung waren es zwanzig Mitglieder; **all together now, on the ~ of three** und jetzt alle zusammen, bei drei geht's los; **he was out for the ~, he took the ~** (Sport) er wurde ausgezählt; (fig) er war k.o.; **he took a ~ of eight** (Sport) er ging bis acht zu Boden.
(b) (Jur: charge) Anklagepunkt m. **on that ~** (fig) in dem Punkt; **on all ~s** in jeder Hinsicht.
(c) no pl (notice) **don't take any ~ of what he says** hören Sie nicht auf das, was er sagt; **she never takes much/any ~ of him** sie nimmt wenig/keine Notiz von ihm.
2 vt (a) (ab)zählen; (~ again) nachzählen; votes (aus)zählen. **to ~ ten** bis zehn zählen; **I only ~ed ten people** ich habe nur zehn Leute gezählt; **to ~ the cost** (lit) auf die Kosten achten, jeden Pfennig umdrehen; **she'll help anyone without ~ing the cost to herself** sie hilft jedem, ohne an sich selbst zu denken.
(b) (consider) ansehen, betrachten; (include) mitrechnen, mitzählen. **to ~ sb (as) a friend/among one's friends** jdn als Freund ansehen/zu seinen Freunden zählen; **you should ~ yourself lucky** to be alive after that crash Sie sollten froh and glücklich sein or Sie können noch von Glück sagen, daß Sie den Unfall überlebt haben; **ten people ~ing/not ~ing the children** zehn Leute, die Kinder mitgerechnet or eingerechnet/nicht mitgerechnet or eingerechnet; **to ~ sth against sb** etw gegen jdn sprechen lassen or anrechnen.
3 vi (a) zählen. ~**ing from today** von heute an (gerechnet).
(b) (be considered) betrachtet or angesehen werden; (be included) mitgerechnet or mitgezählt werden; (be important) wichtig sein. **he ~s as a hero in some countries** in einigen Ländern wird er als Held betrachtet or angesehen; **the children don't ~** die Kinder zählen nicht; **he doesn't ~ amongst her friends** er zählt nicht zu ihren Freunden; **that doesn't ~** das zählt nicht; **every minute/it all ~s** jede Minute ist/das ist alles wichtig; **appearance ~s a lot** es kommt sehr auf die äußere Erscheinung an; **to ~ against sb** gegen jdn sprechen.

♦ **count down 1** vi den Countdown durchführen. **they started ~ing** ~ last night sie haben gestern abend mit dem Countdown angefangen; **to ~ ~ to blast-off** bis zum Abschuß (der Rakete) rückwärts zählen. **2** vt sep **to ~ a rocket ~** den Countdown (für eine Rakete) durchführen.

♦ **count for** vi +prep obj **to ~ ~ a lot** sehr viel bedeuten; **to ~ ~ nothing** nichts gelten.

♦ **count in** vt sep mitzählen; person also mitrechnen, berücksichtigen, einplanen. **to ~ sb ~ on an undertaking** davon ausgehen or damit rechnen, daß jd bei einem Unternehmen mitmacht; **you can ~ me ~!** Sie können mit mir rechnen, da mache ich mit, da bin ich dabei.

♦ **count off** vt sep, vi abzählen.

♦ **count on** vi +prep obj (depend on) rechnen mit, sich verlassen auf (+acc). **to ~ ~ doing sth** die Absicht haben, etw zu tun; **to ~ being able to do sth** damit rechnen, etw tun zu können; **you can ~ ~ him to help you** du kannst auf seine Hilfe zählen.

♦ **count out** vt sep (a) (Sport) auszählen. **(b)** money, books etc abzählen. **(c)** (Brit Parl) **to ~ the House ~** eine Sitzung des Unterhauses wegen zu geringer Abgeordnetenzahl vertagen.

(d) (inf: exclude) (you can) ~ me ~ (of that)! ohne mich!, da mache ich nicht mit!; ~ **him ~ of it** plane ihn besser nicht ein.

♦ **count up** vt sep zusammenzählen or -rechnen.

♦ **count upon** vi +prep obj see **count on**.

count² n Graf m.

countable [ˈkauntəbl] adj zählbar (also Gram).

countdown [ˈkauntdaun] n Countdown m. **to start the ~** mit dem Countdown beginnen.

countenance [ˈkauntinəns] **1** n (a) (old, form: face) Angesicht (old, Eccl), Antlitz (old) nt; (expression) Gesichtsausdruck m. **to keep one's ~** (fig) die Fassung or Haltung bewahren; **to lose ~** (fig) das Gesicht verlieren; **to put sb out of ~** jdn aus der Fassung bringen. **(b)** (support) **to give/lend ~ to sth** etw ermutigen/unterstützen. **2** vt behaviour gutheißen; plan, suggestion also, person unterstützen.

counter [ˈkauntəʳ] **1** n (a) (in shop) Ladentisch, Tresen (N Ger) m; (in café) Theke f; (in bank, post office) Schalter m. **to sell/buy sth under/over the ~** etw unter dem/über den Ladentisch verkaufen/bekommen; **medicines which can be bought over the ~** Medikamente, die man rezeptfrei bekommt; **under-the-~ dealings** (fig) Kungeleien pl (inf), dunkle or undurchsichtige Geschäfte, Schiebereien pl.
(b) (small disc for games) Spielmarke f.
(c) (Tech) Zähler m.
(d) (Sport) Parade f; (Boxing also) Konter m.
(e) (reply) Entgegnung, Erwiderung, Replik (geh) f.
2 vt (retaliate against) antworten auf (+acc), kontern (also Sport). **how dare you ~ my orders!** (countermand) wie können Sie es wagen, meine Anweisungen or (Mil) Befehle aufzuheben; **he ~ed my decision by pointing out that it was impractical** er wandte sich gegen meine Entscheidung mit dem Argument, sie sei undurchführbar; **to ~ the loss** den Verlust wettmachen or ausgleichen.
3 vi kontern (also Sport).
4 adv ~ **to** gegen (+acc); **to go or run ~ to sb's wishes** jds Wünschen (dat) zuwiderlaufen; **the results are running ~ to everyone's expectations** die Ergebnisse widersprechen den Erwartungen aller.

counter: ~**act** vt (make ineffective) neutralisieren; (act in opposition to) entgegenwirken (+dat); disease bekämpfen; ~**action** n see vt Neutralisierung f; Gegenwirkung f; Bekämpfung f; ~**active** adj entgegenwirkend, Gegen-; ~**active measures** Gegenmaßnahmen pl; ~**attack 1** n Gegenangriff m; **2** vt einen Gegenangriff starten gegen; (argue against) kontern, beantworten; **3** vi einen Gegenangriff starten, zurückschlagen; ~**attraction** n Gegenattraktion f (to zu); (on TV etc) Konkurrenzprogramm nt; ~**balance 1** n Gegengewicht nt; **2** vt ausgleichen; ~**charge** n (a) (Jur) Gegenklage f; **(b)** (Mil) Gegenattacke f; ~**check** n Gegenkontrolle f; ~**claim** n (Jur) Gegenanspruch m; ~**clerk** n (in bank, booking office etc) Angestellte(r) mf im Schalterdienst; (in post office etc) Schalterbeamte(r) m/-beamtin f; ~**clockwise** adj, adv (US) see anti-clockwise; ~**espionage** n Gegenspionage, Spionageabwehr f; ~**example** n Gegenbeispiel nt.

counterfeit [ˈkauntəfiːt] **1** adj gefälscht; (fig) falsch. ~ **money/coin** Falschgeld nt. **2** n Fälschung f. **3** vt fälschen; (fig) vortäuschen.

counterfoil [ˈkauntəfɔil] n Kontrollabschnitt m.

counter: ~**intelligence** n see ~espionage; ~**irritant** n (Med) Gegenreizmittel nt; ~**jumper** n (US sl) Ladenschwengel m (hum), Verkäuferin f.

countermand [kauntəˈmɑːnd] vt order aufheben, widerrufen; attack, plan rückgängig machen. **unless ~ed** bis auf gegenteilige Anweisung or (Mil) Order.

counter: ~**march** (Mil) **1** n Rückmarsch m; **2** vi zurückmarschieren; ~**offensive** n (Mil) Gegenoffensive f; ~-**offer** n Gegenangebot nt; ~-**pane** n Tagesdecke f; ~**part** n (equivalent) Gegenüber nt; (complement) Gegenstück, Pendant nt; ~**plot 1** n Gegenanschlag m; **2** vi einen Gegenanschlag planen; ~**point** n (Mus) Kontrapunkt m; ~**poise 1** n (a) (weight) Gegengewicht nt; (force, fig) Gegenkraft f; **(b)** no pl (equilibrium, fig) Gleichgewicht nt; **to be in ~poise** im Gleichgewicht sein; **2** vt (lit, fig) ausgleichen; ~-**productive** adj unsinnig, widersinnig; criticism, measures, policies destruktiv; **that wouldn't help us at all, in fact it would be ~productive** das würde uns nicht weiterbringen, sondern sogar das Gegenteil bewirken; C~**Reformation** n (Hist) Gegenreformation f; ~**revolution** n Gegen- or Konterrevolution f; ~**revolutionary** adj konterrevolutionär; ~**shaft** n (Tech) Vorgelegewelle f; ~**sign 1** n (Mil) Parole f, Kennwort nt; **2** vt cheque etc gegenzeichnen; ~**signature** n Gegenunterschrift f; ~**sink 1** n (tool) Versenker, Spitzsenker m; **2** vt hole senken; screw versenken; ~**tenor** n (Mus) Kontratenor m; ~**weight** n Gegengewicht nt.

countess [ˈkauntis] n Gräfin f.

counting house [ˈkauntiŋhaus] n (old) Kontor nt.

countless [ˈkauntlis] adj unzählig attr, zahllos attr.

count palatine n, pl -s - Pfalzgraf m.

countrified [ˈkʌntrifaid] adj ländlich, bäuerlich, bäu(e)risch (pej).

country [ˈkʌntri] n (a) (state) Land nt; (people also) Volk nt. **his own ~** seine Heimat; **to die for one's ~** für sein Land sterben; **to go to the ~** Neuwahlen ausschreiben.
(b) no pl (as opposed to town) Land nt; (scenery, countryside also) Landschaft f. **in/to the ~** auf dem/aufs Land; **the surrounding ~** das umliegende Land, die Umgebung; **this is good hunting/fishing ~** das ist eine gute Jagd-/Fischgegend; **this is mining ~** dies ist ein Bergbaugebiet; **we're back in familiar ~ again** (fig) wir befinden uns wieder auf vertrautem Boden; **this subject is new ~ to me** das ist Neuland für mich.

country in cpds Land-; ~-**and-western 1** n Country- und Westernmusik f; **2** adj Country- und Western-; ~-**born** adj auf dem Land geboren; **~-bred** adj auf dem Land aufgewachsen; animals auf dem Land gezogen; **~ bumpkin** n (pej) Bauerntölpel (inf), Bauer (pej inf) m; (girl) Bauerntrampel f (inf); **~ club** n Klub m auf dem Lande; **~ cousin** n Vetter m/Base f vom Lande; **~ dance** n Volkstanz m; **~ dancing** n Volkstanz m; to go **~ dancing** zum Volkstanz gehen; **~ dweller** n Landbewohner(in f) m; **~ folk** npl Leute pl vom Lande; **~ gentleman** n Landbesitzer m; **~ gentry** npl Landadel m; **~ house** n Landhaus nt; **~ life** n das Landleben, das Leben auf dem Lande; **~man** n (a) (landsman) Landsmann m; his fellow **~men** seine Landsleute; (b) (country-dweller) **~ people** npl Leute pl vom Land(e); **~ road** n Landstraße f; **~ seat** n Landsitz m; **~side** n (scenery) Landschaft, Gegend f; (rural area) Land nt; it's beautiful **~side** das ist eine herrliche Landschaft or Gegend; to live in the middle of the **~side** mitten auf dem Land leben; **~ town** n Kleinstadt f; **~-wide** adj landesweit, im ganzen Land; **~woman** n (a) (landswoman) Landsmännin f; (b) (country-dweller) Landfrau f.

county ['kauntɪ] **1** n (Brit) Grafschaft f; (US) (Verwaltungs)bezirk m. **2** adj (Brit) family zum Landadel gehörend; accent, behaviour vornehm; occasion für den Landadel.

county: **~ borough** n (Brit) Stadt f mit grafschaftlichen Rechten; **~ council** n (Brit) Grafschaftsrat m; **~ court** n (Brit) Grafschaftsgericht nt; **~ seat** n (US) Hauptstadt f eines Verwaltungsbezirkes; **~ town** n (Brit) Hauptstadt f einer Grafschaft.

coup [kuː] n (a) (successful action) Coup m. (b) (~ d'état) Staatsstreich, Coup d'Etat m.

coup: **~ de grâce** n (lit, fig) Gnadenstoß m; (with gun) Gnadenschuß m; **~ d'état** n see coup (b).

coupé ['kuːpeɪ] n (car) Coupé m.

couple ['kʌpl] **1** n (a) (pair) Paar nt; (married ~) Ehepaar nt. courting **~s** Liebespaare pl; the happy **~** das glückliche Paar; in **~s** paarweise. (b) (inf) a **~** (two) zwei; (several) ein paar, einige; a **~** of letters/friends etc ein paar or einige Briefe/Freunde etc; we had a **~** in the pub wir haben in der Kneipe ein paar getrunken; a **~** of times ein paarmal; it only took a **~** of minutes/hours es hat nur einige or ein paar Minuten/ungefähr zwei Stunden gedauert. **2** vt (a) (link) names, ideas etc verbinden, in Verbindung bringen; carriages etc koppeln; circuit verbinden. (b) (mate) animals paaren. **3** vi (mate) sich paaren.

♦ **couple on** vt sep anhängen.

♦ **couple up** vt sep ankoppeln.

couplet ['kʌplɪt] n Verspaar nt. rhyming **~** Reimpaar nt.

coupling ['kʌplɪŋ] n (a) (linking) Verbindung f; (of carriages etc) Kopplung f. the continual **~** of his name with ... daß sein Name ständig mit ... in Verbindung gebracht wird/wurde. (b) (mating) Paarung f. (c) (linking device) Kupplung f.

coupon ['kuːpɒn] n (a) (voucher) Gutschein m; (ration ~) (Zuteilungs)schein m. (b) (Ftbl) Totoschein, Wettschein m. (c) (Fin) Kupon m.

courage ['kʌrɪdʒ] n Mut m, Courage f (inf). I haven't the **~** to refuse ich habe einfach nicht den Mut, nein zu sagen; take **~**! (liter) nur Mut!; to take **~** from sth sich durch etw ermutigt fühlen; to lose one's **~** den Mut verlieren; to have/lack the **~** of one's convictions Zivilcourage/keine Zivilcourage haben; to take one's **~** in both hands sein Herz in beide Hände nehmen.

courageous [kə'reɪdʒəs] adj mutig; (with courage of convictions) couragiert (inf).

courageously [kə'reɪdʒəslɪ] adv see adj.

courgette ['kuːʒet] n (Brit) Zucchino m usu pl.

courier ['kʊrɪə^r] n (messenger) Kurier m; (tourist guide) Reiseleiter(in f) m.

course[1] [kɔːs] n (a) (direction, path) (of plane, ship) Kurs m; (of river) Lauf m; (fig) (of illness, relationship) Verlauf m; (of history) Lauf m; (of action, way of proceeding) Vorgehensweise f. to set (one's) **~** for or towards a place Kurs auf einen Ort nehmen; to change or alter **~** den Kurs wechseln or ändern; to be on/off **~** auf Kurs sein/vom Kurs abgekommen sein; to let sth take or run its **~** etw (dat) seinen Lauf nehmen lassen; the affair has run its **~** die Angelegenheit ist zu einem Ende gekommen; the **~** of true love ne'er did run smooth (prov) Liebe geht oft seltsame Wege (prov); which **~** of action did you take? wie sind Sie vorgegangen?; that was an unwise **~** (of action) es war unklug, so vorzugehen; the best **~** (of action) would be ... das beste wäre ...; we have no other **~** (of action) but to ... es bleibt uns nichts anderes übrig als zu ...; to take a middle **~** einen gemäßigten Kurs einschlagen; he took or chose the **~** of moving before finding a new position er zog um, bevor er eine neue Stelle hatte; see matter. (b) in the **~** of his life/the next few weeks/the meeting etc während seines Lebens/der nächsten paar Wochen/der Versammlung etc; in the **~** of time/the conversation im Laufe der Zeit/Unterhaltung; it's in the **~** of being done es wird gerade gemacht; in the **~** of shaving/washing the car beim Rasieren/Wagenwaschen; in the ordinary **~** of things, you could expect ... unter normalen Umständen könnte man erwarten ...; things like that are quite in the ordinary **~** of things so etwas ist doch völlig normal; to be in the **~** of nature in der Natur der Sache liegen; see due. (c) of **~** (admittedly) natürlich; (naturally, obviously also) selbstverständlich; of **~**! natürlich!, selbstverständlich!, klar! (inf); of **~** I will! aber natürlich or selbstverständlich!; of **~** I'm coming natürlich or selbstverständlich komme ich, klar, ich komme (inf); don't you like me? — of **~** I do magst du mich nicht? — doch, natürlich; he's rather young, of **~**, but ... er ist natürlich ziemlich jung, aber ... (d) (organized programme) (Sch, Univ) Kurs(us) m; (at work)

Lehrgang m; (Med: of treatment) Kur f. to go to/on a French **~** einen Französischkurs(us) besuchen; a **~** on/in first aid ein Kurs über Erste Hilfe/ein Erste-Hilfe-Kurs; a **~** of lectures, a **lecture** **~** eine Vorlesungsreihe; a **~** of pills/treatment eine Pillenkur/eine Behandlung.

(e) (Sports) (race **~**) Kurs m; (golf **~**) Platz m. to stay or last the **~** (lit) das Rennen durchhalten; (fig) bis zum Ende durchhalten.

(f) (Cook) Gang m. first/main **~** erster Gang/Hauptgericht nt; a three-**~** meal ein Essen mit drei Gängen.

(g) (Build) Schicht f.

(h) (Naut: sail) Untersegel nt.

course[2] **1** vt (Hunt) hare, stag hetzen, jagen. **2** vi (a) (blood, tears) strömen. (b) (Hunt, fig) hetzen, jagen. to go coursing auf Hetzjagd gehen.

courser ['kɔːsə^r] n (a) (dog) Hatz- or Hetzhund m. (b) (poet: horse) (schnelles) Roß (liter).

coursing ['kɔːsɪŋ] n (Sport) Hetzjagd, Hatz, Hetze f.

court [kɔːt] **1** n (a) (Jur) (also **~ of justice or law**) Gericht nt; (body of judges also) Gerichtshof m; (room) Gerichtssaal m. **~ of Session** (Scot) höchstes schottisches Zivilgericht; to appear in **~** vor Gericht erscheinen; the evidence was ruled out of **~** das Beweismaterial wurde nicht zugelassen; his suggestion was ruled out of **~** (fig) sein Vorschlag wurde verworfen; to take sb to **~** jdn verklagen or vor Gericht bringen; to go to **~** over a matter eine Sache vor Gericht bringen, mit einer Sache vor Gericht gehen; the case comes up in **~** next week der Fall wird nächste Woche verhandelt; Sir James is still in **~** Sir James ist noch beim Gericht; see settle.

(b) (royal) Hof m. to be presented at **~** bei Hofe vorgestellt werden; the C**~** of St James der englische Königshof.

(c) (Sport) Platz m; (for squash) Halle f; (marked-off area) Spielfeld nt; (service **~** etc) Feld nt. grass/hard **~** Rasen-/Hartplatz m; on **~** auf dem Platz/in der Halle; out of the **~** außerhalb des Spielfeldes.

(d) (**~yard**, Univ: quadrangle) Hof m. inner **~** Innenhof m.

(e) (old form: courtship) Hof m. to pay **~** to a woman einer Frau (dat) den Hof machen.

2 vt (a) (dated) woman umwerben, werben um, den Hof machen (+dat).

(b) (fig) person's favour werben um, buhlen um (pej); applause sich bemühen um; danger, defeat herausfordern.

3 vi (dated) (man) auf Freiersfüßen gehen (dated, hum). they were **~ing** at the time zu der Zeit gingen sie zusammen; she's **~ing** sie hat einen Freund; are you **~ing**? hast du jemanden?

court: **~ card** n (Brit) Bildkarte f; **~ circular** n Hofnachrichten pl; **~ dress** n Hoftracht f.

courteous adj, **~ly** adv ['kɜːtɪəs, -lɪ] höflich.

courtesan [ˌkɔːtɪ'zæn] n Kurtisane f.

courtesy ['kɜːtɪsɪ] n Höflichkeit f. by **~** of freundlicherweise zur Verfügung gestellt von; would you do me the **~** of shutting up! würden Sie mir den Gefallen tun und den Mund halten!

courtesy: **~ coach** n gebührenfreier Bus; Hotelbus m; **~ light** n (Aut) Innenleuchte f; **~ title** n Höflichkeitstitel m; **~ visit** n Höflichkeitsbesuch m.

court: **~ guide** n Hofkalender m; **~ house** n (Jur) Gerichtsgebäude nt.

courtier ['kɔːtɪə^r] n Höfling m.

courtliness ['kɔːtlɪnɪs] n see adj Höflichkeit f; Vornehmheit f.

courtly ['kɔːtlɪ] adj manners höflich; grace, elegance vornehm. **~ love** Minne f.

court: **~-martial** **1** n, pl **~-martials** or **~s-martial** (Mil) Kriegsgericht nt; to be tried by **~-martial** vor das/ein Kriegsgericht gestellt werden or kommen; **2** vt vor das/ein Kriegsgericht stellen (for wegen); **~room** n (Jur) Gerichtssaal m.

courtship ['kɔːtʃɪp] n (dated) (Braut)werbung f (dated) (of um). during their **~** während er um sie warb or freite (dated); their **~** lasted several years er umwarb sie mehrere Jahre.

court: **~ shoe** n Pumps m; **~ tennis** n (US) Tennis nt; **~yard** n Hof m.

cousin ['kʌzn] n (male) Cousin, Vetter (dated) m; (female) Cousine, Kusine, Base (old) f. Kevin and Susan are **~s** Kevin und Susan sind Cousin und Cousine.

cousinly ['kʌznlɪ] adj verwandtschaftlich.

couture [kuː'tjʊə^r] n Couture f.

couturier [kuː'tjʊərɪə^r] n Couturier m.

cove[1] [kəuv] n (Geog) (kleine) Bucht.

cove[2] n (dated Brit inf: fellow) Kerl m (inf). queer or odd **~** komischer Kauz.

coven ['kʌvn] n Hexenzirkel m; (meeting) Hexensabbat m.

covenant ['kʌvɪnənt] **1** n Schwur m; (Bibl) Bund m; (Jur) Verpflichtung f zu regelmäßigen Spenden. to swear a solemn **~** ... feierlich schwören, daß ... **2** vt to **~** to do sth durch ein Abkommen versprechen, etw zu tun; (Jur) sich vertraglich verpflichten, etw zu tun. **3** vi ein Abkommen/einen Bund schließen.

Coventry ['kɒvəntrɪ] n: to send sb to **~** (Brit inf) jdn schneiden (inf).

cover ['kʌvə^r] **1** n (a) (lid) Deckel m; (of lens) (Schutz)kappe f; (loose **~**: on chair etc) Bezug m; (cloth: for typewriter, umbrella etc) Hülle f; (on lorries, tennis court) Plane f; (sheet: over merchandise, shop counter) Decke f, Tuch nt; (blanket, quilt) (Bett)decke f. the shop assistants put the **~s** on die Verkäufer(innen) deckten die Waren zu; he put a **~** over her/it er deckte sie/es zu.

(b) (of book) Einband m; (of magazine) Umschlag m; (dust ~) (Schutz)umschlag m. to read a book from **~** to **~** ein Buch von Anfang bis Ende or von der ersten bis zur letzten Seite lesen; on the **~** auf dem Einband/Umschlag; (of magazine) auf der Titelseite, auf dem Titel(blatt).

(c) (Comm: envelope) Umschlag m. under separate **~** ge-

trennt; **under plain ~ in** neutralem Umschlag.
(d) *no pl* (*shelter, protection*) Schutz *m* (*from* vor +*dat*, gegen); (*Mil*) Deckung *f* (*from* vor +*dat*, gegen). **to take ~** (*from rain*) sich unterstellen, Schutz suchen (*from* vor +*dat*); (*Mil*) in Deckung gehen (*from* vor +*dat*); **under the ~ of the trees/rocks** im Schutz der Bäume/Felsen; **these plants/the car should be kept under ~ in the winter** diese Pflanzen sollten/das Auto sollte im Winter abgedeckt sein *or* (*under roof*) durch ein Dach geschützt sein; **to get oneself under ~** sich unterstellen; (*for longer period*) Unterschlupf finden; **under ~ of darkness** im Schutz(e) der Dunkelheit; **to give sb ~** (*Mil*) jdm Deckung geben.
(e) (*Hunt*) Deckung *f*. **to break ~** aus der Deckung hervorbrechen.
(f) (*place at meal*) Gedeck *nt*. **she laid ~s for six** sie deckte für sechs Personen, sie legte sechs Gedecke auf.
(g) (*Comm, Fin*) Deckung *f*; (*insurance ~*) Versicherung *f*. **to operate without ~** ohne Deckung arbeiten; **to take out ~ for a car/against fire** ein Auto versichern/eine Feuerversicherung abschließen; **to get ~ for sth** etw versichern (lassen); **do you have adequate ~?** sind Sie ausreichend versichert?
(h) (*assumed identity*) Tarnung *f*; (*front organization also*) Deckung *f*. **he went in the ~ of a clergyman** er ging als Geistlicher getarnt; **under ~ as** getarnt als; **to blow sb's ~** jdn enttarnen.

2 *vt* **(a)** bedecken; (*cover over*) zudecken; (*with loose cover*) *chair etc* beziehen. **a ~ed wagon/way** ein Planwagen *m*/überdachter Weg; **to ~ one's head** den Kopf bedecken; **the car ~ed us in mud** das Auto bespritzte uns von oben bis unten mit Schlamm; **the mountain was ~ed with** *or* **in snow** der Berg war schneebedeckt *or* mit Schnee bedeckt; **you're all ~ed with dog hairs** du bist voller Hundehaare; **to ~ oneself in** *or* **with glory** Ruhm ernten; **~ed in** *or* **with shame** zutiefst beschämt.
(b) (*hide*) *surprise* verbergen; *mistake, tracks also* verdecken. **to ~ one's face in** *or* **with one's hands** sein Gesicht in den Händen verstecken *or* verbergen.
(c) (*Mil, Sport, Chess*): *protect*) decken. **he only said that to ~ himself** er hat das nur gesagt, um sich abzudecken *or* zu decken; **I'll keep you ~ed** ich gebe dir Deckung.
(d) (*point a gun at etc*) *door etc* sichern; *sb* in Schach halten; (*be on guard near*) sichern. **to keep sb ~ed** jdn in Schach halten; **I've got you ~ed!** (*with gun etc*) ich hab auf dich angelegt; (*fig: Chess etc*) ich hab' dich.
(e) (*Fin*) *loan* decken; *expenses, costs also* abdecken; (*Insur*) versichern. **will £3 ~ the petrol?** reichen £ 3 für das Benzin?; **he gave me £3 to ~ the petrol** er gab mir £ 3 für das Benzin.
(f) (*take in, include*) behandeln; (*law also*) erfassen; (*allow for, anticipate*) *possibilities, eventualities* vorsehen.
(g) (*Press: report on*) berichten über (+*acc*).
(h) (*travel*) *miles, distance* zurücklegen.
(i) (*salesman etc*) *territory* zuständig sein für.
(j) (*play a higher card than*) überbieten.
(k) (*animals: copulate with*) decken.

♦**cover for** *vi* +*prep obj* vertreten, einspringen für.
♦**cover in** *vt sep* **(a)** (*fill in*) *grave etc* auffüllen, zuschütten. **(b)** (*roof in*) überdachen.
♦**cover over** *vt sep* **(a)** (*put a cover over*) zudecken; (*for protection*) *tennis court* abdecken. **(b)** (*roof over*) überdachen.
♦**cover up 1** *vi* **(a)** (*wrap up*) sich einmummen. **(b)** (*conceal a fact*) alles vertuschen *or* verheimlichen. **don't try to ~ ~, just admit your mistake** versuchen Sie nicht, Ihren Fehler zu vertuschen, geben Sie's doch einfach zu; **to ~ ~ for sb** jdn decken.
2 *vt sep* **(a)** *child* zudecken; *object also, tennis court* abdecken. **(b)** (*hide*) *truth, facts* vertuschen, verheimlichen.
coverage ['kʌvərɪdʒ] *n* (*Press, Radio, TV*) Berichterstattung *f* (*of* über +*acc*). **to give full ~ to an event** ausführlich über ein Ereignis berichten; **the games got excellent TV ~** die Spiele wurden ausführlich im Fernsehen gebracht.
(b) (*Insur*) Versicherung *f*. **this policy gives you full ~ for ...** diese Police bietet Ihnen volle Deckung bei ...
cover: **~all** *n usu pl* (*US*) Overall *m*; **~ charge** *n* Kosten *pl* für ein Gedeck; **~ girl** *n* Titel(bild)mädchen, Covergirl *nt*.
covering ['kʌvərɪŋ] *n* Decke *f*; (*floor ~*) Belag *m*. **a ~ of dust/snow** eine Staub-/Schneedecke; **what kind of ~ did you put over the hole?** womit haben Sie das Loch ab- *or* zugedeckt?
covering letter *n* Begleitbrief *m*.
coverlet ['kʌvəlɪt] *n* Tagesdecke *f*.
cover: **~ note** *n* Deckungszusage *f*, vorläufiger Versicherungsschein; **~ organization** *n* Deckorganisation *f*; **~ story** *n* (*of paper*) Titelgeschichte *f*; (*of spy*) Geschichte *f*.
covert ['kʌvət] **1** *adj threat, attack* versteckt; *glance also* verstohlen. **2** *n* Versteck *nt*; see **draw²**.
covertly ['kʌvətlɪ] *adv* see *adj* versteckt; verstohlen.
cover-up ['kʌvərʌp] *n* Vertuschung, Verschleierung *f*. **the Watergate ~** die Vertuschung von Watergate.
covet ['kʌvɪt] **1** *vt* begehren. **2** *vi* begehrlich *or* begierig sein.
covetous ['kʌvɪtəs] *adj* begehrlich. **to be ~ of sth** (*liter*) etw begehren; **to cast ~ eyes on sth** begehrliche Blicke auf etw (*acc*) werfen.
covetously ['kʌvɪtəslɪ] *adv* begehrlich.
covetousness ['kʌvɪtəsnɪs] *n* Begierde *f* (*of* auf +*acc*), Begehren *nt* (*of* nach).
covey ['kʌvɪ] *n* (*of partridges*) Kette *f*.
coving ['kəʊvɪŋ] *n* Wölbung *f*.
cow¹ [kaʊ] *n* **(a)** Kuh *f*. **a ~ elephant** eine Elefantenkuh; **till the ~s come home** (*fig inf*) bis in alle Ewigkeit (*inf*); **you'll be waiting till the ~s come home** (*fig inf*) da kannst du warten, bis du schwarz wirst (*inf*). **(b)** (*pej inf: woman*) (*stupid*) Kuh *f* (*inf*); (*nasty*) gemeine Ziege (*inf*).

cow² *vt person, animal* einschüchtern, verschüchtern. **she had a ~ed look about her** sie machte einen eingeschüchterten *or* verschüchterten Eindruck; **to ~ sb into obedience** jdn (durch Einschüchterung) gefügig machen.
coward ['kaʊəd] *n* Feigling *m*.
cowardice ['kaʊədɪs], **cowardliness** ['kaʊədlɪnɪs] *n* Feigheit *f*.
cowardly ['kaʊədlɪ] *adj* feig(e).
cow: **~bell** *n* Kuhglocke *f*; **~boy** *n* Cowboy *m*; **a ~boy outfit** (*fig inf*) ein windiges Unternehmen (*inf*); **they're a bunch of ~boys** (*fig inf*) das sind alles Gauner; **to play ~boys and Indians** Indianer spielen; **~boy hat** *n* Cowboyhut *m*; **~catcher** *n* (*Rail*) Schienenräumer *m*; **~ dung** *n* Kuhmist *m*.
cower ['kaʊə'] *vi* sich ducken; (*squatting*) kauern. **to ~ before sb** vor jdm ducken; **he stood ~ing in a corner** er stand geduckt in einer Ecke; **the ~ing peasants** die geduckten Bauern.
♦**cower away** *vi* (*furchtsam*) ausweichen (*from* dat).
♦**cower down** *vi* sich niederkauern.
cow: **~girl** *n* Cowgirl *nt*; **~hand** *n* Hilfscowboy *m*; (*on farm*) Stallknecht *m*; **~herd** *n* Kuhhirte *m*; **~hide** *n* (a) (*untanned*) Kuhhaut *f*; (*no pl: leather*) Rindsleder *nt*; (b) (*US: whip*) Lederpeitsche *f*.
cowl [kaʊl] *n* (a) (*monk's hood*) Kapuze *f*. (b) (*chimney ~*) (Schornstein)kappe *f*.
cowlick ['kaʊlɪk] *n* Tolle *f*.
cowling ['kaʊlɪŋ] *n* (*Aviat*) Motorhaube *f*.
cowl neck *n* Schalrollkragen *m*.
cowman ['kaʊmən] *n*, *pl* **-men** [-mən] (*farm labourer*) Stallbursche *m*; (*US: cattle rancher*) Viehzüchter *m*.
co-worker ['kəʊ'wɜːkə'] *n* Kollege *m*, Kollegin *f*.
cow: **~parsley** *n* Wiesenkerbel *m*; **~pat** *n* Kuhfladen *m*; **~poke** *n* (*US inf*) Kuhheini (*pej inf*), Cowboy *m*; **~pox** *n* Kuhpocken *pl*; **~puncher** *n* (*US inf*) Cowboy *m*.
cowrie, cowry ['kaʊrɪ] *n* Kaurischnecke *f*.
cow: **~shed** *n* Kuhstall *m*; **~slip** *n* (*Brit: primrose*) Schlüsselblume *f*; (*US: kingcup*) Sumpfdotterblume *f*.
cox [kɒks] **1** *n* Steuermann *m*. **2** *vt crew* Steuermann sein für. **3** *vi* steuern.
coxcomb ['kɒkskəʊm] *n* (*old*) Stutzer *m* (*old*).
coxless ['kɒkslɪs] *adj* ohne Steuermann.
coxswain ['kɒksn] *n* (a) (*in rowing*) see **cox 1.** (b) (*Naut*) Boot(s)führer *m*.
coy *adj* (+*er*), **~ly** *adv* [kɔɪ, -lɪ] (*affectedly shy*) verschämt; (*coquettish*) neckisch, kokett.
coyness ['kɔɪnɪs] *n* see *adj* Verschämtheit *f*; neckisches *or* kokettes Benehmen.
coyote [kɔɪ'əʊtɪ] *n* Kojote *m*.
coypu ['kɔɪpuː] *n* Sumpfbiber *m*.
cozy *adj* (*US*) see **cosy.**
cp *abbr of* **compare** vgl.
crab¹ [kræb] *n* (a) Krabbe *f*; (*small also*) Krebs *m*; (*as food*) Krabbe *f*. **to catch a ~** (*Rowing*) einen Krebs fangen. (b) (*~ louse*) Filzlaus *f*. (c) (*Gymnastics*) Brücke *f*.
crab² *vi* nörgeln.
crab apple *n* (*fruit*) Holzapfel *m*; (*tree*) Holzapfelbaum *m*.
crabbed ['kræbd] *adj* (a) (*person*) griesgrämig, mürrisch. (b) *handwriting* kritzelig, unleserlich.
crabby ['kræbɪ] *adj* (+*er*) see **crabbed** (a).
crab louse *n* Filzlaus *f*.
crack [kræk] **1** *n* (a) (*break*) Riß *m*; (*between floorboards etc*) Ritze *f*; (*wider hole etc*) Spalte *f*; (*fine line: in pottery, glass etc*) Sprung *m*. **leave the window open a ~** laß das Fenster einen Spalt offen; **at the ~ of dawn** in aller Frühe.
(b) (*sharp noise*) (*of wood etc breaking*) Knacks *m*; (*of gun, whip*) Knall(en *nt no pl*) *m*; (*of thunder*) Schlag *m*. **the ~ of doom** (*fig*) die Posaunen des Jüngsten Gerichts; **at the ~ of doom** beim Jüngsten Gericht.
(c) (*sharp blow*) Schlag *m*. **to give sb/oneself a ~ on the head** jdm eins auf den Kopf geben/sich (*dat*) den Kopf anschlagen.
(d) (*inf: gibe*) Stichelei *f*; (*joke*) Witz *m*. **to make a ~ about sb/sth** einen Witz über jdn/etw reißen.
(e) (*inf: attempt*) **to have a ~ at sth** etw mal probieren (*inf*).
2 *adj attr* erstklassig; (*Mil*) Elite-. **~ shot** Meisterschütze *m*.
3 *vt* **(a)** (*make a ~ in*) *glass, china, pottery* einen Sprung machen in (+*acc*); *bone* anbrechen, anknacksen (*inf*); *skin, ground* rissig machen; *ground, ice* einen Riß/Risse machen in (+*acc*). **to ~ one's ribs** sich (*dat*) die Rippen anbrechen.
(b) (*break*) *nuts, safe* (*inf*), (*fig*) *code* knacken; *case* lösen. **to ~ (open) a bottle (with sb)** (mit jdm) einer Flasche den Hals brechen.
(c) *joke* reißen.
(d) *whip* knallen mit; *finger, joint* knacken mit.
(e) (*hit sharply*) schlagen. **he ~ed his head against the pavement** er krachte mit dem Kopf aufs Pflaster.
(f) (*distil*) *petroleum* kracken; **~ing plant** Krackanlage *f*.
4 *vi* **(a)** (*get a ~*) (*pottery, glass*) einen Sprung/Sprünge bekommen, springen; (*ice, road*) einen Riß/Risse bekommen; (*lips, skin*) spröde *or* rissig werden; (*bones*) einen Knacks bekommen; (*break*) brechen. **my lips are ~ing with the cold** meine Lippen werden von der Kälte spröde *or* rissig; **at last his stern face ~ed and he laughed** schließlich verzog sich seine ernste Miene zu einem Lachen.
(b) (*make a ~ing sound*) (*twigs, joints*) knacken, krachen; (*whip, gun*) knallen.
(c) (*hit sharply*) schlagen, krachen.
(d) (*break: voice*) (*with emotion*) versagen. **his voice is ~ing/beginning to ~** (*boy*) er ist im/kommt in den Stimmbruch.
(e) (*inf*) **to get ~ing** los legen (*inf*), sich daran machen; **to get ~ing with** *or* **on sth** mit etw loslegen (*inf*), sich an etw (*acc*) machen; **get ~ing!** los jetzt!; (*speed up*) mach(t) mal ein bißchen Dampf! (*inf*).

(f) see ~ **up 1 (b). the spy ~ed under torture** der Agent ist unter der Folter zusammengebrochen.

♦**crack down** vi **(a)** (whip) niederknallen, niederkrachen. **(b)** (clamp down) hart durchgreifen (on bei).

♦**crack up 1** vi **(a)** (break into pieces) zerbrechen; (road surface, lips) aufspringen, rissig werden; (ice) brechen; (machine, plane) auseinanderbrechen, auseinanderfallen; (make-up) rissig werden.
(b) (fig and inf) (person) durchdrehen (inf); (under strain) zusammenbrechen; (have a mental breakdown) einen Nervenzusammenbruch haben; (organization) auseinanderfallen, zusammenbrechen; (lose ability, strength: athlete etc) abbauen. l/he must be ~ing ~ (hum) so fängt's an (inf); she ~ed ~ in the witness box sie brach auf der Zeugenbank zusammen.
2 vt sep **(a)** (inf) he's/it's not all he's/it's ~ed ~ to be so toll ist er/es dann auch wieder nicht; he's ~ed ~ to be some sort of genius er wird als eine Art Genie gepriesen; to ~ sb/sth ~ to be really good jdn/etw über den grünen Klee loben (inf).

crackajack n, adj (US) see **crackerjack**.

crack: ~ brained ['krækbreɪnd] adj (inf) verrückt, irre; person also bescheuert (inf); **~-down** n (inf) scharfes Durchgreifen; to order a ~-down on sth anordnen, bei etw scharf durchzugreifen.

cracked [krækt] adj **(a)** glass, plate, ice gesprungen; rib, bone angebrochen, angeknackst (inf); (broken) gebrochen; surface, walls, make-up rissig. **(b)** (inf: mad) übergeschnappt (inf).

cracker ['krækər] n **(a)** (biscuit) Kräcker m. **(b)** (fire~) Knallkörper m; (Christmas ~) Knallbonbon nt. **(c)** ~s pl (nut ~s) Nußknacker m. **(d)** (Brit inf) tolle Frau (inf); toller Mann (inf); tolles Ding (inf).

crackerjack, (US) **crackajack** ['krækədʒæk] **1** n (person) Kanone f; (thing) Knüller m (inf). **2** adj bombig (inf).

crackers ['krækəz] adj pred (Brit inf) übergeschnappt (inf). to go ~ überschnappen (inf).

cracking ['krækɪŋ] adj (inf) pace scharf; (dated: good) novel klasse inv (inf), phantastisch.

crack-jaw ['krækdʒɔː] (inf) **1** adj attr word, name zungenbrecherisch. **2** n Zungenbrecher m.

crackle ['krækl] **1** vi (dry leaves) rascheln; (paper also) knistern; (fire) knistern, prasseln; (telephone line) knacken; (machine gun) knattern; (bacon) brutzeln. the line was crackling so much es knackte so stark in der Leitung.
2 vt paper rascheln or knistern mit.
3 n **(a)** (crackling noise) see vi Rascheln nt; Knistern nt; Knistern, Prasseln nt; Knacken nt; Knattern nt; Brutzeln nt. **(b)** (on china, porcelain) Craquelé, Krakelee m or nt.

crackleware ['krækweər] n Craqueléporzellan nt.

crackling ['kræklɪŋ] n, no pl **(a)** see **crackle 3 (a)**. **(b)** (Cook) Kruste f (des Schweinebratens).

cracknel ['kræknl] n (harter) Keks.

crackpot ['krækpɒt] (inf) **1** n Spinner(in f) m (inf), Irre(r) mf. **2** adj verrückt, irre.

cracksman ['kræksmən] n, pl -men [-mən] (sl) Safeknacker m (inf).

crack-up ['krækʌp] n (inf) Zusammenbruch m.

cradle ['kreɪdl] **1** n (cot, fig: birthplace) Wiege f; (support: of phone) Gabel f; (for invalids) Schutzgestell nt (zum Abhalten des Bettzeugs von Verletzungen); (for ship) (Ablauf)schlitten m; (Build, for window-cleaners) Hängegerüst nt; (in sea rescues) Hosenboje f; (for mechanic under car) Schlitten m. from the ~ to the grave von der Wiege bis zur Bahre; right from the ~ von klein auf, von Kindesbeinen an.
2 vt **(a)** (hold closely) an sich (acc) drücken. he was cradling his injured arm er hielt sich (dat) seinen verletzten Arm; to ~ sb/sth in one's arms/lap jdn/etw fest in den Armen/auf dem Schoß halten; the baby lay ~d in her lap das Baby lag (geborgen) in ihrem Schoß; he ~d the telephone under his chin er klemmte sich (dat) den Hörer unters Kinn; the way he ~s the guitar wie er die Gitarre zärtlich hält.
(b) receiver auflegen.

cradle: ~-snatcher n (inf) see baby-snatcher; **~-snatching** n (inf) see baby-snatching; **~-song** n Wiegenlied nt.

craft [krɑːft] n **(a)** (handicraft) Kunst f, Handwerk nt; (trade) Handwerk, Gewerbe nt; (weaving, pottery etc) Kunstgewerbe nt. it's a real ~ das ist eine echte Kunst; see art'. **(b)** (guild) (Handwerker)innung, (Handwerks)zunft (Hist) f. **(c)** no pl (skill) Geschick(lichkeit f) nt, Kunstfertigkeit f. **(d)** no pl (cunning) List f. to obtain sth by ~ sich (dat) etw erlisten, etw durch List bekommen. **(e)** pl - (boat) Boot nt.

craftily ['krɑːftɪlɪ] adv schlau, clever.

craftiness ['krɑːftɪnɪs] n Schlauheit, Cleverness f.

craftsman ['krɑːftsmən] n, pl -men [-mən] Handwerker m. he's a real ~ er ist ein echter Künstler.

craftsmanship ['krɑːftsmənʃɪp] n Handwerkskunst f; (of person also) handwerkliches Können, Kunstfertigkeit f. there's no ~ left these days heutzutage gibt es einfach keine Handwerkskunst mehr.

craft union n Handwerkergewerkschaft f.

crafty ['krɑːftɪ] adj (+er) schlau, clever. he is a ~ one (inf) er ist ein ganz Schlauer (inf); he's as ~ as a fox er ist ein schlauer Fuchs; he took a ~ glance at ... er riskierte einen verstohlenen Blick auf (+acc) ...

crag [kræg] n Fels m.

craggy ['krægɪ] adj (+er) (rocky) felsig; (jagged) zerklüftet; face kantig. he was good-looking in a ~ sort of way er sah auf eine herbe, kantige Art gut aus.

crake [kreɪk] n Ralle f.

cram [kræm] **1** vt **(a)** (fill) vollstopfen, vollpacken; (stuff in) hineinstopfen (in(to) in +acc); people hineinzwängen (in(to) in +acc). the room was ~med der Raum war gestopft voll;

we were all ~med into one room wir waren alle in einem Zimmer zusammengepfercht; he ~med his hat (down) over his eyes er zog sich (dat) den Hut tief ins Gesicht; he ~med his clothes down er drückte seine Kleider zusammen.
(b) (for exam) Latin verbs etc pauken (inf), büffeln (inf); (teach for exam) pupil pauken mit (inf). to ~ sth into sb jdm etw einpauken (inf).
2 vi (swot) pauken (inf), büffeln (inf).

♦**cram in** vi (people) sich hinein-/hereindrängen or -quetschen or -zwängen (-to in +acc).

cram-full ['kræmfʊl] adj (inf) vollgestopft (of mit), gestopft voll (inf).

crammer ['kræmər] n (tutor) Einpauker m; (student) Büffler(in f) m (inf); (book) Paukbuch nt; (school) Paukschule f.

cramp¹ [kræmp] **1** n (Med) Krampf m. to have ~ in one's leg einen Krampf im Bein haben; to have the ~s (US) Krämpfe haben; writer's ~ Schreibkrampf m.
2 vt (also ~ up) persons zusammenpferchen, einpferchen; writing eng zusammenkritzeln.
(b) (fig: hinder) behindern. to ~ sb's style jdm im Weg sein. **(c)** (give cramp to) Krämpfe pl verursachen in (+dat).

cramp² **1** n (also ~ iron) Bauklammer f. **2** vt klammern.

cramped [kræmpt] adj **(a)** space eng, beschränkt. we are very ~ (for space) wir sind räumlich sehr beschränkt. **(b)** position verkrampft. **(c)** handwriting eng zusammengekritzelt.

crampon ['kræmpən] n Steigeisen nt.

cranberry ['krænbəri] n Preiselbeere, Kronsbeere f. ~ sauce Preiselbeersoße f.

crane [kreɪn] **1** n **(a)** (Mech) Kran m. **(b)** (Orn) Kranich m. **2** vt: to ~ one's neck den Hals recken, sich (dat) fast den Hals verrenken (inf). **3** vi (also ~ forward) den Hals or den Kopf recken.

cranefly ['kreɪnflaɪ] n Schnake f.

cranesbill ['kreɪnzbɪl] n (Bot) Storchschnabel m.

crania ['kreɪnɪə] pl of **cranium**.

cranial ['kreɪnɪəl] adj (Anat) Schädel-, kranial (spec).

cranium ['kreɪnɪəm] n, pl **crania** (Anat) Schädel m, Cranium nt (spec).

crank¹ [kræŋk] n (eccentric person) Spinner(in f) m (inf); (US: cross person) Griesgram m.

crank² **1** n (Mech) Kurbel f. **2** vt (also: ~ up) ankurbeln.

crankcase ['kræŋkkeɪs] n (Aut) Kurbelgehäuse nt.

crankiness ['kræŋkɪnɪs] n **(a)** (eccentricity) Verrücktheit f. **(b)** (US: bad temper) Griesgrämigkeit f.

crankshaft ['kræŋkʃɑːft] n (Aut) Kurbelwelle f.

cranky ['kræŋkɪ] adj (+er) **(a)** (eccentric) verrückt. **(b)** (US: bad-tempered) griesgrämig.

cranny ['krænɪ] n Ritze, Spalte f; see nook.

crap [kræp] (vulg) **1** n **(a)** Scheiße f (vulg). to go for/have a ~ scheißen gehen/scheißen (vulg). **(b)** (sl: rubbish) Scheiße f (sl). a load of ~ (sl) große Scheiße (sl). **2** vi scheißen (vulg).

♦**crap out** vi (US sl) kneifen (of vor +dat).

crape n see **crêpe**.

crap game n (US) Würfelspiel nt (mit zwei Würfeln).

crappy ['kræpɪ] adj (+er) (sl) beschissen (sl), Scheiß- (sl).

craps [kræps] n (US) Würfelspiel nt. to shoot ~ Würfel spielen.

crapshooter ['kræpʃuːtər] n Würfelspieler m.

crash [kræʃ] **1** n **(a)** (noise) Krach(en nt) m no pl; (of thunder, cymbals also, of drums) Schlag m. there was a ~ upstairs es hat oben gekracht; the vase fell to the ground with a ~ die Vase fiel krachend zu Boden; a ~ of thunder ein Donnerschlag m; the ~ of the waves against ... das Krachen der Wellen gegen ...
(b) (accident) Unfall m, Unglück nt; (collision also) Zusammenstoß m; (with several cars) Karambolage f; (plane ~) (Flugzeug)unglück nt. to be in a (car) ~ in einen (Auto)unfall verwickelt sein; to have a ~ (mit dem Auto) verunglücken, einen (Auto)unfall haben; (cause it) einen Unfall verursachen or bauen (inf); the impact of the ~ (into another car) die Wucht des Zusammenstoßes; (into a tree, rock, the ground) die Wucht des Aufpralls.
(c) (Fin) Zusammenbruch m.
2 adv krach. he went ~ into a tree er krachte gegen einen Baum; ~, bang, wallop! (inf) bums! (inf), krach! (inf).
3 vt **(a)** car, bicycle einen Unfall haben mit; plane abstürzen mit. if you let him use your car he's bound to ~ it wenn du ihm dein Auto gibst, fährt er es dir bestimmt kaputt (inf); to ~ one's car/plane into sth mit dem Auto/Flugzeug gegen etw krachen or knallen (inf); the car was found ~ed das Auto wurde demoliert aufgefunden.
(b) (with particle: bang) he ~ed it to the ground er knallte es auf den Boden (inf); stop ~ing the plates around hör auf, mit den Tellern zu scheppern (inf); he ~ed the cymbals together er schlug scheppernd die Becken zusammen; he ~ed his head against the windscreen er krachte mit dem Kopf gegen die Windschutzscheibe; he ~ed the car through the barrier er fuhr mit dem Auto stockvoll durch die Absperrung (inf).
(c) (inf: gatecrash) to ~ a party uneingeladen zu einer Party gehen, in eine Party hineinplatzen.
4 vi **(a)** (have an accident) verunglücken, einen Unfall haben; (plane) abstürzen. to ~ into sth gegen etw (acc) krachen or knallen (inf).
(b) (with particle: move with a ~) krachen. to ~ to the ground/through sth zu Boden/durch etw krachen; they went ~ing through the undergrowth sie brachen krachend durchs Unterholz; his fist ~ed into Tom's face seine Faust landete krachend in Toms Gesicht; the whole roof came ~ing down (on him) das ganze Dach krachte auf ihn herunter; his whole world ~ed about him or his ears seine ganze Welt brach zusammen.
(c) (Fin) pleite machen (inf). when Wall Street ~ed als Wall Street zusammenbrach.
(d) (sl: sleep: also ~ out) pofen (sl); (fall asleep) einpofen (sl); (become unconscious) wegtreten (sl).

crash: ~ **barrier** n Leitplanke f; ~ **course** n Schnell- or Intensivkurs m; ~ **diet** n Radikalkur f; ~ **dive** 1 n Schnelltauchmanöver nt; 2 vti schnelltauchen; ~ **helmet** n Sturzhelm m.

crashing ['kræʃɪŋ] adj (inf) he's/it's a ~ bore er/es ist fürchterlich or zum Einschlafen langweilig (inf).

crash: ~**land** 1 vi eine Bruchlandung machen, bruchlanden; 2 vt eine Bruchlandung machen mit, bruchlanden mit; ~**landing** n Bruchlandung f; ~ **programme** n Intensivprogramm nt.

crass [kræs] adj (+er) (stupid, unsubtle) kraß; ignorance also haarsträubend; (coarse) behaviour unfein, derb. **must you be so** ~ **about it?** müssen Sie sich so kraß ausdrücken?

crassly ['kræslɪ] adv kraß; behave unfein.

crassness ['kræsnɪs] n see adj Kraßheit f; Derbheit f.

crate [kreɪt] 1 n (also inf: car, plane) Kiste f. 2 vt goods (in Kisten/eine Kiste) (ver)packen.

crater ['kreɪtəʳ] n Krater m.

cravat(te) [krə'væt] n Halstuch nt.

crave [kreɪv] vt (liter: beg) erbitten; mercy also erflehen; (desire) attention, drink etc sich sehnen nach. **to** ~ **sb's pardon** (form) jdn um Verzeihung anflehen; **ladies and gentlemen, may I** ~ **your indulgence?** (form) meine Damen und Herren, darf ich um Ihre werte Aufmerksamkeit bitten?; **may I** ~ **your indulgence a moment longer?** (form) darf ich Ihre Geduld noch etwas länger in Anspruch nehmen?

♦**crave for** vi +prep obj sich sehnen nach.

craven ['kreɪvən] 1 adj feig(e). **a** ~ **coward** ein elender Feigling, eine feige Memme (geh). 2 n (liter) Memme f (geh).

craving ['kreɪvɪŋ] n Verlangen nt. **to have a** ~ **for sth** Verlangen nach etw haben; **pregnant women have strange** ~**s** schwangere Frauen haben eigenartige Gelüste.

crawfish ['krɔːfɪʃ] n see **crayfish (b)**.

crawl [krɔːl] 1 n (a) (on hands and knees) Kriechen nt; (slow speed) Schnecken- or Kriechtempo nt; (inf: pub ~) Kneipenbummel m. **after the** ~ **through the marsh, he ...** nachdem er durch den Morast gekrochen war ...; **it was a long** ~ wir mußten lange kriechen; (in car) wir sind lange nur im Kriechtempo vorangekommen; **at a** ~ im Schnecken- or Kriechtempo; **we could only go at a** ~ wir kamen nur im Schnecken- or Kriechtempo voran; **to join the** ~ **to the coast** sich der (Auto)schlange zur Küste anschließen.
(b) (swimming stroke) Kraul(stil) m, Kraulen nt. **to do the** ~ kraulen; **she's very fast at the** ~ sie ist sehr schnell im Kraulen.
2 vi (a) kriechen; (baby, insects also) krabbeln; (time also) schleichen. **he tried to** ~ **away** er versuchte wegzukriechen.
(b) (be infested) wimmeln (with von). **the place is** ~**ing!** hier wimmelt es von Ungeziefer!; **the meat was** ~**ing with flies** das Fleisch wimmelte nur so von Fliegen; **the street was** ~**ing with policemen** auf der Straße wimmelte es von Polizisten.
(c) spiders make my flesh or skin ~ wenn ich Spinnen sehe, kriege ich eine Gänsehaut.
(d) (inf: suck up) kriechen (to vor +dat). **he went** ~**ing to teacher** er ist gleich zum Lehrer gerannt.

crawler ['krɔːləʳ] n (a) (inf: sycophant) Kriecher(in f) m. (b) ~**s** pl (rompers) Spielanzug m.

crawler lane n (Brit Aut) Kriechspur f.

crayfish ['kreɪfɪʃ] n (a) (freshwater) Flußkrebs m. (b) (saltwater: also **crawfish**) Languste f.

crayon ['kreɪən] 1 n (a) (pencil) Buntstift m; (wax ~) Wachs(mal)stift m; (chalk ~) Pastellstift m, Malkreide f. (b) (picture) Pastell nt, Kreide- or Pastellzeichnung f. 2 vti (mit Bunt-/Wachsmal-/Pastellstiften) zeichnen or malen.

♦**crayon in** vt sep drawing ausmalen.

craze [kreɪz] 1 n Fimmel m (inf). **it's all the** ~ (inf) das ist große Mode; **there's a** ~ **for collecting old things just now** es ist zur Zeit große Mode, alte Sachen zu sammeln.
2 vt (a) (make insane) wahnsinnig or verrückt machen. **to be half** ~**d with grief** vor Schmerz halb wahnsinnig sein; **he had a** ~**d look on his face** er hatte den Gesichtsausdruck eines Wahnsinnigen.
(b) pottery, glazing rissig machen.
3 vi (pottery) rissig werden.

crazily ['kreɪzɪlɪ] adv (madly) verrückt; lean, tilt unwahrscheinlich.

crazy ['kreɪzɪ] adj (+er) (a) verrückt (with vor +dat). **to send or drive sb** ~ jdn verrückt or wahnsinnig machen; **to go** ~ verrückt or wahnsinnig werden; **what! do you think I'm** ~! was, denkst du, ich bin verrückt!; **that's** ~ das ist doch verrückt!; **like** ~ (inf) wie verrückt (inf).
(b) (inf: enthusiastic) verrückt (inf). **to be** ~ **about sb/sth** ganz verrückt or wild auf jdn/etw sein (inf); **football-**~ Fußballverrückt (inf); **to be** ~ **for sb** verrückt nach jdm sein (inf).
(c) angle, tilt unwahrscheinlich.

crazy: ~ **bone** n (US) Musikantenknochen m; ~ **paving** n Mosaikpflaster nt; ~ **quilt** n (US) Flickendecke f.

creak [kriːk] 1 n Knarren nt no pl; (of hinges, bed springs) Quietschen nt no pl; (of knees etc) Knacken nt no pl. **to give a loud** ~ laut knarren/quietschen/knacken; **a series of** ~**s** (hinges, bed springs) quietschen; (knees etc) knacken.

creaky ['kriːkɪ] adj (+er) see vi knarrend; quietschend; knakkend.

cream [kriːm] 1 n (a) Sahne f, Rahm m (S Ger); (~ pudding, artificial ~) Creme, Krem f. ~ **of tomato/chicken soup** Tomaten-/Hühnercremesuppe f; ~ **of tartar** Weinstein m.
(b) (lotion) Creme f.
(c) (colour) Creme(farbe f) nt. **a skirt in a pale shade of** ~ ein blaß-cremefarbener Rock.
(d) (fig: best) die Besten; (of society also) Crème, Elite f. **our rivals take the** ~ **of the applicants** unsere Konkurrenz sahnt die besten Bewerber ab; **the** ~ **of society** die Crème der Gesellschaft; **to take the** ~ den Rahm abschöpfen.

2 adj (a) (colour) creme inv, cremefarben or -farbig. **a blouse of a light** ~ **colour** eine hellcremefarbene or -farbige Bluse.
(b) (made with ~) Sahne-; Creme-. ~ **soups** Cremesuppen pl.
3 vt (a) (put ~ on) face etc eincremen.
(b) butter, eggs etc cremig rühren; potatoes, fruit pürieren. ~**ed potatoes** Kartoffelpüree nt.
(c) (skim) milk entrahmen.
(d) (allow to form a ~) milk aufrahmen lassen.
4 vi (milk) aufrahmen.

♦**cream off** vt sep (lit) abschöpfen; (fig) profits also, the best absahnen.

cream: ~ **bun** n Eclair nt; ~ **cake** n Sahnetorte f; Cremetorte f; (small) Sahnetörtchen nt; Cremetörtchen nt; ~ **cheese** n (Doppelrahm)frischkäse m.

creamer ['kriːməʳ] n (a) (jug) Sahnekännchen nt. (b) (skimming machine) Milchzentrifuge or -schleuder f. (c) (dried milk) Milchpulver nt.

creamery ['kriːmərɪ] n Molkerei f; (shop) Milchgeschäft nt.

cream: ~ **puff** n Windbeutel m; ~ **soda** n Sodawasser nt mit Vanillegeschmack; ~ **tea** n Nachmittagstee m.

creamy ['kriːmɪ] adj (+er) (a) (tasting of cream) sahnig; (smooth) cremig. **a** ~ **complexion** ein zarter Teint. (b) (creamcoloured) creme(farben or -farbig).

crease [kriːs] 1 n (a) Falte f; (deliberate fold) (in material also) Kniff m; (in paper also) Falz, Kniff m; (ironed: in trousers etc) (Bügel)falte f. **to be a mass of** ~**s** völlig zerknittert sein; **to put a** ~ **in a pair of trousers** eine Falte in ein Paar Hosen bügeln.
(b) (Sport) Linie f.
2 vt (deliberately) clothes Falten/eine Falte machen in (+acc); material, paper Kniffe/einen Kniff machen in (+acc); paper falzen; (unintentionally) zerknittern. **smartly** ~**d trousers** Hosen mit sauberen Bügelfalten.
3 vi knittern. **his face** ~**d with laughter** er fing an zu lachen.

♦**crease up** vi (inf: with laughter) sich kringeln (inf).

crease-proof ['kriːspruːf], **crease-resistant** ['kriːsrɪzɪstənt] adj knitterfrei.

create [kriː'eɪt] 1 vt (a) schaffen; new style, fashion also kreieren; the world, man erschaffen; draught, noise, fuss verursachen; difficulties (person) machen; (action, event) verursachen, machen; problems (person) schaffen; (action, event) verursachen, hervorbringen; impression machen. **to** ~ **a sensation** eine Sensation sein; **to** ~ **a fuss** Theater machen (inf).
(b) (appoint) peer ernennen. **peers can only be** ~**d by the reigning monarch** nur der regierende Monarch kann jemanden in den Adelsstand erheben; **to** ~ **sb baron** jdn zum Baron erheben or ernennen.
2 vi (Brit inf) Theater machen (inf).

creation [kriː'eɪʃən] n (a) no pl see vt Schaffung f; Kreation f; Erschaffung f; Verursachung f; Verursachung f; Schaffen nt; Verursachung f; Erhebung f, Ernennung f.
(b) no pl the C— die Schöpfung; all ~, the whole of ~ die Schöpfung, alle Kreatur f, alle Geschöpfe pl.
(c) (created object) (Art) Werk nt; (Fashion) Kreation f.

creative [kriː'eɪtɪv] adj power, skill etc schöpferisch; approach, attitude, person kreativ. ~ **writing** dichterisches Schreiben; ~ **toys** Spielzeug nt zum Gestalten und Werken.

creativeness [‚kriː'eɪtɪvnɪs], **creativity** [‚kriːeɪ'tɪvɪtɪ] n schöpferische Begabung or Kraft; (of person also, of approach, attitude) Kreativität f.

creator [kriː'eɪtəʳ] n Schöpfer(in f) m.

creature ['kriːtʃəʳ] n (a) (Lebe)wesen nt, Kreatur f. **what a superb** ~! welch ein herrliches Geschöpf!; **all dumb** ~**s** die stumme Kreatur; **she's a poor/funny/beautiful** ~ sie ist ein armes/komisches Ding or Geschöpf/sie ist ein schönes Geschöpf; **there wasn't a** ~ **in sight** nirgends regte sich etwas, kein Lebewesen war zu sehen.
(b) (subordinate person) Geschöpf nt.

creature comforts n pl leibliches Wohl.

crèche [kreɪʃ] n (a) (esp Brit: day nursery) (Kinder)krippe f or -hort m; (esp US: children's home) Kinderheim nt. (b) (crib) Krippe f.

credence ['kriːdəns] n (a) no pl (belief) Glaube m. **to lend** ~ **to sth** etw glaubwürdig erscheinen lassen or machen; **worthy of** ~ glaubwürdig; **to give or attach** ~ **to sth** einer Sache (dat) Glauben schenken; **letter of** ~ Beglaubigungsschreiben nt.
(b) (Eccl: also ~ table) Kredenz f.

credentials [krɪ'denʃəlz] npl (references) Referenzen, Zeugnisse pl; (papers of identity) (Ausweis)papiere pl. **to present one's** ~ seine Papiere vorlegen.

credibility [‚kredə'bɪlɪtɪ] n Glaubwürdigkeit f. ~ **gap** Mangel m an Glaubwürdigkeit; **his** ~ **gap widened** er verlor immer mehr an Glaubwürdigkeit; **his** ~ **rating is pretty low** er wird als nicht sehr glaubwürdig eingestuft.

credible adj, ~**bly** adv ['kredɪbl, -ɪ] glaubwürdig.

credit ['kredɪt] 1 n (a) no pl (Fin) Kredit m; (in pub, hotel, shop etc) Stundung f. **the bank will let me have £5,000** ~ die Bank räumt mir einen Kredit von £ 5.000 ein; **to buy/sell on** ~ auf Kredit kaufen/gegen Kredit verkaufen; **his** ~ **is good** er ist kreditwürdig; (in small shop) or ist vertrauenswürdig; **to give sb (unlimited)** ~ jdm (unbegrenzt) Kredit geben; **we can't give you** ~ (bank) wir können Ihnen keinen Kredit geben; (corner shop etc) wir können Ihnen nichts stunden; **pubs do not usually give** ~ in Lokalen bekommt man normalerweise nichts gestundet; **letter of** ~ Kreditbrief m, Akkreditiv nt.
(b) (Fin: money possessed by person, firm) (Gut)haben nt; (Comm: sum of money) Kreditposten m. **to be in** ~ Geld auf dem Konto haben; **to keep one's account in** ~ sein Konto nicht überziehen; **to place a sum to one's** ~ sich (dat) eine Summe gutschreiben lassen; **the** ~**s and debits** Soll und Haben nt; **how much have we got to our** ~? wieviel haben wir auf dem Konto?

(c) *no pl (standing)* Ansehen *nt.* **a man of good** ~ ein angesehener Mann.

(d) *no pl (honour)* Ehre *f; (recognition)* Anerkennung *f; (Sch, Univ: distinction)* Auszeichnung *f.* **he's to his family er macht seiner Familie Ehre; that's to his** ~ das ehrt ihn; **well, all** ~ **to you for not succumbing** alle Achtung, daß Sie nicht nachgegeben haben; **at least he has this to his** ~ das spricht immerhin für ihn; **to reflect great** ~ **on sb** jdm große Ehre machen; **to come out of sth with** ~ ehrenvoll aus etw hervorgehen; **to get all the** ~ die ganze Anerkennung *or* Ehre einstecken; **I do all the work and he gets all the** ~ ich mache die Arbeit, und ihm wird es als Verdienst angerechnet; **the** ~ **for that should go to him** das ist sein Verdienst; **to take the** ~ **for sth** das Verdienst für etw in Anspruch nehmen; ~ **where** ~ **is due** *(prov)* Ehre, wem Ehre gebührt *(prov).*

(e) *no pl (belief)* Glaube *m.* **to give** ~ **to sth** etw glauben, einer Sache *(dat)* Glauben schenken; **to lend** ~ **to sth** etw glaubwürdig erscheinen lassen *or* machen; **to gain** ~ **an Glaubwürdigkeit gewinnen; I gave you** ~ **for more sense** ich habe Sie für vernünftiger gehalten; **worthy of** ~ glaubwürdig.

(f) *(esp US Univ)* Schein *m.* **to take** *or* **do a** ~ **s** Scheine machen.

(g) ~ **s** *pl (Film etc)* Vor-/Nachspann *m; (in book)* Herausgeber- und Mitarbeiterverzeichnis *nt.*

2 vt (a) *(believe)* glauben. **would you** ~ **it!** ist das denn zu glauben!, ist das denn die Möglichkeit!

(b) *(attribute)* zuschreiben (+*dat*). **I** ~ **ed him with more sense** ich habe ihn für vernünftiger gehalten; **he was** ~ **ed with having invented it/with having found that solution** die Erfindung wurde ihm zugeschrieben/es wurde als sein Verdienst angerechnet *or* es wurde ihm zugute gehalten, diese Lösung gefunden zu haben; **it's** ~ **ed with (having) magic powers** ihm werden Zauberkräfte zugeschrieben; **one is hardly able to** ~ **him with having done such a silly thing** man kann kaum glauben, daß er so etwas Dummes getan hat.

(c) *(Fin)* gutschreiben. **to** ~ **a sum to sb's account** jds Konto *(dat)* einen Betrag gutschreiben (lassen); **he had been** ~ **ed with £100** ihm waren £ 100 gutgeschrieben worden.

creditable [ˈkredɪtəbl] *adj* **(a)** *(praiseworthy)* lobenswert, anerkennenswert. **(b)** *(credible)* glaublich. **I find it hardly** ~ ich finde es höchst unglaublich.

creditably [ˈkredɪtəblɪ] *adv* löblich.

credit: ~ **account** *n* Kreditkonto *nt;* ~ **agency** *n* Kreditschutzverein *m;* ~ **balance** *n* Kontostand, Saldo *m;* ~ **card** *n* Kreditkarte *f;* ~ **facilities** *npl* Kreditmöglichkeiten *pl;* ~ **note** *n* Gutschrift *f.*

creditor [ˈkredɪtə*r*] *n* Gläubiger *m.*

credit: ~ **page** *n* Herausgeber- und Mitarbeiterverzeichnis *nt;* ~ **rating** *n* Kreditwürdigkeit *f;* **to have a good/bad** ~ **rating** als kreditwürdig/als nicht kreditwürdig eingestuft werden; ~ **sales** *npl* Kreditkäufe *pl;* ~ **side** *n (lit, fig)* Habenseite *f;* **on the** ~ **side he's young** für ihn spricht, daß er jung ist; ~ **squeeze** *n* Kreditbeschränkung *or* -knappheit *f;* ~ **terms** *npl* Kreditbedingungen *pl;* ~ **titles** *npl (Film) see* credit 1 (g); ~ **worthiness** *n* Kreditwürdigkeit *f;* ~ **worthy** *adj* kreditwürdig.

credo [ˈkreɪdəʊ] *n (lit, fig)* Kredo, Glaubensbekenntnis *nt.*

credulity [krɪˈdjuːlɪtɪ] *n, no pl* Leichtgläubigkeit *f.*

credulous *adj,* ~ **ly** *adv* [ˈkredjʊləs, -lɪ] leichtgläubig.

creed [kriːd] *n (Eccl)* Glaubensbekenntnis *nt; (as part of service, fig also)* Kredo *nt.*

creek [kriːk] *n (esp Brit: inlet)* (kleine) Bucht; *(US: brook)* Bach *m.* **to be up the** ~ *(inf)* (be in trouble) in der Tinte sitzen *(inf); (be completely wrong)* auf dem falschen Dampfer sein *(inf).*

creel [kriːl] *n* Korb *m.*

creep [kriːp] *(vb: pret, ptp* crept*)* **1 vi (a)** *(move quietly or slowly)* schleichen; *(with the body close to the ground, insects)* kriechen; *(plants)* (horizontally) kriechen; (vertically) klettern, sich ranken. **ivy is a** ~ **ing plant** Efeu ist eine Kletterpflanze; **time's** ~ **ing on** die Zeit verrinnt; ~ **ing paralysis** schleichende Lähmung; **the water-level crept higher and higher** der Wasserspiegel kletterte immer höher.

(b) **the story made my flesh** ~ bei der Geschichte überlief es mich kalt *or* bekam ich eine Gänsehaut.

2 n (a) *(inf) (unpleasant person)* Widerling *m (inf)*, widerlicher *or* fieser Typ *(inf).* **you little** ~ du fieser Typ *(inf).*

(b) *(inf)* **stop giving me the** ~ **s** hör auf, da bekomme ich eine Gänsehaut; **her make-up gives me the** ~ **s** wenn ich ihr Make-up sehe, kriege ich das kalte Grausen *(inf);* **he/this old house gives me the** ~ **s** er ist mir nicht geheuer/in dem alten Haus ist es mir nicht geheuer.

♦ **creep in** *vi (person)* (sich) hinein-/hereinschleichen *(-to* in +*acc); (mistakes, tone of bitterness, doubts)* sich einschleichen *(-to* in +*acc).*

♦ **creep over** *vi* +*prep obj (feeling, doubt etc)* beschleichen, überkommen; *(pleasant feeling)* überkommen.

♦ **creep up** *vi* **(a)** *(person)* sich heranschleichen *(on an* +*acc); (prices)* (in die Höhe) klettern. **(b) to** ~ **on sb** *(time, exam, publication day)* langsam auf jdn zukommen; **old age is** ~ **ing** ~ **on him** er wird langsam alt.

creeper [ˈkriːpə*r*] *n* **(a)** *(plant)* (along ground) Kriechpflanze *f;* (upwards) Kletterpflanze *f.* **(b)** *(bird)* Baumläufer *m.* **(c)** ~ **s** *pl (US)* Schuhe *pl* mit dicken Gummisohlen, Leisetreter *pl (inf).*

creepy [ˈkriːpɪ] *adj* (+*er*) *(frightening)* unheimlich; *story, place also* gruselig.

creepy-crawly [ˈkriːpɪˈkrɔːlɪ] *(inf)* **1** *adj insect* krabbelig *(inf)*, kribbelnd, krabbelnd; *feeling* unheimlich. **2 n** Krabbeltier *nt.*

cremate [krɪˈmeɪt] *vt* einäschern, kremieren *(rare).*

cremation [krɪˈmeɪʃən] *n* Einäscherung, Kremation *f.*

crematorium [ˌkreməˈtɔːrɪəm], *(esp US)* **crematory** [ˈkremətɔːrɪ] *n* Krematorium *nt.*

crème de la crème [ˈkremdəlæˈkrem] *n* Crème de la Crème *f.*

crème de menthe [ˈkremdəˈmɒnt] *n* Pfefferminzlikör *m.*

---

crenellated [ˈkrenɪleɪtɪd] *adj battlements, castle* mit Zinnen versehen, kreneliert *(spec); moulding, pattern* zinnenartig.

crenellation [ˌkrenɪˈleɪʃən] *n usu pl (on castle)* Zinnen *pl*, Krenelierung *f (spec); (on moulding)* Zinnenmuster *nt.*

Creole [ˈkriːəʊl] **1 n (a)** *(language)* Kreolisch *nt.* **(b)** *(person)* Kreole *m*, Kreolin *f.* **2 adj** kreolisch.

creolized [ˈkriːəlaɪzd] *adj* kreolisiert.

creosote [ˈkriːəsəʊt] **1 n** Kreosot *nt.* **2 vt** mit Kreosot streichen.

crêpe, crape [kreɪp] **1 n (a)** *(Tex)* Krepp, Crêpe *m.* **(b)** *see* ~ **rubber.** **(c)** *see* **paper. 2 adj** *(made of* ~*)* Krepp-.

crêpe: ~ **bandage** *n* elastische Binde, elastischer Verband; ~ **de Chine** [ˌkrepdəˈʃiːn] *n* Crêpe de Chine *m;* ~ **paper** *n* Kreppapier *nt;* ~ **rubber 1 n** Kreppgummi *m;* **2 adj** Kreppgummi-; ~ **soled** [kreɪpˈsəʊld] *adj* mit Kreppsohle(n), Krepp-; ~ **suzette** [ˌkrepsuːˈzet] *n* Crêpe Suzette *f.*

crepitate [ˈkrepɪteɪt] *vi (liter)* prasseln.

crept [krept] *pret, ptp of* creep.

crepuscular [krɪˈpʌskjʊlə*r*] *adj (liter)* dämmerig. ~ **animals** *(Zool)* Dämmerungstiere *pl.*

crescendo [krɪˈʃendəʊ] **1 n (a)** *(Mus)* Crescendo *nt; (fig)* Zunahme *f.* ~ **of excitement** Anschwellen *nt* der Aufregung. **2 vi** *(Mus, fig)* anschwellen.

crescent [ˈkresnt] **1 n** Halbmond *m; (in street names)* Weg *m* *(halbmondförmig verlaufende Straße).* **2 adj** ~ **shaped** *adj* halbmond- *or* sichelförmig; **the** ~ **moon** die Mondsichel.

cress [kres] *n* (Garten)kresse *f; (water*~*)* Brunnenkresse *f.*

crest [krest] **1 n (a)** *(of bird)* Haube *f; (of cock)* Kamm *m; (on hat etc)* Federbusch *m; (plume on helmet)* Helmbusch *m.*

(b) *(Her)* Helmzierde *f; (coat of arms)* Wappen *nt.*

(c) *(of wave, hill, Anat: of horse etc)* Kamm *m; (fig: of excitement, popularity)* Höhepunkt, Gipfel *m; (Phys: of oscillation)* Scheitel(punkt) *m.* **he's riding on the** ~ **of a wave** *(fig)* er schwimmt im Augenblick oben.

2 vt *(reach the* ~ *of)* erklimmen.

crested [ˈkrestɪd] *adj notepaper, seal* verziert; *(bird)* Hauben-. ~ **coot** Kammbleßralle *f;* ~ **tit** Haubenmeise *f.*

crestfallen [ˈkrestfɔːlən] *adj* geknickt, niedergeschlagen.

cretaceous [krɪˈteɪʃəs] *adj* Kreide-, kretazeisch *(spec).* **the** ~ **age** *(Geol)* die Kreide(zeit).

Cretan [ˈkriːtən] **1 adj** kretisch. **2 n** Kreter(in *f*) *m.*

Crete [kriːt] *n* Kreta *nt.*

cretin [ˈkretɪn] *n (Med)* Kretin *m; (inf)* Schwachkopf *m (inf).*

cretinism [ˈkretɪnɪzəm] *n (Med)* Kretinismus *m; (inf)* Schwachsinn *m*, Idiotie *f.*

cretinous [ˈkretɪnəs] *adj (Med)* kretinoid; *(inf)* schwachsinnig.

cretonne [kreˈtɒn] *n* Cretonne *f or m.*

crevasse [krɪˈvæs] *n (Gletscher)spalte f.*

crevice [ˈkrevɪs] *n* Spalte *f.*

crew¹ [kruː] **1 n (a)** *(manual)* Mannschaft *(also Sport)*, Crew *f; (including officers: of ship also, of plane, tank)* Besatzung, Crew *f.* **50 passengers and 20** ~ **50 Passagiere und 20 Mann Besatzung; the ground** ~ *(Aviat)* das Bodenpersonal; **is Mary your** ~ macht Mary Vorschotmann?

(b) *(inf: gang)* Bande *f.* **they were a motley** ~ sie waren ein bunt zusammengewürfelter Haufen *(inf).*

2 vi to ~ **for sb** bei jdm den Vorschotmann machen.

3 vt *yacht* die Mannschaft *or* Crew sein von; *(one person in race)* den Vorschotmann machen auf (+*dat*).

crew² *(old) pret of* crow.

crew: ~ **cut** *n* Bürstenschnitt *m;* ~ **member** *n* Mitglied *nt* der Mannschaft, Besatzungsmitglied *nt;* ~ **neck** *n* runder Halsausschnitt; *(also* ~ **neck pullover** *or* **sweater)** Pullover *m* mit rundem Halsausschnitt.

crib [krɪb] **1 n (a)** *(cradle)* Krippe *f; (US: cot)* Kinderbett *nt.* **(b)** *(manger)* Krippe, Raufe *f; (fig: nativity scene)* Krippe *f.* **(c)** *(US: maize bin)* Trockengerüst *nt* für Maiskolben. **(d)** *(Sch: cheating aid)* Spickzettel *m (inf); (inf: plagiary)* Anleihe *f (inf).* **2 vti** *(esp Sch inf)* abschreiben *(inf)*, spicken *(inf).*

cribbage [ˈkrɪbɪdʒ] *n* Cribbage *nt.*

crick [krɪk] **1 n a** ~ **in one's neck/back** ein steifes Genick/ein steifer Rücken. **2 vt to** ~ **one's neck/back** sich *(dat)* ein steifes Genick/einen steifen Rücken zuziehen.

cricket¹ [ˈkrɪkɪt] *n (insect)* Grille *f.*

cricket² *n (Sport)* Kricket *nt.* **that's not** ~ *(fig inf)* das ist nicht fair.

cricket *in cpds* Kricket-; ~ **bat** *n* (Kricket)schlagholz *nt.*

cricketer [ˈkrɪkɪtə*r*] *n* Kricketspieler(in *f*) *m.*

cricket: ~ **match** *n* Kricketspiel *nt;* ~ **pitch** *n* Kricketfeld *nt.*

cri de cœur [ˌkriːdəˈkɜː*r*] *n* verzweifelter Stoßseufzer.

cried [kraɪd] *pret, ptp of* cry.

crier [ˈkraɪə*r*] *n (town* ~*)* Ausrufer *m; (court* ~*)* Gerichtsdiener *m.*

crikey [ˈkraɪkɪ] *interj (dated Brit inf)* Mann *(inf).*

crime [kraɪm] *n* **(a)** Straftat *f; (murder, robbery with violence etc also, fig)* Verbrechen *nt.* **it's not a** ~! das ist nicht verboten; **it's a** ~ **to throw away all that good food** es ist eine Sünde *or* eine Schande, all das gute Essen wegzuwerfen.

(b) *no pl* Verbrechen *pl.* ~ **and punishment** Verbrechen und Verbrechensverfolgung; **to lead a life of** ~ kriminell leben; ~ **is on the increase** die Zahl der Verbrechen nimmt zu; ~ **doesn't pay** Verbrechen lohnen sich nicht.

Crimea [kraɪˈmɪə] *n (Geog) (Insel)* Krim *f; (inf: Crimean War)* der Krimkrieg.

Crimean [kraɪˈmɪən] **1 n (person)** Krimbewohner(in *f*) *m.* **2 adj** Krim-. **she's** ~ sie kommt von der Krim.

crime: ~ **prevention** *n* Verbrechensverhütung *f*, präventive Verbrechensbekämpfung *(form);* ~ **prevention officer** *n* Polizeibeamter, der sich aktiv um die Verhütung von Verbrechen bemüht; ~ **rate** *n* Zahl *f* der Verbrechen, Verbrechensrate *f;* ~ **story** *n* Kriminalgeschichte *f*, Krimi *m (inf);* ~ **wave** *n* Verbrechenswelle *f.*

criminal ['krɪmɪnl] **1** n Straftäter(in f) m (form), Kriminelle(r) mf; (guilty of capital crimes also, fig) Verbrecher(in f) m.
  2 adj **(a)** kriminell, verbrecherisch; action also strafbar. ~ assault Körperverletzung f; **C~ Investigation Department** (Brit) Kriminalpolizei f; ~ **code** Strafgesetzbuch nt; ~ **law** Strafrecht nt; ~ **lawyer** Anwalt m für Strafsachen; (specializing in defence) Strafverteidiger m; ~ **offence** strafbare Handlung; **to take** ~ **proceedings against sb** strafrechtlich gegen jdn vorgehen; **to have a** ~ **record** vorbestraft sein; **C~ Records Office** Kriminaldienststelle f zur Führung der Verbrecherkartei.
  (b) (fig) kriminell. **it's** ~ **to stay indoors in such lovely weather** es ist eine Schande, bei so schönem Wetter drinnen zu bleiben.

criminality [ˌkrɪmɪˈnælɪtɪ] n Kriminalität f.

criminally ['krɪmɪnəlɪ] adv kriminell, verbrecherisch. **he thought she behaved quite** ~ (fig) seiner Meinung nach hat sie sich kriminell verhalten.

criminologist [ˌkrɪmɪˈnɒlədʒɪst] n Kriminologe m, Kriminologin f.

criminology [ˌkrɪmɪˈnɒlədʒɪ] n = Kriminologie f.

crimp [krɪmp] vt hair (mit der Brennschere) wellen.

crimplene ® ['krɪmpliːn] n = knitterfreier Trevira ®.

crimson ['krɪmzn] **1** adj purpurn, purpurrot; sky blutrot, purpurrot (inf); (through blushing) knallrot (inf), dunkelrot. **to turn or go** ~ person, face knallrot (inf) or dunkelrot werden or anlaufen; (sky) sich blutrot färben.
  2 n Purpur, Purpurrot nt.
  3 vt (poet) sky purpurrot or blutrot färben.
  4 vi (poet: sky) sich purpurrot or blutrot färben.

cringe [krɪndʒ] vi **(a)** (shrink back) zurückschrecken (at vor +dat); (fig) schaudern. **to** ~ **before sb** vor jdm zurückweichen or -schrecken; **he** ~**d at the thought** er or ihm schauderte bei dem Gedanken; **he** ~**d when she mispronounced his name** er zuckte zusammen, als sie seinen Namen falsch aussprach.
  (b) (humble oneself, fawn) katzbuckeln, kriechen (to vor +dat). **to go cringing to sb** zu jdm gekrochen kommen; **a cringing person** ein Kriecher m; **cringing behaviour** kriecherisches Benehmen.

crinkle ['krɪŋkl] **1** n (Knitter)falte f; (in skin) Fältchen nt.
  2 vt paper, foil, dress etc (zer)knittern; cardboard, plastic etc knicken; edge of paper wellen. **the paper was all** ~**d** das Papier war ganz zerknittert.
  3 vi (wrinkle) (paper, foil, dress etc) knittern; (face, skin) (Lach)fältchen bekommen; (edges of paper) sich wellen, wellig werden; (curl: hair) sich krausen. **the skin round his eyes** ~**d when he smiled** er bekam tausend Fältchen um die Augen, wenn er lächelte.

crinkly ['krɪŋklɪ] adj (+er) (inf) (wrinkled) paper, foil etc zerknittert; edges wellig; hair krauselig (inf).

crinoline ['krɪnəliːn] n Krinoline f.

cripes [kraɪps] interj (dated Brit inf) Mann (inf).

cripple ['krɪpl] **1** n Krüppel m.
  2 vt person zum Krüppel machen; arm, legs etc verkrüppeln; ship, plane aktionsunfähig machen; (fig) industry, exports lahmlegen, lähmen. **the ship was** ~**d** das Schiff war nicht mehr aktionsfähig; ~**d with rheumatism** von Rheuma praktisch gelähmt; **to be** ~**d for life** lebenslang ein Krüppel sein.

crippling ['krɪplɪŋ] adj taxes, mortgage repayments erdrückend; strikes alles lähmend attr; pain lähmend.

cripplingly ['krɪplɪŋlɪ] adv expensive unerschwinglich.

crisis ['kraɪsɪs] n, pl **crises** ['kraɪsiːz] Krise f (also Med). **to reach** ~ **point** den Höhepunkt erreichen; **that was a** ~ **in his life** (decisive moment) das war ein entscheidender Punkt in seinem Leben; (emotional) ~ das war eine Krise in seinem Leben; **in this time of** ~ in dieser krisenreichen or schweren Zeit; **in times of** ~ in Krisenzeiten.

crisp [krɪsp] **1** adj (+er) apple, lettuce knackig, fest; bread, biscuits, bacon knusprig; snow verharscht; leaves trocken; appearance adrett, frisch; curls, clothes steif; manner, voice, style of writing, remark knapp; air, weather, colour frisch; sound klar; (Sport) shot sauber; pound note brandneu.
  2 n (Brit: potato ~) Chip m. **to burn sth to a** ~ etw verbrutzeln lassen; toast etw schwarz brennen.
  3 vt (also ~ **up**) bread aufbacken.

crispbread ['krɪspbred] n Knäckebrot nt.

crispen (up) ['krɪspn('ʌp)] vt (sep) bread aufbacken; blouse etc auffrischen.

crisper ['krɪspə'] n (in fridge) Gemüsefach nt.

crisply ['krɪsplɪ] adv knackig; baked, fried knusprig; starched steif; dressed adrett, frisch; write, speak knapp. **the snow/leaves crunched** ~ **under his feet** der Schnee knirschte/die Blätter raschelten unter seinen Füßen; **the notes rang out** ~ die Töne kamen klar.

crispness ['krɪspnɪs] n see adj Knackigkeit, Festheit f; Knusprigkeit f; Verharschtheit f; Trockenheit f; Adrettheit, Frische f; Steifheit f; Knappheit f; Frische f; Klarheit f; Sauberkeit f.

crispy ['krɪspɪ] adj (+er) (inf) knusprig.

criss-cross ['krɪskrɒs] **1** n Kreuzundquer nt. **2** adj pattern Kreuz-. **3** adv kreuz und quer. **4** vt mit einem Kreuzmuster versehen.

criterion [kraɪˈtɪərɪən] n, pl **criteria** [kraɪˈtɪərɪə] Kriterium nt. **then, by the same** ~, **he is guilty too** dann ist er ebenso schuldig.

critic ['krɪtɪk] n Kritiker(in f) m. **literary** ~ Literaturkritiker(in f) m; **he's a terrible** ~ (very critical) er kritisiert sich kritisch; **he's his own worst** ~ er kritisiert sich selbst am meisten, er ist sein schlimmster Kritiker; **he is a constant** ~ **of the government** er kritisiert ständig die Regierung or an der Regierung.

critical ['krɪtɪkəl] adj **(a)** (fault-finding, discriminating)

kritisch. **the book enjoyed a** ~ **success** das Buch kam bei den Kritikern an; ~ **reviews** Kritiken pl; ~ **edition** kritische Ausgabe; **to cast a** ~ **eye over sth** sich (dat) etw kritisch ansehen; **to be** ~ **of sb/sth** jdn/etw kritisieren.
  (b) (dangerous, Sci) kritisch; (crucial also) entscheidend.

critically ['krɪtɪkəlɪ] adv **(a)** kritisch. **(b)** ill schwer. **to be** ~ **important** von kritischer Bedeutung sein.

criticism ['krɪtɪsɪzəm] n Kritik f. **literary** ~ Literaturkritik f; **to come in for a lot of** ~ schwer kritisiert werden.

criticize ['krɪtɪsaɪz] vti kritisieren.

critique [krɪˈtiːk] n Kritik f.

critter ['krɪtə'] n (US dial) see **creature**.

croak [krəʊk] **1** n (of frog) Quaken nt no pl; (of raven, person) Krächzen nt no pl. ~, **went the frog/raven** quak, machte der Frosch/krakra, machte der Rabe.
  2 vti **(a)** (frog) quaken; (raven, person) krächzen.
  (b) (sl: die) **he** ~**ed (it)** er ist abgekratzt (sl).

croaky ['krəʊkɪ] adj (+er) (inf) voice krächzend. **you sound a bit** ~ du klingst etwas heiser.

Croat ['krəʊæt] n (person) Kroate m, Kroatin f; (language) Kroatisch nt.

Croatia [krəʊˈeɪʃɪə] n Kroatien nt.

Croatian [krəʊˈeɪʃɪən] **1** n see **Croat**. **2** adj kroatisch.

crochet ['krəʊʃeɪ] **1** n (also ~ **work**) Häkelei f. ~ **hook** Häkelnadel f; **to do a lot of** ~ viel häkeln. **2** vti häkeln.

crock¹ [krɒk] n (jar) Topf m; (pottery chip) Scherbe f.

crock² n (inf) (vehicle) Kiste f (inf); (person) Wrack nt (inf); (horse) Klepper m. **an old** ~**s race** ein Oldtimer-Rennen nt.

♦**crock up** vi (inf) zusammenklappen (inf).

crockery ['krɒkərɪ] n (Brit) Geschirr nt.

crocodile ['krɒkədaɪl] n **(a)** Krokodil nt. **(b)** (Brit Sch) **to walk in a** ~ zwei und zwei hintereinandergehen; **the long** ~ **of little girls** der lange Zug kleiner Mädchen, die zwei und zwei hintereinander gingen/gehen.

crocodile: ~ **clip** n Krokodilklemme f; ~ **tears** npl Krokodilstränen pl.

crocus ['krəʊkəs] n Krokus m.

Croesus ['kriːsəs] n Krösus m. **to be as rich as** ~ ein (richtiger) Krösus sein.

croft [krɒft] n (esp Scot) kleines Pachtgrundstück; (house) Kate f.

crofter ['krɒftə'] n (esp Scot) Kleinpächter(in f) m.

croissant ['krwɑːsɒŋ] n Hörnchen nt.

crone [krəʊn] n Tante f (inf).

crony ['krəʊnɪ] n Freund(in f), Genosse (inf) m, Genossin (inf) f.

crook¹ [krʊk] **1** n **(a)** (dishonest person) Gauner m (inf).
  (b) (staff) (of shepherd) Hirtenstab, Krummstab m; (of bishop also) Bischofsstab m; see **hook**.
  (c) (bend: in road, river) Biegung f; (in arm) Beuge f.
  2 vt finger krümmen; arm beugen. **she only has to** ~ **her (little) finger and he comes running** sie braucht nur mit dem kleinen Finger zu winken, und schon kommt er angerannt.

crook² adj (Austral inf) **(a)** (sick) krank. **he's** ~ **with the flu/a cold** er hat die Grippe/eine Erkältung; **he feels/is** ~ er fühlt sich mies (inf) or lausig (inf)/es geht ihm mies (inf).
  (b) (not functioning) kaputt (inf); (not good) mies (inf).
  (c) (angry) wild (inf). **to go** ~ **at or on sb** wegen jdm wild werden.

crooked ['krʊkɪd] adj (lit) (bent) krumm; (tilted, sloping also), smile schief; (fig inf: dishonest) method krumm; person unehrlich. **your hat's** ~ dein Hut sitzt schief.

croon [kruːn] **1** vt (sing softly) leise or sanft singen; (usu pej: sentimentally) gefühlvoll or schmalzig (pej inf) singen. **2** vi (sing softly) leise or sanft singen; (usu pej: sentimentally) Schnulzen (pej inf) or sentimentale Lieder singen.

crooner ['kruːnə'] n Sänger m (sentimentaler Lieder), Schnulzensänger m (pej inf).

crop [krɒp] **1** n **(a)** (produce) Ernte f; (species grown) (Feld)frucht f; (fig: large number) Schwung m. ~ **rotation** Fruchtwechsel m; cereal ~**s** Getreidearten pl; **the cereal** ~**s were destroyed** die Getreideernte wurde zerstört; **the barley** ~ **is looking good** die Gerste steht gut; **a good** ~ **of fruit/potatoes** eine gute Obst-/Kartoffelernte; **the beef** ~ die Rindfleischproduktion; **to be in or under/out of** ~ bebaut/nicht bebaut sein; **he grows a different** ~ **every year** er baut jedes Jahr etwas anderes an; **to bring the** ~**s in** die Ernte einbringen; **a** ~ **of lies/questions** eine Masse Lügen/Fragen (inf).
  (b) (of bird) Kropf m.
  (c) (of whip) Stock m; (hunting ~) Reitpeitsche f.
  (d) (hairstyle) Kurzhaarschnitt m. **to give sb a close** ~ jdm die Haare gehörig stutzen.
  2 vt hair stutzen; horse's or dog's tail also kupieren. **it's best to keep the grass** ~**ped short** man sollte das Gras kurz halten; **the goat** ~**ped the grass** die Ziege fraß das Gras ab; **the goat kept the grass** ~**ped short** die Ziege hat darauf gesorgt, daß das Gras immer ganz kurz war; ~**ped hair, hair** ~**ped short** kurzgeschnittenes Haar.

♦**crop out** vi auftauchen; (minerals) zutage treten.

♦**crop up** vi aufkommen. **something's** ~**ped** ~ es ist etwas dazwischengekommen; **he was ready for anything that might** ~ ~ er war auf alle Eventualitäten gefaßt.

crop dusting n Schädlingsbekämpfung f (aus dem Flugzeug).

cropper ['krɒpə'] n **(a)** (person) Anbauer m. **these plants are poor** ~**s** diese Pflanzen bringen nicht viel Ertrag. **(b)** (inf) **to come a** ~ (lit: fall) hinfliegen (inf); (fig: fail) auf die Nase fallen.

crop: ~ **sprayer** n (person) Schädlingsbekämpfer m; (plane) Schädlingsbekämpfungsflugzeug nt; (tractor) Schädlingsbekämpfungsfahrzeug, Besprühungsfahrzeug nt; ~ **spraying** n Schädlingsbekämpfung f (durch Besprühen).

croquet ['krəʊkeɪ] n Krocket(spiel) nt. ~ **lawn** Krocketrasen m.

croquette [krəʊ'ket] n Krokette f.

crosier, crozier ['krəʊʒɪə'] n Bischofsstab, Hirtenstab, Krummstab m.

cross¹ [krɒs] **1** n (a) Kreuz nt. to make one's ~ sein Kreuz(chen) machen or setzen; to make the sign of the C~ das Kreuzzeichen machen or schlagen; the C~ and the Crescent Kreuz und Halbmond; to bear/take up one's ~ (fig) sein Kreuz tragen/auf sich (acc) nehmen; we all have our ~ to bear/our little ~es (inf) wir haben alle unser Kreuz zu tragen.

(b) (bias) on the ~ schräg; to be cut on the ~ schräg geschnitten sein.

(c) (hybrid) Kreuzung f; (fig) Mittelding nt.

2 attr (transverse) street, line etc Quer-.

3 vt (a) (go across) (person, train, road) road, river, mountains, Channel überqueren; (on foot) picket line etc überschreiten; country, desert, room durchqueren; (bridge) river, road überqueren, führen über (+acc); (plane) continent, desert überqueren. to ~ the road über die Straße gehen, die Straße überqueren; to ~ sb's path (fig) jdm über den Weg laufen; it ~ed my mind that ... es fiel mir ein, daß ..., mir kam der Gedanke, daß ...; don't ~ your bridges until you come to them (prov) laß die Probleme auf dich zukommen; we'll ~ that bridge when we come to it lassen wir das Problem mal auf uns zukommen, das sind ungelegte Eier (inf).

(b) (put at right-angles, intersect) kreuzen. to ~ one's legs/arms die Beine übereinanderschlagen/die Arme verschränken; the lines are ~ed (Telec) die Leitungen überschneiden sich; line AB ~es line CD at point E AB schneidet CD in E; to ~ sb's palm with silver jdm ein Geldstück in die Hand drücken; keep your fingers ~ed for me! (inf) drück or halt mir die Daumen! (inf); I'm keeping my fingers ~ed (inf) ich drücke or halte die Daumen (inf).

(c) (put a line across) letter, t einen Querstrich machen durch; (Brit) cheque ≈ zur Verrechnung ausstellen. a ~ed cheque ein Verrechnungsscheck m; to ~ sth through etw durchstreichen; see dot.

(d) (make the sign of the C~) to ~ oneself sich bekreuzigen; ~ my/your heart (inf) Ehrenwort, Hand aufs Herz.

(e) (mark with a ~) ankreuzen.

(f) (go against) plans durchkreuzen. to ~ sb jdn verärgern; to be ~ed in love in der Liebe enttäuscht werden.

(g) animal, fruit kreuzen.

4 vi (a) (across road) hinüberfahren, die Straße überqueren; (across Channel etc) hinüberfahren. "~ now" „gehen"; to ~ on the green light bei Grün über die Straße gehen.

(b) (intersect) sich kreuzen; (lines also) sich schneiden. our paths have ~ed several times (fig) unsere Wege haben sich öfters gekreuzt.

(c) (pass: letters etc) sich kreuzen.

♦**cross off** vt sep streichen (prep obj aus, von).

♦**cross out** vt sep ausstreichen.

♦**cross over 1** vi (a) (cross the road) hinübergehen, die Straße überqueren. (b) (change sides) übergehen, überwechseln (to zu). **2** vi +prep obj road, street überqueren.

cross² adj (+er) böse, sauer (inf). to be ~ with sb mit jdm or auf jdn böse sein.

cross: ~-action n (Jur) Widerklage f; ~bar n (of bicycle) Stange f; (Sport) Querlatte f; ~beam n (girder) Querbalken m; (Sport) Schwebebalken m; ~bench n usu pl (Parl) Bank, wo die weder zur Regierungs- noch zur Oppositionspartei gehörenden Abgeordneten sitzen; ~bencher ['krɒsbentʃə'] n (Parl) Abgeordneter, der weder der Regierungs- noch der Oppositionspartei angehört; ~bill n (Orn) Kreuzschnabel m; ~bones npl gekreuzte Knochen pl (unter einem Totenkopf); see skull; ~bow n (Stand)armbrust f; ~bred adj (Zool, Biol) gekreuzt; ~breed (Zool, Biol) **1** n Kreuzung f; **2** vt kreuzen; ~Channel attr ferries, swimmer Kanal-; ~-Channel swim ein Durchschwimmen des Kanals; ~-check **1** n Gegenprobe f; **2** vt facts, figures überprüfen; equation die Gegenprobe machen bei; ~-country **1** adj Querfeldein-; **2** adv querfeldein; **3** n (race) Querfeldeinrennen nt; ~-current n Gegenströmung f; ~-examination n Kreuzverhör nt (of über +acc); ~-examine vt ins Kreuzverhör nehmen; ~-eyed adj schielend; to be ~-eyed schielen; ~-fertilization n, no pl (Bot) Kreuzbefruchtung, Fremdbestäubung f; (fig) gegenseitige Befruchtung; ~-fertilize vt (Bot) kreuzbefruchten; ~fire n Kreuzfeuer nt; to be caught in the ~fire (lit, fig) ins Kreuzfeuer geraten; ~-gartered adj (old) mit kreuzweise geschnürten Waden; ~-grained adj wood quergefasert; (grumpy) mürrisch; (perverse) querköpfig; ~hatch vt mit Kreuzlagen schattieren; ~hatching n Kreuzschattierung f.

crossing ['krɒsɪŋ] n (a) (act) Überquerung f; (sea ~) Überfahrt f. (b) (~ place) Übergang m; (crossroads) Kreuzung f.

cross: ~-keys npl (Her) gekreuzte Schlüssel pl; ~kick n (Ftbl) Querpaß m (nach innen); ~-legged adj, adv mit gekreuzten Beinen; (on ground) im Schneidersitz.

crossly ['krɒslɪ] adv böse, verärgert.

cross: ~over n (Rail) Gleiskreuzung f; ~patch n (inf) Brummbär m (inf); ~piece n (bar) Querstange f; ~ply **1** adj Diagonal-; **2** n (inf) Diagonalreifen m; ~-pollinate vt fremdbestäuben; ~-pollination n Fremdbestäubung f; ~-purposes npl to be or talk at ~-purposes aneinander vorbeireden; he was at ~-purposes with her sie haben aneinander vorbeigeredet; ~-question vt ins ~-examine; ~-refer vt verweisen (to auf +acc); ~-reference **1** n Verweis m (to auf +acc); **2** vt see ~refer; ~roads n sing or pl (lit) Kreuzung f; (fig) Scheideweg m; ~ section n Querschnitt m; to draw sth in ~ section etw im Querschnitt zeichnen; a ~ section of the population ein Querschnitt durch die Bevölkerung; ~-stitch **1** n (Sew) Kreuzstich m; **2** vt im Kreuzstich arbeiten; ~talk n, no pl (a) (witty dialogue) Wortgefecht nt; Wortgefechte pl; (b) (Telec)

Nebensprechen nt; ~-town adj (US) quer durch die Stadt; ~walk n (US) Fußgängerüberweg m; ~ways adv see ~wise; ~wind n Seitenwind m; ~wise adv (transversely) quer; ~word (puzzle) n Kreuzworträtsel nt; ~wort n gewöhnliches Kreuzlabkraut.

crotch [krɒtʃ] n (a) (in tree etc) Gabelung f.

(b) (of trousers) Schritt m; (Anat) Unterleib m. a kick in the ~ ein Tritt zwischen die Beine; she wears her skirts about an inch below the ~ ihre Röcke reichen nur ein Paar Zentimeter über den Po (inf).

crotchet ['krɒtʃɪt] n (a) (Mus) Viertelnote f. ~ rest Viertelpause f. (b) (inf: cross person) Miesepeter m (inf).

crotchety ['krɒtʃɪtɪ] adj (inf: cross) schlecht gelaunt, miesepetrig (inf); child quengelig (inf).

crouch [kraʊtʃ] **1** vi sich zusammenkauern, kauern. to ~ down sich niederkauern. **2** n Hocke f; (of animal) Kauerstellung f.

croup¹ [kru:p] n, no pl (Med) Krupp m, Kehlkopfdiphtherie f.

croup² n (of horse) Kruppe f.

croupier ['kru:pɪeɪ] n Croupier m.

crouton ['kru:tɒn] n Crouton m.

crow¹ [krəʊ] n (a) (Orn) Krähe f. as the ~ flies (in der) Luftlinie; to eat ~ (US inf) zu Kreuze kriechen. (b) (inf) see crowbar.

crow² **1** n (of cock, baby) Krähen nt no pl; (of person) J(a)uchzer m. a ~ of delight ein Freudenjauchzer m.

2 vi (a) pret ~ed or (old) crew, ptp ~ed (cock) krähen.

(b) pret, ptp ~ed (baby) krähen; (person) j(a)uchzen; (fig) (boast) sich brüsten, angeben (about mit); (exalt) hämisch frohlocken (over über +acc).

crow: ~bar n Brecheisen nt; ~berry n Krähenbeere f.

crowd [kraʊd] **1** n (a) Menschenmenge f; (Sport, Theat) Zuschauermenge f. to be swept along by the ~ or in the ~(s) von der or in der Menge mitgerissen werden; to get lost in the ~(s) in der Menge verlorengehen; ~s of people Menschenmassen, große Menschenmengen pl; that would pass in a ~ (fig) das geht (durch), wenn man nicht zu genau hinsieht; to get a good ~ at a match bei einem Spiel eine Menge Zuschauer haben; we were quite a ~ wir waren eine ganze Menge Leute; a whole ~ of us ein ganzer Haufen von uns (inf); ~ scene (Theat) Massenszene f.

(b) (set, of people, clique) Clique f, Haufen m (inf). the university ~ der Uni-Haufen (inf), die Uni-Clique; I'm not in that ~ or one of that ~ ich gehöre nicht zu diesem Haufen (inf) or zu denen; they're a nice ~ sie sind ein netter Haufen (inf).

(c) no pl (the masses) the ~ die (breite) Masse; to go with or follow the ~ mit der Herde laufen; she hates to be just one of the ~ sie geht nicht gern in der Masse unter.

2 vi (sich) drängen. to ~ (a)round/together/in sich herumdrängen/sich zusammendrängen/(sich) hereindrängen; to ~ (a)round sb/sth (sich) um jdn/etw herumdrängen or scharen; memories ~ed in on me Erinnerungen drängten or stürmten auf mich ein.

3 vt (a) to ~ the streets die Straßen bevölkern; to ~ a room with furniture eine Wohnung mit Möbeln vollstopfen; to ~ furniture into a room Möbel in eine Wohnung stopfen; a room ~ed with children ein Zimmer voller Kinder; it will really ~ the office having three new people mit drei neuen Leuten wird es im Büro sicherlich eng werden; to ~ things together Dinge eng zusammendrängen; the holiday was ~ed with incidents die Ferien waren sehr ereignisreich; a mind ~ed with facts eine Ansammlung von Faktenwissen (im Kopf).

(b) (inf: harass) to ~ sb jdn drängen, jdm auf den Füßen stehen (inf); (creditors) jdn bedrängen.

♦**crowd out** vt sep (not let in) wegdrängen; (make leave) herausdrängen; (Press) article etc verdrängen. the pub was ~ed ≈ das Lokal war gerammelt voll (inf) or proppenvoll (inf).

crowded ['kraʊdɪd] adj train, shop etc überfüllt. the streets/shops/trains are ~ es ist voll auf den Straßen in den Geschäften/Zügen; to play to a ~ house (Theat) vor vollem Haus spielen.

crowd-puller ['kraʊdpʊlə'] n Kassenmagnet m.

crowfoot ['krəʊfʊt] n (Bot) Hahnenfuß m.

crown [kraʊn] **1** n (a) Krone f. ~ of thorns Dornenkrone f; the C~ die Krone; to wear the ~ auf dem Thron sitzen; to be heir to the ~ Thronfolger(in) sein; to succeed to the ~ die Thronfolge antreten.

(b) (coin) Krone f.

(c) (top) (of head) Wirbel m; (skull itself) Schädel m; (head measurement) Kopf(umfang) m; (of hat) Kopf m; (of road) Wölbung f; (of arch) Scheitelpunkt m; (of roof) First m; (of tooth, tree) Krone f; (of hill) Kuppe f.

(d) (size of paper) englisches Papierformat (≈ 45 × 38 cm²).

(e) (fig: climax, completion) Krönung f.

2 vt (a) krönen. he was ~ed king er ist zum König gekrönt worden; ~ed head gekröntes Haupt.

(b) (usu pass: top) the hill is ~ed with trees die Bergkuppe ist mit Bäumen bewachsen; the cake was ~ed with marzipan decorations der Kuchen war zur Krönung des Ganzen (noch) mit Marzipanfiguren geschmückt; to be ~ed with success (fig) von Erfolg gekrönt sein.

(c) (fig: complete, form climax to) krönen. to ~ it all it began to snow (inf) zur Krönung des Ganzen begann es zu schneien; that ~s everything! (inf) das ist doch der Gipfel or die Höhe! (inf).

(d) (in draughts etc) eine Dame bekommen mit.

(e) tooth eine Krone machen für. the tooth had already been ~ed before der Zahn hatte schon vorher eine Krone gehabt.

(f) (inf: hit) eine runterhauen (+dat) (inf).

crown: ~ cap n see ~ cork; ~ colony n Kronkolonie f; ~ cork n Kronenkorken m; ~ court n Bezirksgericht nt für Strafsachen.

crowning ['kraʊnɪŋ] **1** n Krönung f. **2** adj success, achievement krönend. her hair was her ~ glory ihr Haar war ihre größte

Zierde; **that symphony was his ~ glory** diese Symphonie war die Krönung seines Werkes.
crown: **~ jewels** npl Kronjuwelen pl; **~ lands** npl königliche Ländereien pl, Ländereien pl der Krone; **~ prince** n Kronprinz m; **~ princess** n Kronprinzessin f; **~ wheel** n Kronenrad, Kammrad nt; **~ witness** n Zeuge m/Zeugin f der Anklage.
crow's: **~ feet** npl Krähenfüße pl; **~ nest** n (Naut) Mastkorb m; (on foremast) Krähennest nt.
crozier n see **crosier**.
crucial ['kru:ʃəl] adj (a) (decisive) entscheidend (to für). (b) (very important) äußert wichtig. (c) (Med) incision etc kreuzförmig, Kreuz-.
crucially ['kru:ʃəlɪ] adv ausschlaggebend; different bedeutend. **~ necessary** äußerst wichtig; **~ important** von entscheidender Bedeutung.
crucible ['kru:sɪbl] n (Schmelz)tiegel m; **~ steel** n Tiegelgußstahl m.
crucifix ['kru:sɪfɪks] n Kruzifix nt.
crucifixion [,kru:sɪ'fɪkʃən] n Kreuzigung f.
cruciform ['kru:sɪfɔ:m] adj kreuzförmig.
crucify ['kru:sɪfaɪ] vt (a) kreuzigen. (b) (fig) play, author verreißen; person in der Luft zerreißen (inf). (c) (mortify) the flesh abtöten.
crude [kru:d] adj (+er) (a) (unprocessed) Roh-, roh. (b) (vulgar) expression, story etc ordinär, derb. (c) (unsophisticated) method, model, implement primitiv; sketch grob; manners ungehobelt, grob; attempt unbeholfen.
crudely ['kru:dlɪ] adv (a) (vulgarly) ordinär, derb. (b) (unsophisticatedly) primitiv; draw grob; behave ungehobelt. **to put it ~** um es ganz grob auszudrücken.
crudeness ['kru:dnɪs], **crudity** ['kru:dɪtɪ] n (a) (vulgarity) Derbheit f. (b) see adj (c) Primitivität f; Grobheit f; Ungehobelte(s) nt (of gen, in +dat); Unbeholfenheit f.
cruel ['kruəl] adj grausam (to zu); remark, wit, critic, winter also unbarmherzig. **to ~ to animals/one's dog** ein Tierquäler sein/seinen Hund quälen; **that is ~ to animals** das ist Tierquälerei; **is taming elephants ~?** ist die Abrichtung von Elefanten Tierquälerei?; **don't be ~!** sei nicht so gemein!; **sometimes you have to be ~ to be kind** manchmal ist es letzten Endes besser, man hat mal hart ist.
cruelly ['kruəlɪ] adv (+vb) grausam; (+adj) auf grausame Art.
cruelty ['kruəltɪ] n see adj Grausamkeit f (to gegenüber); Unbarmherzigkeit f. **~ to children** Kindesmißhandlung f; **~ to animals** Tierquälerei f; **physical/mental ~** Grausamkeit f/ seelische Grausamkeit.
cruet ['kru:ɪt] n (a) (set) Gewürzständer m, Menage f; (for oil) Krügchen nt. **would you pass the ~?** könnten Sie mir bitte die Gewürze reichen? (b) (Eccl) Krügchen nt.
cruise [kru:z] 1 vi (a) eine Kreuzfahrt/Kreuzfahrten machen; (ship also) kreuzen.
(b) (travel at cruising speed) (car) Dauergeschwindigkeit fahren; (aircraft) (mit Reisegeschwindigkeit) fliegen; (athlete) locker laufen; (drive around) herumfahren. **I was cruising at 70** ich bin konstant 70 gefahren; **we were cruising along the road** wir fuhren (gemächlich) die Straße entlang; **we are now cruising at a height/speed of** ... wir fliegen nun in einer Flughöhe/mit einer Reisegeschwindigkeit von ...; **the cyclist ~d down the hill** der Radfahrer rollte den Berg hinunter.
2 vt (ship) befahren; (car) streets fahren auf (+dat); area abfahren.
3 n Kreuzfahrt f. **to go on** or **for a ~** eine Kreuzfahrt machen.
cruiser ['kru:zə'] n (Naut) Kreuzer m; (pleasure ~) Vergnügungsjacht f.
cruiserweight ['kru:zəweɪt] n (Boxing) Halbschwergewicht nt.
cruising ['kru:zɪŋ] n Kreuzfahrten pl. **to go ~** eine Kreuzfahrt/Kreuzfahrten machen.
cruising: **~ speed** n Reisegeschwindigkeit f; **~ yacht** n Vergnügungsjacht f.
cruller ['krʌlə'] n (US) Art f von Berliner.
crumb [krʌm] 1 n (a) (of bread etc) Krümel m, Krume f, Brösel m; (inside of loaf) Krume f. **can you spare a ~?** haben Sie eine Scheibe Brot für einen hungrigen Menschen?; **~s from the rich man's/master's table** Brosamen, die von des Reichen/des Herren Tisch fallen; **~s of wisdom** ein bißchen Weisheit; **a few ~s of information** ein paar Informationsbrocken; **that's one ~ of comfort** das ist (wenigstens) ein winziger Trost.
(b) (sl) (fool) Depp m (inf); (brute) Lump m (inf).
2 interj **~s!** (inf) Mensch! (inf), Mensch Meier! (inf).
3 vt (Cook) fish etc panieren.
crumble ['krʌmbl] 1 vt zerkrümeln, zerbröckeln. **to ~ sth into/onto sth** etw in/auf etw (acc) krümeln or bröckeln.
2 vi (brick, earth) bröckeln; (bread, cake etc) krümeln; (also **~ away**) (earth, building) zerbröckeln; (fig) (resistance, opposition) sich auflösen, schmelzen; (hopes) schwinden; (plans) ins Wanken geraten.
3 n (Cook) Obst nt mit Streusel; (topping) Streusel pl. **apple/rhubarb ~** mit Streuseln bestreutes, überbackenes Apfel/Rhabarberdessert.
crumbly ['krʌmblɪ] adj (+er) stone, earth bröckelig; cake, bread krümelig, bröselig.
crummy ['krʌmɪ] adj (+er) (inf) mies (inf), Scheiß- (sl).
crumpet ['krʌmpɪt] n (a) (Cook) kleiner dicker Pfannkuchen. (b) (esp Brit sl: women) Miezen pl (sl). **he fancied a bit of ~** ihm war nach ein bißchen Sex; **she's a nice bit of ~** sie ist sehr sexy, das ist 'ne dufte Mieze (sl).
crumple ['krʌmpl] 1 vt (also **~ up**) paper, dress, fabric (crease) zer- or verknittern, zerknautschen; (screw up) zusammenknüllen; metal eindrücken. **the force of the impact ~d the car/bonnet** die Wucht des Aufpralls drückte die Kühlerhaube ein/ quetschte das Auto zusammen.

2 vi (lit, fig: collapse) zusammenbrechen; (get creased: paper) krumpeln, knittern; (car, metal) zusammengedrückt werden. **her face** or **features ~d** ihr Gesicht verzog sich (zum Weinen).
crumple zone n Knautschzone f.
crunch [krʌntʃ] 1 vt (a) apple, biscuit etc mampfen (inf).
(b) he **~ed** the beetle/ice/gravel underfoot der Käfer zerknackte/das Eis zersplitterte/der Kies knirschte unter seinen Füßen; **to ~ the gears** (Aut) den Gang/die Gänge einwürgen (inf).
2 vi (a) (gravel, snow etc) knirschen; (gears) krachen. he **~ed across the gravel** er ging mit knirschenden Schritten über den Kies.
(b) **he was ~ing on a carrot** er mampfte eine Möhre (inf); **he ~ed into the apple** er biß knackend in den Apfel.
3 n (a) (sound) Krachen nt; (of footsteps, gravel etc) Knirschen nt. **the two cars collided with a ~** die zwei Autos krachten zusammen (inf); **~!** Krach!
(b) (inf: car crash) Zusammenstoß m. **there was a ~** es hat gebumst (inf).
(c) (inf: moment of reckoning) **the ~** der große Krach; **when it comes to the ~** wenn es darauf ankommt; **this is the ~** jetzt ist der spannende Moment; **it's/we've come to the ~** jetzt kommt es drauf an, jetzt geht es hart auf hart.
♦**crunch up** vt sep (eat) carrot etc zerbeißen; (crush noisily) garbage etc (krachend) zermahlen.
crunchy ['krʌntʃɪ] adj (+er) apple knackig; biscuit knusprig; snow verharscht.
crupper ['krʌpə'] n (a) (of harness) Schweifriemen m. (b) (hindquarters) Kruppe f.
crusade [kru:'seɪd] 1 n (Hist, fig) Kreuzzug m; (evangelical ~) Missionsfeldzug, Glaubensfeldzug m. 2 vi (Hist, fig) einen Kreuzzug/Kreuzzüge führen; (as evangelist) missionieren.
crusader [kru:'seɪdə'] n (Hist) Kreuzritter m; (fig) Apostel m; (evangelical ~) Glaubensjünger m.
crush [krʌʃ] 1 n (a) (crowd) Gedränge nt. **it'll be a bit of a ~** es wird ein bißchen eng werden; **~ barrier** Absperrung, Barrikade f.
(b) (inf) (infatuation) Schwärmerei f; (object of infatuation) Schwarm m. **to have a ~ on sb** für jdn schwärmen, in jdn verschossen sein (inf); **schoolgirl ~** Schulmädchenschwärmerei f.
(c) (drink) Saftgetränk nt.
2 vt (a) (squeeze, press tightly) quetschen; (damage by squeezing) soft fruit etc zerdrücken, zerquetschen; finger, toes etc quetschen; (rock, car etc) sb zerquetschen; (kill) zu Tode quetschen; (grind, break up) spices, garlic (zer)stoßen; ice stoßen; ore, stone zerkleinern, zerstampfen; scrap metal, garbage zusammenpressen; (crease) clothes, paper zerknittern, zerdrücken; (screw up) letter, paper zerknüllen. **~ed pineapple** klein geschnitzelte Ananas; **I was ~ed between two enormous men in the plane** ich war im Flugzeug zwischen zwei fetten Männern eingequetscht or eingeklemmt; **she ~ed the child to her breast** sie drückte das Kind fest an die Brust; **to ~ sb/sth into sth** jdn in etw (acc) quetschen/etw in etw (acc) stopfen.
(b) (fig) enemy, hopes, self-confidence, sb vernichten; revolution, opposition niederschlagen; (oppress) people, peasants unterdrücken. **she ~ed him with one glance** sie vernichtete ihn mit einem Blick; **to ~ sb's spirit** jdn brechen.
3 vi (a) (crowd) (sich) drängen. **to ~ past/round sb** sich an jdm vorbeidrängen/sich um jdn herumdrängen; **they ~ed into the car** sie quetschten or drängten sich in das Auto.
(b) (clothes, fabric) knittern, knautschen (inf).
♦**crush in** 1 vt sep hineinstopfen (prep obj, -to in +acc). 2 vi (sich) hinein-/hereindrängen.
♦**crush out** vt sep juice etc auspressen, ausquetschen (inf).
♦**crush up** vt sep (a) (pulverize) zerstoßen. (b) (pack tightly together) zusammendrücken or -quetschen. **we were (sitting) all ~ed ~** wir saßen alle zusammengequetscht.
crushing ['krʌʃɪŋ] adj defeat zerschmetternd; blow, look, reply vernichtend; experience niederschmetternd.
crush-resistant ['krʌʃrɪzɪstənt] adj knitterfrei.
crust [krʌst] 1 n (all senses) Kruste f. **the earth's ~** die Erdkruste. 2 vi verkrusten. **~ed port** Portwein m mit Kruste.
crustacean [krʌs'teɪʃən] 1 n Schalentier nt, Krustazee f (spec).
2 adj characteristics, class der Schalentiere or Krustazeen (spec); appearance krebsähnlich.
crustily ['krʌstɪlɪ] adv (fig) barsch.
crusty ['krʌstɪ] adj (+er) knusprig; (fig: irritable) barsch.
crutch [krʌtʃ] n (a) (for walking) Krücke f. **to use sb/sth as a ~** (fig) sich an jdn/etw klammern. (b) (Naut) Baumstütze, Baumschere f. (c) see **crotch** (b).
crux [krʌks] n (of matter, problem) Kern m.
cry [kraɪ] 1 n (a) (inarticulate shout) Schrei m; (call) Ruf m. **to give** or **utter a ~** (auf)schreien, einen Schrei ausstoßen; **a ~ of fear/pain** ein Angstschrei m/Schmerzensschrei m; **a ~ for help** ein Hilferuf m; **he gave a ~ for help** er rief um Hilfe; **the ~ of the rag-and-bone man** das Rufen or der Ruf des Lumpensammlers; **within ~** in Rufweite; see **far**.
(b) (of animal) Schrei m; (Hunt: of hounds) Geheul, Gebell nt. **the pack is in full ~** die Meute hetzt laut bellend or heulend hinter der Beute her; **to be in full ~ after sb** (fig) mit großem Geheul auf jdn stürzen.
(c) (slogan) Parole f; (battle ~) Schlachtruf m.
(d) (outcry) **a ~ for/against sth** ein Ruf m nach etw/ein Protest m gegen etw.
(e) (weep) **a ~ will do you good** weine ruhig, das wird dir guttun; **to have a good/little ~** sich einmal richtig ausweinen or ausheulen (inf)/ein bißchen weinen.
2 vi (a) (weep) weinen, heulen (inf); (baby) schreien. **she was ~ing for her teddy bear/lost youth** sie weinte nach ihrem

Teddy/sie weinte ihrer verlorenen Jugend nach; ... or I'll give you something to ~ for or about ... und dann weißt du, warum du heulst (inf).

(b) (call) rufen; (louder, animal, bird) schreien; (Hunt: hounds) heulen. to ~ for help um Hilfe rufen/schreien; she cried for a nurse/for somebody to come sie rief/schrie nach einer Krankenschwester/nach jemandem.

3 vt **(a)** (shout out) rufen; (louder) schreien. to ~ mercy (old, liter) um Gnade flehen; he cried to me to go away er rief mir zu, daß ich verschwinden solle; see shame, wolf.

(b) (announce) ausrufen.

(c) (weep) bitter tears etc weinen. to ~ one's eyes/heart out sich (dat) die Augen ausweinen/herzzerreißend weinen; to ~ oneself to sleep sich in den Schlaf weinen.

♦**cry down** vt sep (decry) herabsetzen.

♦**cry off** vi einen Rückzieher machen, aussteigen (inf). to ~ ~ from sth aus etw aussteigen (inf), etw (wieder) abblasen (inf).

♦**cry out** vi **(a)** aufschreien. to ~ ~ ~ to sb jdm etwas zuschreien; he cried ~ to me to fetch help er schrie mir zu, ich solle Hilfe holen; well for ~ing ~ loud! (inf) na, das darf doch wohl nicht wahr sein! (inf).

(b) (fig) to be ~ing ~ for sth nach etw schreien; (be suitable for also) sich (geradezu) zu etw anbieten; that building is just ~ing ~ to be turned into a pub dieses Gebäude schreit (geradezu) danach, daß man es in ein Lokal verwandelt.

♦**cry up** vt sep it's/he's not all it's/he's cried ~ to be so großartig ist es/er dann auch wieder nicht.

crybaby ['kraɪbeɪbɪ] n (inf) Heulsuse f (inf).

crying ['kraɪɪŋ] 1 adj (fig: outrageous) injustice schreiend; need dringend. it is a ~ shame es ist jammerschade or ein Jammer. 2 n (weeping) Weinen nt; (of baby) Schreien nt.

crypt [krɪpt] n Krypta f; (burial ~) Gruft f.

cryptic ['krɪptɪk] adj remark etc hintergründig, rätselhaft, schleierhaft; clue, riddle etc verschlüsselt. you're being very ~ du drückst dich sehr rätselhaft or schleierhaft aus.

cryptically ['krɪptɪkəlɪ] adv hintergründig, rätselhaft, schleierhaft. ~ worded letter, remark hintergründig etc formuliert; clue verschlüsselt formuliert.

cryptogram ['krɪptəʊgræm] n Kryptogramm nt.

cryptographer [krɪp'tɒgrəfə'], **cryptographist** [krɪp'tɒgrəfɪst] n Kryptograph m.

cryptographic [ˌkrɪptəʊ'græfɪk] adj kryptographisch, in Geheimschrift verschlüsselt.

cryptography [krɪp'tɒgrəfɪ] n Kryptographie f.

crystal ['krɪstl] 1 n **(a)** (Chem) Kristall m. **(b)** (Rad) Kristall m. **(c)** (on watch) (Uhr)glas nt. **(d)** (~ glass) Kristall nt. **(e)** (quartz) (Quarz)kristall m. 2 adj **(a)** (crystalline) Kristall-, kristallin; (like a ~) kristallartig; (~-glass) Kristall-, kristallen; (quartz) Quarzkristall-. **(b)** (fig) waters, lake kristallklar, glasklar.

crystal: ~ ball n Glaskugel f; I don't have a ~ ball (inf) ich bin (doch) kein Hellseher; you didn't see that in your ~ ball, did you? (inf) das hast du wohl nicht vorausgesehen?; ~-ball gazer n Hellseher(in f) m; ~-ball gazing n Hellseherei f; ~-clear adj (lit, fig) glasklar, völlig klar, vollständig klar; ~-detector n (Rad) Kristalldetektor m; ~-gazer n see ~-ball gazer; ~-gazing 1 n see ~-ball gazing; 2 all these ~-gazing so-called experts sind diese sogenannten Experten, die aus dem Kaffeesatz wahrsagen; ~ lattice n Kristallgitter nt.

crystalline ['krɪstəlaɪn] adj Kristall-, kristallin. ~ lens (Augen)linse f.

crystallization [ˌkrɪstəlaɪ'zeɪʃən] n **(a)** (lit) Kristallisierung f; (out of another substance) Auskristallisierung f.

(b) (fig) (Heraus)kristallisierung f; (crystallized form) kristallisierte Form. after the ~ of these ideas into a theory nachdem sich aus diesen Gedanken eine Theorie herauskristallisiert hatte.

crystallize ['krɪstəlaɪz] 1 vt (lit) zum Kristallisieren bringen; (separating out) auskristallisieren; fruit kandieren; (fig) (feste) Form geben (+dat).

2 vi (lit) kristallisieren; (separate out) (sich) auskristallisieren; (fig) feste Form annehmen. this theory ~d out of many years' research diese Theorie hat sich nach jahrelanger Forschung herauskristallisiert.

crystallized ['krɪstəlaɪzd] adj kristallisiert; fruit kandiert.

crystallography [ˌkrɪstə'lɒgrəfɪ] n Kristallographie f.

crystal set n (Rad) Detektorempfänger m.

CSE (Brit) abbr of Certificate of Secondary Education.

CST abbr of Central Standard Time.

ct abbr of cent.

cub [kʌb] 1 n **(a)** (of animal) Junge(s) nt. **(b)** C~ (C~ Scout) Wölfling m. **(c)** (~ reporter) junger Reporter, junge Reporterin. **(d)** (inf: boy) grüner Junge. 2 vi werfen.

Cuba ['kjuːbə] n Kuba nt.

Cuban ['kjuːbən] 1 adj kubanisch. ~ heel Blockabsatz m. 2 n Kubaner(in f) m.

cubby-hole ['kʌbɪhəʊl] n **(a)** (compartment) Fach nt. **(b)** (room) Kabäuschen, Kabuff nt.

cube [kjuːb] 1 n **(a)** (shape, object) Würfel m. ~ sugar Würfelzucker m.

(b) (Math: power of three) dritte Potenz. ~ root Kubikwurzel f; the ~ of 3 is 27 die dritte Potenz von 3 ist 27, 3 hoch 3 ist 27.

2 vt (Math) in die dritte Potenz erheben, hoch 3 nehmen. four ~d vier hoch drei.

(b) (Cook) würfelig or in Würfel schneiden.

cubic ['kjuːbɪk] adj **(a)** (of volume) Kubik-, Raum-. ~ capacity Fassungsvermögen nt; (of engine) Hubraum m; ~ content Raum- or Kubikinhalt m; ~ measure Raum- or Kubikmaß nt; ~ metre/foot/feet Kubikmeter m or nt/Kubikfuß m. **(b)** (Math) kubisch. ~ equation Gleichung f dritten Grades. **(c)** (rare: cube-shaped) würfelförmig.

cubicle ['kjuːbɪkəl] n Kabine f; (in dormitory etc also) Alkoven m; (in toilets) (Einzel)toilette f.

cubiform ['kjuːbɪfɔːm] adj (form) kubisch, würfelförmig.

cubism ['kjuːbɪzəm] n Kubismus m.

cubist ['kjuːbɪst] 1 n Kubist(in f) m. 2 adj kubistisch.

cubit ['kjuːbɪt] n Elle f.

cub: C~ mistress n Wölflingsmutter f; ~ reporter n junger Reporter, junge Reporterin; C~ Scout n Wölfling m.

cuckold ['kʌkəld] 1 n Hahnrei m (old), betrogener Ehemann. 2 vt zum Hahnrei machen (old), betrügen, Hörner aufsetzen (+dat).

cuckoo ['kuku:] 1 n Kuckuck m. 2 adj pred (inf) meschugge (inf). to go ~ überschnappen (inf).

cuckoo: ~ clock n Kuckucksuhr f; ~-pint n (Bot) Gefleckter Aronsstab; ~-spit n (secretion) Kuckucksspeichel m; (insect) Schaumzikade f.

cucumber ['kjuːkʌmbə'] n (Salat)gurke f. as cool as a ~ seelenruhig.

cud [kʌd] n wiedergekäutes Futter. to chew the ~ (lit) wiederkäuen; (fig) vor sich hingrübeln, sinnieren.

cuddle ['kʌdl] 1 n Liebkosung f. to give sb a ~ jdn in den Arm nehmen; to need a ~ Zärtlichkeit brauchen, geknuddelt (inf) or liebkost werden müssen; to have a ~ schmusen. 2 vt in den Arm nehmen; (amorously also) schmusen mit. 3 vi schmusen.

♦**cuddle down** vi sich kuscheln.

♦**cuddle up** vi sich kuscheln (to, against an +acc). to ~ ~ beside sb sich neben jdm zusammenkuscheln; to ~ ~ in bed sich im Bett zusammenkuscheln, sich ins Bett kuscheln; I'm cold — well, ~ ~ then mir ist kalt — na, dann kuschel dich ran (inf); we all had to ~ ~ in the tent to keep warm wir mußten uns alle im Zelt aneinanderkuscheln, um es warm zu haben.

cuddlesome ['kʌdlsəm] adj see cuddly.

cuddly ['kʌdlɪ] adj (+er) (wanting a cuddle) verschmust (inf), anschmiegsam; (good to cuddle) toy, doll zum Liebhaben, knuddelig (inf); person knuddelig (inf). to be in a ~ mood in einer verschmusten Laune or in Schmuselaune sein.

cudgel ['kʌdʒəl] 1 n Knüppel m. to take up the ~s for or on behalf of sb/sth (fig) für jdn/etw eintreten or eine Lanze brechen, für jdn/etw auf die Barrikaden gehen. 2 vt prügeln. to ~ one's brains (fig) sich (dat) das (Ge)hirn zermartern.

cue [kjuː] 1 n (a) (Theat, fig) Stichwort nt; (action) (Einsatz)zeichen nt; (Film, TV) Zeichen nt zum Aufnahmebeginn; (Mus) Einsatz m; (written: preceding bars) Hilfsnoten pl. to give sb his ~ (Theat) jdm das or sein Stichwort geben; (action) jdm das (Einsatz)zeichen geben; (Mus) jdm den Einsatz geben; that sounds like a ~ for a song das hört sich ganz nach einem Lied an; whenever he hears the word "strike" that's his ~ to launch into an attack on the unions das Wort „Streik" ist für ihn jedesmal (das) Stichwort für einen Angriff auf die Gewerkschaften; to take one's ~ from sb sich nach jdm richten; right on ~ (Theat) genau auf's Stichwort; (fig) wie gerufen.

(b) (Billiards) Queue nt.

2 vt (Theat) das Stichwort geben (+dat); (with gesture etc) das Einsatzzeichen geben (+dat); (TV, Film) scene abfahren lassen; (Mus) player den Einsatz geben (+dat); trumpet flourish etc den Einsatz geben für. ~! (Film, TV) ab!

♦**cue in** vt sep den Einsatz geben (+dat); (TV, Film) scene abfahren lassen; tape etc (zur rechten Zeit) einspielen.

cue: ~-ball n Spielball m; ~ card n (TV) Neger m; ~ rest n Stütze f für das Queue.

cuff¹ [kʌf] n **(a)** Manschette f; (turned back also) Stulpe f. off the ~ aus dem Handgelenk, aus dem Stegreif. **(b)** (US: of trousers) (Hosen)aufschlag m. **(c)** usu pl (inf: handcuff) Handschelle f. **(d)** (US inf: credit) on the ~ auf Stottern (inf).

cuff² 1 vt (strike) einen Klaps geben (+dat), eins um die Ohren geben (+dat) (inf). 2 n (blow) Klaps m.

cuff-link ['kʌflɪŋk] n Manschettenknopf m.

cuirass [kwɪ'ræs] n Küraß, Brustharnisch m.

cuirassier [ˌkwɪrə'sɪə'] n Kürassier m.

cuisine [kwɪ'ziːn] n Küche f.

cul-de-sac ['kʌldəsæk] n (esp Brit) Sackgasse f.

culinary ['kʌlɪnərɪ] adj kulinarisch; skill, talents etc Koch-; implements Küchen-.

cull [kʌl] 1 n **(a)** (selection) Auswahl, Auslese f. **(b)** (killing of surplus) ~ of seals Robbenschlag m. **(c)** (rejected item) Ausschuß m. 2 vt **(a)** (pick) flowers pflücken. **(b)** (collect) entnehmen (from dat); legends (zusammen)sammeln (from aus). events ~ed from the writer's own experience Ereignisse, die der Schriftsteller seinem persönlichen Erfahrungsschatz entnommen hat. **(c)** (kill as surplus) to ~ seals Robbenschlag m betreiben.

cullender n see colander.

culminate ['kʌlmɪneɪt] 1 vi (Astron) kulminieren, den or seinen Höchst-/Tiefststand erreichen; (fig) (reach a climax: career, music etc) gipfeln, kulminieren (geh) (in in +dat); (end) herauslaufen (in auf +acc), enden (in mit).

2 vt (US) den Höhepunkt or Gipfel (+gen) darstellen.

culmination [ˌkʌlmɪ'neɪʃən] n (Astron) Kulminationspunkt, Höchst-/Tiefststand m; (fig) (high point: of career etc) Höhepunkt m; (end) Ende nt, Ausgang m.

culottes [kjuː'lɒts] npl Hosenrock m. a pair of ~ ein Hosenrock.

culpability [ˌkʌlpə'bɪlɪtɪ] n (form) Schuld f.

culpable ['kʌlpəbl] adj (form) schuldig. ~ homicide (Jur) fahrlässige Tötung; ~ negligence grobe Fahrlässigkeit.

culprit ['kʌlprɪt] n Schuldige(r) mf; (Jur) Täter(in f) m; (inf: thing, person causing trouble) Übeltäter m.

cult [kʌlt] n (Rel, fig) Kult m. to make a ~ of sth (einen) Kult mit etw treiben.

cultivable ['kʌltɪvəbl] adj kultivierbar.

cultivate ['kʌltɪveɪt] vt **(a)** kultivieren; soil also bebauen; crop,

fruit etc also anbauen; *beard* wachsen lassen.
(b) *(fig) friendship, links etc* pflegen, kultivieren; *art, skill, taste* entwickeln; *sb* sich *(dat)* warmhalten *(inf)*, die Beziehung zu ... pflegen. **a connection like that is definitely worth cultivating** es lohnt sich bestimmt, so eine Verbindung aufrechtzuerhalten; **I decided to ~ him** ich beschloß, ihn mir warmzuhalten *(inf)*; **to ~ one's mind** sich bilden.
cultivated ['kʌltɪveɪtɪd] *adj (Agr, fig)* kultiviert.
cultivation [ˌkʌltɪ'veɪʃən] *n see vt* **(a)** Kultivieren *nt*, Kultivierung *f*; *Anbau m.* **to be under ~** bebaut werden.
(b) Pflege *f (of vn)*; Entwicklung *f*; Bemühung *f (of um)*. **his constant ~ of influential friendships** seine ständigen Bemühungen um einflußreiche Freunde.
(c) *(cultivated state)* Kultiviertheit *f*.
cultivator ['kʌltɪveɪtə'] *n* **(a)** *(machine)* Kultivator, Grubber *m.* **(b)** *(person)* **a ~ of the soil/of new friendships** *etc* jemand, der den Boden bebaut/neue Freundschaften pflegt.
cultural ['kʌltʃərəl] *adj* Kultur-; *differences, resemblances also, events* kulturell. **what sort of ~ activities are there?** was wird kulturell geboten?; **we enjoyed a very ~ evening** wir hatten einen sehr gebildeten Abend; **could you not do something a little more ~ with your spare time?** könntest du deine Freizeit nicht etwas kultivierter gestalten *or* verbringen?
(b) *(Agr)* Kultur-.
culturally ['kʌltʃərəlɪ] *adv* kulturell.
culture ['kʌltʃə'] **1** *n* **(a)** Kultur *f.* **physical ~** *(dated)* Körperkultur *f (dated)*; **a man of ~/of no ~** ein kultivierter/unkultivierter Mann, ein Mann mit/ohne Kultur; **to study German ~** die deutsche Kultur studieren.
(b) *(Agr, Biol, Med)* Kultur *f*; *(of animals)* Zucht *f*.
2 *vt (Biol, Med)* eine Kultur anlegen von.
cultured ['kʌltʃəd] *adj* kultiviert; *(Agr)* Kultur-; *(Biol, Med)* gezüchtet. **~ pearl** Zuchtperle *f*.
culture *in cpds* Kultur-; **~ dish** *n (Biol, Med)* Petrischale *f*; **~ fluid** *n (Biol, Med)* Nährlösung *f*; **~ medium** *n (Biol, Med)* Kulturmedium *nt*, (künstlicher) Nährboden; **~ vulture** *n (hum)* Kulturfanatiker(in *f*) *m*.
culvert ['kʌlvət] *n* unterirdischer Kanal, (Abwasser)kanal *m*; *(for cables)* Kabeltunnel *m*.
cum [kʌm] *prep* in einem, gleichzeitig. **a sort of sofa-~-bed** eine Art von Sofa und Bett in einem.
cumbersome ['kʌmbəsəm] *adj clothing, coat* (be)hinderlich; *suit of armour, spacesuit, movements, gesture, sort of person, style, piece of music* schwerfällig; *vehicle* unhandlich *(inf)*, schwer zu manövrieren; *suitcases, parcels* sperrig, unhandlich; *procedure, regulations* beschwerlich, mühselig. **it's so ~ having to wear all this heavy clothing/having to carry these heavy bags around** es ist so lästig, daß man alle diese schweren Kleidungsstücke tragen muß/diese schweren Taschen herumtragen muß.
cumbersomely ['kʌmbəsəmlɪ] *adv move, write* schwerfällig; *phrased also* umständlich; *dressed* hinderlich.
cumbrous ['kʌmbrəs] *adj see* cumbersome.
cumin ['kʌmɪn] *n* Kreuzkümmel *m*.
cummerbund ['kʌməbʌnd] *n* Kummerbund *m*.
cumulative ['kju:mjʊlətɪv] *adj* gesamt-, kumulativ *(geh)*. **~ evidence** *(Jur)* Häufung *f* von Beweisen/Zeugenaussagen; **~ interest** *(Fin)* Zins und Zinseszins; **~ voting** Wählen *nt* durch Kumulieren *or* Stimmenhäufung *or* nach dem Kumulierungssystem; **the ~ debts of ten years** die Schulden, die sich im Lauf von zehn Jahren angehäuft haben/hatten.
cumulonimbus ['kju:mjʊləʊ'nɪmbəs] *n* Kumulonimbus *m*.
cumulus ['kju:mjʊləs] *n* Kumulus *m*.
cuneiform ['kju:nɪfɔ:m] **1** *adj* keilförmig; *characters, inscription* in Keilschrift, Keilschrift-. **~ writing** Keilschrift *f.* **2** *n* Keilschrift *f*.
cunnilingus [ˌkʌnɪ'lɪŋgəs] *n* Cunnilingus *m*.
cunning ['kʌnɪŋ] **1** *n (cleverness)* Schlauheit, Listigkeit, Gerissenheit *f*; *(liter: skill)* (Kunst)fertigkeit *f*, Geschick *nt*.
2 *adj* **(a)** *plan, idea* schlau; *person also* listig, gerissen; *eyes, smile, expression* verschmitzt, verschlagen *(pej)*; *(ingenious) gadget* schlau *or* clever *(inf)* ausgedacht.
(b) *(US inf)* drollig.
cunningly ['kʌnɪŋlɪ] *adv* schlau; *(with reference to people also)* listig, gerissen; *smile, look* verschmitzt, verschlagen *(pej)*; *(ingeniously)* geschickt. **a ~ designed little gadget** ein geschickt *or* clever ausgedachtes Ding.
cunt [kʌnt] *n (vulg) (vagina)* Fotze *(vulg)*, Möse *(vulg) f*; *(intercourse)* Fick *m (vulg)*; *(term of abuse)* Arsch *m (vulg)*. **she's a nice bit of ~** das ist eine tolle Fotze *(vulg)*.
cup [kʌp] **1** *n* **(a)** Tasse *f*; *(goblet)* Pokal, Kelch *m*; *(mug)* Becher *m*; *(Eccl)* Kelch *m.* **in his ~s** *(dated inf)* angezecht.
(b) *(cupful)* Tasse *f*; *(Cook: standard measure)* 8 fl oz = 0,221. **a ~ of tea/water** eine Tasse Tee/Wasser; **that's just/that's not my ~ of tea** *(fig inf)* das ist genau/ist nicht mein Fall.
(c) *(prize, football ~ etc)* Pokal *m*.
(d) *(drink)* -mix, -becher *m*.
(e) *(Bot: of flower)* Kelch *m*; *(of bra)* Körbchen *nt*; *(Golf)* Metallbüchse *f (im Loch)*; *(Med: ~ping glass)* Schröpfkopf *m*.
(f) *(fig liter: portion)* Kelch *m.* **to drain the ~ of sorrow (to the dregs)** den Kelch des Leidens (bis zur Neige) leeren *(liter)*; **my ~ is overflowing** *(liter) or* **runneth over** *(Bibl)* ich bin über alle Maßen glücklich, mein Glück ist vollkommen.
2 *vt* **(a)** *hands* hohl machen. **~ped hand** hohle Hand; **he ~ped his hands and blew into them** er blies sich *(dat)* in die Hände; **to ~ sth in one's hands** etw in den hohlen Hand halten; **he ~ped his chin in his hand** er stützte das Kinn in die Hand; **to ~ one's ear** *or* **a hand to one's ear** die Hand ans Ohr halten; **to ~ one's hands around sth** etw mit der hohlen Hand umfassen.
(b) *(Med)* schröpfen.
(c) *(Golf)* einlochen mit.

cup: **~-and-ball** *n* Fangbecherspiel *nt*; **~bearer** *n* Mundschenk *m*.
cupboard ['kʌbəd] *n* Schrank *m.* **~ love** fauler Schmus *(inf)*, Zweckfreundlichkeit *f*; **what's all this ~ love, what are you after?** was soll der faule Schmus, worauf willst du hinaus? *(inf)*.
cup: **~-cake** *n kleiner, runder Kuchen*; **C~ Final** *n* Pokalendspiel *nt*; *(international also)* Cupfinale *nt*; **C~ Finalist** *n* Teilnehmer *m* am Pokalendspiel; **~ful** *n*, *pl* **~sful**, **~fuls** Tasse *f*.
cupid ['kju:pɪd] *n* Amorette *f.* **C~** Cupido, Amor *m*; **C~'s dart** *(liter)* Amors Pfeil *(liter)*, Liebespfeil *m*.
cupidity [kju:'pɪdɪtɪ] *n (liter)* Begierde *(pej)*, Gier *(pej) f*.
Cupid's bow ['kju:pɪdz'bəʊ] *adj* bogenförmig geschwungen. **~ mouth** Kußmund, Herzmund *m*.
cup match *n* Pokalspiel *nt*.
cupola ['kju:pələ] *n (Archit)* Kuppel *f*; *(roof also)* Kuppeldach *nt*; *(furnace)* Kupolofen *m*.
cuppa ['kʌpə] *n (Brit inf)* Tasse Tee *f*, Täßchen Tee *nt (inf)*.
cupping ['kʌpɪŋ] *n (Med)* Schröpfen *nt.* **~-glass** Schröpfkopf *m*.
cupreous ['kju:prɪəs] *adj* Kupfer-, kupfern.
cuprite ['kju:praɪt] *n* Kupferoxyd, Rotkupfererz *nt*.
cupronickel ['kju:prəʊ'nɪkl] *n* Kupfernickel *nt*, Kupfer-Nickel-Legierung *f*.
cuprous ['kju:prəs] *adj* Kupfer-, kupfern.
cup: **~ size** *n (of bra)* Körbchengröße *f*; **~ tie** *n* Pokalspiel *nt*.
cupule ['kju:pju:l] *n (Bot)* Becher *m*, Cupula *f (spec)*.
Cup-winners ['kʌpwɪnəz] *npl* Pokalsieger *m.* **~' Cup** *(Ftbl)* Europapokal *m* der Pokalsieger.
cur [kɜ:'] *n (pej) (dog)* Köter *m (pej)*, Töle *f (pej)*; *(old: man)* Kanaille *f (dated pej)*, Hundsfott *m (dated pej)*.
curable ['kjʊərəbl] *adj* heilbar. **is he ~?** ist er zu heilen?
curaçao [ˌkjʊərə'səʊ] *n* Curaçao *m*.
curate ['kjʊərɪt] *n (Catholic)* Kurat *m*; *(Protestant)* Vikar *m.* **it's like the ~'s egg** es ist streckenweise gar nicht so schlecht.
curative ['kjʊərətɪv] **1** *adj* Heil-, heilend. **2** *n* Heilmittel *nt*.
curator [kjʊə'reɪtə'] *n* **(a)** *(of museum etc)* Kustos *m.* **(b)** *(Jur: guardian)* Kurator, Vormund *m*.
curb [kɜ:b] **1** *n* **(a)** *(of harness)* (bit) Kandare *f*; *(chain)* Kinnkette, Kandarenkette *f*.
(b) *(fig)* Behinderung *f*; *(deliberate also)* Beschränkung *f.* **to put a ~ on sb/sth** jdm im Zaum *or* in Schranken halten/etw einschränken; **this acted as a ~ on his musical development** das (be)hinderte seine musikalische Entwicklung.
(c) *(esp US: curbstone)* see **kerb.**
2 *vt* **(a)** *horse* zügeln.
(b) *(fig)* zügeln; *immigration, investment etc* in Schranken halten, bremsen *(inf)*.
curb: **~ bit** *n* Kandare *f*; **~ rein** *n* Kandarenzügel *m*; **~ roof** *n (Archit)* Mansardendach *nt*; **~ service** *n (US)* Bedienung *f* am Fahrzeug; **~stone** *n (esp US)* see **kerbstone.**
curd [kɜ:d] **1** *n (often pl)* Quark *m.* **~ cheese** Weißkäse *m.* **2** *vt* gerinnen lassen. **3** *vi* gerinnen.
curdle ['kɜ:dl] **1** *vt (lit, fig)* gerinnen lassen. **to ~ sb's blood** jdm das Blut in den Adern gerinnen lassen. **2** *vi* gerinnen. **his blood ~d** das Blut gerann ihm in den Adern.
cure [kjʊə'] **1** *vt* **(a)** *(Med) illness, person* heilen, kurieren *(inf)*. **to be/get ~d (of sth)** (von etw) geheilt *or* kuriert *(inf)* sein/werden; **he used to be an alcoholic but he's been ~d** er war früher Alkoholiker, aber jetzt ist er geheilt *or* kuriert *(inf)*; **to ~ sb (of sth/doing sth)** jdn (von etw) heilen *or* kurieren *(inf)*.
(b) *(fig) inflation, ill etc* abhelfen (+*dat*). **to ~ sb of sth/doing sth** jdm etw austreiben, jdn von etw kurieren; **I'll ~ him!** dem werde ich das schon austreiben!
(c) *food* haltbar machen; *(salt)* pökeln; *(smoke)* räuchern; *(dry)* trocknen; *skins, tobacco* trocknen.
2 *vi* **(a)** *(be healed)* heilen.
(b) *(food, bacon, fish)* see *vt* **(c) it is left to ~** es wird zum Pökeln eingelegt/zum Räuchern aufgehängt/zum Trocknen aufgehängt *or* ausgebreitet.
3 *n* **(a)** *(Med) (remedy)* (Heil)mittel *nt (for gegen)*; *(treatment)* Heilverfahren *nt (for sb* für jdn, *for sth* gegen etw); *(recovery)* Heilung *f*; *(health ~)* Kur *f*; *(fig: remedy)* Mittel *nt (for gegen)*. **to take** *or* **follow a ~** zur *or* in Kur gehen, eine Kur machen, sich einer Kur unterziehen *(geh)*; **beyond** *or* **past ~** *(patient)* unheilbar krank; *(illness)* unheilbar; *(fig: state of affairs, laziness etc)* hoffnungslos; **there's no ~ for that** *(lit)* das ist unheilbar; *(fig)* dagegen kann man nichts machen.
(b) *(Eccl: spiritual care)* **the ~ of souls** die Seelsorge; **to have the ~ of souls** (der) Seelsorger sein.
cure-all ['kjʊərɔ:l] *n (lit, fig)* Allheilmittel *nt*.
curettage ['kjʊərətɪdʒ] *n (Med)* Ausschabung, Kürettage *f*.
curet(te) [kjʊə'ret] *n (Med)* Kürette *f*.
curfew ['kɜ:fju:] *n* Ausgangssperre *f*, Ausgehverbot *nt*; *(old: evening bell)* Abendglocke *f.* **to impose a/lift the ~** das Ausgehverbot verhängen/aufheben; **is the ~ still on?** ist noch Ausgangssperre?
curio ['kjʊərɪəʊ] *n* Kuriosität *f*.
curiosity [ˌkjʊərɪ'ɒsɪtɪ] *n* **(a)** *no pl (inquisitiveness)* Neugier *f*; *(for knowledge also)* Wißbegier(de) *f.* **out of** *or* **from ~** aus Neugier; **~ killed the cat** *(Prov)* sei nicht so neugierig. **(b)** *(object, person)* Kuriosität *f.* **~ shop** Kuriositätenladen *m*.
curious ['kjʊərɪəs] *adj* **(a)** *(inquisitive)* neugierig. **I'm ~ to know what he'll do/how he did it** ich bin mal gespannt, was er macht/ich bin neugierig zu erfahren, wie er das gemacht hat; **I'd be ~ to know how you got on** ich wüßte (ganz) gern, wie du zurechtgekommen bist; **the neighbours were ~ to know ...** die Nachbarn wollten zu gerne wissen ...
(b) *(odd)* sonderbar, seltsam, eigenartig. **that's ~, it was there just now** sonderbar *etc*, gerade eben war es noch da; **how ~! wie seltsam!; it's ~ the way he already knew that** sonderbar *etc*, daß er das schon gewußt hat.
curiously ['kjʊərɪəslɪ] *adv* **(a)** *(inquisitively)* neugierig.

(b) (oddly) behave, speak etc seltsam, eigenartig, merkwürdig, sonderbar; disappeared auf sonderbare or seltsame Weise; unconcerned seltsam, merkwürdig. **they are ~ similar** sie ähneln sich merkwürdig or auf seltsame Weise; **it was ~ quiet** es war merkwürdig ruhig; **any sense of humour is ~ absent** seltsamerweise or eigenartigerweise fehlt jeglicher Sinn für Humor; **~ enough** merkwürdigerweise.

curiousness ['kjʊərɪəsnɪs] n **(a)** see **curiosity (a). (b)** (oddness) Merkwürdigkeit, Sonderbarkeit f.

curl [kɜːl] **1** n (of hair) Locke f. **in ~(s)** in Locken, gelockt; (tight) gekräuselt, kraus; **a ~ of smoke/of wood** ein Rauchkringel m/(geringelter) Hobelspan; **with a ~ of his lips** mit gekräuselten Lippen; **its tail was just a little ~** es hatte nur ein kleines Kringelschwänzchen.

2 vt hair locken; (with curlers) in Locken legen; (in tight curls) kräuseln; lips (person) kräuseln; (animal) hochziehen; edges umbiegen. **he ~ed the ball into the back of the net** er zirkelte den Ball mit einem Bogenschuß ins Netz; **the road ~s its way through the hills** die Straße windet or schlängelt sich durch die Hügel.

3 vi **(a)** (hair) sich locken; (tightly) sich kräuseln; (naturally) lockig sein; (paper) sich wellen; (wood) sich verziehen; (road) sich schlängeln, sich winden. **his lips ~ed** er kräuselte die Lippen; **it's enough to make your hair ~** (fig inf) da stehen einem ja die Haare zu Berge (inf).

(b) (Sport) Curling spielen.

♦**curl up 1** vi **(a)** (animal) sich zusammenkugeln; (person also) sich zusammenkuscheln; (hedgehog) sich einigeln; (paper) sich wellen; (metal) sich rollen; (leaf) sich hochbiegen. **his moustache ~s ~ at the ends** sein Schnurrbart ist nach oben gezwirbelt; **to ~ ~ in bed/in an armchair** sich ins Bett/in einen Sessel kuscheln; **to ~ ~ with a good book** es sich (dat) mit einem guten Buch gemütlich machen; **he just ~ed ~ and died** er legte sich einfach hin und starb.

(b) the smoke ~ed der Rauch ringelte sich hoch.

(c) (inf) **the way he behaves just makes me want to ~ ~** es macht mich krank, wie er sich benimmt (inf); **I just wanted to ~ ~ ~ and die** ich wäre am liebsten im Boden versunken.

2 vt sep ends of moustache, piece of paper etc wellen; metal rollen; edges hochbiegen. **to ~ oneself/itself ~** sich zusammenkugeln/zusammenringeln.

curler ['kɜːlə'] n **(a)** (hair ~) Lockenwickel, Lockenwickler m. **to put one's ~s in** sich (dat) die Haare eindrehen or auf (Locken)wickler drehen; **have you never seen her in ~s?** hast du sie noch nie mit Lockenwickeln gesehen?; **I was in ~s, I had my ~s in** ich hatte Lockenwickel or Lockenwickler im Haar.

(b) (Sport) Curlingspieler(in f) m.

curlew ['kɜːljuː] n Brachvogel m.

curlicue ['kɜːlɪkjuː] n Schnörkel m.

curling ['kɜːlɪŋ] n (Sport) Curling, Eisschießen nt. **~ stone** Curlingstein, Eisstock m.

curling-irons ['kɜːlɪŋˌaɪənz] npl or **curling-tongs** ['kɜːlɪŋˌtɒŋz] npl Lockenschere, Brennschere f; (electric) Lockenstab m.

curl paper n (Papier)lockenwickel m.

curly ['kɜːlɪ] **1** adj (+er) hair lockig; (tighter) kraus; tail Ringel-, geringelt; lettuce kraus; leaf gewellt; pattern, writing verschnörkelt, Schnörkel-. **when she was young she was much curlier** als sie jung war, war ihr Haar viel lockiger. **2** n (inf: person) Krauskopf m.

curly: ~**-haired** adj lockig, lockenköpfig; (tighter) krausköpfig; ~**-head** n (inf) Lockenkopf m; (tighter) Krauskopf m; ~**-headed** adj see ~**-haired.**

currant ['kʌrənt] n **(a)** (dried fruit) Korinthe f. **~ bun** Rosinenbrötchen nt. **(b)** (Bot) Johannisbeere f. **~ bush** Johannisbeerstrauch m.

currency ['kʌrənsɪ] n **(a)** (Fin) Währung f. **foreign ~** Devisen pl; **~ appreciation/depreciation** Geldaufwertung f/-abwertung f.

(b) Verbreitung f; (of word, expression) Gebräuchlichkeit f. **to be in ~** in Umlauf sein, verbreitet sein; **to gain ~** sich verbreiten, um sich greifen; **to give ~ to a rumour/theory** ein Gerücht/eine Theorie verbreiten or in Umlauf setzen or in die Welt setzen; **an expression which enjoyed a brief period of ~ in the 60s** ein Ausdruck, der in den 60er Jahren eine kurze Zeit lang allgemein verbreitet or geläufig war.

current ['kʌrənt] **1** adj (present) augenblicklich, gegenwärtig; policy, price aktuell, gegenwärtig, Tages-; research, month, week laufend; edition letzte(r, s); (prevalent) opinion verbreitet; spelling, word gebräuchlich. **to be no longer ~** nicht mehr aktuell sein; (coins) nicht mehr in Umlauf sein; **a ~ rumour** ein Gerücht, das zur Zeit in Umlauf ist; **~ affairs** Tagespolitik f, aktuelle Fragen pl, Aktuelle(s) nt; **in ~ use** allgemein gebräuchlich.

2 n **(a)** (of water) Strömung f, Strom m; (of air) Luftströmung f, Luftstrom m. **with/against the ~** mit dem/gegen den Strom; **air/ocean ~** Luft-/Meeresströmung f or -strom m; **upward/downward ~** Aufwind m/Abwind m.

(b) (Elec) Strom m.

(c) (fig: of events, opinions etc) Tendenz f, Trend m. **to go against/with the ~ of popular opinion** gegen den Strom or die Strömung der öffentlichen Meinung anschwimmen/mit dem Strom or der Strömung der öffentlichen Meinung schwimmen; **if you try to go against the ~ of events** wenn Sie versuchen, gegen den Strom der Ereignisse anzuschwimmen; **the ~ of public feeling is now in favour of/against ...** die öffentliche Meinung tendiert zur Befürwortung/Ablehnung von ...; **a politician who ignores the ~ of popular opinion** ein Politiker, der die Tendenz(en) der öffentlichen Meinung or den Trend (in) der öffentlichen Meinung unbeachtet läßt; **to analyse the change in the ~ of popular opinion** Tendenzwenden pl in der öffentlichen Meinung untersuchen.

current: ~ **account** n Girokonto nt; ~ **assets** npl Umlaufvermögen nt; ~ **collector** n (Rail etc) Stromabnehmer m; ~ **expenses** npl laufende Ausgaben pl.

currently ['kʌrəntlɪ] adv momentan, zur Zeit, gegenwärtig. **it is ~ thought that ...** die aktuelle Meinung ist, daß ...

curricle ['kʌrɪkl] n offener Zweispänner.

curricula [kə'rɪkjʊlə] pl of **curriculum.**

curricular [kə'rɪkjʊlə'] adj activities lehrplanmäßig.

curriculum [kə'rɪkjʊləm] n, pl **curricula** Lehrplan m. **to be on the ~** auf dem Lehrplan stehen; ~ **vitae** Lebenslauf m.

currish ['kɜːrɪʃ] adj (dated) behaviour hundsföttisch (dated).

curry[1] ['kʌrɪ] (Cook) **1** n Curry m or nt. ~**-powder** Currypulver nt; ~ **sauce** Currysauce f. **2** vt mit Curry zubereiten.

curry[2] vt horse striegeln; leather zurichten. **to ~ favour (with sb)** sich (bei jdm) einschmeicheln or lieb Kind machen.

curry-comb ['kʌrɪkəʊm] **1** n Striegel m. **2** vt striegeln.

curse [kɜːs] **1** n **(a)** (malediction) Fluch m. **to be under a ~** unter einem Fluch stehen; **to put sb under a ~** jdn mit einem Fluch belegen, einen Fluch über jdn aussprechen; **to call down ~s on sb** jdn verfluchen; **a ~ or a thousand ~s on him/this pen!** (old, hum) den/den Füller soll doch der Kuckuck holen! (inf), dieser vermaledeite Mensch/Füller (old); ~**s!** (inf) verflucht! (inf).

(b) (swear-word) Fluch m.

(c) (fig: affliction) Fluch m; (inf: nuisance) Plage f (inf). **it's the ~ of my life** das ist der Fluch meines Lebens; **the ~ of drunkenness** der Fluch des Alkohols; **the ~** (inf: menstruation) die Tage pl (inf); **she has the ~** sie hat ihre Tage (inf).

2 vt **(a)** (to put a curse on) verfluchen. ~ **you/it!** (inf) verflucht! (inf), verdammt! (sl), Mist! (inf); **I could ~ you for forgetting it** ich könnte dich verwünschen, daß du das vergessen hast; **where is he now, ~ the man or ~ him!** (inf) wo steckt er jetzt, der verfluchte Kerl (inf); ~ **these trains!** (inf) diese verfluchten Züge! (inf).

(b) (swear at or about) fluchen über (+acc).

(c) (fig: to afflict) **to be ~d with sb/sth** mit jdm/etw geschlagen or gestraft sein.

3 vi fluchen. **he started cursing and swearing** er fing an, wüst zu schimpfen und zu fluchen.

cursed ['kɜːsɪd] adj (inf) verflucht (inf).

cursive ['kɜːsɪv] **1** adj kursiv, Kursiv-. **2** n Kursivschrift f.

cursively ['kɜːsɪvlɪ] adv kursiv.

cursorily ['kɜːsərɪlɪ] adv see adj flüchtig; oberflächlich.

cursoriness ['kɜːsərɪnɪs] n see adj Flüchtigkeit f; Oberflächlichkeit f.

cursory ['kɜːsərɪ] adj glance flüchtig; inspection, investigation also oberflächlich.

curst [kɜːst] adj see **cursed.**

curt [kɜːt] adj (+er) person kurz angebunden; verbal reply also knapp; letter, nod, refusal kurz, knapp. **to be ~ with sb** zu jdm kurz angebunden sein.

curtail [kɜː'teɪl] vt kürzen.

curtailment [kɜː'teɪlmənt] n Kürzung f.

curtain ['kɜːtn] **1** n **(a)** Vorhang m; (on windows also) Gardine f. **to draw or pull the ~s** (open) den Vorhang/die Vorhänge aufziehen; (close) den Vorhang/die Vorhänge zuziehen.

(b) (Theat) Vorhang m. **the ~ rises/falls** der Vorhang hebt sich/fällt; **the ~ rises on a scene of domestic harmony** der Vorhang hebt sich und gibt den Blick auf eine Szene häuslichen Glücks frei; **to take a ~** (inf) vor den Vorhang treten.

(c) (fig) (of mystery) Schleier m. **a ~ of smoke/flames/rain** eine Rauch-/Flammen-/Regenwand; **if you get caught it'll be ~s for you** (inf) wenn sie dich erwischen, ist für dich der Ofen aus (inf) or bist du weg vom Fenster (inf).

2 vt mit Vorhängen/einem Vorhang ausstatten. **a ~ed bed** ein Himmelbett nt.

♦**curtain off** vt sep durch einen Vorhang/Vorhänge abtrennen.

curtain: ~**-call** n (Theat) Vorhang m; **to get/take a ~-call** einen Vorhang bekommen/vor den Vorhang treten; ~ **hook** n Gardinengleithaken m; ~ **rail** n Vorhangschiene f; ~**-raiser** n (Theat) kurzes Vorspiel; ~ **ring** n Gardinenring m; ~ **rod** n Gardinenstange f; ~ **runner** n Vorhangschiene f; (for ~ rings) Gardinenstange f.

curtly ['kɜːtlɪ] adv reply, nod kurz, knapp; refuse kurzerhand.

curtness ['kɜːtnɪs] n see adj Kurzangebundenheit f; Kürze, Knappheit f.

curts(e)y ['kɜːtsɪ] **1** n Knicks m; (to royalty) Hofknicks m. **to drop a ~** einen Knicks/Hofknicks machen. **2** vi knicksen (to or +dat).

curvaceous [kɜː'veɪʃəs] adj üppig; figure, woman also kurvenreich.

curvaceously [kɜː'veɪʃəslɪ] adv swell üppig, prall. **she stretched ~ under the sheet** sie räkelte ihre üppigen Formen unter der Decke.

curvature ['kɜːvətʃə'] n Krümmung f; (misshapen) Verkrümmung f. ~ **of the spine** (normal) Rückgratkrümmung f; (abnormal) Rückgratverkrümmung f; **the ~ of space** die Raumkrümmung.

curve [kɜːv] **1** n Kurve f; (of body, vase etc) Rundung, Wölbung f; (of river) Biegung f; (of archway) Bogen m. **there's a ~ in the road** die Straße macht einen Bogen; **the price ~** die Preiskurve; **her ~s** (inf) ihre Kurven or Rundungen pl (inf).

2 vt biegen; (build with a ~) arch, roof, side of ship wölben. **gravity ~s the path of light** die Gravitation krümmt den Lichtweg; **he ~d the ball around the wall** er zirkelte den Ball um die Mauer herum.

3 vi **(a)** (line, road) einen Bogen machen; (river) eine Biegung machen. **her lips ~d into a smile** ihre Lippen verzogen sich zu einem Lächeln; **the road/river ~d in and out among the hills** die Straße/der Fluß wand or schlängelte sich durch die Berge; **the road ~d down into the valley** die Straße wand sich ins Tal hinunter; **the road ~s around the city** die Straße macht einen

Bogen um die Stadt; **to make a ball ~ (through the air)** einen Ball anschneiden, einem Ball einen Drall geben.

(b) *(be curved) (space, horizon)* gekrümmt sein; *(side of ship, surface, arch)* sich wölben; *(hips, breasts)* sich runden; *(metal strip etc)* sich biegen; *(arch)* sich wölben.

curved [kɜːvd] *adj line* gebogen; *(table-legs etc also* geschwungen; *horizon* gekrümmt; *surface, arch, sides of ship* gewölbt; *hips* rund. **space is** ~ der Raum ist gekrümmt.

curvet [kɜːˈvet] **1** *n* Kruppade *f.* **2** *vi* eine Kruppade springen.

curvilinear [ˈkɜːvɪˈlɪnɪəʳ] *adj (full of curves) tracery etc* mit vielen Rundungen *or* Kurven; *(curved) motion, course* gewunden; *(Geometry) figure* krummlinig begrenzt.

curvy [ˈkɜːvɪ] *adj (+er) (inf) road, figure* kurvenreich.

cushion [ˈkʊʃən] **1** *n* Kissen *nt*; *(pad, fig: buffer)* Polster *nt*; *(Billiards)* Bande *f.* **a stroke off the** ~ ein Stoß gegen die Bande; **a ~ of air/moss** ein Luftkissen *nt*/Moospolster *nt*; ~ **cover** Kissenüberzug, Kissenbezug *m.*

2 *vt* **(a)** *(absorb, soften) fall, blow* auffangen, dämpfen; *(fig) disappointment* dämpfen.

(b) *(fig: protect)* **to ~ sb against sth** jdn gegen etw abschirmen, jdn vor etw *(dat)* behüten; **he ~ed the vase against his chest** er barg die Vase an seiner Brust.

(c) *(Billiards) ball* gegen die Bande spielen.

cushioning [ˈkʊʃənɪŋ] *adj* **to have a ~ effect** (stoß)dämpfend wirken; *(fig)* mildernd wirken.

cushy [ˈkʊʃɪ] *adj (+er) (inf)* bequem. **to have a ~ time of it/be onto a ~ number** eine ruhige Kugel schieben *(inf)*; **a ~ job** ein gemütlicher *or* ruhiger Job; **that job is a ~ number** in dem Job reißt man sich *(dat)* kein Bein aus *(inf)*.

cusp [kʌsp] *n (of tooth)* Höcker *m*; *(of moon)* Spitze *f (*der Mondsichel); *(Astrol)* Eintritt *m* in ein neues Zeichen.

cuspid [ˈkʌspɪd] *n* Eckzahn *m.*

cuspidor [ˈkʌspɪdɔːʳ] *n (US)* Spucknapf *m.*

cuss [kʌs] *(inf)* **1** *n* **(a)** *(person)* Kauz *m (inf).* **(b) he's not worth a (tinker's)** ~ er ist keinen roten Heller wert *(inf)*; **he doesn't care a** ~ **(about it)** das ist ihm völlig Wurst *(inf) or* schnuppe *(inf).* **(c)** *(oath)* Fluch *m.* **2** *vi* fluchen. **to ~ and swear** schimpfen und fluchen.

cussed [ˈkʌsɪd] *adj (inf)* stur.

cussedness [ˈkʌsɪdnɪs] *n (inf)* Sturheit *f.* **out of sheer ~** aus lauter *or* reiner Sturheit.

custard [ˈkʌstəd] *n (pouring ~)* = Vanillesoße *f*; *(set)* = Vanillepudding *m.*

custard: ~ **apple** *n (Bot)* Zimt- *or* Rahmapfel *m*; ~ **cream (biscuit)** *n* Doppelkeks *m* (mit Vanillecremefüllung); ~ **pie** *n* (in slapstick) Sahnetorte *f*; ~ **powder** *n* = Vanillepuddingpulver, Vanillesoßenpulver *nt*; ~**-tart** *n* = Puddingtörtchen *nt.*

custodian [kʌsˈtəʊdɪən] *n (of building, park, museum)* Aufseher, Wächter *m*; *(of treasure)* Hüter *m*; *(of tradition, cultural heritage, world peace, of public morality etc)* Hüter, Gralshüter *(pej) m.*

custody [ˈkʌstədɪ] *n* **(a)** *(keeping, guardianship)* Obhut *f*; *(of person also)* Aufsicht *f (of* über *+acc)*; *(of object also)* Aufbewahrung *f (of* für, über *+acc).* **to put *or* place sth in sb's ~** etw jdm zur Aufbewahrung anvertrauen, etw in jds Obhut *(acc) or* Gewahrsam *(acc)* geben, etw jdm zu treuen Händen übergeben; **the child/money is in safe ~** das Kind/Geld ist gut aufgehoben; **he is in the ~ of his aunt** seine Tante hat die Vormundschaft für *or* über ihn; **the mother was awarded ~ of the children after the divorce** die Kinder wurden (bei der Scheidung) der Mutter zugesprochen; **the souls of his parishioners were, as it were, in his ~** ihm waren die Seelen seiner Gemeinde sozusagen zu treuen Händen anvertraut; **the country's future is placed in the ~ of its teachers** die Zukunft des Landes liegt in den Händen der Lehrer; **whilst these goods are in the ~ of the police** während sich die Gegenstände in Polizeiaufbewahrung befinden.

(b) *(police detention)* (polizeilicher) Gewahrsam, Haft *f.* **to take sb into ~** jdn verhaften; **he will be kept in ~ until ...** er wird inhaftiert bleiben, bis ...

custom [ˈkʌstəm] **1** *n* **(a)** *(established behaviour, convention)* Sitte *f*, Brauch *m.* ~ **demands ...** es ist Sitte *or* Brauch ...; **as ~ has it** wie es Sitte *or* (der) Brauch ist; **our ~s** unsere Bräuche *pl*, unsere Sitten und Gebräuche *pl.*

(b) *(habit)* (An)gewohnheit *f.* **it was his ~ to rest each afternoon** er pflegte am Nachmittag zu ruhen *(geh)*; **as was his ~** wie er es gewohnt war, wie er es zu tun pflegte *(geh).*

(c) *no pl (Comm: patronage)* Kundschaft *f.* **to get sb's ~** jdn als Kunden gewinnen; **to take one's ~ elsewhere** (als Kunde) anderswo hingehen, woanders Kunde werden; **we get a lot of ~ from tourists** wir machen viel Geschäft mit Touristen.

(d) ~**s** *pl (duty, organization)* Zoll *m*; **(the) C~s** der Zoll; **the C~s and Excise Department** die Britische Zollbehörde; **to go through ~s** durch den Zoll gehen; **to get sth through the ~s** etw durch den Zoll bekommen.

(e) *(Jur)* Gewohnheitsrecht *nt.* **that is ~ and practice** das ist allgemein üblich.

2 *adj (US) tailor* Maß-; *suit, shoes also* maßgefertigt; *carpenter* auf Bestellung arbeitend; *car (also Brit)* spezialgefertigt, Spezial-.

customarily [ˈkʌstəmərəlɪ] *adv* normaler- *or* üblicherweise.

customary [ˈkʌstəmərɪ] *adj (conventional)* üblich; *(habitual)* gewohnt. **it's ~ to apologize/to wear a tie** man entschuldigt sich normalerweise *or* gewöhnlich/man trägt normalerweise *or* gewöhnlich eine Krawatte; ~ **laws** Gewohnheitsrecht *nt.*

custom-built [ˈkʌstəmˈbɪlt] *adj* spezialgefertigt.

customer [ˈkʌstəməʳ] *n* **(a)** *(Comm: patron)* Kunde *m*, Kundin *f.* **our ~s** unsere Kundschaft. **(b)** *(inf: person)* Kunde *m (inf).*

customize [ˈkʌstəmaɪz] *vt car etc* individuell aufmachen.

custom-made [ˈkʌstəmmeɪd] *adj clothes, shoes* maßgefertigt,

nach Maß; *furniture, car* spezialangefertigt.

customs: ~ **clearance** *n* Zollabfertigung *f*; **to get ~ clearance for sth** etw zollamtlich abfertigen lassen; ~ **declaration** *n* Zollerklärung *f*; ~ **duty** *n* Zoll(abgabe *f*) *m*; ~ **house** *n* Zollamt *nt*; ~ **inspection** *n* Zollkontrolle *f*; ~ **officer** *n* Zollbeamte(r) *m*; ~ **union** *n* Zollunion *f.*

cut [kʌt] *(vb: pret, ptp ~)* **1** *n* **(a)** *(result of cutting)* Schnitt *m*; *(wound also)* Schnittwunde *f.* **to make a ~ in sth** in etw *(acc)* einen Einschnitt machen.

(b) *(act of cutting, slash, sweep)* Schnitt *m*; *(with sword, axe, whip)* Hieb, Schlag *m.* **his hair could do with a ~** seine Haare könnten mal wieder geschnitten werden; **the ~ and thrust of politics/modern publishing** das Spannungsfeld der Politik/der Trubel des heutigen Verlagswesens; **the ~ and thrust of the debate** die Hitze der Debatte; **a ~ from his sword/whip** ein Schlag mit seinem Schwert/seiner Peitsche.

(c) *(reduction)* *(in gen)* *(in prices)* Senkung, Ermäßigung, Herabsetzung *f*; *(in quality)* Verminderung *f*; *(in quantity, length etc)* Verringerung *f*; *(in expenses, salaries)* Kürzung *f*; *(in working hours, holidays)* (Ver)kürzung *f*; *(in programme, text, film)* Streichung *f* (in *+dat)*; *(in production, output)* Einschränkung *f*; *(in expenditure, budget etc)* Kürzung, Einsparung *f.* **the censor had made so many ~s** die Zensur hatte so viel gestrichen; **he had to take a ~ in (his) salary** er mußte eine Gehaltskürzung hinnehmen.

(d) *(of clothes, hair)* Schnitt *m*; *(of jewel also)* Schliff *m.*

(e) *(of meat)* Stück *nt.* ~**s of meat are different here** das Fleisch wird hier anders geschnitten.

(f) *(inf: share)* Anteil *m*, Teil *m or nt.* **to get one's ~** sein(en) Teil abbekommen.

(g) *(gibe)* Spitze *f*, spitze Bemerkung; *(wounding action)* Beleidigung *f.* **the unkindest ~ of all** *(prov)* der schlimmste Schlag.

(h) *(short route)* Abkürzung *f*; *(connecting alley-way etc)* Verbindungsweg *m.*

(i) *(Sport)* **to give a ~ to the ball** den Ball anschneiden.

(j) *(Elec)* Unterbrechung *f (in gen)*; *(planned)* Sperre *f.* **power/electricity ~** Stromausfall *m*; *(planned)* Stromsperre *f.*

(k) *(Cards)* Abheben *nt.* **it's your ~** du hebst ab.

(l) *(also wood)* Holzschnitt *m.*

(m) he's a ~ above the rest of them er ist den anderen um einiges überlegen.

2 *adj* **(a)** *usu attr flowers, tobacco* Schnitt-; *bread* (auf)geschnitten; *grass* gemäht; *prices* ermäßigt, herabgesetzt, Billig-. **finely ~ features** feingeschnittene Züge *pl*; **a well-~ dress** ein gutgeschnittenes Kleid; ~**-and-dried** *(fig) (fixed beforehand)* abgesprochen, (eine) abgemachte Sache; *(fixed and unchangeable)* festgelegt; ~**-and-dried opinions** festgefahrene Meinungen *pl*; **he wants everything to be ~-and-dried by tomorrow** er möchte, daß morgen alles vom Tisch *or* im Kasten *(inf)* ist; **as far as he's concerned the whole issue is now ~-and-dried** für ihn ist die ganze Angelegenheit erledigt; **it's not all that ~-and-dried** so eindeutig ist das nicht.

(b) *pred (inf: drunken)* voll *(inf).* **to be half ~** einen in der Krone haben *(inf).*

3 *vt* **(a)** *(with knife, scissors)* schneiden; *grass* mähen; *cake* anschneiden; *rope* durchschneiden; *(Naut)* kappen; *(~ out) fabric, suit* zuschneiden; *(~ off)* abschneiden; *(with sword, axe)* abschlagen, abhacken. **to ~ one's finger/lip/leg** sich *(dat)* am Finger/an der Lippe/am Bein schneiden; *(with knife, razor etc also)* sich *(dat)* in den Finger/in die Lippe/ins Bein schneiden; **to ~ one's nails** sich *(dat)* die Nägel schneiden; **to ~ sth in half/three** etw halbieren/dritteln, etw in zwei/drei Teile schneiden; **the road ~s the village in two** die Straße schneidet das Dorf in zwei Teile; **to ~ to pieces** zerstückeln; *sb's reputation* zerstören; *(gunfire) enemy line* auseinanderreißen; **to ~ open** aufschneiden; **he ~ his head open** *(on stone etc)* er hat sich *(dat)* den Kopf aufgeschlagen; *(on nail etc)* er hat sich *(dat)* den Kopf aufgerissen; *(on blade etc)* er hat sich *(dat)* den Kopf aufgeschnitten; **to have *or* get one's hair ~** sich *(dat)* die Haare schneiden lassen; **to ~ sb free/loose** jdn losschneiden.

(b) *(shape) steps* schlagen, hauen; *channel, trench* graben, ausheben; *figure (in wood)* schnitzen (in aus); *(in stone)* hauen (in aus); *glass, crystal, diamond* schleifen; *key* anfertigen; *gramophone record* pressen; *(singer)* machen. **to ~ one's coat according to one's cloth** *(Prov)* sich nach der Decke strecken; **to ~ a fine/sorry figure** eine gute/schlechte Figur machen *or* abgeben; *see* dash.

(c) *(fig: break off) electricity* abstellen; *(interrupt, accidentally)* unterbrechen; *gas also* (ab)sperren; *ties, links* abbrechen. **to ~ all one's ties** *(fig)* alle Verbindungen abbrechen *(with zu)*; **to ~ sb short** *(fig)* jdm das Wort abschneiden; **to ~ sth short** etw vorzeitig abbrechen; **to ~ a long story short** kurz und gut, der langen Rede kurzer Sinn.

(d) *(ignore, avoid) person* schneiden. **to ~ sb dead** jdn wie Luft behandeln.

(e) *(skip, not attend) lecture, class* schwänzen *(inf).*

(f) *(intersect) (line)* schneiden; *(path, road)* kreuzen.

(g) *(reduce) prices* senken, ermäßigen, herabsetzen; *quality* vermindern; *quantity* reduzieren; *working hours, holidays* (ver)kürzen; *expenses, salary, text, programme, film* kürzen; *production, output* verringern, einschränken.

(h) *(eliminate) part of programme or text or film* streichen; *(censor) film* Teile streichen aus. **the ~ version of a film** die zensierte *or* gekürzte Fassung eines Films.

(i) *(cause pain or suffering to)* **it ~ me to the heart *or* to the quick** es schnitt mir ins Herz *or* in die Seele; **the wind ~ his face** der Wind schnitt ihm ins Gesicht.

(j) **to ~ a tooth** zahnen, einen Zahn bekommen; **to ~ one's teeth on sth** *(fig)* sich *(dat)* die (ersten) Sporen an *or* mit etw *(dat)* verdienen.

(k) *(Cards)* to ~ the **cards/the pack** abheben.

(l) *(Sport)* **ball** (an)schneiden.

(m) *(edit)* **film** schneiden, cutten.

(n) *(stop)* **engine** abstellen; *(inf)* **noise** aufhören mit.

(o) *(divide)* **if we ~ the profits three ways** wenn wir den Gewinn dritteln *or* unter drei verteilen *or* aufteilen.

(p) don't ~ it too fine with your revision, it'll take longer than you think laß es mit deiner Wiederholung nicht auf die letzte Minute ankommen, das dauert länger als du denkst; **£10 would be ~ting it rather fine** £ 10 wären etwas knapp (bemessen); **2.20 would be ~ting it a bit fine** 2²⁰ wäre ein bißchen knapp; **aren't you ~ting it a bit fine?** ist das nicht ein bißchen knapp?; **to ~ one's losses** eine Sache abschließen, ehe der Schaden (noch) größer wird; *see* **Gordian, corner.**

4 *vi* **(a)** *(knife, scissors)* schneiden; *(lawnmower also)* mähen. **to ~ both ways** *(fig)* auch umgekehrt zutreffen; *(have disadvantages too)* ein zweischneidiges Schwert sein.

(b) *(material)* **paper ~s easily** Papier läßt sich leicht schneiden.

(c) *(intersect: lines, roads)* sich schneiden.

(d) *(Film)* *(change scenes)* überblenden (*to* zu); *(stop filming)* aufhören, abbrechen. **~!** Schnitt!, aus!

(e) *(Cards)* abheben. **to ~ for dealer** *(durch Ziehen einer Karte)* den Geber auslosen.

(f) *(Sport)* den Ball/die Bälle (an)schneiden. **to ~ at a ball** einen Ball anschneiden.

(g) to ~ and run abhauen *(inf)*, die Beine in die Hand nehmen *(inf)*; **to ~ loose** *(Naut)* losmachen; *(fig)* sich losmachen; *(US inf)* loslegen *(inf)*.

♦**cut across** *vi +prep obj* **(a)** hinüber-/herübergehen *etc (prep obj* über *+acc)*. **you can ~ ~ here** Sie können hier hinüber/herüber; **if you ~ ~ (the fields) it's quicker** wenn Sie über die Felder gehen, ist es kürzer; **to ~ ~ country** querfeldein gehen/fahren *etc*.

(b) *(fig)* **ideas, theory etc** widersprechen *(prep obj dat)*.

♦**cut along** *vi (dated inf)* sich auf die Socken machen *(inf)*.

♦**cut away** *vt sep* wegschneiden. **the dress was ~ ~ at the back** das Kleid war hinten *or* im Rücken *(tief)* ausgeschnitten.

♦**cut back 1** *vi* **(a)** *(go back)* zurückgehen/-fahren; *(Film also)* zurückblenden.

(b) *(reduce expenditure etc)* sich einschränken. **to ~ ~ on expenses etc/production** die Ausgaben *etc* einschränken/die Produktion zurückschrauben; **to ~ ~ on smoking/sweets** weniger rauchen/weniger Süßigkeiten essen.

2 *vt sep* **(a)** **plants, shrubs** zurückschneiden, stutzen.

(b) **production** zurückschrauben; **outgoings** einschränken; **programme** kürzen.

♦**cut down 1** *vt sep* **(a)** **tree** fällen; **corn** schneiden; **person** *(with sword)* (mit dem Schwert) niederstrecken.

(b) *(make smaller)* **number, size, expenses** einschränken; **piece of writing** zusammenstreichen *(to* auf *+acc)*; **clothes** zurechtschneiden, kleiner machen. **to ~ sb ~ to size** jdn auf seinen Platz verweisen.

(c) *usu pass (kill)* dahinraffen *(geh)*. **a young man ~ ~ in his prime** ein junger Mann, der im Frühling seiner Jahre dahingerafft wurde *(liter)*.

2 *vi* **(reduce intake, expenditure etc)** sich einschränken. **to ~ ~ on sth** etw einschränken.

♦**cut in 1** *vi* **(a)** *(interrupt)* sich einschalten. **to ~ ~ on sb/sth** jdn unterbrechen/sich in etw *(acc)* einschalten.

(b) *(cut towards the centre)* **blade** einschneiden. **to ~ ~ on sb's market** sich in jds Revier *(acc)* drängen *(inf)*; **he ~ ~ to the centre of the pitch** er zog ins Mittelfeld herüber.

(c) *(Aut: swerve in front)* sich direkt vor ein anderes/das andere Auto setzen. **to ~ ~ in front of sb** jdn schneiden; **he ~ ~ so sharply that the car behind had to swerve** er zog so schnell herüber, daß das nachfolgende Auto ausweichen mußte.

2 *vt sep* **to ~ sb ~ on sth** jdn an etw *(dat)* beteiligen.

♦**cut into** *vi +prep obj* **(a)** *(make a cut in)* **cake, meat** anschneiden. **(b)** *(interrupt)* **conversation** fallen in *(+acc)*. **(c)** *(swerve into)* **line of traffic** sich drängeln in *(+acc)*; **woods, alley-way** schnell einbiegen in *(+acc)*. **(d)** *(fig: make inroads in)* **savings** ein Loch reißen in *(+acc)*; **holidays** verkürzen.

♦**cut off** *vt sep* **(a)** *(with scissors, knife etc)* abschneiden; *(with axe, sword etc)* abschlagen. **to ~ ~ sb's head** jdm den Kopf abschlagen.

(b) **town, supply, line of escape** abschneiden; **allowance** sperren. **to ~ ~ the enemy's retreat/supplies** dem Feind den Rückzug/die Zufuhr abschneiden; **his deafness ~ him ~ from others** seine Taubheit schnitt ihn von der Umwelt ab; **we're very ~ ~ out here on the moor** wir leben hier draußen auf dem Moor sehr abgeschnitten.

(c) *(disinherit)* enterben. **to ~ sb ~ without a penny** jdn enterben.

(d) *(disconnect)* **gas, telephone etc** abstellen. **operator, I've been ~ ~** wir sind unterbrochen worden.

(e) *(break off)* **discussion, relations, negotiations** abbrechen.

♦**cut out 1** *vi (engine, radio transmission)* aussetzen.

2 *vt sep* **(a)** *(remove by cutting)* ausschneiden; **malignant growth etc** herausschneiden.

(b) *(form by cutting)* **coat, dress** zuschneiden. **they had ~ ~ a path through the jungle** sie hatten *(sich dat)* einen Weg durch den Dschungel geschlagen *or* gebahnt.

(c) *(delete)* *(heraus)streichen; *(not bother with)* verzichten auf *(+acc)*, sich *(dat)* schenken; **smoking, swearing etc** aufhören mit, sein lassen *(inf)*; **rival** ausstechen. **~ it ~!** *(inf)* hör auf damit!, laß das (sein)! *(inf)*; **~ the nonsense** laß den Unsinn; **~ ~ the talking!** *(inf)* halt den Mund! *(inf)*; **and you can ~ ~ the self-pity for a start!** und mit Selbstmitleid brauchst du gar nicht erst zu kommen *or* anzufangen!

(d) *(fig)* **to be ~ ~ for sth** zu etw geeignet *or* gemacht sein; **to**

be ~ ~ to be sth dazu geeignet sein, etw zu sein *or* zu werden; **he's not ~ ~ to be or for a doctor** er ist nicht zum Arzt geeignet, er hat nicht das Zeug zum Arzt.

(e) to have one's work ~ ~ alle Hände voll zu tun haben.

♦**cut through** *vt sep* **he couldn't ~ his way ~** es gelang ihm nicht, durchzukommen; **we ~ ~ the housing estate** wir gingen/fuhren durch die Siedlung.

♦**cut up 1** *vi* **to ~ ~ rough** Krach schlagen *(inf)*. **2** *vt sep* **(a)** **meat** aufschneiden; *(wood)* spalten; *(fig)* **enemy, army** vernichten. **(b)** **pass** *(inf: upset)* **he was very ~ ~ about it** das hat ihn schwer getroffen *or* ziemlich mitgenommen.

cutaneous [kjuːˈteɪnɪəs] *adj* Haut-, kutan *(spec)*.

cutaway [ˈkʌtəweɪ] **1** *n* Cut(away) *m*. **2** *adj* **~ coat** Cut(away) *m*; **~ diagram** Ausschnittzeichnung *f*.

cut-back [ˈkʌtbæk] *n* **(a)** Kürzung *f*. **(b)** *(Film)* Rückblende *f*.

cute [kjuːt] *adj (+er)* **(a)** *(inf: sweet)* süß, niedlich. **(b)** *(esp US inf: clever)* **idea, gadget** dufte *(inf)*, prima *(inf)*; *(shrewd)* **person, move** schlau, gerissen, clever *(inf)*. **that was pretty ~ of him** das hat er ganz schön schlau hingekriegt *(inf)*.

cut glass 1 *n* geschliffenes Glas. **2** *adj* **(a)** *(lit)* aus geschliffenem Glas. **(b)** **accent** vornehm.

cuticle [ˈkjuːtɪkl] *n (of nail)* Nagelhaut *f*; *(Anat)* Epidermis *f*; *(Bot)* Kutikula *f*. **~ remover** Nagelhautentferner *m*.

cutie [ˈkjuːtɪ] *n (esp US inf) (attractive)* flotter Käfer *(inf)*, dufte Biene *(inf)*; *(child)* süßer Fratz *(inf)*; *(shrewd)* gewitzter Kerl, Schlitzohr *(pej) m*.

cutie-pie [ˈkjuːtɪpaɪ] *n (esp US inf)* süßer Fratz *(inf)*.

cutlass [ˈkʌtləs] *n* Entermesser *nt*.

cutler [ˈkʌtlər] *n* Messerschmied *m*.

cutlery [ˈkʌtlərɪ] *n, no pl (esp Brit)* Besteck *nt*.

cutlet [ˈkʌtlɪt] *n* **(a)** *(boneless chop)* Schnitzel *nt*; *(fish fillet)* (Fisch)schnitzel *nt*. **(b)** *(of chopped meat)* (paniertes) Hacksteak.

cut: **~ loaf** *n* aufgeschnittenes Brot; **~-off** *n* **(a)** *(Tech: device)* Ausschaltmechanismus *m*; *(also* **~-off point)** Trennlinie *f*; **~-out 1** *n* **(a)** *(model)* Ausschneidemodell *nt*; *(figure, doll)* Ausschneidepuppe *f*; **~-out book** Ausschneidebogen *m*; **(b)** *(of engine)* Aussetzen *nt*; **it has an automatic ~-out** es setzt automatisch aus; **(c)** *(Elec)* Sperre *f*. **2** *adj* **(a)** **model etc** Ausschneide-; **(b)** *(Elec)* Abschalt-, Ausschalt-; **~-price** *adj* zu Schleuderpreisen; **offer** Billig-; **~-rate** *adj* zu verbilligtem Tarif.

cutter [ˈkʌtər] *n* **(a)** *(tool)* Messer *nt*. **a pair of (wire-)~s** eine Drahtschere; *(Elec)* ein Seitenschneider *m*. **(b)** *(of clothes)* Zuschneider(in *f*) *m*; *(of jewel)* Schleifer(in *f*) *m*; *(of glass)* Glasschneider *m*; *(Film)* Cutter(in *f*) *m*. **(c)** *(boat)* Kutter *m*; *(US: coastguard's boat)* Boot *nt* der Küstenwache. **(d)** *(US: sleigh)* leichter Pferdeschlitten.

cut-throat [ˈkʌtθrəʊt] **1** *n (murderous type)* Strolch, Verbrechertyp *(inf) m*. **2** *adj* **(a)** **competition, business** unbarmherzig, mörderisch. **(b)** **~ razor** (offenes) Rasiermesser.

cutting [ˈkʌtɪŋ] **1** *n* **(a)** *(of grass)* Mähen *nt*; *(of cake)* Anschneiden *nt*; *(of rope)* Durchschneiden, Kappen *nt*; *(with sword)* Abschlagen, Abhauen *nt*; *(of electricity)* Sperrung *f*; *(interruption, accidental)* Unterbrechung *f*; *(of steps)* Schlagen, Hauen *nt*; *(of channel, trench)* Graben *nt*; *(of figure)* *(in wood)* Schnitzen *nt (in aus)*; *(in stone)* Hauen *nt (in aus)*; *(of glass, crystal, jewel)* Schliff *m*; *(of key)* Anfertigung *f*; *(of record)* Pressen *nt*, Herstellung *f*; *(snubbing: of person)* Schneiden *nt*; *(of lecture, class)* Schwänzen *nt (inf)*; *(of prices)* Senkung, Herabsetzung *f*; *(of quality)* Verminderung *f*; *(of quantity)* Reduzierung *f*; *(of working hours)* Verkürzung *f*; *(of expenses, salary)* Kürzung *f*; *(Film)* Schnitt *m*; *(of production)* Drosselung *f*; *(of part of text)* Streichung *f*; *(of ties)* Lösen *nt*, Abbruch *m*.

(b) *(Brit: road, railway ~)* Durchstich *m*.

(c) *(Brit: clipping) (from newspaper)* Ausschnitt *m*; *(of cloth)* Schnipsel *m*, Stückchen (Stoff) *nt*.

(d) *(Hort)* Ableger *m*. **to take a ~** einen Ableger nehmen.

2 *adj* **(a)** **blade, edge** scharf.

(b) *(fig)* **wind, cold** schneidend; **remark also, tongue** scharf, spitz. **to be ~ to sb** jdm gegenüber spitze Bemerkungen machen.

cuttle-bone [ˈkʌtlbəʊn] *n* Schulp *m*.

cuttlefish [ˈkʌtlfɪʃ] *n* Tintenfisch *m*, Sepie *f*, Kuttelfisch *m*.

cwm [kuːm] *n* Kar *nt*.

cwt *abbr of* **hundredweight.**

cyanide [ˈsaɪənaɪd] *n* Zyanid, Blausäuresalz *nt*. **~ poisoning** Blausäurevergiftung *f*.

cybernetics [ˌsaɪbəˈnetɪks] *n sing* Kybernetik *f*.

cyclamen [ˈsɪkləmən] *n* Alpenveilchen, Zyklamen *(spec) nt*.

cycle [ˈsaɪkl] **1** *n* **(a)** *(of seasons also, events)* Zyklus, Kreislauf *m*; *(of poems, songs)* Zyklus *m*; *(Elec)* Periode *f*. **life ~** Lebenszyklus *m* or -kreislauf *m*; **menstrual ~** Monatszyklus, Menstruationszyklus *m*; **the moon's ~** der Mondwechsel, die Lunation *(spec)*. **(b)** *(bicycle)* (Fahr)rad *nt*; *(sl: motorbike)* Maschine *f (sl)*. **2** *vi* mit dem (Fahr)rad fahren. **can you ~?** kannst du radfahren?

cycle path *n* (Fahr)radweg *m*.

cycler [ˈsaɪklər] *n (US) see* **cyclist.**

cycle: **~ race** *n* Radrennen *nt*; **~-track** *n see* **~ path.**

cyclic(al) [ˈsaɪklɪk(əl)] *adj* zyklisch; *(Elec)* periodisch.

cycling [ˈsaɪklɪŋ] *n* Radfahren *nt*. **I enjoy ~** ich fahre gern Rad.

cycling: **~ cape** *n* Radmantel *m*, Radcape *nt*; **~ holiday** *n* Urlaub *m* mit dem Fahrrad; **~ tour** *n* Radtour *f*.

cyclist [ˈsaɪklɪst] *n* (Fahr)radfahrer(in *f*) *m*; *(motor ~)* Motorradfahrer(in *f*) *m*.

cyclometer [saɪˈklɒmɪtər] *n* Kilometerzähler *m*.

cyclone [ˈsaɪkləʊn] *n* Zyklon *m*. **~ cellar** *(US)* tiefer Keller zum Schutz vor Zyklonen.

cyclonic [sar'klɒnɪk] *adj* zyklonartig.
cyclopaedia [ˌsaɪkləʊ'piːdɪə] *n* Enzyklopädie *f*.
Cyclops ['saɪklɒps] *n* Zyklop *m*.
cyclorama [ˌsaɪklə'rɑːmə] *n* Rundhorizont *m*.
cygnet ['sɪgnɪt] *n* Schwanjunge(s) *nt*.
cylinder ['sɪlɪndə'] *n* (*Math, Aut*) Zylinder *m*; (*of revolver, typewriter*) Walze *f*. **a four-~** car ein Vierzylinder *m*, ein vierzylindriges Auto; **to be firing on all four ~s** (*lit*) auf allen vier Zylindern laufen; (*fig*) in Fahrt sein/kommen.
cylinder: ~ block *n* (*Aut*) Zylinderblock *m*; **~ capacity** *n* (*Aut*) Hubraum *m*; **~ head** *n* (*Aut*) Zylinderkopf *m*.
cylindrical *adj*, **~ly** *adv* [sɪ'lɪndrɪkəl, -ɪ] zylindrisch.
cymbal ['sɪmbəl] *n* Beckenteller *m*. **~s** Becken *nt*; **to play the ~s** das Becken schlagen.
cynic ['sɪnɪk] *n* (a) Zyniker(in *f*) *m*. **don't be such a ~** sei nicht so zynisch. (b) **C~** (*Philos*) Kyniker, Zyniker *m*.
cynical ['sɪnɪkəl] *adj* (a) zynisch. **he was very ~ about it** er äußerte sich sehr zynisch dazu. (b) **C~** (*Philos*) kynisch, zynisch.
cynically ['sɪnɪklɪ] *adv* zynisch.
cynicism ['sɪnɪsɪzəm] *n* (a) *no pl* Zynismus *m*. (b) (*cynical remark*) zynische Bemerkung. (c) **C~** (*Philos*) Kynismus, Zynismus *m*.
cynosure ['saɪnəʃʊə'] *n* **to be the ~ of every eye** (*liter*) alle

Blicke auf sich ziehen *or* vereinigen.
cypher *see* **cipher**.
cypress ['saɪprɪs] *n* Zypresse *f*.
Cyprian ['sɪprɪən] *n* (*old*) *see* **Cypriot**.
Cypriot ['sɪprɪət] **1** *adj* zypriotisch, zyprisch. **2** *n* Zypriot(in *f*), Zyprer(in *f*) *m*.
Cyprus ['saɪprəs] *n* Zypern *nt*.
Cyrillic ['sɪrɪlɪk] *adj* kyrillisch.
cyst [sɪst] *n* Zyste *f*.
cystitis [sɪs'taɪtɪs] *n* Blasenentzündung, Zystitis (*spec*) *f*.
cytology [saɪ'tɒlədʒɪ] *n* Zytologie, Zellenlehre *f*.
cytoplasm ['saɪtəʊplæzm] *n* Zytoplasma, Zellplasma *nt*.
czar [zɑː'] *n* Zar *m*.
czarevitch ['zɑːrəvɪtʃ] *n* Zarewitsch *m*.
czarina [zɑː'riːnə] *n* Zarin *f*.
czarism ['zɑːrɪzəm] *n* Zarismus *m*.
czarist ['zɑːrɪst] **1** *adj* zaristisch. **2** *n* Zarist(in *f*) *m*.
Czech [tʃek] **1** *adj* tschechisch. **2** *n* (a) Tscheche *m*, Tschechin *f*. (b) (*language*) Tschechisch *nt*.
Czechoslovak ['tʃekəʊ'sləʊvæk] **1** *adj* tschechoslowakisch. **2** *n* Tschechoslowake *m*, Tschechoslowakin *f*.
Czechoslovakia ['tʃekəʊslə'vækɪə] *n* die Tschechoslowakei.
Czechoslovakian ['tʃekəʊslə'vækɪən] *adj*, *n see* **Czechoslovak**.

D

D, d [diː] *n* D, d *nt*. **D sharp/flat** Dis, dis *nt*/Des, des *nt*; *see also* **major, minor, natural**.
d (*Brit old*) *abbr of* **pence**.
'd = **had, would**.
DA (*US*) *abbr of* **District Attorney**.
D/A *abbr of* **deposit account**.
dab¹ [dæb] **1** *n* (a) (*small amount*) Klecks *m*; (*applied with puff, of cream etc*) Tupfer *m*; (*of liquid, perfume, glue etc*) Tropfen *m*; (*of butter*) Klacks *m*. **a ~ of powder/ointment** *etc* etwas *or* ein bißchen Puder/Salbe *etc*; **to give sth a ~ of paint** etw überstreichen.
(b) **~s** *pl* (*sl: fingerprints*) Fingerabdrücke *pl*.
2 *vt* (*with powder etc*) betupfen; (*with towel etc*) tupfen. **to ~ one's eyes** sich (*dat*) die Augen tupfen; **she ~bed ointment/ powder over her face/the wound** sie betupfte sich (*dat*) das Gesicht/die Wunde mit Salbe/Puder.
♦**dab at** *vi* +*prep obj* betupfen.
♦**dab on** *vt sep* auftragen (*prep obj* auf +*acc*).
dab² *n* (*fish*) Kliesche, Scharbe *f*.
dab³ *adj* (*inf*) **to be a ~ hand at sth/doing sth** gut in etw (*dat*) sein/sich darauf verstehen, etw zu tun; **he is a ~ hand at making something out of nothing** er versteht sich darauf *or* ist sehr geschickt darin, aus nichts etwas zu machen.
dabble ['dæbl] **1** *vt* **to ~ one's hands/feet in the water** mit den Händen/Füßen im Wasser plan(t)schen.
2 *vi* (a) plan(t)schen.
(b) (*fig*) **to ~ in/at sth** sich (*nebenbei*) mit etw beschäftigen; **are you a serious photographer? — no, I only ~ (in it)** beschäftigen Sie sich ernsthaft mit der Photographie? — nein, nur so nebenbei; **he ~s in stocks and shares/antiques** er versucht sich an der Börse/in Antiquitäten.
dabbler ['dæblə'] *n* Amateur *m*.
dabchick ['dæbtʃɪk] *n* Steißfuß *m*.
dace [deɪs] *n*, *pl* - Weißfisch *m*.
dacha ['dætʃə] *n* Datscha, Datsche (*DDR*) *f*.
dachshund ['dækshʊnd] *n* Dackel, Dachshund (*rare*) *m*.
Dacron ® ['dækrɒn] *n* Dacron ® *nt*.
dactyl ['dæktɪl] *n* (*Zool*) Zehe *f*; Finger *m*; (*Liter*) Daktylus *m*.
dactylic [dæk'tɪlɪk] *adj* daktylisch.
dad [dæd] *n* (*inf*) Vater *m*; (*affectionately also*) Vati, Papa *m*.
Dada ['dɑːdɑː] *n* (*Art*) Dada *m*.
Dadaism ['dɑːdaɪɪzm] *n* Dadaismus *m*.
daddy ['dædɪ] *n* (*inf*) Papa, Vati *m* (*inf*). **the ~ of them all** (*esp US inf*) der Größte.
daddy-long-legs [ˌdædɪ'lɒŋlegz] *n*, *pl* - (*Brit*) Schnake *f*; (*US*) Weberknecht *m*.
dado ['deɪdəʊ] *n* (*of pedestal*) Basis *f*; (*of wall*) Paneel *nt*.
daemon ['diːmən] *n* (*liter*) *see* **demon**.
daffodil ['dæfədɪl], **daff** [dæf] (*inf*) *n* Osterglocke, Narzisse *f*.
daffy ['dæfɪ] *adj* (+*er*) (*inf*) *see* **daft**.
daft [dɑːft] *adj* (+*er*) doof, blöd, bekloppt (*all inf*). **~ in the head** (*inf*) blöd (*inf*), bekloppt (*inf*); **what a ~ thing to do** so was Doofes *or* Blödes *or* Beklopptes (*all inf*); **he's ~ about her/football** (*inf*) er ist verrückt nach ihr/nach Fußball (*inf*).
daftie ['dɑːftɪ], **daft ha'porth** ['dɑːfteɪpəθ] *n* (*Brit inf*) Dussel *m* (*inf*).
dagger ['dægə'] *n* (a) Dolch *m*. **to be at ~s drawn with sb** (*fig*)

mit jdm auf (dem) Kriegsfuß stehen; **to look ~s at sb** jdn mit Blicken durchbohren. (b) (*Typ*) Kreuz *nt*.
dago ['deɪgəʊ] *n* (*pej*) Südländer, Kanake (*pej sl*) *m* (*verächtlich für Spanier, Portugiese oder Südamerikaner*).
daguerreotype [də'gerəʊtaɪp] **1** *n* Daguerreotypie *f*. **2** *vt* nach dem Daguerreotypieverfahren photographieren.
dahlia ['deɪlɪə] *n* Dahlie *f*.
Dáil Eireann [dɑɪl'eərən] *n* Unterhaus *nt* der Republik Irland.
daily ['deɪlɪ] **1** *adj* täglich; *wage, newspaper* Tages-. **~ dozen** (*inf*) Morgengymnastik *f*; **~ grind** täglicher Trott; **he is employed on a ~ basis** er ist tageweise angestellt; (*labourer*) er ist als Tagelöhner beschäftigt, er steht im Tagelohn.
2 *adv* täglich.
3 *n* (a) (*newspaper*) Tageszeitung *f*.
(b) (*also* **~ help, ~ woman**) Putzfrau *f*.
daintily ['deɪntɪlɪ] *adv* zierlich; *hold, walk, move* anmutig.
daintiness ['deɪntɪnɪs] *n* Zierlichkeit *f*; (*of movement, manners etc*) Anmutigkeit *f*; Geziertheit *f* (*pej*).
dainty ['deɪntɪ] **1** *adj* (+*er*) (a) zierlich; *lace, handkerchief* fein; *movement, music* anmutig. **she has ~ little ways** bei ihr ist alles fein und zierlich. (b) *food* appetitlich. **~ morsel** Appetithappen *m*. (c) (*refined*) geziert, etepetete (*inf*). **2** *n* Leckerei *f*, Leckerbissen *m*.
daiquiri ['daɪkərɪ] *n* Cocktail *m aus Rum, Limonensaft und Zucker*.
dairy ['deərɪ] *n* Molkerei *f*; (*on farm*) Milchkammer *f*; (*shop*) Milchgeschäft *nt*.
dairy: ~ butter *n* Markenbutter *f*; **~ cattle** *npl* Milchvieh *nt*; **~ cow** *n* Milchkuh *f*; **~ farm** *n* auf Milchviehhaltung spezialisierter Bauernhof; **~ farming** *n* Milchviehhaltung *f*; **~ herd** *n* Herde *f* Milchkühe; **~ ice cream** *n* Milchspeiseeis *nt*.
dairying ['deərɪŋ] *n* Milchwirtschaft *f*.
dairy: ~maid *n* Melkerin *f*; (*worker*) Molkereiangestellte *f*; **~man** *n* Melker *m*; Molkereiangestellte(r) *m*; (*milkman*) Milchmann *m*; **~ produce** *n* Milch- *or* Molkereiprodukte *pl*.
dais ['deɪɪs] *n* Podium *nt*.
daisy ['deɪzɪ] *n* Gänseblümchen *nt*. **~ chain** Kette *f* aus Gänseblümchen; **to be as fresh as a ~** taufrisch sein; **to be pushing up the daisies** (*sl*) sich (*dat*) die Radieschen von unten besehen (*sl*).
dale [deɪl] *n* (*N Engl, liter*) Tal *nt*.
dalesman ['deɪlzmən] *n*, *pl* -men [-mən] Bewohner *m* des Gebiets der Dales in Yorkshire.
dalliance ['dælɪəns] *n* (*liter*) Tändelei *f* (*liter*).
dally ['dælɪ] *vi* (a) (*waste time*) (herum)trödeln, bummeln. **without ~ing** ohne zu trödeln *or* bummeln. (b) (*flirt*) **to ~ with sb/an idea** mit jdm schäkern/mit einem Gedanken liebäugeln *or* spielen.
Dalmatia [dæl'meɪʃə] *n* Dalmatien *nt*.
Dalmatian [dæl'meɪʃən] **1** *adj* dalmatinisch, dalmatisch. **2** *n* (a) (*person*) Dalmatiner(in *f*) *m*. (b) (*dog*) Dalmatiner *m*.
daltonism ['dɔːltənɪzm] *n* Farbenblindheit *f*, Daltonismus *m* (*dated spec*); Rotgrünblindheit *f*.
dam¹ [dæm] **1** *n* (*lit, fig*) Damm *m*; (*reservoir*) Stausee *m*. **2** *vt* (*also* **~ up**) (a) *river, lake* (auf)stauen; *valley* eindämmen. (b) (*fig*) *flow of words* eindämmen; *feelings* aufstauen.
dam² *n* (*mother*) Muttertier *nt*.

damage ['dæmɪdʒ] 1 n (a) Schaden m (to an +dat). to do a lot of ~ großen Schaden anrichten; to do sb/sth a lot of ~ jdm/einer Sache (dat) großen Schaden zufügen; to make good the ~ den Schaden wiedergutmachen; the ~ to his pride/ego/reputation die Verletzung seines Stolzes/Erschütterung seines Selbstbewußtseins/Schädigung seines Rufs; that did a lot of ~ to his reputation das hat seinem Ruf sehr geschadet.
(b) (Jur) ~s Schaden(s)ersatz m.
(c) (inf: cost) what's the ~? was kostet der Spaß? (inf).
2 vt schaden (+dat); machine, car, furniture, fruit, tree beschädigen; health, reputation, relations also schädigen. to ~ one's eyesight sich (dat) die Augen verderben; smoking can ~ your health Rauchen ist gesundheitsschädlich, Rauchen schadet Ihrer Gesundheit; that ~d his chances das hat seine Chancen verdorben; to ~ one's chances sich (dat) die Chancen verderben.

damaging ['dæmɪdʒɪŋ] adj schädlich; remarks abträglich. to be ~ to sth sich auf etw (acc) schädigend or schädlich auswirken, schädlich für etw sein; that was a ~ blow to his opponent's chin/his pride der Schlag ans Kinn seines Gegners saß/das hat seinem Stolz einen empfindlichen Schlag versetzt.

damascene ['dæməsiːn] vt damaszieren. ~d blades Damaszenerklingen pl.

Damascus [dəˈmɑːskəs] n Damaskus nt. ~ steel Damaszener Stahl m.

damask ['dæməsk] 1 n (a) Damast m. (b) ~ (steel) Damaszener Stahl m. (c) ~ rose Damaszenerrose f. 2 adj (a) Damast-, aus Damast. (b) (liter) colour rosig.

dam-buster ['dæmbʌstəʳ] n jemand, der Staudämme in die Luft sprengt.

dame [deɪm] n (a) D~ (Brit) Titel der weiblichen Träger des „Order of the British Empire". (b) (old: lady) Dame f. D~ Fortune Frau Fortuna f. (c) (Theat: in pantomime) (komische) Alte. (d) (US inf) Weib nt (inf).

damfool ['dæmˈfuːl] adj attr (inf) idiotisch (inf).

dammit ['dæmɪt] interj (inf) verdammt (inf), Teufel noch mal (inf). it weighs 2 kilos as near as ~ es wiegt so gut wie 2 Kilo.

damn [dæm] 1 interj (inf) verdammt (inf).
2 n (inf) he doesn't care or give a ~ er schert sich den Teufel or einen Dreck (darum) (inf); I don't give a ~ das ist mir piepegal (inf) or scheißegal (sl); it's not worth a ~ das ist keinen Pfifferling wert.
3 adj attr (inf) verdammt. it's one ~ thing after another ver-dammt noch mal, da kommt aber auch eins nach dem andern; it's a ~ nuisance das ist ein verdammter Mist (inf), das ist wirklich zu blöd (inf); I can't/couldn't see a ~ thing verdammt (noch mal), ich kann überhaupt nichts sehen/das war vielleicht ein Mist (inf), ich konnte überhaupt nichts sehen.
4 adv (inf) verdammt. I should ~ well hope/think so das will ich aber auch stark hoffen/ich doch stark annehmen; a ~ sight better/worse verdammt viel besser/schlechter (inf); ~-all nicht die Bohne (inf); I've done ~-all today verdammt, ich hab heute überhaupt nichts gemacht (inf).
5 vt (a) (Rel) verdammen.
(b) (bring condemnation, ruin on) das Genick brechen (+dat); (evidence) überführen.
(c) (judge and condemn) verurteilen; book etc also ver-reißen. to ~ sb/sth with faint praise jdn/etw auf eine Weise loben, die ihn bloßstellt; to ~ sb to sth jdn zu etw verdammen.
(d) (inf) ~ him/you! (annoyed) verdammt! (inf); (I don't care about him/you) der kann/du kannst mich mal! (inf); ~ him for forgetting so ein (verdammter) Mist, er hat's vergessen (inf); ~ Richard, he's pinched my book der verdammte Richard hat mein Buch geklaut (inf); ~ it! verdammt (noch mal)! (inf); ~ it all! Donnerwetter! (inf); (in surprise) Donnerwetter! (inf), Teufel auch! (inf); well, I'll be ~ed! Donnerwetter! (inf); I'll be ~ed if I'll go there ich denk nicht (im Schlaf) dran (inf), da hin-zugehen; I'll be ~ed if I know weiß der Teufel (inf).

damnable adj, ~bly adv ['dæmnəbl, -ɪ] gräßlich.

damnation [dæmˈneɪʃən] 1 n (Eccl) (act) Verdammung f; (state of ~) Verdammnis f. 2 interj (inf) verdammt (inf).

damned ['dæmd] 1 adj (a) soul verdammt. (b) (inf) see damn 3.
2 adv see damn 4. 3 n (Eccl, liter) the ~ pl die Verdammten pl.

damnedest ['dæmdɪst] n to do or try one's ~ (inf) (verdammt noch mal inf) sein möglichstes tun.

damning ['dæmɪŋ] adj vernichtend; evidence belastend. he was pretty ~ about it er hat sich ziemlich vernichtend darüber geäußert.

Damocles ['dæməkliːz] n: sword of ~ Damoklesschwert nt.

damp [dæmp] 1 adj (+er) feucht. a ~ squib (fig) ein Reinfall m.
2 n (a) Feuchtigkeit f.
(b) (Min) (choke-~) Schlagwetter nt; (fire-~) Grubengas nt.
3 vt (a) befeuchten, anfeuchten; ironing also einsprengen or -spritzen.
(b) (fig) enthusiasm etc dämpfen. to ~ sb's spirits jdm einen Dämpfer aufsetzen.
(c) sounds, vibrations dämpfen; (also ~ down) fire ersticken.

damp course n Dämmschicht f.

dampen ['dæmpən] vt see damp 3 (a, b).

damper ['dæmpəʳ] n (a) (of chimney) (Luft)klappe f; (of piano) Dämpfer m. (b) to put a ~ on sth einer Sache (dat) einen Dämpfer aufsetzen. (c) (Austral: bread) Fladenbrot nt.

dampish ['dæmpɪʃ] adj etwas feucht.

dampness ['dæmpnɪs] n Feuchtigkeit f.

damp-proof ['dæmppruːf] adj feuchtigkeitsbeständig.

damsel ['dæmzəl] n (obs, liter) Maid f (obs, liter).

damsel fly n Seejungfer f, Schlankjungfer f.

damson ['dæmzən] n (fruit) Damaszenerpflaume f; (tree) Damaszenerpflaumenbaum m.

Dan [dæn] n (Sport) Dan m.

dance [dɑːns] 1 n (a) Tanz m. the D~ of Death der Totentanz;

---

may I have the next ~? darf ich um den nächsten Tanz bitten?; she's led him a fine or pretty ~ sie hat ihn ja ganz schön an der Nase herumgeführt; (caused a lot of trouble) ihretwegen hat er sich (dat) die Hacken abgelaufen.
(b) (ball) Tanz m; Tanzabend m. public ~ öffentliche Tanzveranstaltung; end-of-term ~ Semesterball m; to give or hold a ~ einen Tanz(abend) veranstalten; (privately) eine Tanzparty geben; to go to a ~ tanzen gehen, zum Tanzen gehen.
2 vt tanzen. to ~ attendance on sb jdn von hinten und vorn bedienen (inf).
3 vi (a) tanzen. would you like to ~? möchten Sie tanzen?
(b) (move here and there) to ~ about/up and down (herum)tänzeln/auf- und abhüpfen; to ~ for joy einen Freudentanz aufführen.
(c) (fig) tanzen; (boat on waves also) schaukeln.

dance in cpds Tanz-; ~ band n Tanzkapelle f; ~ floor n Tanz-boden m; (in restaurant) Tanzfläche f; ~ hall n Tanzsaal m; ~ music n Tanzmusik f.

dancer ['dɑːnsəʳ] n Tänzer(in f) m.

dancing ['dɑːnsɪŋ] 1 n Tanzen nt. 2 attr Tanz-. ~ dervish tan-zender Derwisch; ~ girl Tänzerin f; ~ shoe Tanzschuh m; put on your ~ shoes! (fig) mach dich hübsch or zurecht!

D and C abbr of dilation and curettage.

dandelion ['dændɪlaɪən] n Löwenzahn m.

dander ['dændəʳ] n (inf): to get sb's/one's ~ up jdn auf die Palme bringen (inf)/seine or die Borsten aufstellen (fig).

dandified ['dændɪfaɪd] adj stutzerhaft.

dandle ['dændl] vt schaukeln (on auf +dat).

dandruff ['dændrəf] n Schuppen pl.

dandy ['dændɪ] 1 n Dandy, Stutzer (dated), Geck (dated) m. 2 adj (esp US inf) prima (inf).

Dane [deɪn] n Däne m, Dänin f.

dang [dæŋ] (dated inf) adj, adv, vt see damn 3, 4, 5 (d).

danger ['deɪndʒəʳ] n (a) Gefahr f. he likes ~ er liebt die Gefahr; to put sb/sth in ~ jdn/etw in Gefahr bringen, jdn/etw gefährden; to run into ~ in Gefahr geraten; to be in ~ of doing sth Gefahr laufen, etw zu tun; the country is in ~ of invasion dem Land droht eine Invasion; out of ~ außer Gefahr; there is a ~ of fire es besteht Feuergefahr; there is a ~ of his getting lost es besteht die Gefahr, daß er sich verirrt; he ran the ~ of being recognized er lief Gefahr, erkannt zu werden; there is no ~ of that die Gefahr besteht nicht; to be a ~ to sb/sth für jdn/etw eine Gefahr bedeuten.
(b) "~" „Achtung, Lebensgefahr!"; (Mot) „Gefahrenstelle"; "~, high-tension cables/road up" „Achtung, Hochspan-nung!/Straßenarbeiten"; "~, ice" „Glatteisgefahr"; "~, keep out" „Zutritt verboten, Lebensgefahr!"; the signal was at ~ (Rail) das Signal stand auf Rot.

danger: ~ area n Gefahrenzone f or -bereich m; ~ list n: on/off the ~ list in/außer Lebensgefahr; ~ money n Gefahrenzulage f; to get ~ money eine Gefahrenzulage kriegen.

dangerous ['deɪndʒrəs] adj gefährlich.

dangerously ['deɪndʒrəslɪ] adv gefährlich. the deadline is getting ~ close der Termin rückt bedenklich nahe.

danger: ~ point n Gefahrengrenze f; to reach ~ point die Gefahrengrenze erreichen; ~ signal n (lit, fig) Warnsignal nt; (Rail) Deckungssignal nt vor Gefahr (spec); ~ zone n Gefahrenzone f.

dangle ['dæŋgl] 1 vt baumeln lassen. to ~ sth in front of or before sb (fig) jdm etw verlockend in Aussicht stellen. 2 vi (a) baumeln. (b) to ~ after sb jdm nachlaufen; to ~ around an important person um eine bedeutende Persönlichkeit herumschwarzenln.

Danish ['deɪnɪʃ] 1 adj dänisch. ~ blue (cheese) (Blau)schimmel-käse m; ~ pastry Plundergebäck nt. 2 n (language) Dänisch nt. the ~ pl (people) die Dänen.

dank [dæŋk] adj (unangenehm) feucht.

Dante ['dæntɪ] n Dante m.

Dantean ['dæntɪən] adj dantisch; works Dantisch.

Dantesque [dænˈtesk] adj dantesk.

Danube ['dænjuːb] n Donau f.

dapper ['dæpəʳ] adj gepflegt, gediegen.

dapple ['dæpl] vt sprenkeln.

dappled ['dæpld] adj gefleckt; (with small flecks) gesprenkelt; sky wolkig; horse scheckig.

dapple grey (horse) n Apfelschimmel m.

Darby and Joan ['dɑːbɪənˈdʒəʊn] npl glückliches, älteres Ehepaar. ~ club Altenclub m.

Dardanelles [ˌdɑːdəˈnelz] npl Dardanellen pl.

dare [dɛəʳ] 1 vi (be bold enough) es wagen; (have the confi-dence) sich trauen. you/he wouldn't ~! du wirst dich/er wird sich schwer hüten; you ~! untersteh dich!; how ~ you! was fällt dir ein!
2 vt (a) to ~ (to) do sth (es) wagen, etw zu tun; sich trauen, etw zu tun; I didn't ~ (to) go upstairs/there ich habe mich nicht getraut, die Treppe hinaufzugehen/dorthin zu gehen, ich habe mich nicht die Treppe hinauf/dorthin getraut; he wouldn't ~ say anything bad about his boss er wird sich hüten or unter-stehen, etwas Schlechtes über seinen Chef zu sagen; he ~ not or ~n't do it das wagt er nicht!; how ~ you say such things? wie kannst du es wagen or was unterstehst du dich, so etwas zu sagen?; don't (you) ~ say that to me untersteh dich, das zu mir zu sagen; ~ you do it? trauen Sie sich?; she ~d a smile/bikini sie riskierte ein Lächeln/wagte es, einen Bikini zu tragen.
(b) I ~ say it gets quite cold here in winter ich könnte mir denken, es ist hier im Winter ziemlich kalt wird; I ~ say he'll be there es kann (gut) sein, daß er dort sein wird; he's bound to be there — I ~ say er ist sicher dort — das kann gut sein; he was very sorry — I ~ say es tat ihm sehr leid — das glaube ich gerne.
(c) (face the risk of) riskieren; danger also trotzen (+dat). to

~ **death/one's life** sein Leben riskieren *or* aufs Spiel setzen. **(d)** (*challenge*) **go on, I** ~ **you!** Feigling!; **are you daring me?** wetten, daß? (*inf*); **(I)** ~ **you to jump off** spring doch, du Feigling!
3 *n* Mutprobe *f.* **to do sth for a** ~ etw als Mutprobe tun.
daredevil ['dɛədevl] **1** *n* Wag(e)hals *m.* **2** *adj* tollkühn, waghalsig.
daring ['dɛərɪŋ] **1** *adj* kühn (*geh*); (*in physical matters*) waghalsig; *remark, attempt* gewagt, kühn (*geh*); *opinion, dress* gewagt. **2** *n* Schneid *m*, Kühnheit *f* (*geh*); (*in physical matters*) Waghalsigkeit *f*, Schneid *m* (*geh*).
daringly ['dɛərɪŋlɪ] *adv* kühn; (*in physical matters*) waghalsig; *dress* gewagt. **he spoke very** ~ **to the boss** er hat in sehr kühnem Ton mit dem Chef gesprochen.
dark [dɑːk] **1** *adj* (+*er*) **(a)** dunkel; *room, night also* finster. **it's getting** *or* **growing** ~ es wird dunkel; (*in evening also*) es wird Nacht; **the sky is getting** ~ der Himmel wird dunkel; (*before storm*) der Himmel verfinstert sich; ~ **blue** dunkelblau; **a** ~ **blue** ein dunkles Blau; **in** ~**est Africa** im tiefsten Afrika. **(b)** (*fig: sinister*) dunkel; *thoughts, threats also* finster. **to keep sth** ~ etw geheimhalten; ~ **deeds** dunkle Geschäfte. **(c)** (*gloomy, sad*) düster. **to look on the** ~ **side of things** schwarzsehen, schwarzseherisch sein.
2 *n* **(a)** Dunkelheit *f*. **after** ~ nach Einbruch der Dunkelheit; **until** ~ bis zum Einbruch der Dunkelheit. **(b)** (*fig: ignorance*) Dunkel *nt*. **to be in the** ~ keine Ahnung haben (*about* von); **he has kept me in the** ~ **as to what they were planning** er hat mich über das, was sie vorhatten, im dunkeln gelassen; **to work in the** ~ im dunkeln *or* finstern tappen; **it was a shot in the** ~ das war nur so auf gut Glück *or* aufs Geratewohl gesagt/getan/geraten.
dark: **D**~ **Ages** *npl* finsteres Mittelalter; ~**-complexioned** ['dɑːkəm,plekʃənd] *adj* mit dunklem Teint; **the D**~ **Continent** *n* der schwarze Erdteil.
darken ['dɑːkən] **1** *vt* **(a)** dunkel machen; *sky also* verdunkeln; (*before storm*) verfinstern; *brilliance also* trüben. **the sun** ~**ed her skin** die Sonne hat ihre Haut gebräunt. **(b)** (*fig*) trüben; *mind also* umnachten; *future also* verdüstern. **an angry frown** ~**ed his brow** ein ärgerliches Runzeln verfinsterte seine Stirn; **never** ~ **my door again!** lassen Sie sich hier nicht mehr blicken!; **his last days were** ~**ed by** ... seine letzten Tage waren von ... verdüstert *or* getrübt.
2 *vi* **see** *vt* **(a)** dunkel werden; sich verdunkeln; sich verfinstern; sich trüben. **(b)** sich trüben; sich umnachten; sich verdüstern; (*brow*) sich verfinstern.
dark: ~**-eyed** ['dɑː,kaɪd] *adj* dunkeläugig; ~ **horse** *n* (*fig*) stilles Wasser (*fig*); (*unexpected winner*) unbekannte Größe.
darkie, darky ['dɑːkɪ] *n* (*pej inf*) Schwarze(r) *mf*.
darkish ['dɑːkɪʃ] *adj* ziemlich dunkel.
darkly ['dɑːklɪ] *adv* (*lit, fig*) dunkel; *think, threaten also* finster.
darkness ['dɑːknɪs] *n* **(a)** Dunkelheit *f*; (*of room, night also*) Finsternis *f*. **in total** ~ in totaler *or* völliger Dunkelheit, in tiefem Dunkel (*geh*); **the house was in** ~ das Haus lag im Dunkeln. **(b)** (*fig: sinisterness*) Finsterkeit *f*. **(c)** (*fig: gloominess, sadness*) Düsterkeit *f*.
dark: ~**room** *n* (*Phot*) Dunkelkammer *f*; ~**-skinned** ['dɑːkskɪnd] *adj* dunkelhäutig.
darky *n* (*pej inf*) **see darkie**.
darling ['dɑːlɪŋ] **1** *n* **(a)** Schatz *m*; (*child also*) Schätzchen *nt*. **he is mother's** ~**/the** ~ **of the public** er ist Mamas Liebling/der Liebling aller; **she's a little** ~ sie ist ein süßer Schatz; **that cat is a little** ~ diese Katze ist ein liebes kleines Tierchen; **be a** ~ **and** ... sei so lieb *or* nett *or* sei ein Schatz und ... **(b)** (*form of address*) Liebling, Schatz *m*, Schätzchen *nt*; (*to child also*) Goldschatz *m*.
2 *adj* *cat, dress etc* süß, goldig; *wife etc* lieb.
darn¹ [dɑːn] (*Sew*) **1** *n* gestopfte Stelle. **2** *vt* stopfen.
darn² (*inf*) **1** *interj* verflixt (*inf*).
2 *adj attr* verflixt (*inf*). **I can't/couldn't see a** ~ **thing** verflixt (noch mal) (*inf*), ich kann überhaupt nichts sehen/das war vielleicht ein Mist (*inf*), ich konnte überhaupt nichts sehen.
3 *adv* verflixt (*inf*). **a** ~ **sight better/worse** ein ganzes Ende besser/schlechter (*inf*).
4 *n* **I don't give a** ~ (*inf*) das ist mir völlig schnurz (*inf*).
5 *vt* ~ **him!** zum Kuckuck mit ihm! (*inf*); ~ **him for coming late** zum Kuckuck mit ihm, warum kommt er auch zu spät!; ~ **it!** verflixt (noch mal) (*inf*); **well I'll be** ~**ed!** Donnerwetter! (*inf*); **I'll be** ~**ed if I** ... das wäre ja noch schöner, wenn ich ... (*inf*); **I'll be** ~**ed if I know** und wenn du dich auf den Kopf stellst, ich weiß es einfach nicht (*inf*).
darned [dɑːnd] *adj, adv* (*inf*) **see darn²** 2, 3.
darning ['dɑːnɪŋ] *n* Stopfen *nt*; (*things to be darned*) Flick- *or* Stopfsachen *pl*, Flickarbeit *f*. **I've a lot of** ~ **to do** ich habe viel zu stopfen; ~ **needle** Stopfnadel *f*; ~ **mushroom** Stopfpilz *m*.
dart [dɑːt] **1** *n* **(a)** (*movement*) Satz *m*. **to make a sudden** ~ **at sb/sth** einen plötzlichen Satz auf jdn/etw zu machen; **the fish made a** ~ **for the shelter of the weeds** der Fisch schnellte ins schützende Seegras; **with a** ~ **of its tongue the chameleon caught its prey** die Zunge schnellte heraus, und das Chamäleon hatte seine Beute gefangen.
(b) (*weapon*) Pfeil *m*; (*fig: of sarcasm etc*) Spitze *f*; (*Sport*) (Wurf)pfeil *m*.
(c) (*liter*) (*of serpent*) (Gift)zahn *m*; (*of bee*) Stachel *m*.
(d) (*Sew*) Abnäher *m*.
2 *vi* flitzen; (*fish*) schnellen. **to** ~ **out** (*person*) heraus-/hinausflitzen; (*fish, tongue*) herausschnellen; **to** ~ **in** (*person*) hinein-/hereinstürzen; (*into water: otter etc*) sich hineinstürzen; **he** ~**ed behind a bush** er hechtete hinter einen Busch; **he** ~**ed off** er flitzte davon; **her eyes** ~**ed round the room** ihre Blicke schossen blitzschnell im Zimmer hin und her; **her**

thoughts were ~**ing here and there** tausend Gedanken schossen ihr durch den Kopf.
3 *vt* **(a)** *glance, look* werfen. **to** ~ **a glance at sb** jdm einen Blick zuwerfen.
(b) (*hit with* ~) mit einem Pfeil schießen auf (+*acc*); *animal* (*with tranquillizer*) mit einem Pfeil betäuben.
dart board *n* Dartscheibe *f*.
darts [dɑːts] *n sing* Darts, Pfeilwurfspiel *nt*. **a game of** ~ ein Dartspiel *nt*.
Darwinian [dɑː'wɪnɪən] **1** *n* Darwinist(in *f*) *m*. **2** *adj* darwinistisch.
Darwinism ['dɑːwɪnɪzəm] *n* Darwinismus *m*.
dash [dæʃ] **1** *n* **(a)** (*sudden rush*) Jagd *f*. **to make a** ~ losstürzen; **he made a** ~ **for the door/across the road** er stürzte auf die Tür zu/über die Straße; **to make a** ~ **for freedom** versuchen, in die Freiheit zu entkommen; **his** ~ **for freedom was unsuccessful** sein Versuch, in die Freiheit zu entkommen, war vergeblich; **she made a** ~ **for it** sie rannte, so schnell sie konnte.
(b) (*hurry*) Hetze *f*.
(c) (*style, vigour*) Schwung, Elan *m*. **to cut a** ~ eine schneidige Figur machen.
(d) (*small amount*) etwas, ein bißchen; (*of wine, vinegar, spirits also*) Schuß *m*; (*of seasoning etc also*) Prise *f*; (*of lemon also*) Spritzer *m*.
(e) (*Typ*) Gedankenstrich *m*.
(f) (*in morse*) Strich *m*.
(g) **see dashboard.**
2 *vt* **(a)** (*throw violently*) schleudern. **to** ~ **sth to pieces** etw in tausend Stücke zerschlagen; **to** ~ **one's head against sth** mit dem Kopf gegen etw schlagen *or* prallen; **the ship was** ~**ed against a rock** das Schiff wurde gegen eine Klippe geschleudert.
(b) (*discourage*) *sb's hopes* zunichte machen. **that** ~**ed his spirits** das hat ihn völlig geknickt; **that** ~**ed him** (*abash*) das hat ihn eingeschüchtert; (*dispirit*) das hat ihn entmutigt.
(c) (*inf*) **see darn²** 5.
3 *vi* **(a)** (*rush*) sausen (*inf*). **to** ~ **into/across a room** in/quer durch ein Zimmer stürzen *or* stürmen; **to** ~ **away/back/up** fort-/zurück-/hinaufstürzen.
(b) (*knock, be hurled*) schlagen; (*waves also*) peitschen.
4 *interj* ~ **(it)!** (*inf*) verflixt! (*inf*), (verflixter) Mist! (*inf*).
◆**dash off 1** *vi* losstürzen. **sorry to have to** ~ ~ **like this** es tut mir leid, daß ich so forthetzen muß. **2** *vt sep letter, essay* hinwerfen; *drawing also* mit ein paar Strichen hinwerfen.
dashboard ['dæʃbɔːd] *n* Armaturenbrett *nt*.
dashed [dæʃt] *adj, adv* **see darn²** 2, 3.
dashing ['dæʃɪŋ] *adj* *person, appearance* flott, schneidig; *behaviour* schneidig.
dashpot ['dæʃpɒt] *n* (*Tech*) Pralltopf *m*.
dastardly ['dæstədlɪ] *adj* niederträchtig, gemein.
data ['deɪtə] *pl of* **datum** *usu with sing vb* Daten *pl*. **a piece of** ~ eine Angabe; (*Math*) ein (Zahlen)wert *m*; **what's the** ~ **on Kowalski?** (*inf*) welche Angaben haben wir über Kowalski?
data: ~ **bank** *n* Datenbank *f*; ~ **capture** *n* Datenbearbeitung *f*; ~ **file** *n* Datei *f*; ~**-handling system** *n* Datenerfassungssystem *nt*; ~ **processing** *n* Datenverarbeitung *f*; ~ **protection** *n* Datenschutz *m*.
date¹ [deɪt] *n* (*fruit*) Dattel *f*; (*tree*) Dattelpalme *f*.
date² [deɪt] *n* Datum *nt*; (*historical* ~) Geschichts- *or* Jahreszahl *f*; (*for appointment*) Termin *m*. ~ **of birth** Geburtsdatum *nt*; **what's the** ~ **today?** der wievielte ist heute?, welches Datum haben wir heute?; **what** ~ **is he coming on?** wann *or* an welchem Tag kommt er?; **what is the** ~ **of that letter?** von wann ist der Brief datiert?; **to** ~ bis heute, bis dato (*form, dated*); **of early/recent** ~ älteren/neueren *or* jüngeren Datums; **see out-of-date, up-to-date.**
(b) (*on coins, medals etc*) Jahreszahl *f*.
(c) (*appointment*) Verabredung *f*; (*with girlfriend etc also*) Rendezvous *nt*. **who's his** ~? mit wem trifft er sich?; **to make a** ~ **with sb** sich mit jdm verabreden; **she's out on a** ~ sie hat eine Verabredung *or* ein Rendezvous.
2 *vt* **(a)** mit dem Datum versehen; *letter etc also* datieren. **letter** ~**d the seventh of August** ein vom siebten August datierter Brief; **a coin** ~**d 1390** eine 1390 geprägte Münze.
(b) (*establish age of*) *work of art etc* datieren. **the features which** ~ **this coin are** ... die Merkmale, nach denen man das Alter dieser Münze bestimmen kann, sind ...; **that really** ~**s you** daran merkt man, wie alt Sie sind.
(c) (*take out*) *girlfriend etc* ausgehen mit; (*regularly also*) gehen mit (*inf*).
3 *vi* **to** ~ **back to** zurückdatieren auf (+*acc*); **to** ~ **from** zurückgehen auf (+*acc*).
(b) (*become old-fashioned*) veralten.
(c) (*have boyfriend etc*) einen Freund/eine Freundin haben; (*couple*) miteinander gehen.
dated ['deɪtɪd] *adj* altmodisch; *clothes, manners also* überholt.
date: ~**less** *adj* **(a)** *manuscript* undatiert, ohne Jahreszahl; **(b)** (*never old-fashioned*) zeitlos; ~ **line** *n* (*Geog*) Datumsgrenze *f*; (*Typ*) Datumszeile *f*; ~ **palm** *n* Dattelpalme *f*; ~**-stamp 1** *n* Datumsstempel *m*; **2** *vt* mit Datumsstempel versehen.
dative ['deɪtɪv] **1** *n* Dativ *m*. **in the** ~ im Dativ. **2** *adj* Dativ-, dativisch. **the** ~ **case** der Dativ.
datum ['deɪtəm] *n, pl* **data** (*rare*) Faktum, Datum *nt*.
daub [dɔːb] **1** *vt* *walls, canvas, face* beschmieren; *paint, slogans, make-up* schmieren; (*coat with grease etc*) *axle* einschmieren; (*coat with mud, clay*) *walls* bewerfen; (*spread on*) *grease, mud, clay* streichen. **she** ~**ed cream all over her face** sie hat sich (*dat*) das ganze Gesicht mit Creme zu- *or* vollgeschmiert; **he** ~**ed grease over the joints, he** ~**ed the joints with grease** er strich *or* schmierte Fett auf die Scharniere, er schmierte die Scharniere mit Fett.

2 n (a) (Build) Bewurf m.
(b) (pej: bad picture) Kleckserei f.
dauber ['dɔːbə'] n (pej) Kleckser m.
daughter ['dɔːtə'] n (lit, fig) Tochter f. **~-in-law** Schwiegertochter f.
daunt [dɔːnt] vt entmutigen. he is never ~ed er ist nie verzagt; nothing ~ed unverzagt.
daunting ['dɔːntɪŋ] adj entmutigend.
dauntless ['dɔːntlɪs] adj unerschrocken, beherzt; courage unbezähmbar.
davenport ['dævnpɔːt] n (a) (esp US: sofa) Sofa nt, Couch f. (b) (Brit: desk) Sekretär m.
David ['deɪvɪd] n David m.
davit ['dævɪt] n (Naut) Davit m or nt.
Davy ['deɪvɪ] n dim of David. to go to ~ Jones' locker den Seemannstod sterben; treasures from ~ Jones' locker Schätze vom Grunde des Meeres; ~ lamp (Gruben-)Sicherheitslampe f.
dawdle ['dɔːdl] vi (be too slow) trödeln; (stroll) bummeln. to ~ on the way unterwegs trödeln; to ~ over one's work bei der Arbeit bummeln or trödeln.
♦ **dawdle along** vi dahinbummeln; (+prep obj) entlangbummeln.
♦ **dawdle away** vt sep time vertrödeln.
dawdler ['dɔːdlə'] n Trödler(in f) m; (as regards work also) Bummelant(in f), Bummler(in f) (inf) m.
dawn [dɔːn] 1 n (lit, fig) (Morgen)dämmerung, Morgenröte (liter) f; (no art: time of day) Tagesanbruch m, Morgengrauen nt. at ~ bei Tagesanbruch, im Morgengrauen; it's almost ~ es ist fast Morgen, es dämmert schon bald; when is ~? wann wird es hell?; from ~ to dusk von morgens bis abends.
2 vi (a) day was already ~ing es dämmerte schon; the day ~ed rainy der Tag fing mit Regen an; the day will ~ when ... (fig) der Tag wird kommen, wo ...
(b) (fig) (new age etc) dämmern, anbrechen; (hope) erwachen.
(c) (inf) ~ (up)on sb jdm dämmern or zum Bewußtsein kommen; the idea ~ed on him that ... es wurde ihm langsam klar, daß ..., es dämmerte ihm, daß ...
dawn: ~ chorus n Morgenkonzert nt der Vögel; ~ patrol n (Aviat) Morgenpatrouille f.
day [deɪ] n (a) Tag m. he's coming in three ~s' time or in three ~s er kommt in drei Tagen; it will arrive any ~ now es muß jeden Tag kommen; what ~ is it today? welcher Tag ist heute?, was haben wir heute?; what ~ of the month is it? der wievielte ist heute?; twice a ~ zweimal täglich or am Tag; the ~ before yesterday vorgestern; the ~ before her birthday der Tag vor ihrem Geburtstag; (on) the ~ after/before, (on) the following/previous ~ am Tag danach/zuvor, am (darauf)folgenden/vorhergehenden Tag; the ~ after tomorrow übermorgen; this ~ week (inf) heute in acht Tagen (inf); from that ~ on(wards) von dem Tag an; from this ~ forth (liter) von diesem Tage an; two years ago to the ~ heute/morgen etc auf den Tag genau vor zwei Jahren; one ~ eines Tages; one ~ we went swimming, and the next ... einen Tag gingen wir schwimmen, und den nächsten ...; one of these ~s irgendwann(einmal), eines Tages; ~ in, ~ out tagein, tagaus; they went to London for the ~ sie machten einen Tagesausflug nach London; for ~s on end tagelang; ~ after ~ Tag für Tag, tagtäglich; ~ by ~ jeden Tag, täglich; the other ~ neulich; at the end of the ~ (fig) letzten Endes; to live from ~ to ~ von einem Tag auf den andern leben; today of all ~s ausgerechnet heute; some ~ soon demnächst; I remember it to this ~ daran erinnere ich mich noch heute; for ~s on end tagelang; he's fifty if he's a ~ er ist mindestens or wenigstens fünfzig; all ~ den ganzen Tag; to travel during the or by ~ tagsüber or während des Tages reisen; at that time of ~ zu der Tageszeit; to work ~ and night Tag und Nacht arbeiten; good ~! guten Tag!; (good-bye) auf Wiedersehen; (the) ~ is done (liter) der Tag ist vorüber; to be paid by the ~ tageweise bezahlt werden; let's call it a ~ machen wir Schluß; some time during the ~ irgendwann im Laufe des Tages; to have a nice/lazy ~ einen schönen Tag verbringen/einen Tag faulenzen; have a nice ~! viel Spaß!; (esp US: said by storekeeper etc) schönen Tag noch!; did you have a nice ~? war's schön?; did you have a good ~ at the office? wie war's im Büro?; to have a good/bad ~ einen guten/schlechten Tag haben; what a ~! (terrible) so ein fürchterlicher Tag!; (lovely) so ein herrlicher Tag!; it's all in the or a ~'s work! das ist (doch) selbstverständlich; to work an eight hour ~ einen Achtstundentag haben, acht Stunden am Tag arbeiten; on a wet ~ an einem regnerischen Tag; that'll be the ~ das möcht' ich sehen or erleben; see make.
(b) (period of time: often pl) these ~s heute, heutzutage; what are you doing these ~s? was machst or treibst du denn so?; in this ~ and age heutzutage; the talking-point of the ~ das Tagesgespräch; in ~s to come künftig, in künftigen Zeiten or Tagen (geh); from his young ~s von Kindesbeinen or frühester Jugend an; in his younger ~s als er noch jünger war; in Queen Victoria's ~, in the ~s of Queen Victoria zu Königin Viktorias Zeiten; the happiest ~s of my life die glücklichste Zeit meines Lebens; those were the ~s das waren noch Zeiten; in the old ~s früher; in the good old ~s in der guten alten Zeit; it's early ~s yet es ist noch zu früh; during the early ~s of the war in den ersten Kriegstagen; he/this material has seen better ~s er/dieser Stoff hat (auch) schon bessere Zeiten or Tage gesehen; to end one's ~s in misery im Elend sterben.
(c) (with poss adj: lifetime, best time) famous in her ~ in ihrer Zeit berühmt; it has had its ~ das hat seine Glanzzeit überschritten; his ~ will come sein Tag wird kommen; everything has its ~ für alles kommt einmal die richtige Zeit.
(d) no pl (contest, battle) to win or carry the ~ den Sieg bringen; to lose/save the ~ (den Kampf) verlieren/retten.

day: ~ bed n Ruhebett nt; ~ boarder n (Brit Sch) Externe(r) mf; ~book n (Comm) Journal, Tagebuch nt; ~ boy n (Sch) Externe(r) m; ~break n Tagesanbruch m; at ~break bei Tagesanbruch; ~ coach n (US) (Eisenbahn)personenwagen m; ~dream 1 n Tagtraum m, Träumerei f; 2 vi (mit offenen Augen) träumen; ~ girl n (Sch) Externe f; ~ labourer n Tagelöhner m.
daylight ['deɪlaɪt] n (a) (daybreak) Tagesanbruch m.
(b) Tageslicht nt. it is still ~ es ist noch hell; it was broad ~ es war heller or hellichter Tag; in broad ~ am hellen or hellichten Tage; I'd like to get there in ~/while it's still ~ ich möchte gern bei Tag ankommen/solange es noch hell ist; I began to see ~ (fig) (to understand) mir ging ein Licht auf; (to see the end appear) so langsam habe ich Land gesehen (inf); to beat the living ~s out of sb (inf) jdn windelweich schlagen (inf); to scare the living ~s out of sb (inf) jdm einen fürchterlichen Schreck einjagen (inf).
daylight: ~ robbery n (inf) Halsabschneiderei f (inf), offener Diebstahl; ~ saving time n (esp US) Sommerzeit f.
day: ~ long adj 24 Stunden-, den ganzen Tag dauernd; ~ nurse n Tagesschwester f; ~ nursery n Kindertagesstätte f; (in private house) Kinderzimmer nt; ~-old adj Eintags-, einen Tag alt; two-/three-~ old zwei/drei Tage alt; ~ pupil n (Sch) Externe(r) mf; ~ release n tageweise Freistellung von Angestellten zur Weiterbildung; ~ release course n Tageskurs m für Berufstätige; ~ return (ticket) n (Brit Rail) Tagesrückfahrkarte f; ~ school n Tagesschule f; ~ shift n Tagschicht f; to be on or work ~ shift Tagschicht arbeiten.
daytime ['deɪtaɪm] 1 n Tag m. in the ~ bei Tage, tagsüber, während des Tages. 2 attr am Tage; course, programme Tages-; raid am hellen or hellichten Tage.
day: ~-to-day adj occurrence alltäglich; way of life Alltags-, täglich; on a ~-to-day basis tageweise; ~ trip n Tagesausflug m; ~ tripper n Tagesausflügler(in f) m.
daze [deɪz] 1 n Benommenheit f. in a ~ ganz benommen. 2 vt benommen machen.
dazed [deɪzd] adj benommen.
dazzle ['dæzl] vt (lit, fig) blenden.
dazzling ['dæzlɪŋ] adj (lit, fig) blendend.
dazzlingly ['dæzlɪŋlɪ] adv (lit, fig) blendend. ~ beautiful strahlend schön.
DC abbr of (a) direct current. (b) District of Columbia.
DD abbr of Doctor of Divinity Dr. Theol.
D-day ['diːdeɪ] n (Hist, fig) der Tag X.
DDT abbr of dichloro-diphenyl-trichloroethane DDT nt.
deacon ['diːkən] n Diakon m.
deaconess ['diːkənes] n Diakonissin f.
deaconry ['diːkənrɪ] n Diakonat nt.
deactivate [diːˈæktɪveɪt] vt entschärfen.
dead [ded] 1 adj (a) tot; plant also abgestorben, eingegangen. he has been ~ for two years er ist seit zwei Jahren tot; to drop (down) or fall down ~ tot umfallen; to shoot sb ~ jdn erschießen or totschießen (inf); to strike sb ~ jdn erschlagen; over my ~ body (inf) nur über meine Leiche (inf).
(b) (not sensitive) limbs abgestorben, taub. my fingers are ~ meine Finger sind wie abgestorben; he is ~ to reason er ist für vernünftige Argumente nicht zugänglich or empfänglich; he is ~ to pity er kennt kein Mitleid; to be ~ from the neck up (inf) nur Stroh im Kopf haben (inf), gehirnamputiert sein (sl); to be ~ to the world vollkommen weggetreten sein (inf).
(c) (without activity etc) town, season tot; business also flau.
(d) (Elec) cable stromlos; (Telec) tot. to go ~ ausfallen.
(e) (burnt out) fire aus pred; match abgebrannt.
(f) (inf: finished with) glass ausgetrunken; (Typ) copy abgesetzt. are these glasses ~? können diese Gläser weg?
(g) (Sport) ball tot.
(h) (obsolete) language etc tot; custom ausgestorben.
(i) (absolute, exact) total, völlig. ~ silence Totenstille f; ~ calm (Naut) absolute or totale Windstille; she was in a ~ faint sie war völlig bewußtlos; to come to a ~ stop völlig zum Stillstand kommen; he's the ~ spit of his father (sl) er ist seinem Vater wie aus dem Gesicht geschnitten; to be on a ~ level with sb mit jdm genau gleichauf sein; to hit sth in the ~ centre etw genau in der Mitte treffen; see cert, set.
(j) colour tot, stumpf, matt; sound dumpf.
(k) (Typ) key Tot-.
(l) (inf: exhausted) tot (inf), völlig kaputt (inf).
2 adv (a) (exactly) genau. ~ straight schnurgerade; to be ~ on time auf die Minute pünktlich kommen; (clock) auf die Minute genau gehen; ~ on course voll or genau auf Kurs; the parachutists landed ~ on target die Fallschirmspringer sind genau im Ziel gelandet.
(b) (inf: very) total (inf), völlig. ~ drunk/tired total betrunken, stockvoll (inf)/todmüde; you're ~ right Sie haben völlig recht; he was ~ lucky er hat Schwein gehabt (inf), er hat irrsinnig Glück gehabt; ~ slow ganz langsam; "~ slow" „Schrittgeschwindigkeit"; to be ~ certain about sth (inf) bei etw todsicher sein; he's ~ against it er ist total or ganz und gar dagegen.
(c) to stop ~ abrupt stehenbleiben or (talking) innehalten.
3 n (a) the ~ pl die Toten pl.
(b) at ~ of night mitten in der Nacht; in the ~ of winter mitten im Winter.
dead: ~-and-alive adj (inf) party, place tot, langweilig; ~-ball line n (Rugby) Feldauslinie f; ~-beat adj (inf) völlig kaputt (inf), total fertig (inf); ~-beat n (down-and-out) Gammler m; (failure) Versager m; ~ duck n to be a ~ duck passé sein; politically he's/it's a ~ duck politisch ist er/es gestorben (inf).
deaden ['dedn] vt shock auffangen; pain mildern; force, blow abschwächen; nerve, passions abtöten; sound, noise dämpfen; mind, feeling abstumpfen.

dead: ~ **end** n Sackgasse f; **to come to a** ~ **end** (*lit*) (*road*) in einer Sackgasse enden; (*driver*) an eine Sackgasse kommen; (*fig*) in eine Sackgasse geraten; **~-end** adj attr **~-end street** (*esp US*) Sackgasse f; **to be in** ~-**end** (*fig*) keine Chancen haben; **~-end kids** Gassenkinder pl; a **~-end job** ein Job m ohne Aufstiegsmöglichkeiten; ~ **heat** n totes Rennen; ~ **letter** n (*lit*) unzustellbarer Brief; (*Jur*) toter Buchstabe; **~line** n (letzter) Termin; **to fix** or **set a ~line** eine Frist setzen; **to work to a ~line** auf einen Termin hinarbeiten; **he was working to a six o'clock ~line** um 6 Uhr mußte er die Arbeit fertig haben; **can you meet the ~line?** können Sie den Termin or die Frist einhalten?

deadliness ['dedlɪnɪs] n (*of poison, weapon*) tödliche Wirkung; (*of wit, sarcasm*) vernichtende Wirkung; (*inf*) (*boringness*) tödliche Langeweile; (*awfulness*) Entsetzlichkeit f.

deadlock ['dedlɒk] n **to reach (a)** ~ sich festfahren, in eine Sackgasse geraten; **to break the** ~ aus der Sackgasse herauskommen; **"union talks: it's** ~" „Verhandlungen mit der Gewerkschaft festgefahren".

deadly ['dedlɪ] **1** adj (+er) (a) poison, hatred, weapon, accuracy tödlich; sin, enemy tödliche Tod-; wit, sarcasm vernichtend. **his aim was** ~ er traf mit tödlicher Sicherheit; **he's in** ~ **earnest** er meint es todernst, es ist sein voller Ernst.
(b) (*inf*) (*boring*) todlangweilig; (*awful*) taste entsetzlich.
2 adv boring tod-. ~ **pale** totenbleich.

deadly nightshade n Tollkirsche f.

dead: ~ **man's handle** n SIFA-Schalttaste, Totmannkurbel f; ~ **march** n Totenmarsch m; ~ **men's shoes** n: **to wait for** ~ **men's shoes** warten, bis ein Platz frei wird.

deadness ['dednɪs] n (*of limbs*) Taubheit f, (*of colour*) Langweiligkeit f. **there is nothing to compare with the** ~ **of Hull** keine Stadt ist so tot wie Hull.

dead: ~**pan** adj face unbewegt; style, humour trocken; **with a ~pan expression** mit unbeweglicher Miene; **2** n (*face, expression*) unbewegliche Miene; ~ **reckoning** n (*Naut*) Koppelung f; **D~ Sea** n Totes Meer; **D~ Sea scrolls** npl Schriftrollen pl vom Toten Meer; ~ **weight** n (*Tech*) Eigen- or Totgewicht nt; **that box/she was a** ~ **weight** die Kiste/sie war furchtbar schwer; ~**wood** n (*lit*) morsches Holz; (*Naut*) Totholz nt; (*fig*) Ballast m; **to cut out the ~wood from the manuscript** allen Ballast im Manuskript abwerfen; **to cut out the ~wood from the staff** die Nieten unter den Mitarbeitern entlassen.

deaf [def] **1** adj (+er) (a) taub. **as ~ as a (door)post** stocktaub.
(b) (*unwilling to listen*) taub (*to gegen*). **he was ~ to her pleas** er blieb gegen alle ihre Bitten taub, er verschloß sich ihren Bitten; **to turn a** ~ **ear to sb/sth** sich jdm/einer Sache (*dat*) gegenüber taub stellen; **our pleas fell on** ~ **ears** unsere Bitten fanden kein Gehör.
2 n the ~ pl die Tauben pl.

deaf: ~-**aid** n Hörgerät nt; ~-**and-dumb** adj taubstumm; language Taubstummen-.

deafen ['defn] vt (*lit*) taub machen; (*fig*) betäuben.

deafening ['defnɪŋ] adj noise ohrenbetäubend; row lautstark. **a** ~ **silence** ein eisiges Schweigen.

deaf-mute ['def'mju:t] n Taubstumme(r) mf.

deafness ['defnɪs] n (*lit, fig*) Taubheit f (*to gegenüber*).

deal¹ [di:l] **1** n (*amount*) Menge f. **a good** or **great** ~ eine Menge, (*ziemlich*) viel; **not a great** ~ nicht (besonders) viel; **there's still a (good** or **great)** ~ **of work left** es ist noch ein schönes Stück or eine Menge Arbeit; **there's a great** or **good** ~ **of truth in what he says** es ist schon ziemlich viel Wahres an dem, was er sagt; **it says a good** ~ **for him** das spricht sehr für ihn; **and that's saying a good** ~ und damit ist schon viel gesagt; **to mean a great** ~ **to sb** jdm viel bedeuten.
2 adv **a good** or **great** ~, **a** ~ (*inf*) (+vb) (ziemlich) viel; (+adj) viel; **not a great** ~ nicht viel; **did you swim much?** — **not a great** ~ seid ihr viel geschwommen? — nicht besonders viel.

deal² (*vb: pret, ptp* **dealt**) **1** n (a) (*Comm: also business* ~) Geschäft nt, Handel m; (*arrangement*) Handel m, Abkommen nt. **to do** or **make a** ~ **with sb** mit jdm ein Geschäft machen or abschließen; **to make a good** ~ ein gutes Geschäft machen; **it's a** ~ abgemacht!; **I'll make** or **do a** ~ **with you** ich schlage Ihnen ein Geschäft vor; **can I suggest a** ~? kann ich einen Vorschlag machen?; **I never make** ~**s** ich lasse mich nie auf Geschäfte ein; **are you forgetting our** ~? hast du unsere Abmachung vergessen?; **a** ~ **on the Stock Exchange** ein Börsengeschäft; *see* **big**.
(b) (*inf*) **to give sb a fair** ~ jdn anständig behandeln; **a better** ~ **for the lower paid** bessere Bedingungen für die schlechter bezahlten Arbeiter; **the Tories/management offered us a new** ~ die Tories haben uns ein neues Programm vorgelegt/die Firmenleitung hat uns ein neues Angebot gemacht.
(c) (*Cards*) it's your ~ Sie geben.
2 vt (a) (*also* ~ **out**) cards geben, austeilen.
(b) *see* **blow¹**.
3 vi (a) **to** ~ **well/badly with sb** jdn gut/schlecht behandeln.
(b) (*Cards*) geben, austeilen.

♦ **deal in** vi +prep obj (*Comm*) handeln mit. **2** vt sep (*Cards*) player Karten geben (+dat).

♦ **deal out** vt sep gifts, money verteilen (*to an* +acc); cards (aus)geben (*to an* +dat). **to** ~ ~ **justice** Recht sprechen; **a judge who was not afraid to** ~ ~ **justice to powerful men** ein Richter, der keine Angst davor hatte, auch mächtige Männer zur Rechenschaft zu ziehen.

♦ **deal with** vi +prep obj (a) (*do business with*) verhandeln mit. **he's not easy to** ~ ~ es ist nicht leicht, mit ihm zu verhandeln or Geschäfte zu machen.
(b) (*manage, handle*) sich kümmern um; (*with job*) befassen mit; (*successfully*) fertigwerden mit; (*Comm*) orders erledigen; (*be responsible for also*) zuständig sein für. **let's** ~ ~ **the adjectives first** behandeln wir zuerst die Adjektive,

befassen wir uns zuerst mit den Adjektiven; **to know how to** ~ ~ **sb** wissen, wie man mit jdm fertig wird or umgeht; **you bad boy, I'll** ~ ~ **you later** (*inf*) dich knöpf' or nehm' ich mir später vor, du Lausebengel! (*inf*); **the problem has been successfully** ~**t** ~ man ist gut mit dem Problem fertiggeworden; **if the government doesn't know how to** ~ ~ **the problem/doesn't** ~ ~ **the problem soon** wenn die Regierung mit dem Problem nicht fertigwerden kann/sich nicht bald mit dem Problem befaßt; **to** ~ ~ **a case** (*judge*) einen Fall verhandeln; (*lawyer*) sich mit einem Fall befassen.
(c) (*be concerned with*) (*book, film etc*) handeln von; (*author*) sich beschäftigen or befassen mit.

deal³ n (*wood*) Kiefern- or Tannenholz nt. **2** adj attr aus Kiefern- or Tannenholz, Kiefern-, Tannen-.

dealer ['di:lə'] n (a) (*Comm*) Händler m; (*wholesaler*) Großhändler m. **a** ~ **in furs** ein Pelzhändler. (b) (*with drugs*) Dealer m. (c) (*Cards*) Kartengeber m.

dealing ['di:lɪŋ] n (a) (*trading*) Handel m; (*on stock exchange also*) Transaktionen pl. **now that all the** ~ **is over** jetzt, wo alle Verhandlungen vorüber sind; **there's some crooked** ~ **involved here** da ist irgend etwas gedreht or gemauschelt (*inf*) worden.
(b) (*of cards*) Geben, Aus- or Verteilen nt.
(c) ~**s** pl (*Comm*) Geschäfte pl; (*generally*) Umgang m; **to have** ~**s with sb** mit jdm zu tun haben; (*Comm also*) Geschäftsbeziehungen zu jdm haben; **he had secret** ~**s with the enemy** er stand heimlich mit dem Feind in Verbindung.

dealt [delt] pret, ptp of **deal²**.

dean [di:n] n (*Eccl, Univ*) Dekan m.

deanery ['di:nərɪ] n (a) Dekanat nt. (b) (*Eccl: house*) Dekanei f.

deanship ['di:nʃɪp] n (*Eccl, Univ*) Dekanat nt.

dear [dɪə'] **1** adj (+er) (a) (*loved*) lieb, teuer (*liter*). **that/she was** ~**est of all to him** das/sie war ihm das Liebste or Teuerste; **I hold him/it** ~ er/es ist mir lieb und teuer; **that is my** ~**est wish** das ist mein sehnlichster or innigster Wunsch; **a** ~ **friend of mine** ein lieber Freund von mir; **my** ~ **chap** mein lieber Freund; **you are very** ~ **to me** du bist mir lieb und teuer; **these memories are very** ~ **to him** diese Erinnerungen sind ihm teuer.
(b) (*lovable, sweet*) child lieb, süß, reizend; thing süß, entzückend, reizend. **what a** ~ **little dress/baby/kitten** was für ein süßes or entzückendes Kleidchen/Kind/Kätzchen!
(c) (*in letter-writing etc*) ~ **Daddy/John** lieber Vati/John!; ~ **Sir/Madam** sehr geehrter Herr X/sehr geehrte Frau X!, sehr verehrte gnädige Frau! (*geh*); (*no name known*) sehr geehrte (Damen und) Herren!; ~ **Mr Kemp** sehr geehrter Herr Kemp!; (*less formal*) lieber Herr Kemp!
(d) (*expensive*) goods, shop teuer; prices hoch. **to get** ~**er** (*goods*) teurer werden; (*prices*) steigen.
2 interj ~ ~!, ~ **me!** (*ach*) du liebe Zeit!, (du) meine Güte!; **oh** ~! oje!, ach du meine Güte or du liebe Zeit!
3 n **hello/thank you** ~ hallo/vielen Dank; **Veronika/Robert** ~ Veronika/Robert; **yes,** ~ (*husband to wife etc*) ja, Schätzchen or Liebling; **Edward, my** ~ (*elderly lady to nephew/brother etc*) mein lieber Eduard, Eduard, mein Lieber; **my** ~**est** meine Teuerste (*geh*), mein Teuerster (*geh*), (meine) Liebste, (mein) Liebster; **are you being served,** ~? (*inf*) werden Sie schon bedient?; **looking for company,** ~? (*inf*) suchen Sie Gesellschaft, Süße?; **give it to me, there's a** ~ (*inf*) gib es mir, sei (doch) so lieb or gut; **be a** ~ (*inf*) sei so lieb or gut; **poor** ~ die Arme, der Arme; **your mother is a** ~ (*inf*) deine Mutter ist ein Engel (*inf*) or richtig lieb; **the little boy is such a little** ~ ihr kleiner Junge ist ein süßer Knopf (*inf*); **this old** ~ **came up to me** dieses Muttchen kam zu mir her (*inf*).
4 adv (*lit, fig*) buy, pay, sell teuer.

dearie, deary ['dɪərɪ] n (*inf usu not translated*); (*woman to child*) Kleine(r, s). **thanks for your help,** ~ (*old woman*) vielen Dank für Ihre Hilfe, mein Kind/Sohn; **coming inside,** ~? (*tart*) kommst du rein, Süßer?

dearly ['dɪəlɪ] adv (a) (*very much*) love von ganzem Herzen. **I should** ~ **like** or **love to live here** ich würde für mein Leben gern hier wohnen. (b) (*lit, fig*) pay etc teuer.

dearness ['dɪənɪs] n (a) (*expensiveness*) hoher Preis. (b) (*being loved*) **her** ~ **to him** daß sie ihm viel bedeutete or lieb und teuer war.

dearth [dɜ:θ] n Mangel m (*of an* +dat); (*of ideas*) Armut f. ~ **of water/ideas** Wassermangel m/Gedankenarmut f; **there is no** ~ **of young men** an jungen Männern ist or herrscht kein Mangel.

deary n see **dearie**.

death [deθ] n Tod m; (*of planet, city, project also, of plans, hopes etc*) Ende nt. ~ **to all traitors!** Tod allen Verrätern!; **D~ is portrayed as ... dem Tod wird als ... dargestellt; **to be afraid of** ~ sich vor dem Tod fürchten; **to be burnt to** ~ verbrennen; (*at stake*) verbrannt werden; **how many** ~**s were there last year?** wieviele Tote or Todesfälle gab es letztes Jahr?; **to die a hero's** ~ den Heldentod sterben; **a fight to the** ~ ein Kampf auf Leben und Tod; **to put sb to** ~ jdn hinrichten; **to do sb to** ~ (*old*) jdn umbringen; **to drink oneself to** ~ sich zu Tode trinken; **to work oneself to** ~ sich totarbeiten; **he works his men to** ~ er schindet seine Leute zu Tode; **to be at** ~'**s door** an der Schwelle des Todes stehen; **to be in at the** ~ (*fig*) das Ende miterleben; **it will be the** ~ **of you** (*inf*) das wird dein Tod sein; **he will be the** ~ **of me** (*inf*) (*he's so funny*) ich lach' mich noch einmal tot über ihn (*inf*); (*he's annoying*) er bringt mich noch ins Grab; **to catch one's** ~ (*of cold*) (*inf*) sich (*dat*) den Tod holen; **I am sick of** ~ **tired to** ~ **of all this** (*inf*) das alles hängt mir gründlich zum Halse raus, ich bin das alles gründlich satt or leid; **he looked like** ~ **warmed up** (*inf*) er sah wie der Tod auf Urlaub aus (*inf*).

death: ~**bed** n Sterbebett nt; ~**bed scene** n Szene f am Sterbebett; ~-**blow** n (*lit, fig*) Todesstoß m; ~ **cell** n Todeszelle f; ~ **certificate** n Sterbeurkunde f, Totenschein m; ~-**dealing** adj *blow, missile* tödlich; ~ **duties** *npl* (*Brit*) Erbschaftssteuern *pl*; ~ **instinct** *n* (*Psych*) Todestrieb *m*; ~**less** *adj* unsterblich; ~**like** *adj* totenähnlich.

deathly ['deθlı] 1 *adj* (+*er*) (a) ~ *hush or stillness* Totenstille *f*; ~ *silence* eisiges Schweigen; ~ *pallor* Totenblässe *f*. (b) *blow etc* tödlich. 2 *adv* ~ *pale* totenbleich, leichenblaß.

death: ~**-mask** *n* Totenmaske *f*; ~ **penalty** *n* Todesstrafe *f*; ~**rate** *n* Sterbeziffer *f*; ~**-rattle** *n* Todesröcheln *nt*; ~**-roll** *n* Verlust- *or* Gefallenenliste *f*; ~ **row** *n* die Todeszellen *pl*; ~ **sentence** *n* Todesurteil *nt*; ~**'s head** *n* (*on flag etc*) Totenkopf *m*; ~**'s head moth** *n* Totenkopf(schwärmer) *m*; ~ **throes** *npl* (*lit, fig*) Todeskampf *m*; ~ **toll** *n* Zahl *f* der (Todes)opfer *or* Toten; ~**-trap** *n* Todesfalle *f*; ~**-warrant** *n* Hinrichtungsbefehl *m*; (*fig*) Todesurteil *nt*; ~**-watch** *n* Totenwache *f*; ~**-watch beetle** *n* Totenuhr *f*, Klopfkäfer *m*; ~**-wish** *n* Wunsch *m* zu sterben.

deb [deb] *n* (*inf*) Debütantin *f*.

débâcle [de'bɑːkl] *n* Debakel *nt* (*over* bei).

debag [,diː'bæg] *vt* (*Brit inf*) die Hosen runterziehen (+*dat*).

debar [dı'bɑːʳ] *vt* (*from club, competition*) ausschließen (*from* von). **to ~ sb from doing sth** jdn davon ausschließen, etw zu tun.

debark [dı'bɑːk] 1 *vi* sich ausschiffen, an Land gehen. 2 *vt* ausschiffen; *troops* landen.

debarkation [,diːbɑː'keıʃən] *n* Ausschiffung, Landung *f*; (*of troops*) Landen *nt*.

debarment [dı'bɑːmənt] *n* Ausschluß *m*. **his ~ from the club/ from taking part** sein Ausschluß aus dem Klub/von der Teilnahme.

debase [dı'beıs] *vt* (a) *person* erniedrigen, entwürdigen. **to ~ oneself by doing sth** sich selbst so weit erniedrigen, daß man etw tut. (b) *virtues, qualities* mindern, herabsetzen. (c) *metal* verschlechtern; *coinage also* den Wert mindern von.

debasement [dı'beısmənt] *n see vt* (a) Erniedrigung, Entwürdigung, Herabwürdigung *f*. (b) Minderung, Herabsetzung *f*. (c) Verschlechterung *f*; Wertminderung *f*. ~ **of the coinage** Münzverschlechterung *f*.

debatable [dı'beıtəbl] *adj* fraglich; *frontier* umstritten. **it's a ~ point whether ...** es ist fraglich, ob ...

debate [dı'beıt] 1 *vt* question debattieren, diskutieren. 2 *vi* debattieren, diskutieren (*with* mit, *about* über +*acc*). **he was debating with himself/his conscience whether to go or not** er überlegte hin und her, ob er gehen sollte. 3 *n* Debatte *f*. **after much ~** nach langer Debatte *or* Diskussion; **the ~ was on** *or* **about ...** die Debatte ging über ... (+*acc*); **the death penalty was under ~** zur Debatte stand die Todesstrafe.

debater [dı'beıtəʳ] *n* Debattierer(in *f*), Debatter (*Press sl*) *m*.

debating [dı'beıtıŋ] 1 *n* Debattieren, Diskutieren *nt*. 2 *adj attr* Debattier-. ~ **society** Debattierklub *m*.

debauch [dı'bɔːtʃ] 1 *vt* verderben. 2 *n* Orgie *f*.

debauched [dı'bɔːtʃt] *adj* person, look verderbt; *life* zügellos, ausschweifend.

debauchee [,debɔː'tʃiː] *n* Wüstling, Lüstling *m*.

debauchery [dı'bɔːtʃərı] *n* Ausschweifung, Debauche (*old*) *f*. **a life of ~** ein zügelloses *or* ausschweifendes Leben.

debenture [dı'bentʃəʳ] *n* (*Fin*) Schuldschein *m*; (*Customs*) Rückzollschein *m*.

debenture: ~ **bond** *n* Schuldverschreibung, Obligation *f*; ~ **stock** *n* Schuldverschreibungen, Obligationen *pl*.

debilitate [dı'bılıteıt] *vt* schwächen.

debilitating [dı'bılıteıtıŋ] *adj* schwächend; *lack of funds etc also* lähmend; *shyness, self-doubt* hinderlich, hemmend.

debility [dı'bılıtı] *n* Schwäche *f*.

debit ['debıt] 1 *n* Schuldposten *m*, Debit *nt*. ~ **account/balance** Debetkonto *nt*/Soll- *or* Debetsaldo *m*; **to enter sth to the ~ side of an account** etw auf die Sollseite verbuchen; **on the ~ side we have the bad weather** (*fig*) auf der Minusseite ist das schlechte Wetter zu erwähnen. 2 *vt* **to ~ sb/sb's account with a sum, to ~ a sum to sb/sb's account** jdn/jds Konto mit einer Summe belasten *or* debitieren (*form*).

debonair [,debə'neəʳ] *adj* flott.

debouch [dı'bautʃ] *vi* (*troops*) hervorbrechen, debouchieren (*old*); (*river*) münden, sich ergießen.

Debrett [də'bret] *n* = Gotha *m*.

debrief [,diː'briːf] *vt* den Einsatz (anschließend) besprechen mit. **to be ~ed** Bericht erstatten.

debriefing [,diː'briːfıŋ] *n* (*also* ~ **session**) Einsatzbesprechung *f* (nach dem Flug *etc*).

debris ['debriː] *n* Trümmer *pl*, Schutt *m*; (*Geol*) Geröll *nt*, Schutt *m*.

debt [det] *n* (*money owed, obligation*) Schuld *f*. ~ **of honour** Ehrenschuld *f*; **National D**~ Staatsschulden *pl*, Verschuldung *f* der öffentlichen Hand; **to be in ~** verschuldet sein (*to* gegenüber); **to be £5 in ~** ~ £ 5 Schulden haben (*to* bei); **he is in my ~** (*for money*) er hat Schulden bei mir; (*for help etc*) er steht in meiner Schuld; **to run or get into ~** Schulden machen; **to be out of ~** aus den Schulden herauskommen; **to be out of ~** schuldenfrei sein; **to repay a ~** (*lit, fig*) eine Schuld begleichen; **I shall always be in your ~** ich werde ewig in Ihrer Schuld stehen; **to pay one's ~** ~ nature das Zeitliche segnen.

debt: ~ **collection agency** *n* Inkassobüro *nt*; ~**-collector** *n* Inkassobeauftragte(r) *mf*, Schuldeneintreiber (*inf*) *m*.

debtor ['detəʳ] *n* Schuldner(in *f*) *m*.

debug [,diː'bʌg] *vt* (a) *mattress* entwanzen. (b) (*remove technical faults from*) die Fehler beseitigen bei. (c) (*remove bugging equipment from*) entwanzen (*sl*).

debunk [,diː'bʌŋk] *vt* den Nimbus nehmen (+*dat*).

début ['deıbjuː] *n* (*lit, fig*) Debüt *nt*. **to make one's ~** (*in society*) in die Gesellschaft eingeführt werden; (*Theat*) debütieren, sein Debüt geben; (*fig*) sein Debüt geben.

débutante ['debjuːtɑːnt] *n* Debütantin *f*.

dec *abbr of* **deceased** gest.

Dec *abbr of* **December** Dez.

decade ['dekeıd] *n* (a) (*ten years*) Jahrzehnt *nt*, Dekade *f*. (b) (*Eccl: of rosary*) Gesätz *nt*.

decadence ['dekədəns] *n* Dekadenz *f*.

decadent ['dekədənt] 1 *adj* dekadent. 2 *n* (*Liter*) Vertreter *m* der Dekadenz, Décadent *m* (*geh*).

decaffeinated [,diː'kæfıneıtıd] *adj* koffeinfrei.

decagramme, **(US) decagram** ['dekəgræm] *n* Dekagramm *nt*.

decal [dı'kæl] *n* (US) Abziehbild *nt*; (*process*) Abziehen *nt*.

decalitre, **(US) decaliter** ['dekə,liːtəʳ] *n* Dekaliter *m or nt*.

decalogue ['dekəlɒg] *n* Dekalog *m*.

decametre, **(US) decameter** ['dekə,miːtəʳ] *n* Dekameter *nt*.

decamp [dı'kæmp] *vi* (a) (*Mil*) das Lager abbrechen. (b) (*inf*) (bei Nacht und Nebel) verschwinden, sich aus dem Staube machen (*inf*).

decant [dı'kænt] *vt* umfüllen, dekantieren (*form*).

decanter [dı'kæntəʳ] *n* Karaffe *f*.

decapitate [dı'kæpıteıt] *vt* enthaupten (*geh*), köpfen, dekapitieren (*form*). **she was ~d in the accident** bei dem Unfall wurde ihr der Kopf abgetrennt.

decapitation [dı,kæpı'teıʃən] *n* Enthauptung *f* (*geh*).

decarbonization ['diː,kɑːbənaı'zeıʃən] *n* (*Aut*) Entkohlung, Dekarbonisierung *f*.

decarbonize [,diː'kɑːbənaız] *vt* pistons etc dekarbonisieren, entkohlen.

decasyllable ['dekəsıləbl] *n* Zehnsilber *m*.

decathlete [dı'kæθliːt] *n* Zehnkämpfer *m*.

decathlon [dı'kæθlɒn] *n* Zehnkampf *m*.

decay [dı'keı] 1 *vi* (a) verfallen, (*building also*) zerfallen; (*rot*) (*dead body, flesh also, vegetable matter*) verwesen; (*food*) schlecht werden, verderben; (*tooth also*) schlecht werden, faulen; (*bones, wood also*) morsch werden; (*Phys: radioactive nucleus*) zerfallen. (b) (*fig*) verfallen; (*health also*) sich verschlechtern; (*beauty also*) verblühen, vergehen; (*civilization, race*) untergehen; (*friendship*) auseinandergehen, zerfallen; (*one's faculties*) verkümmern; (*business, family*) herunterkommen. **a ~ing old actress** eine verblühende alte Schauspielerin. 2 *vt* food schlecht werden lassen, verderben; *tooth* faulen lassen, schlecht werden lassen; *wood* morsch werden lassen. 3 *n* (a) *see vi* (a) Verfall *m*; Zerfall *m*; Verwesung *f*; Schlechtwerden *nt*; Morschwerden *nt*; Zerfall *m*. **it prevents** (*tooth*) ~ es verhindert Zahnverfall; **to fall into ~** in Verfall geraten, verfallen. (b) (~**ed part or area**) Fäule, Fäulnis *f*. (c) (*fig*) Verfall *m*; (*of friendship, civilization*) Zerfall *m*; (*of race, family, business*) Untergang *m*; (*of one's faculties*) Verkümmern *nt*.

decayed [dı'keıd] *adj* wood etc morsch; *tooth* faul; *food* schlecht; *body, vegetable matter* verwest.

decease [dı'siːs] (*Jur, form*) 1 *n* Ableben *nt* (*form*). 2 *vi* sterben, verscheiden (*geh*).

deceased [dı'siːst] (*Jur, form*) 1 *adj* ge- *or* verstorben. **John Brown, ~** John Brown verstorben. 2 *n*: **the ~** der/die Tote *or* Verstorbene; **the ~** die Toten *or* Verstorbenen *pl*.

deceit [dı'siːt] *n* Betrug *m no pl*, Täuschung *f*. **these unending ~s** diese endlosen Täuschungsmanöver; **a character full of evil and ~** ein durch und durch übler und falscher Charakter.

deceitful [dı'siːtful] *adj* falsch, betrügerisch.

deceitfully [dı'siːtfəlı] *adv* betrügerischerweise; *behave* falsch, betrügerisch.

deceitfulness [dı'siːtfulnıs] *n* Falschheit *f*; (*deceitful acts*) Betrügereien *pl*.

deceive [dı'siːv] 1 *vt* täuschen, trügen (*geh*); *one's wife, husband* betrügen. **to ~ sb into doing sth** jdn durch Täuschung dazu bringen, etw zu tun; **are my eyes deceiving me, - is it really you?** täuschen mich meine Augen, oder bist du es wirklich?; **to ~ oneself** sich (*dat*) selbst etwas vormachen; **his hopes were ~d** er sah sich in seinen Hoffnungen betrogen (*geh*). 2 *vi* trügen (*geh*), täuschen.

deceiver [dı'siːvəʳ] *n* Betrüger(in *f*) *m*.

decelerate [diː'seləreıt] 1 *vi* (*car, train*) langsamer werden; (*driver*) die Geschwindigkeit herabsetzen; (*rate also*) abnehmen; (*production*) sich verlangsamen. 2 *vt* verlangsamen.

deceleration [diː,selə'reıʃən] *n see vi* Langsamerwerden *nt*; Herabsetzung *f* der Geschwindigkeit; Abnahme *f*; Verlangsamung *f*.

December [dı'sembəʳ] *n* Dezember *m*; see also **September**.

decency ['diːsənsı] *n* (*good manners etc*) Anstand *m*; (*of dress etc*) Anständigkeit *f*; (*of behaviour*) Schicklichkeit *f*. ~ **demands that ...** der Anstand fordert, daß ...; **it's only common ~ to ...** es gehört sich einfach, zu ...; **have you no sense of ~?** haben Sie denn kein Anstandsgefühl!; **to observe the decencies** den Anstand wahren; **for ~'s sake** anstandshalber; **he could have had/I hope you'll have the ~ to tell me** er hätte es mir anständigerweise auch sagen können/ich hoffe, du wirst die Anständigkeit besitzen, es mir zu sagen.

decent ['diːsənt] *adj* (*all senses*) anständig. **are you ~?** (*inf*) bist du schon salonfähig? (*inf*); **another gin? — very ~ of you** noch ein Gin? — sehr liebenswürdig!

decently ['diːsəntlı] *adv* anständig. **you can't ~ ask him ... Sie** können ihn jetzt kaum bitten ...; **he very ~ offered to help out** es war sehr anständig von ihm, seine Hilfe anzubieten.

decentralization [diː,sentrəlaı'zeıʃən] *n* Dezentralisierung *f*.

decentralize [diː'sentrəlaız] *vti* dezentralisieren.

deception [dı'sepʃən] *n* (a) (*act of deceiving*) Täuschung *f*, Betrug *m no pl* (*of an* +*dat*); (*of wife etc*) Betrug *m*. all the little

~s we practise all die kleinen Betrügereien, die wir verüben.
(b) (*state of being deceived*) Täuschung *f.* **(c)** (*that which deceives*) Täuschung *f.*

deceptive [dɪ'septɪv] *adj* irreführend; *similarity, simplicity* täuschend, trügerisch; *side-step* täuschend. **to be ~** täuschen, trügen (*geh*); *appearances are or can be ~* der Schein trügt.

deceptively [dɪ'septɪvlɪ] *adv* täuschend, trügerisch. **the village looks ~ near** das Dorf scheint täuschend nahe; **he seemed ~ calm** seine Ruhe war täuschend echt.

deceptiveness [dɪ'septɪvnɪs] *n* Täuschende(s), Trügerische(s) (*geh*) *nt.* **the ~ of the effects of perspective** die trügerischen Effekte der Perspektive; **beware of the ~ of statistics** Vorsicht, Statistiken sind irreführend.

decibel ['desɪbel] *n* Dezibel *nt.*

decide [dɪ'saɪd] **1** *vt* **(a)** (*come to a decision*) (sich) entscheiden; (*take it into one's head*) beschließen, sich entschließen. **what did you ~?** (*yes or no*) wie habt ihr euch entschieden?; (*what measures*) was habt ihr beschlossen?; **did you ~ anything?** habt ihr irgendwelche Entscheidungen getroffen?; **you must ~ what to do** du mußt (dich) entscheiden, was du tun willst; **you can't suddenly ~** you're going to leave home just like that du kannst nicht plötzlich beschließen, daß du einfach von zu Hause weggehst; **he seems to have ~d he wants to change the office around** er scheint beschlossen zu haben, im Büro alles umzustellen; **I have ~d we are making a big mistake** ich bin zu der Ansicht gekommen, daß wir einen großen Fehler machen; **I'll ~ what we do!** ich bestimme, was wir tun!; **she always wants to ~ everything** sie will immer alles bestimmen; **the car seems to have ~ed it's not going to start** das Auto scheint beschlossen zu haben, nicht anzuspringen; **the weather hasn't ~d what it's going to do yet** das Wetter hat (sich) noch nicht entschlossen, was es will.
(b) (*settle*) *question, war etc* entscheiden. **to ~ sb's fate or future** jds Schicksal bestimmen, (über) jds Schicksal entscheiden.
(c) to ~ sb to do sth jdn veranlassen *or* jdn dazu bewegen, etw zu tun; **that eventually ~d me** das hat schließlich für mich den Ausschlag gegeben.
2 *vi* (sich) entscheiden. **I don't know, you ~** ich weiß nicht, entscheiden *or* bestimmen Sie!; **I don't know, I can't ~** ich kann mich nicht entscheiden; **to ~ for/against sth** (sich) für/gegen etw entscheiden; **to ~ for or in favour of/against sb/sth** (*Jur*) zu jds Gunsten/Ungunsten *or* für/gegen jdn/etw entscheiden.

♦**decide on** *vi* +*prep obj* sich entscheiden für. **the date which has been ~d ~** der Termin, für den man sich entschieden hat.

decided [dɪ'saɪdɪd] *adj* **(a)** (*clear, definite*) *improvement* entschieden; *difference* deutlich. **there was a ~ smell of burning** es roch entschieden verbrannt.
(b) (*determined*) *person's character, manner* entschlossen, bestimmt; *opinion* entschieden. **it's my ~ opinion that ...** ich bin entschieden der Meinung, daß ....

decidedly [dɪ'saɪdɪdlɪ] *adv* **(a)** (*definitely*) entschieden. **she is ~ lazy** sie ist (ganz) entschieden faul. **(b)** *act* entschlossen.

decider [dɪ'saɪdə^r] *n* **(a) the ~ was that ...** was den Ausschlag gab, war, daß ...; *ausschlaggebend war, daß ...* **(b)** (*game*) Entscheidungsspiel *nt*; (*goal*) Entscheidungstreffer *m.*

deciding [dɪ'saɪdɪŋ] *adj* entscheidend; *factor also* ausschlaggebend; *game, goal also* Entscheidungs-.

deciduous [dɪ'sɪdjʊəs] *adj tree* Laub-; *leaves* die jedes Jahr abfallen; *antler* das abgeworfen wird.

decimal ['desɪməl] **1** *adj* Dezimal-. **to three ~ places** auf drei Dezimalstellen; **to go ~** sich auf das Dezimalsystem umstellen; **~ point** Komma *nt.* **2** *n* Dezimalzahl *f.* **~s** Dezimalzahlen *pl.*

decimalization [ˌdesɪməlaɪ'zeɪʃən] *n* Umstellung *f* auf das Dezimalsystem, Dezimalisierung *f* (*form*).

decimalize ['desɪməlaɪz] *vt system, currency* auf das Dezimalsystem umstellen, dezimalisieren (*form*).

decimate ['desɪmeɪt] *vt* dezimieren.

decipher [dɪ'saɪfə^r] *vt* (*lit, fig*) entziffern.

decipherable [dɪ'saɪfərəbl] *adj* (*lit, fig*) entzifferbar.

decision [dɪ'sɪʒən] *n* **(a)** Entscheidung *f* (*on* über +*acc*), Entschluß *m*; (*esp of committee etc*) Beschluß *m*; (*of judge*) Entscheidung *f.* **to make a ~** eine Entscheidung treffen *or* fällen, einen Entschluß/Beschluß fassen; **she always wants to make all the ~s** sie will immer über alles bestimmen; **I can't make your ~s for you** ich kann nicht für dich entscheiden; **it's your ~** das mußt du entscheiden; **I can't give you a ~ now** ich kann das jetzt nicht entscheiden; **to come to a ~** zu einer Entscheidung kommen; **I've come to the ~ it's a waste of time** ich bin zu dem Schluß gekommen, daß es Zeitverschwendung ist; **~s ~s!** immer diese Entscheidungen!
(b) *no pl* (*of character*) Entschlußkraft, Entschlossenheit *f.* **a man of ~** ein Mann von Entschlußkraft.

decision: **~-maker** *n* Entscheidungsträger *m*; **~-making** *n* Entscheidungsfindung *f*; **to show an aptitude for ~-making** Entschlußkraft zeigen; **he's hopeless at ~-making** er kann einfach keine Entscheidungen treffen; **2** *adj attr* **~-making skills/abilities** Entschlußkraft *f*; **the ~-making function of management** die Aufgabe des Managements, Entschlüsse zu fassen *or* Entscheidungen zu treffen.

decisive [dɪ'saɪsɪv] *adj* **(a)** entscheidend; *factor also* ausschlaggebend; *battle also* Entscheidungs-. **(b)** *manner, answer* bestimmt, entschlossen; *person* entschlußfreudig.

decisively [dɪ'saɪsɪvlɪ] *adv see adj* **(a)** entscheidend. **(b)** bestimmt, entschlossen.

decisiveness [dɪ'saɪsɪvnɪs] *n see adj* **(a)** entscheidende Bedeutung. **a victory of such ~** ein so entscheidender Sieg. **(b)** Bestimmtheit, Entschlossenheit *f.*

deck [dek] **1** *n* **(a)** (*Naut*) Deck *nt.* **on ~** auf Deck; **to go up on ~** an Deck gehen; **to go (down) below ~(s)** unter Deck gehen.
(b) (*of bus, plane*) Deck *nt.* **top or upper ~** Oberdeck *nt.*
(c) (*of cards*) Spiel *nt.*
(d) (*of record-player*) Laufwerk *nt*; (*part of hi-fi unit*) Plattenspieler *m.* **tape ~** Tape-deck *nt.*
2 *vt* (*also ~ out*) schmücken. **to ~ oneself out in one's Sunday best** sich in seinen Sonntagsstaat werfen (*inf*), sich herausputzen; **all ~ed out in his Sunday best** ganz fesch in seinem Sonntagsstaat.

deck: **~ cabin** *n* Deckkabine *f*; **~ cargo** *n* Deckladung *f*; **~chair** *n* Liegestuhl *m.*

-decker ['dekə^r] *n suf* -decker *m.* (*Naut*) **a three-~** ein Dreidecker *m*; *see* **single-decker, double-decker.**

deck: **~-hand** *n* Deckshelfer *m*; **~-house** *n* Deckshaus *nt.*

deckle-edge ['dekledʒ] *n* Büttenrand *m.*

deckle-edged ['dekledʒd] *adj* mit Büttenrand; *paper* Bütten-.

deck tennis *n* Decktennis *nt.*

declaim [dɪ'kleɪm] **1** *vi* deklamieren. **to ~ against sth** gegen etw wettern. **2** *vt* deklamieren, vortragen.

declamation [ˌdeklə'meɪʃən] *n* Deklamation *f*; (*against sth*) Tirade *f.*

declamatory [dɪ'klæmətərɪ] *adj* deklamatorisch, pathetisch.

declarable [dɪ'kleərəbl] *adj goods* verzollbar.

declaration [ˌdeklə'reɪʃən] *n* (*of love, war, income etc*) Erklärung *f*; (*Cards*) Ansage *f*; (*customs also*) Deklaration *f* (*form*). **~ of intent** Absichtserklärung *f*; **~ of war/bankruptcy** Liebeserklärung *f*/Konkursanmeldung *f*; **to make a ~** eine Erklärung abgeben; **~ of the results** (*Pol*) Bekanntgabe des Ergebnisses/der Ergebnisse.

declare [dɪ'kleə^r] **1** *vt* **(a)** *intentions* erklären, kundtun (*geh*); *results* bekanntgeben, veröffentlichen; *goods* angeben, deklarieren (*form*). **have you anything to ~?** haben Sie etwas zu verzollen?; **to ~ one's income** sein Einkommen angeben; **to ~ oneself or one's feelings** (*to a woman*) sich erklären; **to ~ war (on sb)** (jdm) den Krieg erklären; **to ~ sb bankrupt** jdn für bankrott erklären; **I ~ this meeting/motorway officially open** ich erkläre diese Sitzung/diese Autobahn für offiziell eröffnet; **I ~ this meeting closed** ich erkläre die Sitzung für geschlossen; **to ~ sb the winner** jdn zum Sieger erklären.
(b) (*assert*) erklären, beteuern, versichern.
2 *vi* **(a) to ~ for/against sb/sth** sich für/gegen jdn/etw erklären; **well I (do) ~!** (*dated*) ist es denn die Möglichkeit!
(b) (*Sport*) die Runde für beendet erklären.

declared [dɪ'kleəd] *adj* erklärt.

declaredly [dɪ'kleərɪdlɪ] *adv* erklärtermaßen.

declassify [diː'klæsɪfaɪ] *vt information* freigeben.

declension [dɪ'klenʃən] *n* (*Gram*) Deklination *f.*

declinable [dɪ'klaɪnəbl] *adj* (*Gram*) deklinierbar.

decline [dɪ'klaɪn] **1** *n* **(a)** (*in standards, birthrate, business, sales, prices*) Rückgang *m*; (*of empire, a party's supremacy*) Untergang, Niedergang *m.* **to be on the ~** *see vi*; **at the ~ of his life/the day** (*liter*) als sein Leben/der Tag zur Neige ging (*liter*).
(b) (*Med*) Verfall *m.* **she went into a ~** es ging bergab mit ihr.
2 *vt* **(a)** *invitation, honour* ablehnen. **he ~d to come** er hat es abgelehnt, zu kommen.
(b) (*Gram*) deklinieren.
3 *vi* **(a)** (*empire*) verfallen; (*fame*) verblassen; (*health*) sich verschlechtern; (*prices, business*) zurückgehen; (*importance, significance, value*) geringer werden; (*custom*) aussterben; (*popularity, enthusiasm, interest*) abnehmen; (*population, influence*) abnehmen, zurückgehen. **cases of real poverty are declining** Fälle von echter Armut gibt es immer weniger.
(b) (*refuse, say no*) ablehnen.
(c) (*slope: ground*) abfallen.
(d) (*sun*) untergehen; (*liter: life, day*) zur Neige gehen (*liter*). **in his declining years** gegen Ende seiner Tage (*liter*); **in declining health** bei schlechter werdender Gesundheit.
(e) (*Gram*) dekliniert werden.

declivity [dɪ'klɪvɪtɪ] *n* Abschüssigkeit *f.*

declutch [ˌdiː'klʌtʃ] *vi* auskuppeln.

decoction [dɪ'kɒkʃən] *n* Abkochung *f*, Absud *m*; (*Pharm*) Dekokt *nt* (*spec*).

decode [ˌdiː'kəʊd] *vt* dekodieren, dechiffrieren, entschlüsseln.

decoke [diː'kəʊk] *vt* entrußen.

décolletage [ˌdeɪˈkɒltɑːʒ], **décolleté** *n* Dekolleté *nt*, (tiefer) Ausschnitt.

décolleté [deɪ'kɒlteɪ] *adj* dekolletiert, (tief) ausgeschnitten.

decolonize [diː'kɒlənaɪz] *vt* entkolonisieren.

decompose [ˌdiːkəm'pəʊz] **1** *vt* (*Chem, Phys*) zerlegen; (*rot*) zersetzen. **2** *vi* zerlegt werden; (*rot*) sich zersetzen.

decomposition [ˌdiːkɒmpə'zɪʃən] *n* (*Phys: of light*) Zerlegung *f*; (*Chem also*) Aufspaltung *f*, Abbau *m*; (*rotting*) Zersetzung *f*, Verfaulen *nt.*

decompress [ˌdiːkəm'pres] **1** *vt diver* einer Dekompression unterziehen. **2** *vi* (*diver etc*) sich einer Dekompression unterziehen.

decompression [ˌdiːkəm'preʃən] *n* Dekompression, Druckverminderung *f.*

decompression: **~ chamber** *n* Dekompressionskammer *f*; **~ sickness** *n* Dekompressions- *or* Taucherkrankheit *f.*

decongestant [ˌdiːkən'dʒestənt] **1** *adj* abschwellend. **2** *n* abschwellendes Mittel; (*drops etc*) Nasentropfen *pl*/-spray *nt.*

decontaminate [ˌdiːkən'tæmɪneɪt] *vt* entgiften, dekontaminieren (*form*); (*from radioactivity*) entseuchen.

decontamination ['diːkənˌtæmɪ'neɪʃən] *n* Entgiftung, Dekontamination (*form*) *f*; (*from radioactivity*) Entseuchung *f*, Dekontaminieren *nt.*

decontrol [ˌdiːkən'trəʊl] *vt* (*Comm*) *trade, prices* freigeben.

décor ['deɪkɔː^r] *n* (*in room*) Ausstattung *f*; (*Theat*) Dekor *m or nt.* **he did his front room with a 1930s ~** er richtete sein vorderes Zimmer im Stil der dreißiger Jahre ein.

decorate ['dekəreɪt] *vt* **(a)** *cake, hat* verzieren; *street, building, Christmas tree* schmücken; *room* tapezieren; (*paint*) (an)streichen; (*for special occasion*) dekorieren. **(b)** *soldier* dekorieren, auszeichnen.

decorating ['dekəreɪtɪŋ] *n* Tapezieren *nt*; (*painting*) Streichen *nt*.

decoration [ˌdekə'reɪʃən] *n* **(a)** (*action*) *see vt* (*a*) Verzierung *f*; Schmücken *nt*; Tapezieren *nt*; (An)streichen *nt*; Dekoration *f*. **(b)** (*ornament*) (*on cake, hat etc*) Verzierung *f*; (*on Christmas tree, building, in street*) Schmuck *m no pl*. Christmas ~s Weihnachtsdekorationen *pl or* -schmuck *m*; **the office/class-room** ~s **at Christmas** die Weihnachtsdekoration im Büro/Klassenzimmer; **interior** ~ Innenausstattung *f*; **his secretary is just for** ~ seine Sekretärin ist nur zur Dekoration da. **(c)** (*Mil*) Dekoration, Auszeichnung *f*.

decorative ['dekərətɪv] *adj* dekorativ.

decorator ['dekəreɪtə'] *n* (*Brit*) Maler *m*.

decorous ['dekərəs] *adj action, behaviour* geziemend, schicklich; *dress* schicklich.

decorously ['dekərəslɪ] *adv see adj*.

decorum [dɪ'kɔːrəm] *n* Anstand *m*, Dekorum *nt* (*old, form*). **to have a sense of** ~ Gefühl für Anstand haben; **to behave with** ~ sich mit gebührendem Anstand benehmen.

decoy ['diːkɔɪ] **1** *n* (*lit, fig*) Köder *m*; (*person*) Lockvogel *m*. **to act as a** ~ als Köder fungieren; Lockvogel spielen; **police** ~ Lockvogel *m* der Polizei; ~ **manoeuvre** Falle *f*. **2** *vt* **(a)** *bird* anlocken. **(b)** *person* locken. **to** ~ **sb into doing sth** jdn durch Lockmittel dazu bringen, etw zu tun.

decrease [diː'kriːs] **1** *vi* abnehmen, (*figures, output, life expectancy also, birthrate, production*) zurückgehen; (*strength, enthusiasm, intensity*) nachlassen; (*in knitting*) abnehmen. **in decreasing order of importance** in der Reihenfolge ihrer Bedeutung; **it** ~**s in value** es verliert an Wert. **2** *vt* verringern, reduzieren. **3** ['diːkriːs] *n* Abnahme *f*; Rückgang *m*; Nachlassen *nt*; Abnehmen *nt*. ~ **in speed** Verminderung *or* Abnahme *f* der Geschwindigkeit; **to be on the** ~ *see vi*.

decreasingly [diː'kriːsɪŋlɪ] *adv* immer weniger. ~ **popular** immer unbeliebter.

decree [dɪ'kriː] **1** *n* Anordnung, Verordnung, Verfügung *f*; (*Pol, of king etc*) Erlaß *m*; (*Eccl*) Dekret *nt*; (*Jur*) Verfügung *f*; (*of tribunal, court*) Entscheid *m*, Urteil *nt*. **by royal/government** ~ auf königlichen Erlaß/auf Erlaß der Regierung; **to issue a** ~ einen Erlaß herausgeben; ~ **nisi/absolute** vorläufiges/endgültiges Scheidungsurteil. **2** *vt* verordnen, verfügen. **he** ~**d an annual holiday on 1st April** er erklärte den 1. April zum (ständigen) Feiertag.

decrepit [dɪ'krepɪt] *adj staircase etc* altersschwach; *building also* baufällig, heruntergekommen; *person also* klapprig (*inf*).

decrepitude [dɪ'krepɪtjuːd] *n see adj* Altersschwäche *f*; Baufälligkeit *f*; Klapprigkeit *f* (*inf*).

decry [dɪ'kraɪ] *vt* schlechtmachen.

dedicate ['dedɪkeɪt] *vt* **(a)** *church* weihen. **(b)** *book, music* widmen (*to sb* jdm). **to** ~ **oneself** *or* **one's life to sb/sth** sich *or* sein Leben jdm/einer Sache weihen, sein Leben jdm/einer Sache widmen, sich einer Sache hingeben.

dedicated ['dedɪkeɪtɪd] *adj attitude* hingebungsvoll; *service also* treu. **a** ~ **nurse/teacher** *etc* eine Krankenschwester/eine Lehrerin *etc*, die mit Leib und Seele bei der Sache ist; **to become a top-class dancer you have to be really** ~ um ein erstklassiger Tänzer zu werden, muß man wirklich mit Leib und Seele dabei sein; **his work is completely** ~, **he thinks of nothing but his work** er hat sich völlig seiner Arbeit verschrieben, er denkt an nichts anderes; **it's very** ~ **of you to stay on this late, Robinson** das ist sehr aufopfernd von Ihnen, so lange zu bleiben, Robinson.

dedication [ˌdedɪ'keɪʃən] *n* **(a)** (*quality*) Hingabe *f* (*to an* + *acc*). **(b)** (*act*) (*of church*) Einweihung, Weihe *f*. **his** ~ **of his life to helping the poor** daß er sein Leben in den Dienst der Armen gestellt hat. **(c)** (*in book*) Widmung *f*.

deduce [dɪ'djuːs] *vt* folgern, schließen (*from* aus); (*Logic*) deduzieren (*from* von).

deducible [dɪ'djuːsɪbl] *adj* zu schließen, ableitbar (*from* aus); (*Logic*) deduzierbar (*from* von).

deduct [dɪ'dʌkt] *vt* abziehen (*from* von), (*from wages also*) einbehalten. **to** ~ **sth from the price** etw vom Preis ablassen; **to** ~ **sth for expenses** etwas für Spesen zurückbehalten; **to** ~ **income tax at source** Einkommensteuer einbehalten; **after** ~**ing 5%** nach Abzug von 5%.

deductible [dɪ'dʌktəbl] *adj* abziehbar; (*tax* ~) absetzbar.

deduction [dɪ'dʌkʃən] *n* **(a)** (*act of deducting*) Abziehen *nt*, Abzug *m*; (*sth deducted*) (*from price*) Nachlaß *m* (*from* für, auf + *acc*); (*from wage*) Abzug *m*. **(b)** (*act of deducing*) Folgern *nt*, Folgerung *f*; (*sth deduced*) (Schluß)folgerung *f*; (*Logic*) Deduktion *f*. **by a process of** ~ durch Folgern.

deductive [dɪ'dʌktɪv] *adj* deduktiv.

deed [diːd] **1** *n* **(a)** Tat, Handlung *f*; (*feat*) Tat, Leistung *f*. **good** ~ gute Tat; **in word and** ~ in Wort und Tat; **to do a black** *or* **a foul** ~ eine Gemeinheit begehen, etwas Böses *or* Gemeines tun. **(b)** **in** ~ tatsächlich, in der Tat; **he is master in** ~ **if not in name** er ist der eigentliche *or* tatsächliche Herr, wenn auch nicht offiziell *or* nach außen hin. **(c)** (*Jur*) Übertragungsurkunde *f*. **the** ~**s of a house** die Übertragungsurkunde eines Hauses; ~ **of covenant** Vertragsurkunde *f*. **2** *vt* (*US*) überschreiben (*to* auf + *acc*).

deed poll *n* (einseitige) Absichtserklärung.

deejay ['diːdʒeɪ] *n* (*inf*) Diskjockey *m*.

deem [diːm] *vt* **to** ~ **sb/sth (to be) sth** jdn/etw für etw erachten (*geh*) *or* halten; **he was** ~**ed worthy of the honour** (*geh*) er wurde der Ehre (*gen*) für würdig erachtet (*geh*) *or* gehalten.

deep [diːp] **1** *adj* (+ *er*) **(a)** *water, hole, wound* tief. **the pond/snow was 4 metres** ~ der Teich war/der Schnee lag 4

Meter tief; **a two-metre** ~ **trench** ein zwei Meter tiefer Graben; **two metres** ~ **in snow/water** mit zwei Meter Schnee bedeckt/zwei Meter tief unter Wasser; **the** ~ **end** (*of swimming pool*) das Tiefe; **to go off (at) the** ~ **end** (*fig inf*) auf die Palme gehen (*inf*); **to go** *or* **plunge in at the** ~ **end** (*fig*) sich kopfüber in die Sache stürzen; **to be thrown in at the** ~ **end** (*fig*) gleich zu Anfang richtig ranmüssen (*inf*). **(b)** *shelf, cupboard* tief; (*wide*) *border, edge* breit. **a plot of ground 15 metres** ~ ein 15 Meter tiefes Stück Land; **the spectators stood ten** ~ die Zuschauer standen zu zehnt hintereinander. **(c)** *voice, sound, note, colour* tief. **(d)** *breathing, sigh* tief. **(e)** (*fig*) *mystery, sleep, secret, mourning* tief; (*profound*) *thinker, book also, remark, writer* tiefsinnig; (*heartfelt*) *concern, relief, interest* groß; *sorrow* tief (*empfunden*); (*devious*) *person* verschlagen, hintergründig; *dealings* undurchsichtig. ~ **in thought/a book** in Gedanken/in ein Buch vertieft *or* versunken; ~ **in debt** tief verschuldet; **to be in** ~ **trouble** in großen Schwierigkeiten sein; **he's a** ~ **one** (*inf*) er ist ein ganz stilles Wasser, er ist ein ganz verschlagener Kerl. **2** *adv* (+ *er*) tief. ~ **into the night** bis tief in die Nacht hinein; **to drink** ~ (*one draught*) einen tiefen Zug tun; (*all evening*) viel trinken; **to breathe** ~ tief atmen; **he's in it pretty** ~ (*inf*) er steckt *or* hängt ganz schön tief da drin (*inf*). **3** *n* **(a)** (*liter*) **the** ~ das Meer, die See. **(b)** **in the** ~ **of winter** mitten im tiefsten Winter.

deepen ['diːpən] **1** *vt* (*lit, fig*) vertiefen; *concern, sorrow also* vergrößern; *love, friendship also* verstärken; *colour also* dunkler machen; *mystery* vergrößern; *sound* tiefer machen. **2** *vi* (*lit, fig*) sich vergrößern, tiefer werden; (*sorrow, concern, interest*) zunehmen, größer werden; (*colour, sound, voice*) tiefer werden; (*mystery*) größer werden.

deepening ['diːpənɪŋ] **1** *adj sorrow, concern etc* zunehmend, wachsend; *friendship, love also* sich vertiefend; *colour, mystery* sich vertiefend, tiefer werdend. **2** *n* (*of hole*) Vergrößerung *f*; (*of sorrow, interest, concern*) Zunahme *f*; (*of friendship, love*) Vertiefung *f*; (*of mystery*) Vergrößerung *f*. **he watched the** ~ **of the colours in the sunset** er sah zu, wie die Farben beim Sonnenuntergang immer tiefer wurden.

deep: ~**-freeze 1** *n* Tiefkühltruhe *f*; (*upright*) Tiefkühlschrank *m*; **2** *vt* einfrieren; ~**-freezing** *n* Einfrieren, Tiefgefrieren *nt*; ~**-frozen** *adj* tiefgefroren; ~**-frozen foods** Tiefkühlkost *f*; ~**-fry** *vt* fritieren, im schwimmenden Fett herausbacken; ~ **kiss** *n* Zungenkuß *m*; ~**-laid** *adj*, *comp* ~**er-laid** *plot* (sorgfältig) ausgetüftelt (*inf*) *or* ausgearbeitet.

deeply ['diːplɪ] *adv* dig, cut, breathe tief; *think, consider also* gründlich; *drink* schwer. **to go** ~ **into sth** sich gründlich mit etw befassen. **(b)** *grateful, concerned* zutiefst; *offended also, indebted* tief; *love* innig(lich); *interested* höchst; *aware* voll(kommen).

deepness ['diːpnɪs] *n* (*lit, fig*) Tiefe *f*; (*of border, edge*) Breite *f*; (*profundity: of thinker, remark etc*) Tiefsinnigkeit *f*; (*of concern, relief, interest*) Größe *f*.

deep: ~**-ray therapy** *n* Tiefenbestrahlung *f*; ~**-rooted** *adj*, *comp* (*fig*) ~**er-rooted** (*fig*) tiefverwurzelt; ~**-sea** *adj plant, current* Meeres-; *animal also* Tiefsee-; ~**-sea diver** *n* Tiefseetaucher *m*; ~**-sea fishery** *or* **fishing** *n* Hochseefischerei *f*; ~**-seated** *adj*, *comp* ~**er-seated** tiefsitzend; ~**-set** *adj*, *comp* ~**er-set** tiefliegend; **D**~ **South** *n* Tiefer Süden; ~ **space** *n* der äußere Weltraum; ~ **structure** *n* (*Ling*) Tiefenstruktur *f*; ~**-throated** ['diːpˈθrəʊtɪd] *adj* kehlig.

deer [dɪə'] *n*, *pl* - Hirsch *m*; (*roe* ~) Reh *nt*. **the (red/fallow)** ~ **in the forest** das (Rot-/Dam)wild im Wald.

deer: ~**-hound** *n* Deerhound *m*; ~**-park** *n* Wildpark *m*; ~**-skin** *n* Hirsch-/Rehleder *nt*; ~**-stalker** *n* (*a*) (*person*) *jd, der auf die Pirsch geht*; **(b)** (*hat*) = Sherlock-Holmes-Mütze *f*; ~**-stalking** *n* Pirschen *nt*, Pirsch *f*; **to go** ~**-stalking** auf die Pirsch gehen.

de-escalate [ˌdiː'eskəleɪt] *vt* deeskalieren.

de-escalation [ˌdiːeskə'leɪʃən] *n* Deeskalation *f*.

deface [dɪ'feɪs] *vt* verunstalten.

de facto [deɪ'fæktəʊ] *adj, adv* de facto.

defamation [ˌdefə'meɪʃən] *n* Diffamierung, Verleumdung *f*. ~ **of character** Rufmord *m*.

defamatory [dɪ'fæmətərɪ] *adj* diffamierend, verleumderisch.

defame [dɪ'feɪm] *vt* diffamieren, verleumden.

default [dɪ'fɔːlt] **1** *n* **(a)** (*failure to appear*) (*Jur*) Nichterscheinen *nt vor* Gericht; (*Sport*) Nichtantreten *nt*; (*failure to perform duty*) Versäumnis *f*; (*failure to pay*) Nichtzahlung *f*. **judgement by** ~ (*Jur*) Versäumnisurteil *nt*; **to win by** ~ (*Sport*) kampflos gewinnen. **(b)** (*lack, absence*) Mangel *m*. **in** ~ **of, due to** ~ **of** in Ermangelung + *gen*. **2** *vi* (*not appear*) (*Jur*) nicht erscheinen, (*Sport*) nicht antreten; (*not perform duty, not pay*) säumig sein. **to** ~ **in one's payments** seinen Zahlungsverpflichtungen nicht nachkommen.

defaulter [dɪ'fɔːltə'] *n see default 1* nichterscheinende Partei; nichtantretender Spieler, nichtantretende Spielerin; Säumige(r) *mf*; säumiger Zahler; (*Mil, Naut*) Straffällige(r) *mf*.

defeat [dɪ'fiːt] **1** *n* (*defeating*) Besiegung *f*, Sieg *m* (*of* über + *acc*); (*of motion, bill*) Ablehnung *f*; (*of hopes, plans*) Vereitelung *f*; (*being defeated*) Niederlage *f*. **their** ~ **of/by the enemy** ihr Sieg über den Feind/ihre Besiegung *or* Niederlage durch den Feind; **to admit** ~ sich geschlagen geben; **to suffer a** ~ eine Niederlage erleiden. **2** *vt army, team* besiegen, schlagen; *government also* eine (Abstimmungs)niederlage beibringen (+ *dat*); *motion, bill* ablehnen; *hopes, plans* vereiteln. **to** ~ **one's own ends** *or* **object** sich (*dat*) ins eigene Fleisch schneiden; **that would be** ~**ing the**

purpose of the exercise dann verliert die Übung ihren Sinn; it ~s me why ... (inf) es will mir einfach nicht in den Kopf, warum ... (inf).

defeatism [dɪ'fiːtɪzəm] n Defätismus m.

defeatist [dɪ'fiːtɪst] 1 n Defätist m. 2 adj defätistisch.

defecate ['defəkeɪt] vi den Darm entleeren, defäkieren (form).

defecation [,defə'keɪʃən] n Entleerung f des Darms, Defäkation f (form).

defect[1] ['diːfekt] n Fehler, Schaden m; (in mechanism also) Defekt m. physical ~ körperlicher Schaden or Defekt; a character ~ ein Charakterfehler m.

defect[2] [dɪ'fekt] vi (Pol) sich (in den Westen) absetzen; (fig) abtrünnig werden, abfallen. to ~ to the enemy zum Feind übergehen or überlaufen.

defection [dɪ'fekʃən] n (Pol) Überlaufen nt; (fig) Abtrünnigkeit f, Abfall m.

defective [dɪ'fektɪv] 1 adj (a) material etc fehlerhaft; machine also defekt; (fig) reasoning etc fehlerhaft; hearing, sight mangelhaft, gestört. his heart/liver is ~ bei ihm ist die Herz-/Lebertätigkeit gestört.
(b) (Gram) unvollständig, defektiv.
(c) (mentally ~) geistesgestört.
2 n (a) (Gram) Defektivum nt.
(b) (retarded person) Geistesgestörte(r) mf.

defence, (US) **defense** [dɪ'fens] n (a) no pl Verteidigung f no pl. in his ~ zu seiner Verteidigung; to come to sb's ~ jdn verteidigen; to put up a stubborn ~ sich hartnäckig verteidigen; his only ~ was ... seine einzige Rechtfertigung war ....
(b) (form of protection) Abwehr- or Schutzmaßnahme f; (Mil: fortification etc) Befestigung, Verteidigungsanlage f. as a ~ against als Schutz gegen; his ~s were down er vergaß seine normale Zurückhaltung.
(c) (Jur) Verteidigung f.
(d) (Sport) Verteidigung f.

defence: ~ counsel n Verteidiger(in f) m; ~less adj schutzlos; ~ mechanism n (Physiol, Psych) Abwehrmechanismus m; ~ minister n Verteidigungsminister m; ~ witness n Zeuge m/Zeugin f der Verteidigung.

defend [dɪ'fend] vt verteidigen (also Jur) (against gegen). to ~ oneself sich verteidigen.

defendant [dɪ'fendənt] 1 n Angeklagte(r) mf; (in civil cases) Beklagte(r) mf. 2 adj angeklagt; beklagt.

defender [dɪ'fendə^r] n Verteidiger m. D~ of the Faith Fidei Defensor m.

defending [dɪ'fendɪŋ] adj: ~ counsel Verteidiger(in f) m.

defense etc [dɪ'fens] (US) see defence etc.

defensible [dɪ'fensɪbl] adj (a) (lit) wehrhaft. because of its position the town wasn't ~ die Stadt war wegen ihrer Lage nicht zu verteidigen. (b) (justifiable) behaviour, argument vertretbar, zu verteidigen pred.

defensive [dɪ'fensɪv] 1 adj defensiv (also fig), Verteidigungs-. 2 n (Mil) Verteidigungs- or Abwehraktion f. to be on the ~ (Mil, fig) in der Defensive sein.

defer[1] [dɪ'fɜː^r] vt (delay) verschieben; event also verlegen. to ~ doing sth es verschieben, etw zu tun.

defer[2] vi (submit) to ~ to sb/sb's wishes sich jdm beugen or fügen/sich jds Wünschen (dat) fügen.

deference ['defərəns] n Achtung f, Respekt m. out of or in ~ to aus Achtung (dat) or Respekt (dat) vor; with all due ~ to you bei aller schuldigen Achtung or allem schuldigen Respekt Ihnen gegenüber.

deferential [,defə'renʃəl] adj ehrerbietig, respektvoll. to be ~ to sb jdm mit Respekt or Achtung begegnen.

deferentially [,defə'renʃəlɪ] adv see adj.

deferment [dɪ'fɜːmənt] n see defer[1] Verschiebung f; Verlegung f.

deferred [dɪ'fɜːd] adj ~ shares Nachzugsaktien pl; ~ annuity nach bestimmter Zeit fällige Rente; ~ pay (Mil) einbehaltener Sold; (Naut) einbehaltene Heuer; sale on the ~ payment system Verkauf m auf Ratenzahlungsbasis, Ratenzahlungs- or Abzahlungsgeschäft nt; ~ terms Teilzahlung f.

defiance [dɪ'faɪəns] n (a) Trotz m. an act of ~ eine Trotzhandlung.
(b) (act of defying) (of person) Trotz m (of gegenüber +dat); (of order, law also, of death, danger) Mißachtung f (of gen). in ~ of sb/sb's orders jdm/jds Anordnungen zum Trotz, jds Anordnungen mißachtend; that is in ~ of the laws of nature das widerspricht den Gesetzen der Natur.

defiant [dɪ'faɪənt] adj (rebellious, obstreperous) aufsässig; esp child also, answer trotzig; (challenging) manner, attitude herausfordernd.

defiantly [dɪ'faɪəntlɪ] adv see adj.

deficiency [dɪ'fɪʃənsɪ] n (shortage) Mangel m; (Fin) Defizit nt, Fehlbetrag m; (defect: in character, system) Schwäche f. vitamin/iron ~ Vitamin-/Eisenmangel m; ~ disease (Med) Mangelkrankheit f.

deficient [dɪ'fɪʃənt] adj unzulänglich. sb/sth is ~ in sth jdm/einer Sache fehlt es an etw (dat); see mentally.

deficit ['defɪsɪt] n Defizit nt.

defile[1] ['diːfaɪl] 1 n Hohlweg m 2 vi hintereinander marschieren.

defile[2] [dɪ'faɪl] vt (pollute, sully) verschmutzen, verunreinigen; (desecrate) schänden, entweihen.

defilement [dɪ'faɪlmənt] n Verschmutzung, Verunreinigung f; (desecration) Schändung, Entweihung f.

definable [dɪ'faɪnəbl] adj see vt definierbar; bestimmbar; erklärbar.

define [dɪ'faɪn] vt (a) word definieren; conditions, boundaries, powers, duties also bestimmen, festlegen; feeling, attitude also erklären. (b) (show in outline) betonen. clearly/not well ~d scharf/nicht scharf; to be clearly ~d against the sky sich klar or scharf gegen den Himmel abzeichnen.

definite ['defɪnɪt] adj (a) (fixed, concrete, explicit) definitiv; answer, decision, possibility also klar, eindeutig; agreement, date, plan, decision, intention, wish also fest; command, request bestimmt. is that ~? ist das sicher?; (agreed by contract etc also) steht das fest?; we've arranged to meet at 5, that's ~ wir haben fest abgemacht, uns um 5 Uhr zu treffen.
(b) (distinct, pronounced) mark, stain, lisp deutlich; advantage, improvement also klar, eindeutig; problem echt.
(c) (positive, decided) tone, manner bestimmt. she was very ~ about it sie war sich (dat) sehr sicher.
(d) (Gram) bestimmt.

definitely ['defɪnɪtlɪ] adv (a) decide, agree, arrange fest, definitiv. (b) (without doubt) bestimmt. he ~ wanted to come er wollte bestimmt kommen; that's ~ an improvement/advantage das ist zweifelsohne or ganz sicherlich eine Verbesserung/ein Vorteil. (c) (positively, decidedly) speak bestimmt.

definiteness ['defɪnɪtnɪs] n (a) see adj (a) Definitive nt; Klarheit, Eindeutigkeit f. (b) see adj (c) Bestimmtheit f.

definition [,defɪ'nɪʃən] n (a) (of word, concept) Definition f. by ~ per definitionem, definitionsgemäß. (b) (of powers, duties, boundaries) (authoritative) book maßgeblich (on für); (defining) laws Rahmen-; term beschreibend. 2 n (stamp) Briefmarke f einer Dauerserie.

definitive [dɪ'fɪnɪtɪv] 1 adj (decisive) victory, answer entschieden; (authoritative) book maßgeblich (on für); (defining) laws Rahmen-; term beschreibend. 2 n (stamp) Briefmarke f einer Dauerserie.

definitively [dɪ'fɪnɪtɪvlɪ] adv see adj.

deflate [,diː'fleɪt] 1 vt tyre, balloon etwas/die Luft ablassen aus. to ~ the currency (Fin) eine Deflation herbeiführen; he was a bit ~d when ... es war ein ziemlicher Dämpfer für ihn, daß ...; that was rather deflating (for him) das war ein ziemlicher Dämpfer (für ihn). 2 vi (Fin) eine Deflation herbeiführen.

deflation [,diː'fleɪʃən] n (of tyre, ball) Luftablassen nt (of aus); (Fin) Deflation f.

deflationary [,diː'fleɪʃənərɪ] adj (Fin) Deflations-, deflationistisch.

deflect [dɪ'flekt] 1 vt ablenken; ball, bullet also abfälschen; steam, air current also ableiten; (Phys) light beugen. 2 vi (compass needle) ausschlagen; (projectile) abweichen.

deflection [dɪ'flekʃən] n see vb Ablenkung f; Abfälschung f; Ableitung f; Beugung f; Ausschlag m; Abweichung f.

deflective [dɪ'flektɪv] adj ablenkend; (Phys) beugend.

deflector [dɪ'flektə^r] n Deflektor m, Ablenkvorrichtung f.

defloration [,diːflɔː'reɪʃən] n (liter: of girl) Entjungferung, Defloration f.

deflower [,diː'flaʊə^r] vt (liter) girl entjungfern, deflorieren.

defoliant [,diː'fəʊlɪənt] n Entlaubungsmittel nt.

defoliate [,diː'fəʊlɪeɪt] vt entlauben, entblättern.

defoliation [,diːfəʊlɪ'eɪʃən] n Entlaubung f.

deforest [,diː'fɒrɪst] vt abholzen.

deforestation [diː,fɒrɪ'steɪʃən] n Abholzung f.

deform [dɪ'fɔːm] vt deformieren, verunstalten; (Tech) verformen; mind, tastes verderben.

deformation [,diːfɔː'meɪʃən] n see vt Deformierung, Deformation, Verunstaltung f; Verformung f; Verderben nt.

deformed [dɪ'fɔːmd] adj deformiert, verunstaltet; (Tech) verformt; person, limb, body also mißgestaltet; mind krankhaft, abartig.

deformity [dɪ'fɔːmɪtɪ] n see adj Deformität, Verunstaltung f; Verformung f; Mißgestalt f; Krankhaftigkeit, Abartigkeit f.

defraud [dɪ'frɔːd] vt betrügen, hintergehen, defraudieren (dated form). to ~ sb of sth jdn um etw betrügen or bringen.

defrauder [dɪ'frɔːdə^r] n Betrüger(in f), Defraudant(in f) (dated form) m.

defray [dɪ'freɪ] vt tragen, übernehmen.

defrayal [dɪ'freɪəl], **defrayment** [dɪ'freɪmənt] n Übernahme f.

defrock [,diː'frɒk] vt aus dem Priesteramt verstoßen.

defrost [,diː'frɒst] vti fridge, windscreen entfrosten, abtauen; food auftauen.

defroster [,diː'frɒstə^r] n Defroster, Entfroster m.

deft adj (+er), ~ly adv [deft, -lɪ] flink, geschickt.

deftness ['deftnɪs] n Flinkheit, Geschicktheit f.

defunct [dɪ'fʌŋkt] adj person verstorben; (fig) institution etc eingegangen; law außer Kraft.

defuse [,diː'fjuːz] vt (lit, fig) entschärfen.

defy [dɪ'faɪ] vt (a) (refuse to submit to, disobey) person sich widersetzen (+dat); (esp child also) trotzen (+dat); orders, law, death, danger verachten, trotzen (+dat).
(b) (fig: make impossible) widerstehen (+dat). the suitcase defied our efforts to close it der Koffer widerstand unseren Bemühungen, ihn zu schließen; to ~ definition nicht erklärt or definiert werden können; to ~ description jeder Beschreibung spotten.
(c) (challenge) I ~ you to do it/to buy one more cheaply machen Sie es doch/kaufen Sie doch einen billigeren(, wenn Sie können).

degeneracy [dɪ'dʒenərəsɪ], **degenerateness** n Degeneration f.

degenerate [dɪ'dʒenərɪt] 1 adj degeneriert; race, morals also entartet. 2 n degenerierter Mensch. 3 [dɪ'dʒenəreɪt] vi degenerieren; (people, morals also) entarten.

degenerateness [dɪ'dʒenərɪtnɪs] n see degeneracy.

degeneration [dɪ,dʒenə'reɪʃən] n see vi Degeneration f; Entartung f.

degenerative [dɪ'dʒenərətɪv] adj (Med) Abbau-.

degradation [,degrə'deɪʃən] n see vt Erniedrigung f; Degradierung f; Erosion f; Abbau m.

degrade [dɪ'greɪd] vt erniedrigen; (esp Mil: lower in rank) degradieren; (Geol) erodieren; (Chem) abbauen. to ~ oneself sich erniedrigen; **I wouldn't ~ myself by doing that** ich würde mich nicht dazu erniedrigen, das zu tun.

degrading [dɪˈgreɪdɪŋ] *adj* erniedrigend.

degree [dɪˈgriː] *n* (a) (*unit of measurement*) Grad *m no pl.* **an angle of 90 ~s** ein Winkel *m* von 90 Grad; **it was 35 ~s in the shade** es waren 35 Grad im Schatten.
   (b) (*extent*) (*of risk, uncertainty etc*) Maß *nt.* **to some ~, to a** (*certain*) **~** einigermaßen, zu einem gewissen Grad, in gewissem Maße; **to a high ~** in hohem Maße; **to such a ~ that ...** so sehr *or* in solchem Maße, daß ...; **to what ~ was he involved?** wieweit *or* in welchem Maße war er verwickelt?
   (c) (*step in scale*) Grad *m.* **~ of kinship/consanguinity** Verwandschaftsgrad *m*; **by ~s** nach und nach; **first/second ~ murder** (*Jur*) Mord *m* /Totschlag *m.*
   (d) (*Univ*) akademischer Grad. **first/higher** (*academic*) **~** erster/höherer akademischer Grad; **to do a ~** studieren; **when did you do your ~?** wann haben Sie das Examen gemacht?; **I'm taking** *or* **doing a science ~** *or* **a ~ in science** ich studiere Naturwissenschaften; **to get one's ~** seinen akademischen Grad erhalten.
   (e) (*Gram*) **~ of comparison** Steigerungsstufe *f.*
   (f) (*position in society*) Rang, Stand *m.*

degree: **~ course** *n* Universitätskurs, der mit dem ersten akademischen Grad abschließt; **~ day** *n* Tag *m* der Gradverleihung.

dehumanize [ˌdiːˈhjuːmənaɪz] *vt* entmenschlichen.

dehydrate [ˌdiːhaɪˈdreɪt] *vt* Wasser entziehen (+*dat*), dehydrieren (*spec*).

dehydrated [ˌdiːhaɪˈdreɪtɪd] *adj* dehydriert (*spec*); *vegetables, milk also* Trocken-; *milk, eggs also* pulverisiert; *person, skin also* ausgetrocknet.

dehydration [ˌdiːhaɪˈdreɪʃən] *n* Austrocknung, Dehydration (*spec*) *f*; (*of vegetables, milk etc*) Trocknung, Dehydration (*spec*) *f.*

de-ice [ˌdiːˈaɪs] *vt* enteisen.

de-icer [ˌdiːˈaɪsəʳ] *n* Enteiser *m.*

deification [ˌdiːɪfɪˈkeɪʃən] *n* Vergötterung *f.*

deify [ˈdiːɪfaɪ] *vt* vergöttern.

deign [deɪn] *vt* **to ~ to do sth** geruhen *or* sich herablassen, etw zu tun; **he didn't ~ to er** ließ sich nicht dazu herab.

deism [ˈdiːɪzəm] *n* Deismus *m.*

deist [ˈdiːɪst] *n* Deist(in *f*) *m.*

deity [ˈdiːɪtɪ] *n* Gottheit *f.* **the D~** Gott *m.*

déjà vu [ˈdeɪʒɑːˈvjuː] *n* Déjà-vu-Erlebnis *nt.* **a feeling** *or* **sense of ~** das Gefühl, das schon einmal gesehen zu haben.

deject [dɪˈdʒekt] *vt* deprimieren.

dejected *adj*, **~ly** *adv* [dɪˈdʒektɪd, -lɪ] niedergeschlagen, deprimiert.

dejection [dɪˈdʒekʃən] *n* Niedergeschlagenheit, Depression *f.*

de jure [ˌdiːˈdʒʊərɪ] *adj, adv* de jure.

dekko [ˈdekəʊ] *n* (*Brit inf*) kurzer Blick (*at* auf +*acc*). **let's have a ~** (*at it*) (*show me*) laß (das) mal sehen; (*let's go and see it*) gucken wir uns das mal an.

delay [dɪˈleɪ] **1** *vt* (a) (*postpone*) verschieben, aufschieben. **to ~ doing sth** es verschieben *or* aufschieben, etw zu tun; **he ~ed paying until ...** er wartete solange mit dem Zahlen, bis ...; **he ~ed writing the letter** er schob den Brief auf; **rain ~ed play** der Beginn des Spiels verzögerte sich wegen Regens.
   (b) (*hold up*) *person, train, traffic* aufhalten.
   2 *vi* **to ~ in doing sth** es verschieben *or* aufschieben, etw zu tun; **if you ~ too long in booking** wenn Sie zu lange mit der Buchung warten; **he ~ed in paying the bill** er schob die Zahlung der Rechnung hinaus; **don't ~!** verlieren Sie keine Zeit!, tun Sie es unverzüglich!; **don't ~ in sending it in** senden Sie es unverzüglich ein.
   3 *n* (*hold-up*) Aufenthalt *m*; (*to traffic*) Stockung *f*; (*to train, plane*) Verspätung *f*; (*time lapse*) Verzögerung *f.* **to have a ~** aufgehalten werden; **roadworks are causing ~s to traffic of up to 1 hour** Straßenbauarbeiten verursachen Verkehrsstockungen bis zu 1 Stunde; **there are ~s to all trains** alle Züge haben Verspätung; **a split second's ~** eine Verzögerung von einem Bruchteil einer Sekunde; **without ~** unverzüglich; **without further ~** ohne weitere Verzögerung.

delayed-action [dɪˈleɪdˌækʃən] *adj attr bomb, mine* mit Zeitzünder. **~ shutter release** (*Phot*) Selbstauslöser *m.*

delaying [dɪˈleɪɪŋ] *adj action* verzögernd, hinhaltend, Verzögerungs-. **~ tactics** Verzögerungs- *or* Hinhaltetaktik *f.*

delectable [dɪˈlektəbl] *adj* köstlich; (*fig*) reizend.

delectation [ˌdiːlekˈteɪʃən] *n* **for sb's ~** als besonderer Genuß für jdn.

delegate [ˈdelɪgeɪt] **1** *vt person* delegieren; *authority, power, job also* übertragen (*to sb* jdm). **to ~ sb to do sth** jdn dazu abordnen *or* damit beauftragen, etw zu tun. **2** *vi* delegieren. **3** [ˈdelɪgət] *n* Delegierte(r) *mf*, bevollmächtigter Vertreter, bevollmächtigte Vertreterin (*to* für).

delegation [ˌdelɪˈgeɪʃən] *n* Delegation *f* (*to an* +*acc*); (*group of delegates also*) Abordnung *f.*

delete [dɪˈliːt] *vt* streichen (*from* von). "**~ where not applicable**" „Nichtzutreffendes (bitte) streichen".

deleterious [ˌdelɪˈtɪərɪəs] *adj* (*form*) schädlich (*to* für).

deletion [dɪˈliːʃən] *n* Streichung *f.* **who made those ~s?** wer hat das gestrichen?

delft [delft] *n* Delfter Fayencen *pl.*

deli [ˈdelɪ] *n* (*US inf*) *see* **delicatessen.**

deliberate [dɪˈlɪbərɪt] **1** *adj* (a) (*intentional*) absichtlich; *action, insult, lie also* bewußt. (b) (*cautious, thoughtful*) besonnen; *action, judgement* (wohl)überlegt; (*slow*) *movement, step, voice* bedächtig. **2** [dɪˈlɪbəreɪt] *vi* (*ponder*) nachdenken (*on, upon* über +*acc*); (*discuss*) sich beraten (*on, upon* über +*acc*, *wegen*). **3** [dɪˈlɪbəreɪt] *vt* (*ponder*) bedenken, überlegen; (*discuss*) beraten.

deliberately [dɪˈlɪbərɪtlɪ] *adv* (a) (*intentionally*) absichtlich, mit Absicht, bewußt. (b) (*purposefully, slowly*) bedächtig.

deliberateness [dɪˈlɪbərɪtnɪs] *n see adj* Absichtlichkeit *f*; Besonnenheit *f*; Überlegtheit *f*; Bedächtigkeit *f.*

deliberation [dɪˌlɪbəˈreɪʃən] *n* (a) (*consideration*) Überlegung *f* (*on* zu). **after due/careful ~** nach reiflicher/sorgfältiger Überlegung. (b) (*discussion*) Beratungen *pl* (*of, on* in +*dat*, über +*acc*). (c) (*purposefulness, slowness*) Bedächtigkeit *f.*

deliberative [dɪˈlɪbərətɪv] *adj speech* abwägend. **~ assembly** beratende Versammlung.

delicacy [ˈdelɪkəsɪ] *n* (a) *see* **delicateness.** (b) (*food*) Delikatesse *f*, Leckerbissen *m.*

delicate [ˈdelɪkɪt] **1** *adj* (a) (*fine, exquisite, dainty*) fein; *fabric also, bones, colour* zart; (*fragile*) *person, bones, china also* zerbrechlich; *fabric, flower* empfindlich.
   (b) (*Med*) *health, person* zart; *liver* empfindlich. **in a ~ condition** (*dated euph*) in anderen Umständen.
   (c) (*sensitive*) *person* feinfühlig; *manner also* delikat; *instrument* empfindlich; *task* fein; *playing* gefühlvoll; *painting* zart. **he has a ~ touch** (*pianist, artist*) er hat sehr viel Gefühl; (*doctor*) er ist sehr behutsam.
   (d) (*requiring skilful handling*) *operation, subject, situation* heikel, delikat.
   (e) *food* delikat; *flavour* fine.
   2 *n* **~s** *pl* (*fabrics*) Feinwäsche *f.*

delicately [ˈdelɪkɪtlɪ] *adv see adj* (a, c, e).

delicateness [ˈdelɪkɪtnɪs] *n see adj* (a) Feinheit *f*; Zartheit *f*; Zerbrechlichkeit *f*; Empfindlichkeit *f.* (b) Zartheit *f*; Empfindlichkeit *f.* (c) Feingefühl *nt*; Empfindlichkeit *f*; Feinheit *f*; Gefühl(volle) *nt*; Zartheit *f.* (d) Heikle *nt*, Delikatheit *f.* (e) Delikatheit *f*; Feinheit *f.*

delicatessen [ˌdelɪkəˈtesn] *n* Delikatessen- *or* Feinkostgeschäft *nt.*

delicious [dɪˈlɪʃəs] *adj* (a) *food etc* köstlich, lecker (*inf*). (b) (*delightful*) herrlich.

delight [dɪˈlaɪt] **1** *n* (a) (*intense pleasure*) Freude *f.* **to my ~** zu meiner Freude; **he takes great ~ in doing that** es bereitet ihm große Freude, das zu tun; **to give sb ~** jdn erfreuen.
   (b) (*source of pleasure*) Freude *f.* **sensual ~s** Sinnesfreuden *pl*; **he's a ~ to watch, it's a ~ to watch him** es ist eine Freude, ihm zuzusehen.
   2 *vt person, ear, eye etc* erfreuen; *see* **delighted.**
   3 *vi* sich erfreuen (*in an* +*dat*). **she ~s in doing that** es bereitet ihr große Freude, das zu tun.

delighted [dɪˈlaɪtɪd] *adj* (*with* über +*acc*) erfreut, entzückt. **to be ~** sich sehr freuen (*at* über +*acc*, *that* daß); **absolutely ~** hocherfreut, ganz entzückt; **~ to meet you!** sehr angenehm!; **we shall be ~ to accept** (*your invitation*) wir werden Ihrer Einladung gern Folge leisten; **I'd be ~ to help you** ich würde Ihnen sehr gern helfen.

delightful [dɪˈlaɪtfʊl] *adj* reizend; *weather, party, meal* wunderbar.

delightfully [dɪˈlaɪtfəlɪ] *adv* wunderbar.

delimit [diːˈlɪmɪt] *vt* abstecken, abgrenzen.

delimitation [diːˌlɪmɪˈteɪʃən] *n* Abgrenzung *f.*

delineate [dɪˈlɪnɪeɪt] *vt* (*draw*) skizzieren; (*describe*) beschreiben, darstellen. **the mountains were clearly ~d against the sky** die Berge zeichneten sich klar gegen den Himmel ab.

delineation [dɪˌlɪnɪˈeɪʃən] *n see vt* Skizzierung *f*; Beschreibung, Darstellung *f.*

delinquency [dɪˈlɪŋkwənsɪ] *n* Kriminalität, Delinquenz (*spec*) *f.* **an act of ~** eine Straftat; (*fig*) ein Verbrechen *nt.*

delinquent [dɪˈlɪŋkwənt] **1** *adj* (a) straffällig. (b) (*US*) *bill* überfällig; *account* rückständig. **2** *n* Delinquent *m.*

delirious [dɪˈlɪrɪəs] *adj* (*Med*) im Delirium; (*fig*) im Taumel. **to be ~ with joy** im Freudentaumel sein.

deliriously [dɪˈlɪrɪəslɪ] *adv see adj* **~ happy** überglücklich.

delirium [dɪˈlɪrɪəm] *n* (*Med*) Delirium *nt*; (*fig*) Taumel *m.* **~ tremens** Delirium tremens, Säuferwahn(sinn) *m.*

deliver [dɪˈlɪvəʳ] **1** *vt* (a) (*take to destination*) *goods* liefern; *note, message* zustellen, überbringen; (*on regular basis*) *letters, papers etc* zustellen; (*on foot*) austragen; (*by car*) ausfahren. **to ~ sth to sb** jdm etw liefern/zustellen; **~ed free** frei Haus; **to ~ sb/sth into sb's care** jdn/etw in jds Obhut (*acc*) geben; **he ~ed me right to the door** er brachte mich bis zur Tür; **to ~ the goods** (*fig inf*) es bringen (*inf*), es schaffen (*inf*).
   (b) (*liter: rescue*) befreien. **~ us from evil** (*Bibl*) erlöse uns von dem Übel *or* Bösen.
   (c) (*pronounce*) *speech, sermon* halten; *ultimatum* stellen; *verdict* sprechen, verkünden.
   (d) (*Med*) *baby* zur Welt bringen; (*old*) *woman* entbinden. **to be ~ed of a son** (*old*) eines Jungen genesen (*old*).
   (e) (*hand over: also* **~ up**) aushändigen, übergeben. **to ~ a town** (**up**) **into the hands of the enemy** eine Stadt dem Feind ausliefern; *see* **stand.**
   (f) (*aim, throw*) *blow* versetzen, landen (*inf*); *ball* werfen. **Ali ~ed a punch to Bugner's jaw** Ali landete einen Schlag an Bugners Kinn (*inf*); **to ~ a broadside** eine Breitseite abfeuern.
   2 *vi* liefern.

deliverance [dɪˈlɪvərəns] *n* (*liter*) Befreiung, Erlösung (*from* von) *f.*

deliverer [dɪˈlɪvərəʳ] *n* (a) (*Comm*) Lieferant *m.* (b) (*liter: rescuer*) Erlöser, Retter *m.*

delivery [dɪˈlɪvrɪ] *n* (a) (*of goods*) (Aus)lieferung *f*; (*of parcels, letters*) Zustellung *f.* **there is no ~ on Sundays** sonntags gibt es keine Zustellung; **to take ~ of a parcel** ein Paket in Empfang nehmen; **to pay on ~** bei Empfang zahlen.
   (b) (*Med*) Entbindung *f.*
   (c) (*of speaker*) Vortrag *m*, Vortragsweise *f.*

(d) (*liter: rescue*) Rettung, Befreiung *f*.
(e) (*of punch, blow*) Landung *f* (*inf*); (*Cricket*) Wurf *m*.

delivery: ~ **boy** *n* Bote *m*; (*for newspapers*) Träger *m*; ~ **man** *n* Lieferant *m*; ~ **note** *n* Lieferschein *m*; ~ **room** *n* Kreißsaal, Entbindungssaal *m*; ~ **service** *n* Zustelldienst *m*; ~ **van** *n* (*Brit*) Lieferwagen *m*.

dell [del] *n* kleines bewaldetes Tal.

delouse [ˌdiːˈlaus] *vt* entlausen.

Delphic [ˈdelfɪk] *adj* (*lit, fig*) delphisch. **the ~ oracle** das Delphische Orakel, das Orakel von Delphi.

delphinium [delˈfɪnɪəm] *n* Rittersporn *m*.

delta [ˈdeltə] *n* Delta *nt*.

delta: ~ **ray** *n* (*Phys*) Deltastrahl *m*; ~ **rhythm** *or* **wave** *n* (*Physiol*) Deltawelle *f*; ~ **wing** *n* (*Aviat*) Deltaflügel *m*.

delude [dɪˈluːd] *vt* täuschen, irreführen (*with* mit). **to ~ sb into thinking sth** (*incident*) jdn dazu verleiten, etw zu glauben; (*person also*) jdm etw weismachen; **to ~ oneself** sich (*dat*) Illusionen machen, sich (*dat*) etwas vormachen; **stop deluding yourself/don't ~ yourself that** ... mach dir doch nicht vor, vorzumachen, daß .../mach dir doch nicht vor, daß ...; ~**d voller Illusionen; poor ~d creature** armer Irrer, arme Irre.

deluge [ˈdeljuːdʒ] **1** *n* (*lit*) Überschwemmung *f*; (*of rain*) Guß *m*; (*fig: of complaints, letters etc*) Flut *f*. **the D~** (*Bibl*) die Sintflut. **2** *vt* (*lit, fig*) überschwemmen, überfluten.

delusion [dɪˈluːʒən] *n* Illusion *f*, Irrglaube *m no pl*; (*Psych*) Wahnvorstellung *f*. **to be or labour under a ~** in einem Wahn leben; **to have ~s of grandeur** den Größenwahn haben.

delusive [dɪˈluːsɪv], **delusory** [dɪˈluːsərɪ] *adj* irreführend, täuschend, trügerisch.

de luxe [dɪˈlʌks] *adj* Luxus-, De-luxe-.

delve [delv] *vi* **(a)** (*into a subject, the past*) sich eingehend befassen (*into* mit); (*into a book*) sich vertiefen (*into in* +*acc*). **(b)** **to ~ in(to) one's pocket/a drawer** tief in die Tasche/eine Schublade greifen.

demagnetize [ˌdiːˈmægnɪtaɪz] *vt* entmagnetisieren.

demagogic [ˌdeməˈgɒgɪk] *adj* demagogisch.

demagogue, (*US*) **demagog** [ˈdeməgɒg] *n* Demagoge *m*.

demagoguery [ˌdeməˈgɒgərɪ], **demagogy** [ˈdeməgɒgɪ] *n* Demagogie *f*.

demand [dɪˈmaːnd] **1** *vt* verlangen, fordern (*of, from* von); (*situation, task etc*) erfordern, verlangen; *time* beanspruchen. **he ~ed my name/to see my passport** er wollte meinen Namen wissen/meinen Paß sehen; **he ~ed to know what had happened** er verlangte zu wissen, was passiert war.
2 *n* **(a)** Forderung *f*, Verlangen *nt* (*for* nach); (*claim for better pay, of kidnapper etc*) Forderung *f* (*for* nach). **by popular ~** auf allgemeinen Wunsch; **payable on ~** zahlbar bei Vorlage; **to make ~s on sb** Forderungen *or* Ansprüche an jdn stellen; **he makes too many ~s on my patience/time/pocket** er (über)strapaziert meine Geduld/er bedget mich *or* meine Zeit zu sehr mit Beschlag/er liegt mir zu sehr auf der Tasche; **I have many ~s on my time** meine Zeit ist sehr mit Beschlag belegt.
(b) *no pl* (*Comm*) Nachfrage *f*. **to create a ~ for a product** Nachfrage für ein Produkt schaffen; **there's no ~ for it** es ist nicht gefragt, es besteht keine Nachfrage danach; **to be in great ~** (*article, person*) sehr gefragt sein.

demand bill *n see* **demand note**.

demanding [dɪˈmaːndɪŋ] *adj child* anstrengend; *teacher, boss, task also* anspruchsvoll. **physically ~** körperlich anstrengend.

demand: ~ **management** *n* Steuerung *f* der Nachfrage; ~ **note** *n* Zahlungsaufforderung *f*.

demarcate [ˈdiːmaːkeɪt] *vt* abgrenzen, demarkieren.

demarcation [ˌdiːmaːˈkeɪʃən] *n* Abgrenzung, Demarkation *f*. ~**-line** Demarkationslinie *f*; ~ **dispute** Streit *m* um den Zuständigkeitsbereich.

démarche [ˈdeɪmaːʃ] *n* Demarche *f*.

dematerialize [ˌdiːməˈtɪərɪəlaɪz] **1** *vt* entmaterialisieren. **2** *vi* sich entmaterialisieren.

demean [dɪˈmiːn] *vr* **(a)** (*lower*) sich erniedrigen. **I will not ~ myself (so far as) to do that** ich werde mich nicht (dazu) erniedrigen, das zu tun; ~**ing** erniedrigend. **(b)** (*behave*) sich benehmen *or* verhalten.

demeanour, (*US*) **demeanor** [dɪˈmiːnəʳ] *n* (*behaviour*) Benehmen, Auftreten *nt*; (*bearing*) Haltung *f*.

demented [dɪˈmentɪd] *adj* verrückt, wahnsinnig. ~ **with worry** verrückt vor Angst.

dementia [dɪˈmenʃɪə] *n* Schwachsinn *m*, Demenz *f* (*spec*). ~ **praecox** Jugendirresein *nt*, Dementia praecox *f* (*spec*).

demerara (sugar) [ˌdeməˈrɛərə(ˈʃuːgəʳ)] *n* brauner Rohrzucker.

demerit [diːˈmerɪt] *n* Schwäche *f*, Fehler *m*; (*US: black mark*) Minuspunkt *m*.

demesne [dɪˈmeɪn] *n* Grundbesitz *m*. **to hold sth in ~** etw in Besitz haben.

demi [ˈdemɪ-] *pref* Halb-, halb-. ~**god** Halbgott *m*; ~**john** Demijohn *m*; (*in wickerwork also*) bauchige Korbflasche.

demilitarization [ˈdiːˌmɪlɪtəraɪˈzeɪʃən] *n* Ent- *or* Demilitarisierung *f*.

demilitarize [ˌdiːˈmɪlɪtəraɪz] *vt* ent- *or* demilitarisieren.

demise [dɪˈmaɪz] *n* (*death*) Tod *m*; (*of person also*) Ableben *nt* (*geh*); (*fig: of institution, newspaper etc*) Ende *nt*.

demisemiquaver [ˌdemɪsemɪˈkweɪvəʳ] *n* Zweiunddreißigstelnote *f*.

demist [ˌdiːˈmɪst] *vt* *windscreen* freimachen.

demister [ˌdiːˈmɪstəʳ] *n* Gebläse *nt*.

demitasse [ˈdemɪtæs] *n* (*US*) (*cup*) Mokkatasse *f*; (*coffee*) Mokka *m*.

demo [ˈdeməʊ] *n abbr of* **demonstration** Demo(nstration) *f*.

demob [diːˈmɒb] (*Brit*) **1** *n abbr of* **demobilization** Entlassung *f* aus dem Kriegsdienst. **2** *vt abbr of* **demobilize** aus dem Kriegsdienst entlassen, demobilisieren.

demobilization [ˈdiːˌməʊbɪlaɪˈzeɪʃən] *n* (*of army*) Demobilmachung, Demobilisierung *f*; (*of soldier*) Entlassung aus dem Kriegsdienst, Demobilisierung *f*.

demobilize [diːˈməʊbɪlaɪz] *vt* aus dem Kriegsdienst entlassen, demobilisieren.

democracy [dɪˈmɒkrəsɪ] *n* Demokratie *f*.

democrat [ˈdeməkræt] *n* Demokrat(in *f*) *m*.

democratic *adj*, ~**ally** *adv* [ˌdeməˈkrætɪk, -əlɪ] demokratisch.

democratize [dɪˈmɒkrətaɪz] *vt* demokratisieren.

demographer [dɪˈmɒgrəfəʳ] *n* Demograph(in *f*) *m*.

demographic [ˌdeməˈgræfɪk] *adj* demographisch.

demography [dɪˈmɒgrəfɪ] *n* Demographie *f*.

demolish [dɪˈmɒlɪʃ] *vt building* ab- *or* einreißen, abbrechen; *fortifications* niederreißen; (*fig*) *opponent, theory* zunichte machen, vernichten; (*hum*) *cake etc* vertilgen.

demolition [ˌdeməˈlɪʃən] *n* Abbruch *m*.

demolition: ~ **area** *n see* ~ **zone**; ~ **squad** *n* Abbruchkolonne *f*; ~ **zone** *n* Abbruchgebiet *nt*.

demon [ˈdiːmən] *n* Dämon *m*; (*inf: child*) Teufel *m*. **to be a ~ for work** ein Arbeitstier sein; **the D~ Drink** König Alkohol *m*.

demoniac [dɪˈməʊnɪæk] **1** *adj* dämonisch. **2** *n* Besessene(r) *mf*.

demoniacal [ˌdiːməʊˈnaɪəkəl] *adj* dämonisch.

demonic [dɪˈmɒnɪk] *adj* dämonisch.

demonstrable *adj*, ~**bly** *adv* [ˈdemənstrəbl, -ɪ] beweisbar, offensichtlich.

demonstrate [ˈdemənstreɪt] **1** *vt* **(a)** *truth, emotions, needs, good will* zeigen, beweisen; (*by experiment, example also*) demonstrieren. **(b)** *appliance etc* vorführen; *operation also* demonstrieren. **2** *vi* (*Pol etc*) demonstrieren.

demonstration [ˌdemənˈstreɪʃən] **1** *n* **(a)** *see vt* Zeigen *nt*, Beweis *m*; Demonstration *f*; Vorführung *f*; Demonstration *f*. **to give a ~ (of sth)** etw demonstrieren; (*of gadgets*) eine Vorführung machen, etw vorführen.
(b) (*Pol etc*) Demonstration *f*. **to hold a ~** eine Demonstration veranstalten *or* durchführen.
2 *attr car, lesson* Vorführ-, Demonstrations-.

demonstrative [dɪˈmɒnstrətɪv] *adj* demonstrativ; (*Gram*) *adjective also* hinweisend.

demonstrator [ˈdemənstreɪtəʳ] *n* **(a)** (*Comm*) Vorführer(in *f*) *m* (von technischen Geräten), Propagandist(in *f*) *m*; (*Sch, Univ*) Demonstrator *m*. **(b)** (*Pol*) Demonstrant(in *f*) *m*.

demoralization [dɪˌmɒrəlaɪˈzeɪʃən] *n see vt* Entmutigung *f*; Demoralisierung *f*.

demoralize [dɪˈmɒrəlaɪz] *vt* entmutigen; *troops etc* demoralisieren.

demoralizing [dɪˈmɒrəlaɪzɪŋ] *adj see vt* entmutigend; demoralisierend.

demote [dɪˈməʊt] *vt* degradieren (*to* zu). ~**d to captain** zum Hauptmann degradiert.

demotic [dɪˈmɒtɪk] *adj* **(a)** *Greek* demotisch. **(b)** (*of the people*) volkstümlich.

demotion [dɪˈməʊʃən] *n* Degradierung *f*.

demur [dɪˈmɜːʳ] **1** *vi* Einwände erheben, Bedenken haben (*to, at* gegen); (*Jur*) Einspruch erheben *or* einlegen. **2** *n* (*form*) Einwand *m*, Bedenken *pl*; (*Jur*) Einspruch *m*. **without ~** widerspruchslos.

demure [dɪˈmjʊəʳ] *adj* (+*er*) (*coy*) *look, girl, smile* spröde; (*sedate*) ernst, gesetzt; (*sober*) nüchtern, gelassen. **a ~ little hat** ein schlichter kleiner Hut.

demurely [dɪˈmjʊəlɪ] *adv see adj*.

demureness [dɪˈmjʊənɪs] *n see adj* Sprödigkeit *f*; Ernst *m*, Gesetztheit *f*; Nüchternheit, Gelassenheit *f*; Schlichtheit *f*.

demythologize [ˌdiːmɪˈθɒlədʒaɪz] *vt* entmythologisieren.

den [den] *n* **(a)** (*of lion, tiger etc*) Höhle *f*, Versteck *nt*; (*of fox*) Bau *m*. **(b)** ~ **of iniquity** *or* **vice** Lasterhöhle *f*; ~ **of thieves** Spelunke, Räuberhöhle (*hum*) *f*; *see* **gambling, opium den**. **(c)** (*study*) Arbeitszimmer *nt*; (*private room*) gemütliches Zimmer, Bude *f* (*inf*). **hobby ~** Hobbyraum *m*.

denationalization [ˈdiːˌnæʃnəlaɪˈzeɪʃən] *n* Entnationalisierung *f*.

denationalize [ˌdiːˈnæʃnəlaɪz] *vt* entnationalisieren.

denature [ˌdiːˈneɪtʃəʳ] *vt* denaturieren; (*make unfit for eating, drinking also*) ungenießbar machen, vergällen.

denazification [ˈdiːˌnætsɪfɪˈkeɪʃən] *n* Entnazifizierung *f*.

denazify [ˌdiːˈnætsɪfaɪ] *vt* entnazifizieren.

dendrite [ˈdendraɪt] *n* Dendrit *m*.

denial [dɪˈnaɪəl] *n* **(a)** (*of accusation, guilt*) Leugnen *nt*. ~ **of (the existence of) God** Gottesleugnung *f*; **the government issued an official ~** die Regierung gab ein offizielles Dementi heraus. **(b)** (*refusal: of request etc*) Ablehnung *f*, abschlägige Antwort; (*official*) abschlägiger Bescheid; (*of rights*) Verweigerung *f*. **he regarded this as a ~ of his sons** er war der Ansicht, daß seine Söhne übergangen worden waren. **(c)** (*disowning*) Verleugnung *f*. **Peter's ~ of Christ** die Verleugnung des Petrus. **(d)** (*self-~*) Selbstverleugnung *f*.

denier [ˈdenɪəʳ] *n* (*of stockings*) Denier *nt*.

denigrate [ˈdenɪgreɪt] *vt* verunglimpfen.

denigration [ˌdenɪˈgreɪʃən] *n* Verunglimpfung *f*.

denim [ˈdenɪm] **1** *n* **(a)** Jeansstoff, Köper *m*. **(b)** ~**s** *pl* Blue Jeans, Jeans *pl*. **2** *adj attr* Jeans-, Köper-. ~ **jacket** Jeansjacke *f*; ~ **suit** Jeansanzug *m*.

denizen [ˈdenɪzn] *n* Bewohner(in *f*) *m*; (*person*) Einwohner(in *f*) *m*. ~**s of the forest/deep** Waldbewohner *pl*/Bewohner *pl* der Tiefe.

Denmark [ˈdenmaːk] *n* Dänemark *nt*.

denominate [dɪˈnɒmɪneɪt] *vt* benennen, bezeichnen.

denomination [dɪˌnɒmɪˈneɪʃən] *n* **(a)** (*Eccl*) Konfession *f*. **(b)** (*name, naming*) Benennung, Bezeichnung *f*. **(c)** (*of money*) Nennbetrag *m*; (*of weight, measures*) Einheit *f*. **(d)** (*class, kind*) Klasse *f*, Gruppe *f*.

denominational [dɪˌnɒmɪˈneɪʃənl] adj (Eccl) konfessionell, Konfessions-.

denominator [dɪˈnɒmɪneɪtəʳ] n (Math) Nenner m.

denotation [ˌdiːnəʊˈteɪʃən] n (a) (Philos: of term, concept) Denotation f, Begriffsumfang m; (of word) Bedeutung f. (b) (name: of object) Bezeichnung f; (symbol) Symbol nt.

denote [dɪˈnəʊt] vt bedeuten; symbol, word bezeichnen; (Philos) den Begriffsumfang angeben von.

dénouement [dɪˈnuːmɒŋ] n (Theat, Liter) (Auf)lösung f; (fig) Ausgang m.

denounce [dɪˈnaʊns] vt (a) (accuse publicly) anprangern, brandmarken; (inform against) anzeigen, denunzieren (sb to sb jdn bei jdm). (b) (condemn as evil) alcohol, habit etc verurteilen, denunzieren (geh). (c) treaty (auf)kündigen.

denouncement [dɪˈnaʊnsmənt] n see denunciation.

dense [dens] adj (+er) (a) fog, forest, crowd, population dicht. (b) (Phot) negative überbelichtet. (c) (inf: stupid) person beschränkt, unterbelichtet (inf), blöd (inf). are you being ~? stellst du dich dumm?

densely [ˈdenslɪ] adv (a) dicht. ~ wooded/populated dicht bewaldet pred, dichtbewaldet attr/dicht bevölkert pred, dichtbevölkert attr. (b) (inf: stupidly) blöd (inf).

denseness [ˈdensnɪs] n (a) see density. (b) (inf) Beschränktheit, Blödheit (inf) f.

density [ˈdensɪtɪ] n Dichte f. **population** ~ Bevölkerungsdichte f.

dent [dent] 1 n (in metal) Beule, Delle (inf) f; (in wood) Kerbe, Delle (inf) f. that made a ~ in his savings (inf) das hat ein Loch in seine Ersparnisse gerissen; that made a bit of a ~ in his pride das hat seinen Stolz ganz schön angeknackst (inf).
2 vt hat, car, wing einbeulen, verbeulen; wood, table eine Delle machen in (+acc); (inf) pride anknacksen (inf).
3 vi (metal etc) sich einbeulen; (wood, table) eindellen.

dental [ˈdentl] 1 adj (a) Zahn-; treatment zahnärztlich; training zahnmedizinisch (form). ~ floss Zahnseide f; ~ surgeon Zahnarzt m/-ärztin f; ~ technician Zahntechniker(in f) m. (b) (Ling) Dental-, dental. 2 n (Ling) Dental, Zahnlaut m.

dentifrice [ˈdentɪfrɪs] n Zahnpasta f.

dentist [ˈdentɪst] n Zahnarzt m, Zahnärztin f. at the ~('s) beim Zahnarzt.

dentistry [ˈdentɪstrɪ] n Zahnmedizin, Zahnheilkunde f. a nice bit of ~ eine gute (Zahnarzt)arbeit.

dentition [denˈtɪʃən] n (process of teething) Zahnen nt, Dentition f (spec); (arrangement of teeth) Gebißform f.

dentures [ˈdentʃəz] npl (partial ~) Zahnprothese f; (full ~) Gebiß nt.

denude [dɪˈnjuːd] vt (of trees etc) entblößen (of gen); (fig also) berauben (of gen).

denunciation [dɪˌnʌnsɪˈeɪʃən] n see denounce Anprangerung, Brandmarkung f; Denunziation f; Verurteilung f; (Auf)kündigung f. the book is a sustained ~ of ... das Buch ist eine einzige Anklage gegen ...

deny [dɪˈnaɪ] vt (a) charge, accusation etc bestreiten, abstreiten, (ab)leugnen; existence of God leugnen; (officially) dementieren. do you ~ having said that? leugnen or bestreiten Sie, das gesagt zu haben?; there's no ~ing it das läßt sich nicht bestreiten or leugnen; I ~ that there is a real need for it ich bestreite, daß ein echtes Bedürfnis danach besteht.
(b) (refuse) to ~ sb a request/his rights/aid/a privilege/admittance/credit jdm eine Bitte abschlagen/jdm seine Rechte vorenthalten/jdm Hilfe/ein Privileg versagen/jdm den Zugang verwehren/jdm Kredit verweigern; I can't ~ her anything ich kann ihr nichts abschlagen; I had to ~ myself the pleasure of his company ich mußte mir das Vergnügen seiner Gesellschaft versagen; why should I ~ myself these little comforts? warum sollte ich mir das bißchen Komfort nicht gönnen?
(c) (disown) leader, religion, principles verleugnen.
(d) to ~ oneself sich selbst verleugnen; to ~ the flesh der Sinneslust entsagen (liter), sich kasteien.

deodorant [diːˈəʊdərənt] 1 adj desodor(is)ierend. 2 n De(s)odorant nt.

deodorize [diːˈəʊdəraɪz] vt desodor(is)ieren.

deontology [ˌdiːɒnˈtɒlədʒɪ] n Pflichtethik, Deontologie f.

deoxidize [diːˈɒksɪdaɪz] vt desoxydieren.

deoxyribonucleic acid [diːˈɒksɪˌraɪbəʊnjuːˈkleɪɪkˌæsɪd] n Desoxyribonukleinsäure f.

dep abbr of **departure** Abf.

depart [dɪˈpɑːt] 1 vi (a) (go away) weggehen; (on journey) abreisen; (by bus, car etc) wegfahren; (train, bus etc) abfahren. the train at platform 6 ~ing for ... der Zug auf Bahnsteig 6 nach ...; guests are asked to sign the register before they ~ Gäste werden gebeten, vor der Abreise einen Meldezettel auszufüllen; to be ready to ~ (person) start- or abfahrbereit sein; a train ~ing London 1800 hours (form) ein Zug, der um 18⁰⁰ Uhr in London abfährt; the train was/visitors were about to ~ der Zug war im Begriff abzufahren/die Gäste waren im Begriff aufzubrechen; to ~ on one's way (liter, old) sich aufmachen, aufbrechen; this is the point from which we ~ed (fig) das war unser Ausgangspunkt.
(b) (deviate: from opinion etc) abweichen, abgehen.
2 vt (liter) to ~ this world or life aus dieser Welt or diesem Leben scheiden (liter).

departed [dɪˈpɑːtɪd] 1 adj (a) (liter: dead) verstorben, verschieden (geh). (b) (bygone) friends verloren; glory, happiness also vergangen. 2 n the (dear) ~ der/die (liebe) Verstorbene; die (lieben) Verstorbenen pl.

department [dɪˈpɑːtmənt] n (a) (generally) Abteilung f; (Geog: in France) Departement nt; (in civil service) Ressort nt. D~ of Employment (Brit) Arbeitsministerium nt; D~ of State (US) Außenministerium nt; that's not my ~ das ist nicht mein Ressort. (b) (Sch) Fachbereich m; (Univ also) Seminar nt.

departmental [ˌdiːpɑːtˈmentl] adj (a) Abteilungs-. ~ store (dated) Warenhaus nt. (b) (Sch) Fachbereichs-; (Univ also) Seminar-.

departmentalism [ˌdiːpɑːtˈmentəlɪzəm] n Gliederung f in Abteilungen.

departmentalize [ˌdiːpɑːtˈmentəlaɪz] vt in Abteilungen einteilen or (auf)gliedern.

departmentally [ˌdiːpɑːtˈmentəlɪ] adv abteilungsweise.

department store n Kaufhaus, Warenhaus nt.

departure [dɪˈpɑːtʃəʳ] n (a) (of person) Weggang m; (on journey) Abreise f (from aus); (of vehicle) Abfahrt f; (of plane) Abflug m. to be on the point of ~ im Aufbruch (begriffen) sein; there are three ~s daily for Stockholm es gibt täglich drei Flüge nach Stockholm; "~s" "Abfahrt"; (at airport) "Abflug"; at the hour of our ~ from this life (liter) in der Stunde unseres Dahinscheidens (liter).
(b) (fig: from custom, principle) Abweichen, Abgehen nt (from von); (from truth) Abweichen nt.
(c) (fig) (change in policy etc) Richtung f; (in science, philosophy also) Ansatz m. this is a new ~ for us das ist eine neue Richtung für uns.

departure: ~ **gate** n Flugsteig, Ausgang m; ~ **lounge** n Abflughalle f; ~ **platform** n (Abfahrts)bahnsteig m; ~ **signal** n Abfahrtssignal nt; ~ **time** n (Aviat) Abflugzeit f; (Rail, bus) Abfahrtzeit f.

depend [dɪˈpend] vi (a) abhängen (on sb/sth von jdm/etw). it ~s on what you mean by reasonable es kommt darauf an, was Sie unter vernünftig verstehen; it all ~s (on whether ...) das kommt ganz darauf an or das hängt ganz davon ab(, ob ...); that ~s das kommt darauf an, je nachdem; ~ing on his mood/the amount needed/how late we arrive je nach seiner Laune/Höhe des erforderlichen Betrags/je nachdem, wie spät wir ankommen.
(b) (rely) sich verlassen (on, upon auf +acc). you may ~ (up)on his coming Sie können sich darauf verlassen, daß er kommt; you can ~ (up)on it! darauf können Sie sich verlassen!
(c) (person: be dependent on) to ~ on sb/sth angewiesen sein auf (+acc).

dependability [dɪˌpendəˈbɪlɪtɪ] n Zuverlässigkeit, Verläßlichkeit f.

dependable [dɪˈpendəbl] adj zuverlässig, verläßlich.

dependant, dependent [dɪˈpendənt] n Abhängige(r) mf. do you have ~s? haben Sie (abhängige) Angehörige?

dependence [dɪˈpendəns] n (a) (state of depending) Abhängigkeit f (on, upon von). (b) (reliance) I could never put much ~ on him ich habe nie sehr viel von seiner Zuverlässigkeit gehalten.

dependency [dɪˈpendənsɪ] n (a) (country) Schutzgebiet nt, Kolonie f. (b) see dependence (a).

dependent [dɪˈpendənt] 1 adj abhängig (on, upon von). to be ~ on charity/sb's good will auf Almosen/jds Wohlwollen (acc) angewiesen sein. 2 n see dependant.

depersonalize [diːˈpɜːsənəlaɪz] vt entpersönlichen, depersonalisieren (Psych).

depict [dɪˈpɪkt] vt darstellen; (in words also) beschreiben.

depiction [dɪˈpɪkʃən] n see vt Darstellung f; Beschreibung f.

depilatory [dɪˈpɪlətərɪ] 1 adj enthaarend, Enthaarungs-. 2 n Enthaarungsmittel nt.

deplete [dɪˈpliːt] vt (a) (exhaust) erschöpfen; (reduce) vermindern, verringern. our supplies are/the larder is somewhat ~d unsere Vorräte sind ziemlich erschöpft/die Speisekammer ist ziemlich leer; this extra spending has seriously ~d our funds diese Sonderausgaben haben unsere Finanzen stark verringert; the audience had become somewhat ~d die Zuschauerreihen hatten sich ziemlich gelichtet.
(b) (Med) entleeren.

depletion [dɪˈpliːʃən] n see vt Erschöpfung f; Verminderung, Verringerung f; Entleerung f; (of stock also, of membership) Abnahme f.

deplorable [dɪˈplɔːrəbl] adj beklagenswert, bedauerlich.

deplorably [dɪˈplɔːrəblɪ] adv see adj to be in ~ bad taste von bedauernswert schlechtem Geschmack zeugen.

deplore [dɪˈplɔːʳ] vt (regret) bedauern, beklagen; (disapprove of) mißbilligen. his attitude is to be ~d seine Haltung ist bedauerlich.

deploy [dɪˈplɔɪ] 1 vt (a) (Mil: use, employ) einsetzen; (position) aufstellen; (along border etc) auffahrschieren lassen. (b) (fig) resources, staff, arguments einsetzen. 2 vi (Mil) sich aufstellen; aufmarschieren.

deployment [dɪˈplɔɪmənt] n see vb Einsatz m; Aufstellung f; Aufmarsch m.

depoliticize [diːpəˈlɪtɪsaɪz] vt entpolitisieren.

deponent [dɪˈpəʊnənt] 1 n (Ling) Deponens nt; (Jur) vereidigter Zeuge. 2 adj ~ **verb** Deponens nt.

depopulate [ˌdiːˈpɒpjʊleɪt] vt entvölkern.

depopulation [ˈdiːˌpɒpjʊˈleɪʃən] n Entvölkerung f; see rural.

deport [dɪˈpɔːt] 1 vt prisoner deportieren; alien abschieben. 2 vr (behave) sich benehmen or verhalten.

deportation [ˌdiːpɔːˈteɪʃən] n see vt Deportation f; Abschiebung f.

deportee [dɪpɔːˈtiː] n Deportierte(r) mf; (alien awaiting deportation) Abzuschiebende(r) mf.

deportment [dɪˈpɔːtmənt] n Haltung f; (behaviour) Verhalten, Benehmen nt. lessons in ~ Haltungsschulung f; Anstandsunterricht m.

depose [dɪˈpəʊz] 1 vt sovereign entthronen, absetzen; official absetzen. 2 vi (Jur) unter Eid aussagen.

deposit [dɪˈpɒzɪt] 1 vt (a) (put down) hinlegen; (upright) hinstellen. the turtle ~s her eggs in the sand die Schildkröte legt ihre Eier im Sand ab.
(b) money, valuables deponieren (with bei).
(c) (Geol) ablagern.

2 n **(a)** (Fin: in bank) Einlage f, Guthaben nt. **to have £50 on ~** ein Guthaben or eine Einlage von £ 50 haben. **(b)** (Comm) (part payment) Anzahlung f; (returnable security) Sicherheit, Kaution f. **to put down a ~ on a car** eine Anzahlung für ein Auto leisten, (auf) ein Auto anzahlen; **to leave a ~** eine Sicherheit or Kaution hinterlegen; **to lose one's ~** (Pol) seine Kaution verlieren. **(c)** (Chem: in wine, Geol) Ablagerung f; (accumulation of ore, coal, oil) (Lager)stätte f. **to form a ~** sich ablagern.

deposit account n Sparkonto nt.

depositary [dɪˈpɒzɪtərɪ] n Treuhänder(in f) m.

deposition [ˌdiːpəˈzɪʃən] n **(a)** (of sovereign) Entthronung, Absetzung f; (of official) Absetzung f. **(b)** (Jur) Aussage f unter Eid. **(c)** (Art, Rel) ~ from the cross Kreuzabnahme f.

depositor [dɪˈpɒzɪtəʳ] n Deponent(in f), Einzahler(in f) m.

depository [dɪˈpɒzɪtərɪ] n Verwahrungsort m, (warehouse) Lagerhaus nt.

depot [ˈdepəʊ] n **(a)** (bus garage etc) Depot nt; (store also) (Lager)haus nt. **(b)** (US Rail) Bahnhof m.

depot ship n Versorgungsschiff nt.

depravation [ˌdeprəˈveɪʃən] n **(a)** (depraving) Verderbung f. **(b)** (depravity) Verderbtheit, Verworfenheit f.

deprave [dɪˈpreɪv] vt verderben.

depraved [dɪˈpreɪvd] adj verderbt, verkommen, verworfen.

depravity [dɪˈprævɪtɪ] n Verderbtheit, Verworfenheit f.

deprecate [ˈdeprɪkeɪt] vt (form) mißbilligen.

deprecating [ˈdeprɪkeɪtɪŋ] adj **(a)** (disapproving) mißbilligend. **(b)** (apologetic) abwehrend.

deprecatingly [ˈdeprɪkeɪtɪŋlɪ] adv see adj.

deprecation [deprɪˈkeɪʃən] n (form) Mißbilligung f.

deprecatory [ˈdeprɪkətərɪ] n see deprecating.

depreciate [dɪˈpriːʃɪeɪt] **1** vt **(a)** value mindern. **to ~ a currency** die Kaufkraft einer Währung mindern. **(b)** (belittle) herabsetzen or -mindern or -würdigen. **2** vi an Wert verlieren; (currency) an Kaufkraft verlieren.

depreciation [dɪˌpriːʃɪˈeɪʃən] n **(a)** (of property, value) Wertminderung f; (of currency) Kaufkraftverlust m. **(b)** (belittlement) Herabsetzung or -minderung or -würdigung f.

depreciatory [dɪˈpriːʃɪətərɪ] adj abschätzig, herabsetzend.

depredation [depriˈdeɪʃən] n usu pl Verwüstung f.

depress [dɪˈpres] vt **(a)** person deprimieren; (discourage) entmutigen. **(b)** (press down) lever niederdrücken, herunterdrücken; push button drücken, betätigen.

depressant [dɪˈpresnt] **1** n Beruhigungsmittel, Sedativ(um) (spec) nt. **2** adj beruhigend, dämpfend, sedativ (spec).

depressed [dɪˈprest] adj **(a)** person deprimiert, niedergeschlagen; (sad) bedrückt; (discouraged) entmutigt. **(b)** industry notleidend; area Notstands-; market, trade, business schleppend, flau.

depressing [dɪˈpresɪŋ] adj deprimierend, bedrückend. **don't be so ~** hör auf, ständig schwarzzusehen.

depressingly [dɪˈpresɪŋlɪ] adv deprimierend, bedrückend.

depression [dɪˈpreʃən] n **(a)** Depression f; (Med) Depressionen pl. **(b)** (lowering) (of lever) Herunter- or Niederdrücken nt; (of key, push button) Drücken, Betätigen nt, Betätigung f. **(c)** (in ground) Vertiefung, Senke, Mulde f. **(d)** (Met) Tief(druckgebiet) nt. **a deep/shallow ~** ein ausgedehntes/schwaches Tief(druckgebiet). **(e)** (Econ) Flaute f; (St Ex) Baisse f. **the D~** die Weltwirtschaftskrise.

depressive [dɪˈpresɪv] **1** adj depressiv. **2** an Depressionen Leidende(r) mf. **to be a ~** depressiv sein.

deprivation [deprɪˈveɪʃən] n **(a)** (depriving) Entzug m; (loss) Verlust m; (Psych) Deprivation f; (of rights) Beraubung f. **(b)** (state) Entbehrung f; (lack of necessities) Mangel m. **the ~s of the war** die Entbehrungen des Krieges.

deprive [dɪˈpraɪv] vt **to ~ sb of sth** jdm etw entziehen; **they had been ~d of a decent education/the benefit of ...** ihnen wurde eine anständige Erziehung/der Vorteil von ... vorenthalten; **I wouldn't want to ~ you of the pleasure of ...** ich möchte dir das Vergnügen ... nicht vorenthalten; **I don't want to ~ you** ich will dir das/die etc nicht vorenthalten; **those who are ~d of any sense of national identity** die, denen jedes Gefühl für nationale Identität fehlt; **to ~ oneself of sth** sich (dat) etw nicht gönnen.

deprived [dɪˈpraɪvd] adj ~ child benachteiligtes Kind; ~ families benachteiligte or deprivierte (Sociol) Familien; **are you feeling ~?** (inf) fühlst du dich benachteiligt?

dept abbr of department Abt.

depth [depθ] n **(a)** (of water, shelf) Tiefe f. **the ~s of the ocean** die Tiefen des Ozeans; **at a ~ of 3 metres** in einer Tiefe von 3 Metern, in 3 Meter Tiefe; **don't go out of your ~** geh nicht zu tief rein!; **to get out of one's ~** (lit) den Boden unter den Füßen verlieren; (fig also) ins Schwimmen geraten; **sorry, I'm out of my ~ there** es tut mir leid, aber davon habe ich keine Ahnung or da muß ich passen. **(b)** (of knowledge, feeling, colour) Tiefe f. **to sing/act with great ~ of feeling** sehr gefühlvoll singen/sehr einfühlsam spielen; **in ~** eingehend, intensiv; see in-depth. **(c)** (fig) ~(s) Tiefen pl; **in the ~s of despair** in tiefster Verzweiflung; **in the ~s of winter/the forest** im tiefsten Winter/Wald; **from the ~s of the earth** aus den Tiefen der Erde (geh).

depth: ~ **charge** n Wasserbombe f; ~ **of field** n (Phot) Tiefenschärfe, Schärfentiefe f; ~ **psychology** n Tiefenpsychologie f.

deputation [depjʊˈteɪʃən] n (act) Abordnung f; (people also) Delegation f.

depute [dɪˈpjuːt] vt person abordnen, delegieren; power, authority delegieren, übertragen (to sb jdm).

deputize [ˈdepjʊtaɪz] **1** vi vertreten (for sb jdn), als Vertreter

fungieren (for sb für jdn). **2** vt ernennen, abordnen.

deputy [ˈdepjʊtɪ] **1** n **(a)** Stellvertreter(in f) m. **(b)** (member of deputation) Delegierte(r) mf. **(c)** (US: also ~ sheriff) Hilfssheriff m. **(d)** (in France) Deputierte(r) mf; (US: in foreign parliaments) Abgeordnete(r) mf. **2** adj attr stellvertretend.

derail [dɪˈreɪl] **1** vt zum Entgleisen bringen, entgleisen lassen. **to be ~ed** entgleisen. **2** vi entgleisen.

derailleur gears [dɪˈreɪljəˈgɪəz], **derailleurs** [dɪˈreɪljəz] (inf) npl Kettenschaltung f.

derailment [dɪˈreɪlmənt] n Entgleisung f.

derange [dɪˈreɪndʒ] vt **(a)** (make insane) verrückt or wahnsinnig machen. **(b)** plan durcheinanderbringen, umwerfen.

deranged [dɪˈreɪndʒd] adj mind gestört, verwirrt, verstört. **to be (mentally) ~** (person) geistesgestört sein.

derangement [dɪˈreɪndʒmənt] n **(a)** Geistesgestörtheit f. **(b)** (of order) Unordnung f, Durcheinander nt. **I apologize for any ~ to your plans** es tut mir leid, wenn das Ihre Pläne durcheinandergebracht hat.

Derby [ˈdɑːbɪ, (US) ˈdɜːbɪ] n **(a)** (US: also ~ hat) Melone f. **(b)** (local ~) (Lokal)derby nt. **(c)** (Racing) Derby nt.

derelict [ˈderɪlɪkt] **1** adj (abandoned) verlassen, aufgegeben; (ruined) verfallen, heruntergekommen. **2** n **(a)** (Naut) (treibendes) Wrack. **(b)** (person) Obdachlose(r) mf.

dereliction [derɪˈlɪkʃən] n **(a)** (state: of property) Verfall m, Heruntergekommenheit f. **(b)** ~ of duty Pflichtversäumnis nt.

derestricted [ˌdiːrɪˈstrɪktɪd] adj road, area ohne Geschwindigkeitsbegrenzung or -beschränkung.

deride [dɪˈraɪd] vt sich lustig machen über (+acc), verspotten, verhöhnen.

derision [dɪˈrɪʒən] n Hohn, Spott m. **object of ~** Zielscheibe f des Spotts; **to be greeted with ~** mit Spott or spöttisch aufgenommen werden.

derisive adj, ~ly adv [dɪˈraɪsɪv, -lɪ] spöttisch, höhnisch; (malicious) hämisch, verächtlich.

derisory [dɪˈraɪsərɪ] adj **(a)** amount, offer lächerlich. **(b)** see derisive.

derivable [dɪˈraɪvəbl] adj (Ling, Philos, Chem) ableitbar.

derivation [derɪˈveɪʃən] n (Ling, Philos) Ableitung f; (Chem) Derivation f.

derivative [dɪˈrɪvətɪv] **1** adj abgeleitet; (Ling, Chem also) derivativ; (fig) style, composition, literary work etc nachgeahmt, imitiert. **2** n Ableitung f; (Ling also, Chem) Derivat nt.

derive [dɪˈraɪv] **1** vt ideas, names, origins her- or ableiten (from von); profit ziehen (from aus); satisfaction, comfort, pleasure gewinnen (from aus). **this word is ~d from the Greek** dieses Wort stammt aus dem Griechischen. **2** vi **to ~ from** sich her- or ableiten von; (power, fortune) beruhen auf (+dat), herkommen or -rühren von; (ideas) kommen or stammen von; **it all ~s from the fact that ...** das beruht alles auf der Tatsache, daß ...

dermatitis [dɜːməˈtaɪtɪs] n Hautentzündung, Dermatitis f.

dermatologist [dɜːməˈtɒlədʒɪst] n Hautarzt m, Hautärztin f, Dermatologe m, Dermatologin f.

dermatology [dɜːməˈtɒlədʒɪ] n Dermatologie f.

derogate [ˈderəgeɪt] vi **to ~ from sth** (form) einer Sache (dat) Abbruch tun; **without derogating from his authority/merits** ohne seine Autorität/Verdienste schmälern zu wollen.

derogation [derəˈgeɪʃən] n (form: of power, dignity etc) Beeinträchtigung, Schmälerung f, Abbruch m (of, from gen).

derogatory [dɪˈrɒgətərɪ] adj abfällig, abschätzig.

derrick [ˈderɪk] n Derrickkran, Montagekran m; (above oilwell) Bohrturm m.

derring-do [ˈderɪŋˈduː] n (old) Verwegenheit, Tollkühnheit f. **deeds of ~** verwegene or tollkühne Taten.

derringer [ˈderɪndʒəʳ] n Derringer m or f.

derv [dɜːv] n (Brit) Diesel(kraftstoff) m, Dieselöl nt.

dervish [ˈdɜːvɪʃ] n Derwisch m.

DES abbr of Department of Education and Science.

desalinate [diːˈsælɪneɪt] vt entsalzen.

desalination [diːˌsælɪˈneɪʃən], **desalinization** [diːˌsælɪnaɪˈzeɪʃən] n Entsalzung f. ~ **plant** Meerwasserentsalzungsanlage f.

desalinize [diːˈsælɪnaɪz] vt entsalzen.

desalt [diːˈsɔːlt] vt (esp US) entsalzen. ~**ing plant** Meerwasserentsalzungsanlage f.

descale [diːˈskeɪl] vt entkalken.

descant [ˈdeskænt] **1** n (Mus) Diskant m. ~ **recorder** Sopranflöte f. **2** [desˈkænt] vi sich auslassen or verbreiten (upon über +acc), ausgiebig kommentieren.

descend [dɪˈsend] **1** vi **(a)** (go down: person) herunter-/hinuntergehen, hinabschreiten (geh); (lift, vehicle) herunter-/hinunterfahren; (road) herunter-/hinunterführen, herunter-/hinuntergehen; (hill) abfallen; (from horse) absteigen; (Astron) untergehen. **in ~ing order of importance** nach Wichtigkeit geordnet. **(b)** (have as ancestor) abstammen (from von). **(c)** (pass by inheritance) (property) übergehen (from von, to auf +acc); (customs) überliefert werden (from von, to auf +acc); (rights) vererbt werden (from von, to auf +acc). **(d)** (attack suddenly) hereinbrechen (on, upon über +acc), herfallen (on, upon über +acc), überfallen (on, upon sb jdn); (plague) hereinbrechen (on, upon über +acc); (come over: sadness etc) befallen (on, upon sb jdn). **(e)** (inf: visit) **to ~ (up)on sb** jdn überfallen (inf). **(f)** (lower oneself) **to ~ to sth** sich zu etw herablassen or erniedrigen; **I wouldn't ~ to lying** ich würde mich nie dazu herablassen or erniedrigen zu lügen; **he even ~ed to bribery** er scheute selbst vor Bestechung nicht zurück. **2** vt **(a)** stairs hinunter-/heruntergehen or -steigen, hinabschreiten (geh).

(b) to be ~**ed from** abstammen von.
descendant [dɪˈsendənt] n **(a)** Nachkomme m. **(b)** (Astron, Astrol) in the ~ im Deszendenten.
descender [dɪˈsendə^r] n (Typ) Unterlänge f.
descent [dɪˈsent] n **(a)** (going down) (of person) Hinunter-/Heruntergehen, Absteigen nt; (from mountain, of plane, into underworld) Abstieg m; (of gymnast) Abgang m; (slope, of road) Abfall m. **the** ~ **of the mountain** der Abstieg vom Berg; **the road made a sharp** ~ die Straße fiel steil ab; ~ **by parachute** Fallschirmabsprung m; **the** ~ **from the cross** (Art, Rel) die Kreuzabnahme.
(b) (ancestry) Abstammung, Herkunft f. **of noble** ~ von adliger Abstammung or Herkunft; **he is the thirteenth in** ~ **from ...** er ist der dreizehnte Nachkomme von ...
(c) (of property) Vererbung, Übertragung f (to auf +acc); (of customs) Überlieferung f (to auf +acc).
(d) (Mil, fig: attack) Überfall m.
(e) (inf: visit) Überfall m (inf). **sorry about our unannounced** ~ **on you last night** entschuldige, daß wir dich gestern abend so unangemeldet überfallen haben.
(f) (fig: into crime etc) Absinken nt (into in +acc).
describe [dɪˈskraɪb] vt **(a)** scene, person beschreiben, schildern. ~ **him for us** beschreiben Sie ihn uns (dat); **which cannot be** ~**d** was unbeschreiblich ist. **(b)** (+as) bezeichnen. **he** ~**s himself as a doctor** er bezeichnet sich (als) Arzt. **(c)** (Math) beschreiben.
description [dɪˈskrɪpʃən] n **(a)** Beschreibung f; (of event, situation also) Schilderung f. **of a beauty beyond** ~ von unbeschreiblicher Schönheit. **(b)** (+as) Bezeichnung f; see **answer 2 (b). (c)** (sort) Art f. **vehicles of every** ~ Fahrzeuge aller Art. **(d)** (Math) Beschreibung f.
descriptive [dɪˈskrɪptɪv] adj **(a)** beschreibend; account, adjective, passage anschaulich. ~ **writing** Beschreibung f; **to be** ~ **of sth** etw beschreiben. **(b)** philosophy, linguistics, science etc deskriptiv.
descry [dɪˈskraɪ] vt (form, liter) gewahren (geh), erblicken.
desecrate [ˈdesɪkreɪt] vt entweihen, schänden.
desecration [ˌdesɪˈkreɪʃən] n Entweihung, Schändung f.
desegregate [ˌdiːˈsegrɪgeɪt] vt schools desegregieren. ~**d schools** gemischtrassige Schulen pl.
desegregation [ˈdiːˌsegrɪˈgeɪʃən] n Aufhebung f der Rassentrennung (of in +dat), Desegregation f.
desensitize [ˌdiːˈsensɪtaɪz] vt (Phot) lichtunempfindlich machen; (Med) desensibilisieren.
desert[1] [ˈdezət] 1 n (lit, fig) Wüste f. 2 adj attr region, climate Wüsten-. ~ **island** einsame or verlassene Insel; ~ **boots** Boots pl; ~ **rat** (Brit fig inf) Wüstensoldat m.
desert[2] [dɪˈzɜːt] 1 vt (leave) verlassen; wife etc also böswillig verlassen (Jur); cause, party im Stich lassen. **by the time the police arrived the place was** ~**ed** als die Polizei eintraf, war niemand mehr da; **in winter the place is** ~**ed** im Winter ist der Ort verlassen.
2 vi (Mil) desertieren, Fahnenflucht begehen; (fig also) fahnenflüchtig werden. **to** ~ **to the rebels** zu den Rebellen überlaufen.
deserter [dɪˈzɜːtə^r] n (Mil, fig) Deserteur m.
desertion [dɪˈzɜːʃən] n **(a)** (act) Verlassen nt; (Jur: of wife, family) böswilliges Verlassen; (Mil) Desertion, Fahnenflucht f; (fig) Fahnenflucht f. ~ **to the enemy** Überlaufen nt zum Feind. **(b)** (state) Verlassenheit f.
deserts [dɪˈzɜːts] npl Verdienste pl; (reward, also iro) verdiente Belohnung; (punishment) verdiente Strafe. **according to one's** ~ nach seinen Verdiensten; **to get one's just** ~ bekommen, was man verdient, **seine gerechte Belohnung bekommen.**
deserve [dɪˈzɜːv] 1 vt verdienen. **he** ~**s to win** er verdient den Sieg; **he** ~**s to be punished** er verdient es, bestraft zu werden; **he got what he** ~**d** er bekam, was er verdiente. 2 vi **he** ~**s well of his country** (form) sein Land ist ihm zu Dank verpflichtet.
deservedly [dɪˈzɜːvɪdlɪ] adv verdientermaßen. **and** ~ **so** und das verdientermaßen.
deserving [dɪˈzɜːvɪŋ] adj person, action, cause verdienstvoll. **the** ~ **poor** die Bedürftigen; **to be** ~ **of sth** etw verdienen.
deshabille [ˌdezaˈbiːl] n see **dishabille.**
desiccate [ˈdesɪkeɪt] vt trocknen.
desiccated [ˈdesɪkeɪtɪd] adj getrocknet; (fig) vertrocknet.
desiccation [ˌdesɪˈkeɪʃən] n Trocknung f, Trocknen nt.
desideratum [dɪˌzɪdəˈrɑːtəm] n, pl **desiderata** [dɪˌzɪdəˈrɑːtə] Desiderat(um) (liter), Erfordernis nt.
design [dɪˈzaɪn] 1 n **(a)** (planning, shaping etc) (of building, book, picture etc) Entwurf m; (of dress also) Design nt; (of car, machine, plane etc) Konstruktion f. **it's still at the** ~ **stage** es befindet sich noch in der Konstruktion or im Konstruktionsstadium; **a machine with a good/faulty** ~ eine gut/schlecht konstruierte Maschine; **a new** ~ (Aut) ein neues Modell.
(b) no pl (as subject, art of designing) Design nt. **industrial** ~ Konstruktionslehre f.
(c) (pattern: on pottery, material) Muster nt.
(d) (intention) Plan m, Absicht f. **by** ~ absichtlich; **to have** ~**s on sb/sth** mit jdm/etw etwas im Sinn haben, es auf jdn/etw abgesehen haben; **he has** ~**s on her** er hat etwas mit ihr vor.
2 vt (a) entwerfen; machine konstruieren. **a well** ~**ed machine** ein gut durchkonstruierte Maschine.
(b) (intend) **to be** ~**ed for sb/sth** für jdn/etw vorgesehen or bestimmt sein.
3 vi planen, Pläne or Entwürfe machen.
designate [ˈdezɪgneɪt] 1 vt **(a)** (name) kennzeichnen, bezeichnen, benennen; (appoint) bestimmen, ernennen, designieren (form). **to** ~ **sb as sth** jdn zu etw ernennen. **(b)** (indicate, specify, mark) festlegen, bestimmen. 2 [ˈdezɪgnɪt] adj **the Prime Minister** ~ der designierte Premierminister.
designation [ˌdezɪgˈneɪʃən] n see vt Kennzeichnung,

Bezeichnung, Benennung f; Bestimmung, Ernennung f; Festlegung, Bestimmung f.
designedly [dɪˈzaɪnɪdlɪ] adv absichtlich, vorsätzlich.
designer [dɪˈzaɪnə^r] n Designer, Gestalter m; (fashion ~) Modeschöpfer(in f) m; (of machines etc) Konstrukteur m; (Theat) Bühnenbildner(in f) m.
designing [dɪˈzaɪnɪŋ] adj intrigant, hinterhältig.
desirability [dɪˌzaɪərəˈbɪlɪtɪ] n Wünschbarkeit f. **they discussed the** ~ **of the plan** sie erörterten, ob das Vorhaben wünschenswert sei; **in his eyes this only increased her** ~ das machte sie in seinen Augen um so begehrenswerter; **to increase the** ~ **of these houses** um die Attraktivität dieser Häuser zu erhöhen.
desirable [dɪˈzaɪərəbl] adj **(a)** action, progress wünschenswert, erwünscht. **(b)** position, offer, house, area reizvoll, attraktiv. **(c)** woman begehrenswert.
desire [dɪˈzaɪə^r] 1 n (for nach) Wunsch m; (longing) Sehnsucht f; (sexual) Verlangen, Begehren nt. **her sexual** ~**s** ihre sexuellen Wünsche; **a** ~ **for peace** ein Verlangen nach Frieden; **heart's** ~ Herzenswunsch m; **I have no** ~ **to see him** ich habe kein Verlangen, ihn zu sehen; **I have no** ~ **to cause you any trouble** ich möchte Ihnen keine Unannehmlichkeiten bereiten.
2 vt **(a)** (want) wünschen; object sich (dat) wünschen; woman begehren; peace haben wollen, verlangen nach. **it leaves much to be** ~**d** das läßt viel zu wünschen übrig.
(b) (form: request) **to** ~ **sb to do sth** jdn bitten or ersuchen, etw zu tun.
desirous [dɪˈzaɪərəs] adj see vt **to be** ~ **of sth** (form) etw wünschen/wollen/begehren.
desist [dɪˈzɪst] vi (form) Abstand nehmen, absehen (from doing sth davon, etw zu tun, from sth von etw). **would you kindly** ~! unterlassen Sie das gefälligst!
desk [desk] n Schreibtisch m; (for pupils, master) Pult nt; (in shop, restaurant) Kasse f; (in hotel) Empfang m; (Press) Ressort nt. **information** ~ Information(sschalter m) f.
desk: ~**bound** adj an den Schreibtisch gebunden; ~ **clerk** n (US) Empfangschef m; ~ **diary** n Tischkalender m; ~ **editor** n Lektor(in f), Manuskriptbearbeiter(in f) m; (Press) Ressortchef(in f) m; ~ **job** n Bürojob m; ~**work** n Schreibarbeit f.
desolate [ˈdesəlɪt] 1 adj **(a)** place (devastated) verwüstet; (barren) trostlos; (fig) outlook trostlos. **(b)** (grief-stricken) tieftraurig, zu Tode betrübt; (friendless) verlassen; cry verzweifelt, der Verzweiflung. 2 [ˈdesəlet] vt **(a)** country verwüsten. **(b)** person zu Tode betrüben, untröstlich machen.
desolately [ˈdesəlɪtlɪ] adv see adj.
desolation [ˌdesəˈleɪʃən] n **(a)** (of country by war) Verwüstung f. **(b)** (of landscape) Trostlosigkeit f. **(c)** (grief) Trostlosigkeit f; (friendlessness) Verlassenheit f.
despair [dɪˈspeə^r] 1 n Verzweiflung f (about, at über +acc). **to be in** ~ verzweifelt sein; **he was filled with** ~ Verzweiflung überkam or ergriff ihn; **in** ~, **she killed him** sie tötete ihn aus Verzweiflung or in ihrer Verzweiflung; **his** ~ **of ever being able to return home** seine Verzweiflung darüber, vielleicht nie mehr nach Hause zurückkehren zu können; **to be the** ~ **of sb** jdn zur Verzweiflung bringen.
2 vi verzweifeln, alle Hoffnung aufgeben. **to** ~ **of doing sth** alle Hoffnung aufgeben, etw zu tun; **to** ~ **of sth** alle Hoffnung auf etw (acc) aufgeben; **his life was** ~**ed of** man gab ihm keine Überlebenschancen; **to make sb** ~ jdn zur Verzweiflung bringen or treiben.
despairing adj, ~**ly** adv [dɪsˈpeərɪŋ, -lɪ] verzweifelt.
despatch [dɪˈspætʃ] vt, n see **dispatch.**
desperado [ˌdespəˈrɑːdəʊ] n, pl **-(e)s** Desperado m.
desperate [ˈdespərɪt] adj **(a)** verzweifelt; criminal zum Äußersten entschlossen; (urgent) need etc dringend. **to feel** ~ verzweifelt sein; **to get** ~ verzweifeln, in Verzweiflung geraten; **I haven't had a cigarette for hours, I'm getting** ~ (inf) ich habe schon seit Stunden keine mehr geraucht, jetzt brauche ich (aber) dringend eine; **to be** ~ **for sth** etw dringend brauchen or benötigen; **I'm/it's not that** ~! so dringend ist es nicht!; **I was** ~ **to get the job** ich wollte die Stelle unbedingt haben; **don't do anything** ~! lassen Sie sich nicht zu einer Verzweiflungstat hinreißen; **to do something** ~ sich zu einer Verzweiflungstat hinreißen lassen; **amputating the whole leg was a rather** ~ **solution** (gleich) das ganze Bein zu amputieren, war (doch) eine recht extreme Lösung.
(b) (extremely serious or dangerous) situation etc verzweifelt, auswegslos, hoffnungslos. **things are getting** ~ die Lage wird allmählich verzweifelt etc.
(c) (inf: very bad) colour etc schrecklich. **what a** ~ **idiot he is** er ist (doch) wirklich der letzte Idiot (inf).
desperately [ˈdespərɪtlɪ] adv **(a)** verzweifelt, voller Verzweiflung; (urgently) need dringend. ~ **in love** verliebt bis über beide Ohren; ~ **ill** schwerkrank attr, schwer krank pred; **do you want ...?** — **not** ~ möchten Sie ...? — nicht unbedingt; **was it good/are you busy?** — **not** ~ war's schön/hast du zu tun? — nicht gerade übermäßig, es hielt/hält sich in Grenzen.
(b) (inf) cold, frightened, funny fürchterlich attr.
desperation [ˌdespəˈreɪʃən] n Verzweiflung f. **an act of** ~ eine Verzweiflungstat; **in (sheer)** ~ aus (reiner) Verzweiflung; **in** ~ **of ever seeing him** weil sie etc alle Hoffnung aufgegeben hatte, ihn je zu sehen or zu Gesicht zu bekommen; **to drive sb to** ~ jdn zur Verzweiflung bringen; **to be in** ~ verzweifelt sein; **to fight with** ~ verzweifelt kämpfen.
despicable [dɪˈspɪkəbl] adj verabscheuungswürdig; person verachtenswert, widerwärtig, ekelhaft. **don't be so** ~ sei (doch) nicht ekelhaft.
despicably [dɪˈspɪkəblɪ] adv verabscheuungswürdig, widerwärtig, ekelhaft. **he was** ~ **rude** er war so ekelhaft or widerwärtig grob.
despise [dɪˈspaɪz] vt verachten; presents, food also verschmähen.

despising adj, ~ly adv [dɪ'spaɪzɪŋ, -lɪ] verächtlich, voller Verachtung, verachtungsvoll.

despite [dɪ'spaɪt] prep trotz (+gen). in ~ of (old, liter) trotz, ungeachtet (+gen); ~ his warnings seinen Warnungen zum Trotz; ~ what he says trotz allem, was sie sagt.

despoil [dɪ'spɔɪl] vt person berauben (of gen); country plündern. ~ed of all its treasures all seiner Schätze beraubt.

despondence [dɪ'spɒndəns], **despondency** [dɪ'spɒndənsɪ] n Niedergeschlagenheit, Mutlosigkeit f.

despondent [dɪ'spɒndənt] adj niedergeschlagen, mutlos. to be ~ about sth über etw (acc) bedrückt sein; to grow or get ~ den Mut verlieren.

despondently [dɪ'spɒndəntlɪ] adv niedergeschlagen, mutlos.

despot ['despɒt] n (lit, fig) Despot m.

despotic adj, ~ally adv [des'pɒtɪk, -əlɪ] (lit, fig) despotisch, herrisch.

despotism ['despətɪzəm] n Despotie f; (as ideology) Despotismus m.

dessert [dɪ'zɜːt] n Nachtisch m, Dessert nt. for ~ als or zum Nachtisch.

dessert: ~ plate n Dessertteller m; ~spoon n Dessertlöffel m; ~ wine n Dessertwein m.

destination [ˌdestɪ'neɪʃən] n (of person) Reiseziel nt; (of goods) Bestimmungsort m; (fig: of person) Bestimmung f; (of money) Zweck m. port of ~ Bestimmungshafen m; to know one's ~ in life seine Bestimmung kennen.

destine ['destɪn] vt (a) (set apart, predestine) person bestimmen, ausersehen; object bestimmen. to be ~d to do sth dazu bestimmt or ausersehen sein, etw zu tun; the qualities which ~d him for leadership die Eigenschaften, die ihn für Führungsaufgaben prädestinierten.
  (b) usu pass (be fated) we were ~d to meet das Schicksal hat es so gewollt, daß wir uns begegnen; I was ~d never to see them again ich sollte sie nie (mehr) wiedersehen; at the ~d hour zu der vom Schicksal (vor)bestimmten Stunde.

destined ['destɪnd] adj ~ for (ship) unterwegs nach; (goods) für; where is the cargo ~ for? wo geht diese Fracht hin?

destiny ['destɪnɪ] n (a) art (determining power) Schicksal nt, Vorsehung f. D~ das Schicksal, die Vorsehung.
  (b) (individual fate, fated event) Schicksal, Geschick, Los nt. the destinies of Germany during this period die Geschicke Deutschlands während dieser Zeit; to control one's own ~ sein Schicksal selbst in die Hand nehmen; it was his ~ es war sein Schicksal or Los, es war ihm beschieden (zu ...); will it be our ~ to meet again? wird uns das Schicksal (je) wieder zusammenführen?

destitute ['destɪtjuːt] 1 adj (a) (poverty-stricken) mittellos. to be utterly ~ bettelarm sein. (b) (lacking) bar (of gen). 2 npl the ~ die Mittellosen, die, die im Elend leben.

destitution [ˌdestɪ'tjuːʃən] n (bittere) Not, Elend nt; (esp financially) Mittellosigkeit f.

destroy [dɪ'strɔɪ] vt (a) zerstören; (break up, make useless) box, toy, watch etc kaputtmachen; documents, manuscripts etc also vernichten; trace also tilgen; (fire also) verwüsten. to ~ oneself sich zugrunde richten; to be ~ed by fire durch Brand vernichtet werden.
  (b) (kill) vernichten; animal einschläfern.
  (c) (put an end to) zerstören; influence, hopes, chances zunichte machen, vernichten; reputation, mood, beauty ruinieren; morals zersetzen. you'll ~ your appetite du verdirbst dir or das verdirbt dir den Appetit; they are trying to ~ him as party leader sie versuchen, seine Stellung als Parteiführer zu ruinieren.

destroyer [dɪ'strɔɪə'] n (Naut) Zerstörer m.

destruct [dɪ'strʌkt] vi (esp Space) sich selbst zerstören.

destructible [dɪ'strʌktəbl] adj vernichtbar.

destruction [dɪ'strʌkʃən] n (a) (destroying: of town, building, hope) Zerstörung f; (of enemy, people, insects, documents) Vernichtung f; (of reputation also) Ruinierung f; (of character, soul) Verwüstung, Zerstörung f. (b) (damage: caused by war, fire) Verwüstung, Zerstörung f.

destructive [dɪ'strʌktɪv] adj (a) wind, fire, war zerstörerisch; tendencies also destruktiv; urge Zerstörungs-. a ~ child ein Kind, das zum Zerstören neigt, ein destruktives Kind (Psych); to be ~ of sth etw zerstören. (b) (fig) criticism etc destruktiv.

destructively [dɪ'strʌktɪvlɪ] adv destruktiv.

destructiveness [dɪ'strʌktɪvnɪs] n (a) (of fire, war) zerstörende Wirkung; (of person, child etc) Destruktivität f (esp Psych), Zerstörungswut f. (b) (of criticism) Destruktivität f, zersetzende Wirkung.

destructor [dɪ'strʌktə'] n (Tech: also refuse ~) Müllverbrennungsanlage f.

desuetude [dɪ'sjuːɪtjuːd] n (form) to fall into ~ außer Gebrauch kommen.

desultoriness ['desəltərɪnɪs] n see adj Flüchtigkeit f; Halbherzigkeit f; Zwanglosigkeit f.

desultory ['desəltərɪ] adj reading flüchtig; manner, approach, attempt halbherzig; firing vereinzelt, sporadisch. to have a ~ conversation eine zwanglose Unterhaltung führen.

detach [dɪ'tætʃ] vt (a) (separate, unfasten) rope, cart loslösen (from von); section of form, document abtrennen (from von); part of machine, wooden leg, collar, hood abnehmen (from von); lining herausnehmen (from aus); coach from train abhängen (from von). to ~ oneself from a group sich von einer Gruppe lösen or trennen; a section became ~ed from ... ein Teil löste sich von ...; these buildings are ~ed from the main block diese Gebäude stehen gesondert vom Hauptkomplex.
  (b) (Mil, Naut) abkommandieren. troops were ~ed to guard the town Truppen wurden zur Überwachung der Stadt abkommandiert.

detachable [dɪ'tætʃəbl] adj part of machine, collar abnehmbar;

section of document abtrennbar (from von); lining ausknöpfbar; (with zip) ausreißbar; lens auswechselbar.

detached [dɪ'tætʃt] adj (a) (unbiased) opinion unvoreingenommen; (unemotional) manner kühl, distanziert. (b) ~ house alleinstehendes Haus, Einzelhaus nt.

detachment [dɪ'tætʃmənt] n (a) (act of separating) see vt (a) Loslösen nt; Abtrennen nt; Abnehmen nt; Herausnehmen nt; Abhängen nt. (b) (emotionlessness) Distanz f; (objectivity) Abstand m. (c) (Mil) Sonderkommando nt, Abordnung f.

detail ['diːteɪl] 1 n (a) Detail nt; (particular) Einzelheit f; (part of painting, photo etc) Ausschnitt m; (insignificant circumstance) unwichtige Einzelheit. in ~ im Detail, in Einzelheiten; in great ~ in allen Einzelheiten, ausführlich; in every ~ mit or in allen Einzelheiten; every ~ was taken care of jede Kleinigkeit wurde beachtet; there's one little ~ you've forgotten one Kleinigkeit haben Sie (noch) vergessen; please send me further ~s bitte schicken Sie mir nähere or weitere Einzelheiten; I didn't want to hear the ~s ich wollte die Einzelheiten (gar) nicht hören; to go into ~s auf Einzelheiten eingehen, ins Detail gehen; his attention to ~ seine Aufmerksamkeit für das Detail; but that's a ~! das ist doch (wirklich) nur eine (unwichtige) Einzelheit, das ist doch unwichtig!
  (b) (Mil) Sondertrupp m.
  2 vt (a) facts, story ausführlich or genau erzählen or berichten. the specifications are fully ~ed on page 3 die genaue Ausführung wird auf Seite 3 aufgeführt.
  (b) (Mil) troops abkommandieren (for zu, to do um zu tun).

detail drawing n Detailzeichnung f.

detailed ['diːteɪld] adj ausführlich, genau, detailliert.

detain [dɪ'teɪn] vt (keep back) aufhalten; (police) in Haft nehmen. to be ~ed sich in Haft or polizeilichem Gewahrsam befinden.

detainee [diːteɪ'niː] n Häftling m.

detect [dɪ'tekt] vt entdecken, herausfinden; (see, make out) ausfindig machen; culprit entlarven; crime aufdecken; a tone of sadness, movement, noise wahrnehmen; mine, gas aufspüren. do I ~ a note of irony? höre ich da nicht eine gewisse Ironie (heraus)?

detectable [dɪ'tektəbl] adj (able to be found) trace feststellbar. sb/sth is ~ (discernible) jd läßt sich ausfindig machen/etw läßt sich wahrnehmen; no ~ difference kein erkennbarer Unterschied.

detection [dɪ'tekʃən] n (a) (of criminal) Entlarvung f; (of crime) Entdeckung, Aufdeckung f; (of fault) Entdeckung, Feststellung f; (detective work) Ermittlungsarbeit f. to escape ~ (criminal) der Entdeckung or dingfest gemacht werden; (mistake) der Aufmerksamkeit (dat) entgehen; he tried to escape ~ by ... er versuchte, unentdeckt zu bleiben, indem ...; a brilliant piece of ~ ein glänzendes Stück Detektivarbeit.
  (b) (of gases, mines) Aufspürung f.

detective [dɪ'tektɪv] n (police ~) Kriminalbeamte(r) mf; (private ~) Detektiv m; (fig) Detektiv m.

detective: ~ agency n Detektivbüro nt, Detektei f; ~ inspector n Kriminalinspektor m; ~ story n Kriminalgeschichte f, Kriminalroman, Krimi (inf) m.

detector [dɪ'tektə'] n (Rad, Tech) Detektor m; see mine ~.

détente [deɪ'tɑːnt] n Entspannung f, Détente f.

detention [dɪ'tenʃən] n (a) (captivity) Haft f, Gewahrsam m; (act) Festnahme f; (Mil) Arrest m; (Sch) Nachsitzen nt. to give a pupil two hours' ~ einen Schüler zwei Stunden nachsitzen lassen; he's in ~ (Sch) er sitzt nach.
  (b) (being held up, delayed) Verzögerung f, Aufenthalt m.

detention centre n Jugendstrafanstalt f.

deter [dɪ'tɜː'] vt (prevent) abhalten, hindern; (discourage) abschrecken. to ~ sb from sth jdn von etw abhalten or an etw (dat) hindern; he won't be ~red er läßt sich nicht abhalten/abschrecken; don't let him ~ you lassen Sie sich nicht von ihm abhalten or abbringen.

detergent [dɪ'tɜːdʒənt] 1 n Reinigungs- or Säuberungsmittel nt; (soap powder etc) Waschmittel nt. 2 adj reinigend.

deteriorate [dɪ'tɪərɪəreɪt] vi sich verschlechtern; (materials) verderben; (species) entarten; (morals, brickwork) verfallen.

deterioration [dɪ,tɪərɪə'reɪʃən] n see vi Verschlechterung f; Verderben nt; Entartung f; Verfall m.

determinable [dɪ'tɜːmɪnəbl] adj (a) quantity bestimmbar. (b) (Jur) befristet.

determinant [dɪ'tɜːmɪnənt] 1 adj determinierend attr, entscheidend. 2 n ausschlaggebender Faktor; (Math, Biol etc) Determinante f.

determinate [dɪ'tɜːmɪnɪt] adj number, period etc bestimmt, begrenzt; concept also fest(gelegt).

determination [dɪ,tɜːmɪ'neɪʃən] n (a) (firmness of purpose) Entschlossenheit f. he has great ~ er ist ein Mensch von großer Entschlußkraft; an air of ~ eine entschlossene Miene; there is an air of ~ about him er hat etwas Entschlossenes an sich.
  (b) (determining) Determinierung f; (of character, future also) Bestimmung f; (of cause, nature, position) Ermittlung, Bestimmung f; (of frontiers) Festlegung, Festsetzung f.

determine [dɪ'tɜːmɪn] vt (a) (be a decisive factor in) sb's character, future etc bestimmen, determinieren.
  (b) (settle, fix) conditions, price festlegen, festsetzen.
  (c) (ascertain) cause, nature, position ermitteln, bestimmen.
  (d) (resolve) beschließen, sich entschließen.
  (e) (cause to decide) person veranlassen. to ~ sb to do sth jdn dazu veranlassen or bewegen, etw zu tun.
  (f) (Jur) contract beenden.

♦**determine on** vi +prep obj course of action, alternative sich entschließen zu. to ~ ~ doing sth beschließen or sich entschließen, etw zu tun.

determined [dɪ'tɜːmɪnd] adj person, appearance entschlossen. he is ~ that ... er hat fest beschlossen, daß ...; they are ~ to

succeed sie sind (fest) entschlossen, erfolgreich zu sein; **he's ~ to make me lose my temper** (inf) er legt es darauf an, daß ich wütend werde; **you seem ~ to exhaust yourself** du scheinst dich mit aller Gewalt kaputtmachen zu wollen.

determinedly [dɪ'tɜːmɪndlɪ] adv voller Entschlossenheit, entschlossen.

determiner [dɪ'tɜːmɪnəʳ] n (Gram) Bestimmungswort nt.

determining [dɪ'tɜːmɪnɪŋ] adj entscheidend, bestimmend.

determinism [dɪ'tɜːmɪnɪzəm] n Determinismus m.

determinist [dɪ'tɜːmɪnɪst] 1 adj deterministisch. 2 n Determinist(in f) m.

deterministic [dɪˌtɜːmɪ'nɪstɪk] adj deterministisch.

deterrent [dɪ'terənt] 1 n (also Mil) Abschreckungsmittel nt. **to act as a ~** als Abschreckung(smittel) dienen (to für); **to be a ~** abschrecken. 2 adj abschreckend, Abschreckungs-.

detest [dɪ'test] vt verabscheuen, hassen. **I ~ having to get up early** ich hasse es, früh aufstehen zu müssen; **~ed by all** von allen gehaßt.

detestable [dɪ'testəbl] adj widerwärtig, abscheulich; character also verabscheuungswürdig.

detestably [dɪ'testəblɪ] adv widerwärtig, abscheulich.

detestation [ˌdiːtes'teɪʃən] n (a) Abscheu m (of vor +dat). (b) (object of hatred) **to be the ~ of sb** jds Abscheu erregen.

dethrone [diː'θrəʊn] vt entthronen.

dethronement [diː'θrəʊnmənt] n Entthronung f.

detonate ['detəneɪt] 1 vi (fuse) zünden; (bomb also) detonieren. 2 vt explodieren lassen, zur Explosion bringen. **detonating device** Detonator m.

detonation [ˌdetə'neɪʃən] n Zündung f.

detonator ['detəneɪtəʳ] n Zünd- or Sprengkapsel f; (Rail) Nebelsignal nt.

detour ['diːˌtʊəʳ] 1 n (a) (in road, fig) Umweg m; (in river) Schleife f, Bogen m; (from a subject) Abschweifung f. **to make a ~** einen Umweg machen. (b) (for traffic) Umleitung f. 2 vt traffic umleiten.

detract [dɪ'trækt] vi **to ~ from sth** etw beeinträchtigen, einer Sache (dat) Abbruch tun; pleasure, merit also etw schmälern.

detraction [dɪ'trækʃən] n Beeinträchtigung, Schmälerung f (from gen).

detractor [dɪ'træktəʳ] n Gegner m.

detrain [diː'treɪn] 1 vt ausladen. 2 vi (troops, esp US: passengers) aussteigen.

detribalize [diː'traɪbəlaɪz] vt die Stammesstruktur auflösen in (+dat). **as Africa becomes increasingly ~d** mit dem zunehmenden Verfall der Stammesstruktur in Afrika.

detriment ['detrɪmənt] n Schaden, Nachteil m. **to the ~ of** zum Schaden (+gen) or von; **without ~ to** ohne Schaden für; **I don't know anything to his ~** ich weiß nichts Nachteiliges über ihn.

detrimental [ˌdetrɪ'mentl] adj (to health, reputation) schädlich (to dat); effect also nachteilig (to für); (to case, cause, one's interest) abträglich (to dat).

detritus [dɪ'traɪtəs] n (Geol) Geröll nt; (fig) Müll m.

de trop [də'trəʊ] adj fehl am Platz, überflüssig.

deuce¹ [djuːs] n (a) (Cards) Zwei f. (b) (Tennis) Einstand m. **after ten ~s nachdem es zehnmal Einstand gegeben hatte; to be at ~** den Einstand erreicht haben.

deuce² n (dated inf) Teufel, Daus (old) m; for phrases see devil 1 (c).

deuced ['djuːsɪd] (dated inf) 1 adj verteufelt (dated inf), verdammt (inf). **that ~ dog** dieser verdammte Hund (inf). 2 adv **what ~ bad weather** verteufelt schlechtes Wetter! (dated inf).

deucedly ['djuːsɪdlɪ] adv (dated inf) verteufelt (dated inf).

deus ex machina ['deɪseks'mækɪnə] n Deus ex machina m.

deuterium [djuː'tɪərɪəm] n Deuterium nt.

Deuteronomy [ˌdjuːtə'rɒnəmɪ] n das fünfte Buch Mose(s), Deuteronomium nt (spec).

devalue [diː'væljueɪt] vt see devalue.

devaluation [ˌdiːvæljʊ'eɪʃən] n Abwertung f.

devalue [diː'væljuː] vt abwerten.

devastate ['devəsteɪt] vt (a) (lit) town, land verwüsten; (fig) opponent, opposition vernichten. (b) (inf: overwhelm) niederschmettern, umhauen (inf). **I was ~d** das hat mich umgehauen (inf).

devastating ['devəsteɪtɪŋ] adj (a) (destructive) wind, storm verheerend, vernichtend. (b) (fig: overwhelming) power verheerend; passion zerstörerisch; news niederschmetternd; grief überwältigend. (c) (inf: crushing) argument, attack, reply vernichtend; effect, consequences verheerend. (d) (inf: irresistible) wit, humour, charm, woman umwerfend, überwältigend.

devastatingly ['devəsteɪtɪŋlɪ] adv beautiful, funny umwerfend.

devastation [ˌdevə'steɪʃən] n Verwüstung f.

develop [dɪ'veləp] 1 vt (a) mind, body entwickeln. (b) argument, thesis, outlines (weiter)entwickeln, weiter ausführen; original idea (weiter)entwickeln; plot of novel (unfold) entfalten; (fill out) weiterentwickeln, ausbauen; (Mus) theme durchführen. (c) natural resources, region, ground erschließen; old part of a town sanieren; new estate erschließen; new series, new model entwickeln; business (expand) erweitern, ausbauen; (from scratch) aufziehen. **they plan to ~ this area into a ... es ist geplant, dieses Gebiet als ... zu erschließen.** (d) liking, taste, talent entwickeln; cold sich (dat) zuziehen. (e) (Phot, Math) entwickeln. 2 vi (a) (person, region, country) sich entwickeln. **to ~ into sth** sich zu etw entwickeln, etw werden. (b) (illness, tendency, feeling) sich entwickeln; (talent, plot etc) sich entfalten. (c) (Phot) entwickelt werden.

(d) (event, situation) sich entwickeln. **it later ~ed that he had never seen her** später stellte sich heraus or zeigte es sich, daß er sie nie gesehen hatte.

developer [dɪ'veləpəʳ] n (a) see property ~. (b) (Phot) Entwickler m. (c) late ~ Spätentwickler m.

developing [dɪ'veləpɪŋ] 1 adj crisis, storm aufkommend; industry neu entstehend; interest wachsend. 2 n (a) see development (a, d). (b) (Phot) Entwickeln nt.

developing: ~ bath n Entwicklerbad nt; **~ country** n Entwicklungsland nt; **~ tank** n Entwicklerschale f.

development [dɪ'veləpmənt] n (a) (of person, mind, body) Entwicklung f. (b) (way subject, plot etc is developed) Ausführung f; (of interests also) Entfaltung f; (of argument etc) (Weiter)entwicklung f; (Mus) Durchführung f. (c) (change in situation) Entwicklung f. **new ~s in ... neue Entwicklungen in ...; to await ~s** die Entwicklung abwarten. (d) (of area, site, new town) Erschließung f; (of old part of town) Sanierung f; (of industry) (from scratch) Entwicklung f; (expansion) Ausbau m. **we live in a new ~** wir leben in einer neuen Siedlung. (e) (Phot, Math) Entwicklung f.

developmental [dɪveləp'mentl] adj stage Entwicklungs-.

development: ~ area n Entwicklungsgebiet nt; (in town) Erschließungsgebiet nt; (in old town) Sanierungsgebiet nt; **~ company** n (Wohnungs)baugesellschaft f.

deviancy ['diːvɪənsɪ] n abweichendes Verhalten, Devianz f.

deviant ['diːvɪənt] 1 adj behaviour abweichend, deviant (spec). 2 n jd, der von der Norm abweicht, Deviant m (spec).

deviate ['diːvɪeɪt] vi (a) (person: from truth, former statement, routine) abweichen. (b) (ship, plane, projectile) vom Kurs abweichen or abkommen; (deliberately) vom Kurs abgehen.

deviation [ˌdiːvɪ'eɪʃən] n Abweichen nt, Abweichung f.

deviationism [ˌdiːvɪ'eɪʃənɪzəm] n Abweichlertum nt.

deviationist [ˌdiːvɪ'eɪʃənɪst] 1 adj abweichend. 2 n Abweichler(in f) m.

device [dɪ'vaɪs] n (a) (gadget etc) Gerät nt; (extra fitment) Vorrichtung f. **nuclear ~** atomarer Sprengkörper; **a rhetorical ~** ein rhetorischer Kunstgriff. (b) **to leave sb to his own ~s** jdn sich (dat) selbst überlassen. (c) (emblem) Emblem nt; (motto) Motto nt, Devise f.

devil ['devl] 1 n (a) (evil spirit) Teufel m. (b) (inf) (person, child) Teufel m (inf); (object, screw etc) Plage f; (daring person) Teufelskerl m. **you poor ~** (du) armer Teufel!; **he's a ~ with the ladies** er ist ein Weiberheld; **you little ~!** du kleiner Satansbraten!; **shall I have another? — go on, be a ~** soll ich noch einen trinken? etc — los, nur zu, riskier's! (inf); **be a ~ and say yes** riskier mal was und sag ja. (c) (inf: as intensifier) **a ~ of a job** eine Heidenarbeit; **I had the ~ of a job getting here** es war verdammt schwierig, hierher zu kommen; **the ~ of a wind** ein scheußlicher Wind; **a ~ of a fellow** ein Teufelskerl m; **to live a ~ of a long way away** verdammt weit weg wohnen; **how/what/why/who the ~ ...?** wie/was/warum/wer zum Teufel or in drei Teufels Namen ...?; **to work like the ~** wie ein Pferd schuften (inf); **to run like the ~** wie ein geölter Blitz sausen (inf); **to shout like the ~** wie am Spieß brüllen (inf); **they were making the ~ of a noise** sie machten einen Höllenlärm; **to be in a ~ of a mess** ganz schön in der Patsche or Klemme sitzen (inf) or sein (inf); **there will be the ~ to pay** das dicke Ende kommt noch. (d) (in expressions) (to be) **between the D~ and the deep blue sea** (sich) in einer Zwickmühle (befinden); **to play the ~ with sth** (inf) etw ruinieren; **go to the ~!** (inf) scher dich zum Teufel! (inf); **the ~ take him/it** (old inf) der Teufel soll ihn/es holen (old, inf), **hol's der Teufel** (inf); **the ~ finds work for idle hands** (Prov) Müßiggang ist aller Laster Anfang (Prov); **he has the ~ in him today** ihn reitet heute der Teufel; **speak or talk of the ~!** wenn man vom Teufel spricht!; **give the ~ his due** das muß der Neid ihm lassen; **to have the ~'s own luck** (inf) or the luck of the **~** (inf) ein Schweineglück (inf) or unverschämtes Glück haben; **better the ~ you know** (than the **~ you don't**) (prov) von zwei Übeln wählt man besser das, was man schon kennt; **(the) ~ take the hindmost** den Letzten beißen die Hunde (Prov). (e) printer's **~** Setzerjunge m. 2 vi (Jur, Typ, Liter etc) Handlangerdienste tun. 3 vt (Cook) kidneys scharf gewürzt grillen.

devil fish n (ray) Rochen m; (octopus) Tintenfisch m.

devilish ['devlɪʃ] 1 adj (a) invention teuflisch. (b) (inf: terrible) schrecklich. 2 adv (dated inf: very) verteufelt (dated inf); funny, amusing furchtbar.

devilishly ['devlɪʃlɪ] adv (a) behave abscheulich. (b) (dated inf) see devilish 2.

devilishness ['devlɪʃnɪs] n Teuflische(s) nt (of an +dat); (of behaviour) Abscheulichkeit f.

devil-may-care [devlmeɪ'kɛəʳ] adj leichtsinnig, vollständig unbekümmert; (in a selfish way) Nach-mir-die-Sintflut-.

devilment ['devlmənt] n (grober) Unfug. **out of sheer ~** aus lauter Übermut; **a piece of ~** (old) (grober) Unfug; **full of ~** voller Übermut.

devilry ['devlrɪ] n (a) (mischief) (grober) Unfug. **a piece of childish ~** ein Dummejungenstreich m. (b) (black magic) Teufelskunst f. (c) (extreme wickedness, cruelty) Teufelei f.

devil's advocate n des Teufels Advokat, Advocatus Diaboli m.

devious ['diːvɪəs] adj (a) path, argumentation gewunden. **by a ~ route** auf einem Umweg; **he has a very ~ mind** er hat sehr verschlungene Gedankengänge, er denkt immer um viele Ecken (inf). (b) (dishonest) method, manoeuvre, route krumm (inf), fragwürdig; person verschlagen, hinterhältig. **he has a very ~ mind** er ist durch und durch verschlagen.

deviously ['diːvɪəslɪ] adv verschlagen, hinterhältig. **~ worded** verklausuliert.

deviousness ['di:vɪəsnɪs] n see adj (a) Gewundenheit f. (b) Fragwürdigkeit f; Verschlagenheit, Hinterhältigkeit f.

devise [dɪ'vaɪz] 1 vt (a) scheme, style sich (dat) ausdenken. (b) (Jur) hinterlassen, vermachen. 2 n (Jur) Vermächtnis nt, Hinterlassenschaft f.

devitalization [di:ˌvaɪtəlaɪ'zeɪʃən] n Schwächung f.

devitalize [di:'vaɪtəlaɪz] vt schwächen.

devoid [dɪ'vɔɪd] adj: ~ of bar (+gen), ohne.

devolution [di:vəˈlu:ʃən] n (a) (of power) Übertragung f (from ... to von ... auf +acc); (Pol) Dezentralisierung f. (b) (Jur: of property) (active devolving) Übertragung f; (being devolved) Übergang m. (c) (Biol) Rückentwicklung, Degeneration f.

devolve [dɪ'vɒlv] (on, upon auf +acc) 1 vi (duty, property etc) übergehen. 2 vt duty übertragen.

devote [dɪ'vəʊt] vt time, life, oneself, book, chapter, attention widmen (to dat); thought verwenden (to auf +acc); building verwenden (to für); resources bestimmen (to für).

devoted [dɪ'vəʊtɪd] adj ergeben; followers, service, friendship treu; admirer eifrig. he/his time is ~ to his work/children er geht in seiner Arbeit/seinen Kindern auf/seine Zeit ist seiner Arbeit/seinen Kindern gewidmet; your ~ servant/son (old) Ihr ergebener Diener/Sohn (old).

devotedly [dɪ'vəʊtɪdlɪ] adv hingebungsvoll; serve, follow treu; support eifrig.

devotee [ˌdevəʊ'ti:] n Anhänger(in f) m; (of a writer) Verehrer(in f) m; (of music also, poetry) Liebhaber(in f) m.

devotion [dɪ'vəʊʃən] n (a) (to friend, wife etc) Ergebenheit f (to gegenüber); (to work) Hingabe f (to an +acc). ~ to duty Pflichteifer m. (b) (of part of building, time etc) (to für) Verwendung f; (of resources) Bestimmung f. (c) (Rel) ~s pl Andacht f; to be at one's ~s in Andacht versunken sein.

devotional [dɪ'vəʊʃənl] adj book, literature religiös. ~ objects Devotionalien pl.

devour [dɪ'vaʊəʳ] vt (lit, fig) verschlingen. I could ~ you ich habe dich zum Fressen gern, du bist wirklich zum Fressen; to be ~ed by jealousy/an all-consuming passion von Eifersucht/einer unersättlichen Leidenschaft verzehrt werden.

devouring [dɪ'vaʊərɪŋ] adj hunger, passion verzehrend.

devout [dɪ'vaʊt] adj (+er) person fromm; hope sehnlich(st).

devoutly [dɪ'vaʊtlɪ] adv pray fromm; hope sehnlich(st).

dew [dju:] n Tau m.

dew: ~claw n Afterkralle or -klaue f; ~drop n Tautropfen m; ~lap n (on cow) Wamme f; (hum: on person) Doppelkinn nt; ~pond n flacher Teich, der sich aus Regenwasser bildet.

dewy ['dju:ɪ] adj (+er) grass taufeucht; skin taufrisch. her eyes were ~ ihre Augen hatten einen feuchten Schimmer.

dewy-eyed ['dju:ɪaɪd] adj (innocent, naive) naiv; (trusting) vertrauensselig. to go all ~ feuchte Augen bekommen; to look all ~ mit großen Augen in die Welt schauen.

dexterity [deks'terɪtɪ] n (a) Geschick nt. his ~ in or at conducting the negotiations sein Geschick bei der Verhandlungsführung. (b) (right-handedness) Rechtshändigkeit f.

dexterous, dextrous ['dekstrəs] adj (a) (skilful) person, movement geschickt. (b) (rare: right-handed) rechtshändig.

dextrose ['dekstrəʊz] n Dextrose f, Traubenzucker m.

DHSS (Brit) abbr of **Department of Health and Social Security.**

diabetes [ˌdaɪə'bi:ti:z] n Zuckerkrankheit f, Diabetes m, Zucker no art (inf).

diabetic [ˌdaɪə'betɪk] 1 adj (a) zuckerkrank, diabetisch (spec). (b) beer, chocolate Diabetiker-. 2 n Zuckerkranke(r) mf, Diabetiker(in f) m.

diabolic(al) [ˌdaɪə'bɒlɪk(əl)] adj (a) power, invention, action diabolisch, teuflisch. (b) (sl) weather, child, heat saumäßig (sl). it's diabolical! das ist ja saumäßig! (sl).

diabolically [ˌdaɪə'bɒlɪkəlɪ] adv see adj.

diachronic [ˌdaɪə'krɒnɪk] adj diachron.

diacritic [ˌdaɪə'krɪtɪk] 1 adj diakritisch. 2 n diakritisches Zeichen.

diacritical [ˌdaɪə'krɪtɪkəl] adj diakritisch.

diadem ['daɪədem] n Diadem nt.

diaeresis, (US) dieresis [daɪ'erɪsɪs] n Diärese f; (sign) Trema nt.

diagnose ['daɪəgnəʊz] vt (Med, fig) diagnostizieren.

diagnosis [ˌdaɪəg'nəʊsɪs] n, pl **diagnoses** [ˌdaɪəg'nəʊsi:z] Diagnose f. to make a ~ eine Diagnose stellen.

diagnostic [ˌdaɪəg'nɒstɪk] adj diagnostisch.

diagnostician [ˌdaɪəgnɒs'tɪʃən] n Diagnostiker(in f) m.

diagonal [daɪ'ægənl] 1 adj diagonal. 2 n Diagonale f.

diagonally [daɪ'ægənəlɪ] adv cut, fold diagonal; (loosely: crossways) schräg. ~ across sth walk schräg über etw (acc); be placed sth schräg über etw (dat); to be ~ opposite sth einer Sache (dat) schräg gegenüber sein; the car was struck ~ by a lorry das Auto wurde schräg von hinten/vorn von einem Lastwagen gerammt.

diagram ['daɪəgræm] n (Math) Diagramm nt; (of machine etc also) Schaubild nt; (chart: of figures etc) graphische Darstellung. as shown in the ~ wie das Schaubild or Diagramm/die graphische Darstellung zeigt; you don't have to make me a ~ (fig inf) Sie brauchen es mir nicht aufzuzeichnen (inf).

diagrammatic [ˌdaɪəgrə'mætɪk] adj diagrammatisch. in ~ form in einem Schaubild or Diagramm/graphisch dargestellt.

dial ['daɪəl] 1 n (a) (of clock) Zifferblatt nt; (of speedometer, pressure gauge) Skala f; (Telec) Wähl- or Nummernscheibe f; (on radio etc) (Frequenzbereich-)Einstellskala f; see sundial. (b) (sl: face) Visage f (sl). 2 vt (Telec) wählen. to ~ direct durchwählen; you can ~ London direct man kann nach London durchwählen; to ~ 999 den Notruf wählen; to ~ a wrong number eine falsche Nummer wählen, sich verwählen. 3 vi (Telec) wählen.

dialect ['daɪəlekt] 1 n Dialekt m; (local, rural also) Mundart f. the country people spoke in ~ die Landbevölkerung sprach Dialekt; the play is in ~ das Stück ist in Dialekt or Mundart geschrieben. 2 attr word Dialekt-.

dialectal [ˌdaɪə'lektl] adj see n dialektal, Dialekt-; mundartlich, Mundart-.

dialectical [ˌdaɪə'lektɪkəl] adj dialektisch. ~ materialism dialektischer Materialismus.

dialectician [ˌdaɪəlek'tɪʃən] n Dialektiker(in f) m.

dialectic(s) [ˌdaɪə'lektɪk(s)] n (with sing vb) Dialektik f.

dialling ['daɪəlɪŋ]: ~ code n Vorwahl(nummer), Ortsnetzkennzahl (form) f; ~ tone n (Brit Telec) Amtszeichen nt.

dialogue, (US) dialog ['daɪəlɒg] n (all senses) Dialog m. ~ coach Dialogregisseur m.

dial tone n (US Telec) Amtszeichen nt.

dialysis [daɪ'ælɪsɪs] n Dialyse f.

diamanté [ˌdaɪə'mæntɪ] n Straß m; (rare: fabric) mit Pailletten besetzter Stoff.

diameter [daɪ'æmɪtəʳ] n Durchmesser m. to be one metre in ~ einen Durchmesser von einem Meter haben; what's its ~? welchen Durchmesser hat es?, wie groß ist es im Durchmesser?

diametrical [ˌdaɪə'metrɪkəl] adj (Math, fig) diametral.

diametrically [ˌdaɪə'metrɪkəlɪ] adv diametral. ~ opposed (to) diametral entgegengesetzt (+dat).

diamond ['daɪəmənd] n (a) Diamant m. it was a case of ~ cut ~ (Prov) da sind die Richtigen aneinandergeraten; see rough ~. (b) ~s (Cards) Karo pl; the King of ~s der Karokönig. (c) (Baseball) Innenfeld nt. (d) (Math: rhombus) Raute f.

diamond in cpds ring etc Diamant-; ~ cutter n Diamantschneider(in f) m; (Ind) Diamantschleifer(in f) m; ~ cutting n Diamantschleifen nt; ~ drill n Diamantbohrer m; ~ merchant n Diamantenhändler(in f) m; ~-shaped adj rautenförmig; ~ wedding n diamantene Hochzeit.

Diana [daɪ'ænə] n Diana f.

diapason [ˌdaɪə'peɪzən] n (a) Diapason m or nt. (b) (of organ) Diapason m or nt. open/stopped ~ Prinzipal nt/gedacktes Prinzipal.

diaper ['daɪəpəʳ] n (US) Windel f.

diaphanous [daɪ'æfənəs] adj durchscheinend.

diaphragm ['daɪəfræm] n (Anat, Phys, Chem) Diaphragma nt; (abdominal also) Zwerchfell nt; (Phot also) Blende f; (in telephone) Membran f; (contraceptive) Pessar nt.

diarist ['daɪərɪst] n (of personal events) Tagebuchschreiber(in f) m; (of contemporary events) Chronist m.

diarrhoea, (US) diarrhea [ˌdaɪə'rɪə] n Durchfall m, Diarrhöe f. verbal ~ Laberei f (inf); the speaker was suffering from verbal ~ der Redner hatte geistigen Dünnschiß (sl).

diary ['daɪərɪ] n (of personal experience) Tagebuch nt; (for noting dates) (Termin)kalender m. to keep a ~ Tagebuch führen; desk/pocket ~ Schreibtisch-/Taschenkalender m; I've got it in my ~ es steht in meinem (Termin)kalender.

Diaspora ['daɪəspərə] n Diaspora f.

diastole [daɪ'æstəlɪ] n Diastole f.

diatonic [ˌdaɪə'tɒnɪk] adj diatonisch.

diatribe ['daɪətraɪb] n Schmährede f.

dibble ['dɪbl] 1 n Pflanz- or Setzholz nt. 2 vt plant setzen, pflanzen; hole machen, graben.

dice [daɪs] 1 n, pl – Würfel m. to play ~ Würfel spielen, würfeln; ~ cup or box Würfelbecher m; no ~ (sl) (das) ist nicht drin (inf). 2 vi würfeln. to ~ with death mit dem Tode spielen. 3 vt (Cook) würfelig or in Würfel schneiden.

dicey ['daɪsɪ] adj (Brit inf) riskant.

dichotomy [dɪ'kɒtəmɪ] n Trennung, Dichotomie f.

dick [dɪk] n (a) (sl: detective) Schnüffler m (inf). private ~ Privatdetektiv m; see clever. (b) (vulg: penis) Schwanz m (sl).

dickens ['dɪkɪnz] n (euph inf for devil) Teufel m; for phrases see devil 1 (c).

dicker ['dɪkəʳ] vi (US) feilschen.

dickey, dicky ['dɪkɪ] n (a) (inf: on shirt) Hemdbrust f; (bowtie) Fliege f. (b) (also ~ seat) Notsitz m in einem Zweisitzer.

dicky ['dɪkɪ] adj (inf) heart angeknackst (inf). I feel a bit ~ (dated) ich bin ziemlich ab (inf) or erschossen (inf).

dickybird ['dɪkɪbɜːd] n (baby-talk) Piepmatz m (baby-talk). I didn't see a ~ (inf) ich habe überhaupt nichts gesehen.

dicta ['dɪktə] pl of dictum.

dictaphone ® ['dɪktəfəʊn] n Diktaphon nt.

dictate [dɪk'teɪt] 1 vti (all senses) diktieren. 2 ['dɪkteɪt] n usu pl Diktat nt; (of reason) Gebote pl.

♦**dictate to** vi +prep obj person diktieren (+dat), Vorschriften machen (+dat). I won't be ~d ~ ich lasse mir nicht diktieren, ich lasse mir keine Vorschriften machen.

dictation [dɪk'teɪʃən] n (also Sch) Diktat nt. to take a ~ ein Diktat aufnehmen; to read at ~ speed in Diktiertempo lesen.

dictator [dɪk'teɪtəʳ] n (a) (Pol, fig) Diktator m. (b) (of letter, passage) Diktierende(r) mf.

dictatorial adj, ~ly adv [ˌdɪktə'tɔːrɪəl, -ɪ] (Pol, fig) diktatorisch.

dictatorship [dɪk'teɪtəʃɪp] n (Pol, fig) Diktatur f.

diction ['dɪkʃən] n (a) (Liter) Diktion f. poetic ~ poetische Sprache. (b) (way of speaking) Diktion f.

dictionary ['dɪkʃənrɪ] n Wörterbuch nt, Diktionär m (old).

dictum ['dɪktəm] n, pl **dicta** Diktum nt.

did [dɪd] pret of do².

didactic adj, ~ally adv [dɪ'dæktɪk, -əlɪ] didaktisch.

diddle ['dɪdl] vt (inf) übers Ohr hauen (inf), beschummeln. you have been ~d man hat Sie übers Ohr gehauen; to ~ sb out of sth jdm etw abgaunern (inf).

diddler ['dɪdləʳ] n (inf) Spitzbube, Gauner m.

didn't ['dɪdənt] = did not; see do².

diddums ['dɪdəmz] interj (inf) du Armer/Arme.

didst [dɪdst] (obs) = didst thou; see do².

die¹ [daɪ] vi **(a)** sterben; *soldier also* fallen; *(motor, engine)* absterben; *(planet)* vergehen. **to ~ of hunger/pneumonia/grief** Hungers *(geh)* or vor Hunger/an Lungenentzündung/vor or aus Kummer sterben; **to ~ by one's own hand** von eigener Hand sterben, Hand an sich legen; **~d a hero** er starb als Held; **to be dying** im Sterben liegen; **never say ~!** nur nicht aufgeben!; **to ~ laughing** *(inf)* sich totlachen *(inf)*.

(b) to be dying to do sth *(fig)* darauf brennen, etw zu tun, brennend gern etw tun wollen; **I'm dying for a cigarette** ich brauche jetzt unbedingt eine Zigarette; **I'm dying to know what happened** ich bin schrecklich gespannt zu hören, was passiert ist; **he's dying to meet you/to get home** er möchte Sie brennend gern kennenlernen/er brennt darauf, heimzukommen.

(c) *(disappear) (love)* vergehen, ersterben *(geh)*, erlöschen *(geh)*; *(memory)* (ver)schwinden; *(custom)* aussterben; *(empire)* untergehen. **the secret ~d with him** er nahm das Geheimnis mit ins Grab; **rumours ~ hard** Gerüchte sind nicht totzukriegen.

2 vt **to ~ a hero's/a violent death** den Heldentod/eines gewaltsamen Todes sterben; **to ~ the death** *(plan etc)* sterben *(inf)*.

♦**die away** vi *(sound, voice)* schwächer or leiser werden; *(wind)* nachlassen, sich legen; *(anger)* sich legen, vergehen.

♦**die back** vi absterben.

♦**die down** vi nachlassen; *(fire)* herunterbrennen; *(flames)* kleiner werden; *(storm, wind also)* sich legen, schwächer werden; *(noise also)* leiser werden, schwächer werden; *(emotion also)* sich legen; *(quarrel, protest also)* schwächer werden.

♦**die off** vi (hin)wegsterben; *(animals, people also)* (der Reihe nach) sterben.

♦**die out** vi aussterben.

die² n **(a)** pl **dice** Würfel m. **the ~ is cast** *(fig)* die Würfel sind gefallen; *see also* **dice**. **(b)** pl **-s** *(Tech)* Gesenk nt, Gußform f; *(in minting)* Prägestempel m.

die casting n *(article)* Spritzguß(stück nt) m; *(process)* Spritzgußverfahren nt.

die-hard ['daɪhɑːd] **1** n zäher Kämpfer; *(resistant to change)* Ewiggestrige(r) mf. **2** adj zäh; *(pej)* reaktionär.

dieresis n *(US) see* **diaeresis**.

diesel ['diːzəl] n *(train)* Dieseltriebwagen m; *(car)* Diesel m; *(fuel)* Dieselöl nt, Diesel no art.

diesel: **~-electric** adj dieselelektrisch; **~ engine** n Dieselmotor m; **~ oil** n Dieselkraftstoff m; **~ train** n Dieseltriebwagen m.

die sinker n Werkzeugmacher(in f) m.

diet¹ ['daɪət] **1** n **(a)** Nahrung f; *(special ~)* Diät f; *(slimming ~)* Schlankheitskur f. **to put sb on a ~/special ~** jdm eine Schlankheitskur/Diät verordnen; **to be/go on a ~** eine Schlankheitskur machen; **high protein ~** proteinreiche Diät; **~ sheet** Diät-/Schlankheits(fahr)plan m.

2 vi eine Schlankheitskur machen.

diet² n *(assembly)* Abgeordnetenversammlung f. **the German/Japanese ~** der deutsche/japanische Reichstag; **the D~ of Worms** der Reichstag zu Worms.

dietary ['daɪətərɪ] adj Diät-, diätetisch, Ernährungs-.

dietetic [,daɪə'tetɪk] adj Diät-, diätetisch, Ernährungs-.

dietetics [,daɪə'tetɪks] n sing Diätlehre, Diätetik f.

dietician [,daɪə'tɪʃən] n Diätist(in f), Ernährungswissenschaftler(in f) m.

differ ['dɪfəʳ] vi **(a)** *(be different)* sich unterscheiden *(from* von*)*. **they ~ed in one respect** sie unterschieden sich in einer Hinsicht; **tastes ~** die Geschmäcker sind verschieden; **I ~ from you in that ...** ich unterscheide mich von Ihnen darin, daß ...

(b) *(disagree)* **to ~ with sb over sth** über etw anderer Meinung sein als jd; **we ~ed sharply over that** darin waren wir völlig verschiedener Meinung; *see* **agree, beg**.

difference ['dɪfrəns] n **(a)** Unterschied m; *(in age)* (Alters)unterschied m *(in, between* zwischen *+ dat)*. **that makes a big ~ to me** das ist für mich ein großer Unterschied; **to make a ~ to or in sth** einen Unterschied bei etw machen; **that makes a big ~, that makes all the ~** das ändert die Sache völlig, das gibt der Sache *(dat)* ein ganz anderes Gesicht; **a bottle of wine would make all the ~ in the world** da liegt der entscheidende Unterschied; **what ~ does it make if ...** was wäre denn anders or was macht es schon, wenn ...; **what ~ is that to you?** was macht dir das aus?; **it makes no ~ es ist egal** *(inf)*; **it makes no ~ to me** das ist mir egal or einerlei; **it makes a lot of ~** das ist ein erheblicher or gewaltiger Unterschied; **cooperation makes all the ~** Zusammenarbeit macht viel aus; **for all the ~ it makes** obwohl es ja eigentlich egal ist; **a car/dress with a ~** *(inf)* ein Auto/Kleid, das mal was anderes ist.

(b) *(between numbers, amounts)* Differenz f. **to pay the ~** die Differenz or den Rest(betrag) bezahlen.

(c) *(quarrel)* Differenz, Auseinandersetzung f. **a ~ of opinion** eine Meinungsverschiedenheit; **to settle one's ~s** die Differenzen or Meinungsverschiedenheiten beilegen.

different ['dɪfrənt] adj **(a)** andere(r, s), anders pred *(from, to* als*)*; *two people, things* verschieden, unterschiedlich. **completely ~** völlig verschieden; *(changed)* völlig verändert; **that's ~!** das ist was anderes!; **in what way are they ~?** wie unterscheiden sie sich?; **to feel a ~ person** ein ganz anderer Mensch sein; **quite a ~ way of doing sth** eine völlig andere Methode, etw zu tun; **to do something ~** etwas anderes tun; **that's quite a ~ matter** das ist etwas völlig anderes; **she's quite ~ from what you think** sie ist ganz anders, als Sie denken; **he wants to be ~** er will unbedingt anders or etwas Besonderes sein.

(b) *(various)* verschieden.

differential [,dɪfə'renʃəl] **1** adj *(different) rates of pay, treatment* unterschiedlich, verschieden; *(distinguishing) feature* unterscheidend. **~ calculus** Differentialrechnung f; **~ coeffi-**

-cient *(Math)* Ableitung f; **~ gear** Differential(getriebe) nt.

2 n **(a)** *(difference)* Unterschied m; *(Math)* Differential nt. **wage/salary ~** Lohn-/Gehaltsunterschiede or -differenzen pl.

(b) *(Aut)* Differential(getriebe) nt.

differentially [,dɪfə'renʃəlɪ] adv *(Tech)* differential.

differentiate [,dɪfə'renʃɪeɪt] **1** vt *(perceive as different)* unterscheiden, trennen; *(be the difference between)* unterscheiden; *(Math)* differenzieren. **to ~ x and y/x from y** x und y voneinander/x von y unterscheiden.

2 vi *(see difference)* unterscheiden, einen Unterschied machen, differenzieren; *(two things: become different)* sich unterschiedlich or anders entwickeln. **to ~ between people** einen Unterschied zwischen Menschen machen.

differentiation [,dɪfərenʃɪ'eɪʃən] n Unterscheidung, Differenzierung f.

differently ['dɪfrəntlɪ] adv anders *(from* als*)*; *(from one another)* verschieden, unterschiedlich. **he thinks ~ (from you)** er denkt anders (als Sie).

difficult ['dɪfɪkəlt] adj **(a)** schwierig, schwer; *(hard to understand)* schwer, diffizil *(geh)*; *writer* kompliziert, schwierig. **sth is ~ to do** es ist schwierig or schwer, etw zu tun; **it is ~ for me** or **I find it ~ to understand** es fällt mir or ist für mich schwer, das zu glauben; **we'll make things ~ for him** wir werden es ihm schwer or nicht leicht machen; **it's ~ to know whether ...** es ist schwer zu sagen, ob ...; **there's nothing ~ about it** das ist nicht schwierig or schwer; **the ~ thing is ...** die Schwierigkeit liegt darin ...; **it's ~ to deny that ...** es läßt sich kaum leugnen, daß ...; **he's just trying to be ~** er will nur Schwierigkeiten machen.

(b) *neighbour, character, child* schwierig. **she is ~ to get on with** es ist schwer, mit ihr auszukommen, mit ihr ist schwer auskommen.

difficulty ['dɪfɪkəltɪ] n Schwierigkeit f. **with/without ~** mit/ohne Schwierigkeiten pl; **he had ~ in doing that** es fiel ihm schwer or nicht leicht, das zu tun, er hatte Schwierigkeiten dabei; **a slight ~ in breathing** leichte Atembeschwerden pl; **there was some ~ in finding him** es war schwierig or nicht leicht, ihn zu finden; **the ~ is in choosing or to choose** die Wahl ist nicht leicht; **they hadn't appreciated the ~ of finding somewhere to live** sie hatten nicht bedacht, wie schwierig es sein würde, eine Wohnung zu finden; **in ~ or difficulties** in Schwierigkeiten pl; **to get into difficulties** in Schwierigkeiten geraten; **to get out of difficulties** Schwierigkeiten überwinden; **he was working under great difficulties** er arbeitete unter äußerst schwierigen Bedingungen.

diffidence ['dɪfɪdəns] n Bescheidenheit, Zurückhaltung f; *(smile)* Zaghaftigkeit f.

diffident ['dɪfɪdənt] adj zurückhaltend, bescheiden; *smile* zaghaft. **he was very ~ about offering his help** er hat zaghaft seine Hilfe angeboten.

diffidently ['dɪfɪdəntlɪ] adv *see* adj.

diffract [dɪ'frækt] vt beugen.

diffraction [dɪ'frækʃən] n Diffraktion, Beugung f.

diffuse [dɪ'fjuːz] **1** vt *light, heat, gas, rays* ausstrahlen, verbreiten; *fluid* ausgießen, ausschütten; *(Chem)* diffundieren, verwischen; *perfume* verbreiten, verströmen; *knowledge, custom, news* verbreiten.

2 vi ausstrahlen, sich ver- or ausbreiten; *(fluid)* sich ausbreiten; *(Chem)* diffundieren, sich verwischen; *(perfume, odour)* ausströmen; *(custom, news)* sich verbreiten.

3 [dɪ'fjuːs] adj **(a)** *gas, rays, light* diffus. **(b)** *(verbose) style, writer* langatmig, weitschweifig.

diffused [dɪ'fjuːzd] adj verbreitet; *lighting* indirekt.

diffuseness [dɪ'fjuːsnɪs] n *(of style)* Weitschweifigkeit f.

diffuser [dɪ'fjuːzəʳ] n *(for light)* (Licht)diffusor m.

diffusion [dɪ'fjuːʒən] n *(of light, heat, rays, fluid etc)* Ausbreitung f; *(Chem)* Diffusion f; *(of perfume, odour)* Ausströmung f; *(of knowledge, custom, news)* Verbreitung f.

dig [dɪg] *(vb: pret, ptp dug)* **1** vt **(a)** *ground* graben; *trench, hole, tunnel etc also* ausheben. **to ~ potatoes** Kartoffeln roden; **they dug their way out of prison** sie gruben sich *(dat)* einen (Flucht)tunnel aus dem Gefängnis.

(b) *(poke, thrust)* bohren *(sth into sth* etw in etw *acc)*. **to ~ sb in the ribs** jdm or jdn in die Rippen stoßen.

(c) *(sl) (enjoy)* stehen auf *(+dat)* *(inf)*; *(take notice of)* sich *(dat)* angucken; *(understand)* kapieren *(inf)*.

2 vi **(a)** *(person)* graben; *(dog, pig also)* wühlen; *(Tech)* schürfen; *(Archeol)* (aus)graben, Ausgrabungen machen. **to ~ for minerals** Erz schürfen; **to ~ in one's pockets for sth in** seinen Taschen nach etw suchen or wühlen.

(b) *(inf: taunt)* **to ~ at sb** jdn anschießen or anmotzen *(inf)*.

(c) *(dated Brit inf: lodge)* seine Bude haben *(inf)* *(with* bei*)*.

3 n **(a)** *(with hand, elbow)* Puff, Stoß m. **to give sb a ~ in the ribs** jdm einen Rippenstoß geben.

(b) *(sarcastic remark)* Seitenhieb m, Spitze f. **to have a ~ at sb/sth** eine Spitze gegen jdn loslassen *(inf)*, eine spitze Bemerkung über jdn machen.

(c) *(Archeol)* (Aus)grabung f; *(site)* Ausgrabungsstätte f.

♦**dig around** vi *(inf)* herumsuchen.

♦**dig in 1** vi **(a)** *(also ~ oneself ~)* *(Mil, fig)* sich eingraben. **(b)** *(inf: eat)* reinhauen *(inf)*. **2** vt sep **(a)** *compost* unter- or eingraben. **(b)** *(Mil) troops, tanks* eingraben. **(c)** **to ~ one's spurs ~** (den Pferd) die Sporen geben; **to ~ one's heels ~** *(lit)* die Hacken in den Boden stemmen; *(fig)* sich auf die Hinterbeine stellen *(inf)*.

♦**dig into** vi +prep obj **(a)** *(inf) cake, pie* herfallen über *(+acc)* *(inf)*. **(b)** *sb's past* wühlen in *(+dat)*.

♦**dig out** vt sep *(lit, fig)* ausgraben *(of* aus*)*.

♦**dig up** vt sep **(a)** *earth* aufwühlen; *lawn, garden* umgraben. **(b)** *plants, treasure, body, idea* ausgraben; *weeds* (aus)jäten; *(fig) fact, information also* auftun; *solution* finden. **where did you ~ her ~?** *(inf)* wo hast du die denn aufgegabelt? *(inf)*.

digest [daɪˈdʒest] **1** vt (lit, fig) verdauen. **2** vi verdauen. **3** [ˈdaɪdʒest] n **(a)** (of book, facts) Digest m or nt, Auswahl f. **(b)** (Jur) Gesetzessammlung f.

digestible [dɪˈdʒestəbl] adj verdaulich.

digestion [dɪˈdʒestʃən] n Verdauung f.

digestive [dɪˈdʒestɪv] adj Verdauungs-. ~ (biscuit) (Brit) Keks m aus Roggenmehl.

digger [ˈdɪgəʳ] n **(a)** (person) (miner) Bergmann m; Goldgräber m; (navvy) Straßenarbeiter m; (Tech: excavator) Bagger m. **(b)** (sl) australischer/neuseeländischer Soldat; (Austral inf: pal) Kumpel m.

diggings [ˈdɪgɪŋz] npl **(a)** (Min) Bergwerk nt; (minerals) Funde pl; (Archeol) Grabungsort m. **(b)** (US) see digs.

digit [ˈdɪdʒɪt] n **(a)** (finger) Finger m; (toe) Zehe f. **(b)** (Math) Ziffer f. a four-~ number eine vierstellige Zahl.

digital [ˈdɪdʒɪtəl] adj **(a)** clock, computer Digital-. **(b)** (Anat) Finger-. **2** n (of piano, organ) Taste f.

digitalin [ˌdɪdʒɪˈteɪlɪn] n Digitalis f.

digitalis [ˌdɪdʒɪˈteɪlɪs] n Digitalis f.

dignified [ˈdɪgnɪfaɪd] adj person (ehr)würdig; behaviour, manner fein. he maintained a ~ silence er schwieg würdevoll.

dignify [ˈdɪgnɪfaɪ] vt **(a)** ehren, auszeichnen. **(b)** to ~ sth with the name of or by calling it ... etw mit dem anspruchsvollen Namen ... belegen.

dignitary [ˈdɪgnɪtərɪ] n Würdenträger(in f) m. the local dignitaries die Honoratioren am Ort.

dignity [ˈdɪgnɪtɪ] n **(a)** (of person, occasion, work) Würde f. to stand on one's ~ förmlich sein; to lose one's ~ sich blamieren; that would be beneath my ~ das wäre unter meiner Würde. **(b)** (high rank, post) Rang m, (hohe) Stellung; (title) Würde f.

digraph [ˈdaɪgræf] n Digraph m.

digress [daɪˈgres] vi abschweifen. but I ~ doch ich schweife ab.

digression [daɪˈgreʃən] n Abschweifung f, Exkurs m. this by way of ~ aber das nur nebenbei.

digressive [daɪˈgresɪv] adj abschweifend, abweichend.

digs [dɪgz] npl (Brit) Bude f (inf). to be in ~ ein möbliertes Zimmer or eine Bude (inf) haben.

dihedral [daɪˈhiːdrəl] **1** adj zweiflächig. **2** n V-Winkel m; (Aviat) V-Stellung f.

dike [daɪk] n, vt see dyke.

dilapidated [dɪˈlæpɪdeɪtɪd] adj house verfallen, heruntergekommen, baufällig; book schäbig, abgegriffen; clothes verschlissen, schäbig, abgetragen.

dilapidation [dɪˌlæpɪˈdeɪʃən] n **(a)** (of building) Baufälligkeit f, Verfall m; (of book, clothes) Schäbigkeit f. in a state of ~ in schlechtem Zustand. **(b)** (Geol) Verwitterung f.

dilate [daɪˈleɪt] **1** vt weiten, dehnen. **2** vi sich weiten, sich dehnen; (pupils) sich erweitern. ~d pupils erweiterte Pupillen pl; to ~ (up)on (talk at length) sich verbreiten über (+acc).

dilatation [ˌdaɪləˈteɪʃən], **dilation** [daɪˈleɪʃən] n Ausdehnung f, Erweiterung f; (of pupils) Erweiterung f. ~ and curettage Dilation und Kürettage (spec), Ausschabung f.

dilatoriness [ˈdɪlətərɪnɪs] n Langsamkeit f, Zögern nt (in doing sth etw zu tun).

dilatory [ˈdɪlətərɪ] adj **(a)** person langsam; reply verspätet. to be ~ sich (dat) Zeit lassen; he was rather ~ in answering er ließ sich mit der Antwort Zeit. **(b)** (delaying) action, policy Verzögerungs-, Hinhalte-.

dildo [ˈdɪldəʊ] n Godemiché m.

dilemma [daɪˈlemə] n Dilemma nt. to be in a ~ sich in einem Dilemma befinden, in der Klemme sitzen (inf); to place sb in a ~ jdn in ein Dilemma or in ein Dilemma bringen.

dilettante [ˌdɪlɪˈtæntɪ] **1** n, pl dilettanti [ˌdɪlɪˈtæntɪ] Amateur(in f), Dilettant(in f) m; (Art) Kunstliebhaber(in f) m. **2** adj amateurhaft, stümperhaft.

dilettantism [ˌdɪlɪˈtæntɪzəm] n Dilettantismus m; Kunstliebhaberei f.

diligence [ˈdɪlɪdʒəns] n Eifer m; (in work etc also) Fleiß m.

diligent [ˈdɪlɪdʒənt] adj person eifrig; (in work etc also) fleißig; search, work sorgfältig, genau. to be ~ in doing sth etw eifrig or mit großem Eifer tun.

diligently [ˈdɪlɪdʒəntlɪ] adv see adj.

dill [dɪl] n Dill m.

dilly-dally [ˈdɪlɪdælɪ] vi (over work etc) trödeln; (when walking also) bummeln. without ~ing ohne zu trödeln/bummeln; no ~ing! ein bißchen dalli!

dilute [daɪˈluːt] **1** vt orange juice, milk etc verdünnen; colour dämpfen, abschwächen; (fig) mildern, (ab)schwächen. ~ to taste nach Geschmack verdünnen. **2** adj verdünnt.

dilution [daɪˈluːʃən] n see vt Verdünnung f; Dämpfung f, Abschwächung f; Milderung f.

dim [dɪm] **1** adj (+er) **(a)** light schwach, trüb, schummerig (inf); lamp schwach, dunkel, trüb; room, forest etc halbdunkel, dämmerig, schummerig (inf). to grow ~ schwach or dunkel werden; the room grew ~ im Zimmer wurde es dunkel; it's a ~ look-out for him es sieht sehr trübe or schlecht für ihn aus. **(b)** eyesight schwach; colour gedeckt, glanzlos; eyes trüb; metal matt, glanzlos. **(c)** sound, memory schwach, verschwommen; outline, shape undeutlich, verschwommen, unscharf. **(d)** (mentally) begriffsstutzig, beschränkt; (inf: stupid) schwer von Begriff or Kapee (inf). **(e)** (inf) to take a ~ view of sb/sth wenig or nicht viel von jdm/etw halten; he took a ~ view of his selling the car sie hielt nichts davon, daß er das Auto verkaufte.
2 vt **(a)** light dämpfen; lamp verdunkeln. to ~ the lights (Theat) das Licht langsam ausgehen lassen; to ~ one's headlights (esp US) abblenden.
(b) sight, mind, senses trüben; colour dämpfen, decken; metal mattieren; beauty beeinträchtigen; glory beeinträchtigen, verblassen lassen.
(c) sound dämpfen; outline unscharf or undeutlich machen; memory trüben.
3 vi **(a)** (light) schwach or trübe werden; (lamps) verlöschen, dunkler werden.
(b) (sight) nachlassen, getrübt werden; (colour) gedämpft or matter werden; (metal) mattiert werden; (beauty) getrübt werden, (memory) verblassen; (glory) verblassen, vergehen.
(c) (sound) leiser werden; (outline) undeutlich or unscharf werden, verschwimmen; (memory) nachlassen.

♦**dim out** vt sep (US) verdunkeln.

dime [daɪm] n (US) Zehncentstück nt. it's not worth a ~ (inf) das ist keinen (roten) Heller or keine fünf Pfennig or keinen Sechser (dial) wert; they're a ~ a dozen das ist Dutzendware; ~ novel Groschen- or Schundroman m.

dimension [daɪˈmenʃən] n Dimension f; (measurement) Abmessung(en pl) f, Maß nt. a project of vast ~(s) ein Projekt von gewaltigen Ausmaßen or von gewaltiger Größenordnung; it adds a new ~ to ... das gibt ... (dat) eine neue Dimension.

-dimensional [daɪˈmenʃənl] adj suf -dimensional.

diminish [dɪˈmɪnɪʃ] **1** vt **(a)** verringern; price, speed, authority also herabsetzen; value, strength also (ver)mindern; number also verkleinern; (enthusiasm) dämpfen; reputation schmälern. a ~ed staff eine reduzierte Belegschaft; ~ed responsibility (Jur) verminderte Zurechnungsfähigkeit.
(b) (Mus) (um einen Halbton) vermindern. ~ed vermindert.
2 vi sich verringern; (speed, authority, strength also) abnehmen, sich vermindern; (price also) fallen, sinken; (value also) sich vermindern; (number also) sich verkleinern; (enthusiasm) nachlassen; (reputation) schlechter werden. law of ~ing returns (Econ) Gesetz nt von der fallenden Profitrate; to ~ in numbers weniger werden, zahlenmäßig abnehmen; to ~ in price billiger werden, im Preis sinken; to ~ in value im Wert sinken, an Wert verlieren.

diminuendo [dɪˌmɪnjuˈendəʊ] **1** adv diminuendo. **2** n Diminuendo nt.

diminution [ˌdɪmɪˈnjuːʃən] n (of size) Verringerung f; (of reputation) Schmälerung f; (in enthusiasm) Nachlassen nt.

diminutive [dɪˈmɪnjʊtɪv] **1** adj **(a)** person, object, house, garden winzig, klein. **(b)** (Gram) diminutiv. **2** n (Gram) Verkleinerungsform f, Diminutiv(um) nt.

dimity [ˈdɪmɪtɪ] n Dimitz m.

dimly [ˈdɪmlɪ] adv **(a)** shine schwach; hear also gedämpft, undeutlich; remember also undeutlich; see verschwommen; lit schwach. **(b)** (inf: stupidly) einfältig, begriffsstutzig.

dimmer [ˈdɪməʳ] n (Elec) Abblendungsvorrichtung f; (US Aut) Abblendschalter or -hebel m. ~ switch Dimmer m; (US Aut) Abblendschalter m; ~s (US Aut) Abblendlicht nt; (sidelights) Begrenzungsleuchten pl.

dimness [ˈdɪmnɪs] n see adj **(a)** (of light, sight) Schwäche, Trübheit f; Halbdunkel, Dämmerlicht nt.
(b) Schwäche f; Glanzlosigkeit f; Trübheit f; Mattheit, Glanzlosigkeit f.
(c) Schwäche, Verschwommenheit f; Undeutlichkeit, Verschwommenheit, Unschärfe f.
(d) Begriffsstutzigkeit, Beschränktheit f.

dim-out [ˈdɪmaʊt] n (US) Verdunkelung f.

dimple [ˈdɪmpl] **1** n (on cheek, chin) Grübchen nt; (depression) Delle, Vertiefung f; (on water) Kräuselung f.
2 vi (cheeks) Grübchen bekommen; (person) Grübchen zeigen; (surface) sich einbeulen; (water) sich kräuseln.
3 vt a smile ~d her cheeks sie lächelte und zeigte dabei ihre Grübchen.

dimpled [ˈdɪmpld] adj cheek, chin, arm mit Grübchen.

dim- [dɪm] ~wit n (inf) Blödmann m (inf); ~-witted adj (inf) blöd (inf), dämlich (inf).

din [dɪn] **1** n Lärm m, Getöse nt. an infernal ~ ein Höllenlärm or -spektakel m. **2** vt to ~ sth into sb jdm etw einbleuen. **3** vi the noise was still ~ning in his ears der Lärm dröhnte ihm immer noch in den Ohren.

dine [daɪn] **1** vi speisen, dinieren (old, geh) (on etw). to ~ out außer Haus or auswärts speisen; he ~d out on that story for months diese Geschichte hat ihm monatelang Einladungen zum Essen verschafft. **2** vt bewirten, beköstigen.

diner [ˈdaɪnəʳ] n **(a)** (person) Speisende(r) mf; (in restaurant) Gast m. **(b)** (US) Eßlokal nt. **(c)** (Rail) Speisewagen m.

dinette [daɪˈnet] n Eßecke f.

ding-a-ling [ˈdɪŋəlɪŋ] n Klingeling nt; (fire-engine) Tatütata nt.

ding-dong [ˈdɪŋˈdɒŋ] **1** n Bimbam nt. **2** adj (fig) battle hin- und herwogend.

ding(e)y, dinghy [ˈdɪŋgɪ] n Ding(h)i nt; (collapsible) Schlauchboot nt.

dinginess [ˈdɪndʒɪnɪs] n Unansehnlichkeit f.

dingle [ˈdɪŋgl] n baumbestandene Mulde.

dingo [ˈdɪŋgəʊ] n Dingo m, australischer Wildhund.

dingy¹ [ˈdɪndʒɪ] adj place, furniture schmuddelig.

dingy² [ˈdɪŋgɪ] n see ding(e)y.

dining [ˈdaɪnɪŋ]: ~ car n Speisewagen m; ~ chair n Eßzimmerstuhl m; ~ hall n Speisesaal m; ~ room n Eßzimmer nt; (in hotel) Speiseraum m; ~-table n Eßtisch m.

dinkum [ˈdɪŋkəm] (Austral inf) **1** adj ehrlich; person also anständig, redlich. **2** adv ehrlich.

dinky [ˈdɪŋkɪ] adj **(a)** (Brit inf) schnuckelig (inf). **(b)** ® (also D~) car Modell-.

dinner [ˈdɪnəʳ] n (evening meal) (Haupt)mahlzeit f, Abendessen nt; (formal) (Abend)essen nt; (for cat, dog) Fressen nt. to be at ~ beim Essen sein, (gerade) essen; to be eating or having one's ~ zu Abend/Mittag essen; (dog, cat) (gerade) fressen; we're having people to ~ wir haben Gäste zum Essen; ~'s ready das Essen ist fertig; to finish one's ~ zu Ende essen; what time do you finish ~? wann bist du mit dem Essen fertig?; to go out to ~ (in restaurant) auswärts or außer Haus essen (gehen); (*at friends'*) zum Essen eingeladen sein; **to give a ~ in sb's honour** ein Essen zu jds Ehren geben; **a formal ~** ein offizielles Essen.

dinner: ~ **bell** *n* (Essens)glocke *f*; **the ~ bell has gone** es hat (zum Essen) geläutet; ~**dance** *n Abendessen nt mit Tanz*; ~ **duty** *n* to do ~ **duty** Tischaufsicht haben; ~ **jacket** *n* Smokingjacke *f*; ~ **knife** *n* Tafelmesser *nt*; ~ **party** *n* Abendgesellschaft *f* (mit Essen); **to have a small ~ party** ein kleines Essen geben; ~ **plate** *n* Tafelteller *m*; ~ **service** *n* Tafelservice *nt*; ~ **suit** *n* Smoking *m*; ~ **table** *n* Tafel *f*; **we were already sitting at the ~ table** wir hatten schon zum Essen Platz genommen; ~**time** *n* Essenszeit *f*; ~ **trolley** *or* **wagon** *n* Servierwagen *m*.

dinosaur ['daɪnəsɔːʳ] *n* Dinosaurier *m*.

dinosaurian [daɪnə'sɔːrɪən] *adj* Dinosaurier-.

dint [dɪnt] **1** *n* (a) **by ~ of** durch, kraft (+*gen*); **we succeeded by ~ of working 24 hours a day** wir schafften es, indem wir 24 Stunden pro Tag arbeiteten. (b) **see dent. 2** *vt* see **dent**.

diocesan [daɪ'ɒsɪsən] *adj* Diözesan-, Bistums-.

diocese ['daɪəsɪs] *n* Diözese *f*, Bistum *nt*.

diode ['daɪəʊd] *n* Diode *f*.

Dionysian [daɪə'nɪzɪən] *adj* dionysisch.

Dionysus [daɪə'naɪsɪs] *n* Dionysos, Dionys *m*.

dioptre, (*US*) **diopter** [daɪ'ɒptəʳ] *n* Dioptrie *f*.

diorama [daɪə'rɑːmə] *n* Diorama *nt*.

dioxide [daɪ'ɒksaɪd] *n* Dioxyd *nt*.

Dip *abbr of* **diploma**.

dip [dɪp] **1** *vt* (a) (*in*(to) *in* +*acc*) (*into liquid*) tauchen; *pen, hand* eintauchen; *bread* (ein)tunken, stippen (*inf*); *candles* ziehen; *sheep* in Desinfektionslösung baden, dippen.
 (b) (*into bag, basket*) *hand* stecken.
 (c) (*Brit Aut*) *headlights* abblenden. **to drive on ~ped headlights** mit Abblendlicht fahren.
 (d) **to ~ one's flag** (*Naut*) die Flagge dippen.
 2 *vi* (*ground*) sich senken, (*temperature, pointer on scale, prices*) fallen, sinken; (*boat*) tauchen. **the sun ~ped behind the mountains** die Sonne verschwand hinter den Bergen.
 3 *n* (a) (*swim*) **to go for a** *or* **to have a ~** kurz *or* schnell mal schwimmen gehen, kurz reinspringen; **after a/her ~ she lay and sunbathed** nach einem kurzen Bad sonnte sie sich.
 (b) (*liquid*) (*for cleaning animals*) Desinfektionslösung *f*; (*Tech*) Lösung *f*.
 (c) (*in ground*) (*hollow*) Bodensenke *f*; (*slope*) Abfall *m*. **the road took a ~** die Straße fiel ab.
 (d) (*Phys: also angle of ~*) Inklination *f*, Neigungswinkel *m*.
 (e) (*Naut: of flag*) Dippen *nt*.
 (f) (*Cook*) Dip *m*; *see* **lucky**.
 (g) (*candle*) gezogene Kerze.
 (h) (*Sport*) Beugestütz *m*.
 (i) (*sl: pickpocket*) Taschendieb, Langfinger (*inf*) *m*.

♦ **dip into** *vi* +*prep obj* (a) (*lit*) **she ~ped ~ her handbag for money** sie griff in ihre Handtasche, um Geld zu holen. (b) (*fig*) **to ~ ~ one's pocket** tief in die Tasche greifen; **to ~ ~ one's savings** seine Ersparnisse angreifen, an seine Ersparnisse gehen. (c) (*look at quickly*) *book* einen kurzen Blick werfen in (+*acc*).

diphtheria [dɪf'θɪərɪə] *n* Diphtherie *f*.

diphthong ['dɪfθɒŋ] *n* Diphthong *m*.

diphthongize ['dɪfθɒŋgaɪz] *vti* diphthongieren.

diploma [dɪ'pləʊmə] *n* Diplom *nt*. **teacher's ~** Lehrerdiplom *nt*; **to hold a ~ in** ein Diplom haben in (+*dat*).

diplomacy [dɪ'pləʊməsɪ] *n* (*Pol, fig*) Diplomatie *f*. **to use ~** diplomatisch vorgehen.

diplomat ['dɪpləmæt] *n* (*Pol, fig*) Diplomat *m*.

diplomatic *adj*, ~**ally** *adv* [dɪplə'mætɪk, -əlɪ] (*lit, fig*) diplomatisch.

diplomatic: ~ **bag** *n* Diplomatenpost *f*; ~ **corps** *n* diplomatisches Korps; ~ **immunity** *n* Immunität *f*; ~ **pouch** *n* (*US*) see ~ **bag**; ~ **service** *n* diplomatischer Dienst.

diplomatist [dɪ'pləʊmətɪst] *n* see **diplomat**.

dip needle *n* Inklinationsnadel *f*.

dipper ['dɪpəʳ] *n* (a) (*ladle*) Schöpflöffel *m*, Kelle *f*.
 (b) (*Tech: person*) Eintaucher(in *f*) *m*.
 (c) (*Orn*) Taucher *m*, Tauchente *f*.
 (d) (*Tech*) (*bulldozer*) Bagger *m*; (*scoop*) Schaufel *f*.
 (e) (*at fair: also Big D~*) Achterbahn *f*.
 (f) (*Brit Aut: for headlamps*) Abblendschalter *m*.
 (g) (*US Astron*) **the Big** *or* **Great/Little D~** der Große/Kleine Wagen *or* Bär.

dipping needle ['dɪpɪŋniːdl] *n* see **dip needle**.

dippy ['dɪpɪ] *adj* (*inf*) plemplem (*inf*), meschugge (*inf*).

dip rod *n* (*US*) see **dipstick**.

dipso ['dɪpsəʊ] *n abbr of* **dipsomaniac**.

dipsomania [dɪpsəʊ'meɪnɪə] *n* Trunksucht *f*.

dipsomaniac [dɪpsəʊ'meɪnɪæk] *n* Trunksüchtige(r) *mf*.

dip: ~**stick** *n* Ölmeßstab *m*; ~**switch** *n* Abblendschalter *m*.

diptera ['dɪptərə] *npl* Dipteren (*spec*), Zweiflügler *pl*.

dipterous ['dɪptərəs] *adj* zweiflüg(e)lig.

diptych ['dɪptɪk] *n* Diptychon *nt*.

dire [daɪəʳ] *adj* schrecklich, furchtbar, gräßlich; *poverty* äußerste(r, s). ~ **necessity** dringende Notwendigkeit; **to be in ~ need** in großer Verlegenheit sein (*of* nach); *see* **strait**.

direct [daɪ'rekt] **1** *adj* (a) direkt; (*following straight on, uninterrupted*) *link, result, heir, contact also* unmittelbar; *responsibility, cause, danger* unmittelbar; *train* durchgehend; *opposite* genau. **to be a ~ descendant of sb** von jdm in direkter Linie abstammen, ein direkter Nachkomme von jdm sein; ~ **action** direkte Aktion; ~ **grant (school)** (*Brit*) Privatschule *f* mit staatlicher Unterstützung; "**keep away from ~ heat**", vor unmittelbarer Wärmeeinstrahlung schützen"; ~ **heating** Zimmerheizung *f*; ~ **hit** Volltreffer *m*; ~**mail advertising** Postwurfsendung *f*; ~ **method** direkte Methode.

 (b) (*blunt*) *person, remark* direkt, offen; *refusal, denial* glatt.
 (c) (*Gram*) ~ **object** direktes Objekt, Akkusativobjekt *nt*; ~ **speech** *or* **discourse** (*US*) direkte Rede.
 (d) (*Elec*) ~ **current** Gleichstrom *m*.
 2 *vt* (a) (*address, aim*) *remark, letter* richten (*to an* +*acc*); *efforts* richten (*towards* auf +*acc*). **to ~ one's steps to(wards) sb/sth** auf jdn/etw zugehen; **to ~ sb's attention to sth/sth** jds Aufmerksamkeit auf jdn/etw lenken; **can you ~ me to the town hall?** können Sie mir den Weg zum Rathaus sagen?, können Sie mir sagen, wie ich zum Rathaus komme?
 (b) (*supervise, control*) *person's work, business* leiten, lenken; *traffic* regeln.
 (c) (*order*) anweisen (*sb to do sth* jdn, etw zu tun), befehlen (*sb to do sth* jdm, etw zu tun); (*Jur*) *jury* Rechtsbelehrung erteilen (+*dat*). **the judge ~ed the jury to ...** der Richter belehrte die Schöffen darüber, daß ...; **as ~ed** (*Med*) wie verordnet.
 (d) *film* Regie führen bei; *play also* Spielleitung haben von; *group of actors* dirigieren; *radio/TV programme* leiten.
 3 *adv* direkt.

direction [dɪ'rekʃən] *n* (a) (*lit, fig: way*) Richtung *f*. **in every ~** in jede Richtung; **in the wrong/right ~** (*lit, fig*) in die falsche/richtige Richtung; **in the ~ of Hamburg/the star** in Richtung Hamburg/des Sterns; **what ~ did he go in?** in welche Richtung ist er gegangen/gefahren?; **a sense of ~** (*lit*) Orientierungssinn *m*; (*fig*) ein Ziel *nt* im Leben; **new ~s in modern philosophy** neue Wege in der modernen Philosophie.
 (b) (*management: of company etc*) Leitung, Führung *f*.
 (c) (*of film, actors*) Regie *f*; (*of play also*) Spielleitung *f*; (*of radio/TV programme*) Leitung *f*. **under the ~ of** unter der Regie von.
 (d) ~**s** *pl* (*instructions*) Anweisungen *pl*; (*to a place*) Angaben *pl*; (*for use*) (Gebrauchs)anweisung *or* -anleitung *f*; (*in recipe etc*) Hinweise *pl*.

directional [dɪ'rekʃənl] *adj* Richtungs-, gerichtet.

direction: ~ **finder** *n* Peilantenne *f*; ~ **indicator** *n* (*Aut*) Winker *m*; (*flashing*) Blinker *m*.

directive [dɪ'rektɪv] *n* Direktive, Weisung *f*.

directly [dɪ'rektlɪ] **1** *adv* (a) (*without deviating, following straight on*) direkt, unmittelbar; (*in a short time*) sofort, gleich. **to come ~ to the point** direkt *or* ohne Umschweife zur Sache kommen; **to be ~ descended from sb** in direkter Linie *or* direkt von jdm abstammen.
 (b) (*frankly*) *speak* direkt, ohne Umschweife.
 (c) (*completely*) *opposite* genau, unmittelbar; *opposed* völlig.
 2 *conj* sobald, sowie. **he'll come ~ he's ready** er kommt, sobald *or* sowie er fertig ist.

directness [daɪ'rektnɪs] *n* (a) (*of attack*) Direktheit *f*. (b) (*of speech, reply*) Offenheit, Direktheit *f*; (*of person*) Direktheit, Geradheit *f*.

director [dɪ'rektəʳ] *n* (a) (*of company, institution*) Direktor, Leiter *m*; (*Univ*) Rektor *m*. ~ **of studies** Studienberater *m*; ~ **of music** Musikdirektor *m*; ~ **of Public Prosecutions** Leiter *m* der Anklagebehörde; ~ **general** Generaldirektor(in *f*) *m*. (b) (*Rad, TV*) Direktor *m*; (*Film, Theat*) Regisseur *m*. ~**'s chair** Regiestuhl *m*. (c) (*Mil*) Direktor *m*.

directorate [daɪ'rektərɪt] *n* (*period of office*) Dienstzeit *f* als Direktor; (*board of directors*) Aufsichtsrat *m*.

directorship [dɪ'rektəʃɪp] *n* Direktorstelle *f or* -posten *m*. **under his ~** unter seiner Leitung.

directory [dɪ'rektərɪ] *n* (a) Adreßbuch *nt*; (*telephone ~*) Telefonbuch *nt*; (*trade ~*) Branchenverzeichnis *nt*. ~ **enquiries** *or* (*US*) **assistance** (*Telec*) Fernsprechauskunft *f*. (b) (*Hist*) **the D~** das Direktorium.

dirge [dɜːdʒ] *n* Grab- *or* Trauer- *or* Klagegesang *m*.

dirigible ['dɪrɪdʒəbl] **1** *n* (lenkbares) Luftschiff. **2** *adj* lenkbar.

dirk [dɜːk] *n* (*Scot*) Dolch *m*.

dirt [dɜːt] *n* (a) Schmutz *m*; (*soil*) Erde *f*; (*excrement*) Dreck *m*; (*rubbish also*) Unrat, Kehricht *m*. **to be covered in ~** völlig verschmutzt sein; **to eat ~** (*fig*) sich widerspruchslos demütigen *or* beleidigen lassen; **to treat sb like ~** jdn wie (den letzten) Dreck behandeln (*inf*); **he looked at me as though I was a bit of ~** er sah mich an, als wäre ich ein Stück Dreck (*inf*).
 (b) (*fig: obscenity*) Schmutz *m*; (*scandal also*) schmutzige Wäsche. **go and wash the ~ out of your mouth!** schäm dich, solche Worte in den Mund zu nehmen!

dirt-cheap ['dɜːt'tʃiːp] *adj, adv* (*inf*) spottbillig.

dirtily ['dɜːtɪlɪ] *adv* (a) schmutzig; *eat, live* wie ein Ferkel. (b) (*fig*) (*meanly*) gemein, schäbig; (*obscenely*) schmutzig, unanständig.

dirt: ~ **road** *n* unbefestigte Straße; ~ **track** *n* Feldweg *m*; (*Sport*) Aschenbahn *f*; ~-**track racing** *n* Aschenbahnrennen *nt*.

dirty ['dɜːtɪ] **1** *adj* (+*er*) (a) schmutzig; *hands, clothes, shoes etc also, wound* verschmutzt. ~ **weather** Dreckwetter, Sauwetter (*inf*) *nt*; (*Naut*) stürmisches Wetter; **a ~ colour** eine Schmutzfarbe; **to get ~** schmutzig *or* dreckig werden; **to get sth ~** etw schmutzig machen; **to give sb a ~ look** (*fig*) jdm einen bösen *or* giftigen Blick zuwerfen.
 (b) (*fig: obscene*) schmutzig, unanständig; *story, joke also* zotig. **to have a ~ mind** eine schmutzige Phantasie haben; **a ~ old man** fieser alter Kerl, alte Drecksau (*sl*); **you ~ old man!** Sie Schmutzfink!; **the ~ raincoat brigade** (*hum*) = die Spanner *pl*; **they're having a ~ weekend** (*inf*) sie sind zusammen übers Wochenende weggefahren.
 (c) (*fig*) (*despicable*) gemein, niederträchtig; (*Sport*) *player, match* unfair. **a ~ bastard** (*sl*) ein richtiges Schwein (*sl*); ~ **work** Dreck(s)arbeit *f* (*inf*).
 2 *vt* *hands, clothes, reputation* beschmutzen; *machine* verschmutzen.
 3 *n* **to do the ~ on sb** (*Brit inf*) jdn reinlegen (*inf*).

disability [dɪsə'bɪlɪtɪ] *n* (a) (*handicap, injury etc*) Behinderung *f.* ~ **for work** Arbeitsunfähigkeit *f;* **sb's** ~ **to do sth** jds Unfähigkeit *f or* Unvermögen *nt,* etw zu tun; ~ **pension** *n* Invalidenrente *f.* **(b)** *(Jur)* Rechtsunfähigkeit *f.*

disable [dɪsˈeɪbl] *vt* **(a) to** ~ **sb for work** jdn arbeitsunfähig machen. **(b)** *tank, gun* unbrauchbar machen; *ship* kampfunfähig machen. **(c)** *(Jur)* *(make incapable)* rechtsunfähig machen; *(disqualify)* für unfähig erklären *(from doing sth* etw zu tun).

disabled [dɪsˈeɪbld] **1** *adj* **(a)** behindert. ~ **ex-serviceman** Kriegsversehrte(r) *or* -invalide *m.* **(b)** *tank, gun* unbrauchbar; *ship* nicht seetüchtig. **(c)** *(Jur)* nicht rechtsfähig. **2** *npl* **the** ~ die Behinderten *pl;* **the war** ~ die Kriegsversehrten *or* -invaliden *pl.*

disablement [dɪsˈeɪblmənt] *n* **(a)** Behinderung *f.* **(b)** *(of tank, gun, ship)* Unbrauchbarmachen *nt.*

disabuse [ˌdɪsəˈbjuːz] *vt* **to** ~ **sb of sth** jdn von etw befreien.

disadvantage [ˌdɪsədˈvɑːntɪdʒ] *n* **(a)** *(obstacle, unfavourable factor)* Nachteil *m; (detriment also)* Schaden *m.* **to be at a** ~ sich im Nachteil befinden, benachteiligt *or* im Nachteil sein; **to put sb at a** ~ jdn benachteiligen; **to show oneself at a** ~ sich von einer ungünstigen *or* unvorteilhaften Seite zeigen; **he felt his** ~ er empfand seine Benachteiligung; **it would be to your** ~ es wäre zu Ihrem Nachteil.

disadvantaged [ˌdɪsədˈvɑːntɪdʒd] *adj* benachteiligt.

disadvantageous *adj,* ~**ly** *adv* [ˌdɪsˌædvɑːnˈteɪdʒəs, -lɪ] nachteilig.

disaffected [ˌdɪsəˈfektɪd] *adj* entfremdet. **to become** ~ sich entfremden.

disaffection [ˌdɪsəˈfekʃən] *n* Entfremdung *f (from* von).

disagree [ˌdɪsəˈgriː] *vi* **(a)** *(with person, views)* nicht übereinstimmen; *(with plan, suggestion etc)* nicht einverstanden sein; *(two people)* sich nicht einig sein. **(b)** *(quarrel)* eine Meinungsverschiedenheit haben. **(c)** *(be different: figures, reports)* nicht übereinstimmen. **(d)** *(climate, food)* **to** ~ **with sb** jdm nicht bekommen; **mutton** ~**s with me** ich vertrage Hammelfleisch nicht, Hammelfleisch bekommt mir nicht.

disagreeable [ˌdɪsəˈgriːəbl] *adj* smell, work, experience unangenehm; *(bad-tempered) person* unsympathisch.

disagreeableness [ˌdɪsəˈgriːəblnɪs] *n see adj* Unangenehme(s) *nt;* unangenehme Art, unsympathische Art.

disagreeably [ˌdɪsəˈgriːəblɪ] *adv see adj.*

disagreement [ˌdɪsəˈgriːmənt] *n* **(a)** *(with opinion, between opinions)* Uneinigkeit *f.* **my** ~ **with that view** ist das on ... ich bin mit dieser Ansicht nicht einverstanden, weil ...; **there is still** ~ **es herrscht noch Uneinigkeit. (b)** *(quarrel)* Meinungsverschiedenheit *f.* **(c)** *(between figures, reports)* Diskrepanz *f.*

disallow [ˌdɪsəˈlaʊ] *vt* evidence nicht anerkennen; *claim also* zurückweisen; *plan etc* ablehnen; *(Sport)* goal nicht anerkennen, nicht geben.

disappear [ˌdɪsəˈpɪəʳ] *vi* verschwinden; *(worries, fears, difficulties also)* sich in Nichts auflösen; *(rage also)* verrauchen; *(memory)* schwinden; *(objections)* sich zerstreuen. **he** ~**ed from (our) sight** er verschwand; **to make sth** ~ etw verschwinden lassen; **to do one's** ~**ing trick** *(inf)* sich verdünnisieren *(inf),* sich verdrücken *(inf).*

disappearance [ˌdɪsəˈpɪərəns] *n see vi* Verschwinden *nt;* Verrauchen *nt;* Schwinden *nt;* Zerstreuung *f.*

disappoint [ˌdɪsəˈpɔɪnt] *vt* enttäuschen; *hope also, ambition, plan* zunichte machen.

disappointed [ˌdɪsəˈpɔɪntɪd] *adj* person enttäuscht; *hopes* getäuscht. **to be** ~ **in sb/sth** von jdm/etw enttäuscht sein; **to be** ~ **in love** eine Enttäuschung in der Liebe erleben.

disappointing [ˌdɪsəˈpɔɪntɪŋ] *adj* enttäuschend. **how** ~! so eine Enttäuschung!

disappointingly [ˌdɪsəˈpɔɪntɪŋlɪ] *adv* enttäuschend. **rather** ~ **he didn't have the opportunity** es war ziemlich enttäuschend, daß er keine Gelegenheit hatte; **he did** ~ **in the exams** er hat in den Prüfungen enttäuschend abgeschnitten *or* enttäuscht.

disappointment [ˌdɪsəˈpɔɪntmənt] *n* Enttäuschung *f; (of hopes also, ambition)* Nichterfüllung *f.*

disapprobation [ˌdɪsæprəˈbeɪʃən] *n* Mißbilligung *f.*

disapproval [ˌdɪsəˈpruːvl] *n* Mißbilligung *f.* **murmur of** ~ mißbilligendes Gemurmel.

disapprove [ˌdɪsəˈpruːv] **1** *vt* mißbilligen. **2** *vi* dagegen sein. **if you don't** ~, **I'd like to ...** wenn Sie nichts dagegen haben, würde ich gerne ...; **to** ~ **of sth** etw mißbilligen; **he** ~**s of children smoking** er mißbilligt es, wenn Kinder rauchen.

disapproving *adj,* ~**ly** *adv* [ˌdɪsəˈpruːvɪŋ, -lɪ] mißbilligend.

disarm [dɪsˈɑːm] **1** *vt (lit, fig)* entwaffnen. **2** *vi (Mil)* abrüsten.

disarmament [dɪsˈɑːməmənt] *n* Abrüstung *f.*

disarming *adj,* ~**ly** *adv* [dɪsˈɑːmɪŋ, -lɪ] entwaffnend.

disarrange [ˈdɪsəˈreɪndʒ] *vt* durcheinanderbringen; *plans also* umwerfen.

disarranged [ˈdɪsəˈreɪndʒd] *adj* unordentlich; *plans* durcheinandergebracht.

disarray [ˌdɪsəˈreɪ] **1** *n* Unordnung *f.* **to be in** ~ *(troops)* in Auflösung (begriffen) sein; *(thoughts, organization, political party)* durcheinander *or* in Unordnung sein; *(person)* aufgelöst sein; *(clothes)* in unordentlichem Zustand sein. **2** *vt* in Unordnung bringen; *enemy* verwirren.

disassemble [ˈdɪsəˈsembl] *vt* auseinandernehmen; *prefabricated building* abbauen.

disassociate [ˈdɪsəˈsəʊʃɪeɪt] *vt see* **dissociate**.

disaster [dɪˈzɑːstəʳ] *n* Katastrophe *f; (Aviat, Min, Rail also)* Unglück *nt; (fiasco)* Fiasko, Desaster *nt.* **doomed to** ~ zum Untergang verdammt *or* verurteilt.

disaster: ~ **area** *n* Katastrophengebiet *nt; (fig inf: person)* Katastrophe *f;* ~ **fund** *n* Katastrophenfonds *m.*

disastrous *adj,* ~**ly** *adv* [dɪˈzɑːstrəs, -lɪ] katastrophal, verheerend.

disavow [ˌdɪsəˈvaʊ] *vt* verleugnen; *one's words* ableugnen.

disavowal [ˌdɪsəˈvaʊəl] *n see vt* Verleugnung *f;* Ableugnung *f.*

disband [dɪsˈbænd] **1** *vt* auflösen. **2** *vi (army, club)* sich auflösen; *(soldiers, club members)* auseinandergehen.

disbar [dɪsˈbɑːʳ] *vt (Jur)* die Lizenz entziehen *(+dat).*

disbelief [ˈdɪsbəˈliːf] *n* Ungläubigkeit *f; (Rel)* Unglaube *m.* **in** ~ ungläubig.

disbelieve [ˈdɪsbəˈliːv] *vt* nicht glauben.

disbeliever [ˈdɪsbəˈliːvəʳ] *n* Ungläubige(r) *mf.*

disburden [dɪsˈbɜːdn] *vt (lit, fig)* entlasten.

disburse [dɪsˈbɜːs] *vt* aus(be)zahlen.

disbursement [dɪsˈbɜːsmənt] *n* Auszahlung *f.*

disc, *(esp US)* **disk** [dɪsk] *n* **(a)** *(flat, circular object)* (runde) Scheibe; *(Anat)* Bandscheibe *f; (Mil: identity* ~) (Erkennungs)marke *f;* see **slip**. **(b)** *(record, Computers)* Platte *f.*

discard [dɪˈskɑːd] **1** *vt* **(a)** *unwanted article, person* ausrangieren; *idea, plan* verwerfen; *(take off) coat etc* ausziehen; *skin, antlers, leaves* abwerfen. **(b)** *also vi (Cards)* abwerfen. **2** *n* **(a)** *(Cards)* Abwerfen *nt.* **(b)** *(Ind, Comm)* Ausschuß(ware *f) m.*

disc brake *n* Scheibenbremse *f.*

discern [dɪˈsɜːn] *vt (with senses)* wahrnehmen; *(mentally also)* erkennen. **he was too young to** ~ **right from wrong** er war zu jung, um ein Recht von Unrecht unterscheiden zu können.

discernible [dɪˈsɜːnəbl] *adj (with senses)* wahrnehmbar; *(mentally)* erkennbar.

discernibly [dɪˈsɜːnəblɪ] *adv see adj.*

discerning [dɪˈsɜːnɪŋ] *adj* clientele, reader anspruchsvoll, kritisch; *eye, ear* fein.

discernment [dɪˈsɜːnmənt] *n* **(a)** *(ability to discern) (observation)* feines Gespür; *(discriminating taste)* kritisches Urteilsvermögen. **(b)** *(act of discerning)* see *vt* Wahrnehmung *f;* Erkennen *nt.*

discharge [dɪsˈtʃɑːdʒ] **1** *vt* **(a)** employee, prisoner, patient etc entlassen; *accused* freisprechen; *bankrupt* entlasten. **he** ~**d himself (from hospital)** er hat das Krankenhaus auf eigene Verantwortung verlassen. **(b)** *(emit) (Elec)* entladen; *liquid, gas (pipe etc)* ausstoßen; *(workers)* ausströmen lassen; *(Med)* ausscheiden, absondern. **the tanker was discharging its oil into the Channel** das Öl lief aus dem Tanker in den (Ärmel)kanal; **how much oil has been** ~**d?** wieviel Öl ist ausgelaufen?; *(deliberately)* wieviel Öl hat man abgelassen? **(c)** *(unload) ship, cargo* löschen. **the bus** ~**d its load of ...** aus dem Bus strömten die ... **(d)** *(gun)* abfeuern. **(e)** *debt* begleichen; *obligation, duty* nachkommen *(+dat); function* erfüllen.
2 *vi (wound, sore)* eitern.
3 [ˈdɪstʃɑːdʒ] *n* **(a)** *(dismissal)* see *vt* **(a)** Entlassung *f;* Freispruch *m;* Entlastung *f; (of soldier)* Abschied *m.* **(b)** *(Elec)* Entladung *f; (of gas)* Ausströmen *nt; (of liquid, Med: vaginal* ~) Ausfluß *m; (of pus)* Absonderung *f.* **(c)** *(of cargo)* Löschen *nt.* **(d)** *(of debt)* Begleichung *f; (of obligation, duty, function)* Erfüllung *f.*

disc harrow *n* Scheibenegge *f.*

disciple [dɪˈsaɪpl] *n (lit, fig)* Jünger *m; (fig: non-emotional)* Schüler(in *f) m.*

disciplinarian [ˌdɪsɪplɪˈnɛərɪən] *n* Zuchtmeister(in *f) m.* **to be a strict** ~ eiserne Disziplin halten, ein strenger Zuchtmeister sein.

disciplinary [ˈdɪsɪplɪnərɪ] *adj* Disziplinar-, disziplinarisch.

discipline [ˈdɪsɪplɪn] **1** *n (all senses)* Disziplin *f; (punishment)* disziplinarische Maßnahmen *pl.* **to maintain** ~ die Disziplin aufrechterhalten.
2 *vt* **(a)** *(train, make obedient)* disziplinieren; *reactions, emotions* in Zucht *or* unter Kontrolle halten. **to** ~ **sb/oneself to do sth** jdn/sich dazu anhalten *or* zwingen, etw zu tun. **(b)** *(punish)* bestrafen; *(physically)* züchtigen.

disciplined [ˈdɪsɪplɪnd] *adj* diszipliniert; *behaviour, reactions, emotions also* beherrscht. **well/badly** ~ diszipliniert/disziplinlos, undiszipliniert.

disc jockey *n* Diskjockey *m.*

disclaim [dɪsˈkleɪm] *vt* **(a)** abstreiten, (weit) von sich *(dat)* weisen. **to** ~ **all knowledge/responsibility** jede Kenntnis abstreiten *or* von sich weisen/jede Verantwortung von sich weisen. **(b)** *(Jur) a right* verzichten auf *(+acc).*

disclaimer [dɪsˈkleɪməʳ] *n* **(a)** Dementi *nt.* **to issue a** ~ eine Gegenerklärung abgeben; **his** ~ **of responsibility** seine Erklärung, nicht verantwortlich zu sein. **(b) to put in a** ~ **of sth** *(Jur)* eine Verzichterklärung auf etw *(acc)* abgeben.

disclose [dɪsˈkləʊz] *vt* secret enthüllen; *intentions, news* bekanntgeben *or* -machen.

disclosure [dɪsˈkləʊʒəʳ] *n* **(a)** see *vt* Enthüllung *f;* Bekanntgabe *f.* **(b)** *(fact etc revealed)* Mitteilung *f.*

disco [ˈdɪskəʊ] *n* Disko *f.*

discolor *vti (US) see* **discolour**.

discoloration [dɪsˌkʌləˈreɪʃən] *n* Verfärben *nt; (mark)* Verfärbung *f.*

discolour [dɪsˈkʌləʳ] **1** *vt* verfärben. **2** *vi* sich verfärben.

discomfit [dɪsˈkʌmfɪt] *vt* Unbehagen verursachen *(+dat).*

discomfiture [dɪsˈkʌmfɪtʃəʳ] *n* Unbehagen *nt.*

discomfort [dɪsˈkʌmfət] *n (lit)* Beschwerden *pl; (fig: uneasiness, embarrassment)* Unbehagen *nt.* **the injury gives me a little** ~ **now and again** die Verletzung verursacht mir ab und zu leichte Beschwerden.

disconcert [ˌdɪskənˈsɜːt] *vt* aus der Fassung bringen, beunruhigen.

disconcerting *adj,* ~**ly** *adv* [ˌdɪskənˈsɜːtɪŋ, -lɪ] beunruhigend.

disconnect ['dɪskə'nekt] *vt pipe etc* trennen; *TV, iron* ausschalten; (*cut off supply of*) *gas, electricity* abstellen. **to ~ a call** (*Telec*) ein Gespräch unterbrechen; **I've been ~ed** (*for non-payment*) man hat mir das Telefon/den Strom/das Gas etc abgestellt; (*in mid-conversation*) das Gespräch ist unterbrochen worden.

disconsolate [dɪs'kɒnsəlɪt] *adj* niedergeschlagen. **to grow ~** verzweifeln, verzagen.

discontent ['dɪskən'tent] *n* Unzufriedenheit *f*.

discontented ['dɪskən'tentɪd] *adj* unzufrieden (*with, about* mit).

discontentment ['dɪskən'tentmənt] *n* Unzufriedenheit *f*.

discontinuation [dɪskən,tɪnjʊ'eɪʃən] *n see vt* Aufgabe *f*; Abbruch *m*; (Produktions)einstellung *f*; Einstellung *f*.

discontinue ['dɪskən'tɪnju:] *vt* aufgeben; *class, project also, conversation* abbrechen; (*Comm*) *line* auslaufen lassen, die Produktion einstellen von; *production,* (*Jur*) *case* einstellen. **to ~ one's subscription to a newspaper** seine Zeitung abbestellen; **a ~d line** (*Comm*) eine ausgelaufene Serie.

discontinuity [,dɪskɒntɪ'nju:ɪtɪ] *n* mangelnde Kontinuität, Diskontinuität (*geh*) *f*. **a certain amount of ~** ein gewisser Mangel an Kontinuität; **to reduce any ~ to a minimum** die Kontinuität möglichst wenig unterbrechen.

discontinuous *adj,* **~ly** *adv* ['dɪskən'tɪnjʊəs, -lɪ] nicht kontinuierlich.

discord ['dɪskɔːd] *n* (a) Uneinigkeit *f*. (b) (*Mus*) Disharmonie *f*.

discordance [dɪs'kɔːdəns] *n* (a) Uneinigkeit *f*. (b) (*of colours, sounds, music*) Disharmonie *f*.

discordant [dɪs'kɔːdənt] *adj opinions, colours* nicht miteinander harmonierend; *meeting, atmosphere* unharmonisch; (*Mus*) disharmonisch.

discotheque ['dɪskəʊtek] *n* Diskothek *f*.

discount ['dɪskaʊnt] **1** *n* (a) (*on article*) Rabatt *m*; (*for cash*) Skonto *nt or m*. **trade ~** Händlerrabatt *m*; **to give a ~ on sth** Rabatt *or* Prozente (*inf*) auf etw (*acc*) geben; **to give sb a 5% ~** jdm 5% Rabatt/Skonto geben; **at a ~** auf Rabatt/Skonto; **~ for cash** Skonto, Rabatt bei Barzahlung. (b) **to be at a ~** (*Fin*) unter pari sein; (*fig*) nicht *or* wenig gefragt sein.
2 *vt* (a) (*Comm*) *sum of money* nachlassen; *bill, note* diskontieren.
(b) [dɪs'kaʊnt] *person's opinion* unberücksichtigt lassen. **to ~ sth as exaggeration/untrue** etw als Übertreibung/unwahr abtun.

discount house *or* **store** *n* Discountgeschäft *nt or* -laden *m*.

discourage [dɪs'kʌrɪdʒ] *vt* (a) (*dishearten*) entmutigen. **to become ~d** entmutigt werden; (*generally disheartened*) mutlos werden; **he will not be ~d by trifles** er läßt sich nicht so schnell entmutigen.
(b) (*dissuade*) **to ~ sb from sth/from doing sth** jdm von etw abraten/jdm abraten, etw zu tun; (*successfully*) jdn von etw abbringen/jdn davon abbringen, etw zu tun.
(c) (*deter, hinder*) abhalten; *friendship, advances, plan* zu verhindern suchen; *praise, evil* abwehren; *pride* nicht ermutigen. **the weather ~d people from going away** das Wetter hielt die Leute davon ab wegzufahren.

discouragement [dɪs'kʌrɪdʒmənt] *n* (a) (*depression*) Mutlosigkeit *f*.
(b) (*dissuasion*) Abraten *nt*; (*with success*) Abbringen *nt*.
(c) (*deterrence, hindrance*) Abhaltung *f*; (*of friendship*) Verhinderung *f*; (*of praise*) Abwehr *f*.
(d) (*discouraging thing*) **to be a ~** entmutigend sein.

discouraging [dɪs'kʌrɪdʒɪŋ] *adj* entmutigend. **he was rather ~ about her chances** er äußerte sich ziemlich entmutigend über ihre Chancen.

discouragingly [dɪs'kʌrɪdʒɪŋlɪ] *adv see adj*.

discourse ['dɪskɔːs] **1** *n* Diskurs *m* (*geh*). **2** *vi* einen Diskurs geben (*geh*); (*converse*) einen Diskurs führen (*geh*).

discourteous *adj,* **~ly** *adv* [dɪs'kɜːtɪəs, -lɪ] unhöflich.

discourteousness [dɪs'kɜːtɪəsnɪs], **discourtesy** [dɪs'kɜːtɪsɪ] *n* Unhöflichkeit *f*.

discover [dɪs'kʌvəʳ] *vt* entdecken; *culprit* finden; *secret also* herausfinden; (*after search*) *house, book also* ausfindig machen; (*notice*) *mistake, loss also* feststellen, bemerken. **did you ever ~ who ...?** haben Sie jemals herausgefunden, wer ...?

discoverer [dɪs'kʌvərəʳ] *n* Entdecker(in *f*) *m*.

discovery [dɪs'kʌvərɪ] *n* Entdeckung *f*.

discredit [dɪs'kredɪt] **1** *vt* (a) (*cast slur/doubt on*) *report, theory* in Mißkredit bringen; *family, company also* diskreditieren.
(b) (*disbelieve*) keinen Glauben schenken (+*dat*).
2 *n* (a) *no pl* (*dishonour, disbelief*) Mißkredit *m*. **to bring ~ (up)on sb/sth** jdn/etw in Mißkredit bringen; **without any ~ to you** ohne daß Sie dadurch diskreditiert *or* in Mißkredit gebracht werden; **a certain amount of ~ has been cast on that idea** diese Idee ist ziemlich in Mißkredit geraten.
(b) **to be a ~ to sb** eine Schande für jdn sein.

discreditable [dɪs'kredɪtəbl] *adj* diskreditierend. **to be ~ to sb** jdn diskreditieren, jdn in Mißkredit bringen.

discreditably [dɪs'kredɪtəblɪ] *adv see adj*.

discreet [dɪs'kriːt] *adj* diskret; (*in quiet taste also*) dezent.

discreetly [dɪs'kriːtlɪ] *adv* diskret; *dressed also, decorated* dezent.

discreetness [dɪs'kriːtnɪs] *n see adj* Diskretheit *f*; dezente Art.

discrepancy [dɪs'krepənsɪ] *n* Diskrepanz *f* (*between* zwischen +*dat*).

discrete [dɪs'kriːt] *adj* diskret.

discretion [dɪs'kreʃən] *n* (a) Diskretion *f*. **~ is the better part of valour** (*Prov*) Vorsicht ist die Mutter der Porzellankiste (*inf*).
(b) (*freedom of decision*) Ermessen *nt*. **to leave sth to sb's ~** etw in jds Ermessen (*acc*) stellen; **use your own ~** Sie müssen

nach eigenem Ermessen handeln; **to be at sb's ~** in jds Ermessen (*dat*) stehen.

discretionary [dɪ'skreʃənərɪ] *adj* Ermessens-. **~ powers** Ermessensspielraum *m*.

discriminate [dɪ'skrɪmɪneɪt] **1** *vi* (a) (*be discriminating*) kritisch sein; (*distinguish*) unterscheiden (*between* zwischen +*dat*).
(b) (*make unfair distinction*) Unterschiede machen (*between* zwischen +*dat*). **to ~ against/in favour of sb** jdn diskriminieren/bevorzugen.
2 *vt* unterscheiden, einen Unterschied machen zwischen (+*dat*). **to ~ good and/from bad** Gut und Böse/Gut von Böse unterscheiden können.

discriminating [dɪ'skrɪmɪneɪtɪŋ] *adj* (a) *person, judgement, mind* kritisch; *clientele* verwöhnt; *taste* fein. (b) *tariff, duty* Differential-.

discrimination [dɪ,skrɪmɪ'neɪʃən] *n* (a) (*differential treatment*) Diskriminierung *f*. **racial ~** Rassendiskriminierung *f*; **sexual ~** Diskriminierung auf Grund des Geschlechts. (b) (*differentiation*) Unterscheidung *f* (*between* zwischen +*dat*). (c) (*discernment*) kritisches Urteilsvermögen.

discriminatory [dɪ'skrɪmɪnətərɪ] *adj* diskriminierend.

discursive [dɪ'skɜːsɪv], **discursory** [dɪ'skɜːsərɪ] *adj* (a) *style* weitschweifig. (b) (*Philos*) diskursiv.

discus ['dɪskəs] *n* Diskus *m*. **~ thrower** Diskuswerfer(in *f*) *m*; **in the ~** im Diskuswerfen.

discuss [dɪ'skʌs] *vt* besprechen; *politics, theory* diskutieren; *in essay, speech etc* erörtern, diskutieren. **I don't want to ~ it any further** ich möchte darüber nicht weiter reden, ich möchte das nicht weiter diskutieren; **I am not willing to ~ it** ich bin nicht gewillt, darüber zu diskutieren.

discussant [dɪ'skʌsənt] *n* (*US*) Diskussionsteilnehmer(in *f*) *m*.

discussion [dɪ'skʌʃən] *n* Diskussion *f*; (*meeting*) Besprechung *f*. **after a lot of ~** nach langen Diskussionen; **to be under ~** zur Diskussion stehen; **that is still under ~** das ist noch in der Diskussion; **a subject for ~** ein Diskussionsthema *nt or* -gegenstand *m*.

disdain [dɪs'deɪn] **1** *vt sb* verachten; *sth also* verschmähen. **he ~ed to notice them** er hielt es für unter seiner Würde, ihnen Beachtung zu schenken. **2** *n* Verachtung *f*.

disdainful *adj,* **~ly** *adv* [dɪs'deɪnfʊl, -fəlɪ] verächtlich.

disease [dɪ'ziːz] *n* (*lit, fig*) Krankheit *f*.

diseased [dɪ'ziːzd] *adj* (*lit, fig*) *krank; tissue, plant* befallen.

disembark [,dɪsɪm'bɑːk] **1** *vt* ausschiffen. **2** *vi* von Bord gehen.

disembarkation [,dɪsɪmbɑː'keɪʃən] *n* Landung *f*.

disembodied ['dɪsɪm'bɒdɪd] *adj* körperlos; *voice* geisterhaft.

disembowel [,dɪsɪm'baʊəl] *vt* die Eingeweide herausnehmen (+*dat*); (*murder*) den Bauch aufschlitzen (+*dat*).

disenchant ['dɪsɪn'tʃɑːnt] *vt* ernüchtern. **he became ~ed with her/it** sie/es ernüchterte ihn.

disenfranchise ['dɪsɪn'fræntʃaɪz] *vt see* **disfranchise**.

disengage [,dɪsɪn'geɪdʒ] **1** *vt* (a) (*extricate*) losmachen, lösen (*from* aus).
(b) (*Tech*) ausrücken (*form*). **to ~ the clutch** (*Aut*) auskuppeln.
(c) (*Mil*) (*from country*) abziehen; (*from battle also*) abrücken lassen.
2 *vi* (a) (*Tech*) ausrücken (*form*).
(b) (*Mil*) auseinanderrücken; (*opponents*) sich trennen.
(c) (*Fencing*) sich (aus seiner Bindung) lösen.

disengagement [,dɪsɪn'geɪdʒmənt] *n see vt* (a) Lösung *f*. (b) Ausrücken *nt* (*form*). **~ of the clutch** das Auskuppeln. (c) Abzug *m*.

disentail ['dɪsɪn'teɪl] *vt* (*Jur*) das Fideikommiß (+*gen*) auflösen.

disentangle ['dɪsɪn'tæŋgl] *vt* (*lit, fig*) entwirren; *problem, mystery also* enträtseln. **to ~ oneself from sth** (*lit*) sich aus etw lösen; (*fig*) sich von etw lösen.

disestablish ['dɪsɪs'tæblɪʃ] *vt the Church* vom Staat trennen.

disestablishment [,dɪsɪs'tæblɪʃmənt] *n* Trennung *f* (vom Staat).

disfavour, (*US*) **disfavor** [dɪs'feɪvəʳ] *n* (a) (*displeasure*) Ungnade *f*; (*dislike*) Mißfallen *nt*. **to fall into/be in ~** in Ungnade fallen/sein (*with* bei); **to look with ~ upon sb/sth** jdn/etw mit Mißfallen betrachten.
(b) (*disadvantage*) **in/to his ~** zu seinen Ungunsten.

disfigure [dɪs'fɪgəʳ] *vt* verunstalten; *person also* entstellen.

disfigurement [dɪs'fɪgəmənt] *n see vt* Verunstaltung *f*; Entstellung *f*.

disfranchise ['dɪs'fræntʃaɪz] *vt person* die bürgerlichen Ehrenrechte aberkennen (+*dat*); *town* das Recht nehmen, einen Abgeordneten ins Parlament zu senden (+*dat*).

disfranchisement [dɪs'fræntʃaɪzmənt] *n* (*of person*) Aberkennung *f* der bürgerlichen Ehrenrechte; (*of town*) Entzug *m* des Rechts, einen Abgeordneten ins Parlament zu senden.

disgorge [dɪs'gɔːdʒ] **1** *vt food* ausspucken, ausspeien; (*stomach*) ausstoßen; (*fig*) (*spew forth*) ausspeien; (*river*) *waters* ergießen; (*give up*) (*widerwillig*) her(aus)geben *or* herausrücken. **2** *vi* (*river*) aus einer Schlucht austreten.

disgrace [dɪs'greɪs] **1** *n* (a) *no pl* (*dishonour, shame*) Schande *f*. **to bring ~ on sb** jdm Schande machen *or* bringen; **to be in/fall into ~** in Ungnade (gefallen) sein/fallen (*with* bei).
(b) (*cause of shame*) (*thing*) Schande, Blamage *f* (*to* für); (*person*) Schandfleck *m* (*to gen*).
2 *vt* Schande machen (+*dat*); *country, family also* Schande bringen über (+*acc*). **don't ~ us!** mach uns keine Schande!; **blamier uns nicht; to ~ oneself** sich blamieren; (*child, dog*) sich schlecht benehmen; **to be ~d** blamiert sein; (*politician, officer etc*) in Unehre gefallen sein.

disgraceful [dɪs'greɪsfʊl] *adj* erbärmlich (*schlecht*); *behaviour, performance, exam results also* skandalös. **it's quite ~ how/that ...** es ist wirklich eine Schande, wie/daß ....

disgracefully [dɪsˈgreɪsfəlɪ] adv (+adj) erbärmlich; (+vb) erbärmlich schlecht.

disgruntle [dɪsˈgrʌntl] vt verstimmen. ~d verstimmt.

disgruntlement [dɪsˈgrʌntlmənt] n Verstimmung f.

disguise [dɪsˈgaɪz] 1 vt unkenntlich machen; sb, oneself also verkleiden; voice verstellen; vehicle, aircraft, building also tarnen; facts, mistakes, interest, feelings verschleiern.
2 n (lit) Verkleidung f; (of vehicle, aircraft, building) Tarnung f; (fig) Deckmantel m. in ~ verkleidet; getarnt; in the ~ of in der Verkleidung als, verkleidet als/getarnt als/unter dem Deckmantel von or der Maske (+gen).

disgust [dɪsˈgʌst] 1 n Ekel m; (at sb's behaviour) Entrüstung, Empörung f. to go away in ~ sich voller Ekel/Empörung abwenden; much to his ~ he was given raw fish to eat/they left Ekel überkam ihn, als ihm roher Fisch vorgesetzt wurde/sehr zu seiner Empörung gingen sie.
2 vt (person, sight) anekeln, anwidern; (actions) empören.

disgusted [dɪsˈgʌstɪd] adj angeekelt; (at sb's behaviour) empört. I am ~ with you ich bin empört über dich.

disgustedly [dɪsˈgʌstɪdlɪ] adv voller Ekel; (at sb's behaviour) empört.

disgusting [dɪsˈgʌstɪŋ] adj widerlich; (physically nauseating also) ekelhaft; (euph: obscene) mind schmutzig; behaviour, language anstößig; (inf: terrible also) ekelhaft. don't be ~ sei nicht so ordinär; that's ~ das ist eine Schweinerei (inf).

disgustingly [dɪsˈgʌstɪŋlɪ] adv widerlich, ekelhaft; rich stink-.

dish [dɪʃ] 1 n (a) Schale f; (for serving also) Schüssel f.
(b) ~es pl (crockery) Geschirr nt; to do the ~es Geschirr spülen, abwaschen.
(c) (food) Gericht nt.
(d) (Elec) Parabolreflektor m.
(e) (sl) (girl) duftes Mädchen (inf); (man) toller Typ (inf).
2 vt (a) (serve) anrichten.
(b) (inf) zunichte machen; chances also vermasseln (inf).

♦**dish out** vt sep (inf) austeilen.

♦**dish up** 1 vt sep (a) (lit) auf dem Teller anrichten; (in bowls) auftragen. (b) (fig inf) facts auftischen (inf). 2 vi anrichten.

dishabille [ˌdɪsaˈbiːl] n in a state of ~ (woman) im Negligé; (man) halb angezogen.

disharmony [ˈdɪsˈhɑːmənɪ] n (lit, fig) Disharmonie f.

dishcloth [ˈdɪʃklɒθ] n (for drying) Geschirrtuch nt; (for washing) Spüllappen m or -tuch nt.

dishearten [dɪsˈhɑːtn] vt entmutigen. don't be ~ed! nun verlieren Sie nicht gleich den Mut!, nur Mut!

disheartening adj, ~ly adv [dɪsˈhɑːtnɪŋ, -lɪ] entmutigend.

dished [dɪʃt] adj (Tech) konkav (gewölbt); wheels gestürzt.

dishevelled, (US) **disheveled** [dɪˈʃevəld] adj ramponiert (inf), unordentlich; hair zerzaust.

dish mop m Spülbürste f.

dishonest [dɪsˈɒnɪst] adj unehrlich; (cheating also) businessman unredlich; (lying also) verlogen; plan, scheme unlauter.

dishonestly adv see adj.

dishonesty [dɪsˈɒnɪstɪ] n see adj Unehrlichkeit f; Unredlichkeit f; Verlogenheit f; Unlauterkeit f.

dishonour, (US) **dishonor** [dɪsˈɒnəʳ] 1 n Schande, Unehre f. to bring ~ upon sb Schande über jdn bringen.
2 vt (a) schänden, entehren; family Schande machen (+dat).
(b) (Comm, Fin) cheque nicht honorieren; bill nicht bezahlen.
(c) agreement nicht einhalten; promise also nicht einlösen.

dishonourable, (US) **dishonorable** [dɪsˈɒnərəbl] adj unehrenhaft.

dishonourableness, (US) **dishonorableness** [dɪsˈɒnərəblnɪs] n Unehrenhaftigkeit f.

dishonourably, (US) **dishonorably** [dɪsˈɒnərəblɪ] adv see adj. to behave ~ to sb sich jdm gegenüber unehrenhaft or unanständig verhalten.

dish: ~pan hands npl rauhe und rissige Hände; ~ rack n Geschirrständer m; (in ~washer) (Einsatz)korb m; ~ towel n (US, Scot) Geschirrtuch nt; ~washer n (person) Tellerwäscher(in f), Spüler(in f) m; (machine) Geschirrspülmaschine f; ~water n Abwasch- or Spülwasser nt; this coffee is like ~water der Kaffee schmeckt wie Abwasch- or Spülwasser.

dishy [ˈdɪʃɪ] adj (+er) (Brit sl) woman, man dufte (inf).

disillusion [ˌdɪsɪˈluːʒən] 1 vt desillusionieren. I hate to ~ you, but ... es tut mir leid, Ihnen Ihre Illusionen rauben or Sie desillusionieren zu müssen, aber ... 2 n Desillusion f.

disillusionment [ˌdɪsɪˈluːʒənmənt] n Desillusionierung f.

disincentive [ˌdɪsɪnˈsentɪv] n Entmutigung f. to be a ~ to sth keinen Anreiz für etw bieten; it acts as a ~ es hält die Leute ab.

disinclination [ˌdɪsɪnklɪˈneɪʃən] n Abneigung, Unlust f.

disinclined [ˌdɪsɪnˈklaɪnd] adj abgeneigt.

disinfect [ˌdɪsɪnˈfekt] vt desinfizieren.

disinfectant [ˌdɪsɪnˈfektənt] 1 n Desinfektionsmittel nt. 2 adj desinfizierend, Desinfektions-.

disinfection [ˌdɪsɪnˈfekʃən] n Desinfektion f.

disingenuous [ˌdɪsɪnˈdʒenjuːəs] adj unaufrichtig.

disingenuousness [ˌdɪsɪnˈdʒenjuːəsnɪs] n Unaufrichtigkeit f.

disinherit [ˈdɪsɪnˈherɪt] vt enterben.

disinheritance [ˈdɪsɪnˈherɪtəns] n Enterbung f.

disintegrate [dɪsˈɪntɪgreɪt] 1 vi zerfallen; (rock, cement) auseinanderbröckeln; (road surface) rissig werden; (car) sich in seine Bestandteile auflösen; (group also, institution) auflösen; (theory) zusammenbrechen.
2 vt zerfallen lassen; rock, cement auseinanderbröckeln lassen; road surface brüchig werden lassen; group, institution auflösen; theory zusammenbrechen lassen.

disintegration [dɪsˌɪntɪˈgreɪʃən] n see vi Zerfall m; Auseinanderbröckeln nt; Rissigkeit f; Auflösung f in seine Bestandteile; Auflösung f; Zusammenbruch m.

disinter [ˈdɪsɪnˈtɜːʳ] vt ausgraben.

disinterest [dɪsˈɪntrəst] n Desinteresse nt (in an +dat). it's a matter of complete ~ to me die Sache interessiert mich in keiner Weise, ich bin an der Sache völlig desinteressiert.

disinterested [dɪsˈɪntrɪstɪd] adj (a) (unbiased) unvoreingenommen, unparteiisch. (b) (bored) desinteressiert.

disinterestedly [dɪsˈɪntrɪstɪdlɪ] adv see adj.

disinterestedness [dɪsˈɪntrɪstɪdnɪs] n see adj (a) Unvoreingenommenheit f. (b) Desinteresse nt.

disinterment [ˌdɪsɪnˈtɜːmənt] n Ausgrabung f.

disjointed adj, ~ly adv [dɪsˈdʒɔɪntɪd, -lɪ] unzusammenhängend, zusammenhang(s)los.

disjointedness [dɪsˈdʒɔɪntɪdnɪs] n Zusammenhang(s)losigkeit f.

disjunctive [dɪsˈdʒʌŋktɪv] (Gram) 1 adj disjunktiv. 2 n Disjunktion f.

disk n (esp US) see disc.

dislike [dɪsˈlaɪk] 1 vt nicht mögen, nicht gern haben. to ~ doing sth etw ungern or nicht gern tun; to ~ sb doing sth es nicht gern haben or sehen, wenn jd etw tut; I ~ him/it intensely ich mag ihn/es überhaupt nicht; I don't ~ it ich habe nichts dagegen.
2 n Abneigung f (of gegen). to take a ~ to sb/sth eine Abneigung gegen jdn/etw fassen.

dislocate [ˈdɪsləʊkeɪt] vt (Med) ver- or ausrenken; (fig) plans, timetable durcheinanderbringen, in Verwirrung bringen. to ~ one's shoulder sich (dat) den Arm auskugeln.

dislocation [ˌdɪsləʊˈkeɪʃən] n (Med) see vt Verrenkung f; (fig) Durcheinanderbringen nt; Auskugeln nt.

dislodge [dɪsˈlɒdʒ] vt obstruction, stone lösen; (prise, poke out) herausstochern; (knock out) herausschlagen or -klopfen; enemy verdrängen. a few bricks/stones have been ~d einige Ziegelsteine/Steine sind verschoben worden.

disloyal [dɪsˈlɔɪəl] adj illoyal. to be ~ to sb/the cause sich jdm/der Sache gegenüber illoyal verhalten.

disloyalty [dɪsˈlɔɪəltɪ] n Illoyalität f (to gegenüber).

dismal [ˈdɪzməl] adj düster, trist; person trübselig, trübsinnig; failure, result kläglich.

dismally [ˈdɪzməlɪ] adv trostlos; fail kläglich; think, say trübselig. the sky remained ~ overcast der Himmel blieb trüb.

dismantle [dɪsˈmæntl] vt (take to pieces) auseinandernehmen; scaffolding abbauen; (permanently) arms factory, machinery demontieren; ship abwracken.

dismast [dɪsˈmɑːst] vt entmasten.

dismay [dɪsˈmeɪ] 1 n Bestürzung f. in ~ bestürzt. 2 vt bestürzen.

dismember [dɪsˈmembəʳ] vt (lit) animal, body zerstückeln; (Med) zergliedern; (fig) empire zersplittern.

dismemberment [dɪsˈmembəmənt] n (lit) Zergliederung f; (fig) Zersplitterung f.

dismiss [dɪsˈmɪs] vt (a) (from job) employee entlassen; official, officer also den Abschied geben (+dat).
(b) (allow to go) entlassen; assembly auflösen, aufheben. ~! wegtreten!
(c) (brush aside) point, objection abtun.
(d) (Jur) accused entlassen; appeal abweisen. to ~ a case die Klage abweisen.
(e) (Sport) batsman, team ausschlagen. he was ~ed for 52 runs er wurde nach 52 Läufen ausgeschlagen.

dismissal [dɪsˈmɪsəl] n see vt (a) Entlassung f; Abschied m. (b) Entlassung f; Auflösung f. he made a gesture of ~ (to us) er entließ uns mit einer Handbewegung. (c) Abtun nt. (d) Entlassung f; Abweisung f; Einstellung f. (e) Ausschlagen nt.

dismissive [dɪsˈmɪsɪv] adj remark wegwerfend. to be ~ about sth etw abtun; ... he said with a ~ wave of his hand ... sagte er mit einer abweisenden Handbewegung.

dismount [dɪsˈmaʊnt] 1 vi absteigen. 2 vt (a) rider abwerfen. (b) (Tech) machine, gun abmontieren.

disobedience [ˌdɪsəˈbiːdɪəns] n Ungehorsam m (to gegenüber). an act of ~ ungehorsames Verhalten.

disobedient [ˌdɪsəˈbiːdɪənt] adj ungehorsam.

disobey [ˌdɪsəˈbeɪ] vt parents, teacher nicht gehorchen (+dat); officer den Gehorsam verweigern (+dat); rule, law übertreten.

disoblige [ˌdɪsəˈblaɪdʒ] vt keinen Gefallen tun (+dat).

disobliging adj, ~ly adv [ˌdɪsəˈblaɪdʒɪŋ, -lɪ] ungefällig.

disorder [dɪsˈɔːdəʳ] 1 n (a) Durcheinander nt; (in room etc also) Unordnung f. in ~ durcheinander; (in room etc also) in Unordnung f. to throw sth into ~ etw durcheinanderbringen/in Unordnung bringen; to retreat in ~ einen ungeordneten Rückzug antreten.
(b) (Pol: rioting) Unruhen pl.
(c) (Med) Funktionsstörung f. kidney/mental ~ Nieren-/Geistesstörung; stomach ~ Magenbeschwerden pl.
2 vt (a) durcheinanderbringen; room in Unordnung bringen.
(b) (Med) angreifen.

disordered [dɪsˈɔːdəd] adj (a) room, thoughts unordentlich, durcheinander pred; plans, papers also wirr; existence ungeordnet. (b) (Med) stomach, liver angegriffen; mind gestört, verwirrt; imagination wirr.

disorderliness [dɪsˈɔːdəlɪnɪs] n see adj Unordentlichkeit f; Durcheinander nt; Wirrheit f; Ungeordnetheit f.

disorderly [dɪsˈɔːdəlɪ] adj (untidy) desk, room unordentlich; life unsolide; mind wirr; (unruly) crowd aufrührerisch; pupils also ungebärdig, außer Rand und Band; behaviour ungehörig. ~ conduct (Jur) ungebührliches Benehmen; ~ house (brothel) Bordell, Freudenhaus nt; (gambling den) Spielhölle f.

disorganization [dɪsˌɔːgənaɪˈzeɪʃən] n Desorganisation f; (state of confusion also) Durcheinander nt.

disorganize [dɪsˈɔːgənaɪz] vt durcheinanderbringen, desorganisieren (geh).

disorganized [dɪsˈɔːgənaɪzd] adj systemlos; life also, person chaotisch; filing system etc durcheinander pred, ungeordnet. he/the office is completely ~ bei ihm/im Büro geht alles drunter und drüber; he was completely ~ about it er ist dabei völlig unsystematisch vorgegangen.

disorient [dɪs'ɔːrɪənt], **disorientate** [dɪs'ɔːrɪənteɪt] *vt* (*lit, fig*) verwirren.

disown [dɪs'əʊn] *vt* verleugnen; *child also* verstoßen; *signature* nicht (als seine eigene) anerkennen; *suggestion* nicht wahrhaben wollen. **I'll ~ you if you go out in that hat** wenn du mit dem Hut ausgehst, tue ich so, als ob ich dich nicht zu dir gehöre.

disparage [dɪ'spærɪdʒ] *vt* herabsetzen; *work, achievements also* schmälern.

disparagement [dɪ'spærɪdʒmənt] *n see vt* Herabsetzung *f*; Schmälerung *f*.

disparaging *adj*, **~ly** *adv* [dɪ'spærɪdʒɪŋ, -lɪ] abschätzig, geringschätzig.

disparate ['dɪspərɪt] *adj* ungleich, disparat (*geh*).

disparity [dɪs'pærɪtɪ] *n* Ungleichheit, Disparität (*geh*) *f*.

dispassion [dɪs'pæʃən] *n* Objektivität *f*.

dispassionate *adj*, **~ly** *adv* [dɪs'pæʃənɪt, -lɪ] objektiv.

dispatch [dɪ'spætʃ] **1** *vt* (a) senden, schicken; *letter, telegram also* aufgeben; *person, troops etc also* entsenden. **(b)** (*deal with*) *job etc* (prompt) erledigen. **(c)** (*kill*) töten; (*shoot also*) den Todesschuß geben (+*dat*). **(d)** (*inf*) *food* fertig werden mit (*inf*). **2** *n also* ['dɪspætʃ] **(a)** *see vt* (a–c) Senden, Schicken *nt*; Aufgabe *f*; Entsendung *f*; prompte Erledigung; Tötung *f*. **date of ~** Absendedatum *nt*. **(b)** (*message, report*) Depesche *f*; (*Press*) Bericht *m*. **to be mentioned in ~es** (*Mil*) in den Kriegsberichten erwähnt werden. **(c)** (*promptness*) Promptheit *f*. **with ~** prompt. **dispatch:** **~ box** *n* (*Brit Parl*) Depeschenkassette *f*; **~ note** *n* (*in advance*) Benachrichtigungsschein *m*; (*with goods*) Begleitschein *m*; **~ rider** *n* (*Mil*) Meldereiter *or* -fahrer *m*.

dispel [dɪ'spel] *vt clouds, fog* auflösen, vertreiben; *doubts, fears* zerstreuen; *sorrows* vertreiben.

dispensability [dɪ,spensɪ'bɪlɪtɪ] *n* Entbehrlichkeit *f*.

dispensable [dɪ'spensəbl] *adj* entbehrlich.

dispensary [dɪ'spensərɪ] *n* (*in hospital*) (Krankenhaus)apotheke *f*; (*in chemist's*) Apothekenabteilung *f*; (*clinic*) Dispensarium *nt*.

dispensation [,dɪspen'seɪʃən] *n* (a) (*handing out*) Verteilung *f*; (*of charity*) Austeilung *f*. **~ of justice** Rechtsprechung *f*. **(b)** (*exemption, Eccl*) Dispens *m*, Dispensation *f*. **(c)** (*system, regime*) System *nt*; (*Rel*) Glaubenssystem *nt*. **~ of Providence** Fügung *f* der Vorsehung *or* des Schicksals.

dispense [dɪ'spens] **1** *vt* (a) verteilen, austeilen (*to an* +*acc*); *advice also* erteilen. **to ~ one's favours** seine Gunst verschenken; **to ~ justice** Recht sprechen. **(b)** (*Pharm*) *medicine* abgeben; *prescription* zubereiten. **(c)** (*form: exempt*) dispensieren, befreien. **to ~ sb from doing sth** jdn davon befreien *or* dispensieren, etw zu tun. **2** *vi* (*Pharm*) Medizin abgeben, dispensieren (*form*). **dispensing chemist's** Apotheke *f*.

♦**dispense with** *vi* +*prep obj* verzichten auf (+*acc*). **I could/couldn't ~ ~ that** ich könnte darauf gut/nicht verzichten, ich könnte ohne das auskommen/nicht auskommen; **that can be ~d with** das ist entbehrlich.

dispenser [dɪ'spensəʳ] *n* **(a)** (*Pharm*) Apotheker(in *f*) *m*. **(b)** (*container*) Spender *m*; *slot-machine*) Automat *m*.

dispersal [dɪ'spɜːsəl] *n see vt* Verstreuen *nt*; Verteilung *f*; Zerstreuung *f*, Auflösung *f*; Streuung *f*; Dispersion *f*; Verbreitung *f*; (*of efforts*) Verzettelung *f*, Zersplitterung *f*.

dispersant [dɪ'spɜːsənt] *n* Lösungsmittel *nt*.

disperse [dɪ'spɜːs] **1** *vt* (a) (*scatter widely*) verstreuen; (*Bot*) *seed* verteilen; (*dispel*) *crowd, mist* zerstreuen, auflösen; *oil slick* auflösen; (*Opt*) *light* streuen; (*Chem*) *particles* dispergieren; (*fig*) *knowledge etc* verbreiten. **2** *vi* sich zerstreuen *or* auflösen; (*oil slick*) sich auflösen.

dispersion [dɪ'spɜːʃən] *n see* dispersal.

dispirit [dɪ'spɪrɪt] *vt* entmutigen.

dispirited *adj*, **~ly** *adv* [dɪ'spɪrɪtɪd, -lɪ] entmutigt.

dispiriting *adj*, **~ly** *adv* [dɪ'spɪrɪtɪŋ, -lɪ] entmutigend.

displace [dɪs'pleɪs] *vt* **(a)** (*move*) verschieben. **(b)** (*replace*) ablösen, ersetzen. **(c)** (*Naut, Phys*) *water, air etc* verdrängen. **(d)** (*in office*) verdrängen, ausbooten (*inf*).

displaced: **~ emotion** *n* verlagertes Gefühl; **~ person** *n* Verschleppte(r) *mf*, Zwangsvertriebene(r) *mf*.

displacement [dɪs'pleɪsmənt] *n* **(a)** (*act of displacing*) *see vt* Verschiebung *f*; Ablösung *f*, Ersatz *m*; Verdrängung *f*; Verdrängung, Ausbootung (*inf*) *f*. **(b)** (*distance sth is moved*) Verschiebung *f*; (*Geol: of rocks*) Dislokation *f*. **(c)** (*volume displaced*) (*Phys*) verdrängte Menge; (*Naut*) Verdrängung *f*.

displacement: **~ activity** *n* (*Psych*) Ersatzbefriedigung *f*; **~ ton** *n* (*Naut*) Verdrängungstonne *f*.

display [dɪ'spleɪ] **1** *vt* **(a)** zeigen; *interest, courage also* beweisen; *interest, ignorance* an den Tag legen, beweisen; (*ostentatiously*) *new clothes etc also* vorführen; *luxury, sth sensational* zur Schau stellen; *power* demonstrieren; *exam results, notice* aushängen. **(b)** (*Comm*) *goods* ausstellen. **(c)** (*Typ, Press*) hervorheben. **2** *vi* Imponiergehabe zeigen; (*birds also*) balzen. **3** *n also* ['dɪspleɪ] **(a)** Zeigen *nt*; Beweis *m*; Vorführung *f*; Zurschaustellung *f*; Demonstration *f*; Aushängen *nt*. **to make a great ~ of sth/one's feelings** etw groß zur Schau stellen/seine Gefühle deutlich zeigen; **to be on ~** ausgestellt sein; **these are only for ~** die sind nur zur Ansicht; **I hope we don't have another ~ ~ (of temper)** ich hoffe, wir kriegen nicht noch einmal denselben Tanz *or* dieselbe Schau (*inf*). **(b)** (*exhibition of paintings etc*) Ausstellung *f*; (*dancing ~ etc*) Vorführung *f*; (*military, air ~*) Schau *f*.

(c) (*Comm*) Auslage *f*.
(d) (*Typ, Press*) **to give top ~ to sth** etw groß herausbringen.
(e) (*Zool*) Imponiergehabe *nt*; (*of bird also*) Balz *f*.
(f) (*visual ~*) Anzeige *f*.

display *in cpds* (*Comm*) Ausstellungs-; **~ advertising** *n* Großanzeige *f*; **~ cabinet** *n* Schaukasten *m*; **~ case** *n* Vitrine *f*; **~ window** *n* Schaufenster *nt*.

displease [dɪs'pliːz] *vt* mißfallen (+*dat*), nicht gefallen (+*dat*); (*annoy*) verstimmen, verärgern. **he was rather ~d to hear that ...** er hörte nur sehr ungern, daß ...; **he is easily ~d** er ist leicht verstimmt.

displeasing [dɪs'pliːzɪŋ] *adj* unangenehm. **to ~ sb** jdm mißfallen *or* nicht gefallen; (*annoy*) jdn verstimmen *or* verärgern; **the idea was not ~ to her** der Gedanke war ihr gar nicht so unangenehm.

displeasure [dɪs'pleʒəʳ] *n* Mißfallen *nt* (*at über* +*acc*).

disport [dɪs'pɔːt] *vr* (*old*) sich ergötzen (*old*).

disposable [dɪ'spəʊzəbl] *adj* **(a)** (*to be thrown away*) Wegwerf-, wegwerfbar; *handkerchief, nappy also* Papier-; *cup, plate* Papp-/Plastik-; *bottle, syringe* Einweg-. **easily ~** leicht zu vernichten. **(b)** (*available*) *capital, money* verfügbar, disponibel (*spec*). (*Fin*) **~ assets** disponibles (*spec*) *or* frei verfügbares Vermögen; **~ income** verfügbares Einkommen.

disposal [dɪ'spəʊzl] *n* **(a)** *see* dispose of **(a)** Loswerden *nt*; Veräußerung *f*; Beseitigung *f*; Erledigung, Regelung *f*. **(waste) ~ unit** Müllschlucker *m*. **(b)** (*control: over resources, funds, personnel*) Verfügungsgewalt *f*. **the means at one's ~** die jdm zur Verfügung stehenden Mittel; **to put sth at sb's ~** jdm etw zur Verfügung stellen; **we had the entire staff/afternoon at our ~** die ganze Belegschaft/der ganze Nachmittag stand uns zur Verfügung. **(c)** (*form: arrangement*) (*of ornaments, furniture*) Anordnung *f*, Arrangement *nt*; (*Mil: of troops*) Aufstellung *f*.

dispose [dɪ'spəʊz] **1** *vt* **(a)** (*form: arrange*) *shrubs, ornaments* anordnen; *people, troops* aufstellen; *papers* ordnen. **(b)** (*make willing*) **to ~ sb towards sb/sth** jdn für jdn/etw gewinnen; **to ~ sb to do sth** jdn geneigt machen, etw zu tun. **2** *vi see* propose.

♦**dispose of** *vi* +*prep obj* **(a)** (*get rid of*) *furniture* loswerden; (*by selling also*) veräußern; *unwanted person or goods also, litter* beseitigen; *opponent, difficulties* aus dem Weg schaffen; *question, matter, difficulties* erledigen, regeln. **(b)** (*have at disposal*) *fortune, time* verfügen über (+*acc*).

disposed [dɪ'spəʊzd] *adj* bereit. **to be well/ill ~ towards sb** jdm wohlwollen/übelwollen.

disposition [,dɪspə'zɪʃən] *n* **(a)** (*form: arrangement*) (*of buildings, ornaments*) Anordnung *f*; (*of forces*) Aufstellung *f*. **(b)** (*temperament*) Veranlagung *f*. **her cheerful/friendly ~** ihre fröhliche/freundliche Art.

dispossess ['dɪspə'zes] *vt* enteignen.

dispossession [,dɪspə'zeʃən] *n* Enteignung *f*.

disproportion [,dɪsprə'pɔːʃən] *n* Mißverhältnis *nt*.

disproportionate [,dɪsprə'pɔːʃnɪt] *adj* **to be ~ (to sth)** in keinem Verhältnis (zu etw) stehen; **a ~ amount of money/time** ein unverhältnismäßig hoher/niedriger Geldbetrag/eine unverhältnismäßig lange/kurze Zeit.

disproportionately [,dɪsprə'pɔːʃnɪtlɪ] *adv* unverhältnismäßig.

disprovable [dɪs'pruːvəbl] *adj* widerlegbar.

disprove [dɪs'pruːv] *vt* widerlegen.

disputable [dɪs'pjuːtəbl] *adj* sehr zweifelhaft, disputabel.

disputant [dɪ'spjuːtənt] *n* Disputant(in *f*) *m*.

disputation [,dɪspjuː'teɪʃən] *n* (*arguing*) Disput *m*, Kontroverse *f*.

disputatious [,dɪspjuː'teɪʃəs] *adj* streitbar, streitlustig.

dispute [dɪ'spjuːt] **1** *vt* **(a)** (*argue against*) *statement* bestreiten, anfechten; *claim to sth, will* anfechten. **I would ~ that** das möchte ich bestreiten. **(b)** (*debate*) *question, subject* sich streiten über (+*acc*); (*scholars etc also*) disputieren über (+*acc*). **the issue was hotly ~d** das Thema wurde hitzig diskutiert. **(c)** (*contest*) *championship, possession* jdm streitig machen; *territory* beanspruchen. **2** *vi* (*argue*) streiten; (*debate: scholars etc*) disputieren. **3** *n also* [dɪ'spjuːt] **(a)** *no pl* (*arguing, controversy*) Disput *m*, Kontroverse *f*. **a lot of ~** ein größerer Disput, eine größere Kontroverse; **to be beyond ~** außer Frage stehen; **without ~** zweifellos; **beyond** *or* **without ~ he would be ...** er wäre zweifelsohne *or* unbestritten ...; **there is some ~ about which horse won** es ist umstritten, welches Pferd gewonnen hat; **a territory in** *or* **under ~** ein umstrittenes Gebiet; **to be open to ~** anfechtbar *or* umstritten sein; **the case is in** *or* **under ~** (*Jur*) der Fall wird verhandelt. **(b)** (*quarrel, argument*) Streit *m*; (*debate: between scholars etc also*) Kontroverse *f*. **(c)** (*Ind*) Auseinandersetzung *f*. **the union is in ~ (with the management)** zwischen Gewerkschaft und Betriebsleitung bestehen Unstimmigkeiten; **wages ~** Tarifauseinandersetzungen *pl*; **to be in ~** (*on strike*) im Ausstand sein.

disqualification [dɪs,kwɒlɪfɪ'keɪʃən] *n* **(a)** Ausschluß *m*; (*Sport also*) Disqualifizierung, Disqualifikation *f*. **~ (from driving)** Führerscheinentzug *m*. **(b)** (*disqualifying factor*) Grund *m* zur Disqualifikation.

disqualify [dɪs'kwɒlɪfaɪ] *vt* (*make ineligible*) untauglich *or* ungeeignet machen (*from* für); (*Sport etc*) disqualifizieren, ausschließen. **to ~ sb from driving** jdm den Führerschein entziehen; **that disqualifies you from criticizing him** das nimmt Ihnen jedes Recht, ihn zu kritisieren.

disquiet [dɪs'kwaɪət] **1** *vt* beunruhigen. **2** *n* (*also* disquietude) Unruhe *f*.

disquisition [ˌdɪskwɪˈzɪʃən] n (lange, ausführliche) Abhandlung or (speech) Rede (on über +acc).

disregard [ˈdɪsrɪˈgɑːd] 1 vt (a) remark, feelings also nicht beachten, nicht achten auf (+acc); danger, advice, authority also mißachten.
2 n Nichtbeachtung, Mißachtung f (for gen); (for danger also, money) Geringschätzung f (for gen). to show complete ~ for sth etw völlig außer acht lassen.

disrepair [ˈdɪsrɪˈpɛər] n Baufälligkeit f. in a state of ~ baufällig; to fall into ~ verfallen.

disreputable [dɪsˈrepjʊtəbl] adj (dishonest, dishonourable) übel; (not respectable) unfein; clothes unansehnlich; area anrüchig, verrufen, übel.

disreputably [dɪsˈrepjʊtəblɪ] adv behave (dishonourably) übel, gemein; (not respectably) unfein; dress schlecht.

disrepute [ˈdɪsrɪˈpjuːt] n schlechter Ruf. to bring sth into ~ etw in Verruf bringen; to fall into ~ in Verruf kommen or geraten.

disrespect [ˈdɪsrɪsˈpekt] n Respektlosigkeit f (for gegenüber). I don't mean any ~, but ... ich will nicht respektlos sein, aber ...

disrespectful adj, **~ly** adv [ˌdɪsrɪsˈpektfʊl, -fəlɪ] respektlos (to gegenüber).

disrobe [dɪsˈrəʊb] 1 vi (judge) seine Gewänder ablegen; (form, hum: undress) sich entkleiden, sich entblättern (hum inf). 2 vt (form, hum: undress) entkleiden.

disrupt [dɪsˈrʌpt] vt stören; lesson, meeting, conversation, train service, communications also unterbrechen.

disruption [dɪsˈrʌpʃən] n see vt Störung f; Unterbrechung f.

disruptive [dɪsˈrʌptɪv] adj störend. ~ element störendes Element, Störenfried m.

dissatisfaction [ˈdɪsˌsætɪsˈfækʃən] n Unzufriedenheit f.

dissatisfied [dɪsˈsætɪsfaɪd] adj unzufrieden (with mit).

dissect [dɪˈsekt] vt plant präparieren; animal also sezieren; (fig) report, theory sezieren, zergliedern.

dissection [dɪˈsekʃən] n (a) (act) see vt Präparation f; Sektion f; Zergliederung f. (b) (plant, animal) Präparat nt.

dissemble [dɪˈsembl] 1 vt (cover up) verbergen; (feign) vortäuschen, heucheln. 2 vi (liter) sich verstellen; (feign illness) simulieren.

dissembler [dɪˈsemblər] n Heuchler(in f) m.

disseminate [dɪˈsemɪneɪt] vt verbreiten.

dissemination [dɪˌsemɪˈneɪʃən] n Verbreitung f.

dissension [dɪˈsenʃən] n Meinungsverschiedenheit, Differenz f. a great deal of ~ große Differenzen or Meinungsverschiedenheiten pl; to cause ~ zu Meinungsverschiedenheiten or Differenzen führen; (person) Meinungsverschiedenheiten or Differenzen verursachen.

dissent [dɪˈsent] 1 vi (a) anderer Meinung sein, differieren (geh). I strongly ~ from what he says ich muß dem, was er sagt, entschieden widersprechen.
(b) (Eccl) sich weigern, die Staatskirche anzuerkennen.
2 n (a) Dissens m (geh), Nichtübereinstimmung f. to voice/express one's ~ (with sth) erklären, daß man (mit etw) nicht übereinstimmt; in the absence of any ~ da keine Gegenstimme laut wurde; the motion was carried with almost no ~ der Antrag wurde fast ohne Gegenstimmen angenommen.
(b) (Eccl) Weigerung f, die (englische) Staatskirche anzuerkennen.

dissenter [dɪˈsentər] n Dissident m; (Eccl also) Dissenter m.

dissentient [dɪˈsenʃɪənt] adj opinion abweichend. there was not a single ~ voice es wurde keine Gegenstimme laut.

dissertation [ˌdɪsəˈteɪʃən] n wissenschaftliche Arbeit; (for PhD) Dissertation f; (fig) Vortrag m.

disservice [dɪsˈsɜːvɪs] n to do sb a ~ jdm einen schlechten Dienst erweisen; to be a ~/of ~ to sb sich nachteilig für jdn auswirken, jdm schaden.

dissidence [ˈdɪsɪdəns] n Opposition f; (Pol) Dissidententum nt.

dissident [ˈdɪsɪdənt] 1 n Dissident(in f), Regimekritiker(in f) m. 2 adj dissident, regimekritisch.

dissimilar [ˈdɪˈsɪmɪlər] adj unterschiedlich, verschieden (to von); two things verschieden. not ~ (to sb/sth) (jdm/einer Sache) nicht unähnlich or (in appearance) nicht unähnlich.

dissimilarity [ˌdɪsɪmɪˈlærɪtɪ] n Unterschiedlichkeit, Verschiedenheit f; (in appearance also) Unähnlichkeit f.

dissimulate [dɪˈsɪmjʊleɪt] 1 vt verbergen. 2 vi sich verstellen.

dissimulation [dɪˌsɪmjʊˈleɪʃən] n Verstellung, Heuchelei f. by this ~ of his real feelings dadurch, daß er so seine wahren Gefühle verbarg or nicht zeigte.

dissipate [ˈdɪsɪpeɪt] 1 vt (a) (dispel) fog auflösen; doubts, fears zerstreuen. (b) energy, efforts verschwenden, vergeuden; fortune verschwenden, verschleudern (inf). 2 vi (clouds, fog) sich auflösen; (crowd, doubts, fear also) sich zerstreuen.

dissipated [ˈdɪsɪpeɪtɪd] adj behaviour, society zügellos; person also leichtlebig; (in appearance) verlebt; life ausschweifend.

dissipation [ˌdɪsɪˈpeɪʃən] n see vt (a) Auflösung f; Zerstreuung f. (b) Verschwendung, Vergeudung f; Verschwendung f, Verschleudern nt (inf). (c) (debauchery) Ausschweifung f. a life of ~ ein ausschweifendes Leben.

dissociate [dɪˈsəʊʃɪeɪt] vt (a) trennen, dissoziieren (geh). to ~ oneself from sb/sth sich von jdm/etw distanzieren; two aspects which have become largely ~d zwei Aspekte, die sich weitgehend voneinander gelöst haben. (b) (Chem) dissoziieren.

dissociation [dɪˌsəʊsɪˈeɪʃən] n (a) (separation) Trennung, Dissoziation (geh) f. in ~ from getrennt or losgelöst von. (b) (Chem, Psych) Dissoziation f.

dissoluble [dɪˈsɒljʊbl] adj (Chem) löslich, dissolubel (spec).

dissolute [ˈdɪsəluːt] adj person zügellos, freizügig; way of life also ausschweifend; appearance verlebt.

dissoluteness [ˈdɪsəluːtnɪs] n see adj Zügellosigkeit, Freizügigkeit f; Verlebtheit f.

dissolution [ˌdɪsəˈluːʃən] n (a) (Chem, Jur, Pol) Auflösung f. (b)
(of relationship) Auflösung f; (of faith) Abbröckeln nt.

dissolve [dɪˈzɒlv] 1 vt (a) (lit, Jur, Pol, fig) auflösen; marriage also scheiden.
(b) (Film) überblenden (into in or auf +acc).
2 vi (a) (lit, Jur, Pol, fig) sich (auf)lösen; (fig) sich in nichts auflösen. it ~s in water es ist wasserlöslich, es löst sich in Wasser; to ~ into tears in Tränen zerfließen.
(b) (Film) überblenden (into in or auf +acc).
3 n (Film) Überblendung f.

dissolvent [dɪˈzɒlvənt] 1 adj lösend. 2 n Lösungsmittel nt.

dissonance [ˈdɪsənəns] n (Mus, fig) Dissonanz f.

dissonant [ˈdɪsənənt] adj (Mus) dissonant; (fig) opinions, temperaments unvereinbar; colours disharmonisch.

dissuade [dɪˈsweɪd] vt to ~ sb (from sth)/from doing sth jdn von etw abbringen, jdm etw ausreden/jdn davon abbringen or jdm ausreden, etw zu tun; to try to ~ sb from sth jdn von etw abraten, versuchen, jdn von etw abzubringen; he wouldn't be ~d er ließ sich nicht davon abbringen, er ließ sich das nicht ausreden.

dissuasion [dɪˈsweɪʒən] n Abraten nt. no amount of ~ would make him change his mind so sehr man ihm auch abriet, er änderte seinen Entschluß nicht.

dissuasive [dɪˈsweɪsɪv] adj abratend. he was most ~ er riet sehr davon ab; in the most ~ tone he advised her not to go er riet ihr ausdrücklich davon ab, hinzugehen; I found his argument ~ rather than persuasive statt mich dazu zu überreden, brachten mich seine Argumente eher davon ab.

dissuasively [dɪˈsweɪsɪvlɪ] adv see adj.

dissuasiveness [dɪˈsweɪsɪvnɪs] n (of person) Abraten nt. the ~ of his tone/voice/arguments sein abratender Ton/seine abratende Stimme/seine abratenden Argumente.

distaff [ˈdɪstɑːf] n (a) (in spinning) Spinnrocken m, Kunkel f. (b) on the ~ side mütterlicherseits.

distance [ˈdɪstəns] 1 n (a) (in space) Entfernung f; (gap, interval) Abstand m, Distanz f (geh); (distance covered) Strecke f, Weg m. we now measure ~ in metres wir geben Entfernungen jetzt in Metern an; at a ~ of two metres in zwei Meter(n) Entfernung; stopping ~ Bremsweg m; the ~ between the eyes/railway lines der Abstand der Augen or zwischen den Augen/der Abstand zwischen den Eisenbahnschienen; at an equal ~ from each other gleich weit voneinander entfernt or weg; the ~ between London and Glasgow is ... die Entfernung zwischen London und Glasgow beträgt ...; what's the ~ from London to Glasgow? wie weit ist es von London nach Glasgow?; I don't know the exact ~ ich weiß nicht genau, wie weit es ist; we covered the ~ between London and Glasgow in five hours wir haben für die Strecke London-Glasgow fünf Stunden gebraucht; he went with me (for) part of the ~ er ging einen Teil der Strecke or des Weges mit mir; modern transport has reduced the ~ between nations die modernen Verkehrsmittel haben die Entfernungen or den Abstand zwischen den Völkern verringert; in the (far) ~ (ganz) in der Ferne, (ganz) weit weg; he admired her at a ~ (fig) er bewunderte sie aus der Ferne; it's within walking ~ es ist zu Fuß erreichbar; it's no ~ es ist überhaupt nicht weit, es ist nur ein Katzensprung; seen from a ~ it looks different von weitem or aus der Entfernung sieht das ganz anders aus; quite a short ~ (away) ziemlich weit/nicht weit (entfernt or weg); we drove 600 miles — that's quite a ~ wir sind 600 Meilen gefahren — das ist eine ganz schöne Strecke; the race is over a ~ of 3 miles das Rennen geht über eine Distanz von 3 Meilen; the fight went the ~ der Kampf ging über alle Runden; to go the ~ durchhalten, es durchstehen; to keep one's ~ Abstand halten.
(b) (in time) at a ~ of 400 years aus einem Abstand von 400 Jahren; at this ~ in time nach einem so langen Zeitraum.
(c) (fig: in social rank) Unterschied m. to keep sb at a ~ jdn auf Distanz halten; to keep one's ~ (be aloof) auf Distanz bleiben, Abstand or Distanz wahren (geh); he keeps his ~ er bleibt immer auf Distanz, er ist immer sehr distanziert.
2 vt (a) (Sport etc) see outdistance.
(b) to ~ oneself from sb/sth sich von jdm/etw distanzieren.

distance: ~ event n Langstreckenlauf m; ~ runner n Langstreckenläufer(in f) m.

distant [ˈdɪstənt] 1 adj (a) (far away) country weit entfernt, fern. we had a ~ view of the church wir sahen in der Ferne die Kirche; that's not so far ~ from the truth das ist gar nicht so weit von der Wahrheit entfernt.
(b) (in past) age fern, weit zurückliegend; recollection entfernt. that was in the ~ past das liegt weit zurück.
(c) (in future) that's a ~ prospect das ist Zukunftsmusik, das liegt noch in weiter Ferne; in the ~ future in ferner Zukunft; the exams are still very ~ bis zu den Prüfungen ist noch viel Zeit.
(d) relationship, likeness, cousin entfernt.
(e) (fig: aloof) person, manner distanziert, kühl, reserviert.
2 adv entfernt. two miles ~ zwei Meilen entfernt.

distantly [ˈdɪstəntlɪ] adv (a) (lit) entfernt, fern. the lights shone ~ on the horizon die Lichter leuchteten weit weg am Horizont. (b) (fig) resemble entfernt; be related also weitläufig. (c) (fig: aloofly) speak, behave kühl, distanziert, reserviert.

distaste [dɪsˈteɪst] n Widerwille m (for gegen).

distasteful [dɪsˈteɪstfʊl] adj task unangenehm; photo, magazine geschmacklos. to be ~ to sb jdm zuwider or unangenehm sein; he's finding his duties more and more ~ seine Pflichten werden ihm immer mehr zuwider.

distemper[1] [dɪsˈtempər] 1 n (paint) Temperafarbe f. 2 vt mit Temperafarbe streichen.

distemper[2] n (a) (Vet) Staupe f. (b) (old: ill temper) Verstimmung f.

distend [dɪsˈtend] 1 vt balloon (auf)blasen; sails, stomach (auf)blähen. 2 vi sich blähen.

distension [dɪ'stenʃən] n Blähen nt; (of stomach also) (Auf)blähung f.
distil, (US) distill [dɪ'stɪl] **1** vt **(a)** (Chem) destillieren; whisky etc also brennen; (fig) herausarbeiten, (heraus)destillieren.
   (b) (drip slowly) tropfenweise ausscheiden or absondern.
2 vi **(a)** (Chem) sich herausdestillieren; (whisky also) gebrannt werden; (fig also) sich herauskristallisieren.
   (b) (drip slowly) langsam heraustropfen, herauströpfeln.
distillation [ˌdɪstɪ'leɪʃən] n (Chem etc) (act) Destillation f; (of whisky etc also) Brennen nt; (product) Destillat nt; (fig) (act) Verarbeitung f; (product) Destillat nt.
distiller [dɪ'stɪlər] n Destillateur, (Branntwein)brenner m. ~s of whisky/gin Whisky-/Ginbrenner or -destillateure pl.
distillery [dɪ'stɪlərɪ] n Destillation, (Branntwein)brennerei f.
distinct [dɪ'stɪŋkt] adj **(a)** deutlich, klar, distinkt (geh); landmark, shape also deutlich or klar erkennbar; preference also ausgesprochen; likeness also ausgeprägt, ausgesprochen; increase, progress also merklich, entschieden. **I have a ~ memory of him putting it there** ich erinnere mich deutlich daran, daß er es dahin gelegt hat; **a ~ lack of respect** ein deutlicher Mangel an Respekt; **I had the ~ feeling that something bad was going to happen** ich hatte das bestimmte Gefühl, daß etwas Schlimmes passieren würde; **he has a ~ Scottish accent** er hat einen unverkennbar schottischen Akzent; **he has a ~ advantage over her** er ist ihr gegenüber klar or deutlich im Vorteil, er hat ihr gegenüber einen deutlichen Vorteil.
   (b) (different) verschieden; (separate) getrennt. **as ~ from** im Unterschied zu; **to keep sth ~ from sth else** etw und etw auseinanderhalten.
   (c) (distinctive) eigen, individuell. **in his own ~ style** in seinem eigenen unverwechselbaren or unverkennbaren Stil.
distinction [dɪ'stɪŋkʃən] n **(a)** (difference) Unterschied m; (act of distinguishing) Unterscheidung f. **to make a ~ (between two things)** (zwischen zwei Dingen) unterscheiden or einen Unterschied machen; **is there any ~ in meaning here?** liegt hier ein Bedeutungsunterschied vor?
   (b) no pl (preeminence) (hoher) Rang m, Distinktion f (dated geh); (refinement) Vornehmheit f. **she has an air of ~** sie hat etwas Vornehmes or Distinguiertes (geh); **to win ~** sich hervortun or auszeichnen; **a pianist of ~** ein Pianist von Rang.
   (c) (Sch, Univ: grade) Auszeichnung f. **he got a ~ in French** er hat das Französischexamen mit Auszeichnung bestanden; **he was awarded several academic ~s** ihm sind mehrere akademische Auszeichnungen verliehen worden.
distinctive [dɪ'stɪŋktɪv] adj colour, plumage auffällig; (unmistakable) unverwechselbar; gestures, walk, voice, bird call etc unverwechselbar, unverkennbar; characteristic, feature kennzeichnend. **with his ~ irony** mit der ihm eigenen or für ihn charakteristischen Ironie; **it wasn't a very ~ car** es war nichts Besonderes an dem Auto.
distinctively [dɪ'stɪŋktɪvlɪ] adv see adj.
distinctly [dɪ'stɪŋktlɪ] adv **(a)** deutlich, klar; prefer also, alike, rude ausgesprochen; better, increased entschieden. **his accent was ~ Bavarian** sein Akzent war eindeutig bayrisch. **(b)** (differently) verschieden; (separate) getrennt.
distinguish [dɪ'stɪŋgwɪʃ] **1** vt **(a)** (make different) unterscheiden. **only the length of their hair ~es the twins** die Zwillinge unterscheiden sich nur durch ihre Haarlänge.
   (b) (tell apart) unterscheiden, auseinanderhalten. **he can't ~ green from/and red** er kann Rot nicht von Grün unterscheiden, er kann Rot und Grün nicht auseinanderhalten.
   (c) (make out) landmark, shape erkennen, ausmachen.
2 vi **to ~ between** unterscheiden zwischen (+dat), einen Unterschied machen zwischen (+dat).
3 vr sich auszeichnen, sich hervortun.
distinguishable [dɪ'stɪŋgwɪʃəbl] adj **(a)** (which can be differentiated) two things, people unterscheidbar. **to be (easily/scarcely) ~ from sb/sth** (gut/kaum) von jdm/etw zu unterscheiden sein; **the twins are hardly ~** die Zwillinge sind kaum auseinanderzuhalten or voneinander zu unterscheiden.
   (b) (discernible) landmark, shape erkennbar, zu erkennen; change, improvement merklich, deutlich.
distinguished [dɪ'stɪŋgwɪʃt] adj **(a)** (eminent) pianist, scholar von hohem Rang; career hervorragend. **(b)** (refined, elegant) person, manner distinguiert (geh), vornehm; voice gepflegt.
distinguishing [dɪ'stɪŋgwɪʃɪŋ] adj kennzeichnend, charakteristisch. **the ~ feature of his work is ...** was seine Arbeit auszeichnet or kennzeichnet, ist ...
distort [dɪ'stɔːt] vt **(a)** (divert attention of) verzerren (also Phys); truth, words verdrehen; facts verzerrt darstellen, verdrehen; judgement trüben, beeinträchtigen. **a ~ed report/view of life** ein verzerrter Bericht/ein verzerrtes Bild von der Wirklichkeit; **she has a ~ed impression of what is happening** sie sieht die Ereignisse völlig verzerrt.
2 vi verzerrt werden.
distortion [dɪ'stɔːʃən] n see vt Verzerrung f; Verdrehung f; verzerrte Darstellung, Verdrehung f; Trübung, Beeinträchtigung f.
distract [dɪ'strækt] vt **(a)** (divert attention of) ablenken. **the noise ~ed him from his work** der Lärm lenkte ihn von der Arbeit ab. **(b)** (old: amuse) zerstreuen, die Zeit vertreiben (+dat).
distracted [dɪ'stræktɪd] adj (worried, anxious) besorgt, beunruhigt; (grief-stricken, distraught) außer sich (with vor +dat). **she screamed like one ~** sie schrie wie eine Irre.
distractedly [dɪ'stræktɪdlɪ] adv see adj.
distraction [dɪ'strækʃən] n **(a)** no pl (lack of attention) Unaufmerksamkeit f. **in a state of ~** zerstreut.
   (b) (interruption: from work etc) Ablenkung f.
   (c) (entertainment) Zerstreuung f.
   (d) (anxiety) Ruhelosigkeit, Unruhe f; (distraughtness) Ver-

störung f. **to love sb to ~** jdn wahnsinnig lieben; **to drive sb to ~** jdn zum Wahnsinn or zur Verzweiflung treiben.
distrain [dɪ'streɪn] vi (Jur) **to ~ upon sb's goods** jds Eigentum beschlagnahmen.
distraint [dɪ'streɪnt] n (Jur) Beschlagnahmung, Beschlagnahme f.
distraught [dɪ'strɔːt] adj verzweifelt, außer sich (dat) pred; look, voice verzweifelt.
distress [dɪ'stres] **1** n **(a)** Verzweiflung f; (physical) Leiden nt; (mental, cause of ~) Kummer m, Sorge f. **to be in great ~** sehr leiden; (physical also) starke Schmerzen haben; **to cause ~ to sb** jdm Kummer or Sorge/starke Schmerzen bereiten.
   (b) (great poverty) Not f, Elend nt.
   (c) (danger) Not f. **a ship/plane in ~** ein Schiff in Seenot/ein Flugzeug in Not; **~ call** Notsignal nt.
2 vt (worry) Kummer machen (+dat), Sorge bereiten (+dat). **don't ~ yourself** machen Sie sich (dat) keine Sorgen!
distressed [dɪ'strest] adj **(a)** (upset) bekümmert; (grief-stricken) erschüttert (about von). **(b)** (poverty-stricken) **in ~ circumstances** in erbärmlichen or armseligen Umständen or Verhältnissen; **~ area** Notstandsgebiet nt; **~ gentlewoman** verarmte Dame von Stand.
distressing [dɪ'stresɪŋ] adj (upsetting) besorgniserregend; (stronger) erschreckend; (regrettable) bedauerlich, betrüblich.
distressingly [dɪ'stresɪŋlɪ] adv see adj.
distress: **~ rocket** n Notrakete f; **~-signal** n Notsignal nt.
distributary [dɪ'strɪbjʊtərɪ] **1** n (Geog) Nebenarm m, Flußarm m eines Delta. **2** adj network Verteiler-.
distribute [dɪ'strɪbjuːt] vt verteilen; (Comm) goods vertreiben; films verleihen; dividends ausschütten. **to ~ to/amongst** verteilen auf (+acc)/unter (+acc); vertreiben/ausschütten an (+acc); **the incidence of this disease is evenly ~d throughout the classes** diese Krankheit tritt in allen Schichten gleich häufig auf.
distribution [ˌdɪstrɪ'bjuːʃən] n see vt Verteilung f; Vertrieb m; Verleih m; Ausschüttung f.
distributive [dɪ'strɪbjʊtɪv] **1** adj (Gram) distributiv. **2** n (Gram) Distributivum nt.
distributor [dɪ'strɪbjʊtər] n Verteiler m (also Aut); (Comm) Großhändler m; (of films) Verleih(er) m.
district ['dɪstrɪkt] n (of country) Gebiet nt; (of town) Stadtteil m, Viertel nt; (administrative area) (Verwaltungs)bezirk m. **all the girls in the ~** alle Mädchen in der Gegend.
district: **~ attorney** n (US) Bezirksstaatsanwalt m; **D~ Commissioner** n hoher Regierungsbeamter in einer Kolonie; **~ council** n (Brit) = Bezirksregierung f; **~ court** n (US Jur) Bezirksgericht nt; **~ manager** n (Comm) Bezirksdirektor m; **~ nurse** n Gemeindeschwester f; **~ surveyor** n Bauinspektor m, Beamte(r) m des regionalen Bauaufsichtsamtes.
distrust [dɪs'trʌst] **1** vt mißtrauen (+dat). **2** n Mißtrauen nt (of gegenüber).
distrustful [dɪs'trʌstfʊl] adj mißtrauisch (of gegenüber).
disturb [dɪ'stɜːb] **1** vt **(a)** (interrupt, interfere with, bother) person, sleep, silence, balance, concentration stören. **you ~ed my sleep** du hast mich im Schlaf gestört; **I hope I'm not ~ing you** ich hoffe, ich störe (Sie) nicht.
   (b) (alarm) person beunruhigen.
   (c) waters bewegen; sediment aufwirbeln; papers durcheinanderbringen; (fig) peace of mind stören.
2 vi stören. **"please do not ~"** „bitte nicht stören".
disturbance [dɪ'stɜːbəns] n **(a)** (political, social) Unruhe f; (in house, street) (Ruhe)störung f. **to cause or create a ~** Unruhe or eine Ruhestörung verursachen.
   (b) (interruption: in work, routine) Störung f.
   (c) no pl (disarranging) see vt (c) Bewegung f; Aufwirbeln nt; Durcheinanderbringen nt; Störung f.
   (d) no pl (alarm, uneasiness) Unruhe f. **I don't want to cause any ~ but** ... ich will Sie ja nicht beunruhigen, aber ...
disturbed [dɪ'stɜːbd] adj **(a)** (unbalanced) (mentally) geistig gestört; (socially) verhaltensgestört. **his mind is ~** er ist geistig gestört.
   (b) (worried, unquiet) beunruhigt (at, by über +acc, von). **your father was rather ~ to hear of your trouble with the police** dein Vater hat sich sehr beunruhigt, als er von deinen Schwierigkeiten mit der Polizei hörte.
   (c) **to have a ~ night** eine unruhige Nacht verbringen.
   (d) waters unruhig; surface bewegt.
disturbing [dɪ'stɜːbɪŋ] adj (alarming) beunruhigend; (distracting) störend.
disturbingly [dɪ'stɜːbɪŋlɪ] adv see adj.
disulphide, (US) disulfide [daɪ'sʌlfaɪd] n Disulfid nt.
disunite [ˌdɪsju:'naɪt] vt spalten, entzweien.
disunity [ˌdɪs'ju:nɪtɪ] n Uneinigkeit f.
disuse ['dɪs'juːs] n **to fall into ~** nicht mehr benutzt werden; (custom) außer Gebrauch kommen; **rusty from ~** wegen mangelnder Benutzung verrostet.
disused ['dɪs'juːzd] adj building leerstehend; mine, railway line stillgelegt; vehicle, machine nicht mehr benutzt.
disyllabic [ˌdɪsɪ'læbɪk] adj zweisilbig.
ditch [dɪtʃ] **1** n **(a)** Graben m.
   (b) (Aviat sl) Bach m (sl). **the plane came down in the ~** die Maschine fiel in den Bach (sl).
2 vt (sl: get rid of) person abhängen (inf); employee, boyfriend abservieren (inf); plan, project badengehen lassen (sl); car stehenlassen; old manuscript, unwanted object wegschmeißen (inf). **to ~ a plane** eine Maschine im Bach landen (sl).
3 vi (Aviat sl) in den Bach (sl).
dither ['dɪðər] **1** n **to be all of a ~**, **to be in a ~** ganz aufgeregt or am Rotieren (inf) sein.
2 vi zaudern, schwanken. **to ~ over a decision**

mit einer Entscheidung zaudern or nicht zu Potte kommen (inf); **stop** ~**ing (about) and get on with it**! jetzt laß doch dieses ewige Hin und Her und fang endlich mal an.

dithyrambs [ˈdɪθɪræmz] npl Dithyramben pl.

ditto [ˈdɪtəʊ] n **I'd like coffee — ~ (for me)** (inf) ich möchte Kaffee — ich auch, dito (inf); ~ **marks,** ~ **sign** Wiederholungszeichen nt.

ditty [ˈdɪtɪ] n Liedchen nt, Weise f.

diuretic [ˌdaɪjʊəˈretɪk] **1** adj harntreibend, diuretisch (spec). **2** n harntreibendes Mittel, Diuretikum nt (spec).

diurnal [daɪˈɜːnl] **1** adj (liter: of the daytime) Tages-; (Bot, Zool) Tag-. **the sun's** ~ **course** der Tageslauf der Sonne, der tägliche Lauf der Sonne; **this pallid** ~ **moon** dieser blasse Mond am Tageshimmel. **2** n (Eccl) Diurnal(e) nt.

div abbr of **dividend**.

divan [dɪˈvæn] n Diwan m. ~ **bed** Liege f.

dive [daɪv] (vb: pret ~**d** or (US) **dove**, ptp ~**d**) **1** n (a) (by swimmer) Sprung m; (by plane) Sturzflug m; (Ftbl) Hechtsprung, Hechter (inf) m. **divers are only allowed to make two** ~**s a day** Taucher dürfen nur zweimal am Tag unter Wasser; **the deepest** ~ **yet made** die bisher größte Tauchtiefe; **to make a** ~ **for sth** (fig inf) sich auf etw (acc) stürzen; **to take a** ~ (sl: boxer) ein K.O. vortäuschen; (inf: pound, dollar etc: plunge) absacken (inf).
(b) (pej inf: club etc) Spelunke f (inf).
2 vi (a) (person) (from diving-board) springen; (from side of lake, pool etc) (mit dem Kopf voraus) springen, hechten; (under water) tauchen; (submarine) untertauchen; (plane) einen Sturzflug machen. **to** ~ **for pearls** nach Perlen tauchen; **the goalie** ~**d for the ball** der Torwart hechtete nach dem Ball; ~**!** (Naut) Tauchstation!
(b) (inf) **he** ~**d into the crowd/under the table** er tauchte in der Menge unter/verschwand blitzschnell unter dem Tisch; **to** ~ **for cover** eilig in Deckung gehen; **he** ~**d into his car and raced off** er stürzte (sich) ins Auto und raste davon; **he** ~**d into his pocket** er fischte eilig in seiner Tasche.
♦**dive in** vi (a) (swimmer) (mit dem Kopf voraus) hineinspringen. (b) (inf: start to eat) ~ ~**!** hau(t) rein! (inf).

dive-: ~**bomb** vt im Sturzflug bombardieren; ~**bomber** n Sturzkampfbomber, Stuka m; ~**bombing** n Sturzkampfbombardierung f.

diver [ˈdaɪvə^r] n (also bird) Taucher m; (off high board) Turmspringer(in f) m; (off springboard) Kunstspringer(in f) m.

diverge [daɪˈvɜːdʒ] vi abweichen (from von), divergieren (geh, Math); (two things) voneinander abweichen, auseinandergehen.

divergence [daɪˈvɜːdʒəns] n Divergenz f (geh, Math), Auseinandergehen nt; (from a standard etc) Abweichung f.

divergent [daɪˈvɜːdʒənt] adj opinions etc auseinandergehend, divergent (geh, Math), divergierend (geh, Math).

divers [ˈdaɪvɜːz] adj attr mehrere, diverse.

diverse [daɪˈvɜːs] adj verschieden(artig), unterschiedlich.

diversification [daɪˌvɜːsɪfɪˈkeɪʃən] n (change, variety) Abwechslung f; (of business etc) Diversifikation f (spec).

diversify [daɪˈvɜːsɪfaɪ] **1** vt abwechslungsreich(er) gestalten; interests breit(er) fächern; business etc diversifizieren (Comm). **2** vi (Comm) diversifizieren.

diversion [daɪˈvɜːʃən] n (a) (redirecting: of traffic, stream) Umleitung f.
(b) (relaxation) Unterhaltung f. **for** ~ zur Unterhaltung or Zerstreuung; **it's a** ~ **from work** es ist eine angenehme Abwechslung von der Arbeit.
(c) (Mil, fig: that which distracts attention) Ablenkung f. **to create a** ~ ablenken; **as a** ~ um abzulenken.

diversionary [daɪˈvɜːʃnərɪ] adj ablenkend, Ablenkungs-. ~ **tactics** (Mil, fig) eine Reihe von Ablenkungstaktiken/Ablenkungstaktiken pl; **a** ~ **manoeuvre** (Mil, fig) ein Ablenkungsmanöver nt; **the attack was meant to serve a purely** ~ **purpose** der Angriff sollte nur zur Ablenkung dienen; ~ **behaviour** Ablenkungsgebaren nt.

diversity [daɪˈvɜːsɪtɪ] n Vielfalt f. ~ **of opinion** Meinungsvielfalt f.

divert [daɪˈvɜːt] vt (a) traffic, stream umleiten; attention ablenken; conversation in eine andere Richtung lenken; blow abwenden. (b) (amuse) unterhalten.

diverting [daɪˈvɜːtɪŋ] adj unterhaltsam, kurzweilig.

divest [daɪˈvest] vt (a) (of clothes, leaves) berauben (sb of sth jdn einer Sache gen); **the** ~**book of technical expressions** er versuchte, das Buch von Fachausdrücken zu reinigen; ~**ed of its rhetoric the speech says very little** ihrer Rhetorik entkleidet, ist die Rede recht nichtssagend; **he** ~**ed himself of his heavy overcoat** (hum, form) er entledigte sich seines schweren Mantels; **the country has** ~**ed itself of the last traces of imperialism** das Land hat sich der letzten Reste des Imperialismus entledigt.
(b) **to** ~ **sb of office/his authority** jdn des or seines Amtes entkleiden (geh)/seiner Macht entheben; **to** ~ **sb of (his) rank** jdn seiner Würden entkleiden (geh).

divide [dɪˈvaɪd] **1** vt (a) (separate) trennen. **the wall which** ~**s the two offices** die Wand, die die beiden Büros trennt.
(b) (split into parts: also ~ **up**) money, work, property, kingdom, room teilen (into in +acc); (in order to distribute) aufteilen. **the river** ~**s the city into two** der Fluß teilt die Stadt; ~ **the piece of paper into three parts** teilen Sie das Blatt in drei Teile (ein); **she** ~**d the cake into five parts** sie teilte den Kuchen in fünf Stücke (auf); **the book can be** ~**d into three main parts** das Buch kann in drei Hauptteile gegliedert werden.
(c) (share out) money, time, food verteilen. **she** ~**d the food evenly among the children** sie verteilte das Essen gleichmäßig an die Kinder, sie teilte das Essen gleichmäßig unter die Kinder or den Kindern auf; **God's gifts are not very equitably**

~**d** Gottes Gaben sind nicht sehr gleichmäßig verteilt.
(d) (Math) dividieren, teilen. **to** ~ **6 into 36, to** ~ **36 by 6** 36 durch 6 teilen or dividieren; **what is 12** ~**d by 3**? was ist 12 (geteilt or dividiert) durch 3?
(e) (cause disagreement among) friends, political parties entzweien.
(f) (Brit Parl) **to** ~ **the House** durch Hammelsprung abstimmen lassen.
2 vi (a) (river, road, room, cells) sich teilen; (book etc) sich gliedern (into in +acc). **to** ~ **into groups** sich in Gruppen aufteilen; (be classified) sich gliedern lassen; **the policy of** ~ **and rule** die Politik des „divide et impera".
(b) (Math: number) sich teilen or dividieren lassen (by durch). **we're learning to** ~ wir lernen Teilen or Dividieren; **he can't** ~ er kann nicht teilen or dividieren.
(c) (Brit Parl) **the House** ~**d** das Parlament stimmte durch Hammelsprung ab; ~, ~**!** abstimmen!
3 n (Geog) Wasserscheide f. **the Great D**~ (Geog) die (nord)amerikanische Wasserscheide; (fig) die Kluft; (death) der Tod; **to cross the Great D**~ (fig) den Schritt über die Schwelle tun; (die) die Schwelle des Todes überschreiten.
♦**divide off** vi sich (ab)trennen; (be separable) sich (ab)trennen lassen. **2** vt sep (ab)trennen.
♦**divide out** vt sep aufteilen (among unter +acc or dat).
♦**divide up 1** vi see **divide 2 (a). 2** vt sep see **divide 1 (b).**

divided [dɪˈvaɪdɪd] adj (a) (lit) geteilt. ~ **highway** (US) Schnellstraße f; ~ **skirt** Hosenrock m. (b) (in disagreement) opinion, country, self geteilt; couple getrennt. **a people** ~ **against itself** ein unter sich (dat) uneiniges Volk.

dividend [ˈdɪvɪdend] n (a) (Fin) Dividende f. **to pay** ~**s** (fig) sich bezahlt machen. (b) (Math) Dividend m.

dividers [dɪˈvaɪdəz] npl Stechzirkel m.

dividing [dɪˈvaɪdɪŋ] adj ~**trennend.** ~ **wall** Trennwand f; ~ **line** (lit, fig) Trennungslinie f.

divination [ˌdɪvɪˈneɪʃən] n Prophezeiung, Weissagung f.

divine [dɪˈvaɪn] **1** adj (Rel, fig inf) göttlich. ~ **worship** Anbetung f Gottes. **2** n Theologe m; (priest also) Geistliche(r) m. **3** vt (a) (foretell) the future weissagen, prophezeien. (b) (liter: make out) sb's intentions erahnen, erspüren (liter). (c) (find) water, metal aufspüren.

divinely [dɪˈvaɪnlɪ] adv see adj.

diviner [dɪˈvaɪnə^r] n (a) (of future) Wahrsager(in f) m. (b) see **water** ~.

diving [ˈdaɪvɪŋ] n (under water) Tauchen nt; (into water) Springen nt; (Sport) Wasserspringen nt.

diving: ~**bell** n Taucherglocke f; ~**board** n (Sprung)brett nt; ~**suit** n Taucheranzug m.

divining-rod [dɪˈvaɪnɪŋˈrɒd] n Wünschelrute f.

divinity [dɪˈvɪnɪtɪ] n (a) (divine being) göttliches Wesen, Gottheit f. (b) (divine quality) Göttlichkeit f. (c) (theology) Theologie f; (Sch) Religion f. **doctor of** ~ Doktor der Theologie.

divisible [dɪˈvɪzəbl] adj teilbar (by durch).

division [dɪˈvɪʒən] n (a) (act of dividing, state of being divided) Teilung f; (Math) Teilen nt, Division f. **we're still learning** ~ wir sind immer noch beim Teilen; **the** ~ **of labour** die Arbeitsteilung.
(b) (Mil) Division f.
(c) (result of dividing) (in administration) Abteilung f; (in box, case) Fach nt; (part) Teil m; (category) Kategorie f.
(d) (that which divides) (in room) Trennwand f; (fig: between social classes etc) Schranke f; (dividing line: lit, fig) Trennungslinie f. **where does the syllable** ~ **come?** wie ist die Silbentrennung hier?
(e) (fig: discord) Uneinigkeit f.
(f) (Brit Parl) **to call for/insist on a** ~ eine Abstimmung durch Hammelsprung verlangen/auf einer Abstimmung durch Hammelsprung bestehen.
(g) (Sport) Liga f.

division-bell [dɪˈvɪʒənˌbel] n (Parl) Klingel, mit der die Abgeordneten zur Abstimmung gerufen werden.

division sign n (Math) Teilungszeichen nt.

divisive [dɪˈvaɪsɪv] adj **to be** ~ Uneinigkeit schaffen.

divisor [dɪˈvaɪzə^r] n (Math) Divisor m.

divorce [dɪˈvɔːs] **1** n (Jur) Scheidung f (from von); (fig) Trennung f. **he wants a** ~ er will sich scheiden lassen; **to get a** ~ (from sb) sich (von jdm) scheiden lassen; ~ **court** Scheidungsgericht nt; ~ **proceedings** Scheidungsprozeß m.
2 vt (a) husband, wife sich scheiden lassen von. **to get** ~**d** sich scheiden lassen. (b) (fig) trennen.

divorced [dɪˈvɔːst] adj (Jur) geschieden (from von). **to be** ~ **from sth** (fig) keine(rlei) Beziehung zu etw haben.

divorcee [dɪˌvɔːˈsiː] n Geschiedene(r) mf, geschiedener Mann, geschiedene Frau. **he is a** ~ er ist geschieden.

divot [ˈdɪvɪt] n vom Golfschläger etc ausgehacktes Rasenstück.

divulge [daɪˈvʌldʒ] vt preisgeben (sth to sb jdm etw).

dixie [ˈdɪksɪ] n (Brit Mil sl) Gulaschkanone f (inf); (for eating) Eßgeschirr nt.

Dixie n (also ~**land**) Dixieland m.

DIY abbr of **do it yourself**.

dizzily [ˈdɪzɪlɪ] adv (a) (giddily) stagger taumelnd, schwankend. **the pound rose** ~ **to DM 4.20** das Pfund stieg auf schwindelerregende DM 4.20. (b) (inf: foolishly) behave verrückt.

dizziness [ˈdɪzɪnɪs] n Schwindel m. **attack of** ~ Schwindelanfall m.

dizzy [ˈdɪzɪ] adj (+er) (a) (lit, fig) person schwind(e)lig; height, speed schwindelerregend. ~ **spell** Schwindelanfall m; **I feel** ~ mir ist or ich bin schwindlig; **it makes me/one** ~ **to think of it** mir wird/es wird einem ganz schwindlig bei dem Gedanken; **the** ~ **heights of fame** die schwindelerregenden Ruhmeshöhen.
(b) (inf: foolish) verrückt.

DJ *abbr of* (a) **dinner jacket.** (b) **disc jockey.**
D Lit *abbr of* **Doctor of Letters** Dr phil.
DM *abbr of* **Deutschmark; Doctor of medicine** Dr. med.
D Mus *abbr of* **Doctor of Music** Dr. phil.
DNA *abbr of* **de(s)oxyribonucleic acid** DNS *f.*
do¹ [dəʊ] *n* (*Mus*) Do *nt.*
do² [duː] (*vb: pret* **did,** *ptp* **done**) 1 *v aux* (a) (*used to form interrog and neg in present and pret vbs*) ~ **you understand?** verstehen Sie?; **I ~ not** *or* **don't understand** ich verstehe nicht; **didn't you** *or* **did you not know?** haben Sie das nicht gewußt?; **never did I see so many** ich habe noch nie so viele gesehen.
(b) (*for emphasis: with stress on do*) ~ **come!** kommen Sie doch (bitte)!; ~ **shut up!** (nun) sei doch (endlich) ruhig!; ~ **tell him that ...** sagen Sie ihm doch (bitte), daß ...; ~ **I remember him!** und ob ich mich an ihn erinnere!; **but I ~ like it** aber es gefällt mir wirklich; **it's very dear, but I ~ like it** es ist zwar sehr teuer, aber es gefällt mir nun mal; **so you ~ know them!** Sie kennen sie also wirklich *or* tatsächlich!; (*and were lying etc*) Sie kennen sie also doch!; **you don't do meals, do you?** — **yes, we ~ do meals** Essen gibt's bei Ihnen nicht? — doch.
(c) (*used to avoid repeating vb*) **you speak better than I ~** Sie sprechen besser als ich; **he likes cheese and so ~ I** er ißt gern Käse und ich auch; **he doesn't like cheese and neither ~ I** er mag keinen Käse und ich auch nicht; **they said he would go and he did** sie sagten, er würde gehen, und das tat er (dann) auch.
(d) (*in question tags*) oder. **you know him, don't you?** Sie kennen ihn doch?, Sie kennen ihn (doch), oder *or* nicht wahr?; **so you know/don't know him,** ~ **you?** Sie kennen ihn also/also nicht, oder?; **you do understand, don't you?** das verstehen Sie doch (sicherlich)(, nicht wahr *or* oder)?; **he didn't go, did he?** er ist (doch) nicht gegangen, oder?
(e) (*in answers: replacing vb*) **do you see them often?** — **yes, I** ~**/no, I don't** sehen Sie sie oft? — ja/nein; **they speak French** — **oh,** ~ **they?** sie sprechen Französisch — ja?, ach, wirklich *or* tatsächlich?; **they speak French** — ~ **they really?** sie sprechen Französisch — wirklich?; **may I come in?** — ~**!** darf ich hereinkommen? — ja, bitte; **shall I open the window?** — **no, don't!** soll ich das Fenster öffnen? — nein, bitte nicht!; **who broke the window?** — **I did** wer hat das Fenster eingeschlagen? — ich.
2 *vt* (a) (*be busy with, be involved in, carry out*) tun, machen. **what are you** ~**ing (with yourself) on Saturday?** was machen *or* tun Sie am Sonnabend?; **I've got nothing to** ~ ich habe nichts zu tun; **are you** ~**ing anything this evening?** haben Sie heute abend schon etwas vor?; **I shall** ~ **nothing of the sort** ich werde nichts dergleichen tun; **he does nothing but complain** er nörgelt immer nur, er tut nichts als nörgeln (*inf*); **what must I** ~ **to get better?** was soll ich tun, um wieder gesund zu werden?; **what shall we** ~ **for money?** wie machen wir es mit Geld?
(b) (*perform, accomplish*) tun; *homework* machen. **I've done a stupid thing** ich habe da was Dummes gemacht *or* getan; **to** ~ **a play** ein Stück aufführen; **to** ~ **a film** einen Film machen *or* drehen; **to** ~ **one's military service** seinen Wehrdienst ableisten *or* machen (*inf*); **to** ~ **the housework** die Hausarbeit machen; **I'll** ~ **my all** ich werde alles tun, was in meinen Kräften steht; **we'll have to** ~ **something about this/him** wir müssen da etwas tun *or* unternehmen/müssen mit ihm etwas tun *or* unternehmen; **how do you** ~ **it?** wie macht man das?; (*in amazement*) wie machen Sie das bloß?; **what's to be done?** was ist da zu tun?; **what can you** ~**?** was kann man da machen?; **sorry, it's impossible, it can't be done** tut mir leid, (ist) ausgeschlossen, es läßt sich nicht machen; **well,** ~ **what you can** mach *or* tu (eben), was du kannst; **what can I** ~ **for you?** was kann ich für Sie tun?; (*by shop assistant etc*) was darf's sein?; **can you** ~ **it by yourself?** schaffst du das allein, kannst du das allein machen?; **what do you want me to** ~ **(about it)?** und was soll ich da tun *or* machen?; **he knows it's a mistake but he can't** ~ **anything about it** er weiß, daß es ein Fehler ist, aber er kann nichts dagegen machen *or* daran ändern; **to** ~ **sth again** etw noch (ein)mal tun *or* machen; ~ **something for me, will you ...** shut up tu mir bloß den (einen) Gefallen und halt den Mund; **you** ~ **something to me** du hast es mir angetan; **does that** ~ **anything for you?** macht dich das an? (*inf*); **Brecht doesn't** ~ **anything for me** Brecht läßt mich kalt (*inf*) *or* sagt mir nichts; **what have you done to him?** was haben Sie mit ihm gemacht?; **that's done it** (*inf*) so, da haben wir's, da haben wir die Bescherung; **that does it!** jetzt reicht's mir!; **oh God, now what have you done!** ach du Schreck, was hast du jetzt bloß wieder angestellt *or* gemacht?
(c) (*make, produce*) ~ **this letter and six copies** tippen Sie den Brief mit sechs Durchschlägen; **I'll** ~ **a translation for you** ich werde eine Übersetzung für Sie machen; *see* **wonder** *etc.*
(d) (*Sch etc: study*) durchnehmen, haben. **we've done Milton** wir haben Milton gelesen *or* durchgenommen; **I've never done any German** ich habe nie Deutsch gelernt *or* gehabt.
(e) (*solve*) lösen; *sum, crossword, puzzle etc also* machen.
(f) (*arrange*) **to** ~ **the flowers** die Blumen arrangieren; **to** ~ **one's hair** sich frisieren, sich (*dat*) die Haare (zurecht)machen (*inf*); **who does your hair?** zu welchem Friseur gehen Sie?; **who did your hair last time, madam?** wer hat Sie letztes Mal bedient?; **I can't** ~ **my tie** ich kann meine Krawatte nicht binden.
(g) (*clean, tidy*) **to** ~ **one's nails** sich (*dat*) die Nägel schneiden *or* (*varnish*) lackieren; **to** ~ **one's teeth** sich (*dat*) die Zähne putzen; **to** ~ **the shoes** Schuhe putzen; **this room needs** ~**ing today** dieses Zimmer muß heute gemacht werden (*inf*); **to** ~ **the dishes** spülen, den Abwasch machen.
(h) (*deal with*) **the barber said he'd** ~ **me next** der Friseur sagte, er würde mich als Nächsten drannehmen; **who did the choreography/the jacket design?** wer hat die Choreographie/den Umschlagentwurf gemacht?; **you** ~ **the painting**

and **I'll** ~ **the papering** du streichst an und ich tapeziere; **we'll have to get someone to** ~ **the roof** wir müssen jemanden bestellen, der das Dach macht (*inf*); **he does the film crits for the magazine** er schreibt die Filmkritiken für die Zeitschrift; **we only** ~ **one make of gloves** wir haben *or* führen nur eine Sorte Handschuhe; (*produce*) wir stellen nur eine Sorte Handschuhe her; **I'll** ~ **the talking** ich übernehme das Reden; **who's** ~**ing the flowers?** wer besorgt die Blumen?; **who did the food for your reception?** wer hat bei Ihrem Empfang für das Essen gesorgt?; **I'll** ~ **you** (*sl*) der besorg' ich's noch! (*inf*).
(i) (*in pret, ptp only: complete, accomplish*) **the work's done now** die Arbeit ist gemacht *or* getan *or* fertig; **what's done cannot be undone** was geschehen ist, kann man nicht ungeschehen machen; **I haven't done telling you what I think of you** mit dir bin ich noch lange nicht fertig; **done!** abgemacht!; **it's all over and done with** (*is finished*) das ist alles erledigt; (*has happened*) das ist alles vorbei *or* überstanden; **to get done with sth** etw fertigmachen.
(j) (*visit, see sights of*) *city, country, museum* besuchen, abhaken (*inf*); (*take in also*) mitnehmen (*inf*).
(k) (*Aut etc*) fahren, machen (*inf*). **this car does** *or* **can** ~ *or* **will** ~ **100** das Auto fährt *or* macht (*inf*) 100; **we did London to Edinburgh in 8 hours** wir haben es in 8 Stunden von London bis Edinburgh geschafft.
(l) (*inf*) (*be suitable*) passen (*sb* jdm); (*be sufficient for*) reichen (*sb* jdm). **that will** ~ **me nicely** das reicht dicke (*inf*) *or* allemal.
(m) (*Theat*) *part* spielen. **to** ~ **Hamlet** den Hamlet spielen.
(n) (*take off, mimic*) nachmachen.
(o) (*inf: cheat*) übers Ohr hauen (*inf*), reinlegen (*inf*). **you've been done!** du bist reingelegt *or* übers Ohr gehauen worden (*inf*); **I was done for £40 for that table** mit £ 40 für den Tisch hat man mich ganz schön übers Ohr gehauen (*inf*).
(p) (*sl: burgle*) einbrechen in (+*acc*). **the office was done last night** im Büro ist gestern nacht ein Bruch gemacht worden (*sl*).
(q) (*provide service of*) sorry, **we don't** ~ **lunches** wir haben leider keinen Mittagstisch; **we don't** ~ **telegrams** wir können keine Telegramme annehmen.
(r) (*inf: provide food, lodgings for*) **they** ~ **you very well at that hotel/restaurant** in dem Hotel ist man gut untergebracht *or* aufgehoben/in dem Restaurant ißt man sehr gut.
(s) (*Cook*) machen (*inf*); *vegetables etc also* kochen. **to** ~ **the cooking/food** Essen machen; **how do you like your steak done?** wie möchten Sie Ihr Steak?; **well done** durch(gebraten).
(t) (*inf: tire out*) **I'm absolutely done!** ich bin völlig geschafft *or* erledigt *or* fertig (*all inf*).
(u) (*inf: in prison*) **6 years** sitzen, abreißen (*inf*).
(v) (*old, liter: translate*) **done into the English by ...** ins Englische übertragen von ...
3 *vi* (a) (*act*) ~ **as I** ~ mach es wie ich; **he did well to take advice** er tat gut daran, sich beraten zu lassen; **he did right** *or* hat richtig gehandelt, es war richtig von ihm; **he did right/well to go** es war richtig/gut, daß er gegangen ist.
(b) (*get on, fare*) **how are you** ~**ing?** wie geht's (Ihnen)?; **I'm not** ~**ing so badly** es geht mir gar nicht so schlecht; **the patient is** ~**ing very well** dem Patienten geht es recht ordentlich; **he's** ~**ing well at school** er ist gut in der Schule; **his business is** ~**ing well** sein Geschäft geht gut; **the roses are** ~**ing well this year** die Rosen stehen dieses Jahr gut; **I married and did quite well out of it** ich habe geheiratet und bin dabei ganz gut gefahren; **what's** ~**ing?** was ist los?
(c) (*finish*) **the meat, is it done?** ist das Fleisch fertig (gebraten) *or* durch?; **have you done?** sind Sie endlich *or* schon (*iro*) fertig?
(d) (*suit, be convenient*) gehen. **that will never** ~**!** das geht nicht!; **this room will** ~ das Zimmer geht (*inf*) *or* ist in Ordnung; **will it** ~ **if I come back at 8?** geht es, wenn ich um 8 Uhr zurück bin?; **it doesn't** ~ **to keep a lady waiting** es gehört sich *or* geht nicht, daß man eine Dame warten läßt; **will she/it** ~? geht sie/das?; **this coat will** ~ *for* **or** *as* a cover dieser Mantel geht als Decke; **you'll have to make** ~ **with £10** £ 10 müssen Ihnen reichen, Sie werden mit £ 10 auskommen müssen.
(e) (*be sufficient*) reichen. **can you lend me some money?** — **will £1** ~? können Sie mir etwas Geld leihen? — reicht £ 1?; **yes, that'll** ~ ja, das reicht; **that'll** ~**!** jetzt reicht's aber!
(f) (*inf: char*) putzen.
4 *vr* **to** ~ **oneself well** es sich (*dat*) gutgehen lassen.
5 *n* (*inf*) (a) (*Veranstaltung, Sache* (*inf*) *f*; (*party*) Fete *f* (*inf*).
(b) (*Brit: swindle*) **the whole business was a real** ~ **from start to finish** das ganze Geschäft war von Anfang an ein einziger Schwindel.
(c) (*in phrases*) **it's a poor** ~**!** das ist ja schwach (*inf*) *or* ein schwaches Bild! (*inf*); **the** ~**s and don'ts** was man tun und nicht tun sollte (*for als*); (*highway code*) die Ge- und Verbote; **fair** ~**s all round** gleiches Recht für alle.

♦**do away with** *vi* +*prep obj* (a) (*get rid of*) *custom, law* abschaffen; *document* vernichten; *building* abreißen. (b) (*kill*) *person, oneself* umbringen.
♦**do by** *vi* +*prep obj* **to** ~ **well/badly** ~ **sb** jdn gut/schlecht behandeln; **do as you would be done** ~ (*Prov*) was du nicht willst, daß man dir tu, das füg auch keinem andern zu (*Prov*); *see* **hard.**
♦**do down** *vt sep* (*Brit*) heruntermachen, schlechtmachen.
♦**do for** *vi* +*prep obj* (a) (*inf: finish off*) *person* fertigmachen (*inf*); *project* zunichte machen. **to be done** ~ (*person*) erledigt *or* fertig (*inf*) sein; (*project*) gestorben sein (*inf*). (b) (*inf: charlady*) putzen für *or* bei.
♦**do in** *vt sep* (*inf*) (a) (*kill*) um die Ecke bringen (*inf*). (b) (*usu pass: exhaust*) **to be** *or* **feel done** ~ fertig *or* geschafft sein (*inf*).
♦**do out** *vt sep* (a) *room* auskehren *or* -fegen. (b) **to** ~ **sb** ~ **of a job/his rights** jdn um eine Stelle/seine Rechte bringen; **to** ~ **sb**

~ of £100 jdn um £ 100 bringen or erleichtern (inf).
♦**do over** vt sep (a) (redecorate) (neu) herrichten. (b) (sl: beat up) zusammenschlagen. (c) (US: do again) noch einmal machen.
♦**do up 1** vi (dress etc) zugemacht werden.
  2 vt sep (a) (fasten) zumachen. ~ yourself ~, sir! machen Sie Ihre Hose zu!
  (b) (parcel together) goods zusammenpacken. books done ~ in brown paper in Packpapier eingewickelte Bücher; to ~ sth ~ in a parcel etw einpacken.
  (c) house, room (neu) herrichten. to ~ ~ one's face sich schminken; to ~ oneself ~ sich zurechtmachen.
♦**do with** vi +prep obj (a) (with can or could: need) brauchen. do you know what I could ~ ~? weißt du, was ich jetzt brauchen könnte?; it could ~ ~ a clean es müßte mal saubergemacht werden.
  (b) (dial: in neg, with can or could: tolerate) ausstehen, vertragen. I can't be ~ing ~ this noise ich kann den Lärm nicht vertragen or ausstehen.
  (c) he has to ~ ~ the steel industry er hat mit der Stahlindustrie zu tun; what has that got to ~ ~ it? was hat das damit zu tun?; I won't have anything to ~ ~ it! ich möchte nichts damit zu tun haben!; that has or is nothing to ~ ~ you! das geht Sie gar nichts an!; this debate has to ~ ~ ... in dieser Debatte geht es um ...; well, it's to ~ ~ this letter you sent es geht um den Brief, den Sie geschickt haben; money has a lot to ~ ~ it Geld spielt eine große Rolle dabei.
  (d) what have you done ~ my gloves/your face? was haben Sie mit meinen Handschuhen/Ihrem Gesicht gemacht?
  (e) he doesn't know what to ~ ~ himself er weiß nicht, was er mit sich anfangen soll; the children can always find something to ~ ~ themselves die Kinder finden immer etwas, womit sie sich beschäftigen können.
  (f) to be done ~ sb/sth (finished) mit jdm/etw fertig sein.
♦**do without** vi +prep obj auskommen ohne. I can ~ ~ your advice Sie können sich Ihren Rat sparen; I could have done ~ that! das hätte mir (wirklich) erspart bleiben können; you'll have to ~ ~ Sie müssen ohne auskommen.
do³ written abbr of ditto.
DOA abbr of dead on arrival.
doc [dɒk] n (inf) abbr of doctor Herr Doktor m.
docile [ˈdəʊsaɪl] adj sanftmütig; horse fromm; engine schwach.
docility [dəʊˈsɪlɪtɪ] n Sanftmut f.
dock¹ [dɒk] **1** n Dock nt; (for berthing) Pier, Kai m. ~s pl Hafen m; my car is in ~ (inf) mein Wagen ist in der Werkstatt. **2** vt docken; (Space also) ankoppeln. **3** vi (a) (Naut) anlegen. (b) (Space: two spacecraft) docken (spec), ankoppeln.
dock² n (Jur) Anklagebank f. to stand in the ~ auf der Anklagebank sitzen; "prisoner in the ~" „Angeklagte(r)".
dock³ 1 vt (a) dog's tail kupieren; horse's tail stutzen. (b) wages kürzen. to ~ 50p off sb's wages jds Lohn um 50 Pence kürzen. **2** n kupierter Schwanz; (of horse) gestutzer Schweif.
dock⁴ n (Bot) Ampfer m.
docker [ˈdɒkəʳ] n (Brit) Hafenarbeiter, Docker m.
docket [ˈdɒkɪt] **1** n (a) (paper: on document, parcel etc) Warenbegleitschein, Laufzettel m.
  (b) (Jur: judgements register) Urteilsregister nt; (list of cases) Liste f der Gerichtstermine.
  (c) (customs certificate) Zollinhaltserklärung f.
  2 vt (a) contents, (Jur) judgement, information etc zusammenfassen, eine Kurzfassung geben or herstellen von.
  (b) contents angeben; (put ~ on) crate mit einem Warenbegleitschein or Laufzettel versehen.
dock gates npl Hafeneingang m; (in water) Docktor nt.
docking [ˈdɒkɪŋ] n (Space) Docking nt (spec), Ankoppelung f.
docking: ~ manoeuvre n (Space) (An)koppelungsmanöver nt; ~ techniques npl (Space) (An)koppelungstechnik f; ~ time n Liegezeit f.
dock: ~land n Hafenviertel nt; ~ strike n Hafenarbeiterstreik m; ~yard n Werft f.
doctor [ˈdɒktəʳ] **1** n (a) (Med) Arzt m, Ärztin f, Doktor(in f) m (inf). D~ Smith Doktor Schmidt; yes, ~ ja, Herr Doktor; to send for the ~ den Arzt holen; he is a ~ er ist Arzt; a woman ~ eine Ärztin; he's under the ~ (inf) er ist in Behandlung; it's just what the ~ ordered (fig inf) das ist genau das richtige.
  (b) (Univ etc) Doktor m. to take one's ~ degree promovieren, seinen Doktor machen; ~ of Law/of Science etc Doktor der Rechte/der Naturwissenschaften etc; Dear Dr Smith Sehr geehrter Herr Dr./Sehr geehrte Frau Dr. Smith.
  2 vt (a) cold behandeln. she's always ~ing herself sie doktort dauernd an sich (dat) herum.
  (b) (inf: castrate) kastrieren.
  (c) (tamper with) accounts frisieren; text, document verfälschen. the food's/wine's been ~ed dem Essen/Wein ist etwas beigemischt worden.
doctoral [ˈdɒktərəl] adj ~ thesis Doktorarbeit f.
doctorate [ˈdɒktərɪt] n Doktorwürde f. ~ in science/philosophy Doktor(titel) m in Naturwissenschaften/Philosophie; to get one's ~ die Doktorwürde verliehen bekommen; to do one's ~ seinen Doktor machen; he's still doing his ~ er sitzt immer noch an seiner Doktorarbeit.
doctrinaire [ˌdɒktrɪˈneəʳ] adj doktrinär.
doctrinal [dɒkˈtraɪnl] adj doktrinell. on ~ matters in Sachen der Doktrin.
doctrine [ˈdɒktrɪn] n Doktrin, Lehre f.
document [ˈdɒkjʊmənt] **1** n Dokument nt, Urkunde f.
  2 vt (a) case beurkunden, (urkundlich) belegen. his argument/theory is well ~ed sein Argument/seine Theorie ist gut belegt; have you any evidence to ~ that claim? haben Sie Unterlagen, um diese Forderung zu belegen?
  (b) ship mit Papieren versehen.

documentary [ˌdɒkjʊˈmentərɪ] **1** adj (a) dokumentarisch, urkundlich. ~ evidence (Jur) urkundliche Beweise pl. (b) (Film, TV) a ~ film ein Dokumentarfilm m; in ~ form in Form einer Dokumentation. **2** n (Film, TV) Dokumentarfilm m.
documentation [ˌdɒkjʊmenˈteɪʃən] n Dokumentation f.
dodder [ˈdɒdəʳ] vi tapern.
dodderer [ˈdɒdərəʳ] n (inf) Tapergreis (inf), Tattergreis (inf) m.
doddering [ˈdɒdərɪŋ], **doddery** [ˈdɒdərɪ] adj walk unsicher; person taperig. the ~ old fool (inf) der vertrottelte alte Opa (inf).
dodge [dɒdʒ] **1** n (a) (lit) Sprung m zur Seite, rasches Ausweichen; (Ftbl, Boxing) Ausweichen nt.
  (b) (trick) Trick, Kniff m; (ingenious plan) Glanzidee f (inf). to be up to all the ~s mit allen Wassern gewaschen sein.
  2 vt blow, ball, question, difficulty ausweichen (+dat); tax umgehen; (shirk) work, military service sich drücken vor (+dat). to ~ the issue der (eigentlichen) Frage or dem Problem ausweichen or aus dem Weg gehen.
  3 vi ausweichen. to ~ out of sight blitzschnell verschwinden, sich blitzschnell verdrücken (inf); to ~ out of the way zur Seite springen; (to escape notice) blitzschnell verschwinden; to ~ behind a tree hinter einen Baum springen or schlüpfen; to ~ through the traffic sich durch den Verkehr schlängeln.
dodgem [ˈdɒdʒəm] n (Auto)skooter m. did you go on the ~s? bist du (Auto)skooter gefahren?
dodger [ˈdɒdʒəʳ] n (a) (trickster) Schlawiner m (inf); see artful. (b) (Naut) Wetterschutz m.
dodgy [ˈdɒdʒɪ] adj (+er) (Brit inf: tricky) situation vertrackt (inf), verzwickt (inf); (dubious) zweifelhaft; engine nicht einwandfrei, launisch (inf). this translation/his spelling/the carburettor is a bit ~ diese Übersetzung/seine Rechtschreibung/der Vergaser ist nicht einwandfrei.
dodo [ˈdəʊdəʊ] n Dodo m, Dronte f. as dead as the/a ~ schon längst tot.
doe [dəʊ] n (roe deer) Reh(geiß f) nt, Ricke f; (red deer) Hirschkuh f; (rabbit) (Kaninchen)weibchen nt; (hare) Häsin f.
doer [ˈduːəʳ] n (a) (author of deed) Täter(in f) m. he's a great ~ of crosswords (inf) er macht sehr gerne Kreuzworträtsel.
  (b) (active person) Mann m der Tat, Macher m (inf). more of a ~ than a thinker eher ein Mann der Tat als der Theorie.
does [dʌz] 3rd pers sing of do².
doeskin [ˈdəʊskɪn] n Rehfell nt; (treated) Rehleder nt.
doesn't [ˈdʌznt] contr of does not.
doff [dɒf] vt hat einen, lüften; (old) garment ablegen.
dog [dɒg] **1** n (a) Hund m. the ~s (Brit Sport) das Hunderennen.
  (b) (fig phrases) to lead a ~'s life ein Hundeleben führen, wie ein Hund leben; it's a ~'s life es ist ein Hundeleben; to go to the ~s (person, business, district, institution) vor die Hunde gehen (inf); give a ~ a bad name (and hang him) wer einmal ins Gerede or in Verruf kommt(, dem hängt das sein Leben lang an); ~ in the manger Spielverderber(in f) m; ~-in-the-manger attitude mißgünstige Einstellung; every ~ has his day jeder hat einmal Glück im Leben; it's (a case of) ~ eat ~ es ist ein Kampf aller gegen alle; you can't teach an old ~ new tricks der Mensch ist ein Gewohnheitstier; she was done up like a ~'s dinner (inf) sie war aufgetakelt wie eine Fregatte (inf); to put on the ~ (US inf) auf fein machen (inf); ~'s breakfast (fig inf) Schlamassel m (inf).
  (c) (male fox, wolf) Rüde m.
  (d) (inf: man) lucky ~ Glückspilz m; gay ~ lockerer Vogel (inf); dirty ~ gemeiner Hund; sly ~ gerissener Hund (inf); there's life in the old ~ yet noch kann man ihn nicht zum alten Eisen werfen; Tom Jones, you old ~! Tom Jones, du alter Schwerenöter!; see top ~.
  (e) (Tech: clamp) Klammer f.
  (f) ~s pl (sl: feet) Quanten pl (sl).
  (g) (US inf: failure) Pleite f (inf).
  2 vt (a) (follow closely) to ~ sb or sb's footsteps jdm hart auf den Fersen sein/bleiben.
  (b) (harass) verfolgen. ~ged by misfortune vom Pech verfolgt.
dog: ~ biscuit n Hundekuchen m; ~cart n Dogcart m; ~-collar n (lit) Hundehalsband nt; (vicar's) steifer, hoher Kragen; ~ days npl Hundstage pl; ~-eared [ˈdɒgɪəd] adj mit Eselsohren; ~-fancier n Hundeliebhaber(in f), Hundefreund(in f) m; (breeder, seller) Hundezüchter(in f) m; ~fight n (Aviat) Luftkampf m; ~fish n Hundshai m; ~ food n Hundefutter nt; ~ fox n Fuchsrüde m.
dogged adj, ~ly adv [ˈdɒgɪd, -lɪ] beharrlich, zäh.
doggedness [ˈdɒgɪdnɪs] n Beharrlichkeit, Zähigkeit f.
doggerel [ˈdɒgərəl] n (also ~ verse) Knittelvers m.
doggie, doggy [ˈdɒgɪ] **1** n (inf) kleiner Hund, Hündchen nt. **2** adj smell Hunde-; (dog loving) hundenärrisch.
doggie bag n Beutel m für Essensreste, die nach Hause mitgenommen werden.
doggo [ˈdɒgəʊ] adv (inf): to lie ~ sich nicht mucksen (inf); (go underground) von der Bildfläche verschwinden (inf).
doggone [ˈdɒgˈgɒn] interj (US sl) ~ (it)! verdammt noch mal!
doggoned [ˌdɒgˈgɒn(d)] adj (US sl) verdammt.
dog: ~house n Hundehütte f; he's in the ~house (inf) er ist in Ungnade; (with wife) bei ihm hängt der Haussegen schief; ~ Latin n Küchenlatein nt; ~ licence n Hundemarke f; a ~ licence costs ... die Hundesteuer beträgt ...; ~like adj Hunde-, hundeähnlich; ~like devotion hündische Ergebenheit.
dogma [ˈdɒgmə] n Dogma nt.
dogmatic [dɒgˈmætɪk] adj dogmatisch. D~ theology Dogmatik f; to be very ~ about sth in etw (dat) sehr dogmatisch sein.
dogmatically [dɒgˈmætɪkəlɪ] adv see adj.
dogmatism [ˈdɒgmətɪzəm] n Dogmatismus m.
dogmatize [ˈdɒgmətaɪz] **1** vi (Rel, fig) dogmatisch sein/dog-

matische Behauptungen aufstellen. **2** *vt* (*Rel, fig*) dogmatisieren, zum Dogma erheben.

do-gooder ['du:'gudə'] *n* (*pej*) Weltverbesserer *m*.

dog: ~ **paddle** *n* to do (the) ~ **paddle** paddeln, Hundepaddeln machen; ~**rose** *n* Hundsrose *f*.

dogsbody ['dɒgzbɒdɪ] *n* **she's/he's the general** ~ sie/er ist (das) Mädchen für alles; **fed up with being the office** ~ he ... er hatte es satt, im Büro das Mädchen für alles zu sein und ...

dog: ~ **show** *n* Hundeausstellung *f*; ~ **sled** *n* Hundeschlitten *m*; ~ **star** *n* Hundsstern, Sirius *m*; ~ **tag** *n* (*US Mil inf*) Erkennungsmarke, Hundemarke (*inf*) *f*; ~**tired** *adj* hundemüde; ~**tooth** *n* (*Archit*) Hundszahn *m*; ~ **track** *n* Hunderennbahn *f*; ~**trot** *n* gemächlicher *or* leichter Trott; ~**watch** *n* (*Naut*) Hundewache *f*; ~**wood** *n* Hartriegel, Hornstrauch *m*.

doily ['dɔɪlɪ] *n* (Spitzen- *or* Zier)deckchen *nt*.

doing ['du:ɪŋ] *n* **(a)** Tun *nt*. **this is your** ~ das ist dein Werk; **it was none of my** ~ ich hatte nichts damit zu tun; **that takes some** ~ da gehört (schon) etwas dazu; **there is a difference between** ~ **and saying** zwischen Taten und Worten besteht ein Unterschied. **(b)** (*inf*) ~**s** *pl* Handlungen, Taten *pl*.

doings ['du:ɪŋz] *n sing* (*Brit inf*) Dingsbums *nt* (*inf*).

do-it-yourself ['du:ɪtjə'self] **1** *adj shop* Bastler-, Hobby-. ~ **fan** Heimwerker(in *f*), Bastler(in *f*) *m*; **the** ~ **craze** die Do-it-yourself-Bewegung; ~ **kit** (*for household jobs*) Heimwerkerausrüstung *f*; (*for radio etc*) Bausatz *m*. **2** *n* Heimwerken, Do-it-yourself *nt*.

dol *abbr* of **dollar**.

doldrums ['dɒldrəmz] *npl* **(a)** (*Geog*) (*area*) Kalmengürtel *m or* -zone *f*; (*weather*) Windstille, Kalme *f*. **(b) to be in the** ~ (*people*) Trübsal blasen; (*business etc*) in einer Flaute stecken.

dole [dəʊl] *n* (*Brit inf*) Stempelgeld *nt* (*inf*). **to go/be on the** ~ stempeln (gehen).

♦**dole out** *vt sep* austeilen, verteilen.

doleful ['dəʊlfʊl] *adj* traurig; *face, expression, prospect also* trübselig; *tune, song also* klagend.

dolefully ['dəʊlfəlɪ] *adv* see *adj*.

dolichocephalic ['dɒlɪkəʊsə'fælɪk] *adj* dolichozephal.

doll [dɒl] *n* **(a)** Puppe *f*. ~'s **house** Puppenhaus *nt*; ~'s **pram** Puppenwagen *m*. **(b)** (*esp US inf: girl*) Mädchen *nt*; (*pretty girl*) Puppe *f* (*inf*). **thanks Betty, you're a** ~ danke Betty, du bist klasse (*inf*).

♦**doll up** *vt sep* (*inf*) herausputzen. **to** ~ **oneself** ~, **to get** ~**ed** ~ sich herausputzen *or* aufdonnern (*inf*).

dollar ['dɒlə'] *n* Dollar *m*.

dollar: ~ **area** *n* Dollar-Raum *m*; ~ **diplomacy** *n* Finanzdiplomatie *f*; ~ **gap** *n* Dollar-Lücke *f*.

dollop ['dɒləp] *n* (*inf*) Schlag *m* (*inf*).

dolly ['dɒlɪ] **1** *n* **(a)** (*inf: doll*) Püppchen *nt*. **(b)** (*wheeled frame*) (Transport)wagen *m*; (*Film, TV*) Dolly, Kamerawagen *m*; (*Rail*) Schmalspurrangierlokomotive *f*. **(c)** (*for washing clothes*) Wäschestampfer *m*. **(d)** (*Tech: for rivet*) Gegenhalter *m*. **(e)** (*inf: girl: also* ~**-bird**) Puppe *f*. **(f)** (*Sport inf*) lahmer Ball (*inf*). **2** *adj* (*Sport inf*) *shot* lahm; *catch* leicht.

♦**dolly in** *vti sep* (*Film, TV*) vorfahren.

♦**dolly out** *vti sep* (*Film, TV*) zurückfahren.

dolly-bird ['dɒlɪbɜ:d] **1** *n* (*inf*) Puppe *f*. **2** *adj attr* puppig.

dolman ['dɒlmən] *n* Dolman *m*. ~ **sleeve** angeschnittener Ärmel.

dolomite ['dɒləmaɪt] *n* Dolomit *m*. **the D**~**s** die Dolomiten *pl*.

dolphin ['dɒlfɪn] *n* Delphin *m*.

dolt [dəʊlt] *n* Tölpel *m*.

domain [dəʊ'meɪn] *n* **(a)** (*lit: estate*) Gut *nt*; (*belonging to state, Crown*) **the Crown** ~**s** die Ländereien der Krone. **(b)** (*fig*) Domäne *f*. **(c)** (*Math*) Funktionsbereich *m*.

dome [dəʊm] *n* **(a)** (*Archit: on building*) Kuppel *f*. **(b)** (*of heaven, skull*) Gewölbe *nt*; (*of hill*) Kuppe *f*; (*of branches*) Kuppel *f*. **(c)** (*lid, cover etc*) Haube *f*.

domed [dəʊmd] *adj forehead* gewölbt.

domestic [də'mestɪk] **1** *adj* **(a)** *duty, bliss, life* häuslich. ~ **servants** Hauspersonal *pl*, Hauspersonal *nt*; **she was in** ~ **service** sie arbeitete als Hausmädchen, sie war Hausgehilfin; **everything of a** ~ **nature** alles, was den Haushalt angeht; **wedding presents are generally things of a** ~ **nature** Hochzeitsgeschenke sind normalerweise Dinge für den Haushalt. **(b)** (*Pol, Econ*) *policy, politician* Innen-; *news* Inland-, aus dem Inland; *produce* einheimisch; *trade* Binnen-; *flight* Inland-. ~ **quarrels** innenpolitische Auseinandersetzungen *pl*; ~ **affairs** Inneres *nt*, innere Angelegenheiten *pl*. **(c)** *animal* Haus-.
2 *n* Domestik *m* (old), Hausangestellte(r) *mf*.

domesticate [də'mestɪkeɪt] *vt wild animal*, (*hum*) *person* domestizieren; (*house-train*) *dog, cat* stubenrein machen.

domesticated [də'mestɪkeɪtɪd] *adj* domestiziert; *cat, dog* stubenrein. **she's very** ~ sie ist sehr häuslich.

domestication [dəmestɪ'keɪʃən] *n see vt* Domestikation, Domestizierung *f*; Gewöhnung *f* ans Haus.

domesticity [dəʊmes'tɪsɪtɪ] *n* häusliches Leben. **a life of simple** ~ ein (gut)bürgerliches Leben.

domestic science *n* Hauswirtschaftslehre *f*. ~ **college** Frauenfachschule *f*.

domicile ['dɒmɪsaɪl] **1** *n* (*Admin*) Wohnsitz *m*; (*Fin*) Zahlungs- *or* Erfüllungsort *m*. **2** *vt* (*Admin*) unterbringen (*with* bei, in +*dat*); (*Fin*) domizilieren (*at* bei).

domiciliary [dɒmɪ'sɪlɪərɪ] *adj* (*Admin*) *expenses* Haushalts-; *care of invalids* Haus-. ~ **visit** *of a doctor* Hausbesuch *m*.

dominance ['dɒmɪnəns] *n* Vorherrschaft, Dominanz *f* (*also Biol*) (*over* über +*acc*); (*Biol*) Dominanz *f*.

dominant ['dɒmɪnənt] **1** *adj* **(a)** (*controlling, masterful*) dominierend; *nation also* vorherrschend, mächtig; *gene*

dominant, überdeckend; (*more prominent*) *colour, building, industry, mountain* beherrschend, dominierend; *feature also* hervorstechend, herausragend. **he was the** ~ **personality at the conference** er war die dominierende *or* überragende Persönlichkeit der Konferenz. **(b)** (*Mus*) dominant. ~ **seventh** Dominantseptakkord *m*. **2** *n* (*Mus*) Dominante *f*.

dominate ['dɒmɪneɪt] **1** *vi* dominieren. **2** *vt* beherrschen; (*colour, feature also, species, gene*) dominieren.

domination [dɒmɪ'neɪʃən] *n* (Vor)herrschaft *f*. **under the** ~ **of the Romans** unter römischer Herrschaft; **his** ~ **of his younger brothers** sein dominierendes Verhalten seinen jüngeren Brüdern gegenüber; **her** ~ **of the conversation** die Tatsache, daß sie die Unterhaltung beherrschte.

domineer [dɒmɪ'nɪə'] *vi* tyrannisieren (*over sb* jdn).

domineering [dɒmɪ'nɪərɪŋ] *adj* herrisch; *mother-in-law, husband etc also* herrschsüchtig.

Dominican[1] [də'mɪnɪkən] (*Geog*) **1** *adj* dominikanisch. ~ **Republic** Dominikanische Republik. **2** *n* Dominikaner(in *f*) *m*.

Dominican[2] (*Eccl*) **1** *n* Dominikaner *m*. **2** *adj* Dominikaner-, dominikanisch.

dominion [də'mɪnɪən] *n* **(a)** *no pl* Herrschaft *f* (*over* über +*acc*). **to have** ~ **over sb** Macht über jdn haben. **(b)** (*territory*) Herrschaftsgebiet *nt*. **overseas** ~**s** überseeische Gebiete *pl*; **the D**~ **of Canada** das Dominion Kanada; **D**~ **Day** gesetzlicher Feiertag *in Kanada zur Erinnerung an die* Übertragung der vollen politischen Autonomie.

domino ['dɒmɪnəʊ] *n, pl* -es **(a)** Domino(stein) *m*. **a game of** ~**es** ein Dominospiel *nt*; **to play** ~**es** Domino spielen. **(b)** (*costume, mask*) Domino *m*.

don[1] [dɒn] *n* (*Brit Univ*) Universitätsdozent *m*, besonders in Oxford und Cambridge.

don[2] *vt garment* anziehen, anlegen (*dated*); *hat* aufsetzen.

donate [dəʊ'neɪt] *vt blood, kidney* spenden; *money, gifts to a charity also* stiften.

donation [dəʊ'neɪʃən] *n* (*act of giving*) (*of money, gifts*) Spenden *nt*; (*on large scale*) Stiften *nt*; (*of blood*) Spenden *nt*; (*gift*) Spende *f*; (*large scale*) Stiftung *f*. **to make a** ~ **of 50p/£1,000** 50 Pence spenden/£ 1.000 stiften.

done [dʌn] **1** *ptp* of **do**[2].
2 *adj* **(a)** (*finished*) *work* erledigt; (*cooked*) *vegetables* gar; *meat* durch. **to get sth** ~ (*finished*) etw fertigkriegen; **is that** ~ **yet?** ist das schon erledigt? **(b)** (*inf: tired out*) **I'm** ~ ich bin geschafft (*inf*) *or* fertig. **(c)** **it's not the** ~ **thing, that's not** ~ das tut man nicht. **(d)** (*inf: used up*) **the butter is** ~ die Butter ist alle.

dong [dɒŋ] *n* (*US sl: penis*) Apparat *m* (*inf*).

Don Juan [dɒn'dʒu:ən] *n* (*lit, fig*) Don Juan *m*.

donkey ['dɒŋkɪ] *n* Esel *m*. ~'s **years** (*inf*) eine Ewigkeit, ewig und drei Tage (*inf*); **she's been here for** ~'s **years** (*inf*) sie ist schon ewig und drei Tage (*inf*) *or* eine Ewigkeit hier.

donkey: ~ **engine** *n* (*Rail*) (kleines) Hilfsaggregat; ~ **jacket** *n* dicke (gefütterte) Jacke; ~ **ride** *n* Ritt *m* auf dem/einem Esel, Eselsritt *m*, Eselreiten *nt*; ~ **work** *n* Routinearbeit, Dreckarbeit (*inf*) *f*.

donnish ['dɒnɪʃ] *adj* gebildet; *tone* belehrend.

donor ['dəʊnə'] *n* (*Med: of blood, organ for transplant*) Spender(in *f*) *m*; (*to charity etc also*) Stifter(in *f*) *m*.

don't [dəʊnt] *contr* of **do not**.

don't-know [dəʊnt'nəʊ] *n* (*in opinion poll*) **30% were** ~**s** 30% hatten keine Meinung.

donut ['dəʊnʌt] *n* (*esp US*) see **doughnut**.

doodah ['du:da:] *n* (*inf*) Dingsbums (*inf*), Dingsda (*inf*) *nt*.

doodle ['du:dl] **1** *vi* Männchen malen. **2** *vt* kritzeln. **3** *n* Gekritzel *nt*.

doodlebug ['du:dlbʌg] *n* **(a)** (*Brit: bomb*) V1-Rakete *f*. **(b)** (*US: larva*) Ameisenlarve *f*.

doom [du:m] **1** *n* (*fate*) Schicksal *nt*; (*ruin*) Verhängnis *nt*. **to go to one's** ~ seinem Verhängnis entgegengehen; **to send sb to his** ~ jdn ins Verhängnis stürzen; **he met his** ~ das Schicksal ereilte ihn.
2 *vt* verurteilen, verdammen. **to be** ~**ed** verloren sein; **the project was** ~**ed from the start** das Vorhaben war von Anfang an zum Scheitern verurteilt; **the** ~**ed ship** das dem Untergang geweihte Schiff; ~**ed to die** dem Tode geweiht; ~**ed to failure/to perish** zum Scheitern/Untergang verurteilt; **this country was** ~**ed to become a second-rate nation** dieses Land war dazu verdammt, zur Zweitrangigkeit abzusinken.

doomsday ['du:mzdeɪ] *n* der Jüngste Tag. ... **otherwise we'll all be here till** ~ (*inf*) ... sonst sind wir alle in zwanzig Jahren noch hier.

door [dɔ:'] *n* **(a)** Tür *f*; (*entrance: to cinema etc*) Eingang *m*. **there's someone at the** ~ da ist jemand an der Tür; **was that the** ~? hat es geklingelt/geklopft?; **to stand in the** ~ in der Tür stehen; **to pay at the** ~ (*Theat etc*) an der (Abend)kasse zahlen; "~**s open 2.20**" „Einlaß 14.[20] Uhr"; **to go from** ~ **to** ~ (*salesman etc*) von Tür zu Tür gehen, Klinken putzen (*inf*); **he lives three** ~**s away** er wohnt drei Häuser weiter. **(b)** (*phrases*) **the** ~ **to success** der Schlüssel zum Erfolg; **to lay sth at sb's** ~ jdm etw vorwerfen *or* anlasten; **to leave the** ~ **open to** *or* **for further negotiations** die Tür zu weiteren *or* für weitere Verhandlungen offen lassen; **to open the** ~ **to sth** einer Sache (*dat*) Tür und Tor öffnen; **to show sb the** ~ jdm die Tür weisen; **to shut** *or* **close the** ~ **on sth** etw ausschließen; **we don't want to shut any** ~**s** wir möchten uns (*dat*) keine Möglichkeiten verbauen; **when one** ~ **shuts, another** ~ **opens** (*prov*) irgendwie geht es immer weiter; **out of** ~**s** im Freien.

door *in cpds* Tür-; ~**bell** *n* Türglocke *or* -klingel *f*; **there's the** ~**bell** es hat geklingelt.

do-or-die ['du:ɔ:r'daɪ] *adj* verbissen.

door: ~**frame** *n* Türrahmen *m*, Zarge *f*; ~ **handle,** ~ **knob,**

Türklinke f, Türknauf m; ~**keeper**, ~**man** n (of hotel, block of flats) Portier m; ~**knocker** n Türklopfer m; ~**mat** n Fußmatte f, Abtreter m; (fig) Fußabtreter m; ~**nail** n: **as dead as a** ~**nail** mausetot; ~**plate** n Türschild nt; ~**post** n Türpfosten m; **deaf as a** ~**post** stocktaub; ~**step** n Eingangsstufe f; (hum: hunk of bread) dicke Scheibe Brot; **the bus stop is just on my** ~**step** (fig) die Bushaltestelle ist direkt vor meiner Tür; ~**stop(per)** n Türanschlag m; ~**-to-**~ adj (a) ~**-to-**~ **salesman** Vertreter m; (b) delivery von Haus zu Haus; **how's that for** ~**-to-**~ **service?** na, ist das nicht ein Service?; ~**way** n (of room) Tür f; (of building, shop) Eingang m; (fig: to success etc) Weg m.

dope [dəʊp] **1** n (a) no pl (inf: drugs) Rauschgift nt, Stoff m (inf), Drogen pl; (Sport) Anregungs- or Aufputschmittel nt. **to test for** ~ eine Dopingkontrolle machen.
  (b) no pl (inf: information) Information(en pl) f. **to give sb the** ~ jdn informieren, jdm etw stecken (sl) (on über +acc); **what's the** ~ **on ...?** was wissen wir über (+acc) ...?
  (c) (inf: stupid person) Esel (inf), Trottel (inf) m.
  (d) (varnish) Lack m.
  (e) (for explosives) Benzinzusatz(mittel nt) m.
  2 vt horse, person dopen; food, drink präparieren, ein Betäubungsmittel untermischen (+dat).

dope: ~ **fiend** n Drogensüchtige(r) mf; ~ **peddler** or **pusher** n Drogenhändler, Dealer (sl), Pusher (sl) m.
dopey, dopy [ˈdəʊpɪ] adj (+er) (inf) (stupid) bekloppt (inf), blöd (inf); (sleepy, half-drugged) benommen, benebelt (inf).
doping [ˈdəʊpɪŋ] n (Sport) Doping nt.
Doppler effect [ˈdɒplərɪˌfekt] n Dopplereffekt m.
Doric [ˈdɒrɪk] adj (Archit) dorisch.
dorm [dɔːm] (inf) abbr of **dormitory**.
dormant [ˈdɔːmənt] adj (Zool, Bot) ruhend; volcano untätig; energy verborgen, latent; passion schlummernd; (Her) liegend. **to let a matter lie** ~ eine Sache ruhen or liegen lassen; **to lie** ~ (evil etc) schlummern.
dormer (window) [ˈdɔːmə(ˈwɪndəʊ)] n Mansardenfenster nt.
dormitory [ˈdɔːmɪtrɪ] n Schlafsaal m; (US; building) Wohnheim nt. ~ **suburb** or **town** n Schlafstadt f.
dormobile ® [ˈdɔːməbiːl] n Campomobil nt, Camper m.
dormouse [ˈdɔːmaʊs] n, pl **dormice** [ˈdɔːmaɪs] Haselmaus f.
dorsal [ˈdɔːsl] **1** adj Rücken-, dorsal (spec). **2** n (Phon) Dorsal-(laut) m.
dory [ˈdɔːrɪ] n (US) amerikanisches Ruderboot mit spitzem Bug und schmalem Heck.
dosage [ˈdəʊsɪdʒ] n Dose, Dosis f; (giving of medicine) Dosierung f.
dose [dəʊs] **1** n (a) (Med) Dosis f; (fig: of punishment, flattery etc) Ration f. **give him a** ~ **of medicine** gib ihm Medizin; **in small/large** ~s (fig) in kleinen/großen Mengen; **she's all right in small** ~s sie ist nur (für) kurze Zeit zu ertragen; **I can stand this weather in small** ~s ich kann dies Wetter nicht auf die Dauer or nur für kurze Zeit vertragen.
  (b) (inf: venereal disease) Tripper m. **to catch a** ~ sich (dat) etwas holen (inf), sich (dat) den Tripper holen.
  (c) (inf: bout of illness) Anfall m. **she's just had a** ~ **of the flu** sie hat gerade Grippe gehabt.
  2 vt person geben (+dat). **she's always dosing herself** sie nimmt or schluckt ständig Medikamente; **I've tried dosing myself with cough mixture** ich habe versucht, mich mit Hustensaft zu kurieren.
doss [dɒs] (Brit sl) **1** n Schlafplatz m, Bleibe f (inf). **2** vi (also ~ **down**) pennen (inf), sich hinhauen (inf). **to** ~ **down for the night** sich für die Nacht einquartieren (inf), für die Nacht unterkriechen (inf).
dosser [ˈdɒsəʳ] n (Brit sl) Penner(in f), Stadtstreicher(in f) m.
dosshouse [ˈdɒshaʊs] n (Brit sl) Penne (sl), Unterkunft f.
dossier [ˈdɒsɪeɪ] n Dossier m or nt. **they are keeping a** ~ **on him** sie haben ein Dossier über ihn angelegt.
dost [dʌst] (obs) 2nd pers sing of **do**².
dot [dɒt] **1** n (a) Punkt m; (over i also) Pünktchen, Tüpfelchen m; (on material) Tupfen, Punkt m. **morse code is made up of** ~s **and dashes** das Morsealphabet besteht aus kurzen und langen Signalen, ~, **dash**, ~ (morse) kurz, lang, kurz; ~, ~, ~ (in punctuation) drei Punkte.
  (b) (phrases) **to arrive on the** ~ auf die Minute pünktlich (an)kommen; **at 3 o'clock on the** ~ haargenau or auf die Minute genau um 3 Uhr; **in the year** ~ (inf) Anno dazumal (inf) or Tobak (inf); **she has lived here since the year** ~ sie lebt schon ewig hier or schon seit ewigen Zeiten hier.
  2 vt (a) **to** ~ **an i** einen i-Punkt setzen; **to** ~ **one's i's and cross one's t's** peinlich genau or penibel sein; **to** ~ **the line** punktierte Linie; **to tear along the** ~**ted line** an der or entlang der punktierten Linie abtrennen; **to sign on the** ~**ted line** (fig) seine formelle Zustimmung geben, formell zustimmen.
  (b) (sprinkle) verstreuen. **a field** ~**ted with flowers** ein mit Blumen übersätes Feld; **cars were** ~**ted along the side of the road** an der Straße entlang stand hier und da ein Auto; **the firm has various branches** ~**ted about the country** die Firma hat mehrere über das ganze Land verstreute Niederlassungen; **he has friends** ~**ted about all over Germany** seine Freunde leben über ganz Deutschland verteilt.
  (c) **to** ~ **sb one** (inf) jdm eine langen (inf).
dotage [ˈdəʊtɪdʒ] n Senilität, Altersschwäche f. **to be in one's** ~ in seiner zweiten Kindheit sein, senil sein.
dote on [ˈdəʊtɒn] vi +prep obj abgöttisch lieben.
doth [dʌθ] (obs) 3rd pers sing of **do**².
doting [ˈdəʊtɪŋ] adj her ~ **parents** ihre sie vergötternden or abgöttisch liebenden Eltern.
dottle [ˈdɒtl] n Tabakrest m.
dotty [ˈdɒtɪ] adj (+er) (Brit inf) kauzig, schrullig. **to be** ~ **about sb/sth** (like) nach jdm/etw verrückt sein.
double [ˈdʌbl] **1** adj (a) (twice as much, twofold) doppelt;

(having two similar parts, in pairs) Doppel-. **he got a** ~ **amount of work** er mußte die doppelte Arbeit tun, er erhielt doppelt soviel Arbeit; **a** ~ **whisky** ein doppelter Whisky; **her salary is** ~ **what it was ten years ago** ihr Gehalt hat sich in den letzten zehn Jahren verdoppelt, sie bekommt doppelt soviel Gehalt wie vor zehn Jahren; ~ **bottom** doppelter Boden; ~ **consonant** Doppelkonsonant m; ~ **knot** doppelter Knoten; ~ **track** (Rail) zweigleisige Strecke; **an egg with a** ~ **yolk** ein Ei mit zwei Dottern; **it is spelt with a** ~ "p" es wird mit Doppel-p or mit zwei „p" geschrieben; ~ **six** (in ludo etc) Doppelsechs f; (in dominoes, dice) Sechserpasch m; ~ **seven five four/**~ **seven five** (Telec) siebenundsiebzig vierundfünfzig/sieben sieben fünf.
  (b) (made for two) Doppel-. ~ **room** Doppelzimmer nt.
  (c) (dual, serving two purposes) doppelt. **it has a** ~ **meaning/interpretation** es ist zwei- or doppeldeutig/läßt zwei Auslegungen zu; ~ **standards** Doppelmoral f; **society applies** ~ **standards** die Gesellschaft mißt mit zweierlei Maß or legt zwei (verschiedene) Maßstäbe an.
  (d) (underhand, deceptive) doppelt. **to lead a** ~ **life** ein Doppelleben führen; **to play a** ~ **game** ein Doppelspiel treiben.
  (e) (Bot) gefüllt.
  (f) ~ **time** (Mil) Laufschritt m.
  2 adv (a) (twice) doppelt. **that costs** ~ **what it did last year** das kostet doppelt soviel wie letztes Jahr; **I have** ~ **what you have** ich habe doppelt soviel wie du; **he did it in** ~ **the time** it **took me** er brauchte doppelt so lange wie ich; **he's** ~ **your age** er ist doppelt so alt wie du; ~ **six is twelve** zweimal sechs ist zwölf; **to see** ~ doppelt sehen.
  (b) **to be bent** ~ **with pain** sich vor Schmerzen krümmen, vor Schmerz gekrümmt sein; **fold the paper** ~ falte das Papier (einmal).
  3 n (a) (twice a quantity, number, size etc) das Doppelte, das Zweifache. ~ **or quits** doppelt oder nichts; **he earns the** ~ **of what I do** er verdient doppelt soviel wie ich.
  (b) (person) Ebenbild nt, Doppelgänger(in f) m; (Film, Theat: stand-in) Double nt; (actor taking two parts) Schauspieler, der eine Doppelrolle spielt. **I've got the** ~ **of that clock** ich habe genau die gleiche Uhr.
  (c) **at the** ~ (also Mil) im Laufschritt; (fig) auf der Stelle.
  (d) (Cards) (increase) Verdoppelung f; (hand) Blatt, das Verdoppelung rechtfertigt; (in racing) Doppelwette f; (in dice) Pasch m; (in dominoes also) Doppelstein m.
  4 vt (a) (increase twofold) verdoppeln.
  (b) (fold in two) piece of paper (einmal) falten.
  (c) (Film, Theat) he ~s **the parts of courtier and hangman** er hat die Doppelrolle des Höflings und Henkers; **the producer decided to** ~ **the parts of pimp and judge** der Produzent beschloß, die Rollen des Zuhälters und des Richters mit demselben Schauspieler zu besetzen; **who is doubling for him?** wer doubelt ihn?, wer ist sein Double?
  (d) (Naut: sail round) umsegeln.
  (e) (Cards) one's opponent, his call verdoppeln.
  5 vi (a) (increase twofold) sich verdoppeln; (price also) um das Doppelte steigen.
  (b) (Mus) zwei Instrumente spielen. **he** ~s **on flute and clarinet** er spielt Flöte und Klarinette.
  (c) (Film, Theat) **to** ~ **for sb** jds Double sein, jdn doubeln; **he** ~s **as the butler and the duke** er hat die Doppelrolle des Butlers und Herzogs.
  (d) (Cards) verdoppeln; (Bridge) kontrieren.
♦**double back 1** vi (person) kehrtmachen, zurückgehen/-fahren; (animal) kehrtmachen, zurücklaufen; (road, river) sich zurückwinden or -schlängeln. **2** vt sep blanket umschlagen; page umknicken.
♦**double over 1** vi see **double up 1** (a). **2** vt sep see **double back 2**.
♦**double up 1** vi (a) (bend over) sich krümmen; (with laughter) sich biegen, sich kringeln (inf). **he** ~**d** ~ **when the bullet hit him** er klappte (inf) or brach zusammen, als die Kugel ihn traf.
  (b) (share room) das Zimmer/Büro etc gemeinsam benutzen; (share bed) in einem Bett schlafen. **you'll have to** ~ ~ **with Mary** du mußt dir ein Zimmer mit Mary teilen.
  (c) (Brit Betting) den Einsatz bis zum ersten Gewinn verdoppeln.
  2 vt sep (a) paper falten, knicken; blanket zusammenlegen.
  (b) **the bullet/blow** ~**d him** ~ von der Kugel/dem Schlag getroffen, brach er zusammen.
double: ~**-acting** adj engine doppelwirkend; ~ **agent** n Doppelagent m; ~ **bar** n (Mus) Doppelstrich m; ~**-barrelled**, (US) ~**-barreled** [ˌdʌblˈbærəld] adj surname Doppel-; ~**-barrel(l)ed shotgun** n doppelläufiges Gewehr, Zwilling m; ~ **bass** n Kontrabaß m; ~ **bassoon** n Kontrafagott nt; ~ **bed** n Doppelbett nt; ~ **bend** n S-Kurve f; ~ **boiler** n (US) Turmtopf m; ~**-breasted** adj zweireihig; ~**-breasted jacket/suit** Zweireiher m; ~**-check** vti noch einmal (über)prüfen; ~ **chin** n Doppelkinn nt; ~ **cream** n stark fetthaltige Schlagsahne; ~**-cross** (inf) **1** vt ein Doppelspiel or falsches Spiel treiben mit; **the** ~**-crossing swines!** diese falschen Hunde! (inf); **2** n Doppelspiel m; ~**-crosser** n (inf) falscher Freund or Hund (inf); ~**-dealer** n Betrüger m; ~**-dealing** n Betrügerei(en pl) f; **2** adj betrügerisch; ~**-decker** n (all senses) Doppeldecker m; ~**-declutch** vi (Aut) mit Zwischengas schalten; ~**-dutch** (Brit) Kauderwelsch nt; **to talk** ~ **dutch** Unsinn or Kauderwelsch reden; **it was** ~ **dutch to me** das waren für mich böhmische Dörfer; ~ **eagle** n (US) alte amerikanische Goldmünze mit einem Wert von $ 20; ~**-edged** adj (lit, fig) zweischneidig; ~ **entendre** [ˈduːblãːˈtãːndr] n Zweideutigkeit f; ~**-entry book-keeping** n doppelte Buchführung f; ~ **exposure** n doppelt belichtetes Foto; ~ **fault** n (Tennis) Doppelfehler m; ~ **feature** n Programm nt mit zwei Hauptfilmen; ~ **first** n

(*Brit Univ*) he got a ~ first er bestand beide Fächer mit „sehr gut" (*in einem honours degree course*); ~ **flat** n (*Mus*) Doppel-b nt; ~**-glaze** vt mit Doppelverglasung versehen; ~ **glazing** n doppelt verglaste Fenster pl; ~ **Gloucester** n *englische Käsesorte*; ~ **honours (course)** n (*Brit Univ*) = Doppelstudium nt; ~**-jointed** adj äußerst elastisch, sehr gelenkig; ~**-knitting (wool)** n = Sportwolle f; ~ **lock** n Doppelschloß nt; ~**-lock** vt zweimal abschließen; ~ **negative** n doppelte Verneinung; ~**-page spread** n Doppelseite f; ~ **park** vi in der zweiten Reihe parken; ~ **parking** n Parken nt in der zweiten Reihe; ~ **pneumonia** n doppelseitige Lungenentzündung; ~**-quick** (*inf*) 1 adv sehr schnell; 2 adj in ~**-quick time** im Nu, in Null Komma nichts (*inf*).

doubles ['dʌblz] n sing or pl (*Sport*) Doppel nt.

double: ~ **saucepan** n Turmtopf m; ~**-sharp** n (*Mus*) Doppelkreuz nt; ~ **spacing** n doppelter Zeilenabstand; ~ **star** n Doppelstern m; ~ **stop** 1 n (*Mus*) Doppelgriff m; 2 vi mit Doppelgriff spielen.

doublet ['dʌblɪt] n (a) Wams nt. (b) (*Ling*) Dublette f.

double: ~ **take** n he did a ~ take er mußte zweimal hingucken; ~**talk** n (*ambiguous*) zwei- or doppeldeutiges Gerede; (*deceitful*) doppelzüngiges Gerede; ~**think** n widersprüchliches Denken; ~ **time** n (*in wages*) doppelter Lohn; ~**-tongue** vi (*Mus*) mit Doppelzunge blasen; ~**-tonguing** n Doppelzunge f.

doubloon [dʌ'blu:n] n Dublone f.

doubly ['dʌblɪ] adv doppelt. this road is dangerous, ~ so when it's icy diese Straße ist gefährlich, vor allem bei Glatteis.

doubt [daʊt] 1 n Zweifel m. his honesty is in ~ seine Ehrlichkeit wird angezweifelt; I am in (some) ~ about his honesty ich habe Zweifel an seiner Ehrlichkeit; to be in great ~ as to sth schwere Bedenken hinsichtlich einer Sache (*gen*) haben; I am in ~ as to whether ... ich habe so meine Zweifel, ob ...; it is still in ~ es ist noch zweifelhaft; I am in no ~ as to what or about what he means ich bin mir völlig im klaren darüber, was er meint; to have one's ~s as to or about sth (so) seine Bedenken hinsichtlich einer Sache (*gen*) haben; I have my ~s whether he will come ich bezweifle, daß er kommt; to cast ~ on sth etw in Zweifel ziehen; there is room for ~ es ist durchaus nicht sicher; there's no ~ about it daran gibt es keinen Zweifel; I have no ~ about it ich bezweifle das nicht; I have no ~s about taking the job ich habe keine Bedenken, die Stelle anzunehmen; no ~ he will come tomorrow höchstwahrscheinlich kommt er morgen; without (a) ~ ohne Zweifel; yes, no ~, but ... ja, zweifelsohne, aber ...; it's beyond ~ that ... es steht außer Zweifel, daß ...; when in ~ im Zweifelsfall.

2 vt bezweifeln; sb's honesty, truth of statement anzweifeln, Zweifel haben an (+*dat*). I'm sorry I ~ed you (*what you said*) es tut mir leid, daß ich dir nicht geglaubt habe; (*your loyalty etc*) es tut mir leid, daß ich an dir gezweifelt habe; I ~ it (*very much*) das möchte ich (doch stark) bezweifeln, das bezweifle ich (sehr); I don't ~ it das bezweifle ich (auch gar) nicht; I ~ whether he will come ich bezweifle, daß er kommen wird; I ~ if that is what she wanted ich bezweifle, daß das ihrem Wunsch entspricht.

3 vi Zweifel haben or hegen. ~ing Thomas ungläubiger Thomas.

doubter ['daʊtər] n Skeptiker, Zweifler m.

doubtful ['daʊtfʊl] adj (a) (*uncertain*) unsicher, zweifelhaft; outcome, result, future ungewiß. to be ~ about sb/sth jdm/einer Sache gegenüber Zweifel hegen or voller Zweifel sein; to be ~ about doing sth zweifeln or Bedenken haben, ob man etw tun soll; he might do it, but I'm a bit ~ es kann sein, daß er es macht, aber ganz sicher bin ich nicht; to look ~ (*person*) skeptisch aussehen; the weather was or looked a bit ~ es sah nach schlechtem Wetter aus; it is ~ whether/that ... es ist unsicher or zweifelhaft, ob ...; he's a ~ starter (*in race*) es ist zweifelhaft, ob er starten wird or (*for job etc*) ob er anfangen wird. (b) (*of questionable character*) zweifelhaft; person, affair also zwielichtig; reputation also fragwürdig; joke zweideutig.

doubtfully ['daʊtfəlɪ] adv skeptisch, voller Zweifel.

doubtfulness ['daʊtfʊlnɪs] n see adj (a) Unsicherheit f; Ungewißheit f. because of the ~ of the weather weil es nach schlechtem Wetter aussah. (b) Zweifelhaftigkeit f; Zwielichtigkeit f; Fragwürdigkeit f; Zweideutigkeit f.

doubtless ['daʊtlɪs] adv ohne Zweifel, zweifelsohne.

douche [du:ʃ] 1 n Spülung, Irrigation (*spec*) f; (*instrument*) Irrigator m. like a cold ~ (*inf*) wie eine kalte Dusche. 2 vi eine Spülung machen. 3 vt spülen.

dough [dəʊ] n (a) Teig m. (b) (*sl: money*) Kohle f, Kies, Zaster m (*all inf*).

dough: ~**ball** n Kloß m; ~**boy** n (*US Mil sl*) Landser m (*inf*); ~**nut** n Berliner (Pfannkuchen), Krapfen (*S Ger*) m.

doughty ['daʊtɪ] adj (*liter*) kühn, tapfer.

doughy ['dəʊɪ] adj (a) consistency zäh, teigig; (*pej*) bread klitschig, nicht durchgebacken. (b) (*pej*) complexion käsig.

Douglas fir [,dʌgləs'fɜ:r] or **pine** [-'paɪn] n Douglastanne f.

dour ['dʊər] adj (*silent, unfriendly*) mürrisch, verdrießlich; struggle hart, hartnäckig. to be ~-faced mürrisch or verdrießlich aussehen.

douse [daʊs] vt (a) (*pour water over*) Wasser schütten über (+*acc*); (*put into water*) ins Wasser tauchen; plants reichlich wässern. (b) light ausmachen, löschen. ~ that light! Licht aus!

dove¹ [dʌv] n (*lit, fig*) Taube f.

dove² [dəʊv] (*US*) pret of dive.

dove [dʌv-]: ~**-coloured** adj taubenblau; ~**cot(e)** n ['dʌvkɒt] Taubenschlag m; ~ **grey** adj taubengrau.

dovetail ['dʌvteɪl] 1 n Schwalbenschwanz m. ~ **joint** n Schwalbenschwanzverbindung f. 2 vt (schwalbenschwanzförmig) überblattern. we must ~ our plans with yours wir müssen unsere Pläne koordinieren or aufeinander abstimmen. 3 vi (*plans*) übereinstimmen.

dowager ['daʊədʒər] n (adlige) Witwe. ~ **duchess** Herzoginwitwe f.

dowdiness ['daʊdɪnɪs] n absoluter Mangel an Schick.

dowdy ['daʊdɪ] adj (+er) ohne jeden Schick.

dowel ['daʊəl] n Dübel m.

dower house ['daʊəhaʊs] n Haus nt für eine Witwe.

down¹ [daʊn] 1 adv (a) (*indicating movement*) (*towards speaker*) herunter; (*away from speaker*) hinunter; (*downstairs also*) nach unten. ~! (*to dog*) Platz!; ~ it goes! (*taking medicine, child eating*) nun schluck mal schön runter; (*of stone, tree etc*) da fällt er; to fall ~ hinunter-/herunterfallen; and ~ he fell und da fiel er hinunter/herunter; to run/look/jump/climb ~ hinunter-/herunterlaufen/-sehen/-springen/-klettern; ~ with school/traitors! nieder mit der Schule/den Verrätern!; on his way ~ from the hilltop auf seinem Weg vom Gipfel herab/hinab; all the way ~ to the bottom bis ganz nach unten.

(b) (*indicating static position*) unten. ~ there da unten; I shall stay ~ here ich bleibe hier unten; ~ in the valley unten im Tal; he's ~ in the cellar er ist (unten) im Keller; it needs a bit of paint ~ at the bottom es muß unten herum neu gestrichen werden; don't kick or hit a man when he's ~ man soll jemanden nicht fertigmachen, wenn er schon angeschlagen ist or wenn's ihm dreckig geht (*inf*); head ~ mit dem Kopf nach unten; the sun is ~ die Sonne ist untergegangen; the sun was well ~ in the sky die Sonne stand schon ziemlich tief; the blinds were ~ die Jalousien waren unten or heruntergelassen; John isn't ~ yet (*hasn't got up*) John ist noch nicht unten; I'll be ~ in a minute ich komme sofort runter; to be ~ for the count (*Boxing*) ausgezählt werden; I've been ~ with flu ich habe mit Grippe (im Bett) gelegen; he was (feeling) a bit ~ er fühlte sich ein wenig niedergeschlagen or down (*inf*).

(c) (*to or at another place*) usu not translated he came ~ from London yesterday er kam gestern aus London; (*to south also*) er ist gestern von London runtergekommen (*inf*); on the way ~ from London auf dem Weg von London hierher or runter (*inf*); he's ~ in London er ist in London; ~ South im Süden/in den Süden; ~ here in Italy hier unten in Italien; we're going ~ to the sea/to Dover wir fahren an die See/nach Dover; ~ in Australia in Australien; he's ~ at his brother's er ist bei seinem Bruder.

(d) (*in volume, degree, activity, status*) his shoes were quite worn ~ seine Schuhe waren ziemlich abgetragen; the tyres are ~ die Reifen sind platt; his temperature has gone ~ sein Fieber ist zurückgegangen; the price of meat is ~ on last week der Fleischpreis ist gegenüber der letzten Woche gefallen; I'm £2 ~ on what I expected ich habe £2 weniger, als ich dachte; their team is three points ~ (on last week/on their opponents) ihre Mannschaft liegt (verglichen mit letzter Woche/ihren Gegnern) um drei Punkte zurück; they're still three goals ~ sie liegen immer noch mit drei Toren zurück.

(e) (*in writing, planning*) to write sth ~ etw aufschreiben; I've got it ~ in my diary ich habe es in meinem Kalender notiert; let's get it ~ on paper schreiben wir es auf, halten wir es schriftlich fest; when you see it ~ on paper wenn man es schwarz auf weiß sieht; to be ~ for the next race für das nächste Rennen gemeldet sein; it's ~ for next month es steht für nächsten Monat auf dem Programm/Stundenplan etc.

(f) (*indicating succession of things, events, in hierarchy*) usu not translated from 1700 ~ to the present seit 1700 bis zur Gegenwart; (all or right) ~ through the ages von jeher; right ~ to the present day bis zum heutigen Tag; from the biggest ~ vom Größten angefangen; from the biggest ~ to the smallest von Größten bis zum Kleinsten; from the king (all the way) ~ to the poorest beggar vom König bis (herunter) zum ärmsten Bettler.

(g) to pay £2 ~ £2 anzahlen; how much do they want ~? was verlangen sie als Anzahlung?; to be ~ on sb jdn schikanieren or triezen (*inf*).

2 prep (a) (*indicating movement to*) to go/come ~ the hill/street etc den Berg/die Straße etc hinuntergehen/herunterkommen; she let her hair fall ~ her back sie ließ ihr Haar über die Schultern fallen; he ran his finger ~ the list er ging (mit dem Finger) die Liste hinab.

(b) (*at a lower part of*) he's already ~ the hill er ist schon unten; the other skiers were further ~ the slope die anderen Skifahrer waren weiter unten; she lives ~ the street (*from us*) sie wohnt ein Stückchen weiter die Straße entlang.

(c) ~ the ages/centuries durch die Jahrhunderte (hindurch).

(d) (*along*) he was walking/coming ~ the street er ging/kam die Straße entlang; looking ~ this road, you can see ... wenn Sie die Straße hinunterblicken, können Sie ... sehen.

(e) (*Brit inf: to, in, at*) he's gone ~ the pub er ist in die Kneipe gegangen; she's ~ the shops sie ist einkaufen gegangen; he works ~ the garage er arbeitet in der Autowerkstatt; let's go ~ Jimmy's place gehen wir doch zu Jimmy.

3 n to have a ~ on sb (*inf*) jdn auf dem Kieker haben (*inf*); ~ up.

4 vt opponent niederschlagen, zu Fall bringen; enemy planes abschießen, (he)runterholen (*inf*); beer etc runterkippen or -schütten (*inf*). to ~ tools die Arbeit niederlegen.

down² n (*feathers*) Daunen, Flaumfedern pl; (*youth's beard*) Flaum m.

down³ n usu pl (*Geog*) Hügelland nt no pl. on the ~(s) im Hügelland.

down: ~**-and-out** 1 n (*tramp*) Penner m (*inf*); 2 adj heruntergekommen; appearance also abgerissen; ~**-beat** 1 n Taktstockführung f, die den ersten betonten Taktteil anzeigt, erster Taktteil; 2 adj (*fig*) ending undramatisch; ~**-bow** n (*Mus*) Abstrich m; ~**cast** 1 adj (a) (*depressed*) person, expression niedergedrückt, entmutigt; (b) eyes niedergeschlagen;

look gesenkt; **2** *n* (*Min*) Wetterschacht *m*; **~ draught**, (*US*) **~ draft** *n* (*Met*) Fallwind *m*; (*Tech*) Fallstrom *m*.

downer ['daʊnəʳ] *n* (*sl*) Downer *m* (*sl*), Beruhigungsmittel *nt*.

down: **~fall** *n* (**a**) Sturz, Fall *m*; (*of empire also*) Untergang *m*; (*cause of ruin: drink etc*) Ruin *m*; (**b**) (*of rain*) heftiger Niederschlag, Platzregen *m*; **~grade 1** *n* (*Rail*) Gefälle *nt*; **to be on the ~grade** (*fig*) auf dem absteigenden Ast sein; (*health, quality*) sich verschlechtern; **2** *vi hotel, job, work* herunterstufen; *person also* degradieren; **~-hearted** *adj* niedergeschlagen, entmutigt; **~hill 1** *adv* **to go ~hill** (*road*) bergab führen *or* gehen; (*car*) hinunter *or* herunterfahren; (*person*) hinunter- *or* heruntergehen; (*fig*) (*person*) auf dem absteigenden Ast sein; (*work, health*) sich verschlechtern; **2** *adj* (*lit*) abfallend *attr*, bergab führend *attr*; **the path is ~hill for 2 miles** der Weg führt zwei Meilen bergab; **the ~hill path to drug addiction** der abschüssige Weg in die Drogensucht; **~ line** *n* (*Rail*) Eisenbahnlinie *f* von der Stadt aufs Land oder aus der Hauptstadt heraus; **~market** *adj* product für den Massenmarkt; *area* weniger anspruchsvoll; **~ payment** *n* (*Fin*) Anzahlung *f*; **~pipe** *n* Abflußrohr, Fallrohr *nt*; **~pour** *n* Platzregen, Wolkenbruch *m*; **~right 1** *adj refusal, lie* glatt; *rudeness, scoundrel, liar* ausgesprochen; **2** *adv* rude, angry ausgesprochen; **~river** *adv* flußabwärts (*from* von); **~river from Bonn** unterhalb von Bonn; **~spout** *n* Abflußrohr, Fallrohr *nt*; **~stage** *adv* (*at the front*) im vorderen Teil der Bühne; (*towards the front*) zum vorderen Teil der Bühne; **he was standing ~stage from her** er stand von ihr aus gesehen weiter vorne auf der Bühne; **~stairs 1** *adv* go, come nach unten; be unten; **the people ~stairs** die Leute unter uns *or* von unten; **2** *adj* flat Parterre-; **the ~stairs rooms** die unteren Zimmer, die Zimmer unten; **our ~stairs neighbours** die Nachbarn unter uns; **3** *n* Parterre *nt*; **~stream** *adv* fluß- *or* stromabwärts (*from* von); **~stroke** *n* (*in writing*) Abstrich *m*; (*Mech: of piston*) Ansaugtakt *m*; **~ swing** *n* Abwärtsschwingen *nt*; **~-to-earth** *adj* nüchtern; **~town 1** *adj* **~town district** Zentrum *nt*, Innenstadt *f*; (*US*) Geschäftsviertel *nt*; **~town Chicago** das Zentrum *or* die City *or* Innenstadt von Chicago; **2** *adv* **to go ~town** in die (Innen)stadt *or* ins Zentrum gehen; **to live ~town** im (Stadt)zentrum *or* in der Innenstadt wohnen; **~ train** *n* Zug, der von der Stadt aufs Land fährt oder von der Hauptstadt abgeht; **~trodden** *adj people* unterdrückt, geknechtet; **~turn** *n* (*in prices, business*) Rückgang *m*, Abflauen *nt*; **to take a ~turn** zurückgehen, abflauen; **his fortunes took a ~turn** sein Glücksstern sank; **~ under** (*Brit inf*) **1** *n* Australien *nt*; **2** *adv* in/nach Australien.

downward ['daʊnwəd] **1** *adj movement, pull* nach unten; *slope* abfallend. **he's on the ~ path** (*fig*) mit ihm geht's bergab. **2** *adv* (*also* **downwards**) (**a**) *go, look* nach unten. **to slope gently ~** sanft abfallen. (**b**) (*fig*) **from the 10th century ~** seit dem 10. Jahrhundert; **from the king ~** beim König angefangen.

downwind ['daʊnwɪnd] *adv* in Windrichtung (*of or from sth* einer Sache *gen*).

downy ['daʊnɪ] *adj* (+*er*) *skin, leaf, peach* flaumig, mit (feinen) Härchen bedeckt; *cushion* Daunen-; *softness* flaumweich, daunenweich.

dowry ['daʊrɪ] *n* Mitgift *f*.

dowse¹ [daʊz] *vt see* **douse**.

dowse² [daʊz] *vi* (*divine*) mit einer Wünschelrute suchen. **dowsing rod** Wünschelrute *f*.

dowser ['daʊzəʳ] *n* Wünschelrutengänger(in *f*) *m*.

doxology [dɒk'sɒlədʒɪ] *n* Lobpreisung *f*, Verherrlichung *f* Gottes.

doyen ['dɔɪən] *n* (*senior and expert member of group*) Nestor *m*; (*of diplomatic corps*) Doyen *m*.

doyenne ['dɔɪen] *n* Doyenne *f*.

doz *abbr of* **dozen**.

doze [daʊz] **1** *n* Nickerchen *nt*. **to have a ~** dösen, ein Nickerchen machen. **2** *vi* (*vor sich hin*) dösen.

♦doze off *vi* einschlafen, einnicken.

dozen ['dʌzn] *n* Dutzend *nt*. **20p a ~** 20 Pence das Dutzend; **half a ~** sechs, ein halbes Dutzend; (*fig inf*) eine ganze Menge; **~s of times** (*inf*) x-mal (*inf*), tausendmal; **there are ~s like that** (*inf*) das gibt's wie Sand am Meer; **how many has he got?** — **~s** (*inf*) wieviel hat er? — jede Menge; **~s of people came** (*inf*) Dutzende von Leute kamen.

dozily ['dəʊzɪlɪ] *adv* verschlafen, schläfrig.

dozy ['dəʊzɪ] *adj* (+*er*) (*sleepy*) schläfrig, verschlafen. (**b**) (*sl: stupid*) dösig (*inf*).

D Phil *abbr of* **Doctor of Philosophy** Dr. phil.

DPP *abbr of* **Director of Public Prosecutions**.

dpt *abbr of* **department** Abt.

Dr *abbr of* **doctor** Dr.

drab [dræb] **1** *adj* (+*er*) trist; *colour also* düster; *town also* grau. **2** *n, no pl* (*Tex*) grober, graubrauner Wollstoff.

drably ['dræblɪ] *adv see adj*.

drabness ['dræbnɪs] *n see adj* Tristheit *f*; Düsterkeit *f*; Grauheit *f*.

drachma ['drækmə] *n, pl* **-e** ['drækmiː] *or* **-s** Drachme *f*.

draconian [drə'kəʊnɪən] *adj* drakonisch.

draft [drɑːft] **1** *n* (**a**) (*rough outline*) Entwurf *m*. (**b**) (*Fin, Comm*) Wechsel *m*, Tratte *f*. (**c**) (*Mil: group of men*) Sonderkommando *nt*. (**d**) (*US Mil: group of conscripts*) Rekruten *pl*; (*conscription*) Einberufung (zum Wehrdienst). (**e**) (*US*) *see* **draught**. **2** *vt* (**a**) *letter, speech, bill, contract* entwerfen. (**b**) (*US Mil*) *conscript* einziehen, einberufen. **he was ~ed into the Engineers** er wurde zu den Pionieren einberufen *or* eingezogen; **he was ~ed into the Cabinet** (*fig*) er wurde ins Kabinett berufen; **to ~ sb to do sth** (*Mil*) jdn dazu abkommandieren, etw zu tun; (*fig*) jdn beauftragen, etw zu tun.

draft: **~ board** *n* (*US Mil*) Einberufungsbehörde *f*; (*panel*)

Einberufungsausschuß *m*; **~ card** *n* (*US Mil*) Wehrpaß *m*; **~ dodger** *n* (*US Mil*) Wehrpflichtiger, der sich vor dem Wehrdienst drückt, Drückeberger *m* (*pej inf*).

draftee ['drɑːftiː] *n* (*US Mil*) Eingezogene(r), Wehrpflichtige(r) *m*.

draftiness *etc* (*US*) *see* **draughtiness** *etc*.

draft: **~ letter** *n* Entwurf *m* eines/des Briefes; **~ version** *n* Entwurf *m*.

drag [dræg] **1** *n* (**a**) (*object pulled along*) (*for dredging etc*) Suchanker *m*; (*Naut: cluster of hooks*) Dregganker, Draggen *m*; (*~-net*) Schleppnetz *nt*; (*heavy sledge*) Lastschlitten *m*; (*Agr: harrow*) schwere Egge. (**b**) (*resistance*) (*Aviat*) Luft- *or* Strömungswiderstand *m*; (*Naut*) Wasserwiderstand *m*. (**c**) (*brake*) Hemmklotz, Hemmschuh *m*. (**d**) (*slow laborious progress*) **it was a long ~ up to the top of the hill** es war ein langer, mühseliger Aufstieg zum Gipfel, der Aufstieg auf den Gipfel war ein furchtbarer Schlauch (*inf*). (**e**) (*inf: hindrance*) **to be a ~ on sb** für jdn ein Klotz am Bein *or* ein Hemmschuh sein; **this extra work's going to be a bit of a ~ on us** diese zusätzliche Arbeit bedeutet eine ganz schöne Mehrbelastung für uns. (**f**) (*inf*) **what a ~!** (*boring*) Mann, ist der/die/das langweilig! (*inf*); (*nuisance*) so'n Mist (*inf*); **what a ~ having to go back!** so'n Mist, daß wir zurückmüssen (*inf*); **the film was a ~** der Film war stinklangweilig (*inf*); **he suddenly decided that his girlfriend was a real ~** es wurde ihm plötzlich klar, daß seine Freundin ihn anödete (*inf*). (**g**) (*inf: pull on cigarette*) Zug *m* (*on, at* an +*dat*). **give me a ~** laß mich mal ziehen, gib mir mal'n Zug (*inf*). (**h**) (*inf: women's clothing worn by men*) (*von Männern getragene*) Frauenkleidung *f*. **in** *or* **wearing ~** in Frauenkleidung, im Fummel (*sl*), als Tunte (*sl*). (**i**) (*US inf: influence*) Einfluß *m*. **to use one's ~** seinen Einfluß ausüben. **2** *vt* (**a**) *person, object* schleppen, schleifen, ziehen. **the dog was ~ging its broken leg** der Hund schleifte sein gebrochenes Bein hinter sich her; **to ~ one's feet** (*lit*) (mit den Füßen) schlurfen; (*fig*) alles/die Sache schleifen lassen; **to ~ anchor** (*Naut*) vor Anker treiben; **to ~ the truth out of sb** aus jdm die Wahrheit mühsam herausholen; **he ~ged the words out of him** er mußte ihm jedes Wort einzeln aus der Nase ziehen (*inf*). (**b**) *river* absuchen. **3** *vi* (**a**) schleifen; (*feet*) schlurfen; (*Naut: anchor*) treiben. (**b**) (*lag behind: person*) hinterherhinken. (**c**) (*fig*) (*time, work*) sich hinziehen; (*play, book*) sich in die Länge ziehen; (*conversation*) sich (mühsam) hinschleppen.

♦drag along *vt sep person* mitschleppen. **to ~ oneself ~** sich mühsam dahinschleppen; **to ~ sth ~ behind one** etw hinter sich (*dat*) her schleppen *or* schleifen.

♦drag apart *vt sep* auseinanderzerren, trennen.

♦drag away *vt sep* (*lit, fig*) wegschleppen *or* -ziehen. **you'll have to ~ him ~ from the television** den muß man mit Gewalt vom Fernsehen wegziehen; **if you can ~ yourself ~ from the television for a second** ... wenn du dich vielleicht mal für eine Sekunde vom Fernsehen losreißen könntest ...

♦drag behind 1 *vt* + *prep obj* **to ~ sth/sb ~** one jdn/etw hinter sich (*dat*) herschleppen *or* herschleifen. **2** *vi* (*in class*) zurück sein, hinterherhinken; (*in race*) hinterherlaufen *or* -fahren; (*on a walk*) zurückbleiben, hinterhertrödeln.

♦drag down *vt sep* (*lit*) herunterziehen; (*fig*) mit sich ziehen. **to ~ sb ~ to one's own level** (*fig*) jdn auf sein eigenes Niveau herabziehen; **his illness is ~ging him ~** seine Krankheit macht ihn fertig (*inf*); **you shouldn't let these things ~ you ~** so du solltest dich dadurch nicht so entmutigen lassen.

♦drag in *vt sep* (**a**) (*lit*) hineinziehen. (**b**) (*fig*) *subject* aufs Tapet bringen; *remark* anbringen.

♦drag off *vt sep* (*lit*) wegzerren *or* -ziehen; (*fig*) wegschleppen. **to ~ sb ~ to a concert** jdn in ein Konzert schleppen.

♦drag on *vi* sich in die Länge ziehen; (*meeting, lecture also*) sich hinziehen; (*conversation*) sich hinschleppen. **it ~ged on for 3 hours** es zog sich über 3 Stunden hin.

♦drag out *vt sep meeting, discussion etc* in die Länge ziehen.

♦drag up *vt sep* (**a**) *scandal, story* ausgraben; *person* aufgabeln (*inf*), auftun (*inf*). (**b**) (*inf*) *child* mehr schlecht als recht aufziehen. **~ged ~ rather than brought up** mehr schlecht als recht aufgezogen.

drag artist *n* (*inf*) Künstler, der in Frauenkleidung auftritt.

dragée ['dræʒeɪ] *n* (*Med*) Dragee *nt*.

draggy ['drægɪ] *adj* (*sl*) anödend (*inf*).

dragnet ['drægnet] *n* (*for fish*) Schleppnetz *nt*; (*police hunt*) großangelegte Polizeiaktion. **to slip through the ~** (der Polizei) durch die Maschen schlüpfen.

dragoman ['drægəʊmən] *n* Dragoman *m*.

dragon ['drægən] *n* (*lit, fig inf*) Drache *m*.

dragonfly ['drægənflaɪ] *n* Libelle *f*.

dragoon [drə'guːn] **1** *n* (*Mil*) Dragoner *m*. **2** *vt* **to ~ sb into doing sth** jdn zwingen *or* mit Gewalt dazu bringen, etw zu tun.

drag: **~ queen** *n* (*sl*) Fummeltrine (*sl*), Tunte (*sl*) *f*; **~ race** *n* Beschleunigungsrennen *nt*; **~rope** *n* Schlepptau *nt*; **~ show** *n* Transvestitenshow *f*.

dragster ['drægstəʳ] *n* Dragster *m* (*sl*).

drain [dreɪn] **1** *n* (**a**) (*pipe*) Rohr *nt*; (*under sink etc*) Abfluß(rohr *nt*) *m*; (*under the ground*) Kanalisationsrohr *nt*; (*grill in gutter etc*) Gully *m*. **open ~** (*Abfluß*)rinne *f*; **to throw one's money down the ~** (*fig*) das Geld zum Fenster hinauswerfen; **all his hopes have gone down the ~ now** (*inf*) er hat alle seine Hoffnungen begraben (müssen); **this country's going down the ~** (*inf*) dieses Land geht vor die Hunde (*inf*); **I had to watch all our efforts go down the ~** ich mußte zusehen, wie alle unsere Bemühungen zunichte (gemacht) wurden; **to laugh like**

a ~ (inf) sich vor Lachen ausschütten wollen.
  (b) (on resources etc) Belastung f (on gen). **looking after her father has been a great** ~ **on her strength** die Pflege ihres Vaters hat sehr an ihren Kräften gezehrt; see **brain** ~.
  2 vt (a) drainieren; land, marshes also entwässern; vegetables abgießen; (let ~) abtropfen lassen; mine auspumpen; reservoir trockenlegen; boiler, radiator das Wasser ablassen aus; engine oil ablassen.
  (b) (fig) **to** ~ **sb of strength** an jds Kräften (acc) zehren; **to feel** ~ed **(of energy)** sich ausgelaugt fühlen; **to** ~ **a country of resources** ein Land auslaugen or auspowern (sl); **to** ~ **sb dry** jdn ausnehmen (inf).
  (c) glass austrinken, leeren.
  3 vi (vegetables, dishes) abtropfen; (land into river) entwässert werden.
♦drain away 1 vi (liquid) ablaufen; (strength) dahinschwinden. 2 vt sep liquid ableiten.
♦drain off vt sep abgießen; (let drain) abtropfen lassen.
drainage ['dreɪnɪdʒ] n (a) (draining) Dränage f; (of land also) Entwässerung f. (b) (system) Entwässerungssystem nt; (in house, town) Kanalisation f. (c) (sewage) Abwasser nt. (d) (Geol) Drän(ier)ung (spec), Entwässerung f.
drainage: ~ **area,** ~ **basin** n (Geol) Einzugsgebiet f; ~ **channel** n (Build) Entwässerungsgraben, Abzugsgraben m.
drain: ~**ing board,** (US) ~ **board** n Ablauf m; ~ **pipe** n Kanalisations-/Abflußrohr nt; ~**pipes,** ~**pipe trousers** npl Röhrenhosen pl.
drake [dreɪk] n Erpel, Enterich m; see **duck**[1].
dram [dræm] n (a) (measure, Pharm) = Drachme f (old). (b) (small drink) Schluck m (Whisky).
drama ['drɑːmə] n (art, play, incident) Drama nt; (no pl: quality of being dramatic) Dramatik f. **18th-century German** ~ das deutsche Drama des 18. Jahrhunderts.
drama: ~ **critic** n Theaterkritiker(in f) m; ~ **school** n Schauspielschule f; ~ **student** n Schauspielschüler(in f) m.
dramatic [drə'mætɪk] adj dramatisch; criticism Theater-; ability of actor schauspielerisch.
dramatically [drə'mætɪkəlɪ] adv dramatisch; (in a theatrical manner) theatralisch. **he flung his book** ~ **to the ground** mit theatralischer Geste schleuderte er sein Buch auf den Boden; **it's not** ~ **different** so dramatisch ist der Unterschied nicht.
dramatics [drə'mætɪks] npl (a) (Theat) Dramaturgie f; see **amateur.** (b) (fig) theatralisches Gehabe.
dramatis personae ['dræmətɪspɜː'səʊnaɪ] npl Personen der Handlung, dramatis personae (old) pl.
dramatist ['dræmətɪst] n Dramatiker m.
dramatization [ˌdræmətaɪ'zeɪʃən] n see vt Bühnen-/Fernsehbearbeitung f; Dramatisierung f.
dramatize ['dræmətaɪz] 1 vt (a) novel für die Bühne/das Fernsehen bearbeiten, dramatisieren. (b) (make vivid) event dramatisieren. 2 vi (novel etc) sich für die Bühne/das Fernsehen bearbeiten lassen. (b) (exaggerate) übertreiben.
drank [dræŋk] pret of **drink.**
drape [dreɪp] 1 vt (a) drapieren; window mit Vorhängen versehen; person hüllen; altar also behängen.
  (b) curtain, length of cloth drapieren. **to** ~ **sth over sth** etw über etw (acc) drapieren; **she** ~**d herself over the sofa** (inf) sie drapierte sich malerisch auf das Sofa.
  2 n (a) ~s pl (US) Gardinen pl. (b) (way sth hangs) Fall m.
draper ['dreɪpər] n (Brit) Textilkaufmann m. ~**'s (shop)** Textilgeschäft nt.
drapery ['dreɪpərɪ] n (a) (Brit) (cloth etc) Stoff m; (business: also ~ **shop**) Stoffladen m. (b) (hangings) Draperie f (old); (on wall also) Behang m; (around bed etc) Vorhänge pl; (clothing, fig liter) Gewand nt.
drastic ['dræstɪk] adj (a) drastisch. **it was rather** ~ **of you to fire him** es war eine ziemlich drastische Maßnahme, ihn zu feuern; **you'll have to do something** ~ Sie werden da drastische Maßnahmen ergreifen müssen; **there's no need to be so** ~ man braucht nicht so radikal or drastisch vorzugehen; **he's had a very** ~ **haircut** (inf) er hat sich die Haare radikal abschneiden lassen.
  (b) (urgent, serious) bedrohlich. **things are getting** ~ die Sache wird bedrohlich; **there's a** ~ **need for medical supplies** es besteht dringender Bedarf an Medikamenten.
drastically ['dræstɪkəlɪ] adv see adj (a) drastisch. (b) bedrohlich. **they're** ~ **short of supplies** ihre Vorräte sind bedrohlich knapp.
drat [dræt] interj (inf) ~ **(it)!** verflixt! (inf); ~ **the child!** dieses verflixte Kind! (inf).
dratted ['drætɪd] adj (inf) verflixt (inf).
draught, (US) **draft** [drɑːft] n (a) (Luft)zug m; (through ~) Durchzug m; (for fire) Zug m. **there's a terrible** ~ **in here** hier zieht es fürchterlich; **what a** ~! das zieht ja fürchterlich!; **I'm sitting in a** ~ ich sitze im Zug; **are you in a** ~? zieht's Ihnen?; **I've got a** ~ **blowing round the back of my neck** mir zieht's im Genick; **open the window so we'll get a nice cool** ~ **in here** mach mal das Fenster auf, damit wir etwas frische Luft bekommen; **open the flues to increase the** ~ mach die Klappen auf, damit der Ofen mehr Zug bekommt; **he's beginning to feel the** ~ (fig inf) ihm wird allmählich das Geld knapp.
  (b) (swallow, drink) Zug m. **a** ~ **of mead** ein Schluck Met.
  (c) (~ beer) Faß- or Schankbier nt. **on** ~ vom Faß.
  (d) (Naut) Tiefgang m.
  (e) (of fish) Fischzug m.
  (f) (Brit: game) ~s (+ sing vb) Damespiel nt; (+ pl vb: pieces) Damesteine pl.
  (g) (rough sketch) see **draft** 1 (a).
draught: ~ **animal** n Zugtier nt; ~ **beer** n Faßbier nt, Bier nt vom Faß; ~**-board** n Damebrett nt; ~ **excluder** n Dichtungsmaterial nt.

draughtiness, (US) **draftiness** ['drɑːftɪnɪs] n Zugigkeit f.
draughtsman ['drɑːftsmən] n, pl -**men** [-mən] (a) (US **draftsman**) (of plans) Zeichner m; (of documents, treaty etc) Verfasser m. (b) (Brit: in game) Damestein m.
draughtsmanship, (US) **draftsmanship** ['drɑːftsmənʃɪp] n **you can tell by the** ~ **that it was done by an expert** an der Qualität der Zeichnung/des Entwurfs kann man sehen, daß das ein Fachmann gemacht hat; **the skills of** ~ das zeichnerische Können; **an excellent piece of** ~ ein hervorragendes Beispiel zeichnerischen Könnens.
draughty, (US) **drafty** ['drɑːftɪ] adj (er) zugig. **it's** ~ **in here** hier zieht es.
draw[1] [drɔː] pret **drew,** ptp **drawn** 1 vt (lit, fig) zeichnen; line ziehen. **we must** ~ **the line somewhere** (fig) irgendwo muß Schluß sein; **I** ~ **the line there** da ist bei mir Schluß, da hört's bei mir auf; **I** ~ **the line at scrubbing floors** beim Schrubben von Fußböden ist bei mir Schluß or hört's bei mir auf; **some people just don't know where to** ~ **the line** manche Leute wissen einfach nicht, wie weit sie gehen können.
  2 vi zeichnen.
draw[2] (vb: pret **drew,** ptp **drawn**) 1 vt (a) (move by pulling) ziehen; bolt zurückschieben; bow spannen; curtains (open) aufziehen; (shut) zuziehen; (Med) abscess schneiden. **he drew the book towards him** er zog das Buch näher (zu sich heran); **he drew his finger along the edge of the table** er fuhr mit dem Finger die Tischkante entlang; **he drew his hat over his eyes** er zog sich (dat) den Hut ins Gesicht; **to** ~ **one's belt tighter** den Gürtel enger schnallen; **he drew the smoke down into his lungs** er machte einen (tiefen) Lungenzug.
  (b) (move by pulling behind) coach, cart ziehen.
  (c) (extract, remove) teeth, sword ziehen; cork herausziehen. **with** ~**n sword** mit gezogenem or gezücktem Schwert.
  (d) (obtain from source) holen; wine also (from barrel) zapfen. **to** ~ **a bath** das Badewasser einlassen; **to** ~ **money from the bank** Geld (vom Konto) abheben; **he's bitten her — she he** ~**n blood?** er hat sie gebissen — blutet sie?; **to** ~ **a cheque on a bank** einen Scheck auf eine Bank ausstellen; **to** ~ **first prize** den ersten Preis gewinnen; **to** ~ **inspiration from sb/sth/somewhere** sich von jdm/von etw/von irgendwas inspirieren lassen; **to** ~ **comfort from sth** sich mit etw trösten; **her singing drew tears from the audience** ihr Singen rührte die Zuhörer zu Tränen; **her singing drew tremendous applause from the audience** ihr Singen rief brausenden Beifall hervor; **to** ~ **a big salary/the dole** ein großes Gehalt/Arbeitslosenunterstützung beziehen; **to** ~ **a smile/a laugh from sb** jdm ein Lächeln/ein Lachen entlocken.
  (e) (attract) interest erregen; customer, crowd anlocken. **the play has** ~**n a lot of criticism** das Theaterstück hat viel Kritik auf sich (acc) gezogen; **to feel** ~**n towards sb** sich zu jdm hingezogen fühlen; **to** ~ **sb into sth** jdn in etw (acc) hineinziehen or verwickeln; **to** ~ **sb away from sb/sth** jdn von jdm/etw weglocken; **I was irresistibly** ~**n to** the conclusion that ... ich kam unweigerlich zu dem Schluß, daß ...; **her shouts drew me to the scene** ihr Rufen brachte mich an den Ort des Geschehens.
  (f) **to** ~ **a (deep) breath** (tief) Luft holen; **to** ~ **a long breath** einmal tief Luft holen.
  (g) (cause to speak, to disclose feelings) **I could** ~ **no reply from him** ich konnte keine Antwort aus ihm herausbringen; **he refuses to be** ~**n (will not speak)** aus ihm ist nichts herauszubringen; (will not be provoked) er läßt sich auf nichts ein; **I won't be** ~**n on that one** dazu möchte ich mich nicht äußern; **I is able to** ~ **him out of himself** sie kann ihn dazu bringen, aus sich herauszugehen.
  (h) (establish, formulate) conclusion, comparison ziehen; distinction treffen. **well,** ~ **your own conclusions!** zieh deine eigenen Schlüsse!; **you can** ~ **whatever conclusion you like** du kannst daraus schließen, was du willst.
  (i) (Naut) **the boat** ~**s 4 metres** das Boot hat 4 m Tiefgang.
  (j) (Sport) **to** ~ **a match** sich unentschieden trennen, unentschieden spielen.
  (k) **we've been** ~**n (to play) away/at home** wir sind für ein Auswärtsspiel/Heimspiel gezogen worden; **France has been** ~**n against Scotland** Frankreich ist für ein Spiel gegen Schottland gezogen worden.
  (l) (Cards) **to** ~ **a card from the pack** eine Karte vom Haufen abheben or nehmen; **to** ~ **trumps** Trümpfe herauszwingen.
  (m) (Cook) fowl ausnehmen; see **hang.**
  (n) (Hunt) fox aufstöbern. **to** ~ **a covert** ein Tier aus seinem Versteck aufstöbern or aufjagen.
  (o) **to** ~ **sth to a close** etw zu Ende bringen or beenden.
  2 vi (a) (move, come: of person, time, event) kommen. **he drew towards the door** er bewegte sich auf die Tür zu; **he drew to one side** er ging/fuhr zur Seite; **to** ~ **round the table** sich um den Tisch versammeln; **to** ~ **to a close** dem Ende zugehen, sich dem Ende zuneigen; **the day is** ~**ing to a close** der Tag geht zu Ende or zur Neige (liter); **to** ~ **to an end** zu Ende gehen; **he drew ahead of the other runners** er zog den anderen Läufern davon; **the two horses drew level** die beiden Pferde zogen gleich; **to** ~ **near** herankommen (to an + acc); **to** ~ **nearer** (immer) näher (heran)kommen (to an + acc); see **near.**
  (b) (allow airflow: of chimney, pipe) ziehen.
  (c) (Sport: of teams in matches) unentschieden spielen. **they drew 2-2** sie trennten sich or spielten 2:2 unentschieden; **the teams drew for second place** im Kampf um den 2. Platz trennten sich die Mannschaften unentschieden.
  (d) (Cards) **to** ~ **for partners** die Partner durch Kartenziehen bestimmen.
  (e) (infuse: tea) ziehen.
  3 n (a) (lottery) Ziehung, Ausspielung f; (for sports competitions) Auslosung, Ziehung f; see **luck.**
  (b) (Sport) Unentschieden nt. **the match ended in a** ~ das

Spiel endete unentschieden *or* mit einem Unentschieden; **the team had five wins and two ~s** die Mannschaft hat fünfmal gewonnen und zweimal unentschieden gespielt.
  (c) *(attraction: play, film etc)* (Kassen)schlager, Knüller *(inf) m; (person)* Attraktion *f*.
  (d) to be quick on the ~ *(lit)* schnell mit der Pistole sein, schnell (den Revolver) ziehen; *(fig)* schlagfertig sein.

♦**draw alongside** *vi* heranfahren/-kommen (+*prep obj* an +*acc*).

♦**draw apart 1** *vi (move away)* sich lösen; *(couple)* sich auseinanderleben; *(from political party etc)* abrücken. **2** *vt sep person* beiseite nehmen.

♦**draw aside** *vt sep person* beiseite nehmen; *curtains* zur Seite ziehen.

♦**draw away 1** *vi* **(a)** *(move off: car etc)* losfahren; *(procession)* sich entfernen.
  (b) *(move ahead: runner, racehorse etc)* davonziehen *(from sb* jdm).
  (c) *(move away: person)* sich entfernen. **she drew ~ from him when he put his arm around her** sie rückte von ihm ab, als er den Arm um sie legte.
  2 *vt sep person* weglocken; *object* wegnehmen.

♦**draw back 1** *vi* zurückweichen. **2** *vt sep* zurückziehen; *curtains also* aufziehen.

♦**draw down** *vt sep blinds* herunterlassen.

♦**draw in 1** *vi* **(a)** *(train)* einfahren; *(car)* anhalten. **to ~ ~ at the kerb** am Bordstein (an)halten.
  (b) *(get shorter: days)* kürzer werden.
  2 *vt sep* **(a)** *breath, air* einziehen.
  (b) *(attract, gain) crowds* anziehen. **the play is ~ing ~ huge returns** das Stück spielt hohe Summen ein; **to ~ sb ~ on a project** jdn für ein Projekt gewinnen; **I don't want to be ~n ~ into your problems** ich möchte nicht in Ihre Probleme verwickelt *or* hineingezogen werden.
  (c) to ~ ~ one's claws *(lit, fig)* die Krallen einziehen; *see* horn.
  (d) *(pull on) reins* anziehen. **to ~ ~ one's belt** den Gürtel enger schnallen.

♦**draw off 1** *vi (car)* losfahren. **2** *vt sep* **(a)** *(remove) gloves, garment* ausziehen. **(b)** *excess liquid* abgießen; *(Med) blood* abnehmen.

♦**draw on 1** *vi* **as the night drew ~** mit fortschreitender Nacht; **winter ~s ~** der Winter naht; **time is ~ing ~** es wird spät.
  2 *vi +prep obj (use as source: also ~ upon)* sich stützen auf (+*acc*). **he ~s heavily ~ classical literature/Marx** er stützt sich stark auf klassische Literatur/Marx; **you need to ~ ~ your powers of imagination** Sie müssen Ihre Phantasie zu Hilfe nehmen; **the author ~s ~ his experiences in the desert** der Autor schöpft aus seinen Erfahrungen in der Wüste.
  3 *vt sep (put on) stockings, gloves, garments, shoes* anziehen.

♦**draw out 1** *vi* **(a)** *(train)* ausfahren; *(car)* herausfahren *(of* aus).
  (b) *(become longer: days)* länger werden.
  2 *vt sep* **(a)** *(take out)* herausziehen.
  (b) *(make longer)* ziehen. **he drew the elastic ~ as far as it would go** er zog das Gummi so lang, wie es ging.
  (c) *(prolong)* in die Länge ziehen, hinausziehen. **a long-~n-~ meeting** eine sehr in die Länge gezogene Konferenz.
  (d) *(cause to speak)* **to ~ sb ~/sb ~ of his shell** jdn aus der Reserve locken.

♦**draw over** *vi* **the policeman told the motorist to ~ ~ (to the side of the road)** der Polizist sagte dem Autofahrer, er solle an den Straßenrand fahren.

♦**draw together** *vt sep threads* miteinander verknüpfen; *bits of argument also* in einen Zusammenhang bringen.

♦**draw up 1** *vi (stop: car)* (an)halten.
  2 *vt sep* **(a)** *(formulate)* entwerfen; *contract, agreement also, will* aufsetzen; *list* aufstellen.
  (b) *chair* heranziehen; *boat* aufschleppen *(spec)*, an Land ziehen. **to ~ oneself ~ (to one's full height)** sich (zu seiner vollen Größe) aufrichten.
  (c) *(set in line) troops* aufstellen.
  (d) *(make stop)* **this thought drew him ~ sharp** dieser Gedanke ließ ihn mit einem Ruck innehalten.

♦**draw upon** *vi +prep obj see* **draw on 2.**

draw: **~back** *n* Nachteil *m*; **~bridge** *n* Zugbrücke *f*.
drawee [drɔːˈiː] *n (Fin)* Bezogene(r) *mf*; Trassat *m (spec)*.
drawer *n* **(a)** [drɔːʳ] *(in desk etc)* Schublade *f*. **(b)** [ˈdrɔːəʳ] *(person: of pictures)* Zeichner *m*. **(c)** [ˈdrɔːə] *(of cheque etc)* Aussteller, Trassant *m (spec)*. **m (d)** [drɔːz] *(dated, hum)* **~s** *pl (for men)* Unterhosen *pl; (for women also)* Schlüpfer *pl*.
drawing [ˈdrɔːɪŋ] *n* Zeichnung *f*. **I'm no good at ~** ich bin nicht gut im Zeichnen, ich kann nicht gut zeichnen.
drawing: **~-board** *n* Reißbrett *nt*; **the scheme is still on the ~-board** *(fig)* das Projekt ist noch in der Planung; **well, it's back to the ~-board** *(fig)* das muß noch einmal ganz neu überdacht werden; **~ paper** *n* Zeichenpapier *nt*; **~ pen** *n* Zeichenfeder *f*; **~-pin** *n (Brit)* Reißzwecke *f*; **~ room** *n* Wohnzimmer *nt; (in mansion)* Salon *m*.
drawl [drɔːl] **1** *vi* schleppend sprechen. **2** *vt* schleppend aussprechen. **a Texan/Southern ~** schleppendes Texanisch/ein schleppender südlicher Dialekt.
drawn [drɔːn] **1** *ptp of* **draw¹, draw².** **2** *adj* **(a)** *(haggard) (from tiredness)* abgespannt; *(from worry)* abgehärmt, verhärmt. **his face ~ with pain** sein vor Schmerzen verzerrtes Gesicht. **(b)** *(equal)* **game, match** unentschieden.
drawstring [ˈdrɔːstrɪŋ] *n* Kordel *f* zum Zuziehen.
dray [dreɪ] *n* Rollwagen *f*.
dray: **~-horse** *n* Zugpferd *nt; (in brewery)* Brauereipferd *nt*; **~man** *n* Rollkutscher *m*.

dread [dred] **1** *vt* sich fürchten vor (+*dat*), große Angst haben vor (+*dat*). **his violent temper was ~ed by the whole school** seine Wutausbrüche waren von der ganzen Schule gefürchtet; **the ~ed monster from outer space** das gefürchtete Ungeheuer aus dem All; **and the ~ed moment, here are the exam results** der mit Schrecken erwartete Augenblick ist da, hier sind die Examensergebnisse; **I ~ to think what may happen** ich wage nicht daran zu denken, was passieren könnte; **I ~ or I'm ~ing seeing her again** ich denke mit Schrecken an ein Wiedersehen mit ihr; **he ~s going to the dentist** er hat schreckliche Angst davor, zum Zahnarzt zu gehen; **I ~ to think of it** *(inf)* das wage ich nicht, mir vorzustellen.
  2 *n* **an object of ~ to the whole world** etwas, was der ganzen Welt Furcht und Schrecken einjagt; **to go or live in ~ of the secret police/being found out** in ständiger Angst vor der Geheimpolizei leben/in ständiger Angst davor leben, entdeckt zu werden.
  3 *adj (liter)* gefürchtet.
dreadful [ˈdredfʊl] *adj* schrecklich, furchtbar. **what a ~ thing to happen** wie entsetzlich *or* furchtbar, daß das passieren mußte; **tell me the ~ truth** sag mir schon, ich bin auf das Schlimmste gefaßt; **I feel ~** *(ill)* ich fühle mich schrecklich *or* scheußlich; *(mortified)* es ist mir schrecklich (peinlich).
dreadfully [ˈdredfəlɪ] *adv* schrecklich. **are you keen to come? — not —** *(inf)* möchten Sie gern kommen? — nicht übermäßig.
dreadnought [ˈdrednɔːt] *n (Naut)* Dreadnought *m*.
dream [driːm] *(vb: pret, ptp* **dreamt** *or* **~ed) 1** *n* **(a)** Traum *m*. **to have a bad ~** schlecht träumen; **the whole business was like a bad ~** die ganze Angelegenheit war wie ein böser Traum; **sweet ~s!** träum was Schönes!, träume süß!; **to have a ~ about sb/sth** von jdm/etw träumen; **to see sb/sth in a ~** jdn/etw im Traum sehen; **it's life is but a ~** das Leben ist nur ein Traum; **it worked like a ~** *(inf)* das ging wie im Traum.
  (b) *(when awake)* lost in ~s traumverloren; **she goes round in a ~** sie lebt wie im Traum; **to be in a ~** *(with offenen Augen)* träumen; **she was walking down the street in a ~** sie ging die Straße wie im Traum entlang; **to go into a ~** zu träumen anfangen; **sorry, I didn't hear you, I was in a ~** Entschuldigung, ich habe Sie nicht gehört, ich habe geträumt.
  (c) *(fantasy, vision)* Traum *m*. **the house of his ~s** das Haus seiner Träume, sein Traumhaus; **she was happy beyond her wildest ~s** sie war so glücklich, wie sie es in ihren kühnsten Träumen nicht für möglich gehalten hätte; **to have ~s of becoming rich** davon träumen, reich zu werden; **all his ~s came true** all seine Träume gingen in Erfüllung; **I have a ~ of a better world** ich träume von einer besseren Welt; **all his planning and big talk, it's just idle ~s** all seine Pläne und sein Reden sind nichts als Wunschträume *or* Phantastereien.
  (d) *(inf)* Schatz *m*. **darling, you're a ~!** Liebling, du bist ein Schatz; **a ~ of a hat** ein traumhaft schöner Hut; **a ~ of a girl** ein Schatz von einem Mädchen; **a ~ of a father** ein toller Vater.
  2 *vi (lit, fig)* träumen *(about, of* von). **I'm sorry, I was ~ing** es tut mir leid, ich habe geträumt.
  3 *vt (lit, fig)* träumen; *dream* haben. **he ~s of being free one day** er träumt davon, eines Tages frei zu sein; **I should never have ~t of doing such a thing** ich hätte nicht im Traum daran gedacht, so etwas zu tun; **I wouldn't ~ of it/of telling her** das würde mir nicht im Traum einfallen/es fiele mir nicht im Traum ein, es ihr zu erzählen; **I little ~t that** ich hätte mir nicht träumen lassen, daß es so kompliziert sein würde; **I never ~t (that) he would come** ich hätte mir nie *or* nicht träumen lassen, daß er kommen würde.
  4 *adj attr car, holiday* Traum-. **~boat** *(dated sl)* Traumfrau *f/* -mann *m;* **~land** *n* Traumland *nt;* **~ world** Traumwelt *f*.

♦**dream away** *vt sep time* verträumen; *one's life* mit Träumen verbringen.

♦**dream up** *vt sep (inf) idea* sich *(dat)* einfallen lassen *or* ausdenken. **where did you ~ that ~?** wie bist du denn bloß darauf gekommen?
dreamer [ˈdriːməʳ] *n* Träumer(in *f) m*.
dreamily [ˈdriːmɪlɪ] *adv* verträumt.
dreamless [ˈdriːmlɪs] *adj sleep* traumlos.
dreamlike [ˈdriːmlaɪk] *adj* traumähnlich; *music* traumhaft.
dreamt [dremt] *pret, ptp of* **dream.**
dreamy [ˈdriːmɪ] *adj (+er)* **(a)** *person* verträumt; *expression also* versonnen. **(b)** *music* zum Träumen. **soft ~ colours** weiche, verträumte Farben; **the ~ quality of the music** die Verträumtheit der Musik. **~** *(inf: lovely)* traumhaft.
drear [drɪəʳ] *adj (poet) see* **dreary.**
drearily [ˈdrɪərɪlɪ] *adv* eintönig, langweilig; *say, stare* trüb. **the music droned on ~ for another hour** die Musik plärrte noch eine Stunde weiter; **it rained ~ all day** den ganzen Tag über war es trüb und regnerisch.
dreariness [ˈdrɪərɪnɪs] *n see adj* Eintönigkeit *f*; Trübheit *f*; Langweiligkeit, Farblosigkeit *f*.
dreary [ˈdrɪərɪ] *adj (+er)* eintönig; *weather* trüb; *person, speech* langweilig, farblos. **how ~ for you!** wie langweilig für Sie.
dredge¹ [dredʒ] **1** *n* Bagger *m; (net)* Schleppnetz *nt; (vessel) see* **dredger¹. 2** *vt river, canal* ausbaggern, schlämmen.

♦**dredge up** *vt sep (lit)* ausbaggern; *(fig) unpleasant facts* ans Licht zerren.
dredge² *vt (Cook)* bestäuben, bestreuen.
dredger¹ [ˈdredʒəʳ] *n (ship)* Schwimmbagger *m; (machine)* Bagger *m*.
dredger² *n (Cook)* Streuer *m; (also sugar ~)* Zuckerstreuer *m*.
dredging¹ [ˈdredʒɪŋ] *n* Ausbaggern *nt*.
dredging² *n (Cook)* Bestreuen *nt*.
dregs [dregz] *npl* **(a)** *(Boden)satz m*. **to drink sth to the ~** etw bis auf den letzten Tropfen austrinken. **(b)** *(fig)* Abschaum *m*. **the ~ of society** der Abschaum der Gesellschaft.
drench [drentʃ] *vt* **(a)** durchnässen. **I'm absolutely ~ed** ich bin

durch und durch naß *or* naß bis auf die Haut; **to get ~ed to the skin** bis auf die Haut naß werden; **sprinkle some water on it, don't ~ it** besprengen Sie es mit Wasser, aber ersäufen Sie es nicht (*inf*).

  (**b**) (*Vet*) einem Tier Arznei einflößen.

drenching ['drentʃɪŋ] **1** *n* **to get a ~** bis auf die Haut naß werden. **2** *adj:* **~ rain** Regen, der bis auf die Haut durchgeht; **he's been working out in the ~ rain all day** er hat den ganzen Tag draußen im strömenden Regen gearbeitet.

Dresden ['drezdən] *n* (*also ~ china*) = Meißner Porzellan *nt*.

dress [dres] **1** *n* (**a**) (*for woman*) Kleid *nt*.

  (**b**) *no pl* (*clothing*) Kleidung *f*. **articles of ~** Kleidungsstücke *pl*; **to be in eastern ~** orientalisch gekleidet sein.

  (**c**) *no pl* (*way of dressing*) Kleidung *f*, Kleider *pl*. **to be modest/careless in one's ~** sich einfach/nachlässig kleiden.

  2 *vt* (**a**) (*clothe*) *child* ankleiden; *family* kleiden; *recruits etc* einkleiden. **to get ~ed** sich anziehen; **are you ~ed?** bist du schon angezogen?; **he's old enough to ~ himself** er ist alt genug, um sich allein anzuziehen; **to ~ sb in sth** jdm etw anziehen; **she ~es herself with great fastidiousness** sie kleidet sich sehr sorgfältig; **~ed in black** in Schwarz, schwarz gekleidet; **~ed in a sailor's uniform** im Matrosenanzug; **to be ~ed for the country/town/tennis** fürs Land/für die Stadt/zum Tennisspielen angezogen sein.

  (**b**) (*Theat*) *play* Kostüme entwerfen für.

  (**c**) (*arrange, decorate*) (*Naut*) *ship* beflaggen; (*Comm*) *shop-window* dekorieren. **to ~ sb's hair** jdm das Haar frisieren, jdn frisieren.

  (**d**) (*Cook*) *salad* anmachen; *food for table* anrichten; *chicken* brat- *or* kochfertig machen. **~ed crab** farcierter Krebs.

  (**e**) *skins* gerben; *material* appretieren; *timber* hobeln; *stone* schleifen.

  (**f**) *wound* verbinden.

  (**g**) *troops* ausrichten.

  (**h**) (*Agr*) *fields* vorbereiten.

  3 *vi* (**a**) sich anziehen *or* kleiden. **to ~ in black** sich schwarz kleiden; **she ~es very well** sie zieht sich sehr gut an *or* kleidet sich sehr gut; **to ~ for dinner** sich zum Essen umziehen.

  (**b**) (*soldiers*) sich ausrichten. **right, ~!** rechts, richt't euch!

♦**dress down** *vt sep* (**a**) *horse* striegeln. (**b**) *see* **dressing down**.

♦**dress up 1** *vi* (**a**) (*put on smart clothes*) sich feinmachen, sich schön anziehen.

  (**b**) (*put on fancy dress*) sich verkleiden. **he came ~ed ~ as Father Christmas** er kam als Weihnachtsmann (verkleidet); **to ~ ~ as a pirate** sich als Pirat verkleiden.

  2 *vt sep* (**a**) (*disguise*) verkleiden. **it's just his old plan ~ed ~ in a new way** (*fig*) das ist bloß sein alter Plan in einem neuen Gewand.

  (**b**) (*smarten*) *sb* herausputzen. **~ yourself ~ a bit!** mach dich ein bißchen schön!

dressage ['dresɑːʒ] *n* Dressur *f*.

dress: **~ circle** *n* erster Rang; **~ coat** *n* Frack *m*; **~ designer** *n* Modezeichner(in *f*) *m*.

dresser[1] ['dresə'] *n* (**a**) (*Theat*) Garderobier *m*, Garderobiere *f*. (**b**) (*Med*) **his ~** sein Assistent bei der Operation. (**c**) (*tool: for wood*) Hobel *m*; (*for stone*) Schleifstein *m*. (**d**) (*Comm: also* **window-~**) Dekorateur(in *f*) *m*. (**e**) **she's a stylish ~** sie kleidet sich stilvoll.

dresser[2] *n* (**a**) Anrichte *f*. (**b**) (*US: dressing-table*) Frisierkommode *f*.

dressing ['dresɪŋ] *n* (**a**) (*act*) Anziehen, Ankleiden *nt*. **~ always takes me a long time** ich brauche immer lange zum Anziehen.

  (**b**) (*Med: bandage, ointment*) Verband *m*.

  (**c**) (*Cook*) Soße *f*.

  (**d**) (*Agr*) Dünger *m*. **a ~ of phosphate** Phosphatdünger *m*.

  (**e**) (*of material*) Appretieren *nt*; (*of stone*) Schleifen *nt*; (*of leather*) Gerben *nt*; (*of wood*) Hobeln *nt*; (*for material*) Appreturmittel *nt*; (*for leather*) Gerbmittel *nt*.

dressing: **~ down** *n* (*inf*) Standpauke *f* (*inf*); **to give sb a ~ down** jdn herunterputzen (*inf*), jdm eine Standpauke halten; **to get a ~ down** eins auf den Deckel *or* das Dach kriegen (*inf*); **~-gown** *n* (*in towelling: for bather, boxer, etc*) Bademantel *m*; (*for women: négligé*) Morgenrock *m*; **~-room** *n* (*in house*) Ankleidezimmer *nt*; (*Theat*) (Künstler)garderobe *f*; (*Sport*) Umkleidekabine *f*; **~-station** *n* Verbandsplatz *m*; **~-table** *n* Frisiertoilette *or* -kommode *f*; **~-table set** Toilettengarnitur *f*.

dress: **~maker** *n* (Damen)schneider(in *f*) *m*; **~making** *n* Schneidern *nt*; **~ rehearsal** *n* (*lit, fig*) Generalprobe *f*; **~ shield** *n* Arm- *or* Schweißblatt *nt*; **~ shirt** *n* Frackhemd *nt*; **~ suit** *n* Abendanzug *m*; **~ uniform** *n* Galauniform *f*.

dressy ['dresɪ] *adj* (*+ er*) (*inf*) *person* fein angezogen, aufgedonnert (*pej*). **she's a very ~ person** sie ist immer sehr fein angezogen; **do you think I look a bit too ~?** meinst du, daß ich zu fein angezogen bin?; **a long skirt would be a bit too ~** ein langer Rock wäre etwas übertrieben; **you need something a bit more ~** es müßte etwas Eleganteres sein.

drew [druː] *pret of* **draw**[1], **draw**[2].

dribble ['drɪbl] **1** *vi* (**a**) (*liquids*) tropfen. (**b**) (*baby, person*) sabbern; (*animal*) geifern.

  (**c**) (*Sport*) dribbeln.

  (**d**) (*people*) **to ~ back/in** *etc* kleckerweise (*inf*) zurückkommen/hereinkommen *etc*.

  2 *vt* (**a**) (*Sport*) **to ~ the ball** mit dem Ball dribbeln.

  (**b**) (*baby etc*) kleckern. **to ~ saliva** sabbern; **he ~d his milk all down his chin** er kleckerte sich (*dat*) Milch übers Kinn.

  3 *n* (**a**) (*of water*) ein paar Tropfen. **a slow ~ of water was still coming out of the pipe** es tröpfelte immer noch etwas aus der Leitung. (**b**) (*of saliva*) Tropfen *m*. **don't expect me to clean up all your dog's ~** erwarten Sie nicht, daß ich dauernd aufwische, wo Ihr Hund gesabbert hat.

  (**c**) (*Sport*) Dribbling *nt*.

driblet ['drɪblɪt] *n* (*drop*) Tropfen *m*. **in ~s** (*money*) in kleinen Raten, kleckerweise (*inf*); **~s of intelligence began to come through** Informationen fingen an durchzusickern.

dribs and drabs ['drɪbzən'dræbz] *npl:* **in ~** kleckerweise (*inf*); **it's better to do the work all at once rather than in ~** es ist besser, die Arbeit in einem Zug statt kleckerweise zu machen (*inf*).

dried [draɪd] *adj* getrocknet; *fruit also* Dörr-. **~ eggs/milk** Trockenei -milch *f*, Ei-/Milchpulver *nt*.

drier *n see* **dryer**.

drift [drɪft] **1** *vi* (**a**) (*Naut, Aviat, snow*) treiben; (*sand*) wehen; (*Rad*) verschwimmen. **to ~ off course** abtreiben; **rally drivers have a special technique of ~ing round corners** Rallye-Fahrer haben eine bestimmte Technik, sich durch Kurven tragen zu lassen.

  (**b**) (*fig: person*) sich treiben lassen. **to let things ~** die Dinge treiben lassen; **he ~ed into marriage** er ist in die Ehe hineingeschlittert (*inf*); **he ~ed from job to job** er ließ sich planlos von Job zu Job treiben; **he was ~ing aimlessly along** er wanderte ziellos umher; (*in life etc*) er lebte planlos in den Tag hinein, er ließ sich plan- und ziellos treiben; **the nation was ~ing towards a crisis** das Land trieb auf eine Krise zu; **young people are ~ing away from the villages** junge Leute wandern aus den Dörfern ab; **to ~ apart** (*people*) sich auseinanderleben; **we're ~ing apart** wir leben uns immer mehr auseinander; **as the smoke ~ed away** als sich der Rauch verzog; **the audience started ~ing away** das Publikum begann wegzugehen.

  2 *vt* treiben; (*wind*) *clouds, snow also* vor sich her treiben.

  3 *n* (**a**) (*of air, water current*) Strömung *f*. **the ~ of the current** (*speed*) die (Stärke der) Strömung; (*direction*) die Strömung(srichtung).

  (**b**) (*mass caused by ~ing*) (*of sand, fallen snow*) Verwehung *f*; (*of leaves*) Haufen *m*.

  (**c**) (*of ship, aircraft*) (Ab)drift, Abweichung *f*. **to allow for ~** Abdriften *or* Abweichungen (mit) einkalkulieren.

  (**d**) (*Geol: deposits*) Geschiebe *nt*. **glacial ~** Moräne *f*; **continental ~** Kontinentalverschiebung *or* -drift *f*.

  (**e**) (*tendency*) **the ~ to the city** der Drang in die Stadt; **moving with the general ~ of events** dem allgemeinen Zug der Ereignisse folgend; **the ~ of opinion away from this view** das (allmähliche) Abrücken von dieser Ansicht.

  (**f**) (*general meaning: of questions*) Richtung, Tendenz *f*. **I caught the ~ of what he said** ich verstand, worauf er hinauswollte; **if I get your ~** wenn ich Sie recht verstehe.

  (**g**) (*Ling*) Tendenz *f*.

drift anchor *n* (*Naut*) Treibanker *m*.

drifter ['drɪftə'] *n* (**a**) (*person*) Gammler *m*. **he's a bit of a ~** ihn hält's nirgends lange; **there's no place for ~s in this business** ziellose und unentschlossene Leute haben in diesem Geschäft keinen Platz. (**b**) (*boat*) Drifter *m*.

drift: **~-ice** *n* Treibeis *nt*; **~ing mine** *n* Treibmine *f*; **~-net** *n* Treibnetz *nt*; **~sand** *n* Treibsand *m*; **~wood** *n* Treibholz *nt*.

drill[1] [drɪl] **1** *n* (*for metal, wood, oil, dentist's*) Bohrer *m*. **2** *vti* bohren. **to ~ for oil** nach Öl bohren; **have they started ~ing yet?** haben sie schon mit den Bohrungen angefangen?; **they ~ed 60 feet into the earth** sie haben 60 Fuß tief in die Erde gebohrt.

♦**drill down** *vi* (in die Tiefe) bohren. **we kept ~ing ~ until we hit oil** wir bohrten bis wir auf Öl stießen; **we ~ed ~ 500 feet** wir bohrten in eine Tiefe von 500 Fuß.

drill[2] **1** *n* (**a**) *no pl* (*esp Mil, fig*) Drill *m*; (*marching etc*) Exerzieren *nt*. **we get ~ every morning** jeden Morgen müssen wir exerzieren.

  (**b**) (*in grammar etc*) Drillübung *f*. **pattern ~** Patterndrill *m*.

  (**c**) (*inf: procedure*) **what's the ~?** wie geht das?, wie macht man das?; **he doesn't know the ~** er weiß nicht, wie der Laden läuft (*inf*) *or* wie die Sache angefaßt werden muß.

  2 *vt* (**a**) *soldiers* drillen; (*in marching etc*) exerzieren.

  (**b**) **to ~ pupils in grammar** mit den Schülern Grammatik pauken.

  (**c**) **to ~ good manners into a child** einem Kind gute Manieren eindrillen (*inf*); **I ~ed it into him that he must not ... ich** habe es ihm eingebläut (*inf*), daß er nicht ... darf.

  3 *vi* (*Mil*) gedrillt werden; (*marching etc*) exerzieren.

drill[3] (*Agr*) **1** *n* (**a**) (*furrow*) Furche *f*. (**b**) (*machine*) Drillmaschine *f*. **2** *vt* drillen.

drill[4] *n* (*Tex*) Drillich *m*.

drill ground *n* Exerzierplatz *m*.

drilling ['drɪlɪŋ] *n* (*for oil*) Bohrung *f*; (*by dentist*) Bohren *nt*. **when does ~ start?** wann fangen die Bohrungen an?; **~ operations begin next week** die Bohrungen fangen nächste Woche an; **~ rig** Bohrturm *m*; (*at sea*) Bohrinsel *f*.

drill sergeant *n* Ausbilder *m*.

drily ['draɪlɪ] *adv see* **dryly**.

drink [drɪŋk] (*vb: pret* **drank**, *ptp* **drunk**) **1** *n* (**a**) (*liquid to ~*) Getränk *nt*. **food and ~** Essen und Getränke; **may I have a ~?** kann ich etwas zu trinken haben?; **would you like a ~ of water?** möchten Sie etwas Wasser?; **to give sb a ~** jdm etwas zu trinken geben.

  (**b**) (*glass of alcoholic ~*) Glas *nt*, Drink *m*. **have a ~!** trink doch was *or* einen!; **let's have a ~** trinken wir was; **I need a ~!** ich brauche was zu trinken!; **he likes a ~** er trinkt gern (einen); **to ask friends in for ~s** Freunde auf ein Glas *or* einen Drink einladen; **afterwards there will be ~s** anschließend Getränke; **he's got a few ~s in him** (*inf*) er hat einige intus (*inf*).

  (**c**) *no pl* (*alcoholic liquor*) Alkohol *m*. **the ~ problem** der Alkoholismus; **he has a ~ problem** er trinkt; **~ was his ruin** der Alkohol hat ihn ruiniert; **to be the worse for ~** betrunken sein; **to take to ~** zu trinken anfangen; **his worries/she drove him to ~** vor lauter Sorgen fing er an zu trinken/sie war der

Grund, warum er zu trinken anfing; **it's enough to drive you to ~!** da könnte man wirklich zum Trinker werden.
  (d) (esp Naut, Aviat sl: sea) Bach m (sl). **three planes went down into the ~** drei Flugzeuge gingen in den Bach or gingen baden (sl).
  2 vt trinken. **would you like something to ~?** möchten Sie etwas zu trinken (haben)?; **is the water fit to ~?** ist das Trinkwasser?, kann man das Wasser trinken?; **this coffee isn't fit to ~** diesen Kaffee kann man nicht trinken; **he ~s all his wages** er vertrinkt seinen ganzen Lohn; **to ~ oneself into debt** Haus und Hof versaufen (inf); **to ~ oneself silly** sich dumm und dämlich trinken (inf) or saufen (inf); **this car ~s petrol** dieses Auto säuft das Benzin nur so (inf); **they drank the pub dry** sie tranken die Kneipe leer.
  3 vi trinken. **he doesn't ~** er trinkt nicht, er trinkt keinen Alkohol; **his father drank** sein Vater hat getrunken or war Trinker; **to go out ~ing** einen trinken gehen; **one shouldn't ~ and drive** nach dem Trinken soll man nicht fahren; **~ing and driving** Alkohol am Steuer; **to ~ to sb** auf jdn trinken; (to one's neighbour at table etc) jdm zuprosten or zutrinken; **to ~ to sth** auf etw (acc) trinken; **I'll ~ to that** darauf trinke ich.
♦**drink away** vt sep fortune vertrinken; sorrows im Alkohol ersäufen.
♦**drink down** vt sep hinuntertrinken, hinunterschlucken.
♦**drink in** vt sep (a) (plants etc) water aufsaugen; (person) air einsaugen, einatmen; sunshine in sich (acc) aufsaugen. (b) (fig) a sight, his words etc (begierig) in sich aufnehmen.
♦**drink off** vt sep austrinken, leeren. **he drank ~ the wine in one long gulp** er trank den Wein in einem Zug aus.
♦**drink up** 1 vi austrinken. **~!** trink aus! 2 vt sep austrinken.
drinkable ['drɪŋkəbl] adj (a) (not poisonous) water trinkbar, Trink-. (b) (palatable) genießbar, trinkbar. **a very ~ little wine** ein sehr süffiges Weinchen.
drinker ['drɪŋkəʳ] n Trinker(in f) m.
drinking ['drɪŋkɪŋ] n (a) (act) Trinken nt. (b) (drunkenness) das Trinken, das Saufen (inf).
drinking: ~ **bout** n Sauftour f (inf); **to go on a ~ bout** auf Sauftour gehen (inf); **when his wife died he went on a ~ bout for three months** als seine Frau starb, hat er drei Monate lang nur getrunken; ~ **companion** n Saufbruder (inf), Zechkumpan m; ~ **fountain** n Trinkwasserbrunnen m; **~-song** n Trinklied nt; ~ **trough** n Tränke f; **~-up time** n (Brit) die letzten zehn Minuten vor der Polizeistunde; **~-water** n Trinkwasser nt.
drip [drɪp] **1** vi (water, sweat, rain, tap) tropfen. **careful with that beer, you're ~ping!** paß auf mit dem Bier, es tropft!; **to be ~ping with sweat/blood** schweißüberströmt or schweißgebadet sein/von Blut triefen; **sweat was ~ping off his forehead** der Schweiß triefte ihm von der Stirn; **the walls were ~ping (with water)** die Wände waren triefnaß; **the film positively ~s with sentimentality** der Film trieft förmlich vor Schmalz.
  2 vt liquid träufeln, tropfen. **he was ~ping water/blood all over the carpet** Wasser/sein Blut tropfte überall auf den Teppich; **his clothes were ~ping water/his wound was ~ping blood all over the carpet** von seinen Kleidern tropfte Wasser/aus seiner Wunde tropfte Blut überall auf den Teppich; **careful, you're ~ping paint over my coat** paß auf, die Farbe tropft mir auf den Mantel!
  3 n (a) (sound: of water, rain, tap) Tropfen nt.
  (b) (drop) Tropfen m.
  (c) (Med) Infusionsapparat, Tropf (inf) m. **to be on a ~** eine Infusion bekommen, am Tropf hängen (inf).
  (d) (inf: silly person) Flasche f (inf).
drip: **~-dry** 1 adj shirt bügelfrei; 2 vt tropfnaß aufhängen; 3 vi bügelfrei sein; **~-dry** (on label) bügelfrei; **let it ~-dry** hängen Sie es tropfnaß auf; **~-feed** (Med) **1** n künstliche Ernährung; **2** vt künstlich ernähren.
dripping ['drɪpɪŋ] **1** n (a) (Cook) Bratenfett nt.
  (b) (action: of water etc) Tropfen nt.
  2 adj ~ tap, trees tropfend; washing tropfnaß.
  (b) (inf: very wet) coat, clothes triefend, klatschnaß. **I'm absolutely ~!** ich bin klatschnaß!; ~ **wet** triefnaß, klatschnaß.
  (c) ~ **pan** (Cook) Fettpfanne f.
drippy ['drɪpɪ] adj (+er) (inf) person müde (inf); (sentimental) singer, film, novel schmalzig; (US) day regnerisch.
drive [draɪv] (vb: pret drove, ptp driven) **1** n (a) (Aut: journey) (Auto)fahrt f. **to go for a ~** eine bißchen (raus)fahren; **to go for a ~ to the coast** ans Meer fahren; **he took her for a ~ in his new car** er machte mit ihr eine Spazierfahrt in seinem neuen Auto; **it's about one hour's ~ from London** es ist etwa eine Stunde Fahrt von London or eine Autostunde von London (entfernt).
  (b) (into house: also **~way**) Einfahrt f; (longer) Auffahrt, Zufahrt f.
  (c) (Golf, Tennis) Treibschlag m.
  (d) (Psych etc) Trieb m. **the sex ~** der Geschlechtstrieb, der Sexualtrieb.
  (e) (energy) Schwung, Elan, Tatendrang m. **you're losing your ~** Ihr Elan or Schwung läßt nach; **he has no ~ to improve his job** ihm fehlt es an Elan or Schwung, sich beruflich zu verbessern.
  (f) (Comm, Pol etc) Aktion f. **this is part of a ~ for new members** das ist Teil einer Mitgliederwerbeaktion; **fund-raising ~** Sammelaktion f; **sales ~** Verkaufskampagne f; see export.
  (g) (Mil: offensive) kraftvolle Offensive.
  (h) (Mech: power transmission) Antrieb m. **front-wheel/rear-wheel ~** Vorderrad-/Hinterradantrieb m.
  (i) (Aut) Steuerung f. **left-hand ~** Linkssteuerung f.
  (j) (Cards) see whist.
  2 vt (a) (cause to move) people, animals, dust, clouds etc treiben. **to ~ sb out of the country** jdn aus dem Land (ver)-

treiben; **Christ drove them out of the temple** Jesus vertrieb or jagte sie aus dem Tempel; **to ~ a nail/stake into sth** einen Nagel/Pfahl in etw (acc) treiben; **to ~ sth into sb's head** (fig) jdm etw einhämmern or einbläuen or eintrichtern; **the gale drove the ship off course** der Sturm trieb das Schiff vom Kurs ab.
  (b) cart, car, train fahren. **he ~s a taxi (for a living)** er ist Taxifahrer, er fährt Taxi (inf).
  (c) (convey in vehicle) person fahren. **I'll ~ you home** ich fahre Sie nach Hause; **could you ~ us there?** können Sie uns dahin fahren?
  (d) (provide power for, operate) motor (belt, shaft) antreiben; (electricity, fuel) betreiben. **steam-~n train** Zug m mit Dampflokomotive; **machine ~n by electricity** elektrisch betriebene Maschine, Maschine mit Elektroantrieb.
  (e) (Tennis, Golf) ball driven (spec), einen Treibball spielen.
  (f) (cause to be in a state or to become) treiben. **to ~ sb/oneself mad** or round the bend (inf) jdn/sich selbst verrückt machen; **to ~ sb to desperation** jdn zur Verzweiflung treiben; **to ~ sb to rebellion** jdn in die Rebellion treiben; **I was ~n to it** ich wurde dazu getrieben; **who/what drove you to do that?** wer/was trieb or brachte Sie dazu(, das zu tun)?; see drink.
  (g) (force to work hard) person hart herannehmen, schinden (pej). **you're driving him too hard** Sie nehmen ihn zu hart ran, Sie schinden ihn zu sehr; **you don't ~ them hard enough** Sie nehmen sie nicht hart genug ran; **he ~s himself very hard** er fordert sich selbst sehr stark.
  (h) tunnel treiben; well ausheben; nail schlagen.
  3 vi (a) (travel in vehicle) fahren. **he's learning to ~** er lernt Auto fahren; **to ~ at 50 km an hour** mit (einer Geschwindigkeit von) 50 km in der Stunde fahren; **to ~ on the right** rechts fahren; **did you come by train? — no, we drove** sind Sie mit der Bahn gekommen? — nein, wir sind mit dem Auto gefahren; **it's cheaper to ~** mit dem Auto ist es billiger.
  (b) (move violently) schlagen, peitschen. **the rain was driving in our faces** der Regen peitschte uns (dat) ins Gesicht.
♦**drive along** **1** vi (vehicle, person) dahinfahren. **2** vt sep (wind, current) person, boat (voran)treiben. **he was ~n by** the wind der Wind trieb ihn voran.
♦**drive at** vi +prep obj (fig: intend, mean) hinauswollen auf (+acc). **what are you driving ~?** worauf wollen Sie hinaus?; **I don't see what he's driving ~ in this article** of his ich weiß nicht, worauf er in seinem Artikel hinauswill.
♦**drive away** **1** vi (car, person) wegfahren. **2** vt sep (lit, fig) person, cares vertreiben; suspicions zerstreuen.
♦**drive back** **1** vi (car, person) zurückfahren. **2** vt sep (a) (cause to retreat) person zurückdrängen; enemy also zurücktreiben. (b) (convey back in vehicle) person zurückfahren.
♦**drive home** vt sep nail einschlagen, einhämmern; argument einhämmern. **she drove ~ her point that ...** sie legte eindringlich und überzeugend dar, daß ...; **how can I ~ it ~ to him that it's urgent?** wie kann ich (es) ihm nur klarmachen, daß es dringend ist?
♦**drive in** **1** vi (car, person) (hinein)fahren. **he drove ~to the garage** er fuhr in die Garage. **2** vt sep nail (hin)einschlagen, (hin)einhämmern; screw (r)eindrehen.
♦**drive off** **1** vi (a) (person, car) weg- or abfahren. (b) (Golf) abschlagen. **2** vt sep (a) person, enemy vertreiben. (b) **she was ~n ~ in a big Mercedes/an ambulance** sie wurde in einem großen Mercedes weg/sie wurde in einem Krankenwagen weggebracht or abtransportiert.
♦**drive on** **1** vi (person, car) weiterfahren. **2** vt sep (incite, encourage) person antreiben; (to do sth bad) anstiften.
♦**drive out** **1** vi heraus-/hinausfahren. **he drove ~ onto the street** er fuhr auf die Straße (hinaus). **2** vt sep person hinaustreiben or jagen; evil thoughts austreiben.
♦**drive over** **1** vi hinüberfahren. **2** vt always separate (in car) person hinüberfahren. **he drove his family ~ to see us** er hat seine Familie (mit dem Auto) zu uns gebracht. **3** vi +prep obj dog überfahren.
♦**drive up** vi (car, person) vorfahren. **a car drove ~ outside the house** ein Auto fuhr vor dem Haus vor.
drive: ~ **belt** n Treibriemen m; **~-in** adj: **~-in cinema** Autokino nt; **~-in bank** Autoschalter m.
drivel ['drɪvl] **1** n (pej) Blödsinn, Kokolores (inf) m. **what utter ~!** das ist ja kompletter Blödsinn!; **meaningless ~** leeres Gefasel. **2** vi (pej) Unsinn reden. **what's he ~ling (on) about?** was faselt er da?, worüber labert er da? (inf).
driven ['drɪvn] ptp of drive.
driver ['draɪvəʳ] n (a) (of car, taxi, lorry, bus) Fahrer(in f) m; (Brit: of locomotive) Führer m; (of coach) Kutscher m. **to be in the ~'s seat** (fig) das Steuer führen, die Zügel in der Hand haben. (b) (of animals) Treiber m. (c) (golf-club) Driver m.
driver's license n (US) Führerschein m.
drive: ~ **shaft** n Antriebswelle f; (Aut) Kardanwelle f; **~way** n Auffahrt f; (longer) Zufahrtsstraße f or -weg m; ~ **wheel** n Antriebsrad, Treibrad nt.
driving ['draɪvɪŋ] **1** n Fahren nt. **his ~ is awful** er fährt schrecklich (schlecht); **that was a very bad piece of ~** da sind Sie/ist er etc aber wirklich schlecht gefahren; **I do a lot of ~ in my job** in meinem Beruf muß ich sehr viel fahren; **~ is his hobby** Autofahren ist sein Hobby; **I don't like ~** ich fahre nicht gern (Auto); **dangerous ~** (Jur) rücksichtsloses Fahren.
  2 adj (a) **he was the ~ force behind it all** bei der ganzen Angelegenheit war er die treibende Kraft.
  (b) ~ rain peitschender Regen.
driving: ~ **instructor** n Fahrlehrer(in f) m; ~ **iron** n (Golf) Driving-Iron m; ~ **lesson** n Fahrstunde f; ~ **licence** n (Brit) Führerschein m; ~ **mirror** n Rückspiegel m; ~ **range** n (Golf) Drivingrange nt; ~ **school** n Fahrschule f; ~ **test** n Fahrprüfung f; **to take/fail/pass one's ~ test** die Fahrprüfung

machen/nicht bestehen/bestehen; ~ **wheel** *n* Antriebsrad, Treibrad *nt*.

drizzle ['drɪzl] **1** *n* Nieselregen, Sprühregen *m*. **2** *vi* nieseln.

drizzly ['drɪzlɪ] *adj weather* Niesel-. **it was such a** ~ **afternoon** es hat den ganzen Nachmittag so genieselt.

dromedary ['drɒmɪdərɪ] *n* Dromedar *nt*.

drone [drəʊn] **1** *n* **(a)** (*bee*, *fig*) Drohne *f*.

(b) (*sound*) (*of bees*) Summen *nt*; (*of engine, aircraft*) Brummen *nt*.

(c) (*monotonous way of speaking*) monotone Stimme.

(d) (*Mus*) (*bass voice part*) Baß *m*; (*of bagpipes*) Brummer *m*; (*sound*) Bordun(ton) *m*.

(e) (*Aviat: robot plane*) ferngesteuertes Flugzeug.

2 *vi* **(a)** (*bee*) summen; (*engine, aircraft*) brummen.

(b) (*speak monotonously: also* ~ **away** *or* **on**) eintönig sprechen; (*in reciting*) leiern. **he** ~**d on and on for hours** er redete stundenlang in seinem monotonen Tonfall; **we had to listen to him droning on** wir mußten seinem monotonen Geschwafel zuhören (*inf*).

♦**drone out** *vt sep speech* monoton vortragen; (*reciting*) leiern.

drool [druːl] *vi* sabbern.

♦**drool over** *vi* +*prep obj* richtig verliebt sein in (+*acc*). **the young mother** ~**s** ~ **her little boy** die junge Mutter ist ganz vernarrt in ihren kleinen Jungen; **he sat there** ~**ing** ~ **a copy of Playboy** er geilte sich an einem Playboyheft auf (*sl*).

droop [druːp] **1** *vi* **(a)** (*lit*) (*person*) vornüber gebeugt stehen, krumm stehen, sich schlecht halten; (*shoulders*) hängen; (*head*) herunterfallen; (*eyelids*) herunterhängen; (*with sleepiness*) zufallen; (*flowers*) die Köpfe hängen lassen; (*feathers, one's hand, breasts*) schlaff herunterhängen; (*rope, roof etc*) durchhängen. **the corpse** ~**ed over the railing** die Leiche hing schlaff über dem Geländer; **stand up straight, don't** ~ **halte dich aufrecht, steh nicht so krumm.

(b) (*fig: one's interest, energy*) erlahmen; (*audience etc*) erschlaffen, schlaff werden. **his spirits were beginning to** ~ sein Mut begann zu schwinden *or* sinken; **don't let your spirits** ~ **laß den Mut nicht sinken; **the heat made him** ~ die Hitze machte ihn schlaff *or* matt.

2 *vt head* hängen lassen.

3 *n* (*lit*) (*of body*) Gebeugtsein *nt*; (*of eyelids*) Schwere *f*. **I recognized her by the familiar** ~ **of her shoulders** ich habe sie an ihren hängenden Schultern erkannt.

drooping ['druːpɪŋ] *adj* (*as head, shoulders, breasts, feathers, leaves, tail*) hängend; (*flowers*) welk; (*hand*) herunterhängend; (*eyelids*) herunterhängend; (*with sleep*) sinken; (*roof*) durchhängend. **(b)** (*a drink to revive his* ~ **spirits** ein Schluck, um seine (geschwundenen) Lebensgeister wieder zu wecken.

drop [drɒp] **1** *n* **(a)** (*of liquid, also fig*) Tropfen *m*. ~ **by** ~ tropfenweise; **a** ~ **of blood** ein Blutstropfen *m*, ein Tropfen Blut; **it's a** ~ **in the ocean** *or* **bucket** (*fig*) das ist ein Tropfen auf den heißen Stein.

(b) (*alcohol*) Tropfen *m*. **just a** ~ **for me** für mich nur einen Tropfen; **this is a nice little** ~ das ist ein guter Tropfen; **a** ~ **of wine?** ein Schlückchen Wein?; **he's had a** ~ **too much** er hat einen über den Durst getrunken; **he likes a** ~ er trinkt ganz gern mal einen.

(c) (*sweet*) Drops *m*.

(d) (*fall: in temperature, prices*) Rückgang *m*; (*sudden*) Sturz *m*. **a** ~ **in prices** ein Preissturz *m*/-rückgang *m*; **20% is quite a** ~ 20%, das ist stark gefallen; **he took a large** ~ **in salary when he changed jobs** als er die Stelle wechselte, nahm er eine beträchtliche Gehaltsverschlechterung in Kauf; **a sudden/noticeable** ~ **in the temperature** ein plötzlicher/merklicher Temperaturabfall; ~ **in the voltage** Spannungsabfall *m*.

(e) (*difference in level*) Höhenunterschied *m*; (*fall*) Sturz, Fall *m*; (*parachute jump*) (Ab)sprung *m*. **a** ~ **of ten metres** ein Höhenunterschied von zehn Metern; **there's a** ~ **of ten metres down to the ledge** bis zu dem Felsvorsprung geht es zehn Meter hinunter; **it was only a short** ~ **off the wall** es war nur ein kleiner Sprung von der Mauer; **it's a long** ~ es geht tief hinunter; **it was a sheer** ~ **from the top of the cliff into the sea** die Klippen fielen schroff zum Meer ab; **careful, it's a nasty** ~ **paß auf, da geht es tief hinunter.

(f) (*of supplies, arms*) Abwurf *m*. **the Red Cross made a** ~ **of medical supplies into the flood zone** das Rote Kreuz warf Medikamente über dem Überschwemmungsgebiet ab.

(g) (*of gallows*) Falltür *f*.

(h) (*Theat: also* ~-**curtain**) Vorhang *m*.

2 *vt* **(a)** (*cause to fall in* ~**s**) liquid tropfen.

(b) (*allow to fall*) fallen lassen; *bomb, supplies, pamphlets, burden* abwerfen; *parachutist* absetzen; *lampshade* (*from ceiling*) aufhängen; *curtsy* machen; *voice* senken; (*Knitting*) *stitch* fallen lassen; (*lower*) *hemline* herunterlassen; (*Theat*) *curtain* herunterlassen. **I** ~**ped my watch** meine Uhr ist runtergefallen; **don't** ~ **it!** laß es nicht fallen!; **he** ~**ped his heavy cases on the floor** er setzte *or* stellte seine schweren Koffer auf dem Boden ab; ~ **that gun!** wirf die Pistole weg!, laß die Pistole fallen!; **to** ~ **a letter in the postbox** einen Brief einwerfen *or* in den Briefkasten werfen; **he** ~**ped the ball into the back of the court** (*Tennis*) er schlug einen hohen Ball in die hintere Hälfte des Feldes.

(c) (*kill*) *bird* abschießen; (*sl*) *person* abknallen (*sl*); (*send sprawling*) zu Fall bringen, zu Boden strecken.

(d) (*set down*) (*from car*) *person* absetzen; *thing* abliefern; (*from boat*) *cargo* löschen.

(e) (*utter casually*) *remark, name* fallenlassen; *clue* geben; *hint* machen. **to** ~ **a word in sb's ear** mal mit jdm reden, es jdm stecken (*inf*); **he let** ~ **that he was going to be married** (*by mistake*) es rutschte ihm raus (*inf*), daß er heiraten wollte; (*deliberately*) er erwähnte so nebenbei, daß er heiraten wollte.

(f) (*send, write casually*) *postcard, note, line* schreiben. **to** ~

sb a note *or* **a line** jdm ein paar Zeilen schreiben.

(g) (*omit*) *word, reference* auslassen; (*deliberately also*) weglassen (*from* in +*dat*); *programme* absetzen. **this word** ~**s the "e" in the plural** bei diesem Wort fällt das „e" im Plural weg; **the newspaper editor refused to** ~ **the story** der Herausgeber der Zeitung weigerte sich, den Artikel herauszunehmen; **he** ~**s his h's** er verschluckt immer das „h"; **to** ~ **sb from a team** jdn aus einer Mannschaft nehmen.

(h) (*cease to associate with, dismiss*) *candidate, minister, friend* fallenlassen; *girlfriend* Schluß machen mit.

(i) (*give up*) *work, habit, style* aufgeben; *idea, plan also* fallenlassen; *discussion, conversation also* abbrechen; (*Jur*) *case* niederschlagen. **you'll find it hard to** ~ **the habit** es wird Ihnen schwerfallen, sich (*dat*) das abzugewöhnen; **let's** ~ **the subject** lassen wir das Thema; **you'd better** ~ **the idea** schlagen Sie sich (*dat*) das aus dem Kopf; ~ **it!** (*inf*) hör auf (damit)!; ~ **everything!** (*inf*) laß alles stehen und liegen!

(j) (*lose*) *money* verlieren, loswerden (*inf*). **she** ~**ped the first three games** (*Tennis*) sie gab die ersten drei Spiele ab.

(k) (*give birth to: animal*) werfen.

3 *vi* **(a)** (*drip: liquid*) (herunter)tropfen.

(b) (*fall: object*) (herunter)fallen; (*Theat: curtain*) fallen. **don't let it** ~ laß es nicht fallen; *see* **penny, pin.**

(c) (*fall: rate, temperature etc*) sinken; (*wind*) sich legen; (*voice*) sich senken. **to** ~ **astern** (*Naut*) zurückfallen.

(d) (*to the ground: person*) fallen; (*collapse*) umfallen, umkippen (*inf*). **to** ~ **to the ground** sich zu Boden fallen lassen; **to** ~ **to one's knees** auf die Knie fallen *or* sinken; **I'm ready to** ~ (**with fatigue**) ich bin zum Umfallen müde; **she** ~**ped into an armchair** sie sank in einen Sessel, sie ließ sich in einen Sessel fallen; **to** ~ (**down**) **dead** tot umfallen; ~ **dead!** (*sl: expressing contempt*) geh zum Teufel! (*inf*); (*in games*) du bist tot!

(e) (*come to an end: conversation, correspondence*) aufhören. **you can't just let the matter** ~ Sie können die Sache nicht einfach auf sich beruhen lassen; **shall we let it** ~? sollen wir es darauf beruhen lassen?; **there the matter** ~**ped** dabei ist es dann geblieben.

♦**drop across** *or* **around** *vi* (*inf*) vorbeikommen/-gehen. **we** ~**ped** ~ **to see him** wir sind bei ihm vorbeigegangen; ~ ~ **and see us** some time kommen Sie doch mal (bei uns) vorbei.

♦**drop away** *vi* **(a)** (*become fewer: numbers*) **people have been** ~**ping** ~ **at recent meetings** in letzter Zeit sind immer weniger Leute zu den Versammlungen gekommen. **(b)** (*cliffs*) jäh *or* steil *or* schroff abfallen.

♦**drop back** *vi* zurückfallen.

♦**drop behind 1** *vi* zurückfallen. **2** *vi* +*prep obj* **to** ~ ~ **sb** hinter jdn zurückfallen.

♦**drop by** *vi* (*inf*) vorbeikommen, hereinschauen.

♦**drop down 1** *vi* (*fruit, monkeys*) herunterfallen. **we** ~**ped** ~ **behind the hedge** er duckte sich hinter die Hecke; **we** ~**ped** ~ **to the coast for a few days** wir sind für ein paar Tage an die Küste gefahren; **he** ~**ped** ~ **onto his knees** er sank in *or* fiel auf die Knie; **the hawk** ~**ped** ~ **out of the sky and caught the rabbit** der Habicht stürzte sich aus der Luft (herunter) auf das Kaninchen; **the cliffs** ~ ~ **to the sea** die Klippen fallen jäh *or* steil zum Meer (hin) ab.

2 *vt sep* fallen lassen.

♦**drop in** *vi* (*inf: visit casually*) vorbeikommen, hereinschauen. ~ ~ **on the Smiths** schauen Sie doch mal bei den Smiths herein; **to** ~ ~ **at the grocer's** beim Lebensmittelgeschäft vorbeigehen; **I've just** ~**ped** ~ **for a minute** ich wollte nur mal kurz hereinschauen.

♦**drop off 1** *vi* **(a)** (*fall off*) abfallen; (*come off*) abgehen. **(b)** (*fall asleep*) einschlafen; (*for brief while*) einnicken. **(c)** (*sales*) zurückgehen; (*speed, interest, popularity also*) nachlassen; (*friends*) abfallen. **2** *vt sep* (*set down from car etc*) *person* absetzen; *parcel* abliefern.

♦**drop out** *vi* **(a)** (*of box etc*) herausfallen (*of* aus). **(b)** (*from competition etc*) ausscheiden (*of* aus). **to** ~ ~ **of a race** (*before it*) an einem Rennen nicht teilnehmen; (*during it*) aus dem Rennen ausscheiden; **he** ~**ped** ~ **of the philosophy course** er gab den Kurs in Philosophie auf, er hängte den Philosophiekurs an den Nagel (*inf*); **to** ~ ~ **of society/university** ausflippen (*inf*), aus der Gesellschaft ausbrechen/sein Studium abbrechen, aus dem Studium aussteigen (*inf*), **he decided to** ~ ~ er beschloß, auszusteigen (*inf*).

(c) **the "t"** ~**s** ~ das „t" fällt weg.

♦**drop over** *vi* (*inf*) *see* **drop across.**

drop: ~ **ceiling** *n* Hängedecke *f*; ~ **curtain** *n* (*Theat*) (Fall)vorhang *m*; ~ **hammer** *n* Fallhammer *m*; ~-**leaf table** *n* Tisch *m* mit herunterklappbaren Seitenteilen.

droplet ['drɒplɪt] *n* Tröpfchen *nt*.

dropout ['drɒpaʊt] *n* (*from society*) Aussteiger (*inf*), Drop-out (*sl*) *m*; (*pej*) Asoziale(r) *mf*; (*university* ~) Studienabbrecher(in *f*) *m*. **at 25 he became a** ~ mit 25 ist er ausgeflippt (*sl*); **the** ~ **rate at universities** die Zahl der Studienabbrecher.

dropper ['drɒpə'] *n* (*Med*) Pipette *f*; (*on bottle*) Tropfer *m*.

droppings ['drɒpɪŋz] *npl* Kot *m*; (*of horse*) Äpfel *pl* (*inf*); (*of sheep*) Bohnen, Köttel (*inf*) *pl*.

drop: ~ **scene** *n* (*Theat*) (Zwischen)vorhang *m*; ~ **shot** *n* (*Tennis*) Stoppball *m*.

dropsical ['drɒpsɪkəl] *adj* wassersüchtig.

dropsy ['drɒpsɪ] *n* Wassersucht *f*.

drop zone *n* (*for supplies*) Abwurfgebiet *nt*; (*for parachutists*) Absprunggebiet *nt*.

drosophila [drɒˈsɒfɪlə] *n* Drosophila, Taufliege *f*.

dross [drɒs] *n, no pl* (*Metal*) Schlacke *f*; (*fig*) Tand *m*. **wealth and fame are but** ~ Reichtum und Ruhm sind eitel und nichtig; **everything else is but** ~ alles andere ist eitel und nichtig.

drought [draʊt] *n* Dürre *f*. **three** ~**s in three years** drei Dürrekatastrophen in drei Jahren.

drove[1] [drəʊv] n (of animals) Herde f; (of people) Schar f. they came in ~s sie kamen in hellen Scharen.

drove[2] pret of drive.

drover ['drəʊvə'] n Viehtreiber m.

drown [draʊn] 1 vi ertrinken.
2 vt (a) person, animal ertränken. to be ~ed ertrinken; he looks like a ~ed rat (inf) er sieht wie eine gebadete Maus aus (inf); to ~ one's sorrows (in drink) seine Sorgen (in Alkohol) ertränken; to ~ one's whisky seinen Whisky verwässern.
(b) (submerge, flood) land überschwemmen, überfluten. with her face ~ed in tears mit tränenüberströmtem Gesicht.
(c) (render inaudible: also ~ out) noise, voice übertönen; speaker niederschreien.

drowning ['draʊnɪŋ] 1 adj person ertrinkend. a ~ man will clutch at a straw (Prov) dem Verzweifelten ist jedes Mittel recht. 2 n Ertrinken nt. there were three ~s here last year im letzten Jahr sind hier drei Leute ertrunken.

drowse [draʊz] 1 vi (vor sich (acc) hin) dösen or dämmern. 2 n Halbschlaf, Dämmerschlaf m.
♦**drowse off** vi eindämmern, eindösen (inf).

drowsily ['draʊzɪlɪ] adv schläfrig, dösig (inf); (after sleeping) verschlafen.

drowsiness ['draʊzɪnɪs] n Schläfrigkeit f. to cause ~ schläfrig machen.

drowsy ['draʊzɪ] adj (+er) (a) person schläfrig, dösig (inf); (after sleep) verschlafen. to grow/get ~ schläfrig werden; to feel ~ schläfrig sein. ~ afternoon träge; atmosphere schläfrig. I had a ~ afternoon ich habe den Nachmittag verdöst.

drub [drʌb] vt (thrash) person (ver)prügeln, schlagen.

drubbing ['drʌbɪŋ] n (a) (thrashing) Prügel pl. to give sb a sound ~ jdm eine Tracht Prügel verpassen. (b) (defeat) Niederlage f. to take a good ~ ganz schön Prügel kriegen (inf).

drudge [drʌdʒ] 1 n (person) Arbeitstier nt (inf); (job) stumpfsinnige Plackerei or Schufterei (inf). is the lexicographer a harmless ~? ist der Lexikograph ein Mensch, der nur brav vor sich hin schuftet? 2 vi sich placken, schuften (inf).

drudgery ['drʌdʒərɪ] n stumpfsinnige Plackerei or Schufterei (inf). it's sheer ~ es ist eine einzige Plackerei; the ~ of working in a hotel kitchen die stumpfsinnige Plackerei or Schufterei (inf) in einer Hotelküche.

drug [drʌg] 1 n (a) (Med, Pharm) Medikament, Arzneimittel nt. he's been on ~s since Christmas seit Weihnachten muß er Medikamente nehmen; to put sb on ~s jdm Medikamente verordnen.
(b) (addictive substance) Droge f, Rauschgift nt. to be on ~s/to take ~s drogen- or rauschgiftsüchtig sein/Drogen or Rauschgift nehmen; see hard ~, soft.
(c) (inducing unconsciousness) Betäubungsmittel nt.
(d) (Comm: unsaleable goods) a ~ on the market unverkäufliche Ware; (in shop) ein Ladenhüter m.
2 vt (a) (render unconscious by ~s) person betäuben. to be in a ~ged sleep in tiefer Betäubung liegen; to be ~ged with sleep (fig) schlaftrunken sein; to be ~ged from lack of sleep vor Müdigkeit ganz benommen sein.
(b) (food, drink) to ~ sth ein Betäubungsmittel in etw (acc) mischen. her whisky was ~ged in ihrem Whisky war ein Betäubungsmittel.
(c) (Med) patient Medikamente geben (+dat). to be/get ~ged up to the eyeballs on tranquillizers (inf) mit Beruhigungsmittel vollgepumpt sein (inf)/sich mit Beruhigungsmitteln vollpumpen (inf).

drug: ~ addict n Drogen- or Rauschgiftsüchtige(r), Drogen- or Rauschgiftabhängige(r) mf; ~ addiction n Rauschgiftsucht, Drogenabhängigkeit or -sucht f; ~ culture n Drogenkultur f.

druggist ['drʌgɪst] n (US) Drogist(in f) m.

drug: ~ pusher n Dealer (sl), Pusher (sl) m; ~store n (US) Drugstore m; ~ taker n jd, der Drogen or Rauschgift nimmt; ~ taking n Einnehmen nt von Drogen or Rauschgift; ~ traffic, ~ trafficking n Drogenhandel m.

druid ['druːɪd] n Druide m.

drum [drʌm] 1 n (a) (Mus) Trommel f. Joe Jones on ~s am Schlagzeug: Joe Jones; the ~s die Trommeln pl; (pop, jazz) das Schlagzeug; to beat the ~ for sb/sth (fig) die Trommel für jdn/etw rühren.
(b) (for oil, petrol) Tonne f; (cylinder for wire) Trommel, Rolle f; (Tech: machine part) Trommel, Walze f; (Phot) Entwicklertrommel f; (Archit) (wall) Tambour m, Trommel f; (shaft) Säulentrommel f.
(c) (Anat: also ear~) Trommelfell nt.
2 vi (a) (Mus) trommeln.
(b) (fig) (with fingers, rain etc) trommeln. the noise is still ~ming in my ears das Geräusch dröhnt mir noch in den Ohren.
3 vt to ~ one's fingers on the table mit den Fingern auf den Tisch trommeln.
♦**drum into** vt always separate to ~ sth ~ sb or sb's head jdm etw eintrichtern (inf) or einpauken (inf).
♦**drum out** vt sep (out of army, club) ausstoßen.
♦**drum up** vt sep enthusiasm erwecken; support auftreiben. to ~ ~ business Aufträge anbahnen.

drum: ~beat n Trommelschlag m; ~ brake n Trommelbremse f; ~fire n (Mil) Trommelfeuer nt; ~head n Trommelfell nt; ~head court martial n Standgericht nt; ~ major n Tambourmajor m; ~-majorette n (US) Tambourmajorin f.

drummer ['drʌmə'] n (a) (in orchestra) Trommelschläger m; (in band, pop-group) Schlagzeuger m; (Mil, in parade etc also) Trommler m. (b) (US inf) Vertreter m.

drummer boy n Trommler m.

drumstick ['drʌmstɪk] n (a) (Mus) Trommelschlegel or -stock m. (b) (on chicken etc) Keule f.

drunk [drʌŋk] 1 ptp of drink.
2 adj (a) betrunken. I'm going out to get ~ ich gehe mich jetzt

betrinken or besaufen (inf); to get ~ (on) betrunken werden (von); (on purpose) sich betrinken (mit); he gets ~ on two pints of beer er ist schon nach zwei Halben betrunken; to get sb ~ jdn betrunken or blau (inf) machen; ~ and disorderly (Jur) durch Trunkenheit öffentliches Ärgernis erregend; as ~ as a lord blau wie ein Veilchen (inf), voll wie ein Amtmann (inf).
(b) (fig) trunken, berauscht. ~ with blood killers etc im Blutrausch; ~ with joy freudetrunken; ~ with success erfolgsselig, vom Erfolg berauscht.
3 n Betrunkene(r) mf; (habitually) Trinker(in f), Säufer(in f) (inf) m.

drunkard ['drʌŋkəd] n Trinker(in f), Säufer(in f) m.

drunken ['drʌŋkən] adj person betrunken, blau (inf). a ~ old fool ein alter Saufkopp (inf); ~ driving (Jur) Trunkenheit f am Steuer. (b) orgy feucht-fröhlich, Sauf-; brawl mit/von Betrunkenen; fury betrunken; voice betrunken, besoffen (inf). I can't read this ~ scrawl ich kann nicht lesen, was er in seinem betrunkenen Zustand da geschmiert hat.

drunkenly ['drʌŋkənlɪ] adv betrunken; stagger blau, wie er etc war (inf); behave wie ein Betrunkener or eine Betrunkene.

drunkenness ['drʌŋkənnɪs] n (state) Betrunkenheit f; (habit, problem) Trunksucht f.

drunkometer [drʌŋ'kɒmɪtə'] n (US) see breathalyzer.

dry [draɪ] 1 n come into the ~ komm ins Trockene; to give sth a ~ etw trocknen.
2 adj (+er) (all senses) trocken. to wipe sth ~ etw trockenwischen; the river ran ~ der Fluß trocknete aus; as ~ as a bone land, clothes knochentrocken (inf); mouth, ditches völlig ausgetrocknet; ~ bread trocken(es) Brot; to feel/to be ~ (thirsty) durstig sein, eine trockene Kehle haben (inf); the cow has gone ~ die Kuh steht trocken.
3 vt trocknen; (~ out) skin austrocknen; fruit also dörren; (with cloth) dishes, one's hands (ab)trocknen. to ~ one's eyes sich (dat) die Tränen abwischen; the dishes will ~ themselves das Geschirr trocknet von selbst; to ~ oneself sich abtrocknen.
4 vi trocknen, trocken werden.
♦**dry off** vi (clothes etc) trocknen, trocken werden.
♦**dry out** 1 vi (a) (clothes) trocknen; (ground, skin etc) austrocknen. (b) (inf: alcoholic) eine Entziehungskur machen. 2 vt sep clothes trocknen; ground, skin austrocknen.
♦**dry up** 1 vi (a) (stream, well) austrocknen, versiegen; (moisture) trocknen; (inspiration, source of income) versiegen; (author) keine Ideen mehr haben. then business started ~ing ~ dann wurden die Aufträge immer spärlicher.
(b) (dishes) abtrocknen.
(c) (actor) steckenbleiben (inf); (speaker also) den Faden verlieren.
(d) (inf: be quiet) ~ ~! halt den Mund! (inf); to make sb ~ ~ jdn zum Schweigen bringen.
2 vt sep mess aufwischen; dishes abtrocknen; (sun) well austrocknen.

dryad ['draɪæd] n Dryade f.

dry: ~-as-dust adj fürchterlich trocken, staubtrocken; ~ battery n (Elec) Trockenbatterie f; ~ cell n (Elec) Trockenelement nt; ~ cell battery n Trockenbatterie f; ~-clean 1 vt chemisch reinigen; to have a dress ~-cleaned ein Kleid chemisch reinigen lassen; ~-clean only (on label) chemisch reinigen!; 2 vi will it ~-clean? läßt es sich chemisch reinigen?; ~-cleaner's n chemische Reinigung; ~-cleaning n chemische Reinigung; ~ dock n (Naut) Trockendock nt.

dryer, drier ['draɪə'] n (for clothes) Wäschetrockner m; (spin ~) Wäscheschleuder f; (for hair) Fön, Haartrockner m; (over head) Trockenhaube f; (in paint) Trockenstoff m.

dry: ~ farming n Trockenfarmsystem nt; ~-fly fishing n Trockenfliegenfischen nt; ~ goods npl (Comm) Kurzwaren pl; ~ ice n Trockeneis nt.

drying ['draɪɪŋ]: ~ cupboard n (Wäsche)trockenschrank m; ~ room n Trockenboden m; Trockenkeller m; ~-up n Abtrocknen nt; to do the ~-up abtrocknen.

dry land n fester Boden. I'll be glad to be on ~ again ich bin froh, wenn ich erst mal wieder festen Boden unter den Füßen habe.

dryly ['draɪlɪ] adv trocken.

dry measure n Trockenmaß nt.

dryness ['draɪnɪs] n (all senses) Trockenheit f.

dry: ~ nurse n Säuglingsschwester f; ~ rot n (Haus- or Holz)schwamm m; ~ run n Probe f; (Mil) Trockentraining nt; ~ shampoo n Trockenshampoo nt; ~ ski slope n Trockenskipiste f; ~ spell n (Met) Trockenperiode f; ~-stone wall n Bruchsteinmauer f; ~ valley n Trockental nt.

DSC abbr of Distinguished Service Cross.

DSc abbr of Doctor of Science Dr. rer. nat.

DSM abbr of Distinguished Service Medal.

DSO abbr of Distinguished Service Order.

DST (US) abbr of daylight saving time.

DTs [di:'ti:z] abbr of delirium tremens. to have the ~ vom Saufen den Tatterich haben (inf).

dual ['djuːəl] adj (double) doppelt, Doppel-; (two kinds of) zweierlei. in his ~ rôles of ... in seiner Doppelrolle als ...; it has a ~ function es hat doppelte or zweierlei Funktion; the ~ criteria of quality and price die zwei Kriterien Qualität und Preis; ~ carriageway (Brit) Straße f mit Mittelstreifen und Fahrbahnen in beiden Richtungen; ~ Schnellstraße f; ~ control (Aut) Doppelsteuerung f; ~ nationality doppelte Staatsangehörigkeit; the company is under ~ ownership die Firma hat zwei Eigentümer; ~ personality gespaltene Persönlichkeit.

dualism ['djuːəlɪzəm] n Dualismus m.

dualist ['djuːəlɪst] n Dualist m.

dualistic [djuːə'lɪstɪk] adj dualistisch.

duality [djuː'ælɪtɪ] n Dualität f.

dual-purpose ['djuːəl'pɜːpəs] adj zweifach verwendbar.

dub[1] [dʌb] *vt* (a) to ~ sb (a) **knight** jdn zum Ritter schlagen. (b) (*nickname*) taufen. (c) *film* synchronisieren.
♦**dub in** *vt sep* (*Film*) synchron (zum Bild) aufnehmen.
dub[2] *n* (*US inf*) Tolpatsch *m*.
dubbin [ˈdʌbɪn] *n* Lederfett *nt*.
dubbing [ˈdʌbɪŋ] *n* (*Film*) Synchronisation *f*.
dubiety [djuˈbaɪətɪ] *n* (*form*) Zweifel *pl*.
dubious [ˈdjuːbɪəs] *adj* (a) (*uncertain*) *matter etc* zweifelhaft, ungewiß; *look* zweifelnd he's ~ whether ... er weiß nicht *or* ist im Zweifel, ob ...; I'm very ~ about it ich habe da (doch) starke Zweifel; he gave me a ~ look er sah mich zweifelnd an.
  (b) *people, company, reputation* zweifelhaft, fragwürdig.
  (c) (*questionable*) *honour, advantage* zweifelhaft, fragwürdig. he was given the ~ honour of signing the surrender ihm wurde die zweifelhafte Ehre zuteil, die Kapitulation unterzeichnen zu dürfen.
dubiously [ˈdjuːbɪəslɪ] *adv look* zweifelnd, ungewiß; *behave* zweifelhaft, fragwürdig.
dubiousness [ˈdjuːbɪəsnɪs] *n see adj* (a) Zweifelhaftigkeit, Ungewißheit *f*. there was a certain ~ in his voice es lag ein gewisser Zweifel in seiner Stimme.
  (b) Zweifelhaftigkeit, Fragwürdigkeit *f*.
  (c) Zweifelhaftigkeit, Fragwürdigkeit *f*.
ducal [ˈdjuːkəl] *adj* herzoglich; *palace also* Herzogs-.
ducat [ˈdʌkɪt] *n* (*Hist*) Dukaten *m*.
duchess [ˈdʌtʃɪs] *n* Herzogin *f*.
duchy [ˈdʌtʃɪ] *n* Herzogtum *nt*.
duck[1] [dʌk] 1 *n* (a) (*bird*) Ente *f*. wild ~ Wildente *f*; roast ~ gebratene Ente, Entenbraten *m*; to play ~s and drakes Steine (über das Wasser) springen lassen; to play ~s and drakes with sth (*squander*) mit etw furchtbar aasen (*inf*); to take to sth like a ~ to water bei etw gleich in seinem Element sein; it's like water off a ~'s back das läuft alles an ihm/ihr *etc* ab.
  (b) (*Brit sl*) *see* duckie.
  (c) (*sl*) Tante *f* (*inf*). she's a funny/nice old ~ sie ist eine komische/nette alte Tante (*inf*).
  (d) (*Mil inf*) Amphibienfahrzeug *nt*.
  (e) (*Cricket*) he made *or* scored a ~ er hat keinen Punkt gemacht; to be out for a ~ ohne Punktgewinn aus sein.
  2 *vi* (a) (*also* ~ **down**) sich ducken. he ~ed down out of sight er duckte sich, so daß man ihn nicht mehr sehen konnte; he ~ed under the water er tauchte (im Wasser) unter.
  (b) he ~ed out of the room when he ... er verschwand aus dem Zimmer, als er ....
  3 *vt* (a) (*push under water*) untertauchen.
  (b) to ~ one's head den Kopf einziehen.
  (c) (*avoid*) *difficult question etc* ausweichen (+*dat*).
duck[2] *n* (*Tex*) Segeltuch *nt*. ~s Segeltuchhosen *pl*.
duck: ~-**bill,** ~-**billed platypus** *n* Schnabeltier *nt*; ~**board** *n* Laufrost *m*; ~-**egg blue** *n* zartes Blau.
duckie [ˈdʌkɪ] *n* (*Brit sl: also* **duck, ducks**) *often not translated* (*bus conductress to passenger*) junger Mann, junge Frau; (*actors, homosexuals, prostitute client*) Süße (r) *mf*. he is a ~ er ist süß *or* ein süßer Knopf (*inf*).
ducking [ˈdʌkɪŋ] *n* Untertauchen, Tauchen *nt*. to give sb a ~ jdn untertauchen *or* tunken.
ducking-stool [ˈdʌkɪŋstuːl] *n* Sitz *m* auf einem Balken, mit dem Übeltäter zur Strafe ins Wasser getaucht wurden.
duckling [ˈdʌklɪŋ] *n* Entenküken, Entlein *nt*. roast ~ gebratene junge Ente; *see* ugly.
duck pond *n* Ententeich *m*.
ducks [dʌks] *n* (*Brit sl*) *see* duckie.
duck: ~ **shooting** *n* Entenjagd *f*; ~**weed** *n* Entenflott *nt*, Entengrütze, Wasserlinse *f*.
ducky *n* (*Brit sl*) *see* duckie.
duct [dʌkt] *n* (a) (*Anat*) Röhre *f*. tear ~ Tränenkanal *m*.
  (b) (*for liquid, gas*) (Rohr)leitung *f*, Rohr *nt*; (*Elec*) Rohr *nt*, Röhre *f*.
ductile [ˈdʌktaɪl] *adj* (a) *metal* hämmerbar; (*stretchable*) dehnbar, streckbar. (b) (*fig liter*) *person* leicht lenkbar.
ductless gland [ˈdʌktlɪsˈglænd] *n* endokrine *or* innersekretorische Drüse.
dud [dʌd] (*inf*) 1 *adj* (a) ~ **shell/bomb** Blindgänger *m*.
  (b) *tool* nutzlos; *saw* stumpf; *actor, teacher* mies (*inf*), schlecht; *coin* falsch; *cheque* ungedeckt; (*forged*) gefälscht. ~ **note** Blüte *f* (*inf*); **we had pretty** ~ **holidays** unsere Ferien waren ein ziemlicher Reinfall *or* waren ziemlich mies (*inf*).
  2 *n* (a) (*shell, bomb*) Blindgänger *m*.
  (b) (*cheque*) ungedeckter *or* (*forged*) gefälschter Scheck; (*note*) Blüte *f* (*inf*).
  (c) (*person*) Blindgänger (*inf*), Versager *m*.
dude [djuːd] *n* (*US*) (a) (*dandy*) Dandy *m*. (b) (*city type*) Städter *m*, feiner Stadtpinkel (*pej inf*). (c) (*inf: man*) Kerl *m* (*inf*).
dude ranch *n* (*US*) Touristenranch, Ferienranch *f*.
dudgeon [ˈdʌdʒən] *n*: **in high** ~ sehr empört, sehr aufgebracht.
duds [dʌdz] *npl* (*sl: clothes*) Klamotten *pl* (*inf*).
due [djuː] 1 *adj* (a) (*to be paid, owing*) fällig. **the sum/respect which is** ~ **to him** die Summe, die ihm zusteht/der Respekt, der ihm gebührt; **the amount** ~ **as compensation** der Betrag, der als Schadenersatz gezahlt werden soll; **to fall** ~ fällig werden *or* sein; **I am** ~ **six days off/(for) a rise** mir stehen sechs Tage Urlaub zu/mir steht eine Gehaltserhöhung zu; **I was** ~ **a bit of luck** es wurde auch Zeit, daß ich ein bißchen Glück hatte.
  (b) (*expected, scheduled*) to be ~ **to do sth** etw tun sollen; **the train is** ~ *or* ~ **to arrive at midday** der Zug soll laut Fahrplan um zwölf Uhr ankommen; **where are we** ~ *or* **when are we** ~? wann sollen wir dasein?; **I'm** ~ **in London tomorrow** ich soll morgen in London sein; **he's** ~ **back tomorrow** er müßte morgen zurück sein; **this building is** ~ **to be demolished** dies Gebäude soll demnächst abgerissen werden; **when is the baby/she** ~? wann wird das Baby kommen/bekommt sie

ihr Baby?; **his next novel is about** ~ sein nächster Roman ist demnächst fällig.
  (c) (*proper, suitable*) *respect, regard* gebührend, geziemend (*geh*), nötig. **with all** ~ **respect** bei allem Respekt; **buried with all honour** ~ **to his rank** mit allen Ehren begraben, die ihm rangmäßig zustehen; **with the respect** ~ **from a son to his father** mit allem Respekt, den ein Sohn seinem Vater schuldet; **in** ~ **form** in geziemender (*geh*) *or* gebührender Form; **we'll let you know in** ~ **course** *or* **time** wir werden Sie zu gegebener Zeit benachrichtigen; **the man who was, in** ~ **course, to become** ... derjenige, der dann im Laufe der Zeit ... wurde; **after** ~ **consideration** nach reiflicher Überlegung; **after** ~ **process of law** nach einem ordentlichen (Gerichts)verfahren.
  (d) ~ **to** aufgrund (+*gen*), wegen (+*gen or dat*); **what's it** ~ **to?** worauf ist dies zurückzuführen?; **his failure was entirely** ~ **to himself/his carelessness** an seinem Versagen war nur er selbst/seine Sorglosigkeit schuld; **it is** ~ **to you that we lost/are alive today** wir haben es euch zu verdanken, daß wir verloren haben/heute am Leben sind.
  2 *adv* ~ **west** direkt nach Westen; ~ **east of the village** genau im Osten *or* östlich des Dorfes.
  3 *n* (a) ~s *pl* (*fees*) Gebühr *f*, Gebühren *pl*.
  (b) *no pl* (**to**) **give the man his** ~, **it was an extremely difficult task** man muß gerechterweise zugeben, daß es äußerst schwierig war; **give him his** ~, **he did have some success das muß der Neid ihm lassen, er hatte doch einigen Erfolg; (**to**) **give him his** ~, **he did try hard** das muß man ihm lassen, er hat sich wirklich angestrengt; *see* devil.
duel [ˈdjuəl] 1 *n* (*lit, fig*) Duell *nt*. ~**ling pistols** Duellierpistolen *pl*; **students'** ~ Mensur *f*; ~ **of wits** geistiger Wettstreit. 2 *vi* sich duellieren; (*German students*) eine Mensur schlagen.
duellist [ˈdjuəlɪst] *n* Duellant *m*.
duet [djuːˈet] *n* Duo *nt*; (*for voices*) Duett *nt*. **violin** ~ Geigenduo.
duff[1] [dʌf] *n* (*Cook*) Mehlpudding *m*; *see* plum ~.
duff[2] *adj* (*Brit sl*) Scheiß- (*sl*); *suggestion, idea* doof (*inf*).
♦**duff up** *vt sep* (*Brit sl*) zusammenschlagen (*inf*).
duffel [ˈdʌfl]: ~ **bag** *n* Matchbeutel *or* -sack *m*; ~-**coat** *n* Dufflecoat *m*.
duffer [ˈdʌfəʳ] *n* (*Brit sl*) (a) (*esp Sch*) Blödmann *m* (*inf*). **to be a** ~ **at football/French** eine Flasche im Fußball sein (*inf*)/eine Niete in Französisch sein (*inf*). (b) (*silly old man*) (alter) Trottel (*inf*).
dug[1] [dʌg] *n* (*of animal*) Zitze *f*.
dug[2] *pret, ptp of* dig.
dugout [ˈdʌɡaʊt] *n* (*Mil*) Schützengraben, Unterstand *m*; (*also* ~ **canoe**) Einbaum *m*.
duke [djuːk] *n* Herzog *m*.
dukedom [ˈdjuːkdəm] *n* (*territory*) Herzogtum *nt*; (*title*) Herzogswürde *f*.
dukes [djuːks] *npl* (*dated sl: fists*) Fäuste *pl*. **put up your** ~ zeig mal deine Fäuste (*inf*).
dulcet [ˈdʌlsɪt] *adj* (*liter, hum, iro*) wohlklingend, melodisch. **so nice to hear your** ~ **tones again** (*hum, iro*) wie nett, deine liebliche *or* (*to man*) sonore Stimme wieder zu hören (*hum, iro*).
dulcimer [ˈdʌlsɪməʳ] *n* Cymbal, Hackbrett *nt*.
dull [dʌl] 1 *adj* (+*er*) (a) (*slow-witted*) *person* langsam, schwerfällig. **the** ~ **ones** (*Sch*) die schwächeren *or* langsameren Schüler *pl*; **his senses/intellectual powers are growing** ~ seine Sinne/geistigen Kräfte lassen langsam nach.
  (b) (*boring*) langweilig; *person, book, evening etc also* lahm (*inf*). **as** ~ **as ditchwater** stinklangweilig (*inf*).
  (c) (*lacking spirit*) *person, mood, humour* lustlos. **he felt very** ~ **all day** er hatte den ganzen Tag zu nichts so richtig Lust.
  (d) (*dim, not vivid*) *colour, light* trüb; *eyes also* glanzlos, matt; *mirror* blind; (*matt*) *colour* matt; (*tarnished*) *metal* angelaufen, stumpf.
  (e) (*overcast*) *weather* trüb, grau; *sky also* verhangen, bedeckt. **it's** ~ **today** es ist trüb(es Wetter) heute.
  (f) (*muffled*) *sound* dumpf. **he fell to the ground with a** ~ **thud** er schlug dumpf auf den Boden auf.
  (g) (*blunted*) *blade* stumpf; (*fig*) *pain* dumpf.
  (h) (*St Ex*) *market* flau; (*Comm*) *trade, business* träge, schleppend.
  2 *vt* (a) (*cause to function less well*) *senses, powers of memory* trüben, schwächen; *mind* abstumpfen. **emotionally** ~**ed** (*emotional*) abgestumpft.
  (b) (*lessen impact of*) *pain, grief* betäuben; *pleasure* dämpfen.
  (c) (*muffle*) *sound* dämpfen.
  (d) (*blunt*) *edge, blade* stumpf machen.
  (e) (*make less bright*) *colour* dämpfen; *mirror* blind *or* matt machen; *metal* stumpf werden lassen, anlaufen lassen.
dullard [ˈdʌləd] *n* Dummkopf *m*.
dullness [ˈdʌlnɪs] *n see adj* (a) Langsamkeit, Schwerfälligkeit *f*.
  (b) Langweiligkeit *f*; Lahmheit *f* (*inf*).
  (c) Lustlosigkeit *f*.
  (d) Trübheit *f*; Glanzlosigkeit, Mattheit *f*, Blindheit *f*; Mattheit *f*; Stumpfheit *f*.
  (e) Trübheit, Grauheit *f*; Bedecktheit *f*.
  (f) Dumpfheit *f*.
  (g) Stumpfheit *f*; Dumpfheit *f*.
  (h) Flauheit *f*.
dully [ˈdʌlɪ] *adv* (a) (*in a listless way*) *look* lustlos. (b) (*boringly*) *talk, write* langweilig, einfallslos. (c) (*dimly*) *shine* matt, schwach; *sense, perceive* dumpf.
duly [ˈdjuːlɪ] *adv* entsprechend; (*properly*) gebührend, wie es sich gehört; (*according to regulations etc*) ordnungsgemäß, vorschriftsmäßig. he was ~ **surprised** er war entsprechend überrascht; **when all the details have been** ~ **considered** wenn alle Einzelheiten gebührend bedacht sind; **and the parcel** ~ **arrived the next morning** und das Paket kam dann auch am

nächsten Morgen; **has the witness been ~ sworn in?** ist der Zeuge ordnungsgemäß vereidigt worden?

dumb [dʌm] *adj* (+ *er*) **(a)** stumm. **a ~ person** ein Stummer, eine Stumme; **the ~ die Stummen** *pl*; **~ animals** die Tiere *pl*; **our ~ friends** unsere stummen Freunde (*geh*); **that's cruelty to ~ animals** (*fig*) das ist ja Tierquälerei!; **to strike sb ~** (*lit*) jdm die Sprache nehmen; **he was (struck) ~ with fear/horror** es hatte ihm vor Furcht/Schreck die Sprache verschlagen.
(b) (*esp US inf: stupid*) doof (*inf*), dumm. **that's a pretty ~ thing to do** wie kann man nur so was Doofes machen!; **a ~ blonde** eine doofe Blondine; **to act ~** sich dumm stellen.
dumb-bell ['dʌmbel] *n* (*Sport*) Hantel *f*.
dumbfound ['dʌmfaund] *vt* verblüffen. **I'm ~ed!** ich bin sprachlos.
dumbness ['dʌmnɪs] *n* **(a)** Stummheit *f*. **(b)** (*esp US inf. stupidity*) Doofheit (*inf*), Dummheit *f*.
dumb: ~ show *n* (*Theat*) pantomimische Einlage in einem Stück; **in ~ show** in Mimik; **~ waiter** *n* Speiseaufzug *m*; (*trolley*) Serviertisch *m*.
dum-dum ['dʌmdʌm] *n* (*inf*) Doofie *m* (*inf*).
dumdum (bullet) *n* Dumdum(geschoß) *nt*.
dummy ['dʌmɪ] **1** *n* **(a)** (*sham object*) Attrappe *f*; (*Comm also*) Schaupackung *f*; (*for clothes*) (Schaufenster- *or* Kleider)-puppe *f*; (*of book*) Blindband *m*. **the manager is only a ~** der Direktor ist nur ein Strohmann; *see* **tailor.**
(b) (*Brit: baby's teat*) Schnuller *m*.
(c) (*Cards*) (*person*) Strohmann *m*; (*cards*) Tisch *m*.
(d) (*inf: fool*) Dummkopf, Idiot (*inf*), Doofie (*inf*) *m*.
(e) (*Ftbl etc*) Finte *f*. **to sell sb a ~** jdn antäuschen.
2 *adj attr* (*not real*) unecht. **it's just a ~ ...** das ist nur die Attrappe eines/einer ...; **a ~ rifle** eine Gewehrattrappe; **~ run** Probe *f*; (*of air attack*) Übung *f*.
dump [dʌmp] **1** *n* **(a)** (*pile of rubbish*) Schutthaufen, Abfallhaufen *m*; (*place*) Müllplatz *m*, Müllkippe *f*.
(b) (*Mil*) Depot *nt*.
(c) (*pej inf: town*) Kaff *nt* (*inf*); (*house, building*) Dreckloch *nt* (*pej inf*); (*school etc*) Sauladen *m* (*pej sl*).
(d) (*inf*) **to be (down) in the ~s** deprimiert *or* down (*sl*) sein.
2 *vt* **(a)** (*get rid of*) rubbish abladen. **they ~ed the cargo/bodies overboard** sie warfen die Ladung/Leichen über Bord.
(b) (*put down, let fall*) load, rubbish abladen; sand, bricks *also* kippen; bags etc (*drop*) fallen lassen; (*leave*) lassen. **where can I ~ these books?** wo kann ich diese Bücher lassen?
(c) (*inf: abandon, get rid of*) person, girlfriend abschieben; sth unwanted abladen.
(d) (*Comm*) goods zu Dumpingpreisen verkaufen.
◆**dump down** *vt sep* fallen lassen.
◆**dump off** *vt sep* (*inf*) **will you ~ me ~ on the way home?** kannst du mich auf der Rückfahrt absetzen?
dumper ['dʌmpə'] *n* (*also* **dump truck**) Kipper *m*.
dumping ['dʌmpɪŋ] *n* **(a)** (*of load, rubbish*) Abladen *nt*. **"no ~ "** „Schuttabladen verboten!" **(b)** (*Comm*) Dumping *nt*.
dumping ground *n* Müllkippe *f*, Schuttabladeplatz *m*; (*fig*) Abladeplatz *m*.
dumpling ['dʌmplɪŋ] *n* **(a)** (*Cook*) Kloß, Knödel *m*. **apple ~** Apfel *m* im Schlafrock. **(b)** (*inf: person*) Dickerchen (*inf*) *nt*.
dump truck *n* Kipper *m*.
dumpy ['dʌmpɪ] *adj* pummelig; glasses klein und massiv.
dun¹ [dʌn] **1** *adj* graubraun. **2** *n* Graubraun *nt*.
dun² *vt* mahnen. **to ~ sb for the money he owes** bei jdm seine Schulden anmahnen.
dunce [dʌns] *n* (*Sch*) langsamer Lerner *or* Schüler; (*stupid person*) Dummkopf *m*. **to be a ~ at maths** eine Niete *or* schlecht in Mathe sein (*inf*); **the ~ of the class** das Schlußlicht der Klasse; **~'s cap** spitzer Papierhut, der früher zur Strafe dem schlechtesten Schüler aufgesetzt wurde.
dunderhead ['dʌndəhed] *n* Dummkopf, Dummerjan (*inf*) *m*.
dune [dju:n] *n* Düne *f*.
dung [dʌŋ] **1** *n* **(a)** (*excrement*) Dung *m*; (*of birds*) Dreck *m*. **(b)** (*Agr: manure*) Dung, Mist, Dünger *m*. **2** *vt* field düngen, misten.
dungarees [ˌdʌŋgəˈriːz] *npl* (*workman's, child's*) Latzhosen *pl*. **a pair of ~** eine Latzhose.
dung: ~ beetle *n* Mistkäfer *m*; **~ cart** *n* Mistkarren *m*.
dungeon ['dʌndʒən] *n* Verlies *nt*, Kerker *m*.
dunghill ['dʌŋhɪl] *n* Mist- *or* Dunghaufen *m*.
dunk [dʌŋk] *vt* (ein)tunken.
dunning letter ['dʌnɪŋˌletə'] *n* Mahnbrief *m*.
dunno ['dʌnəʊ] = (**I**) **don't know.**
duo ['dju:əʊ] *n* Duo *nt*.
duodenal [ˌdju:əʊˈdi:nl] *adj* Duodenal- (*form*). **~ ulcer** Zwölffingerdarmgeschwür *nt*.
duodenum [ˌdju:əʊˈdi:nəm] *n* Zwölffingerdarm *m*, Duodenum *nt* (*spec*).
dupe [dju:p] *vt* betrügen, überlisten, übertölpeln. **he was ~d/into believing it** er fiel darauf rein. **2** *n* Betrogene(r) *mf*.
duple ['dju:pl] *adj* (*Mus*) **~ time** Zweiertakt *m*.
duplex ['dju:pleks] **1** *adj* **(a)** (*Elec, Tech*) doppelt, Doppel-, Duplex-. **(b)** **~ apartment** (*US*) zweistöckige Wohnung; **~ house** (*US*) Zweifamilienhaus *nt*. **2** *n* (*US*) *see* **(b).**
duplicate ['dju:plɪkeɪt] **1** *vt* **(a)** (*make a copy of*) document ein Duplikat *nt or* eine Zweitschrift anfertigen von.
(b) (*make copies of: on machine*) kopieren, vervielfältigen.
(c) (*repeat*) action etc wiederholen, noch einmal machen. **(wastefully)** doppelt *or* zweimal machen. **that is merely duplicating work already done** da wird doch nur schon Erledigtes noch einmal gemacht.
2 ['dju:plɪkɪt] *n* (*of document*) Duplikat *nt*, Kopie *f*; (*of work of art*) Kopie *f*; (*of key etc*) Zweitschlüssel *m*. **I have a watch which is the exact ~ of yours** ich habe genau die gleiche Uhr wie Sie; **in ~** in doppelter Ausfertigung.

3 ['dju:plɪkɪt] *adj* doppelt, zweifach. **a ~ copy of the text** ein Duplikat *nt or* eine Kopie des Textes; **a ~ receipt** eine Empfangsbescheinigung in doppelter Ausfertigung; **~ bus/coach** zweite(r) Bus; **a ~ cheque** ein Scheckduplikat *nt*; **a ~ key** ein Zweitschlüssel *m*.
duplicating machine ['dju:plɪkeɪtɪŋməʃi:n], **duplicator** *n* Vervielfältigungsapparat *m*.
duplication [ˌdju:plɪˈkeɪʃən] *n* (*of documents*) (*act*) Vervielfältigung *f*; (*thing also*) Kopie *f*; (*double*) Doppel *nt*; (*of efforts, work*) Wiederholung *f*. **save expenses by avoiding ~ of efforts** tun Sie nichts zweimal, sparen Sie Kosten.
duplicator ['dju:plɪkeɪtə'] *n see* **duplicating machine.**
duplicity [dju:ˈplɪsɪtɪ] *n* Doppelspiel *nt*.
durability [ˌdjʊərəˈbɪlɪtɪ] *n see adj* Dauer *f*; Haltbarkeit *f*; Widerstandsfähigkeit *f*.
durable ['djʊərəbl] *adj* friendship dauerhaft; material haltbar; metal widerstandsfähig.
duration [djʊəˈreɪʃən] *n* (*of play, war etc*) Länge, Dauer *f*. **of long/short ~** von langer/kurzer Dauer; **after a struggle of six years'** ~ nach sechsjährigem Kampf; **~ of life** Lebensdauer *f*; **he joined up for the ~** er hat sich bis zum Ende verpflichtet; **it looks as though we are here for the ~** (*inf*) es sieht so aus, als ob wir bis zum Ende hier sind.
duress [djʊəˈres] *n* Zwang *m*. **he signed the form under ~** er hat die Unterschrift unter Zwang geleistet.
durex ® ['djʊəreks] *n* Gummi (*inf*), Fromms ® *m*.
during ['djʊərɪŋ] *prep* während (+ *gen*).
durst [dɜ:st] (*obs*) *pret of* **dare.**
dusk [dʌsk] *n* (*twilight*) (Abend)dämmerung *f*; (*gloom*) Finsternis *f*. **at ~** bei Einbruch der Dunkelheit.
duskiness ['dʌskɪnɪs] *n* Dunkelheit *f*.
dusky ['dʌskɪ] *adj* (+ *er*) dunkel. **~ maidens** dunkelhäutige Mädchen *pl*; **~ pink** altrosa.
dust [dʌst] **1** *n, no pl* (*on furniture, ground*) Staub *m*. **covered in ~** staubbedeckt; **furniture etc also** ganz verstaubt; **to make or raise a lot of ~** (*lit, fig*) eine Menge Staub aufwirbeln; **a bit of ~** ein Staubkorn, ein Körnchen Staub *nt*; **clouds of interstellar ~** staubförmige interstellare Materie; **I'd like to get home and wash the ~ of the office/city off my hands and face** ich möchte gern nach Haus, um den Bürostaub/den Staub der Stadt abzuwaschen; **when the ~ had settled** (*fig*) als sich die Wogen wieder etwas geglättet hatten; *see* **bite, shake off.**
(b) **to give sb a ~** etw abstauben.
2 *vt* **(a)** furniture abstauben; room Staub wischen in (+ *dat*).
(b) (*Cook*) bestäuben.
3 *vi* (*housewife etc*) Staub wischen, abstauben. **she spent the morning ~ing** sie verbrachte den Morgen mit Staubwischen *or* Abstauben.
◆**dust down** *vt sep* person, sb's clothes (with brush) abbürsten; (with hand) abklopfen. **to ~ oneself ~** sich abbürsten; sich (*dat*) den Staub abklopfen.
◆**dust off** *vt sep* dirt abwischen, wegwischen; table, surface abstauben.
◆**dust out** *vt sep* box, cupboard auswischen.
dust: ~bath *n* Staubbad *nt*; **~bin** *n* (*Brit*) Mülltonne *f*; **~ bowl** *n* Trockengebiet *nt*; **~cart** *n* (*Brit*) Müllwagen *m*; **~ cloud** *n* Staubwolke *f*; **~coat** *n* Kittel *m*; **~cover** *n* (*on book*) (Schutz)-umschlag *m*; (*on furniture*) Schonbezug *m*.
duster ['dʌstə'] *n* **(a)** Staubtuch *nt*; (*Sch*) (Tafel)schwamm *m*. **(b)** (*Naut*) Schiffsflagge; *see* **red ~ . (c)** (*US: ~coat*) Kittel *m*.
dustfree ['dʌstfri:] *adj* staubfrei.
dusting ['dʌstɪŋ] *n* **(a)** (*of furniture*) Staubwischen, Abstauben *nt*. **to give sth a ~** etw abstauben, von etw den Staub abwischen; **to do the ~** Staub wischen, abstauben; **when I've finished the ~** wenn ich mit Staubwischen fertig bin.
(b) (*Cook etc: sprinkling*) (Be)stäuben *nt*.
(c) (*dated inf*) the colonel gave his officers a good ~ down der Oberst putzte seine Offiziere gründlich herunter (*inf*).
dust: ~ jacket *n* (Schutz)umschlag *m*; **~man** *n* (*Brit*) Müllmann, Müllkutscher (*inf*, *old*) *m*; **the ~men come on Fridays** freitags ist Müllabfuhr; **~pan** *n* Kehr- *or* Müllschaufel *f*; **~proof** *adj* staubdicht; **~sheet** *n* Tuch *nt* (*zum Abdecken unbenutzter Möbel*); **~ storm** *n* Staubsturm *m*; **~-trap** *n* Staubfänger *m*; **~-up** *n* (*dated inf*) Streit *m*, (handgreifliche) Auseinandersetzung.
dusty ['dʌstɪ] *adj* (+ *er*) table, path staubig. **to get ~** staubig werden; **the furniture gets very ~ in this room** die Möbel verstauben in diesem Zimmer sehr; **to get a ~ answer** (*dated inf*) eine unklare Antwort bekommen; **not so ~** (*dated inf*) gar nicht so übel *or* unflott (*inf*).
Dutch [dʌtʃ] **1** *adj* holländisch, niederländisch (*esp form*). **the ~ School** (*Art*) die Niederländische Schule; **~ cheese** Holländer Käse; **~ barn** (*Brit*) (offene) Scheune; **that's just ~ courage** (*inf*) er hat sich (*dat*) Mut angetrunken; **I need a little ~ courage** (*inf*) ich muß mir ein bißchen Mut antrinken; **~ door** quergeteilte Tür; **~ elm disease** Ulmensterben *nt*; **to talk to sb like a ~ uncle** (*inf*) jdm eine Standpauke halten.
2 *adv* **to go ~** (*inf*) getrennte Kasse machen.
3 *n* **(a)** the **~** die Holländer *or* Niederländer *pl*.
(b) (*language*) Holländisch, Niederländisch (*esp form*) *nt*.
(c) **my old ~** (*Brit sl*) meine gute Alte (*inf*).
Dutchman ['dʌtʃmən] *n, pl* **-men** [-mən] Holländer, Niederländer (*esp form*) *m*. **he did say that or I'm a ~** (*inf*) ich fresse einen Besen, wenn er das nicht gesagt hat (*inf*).
Dutchwoman ['dʌtʃˌwʊmən] *n, pl* **-women** [-ˌwɪmɪn] Holländerin, Niederländerin (*esp form*) *f*.
dutiable ['dju:tɪəbl] *adj* zollpflichtig.
dutiful ['dju:tɪfʊl] *adj* child gehorsam; husband, employee pflichtbewußt. **your ~ son** (*old, form: in letters*) Dein treuer Sohn (*old, form*).
dutifully ['dju:tɪfəlɪ] *adv* obey gehorsam; act pflichtbewußt.

duty ['djuːtɪ] n (a) Pflicht f. to do one's ~ seine Pflicht tun; to do one's ~ by sb seine Pflicht gegenüber jdm tun or erfüllen; it is my ~ to say or I am (in) ~ bound to say that ... es ist meine Pflicht zu sagen, daß ...; one's ~ to one's parents seine Pflicht (und Schuldigkeit) seinen Eltern gegenüber; it is my painful ~ to admit ... ich habe die schwere or traurige Pflicht, Ihnen zu gestehen ...; you don't know? but it's your ~ to know! du weißt das nicht? aber es ist deine verdammte Pflicht und Schuldigkeit, es zu wissen! (inf); to make it one's ~ to do sth es sich (dat) zur Pflicht machen, etw zu tun.
(b) (often pl: responsibility) Aufgabe, Pflicht f. to take up one's duties seine Pflichten aufnehmen; my duties consist of ... zu meinen Aufgaben or Pflichten gehört ...; to be on ~ (doctor etc) im Dienst sein; (Sch etc) Aufsicht haben; who's on ~ tomorrow? wer hat morgen Dienst/Aufsicht? he's off ~ nicht im Dienst sein; he comes off ~ at 9 sein Dienst endet um 9; Tuesday I'm off ~ Dienstag habe ich dienstfrei; he was called for overseas ~ er wurde nach Übersee eingezogen; to return to ~ den Dienst wieder aufnehmen; night ~ Nachtdienst m; he's been neglecting his duties as a husband er hat seine ehelichen Pflichten vernachlässigt; the box does ~ for a table die Kiste dient als Tisch.
(c) (Fin: tax) Zoll m. to pay ~ on sth Zoll auf etw (acc) zahlen; see estate ~ etc.

duty: ~ call n: a ~ call ein Höflichkeitsbesuch m; ~-free 1 adj zollfrei; ~-free shop Duty-free-Shop m; 2 n zollfreie Ware; ~ NCO n UvD m; ~ officer n Offizier m vom Dienst; ~ roster n Dienstplan m.

DV abbr of **deo volente** so Gott will.

dwarf [dwɔːf] 1 n, pl **dwarves** [dwɔːvz] Zwerg m; (tree) Zwergbaum m; (star) Zwergstern m.
2 adj person zwergenhaft; tree, star Zwerg-.
3 vt (a) klein erscheinen lassen, überragen; (through achievements, ability etc) in den Schatten stellen.
(b) (Hort) tree klein züchten.

dwell [dwel] pret, ptp **dwelt** vi (a) (liter: live) weilen (geh), leben, wohnen. (b) (fig) the thought dwelt in his mind der Gedanke haftete in seinem Gedächtnis.

♦**dwell (up)on** vi +prep obj (a) verweilen bei, sich länger aufhalten bei; (in thought) verweilen bei, länger nachdenken über (+acc). to ~ ~ the past sich ständig mit der Vergangenheit befassen; don't let's ~ ~ it wir wollen uns nicht (länger) damit aufhalten. (b) (Mus) note halten.

dweller ['dwelər] n Bewohner(in f) m; see country ~, flat-dweller.

dwelling ['dwelɪŋ] n (form: also ~ place) Wohnsitz m (form), Wohnung f. ~ house n Wohnhaus nt.

dwelt [dwelt] pret, ptp of **dwell**.

dwindle ['dwɪndl] vi (strength, interest, relevance) schwinden, abnehmen; (numbers, audiences) zurückgehen, abnehmen; (supplies) schrumpfen, zur Neige gehen.

♦**dwindle away** vi (strength, person) dahinschwinden; (supplies) zusammenschrumpfen.

dwindling ['dwɪndlɪŋ] n (of strength) Schwinden nt, Abnahme f; (of supplies) Schwinden nt; (of interest) Nachlassen nt, Abnahme f. 2 adj schwindend; resources versiegend.

dye [daɪ] 1 n Farbstoff m. hair ~ Haarfärbmittel nt; the ~ will come out in the wash die Farbe geht bei der Wäsche heraus; a crime of so deep a ~ (liter) ein derart abscheuliches or verwerfliches Verbrechen; a villain of the deepest ~ (liter) ein Schurke übelster or schlimmster Sorte.
2 vt färben.
3 vi (cloth etc) sich färben lassen.

dyed-in-the-wool ['daɪdɪnðə‚wʊl] adj durch und durch pred; attitude eingefleischt, in der Wolle gefärbt attr (geh).

dyer ['daɪər] n Färber(in f) m. ~'s and cleaner's Färberei und Reinigung.

dye: ~stuffs npl Farbstoffe pl; ~works n sing or pl Färberei f.

dying ['daɪɪŋ] 1 adj person sterbend; tradition, art, race, civilization aussterbend; embers verglühend; civilization untergehend; year ausklingend. he's a ~ man er liegt im Sterben; to my ~ day bis an mein Lebensende, bis zu meinem Tode; ~ wish letzter Wunsch; ~ words letzte Worte.
2 n the ~ die Sterbenden.

dyke, dike [daɪk] 1 n (a) (channel) (Entwässerungs)graben, Kanal m. (b) (barrier) Deich, Damm m; (causeway) Fahrdamm m. (c) (sl: lesbian) Lesbe f (sl). 2 vt land eindeichen; river eindämmen.

dynamic adj, ~ally adv [daɪ'næmɪk, -əlɪ] dynamisch.

dynamics [daɪ'næmɪks] n sing or pl Dynamik f.

dynamism ['daɪnəmɪzəm] n Dynamismus m; (of person) Dynamik f.

dynamite ['daɪnəmaɪt] 1 n (lit) Dynamit nt; (fig) Zünd- or Sprengstoff m. this new actress is ~ diese neue Schauspielerin ist eine Wucht (inf); this new piece of evidence is ~ dieses neue Beweisstück wird wie eine Bombe einschlagen; that story is ~ diese Geschichte ist der reinste Zündstoff.
2 vt rocks, bridge sprengen.

dynamo ['daɪnəməʊ] n Dynamo m.

dynastic [daɪ'næstɪk] adj dynastisch.

dynasty ['dɪnəstɪ] n Dynastie f.

dysentery ['dɪsɪntrɪ] n Dysenterie, Ruhr f.

dysfunction [dɪs'fʌnkʃən] n Funktionsstörung, Fehlfunktion f.

dyslexia [dɪs'leksɪə] n Legasthenie f.

dyslexic [dɪs'leksɪk] 1 adj legasthenisch. 2 n Legastheniker (in f) m.

dyspepsia [dɪs'pepsɪə] n Dyspepsie, Verdauungsstörung f.

dyspeptic [dɪs'peptɪk] 1 adj dyspeptisch. 2 n jd, der an Dyspepsie leidet.

dystrophy ['dɪstrəfɪ] n Dystrophie, Ernährungsstörung f. muscular ~ Muskelschwund m.

E

E, e [iː] n E, e nt; (Mus) E, e nt. **E flat/sharp** Es, es nt/Eis, eis nt; see also **major, minor, natural.**

E abbr of **east** O.

each [iːtʃ] 1 adj jede(r, s). ~ one of us/ ~ and every one of us jeder einzelne von uns; ~ and every boy jeder einzelne Junge (ohne Ausnahme); to back a horse ~ way auf alle drei Gewinnplätze setzen.
2 pron (a) jede(r, s). ~ of them gave their (inf) or his opinion sie sagten alle ihre Meinung, jeder (von ihnen) sagte seine Meinung; a little of ~ please ein bißchen von jedem, bitte; we ~ had our own ideas about it jeder von uns hatte seine eigene Vorstellung davon.
(b) ~ other sich, einander (geh); they get on ~ other's nerves sie gehen sich (dat) or einander auf die Nerven; they haven't seen ~ other for a long time sie haben sich or einander lange nicht gesehen; they wrote (to) ~ other sie haben sich (dat) or einander geschrieben; we visit ~ other wir besuchen uns (gegenseitig), wir besuchen einander; they were sorry for ~ other sie bedauerten sich gegenseitig, sie bedauerten einander; the respect/love they have for ~ other die Achtung, die sie voreinander haben/die Liebe, die sie füreinander empfinden; you must help ~ other ihr müßt einander helfen or euch gegenseitig helfen; on top of ~ other/next to ~ other aufeinander/nebeneinander.
3 adv je. we gave them one apple ~ wir haben ihnen je einen Apfel gegeben; two classes of 20 pupils ~ zwei Klassen mit je 20 Schülern; the books are £1 ~ die Bücher kosten je £ 1; carnations at one mark ~ Nelken zu einer Mark das Stück.

eager ['iːgər] adj person, discussion, pursuit eifrig. the ~ looks on their faces der erwartungsvolle Ausdruck in ihren Gesichtern; to be ~ to do sth darauf erpicht sein, etw zu tun, etw unbedingt tun wollen; he was ~ to please her/to help er war eifrig bedacht, sie zufriedenzustellen/äußerst willig zu helfen; children who are ~ to learn Kinder, die lerneifrig or lernbegierig or lernwillig sind; to be ~ for sth auf etw (acc) erpicht or aus sein; ~ for knowledge wißbegierig; he was ~ for happiness/affection es verlangte ihn nach Glück/Liebe; ~ beaver (inf) Arbeitstier nt (inf).

eagerly ['iːgəlɪ] adv eifrig; look, wait voll gespannter Ungeduld. we look forward ~ to the day when ... wir warten ungeduldig auf den Tag, an dem ...; they agreed so ~ it was suspicious sie stimmten so bereitwillig zu, daß es schon verdächtig war.

eagerness ['iːgənɪs] n Eifer m. ~ for knowledge/profit/power/vengeance/independence Wißbegierde f/Profit-/Machtgier f/Rachgier f/Unabhängigkeitsstreben nt; such was his ~ to please/help er war so darauf bedacht zu gefallen/seine Bereitwilligkeit zu helfen war so groß, ...

eagle ['iːgl] n Adler m; (Golf) Eagle nt.

eagle-eyed ['iːglaɪd] adj the ~ detective der Detektiv mit seinen Adleraugen.

eaglet ['iːglɪt] n Adlerjunge(s) nt.

ear[1] [ɪər] n (a) (Anat, fig) Ohr nt. to keep one's ~s open die Ohren offenhalten; to keep an ~ to the ground die Ohren aufsperren or offenhalten; to be all ~s ganz Ohr sein; your ~s must have been burning Ihnen müssen die Ohren geklungen haben; to lend an ~ to sb jdm sein Ohr leihen; if that came to or reached his ~s wenn ihm das zu Ohren kommt; he has the ~ of the king der König hört auf ihn; it goes in one ~ and out the other das geht zum einen Ohr hinein und zum anderen wieder hinaus; to be up to the ~s in debt bis über die or beide Ohren in

Schulden stecken; **to set two people by the ~s** zwei Leute gegeneinander aufbringen; **he'll be out on his ~** (*inf*) dann fliegt er raus (*inf*).

(b) (*sense of hearing*) Gehör, Ohr *nt*. **to have a good ~ for music** ein feines Gehör für Musik haben; **to play by ~** (*lit*) nach (dem) Gehör spielen; **to play it by ~** (*fig*) improvisieren; **these sounds are pleasing to the ~** diese Klänge schmeicheln dem Ohr *or* sind ein Ohrenschmaus *m*; **it is not exactly pleasing to the ~** das ist nicht gerade ein Ohrenschmaus *m*.

ear² [ɪəˊ] *n* (*of grain, plant*) Ähre *f*; (*of maize*) Kolben *m*.

ear: **~ache** *n* Ohrenschmerzen *pl*; **~drum** *n* Trommelfell *nt*.

-eared [-ɪəd] *adj suf* **long-/short-~** lang-/kurzohrig.

ear: **~ flap** *n* Ohrenklappe *f*; **~ful** *n* (*inf*) **to get an ~ful** mit einer Flut von Beschimpfungen überschüttet werden.

earl [ɜːl] *n* Graf *m*.

earldom [ˊɜːldəm] *n* (*land*) Grafschaft *f*; (*title*) Grafentitel *m*; (*rank*) Grafenstand *m*.

earlobe [ˊɪələʊb] *n* Ohrläppchen *nt*.

early [ˊɜːlɪ] **1** *adj* (+*er*) **(a) it was ~ in the morning** es war früh am Morgen; **to be an ~ riser** ein Frühaufsteher sein; **the ~ bird catches the worm** (*Prov*) Morgenstund hat Gold im Mund (*Prov*); (*first come first served*) wer zuerst kommt, mahlt zuerst (*Prov*); **~ to bed, ~ to rise (makes Jack healthy, wealthy and wise)** (*Prov*) früh ins Bett und früh heraus, frommt dem Leib, dem Geist, dem Haus (*Prov*); **in the ~ hours** in den frühen Morgenstunden; *see* **day.**

(b) (*near to beginning of period of time*) **in the ~ morning/afternoon** am frühen Morgen/Nachmittag; **in ~ spring** zu Anfang des Frühjahrs; **in his ~ youth** in seiner frühen Jugend; **in his earlier years he had ...** in jüngeren Jahren hatte er ...; **from an ~ age** von frühester Jugend *or* Kindheit an; **she's in her ~ forties** sie ist Anfang Vierzig; **in the ~ part of the century** Anfang des Jahrhunderts; **an ~ Baroque church** eine frühbarocke Kirche, eine Kirche aus dem Frühbarock.

(c) (*first, primitive*) **E~ Church** Urkirche *f*; **the ~ masters** (*Art*) die frühen Meister; **this is an ~ form of writing** das ist eine frühe Schriftform; **the mystery plays as an ~ form of moral education** die Mysterienspiele als Frühform der Moralerziehung.

(d) (*sooner than expected*) zu früh; *fruit, vegetable* Früh-.

(e) (*in the future*) **at an ~ date** bald; **at an earlier date** früher, eher; **at the earliest possible moment** so bald wie (irgend) möglich, möglichst bald; **to promise ~ delivery** baldige Lieferung versprechen.

2 *adv* früh(zeitig). **good morning, you're ~ today** guten Morgen, Sie sind heute ja früh dran; **post ~** geben Sie Ihre Post früh(zeitig) auf; **I get up earlier in summer** im Sommer stehe ich früher *or* zeitiger auf; **I cannot come earlier than Thursday** ich kann nicht vor Donnerstag *or* eher als Donnerstag kommen; **he told me earlier on this evening** er hat es mir früher am Abend gesagt; **I saw him earlier on this week** ich habe ihn Anfang der Woche gesehen; **earlier on that year** Jim had ... Jim hatte früher in dem Jahr ...; **the earliest he can come is ...** er kann frühestens ... kommen; **earlier on in the novel** an einer früheren Stelle in dem Roman; **~ in the morning** früh am Morgen; **~ in the year/in winter** Anfang des Jahres/Winters; **~ in May** Anfang Mai; **I learned that ~ in life** ich habe das früh im Leben gelernt; **too ~** zu früh; **as ~ as possible** so früh wie möglich, möglichst früh; **she left ten minutes ~** sie ist zehn Minuten früher gegangen; **he was half an hour ~ for the meeting** er kam eine halbe Stunde zu früh zur Versammlung.

early: **~ bird** *n* (*in morning*) Frühaufsteher(in *f*) *m*; (*arriving etc*) Frühankömmling *m*; **~ closing** *n* **it's ~ closing today** die Geschäfte haben *or* sind heute nachmittag geschlossen *or* zu (*inf*); **~-warning system** *n* Frühwarnsystem *nt*.

ear: **~mark** **1** *n* (*on animal*) Ohrmarke *f*; **2** *vt* (*fig*) vorsehen, bestimmen; **~-muffs** *npl* Ohrenschützer *pl*.

earn [ɜːn] *vt money, praise, rest* verdienen; (*Fin*) *interest* bringen. **this ~ed him a lot of money/respect** das trug ihm viel Geld/große Achtung ein, damit verdiente er sich (*dat*) viel Geld/große Achtung; **he's ~ed it** das hat er sich (*dat*) verdient; **~ed income** Einkommen *nt* aus Arbeit; **~ing capacity** Verdienstmöglichkeiten *pl*.

earnest [ˊɜːnɪst] **1** *adj* **(a)** (*serious, determined*) ernsthaft.

(b) *hope etc* aufrichtig; *prayer, desire also* ernstgemeint.

2 in ~ (*with determination*) ernsthaft; (*without joking*) im Ernst; **this time I'm in ~** diesmal meine ich es ernst, das ist mein Ernst; **it is snowing in ~** nun jetzt schneit es richtig.

earnestly [ˊɜːnɪstlɪ] *adv speak* ernsthaft; *beseech* ernstlich; *hope* aufrichtig.

earnestness [ˊɜːnɪstnɪs] *n* Ernsthaftigkeit *f*; (*of voice*) Ernst *m*.

earnings [ˊɜːnɪŋz] *npl* (*of person*) Verdienst *m*; (*of a business also*) Ertrag *m*.

ear: **~, nose and throat** *adj attr* Hals-, Nasen- und Ohren-; **~phones** *npl* Kopfhörer *pl*; **~-piece** *n* Hörer *m*; **~-plug** *n* Ohrwatte *f*, Ohropax ® *nt*; **~-ring** *n* Ohrring *m*; **~shot** *n*: **out of/within ~shot** außer/in Hörweite; **~-splitting** *adj sound, scream* ohrenbetäubend; *din* Höllen-.

earth [ɜːθ] **1** *n* **(a)** (*world*) Erde *f*. **the ~, E~** die Erde; **on ~** auf der Erde, auf Erden (*liter*); **to the ends of the ~** bis ans Ende der Welt; **where/who** *etc* **on ~?** (*inf*) wo/wer *etc* ... bloß?; **what on ~?** (*inf*) was in aller Welt (*inf*), was bloß (*inf*); **nothing on ~ will stop me now** keine Macht der Welt hält mich jetzt noch auf; **heaven on ~** der Himmel auf Erden; **it cost the ~** (*inf*) das hat eine schöne Stange Geld gekostet (*inf*); **it won't cost the ~** (*inf*) es wird schon nicht die Welt kosten (*inf*).

(b) (*ground*) Erde *f*. **to fall to ~** zur Erde fallen; **to come back** *or* **down to ~ (again)** (*fig*) wieder auf den Boden der Tatsachen (zurück)kommen; **to bring sb down to ~ (with a bump)** (*fig*) jdn (unsanft) wieder auf den Boden der Tatsachen zurückholen.

(c) (*soil*) Erde *f*.

(d) (*Elec*) Erde *f*.

(e) (*of fox, badger etc*) Bau *m*. **to go to ~** (*fox*) im Bau verschwinden; (*criminal etc*) untertauchen; **to run sb/sth to ~** (*fig*) jdn/etw ausfindig machen *or* aufstöbern.

2 *vt* (*Elec*) erden.

♦**earth up** *vt sep plant* ausgraben.

earth: **~-bound** *adj* **(a)** erdgebunden; **(b) the spacecraft is on its ~-bound journey** das Raumschiff ist auf dem Rückflug zur Erde; **~ closet** *n* Trockenabort *m*.

earthen [ˊɜːθən] *adj* irden.

earthenware [ˊɜːθənwɛəˊ] **1** *n* (*material*) Ton *m*; (*dishes etc*) Tongeschirr *nt*. **2** *adj* aus Ton, Ton-.

earthiness [ˊɜːθɪnɪs] *n* Derbheit *f*.

earthling [ˊɜːθlɪŋ] *n* (*pej*) Erdenwurm *m*.

earthly [ˊɜːθlɪ] **1** *adj* **(a)** (*of this world*) irdisch.

(b) (*inf: possible*) **there is no ~ reason to think ...** es besteht nicht der geringste Grund für die Annahme ...; **for no ~ reason** ohne den geringsten Grund; **he hasn't an ~ chance of succeeding** er hat nicht die geringste Aussicht auf Erfolg; **this thing is of no ~ use** das Ding hat nicht den geringsten Nutzen.

2 *n* (*inf*) **she hasn't got an ~** sie hat ja im Leben keine Chance.

earth: **~-moving equipment** *n* Maschinen *pl* für Erdbewegungen; **~quake** *n* Erdbeben *nt*; **~ tremor** *n* Erdstoß *m*; **~ward(s)** *adv* auf die Erde zu, in Richtung Erde, erdwärts (*geh*); **~work** *n* (*Build*) Erdarbeiten *pl*; (*Mil*) Schanzwerk *nt*, Schanze *f*; **~worm** *n* Regenwurm *m*.

earthy [ˊɜːθɪ] *adj* (+*er*) **(a)** *taste, smell* erdig. **(b)** *person, humour* derb.

ear: **~-trumpet** *n* Hörrohr *nt*; **~-wax** *n* Ohrenschmalz *nt*; **~wig** *n* Ohrwurm *m*.

ease [iːz] **1** *n* **(a)** (*freedom from discomfort*) Behagen *nt*. **I am never at ~ in this dress** ich fühle mich in diesem Kleid nie ganz wohl; **I am never at ~ in his company** in seiner Gesellschaft fühle ich mich immer befangen *or* fühle ich mich nie frei und ungezwungen; **to put** *or* **set sb at his ~** jdn die Befangenheit nehmen; **to put** *or* **set sb's mind at ~** jdn beruhigen; **my mind is at ~ now** jetzt bin ich beruhigt; **to take one's ~** es sich (*dat*) bequem machen; (*Mil*) (**stand**) **at ~!** rührt euch!

(b) (*absence of difficulty*) Leichtigkeit *f*. **with ~** mit Leichtigkeit; **I admire the ~ of his manners** seine Ungezwungenheit imponiert mir.

(c) (*absence of work*) Muße *f*. **he lives a life of ~** er führt ein Leben der Muße.

2 *vt* **(a)** (*relieve*) *pain* hindern; *mind* erleichtern. **to ~ sb of a burden/a few pounds** (*hum inf*) jdm eine Last abnehmen, jdm eine Last von der Seele nehmen/jdn um ein paar Pfund erleichtern (*hum inf*).

(b) (*make less, loosen*) *rope, strap* lockern, nachlassen; *dress etc* weiter machen; *pressure, tension* verringern.

(c) to ~ a key into a lock einen Schlüssel behutsam in ein Schloß stecken *or* einführen; **to ~ in the clutch** (*Aut*) die Kupplung behutsam kommen lassen; **he ~d the car into gear** er legte behutsam einen Gang ein; **he ~d out the screw** er drehte die Schraube behutsam heraus; **he ~d the lid off** er löste den Deckel behutsam ab; **he ~d his broken leg up onto the stretcher** er hob sein gebrochenes Bein behutsam auf die Trage.

3 *vi* nachlassen; (*situation*) sich entspannen; (*prices also*) nachgeben. **he ~d down into second gear** er schaltete behutsam in den zweiten Gang zurück.

♦**ease off** *or* **up** *vi* **(a)** (*slow down, relax*) langsamer werden; (*driver*) verlangsamen; (*situation*) sich entspannen. **~ a bit!** (etwas) langsamer!, sachte, sachte!; **the doctor told him to ~ a bit at work** der Arzt riet ihm, bei der Arbeit etwas kürzer zu treten; **things usually ~ ~ a little just after Christmas** nach Weihnachten wird es normalerweise etwas ruhiger *or* geruhsamer; **there'll be no easing ~ until we've finished!** es wird keine Ruhepause geben, bis wir fertig sind.

(b) (*pain, rain*) nachlassen.

easel [ˊiːzl] *n* Staffelei *f*.

easily [ˊiːzɪlɪ] *adv* **(a)** (*without difficulty*) leicht. **he learnt to swim ~** er lernte mühelos schwimmen; **he can run 3 miles ~** er läuft leicht *or* mit Leichtigkeit drei Meilen.

(b) (*without doubt*) gut und gerne. **he is ~ the best/winner** er ist mit Abstand der beste/der Sieger; **it's ~ 25 miles** es sind gut und gerne 25 Meilen.

(c) (*possibly*) leicht. **he may ~ change his mind** er kann es sich (*dat*) leicht noch anders überlegen.

(d) (*calmly*) gelassen.

easiness [ˊiːzɪnɪs] *n* Leichtigkeit *f*.

east [iːst] **1** *n* **(a)** (*Osten m*). **in/to the ~** im Osten/nach *or* gen (*old, poet*) Osten; **from the ~** von Osten; **to the ~ of** östlich von; **the wind is blowing from the ~** der Wind kommt von Ost(en) *or* aus (dem) Osten.

(b) (*Geog, Pol*) **the E~** der Osten; **from the E~** aus dem Osten; *see* **Far ~, Middle ~, Near ~.**

2 *adv* nach Osten, ostwärts. **~ of** östlich von.

3 *adj* östlich, Ost-. **~ wind** Ostwind *m*.

east: **E~ Africa** *n* Ostafrika *nt*; **E~ Berlin** *n* Ostberlin *nt*; **~bound** *adj traffic, carriageway* (in) Richtung Osten; **E~ End** *n*: **the E~ End** der (Londoner) Osten.

Easter [ˊiːstəˊ] **1** *n* Ostern *nt*. **at ~** an *or* zu Ostern. **2** *adj attr week, egg* Oster-. **~ Island** Osterinsel *f*; **~ Monday** Ostermontag *m*; **~ Sunday, ~ Day** Ostersonntag *m*.

easterly [ˊiːstəlɪ] *adj* östlich, Ost-. **in an ~ direction** in östlicher Richtung.

eastern [ˊiːstən] *adj* Ost-, östlich; *attitude* orientalisch. **the ~ bloc** der Ostblock.

easterner [ˊiːstənəˊ] *n* (*esp US*) Oststaatler(in *f*) *m*. **he's an ~** er kommt aus dem Osten.

easternmost [ˊiːstənməʊst] *adj* östlichst.

east: **E~ German** *adj* ostdeutsch, DDR-; **E~ Germany** *n*

Ostdeutschland *nt*, die DDR; **E~ Indies** *npl* Ostindien *nt* (*old*), der Malaiische Archipel; **~ward, ~wardly 1** *adj* östlich; **in an ~wardly direction** nach Osten, (in) Richtung Osten; **2** *adv* (*also* **~wards**) ostwärts, nach Osten.

easy ['iːzɪ] **1** *adj* (+*er*) **(a)** (*not difficult*) leicht. **it is as ~ as anything** das ist kinderleicht; **it is ~ to see that ...** es ist leicht zu sehen, daß ...; **it is ~ for him to do that** das ist leicht für ihn; **it's ~ for you to say that** du hast leicht reden; **he was an ~ winner, he came in an ~ first** es war ihm ein leichtes zu gewinnen (*geh*), er hat mühelos gewonnen; **he is ~ to work with** man kann gut mit ihm arbeiten; **he is ~ to get on with** mit ihm kann man gut auskommen; **~ money** leicht verdientes Geld.

(b) (*free from discomfort etc*) bequem, leicht; *manners, movement* ungezwungen; *style* flüssig. **in ~ stages** in gemütlichen Etappen; (*pay, persuade sb*) nach und nach; **on ~ terms** (*Comm*) zu günstigen Bedingungen; **I'm ~** , (*inf*) mir ist alles recht; **at an ~ pace** in gemütlichem Tempo; **a colour which is ~ on the eyes** eine Farbe, die angenehm für die Augen ist.

(c) (*St Ex*) *market* ruhig.

2 *adv* ~!, ~ **now!, ~ does it!** immer sachte!; **to take things *or* it ~** (*healthwise*) sich schonen; **take it ~ !** (*don't worry*) nimm's nicht so schwer; (*don't get carried away, don't rush*) immer mit der Ruhe!; **to go ~ on *or* with sth** sparsam mit etw umgehen; **to go ~ on the brakes/one's liver** die Bremsen/seine Leber schonen; **to go ~ on sb** nicht zu hart *or* streng mit jdm sein; **look, go ~, that's got to last us all night** sachte, sachte (*inf*), das muß die ganze Nacht reichen; **stand ~!** (*Mil*) rührt euch!

easy: **~ chair** *n* Sessel *m*; **~ come ~ go 1** *interj* wie gewonnen, so zerronnen (*Prov*); **2** *adj* ~**-come ~-go** unbekümmert; **~-going** *adj* (*not anxious*) gelassen; (*lax*) lax, lässig.

eat [iːt] (*vb*: *pret* **ate**, *ptp* **eaten**) **1** *vt* (*pej*) essen, fressen (*pej inf*); (*animal*) fressen. **to ~ one's breakfast** frühstücken; **" ~ before July 2"** zu verzehren bis: 2. Juli"; **he ate his way through ...** er aß sich durch ...; **he's ~ing us out of house and home** (*inf*) der (fr)ißt uns noch arm *or* die Haare vom Kopf (*inf*); **to ~ one's words** (alles), was man gesagt hat, zurücknehmen; **I'll make him ~ his words** ich bringe ihn dazu, daß er das zurücknimmt; **he won't ~ you** (*inf*) er wird dich schon nicht fressen (*inf*); **what's ~ing you?** (*inf*) was hast du denn?

2 *vi* essen, fressen (*pej inf*); (*animal*) fressen. **I haven't ~en for ages** ich habe schon ewig nichts mehr gegessen.

3 *n* (*inf*) ~**s** *pl* Fressalien *pl* (*inf*); **time for ~s!** Fütterung der Raubtiere! (*inf*).

♦ eat away *vt sep* (*sea*) auswaschen; (*acid*) zerfressen.

♦ eat into *vt +prep obj* *metal* anfressen; *capital* angreifen.

♦ eat out 1 *vi* zum Essen ausgehen. **2** *vt sep* **to ~ one's heart ~** Trübsal blasen, sich vor Gram verzehren (*geh*); **Michael Parkinson, ~ your heart ~** Michael Parkinson, da kannst du vor Neid erblassen.

♦ eat up 1 *vt sep* **(a)** aufessen; (*animal*) auffressen. **(b)** (*fig*: *use up, consume*) verbrauchen, fressen (*inf*). **this car ~s ~ the miles** der Wagen gibt ganz schön was her (*inf*). **(c)** **he was ~en ~ with envy** der Neid nagte *or* zehrte an ihm.

2 *vi* aufessen.

eatable ['iːtəbl] *adj* eßbar, genießbar. **it's very ~** das ist durchaus genießbar.

eat-by date ['iːtbaɪdeɪt] *n* Haltbarkeitsdatum *nt*.

eaten ['iːtn] *ptp of* **eat.**

eater ['iːtəʳ] *n* **(a)** Esser(in *f*) *m*. **(b)** (*apple*) Eßapfel *m*.

eating ['iːtɪŋ] *n* Essen *nt*. **to make good ~** gut zum Essen sein.

eating: **~ apple** *n* Eßapfel *m*; **~-house** *n* Gasthaus *nt*; **~ place** *n* Eßlokal *nt*.

eau de Cologne ['əʊdəkə'ləʊn] *n* Kölnisch Wasser, Eau de Cologne *nt*.

eaves ['iːvz] *npl* Dachvorsprung *m*.

eavesdrop ['iːvzdrɒp] *vi* (heimlich) lauschen. **to ~ on a conversation** ein Gespräch belauschen.

eavesdropper ['iːvzdrɒpəʳ] *n* Lauscher *m*.

ebb [eb] **1** *n* Ebbe *f*. **~ and flow** Ebbe und Flut *f*; (*fig*) Auf und Ab *nt*; **~ tide** Ebbe; **at a low ~** (*fig*) auf einem Tiefstand. **2** *vi* **(a)** (*tide*) zurückgehen. **to ~ and flow** (*lit*, *fig*) kommen und gehen. **(b)** (*fig*: *also* **~ away**) (*enthusiasm etc*) ab- *or* verebben.

ebonite ['ebənaɪt] *n* Ebonit *nt*.

ebony ['ebənɪ] **1** *n* Ebenholz *nt*. **2** *adj* *colour* schwarz wie Ebenholz; *material* aus Ebenholz.

ebullience [ɪ'bʌlɪəns] *n* Überschwenglichkeit *f*. **the ~ of youth** jugendlicher Überschwang.

ebullient [ɪ'bʌlɪənt] *adj* *person* überschwenglich; *spirits, mood* übersprudelnd.

eccentric [ɪk'sentrɪk] **1** *adj* **(a)** *person* exzentrisch. **(b)** *load* schief, ungleich; *orbit, curve, circles* exzentrisch. **2** *n* **(a)** (*person*) Exzentriker(in *f*) *m*. **(b)** (*Tech*) Exzenter *m*.

eccentrically [ɪk'sentrɪkəlɪ] *adv* exzentrisch.

eccentricity [.eksən'trɪsɪtɪ] *n* (*all senses*) Exzentrizität *f*.

Ecclesiastes [ɪ.kliːzɪ'æstiːz] *n* (der Prediger) Salomo *m*.

ecclesiast [ɪ.kliːzɪ'æst] *n* Kleriker *m*.

ecclesiastical [ɪ.kliːzɪ'æstɪkəl] *adj* kirchlich.

ECG *abbr of* **electrocardiogram** EKG *nt*.

echelon ['eʃəlɒn] *n* (*Mil*) (*formation*) Staffelung *f*, Echelon *m* (*old*). **the higher ~s** die höheren Ränge *pl*.

echo ['ekəʊ] **1** *n* Echo *nt*, Widerhall *m*; (*fig*) Anklang *m* (*of an* +*acc*). **he was cheered to the ~** er bekam brausenden *or* rauschenden Beifall. **2** *vt* **(a)** (*wall, mountain*) *sound* zurückwerfen. **(b)** (*fig*) wiedergeben. **3** *vi* (*sounds*) widerhallen; (*room*) hallen. **to ~ with sth** von etw widerhallen; **it ~s in here** hier ist ein Echo.

echo: **~ chamber** *n* Hallraum *m*; (*for electric guitar*) Nachhall-Erzeuger *m*; **~-sounder** *n* Echolot *nt*.

éclair [eɪ'kleəʳ] *n* Eclair *nt*, Liebesknochen *m*.

eclectic [ɪ'klektɪk] *adj* eklektisch.

eclecticism [ɪ'klektɪsɪzəm] *n* Eklektizismus *m*.

eclipse [ɪ'klɪps] **1** *n* (*Astron*) Eklipse (*spec*), Finsternis *f*; (*fig*) (*of fame, theory*) Verblassen *nt*; (*of person*) Niedergang *m*. **~ of the sun/moon** Sonnen-/Mondfinsternis *f*; **to be in ~** (*sun, moon*) verfinstert sein; (*fig*) in der Versenkung verschwunden sein.

2 *vt* (*Astron*) verfinstern; (*fig*) in den Schatten stellen.

ecological [.iːkə'lɒdʒɪkəl] *adj* ökologisch.

ecologist [ɪ'kɒlədʒɪst] *n* Ökologe *m*, Ökologin *f*.

ecology [ɪ'kɒlədʒɪ] *n* Ökologie *f*.

economic [.iːkə'nɒmɪk] *adj* (*all senses*) wirtschaftlich, ökonomisch; *development, factor, system also, geography* Wirtschafts-.

economical [.iːkə'nɒmɪkəl] *adj* wirtschaftlich, ökonomisch; *person also* sparsam. **to be ~ with sth** mit etw haushalten *or* sparsam umgehen; **he's a very ~ runner** er geht beim Laufen sehr sparsam mit seinen Kräften um; **to be ~ (to run)** (*car*) (in der Haltung) wirtschaftlich sein.

economically [.iːkə'nɒmɪkəlɪ] *adv* wirtschaftlich; (*thriftily*) sparsam. **to use sth ~** mit etw wirtschaftlich umgehen/etw sparsam verwenden, mit etw sparsam umgehen; **one has to be ~ minded** man muß wirtschaftlich *or* ökonomisch denken; **~ yes but ... in** wirtschaftlicher Hinsicht schon, aber ...

economics [.iːkə'nɒmɪks] *n* **(a)** *with sing or pl vb* Volkswirtschaft *f*, Wirtschaftswissenschaften *pl*, Ökonomie *f*; (*social ~*) Volkswirtschaft *f*; (*in management studies*) Betriebswirtschaft *f*.

(b) *pl* (*economic aspect*) Wirtschaftlichkeit, Ökonomie *f*. **the ~ of the situation** die wirtschaftliche Seite der Situation.

economist [ɪ'kɒnəmɪst] *n* *see* **economics** Wirtschaftswissenschaftler(in *f*), Ökonom *m* (*dated*); Volkswirt(in *f*), Volkswirtschaftler(in *f*) *m*; Betriebswirt(in *f*), Betriebswirtschaftler(in *f*) *m*.

economize [ɪ'kɒnəmaɪz] *vi* sparen.

♦ economize on *vi +prep obj* sparen.

economy [ɪ'kɒnəmɪ] *n* **(a)** (*system*) Wirtschaft *f* *no pl*; (*from a monetary system*) Konjunktur *f*. **what is the state of the ~?** wie ist die Wirtschaftslage/Konjunktur?; **to improve our economies** um die Wirtschaft (unserer Länder) zu verbessern/Konjunktur (in unseren Ländern) anzukurbeln.

(b) (*in time, money*) Sparmaßnahme, Einsparung *f*. **an ~ in time** eine Zeitersparnis; **a false ~** Sparen *nt* am falschen Ende, falsche Sparsamkeit.

(c) (*thrift*) Sparsamkeit *f*. **housewives should practise ~** Hausfrauen sollten Sparsamkeit walten lassen; **his ~ of style** sein knapper Stil; **he has run the race with great ~** er hat seine Kräfte gut eingeteilt; **with ~ of effort** mit sparsamem Kräfteaufwand.

economy: **~ class** *n* Touristenklasse *f*; **~ drive** *n* Sparmaßnahmen *pl*; **we'll have to have an ~ drive** wir werden Sparmaßnahmen ergreifen müssen; **~ size** *n* Sparpackung *f*.

ecru [e'kruː] *adj* (*US*) naturfarben, ekrü.

ecstasy ['ekstəsɪ] *n* Ekstase, Verzückung *f*. **to go into/to be in ecstasies over sth** über etw (*acc*) in Ekstase *or* Verzückung geraten; **~! she sighed** welche Wonne! seufzte sie.

ecstatic *adj*, **~ally** *adv* [eks'tætɪk, -əlɪ] ekstatisch, verzückt.

ECT *abbr of* **electro-convulsive therapy** Elektroschock *m*, Elektrokrampftherapie *f*.

ectomorph ['ektəʊmɔːf] *n* ektomorpher Konstitutionstyp.

ectoplasm ['ektəʊplæzəm] *n* Ektoplasma *nt*.

Ecuador ['ekwədɔːʳ] *n* Ecuador, Ekuador *nt*.

Ecuador(i)an [.ekwə'dɔːr(ɪ)ən] **1** *adj* ecuadorianisch, ekuadorianisch. **2** *n* Ecuadorianer(in *f*), Ekuadorianer(in *f*) *m*.

ecumenical [.iːkjuː'menɪkəl] *adj* ökumenisch. **E~ Council** Ökumenischer Rat.

eczema ['eksɪmə] *n* Ekzem *nt*, (Haut)ausschlag *m*.

ed *abbr of* **editor** Verf, Verfasser *m*; **edition** Ausg, Ausgabe *f*; **edited** hg, herausgegeben.

Edam ['iːdæm] *n* Edamer (Käse) *m*.

eddy ['edɪ] **1** *n* Wirbel *m*; (*of water also*) Strudel *m*. **the wind swept the leaves in eddies down the avenue** der Wind wirbelte die Blätter durch die Allee. **2** *vi* wirbeln; (*water also*) strudeln.

edelweiss ['eɪdlvaɪs] *n* Edelweiß *nt*.

edema [ɪ'diːmə] *n* (*esp US*) Ödem *nt*.

Eden ['iːdn] *n* (*also fig*): **Garden of ~** Garten *m* Eden.

edge [edʒ] **1** *n* **(a)** (*of knife, razor*) Schneide *f*. **to put an ~ on a knife** ein Messer schleifen; **to take the ~ off** a blade eine Klinge stumpf machen; **to take the ~ off sth** (*fig*) *sensation* etw der Wirkung (*gen*) berauben; *pain* etw lindern; **that took the ~ off my appetite** das nahm mir erst einmal den Hunger; **the noise/taste sets my teeth on ~** das Geräusch geht mir durch und durch/der Geschmack ist mir unangenehm an den Zähnen; **to be on ~** nervös sein; **my nerves are all on ~** ich bin schrecklich nervös; **to have the ~ on sb/sth** jdm/etw überlegen sein; **but the professional had just that little extra ~** aber der Profi war eben doch noch etwas besser; **it gives her/it that extra ~** darin besteht eben der kleine Unterschied.

(b) (*outer limit*) Rand *m*; (*of cloth, table also, of brick, cube*) Kante *f*; (*of lake, river also, of sea*) Ufer *nt*; (*of estates etc*) Grenze *f*. **a book with gilt ~s** ein Buch mit Goldschnitt; **the trees at the ~ of the road** die Bäume am Straßenrand; **to be on the ~ of disaster** am Rande des Untergangs stehen.

2 *vt* **(a)** (*put a border on*) besetzen, einfassen **to ~ a coat with fur** einen Mantel mit Pelz verbrämen.

(b) (*sharpen*) *tool, blade* schärfen, schleifen, scharf machen.

(c) **to ~ one's way towards sth/forwards** (*slowly*) sich allmählich auf etw (*acc*) zubewegen/sich allmählich vorwärts bewegen; (*carefully*) sich vorsichtig auf etw (*acc*) zubewegen/sich vorsichtig vorwärts bewegen; **she ~d her way through the guests** sie schlängelte sich durch die Gäste; **the prisoner ~d his way along the wall** der Gefangene schob sich langsam der Wand entlang; **he ~d his chair nearer the door** er rückte mit seinem Stuhl allmählich auf die Tür zu.

3 *vi* sich schieben. **to ~ out of a room** sich aus einem Zimmer stehlen; **to ~ away from sb/sth** sich allmählich immer weiter von jdm/etw entfernen; **I could see him edging away towards the perimeter fence** ich beobachtete, wie er sich allmählich immer weiter in Richtung Grenzzaun entfernte; **to ~ up to sb** sich an jdn heranmachen; **he ~d past me** er drückte *or* schob sich an mir vorbei.

edgeways ['edʒweɪz] *adv* mit der Schmalseite voran. **to stand a brick ~** einen Ziegel hochkant stellen; **I couldn't get a word in ~** ich bin überhaupt nicht zu Wort gekommen.

edging ['edʒɪŋ] *n* Borte, Einfassung *f*; *(of ribbon, silk also)* Paspel *f*. **~-shears** Rasenschere *f*.

edgy ['edʒɪ] *adj (+er) person* nervös.

edible ['edɪbl] *adj* eßbar, genießbar. **very ~!** durchaus genießbar!

edict ['iːdɪkt] *n* Erlaß *m*; *(Hist)* Edikt *nt*.

edification [ˌedɪfɪ'keɪʃən] *n* Erbauung *f*. **for the ~ of ...** zur Erbauung der ...

edifice ['edɪfɪs] *n* (*lit, fig*) Gebäude *nt*; (*fig also*) Gefüge *nt*.

edify ['edɪfaɪ] *vt* erbauen.

edifying ['edɪfaɪɪŋ] *adj* erbaulich.

edit ['edɪt] **1** *vt series, author, newspaper, magazine* herausgeben, edieren; *newspaper story, book, text* redigieren; *film, tape* schneiden, cutten, montieren; *(editing terminal) data* zum Druck aufbereiten; *tape* redigieren. **~ed by: ...** *(Film)* Schnitt: ... **2** *vi* redigieren, redaktionell arbeiten.

♦**edit out** *vt sep* herausnehmen; *(from film, tape)* herausschneiden; *character from story* herausstreichen.

editing terminal *n* Redigiertastatur *f*.

edition [ɪ'dɪʃən] *n* Ausgabe, Edition *f*; *(impression)* Auflage *f*.

editor ['edɪtəʳ] *n (of text, newspaper, magazine, series, author)* Herausgeber(in *f*) *m*; *(publisher's)* (Verlags)lektor(in *f*) *m*; *(Film)* Cutter(in *f*) *m*; *(Computers)* Editor *m*. **political/sports ~** politischer Redakteur/Sportredakteur *m*; **~-in-chief** Herausgeber *m*; *(of newspaper)* Chefredakteur *m*; **the ~s in our educational department** die Redaktion unserer Schulbuchabteilung; **the ~ of this passage obviously misunderstood** der, der diese Stelle redigierte, hat offensichtlich nicht richtig verstanden.

editorial [ˌedɪ'tɔːrɪəl] **1** *adj* redaktionell, Redaktions-. **~ assistant** Redaktionsassistent(in *f*) *m*; **~ office** Redaktion *f*; *(Publishing also)* (Verlags)lektorat *nt*; **~ staff** Redaktion(sangestellte *pl*) *f*; **he is ~ staff** er arbeitet in der Redaktion; **there's an ~ job going in the Bible Department** in der Bibelabteilung ist eine Lektorenstelle zu besetzen; **some tricky ~ problems in the text** einige knifflige redaktionelle Textprobleme.
2 *n* Leitartikel *m*.

editorially [ˌedɪ'tɔːrɪəlɪ] *adv* redaktionell.

editorship ['edɪtəʃɪp] *n (of newspaper, magazine)* Chefredaktion, Schriftleitung *f*. **under the general ~ of ...** unter ... als Herausgeber; **skills of ~** Fähigkeiten als Redakteur/Verlagslektor.

educable ['edjʊkəbl] *adj* erziehbar; *(academically)* ausbildbar.

educate ['edjʊkeɪt] *vt* **(a)** erziehen. **he was ~d at Eton** er ist in Eton zur Schule gegangen; **the public must first be ~d about the health risks** die Öffentlichkeit muß zuerst einmal über die gesundheitlichen Gefahren aufgeklärt werden.
(b) *the mind* schulen; *one's tastes* (aus)bilden. **an influence which has clearly ~d the general public's taste** ein Einfluß, der den allgemeinen Geschmack deutlich geprägt hat.

educated ['edjʊkeɪtɪd] *adj* gebildet. **to make an ~ guess** eine fundierte *or* wohlbegründete Vermutung anstellen.

education [ˌedjʊ'keɪʃən] *n* Erziehung *f*; *(studies, training)* Ausbildung *f*; *(knowledge, culture)* Bildung *f*. **Ministry of E~** Ministerium *nt* für Erziehung und Unterricht, Kultusministerium *nt*; **lecturer in ~** Dozent(in *f*) *m* für Pädagogik; **College of E~** Pädagogische Hochschule; *(for graduates)* Studienseminar *nt*; **to study ~** Pädagogik *or* Erziehungswissenschaften studieren; **if the Government neglects ~** wenn die Regierung das Erziehungs- und Ausbildungswesen vernachlässigt; **the ~ budget** der Etat für das Erziehungs- und Ausbildungswesen; **~ is free** die Schulausbildung ist kostenlos; **his ~ was interrupted** seine Ausbildung wurde unterbrochen; **the ~ which he received at school** seine Schulbildung; **haven't you got any ~?** hast du denn überhaupt keine Bildung?; **a good literary/scientific ~** ein gute literarische/naturwissenschaftliche Bildung; **the ~ of one's taste buds** to appreciate ... (Aus)bildung seines Geschmacks für ...

educational [ˌedjʊ'keɪʃənl] *adj pädagogisch; methods, work also* Erziehungs-; *films, games also* Lehr-; *role, function also* erzieherisch; *publisher also* Schulbuch-, Lehrbuch-. **a very ~ experience** eine sehr lehrreiche Erfahrung.

education(al)ist [ˌedjʊ'keɪʃn(ə)lɪst] *n* Pädagoge *m*, Pädagogin *f*, Erziehungswissenschaftler(in *f*) *m*.

educationally [ˌedjʊ'keɪʃnəlɪ] *adj* pädagogisch.

educative ['edjʊkətɪv] *adj* erzieherisch.

educator ['edjʊkeɪtəʳ] *n* Pädagoge, Erzieher *m*. **an ~ of the people** ein Erzieher des Volkes.

educe [ɪ'djuːs] *vt (form)* ableiten *(from sth von etw)*; entlocken *(from sb jdm)*.

Edward ['edwəd] *n* Eduard *m*.

Edwardian [ed'wɔːdɪən] **1** *adj* aus der Zeit Eduards VII. **in ~ days** unter Eduard VII., im ersten Jahrzehnt des 20. Jahrhunderts. **2** *n* Zeitgenosse *m* Eduards VII.

EEC *abbr of* **European Economic Community** EWG *f*.

eel [iːl] *n* Aal *m*; *see* **slippery**.

e'en [iːn] *adv (poet) contr of* **even**[1].

e'er [eəʳ] *adv (poet) contr of* **ever**.

eerie, eery *adj (+er)*, **eerily** *adv* ['ɪərɪ, -lɪ] unheimlich; *sound also* schaurig.

---

efface [ɪ'feɪs] *vt* auslöschen. **to ~ oneself** sich zurückhalten.

effect [ɪ'fekt] **1** *n* **(a)** *(result)* Wirkung *f*, Effekt *m*; *(repercussion)* Auswirkung *f*. **the ~ of an acid on metal** die Wirkung einer Säure auf Metall; **alcohol has the ~ of dulling your senses** Alkohol bewirkt eine Abstumpfung der Sinne; **the ~ of this rule will be to prevent ...** diese Regelung wird die Verhinderung von ... bewirken *or* zur Folge haben; **the ~ of this is that ...** das hat zur Folge, daß ...; **the ~s of radioactivity on the human body** die Auswirkungen radioaktiver Strahlen auf den menschlichen Körper; **to feel the ~s of an accident/of drink** die Folgen eines Unfalls/des Trinkens spüren; **to no ~** erfolglos, ergebnislos; **our warning was to no ~** unsere Warnung hatte keine Wirkung; **to such good ~ that** so wirkungsvoll, daß ...; **to put one's knowledge into ~** seine Kenntnisse anwenden; **to have an ~ on sb/sth** eine Wirkung auf jdn/etw haben; **to have no ~** keine Wirkung haben; **to take ~** *(drug)* wirken.
(b) *(impression)* Wirkung *f*, Effekt *m*. **to create an ~** eine Wirkung *or* einen Effekt erzielen; **to give a good ~** einen guten Effekt ergeben; **literary ~** literarischer Effekt; **~s of light** *(Art)* Lichteffekte *pl*; **the sword was only for ~** der Degen war nur zum Effekt da; **it's all done solely for ~** es wird alles bloß des Effekts wegen *or* aus Effekthascherei *(pej)* getan.
(c) *(meaning)* **his letter is to the ~ that ...** sein Brief hat zum Inhalt, daß ...; **we received his letter to the ~ that ...** wir erhielten sein Schreiben des Inhalts, daß ...; **an announcement to the ~ that ...** eine Erklärung des Inhalts, daß ...; **he used words to that ~** ... sinngemäß drückte er sich so aus; **... or words to that ~** ... oder etwas in diesem Sinne *or* etwas ähnliches; **could you please finish the letter with "we look forward to hearing your decision" or words to that ~** könnten Sie bitte mit „wir sehen Ihrer Entscheidung entgegen" oder so ähnlich schließen.
(d) **~s** *pl (property)* Effekten *pl*.
(e) *(reality)* **in ~** in Wirklichkeit, im Effekt.
(f) *(of laws)* **to be in ~** gültig *or* in Kraft sein; **to come into ~** in Kraft treten; **to put sth into ~** etw in Kraft setzen; **to take ~** in Kraft treten.
2 *vt* **(a)** bewirken, herbeiführen. **to ~ one's purpose** seine Absicht verwirklichen *or* in die Tat umsetzen; **to ~ an entry** *(form)* sich *(dat)* Zutritt verschaffen.
(b) *(form) sale, purchase* tätigen; *payment* leisten; *insurance* abschließen; *settlement* erzielen.

effective [ɪ'fektɪv] *adj* **(a)** *(achieving a result)* wirksam, effektiv. **to become ~** *(law)* in Kraft treten, wirksam werden; *(drug)* wirken.
(b) *(creating a striking impression)* wirkungsvoll, effektvoll. **a very ~ use of colours** eine sehr wirkungsvolle Farbgebung.
(c) *(real) aid, contribution* tatsächlich; *profit, performance also* effektiv. **~ troops** einsatzbereite Truppen.

effectively [ɪ'fektɪvlɪ] *adv see adj* **(a)** wirksam, effektiv. **(b)** wirkungsvoll, effektvoll. **(c)** effektiv. **but they are ~ the same** aber effektiv sind sie gleich.

effectiveness [ɪ'fektɪvnɪs] *n see adj* **(a)** Wirksamkeit, Effektivität *f*. **(b)** Wirkung *f*, Effekt *m*.

effectual *adj*, **~ly** *adv* [ɪ'fektjʊəl, -ɪ] wirksam.

effectuate [ɪ'fektjʊeɪt] *vt* bewirken.

effeminacy [ɪ'femɪnəsɪ] *n* Unmännlichkeit *f*, weibisches Wesen, Effemination *f (geh)*.

effeminate [ɪ'femɪnɪt] *adj* unmännlich, weibisch, effeminiert *(geh)*.

effervesce [ˌefə'ves] *vi* sprudeln; *(fig: person)* übersprudeln, überschäumen.

effervescence [ˌefə'vesns] *n (lit)* Sprudeln *nt*; *(fig)* Übersprudeln, Überschäumen *nt*; überschäumendes Temperament.

effervescent [ˌefə'vesnt] *adj* sprudelnd; *(fig)* überschäumend, übersprudelnd.

effete [ɪ'fiːt] *adj* schwach; *person* saft- und kraftlos.

efficacious [ˌefɪ'keɪʃəs] *adj* wirksam.

efficacy ['efɪkəsɪ] *n* Wirksamkeit *f*.

efficiency [ɪ'fɪʃənsɪ] *n (of person)* Fähigkeit, Tüchtigkeit *f*; *(of machine, engine, factory)* Leistungsfähigkeit *f*; *(of method, organization)* Rationalität, Effizienz *(geh)* *f*. **driving ~** Fahrtüchtigkeit *f*; **~-minded** leistungsorientiert; **when jobs are lost for the sake of ~** wenn Stellen wegrationalisiert werden.

efficient [ɪ'fɪʃənt] *adj person* fähig, effizient *(geh)*; *worker, secretary etc also* tüchtig; *machine, engine, factory, company, department* leistungsfähig; *method, organization* rationell, effizient *(geh)*. **to be ~ at sth/at doing sth** etw gut verstehen/es gut verstehen, etw zu tun, in etw *(dat)* tüchtig sein; **he's quite an ~ bachelor** er ist ein Junggeselle, der sich recht gut selbst versorgen kann; **the ~ working of a mechanism** das gute Funktionieren eines Mechanismus.

efficiently [ɪ'fɪʃəntlɪ] *adj* gut, effizient *(geh)*. **the new machines were installed smoothly and ~** die neuen Maschinen wurden glatt und reibungslos eingebaut.

effigy ['efɪdʒɪ] *n* Bildnis *nt*. **to burn sb in ~** jds Puppe verbrennen.

effing ['efɪŋ] *adj (euph vulg)* Scheiß- *(sl)*.

efflorescent [ˌeflɔː'resnt] *adj (Chem)* ausblühend, efflores zierend *(spec)*; *(Bot)* aufblühend.

effluence ['efluəns] *n* Abwasser *nt*.

effluent ['efluənt] **1** *adj* ausfließend; *gas* ausströmend. **2** *n (from a lake)* Ausfluß *m*; *(sewage)* Abwasser *nt*.

effluvium [e'fluːvɪəm] *n* Ausdünstung *f*.

eff off ['ef'ɒf] *vi (euph vulg)* sich verpissen *(sl)*.

effort ['efət] *n* **(a)** *(attempt)* Bemühung *f*; *(strain, hard work)* Anstrengung, Mühe *f*; *(Mech)* Leistung *f*. **to make an ~ to do sth** sich bemühen *or* anstrengen, etw zu tun; **to make every ~ or a great ~ to do sth** sich sehr bemühen *or* anstrengen, etw zu tun;

to make every possible ~ to do sth jede nur mögliche Anstrengung or große Anstrengungen unternehmen or machen, etw zu tun; he made no ~ to be polite machte sich (dat) nicht die Mühe, höflich zu sein; it's an ~ (to get up in the morning) es kostet einige Mühe or Anstrengung(, morgens aufzustehen); it's an awful ~ to start working again es kostet große Mühe, wieder mit der Arbeit anzufangen; I'll try to persuade him but it'll be an ~ ich will versuchen, ihn zu überreden, aber es wird einige Mühe kosten; with an ~ mühsam; he had to double his ~s er mußte seine Anstrengungen verdoppeln; the government's ~s to avoid a crisis die Bemühungen der Regierung, eine Krise zu vermeiden; if it's not too much of an ~ for you (iro) wenn es dir nicht zu viel Mühe macht; you could make a little more ~ Sie könnten sich ein bißchen mehr Mühe geben; come on, make an ~ komm, streng dich an.
  (b) (inf) Unternehmen nt. it was a pretty poor ~ das war eine ziemlich schwache Leistung; he made a pretty poor ~ of the repair er hat bei der Reparatur ziemlich gepfuscht or ziemliche Pfuscharbeit geleistet; it's not bad for a first ~ das ist nicht schlecht für den Anfang; what did you think of his latest ~? was halten Sie von seinem jüngsten Unternehmen?; do you understand those rationalization ~s? verstehen Sie diese Rationalisierungsbestrebungen?; his first ~ at making a film sein erster Versuch, einen Film zu drehen; what's this peculiar cylinder ~? was ist denn das Zylinder-Ding da? (inf).

effortless ['efətlıs] adj mühelos, leicht; style leicht, flüssig.
effortlessly ['efətlıslı] adv mühelos, leicht.
effrontery [ı'frʌntərı] n Unverschämtheit f. how can you have the ~ to deny the charge? daß Sie die Frechheit besitzen, den Vorwurf abzustreiten!
effusion [ı'fju:ʒən] n (lit, fig) Erguß m.
effusive [ı'fju:sıv] adj überschwenglich; person, character, style also exaltiert.
effusively [ı'fju:sıvlı] adv überschwenglich.
effusiveness [ı'fju:sıvnıs] n Überschwenglichkeit f.
EFTA ['eftə] abbr of **European Free Trade Association** EFTA f.
eg abbr of **for example** z.B.
egad [ı'gæd] interj (old, hum) fürwahr (old, hum).
egalitarian [ı,gælı'teərıən] **1** n Verfechter(in f) m des Egalitarismus. **2** adj person egalitär (geh); principle also Gleichheits-.
egalitarianism [ı,gælı'teərıənızəm] n Egalitarismus m.
egg [eg] n Ei nt. to put all one's ~s in one basket (Prov) alles auf eine Karte setzen; as sure as ~s is ~s (inf) so sicher wie das Amen in der Kirche (inf); to have ~ all over one's face (fig inf) belemmert aus der Wäsche gucken (inf); he's a good/bad ~ (dated inf) er ist ein famoser Kerl (dated)/ein übler Kunde (inf); the plan is still in the ~ der Plan ist noch im Entstehen.
  ♦**egg on** vt sep anstacheln. don't ~ him ~! jetzt stachel ihn doch nicht auch noch an!
egg: ~ and dart n Eierstab m (spec); ~-beater n Schneebesen m; ~-cup n Eierbecher m; ~-flip n Ei-Flip m; ~-head n (pej inf) Intellektuelle(r) mf, Eierkopf m (inf); ~-plant n Aubergine f; ~-shell n Eierschale f; **2** adj Eierschalen-; ~ spoon n Eierlöffel m; ~-timer n Eieruhr f; ~-whisk n Schneebesen m; ~-white n Eiweiß nt; ~ yolk n Eidotter m, Eigelb nt.
eglantine ['egləntaın] n Weinrose f.
ego ['i:gəʊ] n (Psych) Ego, Ich nt; (inf) Selbstbewußtsein nt; (conceit) Einbildung f. this will boost his ~ das wird sein Selbstbewußtsein stärken, das wird ihm Auftrieb geben; his ~ won't allow him to admit that he is wrong sein Stolz läßt ihn nie zugeben, daß er unrecht hat.
egocentric(al) [,egəʊ'sentrık(əl)] adj egozentrisch, ichbezogen.
egoism ['egəʊızəm] n Egoismus m, Selbstsucht f.
egoist ['egəʊıst] n Egoist m, selbstsüchtiger Mensch.
egoistical [,egəʊ'ıstıkəl] adj egoistisch, selbstsüchtig, eigennützig.
egotism ['egəʊtızəm] n Ichbezogenheit f, Egotismus m.
egotist ['egəʊtıst] n Egotist m, ichbezogener Mensch.
egotistic(al) [,egəʊ'tıstık(əl)] adj von sich eingenommen, ichbezogen, egotistisch.
ego-trip ['i:gəʊtrıp] n (inf) I can't stand him when he's on one of these ~s ich kann es nicht ausstehen, wenn er so angibt; it won't last long, it's just some sort of ~ das hält nicht lange an, er tut das nur zur Befriedigung seines Selbstgefühls.
egregious [ı'gri:dʒəs] adj ausgemacht, ungeheuerlich.
egret ['i:grıt] n (a) (Orn) Reiher m. (b) (ornament) Reiherfeder f.
Egypt ['i:dʒıpt] n Ägypten nt.
Egyptian [ı'dʒıpʃən] **1** adj ägyptisch. **2** n (a) Ägypter(in f) m. (b) (language) Ägyptisch nt.
Egyptology [,i:dʒıp'tɒlədʒı] n Ägyptologie f.
eh [eı] interj (a) (inviting repetition) I've found a gold mine — ~? ich habe eine Goldmine entdeckt — was?, hä? (b) (inviting agreement) it's good, ~? gut, nicht?
eider ['aıdə^r] n Eiderente f.
eiderdown ['aıdədaʊn] n (quilt) Federbett, Daunenbett nt; (feathers) Daunen, Flaumfedern pl.
eidetic [aı'detık] adj eidetisch.
eight [eıt] **1** adj acht; see six. **2** n (a) Acht f; see six. (b) (Rowing) Achter m. (c) to have had one over the ~ (inf) einen über den Durst or einen zuviel getrunken haben (inf).
eighteen ['eı'ti:n] **1** adj achtzehn. **2** n Achtzehn f.
eighteenth ['eı'ti:nθ] **1** adj achtzehnte(r, s). **2** n (fraction) Achtzehntel nt; (of series) Achtzehnte(r, s); see sixteenth.
eighth [eıtθ] **1** adj achte(r, s). **2** n (fraction) Achtel nt; (of series) Achte(r, s); see sixth.
eighth-note ['eıtθnəʊt] n (US Mus) Achtelnote f, Achtel nt.
eightieth ['eıtııθ] **1** adj achtzigste(r, s). **2** n (fraction)

Achtzigstel nt; (of series) Achtzigste(r, s); see sixtieth.
eightsome (reel) ['eıtsəm('ri:l)] n schottischer Volkstanz für 8 Tänzer.
eighty ['eıtı] **1** adj achtzig. **2** n Achtzig f; see sixty.
Eire ['eərə] n Irland, Eire nt.
either ['aıðə^r] **1** adj, pron (a) (one or other) eine(r, s) (von beiden). there are two boxes on the table, take ~ auf dem Tisch liegen zwei Schachteln, nimm eine davon; if on ~ side of the road there is a line of trees wenn eine Straßenseite mit Bäumen bestanden ist.
  (b) (each, both) jede(r, s), beide pl. ~ day would suit me beide Tage passen mir; which bus will you take? — ~ (will do) welchen Bus wollen Sie nehmen? — das ist egal; I don't admire ~ ich bewundere keinen von beiden, ich bewundere beide nicht; she had flowers in ~ hand sie hatte in beiden Händen Blumen; on ~ side of the street auf beiden Seiten der Straße; it wasn't in ~ (box) es war in keiner der beiden (Kisten).
  2 adv, conj (a) (after neg statement) auch nicht. he sings badly and he can't act ~ er ist ein schlechter Sänger, und spielen kann er auch nicht; I have never heard of him — no, I haven't ~ ich habe noch nie von ihm gehört — ich auch nicht.
  (b) ~ ... or entweder ... oder. ~ (after a negative) weder ... noch; he must be ~ lazy or stupid er muß entweder faul oder dumm sein; ~ be quiet or go out! entweder bist du ruhig oder du gehst raus!; I have never been to ~ Paris or Rome ich bin weder in Paris noch in Rom gewesen.
  (c) (moreover) she inherited a sum of money and not such a small one ~ sie hat Geld geerbt, und (zwar) gar nicht so wenig.
ejaculate [ı'dʒækjuleıt] **1** vi (cry out) aufschreien; (Physiol) ejakulieren. **2** vt (utter) ausstoßen, ausrufen; (Physiol) ejakulieren, ausspritzen. **3** [ı'dʒækjulıt] n Ejakulat m.
ejaculation [ı,dʒækju'leıʃən] n (a) (cry) Ausruf m. (b) (Physiol) Ejakulation f, Samenerguß m.
ejaculatory [ı'dʒækjulətərı] adj style, language stoßhaft; (Physiol) Ejakulations-.
eject [ı'dʒekt] **1** vt (a) (throw out) heckler, tenant hinauswerfen. (b) smoke, flames ausstoßen; cartridge auswerfen; (Tech) ausstoßen, auswerfen; pilot herausschleudern. **2** vi (pilot) den Schleudersitz betätigen.
ejection [ı'dʒekʃən] n Hinauswurf m; (of cartridge) Auswerfen nt; (Tech) Auswerfen nt, Ausstoß m. ~ is the pilot's last resort Betätigung des Schleudersitzes ist die letzte Rettung für den Piloten.
ejector [ı'dʒektə^r] n (on gun) Auswerfer, Ejektor m. ~ seat (Aviat) Schleudersitz m.
♦**eke out** vt sep food, supplies strecken, verlängern; money, income aufbessern. to ~ ~ a living sich (recht und schlecht) durchschlagen.
elaborate [ı'læbərıt] **1** adj design, hairstyle, pattern, drawing kunstvoll, kompliziert; style (of writing) also, document ausführlich, detailliert; plan ausgefeilt, ausgeklügelt; sculpture, style kunstvoll; preparations also umfangreich; clothes, meal üppig; joke ausgeklügelt. I could cook something a little more ~ ich könnte etwas Anspruchsvolleres kochen; an ~ meal ein großes Menü.
  2 [ı'læbəreıt] vt (work out in detail) ausarbeiten; (describe in detail) ausführen.
  3 [ı'læbəreıt] vi could you ~? könnten Sie das etwas näher ausführen?; there's no need to ~ Sie brauchen nichts weiter zu sagen.
♦**elaborate on** vi +prep obj näher ausführen.
elaborately [ı'læbərıtlı] adv designed, drawn, structured kunstvoll, kompliziert; detailed ausführlich; worked out detailliert; prepared umfangreich.
elaborateness [ı'læbərıtnıs] n see adj Kompliziertheit f; Ausführlichkeit, Detailliertheit f; Umfang m; Üppigkeit f.
elaboration [ı,læbə'reıʃən] n (working out in detail) (of plan) Ausfeilung f; (description: of details etc) nähere Ausführung; (that which elaborates: details etc) Ausschmückung f. an author who goes in for a great deal of tedious ~ ein Schriftsteller, der eine Menge langatmiger Beschreibungen bringt.
élan [eı'læn] n Elan m.
elapse [ı'læps] vi vergehen, verstreichen.
elastic [ı'læstık] **1** adj (lit, fig) elastisch. ~ band (Brit) Gummiband nt; ~ stockings Gummistrümpfe pl. **2** n Gummi(band nt) m; (US: rubber band) Gummi m.
elasticity [,i:læs'tısıtı] n Elastizität f.
Elastoplast ® [ı'læstəʊplɑːst] n (Brit) Hansaplast ® nt.
elate [ı'leıt] vt begeistern, in Hochstimmung versetzen.
elated [ı'leıtıd] adj begeistert. ~ mood Hochstimmung f.
elation [ı'leıʃən] n Begeisterung f (at über +acc), Hochstimmung f; (of crowd also) Jubel m. a mood of such ~ eine solche Hochstimmung.
elbow ['elbəʊ] **1** n (a) Ellbogen m. ~s in! lümmel dich nicht so!, mach dich nicht so breit!; out at the ~s an den Ellbogen durchgewetzt; since he's been rubbing ~s with senators (esp US) seit er sich in Senatorenkreisen bewegt.
  (b) (of piping, river, road) Knie nt.
  2 vt to ~ one's way through/forward sich durchboxen or -drängen; he just ~ed his way through the crowd er boxte sich einfach durch die Menge; to ~ sb aside jdn beiseite stoßen; he ~ed me in the stomach er stieß mir or mich mit dem Ellbogen in den Magen.
♦**elbow out** vt sep (fig) hinausdrängeln.
elbow: ~-grease n (inf) Muskelschmalz nt (inf); ~-rest n Armstütze f; ~-room n (inf: lit, fig) Ellbogenfreiheit f (inf).
elder[1] ['eldə^r] **1** adj attr comp of **old** (a) (older) brother etc ältere(r, s). (b) (senior) Pliny the ~ Plinius der Ältere, der ältere Plinius. (c) ~ statesman (alt)erfahrener Staatsmann. **2** n (a) respect your ~s and betters du mußt Respekt vor Älteren haben.

(b) (of tribe, Church) Älteste(r) m.

(c) (Presbyterian) Gemeindeälteste(r), Presbyter m.

elder² ['eldə'] n (Bot) Holunder m.

elderberry ['eldə͵berɪ] n Holunderbeere f. ~ **wine** Holunderbeerwein m.

elderly ['eldəlɪ] adj ältlich, ältere(r, s) attr.

eldest ['eldɪst] adj attr superl of **old** älteste(r, s). **their** ~ **ihr** Ältester/ihre Älteste.

elec abbr of (a) electricity. (b) electric elektr.

elect [ɪ'lekt] **1** vt (a) wählen. **he was ~ed chairman/MP** er wurde zum Vorsitzenden/Abgeordneten gewählt; **to** ~ **sb to the Senate** jdn in den Senat wählen.

(b) (choose) (er)wählen, sich entscheiden für. **to** ~ **to do sth** sich dafür entscheiden, etw zu tun; **to** ~ **French nationality** sich für die französische Staatsangehörigkeit entscheiden.

2 adj **the president/bishop** ~ der designierte or künftige Präsident/Bischof.

3 npl (esp Rel) **the** ~ die Auserwählten pl.

election [ɪ'lekʃən] n Wahl f.

election in cpds Wahl-; ~ **campaign** n Wahlkampagne f or -kampf m.

electioneer [ɪ͵lekʃə'nɪə'] vi als Wahlhelfer arbeiten, Wahlhilfe leisten. **he's just ~ing for X** er macht nur Wahlpropaganda für X.

electioneering [ɪ͵lekʃə'nɪərɪŋ] **1** n (campaign) Wahlkampf m; (propaganda) Wahlpropaganda f. **2** adj campaign Wahl-; speech Wahlkampf-.

elective [ɪ'lektɪv] **1** adj (a) Wahl-. ~ **assembly** Wahlversammlung f. (b) (Chem) ~-**attraction** Wahlverwandtschaft f; (fig) ~- **affinity** Wahlverwandtschaft f. (c) (US) class, course wahlfrei.

2 n (US) Wahlfach nt.

elector [ɪ'lektə'] n (a) Wähler(in f) m. (b) (Hist) E~ Kurfürst m. (c) (US) Wahlmann m.

electoral [ɪ'lektərəl] adj Wahl-. ~ **college** (US) Wahlmänner-Kollegium nt; ~ **district** or **division** Wahlbezirk m; ~ **roll** Wählerverzeichnis nt.

electorate [ɪ'lektərɪt] n Wähler pl, Wählerschaft f.

electric [ɪ'lektrɪk] adj appliance, current, wire elektrisch; generator Strom-. **the atmosphere was** ~ es herrschte große Spannung; **the effect was** ~ (inf) das hatte eine tolle Wirkung.

electrical [ɪ'lektrɪkəl] adj Elektro-, elektrisch. ~ **engineer** Elektrotechniker m; (with Univ etc degree) Elektroingenieur m; ~ **engineering** Elektrotechnik f.

electric: ~ **blanket** n Heizdecke f; ~ **blue 1** n Stahlblau nt; 2 adj stahlblau; ~ **chair** n elektrischer Stuhl; ~ **cooker** n Elektroherd m; ~ **eel** n Zitteraal m; ~ **eye** n Photozelle f; ~ **field** n elektrisches Feld; ~ **fire**, ~ **heater** n elektrisches Heizgerät; ~ **guitar** n elektrische Gitarre.

electrician [ɪlek'trɪʃən] n Elektriker m.

electricity [ɪlek'trɪsɪtɪ] n Elektrizität f; (electric power for use) (elektrischer) Strom. **to have** ~ **installed** Stromanschluß or elektrischen Strom bekommen; **to turn on/off the** ~ den Strom an-/abschalten.

electricity: ~ (**generating**) **board** (Brit) n Elektrizitätswerk nt; ~ **meter** n Stromzähler m.

electric: ~ **light** n elektrisches Licht; ~ **motor** n Elektromotor m; ~ **organ** n elektrische Orgel; ~ **ray** n (Zool) Zitterrochen m; ~ **shock 1** n elektrischer Schlag, Stromschlag m; (Med) Elektroschock m; 2 adj attr ~ **shock treatment** (Elektro)schocktherapie f; **to give sb** ~ **shock treatment** jdn mit (Elektro)schock behandeln.

electrification [ɪ͵lektrɪfɪ'keɪʃən] n Elektrifizierung f.

electrify [ɪ'lektrɪfaɪ] vt (a) (Rail) elektrifizieren. (b) (charge with electricity) unter Strom setzen. (c) (fig) elektrisieren.

electrifying [ɪ'lektrɪfaɪɪŋ] adj (fig) elektrisierend.

electro- [ɪ'lektrəʊ-] pref Elektro-. ~**cardiogram** Elektrokardiogramm nt; ~**cardiograph** Elektrokardiograph m.

electrocute [ɪ'lektrəkjuːt] vt durch einen (Strom)schlag töten; (execute) durch den or auf dem elektrischen Stuhl hinrichten.

electrocution [ɪ͵lektrə'kjuːʃən] n see vt (a) Tötung f durch Stromschlag; Hinrichtung f durch den elektrischen Stuhl.

electrode [ɪ'lektrəʊd] n Elektrode f.

electro: ~**dynamics** n Elektrodynamik f; ~**encephalogram** n Elektroenzephalogramm nt; ~**encephalograph** n Elektroenzephalograph m.

electrolysis [ɪlek'trɒlɪsɪs] n Elektrolyse f.

electrolyte [ɪ'lektrəʊlaɪt] n Elektrolyt m.

electromagnet [ɪ'lektrəʊ'mægnɪt] n Elektromagnet m.

electromagnetic [ɪ'lektrəʊmæg'netɪk] adj elektromagnetisch.

electron [ɪ'lektrɒn] n Elektron nt. ~ **beam** Elektronenstrahl m; ~ **microscope** n Elektronenmikroskop nt.

electronic [ɪlek'trɒnɪk] adj elektronisch. ~ **brain** n Elektronen(ge)hirn nt.

electronics [ɪlek'trɒnɪks] n (a) sing (subject) Elektronik f. (b) pl (of machine etc) Elektronik f.

electroplate [ɪ'lektrəʊpleɪt] **1** vt galvanisieren. **2** n, no pl Galvanisierung f. **is it silver?** — **no,** ~ **ist das Silber?** — nein, nur versilbert.

electroplated [ɪ'lektrəʊpleɪtɪd] adj (galvanized) versilbert/ verchromt etc.

elegance ['elɪgəns] n Eleganz f.

elegant adj, ~**ly** adv ['elɪgənt, -lɪ] elegant.

elegiac [͵elɪ'dʒaɪək] **1** adj elegisch. **2** n ~**s** pl elegische Verse pl, Verse pl im elegischen Versmaß.

elegize ['elɪdʒaɪz] vi (in Elegien) klagen (upon über +acc).

elegy ['elɪdʒɪ] n Elegie f.

element ['elɪmənt] n (all senses) Element nt; (Chem also) Grundstoff m; (usu pl: of a subject also) Grundbegriff m. **the ~s of mathematics** die Grundbegriffe or Anfangsgründe (geh) pl der Mathematik; **an** ~ **of danger** ein Gefahrenelement nt;

---

the ~ **of chance** das Zufallselement; **an** ~ **of truth** eine Spur or ein Element nt von Wahrheit; **the personal** ~ das persönliche Element; **undesirable** ~**s** unerwünschte Elemente pl; **the** (**four**) ~**s** die (vier) Elemente; **to be in one's** ~ in seinem Element sein; **to be out of one's** ~ (with group of people) sich fehl am Platze fühlen; (with subject) nicht zu Hause sein.

elemental [͵elɪ'mentl] adj (a) (concerning the four elements) force, power, gods elementar. (b) (simple) einfach, elementar. ~ **truth** einfache Wahrheit. (c) (Chem, Phys) Grundstoff-.

elementary [͵elɪ'mentərɪ] adj (a) (simple) einfach, simpel, elementar.

(b) (first, basic) elementar, Grund-. ~ **education** Elementarunterricht m; ~ **geometry course** Geometrie-Grundkursus m; ~ **particle** (Phys) Elementarteilchen nt; ~ **politeness requires that** ... es ist ein einfaches Gebot der Höflichkeit, daß ...; **still in the** ~ **stages** noch in den Anfängen; ~ **school** Grundschule f; ~ **science** elementare Naturwissenschaften pl; (Sch) Grundkurs m in Naturwissenschaften.

elephant ['elɪfənt] n Elefant m; see pink, white ~.

elephantiasis [͵elɪfən'taɪəsɪs] n Elephantiasis f.

elephantine [͵elɪ'fæntaɪn] adj (heavy, clumsy) movements schwerfällig, wie ein Elefant; (large) mammuthaft, Mammut-.

elevate ['elɪveɪt] vt (a) heben. **by elevating the house a full 3 metres above** ... indem man das Haus ganze 3 Meter über (+acc) ... setzt.

(b) (fig) mind erbauen; soul erheben. **elevating reading** erbauliche Lektüre.

(c) **to** ~ **sb to the peerage** jdn in den Adelsstand erheben; **since he's been** ~**d to top management** (hum) seit er ins Spitzenmanagement berufen worden ist.

elevated ['elɪveɪtɪd] adj (a) position hoch(liegend), höher; platform erhöht. ~ **railway** Hochbahn f; ~ **motorway** (Brit) Hochstraße f. (b) (fig) position, style gehoben; thoughts erhaben.

elevation [͵elɪ'veɪʃən] n (a) (lit) Hebung f; (to higher rank) Erhebung f (to in +acc); (Eccl) Elevation f.

(b) (of thought) Erhabenheit f; (of position, style) Gehobenheit f.

(c) (above sea level) Höhe f über dem Meeresspiegel or über N.N.; (hill etc) (Boden)erhebung, Anhöhe f.

(d) angle of ~ Höhen- or Elevationswinkel m.

(e) (of gun) Elevation, Erhöhung f.

(f) (Archit: drawing) Aufriß m. **front** ~ Frontansicht f, Fassadenaufriß m.

elevator ['elɪveɪtə'] n (a) (US) Fahrstuhl, Lift, Aufzug m. (b) (storehouse) Silo m. (c) (Aviat) Höhenruder nt. (d) (with buckets etc) Aufzug m; (hoist) Winde f.

eleven [ɪ'levn] **1** n (a) (number) Elf f. **the** ~ **plus** (old Brit Sch) Aufnahmeprüfung in eine weiterführende Schule. (b) (Sport) Elf f. **the West German** ~ die bundesdeutsche (National)elf; **the second** ~ die zweite Mannschaft. **2** adj elf; see also six.

elevenses [ɪ'levnzɪz] n sing or pl (Brit) zweites Frühstück.

eleventh [ɪ'levnθ] **1** adj elfte(r, s). **at the** ~ **hour** (fig) in letzter Minute, fünf Minuten vor zwölf. **2** n (fraction) Elftel nt; Elfte(r, s); (of series) Elfte(r, s); see also sixth.

elf [elf] n, pl **elves** Elf m, Elfe f; (mischievous) Kobold m.

elfin ['elfɪn] adj light, music Elfen-, elfisch.

elfish ['elfɪʃ] adj elfisch; (mischievous) koboldhaft.

elicit [ɪ'lɪsɪt] vt Reaktion hervorrufen (from ab jdm).

elide [ɪ'laɪd] **1** vt elidieren, auslassen. **2** vi elidiert werden, wegor ausfallen.

eligibility [͵elɪdʒə'bɪlɪtɪ] n (a) Berechtigung f. **because of his undoubted** ~ **for the post** da er für die Stelle zweifelsohne in Frage kommt/kam. (b) Wählbarkeit f.

eligible ['elɪdʒəbl] adj (a) in Frage kommend; (for competition etc also) teilnahmeberechtigt; (for student flights, grants etc also) berechtigt; (for membership) aufnahmeberechtigt. **to be** ~ **for a job/an office/a pension** für einen Posten/ein Amt in Frage kommen/pensionsberechtigt sein; **an** ~ **bachelor** ein begehrter Junggeselle. (b) (able to be elected) wählbar.

eliminate [ɪ'lɪmɪneɪt] vt (a) ausschließen; alternative also ausscheiden; possibility of error also, competitor ausschalten; (Physiol) ausscheiden, eliminieren; (Math) eliminieren. **our team/candidate was** ~**d in the second round** unsere Mannschaft/unser Kandidat m schied in der zweiten Runde aus. (b) (kill) enemy ausschalten, eliminieren.

elimination [ɪ͵lɪmɪ'neɪʃən] n see vt (a) Ausschluß m; Ausscheidung f; Ausschaltung f; Ausscheidung, Elimination f; Elimination f. **by** ~ **a process of** ~ durch negative Auslese; our ~ **at the hands of the German team** die Ausschaltung unserer Mannschaft durch die deutsche. (b) Ausschaltung, Eliminierung f.

elision [ɪ'lɪʒən] n Elision f.

élite [er'liːt] n Elite f.

élitism [er'liːtɪzəm] n Elitedenken nt.

élitist [er'liːtɪst] adj elitär.

elixir [ɪ'lɪksə'] n Elixier nt, Auszug m. ~ **of life** Lebenselixier nt.

Elizabeth [ɪ'lɪzəbəθ] n Elisabeth f.

Elizabethan [ɪ͵lɪzə'biːθən] **1** adj elisabethanisch. **2** n Elisabethaner(in f) m.

elk [elk] n Elch m. **Canadian** ~ Wapiti(-Hirsch) m.

ellipse [ɪ'lɪps] n Ellipse f.

ellipsis [ɪ'lɪpsɪs] n, pl **ellipses** [ɪ'lɪpsiːz] (Gram) Ellipse f.

elliptic(al) [ɪ'lɪptɪk(əl)] adj (Math, Gram) elliptisch.

elm [elm] n Ulme f.

elocution [͵elə'kjuːʃən] n Sprechtechnik f. **teacher of** ~ Sprecherzieher(in f) m; ~ **classes** Sprecherziehung f.

elocutionist [͵elə'kjuːʃənɪst] n Sprecherzieher(in f) m.

elongate ['iːlɒŋgeɪt] **1** vt verlängern; (stretch out) langziehen, strecken. **2** vi länger werden.

elongated ['iːlɒŋgeɪtɪd] adj (extra length added) verlängert; (stretched) neck ausgestreckt; shape länglich.

elongation [ˌiːlɒŋˈgeɪʃən] n Verlängerung f; (stretching) Ausstrecken nt.

elope [ɪˈləʊp] vi durchbrennen (inf), ausreißen (inf).

elopement [ɪˈləʊpmənt] n Durchbrennen, Ausreißen (inf) nt.

eloquence [ˈeləkwəns] n see adj Beredsamkeit, Eloquenz (geh), Wortgewandtheit f; Gewandtheit f; Wohlgesetztheit f; Beredtheit f. **phrased with such** ~ mit einer solchen Eloquenz ausgedrückt.

eloquent [ˈeləkwənt] adj person beredt, beredsam, wortgewandt; words gewandt; speech wohlgesetzt; (fig) look, gesture beredt, vielsagend. **this is** ~ **proof of** ... das spricht wohl deutlich dafür, daß ...

eloquently [ˈeləkwəntlɪ] adv wortgewandt, mit beredten Worten. **very** ~ **put** or **phrased** sehr gewandt ausgedrückt.

else [els] adv (a) (after pron) andere(r, s). **anybody** ~ **would have done it** jeder andere hätte es gemacht; **is there anybody** ~ **there**? (in addition) ist sonst (noch) jemand da?; **since John doesn't want it, does anybody** ~ **want it**? da John es nicht will, will jemand anders es haben?; **may I speak to somebody** ~? kann ich mit jemand anders or sonst jemand sprechen?; **I'd prefer something** ~ ich möchte lieber etwas anderes; **I'd prefer anything** ~ alles andere wäre mir lieber; **have you anything** ~ **to say**? haben Sie sonst noch etwas zu sagen?; **do you find this species anywhere** ~? findet man die Gattung sonstwo or auch anderswo?; **but they haven't got anywhere** ~ **to go** aber sie können sonst nirgends anders hingehen; **somebody** ~ sonst jemand, jemand anders; **is there somebody** ~?, **she** asked ist da jemand anders?, fragte sie; **this is somebody** ~'s **umbrella** dieser Schirm gehört jemand anders; **something** ~ etwas anderes, sonst etwas; **if all** ~ **fails** wenn alle Stricke reißen; **will there be anything** ~, **sir**? (in shop) darf es sonst noch etwas sein?; (butler) haben Sie sonst noch Wünsche?

(b) **somewhere** ~, **someplace** ~ (esp US) woanders, anderswo; (with motion) woandershin, anderswohin; **from somewhere** ~ anderswoher, woandersher, von woanders.

(c) (after pron, neg) **nobody** ~, **no one** ~ sonst niemand, niemand anders; **nobody** ~ **understood** sonst hat es niemand verstanden, niemand anders hat es verstanden; **nothing** ~ sonst nichts, nichts anderes; **nothing** ~ **would be good enough** alles andere wäre nicht gut genug; **what do you want**? — **nothing** ~, **thank you** was möchten Sie? — danke, nichts weiter; **that this is a result of the cold and nothing** ~ daß dies allein auf die Kälte zurückzuführen ist; **nowhere** ~ sonst nirgends or nirgendwo, nirgendwo anders; (with motion) sonst nirgendwohin, nirgendwo andershin; **there's nowhere** ~ **for it but to** ... da gibt es keinen anderen Ausweg, als zu ...

(d) (after interrog) **where** ~? wo sonst?, wo anders?; **who** ~? wer sonst?; **who** ~ **but John could have done a thing like that**? wer anders als John hätte so etwas tun können?; **what** ~? was sonst?; **how** ~ **can I do it**? wie kann ich es denn sonst or anders machen?; **what** ~ **could I do**? was könnte ich sonst tun?

(e) (adv of quantity) **they sell books and toys and much** ~ sie führen Bücher, Spielzeug und vieles andere; **there is little** ~ **to be done** da bleibt nicht viel zu tun übrig.

(f) (otherwise, if not) sonst, andernfalls. **do what you're told or** ~ **go to bed** mach, was man dir sagt oder geh ins Bett or sonst gehst du ins Bett; **do it now (or)** ~ **you'll be punished** tu es jetzt, sonst setzt es Strafe or setzt es Strafe; **do it or** ~ ...! mach das, sonst or oder ...!; **you better had, or** ~ ...! mach das bloß, sonst or oder ...!

elsewhere [ˌelsˈwɛəʳ] adv woanders, anderswo; (to another place) woandershin, anderswohin. **from** ~ von woanders (her), woandersher; ... **which is found in Wales and** ~ das unter anderem in Wales gefunden wird; **my mind was** ~ ich war mit meinen Gedanken woanders.

elucidate [ɪˈluːsɪdeɪt] vt text erklären; mystery aufklären, aufhellen.

elucidation [ɪˌluːsɪˈdeɪʃən] n see vt Erklärung f; Aufklärung f, Aufhellung f.

elucidatory [ɪˈluːsɪdətərɪ] adj erklärend.

elude [ɪˈluːd] vt observation, pursuit, justice sich entziehen (+dat); sb's gaze, question ausweichen (+dat); police, enemy entkommen (+dat), entwischen (+dat). **to** ~ **sb's grasp** sich nicht fassen lassen; **the name** ~s **me** der Name ist mir entfallen.

elusive [ɪˈluːsɪv] adj schwer faßbar; concept, meaning also schwer definierbar; thoughts, memory flüchtig; happiness unerreichbar; answer ausweichend; fox etc schwer zu fangen. **he tried hard but success was** or **remained** ~ er gab sich (dat) alle Mühe, aber der Erfolg wollte sich nicht einstellen.

elusively [ɪˈluːsɪvlɪ] adv answer ausweichend. **but the fox slipped** ~ **past the traps** aber der Fuchs schlüpfte an den Fallen vorbei; **this prospect of happiness which hovered** ~ **before him** diese Aussicht auf ein Glück, das so nah und doch nicht faßbar war; **but a single true definition of the concept will always slip** ~ **away** aber der Begriff wird sich immer einer eindeutigen, der Wahrheit entsprechenden Definition entziehen.

elusiveness [ɪˈluːsɪvnɪs] n (of thoughts) Flüchtigkeit f; (of happiness) Unerreichbarkeit f; (of answer) Ausweichen nt. **the** ~ **of this concept** die Schwierigkeit, diesen Begriff zu definieren.

elves [elvz] pl of elf.

'em [əm] pron (inf) = them.

emaciated [ɪˈmeɪsɪeɪtɪd] adj ab- or ausgezehrt, stark abgemagert. **to become** ~ stark abmagern.

emaciation [ɪˌmeɪsɪˈeɪʃən] n Auszehrung f, starke Abmagerung.

emanate [ˈeməneɪt] vi ausgehen (from von); (light also) ausstrahlen (from von); (odour also) ausströmen (from von); (documents, instructions etc) stammen (from aus). **according to instructions emanating from regional headquarters** (form)

nach Anweisungen der Bezirksstelle.

emanation [ˌeməˈneɪʃən] n see vi Ausgehen nt; Ausstrahlung f; Ausströmen nt, (Rel) Emanation f.

emancipate [ɪˈmænsɪpeɪt] vt women emanzipieren; slaves freilassen; (fig) emanzipieren, befreien, frei machen.

emancipated [ɪˈmænsɪpeɪtɪd] adj woman, outlook emanzipiert; slave freigelassen.

emancipation [ɪˌmænsɪˈpeɪʃən] n (lit, fig) Emanzipation f; (of slave) Freilassung f.

emasculate [ɪˈmæskjʊleɪt] vt (a) (weaken) entkräften. (b) (lit) man entmannen.

emasculated [ɪˈmæskjʊleɪtɪd] adj style etc (saft- und) kraftlos.

embalm [ɪmˈbɑːm] vt corpse einbalsamieren. ~**ing oil** Balsamieröl nt.

embankment [ɪmˈbæŋkmənt] n (Ufer)böschung f; (along path, road) Böschung f; (for railway) Bahndamm m; (holding back water) (Ufer)damm, Deich m; (roadway beside a river) Ufer(straße f) nt.

embargo [ɪmˈbɑːgəʊ] n, pl -es (a) Embargo nt. **to lay** or **place** or **put an** ~ **on sth** etw mit einem Embargo belegen, ein Embargo über etw (acc) verhängen; **there's still an** ~ **on petrol, petrol is still under an** ~ es besteht immer noch ein Embargo für Benzin.

(b) (fig) Sperre f. **to put an** ~ **on further spending** alle weiteren Ausgaben sperren.

embark [ɪmˈbɑːk] **1** vt einschiffen; goods also verladen. **2** vi (a) (Naut) sich einschiffen; (troops) eingeschifft werden. (b) (fig) **to** ~ **up(on) sth** etw anfangen, etw beginnen.

embarkation [ˌembɑːˈkeɪʃən] n (a) Einschiffung f. ~ **officer** Verladeoffizier m; ~ **papers** Bordpapiere pl. (b) (of cargo) Verladung, Übernahme f.

embarrass [ɪmˈbærəs] vt (a) in Verlegenheit bringen, verlegen machen; (generosity etc also) beschämen. **to look** ~ed verlegen aussehen; **I feel so** ~ed **about it** das ist mir so peinlich; **she was** ~ed **by the question** die Frage war ihr peinlich; **there's no need to feel** ~ed, **here, take the money** das braucht Ihnen gar nicht peinlich zu sein, hier, nehmen Sie das Geld.

(b) **to be** ~ed **by lack of money** in einer finanziellen Verlegenheit sein; **I am** ~ed **as to which one to choose** die Wahl bringt mich in Verlegenheit.

(c) ~ed **by his cumbersome greatcoat** durch seinen unförmigen Übermantel behindert.

embarrassed [ɪmˈbærəst] adj verlegen.

embarrassing [ɪmˈbærəsɪŋ] adj peinlich; generosity etc also beschämend.

embarrassingly [ɪmˈbærəsɪŋlɪ] adv see adj **he said a few rather** ~ **candid things** er machte ein paar Bemerkungen, deren Offenheit schon peinlich war.

embarrassment [ɪmˈbærəsmənt] n Verlegenheit f; (through generosity also) Beschämung f. **to cause** ~ **to sb** jdn in Verlegenheit bringen, jdn verlegen machen; **to be a source of** ~ **to sb** jdn ständig in Verlegenheit bringen; (thing also) jdm peinlich sein; **much to my** ~ **she** ... **sie** ..., was mir sehr peinlich war; **she's an** ~ **to her family** sie blamiert die ganze Familie (inf); **financial** ~ finanzielle Verlegenheit.

embassy [ˈembəsɪ] n Botschaft f.

embattled [ɪmˈbætld] adj army kampfbereit; building (mit Zinnen) bewehrt, befestigt.

embed [ɪmˈbed] vt einlassen. **the screws/tyres were so firmly** ~ded **that** ... die Schrauben/Reifen steckten so fest, daß ...; **the bullet** ~ded **itself in the wall** die Kugel bohrte sich in die Wand; **to be** ~ded **in sth** (fig) fest in etw (dat) verwurzelt sein; **the belief is now firmly** ~ded **in their minds** der Glaube ist jetzt fest in ihrem Denken verankert.

embellish [ɪmˈbelɪʃ] vt (adorn) schmücken, verschönern; (fig) tale, account ausschmücken; truth beschönigen.

embellishment [ɪmˈbelɪʃmənt] n Schmuck m; (act also) Verschönerung f; (of story) Ausschmückung f; (of truth) Beschönigung f; (of handwriting) Verzierung f; Schnörkel m; (Mus) Verzierung f.

embers [ˈembəz] npl Glut f; see fan¹.

embezzle [ɪmˈbezl] vt unterschlagen, veruntreuen.

embezzlement [ɪmˈbezlmənt] n Unterschlagung f, Veruntreuung f.

embezzler [ɪmˈbezləʳ] n jd, der eine Unterschlagung begangen hat. **he was accused of being an** ~ er wurde beschuldigt, Geld unterschlagen or veruntreut zu haben.

embitter [ɪmˈbɪtəʳ] vt person verbittern; relations trüben, vergiften.

emblazon [ɪmˈbleɪzən] vt (a) (Her) schmücken, (ver)zieren. (b) (display boldly) name stolz hervorheben. **the name "Jones" was** ~ed **on the cover** der Name „Jones" prangte auf dem Umschlag. (c) (extol) überschwenglich preisen, rühmen, verherrlichen.

emblem [ˈembləm] n Emblem nt; (of political party, trade also) Wahrzeichen nt.

emblematic [ˌembləˈmætɪk] adj emblematisch (of für).

embodiment [ɪmˈbɒdɪmənt] n (a) Verkörperung f. **to be the** ~ **of virtue** die Tugend in Person sein. (b) (inclusion) Aufnahme, Eingliederung f.

embody [ɪmˈbɒdɪ] vt (a) (give form to) one's thoughts ausdrücken, Ausdruck geben (+dat), in Worte kleiden. (b) one's ideal verkörpern. (c) (include) enthalten. **to become embodied in sth** in etw (acc) aufgenommen werden.

embolden [ɪmˈbəʊldən] vt ermutigen, Mut machen (+dat). **to** ~ **sb to do sth** jdn dazu ermutigen or jdm Mut machen, etw zu tun.

embolism [ˈembəlɪzəm] n (Med) Embolie f.

embonpoint [ˌɒmbɒ̃ˈpwaːŋ] n (hum, euph) Embonpoint m or nt (dated), Leibesfülle f.

emboss [ɪmˈbɒs] vt metal, leather prägen; silk, velvet gaufrieren. ~**ed wallpaper** Prägetapete f; ~**ed writing paper**

Briefpapier mit geprägtem Kopf; **a silver vase ~ed with a design** eine silberne Vase mit erhaben herausgearbeitetem Muster; **an ~ed silver tray** ein Silbertablett mit Relief.

embouchure ['ɒmbuʃʊəʳ] n (*Mus*) Mundstück nt; (*of player*) Mundstellung f.

embrace [ɪm'breɪs] **1** vt (a) (*hug*) umarmen, in die Arme schließen.
   (b) (*seize eagerly*) *religion* annehmen; *opportunity* wahrnehmen, ergreifen; *cause* sich annehmen (+*gen*); *offer* annehmen, ergreifen. **he ~d the cause of socialism** er machte die Sache des Sozialismus zu seiner eigenen.
   (c) (*include*) umfassen, erfassen. **an all-embracing review** eine allumfassende Besprechung.
   2 vi sich umarmen.
   3 n (*hug*) Umarmung f. **a couple in a tender ~** ein Paar in zärtlicher Umarmung; **he held her in his ~** er hielt sie umschlungen; **death's ~** (*liter*) die Arme des Todes.

embrasure [ɪm'breɪʒəʳ] n (*in parapet*) Schießscharte f; (*of door, window*) Laibung f.

embrocation [ˌembrəʊ'keɪʃən] n Einreibemittel nt.

embroider [ɪm'brɔɪdəʳ] **1** vt (a) *garment, cloth* besticken; *pattern, design* sticken. (b) (*fig*) *facts, truth, story* ausschmücken. **2** vi sticken.

embroidery [ɪm'brɔɪdərɪ] n (a) Stickerei f. (b) (*fig*) Ausschmückungen pl.

embroidery: **~ frame** n Stickrahmen m; **~ thread** n Stickgarn nt.

embroil [ɪm'brɔɪl] vt **to ~ sb in sth** jdn in etw (*acc*) hineinziehen; **to become ~ed in a dispute** in einen Streit verwickelt or hineingezogen werden.

embroilment [ɪm'brɔɪlmənt] n Verwicklung f (*in* in +*acc*).

embryo ['embrɪəʊ] n (*lit, fig*) Embryo m; (*fig also*) Keim m. **in ~** (*lit*) im Keim; (*animal*) als Embryo; (*fig*) im Keim.

embryonic [ˌembrɪ'ɒnɪk] adj (*lit, fig*) embryonisch; (*fig also*) keimhaft.

emcee ['em'si:] **1** n Conférencier m; (*on TV also*) Showmaster m; (*at private functions*) Zeremonienmeister, Maître de plaisir (*old, hum*) m. **2** vt *show* als Conférencier *etc* leiten.

emend [ɪ'mend] vt *text* verbessern, korrigieren.

emendation [ˌi:men'deɪʃən] n Verbesserung, Korrektur f.

emerald ['emərəld] **1** n (a) (*stone*) Smaragd m. (b) (*colour*) Smaragdgrün nt. **2** adj smaragden, Smaragd-; *colour also* smaragdgrün. **the E~ Isle** die Grüne Insel.

emerge [ɪ'mɜːdʒ] vi (a) auftauchen. **he ~d victorious/the winner** er ging als Sieger/siegreich hervor; **we ~d into the bright daylight** wir kamen heraus in das helle Tageslicht; **he ~d behind the shed** er tauchte hinter dem Schuppen auf; **one arm ~d from beneath the blanket** ein Arm tauchte unter der Decke hervor.
   (b) (*come into being: life, new nation*) entstehen. **life ~d from the sea** das Leben entstammt dem or kommt aus dem Meer.
   (c) (*truth, nature of problem etc*) sich herausstellen, herauskommen (*from* bei); (*facts*) sich herausstellen, an den Tag kommen. **it ~s that ...** es stellt sich heraus, daß ...; **but what ~s from all this?** aber was ergibt sich aus all dem?

emergence [ɪ'mɜːdʒəns] n Auftauchen nt; (*of new nation etc*) Entstehung f; (*of theory, school of thought*) Aufkommen nt.

emergency [ɪ'mɜːdʒənsɪ] **1** n Notfall m; (*state of ~*) Notlage f. **in case of ~, in an ~** im Notfall; **to be prepared for any ~** für den Notfall vorbereitet sein; **to declare a state of ~** den Notstand erklären or ausrufen; **to declare a state of ~ in an area** eine Gegend zum Notstandsgebiet erklären; **there's always an ~ just before publication** kurz vor der Veröffentlichung kommt es immer zur Panik; **the doctor's been called out on an ~** der Arzt ist zu einem Notfall gerufen worden.
   2 adj attr *case, fund* Not-. **for ~ use only** nur für den Notfall.

emergency in cpds Not-; **~ brake** n Notbremse f; **~ call** n Notruf m; **~ centre** n Rettungszentrum nt des Noteinsatzes; **~ exit** n Notausgang m; **~ landing** n Notlandung f; **~ powers** npl Notstandsvollmachten pl; **~ rations** npl Notverpflegung f, eiserne Ration f; **~ service** n Not- or Hilfsdienst m; **~ services** npl Notdienst m; **~ ward** n Unfallstation f.

emergent [ɪ'mɜːdʒənt] adj *nations* jung, aufstrebend.

emeritus [ɪ'merɪtəs] adj emeritiert.

emery ['emərɪ] n Schmirgel m.

emery: **~ board** n Papiernagelfeile f; **~ cloth** n Schmirgelleinwand f; **~ paper** n Schmirgelpapier nt.

emetic [ɪ'metɪk] n Brechmittel, Emetikum (*spec*) nt.

emigrant ['emɪgrənt] **1** n Auswanderer m; (*esp for political reasons*) Emigrant(in f) m. **2** adj attr Auswanderer-; Emigranten-. **~ labourers** Arbeitsemigranten pl.

emigrate ['emɪgreɪt] vi auswandern, (*esp for political reasons*) emigrieren.

emigration [ˌemɪ'greɪʃən] n Auswanderung f; (*esp for political reasons*) Emigration f.

émigré ['emɪgreɪ] n Emigrant(in f) m.

eminence ['emɪnəns] n (a) (*distinction*) hohes Ansehen. **doctors of ~** (hoch)angesehene Ärzte pl. (b) (*of ground*) Erhebung, Anhöhe f. (c) (*Eccl*) **His/Your E~** Seine/Eure Eminenz.

éminence grise ['emɪnəns'griːz] n graue Eminenz.

eminent ['emɪnənt] adj *person* (hoch)angesehen, berühmt; *suitability, fairness* ausgesprochen, eminent.

eminently ['emɪnəntlɪ] adv ausgesprochen, außerordentlich. **~ respectable** hochangesehen attr, hoch angesehen pred, hochgeachtet attr, hoch geachtet pred.

emir [e'mɪəʳ] n Emir m.

emirate [e'mɪərɪt] n Emirat nt.

emissary ['emɪsərɪ] n Emissär m, Abgesandte(r) mf.

emission [ɪ'mɪʃən] n Ausstrahlung, Abstrahlung f; (*of light also, of fumes, X-rays*) Emission f (*spec*); (*of heat also, of sound*) Abgabe f; (*of gas also, of smell*) Verströmen,

Ausströmen nt; (*of liquid*) Ausströmen nt; (*gradual*) Absonderung, Abscheidung f; (*of vapour, smoke*) (*continuous*) Abgabe f; (*of lava*) Ausstoßen nt; (*of sparks*) Versprühen nt. **~ of semen** Samenerguß m.

emit [ɪ'mɪt] vt (a) *light* ausstrahlen, abstrahlen; *radiation also* aussenden, emittieren; *heat also, sound* abgeben; *gas also, smell* verströmen, ausströmen; *vapour, smoke* (*continuous*) abgeben; *lava, cry* ausstoßen; *liquid* (*gradually*) absondern, abscheiden; *sparks* versprühen. (b) *banknotes* ausgeben.

emollient [ɪ'mɒlɪənt] (*Med*) **1** n Linderungsmittel nt. **2** adj lindernd.

emolument [ɪ'mɒljumənt] n (*usu pl: form*) Vergütung f; (*fee*) Honorar nt; (*salary*) Bezüge pl.

emote [ɪ'məʊt] vi seine Gefühle ausdrücken; (*actor*) Gefühle mimen. **she's just emoting** (*inf*) sie spielt nur Theater (*inf*).

emotion [ɪ'məʊʃən] n (a) Gefühl nt, Gefühlsregung, Emotion f.
   (b) no pl (*state of being moved*) (Gemüts)bewegung, Bewegtheit f. **to show no ~** unbewegt bleiben; **in a voice full of ~** mit bewegter Stimme; **there was absolutely no ~ in his voice** seine Stimme war völlig emotionslos; **one should not allow ~ to interfere with reason in matters this serious** bei so wichtigen Dingen sollte der Verstand nicht durch das Gefühl beeinflußt werden.

emotional [ɪ'məʊʃənl] adj (a) emotional, emotionell; *shock also* seelisch, Gefühls-; *story, film, speech also* gefühlsbetont; *moment, writing also* gefühlvoll; *decision also* gefühlsmäßig; *day, experience* erregend; *letter* erregt. **~ state** Zustand m der Erregung; **~ disturbance** Störung f des Gefühlslebens; **it has an ~ appeal** es appelliert an das Gefühl; **sex without ~ involvement** Sex ohne echtes Gefühl.
   (b) *person, character, disposition* (leicht) erregbar, emotional. **don't get so ~ about it** reg dich nicht so darüber auf.

emotionalism [ɪ'məʊʃnəlɪzəm] n Gefühlsbetontheit, Rührseligkeit f. **the article was sheer ~** der Artikel war reine Gefühlsduselei.

emotionally [ɪ'məʊʃnəlɪ] adv *behave, react* gefühlsmäßig, emotional; (*with feeling*) *speak* gefühlvoll; (*showing one is upset*) *respond etc* erregt. **an ~ deprived child** ein Kind ohne Nestwärme; **to be ~ disturbed** seelisch gestört sein; **you're ~ deprived!** du bist ja total gefühlsarm!; **I don't want to get ~ involved (with her)** ich will mich (bei ihr) nicht ernsthaft engagieren.

emotionless [ɪ'məʊʃənlɪs] adj *face etc* ausdruckslos; *person* gefühllos, emotionslos.

emotive [ɪ'məʊtɪv] adj gefühlsbetont; *word also* emotional gefärbt; *force of a word* emotional.

empanel vt see **impanel**.

empathize ['empəθaɪz] vi sich hineinversetzen or einfühlen (*with* in +*acc*).

empathy ['empəθɪ] n Einfühlungsvermögen nt, Empathie f.

emperor ['empərəʳ] n Kaiser m; (*in Rome also*) Imperator m.

emperor penguin n Kaiserpinguin m.

emphasis ['emfəsɪs] n (a) (*vocal stress*) Betonung f. **the ~ is on the first syllable** die Betonung or der Ton liegt auf der ersten Silbe; **to lay or put ~ on a word** ein Wort betonen; **to say sth with ~** etw mit Nachdruck or nachdrücklich betonen.
   (b) (*importance*) Betonung f, (Schwer)gewicht nt. **to lay ~ or put the ~ on sth** etw betonen; **this year the ~ is on masculinity** dieses Jahr liegt der Akzent or die Betonung auf Männlichkeit; **there is too much ~ on ... ...** wird zu sehr betont; **a change of ~** eine Akzentverschiebung.

emphasize ['emfəsaɪz] vt *word, syllable, hips* betonen; *point, importance, need also* hervorheben. **this point cannot be too strongly ~d** das kann man gar nicht genug betonen.

emphatic [ɪm'fætɪk] adj *tone, manner* nachdrücklich, entschieden, emphatisch (*geh*); *denial also* energisch; *person* bestimmt, entschieden. **I am ~ about this point** ich bestehe auf diesem Punkt.

emphatically [ɪm'fætɪkəlɪ] adv *state* mit Nachdruck, ausdrücklich, emphatisch (*geh*); *deny, refuse* strikt, energisch. **most ~ not** auf gar keinen Fall.

empire ['empaɪəʳ] **1** n (a) Reich nt; (*ruled by Kaiser, emperor also*) Kaiserreich nt; (*world-wide*) Weltreich, Imperium nt. **the responsibilities of ~** die Verantwortung einer Weltmacht; **the Holy Roman E~** das Heilige Römische Reich (deutscher Nation); **the British E~** das Britische Weltreich, das Empire.
   (b) (*fig: esp Comm*) Imperium nt.
   2 adj attr E~ *costume, furniture, style* Empire-.

empire: **~-builder** n (*fig*) jd, der sich ein kleines Imperium aufbaut; **~-building** n (*fig*) Schaffung f eines eigenen kleinen Imperiums.

empiric [em'pɪrɪk] **1** adj see **empirical**. **2** n Empiriker m.

empirical [em'pɪrɪkəl] adj empirisch, Erfahrungs-.

empirically [em'pɪrɪkəlɪ] adv *tested, testable* empirisch; *based* auf Erfahrung.

empiricism [em'pɪrɪsɪzəm] n Empirismus m; (*method*) Empirie f.

empiricist [em'pɪrɪsɪst] n Empiriker m.

emplacement [ɪm'pleɪsmənt] n (*Mil*) Stellung f.

employ [ɪm'plɔɪ] **1** vt (a) *person* beschäftigen; (*take on*) anstellen; *private detective* beauftragen. **he has been ~ed with us for 15 years** er ist schon seit 15 Jahren bei uns.
   (b) (*use*) *means, method, force, cunning* anwenden, einsetzen; *skill also, word, concept* verwenden; *time* verbringen. **you can surely find a better way of ~ing your time** Sie können doch bestimmt Besseres mit Ihrer Zeit anfangen.
   (c) **to be ~ed in doing sth** damit beschäftigt sein, etw zu tun.
   2 n **to be in the ~ of sb** (*form*) bei jdm beschäftigt sein, in jds Diensten stehen (*geh*).

employable [ɪm'plɔɪəbl] adj *person* anstellbar, zu beschäftigen pred; (*useable*) *method etc* anwendbar; *word* verwendbar.

employee [ˌɪmplɔɪˈiː] n Angestellte(r) mf. ~s and employers Arbeitnehmer und Arbeitgeber; the ~s (of one firm) die Belegschaft, die Beschäftigten pl.

employer [ɪmˈplɔɪəʳ] n Arbeitgeber(in f), Brötchengeber (hum inf) m; (Comm, industry also) Unternehmer(in f) m; (of domestics, servants, civil servants also) Dienstherr m. ~s' federation Arbeitgeberverband m; ~'s contribution Arbeitgeberanteil m; ~'s liability insurance Betriebshaftpflicht(versicherung) f.

employment [ɪmˈplɔɪmənt] n (a) (An)stellung, Arbeit f. to take up ~ with sb eine Stelle bei jdm annehmen; to be without ~ stellungslos or ohne Arbeit sein; to seek ~ Arbeit or eine Stelle suchen; to seek ~ with sb sich bei jdm bewerben; out of ~ stellungslos, arbeitslos; to throw workers out of ~ Arbeiter um ihren Arbeitsplatz bringen; how long is it since you were last in ~? wann hatten Sie Ihre letzte Stellung?; conditions/contract/place of ~ Arbeitsbedingungen pl/-vertrag m/-platz m; to find ~ for sb Arbeit or eine Anstellung für jdn finden; what sort of ~ are you looking for? welche Art von Tätigkeit suchen Sie?; what's your ~? als was sind Sie tätig?
(b) (act of employing) Beschäftigung f; (taking on) Anstellung f, Einstellen nt.
(c) (use) (of means, method, force, cunning) Anwendung f, Einsatz m; (of skill also, word, concept) Verwendung f.

employment: ~ agency n Stellenvermittlung f; ~ exchange n Arbeitsamt nt.

emporium [emˈpɔːrɪəm] n Warenhaus nt.

empower [ɪmˈpaʊəʳ] vt to ~ sb to do sth jdn ermächtigen or (Jur) jdm (die) Vollmacht erteilen, etw zu tun; to be ~ed to do sth ermächtigt or befugt sein/die Vollmacht haben, etw zu tun.

empress [ˈemprɪs] n Kaiserin f.

emptiness [ˈemptɪnɪs] n Leere, Leerheit f; (of life etc) Leere f.

empty [ˈemptɪ] **1** adj (+er) (all senses) leer; (not occupied) house etc leerstehend attr; head hohl. ~ of ohne, bar (+gen) (liter); to be taken on an ~ stomach auf nüchternen Magen zu nehmen; I just feel ~ ich fühle mich innerlich völlig leer; ~ vessels make most noise (Prov) die am wenigsten zu sagen haben, reden am meisten; to look into ~ space ins Leere blicken.
2 n usu pl Leergut nt no pl.
3 vt (a) leeren, leer machen; container (ent)leeren; box, room also ausräumen; house räumen; glass, bottle also (by drinking) austrinken; pond, tank also ablassen; lorry abladen. her singing emptied the hall in ten minutes flat mit ihrem Singen schaffte sie es, daß der Saal innerhalb von zehn Minuten leer war; the burglars emptied the shop die Einbrecher haben den Laden ausgeräumt; as though he had now emptied himself of all emotion als ob er nun jegliches Gefühl verloren hätte.
(b) liquid also ausgießen, leeren. he emptied it into another container er goß es in ein anderes Gefäß um.
4 vi (water) auslaufen, abfließen; (rivers) münden, sich ergießen (liter) (into in +acc); (theatre, streets) sich leeren. the sink is not ~ing properly der Ausguß läuft nicht richtig ab.
♦**empty out** vt sep ausleeren; pockets also ausräumen.

empty: ~-handed adj to return ~-handed mit leeren Händen zurückkehren, unverrichteterdinge zurückkehren; ~-headed adj strohdumm; she's an ~-headed girl sie hat Stroh im Kopf.

emu [ˈiːmjuː] n Emu m.

emulate [ˈemjʊleɪt] vt nacheifern (+dat), nachstreben (+dat). I tried to ~ his success ich versuchte, es ihm gleichzutun.

emulation [ˌemjʊˈleɪʃən] n Nacheiferung f. in ~ of sb in dem Bestreben, es jdm gleichzutun.

emulsifier [ɪˈmʌlsɪfaɪəʳ] n Emulgator m.

emulsify [ɪˈmʌlsɪfaɪ] vt emulgieren, zu einer Emulsion verbinden.

emulsion [ɪˈmʌlʃən] n (a) Emulsion f. (b) (also ~ paint) Emulsionsfarbe f.

enable [ɪˈneɪbl] vt (a) (make able) to ~ sb to do sth es jdm ermöglichen or möglich machen, etw zu tun, jdn in den Stand setzen, etw zu tun (geh); what ~s the seal to stay under water so long? wodurch ist der Seehund fähig, so lange unter Wasser zu bleiben?; the good weather ~d us to go out das schöne Wetter machte es uns möglich auszugehen.
(b) (Jur: authorize) to ~ sb to do sth jdn (dazu) ermächtigen, etw zu tun.

enabling act [ɪˈneɪblɪŋˌækt] n (Parl) Ermächtigungsgesetz nt.

enact [ɪˈnækt] vt (a) (Pol) law erlassen. it is hereby ~ed that ... es wird hiermit verfügt, daß ... (b) (perform) play aufführen; rôle darstellen, spielen. the drama which was ~ed yesterday (fig) das Drama, das sich gestern abgespielt hat.

enactment [ɪˈnæktmənt] n (of law) Erlaß m; (law also) Verordnung, Verfügung f.

enamel [ɪˈnæməl] **1** n Email nt, Emaille f (inf); (paint) Email-(le)lack m; (of tiles etc) Glasur f; (of teeth) Zahnschmelz m; (nail ~) Nagellack m. **2** vt emaillieren. **3** adj pot, pan Email-(le)-. ~ paint Email(le)lack m; ~ painting Email(le)malerei f.

enamelled [ɪˈnæməld] adj emailliert; tile glasiert.

enamelware [ɪˈnæməlˌweəʳ] n Email(le)waren pl.

enamour, (US) **enamor** [ɪˈnæməʳ] vt to be ~ed of sb/sth (in love with) in jdn/etw verliebt sein; (taken by) von jdm/etw angetan or entzückt sein; she was not exactly ~ed of the idea sie war von der Idee nicht gerade begeistert.

encamp [ɪnˈkæmp] **1** vi das Lager aufschlagen. **2** vt where the troops were ~ed wo die Truppen im Lager bezogen hatten.

encampment [ɪnˈkæmpmənt] n Lager nt.

encapsulate [ɪnˈkæpsjʊleɪt] vt (Pharm) in Kapseln abfüllen; (express in condensed form) zusammenfassen.

encase [ɪnˈkeɪs] vt verkleiden (in mit); wires umgeben (in mit); cake überziehen (in mit).

encephalitis [ˌensefəˈlaɪtɪs] n Gehirnentzündung f.

enchain [ɪnˈtʃeɪn] vt (lit) in Ketten legen. to be ~ed in Ketten liegen; (fig) gefangen sein; so ~ed was he by these passions die Leidenschaft hielt ihn so gefangen.

enchant [ɪnˈtʃɑːnt] vt (a) (delight) bezaubern, entzücken. to be ~ed with sth von etw or über etw (acc) entzückt sein. (b) (put under spell) verzaubern. the ~ed wood der Zauberwald.

enchanting adj, ~ly adv [ɪnˈtʃɑːntɪŋ, -lɪ] bezaubernd, entzückend.

enchantment [ɪnˈtʃɑːntmənt] n (a) (delight) Entzücken nt. (b) (charm) Zauber m.

enchantress [ɪnˈtʃɑːntrɪs] n Zauberin f; (enchanting woman) bezaubernde Frau.

encipher [ɪnˈsaɪfəʳ] vt chiffrieren.

encircle [ɪnˈsɜːkl] vt (surround) umgeben, umfassen; (wall, belt also) umschließen; (troops) einkreisen, umfassen; building umstellen. his arm ~d her waist er hielt ihre Taille umfaßt; the house is ~d by trees das Haus ist von Bäumen umstanden.

encirclement [ɪnˈsɜːklmənt] n (Mil) Einkreisung, Umfassung f; (in a valley also) Einkesselung f; (of building) Umstellung f.

encircling [ɪnˈsɜːklɪŋ] **1** n (Mil) Umfassung f, Einkreisen nt; (in valley) Einkesseln nt; (of building) Umstellung f. **2** adj walls etc umgebend; (liter) night alles umgebend or umfassend; ~ movement (Mil) Einkreisungs- or Umfassungsmanöver nt.

enc(l) abbr of enclosure(s) Anl.

enclave [ˈenkleɪv] n Enklave f.

enclitic [ɪnˈklɪtɪk] n Enklitikon n.

enclose [ɪnˈkləʊz] vt (a) (shut in) einschließen; (surround) umgeben; (with fence etc) ground umgeben, einfrieden (geh). the garden is completely ~d der Garten ist völlig abgeschlossen.
(b) (in a parcel, envelope) beilegen, beifügen. please find ~d a cheque for £20 als Anlage or anbei übersenden wir Ihnen einen Scheck über £ 20; a banknote was ~d in the letter dem Brief lag ein Geldschein bei; to ~ sth in a letter einem Brief etw beilegen; letter enclosing a receipt Brief mit einer Quittung als Anlage; the ~d cheque der beiliegende Scheck; I ~d your letter with mine ich habe Ihren Brief mitgeschickt.

enclosure [ɪnˈkləʊʒəʳ] n (a) (ground enclosed) eingezäuntes Grundstück or Feld, Einfried(ig)ung f (geh); (for animals) Gehege nt. (on racecourse) the ~ der Zuschauerbereich; royal ~ abgeteilter Zuschauerbereich für die königliche Familie.
(b) (act) Einzäunung, Einfried(ig)ung (geh) f.
(c) (fence etc) Umzäunung f. ~ wall Umfassungsmauer f.
(d) (document etc enclosed) Anlage f.

encomium [ɪnˈkəʊmɪəm] n (form) Lobrede, Laudatio (geh) f.

encompass [ɪnˈkʌmpəs] vt (a) (liter: surround) umfassen (with mit). (b) (include) umfassen. (c) (liter: bring about) downfall herbeiführen.

encore [ˈɒŋkɔːʳ] **1** interj da capo, Zugabe. **2** n Zugabe f, Dacapo nt. to call for/give an ~ eine Zugabe verlangen/machen (inf) or singen/spielen etc. **3** vt singer, artist um eine Zugabe bitten.

encounter [ɪnˈkaʊntəʳ] **1** vt enemy, opposition treffen on or stoßen auf (+acc); difficulties stoßen auf (+acc); danger geraten in (+acc); (liter) person begegnen (+dat), treffen. to ~ enemy fire unter feindlichen Beschuß geraten.
2 n Begegnung f, Treffen nt; (in battle) Zusammenstoß m. ~ group (Psych) Encountergruppe f.

encourage [ɪnˈkʌrɪdʒ] vt person ermutigen, ermuntern (to zu); (motivate) anregen; (give confidence also) Mut machen (+dat); arts, industry, projects fördern; (Sport) team, competitor also anfeuern, anspornen; sb's bad habits unterstützen. he's lazy enough as it is, please don't ~ him er ist schon faul genug, bitte ermuntern or unterstützen Sie ihn nicht noch; that will only ~ bad habits das wird nur zu schlechten Gewohnheiten führen; to ~ sb in a belief jdn in einem Glauben bestärken; you'll only ~ him to think there's still hope er wird dann nur noch eher glauben, daß noch Hoffnung besteht; this ~s me to think that maybe ... das läßt mich vermuten, daß vielleicht ...

encouragement [ɪnˈkʌrɪdʒmənt] n Ermutigung, Ermunterung f; (motivation) Anregung f; (support) Unterstützung, Förderung f. to give sb ~ jdn ermuntern; it's an ~ to know ... es ist ein Ansporn, zu wissen ...; he doesn't need much ~ ihn braucht man nicht groß zu ermuntern.

encouraging [ɪnˈkʌrɪdʒɪŋ] adj ermutigend. you are not very ~ du machst mir/uns etc nicht gerade Mut.

encouragingly [ɪnˈkʌrɪdʒɪŋlɪ] adv see adj.

encroach [ɪnˈkrəʊtʃ] vi to ~ (up)on land vordringen in (+acc); sphere, rights eingreifen in (+acc); privileges übergreifen auf (+acc); time in Anspruch nehmen.

encroachment [ɪnˈkrəʊtʃmənt] n see vi Vordringen nt; Eingriff m; Übergriff m; Beanspruchung f.

encrust [ɪnˈkrʌst] vi (with earth, cement) überkrusten; (with pearls, ice etc) überziehen.

encrustation [ˌɪnkrʌsˈteɪʃən] n Kruste f. with ~s of diamonds diamant(en)besetzt.

encumber [ɪnˈkʌmbəʳ] vt beladen; (with responsibility, debts also) belasten. to be ~ed with sth (person) mit etw beladen/belastet sein; (room) mit etw überladen sein; ~ed by heavy clothes durch schwere Kleidung behindert.

encumbrance [ɪnˈkʌmbrəns] n (also Jur) Belastung f; (person also) Last f. to be an ~ to sb (luggage) jdn behindern; (person) eine Last für jdn sein; (dependent, responsibility) eine Belastung für jdn sein.

encyclical [ɪnˈsɪklɪkəl] n Enzyklika f.

encyclop(a)edia [ɪnˌsaɪkləʊˈpiːdɪə] n Lexikon nt, Enzyklopädie f.

encyclop(a)edic [ɪnˌsaɪkləʊˈpiːdɪk] adj enzyklopädisch.

end [end] **1** n (a) Ende nt; (of finger) Spitze f. at the ~ of the procession am Schluß or Ende der Prozession; the fourth from the ~ der/die/das vierte von hinten; to the ~s of the earth bis ans Ende der Welt; from ~ to ~ von einem Ende zum anderen; to keep one's ~ up (inf) (stay cheerful) sich nicht unterkriegen lassen (inf); (do one's share) das Seine tun; to stand on ~ ...

(*barrel, box etc*) hochkant stehen; (*hair*) zu Berge stehen; **two hours on** ~ zwei Stunden ununterbrochen; **for hours on** ~ stundenlang ununterbrochen; **the ships collided** ~**-on die Schiffe fuhren aufeinander auf;** ~ **to** ~ mit den Enden aneinander; **to change** ~s (*Sport*) die Seiten wechseln; **to make** (**both**) ~s **meet** (*fig*) durchkommen (*inf*); **to see no further than the** ~ **of one's nose** nicht weiter sehen als seine Nase (reicht); **to begin at the wrong** ~ am falschen Ende beginnen, das Pferd beim Schwanz aufzäumen; **to have one's** ~ **away** (*vulg*) einen wegstecken (*sl*).

(**b**) (*remnant*) (*of rope*) Ende *nt*, Rest *m*; (*of candle, cigarette*) Stummel *m*. **just a few odd** ~**s left** nur noch ein paar Reste.

(**c**) (*conclusion*) Ende *nt*. **the** ~ **of the month** das Monatsende; **at/towards the** ~ **of December** Ende/gegen Ende Dezember; **at the** ~ **of (the) winter/the war/the opera/the book** am Ende des Winters/des Krieges/am Schluß der Oper/des Buches; **at the** ~ **of three weeks** nach drei Wochen; **is there no** ~ **to this?** hört das denn nie auf?; **as far as I'm concerned, that's the** ~! für mich ist die Sache erledigt; **we shall never hear the** ~ **of it** das werden wir noch lange zu hören kriegen; **to be at an** ~ zu Ende sein; **to be at the** ~ **of one's patience/strength** mit seiner Geduld/seinen Kräften am Ende sein; **to read a film/read a book to the** ~ einen Film/ein Buch bis zu Ende sehen/lesen; **that's the** ~ **of him** er ist erledigt *or* fertig (*inf*); **that's the** ~ **of that** das ist damit erledigt; **to bring to an** ~ *speech, writing* zu Ende bringen, beenden; *relations* ein Ende setzen (+ *dat*), beenden; **to come to an** ~ zu Ende gehen; **to get to the** ~ **of the road/book/job/money** ans Ende der Straße/zum Schluß des Buches kommen/mit der Arbeit fertig werden/das Geld ausgegeben haben; **in the** ~ schließlich, zum Schluß; **to put an** ~ **to sth** einer Sache (*dat*) ein Ende setzen, mit einer Sache Schluß machen; **to come to a bad** ~ ein böses Ende nehmen; **to meet one's** ~ den Tod finden; **were you with him at the** ~? warst du zum Schluß *or* am Ende bei ihm?

(**d**) (*inf phrases*) **we met no** ~ **of famous people** wir trafen irrsinnig viel berühmte Leute (*inf*); **he's no** ~ **of a nice chap** er ist ein irrsinnig netter Kerl (*inf*); **it's done him no** ~ **of harm** es hat ihm irrsinnig (*inf*) *or* maßlos geschadet; **to think no** ~ **of sb** große Stücke auf jdn halten; **it pleased her no** ~ das hat ihr maßlos *or* irrsinnig (*inf*) gefallen; **you're the** ~ (*annoying*) du bist der letzte Mensch (*inf*); (*funny*) du bist zum Schreien (*inf*).

(**e**) (*purpose*) Ziel *nt*, Zweck *m*. **with** ~ **in view** mit diesem Ziel vor Augen; **to what** ~? (*form*) zu welchem Zweck?; **an** ~ **in itself** Selbstzweck *no art*; **the** ~ **justifies the means** (*prov*) der Zweck heiligt die Mittel (*prov*).

2 *adj attr* letzte(r, s); *house also* End-.

3 *vt* beenden; *speech, broadcast, series, one's days also* beschließen. **the novel to** ~ **all novels** der größte Roman aller Zeiten; **the howler to** ~ **all howlers** der schlimmste Schnitzer aller Zeiten.

4 *vi* enden. **we'll have to** ~ **soon** wir müssen bald Schluß machen; **we** ~**ed with a song** zum Schluß sangen wir ein Lied; **to be** ~**ing** zu Ende gehen; **where's it all going to** ~? wo soll das nur enden?; **how will it all** ~? wie wird das alles enden?; **to** ~ **in an "s"** auf "s" enden; **a post which** ~**s in a point** ein zugespitzter Pfahl; **an argument which** ~**ed in a fight** ein Streit, der mit einer Schlägerei endete.

♦ **end off** *vt sep* abschließen, beschließen.

♦ **end up** *vi* enden, landen (*inf*). **to** ~ ~ **doing sth** schließlich etw tun; **to** ~ ~ **as a lawyer/an alcoholic** schließlich Rechtsanwalt werden/als Alkoholiker enden; **we** ~**ed** ~ **at Joe's** wir waren *or* landeten (*inf*) schließlich bei Joe; **you'll** ~ ~ **in trouble** Sie werden noch Ärger bekommen.

endanger [ɪnˈdeɪndʒəʳ] *vt* gefährden.

endear [ɪnˈdɪəʳ] *vt* beliebt machen (*to* bei).

endearing [ɪnˈdɪərɪŋ] *adj smile* lieb, gewinnend; *personality, characteristic also* liebenswert.

endearingly [ɪnˈdɪərɪŋlɪ] *adv* lieb.

endearment [ɪnˈdɪəmənt] *n* **term of** ~ Kosename *m*, Kosewort *nt*; **words of** ~ liebe Worte *pl*.

endeavour [ɪnˈdevəʳ] **1** *n* (*attempt*) Anstrengung, Bemühung *f*; (*liter: striving*) (Be)streben *nt no pl* (*geh*). **to make an** ~ **to do sth** sich anstrengen *or* bemühen, etw zu tun; **to make every** ~ **to do sth** sich nach Kräften bemühen, etw zu tun; **in an** ~ **to please her** um ihr eine Freude zu machen. **2** *vt* sich anstrengen, sich bemühen, bestrebt sein (*geh*).

endemic [enˈdemɪk] *adj* (*lit, fig*) endemisch. **petty embezzling seems to be** ~ **here** kleine Unterschlagungen scheinen hier eine Krankheit zu sein.

end game *n* Endspiel *nt*.

ending [ˈendɪŋ] *n* (*of story, book, events*) Ausgang *m*; (*of day*) Abschluß *m*; (*last part*) Ende *nt*, Schluß *m*; (*of word*) Endung *f*. **a story with a happy** ~ eine Geschichte mit einem Happy End; **the events had a happy** ~ alles ging gut aus.

endive [ˈendaɪv] *n* (*Winter*)endivie *f*, Endiviensalat *m*.

endless [ˈendlɪs] *adj* endlos; *attempts also, times* unzählig; *patience also, possibilities* unendlich. **this job is** ~ diese Arbeit nimmt kein Ende; ~ **belt** endloses Transportband, Endlosband *nt*.

endlessly [ˈendlɪslɪ] *adv stretch out* endlos; *patient, generous* unendlich.

endocrine [ˈendəʊkraɪn] *adj* endokrin. ~ **gland** endokrine Drüse.

endomorph [ˈendəʊmɔːf] *n* Pykniker *m*.

endomorphic [endəʊˈmɔːfɪk] *adj* pyknisch.

endorse [ɪnˈdɔːs] *vt* (**a**) *document, cheque* auf der Rückseite unterzeichnen, indossieren.

(**b**) (*Brit Jur*) *driving licence* eine Strafe vermerken auf (+ *dat*). **I had my licence** ~**d** ich bekam einen Strafvermerk auf meinem Führerschein.

(**c**) (*approve*) billigen, unterschreiben (*inf*). **I** ~ **that dem**

stimme ich zu, dem pflichte ich bei.

endorsee [ɪndɔːˈsiː] *n* (*Fin*) Indossatar *m*.

endorsement [ɪnˈdɔːsmənt] *n* (**a**) (*on cheque, bill of exchange*) Indossament *nt*; (*on policy*) Zusatz, Nachtrag *m*. (**b**) (*Brit Jur: on driving licence*) Strafvermerk *m* auf dem Führerschein. (**c**) (*of opinion*) Billigung *f*. **management's** ~ **of our suggestion** die Billigung unseres Vorschlags durch die Betriebsleitung.

endorser [ɪnˈdɔːsəʳ] *n* (*Fin*) Indossar *m*.

endow [ɪnˈdaʊ] *vt* (**a**) *institution, church* eine Stiftung machen an (*acc*); (*Univ, Sch*) *prize, chair* stiften. **he** ~**ed the church with a large sum of money** er stiftete der Kirche eine große Summe; **an** ~**ed school** eine mit Stiftungsgeldern gebaute und finanzierte Schule.

(**b**) (*fig*) *usu pass* **to** ~ **sb with sth** jdm etw geben *or* schenken; **to be** ~**ed with a natural talent for singing** ein sängerisches Naturtalent sein; **the poor lad is not very well** ~**ed** (*inf*) mit dem armen Bengel ist nicht viel los; **she's well** ~**ed** (*hum*) sie ist von der Natur reichlich ausgestattet (worden).

endowment [ɪnˈdaʊmənt] *n* (**a**) Stiftung *f*. ~**s** Stiftungsgelder *pl*. (**b**) (*natural talent etc*) Begabung *f*. **his/her physical** ~**s** (*hum*) womit ihn/sie die Natur ausgestattet hat.

endowment: ~ **assurance** *n* Versicherung *f* auf den Erlebensfall, Erlebensversicherung *f*; ~ **mortgage** *n* Versicherungsdarlehen *nt*; ~ **policy** *n* Lebensversicherungspolice *f*.

end: ~**papers** *npl* Vorsatzblätter *pl*; ~ **product** *n* Endprodukt *nt*; (*fig*) Produkt *nt*; ~ **result** *n* Endergebnis *nt*.

endue [ɪnˈdjuː] *vt* versehen, begaben (*liter*). **to be** ~**d with sth** über etw (*acc*) verfügen, mit etw begabt sein.

endurable [ɪnˈdjʊərəbl] *adj* erträglich.

endurance [ɪnˈdjʊərəns] *n* Durchhaltevermögen *nt*. **to have great powers of** ~ großes Durchhaltevermögen haben; **to have great powers of** ~ **against the cold** sehr widerstandsfähig gegen Kälte sein; **what a feat of** ~ welche Ausdauer!; **he was tried beyond** ~ er wurde über die Maßen gereizt; **this is beyond** ~ das ist ja nicht auszuhalten.

endurance: ~ **race** *n* (*Sport*) Rennen *nt*, **bei dem es vor allem auf die Ausdauer ankommt;** ~ **test** *n* Belastungsprobe *f*; (*fig also*) Durchhaltetest *m*.

endure [ɪnˈdjʊəʳ] **1** *vt* (**a**) (*undergo*) *pain, insults, tribulations, hardship* (er)leiden. (**b**) (*put up with*) ertragen; *pains also* aushalten. **she can't** ~ **being laughed at** sie kann es nicht vertragen *or* haben (*inf*), wenn man über sie lacht. **2** *vi* bestehen, (*work, memories also*) Bestand haben.

enduring [ɪnˈdjʊərɪŋ] *adj value, fame* bleibend, dauernd; *friendship, peace also* dauerhaft; *illness* langwierig; *hardship* anhaltend.

endways [ˈendweɪz], **endwise** [ˈendwaɪz] *adv* mit dem Ende nach vorne *or* zuerst; (*end to end*) mit den Enden aneinander. **put it** ~ **on** legen Sie es mit dem Ende *or* der Spitze an.

ENE *abbr of* **east-north-east** ONO.

enema [ˈenɪmə] *n* (**a**) Klistier *nt*. (**b**) (*syringe*) Klistierspritze *f*.

enemy [ˈenəmɪ] **1** *n* (*lit, fig*) Feind *m*. **to make enemies** sich (*dat*) Feinde machen *or* schaffen; **to make an** ~ **of sb** sich (*dat*) jdn zum Feind(e) machen; **he is his own worst** ~ er schadet sich (*dat*) selbst am meisten; ~**-occupied** vom Feind besetzt. **2** *adj attr* feindlich; *position, advance, morale* des Feindes. **destroyed by** ~ **action** vom Feind *or* durch Feindeinwirkung (*form*) zerstört.

energetic [enəˈdʒetɪk] *adj* (**a**) voller Energie, energiegeladen; (*active*) aktiv; *manager, government* tatkräftig, aktiv; *dancer, dancing, music, prose* schwungvoll. **she is a very** ~ **person** sie ist immer sehr aktiv, sie steckt voller Energie; **if I'm feeling** ~ wenn ich die Energie habe; **I've had a very** ~ **day** ich hatte einen anstrengenden Tag.

(**b**) *denial, refusal, protest* energisch, entschlossen.

energetically [enəˈdʒetɪkəlɪ] *adv* voller Energie; *dance* schwungvoll; *express oneself* energisch, entschieden. **he has worked competently and** ~ er hat mit sehr viel Kompetenz und Schwung gearbeitet.

energize [ˈenədʒaɪz] *vt rocket motor, particle* Antrieb geben (+ *dat*); (*Elec*) unter Strom setzen.

energy [ˈenədʒɪ] *n* Energie *f*. **he put his speech over with a lot of** ~ er hielt seine Rede mit viel Schwung; **chocolate gives you** ~ Schokolade gibt neue Energie; **to apply all one's energies to sth** seine ganze Energie *or* Kraft für etw einsetzen; **I haven't the** ~ ich habe nicht die (nötige) Energie dazu, mir fehlt die Energie dazu; **to conserve one's energies** mit seinen Kräften haushalten *or* sparsam umgehen, Energie sparen (*inf*).

energy: ~ **crisis** *n* Energiekrise *f*; ~**-giving** *adj food* energiespendend; ~ **supplies** *npl* Energievorräte *pl*.

enervate [ˈenɜːveɪt] *vt* (*physically*) entkräften, schwächen; (*mentally*) entnerven, enervieren (*geh*).

enervating [ˈenɜːveɪtɪŋ] *adj* strapazierend.

enfant terrible [ɒnfɒntɛˈriːblə] *n, pl* ~**s** ~**s** Enfant terrible *nt*.

enfeeble [ɪnˈfiːbl] *vt* schwächen.

enfeeblement [ɪnˈfiːblmənt] *n* Schwächung *f*.

enfold [ɪnˈfəʊld] *vt* einhüllen (*in* in + *acc*). **to** ~ **sb in one's arms** jdn in die Arme schließen.

enforce [ɪnˈfɔːs] *vt* (**a**) durchführen, Geltung verschaffen (+ *dat*); *one's claims, rights* geltend machen; *silence, discipline* sorgen für, schaffen; *obedience* sich (*dat*) verschaffen. **the police** ~ **the law** die Polizei sorgt für die Einhaltung der Gesetze; **to** ~ **silence/obedience** Ruhe/Gehorsam erzwingen; **a gun might** ~ **obedience** mit einer Pistole kann man sich vielleicht Gehorsam, aber keinen Respekt (ver)schaffen; **to** ~ **sth (up)on sb** jdm etw aufzwingen.

(**b**) (*rare: give force to*) *demand* Nachdruck verschaffen (+ *dat*); *argument* stützen, untermauern.

enforceable [ɪnˈfɔːsəbl] *adj* durchsetzbar, durchzusetzen *pred*.

enforcement [ɪnˈfɔːsmənt] *n* (*of law, policy, ruling*) Durchführung f; (of obedience) Erzwingung f.

enfranchise [ɪnˈfræntʃaɪz] vt (a) (give vote to) das Wahlrecht geben or erteilen (+dat). to be ~d wahlberechtigt sein. (b) (set free) slaves freilassen.

enfranchisement [ɪnˈfræntʃɪzmənt] n (a) (Pol) Erteilung f des Wahlrechts. after the ~ of women nachdem die Frauen das Wahlrecht erhalten hatten. (b) (of slave) Freilassung f.

engage [ɪnˈgeɪdʒ] 1 vt (a) servant, workers an- or einstellen; singer, performer engagieren; lawyer sich (dat) nehmen.
(b) room mieten, sich (dat) nehmen.
(c) the attention in Anspruch nehmen; interest also fesseln. to ~ sb in conversation jdn in ein Gespräch verwickeln.
(d) to ~ oneself to do sth (form) sich verpflichten, etw zu tun.
(e) the enemy angreifen, den Kampf eröffnen gegen.
(f) (Tech) gear wheels ineinandergreifen lassen. to ~ a gear (Aut) einen Gang einlegen; to ~ the clutch (ein)kuppeln.
2 vi (a) (form: promise) sich verpflichten (to do zu tun).
(b) (gear wheels) ineinandergreifen; (clutch) fassen.
(c) to ~ in sich an etw (dat) beteiligen; to ~ in politics sich politisch betätigen; to ~ in controversy sich an einem Streit beteiligen, sich auf einen Streit einlassen; to ~ in competition with sb in Wettbewerb mit jdm treten.
(d) (Mil) angreifen.

engaged [ɪnˈgeɪdʒd] adj (a) (betrothed) verlobt. ~ to be married verlobt; to become ~ sich verloben (to mit); the ~ couple die Verlobten pl.
(b) (occupied) beschäftigt.
(c) the parties ~ in this dispute die streitenden or am Streit beteiligten Parteien; ~ in bitter conflict in erbittertem Streit.
(d) seat, taxi, toilet, (Brit Telec) number, line besetzt. ~ tone (Brit Telec) Besetztzeichen nt.

engagement [ɪnˈgeɪdʒmənt] n (a) (appointment) Verabredung f; (of actor etc) Engagement nt. public/social ~s öffentliche/gesellschaftliche Verpflichtungen pl; a dinner ~ eine Verabredung zum Essen. (b) (betrothal) Verlobung f. (c) (form: undertaking) Verpflichtung f. (d) (Mil) Gefecht nt, Kampf m. (e) (of parts of machine) Ineinandergreifen nt.

engagement: ~ diary n Terminkalender m; ~ ring n Verlobungsring m.

engaging [ɪnˈgeɪdʒɪŋ] adj personality einnehmend; smile, look, tone gewinnend.

en garde [ɒŋˈgɑːd] interj en garde.

engender [ɪnˈdʒendəʳ] vt (fig) erzeugen.

engenderment [ɪnˈdʒendəmənt] n Erzeugung f.

engine [ˈendʒɪn] n (a) Maschine f; (of car, plane etc) Motor m; (of ship) Maschine f. (b) (Rail) Lokomotive, Lok f.

engine block n Motorblock m.

-engined [-ˈendʒɪnd] adj suf -motorig.

engine driver n (Brit) Lok(omotiv)führer(in f) m.

engineer [ˌendʒɪˈnɪəʳ] 1 n (a) Techniker(in f) m; (with university degree etc) Ingenieur(in f) m. the E~s (Mil) die Pioniere pl.
(b) (Naut: on merchant ships) Maschinist m; (in Navy) (Schiffs)ingenieur m. ~ officer Technischer Offizier.
(c) (US Rail) Lokführer m.
(d) (fig: of scheme) Arrangeur m.
2 vt (a) konstruieren.
(b) (fig) election, campaign organisieren; downfall, plot arrangieren, einfädeln; success, victory in die Wege leiten; (Sport) goal einfädeln. to ~ a scheme einen Plan aushecken.

engineering [ˌendʒɪˈnɪərɪŋ] n (a) Technik f; (mechanical ~) Maschinenbau m; (engineering profession) Ingenieurwesen nt. the ~ of the Tay Bridge die Konstruktion der Tay-Brücke; he's in some sort of ~ er ist irgend etwas Technisches (inf); a brilliant piece of ~ eine Meisterkonstruktion; a triumph of ~ ein Triumph m der Technik.
(b) (fig) see vt (b) Organisation f; Arrangement nt; (manoeuvring) Arrangements pl. he was responsible for the ~ of this success/victory/goal er hat diesen Erfolg/Sieg zuwege gebracht/dieses Tor eingefädelt.

engineering: ~ department n technische Abteilung; (mechanical) Abteilung f für Maschinenbau; ~ faculty n (Univ) Fakultät f für Maschinenbau; ~ industries npl Maschinenindustrie f; ~ worker n Techniker(in f) m; ~ works n sing or pl Maschinenfabrik f.

engine: ~ room n (Naut) Maschinenraum m; ~ shed n (Brit) Lokomotivschuppen m.

England [ˈɪŋglənd] 1 n England nt. 2 adj attr the ~ team die englische Mannschaft.

English [ˈɪŋglɪʃ] 1 adj englisch. he is ~ er ist Engländer; our ~ teacher (teaching ~) unser Englischlehrer; (~ by nationality) unser englischer Lehrer; ~ translator englischer Übersetzer; (foreign) Übersetzer m für Englisch.
2 n (a) the ~ pl die Engländer pl.
(b) Englisch nt; (the ~ language in general, ~ grammar also) das Englische; (as university subject) Anglistik f. can you speak ~? können Sie Englisch?; he doesn't speak ~ er spricht kein Englisch; "~ spoken" „hier wird Englisch gesprochen"; they were speaking ~ sie sprachen englisch; they were talking (in) ~ to each other sie unterhielten sich auf englisch; he speaks (a) very clear ~ er spricht (ein) sehr klares Englisch; in ~ auf or in (inf) Englisch or englisch; in good/modern-day ~ in gutem/modernem Englisch; to translate sth into/from (the) ~ etw ins Englische/aus dem Englischen übersetzen; the ~ structures in ~ die Verbstruktur im Englischen; is that ~? (correct) ist das richtig?; that's not ~ das ist verkehrt, das ist falsches Englisch; ~/teaching ~ as a foreign language (abbr EFL/TEFL) Englisch als Fremdsprache; the head of ~ der Fachbereichsleiter für Englisch or (Univ) Anglistik; King's/Queen's ~ die englische Hochsprache; see old ~, plain.

English: ~ Channel n Ärmelkanal m; ~man n Engländer m; an

~man's home is his castle (Prov) für den Engländer ist sein Haus seine Burg; ~woman n Engländerin f.

engorge [ɪnˈgɔːdʒ] vi anschwellen.

engraft [ɪnˈgrɑːft] vt (Hort, fig) aufpropfen (into, on auf +acc); (Med) einpflanzen (into in +acc); passage into book etc einfügen (into in +acc).

engrave [ɪnˈgreɪv] vt eingravieren; (on rock, stone) einmeißeln; (on wood) einschnitzen, einkerben; (fig) einprägen. this picture is ~d on my memory dieses Bild hat sich mir (unauslöschlich) eingeprägt.

engraver [ɪnˈgreɪvəʳ] n Graveur(in f) m; (on stone) Steinhauer(in f) m; (on wood) Holzschneider(in f) m, Hersteller m von Druckstöcken.

engraving [ɪnˈgreɪvɪŋ] n (a) (process) see vt Gravieren nt; Einmeißeln nt; Einschnitzen, Einkerben nt. ~ needle Graviernadel f. (b) (copy) (Kupfer-/Stahl)stich m; (from wood) Holzschnitt m; (design) Gravierung f; (on wood, stone) eingemeißelte Verzierung/Schrift etc.

engross [ɪnˈgrəus] vt person, attention gefangennehmen. to become ~ed in one's book sich in sein Buch vertiefen; to be ~ed in one's own thoughts in Gedanken vertieft sein.

engrossing [ɪnˈgrəusɪŋ] adj fesselnd.

engulf [ɪnˈgʌlf] vt verschlingen. to be ~ed by the sea von den Wellen verschlungen werden (liter); he was ~ed by a pile of work er war mit Arbeit überhäuft; his coat ~s him completely er verschwindet völlig in seinem Mantel; he was ~ed in or by the crowd er wurde von der Menge verschlungen.

enhance [ɪnˈhɑːns] vt verbessern; chances also, price, value, attraction erhöhen.

enigma [ɪˈnɪgmə] n Rätsel nt.

enigmatic adj, ~ally adv [ˌenɪgˈmætɪk, -əlɪ] rätselhaft.

enjambement [ɪnˈdʒæmmənt] n (Poet) Enjambement nt.

enjoin [ɪnˈdʒɔɪn] vt (form) to ~ sb to silence/caution, to ~ silence/caution on sb jdn eindringlich zur Ruhe/zur Vorsicht mahnen; to ~ on sb the need for sth jdm die Notwendigkeit einer Sache eindringlich vor Augen stellen; to ~ sb to do sth jdn eindringlich mahnen, etw zu tun.

enjoy [ɪnˈdʒɔɪ] 1 vt (a) (take pleasure in) genießen. he ~s swimming/reading er schwimmt/liest gern, Lesen/Schwimmen macht ihm Spaß; he ~s being rude to people es macht ihm Spaß or ihm macht es Spaß, zu Leuten unhöflich zu sein; he ~ed reading the book er hat das Buch gern gelesen; I ~ed the book/concert/film das Buch/Konzert/der Film hat mir gefallen; he ~ed the meal das Essen hat ihm gut geschmeckt; I've ~ed talking to you es war mir eine Freude, mich mit Ihnen zu unterhalten, es war nett, sich mit Ihnen zu unterhalten; I didn't ~ it at all es hat mir überhaupt keinen Spaß gemacht; the author didn't mean his book to be ~ed dem Verfasser ging es nicht darum, daß man an seinem Buch Spaß or Vergnügen haben sollte; to ~ life das Leben genießen; I ~ed a very pleasant weekend in the country ich habe ein sehr angenehmes Wochenende auf dem Land verbracht; did you ~ your holidays? hat es Ihnen im Urlaub gefallen?; I really ~ed my holidays ich habe meinen Urlaub richtig genossen.
(b) good health sich erfreuen (+gen) (geh); rights, advantages, respect, confidence also genießen; income also haben.
2 vr to ~ oneself sich amüsieren; ~ yourself! viel Spaß!, amüsieren Sie sich gut!

enjoyable [ɪnˈdʒɔɪəbl] adj nett; film, book also unterhaltsam, amüsant; evening also, meal angenehm.

enjoyably [ɪnˈdʒɔɪəblɪ] adv angenehm.

enjoyment [ɪnˈdʒɔɪmənt] n (a) Vergnügen nt, Spaß m (of an +dat). he got a lot of ~ from this book/from bird-watching das Buch machte ihm großen Spaß/es machte ihm großen Spaß or er fand großen Spaß daran, Vögel zu beobachten.
(b) (of rights, income, fortune) Genuß m.

enlarge [ɪnˈlɑːdʒ] 1 vt vergrößern; empire, influence also ausdehnen; hole, field of knowledge, (Med) organ, pore also erweitern; membership, numbers, majority also erhöhen. ~d edition erweiterte Ausgabe.
2 vi (a) (get bigger) sich vergrößern; sich ausdehnen; sich erweitern; sich erhöhen.
(b) to ~ (up)on sth sich über etw (acc) genauer äußern.

enlargement [ɪnˈlɑːdʒmənt] n (a) (Phot) Vergrößerung f. (b) (enlarging) see vt Vergrößerung f; Ausdehnung f; Erweiterung f; Erhöhung f.

enlarger [ɪnˈlɑːdʒəʳ] n (Phot) Vergrößerungsapparat m.

enlighten [ɪnˈlaɪtn] vt aufklären (on, as to, about über +acc); (spiritually) erleuchten. let me ~ you darf ich es Ihnen erklären?

enlightened [ɪnˈlaɪtnd] adj aufgeklärt; (spiritually) erleuchtet.

enlightening [ɪnˈlaɪtnɪŋ] adj aufschlußreich.

enlightenment [ɪnˈlaɪtnmənt] n Aufklärung f; (spiritual) Erleuchtung f. the E~ die Aufklärung; the age of E~ das Zeitalter der Aufklärung.

enlist [ɪnˈlɪst] 1 vi (Mil etc) sich melden (in zu).
2 vt soldiers einziehen; recruits also einstellen; supporters, collaborators anwerben, gewinnen; assistance, sympathy, support gewinnen. could I ~ your aid? darf ich Sie um Hilfe bitten?; ~ed man (US) gemeiner Soldat.

enlistment [ɪnˈlɪstmənt] n see vb (a) Meldung f. (b) Einziehung f; Einstellung f; Anwerbung, Gewinnung f; Gewinnung f.

enliven [ɪnˈlaɪvn] vt beleben.

enmesh [ɪnˈmeʃ] vt (lit) in einem Netz fangen; (fig) verstricken. to get ~ed in sth (fig) in etw (acc) verstrickt werden.

enmity [ˈenmɪtɪ] n Feindschaft f.

ennoble [ɪˈnəubl] vt (lit) adeln, in den Adelsstand erheben; (fig) mind, person erheben (geh).

enormity [ɪˈnɔːmɪtɪ] n (a) no pl (of action, offence) ungeheures Ausmaß. (b) (crime) Ungeheuerlichkeit f.

enormous [ɪˈnɔːməs] adj gewaltig, enorm; person enorm groß;

patience enorm. **an ~ number of people** ungeheuer viele Menschen; **an ~ amount of money/time** eine Unsumme (*inf*), eine Unmenge Geld/Zeit.

enormously [ɪˈnɔːməslɪ] *adv* enorm, ungeheuer.

enough [ɪˈnʌf] **1** *adj* genug, genügend *attr.* **to be ~** genügen, reichen; **is there ~ milk?, is there milk ~?** ist genug *or* genügend Milch da?, reicht die Milch?; **have you ~ to pay with?** haben Sie genug, um zu bezahlen?; **we have ~ to live on** wir haben genug zum Leben, es reicht uns zum Leben; **more than ~** mehr als genug; **I've had ~, I'm going home** mir reicht's *or* jetzt reicht's mir aber, ich gehe nach Hause; **I've had ~ of this novel** jetzt habe ich genug von diesem Roman; **I've had ~ of your impudence** jetzt habe ich aber genug von deiner Frechheit, jetzt reicht es mir aber mit deiner Frechheit; **one can never have ~ of this music** von dieser Musik kann man nie genug kriegen; **that's ~, thanks** danke, das ist genug *or* das reicht; **now children, that's ~!** Kinder, jetzt ist es aber genug *or* jetzt reicht es aber!; **~ of this!** genug davon!; **this noise is ~ to drive me mad** dieser Lärm macht mich noch ganz verrückt; **one song was ~ to show he couldn't sing** ein Lied genügte, um zu zeigen, daß er nicht singen konnte; **it is ~ for us to know that ...** es genügt uns zu wissen, daß ...; **~ is as good as a feast** (*prov*) allzuviel ist ungesund (*prov*); **~ is ~** was zuviel ist, ist zuviel.
2 *adv* **(a)** (*sufficiently*) (*+adj*) genug; (*+vb also*) genügend. **not big ~** nicht groß genug; **this meat is not cooked ~** das Fleisch ist nicht richtig durch; **that's a good ~ excuse** die Entschuldigung kann man gelten lassen; **he knows well ~ what I said** er weiß ganz genau, was ich gesagt habe. **(b)** (*tolerably*) **she is clever/pleasant ~** sie ist so weit ganz intelligent/nett; **he writes/sings well ~** er schreibt/singt ganz ordentlich; **it's good ~ in its way** es ist in seiner Art ganz ordentlich; **I like it well ~** mir gefällt es ganz gut. **(c)** (*as intensifier*) **oddly/funnily ~, I saw him too** sonderbarerweise/komischerweise habe ich ihn auch gesehen; **and sure ~, he didn't come** und er kam auch prompt nicht.

enquire, inquire [ɪnˈkwaɪə^r] **1** *vt* **the time, a name, the way** sich erkundigen nach, fragen nach. **to ~ sth of sb** sich bei jdm nach etw erkundigen; **he ~d what/whether/when etc ...** er erkundigte sich *or* fragte, was/ob/wann *etc* ...
2 *vi* sich erkundigen (*about* nach), fragen (*about* nach, wegen). **"~ within"** „Näheres im Geschäft".

♦**enquire after** *vi + prep obj* **person, sb's health** sich erkundigen nach.

♦**enquire for** *vi + prep obj* **person** fragen nach.

♦**enquire into** *vi + prep obj* untersuchen.

enquirer [ɪnˈkwaɪərə^r] *n* Fragende(r) *mf*.

enquiring [ɪnˈkwaɪərɪŋ] *adj* fragend; **mind** forschend.

enquiry, inquiry [ɪnˈkwaɪərɪ, (*US*) ˈɪnkwɪrɪ] *n* **(a)** (*question*) Anfrage *f* (*about* über *+acc*); (*for tourist information, direction etc*) Erkundigung *f* (*about* über *+acc*, nach). **to make enquiries** Erkundigungen einziehen; (*police etc*) Nachforschungen anstellen (*about sb* über jdn, *about sth* nach etw); **all enquiries to ...** alle Anfragen an (*+acc*) ...; **E~s** (*office*) Auskunft *f*. **(b)** (*investigation*) Untersuchung *f*. **to hold an ~ into the cause of the accident** eine Untersuchung der Unfallursache durchführen; **court of ~** Untersuchungskommission *f*.

enrage [ɪnˈreɪdʒ] *vt* wütend machen. **it ~s me to think that ...** es macht mich wütend, wenn ich daran denke, daß ...

enrapture [ɪnˈræptʃə^r] *vt* entzücken, bezaubern.

enrich [ɪnˈrɪtʃ] *vt* bereichern; **soil, food** anreichern.

enrichment [ɪnˈrɪtʃmənt] *n* Bereicherung *f*; (*of soil*) Anreicherung *f*.

enrol, (US) enroll [ɪnˈrəʊl] **1** *vt* einschreiben; **members** *also* aufnehmen; **schoolchild** (*school, headmaster*) aufnehmen; (*parents*) anmelden; (*Univ*) immatrikulieren.
2 *vi* sich einschreiben; (*in the army*) sich melden (*in* zu); (*as member also*) sich einschreiben lassen; (*for course also, at school*) sich anmelden; (*Univ also*) sich immatrikulieren.

enrolment [ɪnˈrəʊlmənt] *n* **(a)** (*enrolling*) *see vt* Einschreibung *f*; Aufnahme *f*; Anmeldung *f*; Immatrikulation *f*. **(b)** (*being enrolled*) *see vi* Einschreibung *f*; Meldung *f*; Einschreibung *f*; Anmeldung *f*; Immatrikulation *f*. **(c) an evening class/a university/school with a total ~ of ...** ein Abendkurs mit einer (Gesamt)teilnehmerzahl von .../eine Universität mit ... immatrikulierten Studenten/eine Schule mit einer (Gesamt)schülerzahl von ...

en route [ɒŋˈruːt] *adv* unterwegs, en route (*geh*). **we can see it ~ to Paris** wir können es auf dem Weg nach Paris sehen.

ensconce [ɪnˈskɒns] *vr* sich niederlassen, sich häuslich niederlassen (*in in + dat*). **he was ~d in the front room** er hatte sich in dem vorderen Zimmer (häuslich) niedergelassen.

ensemble [ãːnˈsãːmbl] *n* (*Mus, Fashion*) Ensemble *nt*.

enshrine [ɪnˈʃraɪn] *vt* (*fig*) bewahren.

ensign [ˈensaɪn] *n* **(a)** (*flag*) Nationalflagge *f*. **(b)** (*Mil Hist*) Fähnrich *m*. **(c)** (*US Naut*) Fähnrich *m* zur See.

enslave [ɪnˈsleɪv] *vt* zum Sklaven machen. **he is ~d by tradition** er ist der Tradition sklavisch verhaftet; **he was ~d by her beauty** ihre Schönheit hat ihn zu ihrem Sklaven gemacht.

enslavement [ɪnˈsleɪvmənt] *n* (*lit*) Versklavung *f*; (*fig*) sklavische Abhängigkeit.

ensnare [ɪnˈsnɛə^r] *vt* (*lit*) fangen; (*fig*) (*woman*) umgarnen; (*charms*) berücken, bestricken. **his leg became ~d in the ropes** sein Bein verfing sich in den Seilen.

ensue [ɪnˈsjuː] *vi* folgen (*from, on* aus). **it ~s that ...** daraus folgt, daß ...; **what ~d?** was folgte darauf(hin)?

ensuing [ɪnˈsjuːɪŋ] *adj* **year, day** folgend; **events** nachfolgend.

ensure [ɪnˈʃʊə^r] *vt* sicherstellen; (*secure*) sichern. **he did everything to ~ that the work was finished in time** er tat alles, um sicherzustellen, daß die Arbeit rechtzeitig fertig wurde; **can I ~ that I will have a seat?** kann ich sicher sein *or* sichergehen, daß ich einen Platz bekomme?

entablature [ɪnˈtæblətjʊə^r] *n* Gebälk *nt*.

entail [ɪnˈteɪl] *vt* **(a)** (*cause, make necessary*) *expense, inconvenience, suffering* mit sich bringen; *risk, difficulty also* verbunden sein mit; (*involve*) *work* **stages** *also* erforderlich machen. **what is ~ed in doing that/buying a house?** was ist dazu/zum Hauskauf alles erforderlich?; **this will ~ (my) buying a new car** das bringt mit sich *or* macht es erforderlich, daß ich mir ein neues Auto kaufen muß. **(b)** (*Logic*) **if a = b, not a ~s not b** wenn a = b ist, so folgt daraus, daß nicht a = nicht b ist. **(c)** (*Jur*) **to ~ an estate** ein Gut als Fideikommiß vererben; **~ed estate** unveräußerliches Erbgut, Fideikommiß *nt*.

entangle [ɪnˈtæŋgl] *vt* **(a)** (*snare, catch up*) verfangen. **to become ~d in sth** sich in etw (*dat*) verfangen; **their feet were ~d in the ropes** sie hatten sich mit den Füßen in den Seilen verfangen. **(b)** (*get into a tangle*) *hair* verwirren; *wool, thread, ropes also* verwickeln. **to become ~d** sich verwirren; sich verwickeln *or* verheddern (*inf*); (*branches*) ineinanderwachsen. **(c)** (*fig: in affair etc*) verwickeln, verstricken (*in in +acc*). **he became ~d in his lies/explanations** er hat sich in Lügen verstrickt/sich bei seinen Erklärungen verheddert (*inf*).

entanglement [ɪnˈtæŋglmənt] *n* **(a)** (*lit*) (*no pl: enmeshing*) Verfangen *nt*; (*tangle*) (*of ropes etc*) Durcheinander *nt*; (*esp Mil: of barbed wire*) Verhau *m*. **(b)** (*fig*) (*in affair etc*) Verwicklung *f*. **legal ~** Rechtskonflikt *m*; **he wanted to avoid any ~ with the police** er wollte auf keinen Fall etwas mit der Polizei zu tun kriegen; **emotional ~** gefühlsmäßiges Engagement; **she didn't want any emotional ~** sie wollte sich gefühlsmäßig nicht engagieren.

enter [ˈentə^r] **1** *vt* **(a)** (*towards speaker*) hereinkommen in (*+acc*); (*away from speaker*) hineingehen in (*+acc*); (*walk into*) *building etc also* betreten, eintreten in (*+acc*); (*drive into*) *car park, motorway* einfahren in (*+acc*); (*turn into*) *road etc* einbiegen in (*+acc*); (*flow into: river, sewage etc*) münden in (*+acc*); (*penetrate: bullet etc*) eindringen in (*+acc*); (*climb into*) *bus* einsteigen in (*+acc*); (*cross border of*) *country* einreisen in (*+acc*). **to ~ harbour** (in den Hafen) einlaufen; **he is ~ing his 60th year** er tritt ins sechzigste Lebensjahr ein; **the thought never ~ed my head** *or* **mind** so etwas wäre mir nie eingefallen; **that idea had ~ed my mind** (*iro*) auf diesen Gedanken bin ich tatsächlich gekommen. **(b)** (*join, become a member of*) eintreten in (*+acc*). **to ~ the Army/Navy** zum Heer/zur Marine gehen; **to ~ the Church** Geistlicher werden; **to ~ a school/the university** in eine Schule eintreten/die Universität beziehen; **to ~ a profession** einen Beruf ergreifen. **(c)** (*write down, record*) eintragen (*in in +acc*). **to ~ a/one's name (on a list)** einen Namen/sich (in eine Liste) eintragen; **~ these purchases to me** (*Comm*) tragen Sie diese Käufe auf meinen Namen ein. **(d)** (*enrol*) (*for school, exam etc, pupil*) anmelden; (*athlete, competitor also, horse, for race, contest etc*) melden. **(e)** (*go in for*) *race, contest* sich beteiligen an (*+dat*). **only amateurs could ~ the race** es konnten nur Amateure an dem Rennen teilnehmen. **(f)** (*submit*) *appeal, plea* einlegen. **to ~ an action against sb** (*Jur*) gegen jdn einen Prozeß anstrengen *or* einleiten.
2 *vi* **(a)** (*towards speaker*) hereinkommen; (*away from speaker*) hineingehen; (*walk in*) eintreten; (*into bus etc*) einsteigen; (*drive in*) einfahren; (*penetrate: bullet etc*) eindringen; (*cross into country*) einreisen. **(b)** (*Theat*) auftreten. **(c)** (*for race, exam etc*) sich melden (*for* zu).

♦**enter into** *vi + prep obj* **(a)** *relations, negotiations, discussions* aufnehmen; *contract, alliance* schließen, eingehen. **to ~ ~ conversation/a correspondence with sb** ein Gespräch mit jdm anknüpfen/mit jdm in Briefwechsel treten; *see* spirit. **(b)** (*figure in*) eine Rolle spielen bei. **that possibility did not ~ ~ our calculations** diese Möglichkeit war in unseren Berechnungen nicht einkalkuliert *or* eingeplant.

♦**enter up** *vt sep* eintragen.

♦**enter (up)on** *vi + prep obj* (*begin*) *career, duties* antreten; *new era, time of prosperity* eintreten in (*+acc*); *subject* eingehen auf (*+acc*).

enteric [enˈterɪk] *adj* Darm-. **~ fever** (Unterleibs)typhus *m*.

enteritis [ˌentəˈraɪtɪs] *n* Dünndarmentzündung *f*.

enterprise [ˈentəpraɪz] *n* **(a)** *no pl* (*initiative, ingenuity*) Initiative *f*; (*adventurousness*) Unternehmungsgeist *m*. **(b)** (*project, undertaking, Comm: firm*) Unternehmen *nt*. **free/public/private ~** (*system*) freies/öffentliches/Privatunternehmertum *nt*.

enterprising [ˈentəpraɪzɪŋ] *adj* **person** (*with initiative, ingenious*) einfallsreich, erfindungsreich; (*adventurous*) unternehmungslustig, unternehmend; **idea, venture** kühn.

enterprisingly [ˈentəpraɪzɪŋlɪ] *adv see adj* einfallsreich, erfindungsreich; unternehmungslustig, unternehmend; kühn. **he very ~ started his own business** unternehmungslustig, wie er war, machte er sein eigenes Geschäft auf.

entertain [ˌentəˈteɪn] **1** *vt* **(a)** (*offer hospitality to*) einladen; (*to meal*) bewirten. **to ~ sb to dinner** jdn zum Essen einladen. **(b)** (*amuse*) unterhalten; (*humorously: joke*) belustigen. **(c)** *thought, intention* sich tragen mit; *suspicion, doubt* hegen; *hope* nähren; *suggestion, proposal, offer* erwägen, in Erwägung ziehen. **2** *vi* **(a)** (*have visitors*) Gäste haben. **(b)** (*comedian, conjurer etc*) unterhalten.

entertainer [ˌentəˈteɪnə^r] *n* Unterhalter(in *f*), Entertainer(in *f*) *m*.

entertaining [ˌentəˈteɪnɪŋ] **1** *adj* amüsant, unterhaltsam. **2** *n* **she does a lot of ~** sie hat sehr oft Gäste.

entertainingly [ˌentəˈteɪnɪŋlɪ] *adv* amüsant, unterhaltsam.

entertainment [ˌentəˈteɪnmənt] n (a) (amusement) Unterhaltung f; (professional also) Entertainment nt. much to the ~ of the onlookers sehr zur Belustigung der Zuschauer; for my own ~ nur so zum Vergnügen, zu meinem Privatvergnügen; the cinema is my favourite ~ zur Unterhaltung gehe ich am liebsten ins Kino; he/the film is good ~ er/der Film ist sehr unterhaltend; the world of ~ die Unterhaltungsbranche.
  (b) (performance) Darbietung f. a musical ~ eine musikalische Darbietung or Unterhaltung.

entertainment: ~ allowance n = Aufwandspauschale f; ~ tax n Vergnügungssteuer f; ~ value n to be good ~ value großen Unterhaltungswert haben; (person) sehr unterhaltend sein.

enthral(l) [ɪnˈθrɔːl] vt begeistern, berücken (geh); (exciting story etc also) packen, fesseln. (held) ~led by her beauty von ihrer Schönheit gefesselt or bezaubert or berückt (geh).

enthralling [ɪnˈθrɔːlɪŋ] adj spannend; story, film also packend, fesselnd.

enthrone [ɪnˈθrəʊn] vt inthronisieren; king also auf den Thron erheben; bishop also feierlich einsetzen. to sit ~d thronen.

enthuse [ɪnˈθjuːz] vi schwärmen (over von).

enthusiasm [ɪnˈθjuːzɪæzəm] n Begeisterung f, Enthusiasmus m (for für). I can't rouse or find any ~ for going out ich kann mich gar nicht dafür begeistern, auszugehen; I can't rouse any ~ for the idea ich kann mich für die Idee nicht erwärmen or begeistern.

enthusiast [ɪnˈθjuːzɪæst] n Enthusiast m. sports/football/rock-and-roll ~ begeisterter Sportler/Fußballfreund m/Rock'n'roll-Anhänger m.

enthusiastic [ɪnˌθjuːzɪˈæstɪk] adj begeistert, enthusiastisch. to be/get ~ about sth von etw begeistert sein/sich für etw begeistern; to become or get ~ in Begeisterung geraten.

enthusiastically [ɪnˌθjuːzɪˈæstɪkəlɪ] adv begeistert, enthusiastisch, mit Begeisterung.

entice [ɪnˈtaɪs] vt locken, (lead astray) verführen, verleiten. to ~ sb to do sth or into doing sth jdn dazu verführen or verleiten, etw zu tun; to ~ sb away jdn weglocken.

enticement [ɪnˈtaɪsmənt] n (act) Lockung f; (leading astray) Verführung f; (lure) Lockmittel nt; (fig) Verlockung f.

enticing [ɪnˈtaɪsɪŋ] adj verlockend; prospect also, look verführerisch.

entire [ɪnˈtaɪər] adj (a) ganz; set, waste of time vollständig. the ~ week/edition die ganze Woche/Auflage; he has my ~ confidence er hat mein ganzes or vollstes Vertrauen. (b) (unbroken) ganz, heil.

entirely [ɪnˈtaɪəlɪ] adv ganz. the money was given ~ to charity das gesamte Geld wurde für wohltätige Zwecke ausgegeben; I'm not ~ surprised das kommt für mich nicht ganz überraschend; the house has been ~ rebuilt das Haus ist ganz or völlig neu gebaut worden; it's ~ different es ist völlig or ganz anders; I don't ~ agree ich bin nicht ganz der (gleichen) Meinung; it's ~ revolting es ist ausgesprochen widerlich.

entirety [ɪnˈtaɪərətɪ] n Gesamtheit f. in its ~ in seiner Gesamtheit.

entitle [ɪnˈtaɪtl] vt (a) book betiteln. it is ~d ... es hat den Titel ...
  (b) (give the right) to ~ sb to sth/to do sth jdn zu etw berechtigen/jdn dazu berechtigen, etw zu tun; (to compensation, legal aid, taking holiday) jdm den Anspruch auf etw (acc) geben/jdm den Anspruch darauf or das Anrecht dazu geben, etw zu tun; to be ~d to sth/to do sth das Recht auf etw (acc) haben/das Recht haben, etw zu tun; (to compensation, legal aid, holiday) Anspruch auf etw (acc) haben/Anspruch darauf haben, etw zu tun; he is ~d to two weeks' holiday ihm stehen zwei Wochen Urlaub zu, er hat Anspruch auf zwei Wochen Urlaub.

entitlement [ɪnˈtaɪtlmənt] n Berechtigung f (to zu); (to compensation, legal aid, holiday etc) Anspruch m (to auf +acc). what is your holiday ~? wieviel Urlaub steht Ihnen zu?

entity [ˈentɪtɪ] n Wesen nt. legal ~ juristische Person.

entomb [ɪnˈtuːm] vt beisetzen, bestatten. the mausoleum which ~s his body das Mausoleum, in dem er beigesetzt ist.

entomologist [ˌentəˈmɒlədʒɪst] n Entomologe m, Entomologin f.

entomology [ˌentəˈmɒlədʒɪ] n Entomologie f, Insektenkunde f.

entourage [ˌɒntʊˈrɑːʒ] n Gefolge nt, Entourage f (geh).

entr'acte [ˈɒntrækt] n Zwischenspiel nt; (Mus also) Zwischenaktsmusik f.

entrails [ˈentreɪlz] npl (lit) Eingeweide pl; (fig: of watch etc also) Innereien pl (hum).

entrain [ɪnˈtreɪn] 1 vt troops (in Eisenbahnwaggons) verladen. 2 vi (in den Zug) einsteigen.

entrance[1] [ɪnˈtrɑːns] vt in Entzücken or Verzückung versetzen. to be ~d verzückt sein; to be ~d by/at sth von etw entzückt sein.

entrance[2] [ˈentrəns] n (a) (way in) Eingang m; (for vehicles) Einfahrt f; (hall) Eingangshalle f, Entree nt (geh).
  (b) (entering) Eintritt m; (Theat) Auftritt m. on his ~ bei seinem Eintritt/Auftritt; to make an ~ in Erscheinung treten; to make one's ~ (Theat) auftreten; (fig also) erscheinen; a door which gives ~ to a room (form) eine Tür, die Zugang zu einem Zimmer bietet (geh).
  (c) (admission) Eintritt m (to in +acc); (to club etc) Zutritt m (to zu); (to school) Aufnahme f (to in +acc). to gain ~ to a university die Zulassung zu einer Universität erhalten.

entrance: ~ card n Eintrittskarte f; ~ examination n Aufnahmeprüfung f; ~ fee n (for museum etc) Eintrittsgeld nt; (for competition) Teilnahmegebühr f; (for club membership) Aufnahmegebühr f; ~ ticket n Eintrittskarte f; ~ visa n Einreisevisum nt.

entrancing [ɪnˈtrɑːnsɪŋ, -lɪ] adj, ~ly adv bezaubernd.

entrant [ˈentrənt] n (to profession) Berufsanfänger(in f) m (to in +dat); (in competition) Teilnehmer(in f) m; (in exam) Prüfling m.

entreat [ɪnˈtriːt] vt inständig or dringend bitten, anflehen (for um). listen to him, I ~ you ich bitte Sie inständig or ich

flehe Sie an, ihn anzuhören.

entreatingly [ɪnˈtriːtɪŋlɪ] adv flehentlich.

entreaty [ɪnˈtriːtɪ] n dringende or flehentliche Bitte. they remained deaf to my entreaties sie blieben gegen alle meine Bitten taub; a look of ~ ein flehender Blick.

entrecôte (steak) [ˈɒntrəkəʊt(ˌsteɪk)] n Entrecote nt.

entrée [ˈɒntreɪ] n (a) Hauptgericht nt. (b) (to club etc) Zutritt m.

entrench [ɪnˈtrentʃ] vt (a) (Mil) eingraben, verschanzen.
  (b) (fig) to be/become ~ed in sth (word, custom) sich in etw (dat) eingebürgert haben/einbürgern; (idea, prejudice) sich in etw (dat) festgesetzt haben/festsetzen; (belief) in etw (dat) verwurzelt sein/sich in etw (dat) verwurzeln.

entrenchment [ɪnˈtrentʃmənt] n (Mil) Verschanzung f.

entrepôt [ˈɒntrəpəʊ] n (warehouse) Lagerhalle f; (port) Umschlaghafen m.

entrepreneur [ˌɒntrəprəˈnɜː] n Unternehmer m.

entrepreneurial [ˌɒntrəprəˈnɜːrɪəl] adj unternehmerisch.

entropy [ˈentrəpɪ] n Entropie f.

entrust [ɪnˈtrʌst] vt anvertrauen (to sb jdm). to ~ a child to sb's care ein Kind jds Obhut anvertrauen; to ~ sb with a task/a secret/one's valuables etc jdn mit einer Aufgabe betrauen/jdm ein Geheimnis/seine Wertgegenstände anvertrauen.

entry [ˈentrɪ] n (a) (into in +acc) (coming or going in) Eintritt m; (by car etc) Einfahrt f; (into country) Einreise f; (into club, school etc) Aufnahme f; (Theat) Auftritt m. point of ~ (of bullet etc) Einschußstelle f; (of inlet pipe etc) Anschlußstelle f; port of ~ Einreisehafen m; (airport) Landeflughafen m; to make an/one's ~ auftreten; "no ~" (on door etc) „Zutritt verboten"; (on one-way street) „keine Einfahrt"; on ~ into the earth's atmosphere beim Eintritt in die Erdatmosphäre.
  (b) (way in, doorway: of building, mine etc) Eingang m; (for vehicles) Einfahrt f.
  (c) (in diary, account book, dictionary etc) Eintrag m. the dictionary has 30,000 entries das Wörterbuch enthält 30.000 Stichwörter; to make an ~ against sb einen Betrag von jds Konto abbuchen.
  (d) (for race etc: competitor) Meldung f. there is a large ~ for the 200 metres für die 200 m sind viele Meldungen eingegangen.

entry: ~ form n Anmeldeformular nt; ~ permit n Passierschein m; (into country) Einreiseerlaubnis f; ~way n (US) Eingang m; (for vehicles) Einfahrt f.

entwine [ɪnˈtwaɪn] 1 vt (twist together) stems, ribbons ineinanderschlingen. they ~d their hands sie schlangen ihre Hände ineinander. 2 vi sich ineinanderschlingen or -winden.

enumerate [ɪˈnjuːməreɪt] vt aufzählen.

enumeration [ɪˌnjuːməˈreɪʃən] n Aufzählung f.

enunciate [ɪˈnʌnsɪeɪt] vti artikulieren.

enunciation [ɪˌnʌnsɪˈeɪʃən] n Artikulation f.

enuresis [ˌenjəˈriːsɪs] n (spec) Enurese f.

envelop [ɪnˈveləp] vt einhüllen. flames ~ed the house das Haus war von Flammen eingehüllt; he came ~ed in a big coat er kam in einen großen Mantel gehüllt.

envelope [ˈenvələʊp] n (a) (Brief)umschlag m; (large, for packets etc) Umschlag m. (b) (of balloon, Biol) Hülle f; (of airship) Außenhaut f; (of insect) Hautpanzer m.

enveloping [ɪnˈveləpɪŋ] adj alles umhüllend. the all-~ fog/silence die dichte Nebelhülle/die Hülle des Schweigens.

envelopment [ɪnˈveləpmənt] n Einhüllung f.

envenom [ɪnˈvenəm] vt (lit, fig) vergiften.

enviable adj, ~bly adv [ˈenvɪəbl, -lɪ] beneidenswert.

envious [ˈenvɪəs] adj neidisch (of auf +acc).

enviously [ˈenvɪəslɪ] adv neidisch; speak, think also voll Neid.

environment [ɪnˈvaɪərənmənt] n Umwelt f; (of town etc, physical surroundings) Umgebung f; (social, cultural surroundings also) Milieu nt. working-class ~ Arbeitermilieu nt; cultural/hostile ~ kulturelle/feindliche Umwelt; Department of the E~ (Brit) Umweltministerium nt.

environmental [ɪnˌvaɪərənˈmentl] adj Umwelt-; (relating to social, cultural environment also) Milieu-.

environmentalist [ɪnˌvaɪərənˈmentəlɪst] n Umweltschützer(in f) m.

environmentally [ɪnˌvaɪərənˈmentəlɪ] adv im Hinblick auf die Umwelt. ~ beneficial/damaging umweltfreundlich/-feindlich.

environs [ɪnˈvaɪərənz] npl Umgebung f. Rome and its ~ Rom und Umgebung.

envisage [ɪnˈvɪzɪdʒ] vt sich (dat) vorstellen. do you ~ any price rises in the near future? halten Sie Preisanstiege in nächster Zukunft für wahrscheinlich?

envoy [ˈenvɔɪ] n Bote m; (diplomat) Gesandte(r) mf.

envy [ˈenvɪ] n Neid m. his house was the ~ of his friends seine Freunde beneideten ihn um sein Haus; a laboratory which would be the ~ of every scientist im Labor, das der Neid eines jeden Wissenschaftlers wäre. 2 vt person beneiden. to ~ sb sth jdn um or wegen etw beneiden; that's a job I don't ~ das ist eine Arbeit, um die ich niemanden beneide.

enzyme [ˈenzaɪm] n Enzym, Ferment nt.

Eolithic [ˌiːəʊˈlɪθɪk] adj eolithisch.

eon [ˈiːɒn] n see aeon.

EP n Schallplatte f mit verlängerter Spieldauer.

epaulette [ˈepɔːlet] n Epaulette f, Schulterstück nt.

épée [ˈeɪpeɪ] n (Fecht)degen m.

ephebe [ɪˈfiːb] n Ephebe m.

ephemeral [ɪˈfemərəl] adj ephemer (geh, Zool), kurzlebig; happiness also flüchtig.

epic [ˈepɪk] 1 adj poetry episch; film, novel monumental, Monumental-; performance, match gewaltig; journey lang and abenteuerlich. 2 n (poem) Epos, Heldengedicht nt; (film, novel) Epos nt, monumentaler Film/Roman; (match) gewaltiges Spiel. an ~ of the screen (Film) ein Filmepos nt.

epicentre, (US) **epicenter** ['epɪsentəʳ] n Epizentrum nt.

epicure ['epɪkjʊəʳ] n Feinschmecker(in f) m.

epicurean [ˌepɪkjʊə'riːən] **1** adj epikureisch (geh). **2** n Epikureer (geh), Genußmensch m.

epicycle ['epɪsaɪkl] n Epizykel m.

epicyclic [ˌepɪ'saɪklɪk] adj epizykel-, epizyklisch.

epidemic [epɪ'demɪk] **1** n Epidemie (also fig), Seuche f. **2** adj epidemisch.

epidermis [ˌepɪ'dɜːmɪs] n Epidermis, Oberhaut f.

epidural [ˌepɪ'djʊərəl] **1** adj epidural. **2** n Epiduralanästhesie f.

epiglottis [ˌepɪ'glɒtɪs] n Kehldeckel m, Epiglottis f (spec).

epigram ['epɪgræm] n (saying) Epigramm, Sinngedicht nt.

epigrammatic(al) [ˌepɪgrə'mætɪk(əl)] adj epigrammatisch.

epigraph ['epɪgrɑːf] n Epigraph m, Inschrift f; (at beginning of book, chapter) Motto nt, Sinnspruch m.

epilepsy ['epɪlepsɪ] n Epilepsie f.

epileptic [ˌepɪ'leptɪk] **1** adj epileptisch. ~ **fit** epileptischer Anfall. **2** n Epileptiker(in f) m.

epilogue ['epɪlɒg] n Epilog m, Nachwort nt; (Rad, TV) Wort nt zum Tagesausklang.

Epiphany [ɪ'pɪfənɪ] n das Dreikönigs- or Erscheinungsfest.

episcopal [ɪ'pɪskəpəl] adj bischöflich, Bischofs-, episkopal (spec). **the E~ church** die Episkopalkirche.

episcopalian [ɪˌpɪskə'peɪlɪən] **1** adj zur Episkopalkirche gehörig. **2** n E~ Mitglied der Episkopalkirche, Episkopale(r) mf (form); **the E~s** die Episkopalkirche.

episiotomy [əˌpiːzɪ'ɒtəmɪ] n Dammschnitt m, Episiotomie f.

episode ['epɪsəʊd] n Episode f; (of story, TV, Rad) Fortsetzung f; (incident also) Begebenheit f, Vorfall m.

episodic [ˌepɪ'sɒdɪk] adj episodenhaft, episodisch; novel in Episoden.

epistemology [ɪˌpɪstə'mɒlədʒɪ] n Erkenntnistheorie, Epistemologie (spec) f.

epistle [ɪ'pɪsl] n (old, iro) Epistel f; (Bibl) Brief m (to an +acc).

epistolary [ɪ'pɪstələrɪ] adj Brief-.

epitaph ['epɪtɑːf] n Epitaph nt; (on grave also) Grabinschrift f.

epithet ['epɪθet] n Beiname m, Epitheton nt (geh); (insulting name) Schimpfname m.

epitome [ɪ'pɪtəmɪ] n (a) (of virtue, wisdom etc) Inbegriff m (of gen, an +dat). (b) (rare: of book) Epitome f (spec).

epitomize [ɪ'pɪtəmaɪz] vt verkörpern.

epoch ['iːpɒk] n Zeitalter nt (also Geol), Epoche f.

epoch-making ['iːpɒkˌmeɪkɪŋ] adj epochemachend, epochal.

epoxy resin [ɪ'pɒksɪ'rezɪn] n Epoxydharz nt.

Epsom salts ['epsəm'sɔːlts] npl (Epsomer) Bittersalz nt.

equable ['ekwəbl] adj gleichmäßig, ausgeglichen pred.

equably ['ekwəblɪ] adv gleichmäßig.

equal ['iːkwəl] **1** adj (a) gleich (to +dat). **the two groups were ~ in number** die beiden Gruppen waren zahlenmäßig gleich groß; **they are about ~ in value** sie haben ungefähr den gleichen Wert; **an ~ sum of money** eine gleich große or gleiche Summe Geld; **to divide sth into ~ parts** etw in gleiche Teile teilen; **two halves are ~ to one whole** zwei Halbe sind gleich ein Ganzes; **she received blame and praise with ~ indifference** sie nahm Lob und Tadel mit derselben Gleichgültigkeit entgegen; **to be on an ~ footing or on ~ terms** auf der gleichen Stufe stehen (with mit); **~ pay for ~ work** gleicher Lohn für gleiche Arbeit; **~ opportunities** Chancengleichheit f; **(all) other things being ~** wenn nichts dazwischenkommt; **now we're ~** jetzt sind wir quitt; **all men are ~,** but some are more ~ **than others** (hum) alle Menschen sind gleich, nur einige sind gleicher.

(b) to be ~ to the situation/task der Situation/Aufgabe gewachsen sein; **to feel ~ to sth** sich zu etw imstande or in der Lage fühlen.

2 n (in rank) Gleichgestellte(r) mf; (in birth also) Artgenosse m/-genossin f. **she is his ~** sie ist ihm ebenbürtig; **he has no ~** er hat nicht seinesgleichen; **our ~s** unseresgleichen; **to treat sb as an ~** jdn als ebenbürtig behandeln.

3 vt (be same as, Math) gleichen; (match, measure up to) gleichkommen (+dat). **three times three ~s nine** drei mal drei (ist) gleich neun; **let x ~ 3** wenn x gleich 3 ist; **he ~led his brother in generosity** er kam seinem Bruder an Großzügigkeit gleich; **not to be ~led** unvergleichlich; **this show is not to be ~led by any other** diese Show hat nicht ihresgleichen; **there is nothing to ~ it** nichts kommt dem gleich.

equality [ɪ'kwɒlɪtɪ] n Gleichheit f.

equalize ['iːkwəlaɪz] **1** vt chances, opportunities ausgleichen; incomes angleichen. **2** vi (Sport) ausgleichen. **the equalizing goal** das Ausgleichstor.

equalizer ['iːkwəlaɪzəʳ] n (Sport) Ausgleich m; (Ftbl etc also) Ausgleichstor nt or -treffer m. **to score or get the ~** den Ausgleich erzielen.

equally ['iːkwəlɪ] adv (a) ~ **gifted** gleich begabt pred, gleichbegabt attr, gleichermaßen begabt; ~ **paid** gleich bezahlt pred, gleichbezahlt attr; ~ **guilty** gleich schuldig pred, gleichermaßen schuldig.

(b) divide, distribute gleichmäßig.

(c) (just as) genauso. **he is ~ unsuited** er ist genauso ungeeignet.

(d) but then, ~ **one must concede ...** aber dann muß man ebenso zugestehen, daß ...

equals sign ['iːkwəlz'saɪn] n Gleichheitszeichen nt.

equanimity [ˌekwə'nɪmɪtɪ] n Gleichmut m, Gelassenheit f. **to recover one's ~** seine Gelassenheit wiedergewinnen, das seelische Gleichgewicht wiederfinden.

equate [ɪ'kweɪt] vt (a) (identify) gleichsetzen, identifizieren (with mit); (compare, treat as the same) auf die gleiche Stufe stellen, als gleichwertig hinstellen or betrachten. **do not ~ physical beauty with moral goodness** du mußt or darfst Schönheit nicht mit gutem Charakter gleichsetzen; **to ~ Eliot and Shakespeare** Eliot und Shakespeare auf eine Stufe stellen.

(b) (Math) gleichsetzen (to mit).

equation [ɪ'kweɪʒən] n (Math, fig) Gleichung f. ~ **of supply and demand** Ausgleich m von Angebot und Nachfrage; **work and leisure, how to get the ~ right** wie man Arbeit und Freizeit ins rechte Gleichgewicht bringt.

equator [ɪ'kweɪtəʳ] n Äquator m. **at the ~** am Äquator.

equatorial [ˌekwə'tɔːrɪəl] adj äquatorial, Äquatorial-.

equerry [ɪ'kwerɪ] n (personal attendant) persönlicher Diener (eines Mitgliedes der königlichen Familie); (in charge of horses) königlicher Stallmeister.

equestrian [ɪ'kwestrɪən] adj Reit-, Reiter-. ~ **act** (Kunst)reit- or Pferdenummer f; ~ **events** Reitveranstaltung f; (tournament) Reitturnier nt; ~ **prowess** Reitkunst f; ~ **statue** Reiterstandbild nt.

equestrianism [ɪ'kwestrɪənɪzəm] n Pferdesport m, Reiten nt.

equidistant ['iːkwɪ'dɪstənt] adj gleich weit entfernt (from von).

equilateral ['iːkwɪ'lætərəl] adj gleichseitig.

equilibrium [ˌiːkwɪ'lɪbrɪəm] n Gleichgewicht nt. **the political ~ of East Asia** das politische Gleichgewicht in Ostasien; **to lose one's ~** das Gleichgewicht halten/verlieren; **in ~** im Gleichgewicht.

equine ['ekwaɪn] adj Pferde-.

equinoctial [ˌiːkwɪ'nɒkʃəl] adj gales, tides äquinoktial.

equinox ['iːkwɪnɒks] n Tagundnachtgleiche f, Äquinoktium nt.

equip [ɪ'kwɪp] vt ship, soldier, astronaut, army, worker ausrüsten; household, kitchen ausstatten. **to ~ a room as a laboratory** ein Zimmer als Labor einrichten; **to ~ a boy for life** (fig) einem Jungen das (nötige) Rüstzeug fürs Leben mitgeben; **he is well ~ped for the job** (fig) er hat die nötigen Kenntnisse or das nötige Rüstzeug für die Stelle; **you are better ~ped than I to tackle chemistry translations** du bringst für Chemieübersetzungen das bessere Rüstzeug mit.

equipage ['ekwɪpɪdʒ] n Equipage f.

equipment [ɪ'kwɪpmənt] n, no pl (a) (objects) (of person) Ausrüstung f; laboratory ~ Laborausstattung f; office ~ Büroeinrichtung f; electrical ~ Elektrogeräte pl; kitchen/domestic ~ Küchen-/Haushaltsgeräte pl.

(b) (action) see vt Ausrüstung f; Ausstattung f.

(c) (mental, intellectual) (geistiges) Rüstzeug.

equipoise ['ekwɪpɔɪz] n (state) Gleichgewicht nt; (thing) Gegengewicht nt.

equitable ['ekwɪtəbl] adj fair, gerecht, recht und billig.

equitableness ['ekwɪtəblnɪs] n Fairneß, Billigkeit f.

equitably ['ekwɪtəblɪ] adv fair, gerecht.

equity ['ekwɪtɪ] n (a) Fairneß, Billigkeit f. (b) (Fin) equities pl Stammaktien pl, Dividendenpapiere pl; ~ **capital** Eigenkapital nt, Nettoanteil m. (c) (Jur) Billigkeitsrecht nt, billiges Recht. (d) (Brit Theat) E~ Gewerkschaft f der Schauspieler.

equivalence [ɪ'kwɪvələns] n Äquivalenz, Entsprechung f.

equivalent [ɪ'kwɪvələnt] **1** adj (a) (equal) gleich, gleichwertig, äquivalent. **three more or less ~ translations** drei mehr oder weniger gleichwertige Übersetzungen; **that's ~ to saying ...** das ist gleichbedeutend damit, zu sagen ...; **to be ~ in meaning** die gleiche Bedeutung haben; **no two words are exactly ~ in meaning** zwei Wörter haben niemals genau die gleiche Bedeutung.

(b) (corresponding) entsprechend. **the ~ institution in America** die entsprechende Einrichtung in Amerika, das amerikanische Äquivalent dazu; **an ~ salary in 1935 would have been ...** ein entsprechendes Gehalt wäre im Jahre 1935 ... gewesen; **it is ~ to £30** das entspricht £ 30; **an ace is ~ to ... ein** As entspricht ...; **... or the ~ value in francs** ... oder der Gegenwert in Francs.

(c) (Chem) gleichwertig; (Geometry) äquivalent.

(d) that's ~ **to lying** das ist soviel wie gelogen; **as au pair girl she is ~ to nanny, maid and tutor all in one** als Au-pair-Mädchen ist sie soviel wie Kindermädchen, Dienstmädchen und Hauslehrerin in einer Person.

2 n Äquivalent nt; (counterpart) (thing also) Gegenstück, Pendant nt; (person also) Pendant nt. **what is the ~ in German marks?** was ist der Gegenwert in DM?; **the American ~ of the British public school** das amerikanische Gegenstück or Pendant zur britischen Public School; **the German ~ of the English word** die deutsche Entsprechung des englischen Wortes; ... or **the ~ in cash** ...oder der/den Gegenwert in bar; **the ~ from another company** das gleiche von einer anderen Firma.

equivocal [ɪ'kwɪvəkəl] adj behaviour zweideutig; words doppeldeutig; outcome nicht eindeutig; (vague) unklar, unbestimmt.

equivocally [ɪ'kwɪvəkəlɪ] adv see adj.

equivocate [ɪ'kwɪvəkeɪt] vi ausweichen, ausweichend antworten.

equivocation [ɪˌkwɪvə'keɪʃən] n Ausflucht f, doppelsinnige or ausweichende Formulierung/Antwort. **without so much ~** ohne so viele Ausflüchte.

ER abbr of Elizabeth Regina.

era ['ɪərə] n Ära, Epoche f; (Geol) Erdzeitalter nt. **the Christian ~** (die) christliche Zeitrechnung; **the end of an ~** das Ende einer Ära.

eradicate [ɪ'rædɪkeɪt] vt ausrotten.

eradication [ɪˌrædɪ'keɪʃən] n Ausrottung f.

erase [ɪ'reɪz] vt ausradieren; (from tape, computer) löschen; (from the mind) streichen (from aus); (sl: kill) erledigen (sl).

eraser [ɪ'reɪzəʳ] n Radiergummi nt or m; (for blackboard) Schwamm m.

erasure [ɪ'reɪʒəʳ] n (act) Auslöschen, Ausradieren nt; (from tape) Löschen nt; (sth erased) ausradierte Stelle, Radierstelle f; (on tape) gelöschte Stelle.

ere [ɛəʳ] (old, poet) **1** prep ehe, bevor. ~ **now** bisher; ~ **then** vordem, schon vorher; ~ **long** binnen kurzem. **2** conj ehe, bevor.

erect [ɪˈrekt] **1** adj aufrecht, gerade; *penis etc* erigiert, steif. **to hold oneself ~** sich gerade halten; **he went forward, his head ~** er ging mit hocherhobenem Kopf nach vorn; **with tail ~** mit hocherhobenem Schwanz.
  2 vt *temple, edifice* (er)bauen, errichten (*to sb* jdm); *wall, flats, factory* bauen; *statue, altar* errichten (*to sb* jdm); *machinery, traffic signs, collapsible furniture* aufstellen; *scaffolding* aufstellen, aufbauen; *tent* aufschlagen; *mast, flagpole* aufrichten; (*fig*) *barrier* errichten, aufbauen; *theoretical system* aufstellen.

erectile [ɪˈrektaɪl] adj Schwell-, erektil.

erection [ɪˈrekʃən] n (a) see vt (Er)bauen, Errichten nt; Bauen nt; Errichten nt; Aufstellen nt; Aufbauen nt; Aufschlagen nt; Aufrichten nt; Errichten nt; Aufstellen nt. (b) (*the building, structure*) Gebäude nt, Bau m. (c) (*Physiol*) Erektion f.

erectly [ɪˈrektlɪ] adv *sit etc* gerade, aufrecht.

erg [ɜːg] n Erg nt.

ergonomics [ˌɜːgəʊˈnɒmɪks] n sing Arbeitswissenschaft, Ergonomik, Ergonomie f.

ergot [ˈɜːgət] n Mutterkorn, Hungerkorn nt.

ergotism [ˈɜːgətɪzəm] n (*Med*) Mutterkornvergiftung f, Ergotismus m.

Erin [ˈɪərɪn] n (*poet*) Irland nt.

ermine [ˈɜːmɪn] n (*animal*) Hermelin nt; (*fur*) Hermelin m.

ERNIE abbr of **Electronic Random Number Indicator Equipment.**

erode [ɪˈrəʊd] vt (*glacier, water, sea*) auswaschen, erodieren (*spec*); (*acid*) ätzen; (*rust*) wegfressen, anfressen; (*fig*) *confidence, sb's beliefs* untergraben; *differentials* aushöhlen.

erogenous [ɪˈrɒdʒənəs] adj erogen.

erosion [ɪˈrəʊʒən] n (*by water, glaciers, rivers*) Erosion, Abtragung f; (*by acid*) Ätzung f; (*fig: of value etc*) Schwinden nt; (*of differentials*) Aushöhlen nt. **an ~ of confidence in the pound** ein Vertrauensverlust or -schwund des Pfundes.

erosive [ɪˈrəʊzɪv] adj *effect of sea etc* abtragend; *effect of acid* ätzend.

erotic [ɪˈrɒtɪk] adj aufreizend; *literature, film* erotisch. **he's a very ~ person** er wirkt sehr erotisch.

erotica [ɪˈrɒtɪkə] npl Erotika pl.

erotically [ɪˈrɒtɪkəlɪ] adv aufreizend; *written, photographed* erotisch.

eroticism [ɪˈrɒtɪsɪzəm] n Erotik f.

err [ɜː] vi (a) (*be mistaken*) sich irren. **to ~ in one's judgement** in seinem Urteil fehlgehen, sich in seinem Urteil irren; **to ~ is human(, to forgive divine)** (*Prov*) Irren ist menschlich(, Vergeben göttlich); **it is better to ~ on the side of caution** man sollte im Zweifelsfall lieber zu vorsichtig sein.
  (b) (*sin*) sündigen, Verfehlungen begehen.
  (c) (*Rel: stray*) abgehen, in die Irre gehen. **to ~ from the path of righteousness** vom Pfad der Tugend abweichen or abgehen.

errand [ˈerənd] n (*shopping etc*) Besorgung f; (*to give a message etc*) Botengang m; (*task*) Auftrag m. **to send sb on an ~** jdn auf Besorgungen/einen Botengang schicken; **to go on or run ~s (for sb)** (für jdn) Besorgungen/Botengänge machen; **to give sb an ~ to do** jdm etw auftragen; **you can't trust him with any ~s** man kann ihm nichts auftragen; **to be on an ~** Besorgungen/einen Botengang machen, etwas erledigen; **~ of mercy** Rettungsaktion f; **~ boy** Laufbursche, Laufjunge m.

errant [ˈerənt] adj (a) *knight* fahrender Ritter. (b) (*erring*) *ways* sündig, verfehlt; *husband* abtrünnig; (*hum*) *Marxist, Freudian* fehlgeleitet, auf Irrwegen.

errata [eˈrɑːtə] pl of **erratum**.

erratic [ɪˈrætɪk] adj (a) unberechenbar; *person also* sprunghaft; *moods also* schwankend; *results also* stark abweichend, stark schwankend; *work, performance* ungleichmäßig, unregelmäßig; *working of machine, freezer, weather also* launisch. (b) (*Geol*) erratisch.

erratically [ɪˈrætɪkəlɪ] adv *act* unberechenbar, launenhaft; *work* (*machine*) unregelmäßig; (*person*) ungleichmäßig; *drive* unberechenbar.

erratum [eˈrɑːtəm] n, pl **errata** Erratum nt.

erring [ˈɜːrɪŋ] adj see errant (b).

erroneous [ɪˈrəʊnɪəs] adj falsch; *assumption, belief* irrig.

erroneously [ɪˈrəʊnɪəslɪ] adv fälschlicherweise; *accuse* fälschlich. **~ known as ...** fälschlich als ... bekannt; **~ labelled** falsch etikettiert.

error [ˈerəʳ] n (a) (*mistake*) Fehler m. **the elimination of ~** das Ausmerzen von Fehlern, die Ausmerzung von Fehlern; **~ in calculation** Rechenfehler m; **compass ~** (magnetische) Abweichung; **a navigational ~** ein Navigationsfehler m; **~s and omissions excepted** (*Comm*) Irrtum vorbehalten; **a pilot's ~** ein Fehler des Piloten; **the ~ rate** die Fehlerquote, die Fehlerrate; see **margin**.
  (b) (*wrongness*) Irrtum m. **to be in ~** im Irrtum sein, sich im Irrtum befinden; **in ~** (*wrongly, accidentally*) aus Versehen; **to see the ~ of one's ways** seine Fehler irrtümlicherweise; **to see the ~ of one's ways** seine Fehler einsehen.

ersatz [ˈeəzæts] **1** adj Ersatz-. **~ religion** Ersatzreligion f; **~ coffee** Kaffee-Ersatz m. **2** n Ersatz m.

erstwhile [ˈɜːstwaɪl] **1** adj (*old, liter*) vormalig, einstig, ehemalig. **2** adv (*old, liter*) vormals, ehedem, einst.

eructate [ɪˈrʌkteɪt] vi (*hum, form*) aufstoßen.

eructation [ˌɪrʌkˈteɪʃən] n (*hum, form*) Aufstoßen nt. **an ~** ein Rülpser m (*inf*).

erudite [ˈerʊdaɪt] adj gelehrt; *person also* gebildet, belesen.

eruditely [ˈerʊdaɪtlɪ] adv gelehrt.

erudition [ˌerʊˈdɪʃən] n Gelehrsamkeit f. **a book of great ~** ein sehr gelehrtes Buch.

erupt [ɪˈrʌpt] vi (*volcano, war, quarrel*) ausbrechen; (*spots*) zum Vorschein kommen; (*teeth*) durchkommen, durchstoßen; (*fig:*

person) explodieren. **he ~ed into a fit of rage** er bekam einen Wutanfall; **he ~ed into the room** er platzte ins Zimmer; **she/her face ~s in spots** sie bekommt im ganzen Gesicht Pickel.

eruption [ɪˈrʌpʃən] n (*of volcano, anger, violence*) Ausbruch m; (*Med*) (*of spec, rash*) Eruption f (*spec*), Ausbruch m, Auftreten nt; (*rash etc*) Hautausschlag m, Eruption f (*spec*).

erysipelas [ˌerɪˈsɪpɪləs] n (*Wund*)rose f.

escalate [ˈeskəleɪt] **1** vt *war* ausweiten, eskalieren; *costs* sprunghaft erhöhen. **2** vi sich ausweiten, um sich greifen, eskalieren; (*costs*) sprunghaft ansteigen, in die Höhe schnellen.

escalation [ˌeskəˈleɪʃən] n Eskalation f.

escalator [ˈeskəleɪtəʳ] n Rolltreppe f.

escalope [ˈeskæləp] n Schnitzel nt.

escapade [ˌeskəˈpeɪd] n Eskapade f.

escape [ɪˈskeɪp] **1** vi (a) flüchten (*from* aus), entfliehen (*geh*) (*from* dat); (*from pursuers*) entkommen (*from* dat); (*from prison, camp, cage, stall etc*) ausbrechen (*from* aus); (*bird*) entfliegen (*from* dat); (*water*) auslaufen (*from* aus); (*gas*) ausströmen (*from* aus). **to stop the prisoners escaping** um Gefängnisausbrüche zu verhindern; **he was shot while trying to ~** er wurde bei einem Fluchtversuch erschossen; **he's trying to ~ from his life in the suburbs** er versucht, seinem Leben in der Vorstadt zu entfliehen or zu entkommen; **in order to let sb ~** um die Königin davonkommen zu lassen; **an ~d prisoner/tiger** ein entsprungener Häftling/Tiger; **he ~d from the fire** er entkam dem Feuer; **I've got you now,** she said, **and I won't let you ~** jetzt habe ich dich, sagte sie, und du entkommst mir so schnell nicht; **you cannot ~ from the passage of time** man kann dem Lauf der Zeit nicht entrinnen; **I just feel I have to ~ from this job/place** ich habe einfach das Gefühl, daß ich hier weg muß; **she has to be able to ~ from her family sometimes** sie muß ab und zu die Möglichkeit haben, ihrer Familie zu entfliehen; **a room which I can ~ to** ein Zimmer, in das ich mich zurückziehen kann; **to ~ from oneself** vor sich (dat) selber fliehen; **it's no good trying to ~ from the world** es hat keinen Zweck, vor der Welt fliehen zu wollen.
  (b) (*get off, be spared*) davonkommen. **to ~ with a warning/a few cuts** mit einer Verwarnung/ein paar Schnittwunden davonkommen; **these cuts will affect everyone, nobody will ~** diese Kürzungen betreffen alle, keiner wird ungeschoren davonkommen; **the others were killed, but he ~d** die anderen wurden getötet, aber er kam mit dem Leben davon.

  2 vt (a) *pursuers* entkommen (+dat).
  (b) (*avoid*) *consequences, punishment, disaster* entgehen (+dat). **no department will ~ these cuts** keine Abteilung wird von diesen Kürzungen verschont bleiben; **he narrowly ~d danger/death** er ist der Gefahr/dem Tod mit knapper Not entronnen; **he narrowly ~d being run over** er wäre um ein Haar or um Haaresbreite überfahren worden; **but you can't ~ the fact that ...** aber du kannst nicht leugnen or abstreiten, daß ...; **there's no escaping this remorseless logic** man kann sich dieser unbarmherzigen Logik nicht entziehen.
  (c) (*be unnoticed, forgotten by*) **his name/the word ~s me** sein Name/das Wort ist mir entfallen; **nothing ~s him** ihm entgeht nichts; **to ~ observation or notice** unbemerkt bleiben; **it had not ~d her notice** es war ihr nicht entgangen; **the thoughtless words which ~d me** die unbedachten Worte, die mir herausgerutscht or entfahren sind.

  3 n (a) (*from prison etc*) Ausbruch m, Flucht f; (*attempted ~*) Ausbruchsversuch, Fluchtversuch m; (*from a country*) Flucht f; (*fig: from reality, one's family etc*) Flucht f. **to plan an ~** ausbrechen or einen Ausbruch planen; **to make an ~** ausbrechen, entfliehen; **somebody must have told the guards about the ~** irgend jemand muß den Wachen von dem Ausbruchsplan berichtet haben; **the ~ was successful** der Ausbruch- or Fluchtversuch glückte or war erfolgreich; **there's been an ~** jemand ist ausgebrochen; **there were two ~s from this prison last month** im letzten Monat sind aus diesem Gefängnis zweimal Leute ausgebrochen; **the increasing number of ~s** die zunehmende Zahl von Ausbruchsfällen; **with this security system ~ is impossible** dieses Sicherheitssystem macht Ausbrechen unmöglich; **what are their chances of ~?** wie sind ihre Fluchtmöglichkeiten?, wie sind ihre Chancen zu entkommen?; **have you had any ~s at this zoo?** sind Ihnen aus dem Zoo schon Tiere ausgebrochen?; **there's been an ~ at London Zoo** aus dem Londoner Zoo ist ein Löwe/Tiger etc ausgebrochen; **to have a miraculous ~** (*from accident, illness*) auf wunderbare Weise davonkommen; **an ~ from reality** eine Flucht vor der Realität; **fishing/music is his ~** Angeln/Musik ist seine Zuflucht; **otherwise I don't get any ~ from my routine life/the demands of my family** sonst habe ich überhaupt keine Abwechslung mit meiner Routine/von den Ansprüchen meiner Familie; **there's no ~** (*fig*) es gibt keinen Ausweg or kein Entrinnen (*geh*); see **lucky**.
  (b) (*of water*) Ausfließen nt; (*of gas*) Ausströmen nt; (*of steam, gas, in a machine*) Entweichen nt. **due to an ~ of gas** aufgrund ausströmenden Gases.

escape: **~ artist** n Entfesselungskünstler(in f) m; **~ attempt, ~ bid** n Fluchtversuch m; **~ clause** n (*Jur*) Befreiungsklausel f.

escapee [ɪskeɪˈpiː] n entwichener Häftling or Gefangener.

escape: **~ hatch** n (*Naut*) Notluke f; **~ mechanism** n Abwehrmechanismus m.

escapement [ɪˈskeɪpmənt] n (*of clock*) Hemmung f.

escape: **~ pipe** n Überlaufrohr nt; (*for gas, steam*) Abzugsrohr nt; **~ plan** n Fluchtplan m; **~-proof** adj ausbruchsicher; **~ road** n Ausweichstraße f; **~ route** n Fluchtweg m; **~ valve** n Sicherheitsventil nt; **~ velocity** n (*Space*) Fluchtgeschwindigkeit f.

escapism [ɪˈskeɪpɪzəm] n Wirklichkeitsflucht f, Eskapismus m (*spec*) m.

escapist [ɪˈskeɪpɪst] **1** n jd, der vor der Wirklichkeit flieht, Eskapist m (spec). **2** adj ~ **visions** unrealistische Träume pl; ~ **literature** unrealistische, eine Phantasiewelt vorgaukelnde Literatur.

escapologist [ˌeskəˈpɒlədʒɪst] n Entfesselungskünstler(in f) m.

escarpment [ɪˈskɑːpmənt] n Steilhang m; (Geol) Schichtstufe f; (as fortification) Böschung f.

eschatological [ˌeskətəˈlɒdʒɪkəl] adj eschatologisch.

eschatology [ˌeskəˈtɒlədʒɪ] n Eschatologie f.

eschew [ɪsˈtʃuː] vt (old, liter) scheuen, (ver)meiden; **wine etc** sich enthalten (+gen); **temptation** aus dem Wege gehen (+dat).

escort [ˈeskɔːt] **1** n (a) Geleitschutz m; (escorting vehicles, ships etc) Eskorte f; Geleitschiff nt/-schiffe pl; (police ~) Begleitmannschaft, Eskorte f; (guard of honour) Eskorte f. **under ~** unter Bewachung; **motor-cycle ~** Motorradeskorte f. (b) (male companion) Begleiter m; (hired female) Hostess f. **2** [ɪˈskɔːt] vt begleiten; (Mil, Naut) general eskortieren, Geleit(schutz) geben (+dat).

escort: ~ **agency** n Hostessenagentur f; ~ **duty** n Geleitdienst m; **to be on** ~ **duty** Geleitschutz geben müssen; ~ **fighter** n (Aviat) Begleitjäger m; ~ **party** n Eskorte f; ~ **vessel** n (Naut) Geleitschiff nt.

escutcheon [ɪˈskʌtʃən] n Wappen nt. **it is a blot on his** ~ das ist ein Fleck auf seiner weißen Weste.

ESE abbr of **east-south-east** OSO.

Eskimo [ˈeskɪməʊ] **1** adj Eskimo-, eskimoisch. **2** n (a) Eskimo m, Eskimofrau f. (b) (language) Eskimosprache f.

ESN abbr of **educationally subnormal**.

esophagus n (esp US) see **oesophagus**.

esoteric [ˌesəʊˈterɪk] adj esoterisch.

ESP abbr of **extra-sensory perception** ASW f, Außersinnliche Wahrnehmung.

espalier [ɪˈspæljəʳ] n (trellis) Spalier nt; (tree) Spalierbaum m; (method) Anbau m von Spalierobst.

especial [ɪˈspeʃəl] adj besondere(r, s).

especially [ɪˈspeʃəlɪ] adv besonders. **everyone should come,** ~ **you** alle sollten kommen, vor allen Dingen du or du besonders; **you** ~ **ought to know** gerade du solltest wissen; **more** ~ **as** besonders da, zumal; **why me** ~? warum unbedingt or gerade ich/mich?; **I came** ~ **to see you** ich bin speziell gekommen, um dich zu besuchen; ~ **in the summer** besonders or zumal im Sommer.

Esperanto [ˌespəˈræntəʊ] n Esperanto nt.

espionage [ˌespɪəˈnɑːʒ] n Spionage f.

esplanade [ˌespləˈneɪd] n (Strand)promenade f.

espousal [ɪˈspaʊzəl] n (a) (old) (marriage) Vermählung f; (betrothal) Verlobung f. (b) (of cause etc) Parteinahme f (of für).

espouse [ɪˈspaʊz] vt (a) (old, form) woman sich vermählen mit, zur Frau nehmen; (get betrothed to) sich anverloben (+dat) (old). **to become** ~**d to sb** jdm angetraut/anverlobt werden. (b) (fig) cause Partei ergreifen für, eintreten für.

espresso [eˈspresəʊ] n Espresso m. ~ **bar** Espresso(bar f) nt.

esprit de corps [eˈspriːdəˈkɔːʳ] n Korpsgeist m.

espy [ɪˈspaɪ] vt (old, liter) erspähen, erblicken.

esquire [ɪˈskwaɪəʳ] n (Brit: on envelope, abbr **Esq**) als Titel nach dem Namen, wenn kein anderer Titel angegeben wird. **James Jones, Esq** Herrn James Jones.

essay¹ [eˈseɪ] (form) **1** vt (try) (aus)probieren. **2** n Versuch m.

essay² [ˈeseɪ] n Essay m or nt; (esp Sch) Aufsatz m.

essayist [ˈeseɪɪst] n Essayist m.

essence [ˈesəns] n (a) (Philos) Wesen nt, Essenz f; (substratum) Substanz f. (b) (most important quality) Wesen, Wesentliche(s) nt, Kern m. **in** ~ **the theories are very similar** die Theorien sind im Wesentlichen or in ihrem Kern or essentiell (geh) sehr ähnlich; **how would you describe the situation, in** ~? wie würden Sie die Situation im wesentlichen beschreiben?; **well that's it, in** ~ nun, das wäre es im wesentlichen; **good management is of the** ~ gutes Management ist von entscheidender or ausschlaggebender Bedeutung; **the** ~ **of his thought** der Kern or die Essenz seines Denkens; **the note contained the** ~ **of what he had said** die Notiz enthielt den Kern dessen, was er gesagt hatte; **the** ~ **of stupidity/tact** der Inbegriff der Dummheit/des Taktes; **the** ~ **of Liberalism** die Essenz des Liberalismus. (c) (extract: Chem, Cook) Essenz f. **meat** ~ Fleischextrakt m.

essential [ɪˈsenʃəl] **1** adj (a) (necessary, vital) (unbedingt or absolut) erforderlich or notwendig. **it is** ~ **to act quickly** schnelles Handeln ist unbedingt or absolut erforderlich, schnelles Handeln tut not; **it is** ~ **that he comes** es ist absolut or unbedingt erforderlich, daß er kommt, er muß unbedingt kommen; **it is** ~ **that you understand this** du mußt das unbedingt verstehen; **do it now — is it really** ~? mach es jetzt — ist das wirklich unbedingt nötig?; **this is of** ~ **importance** dies ist von entscheidender Bedeutung; **it's** ~ **for a happy life** dies ist eine notwendige Voraussetzung für ein glückliches Leben; **sleep is** ~ **for a healthy life** Schlaf ist die wesentliche Voraussetzung or eine unabdingbare Voraussetzung für ein gesundes Leben; **she's become** ~ **to me** sie ist mir unentbehrlich geworden; **the** ~ **thing is to ...** wichtig ist vor allem, zu ... (b) (of the essence, basic) wesentlich, essentiell (geh) (Philos) essentiell, wesenhaft; question entscheidend. ~ **features** wesentliche Eigenschaften pl; **I don't doubt his** ~ **goodness** ich zweifle nicht an, daß er im Grunde ein guter Mensch ist; **he has an** ~ **honesty** er ist im Grunde (genommen) ehrlich; **there is no** ~ **difference** da gibt es keinen wesentlichen Unterschied; **the** ~ **feature of his personality** der Grundzug or der grundlegende Zug seiner Persönlichkeit. (c) (Chem) ~ **oils** ätherische Öle pl.

2 n (a) (necessary thing) **an ice-axe is an** ~ **for mountain climbing** ein Eispickel ist zum Bergsteigen unerläßlich, ein Eispickel ist unbedingt notwendig zum Bergsteigen; **accuracy is an** ~ or **one of the** ~**s in this type of work** Genauigkeit ist für diese Art (von) Arbeit unabdingbar; **just bring the** ~**s** bring nur das Allernotwendigste mit; **with only the bare** ~**s** nur mit dem Allernotwendigsten ausgestattet. (b) ~**s** pl (most important points) wichtige Punkte pl, Essentials pl, **the** ~**s of German grammar** die Grundlagen or Grundzüge der deutschen Grammatik.

essentially [ɪˈsenʃəlɪ] adv (basically) im Grunde genommen, im Prinzip; (in essence) dem Wesen nach, im wesentlichen. **he's** ~ **a nervous person** im Grunde seines Wesens ist er ein nervöser Mensch; **our points of view are** ~ **similar** unsere Ansichten gleichen einander im Wesentlichen; **what are the** ~ **French characteristics that he reveals?** welche im wesentlichen französischen Eigenschaften zeigt er?; **an** ~ **optimistic view** eine im wesentlichen optimistische Einstellung.

EST (US) abbr of **Eastern Standard Time**.

est abbr of **established**.

establish [ɪˈstæblɪʃ] **1** vt (a) (found, set up) gründen; government bilden; religion also stiften; laws geben, schaffen; custom, new procedure einführen; relations herstellen, aufnehmen; post einrichten, schaffen; power, authority sich (dat) verschaffen; peace stiften; order (wieder)herstellen; list (in publishing) aufstellen, zusammenstellen; reputation sich (dat) verschaffen; precedent setzen; committee einsetzen. **once he had** ~**ed his power as Emperor** als er seine Macht als Kaiser begründet hatte; **his father** ~**ed him in business** sein Vater ermöglichte ihm den Start ins Geschäftsleben; **he offered to** ~ **me in business** er bot an, mir beim Start ins Geschäftsleben behilflich zu sein; **to** ~ **one's reputation as a scholar/writer** sich (dat) einen Namen als Wissenschaftler/Schriftsteller machen. (b) (prove) fact, innocehce beweisen, nachweisen; claim unter Beweis stellen. **we have** ~**ed that ...** wir haben bewiesen or gezeigt, daß ...; **having** ~**ed his indispensability** nachdem er seine Unentbehrlichkeit unter Beweis gestellt hatte. (c) (determine) identity, facts ermitteln, feststellen. (d) (gain acceptance for) product, theory, ideas Anklang or Anerkennung finden für; one's rights Anerkennung finden für. **if we can** ~ **our product on the market** wenn wir unser Produkt auf dem Markt etablieren können; **we have tried to** ~ **our product as the number-one model** wir haben versucht, unser Produkt als das Spitzenmodell einzuführen; **after years of opposition he finally saw his ideas** ~**ed** nach Jahren des Widerstandes sah er endlich, wie seine Ideen Anerkennung fanden.

2 vr (in business, profession) sich etablieren, sich niederlassen. **he has now firmly** ~**ed himself within the company** er ist jetzt in der Gesellschaft fest etabliert; **he seems to have** ~**ed himself as an expert** er scheint sich (dat) einen Ruf als Experte verschafft zu haben.

established [ɪˈstæblɪʃt] adj (a) (on firm basis) reputation gesichert, gefestigt. **well-**~ business gut eingeführte or alteingesessene Firma. (b) (accepted) fact feststehend, akzeptiert; truth akzeptiert, anerkannt; custom althergebracht; procedure anerkannt; belief überkommen, herrschend; government herrschend; laws bestehend, geltend; order bestehend, etabliert. **an** ~ **scientific fact** eine wissenschaftlich erwiesene Tatsache; **is there an** ~ **procedure for this?** gibt es dafür ein handelsübliches or allgemeinübliches Verfahren?; **he deviated somewhat from the** ~ **procedure** er wich ein wenig vom üblichen or sonst allgemeinüblichen Verfahren ab. (c) (Eccl) **the** ~ **Church** die Staatskirche.

establishment [ɪˈstæblɪʃmənt] n (a) see vt (a) Gründung f; Bildung f; Stiftung f; Schaffung f, Erlassen nt; Einführung f; Herstellung, Aufnahme f; Einrichtung, Schaffung f; (of power, authority) Festigung f; Stiftung f; (Wieder)herstellung f; Aufstellung f, Zusammenstellen nt; (of reputation) Begründung f; Setzen nt; Einsetzen nt. (b) (proving) Beweis m. **the lawyer devoted a lot of time to the** ~ **of a few basic facts** der Rechtsanwalt verwandte viel Zeit darauf, ein paar Tatsachen unter Beweis zu stellen. (c) (determining) Ermittlung f. ~ **of truth** Wahrheitsfindung f. (d) (institution etc) Institution f; (hospital, school etc also) Anstalt f. **that big house on the corner is a very dubious** ~ das große Haus an der Ecke ist ein sehr zweifelhaftes Etablissement; **commercial** ~ kommerzielles Unternehmen. (e) (household) Haus nt, Haushalt m. **to keep up a large** ~ ein großes Haus führen. (f) (Mil, Naut etc: personnel) Truppenstärke f. **war/peace** ~ Kriegs-/Friedensstärke f. (g) (Brit) **the E-**~ das Establishment.

estate [ɪˈsteɪt] n (a) (land) Gut nt. **to retire to one's country** ~ sich auf sein Landgut zurückziehen; **family** ~ Familienbesitz m. (b) (Jur: possessions) Besitz(tümer pl) m, Eigentum nt; (of deceased) Nachlaß m, Erbmasse f. **to leave one's** ~ **to sb** jdm seinen ganzen Besitz vermachen or hinterlassen; **personal** ~ persönliches Eigentum; see **real**. (c) (esp Brit) (housing) ~ Siedlung f; (trading ~) Industriegelände nt. (d) (order, rank) Stand m. **the three** ~**s** die drei Stände; **person of high** ~ (old) Standesperson f (old); **the holy** ~ **of matrimony** (Rel) der heilige Stand der Ehe; **to reach man's** ~ (liter) in den Mannesstand treten (old).

estate: ~ **agent** n (Brit) Grundstücks- or Immobilienmakler(in f) m; ~ **car** n (Brit) Kombi(wagen) m; ~ **duty** n Erbschaftssteuer f.

esteem [ɪˈstiːm] **1** vt (a) (consider) ansehen, betrachten. **I** ~ **it an honour** ich sehe es als eine Ehre an, ich betrachte es als Ehre.

(b) (*think highly of*) person hochschätzen; *qualities* schätzen. **my** ~ed **colleague** (*form*) mein verehrter Herr Kollege (*form*). **2** *n* Wertschätzung *f.* **to hold sb/sth in (high)** ~ jdn/etw (hoch)schätzen, von jdm/etw eine hohe Meinung haben; **to be held in low/great** ~ wenig/sehr geschätzt werden; **he went down in my** ~ er ist in meiner Achtung gesunken.

esthete *etc* (*esp US*) *see* **aesthete** *etc*.

Esthonia [e'stəʊnɪə] *n* Estland *nt.*

Esthonian [e'stəʊnɪən] **1** *adj* estnisch. **2** *n* (a) Este *m*, Estin *f.* (b) (*language*) Estnisch *nt.*

estimable ['estɪməbl] *adj* (a) (*deserving respect*) schätzenswert. (b) (*that can be estimated*) (ab)schätzbar.

estimate ['estɪmɪt] **1** *n* (a) (*approximate calculation*) Schätzung *f*; (*valuation: by antique dealer etc*) Taxierung *f.* **what's your** ~ **of our chances of success?** wie schätzen Sie unsere Erfolgschancen ein?; **to form an** ~ **of sb's capabilities** sich (*dat*) ein Bild von jds Fähigkeiten machen, jds Fähigkeiten einschätzen; **£100 is just an** ~ £ 100 ist nur geschätzt; **it's just an** ~ das ist nur geschätzt; **at a rough** ~ grob geschätzt, über den Daumen gepeilt (*inf*); **at the lowest** ~ mindestens, wenigstens.

(b) (*Comm: of cost*) (Kosten)voranschlag *m.* **to get an** ~ einen (Kosten)voranschlag einholen.

(c) (*government costs*) ~s *pl* Haushalt *m*, Budget *nt.*

2 ['estɪmeɪt] *vt cost, price* (ein)schätzen; *distance, speed* schätzen. **his wealth is** ~**d at ...** sein Vermögen wird auf ... geschätzt; **it's hard to** ~ es läßt sich schwer (ab)schätzen; **I** ~ **she must be 40** ich schätze sie auf 40, ich schätze, daß sie 40 ist; **I would** ~ **we'd need 30 people/£300** ich schätze, wir brauchen 30 Leute/£ 300.

3 ['estɪmeɪt] *vi* schätzen. **I'm just estimating** das schätze ich nur.

estimation [,estɪ'meɪʃən] *n* (a) Einschätzung *f.* **in my** ~ meiner Einschätzung nach.

(b) (*esteem*) Achtung *f.* **to hold sb in high** ~ jdn hochachten, viel von jdm halten; **he went up/down in my** ~ er ist in meiner Achtung gestiegen/gesunken.

estivate *etc* (*US*) *see* **aestivate** *etc.*

estrange [ɪ'streɪndʒ] *vt person* entfremden (*from* +*dat*). **to be/become** ~d **from sb** sich jdm entfremdet haben/entfremden; **to be** ~d **from one's wife/husband** sich seiner Frau/seinem Mann entfremdet haben; **they are** ~d (*married couple*) sie haben sich auseinandergelebt.

estrangement [ɪ'streɪndʒmənt] *n* Entfremdung *f* (*from* von).

estrogen ['i:strəʊdʒən] *n* (*US*) Östrogen *nt.*

estuary ['estjʊərɪ] *n* Mündung *f.*

ETA *abbr of* **estimated time of arrival** gesch. Ank, geschätzte Ankunft.

et al [et'æl] *adv* et al.

etcetera [ɪt'setərə] *adv* (*abbr etc*) und so weiter, et cetera.

etch [etʃ] *vti* ätzen; (*in copper*) kupferstechen; (*in other metals*) radieren. **the event was** ~ed **or had** ~ed **itself on her mind** das Ereignis hatte sich ihr ins Gedächtnis eingegraben.

etching ['etʃɪŋ] *n see vb* (a) Ätzen *nt*; Kupferstechen *nt*; Radieren *nt.* (b) (*picture*) Ätzung *f*; Kupferstich *m*; Radierung *f.* **come up and see my** ~s (*hum*) wollen Sie noch mit heraufkommen und sich (*dat*) meine Briefmarkensammlung ansehen? (*hum*).

eternal [ɪ'tɜ:nl] **1** *adj* (a) ewig. **the E** ~ **City** die Ewige Stadt; **the** ~ **triangle** (*fig*) das Dreiecksverhältnis. (b) (*complaints, gossiping*) ewig. **2** *n* **the E**~ das Ewige; (*God*) der Ewige.

eternally [ɪ'tɜ:nəlɪ] *adv* ewig, immer; (*unceasingly*) ewig.

eternity [ɪ'tɜ:nɪtɪ] *n* (*lit, fig inf*) Ewigkeit *f*; (*Rel: the future life*) das ewige Leben. **from here to** ~ bis in alle Ewigkeit; **will we meet again in** ~? werden wir uns im Jenseits wiedersehen?; **the hours I spent there seemed an** ~ die Stunden, die ich da verbrachte, kamen mir wie eine Ewigkeit vor; ~ **ring** Memoire-Ring *m.*

ethane ['i:θeɪn] *n* Äthan *nt.*

ethanol ['eθənɒl] *n* Äthanol *nt.*

ether ['i:θər] *n* (*Chem, poet*) Äther *m.*

ethereal [ɪ'θɪərɪəl] *adj* (a) (*light, delicate, spiritual*) ätherisch. (b) (*of the upper air*) regions himmlisch.

ethic ['eθɪk] *n* Ethik *f*, Ethos *m.*

ethical ['eθɪkəl] *adj* (a) (*morally right*) ethisch *attr*; (*of ethics*) *judgement, philosophy etc* Moral-. ~ **values** moralische Werte *pl*; **it is not** ~ **to ...** es ist unethisch *or* unmoralisch, zu ... (b) *medicine etc* verschreibungspflichtig.

ethically ['eθɪkəlɪ] *adv* ethisch, moralisch.

ethics ['eθɪks] *n* (a) *sing* (*study, system*) Ethik *f.* (b) *pl* (*morality*) Moral *f.* **the** ~ **of abortion** die moralischen *or* ethischen Aspekte der Abtreibung.

Ethiopia [,i:θɪ'əʊpɪə] *n* Äthiopien *nt.*

Ethiopian [,i:θɪ'əʊpɪən] **1** *adj* äthiopisch. **2** *n* (a) Äthiopier(in *f*) *m.* (b) (*language*) Äthiopisch(e) *nt.*

ethnic ['eθnɪk] *adj* ethnisch, Volks-; *atmosphere, pub* urtümlich, urwüchsig; *clothes* folklorisch. ~ **groups/minority** ethnische Gruppen *pl*/Minderheit *f*; ~ **Germans** Volksdeutsche *pl.*

ethnographer [eθ'nɒgrəfər] *n* Völkerkundler(in *f*) *m.*

ethnography [eθ'nɒgrəfɪ] *n* (beschreibende) Völkerkunde, Ethnographie *f.*

ethnologist [eθ'nɒlədʒɪst] *n* Ethnologe *m*, Ethnologin *f.*

ethnology [eθ'nɒlədʒɪ] *n* (vergleichende) Völkerkunde, Ethnologie *f.*

ethologist [ɪ'θɒlədʒɪst] *n* Verhaltensforscher(in *f*) *m.*

ethology [ɪ'θɒlədʒɪ] *n* Verhaltensforschung, Ethologie *f.*

ethos ['i:θɒs] *n* Gesinnung *f*, Ethos *m.*

ethyl ['i:θaɪl] *n* Äthyl *nt.*

ethylene ['eθɪli:n] *n* Äthylen *nt.*

etiolate ['i:tɪəʊleɪt] *vt* (*Bot*) etiolieren (*spec*); (*enfeeble*) auszehren.

etiology *etc* (*esp US*) *see* **aetiology** *etc.*

etiquette ['etɪket] *n* Etikette *f.* **court** ~ Hofetikette *f*; **that's not in accordance with medical** ~ das entspricht nicht dem Berufsethos eines Arztes.

Eton collar ['i:tənkɒlə] *n* breiter, steifer, weißer Umlegekragen.

Eton crop ['i:tənkrɒp] *n* Bubikopf *m*, Herrenschnitt *m.*

Etruscan [ɪ'trʌskən] **1** *adj* etruskisch. **2** *n* (a) Etrusker(in *f*) *m.* (b) (*language*) Etruskisch *nt.*

etymological *adj*, ~**ly** *adv* [,etɪmə'lɒdʒɪkəl, -ɪ] etymologisch.

etymology [,etɪ'mɒlədʒɪ] *n* Etymologie *f.*

eucalyptus [,ju:kə'lɪptəs] *n* Eukalyptus *m.* ~ (**oil**) Eukalyptusöl *nt.*

Eucharist ['ju:kərɪst] *n* (*Eccl*) (*service*) Abendmahlsgottesdienst *m.* **the** ~ das (heilige) Abendmahl, die Eucharistie.

Euclid ['ju:klɪd] *n* Euklid *m.*

Euclidean [ju:'klɪdɪən] *adj* euklidisch.

eugenics [ju:'dʒenɪks] *n sing* Eugenik *f.*

eulogize ['ju:lədʒaɪz] *vt* eine Lobesrede halten auf (+*acc*).

eulogy ['ju:lədʒɪ] *n* Lobesrede, Eloge (*liter*) *f.*

eunuch ['ju:nək] *n* Eunuch *m.*

euphemism ['ju:fəmɪzəm] *n* Euphemismus *m*, Hüllwort *nt.*

euphemistic *adj*, ~**ally** *adv* [,ju:fə'mɪstɪk, -əlɪ] euphemistisch, verhüllend.

euphonic [ju:'fɒnɪk], **euphonious** [ju:'fəʊnɪəs] *adj* euphonisch, wohlklingend.

euphonium [ju:'fəʊnɪəm] *n* Euphonium *nt.*

euphony ['ju:fənɪ] *n* (*Mus, Ling*) Euphonie *f*, Wohlklang *m.*

euphoria [ju:'fɔ:rɪə] *n* Euphorie *f.*

euphoric [ju:'fɒrɪk] *adj* euphorisch.

Euphrates [ju:'freɪti:z] *n* Euphrat *m.*

Eurasia [jʊə'reɪʃə] *n* Eurasien *nt.*

Eurasian [jʊə'reɪʃən] **1** *adj* eurasisch. **2** *n* Eurasier(in *f*) *m.*

Euratom [jʊə'rætəm] *abbr of* **European Atomic Energy Community** Euratom *f.*

eureka [jʊə'ri:kə] *interj* heureka, ich hab's!

eurhythmics [ju:'rɪðmɪks] *n sing* Eurhythmie *f.*

Eurocrat [jʊərəʊkræt] *n* Eurokrat(in *f*) *m.*

Eurodollar ['jʊərəʊdɒlər] *n* Eurodollar *m.*

Europe ['jʊərəp] *n* Europa *nt.*

European [,jʊərə'pi:ən] **1** *adj* europäisch. ~ **Economic Community** Europäische Wirtschaftsgemeinschaft. **2** *n* Europäer(in *f*) *m.*

Eurovision [jʊərəʊvɪʒn] *n* Eurovision *f.* ~ **Song Contest** Eurovisions-Schlagerwettbewerb *m.*

Eustachian tube [ju:'steɪʃənˈtju:b] *n* Eustachische Röhre.

euthanasia [,ju:θə'neɪzɪə] *n* Euthanasie *f.*

evacuate [ɪ'vækjʊeɪt] *vt* (a) (*leave*) fort, house räumen. (b) (*clear*) danger area räumen; civilians, women, children evakuieren. (c) bowels entleeren.

evacuation [ɪ,vækjʊ'eɪʃən] *n see vt* Räumung *f*; Evakuierung *f.*

evacuee [ɪ,vækjʊ'i:] *n* Evakuierte(r) *mf.*

evade [ɪ'veɪd] *vt* (a) *blow* ausweichen (+*dat*); *pursuit, pursuers* sich entziehen (+*dat*), entkommen (+*dat*). (b) *obligation, justice* sich entziehen (+*dat*); *military service* also umgehen; *question, issue* ausweichen (+*dat*); *difficulty, person, sb's glance* ausweichen (+*dat*), (ver)meiden; *sb's vigilance* entgehen (+*dat*). **to** ~ **taxes** Steuern hinterziehen; **he successfully** ~d **the tax authorities for several years** mehrere Jahre kam das Finanzamt ihm nicht auf die Spur; **if you try to** ~ **paying import duty** wenn Sie versuchen, den Einfuhrzoll zu umgehen; **a concept which somehow** ~s **precise definition** ein Begriff, der sich einer genauen Definition entzieht.

evaluate [ɪ'væljʊeɪt] *vt house, painting, worth etc* schätzen (*at* auf +*acc*); *damages* festsetzen (*at* auf +*acc*); *chances, effectiveness, usefulness* einschätzen, beurteilen; *evidence, results* auswerten; *pros and cons* (gegeneinander) abwägen; *contribution, achievement* bewerten, beurteilen. **to** ~ **sth at £100** etw auf £ 100 taxieren *or* schätzen.

evaluation [ɪ,væljʊ'eɪʃən] *n see vt* (Ein)schätzung *f*; Festsetzung *f*; Einschätzung, Beurteilung *f*; Auswertung *f*; Abwägung *f*; Bewertung *f.* **in my** ~ nach meiner Schätzung; **on** ~ **of the evidence it became clear that ...** die Auswertung *or* Sichtung des Beweismaterials machte klar, daß...

evanescence [,i:və'nesəns] *n* Vergänglichkeit *f.*

evanescent [,i:və'nesənt] *adj* vergänglich.

evangelic(al) [,i:vænˈdʒelɪk(əl)] *adj* evangelisch.

evangelist [ɪ'vændʒəlɪst] *n* (*Bibl*) Evangelist(in *f*) *m*; (*preacher*) Prediger(in *f*) *m*; (*itinerant*) Wanderprediger(in *f*) *m.*

evangelize [ɪ'vændʒəlaɪz] **1** *vt* evangelisieren, bekehren. **2** *vi* das Evangelium predigen.

evaporate [ɪ'væpəreɪt] **1** *vi* (a) (*liquid*) verdampfen, verdunsten. (b) (*fig*) (*disappear*) sich in nichts *or* in Luft auflösen; (*hopes*) sich zerschlagen, schwinden. **2** *vt liquid* verdampfen *or* verdunsten (lassen). ~d **milk** Kondens- *or* Büchsenmilch *f*; **evaporating dish** Abdampfschale *f.*

evaporation [ɪ,væpə'reɪʃən] *n* Verdampfung *f*, Verdampfen *nt*; (*fig*) Schwinden *nt.*

evasion [ɪ'veɪʒən] *n* (a) (*of responsibility, question*) Ausweichen *nt* (*of* vor +*dat*). (b) (*evasive answer etc*) Ausflucht *f.*

evasive [ɪ'veɪzɪv] *adj answer* ausweichend; *meaning, truth* schwer zu fassen, schwer zu greifen; *prey* schwer zu fangen. **don't be so** ~ weich nicht aus; **he was very** ~ **about it** er wollte (dazu) nicht mit der Sprache herausrücken, er wich dauernd aus; **to take** ~ **action** (*Mil, fig*) ein Ausweichmanöver machen.

evasively [ɪ'veɪzɪvlɪ] *adv say, answer* ausweichend.

Eve [i:v] *n* Eva *f.*

eve[1] [i:v] *n* Vorabend *m.* **on the** ~ **of** am Tage vor (+*dat*); am Vorabend (+*gen*, von).

eve[2] *n* (*obs, poet*) Abend *m.*

even[1] ['i:vən] **1** *adj* **(a)** *surface, ground* eben. **to make sth ~ ground, earth** etw ebnen; **can you make all these piles ~?** können Sie alle diese Haufen gleich hoch machen?; **they made the top of the cupboard ~ with the top of the oven** sie machten den Schrank genau so hoch wie den Herd; **the concrete has to be ~ with the ground** der Beton muß eben mit dem Boden abschließen.

(b) *(regular) layer etc* gleichmäßig; *progress* stetig; *breathing, pulse also* regelmäßig; *temper* ausgeglichen. **his work is not ~** seine Leistung ist schwankend *or* ungleichmäßig.

(c) *quantities, distances, values* gleich. **the score is ~** steht unentschieden; **they are an ~ match** sie sind einander ebenbürtig; **I will get ~ with you for that** das werde ich dir heimzahlen; **that makes us ~** *(in game)* damit steht es unentschieden; *(fig)* damit sind wir quitt; **the odds** *or* **chances are about ~** die Chancen stehen etwa fifty-fifty; **to break ~** sein Geld wieder herausbekommen.

(d) *number* gerade. **~ money** Wette, *bei der die doppelte Einsatzsumme als Gewinn ausgezahlt wird*; **I'll give you ~ money** he's late *(inf)* ich gehe jede Wette mit dir ein, daß er zu spät kommt.

(e) *(exact)* genau. **let's make it an ~ hundred** nehmen wir eine runde Zahl und sagen 100.

2 *adv* **(a)** sogar, selbst. **~ for a fast car that's good going** sogar *or* selbst für ein schnelles Auto ist das allerhand; **they ~ denied its existence** sie leugneten sogar seine Existenz; **it'll be difficult, impossible ~** das wird schwierig sein, oder sogar *or* wenn nicht (so)gar unmöglich.

(b) *(with comp adj)* sogar noch. **that's ~ better/more beautiful** das ist sogar (noch) besser/schöner.

(c) *(with neg)* **not ~** nicht einmal; **with not ~ a smile** ohne auch nur zu lächeln; **he didn't ~ answer the letter** er hat den Brief (noch) nicht einmal beantwortet.

(d) **~ if/though** sogar *or* selbst wenn; **~ if you were a millionaire** sogar *or* selbst wenn du ein Millionär wärst; **but ~ then** aber sogar *or* selbst dann; **~ as I spoke someone knocked at the door** noch während ich redete, klopfte es an der Tür; **~ as he had wished** genau, wie er es sich gewünscht hatte; **~ as** ... so *(old)* genau wie ... so; **~ so** (aber) trotzdem.

3 *vt surface* glatt *or* eben machen, glätten.

◆**even out 1** *vi* **(a)** *(prices)* sich einpendeln. **(b)** *(ground)* eben werden, sich ebnen.

2 *vt sep* **(a)** *prices* ausgleichen. **(b)** *ground, cement* ebnen, glätten; *(mechanically also)* planieren. **(c)** *taxation burden, wealth* gerecht *or* gleichmäßig verteilen. **that should ~ things ~ a bit** dadurch müßte ein gewisser Ausgleich erzielt werden; **that will ~ things ~ between us** damit sind wir wohl wieder quitt.

◆**even up 1** *vt sep sum* aufrunden *(to auf +acc)*. **that will ~ things ~** das wird die Sache etwas ausgleichen. **2** *vi (pay off debt)* Schulden begleichen *(with bei)*. **can we ~ ~ later?** können wir später abrechnen?

even[2] *n (obs, poet)* Abend *m*.

evening ['i:vnɪŋ] *n* Abend *m*. **in the ~** abends, am Abend; **this/tomorrow/yesterday ~** heute/morgen/gestern abend; **that ~** an jenem Abend; **that ~ was** ... jener Abend war ...; **on the ~ of the twenty-ninth** am Abend des 29., am 29. abends; **one ~ as I** ... eines Abends, als ich ...; **every Monday ~** jeden Montagabend; **all ~** den ganzen Abend (lang *or* über); **the ~ of his life** *(liter)* sein Lebensabend.

evening *in cpds* Abend-; **~ class** *n* Abendkurs *m*; **to do ~ classes** *or* **an ~ class in French** einen Abendkurs in Französisch besuchen; **~ dress** *n (men's)* Abendanzug, Gesellschaftsanzug *m*; *(women's)* Abendkleid *nt*; **~ gown** *n* Abendkleid *nt*.

evenly ['i:vənlɪ] *adv spread, breathe, space, distribute, divide* gleichmäßig; *say* gelassen. **the two contestants were ~ matched** die beiden Gegner waren einander ebenbürtig.

evenness ['i:vnnɪs] *n* **(a)** *(of ground)* Ebenheit *f*. **(b)** *(regularity)* Gleichmäßigkeit *f*; *(of progress)* Stetigkeit *f*; *(of breathing, pulse also)* Regelmäßigkeit *f*; *(of temper)* Ausgeglichenheit *f*.

evensong ['i:vənsɒŋ] *n* Abendgottesdienst *m*.

event [ɪ'vent] *n* **(a)** *(happening)* Ereignis *nt*. **~s are taking place in Belfast which** ... in Belfast ereignen sich *or* geschehen Dinge, die ...; **in the normal course of ~s** normalerweise; **to be overtaken by ~s** von den Ereignissen überholt werden; **~s have proved us right** die Ereignisse haben uns recht gegeben; **it's quite an ~** das ist wirklich ein Ereignis; **it's easy to be wise after the ~** hinterher ist man immer klüger; **be happy.**

(b) *(organized function)* Veranstaltung *f*; *(Sport)* Wettkampf *m*. **what is your best ~?** in welcher Disziplin sind Sie am besten?

(c) *(case)* Fall *m*. **in the ~ of her death** im Falle ihres Todes; **in the ~ of war/fire** im Falle eines Krieges/Brandes, im Kriegs-/Brandfall; **he said he wouldn't come, but in the ~ he did** er sagte, er würde nicht kommen, aber er kam dann schließlich *or* im Endeffekt doch; **in the unlikely ~ that** ... falls, was sehr unwahrscheinlich ist, ...; **but in any ~ I can't give you my permission** aber ich kann dir ohnehin *or* sowieso nicht meine Erlaubnis geben; **but in any ~ you have my permission** aber Sie haben auf alle Fälle meine Erlaubnis; **in either ~** in jedem Fall; **at all ~s** auf jeden Fall.

even-tempered ['i:vən'tempəd] *adj* ausgeglichen.

eventful [ɪ'ventfʊl] *adj* ereignisreich; *life, period also* bewegt.

eventide ['i:vəntaɪd] *n (obs, poet)* Abendzeit *f*.

eventual [ɪ'ventʃʊəl] *adj* **the decline and ~ collapse of the Roman Empire** der Niedergang und schließlich vollkommene Zerfall des Römischen Reiches; **he predicted the ~ fall of the government** er hat vorausgesagt, daß die Regierung am Ende *or* schließlich zu Fall kommen würde; **his ~ arrival caused great rejoicing** es rief große Freude hervor, als er schließlich

kam; the ~ success of the project is not in doubt es besteht kein Zweifel, daß das Vorhaben letzten Endes Erfolg haben wird.

eventuality [ɪˌventʃʊ'ælɪtɪ] *n (möglicher)* Fall, Eventualität *f*. **in the ~ of fire** im Brandfall; **be ready for any ~** sei auf alle Eventualitäten gefaßt.

eventually [ɪ'ventʃʊəlɪ] *adv* schließlich, endlich. **it ~ turned out that** ... es hat sich schließlich *or* zum Schluß herausgestellt, daß ...; **he will get used to it ~** er wird sich schließlich daran gewöhnen; **of course ~ he always changed his mind** natürlich hat er es sich (dann) zum Schluß immer noch einmal anders überlegt.

ever ['evə^r] *adv* **(a)** je(mals). **not ~** nie; **nothing ~ happens** es passiert nie etwas; **it hardly ~ snows here** hier schneit es kaum (jemals); **if I ~ catch you doing that again** wenn ich dich noch einmal dabei erwische; **if you ~ see her** wenn Sie sie je sehen sollten; **seldom, if ~** selten, wenn überhaupt; **he's a rascal if ~ there was one** er ist ein richtiggehender kleiner Halunke; **as if I ~ would** als ob ich das jemals täte; **don't you ~ say that again!** sag das ja nie mehr!; **have you ~ ridden a horse?** bist du schon einmal (auf einem Pferd) geritten?; **have you ~ been to Glasgow?** bist du schon einmal in Glasgow gewesen?; **have you ~ known him tell a lie?** haben Sie ihn (schon) jemals lügen hören?; **more beautiful than ~** schöner denn je; **the best soup I have ~ eaten** die beste Suppe, die ich je(mals) gegessen habe; **the first ~** der *etc* allererste; **the first man ~ to step on the moon** der erste Mensch, der je(mals) den Mond betrat; **the coldest night ~** die kälteste Nacht seit Menschengedenken.

(b) *(at all times)* **since I was a boy** seit ich ein Junge war; **~ since I have lived here** ... seitdem ich hier lebe ...; **~ since then** seit der Zeit, seitdem; **for ~** für immer, für alle Zeit(en); **it ~ seemed to go on for ~ (and ~)** es schien ewig zu dauern; **for ~ and a day** für alle Zeiten, ewig und drei Tage *(inf)*; **~ increasing powers** ständig wachsende Macht; **an ~ present feeling** ein ständiges Gefühl; *see* **forever.**

(c) *(intensive)* **he be ~ so charming** wenn er auch noch so liebenswürdig ist, sei er auch noch so liebenswürdig; **no government be it ~ so powerful** keine noch so mächtige Regierung; **come as quickly as ~ you can** komm so schnell du nur kannst; **she's the best grandmother ~** sie ist die beste Großmutter, die es gibt; **did you ~!** *(inf)* also so was!

(d) **what ~ shall we do?** was sollen wir bloß machen?; **when ~ will they come?** wann kommen sie denn bloß *or* endlich?; **why ~ not?** warum denn bloß nicht?; *see* **whatever, wherever** etc.

(e) *(inf)* **~ so/such** unheimlich; **~ so slightly drunk** ein ganz klein wenig betrunken; **he's ~ such a nice man** er ist ein ungemein netter Mensch; **I am ~ so sorry** es tut mir schrecklich leid; **thank you ~ so much** ganz herzlichen Dank.

(f) *(old: always)* allzeit *(old, liter)*.

(g) *(in letters)* **yours ~, Wendy** viele Grüße, Ihre Wendy.

everglade ['evəgleɪd] *n (US)* sumpfiges Flußgebiet.

evergreen ['evəgri:n] **1** *adj trees, shrubs* immergrün; *(fig) topic* immer aktuell. **~ song** Evergreen *m*. **2** *n* Nadelbaum *m*; immergrüner Busch.

everlasting [ˌevə'lɑːstɪŋ] **1** *adj* **(a)** *God* ewig; *gratitude* immerwährend; *glory* unvergänglich. **~ flower** Strohblume, Immortelle *f*. **(b)** *(inf: constant)* ewig *(inf)*. **2** *n*: **from ~ to ~** thou art God du bist Gott von Ewigkeit zu Ewigkeit.

everlastingly [ˌevə'lɑːstɪŋlɪ] *adv* ewig.

evermore [ˌevə'mɔː^r] *adv* immer, stets. **for ~** auf alle Zeiten, in (alle) Ewigkeit *(esp Rel)*, auf immer; **their name liveth for ~** ihr Name wird ewig fortleben.

every ['evrɪ] *adj* **(a)** jede(r, s). **he's read ~ book in the library** er hat jedes Buch in der Bibliothek gelesen; **I have ~ reason to believe that** ... ich habe allen Grund anzunehmen, daß ...; **you must examine ~ one** Sie müssen jeden (einzelnen) untersuchen; **~ man for himself** jeder für sich; **in ~ way** *(in all respects)* in jeder Hinsicht; *(by ~ means)* mit allen Mitteln; **he is ~ bit as clever as his brother** er ist ganz genauso schlau wie sein Bruder; **~ bit as much** ganz genauso viel; **~ single time** jedes einzelne Mal; **~ single time I** ... immer wenn ich ...

(b) *(all possible)* **I have ~ confidence in him** ich habe unbedingtes *or* uneingeschränktes Vertrauen zu ihm; **I have ~ hope that** ... ich habe allen Grund/es besteht aller Grund zu der Hoffnung, daß ...; **we wish you ~ success/happiness** wir wünschen Ihnen alles (nur erdenklich) Gute/viel Glück und Zufriedenheit; **there was ~ prospect of success** es bestand alle Aussicht auf Erfolg.

(c) *(indicating recurrence)* **~ fifth day, ~ five days** jeden fünften Tag, alle fünf Tage; **~ other day** jeden zweiten Tag, alle zwei Tage; **write on ~ other line** bitte eine Zeile Zwischenraum lassen; **once ~ week** einmal jede *or* pro Woche; **~ so often, ~ once in a while, ~ now and then** *or* **again** hin und wieder, ab und zu, gelegentlich.

(d) *(after poss adj)* **his ~ action** jede seiner Handlungen; **his ~ word** jedes seiner Worte, jedes Wort, das er sagte.

everybody ['evrɪbɒdɪ] *pron* jeder(mann), alle *pl*. **~ has finished** alle sind fertig; **it's not ~ who can afford a deep-freeze** nicht jeder kann sich *(dat)* eine Tiefkühltruhe leisten; **~ knows ~ else here** hier kennt jeder jeden; **~ knows** (doch) jeder.

everyday ['evrɪdeɪ] *adj* alltäglich; *language* Alltags-, Umgangs-. **words in ~ use** Wörter der Alltags- *or* Umgangssprache.

everyone ['evrɪwʌn] *pron see* **everybody.**

everything ['evrɪθɪŋ] *n* alles. **~ possible/old** alles Mögliche/Alte; **~ you have** alles, was du hast; **time is ~** Zeit ist kostbar; **money isn't ~** Geld ist nicht alles; **money is ~ to him** Geld bedeutet ihm alles.

everywhere ['evrɪweə^r] *adv* überall; *(with direction)* überallhin. **from ~** überallher *or* von überall; **~ you look there's a mistake** wo man auch hinsieht, findet man Fehler.

evict [ɪ'vɪkt] *vt tenants* zur Räumung zwingen (*from gen*).

eviction [ɪ'vɪkʃən] *n* Exmittierung *f* (*form*). ~ **order** Räumungsbefehl *m*.

evidence ['evɪdəns] **1** *n* **(a)** Beweis(e *pl*) *m*. **what** ~ **is there for this belief?** welche Anhaltspunkte gibt es für diese Annahme?; **show me your** ~ welche Beweise haben Sie?; **according to the** ~ **of our senses** nach dem, was wir mit unseren Sinnen erkennen können; **these marks are** ~ **of life on Mars** diese Spuren sind Beweis *or* ein Zeichen *nt* dafür, daß es auf dem Mars Leben gibt; **the car bore** ~ **of having been in an accident** das Auto trug deutliche Spuren eines Unfalls.
(b) (*Jur*) Beweismaterial *nt*; (*object, dagger etc also*) Beweisstück *nt*; (*testimony*) Aussage *f*. **the lawyers are still collecting** ~ die Anwälte holen immer noch Beweise ein; **we haven't got any** ~ wir haben keinerlei Beweise; **there wasn't enough** ~ **die Beweise** *or* Indizien reichten nicht aus; **for lack of** ~ aus Mangel an Beweisen, mangels Beweisen (*form*); **on the** ~ **available ...** auf Grund des vorhandenen Beweismaterials ...; **not admissible as** ~ als Beweismittel nicht zulässig; **all the** ~ **was against his claim** alles sprach *or* die Tatsachen sprachen gegen seine Behauptung; **to give** ~ (**for/against sb**) (für/gegen jdn) aussagen; **the** ~ **for the defence/prosecution** die Beweisführung für die Verteidigung/für die Anklage; **a piece of** ~ (*statement*) Zeugenaussage *f*; (*object*) Beweisstück *or* -mittel *nt*; **a fingerprint was the only** ~ ein Fingerabdruck war der einzige Beweis; *see* Queen's ~, State's ~.
(c) to be in ~ sichtbar sein; **political ideas which have been very much in** ~ recently politische Ideen, die in letzter Zeit deutlich in Erscheinung getreten sind; **his father was nowhere in** ~ sein Vater war nirgends zu sehen; **she likes to be very much in** ~ sie hat es gern, gesehen und beachtet zu werden; **a statesman very much in** ~ **at the moment** ein Staatsmann, der zur Zeit stark beachtet wird.
2 *vt* zeugen von.

evident *adj*, ~**ly** *adv* ['evɪdənt, -lɪ] offensichtlich.

evil ['iːvl] **1** *adj; person also, reputation, example, advice, influence* schlecht; *consequence also*, (*inf*) *smell* übel. **the E~ One** der Böse; **to fall on** ~ **days** in eine unglückliche Lage geraten.
2 *n* Böse *nt*; (*evil thing, circumstance etc*) Übel *nt*. **the struggle of good against** ~ der Kampf des Guten gegen das Böse *or* zwischen Gut und Böse; **the** ~**s of war and disease** die Übel von Krieg und Krankheit; **to choose the lesser of two** ~**s** von zwei Übeln das kleinere wählen; **social** ~**s** soziale Mißstände; **he fell victim to the** ~**s of drink** er fiel dem Laster des Trinkens zum Opfer; **we must combat the** ~**s of alcoholism** wir müssen das Übel der Trunksucht bekämpfen.

evil: ~**-doer** *n* Übeltäter(in *f*) *m*, Bösewicht *m* (*dated*); **the** ~ **eye** *n* der böse Blick; ~**-minded** *adj* bösartig; ~**-smelling** *adj* übelriechend.

evince [ɪ'vɪns] *vt* an den Tag legen; *surprise, desire also* bekunden.

eviscerate [ɪ'vɪsəreɪt] *vt* ausnehmen; (*person*) entleiben.

evocation [ˌevə'keɪʃən] *n* Heraufbeschwören, Wachrufen *nt*.

evocative [ɪ'vɒkətɪv] *adj* evokativ (*geh*). **an** ~ **style/scent** ein Stil/Geruch, der Erinnerungen/Gedanken *etc* wachruft *or* heraufbeschwört; **to be** ~ **of sth** etw heraufbeschwören.

evoke [ɪ'vəuk] *vt* evozieren (*geh*), heraufbeschwören; *memory also* wachrufen; *admiration* hervorrufen.

evolution [ˌiːvə'luːʃən] *n* **(a)** (*development, Biol*) Evolution, Entwicklung *f*. **the** ~ **of events in Vietnam** die Entwicklung in Vietnam; **political** ~ **rather than revolution** eher politische Evolution als Revolution; **theory of** ~ Evolutionstheorie *f*.
(b) *often pl* (*of troops*) Bewegung *f*; (*of dancers, skaters*) Figur, Bewegung *f*.

evolutionary [ˌiːvə'luːʃnərɪ] *adj* evolutionär; *theory* Evolutions-.

evolve [ɪ'vɒlv] **1** *vt; system, theory, plan* entwickeln. **2** *vi* sich entwickeln, sich herausbilden.

ewe [juː] *n* Mutterschaf *nt*.

ewer ['juːəʳ] *n* Wasserkrug *m*.

ex¹ [eks] *n* (*inf*) Verflossene(r) *mf* (*inf*).

ex² *abbr of* **example** Bsp, Beispiel *nt*.

ex- [eks-] *pref* **(a)** ehemalig, Ex- (*inf*). ~**-president** früherer Präsident, Expräsident *m* (*inf*); ~**-wife** frühere Frau, Exfrau *f* (*inf*). **(b)** ~**-dividend** ohne Anrecht auf Dividende; ~**-factory**, ~**-works** ab Werk; *see* **ex-officio**.

exacerbate [ek'sæsəbeɪt] *vt; person* verärgern; *pain, disease* verschlimmern; *hate* vergrößern; *resentment, discontent* vertiefen; *situation* verschärfen.

exacerbation [ek,sæsə'beɪʃən] *n* (*of pain, disease*) Verschlimmerung *f*; (*of situation*) Verschärfung *f*.

exact [ɪg'zækt] **1** *adj* genau; *figures, analysis etc also* exakt. **that's the** ~ **word I was looking for** das ist genau das Wort, nach dem ich gesucht habe; **at that** ~ **moment** genau in dem Augenblick; **sorry I can't be more** ~ leider kann ich es nicht genau sagen; **47 to be** ~ 47, um genau zu sein; **or, to be (more)** ~ oder, genauer gesagt ...; **the** ~ **sciences** die exakten Wissenschaften; **to give** ~ **attention to details** sehr genau auf Details achten; **to be very** ~ **in one's work** peinlich genau arbeiten.
2 *vt* **(a)** *money, ransom* fordern (*from* von); *taxes also* auferlegen (*from dat*); *payment* eintreiben (*from* von). **(b)** *obedience* fordern; *care, attentiveness* erfordern; *promise* abverlangen (*from sb* jdm).

exacting [ɪg'zæktɪŋ] *adj; person, work* anspruchsvoll. **to be too/very** ~ **with sb** zu viel/sehr viel von jdm verlangen; **he's very** ~ **about cleanliness** er ist peinlich genau, was Sauberkeit angeht, er nimmt es mit der Sauberkeit sehr genau.

exactingness [ɪg'zæktɪŋnɪs] *n because of his* ~ *as a teacher* da er ein so anspruchsvoller Lehrer ist/war.

exaction [ɪg'zækʃən] *n* **(a)** (*act*) (*of money*) Eintreiben *nt*; (*of promises*) Abverlangen *nt*; (*of obedience*) Fordern *nt*. **(b)** (*money exacted*) Forderung *f*; (*excessive demand*) übertriebene/überzogene Forderung.

exactitude [ɪg'zæktɪtjuːd] *n* Genauigkeit, Exaktheit *f*.

exactly [ɪg'zæktlɪ] *adv* **(a)** (*with exactitude*) genau. **(b)** (*quite, precisely*) (ganz) genau. **we don't** ~ **know** wir wissen es nicht genau; **I'm not** ~ **sure who he is** ich bin mir nicht ganz sicher, wer er ist; **that's** ~ **what I thought** genau das habe ich gedacht; **it is three o'clock** ~ es ist genau *or* Punkt drei Uhr; ~**!** genau!; ~ **so!** ganz recht!, genau!; **not** ~ nicht ganz; (*hardly*) nicht direkt *or* gerade; **it's not** ~ **a detective story** es ist eigentlich keine Kriminalgeschichte; **he wasn't** ~ **pleased** er war nicht gerade erfreut.

exactness [ɪg'zæktnɪs] *n* Genauigkeit *f*.

exaggerate [ɪg'zædʒəreɪt] **1** *vt* **(a)** (*overstate*) übertreiben. **he** ~**d what really happened** er hat das, was wirklich geschehen war, übertrieben dargestellt. **(b)** (*intensify*) *effect* verstärken; *similarity* hervorheben. **2** *vi* übertreiben.

exaggerated [ɪg'zædʒəreɪtɪd] *adj* übertrieben. **to have an** ~ **opinion of oneself** eine übertrieben hohe Meinung von sich selbst haben.

exaggeration [ɪg,zædʒə'reɪʃən] *n* Übertreibung *f*. **a bit of an** ~ eine leichte Übertreibung, leicht übertrieben.

exalt [ɪg'zɔːlt] *vt* **(a)** (*in rank or power*) erheben. **(b)** (*praise*) preisen.

exaltation [ˌegzɔː'teɪʃən] *n* (*feeling*) Begeisterung, Exaltation (*liter*) *f*.

exalted [ɪg'zɔːltɪd] *adj* **(a)** *position, style* hoch. **the** ~ **ranks of ...** die erhabenen Ränge der ... **(b)** *mood, person* exaltiert, überschwenglich.

exam [ɪg'zæm] *n* Prüfung *f*.

examination [ɪg,zæmɪ'neɪʃən] *n* **(a)** (*Sch etc*) Prüfung *f*; (*Univ also*) Examen *nt*. **geography** ~ Geographieprüfung *f*.
(b) (*study, inspection*) Prüfung, Untersuchung *f*; (*of machine, premises, passports*) Kontrolle *f*; (*of question*) Untersuchung *f*; (*of accounts*) Prüfung *f*. **on closer** ~ bei genauer(er) Prüfung *or* Untersuchung; **it was found on** ~ **that ...** die Untersuchung ergab, daß ...; **the matter is still under** ~ die Angelegenheit wird noch geprüft *or* untersucht; *see* **medical**.
(c) (*Jur: of suspect, accused, witness*) Verhör *nt*; (*of case, documents*) Untersuchung *f*. **legal** ~ Verhör *nt*.

examine [ɪg'zæmɪn] *vt* **(a)** (*for auf* +*acc*) untersuchen; *documents, accounts* prüfen; *machine, passports, luggage* kontrollieren. **you want to have your head** ~**d** (*inf*) du solltest dich mal auf deinen Geisteszustand untersuchen lassen.
(b) *pupil, candidate* prüfen (*in* in +*dat*, *on* über +*acc*).
(c) (*Jur*) *suspect, accused, witness* verhören.

examinee [ɪg,zæmɪ'niː] *n* (*Sch*) Prüfling *m*; (*Univ*) (Examens)kandidat(in *f*) *m*.

examiner [ɪg'zæmɪnəʳ] *n* (*Sch, Univ*) Prüfer *m*. **board of** ~**s** Prüfungsausschuß *m*.

example [ɪg'zɑːmpl] *n* Beispiel *nt*. **for** ~ zum Beispiel; **to set a good/bad** ~ ein gutes/schlechtes Beispiel geben, mit gutem/schlechtem Beispiel vorangehen; **his conduct should be an** ~ **to us** sein Verhalten sollte uns ein Beispiel sein; **a leader who is an** ~ **to his men** ein Führer, der seinen Männern als Beispiel dient *or* mit leuchtendem Beispiel vorangeht; **to take sb as an** ~ sich (*dat*) an jdm ein Beispiel nehmen; **to make an** ~ **of sb** an jdm ein Exempel statuieren; **to punish sb as an** ~ **to others** jdn exemplarisch bestrafen.

exasperate [ɪg'zɑːspəreɪt] *vt* zur Verzweiflung bringen, auf die Palme bringen (*inf*). **to become** *or* **get** ~**d** verzweifeln (*with* an +*dat*), sich aufregen (*with* über +*acc*); ~**d at** *or* **by his lack of attention** verärgert über seine mangelnde Aufmerksamkeit.

exasperating [ɪg'zɑːspəreɪtɪŋ] *adj* ärgerlich; *delay, difficulty, job* leidig *attr.* **it's so** ~ **not to be able to buy any petrol** es ist wirklich zum Verzweifeln, daß man kein Benzin bekommen kann; **you can be** ~! du kannst einen wirklich zur Verzweiflung *or* auf die Palme (*inf*) bringen!

exasperatingly [ɪg'zɑːspəreɪtɪŋlɪ] *adv* **this train/student is** ~ **slow** es ist zum Verzweifeln, wie langsam dieser Zug fährt/dieser Student ist.

exasperation [ɪg,ɑːspə'reɪʃən] *n* Verzweiflung *f* (*with an* +*dat*). **he cried out in** ~ er schrie verzweifelt auf; **the negotiations ended with everyone in a state of** ~ am Ende der Verhandlungen waren alle völlig frustriert.

excavate ['ekskəveɪt] **1** *vt; ground* ausschachten; (*machine*) ausbaggern; (*Archeol*) *remains* ausgraben; *trench* ausheben. **2** *vi* (*Archeol*) Ausgrabungen machen.

excavation [,ekskə'veɪʃən] *n* **(a)** (*Archeol*) (Aus)grabung *f*. ~**s** (*site*) Ausgrabungsstätte *f*; **to carry out** ~**s** Ausgrabungen machen. **(b)** (*of tunnel etc*) Graben *nt*.

excavator ['ekskəveɪtəʳ] *n* (*machine*) Bagger *m*; (*Archeol: person*) Ausgräber(in *f*).

exceed [ɪk'siːd] *vt* **(a)** (*in value, amount, length of time*) übersteigen, überschreiten (*by* um). **to** ~ **40 in number** die Zahl 40 übersteigen *or* überschreiten; **the guests** ~**ed 40 in number** die Zahl der Gäste überstieg 40; **to** ~ **5 kilos in weight** das Gewicht von 5 kg übersteigen *or* überschreiten; **a fine not** ~**ing £50** eine Geldstrafe bis zu £ 50.
(b) (*go beyond*) hinausgehen über (+*acc*); *expectations, desires also* übertreffen, übersteigen; *limits, powers also, speed limit* überschreiten.

exceedingly [ɪk'siːdɪŋlɪ], **exceeding** (*old*) [ɪk'siːdɪŋ] *adv* äußerst.

excel [ɪk'sel] **1** *vi* sich auszeichnen, sich hervortun. **to** ~ **in** *or* **at mathematics/tennis** sich in Mathematik/als Tennis hervortun *or* auszeichnen; **he doesn't exactly** ~ **in Latin** er tut sich in Latein nicht gerade hervor, er ist nicht gerade eine Leuchte in Latein (*inf*).

2 *vt* übertreffen (*in* in +*dat*, an +*dat*). **to ~ oneself** (*oft iro*) sich selbst übertreffen.

excellence ['eksələns] *n* **(a)** (*high quality*) hervorragende Qualität, Vorzüglichkeit *f*. **the ~ of the essay/weather** der ausgezeichnete *or* hervorragende Aufsatz/das ausgezeichnete *or* hervorragende Wetter; **we aim at ~** wir streben hervorragende Qualität an. **(b)** (*excellent feature*) Vorzug *m*, hervorragende Eigenschaft.

Excellency ['eksələnsɪ] *n* Exzellenz *f*. **Your/His ~** Eure/Seine Exzellenz.

excellent ['eksələnt] *adj* ausgezeichnet, hervorragend.

excellently ['eksələntlɪ] *adv* ausgezeichnet, hervorragend. **you did ~** das hast du ausgezeichnet gemacht.

excelsior [ek'selsɪɔːʳ] *n* (*US: shavings*) Holzwolle *f*.

except [ɪk'sept] **1** *prep* **(a)** außer.
  (b) (*after neg clause*) außer; (*after questions also*) (anders ...) als. **what can they do ~ wait?** was können sie anders tun als warten?; **nobody ~ you can do it** niemand außer Ihnen kann das (tun); **who would have done it ~ him?** wer hätte es außer ihm denn getan?
  (c) **~ for** abgesehen von, bis auf (+*acc*); **~ that ...** außer *or* nur daß ...; **~ for the fact that** abgesehen davon, daß ...; **~ if** es sei denn(, daß), außer wenn; **~ when** außer wenn.
  2 *conj* **(a)** (*old, form: unless*) es sei denn(, daß). **~ he be a traitor** es sei denn, er wäre ein Verräter.
  (b) (*only*) doch. **I'd refuse ~ I need the money** ich würde ablehnen, doch ich brauche das Geld.
  3 *vt* ausnehmen. **to ~ sb from sth** jdn bei etw ausnehmen; **none ~ed** ohne Ausnahme.

excepting [ɪk'septɪŋ] *prep* außer. **not** *or* **without ~ X** ohne X auszunehmen *or* auszuschließen, X nicht ausgenommen; **always ~ ...** natürlich mit Ausnahme (+*gen*).

exception [ɪk'sepʃən] *n* **(a)** Ausnahme *f*. **to make an ~** eine Ausnahme machen; **to make an ~ of/for sb** eine Ausnahme bei jdm/für jdn machen; **without ~** ohne Ausnahme; **with the ~ of** mit Ausnahme von; **this case is an ~ to the rule** dieser Fall ist eine Ausnahme, das ist ein Ausnahmefall; **the ~ proves the rule** (*prov*) Ausnahmen bestätigen die Regel (*prov*); **these strokes of luck are the ~** diese Glückstreffer sind die Ausnahme; **with this ~** mit der einen Ausnahme.
  (b) to take ~ to sth Anstoß *m* an etw (*dat*) nehmen, sich an etw (*dat*) stören.

exceptional [ɪk'sepʃənl] *adj* außergewöhnlich. **apart from ~ cases** abgesehen von Ausnahmefällen.

exceptionally [ɪk'sepʃənəlɪ] *adv* (*as an exception*) ausnahmsweise; (*outstandingly*) außergewöhnlich.

excerpt ['eksɜːpt] *n* Auszug *m*, Exzerpt *nt*.

excess [ɪk'ses] *n* **(a)** Übermaß *nt* (*of an* +*dat*). **an ~ of caution/ details** allzuviel Vorsicht/allzu viele Einzelheiten; **to eat/drink to ~** übermäßig essen/trinken; **to carry sth to ~** etw übertreiben; **don't do anything to ~** man soll nichts übertreiben; **he does everything to ~** er übertreibt bei allem.
  (b) ~es *pl* Exzesse *pl*; (*drinking, sex etc also*) Ausschweifungen *pl*; (*brutalities also*) Ausschreitungen *pl*.
  (c) (*amount left over*) Überschuß *m*.
  (d) to be in ~ of hinausgehen über (+*acc*), überschreiten; **a figure in ~ of ...** eine Zahl über (+*dat*).

excess *in cpds* weight, production Über-; profit Mehr-; **~ baggage** *n* Übergewicht *nt*; **~ charge** *n* zusätzliche Gebühr; (*for letter etc*) Nachgebühr *f*; **~ fare** *n* Nachlösegebühr *f*; **I had to pay ~ fare** ich mußte nachlösen; **~ fat** *n* Fettpolster *nt*, überschüssiges Fett.

excessive [ɪk'sesɪv] *adj* übermäßig; demands, price, praise *also* übertrieben. **~ use of the clutch** zu häufiger Gebrauch der Kupplung; **isn't that rather ~?** ist das nicht etwas übertrieben?; **I think you're being ~** ich finde, Sie übertreiben.

excessively [ɪk'sesɪvlɪ] *adv* **(a)** (*to excess*) (+*vb*) eat, drink, spend übermäßig, allzuviel; (+*adj*) optimistic, worried, severe allzu. **(b)** (*extremely*) pretty, ugly, boring äußerst, ungemein.

excess postage *n* Nachgebühr *f*, Strafporto *nt* (*inf*).

exchange [ɪks'tʃeɪndʒ] **1** *vt* things, seats tauschen; *foreign currency* wechseln, umtauschen (*for* in +*acc*); letters, glances, courtesies wechseln, austauschen; ideas, experiences etc austauschen. **to ~ words/blows** einen Wortwechsel haben/sich schlagen; **to ~ one thing for another** eine Sache gegen eine andere austauschen *or* (*in shop*) umtauschen.
  2 *n* **(a)** (*of goods, stamps*) Tausch *m*; (*of prisoners, views, secrets, diplomatic notes*) Austausch *m*; (*of one bought item for another*) Umtausch *m*. **in ~ dafür**; **in ~ for money** gegen Geld *or* Bezahlung; **in ~ for a table/for lending me your car** für einen Tisch/dafür, daß Sie mir Ihr Auto geliehen haben; **that's not a fair ~ for my bike** das ist kein fairer Tausch für mein Rad; **to lose by the ~** einen schlechten Tausch machen; **fair ~ is no robbery** (*prov*) Tausch ist kein Raub (*Prov*).
  (b) (*Fin*) (*act*) Umtausch *m*; (*place*) Wechselstube *f*. **~ control** Devisenkontrolle *f*; **~ rate** Wechselkurs *m*.
  (c) (*St Ex*) Börse *f*.
  (d) (*telephone*) **~** Fernvermittlungsstelle *f* (*form*), Fernamt *nt*; (*in office etc*) (Telefon)zentrale *f*.
  (e) (*altercation*) Wortwechsel *m*.
  3 *adj attr* student, teacher Austausch-.

exchangeable [ɪks'tʃeɪndʒəbl] *adj* austauschbar (*for* gegen); goods bought umtauschbar (*for* gegen). **goods bought in the sale are not ~** Ausverkaufsware ist vom Umtausch ausgeschlossen.

exchequer [ɪks'tʃekəʳ] *n* Finanzministerium *nt*; (*esp in GB*) Schatzamt *nt*; (*inf: personal*) Finanzen *pl* (*inf*); see **chancellor**.

excisable [ek'saɪzəbl] *adj* steuerpflichtig.

excise¹ ['eksaɪz] *n* **(a)** Verbrauchssteuer *f* (*on auf* +*acc*, für). **~ on beer/tobacco** Bier-/Tabaksteuer *f*. **(b)** (*Brit: department*) Verwaltungsabteilung *f* für indirekte Steuern.

excise² [ek'saɪz] *vt* (*Med*) herausschneiden, entfernen (*also fig*).

excise ['eksaɪz]: **~ duties** *npl* Verbrauchssteuern *pl*; **~man** *n* Steuereinnehmer *m*.

excision [ek'sɪʒən] *n* (*Med, fig*) Entfernung *f*.

excitability [ɪk,saɪtə'bɪlɪtɪ] *n see adj* Erregbarkeit *f*; Reizbarkeit *f*.

excitable [ɪk'saɪtəbl] *adj* (leicht) erregbar; (*Physiol also*) reizbar.

excite [ɪk'saɪt] *vt* **(a)** aufregen, aufgeregt machen; (*rouse enthusiasm in*) begeistern. **the news had clearly ~d him** er war wegen der Nachricht sichtlich aufgeregt; **the whole village was ~d by the news** das ganze Dorf war über die Nachricht in Aufregung; **the prospect doesn't exactly ~ me** ich finde die Aussicht nicht gerade begeisternd.
  (b) (*Physiol*) nerve reizen; (*sexually*) erregen.
  (c) sentiments, passion, admiration erregen; interest, curiosity *also* wecken; imagination, appetite anregen.

excited [ɪk'saɪtɪd] *adj* aufgeregt; (*worked up, not calm also*) erregt; (*sexually*) erregt. **don't get ~!** (*angry etc*) reg dich nicht auf!; **don't get ~, I only said "perhaps"** sei nicht gleich so aufgeregt, ich habe nur „vielleicht" gesagt; **aren't you ~ about these developments?** finden Sie diese Entwicklungen nicht aufregend?; **aren't you ~ about what might happen?** sind Sie nicht gespannt, was passieren wird?; **he's very ~ about your idea** er ist sehr von deiner Idee begeistert; **the critics are very ~ about this new writer** die Kritiker sind von dem neuen Schriftsteller begeistert.

excitedly [ɪk'saɪtɪdlɪ] *adv see adj* aufgeregt; erregt. **we're waiting ~ to see what will happen** wir warten gespannt darauf, was passiert.

excitement [ɪk'saɪtmənt] *n* **(a)** Aufregung *f*; (*not being calm etc also*) Erregung *f*. **the ~ of the elections** die Aufregung der Wahlen; **a mood of ~** eine Spannung; **a shriek of ~** ein aufgeregter Schrei; **in the ~ of the match** in der Aufregung des Spiels, im Eifer des Gefechts; **the ~ of a day in the office** der aufregende Tagesablauf im Büro; **she only did it for ~** sie hat es nur getan, um ein bißchen Aufregung zu haben; **what's all the ~ about?** wozu die ganze Aufregung?; **to be in a state of great ~** in heller Aufregung sein; **his novel has caused great ~** sein Roman hat große Begeisterung ausgelöst.
  (b) (*Physiol*) Reizung *f*; (*sexual*) Erregung *f*.

exciting [ɪk'saɪtɪŋ] *adj* moment, week, life, prospects, idea aufregend; story, film, event, adventure *also* sensationell; (*sexually*) erregend. **a letter for me? how ~!** ein Brief für mich? prima!; **it looks as though it might work out, isn't that ~!** es sieht so aus, als ob es klappen würde, ist das nicht prima?; **how ~ for you** prima!, wie aufregend (*also iro*).

excl *abbr of* **(a)** excluding. **(b)** exclusive exkl.

exclaim [ɪk'skleɪm] **1** *vi* **he ~ed in surprise when he saw it** er schrie überrascht auf, als er es sah. **2** *vt* ausrufen. **at last! she ~ed endlich!** rief sie (aus).

exclamation [,eksklə'meɪʃən] *n* Ausruf *m* (*also Gram*). **~ mark** *or* **point** (*US*) Ausrufezeichen *nt*; **an ~ of horror** ein Schreckenschrei *m*.

exclamatory [ɪk'sklæmətərɪ] *adj* Ausrufe-; style exklamatorisch. **~ remarks** Ausrufe *pl*.

exclude [ɪk'skluːd] *vt* ausschließen. **to ~ sb from the team/an occupation** jdn aus der Mannschaft/von einer Beschäftigung ausschließen; **if we ~ all cases in which ...** wenn wir alle Fälle ausnehmen, in denen ...; **everything excluding petrol** alles außer *or* ausgenommen Benzin.

exclusion [ɪk'skluːʒən] *n* Ausschluß *m* (*from* von). **you can't just think about your job to the ~ of everything else** du kannst nicht ausschließlich an deine Arbeit denken.

exclusive [ɪk'skluːsɪv] **1** *adj* **(a)** group, club etc exklusiv; right, interview *also* Exklusiv-. **this garage has ~ rights for VW** das ist eine VW-Vertragswerkstatt; **the two possibilities are mutually ~** die beiden Möglichkeiten schließen einander aus.
  (b) (*fashionable, sophisticated*) vornehm, elegant.
  (c) (*sole*) ausschließlich, einzig.
  (d) (*not including*) **from 15th to 20th June ~** vom 15. bis zum 20. Juni ausschließlich; **~ of** (+*gen*), exklusive (+*gen*); **the price is ~ of transport charges** der Preis enthält keine Transportkosten *or* ist ausschließlich der Transportkosten; **£30 ~ of postage** £ 30 exklusive Porto.
  2 *n* (*Press, TV*) Exklusivinterview *nt*.

exclusively [ɪk'skluːsɪvlɪ] *adv* ausschließlich.

excommunicate [,ekskə'mjuːnɪkeɪt] *vt* exkommunizieren.

excommunication ['ekskə,mjuːnɪ'keɪʃən] *n* Exkommunikation *f*.

ex-convict [,eks'kɒnvɪkt] *n* ehemaliger Häftling.

excrement ['ekskrɪmənt] *n* Kot *m*, Exkremente *pl*.

excrescence [ɪks'kresns] *n* Gewächs *nt*, Auswuchs *m* (*also fig*).

excreta [ɪks'kriːtə] *npl* Exkremente *pl*.

excrete [ɪks'kriːt] *vt* ausscheiden, absondern.

excretion [ɪks'kriːʃən] *n* (*act*) Ausscheidung, Exkretion *f*; (*substance*) Exkret *nt*.

excruciating [ɪks'kruːʃɪeɪtɪŋ] *adj* pain, noise gräßlich, fürchterlich, entsetzlich. **it was ~** (*inf*) (*embarrassing, boring*) es war gräßlich *or* fürchterlich; (*hilarious*) es war zum Schreien (*inf*); (*painful*) es hat scheußlich weh getan (*inf*).

excruciatingly [ɪks'kruːʃɪeɪtɪŋlɪ] *adv see adj* **it was ~ painful** es hat scheußlich weh getan (*inf*); **~ funny** urkomisch.

exculpate ['ekskʌlpeɪt] *vt* (*form*) person freisprechen, exkulpieren (*liter*) (*from* von). **to ~ oneself** sich rechtfertigen.

excursion [ɪk'skɜːʃən] *n* Ausflug *m*; (*fig: into a subject also*) Exkurs *m*. **to go on an ~** einen Ausflug machen.

excursionist [ɪk'skɜːʃənɪst] *n* Ausflügler(in *f*) *m*.

excursion: **~ ticket** *n* verbilligte Fahrkarte (zu einem Ausflugsort); **we are going on an ~ ticket** wir fahren zum Ausflugstarif; **~ train** *n* Sonderzug *m*.

excusable [ɪk'skjuːzəbl] *adj* verzeihlich, entschuldbar.

excuse [ɪk'skjuːz] **1** *vt* **(a)** *(seek to justify) action, person* entschuldigen. **such rudeness cannot be ~d** so ein schlechtes Benehmen ist nicht zu entschuldigen; **to ~ oneself** sich entschuldigen *(for sth für or wegen etw)*; **he ~d himself for being late** er entschuldigte sich, daß er zu spät kam.

(b) *(pardon)* **to ~ sb** jdm verzeihen; **to ~ sb's insolence** jds Frechheit entschuldigen; **jdm seine Frechheit verzeihen**; **to ~ sb for having done sth** entschuldigen, daß jd etw getan hat, jdm verzeihen, daß er etwas getan hat; **well, I think I can be ~d for believing him** nun, man kann es mir wohl nicht übelnehmen, daß ich ihm geglaubt habe; **if you will ~ the expression** wenn Sie mir den Ausdruck gestatten; **~ me for laughing** entschuldigen *or* verzeihen Sie, daß *or* wenn ich lache; **~ me!** *(to get attention, sorry)* Entschuldigung!, entschuldigen Sie!; *(indignant)* erlauben Sie mal!; **~ me for not coming down with you** entschuldigen Sie, daß ich nicht mit Ihnen hinuntergehe; **well, ~ me for asking!** entschuldige, daß ich gefragt habe!

(c) *(set free from obligation)* **to ~ sb from (doing) sth** jdn von einer Sache befreien, jdm etw erlassen; **he is ~d boots** er ist davon befreit worden, Stiefel zu tragen; **you are ~d** *(to children)* ihr könnt gehen; **can I be ~d?** darf ich mal verschwinden *(inf)*?; **and now if you will ~ me** I have work to do und nun entschuldigen Sie mich bitte, ich habe zu arbeiten.

2 [ɪks'kjuːs] *n* **(a)** *(justification)* Entschuldigung *f*. **there's no ~ for it** dafür gibt es keine Entschuldigung; **to give sth as an ~ etw** zu seiner Entschuldigung anführen *or* vorbringen; **the reasons he gave in ~ of his action** die Gründe, die er zu seiner Entschuldigung *or* als Entschuldigung für seine Tat anführte.

(b) *(pretext)* Ausrede, Entschuldigung *f*. **to make up ~s for sb** jdn herausreden; **to make ~s for sb** jdn entschuldigen; **I have a good ~ for not going** ich habe eine gute Ausrede *or* Entschuldigung, warum ich nicht hingehen kann; **it was raining — well, that's your ~** es hat geregnet — das ist wohl deine Ausrede *or* Entschuldigung; **~s, ~s!** nichts als Ausreden!; **you're full of ~s** du hast immer eine Ausrede; **he's only making ~s** er sucht nur nach einer Ausrede; **a good ~ for a party** ein guter Grund, eine Party zu feiern.

(c) **~s** *pl (apology)* Entschuldigung *f*; **to offer one's ~s** sich entschuldigen.

(d) **an ~ for steak/a heating system** ein jämmerliches *or* armseliges Steak/eine jämmerliche Heizung, eine Krankheit *(inf)*.

excuse-me [ɪk'skjuːmiː] *n (dance)* Tanz *m* mit Abklatschen.

ex-directory [ˌeksdaɪ'rektərɪ] *adj (Brit)* **to be ~** nicht im Telefonbuch stehen.

execrable *adj*, **~bly** *adv* ['eksɪkrəbl, -ɪ] scheußlich, abscheulich.

execrate ['eksɪkreɪt] *vt* **(a)** *(hate)* verabscheuen. **(b)** *(curse)* verfluchen, verwünschen.

execration [ˌeksɪ'kreɪʃən] *n* **(a)** *(hatred)* Abscheu *m*. **to hold in ~** verabscheuen. **(b)** *(curse)* Fluch *m*, Verwünschung *f*.

executant [ɪg'zekjutənt] *n* Ausführende(r) *mf*.

execute ['eksɪkjuːt] *vt* **(a)** *plan, order, task etc* durchführen, ausführen; *movement, dance* ausführen; *duties* erfüllen, wahrnehmen; *purpose* erfüllen.

(b) *(Mus) (perform)* vortragen; *cadenza etc* ausführen.

(c) *criminal* hinrichten.

(d) *(Jur) will* vollstrecken, ausführen; *contract* ausfertigen; *(sign) document* unterzeichnen.

execution [ˌeksɪ'kjuːʃən] *n* **(a)** *see vt* **(a)** Durchführung, Ausführung *f*; Ausführung *f*; Erfüllung, Wahrnehmung *f*; Erfüllung *f*. **to put sth into ~** etw ausführen; **in the ~ of his duties** bei der Ausübung seines Amtes.

(b) *(Mus)* Vortrag *m*; *(musician's skill)* Ausführung *f*.

(c) *(as punishment)* Hinrichtung, Exekution *f*.

(d) *(Jur) (of will, judgement)* Vollstreckung *f*; *(of contract)* Ausfertigung *f*; *(signing)* Unterschreiben *nt*.

executioner [ˌeksɪ'kjuːʃnəʳ] *n* Henker, Scharfrichter *m*.

executive [ɪg'zekjutɪv] **1** *adj powers, committee etc* exekutiv, Exekutiv-; *(Comm)* geschäftsführend. **~ position** leitende Stellung *or* Position; **~ ability** Führungsqualität *f*; **I think he's ~ material** ich glaube, er hat das Zeug zum Manager.

2 *n* **(a)** *(of government)* Exekutive *f*; *(of association, trades union)* Vorstand *m*. **(b)** *(person in business)* leitender Angestellter, leitende Angestellte, Manager *m*.

executive: **~ (brief)case** *n* Diplomatenaktentasche *f*; **~ committee** *n* Vorstand *m*; **~ jet** *n* Privatjet *m* (für Manager); **~ officer** *n* Erster Offizier; **~ suite** *n (in office)* Vorstandsetage *f*.

executor [ɪg'zekjutəʳ] *n (of will)* Testamentsvollstrecker *m*.

executrix [ɪg'zekjutrɪks] *n* Testamentsvollstreckerin *f*.

exegesis [ˌeksɪ'dʒiːsɪs] *n* Exegese, Auslegung *f*.

exegetical [ˌeksɪ'dʒetɪkəl] *adj* exegetisch.

exemplary [ɪg'zempləri] *adj conduct, virtue, pupil* vorbildlich, beispielhaft. **~ punishment** exemplarische Strafe; **~ damages** über den verursachten Schaden hinausgehende Entschädigung, Bußgeld *nt*.

exemplification [ɪgˌzemplɪfɪ'keɪʃən] *n* Erläuterung, Veranschaulichung, Exemplifizierung *(geh)* *f*.

exemplify [ɪg'zemplɪfaɪ] *vt* erläutern, veranschaulichen.

exempt [ɪg'zempt] **1** *adj* befreit *(from* von). **diplomats are ~** Diplomaten sind ausgenommen; **could I be made ~ (from that)?** könnte ich davon befreit werden? **2** *vt person* befreien. **to ~ sb from doing sth** jdn davon befreien, etw zu tun.

exemption [ɪg'zempʃən] *n* Befreiung *f*. **~ from taxes** Steuerfreiheit *f*.

exercise ['eksəsaɪz] **1** *n* **(a)** *no pl (of right)* Wahrnehmung *f*; *(of physical, mental power)* Ausübung *f*; *(of patience, mental faculties)* Übung *f*; *(of imagination)* Anwendung *f*. **in the ~ of his duties** bei der Ausübung seiner Pflichten.

(b) *(bodily or mental, drill, Mus etc)* Übung *f*. **to do one's ~s in the morning** Morgengymnastik machen.

(c) *no pl (physical)* Bewegung *f*. **physical ~** *(körperliche)* Bewegung; **~ is good for you** Bewegung ist gesund; **a dog needs a lot of ~** ein Hund braucht viel Bewegung; **people who don't take or get enough ~** Leute, die sich nicht genug bewegen *or* die nicht genug Bewegung bekommen; **shall we go out and get some ~?** wollen wir rausgehen und uns ein wenig Bewegung verschaffen?; **what do you do for ~?** wie halten Sie sich fit?

(d) *(Mil: usu pl)* Übung *f*. **to go on ~s** eine Übung machen.

(e) **~s** *pl (US: ceremonies)* Zeremoniell *nt*, Feierlichkeiten *pl*.

2 *vt* **(a)** *body, mind* üben, trainieren; *(Mil) troops* exerzieren; *horse* bewegen; *dog* spazierenführen. **I'm not saying this just to ~ my voice** ich sage das nicht zum Spaß.

(b) *(use) one's authority, control, power* ausüben; *a right also* geltend machen; *patience, tact, discretion* üben; *influence* ausüben *(on* auf *+acc)*; *talents* Gebrauch machen von. **to ~ care in doing sth** Vorsicht walten lassen, wenn man etw tut.

3 *vi* **if you ~ regularly** ... wenn Sie sich viel bewegen ...; **you don't ~ enough** du hast zuwenig Bewegung; **he was exercising on the parallel bars** er turnte (gerade) am Barren.

exercise book *n* Heft *nt*.

exerciser ['eksəsaɪzə] *n* Trainingsgerät *nt*.

exercise yard *n* Hof *m*.

exert [ɪg'zɜːt] **1** *vt pressure* ausüben *(on* auf *+acc)*; *influence also* aufbieten; *authority, einsetzen (on* bei); *force* gebrauchen, anwenden. **to ~ a force on sth** eine Kraft auf etw *(acc)* ausüben. **2** *vr* sich anstrengen.

exertion [ɪg'zɜːʃən] *n* **(a)** *(effort)* Anstrengung *f*.

(b) *(of force, strength)* Anwendung *f*, Einsatz *m*; *(of authority)* Aufgebot *nt*, Einsatz *m*; *(of influence)* Aufgebot *nt*. **the ~ of force/pressure on sth** die Ausübung von Kraft/Druck auf etw *(acc)*; **the ~ of an influence on sb** die Ausübung eines Einflusses auf jdn; **by the ~ of a little pressure** durch Ausübung *or* Anwendung von etwas Druck; **rugby requires a lot of ~** Rugby fordert viel Einsatz; **by one's own ~s** durch eigene Anstrengungen; **after the day's ~s** nach des Tages Mühen.

exeunt ['eksɪʌnt] *(in stage directions)* ab. **~ Brutus and Cassius** Brutus und Cassius ab.

ex gratia [eks'greɪʃə] *adj* payment Sonder-.

exhale [eks'heɪl] **1** *vt* **(a)** *(breathe out)* ausatmen. **(b)** *(give off) smoke* abgeben; *gas, vapour also* ablassen. **2** *vi* ausatmen.

exhaust [ɪg'zɔːst] **1** *vt* **(a)** *(use up completely)* erschöpfen. **my patience is ~ed** meine Geduld ist erschöpft *or* zu Ende.

(b) *(tire)* erschöpfen. **the children are/this job is ~ing me** die Kinder sind/diese Arbeit ist eine Strapaze für mich.

2 *n* *(Aut etc)* Auspuff *m*; *(gases)* Auspuffgase *pl*.

exhausted [ɪg'zɔːstɪd] *adj* erschöpft.

exhaust fumes *npl* Auspuffgase, Abgase *pl*.

exhausting [ɪg'zɔːstɪŋ] *adj activity, work, person* anstrengend, strapaziös. **the climate is ~** das Klima erschöpft einen.

exhaustion [ɪg'zɔːstʃən] *n* Erschöpfung *f*.

exhaustive *adj*, **~ly** *adv* [ɪg'zɔːstɪv, -lɪ] erschöpfend.

exhaust: **~ pipe** *n* Auspuffrohr *nt*; **~ system** *n* Auspuff *m*.

exhibit [ɪg'zɪbɪt] **1** *vt* **(a)** *paintings, handicrafts* ausstellen; *merchandise also* auslegen; *documents, membership card* vorzeigen, vorweisen.

(b) *skill, ingenuity* zeigen, beweisen, an den Tag legen. **2** *vi* ausstellen.

3 *n* **(a)** *(in an exhibition)* Ausstellungsstück *nt*.

(b) *(Jur)* Beweisstück *nt*.

exhibition [ˌeksɪ'bɪʃən] *n* **(a)** *(of paintings, furniture etc)* Ausstellung *f*; *(of articles for sale)* Auslage *f*.

(b) *(act of showing: of a technique, trick etc)* Vorführung *f*.

(c) **what an ~ of bad manners!** was für schlechte Manieren!; **did you see her at the party last night? — what an ~!** hast du sie auf der Party gestern abend gesehen? — die hat sich vielleicht aufgeführt!; **to make an ~ of oneself** ein Theater machen *(inf)*; **am I making an ~ of myself?** benehm ich mich daneben?

(d) *(Brit Univ: grant)* Stipendium *nt*.

exhibitioner [ˌeksɪ'bɪʃənəʳ] *n (Brit Univ)* Stipendiat(in *f*) *m*.

exhibitionism [ˌeksɪ'bɪʃənɪzəm] *n* Exhibitionismus *m*.

exhibitionist [ˌeksɪ'bɪʃənɪst] **1** *n* Exhibitionist(in *f*) *m*. **2** *adj* exhibitionistisch.

exhibitor [ɪg'zɪbɪtəʳ] *n* Aussteller *m*.

exhilarate [ɪg'zɪləreɪt] *vt* in Hochstimmung versetzen; *(news also)* (freudig) erregen; *(sea air etc)* beleben, erfrischen.

exhilarated [ɪg'zɪləreɪtɪd] *adj laugh* erregt, aufgeregt. **to feel ~** in Hochstimmung sein.

exhilarating [ɪg'zɪləreɪtɪŋ] *adj sensation, speed* erregend, berauschend; *conversation, music, work* anregend; *air, wind etc* belebend, erfrischend.

exhilaration [ɪgˌzɪlə'reɪʃən] *n* Hochgefühl *nt*. **the ~ of flying** das Hochgefühl beim Fliegen; **to fill sb with a feeling of ~** jdn in Hochstimmung versetzen.

exhort [ɪg'zɔːt] *vt* ermahnen.

exhortation [ˌegzɔː'teɪʃən] *n* Ermahnung *f*.

exhumation [ˌekshjuː'meɪʃən] *n* Exhumierung, Exhumation *f*.

exhume [eks'hjuːm] *vt* exhumieren.

exigence ['eksɪdʒəns], **exigency** [ɪg'zɪdʒənsɪ] *n* **(a)** *usu pl (requirement)* (An)forderung *f*; *(of situation also)* Erfordernis *nt*. **(b)** *(emergency)* Notlage *f*. **(c)** *(urgency)* Dringlichkeit *f*.

exigent ['eksɪdʒənt] *adj (urgent)* zwingend, dringend; *(exacting) master* streng, gestreng *(old)*.

exiguity [ˌegzɪ'gjuːɪtɪ] *n (form)* Winzigkeit *f*; *(meagreness)* Knappheit *f*.

exiguous [ɪg'zɪgjʊəs] *adj (form) space* klein, winzig; *income* gering, dürftig.

exile ['eksaɪl] **1** *n* **(a)** *(person)* Verbannte(r) *mf*. **(b)** *(banishment)* Exil *nt*, Verbannung *f*. **to go into ~** ins Exil gehen; **in ~** im Exil. **2** *vt* verbannen *(from* aus), ins Exil schicken.

exist [ɪgˈzɪst] vi (a) (to be) existieren, bestehen. everything that ~s alles, was ist or existiert; it only ~s in her imagination das gibt es or das existiert nur in ihrer Phantasie; I want to live, not just ~ ich möchte leben, nicht einfach nur existieren; it doesn't ~ das gibt es nicht; to cease to ~ zu bestehen aufhören; to continue to ~ fort- or weiterbestehen; doubts still ~ noch bestehen Zweifel; the understanding which ~s between the two countries das Einvernehmen zwischen den beiden Ländern; there ~s a tradition that ... es gibt den Brauch, daß ...
　(b) (live) existieren, leben. we cannot ~ without water wir können ohne Wasser nicht leben or existieren; can life ~ on Mars? kann auf dem Mars Leben existieren?; she ~s on very little sie kommt mit sehr wenig aus; we manage to ~ wir kommen gerade aus; is it possible to ~ on such a small salary? kann man denn von so einem kleinen Gehalt leben?
　(c) (be found) vorkommen.

existence [ɪgˈzɪstəns] n (a) Existenz f; (of custom, tradition, institution also) Bestehen nt. to be in ~ existieren, bestehen; to come into ~ entstehen; (person) auf die Welt kommen; to go out of ~ zu bestehen or existieren aufhören; do you believe in the ~ of angels? glauben Sie daran, daß es Engel gibt?, glauben Sie an die Existenz von Engeln?; the continued ~ of such a procedure das Weiterbestehen or der Fortbestand eines solchen Verfahrens; the only one in ~ der einzige, den es gibt.
　(b) (life) Dasein, Existenz nt, Existenz f. a miserable ~ ein elendes Leben, ein trostloses Dasein; what are your means of ~? wie verdienen Sie Ihren Lebensunterhalt?

existent [ɪgˈzɪstənt] adj existent; conditions, laws bestehend. to be ~ existieren; dinosaurs are no longer ~ Saurier gibt es nicht mehr.

existential [ˌegzɪsˈtenʃəl] adj existentiell.

existentialism [ˌegzɪsˈtenʃəlɪzəm] n Existentialismus m.

existentialist [ˌegzɪsˈtenʃəlɪst] 1 n Existentialist(in f) m. 2 adj existentialistisch.

existing [ɪgˈzɪstɪŋ] adj law bestehend; director gegenwärtig.

exit [ˈeksɪt] 1 n (a) (from stage, life) Abgang m; (from room also) Hinausgehen nt (from aus); (from sb's life) Scheiden nt (geh). to make one's ~ (from stage) abgehen; (from room) hinausgehen; he made a very dramatic ~ sein Abgang war sehr dramatisch.
　(b) (way out) Ausgang m; (for vehicles) Ausfahrt f.
　2 vi hinausgehen; (from stage) abgehen. ~ the king (stage direction) der König (tritt) ab.
　3 vt (US) bus etc verlassen, aussteigen aus.

exit: ~ permit n Ausreisegenehmigung f; ~ visa n Ausreisevisum nt.

exodus [ˈeksədəs] n (a) Auszug m; (Bibl: of Hebrews, fig) Exodus m. general ~ allgemeiner Aufbruch; the ~ of city dwellers to the sea in summer die sommerliche Völkerwanderung der Städter an die See. (b) ~ of capital Kapitalabwanderung f. (c) (Bibl) E~ 2. Buch Mosis or Mose, Exodus m.

ex-officio [ˌeksəˈfɪʃɪəʊ] 1 adj to be ~ commander/an ~ member vom Amts wegen Kommandant/Mitglied sein. 2 adv ex officio. to act ~ kraft seines Amtes handeln.

exonerate [ɪgˈzɒnəreɪt] vt entlasten (from von).

exoneration [ɪgˌzɒnəˈreɪʃən] n Entlastung f (from von).

exorbitance [ɪgˈzɔːbɪtəns] n (of price) Unverschämtheit f; (of demands also) Maßlosigkeit, Übertriebenheit f.

exorbitant [ɪgˈzɔːbɪtənt] adj price astronomisch, unverschämt, exorbitant (geh); demands maßlos, übertrieben. £50 for that is ~! £ 50 dafür ist Wucher.

exorcism [ˈeksɔːsɪzəm] n Geisterbeschwörung f, Exorzismus m, Austreibung f böser Geister.

exorcist [ˈeksɔːsɪst] n Exorzist m.

exorcize [ˈeksɔːsaɪz] vt exorzieren; evil spirit also austreiben.

exoskeleton [ˌeksəʊˈskelɪtən] n Außenskelett nt.

exoteric [ˌeksəʊˈterɪk] adj exoterisch.

exotic [ɪgˈzɒtɪk] 1 adj exotisch. 2 n (Bot) exotische Pflanze.

exotica [ɪgˈzɒtɪkə] npl Exotika pl. a museum of ~ (fig) ein Raritätenkabinett nt.

exotically [ɪgˈzɒtɪkəlɪ] adv see adj.

exoticism [ɪgˈzɒtɪsɪzəm] n Exotik f, Exotische nt.

expand [ɪkˈspænd] 1 vt metal, gas, liquid, empire, chest ausdehnen, expandieren; business, trade, production also erweitern, ausweiten; knowledge, mind, algebraic formula erweitern; influence also, experience vergrößern; summary, notes weiter ausführen; ideas entwickeln.
　2 vi (solids, gases, liquids, universe) sich ausdehnen, expandieren; (business, trade, empire) expandieren, sich ausweiten; (volume of trade, exports, production) zunehmen, wachsen; (knowledge, experience, influence) zunehmen, wachsen; (fields of knowledge, study, mind) breiter werden; (horizons) sich erweitern. we want to ~ wir wollen expandieren or (uns) vergrößern; the market is ~ing der Markt wächst; could you ~ on that? könnten Sie das weiter ausführen?; ~ing watch-strap Gliederarmband nt.

expander [ɪkˈspændə] n Expander m.

expanse [ɪkˈspæns] n Fläche f; (of ocean etc) Weite f no pl. an ~ of grass/woodland eine Grasfläche/ein Waldgebiet nt.

expansion [ɪkˈspænʃən] n (of liquid, gas, metal, universe, property) Ausdehnung, Expansion f; (of business, trade, production) Erweiterung, Ausweitung f; (of empire, territorial, economic, colonial) Expansion f; (of subject, idea) Entwicklung f; (Math) Erweiterung f; (of knowledge) Erweiterung f; (of experience, influence) Vergrößerung f; (of summary, notes) Ausweitung f.

expansionism [ɪkˈspænʃənɪzəm] n Expansionspolitik f.

expansionist [ɪkˈspænʃənɪst] 1 adj expansionistisch. Expansions-. 2 n Expansionspolitiker(in f) m.

expansive [ɪkˈspænsɪv] adj (a) person mitteilsam. to be in an ~ mood mitteilsam sein. (b) (Phys) expansiv.

expatiate [ɪkˈspeɪʃɪeɪt] vi sich verbreiten (on über + acc).

expatiation [ɪkˌspeɪʃɪˈeɪʃən] n weitläufige Erörterung.

expatriate [eksˈpætrɪeɪt] 1 vt ausbürgern, expatriieren.
　2 [eksˈpætrɪət] adj person im Ausland lebend. ~ community Auslandsgemeinde, Kolonie f; there are a lot of ~ Englishmen/workers here hier leben viele Engländer/ausländische Arbeitskräfte; ~ German Auslandsdeutsche(r) mf.
　3 [eksˈpætrɪət] n im Ausland Lebende(r) mf. the ~s in Abu Dhabi die Ausländer in Abu Dhabi; Hemingway would go drinking with other ~s Hemingway pflegte mit anderen Exilamerikanern trinken zu gehen; I'm an ~ too ich bin hier auch im Exil (hum).

expect [ɪkˈspekt] 1 vt (a) (anticipate) erwarten; esp sth bad also rechnen mit. that was to be ~ed das war zu erwarten, damit war zu rechnen; I know what to ~ ich weiß, was mich erwartet; I did not ~ that from him das habe ich nicht von ihm erwartet; we were ~ing war in 1939 1939 haben wir mit Krieg gerechnet; to ~ the worst mit dem Schlimmsten rechnen; I ~ed as much das habe ich erwartet, damit habe ich gerechnet; he failed as (we had) ~ed er fiel, wie erwartet, durch; he got first prize as was to be ~ed wie erwartet, bekam er den ersten Preis; to ~ to do sth erwarten or damit rechnen, etw zu tun; I didn't ~ to gain his sympathy ich habe kein Mitleid von ihm erwartet; he ~s to be elected er rechnet damit, gewählt zu werden; it is ~ed that ... es wird erwartet or man erwartet, daß ..., man rechnet damit, daß ...; it is hardly to be ~ed that es ist kaum zu erwarten or damit zu rechnen, daß; I do not ~ her to be discreet ich erwarte von ihr gar keine Diskretion; I was ~ing him to come ich habe eigentlich erwartet, daß er kommt; you can't ~ me to agree to that! Sie erwarten doch wohl nicht, daß ich dem zustimme!; I'll ~ to see you tomorrow then dann sehen wir uns also morgen.
　(b) (suppose) denken, glauben. will they be on time? — yes, I ~ so nehmen sie pünktlich? — ja, ich glaube schon or denke doch; this work is very tiring — yes, I ~ it is diese Arbeit ist sehr anstrengend — (ja,) das glaube ich; I ~ it will rain höchstwahrscheinlich wird es regnen, es wird wohl regnen; I ~ you'd like a drink Sie möchten sicher etwas trinken, ich nehme an, Sie möchten etwas trinken; I ~ you're tired Sie werden sicher müde sein; I ~ he turned it down er hat wohl abgelehnt, ich nehme an, er hat abgelehnt; well, I ~ he's right er wird schon recht haben; well, I ~ it's all for the best das ist wohl nur gut so; I ~ he will soon be finished er ist sicher bald fertig; I ~ it was your father who telephoned ich nehme an, es war dein Vater, der angerufen hat.
　(c) (demand) to ~ sth of or from sb etw von jdm erwarten; to ~ sb to do sth erwarten, daß jd etw tut; I ~ you to be obedient ich erwarte von dir Gehorsam; what do you ~ me to do about it? was soll ich da tun?; don't ~ me to feel sorry erwarte von mir kein Mitleid; are we ~ed to tip the waiter? müssen wir dem Kellner Trinkgeld geben?
　(d) (await) person, thing, action erwarten; baby also bekommen. I will be ~ing you tomorrow ich erwarte dich morgen; I am ~ing them for supper ich erwarte sie zum Abendessen; we'll ~ you when we see you (inf) wenn ihr kommt, dann kommt ihr (inf); you'll have to ~ me when you see me (inf) wenn ich da bin, bin ich da! (inf).
　2 vi she's ~ing sie ist in anderen Umständen, sie bekommt or erwartet ein Kind.

expectancy [ɪkˈspektənsɪ] n Erwartung f.

expectant [ɪkˈspektənt] adj erwartungsvoll; mother werdend.

expectantly [ɪkˈspektntlɪ] adv erwartungsvoll. to wait ~ gespannt or ungeduldig warten.

expectation [ˌekspekˈteɪʃən] n (a) (act of expecting) Erwartung f. in ~ of in Erwartung (+ gen); in the confident ~ of an easy victory fest mit einem leichten Sieg rechnend.
　(b) (that expected) Erwartung f. contrary to all ~(s) wider Erwarten; beyond all ~(s) über Erwarten, über alle Erwartung; to come up to sb's ~s jds Erwartungen entsprechen.
　(c) (prospect) Aussicht f.
　(d) ~ of life Lebenserwartung f.

expectorant [ɪkˈspektərənt] n Expektorans nt (spec).

expectorate [ɪkˈspektəreɪt] vti (form) ausspeien.

expedience [ɪkˈspiːdɪəns], **expediency** [ɪkˈspiːdɪənsɪ] n (a) (self-interest) Zweckdenken nt, Berechnung f. (b) (of measure etc) (politic nature) Zweckdienlichkeit f; (advisability) Ratsamkeit f.

expedient [ɪkˈspiːdɪənt] 1 adj (politic) zweckdienlich; (advisable) angebracht, ratsam. 2 n Notbehelf m, Hilfsmittel nt.

expedite [ˈekspɪdaɪt] vt (a) (hasten) beschleunigen, vorantreiben. see what you can do to ~ matters sehen Sie zu, daß Sie die Sache beschleunigen or vorantreiben. (b) (rare) letters expedieren (spec).

expedition [ˌekspɪˈdɪʃən] n (a) Expedition f; (scientific also) Forschungsreise f; (Mil) Feldzug m. shopping ~ Einkaufstour f; to go on an ~/a shopping ~ auf (eine) Expedition or Forschungsreise gehen/eine Einkaufstour machen. (b) no pl (old, form: speed) Eile f. with all possible ~ eilends (old, form).

expeditionary [ˌekspɪˈdɪʃənrɪ] adj Expeditions-. ~ force (Mil) Expeditionskorps nt.

expeditious adj, ~ly adv [ˌekspɪˈdɪʃəs, -lɪ] schnell, prompt.

expel [ɪkˈspel] vt (a) vertreiben; (officially: from country, school etc) ausweisen (from aus), verweisen (from gen); (from society) ausstoßen, ausschließen. (b) gas, liquid ausstoßen.

expend [ɪkˈspend] vt (a) (spend, employ) money ausgeben, aufwenden; time, energy, care aufwenden (on für, on doing sth um etw zu tun), verwenden (on auf + acc, on doing sth darauf, etwas zu tun). (b) (use up) resources verbrauchen.

expendable [ɪkˈspendəbl] adj entbehrlich; people überflüssig.

expenditure [ɪkˈspendɪtʃə] n (a) (money spent) Ausgaben pl. (b) (spending) (of money) Ausgabe f; (of time, energy) Aufwand m (on an + dat). the ~ of money on ... Geld auszugeben für ...; ~ of time/energy Zeit-/Energieaufwand *m*.

expense [ɪk'spens] *n* **(a)** Kosten *pl*. **at** my ~ auf meine Kosten; **at the public** ~ auf Staatskosten; **at little/great** ~ mit geringen/hohen Kosten; **but consider the** ~ aber denken Sie an die Kosten *pl*; **it's a big** ~ es ist eine große Ausgabe; **to go to the** ~ **of buying a car** (viel) Geld für ein Auto anlegen; **to go to great** ~ **to repair the house** es sich (*dat*) etwas kosten lassen, das Haus instand zu setzen; **don't go to any** ~ **over our visit** stürz dich nicht in Unkosten wegen unseres Besuchs.

(b) (*Comm: usu pl*) Spesen *pl*. **to incur** ~s Unkosten haben; **your** ~s **will be entirely covered** alle Unkosten werden Ihnen vergütet; **put it on** ~s schreiben Sie es auf die Spesenrechnung; **it's all on** ~s das geht alles auf Spesen.

(c) (*fig*) **at sb's** ~/**at the** ~ **of sth** auf jds Kosten (*acc*)/auf Kosten einer Sache (*gen*); **to get rich at somebody else's** ~/**at the** ~ **of others** sich auf Kosten eines anderen/anderer bereichern; **at the** ~ **of a decrease in quality** auf Kosten der Qualität; **at the** ~ **of great sacrifices** unter großen Opfern; **at the** ~ **of great personal suffering** unter großen persönlichen Verlusten.

expense: ~ **account 1** *n* Spesenkonto *nt*; **this will go on his** ~ **account** das geht auf Spesen; **2** *adj attr* ~-**account lunch** Mittagessen *nt* auf Spesen; ~-**account living** Leben *nt* auf Spesen; **it's only** ~-**account types who stay in this hotel** (*inf*) in diesem Hotel wohnen nur Spesenreiter (*inf*); ~s **form** *n* Spesenrechnung *f*; ~s-**paid** *adj* auf Geschäftskosten.

expensive [ɪk'spensɪv] *adj* teuer; *goods, undertaking also* kostspielig.

expensively [ɪk'spensɪvlɪ] *adv* teuer. ~ **priced** teuer.

expensiveness [ɪk'spensɪvnɪs] *n* (*of goods, travel, services etc*) hoher Preis, Kostspieligkeit *f*; (*of living here etc*) Kostspieligkeit *f*. **the** ~ **of her tastes** ihr teurer Geschmack; **the increasing** ~ **of basic commodities** die ständige Verteuerung von Grundbedarfsmitteln.

experience [ɪk'spɪərɪəns] **1** *n* **(a)** (*knowledge, wisdom acquired*) Erfahrung *f*. ~ **of life** Lebenserfahrung *f*; ~ **shows or proves that** ... die Erfahrung lehrt, daß ...; **to know sth by or from** ~ etw aus Erfahrung wissen; **from my own personal** ~ aus eigener Erfahrung; **a fact established by** ~ eine Erfahrungstatsache, eine auf Erfahrung beruhende Tatsache; **he has no** ~ **of real grief** er hat nie wirklichen Kummer erfahren *or* erlebt; **he has no** ~ **of living in the country** er kennt das Landleben nicht; **I gained a lot of useful** ~ ich habe viele nützliche Erfahrungen gemacht; **to have an** ~ eine Erfahrung machen.

(b) (*practice, skill*) Erfahrung *f*. **he has had no practical** ~ ihm fehlt die Praxis, er hat keine praktischen Kenntnisse, er hat keine Erfahrung; **to have** ~ **of a technique** Erfahrung in einer Methode haben; **have you had some** ~ **of driving a bus?** haben Sie Erfahrung im Busfahren?; ~ **in a trade/in business** Berufs-/Geschäftserfahrung *f*; **to have a lot of teaching** ~ große Erfahrung als Lehrer haben; **he lacks** ~ ihm fehlt die Praxis *or* praktische Erfahrung; **have you any previous** ~ **in this kind of work?** haben Sie schon Erfahrung (auf diesem Gebiet)?; **he is working in a factory to gain** ~ er arbeitet in einer Fabrik, um praktische Erfahrungen zu sammeln.

(c) (*event experienced*) Erlebnis *nt*. **I had a nasty** ~ mir ist etwas Unangenehmes passiert; **the trial was a very nasty** ~ der Prozeß war eine sehr unangenehme Sache; **to go through or have a painful** ~ Schreckliches erleben; **to go through some terrible** ~s viel durchmachen; **what an** ~! das war vielleicht was!; **it was a new** ~ **for me** es war völlig neu für mich.

2 *vt* **(a)** erleben; (*suffer, undergo*) *pain, grief, hunger also* erfahren; *difficult times also* durchmachen. **to** ~ **difficulties** auf Schwierigkeiten stoßen, Schwierigkeiten haben.

(b) (*feel*) fühlen, spüren, empfinden.

experienced [ɪk'spɪərɪənst] *adj* erfahren; *eye, ear* geschult. **to be** ~ **in sth** erfahren in etw (*dat*) sein.

experiential [ɪk,spɪərɪ'enʃəl] *adj* auf Erfahrung beruhend, Erfahrungs-.

experiment [ɪk'sperɪmənt] **1** *n* (*Chem, Phys, fig*) Versuch *m*, Experiment *nt*. **to do an** ~ einen Versuch *or* ein Experiment machen; **as an** ~ versuchsweise, als Versuch. **2** *vi* (*Chem, Phys, fig*) experimentieren.

experimental [ɪk,sperɪ'mentl] *adj* **(a)** (*based on experiments*) *research, method, science, evidence* experimentell, Experimental-. **(b)** *laboratory, farm, engine, prototype, period* Versuchs-, Test-; *novel* experimentell; *theatre, cinema* Experimentier-, experimentell. **at the** ~ **stage** im Versuchsstadium; **on an** ~ **basis** auf Versuchsbasis.

experimentally [ɪk,sperɪ'mentəlɪ] *adv* **(a)** (*by experiment*) *test, discover* durch Versuche, experimentell. **(b)** (*as an experiment*) versuchsweise, als Versuch.

experimentation [ɪk,sperɪmen'teɪʃən] *n* Experimentieren *nt*.

expert ['ekspɜːt] **1** *n* Fachmann, Experte *m*, Expertin *f*; (*Jur*) Sachverständige(r) *mf*. **he is an** ~ **on the subject/that sort of negotiation** er ist Fachmann *or* Experte auf diesem Gebiet/für solche Verhandlungen; ~ **in geology** Fachmann *m* für Geologie, Geologieexperte *m*; **an** ~ **at chess** ein Schachexperte *m*; **he's an** ~ **at saying the wrong thing** er versteht es meisterhaft, genau das Falsche zu sagen; **with the eye of an** ~ mit fachmännischem Blick; **to get the advice of** ~s Experten *or* Fachleute/Sachverständige zu Rate ziehen; **OK, you do it, you're the** ~, gut, machen Sie's, Sie sind der Fachmann.

2 *adj work* ausgezeichnet, geschickt; *driver etc* erfahren, geschickt; *approach, advice* fachmännisch; *opinion* eines Fachmanns/Sachverständigen. **to be** ~ **in an art/a science** sich in einer Kunst/Wissenschaft sehr gut auskennen; ~ **witness** sachverständiger Zeuge; **what's your** ~ **opinion?** (*also iro*) was meinen Sie als Fachmann *or* Experte dazu?; **the** ~ **touch** die Meisterhand; **he is** ~ **in handling a boat/in repairing cars** er

kann meisterhaft mit einem Boot umgehen/er ist ein Experte für Autoreparaturen; **to cast an** ~ **eye over sth** etw fachmännisch begutachten.

expertise [,ekspə'tiːz] *n* Sachverstand *m*, Sachkenntnis *f* (*in* + *dat*, auf dem Gebiet + *gen*); (*manual skills*) Geschick *nt* (*in* bei).

expertly ['ekspɜːtlɪ] *adv* meisterhaft; *drive, dribble* geschickt, gekonnt; *judge, examine* sachverständig, mit Sachverstand.

expiate ['ekspɪeɪt] *vt* sühnen.

expiation [,ekspɪ'eɪʃən] *n* **in** ~ **of** als Sühne für.

expiatory ['ekspɪətərɪ] *adj offering, sacrifice* Sühne-, sühnend.

expiration [,ekspaɪə'reɪʃən] *n* **(a)** see **expiry**. **(b)** (*of breath*) Ausatmen *nt*, Ausatmung *f*.

expire [ɪk'spaɪə'] *vi* **(a)** (*lease, passport*) ablaufen, ungültig werden; (*time limit*) ablaufen, zu Ende gehen. **(b)** (*liter: die*) seinen Geist aufgeben (*liter*). **(c)** (*breathe out*) ausatmen.

expiry [ɪk'spaɪərɪ] *n* Ablauf *m*. **on the** ~ **of** nach Ablauf (+*gen*); **date of** ~, ~ **date** Ablauftermin *m*; (*of voucher, special offer*) Verfallsdatum *nt*.

explain [ɪk'spleɪn] **1** *vt* erklären (*to sb* jdm); *motives, situation, thoughts also* erläutern; *mystery* aufklären. **it's all right, I can** ~ **everything** schon gut, ich kann das alles erklären; **that is easy to** ~, **that is easily** ~**ed** es läßt sich leicht erklären; **he wanted to see me but wouldn't** ~ **why** er wollte mich sehen, sagte aber nicht, warum *or* aus welchem Grunde; **the bad weather** ~s **why he is absent** das schlechte Wetter erklärt seine Abwesenheit; **so that** ~s **why he didn't react** ach, das erklärt, warum er nicht reagiert hat.

2 *vr* (*justify*) sich rechtfertigen. **he'd better** ~ **himself** ich hoffe, er kann das erklären; **listen, my boy, I think you'd better start** ~**ing yourself** was hast du zu deiner Entschuldigung zu sagen, mein Junge?; **what do you mean "stupid"!** ~ **yourself!** was meinst du mit „dumm"! erkläre mir/uns das!; ~ **yourself!** was soll das?, kannst du es/das erklären?

3 *vi* es/alles erklären. **please** ~ **bitte erklären Sie das; I think you've got a little** ~**ing to do** ich glaube, Sie müssen da einiges erklären.

♦**explain away** *vt sep* eine (einleuchtende) Erklärung finden für, wegerklären (*inf*).

explainable [ɪk'spleɪnəbl] *adj* erklärlich. **this is easily** ~ das läßt sich leicht erklären; **that is** ~ **by** ... das läßt sich durch ... erklären.

explanation [,eksplə'neɪʃən] *n* **(a)** see *vt* Erklärung *f*; Erläuterung *f*; Aufklärung *f*. **it needs some/a little** ~ es bedarf einer/einer kurzen Erklärung, man muß das etwas/ein wenig erklären; **he gave a long** ~ **of what he meant** er erklärte lange, was er meinte; **what is the** ~ **of this?** wie ist das zu erklären? **(b)** (*justification*) Erklärung, Rechtfertigung *f*. **has he anything to say in** ~ **of his conduct?** kann er irgend etwas zur Erklärung seines Verhaltens vorbringen?; **what is the** ~ **of this?** was soll das heißen?

explanatory [ɪk'splænətərɪ] *adj* erklärend; *remarks etc also* erläuternd. **a few** ~ **remarks** ein paar Worte zur Erklärung.

expletive [ɪk'spliːtɪv] **1** *n* (*exclamation*) Ausruf *m*; (*oath*) Kraftausdruck, Fluch *m*; (*Gram: filler word*) Füllwort *nt*. **2** *adj* ~ **word** (*Gram*) Füllwort *nt*.

explicable [ɪk'splɪkəbl] *adj* erklärbar.

explicate ['eksplɪkeɪt] *vt* (*form*) erläutern, ausführen.

explication [,eksplɪ'keɪʃən] *n* (*form*) Erläuterung, Ausführung *f*.

explicit [ɪk'splɪsɪt] *adj* deutlich, explizit (*geh*); *text, meaning also* klar; *sex scene* deutlich, unverhüllt. **in** ~ **terms** klar und deutlich; **there's no need to be quite so** ~ Sie brauchen nicht so deutlich zu werden; **he was** ~ **on this point** er wurde an diesem Punkt ziemlich deutlich; ~ **denial** deutliches Abstreiten.

explicitly [ɪk'splɪsɪtlɪ] *adv* deutlich, explizite (*geh*); (*clearly also*) klar.

explode [ɪk'spləʊd] **1** *vi* **(a)** explodieren; (*powder, booby-trap, mine*) in die Luft fliegen (*inf*). **(b)** (*fig: with anger*) explodieren, vor Wut platzen (*inf*), in die Luft gehen (*inf*). **to** ~ **with laughter** in schallendes Gelächter ausbrechen, losplatzen (*inf*).

2 *vt* **(a)** *bomb, mine, plane* sprengen; *dynamite, gas* zur Explosion bringen. **(b)** (*fig*) *theory, argument* zu Fall bringen. **to** ~ **a popular fallacy** einen weitverbreiteten Irrtum aufdecken.

exploded [ɪk'spləʊdɪd] *adj* ~ **diagram** Explosionszeichnung *f*.

exploit ['eksplɔɪt] **1** *n* (*heroic*) Heldentat *f*. ~s (*adventures*) Abenteuer *pl*. **2** [ɪks'plɔɪt] *vt* **(a)** (*use unfairly*) *workers* ausbeuten; *friend, sb's credulity, good nature* ausnutzen. **(b)** (*make use of*) *talent, the situation* ausnutzen, ausnützen (*dial*); *coal seam* ausbeuten; *land, natural resources* nutzen.

exploitation [,eksplɔɪ'teɪʃən] *n* see *vt* Ausbeutung *f*; Ausnutzung *f*; Ausnutzung *f*; Ausbeutung *f*; Nutzung *f*.

exploration [,eksplɔː'reɪʃən] *n* (*of country, area*) Erforschung, Exploration (*geh*) *f*; (*of small area, town*) Erkundung *f*; (*of topic, possibilities*) Erforschung, Untersuchung, Sondierung *f*; (*Med*) Untersuchung, Exploration *f*. **a voyage of** ~ (*lit, fig*) eine Entdeckungsreise; **on his** ~s auf seinen Forschungsreisen/Erkundungen.

exploratory [ɪk'splɔːrətərɪ] *adj drilling* Probe-; *excursion* Forschungs-. ~ **operation** (*Med*) Explorationsoperation *f*; ~ **talks** Sondierungsgespräche *pl*.

explore [ɪk'splɔː'] **1** *vt* **(a)** *country, forest, unknown territory* erforschen, erkunden, explorieren (*geh*); (*Med*) untersuchen. **(b)** (*fig*) *question, possibilities* erforschen, untersuchen, sondieren. **talks to** ~ **the ground** Sondierungsgespräche *pl*.

2 *vi* **to go exploring** auf Entdeckungsreise gehen. **he went off into the village to** ~ er ging auf Entdeckungsreise ins Dorf.

explorer [ɪk'splɔːrə'] *n* Forscher(in *f*) *m*, Forschungsreisende(r) *mf*.

explosion [ɪk'spləʊʒən] n (a) Explosion f; (noise also) Knall m. (b) (fig: of anger) Wutausbruch m. (c) (fig: in prices, figures etc) Explosion f.

explosive [ɪk'spləʊzɪv] 1 adj (a) gas, matter, mixture, weapons, force explosiv, Explosiv-, Spreng-. ~ **device** Sprengkörper m. (b) (fig) situation, combination explosiv; temper also leicht aufbrausend. 2 n Sprengstoff m.

exponent [ɪk'spəʊnənt] n (a) (of theory) Vertreter(in f), Exponent(in f) m. (b) (Math) Exponent m, Hochzahl f.

exponential [ˌekspəʊ'nenʃəl] adj Exponential-.

export 1 [ɪk'spɔːt] vti exportieren, ausführen. **countries which** ~ **oil** Ölexportierende or Ölexport-Länder.
2 ['ekspɔːt] n Export m, Ausfuhr f. **ban on** ~**s** Exportverbot, Ausfuhrverbot nt.
3 ['ekspɔːt] adj attr Export-, Ausfuhr-. ~ **duty** Export- or Ausfuhrzoll m; ~ **drive** Exportkampagne f; ~ **licence** Ausfuhrgenehmigung or -lizenz, Exportgenehmigung f; ~ **permit** Ausfuhrerlaubnis, Exporterlaubnis f; ~ **trade** Exporthandel m.

exportable [ɪk'spɔːtəbl] adj exportfähig.

exportation [ˌekspɔː'teɪʃən] n Export m, Ausfuhr f.

exporter [ɪk'spɔːtəʳ] n (person) Exporteur m (of von); (country also) Exportland nt (of für).

expose [ɪk'spəʊz] vt (a) (uncover) rocks, remains freilegen; electric wire, nerve also bloßlegen. **a dress which leaves the back** ~**d** ein Kleid, bei dem der Rücken frei bleibt; **to be** ~**d to view** den Blicken ausgesetzt sein, offen daliegen; ~**d position** (Mil) exponierte Stellung.
(b) (to danger, rain, sunlight, radiation) aussetzen (to dat); baby aussetzen. **not to be** ~**d to heat** vor Hitze (zu) schützen; **to** ~ **oneself to criticism** sich der Kritik aussetzen.
(c) (display) one's ignorance offenbaren; one's wounds (vor)-zeigen; (indecently) oneself entblößen. **darling, you're exposing yourself** du zeigst etwas viel, Liebling.
(d) abuse, treachery aufdecken; scandal, plot also enthüllen; person, imposter bloßstellen, entlarven; murderer, thief entlarven. **to** ~ **sb/sth to the press** jdn/etw der Presse ausliefern.
(e) (Phot) belichten.

exposé [ek'spəʊzeɪ] n Exposé nt; (of scandal etc) Aufdeckung f.

exposed [ɪk'spəʊzd] adj (a) (to weather) place ungeschützt. ~ **to the wind** dem Wind ausgesetzt; **it's quite** ~ **where you live** Sie wohnen ziemlich ungeschützt; **this house is very** ~ dieses Haus steht sehr frei or ungeschützt.
(b) (insecure) to feel ~ sich allen Blicken ausgesetzt fühlen.
(c) (to view) sichtbar. **the** ~ **parts of a motor** die frei liegenden Teile eines Motors.

exposition [ˌekspə'zɪʃən] n (a) (of facts, theory) Darlegung, Exposition (geh) f; (explanatory) Erklärung, Erläuterung f; (of literature, text) Kommentar m (of zu), Erläuterung f; (Mus) Exposition f. (b) (exhibition) Ausstellung f.

expository [ɪk'spɒzɪtərɪ] adj darlegend.

expostulate [ɪk'spɒstjʊleɪt] vi protestieren. **to** ~ **with sb** mit jdm disputieren.

expostulation [ɪkˌspɒstjʊ'leɪʃən] n Protest m.

exposure [ɪk'spəʊʒəʳ] n (a) (to sunlight, air, danger) Aussetzung f (to dat). ~ **of the body to strong sunlight** wenn man den Körper starkem Sonnenlicht aussetzt; **to be suffering from** ~ an Unterkühlung leiden; **to die of** ~ erfrieren.
(b) (displaying) Entblößung f. **indecent** ~ Erregung f öffentlichen Ärgernisses.
(c) (unmasking: of person) Bloßstellung f; (of thief, murderer) Entlarvung f; (of abuses, plots, vices, scandals, crime) Aufdeckung f. **to threaten sb with** ~ drohen, jdn bloßzustellen/zu entlarven.
(d) (position of building) Lage f. **southern** ~ Südlage f.
(e) (Phot) Belichtung(szeit) f. ~ **meter** Belichtungsmesser m.
(f) (Media) Publicity f. **his new film has been given a lot of** ~ sein neuer Film hat viel Publicity bekommen.

expound [ɪk'spaʊnd] vt theory, one's views darlegen, erläutern, auseinandersetzen.

express [ɪk'spres] 1 vt (a) ausdrücken, zum Ausdruck bringen; (in words) wish, one's sympathy, appreciation also aussprechen. **to** ~ **sth in figures/another language** etw in Zahlen/einer anderen Sprache ausdrücken; **to** ~ **oneself** sich ausdrücken; **this** ~**es exactly the meaning of the word** das gibt genau die Bedeutung des Wortes wieder; **I haven't the words to** ~ **my thoughts** mir fehlen die Worte, um meine Gedanken auszudrücken; **the thought/feeling which is** ~**ed here** der Gedanke, der/das Gefühl, das hier zum Ausdruck kommt.
(b) (be expressive of) ausdrücken. **a face which** ~**es candour/pride** ein Gesicht, das Aufrichtigkeit/Stolz ausdrückt.
(c) (form) juice, milk auspressen, ausdrücken.
(d) letter etc per Expreß or als Eilsendung schicken.
2 adj (clear) instructions ausdrücklich; intention bestimmt. **with the** ~ **purpose of seeing him** mit der bestimmten Absicht, ihn zu sprechen.
3 adv **to send sth** ~ etw per Expreß or als Eilgut schicken.
4 n (a) (train) Schnellzug m; Expreß m (dated).
(b) **to send goods by** ~ Waren per Expreß schicken.

express: ~ **company** n (US) Spedition f (für Preßgut); ~ **delivery** n (Brit) Eilzustellung f.

expression [ɪk'spreʃən] n (a) (expressing: of opinions, friendship, affection, joy) Äußerung f, Ausdruck m. **as an** ~ **of our gratitude** zum Ausdruck unserer Dankbarkeit; **to give** ~ **to sth** etw zum Ausdruck bringen; **feelings which found** ~ **in tears** Gefühle, die sich in Tränen äußerten or die in Tränen zum Ausdruck kamen.
(b) (feeling: in music, art etc) Ausdruck m. **you need to put more** ~ **into it/your voice** Sie müssen das ausdrucksvoller spielen/vortragen; **to play with** ~ ausdrucksvoll spielen.
(c) (phrase etc) Ausdruck m
(d) (of face) (Gesichts)ausdruck m. **you could tell by his** ~ **that ...** man konnte an seinem Gesichtsausdruck erkennen, daß ...
(e) (Math) Ausdruck m.

expressionism [ɪk'spreʃənɪzəm] n Expressionismus m.

expressionist [ɪk'spreʃənɪst] 1 n Expressionist(in f) m. 2 adj expressionistisch.

expressionistic [ɪkˌspreʃə'nɪstɪk] adj expressionistisch.

expressionless [ɪk'spreʃənlɪs] adj ausdruckslos.

expressive [ɪk'spresɪv] adj ausdrucksvoll, expressiv (geh); face also ausdrucksfähig. **a poem** ~ **of despair** (liter) ein Verzweiflung ausdrückendes Gedicht.

expressively [ɪk'spresɪvlɪ] adv ausdrucksvoll.

expressiveness [ɪk'spresɪvnɪs] n Ausdruckskraft f; (of face also) Ausdrucksfähigkeit f.

express letter n Eil- or Expreßbrief m.

expressly [ɪk'spreslɪ] adv (a) (explicitly) deny, prohibit ausdrücklich. (b) (on purpose) **he did it** ~ **to annoy me** er hat es absichtlich getan, um mich zu ärgern.

express: ~ **train** n Schnellzug m; ~**way** n Schnellstraße f.

expropriate [eks'prəʊprɪeɪt] vt enteignen.

expropriation [eksˌprəʊprɪ'eɪʃən] n Enteignung, Expropriation (dated) f.

expulsion [ɪk'spʌlʃən] n (from a country) Ausweisung f (from aus); (driving out) Vertreibung f (from aus); (from school) Verweisung f (von der Schule). ~ **order** Ausweisungsbefehl m.

expunge [ɪk'spʌndʒ] vt (form) ausstreichen (from aus); (from record also) auslöschen (from aus).

expurgate ['ekspəːgeɪt] vt zensieren, die anstößigen Stellen entfernen aus. ~**d edition** gereinigte Fassung.

exquisite [ɪk'skwɪzɪt] adj (a) (excellent) workmanship, sewing ausgezeichnet, vorzüglich; woman, dress, painting exquisit; food, wine exquisit, köstlich; taste, wine gepflegt; view einmalig, herrlich; sensibility, politeness fein, außerordentlich; sense of humour köstlich.
(b) (keenly felt) thrill, satisfaction, pleasure, pain köstlich.

exquisitely [ɪk'skwɪzɪtlɪ] adv (a) paint, embroider, decorate, express ausgezeichnet, vorzüglich; dress, dine exquisit, gepflegt. **she has the most** ~ **delicate hands** sie hat wunderbar zarte Hände. (b) (extremely) äußerst.

ex-serviceman [eks'sɜːvɪsmən] n, pl -**men** [-mən] altgedienter Soldat, Veteran m.

ext abbr of **extension** App, Apparat m.

extant [ek'stænt] adj (noch) vorhanden or existent.

extemporaneous [ɪkˌstempə'reɪnɪəs], **extemporary** [ɪk'stempərɪ] adj unvorbereitet, aus dem Stegreif.

extempore [ɪks'tempərɪ] 1 adv speak aus dem Stegreif, unvorbereitet. 2 adj **to give an** ~ **speech** eine Rede aus dem Stegreif halten, extemporieren (geh).

extemporize [ɪk'stempəraɪz] vti aus dem Stegreif sprechen, extemporieren (geh); (Mus, with makeshift) improvisieren.

extend [ɪk'stend] 1 vt (a) (stretch out) arms ausstrecken. **to** ~ **one's hand to sb** jdm die Hand reichen; **to** ~ **a wire between two posts** einen Draht zwischen zwei Pfosten spannen.
(b) (prolong) street, line, visit, passport, holidays verlängern. ~**ed credit** verlängerter Kredit.
(c) (enlarge) research, powers, franchise ausdehnen, erweitern; knowledge erweitern, vergrößern; house anbauen an (+acc); property also vergrößern; limits erweitern; frontiers of a country ausdehnen. ~**ed play record** (45er) Schallplatte mit verlängerter Spielzeit; ~**ed family** Großfamilie f; **in an** ~**ed sense of the word** im weiteren Sinne des Wortes.
(d) (offer) (to sb jdm) help gewähren; hospitality, friendship erweisen; invitation, thanks, condolences, congratulations aussprechen. **to** ~ **a welcome to sb** jdn willkommen heißen.
(e) (usu pass: make demands on) person, pupil, athlete fordern. **in this job he is fully** ~**ed** in diesem Beruf wird sein ganzes Können gefordert.
2 vi (a) (wall, estate, garden) sich erstrecken, sich ausdehnen (to, as far as bis); (ladder) sich ausziehen lassen; (meetings etc: over period of time) sich ausdehnen or hinziehen.
(b) (reach to) enthusiasm which ~s even to the children Begeisterung, die sich sogar auf die Kinder überträgt; **does that** ~ **to me?** betrifft das auch mich?

extensible [ɪk'stensɪbl] adj telescope ausziehbar; time-limit ausdehnbar.

extension [ɪk'stenʃən] n (a) (of property) Vergrößerung f; (of business, knowledge also) Erweiterung f; (of powers, franchise, research, frontiers) Ausdehnung f; (of road, line, period of time) Verlängerung f; (of house) Anbau m; (of time limit) Verlängerung f, Aufschub m.
(b) (addition to length of sth: of road, line) Verlängerung f; (of table, holidays, leave etc) Verlängerung f; (of house) Anbau m.
(c) (telephone in offices, in private houses) (Neben)anschluß m. ~ **3714** Apparat 3714.
(d) (Logic: of word, concept) Extension f.

extension: ~ **course** n (Univ) weiterführender Kurs; ~ **ladder** n Ausziehleiter f.

extensive [ɪk'stensɪv] adj land, forest ausgedehnt, weit; view weit; knowledge, press coverage umfassend, umfangreich; study, research, enquiries umfangreich, ausgedehnt; investments, operations, alterations umfangreich; damage beträchtlich; use häufig; plans, reforms, business, influence weitreichend. ~ **use is made of the cottage** die Hütte wird häufig or viel benutzt.

extensively [ɪk'stensɪvlɪ] adv weit; study, investigate, cover ausführlich; altered, reformed, damaged beträchtlich; used häufig, viel. **he has travelled** ~ **in the South of France** er ist viel in Südfrankreich herumgefahren.

extensor [ɪk'stensəʳ] n Streckmuskel m.

extent [ɪk'stent] n (a) (length) Länge f; (size) Ausdehnung f. an avenue bordered with trees along its entire ~ eine Allee, die in ihrer ganzen Länge von Bäumen gesäumt ist; we could see the full ~ of the park wir konnten den Park in seiner ganzen Ausdehnung sehen.
  (b) (range, scope) (of knowledge, alterations, power, activities) Umfang m; (of damage, commitments, losses also) Ausmaß nt. debts to the ~ of £500 Schulden in Höhe von £ 500.
  (c) (degree) Grad m, Maß nt. to some ~ bis zu einem gewissen Grade; to what ~ inwieweit; to a certain ~ in gewissem Maße; to a large/slight ~ in hohem/geringem Maße; to such an ~ that ... dermaßen or derart, daß ...; such was the ~ of the damage so groß war der Schaden.

extenuate [ɪk'stenjʊeɪt] vt guilt verringern, mindern; offence, conduct beschönigen. extenuating circumstances mildernde Umstände.

extenuation [ɪk,stenjʊ'eɪʃən] n (act) Verringerung, Minderung f; Beschönigung f; (extenuating factor) mildernde Umstände pl. he pleaded ... in ~ of his crime (form) er führte ... als mildernden Umstand an.

exterior [ɪk'stɪərɪəʳ] 1 adj surface äußere(r, s), Außen-; decorating, angle Außen-. 2 n (a) (of house, box etc) Außenseite f, Äußere(s) nt; (of person) Äußere(s) nt. on the ~ außen, an der Außenseite. (b) (Film) Außenaufnahme f.

exterminate [ɪk'stɜːmɪneɪt] vt ausrotten, vernichten; pests also vertilgen; disease ausrotten; beliefs, ideas ausrotten, austilgen.

extermination [ɪk,stɜːmɪ'neɪʃən] n see vt Ausrottung, Vernichtung f; Vertilgung f; Austilgung f.

exterminator [ɪk'stɜːmɪneɪtəʳ] n (person) (of rats etc) Entweser m (form); (of pests) Kammerjäger m; (poison etc) Vernichtungsmittel nt.

external [ɪk'stɜːnl] 1 adj wall äußere(r, s), Außen-; factors, help extern. for ~ use only (Med) nur äußerlich (anzuwenden); ~ examiner (Brit Univ) externer Prüfer; ~ degree Fernstudium nt; he has an ~ degree in Maths er hat ein Fernstudium in Mathematik abgeschlossen; the ~ world (Philos) die Außenwelt or äußere Welt; ~ trade Außenhandel m; this is ~ to our present enquiry das liegt außerhalb des Bereichs unserer momentanen Untersuchung.
  2 n (fig) ~s pl Äußerlichkeiten pl.

externalize [ek'stɜːnəlaɪz] vt externalisieren.

externally [ek'stɜːnəlɪ] adv äußerlich. he remained ~ calm er blieb äußerlich ruhig; some of the work is done ~ ein Teil der Arbeit wird außer Haus erledigt.

extinct [ɪk'stɪŋkt] adj volcano, love erloschen; species ausgestorben. to become ~ aussterben; volcano erlöschen.

extinction [ɪk'stɪŋkʃən] n (of fire) Löschen nt; (of race, family) Aussterben nt; (annihilation) Auslöschung, Vernichtung f.

extinguish [ɪk'stɪŋgwɪʃ] vt fire, candle (aus)löschen; light löschen; hopes, passion zerstören; debt tilgen.

extinguisher [ɪk'stɪŋgwɪʃəʳ] n Feuerlöscher m, Löschgerät nt.

extirpate ['ekstɜːpeɪt] vt (lit, fig) (mit der Wurzel) ausrotten, (gänzlich) beseitigen.

extirpation [,ekstɜː'peɪʃən] n (lit, fig) Ausrottung f.

extol [ɪk'stəʊl] vt preisen, rühmen.

extort [ɪk'stɔːt] vt money erpressen (from von); confession also erzwingen (from von); secret abpressen (from dat).

extortion [ɪk'stɔːʃən] n (of money, taxes) Erpressung f; (of signature) Erzwingung f. this is sheer ~! (inf) das ist ja Wucher!

extortionate [ɪk'stɔːʃənɪt] adj prices Wucher-; tax, demand ungeheuer.

extortioner [ɪk'stɔːʃənəʳ] n Erpresser(in f) m; (charging high prices) Wucherer(in f) m.

extra ['ekstrə] 1 adj (a) (additional) zusätzlich; bus Einsatz-, zusätzlich. we need an ~ chair wir brauchen noch einen Stuhl; to work ~ hours Überstunden machen; to make an ~ effort sich besonders anstrengen; I have had ~ work this week ich habe in dieser Woche zusätzliche Arbeit gehabt; to order an ~ helping eine zusätzliche Portion or eine Portion extra bestellen; ~ charge Zuschlag m; to make an ~ charge Zuschlag berechnen; there is an ~ charge for wine der Wein wird extra berechnet; there will be no ~ charge das wird nicht extra berechnet; for ~ whiteness für ein strahlendes Weiß; ~ time (Brit Ftbl) Verlängerung f; we had to play ~ time es gab eine Verlängerung, es wurde nachgespielt; ~ pay eine Zulage; for ~ safety zur größeren Sicherheit; we need an ~ 10 minutes wir brauchen 10 Minuten mehr or extra; could you give me an ~ £3? könnten Sie mir £ 3 mehr or extra geben?; I have set an ~ place at the table ich habe ein Gedeck mehr or extra aufgelegt.
  (b) (spare) Reserve-, übrig. I bought a few ~ tins ich habe ein paar Dosen mehr or extra gekauft; I have brought an ~ pair of shoes ich habe ein Paar Schuhe extra mitgebracht; these copies are ~ diese Exemplare sind übrig; are there any ~ helpings? gibt es Nachschlag? (inf), kann man noch eine Portion haben?; go and get some ~ potatoes from the kitchen hol noch ein paar Kartoffeln aus der Küche.
  2 adv (a) (especially) extra, besonders. she was ~ kind that day sie war besonders freundlich an diesem Tag.
  (b) (in addition) extra. postage and packing ~ zuzüglich Porto- und Versandkosten; the wine is ~ der Wein wird extra berechnet.
  (c) (inf: more) to work ~ länger arbeiten.
  3 n (a) (perk) Zusatzleistung f; (for car) Extra nt. they regard it as an ~ sie betrachten es als Luxus; singing and piano are (optional) ~s Gesang- und Klavierunterricht sind Wahl- or Zusatzfächer pl.
  (b) ~s pl (~ expenses) zusätzliche Kosten pl, Nebenkosten pl; (in restaurant) Zusätzliches nt; (food) Beilagen pl.

  (c) (Film, Theat) Statist(in f), Komparse m, Komparsin f.
  (d) (remainder) what shall we do with the ~? was sollen wir mit dem Rest machen?

extra- pref (a) (outside) außer-; (esp with foreign words) extra-.
  (b) (especially) besonders, extra. ~dry wine herb; champagne extra dry; ~fine besonders fein, extrafein; ~smart besonders schick, todschick (inf); see also extra 2 (a).

extract [ɪk'strækt] 1 vt (a) herausnehmen; cork etc (heraus)ziehen (from aus); juice, minerals, oil gewinnen (from aus); tooth also ziehen, extrahieren (spec); bullet, foreign body also entfernen. she ~ed herself from his arms sie befreite sich aus seinen Armen.
  (b) (fig) information, secrets, confession herausholen, herausziehen (from aus); permission also, promise abringen, abnehmen, entlocken (from dat); money herausholen (from aus); the meaning, moral of a text herausarbeiten, herausholen (from aus). to ~ sounds from an instrument einem Instrument Töne entlocken.
  (c) (Math) square root ziehen.
  (d) quotation, passage herausziehen, exzerpieren (geh).
  2 ['ekstrækt] n (a) (from book etc) Auszug m, Exzerpt nt.
  (b) (Med, Cook) Extrakt m. beef ~ Fleischextrakt m.

extraction [ɪk'strækʃən] n (a) see vt Herausnehmen nt; (Heraus)ziehen nt; Gewinnung f; (Zahn)ziehen nt, Extraktion f (spec); Entfernung f; Herausholen, Herausziehen nt; Abnahme, Entlockung f; Herausholen nt; Herausarbeiten, Herausholen nt; Wurzelziehen nt. he had to have three ~s ihm mußten drei Zähne gezogen werden.
  (b) (descent) Herkunft, Abstammung f. of Spanish ~ spanischer Herkunft or Abstammung.

extractor [ɪk'stræktəʳ] n (for juice) Presse f, Entsafter m; (for dust) Sauganlage f; (of gun) Auszieher m. ~ fan Zentrifugalventilator, Fliehkraftlüfter m.

extracurricular ['ekstrəkə'rɪkjʊləʳ] adj außerhalb des Stundenplans.

extraditable ['ekstrədaɪtəbl] adj offence auslieferungsfähig; person auszuliefern pred, auszuliefernd attr.

extradite ['ekstrədaɪt] vt ausliefern.

extradition [,ekstrə'dɪʃən] n Auslieferung f. ~ treaty Auslieferungsvertrag m.

extramarital ['ekstrə'mærɪtl] adj außerehelich.

extramural ['ekstrə'mjʊərəl] adj courses Volkshochschul-.

extraneous [ɪk'streɪnɪəs] adj (a) (from outside) influence von außen (her), extern. (b) (unrelated) ~ to irrelevant für, ohne Beziehung zu. (c) (not essential) detail unwesentlich.

extraordinarily [ɪk'strɔːdnrɪlɪ] adv außerordentlich; rude also höchst. how ~ odd! wie überaus seltsam!

extraordinary [ɪk'strɔːdnrɪ] adj (a) (beyond what is common) außerordentlich; (not usual) ungewöhnlich. there's nothing ~ about that daran ist gar nichts Ungewöhnliches.
  (b) (odd, peculiar) sonderbar, seltsam. I find it rather ~ that he hasn't replied ich finde es recht seltsam, daß er nicht geantwortet hat; it's ~ to think that ... es ist (schon) seltsam or sonderbar, wenn man denkt, daß ...; you are a most ~ person! du bist wirklich sonderbar or seltsam!; the ~ fact is that he succeeded das Merkwürdige an der Sache ist, daß er Erfolg hatte; it's ~ how much he resembles his brother es ist erstaunlich, wie sehr er seinem Bruder ähnelt; how ~! ist das nicht seltsam!
  (c) (specially employed or arranged) Sonder-. envoy ~ Sonderbeauftragter m; an ~ meeting eine Sondersitzung.

extrapolate [ek'stræpəleɪt] vti extrapolieren (from aus).

extrapolation [ek,stræpə'leɪʃən] n Extrapolation f.

extrasensory ['ekstrə'sensərɪ] adj außersinnlich. ~ perception außersinnliche Wahrnehmung.

extra-special ['ekstrə'speʃəl] adj ganz besondere(r, s). to take ~ care over sth sich (dat) besonders viel Mühe mit etw geben; ~ occasion ganz besondere Gelegenheit; to make something ~ to eat etwas ganz Besonderes zu essen machen.

extraterrestrial ['ekstrətɪ'restrɪəl] adj außerirdisch, extraterrestrisch. 2 n außerirdisches Lebewesen.

extraterritorial ['ekstrə,terɪ'tɔːrɪəl] adj exterritorial.

extravagance [ɪk'strævəgəns] n (a) (with money) Luxus m no pl. her ~ ihre Verschwendungssucht; if you can't forgive her occasional ~s wenn Sie es ihr nicht verzeihen können, daß sie sich ab und zu einen Luxus leistet; the ~ of her tastes ihr kostspieliger or teurer Geschmack; a life of such ~ ein derart luxuriöser Lebensstil; the ~ of this big wedding der Aufwand einer solch großen Hochzeitsfeier.
  (b) (wastefulness) Verschwendung f.
  (c) (of ideas, theories) Extravaganz, Ausgefallenheit f; (of claim, demand) Übertriebenheit f.
  (d) (extravagant action or notion) Extravaganz f. the ~s of Nero die Extravaganzen eines Nero.

extravagant [ɪk'strævəgənt] adj (a) (with money) taste, habit teuer, kostspielig; wedding, lifestyle aufwendig, luxuriös; price überhöht. she is ~ sie gibt das Geld mit vollen Händen aus; it was very ~ of him to buy me this bracelet es war gar zu großzügig, daß er mir dieses Armband gekauft hat; isn't it rather ~ to have two cars? ist das nicht ein Luxus, zwei Autos zu haben?; I'll be ~ and treat myself to a new coat ich leiste mir den Luxus und kaufe mir einen neuen Mantel; go on, be ~ gönn dir doch den Luxus.
  (b) (wasteful: in consumption etc) verschwenderisch.
  (c) behaviour extravagant; ideas, theories, tie, pattern also ausgefallen; claim, demand übertrieben. he was given to indulging in rather ~ talk er neigte dazu, lose Reden zu führen; it would be ~ of me to claim that ... es wäre eine Anmaßung, wenn ich behauptete, daß ...

extravagantly [ɪk'strævəgəntlɪ] adv (a) (lavishly, with much expense) furnished luxuriös; spend mit vollen Händen; live auf großem Fuß, luxuriös. I rather ~ bought myself a gold watch

ich habe mir den Luxus einer goldenen Uhr geleistet.
(b) *(wastefully)* *use, consume etc* verschwenderisch.
(c) *(excessively, flamboyantly)* *furnish, dress* extravagant; *praise, act* überschwenglich; *demand, claim* übertrieben. **to talk ~** lose Reden führen.
extravaganza [ɪkˌstrævə'gænzə] *n* phantastische Dichtung *or* *(Mus)* Komposition; *(show)* Ausstattungsstück *nt*.
extreme [ɪk'striːm] **1** *adj* **(a)** *(furthest off)* *limit* äußerste(r, s). **to the ~** right ganz rechts; **at the ~** left of the photograph ganz links im Bild; **at the ~** end of the path ganz am Ende des Weges; **the ~** opposite genau das Gegenteil; **they are ~** opposites sie sind Extreme, sie sind völlig gegensätzliche Charaktere.
(b) *(of the highest degree)* *courage, pleasure, kindness, simplicity* äußerste(r, s); *rudeness* also maßlos, extrem; *urgency* also extrem; *penalty* höchste(r, s). **with ~** pleasure mit größtem Vergnügen; **~** old age im äußerst hohes Alter; **in ~** danger in größter *or* höchster Gefahr; **the most ~** poverty die bitterste *or* größte Armut; **an ~** case ein Extremfall *m*.
(c) *(exaggerated, drastic, Pol)* extrem; *praise, flattery* übertrieben; *exaggeration, demands* maßlos. **to be ~** in one's opinions extreme Ansichten haben; **he was rather ~** in his praise er hat bei seinem Lob ziemlich übertrieben; **the ~** right/left *(Pol)* die äußerste *or* extreme Rechte/Linke; *see* unction.
2 *n* Extrem *nt*. **the ~s of happiness and despair** höchstes Glück und tiefste Verzweiflung; **~s of temperature** extreme Temperaturen *pl*; **in the ~** im höchsten Grade; **it is bewildering in the ~** es ist höchst *or* im höchsten Grade verwirrend; **to go from one ~ to the other** von einem Extrem ins andere fallen; **to go to ~s** es übertreiben; **I wouldn't go to that ~** so weit würde ich nicht gehen; **to drive sb to ~s** jdn zum Äußersten treiben.
extremely [ɪk'striːmlɪ] *adv* höchst, extrem. **was it difficult? — ~** war es schwierig? — sehr!
extremism [ɪk'striːmɪzəm] *n* Extremismus *m*.
extremist [ɪk'striːmɪst] **1** *adj* *view, opinion* extremistisch. **2** *n* Extremist(in *f*) *m*.
extremity [ɪk'stremɪtɪ] *n* **(a)** *(furthest point)* äußerstes Ende. **at the northernmost ~ of the continent** am nördlichsten Zipfel des Kontinents.
(b) *(extreme degree)* **in the ~ of his despair** in tiefster *or* äußerster Verzweiflung; **the ~ to which he had taken the theory** die Entwicklung der Theorie bis zu ihrem Extrem.
(c) *(state of need, distress)* Not *f*. **to help sb in his ~** jdm in seiner Not helfen; **to be reduced to a sad ~** sich in einer Notlage befinden; **I haven't yet been reduced to that ~** es ist noch nicht so weit mit mir gekommen; **he was reduced to the ~ of having to sell his business** er mußte zum äußersten Mittel schreiten und sein Geschäft verkaufen.
(d) *(extreme actions)* **to resort to extremities** zu äußersten *or* extremen Mitteln greifen; **to drive sb to extremities** jdn zum Äußersten treiben.
(e) **extremities** *pl* *(hands and feet)* Extremitäten *pl*.
extricate ['ekstrɪkeɪt] *vt* *object* befreien. **to ~ oneself from sth** sich aus etw befreien.
extrinsic [ek'strɪnsɪk] *adj* *value, qualities* äußerlich; *considerations* nicht hereinspielend. **considerations ~ to the argument** Überlegungen, die in keinem direkten Zusammenhang mit der Frage stehen.
extroversion [ˌekstrəʊ'vɜːʃən] *n* Extravertiertheit *f*.
extrovert ['ekstrəʊvɜːt] **1** *adj* extravertiert. **2** *n* extravertierter Mensch, Extravertierte(r) *mf*.
extrude [ɪk'struːd] **1** *vt* *sb, sth* ausstoßen; *metal, plastic* herauspressen. **2** *vi* herausstehen *(from* aus). **this bit of land ~s into our territory** dieses Stückchen Land ragt in unser Gebiet.
exuberance [ɪg'zuːbərəns] *n* **(a)** *(of person)* Überschwenglichkeit *f*; *(of joy, youth, feelings)* Überschwang *m*; *(joy)* überschwengliche Freude *(at* über *+acc)*. **in his ~** *(rejoicing)* in seiner überschwenglichen Freude, im Überschwang der Gefühle; **in their youthful ~** *(high spirits)* in ihrem jugendlichen Überschwang.
(b) *(vitality: of prose, style)* Vitalität *f*, (übersprudelnde) Lebendigkeit.
(c) *(abundance)* Fülle *f*, Reichtum *m*.
exuberant [ɪg'zuːbərənt] *adj* überschwenglich; *imagination* übersprudelnd; *style* übersprudelnd, vital; *painting, colour* lebendig; *music, melody* mitreißend. **they were ~ after their victory** nach ihrem Sieg waren sie in Jubelstimmung.
exude [ɪg'zjuːd] **1** *vi* *(liquid)* austreten *(from* aus); *(blood, pus etc)* abgesondert werden *(from* von). **2** *vt* **(a)** *(liquid)* ausscheiden; *dampness, sap* also ausschwitzen. **(b)** *(fig: radiate)* *confidence* ausstrahlen; *(pej)* *charm* triefen vor.
exult [ɪg'zʌlt] *vi* frohlocken. **~ing at his own success** über seinen eigenen Erfolg jubelnd.
exultant [ɪg'zʌltənt] *adj* jubelnd; *shout* also Jubel-. **to be ~, to be in an ~** mood jubeln, in Jubelstimmung sein; **I had never seen her so ~** ich hatte sie noch nie in solcher Jubelstimmung gesehen; **exhausted but ~** erschöpft, aber triumphierend.
exultation [ˌegzʌl'teɪʃən] *n* Jubel *m*. **sing in ~** *(Rel)* jauchzet und frohlocket; **their ~ at finding it** ihr Jubel, als sie es fanden.
eye [aɪ] **1** *n* **(a)** *(of human, animal, electronic)* Auge *nt*. **with tears in her ~s** mit Tränen in den Augen; **with one's ~s closed/open** mit geschlossenen/offenen Augen; *(fig)* blind/mit offenen Augen; **an ~ for an ~** for an eye Auge um Auge; **~s right!** *(Mil)* (die) Augen rechts!; **~s front!** *(Mil)* Augen geradeaus!; **to be all ~s** große Augen machen; **they were all ~s watching the magician** sie beobachteten den Zauberer mit großen Augen; **that's one in the ~ for him** *(inf)* da hat er eins aufs Dach gekriegt *(inf)*; **to do sb in the ~** *(inf)* jdn übers Ohr hauen *(inf)*; **to cast or run one's ~s over sth** etw überfliegen; **to cast one's ~s round a room** seine Blicke durch ein Zimmer wandern *or* schweifen lassen; **his ~ fell on a small door** sein Blick fiel auf eine kleine Tür; **to let one's ~ rest on sth** seine Augen *or* den Blick auf

etw *(dat)* ruhen lassen; **to look sb (straight) in the ~** jdm in die Augen sehen; **to set or clap** *(inf)* **~s on sb/sth** jdn/etw zu Gesicht bekommen; **to have a keen ~** ein scharfes Auge haben, einen scharfen Blick haben; **a strange sight met our ~s** ein seltsamer Anblick bot sich uns; **(why don't you) use your ~s!** hast du keine Augen im Kopf?; **with one's own ~s** mit eigenen Augen; **before my very ~s** *(direkt)* vor meinen Augen; **it was there all the time right in front of my ~s** es lag schon die ganze Zeit da, direkt vor meiner Nase; **under the watchful ~ of the guard/their mother** unter der Aufsicht des Wächters/ihrer Mutter; **to keep an ~ on sb/sth** *(look after)* auf jdn/etw aufpassen; **to keep one's ~ on the ball/main objective** sich auf den Ball/die Hauptsache konzentrieren; **to have one's ~s fixed on sth** etw nicht aus den Augen lassen; **never to take one's ~s off sb/sth** kein Auge von jdm/etw wenden; **to keep one's ~s open or peeled** *(inf)* **or skinned** *(inf)* die Augen offenhalten; **to keep an ~ open or out for a hotel** nach einem Hotel Ausschau halten; **to keep a watchful ~ on the situation** die Sache im Auge behalten; **to keep an ~ on expenditure** auf seine Ausgaben achten *or* aufpassen; **to open sb's ~s to sth/sb** jdm die Augen über jdn/etw öffnen; **to close one's ~s to sth** die Augen vor etw *(dat)* verschließen; **to see ~ to ~ with sb** mit jdm einer Meinung sein; **to make ~s at sb** jdm schöne Augen machen; **to catch sb's ~** jds Aufmerksamkeit erregen; **that colour caught my ~** die Farbe fiel *or* stach mir ins Auge; **she would buy anything that caught her ~** sie kaufte alles, was ihr ins Auge fiel; **he was a monster in their ~s** in ihren Augen war er ein Scheusal; **through somebody else's ~s** mit den Augen eines anderen; **to look at a question through the ~s of an economist** eine Frage mit den Augen *or* aus der Sicht eines Volkswirts betrachten; **in the ~s of the law** in den Augen des Gesetzes; **with a critical/jealous/an uneasy ~** mit kritischem/scheelem/ besorgtem Blick; **with an ~ to the future** im Hinblick auf die Zukunft; **with an ~ to buying sth** in der Absicht, etw zu kaufen; **to have an ~ to the main chance** jede Gelegenheit ausnutzen; **to take one's ~s off sb/sth** die Augen *or* den Blick von jdm/etw abwenden; **take your ~s off that woman!** starr die Frau nicht so an!; **he couldn't take his ~s off her/the cake** er konnte einfach den Blick nicht von ihr/dem Kuchen lassen; **don't take your ~ off the ball** konzentrier dich auf den Ball; **have you got your ~ on the ball all the time you're playing?** konzentrierst du dich auch während des ganzen Spiels auf den Ball?; **don't take your ~s off the magician's left hand** lassen Sie die linke Hand des Zauberkünstlers nicht aus den Augen; **just watch it, my boy, I've got my ~ on you** paß bloß auf, mein Freund, ich beobachte dich genau; **to have one's ~ on sth** *(want)* auf etw *(acc)* ein Auge geworfen haben; **to have an ~ on sb for a job** jdn für eine Stelle im Auge haben; **I only have ~s for you** ich habe nur Augen für dich; **she has an ~ for a bargain** sie hat einen Blick *or* ein Auge für günstige Käufe; **he has no ~ for beauty** ihm fehlt der Blick für Schönheit; **he has a good ~ for colour/form** er hat ein Auge für Farbe/Form; **you need an ~ for detail** man muß einen Blick fürs Detail haben; **to get one's ~ in** *(shooting)* sich einschießen; *(playing tennis etc)* sich einspielen; **to be up to the ~s in work** *(inf)* in Arbeit ersticken *(inf)*; **he's in it up to the ~s** *(inf)* er steckt bis zum Hals drin *(inf)*; **my ~!** *(inf)* Unsinn!; **that's all my ~** *(inf)* das ist doch alles Gewäsch *(inf)*.
(b) *(of needle)* Öhr *nt*; *(of potato, on peacock's tail)* Auge *nt*; *(of hurricane)* Auge *nt*. **in the ~ of the wind** *(Naut)* in *or* gegen den Wind; *see* hook and eye.
2 *vt* anstarren. **to ~ sb up and down** jdn von oben bis unten mustern.
♦eye up *vt sep* *girls, boys* mustern, begutachten.
eye *in cpds* Augen-; **~ball** *n* Augapfel *m*; **to be/meet ~ball to ~ball** sich direkt gegenüberstehen; **~bath** *n* Augenbad *nt*; *(container)* Augenbadewanne *f*; **~brow** *n* Augenbraue *f*; **to raise one's ~brows** die Augenbrauen hochziehen; **he never raised an ~brow** er hat sich nicht einmal gewundert; **that will raise a few ~brows, there will be a few raised ~brows** (at that) da werden sich einige wundern; **~brow pencil** *n* Augenbrauenstift *m*; **~catcher** *n* *(thing)* Blickfang *m*; **she's quite an ~catcher** sie zieht alle Blicke auf sich; **~catching** *adj* auffallend; *publicity, poster* also auffällig, ins Auge springend *or* stechend; **that's rather ~catching** das fällt *or* springt ins Auge; **~cup** *n* *(US)* Augenbadewanne *f*.
-eyed [-aɪd] *adj suf* -äugig.
eye drops ['aɪdrɒps] *npl* Augentropfen *pl*.
eyeful ['aɪfʊl] *n* **he got an ~ of soda water** er bekam Selterswasser ins Auge; **she's quite an ~** *(inf)* sie hat allerhand zu bieten *(inf)*; **I opened the bathroom door and got quite an ~** ich öffnete die Badezimmertür und sah allerhand *(inf)*.
eye: **~glass** *n* *(old)* Augenglas *nt* *(old)*; **~lash** *n* Augenwimper *f*; **~let** ['aɪlɪt] *n* Öse *f*; **~-level** *adj attr* grill in Augenhöhe; **~lid** *n* Augenlid *nt*; **~ liner** *n* Eyeliner *m*; **~-opener** *n* **(a)** *that was a real ~-opener to me** das hat mir die Augen geöffnet; **(b)** *(US inf: drink)* (alkoholischer) Muntermacher; **~ patch** *n* Augenklappe *f*; **~piece** *n* Okular *nt*; **~shade** *n* Augenblende *f*, Schild *m*; **~shadow** *n* Lidschatten *m*; **~sight** *n* Sehkraft *f*, Sehvermögen *nt*; **to have good ~sight** gute Augen haben; **to lose one's ~sight** das Augenlicht verlieren *(geh)*, erblinden; **his ~sight is failing** seine Augen lassen nach, sein Sehvermögen läßt nach; **~sore** *n* Schandfleck *m*; **this carpet is a real ~sore** dieser Teppich beleidigt das Auge; **~strain** *n* Überanstrengung *or* Ermüdung *f* der Augen; **~ test** *n* Augentest *m or* -untersuchung *f*.
Eyetie ['aɪtaɪ] *n* *(sl)* Spaghettifresser *(pej inf)*, Itaker *(pej sl)* *m*.
eye: **~ tooth** *n* Eckzahn, Augenzahn *m*; **I'd give my ~ teeth for that** darum würde ich alles geben; **~wash** *n* *(Med)* Augenwasser *m or* -bad *nt*; *(fig inf)* Gewäsch *nt* *(inf)*; *(deception)* Augenwischerei *f*; **~witness** *n* Augenzeuge *m*.
eyrie ['ɪərɪ] *n* Horst *m*.
Ezekiel [ɪ'ziːkɪəl] *n* *(Bibl)* Hesekiel, Ezechiel *m*.

F

F, f [ef] n F, f nt. ~ **sharp/flat** Fis, fis nt/Fes, fes nt; see also major, minor, natural.

F abbr of **Fahrenheit** F.

f abbr of **(a) foot, feet. (b) feminine** f.

FA abbr of **Football Association.**

fa [fɑː] n (Mus) Fa nt.

fab [fæb] adj (dated sl) abbr of **fabulous** toll (inf), dufte (inf).

fable ['feɪbl] n Fabel f; (legend, body of legend) Sage f; (fig: lie) Märchen nt. **to sort out fact from ~** Dichtung und Wahrheit unterscheiden.

fabled ['feɪbld] adj sagenhaft. **Cleopatra, ~ for her beauty** Kleopatra, berühmt für ihre Schönheit.

fabric ['fæbrɪk] n (a) (Tex) Stoff m. (b) (basic structure) the ~ **of the building/church** das Gebäude/Kirchengebäude als solches war ganz gut. (c) (fig: of society etc) Gefüge nt, Struktur f.

fabricate ['fæbrɪkeɪt] vt (a) (invent) story erfinden, ersinnen (geh). (b) (manufacture) herstellen, fabrizieren.

fabrication [ˌfæbrɪ'keɪʃən] n (a) (act of inventing) Erfindung f; (story invented also) Lügengeschichte f, Lügenmärchen nt. **it's (a) pure ~** das ist ein reines Märchen or (eine) reine Erfindung. (b) (manufacture) Herstellung, Fabrikation f.

Fabrikoid ® ['fæbrɪkɔɪd] n (US) Kunstleder, Skai ® nt.

fabulist ['fæbjʊlɪst] n (a) Fabeldichter(in f), Fabulist (old) m. (b) (liar) Fabulant(in f) (geh), Lügner(in f) m.

fabulous ['fæbjʊləs] adj sagenhaft; (inf: wonderful also) toll (inf), fabelhaft.

fabulously ['fæbjʊləslɪ] adv sagenhaft.

façade [fə'sɑːd] n (lit, fig) Fassade f.

face [feɪs] **1** n (a) Gesicht nt. **I don't want to see your ~ here again** ich möchte Sie hier nie wieder sehen; **we were standing ~ to ~** wir standen einander Auge in Auge or von Angesicht zu Angesicht (geh) gegenüber; **next time I see him ~ to ~** das nächste Mal, wenn ich ihm begegne or wenn er mir unter die Augen kommt; **to bring two people ~ to ~** zwei Leute einander gegenüberstellen or miteinander konfrontieren; **to come ~ to ~ with sb/one's Maker/death** jdn treffen/Gott von Angesicht zu Angesicht sehen/dem Tod ins Auge sehen; **he told him so to his ~** er sagte ihm das (offen) ins Gesicht; **he shut the door in my ~** er schlug mir die Tür vor der Nase zu; **he laughed in my ~** er lachte mir ins Gesicht; **to look/be able to look sb in the ~** jdn ansehen/jdm in die Augen sehen können; **to fling or throw a remark back in sb's ~** jdm seine eigene Bemerkung wieder auftischen; **in the ~ of great difficulties/much opposition** etc angesichts or (despite) trotz größter Schwierigkeiten/starker Opposition etc; **courage in the ~ of the enemy** Tapferkeit vor dem Feind; see **flat¹.**

(b) (expression) Gesicht(sausdruck m) nt. **to make or pull a ~** das Gesicht verziehen; **to make or pull ~s/a funny ~** Gesichter or Grimassen/eine Grimasse machen or schneiden (at sb jdm); **to put a good ~ on it** gute Miene zum bösen Spiel machen; **to put a brave ~ on it** sich (dat) nichts anmerken lassen; (do sth one dislikes) (wohl oder übel) in den sauren Apfel beißen; **he has set his ~ against that** er stemmt sich dagegen.

(c) (prestige) loss of ~ Gesichtsverlust m; **to save (one's)/lose ~** das Gesicht wahren/verlieren.

(d) (of clock) Zifferblatt nt; (rock ~) (Steil)wand f; (coal~) Streb m; (type~) Schriftart f; (of playing card) Bildseite f; (of coin) Vorderseite f; (of house) Fassade f. **to put sth ~ up(wards)/down(wards)** Bildseite f etw mit der Vorderseite nach oben/unten legen; **to be ~ up(wards)/down(wards)** (person) mit dem Gesicht nach oben/unten liegen; (thing) mit der Vorderseite nach oben/unten liegen; (book) mit der aufgeschlagenen Seite nach oben/unten liegen; **to work at the (coal)~** vor Ort arbeiten; **to change the ~ of a town** das Gesicht or Aussehen einer Stadt verändern; **he/it vanished off the ~ of the earth** (inf) er/es war wie vom Erdboden verschwunden; **on the ~ of it so**, wie es aussieht.

(e) (inf: effrontery) **to have the ~ to do sth** die Stirn haben, etw zu tun.

2 vt (a) (be opposite, have one's face towards) gegenübersein/-stehen/-liegen etc (+dat); (window, door) north, south gehen nach; street, garden etc liegen zu; (building, room) north, south liegen nach; park, street liegen zu. **to ~ the wall/light** zur Wand gekehrt/dem Licht zugekehrt sein; (person) mit dem Gesicht zur Wand/zum Licht stehen/sitzen etc; **sit down and ~ the front!** setz dich und sieh nach vorn!; **~ this way!** bitte sehen Sie hierher!; **he was facing me at dinner** er saß mir beim Essen gegenüber; **the picture/wall facing you** das Bild/die Wand Ihnen gegenüber; **facing one another** einander gegenüber; **the picture facing page 16** die Abbildung gegenüber Seite 16; **to sit facing the engine/front of the bus** in Fahrtrichtung sitzen.

(b) (fig) possibility, prospect rechnen müssen mit. **to be ~d with sth** sich einer Sache (dat) gegenübersehen; **the problem facing us** das Problem, dem wir gegenüberstehen or mit dem wir konfrontiert sind; **you'll ~ a lot of criticism if you do that** Sie setzen sich großer Kritik aus, wenn Sie das tun; **to be ~d with a bill for £10** eine Rechnung über £ 10 präsentiert

bekommen; **he is facing/will ~ a charge of murder** er steht unter Mordanklage, er ist/wird wegen Mordes angeklagt.

(c) (meet confidently) situation, danger, criticism sich stellen (+dat); person, enemy gegenübertreten (+dat). **he ~d defeat bravely** er hat sich tapfer mit der Niederlage abgefunden; **to ~ (the) facts** den Tatsachen ins Auge sehen; **let's ~ it** machen wir uns doch nichts vor; **you'd better ~ it, you're not going to get it** du mußt dich wohl damit abfinden, daß du das nicht bekommst; **why don't you ~ it, ...** mach dir doch nichts vor, ...

(d) (inf: put up with, bear) verkraften (inf); **another drink, cake etc** runterkriegen (inf). **to ~ doing sth** es fertigbringen (inf) or es über sich (acc) bringen, etw zu tun; **I can't ~ it** (inf) ich bringe es einfach nicht über mich.

(e) building, wall verblenden, verkleiden; (Sew) garment (mit Besatz) verstürzen.

(f) (Cards) aufdecken.

(g) stone glätten, (plan) schleifen.

3 vi (house, room) liegen; **towards park** dem Park zu; **onto road** zur Straße; **away from road** nicht zur Straße; (window) gehen (onto, towards auf +acc, zu, away from nicht auf +acc). **he was sitting facing away from me** er saß mit dem Rücken zu mir; **they were all facing towards the window** sie saßen alle mit dem Gesicht zum Fenster (hin); **the house ~s away from the sea** das Haus liegt nicht aufs Meer zu; **in which direction was he facing?** in welche Richtung stand er?; **you've parked facing in the wrong direction** Sie haben in der falschen Richtung geparkt; **the side of the house that ~s onto the road** die der Straße zugekehrte Seite des Hauses; **why was the house built facing away from the park?** warum wurde das Haus nicht mit Blick auf den Park gebaut?; **right ~!** (Mil) rechts um!

♦**face about** vi (US Mil) kehrtmachen.

♦**face out** vt sep durchstehen.

♦**face up to** vi +prep obj fact, truth ins Gesicht sehen (+dat); danger ins Auge sehen or blicken (+dat); possibility sich abfinden mit; responsibility auf sich (acc) nehmen. **he won't ~ ~ the fact that ...** er will es nicht wahrhaben, daß ...

face in cpds Gesichts-; ~ **card** n Bild(er)karte f; ~**cloth** n Waschlappen m; ~ **cream** n Gesichtscreme f; ~ **guard** n Schutzmaske f; ~**less** adj drawing gesichtslos; (fig) anonym; ~**lift** n (lit) Gesichts(haut)straffung f, Facelift(ing) nt; (fig: for car, building etc) Verschönerung f; **to have a ~lift** sich (dat) das Gesicht liften or straffen lassen; (fig) neues Aussehen bekommen; **to give the house a ~lift** das Haus renovieren, das Haus einer Verschönerungsaktion unterziehen; ~ **pack** n Gesichtspackung f; ~ **powder** n Gesichtspuder m.

facer ['feɪsəʳ] n (Brit inf: difficulty) harte Nuß (inf).

face: ~-**saver** n Ausrede f, um das Gesicht zu wahren; ~-**saving** adj a ~-**saving excuse/remark/tactic** eine Entschuldigung/Bemerkung/Taktik, um das Gesicht zu wahren.

facet ['fæsɪt] n (lit) Facette f; (fig) Seite f, Aspekt m.

faceted ['fæsɪtɪd] adj (Zool) Facetten-; (Miner also) facettiert.

faceting ['fæsɪtɪŋ] n (Miner) Facettenschliff m.

facetious [fə'siːʃəs] adj remark, speech, tone witzelnd, spöttisch, mokant. **to be ~ (about sth)** (über etw acc) Witze machen, sich (über etw acc) mokieren; ~ **humour** Blödeleien pl; **if satire is merely ~** wenn Satire zur Blödelei wird; **I was just being ~** das war doch nur ein Witz or so eine Blödelei (inf).

facetiously [fə'siːʃəslɪ] adv albern, witzelnd.

face: ~-**to-** ~ adj persönlich, von Angesicht zu Angesicht (geh); confrontation direkt; ~ **value** n (Fin) Nennwert, Nominalwert m; **to take sth at (its) ~ value** (fig) etw für bare Münze nehmen; **to take sb at ~ value** jdm unbesehen glauben; ~-**worker** n (Min) Hauer m.

facial ['feɪʃəl] **1** adj Gesichts-. **2** n (inf) kosmetische Gesichtsbehandlung.

facile ['fæsaɪl] adj (a) (glib, superficial) oberflächlich; emotions, mind also ohne Tiefgang; piece of writing also seicht, ohne Tiefgang. **he made a few ~ remarks** er hat einige nichtssagende Bemerkungen gemacht. (b) (flowing) style flüssig, gewandt. (c) (easy) task, victory leicht.

facilitate [fə'sɪlɪteɪt] vt erleichtern; (make possible) ermöglichen. **it would ~ matters** es würde die Sache erleichtern.

facility [fə'sɪlɪtɪ] n (a) Einrichtung f. **to offer facilities** Möglichkeiten bieten; **to give sb every ~** jdm jede Möglichkeit bieten; **you will have every ~ or all facilities for study** es wird Ihnen alles zur Verfügung stehen, was Sie zum Studium brauchen; **cooking facilities** Kochgelegenheit f.

(b) no pl (ease) Leichtigkeit f, Mühelosigkeit f; (dexterity) Gewandtheit, Geschicklichkeit f. ~ **in learning** (leichte) Auffassungsgabe.

facing ['feɪsɪŋ] n (a) (on wall) Verblendung, Verkleidung f. (b) (Sew) Besatz m.

facsimile [fæk'sɪmɪlɪ] n Faksimile nt; (Rad) Faksimileübertragung f.

fact [fækt] n (a) Tatsache f, Faktum nt (geh); (historical, geographical etc) Faktum nt. **hard ~s** nackte Tatsachen pl; **the true ~s** der wahre Sachverhalt; **to know for a ~ that** (es) ganz genau or sicher wissen, daß; **the ~ is that ...** die Sache ist die, ...

daß ...; **to stick to the ~s** bei den Tatsachen bleiben, sich an die Tatsachen or Fakten halten; (*not speculate also*) auf dem Boden der Tatsachen bleiben; **to look (the) ~s in the face** der Wirklichkeit or den Tatsachen (*dat*) ins Auge sehen; **the ~s of the case** (*Jur*) der Tatbestand, der Sachverhalt; **... and that's a ~ darüber besteht kein Zweifel!, Tatsache! (*inf*); is that a ~? tatsächlich?, Tatsache? (*inf*); see face 2 (c).

(**b**) *no pl* (*reality*) Wirklichkeit, Realität *f*. **~ and fiction** Dichtung und Wahrheit; **founded on ~** auf Tatsachen beruhend.

(**c**) **in** (*point of or actual*) **~** eigentlich; (*in reality*) tatsächlich, in Wirklichkeit; (*after all*) (dann) doch; (*to make previous statement more precise*) nämlich; **in ~, as a matter of ~** eigentlich; (*to intensify previous statement*) sogar; **I don't suppose you know him/you want it? — in** (*point of or actual*) **~ or as a matter of ~ I do** Sie kennen ihn/möchten das nicht zufällig? — doch, eigentlich schon; **do you know him/want it? — in** (*point of or actual*) **~ or as a matter of ~ I do** kennen Sie ihn/möchten Sie das? — jawohl; **but in** (*point of or actual*) **~ he didn't do it/there were a lot more** aber in Wirklichkeit hat er es gar nicht getan/ waren viel mehr da; **I'd meant to do some work but in ~ I was too tired** ich wollte eigentlich etwas arbeiten, war aber dann zu müde; **but in** (*point of or actual*) **~ he didn't arrive till late/it was awful** er ist dann aber erst spät angekommen/es war dann aber fürchterlich; **I thought I could give you a lift, but in** (*point of or actual*) **~ I won't be going/won't have a car** ich dachte, ich könnte dich mitnehmen, aber ich gehe doch nicht/habe doch kein Auto; **but in** (*point of or actual*) **~ I could do it/he did come** ich konnte es dann doch/er ist dann doch gekommen; **I'm going soon, in** (*point of or actual*) **~** tomorrow ich gehe bald, nämlich morgen; **it won't be easy, in ~ or as a matter of ~ it'll be very difficult** es wird nicht einfach sein, es wird sogar sehr schwierig sein; **does it hurt? — as a matter of ~ it's very painful** tut's weh? — ja, und sogar ganz schön; **I bet you haven't done that! — as a matter of ~ I have!** du hast das bestimmt nicht gemacht! — und ob, aber ja doch!; **as matter of ~ we were just talking about you** wir haben (nämlich) eben von Ihnen geredet; **I can't find it, as a matter of ~/in ~ I think I've lost it** ich kann's nirgends finden, ich glaube fast/sogar, ich habe es verloren; **do you know Sir Charles? — as a matter of ~ he's my uncle/yes, in ~ he's my uncle** kennen Sie Sir Charles? — ja, und er ist sogar/ja, er ist nämlich mein Onkel.

(**d**) (*Jur*) **to be an accessory before/after the ~** sich der Beihilfe/Begünstigung schuldig machen.

fact-finding ['fæktfaɪndɪŋ] *adj* **commission** Untersuchungs-; **mission** Erkundungs-.

faction ['fækʃən] *n* (**a**) (*group*) (Partei)gruppe *f*; (*splinter group*) Splittergruppe *f*. (**b**) *no pl* (*strife*) interne Unstimmigkeiten *pl*; (*Pol also*) Parteihader *m*.

factious ['fækʃəs] *adj* (*liter*) streitsüchtig, händelsüchtig; *quarrelling* kleinlich, engherzig.

factitious [fæk'tɪʃəs] *adj* künstlich, unecht; *demand for goods* hochgespielt.

fact of life *n* (**a**) (*reality*) harte Tatsache. **that's just a ~** so ist es nun mal im Leben. (**b**) **~s ~ ~** *pl* (*sexual*) Aufklärung *f*; **to tell/teach sb the ~s ~ ~** jdn aufklären; **to know the ~s ~ ~** aufgeklärt sein.

factor ['fæktər] *n* (**a**) Faktor *m*. (**b**) (*Biol*) Erbfaktor *m*. (**c**) (*agent*) Makler *m*.

factorize ['fæktəraɪz] *vt* in Faktoren zerlegen, faktorisieren.

factory ['fæktərɪ] *n* Fabrik *f*; (*plant also*) Werk *nt*.

factory: F~ Act *n* Arbeitsschutzgesetz *nt*; ~ **hand** *n* Fabrikarbeiter(in *f*) *m*; ~ **inspector** *n* Gewerbeaufsichtsbeamte(r) *m*; ~ **ship** *n* Fabrikschiff *nt*; ~ **worker** *n* Fabrikarbeiter(in *f*) *m*.

factotum [fæk'təʊtəm] *n* Faktotum *nt*, Mädchen *nt* für alles (*inf*).

factual ['fæktjʊəl] *adj* sachlich, Tatsachen-; (*real*) tatsächlich. ~ **error** Sachfehler *m*.

factually ['fæktjʊəlɪ] *adv* sachlich.

faculty ['fækəltɪ] *n* (**a**) (*power of mind*) Vermögen *nt*, Fähigkeit, Kraft *f*; (*ability, aptitude*) Begabung *f*, Talent *nt*. ~ **of reason** Vernunft *f*; ~ **of speech/thought/sight** Sprech-/Denk-/ Sehvermögen *nt*; **the mental faculties** die Geisteskräfte *pl*; **to be in (full) possession of (all) one's faculties** im Vollbesitz seiner Kräfte sein; **to have a ~ for doing sth** ein Talent dafür haben, etw zu tun; **to have a ~ for learning languages** sprachbegabt sein.

(**b**) (*Univ*) Fakultät *f*. **the medical ~, the ~ of medicine** die Medizinische Fakultät; **the F~** (*staff*) der Lehrkörper.

(**c**) (*Eccl*) Vollmacht *f*.

fad [fæd] *n* Fimmel (*inf*), Tick (*inf*) *m*; (*fashion*) Masche *f* (*inf*). **it's just a ~** das ist nur ein momentaner Fimmel (*inf*) or Tick (*inf*); **that's the latest fashion ~** das ist die neuste Modemasche (*inf*); **his ~ for caviar/wearing one earring** sein Kaviarfimmel (*inf*)/sein Tick or Fimmel, nur einen Ohrring zu tragen (*inf*).

faddish ['fædɪʃ], **faddy** ['fædɪ] (*inf*) *adj* wählerisch.

fade [feɪd] **1** *vi* (**a**) verblassen; (*material, colour also*) verbleichen; (*on exposure to light*) verschießen; (*flower also*) verblühen; (*lose shine*) seinen Glanz verlieren. **guaranteed non-~ or not to ~** garantiert farbecht.

(**b**) (*fig*) (*memory*) verblassen; (*sight, strength, inspiration, feeling*) nachlassen, schwinden (*geh*); (*hopes*) zerrinnen; (*smile*) vergehen, verschwinden; (*beauty*) verblühen; (*sound*) verklingen, verhallen; (*radio signal*) schwächer werden.

(**c**) (*Rad, TV, Film*) (*scene*) ausgeblendet werden; (*cameraman*) ausblenden. **to ~ to another scene** (allmählich) zu einer anderen Szene überblenden.

(**d**) (*Tech: brakes*) nachlassen.

2 *vt* (**a**) (*cause to lose colour*) ausbleichen.

(**b**) (*Rad, TV, Film*) ausblenden. **to ~ one scene (in)to another** von einer Szene (allmählich) in eine andere überblenden.

3 *n* (*Rad, TV, Film*) Abblende *f*.

♦**fade away** *vi* (*sight*) schwinden (*geh*); (*memory also*) verblassen; (*hopes also*) zerrinnen; (*interest, strength, inspiration also*) nachlassen; (*sound*) verklingen, verhallen; (*person*) immer weniger or schwächer werden, verhallen; (*from memory of the public*) aus dem Gedächtnis schwinden.

♦**fade in** (*Rad, TV, Film*) **1** *vi* allmählich eingeblendet werden. **2** *vt sep* allmählich einblenden.

♦**fade out** *vi* (*Rad, TV, Film*) abblenden. (**b**) **to ~ of sb's life** aus jds Leben verschwinden. **2** *vt sep* (*Rad, TV, Film*) abblenden.

♦**fade up** *vt sep* (*Rad, TV, Film*) aufblenden; *sound* lauter werden lassen, anschwellen lassen.

faded ['feɪdɪd] *adj* verblaßt, verblichen; *material* (*after exposure to light*) verschossen; *flowers, beauty* verblüht.

fade: ~-**in** *n* (*Rad, TV, Film*) Aufblendung *f*; ~-**out** *n* (*Rad, TV, Film*) Abblende *f*.

faeces, (*US*) **feces** ['fiːsiːz] *pl* Kot *m*.

faerie, faery ['feərɪ] (*old*) **1** *n* Fee *f*. **2** *adj* Feen-, Elfen-. ~ **king/ queen** Elfenkönig *m*/-königin *f*.

faff about ['fæfəˌbaʊt] *vi* (*Brit inf*) herumbosseln (*inf*).

fag [fæg] (*inf*) **1** *n* (**a**) *no pl* (*drudgery*) Schinderei, Plackerei *f*.

(**b**) (*Brit: cigarette*) Kippe *f* (*inf*), Glimmstengel *m* (*inf*).

(**c**) (*Brit Sch*) junger Internatsschüler, der einem älteren bestimmte Dienste zu leisten hat.

(**d**) (*sl: homosexual*) Schwule(r) *m* (*inf*).

2 *vt* (*also* ~ **out**) (*inf*) erschöpfen, schlauchen (*inf*). **to ~ oneself (out)** sich abschinden, sich abrackern (*inf*); **to be ~ged (out)** kaputt or geschafft sein (*inf*).

3 *vi* (**a**) (*also* ~ **away**) sich abrackern (*inf*), sich abplagen.

(**b**) (*Brit Sch*) einem älteren Schüler Dienste leisten.

fag end *n* (**a**) (*Brit inf: cigarette end*) Kippe *f* (*inf*), Stummel *m*.

(**b**) (*inf: last part*) letztes Ende. **the ~ of a conversation** die letzten Fetzen einer Unterhaltung; **at the ~ of the concert** ganz zum Schluß des Konzerts.

faggot, (*US*) **fagot** ['fægət] *n* (**a**) Reisigbündel *nt*. (**b**) (*Cook*) Frikadelle *f*. (**c**) (*inf: person*) Blödmann *m* (*inf*). **you lazy ~** du Faulpelz (*inf*). (**d**) (*esp US sl: homosexual*) Schwule(r) *m* (*inf*).

Fahrenheit ['færənhaɪt] *n* Fahrenheit *nt*.

fail [feɪl] **1** *vi* (**a**) (*be unsuccessful*) keinen Erfolg haben; (*in mission, life etc*) versagen, scheitern; (*campaign, efforts, negotiations also, plan, experiment, marriage*) fehlschlagen, scheitern; (*undertaking, attempt*) fehlschlagen, mißlingen, mißglücken; (*applicant, application*) nicht angenommen werden; (*election candidate, Theat: play*) durchfallen; (*business*) eingehen; (*charm, attempts at persuasion etc also*) vergeblich or umsonst sein. **I/he/they etc ~ed (in doing sth)** es gelang mir/ihm/ihnen etc nicht(, etw zu tun); **I don't like ~ing** ich habe nicht gern Mißerfolge; **he ~ed in his attempt** sein Versuch schlug fehl or blieb erfolglos or mißglückte; **he ~ed in his application for the post** seine Bewerbung wurde nicht angenommen; **to ~ in one's duty** seine Pflicht nicht tun; **to ~ by 5 votes** (*motion*) mit 5 Stimmen Mehrheit abgelehnt werden; (*person*) um 5 Stimmen geschlagen werden; **if all else ~s** wenn alle Stricke reißen.

(**b**) (*not pass exam*) durchfallen.

(**c**) (*fall short*) where he/the essay ~s is in not being detailed enough sein Fehler/der Fehler des Aufsatzes ist, daß er nicht ausführlich genug ist; **this report ~s in that it comes up with no clear proposals** dieser Bericht läßt es an klaren Vorschlägen fehlen; **where you ~ is that you lack experience** Ihnen fehlt es an der notwendigen Erfahrung.

(**d**) (*grow feeble*) (*health*) sich verschlechtern; (*hearing, eyesight also*) nachlassen; (*invalid*) schwächer werden. **he is ~ing fast** sein Zustand verschlechtert sich zusehends.

(**e**) (*stop working, be cut off etc*) (*generator, battery, radio, electricity*) ausfallen; (*pump, engine also, brakes*) versagen; (*supply, wind*) ausbleiben; (*heart*) versagen, aussetzen. **the crops ~ed** es gab ein Mißernte; (*completely*) die Ernte fiel aus.

2 *vt* (**a**) *candidate* durchfallen lassen. **to ~ an exam** eine Prüfung nicht bestehen, in einer Prüfung durchfallen, durch eine Prüfung fallen.

(**b**) (*let down: person, memory*) im Stich lassen; (*not live up to sb's expectations*) enttäuschen. **his heart ~ed him** sein Herz setzte aus; **words ~ me** mir fehlen die Worte.

(**c**) **to ~ to do sth** etw nicht tun; (*neglect*) (es) versäumen, etw zu tun; **I ~ to see why** es ist mir völlig unklar, warum; (*indignantly*) ich sehe gar nicht ein, warum.

3 *n* (**a**) **without ~** ganz bestimmt, auf jeden Fall; (*inevitably*) garantiert, grundsätzlich.

(**b**) (*failed candidate, exam*) there were ten ~s zehn sind durchgefallen or durchgerasselt (*inf*); **she got a ~ in history** in Geschichte ist sie durchgefallen or hängengeblieben (*inf*).

failing ['feɪlɪŋ] **1** *n* Schwäche *f*, Fehler *m*.

2 *prep* ~ **an answer** mangels (einer) Antwort (*geh*); **ask John if he knows,** ~ **him try Harry** fragen Sie John (danach), und wenn er es nicht weiß, versuchen Sie es bei Harry; ~ **this/that** (oder) sonst, und wenn das nicht möglich ist; ~ **which** ansonsten, widrigenfalls (*form*).

fail-safe ['feɪlseɪf] *adj* (ab)gesichert; *method* hundertprozentig sicher.

failure ['feɪljər] *n* (**a**) (*lack of success*) Mißerfolg *m*; (*of campaign, efforts, negotiations also, of plan, experiment, marriage*) Fehlschlag *m*, Scheitern *nt*; (*of undertaking, attempt*) Fehlschlag *m*; (*of application*) Ablehnung *f*; (*in exam, Theat: of play also*) Durchfall *m*; (*of business*) Eingehen *nt*. ~ **to do sth** vergeblicher Versuch, etw zu tun.

(**b**) (*unsuccessful person*) Versager *m*, Niete *f* (*inf*) (*at in* +*dat*); (*unsuccessful thing*) Mißerfolg, Reinfall (*inf*) *m*, Pleite *f* (*inf*). **sb is a ~ at doing sth** jd ist in etw (*dat*) eine Niete (*inf*), es gelingt jdm nicht, etw zu tun; **I'm a bit of a ~ at making my own clothes** ich bin nun eine ziemliche Niete, wenn es darum geht, meine eigenen Kleider zu nähen (inf).

(c) (omission, neglect) **because of his ~ to reply/act** weil er nicht geantwortet/gehandelt hat, weil er es versäumt or unterlassen hat zu antworten/zu handeln; **his ~ to notice anything** weil er nichts bemerkt hat; **~ to pay will result in prosecution** im Nichteinbringungsfall erfolgt Anzeige (form); **~ to perform one's duty** Nichterfüllung f seiner Pflicht; **~ to appear** Nichterscheinen nt (form); **~ to observe a law** Nichtbeachtung f eines Gesetzes.

(d) (of health) Verschlechterung f; (of hearing, eyesight also) Nachlassen nt; (of invalid) Nachlassen nt der Kräfte.

(e) (breakdown) (of generator, engine, electricity) Ausfall m; (of pump, engine also, of brakes) Versagen nt; (of supply, wind) Ausbleiben nt; (of heart) Versagen, Aussetzen nt. **~ of crops** Mißernte f; (complete) Ernteausfall m.

fain [feɪn] adv (obs) gern.

faint [feɪnt] **1** adj (+er) **(a)** schwach; colour, recollection also blaß; suspicion, hope, sound also, wish leise attr; smell, tracks, line, smile also, amusement leicht attr; resemblance also entfernt; voice (feeble) matt, schwach; (distant, not loud) leise. **a ~ idea** eine leise Ahnung; **I haven't the ~est (idea)** ich habe keinen blassen (Schimmer) (inf); **I haven't the ~est idea about it** davon habe ich nicht die leiseste Ahnung.

(b) (pred: about to swoon) **I feel a bit ~** mir ist ganz schwach; **she felt ~** ihr wurde schwach; **she looked ~** sie schien einer Ohnmacht nahe; **I feel ~ with hunger** mir ist (ganz) schwach vor Hunger.

(c) (timid) **~ heart never won fair lady** (Prov) wer nicht wagt, der nicht gewinnt (Prov).

2 n Ohnmacht f. **to fall in a ~** in Ohnmacht fallen, ohnmächtig werden.

3 vi ohnmächtig werden, in Ohnmacht fallen (with, from vor +dat).

faint-hearted [ˈfeɪntˈhɑːtɪd] adj zaghaft.

fainting fit [ˈfeɪntɪŋfɪt] n Ohnmachtsanfall m.

faintly [ˈfeɪntlɪ] adv schwach; visible also kaum; suspect, hope, attempt, sound leise; smell, smile leicht; similar, resemble entfernt; (slightly) interested, disappointed leicht.

faintness [ˈfeɪntnɪs] n **(a)** see adj **such was the ~ of his voice/the colour/the smell/the resemblance etc ...** seine Stimme war so schwach/die Farbe war so blaß/der Geruch war so schwach/die Ähnlichkeit war so schwach or entfernt etc ...

(b) (dizziness) flaues Gefühl, Schwächegefühl nt.

(c) **~ of heart** (liter) Verzagtheit f.

fair¹ [fɛəʳ] **1** adj (+er) **(a)** (just) gerecht, fair (to/on sb jdm gegenüber, gegen jdn). **to be ~ to/on sb** (not unjust) jdm gegenüber fair or gerecht sein or (not mean) anständig handeln; **he tried to be ~ to everybody** er versuchte, gegen alle gerecht zu sein or (give everybody his due) allen gerecht zu werden; **that's a ~ comment** das stimmt, das läßt sich nicht abstreiten; **it's only ~ for him to earn more than us** es ist doch nur gerecht or fair, daß er mehr verdient als wir; **it's only ~ to ask him/to give him a hand etc** man sollte ihn fairerweise fragen/ihm fairerweise helfen etc; **it's only ~ to expect ...** man kann doch wohl zu Recht erwarten ...; **~ enough!** na schön, na gut; **that's ~ enough** das ist nur recht und billig; **as is (only) ~** was nur recht und billig ist; **~'s ~!** wir wollen doch fair bleiben; **by ~ means or foul** ohne Rücksicht auf Verluste (inf); **~ and square** offen und ehrlich, redlich; **that's a ~ sample of ...** das ist ziemlich typisch für ...

(b) (reasonable) ganz ordentlich. **only ~** nur mäßig or mittelprächtig (inf), soso lala (inf); **~ to middling** gut bis mittelmäßig; **he's a ~ judge of character** er hat eine gute Menschenkenntnis; **to have a ~ idea of sth** eine ungefähre Vorstellung von etw haben; **to have a ~ idea (of) what/how etc ...** sich (dat) ziemlich gut vorstellen können, was/wie etc ...; **to have a ~ idea that ...** den leisen Verdacht haben, daß ...; **a ~ chance of success** recht gute Erfolgsaussichten pl.

(c) (reasonably large, fast, strong) sum, number, speed ziemlich, ansehnlich; wind frisch. **a ~ amount** ziemlich viel; **to go at a ~ pace** ziemlich schnell gehen/fahren etc, ein ganz schönes Tempo drauf haben (inf).

(d) (fine) weather heiter, schön. **set ~** beständig; **the barometer/weather is set ~** das Barometer steht auf Schönwetter/das Wetter ist beständig.

(e) person (light-haired) blond; (light-skinned) hell.

(f) (old: beautiful) hold (old), liebreizend (liter). **the ~ sex** (not old) das schöne Geschlecht, die holde Weiblichkeit (hum); **her ~ name** (liter) ihr unbescholtener Name (geh).

(g) **to be in a ~ way to doing sth** (inf) auf dem besten Wege sein, etw zu tun.

2 adv **(a)** **to play ~** (Sport) fair spielen; (fig also) fair sein.

(b) **~ and square** (honestly) offen und ehrlich; (accurately, directly) genau, direkt; **he struck him ~ and square in the face** er schlug ihm mitten ins Gesicht.

(c) (dial: pretty well) ganz schön (inf), vielleicht (inf). **it ~ took my breath away** das hat mir glatt den Atem verschlagen.

fair² n (Jahr)markt m; (fun ~) Volksfest nt, Rummel m (inf); (Comm) Messe f.

fair: **~ copy** n Reinschrift f; **to write out a ~ copy of sth** etw ins reine schreiben; **~ game** n (lit) jagdbares Wild; (fig) Freiwild nt; **the grouse is ~ game between the months of ...** das Moorhuhn darf in den Monaten ... bejagt (spec) or gejagt werden; **~ground** n see fair² Markt(platz) m; Rummel- or Festplatz m; **~-haired** adj, comp **~er-haired** blond; **~-haired boy** n (US) Lieblingskind nt, Liebling m.

fairing [ˈfɛərɪŋ] n (Aviat, Aut) Stromlinien-Verkleidung f.

fairly [ˈfɛəlɪ] adv **(a)** (justly) gerecht. **~ and squarely beaten** nach allen Regeln der Kunst geschlagen. **(b)** (rather) ziemlich, recht. **(c)** (pretty well) see **fair¹** 2 (c).

fair-minded [ˈfɛəˈmaɪndɪd] adj gerecht.

fairness [ˈfɛənɪs] n **(a)** (justice) Gerechtigkeit, Fairneß f. **in all ~ gerechterweise, fairerweise; **in (all) ~ to him we should wait** wir sollten fairerweise warten. **(b)** (lightness) (of hair) Blondheit f; (of skin) Hellhäutigkeit f. **(c)** (of weather) Schönheit f. **(d)** (old: beauty) Liebreiz m (old).

fair: **~ play** n (Sport, fig) faires Verhalten, Fair play nt; **that's not ~ play** (fig) das ist nicht fair or gerecht; **~-sized** adj recht groß; **~way** n (Naut) Fahrwasser nt or -rinne f; **(b)** (Golf) Fairway nt; **~-weather** adj friends nur in guten Zeiten.

fairy [ˈfɛərɪ] n **(a)** Fee f. **he's away with the fairies** (sl) der hat einen Haschmich (sl) or Stich (inf). **(b)** (pej inf: homosexual) Homo (inf), Schwule(r) (inf) m.

fairy: **~ cycle** n Kinderfahrrad nt; **~ footsteps** npl (iro inf) Stapfen nt; **~ godmother** n (lit, fig) gute Fee; **~land** n Märchenland nt; **~ lights** npl bunte Lichter pl; **~-like** adj feenhaft; **~ queen** n Elfenkönigin f; **~ ring** n Hexentanzplatz m; (of mushrooms) Hexenring m; **~ story, ~-tale** n (lit, fig) Märchen nt.

fait accompli [ˌfeɪtəˈkɒmpliː] n vollendete Tatsache, Fait accompli nt (geh). **to present sb with a ~** jdn vor vollendete Tatsachen stellen.

faith [feɪθ] n **(a)** (trust) Vertrauen nt (in zu); (in human nature, medicine, science etc, religious ~) Glaube m (in an + acc). **~ in God** Gottvertrauen nt; **to have ~ in sb** auf jdn vertrauen, jdm (ver)trauen; **to have ~ in sth** Vertrauen in etw (acc) haben, einer Sache (dat) trauen; **have ~** haben Sie Vertrauen!; **act of ~** Vertrauensbeweis m; **it was more an act of ~ than a rational decision** das war mehr auf gut Glück gemacht als eine rationale Entscheidung.

(b) (religion) Glaube m no pl, Bekenntnis nt.

(c) (promise) **to keep/break ~ with sb** jdm treu bleiben/untreu werden, jdm die Treue halten/brechen (geh).

(d) (sincerity, loyalty) Treue f. **to act in good/bad ~** in gutem Glauben/böser Absicht handeln.

faith cure n Heilung f durch Gesundbeten.

faithful [ˈfeɪθful] **1** adj **(a)** treu. **~ to one's promise** seinem Versprechen getreu. **(b)** (accurate) account, translation genau, getreu. **2** npl **the ~** (Rel) die Gläubigen pl.

faithfully [ˈfeɪθfəlɪ] adv **(a)** treu; promise fest, hoch und heilig (inf). **yours ~** mit freundlichen Grüßen; (more formally) hochachtungsvoll. **(b)** report etc genau, getreu; translate wortgetreu, genau.

faithfulness [ˈfeɪθfulnɪs] n (loyalty) Treue f (to zu); (of servant, dog etc also) Ergebenheit f (to gegenüber); (of translation) Genauigkeit f; (of reproduction) Originaltreue f.

faith: **~ healer** n Gesundbeter(in f) m; **~ healing** n Gesundbeten nt; **~less** adj treulos; **~lessness** n Treulosigkeit f.

fake [feɪk] **1** n **(a)** (object) Fälschung f; (jewellery) Imitation f; (person) (trickster) Schwindler m; (feigning illness) Simulant m. **he's just a big ~!** (inf) das ist doch alles nur Schau! (inf). **2** vt vortäuschen; picture, document, results etc fälschen; bill, burglary, crash fingieren; jewellery imitieren, nachmachen; elections manipulieren. **to ~ an illness** (eine Krankheit) simulieren or vortäuschen.

♦fake up vt sep story erfinden; picture, passport fälschen; jewellery imitieren.

fakir [ˈfɑːkɪəʳ] n Fakir m.

falcon [ˈfɔːlkən] n Falke m.

falconer [ˈfɔːlkənəʳ] n Falkner, Falkenier (old) m.

falconry [ˈfɔːlkənrɪ] n (sport) Falkenjagd or -beize f.

fall [fɔːl] (vb: pret **fell**, ptp **fallen**) **1** n **(a)** Fall no pl, Sturz m; (decline: of empire etc) Untergang m. **the F~ (of Man)** (Eccl) der Sündenfall; **to break sb's ~** jds Fall auffangen; **to have a ~** (hin)fallen, stürzen; **he had several ~s** er ist mehrmals hingefallen or gestürzt; **it's a long ~ from up here** von hier oben geht es tief hinunter; **to head or ride for a ~** in sein Verderben rennen.

(b) (defeat) (of town, fortress etc) Einnahme, Eroberung f; (of Troy) Fall m; (of country) Zusammenbruch m; (of government) Sturz m.

(c) **~ of rain/snow** Regen-/Schneefall m; **~ of rock** Steinschlag m; **there was another heavy ~ last night** es hat heute nacht wieder viel geschneit.

(d) (of night) Einbruch m.

(e) (in gen) (lowering) Sinken nt; (in temperature also) Abfall m; (sudden) Sturz m; (of barometer) Fallen nt; (sudden) Sturz m; (in wind) Nachlassen nt; (in revs, population, membership) Abnahme f; (in graph) Abfall m; (in morals) Verfall m; (of prices, currency) (gradual) Verfall m; (sudden) Sturz m. **~ in altitude** Höhenverlust m.

(f) (slope) (of roof, ground) Gefälle nt; (steeper) Abfall m.

(g) (water~: also **~s**) Wasserfall m. **the Niagara F~s** der Niagarafall.

(h) (Wrestling) Schultersieg m.

(i) (hang: of curtains etc) Fall m.

(j) (US: autumn) Herbst m. **in the ~** im Herbst.

2 vi **(a)** fallen; (Sport, from a height, badly) stürzen; (object: to the ground) herunter-/hinunterfallen. **to ~ to one's death** tödlich abstürzen; **to ~ into a trap** in die Falle gehen.

(b) (hang down: hair, clothes etc) fallen. **his tie kept ~ing into the soup** seine Krawatte hing ihm dauernd in die Suppe.

(c) (drop) (temperature, price) fallen, sinken; (population, membership etc) abnehmen; (voice) sich senken; (wind) sich legen, nachlassen; (land) abfallen; (graph, curve, rate) abnehmen; (steeply) abfallen. **her eyes fell** sie schlug die Augen nieder (geh); **his face fell** er machte ein langes Gesicht; **to ~ in sb's estimation or eyes** in jds Achtung (dat) sinken.

(d) (be defeated) (country) eingenommen werden; (city, fortress also) fallen, erobert werden; (government, ruler) gestürzt werden. **to ~ to the enemy** vom Feind eingenommen werden; (fortress, town also) vom Feind erobert werden.

(e) *(be killed)* fallen. to ~ in battle fallen.
(f) *(night)* hereinbrechen; *(silence)* eintreten.
(g) *(Bibl)* den Sündenfall tun; *(old: girl)* die Unschuld *or* Ehre verlieren *(dated).* when Adam fell nach Adams Sündenfall.
(h) *(occur)* *(birthday, Easter etc)* fallen *(on auf +acc);* *(accent)* liegen *(on auf +dat);* *(be classified)* gehören *(under in +acc),* fallen *(under unter +acc).* it ~s under another category das gehört in *or* fällt in eine andere Kategorie; to ~ outside/within the scope ... das fällt nicht in/in den Bereich ..., das liegt außerhalb/innerhalb des Bereichs ...
(i) *(be naturally divisible)* zerfallen, sich gliedern *(into in +acc).* to ~ into three sections sich in drei Teile gliedern; to ~ into categories sich in Kategorien gliedern lassen.
(j) *(fig)* no word fell from his lips kein Wort kam über seine Lippen; her eyes fell on a strange object ihr Blick fiel auf einen merkwürdigen Gegenstand; the responsibility ~s on you Sie tragen *or* haben die Verantwortung; the blame for that ~s on him ihn trifft die Schuld daran; where do you think the responsibility/blame for that will ~? wem wird Ihrer Meinung nach die Verantwortung dafür/die Schuld daran gegeben?
(k) *(become)* werden. to ~ asleep einschlafen; to ~ ill krank werden, erkranken *(geh);* to ~ in/out of love with sb sich in jdn verlieben/aufhören, jdn zu lieben; she's forever ~ing in and out of love sie verliebt sich dauernd neu; to ~ silent still werden, verstummen.
(l) *(pass into a certain state)* to ~ into despair verzweifeln; to ~ into a deep sleep in tiefen Schlaf fallen *or* sinken; to ~ into a state of unconsciousness/into a coma das Bewußtsein verlieren, in Ohnmacht/in ein Koma fallen; to ~ into bad ways auf die schiefe Bahn geraten; to ~ apart *or* to pieces *(chairs, cars, book etc)* aus dem Leim gehen *(inf);* *(clothes, curtains)* sich in Wohlgefallen auflösen *(inf);* *(house)* verfallen; *(system, company, sb's life)* aus den Fugen geraten *or* gehen.
(m) to ~ to doing sth anfangen, etw zu tun; they fell to fighting amongst themselves sie fingen an, untereinander zu streiten.
(n) *(in set constructions see also n, adj etc)* to ~ into the hands of sb jdm in die Hände fallen; to ~ among thieves unter die Räuber fallen *or* geraten.
3 *vt* to ~ prey/a victim to sb/sth jdm/einer Sache zum Opfer fallen.

♦**fall about** *(also ~ ~ laughing)* *vi* sich krank lachen *(inf).*
♦**fall away** *vi* **(a)** *(ground)* abfallen. **(b)** *(come away, crumble: plaster, bricks, river bank)* abbröckeln *(from von).* **(c)** see fall off **(b).** **(d)** *(anxiety, fears)* weichen *(geh) (from von).* **(e)** *(from party, church)* abfallen.
♦**fall back** *vi* zurückweichen *(also Mil).*
♦**fall back (up)on** *vi +prep obj* zurückgreifen auf *(+acc).*
♦**fall behind** *vi* **(a)** *(race, school etc)* zurückbleiben *(prep obj hinter +dat),* zurückfallen *(prep obj hinter +acc).* **(b)** *(with rent, work etc)* in Rückstand *or* Verzug geraten.
♦**fall down** *vi* **(a)** *(person)* hinfallen; *(statue, vase)* herunter-/hinunterfallen; *(collapse: house, scaffolding etc)* einstürzen. **(b)** *(down stairs, cliff face)* hinunterfallen *(prep obj acc).* he fell right ~ to the bottom er ist bis ganz nach unten gefallen. **(c)** *(fig: be inadequate: person, theory, plan)* versagen. where he/the plan ~s ~ is ... woran es ihm/dem Plan fehlt, ist ..., woran es bei ihm/dem Plan hapert, ist ... *(inf);* he fell ~ badly that time er hat damals übel versagt; that was where we fell ~ daran sind wir gescheitert.
♦**fall for** *vi +prep obj* **(a)** I really fell ~ him/that er/das hatte es mir angetan. **(b)** *(be taken in by)* sales talk, propaganda hereinfallen auf *(+acc).*
♦**fall in** *vi* **(a)** *(into water etc)* hineinfallen. to ~ ~(to) sth in etw *(acc)* fallen. **(b)** *(collapse)* einstürzen; *(building also)* zusammenbrechen. **(c)** *(Mil)* troops *(in Reih und Glied)* antreten; *(one soldier)* ins Glied treten. ~ ~! antreten!; to ~ ~ beside *or* alongside sb sich dem anschließen.
♦**fall in with** *vi +prep obj* **(a)** *(meet, join up with)* sich anschließen *(+dat);* bad company geraten in *(+acc).* **(b)** *(agree to)* mitmachen bei; *request* unterstützen.
♦**fall off** *vi* **(a)** *(lit)* *(person, cup etc)* herunter-/hinunterfallen *(prep obj von).* **(b)** *(decrease)* zurückgehen, abnehmen; *(supporters)* abfallen; *(speed also)* sich verringern; *(support, enthusiasm)* nachlassen.
♦**fall on** *vi +prep obj* **(a)** *(trip on)* stone fallen über *(+acc).* **(b)** *(be the responsibility of, be borne by)* *(duty, decision, task)* zufallen *(+dat);* *(blame)* treffen *(+acc).* **(c)** *(attack)* herfallen über *(+acc).* **(d)** *(find)* stoßen auf *(+acc).*
♦**fall out** *vi* **(a)** *(of bed, boat, window)* heraus-/hinausfallen. to ~ ~ of sth aus etw fallen. **(b)** *(quarrel)* sich *(zer)streiten.* **(c)** *(Mil)* wegtreten. **(d)** *(happen)* sich ergeben. just wait and see how things ~ ~ wart erst mal ab, wie alles wird; if everything ~s ~ all right wenn alles wunschgemäß verläuft *or* nach Wunsch geht; it fell ~ that ... *(liter)* es erwies sich, daß ... *(geh).*
♦**fall over** *vi* **(a)** *(person)* hinfallen; *(collapse)* umfallen; *(statue, vase also)* umkippen.
(b) *+prep obj* *(trip over)* stone, sb's legs fallen über *(+acc).* he was always ~ing ~ himself er stolperte ständig über seine eigenen Füße; they were ~ing ~ each other to get the book sie drängelten sich, um das Buch zu bekommen.
(c) to ~ ~ oneself to do sth *(inf)* umbringen *(inf) or* sich *(dat)* die größte Mühe geben, etw zu tun; to ~ ~ backwards to do sth *(förmlich)* überschlagen, etw zu tun *(inf).*
♦**fall through** *vi* *(plan)* ins Wasser fallen, fehlschlagen.
♦**fall to** *vi* **(a)** *(inf)* *(start eating)* sich dranmachen *(inf),* reinhauen *(inf);* *(start fighting, working)* loslegen *(inf).* **(b)** *(be the responsibility of)* zufallen *(+dat),* obliegen *(+dat) (geh).*
♦**fall upon** *vi +prep obj* see **fall on (b-d).**
fallacious [fəˈleɪʃəs] *adj* irrig; *argument* trugschlüssig.
fallacy [ˈfæləsɪ] *n* Irrtum *m;* *(in logic)* Fehlschluß, Trugschluß

m. a popular ~ ein weitverbreiteter Irrtum; it's a ~ to think that ... es ist ein Irrtum zu meinen, daß ...
fallen [ˈfɔːlən] **1** *ptp of* fall. **2** *adj women, soldier, angel* gefallen; *leaf* abgefallen. **3** *npl* the F~ *(Mil)* die Gefallenen *pl.*
fall guy *n (esp US inf)* *(victim)* armes Opfer, Angeschmierte(r) *(inf) mf;* *(scapegoat)* Sündenbock *m.*
fallibility [ˌfælɪˈbɪlɪtɪ] *n* Fehlbarkeit *f.*
fallible [ˈfælɪbl] *adj* nicht unfehlbar.
falling [ˈfɔːlɪŋ]: ~ sickness *n (old)* Fallsucht *f (old);* ~ star *n* Sternschnuppe *f.*
fall: ~ line *n (Sci)* Fall-Linie *f;* ~-off *n (in gen)* Rückgang *m,* Abnahme *f; (in numbers, attendances)* Abfall *m; (in speed)* Verringerung *f; (in enthusiasm, support)* Nachlassen *nt.*
Fallopian tube [fəˈləʊpɪənˈtjuːb] *n* Eileiter *f.*
fall-out [ˈfɔːlaʊt] *n* radioaktiver Niederschlag, Fall-out *m (spec).* ~ shelter Atombunker *m.*
fallow[1] [ˈfæləʊ] *adj* land brach. to lie ~ brachliegen.
fallow[2] *adj* falb, gelbbraun. ~ deer Damwild *nt.*
false [fɔːls] **1** *adj* falsch; *friend also, lover* treulos; *ceiling, floor* Einschub-, Zwischen-. to put a ~ interpretation on sth etw falsch auslegen *or* deuten; ~ labour Vorwehen *pl;* a ~ move/step eine falsche Bewegung/ein falscher Schritt; to put sb in a ~ position jdn in eine Position drängen, die er sonst nicht vertritt; to sail under ~ colours unter falscher Flagge segeln; to bear ~ witness *(Bibl)* falsch(es) Zeugnis reden *(Bibl);* under ~ pretences unter Vorspiegelung falscher Tatsachen; to be ~ to one's wife/word seine Frau hintergehen/sein Wort brechen; a box with a ~ bottom eine Kiste mit doppeltem Boden.
2 *adv:* to play sb ~ mit jdm ein falsches Spiel treiben.
false: ~ alarm *n* falscher *or* blinder Alarm; ~ dawn *n* Zodiakal- *or* Tierkreislicht *nt;* ~-hearted *adj* falsch, treulos.
falsehood [ˈfɔːlshʊd] *n* **(a)** *(lie)* Unwahrheit *f.* **(b)** no pl *(of statement etc)* Unwahrheit *f.*
falsely [ˈfɔːlslɪ] *adv interpret, understand* falsch; *believe, claim, declare* fälschlicherweise; *accuse* zu Unrecht; *smile* unaufrichtig; *deceive, act* treulos. to promise ~ to do sth sein Versprechen, etw zu tun, nicht ernst meinen.
falseness [ˈfɔːlsnɪs] *n (of statement etc)* Unrichtigkeit, Falschheit *f; (of promise)* Unaufrichtigkeit, Falschheit *f; (artificiality: of pearls, eyelashes etc)* Unechtheit *f; (unfaithfulness: of lover etc)* Untreue, Treulosigkeit *f.*
false: ~ rib *n* falsche Rippe; ~ start *n* Fehlstart *m;* ~ teeth *npl* (künstliches) Gebiß.
falsetto [fɔːlˈsetəʊ] **1** *n (voice)* Fistelstimme *f; (Mus also)* Falsett *nt; (person)* Falsettist *m.* **2** *adj* Fistel-; *(Mus)* Falsett-. **3** *adv sing* im Falsett.
falsies [ˈfɔːlsɪz] *npl (inf)* Gummibusen *m (inf).*
falsifiable [ˈfɔːlsɪfaɪəbl] *adj (disprovable)* widerlegbar, falsifizierbar *(spec).*
falsification [ˌfɔːlsɪfɪˈkeɪʃən] *n* **(a)** *(Ver)fälschung f.* **(b)** *(disproving)* Widerlegung, Falsifikation *(spec) f.*
falsify [ˈfɔːlsɪfaɪ] *vt* **(a)** *records, evidence, document* fälschen; *report, story* entstellen. **(b)** *(disprove)* widerlegen, falsifizieren *(spec).*
falsity [ˈfɔːlsɪtɪ] *n (incorrectness)* Unrichtigkeit *f; (artificiality: of smile)* Falschheit *f; (unfaithfulness)* Treulosigkeit *f.*
falter [ˈfɔːltəʳ] *vi (speaking)* stocken; *(steps, horse)* zögern.
faltering [ˈfɔːltərɪŋ] *adj voice* stockend, stammelnd; *(hesitating, wavering)* zögernd; *(unsteady)* taumelnd.
falteringly [ˈfɔːltərɪŋlɪ] *adv see adj.*
fame [feɪm] *n* Ruhm *m.* of ill ~ von üblem Ruf, berüchtigt; to come to ~ Ruhm erlangen, zu Ruhm kommen; to win ~ for oneself sich *(dat)* einen Namen machen; is that the Joseph Heller of "Catch-22" ~? ist das der berühmte Joseph Heller, der „Catch-22" geschrieben hat?; Borg of Wimbledon 1979 ~ Borg, der sich 1979 in Wimbledon einen Namen gemacht hat.
famed [feɪmd] *adj* berühmt.
familiar [fəˈmɪljəʳ] **1** *adj* **(a)** *(usual, well-known)* surroundings, sight, scene* gewohnt, vertraut; *street, phrase, title, song* geläufig, bekannt; *complaint, event, protest* häufig. he's a ~ figure in the town er ist in der Stadt eine bekannte Gestalt; his face is ~ das Gesicht ist mir bekannt; among ~ faces unter vertrauten Gesichtern; to be/seem ~ to sb jdm bekannt sein/vorkommen; it looks very ~ es kommt mir sehr bekannt vor; to sound ~ sich bekannt anhören *(to sb jdm);* that sounds ~ das habe ich doch schon mal gehört; to be on ~ ground Bescheid wissen; to be on ~ ground with sth *(dat)* zu Hause sein.
(b) *(conversant)* I am ~ with the word/the town/him das Wort/die Stadt/er ist mir bekannt *or (more closely)* vertraut; I am not ~ with Ancient Greek/computer language ich kann kein Altgriechisch/ich bin mit der Computersprache nicht vertraut; are you ~ with these modern techniques? wissen Sie über diese modernen Techniken Bescheid?; is he ~ with our customs? ist er mit unseren Bräuchen vertraut?; to make oneself ~ with sth sich mit etw vertraut machen.
(c) *(friendly)* language, way of talking familiär; *greeting* freundschaftlich; *gesture* familiär, vertraulich; *(overfriendly)* familiär, plump-vertraulich. the ~ term of address die Anrede für Familie und Freunde, die vertraute Anrede; to be on ~ terms with sb mit jdm auf vertrautem Fuß stehen; we're all on pretty ~ terms wir haben ein ziemlich ungezwungenes Verhältnis zueinander; ~ language/expressions Umgangssprache f/umgangssprachliche Ausdrücke pl; there's no need to get ~ kein Grund, gleich (plump-)vertraulich *or* familiär zu werden; if you're too ~ with your staff wenn man zu seinen Untergebenen ein zu vertrauliches Verhältnis hat; they're not the kind of people one wishes to become too ~ with mit solchen Leuten möchte man sich nicht unbedingt näher einlassen.
2 *n* **(a)** *(liter: friend)* Vertraute(r) *mf (liter),* Intimus *m (geh),* Intima *f (geh).*

(b) (*of witch etc*) Hausgeist *m*.

familiarity [fə‚mɪlɪˈærɪtɪ] *n* **(a)** *no pl* Vertrautheit *f*.

(b) (*between people*) vertrautes Verhältnis; (*between colleagues etc*) ungezwungenes *or* familiäres Verhältnis; (*of language etc*) Familiarität *f*; (*of greeting*) Freundschaftlichkeit *f*; (*of gesture*) Vertraulichkeit, Familiarität *f*; (*pej*) plumpe Vertraulichkeit, Familiarität *f*. ~ **breeds contempt** (*Prov*) allzu große Vertrautheit erzeugt Verachtung.

(c) *usu pl* (*overfriendly action*) (plumpe) Vertraulichkeit.

familiarization [fə‚mɪlɪərarˈzeɪʃən] *n* process of ~ Gewöhnungsprozeß *m*; **he is responsible for the** ~ **of all new employees with ...** er ist dafür verantwortlich, daß alle neuen Angestellten mit ... vertraut gemacht werden.

familiarize [fəˈmɪliəraɪz] *vt* to ~ **sb/oneself with sth** jdn/sich mit etw vertraut machen; *newcomer, new staff also* jdn in etw (*acc*) einweisen; **once you've** ~**d yourself with the job** wenn Sie sich eingearbeitet haben.

familiarly [fəˈmɪljəlɪ] *adv speak, behave* familiär, vertraulich; (*pej*) familiär, plump-vertraulich. ~ **known as** besser allgemein bekannt als; **more** ~ **known as** besser bekannt als.

family [ˈfæmɪlɪ] **1** *n* **(a)** Familie *f*; (*including cousins, aunts etc*) Verwandtschaft *f*; (*lineage*) Familie *f*, Haus, Geschlecht (*geh*) *nt*. **to start a** ~ eine Familie gründen; **they plan to add to their** ~ sie planen Familienzuwachs; **has he any** ~? hat er Familie?; **it runs in the** ~ das liegt in der Familie; **of good** ~ aus guter Familie *or* gutem Hause; **he's one of the** ~ er gehört zur Familie; **with just the immediate** ~ im engsten Familienkreis.

(b) (*of plants, animals, languages etc*) Familie *f*. **the** ~ **of man** die Menschheit.

2 *attr* Familien-. **a** ~ **friend** ein Freund des Hauses *or* der Familie; **she's in the** ~ **way** (*inf*) sie ist in anderen Umständen.

family: ~ **allowance** *n* Kindergeld *nt*; ~ **butcher** *n* D. Crosby, F~ Butcher D. Crosby, Fleischermeister; **our/their/the** ~ **butcher** unsere/ihre/die Stammfleischerei; ~ **doctor** *n* Hausarzt *m*/-ärztin *f*; ~ **hotel** *n* Familienpension *f*; ~ **man** *n* (*home-loving*) häuslich veranlagter Mann; (*with a* ~) Familienvater *m*; ~ **planning** *n* Familienplanung *f*; ~ **planning clinic** *n* Familienberatungsstelle *f*; ~**-size** *adj* in Haushaltsgröße; *car, packets* Familien-; *house* Einfamilien-; *refrigerator* Haushalts-; ~ **tree** *n* Stammbaum *m*.

famine [ˈfæmɪn] *n* (*lit*) Hungersnot *f*; (*fig*) Knappheit *f*. **to die of** ~ verhungern.

famish [ˈfæmɪʃ] *vi* (*inf*) verhungern.

famished [ˈfæmɪʃt] *adj* (*inf*) verhungert, ausgehungert. **I'm absolutely** ~ ich sterbe vor Hunger (*inf*).

famous [ˈfeɪməs] *adj* **(a)** berühmt (*for* durch, für). **(b)** (*dated inf: splendid*) famos (*dated*).

famously [ˈfeɪməslɪ] *adv* (*dated inf*) famos (*dated*), prächtig.

famulus [ˈfæmjʊləs] *n* Famulus *m*.

fan¹ [fæn] **1** *n* **(a)** (*hand-held*) Fächer *m*; (*mechanical, extractor* ~, *Aut: to cool engine*) Ventilator *m*; (*on scooter*) Lüfterrad *nt*; (*Aut: booster*) Gebläse *nt*.

(b) (*of peacock, fig*) Fächer *m*. **to spread sth out in a** ~ etw fächerförmig ausbreiten.

2 *vt* **(a)** (*wind*) umwehen; (*person*) fächeln (+*dat*); (*fig*) *enthusiasm, interest* anfachen. **to** ~ **sb/oneself** jdm/sich (Luft) zufächeln; **to** ~ **the embers** die Glut anfachen; (*fig also*) das Feuer entfachen; **to** ~ **the flames** (*fig*) Öl ins Feuer gießen; **to** ~ **the flames of passion** das Feuer der Leidenschaft (noch) schüren.

(b) *cards* fächerförmig ausbreiten. **the peacock** ~**ned its tail** der Pfau schlug ein Rad.

♦**fan out 1** *vi* (*troops, searchers*) ausschwärmen. **2** *vt sep tail feathers* fächerförmig aufstellen; *playing cards* fächerförmig ausbreiten.

fan² *n* (*supporter*) Fan *m*. **I'm quite a** ~ **of yours** ich bin ein richtiger Verehrer von Ihnen.

fanatic [fəˈnætɪk] *n* Fanatiker(in *f*) *m*.

fanatic(al) *adj*, **fanatically** *adv* [fəˈnætɪk(əl), fəˈnætɪkəlɪ] fanatisch.

fanaticism [fəˈnætɪsɪzəm] *n* Fanatismus *m*.

fan belt *n* Keilriemen *m*.

fancied [ˈfænsɪd] *adj* (*imaginary*) eingebildet.

fancier [ˈfænsɪəʳ] *n* Liebhaber(in *f*) *m*.

fanciful [ˈfænsɪfʊl] *adj story, idea* phantastisch, abstrus; (*fancy*) *costume* reich verziert; *pattern* phantasievoll. **I think you're being somewhat** ~ ich glaube, das ist etwas weit hergeholt; **and I don't think it's** ~ **to claim that ...** und ich glaube nicht, daß es verstiegen ist zu behaupten, daß ...

fancifulness [ˈfænsɪfʊlnɪs] *n* (*of story etc*) Seltsamkeit *f*; (*of person*) blühende Phantasie; (*of costume*) reiche Verzierung; (*of pattern*) Phantasiereichtum *m*.

fan club *n* Fanclub *m*.

fancy [ˈfænsɪ] **1** *n* **(a)** (*liking*) to have a ~ **for sth** Lust zu etw *or* (*to eat or drink*) auf etw (*acc*) haben; **he had a** ~ **for sports cars** er hatte eine Vorliebe für Sportwagen; **a passing** ~ nur so eine Laune; **he's taken a** ~ **to her/this car/the idea** sie/das Auto/die Idee hat es ihm angetan; **they took a** ~ **to each other** sie fanden sich sympathisch; **to take** *or* **catch sb's** ~ jdn ansprechen, jdm gefallen; **he took a** ~ **to go swimming** er hatte Lust, schwimmen zu gehen; **to tickle sb's** ~ jdn reizen; **just as the** ~ **takes me/you** ganz nach Lust und Laune; **he only works when the** ~ **takes him** er arbeitet nur, wenn ihm gerade danach ist.

(b) (*no pl: imagination*) Phantasie *f*; (*thing imagined also*) Phantasievorstellung *f*. **that was just his** ~ das hat er sich (*dat*) nur eingebildet.

(c) (*notion, whim*) I have a ~ **that ...** ich habe so ein Gefühl, daß ...; **he had a sudden** ~ **to go to Spain** ihn überkam eine plötzliche Laune, nach Spanien zu fahren.

2 *vt* **(a)** (*in exclamations*) ~ **doing that!** so was(, das) zu tun!; (*shocked also*) wie kann/konnte man so was bloß tun!; ~ **him**

doing that nicht zu fassen *or* nein, daß er das tut/getan hat!; ~ **that!** (*inf*), (**just**) ~! (*inf*) (nein) so was!, denk mal an! (*inf*); **just** ~, **he ...** stell dir vor *or* denk dir, er ...; ~ **seeing you here!** so was, Sie hier zu sehen!; ~ **him winning!** wer hätte gedacht, daß er gewinnt!

(b) (*imagine*) meinen, sich (*dat*) einbilden; (*think*) glauben. **he fancied he heard footsteps** er bildete sich ein *or* meinte, Schritte zu hören; **I rather** ~ **he has gone out** ich glaube, er ist weggegangen.

(c) (*like, be attracted by*) **he fancies that car/the idea/her** (*likes*) das Auto/die Idee/sie gefällt ihm *or* hat es ihm angetan; **he fancies a house on Crete/her as a wife/her as his MP** (*would like to have*) er hätte gern ein Haus auf Kreta/er hätte sie gern zur Frau/als seine Abgeordnete; **he fancies a walk/steak/beer** (*feels like*) er hat Lust zu einem Spaziergang/auf ein Steak/ Bier; **he fancies (the idea of) doing that** er würde *or* möchte das gern tun; (*feels like it*) er hätte Lust, das zu tun; (**do you**) ~ **a walk?** hast du Lust zu einem Spaziergang?; **count me out, I don't** ~ **the idea** ohne mich, das nicht für mich; **I don't** ~ **the idea, but I'll have to do it** ich habe gar keine Lust dazu, aber ich muß es ja wohl tun; **I don't** ~ **that** (**idea**)**!** nur das nicht, nein, das finde ich nicht gut; **I didn't** ~ **that job/that party** die Stelle/die Party hat mich nicht gereizt; **I don't** ~ **a house in Glasgow** ich möchte kein Haus in Glasgow haben; **he fancies his chances** er meint, er hätte Chancen; **I don't** ~ **my chances of getting that job** ich rechne mir keine großen Chancen aus, die Stelle zu bekommen; **a bit of what you** ~ **does you good** man muß sich auch mal was Gutes gönnen.

3 *vr* von sich eingenommen sein, sich für wunder was halten (*inf*). **he fancies himself as an actor/expert on that** er hält sich für einen (guten) Schauspieler/einen Experten auf dem Gebiet; **do you** ~ **yourself as a teacher?** kannst du dir dich als Lehrer vorstellen?

4 *adj* **(a)** (+*er*) (*elaborate*) *hairdo, dancing steps, footwork* kunstvoll; (*unusual*) *food, pattern, decorations, cigarettes, furnishings* ausgefallen; *baking, cakes, bread* fein; (*inf*) *gadget, car, girlfriend etc* toll, schick (*inf*). **nothing** ~ etwas ganz Einfaches; (*dress, furniture etc also*) etwas ganz Schlichtes; **a big** ~ **car** ein toller Schlitten (*inf*); **he always uses these big** ~ **words** er drückt sich immer so geschwollen aus; **that was a** ~ **bit of driving** das war ein gewagtes Manöver; **do you like my new stereo/dress? — very** ~ gefällt dir meine neue Stereoanlage/mein neues Kleid? — toll, toll; **that's too** ~ **for me** das ist mir etwas zu übertrieben; **you won't get me eating any of these** ~ **German sausages** du kriegst mich nicht dazu, diese komischen deutschen Würste zu essen.

(b) (*fig pej*) *idea* überspannt, verstiegen; *cure* seltsam; *price* gepfeffert, stolz *attr*.

(c) (*US: extra good*) *goods, foodstuffs* Delikateß-.

fancy: ~ **dress** *n* (Masken)kostüm *nt*; **is it** ~ **dress?** geht man da verkleidet hin?; **they came in** ~ **dress** sie kamen verkleidet *or* kostümiert; ~**-dress ball/party** *n* Maskenball *m*/Kostümfest *nt*; ~**-free** *adj* frei und ungebunden; ~ **goods** *npl* Geschenkartikel *pl*; ~ **man** *n* (*pimp*) Zuhälter *m*; (*lover*) Liebhaber *m*; ~ **woman** *n* Freundin *f*, Weibchen *nt* (*inf*); ~**work** *n* feine Handarbeit.

fandango [fænˈdæŋgəʊ] *n* Fandango *m*.

fanfare [ˈfænfeə] *n* Fanfare *f*. **bugle** ~ Fanfarenstoß *m*.

fang [fæŋ] *n* (*of snake*) Giftzahn *m*; (*of wolf, dog*) Fang *m*; (*of vampire*) Vampirzahn *m*; (*hum: of person*) Hauer *m* (*hum*).

fan: ~**light** *n* Oberlicht *nt*; ~ **mail** *n* Verehrerpost *f*.

fanny [ˈfænɪ] *n* **(a)** (*esp US inf*) Po *m* (*inf*). **(b)** (*Brit vulg*) Möse *f* (*vulg*).

fan: ~**-shaped** *adj* fächerförmig; ~**tail** *n* (*pigeon*) Pfautaube *f*.

fantasia [fænˈteɪzjə] *n* Fantasie *f*.

fantasize [ˈfæntəsaɪz] *vi* phantasieren; (*dream*) Phantasievorstellungen haben (*about* von).

fantastic [fænˈtæstɪk] *adj* **(a)** (*also* ~**al**) phantastisch, skurril; *garment also* extravagant. **(b)** (*incredible*) phantastisch, unwahrscheinlich. **(c)** (*inf: wonderful*) toll (*inf*), phantastisch.

fantastically [fænˈtæstɪkəlɪ] *adv see adj*.

fantasy [ˈfæntəzɪ] *n* **(a)** (*imagination*) Phantasie *f*. **(b)** (*illusion*) Phantasie *f*, Hirngespinst *nt* (*pej*). **that's pure** ~ *or* **a** ~ das ist reine Phantasie *or* bloß ein Hirngespinst. **(c)** (*Mus, Liter*) Fantasie *f*.

fan: ~ **tracery** *n* fächerförmiges Maßwerk; ~ **vaulting** *n* Fächergewölbe *nt*.

far [fɑːʳ] *see also comp* **further, farther,** *superl* **furthest, farthest 1** *adv* **(a)** (*in place*) weit. **we don't live** ~ *or* **we live not** ~ **from here** wir wohnen nicht weit von hier; **how** ~ **are you going?** wie weit gehen/fahren Sie?; **I'll go with you as** ~ **as the gate** ich komme/gehe bis zum Tor mit; ~ **and wide** weit und breit; **from** ~ **and near** *or* **wide** von nah und fern; ~ **above** hoch *or* weit über (+*dat*); ~ **away** weit entfernt *or* weg; ~ **away in the distance** weit in der Ferne; **it's** ~ **beyond the forest** es ist weit über den Wald hinaus; ~ **into the jungle** weit in den Dschungel hinein; **I won't be** ~ **off** *or* **away** ich bin ganz in der Nähe; ~ **out** weit draußen; **have you come** ~? kommen Sie von weit her?

(b) (*in time*) **as** ~ **back as I can remember** so weit ich (zurück)denken *or* mich erinnern kann; **as** ~ **back as 1945;** **schon** (im Jahr) 1945; ~ **into the night** bis spät in die Nacht; ~ **into the future** bis weit in die Zukunft.

(c) (*in degree, extent*) weit. **how** ~ **have you got with your plans?** wie weit sind Sie mit Ihren Plänen (gekommen)?; ~ **longer/better** weit länger/besser; **it's** ~ **beyond what I can afford** das übersteigt meine Mittel bei weitem.

(d) (*in set phrases*) **as or so** ~ **as I'm concerned** was mich betrifft; **it's all right as** ~ **as it goes** das ist soweit ganz gut; **in so** ~ **as insofern als;** ~ **and away the best, by** ~ **the best, the best** **by** ~ bei weitem *or* mit Abstand der/die/das Beste; **better by** ~ weit besser; ~ **from satisfactory** alles andere als befriedigend; ~ **from liking him I find him quite unpleasant** nicht nur, daß ich ihn nicht leiden kann, ich finde ihn sogar ausgesprochen unsympathisch; ~ **from** it! ganz und gar nicht, (ganz) im Gegenteil; ~ **be it from me to** ... es sei mir ferne, zu ...; **so** ~ (*up to now*) bisher, bis jetzt; (*up to this point*) soweit; **so** ~ **this week** I've seen him once/three times/I haven't seen him at all diese Woche habe ich ihn erst einmal/schon dreimal/noch nicht gesehen; **so** ~ **so good** so weit, so gut; **so** ~ **and no further** bis hierher und nicht weiter; **to go** ~ (*money, supplies etc*) weit *or* (*last a long time also*) lange reichen; (*person: succeed*) es weit bringen; (*measures*) weit reichen; **these measures won't go very** ~ **towards stemming rising costs** diese Maßnahmen werden nicht viel dazu beitragen, die steigenden Kosten aufzuhalten; **I would go so** ~ **as to say** ... ich würde so weit gehen zu sagen ...; **that's going too** ~ das geht zu weit; **to carry a joke too** ~ einen Spaß zu weit treiben; **that's carrying a joke too** ~ da hört der Spaß auf; **not** ~ **out** (*in guess*) nicht schlecht; ~ **out** (*sl: fantastic*) einsame Klasse (*sl*); **not** ~ **off** (*in guess, aim*) fast (getroffen); (*almost*) nicht viel weniger; ~ **gone** (*inf*) schon ziemlich hinüber (*inf*).

2 *adj* (a) (*more distant of two*) weiter entfernt, hintere(r, s). **the** ~ **end of the room** das andere Ende des Zimmers; **the** ~ **window/door/wall** das Fenster/die Tür/Wand am anderen Ende des Zimmers; **at the** ~ **end of the road** am anderen Ende der Straße; **on the** ~ **side of** auf der anderen Seite von; **when he reached the** ~ **bank** als er am anderen Ufer ankam; **which of these cars is yours?** — **the** ~ **one** welches ist das Auto? — das, das weiter weg ist; **which bed will you have?** — **the** ~ **one** welches Bett möchtest du? — das da drüben.

(b) (~-*off*) *country, land* weitentfernt *attr.* **in the** ~ **distance** in weiter Ferne; **it's a** ~ **cry from** ... (*fig*) das ist etwas ganz anderes als ...; **it's a** ~ **cry from what she promised** at first ursprünglich hat sie etwas ganz anderes versprochen.

faraway [ˈfɑːrəweɪ] *adj attr place* abgelegen; (*fig: dreamy*) verträumt, versonnen. **a** ~ **voice** (*distant*) eine Stimme in *or* aus der Ferne; (*dreamy*) eine verträumte Stimme.

farce [fɑːs] *n* (*Theat, fig*) Farce *f*.

farcemeat [ˈfɑːsmiːt] *n see* **forcemeat.**

farcical [ˈfɑːsɪkəl] *adj* (*Theat*) possenhaft; (*fig: absurd*) absurd, grotesk.

fare [fɛəʳ] **1** *n* (a) (*charge*) Fahrpreis *m*; (*on plane*) Flugpreis *m*; (*on boat*) Preis *m* für die Überfahrt; (*money*) Fahrgeld *nt*. **what is the** ~? was kostet die Fahrt/der Flug/die Überfahrt?; ~s **please!** noch jemand ohne (*inf*), noch jemand zugestiegen?; **have you got the right** ~? haben Sie das Fahrgeld passend?; **he gave me (the cost of/money for) the** ~ er gab mir das Fahrgeld.

(b) (*passenger*) Fahrgast *m*.

(c) (*old, form: food*) Kost *f*.

2 *vi* **he** ~**d well** es ging *or* erging (*geh*) ihm gut; **we all** ~**d the same** es ging uns allen gleich; ~ **thee well** (*old*) leb(e) wohl (*old*).

Far East *n* **the** ~ der Ferne Osten.

fare stage *n* Fahrzone, Teilstrecke, Zahlgrenze *f*.

farewell [fɛəˈwel] **1** *n* Abschied *m*. **to make one's** ~s sich verabschieden; (*before a longer absence*) Abschied nehmen; **to bid sb** ~ jdm auf Wiedersehen *or* Lebewohl (*old*) sagen. **2** *interj* (*old*) lebt wohl (*old*); (*to friend, sweetheart*) leb(e) wohl (*old*).

farewell *in cpds* Abschieds-.

far: ~-**fetched** *adj* weithergeholt *attr*, weit hergeholt *pred*, an den Haaren herbeigezogen; ~-**flung** *adj* (a) (*distant*) abgelegen; (b) (*widely spread*) weit auseinandergezogen.

farinaceous [ˌfærɪˈneɪʃəs] *adj* mehlhaltig.

farm [fɑːm] **1** *n* Bauernhof *m*; (*bigger*) Gut(shof *m*) *nt*; (*in US, Australia, health* ~) Farm *f*; (*fish* ~) Fischzucht, Teichwirtschaft (*form*) *f*; (*mink* ~ *etc*) (Pelztier)zuchtfarm *f*.

2 *attr house* Bauern-; *produce, buildings,* landwirtschaftlich, Landwirtschafts-; *labourer* Land-. ~ **animals** Tiere auf dem Bauernhof.

3 *vt land* bebauen; *livestock* halten; *trout, mink etc* züchten.

4 *vi* Landwirtschaft betreiben. **man has been** ~**ing for thousands of years** der Mensch hat (be)treibt schon seit Jahrtausenden Ackerbau und Viehzucht.

♦**farm out** *vt sep work* vergeben (*on, to an* +*acc*); *children* in Pflege geben (*to dat, bei*).

farmer [ˈfɑːməʳ] *n* Bauer, Landwirt *m*; (*in US, Australia*) Farmer *m*; (*mink* ~) Züchter *m*; (*fish* ~) Teichwirt *m* (*form*); (*gentleman* ~) Gutsherr *m*; (*tenant* ~) Pächter *m*. ~'s **wife** Bäuerin *f*; ~'s **co-operative** landwirtschaftliche Genossenschaft.

farm: ~**hand** *n* Landarbeiter *m*; (*living on small farm*) Knecht *m*; ~**house** *n* Bauernhaus *nt*.

farming [ˈfɑːmɪŋ] *n* Landwirtschaft *f*; (*of crops also*) Ackerbau *m*; (*animals also*) Viehzucht *f*.

farm: ~ **land** *n* Ackerland *nt*; ~**stead** *n* Bauernhof *m*, Gehöft *nt*; ~**yard** *n* Hof *m*.

Far North *n* **the** ~ der Hohe Norden.

faro [ˈfɛərəʊ] *n* Phar(a)o *nt*.

far-off [fɑːˈrɒf] *adj* (weit)entfernt.

farrago [fəˈrɑːgəʊ] *n* Gemisch, Allerlei *nt*.

far-reaching [ˈfɑːˌriːtʃɪŋ] *adj* weitreichend.

farrier [ˈfærɪəʳ] *n* Hufschmied *m*.

farrow [ˈfærəʊ] **1** *vt piglets* werfen. **2** *vi* ferkeln. **3** *n* Wurf *m*.

far: ~-**seeing** *adj* weitblickend; ~-**sighted** *adj* (a) (*lit*) weitsichtig; (b) (*fig*) *person* weitblickend; (*taking precautionary measures*) umsichtig; *measures* auf weite Sicht geplant; ~-**sightedness** *n see adj* (a) Weitsichtigkeit *f*; (b) Weitblick *m*; Umsicht *f*; **the** ~-**sightedness of these measures** diese Maßnahmen, die Weitblick verraten.

fart [fɑːt] (*vulg*) **1** *n* Furz *m* (*inf*). **2** *vi* furzen (*inf*).

♦**fart about** *or* **around** *vi* (*vulg*) wie ein Furz an der Gardinenstange hin und her sausen (*sl*).

farther [ˈfɑːðəʳ] *comp of* **far 1** *adv see* **further 1** (a). **2** *adj* weiter entfernt, hintere(r, s). **at the** ~ **end** am anderen Ende.

farthermost [ˈfɑːðəməʊst] *adj see* **furthermost.**

farthest [ˈfɑːðɪst] *adj, adv superl of* **far** *see* **furthest 1, 2.**

farthing [ˈfɑːðɪŋ] *n* Farthing *m* (*ein Viertelpenny*). **I haven't a** ~ ich habe keinen roten Heller (*dated*).

farthingale [ˈfɑːðɪŋgeɪl] *n* Reifrock *m*, Krinoline *f*.

fascia [ˈfeɪʃə] *n* (*Brit Aut*) Armaturentafel *f*.

fascicle [ˈfæsɪkl], **fascicule** [ˈfæsɪkjuːl] *n* (a) (*Bot*) Büschel *nt*; (*Anat*) Bündel *nt*. (b) (*of book*) Lieferung *f*, Faszikel (*old*) *m*.

fascinate [ˈfæsɪneɪt] *vt faszinieren* (*geh*); (*enchant: skill, beauty, singer etc also*) begeistern, bezaubern; (*hold spellbound: book, film, magician also*) fesseln; (*snake etc*) hypnotisieren. **old houses** ~/**this subject** ~s **me** ich finde alte Häuser/dieses Gebiet hochinteressant *or* faszinierend (*geh*); **the audience watched/listened** ~**d** das Publikum sah/hörte gebannt zu; **it** ~s **me how skilfully he does these things** ich finde es erstaunlich, wie geschickt er das macht.

fascinating [ˈfæsɪneɪtɪŋ] *adj* faszinierend (*geh*); *subject, book, speaker, facts also* hochinteressant; *beauty, display, rhythm also* bezaubernd; *idea, person* außerordentlich, interessant; *selection* erstaunlich. **I find it** ~ **how quickly he does it** ich finde es erstaunlich, wie schnell er das macht; ~! (*iro*) umwerfend (*iro inf*), faszinierend (*iro geh*).

fascinatingly [ˈfæsɪneɪtɪŋlɪ] *adv* faszinierend (*geh*); *talk, describe* hochinteressant, fesselnd; *beautiful* bezaubernd.

fascination [ˌfæsɪˈneɪʃən] *n* Faszination *f* (*geh*); (*fascinating quality also*) Reiz *m*. **to listen/watch in** ~ gebannt zuhören/ zusehen; **to have** *or* **hold a** ~ **for sb** auf jdn einen besonderen Reiz ausüben; **his** ~ **with the cinema** der Reiz, den das Kino für ihn hat, die Faszination, die das Kino auf ihn ausübt (*geh*).

fascism [ˈfæʃɪzəm] *n* Faschismus *m*.

fascist [ˈfæʃɪst] **1** *n* Faschist(in *f*) *m*. **2** *adj* faschistisch.

fash [fæʃ] *vt* (*Scot*) (*trouble*) ärgern; (*worry*) aufregen.

fashion [ˈfæʃən] **1** *n* (a) *no pl* (*manner*) Art (und Weise) *f*. (**in the**) **Indian** ~ auf Indianerart, nach Art der Indianer; **in the usual** ~ wie üblich; **to behave/walk in a peculiar** ~ sich merkwürdig verhalten/merkwürdig gehen; **after** *or* **in a** ~ in gewisser Weise; **were you successful/have you translated it?** — **well, after a** ~ hast du Erfolg gehabt/es übersetzt? — na ja, so einigermaßen; **to do sth after** *or* **in a** ~ etw recht und schlecht machen; **a novel after** *or* **in the** ~ **of D.H. Lawrence** ein Roman im Stil von D.H Lawrence; **after** *or* **in this** ~ auf diese Weise, so.

(b) (*in clothing, latest style*) Mode *f*. **in** ~ modern; **it's the/all the** ~ es ist Mode/große Mode; **to come into/go out of** ~ in Mode/aus der Mode kommen; **a man of** ~ ein modischer Herr; **the Paris** ~s die Pariser Mode; ~s **in women's clothes** die Damenmode; **to set a** ~ eine Mode aufbringen.

(c) (*custom*) (*of society*) Sitte *f*, Brauch *m*; (*of individual*) Gewohnheit *f*. **it was the** ~ **in those days** das war damals Sitte *or* Brauch; **as was his** ~ (*old*) wie er zu tun pflegte (*geh*).

2 *vt* formen, gestalten. **to** ~ **sth after** *or* **sth** etw einer Sache (*dat*) nachbilden.

fashionable [ˈfæʃnəbl] *adj* (*stylish*) *clothes, person* modisch; *custom* modern; *illness, colour* Mode-; (*patronized by* ~ *people*) *area, address* vornehm; *pub, artist, author* in Mode. **all the** ~ **people go there** die Schickeria geht dahin; **a very** ~ **expression/artist** ein Modeausdruck/Mode- *or* Erfolgsautor; **it's (very)** ~ es ist (große) Mode.

fashionably [ˈfæʃnəblɪ] *adv* modisch; *behave* modern.

fashion *in cpds* Mode-; ~ **designer** *n* Modezeichner(in *f*) *m*; ~ **magazine** *n* Mode(n)heft *nt or* -zeitschrift *f*; ~ **model** *n* Mannequin *nt*; (*mann*) Dressman *m*; ~ **parade** *n* Mode(n)schau *f*; ~ **plate** *n* Modezeichnung *f*; **she looked like a** ~ **plate** sie sah aus wie aus der Modezeitung; ~ **show** *n* Mode(n)schau *f*.

fast¹ [fɑːst] **1** *adj* (+*er*) (a) (*quick*) schnell. **he's a** ~ **worker** (*lit*) er arbeitet schnell, (*fig*) er geht mächtig ran (*inf*); **to pull a** ~ **one on sb** (*inf*) jdn übers Ohr hauen (*inf*); ~ **lane** Überholspur *f*; ~ **train** D-Zug *m*.

(b) **to be** ~/**five minutes** ~ (*clock, watch*) vorgehen/fünf Minuten vorgehen.

(c) *tennis court, squash ball etc* schnell.

(d) (*Phot*) *film* hochempfindlich; *lens* lichtstark.

(e) (*fig: immoral*) *behaviour, person* locker, flott, ausschweifend (*pej*). ~ **woman** leichtlebige Frau.

2 *adv* (a) schnell.

(b) (*fig*) **to live** ~ flott *or* locker leben.

(c) (*old*) ~ **by** (*close by*) dicht bei; **to follow** ~ **on sth** dicht auf etw (*acc*) folgen.

fast² [fɑːst] **1** *adj* (a) (*film, secure*) fest. **is the rope** ~? ist das Tau fest(gemacht)?; **to make a boat** ~ ein Boot festmachen *or* vertäuen.

(b) *colour, dye* farbecht; (*against light also*) lichtecht; (*against washing also*) waschecht.

(c) (*staunch*) *friend* gut.

2 *adv* (a) (*firmly, securely*) fest. **to stick** ~ festsitzen; (*with glue*) festkleben; **to stand** ~ standhaft *or* fest bleiben; **to stand** ~ **by sb/sth** (*inf*) zu jdm stehen/an etw (*dat*) festhalten; **to hold** ~ **to sth** an etw (*dat*) festhalten; **to play** ~ **and loose with sb** mit jdm ein falsches *or* doppeltes Spiel treiben.

(b) (*soundly*) **to be** ~ **asleep** tief *or* fest schlafen.

fast³ **1** *vi* (*not eat*) fasten. **2** *n* Fasten *nt*; (*period of fasting*) Fastenzeit *f*. ~ **day** *n* Fasttag *m*; **to break one's** ~ das Fasten brechen.

fast: ~-**back** *n* (Wagen *m* mit) Fließheck *nt*; ~ **breeder reactor** *n* schneller Brüter.

fasten [ˈfɑːsn] **1** *vt* (a) (*attach*) festmachen, befestigen (*to, onto* an +*dat*); (*do up*) *parcel etc* zuschnüren; *buttons, buckle, dress etc* zumachen; (*tighten*) *screw etc* anziehen; (*lock*) *door* (ab)schließen. **to** ~ **two things together** zwei Dinge zusammenmachen (*inf*) *or* aneinander befestigen.

(b) (*fig*) *thoughts, attention* zuwenden (*on sb* jdm). **to** ~ **the** blame on sb die Schuld auf jdn schieben, jdm die Schuld in die Schuhe schieben (*inf*); **to ~ one's eyes on sth** die Augen *or* den Blick auf etw (*acc*) heften.

2 *vi* **sich schließen lassen. the dress ~s at the back** das Kleid wird hinten zugemacht; **the door won't ~** die Tür läßt sich nicht schließen; **these two pieces ~ together** diese zwei Teile werden miteinander verbunden; **this piece ~s in here** dieses Teil wird hier befestigt *or* gehört hier hinein.

◆**fasten down** *vt sep* festmachen.

◆**fasten in** *vt sep* festschnallen (*+prep obj* in *+dat*).

◆**fasten on 1** *vt sep* festmachen, festmachen (*+prep obj, -to* an *+dat*); *flower, badge* anheften (*+prep obj, -to* an *+dat*). **2** *vi* *+prep obj* (*fig*) **the teacher always ~s ~ Smith** der Lehrer hackt immer auf Smith herum (*inf*).

◆**fasten onto** *vi +prep obj* (*fig*) **to ~ ~ sb** sich an jdn hängen.

◆**fasten up** *vt sep dress etc* zumachen. **would you ~ me ~?** (*inf*) kannst du mir zumachen? (*inf*).

fastener ['fɑːsnə'], **fastening** ['fɑːsnɪŋ] *n* Verschluß *m*.

fastidious [fæs'tɪdɪəs] *adj* heikel, pingelig (*inf*) (*about* in bezug auf *+acc*).

fastness ['fɑːstnɪs] *n* (a) (*stronghold*) Feste *f*. **mountain ~** Bergfeste *f*. (b) (*of colours*) Farbechtheit *f*; (*against light also*) Lichtechtheit *f*. (c) (*immorality*) Liederlichkeit *f*.

fat [fæt] **1** *n* (*Anat, Cook, Chem*) Fett *nt*. **now the ~'s in the fire** jetzt ist der Teufel los (*inf*); **to live off the ~ of the land** (*fig*) wie Gott in Frankreich *or* wie die Made im Speck (*inf*) leben; **to put on ~** Speck ansetzen; **to run to ~** in die Breite gehen (*inf*).

2 *adj* (*+er*) (a) (*plump*) dick, fett (*pej*). **to get ~** dick werden; **she has got a lot ~ter** sie hat ziemlich zugenommen.

(b) (*containing fat*) *meat* fett.

(c) (*fig*) *volume* dick, umfangreich; *wallet, cigar* dick; *salary, cheque, profit* üppig, fett (*inf*); *part in play* umfangreich.

(d) (*iro inf*) **a ~ lot of good you are!** Sie sind ja 'ne schöne Hilfe! (*iro inf*); **a ~ lot he knows!** was der alles *or* nicht weiß (*iro inf*); **a ~ chance he's got** da hat er ja Mordschancen (*inf*).

(e) *land* fett.

fatal ['feɪtl] *adj* (*lit*) tödlich (*to* für); (*fig*) verheerend, fatal, verhängnisvoll; (*fateful*) *day, decision* schicksalsschwer. **that would be ~** das wäre das Ende (*to gen*), das wäre tödlich (*inf*); **to be a ~ blow to sb/sth** ein schwerer Schlag für jdn/etw sein; **to deal sb/sth a ~ blow** jdm/einer Sache einen schweren Schlag versetzen; **an incident that proved ~ to** their diplomatic relations ein Vorfall, der verheerende Auswirkungen auf ihre diplomatischen Beziehungen hatte; **it's ~ to say that** das ist fatal, so was zu sagen.

fatalism ['feɪtəlɪzəm] *n* Fatalismus *m*.

fatalist ['feɪtəlɪst] *n* Fatalist(in *f*) *m*.

fatalistic *adj*, **~ally** *adv* [feɪtə'lɪstɪk, -əlɪ] fatalistisch.

fatality [fə'tælɪtɪ] *n* (a) Todesfall *m*; (*in accident, war etc*) (Todes)opfer *nt*. (b) (*liter: inevitability*) Unabwendbarkeit *f*.

fatally ['feɪtəlɪ] *adv wounded* tödlich. **to be ~ attracted to sb** jdm hoffnungslos verfallen sein.

fata morgana [fɑːtəmɔː'gɑːnə] *n* Fata Morgana *f*.

fate [feɪt] *n* Schicksal *nt*. **the F~s** *pl* (*Myth*) die Parzen *pl*; **~ decided otherwise** das Schicksal wollte es anders, das Schicksal hat es anders bestimmt; **the examiners meet to decide our ~** next week die Prüfer kommen nächste Woche zusammen, um über unser Schicksal zu entscheiden; **to leave sb to his ~** jdn seinem Schicksal überlassen; **to go to meet one's ~** seinem Schicksal entgegentreten; **to meet one's ~** vom Schicksal heimgesucht *or* ereilt (*geh*) werden; **as sure as ~** it will go wrong/it went wrong das ganz garantiert schief/das ist natürlich prompt schiefgegangen.

fated ['feɪtɪd] *adj* unglückselig; *project, plan* zum Scheitern verurteilt. **to be ~** unter einem ungünstigen Stern stehen; **to be ~ to fail** *or* **be unsuccessful** zum Scheitern verurteilt sein; **they were ~ never to meet again** es war ihnen bestimmt, sich nie wiederzusehen; **their plans were ~ to be forgotten** ihre Pläne waren dazu verurteilt, vergessen zu werden.

fateful ['feɪtfʊl] *adj* (*disastrous*) verhängnisvoll; (*momentous*) schicksalsschwer.

fat-: ~head *n* (*inf*) Dummkopf, Blödian (*inf*) *m*; **~headed** *adj* (*inf*) dumm, blöd (*inf*).

father ['fɑːðə'] **1** *n* (a) (*lit, fig*) Vater *m* (*to sb* jdm). **from ~ to son** vom Vater auf den Sohn; **like ~ like son** der Apfel fällt nicht weit vom Stamm; (*Old*) **F~ Time** die Zeit (*als Allegorie*).

(b) **~s** *pl* (*ancestors*) Väter *pl*.

(c) (*founder*) Vater *m*; (*leader*) Führer, Vater (*liter*) *m*. **the F~s of the Church** die Kirchenväter *pl*.

(d) (*God*) **F~** Vater *m*.

(e) (*priest*) Pfarrer *m*; (*monk*) Pater *m*. **good morning, ~** guten Morgen, Herr Pfarrer/Pater X; **the Holy F~** der Heilige Vater; **~ confessor** Beichtvater *m*.

2 *vt* (a) *child* zeugen; (*admit paternity*) die Vaterschaft anerkennen für; (*fig*) *idea, plan* Urheber (*+gen*) sein.

(b) (*saddle with responsibility*) **to ~ sth on sb** jdm die Verantwortung für etw aufhalsen (*inf*) *or* aufbürden (*inf*); **to ~ the blame on sb** jdm die Schuld in die Schuhe schieben (*inf*).

father-: F~ Christmas *n* der Weihnachtsmann; **~-figure** *n* Vaterfigur *f*; **~hood** *n* Vaterschaft *f*; **~-in-law** *n* Schwiegervater *m*; **~land** *n* Vaterland *nt*; **~less** *adj* vaterlos.

fatherly ['fɑːðəlɪ] *adj* väterlich, wie ein Vater.

fathom ['fæðəm] **1** *n* Faden *m*. **2** *vt* (a) (*lit*) ausloten. (b) (*understand*) ermessen (*geh*); (*inf: also* **~ out**) verstehen. **I just can't ~ him** (out) er ist mir ein Rätsel; **I couldn't ~ it** (out) ich kann der Sache nicht auf den Grund, ich kann nicht dahinter (*inf*).

fathomable ['fæðəməbl] *adj* (*fig*) faßbar. **not ~** unerforschlich.

fathomless ['fæðəmlɪs] *adj* (*lit*) abgründlich; (*fig*) (*boundless*) unermeßlich; (*incomprehensible*) unergründlich.

fatigue [fə'tiːg] **1** *n* (a) Abspannung, Erschöpfung, Ermüdung *f*. (b) (*Tech: metal ~*) Ermüdung *f*. (c) (*Mil: ~ duty*)

to be on ~ (*Mil*) Arbeitsdienst haben. (d) **~s** *pl* (*Mil*) see **~ dress**. 2 *vt* (a) (*tire*) ermüden; (*exhaust*) erschöpfen. (b) (*Tech*) *metal* ermüden. 3 *vi* ermüden.

fatigue: ~ dress *n* Arbeitsanzug *m*; **in ~ dress** im Arbeitsanzug; (*on duty*) in Arbeitseinsatz, Arbeitsdienst *m*; **~ party** *n* Arbeitskommando *nt*.

fatiguing [fə'tiːgɪŋ] *adj* (*tiring*) ermüdend; (*exhausting*) erschöpfend.

fatness ['fætnɪs] *n see adj* (*a-c*) (a) Dicke, Fettheit (*pej*) *f*. (b) Fettigkeit *f*. (c) Umfang *m*; Dicke *f*; Üppigkeit, Fettheit (*inf*) *f*; Umfang *m*. (d) (*fig: of land*) Fruchtbarkeit *f*.

fatso ['fætsəʊ] *n* (*inf*) Dicke(r) (*inf*), Fettsack (*pej inf*) *m*.

fat stock *n* Mastvieh *nt*.

fatted ['fætɪd] *adj*: **to kill the ~ calf** einen Willkommensschmaus veranstalten.

fatten ['fætn] **1** *vt* (*also* **~ up**) *animals* mästen; *people* herausfüttern (*inf*). **are you trying to ~ me up?** (*inf*) du willst mich wohl mästen? (*inf*).

2 *vi* (*also* **~ up** *or* **out**) (*animal*) fett werden; (*person*) dick werden; (*through overeating*) sich mästen (*inf*).

fattening ['fætnɪŋ] *adj food* dick machend. **chocolate is ~** Schokolade macht dick.

fatty ['fætɪ] **1** *adj* fett; *food also* fetthaltig; (*greasy*) fettig; *acid, tissue* Fett-. **~ degeneration** (*Med*) Verfettung *f*; **~ tumour** Fettgeschwulst *f*. **2** *n* (*inf*) Dickerchen *nt* (*inf*).

fatuity [fə'tjuːɪtɪ] *n* Albernheit *f*; (*remark, action also*) törichte Bemerkung/Tat (*geh*).

fatuous ['fætjʊəs] *adj* töricht (*geh*), albern.

faucet ['fɔːsɪt] *n* (*US*) Hahn *m*.

faugh [fɔː] *interj* (*old*) pfui.

fault [fɔːlt] **1** *n* (a) (*mistake, defect*) Fehler *m*; (*Tech also*) Defekt *m*; (*in sth bought also*) Mangel *m*. **generous to a ~** übermäßig großzügig; **to find ~ with sb/sth** etwas an jdm/etw auszusetzen haben; **he/my memory was at ~** er war im Unrecht/mein Gedächtnis hat mich getrogen; **you were at ~ in not telling me** es war nicht recht von Ihnen, daß Sie mir das nicht gesagt haben.

(b) *no pl* **it won't be my/his ~ if ...** es ist nicht meine/seine Schuld, wenn ..., ich bin/er ist nicht schuld, wenn ...; **whose ~ is it?** wer ist schuld (daran)?; **it's all your own ~** das ist Ihre eigene Schuld, Sie sind selbst schuld.

(c) (*Geol*) Verwerfung *f*.

(d) (*Tennis, Horseriding*) Fehler *m*.

2 *vt* (a) Fehler finden an (*+dat*), etwas auszusetzen haben an (*+dat*). **I can't ~ it** ich habe nichts daran auszusetzen; (*can't disprove it*) ich kann es nicht widerlegen.

(b) (*Geol*) eine Verwerfung verursachen in (*+dat*).

3 *vi* (*Geol*) sich verwerfen.

fault: ~-finder *n* Krittler(in *f*) *m*; **~-finding 1** *adj* krittelig; **2** *n* Krittelei *f*.

faultily *adv* falsch.

faultless ['fɔːltlɪs] *adj appearance* tadellos, einwandfrei; (*without mistakes*) fehlerlos; *English* fehlerfrei, fehlerlos.

faulty ['fɔːltɪ] *adj* (*+er*) (*Tech*) defekt; (*Comm*) fehlerhaft; *reasoning, logic* falsch, fehlerhaft.

faun [fɔːn] *n* (*Myth*) Faun *m*.

fauna ['fɔːnə] *n* Fauna *f*.

faux pas [fəʊ'pɑː] *n* Fauxpas *m*.

favour, (*US*) **favor** ['feɪvə'] **1** *n* (a) *no pl* (*goodwill*) Gunst *f*, Wohlwollen *nt*. **to win/lose sb's ~** jds Gunst (*acc*) erlangen (*geh*)/verscherzen; **to find ~ with sb** bei jdm Anklang finden; **to get back in(to) sb's ~** von jdm wieder in Gnaden aufgenommen werden; **to be in ~ with sb** bei jdm gut angeschrieben sein; (*fashion, pop star, writer etc*) bei jdm beliebt sein, bei jdm gut ankommen; **to be/fall out of ~** in Ungnade (*gefallen*) sein/fallen; (*fashion, pop star, writer etc*) nicht mehr beliebt sein (*with bei*)/nicht mehr ankommen (*with bei*).

(b) **to be in ~ of sth** für etw sein; **a point in his ~** ein Punkt zu seinen Gunsten, ein Punkt, der für ihn spricht; **all those in ~ raise their hands** alle, die dafür sind, Hand hoch; **see balance**.

(c) (*partiality*) Vergünstigung *f*. **to show ~ to sb** jdn bevorzugen.

(d) (*act of kindness*) Gefallen *m*, Gefälligkeit *f*. **to ask a ~ of sb** jdn um einen Gefallen bitten; **to do sb a ~** jdm einen Gefallen tun; **do me a ~!** (*inf*) sei so gut!; **would you do me the ~ of returning my library books?** wären Sie bitte so freundlich und würden meine Bücher in die Bücherei zurückbringen?; **do me the ~ of shutting up!** (*inf*) tu mir einen Gefallen und halt den Mund!; **as a ~** aus Gefälligkeit; **as a ~ to him** ihm zuliebe.

(e) (*old: ribbon etc*) Schleife *f*.

(f) **to enjoy sb's ~s** jds (*Liebes*)gunst genießen (*dated geh*).

(g) (*on wedding cake*) Verzierung, (*Kuchen*)dekoration *f*.

2 *vt* (a) *plan, idea* (*be in ~ of*) für gut halten; (*think preferable*) bevorzugen. **I don't ~ the idea** ich halte nichts von der Idee; **I ~ the second suggestion** ich bin für den zweiten Vorschlag.

(b) (*show preference*) bevorzugen; (*king etc*) begünstigen.

(c) (*oblige, honour*) beehren (*form*). **to ~ sb with one's attention/a smile** an interview jdm gütigerweise seine Aufmerksamkeit/ein Lächeln/ein Interview gewähren (*geh*).

(d) (*be favourable for*) begünstigen.

(e) (*US: resemble*) ähneln (*+dat*).

favourable, (*US*) **favorable** ['feɪvərəbl] *adj* günstig, vorteilhaft (*for, to* für); (*expressing approval*) positiv.

favourableness, (*US*) **favorableness** ['feɪvərəblnɪs] *n* Günstigkeit *f*. **the ~ of his reply/report** seine positive Antwort/sein positiver Bericht.

favourably, (*US*) **favorably** ['feɪvərəblɪ] *adv see adj* vorteilhaft, positiv. **to be ~ inclined to sb/sth** sich positiv zu jdm/etw stellen, jdm/einer Sache gewogen sein (*geh*).

favoured, (US) **favored** ['feɪvəd] adj the/a ~ few die wenigen Auserwählten/einige (wenige) Auserwählte; a ~ friend ein besonderer Freund.

favourite, (US) **favorite** ['feɪvərɪt] **1** n (a) (person) Liebling m; (Hist, pej) Günstling m. he is a universal ~ er ist allgemein beliebt; **which of her children/suitors is her ~?** welches Kind/welchen Verehrer mag sie am liebsten?, welches ihrer Kinder ist ihr Liebling/welcher Verehrer ist der Favorit?

(b) (thing) this one is my ~ das habe ich am liebsten; this film/dress/photograph is my ~ das ist mein Lieblingsfilm/-kleid/-bild; we sang all the old ~s wir haben all die alten Lieder gesungen.

(c) (Sport) Favorit(in f) m. Chelsea are the ~s Chelsea ist (der) Favorit.

2 adj attr Lieblings-. ~ son (US Pol) regionaler Spitzenkandidat.

favouritism, (US) **favoritism** ['feɪvərɪtɪzəm] n Vetternwirtschaft (inf), Günstlingswirtschaft f; (in school) Schätzchenwirtschaft (inf), Lieblingswirtschaft f.

fawn¹ [fɔːn] **1** n (a) Hirschkalb nt; (of roe deer) Rehkitz nt. **(b)** (colour) Beige nt. **2** adj colour beige.

fawn² vi (dog) (mit dem Schwanz) wedeln; (fig: person) katzbuckeln (on, upon vor +dat), herumschwänzeln (on, upon um).

fawning ['fɔːnɪŋ] adj person, manner kriecherisch, liebedienernd; dog schwanzwedelnd.

fay [feɪ] n (liter: fairy) Fee f.

faze [feɪz] vt (US inf) verdattern (inf). it didn't ~ me es hat mich nicht gejuckt (sl).

FBI (US) abbr of **Federal Bureau of Investigation** FBI m.

FC abbr of **football club** FC m.

Feb abbr of **February** Febr.

fealty ['fiːəltɪ] n (Hist) Lehnstreue f.

fear [fɪər] **1** n (a) Angst, Furcht f (or vor +dat). he has ~s for his sister's life er fürchtet für or um das Leben seiner Schwester; **have no ~** (old, hum) fürchte dich nicht (old, hum); **in ~ and trembling** mit schlotternden Knien; **to be/go in ~ of sb/sth** Angst vor jdm/etw haben/in (ständiger) Angst vor jdm/etw leben; **to be/go in ~ of one's life** um sein/ständig um sein Leben bangen; **for ~ that ...** aus Angst, daß ...; **she asked us to be quiet/she talked quietly for ~ of waking the child** sie bat uns, leise zu sein, damit wir das Kind nicht wecken/sie sprach leise, um das Kind nicht aufzuwecken; **without ~ or favour** ganz gerecht.

(b) no pl (risk, likelihood) no ~! (inf) nie im Leben! (inf); there's no ~ of that happening again keine Angst, das passiert so leicht nicht wieder; there's not much ~ of his coming wir brauchen kaum Angst zu haben, daß er kommt.

(c) (awe: of God) Scheu, Ehrfurcht f. to put the ~ of God into sb (inf) jdm gewaltig Angst einjagen (inf).

2 vt (a) (be)fürchten. I ~ the worst ich befürchte das Schlimmste; he's a man to be ~ed er ist ein Mann, vor dem man Angst haben muß; they did not ~ to die (liter) sie fürchteten den Tod nicht.

(b) (feel awe for) God Ehrfurcht haben vor (+dat).

3 vi to ~ for fürchten für or um; never ~! keine Angst!

fearful ['fɪəfʊl] adj (a) (frightening, inf: terrible) furchtbar, schrecklich.

(b) (apprehensive) ängstlich, bang. he was ~ lest he fail/be discovered (old) ihm bangte davor zu versagen/entdeckt zu werden; to be ~ for one's/sb's life um sein/jds Leben fürchten; I was ~ of waking her ich befürchtete, daß ich sie aufwecken würde.

fearfully ['fɪəfʊlɪ] adv see adj.

fearfulness ['fɪəfʊlnɪs] n see adj Furchtbarkeit, Schrecklichkeit f; Ängstlichkeit f.

fearless ['fɪəlɪs] adj furchtlos. ~ of sth ohne Angst or Furcht vor etw (dat); to be ~ of heights/the consequences keine Angst vor Höhen/vor den Folgen haben, Höhen/die Folgen nicht fürchten.

fearlessly ['fɪəlɪslɪ] adv see adj.

fearlessness ['fɪəlɪsnɪs] n Furchtlosigkeit f.

fearsome adj, **~ly** adv ['fɪəsəm, -lɪ] furchterregend.

feasibility [,fiːzə'bɪlɪtɪ] n (a) (practicability: of plan etc) Durchführbarkeit, Machbarkeit f. ~ study Machbarkeitsstudie f; the ~ of doing sth die Möglichkeit, etw zu tun; I doubt the ~ of doing that ich glaube nicht, daß das möglich or machbar ist.

(b) (plausibility: of story etc) Wahrscheinlichkeit f.

feasible ['fiːzəbl] adj (a) (possible) möglich, machbar; plan also durchführbar, realisierbar; route gangbar, möglich. **(b)** (likely, probable) excuse, story, theory plausibel, wahrscheinlich.

feasibly ['fiːzəblɪ] adv (a) if it can ~ be done wenn es machbar ist or praktisch möglich ist; it can't ~ be done es ist praktisch nicht möglich, es ist nicht machbar. **(b)** plausibel. that could ~ be true das könnte durchaus stimmen.

feast [fiːst] **1** n (a) (banquet) Festmahl, Festessen nt; (Hist) Festgelage nt. a ~ for the eyes eine Augenweide.

(b) (Eccl, Rel) Fest nt. ~ day n Festtag, Feiertag m; movable/immovable ~ beweglicher/unbeweglicher Feiertag.

2 vi (lit) Festgelage pl/ein Festgelage halten. to ~ on sth sich an etw (dat) gütlich tun; (person also) in etw (dat) schwelgen; (fig) sich an etw (dat) weiden.

3 vt (a) guest festlich bewirten. to ~ oneself sich gütlich tun (on an +dat); (person also) schwelgen (on in +dat).

(b) to ~ one's eyes on sb/sth seine Augen an jdm/etw weiden.

feat [fiːt] n Leistung f; (heroic, courageous etc) Heldentat f; (skilful) Kunststück nt, Meisterleistung f. a ~ of courage/daring eine mutige/wagemutige Tat; a ~ of strength eine Kraftleistung.

feather ['feðər] **1** n Feder f. ~s (plumage) Gefieder nt; (on dart, arrow also) Befiederung f; as light as a ~ federleicht; in fine ~ (inf) in guter Laune; (in top form) in Hoch-

form; that's a ~ in his cap das ist ein Ruhmesblatt nt für ihn; you could have knocked me down with a ~ (inf) ich war wie vom Donner gerührt; that'll make the ~s fly das wird die Gemüter bewegen; birds of a ~ flock together (Prov) gleich und gleich gesellt sich gern (Prov); see white ~.

2 vt (a) arrow etc mit Federn versehen. to ~ one's nest (fig) sein Schäfchen ins trockene bringen.

(b) (Aviat) propeller auf Segelstellung bringen.

(c) (Rowing) oar flachdrehen.

3 vi (Rowing) das Ruderblatt flachdrehen.

feather: ~-bed **1** n mit Federn gefüllte Matratze; **2** vt (fig) person verhätscheln; (Ind) (with grants) verhätscheln; (by overmanning) unnötige Arbeitskräfte zugestehen (+dat); ~brain n Spatzenhirn nt; ~brained adj dümmlich; ~ duster n Staubwedel m.

feathered ['feðəd] adj gefiedert.

feather: ~ headdress n Kopfschmuck m aus Federn; ~weight (Boxing) **1** n Federgewicht nt; (fig) Leichtgewicht nt; **2** adj Federgewicht-.

feathery ['feðərɪ] adj (+er) fed(e)rig; feel zart.

feature ['fiːtʃər] **1** n (a) (facial) (Gesichts)zug m.

(b) (characteristic) Merkmal, Kennzeichen, Charakteristikum nt; (of sb's character) Grundzug m. a ~ of his style is ... sein Stil ist durch ... gekennzeichnet; a ~ of this book is ... das Buch zeichnet sich durch ... aus.

(c) (focal point: of room, building etc) Charakteristikum nt. to make a ~ of sth etw besonders betonen or hervorheben.

(d) (Press) (Sonder)beitrag m, Feature nt or f; (Rad, TV) (Dokumentar)bericht m, Feature nt or f.

(e) (film) Spielfilm m.

2 vt (a) (Press) story, picture bringen.

(b) (film) this film ~s an English actress in diesem Film spielt eine englische Schauspielerin mit.

3 vi vorkommen. **(b)** (Film) (mit)spielen.

feature: ~ article n Sonderbeitrag m, Feature nt or f; ~ film n Spielfilm m; ~ fireplace n offener Kamin; ~-length adj film mit Spielfilmlänge; ~less adj ohne besondere Merkmale; ~ story n Sonderbericht m, Feature nt or f; ~ writer n Journalist, der Features schreibt.

febrile ['fiːbraɪl] adj fiebrig, fieberhaft.

February ['februərɪ] n Februar m; see September.

feces ['fiːsiːz] npl (US) see faeces.

feckless ['fekɪs] adj nutzlos.

fecund ['fiːkənd] adj (lit, fig) fruchtbar.

fecundate ['fiːkəndeɪt] vt befruchten.

fecundity [fɪ'kʌndɪtɪ] n (lit, fig) Fruchtbarkeit f.

fed¹ [fed] pret, ptp of **feed**.

fed² n (US inf) FBI-Agent m.

federal ['fedərəl] adj (a) Bundes-; system etc föderativ, föderal; (US Hist) föderalistisch. ~ state (in US) (Einzel)staat m; the F~ Republic of Germany die Bundesrepublik Deutschland. **2** n (US Hist) Föderalist m; (US inf) FBI-Mann m.

federalism ['fedərəlɪzəm] n Föderalismus m.

federalist ['fedərəlɪst] **1** adj föderalistisch. **2** n Föderalist m.

federate ['fedəreɪt] **1** vt zu einem Bund vereinigen or zusammenschließen, föderieren (rare). **2** vi sich zu einem Bund vereinigen or zusammenschließen. **3** ['fedərɪt] adj verbündet, föderiert.

federation [,fedə'reɪʃən] n (a) (act) Zusammenschluß m, Föderation f (rare). **(b)** (league) Föderation f, Bund m.

fed up (inf) I'm ~ ich habe die Nase voll (inf); I'm ~ with him/it er/es hängt mir zum Hals heraus (inf), ich habe ihn/es satt; you're looking pretty ~ du siehst so aus, als hättest du die Nase voll (inf); I'm ~ waiting for him ich habe es satt or ich bin es leid, auf ihn zu warten.

fee [fiː] n (a) Gebühr f; (of doctor, lawyer, artist, tutor) Honorar nt; (of stage performer) Gage f; (of director, administrator etc) Bezüge pl; (membership ~) Beitrag m. (school) ~s Schulgeld nt; on payment of a small ~ gegen geringe Gebühr. **(b)** land held in ~ simple (Jur) unbeschränkt vererbbares Land.

feeble ['fiːbl] adj (+er) schwach; voice, smile also matt; attempt kläglich, schwach.

feeble: ~-minded adj dümmlich; ~ness n see adj Schwäche f; Mattheit f; Kläglichkeit f.

feebly ['fiːblɪ] adv see adj schwach; matt; kläglich.

feed [fiːd] (vb: pret, ptp fed) **1** n (a) (meal) (of animals) Fütterung f; (of baby, inf: of person) Mahlzeit f; (food) (of animals) Futter nt; (inf: of person) Essen nt. when is the baby's next ~? wann wird das Baby wieder gefüttert?; to have a good ~ (inf) tüchtig futtern (inf); he's off his ~ (hum) er hat keinen Appetit.

(b) (Theat) Stichwort nt. a bad ~ spoilt his lines ein schlecht gegebenes Stichwort verdarb ihm seinen Text.

(c) (Tech) (to machine) Versorgung f (to gen); (to furnace) Beschickung f (to gen); (to computer) Eingabe f (into in +acc).

2 vt (a) (provide food for) person verpflegen; family, army also ernähren. to ~ oneself sich selbst verpflegen; he ~s himself well er ißt gut.

(b) (give food to) baby, invalid, animal füttern. to ~ oneself (child) allein or ohne Hilfe essen (können); to ~ sth to sb/an animal jdm/einem Tier etw zu essen/fressen geben; they were fed to the lions sie wurden den Löwen zum Fraß vorgeworfen.

(c) (supply) machine versorgen; furnace beschicken; computer füttern; meter Geld einwerfen in (+acc), füttern (hum); (fire) unterhalten, etwas legen auf (+acc); (fig) hope, imagination, rumour nähren, Nahrung geben (+dat). two rivers ~ this reservoir dieses Reservoir wird von zwei Flüssen gespeist; to ~ sth into a machine etw in eine Maschine geben; to ~ coolant into a machine einer Maschine (dat) Kühlmittel zuführen; to ~ information to sb, to ~ sb with information jdm Informationen zustecken, jdn mit Informationen versorgen.

(d) (*Tech: insert*) führen. **to ~ sth along/through a tube** etw an einem Röhrchen entlang/durch ein Röhrchen führen.

(e) (*Theat, fig*) **to ~ sb (with) the right lines** jdm die richtigen Stichworte geben.

3 *vi* (*animal*) fressen; (*baby*) gefüttert werden; (*hum: person*) futtern (*inf*).

♦**feed back** *vt sep facts, information* zurückleiten (*to an* +*acc*); (*Elec*) rückkoppeln. **by the time the information had been fed ~ to him** als die Informationen schließlich zu ihm zurückkamen; **to ~ sth ~ into the computer** dem Computer etw wieder eingeben.

♦**feed in** *vt sep tape, wire etc* einführen (*prep obj in* +*acc*); *facts, information* eingeben (*prep obj in* +*acc*).

♦**feed on 1** *vi* +*prep obj* sich (er)nähren von; (*fig*) sich nähren von. **2** *vt sep* +*prep obj animal, baby* füttern mit; *person* ernähren mit.

♦**feed up** *vt sep animal* mästen. **to ~ sb ~** jdn aufpäppeln; *see also* **fed up**.

feed: ~**back** *n* (*Psych, Computers*) Feedback *nt*, Rückmeldung *f*; (*Elec*) Rückkoppelung *f*; (*fig*) Reaktion *f*, Feedback *nt*; ~**back of information** Rückinformation *f*. **in our discussion group each participant should try to get as much ~back as possible from the others** in unserer Diskussionsgruppe sollte jeder Teilnehmer von den anderen möglichst viel zurückbekommen; **to provide more ~back about sth** ausführlicher über etw (*acc*) berichten; **to put on the ~bag** (*inf*) **to put on the ~bag** (*inf*) eine Mahlzeit einlegen.

feeder ['fiːdə'] **1** *n* (**a**) (*person*) Versorger *m*; (*bottle*) Flasche *f*. **automatic ~** Futterautomat *m*.
(**b**) (*eater*) Esser(in *f*) *m*. **the cow is a good ~** die Kuh frißt gut.
(**c**) (*supplying machine*) (*person*) Material zuführende Person; (*device*) Zubringer *m*.
(**d**) (*contributory source*) (*river*) Zu(bringer)fluß *m*; (*road*) Zubringer(straße *f*) *m*; (*air, bus, rail service*) Zubringerlinie *f*; (*Elec*) Speiseleitung *f*, Feeder *m*. ~ **pipe** Zuleitungsrohr *nt*.
2 *attr plane etc* Zubringer-.

feeding ['fiːdɪŋ] ~ **bottle** *n* Flasche *f*; ~ **time** *n* (*for animal*) Fütterungszeit *f*; (*for baby*) Zeit *f* für die Mahlzeit.

feel [fiːl] (*vb: pret, ptp* **felt**) **1** *vt* (**a**) (*touch*) fühlen; (*examining*) befühlen. **to ~ one's way** sich vortasten; **I'm still ~ing my way around** ich versuche noch, mich zu orientieren; **to ~ one's way into sth** sich in etw (*acc*) einfühlen.
(**b**) (*be aware of by touching, feeling*) *prick, sun etc* fühlen, spüren. **I can't ~ anything in my left leg** ich habe kein Gefühl im linken Bein; **I felt it move** ich spürte, wie es sich bewegte.
(**c**) (*be conscious of in oneself*) *regret, joy, fear etc* fühlen, verspüren, empfinden; *effects* spüren. **I could ~ him getting angry** ich merkte or spürte, daß er wütend wurde; **we all felt the ignominy he suffered** wir spürten or fühlten alle, welche Schmach das für ihn war; **he felt a sense of regret** er empfand Bedauern; **can't you ~ the sadness in this music?** können Sie nicht empfinden, wie traurig diese Musik ist?
(**d**) (*be affected by*) *heat, cold, insult* leiden unter (+*dat*); *loss also* empfinden. **I don't ~ the cold as much as he does** die Kälte macht mir nicht so viel aus wie ihm; **a right hook which he really felt** ein rechter Haken, der saß; **she's fallen, I bet she felt that!** sie ist hingefallen, das hat bestimmt weh getan.
(**e**) (*think*) glauben. **what do you ~ about him/it?** was halten Sie von ihm/davon?; **it was felt that ...** man war der Meinung, daß ...; **he felt it necessary or** hielt es für notwendig; **don't ~ you have to ...** glauben Sie nicht, Sie müßten ...

2 *vi* (**a**) (*indicating physical or mental state: person*) sich fühlen. **to ~ well/ill/secure/apprehensive/relaxed/depressed** sich wohl/elend/sicher/unsicher/entspannt/deprimiert fühlen; **how do you ~ today?** wie fühlen Sie sich heute?; **to ~ convinced/certain** überzeugt/sicher sein; **to ~ hungry/thirsty/sleepy** hungrig/durstig/müde sein, Hunger/Durst/Schlaf haben; **I ~ hot/cold** mir ist heiß/kalt; **I felt very touched at or by his remarks** ich war sehr gerührt von seinen Bemerkungen; **I ~ much better** ich fühle mich viel besser, es geht mir viel besser; **you'll ~ all the better for a holiday** ein Urlaub wird Ihnen guttun; **he doesn't ~ quite himself today** er ist heute nicht ganz auf der Höhe; **I felt as if I was going to faint** ich fühlte mich einer Ohnmacht nahe; **I felt strange mir** war traurig/komisch zumute; **I felt as though I'd never been away/I'd seen him before** mir war, als ob ich nie weggewesen wäre/als ob ich ihn schon mal gesehen hätte; **I felt as if I was going to be sick/to explode** ich dachte, mir würde schlecht werden/ich würde gleich explodieren; **how do you ~ about him?** (*emotionally*) was empfinden Sie für ihn?; **you can imagine what I felt like or how I felt** Sie können sich (*dat*) vorstellen, wie mir zumute war.
(**b**) (~ **to the touch:** *material, ground, bricks etc*) sich anfühlen. **to ~ hard/soft/rough etc** sich hart/weich/rauh *etc* anfühlen; **the room/air ~s warm** das Zimmer/die Luft kommt einem warm vor; **my skin ~s tight** mir spannt die Haut.
(**c**) (*think, have opinions*) meinen. **I ~ something should be done about it** ich bin der Meinung or ich meine, daß da etwas getan werden müßte; **how do you ~ about him/the idea/going for a walk?** was halten Sie von ihm/der Idee/von einem Spaziergang or davon spazierenzugehen?; **how do you ~ about these developments?** was meinen Sie zu dieser Entwicklung?; **that's just how I ~** das meine ich auch, ich bin genau derselben Meinung.
(**d**) **to ~ like** (*have desire for*) Lust haben auf (+*acc*); (*for food also*) Appetit haben auf (+*acc*); **I ~ like eating something/going for a walk** ich könnte jetzt etwas essen/ich habe Lust spazierenzugehen; **I felt like screaming/crying/giving up** ich hätte am liebsten geschrien/geheult/aufgegeben, ich hätte schreien/heulen/aufgeben können; **if you ~ like it** wenn Sie Lust haben, wenn Sie wollen or gern möchten.

(**e**) *impers* **what does it ~ like or how does it ~ to be all alone?** wie fühlt man sich or wie ist das so ganz allein?; **what does it ~ like or how does it ~ to be the boss?** wie fühlt man sich als Chef?, was ist das für ein Gefühl, Chef zu sein?; **what does it ~ like or how does it ~ to drive a racing car?** wie fühlt man sich or wie ist es, wenn man einen Rennwagen fährt?; **it ~s like flying** es ist wie Fliegen.

3 *n, no pl* (**a**) **let me have a ~** (of it)! laß (mich) mal fühlen!
(**b**) (*quality when touched*) **it has a velvety/scaly ~** es fühlt sich samten/schuppig an; **he recognizes things by their ~** er erkennt Dinge daran, wie sie sich anfühlen; **I don't like the ~ of wool against my skin** ich mag Wolle nicht auf der Haut.
(**c**) (*fig*) **to get/have a ~ for sth** ein Gefühl für etw bekommen/haben; **to get the ~ for sth** ein Gefühl für etw bekommen; **you must get the ~ of the poem** Sie müssen sich in das Gedicht einfühlen.

♦**feel about** or **around** *vi* umhertasten; (*in drawer, bag etc*) herumsuchen.

♦**feel for** *vi* +*prep obj* (**a**) (*sympathize with*) (mit)fühlen mit, Mitgefühl haben mit. **I ~ ~ you** Sie tun mir leid. (**b**) (*search or grope for*) tasten nach; (*in pocket, bag etc*) kramen nach.

♦**feel up to** *vi* +*prep obj* sich gewachsen fühlen (+*dat*).

feeler ['fiːlə'] *n* (**a**) (*Zool*) Fühler *m*; (*of sea animal*) Tentakel *m or nt*. (**b**) (*fig*) Fühler *m*. **to throw or put out ~s/a ~** seine Fühler ausstrecken. (**c**) ~**s** *pl* (*also ~ gauge*) Fühl(er)lehre *f*.

feeling ['fiːlɪŋ] *n* (**a**) (*sense of touch*) Gefühl *nt*, Empfindung *f*. **I've lost all ~ in my right arm** ich habe kein Gefühl mehr im rechten Arm.
(**b**) (*physical, mental sensation, emotion*) Gefühl *nt*. **a ~ of pain/warmth** ein Gefühl des Schmerzes/der Wärme; **I had a ~ of isolation** ich kam mir ganz isoliert vor; **he doesn't have much ~ for his sister** er hat nicht viel für seine Schwester übrig.
(**c**) (*presentiment*) (Vor)gefühl *nt*. **I've a funny ~ she won't come** ich hab so das Gefühl, daß sie nicht kommt.
(**d**) (*opinion: also ~s*) Meinung, Ansicht *f* (*on zu*). **there was a general ~ that ...** man war allgemein der Ansicht, daß ...; **ill or bad/good ~** Verstimmung *f*/Wohlwollen *nt*; **there's been a lot of bad ~ about this decision** wegen dieser Entscheidung hat es viel böses Blut gegeben.
(**e**) ~**s** Gefühle *pl*; **you've hurt his ~s** Sie haben ihn verletzt; **no hard ~s!** ich nehme es dir nicht übel; **no hard ~s?** nimm es mir nicht übel.

feet [fiːt] *pl of* **foot**.

feign [feɪn] *vt* vortäuschen; *friendship, interest, sympathy, feelings also* heucheln. **to ~ illness/madness/death** simulieren, sich krank/verrückt/tot stellen; **to ~ urgent business** dringende Geschäfte vorgeben or vorschützen.

feigned [feɪnd] *adj* vorgeblich *attr*; *illness also* simuliert; *interest, sympathy etc also* vorgetäuscht, geheuchelt.

feint [feɪnt] **1** *n* (*Sport*) Finte *f*; (*Mil*) Täuschungsmanöver *nt*, Scheinangriff *m*. **he made a ~ to the left and shot to the right** er hat links angetäuscht und nach rechts geschossen; **to make a ~** eine Finte anwenden (*at* gegenüber).
2 *vi* (*Sport*) fintieren, eine Finte anwenden (*also fig*); (*Mil*) einen Scheinangriff machen. **he ~ed with the left and hit with the right** er hat links angetäuscht und rechts zugeschlagen.

feint(-ruled) ['feɪnt(ruːld)] *adj* fein liniert.

felicitate [fɪˈlɪsɪteɪt] *vt* (*form*) beglückwünschen (*sb on sth* jdn zu etw), gratulieren (*sb on sth* jdm zu etw).

felicitation [fɪˌlɪsɪˈteɪʃən] *n usu pl* (*form*) Glückwunsch *m*. **my ~s** herzliche Glückwünsche, ich gratuliere.

felicitous *adj*, ~**ly** *adv* [fɪˈlɪsɪtəs, -lɪ] (*form*) glücklich.

felicity [fɪˈlɪsɪtɪ] *n* (*form*) (**a**) (*happiness*) Glück *nt*, Glückseligkeit *f* (*geh*). (**b**) (*aptness*) **he expresses himself with ~** er drückt sich sehr glücklich aus; **the ~ of the expression** die glückliche Wahl des Ausdrucks.

feline ['fiːlaɪn] **1** *adj* (*lit*) Katzen-; *species* der Katzen; (*fig*) *grace, suppleness* katzenartig, katzenhaft. **she gave a ~ purr** sie schnurrte wie eine Katze. **2** *n* Katze *f*.

fell[1] [fel] *pret of* **fall**.

fell[2] *n* (*skin*) Fell *nt*, Balg *m*.

fell[3] *adj* (*liter*) fürchterlich. **with one ~ blow** (*not liter*) mit einem einzigen gewaltigen or mächtigen Hieb; *see* **swoop**.

fell[4] *vt tree* fällen, schlagen; *person* niederstrecken, zu Boden strecken; *animal* zur Strecke bringen.

fell[5] *n* (*N Engl*) (*mountain*) Berg *m*; (*moor*) Moorland *nt*.

fellah ['fela'] *n* (**a**) Fellache *m*, Fellachin *f*. (**b**) *see* **fellow**.

fellatio [fɪˈleɪʃɪəʊ] *n* Fellatio *f*.

fellow[1] ['feləʊ] *n* (**a**) Mann, Kerl (*usu pej*), Typ (*sl*) *m*; (*inf: boyfriend*) Freund, Typ (*sl*) *m*. **a poor/nice/rude/an intelligent/a clever ~** ein armer/netter/unverschämter Kerl/ein kluger Kopf *or* Bursche/ein gescheiter Bursche, ein cleverer Typ (*sl*); **poor little ~** das arme Kerlchen; **listen to me, ~** (*US inf*) hör mal her, Mann (*inf*); **an old ~** ein alter Mann or Knabe (*inf*); **look here, old ~** hör mal her, alter Junge (*inf*); **young ~** junger Spund (*inf*) or Bursche; **this journalist ~** diese komische Journalistentype (*sl*); **my dear ~** mein lieber Freund or Mann (*inf*); **who is this ~?** wer ist denn der Typ (*sl*) or Kerl da?; **this ~ here** dieser Herr/junge Mann, dieser Typ (*sl*); (*rude*) dieser Kerl hier; **I'm not the sort of ~ who ...** ich bin nicht der Typ, der ...; **a ~ needs a bit of rest sometimes** (*inf*) man braucht doch auch mal 'ne Pause (*inf*).
(**b**) (*comrade*) Kamerad, Kumpel (*inf*) *m*; (*colleague*) Kollege *m*, Kollegin *f*. ~**s in misfortune** Leidensgenossen *pl*; **to get together with one's ~s** mit seinesgleichen zusammenkommen; **the company of his/their ~s** die Gesellschaft mit seines-/ihresgleichen.
(**c**) (*Univ*) Fellow *m*; *see* **research ~**.
(**d**) (*of a society*) Mitglied *nt*.
(**e**) (*of things: one of a pair*) Gegenstück *nt*, Kamerad *m* (*inf*). **its ~** das Gegenstück dazu, sein Kamerad (*inf*).

fellow² *pref* our ~ **bankers/doctors** unsere Kollegen (im Bankwesen/in der Ärzteschaft), unsere Berufskollegen *pl*; ~ **writers** Schriftstellerkollegen *pl*; he is a ~ **lexicographer** er ist auch Lexikograph; our ~ **communists/royalists** unsere kommunistischen/royalistischen Gesinnungsgenossen.

fellow: ~ **being** *n* Mitmensch *m*; ~ **citizen** *n* Mitbürger(in *f*) *m*; ~ **countryman** *n* Landsmann *m*/-männin *f*; ~ **countrymen** *npl* Landsleute *pl*; ~ **creature** *n* Mitmensch *m*; ~ **feeling** *n* Mitgefühl *nt*; (*togetherness*) Zusammengehörigkeitsgefühl *nt*; ~ **member** *n* (*in club*) Klubkamerad(in *f*) *m*; (*in party*) Parteigenosse *m*/-genossin *f*; ~ **men** *npl* Mitmenschen *pl*; ~ **passenger** *n* Mitreisende(r) *mf*.

fellowship ['felǝʊʃɪp] *n* (a) *no pl* Kameradschaft *f*; (*company*) Gesellschaft *f*; (*Eccl*) Gemeinschaft *f*. ... who lived without the ~ of other men ..., der keinen Umgang mit anderen Menschen hatte; **there's no sense of** ~ **here** hier herrscht kein kameradschaftlicher Geist.
(b) (*society, club etc*) Gesellschaft *f*.
(c) (*Univ: scholarship*) Forschungsstipendium *nt*; (*job*) Position *f* eines Fellow.

fellow: ~ **student** *n* Kommilitone *m*, Kommilitonin *f*; ~ **sufferer** *n* Leidensgenosse *m*/-genossin *f*; ~ **traveller** *n* (a) (*lit*) Mitreisende(r) *mf*; (b) (*Pol*) Sympathisant *m*; ~ **worker** *n* Kollege *m*, Mitarbeiter(in *f*) *mf*.

fell-runner ['felrʌnǝʳ] *n* Geländeläufer(in *f*) *m über bergiges Gebiet*.

felon ['felǝn] *n* (Schwer)verbrecher *m*.

felonious [fɪ'lǝʊnɪǝs] *adj* verbrecherisch.

felony ['felǝnɪ] *n* (schweres) Verbrechen *nt*.

felspar ['felspɑːʳ] *n* Feldspat *m*.

felt¹ [felt] *pret, ptp of* **feel**.

felt² 1 *n* Filz *m*; *see* **roofing**. 2 *adj attr* hat etc Filz-. 3 *vi* (*wool etc*) (ver)filzen.

felt-tip (pen) ['felttɪp('pen)] *n* Filzstift, Filzschreiber *m*.

felucca [fe'lʌkǝ] *n* Feluke *f*.

female ['fiːmeɪl] 1 *adj* (a) weiblich; *labour, rights* Frauen-. **a** ~ **doctor/student/slave/dog** eine Ärztin/Studentin/Sklavin/Hündin; ~ **bear/fish/ant** Bären-/Fisch-/Ameisenweibchen *nt*; ~ **bee** Biene *f*; **a** ~ **companion** eine Gesellschafterin; **a** ~ **football team** eine Damenfußballmannschaft; ~ **impersonator** Damen-Imitator *m*; **a typical** ~ **attitude** typisch Frau.
(b) (*Tech*) ~ **screw** (Schrauben)mutter, Mutterschraube *f*; ~ **thread** Mutter- *or* Innengewinde *nt*.
2 *n* (a) (*animal*) Weibchen *nt*.
(b) (*inf: woman*) Tante *f* (*inf*); (*pej*) Weib (*pej*), Weibsbild (*pej inf*) *nt*. **a typical** ~ eine typische Frau; **to eye up all the** ~**s** die Frauen *or* Miezen (*inf*) beäugen.

feminine ['femɪnɪn] 1 *adj* (*also Gram*) feminin, weiblich; *rhyme* weiblich, klingend; (*effeminate*) weibisch (*pej*), feminin. 2 *n* (*Gram*) Femininum *nt*. **in the** ~ in der femininen *or* weiblichen Form.

femininity [femɪ'nɪnɪtɪ] *n* Weiblichkeit *f*.

feminism ['femɪnɪzǝm] *n* Feminismus *m*, Frauenrechtlertum *nt*.

feminist ['femɪnɪst] *n* Feminist(in *f*), Frauenrechtler(in *f*) *m*.

femur ['fiːmǝʳ] *n* Oberschenkelknochen *m*.

fen [fen] *n* Moor- *or* Sumpfland *nt*. **the F~s** *die Niederungen pl in East Anglia*.

fence [fens] 1 *n* (a) Zaun *m*; (*Sport*) Hindernis *nt*. **to sit on the** ~ (*fig*) (*neutral*) neutral bleiben, nicht Partei ergreifen; (*irresolute*) unschlüssig sein, zaudern; **on the right side of the** ~ (*fig*) auf der richtigen Seite.
(b) (*inf: receiver of stolen goods*) Hehler *m*.
2 *vt* (a) (*also* ~ **in**) land ein- *or* umzäunen.
(b) (*Sport*) fechten gegen.
(c) (*inf*) hehlen. **until we find somebody to** ~ **these jewels** ... bis wir einen Hehler für diese Juwelen finden ...
3 *vi* (a) (*Sport*) fechten.
(b) (*fig*) ausweichen. **to** ~ **with a question** einer Frage ausweichen.
(c) (*inf: receive stolen goods*) hehlen, mit Diebesgut handeln.

♦**fence in** *vt sep* ein- *or* umzäunen, mit einem Zaun umgeben. (b) (*fig*) **to** ~ **sb** ~ jdn in seiner Freiheit ein- *or* beschränken, jds Freiheit beschneiden *or* einengen; **don't** ~ **me** ~ laß mir meine Freiheit, **to feel** ~**d** ~ **by restrictions** sich von Beschränkungen eingeengt fühlen.

♦**fence off** *vt sep* (a) *piece of land* abzäunen. (b) *attack, blow, question* abwehren, parieren.

fencer ['fensǝʳ] *n* Fechter(in *f*) *m*.

fencing ['fensɪŋ] *n* (a) (*Sport*) Fechten *nt*. ~ **instructor** Fechtlehrer(in *f*) *or* -meister *m*; ~ **school** Fechtschule *f*. (b) (*fences, material*) Zaun *m*, Einzäunung *f*.

fend [fend] *vi* **to** ~ **for oneself** (*provide*) für sich (selbst) sorgen, sich allein durchbringen; (*defend*) sich (selbst) verteidigen; **could she** ~ **for herself in the big city?** konnte sie sich in der großen Stadt allein durchschlagen?

♦**fend off** *vt sep* abwehren; *attacker also* vertreiben.

fender ['fendǝʳ] *n* (a) (*in front of fire*) Kamingitter *nt*. (b) (*US Aut*) Kotflügel *m*; (*of bicycle etc*) Schutzblech *nt*. (c) (*Naut*) Fender *m*. (d) (*US: on train, streetcar*) Puffer *m*.

fenestration [fenɪs'treɪʃǝn] *n* (a) (*Archit*) Fensteranordnung *f*. (b) (*Med*) Fensterungsoperation *f*.

fennel ['fenl] *n* (*Bot*) Fenchel *m*.

feoff [fiːf] *n* (*old, form: land*) Lehen *nt*.

feral ['ferǝl] *adj* (*form*) (*wild*) wild; *animals also* ungezähmt.

ferment ['fɜːment] 1 *n* (a) (*fermentation*) Gärung *f*; (*substance*) Ferment *nt*, Gärstoff *m*.
(b) (*fig*) Unruhe, Erregung *f*. **the city/he was in a state of** ~ es brodelte *or* gärte in der Stadt/in ihm.
2 [fǝ'ment] *vi* (*lit, fig*) gären; (*plan also*) (aus)reifen.

3 [fǝ'ment] *vt* (*lit*) fermentieren, zur Gärung bringen; (*fig*) anwachsen lassen.

fermentation [fɜːmen'teɪʃǝn] *n* (a) Gärung *f*; (*fig: of plan etc*) Ausreifen *nt*. ~ **lock** Gärventil *nt*. (b) (*fig: excitement*) Aufregung, Unruhe *f*.

fern [fɜːn] *n* Farn(kraut *nt*) *m*.

ferocious [fǝ'rǝʊʃǝs] *adj appearance* wild, grimmig; *glance, look* böse, grimmig; *dog, animal* wild; *criticism, competition* scharf; *fight, resistance, temper* heftig; *attack* heftig, scharf; *virus* bösartig.

ferociously [fǝ'rǝʊʃǝslɪ] *adv* grimmig; *growl, bare teeth* wild; *fight, attack, resist* heftig; *criticize* scharf.

ferocity [fǝ'rɒsɪtɪ] *n see adj* Wildheit, Grimmigkeit *f*; Grimmigkeit *f*; Wildheit, Bissigkeit *f*; Schärfe *f*; Heftigkeit *f*; Heftigkeit, Schärfe *f*; Bösartigkeit *f*.

ferret ['ferɪt] 1 *n* Frettchen *nt*.
2 *vi* (a) (*Sport: also* go ~**ing**) mit dem Frettchen jagen.
(b) (*also* ~ **around**) herumstöbern *or* -schnüffeln (*pej*). **she was** ~**ing** (**about** *or* **around**) **among my books** sie schnüffelte in meinen Büchern (herum); **he was** ~**ing for information** er schnüffelte nach Informationen.

♦**ferret out** *vt sep* aufstöbern, aufspüren.

ferric ['ferɪk] *adj* Eisen-, Eisen(III)- (*spec*).

Ferris wheel ['ferɪs,wiːl] *n* Riesenrad *nt*.

ferrite ['feraɪt] *n* Ferrit *m*. ~ **rod** Ferritstab *m*; ~ **rod aerial** Ferritantenne *f*.

ferroconcrete ['ferǝʊ'kɒŋkriːt] *n* Eisen- *or* Stahlbeton *m*.

ferrous ['ferǝs] *adj* Eisen-, Eisen(II)- (*spec*). ~ **chloride** Eisenchlorid *nt*.

fer(r)ule ['feruːl] *n* (*of umbrella, cane*) Zwinge *f*, Ring *m*.

ferry ['ferɪ] 1 *n* Fähre *f*.
2 *vt* (a) (*by boat: also* ~ **across** *or* **over**) übersetzen; (*by plane, car etc*) transportieren, bringen. **to** ~ **sb across** *or* **over a river** jdn über einen Fluß setzen; **to** ~ **sb/sth back and forth** jdn/etw hin- und herbringen; **he ferried voters to and from the polls** er fuhr Wähler zum Wahllokal und wieder nach Hause.
(b) (*deliver*) *plane* überführen.

ferry: ~**boat** *n* Fährboot *nt*; ~**man** *n* Fährmann *m*.

fertile ['fɜːtaɪl] *adj* (*lit, fig*) fruchtbar; *land, soil also* ertragreich. **one of the more** ~ **areas of research** eines der fruchtbareren *or* ergiebigeren Forschungsgebiete; **the idea fell on** ~ **ground** der Gedanke fiel auf fruchtbaren Boden.

fertility [fǝ'tɪlɪtɪ] 1 *n* (*lit, fig*) Fruchtbarkeit *f*; (*of soil, seed also*) Ergiebigkeit *f*. 2 *attr cult, symbol* Fruchtbarkeits-. ~ **drug** Fruchtbarkeitspille *f*.

fertilization [fɜːtɪlaɪ'zeɪʃǝn] *n* Befruchtung *f*; (*of soil*) Düngung *f*.

fertilize ['fɜːtɪlaɪz] *vt animal, egg, flower* befruchten; *land, soil* düngen.

fertilizer ['fɜːtɪlaɪzǝʳ] *n* Dünger *m*, Düngemittel *nt*. **artificial** ~ Kunstdünger *m*.

ferule ['feruːl] *n* (a) Stock *m*. (b) *see* **fer(r)ule**.

fervency ['fɜːvǝnsɪ] *n see* **fervour**.

fervent ['fɜːvǝnt], **fervid** ['fɜːvɪd] *adj* leidenschaftlich; *desire, wish, hope also* inbrünstig, glühend; *tone of voice, expression, prayer also* inbrünstig.

fervently ['fɜːvǝntlɪ], **fervidly** ['fɜːvɪdlɪ] *adv* inbrünstig, leidenschaftlich.

fervour, (*US*) **fervor** ['fɜːvǝʳ] *n* Inbrunst *f*; (*of public speaker also*) Leidenschaft *f*; (*of lover*) Leidenschaftlichkeit *f*.

fester ['festǝʳ] *vi* eitern, schwären (*old*); (*fig: insult, resentment etc*) nagen, fressen. ~**ing sore** (*fig*) Eiterbeule *f*.

festival ['festɪvǝl] *n* (a) (*Eccl etc*) Fest *nt*. **Church** ~**s** kirchliche Feste, kirchliche Feiertage *pl*; **F~ of Lights** Lichterfest *nt*. (b) (*cultural*) Festspiele *pl*, Festival *nt*; (*lasting several days also*) Festwoche *f*. **the Edinburgh/Salzburg F~** das Edinburgh-Festival/die Salzburger Festspiele *pl*.

festive ['festɪv] *adj* festlich. **the** ~ **season** die Festzeit; **he was in** (**a**) ~ **mood** er war in festlicher Stimmung *or* in Festtagslaune.

festivity [fe'stɪvɪtɪ] *n* (a) (*gaiety*) Feststimmung, Feiertagsstimmung *f*. **there was an air of** ~ **in the office** im Büro herrschte Feststimmung *f*. (b) (*celebration*) Feier *f*. **festivities** *pl* (*festive proceedings*) Feierlichkeiten, Festivitäten (*hum*) *pl*.

festoon [fe'stuːn] 1 *n* Girlande *f*; (*in curtain etc, Archit*) Feston *m*. 2 *vt* **to** ~ **sb/sth with sth** jdn mit etw behängen/etw mit etw schmücken *or* zieren; **to be** ~**ed with sth** mit etw behängt sein; **garlands** ~**ed the room** Girlanden schmückten den Raum.

fetal *adj* (*esp US*) *see* **foetal**.

fetch [fetʃ] 1 *vt* (a) (*bring*) holen; (*collect*) *person, thing* abholen. **would you** ~ **me a handkerchief for me** *or* ~ **me a handkerchief?** kannst du mir ein Taschentuch holen (gehen)?; **I'll** ~ **her from the station** ich hole sie vom Bahnhof ab; **he** ~**ed out a handkerchief from his pocket** er zog *or* holte ein Taschentuch aus der Tasche; **she** ~**ed in the washing** sie holte die Wäsche herein; **he's upstairs, I'll** ~ **him down** er ist oben, ich hole ihn herunter.
(b) *sigh, groan* ausstoßen.
(c) (*bring in*) *money* (ein)bringen.
(d) (*inf*) **to** ~ **sb a blow/one** jdm eine langen (*inf*); (*accidentally: with rucksack etc*) jdn erwischen (*inf*).
2 *vi* (a) **to** ~ **and carry for sb** bei jdm Mädchen für alles sein, bei jdm die Minna (fürs Grobe) sein (*hum*).
(b) (*Naut*) Kurs halten; (*change course*) Kurs nehmen.

♦**fetch up** 1 *vi* (*inf*) landen (*inf*). 2 *vt sep* (*Brit: vomit*) wieder von sich geben, erbrechen.

fetching ['fetʃɪŋ] *adj* bezaubernd, reizend; *hat, dress also* entzückend; *smile also* gewinnend, einnehmend.

fête [feɪt] 1 *n* Fest *nt*. **village** ~ Dorffest *nt*. 2 *vt* (*make much of*) *sb, sb's success* feiern. **to** ~ **sb** (*entertain*) zu jds Ehren ein Fest geben; **a much** ~**d actress** eine gefeierte Schauspielerin.

fetid ['fetɪd] *adj* übelriechend.

fetish ['fetɪʃ] n (all senses) Fetisch m. to have a ~ about leather/cleanliness einen Leder-/Sauberkeitsfetisch haben (inf), ein Leder-/Sauberkeitsfetischist sein; to make a ~ of sth einen Kult mit etw treiben, etw zum Fetisch machen or erheben.

fetishism ['fetɪʃɪzəm] n Fetischismus m.

fetishist ['fetɪʃɪst] n Fetischist m.

fetlock ['fetlɒk] n Fessel f; (joint) Fesselgelenk nt.

fetter ['fetər] 1 vt prisoner fesseln; goat anpflocken; (fig) in Fesseln legen. 2 n ~s pl (Fuß)fesseln pl; (fig) Fesseln pl; to put a prisoner in ~s einen Gefangenen in Fesseln legen.

fettle ['fetl] n to be in fine or good ~ in bester Form sein; (as regards health also) in bester Verfassung or topfit sein (inf).

fetus n (US) see **foetus**.

feu [fjuː] n (Scot) Lehen nt. ~ duty Lehnsabgabe f.

feud [fjuːd] 1 n (lit, fig) Fehde f. to have a ~ with sb mit jdm in Fehde liegen. 2 vi (lit, fig) sich befehden, in Fehde liegen.

feudal ['fjuːdl] adj Feudal-, feudal, Lehns-.

feudalism ['fjuːdəlɪzəm] n Feudalismus m, Lehnswesen nt.

fever ['fiːvər] n (a) Fieber nt no pl. tropical ~s tropische Fieberkrankheiten pl; to have a ~ eine Fieberkrankheit haben; (high temperature) Fieber haben.
(b) (fig) Aufregung, Erregung f, Fieber nt. election ~ Wahlfieber nt, Wahlrausch m; in a ~ of excitement in fieberhafter Erregung; to go into a ~ of excitement von fieberhafter Erregung ergriffen or befallen werden; ~ pitch Siedepunkt m; to reach ~ pitch am Siedepunkt angelangt sein, den Siedepunkt erreichen; to be working at ~ pitch auf Hochtouren arbeiten.

feverish ['fiːvərɪʃ] adj (Med) fiebernd attr; (fig) activity fieberhaft; atmosphere fiebrig. he's still ~ er fiebert noch, er hat noch Fieber.

feverishly ['fiːvərɪʃlɪ] adv fieberhaft.

few [fjuː] 1 adj (+er) (a) (not many) wenige. ~ people come to see him nur wenige Leute besuchen ihn; with ~ exceptions mit wenigen Ausnahmen; we are very ~ wir sind nur sehr wenige or nur ein kleines Häufchen; ~ and far between dünn gesät; as ~ books as you genauso wenig(e) Bücher wie du; as ~ as six objections bloß sechs Einwände, nicht mehr als sechs Einwände; how ~ they are! wie wenige das sind!; so ~ books so wenige Bücher; too ~ cakes zu wenige Kuchen; there were 3 too ~ es waren 3 zuwenig da; 10 would not be too ~ 10 wären nicht zuwenig; he is one of the ~ people who ... er ist einer der wenigen, die ...; the exceptions are ~ es gibt nur wenige Ausnahmen; such occasions are ~ solche Gelegenheiten sind selten or rar; its days are ~ es hat nur ein kurzes Leben; the remaining ~ minutes die wenigen verbleibenden Minuten.
(b) a ~ ein paar; a ~ more days noch ein paar Tage; a ~ times ein paar Male; there were quite a ~ waiting ziemlich viele warteten; he has quite a ~ girl-friends er hat eine ganze Menge or ziemlich viele Freundinnen; he's had a good ~ drinks er hat ziemlich viel getrunken; quite a ~ books ziemlich viele Bücher, eine ganze Menge Bücher; I saw a good ~ or quite a ~ people ich habe ziemlich viele Leute or eine ganze Menge Leute gesehen; we'll go in a ~ minutes wir gehen in ein paar Minuten; in the next/past ~ days in den nächsten/letzten paar Tagen; every ~ days alle paar Tage.
2 pron (a) (not many) wenige. ~ of them came wenige von ihnen kamen; some ~ gar nicht so wenige; the F~ Kampfflieger, die an der Luftschlacht um England im zweiten Weltkrieg teilnahmen; the lucky ~ die wenigen Glücklichen; as ~ as you genauso wenig wie du; how ~ there are! wie wenige das sind!; however ~ there may be wie wenig auch immer da ist; I've got so/too ~ as it is ich habe sowieso schon so/zu wenig(e); so ~ have been sold so wenige sind bis jetzt verkauft worden; there are too ~ of you ihr seid zu wenige.
(b) a ~ ein paar; a ~ thought otherwise ein paar (Leute) dachten anders; I'll take just a ~ ich nehme nur ein paar; a ~ more ein paar mehr; quite a ~ did not believe him eine ganze Menge Leute or ziemlich viele Leute glaubten ihm nicht; there were quite a ~ waiting es warteten ziemlich viele; quite a ~ eine ganze Menge; some ~ einige; there are always the ~ who ... es gibt immer einige wenige Leute or ein paar Leute, die ...; the ~ who knew him die wenigen, die ihn kannten.

fewer ['fjuːər] adj, pron comp of **few** weniger. no ~ than nicht weniger als.

fewest ['fjuːɪst] superl of **few** 1 adj die wenigsten. the ~ occasions possible so wenig wie möglich, so selten wie möglich. 2 pron die wenigsten, am wenigsten.

fey [feɪ] adj (Scot) todgeweiht; (clairvoyant) hellseherisch.

fez [fez] n Fes m.

ff abbr of **following** ff.

fiancé [fɪ'ɑ̃ːŋseɪ] n Verlobte(r) m.

fiancée [fɪ'ɑ̃ːŋseɪ] n Verlobte f.

fiasco [fɪ'æskəʊ] n, pl -s, (US also) -es Fiasko nt. what a ~ of a reception was für ein Fiasko dieser Empfang ist/war.

fiat ['faɪæt] n (a) (decree) Befehl, Erlaß m, Anordnung f. you can't just get it done by ~ das erledigt sich nicht so einfach auf Befehl (von selbst). (b) (authorization) Billigung f, Einverständnis nt, Plazet nt.

fib [fɪb] (inf) 1 n Flunkerei (inf), Schwindelei (inf) f. (that's a) ~! das ist geflunkert! (inf); don't tell ~s flunker or schwindel nicht! (inf); it's all a big ~ das ist alles (ein) großer Schwindel! 2 vi flunkern (inf), schwindeln (inf).

fibber ['fɪbər] n (inf) Flunkerer (inf), Schwindler (inf) m.

fibbing ['fɪbɪŋ] n (inf) Flunkerei f (inf).

fibre, (US) **fiber** ['faɪbər] n (a) Faser f. (b) (fig) moral ~ Charakterstärke f; he has no moral ~ er hat keinen inneren Halt, er hat kein Rückgrat nt.

fibreglass ['faɪbəglɑːs] 1 n Fiberglas nt. 2 adj Fiberglas-, aus Fiberglas.

fibrositis [ˌfaɪbrə'saɪtɪs] n Bindegewebsentzündung f.

fibrous ['faɪbrəs] adj faserig.

fibula ['fɪbjʊlə] n Wadenbein nt.

fickle ['fɪkl] adj unbeständig, launenhaft; person also wankelmütig; weather also wechselhaft.

fickleness ['fɪklnɪs] n Wechselhaftigkeit, Unbeständigkeit f; (of person also) Wankelmütigkeit f.

fiction ['fɪkʃən] n (a) no pl (Liter) Erzähl- or Prosaliteratur f. you'll find that under ~ das finden Sie unter Belletristik; work of ~ Erzählung f; (longer) Roman m; light ~ (leichte) Unterhaltungsliteratur; romantic ~ Liebesromane pl.
(b) (invention) (freie) Erfindung, Fiktion f. that's pure ~ das ist frei erfunden; the unicorn is a ~ das Einhorn ist eine Fiktion.
(c) legal ~ juristische Fiktion.

fictional ['fɪkʃənl] adj erdichtet, erfunden. all these events are purely ~ alle diese Ereignisse sind frei erfunden; his ~ writing seine erzählenden Schriften; a ~ representation of historical events eine dichterische Darstellung historischer Ereignisse; a ~ character eine Gestalt aus der Literatur.

fictitious [fɪk'tɪʃəs] adj (a) (imaginary) fiktiv, frei erfunden. all characters in this film are ~ alle Gestalten in diesem Film sind frei erfunden. (b) (false) falsch. (c) ~ person (Jur) juristische Person.

fiddle ['fɪdl] 1 n (a) (Mus inf) Fiedel f, Geige f. first ~ erste Geige; to play second ~ (to sb) (fig) in jds Schatten (dat) stehen; he refuses to play second ~ (fig) er will immer die erste Geige spielen; as fit as a ~ kerngesund; he had a face as long as a ~ er machte ein Gesicht wie drei Tage Regenwetter.
(b) (Brit inf: cheat, swindle) Manipulation, Schiebung f; (with money) faule Geschäfte pl (inf). it's a ~ das ist Schiebung!; he only got that job through some ~ er hat die Stelle nur durch Trickserei gekriegt (inf); there are so many ~s going on es wird so viel getrickst (inf) or manipuliert; the accountants were well aware there had been some sort of ~ die Buchprüfer wußten ganz genau, daß da irgend etwas manipuliert or frisiert (inf) worden war; tax ~ Steuermanipulation f; to be on the ~ faule Geschäfte or krumme Dinger machen (inf).
2 vi (a) (Mus inf) fiedeln (inf), geigen.
(b) (fidget, play around) herumspielen. don't ~ with the engine if you don't know what you're doing spiel nicht am Motor herum, wenn du dich damit nicht auskennst; he sat there nervously fiddling with his tie/cigarette lighter er saß da und spielte nervös an seinem Schlips herum/spielte mit seinem Feuerzeug herum; put that thing down and stop fiddling! leg das Ding weg und hör endlich mit dem Herumspielen auf!
(c) (split hairs, be over-precise etc) Haare spalten, pingelig sein (inf). that would just be fiddling das wäre reine Haarspalterei or bloße Pingeligkeit (inf).
3 vt (inf) (a) accounts, results frisieren (inf); election manipulieren. he ~d some money out of the firm er hat der Firma ein bißchen Geld abgegaunert (inf); he ~d it so that ... er hat es so hingebogen or getrickst (inf), daß ...
(b) tune fiedeln (inf), geigen.
4 interj ach du liebe Zeit, ach du liebes Lottchen (hum inf).

♦**fiddle about** or **around** vi to ~ ~ with sth an etw (dat) herumspielen or herumfummeln (inf); (fidget with) mit etw herumspielen; he dived under the bonnet and ~d ~ for a while er verschwand unter der Kühlerhaube und fummelte eine Weile herum (inf); I'm not spending all day just fiddling ~ with this one little job! ich werde doch nicht den ganzen Tag damit zubringen, an dieser einen Kleinigkeit rumzufummeln! (inf); he wasn't really playing a tune, just fiddling ~ er spielte keine richtige Melodie, er spielte nur so rum (inf); he ~d ~ with a couple of chords until a tune began to emerge er klimperte ein paar Akkorde, bis sich eine Melodie herauslöste.

fiddle-faddle ['fɪdlfædl] interj (dated: nonsense) Quatsch (inf).

fiddler ['fɪdlər] n (a) (Mus inf) Geiger m. (b) you little ~, now you've broken it du mit deiner ewigen Herumspielerei, jetzt ist es kaputt. (c) (inf: cheat) Schwindler, Betrüger m.

fiddler crab n Winkerkrabbe f.

fiddlesticks ['fɪdlstɪks] interj (nonsense) Unsinn, Quatsch (inf); (bother) du liebe Zeit, du liebes Lottchen (hum inf).

fiddliness ['fɪdlɪnɪs] n (inf: intricacy) Kniffligkeit f (inf).

fiddling ['fɪdlɪŋ] adj (trivial) läppisch.

fiddly ['fɪdlɪ] adj (+er) (inf: intricate) knifflig (inf).

fidelity [fɪ'delɪtɪ] n (a) Treue f (to zu). (b) (of translation etc) Genauigkeit f; (Rad etc) Klangtreue f.

fidget ['fɪdʒɪt] 1 vi (be restless) zappeln. to ~ with sth mit etw herumspielen or herumfummeln; don't ~ zappel nicht so rum; he sat there ~ing on his chair er rutschte auf seinem Stuhl hin und her.
2 n (a) (person) Zappelphilipp m (inf).
(b) (inf) to give sb the ~s jdn zappelig or kribbelig machen; have you got the ~s? was bist du für ein Zappelphilipp! (inf); to get the ~s zappelig werden.

fidgety ['fɪdʒɪtɪ] adj zappelig; audience etc unruhig.

fiduciary [fɪ'djuːʃɪərɪ] 1 adj treuhänderisch; currency ungedeckt. 2 n Treuhänder m.

fie [faɪ] interj (old) pfui. ~ upon you pfui!

fief [fiːf] n (Hist) Lehen nt.

field [fiːld] 1 n (a) (Agr) Feld nt, Acker m; (area of grass) Wiese f; (for cows, horses etc) Weide f. corn/wheat ~ Getreide-/Weizenfeld nt; potato ~ Kartoffelacker m; we had a picnic in a ~ wir machten auf einer Wiese Picknick; he's working in the ~s er arbeitet auf dem Feld or Acker; the farm has 20 ~s der Hof hat 20 Felder; beasts of the ~ Feldtiere pl; to cut across the ~s quer über die Felder gehen.
(b) (coal~, ice~, oil~ etc) Feld nt.
(c) (for football etc: ground) Platz m. sports or games ~ Sportplatz m; to take the ~ auf den Platz kommen, einlaufen.
(d) (Mil) ~ of battle Schlachtfeld nt; noted for his bravery in the ~ für seine Tapferkeit im Feld bekannt; to take the ~ zur

Schlacht antreten; **to hold the ~** das Feld behaupten; **the ~ was ours** der Sieg war unser (geh); **he died on the ~ of honour** er ließ sein Leben auf dem Feld der Ehre.

(e) (of study, work etc) Gebiet, Feld nt. **to be first in the ~ with sth** (Comm) als Erster etw auf den Markt bringen; **in all the ~s of human endeavour** (liter) im gesamten menschlichen Trachten (liter); **studies in the ~ of medicine** Studien auf dem Gebiet der Medizin; **this is, of course, a very broad ~** das ist natürlich ein weites Feld; **what ~ are you in?** auf welchem Gebiet or in welchem Feld arbeiten Sie?; **his ~ is Renaissance painting** sein Spezialgebiet ist die Malerei der Renaissance.

(f) (area of practical observation or operation) Praxis f. **when a salesman goes out into the ~** wenn ein Verkäufer in den Außeneinsatz geht; **work in the ~** Feldforschung f; (of sales rep) Außendienst m; **to test sth in the ~** etw in der Praxis or vor Ort ausprobieren.

(g) (Phys, Opt) Feld nt. **~ of vision** Blick- or Gesichtsfeld nt; **gravitational ~** Gravitationsfeld, Schwerefeld nt; **~ of force** Kraftfeld nt; **magnetic ~** Magnetfeld nt, magnetisches Feld.

(h) (Sport: competitors) Feld nt; (Hunt also) rotes Feld; (Cricket, Baseball) Fängerpartei f. **there's quite a strong ~ for this year's chess contest** das Teilnehmerfeld für den diesjährigen Schachwettbewerb ist ziemlich stark.

(i) (Computers) Datenfeld nt; (on punch card) Feld nt.

(j) (on flag, Her) Feld nt, Grund m.

2 vt **(a)** (Cricket, Baseball etc) ball auffangen und zurückwerfen; (fig) question etc abblocken, abwehren.

(b) team, side aufs Feld or auf den Platz schicken.

3 vi (Cricket, Baseball etc) als Fänger spielen. **when we go out to ~** wenn wir die Fänger(partei) stellen; **he bats well but he can't ~** er ist ein guter Schlagmann, aber als Fänger nicht zu gebrauchen.

field: **~ ambulance** n (Mil) Sanka, Sanitätskraftwagen m; **~ artillery** n Feldartillerie f; **~ day** n **(a)** Manöver nt; **(b)** (fig) **I had a ~ day** ich hatte meinen großen Tag; **to have a ~ day** einen inneren Reichsparteitag haben (inf); **with the score at 6–0 the Scots are having a ~ day against the English** beim Stand von 6:0 machen die Schotten jetzt die Engländer nach allen Regeln der Kunst fertig (inf).

fielder ['fiːldə'] n (Cricket, Baseball etc) Fänger m.

field: **~ event** n (Athletics) Disziplin, die nicht auf der Aschenbahn ausgetragen wird; **~ games** npl Feldspiele pl; **~ glasses** npl Feldstecher m; **~ goal** n (US) (Basketball) Korbwurf m aus dem Spielgeschehen; (Ftbl) Feldtor nt; **~ gun** n (Mil) Feldgeschütz nt; **~ hockey** n (US) Hockey nt; **~ hospital** n (Mil) (Feld)lazarett nt; **~ kitchen** n (Mil) Feldküche f; **~ marshal** n (Mil) Feldmarschall m; **~mouse** n Feldmaus f; **~notes** npl Arbeits- or Beobachtungsnotizen pl; **~piece** n (Mil) Feldgeschütz nt.

fieldsman ['fiːldzmən] n, pl **-men** [-mən] (Cricket) Fänger m.

field: **~ sports** npl **(a)** Sport m im Freien (Jagen und Fischen); **(b) see ~ games**; **~ study** n Feldforschung f; **a ~ study** eine Feldstudie; **~work** n **(a)** (of geologist, surveyor etc) Arbeit f im Gelände; (of sociologist etc) Feldarbeit, Feldforschung f; **(b)** (Mil) Feldbefestigung, Schanze f; **~worker** n Praktiker m.

fiend [fiːnd] n **(a)** (evil spirit) Teufel, Dämon m; (person) Teufel m. **the F~** der böse Feind; **"sex ~ strikes again"** „Sexungeheuer schlägt wieder zu".

(b) (inf: addict) Fanatiker(in f) m. **he's a real ~ for Verdi** er ist ein richtiger Verdinarr or -fanatiker; **tennis ~** Tennisnarr m; **a fresh-air ~** ein Frischluftfanatiker m.

fiendish ['fiːndɪʃ] adj teuflisch; cruelty also unmenschlich; (inf) pace, heat höllisch (inf), Höllen- (inf); (inf) problem verteufelt (inf), verzwickt. **to take a ~ delight in doing sth** seine höllische Freude daran haben, etw zu tun (inf).

fiendishly ['fiːndɪʃlɪ] adv grin, chuckle teuflisch; (dated inf) difficult, complicated verteufelt (inf).

fierce [fɪəs] adj (+ er) appearance wild, grimmig; glance, look böse, grimmig; dog blissig; lion, warrior wild; criticism, competition scharf; fight, resistance, temper heftig; attack (lit, fig) heftig, scharf; heat glühend; sun grell, glühend.

fiercely ['fɪəslɪ] adv see adj.

fierceness ['fɪəsnɪs] n see adj (savageness) Wildheit, Grimmigkeit f; Grimmigkeit f; Bissigkeit f; Wildheit f; Schärfe f; Heftigkeit f; Heftigkeit, Schärfe f; Glut f; Grellheit, Glut f.

fiery ['faɪərɪ] adj (+ er) feurig, glühend; sunset rotglühend; (fig) person, temper feurig, hitzig; curry feurig. **to have a ~ temper/to be ~** im Kopf m sein; **~ liquor** feuriger Schnaps.

fiesta [fɪ'estə] n Fiesta f.

FIFA ['fiːfə] abbr of **Federation of International Football Associations** FIFA f.

fife [faɪf] n (Mus) Querpfeife f.

fifteen ['fɪf'tiːn] **1** adj fünfzehn. **2** n **(a)** Fünfzehn f; see also **sixteen**. **(b) a rugby ~** eine Rugbymannschaft; **the Welsh ~** die Rugbynationalmannschaft von Wales.

fifteenth ['fɪf'tiːnθ] **1** adj fünfzehnte(r, s). **2** n Fünfzehnte(r, s); (part, fraction) Fünfzehntel nt; see also **sixteenth**.

fifth [fɪfθ] **1** adj fünfte(r, s). **~ column** fünfte Kolonne; **~ columnist** Angehörige(r) mf der fünften Kolonne; **~ rate** fünftrangig. **2** n Fünfte(r, s); (part, fraction) Fünftel nt; (Mus) Quinte f; see also **sixth**.

fiftieth ['fɪftɪθ] **1** adj fünfzigste(r, s). **2** n Fünfzigste(r, s); (part, fraction) Fünfzigstel nt.

fifty ['fɪftɪ] **1** adj fünfzig. **2** n Fünfzig f; see also **sixty**.

fifty-fifty ['fɪftɪ'fɪftɪ] **1** adj halbe-halbe, fifty-fifty. **we have a ~ chance of success** unsere Chancen stehen fifty-fifty. **2** adv **to go ~ (with sb)** (mit jdm) halbe-halbe or fifty-fifty machen. **3** n Halbe-Halbe, Fifty-Fifty nt.

fiftyish ['fɪftɪɪʃ] adj um die Fünfzig.

fig abbr of **figure(s)** Abb.

fig [fɪg] n Feige f. **I don't care a ~** (inf) ich kümmere mich einen

Dreck darum (inf); **I don't give a ~ for what he thinks!** seine Meinung kümmert mich einen (feuchten) Dreck (inf); **not worth a ~** keinen Deut wert; **a ~ for your honour, sir!** (old) ich gebe keinen Deut für Ihre Ehre, mein Herr!

fight [faɪt] (vb: pret, ptp **fought**) **1** n **(a)** (lit, fig) Kampf m; (fist ~, scrap) Rauferei, Prügelei, Schlägerei f; (Mil) Gefecht nt; (argument, row) Streit m. **to have a ~ with sb** sich mit jdm schlagen; (argue) sich mit jdm streiten; **to give sb a ~** (lit, fig) jdm einen Kampf liefern; **to put up a ~** (lit, fig) sich zur Wehr setzen; **to put up a good ~** (lit, fig) sich tapfer zur Wehr setzen, sich tapfer schlagen; **do you want a ~?** willst du was?, du willst dich wohl mit mir anlegen?; **if he wants a ~, then ...** (lit, fig) wenn er Streit sucht, dann ...; **a politician who enjoys a good ~** ein streitlustiger Politiker; **he won't give in without a ~** er ergibt sich nicht kampflos; **in the ~ against disease** im Kampf gegen die Krankheit; **the big ~** (Boxing) der große Kampf.

(b) (~ing spirit) Kampfgeist m. **there was no ~ left in him** sein Kampfgeist war erloschen; **to show ~** Kampfgeist zeigen.

2 vi kämpfen; (have punch-up etc) raufen, sich prügeln, sich schlagen; (argue, with wife etc) sich streiten or zanken. **the dogs were ~ing over a bone** die Hunde rauften um eine ganzen Knochen; **to ~ against disease** Krankheiten bekämpfen; **to ~ for sb/sth** um jdn/etw kämpfen; **to ~ for what one believes in** für seine Überzeugungen eintreten or streiten; **to ~ for one's life** um sein Leben kämpfen; **to go down ~ing** sich nicht kampflos ergeben; **to ~ shy of sth** einer Sache (dat) aus dem Weg gehen; **I've always fought shy of claiming that ...** ich habe immer bewußt vermieden, zu behaupten ...

3 vt **(a)** person kämpfen mit or gegen; (have punch-up with) sich schlagen mit, sich prügeln mit; (in battle) kämpfen mit, sich (dat) ein Gefecht nt liefern mit. **I'm prepared to ~ him/the government** (argue with, take on) ich bin bereit, das mit ihm/der Regierung durchzukämpfen; **I'll ~ him on that one** dazu nehme ich es mit ihm auf; **you can't ~ the whole company** du kannst es nicht mit der ganzen Firma aufnehmen.

(b) fire, disease, cuts, policy bekämpfen; decision ankämpfen gegen. **there's no point in ~ing it, this thing is bigger than both of us** es hat keinen Zweck, dagegen anzukämpfen, dieses Gefühl ist stärker als wir beide.

(c) to ~ **a duel** ein Duell nt austragen, sich duellieren; **to ~ an action at law** einen Prozeß vor Gericht durchkämpfen or durchfechten; **to ~ one's way out of the crowd** sich aus der Menge freikämpfen; see **battle**.

(d) (Mil, Naut: control in battle) army, ships kommandieren.

♦**fight back 1** vi (in fight) zurückschlagen; (Mil) sich verteidigen, Widerstand leisten; (in argument) sich wehren, sich zur Wehr setzen; (after illness) zu Kräften kommen; (Sport) zurückkämpfen.

2 vt sep tears etc unterdrücken; doubts also zu besiegen versuchen. **he fought his way ~ into the match/to the top** er hat sich ins Spiel/wieder an die Spitze zurückgekämpft.

♦**fight down** vt sep anxiety unterdrücken, bezwingen.

♦**fight off** vt sep (Mil, fig) attack, disease abwehren; sleep ankämpfen gegen; a cold erfolgreich bekämpfen. **I'm still trying to ~ this cold** ich kämpfe immer noch mit dieser Erkältung; **she has to keep ~ing men** sie muß dauernd Männer abwimmeln.

♦**fight on** vi weiterkämpfen.

♦**fight out** vt sep **to ~ it** es untereinander ausfechten.

fightback ['faɪtbæk] n Comeback nt.

fighter ['faɪtə'] n **(a)** Kämpfer, Streiter m; (Boxing) Fighter m. **he's a ~** (fig) er ist eine Kämpfernatur. **(b)** (Aviat: plane) Jagdflugzeug nt, Jäger m.

fighter: **~-bomber** n Jagdbomber m; **~-interceptor** n Abfangjäger m; **~-pilot** n Jagdflieger m.

fighting ['faɪtɪŋ] **1** n (Mil) Kampf m, Gefecht nt; (punch-ups, scrapping etc) Prügeleien, Raufereien pl; (arguments between husband and wife etc) Streit, Zank m. **~ broke out** Kämpfe brachen aus; see **street ~**. **2** adj attr person kämpferisch, streitlustig; (Mil) troops Kampf-.

fighting: **~ chance** n faire Chancen pl; **he's in with or he has a ~ chance** er hat eine Chance, wenn er sich anstrengt; **~ cock** n (lit, fig) Kampfhahn m; **~ forces** npl Kampftruppen pl; **~ line** n Front f; **~ man** n Krieger, Kämpfer m; **~ spirit** n Kampfgeist m; **to have a lot of ~ spirit** großen Kampfgeist haben; **~ strength** n (Mil) Kampf- or Einsatzstärke f.

figleaf ['fɪglɪːf] n (lit, fig) Feigenblatt nt.

figment ['fɪgmənt] n **a ~ of the imagination** pure Einbildung, ein Hirngespinst nt; **it's all a ~ of his imagination** das ist alles eine Ausgeburt seiner Phantasie.

fig tree n Feigenbaum m.

figurative ['fɪgjʊrətɪv] adj **(a)** language bildlich; use, sense übertragen, figürlich. **(b)** (Art) gegenständlich.

figuratively ['fɪgjʊrətɪvlɪ] adv im übertragenen or figürlichen Sinne. **~ speaking, of course** natürlich nicht im wörtlichen Sinn.

figure ['fɪgə'] **1** n **(a)** (number) Zahl; (digit also) Ziffer f; (sum) Summe f. **could you put some sort of ~ on the salary?** können Sie mir ungefähr die Höhe meines Gehaltes angeben?; **he's good at ~s** er ist ein guter Rechner; **a mistake in the ~s** eine Unstimmigkeit in den Zahlen; **have you seen last year's ~s?** haben Sie die Zahlen vom Vorjahr gesehen?; **Miss Jones, could you bring in the ~s for the Fotheringham contract?** Fräulein Jones, könnten Sie das Zahlenmaterial zum Fotheringham-Vertrag bringen?; **to get into double ~s** sich auf zweistellige Beträge belaufen, in die zweistelligen Zahlen gehen; **three-~ number** dreistellige Zahl; **to sell for a high ~** für eine hohe Summe verkauft werden; **he earns well into four ~s** er hat gut und gern ein vierstelliges Einkommen.

(b) (in geometry, dancing, skating) Figur f. **~ of eight** Acht f.

(c) (human form) Gestalt f.

(d) (*shapeliness*) Figur *f*. **she has a good** ~ sie hat eine gute Figur; **I'm dieting to keep my** ~ ich lebe Diät, um meine Figur zu behalten; **what a** ~! (was für) eine tolle Figur!; **she's a fine** ~ **of a woman** sie ist eine stattliche Frau; **he's a fine** ~ **of a man** er ist ein Bild von einem Mann; *see* cut.

(e) (*personality*) Persönlichkeit *f*; (*character in novel etc*) Gestalt *f*. **the great** ~**s of history** die Großen der Geschichte; **a great public** ~ eine bedeutende Persönlichkeit des öffentlichen Lebens; ~ **of fun** Witzfigur *f*, lächerliche Erscheinung.

(f) (*statuette, model etc*) Figur *f*.

(g) (*Liter*) ~ **of speech** Redensart, Redewendung *f*; **it's just a** ~ **of speech** das ist doch nur eine (leere) Redensart, das sagt man doch nur so.

(h) (*Mus*) Figur, Phrase *f*; (*notation*) Ziffer *f*.

2 *vt* **(a)** (*decorate*) *silk etc* bemalen, mustern. ~**d velvet** bedruckter Samt.

(b) (*Mus*) *bass* beziffern; *melody* verzieren.

(c) (*imagine*) sich (*dat*) vorstellen, sich (*dat*) denken.

(d) (*US inf: think, reckon*) glauben, schätzen (*inf*).

(e) (*US inf:* ~ **out**) schlau werden aus, begreifen.

3 *vi* **(a)** (*appear*) erscheinen, auftauchen. **where does pity** ~ **in your scheme of things?** wo rangiert Mitleid in deiner Weltordnung?; **he** ~**d in a play** er trat in einem Stück auf; **he** ~**d prominently in the talks** er spielte eine bedeutende Rolle bei den Gesprächen.

(b) (*inf: make sense*) hinkommen (*inf*), hinhauen (*inf*). **that** ~**s** das hätte ich mir denken können; **it doesn't** ~ das paßt *or* stimmt nicht zusammen; **it** ~**s that he would do that** typisch, daß er das getan hat.

◆**figure on** *vi* +*prep obj* (*esp US*) rechnen mit.

◆**figure out** *vt sep* **(a)** (*understand, make sense of*) begreifen, schlau werden aus. **I can't** ~ **him** ~ **at all** ich werde überhaupt nicht schlau aus ihm; **I can't** ~ **it** ~ ich werde daraus nicht schlau.

(b) (*work out*) ausrechnen; *answer, how to do sth* herausbekommen; *solution* finden; **I** ~**d** ~ **how long it would take** ich habe ausgerechnet, wie lange das dauert; ~ **it** ~ **for yourself** das kannst du dir (leicht) selbst ausrechnen.

figure: ~**-conscious** *adj* figurbewußt; ~**head** *n* (*Naut, fig*) Galionsfigur *f*; ~**-skate** *vi* eiskunstlaufen; ~**-skater** *n* Eiskunstläufer(in *f*) *m*; ~**-skating** *n* Eiskunstlaufen *nt*.

figurine [ˈfɪgəriːn] *n* Figurine *f*.

Fiji [ˈfiːdʒiː] *n* Fidschiinseln *pl*.

Fijian [fiˈdʒiːən] **1** *adj* fidschianisch. **2** *n* **(a)** Fidschiinsulaner(in *f*) *m*. **(b)** (*language*) Fidschianisch *nt*.

filament [ˈfɪləmənt] *n* (*Elec*) (Glüh- *or* Heiz)faden *m*; (*Bot*) Staubfaden *m*.

filch [fɪltʃ] *vt* filzen, mopsen, mausen (*all inf*).

file¹ [faɪl] **1** *n* (*tool*) Feile *f*. **2** *vt* feilen. **to** ~ **one's fingernails** sich (*dat*) die Fingernägel feilen.

◆**file away** *vt sep* abfeilen.

◆**file down** *vt sep* abfeilen.

file² **1** *n* **(a)** (*holder*) (Akten)hefter, Aktenordner *m*; (*for card index*) Karteikasten *m*. **would you go to the** ~**s and get ...** könnten Sie bitte ... aus der Kartei holen; **it's in the** ~**s** somewhere das muß irgendwo bei den Akten sein.

(b) (*documents, information*) Akte *f* (*on sb* über jdn, *on sth* zu etw). **on** ~ aktenkundig, bei den Akten; **have we got that on** ~? haben wir das bei den Akten?; **to open** *or* **start a** ~ **on sb/sth** eine Akte über jdn/zu etw anlegen; **to keep a** ~ **on sb/sth** eine Akte über jdn/zu etw führen; **to close the** ~ **on sb/sth** jds Akte schließen/die Akte zu einer Sache schließen; **the Kowalski** ~ die Akte Kowalski.

(c) (*Computers*) Datenblock *m* mit Adresse. **data on** ~ unter einer Adresse *or* auf Abruf gespeicherte Daten.

2 *vt* **(a)** (*put in* ~) *letters* ablegen, abheften. **it's** ~**d under "B"** das ist unter „B" abgelegt.

(b) (*Jur*) einreichen, erheben. **to** ~ **a petition at court** (*Jur*) ein Gesuch *nt* bei Gericht einreichen.

◆**file away** *vt sep* *papers* zu den Akten legen.

file³ **1** *n* (*row*) Reihe *f*. **in Indian** *or* **single** ~ im Gänsemarsch; (*Mil*) in Reihe; *see* rank¹.

2 *vi* **to** ~ **in** hereinmarschieren *or* -kommen; **they** ~**d out of the classroom** sie gingen/kamen hintereinander *or* nacheinander aus dem Klassenzimmer; **the procession** ~**d under the archway** die Prozession zog unter dem Torbogen hindurch; **long lines of spectators** ~**d slowly into the stadium** lange Zuschauerreihen kamen langsam ins Stadion; **they** ~**d through the turnstile** sie kamen nacheinander durch das Drehkreuz; **the troops** ~**d past the** general die Truppen marschierten *or* defilierten am General vorbei; **the children** ~**d past the head-master** die Kinder gingen in einer Reihe am Direktor vorbei; **a long line of refugees** ~**d over the bridge** eine lange Reihe von Flüchtlingen zog über die Brücke.

file clerk *n* (*US*) Angestellte(r) *mf* in der Registratur.

filial [ˈfɪlɪəl] *adj* Kindes-; *duty also* töchterlich, Sohnes-. **with due** ~ **respect** mit dem Respekt, den eine Tochter/ein Sohn schuldig ist.

filibuster [ˈfɪlɪbʌstəʳ] (*esp US*) **1** *n* **(a)** (*speech*) Obstruktion, Dauerrede *f*; (*person*) Filibuster, Dauerredner, Obstruktionist *m*. **2** *vi* filibustern, Obstruktion betreiben.

filibusterer [ˈfɪlɪbʌstərəʳ] *n* (*esp US*) Filibuster, Dauerredner, Obstruktionist *m*.

filibustering [ˈfɪlɪbʌstərɪŋ] *n* Verschleppungstaktik *f*, Obstruktionismus *m*.

filigree [ˈfɪlɪgriː] **1** *n* Filigran(arbeit *f*) *nt*. **2** *adj* Filigran-.

filing [ˈfaɪlɪŋ] *n* **(a)** (*of documents*) Ablegen, Abheften *nt*. **who does your** ~? wer ist bei Ihnen für die Ablage zuständig?; **have you done the** ~? haben Sie die Akten schon abgelegt? **(b)** (*Jur*) Einreichung *f*.

filing: ~ **cabinet** *n* Aktenschrank *m or* -regal *nt*; ~ **clerk** *n* (*Brit*)

Angestellte(r) *mf* in der Registratur.

filings [ˈfaɪlɪŋz] *npl* Späne *pl*.

Filipino [fɪlɪˈpiːnəʊ] *n* Filipino *m*.

fill [fɪl] **1** *vt* **(a)** *bottle, bucket, hole* füllen; *pipe* stopfen; *teeth also* plombieren; (*wind*) *sails* blähen; (*fig*) (aus)füllen. **I had three teeth** ~**ed** ich bekam drei Zähne plombiert *or* gefüllt.

(b) (*permeate*) erfüllen. ~**ed with anger/admiration/longing** voller Zorn/Bewunderung/Verlangen, von Zorn/Bewunderung/Verlangen erfüllt (*geh*); **the thought** ~**ed him with horror** der Gedanke erfüllte ihn mit Entsetzen.

(c) *post, position* (*employer*) besetzen; (*employee*) (*take up*) einnehmen; (*be in*) innehaben; *need* entsprechen (+*dat*). **we are looking for a young man to** ~ **the post of ...** wir suchen einen jungen Mann, der den Posten eines ... einnehmen soll; **I think he will** ~ **the job very nicely** ich denke, er wird die Stelle sehr gut ausfüllen *or* er ist der richtige Mann für den Job; **the position is already** ~**ed** die Stelle ist schon besetzt *or* vergeben.

2 *vi* sich füllen.

3 to drink one's ~ seinen Durst löschen; **to eat one's** ~ sich satt essen; **to have had one's** ~ gut satt sein; **I've had my** ~ **of him/it** (*inf*) ich habe von ihm/davon die Nase voll (*inf*), ich habe ihn/das satt; **a** ~ **of tobacco** eine Pfeife Tabak.

◆**fill in 1** *vi* **to** ~ **for sb** für jdn einspringen.

2 *vt sep* **(a)** *hole* auffüllen; *door, fireplace* zumauern. **to** ~ ~ **the gaps in one's knowledge** seine Wissenslücken stopfen; **he's just** ~**ing** ~ **time until he gets another job** er überbrückt nur die Zeit, bis er eine andere Stelle bekommt.

(b) *form, questionnaire* ausfüllen; *name, address, details, missing word* eintragen.

(c) to ~ **sb** ~ (**on sth**) jdn (über etw *acc*) aufklären *or* ins Bild setzen.

◆**fill out 1** *vi* **(a)** (*sails etc*) sich blähen. **(b)** (*person: become fatter*) fülliger werden; *cheeks, face* runder *or* voller werden.

2 *vi sep form* ausfüllen; *essay, article etc* strecken.

◆**fill up 1** *vi* **(a)** (*Aut*) (auf)tanken.

(b) (*hall, barrel etc*) sich füllen.

2 *vt sep* **(a)** *tank, cup* vollfüllen; (*driver*) volltanken; *hole* füllen, stopfen. **to** ~ **sth right** ~ etw bis zum Rand (an)füllen; **he** ~**ed the glass** ~ **to the brim** er füllte das Glas randvoll; ~ **her** ~! (*Aut inf*) volltanken bitte!; **that pie has really** ~**ed me** ~ ich fühle mich wirklich voll nach dieser Pastete; **you need something to** ~ **you** ~ du brauchst was Sättigendes.

(b) *form* ausfüllen.

filler [ˈfɪləʳ] *n* **(a)** (*funnel*) Trichter *m*. **(b)** (*Build: paste for cracks*) Spachtelmasse *f*. **(c)** (*Press, TV*) Füllsel *nt*, (Lücken)-füller *m*. **(d)** (*Chem: for plastics*) Füllstoff *m*.

fillet [ˈfɪlɪt] **1** *n* **(a)** (*Cook: of beef, fish*) Filet *nt*. ~ **steak** Filetsteak *nt*. **(b)** (*for the hair*) (Haar)band *nt*. **2** *vt* (*Cook*) filetieren; *meat also* in Filets schneiden. ~**ed sole** Seezungenfilet *nt*.

filling [ˈfɪlɪŋ] **1** *n* **(a)** (*in tooth*) Füllung, Plombe *f*. **my** ~**'s come out** ich hab eine Füllung *or* Plombe verloren; **I had to have three** ~**s** ich mußte mir drei Zähne plombieren *or* füllen lassen. **(b)** (*Cook: in pie, tart*) Füllung *f*. **2** *adj food* sättigend.

filling station *n* Tankstelle *f*.

fillip [ˈfɪlɪp] *n* (*fig*) Ansporn *m*, Aufmunterung *f*. **to give sb/sth a** ~ jdn aufmuntern *or* anspornen/einer Sache (*dat*) (neuen) Schwung geben; **this gave a** ~ **to our business** dadurch hat unser Geschäft einen Aufschwung genommen.

fill-up [ˈfɪlʌp] *n* (*inf*) **to give sb a** ~ jdm nachschenken; **do you want a** ~? soll ich nachschenken?; **he's already had three** ~**s** ich habe ihm schon dreimal nachgeschenkt.

filly [ˈfɪlɪ] *n* Stutfohlen *nt*; (*dated inf*) Mädel *nt* (*dated*).

film [fɪlm] **1** *n* **(a)** Film *m*; (*of dust*) Schicht *f*; (*of ice on water*) Schicht *f*; (*of mist, on the eye*) Schleier *m*; (*thin membrane*) Häutchen *nt*; (*on teeth*) Belag *m*; (*fine web*) feines Gewebe.

(b) (*Phot*) Film *m*. **get your holiday on** ~ bannen Sie Ihre Ferien auf den Film; **I wish I'd got that on** ~ ich wünschte, ich hätte das aufnehmen können; **to take a** ~ **of sth** einen Film über etw (*acc*) drehen *or* machen.

(c) (*motion picture*) Film *m*. **to make** *or* **shoot a** ~ einen Film drehen *or* machen; **to make a** ~ (*actor*) einen Film machen; **to go to the** ~**s** ins Kino gehen; **he's in** ~**s** er ist beim Film; **to go into** ~**s** zum Film gehen.

2 *vt play* verfilmen; *scene* filmen; *people* einen Film machen von. **he didn't know he was being** ~**ed** er wußte nicht, daß er gefilmt wurde.

3 *vi* **she** ~**s well** sie ist sehr fotogen; **the story** ~**ed very well** die Geschichte ließ sich gut verfilmen; ~**ing starts tomorrow** die Dreharbeiten fangen morgen an.

◆**film over** *or* **up** *vi* (*mirror, glass*) anlaufen.

film: ~ **archives** *npl* Filmarchiv(e *pl*) *nt*; ~ **camera** *n* Filmkamera *f*; ~ **clip** *n* Filmausschnitt *m*; ~ **fan** *n* Filmliebhaber(in *f*) *m*, Filmfan *m*; ~ **library** *n* Cinemathek *f*; ~ **rights** *npl* Filmrechte *pl*; ~ **script** *n* Drehbuch *nt*; ~**-set** *n* (*Brit Typ*) lichtsetzen, photosetzen; ~**-setting** *n* (*Brit Typ*) Lichtsatz, Photosatz *m*; ~**star** *n* Filmstar *m*; ~**strip** *n* Filmstreifen *m*; ~ **studio** *n* Filmstudio *nt*; ~ **test** *n* Probeaufnahmen *pl*; **to give sb a** ~ **test** Probeaufnahmen von jdm machen; ~ **version** *n* Verfilmung *f*.

filmy [ˈfɪlmɪ] *adj* (+*er*) *material* dünn, zart.

filter [ˈfɪltəʳ] **1** *n* **(a)** Filter *m*; (*Phot, Rad, Mech*) Filter *nt or m*. **(b)** (*Brit: for traffic*) grüner Pfeil (*für Abbieger*). **2** *vt liquids, air* filtern. **3** *vi* **(a)** (*light*) durchscheinen, durchschimmern; (*liquid, sound*) durchsickern. **(b)** (*Brit Aut*) sich einordnen. **to** ~ **to the left** sich links einordnen.

◆**filter back** *vi* (*refugees, prisoners etc*) allmählich zurückkommen.

◆**filter in** *vi* (*people*) langsam *or* allmählich eindringen; (*news*) durchsickern.

◆**filter out 1** *vi* (*people*) einer nach dem anderen herausgehen/-kommen. **2** *vt sep* (*lit*) herausfiltern; (*fig*) heraussieben.

♦**filter through** vi (*liquid, sound, news*) durchsickern; (*light*) durchschimmern, durchscheinen.

filter: ~ **bed** n Klärbecken nt; ~ **lane** n (*Brit*) Spur f zum Einordnen, Abbiegspur f; ~ **paper** n Filterpapier nt; ~ **tip** n Filter m; ~**-tipped** adj cigarette Filter-.

filth [fɪlθ] n (*lit*) Schmutz, Dreck m; (*fig*) Schweinerei, Sauerei (*sl*) f; (*people*) Dreckspack, (Lumpen)gesindel nt. **all the** ~ **they wrote about him in the papers** all der Unflat, der über ihn in der Zeitung geschrieben wurde; **none of your** ~! keine Schweinereien, bitte!; **to talk** ~ unflätig reden.

filthy ['fɪlθɪ] adj (+er) schmutzig, dreckig; (*inf*) weather Drecks- (*inf*), Sau- (*sl*); day Mist-; temper übel; (*obscene*) unanständig, schweinisch (*inf*). **your hands are** ~! deine Hände sind ja ganz dreckig (*inf*) or völlig verdreckt; **he's got a** ~ **mind** er hat eine schmutzige or schweinische (*inf*) Phantasie; **don't be** ~ (*to child*) du Ferkel!; (*to grown-up*) Sie Schmutzfink!; **you** ~ **little boy!** du bist vielleicht ein Ferkel!; **you** ~ **swine!** du dreckiges Schwein! (*inf*), du Drecksau! (*sl*); **a** ~ **habit** eine widerliche Angewohnheit; ~ **rich** (*inf*) stinkreich (*inf*).

fin [fɪn] n (a) (*of fish*) Flosse f. (b) (*Aviat*) Seitenleitwerk nt, Seitenflosse f; (*of bomb, rocket, ship*) Stabilisierungsfläche f. (c) (*Aut: of radiator*) Kühlrippe f. (d) (*for swimming*) Schwimmflosse f.

final ['faɪnl] **1** adj (a) (*last*) letzte(r, s); instalment, chapter, act also, examination, chord Schluß-.
  (b) (*ultimate, result*) letztendlich, End-; version endgültig, letzte(r, s); offer (aller)letzte(r, s); ~ **score** Schlußstand m, Endergebnis nt.
  (c) (*definite*) endgültig. ~ **word** letztes Wort; **we'll probably leave at 10, but that's not** ~ **yet** wir gehen wahrscheinlich um 10, aber das steht noch nicht endgültig fest; **you're not going and that's** ~ du gehst nicht, und damit basta (*inf*).
  (d) ~ **cause** (*Philos*) Urgrund m; ~ **clause** (*Gram*) Finalsatz m.

  2 n (a) ~**s** pl (*Univ*) Abschlußprüfung f.
  (b) (*Sport*) Finale, Endspiel nt; (*in quiz*) Finale nt, Endrunde f. **the** ~**s** das Finale.
  (c) (*Press*) Spätausgabe f. **late-night** ~ letzte Nachtausgabe.

finale [fɪ'nɑːlɪ] n (*Mus, in opera*) Finale nt; (*Theat*) Schlußszene f; (*fig*) Finale nt (*geh*), (Ab)schluß m.

finalist ['faɪnəlɪst] n (*Sport*) Endrundenteilnehmer(in f), Finalist(in f) m; (*Univ*) Examenskandidat(in f) m.

finality [faɪ'nælɪtɪ] n (*of decision etc*) Endgültigkeit f; (*of tone of voice*) Entschiedenheit, Bestimmtheit f.

finalization [ˌfaɪnəlaɪ'zeɪʃən] n see vt Beendigung f; endgültige Festlegung; endgültiger Abschluß; endgültige Formgebung.

finalize ['faɪnəlaɪz] vt fertigmachen, beenden; (*determine*) plans, arrangements endgültig festlegen; deal (endgültig) abschließen, zum Abschluß bringen; draft eine endgültige Form geben (+dat). **to** ~ **a decision** eine endgültige Entscheidung treffen.

finally ['faɪnəlɪ] adv (a) (*at last, eventually*) schließlich; (*expressing relief etc*) endlich. **at last he's** ~ **understood!** nun hat er es endlich verstanden!
  (b) (*at the end, lastly*) schließlich, zum Schluß.
  (c) (*in a definite manner*) endgültig. **he said it very** ~ er hat es in sehr bestimmtem or entschiedenem Ton gesagt.
  (d) **we are,** ~, **all human beings** wir sind doch letztlich or schließlich alle Menschen.

finance [faɪ'næns] **1** n (a) Finanzen pl, Finanz- or Geldwesen nt. **high** ~ Hochfinanz f; **to study** ~ (*academically*) Finanzwissenschaft studieren; (*as training*) eine Finanzfachschule besuchen.
  (b) (*money*) Geld nt, (Geld)mittel pl. **it's a question of** ~ das ist eine Geldfrage or Frage der Finanzen; ~**s** Finanzen pl, Finanz- or Einkommenslage f; **his** ~**s aren't sound** seine Finanzlage ist nicht gesund, seine Finanzen stehen nicht gut.
  2 vt finanzieren.

finance: ~ **company** n Finanz(ierungs)gesellschaft f; ~ **director** n Leiter m der Finanzabteilung.

financial [faɪ'nænʃəl] adj finanziell; situation also, crisis Finanz-; news, page Wirtschafts-. ~ **paper** Börsenblatt nt; ~ **director** Leiter m der Finanzabteilung; **the** ~ **year** das Rechnungsjahr.

financially [faɪ'nænʃəlɪ] adv finanziell. **the company is** ~ **sound** die Finanzlage der Firma ist gesund; **the planning was** ~ **disastrous** die Planung war ein finanzielles Fiasko.

financier [faɪ'nænsɪəʳ] n Finanzier m.

finch [fɪntʃ] n Fink m.

find [faɪnd] (*vb: pret, ptp* **found**) **1** vt (a) finden. **it's not to be found** es läßt sich nicht finden or auftreiben (*inf*); **to** ~ **sb out or away** jdn nicht (zu Hause) antreffen; **hoping this letter** ~**s you in good health** in der Hoffnung, daß Sie gesund sind; **we left everything as we found it** wir haben alles so gelassen, wie wir es vorgefunden haben; **he was found dead in bed** er wurde tot im Bett aufgefunden; **I can never** ~ **anything to say to him** ich weiß nie, was ich zu ihm sagen soll; **where am I going to** ~ **the money/time?** wo nehme ich nur das Geld/die Zeit her?; **you must take us as you** ~ **us** Sie müssen uns so nehmen, wie wir sind; **if you can** ~ **it in you to ...** wenn Sie es irgend fertigbringen, zu ...
  (b) (*supply*) besorgen (sb sth jdm etw). **go and** ~ **me a needle** hol mir doch mal eine Nadel; **did you** ~ **him what he wanted?** haben Sie bekommen, was er wollte?; **we'll have to** ~ **him a car/secretary** wir müssen ihm ein Auto besorgen/eine Sekretärin für ihn finden.
  (c) (*discover, ascertain*) feststellen; cause also (heraus)finden. **we found the car wouldn't start** es stellte sich heraus, daß das Auto nicht ansprang; **I** ~ **I'm unable to ...** ich stelle fest, daß ich ... nicht kann; **if you still** ~ **you can't do it** wenn Sie feststellen, daß Sie es immer noch nicht können; **you will** ~ **that**

I am right Sie werden sehen, daß ich recht habe; **it has been found that this is so** es hat sich herausgestellt, daß es so ist.
  (d) (*consider to be*) finden. **I** ~ **Spain too hot** ich finde Spanien zu heiß; **I don't** ~ **it easy to tell you this** es fällt mir nicht leicht, Ihnen das zu sagen; **he always found languages easy/hard** ihm fielen Sprachen immer leicht/schwer; **I found all the questions easy** ich fand, daß die Fragen alle leicht waren; **did you** ~ **her a good worker?** fanden Sie, daß sie gut arbeitet?; **I** ~ **it impossible to understand him** ich kann ihn einfach nicht verstehen.
  (e) **I** ~ **myself in an impossible situation/in financial difficulties** ich befinde mich in einer unmöglichen Situation/in finanziellen Schwierigkeiten; **one day he suddenly found himself a rich man/out of a job** eines Tages war er plötzlich ein reicher Mann/arbeitslos; **he awoke to** ~ **himself in prison/hospital** er erwachte und fand sich im Gefängnis/Krankenhaus wieder; **I found myself quite competent to deal with it** ich stellte fest, daß ich durchaus fähig war, damit zurechtzukommen; **I found myself unable/forced to ...** ich sah mich außerstande/gezwungen, zu .../umringt; **at the end of the tunnel I found myself in ...** am Ende des Tunnels fand ich mich in ...; **how do you** ~ **yourself this morning?** wie geht es Ihnen or befinden Sie sich (*geh*) heute morgen?
  (f) **this flower is found all over England** diese Blume findet man in ganz England; **you don't** ~ **bears here any more** man findet hier keine Bären mehr; **do you know where there is a chemist's to be found?** wissen Sie, wo hier eine Apotheke ist?; **there wasn't one to be found** es war keine(r) etc zu finden.
  (g) **£100 per week all found** £ 100 pro Woche, (und freie) Kost und Logis or (in institution) bei freier Station.
  (h) (*Jur*) ~ **sb guilty** jdn für schuldig befinden, jdn schuldig sprechen; **how do you** ~ **the accused?** wie lautet Ihr Urteil?; **the court has found that ...** das Gericht hat befunden, daß ...

  2 vi (*Jur*) **to** ~ **for/against the accused** den Angeklagten freisprechen/verurteilen, für/gegen den Angeklagten entscheiden.

  3 n Fund m.

♦**find out 1** vt sep (a) answer, sb's secret herausfinden.
  (b) (*discover the misdeeds etc of*) person erwischen; (*come to know about*) auf die Schliche kommen (+dat) (*inf*). **his wife has found him** ~ seine Frau ist dahintergekommen; **don't get found** ~ laß dich nicht erwischen; **you've been found** ~ du bist entdeckt or ertappt (*inf*); **your sins will** ~ **you** ~ (*liter*) die Sonne bringt es an den Tag (prov).
  2 vi es herausfinden; (*discover misdeeds, dishonesty etc also*) dahinterkommen. **where is it?** — ~ ~ **for yourself!** wo ist es? — sieh doch selbst nach!; **where have you hidden it?** — ~ ~! wo hast du es versteckt? — such's doch!

finder ['faɪndəʳ] n (a) (*of lost object*) Finder(in f) m. ~**s keepers** (*inf*) wer's findet, dem gehört's. (b) (*of telescope*) Sucher m.

finding ['faɪndɪŋ] n (a) ~**s** pl Ergebnis(se pl) nt; (*medical*) Befund m; **the** ~**s of the commission of enquiry were as follows** die Untersuchungskommission kam zu folgendem Ergebnis.
  (b) (*Jur: verdict*) Urteil(sspruch m) nt.

fine[1] [faɪn] adv: **in** ~ (*liter*) kurz und gut, kurzum.

fine[2] **1** n (*Jur*) Geldstrafe f; (*for less serious offences also*) Geldbuße f; (*driving also*) Bußgeld nt; (*for minor traffic offences*) (gebühren)pflichtige) Verwarnung f.
  2 vt see n zu einer Geldstrafe verurteilen, mit einer Geldstrafe/-buße belegen; Bußgeld verhängen gegen; eine (gebühren)pflichtige) Verwarnung erteilen (+dat). **he was** ~**d £10** er mußte £ 10 Strafe bezahlen; **he was** ~**d for speeding** er hat einen Strafzettel für zu schnelles Fahren bekommen.

fine[3] **1** adj (+er) (a) weather schön. **it's going to be** ~ **this afternoon** heute nachmittag wird es schön; **we'll go if it's** ~ wir gehen, wenn das Wetter schön ist; **one** ~ **day** eines schönen Tages; **I hope it keeps** ~ **for you!** ich hoffe, Sie haben schönes Wetter!; (*dated inf*) alles Gute!
  (b) (*good*) gut; example, selection, workmanship also, person, character fein; specimen, chap, woman prächtig; mind fein, scharf; pianist, novel, painting, shot großartig; complexion, holiday schön; holiday, meal, view herrlich; (*elegant*) clothes, manners etc fein, vornehm. **our** ~**st hour** unsere größte Stunde; **he did a** ~ **job there** da hat er gute Arbeit geleistet; **that's a** ~ **excuse** (*iro*) das ist ja eine schöne Ausrede; **a** ~ **time to ...** (*iro*) ein feiner Augenblick, zu ...; **a** ~ **friend you are** (*iro*) du bist nur ein schöner Freund!; **that's a** ~ **thing to say** (*iro*) das ist ja wirklich nett, so was zu sagen! (*iro*); **that's all very** ~ **but ...** das ist ja alles schön und gut, aber ...; **this is a** ~ **state of affairs** (*iro*) das sind ja schöne Zustände; **she likes to play at being the** ~ **lady** sie spielt sich gern als feine Dame auf.
  (c) (*OK, in order*) gut, in Ordnung. **more soup?** — **no thanks, I'm** ~ noch etwas Suppe? — nein danke, ich habe genug; **everything was** ~ **until he came along** alles ging gut, bis er kam; **that's** ~ **by me** ich habe nichts dagegen; (*that's*) ~ gut or in Ordnung; ~, **fantastic!** gut, ausgezeichnet!; ~, **let's do that then** ja or gut, machen wir das; **I got the tickets** — **oh that's** ~, **then** ich habe die Karten bekommen — fein or schön; **4 o'clock OK?** — ~ ~ geht es um 4? — ja, das ist gut or in Ordnung.
  (d) (*healthwise, mentally*) sb is or feels ~ jdm geht es gut; **I'm/he is** ~ **now** es geht mir/ihm wieder gut; **how are you?** — ~ **wie geht's?** — gut.
  (e) (*delicate*) workmanship fein; material, china also zart. ~ **feelings** Feingefühl nt; **to appeal to sb's** ~**r feelings** an jds besseres Ich appellieren; **it's no good trying to appeal to his** ~**r feelings** es hat keinen Wert, an seine Gefühle zu appellieren.
  (f) dust, sand fein; rain also Niesel-.
  (g) (*thin*) fein, dünn; (*sharp*) scharf; handwriting fein, zierlich. ~ **nib** spitze Feder; see point.
  (h) (*Metal*) Fein-.

(i) (*discriminating*) *distinction, ear* fein. **there's a very ~ line between ...** es besteht ein feiner Unterschied zwischen ...

2 *adv* **(a)** (*well*) gut, prima (*inf*). **these ~-sounding adjectives** diese wohlklingenden Adjektive.

(b) (*+er*) **to chop sth up ~** etw fein (zer)hacken; *see* cut.

♦**fine down** *vt sep wood etc* abhobeln/-feilen; *text, novel etc* straffen (*to* zu); *theory* reduzieren (*to* auf +*acc*).

fine: ~ **art** *n* (*a*) *usu pl* schöne Künste *pl*; (**b**) (*skill*) Kunststück *nt*, echte Kunst; **he's got it down to a ~ art** er hat den Bogen heraus (*inf*); ~**-drawn** *adj* (**a**) *thread* fein gesponnen *or* (*synthetic*) gezogen; *wire* fein gezogen; (**b**) *features* fein (geschnitten); ~**-grained** *adj wood* fein gemasert; *photographic paper* feinkörnig.

finely ['faɪnlɪ] *adv* fein; *worked, made* schön; *detailed* genau; *sliced also* dünn.

fineness ['faɪnnɪs] *n* (**a**) Schönheit *f*.

(b) (*of quality*) Güte *f*; (*of mind, novel*) Großartigkeit *f*; (*elegance*) Feinheit *f*.

(c) (*of piece of work*) Feinheit *f*; (*of material, feelings*) Zartheit *f*.

(d) (*of dust, sand*) Feinheit, Feinkörnigkeit *f*.

(e) (*thinness*) Feinheit, Dünnheit, Dünne *f*; (*sharpness*) Schärfe *f*; (*of handwriting*) Feinheit *f*; (*of nib*) Spitze *f*.

(f) (*of metal*) Feingehalt *m*.

(g) (*of distinction*) Feinheit *f*.

finery ['faɪnərɪ] *n* (**a**) (*of dress*) Staat *m*; (*liter: of nature etc also*) Pracht *f*. **she had never seen so much ~** sie hatte noch nie so viel Eleganz gesehen. (**b**) (*Metal: furnace*) Frischofen *m*.

finesse [fɪ'nes] **1** *n* (**a**) (*skill, diplomacy*) Gewandtheit *f*, Geschick *nt*. (**b**) (*cunning*) Schlauheit, Finesse *f*. (**c**) (*Cards*) Schneiden *nt*. **2** *vti* (*Cards*) schneiden.

fine-tooth comb ['faɪn'tuːθkəʊm] *n*: **to go through sth with a ~** etw genau unter die Lupe nehmen.

finger ['fɪŋgə'] **1** *n* Finger *m*. **she can twist him round her little ~** sie kann ihn um den (kleinen) Finger wickeln; **to have a ~ in every pie** überall die Finger drin *or* im Spiel haben (*inf*), überall mitmischen (*inf*); **I forbid you to lay a ~ on him** ich verbiete Ihnen, ihm auch nur ein Härchen zu krümmen; **I didn't lay a ~ on her** ich habe sie nicht angerührt; **he wouldn't lift a ~ to help me** er würde keinen Finger rühren, um mir zu helfen; **he didn't lift a ~** er hat keinen Finger krumm gemacht (*inf*); **to point one's ~ at sb** mit dem Finger auf jdn zeigen; **to point the ~ at sb** (*fig*) mit Fingern auf jdn zeigen; **I can't put my ~ on it, but ...** ich kann es nicht genau ausmachen, aber ...; **you've put your ~ on it** there da haben Sie den kritischen Punkt berührt; **to put the ~ on sb** (*sl*) jdn verpfeifen (*inf*); **to get** *or* **pull one's ~ out** (*sl*) Nägel mit Köpfen machen (*sl*); **pull your ~ out!** (*sl*) es wird Zeit, daß du Nägel mit Köpfen machst! (*sl*); *see* cross.

2 *vt* (**a**) anfassen; (*toy, meddle with*) befingern, herumfingern an (+*dat*).

(b) (*Mus: mark for ~ing*) mit einem Fingersatz versehen. **to ~ the keys/strings** in die Tasten/Saiten greifen.

finger: ~ **alphabet** *n* Fingeralphabet *nt*; ~ **board** *n* Griffbrett *nt*; ~**bowl** *n* Fingerschale *f*; ~ **exercise** *n* Fingerübung *f*.

fingering ['fɪŋgərɪŋ] *n* (**a**) (*Mus*) (*in the notation*) Fingersatz *m*; (*of keys, strings*) (Finger)technik *f*. **the ~ is very difficult** die Griffe sind sehr schwierig.

(b) (*of goods in shop etc*) Anfassen, Berühren *nt*; (*toying, meddling*) Befingern *nt* (*of, with gen*), Herumfingern *nt* (*of, with an* +*dat*).

(c) (*Tex*) Strumpfwolle *f*.

finger: ~**mark** *n* Fingerabdruck *m*; ~**nail** *n* Fingernagel *m*; ~**print** **1** *n* Fingerabdruck *m*; **2** *vt* **to ~print sb/sth** jdm die Fingerabdrücke *pl* abnehmen/von etw Fingerabdrücke *pl* abnehmen; ~**print expert** *n* Sachverständige(r) *mf* für Fingerabdrücke; ~**stall** *n* Fingerling *m*; ~**tip** *n* Fingerspitze *f*; **to have sth at one's ~tips** (*fig*) (*know very well*) etw aus dem Effeff kennen (*inf*); (*have at one's immediate disposal*) etw im kleinen Finger (*inf*) *or* parat haben; **to one's ~tips** (*fig*) durch und durch; ~**tip control** *n* (*of steering wheel etc*) mühelose Steuerung; **to have ~tip control** sich mühelos bedienen lassen.

finickiness ['fɪnɪkɪnɪs] *n* (*of person*) Pingeligkeit *f* (*inf*); (*about language also*) Wortklauberei, Haarspalterei *f*; (*of task*) Kniff(e)ligkeit *f* (*inf*). **because of his ~ about what he eats** weil er so wählerisch *or* heikel (*dial inf*) im Essen ist.

finicky ['fɪnɪkɪ] *adj person* schwer zufriedenzustellen, pingelig (*inf*); (*about language also*) wortklauberisch, haarspalterisch; (*about food, clothes etc also*) wählerisch, heikel (*dial inf*); *work, job* kniff(e)lig (*inf*); *detail* winzig.

finish ['fɪnɪʃ] **1** *n* (**a**) (*end*) Schluß *m*, Ende *nt*; (*of race*) Finish *nt*; (~*ing line*) Ziel *nt*. **they never gave up, right to the ~** sie haben bis zum Schluß nicht aufgegeben; **he's got a good ~** (*Sport*) er hat einen starken Endspurt; **to be in at the ~** (*fig*) beim Ende dabeisein; **to fight to the ~** bis zum letzten Augenblick kämpfen.

(b) (*perfection: of manners*) Schliff *m*; (*of things*) Verarbeitung, Ausfertigung *f*. **factory-made objects lack the ~ of the handmade ones** industriell hergestellte Waren sind nicht so sorgfältig *or* sauber verarbeitet wie handgemachte; **it has a poor ~** die Verarbeitung *or* Ausfertigung ist nicht gut; **the style lacks ~** dem Stil fehlt der Schliff.

(c) (*of industrial products*) Finish *nt*; (*final coat of paint*) Deckanstrich *m*; (*of material*) Appretur *f*; (*of paper*) Oberflächenfinish *nt*; (*of pottery*) Oberfläche *f*; (*ornamental work*) Verzierung *f*. **paper with a gloss/matt ~** Hochglanz-/Mattglanzpapier *nt*; **paint with a gloss/matt ~** Farbe mit Hochglanzeffekt/mattem Glanz; **highly polished to give it a good ~** hoch poliert, um Glanz zu erzielen.

2 *vt* (**a**) beenden; *education, course also* abschließen; *work, business also* erledigen, abschließen. **he's ~ed the painting/novel/job** er hat das Bild/den Roman/die Arbeit fertig(gemalt/

-geschrieben/-gemacht); **to ~/have ~ed doing sth** mit etw fertig werden/sein; **to ~ writing/reading sth** etw zu Ende schreiben/lesen, etw fertigschreiben/-lesen; **let me ~ eating** laß mich zu Ende essen, laß mich fertigessen; **to have ~ed sth** etw fertig haben; *task, course* mit etw fertig sein, etw beendet haben; **when do you ~ work?** wann machen Sie Feierabend *or* Schluß?; **I'm in a hurry to get this job ~ed** ich möchte diese Sache so schnell wie möglich zu Ende bringen; **she never lets him ~ what he's saying** sie läßt ihn nie ausreden; **daddy, will you ~ (telling) that story?** Papa, erzählst du die Geschichte zu Ende *or* fertig?; **can I have that book when you've ~ed it?** kann ich das Buch haben, wenn es ausgelesen hast?; **give me time to ~ my drink** laß mich austrinken; **~ what you're doing and we'll go** mach fertig, was du angefangen hast, und dann gehen wir; **that last kilometre nearly ~ed me** (*inf*) dieser letzte Kilometer hat mich beinahe geschafft (*inf*).

(b) (*give ~ to*) den letzten Schliff geben (+*dat*); *piece of handiwork* verarbeiten; *surface* eine schöne Oberfläche geben (+*dat*); *industrial product* ein schönes Finish geben (+*dat*). **the paintwork isn't very well ~ed** der Lack hat keine besonders schöne Oberfläche; **to ~ sth with a coat of varnish** etw zum Schluß lackieren; **the metal is ~ed with a high-speed disc** das Metall wird zum Schluß mit einer schnell rotierenden Scheibe poliert; **the paper is ~ed on the glazing rollers** das Papier wird zum Schluß mit dem Kalander bearbeitet.

3 *vi* (**a**) zu Ende *or* aus sein; (*person: with task etc*) fertig sein; (*come to an end, ~ work*) aufhören; (*piece of music, story etc*) enden. **when does the film ~?** wann ist der Film aus?; **my holiday ~es this week** mein Urlaub geht diese Woche zu Ende; **we'll ~ by singing a song** wir wollen mit einem Lied schließen, zum Schluß singen wir ein Lied; **I've ~ed** ich bin fertig.

(b) (*Sport*) das Ziel erreichen. **to ~ first/second** als erster/zweiter durchs Ziel gehen.

♦**finish off 1** *vi* (**a**) aufhören, Schluß machen.

(b) **to ~ with a glass of brandy** zum (Ab)schluß ein Glas Weinbrand trinken; **we ~ed ~ by singing** ... wir schlossen mit dem Lied ..., wir sangen zum (Ab)schluß ...

2 *vt sep* (**a**) *piece of work* fertigmachen; *job also* erledigen. **to ~ ~ a painting/letter/story** ein Bild zu Ende malen/einen Brief zu Ende schreiben/eine Geschichte zu Ende erzählen.

(b) *food, meal* aufessen; *drink* austrinken.

(c) (*kill*) *wounded animal, person* den Gnadenstoß geben (+*dat*); (*by shooting*) den Gnadenschuß geben (+*dat*).

(d) (*do for*) *person* den Rest geben (+*dat*), erledigen (*inf*). **the last two miles just about ~ed me** (*inf*) die letzten beiden Meilen haben mich ziemlich fertiggemacht (*inf*) *or* geschafft (*inf*).

♦**finish up 1** *vi* (**a**) *see* finish off 1 (a, b).

(b) (*end up in a place*) landen (*inf*). **he ~ed ~ a nervous wreck** er war zum Schluß ein Nervenbündel; **he ~ed ~ in third place** er landete auf dem dritten Platz (*inf*); **you'll ~ ~ wishing you'd never started** du wünschst dir bestimmt noch, du hättest gar nicht erst angefangen; **I'll just ~ ~ by doing it all again** zum Schluß muß ich doch alles noch mal machen.

2 *vt sep see* **finish off 2** (**b**).

♦**finish with** *vi* +*prep obj* (**a**) (*no longer need*) nicht mehr brauchen. **I've ~ed ~ the paper/book** ich habe die Zeitung/das Buch fertiggelesen; **I won't be ~ed ~ him/it for some time yet** ich werde noch eine Weile mit ihm/damit zu tun haben.

(b) (*want no more to do with*) nichts mehr zu tun haben wollen mit, fertig sein mit (*inf*); (*with boy/girlfriend*) Schluß machen mit. **I've ~ed ~ him** ich will nichts mehr mit ihm zu tun haben, ich bin fertig mit ihm (*inf*); ich habe mit ihm Schluß gemacht.

(c) **you wait till I've ~ed ~ you!** (*inf*) wart nur, dich köpfe ich mir noch vor (*inf*).

finished ['fɪnɪʃt] *adj* (**a**) *item, product* fertig; *woodwork, metal* fertig bearbeitet; (*polished also*) poliert; (*varnished, lacquered also*) lackiert; *performance* ausgereift, makellos; *appearance* vollendet. **~ goods** Fertigprodukte *pl*; **beautifully ~ dolls** wunderschön gearbeitete Puppen.

(b) **to be ~** (*person, task etc*) fertig sein; (*exhausted, done for etc*) erledigt sein; **the wine is/the chops are ~** es ist kein Wein/es sind keine Koteletts mehr da; Wein ist/die Koteletts sind aus *or* alle (*inf*); **those days are ~** die Zeiten sind vorbei; **he's ~ as a politician** als Politiker ist er erledigt; **if you tell him that, you're ~** wenn Sie ihm das sagen, sind Sie erledigt; **I'm ~ with him/this company** er/diese Firma ist für mich erledigt *or* gestorben; **I'm ~ with politics/the theatre** mit der Politik/dem Theater ist es für mich vorbei; **it's all ~ (between us)** es ist alles aus (zwischen uns).

finishing ['fɪnɪʃɪŋ] *n*: ~ **line** *n* Ziellinie *f*; ~ **school** *n* (Mädchen)pensionat *nt*.

finite ['faɪnaɪt] *adj* (**a**) begrenzt. **a ~ number** eine endliche Zahl.

(b) ~ **verb** (*Gram*) finites Verb, Verbum finitum *nt* (*spec*).

fink [fɪŋk] *n* (*US sl*) (**a**) (*strikebreaker*) Streikbrecher *m*. (**b**) (*contemptible person*) Saftsack *m* (*sl*).

Finland ['fɪnlənd] *n* Finnland *nt*.

Finn [fɪn] *n* Finne *m*, Finnin *f*.

Finnish ['fɪnɪʃ] **1** *adj* finnisch. **2** *n* Finnisch *nt*.

fiord [fjɔːd] *n* Fjord *m*.

fir [fɜː'] *n* Tanne *f*; (~ *wood*) Tanne(nholz *nt*) *f*. ~ **cone** Tannenzapfen *m*.

fire [faɪə'] **1** *n* (**a**) Feuer *nt*. **the house was on ~** das Haus brannte; **to set ~ to sth, to set sth on ~** etw anzünden; (*so as to destroy*) etw in Brand stecken; (*deliberately also*) Feuer an etw (*acc*) legen; **to catch ~** Feuer fangen; (*building, forest etc also*) in Brand geraten; **when man discovered ~** als der Mensch das Feuer entdeckte; **you're playing with ~** (*fig*) du spielst mit dem Feuer; **to fight ~ with ~** (*fig*) mit den gleichen Waffen kämpfen; **to go through ~ and water for sb** (*fig*) für jdn durchs Feuer gehen; *see* house.

   (b) (*house* ~, *forest* ~ *etc*) Brand *m*. there was a ~ next door nebenan hat es gebrannt; ~! Feuer!, feurio (*old*); Glasgow has more ~s than any other city in Glasgow brennt es häufiger als in anderen Städten; to insure oneself against ~ eine Feuerversicherung abschließen.

   (c) (*in grate*) (Kamin)feuer *nt*; (*electric* ~, *gas* ~) Ofen *m*. they have an open ~ sie haben einen offenen Kamin *or* ein Kaminfeuer *nt*.

   (d) (*Mil*) Feuer *nt*. ~! Feuer!; to come between two ~s (*lit, fig*) zwischen zwei Feuer geraten; to come under ~ (*lit, fig*) unter Beschuß geraten; he came under ~ from the critics er wurde von den Kritikern unter Beschuß genommen; to be in the line of ~ (*lit, fig*) in der Schußlinie stehen.

   (e) (*passion*) Feuer *nt*. he spoke with ~ er sprach mit Leidenschaft.

   2 *vt* (a) (*burn to destroy*) in Brand stecken.

   (b) *pottery* brennen.

   (c) *furnace* befeuern; *see* oil-fired, gas-fired.

   (d) (*fig*) *imagination* beflügeln; *passions* entzünden, entfachen (*geh*); *enthusiasm* befeuern. to ~ sb with enthusiasm jdn begeistern, jdn in Begeisterung versetzen.

   (e) *gun* abschießen; *shot* abfeuern, abgeben; *rocket* zünden, abfeuern. to ~ a gun at sb auf jdn schießen; to ~ a salute schießen; to ~ questions at sb Fragen auf jdn abfeuern.

   (f) (*inf: dismiss*) feuern (*inf*).

   3 *vi* (a) (*shoot*) feuern, schießen (*at* auf +*acc*). ~! (gebt) Feuer!

   (b) (*engine*) zünden. the engine is only firing on three cylinders der Motor läuft nur auf drei Zylindern.

♦**fire away** *vi* (*inf: begin*) losschießen (*inf*).

♦**fire off** *vt sep gun, round, shell, questions* abfeuern.

fire: ~ alarm *n* Feueralarm *m*; (*apparatus*) Feuermelder *m*; ~arm *n* Feuer- *or* Schußwaffe *f*; ~ assurance *n see* ~ insurance; ~ball *n* (a) (*of nuclear explosion*) Feuerball *m*; (*lightning*) Kugelblitz *m*; (b) (*meteor*) Feuerkugel *f*; (c) (*fig inf: person*) Energiebündel *nt* (*inf*); ~brand *n* (a) Feuerbrand *m* (*old*); (b) (*mischief-maker*) Unruhestifter, Aufwiegler *m*; ~break *n* (*strip of land*) Feuerschneise *f*; (*wall*) Brandmauer *f*; (*sandbags etc*) (Schutz)wall *m gegen die Ausbreitung eines Feuers*; ~brick *n* Schamottstein *m*; ~ brigade *n* Feuerwehr *f*; ~bug *n* (*inf*) Feuerteufel *m* (*inf*); ~clay *n* Schamotte *f*; ~cracker *n* Knallkörper *m*; ~damp *n* (*Min*) Grubengas *nt*, schlagende Wetter *pl*; ~ department *n* (*US*) Feuerwehr *f*; ~dog *n* Kaminbock *m*; ~ door *n* Feuertür *f*; ~ drill *n* (*for firemen*) Feuerwehrübung *f*; (*for passengers, people in a big building etc*) Probealarm *m*; ~-eater *n* Feuerfresser *or* -schlucker *m*; ~-engine *n* Feuerwehrauto *nt*; ~ escape *n* (*staircase*) Feuertreppe *f*; (*ladder*) Feuerleiter *f*; ~ extinguisher *n* Feuerlöscher *m*; ~-fighter *n* (*fireman*) Feuerwehrmann *m*; (*voluntary help*) freiwilliger Helfer (bei der Feuerbekämpfung); ~-fighting *adj attr techniques* Feuerbekämpfungs-; *equipment* (Feuer)-lösch-; ~fly *n* Leuchtkäfer *m*; ~ guard *n* (Schutz)gitter *nt* (*vor dem Kamin*); ~ hazard *n* to be a ~ hazard feuergefährlich sein; these old houses are a ~ hazard bei diesen alten Häusern besteht Brandgefahr; ~ hose *n* Feuerwehrschlauch *m*; ~ house *n* (*US*) Feuerwache, Feuerwehrzentrale *f*; ~ hydrant *n* Hydrant *m*; ~ insurance *n* Feuer- *or* Brandversicherung *f*; ~ irons *npl* Kaminbesteck *nt*; ~light *n* Schein *m* des Feuers *or* der Flammen; ~lighter *n* Feueranzünder *m*; ~man *n* (a) Feuerwehrmann *m*; (b) (*Rail*) Heizer *m*; ~place *n* Kamin *m*; ~plug *n* (*US*) Hydrant *m*; ~power *n* (*of guns, aircraft, army*) Feuerkraft *f*; ~proof 1 *adj* feuerfest; 2 *vt materials* feuerfest machen; ~raiser *n* Brandstifter *m*; ~raising *n* Brandstiftung *f*; ~screen *n* Ofenschirm *m*; F~ Service *n* Feuerwehr *f*; ~side *n* to sit by the ~side am Kamin sitzen; ~side chair *n* Lehnsessel *m*; ~ station *n* Feuerwache, Feuerwehrzentrale *f*; ~storm *n* Feuersturm *m*; ~trap *n* Feuerfalle *f*; ~wall *n* Brandmauer *f*; ~warden *n* Feuerwache *f*; ~water *n* (*inf*) Feuerwasser *nt* (*inf*); ~wood *n* Brennholz *nt*; ~works *npl* Feuerwerkskörper *pl*; (*display*) Feuerwerk *nt*; there'll be ~works if he finds out (*inf*) wenn er das erfährt, ist Feuer unterm Dach (*inf*); there's going to be ~works at the meeting (*inf*) bei dem Treffen werden die Funken fliegen.

firing ['faɪrɪŋ] *n* (a) (*of pottery*) Brennen *nt*. (b) (*Mil*) Feuer *nt*; (*of gun, shot, rocket*) Abfeuern *nt*. the ~ of a salute Salutschüsse *pl*. (c) (*inf: dismissal*) Rausschmiß *m* (*inf*). (d) (*Aut: of engine*) Zündung *f*.

firing: ~ line *n* (*Mil*) Feuer- *or* Schußlinie *f*; (*fig*) Schußlinie *f*; ~ pin *n* Schlagbolzen *m*; ~ squad *n* Exekutionskommando *nt*.

firm¹ ['fɜːm] *n* Firma *f*. ~ of solicitors Rechtsanwaltsbüro *nt*.

firm² 1 *adj* (+*er*) (a) *base also* stabil; *look also* entschlossen; *friendship also* beständig; *hold, basis also* sicher. to be ~ with sb jdm gegenüber bestimmt auftreten. (b) (*Comm*) fest; *market* stabil. 2 *adv* to stand ~ on sth (*fig*) fest *or* unerschütterlich bei etw bleiben.

♦**firm up** *vt sep wall etc* (ab)stützen; *deal etc* unter Dach und Fach bringen.

firmament ['fɜːməmənt] *n* Firmament *nt*.

firmly ['fɜːmlɪ] *adv* fest. no, she said ~ nein, sagte sie in bestimmtem *or* entschiedenem Ton.

firmness ['fɜːmnɪs] *n see adj* (a) Festigkeit *f*; Stabilität *f*; Entschlossenheit *f*; Beständigkeit *f*; Sicherheit *f*. ~ of character Charakterstärke *f*. (b) Festigkeit *f*; Stabilität *f*.

first [fɜːst] 1 *adj* (+*er, s*). he was ~ in the queue/in Latin/to do that er war der erste in der Schlange/er war der Beste in Latein/er war der erste, der das gemacht hat; who's ~? wer ist der erste?; I'm ~, I've been waiting longer than you du bist ja zuerst an der Reihe, ich warte schon länger als Sie; (let's put) ~ things ~ eins nach dem anderen, immer (hübsch) der Reihe nach; you have to put ~ things ~ du mußt wissen, was dir am wichtigsten ist; he doesn't know the ~ thing about it/cars

davon/von Autos hat er keinen blassen Schimmer (*inf*); we did it the very ~ time wir haben es auf Anhieb geschafft; in the ~ place zunächst *or* erstens einmal; why didn't you say so in the ~ place? warum hast du denn das nicht gleich gesagt?

   2 *adv* (a) zuerst; (*before all the others*) arrive, leave als erste(r, s). ~, take three eggs zuerst *or* als erstes nehme man drei Dier; ~ come ~ served (*prov*) wer zuerst kommt, mahlt zuerst (Prov); women and children ~ Frauen und Kinder zuerst; ladies ~ Ladies first!, den Damen der Vortritt; he says ~ one thing then another er sagt mal so, mal so, er sagt mal hü, mal hott; before he says anything I want to get in ~ with a few comments bevor er irgend etwas sagt, möchte ich einige Bemerkungen anbringen; that's not what you said ~ zuerst hast du etwas anderes gesagt; you ~ du zuerst; which things come ~ in your order of priorities? was steht bei Ihnen an erster Stelle?, was ist Ihnen am wichtigsten?; but darling, you know you always come ~ aber, mein Schatz, du weißt doch, daß du bei mir immer an erster Stelle stehst; he always puts his job ~ seine Arbeit kommt bei ihm immer vor allem anderen.

   (b) (*before all else*) als erstes, zunächst; (*in listing*) erstens. ~ of all (*before all else, mainly*) vor allem; ~ of all I am going for a swim als erstes *or* zuallererst gehe ich schwimmen; why can't I? — well, ~ of all it's not yours and ... warum denn nicht? — nun, zunächst *or* erstens einmal gehört es nicht dir und ...; ~ and foremost zunächst, vor allem; ~ and last in erster Linie.

   (c) (*for the* ~ *time*) zum ersten Mal, das erste Mal. when did you ~ meet him? wann haben Sie ihn das erste Mal getroffen?; when this model was ~ introduced zu Anfang *or* zuerst, als das Modell herauskam; when it ~ became known that ... als zuerst bekannt wurde, daß ...

   (d) (*before: in time*) (zu)erst. I must finish this ~ ich muß das erst fertigmachen; think ~ before you sign anything überlegen Sie es sich, bevor Sie etwas unterschreiben.

   (e) (*in preference*) eher, lieber. I'd die ~! eher *or* lieber würde ich sterben!

   3 *n* (a) the ~ der/die/das Erste; he was among the very ~ to arrive er war unter den ersten, die ankamen; they were the ~ to come sie kamen als erste; he was the ~ home/finished er war als erster zu Hause/fertig.

   (b) this is the ~ I've heard of it das ist mir ja ganz neu.

   (c) at ~ zuerst, zunächst; from the ~ von Anfang an; from ~ to last von Anfang bis Ende.

   (d) (*Brit Univ*) Eins *f*, die Note „Eins". he got a ~ er bestand (sein Examen) mit „Eins" *or* „sehr gut"; he was supposed to get a ~ er war ein Einserkandidat.

   (e) (*Aut*) ~ (gear) der erste (Gang). in ~ im ersten (Gang).

   (f) (*US: Baseball*) erstes Base *or* Mal; *see also* sixth.

first: ~ aid *n* Erste Hilfe; to give ~ aid Erste Hilfe leisten; ~ aid box *n* Verbandskasten *m*; ~ aid kit *n* Erste-Hilfe-Ausrüstung *f*; ~ aid post *or* station *n* Sanitätswache *f*; (*at race-track also*) Ärztezelt *nt*; ~-born 1 *adj* erstgeboren; 2 *n* Erstgeborene(r) *mf*; ~-class 1 *adj* (a) erstklassig; ~-class compartment Erste(r)-Klasse-Abteil *nt*, Abteil *nt* erster Klasse; ~-class carriage Erste(r)-Klasse-Wagen *m*; ~-class mail bevorzugt beförderte Post; ~-class ticket Erster-Klasse-Fahrkarte *f*, Fahrkarte *f* für die erste Klasse; (b) (*excellent*) erstklassig; he's ~-class at tennis/cooking er ist ein erstklassiger Tennisspieler/Koch; that's absolutely ~-class das ist einfach Spitze (*inf*); oh ~-class! (*dated*) oh pfundig! (*dated inf*); ~-class (*Brit Univ*) ~-class degree sehr gutes Examen; 2 *adv travel* erster Klasse; ~ cousin *n* Vetter *m* ersten Grades; ~-day cover *n* Ersttagsbrief *m*; ~ edition *n* Erstausgabe *f*; ~ form *n* (*Brit Sch*) erste Klasse; ~-former *n* (*Brit Sch*) Erstkläßler(in *f*) *m*; ~-generation *adj citizen, computer* der ersten Generation; ~-hand *adj, adv* aus erster Hand; F~ Lady *n* First Lady *f*; ~ lieutenant *n* Oberleutnant *m*.

firstly ['fɜːstlɪ] *adv* erstens, zunächst (einmal).

first: ~ mate *n* (*Naut*) Erster Offizier; (*on small boats*) Bestmann *m*; ~ name *n* Vorname *m*; they're on ~ name terms sie reden sich mit Vornamen an; ~ night *n* (*Theat*) Premiere *f*; ~ night nerves Premierenfieber *nt*; ~-nighter *n* Premierenbesucher(in *f*) *m*; ~ offender *n* noch nicht Vorbestrafte(r) *mf*; he is a ~ offender er ist nicht vorbestraft; ~ officer *n* (*Naut*) Erster Offizier; ~ performance *n* (*Theat*) Uraufführung *f*; (*Mus also*) Erstaufführung *f*; ~ person *n* erste Person; ~-person *adj narrative* Ich-; ~ principles *npl* Grundprinzipien *pl*; to get down to ~ principles den Dingen auf den Grund gehen; ~-rate *adj see* ~-class 1 (b); ~ violin *n* erste Geige; he is a ~ violin er spielt in der ersten Geige.

firth [fɜːθ] *n* (*Scot*) Förde *f*, Meeresarm *m*.

fir tree *n* Tannenbaum *m*.

fiscal ['fɪskəl] 1 *adj* Finanz-. 2 *n* (*Scot Jur*) Staatsanwalt *m*.

fish [fɪʃ] 1 *n, pl* - *or* (*esp for different types*) ~es (a) Fisch *m*. ~ and chips Fisch und Pommes frites; to drink like a ~ (*inf*) wie ein Loch saufen (*inf*), wie ein Bürstenbinder trinken; to have other ~ to fry (*fig inf*) wichtigere Dinge *or* Wichtigeres zu tun haben; like a ~ out of water wie ein Fisch auf dem Trockenen; neither ~ nor fowl (*fig*) weder Fisch noch Fleisch; he's a queer ~! (*inf*) er ist ein komischer Kauz; there are plenty more ~ in the sea (*fig inf*) es gibt noch mehr (davon) auf der Welt; a big ~ in a little pond der Hahn im Korb; a little ~ in a big pond nur einer von vielen.

   (b) The F~es (*Astron*) die Fische *pl*.

   2 *vi* fischen; (*with rod also*) angeln. to go ~ing fischen/angeln gehen; to go salmon ~ing auf Lachsfang gehen.

   3 *vt* (a) fischen; (*with rod also*) angeln.

   (b) to ~ a river/pool in einem Fluß/Teich fischen/angeln; to ~ a river dry einen Fluß abfischen.

♦**fish for** *vi* +*prep obj* (a) fischen/angeln, fischen/angeln auf (+*acc*) (*spec*). (b) (*fig*) compliments fischen nach. to ~ ~ information from sb jdn auszuhorchen versuchen; they were

~ing ~ information sie waren auf Informationen aus.

♦**fish out** vt sep herausfischen or -angeln (of or from sth aus etw). **he ~ed it ~ from behind the cupboard** er angelte es hinter dem Schrank hervor.

♦**fish up** vt sep auffischen, herausziehen; (fig) (from memory etc) hervorkramen or -holen.

fish: ~**bone** n (Fisch)gräte f; ~**cake** n Fischfrikadelle f.

fisher ['fɪʃə'] n (a) (old: ~man) Fischer m. ~**s of men** (Bibl) Menschenfischer pl (Bibl). **(b)** (animal) Fischfänger m.

fisherman ['fɪʃəmən] n, pl **-men** [-mən] Fischer m; (amateur) Angler m; (boat) Fischereiboot nt.

fishery ['fɪʃərɪ] n (area) Fischereizone f or -gewässer nt; (industry) Fischerei f.

fish: ~ **farm** n Fischzucht(anlage) f; ~ **farming** n Teichwirtschaft f; ~ **finger** n Fischstäbchen nt; ~ **glue** n Fischleim m; ~**hook** n Angelhaken m.

fishing ['fɪʃɪŋ] n Fischen nt; (with rod) Angeln nt; (as industry) Fischerei f. ~ **(is) prohibited** Angeln verboten!

fishing: ~ **boat** n Fischerboot nt; ~ **fleet** n Fischereiflotte f; ~ **grounds** npl Fischgründe pl; ~ **industry** n Fischindustrie f; ~-**line** n Angelschnur f; ~ **net** n Fischnetz nt; ~ **port** n Fischereihafen m; ~-**rod** n Angelrute f; ~ **tackle** n (for sport) Angelgeräte pl; (for industry) Fischereigeräte pl; ~ **village** n Fischerdorf nt.

fish: ~ **ladder** n Fischleiter f; ~ **market** n Fischmarkt m; ~**monger** n (Brit) Fischhändler(in f) m; ~**monger's** n (Brit) Fischgeschäft nt; ~-**net stockings** npl Netzstrümpfe pl; ~ **paste** n Fischpaste f; ~**plate** n (Rail) Lasche f; ~**pond** n Fischteich m; ~ **slice** n (Braten)wender m; ~ **story** n (US inf) Seemannsgarn nt; ~**wife** n Fischfrau f; (fig pej) Marktweib nt.

fishy ['fɪʃɪ] adj (+er) (a) smell Fisch-. **it smells rather ~** es riecht ziemlich nach Fisch. **(b)** (inf) verdächtig; excuse, story faul (inf). **there's something ~ about his story** an der Geschichte ist was faul (inf).

fissile ['fɪsaɪl] adj spaltbar.

fission ['fɪʃən] n (Phys) Spaltung f; (Biol) (Zell)teilung f. ~ **bomb** (konventionelle) Atombombe.

fissionable ['fɪʃnəbl] adj spaltbar.

fissure ['fɪʃə'] n Riß m; (deep) Kluft f; (narrow) Spalt(e f) m.

fissured ['fɪʃəd] adj rissig; (with deep fissures) zerklüftet.

fist [fɪst] n Faust f. **to put up one's ~s** die Fäuste hochnehmen, in (Box)kampfstellung gehen.

fistful ['fɪstfʊl] n Handvoll f. **a ~ of pound notes** eine Handvoll Pfundnoten.

fisticuffs ['fɪstɪkʌfs] npl (dated inf) (fighting) Handgreiflichkeiten pl; (boxing) Boxen nt. **I'm not much good at ~** ich tauge nicht viel mit den Fäusten; **resorting to ~ is no solution** handgreiflich (zu) werden ist keine Lösung.

fit[1] [fɪt] **1** adj (+er) (a) (suitable, suited for sth) geeignet; time, occasion also günstig. **~ to eat** eßbar; **is this meat still ~ to eat?** kann man dieses Fleisch noch essen?; ~ **for habitation** bewohnbar; **to be ~ to be seen** sich sehen lassen können; **to be ~ for a job** sich für eine Stelle eignen, für eine Stelle geeignet sein; **the coat is ~ for nothing but the dustbin** der Mantel taugt nur noch für den Mülleimer.

(b) (deserving) **a man like that is not ~ to have such a good wife** ein Mann wie er verdient so eine gute Frau nicht or ist eine so gute Frau nicht wert; **you're not ~ to be spoken to** du bist es nicht wert or verdienst es nicht, daß man sich mit dir unterhält.

(c) (right and proper) angebracht, richtig. **I'll do as I think ~** ich handle, wie ich es für richtig halte; **to see ~ to do sth** es für richtig or angebracht halten, etw zu tun; **as is only ~** wie es sich gebührt; **it is only ~** es ist nur recht und billig; **he did not see ~ to apologize** er hat es nicht für nötig gehalten, sich zu entschuldigen.

(d) (in health) gesund; sportsman etc fit, in Form. **she is not yet ~ to travel** sie ist noch nicht reisefähig; **only the ~test survive** nur die Geeignetsten überleben; (people) nur die Gesunden überleben; (in business etc) nur die Starken können sich halten.

(e) to laugh ~ to burst vor Lachen beinahe platzen; **to be ~ to drop (with tiredness)** zum Umfallen müde sein.

2 n (of clothes) Paßform f. **it is a very good/bad ~** es sitzt or paßt wie angegossen/nicht gut; **it's a bit of a tight ~** (clothes) es ist etwas eng; (suitcase, timing, parking) es geht gerade (noch).

3 vt (a) (cover, sheet, nut etc) passen auf (+acc); (key etc) passen in (+acc); (clothes etc) passen (+dat). **this coat ~s you better** dieser Mantel paßt Ihnen besser or sitzt besser; **this spanner doesn't ~ this nut** dieser Schraubenschlüssel paßt nicht für diese Mutter; **that part won't ~ this machine** das Teil paßt nicht für diese Maschine; **to make a ring ~ sb** jdm einen Ring anpassen.

(b) (be suitable for) sb's plans, a theory etc passen in (+acc).

(c) to ~ a dress on sb jdm ein Kleid anprobieren.

(d) (put on, attach) anbringen (to an +dat); tyre, lock also montieren; double-glazing also einsetzen; (put in) einbauen (in in +acc); (furnish, provide with) ausstatten. **to ~ a key in the lock/a bulb in its socket** einen Schlüssel ins Schloß stecken/eine Glühbirne in die Fassung drehen or schrauben; **to ~ a knob on a door** eine Tür mit einem Knauf versehen.

(e) (match) description, facts entsprechen (+dat); (person also) passen auf (+acc). **to make the punishment ~ the crime** eine dem Vergehen angemessene Strafe verhängen.

(f) to ~ oneself for a job/a hard winter sich für eine Stelle/einen strengen Winter rüsten; **the qualifications that ~ him for the post** die Qualifikationen, die ihn zu dem Posten befähigen.

4 vi (a) passen.

(b) (correspond) zusammenstimmen or -passen. **the facts don't ~** die Fakten sind widersprüchlich; **it all ~s** es paßt alles zusammen; **there's still one piece of evidence that doesn't**

~ da ist immer noch ein Indiz, das nicht dazupaßt.

♦**fit in 1** vt sep (a) (find space for) unterbringen.

(b) (find time for) person einen Termin geben (+dat); meeting unterbringen; (squeeze in also) einschieben; (for treatment also) drannehmen (inf). **Sir Charles could ~ you ~ at 3 um 3 Uhr** hätte Sir Charles Zeit für Sie; **can you ~ this meeting ~(to) your schedule?** können Sie diese Konferenz noch in Ihrem Terminkalender unterbringen?

(c) (make harmonize) **to ~ sth ~ with sth** etw mit etw in Einklang bringen.

(d) (fit, put in) einsetzen, einbauen.

2 vi (a) (go into place) hineinpassen.

(b) (plans, ideas, word) passen; (facts etc) übereinstimmen; (match) dazupassen. **there is one fact that doesn't ~ ~** da ist ein Punkt, der nicht ins Ganze paßt; **how does this ~ ~?** wie paßt das ins Ganze?; **I see, it all ~s ~** now jetzt paßt alles zusammen; **you can't force the facts to ~ ~** Sie können den Tatsachen nicht einfach Gewalt antun; **to ~ ~ with sth** (plans, ideas) in etw (acc) passen; (facts) mit etw übereinstimmen; (match) zu etw passen; **does that ~ ~ with your plans?** läßt sich das mit Ihren Plänen vereinbaren?; **he wants everybody to ~ ~ with him/his plans/his wishes** er will, daß sich jedermann nach ihm/ seinen Plänen/Wünschen richtet.

(c) (people: harmonize) **he doesn't ~ ~ here/with the others/with such a firm** er paßt hier nicht her/nicht zu den anderen/ nicht in eine solche Firma; **she's the sort who ~s ~ easily in any group** sie ist der Typ, der sich in jede Gruppe leicht einfügt; **the new director didn't ~ ~** der neue Direktor hat nicht in die Firma gepaßt or nicht reingepaßt (inf); **try to ~ ~** (with the others) versuche, dich den anderen anzupassen or dich einzufügen.

♦**fit on 1** vi (a) passen. **will it ~ ~?** paßt es (darauf)? **(b)** (be fixed) befestigt or angebracht sein. **where does this part ~ ~?** wo gehört dieses Teil drauf?, wo wird dieses Teil befestigt? **2** vt sep (a) dress anprobieren; (tailor) anpassen (prep obj dat).

(b) (put in place, fix on) anbringen.

♦**fit out** vt sep expedition, person (for an expedition) ausrüsten; person, ship ausstatten.

♦**fit up** vt sep (a) (fix up) anbringen; (assemble) zusammensetzen or -bauen. **(b)** (supply with) ausstatten, mit allem Nötigen versehen; (with clothes also) ausstaffieren; (with implements, weapons etc also) ausrüsten. **to ~ sb/sth ~ with sth** jdn/etw mit etw versehen or ausstatten.

fit[2] n (Med, fig) Anfall m. ~ **of coughing/anger** Husten-/ Wutanfall m; **in a ~ of anger** in einem Anfall von Wut; ~ **of energy/generosity/repentance** Anwandlung or Anfall von Aktivität/Großzügigkeit/Reue; **in or by ~s and starts** stoßweise; **he wrote this novel in ~s and starts** er hat diesen Roman in mehreren Anläufen geschrieben; **to be in ~s of laughter** sich vor Lachen biegen or kugeln (inf); **he'd have a ~** (fig inf) er würde (ja) einen Anfall kriegen (inf); **don't tell him, you'll give him a ~** (fig inf) sag es ihm nicht, er kriegt sonst einen Anfall (inf); **he'd do anything when the ~ was on him** wenn es ihn gepackt hat, war er zu allem fähig (inf).

fitful ['fɪtfʊl] adj unbeständig; working, progress stoßweise; sleep unruhig; sun launenhaft (geh); enthusiasm sporadisch.

fitfully ['fɪtfəlɪ] adv progress stoßweise; work also, blow sporadisch; sleep unruhig. **the sun shone ~** die Sonne kam vereinzelt durch.

fitment ['fɪtmənt] n (furniture) Einrichtungsgegenstand m; (of machine, car) Zubehörteil nt.

fitness ['fɪtnɪs] n (a) (health) Gesundheit f; (condition) Fitness, Fitneß, Kondition f. ~ **training** Fitneßtraining nt. **(b)** (suitability) Geeignetheit f; (for job also) Eignung f; (of remark etc) Angemessenheit f.

fitted ['fɪtɪd] adj (a) garment tailliert. ~ **carpet** Teppichboden m; ~ **kitchen/cupboards** Einbauküche f/Einbauschränke pl; ~ **sheet** Spannbettuch nt. **(b)** person geeignet (for für).

fitter ['fɪtə'] n (for clothes) Schneider(in f) m. **(b)** (Tech) (of engines) Monteur m; (for machines) (Maschinen)schlosser m; (not specially qualified) Montagearbeiter(in f) m; (of pipes etc) Installateur m.

fitting ['fɪtɪŋ] **1** adj (suitable) passend; expression also angebracht; time also geeignet; (seemly, becoming) schicklich (dated). **it is not ~ for a young lady ...** es schickt sich nicht or ist nicht schicklich (dated) für eine junge Dame ...

2 n (a) Anprobe f. ~ **room** Anproberaum m; (cubicle) Anprobekabine f; **to go in for a ~** zur Anprobe gehen.

(b) (part) Zubehörteil nt. ~**s** Ausstattung f; (furniture also) Einrichtung f; (pipes) Installation f; **bathroom/office.** ~**s** Badezimmer-/Büroeinrichtung f; **electrical** ~**s** Elektroinstallationen.

fittingly ['fɪtɪŋlɪ] adv see adj.

five [faɪv] **1** adj fünf. **2** n Fünf f; see also **six.**

five: ~-**and-ten** n (US) billiges Kaufhaus; ~**fold** adj, adv fünffach; ~-**o'clock shadow** n nachmittäglicher Anflug von Bartstoppeln.

fiver ['faɪvə'] n (inf) Fünfpfund-/Fünfdollarschein m.

five: ~**spot** n (US inf) Fünfdollarschein m; ~-**star hotel** n Fünf-Sterne-Hotel nt; ~-**year plan** n Fünfjahresplan m.

fix [fɪks] **1** vt (a) (make firm) befestigen, festmachen (sth to sth etw an/auf etw +dat); (put on, install) new aerial, new dynamo anbringen; (fig) ideas, images verankern, festsetzen. **to ~ a stake in the ground** einen Pfahl in den Boden rammen; **to ~ the blame on sb** die Schuld auf jdn schieben, jdm die Schuld geben; **this image was firmly ~ed in his memory** diese Vorstellung war fest in seinem Gedächtnis verankert; **to ~ sth in one's mind** (dat) etw fest einprägen; **to ~ bayonets** die Bajonette aufpflanzen.

(b) eyes, attention richten (on, upon auf +acc). **she kept all eyes/everybody's attention ~ed on her** alle sahen sie wie gebannt an; **to ~ sb with an angry stare** (*liter*) jdn mit ärgerlichen Blicken durchbohren.

(c) *date, price, limit* festsetzen, festlegen; *(agree on)* ausmachen, beschließen. **nothing has been ~ed yet** es liegt noch nichts fest; es ist noch nichts fest (ausgemacht *or* beschlossen worden).

(d) *(arrange)* arrangieren; *tickets, taxi etc* besorgen, organisieren (*inf*). **try and ~ things so that they don't meet** versuch's so zu arrangieren, daß sie sich nicht treffen; **have you got anything ~ed for tonight?** haben Sie (für) heute abend schon etwas vor?

(e) *(straighten out, sort out)* in Ordnung bringen, regeln. **don't worry I'll ~ things with him** mach dir keine Gedanken, ich regle das mit ihm *or* ich bringe das in Ordnung.

(f) (*inf: get even with, sort out*) **I'll ~ him** dem werd' ich's besorgen (*inf*); **the Mafia will ~ him** den wird sich (*dat*) die Mafia vornehmen (*inf*) *or* vorknöpfen (*inf*).

(g) *(repair)* in Ordnung bringen, (*ganz*) machen (*inf*); *(put in good order, adjust)* machen (*inf*).

(h) *drink, meal* machen. **to ~ one's hair** sich frisieren.

(i) *(inf) race, fight* manipulieren; *jury also* bestechen. **the whole discussion/interview was ~ed** die Diskussion/das Interview war gestellt; **the whole thing was ~ed** das war eine abgekartete Sache (*inf*).

(j) *(US inf: intend)* vorhaben. **I'm ~ing on getting married soon** ich habe vor, bald zu heiraten.

(k) *(Chem, Phot)* fixieren.

(l) *(Naut, Aviat) position* bestimmen; *submarine etc also* orten.

2 *n* **(a)** *(inf: tricky situation)* Patsche (*inf*), Klemme (*inf*) *f.* **to be in a ~** in der Patsche *or* Klemme sitzen (*inf*); **to get oneself into a ~** sich (*dat*) eine schöne Suppe einbrocken (*inf*).

(b) *(Naut)* Position *f*, Standort *m.* **to take a ~ on sth** etw orten.

(c) *(sl: of drugs)* Fix *m* (*sl*). **to give oneself a ~** fixen (*sl*).

(d) *(inf)* **the fight/competition was a ~** der Kampf/Wettbewerb war eine abgekartete Sache (*inf*).

♦**fix down** *vt sep* befestigen.

♦**fix on 1** *vt sep* festmachen (*prep obj* auf +*dat*); *badge etc also* anheften, anstecken; *(fit on)* anbringen; *(by sewing)* annähen. **2** *vi +prep obj (decide on)* sich entscheiden für.

♦**fix together** *vt sep* zusammenmachen (*inf*).

♦**fix up** *vt sep* **(a)** *shelves* anbringen; *tent* aufstellen.

(b) *(arrange)* arrangieren; *holidays etc* festmachen; *(book)* organized tour, hotel etc buchen. **it's all ~ed** ~ es ist (schon) alles arrangiert/fest (*inf*) *or* festgemacht/fest gebucht; **have you got anything ~ed ~ for this evening?** haben Sie (für) heute abend schon etwas vor?

(c) **to ~ sb ~ with sth** jdm etw besorgen *or* verschaffen; **we ~ed them ~ for the night** wir haben sie für die Nacht untergebracht; **I stayed with him until I got myself ~ed ~ (with a room)** ich habe bei ihm gewohnt, bis ich ein Zimmer hatte.

(d) *(straighten out, sort out)* in Ordnung bringen, regeln.

fixated [fɪk'seɪtɪd] *adj* fixiert (*on* auf +*acc*).

fixation [fɪk'seɪʃən] *n* **(a)** *(Psych)* Fixierung *f.* **she has this ~ about cleanliness** sie hat einen Sauberkeitsfimmel (*inf*). **(b)** *(Chem)* Fixierung *f.*

fixative ['fɪksətɪv] *n* Fixativ *nt.*

fixed [fɪkst] *adj* **(a)** *fest;* *idea* fix; *smile* starr. **~ assets** feste Anlagen *pl;* **~ capital** Anlagevermögen, Anlagekapital *nt;* **~ menu** Tagesmenü *nt;* **~ price** Festpreis *m;* (*Econ also*) gebundener Preis; **~ star** Fixstern *m.*

(b) *(inf)* **how are you ~ for time/food/money etc?** wie sieht's bei dir mit der Zeit/dem Essen/dem Geld etc aus? (*inf*), wie steht's (denn) bei dir mit Zeit/Essen/Geld etc? (*inf*); **how are you ~ for tonight?** was hast du (für) heute abend vor?

fixedly ['fɪksɪdlɪ] *adv stare, look* starr, unbeweglich.

fixer ['fɪksə'] *n (Phot)* Fixiermittel *nt;* (*sl*) Schieber *m.*

fixing bath ['fɪksɪŋ-] *n* Fixierbad *nt.*

fixings ['fɪksɪŋz] *npl (US Cook)* Beilagen *pl.*

fixity ['fɪksɪtɪ] *n (liter)* **his ~ of purpose** seine Zielstrebigkeit.

fixture ['fɪkstʃə'] *n* **(a)** *(of a building etc)* **~s** Ausstattung *f*, unbewegliches Inventar (*form*); **~s and fittings** Anschlüsse und unbewegliches Inventar (*form*); **lighting ~s** elektrische Anschlüsse; **to be a ~** *(fig hum: person)* zum Inventar gehören.

(b) *(Brit Sport)* Spiel *nt.* **~ list** Spielplan *m.*

fizz [fɪz] **1** *vi (champagne etc)* perlen, sprudeln, moussieren. **2** *n* **(a)** *(of champagne etc)* Perlen, Moussieren *nt.* **(b)** *(drink)* Sprudel *m;* *(flavoured also)* (Brause)limonade, Brause *f.* **(c)** *(dated Brit inf: champagne)* Schampus *m (dated inf).*

♦**fizz up** *vi* (auf)sprudeln.

fizzle ['fɪzl] *vi* zischen, spucken (*inf*).

♦**fizzle out** *vi (firework, enthusiasm)* verpuffen; *(rocket)* vorzeitig verglühen; *(plan)* im Sande verlaufen.

fizzy ['fɪzɪ] *adj* (+*er*) sprudelnd. **to be ~** sprudeln; **it's too ~** da ist zu viel Kohlensäure drin; **the soda water makes it ~** durch das Sodawasser sprudelt es; **a ~ drink** eine Brause.

fjord [fjɔːd] *n* Fjord *m.*

flab [flæb] *n (inf)* Speck *m.* **to fight the ~** *(hum)* etwas für die schlanke Linie tun, sich trimmen.

flabbergast ['flæbəgɑːst] *vt (inf)* verblüffen, umhauen (*inf*). **I was ~ed to see him/at the price** ich war platt (*inf*) *or* von den Socken (*sl*), als ich ihn sah/als ich den Preis erfuhr.

flabbergasting ['flæbəgɑːstɪŋ] *adj pred (inf)* unglaublich.

flabbily ['flæbɪlɪ] *adv written* schwammig.

flabbiness ['flæbɪnɪs] *n see adj* Schlaffheit *f;* Schwammigkeit *f;* Farblosigkeit *f;* Schwammigkeit, Wabbeligkeit (*inf*) *f.*

flabby ['flæbɪ] *adj* (+*er*) schlaff; *prose, argument, thesis* schwammig; *person, character* ohne Saft und Kraft, farblos; *(fat) stomach* schwammig, wabbelig (*inf*). **he's getting ~ round the middle** er setzt um die Taille Speck an.

flaccid ['flæksɪd] *adj (liter)* schlaff; *prose* saft- und kraftlos.

flag¹ [flæg] **1** *n* **(a)** Fahne *f;* *(small, on map, chart etc)* Fähnchen *nt;* *(national also, Naut)* Flagge *f;* *(for semaphore)* Signalflagge *or* -fahne *f.* **to go down with ~s flying** *(lit)* bis zum letzten kämpfen; *(fig)* mit Glanz und Gloria untergehen; **to keep the ~ flying** *(lit, fig)* die Stellung halten; **to show the ~** seine Präsenz *or (fig also)* seine Anwesenheit dokumentieren.

(b) *(for charity)* Fähnchen *nt.*

(c) *(of taxi)* **the ~ was down** das Taxi war besetzt; **he put the ~ down** er stellte auf „besetzt".

(d) *(paper marker)* Reiter *m.*

2 *vt* beflaggen.

♦**flag down** *vt sep taxi etc* anhalten.

♦**flag up** *vt sep (inf: mark, indicate)* markieren.

flag² *vi* erlahmen; *(interest, enthusiasm, strength etc also)* nachlassen; *(person also)* ermüden; *(plant)* den Kopf/die Blätter hängen lassen.

flag³ *n (Bot)* Schwertlilie *f;* *(sweet ~)* Kalmus *m.*

flag⁴ **1** *n (also ~stone)* Steinplatte *f;* *(for floor also)* Fliese *f.* **2** *vt* mit Steinplatten/Fliesen belegen; *floor also* fliesen.

flag day *n* **(a)** *(Brit)* Tag *m*, an dem eine Straßensammlung für einen wohltätigen Zweck durchgeführt wird. **(b)** F~ D~ *(US)* 14. Juni, Gedenktag der Einführung der amerikanischen Nationalflagge.

flagellate ['flædʒəleɪt] *vt* geißeln.

flagellation [ˌflædʒə'leɪʃən] *n* Geißelung *f.*

flag officer *n (Naut)* Flaggoffizier *m.*

flagon ['flægən] *n (bottle)* Flasche *f;* *(jug)* Krug *m.*

flagpole ['flægpəʊl] *n* Fahnenstange *f.*

flagrance ['fleɪgrəns], **flagrancy** ['fleɪgrənsɪ] *n* eklatante *or* krasse Offensichtlichkeit; *(of affair, defiance, disregard)* Unverhohlenheit *f.* **such was the ~ of this injustice** ... das war eine derart eklatante *or* krasse *or* himmelschreiende Ungerechtigkeit ...; **the unabashed ~ of his abuse of privilege** die unverhohlene Art, mit der er seine Privilegien mißbrauchte.

flagrant ['fleɪgrənt] *adj* eklatant, kraß; *injustice, crime also* himmelschreiend; *breach, violation also* flagrant (*geh*); *disregard, defiance also, affair* unverhohlen, offenkundig.

flagrantly ['fleɪgrəntlɪ] *adv* ganz eindeutig *or* offensichtlich; *abuse, flirt, disregard* unverhohlen, ganz offenkundig. **he ~ parked right outside the police station** er hat ganz ungeniert *or* unverfroren direkt vor der Polizeiwache geparkt; **a ~ modernistic style** ein kraß modernistischer Stil.

flag: **~ship** *n* Flaggschiff *nt;* **~staff** *n* Fahnen- *or* Flaggenmast *m;* **~stone** *n* (Stein)platte *f;* *(on floor also)* Fliese *f;* **~waver** *n* Hurrapatriot(in *f*) *m*, Chauvinist *m;* **~waving 1** *n* Hurrapatriotismus, Chauvinismus *m;* **2** *adj speech* chauvinistisch.

flail [fleɪl] **1** *n (Dresch)flegel m.* **2** *vt* dreschen. **he wildly ~ed his arms about** er schlug (mit den Armen) wild um sich. **3** *vi* **to ~ about** herumfuchteln; **the dying deer with its legs ~ing in all directions** das verendende Reh, das mit seinen Läufen nach allen Richtungen ausschlug.

flail tank *n* Minenräumpanzer *m.*

flair [fleə'] *n (for selecting the best etc)* Gespür *nt*, (feine) Nase (*inf*), Riecher *m (inf);* *(talent)* Talent *nt;* *(stylishness)* Flair *nt.* **his great ~ for business** sein großes Geschäftstalent.

flak [flæk] *n* Flakfeuer *nt.* **~ jacket** kugelsichere Weste.

flake [fleɪk] **1** *n (of snow, soap)* Flocke *f;* *(of paint, rust)* Splitter *m;* *(of plaster)* abgebröckelte Stückchen; *(of metal, wood)* Span *m;* *(of skin)* Schuppe *f.* **~s of paint/plaster were falling off the ceiling** die Farbe an der Decke blätterte ab/der Gips bröckelte von der Decke ab.

2 *vi (stone, plaster etc)* abbröckeln; *(paint)* abblättern.

3 *vt (Cook)* chocolate, almonds raspeln.

♦**flake off** *vi (plaster)* abbröckeln; *(paint, rust etc)* abblättern, absplittern; *(skin)* sich schälen, sich abschuppen.

♦**flake out** *vi (inf) (become exhausted)* abschlaffen (*inf*); *(pass out)* aus den Latschen kippen (*sl*); *(fall asleep)* einschlafen, einpennen (*sl*).

flaky ['fleɪkɪ] *adj* (+*er*) *potatoes* flockig; *paint, plaster etc* brüchig; *crust* blättrig; *skin* schuppig. **~ pastry** Blätterteig *m.*

flamboyance [flæm'bɔɪəns] *n* Extravaganz *f;* *(of life style also)* Üppigkeit *f;* *(of colour)* Pracht *f;* *(of gesture)* Großartigkeit *f.*

flamboyant [flæm'bɔɪənt] *adj* extravagant; *life style also* üppig, aufwendig; *plumage* farbenprächtig; *colours* prächtig; *gesture* großartig. **~ style** *(Archit)* Flamboyantstil *m;* **in the ~ court of Louis XIV** am prunkvollen Hof Ludwigs XIV.

flamboyantly [flæm'bɔɪəntlɪ] *adv* extravagant. **in Hollywood, where nothing that is done is not done ~** in Hollywood, wo alles in großem Stil *or* Rahmen gemacht wird.

flame [fleɪm] **1** *n* **(a)** Flamme *f.* **the house was in ~s** das Haus stand in Flammen.

(b) *(of passion)* Flamme *f (geh)*, Feuer *nt no pl.* **the ~ of anger in his eye** *(liter)* die Zornesglut in seinen Augen (*liter*).

(c) *(inf: sweetheart)* Flamme *f (inf).*

2 *vi (fire)* lodern, flammen (*geh*); *(liter: colour)* leuchten; *(gem)* funkeln, gleißen (*liter*).

♦**flame up** *vi (a) (fire)* auflodern. **(b)** *(fig) (person)* in Wut *or* Rage geraten; *(anger etc)* aufflammen, auflodern.

flame-coloured ['fleɪmkʌləd] *adj* feuerfarben.

flamenco [flə'meŋkəʊ] **1** *n* Flamenco *m.* **2** *adj* Flamenco-.

flame: **~ red 1** *n* Feuerrot *nt;* **2** *adj* feuerrot; **~thrower** *n* Flammenwerfer *m.*

flaming ['fleɪmɪŋ] *adj* **(a)** brennend, lodernd; *(fig) colour* leuchtend; *rage* hell; *passion* glühend.

(b) *(Brit inf: angry)* **she was absolutely ~** sie kochte (vor Wut) (*inf*).

(c) *(Brit sl: bloody)* verdammt (*inf*), Scheiß- (*sl*). **it's a ~ nuisance/waste of time** Mensch, das ist vielleicht ein Mist/das ist die reinste Zeitverschwendung (*inf*); **it was there all the ~ time** Mensch (*inf*) *or* Scheiße (*sl*), das war die ganze Zeit da; **just a ~ minute** Mensch *or* Mann *or* Herrgott, nun wart doch mal (*inf*); **who does he ~ well think he is?** Mensch *or* verdammt noch mal, für wen hält der sich eigentlich? (*sl*).

flamingo [flə'mɪŋgəʊ] *n, pl* **-(e)s** Flamingo *m*.

flammable ['flæməbl] *adj* leicht entzündbar, feuergefährlich.

flan [flæn] *n* Kuchen *m*. **fruit ~** Obstkuchen *m*; **~ case** Tortenboden *m*.

Flanders ['flɑːndəz] *n* Flandern *nt*.

flange [flændʒ] *n* (*on wheel etc*) Spurkranz *m*; (*Tech: ring, collar*) Winkelring, Flansch, Bördelrand *m*.

flanged [flændʒd] *adj* gebördelt; *tube etc also* geflanscht.

flank [flæŋk] **1** *n* (*of animal, Mil*) Flanke *f*; (*of mountain, building*) Seite, Flanke (*old*) *f*. **2** *vt* (a) flankieren. (b) (*Mil*) *the enemy* seitlich umgehen.

flanking movement ['flæŋkɪŋ'muːvmənt] *n* (*Mil*) Flankenbewegung *f*.

flannel ['flænl] **1** *n* (a) Flanell *m*. **~s** *pl* (*trousers*) Flanellhose *f*. (b) (*Brit: face-~*) Waschlappen *m*. (c) (*Brit inf: waffle*) Geschwafel (*inf*), Gelaber (*inf*) *nt*. **2** *adj trousers etc* Flanell-. **3** *vi* (*Brit inf: waffle*) schwafeln (*inf*), labern (*inf*).

flannelette [ˌflænə'let] *n* Baumwollflanell *m*. **~ sheet** Biberbettuch *nt*.

flap [flæp] **1** *n* (a) (*of pocket*) Klappe *f*; (*of table*) ausziehbarer Teil; (*Aviat*) (Lande)klappe *f*. **a ~ of skin** ein Hautfetzen *m*; (*Med*) ein Hautlappen *m*. (b) (*sound*) (*of sails, sheeting etc*) Flattern, Knattern *nt*; (*of wings*) Schlagen *nt*. (c) (*motion*) **to give sth a ~** leicht auf etw (*acc*) klatschen. (d) (*inf*) helle Aufregung, Panik *f*. **to get in(to) a ~** in helle Aufregung geraten, ins Flattern geraten (*inf*); **there's a big ~ on** es herrscht große Panik, alles ist in heller Aufregung. (e) (*Phon*) geschlagener Laut. **2** *vi* (a) (*wings*) schlagen; (*door, shutters also*) klappern; (*sails, tarpaulin etc*) flattern. **his coat ~ped about his legs** der Mantel schlackerte ihm um die Beine (*inf*); **his ears were ~ping** (*inf*) er spitzte die Ohren. (b) (*inf*) in heller Aufregung sein. **to start to ~** in helle Aufregung geraten; **don't ~** reg dich nicht auf; **there's no need to ~** (das ist) kein Grund zur Aufregung; **she's been ~ping around all morning** sie rennt schon den ganzen Morgen wie ein aufgescheuchtes Huhn durch die Gegend (*inf*). **3** *vt* **to ~** his wings mit den Flügeln schlagen; **he ~ped the newspaper at the fly** er schlug *or* klatschte mit der Zeitung nach der Fliege; **he ~ped the fly with the newspaper** er schlug *or* klatschte mit der Zeitung auf die Fliege.

♦**flap away** *vi* (*bird*) davonfliegen.

flapjack ['flæpdʒæk] *n* Pfannkuchen *m*.

flapper ['flæpəʳ] *n* modisches Mädchen in den 20er Jahren.

flare [flɛəʳ] **1** *n* (a) Auflodern *nt*; (*fig: of anger*) Aufflackern *nt*. (b) (*signal*) Leuchtsignal *nt*; (*from pistol etc*) Leuchtrakete, Leuchtkugel *f*; (*fire, landing ~*) Leuchtfeuer *nt*. (c) (*Fashion*) ausgestellter Schnitt. **a skirt with a slight ~** ein leicht ausgestellter Rock; **trousers with ~s** ausgestellte Hose/Hosen, Hose *f*/Hosen *pl* mit Schlag. (d) (*solar ~*) Sonneneruption, Fackel *f*. (e) (*Phot*) Reflexlicht *nt*. **2** *vi* (a) (*match, torch*) aufleuchten; (*sunspot also*) aufblitzen. (b) (*trousers, skirts*) ausgestellt sein. (c) (*nostrils*) sich blähen.

♦**flare up** *vi* (*lit, fig: situation, affair*) aufflackern, auflodern; (*fig*) (*person*) aufbrausen, auffahren; (*fighting, epidemic*) ausbrechen; (*anger*) zum Ausbruch kommen. **she ~d ~ at me** sie fuhr mich an.

flared [flɛəd] *adj trousers, skirt* ausgestellt.

flare: **~ path** *n* (*Aviat*) Leuchtpfad *m*; **~ pistol** *n* Leuchtpistole *f*; **~-up** *n see* **~ up** Aufflackern, Auflodern *nt*; Aufbrausen *nt*; Ausbruch *m*; (*sudden dispute*) (plötzlicher) Krach .

flash [flæʃ] **1** *n* (a) Aufblinken *nt no pl*; (*very bright*) Aufblitzen *nt no pl*; (*of metal, jewels etc*) Blitzen, Blinken *nt no pl*; (*Mot*) Lichthupe *f no pl*. **to give sb a ~** (*Mot*) jdn (mit der Lichthupe) anblinken; **~ of lightning** Blitz *m*; **he gave two quick ~es with his torch** er blinkte zweimal kurz mit der Taschenlampe; **the ~es come at regular intervals** es blinkt in regelmäßigen Abständen; **three short ~es are the Morse sign for S** dreimal kurz Blinken ist *or* drei kurze Blinkzeichen sind das Morsezeichen für S. (b) (*fig*) (*news ~*) Kurzmeldung *f*; (*interrupting programme also*) Zwischenmeldung *f*. **~ of wit/inspiration** Geistesblitz *m*; **in a ~** blitzartig, wie der Blitz; **as quick as a ~** blitzschnell; **a ~ in the pan** (*inf*) ein Strohfeuer *nt*. (c) (*Mil: on uniform*) Abzeichen *nt*. (d) (*Phot*) Blitz(licht *nt*) *m*. **to use a ~** Blitzlicht benutzen. (e) (*US inf: torch*) Taschenlampe *f*. **2** *vi* (a) aufblinken; (*very brightly*) aufblitzen; (*repeatedly: indicators etc*) blinken; (*metal, jewels, eyes*) blitzen, blinken; (*Mot*) die Lichthupe benutzen. (b) (*move quickly*) (*vehicle*) sausen, schießen, flitzen (*all inf*); (*person also*) huschen. **to ~ in and out** rein und raus sausen *etc*; **a smile ~ed across his face** ein Lächeln huschte über sein Gesicht; **to ~ past** *or* **by** vorbeisausen *etc*; (*holidays etc*) vorbeifliegen; **the time ~ed past** die Zeit verflog im Nu; **the news ~ed round** die Nachricht ging wie ein Lauffeuer um; **the thought ~ed through my mind that ...** mir kam plötzlich der Gedanke, daß ..., es schoß mir durch den Kopf, daß ... **3** *vt* (a) *light* aufblitzen *or* aufleuchten lassen; *SOS, message* blinken. **to ~ a torch on sb/sth** jdn/etw mit der Taschenlampe anleuchten; **to ~ one's headlights** die Lichthupe betätigen; **to ~ one's headlights at sb, to ~ sb** jdn mit der Lichthupe anblinken; **she ~ed him a look of contempt/gratitude** sie blitzte ihn verächtlich/dankbar an.

(b) (*inf: show, wave: also ~ around*) schwenken (*inf*), protzen mit; *diamond ring* blitzen lassen. **don't ~ all that money around** wedel nicht so mit dem vielen Geld herum (*inf*). **4** *adj* (*inf*) (*showy*) protzig (*pej*); (*smart*) schick.

♦**flash back** *vi* (*Film*) zurückblenden (*to auf* +*acc*).

flash: **~back** *n* (*Film*) Rückblende *f*; **~bulb** *n* (*Phot*) Blitzbirne *f*; **~ burn** *n* Verbrennung *f* (*durch kurzzeitige Strahlungshitze*); **~ card** *n* (*Sch*) Leselernkarte *f*; **~cube** *n* (*Phot*) Blitz(licht)würfel *m*.

flasher ['flæʃəʳ] *n* (a) (*Mot*) Lichthupe *f*. (b) (*Brit inf: person exposing himself*) Exhibitionist *m*.

flash: **~ flood** *n* flutartige Überschwemmung; **~ gun** *n* Elektronenblitzgerät *nt*; **~ Harry** *n* (*inf*) Lackaffe *m* (*pej inf*); **~light** *n* (a) (*Phot*) Blitzlicht *nt*; (b) (*esp US: torch*) Taschenlampe *f*; (c) (*signal lamp*) Leuchtfeuer *nt*; **~ point** *n* (*Chem*) Flammpunkt *m*; (*fig*) Siedepunkt *m*.

flashy ['flæʃɪ] *adj* (+*er*) auffallend, auffällig.

flask [flɑːsk] *n* Flakon *m*; (*Chem*) Glaskolben *m*; (*for spirits, carried in pocket*) Flachmann *m* (*inf*), Reiseflasche *f*; (*vacuum ~*) Thermosflasche *f*.

flat¹ [flæt] **1** *adj* (+*er*) (a) flach; *countryside also, tyre, nose, feet* platt; *surface* eben. **make sure the paper/book is ~** achten Sie darauf, daß das Papier/Buch flach ist *or* liegt; **he stood ~ against the wall** er stand platt gegen die Wand gedrückt; **as ~ as a pancake** (*inf*) (*tyre*) total platt; (*countryside*) total flach; (*girl*) flach wie ein (Plätt)brett, platt wie eine Flunder; **~ roof** Flachdach *nt*; **to fall ~ on one's face** auf die Nase fallen; **to lie ~** flach *or* platt liegen; **lay the book ~ on the table** leg das Buch flach auf den Tisch; **the earthquake laid the whole city ~** das Erdbeben machte die ganze Stadt dem Erdboden gleich.

(b) (*fig*) fad(e); *painting, photo also* flach, kontrastarm; *colour* matt, stumpf, glanzlos; *joke, remark* abgedroschen, öde, müde; *trade, market* lau, lahm, lustlos; (*stale*) *beer, wine* schal, abgestanden. **she felt a bit ~** sie fühlte sich ein bißchen daneben (*inf*), sie hatte zu nichts Lust; **to fall ~** (*joke*) nicht ankommen; (*play etc*) durchfallen. (c) *refusal, denial* glatt, deutlich. **and that's ~** und damit basta. (d) (*Mus*) *instrument* zu tief (gestimmt); *voice* zu tief. (e) (*Comm*) Pauschal-. **~ rate of pay** Pauschallohn *m*; **~ rate** Pauschale *f*; **to pay a ~ rate of income tax** eine Einkommenssteuerpauschale bezahlen; **to get a ~ rate of pay** pauschal bezahlt werden. (f) (*US inf: broke*) pleite (*inf*).

2 *adv* (+*er*) (a) *turn down, refuse* rundweg, kategorisch. **he told me ~ that ...** er sagte mir klipp und klar, daß ... (b) (*Mus*) **to sing/play ~** zu tief singen/spielen. (c) **in ten seconds ~** in sage und schreibe (nur) zehn Sekunden. (d) **~ broke** (*Brit inf*) total pleite (*inf*). (e) **~ out** (*inf*) (*exhausted*) total erledigt (*inf*); (*asleep, drunk*) hinüber (*inf*); **to go ~ out** voll aufdrehen (*inf*); (*in car also*) Spitze fahren (*inf*); **to work** *or* **go ~ out** auf Hochtouren arbeiten; **to be lying ~ out** platt am Boden liegen.

3 *n* (a) (*of hand*) Fläche *f*; (*of blade*) flache Seite. (b) (*Geog*) Ebene *f*. (c) (*Mus*) Erniedrigungszeichen, b *nt*. **you played E natural instead of a ~** du hast e statt es gespielt. (d) (*Aut*) Platte(r) *m* (*inf*), (Reifen)panne *f*. (e) (*Theat*) Kulisse *f*. (f) (*Sport*) **the ~** das Flachrennen; (*season*) die Flachrennsaison.

flat² *n* (*Brit*) Wohnung *f*.

flat: **~-bottomed** ['flæt,bɒtəmd] *adj boat* flach; **~-chested** *adj* flachbrüstig; **~-dweller** *n* (*Brit*) Wohnungsbewohner(in *f*) *m*; **~ feet** *npl* Plattfüße *pl*; **~fish** *n* Plattfisch *m*; **~-footed** *adj* plattfüßig; **~-hunting** *n* (*Brit*) Wohnungssuche *f*. **to go/be ~-hunting** auf Wohnungssuche gehen/sein; **~-iron** *n* (*old*) Plätteisen *nt*; **~let** *n* (*Brit*) kleine Wohnung.

flatly ['flætlɪ] *adv deny, refuse* rundweg, kategorisch; *say* klipp und klar, schlankweg.

flatmate ['flætmeɪt] *n* (*Brit*) Mitbewohner(in *f*) *m*.

flatness ['flætnɪs] *n see adj* (a-c) (a) Flachheit *f*; Plattheit *f*; Ebenheit *f*. (b) Fadheit *f*; Flachheit, Kontrastarmut *f*; Stumpfheit *f*; Abgedroschenheit *f*; Lustlosigkeit *f*; Schalheit *f*. (c) Deutlichkeit, Direktheit *f*.

flat: **~ race** *n* Flachrennen *nt*; **~ racing** *n* Flachrennen *nt*; **~ season** *n* Flachrennsaison *f*.

flatten ['flætn] **1** *vt* (a) *path, road, field* ebnen, planieren; *metal* flach *or* platt hämmern *or* schlagen; (*storm etc*) *crops* zu Boden drücken, niederdrücken; *trees* umwerfen; *town* dem Erdboden gleichmachen. (b) (*inf: demoralize, snub*) zu nichts reduzieren. **that'll ~ him** das wird bei ihm die Luft rauslassen (*inf*). **2** *vr* **to ~ oneself against sth** sich platt gegen *or* an etw drücken.

♦**flatten out 1** *vi* (*countryside*) flach(er) *or* eben(er) werden; (*road*) eben(er) werden; (*Aviat*) ausschweben. **2** *vt sep path* ebnen; *metal* glatt hämmern; *map, paper, fabric* glätten.

flatter ['flætəʳ] *vt* schmeicheln (+*dat*). **it ~s your figure** das ist sehr vorteilhaft; **I was very ~ed by his speech** ich fühlte mich von seiner Rede sehr geschmeichelt; **you can ~ yourself on being ...** Sie können sich (*dat*) etwas darauf einbilden, daß Sie ...; **he ~s himself he's a good musician** er schmeichelt sich (*dat*) *or* er bildet sich (*dat*) ein, ein guter Musiker zu sein.

flatterer ['flætərəʳ] *n* Schmeichler(in *f*) *m*.

flattering ['flætərɪŋ] *adj* schmeichelhaft; *words also* schmeichlerisch; *clothes* vorteilhaft.

flatteringly ['flætərɪŋlɪ] *adv say* schmeichlerisch; *posed, dressed* vorteilhaft.

flattery ['flætərɪ] *n* (*compliments*) Schmeicheleien *pl*. **~ will get you nowhere** mit Schmeicheln kommst du nicht weiter.

flatulence ['flætjʊləns] n Blähung(en pl), Flatulenz (spec) f. **to cause ~** Blähungen verursachen, blähen.

flatulent ['flætjʊlənt] adj aufgebläht; food blähend.

flat: **~ware** n (US) (cutlery) Besteck nt; (plates etc) Geschirr nt; **~work** n (US) Mangelwäsche f; **~worm** n Plattwurm m.

flaunt [flɔːnt] vt wealth, knowledge zur Schau stellen, protzen mit. **she ~ed her femininity/independence at him** sie ließ ihre Reize vor ihm spielen/sie rieb ihm ihre Unabhängigkeit unter die Nase; **to ~ oneself** sich groß in Szene setzen.

flautist ['flɔːtɪst] n Flötist(in f) m.

flavour, (US) **flavor** ['fleɪvəʳ] **1** n (taste) Geschmack m; (flavouring) Aroma nt; (fig) Beigeschmack m. **with a rum ~** mit Rumgeschmack; **20 different ~s** 20 verschiedene Geschmackssorten; **the film gives the ~ of Paris in the twenties** der Film vermittelt die Atmosphäre des Paris der zwanziger Jahre.
2 vt Geschmack verleihen (+dat) or geben (+dat). **pineapple-~ed** mit Ananasgeschmack.

flavouring, (US) **flavoring** ['fleɪvərɪŋ] n (Cook) Aroma(stoff m) nt. **vanilla/rum ~** Vanille-/Rumaroma nt.

flavourless, (US) **flavorless** ['fleɪvəlɪs] adj fad(e), geschmacklos.

flaw [flɔː] **1** n (lit) Fehler m; (fig also) Mangel m; (in sb's character also) Mangel, Defekt m; (Jur: in contract etc) (Form)fehler m. **to pick out the ~s in an argument** die Fehler or Mängel eines Argumentes herausstellen.
2 vt argument, plan einen Fehler aufzeigen or finden in (+dat). **his logic couldn't be ~ed** man konnte in seiner Logik keinen Fehler aufzeigen or finden.

flawed [flɔːd] adj fehlerhaft.

flawless ['flɔːlɪs] adj performance fehlerlos; behaviour untadelig, tadellos; complexion makellos; diamond lupenrein. **~ English** fehlerloses or einwandfreies or tadelloses Englisch.

flax [flæks] n (Bot) Flachs m.

flaxen ['flæksən] adj hair flachsfarben, Flachs-; (Tex) flächse(r)n. **~-haired** flachsblond.

flay [fleɪ] vt (a) (skin) animal abziehen, häuten; (beat) verdreschen; (whip) auspeitschen. **to ~ sb alive** jdn gründlich verdreschen. **(b)** (fig: criticize) kein gutes Haar lassen an (+dat), heruntermachen (inf).

flea [fliː] n Floh m. **to send sb off with a ~ in his/her ear** (inf) jdn wie einen begossenen Pudel abziehen lassen.

flea: **~bag** n (a) (US inf: hotel) Flohbude (inf), Absteige f; **(b)** (Brit inf: person) Schrulle f (inf); **~ bite** n Flohbiß m; **it's a mere ~ bite** (fig) es ist eine Kleinigkeit; **~-bitten** adj voller Flohbisse; (inf) vergammelt (inf); **~ circus** n Flohzirkus m; **~ market** n Flohmarkt m; **~pit** n (Brit inf) Flohkino nt (inf).

fleck [flek] **1** n (of red etc) Tupfen m; (of mud, paint) (blotch) Fleck(en) m; (speckle) Spritzer m; (of fluff, dust) Teilchen m, Flöckchen nt. **a ~ of dandruff** eine Schuppe.
2 vt sprenkeln; (with mud etc) bespritzen. **~ed wool** melierte Wolle; **blue ~ed with white** blau mit weißen Tupfen or Punkten, blau und weiß gesprenkelt; **the sky was ~ed with little clouds** der Himmel war mit Schäfchenwolken übersät.

fled [fled] pret, ptp of flee.

fledged [fledʒd] adj bird flügge; see fully-fledged.

fledg(e)ling ['fledʒlɪŋ] n (a) (bird) Jungvogel m. **(b)** (fig: inexperienced person) Grünschnabel m.

flee [fliː] pret, ptp fled **1** vi fliehen, flüchten (from vor +dat). **she fled to answer the door** sie eilte zur Tür, um aufzumachen; **he fled when he saw her coming** als er sie kommen sah, flüchtete or floh er; **to ~ from temptation** der Versuchung entfliehen.
2 vt town, country fliehen or flüchten aus; temptation, danger entfliehen (+dat).

fleece [fliːs] **1** n Vlies, Schaffell nt; (fabric) (natural) Schaffell nt; (artificial) Webpelz, Flausch m; see Golden F~. **2** vt (a) sheep scheren. **(b)** (fig inf) **to ~ sb of his money** jdn schröpfen.

fleecy ['fliːsɪ] adj (+er) blanket flauschig; snow flockig. **~ clouds** Schäfchenwolken pl.

fleet¹ [fliːt] n (a) (Naut) Geschwader nt; (entire naval force) Flotte f. **F~ Air Arm** Marineluftwaffe f; **merchant ~** Handelsflotte f. **(b)** (of cars, coaches, buses etc) (Fuhr)park m. **he owns a ~ of lorries** er hat eine Lastwagenflotte f.

fleet² adj (+er) schnell, flink. **~ of foot**, **~-footed** schnell- or leichtfüßig.

fleet admiral n (US) Großadmiral m.

fleeting ['fliːtɪŋ] adj flüchtig; beauty vergänglich. **a ~ visit** eine Stippvisite; **the ~ years** die entfliehenden Jahre pl.

Fleming ['flemɪŋ] n Flame m, Flamin, Flämin f.

Flemish ['flemɪʃ] **1** adj flämisch. **2** n (a) **the ~** pl die Flamen pl. **(b)** (language) Flämisch nt.

flesh [fleʃ] n (a) Fleisch nt; (of fruit) (Frucht)fleisch nt; (of vegetable) Mark nt. **to put on ~** (animals) zunehmen; (person also) Fleisch auf die Rippen bekommen (inf); **all that bare ~ on the beach** diese Fleischbeschau am Strand.
(b) (fig) **one's own ~ and blood** sein eigen(es) Fleisch und Blut; **it was more than ~ and blood could bear** das war einfach nicht zu ertragen; **creatures of ~ and blood** Menschen von Fleisch und Blut; **I'm only ~ and blood** ich bin auch nur aus Fleisch und Blut; **in the ~** in Person, in natura; **he's gone the way of all ~** er ist den Weg allen Fleisches gegangen.
(c) (Rel) Fleisch nt. **sins of the ~** Sünden pl des Fleisches.

flesh: **~ colour** n Fleischfarbe f; **~-coloured** adj fleischfarben; **~-eating** adj fleischfressend.

fleshings ['fleʃɪŋz] npl (tights) Trikotstrumpfhose(n pl) f.

flesh: **~pots** npl Fleischtöpfe pl; **~ tints** pl Fleischtöne pl; **~ wound** n Fleischwunde f.

fleshy ['fleʃɪ] adj (+er) fleischig; vegetable Mark-.

fletch [fletʃ] vt arrow befiedern.

fletcher ['fletʃəʳ] n Pfeilmacher m.

fleur de lys [ˌflɜːdəˈliː] n, pl **-s - -** [ˌflɜːdəˈliːz] bourbonische Lilie.

flew [fluː] pret of fly², fly³.

flex [fleks] **1** n (Brit) Schnur f; (heavy duty) Kabel nt. **2** vt body, knees beugen. **to ~ one's muscles** (lit, fig) seine Muskeln spielen lassen.

flexibility [ˌfleksɪˈbɪlɪtɪ] n see adj (a) Biegsamkeit f; Elastizität f. **(b)** Flexibilität f; Modulationsfähigkeit f.

flexible ['fleksəbl] adj (a) wire biegsam; material, plastic, branch also elastisch. **(b)** (fig) flexibel; voice modulationsfähig. **~ working hours** gleitende Arbeitszeit, Gleitzeit f.

flexion ['flekʃən] n (Gram) Flexion, Beugung f.

flexional ['flekʃənl] adj ending Flexions-.

flex(i)time ['fleks(ɪ)taɪm] n Gleitzeit f.

flexor (muscle) ['fleksə(mʌsl)] n Beuger m.

flibbertigibbet ['flɪbətɪˈdʒɪbɪt] n (junges) Gänschen.

flick [flɪk] **1** n (with finger) Schnipsen nt no pl; (of tail) kurzer Schlag; (with whip) Schnalzen nt no pl. **with a ~ of his fingers/whip** mit einem Fingerschnalzen/Peitschenschnalzen; **one ~ of his fingers and the dog came running** er schnipste nur einmal mit dem Finger, und der Hund kam angerannt; **a ~ of the wrist** eine schnelle Drehung des Handgelenks; **she gave the room a quick ~ with the duster** sie ging kurz mit dem Staublappen durch das Zimmer.
2 vt whip schnalzen or knallen mit; fingers schnalzen mit; (with whip) horse etc leicht schlagen; (with fingers) switch anknipsen; dust, ash wegschnippen; (with cloth) wegwedeln. **she ~ed her hair out of her eyes** sie strich sich (dat) die Haare aus den Augen; **I'll just ~ a duster round the sitting-room** (inf) ich wedel' or geh' eben mal mit dem Staubtuch durchs Wohnzimmer (inf); **he ~ed the pages of the book over** er blätterte flüchtig durch das Buch.
3 vi **the snake's tongue ~ed in and out** die Schlange züngelte.
♦**flick off** vt sep wegschnippen; (with duster) wegwedeln.
♦**flick through** vi +prep obj (schnell) durchblättern.

flicker ['flɪkəʳ] **1** vi (flame, candle) flackern; (light, TV also) flimmern; (needle on dial) zittern; (smile) zucken; (eyelid) flattern, zucken. **the snake's tongue ~ed in and out** die Schlange züngelte.
2 n see vi Flackern nt; Flimmern nt; Zittern nt; Zucken nt; Flattern, Zucken nt. **a ~ of hope** ein Hoffnungsschimmer m; **without a ~** ohne mit der Wimper zu zucken; **with not so much as the ~ of a smile** ohne (auch nur) das geringste Anzeichen eines Lächelns.

flick knife n Klappmesser, Schnappmesser nt.

flicks [flɪks] npl (Brit inf) Kintopp m or nt (inf). **to/at the ~** in den or ins Kintopp (inf)/im Kintopp (inf).

flier ['flaɪəʳ] n (a) (Aviat: pilot) Flieger(in f) m. **to be a good/bad ~** (person) Fliegen gut/nicht vertragen; (bird) ein guter/schlechter Flieger sein.
(b) (US) (train) Schnellzug m; (fast coach) Expreßbus m.
(c) **to take a ~** (leap) einen Riesensprung or -satz machen; (fall) der Länge nach hinfallen.
(d) (flying start) fliegender Start. **he got a ~** er hat einen fliegenden Start gemacht.

flight¹ [flaɪt] n (a) Flug m. **in ~** (birds) im Flug; (Aviat) in der Luft; **to take ~** (bird) davonfliegen, auffliegen; **the principles of ~** die Prinzipien des Fliegens.
(b) (group) (of birds) Schwarm m, Schar f; (of aeroplanes) Geschwader nt, Formation f. **to be in the first or top ~** (fig) zur Spitze gehören; **the first or top ~ of scientists/novelists** die Spitzenwissenschaftler pl/-schriftsteller pl.
(c) (of fancy, imagination) Höhenflug m. **~s of fancy** geistige Höhenflüge pl; **~s of oratory** rednerische Höhenflüge pl.
(d) **~ (of stairs)** Treppe f; **he lives six ~s up** er wohnt sechs Treppen hoch; **a ~ of hurdles** eine Gruppe von Hürden; **he fell at the second ~** er fiel bei der zweiten Hürde; **a ~ of terraces** (eine Gruppe von) Terrassen pl.
(e) (on dart, arrow) Steuerfeder f.

flight² n Flucht f. **to put the enemy to ~** den Feind in die Flucht schlagen; **to take (to) ~** die Flucht ergreifen; **the ~ of capital abroad** die Kapitalflucht ins Ausland.

flight: **~ bag** n Schultertasche f; **~ deck** n (a) (Naut) Flugdeck nt; (b) (Aviat) Cockpit nt; **~ engineer** n Bordingenieur m; **~ feather** n Schwungfeder f; **~less** adj nicht flugfähig; **~ log** n Bordbuch nt; **~ mechanic** n Bordmechaniker m; **~ path** n Flugbahn f; (of individual plane) Flugroute f; **~ incoming/outgoing ~ path** Einflug-/Ausflugschneise f; **~ plan** n Flugablaufplan m; **~ recorder** n Flugschreiber m; **~ sergeant** n Haupt- or Oberfeldwebel m (der Luftwaffe); **~ simulator** n Simulator m; **~-test** n Flugtest m; **2** vt im Flug testen, flugtesten.

flighty ['flaɪtɪ] adj (+er) (fickle) unbeständig, flatterhaft; (empty-headed) gedankenlos.

flim-flam ['flɪmflæm] n (inf) (rubbish) Blödsinn m; (lies) Schwindel m.

flimsily ['flɪmzɪlɪ] adv dressed leicht; built, constructed also nicht solide. **a ~ bound book** ein schlecht gebundenes Buch.

flimsiness ['flɪmzɪnɪs] n (a) see adj (a) Dünne f; Leichtigkeit, Dürftigkeit f; leichte or wenig solide Bauweise; (of book) schlechte or billige Aufmachung; schlechte Qualität. **in spite of the ~ of the wings** trotz der leichten Bauweise der Tragflächen.
(b) (of excuse) Fadenscheinigkeit f; (of reasoning) mangelnde Stichhaltigkeit, Dürftigkeit f.

flimsy ['flɪmzɪ] **1** adj (+er) (a) material dünn; clothing leicht, dürftig; house, aircraft leicht gebaut, nicht stabil gebaut; book schlecht gebunden; binding schlecht. **a ~ dress** ein Fähnchen nt; **these ~ houses** diese Billighäuser pl (pej).
(b) excuse fadenscheinig, schwach; reasoning also nicht stichhaltig, dürftig.

2 n (paper) Durchschlagpapier nt.

flinch [flɪntʃ] vi (a) (wince) zurückzucken. **without ~ing** ohne mit der Wimper zu zucken. (b) (fig) **to ~ from a task** vor einer Aufgabe zurückschrecken; **he ~ed from telling her the truth** er scheute sich, ihr die Wahrheit zu sagen.

fling [flɪŋ] (vb: pret, ptp **flung**) 1 n (a) (act of ~ing) Wurf m, Schleudern nt no pl.

(b) (fig inf) Anlauf m. **to have a ~ at sth, to give sth a ~** sich an etw (dat) versuchen, etw (aus)probieren; **to have a ~ at doing sth** einen Anlauf machen, etw zu tun (inf); **youth must have its ~** die Jugend muß sich austoben; **to have a ~ or one's ~** sich austoben; **he'll drop her when he's had his ~** wenn er erst mal seinen Spaß gehabt hat, läßt er sie fallen; **to go on a ~** einen draufmachen (inf); (in shops) sehr viel Geld ausgeben.

(c) see **Highland ~**.

2 vt (lit, fig) schleudern. **to ~ the window open/shut** das Fenster aufstoßen/zuwerfen; **the door was flung open** die Tür flog auf; **to ~ one's arms round sb's neck** jdm die Arme um den Hals werfen; **he flung himself at the intruder** er stürzte sich or warf sich auf den Eindringling; **to ~ a coat round one's shoulders** sich (dat) einen Mantel über die Schulter(n) werfen; **to ~ on one's coat** (sich dat) den Mantel überwerfen; **to ~ oneself into a job** sich auf eine Aufgabe stürzen; **to ~ oneself out of the window/into a chair** sich aus dem Fenster stürzen/sich in einen Sessel werfen; **you shouldn't just ~ yourself at him** (fig inf) du solltest dich ihm nicht so an den Hals werfen.

♦**fling away** vt sep wegwerfen, wegschmeißen (inf); (fig) money, time vergeuden, verschwenden.

♦**fling back** vt sep one's head zurückwerfen.

♦**fling down** vt sep (lit) runterschmeißen (inf). **to ~ a challenge** den Fehdehandschuh hinwerfen or hinschleudern.

♦**fling off** vt sep (lit) coat abwerfen; opponent abschütteln; (fig) remark hinwerfen; essay hinhauen (inf); restraints von sich werfen.

♦**fling out** vt sep unwanted object wegwerfen, wegschmeißen (inf); person hinauswerfen, rausschmeißen (inf).

♦**fling up** vt sep (a) hochwerfen. **to ~ one's arms ~ in horror** entsetzt die Hände über dem Kopf zusammenschlagen. (b) (fig inf) **to ~ sth ~ at sb** jdm etw unter die Nase reiben.

flint [flɪnt] n (a) (for cigarette-lighter) Feuerstein m. (b) (stone) Feuerstein, Flint(stein) m.

flint: **~ axe** n (Feuer)steinbeil nt; **~ glass** n Flintglas nt; **~lock** n Steinschloßgewehr nt.

flinty [ˈflɪntɪ] adj soil, rocks aus Feuerstein; (like flint) wie Feuerstein; (fig) heart steinern.

flip [flɪp] 1 n (a) Schnipser m. **to give sth a ~** etw in die Luft schnellen.

(b) (somersault) Salto m. **backwards ~** Salto rückwärts.

(c) (Aviat inf) Rundflug m.

(d) (drink) Flip m.

2 adj (inf: flippant) schnodderig (inf).

3 vt schnippen, schnipsen; (inf) record rumdrehen (inf). **to ~ a book open** ein Buch aufklappen or aufschlagen; **to ~ one's lid** (inf) durchdrehen (inf), aus dem Häuschen geraten (inf).

4 vi (sl) durchdrehen (inf).

5 interj (Brit inf) verflixt (inf).

♦**flip off** vt sep wegschnipsen; ash from cigarette abtippen.

♦**flip over** 1 vt sep umdrehen; pages of book wenden. 2 vi sich (um)drehen; (plane) sich in der Luft (um)drehen.

♦**flip through** vi +prep obj book durchblättern.

flip-flop [ˈflɪpflɒp] n (a) (Sport) Flickflack m. (b) (Elec) Flipflop m. (c) (sandal) Gummilatsche f (inf).

flip pack n Klappschachtel f.

flippancy [ˈflɪpənsɪ] n Frivolität, Leichtfertigkeit f.

flippant [ˈflɪpənt] adj leichtfertig, schnodderig (inf); remarks unernst, schnodderig (inf); **you shouldn't be so ~ (about it)** du solltest das etwas ernster nehmen.

flippantly [ˈflɪpəntlɪ] adv see adj.

flipper [ˈflɪpər] n Flosse f; (of diver) (Schwimm)flosse f.

flipping [ˈflɪpɪŋ] adj, adv (Brit inf) verflixt.

flip: **~side** n (of record) B-Seite f; **~ top** n Klappdeckel m.

flirt [flɜːt] 1 vi flirten. **to ~ with an idea** mit einem Gedanken liebäugeln or spielen; **to ~ with death/disaster** den Tod/das Unglück herausfordern. 2 n he/she is just a ~ er/sie will nur flirten; **I'm a bit of a ~** ich flirte (für mein Leben) gern; **he's a great ~** er ist ein großer Charmeur.

flirtation [flɜːˈteɪʃən] n Flirt m. his ~ with death/danger sein Spiel mit dem Tod/der Gefahr.

flirtatious [flɜːˈteɪʃəs] adj kokett.

flit [flɪt] 1 vi (a) (bats, butterflies etc) flattern, huschen; (ghost, person, image) huschen. **to ~ in and out** (person) rein- und rausflitzen; **an idea ~ted through my mind** ein Gedanke schoß mir or huschte mir durch den Kopf.

(b) (Brit: move house secretly) bei Nacht und Nebel ausziehen, sich bei Nacht und Nebel davonmachen.

(c) (Scot, N Engl: move house) umziehen.

2 n (Brit) **to do a (moonlight) ~** bei Nacht und Nebel umziehen.

flitch [flɪtʃ] n Speckseite f; (of halibut) Heilbuttschnitte f.

float [fləʊt] 1 n (a) (on fishing-line, in cistern, carburettor, on aeroplane) Schwimmer m; (anchored raft) (verankertes) Floß, Schwimmplattform f; (as swimming aid) Schwimmkork m; (of fish) Schwimmblase f; (on trawl net) Korken m.

(b) (vehicle) (in procession) Festwagen m; (for deliveries) kleiner Elektrolieferwagen.

(c) (ready cash: in till) Wechselgeld nt no indef art (zu Geschäftsbeginn); (loan to start business) Startkapital nt.

2 vi (a) (on water) schwimmen; (move gently) treiben; (in air) schweben. **the corpse ~ed up to the surface** die Leiche trieb an die Wasseroberfläche; **it ~ed downriver** es trieb flußabwärts.

(b) (Comm: currency) floaten.

3 vt (a) boat zu Wasser bringen. **they ~ed the logs downstream** sie flößten die Baumstämme flußabwärts.

(b) (Comm, Fin) company gründen; loan lancieren; shares auf den Markt bringen; bond issue ausgeben; currency freigeben, floaten lassen; (fig) ideas, suggestion in den Raum stellen, zur Debatte stellen. **the ~ing of the pound** die Freigabe or das Floaten or das Floating des Pfundes.

♦**float (a)round** vi (rumour, news) im Umlauf sein; (person) herumschweben (inf); (things) herumfliegen (inf).

♦**float away** or **off** vi (on water) abtreiben, wegtreiben; (in air) davonschweben; (fig person) hinwegschweben.

floating [ˈfləʊtɪŋ] adj (a) raft, logs treibend. **~ bridge** Schiffsbrücke f; **~ dock** Schwimmdock m.

(b) (fig) population wandernd. **~ voter** Wechselwähler m.

(c) (Fin) currency freigegeben. **~ capital** Umlauf- or Betriebskapital nt; **~ debt** schwebende Schuld.

(d) (Math) decimal point Gleit-.

(e) (Med) kidney Wander-; rib frei.

flock¹ [flɒk] 1 n (a) (of sheep, geese) Herde f; (of birds) Schwarm m, Schar f.

(b) (of people) Schar f, Haufen m (inf). **they came in ~s** kamen haufenweise (inf) or in hellen Scharen.

(c) (Eccl) Herde f.

2 vi in Scharen kommen. **to ~ in** hinein-/hereinströmen or -drängen; **to ~ out** hinaus-/herausströmen or -drängen; **to ~ together** zusammenströmen, sich versammeln; **to ~ around sb** sich um jdn scharen or drängen.

flock² n (Tex) Flocke f. **~ wallpaper** Velourstapete f.

floe [fləʊ] n Treibeis nt, Eisscholle f.

flog [flɒg] vt (a) prügeln, schlagen; thief, mutineer auspeitschen. **you're ~ging a dead horse** (inf) Sie verschwenden Ihre Zeit; **to ~ sth to death** (fig) etw zu Tode reiten.

(b) (Brit inf) verkloppen, verscherbeln, losschlagen (all inf).

flogging [ˈflɒgɪŋ] n Tracht f Prügel; (Jur) Prügelstrafe f; (of thief, mutineer) Auspeitschen nt. **he was given a ~** er bekam eine Tracht Prügel; (Jur) er wurde zu (einer) Prügelstrafe verurteilt; er wurde ausgepeitscht; **to bring back ~** die Prügelstrafe wiedereinführen; **a public ~** eine öffentliche Auspeitschung.

flood [flʌd] 1 n (a) (of water) Flut f. **~s** Überschwemmung f, Hochwasser nt; (in several places) Überschwemmungen pl, Hochwasser nt; **the F~** die Sintflut; **the river is in ~** der Fluß führt Hochwasser; **she had a ~ in the kitchen** ihre Küche stand unter Wasser.

(b) (fig) Flut f, Schwall m. **~s of tears** ein Strom von Tränen. **she was in ~s of tears** sie war in Tränen gebadet; **the scene was bathed in a ~ of light** die Szene war lichtüberflutet.

(c) (also ~-tide) Flut f.

2 vt (a) fields, town überschwemmen, unter Wasser setzen. **the village/cellar was ~ed** das Dorf/der Keller war überschwemmt or stand unter Wasser; **to ~ the carburettor** den Motor absaufen lassen (inf).

(b) (storm, rain) river, stream über die Ufer treten lassen.

(c) (fig) überschwemmen, überfluten. **~ed with light** lichtdurchflutet, von Licht durchflutet.

(d) (Comm) **to ~ the market** den Markt überschwemmen.

3 vi (a) (river) über die Ufer treten; (bath etc) überfließen, überlaufen; (cellar) unter Wasser stehen; (garden, land) überschwemmt werden.

(b) (people) strömen, sich ergießen (geh). **the crowd ~ed into the streets** die Menge strömte auf die Straßen.

♦**flood in** vi (people, sunshine) hinein-/hereinströmen; (water also) hinein-/hereinfluten. **the letters just ~ed ~** wir/sie hatten eine Flut von Briefen.

♦**flood out** vt sep house überfluten, unter Wasser setzen. **the villagers were ~ed ~** die Dorfbewohner wurden durch das Hochwasser obdachlos.

flood: **~ control** n Hochwasserschutz m; **~ disaster** n Flutkatastrophe f; **~gate** n Schleusentor nt; **to open the ~gates** (fig) Tür und Tor öffnen (to dat).

flooding [ˈflʌdɪŋ] n Überschwemmung f.

flood: **~light** (vb: pret, ptp **~lit**) 1 vt buildings anstrahlen; football pitch mit Flutlicht beleuchten; (fig: light brightly) beleuchten; 2 n (device) Scheinwerfer m; (light) Flutlicht nt; under **~lights, by ~light** unter or bei Flutlicht; **~lighting** n (a) Flutlicht(anlage f) nt; (b) (of building etc) Beleuchtung f; **~lit** 1 pret, ptp of **~light**; 2 adj **~lit football** Fußball bei or unter Flutlicht; **~ plain** n Schwemmebene f; **~-tide** n Flut f.

floor [flɔːr] 1 n (a) (of room) Boden m; (of room) (Fuß)boden m; (dance-~) Tanzboden m, Tanzfläche f. stone/tiled **~** Stein-/Fliesenboden m; **to take the ~** (dance) aufs Parkett or auf den Tanzboden gehen; (speak) das Wort ergreifen; **to hold or have the ~** (speaker) das Wort haben.

(b) (storey: in apartment block etc) Stock(werk nt) m. **first ~** (Brit) erster Stock; (US) Erdgeschoß nt; **on the second ~** (Brit) im zweiten Stock; (US) im ersten Stock.

(c) (of prices etc) Minimum nt.

(d) (main part of chamber) Plenar- or Sitzungssaal m (also Parl); (of stock exchange) Parkett nt; (people present) Zuhörerschaft f; (Parl) Abgeordnete pl, Haus nt. **a question from the ~** (of the House) eine Frage aus der Zuhörerschaft; (Parl) eine Frage aus dem Haus; **~ of the House** Plenarsaal m des Unterhauses; **to cross the ~** (Parl) die Partei wechseln.

2 vt (a) room etc mit einem (Fuß)boden versehen. **to ~ a room in or with parquet** ein Zimmer mit Parkettboden auslegen.

(b) (knock down) opponent zu Boden schlagen.

(c) (silence) die Sprache verschlagen (+dat); (bewilder, puzzle) verblüffen; (defeat: question, problem, task etc) schaffen (inf). **to be ~ed by a problem** mit einem Problem überhaupt nicht zu Rande kommen (inf); **he looked completely ~ed** er sah völlig perplex aus.

floor: ~board n Diele, Bohle f; ~cloth n Scheuer- or Putzlappen m; ~ exercise n Bodenübung f; ~ lamp n Stehlampe f; ~ manager n (in store) Abteilungsleiter(in f) m (im Kaufhaus); (TV) Aufnahmeleiter(in f) m; ~ plan n Grundriß m (eines Stockwerkes); ~ polish n Bohnerwachs nt; ~ polisher n (tool) Bohnerbesen m; ~ show n Show, Vorstellung f (im Nachtklub oder Kabarett); ~ space n Stellraum m; if you've got a sleeping bag we have plenty of ~ space wenn du einen Schlafsack hast, wir haben viel Platz auf dem Fußboden; ~-walker n (Comm) Ladenaufsicht f; ~ wax n Bohnerwachs nt.

floozie, floozy ['flu:zɪ] n (inf) Flittchen nt (inf), Schickse f (inf).

flop [flɒp] 1 vi (a) (lose) fallen; (hard object) knallen, plumpsen; (inf: person) sich fallenlassen, sich hinplumpsen lassen. the fish ~ped feebly in the basket der Fisch zappelte matt im Korb; he ~ped down on the bed er ließ sich aufs Bett plumpsen or fallen; I'm ready to ~ (inf) ich falle gleich um.
(b) (inf: fail) (play, book) durchfallen; (actor, artiste) nicht ankommen; (party, picnic, scheme) ein Reinfall sein.
2 n (a) (inf: failure) Reinfall m; (person) Versager m, Niete f.
(b) (movement, sound) Plumps m.
3 adv the whole business went ~ (inf) das ganze Geschäft ging hops (inf).

♦**flop around** vi herumzappeln; (person: in slippers etc) herumschlappen.

flophouse ['flɒphaʊs] n billige Absteige, Penne f.

floppy ['flɒpɪ] adj (+er) schlaff, schlapp; hat, ears Schlapp-; movement schlaksig; clothes weit. ~ disk flexible Magnetplatte, Floppy Disk f.

flora ['flɔːrə] n Flora f.

floral ['flɔːrəl] adj arrangement, perfume Blüten-; fabric, dress geblümt, mit Blumenmuster.

Florence ['flɒrəns] n Florenz nt.

Florentine ['flɒrəntaɪn] adj florentinisch.

florescence [flɔ'resəns] n Blüte f.

floret ['flɒrət] n (of flower) (Einzel)blütchen nt; (of cauliflower) Röschen nt.

florid ['flɒrɪd] adj (a) complexion kräftig. his ~ face seine kräftigen (Gesichts)farben. (b) (overelaborate) überladen; style, writing blumig, schwülstig; architecture, music also zu reich verziert.

florin ['flɒrɪn] n Florin m; (Dutch) Gulden m; (dated Brit) Zweishillingstück nt.

florist ['flɒrɪst] n Blumenhändler(in f), Florist(in f) m. ~'s shop Blumengeschäft nt.

floss [flɒs] n Flockseide, Schappe f; (thread) Florettgarn nt, ungezwirntes Seidengarn; (dental ~) Zahnseide f. ~ silk Schappeseide, Florettseide f.

flotation [fləʊ'teɪʃən] n (of ship) Flottmachen nt; (of log) Flößen nt; (Comm: of firm) Gründung f; (Metal) Flotation, Schwimmaufbereitung f. ~ collar (Space) Schwimmkragen m.

flotilla [fləʊ'tɪlə] n Flotille f.

flotsam ['flɒtsəm] n Treibgut nt. ~ and jetsam (floating) Treibgut nt; (washed ashore) Strandgut nt; the ~ and jetsam of our society das Strandgut unserer Gesellschaft.

flounce¹ [flaʊns] 1 vi stolzieren. to ~ in/out/around herein-/heraus-/herumstolzieren. 2 n she turned on her heel/left the room with a ~ sie drehte sich pikiert auf dem Absatz um/sie stolzierte aus dem Zimmer.

flounce² 1 n (frill) Volant m, Rüsche f. 2 vt mit einem Volant/Volants or Rüschen besetzen.

flounced [flaʊnst] adj skirt, dress mit einem Volant/Volants or Rüschen besetzt.

flounder¹ ['flaʊndə'] n (fish) Flunder f.

flounder² vi (a) sich abstrampeln, sich abzappeln. a stranded whale ~ing on the beach ein gestrandeter Wal, der sich am Strand abquält; we ~ed along in the mud wir quälten uns mühselig durch den Schlamm.
(b) (fig) sich abzappeln (inf), sich abstrampeln (inf). to start to ~ ins Schwimmen kommen; to ~ through sth sich durch etw wursteln (inf) or mogeln (inf); he ~ed on er wurstelte weiter.

flour ['flaʊə'] 1 n Mehl nt. 2 vt (Cook) dough, rolling-pin etc mit Mehl bestäuben; one's hands also mehlen.

flour: ~bin n Mehlbüchse f; ~ dredger n Mehlstreuer m.

flourish ['flʌrɪʃ] 1 vi (plants etc, person) (prächtig) gedeihen; (business) blühen, florieren; (type of literature, painting etc) seine Blütezeit haben; (writer, artist etc) großen Erfolg haben, erfolgreich sein. nothing ~es in this soil auf diesem Boden gedeiht nichts.
2 vt (wave about) stick, book etc herumwedeln or -fuchteln mit, schwenken.
3 n (a) (curve, decoration etc) Schnörkel m.
(b) (movement) schwungvolle Bewegung, eleganter Schwung. with a ~ of his stick seinen Stock schwenkend.
(c) (Mus) (fanfare) Fanfare f; (decorative passage) Verzierung f. with a ~ of trumpets mit einem Fanfarenstoß.

flourishing ['flʌrɪʃɪŋ] adj plant, person blühend attr; business gutgehend attr, florierend attr.

flour: ~ mill n (Korn)mühle f; ~ shaker n Mehlstreuer m.

floury ['flaʊərɪ] adj face, hands, potatoes mehlig; dish bemehlt.

flout [flaʊt] vt sich hinwegsetzen über (+acc), mißachten; convention, society pfeifen auf (+acc).

flow [fləʊ] 1 vi (a) (lit, fig) fließen; (tears also) strömen; (prose) flüssig sein. where the river ~s into the sea wo der Fluß ins Meer mündet; tears were ~ing down her cheeks Tränen liefen or flossen or strömten ihr übers Gesicht; to keep the conversation ~ing das Gespräch in Gang halten; to keep the traffic ~ing den Verkehr nicht ins Stocken kommen lassen; try and keep the work ~ing smoothly versuchen Sie, die Arbeit stetig vorangehen zu lassen; to ~ in (water, people, money etc) hinein-/hereinströmen; to ~ out of herausströmen aus.
(b) (dress, hair etc) fließen, wallen.

(c) (tide) steigen, hereinkommen.
2 n (a) Fluß m. the ~ of blood/traffic/information der Blut-/Verkehrs-/Informationsfluß; against the ~ of the river gegen den Strom; see cash-flow.
(b) the tide is on the ~ die Flut kommt.
(c) (of words etc) Redefluß m. the ~ of his style sein flüssiger Stil; the powerful ~ of his prose seine wortgewaltige Prosa.

flow chart n Flußdiagramm nt.

flower ['flaʊə'] 1 n (a) Blume f; (blossom) Blüte f. in ~ in Blüte; to say sth with ~s etw mit Blumen sagen; "say it with ~s" „laßt Blumen sprechen"; no ~s by request wir bitten von Blumenspenden abzusehen.
(b) no pl (fig) Blüte f. to be in the ~ of youth in der Blüte seiner Jugend stehen; the ~ of the army die Blüte des Heeres; ~s of rhetoric blumenreiche Ausdrücke pl.
(c) (Chem) ~s of sulphur Schwefelblume or -blüte f.
2 vi (lit, fig) blühen.

flower: ~ arrangement n Blumengesteck nt; ~-arranging n Blumenstecken nt; ~bed n Blumenbeet nt; ~ child n Blumenkind nt.

flowered ['flaʊəd] adj shirt, wallpaper geblümt.

flower: ~ garden n Blumengarten m; ~ girl n (a) (seller) Blumenmädchen nt; (b) (at wedding etc) Streukind nt; ~head n Blütenkopf m.

flowering ['flaʊərɪŋ] adj plant Blüten-; cherry, shrub Zier-.

flower: ~ people npl Blumenkinder pl; ~pot n Blumentopf m; ~ power n Flower-power f; ~ shop n Blumenladen m, Blumengeschäft nt; ~ show n Blumenschau f.

flowery ['flaʊərɪ] adj (a) meadow Blumen-, mit Blumen übersät; perfume blumig; dress, material geblümt. (b) (fig) language etc blumig.

flowing ['fləʊɪŋ] adj fließend; dress, hair also wallend; style of writing, painting flüssig; tide auflaufend, hereinkommend.

flown [fləʊn] ptp of fly¹, fly³.

flu, 'flu [flu:] n Grippe f. to have (the) ~ (die or eine) Grippe haben.

fluctuate ['flʌktjʊeɪt] vi schwanken; (in number also) fluktuieren.

fluctuation [ˌflʌktjʊ'eɪʃən] n Schwankung f, Schwanken nt no pl; (in number also) Fluktuation f; (fig: of opinions) Schwanken nt no pl.

flue [flu:] n Rauchfang, Rauchabzug m; (Mus: of organ) (pipe) Labialpfeife f; (opening) Kernspalt m. ~ brush Stoßbesen m.

fluency ['flu:ənsɪ] n Flüssigkeit f; (of speaker) Gewandtheit f. his ~ in English ... daß er fließend Englisch spricht/sprach.

fluent ['flu:ənt] adj style flüssig; speaker, writer gewandt. to be ~ in Italian, to speak ~ Italian fließend Italienisch sprechen; his ~ Italian sein gutes Italienisch.

fluently ['flu:əntlɪ] adv speak a language fließend; write flüssig, gewandt; express oneself gewandt.

fluff [flʌf] 1 n, no pl (on birds, young animals) Flaum m; (from material) Fusseln pl; (dust) Staubflocken pl. a ball of ~ eine Staubflocke/eine or ein Fussel; (hum inf) eine Mieze (inf). 2 vt (a) (also ~ out) feathers aufplustern; pillows aufschütteln. (b) opportunity, lines in play, entrance vermasseln (inf).

fluffy ['flʌfɪ] adj (+er) bird flaumig; material, toy also kuschelig, weich; hair locker, duftig.

fluid ['flu:ɪd] 1 adj substance flüssig; drawing, outline fließend; style flüssig; (fig) situation ungewiß. the situation is still ~ die Dinge sind noch im Fluß. 2 n Flüssigkeit f.

fluidity [flu:'ɪdɪtɪ] n no pl see adj Flüssigkeit f; Fließende(s) nt; Flüssigkeit f; Ungewißheit f.

fluke¹ [flu:k] n (inf) Dusel m (inf), Schwein nt (inf). by a ~ durch Dusel (inf); it was a (pure) ~ das war (einfach) Dusel (inf).

fluke² n (Naut) Flunke m; (of a whale's tail) Fluke f; (Fishing: flounder) Flunder f; (Zool: flatworm) Plattwurm m.

fluky ['flu:kɪ] adj (inf) wind wechselnd. that was a ~ shot das war ein Zufallstreffer.

flummox ['flʌməks] vt (inf) person durcheinanderbringen, aus dem Konzept bringen (inf). to be ~ed durcheinander sein.

flung [flʌŋ] pret, ptp of fling.

flunk [flʌŋk] (inf) 1 vi durchfallen (inf), durchrasseln (sl), durch die Prüfung fliegen (inf). 2 vt exam verhauen (inf); candidate durchfallen (inf) or durchrasseln (sl) lassen. to ~ German/an exam in Deutsch/bei einer Prüfung durchfallen.

flunk(e)y ['flʌŋkɪ] n Lakei m; (flatterer) Radfahrer m (inf).

fluorescent [flʊə'resənt] adj Leucht-, fluoreszierend (spec); lighting, tube Neon-.

fluoridate ['flʊərɪdeɪt] vt mit Fluor versetzen, fluorieren.

fluoridation [ˌflʊərɪ'deɪʃən] n Fluorzusatz m (of zu).

fluoride ['flʊəraɪd] n Fluorid nt. ~ toothpaste Fluorzahnpasta f.

fluorine ['flʊəri:n] n Fluor nt.

flurried ['flʌrɪd] adj to get ~ sich aufregen, nervös werden.

flurry ['flʌrɪ] 1 n (a) (of snow) Gestöber nt; (of rain) Guß m; (of wind) Stoß m. a ~ of blows ein Hagel m von Schlägen.
(b) (fig) Aufregung, Nervosität f. all in a ~ ganz aufgescheucht, in großer Aufregung; a ~ of activity eine Hektik; in a ~ of excitement in hektischer Aufregung.
2 vt nervös machen, aufregen; see flurried.

flush¹ [flʌʃ] 1 n (a) (lavatory ~) (Wasser)spülung f; (water) Schwall m.
(b) (blush) Röte f. hot ~es (Med) fliegende Hitze; the ~ of blood to her cheeks wie ihr das Blut in die Wangen schießt/schoß.
(c) (of beauty, youth) Blüte f; (of joy) Anfall m; (of excitement) Welle f. in the (first) ~ of victory im (ersten) Siegestaumel; in the first ~ of youth in der ersten Jugendblüte; she was in the full ~ of health sie sah blühend aus.
2 vi (person, face) rot werden, rot anlaufen (with vor + dat). to ~ crimson dunkelrot anlaufen or werden.

3 vt (a) spülen; (also ~ out) drain durch- or ausspülen. to ~ the lavatory spülen, die Wasserspülung betätigen; to ~ a wall down eine Wand abspritzen; to ~ sth down the lavatory etw die Toilette hinunterspülen.
(b) face röten.

♦**flush away** vt sep waste matter etc wegspülen.

♦**flush out** vt sep (a) (with water) sink, bottle ausspülen, auswaschen; dirt wegspülen, wegschwemmen. (b) thieves, spies aufstöbern, aufspüren.

flush² adj pred (a) bündig; (horizontally also) in gleicher Ebene. cupboards ~ with the wall Schränke, die mit der Wand abschließen; ~ against the wall direkt an die/der Wand.
(b) (inf) to be ~ gut bei Kasse sein (inf).

flush³ vt game, birds aufstöbern, aufscheuchen.

flush⁴ n (Cards) Flöte, Sequenz f; (Poker) Flush m.

flushed ['flʌʃt] adj person rot (with vor); face rosa, (with fever) gerötet. he came out of the meeting rather ~ er kam mit rotem Kopf aus der Besprechung; they were ~ with happiness/success sie strahlten förmlich vor Glück/über ihren Erfolg.

fluster ['flʌstəʳ] **1** vt nervös machen; (confuse) durcheinanderbringen. don't ~ me! machen Sie mich nicht nervös!; she got ~ed sie wurde nervös; das brachte sie durcheinander; to be ~ed nervös or aufgeregt sein; durcheinander sein.
2 n in a (real) ~ (ganz) nervös or aufgeregt; (confused) (völlig) durcheinander.

flute [fluːt] **1** n (Mus) Querflöte f; (organ stop) Flötenregister nt.
2 vt column, pillar kannelieren.

fluted ['fluːtɪd] adj column, pillar kanneliert; border, edge Bogen-, bogenförmig.

fluting ['fluːtɪŋ] n (Archit) Kannelierung f, Kanneluren pl; (of border, edge) Bogenform f.

flutist ['fluːtɪst] n (US) see flautist.

flutter ['flʌtəʳ] **1** vi (a) flattern (also Med). her heart ~ed as he entered the room sie bekam Herzklopfen, als er das Zimmer betrat; to ~ away or off davonflattern.
(b) (person) tänzeln; (nervously) flatterig sein. to ~ around herumtänzeln; nervös herumfuhrwerken (inf); she ~ed into/out of the room sie tänzelte ins Zimmer/aus dem Zimmer.
2 vt fan, piece of paper wedeln mit; (birds) wings flattern mit; one's eyelashes klimpern mit (hum inf). to ~ one's eyelashes at sb mit den Wimpern klimpern, jdn mit einem tollen Augenaufschlag bezirzen.
3 n (a) Flattern nt (also Med). this caused a ~ among the audience dies verursachte leichte Unruhe im Publikum.
(b) (nervousness) (all) in or of a ~ in heller Aufregung.
(c) (Brit inf: gamble) to have a ~ sein Glück (beim Wetten) versuchen; he likes his little ~ on a Friday night er versucht Freitag abends gern sein Glück beim Wetten.
(d) (Aviat) Flattern nt.

flutter kick n Wechselschlag m (beim Kraulen).

fluty ['fluːtɪ] adj (+er) voice flötend.

fluvial ['fluːvɪəl] adj in Flüssen, fluvial (spec). ~ water Flußwasser nt.

flux [flʌks] n (a) (state of change) Fluß m. things are in a state of ~ die Dinge sind im Fluß. (b) (Med: no pl) Ausfluß m; (Phys) Fluß m. (c) (Metal) Flußmittel nt.

fly¹ [flaɪ] n Fliege f. the epidemic killed them off like flies sie starben während der Epidemie wie die Fliegen; he wouldn't hurt a ~ er könnte keiner Fliege etwas zuleide tun; there's a ~ in the ointment (inf) da ist ein Haar in der Suppe; he's the ~ in the ointment er ist Sand im Getriebe; there are no flies on him (inf) ihn legt man nicht so leicht rein (inf).

fly² (vb: pret flew, ptp flown) **1** vi (a) fliegen.
(b) (move quickly) (time) (ver)fliegen; (people) sausen (inf), fliegen; (sparks) stieben, fliegen. time flies! wie die Zeit vergeht!; to ~ past (car, person) vorbeisausen (inf) or -flitzen; I am already late, I must ~ ich bin schon spät dran, ich muß jetzt wirklich sausen (inf); the door flew open die Tür flog auf; to ~ to sb's assistance jdm zu Hilfe eilen; to ~ into a rage einen Wutanfall bekommen; to ~ at sb (inf) auf jdn losgehen; to ~ at sb's throat jdm an die Kehle fahren; to let ~ at sb auf jdn losgehen; he really let ~ er legte kräftig los; (verbally also) er zog kräftig vom Leder; to let ~ a stone einen Stein schleudern; I sent him ~ing ich habe ihn umgeschmissen (inf) or umgeworfen; to knock or send sth ~ing etw umschmeißen (inf) or umwerfen; he sent the ball ~ing over the wall er schleuderte or schmiß (inf) den Ball über die Mauer; to send a plate ~ing einen Teller herunterschmeißen (inf).
(c) to ~ in the face of authority sich über jede Autorität hinwegsetzen; to ~ in the face of reason (person, organization) sich über jede Vernunft hinwegsetzen; (idea, theory etc) jeder Vernunft entbehren; to ~ in the face of the evidence in krassem Widerspruch zu den Tatsachen stehen.
(d) (flag) wehen.
2 vt (a) aircraft fliegen; kite steigen lassen.
(b) passengers, route, plane fliegen; Atlantic überfliegen.
(c) flag führen, wehen lassen; see flag¹.
3 n to go for a ~ fliegen.

♦**fly away** vi (person, plane, bird) weg- or fortfliegen; (plane, person also) abfliegen; (fig: hopes, cares) schwinden.

♦**fly in 1** vi (troops, president, rescue plane etc) einfliegen. we flew ~to Heathrow at night wir sind abends in Heathrow angekommen; she flew ~ from New York this morning sie ist heute morgen mit dem Flugzeug aus New York angekommen. **2** vt sep supplies, troops einfliegen.

♦**fly off** vi (a) (plane, person) abfliegen, wegfliegen; (bird) wegfliegen, fortfliegen. to ~ ~ to the south nach Süden fliegen; a search plane flew ~ to look for them ein Suchflugzeug flog los, um nach ihnen Ausschau zu halten; as the plane flew ~ into the sunset während das Flugzeug der untergehenden Sonne entgegenflog.

(b) (come off: hat, lid etc) wegfliegen; (button) abspringen.

♦**fly out 1** vi (troops, president, troop-plane) ausfliegen. as we flew ~ of Heathrow als wir von Heathrow abflogen; I'll ~ ~ and come back by ship ich werde hin fliegen und mit dem Schiff zurückkommen.
2 vt sep troops (to an area) hinfliegen; (out of an area) ausfliegen. troops were flown ~ to the trouble area Truppen wurden in das Krisengebiet geflogen; the company will ~ you ~ die Firma wird Sie hinfliegen.

♦**fly past** vi (a) + prep obj to ~ sb an etw (dat) vorbeifliegen. (b) (ceremonially) vorbeifliegen. (c) (time) verfliegen.

fly³ pret flew, ptp flown **1** vi (flee) fliehen, flüchten. to ~ for one's life um sein Leben laufen/fahren etc. **2** vt to ~ the country aus dem Land niehen.

fly⁴ n (a) (on trousers: also flies) (Hosen)schlitz m. (b) see flysheet. (c) (Theat) flies pl Obermaschinerie f. (d) see flywheel.

fly⁵ adj (inf) clever, gerissen.

fly-away ['flaɪəweɪ] adj hair fliegend, schwer zu bändigen.

fly-by-night ['flaɪbaɪnaɪt] **1** n (a) (irresponsible man) Windhund m (inf); (woman) leichtsinniges Ding (inf). (b) (decamping debtor) flüchtiger Schuldner. **2** adj (a) person unzuverlässig, unbeständig. (b) (Fin, Comm) firm, operation zweifelhaft, windig (inf).

fly: ~catcher n (a) Fliegenschnäpper m; (b) (trap for flies) Fliegenfänger m; ~fishing n Fliegenfischen nt; ~-half n (Rugby) Halbspieler m.

flying ['flaɪɪŋ] n Fliegen nt. he likes ~ er fliegt gerne.

flying: ~ ambulance n (helicopter) Rettungshubschrauber m; (plane) Rettungsflugzeug n; ~ boat n Flugboot nt; ~-bomb n V-Rakete f; ~ buttress n (Archit) Strebebogen m; ~ colours npl to come through/pass etc with ~ colours glänzend abschneiden; ~ doctor n fliegender Arzt (esp in Australien); the F~ Dutchman n der Fliegende Holländer; ~ fish n fliegender Fisch; ~ insect n Fluginsekt nt; ~ jump n (großer) Satz; to take a ~ jump einen großen Satz machen; ~ machine n (old, hum) Flugmaschine f; ~ officer n (Brit) Oberleutnant m; ~ saucer n fliegende Untertasse; ~ squad n Bereitschaftsdienst m; ~ start n (Sport) fliegender Start; to get off to a ~ start (Sport) hervorragend wegkommen (inf); (fig) einen glänzenden Start haben; ~-time n Flugzeit f; ~ trapeze n Trapez, Schwebereck nt; ~ visit n Blitzbesuch m, Stippvisite f.

fly: ~leaf n Vorsatzblatt nt; ~over n Überführung f; ~paper n Fliegenfänger m; ~-past n Luftparade f; ~sheet n (entrance) Überdach nt; (outer tent) Überzelt nt; ~-spray n Fliegenspray m; ~-swat(ter) n Fliegenklatsche f; ~weight n (Boxing) Fliegengewicht nt; ~wheel n Schwungrad nt.

FM abbr of (a) frequency modulation. (b) field marshal.

foal [fəʊl] **1** n Fohlen, Füllen nt. in ~ trächtig. **2** vi fohlen.

foam [fəʊm] **1** n Schaum m; (of sea also) Gischt f. **2** vi schäumen. to ~ at the mouth (lit) Schaum vorm Mund/Maul haben; (fig: person) schäumen.

♦**foam up** vi (liquid in container) schäumen.

foam: ~ rubber n Schaumgummi m; ~ sprayer n Schaumlöscher m.

foamy ['fəʊmɪ] adj (+er) schäumend.

fob¹ ['efəʊbiː] abbr of free on board.

fob² [fɒb] **1** vt to ~ sb off (with promises) jdn (mit leeren Versprechungen) abspeisen; to ~ sth off on sb, to ~ sb off with sth jdm etw andrehen. **2** n (old: also ~ pocket) Uhrtasche f. ~ watch Taschenuhr f.

focal ['fəʊkəl] adj (fig) im Brennpunkt (stehend), fokal (geh).

focal: ~ length n Brennweite f; ~ plane n Brennebene f; ~ point n (lit, fig) Brennpunkt m.

fo'c'sle ['fəʊksl] n see forecastle.

focus ['fəʊkəs] **1** n, pl foci ['fəʊkaɪ] (Phys, Math, fig) Brennpunkt m; (of storm) Zentrum nt; (of earthquake, Med) Herd m. in ~ camera (scharf) eingestellt; photo scharf; to bring into ~ (lit) klar or scharf einstellen; (fig) topic in den Brennpunkt rücken; out of ~ (lit) camera unscharf eingestellt; photo unscharf; (fig) ideas vage; to come into ~ ins Blickfeld rücken; he was the ~ of attention er stand im Mittelpunkt.
2 vt instrument einstellen (on auf + acc); light, heat rays bündeln; (fig) one's efforts konzentrieren (on auf + acc). to ~ one's eyes on sth den Blick auf etw (acc) richten; all eyes were ~ed on him alle Blicke waren auf ihn gerichtet; to ~ one's attention sich konzentrieren; I should like to ~ your attention (up)on a new problem ich möchte Ihre Aufmerksamkeit auf ein neues Problem lenken.
3 vi (light, heat rays) sich bündeln. to ~ on sth sich auf etw (acc) konzentrieren; his eyes ~ed on the book sein Blick richtete sich auf das Buch; I can't ~ properly ich kann nicht mehr klar sehen.

fodder ['fɒdəʳ] n (lit, fig) Futter nt.

foe [fəʊ] n (liter) Feind, Widersacher (geh) m.

foetal ['fiːtl] adj see fetal.

foetid ['fiːtɪd] adj see fetid.

foetus, (esp US) **fetus** ['fiːtəs] n Fötus, Fetus m.

fog [fɒg] **1** n (a) Nebel m. I am still in a ~ about it (dated inf) das ist mir immer noch nicht klar.
(b) (Phot) (Grau)schleier m.
2 vt (a) (also ~ up or over) mirror, glasses beschlagen.
(b) (Phot) verschleiern.
(c) (fig) to ~ the issue die Sache vernebeln; I was really ~ged ich war wirklich ratlos.
3 vi (a) (also ~ up or over) (mirror, glasses) beschlagen.
(b) (Phot: negative) einen Grauschleier bekommen.

fog: ~ bank n Nebelbank f; ~bound adj ship, plane durch Nebel festgehalten; airport wegen Nebel(s) geschlossen; the motorway is ~bound auf der Autobahn herrscht dichter Nebel.

fogey ['fəʊgɪ] n (inf) old ~ alter Kauz (inf); (woman) Schrulle f (inf).

foggy ['fɒgɪ] adj (+er) **(a)** landscape, weather neb(e)lig. **(b)** (fig) ideas, reasoning unklar, vage. **I haven't the foggiest (idea)** (inf) ich habe keinen blassen Schimmer (inf).

fog: ~horn n (Naut) Nebelhorn nt; **a voice like a ~horn** (inf) eine dröhnende Stimme; ~ **lamp,** ~ **light** n Nebellampe f; ~ **signal** n (Naut, Rail) Nebelsignal nt.

foible ['fɔɪbl] n Eigenheit f.

foil¹ [fɔɪl] n **(a)** (metal sheet) Folie f; (of a mirror) Spiegelfolie f; **see cooking ~, kitchen ~. (b)** (fig) Hintergrund m, Folie f. **to act as a ~ to sb** jdm als Hintergrund or Folie dienen.

foil² n (Fencing) Florett nt.

foil³ vt plans durchkreuzen; attempts vereiteln; person einen Strich durch die Rechnung machen (+dat); **~ed again!** (hum) wieder nichts!; **he was ~ed in his plans/attempts** ihm wurde ein Strich durch die Rechnung gemacht.

foist [fɔɪst] vt **(a) to ~ sth (off) on sb** goods jdm etw andrehen; task etw an jdn abschieben. **(b) to ~ oneself on(to) sb** sich jdm aufdrängen.

fold¹ [fəʊld] **1** n Falte f; (Geol: of the earth) (Boden)falte f.
  2 vt **(a)** (bend into ~s) paper (zusammen)falten; blanket also zusammenlegen. **to ~ a newspaper in two/four** eine Zeitung falten/zweimal falten.
  (b) to ~ one's arms die Arme verschränken.
  (c) (wrap up) einwickeln, einschlagen (in in +acc). **he ~ed the book in some paper** er schlug das Buch in Papier ein.
  (d) to ~ sb in one's arms jdn in die Arme schließen; **to ~ sb to one's heart** (liter) jdn ans Herz drücken.
  3 vi **(a)** (chair, table) sich zusammenklappen lassen; (accidentally) zusammenklappen. **how does this map ~?** wie wird die Karte gefaltet?
  (b) (close down: business) see **fold up.**

◆**fold away 1** vi (table, bed) zusammenklappbar sein, sich zusammenlegen lassen. **2** vt sep table, bed zusammenklappen; clothes zusammenlegen; newspaper zusammenfalten.

◆**fold back 1** vt sep shutters, door zurückfalten; sheet, bedclothes auf- or zurückschlagen. **2** vi (door, shutters) zurückfalten, sich zurückfalten lassen.

◆**fold down** vt sep chair zusammenklappen; corner kniffen.

◆**fold over** vt sep paper umknicken; blanket umschlagen.

◆**fold up 1** vi **(a)** (newspaper, business venture) eingehen (inf); (Theat: play) abgesetzt werden. **to ~ with laughter** sich vor Lachen biegen. **2** vt sep paper, blanket etc zusammenfalten; blanket also zusammenlegen.

fold² n (pen) Pferch m; (Eccl) Herde, Gemeinde f. **to return to the ~** (fig) in den Schoß der Gemeinde zurückkehren.

foldaway ['fəʊldəweɪ] adj attr zusammenklappbar.

folder ['fəʊldə'] n **(a)** (for papers) Aktendeckel m, Aktenmappe f. **(b)** (brochure) Informationsblatt nt.

folding ['fəʊldɪŋ] adj attr ~ boat Faltboot nt; ~ bed Klappbett nt; ~ chair Klappstuhl m; ~ doors Falttür f; (concertina doors also) Harmonikatür f; (grille on lift) Scherengittertür f; ~ table Klapptisch m.

foliage ['fəʊlɪɪdʒ] n Blätter pl; (of tree also) Laub(werk) nt.

foliation [ˌfəʊlɪ'eɪʃən] n **(a)** (Bot) Blattanordnung f; (development) Blattbildung f. **(b)** (of book) Foliierung, Blattzählung f. **(c)** (Geol) Schichtung f. **(d)** (Archit) Laubwerk nt.

folio ['fəʊlɪəʊ] n **(a)** (sheet) Folio nt. **(b)** (volume) Foliant m.

folk [fəʊk] npl **(a)** (also ~s nt) (people) Leute pl; (people in general) die Leute, man. **a lot of ~(s) believe ...** viele (Leute) glauben ...; **there were a lot of ~ at the concert** es waren eine Menge Leute bei dem Konzert; **come on ~(s)** (inf) na los, Leute!; **the young/old ~** die Jungen/Alten; **old ~ can't ...** alte Menschen können nicht ...
  (b) (inf: relatives: also ~s) **my ~s** meine Leute (inf); **the old ~(s) stayed at home** die alten Herrschaften blieben zu Haus.

folk: ~-dance n Volkstanz m; ~lore n Folklore, Volkskunde f; ~music n Volksmusik f; ~-singer n Sänger(in f) m von Volksliedern/Folksongs; ~-song n Volkslied nt; (modern) Folksong m.

folksy ['fəʊksɪ] adj volkstümlich.

folk-tale ['fəʊkteɪl] n Volksmärchen nt.

follow ['fɒləʊ] **1** vt **(a)** folgen (+dat), nachgehen/-fahren etc (+dat); (pursue also) verfolgen; (succeed) folgen (+dat), kommen nach. **he ~ed me about** er folgte mir überall hin; er ging mir überall(hin) nach; **he ~ed me out** er folgte mir nach draußen, er ging mir nach draußen nach; ~ **me** folgen Sie mir; (by car also) fahren Sie mir nach; **we're being ~ed** wir werden verfolgt; **to have sb ~ed** jdn verfolgen lassen; **he arrived first, ~ed by the ambassador** er kam als erster, gefolgt vom Botschafter; **he ~ed his father into the business** er folgte seinem Vater im Geschäft; **the earthquake was ~ed by an epidemic** auf das Erdbeben folgte eine Epidemie; **the dinner will be ~ed by a concert** im Anschluß an das Essen findet ein Konzert statt; **the toast was ~ed by a vote of thanks** auf den Trinkspruch folgten Worte des Dankes; **the years ~ one another** ein Jahr folgt auf das andere; **the years ~ one another in rapid succession** die Jahre vergehen in rascher Folge; **to ~ the hounds** (mit den Hunden) auf die Jagd gehen.
  (b) (keep to) road, path folgen (+dat), entlanggehen/-fahren etc. **to ~ one's nose** der Nase nach gehen (inf); **the boat ~ed the coast** das Boot fuhr die Küste entlang; **the road ~s the valley** die Straße folgt dem Tal.
  (c) (understand) folgen (+dat). **do you ~ me?** können Sie mir folgen?
  (d) profession ausüben, nachgehen (+dat); course of study, career verfolgen. **to ~ the sea/plough** (liter) zur See fahren/Bauersmann sein.
  (e) (conform to) fashion mitmachen; advice, instructions befolgen, folgen (+dat); party line folgen (+dat). **to ~ (the dic-**

tates of) **one's heart/conscience** auf die Stimme seines Herzens/Gewissens hören.
  (f) (read, watch regularly) serial verfolgen; strip cartoon regelmäßig lesen; (take an interest in) progress, development, news verfolgen; athletics, swimming etc sich interessieren für; (listen to attentively) speech (genau) verfolgen. **to ~ the horses** sich für Pferderennen interessieren; **which team do you ~?** für welchen Verein sind Sie?
  2 vi **(a)** (come after) folgen (on sth auf etw acc). **as ~s** wie folgt; **his argument was as ~s** er argumentierte folgendermaßen; **to ~ in sb's footsteps** (fig) in jds Fußstapfen (acc) treten; **what is there to ~?** (at meals) was gibt es noch or (planning the meal) hinterher or anschließend?; **what ~s das Folgende.**
  (b) (results, deduction) folgen (from aus). **it ~s from this that ...** hieraus folgt, daß ...; **it doesn't ~ that ...** daraus folgt nicht, daß ...; **that doesn't ~** nicht unbedingt!; **your conclusion doesn't ~** Ihr Schluß ist nicht folgerichtig.
  (c) (understand) folgen. **I don't ~** das verstehe ich nicht, da komme ich nicht mit.

◆**follow on** vi **(a)** (come after) später folgen or kommen; (person also) nachkommen.
  (b) (results) folgen, sich ergeben (from aus).
  (c) (continue) **the story ~s** from his death die Geschichte geht nach seinem Tod weiter; **she will ~ ~ from where he left off** sie wird da weitermachen, wo er aufgehört hat.
  (d) (Cricket) zwei Innenrunden hintereinander spielen.

◆**follow out** vt sep idea, plan zu Ende verfolgen, durchziehen.

◆**follow through 1** vt sep argument durchdenken, (zu Ende) verfolgen; idea, plan, undertaking (zu Ende) verfolgen, durchziehen. **2** vi (Sport) durchschwingen.

◆**follow up 1** vt sep **(a)** (pursue, take further action on) request nachgehen (+dat); offer, suggestion also aufgreifen.
  (b) (investigate further) sich näher beschäftigen or befassen mit; suspect also Erkundigungen einziehen über (+acc); candidate also in die engere Wahl nehmen; matter also weiterverfolgen; rumour nachgehen (+dat); patient nachuntersuchen; (not lose track of) matter im Auge behalten.
  (c) (reinforce) success, victory fortsetzen, ausbauen. **to ~ ~ insults with threats** auf Beleidigungen Drohungen folgen lassen; **he ~ed ~ his remark by punching him/by handing her a bouquet** er versetzte ihm zur Bekräftigung einen Schlag/er überreichte ihr zur Bekräftigung einen Blumenstrauß.
  (d) (get further benefit from) advantage ausnutzen.
  2 vi **(a) to ~ ~ with sth** etw folgen lassen.
  (b) (Sport) nachziehen.

follower ['fɒləʊə'] n (disciple) Anhänger(in f) m, Schüler(in f) m; (old: servant) Gefolgsmann m. **to be a ~ of fashion** sehr modebewußt sein; **a ~ of Rangers** ein Rangers-Anhänger m.

following ['fɒləʊɪŋ] **1** adj **(a)** folgend. **the ~ day** der nächste or (darauf)folgende Tag; **he made the ~ remarks** er bemerkte folgendes.
  (b) a ~ wind Rückenwind m.
  2 n **(a)** (followers) Anhängerschaft, Gefolgschaft f.
  (b) he said the ~ er sagte folgendes; **see the ~ for an explanation** (in documents etc) Erläuterungen hierzu finden Sie im folgenden, Erklärungen im folgenden; **the ~ is/are of note** folgendes ist/folgende (Tatsachen etc) sind wichtig.

follow-through [ˌfɒləʊ'θruː] n (Sport) Durchziehen nt.

follow-up ['fɒləʊˌʌp] n **(a)** (Med) Weiterverfolgen, Weiterführen nt; (event, programme etc coming after) Fortsetzung f (to gen).
  (b) (letter) Nachfaßschreiben nt; (Press) Fortsetzung f.
  (c) (Med) Nachuntersuchung f.

follow-up: ~ advertizing n Nachfaßwerbung f; ~ care n (Med) Nachbehandlung f.

folly ['fɒlɪ] n (foolishness, foolish thing) Torheit, Verrücktheit f; (building) exzentrischer, meist völlig nutzloser Prachtbau. **it is sheer ~ (to do that)** es ist der reinste Wahnsinn(, das zu tun).

foment [fəʊ'ment] vt trouble, discord schüren; (Med) mit feuchten Umschlägen behandeln.

fomentation [ˌfəʊmen'teɪʃən] n see vt Schüren nt; feuchte Umschläge pl.

fond [fɒnd] adj (+er) **(a) to be ~ of sb** jdn gern haben or mögen; **to be ~ of sth** etw mögen; **to be ~ of doing sth** etw gern tun.
  (b) (loving) husband, friend, parent, look liebevoll, zärtlich; hope sehnsüchtig, leise; ambition leise. **his ~est wish** sein Herzenswunsch m; ~**est regards** mit lieben Grüßen, liebe Grüße.
  (c) (indulgent) parent, husband allzu nachsichtig.
  (d) (unlikely to be realized) hope, ambition (allzu) kühn.

fondant ['fɒndənt] n Fondant m.

fondle ['fɒndl] vt (zärtlich) spielen mit; (stroke) streicheln; person schmusen mit.

fondly ['fɒndlɪ] adv see adj (b-d).

fondness ['fɒndnɪs] n **(a)** Begeisterung f; (for people) Zuneigung, Liebe f (for zu); (for food, place, writer etc) Vorliebe f (for für). **his ~ for or of swimming** daß er gern schwimmen ging/geht.

fondue ['fɒnduː] n Fondue nt. ~ **set** Fondueset nt.

font [fɒnt] n **(a)** (Eccl) Taufstein m. **(b)** (US Typ) Schrift f.

food [fuːd] n **(a)** (Eccl) Essen nt; (for animals) Futter nt; (nourishment) Nahrung f; (~stuff) Nahrungsmittel nt; (groceries) Lebensmittel pl. **the ~** is awful here das Essen hier ist schrecklich; **dog and cat ~** Hunde- und Katzenfutter; ~ **and drink** Essen und Trinken; **milk is a ~ rather than a drink** Milch ist eher ein Nahrungsmittel als ein Getränk; **canned ~** Konserven pl; **I haven't any ~ in the house** ich habe nichts zu essen im Haus; **to be off one's ~** keinen Appetit haben; **at last, ~!** endlich etwas zu essen; **the very thought of ~ made her ill** wenn sie nur ans Essen dachte, wurde ihr schon schlecht.
  (b) (fig) Nahrung f. ~ **for thought** Stoff m zum Nachdenken.

food: ~-chain n (Biol) Ernährungskette f; ~ **parcel** n

Lebensmittelpaket *nt*; ~ **poisoning** *n* Lebensmittelvergiftung *f*; ~ **rationing** *n* Lebensmittelrationierung *f*; ~**stuff** *n* Nahrungsmittel *nt*; ~ **value** *n* Nährwert *m*.

fool¹ [fuːl] **1** *n* **(a)** Dummkopf, Narr *m*. **don't be a ~!** sei nicht (so) dumm!; **some ~ of a** civil servant irgend so ein blöder *or* doofer (*inf*) Beamter; **I was a ~ not to realize** wie konnte ich nur so dumm sein und das nicht merken; **have I been a ~!** war ich vielleicht dumm *or* blöd!, ich Idiot!; **he was a ~ not to accept** es war dumm von ihm, nicht anzunehmen; **to be ~ enough to ...** so dumm *or* blöd sein, zu ...; **to play** *or* **act the ~** Unsinn machen, herumalbern; **he made himself look a ~ in front of everyone** er machte sich vor allen lächerlich; **to make a ~ of sb** (*with ridicule*) jdn lächerlich machen; (*with a trick*) jdn zum besten *or* zum Narren haben; **he made a ~ of himself in the discussion** er hat sich in der Diskussion blamiert; **to go on a ~'s errand** einen nutzlosen Gang tun; **to live in a ~'s paradise** in einem Traumland leben; **there's no ~ like an old ~** (*prov*) Alter schützt vor Torheit nicht (*Prov*); **~'s gold** Katzengold *nt*; **~s rush in (where angels fear to tread)** (*prov*) blinder Eifer schadet nur (*prov*); *see* **more**, **nobody**.
(b) (*jester*) Narr *m*.

2 *adj* (*esp US*) *inf* doof (*inf*), schwachsinnig (*inf*).

3 *vi* herumalbern, Blödsinn machen. **stop ~ing (about)!** laß den Blödsinn!; **I was only ~ing** das war doch nur Spaß.

4 *vt* zum Narren haben *or* halten; (*trick*) hereinlegen (*inf*); (*disguise, phoney accent etc*) täuschen. **you won't ~ me so easily** so leicht können Sie mich nicht hereinlegen (*inf*); **I admit I was completely ~ed** ich gebe zu, ich bin darauf hereingefallen; **you had me ~ed** ich habe das tatsächlich geglaubt; **who are you trying to ~?** wem willst du das weismachen?; **they ~ed him into believing that ...** sie haben ihm weisgemacht, daß ...; **they ~ed him into believing it** er hat es ihnen tatsächlich abgenommen.

♦**fool about** *or* **around** *vi* **a** (*waste time*) herumtrödeln. **he spends his time ~ing ~ with the boys** er verschwendet seine ganze Zeit mit den Jungs. **(b)** (*play the fool*) herumalbern. **(c)** **to ~ ~ with sb** mit etw Blödsinn machen. **(d)** **he's just ~ing ~ with her** er treibt nur seine Spielchen mit ihr.

fool² *n* (*Brit Cook*) Sahnespeise *f* aus Obstpüree.
foolery [ˈfuːlərɪ] *n* Albernheit *f*.
foolhardiness [ˈfuːlˌhɑːdɪnɪs] *n* Tollkühnheit *f*.
foolhardy [ˈfuːlˌhɑːdɪ] *adj* tollkühn.
foolish [ˈfuːlɪʃ] *adj* dumm, töricht. **it is ~ to believe him** es ist dumm, ihm zu glauben; **to look ~** dumm aussehen *or* dreinsehen; **he's afraid of looking ~** er will sich nicht blamieren; **it made him look ~** dann stand er dumm da; **I felt very ~** ich kam mir sehr dumm vor.
foolishly [ˈfuːlɪʃlɪ] *adv* dumm, töricht. **~, I assumed ...** törichterweise habe ich angenommen ...
foolishness [ˈfuːlɪʃnɪs] *n* Dummheit, Torheit *f*. **enough of this ~** lassen wir diese Dummheiten *pl*.
foolproof [ˈfuːlpruːf] *adj* narrensicher, idiotensicher (*inf*).
foolscap [ˈfuːlskæp] *n* (*also* ~ **paper**) ≃ Kanzleipapier *nt*, britisches Papierformat 13¼ × 16¼ *Inches*. **a ~ sheet** ein Blatt *nt* Kanzleipapier.

foot [fʊt] **1** *n*, *pl* **feet** *m*. **to be on one's feet** (*lit*, *fig*) auf den Beinen sein; **to put sb (back) on his feet (again)** jdm (wieder) auf die Beine helfen; **on ~** zu Fuß; **to set ~ on dry land** den Fuß auf festen Boden setzen, an Land gehen; **I'll never set ~ here again!** hier kriegen mich keine zehn Pferde mehr her! (*inf*); **the first time he set ~ in the office** als er das erste Mal das Büro betrat; **to rise/jump to one's feet** aufstehen/aufspringen; **to put one's feet up** (*lit*) die Füße hochlegen; (*fig*) es sich (*dat*) bequem machen; **he never puts a ~ wrong** (*gymnast, dancer*) bei ihm stimmt jeder Schritt; (*fig*) er macht nie einen Fehler; **to catch sb on the wrong ~** (*Sport*) jdn auf dem falschen Fuß erwischen; (*fig*) jdn überrumpeln.
(b) (*fig uses*) **to put one's ~ down** (*act with decision or authority*) ein Machtwort sprechen; (*forbid, refuse*) es strikt verbieten; (*Aut*) Gas geben, voll aufs Gas steigen (*inf*); **to put one's ~ in it** ins Fettnäpfchen treten; **to put one's best ~ forward** (*hurry*) die Beine unter den Arm nehmen; (*do one's best*) sich anstrengen; **to find one's feet** sich eingewöhnen, sich zurechtfinden; **to fall on one's feet** auf die Beine fallen; **to have one's** *or* **both feet (firmly) on the ground** mit beiden Beinen (fest) auf der Erde stehen; **to have one ~ in the grave** mit einem Bein im Grabe stehen; **to get/be under sb's feet** jdm im Wege stehen *or* sein; (*children also*) jdm vor den Füßen herumlaufen; **to get off on the right/wrong ~** einen guten/schlechten Start haben; **to have a/get one's** *or* **a ~ in the door** mit einem Fuß *or* Bein drin sein/mit einem Fuß *or* Bein hineinkommen; **to stand on one's own feet** auf eigenen Füßen *or* Beinen stehen; **to sit at sb's feet** jds Jünger sein.
(c) (*of stocking, list, page, stairs, hill etc*) Fuß *m*; (*of bed also*) Fußende *nt*; (*of sewing machine also*) Füßchen *nt*.
(d) (*measure*) Fuß *m*. **3 ~** *or* **feet wide/long** 3 Fuß breit/lang.
(e) (*Poet*) (Vers)fuß *m*.
(f) *no pl* (*Mil*) Infanterie *f*. **the 15th ~** das 15. Infanterieregiment; **ten thousand ~** zehntausend Fußsoldaten *pl*.

2 *vt* **(a)** **to ~ it** (*inf*) marschieren (*inf*); (*dance*) tanzen.
(b) **bill** bezahlen, begleichen.

foot-and-mouth (disease) [ˌfʊtənˈmaʊθ(dɪˌziːz)] *n* Maul- und Klauenseuche *f*.
football [ˈfʊtbɔːl] *n* **(a)** Fußball(spiel *nt*) *m*; (*American* ~) Football *m*, amerikanischer Fußball. ~ **boot** Fußballschuh, Fußballstiefel *m*; ~ **pools** Fußballtoto *m*; *see* **pool¹** (**c**). **(b)** (*ball*) Fußball *m*, Leder (*inf*) *nt*.
footballer [ˈfʊtbɔːlə] *n* Fußball(spiel)er *m*; (*in American football*) Football-Spieler *m*.
foot: ~**bath** *n* Fußbad *nt*; ~**board** *n* (*Rail, on coach*) Trittbrett *nt*; ~ **brake** *n* Fußbremse *f*; ~**bridge** *n* Fußgängerbrücke *f*.

-footed [-fʊtɪd] *adj suf* -füßig. **four-~** vierfüßig.
foot: ~**fall** *n* Schritt *m*; ~**hills** *npl* (Gebirgs)ausläufer *pl*; ~**hold** *n* Stand, Halt *m*; (*fig*) sichere (Ausgangs)position; **he got a ~hold on the rock** er fand mit den Füßen Halt am Felsen; **to lose one's ~hold** (*lit*, *fig*) den Halt verlieren.
footing [ˈfʊtɪŋ] *n* **(a)** (*lit*) Stand, Halt *m*. **to lose one's ~** den Halt verlieren; **to miss one's ~** danebentreten.
(b) (*fig: foundation, basis*) Basis *f*; (*relationship*) Beziehung *f*, Verhältnis *nt*. **the business was on a secure ~** das Geschäft stand auf einer sicheren Basis; **to be on a friendly ~ with sb** mit jdm auf freundschaftlichem Fuße stehen; **on an equal ~ (with each other)** auf gleicher Basis; **to be on a war ~** sich im Kriegszustand befinden; **to get a ~ in society** von der Gesellschaft akzeptiert werden.
(c) (*Archit*) Sockel *m*.
footle [ˈfuːtl] *vi* **to ~ about** (*inf*) herumpusseln.
footlights [ˈfʊtlaɪts] *npl* (*Theat*) Rampenlicht *nt*. **the lure of the ~** (*fig*) die Anziehungskraft der Bühne *or* der Bretter.
footling [ˈfuːtlɪŋ] *adj* albern, dumm, läppisch.
foot: ~**loose** *adj* ungebunden, unbeschwert; ~**loose and fancy-free** frei und ungebunden; ~**man** *n* Lakai *m*; ~**mark** *n* Fußabdruck *m*; ~**note** *n* Fußnote *f*; (*fig*) Anmerkung *f*; ~**path** *n* (**a**) (*path*) Fußweg *m*; **(b)** (*Brit: pavement*) Bürgersteig *m*; ~**plate** *n* Führerstand *m*; ~**platemen**, ~**plate workers** *npl* Lokomotivführer *pl*; ~**pound** *n* britische Maßeinheit für Drehmoment und Energie; ~**print** *n* Fußabdruck *m*; ~**prints** *npl* Fußspuren *pl*; ~ **pump** *n* Fußpumpe *f*, Blasebalg *m*; ~**rest** *n* Fußstütze *f*.
footsie [ˈfʊtsɪ] *n* (*inf*) **to play ~ with sb** mit jdm füßeln.
foot: ~**slog** *vi* (*inf*) latschen (*inf*), marschieren; ~**slogger** *n* (*Mil sl*) Fußsoldat, Infanterist *m*; ~**sloggers** (*Mil sl*) Fußvolk *nt*; (*inf: walkers*) Spaziergänger, Tippler (*inf*) *pl*; ~ **soldier** *n* Fußsoldat, Infanterist *m*; ~**sore** *adj* **to be ~sore** wunde Füße haben; **the ~sore soldier staggered into camp** mit wunden Füßen wankte der Soldat ins Lager; ~**step** *n* Schritt *m*; *see* **follow**; ~**stool** *n* Schemel *m*, Fußbank *f*; ~**wear** *n* Schuhe *pl*, Schuhwerk *nt*; ~**work** *n*, *no pl* (*Boxing*) Beinarbeit *f*.
fop [fɒp] *n* (*dated*) Geck, Stutzer (*dated*) *m*.
foppish [ˈfɒpɪʃ] *adj* geckenhaft, stutzerhaft (*dated*).
for [fɔːr] **1** *prep* **a** (*intention*) für; (*purpose also*) zu; (*destination*) nach. **a letter ~ me** ein Brief für mich; **clothes ~ children** Kleidung für Kinder, Kinderkleidung *f*; **destined ~ greatness** zu Höherem bestimmt; **he is eager ~ praise** er ist lobeshungrig; **to go ~ a walk** spazierengehen, einen Spaziergang machen; **to work ~ one's living** seinen Unterhalt verdienen; **what ~?** wofür?, wozu?; **what is this knife ~?** wozu dient dieses Messer?; **he does it ~ pleasure** er macht es zum *or* aus Vergnügen; **what did you do that ~?** warum *or* wozu haben Sie das getan?; **a room ~ working in/sewing ein Zimmer zum Arbeiten/Nähen**; **a bag ~ carrying books (in)** eine Tasche zum Büchertragen, eine Tasche, um Bücher zu tragen; **fit ~ nothing** zu nichts nutze *or* zu gebrauchen; **to work ~ one's exams** für sein Examen arbeiten; **to get ready ~ a journey** sich auf eine Reise fertigmachen, sich auf eine Reise vorbereiten; **ready ~ anything** zu allem bereit; **this will do ~ a hammer** das kann man als Hammer nehmen; **to go to Yugoslavia ~ one's holidays** nach Jugoslawien in Urlaub fahren; **train ~ Stuttgart** Zug nach Stuttgart; **to leave ~ the USA** in die USA *or* nach Amerika abreisen; **he swam ~ the shore** er schwamm auf die Küste zu, er schwamm in Richtung Küste; **to make ~ home** sich auf den Heimweg machen.
(b) (*indicating suitability*) **it's not ~ you to blame him** Sie haben kein Recht, ihm die Schuld zu geben; **it's not ~ me to say** es steht mir nicht zu, mich dazu zu äußern; **she's the woman** *or* **the one ~ me** sie ist die (richtige) Frau für mich.
(c) (*representing, instead of*) **I'll see her ~ you** if you like wenn Sie wollen, gehe ich an Ihrer Stelle *or* für Sie zu ihr; **to act ~ sb** für jdn handeln; **D ~ Daniel** D wie Daniel; **member** *or* **MP ~ Birmingham** Abgeordneter für Birmingham; **agent ~ Renault** Vertreter für Renault.
(d) (*in defence, in favour of*) für. **are you ~ or against it?** sind Sie dafür oder dagegen?; **the committee were/voted ~ the proposed amendment** das Komitee war/stimmte für den Vorschlag; **I'm all ~ it** ich bin ganz *or* sehr dafür; **I'm all ~ helping him** ich bin sehr dafür, ihm zu helfen.
(e) (*with regard to*) **anxious ~ sb** um jdn besorgt; ~ **my part** was mich betrifft; **as ~ him/that** was ihn/das betrifft; **warm/cold ~ the time of year** warm/kalt für die Jahreszeit; **young ~ a president** jung für einen Präsidenten; **it's all right** *or* **all very well ~ you (to talk)** Sie haben gut reden.
(f) (*because of*) aus. ~ **this reason** aus diesem Grund; **he did it ~ fear of being left** er tat es aus Angst, zurückgelassen zu werden; **he is noted ~ his jokes/famous ~ his big nose** er ist für seine Witze bekannt/er ist wegen seiner großen Nase berühmt; **to shout ~ joy** aus *or* vor Freude jauchzen; **to go to prison ~ theft** wegen Diebstahls ins Gefängnis wandern; **to choose sb ~ his ability** jdn wegen seiner Fähigkeiten wählen; **if it were not ~ him** wenn er nicht wäre; **do it ~ me** tu es für mich.
(g) (*in spite of*) trotz (+*gen* *or* (*inf*) +*dat*). ~ **all his wealth** trotz all seines Reichtums; ~ **all that, you should have warned me** Sie hätten mich trotz allem warnen sollen.
(h) (*in exchange*) für. **to pay two marks ~ a ticket** zwei Mark für eine Fahrkarte zahlen; **how much did you pay ~ that?** wieviel haben Sie dafür bezahlt?; **he'll do it ~ five pounds** er macht es für fünf Pfund.
(i) (*in contrast*) ~ **one man who would do it there are ten who wouldn't** auf einen, der es tun würde, kommen zehn, die es nicht tun würden.
(j) (*in time*) seit; (*with future tense*) für. **I have not seen her ~ two years** ich habe sie seit zwei Jahren nicht gesehen; **I've been here ~ ten days** er ist seit zehn Tagen hier; **I had/have known her ~ years** ich kannte/kenne sie schon seit Jahren; **then I did**

not see her ~ two years dann habe ich sie zwei Jahre lang nicht gesehen; he walked ~ two hours er ist zwei Stunden lang marschiert; I am going away ~ a few days ich werde (für or auf) ein paar Tage wegfahren; I shall be away ~ a month ich werde einen Monat (lang) weg sein; he won't be back ~ a week er wird erst in einer Woche or nicht vor Ablauf einer Woche zurück sein; can you get it done ~ Monday/this time next week? können Sie es bis or für Montag/bis in einer Woche fertig haben?; I've got a job for you ~ next week ich habe für nächste Woche Arbeit für dich; ~ a while/time (für) eine Weile/einige Zeit.

(k) (distance) the road is lined with trees ~ two miles die Straße ist auf or über zwei Meilen mit Bäumen gesäumt; we walked ~ two miles wir sind zwei Meilen weit gelaufen; ~ miles (ahead/around) meilenweit (vor/um uns etc); ~ mile upon mile Meile um Meile.

(l) (with verbs) to pray ~ peace für den or um Frieden beten; to hope ~ news auf Nachricht hoffen; to look ~ sth (nach) etw suchen; see vbs.

(m) (after n indicating liking, aptitude etc) für. a weakness ~ sweet things eine Schwäche für Süßigkeiten; a gift ~ languages eine Begabung für Sprachen; his genius ~ saying the wrong thing sein Talent, das Falsche zu sagen.

(n) (with infin clauses) ~ this to be possible damit dies möglich wird/wurde; it's easy ~ him to do it für ihn ist es leicht, das zu tun, er kann das leicht tun; I brought it ~ you to see ich habe es mitgebracht, damit Sie es sich (dat) ansehen können; the best would be ~ you to go das beste wäre, wenn Sie weggingen; there's still time ~ him to come er kann immer noch kommen; their one hope is ~ him to return ihre einzige Hoffnung ist, daß er zurückkommt.

(o) (phrases) to do sth ~ oneself etw alleine tun; ~ example zum Beispiel; you're ~ it! (inf) jetzt bist du dran! (inf); oh ~ a cup a tea! jetzt eine Tasse Tee – das wäre schön!

2 conj denn.

3 adj pred (in favour) dafür. 17 were ~, 13 against 17 waren dafür, 13 dagegen; how many ~? wieviele sind/waren dafür?

forage ['fɔrɪdʒ] **1** n (a) (fodder) Futter nt. (b) (search for fodder) Futtersuche f; (Mil) Überfall m. **2** vi nach Futter suchen; (Mil) einen Überfall/Überfälle machen; (fig: rummage) herumwühlen, herumstöbern (for nach). ~-cap Schiffchen nt.

foray ['fɔreɪ] **1** n (Raub)überfall m; (fig) Exkurs m (into in +acc). to make or go on a ~ auf Raubzug gehen. **2** vi einen Raubüberfall/Raubüberfälle machen.

forbad(e) [fɔ'bæd] pret of forbid.

forbear [fɔ'bεə'] pret forbore, ptp forborne vti (form) I forbore from expressing my opinion ich verzichtete darauf or nahm Abstand davon, meine Meinung zu äußern; he forbore to make any comment er enthielt sich jeden Kommentars; we begged him to ~ wir baten ihn, darauf zu verzichten.

forbearance [fɔ'bεərəns] n Nachsicht f.

forbears ['fɔːbεəz] npl (form) Vorfahren, Ahnen pl.

forbid [fə'bɪd] pret forbad(e), ptp forbidden vt (a) (not allow) verbieten. to ~ sb to do sth jdm verbieten, etw zu tun; to ~ sb alcohol jdm Alkohol verbieten; smoking ~den Rauchen verboten; it is ~den to ... es ist verboten, zu ... (b) (prevent) verhindern, nicht erlauben. my health ~s my attending the meeting meine Gesundheit erlaubt es nicht, daß ich an dem Treffen teilnehme; God ~! Gott behüte or bewahre!

forbidden [fə'bɪdn] adj ~ fruit verbotene Früchte pl.

forbidding [fə'bɪdɪŋ] adj rocks, cliffs bedrohlich, furchterregend; sky düster; landscape unfreundlich; prospect grauenhaft; look, person streng.

forbore [fɔ'bɔː'] pret of forbear.

forborne [fɔ'bɔːn] ptp of forbear.

force [fɔːs] **1** n no pl (physical strength, power) Kraft f; (of blow also, of impact, collision) Wucht f; (physical coercion) Gewalt f; (Phys) Kraft f. to resort to ~ Gewalt anwenden; to settle sth by ~ etw gewaltsam or durch Gewalt beilegen; by sheer ~ durch reine Gewalt; by sheer ~ of numbers aufgrund zahlenmäßiger Überlegenheit; there is a ~ 5 wind blowing es herrscht Windstärke 5; the ~ of the wind was so great he could hardly stand der Wind war so stark, daß er kaum stehen konnte; they were there/came in ~ sie waren in großer Zahl or Stärke da/sie kamen in großer Zahl or Stärke.

(b) no pl (fig) (of argument) Überzeugungskraft f; (of music, phrase) Eindringlichkeit f; (of character) Stärke f; (of words, habit) Macht f. by ~ of will-power durch Willensanstrengung or Willenskraft; (the) ~ of circumstances (der) Druck der Verhältnisse; I see the ~ of that/of what he is saying ich sehe ein, das ist zwingend/was er sagt, ist zwingend.

(c) (powerful thing, person) Macht f. F~s of Nature Naturgewalten pl; there are various ~s at work here hier sind verschiedene Kräfte am Werk; he is a powerful ~ in the trade union movement er ist ein einflußreicher Mann in der Gewerkschaftsbewegung; see life ~.

(d) (body of men) the ~s (Mil) die Streitkräfte pl; work ~ Arbeitskräfte pl; sales ~ Verkaufspersonal nt; the (police) ~ die Polizei; to join or combine ~s sich zusammentun.

(e) to come into/be in ~ in Kraft treten/sein.

2 vt (a) (compel) zwingen. to ~ sb/oneself to do sth jdn/sich zwingen, etw zu tun; he was ~d to resign er wurde gezwungen zurückzutreten; (felt obliged to) er sah sich gezwungen zurückzutreten; he was ~d to conclude that ... er sah sich zu der Folgerung gezwungen or gedrängt, daß ...

(b) (extort, obtain by ~) erzwingen. he ~d a confession out of or from me er erzwang ein Geständnis von mir; to ~ an error (Sport) den Gegner/jdn ausspielen.

(c) to ~ sth (up)on sb present, one's company jdm etw aufdrängen; conditions, obedience jdm etw auferlegen; condi-

tions, decision, war jdm etw aufzwingen; I don't want to ~ myself on you ich möchte mich Ihnen nicht aufdrängen.

(d) (break open) aufbrechen. to ~ an entry sich (dat) gewaltsam Zugang or Zutritt verschaffen.

(e) (push, squeeze) to ~ books into a box Bücher in eine Kiste zwängen; to ~ a splinter out einen Splitter herausdrücken; the liquid is ~d up the tube by a pump die Flüssigkeit wird von einer Pumpe durch das Rohr nach oben gepreßt; if it won't open/go in, don't ~ it wenn es nicht aufgeht/paßt, wende keine Gewalt an; he ~d himself through the hole in the wall er zwängte sich durch das Loch in der Mauer; to ~ one's way into sth sich (dat) gewaltsam Zugang zu etw or in etw (acc) verschaffen; to ~ one's way through sich gewaltsam einen Weg bahnen; to ~ a car off the road ein Auto von der Fahrbahn drängen; to ~ a bill through parliament eine Gesetzesvorlage durch das Parlament peitschen; to ~ sb into a corner (lit) jdn in eine Ecke drängen; (fig) jdn in die Enge treiben.

(f) plants treiben.

(g) (produce with effort) to ~ a smile gezwungen lächeln; to ~ the pace das Tempo forcieren; she can't sing top C without forcing her voice sie kann das hohe C nur singen, wenn sie ihrer Stimme Gewalt antut; it's just about possible to use the word like that, but it's forcing it a bit man kann das Wort unter Umständen so verwenden, tut ihm aber damit ein bißchen Gewalt an; don't ~ it erzwingen Sie es nicht.

♦**force back** vt sep zurückdrängen; tears unterdrücken.

♦**force down** vt sep food sich (dat) hinunterquälen; aeroplane zur Landung zwingen; price drücken; laugh unterdrücken; lid of suitcase etc mit Gewalt zumachen.

♦**force off** vt sep lid mit Gewalt abmachen.

♦**force up** vt sep prices hochtreiben.

forced [fɔːst] adj smile gezwungen, gequält; plant getrieben; wording, translation gezwungen, unnatürlich. ~ landing Notlandung f; ~ march Gewaltmarsch m.

force-feed ['fɔːsfiːd] **1** vt zwangsernähren. **2** n (Tech) Druckschmierung f.

forceful ['fɔːsfʊl] adj person energisch, kraftvoll; manner überzeugend; character stark; language, style eindringlich, eindrucksvoll; argument wirkungsvoll, stark; reasoning eindringlich.

forcefully ['fɔːsfəlɪ] adv speak, write, argue, reason eindringlich, eindrucksvoll; behave überzeugend.

forcefulness ['fɔːsfʊlnɪs] n see adj Durchsetzungsvermögen nt, energische or kraftvolle Art; überzeugende Art; Stärke f; Eindringlichkeit f; Stärke f; Eindringlichkeit f.

force majeure [ˌfɔːsmæˈʒɜːʳ] n höhere Gewalt. to bow to ~ sich höherer Gewalt (dat) beugen.

forcemeat ['fɔːsmiːt] n (Cook) Fleischfüllung, Farce f.

forceps ['fɔːseps] npl (also pair of ~) Zange f. ~ delivery Zangengeburt f.

forcible ['fɔːsəbl] adj (a) entry gewaltsam. ~ feeding Zwangsernährung f. (b) language, style eindringlich, eindrucksvoll; argument, reason zwingend, überzeugend; warning eindringlich, nachdrücklich.

forcibly ['fɔːsəblɪ] adv (a) (by force) mit Gewalt. he was ~ fed er wurde zwangsernährt. (b) (vigorously) warn, object eindringlich, nachdrücklich; argue, speak überzeugend.

ford [fɔːd] **1** n Furt f. **2** vt durchqueren; (on foot also) durchwaten.

fore [fɔːʳ] **1** adj (esp Naut) vordere(r, s), Vorder-. ~ of the bridge oberhalb der Brücke; ~ and aft sail Schratsegel nt.

2 n (a) (Naut) Vorderteil nt, Bug m. at the ~ am Bug. (b) (fig) to the ~ im Vordergrund, an der Spitze; to come to the ~ ins Blickfeld geraten.

3 adv (Naut) vorn. ~ and aft längsschiffs.

4 interj (Golf) Achtung.

forearm[1] ['fɔːrɑːm] n Unterarm m.

forearm[2] [fɔːr'ɑːm] vt vorbereiten. to ~ oneself sich wappnen; he came ~ed er kam vorbereitet; see forewarn.

forebear[1] ['fɔːbεəʳ] n Vorfahr(in f), Ahn(e f) m.

forebear[2] [fɔːr'bεəʳ] vt see forbear.

forebode [fɔː'bəʊd] vt (be portent of) ein Zeichen or Omen sein für, ahnen lassen, deuten auf (+acc).

foreboding [fɔː'bəʊdɪŋ] n (presentiment) (Vor)ahnung f, Vorgefühl nt; (feeling of disquiet) ungutes Gefühl.

forebrain ['fɔːbreɪn] n Vorderhirn nt.

forecast ['fɔːkɑːst] **1** vt vorhersehen, voraussagen; (Met) voraussagen, vorhersagen. **2** n Voraussage, Vorhersage, Prognose f; (Met) Voraus- or Vorhersage f. the ~ is good der Wetterbericht or die Wettervorhersage ist günstig.

forecaster ['fɔːkɑːstəʳ] n (Met) Meteorologe m, Meteorologin f.

forecastle ['fəʊksl] n (Naut) Vorschiff, Vorderdeck nt; (in Merchant Navy) Logis nt.

foreclose [fɔː'kləʊz] **1** vt loan, mortgage kündigen. to ~ sb jds Kredit/Hypothek kündigen. **2** vi (on loan, mortgage) ein Darlehen/eine Hypothek kündigen. to ~ on sth etw kündigen.

forecourt ['fɔːkɔːt] n Vorhof m.

foredeck ['fɔːdek] n Vor(der)deck nt.

forefather ['fɔːˌfɑːðəʳ] n Ahr, Vorfahr m.

forefinger ['fɔːˌfɪŋgəʳ] n Zeigefinger m.

forefoot ['fɔːfʊt] n Vorderfuß m.

forefront ['fɔːfrʌnt] n in the ~ of im Vorfeld (+gen).

foregather [fɔː'gæðəʳ] vi zusammentreffen, sich versammeln.

forego [fɔː'gəʊ] pret forewent, ptp foregone verzichten auf (+acc).

foregoing ['fɔːgəʊɪŋ] adj vorhergehend, vorangehend. it can be seen from the ~ that ... aus dem bisher Gesagten kann entnommen werden, daß ...

foregone [fɔː'gɒn] **1** ptp of forego. **2** ['fɔːgɒn] adj: it was a ~ conclusion es stand von vornherein fest.

foreground ['fɔːgraʊnd] n (Art, Phot) Vordergrund m. in the ~ im Vordergrund.

forehand ['fɔːhænd] (Sport) **1** n Vorhand f. **2** attr Vorhand-.

forehead ['fɔːhed, 'fɒrɪd] n Stirn f.

foreign ['fɒrən] adj (a) ausländisch; customs, appearance fremdartig, fremdländisch; policy, trade Außen-. is he ~? ist er Ausländer?; ~ person Ausländer(in f) m; ~ countries das Ausland; he came from a ~ country er kam aus dem Ausland.
(b) (not natural) fremd. lying is quite ~ to him/his nature Lügen ist seiner Natur fremd.

foreign: ~ affairs npl Außenpolitik f; spokesman on ~ affairs außenpolitischer Sprecher; ~ agent n (in espionage) ausländischer Agent; (Comm etc) Auslandsvertreter(in f) m; ~-born adj im Ausland geboren; ~ correspondent n Auslandskorrespondent(in f) m; ~ currency n Devisen pl.

foreigner ['fɒrənə'] n Ausländer(in f) m.

foreign: ~ exchange n Devisen pl; ~ exchange market n Devisenmarkt m; ~ language **1** n Fremdsprache f. it was a ~ language to me (fig) es war eine Sprache, die ich nicht verstand; **2** attr Fremdsprachen-; ~ legion n Fremdenlegion f; F~ Minister n Außenminister m; ~ national n ausländische(r) Staatsangehörige(r) mf; F~ Office n (Brit) Auswärtiges Amt; F~ Secretary n (Brit) Außenminister m.

foreknowledge [,fɔː'nɒlɪdʒ] n vorherige Kenntnis.

foreland ['fɔːlənd] n Vorland nt; (promontory) Landspitze f.

foreleg ['fɔːleg] n Vorderbein nt.

forelimb ['fɔːlɪm] n Vorderglied nt.

forelock ['fɔːlɒk] n Stirnlocke f, Stirnhaar nt. to touch or tug one's ~ (to sb) jdm Reverenz erweisen; to take time by the ~ die Zeit (voll) nutzen.

foreman ['fɔːmən] n, pl -men [-mən] (in factory) Vorarbeiter m; (on building site) Polier m; (Jur: of jury) Obmann m.

foremast ['fɔːmɑːst] n (Naut) Fockmast m.

foremost ['fɔːməʊst] **1** adj (lit) erste(r, s), vorderste(r, s); (fig) writer, politician etc führend. the problem/thought which was ~ in his mind das Problem, das/der Gedanke, der ihn hauptsächlich beschäftigte. **2** adv see first.

forename ['fɔːneɪm] n Vorname m.

forenoon ['fɔːnuːn] n (form) Vormittag m.

forensic [fə'rensɪk] adj forensisch; (Med also) gerichtsmedizinisch. ~ science Kriminaltechnik f; ~ medicine Gerichtsmedizin f, forensische Medizin; ~ expert Spurensicherungsexperte m; ~ laboratory Polizeilabor nt.

foreordain [,fɔːrɔː'deɪn] vt see preordain.

foreplay ['fɔːpleɪ] n Vorspiel nt.

forequarters ['fɔːkwɔːtəz] npl Vorderstücke pl.

forerunner ['fɔːrʌnə'] n Vorläufer m. a ~ of disaster ein Vorbote m des Unglücks.

foresaid ['fɔːsed] adj see aforesaid.

foresail ['fɔːseɪl] n (Naut) Focksegel nt.

foresee [fɔː'siː] pret **foresaw** [fɔː'sɔː], ptp **foreseen** [fɔː'siːn] vt vorhersehen, voraussehen.

foreseeable [fɔː'siːəbl] adj voraussehbar, absehbar. in the ~ future in absehbarer Zeit.

foreshadow [fɔː'ʃædəʊ] vt ahnen lassen, andeuten.

foresheet ['fɔːʃiːt] n (Naut) Fockschot f.

foreshore ['fɔːʃɔː'] n Küstenvorland nt; (beach) Strand m.

foreshorten [fɔː'ʃɔːtn] vt (Art, Phot) perspektivisch zeichnen/photographieren. this has a ~ing effect das läßt es kürzer erscheinen.

foreshortening [fɔː'ʃɔːtnɪŋ] n (Art, Phot) zeichnerische/photographische Verkürzung.

foresight ['fɔːsaɪt] n Weitblick m.

foreskin ['fɔːskɪn] n Vorhaut f.

forest ['fɒrɪst] n Wald m; (for lumber etc) Forst m; (fig) (of TV aerials etc) Wald m; (of ideas, suggestions etc) Wust m, Menge f. ~ ranger Förster m.

forestall [fɔː'stɔːl] vt sb, rival zuvorkommen (+dat); accident, eventuality vorbeugen (+dat); wish, desire im Keim ersticken; objection vorwegnehmen.

forestage ['fɔːsteɪdʒ] n Vorbühne f.

forestation [fɒrɪ'steɪʃən] n see afforestation.

forestay ['fɔːsteɪ] n Fockstag nt.

forested ['fɒrɪstɪd] adj bewaldet.

forester ['fɒrɪstə'] n Förster m.

forestry ['fɒrɪstrɪ] n Forstwirtschaft f. F~ Commission (Brit) Forstverwaltung f.

foretaste ['fɔːteɪst] n Vorgeschmack m.

foretell [fɔː'tel] pret, ptp **foretold** [fɔː'təʊld] vt vorhersagen, voraussagen.

forethought ['fɔːθɔːt] n Vorbedacht m.

forever [fər'evə'] adv (a) (constantly) immer, ständig, ewig (inf). he was ~ falling over er fiel immer or ständig or ewig (inf) hin. (b) (esp US: eternally) = for ever; see ever.

forevermore [fər,evə'mɔː'] adv (esp US) = for evermore; see evermore.

forewarn [fɔː'wɔːn] vt vorher warnen. that should have ~ed him das hätte ihm eine Vorwarnung sein sollen; ~ed is forearmed (Prov) Gefahr erkannt, Gefahr gebannt (prov).

forewent [fɔː'went] pret of forego.

forewing ['fɔːwɪŋ] n Vorderflügel m.

forewoman ['fɔːwʊmən] n, pl -women [-wɪmɪn] Vorarbeiterin f.

foreword ['fɔːwɜːd] n Vorwort nt.

forfeit ['fɔːfɪt] **1** vt (a) (esp Jur) verwirken; one's rights also verlustig gehen (+gen).
(b) (fig) one's life, health, honour, sb's respect einbüßen. to ~ the right to criticize sb sich (dat) das Recht verscherzen, jdn zu kritisieren.
2 n (esp Jur) Strafe, Buße f; (fig) Einbuße f; (in game) Pfand nt. ~s sing (game) Pfänderspiel nt; to pay a ~ (in game) ein

Pfand (ab)geben; his health was the ~ he paid er zahlte mit seiner Gesundheit dafür.
3 adj to be ~ (Jur) verfallen sein; (fig) verwirkt sein.

forfeiture ['fɔːfɪtʃə'] n (Jur, fig) Verlust m, Einbuße f; (of claim) Verwirkung f.

forgather [fɔː'gæðə'] vi see foregather.

forgave [fə'geɪv] pret of forgive.

forge [fɔːdʒ] **1** n (workshop) Schmiede f; (furnace) Esse f.
2 vt (a) metal, alliance plan schmieden.
(b) (counterfeit) signature, banknote fälschen.
3 vi to ~ ahead Fortschritte machen, vorwärtskommen; (in one's career) seinen Weg machen; (Sport) vorstoßen; he started to ~ ahead of the rest of the field er setzte sich weit vor die anderen.

forger ['fɔːdʒə'] n Fälscher(in f) m.

forgery ['fɔːdʒərɪ] n (a) (act) Fälschen nt. to be prosecuted for ~ wegen Fälschung angeklagt sein. (b) (thing) Fälschung f.

forget [fə'get] pret **forgot**, ptp **forgotten 1** vt vergessen; ability, language also verlernen. never to be forgotten unvergeßlich, unvergessen; and don't you ~ it! und daß du das ja nicht vergißt!; he never lets you ~ it either er sorgt dafür, daß du auch immer daran denkst; don't ~ the guide vergessen Sie nicht, dem Führer ein Trinkgeld zu geben; I was ~ting you knew him ich habe ganz vergessen, daß Sie ihn kennen; I ~ his name sein Name ist mir entfallen; I ~ what I wanted to say es ist mir entfallen, was ich sagen wollte; to ~ past quarrels vergangene Streitigkeiten ruhen lassen; ~ it! schon gut!; you might as well ~ it (inf) das kannst du vergessen (inf).
2 vi vergessen. don't ~! vergiß (es) nicht!; I never ~ ich vergesse nie etwas; where is he? — I ~ wo ist er? — ich habe es vergessen or es ist mir entfallen.
3 vr (behave improperly) sich vergessen, aus der Rolle fallen; (act unselfishly) sich selbst vergessen.

♦**forget about** vi +prep obj vergessen. I've forgotten all ~ what he did ich habe völlig vergessen, was er getan hat.

forgetful [fə'getfʊl] adj (absent-minded) vergeßlich; (of one's duties etc) achtlos, nachlässig (of gegenüber).

forgetfulness [fə'getfʊlnɪs] n see adj Vergeßlichkeit f; Achtlosigkeit, Nachlässigkeit f (of gegenüber). in a moment of ~ in einem Augenblick geistiger Abwesenheit.

forget-me-not [fə'getmɪnɒt] n (Bot) Vergißmeinnicht nt.

forgettable [fə'getəbl] adj some things just aren't ~ manche Sachen kann man einfach nicht vergessen; an eminently ~ second novel ein zweiter Roman, den man getrost vergessen kann.

forgivable [fə'gɪvəbl] adj verzeihlich, verzeihbar.

forgive [fə'gɪv] pret **forgave**, ptp **forgiven** [fə'gɪvn] vti mistake, clumsiness verzeihen, vergeben; person verzeihen (+dat), vergeben (+dat); (esp Eccl) sin vergeben, erlassen. to ~ sb sth jdm etw verzeihen or vergeben; (Eccl) jdm etw vergeben or erlassen; to ~ sb for sth jdm etw verzeihen or vergeben; to ~ sb for doing sth jdm verzeihen or vergeben, daß er etw getan hat; ~ me, but ... Entschuldigung, aber ...; to ~ and forget vergeben und vergessen.

forgiveness [fə'gɪvnɪs] n, no pl (quality, willingness to forgive) Versöhnlichkeit f. to ask/beg (sb's) ~ (jdn) um Verzeihung or Vergebung (esp Eccl) bitten; her willing ~ of his rudeness surprised him es überraschte ihn, daß sie ihm seine Grobheit so bereitwillig verzieh; the ~ of sins (Eccl) die Vergebung der Sünden; full of ~ versöhnlich.

forgiving [fə'gɪvɪŋ] adj versöhnlich, nicht nachtragend.

forgo pret forwent, ptp **forgone** vt see forego.

forgot [fə'gɒt] pret of forget.

forgotten [fə'gɒtn] ptp of forget.

fork [fɔːk] **1** n (a) (implement) Gabel f. (b) (in tree) Astgabel f; (in road, railway) Gabelung f. take the left ~ nehmen Sie die linke Abzweigung. **2** vt (a) ground mit einer Gabel umgraben; hay (turn over) wenden. to ~ hay onto a cart Heu mit einer Gabel auf einen Wagen werfen. (b) food gabeln (inf). **3** vi (roads, branches) sich gabeln. to ~ (to the) right (road) nach rechts abzweigen; (driver) nach rechts abbiegen.

♦**fork out** vti sep (inf) blechen (inf).

♦**fork over** vt sep ground lockern; hay wenden.

♦**fork up** vt sep soil mit einer Gabel umgraben; hay hochheben; food gabeln (inf).

forked [fɔːkt] adj branch, road gegabelt; (with lots of forks) verästelt; lightning zickzackförmig; tongue gespalten. to speak with ~ tongue mit gespaltener Zunge reden.

fork: ~-lift truck, ~-lift (inf) n Gabelstapler m; ~-luncheon n (Brit) Gabelfrühstück nt.

forlorn [fə'lɔːn] adj (deserted) verlassen; person einsam und verlassen; (desperate) attempt verzweifelt; (hope) schwach. ~ appearance (of house etc) desolates or trostloses Aussehen.

form [fɔːm] **1** n (a) Form f. ~ of government Regierungsform f; ~ of life Lebensform f; the various ~s of energy die verschiedenen Energieformen; ~ of address Anrede f; to choose another ~ of words es anders formulieren; ~s of worship Formen der Gottesverehrung; a ~ of apology/punishment eine Art der Entschuldigung/eine Form or Art der Bestrafung.
(b) (condition, style, guise) Form, Gestalt f. in the ~ of in Form von or +gen; (with reference to people) in Gestalt von or +gen; medicine in tablet ~ Arznei in Tablettenform; water in the ~ of ice Wasser in Form von Eis; the same thing in a new ~ das gleiche in neuer Form or Gestalt; the first prize will take the ~ of a trip to Rome der erste Preis ist eine Reise nach Rom; what ~ should my application take? in welcher Form soll ich mich bewerben?; their discontent took various ~s ihre Unzufriedenheit äußerte sich in verschiedenen Formen.
(c) (shape) Form f. to take ~ (lit, fig) Form or Gestalt annehmen; a ~ approached in the fog eine Gestalt näherte sich im Nebel.

(d) (*Art, Mus, Liter: structure*) Form *f*. ~ **and content** Form und Inhalt.
(e) (*Philos*) Form *f*. **the world of** ~s die Ideenwelt.
(f) (*Gram*) Form *f*. **the plural** ~ die Pluralform, der Plural.
(g) *no pl* (*etiquette*) (Umgangs)form *f*. **he did it for** ~'**s sake** er tat es der Form halber; **it's bad** ~ so etwas tut man einfach nicht; **he pays attention to the** ~s **er legt großen Wert auf Form**; **what's the** ~? (*inf*) was ist üblich?
(h) (*questionnaire, document*) Formular *nt*, Vordruck *m*. **telegraph** ~ Telegrammformular *nt*; **printed** ~ vorgedrucktes Formular; **application** ~ Bewerbungsbogen *m*.
(i) (*physical condition*) Form, Verfassung *f*. **to be in fine/good** ~ gut in Form sein, in guter Form *or* Verfassung sein; **to be on/off** ~ in/nicht in *or* außer Form sein; **he was in great** ~ **that evening** er war an dem Abend in Hochform; **to study (the)** ~ (*Horse-racing*) die Form prüfen; **past** ~ Papierform *f*; **on past** ~ auf dem Papier.
(j) (*esp Brit: bench*) Bank *f*.
(k) (*Brit Sch*) Klasse *f*.
(l) *no pl* (*sl: criminal record*) **to have** ~ vorbestraft sein.
(m) (*Tech: mould*) Form *f*.
(n) (*US Typ*) see **forme.**
(o) (*of hare*) Nest *nt*, Sasse *f* (*spec*).
2 *vt* **(a)** (*shape*) formen, gestalten (*into* zu); (*Gram*) *plural, negative* bilden. **he** ~s **his sentences well** er bildet wohlgeformte Sätze *pl*; **he** ~s **his style on that of** 19th century writers er lehnt sich in seinem Stil an die Schriftsteller des neunzehnten Jahrhunderts an.
(b) (*train, mould*) *child, sb's character* formen.
(c) (*develop*) *liking, desire, idea* entwickeln; *habit also* annehmen; *friendship* schließen, anknüpfen; *opinion* sich (*dat*) bilden; *impression* gewinnen; *plan* ausdenken, entwerfen.
(d) (*set up, organize*) *government, committee* bilden; *company, society* gründen, ins Leben rufen.
(e) (*constitute, make up*) *part, basis* bilden. **the committee is** ~**ed of ...** der Ausschuß wird von ... gebildet.
(f) (*take the shape or order of*) *queue, circle, pattern* bilden.
3 *vi* **(a)** (*take shape*) Gestalt annehmen. **the idea** ~**ed in my mind** die Idee nahm Gestalt an.
(b) (*esp Mil: also* ~ **up**) sich aufstellen *or* formieren, antreten. **to** ~ **into a queue/into two lines** eine Schlange/zwei Reihen bilden; **to** ~ **into a square** sich im Karree aufstellen; **to** ~ **into battle order** sich zur Schlachtordnung formieren.

formal ['fɔːməl] *adj* **(a)** formell; *person, manner, language etc also* förmlich; *reception, welcome (for head of state etc)* feierlich; *education, training* offiziell. ~ **dance/dress** Gesellschaftstanz *m*/-kleidung *f*.
(b) (*in form*) *distinction etc* formal (*also Philos*). ~ **grammar** formalisierte Grammatik; ~ **logic** formale Logik.
formaldehyde [fɔː'mældɪhaɪd] *n* Formaldehyd *m*.
formalin(e) ['fɔːməlɪn] *n* Formalin *nt*.
formalism ['fɔːməlɪzəm] *n* Formalismus *m*.
formality [fɔː'mælɪtɪ] *n* **(a)** *no pl* (*of person, dress, greeting, language, ceremony etc*) Förmlichkeit *f*.
(b) (*matter of form*) Formalität *f*. **it's a mere** ~ es ist (eine) reine Formsache *or* Formalität; **let's dispense with the formalities** lassen wir die Formalitäten beiseite.
formalize ['fɔːməlaɪz] *vt rules, grammar* formalisieren; *agreement, relationship* formell machen.
formally ['fɔːməlɪ] *adv* **(a)** formell; *behave, talk, agree, permit, invite etc also* förmlich; *welcome officially also* feierlich; *educated, trained* offiziell. **to be** ~ **dressed** Gesellschaftskleidung tragen. **(b)** (*in form*) *alike, different, analyzed* formal.
format ['fɔːmæt] *n* (*as regards size*) Format *nt*; (*as regards content*) Aufmachung *f*; (*Rad, TV: of programme*) Struktur *f*.
formation [fɔː'meɪʃən] *n* **(a)** (*act of forming*) Formung, Gestaltung *f*; (*Gram: of plural etc*) Bildung *f*; (*of character*) Formung *f*; (*of government, committee*) Bildung *f*; (*of company, society*) Gründung *f*; (*of desire, idea, impression, habit etc*) Entwicklung *f*; (*of friendship*) Schließen *nt*, Anknüpfung *f*; (*of opinion*) Bildung *f*; (*of plan*) Entwurf *m*.
(b) (*of aircraft, dances*) Formation *f*; (*of troops also*) Aufstellung *f*. **battle** ~ Gefechtsaufstellung *f*; **in close** ~ (*Aviat*) im geschlossenen Verband; ~ **flying** Formationsflug *m*; **to dance in** ~ in Formation tanzen; ~ **dancing** Formationstanzen *nt*.
(c) (*Geol*) Formation *f*.
formative ['fɔːmətɪv] **1** *adj* formend, bildend; (*Gram*) Bildungs-; (*Biol*) morphogenetisch. ~ **element** (*Gram*) Wortbildungselement, Formativ *nt*; ~ **years** entscheidende Jahre *pl*. **2** *n* (*Gram*) Wortbildungselement, Formativ *nt*.
forme [fɔːm] *n* (*Brit Typ*) (Satz)form *f*.
former ['fɔːmə^r] **1** *adj* **(a)** (*of an earlier period*) früher, ehemalig. **the** ~ **mayor** der ehemalige Bürgermeister; **in a** ~ **life** in einem früheren Leben; **in** ~ **times/days** früher.
(b) (*first-mentioned*) erstere(r, s), erstgenannte(r, s).
2 *n* **the** ~ **der/die/das erstere**; **of these two theories I prefer the** ~ von diesen beiden Theorien ziehe ich (die) erstere vor.
-former *n suf* (*Brit Sch*) -kläßler(in *f*) *m*.
formerly ['fɔːməlɪ] *adv* früher. **we had** ~ **agreed that ...** wir hatten uns seinerzeit darauf geeinigt, daß ...; ~ **known as ...** früher *or* ehemals als ... bekannt; **Mrs X,** ~ **Mrs Y** Frau X, die ehemalige *or* frühere Frau Y.
form-fitting ['fɔːmfɪtɪŋ] *adj* enganliegend.
formica ® [fɔː'maɪkə] *n* Resopal ® *nt*.
formic acid ['fɔːmɪk'æsɪd] *n* Ameisensäure *f*.
formidable ['fɔːmɪdəbl] *adj* **(a)** *person; rock-face* furchterregend; *enemy, opponent also* bedrohlich, gefährlich; *height also* gewaltig; *opposition* übermächtig; *obstacles, debts, problems, task* gewaltig, enorm; *piece of work, theory* beeindruckend, beachtlich. **(b)** *achievement* gewaltig, ungeheuer.
form: ~**less** *adj* formlos; ~**lessness** *n* Formlosigkeit *f*.

formula ['fɔːmjʊlə] *n, pl* **-s** *or* **-e** ['fɔːmjuːliː] Formel *f* (*also Sci*); (*for lotion, medicine, soap powder*) Rezeptur *f*. **there's no sure** ~ **for success** es gibt kein Patentrezept *nt* für Erfolg; **they changed the** ~ **of the programme** sie änderten die Aufmachung des Programms; **all his books use the same** ~ alle seine Bücher sind nach demselben Rezept geschrieben.
formulate ['fɔːmjʊleɪt] *vt* formulieren.
formulation [,fɔːmjʊ'leɪʃən] *n* Formulierung *f*.
fornicate ['fɔːnɪkeɪt] *vi* Unzucht treiben.
fornication [,fɔːnɪ'keɪʃən] *n* Unzucht *f*.
fornicator ['fɔːnɪkeɪtə^r] *n* Hurer (*inf*), Hurenbock (*inf*) *m*.
forsake [fə'seɪk] *pret* **forsook** [fə'sʊk], *ptp* **forsaken** [fə'seɪkn] *vt* verlassen; *bad habits* aufgeben, entsagen (+*dat*) (*geh*). **my willpower/courage** ~s **me on these occasions** meine Willenskraft/mein Mut läßt mich bei diesen Gelegenheiten im Stich; *see* **godforsaken.**
forswear [fɔː'sweə^r] *pret* **forswore** [fɔː'swɔː^r], *ptp* **forsworn** [fɔː'swɔːn] *vt* **(a)** (*renounce*) abschwören (+*dat*). **he has forsworn smoking** er hat hoch und heilig versprochen, nicht mehr zu rauchen. **(b)** (*deny*) unter Eid verneinen *or* leugnen.
forsythia [fɔː'saɪθɪə] *n* Forsythie *f*.
fort [fɔːt] *n* (*Mil*) Fort *nt*. **to hold the** ~ (*fig*) die Stellung halten.
forte ['fɔːtɪ] *n* (*strong point*) Stärke *f*, starke Seite.
forth [fɔːθ] *adv* **(a)** **to set** ~ (*liter*) ausziehen (*liter*); **to stretch** ~ **one's hand** (*liter*) die Hand ausstrecken; *see vbs.* **(b)** (*in time*) **from this/that day** ~ (*liter*) von diesem/jenem Tag an. **(c) and so** ~ und so weiter.
forthcoming [fɔːθ'kʌmɪŋ] *adj* **(a)** *event* bevorstehend; *book* in Kürze erscheinend; *film, play* in Kürze anlaufend. ~ **events/attractions** Programmvorschau *f*; ~ **books** *or* **titles** geplante Neuerscheinungen *pl*; **our** ~ **titles for next year** Titel, die nächstes Jahr erscheinen.
(b) **to be** ~ (*money*) kommen; (*help*) erfolgen.
(c) (*esp Brit: frank, informative*) mitteilsam.
forthright ['fɔːθraɪt] *adj* offen; *answer also* unverblümt; *manner also* direkt.
forthwith [,fɔːθ'wɪθ] *adv* (*form*) umgehend, unverzüglich.
fortieth ['fɔːtɪɪθ] **1** *adj* vierzigste(r, s). **2** *n* (*fraction*) Vierzigstel *nt*; (*in series*) Vierzigste(r, s).
fortification [,fɔːtɪfɪ'keɪʃən] *n* **(a)** *see vt* (*act of fortifying*) Befestigung *f*; Vergärung *f*; Anreicherung *f*; Bestärkung *f*. **(b)** (*often pl: Mil*) Befestigungen *pl*, Festungsanlagen *pl*.
fortify ['fɔːtɪfaɪ] *vt* (*Mil*) *town* befestigen; *wine* mit zuckerreichem Most vergären; *food* anreichern; *person* bestärken; (*food, drink*) stärken. **fortified place** befestigte Stellung; **fortified wine** weinhaltiges Getränk, Südwein *m*; **have a drink to** ~ **you** nehmen Sie einen Schluck zur Stärkung.
fortitude ['fɔːtɪtjuːd] *n* (innere) Kraft *or* Stärke.
fortnight ['fɔːtnaɪt] *n* (*esp Brit*) vierzehn Tage, zwei Wochen. **we are going away for a** ~ wir fahren (für) vierzehn Tage *or* zwei Wochen weg; **a** ~'**s holiday** zwei Wochen *or* vierzehn Tage Urlaub.
fortnightly ['fɔːtnaɪtlɪ] (*esp Brit*) **1** *adj* vierzehntägig, zweiwöchentlich. **2** *adv* alle vierzehn Tage, alle zwei Wochen, vierzehntägig, zweiwöchentlich.
FORTRAN ['fɔːtræn] *n* Fortran *nt*.
fortress ['fɔːtrɪs] *n* Festung *f*.
fortuitous *adj*, ~**ly** *adv* [fɔː'tjuːɪtəs, -lɪ] zufällig.
fortuitousness [fɔː'tjuːɪtəsnɪs], **fortuity** [fɔː'tjuːɪtɪ] *n* Zufall *m*.
fortunate ['fɔːtʃənɪt] *adj* *circumstances, coincidence etc* glücklich. **to be** ~ (*person*) Glück haben; **you are very** ~ *or* **you're a** ~ **man** to be alive still du kannst von Glück reden *or* dich glücklich schätzen, daß du noch lebst; **it was** ~ **that ...** es war (ein) Glück, daß ...; **we were** ~ **enough to meet him** wir hatten das Glück, ihn zu treffen; **how** ~! welch ein Glück!
fortunately ['fɔːtʃənɪtlɪ] *adv* glücklicherweise, zum Glück. **he was more** ~ **situated** ihm ging es besser.
fortune ['fɔːtʃuːn] *n* **(a)** (*fate*) Schicksal, Geschick *nt*; (*chance*) Zufall *m*. **she followed his** ~s **with interest** sie verfolgte sein Geschick mit Interesse; **the** ~s **of war** das Auf und Ab des Krieges; **he had the good** ~ **to have rich parents** er hatte das Glück, reiche Eltern zu haben; **by good** ~ glücklicherweise, zum Glück; **by sheer good** ~ rein zufällig; ~ **has favoured him** das Glück war ihm hold; ~ **favours the brave** *or* **bold** (*Prov*) das Glück ist nur dem Tüchtigen hold.
(b) (*money*) Reichtum *m*, Vermögen *nt*. **to come into/make a** ~ ein Vermögen erben/erwerben *or* machen; **to seek/make one's** ~ sein Glück versuchen/machen; **to marry a** ~ eine gute Partie machen, reich heiraten; **it costs a** ~ es kostet ein Vermögen; **she spends a (small)** ~ **on clothes** sie gibt ein (kleines) Vermögen für Kleidung aus.
fortune: ~ **hunter** *n* Mitgiftjäger *m*; ~**-teller** *n* Wahrsager(in *f*) *m*.
forty ['fɔːtɪ] **1** *adj* vierzig. **to have** ~ **winks** (*inf*) ein Nickerchen machen (*inf*). **2** *n* Vierzig *f*; *see also* **sixty.**
forty-niner [,fɔːtɪ'naɪnə^r] *n* Goldgräber, *der im Zuge des Goldrausches 1849 nach Kalifornien ging.*
forum ['fɔːrəm] *n* Forum *nt*.
forward ['fɔːwəd] **1** *adv* **(a)** (*also* ~s) (*onwards, ahead*) vorwärts; (*to the front, to particular point, out of line*) nach vorn. **please step** ~ bitte vortreten; **to take two steps** ~ zwei Schritte vortreten; **to rush** ~ sich vorstürzen; **to go straight** ~ geradeaus gehen; ~! vorwärts!; **he went backward(s) and** ~(s) **between the station and the house** er ging/fuhr *etc* zwischen Haus und Bahnhof hin und her.
(b) (*in time*) **from this time** ~ (*from then*) seitdem; (*from now*) von jetzt an; **if we think** ~ **to the next stage** wir an die vor uns liegende nächste Stufe denken.
(c) (*into prominence*) **to come** ~ sich melden; **to bring** ~ **new proof** neue Beweise *pl* vorlegen.

2 adj **(a)** (in place) vordere(r, s); (in direction) Vorwärts-. ~ march Vormarsch m; ~ gears (Aut) Vorwärtsgänge pl; ~ pass (Sport) Vorwärtspaß m; ~ post (Mil) Vorposten m; **this seat is too far** ~ dieser Sitz ist zu weit vorn. **(b)** (in time) planning Voraus-; (Comm) buying, price Termin-; (well-advanced) season (weit) fortgeschritten; plants Früh-, früh pred; children frühreif. **I'd like to be further** ~ **with my work** ich wollte, ich wäre mit meiner Arbeit schon weiter; **good** ~ **thinking, Jones** gute Voraussicht, Jones. **(c)** (presumptuous, pert) dreist.

3 n (Sport) Stürmer m.

4 vt **(a)** (advance) plans etc vorantreiben; **we'll** ~ **your suggestions to the committee** wir werden Ihre Vorschläge an den Ausschuß weiterleiten. **(b)** (dispatch) goods befördern, senden; (send on) letter, parcel nachsenden. **please** ~ bitte nachsenden.

forwarding ['fɔːwədɪŋ]: ~ **address** n Nachsendeadresse f; ~ **agent** n Spediteur m; ~ **instructions** npl (for goods) Lieferanweisungen pl; (for sending on mail) Nachsendeanweisungen pl.

forward: ~**-line** n (Sport) Sturm m, Stürmerreihe f; ~**-looking** adj person fortschrittlich, progressiv; plan vorausblickend.

forwardness ['fɔːwədnɪs] n (presumption) Dreistigkeit f.

forwards ['fɔːwədz] adv see forward 1 (a).

forwent [fɔː'went] pret of forgo.

fossil ['fɒsl] **1** n (lit) Fossil nt. **he's an old** ~! (inf) er ist so verknöchert. **2** adj versteinert. ~ **fuels** fossile Brennstoffe pl.

fossilized ['fɒsɪlaɪzd] adj versteinert; (fig) person verknöchert; customs verkrustet, starr.

foster ['fɒstəʳ] vt **(a)** child (parents) in Pflege nehmen; (authorities: ~ out) in Pflege geben (with bei); **two of the children are their own, the others are** ~**ed** zwei der Kinder sind ihre eigenen, die anderen sind Pflegekinder. **(b)** (encourage, promote) fördern. **(c)** (have in one's mind) idea, thought hegen.

♦**foster out** vt sep in Pflege geben (with bei).

foster: ~**-brother** n (a) Pflegebruder m; (b) (fed by same mother) Milchbruder m; ~**-child** n Pflegekind nt; ~**-father** n Pflegevater m; ~ **home** n Pflegeheim nt; ~**-mother** n (a) (Jur) Pflegemutter f; (b) (wet-nurse) Amme f; (c) (apparatus) Brutkasten m; ~**-sister** n Pflegeschwester f.

fought [fɔːt] pret, ptp of fight.

foul [faul] **1** adj (+er) **(a)** (putrid, stinking) smell übel, schlecht; water faulig; air schlecht, stinkig (inf); food übelriechend, verdorben. ~ **deed** böse or schlechte Tat. **(b)** (horrible) day, weather, mood ekelhaft, mies (inf); person, behaviour gemein, fies (inf). **he was really** ~ **to her** er war wirklich gemein or fies (inf) zu ihr; **he has a** ~ **temper** er ist ein ganz übellauniger Mensch. **(c)** language unflätig. **(d)** (Sport) serve, throw-in ungültig; punch unerlaubt, verboten. **he was sent off for** ~ **play** er wurde wegen eines Fouls or wegen Regelverstößen vom Platz gestellt; **there was a lot of** ~ **play in that match** es gab eine Menge Fouls or Regelverstöße in diesem Spiel. **(e)** **the police suspect** ~ **play** es besteht Verdacht auf einen unnatürlichen or gewaltsamen Tod; **is there any possibility of** ~ **play?** könnte der Verdacht auf einen unnatürlichen or gewaltsamen Tod vorliegen? **(f)** (entangled) verwickelt. **to fall** or **run** ~ **of sb/the law** mit jdm/dem Gesetz in Konflikt geraten.

2 n (Sport) Foul nt, Regelverstoß m; (Boxing) unerlaubter or verbotener Schlag.

3 vt **(a)** (pollute) air verpesten; (clog) pipe, chimney, gunbarrel verstopfen; (dog) pavement verunreinigen; (fig) reputation lädieren, beschmutzen. **(b)** (entangle) fishing line verheddern; propeller (seaweed etc) sich verheddern in (+dat); (collide with) ship rammen. **be careful not to** ~ **the propeller** paß auf, daß sich die Schraube nicht verheddert. **(c)** (Sport) foulen.

4 vi **(a)** (Sport) foulen, regelwidrig spielen. **(b)** (rope, line) sich verwickeln, sich verheddern.

foully ['faulɪ] adv (horribly) übel, schlimm.

foul-mouthed ['faulmauðd] adj unflätig, vulgär.

foulness ['faulnɪs] n **(a)** (putridness, stink) (of water) Fauligkeit f; (of food) Verdorbenheit f. **the** ~ **of the smell/air** der üble or schlechte Geruch/die schlechte Luft. **(b)** (horribleness) **the** ~ **of the weather/wine** etc das schlechte Wetter/der schlechte Wein etc; **his** ~ **to her** sein gemeines Verhalten or seine Gemeinheit ihr gegenüber. **(c)** (of language) Unflätigkeit f.

foul-smelling ['faulsmelɪŋ] adj übelriechend attr.

found¹ [faund] pret, ptp of find.

found² vt **(a)** (set up) gründen; town, school, hospital also errichten. **(b)** **to** ~ **sth (up)on sth** opinion, belief etw auf etw (dat) gründen or stützen; **our society is** ~**ed on this** darauf beruht or basiert unsere Gesellschaft, das ist die Grundlage unserer Gesellschaft; **the novel is** ~**ed on fact** der Roman beruht or basiert auf Tatsachen.

found³ vt (Metal) metal, glass schmelzen und in eine Form gießen; object gießen.

foundation [faun'deɪʃən] n **(a)** (act of founding) (of business, colony) Gründung f; (of town, school also) Errichtung f. **(b)** (institution) Stiftung f. **(c)** ~**s** pl (Build) (of house etc) Fundament nt; (of road) Unterbau m. **(d)** (fig: basis) Grundlage f. **(e)** (make-up) Grundierungscreme f.

foundation: ~ **cream** n Grundierungscreme f; **F~ Day** n (Austral) australischer gesetzlicher Feiertag zur Erinnerung an die Landung der Briten am 26. Januar 1788; ~ **garment** n

Mieder nt; ~ **stone** n Grundstein m.

founder¹ ['faundəʳ] n (of school, colony, organization etc) Gründer(in f) m; (of charity, museum) Stifter(in f) m.

founder² vi **(a)** (ship: sink) sinken, untergehen. **(b)** (horse etc: stumble) straucheln, stolpern. **(c)** (fig: fail) (plan, project) scheitern, fehlschlagen; (hopes) auf den Nullpunkt sinken.

founder³ n (Metal) Gießer m.

Founding Fathers ['faundɪŋ,faːðəz] npl (US) Väter pl.

foundling ['faundlɪŋ] n Findling m, Findelkind nt. ~ **hospital** Findelhaus, Findelheim nt.

foundry ['faundrɪ] n Gießerei f.

fount [faunt] n **(a)** (liter) (fountain) Born m (poet), Quelle f; (fig: source) Quelle f. **(b)** (Typ) Schrift f.

fountain ['fauntɪn] n Brunnen m; (with upward jets also) Springbrunnen m; (jet, spurt: of water, lava etc) Fontäne f; (drinking ~) (Trinkwasser)brunnen m; (fig: source) Quelle f. ~ **of youth** Jungbrunnen m.

fountain: ~**-head** n (of river) Quelle f; (fig) Quelle f, Ursprung m; ~**-pen** n Füllfederhalter, Füller m.

four [fɔːʳ] **1** adj vier. **open to the** ~ **winds** Wind und Wetter ausgesetzt; **the** ~ **hundred** (US) ≃ die oberen Zehntausend. **2** n Vier f. **on all** ~**s** auf allen vieren; **will you make up a** ~ **for bridge?** haben Sie Lust, beim Bridge den vierten Mann zu machen?; see also six.

four: ~**-ball** n (Golf) Vierer m; ~**-colour** adj (Typ) Vierfarb-; ~**-cycle** adj (US) see ~**-stroke**; ~**-dimensional** adj vierdimensional; ~**-door** attr viertürig; ~**-figure** attr vierstellig; ~**-fold 1** adj vierfach; **2** adv um das Vierfache; ~**-footed** adj vierfüßig; ~**-four time** n (Mus) Viervierteltakt m; ~**-handed** adj (Mus) vierhändig, für vier Hände, zu vier Händen; ~**-in-hand** n Vierspänner m; ~**-leaf clover**, ~**-leaved clover** n vierblättriges Kleeblatt; ~**-letter word** n Vulgärausdruck m; ~**-minute mile** n Vierminutenmeile f; ~**-part** attr serial, programme vierteilig; (Mus) für vier Stimmen; ~**-poster (bed)** n Himmelbett nt; ~**-score** adj achtzig; ~**-seater 1** adj viersitzig; **2** n Viersitzer m; ~**-some** n Quartett nt; (Sport) Viererspiel nt; **to go out in a** ~**some** zu viert ausgehen; ~**-square** adj (a) (square) viereckig, quadratisch; (b) (firm, unyielding) attitude, decision entschlossen, fest; (c) (forthright) account, assessment offen und ehrlich, direkt; ~**-star** adj hotel etc, (US) general Vier-Sterne-; (Brit) petrol Super-; ~**-stroke** adj engine Viertakt-.

fourteen ['fɔː'tiːn] **1** adj vierzehn. **2** n Vierzehn f; see also sixteen.

fourteenth ['fɔː'tiːnθ] **1** adj vierzehnte(r, s). **2** n (fraction) Vierzehntel nt; (of series) Vierzehnte(r, s); see also sixteenth.

fourth [fɔːθ] **1** adj vierte(r, s). **the** ~ **dimension** die vierte Dimension; **the** ~ **estate** die Presse. **2** n (fraction) Viertel nt; (in series) Vierte(r, s). **to drive in** ~ im vierten Gang fahren; **we need a** ~ **for our game of bridge** wir brauchen noch einen vierten zum Bridge; see also sixth.

fourthly ['fɔːθlɪ] adv viertens.

four: ~**-way** adj zu viert; valve Vierwege-; ~**-wheel drive** n Vierradantrieb m.

fowl [faul] **1** n **(a)** (poultry) Geflügel nt; (one bird) Huhn nt; Gans f; Truthahn m etc. **to keep** ~ Hühner etc halten; roast ~ (Cook) Brathuhn nt. **(b)** **the** ~**s of the air** (liter) die Vögel des Himmels. **2** vi (also **to go** ~**ing**) auf Vogeljagd gehen.

fowling piece ['faulɪŋpiːs] n Schrotflinte f.

fowl pest n Hühnerpest f.

fox [fɒks] **1** n **(a)** (lit, fig) Fuchs m. **he's a sly** ~ (fig) er ist ein schlauer Fuchs. **(b)** (~ fur) Fuchs(pelz) m. **2** vt (deceive) täuschen, reinlegen (inf); (bewilder) verblüffen. **that's** ~**ed you, hasn't it?** da bist du baff, was? (inf).

fox: ~ **cub** n Fuchsjunge(s) nt, Fuchswelpe m; ~**glove** n (Bot) Fingerhut m; ~**-hole** n (a) Fuchsbau m; (b) (Mil) Schützengraben m, Schützenloch nt; ~**hound** n Fuchshund m; ~**-hunt 1** n Fuchsjagd f; **2** vi auf (die) Fuchsjagd gehen; ~**-hunting** n Fuchsjagd f; **to go** ~**-hunting** auf die or zur Fuchsjagd gehen; ~ **terrier** n Foxterrier m; ~**trot** n Foxtrott m.

foxy ['fɒksɪ] adj (+er) (wily) listig, pfiffig, verschlagen.

foyer ['fɔɪeɪ] n (in theatre) Foyer nt; (in hotel also) Empfangshalle f; esp US: in apartment house) Diele f.

Fr abbr of **(a)** Father. **(b)** Friar.

fracas ['frækaː] n Aufruhr, Tumult m.

fraction ['frækʃən] n **(a)** (Math) Bruch m. **(b)** (fig) Bruchteil m. **a** ~ **better/shorter** (um) eine Spur besser/kürzer; **move it just a** ~ verrücke es (um) eine Spur; **for a** ~ **of a second** einen Augenblick lang; **it missed me by a** ~ **of an inch** es verfehlte mich um Haaresbreite; **she only moved it a** ~ **of an inch** sie verrückte es nur um eine Spur. **(c)** (Eccl) Brechen nt des Brotes.

fractional ['frækʃənl] adj **(a)** (Math) Bruch-; (fig) geringfügig. ~ **part** Bruchteil m. **(b)** (Chem) distillation fraktioniert.

fractious ['frækʃəs] adj verdrießlich, mürrisch; child aufsässig.

fractiousness ['frækʃəsnɪs] n see adj Verdrießlichkeit f; Aufsässigkeit f.

fracture ['fræktʃəʳ] **1** n Bruch m; (Med also) Fraktur f (spec). **2** vti brechen. **he has or has broken his shoulder** er hat sich (dat) die Schulter gebrochen; ~**d skull** Schädelbruch m.

fragile ['frædʒaɪl] adj china, glass zerbrechlich; butterfly's wing also, material, plant, leaf, complexion zart; (through age) brüchig; (fig) person (in health) gebrechlich; health anfällig; self-confidence, ego labil, wackelig (inf). "~, **handle with care**" „Vorsicht, zerbrechlich"; **he's feeling a bit** ~ **this morning** (inf) er fühlt sich heute morgen ein bißchen delikat.

fragility [frə'dʒɪlɪtɪ] n see adj Zerbrechlichkeit f; Zartheit f; Brüchigkeit f; Gebrechlichkeit f; Anfälligkeit f; Labilität, Wackeligkeit (inf) f.

fragment ['frægmənt] **1** n **(a)** Bruchstück nt; (of china, glass) Scherbe f; (of shell) Stückchen nt; (of paper, letter) Schnipsel

m; *(of programme, opera etc)* Bruchteil *m*. he smashed it to ~s er schlug es in Stücke; ~s of conversation Gesprächsfetzen *pl*.
  (b) *(esp Liter, Mus: unfinished work)* Fragment *nt*.
  2 [fræg'ment] *vi (rock, glass)* (zer)brechen, in Stücke brechen; *(fig) (hopes)* sich zerschlagen; *(society)* zerfallen.
  3 *vt rock, glass* in Stücke brechen; *(with hammer etc)* in Stücke schlagen; *(fig) society, hopes* zerschlagen.
fragmentary ['frægmentəri] *adj (lit, fig)* fragmentarisch, bruchstückhaft.
fragmentation [.frægmen'teiʃən] *n see vb* Zerbrechen *nt*; Zerschlagung *f*. ~ **bomb** Splitterbombe *f*.
fragmented [fræg'mentid] *adj* bruchstückhaft; *(broken up)* unzusammenhängend, ohne Zusammenhang.
fragrance ['freigrəns] *n* Duft, Wohlgeruch *m*.
fragrant ['freigrənt] *adj* duftend, wohlriechend; *(fig liter)* memories köstlich. ~ **smell** Duft *m*.
frail [freil] *adj* (+er) zart; *dried flowers, butterfly's wing, appearance also, old lady* zerbrechlich; *health also* anfällig; *old lace, old book* brüchig; *(fig) flesh, hope* schwach.
frailty ['freilti] *n see adj* Zartheit *f*; Zerbrechlichkeit *f*; Anfälligkeit *f*; Brüchigkeit *f*; Schwäche *f*. ~, **thy name is woman** Schwachheit, dein Name ist Weib.
frame [freim] **1** *n* **(a)** *(basic structure, border of picture)* Rahmen *m*; *(of building)* (Grund)gerippe *nt*; *(of ship)* Gerippe *nt*; *(Typ)* Setzregal *nt*; *(Hort)* Mistbeet, Frühbeet *nt*; *(of spectacles: also* ~s) Gestell *nt*; *(Billiards)* *(single game)* Spiel *nt*; *(triangle)* Rahmen *m*.
  (b) *(of human, animal)* Gestalt *f*. her ~ was shaken by sobs ihr Körper wurde von Schluchzen geschüttelt.
  (c) ~ **of mind** *(mental state)* Verfassung *f*; *(mood)* Stimmung, Laune *f*; in a cheerful ~ of mind in fröhlicher Stimmung or Laune; I am not in the right ~ of mind for singing ich bin nicht in der (richtigen) Laune or Stimmung zum Singen.
  (d) *(fig: framework, system)* grundlegende Struktur. ~ of reference *(lit, fig)* Bezugssystem *nt*; within the ~ of ... im Rahmen (+gen) ...
  (e) *(Film, Phot)* (Einzel)bild *nt*; *(in comic strip)* Bild(chen) *nt*.
  (f) *(TV)* Abtastbild, Rasterbild *nt*.
  (g) *(Telec, Computers)* Impulsfolge, Impulskette *f*.
  2 *vt* **(a)** *picture* rahmen; *(fig) face etc* ein- or umrahmen. he appeared ~d in the door er erschien im Türrahmen.
  (b) *(draw up, construct) constitution, law, plan* entwerfen; *idea* entwickeln; *(express) answer, excuse* formulieren; *sentence* bilden; *words* bilden, formen.
  (c) *(sl: incriminate falsely)* he said he had been ~d er sagte, man habe ihm die Sache angehängt *(inf)*.
  3 *vi (develop)* sich entwickeln. his plans are framing well/badly seine Pläne machen gute/keine Fortschritte *pl*.
frame-house ['freimhaus] *n* Holzhaus, Haus *nt* mit Holzrahmen.
framer ['freimə^r] *n* (Bilder)rahmer(in *f*) *m*.
frame: ~ **rucksack** *n* Rucksack *m* mit Traggestell; ~-**saw** *n* Bügelsäge *f*; ~-**up** *n (inf)* Komplott *nt*; ~**work** *n (lit)* Grundgerüst *nt*; *(fig) (of essay, novel etc also)* Gerippe *nt*; *(of society, government etc)* grundlegende Struktur; within the ~**work of** ... im Rahmen (+gen) ...; **outside the** ~**work of** ... außerhalb des Rahmens (+gen) ...
franc [fræŋk] *n* Franc *m*.
France [frɑːns] *n* Frankreich *nt*.
franchise ['fræntʃaiz] *n (Pol)* Wahlrecht *nt*; *(Comm)* Konzession *f*.
Francis ['frɑːnsis] *n* Franz *m*. **St** ~ **of Assisi** der heilige Franziskus von Assisi.
Franciscan [fræn'siskən] **1** *n* Franziskaner *m*. **2** *adj* Franziskaner-.
Franco- ['fræŋkəu-] *in cpds* Französisch-; ~-**German** *adj* deutsch-französisch.
Franconia [fræŋ'kəuniə] *n* Franken *nt*.
Franconian [fræŋ'kəuniən] **1** *n (person)* Franke *m*, Fränkin *f*; *(dialect)* Fränkisch *nt*. **2** *adj* fränkisch.
franco-: ~**phile** *n* he is a ~phile er ist frankophil; ~**phobe** *n* Franzosenfeind *m*; ~**phone** *adj* französischsprechend; **the F**~-**Prussian War** der Deutsch-Französische Krieg.
frangipane ['frændʒipein], **frangipani** [.frændʒi'pæni] *n* *(shrub)* Roter Jasmin(baum); *(perfume)* Jasminparfüm *nt*.
Franglais ['frɑ̃ːŋglei] *n* Französisch *nt* mit vielen englischen Ausdrücken.
Frank [fræŋk] *n (Hist)* Franke *m*.
frank¹ [fræŋk] *adj* (+er) offen; *opinion also* ehrlich; *desire, distaste, dislike* unverhohlen. to be ~ **with sb** mit jdm offen sein, zu jdm ehrlich sein; he wasn't very ~ about it er äußerte sich nicht sehr offen dazu; to be (perfectly) ~ ehrlich gesagt.
frank² *vt letter* frankieren; *(postmark, cancel)* stamp, letter stempeln.
frankfurter ['fræŋkfɜːtə^r] *n (sausage)* Frankfurter (Würstchen) *nt*.
frankincense ['fræŋkinsens] *n* Weihrauch *m*.
franking-machine ['fræŋkiŋmə'ʃiːn] *n* Frankiermaschine *f*.
Frankish ['fræŋkiʃ] **1** *adj* fränkisch. **2** *n (Ling)* Fränkisch *nt*.
franklin ['fræŋklin] *n (Hist)* Freisasse *m*.
frankly ['fræŋkli] *adv* offen; *(to tell the truth)* ehrlich gesagt.
frankness ['fræŋknis] *n see adj* Offenheit *f*; Ehrlichkeit *f*; Unverhohlenheit *f*.
frantic ['fræntik] *adj effort, cry, scream* verzweifelt; *activity* fiebrig, rasend; *agitation* hell, höchste(r, s); *desire* übersteigert; *person* außer Fassung, außer sich. ~ **with pain/worry** außer sich or rasend vor Schmerzen/außer sich vor Sorge(n); to **go** ~ außer sich geraten; *(with worry)* am Rande der Verzweiflung sein; to **drive sb** ~ jdn zur Verzweiflung treiben, jdn wahnsinnig machen; he was **driven** ~ **by anxiety** er war außer sich vor Sorge.

frantically ['fræntikəli] *adv try, scream* verzweifelt; *gesticulate, rush around* wild, wie wildgeworden *(inf)*; *busy, worried* rasend; *(inf: terribly)* rasend, furchtbar.
frappé ['fræpei] *n* Frappé *nt*.
fraternal [frə'tɜːnl] *adj* brüderlich. ~ **twins** zweieiige Zwillinge *pl*.
fraternity [frə'tɜːniti] *n* **(a)** *no pl* Brüderlichkeit *f*. **(b)** *(community)* Vereinigung, Zunft *f*; *(Eccl)* Bruderschaft *f*; *(US Univ)* Verbindung *f*. the **legal/medical/teaching** ~ die Juristen *pl*/Mediziner *pl*/Lehrer *pl*.
fraternization [.frætənai'zeiʃən] *n* (freundschaftlicher) Umgang, Verbrüderung *f (pej)*; *(Mil also)* Fraternisieren *nt*.
fraternize ['frætənaiz] *vi* (freundschaftlichen) Umgang haben; *(Mil also)* fraternisieren.
fratricide ['frætrisaid] *n* Brudermord *m*; *(person)* Brudermörder(in *f*) *m*.
fraud [frɔːd] *n* **(a)** *(no pl: trickery)* Betrug *m*; *(trick also)* Schwindel *m*. ~s Betrügereien, Schwindeleien *pl*; ~ **squad** Betrugsdezernat *nt*.
  (b) *(fraudulent person)* Betrüger(in *f*), Schwindler(in *f*) *m*; *(feigning illness)* Simulant(in *f*) *m*; *(fraudulent thing)* (reiner) Schwindel, fauler Zauber *(inf)*. you're not really angry, you big ~ du bist ja gar nicht wütend, du tust ja nur so; the **whole thing was a** ~ das ganze war (ein einziger) Schwindel or reiner Schwindel; to **obtain sth by** ~ sich *(dat)* etw erschwindeln.
fraudulence ['frɔːdjuləns], **fraudulency** ['frɔːdjulənsi] *n* Betrügerei *f*; *(of action)* betrügerische Art.
fraudulent ['frɔːdjulənt] *adj* betrügerisch.
fraught [frɔːt] *adj* geladen *(with mit)*. ~ **with danger** gefahrvoll; ~ **with hatred** haßerfüllt; ~ **with meaning** bedeutungsvoll or -schwer; ~ **with tension** spannungsgeladen; the **situation/atmosphere was a bit** ~ *(inf)* die Situation/Atmosphäre war ein bißchen gespannt.
fray¹ [frei] *n* Schlägerei *f*; *(Mil)* Kampf *m*. **ready for the** ~ *(lit, fig)* kampfbereit, zum Kampf bereit; to **be eager for the** ~ *(lit, fig)* kampflustig sein; to **enter the** ~ *(lit)* sich in den Kampf stürzen; *(fig)* sich in den Kampf or Streit einschalten.
fray² **1** *vt cloth* ausfransen; *cuff, rope* durchscheuern. **2** *vi (cloth)* (aus)fransen; *(cuff, trouser turn-up, rope)* sich durchscheuern. **tempers began to** ~ die Gemüter begannen sich zu erhitzen or zu erregen.
frayed [freid] *adj (fig)* gereizt, angespannt. **my nerves are quite** ~ ich bin mit den Nerven runter *(inf)* or am Ende *(inf)*; **tempers were** ~ die Gemüter waren angespannt or erhitzt.
frazzle ['fræzl] **1** *n (inf)* **worn to a** ~ *(exhausted)* am Boden zerstört *(inf)*, völlig kaputt *(inf)*; **burnt to a** ~ *(toast, meat)* völlig verkohlt; *(sunburnt)* von der Sonne total verbrannt. **2** *vt (US inf)* **(a)** *(fray)* ausfransen. **(b)** *(fig: tire)* völlig erschöpfen or ermüden.
freak [friːk] **1** *n* **(a)** *(abnormal plant)* Mißbildung *f*; *(person, animal also)* Mißgeburt *f*. ~ **of nature** Laune *f* der Natur.
  (b) *(abnormal event)* außergewöhnlicher Zufall; *(snowstorm etc)* Anomalie *f*. ~ **of fortune** Laune *f* des Zufalls.
  (c) *(sl: hippy)* ausgeflippter Typ *(sl)*. he's an **acid** ~ er ist ein Säurekopf *m (inf)*, er nimmt LSD.
  (d) *(sl)* **jazz** ~ Jazzfan *m*; **movie** ~ Kinofan *m*; **health** ~ Gesundheitsapostel *m (inf)*.
  (e) *(inf: weird person)* Irre(r) *mf*. he **looked at me as though I was some sort of** ~ er sah mich an, als ob ich vom Mond wäre.
  2 *adj weather, conditions* anormal, abnorm; *error* verrückt; *(Statistics) values* extrem; *victory* Überraschungs-.
♦freak out *vi (sl)* ausflippen *(sl)*; *(of society also)* aussteigen.
freakish ['friːkiʃ] *adj* **(a)** *see* **freak 2**. **(b)** *(changeable)* weather verrückt *(inf)*, launisch, unberechenbar; *person* (aus)geflippt *(sl)*; *hairstyle, idea* verrückt *(inf)*, irre *(inf)*.
freak: ~-**out** *n (sl)* *(party)* Haschparty *f (inf)*, *(drug trip)* (Wahnsinns)trip *m (sl)*; ~ **show** *n* Monstrositätenschau *f*.
freaky ['friːki] *adj* (+er) *(sl)* irre *(sl)*.
freckle ['frekl] *n* Sommersprosse *f*.
freckled ['frekld], **freckly** ['frekli] *adj* sommersprossig.
Frederick ['fredrik] *n* Friedrich *m*.
free [friː] **1** *adj* (+er) **(a)** *(at liberty, unrestricted)* person, animal, state, activity, translation, choice frei. to **set a prisoner** ~ einen Gefangenen freilassen or auf freien Fuß setzen; to **go** ~ *(not be imprisoned)* frei ausgehen; *(be set free)* freigelassen werden; he **is** ~ to **go es steht ihm frei zu gehen; the **fishing is** ~ here diese Stelle hier ist zum Fischen freigegeben; you're ~ to **choose** die Wahl steht Ihnen frei; you're ~ to **come too/to ask** him Sie können ruhig auch kommen/Sie können ihn ruhig fragen; you're ~ to **refuse** Sie können auch ablehnen; you're ~ to **go now/decide** Sie können jetzt gehen(, wenn Sie wollen)/Sie können das selbst entscheiden; I'm **not** ~ to **do it es steht mir nicht frei, es zu tun; do **feel** ~ to **help yourself** nehmen Sie sich ruhig; **feel** ~! *(inf)* bitte, gerne!; to **give sb a** ~ **hand** jdm freie Hand lassen; he **left one end of the string** ~ er ließ ein Ende des Bindfadens lose; his **arms were left** ~ *(not tied)* seine Arme waren frei(gelassen); ~ **and easy** ungezwungen.
  (b) (+prep) ~ **from pain/worry** schmerzfrei/sorgenfrei or -los; ~ **from blame/responsibility** frei von Schuld/Verantwortung; ~ **of sth** frei von etw; we **chose a spot** ~ of **tourists/flies** wir suchten uns *(dat)* einen Platz ohne Touristen/Fliegen; **in two hours we were** ~ of **the city** nach zwei Stunden hatten wir die Stadt hinter uns.
  (c) *(costing nothing)* kostenlos, Gratis-; *ticket also* frei, Frei-; *(Comm)* gratis. it's ~ das kostet nichts; **admission** ~ Eintritt frei; to **get sth** ~ umsonst bekommen; we **got it** ~ or **for** ~ *(inf)* wir kamen umsonst rein; they'll **send it** ~ **on request** sie schicken es gratis or kostenlos auf Anfrage; ~, **gratis and for nothing** gratis und umsonst; I **can tell you that for** ~ *(inf)* das kann ich dir gratis sagen; ~ **delivery** (porto)freier Versand; ~ **gift** (Gratis)geschenk *nt*; ~ **list** *(Theat)* Liste *f* der Empfänger

von Freikarten; ~ **sample** Gratisprobe f; ~ **alongside ship** (Comm) franko Kai; ~ **on board** (Comm) frei Schiff.

(d) (not occupied) room, seat, hour, person frei. **there are two** ~ **rooms** left es sind noch zwei Zimmer frei; **I wasn't able to get** ~ **earlier** ich konnte mich nicht eher freimachen; **to have one's hands** ~ (lit) die Hände frei haben; (fig: have no work to do) nichts zu tun haben; **if you've got a** ~ **hand could you carry this?** wenn du eine Hand frei hast, kannst du mir das tragen?

(e) (lavish, profuse) großzügig, freigebig; (licentious, improper) language, behaviour frei, lose; (over-familiar) plump-vertraulich. **to be** ~ **with one's money** großzügig mit seinem Geld umgehen; **to make** ~ **with other people's property** sich großzügig anderer Leute Sachen (gen) bedienen.

2 vt prisoner (release) freilassen; (help escape) befreien; caged animal freilassen; nation befreien; (untie) person losbinden; knot, tangle (auf)lösen; pipe freimachen; seized brakes, rusty screw, caught fabric lösen. **to** ~ **sb from anxiety** jdn von seiner Angst befreien; **to** ~ **oneself from sth** sich von etw frei machen.

-free adj suf -frei.

free: ~ **association** n freie Assoziation; ~**board** n Freibord nt; ~**booter** n Freibeuter m; ~**born** adj frei geboren; F~ **Church** n Freikirche f; ~ **collective bargaining** n Tarifautonomie f.

freedman ['fri:dmæn] n, pl **-men** [-mən] befreiter or freigelassener Sklave.

freedom ['fri:dəm] n **(a)** Freiheit f. ~ **of action/speech/worship** Handlungs-/Rede-/Religionsfreiheit f; ~ **of the press** Pressefreiheit f; ~ **of the seas** Freiheit f der Meere; **to give sb** ~ **to do as he wishes** jdm (völlige) Freiheit lassen, zu tun, was er will; ~ **from sth** Freiheit von etw.

(b) (frankness) Offenheit f; (over-familiarity) plumpe (inf) or zu große Vertraulichkeit. **to speak with** ~ offen reden.

(c) (permission to use freely) the ~ **of the city** die (Ehren)bürgerrechte pl; **to give sb the** ~ **of one's house** jdm sein Haus zur freien Verfügung stellen.

freedom fighter n Freiheitskämpfer(in f) m.

free: ~ **elections** npl freie Wahlen pl; ~ **enterprise** n freies Unternehmertum; ~**fall** 1 n freier Fall; in ~**-fall** (Space) in freiem Fall; **2** vi frei fallen; (fight) n allgemeine Schlägerei; ~-**for-all** n Gerangel nt (inf); (fight) Schlägerei f; **wages** ~-**for-all** Tarifgerangel nt; **to stop the situation becoming a** ~**-for-all** es unterbinden, daß jeder mitmischen kann; ~**-hand** 1 adj drawing Freihand-; **2** adv freihand, aus der Hand; ~**-handed** adj (generous) großzügig, freigebig; ~**hold** n **to own sth** ~**hold** etw besitzen; **the house** ~**hold** the ~**hold on the house** er hat das Haus gekauft; ~**hold property** n (freier) Grundbesitz; ~ **house** n (Brit) Wirtshaus, das nicht an eine bestimmte Brauerei gebunden ist; ~ **kick** n (Sport) Freistoß m; ~ **labour** n (non-unionized) nicht organisierte Arbeiter(schaft f) pl; ~**-lance** 1 n Freiberufler(in f) m, freischaffender or freier Journalist/Schriftsteller etc, freischaffende or freie Journalistin/Schriftstellerin etc; (with particular firm) freier Mitarbeiter, freie Mitarbeiterin; **2** adj journalist, designer etc frei(schaffend), freiberuflich tätig; **3** adv freiberuflich; **to work** ~**lance** see vi; **4** vi freiberuflich tätig sein, frei arbeiten; (with particular firm) als freier Mitarbeiter/als freie Mitarbeiterin tätig sein; ~**load** vi (US inf) schmarotzen, nassauern (inf) (on bei); ~**loader** n (US inf) Schmarotzer(in f), Nassauer (inf) m; ~ **love** n freie Liebe.

freely ['fri:lɪ] adv **(a)** (lavishly) give reichlich, großzügig. **he spends his money** ~ er gibt sein Geld mit vollen Händen aus. **(b)** (unrestrictedly) speak frei; move ungehindert.

free: ~**man** n **(a)** (not a slave) Freie(r) m; **(b)** ~**man of a city** Ehrenbürger m einer Stadt; ~**mason** n Freimaurer m; ~**masonry** n Freimaurerei f; ~ **port** n Freihafen m; ~**-range** adj (Brit) chicken Farmhof-; eggs Land-.

freesia ['fri:zɪə] n (Bot) Freesie f.

free: ~ **speech** n Redefreiheit f; ~**-spoken** adj freimütig; ~**standing** adj frei stehend; ~**style** 1 n Kür f; (Swimming) Freistil m; **the 200 metres** ~**style** die 200 Meter Freistil; **2** attr Kür-; swimming, wrestling Freistil-; ~**thinker** n Freidenker, Freigeist m; ~**thinking** adj person freidenkerisch, freigeistig; ~**-trade** n Freihandel m; ~**-trader** n Freihändler m; ~ **verse** n freie Rythmen pl; ~**way** n (US) Autobahn f; ~**wheel** 1 vi im Freilauf fahren; **2** n Freilauf m; ~ **will** n (Philos) freier Wille; **he did it of his own** ~ **will** er hat es aus freien Stücken getan; **the F**~ **World** n die freie Welt.

freeze [fri:z] (vb: pret **froze**, ptp **frozen**) **1** vi **(a)** (Met) frieren; (water, liquids) gefrieren; (lakes, rivers) zufrieren; (pipes) einfrieren. **it's freezing hard** es herrscht starker Frost, **es friert stark** (inf); **it'll** ~ **hard tonight** es wird heute nacht starken Frost geben; **frozen solid** völlig gefroren/zugefroren/eingefroren; **I am/my hands are freezing** mir ist/meine Hände sind eiskalt; **to** ~ **to death** (lit) erfrieren; (fig) sich zu Tode frieren; see **frozen**.

(b) (fig) (blood) erstarren, gerinnen; (heart) aussetzen; (smile) erstarren, gefrieren. **it made my blood** ~ es ließ mir das Blut in den Adern gerinnen.

(c) (keep still) in der Bewegung verharren or erstarren. **he froze in his tracks** er blieb wie angewurzelt stehen; ~! keine Bewegung!

(d) (Cook) meat ~s well Fleisch läßt sich gut einfrieren.

2 vt **(a)** water gefrieren; (Med, Cook) einfrieren. **(b)** (Econ) assets festlegen; credit, wages einfrieren, stoppen; (stop) film anhalten. **(c)** (Med) wound vereisen. **(d)** (fig) **to** ~ **sb with a look** jdm einen eisigen Blick zuwerfen.

3 n **(a)** (Met) Frost m. **the big** ~ der harte Frost. **(b)** (Econ) Stopp m. **a wages** ~, **a** ~ **on wages** ein Lohnstopp m.

♦**freeze off** vt sep die kalte Schulter zeigen (+dat).

♦**freeze onto** vi +prep obj (US inf) **to** ~ ~ **sb** sich wie eine Klette an jdn hängen or heften.

♦**freeze out** vt sep (US inf) person herausekeln (inf).

♦**freeze over** vi (lake, river) überfrieren; (windscreen, windows) vereisen.

♦**freeze up 1** vi zufrieren; (lock, car door etc also, pipes) einfrieren; (windscreen, windows) vereisen. **2** vt sep **we were frozen** ~ **last winter** letztes Jahr waren alle unsere Leitungen eingefroren.

freeze-dry ['fri:zdraɪ] vt gefriertrocknen.

freezer ['fri:zə'] n (Tief)gefriertruhe f; (upright) Gefrierschrank m; (ice compartment of fridge) Eisfach, (Tief)kühlfach, Gefrierfach nt.

freeze-up ['fri:zʌp] n **(a)** (Met) Dauerfrost m. **(b)** (esp US: of lakes, rivers etc) during the ~ **a lot of birds perish während Seen und Flüsse zugefroren sind, kommen viele Vögel ums Leben.

freezing ['fri:zɪŋ] **1** adj weather eiskalt. **2** n **(a)** (Cook) Einfrieren nt. **(b)** (~ **point**) **below** ~ unter Null, unter dem Gefrierpunkt.

freezing point n Gefrierpunkt m. **below** ~ unter Null, unter dem Gefrierpunkt.

freight [freɪt] **1** n (goods transported) Fracht(gut nt) f; (charge) Frachtkosten pl, Fracht(gebühr) f. ~ **is less expensive than express** Frachtgut ist billiger als Expressgut; **to send sth** ~ etw als Frachtgut verschicken; ~ **charges** Frachtkosten pl. **2** vt **(a)** (transport) goods verfrachten. **(b)** (load) boat beladen.

freightage ['freɪtdʒ] n (charge) Fracht(gebühr) f.

freight car n (US Rail) Güterwagen m.

freighter ['freɪtə'] n (Naut) Frachter m, Frachtschiff nt; (Aviat) Frachtflugzeug nt.

freight: ~ **plane** n Frachtflugzeug nt; ~ **train** n Güterzug m.

French [frentʃ] **1** adj französisch. **the** ~ **people** die Franzosen pl, das französische Volk. **2** n **(a)** the ~ pl die Franzosen pl. **(b)** (language) Französisch nt; see also **English**.

French: ~ **bean** n grüne Bohne; ~**-Canadian** 1 adj frankokanadisch, kanadisch-französisch; **2** n (a) Frankokanadier(in f) m; **(b)** (language) kanadisches Französisch; ~ **chalk** n Schneiderkreide f; ~ **doors** npl (US) see ~ **window(s)**; ~ **dressing** n Salatsoße, Vinaigrette f; ~ **fried potatoes**, ~ **fries** npl Pommes frites pl; ~ **horn** n (Mus) (Wald)horn nt.

frenchify ['frentʃɪfaɪ] vt französisieren; clothes, restaurant also auf französisch machen (inf). **frenchified ways** französisierte or welsche (pej) Manieren.

French: ~ **kiss** n Zungenkuß m; ~ **leave** n **to take** ~ **leave** sich (auf) französisch empfehlen; ~ **letter** n (Brit inf) Pariser m (inf); ~ **loaf** n Baguette f; ~**man** n Franzose m; ~ **pleat** or **roll** n Damenfrisur, bei der das Haar seitlich zurückgekämmt und in einer länglichen Rolle aufgesteckt wird; ~ **polish** 1 n Möbelpolitur f mit Schellack; **2** vt lackieren; ~ **seam** n (Sew) französische Naht; ~ **stick** n Baguette f; ~ **toast** n nur auf einer Seite gerösteter Toast; (with egg) in Ei getunktes gebratenes Brot; ~ **window(s** pl) n Verandatür f; ~**woman** n Französin f.

frenetic [frə'netɪk] adj frenetisch, rasend.

frenzied ['frenzɪd] adj wahnsinnig; applause, activity rasend.

frenzy ['frenzɪ] n Raserei f, Rasen nt. **in a** ~ in heller or wilder Aufregung; **he worked himself/the audience up into a** ~ er steigerte sich in eine Raserei (hinein)/er brachte die Menge zur Raserei or zum Rasen; ~ **of delight** Freudentaumel m.

frequency ['fri:kwənsɪ] n Häufigkeit f; (Statistics also, Phys) Frequenz f. **high/low** ~ Hoch-/Niederfrequenz f.

frequency: ~ **band** n Frequenzband nt; ~ **distribution** n Häufigkeitsverteilung f; ~ **modulation** n Frequenzmodulation f.

frequent ['fri:kwənt] **1** adj häufig; objection, criticism häufig geäußert; practice landläufig. **it's quite a** ~ **occurrence/state of affairs** es kommt recht häufig vor; **he is a** ~ **visitor to our house** er kommt uns oft or häufig besuchen. **2** vt [frɪ'kwent] vt oft or häufig besuchen, frequentieren (geh).

frequenter [frɪ'kwentə'] n (of a house) häufig gesehener Gast; (of a pub) Stammgast m. **he's not a** ~ **of pubs** er geht nicht oft or regelmäßig ins Wirtshaus.

frequently ['fri:kwəntlɪ] adv oft, häufig. **I have** ~ **said** ... ich habe schon oft gesagt ...; **I don't go to the cinema very** ~ ich gehe nicht oft ins Kino.

fresco ['freskəu] n (technique) Freskomalerei f; (painting) Fresko(gemälde) nt.

fresh [freʃ] **1** adj (+er) **(a)** (newly made, not stale or dirty or tinned or tired etc) frisch. **that news isn't very** ~ **any more** diese Nachrichten sind auch nicht mehr gerade taufrisch (inf); **to keep one's clothes (looking)** ~ seine Kleidung sauber und ordentlich halten; **it's still** ~ **in my memory/mind** es ist mir noch frisch in Erinnerung or im Gedächtnis; ~ **water** (not salt) Süßwasser nt; **in the** ~ **air** an der frischen Luft; **let's have some** ~ **air in here** wir können wir hier mal lüften?; see **daisy**.

(b) (new, different, original) supplies, sheet of paper, arrival, ideas, approach, courage neu. **it needs a** ~ **coat of paint** das muß frisch gestrichen werden, das hat einen neuen Anstrich nötig; **to make a** ~ **start** einen neuen Anfang machen, neu anfangen; **to start a** ~ **job/life** eine neue Stelle antreten/ein neues Leben anfangen; **a** ~ **arrival** ein Neuankömmling m.

(c) (esp US: cheeky) frech, mopsig (inf), pampig (inf). **don't get** ~ **with me!** werd nicht frech!, komm mir bloß nicht frech!

(d) (cool) frisch. light breeze, becoming ~ **towards the evening** leichte, gegen Abend auffrischende Winde pl; ~ **breeze** (Met, Naut) frische Brise.

2 adv (+er) baked, picked etc frisch. ~ **from the oven** ofenfrisch, frisch aus dem Ofen; ~ **out of college** frisch von der Schule; ~ **off the presses** druckfrisch, frisch von der Presse; **to come** ~ **to sth** neu zu etw kommen; **we're** ~ **out of eggs** (sl)

uns sind die Eier ausgegangen; sorry, we're ~ out (sl) tut mir leid, davon ist leider nichts mehr da.
♦**fresh up** vtir (US) see **freshen up.**
freshen ['freʃn] 1 vi (wind) auffrischen; (weather, air) frisch werden. 2 vt shirt etc aufbügeln; bread aufbacken.
♦**freshen up** 1 vir to ~ (oneself) → (person) sich frischmachen. 2 vt sep (a) child, invalid etc frischmachen. that will ~ you → das wird Sie erfrischen. (b) see **freshen 2.**
fresher ['freʃə'] n (Brit Univ inf) Erstsemester nt (inf).
freshly ['freʃlı] adv frisch.
freshman ['freʃmən] n, pl -men [-mən] (US) see **fresher.**
freshness ['freʃnis] n (a) (of food, fruit, wind, dress etc) Frische f; (of approach also, of outlook) Neuheit f. (b) (esp US: cheekiness) Frechheit, Mopsigkeit (inf) f.
freshwater ['freʃwɔːtə'] adj attr Süßwasser-.
fret¹ [fret] 1 vi (a) (become anxious) sich (dat) Sorgen machen; (baby) unruhig sein. don't ~ beruhige dich; the child is ~ting for his mother das Kind jammert nach seiner Mutter.
  (b) (horse) to ~ (at the bit) sich (am Biß) reiben or scheuern. 2 vt nagen an (+dat).
  3 vr sich (dat) Sorgen machen, sich aufregen.
  4 to be in a ~ sich (dat) Sorgen machen, in Sorge sein.
fret² vt wood etc laubsägen.
fret³ n (on guitar etc) Bund m.
fretful ['fretful] adj (worried) besorgt, in Sorge; (peevish) child quengelig; baby unruhig.
fretfulness ['fretfulnis] n see adj Besorgtheit f; Quengeligkeit f; Unruhe f.
fret: ~ **saw** n Laubsäge f; ~**work** n (in wood) Laubsägearbeit f; (Archit) Mäander m.
Freudian ['frɔɪdɪən] 1 adj (Psych, fig) Freudsch attr, freudianisch. ~ **slip** Freudsche Fehlleistung, Freudscher Versprecher; very ~! was Freud wohl dazu sagen würde! 2 n Freudianer(in f) m.
Fri abbr of **Friday** Fr.
friable ['fraɪəbl] adj bröckelig, krümelig.
friableness ['fraɪəblnis] n Bröckeligkeit f, Krümeligkeit f.
friar ['fraɪə'] n Mönch m. F~ **John** Bruder John; **Black/Grey/ White F~s** Dominikaner/Franziskaner/Karmeliter pl.
friary ['fraɪərɪ] n Mönchskloster nt.
fricassee ['frɪkəsɪ] 1 n Frikassee nt. 2 vt zu Frikassee verarbeiten, frikassieren.
fricative ['frɪkətɪv] 1 adj Reibe-. ~ **consonant** Reibelaut m. 2 n Reibelaut m.
friction ['frɪkʃən] n (a) Reibung f; (Phys also) Friktion f. ~ **clutch** Friktionskupplung, Reibungskupplung f; ~ **tape** (US) Isolierband nt. (b) (fig) Reibung f, Reibereien pl. there is a lot of ~ between them sie reiben sich ständig aneinander.
Friday ['fraɪdɪ] n Freitag m; see also **Tuesday.**
fridge [frɪdʒ] n (Brit) Eisschrank, Kühlschrank m.
fried [fraɪd] adj Brat-; egg Spiegel-.
friend [frend] n (a) Freund(in f) m; (less intimate) Bekannte(r) mf. to make ~s with sb sich mit jdm anfreunden, mit jdm Freundschaft schließen; to make a ~ of sb sich (dat) jdn zum Freund machen; he makes ~s easily er findet leicht Freunde; a ~ of mine ein Freund/eine Freundin von mir; ein Bekannter/eine Bekannte; he's no ~ of mine er ist nicht mein Freund; to be ~s with sb mit jdm befreundet sein, jds Freund(in) sein; be a ~ sei so lieb; I'm not ~s with you any more (inf) du bist nicht mehr mein Freund/meine Freundin; we're just (good) ~s da ist nichts, wir sind nur gut befreundet; my honourable (Parl)/learned (Jur) ~ mein verehrter (Herr) Kollege; a ~ at court (fig) ein einflußreicher Freund; he has been a true ~ to us er ist uns immer ein guter Freund gewesen; a ~ in need is a ~ indeed (Prov) Freunde in der Not gehen tausend auf ein Lot (Prov).
  (b) (helper, supporter) Freund m. ~ **of the poor** Helfer or Freund der Armen; ~ **of the arts** Förderer der schönen Künste.
  (c) (Rel) F~ Quäker(in f) m; **Society of F~s** Quäker pl.
friendless ['frendlis] adj ohne Freunde.
friendliness ['frendlinis] n see adj Freundlichkeit f; Freundschaftlichkeit f.
friendly ['frendlı] 1 adj (+er) person, smile, welcome freundlich; attitude also, advice, feelings freundschaftlich; breeze angenehm. to be ~ to sb zu jdm freundlich sein; to be ~ with sb mit jdm befreundet sein; that wasn't a very ~ thing to do das war nicht gerade sehr freundlich; F~ **Society** (Brit) Versicherungsverein m auf Gegenseitigkeit, Hilfskasse f.
  (b) (Sport) match Freundschafts-.
  2 n (Sport) Freundschaftsspiel nt.
Friendly Islands npl Freundschafts-Inseln pl.
friendship ['frendʃɪp] n Freundschaft f.
Friesian ['friːʒən] 1 adj (a) friesisch. ~ **Islands** Friesische Inseln pl. (b) cattle holstein-friesisch. 2 n (a) Friese m, Friesin f. (b) (language) Friesisch nt. (c) (cow) Holstein-Friese m/-Friesin f.
Friesland ['friːslənd] n Friesland nt.
frieze¹ [friːz] n (Archit) (picture) Fries m; (thin band) Zierstreifen m.
freize² [friːz] n (Tex) Fries m.
frigate ['frɪgɪt] n (Naut) Fregatte f.
frigging ['frɪgɪŋ] adj, adv (sl) see **fucking.**
fright [fraɪt] n (a) Schreck(en) m. to get or have a ~ sich erschrecken, einen Schreck bekommen; to give sb a ~ jdm einen Schreck(en) einjagen, jdn erschrecken; to take ~ es mit der Angst zu tun bekommen.
  (b) (inf: person) Vogelscheuche (inf) f. she looks a ~ in that hat mit dem Hut sieht sie verboten or zum Fürchten aus (inf).
frighten ['fraɪtn] 1 vt (give a sudden fright) erschrecken, Angst einjagen (+dat); (make scared) Angst machen (+dat), Angst einjagen (+dat); (idea, thought) ängstigen, Angst or Furcht

einflößen (+dat). I'm not easily ~ed ich fürchte mich nicht so schnell, ich habe nicht so schnell Angst; (with threats etc) so schnell kann man mir keine Angst machen; ... he said in a ~ed voice ... sagte er mit angsterfüllter Stimme; to be ~ed by sth vor etw (dat) erschrecken; to be ~ed of sth vor etw (dat) Angst haben; don't be ~ed (hab) keine Angst; to be ~ed of doing sth Angst davor haben or sich davor fürchten, etw zu tun; I was ~ed out of my wits/to death ich war zu Tode erschrocken.
  2 vi she doesn't ~ easily so leicht fürchtet sie sich nicht; (with threats etc) so leicht kann man ihr keine Angst machen.
♦**frighten away** or **off** vt sep abschrecken; (deliberately) verscheuchen.
frightening ['fraɪtnɪŋ] adj furchterregend, schreckenerregend.
frighteningly ['fraɪtnɪŋlı] adv schrecklich, fürchterlich.
frightful ['fraɪtful] adj (lit, fig) schrecklich, furchtbar.
frightfulness ['fraɪtfulnis] n Schrecklichkeit, Furchtbarkeit f.
frigid ['frɪdʒɪd] adj manner, welcome kühl, frostig; (Physiol, Psych) frigid(e); (Geog) arktisch.
frigidity [frɪ'dʒɪdɪtɪ] n Kühle f; (Physiol, Psych) Frigidität f.
frill [frɪl] n (a) (on dress, shirt etc) Rüsche f; (on animal, bird) Kragen m; (round meat, on plant pot etc) Manschette f.
  (b) ~**s** pl (fig: ornaments) Kinkerlitzchen (inf), Verzierungen pl; **with all the** ~**s** mit allem Drum und Dran (inf); **a simple meal without any** ~**s** ein schlichtes Essen.
frilly ['frɪlı] adj (+er) mit Rüschen, Rüschen-; (fig) speech, style blumig.
fringe [frɪndʒ] 1 n (a) (on shawl) Fransenkante f, Fransen pl.
  (b) (Brit: hair) Pony(fransen pl) m.
  (c) (fig: periphery) Rand m. **on the** ~ **of the forest** am Waldrand; **there is a** ~ **of the Labour Party which** ... es gibt eine Randgruppe der Labour-Party, die ...; **to live on the** ~(s) **of society** am Rande der Gesellschaft leben; **the outer** ~**s of a town** die Randbezirke einer Stadt; see **lunatic.**
  2 vt mit Fransen versehen. ~**d with silk** mit Seidenfransen; **a lawn** ~**d with trees** ein von Bäumen umsäumtes Rasenstück.
fringe: ~ **benefits** npl zusätzliche Leistungen pl; ~ **group** n Randgruppe f.
frippery ['frɪpərɪ] n (pej) (cheap ornament) Flitter m, Kinkerlitzchen pl (inf); (on dress) Tand, Flitterkram (inf) m.
frisbee ® ['frɪzbɪ] n Frisbee ® nt.
Frisian ['frɪzɪən] adj, n see **Friesian 1** (a), **2** (a, b).
frisk [frɪsk] 1 vi (leap about) umhertollen. 2 vt suspect etc durchsuchen, filzen (inf).
friskiness ['frɪskɪnɪs] n Verspieltheit f.
frisky ['frɪskɪ] adj (+er) verspielt.
fritillary [frɪ'tɪlərɪ] n (butterfly) Perlmutterfalter m.
fritter¹ ['frɪtə'] vt (also ~ away) money, time vertun (inf), vergeuden, verplempern (inf).
fritter² n (Cook) Beignet m, Schmalzgebackenes nt no pl mit Füllung. **apple** ~ Apfel-Beignet m.
frivolity [frɪ'vɒlɪtɪ] n Frivolität f.
frivolous ['frɪvələs] adj frivol; person, life, remark also leichtsinnig, leichtfertig.
frivolously ['frɪvələslı] adv frivol; remark also leichtfertig.
frizz [frɪz] 1 vt hair kräuseln. 2 vi sich kräuseln, kraus werden.
frizzle ['frɪzl] 1 vi (sizzle) brutzeln. 2 vt bacon etc knusprig braten. **the meat was all** ~**d up** das Fleisch war ganz verbraten.
frizz(ly) ['frɪz(l)ɪ] adj (+er) hair kraus.
fro [frəʊ] adv see **to, to-ing** and **fro-ing.**
frock [frɒk] n Kleid nt; (of monk) Kutte f.
frock coat n Gehrock m.
frog¹ [frɒg] n (a) Frosch m. **to have a** ~ **in one's throat** einen Frosch im Hals haben. (b) F~ (Brit pej sl: French person) Franzmann m (inf).
frog² n (fastening) Paspelverschluß m.
frog: ~ **kick** n Beinschlag m beim Brustschwimmen; ~**man** n Froschmann m; ~**march** vt (Brit) (ab)schleppen (inf), (weg)schleifen; (carry) zu viert wegtragen; **they** ~**marched him in** sie schleppten ihn herein (inf); ~**spawn** n Froschlaich m.
frolic ['frɒlɪk] (vb: pret, ptp ~**ked**) 1 vi (also ~ **about** or **around**) umhertollen, umhertoben. 2 n (romp) Herumtollen, Herumtoben nt; (gaiety) Ausgelassenheit f; (prank) Jux, Scherz, Spaß m. **the children had a** ~ **on the lawn** die Kinder tobten or tollten auf dem Rasen herum.
frolicsome ['frɒlɪksəm] adj übermütig, ausgelassen.
from [frɒm] prep (a) (indicating starting place) von (+dat); (indicating place of origin) aus (+dat). **he/the train has come** ~ **London** er/der Zug ist von London gekommen; **he/this wine comes** or **is** ~ **Germany** er/dieser Wein kommt or ist aus Deutschland; **where has he come** ~ **today?** von wo ist er heute gekommen?; **where does he come** ~? woher or where ist er ~? woher kommt or stammt er?; **the train** ~ **Manchester** der Zug aus Manchester; **the train** ~ **Manchester to London** der Zug von Manchester nach London; ~ **London to Edinburgh** von London nach Edinburgh; ~ **house to house** von Haus zu Haus.
  (b) (indicating time) (in past) seit (+dat); (in future) ab (+dat), von (+dat) ... an. ~ **last week** until or **to yesterday** von letzter Woche bis gestern; ~ **1917** until or **to 1970** von 1917 bis 1970; ~ **tomorrow until Thursday** von morgen bis Donnerstag; ~ ... **on** ab ...; ~ **now on** von jetzt an, ab jetzt; ~ **then on** von da an; (in past also) seither; ~ **his childhood** von Kindheit an, klein auf; **he comes** ~ **time to time** er kommt von Zeit zu Zeit; **commencing as** ~ **the 6th May** vom 6. Mai an, ab (dem) 6. Mai.
  (c) (indicating distance) von (+dat) (... weg); (from town etc also) von (+dat) ... entfernt. **the house is 10 km** ~ **the coast** das Haus ist 10 km von der Küste entfernt; **to go away** ~ **home** von zu Haus weg- or fortgehen.
  (d) (indicating sender, giver) von (+dat). **tell him** ~ **me** richten Sie ihm von mir aus; **an invitation** ~ **the Smiths** eine Einladung von den Smiths; "~ ..." (on envelope, parcel) „Absender ...", „Abs. ...".

(e) (*indicating removal*) von (+*dat*); (*out of: from pocket, cupboard etc*) aus (+*dat*). **to take/grab** *etc* **sth ~ sb** jdm etw wegnehmen/wegreißen *etc*; **to steal sth ~ sb** jdm etw stehlen; **he took it ~ the top/middle/bottom of the pile** er nahm es oben vom Stapel/aus der Mitte des Stapels/unten vom Stapel weg.

(f) (*indicating source*) von (+*dat*); (*out of*) aus (+*dat*). **where did you get that ~?** wo hast du das her?, woher hast du das?; **I got that ~ the corner shop/the library/Kathy** ich habe das aus dem Laden an der Ecke/aus der Bücherei/von Kathy; **to drink ~ a stream/glass** aus einem Bach/Glas trinken; **quotation ~ Hamlet/the Bible/Shakespeare** Zitat *nt* aus Hamlet/aus der Bibel/nach Shakespeare; **translated ~ the English** aus dem Englischen übersetzt.

(g) (*modelled on*) nach (+*dat*). **painted ~ life** nach dem Leben gemalt; **~ a picture by Ruysdael** nach einem Gemälde von Ruysdael.

(h) (*indicating lowest amount*) ab (+*dat*). **~ £2/the age of 16** (upwards) ab £ 2/ab 16 Jahren (aufwärts); **dresses (ranging) ~ £20 to £30** Kleider *pl* zwischen £ 20 und £ 30; **there were ~ 10 to 15 people there** es waren zwischen 10 und 15 Leute da.

(i) (*indicating escape*) **he fled ~ the enemy** er floh vor dem Feind; **he got away ~ his pursuers** er entkam seinen Verfolgern; **he ran away ~ home** er rannte von zu Hause weg; **he escaped ~ prison** er entkam aus dem Gefängnis.

(j) (*indicating change*) **things went ~ bad to worse** es wurde immer schlimmer; **he went ~ office boy to director** er stieg vom Laufjungen zum Direktor auf; **a price increase ~ 1 mark to 1.50 marks** eine Preiserhöhung von 1 DM auf 1,50 DM; **~ log cabin to White House** aus der Blockhütte ins Weiße Haus.

(k) (*indicating difference*) **he is quite different ~ the others** er ist ganz anders als die andern; **to tell black ~ white** Schwarz und Weiß auseinanderhalten.

(l) (*because of, due to*) **to act ~ conviction** aus Überzeugung handeln; **to die ~ fatigue** an Erschöpfung sterben; **weak ~ hunger/tiredness** schwach vor Hunger/Müdigkeit.

(m) (*on the basis of*) **~ experience** aus Erfahrung; **to judge ~ appearances** nach dem Äußeren urteilen; **~ your point of view** von Ihrem Standpunkt aus (gesehen); **to conclude ~ the information** aus den Informationen einen Schluß ziehen, von den Informationen schließen; **~ what I heard** nach dem, was ich gehört habe; **~ what I can see** ... nach dem, was ich sehen kann, ...; **~ the look of things** ... (so) wie die Sache aussieht, ...

(n) (*in set phrases*) *see also other element to prevent/stop sb ~ doing sth* jdn daran hindern/davor zurückhalten, etw zu tun; **that's not far ~ the truth** das ist nicht allzu weit von der Wahrheit (entfernt); **he prevented me ~ coming** er hielt mich davon ab, zu kommen; **the news was kept ~ her** die Nachricht wurde von ihr ferngehalten; **to shelter ~ the rain** sich vor dem Regen unterstellen, vor dem Regen Zuflucht suchen.

(o) (+*adv*) von. **~ inside/underneath** von innen/unten.

(p) (+*prep*) **~ above** or **over/across sth** über etw (*acc*) hinweg; **~ beneath** or **underneath sth** unter etw (*dat*) hervor; **~ out of sth** aus etw heraus; **~ before his mother's death** aus der Zeit vor dem Tod seiner Mutter; **~ among the trees** zwischen den Bäumen hervor; **~ inside/outside the house** von drinnen/draußen; **~ beyond the grave** aus dem Jenseits.

frond [frɒnd] *n* (*of fern*) Farnwedel *m*; (*of palm*) Palmwedel *m*.

front [frʌnt] **1** *n* **(a)** (*forward side, exterior*) Vorderseite *f*; (*forward part, including interior*) Vorderteil *nt*; (*of house etc: façade*) Vorderfront, Stirnseite *f*; (*of shirt, dress*) Vorderteil *nt*; (*dickey*) Hemdbrust *f*; (*Theat: auditorium*) Zuschauerraum *m*. **in ~** vorne; (*in line, race etc also*) an der Spitze; **in ~ of sb/sth** vor jdm/etw; **at the ~ of** (*inside*) vorne in (+*dat*); (*outside*) vor (+*dat*); (*at the head of*) an der Spitze (+*gen*); **to be in ~** vorne sein; (*Sport*) vorn(e) or an der Spitze liegen; **look in ~ of you** blicken Sie nach vorne; **in ~ of you you see** ... vor sich (*dat*) sehen Sie ...; **a room in** or **at the ~ of the house** ein Zimmer vorne im Haus or auf der Vorderseite des Hauses or nach vorne heraus; **in** or **at the ~ of the train/class** vorne im Zug/Klassenzimmer; **he reached the ~ of the queue** er erreichte die Spitze der Schlange; **she spilt tea down the ~ of her dress** sie verschüttete Tee vorn über ihr Kleid.

(b) (*Mil, Pol, Met*) Front *f*. **he fell at the ~** er ist an der Front gefallen; **there was fighting on several ~s** es wurde an mehreren Fronten gekämpft; **they were attacked on all ~s** (*Mil*) sie wurden an allen Fronten angegriffen; (*fig*) sie wurden von allen Seiten angegriffen; **cold ~** (*Met*) Kalt(luft)front *f*; **we must present a common/united ~** wir müssen eine gemeinsame/geschlossene Front bieten or präsentieren; **on the wages ~** was die Löhne betrifft.

(c) (*Brit*) (*of sea*) Strandpromenade *f*; (*of lake*) Uferpromenade *f*.

(d) (*outward appearance*) Fassade *f*. **to put on a bold ~** eine tapfere Miene zur Schau stellen; **to preserve a calm ~** nach außen hin ruhig bleiben; **it's just a ~** das ist nur Fassade.

(e) (*cover for illicit activity*) Tarnung, Fassade *f*.

(f) (*US: figurehead of organization*) Strohmann *m*, Aushängeschild *nt*.

(g) *no pl* (*effrontery*) Stirn *f*. **to have the ~ to do sth** die Unverschämtheit or Frechheit besitzen, etw zu tun, die Stirn haben, etw zu tun.

(h) (*poet: brow, face*) Antlitz *nt* (*poet*).

2 *adv* **up ~** vorne; **to move up ~** nach vorne rücken; **to attack ~ and rear** von vorn und hinten angreifen; **eyes ~!** (*Mil*) Augen geradeaus!

3 *vi* **the house/windows ~ onto the street** die Häuser liegen/die Fenster gehen auf die Straße hinaus.

4 *adj* vorderste(r, s); **row, page** *also* erste(r, s); **tooth, wheel, room, plan, elevation, view** Vorder-; (*Phon*) *vowel* Vorderzungen-. **~ seat** Platz *m* in der ersten Reihe; (*Aut*) Vordersitz *m*; (*fig*) Logenplatz *m*; **~ garden** Vorgarten *m*;

---

the ~ end of the train die Spitze des Zuges; **~ view** Vorderansicht *f*; (*Tech*) Aufriß *m*.

frontage ['frʌntɪdʒ] *n* (*of building*) Front, Vorderseite *f*; (*ground in front of house*) Grundstück or Gelände *nt* vor dem Haus. **the shop has a ~ on two streets** der Laden hat Schaufenster auf or zu zwei Straßen hinaus; **because of its ~ onto the sea** weil es zur See hinaus liegt.

frontal ['frʌntl] *adj* (*Mil*) Frontal-; (*Anat*) Stirn-; *see* **full ~**.

front: ~ bench *n* (*Parl*) vorderste or erste Reihe (*wo die führenden Politiker sitzen*); **~ door** *n* Haustür *f*.

frontier ['frʌntɪəʳ] *n* Grenze, Landesgrenze *f*; (*boundary area*) Grenzgebiet *nt*; (*fig: of knowledge*) Grenze *f*. **to push back the ~s of science** auf wissenschaftliches Neuland vorstoßen.

frontier *in cpds* **post, town, zone** Grenz-; **~ dispute** *n* Grenzstreitigkeiten *pl*; **~ station** *n* Grenzposten *m*.

frontiersman ['frʌntɪəzmən] *n, pl* **-men** [-mən] Grenzbewohner, Grenzer *m*.

frontispiece ['frʌntɪspiːs] *n* Stirnseite *f*, Frontispiz *nt* (*obs*).

front: ~ line *n* Front(linie) *f*; **~ man** *n* Mann *m* an der Spitze; (*pej*) Strohmann *m*; **~ matter** *n* Titelei *f*; **~ organization** *n* Tarn- or Deckorganisation *f*; **~-page 1** *adj news* auf der ersten Seite; **it's not exactly ~-page news** das wird nicht gerade Schlagzeilen machen; **2** *n* **~ page** erste Seite, Titelseite *f*; **to hit the ~ page** Schlagzeilen machen; **~ rank** *n* **to be in the ~ rank** (*fig*) zur Spitze zählen; **~-runner** *n* **(a)** Läufer(in *f*) *m* an der Spitze; **he's by nature a ~-runner** er läuft am liebsten an der Spitze; **(b)** (*fig*) Spitzenreiter, Favorit *m*; **~-wheel drive** *n* Vorderradantrieb *m*.

frost [frɒst] **1** *n* **(a)** Frost *m*; (*on leaves etc*) Rauhreif *m*. **late ~s** späte Frostperioden *pl*; **ten degrees of ~** zehn Grad Kälte.

(b) (*fig: cold manner*) Kühle, Kälte, Frostigkeit *f*.

(c) (*dated sl: failure*) Pleite *f* (*inf*), Reinfall *m*.

2 *vt* **(a)** *glass* mattieren.

(b) (*esp US*) *cake* mit Zuckerguß überziehen, glasieren.

(c) (*quick-freeze*) einfrieren, tiefkühlen.

frost: ~bite *n* Frostbeulen *pl*; (*more serious*) Erfrierungen *pl*; **to get ~bite on one's hands** Frostbeulen an den Händen bekommen; sich (*dat*) die Hände erfrieren; **~bitten** *adj hands, feet* erfroren; **~bound** *adj ground* hartgefroren.

frosted ['frɒstɪd] *adj* **(a)** **~ glass** Milchglas *nt*. **(b)** (*esp US Cook*) *cake* mit Zuckerguß überzogen, glasiert. **~ icing** Zuckerguß *m*. **(c)** (*quick-frozen*) *food* tiefgekühlt, Tiefkühl-. **(d)** (*spoilt by frost*) *plants, vegetables* erfroren.

frostiness ['frɒstɪnɪs] *n* (*of weather, welcome*) Frostigkeit *f*.

frosting ['frɒstɪŋ] *n* (*esp US: icing*) Zuckerguß *m*.

frosty ['frɒstɪ] *adj* (+*er*) *weather* frostig; *window* bereift, mit Eisblumen bedeckt; (*fig*) *welcome* frostig; *look* eisig.

froth [frɒθ] **1** *n* **(a)** (*on liquids, Med*) Schaum *m*.

(b) (*light conversation, frivolities*) Firlefanz *m*.

2 *vi* schäumen. **the beer ~ed over the edge of the glass** der Schaum floß über den Rand des Bierglases; **the dog was ~ing at the mouth** der Hund hatte Schaum vor dem Maul; **he was ~ing at the mouth (with rage)** er schäumte vor Wut.

frothy ['frɒθɪ] *adj* (+*er*) *beer, liquid, sea* schäumend *attr*; *cream* schaumig, locker; *clouds* duftig; *talk etc* hohl, leer, seicht.

frown [fraʊn] **1** *n* Stirnrunzeln *nt no pl*. **to give a ~** die Stirn(e) runzeln; **... he said with a ~** ... sagte er mit einem Stirnrunzeln; **angry ~** finsterer Blick; **worried/puzzled ~** sorgenvoller/verdutzter Gesichtsausdruck, sorgenvolles/verdutztes Gesicht; **his worried ~** seine sorgenvoll gerunzelte Stirn.

2 *vi* (*lit, fig*) die Stirn(e) runzeln (*at* über +*acc*).

♦**frown (up)on** *vi* +*prep obj* (*fig*) *suggestion, drinking etc* mißbilligen, mit Stirnrunzeln betrachten. **not wearing a tie is ~ed ~** es wird beanstandet, wenn man keinen Schlips trägt.

frowning ['fraʊnɪŋ] *adj face, looks* finster; (*disapproving*) mißbilligend; (*fig*) *cliff* drohend, düster.

frowsy, frowzy ['fraʊzɪ] *adj* (+*er*) (*unkempt*) schlampig, schlud(e)rig.

froze [frəʊz] *pret of* **freeze**.

frozen ['frəʊzn] **1** *ptp of* **freeze**.

2 *adj* **(a)** *river* zugefroren, vereist; *North* eisig; *wastes* Eis-; *person* eiskalt; *body* erfroren; *pipes* eingefroren. **I am ~** mir ist eiskalt; **I'm absolutely ~ stiff** ich bin total steifgefroren; **my hands are ~** meine Hände sind eiskalt or steifgefroren; **your tiny hand is ~** wie eiskalt ist dies Händchen.

(b) **~ foods** Tiefkühlkost *f*; **~ peas/beans** tiefgekühlte or gefrorene Erbsen *pl*/Bohnen *pl*; **~ fish/meat** Gefrierfisch *m*/-fleisch *nt*.

(c) (*pegged*) *prices, wages* eingefroren. **~ assets** (*Fin*) festliegendes Kapital.

FRS *abbr of* **Fellow of the Royal Society.**

fructification [ˌfrʌktɪfɪˈkeɪʃən] *n* (*lit, fig: making fruitful*) Befruchtung *f*; (*forming fruit*) Fruchtbildung *f*.

fructify ['frʌktɪfaɪ] **1** *vt* (*lit, fig*) *seed, imagination* befruchten. **2** *vi* Früchte tragen.

frugal ['fruːgəl] *adj person* sparsam, genügsam; *meal* einfach, schlicht, frugal (*geh*).

frugality [fruːˈgælɪtɪ] *n* (*thrift*) Sparsamkeit *f*; (*of meal*) Schlichtheit, Frugalität (*geh*) *f*.

fruit [fruːt] **1** *n* **(a)** (*as collective*) Obst *nt*; (*fig*) Frucht *f*; (*Bot*) Frucht *f*. **is it a ~ or a vegetable?** ist es Obst oder Gemüse?; **what is your favourite ~?** welches Obst magst du am liebsten?; **southern ~s** Südfrüchte *pl*; **the ~s of the earth** die Früchte *pl* des Feldes; **to bear ~** (*lit, fig*) Früchte tragen; **the ~(s) of my labour** die Früchte *pl* meiner Arbeit.

(b) (*dated Brit inf*) **old ~** alter Knabe (*inf*).

(c) (*esp US inf: homosexual*) Süße(r) *m* (*inf*), warmer Bruder (*inf*).

2 *vi* Früchte tragen.

fruit: ~ bat *n* Flughund *m*; **~ cake** *n* englischer Kuchen; (*sl: eccentric*) Spinner *m* (*inf*); **as nutty as a ~ cake** (*inf*) total verrückt; ~ **cup** n (a) (drink) Cocktail m mit Früchten; (b) (US) Frucht- or Früchtebecher m; ~ **dish** n Obstteller m; ~ **drop** n Drops m, Früchtebonbon m or nt.

fruiterer ['fruːtərəʳ] n (esp Brit) Obsthändler m.

fruit fly n Fruchtfliege, Taufliege f.

fruitful ['fruːtfʊl] adj (a) plant, soil fruchtbar, ertragreich. (b) (fig) life, time at university, discussion fruchtbar; attempt erfolgreich. **were your enquiries** ~? waren Ihre Erkundigungen erfolgreich or von Erfolg gekrönt (geh)?

fruitfully ['fruːtfəlɪ] adv see adj (b).

fruitfulness ['fruːtfʊlnɪs] n (lit, fig) Fruchtbarkeit f.

fruition [fruːˈɪʃən] n (of aims, plans, ideas) Erfüllung, Verwirklichung f. **to come to** ~ sich verwirklichen; **to bring sth to** ~ etw verwirklichen.

fruit knife n Obstmesser nt.

fruitless ['fruːtlɪs] adj (a) plant unfruchtbar. (b) (fig) attempt, discussion, investigation fruchtlos, ergebnislos. **it would be** ~ **to try** ein Versuch wäre zwecklos.

fruit: ~ **machine** n (Brit) Spielautomat m; ~ **salad** n Obstsalat m; (fig inf) Lametta nt; ~ **tree** n Obstbaum m.

fruity ['fruːtɪ] adj (+er) (a) (like fruit) fruchtartig, obstartig; taste, smell Frucht-, Obst-; wine fruchtig. **it has a** ~ **taste** es schmeckt nach Obst; **it has a** ~ **smell** es riecht wie Obst. (b) (esp Brit inf) story gesalzen, gepfeffert (inf). **to get** ~ keck werden. (c) voice rauchig. (d) (US inf: homosexual) schwul (sl).

frump [frʌmp] n (pej) Vogelscheuche f (inf). **old** ~ alte Schachtel (inf).

frumpish ['frʌmpɪʃ] adj (pej) tuntig (inf), tantenhaft.

frustrate [frʌˈstreɪt] vt hopes zunichte machen; plans, plot durchkreuzen, zerstören; person frustrieren. **he was** ~d **in his efforts** seine Anstrengungen waren umsonst or vergebens.

frustrated [frʌˈstreɪtɪd] adj person frustriert.

frustrating [frʌˈstreɪtɪŋ] adj frustrierend. **it's so** ~ das ist alles so frustrierend, so ein Frust (sl).

frustratingly [frʌˈstreɪtɪŋlɪ] adv slow, complex frustrierend.

frustration [frʌˈstreɪʃən] n Frustration f no pl; (of hopes, plans, plot) Zerschlagung f. **the** ~s **of life in a city** die Frustration or der Frust (sl) eines Lebens in der Stadt; **he has had a number of** ~s **during the course of this project** er hat im Verlauf dieses Projektes eine Reihe von Rückschlägen gehabt.

fry¹ [fraɪ] npl (fish) junge or kleine Fische pl. **small** ~ (unimportant people) kleine Fische (inf) or Leute pl; (children) Kroppzeug nt (inf).

fry² **1** vt (a) meat (in der Pfanne) braten. **to** ~ **an egg** ein Spiegelei machen, ein Ei in die Pfanne schlagen; **fried eggs** Spiegeleier pl; **fried potatoes** Bratkartoffeln pl.
(b) (US sl: electrocute) auf dem elektrischen Stuhl hinrichten.
2 vi (a) braten. **we're absolutely** ~ing **in this heat** (inf) wir schmoren (in dieser Hitze) (inf).
(b) (US sl) auf dem elektrischen Stuhl hingerichtet werden.
3 n (US) Barbecue nt.

♦**fry up** vt sep (auf)braten, in die Pfanne hauen (inf).

frying pan ['fraɪ ŋˌpæn] n Bratpfanne f. **to jump out of the** ~ **into the fire** (Prov) vom Regen in die Traufe kommen (Prov).

ft abbr of **foot** ft; **feet** ft.

FTC (US) abbr of **Federal Trade Commission**.

fuchsia ['fjuːʃə] n Fuchsie f.

fuck [fʌk] (vulg) **1** vt (a) (lit) ficken (vulg).
(b) **you can get** ~ed/~ **you!** leck mich am Arsch (vulg); ~ **him!** der kann mich doch am Arsch lecken (vulg); ~ **what he thinks!** ich scheiß was auf seine Meinung (sl); ~ **this car!** dieses Scheißauto! (sl); ~ **me, he didn't say that, did he?** leck mich am Arsch, das hat der wirklich gesagt? (sl).
2 vi ficken (vulg).
3 n (a) Fick m (vulg). **to have a** ~ ficken (vulg); **she's a good** ~ sie fickt gut (vulg).
(b) **I don't give** or **care a** ~ ich kümmere mich einen Scheiß darum (sl); **who/what/where the** ~ **is that?** wer/was/wo ist denn das, verdammt noch mal? (sl).
4 interj (verdammte) Scheiße (sl), verdammt und zugenäht (sl), Herrgottsack (S Ger vulg).

♦**fuck about** or **around** (vulg) **1** vi rumgammeln (inf). **to** ~ ~ **with sb** jdn verarschen (sl); **someone's been** ~ing ~ **with the engine** da hat irgend so ein Arsch am Motor rumgefummelt (sl). **2** vt sep verarschen (sl).

♦**fuck off** vi (vulg) sich verpissen (sl). ~ ~! verpiß dich! (sl), hau ab, du Arsch! (sl).

♦**fuck up** vt sep (vulg) versauen (sl); engine, piece of work also Scheiße bauen mit (sl).

fuck-all ['fʌkaːl] (vulg) **1** n einen Scheiß (sl). **he knows** ~ **about it** der hat keinen Schiß Ahnung davon (sl); **it's got** ~ **to do with him** einen Scheiß hat das mit ihm zu tun (sl); **there was** ~ **to drink** in dem ganzen Puff gab's nichts zu trinken (sl); **I've done** ~ **all day** ich hab den ganzen Tag nichts geschafft gekriegt (inf); ~ **you care!** einen Scheiß kümmert es dich! (sl).
2 adj attr **that's** ~ **use** das ist ja vielleicht ein Scheiß (sl) or total bekackt (vulg) or für'n Arsch (vulg); **he was** ~ **help** was der gemacht hat, war für'n Arsch (vulg); **he's got** ~ **idea how to do it** er hat keinen Schiß Ahnung, wie er das machen soll (sl).

fucker ['fʌkəʳ] n (vulg) Arsch(loch nt) (vulg), Saftsack (vulg) m.

fucking ['fʌkɪŋ] (vulg) **1** adj verdammt (sl), Scheiß- (sl). **all the** ~ **time** die ganze verdammte Zeit (über) (sl); **he doesn't have a** ~ **chance** für den ist nichts drin (sl); ~ **hell!** verdammte Scheiße! (sl), verdammt noch mal! (sl); **it's a** ~ **nuisance** es ist eine verdammte Landplage (sl); **he's a** ~ **idiot/genius/millionaire** der ist ein verdammter Idiot/er ist ein Genie/Millionär, verdammt noch mal! (all sl).
2 adv **it's** ~ **raining again** verdammte Scheiße, das regnet schon wieder (sl).

fuddled ['fʌdld] adj (muddled) verwirrt, verdattert (inf); (tipsy) bedüdelt (inf), beschwipst, angesäuselt.

fuddy-duddy ['fʌdɪˌdʌdɪ] (inf) **1** adj verknöchert, verkalkt. **2** n komischer Kauz (inf). **an old** ~ ein alter Kauz.

fudge [fʌdʒ] **1** n (a) (Cook) Fondant m.
(b) (Press) (space for stop press) Spalte f für letzte Meldungen; (stop press news) letzte Meldungen pl.
2 vt (a) (fake up) story, excuse sich (dat) aus den Fingern saugen, (frei) erfinden.
(b) (dodge) question, issue ausweichen (+dat), aus dem Wege gehen (+dat).

fuel [fjʊəl] **1** n Brennstoff m, Brennmaterial nt; (for vehicle) Kraftstoff m; (petrol) Benzin nt; (Aviat, Space) Treibstoff m; (fig) Nahrung f. **lighter** ~ Feuerzeugbenzin nt; **to add** ~ **to the flames** or **fire** (fig) Öl in die Flammen or ins Feuer gießen; **what kind of** ~ **do you use in your central heating?** womit betreiben Sie Ihre Zentralheizung?; see **solid** ~.
2 vt stove, furnace etc (fill) mit Brennstoff versorgen; (use for ~) betreiben; ships etc (fill) auftanken, betanken; (drive, propel) antreiben. **they are now** ~led **atomically** sie sind jetzt atomgetrieben.
3 vi (ship, engine, aircraft) Brennstoff/Treibstoff m etc aufnehmen, (auf)tanken. ~ling **station** (US) Tankstelle f; ~ling **stop** Landung f zum Auftanken.

fuel: ~ **cell** n Brennstoffzelle f, Brennstoffelement nt; ~ **gauge** n Benzinuhr, Tankuhr f; ~ **injection** n (Benzin)einspritzung f; **engine with** ~ **injection** Einspritzmotor m; ~ **oil** n Gasöl nt; ~ **pump** n Benzinpumpe f; ~ **shortage** n Brennstoffknappheit f; ~ **tank** n Öltank m.

fug [fʌg] n (esp Brit inf) Mief m (inf).

fuggy ['fʌgɪ] adj (+er) (esp Brit inf) muffig, miefig (inf).

fugitive ['fjuːdʒɪtɪv] **1** n Flüchtling m. **he is a** ~ **from the law** er ist auf der Flucht vor dem Gesetz. **2** adj (a) (runaway) flüchtig, auf der Flucht. (b) (liter) thought, happiness, hour flüchtig.

fugue [fjuːg] n (Mus) Fuge f.

fulcrum ['fʌlkrəm] n Dreh- or Stützpunkt m; (fig: of argument, plan, organization) Angelpunkt m.

fulfil, (US) **fulfill** [fʊlˈfɪl] vt condition, desire, one's duties, hopes erfüllen; task, order ausführen. **the prophecy was** ~led **die Prophezeiung erfüllte sich; being a mother didn't** ~ **her sie fand im Muttersein keine Erfüllung; to be** or **feel** ~led **Erfüllung finden; to** ~ **oneself sich selbst verwirklichen.

fulfilling [fʊlˈfɪlɪŋ] adj a ~ job ein Beruf, in dem man Erfüllung findet.

fulfilment, (US) **fulfillment** [fʊlˈfɪlmənt] n Erfüllung f. **to bring sth to** ~ etw zur Erfüllung bringen; **to come to** ~ in Erfüllung gehen; (life's work) seine Erfüllung finden.

full [fʊl] **1** adj (+er) (a) (filled) room, theatre, train voll. **to be** ~ **of** ... voller (+gen) or voll von ... sein, voll sein mit ...; **he's** ~ **of good ideas** er steckt voll(er) guter Ideen; **a look** ~ **of hate** ein haßerfüllter Blick, ein Blick voller Haß; **his heart was** ~ (liter) das Herz lief ihm über; ~ **house** (Theat) (Vorstellung) ausverkauft; (Cards) Full house nt; **each night they played to** ~ **houses** sie spielten jeden Abend vor vollem Haus; **I am** ~ **(up)** (inf) ich platze gleich (inf), ich bin (papp)satt, ich bin voll (bis obenhin) (inf); **we are** ~ **up for July** wir sind für Juli völlig ausgebucht.
(b) (maximum, complete) voll; description, report vollständig; understanding, sympathy vollste(r, s). **at** ~ **speed** in voller Fahrt; **to fall** ~ **length** der Länge nach hinfallen; **roses in** ~ **bloom** Rosen in voller Blüte; **that's a** ~ **day's work** damit habe ich etc den ganzen Tag zu tun; **I need a** ~ **night's sleep** ich muß mich (ein)mal gründlich ausschlafen; **to be in** ~ **flight** kopflos fliehen; **to pay** ~ **fare** den vollen Preis bezahlen; **battalion at** ~ **strength** Bataillon in Sollstärke; **I waited two** ~ **hours** ich habe geschlagene zwei or zwei ganze Stunden gewartet; **the** ~ **particulars** die genauen or die Einzelheiten; **a** ~ **colonel** ein Oberst m; ~ **employment** Vollbeschäftigung f; ~ **member** vollberechtigtes Mitglied; ~ **name** Vor- und Zuname m; **to run** ~ **tilt into sth** mit voller Wucht or in voller Fahrt in etw (acc) or auf etw (acc) rennen; **to go at** ~ **tilt rasen, Volldampf (inf) or volle Pulle (inf) fahren; a very ~ colour eine (sehr) satte Farbe; it's in ~ colour das ist in Farbe; shots of the Rocky Mountains in ~ colour schöne Farbaufnahmen von den Rocky Mountains.
(c) (preoccupied) **to be** ~ **of oneself** von sich (selbst) eingenommen sein, nur sich selbst im Kopf haben; **she was** ~ **of the news** sie platzte vor Neuigkeiten; **she was** ~ **of it** sie hat gar nicht mehr aufgehört, davon zu reden; **the papers were** ~ **of it** for weeks die Zeitungen waren wochenlang voll davon; **he's always so** ~ **of what he's going to do** er ist dauernd von seinen Plänen dran (inf).
(d) (rounded) lips, face voll; figure, skirt etc füllig; (Naut) sails voll, gebläht.
2 adv (a) (at least) **it is a** ~ **five miles from here** es sind volle or gute fünf Meilen von hier.
(b) (very, perfectly) **I know it** ~ **well** ich weiß es sehr wohl.
(c) (directly) **to hit sb** ~ **in the face** jdn voll or mitten ins Gesicht schlagen; **to look sb** ~ **in the face** jdm voll in die Augen sehen.
(d) ~ **out** work auf Hochtouren; drive mit Vollgas.
3 n (a) **in** ~ ganz, vollständig; **to write one's name in** ~ seinen Namen ausschreiben; **to pay in** ~ den vollen Betrag bezahlen.
(b) **to the** ~ vollständig, total, bis zur Neige.

full: ~-**back** n (Sport) Verteidiger m; ~-**blooded** adj (vigorous) kräftig; person also Vollblut-; ~-**blown** adj (a) flower voll aufgeblüht; (b) (fig) doctor, theory reinrassig, ausgewachsen (inf); ~-**bodied** adj wine schwer, vollmundig.

full-dress ['fʊldres] adj (a) clothes Gala-. (b) (fig: important, ceremonious) ~ **debate** wichtige Debatte.

fuller's earth ['fʊləz,3:θ] n Fullererde, Bleicherde f.

full: ~ **face** adj portrait mit zugewandtem Gesicht; ~**-faced** ['fʊlfeɪst] adj rundgesichtig; ~**-fledged** adj (US) see **fully-fledged**; ~ **frontal** 1 n Nacktdarstellung f, Oben-und-Unten-Ohne nt no pl (inf); 2 adj oben und unten ohne (inf); **the** ~ **frontal nudity in this play** die völlig nackten Schauspieler in diesem Stück; ~**-grown** adj ausgewachsen; ~**-length** adj portrait lebensgroß; film abendfüllend; ~**-lipped** adj volllippig; ~ **moon** n Vollmond m.

ful(l)ness ['fʊlnɪs] n (of detail) Vollständigkeit f; (of voice) Klangfülle f; (of colour) Sattheit f; (of sound) Fülle f; (of skirt) Fülle, Weite f. **out of the** ~ **of his heart** (liter) aus der Fülle seines Herzens (liter); **out of the** ~ **of his sorrow** (liter) aus der Tiefe seines Leides or Schmerzes (liter); **in the** ~ **of time** (eventually) zu gegebener Zeit; (at predestined time) da or als die Zeit gekommen war, da or als die Zeit erfüllt war.

full: ~**-page** adj advertisement etc ganzseitig; ~**-scale** adj (a) drawing, replica in Originalgröße; (b) operation, search groß angelegt; revision, reorganization umfassend, total; retreat auf der ganzen Linie; war richtiggehend, ausgewachsen (inf); **the factory starts** ~**-scale operation next month** die Fabrik nimmt den vollen Arbeitsbetrieb nächsten Monat auf; ~ **size(d)** adj bicycle, violin etc richtig (groß); ~**-sized** adj model, drawing lebensgroß; ~ **stop** n Punkt m; **to come to a** ~ **stop** zum völligen Stillstand kommen; **I'm not going,** ~ **stop!** (inf) ich gehe nicht und damit basta (inf); ~**-time** 1 adv work ganztags; 2 adj employment Ganztags-, ganztägig; **it's a** ~**-time job** (fig) das kann einen den ganzen Tag or rund um die Uhr auf Trab halten (inf); 3 n (Sport) **to blow for** ~**-time** das Spiel abpfeifen.

fully ['fʊlɪ] adv (a) (entirely) völlig, voll und ganz. (b) (at least) **it is** ~ **two hours since he went out** es ist volle zwei Stunden her, daß er weggegangen ist; **it's** ~ **a year ago** es ist gut ein Jahr her.

fully: ~**-fashioned** ['fʊlɪˈfæʃnd] adj stocking, jumper mit Paßform; ~**-fledged** adj (a) bird flügge; (b) (fig: qualified) doctor, architect etc richtiggehend, ausgewachsen (inf); ~**-qualified** adj vollqualifiziert attr.

fulmar ['fʊlmə'] n Eissturmvogel m.

fulminate ['fʌlmɪneɪt] vi (fig) wettern, donnern.

fulsome ['fʊlsəm] adj praise übertrieben; (very full) uneingeschränkt; manner übertrieben.

fumble ['fʌmbl] 1 vi (also ~ **about** or **around**) umhertasten or -tappen. **to** ~ **in the dark** im Dunkeln herumtasten or -tappen; **to** ~ **in one's pockets** in seinen Taschen wühlen; **to** ~ **(about) for sth** nach etw suchen or tasten; (in case, pocket, drawer) nach etw wühlen; **to** ~ **with sth** an etw (dat) herumfummeln; **to** ~ **for words** nach Worten suchen or ringen.
2 vt vermasseln (inf), verpfuschen (inf). **to** ~ **the ball** den Ball nicht sicher fangen.

fumbler ['fʌmblə'] n Stümper m.

fume [fjuːm] vi (a) (liquids) dampfen, rauchen; (gases) aufsteigen. (b) (fig inf: person) wütend sein, kochen (inf).

fumes [fjuːmz] npl Dämpfe pl; (of car) Abgase pl. **petrol** ~ Benzindämpfe pl.

fumigate ['fjuːmɪgeɪt] vt ausräuchern.

fun [fʌn] 1 n (amusement) Spaß m. **to have great** ~ **doing sth** viel Spaß daran haben, etw zu tun, viel Spaß an etw (dat) haben; **for or in** ~ (as a joke) im or als Scherz; **this is** ~! das macht Spaß or Freude!; **it's** ~ es macht Spaß or Freude; **I'm not doing it for the** ~ **of it** ich mache das nicht aus or zu meinem Vergnügen; **we just did it for** ~ wir haben das nur aus or zum Spaß gemacht; **to spoil the** ~ den Spaß verderben; **it's** ~ **doing this/being with him** es macht Spaß, das zu tun/mit ihm zusammen zu sein; **it's not much** ~ **for the others though** es ist allerdings für die anderen nicht gerade ein Vergnügen; **it takes all the** ~ **out of life/work** das nimmt einem den Spaß or die Freude am Leben/an der Arbeit; **life's not much** ~ **sometimes** das Leben ist manchmal nicht gerade das reinste Vergnügen; **it's no** ~ **living on your own/being broke** es macht nicht gerade Spaß, allein zu leben/pleite (inf) zu sein; **he is great** ~ man kriegt mit ihm viel Spaß (inf) or viel zu lachen (inf); **but the children thought him great** ~ aber die Kinder fanden ihn sehr lustig; **the visit was good** ~ der Besuch hat viel Spaß gemacht; **what** ~! was für ein Spaß!; **you're no** ~ **to be with any more** es macht keinen Spaß mehr, mit dir zusammen zu sein; **that sounds like** ~ das klingt gut; **I wasn't serious, I was just having a bit of** ~ das hab ich nicht ernst gemeint, ich hab doch nur Spaß gemacht; **the children had** ~ **and games at the picnic** die Kinder haben beim Picknick viel Spaß gehabt; **there'll be** ~ **and games over this decision** (inf) mit dieser Entscheidung wird es noch Spaß geben; **that should be** ~ **and games** das kann ja (noch) heiter werden (inf); **he's having** ~ **and games with the au-pair girl** (inf) er amüsiert sich mit dem Au-pair-Mädchen, er hat seinen Spaß mit dem Au-pair-Mädchen; **to make** ~ **of or poke** ~ **at sb/sth** sich über jdn/etw lustig machen; **we had a bit of** ~ **getting the car started** (inf) wir hatten ein bißchen Theater, ehe das Auto ansprang (inf); **like** ~ (US inf) (ja,) Pustekuchen! (inf).
2 adj attr (sl) **squash is a** ~ **game** Squash macht Spaß; **he's a real** ~ **person** er ist wirklich ein lustiger Kerl; **that sounds like a** ~ **idea** das hört sich prima an (inf).

function ['fʌŋkʃən] 1 n (a) (of heart, tool, word etc) Funktion f. (b) (of person) Aufgaben, Pflichten pl. **in his** ~ **as judge** in seiner Eigenschaft als Richter; **his** ~ **in life** seine Lebensaufgabe. (c) (meeting) Veranstaltung f; (reception) Empfang m; (official ceremony) Feier f. (d) (Math) Funktion f.
2 vi funktionieren; (heart, kidney, brain also) arbeiten. **this line in the poem** ~**s in two separate ways** diese Zeile im Gedicht wirkt auf zweierlei Weise; **he can't** ~ **without his morning coffee** ohne seinen Kaffee am Morgen ist er nicht funktions-

fähig; **to** ~ **as** fungieren als; (person also) die Rolle des/der ... spielen or ausfüllen; (thing also) dienen als.

functional ['fʌŋkʃənəl] adj (a) (able to operate) funktionsfähig. (b) (utilitarian) zweckmäßig, funktionell. (c) (Med) Funktions-. ~ **disease/disorder** Funktionsstörung f.

functionalism ['fʌŋkʃənəlɪzəm] n Funktionalismus m.

functionary ['fʌŋkʃənərɪ] n Funktionär m.

fund [fʌnd] 1 n (a) (Fin) Fonds m. **to start a** ~ einen Fonds einrichten or gründen.
(b) ~**s** pl Mittel, Gelder pl; **the public** ~**s** die öffentlichen Mittel, die Staatsgelder pl; **no** ~**s** (Banking) keine Deckung; **to be in** ~**s** zahlungsfähig or bei Kasse (inf) sein; **to be pressed for or short of** ~**s** knapp bei Kasse sein (inf); **at the moment I haven't the** ~**s** mir fehlen zur Zeit die Mittel or Gelder pl; **how are we off for** ~**s at the moment?** wie steht die Kasse zur Zeit?
(c) (supply: of wisdom, humour etc) Schatz (of von, gen), Vorrat (of an +dat) m.
(d) ~**s** pl (Brit: government securities) Staatspapiere pl.
2 vt (a) debt ausgleichen, bezahlen; (put up money for) scheme, project das Kapital aufbringen für.
(b) (invest) Geld anlegen, investieren.

fundamental [,fʌndə'mentl] 1 adj (basic) grundlegend; presupposition, importance, error also, indifference, problem grundsätzlich, fundamental; role, characteristics also wesentlich; (elementary) Grund-; beliefs also, likes elementar; nature eigentlich. **to be** ~ **to sth** für etw von grundlegender Bedeutung or Wichtigkeit sein; **his** ~ **ignorance of this subject** seine fundamentale Unkenntnis auf diesem Gebiet; **our** ~ **needs/beliefs** unsere Grundbedürfnisse pl or elementaren Bedürfnisse pl/unsere Grundüberzeugungen pl; ~ **tone** (Mus) Grundton m; ~ **research** Grundlagenforschung f.
2 n usu pl Grundlage f.

fundamentally [,fʌndə'mentəlɪ] adv grundlegend; (in essence) im Grunde (genommen), im wesentlichen. **there is something** ~ **wrong with his argument** sein Argument enthält einen grundlegenden Fehler; **is man** ~ **good?** ist der Mensch im Grunde or im wesentlichen gut?; **this is quite** ~ **important for us** dies ist von grundlegender Bedeutung für uns; **we differ quite** ~ **on this** wir sind uns hierzu von Grund auf uneinig.

funeral ['fjuːnərəl] n Begräbnis nt, Beerdigung, Beisetzung (form) f. **to go to sb's** ~ zu jds Beerdigung etc gehen; **were you at his** ~? waren Sie auf seiner Beerdigung?; **that's his** ~ **if he wants to do it** (inf) wenn er das machen will, ist das sein Problem (inf); **well that's your** ~ (inf) na ja, das ist dein persönliches Pech (inf), das ist dein Problem (inf).

funeral: ~ **director** n Beerdigungsunternehmer m; ~ **home** n (US) Leichenhalle f; ~ **march** n Trauermarsch m; ~ **parlour** n Leichenhalle f; ~ **procession** n Leichenzug m; ~ **pyre** n Scheiterhaufen m; ~ **service** n Trauergottesdienst m.

funereal [fjuː'nɪərəl] adj traurig, trübselig; voice Trauer-.

funfair ['fʌnfeə'] n Kirmes f.

fungi ['fʌŋgaɪ] pl of **fungus**.

fungicide ['fʌŋgɪsaɪd] n pilztötendes Mittel.

fungoid ['fʌŋgɔɪd], **fungous** ['fʌŋgəs] adj schwammartig.

fungus ['fʌŋgəs] n, pl **fungi** (Bot, Med) Pilz m; (hum sl: whiskers etc) Sauerkohl m (inf).

funicular (railway) [fjuː'nɪkjʊlə'('reɪlweɪ)] n Seilbahn, Kettenbahn f.

funk [fʌŋk] 1 n (esp Brit inf: fear) Schiß (inf), Bammel (inf) m. **to be in a (blue)** ~ (vor Angst) die Hosen voll haben (inf), mächtig or ganz schön Schiß or Bammel haben (inf); **to go into a (blue)** ~ mächtig Schiß or Bammel kriegen (inf); **to put sb in a blue** ~ jdm mächtig Bammel einjagen (inf).
2 vt kneifen vor (+dat) (inf). **he** ~**ed it** er hat (davor) gekniffen (inf).

funky ['fʌŋkɪ] adj (+er) (a) (esp Brit inf: cowardly) feige, ängstlich. (b) (sl) music irre (sl).

fun-loving ['fʌnlʌvɪŋ] adj lebenslustig. **a** ~ **girl** (euph) ein lebenshungriges Mädchen.

funnel ['fʌnl] 1 n (a) (for pouring) Trichter m. (b) (Naut, Rail) Schornstein m. **two-**~**led steamer** Dampfer m mit zwei Schornsteinen. (c) (US: ventilation shaft etc) Luftschacht m. 2 vt liquid, grain leiten; attention, energies also schleusen, kanalisieren; information, traffic also schleusen.

funnies ['fʌnɪz] npl (US: comic strips) Witze pl, Witzseite f.

funnily ['fʌnɪlɪ] adv see adj. ~ **enough** lustigerweise, komischerweise.

funny ['fʌnɪ] adj (+er) (a) (comic) komisch, lustig. **I suppose you think that's** ~ das hältst du wohl für komisch?; **are you trying to be** ~? are you being ~? das soll wohl ein Witz sein?; **don't you get** ~ **with me!** komm du mir bloß nicht komisch (inf); **it's not** ~ das ist or das finde ich überhaupt nicht komisch.
(b) (strange) seltsam, komisch. **he is** ~ **that way** (inf) in der Beziehung ist er komisch; **don't get any** ~ **ideas** komm bloß nicht auf komische Gedanken; **the meat tastes** ~ das Fleisch schmeckt komisch or seltsam; **it's a** ~ **thing, only last week ...** (das ist doch) komisch, erst letzte Woche ...; ~, **it was here just now** komisch, gerade war es noch da.
(c) (inf: suspicious) ~ **business** faule Sache (inf); **none of your** ~ **tricks!** keine faulen Tricks! (inf); **there's something** ~ **going on here** hier ist doch was faul (inf).
(d) (inf: unwell) **I felt all** ~ mir war ganz komisch or mulmig.

funny: ~ **bone** n Musikantenknochen m; ~ **farm** n (inf) Klapsmühle f (inf); ~ **paper** n (US) Witzseiten pl.

fur [fɜː'] 1 n (a) (on animal) Fell nt, Pelz m; (for clothing) Pelz m. **that will really make the** ~ **fly** (inf) da werden die Fetzen fliegen (inf); **a** ~**-lined coat** ein pelzgefütterter Mantel. (b) ~**s** pl Pelze pl. (c) (in kettle etc) Kesselstein m; (Med: on tongue) Belag m. 2 attr coat, collar Pelz; rug Fell-.

♦**fur up** vi (kettle, boiler) verkalken, Kesselstein ansetzen; (tongue) pelzig werden. **to be** ~**red** ~ belegt or pelzig sein.

furbelow ['fɜ:bɪləʊ] n (a) (old) Falbel f, Faltenbesatz m. (b) usu pl ~s (pej) Firlefanz m.

furbish ['fɜ:bɪʃ] vt (a) (polish) blank reiben, (auf)polieren. (b) (smarten up) aufpolieren.

furious ['fjʊərɪəs] adj person wütend; storm, sea stürmisch, wild; struggle wild; speed rasend, rasant. fast and ~ rasant; things at the party were going fast and ~ die Party war richtig in Schwung or Fahrt gekommen; the jokes/punches came fast and ~ die Witze kamen Schlag auf Schlag/es hagelte Schläge.

furiously ['fjʊərɪəslɪ] adv see adj.

furl [fɜ:l] vt sail, flag aufrollen, einrollen; umbrella zusammenrollen.

furlong ['fɜ:lɒŋ] n Achtelmeile f.

furlough ['fɜ:ləʊ] n (Mil, Admin) Urlaub m. to go on ~ in Urlaub gehen.

furn abbr of furnished möbl.

furnace ['fɜ:nɪs] n Hochofen m; (Metal) Schmelzofen m. this room is like a ~ dieses Zimmer ist ja das reinste Treibhaus.

furnish ['fɜ:nɪʃ] vt (a) house einrichten. ~ed room möbliertes Zimmer; to live in ~ed accommodation zur Untermiete wohnen; ~ing fabrics Dekorationsstoffe pl. (b) information, reason, excuse liefern, geben. to ~ sb with sth jdn mit etw versorgen, jdm etw liefern; with reason, excuse jdm etw liefern.

furnishings ['fɜ:nɪʃɪŋz] npl Mobiliar nt; (with carpets etc) Einrichtung f. with ~ and fittings voll eingerichtet.

furniture ['fɜ:nɪtʃər] n Möbel pl. a piece of ~ ein Möbelstück nt; I must buy some ~ ich muß Möbel kaufen; one settee and three chairs were all the ~ die Einrichtung bestand nur aus einem Sofa und drei Stühlen; he treats her as part of the ~ er behandelt sie, als gehöre sie zur Einrichtung; if I stay here much longer, I'll become a part of the ~ wenn ich noch viel länger hier bleibe, gehöre ich bald zum Inventar.

furniture: ~ depository, ~ depot (US) n Möbellager nt; ~ remover n Möbelspediteur m; ~ van n (Brit) Möbelwagen m.

furore [fjʊəˈrɔːrɪ], (US) **furor** ['fjʊərɔːr] n Protest(e pl) m. the new play caused a ~ das neue Stück machte Furore.

furred [fɜ:d] adj (tongue) belegt, pelzig.

furrier ['fʌrɪər] n Kürschner m.

furrow ['fʌrəʊ] 1 n (Agr) Furche f; (Hort: for flowers etc) Rinne f; (on brow) Runzel f; (on sea) Furche f.
  2 vt earth pflügen, Furchen ziehen in (+dat); brow runzeln; (worries etc) furchen; (boats) sea Furchen ziehen in (+dat). the old man's ~ed brow die zerfurchte Stirn des alten Mannes.

furry ['fɜ:rɪ] adj (+er) animal Pelz-; toy Plüsch-; tongue pelzig, belegt. the little kitten is so soft and ~ das Kätzchen ist so weich und kuschelig; the soft ~ skin of the seal das weiche Fell des Seehundes; it has a ~ feel es fühlt sich wie Pelz or Fell an.

further ['fɜ:ðər] 1 adv, comp of far (a) (in place, time, fig) weiter. ~ on weiter, weiter entfernt; ~ back (in place, time) weiter zurück; (in time) früher; he is ~ on than his brother (fig) er ist weiter als sein Bruder; nothing could be ~ from the truth nichts könnte weiter von der Wahrheit entfernt sein; to get ~ and ~ away sich immer weiter entfernen; we're no ~ advanced now viel weiter sind wir jetzt (auch) nicht; if we take this line of reasoning ~ wenn wir diese Argumente weiterverfolgen; but then, going one step ~ aber dann, wenn man einen Schritt weiter geht; nothing is ~ from my thoughts nichts liegt mir ferner; to make the soup go ~ die Suppe strecken.
  (b) (more) he didn't question me ~ er hat mich nicht weiter or mehr gefragt; until you hear ~ bis auf weiteres; and ~ ... und darüberhinaus ...; ~ I want to say that ... darüberhinaus möchte ich sagen, daß ...; ~ to your letter of ... (Comm) bezugnehmend auf or in bezug auf Ihren Brief vom ... (form).
  2 adj (a) see farther.
  (b) (additional) weiter. until ~ notice bis auf weiteres; to remand a case for ~ enquiry (Jur) einen Fall zurückstellen, bis weitere Nachforschungen angestellt sind; without ~ loss of time ohne weiteren Zeitverlust; will there be anything ~? kann ich sonst noch etwas für Sie tun?; ~ particulars nähere or weitere Einzelheiten pl; ~ education Weiterbildung, Fortbildung f.
  3 vt one's interests, a cause fördern.

furtherance ['fɜ:ðərəns] n Förderung f. in ~ of sth zur Förderung einer Sache (gen).

furthermore [fɜ:ðəˈmɔːr] adv überdies, außerdem.

furthermost ['fɜ:ðəməʊst] adj äußerste(r, s).

furthest ['fɜ:ðɪst] 1 adv the ~ north you can go soweit nach Norden wie möglich; he went the ~ er ging am weitesten; of all the candidates he went ~ into this question von allen Kandidaten drang er am tiefsten in diese Frage ein.
  2 adj in the ~ depths of the forest in den tiefsten Tiefen des Waldes; 5 km at the ~ höchstens 5 km; the ~ way round den längsten Weg; at the ~ point from the centre an dem vom Zentrum am weitesten entfernten Punkt.

furtive ['fɜ:tɪv] adj action heimlich; behaviour heimlichtuerisch; (suspicious) verdächtig; look verstohlen; person heimlichtuerisch.

furtively ['fɜ:tɪvlɪ] adv peer, creep, slink verstohlen; (suspiciously) behave verdächtig.

furtiveness ['fɜ:tɪvnɪs] n see adj Heimlichkeit f; Heimlichtuerei f; Verdacht erregende(s) nt; Verstohlenheit f; Heimlichtuerei f.

fury ['fjʊərɪ] n (a) (of person) Wut f; (of storm also) Ungestüm nt; (of struggle, wind, passion) Heftigkeit f. she flew into a ~ sie kam in Rage; like ~ (inf) wie verrückt (inf). (b) (Myth) the Furies die Furien pl; she's a little ~ sie ist ein kleiner Hitzkopf.

furze [fɜ:z] n Stechginster m.

fuse, (US) **fuze** [fju:z] 1 vt (a) metals verschmelzen.
  (b) (Brit Elec) to ~ the lights/the iron die Sicherung durch-

brennen lassen; I've ~d the lights die Sicherung ist durchgebrannt.
  (c) (fig) vereinigen, verbinden; (Comm) fusionieren.
  2 vi (a) (metals) sich verbinden; (atoms) verschmelzen.
  (b) (Brit Elec) durchbrennen. the lights/the toaster ~d die Sicherung war durchgebrannt/am Toaster war die Sicherung durchgebrannt.
  (c) (fig: also ~ together) sich vereinigen, verschmelzen.
  3 n (a) (Elec) Sicherung f. to blow the ~s die Sicherung durchbrennen lassen; he'll blow a ~ (fig inf) bei dem brennen die Sicherungen durch (inf).
  (b) (Brit Elec: act of fusing) there's been a ~ somewhere irgendwo hat es einen Kurzschluß gegeben, da ist irgendwo ein Kurzschluß or Kurzer (inf).
  (c) (in bombs etc, Min) Zündschnur f.

fuse box n Sicherungskasten m.

fuselage ['fju:zəlɑ:ʒ] n (Flugzeug)rumpf m.

fuse wire n Schmelzdraht m.

fusilier [ˌfju:zɪˈlɪər] n (Brit) Füsilier m.

fusillade [ˌfju:zɪˈleɪd] n Salve f.

fusion ['fju:ʒən] n (of metal, fig) Verschmelzung, Fusion f; (Phys: also nuclear ~) (Kern)fusion, Kernverschmelzung f.

fuss [fʌs] 1 n Theater nt (inf); (bother also) Umstände pl (inf), Aufheben(s) nt; (lavish attention also) Wirbel (inf), Wind (inf) m, Getue (inf) nt (of um). don't go to a lot of ~ mach dir keine Umstände, mach nicht viel Theater (inf) or Aufhebens; we had a bit of a ~ to get our money back wir hatten ein bißchen Theater, ehe wir unser Geld zurückbekamen (inf); to make a ~, to kick up a ~ Krach schlagen (inf); to make a ~ about or over sth viel Aufhebens or Wind (inf) or Wirbel (inf) um etw machen; to avoid a ~ Streit or Krach (inf) vermeiden; to make a ~ of sb um jdn viel Wirbel (inf) or Wind (inf) or Getue (inf) machen; to be in/get into a ~ Zustände haben/kriegen (inf); a lot of ~ about nothing viel Wind or Lärm um nichts.
  2 vi sich (unnötig) aufregen; (get into a ~) Umstände pl machen. there's no need to ~ if your son doesn't wear a vest Sie brauchen sich nicht gleich Zustände zu kriegen, nur weil Ihr Sohn kein Unterhemd anhat (inf); don't ~, mother! ist ja gut, Mutter!; a mother who ~es unnecessarily eine übertrieben besorgte Mutter; the mother bird starts to ~ when she senses the fox die Vogelmutter wird ganz aufgeregt, wenn sie den Fuchs spürt; with a crowd of attendants ~ing busily around her mit einer Menge Bediensteter, die eifrig um sie herumhuschten or herumfuhrwerkten (inf).
  3 vt person nervös machen; (pester) keine Ruhe lassen (dat). don't ~ me laß mich in Ruhe, laß mir meine Ruhe.

◆**fuss about** or **around** vi herumfuhrwerken (inf).

◆**fuss over** vi +prep obj person bemuttern; guests sich (dat) große Umstände machen mit.

fussbudget ['fʌsbʌdʒɪt] n (US inf) see fusspot.

fussily ['fʌsɪlɪ] adv see adj.

fussiness ['fʌsɪnɪs] n see adj (a) Kleinlichkeit, Pingeligkeit (inf) f. because of his incredible ~ about what he eats weil er so eigen ist, was das Essen angeht. (b) Verspieltheit f; Ausgeklügeltheit f; Übergenauigkeit f.

fusspot ['fʌspɒt] n (Brit inf) Umstandskrämer m (inf); (nag) Nörgler(in f) m.

fussy ['fʌsɪ] adj (+er) (a) (finicky) kleinlich, pingelig (inf). she is very ~ about what she eats/wears sie ist sehr eigen, was das Essen/ihre Kleidung angeht; don't be so ~ seien Sie nicht so pingelig (inf) or kleinlich, stellen Sie sich nicht so an (inf); what do you want to do? — I'm not ~ was willst du machen? — ist mir egal; you should be more ~ Sie sollten etwas wählerischer sein.
  (b) (elaborate) dress, pattern, architecture etc verspielt; style of writing ausgeklügelt; distinction übergenau.

fustian ['fʌstɪən] 1 n (Tex) Barchent m. 2 adj (a) (Tex) Barchent-. (b) (fig: pompous) schwülstig.

fusty ['fʌstɪ] adj (+er) (lit, fig) muffig.

futile ['fju:taɪl] adj sinnlos; plan, idea, suggestion nutzlos; effort, attempt (usu attr: in vain) vergeblich; (usu pred: pointless) nutzlos.

futility [fju:ˈtɪlɪtɪ] n see adj Sinnlosigkeit f; Nutzlosigkeit f; Vergeblichkeit f; Nutzlosigkeit f.

future ['fju:tʃər] 1 n (a) Zukunft f. in ~ in Zukunft, künftig; in the near ~ bald, in der nahen Zukunft; that is still very much in the ~ das liegt noch in weiter Ferne; there's no ~ in this type of work diese Art (von) Arbeit hat keine Zukunft; he definitely has a ~ as an actor er hat eine Zukunft als Schauspieler.
  (b) (Gram) Zukunft f, Futur nt. in the ~ in der Zukunft, im Futur; ~ perfect vollendete Zukunft.
  2 adj (a) zukünftig. at some ~ date zu or an einem zukünftigen or späteren Zeitpunkt.
  (b) the ~ tense (Gram) das Futur(um), die Zukunft.

futurism ['fju:tʃərɪzəm] n Futurismus m.

futuristic [ˌfju:tʃəˈrɪstɪk] adj futuristisch.

futurology [ˌfju:tʃəˈrɒlədʒɪ] n Futurologie f.

fuze n (US) see fuse.

fuzz [fʌz] n (a) (on peach, youth's chin etc) Flaum m; (inf) (bushy beard etc) Gemüse nt (inf); (frizzy hair) Wuschelkopf m.
  (b) (inf: blur, blurred sound) Unschärfen pl.
  (c) (sl: policeman) Bulle (pej sl), Polyp (sl) m. the ~ (collective) die Bullen (pej sl), die Polypen (sl) pl.

fuzzy ['fʌzɪ] adj (+er) (a) hair kraus. (b) (blurred) picture, sound, memory etc verschwommen.

fuzzy-headed ['fʌzɪˌhedɪd] adj (inf) (a) (not clear-thinking) nicht (ganz) klar im Kopf; (from headache, drugs, drink also) benebelt. (b) (curly-haired) wuschelköpfig.

fuzzy-wuzzy ['fʌzɪˌwʌzɪ] n (pej sl) Krauskopf m (inf).

G

G, g [dʒiː] n (a) G, g nt. (b) g's pl (*gravitational force*) g nt. (c) G (*US sl: one thousand dollars*) tausend Dollar pl. (d) (*Mus*) G, g nt. ~ **sharp/flat** Gis, gis nt/Ges, ges nt; *see also* **major, minor, natural.**

G (*US*) abbr of **general.**

g abbr of **gram(s), gramme(s)** g.

gab [gæb] (*inf*) 1 n Gequassel (*inf*), Geschwätz nt. **he's all** ~ er ist ein Schwätzer (*inf*); **to have the gift of the** ~ (*talk a lot*) wie ein Wasserfall reden (*inf*); (*be persuasive*) reden können, nicht auf den Mund gefallen sein. 2 vi quatschen (*inf*), quasseln (*inf*).

gabardine, gaberdine [ˌgæbəˈdiːn] n Gabardine m.

gabble [ˈgæbl] 1 vi (*person*) brabbeln (*inf*); (*geese*) schnattern. **he** ~**d through grace in two seconds flat** er rasselte das Tischgebet in zwei Sekunden herunter (*inf*).
  2 vt poem, prayer herunterrasseln (*inf*); excuse, explanation brabbeln (*inf*).
  3 n Gebrabbel nt (*inf*); (*of geese*) Geschnatter nt. **the speaker ended in a** ~ der Redner rasselte das Ende herunter (*inf*).
♦ **gabble away** vi (*geese, people*) drauflosschnattern (*inf*).
♦ **gabble on** vi reden und reden, quasseln und quasseln (*inf*).

gabby [ˈgæbɪ] adj (*inf*) geschwätzig, schwatzhaft.

gable [ˈgeɪbl] n Giebel m. ~ **end** Giebelwand or -seite f; ~ **window** Giebelfenster nt.

gabled [ˈgeɪbld] adj Giebel-.

gad [gæd] interj (by) ~! (*old*) bei Gott! (*old*).
♦ **gad about** or **around** vi herumziehen. **he's always** ~**ding** ~ er ist ständig auf Achse (*inf*); **to** ~ ~ **the country** im Land herumziehen or -reisen.

gadabout [ˈgædəbaʊt] n rastloser Geist; (*who likes travelling*) Reiseonkel m/-tante f. **you've been a bit of a** ~ **recently** Sie sind in letzter Zeit ja sehr viel herumgekommen or auf Achse gewesen (*inf*); **she's a real** ~, **out somewhere every evening** sie ist sehr unternehmungslustig, jeden Abend ist sie irgendwo anders.

gadfly [ˈgædflaɪ] n (Vieh)bremse f.

gadget [ˈgædʒɪt] n Gerät nt, Vorrichtung f, Apparat m. **with a lot of** ~**s** mit allen Schikanen (*inf*).

gadgetry [ˈgædʒɪtrɪ] n Vorrichtungen, Geräte pl; (*superfluous equipment*) technische Spielereien, Kinkerlitzchen (*inf*) pl.

gadzooks [gædˈzuːks] interj (*old*) Kruzitürken (*old*).

Gael [geɪl] n Gäle m, Gälin f.

Gaelic [ˈgeɪlɪk] 1 adj gälisch. ~ **coffee** Irish Coffee m. 2 n (*language*) Gälisch nt.

gaff[1] [gæf] 1 n (a) (*Fishing*) Landungshaken m, Gaff nt. (b) (*Naut*) Gaffel f. 2 vt (*Fishing*) mit dem (Landungs)haken or Gaff an Land ziehen.

gaff[2] n: **to blow the** ~ (*sl*) nicht dichthalten (*inf*); **he blew the** ~ (**on it**) **to Joe** er hat es Joe auf die Nase gebunden (*inf*); **to blow the** ~ **on sth** etw ausquatschen (*sl*).

gaffe [gæf] n Fauxpas m; (*verbal*) taktlose Bemerkung. **to make a** ~ einen Fauxpas begehen; (*by saying sth*) ins Fettnäpfchen treten (*inf*).

gaffer [ˈgæfəʳ] n (*inf*) (a) (*Brit*) (*foreman*) Vorarbeiter, Vormann, Kapo (S Ger) m; (*boss*) Chef, Boß (*inf*), Alte(r) (*inf*) m. (b) (*old man*) Alte(r), Opa (*inf*) m.

gag [gæg] 1 n (a) Knebel m; (*Med*) Mundsperre f.
  (b) (*inf: joke*) Gag m.
  2 vt knebeln; (*Med*) die Mundsperre einlegen (+*dat*); (*fig*) person zum Schweigen bringen; press etc mundtot machen, knebeln.
  3 vi (a) (*inf: joke*) Witze machen; (*comedian, actor*) Gags machen. ..., **he** ~**ged** ..., witzelte er.
  (b) (*esp US: retch*) würgen (*on an* +*dat*).

gaga [ˈgɑːgɑː] adj (*inf*) plemplem (*inf*), meschugge (*inf*); old person verkalkt (*inf*).

gage n, vt (*US*) see **gauge.**

gaggle [ˈgægl] 1 n (*of geese*) Herde f; (*hum: of girls, women*) Schar, Horde f. 2 vi schnattern.

gaiety [ˈgeɪɪtɪ] n (*cheerfulness*) Fröhlichkeit, Heiterkeit f; (*usu pl: merrymaking*) Vergnügung f; (*bright appearance*) Fröhlichkeit, Farbenfreudigkeit f.

gaily [ˈgeɪlɪ] adv fröhlich; (*fig*) unbekümmert; (*colourfully*) farbenfroh. ~ **coloured** farbenfroh or -prächtig, lustig bunt.

gain [geɪn] 1 n (a) no pl (*advantage*) Vorteil m; (*profit*) Gewinn, Profit m. **it will be to your** ~ es wird zu Ihrem Vorteil sein; **the love of** ~ Profitgier f (*pej*); **to do sth for** ~ etw aus Berechnung (*dat*) or zum eigenen Vorteil tun; (*for money*) etw des Geldes wegen tun; **his loss is our** ~ sein Verlust ist unser Gewinn, wir profitieren von seinem Verlust.
  (b) ~**s** pl (*winnings*) Gewinn m; (*profits also*) Gewinne pl.
  (c) (*increase*) (*in gen*) Zunahme f; (*in speed also*) Erhöhung f; (*in wealth also*) Steigerung f; (*in health*) Besserung f; (*in knowledge*) Erweiterung, Vergrößerung f. ~ **in numbers** zahlenmäßiger Zuwachs; **a** ~ **in weight/productivity/height** eine Gewichtszunahme/eine Produktionssteigerung/ein Höhengewinn m.
  2 vt (a) (*obtain, win*) gewinnen; knowledge, wealth erwerben; advantage, respect, entry sich (*dat*) verschaffen; the lead übernehmen; marks, points erzielen; sum of money (*in*

deal) verdienen; liberty erlangen; (*achieve*) nothing, a little etc erreichen. **that** ~**ed something for us damit haben wir etwas erreicht; what does he hope to** ~ **by it?** was verspricht or erhofft er sich (*dat*) davon?; **to** ~ **sb's goodwill** jdn wohlwollend stimmen; **to** ~ **experience** Erfahrungen sammeln; **he** ~**ed a better view by climbing onto a wall** dadurch, daß er auf eine Mauer kletterte, hatte er einen besseren Ausblick; **they didn't** ~ **entry** sie wurden nicht eingelassen; **we** ~**ed an advantage over him** wir waren ihm gegenüber im Vorteil; **we stood to** ~ **over the others** wir waren den anderen gegenüber im Vorteil; **to** ~ **ground** (an) Boden gewinnen; (*disease*) um sich greifen, sich verbreiten; (*rumours*) sich verbreiten; **to** ~ **ground on sb** (*get further ahead*) den Vorsprung zu jdm vergrößern; (*catch up*) jdn langsam einholen, jdm gegenüber aufholen; **how did he** ~ **such a reputation?** wie ist er zu diesem Ruf gekommen?; **he** ~**ed a reputation for himself as ...** er hat sich (*dat*) einen Namen als ... gemacht.
  (b) (*reach*) other side, shore, summit erreichen.
  (c) (*increase*) **to** ~ **height** (an) Höhe gewinnen, höher steigen; **to** ~ **speed** schneller werden, beschleunigen; **she has** ~**ed weight/3 kilos** sie hat zugenommen/3 Kilo zugenommen; **as he** ~**ed confidence** als er sicherer wurde, als seine Selbstsicherheit wuchs or zunahm; **my watch** ~**s five minutes each day** meine Uhr geht fünf Minuten pro Tag vor.
  3 vi (a) (*watch*) vorgehen.
  (b) (*get further ahead*) den Vorsprung vergrößern; (*close gap*) aufholen.
  (c) (*profit: person*) profitieren (*by* von). **you can only** ~ **by it** das kann nur Ihr Vorteil sein, Sie können dabei nur profitieren; **his reputation** ~**ed greatly by that** dadurch wuchs sein Ansehen enorm; **society/the university would** ~ **from that** das wäre für die Gesellschaft/die Universität von Vorteil.
  (d) **to** ~ **in knowledge/wealth** mehr Wissen/Reichtum erwerben, sein Wissen/seinen Reichtum vergrößern; **to** ~ **in confidence** mehr Selbstvertrauen bekommen; **to** ~ **in speed** schneller werden; **to** ~ **in height** (an) Höhe gewinnen; **to** ~ **in weight** zunehmen; **to** ~ **in prestige** an Ansehen gewinnen, sich (*dat*) größeres Ansehen verschaffen.
♦ **gain (up)on** vi +prep obj (*get further ahead*) den Vorsprung zu ... vergrößern; (*close gap*) einholen; (*catch up with*) work, rust etc fertigwerden mit. **he gradually** ~**ed** ~ **the other runners** er holte die anderen Läufer langsam ein; **it is** ~**ing/constantly** ~**ing** ~ **me** ich komme dagegen nicht (mehr)/immer weniger an; **the cold was** ~**ing** ~ **them, they could hardly move/they couldn't get the building finished** die Kälte übermannte sie, und sie konnten sich kaum bewegen/die Kälte brach herein, und sie konnten den Bau nicht fertig stellen.

gainer [ˈgeɪnəʳ] n I/she etc was the ~ ich habe/sie hat etc dabei profitiert, es war eigentlich ein Gewinn für mich/sie etc; **to be the** ~ **by doing sth** davon profitieren or einen Vorteil davon haben, daß man etw tut.

gainful [ˈgeɪnfʊl] adj occupation etc einträglich. **to be in** ~ **employment** erwerbstätig sein.

gainsay [ˌgeɪnˈseɪ] vt pret, ptp **gainsaid** [ˈgeɪnˈsed] widersprechen (+*dat*); fact (ab)leugnen, bestreiten; evidence, argument widerlegen. **it cannot be gainsaid** es läßt sich nicht leugnen; **there is no** ~**ing his honesty** seine Ehrlichkeit läßt sich nicht leugnen.

'gainst [geɪnst] prep see **against.**

gait [geɪt] n Gang m; (*of horse*) Gangart f. **with unsteady** ~ mit unsicheren Schritten.

gaiter [ˈgeɪtəʳ] n Gamasche f.

gal[1] [gæl] n (*dated inf*) Mädel nt (*dated*).

gal[2] abbr of **gallon(s)** gal, gall.

gala [ˈgɑːlə] n (*festive occasion*) großes Fest; (*Theat, Film, ball*) Galaveranstaltung f. **swimming/sports** ~ großes Schwimm-/Sportfest; ~ **day** Festtag m; (*for person*) großer Tag; ~ **dress** Gala f; (*uniform also*) Galauniform f or -anzug m; ~ **night** Galaabend m; ~ **occasion** festliche Veranstaltung; ~ **performance** Galavorstellung, Festvorstellung f.

galactic [gəˈlæktɪk] adj galaktisch.

Galahad [ˈgæləhæd] n Galahad m; (*fig*) Kavalier, Ritter m.

galantine [ˈgæləntiːn] n kalt servierte, glasierte Fleisch- oder Geflügelroulade.

galaxy [ˈgæləksɪ] n (a) (*Astron*) Milchstraße f, Sternsystem nt, Galaxis f (*spec*). **the G~** die Milchstraße or Galaxis (*spec*). (b) (*fig*) Schar f, Heer nt.

gale [geɪl] n (a) Sturm m. **it was blowing a** ~ es stürmte, ein Sturm tobte or wütete; ~ **force 8** Sturmstärke 8; ~**-force winds** orkanartige Winde; ~ **warning** Sturmwarnung f; **warnings of** ~**s in the English Channel** Sturmwarnungen für den Ärmelkanal.
  (b) (*fig*) ~**s of laughter** Lachsalven pl, stürmisches Gelächter.

Galicia [gəˈlɪsɪə] n (a) (*in Soviet Union*) Galizien nt. (b) (*in Spain*) Galicien nt.

Galician [gəˈlɪsɪən] see **Galicia 1** adj (a) galizisch. (b) galicisch. 2 n (a) Galizier(in f) m. (b) Galicier(in f) m.

Galilean [ˌgæləˈliːən] 1 adj galiläisch. 2 n Galiläer(in f) m.

Galilee ['gælɪliː] n Galiläa nt. the Sea of ~ der See Genezareth, das Galiläische Meer.

gall [gɔːl] 1 n (a) (Physiol) Galle(nsaft m) f. to dip one's pen in ~ (fig) seine Feder spitzen, seine Feder in Galle tauchen (liter); he wrote with a pen dipped in ~ er versprizte Gift und Galle. (b) (sore) Wundstelle f; (Bot) Galle f; (nut-shaped) Gallapfel m. (c) (fig liter) Bitternis f (geh). (d) (inf) Frechheit f. of all the ~! so eine Frechheit or Unverschämtheit! 2 vt (chafe) wund reiben or scheuern; (fig) maßlos ärgern.

gallant ['gælənt] 1 adj (brave) tapfer; (chivalrous, noble) edel, ritterlich; boat, appearance stattlich; sight, display prächtig; (attentive to women) person galant, ritterlich; poetry galant. 2 n (dashing man) schneidiger Kavalier; (ladies' man also) Charmeur m; (obs: suitor) Galan m (old, hum).

gallantly ['gæləntlɪ] adv (bravely) tapfer; (nobly) edelmütig; (chivalrously, courteously) galant.

gallantry ['gæləntrɪ] n (a) (bravery) Tapferkeit f; (chivalry) Edelmut m. (b) (attentiveness to women) Ritterlichkeit, Galanterie f. (c) (compliment) Galanterie, Artigkeit (dated) f.

gall bladder n Gallenblase f.

galleon ['gælɪən] n Galeone f.

gallery ['gælərɪ] n (a) (balcony, corridor) Galerie f; (in church) Empore f; (Theat) oberster Rang, Balkon m, Galerie f. to play to the ~ (fig) sich in Szene setzen. (b) (Art) (Kunst)galerie f. (c) (underground) Stollen m.

galley ['gælɪ] n (a) (Naut) (ship) Galeere f; (kitchen) Kombüse f. ~ slave Galeerensklave m. (b) (Typ) (tray) (Setz)schiff nt; (also ~ proof) Fahne(nabzug m) f.

Gallic ['gælɪk] adj gallisch.

gallicism ['gælɪsɪzəm] n Gallizismus m.

gallicize ['gælɪsaɪz] vt französisieren.

galling ['gɔːlɪŋ] adj äußerst ärgerlich; person unausstehlich.

gallivant [,gælɪ'vænt] vi sich amüsieren. to ~ about or around sich herumtreiben, herumzigeunern; to ~ off losziehen (inf); I was out ~ing last night ich war gestern abend bummeln or auf Achse (inf).

gallon ['gælən] n Gallone f.

gallop ['gæləp] 1 n Galopp m. at a ~ im Galopp; at full ~ im gestreckten Galopp; to go for a ~ ausreiten, einen strammen Ritt machen. 2 vi galoppieren, im Galopp reiten. to ~ away davongaloppieren; we ~ed through our work/the agenda wir haben die Arbeit im Galopp erledigt (inf)/die Tagesordnung im Galopp abgehandelt (inf); to ~ through a book/meal ein Buch in rasendem Tempo lesen (inf)/eine Mahlzeit hinunterschlingen. 3 vt horse galoppieren lassen.

galloping ['gæləpɪŋ] adj (lit, fig) galoppierend.

gallows ['gæləʊz] n Galgen m. to send/bring sb to the ~ jdn an den Galgen bringen; he was sentenced to the ~ er wurde zum Tod am Galgen or durch den Strang verurteilt; ~ bird (inf) Galgenvogel m (inf).

gallstone ['gɔːlstəʊn] n Gallenstein m.

Gallup poll ['gæləp,pəʊl] n Meinungsumfrage f.

galore [gə'lɔːʳ] adv in Hülle und Fülle.

galoshes [gə'lɒʃəz] npl Gummischuhe, Galoschen pl.

galumph [gə'lʌmf] vi (inf) trapsen (inf).

galvanic [gæl'vænɪk] adj (a) (Elec) galvanisch. (b) (fig) movement zuckend; (stimulating) mitreißend, elektrisierend.

galvanism ['gælvənɪzəm] n Galvanismus m.

galvanization [,gælvənaɪ'zeɪʃən] n Galvanisierung, Galvanisation f.

galvanize ['gælvənaɪz] vt (a) (Elec) galvanisieren. (b) (fig) elektrisieren. to ~ sb into action jdn plötzlich aktiv werden lassen; to ~ sb into doing sth jdm einen Stoß geben, etw sofort zu tun; he was ~d into life by the news die Nachricht hat ihm enormen Auftrieb gegeben.

galvanized ['gælvənaɪzd] adj iron, steel galvanisiert.

galvanometer [,gælvə'nɒmɪtəʳ] n Galvanometer nt.

Gambia ['gæmbɪə] n (the) ~ Gambia nt.

Gambian ['gæmbɪən] 1 adj gambisch. 2 n Gambier(in f) m.

gambit ['gæmbɪt] n (a) (Chess) Gambit nt. (b) (fig) (Schach)zug m. his favourite ~ was to ... was er am liebsten machte, war ...; his favourite conversational ~ is ... er fängt gern eine Unterhaltung mit ... an.

gamble ['gæmbl] 1 n (a) (lit) I like the occasional ~ ich versuche gern mal mein Glück (im Spiel/bei Pferdewetten/bei Hundewetten etc); to have a ~ on the horses/dogs/stock exchange auf Pferde/Hunde wetten/an der Börse spekulieren. (b) (fig) Risiko nt. it's a ~ es ist riskant or eine riskante Sache; I'll take a ~ on it ich riskiere es; he took a ~ in buying this house bei dem Hauskauf ist er ein Risiko eingegangen. 2 vi (a) (lit) (um Geld) spielen (with mit), sich an Glücksspielen beteiligen; (on horses etc) wetten. to ~ on the horses/stock exchange bei Pferderennen wetten/an der Börse spekulieren; he made a lot of money gambling at cards or hat beim Kartenspiel viel Geld gewonnen. (b) (fig) to ~ on sth sich auf etw (acc) verlassen; she was gambling on his or him being late sie hat sich darauf verlassen, daß er sich verspäten würde; to ~ with sth mit etw spielen, etw aufs Spiel setzen. 3 vt (a) fortune einsetzen. to ~ sth on sth etw auf etw (acc) setzen. (b) (fig) aufs Spiel setzen.

◆**gamble away** vt sep verspielen.

gambler ['gæmbləʳ] n (lit, fig) Spieler(in f) m. he's a born ~ er ist eine Spielernatur.

gambling ['gæmblɪŋ] n Spielen nt (um Geld); (on horses etc) Wetten nt. to disapprove of ~ gegen das Glücksspiel/Wetten sein; ~ debts Spielschulden pl; ~ den or joint (US) or hell (old) Spielhölle f.

gambol ['gæmbəl] 1 n Tollen nt, Tollerei f; (of lambs)

Herumspringen or -hüpfen nt. to have a ~ herumtollen; herumspringen or -hüpfen. 2 vi herumtollen; herumspringen or -hüpfen.

game¹ [geɪm] 1 n (a) Spiel nt; (sport) Sport(art f) m; (single ~) (of team sports, tennis) Spiel nt; (of table tennis) Satz m; (of billiards, board-games etc, informal tennis match) Partie f. to have or play a ~ of football/tennis/chess etc Fußball/Tennis/Schach etc spielen; do you fancy a quick ~ of football/cards/tennis/chess etc? hättest du Lust, ein bißchen Fußball/Karten/Tennis/Schach etc zu spielen?, hättest du Lust auf eine Partie Tennis/Schach?; he plays a good ~ er spielt gut; shall we play a ~ now? wollen wir jetzt ein Spiel machen?; to have a ~ with sb, to give sb a ~ mit jdm spielen; winning the second set put him back in the ~ again nachdem er den zweiten Satz gewonnen hatte, hatte er wieder Chancen; to be off one's ~ nicht in Form sein; ~ of chance/skill Glücksspiel nt/ Geschicklichkeitsspiel nt; ~ set and match to X Satz und Spiel (geht an) X; ~ to X Spiel X; that's ~ Spiel; one ~ all eins beide. (b) (fig) Spiel nt; (scheme, plan) Absicht f, Vorhaben nt. to play the ~ sich an die Spielregeln halten; to play ~s with sb mit jdm spielen; the ~ is up das Spiel ist aus; to play sb's ~ jdm in die Hände spielen; to play a deep/double ~ ein undurchsichtiges/doppeltes Spiel or Doppelspiel treiben; two can play at that ~, that's a ~ (that) two can play wie du mir, so ich dir (inf); to beat sb at his own ~ jdn mit den eigenen Waffen schlagen; to give the ~ away alles verderben; to see through sb's ~ jds Spiel durchschauen, jdm auf die Schliche kommen; to spoil sb's little ~ jdm das Spiel verderben, jdm die Suppe versalzen (inf); I wonder what the PM's ~ is? ich frage mich, was der Premier vorhat or im Schilde führt; so that's your ~, is it? darauf willst du also hinaus!; what's your little ~? was führst du im Schilde? (c) ~s pl (Sports event) Spiele pl. (d) ~s sing (Sch) Sport m; to be good at ~s gut in Sport sein; gym on Tuesdays, ~s on Wednesdays Turnen am Dienstag, Ballspiele/Leichtathletik etc am Mittwoch. (e) (inf: business, profession) Branche f. how long have you been in this ~? wie lange machen Sie das schon?; is he still in this ~? macht er das immer noch?, ist er immer noch dabei?; the publishing ~ das Verlagswesen; he's in the second-hand car ~ er macht in Gebrauchtwagen (inf); to be/go on the ~ auf den Strich gehen (inf). (f) (inf: difficult time) Theater nt (inf). I had quite a ~ getting the tickets das war (vielleicht) ein Theater, bis ich die Karten bekam! (inf). (g) (Hunt) Wild nt; (Cook also) Wildbret nt. 2 vi (um Geld) spielen. 3 vt (also ~ away) verspielen.

game² adj (brave) mutig. to be ~ (willing) mitmachen, dabeisein; to be ~ for sth (bei) etw mitmachen; to be ~ to do sth bereit sein, etw zu tun; to be ~ for anything für alles zu haben sein, zu allen Schandtaten bereit sein (hum inf).

game³ adj (crippled) lahm.

game: ~bag n Jagdtasche f; ~ bird n Federwild nt no pl; the pheasant is a ~ bird der Fasan gehört zum Federwild; ~cock n Kampfhahn m; ~ fish n Sportfisch m; ~keeper n Wildhüter m; ~ laws npl Jagdgesetz nt; ~ licence n Jagdschein m; ~ pie n Wildpastete f; ~ point n Spielpunkt m; ~ preserve n Wildhegegebiet nt; ~ reserve n Wildschutzgebiet or -reservat nt.

games [geɪmz] n: ~manship n Täuschungsmanöver pl; ~ master n Sportlehrer m; ~ mistress n Sportlehrerin f.

gamester ['geɪmstəʳ] n Spieler(in f) m.

gamewarden ['geɪmwɔːdn] n Jagdaufseher m.

gamin ['gæmɛ̃] 1 n Straßenjunge m. 2 attr jungenhaft, knabenhaft.

gaming ['geɪmɪŋ] n see gambling. ~ machine (form) Münzspielgerät nt (form).

gamma ray ['gæmə'reɪ] n Gammastrahl m.

gammon ['gæmən] n (bacon) leicht geräucherter Vorderschinken; (ham) (gekochter) Schinken. ~ steak dicke Scheibe Vorderschinken zum Braten oder Grillen.

gammy ['gæmɪ] adj (inf) see game³.

gamp [gæmp] n (dated hum) Regenschirm m, Musspritze f (dated hum).

gamut ['gæmət] n (Mus) Noten- or Tonskala f; (fig) Skala f. to run the (whole) ~ of emotion(s) die ganze Skala der Gefühle durchlaufen.

gamy ['geɪmɪ] adj nach Wild schmeckend; (high) angegangen. ~ taste Wildgeschmack m; (high) Hautgout m (geh), angegangener Geschmack.

gander ['gændəʳ] n (a) Gänserich, Ganter (dial) m. (b) (inf) to have or take a ~ at sth auf etw (acc) einen Blick werfen; let's have a ~! gucken wir mal! (inf); (let me/us look) laß mal sehen.

gang [gæŋ] n Haufen m, Schar f (of workers, prisoners) Kolonne f, Trupp m; (of criminals, youths, terrorists) Bande, Gang f; (of friends etc, clique) Clique f, Haufen m (inf). there was a whole ~ of them es war ein ganzer Haufen; ~ bang (inf) Gruppenvergewaltigung f; ~ land (inf) die Unterwelt.

◆**gang up** vi sich zusammentun. to ~ ~ against or on sb sich verbünden or verschwören gegen; (to fight) geschlossen losgehen auf (+acc) or gegen.

ganger ['gæŋəʳ] n Vorarbeiter, Vormann m.

Ganges ['gændʒiːz] n Ganges m.

ganglia ['gæŋglɪə] pl of ganglion.

gangling ['gæŋglɪŋ] adj schlaksig, hochaufgeschossen.

ganglion ['gæŋglɪən] n, pl ganglia (a) (Anat) Ganglion nt; (Med also) Überbein nt. (b) (fig: of activity) Zentrum nt.

gangplank ['gæŋplæŋk] n Laufplanke f, Landungssteg m.

gangrene ['gæŋgriːn] n Brand m, Gangrän f or nt (spec).

gangrenous ['gæŋgrɪnəs] adj brandig, gangränös (spec).

gangster ['gæŋstəʳ] n Gangster, Verbrecher m.

gangsterism ['gæŋstərizəm] n Gangstertum, Verbrechertum nt.

gangway ['gæŋweɪ] **1** n (a) (Naut) (gangplank) Landungsbrücke, Gangway f; (ladder) Fallreep nt. (b) (passage) Gang m. **2** interj Platz da.

gannet ['gænɪt] n (Zool) Tölpel m.

gantry ['gæntrɪ] n (for crane) Portal nt; (on motorway) Schilderbrücke f; (Rail) Signalbrücke f; (for rocket) Abschußrampe f.

gaol [dʒeɪl] n, vt see **jail.**

gaoler ['dʒeɪlə'] n see **jailer.**

gap [gæp] n (lit, fig) Lücke f; (chink) Spalt m; (in surface) Spalte f, Riß m; (Geog) Spalte f; (Tech: spark ~) Abstand m; (fig) (in conversation, narrative) Pause f; (gulf) Kluft f. a ~ in sb's education/memory eine Bildungs-/Gedächtnislücke.

gape [geɪp] **1** vi (a) (open mouth wide) (person) den Mund aufreißen or -sperren; (bird) den Schnabel aufsperren; (chasm etc) gähnen, klaffen; (seam, wound) klaffen.
(b) (stare: person) starren, gaffen. to ~ at sb/sth jdn/etw (mit offenem Mund) anstarren; to ~ up/down at sb/sth zu jdm/etw hinaufstarren/auf jdn/etw hinunterstarren; the people stood and ~d die Leute sperrten Mund und Nase auf (inf).
2 n (a) (hole) gähnendes or klaffendes Loch; (in seam) geplatzte Stelle; (chasm) gähnender Abgrund. the menacing ~ of the ravine der drohend gähnende Abgrund.
(b) (stare) Starren, Gaffen nt. the astonished ~(s) of the children wie die Kinder erstaunt Mund und Nase aufsperrten (inf).

gaping ['geɪpɪŋ] adj (a) klaffend; chasm also gähnend; wound weit geöffnet; beaks weit aufgesperrt. (b) (staring) gaffend; (astonished) staunend.

gap: ~less adj lückenlos; ~-toothed adj mit weiter Zahnstellung; (with teeth missing) mit Zahnlücken.

garage ['gærɑːʒ, (US) gə'rɑːʒ] **1** n (for parking) Garage f; (for petrol) Tankstelle f; (for repairs etc) (Reparatur)werkstatt f. ~ **mechanic** Kraftfahrzeug- or Kfz-Mechaniker m. **2** vt (in einer Garage) ab- or unterstellen; (drive into ~) in die Garage fahren. the car is kept ~d das Auto wird in einer Garage aufbewahrt.

garb [gɑːb] **1** n Gewand nt; (inf) Kluft f (inf). **2** vt kleiden.

garbage ['gɑːbɪdʒ] n (lit: esp US) Abfall, Müll m; (fig) (useless things) Schund, Mist (inf) m; (nonsense) Blödsinn, Quatsch m (inf).

garbage: ~ **can** n (US) Müll- or Abfalleimer m; (outside) Mülltonne f; ~ **collector** or **man** n (US) Müllarbeiter m; ~ **collectors** npl Müllabfuhr f; ~ **disposal unit** n Müllschlucker m.

garble ['gɑːbl] vt to ~ one's words sich beim Sprechen überschlagen.

garbled ['gɑːbld] adj wirr. the message got ~ on its way die Nachricht kam völlig entstellt an; the facts got a little ~ die Tatsachen sind etwas durcheinandergebracht worden or durcheinandergeraten.

garden ['gɑːdn] **1** n (a) Garten m. the G~ of Eden der Garten Eden. (b) (often pl: park) Park m, Gartenanlagen pl. **2** vi im Garten arbeiten, Gartenarbeit machen, gärtnern.

gardener ['gɑːdnə'] n Gärtner(in f) m.

gardenia [gɑː'diːnɪə] n Gardenie f.

gardening ['gɑːdnɪŋ] n Gartenarbeit f. she loves ~ sie arbeitet gerne im Garten, sie gärtnert gerne; ~ **tools** Gartengeräte pl.

garden in cpds Garten-; ~ **party** n Gartenparty f or -fest nt; ~-**party** hat n breitrandiger Sommerhut; ~ **shears** npl Heckenschere f.

gargantuan [gɑː'gæntjʊən] adj gewaltig, enorm.

gargle ['gɑːgl] **1** vi gurgeln. **2** n (liquid) Gurgelwasser nt. to have a ~ gurgeln.

gargoyle ['gɑːgɔɪl] n Wasserspeier m.

garish ['gɛərɪʃ] adj lights, illuminations etc grell; colour, decorations etc also knallig (inf); colour also schreiend; clothes knallbunt, auffallend.

garishly ['gɛərɪʃlɪ] adv in grellen or schreienden Farben; colourful auffallend, knallig (inf); illuminated grell.

garishness ['gɛərɪʃnɪs] n grelle or schreiende Farben; (of colours, illuminations) Grellheit f.

garland ['gɑːlənd] **1** n Kranz m; (festoon) Girlande f. **2** vt bekränzen.

garlic ['gɑːlɪk] n Knoblauch m.

garment ['gɑːmənt] n Kleidungsstück nt; (robe) Gewand nt (liter). all her ~s ihre ganzen Kleider; ~ **industry** (US) Bekleidungsindustrie f.

garner ['gɑːnə'] vt (lit, fig) (gather) sammeln; knowledge erwerben; (store) speichern. **memories** ~ed in the Far East Erinnerungen pl an Erlebnisse im Fernen Osten; all his memories are ~ed in this book all seine Erinnerungen sind in diesem Buch zusammengetragen.

garnet ['gɑːnɪt] n Granat m.

garnish ['gɑːnɪʃ] **1** vt garnieren, verzieren; (fig) story also, style ausschmücken. **2** n Garnierung f.

garnishing ['gɑːnɪʃɪŋ] n (Cook) Garnierung f; (act also) Garnieren nt; (fig: of style, story etc) Ausschmückung f.

garret ['gærət] n (attic room) Mansarde f, Dachkammer f; (attic) Dachboden m.

garrison ['gærɪsən] **1** n Garnison f. ~ **duty/town** Garnisonsdienst m/Garnisonstadt f. **2** vt troops in Garnison legen; town mit einer Garnison belegen. to be ~ed in Garnison liegen.

garrotte [gə'rɒt] **1** vt (execute) garrottieren, mit der Garrotte hinrichten; (strangle) erdrosseln. **death by garrotting** Tod durch die Garrotte. **2** n Garrotte f.

garrulity [gə'ruːlɪtɪ] n Geschwätzigkeit, Schwatzhaftigkeit f.

garrulous ['gærʊləs] adj geschwätzig, schwatzhaft.

garrulously ['gærʊləslɪ] adv to talk/chat etc ~ schwatzen, plappern.

garter ['gɑːtə'] n Strumpfband nt; (US: suspender) Strumpfhalter m. **the (Order of the) G~** der Hosenbandorden.

garter: ~ **belt** n (US) Strumpf- or Hüftgürtel m; ~ **snake** n (US) Ringelnatter f; ~ **stitch** n gerippt or rechts-rechts gestricktes Muster; **5 rows** ~ **stitch** 5 Reihen rechts-rechts gestrickt.

gas [gæs] **1** n (a) Gas nt. **to cook by** or **with** or **on** ~ mit Gas kochen; **to cook on a slow** ~ auf niedriger Flamme kochen.
(b) (US: petrol) Benzin nt.
(c) (anaesthetic) Lachgas nt. **to have** ~ Lachgas bekommen; **to have a tooth out with** ~ sich (dat) einen Zahn unter Lachgasnarkose ziehen lassen.
(d) (Mil) (Gift)gas nt.
(e) (inf: talk) leeres Gerede or Gefasel (inf); (boastful) großspuriges Gerede, Angeberei f. **to have a good** ~ einen Schwatz halten.
(f) (sl) **it's/he's a** ~ (fantastic) es/er ist Klasse or dufte or 'ne Wucht (all sl); (hilarious) es/er ist zum Schreien (inf).
2 vt vergasen. **they were** ~**sed accidentally during their sleep** sie starben im Schlaf an Gasvergiftung; **to** ~ **oneself** den Gashahn aufdrehen, sich mit Gas vergiften.
3 vi (inf: talk) schwafeln (inf), faseln (inf).

gas in cpds Gas-; ~ **bag** n (inf) Quasselstrippe f (inf); ~ **bracket** n Gasanschluß(stelle f) m, Gaszuleitungsrohr nt; (for light) Wandarm m; ~ **chamber** n Gaskammer f; ~ **cooker** n Gasherd m; ~ **engine** n Gasmaschine f or -motor m.

gaseous ['gæsɪəs] adj gasförmig.

gas: ~ **field** n Erdgasfeld nt; ~ **fire** n Gasofen m; ~-**fired** adj Gas-, gasbefeuert (form); ~ **fitter** n Gasinstallateur m; ~ **fittings** npl Gasgeräte pl; ~ **fixture** n festinstalliertes Gasgerät; ~ **guzzler** n (US inf) Säufer, Benzinschlucker (inf) m.

gash [gæʃ] **1** n (wound) klaffende Wunde; (in earth, tree) (klaffende) Spalte; (slash) tiefe Kerbe; (in upholstery) tiefer Schlitz. **2** vt aufschlitzen; furniture, wood tief einkerben. **he fell and** ~**ed his head/knee** er ist gestürzt und hat sich (dat) dabei den Kopf/das Knie aufgeschlagen; **I** ~**ed my foot open** ich habe mir den Fuß aufgeschlitzt.

gas: ~ **heater** n Gasofen m; ~-**holder** n Gasometer m, (Groß)gasbehälter m; ~ **jet** n Gasdüse f.

gasket ['gæskɪt] n (Tech) Dichtung f.

gas: ~ **lamp** n Gaslampe f; (in streets) Gaslaterne f; ~-**light** n (a) see ~ **lamp**; (b) no pl Gaslicht nt or -beleuchtung f; ~ **lighter** n (a) Gasanzünder m; (b) (for cigarettes etc) Gasfeuerzeug nt; ~-**lit** adj mit Gasbeleuchtung; ~ **main** n Gasleitung f; ~**man** n Gasmann m (inf); ~ **mantle** n (Gas)glühstrumpf m; ~ **mask** n Gasmaske f; ~ **meter** n Gaszähler m or -uhr f or -messer m.

gasoline ['gæsəʊliːn] n (US) Benzin nt.

gasometer [gæ'sɒmɪtə'] n Gasometer m, (Groß)gasbehälter m.

gas oven n Gasherd m; (gas chamber) Gaskammer f. **to put one's head in the** ~ (kill oneself) den Gashahn aufdrehen.

gasp [gɑːsp] **1** n (for breath) tiefer Atemzug. **the** ~**s of the runner** das Keuchen des Läufers; **to give a** ~ (of surprise/fear etc) (vor Überraschung/Angst etc) die Luft anhalten or nach Luft schnappen (inf); **a** ~ **went up at his audacity** seine Verwegenheit verschlug den Leuten den Atem; **to be at one's last** ~ in den letzten Zügen liegen; (exhausted etc) auf dem letzten Loch pfeifen (inf).
2 vi (continually) keuchen; (once) tief einatmen; (with surprise etc) nach Luft schnappen (inf). **to make sb** ~ jdm den Atem nehmen; (fig also) jdm den Atem verschlagen; **to** ~ **for breath** nach Atem ringen, nach Luft schnappen (inf); **he** ~**ed with astonishment** er war so erstaunt, daß es ihm den Atem verschlug; **heavens, no!, she** ~**ed** um Himmels willen, nein!, stieß sie hervor.

♦ **gasp out** vt sep hervorstoßen.

gasper ['gɑːspə'] n (Brit sl) Lungenbrötchen nt (sl).

gas: ~ **pipe** n Gasrohr nt or -leitung f; ~ **ring** n Gasbrenner m; (portable) Gaskocher m; ~ **station** n (US) Tankstelle f; ~ **stove** n Gasherd m; (portable) Gaskocher m.

gassy ['gæsɪ] adj (+er) (a) (Sci) gasförmig. **it smells** ~ es riecht nach Gas. (b) drink kohlensäurehaltig. (c) (inf) person geschwätzig.

gas: ~ **tank** n (US) Benzintank m; ~ **tap** n Gashahn m; ~**tight** adj gasdicht.

gastric ['gæstrɪk] adj Magen-, gastrisch (spec).

gastric: ~ **flu** or **influenza** n Darmgrippe f; ~ **juices** npl Magensäfte pl; ~ **ulcer** n Magengeschwür nt.

gastritis [gæs'traɪtɪs] n Magenschleimhautentzündung, Gastritis f.

gastro- ['gæstrəʊ-] pref Magen-, Gastro- (spec). ~**enteritis** Magen-Darm-Entzündung, Gastroenteritis (spec) f.

gastronome ['gæstrənəʊm] n Feinschmecker m.

gastronomic [gæstrə'nɒmɪk] adj gastronomisch, kulinarisch.

gastronomy [gæs'trɒnəmɪ] n Gastronomie f.

gastropod ['gæstrəpɒd] n Bauchfüß(l)er m, Gastropode (spec) m.

gasworks ['gæswɜːks] n sing or pl Gaswerk nt.

gat [gæt] n (US sl) Kanone, Knarre (sl) f.

gate [geɪt] **1** n (a) Tor nt; (small, garden ~) Pforte f; (five-barred ~) Gatter nt; (in station) Sperre f; (in airport) Flugsteig m; (level-crossing) Schranke f; (Sport: starting ~) Startmaschine f; (sports ground entrance) Einlaß, Eingang m. **to open/shut the** ~**s** das Tor etc öffnen/schließen; **the** ~**s of heaven** das Himmelstor, die Himmelstür or -pforte.
(b) (Sport) (attendance) Zuschauerzahl f; (entrance money) Einnahmen pl.
2 vt pupil, student Ausgangssperre erteilen (+dat). **to be** ~**d** Ausgangssperre haben.

gateau ['gætəʊ] n Torte f.

gate: ~**crash** (inf) **1** vt to ~**crash a party/meeting** eine Party/Versammlung reinplatzen (inf); (crowd: to disrupt it) eine Party/Versammlung stürmen; **2** vi einfach so hingehen (inf); ~**crasher** n ungeladener Gast; (at meeting) Eindringling m; ~**house** n Pförtnerhaus or -häuschen nt; ~**keeper** n Pförtner m; (Rail) Schrankenwärter m; ~-**leg(ged) table** n Klapptisch m; ~ **money** n (Sport) Einnahmen pl; ~**post** n Torpfosten m; **between you, me and the** ~**post** (inf) unter uns gesagt, unter uns Pastorentöchtern (hum inf); ~**way** n (lit, fig) Tor nt (to zu); (archway, ~ frame) Torbogen m.

gather ['gæðə'] **1** vt **(a)** (collect, bring together) sammeln; crowd, people versammeln; flowers, cultivated fruit pflücken; potatoes, corn etc ernten; harvest einbringen; taxes einziehen; (collect up) broken glass, pins etc zusammenlegen, aufsammeln; one's belongings, books, clothes (zusammen)packen; an impression gewinnen. **to** ~ **one's strength/thoughts** Kräfte sammeln/seine Gedanken ordnen, sich sammeln; **velvet curtains** ~ **dust/dirt** Samtvorhänge sind Staub-/Schmutzfänger; **it just sat there** ~**ing dust** es stand nur da und verstaubte; **to be** ~**ed to one's fathers** (liter) heimgehen (liter).

(b) (increase) **to** ~ **speed** schneller werden, an Geschwindigkeit gewinnen; **to** ~ **strength** stärker werden; **to** ~ **volume** lauter werden, an Lautstärke zunehmen.

(c) (infer) schließen (from aus). **I** ~**ed that** das dachte ich mir; **I** ~ **from the papers that he has** ... wie ich aus den Zeitungen ersehe, hat er ...; **as far as I can** ~ (so) wie ich es sehe; **I** ~ **she won't be coming** ich nehme an, daß sie nicht kommt; **as you will have/might have** ~**ed** ... wie Sie bestimmt/vielleicht bemerkt haben ...; **as will be** ~**ed from my report** wie aus meinem Bericht hervorgeht or zu ersehen ist.

(d) to ~ **sb into one's arms** jdn in die Arme nehmen or schließen; **she** ~**ed her mink around her** sie hüllte sich in ihren Nerz.

(e) (Sew) kräuseln, raffen; (at seam) fassen.

(f) (Typ) zusammentragen, kollationieren (spec).

2 vi **(a)** (collect) (people) sich versammeln; (crowds also) sich ansammeln; (objects, dust etc) sich (an)sammeln; (clouds) sich zusammenziehen; (storm) sich zusammenbrauen. **tears** ~**ed in her eyes** ihre Augen füllten sich mit Tränen.

(b) (increase: darkness, force etc) zunehmen (in an +dat).

(c) (abscess etc) sich mit Eiter füllen; (pus) sich sammeln.

3 n (Sew) Fältchen nt. **there were** ~**s at the waist (of the skirt)** der Rock war in der Taille gekräuselt or gerafft or gefaßt.

♦ **gather in** vt sep **(a)** einsammeln; crops einbringen; taxes einziehen; animals zusammentreiben. **(b)** cloth fassen.

♦ **gather round** vi zusammenkommen. **come on, children,** ~ ~! kommt alle her, Kinder!; **they** ~**ed** ~ **the fire** sie versammelten or scharten sich um das Feuer.

♦ **gather together 1** vi zusammenkommen, sich versammeln.

2 vt sep einsammeln; one's belongings, books zusammenpacken; people versammeln; team zusammenstellen; animals zusammentreiben. **the music** ~**ed a crowd** ~ die Musik lockte eine Menschenmenge an; **to** ~ **oneself** ~ zu sich kommen; (for jump etc) sich bereit machen (for zu).

♦ **gather up** vt sep aufsammeln; one's belongings zusammenpacken; hair hochstecken; skirts (hoch)raffen; (fig) pieces auflesen. **he** ~**ed himself** ~ **to his full height** er reckte sich zu voller Größe auf.

gathering ['gæðərɪŋ] n **(a)** (people at meeting etc) Versammlung f; (meeting) Treffen nt; (small group) Gruppe f, Häufchen nt; (of curious onlookers) Ansammlung f. **(b)** (Sew: gathers) Krause f.

GATT [gæt] abbr of **General Agreement on Tariffs and Trade** GATT.

gauche adj, ~**ly** adv (gauʃ, -lɪ) (socially) unbeholfen, tölpelhaft; remark ungeschickt; (clumsy) linkisch, ungeschickt.

gaucheness ['gəʊʃnɪs] n Unbeholfenheit, Tölpelhaftigkeit f; Ungeschicktheit f.

gaucherie ['gəʊʃərɪ] n **(a)** see gaucheness. **(b)** (act) Tölpelei f; (remark) ungeschickte Bemerkung.

gaucho ['gaʊtʃəʊ] n Gaucho m.

gaudily ['gɔːdɪlɪ] adv see adj.

gaudiness ['gɔːdɪnɪs] n Knalligkeit (inf), Buntheit f; Auffälligkeit f.

gaudy ['gɔːdɪ] adj (+er) knallig (inf), auffällig bunt; colours auffällig, knallig (inf).

gauge [geɪdʒ] **1** n **(a)** (instrument) Meßgerät or -instrument nt; (to measure diameter, width etc) (Meß)lehre f; (for rings) Ringmaß nt; (to measure water level) Pegel m. **pressure/wind** ~ Druck-/Windmesser m; **temperature** ~ Temperaturanzeiger m; **petrol** ~ Benzinuhr f; **oil** ~ Ölstandsanzeiger or -messer m.

(b) (thickness, width) (of wire, sheet metal etc) Stärke f; (of bullet) Durchmesser m, Kaliber nt; (Rail) Spurweite f. **standard/narrow/broad** ~ Normal- or Regel-/Schmal-/Breitspur f.

(c) (fig) Maßstab m (of für).

2 vt **(a)** (Tech: measure) messen.

(b) (fig: appraise) person's capacities, character beurteilen; reaction, course of events abschätzen; situation abwägen; (guess) schätzen.

Gaul [gɔːl] n (country) Gallien nt; (person) Gallier(in f) m.

gaunt [gɔːnt] adj (+er) hager; (from suffering) abgezehrt, ausgemergelt; trees dürr und kahl; landscape öde, karg.

gauntlet[1] ['gɔːntlɪt] n **(a)** (of armour) Panzerhandschuh m. **to throw down/pick up or take up the** ~ (fig) den Fehdehandschuh hinwerfen/aufnehmen. **(b)** (glove) (Stulpen)handschuh m; (part of glove) Stulpe f.

gauntlet[2] n: **to run the** ~ (fig) Spießruten laufen; **to (have) to run the** ~ **of sth** einer Sache (dat) ausgesetzt sein; **the child had to run the** ~ **of his tormentors** das Kind mußte einen Spießrutenlauf durch die Reihen seiner Peiniger veranstalten.

gauntness ['gɔːntnɪs] n see adj Hagerkeit f; Abgezehrtheit, Ausgemergeltheit f; Kahlheit f; Öde, Kargheit f.

gauze [gɔːz] n Gaze f; (Med also) (Verbands)mull m. **wire** ~ Drahtgaze f or -netz nt.

gauzy ['gɔːzɪ] adj (+er) hauchfein or -zart.

gave [geɪv] pret of **give**.

gavel ['gævl] n Hammer m.

gavotte [gə'vɒt] n Gavotte f.

gawk [gɔːk] (inf) **1** n Schlaks m (inf). **2** vi see **gawp**.

gawkily ['gɔːkɪlɪ] adv see adj.

gawkiness ['gɔːkɪnɪs] n see adj Schlaksigkeit, Staksigkeit (inf) f; Unbeholfenheit f.

gawky ['gɔːkɪ] adj (+er) person, movement schlaksig, staksig (inf), linkisch; animal unbeholfen, staksig (inf); appearance unbeholfen.

gawp [gɔːp] vi (inf) glotzen (inf), gaffen. **to** ~ **at sb/sth** jdn/etw anglotzen (inf) or angaffen; **what are you** ~**ing at?** was glotzt du da? (inf).

gay [geɪ] **1** adj (+er) **(a)** (happy) fröhlich; colours also bunt; one colour also lebhaft; company, occasion lustig. ~ **with lights** bunt beleuchtet; **the park/room was** ~ **with flowers** bunte Blumen schmückten den Park/das Zimmer; **with** ~ **abandon** hingebungsvoll.

(b) (pleasure-loving) lebenslustig; life flott. ~ **dog** (inf) lockerer Vogel (inf).

(c) (homosexual) schwul (inf).

2 n Schwule(r) mf. **G**~ **Lib** Homosexuellenbewegung f, Homosexuelle Aktion.

gaze [geɪz] **1** n Blick m. **2** vi starren. **to** ~ **at sb/sth** jdn/etw anstarren.

♦ **gaze about** or **around** vi um sich blicken. **he** ~**d** ~ **(him) at the strange scene** er sah sich (dat) erstaunt die seltsame Szene an.

gazebo [gə'ziːbəʊ] n Gartenlaube f.

gazelle [gə'zel] n Gazelle f.

gazette [gə'zet] **1** n (magazine) Zeitung f; (as title also) Anzeiger m; (government publication) Staatsanzeiger m, Amtsblatt nt. **2** vt im Staatsanzeiger bekanntgeben.

gazetteer [ˌgæzɪ'tɪə'] n alphabetisches Ortsverzeichnis (mit Ortsbeschreibung).

gazump [gə'zʌmp] vt (Brit) entgegen mündlicher Zusage ein Haus an einen Höherbietenden verkaufen.

GB abbr of **Great Britain** GB, Großbritannien nt.

gbh abbr of **grievous bodily harm**.

GC (Brit) abbr of **George Cross**.

GCE (Brit) abbr of **General Certificate of Education**.

Gdns abbr of **Gardens**.

GDR abbr of **German Democratic Republic** DDR f.

gear [gɪə'] **1** n **(a)** (Aut etc) Gang m. ~**s** pl (mechanism) Getriebe nt; (on bicycle) Gangschaltung f; **a bicycle with three-speed** ~**s** ein Fahrrad mit Dreigangschaltung; **to put the car into** ~ einen Gang einlegen; **the car is/you're in/out of** ~ der Gang ist eingelegt or drin (inf)/das Auto ist im Leerlauf, es ist kein Gang drin (inf); **to leave the car in/out of** ~ den Gang eingelegt lassen/das Auto im Leerlauf lassen; **to change** ~ schalten; **to change into third** ~ in den dritten Gang schalten, den dritten Gang einlegen; **the car jumps out of** or **won't stay in** ~ der Gang springt heraus; **I usually function in low** ~ **in the mornings** morgens dauert bei mir alles länger.

(b) (equipment) Ausrüstung f, Zeug nt (inf), Sachen pl (inf); (tools) Gerät, Zeug (inf) nt; (belongings) Sachen pl (inf), Zeug(s) nt (inf); (clothing) Sachen pl (inf).

(c) (Tech) Vorrichtung f; see landing ~, steering ~.

2 vt (fig) abstellen, ausrichten (to auf +acc). **to be** ~**ed to sth** auf etw (acc) abgestellt sein; (person, ambition) auf etw (acc) ausgerichtet sein; (have facilities for) auf etw (acc) eingerichtet sein.

3 vi (Tech) eingreifen, im Eingriff sein.

♦ **gear down 1** vi (driver) herunterschalten, in einen niedrigeren Gang schalten. **2** vt sep engine niedertouriger auslegen or machen; (fig) drosseln.

♦ **gear up** vi heraufschalten, in einen höheren Gang schalten. **2** vt sep engine höhertourig auslegen or machen. **to** ~ **oneself** ~ (fig) sich bereit machen; **to** ~ **oneself** ~ **for sth** (fig) sich auf etw (acc) einstellen.

gear: ~**box** n Getriebe nt; ~ **change** n Schalten f.

-**geared** [-gɪəd] adj suf -tourig.

gearing ['gɪərɪŋ] n Auslegung f (der Gänge).

gear: ~**lever** n Schaltknüppel m; (column-mounted) Schalthebel m; ~ **ratio** n Übersetzung(sverhältnis nt) f; ~ **shift** (US), ~ **stick** n see ~ **lever**; ~ **wheel** n Zahnrad nt.

gee [dʒiː] interj ja (esp US inf) Mensch (inf), Mann (inf). ~ **whiz!** Mensch Meier! (inf). **(b)** (to horse) ~ **up!** hü!

gee-gee ['dʒiːdʒiː] n (baby-talk) Hottehü nt (inf).

geese [giːs] pl of **goose**.

geezer ['giːzə'] n (sl) Typ (sl), Kerl (inf) m. **old** ~ Opa m (inf).

Geiger counter ['gaɪgəˌkaʊntə'] n Geigerzähler m.

geisha (girl) ['geɪʃə(gɜːl)] n Geisha f.

gel [dʒel] **1** n Gel nt. **2** vi gelieren; (jelly etc also) fest werden; (fig: plan, idea) Gestalt annehmen.

gelatin(e) ['dʒelətiːn] n Gelatine f.

gelatinous [dʒɪ'lætɪnəs] adj gelatine- or gallertartig.

geld [geld] vt kastrieren, verschneiden.

gelding ['geldɪŋ] n kastriertes Tier, Kastrat m (spec); (horse) Wallach m.

gelignite ['dʒelɪgnaɪt] n Plastiksprengstoff m.

gem [dʒem] n Edelstein m; (cut also) Juwel nt (geh); (fig) (person) Juwel nt; (of collection etc) Prachtstück or -exemplar nt. **be a** ~ **and** ... sei ein Schatz und ...; **that joke/story/this recording is a real** ~ der Witz/die Geschichte/die Aufnahme ist Spitzenklasse (inf) or einmalig gut; **every one a** ~ (inf) einer besser als der andere; **a** ~ **of a book/painting/watch** (splendid) ein meisterhaftes Buch/Gemälde/eine prachtvolle Uhr; (sweet, amusing) ein entzückendes Büchlein/Bildchen/Ührchen.

Gemini ['dʒemɪniː] n Zwilling pl. **he's a** ~ er ist Zwilling.

gemstone ['dʒemstəʊn] n Edelstein m.

Gen *abbr of* **General** Gen.

gen [dʒen] *n* (*Brit inf*) Informationen *pl.* **to give sb the ~ on** *or* **about sth** jdn über etw (*acc*) informieren; **what's the ~ on this?** worum geht es hier?

♦**gen up** (*Brit inf*) **1** *vi* **to ~ ~ on sth** sich über etw (*acc*) informieren. **2** *vt sep* **to ~ sb ~/get ~ned ~ on sth** jdn/sich über etw (*acc*) informieren; **to be (all) ~ned ~ on** *or* **about sth** sich (sehr gut) auskennen in etw (*dat*).

gender [ˈdʒendəʳ] *n* Geschlecht, Genus *nt*. **what ~ is this word?** welches Geschlecht *or* Genus hat dieses Wort?; **the feminine/masculine ~** das Femininum/Maskulinum.

gene [dʒiːn] *n* Gen *nt*, Erbfaktor *m*. **~ pool** Erbmasse *f*.

genealogical [ˌdʒiːnɪəˈlɒdʒɪkəl] *adj* genealogisch. **~ tree** Stammbaum *m*.

genealogist [ˌdʒiːnɪˈælədʒɪst] *n* Genealoge *m*, Genealogin *f*, Stammbaumforscher(in *f*) *m*.

genealogy [ˌdʒiːnɪˈælədʒɪ] *n* Genealogie, Stammbaumforschung *f*; (*ancestry*) Stammbaum *m*.

genera [ˈdʒenərə] *pl of* **genus**.

general [ˈdʒenərəl] **1** *adj* (**a**) allgemein; *view, enquiry, discussion also* generell; *manager, director, agent, agency* General-; *meeting* Voll-; (*of shareholders*) Haupt-; *user, reader* Durchschnitts-; *trader, dealer, store* Gemischtwaren-. **as a ~ rule,** in the ~ **way (of things)** im allgemeinen; **it is ~ practice** *or* **a ~ custom** es ist allgemein üblich; **in ~ use** allgemein in Gebrauch; **for ~ use** für den allgemeinen *or* normalen Gebrauch; (*for use by everybody*) für die Allgemeinheit; **to be a ~ favourite** allgemein beliebt sein; **that is a ~ problem, that problem is quite ~** das ist ein allgemeines Problem; **we just had a ~ chat** wir haben uns ganz allgemein unterhalten; **~ headquarters** Hauptquartier *nt*; (*Mil*) Generalhauptquartier *nt*; **~ editor** Allgemeinredakteur *m*; (*of particular book*) Herausgeber *m*; **to grant a ~ pardon** eine Generalamnestie erlassen (*to für*); **to explain sth in ~ terms** etw allgemein erklären; **the ~ plan** *or* **idea is that ...** wir/sie *etc* hatten uns/sich (*dat*) das so gedacht, daß ...; **the ~ idea of that is to ...** damit soll bezweckt werden *or* es geht dabei darum, daß ...; **that was the ~ idea** so war das (auch) gedacht; **the ~ idea is to wait and see** wir/sie *etc* wollen einfach mal abwarten; **I've got the ~ idea of** it ich habe eine Vorstellung *or* ich weiß so ungefähr, worum es geht; **to give sb a ~ idea/outline of a subject** jdm eine ungefähre Vorstellung von einem Thema geben/ein Thema in groben Zügen umreißen; **to be ~** (*not detailed or specific: clause, wording, translation, proposals*) allgemein gehalten sein; (*vague*) unbestimmt *or* vage sein; (*promises, clause*) unverbindlich sein; (*widespread: custom, weather etc*) weit verbreitet sein; (*customary*) allgemein üblich sein; **to make the wording/clause** *etc* **more ~** die Formulierung/Klausel *etc* allgemeiner fassen; **that would be more ~ as a translation** das wäre als Übersetzung allgemeiner anwendbar.

(**b**) (*after official title*) Ober-. **Consul ~** Generalkonsul *m*.

2 *n* (**a**) **in ~** im allgemeinen; **to go from the ~ to the particular** vom Allgemeinen ins Besondere gehen.

(**b**) (*Mil*) General *m*; (*Caesar, Napoleon etc*) Feldherr *m*.

general: **~ anaesthetic** *n* Vollnarkose *f*; **G~ Assembly** *n* (*of United Nations*) Voll- *or* Generalversammlung *f*; (*Eccl*) Generalsynode *f*; **G~ Certificate of Education** *n* (*Brit*) (*O-level*) ≈ Mittlere Reife; (*A-level*) ≈ Reifezeugnis, Abitur *nt*; **~ degree** *n* nicht spezialisierter Studienabschluß; **~ election** *n* Parlamentswahlen *pl*.

generalissimo [ˌdʒenərəˈlɪsɪməʊ] *n* Generalissimus *m*.

generality [ˌdʒenəˈrælɪtɪ] *n* (**a**) **to talk in/of generalities** ganz allgemein sprechen/sich über Allgemeines *or* Allgemeinheiten unterhalten.

(**b**) (*general quality*) Allgemeinheit *f*; (*general applicability*) Allgemeingültigkeit *f*. **a rule of great ~** eine fast überall anwendbare Regel.

generalization [ˌdʒenərəlaɪˈzeɪʃən] *n* Verallgemeinerung *f*.

generalize [ˈdʒenərəlaɪz] *vti* verallgemeinern. **to ~** (**a conclusion**) **from sth** allgemeine Schlüsse aus etw ziehen; **to ~ about sth** etw verallgemeinern.

general knowledge 1 *n* Allgemeinwissen *nt* *or* -bildung *f*. **2** *attr* zur Allgemeinbildung.

generally [ˈdʒenərəlɪ] *adv* (*usually*) im allgemeinen; (*for the most part also*) im großen und ganzen; (*widely, not in detail*) allgemein. **~ speaking** im allgemeinen, im großen und ganzen.

general: **G~ Post Office** *n* (*Brit*) (*building*) Hauptpost(amt *nt*) *f*; (*organization*) Post *f*; **~ practice** *n* (*Med*) Allgemeinmedizin *f*; **~ practitioner** *n* Arzt *m*/Ärztin *f* für Allgemeinmedizin, praktischer Arzt, praktische Ärztin; **~ public** *n* Öffentlichkeit, Allgemeinheit *f*; **~-purpose** *adj* Mehrzweck-, Universal-.

generalship [ˈdʒenərəlʃɪp] *n* (*Mil*) (**a**) (*office*) Generalsrang *m*; (*period of office*) Dienstzeit *f* als General. **under his ~** als *er* General war. (**b**) (*skill*) Feldherrnkunst *f*.

general: **~ staff** *n* (*Mil*) Generalstab *m*; **~ store** *n* Kaufmannsladen *m*; **~ strike** *n* Generalstreik *m*.

generate [ˈdʒenəreɪt] *vt* (*lit, fig*) erzeugen; *heat, fumes also* entwickeln. **to ~ electricity from coal** aus Kohle Energie erzeugen *or* gewinnen; **generating station** Kraftwerk, Elektrizitätswerk *nt*.

generation [ˌdʒenəˈreɪʃən] *n* (**a**) (*lit, fig*) Generation *f*; (*period of time also*) Menschenalter *nt*. **~ gap** Generationsproblem *nt* *or* -konflikt *m*.

(**b**) (*act of generating*) Erzeugung *f*.

generative [ˈdʒenərətɪv] *adj* (*Ling*) generativ; (*Biol*) Zeugungs-, generativ (*spec*); (*Elec*) Erzeugungs-.

generator [ˈdʒenəreɪtəʳ] *n* Generator *m*.

generic [dʒɪˈnerɪk] *adj* artmäßig; (*Biol*) Gattungs-. **~ name** *or* **term** Oberbegriff *m*; (*Biol*) Gattungsbegriff *or* -name *m*; **~ group** Gattung *f*.

generically [dʒɪˈnerɪkəlɪ] *adv* (*Biol*) gattungsmäßig. **they could**

be ~ described as ... sie könnten unter dem Oberbegriff ... zusammengefaßt werden.

generosity [ˌdʒenəˈrɒsɪtɪ] *n* Großzügigkeit *f*; (*nobleness*) Großmut *m*.

generous [ˈdʒenərəs] *adj* (**a**) *person, action, gift* großzügig; (*noble-minded*) großmütig. **he has a ~ mind** er ist großmütig. (**b**) (*large, plentiful*) reichlich; *figure* üppig. **a ~ size 14** eine groß ausgefallene Größe 14.

generously [ˈdʒenərəslɪ] *adv see adj*. **a ~ cut dress** ein groß ausgefallenes Kleid.

generousness [ˈdʒenərəsnɪs] *n* (**a**) *see* **generosity**. (**b**) *see adj* (**b**) Reichlichkeit *f*; Üppigkeit *f*.

genesis [ˈdʒenɪsɪs] *n, pl* **geneses** [ˈdʒenɪsiːz] Entstehung, Genese (*spec*) *f*. (**the Book of**) **G~** (die) Genesis, die Schöpfungsgeschichte.

genetic [dʒɪˈnetɪk] *adj* genetisch. **does crime have a ~ cause?** ist Kriminalität erblich bedingt?; **~ engineering** experimentelle Genetik.

geneticist [dʒɪˈnetɪsɪst] *n* Vererbungsforscher(in *f*), Genetiker(in *f*) *m*.

genetics [dʒɪˈnetɪks] *n sing* Vererbungslehre, Genetik *f*.

Geneva [dʒɪˈniːvə] *n* Genf *nt*. **Lake ~** der Genfer See; **~ Convention** Genfer Konvention *f*.

genial [ˈdʒiːnɪəl] *adj* (*lit, fig*) freundlich; *person also* leutselig; *smile also* liebenswert; *atmosphere, climate also, company* angenehm; *warmth, influence* wohltuend.

geniality [ˌdʒiːnɪˈælɪtɪ] *n* (*lit, fig*) Freundlichkeit *f*; (*of person also*) Leutseligkeit *f*; (*of company*) Angenehmheit *f*.

genially [ˈdʒiːnɪəlɪ] *adv see adj*.

genie [ˈdʒiːnɪ] *n* dienstbarer Geist.

genii [ˈdʒiːnɪaɪ] *pl of* **genius**.

genital [ˈdʒenɪtl] *adj* Geschlechts-, Genital-, genital.

genitals [ˈdʒenɪtlz] *npl* Geschlechtsorgane *or* -teile, Genitalien *pl*.

genitive [ˈdʒenɪtɪv] **1** *n* (*Gram*) Genitiv *m*. **in the ~** im Genitiv. **2** *adj* Genitiv-. **~ case** Genitiv *m*.

genius [ˈdʒiːnɪəs] *n, pl* **-es** *or* **genii** (**a**) (*mental or creative capacity also*) Genius *m*, Schöpferkraft *f*. **a man of ~** ein genialer Mensch, ein Genie *nt*; **to have a ~ for sth** eine besondere Gabe für etw haben; **his ~ for organization/languages** sein Organisationstalent *nt*/seine hohe Sprachbegabung; **he has a ~ for saying the wrong thing** er hat ein Talent *or* die Gabe, immer das Falsche zu sagen.

(**b**) (*spirit: of period, country etc*) (Zeit)geist *m*.

(**c**) (*bad influence*) **evil ~** böser Geist.

Genoa [ˈdʒenəʊə] *n* Genua *nt*. **~ cake** mandelverzierter Früchtekuchen.

genocide [ˈdʒenəʊsaɪd] *n* Völkermord *m*, Genozid *nt* (*geh*).

Genoese [ˌdʒenəʊˈiːz] **1** *adj* genuesisch. **2** *n* Genuese(r) *m*, Genueserin *f*.

genre [ˈʒɑːŋrə] *n* Genre *nt* (*geh*), Gattung *f*; (*Art: also ~ painting*) Genremalerei *f*.

gent [dʒent] *n* (*inf*) *abbr of* **gentleman**. **~s' shoes/outfitter** (*Comm*) Herrenschuhe *pl*/-ausstatter *m*; **"G~s"** (*Brit: lavatory*) „Herren"; **where is the ~s?** wo ist die Herrentoilette?

genteel [dʒenˈtiːl] *adj* vornehm, fein; (*affected*) *manners* geziert. **to live in ~ poverty** arm, aber vornehm leben.

genteelly [dʒenˈtiːlɪ] *adv* vornehm; (*affectedly*) geziert. **she coughed ~** sie hüstelte.

gentian [ˈdʒenʃɪən] *n* Enzian *m*.

Gentile [ˈdʒentaɪl] **1** *n* Nichtjude *m*. **2** *adj* nichtjüdisch.

gentility [dʒenˈtɪlɪtɪ] *n* Vornehmheit *f*. **to live in shabby ~** trotz Armut den Schein der Vornehmheit wahren.

gentle [ˈdʒentl] *adj* (+ *er*) (**a**) sanft; (*not hard, vigorous*) *smack, breeze also, exercise* leicht; (*not loud*) *knock, sound* leise, zart; (*delicate*) *kiss, caress also, hint, reminder* zart; (*not harsh*) *words, humour* liebenswürdig, freundlich; *rebuke also, heat* mild; *person, disposition also* sanftmütig; *animal also* fromm, zahm; *heart* weich. **~ reader** (*old*) geneigter Leser (*old*); **the ~ sex** das zarte Geschlecht; **to be ~ with sb** sanft *or* nett zu jdm sein; (*physically*) mit jdm sanft *or* behutsam umgehen; **to be ~ with sth** mit etw behutsam *or* vorsichtig umgehen; **to be ~ with one's hands** (*nurse, doctor*) behutsam sein; (*horseman*) eine leichte Hand haben; **~ as a lamb** sanft wie ein Lamm. (**b**) (*old: well-born*) *knight, maiden* edel (*old*). **of ~ birth** *or* **blood** von edler *or* vornehmer Geburt (*dated*).

gentlefolk [ˈdʒentlfəʊk] *npl* (*dated*) vornehme *or* feine Leute *pl*.

gentleman [ˈdʒentlmən] *n, pl* **-men** [-mən] (**a**) (*well-mannered, well-born*) Gentleman, Herr *m*; (*trustworthy also*) Ehrenmann *m*. **he's a real ~ in everything** he does bei allem, was er tut, verhält er sich wie ein richtiger Gentleman; **gentlemen's agreement** Gentlemen's Agreement *nt*; (*esp in business*) Vereinbarung *f* auf Treu und Glauben.

(**b**) (*man*) Herr *m*. **gentlemen!** meine Herren!; (*in business letter*) sehr geehrte Herren!; **gentlemen of the jury/press!** meine Herren Geschworenen/von der Presse!

(**c**) (*dated: with private income*) Privatier *m*; (*Hist: rank*) Mann *m* von Stand; (*at court*) Höfling *m*. **~ farmer** Gutsbesitzer *m*; **~-in-waiting** Kammerherr *m*.

gentlemanly [ˈdʒentlmənlɪ] *adj* *person, manners* zuvorkommend, gentlemanlike *pred*; *appearance* eines Gentleman, gentlemanlike *pred*.

gentleness [ˈdʒentlnɪs] *n see adj* Sanftheit *f*; Leichtheit *f*; Zartheit *f*; Zartheit *f*; Liebenswürdigkeit, Freundlichkeit *f*; Milde *f*; Sanftmut *f*; Zahmheit *f*; Weichheit *f*.

gentlewoman [ˈdʒentlwʊmən] *n, pl* **-women** [-wɪmɪn] (*dated*) Dame *f* (von Stand); (*at court*) Hofdame *f*; (*Hist: attendant*) Zofe *f*.

gently [ˈdʒentlɪ] *adv see adj*. **to handle sb/sth ~** mit jdm/etw behutsam umgehen; **~ does it!** sachte, sachte!

gentry ['dʒentrɪ] npl (a) Gentry f (niederer Adel und Stände). all the ~ were there alles, was Rang und Namen hatte, war da. (b) (dated pej: people) Leute pl.

genuflect ['dʒenjuflekt] vi (Rel) eine Kniebeuge machen.

genuflection, genuflexion [,dʒenju'flekʃən] n (Rel) Kniebeuge f.

genuine ['dʒenjuɪn] adj echt; manuscript authentic, Original-; offer ernstgemeint, ernsthaft; (sincere) sorrow, joy, willingness, disbelief also, belief aufrichtig; laughter, person natürlich, ungekünstelt. the ~ article (not a copy) das Original; that's the ~ article! das ist das Wahre!; (not imitation) das ist echt!; she has a ~ belief in the supernatural sie glaubt ernsthaft an das Übernatürliche.

genuinely ['dʒenjuɪnlɪ] adv wirklich; (sincerely also) aufrichtig; (authentically) old, antique echt.

genuineness ['dʒenjuɪnnɪs] n see adj Echtheit f; Ernsthaftigkeit f; Aufrichtigkeit f; Natürlichkeit, Ungekünsteltheit f.

genus ['dʒenəs] n, pl **genera** (Biol) Gattung f.

geocentric [,dʒiːəʊ'sentrɪk] adj geozentrisch.

geochemistry [,dʒiːəʊ'kemɪstrɪ] n Geochemie f.

geodesic [,dʒiːəʊ'desɪk] adj geodätisch. ~ dome Traglufthalle f.

geodesy [dʒiː'ɒdɪsɪ] n Geodäsie f.

geographer [dʒɪ'ɒgrəfəʳ] n Geograph(in f) m.

geographic(al) [dʒɪə'græfɪk(əl)] adj, **geographically** [dʒɪə'græfɪkəlɪ] adv geographisch.

geography [dʒɪ'ɒgrəfɪ] n Geographie f; (Sch also) Erdkunde f. the ~ of an area die Geographie or geographische Beschaffenheit eines Gebietes.

geological adj, ~ly adv [dʒiːəʊ'lɒdʒɪkəl, -ɪ] geologisch.

geologist [dʒɪ'ɒlədʒɪst] n Geologe m, Geologin f.

geology [dʒɪ'ɒlədʒɪ] n Geologie f.

geomancy [dʒiːəʊ'mænsɪ] n Geomantie f.

geometric(al) [dʒiːəʊ'metrɪk(əl)] adj, **geometrically** [dʒiːəʊ'metrɪkəlɪ] adv geometrisch.

geometrician [,dʒiːəmə'trɪʃən] n Fachmann m für Geometrie, Geometer (old) m.

geometry [dʒɪ'ɒmɪtrɪ] n (Math) Geometrie f. ~ set (Reißzeug nt or Zirkelkasten m mit) Zeichengarnitur f.

geophysics [,dʒiːəʊ'fɪzɪks] n sing Geophysik f.

geopolitics [,dʒiːəʊ'pɒlɪtɪks] n sing Geopolitik f.

Geordie ['dʒɔːdɪ] n (inf) Bewohner(in f) m/Dialekt m der Bewohner von Newcastle upon Tyne und Umgebung.

George [dʒɔːdʒ] n Georg m. by ~! (Brit dated) potz Blitz! (dated inf); (indicating determination) bei Gott! (dated).

georgette [dʒɔː'dʒet] n Georgette f or m.

Georgia ['dʒɔːdʒɪə] n (US) Georgia nt; (USSR) Georgien nt.

Georgian ['dʒɔːdʒɪən] adj (Brit Hist) georgianisch; (US) in/aus/von Georgia; (USSR) georgisch.

geranium [dʒɪ'reɪnɪəm] n Geranie f.

gerbil ['dʒɜːbɪl] n Wüstenspringmaus f.

geriatric [,dʒerɪ'ætrɪk] 1 adj geriatrisch, Greisen- (often hum); nurse, nursing Alten-; home Alters-; patient alt. ~ medicine Altersheilkunde f; ~ ward geriatrische Abteilung, Pflegestation f. 2 n alter Mensch, Greis m (often hum).

geriatrician [,dʒerɪə'trɪʃən] n Facharzt m/-ärztin f für Geriatrie, Geriater m.

geriatrics [,dʒerɪ'ætrɪks] n sing Geriatrie, Altersheilkunde f.

germ [dʒɜːm] n (lit, fig) Keim m; (of particular illness also) Krankheitserreger m; (esp of cold) Bazillus m. don't spread your ~s around behalte deine Bazillen für dich; that contained the ~(s) of later conflict darin lag der Keim für spätere Konflikte.

German ['dʒɜːmən] 1 adj deutsch. 2 n (a) Deutsche(r) mf. (b) (language) Deutsch nt; see English.

German Democratic Republic n Deutsche Demokratische Republik.

germane [dʒɜː'meɪn] adj (form) von Belang (geh) (to für).

Germanic [dʒɜː'mænɪk] adj germanisch.

germanize ['dʒɜːmənaɪz] vt germanisieren; word eindeutschen.

German: ~ measles n sing Röteln pl; ~ shepherd (dog) n (esp US) deutscher Schäferhund.

Germany ['dʒɜːmənɪ] n Deutschland nt; (Hist) Germanien nt.

germ: ~ carrier n Bazillenträger m; ~ cell n (Biol) Keimzelle f; ~-free adj keimfrei.

germicidal [,dʒɜːmɪ'saɪdl] adj keimtötend.

germicide ['dʒɜːmɪsaɪd] n keimtötendes Mittel.

germinal ['dʒɜːmɪnəl] adj (fig) aufkeimend (geh).

germinate ['dʒɜːmɪneɪt] 1 vi keimen; (fig) aufkeimen (geh). he let the idea ~ in his mind er ließ die Idee in sich (dat) keimen. 2 vt (lit, fig) keimen lassen.

germination [,dʒɜːmɪ'neɪʃən] n (lit) Keimen nt; (fig) Aufkeimen nt (geh).

germ: ~-killer n keimtötendes Mittel; ~ warfare n bakteriologische Kriegsführung, Bakterienkrieg m.

gerontologist [,dʒerɒn'tɒlədʒɪst] n Gerontologe m, Gerontologin f.

gerontology [,dʒerɒn'tɒlədʒɪ] n Gerontologie f.

gerrymander ['dʒerɪmændəʳ] (US Pol) 1 vt to ~ election districts Wahlkreisschiebungen vornehmen. 2 n Wahlkreisschiebung f.

gerrymandering ['dʒerɪmændərɪŋ] n (US Pol) Wahlkreisschiebungen pl.

gerund ['dʒerɒnd] n Gerundium nt.

gerundive [dʒɪ'rʌndɪv] n Gerundivum nt.

gestalt psychology [gə'ʃtæltsaɪ'kɒlədʒɪ] n Gestaltpsychologie f.

Gestapo [ge'stɑːpəʊ] n Gestapo f.

gestate [dʒe'steɪt] 1 vi (lit form) (animal) trächtig sein, tragen (form); (human) schwanger sein; (fig) reifen. 2 vt tragen; (fig)

in sich (dat) reifen lassen; plan, idea sich tragen mit (geh).

gestation [dʒe'steɪʃən] n (lit form) (of animals) Trächtigkeit f; (of humans) Schwangerschaft f; (fig) Reifwerden nt. his book was 10 years in ~ der Reifungsprozeß seines Buches dauerte 10 Jahre.

gesticulate [dʒe'stɪkjʊleɪt] vi gestikulieren.

gesticulation [dʒe,stɪkjʊ'leɪʃən] n (act) Gestikulieren nt; (instance) Gebärde (geh), Geste f. all his ~s all sein Gestikulieren.

gesture ['dʒestʃəʳ] 1 n (lit, fig) Geste f. a ~ of denial/approval eine verneinende/zustimmende Geste; as a ~ of support als Zeichen der Unterstützung; his use of ~ seine Gestik. 2 vi gestikulieren. 3 vt to ~ sb to do sth jdm bedeuten, etw zu tun.

get [get] pret, ptp **got**, (US) ptp **gotten** 1 vt (a) (receive) bekommen, kriegen (inf); sun, light, full force of blow or anger abbekommen, abkriegen (inf); wound also sich (dat) zuziehen; wealth, glory kommen zu; time, personal characteristics haben (from von). where did you ~ it (from)? woher hast du das?; this country ~s very little rain in diesem Land regnet es sehr wenig; the car got it on one wing (inf) das Auto hat am Kotflügel etwas abbekommen or abgekriegt (inf); he wanted to ~ all the glory er wollte all den Ruhm (haben); he got the idea for his book while he was abroad/from some old document die Idee zu dem Buch kam ihm, als er im Ausland war/er hatte die Idee zu seinem Buch von einem alten Dokument; where do you ~ that idea (from)? wie kommst du denn auf die Idee?; I got quite a surprise/shock ich war ziemlich überrascht/ich habe einen ziemlichen Schock bekommen or gekriegt (inf); to ~ sth cheap/for nothing etw billig/umsonst bekommen or kriegen (inf); you'll ~ it! (inf: be in trouble) du wirst was erleben! (inf).

(b) (obtain by one's own efforts) object sich (dat) besorgen; visa, money also sich (dat) beschaffen; (find) staff, financier, partner, job finden; (buy) kaufen; (buy and keep) large item, car, cat sich (dat) anschaffen. not to be able to ~ sth etw nicht bekommen or kriegen (inf); to ~ sb/oneself sth, to ~ sth for sb/oneself jdm/sich etw besorgen; job jdm/sich etw verschaffen; she tried to ~ a partner for her friend sie hat versucht, einen Partner für ihre Freundin zu finden; to need to ~ sth etw brauchen; I've still three to ~ ich brauche noch drei; you'll have to ~ a job/flat/more staff Sie müssen zusehen, daß Sie eine Stelle/eine Wohnung/mehr Personal bekommen or finden; he's been trying to ~ a house/job/partner er hat versucht, ein Haus/eine Stelle/einen Partner zu bekommen; why don't you ~ a flat of your own? warum schaffen Sie sich (dat) nicht eine eigene Wohnung an?; (rent) warum nehmen Sie sich (dat) nicht eine eigene Wohnung?; he got himself a wife/a fancy car/job er hat sich (dat) eine Frau zugelegt (inf)/ein tolles Auto angeschafft or zugelegt/einen tollen Job verschafft; what are you ~ting her for Christmas? was schenkst du ihr zu Weihnachten?; I got her a doll for Christmas ich habe für sie eine Puppe zu Weihnachten besorgt; we could ~ a taxi wir könnten (uns dat) ein Taxi nehmen; could you ~ me a taxi? könnten Sie mir ein Taxi rufen or besorgen?

(c) (fetch) person, doctor, object holen. to ~ sb from the station jdn vom Bahnhof abholen; I got him/myself a drink ich habe ihm/mir etwas zu trinken geholt; can I ~ you a drink? möchten Sie etwas zu trinken?; why don't you ~ a dictionary/the contract and look it up? warum sehen Sie nicht in einem Wörterbuch/im Vertrag nach?

(d) (catch) bekommen, kriegen (inf); cold, illness also sich (dat) holen; (in children's game) fangen. to ~ sb by the arm/leg jdn am Arm/Bein packen; it or the pain ~s me here/when I move (inf) es tut hier weh/es tut weh, wenn ich mich bewege; I got my back when I stretched then (inf) mich hat's im Kreuz erwischt, als ich mich da gestreckt habe (inf); he's got it bad (inf) den hat's übel erwischt (inf); ~ him/it! (to dog) faß!; (I've) got him/it! (inf) (ich) hab' ihn/ich hab's (inf); got you! (inf) hab' dich (erwischt)! (inf); ha, ha, can't ~ me! ha, ha, mich kriegst du nicht! (inf); my big brother will ~ you! mein großer Bruder, der zeigt's dir or macht dich fertig! (inf); he's out to ~ you (inf) er hat's auf dich abgesehen (inf); we'll ~ them yet! (inf) die werden wir schon noch kriegen! (inf); I'll ~ you for that! (inf) das wirst du mir büßen!; you've got me there! (inf) da bin ich auch überfragt (inf); that'll/that question will ~ him da/bei der Frage weiß er bestimmt auch nicht weiter.

(e) (hit) treffen, erwischen (inf). the car got the lamppost with the front wing das Auto hat den Laternenpfahl mit dem vorderen Kotflügel erwischt (inf).

(f) (Rad, TV) bekommen, kriegen (inf). our TV doesn't ~ BBC 2 mit unserem Fernseher bekommen or kriegen (inf) wir BBC 2 nicht.

(g) (Telec) (contact) erreichen; number bekommen; (put through to, get for sb) geben. I'll ~ the number (for you) ich wähle die Nummer (für Sie); (switchboard) ich verbinde Sie mit der Nummer; ~ me 339/Mr Johnston please (to secretary) geben Sie mir bitte 339/Herrn Johnston; (to switchboard) verbinden Sie mich bitte mit 339/Herrn Johnston; I must have got the wrong number ich bin/war wohl falsch verbunden.

(h) (prepare) meal machen. I'll ~ you/myself some breakfast ich mache dir/mir etwas zum Frühstück.

(i) (eat) essen. to ~ breakfast/lunch etc frühstücken/zu Mittag essen etc; to ~ a snack eine Kleinigkeit essen.

(j) (send, take) bringen. to ~ sb to hospital jdn ins Krankenhaus bringen; to ~ sth to sb jdm etw zukommen lassen; (take it oneself) jdm etw bringen; where does that ~ us? (inf) was bringt uns (dat) das? (inf); this discussion isn't ~ting us anywhere diese Diskussion führt zu nichts; tell him to ~ it there as quickly as possible er soll zusehen, daß das so schnell wie möglich dort ist; (take it himself also) er soll das möglichst schnell dort hinbringen; we'll ~ you there somehow irgendwie kriegen wir dich schon dahin (inf).

(k) (*manage to move*) kriegen (*inf*). **we'll never ~ this piano upstairs** das Klavier kriegen wir nie nach oben (*inf*); **he couldn't ~ her/himself up the stairs** er kriegte sie nicht die Treppe rauf (*inf*)/er kam nicht die Treppe rauf.

(l) (*understand*) kapieren (*inf*), mitbekommen (*inf*); (*hear*) mitbekommen, mitkriegen (*inf*); (*make a note of*) notieren. **I don't ~ it/you** *or* **your meaning** (*inf*) da komme ich nicht mit (*inf*)/ich verstehe nicht, was du meinst; **~ it?** kapiert? (*inf*).

(m) (*profit, benefit*) **what do you ~ from that?** was hast du davon?, was bringt dir das? (*inf*); **I don't ~ much from his lectures** seine Vorlesungen geben mir nicht viel; **he's only in it for what he can ~** er will nur dabei profitieren.

(n) (*iro inf*) **~ (a load of) that!** was sagst du dazu! (*inf*), hat man Töne! (*inf*); **~ you!** (*regarding looks*) sag bloß! (*inf*), **Junge, Junge!** (*inf*); (*regarding ideas*) was du nicht sagst! (*inf*); **~ her!** (*regarding looks*) was sagst du zu der da? (*inf*); (*iro*) sieh dir bloß die mal an! (*inf*); (*regarding ideas*) die ist ja ganz schön clever! (*inf*); (*iro*) hör dir bloß das mal an! (*inf*).

(o) (*inf*) (*annoy*) ärgern, aufregen; (*upset*) an die Nieren gehen (+*dat*) (*inf*); (*thrill*) packen (*inf*); (*amuse*) amüsieren. **it ~s you there!** das packt einen so richtig! (*inf*).

(p) to ~ sb to do sth (*have sth done by sb*) etw von jdm machen lassen; (*persuade sb*) jdn dazu bringen, etw zu tun; **I'll ~ him to phone you back** (*inf*) ich werde zusehen, daß er zurückruft; (*make him*) ich werde zusehen, daß er zurückruft; **you'll never ~ him to understand** du wirst es nie schaffen, daß er das versteht.

(q) (+*ptp*) (*cause to be done*) lassen; (*manage to ~ done*) kriegen (*inf*). **to ~ sth made for sb/oneself** jdm/sich etw machen lassen; **to ~ one's hair cut** sich (*dat*) die Haare schneiden lassen; **I'll ~ the grass cut/house painted soon** der Rasen wird bald gemäht/das Haus wird bald gestrichen; (*by sb else*) ich lasse bald den Rasen mähen/das Haus streichen; **to ~ sth done** etw gemacht kriegen (*inf*); **to ~ the washing/dishes/some work done** die Wäsche waschen/abwaschen/Arbeit erledigen; **I'm not going to ~ much done** ich werde nicht viel schaffen *or* fertigbringen (*inf*); **we ought to ~ it done soon** das müßte bald gemacht werden, wir sollten das bald gemacht kriegen (*inf*); **to ~ things done** was fertigkriegen (*inf*); **can you ~ these things done for me?** können Sie das für mich erledigen?; **~ your fare paid by them** lassen Sie sich (*dat*) Ihre Fahrtkosten von ihnen bezahlen; **did you ~ the fare paid/question answered?** haben Sie die Fahrtkosten bezahlt/eine Antwort auf die Frage bekommen *or* gekriegt? (*inf*); **you'll ~ me/yourself thrown out** du bringst es so weit, daß ich hinausgeworfen werde/du hinausgeworfen wirst; **that'll ~ him thrown out** da fliegt er hinaus.

(r) (+*infin or prp: cause to be*) kriegen (*inf*). **he can't ~ the sum to work out/lid to stay open** er kriegt es nicht hin, daß die Rechnung aufgeht/daß der Deckel aufbleibt (*inf*); **I can't ~ the car to start/door to open** ich kriege das Auto nicht an (*inf*)/die Tür nicht auf (*inf*); **can you ~ these two pieces to fit together/the wound to stop bleeding?** kriegen Sie die beiden Teile zusammen/können Sie etwas machen, daß die Wunde nicht mehr blutet?; **how do I ~ these two parts to stick together?** wie kriege ich die beiden Teile zusammengeklebt? (*inf*); **once I've got this machine to work** wenn ich die Maschine erst einmal zum Laufen gebracht habe; **to ~ the fire to burn** das Feuer zum Brennen bringen; **to ~ sth going** *or* **to go** etw in Gang bringen *or* bekommen; **party etc** etw in Schwung bringen; **that really got him going** da ist er aber in Fahrt gekommen (*inf*); **to ~ sb talking** jdn zum Sprechen bringen.

(s) (*cause to be*) (+*adj*) machen; (*manage to make*) kriegen (*inf*); (+*adv phrase*) tun. **to ~ sth/oneself ready** jdn/etw/sich fertigmachen; **to ~ sth clean/open/shut** (*person*) etw sauber-/auf-/zukriegen (*inf*); **that'll ~ it clean/open/shut** damit wird es sauber/geht es auf/zu; **to ~ sb drunk** jdn betrunken machen/kriegen (*inf*); **has she got the baby dressed yet?** hat sie das Baby schon angezogen?; **to ~ one's arm broken** sich (*dat*) den Arm brechen; **to ~ one's hands dirty** sich (*dat*) die Hände schmutzig machen; **to ~ one's things packed** seine Sachen packen; **~ the cat back in its box/out of the room** tu die Katze ins Körbchen zurück/aus dem Zimmer (*inf*); **~ the children to bed** bring die Kinder ins Bett.

(t) to have got sth (*Brit: have*) etw haben.

(u) in set phrases see n, adj etc.

2 vi (a) (*go, arrive*) kommen; gehen. **to ~ home/here** nach Hause kommen/hier ankommen; **to ~ to the top** (*of mountain etc*) zum Gipfel kommen, hinaufkommen; (*in career*) (ganz) nach oben kommen; **I've got as far as page 16** ich bin auf Seite 16; **to ~ far** (*lit*) weit kommen; (*fig*) es weit bringen; **~ (lost)!** verschwinde!

(b) (*fig inf*) **to ~ there** (*succeed*) es schaffen (*inf*); (*understand*) dahinterkommen (*inf*); **now we're ~ting there** (*to the truth*) jetzt kommt's raus! (*inf*); **how's the work going?** — **we're slowly ~ting there** wie geht die Arbeit voran? — langsam wird's was (*inf*); **to ~ somewhere/nowhere** (*in job, career etc*) es zu etwas/nichts bringen; (*with work, in discussion etc*) weiterkommen/nicht weiterkommen; **to ~ somewhere/nowhere (with sb)** (bei jdm) etwas/nichts erreichen; **we're not ~ting anywhere by arguing like this** wir erreichen doch gar nichts, wenn wir uns streiten; **now we're ~ting somewhere** jetzt wird die Sache (*inf*); (*in interrogation, discussion etc*) jetzt kommen wir der Sache schon näher; **to ~ nowhere fast** (*inf*) absolut nichts erreichen.

(c) (*become, be, to form passive*) werden. **to ~ old/tired/paid etc** alt/müde/bezahlt etc werden; **I'm/the weather is ~ting cold/warm** mir wird es/es wird kalt/warm; **to ~ dressed/shaved/washed etc** sich anziehen/rasieren/waschen etc; **to ~ married** heiraten; **to ~ used** *or* **accustomed to sth** sich an etw (*acc*) gewöhnen; **how do people ~ like that** *or* **that way?** (*inf*) wie wird man nur so? (*inf*).

(d) (+*infin*) **to ~ to know sb** jdn kennenlernen; **how did you ~ to know that?** wie hast du das erfahren?; **to ~ to like sb/sth** jdn sympathisch finden/an etw (*dat*) Gefallen finden; **after a time you ~ to realize ...** nach einiger Zeit merkt man ...; **to ~ to do sth** (~ *around to*) dazu kommen, etw zu tun; (~ *chance to*) die Möglichkeit haben, etw zu tun; **to ~ to be ...** (mit der Zeit) ... werden; **to ~ to see sb/sth/etw** zu sehen bekommen; **to ~ to work** sich an die Arbeit machen.

(e) (+*prp or ptp*) **to ~ working/scrubbing etc** anfangen zu arbeiten/schrubben etc; **you lot, ~ cleaning/working!** ihr da, putzt/arbeitet!; **I got talking to him** ich kam mit ihm ins Gespräch; **to ~ going** (*person*) (*leave*) aufbrechen; (*start working*) sich daran machen; (*start talking*) loslegen (*inf*); (*party etc*) in Schwung kommen; (*machine, fire etc*) in Gang kommen; **~ going!** fang an!; (*leave*) geh schon!; **let's ~ started** fangen wir an!

(f) (*inf: start*) **we got to talking about that** wir kamen darauf zu sprechen; **I got to thinking ...** ich habe mir überlegt, ...

(g) **to have got to do sth** (*be obliged to*) etw tun müssen; **I've got to** ich muß.

3 vr see also vt (b, c, h, k) (a) (*convey oneself*) kommen. **I had to ~ myself to the hospital** ich mußte selbst ins Krankenhaus (gehen); **how did you ~ yourself home?** wie bist du nach Hause gekommen?; **~ yourself over here/out of here** komm hier rüber (*inf*)/mach, daß du hier rauskommst (*inf*).

(b) (+*adj*) sich machen. **to ~ oneself dirty/clean** sich schmutzig machen/sich saubermachen; **to ~ oneself pregnant/fit** schwanger/fit werden.

(c) (+*ptp*) **to ~ oneself washed/dressed** sich waschen/anziehen; **to ~ oneself married** heiraten; **he managed to ~ himself promoted** er hat es geschafft, daß er befördert wurde; **he got himself hit in the leg** er wurde am Bein getroffen.

◆ **get about** vi (*prep obj* in +*dat*) **(a)** sich bewegen können; (*to different places*) herumkommen. **(b)** (*news*) sich herumsprechen; (*rumour*) sich verbreiten.

◆ **get across 1** vi **(a)** (*cross*) hinüber-/herüberkommen; (+*prep obj*) *road, river* kommen über (+*acc*). **to ~ ~ to the other side** auf die andere Seite kommen *or* gelangen.

(b) (*communicate*) (*play, joke, comedian etc*) ankommen (*to bei*); (*teacher etc*) sich verständlich machen (*to dat*); (*idea, meaning*) klarwerden, verständlich werden (*to dat*).

2 vt always separate (a) (*transport*) hinüber-/herüberbringen; (*manage to ~*) hinüber-/herüberbekommen; (+*prep obj*) (hinüber-/herüber)bringen über (+*acc*); (hinüber-/herüber)bekommen über (+*acc*).

(b) (*communicate*) *play, joke* ankommen mit (*to bei*); *one's ideas, concepts* verständlich machen, klarmachen (*to sb jdm*).

◆ **get ahead** vi **(a)** (*make progress*) vorankommen (*in in* +*dat*); (*in race*) sich (*dat*) einen Vorsprung verschaffen; (*from behind*) nach vorn kommen. **to ~ ~ of sb** jdn überflügeln; (*in race*) einen Vorsprung zu jdm gewinnen; (*overtake*) jdn überholen; **if he ~s too far ~ in his reading** wenn er im Lesen den anderen zu weit voraus ist; **to ~ ~ of schedule** schneller als geplant vorankommen.

◆ **get along** vi **(a)** (*go*). **I must be ~ting** ich muß jetzt gehen, ich muß mich auf den Weg machen; **~ ~ now!** nun geh/geht schon!; **~ ~ with you!** (*inf*) jetzt hör aber auf! (*inf*).

(b) (*manage*) zurechtkommen. **to ~ ~ without sb/sth** ohne jdn/etw auskommen *or* zurechtkommen.

(c) (*progress*) vorankommen; (*work, patient, wound etc*) sich machen.

(d) (*be on good terms*) auskommen (*with mit*). **they ~ ~ quite well** sie kommen ganz gut miteinander aus.

2 vt always separate to ~ sb ~ to sb/sth (*send*) jdn zu jdm/etw schicken; (*take*) jdn zu jdm/etw mitnehmen/mitbringen; **to ~ sth ~ to sb** jdm etw zukommen lassen; (*take*) jdm etw bringen.

◆ **get around 1** vi see **get about**. **2 vti** +*prep obj* see **get round 1 (b, d), 2 (c, d)**.

◆ **get around to** vi +*prep obj* see **get round to**.

◆ **get at** vi +*prep obj* **(a)** (*gain access to, reach*) herankommen an (+*acc*); *town, house* erreichen, (hin)kommen zu; (*take, eat etc*) *food, money* gehen an (+*acc*). **put it where the dog/child won't ~ ~ it** stellen Sie es irgendwohin, wo der Hund/das Kind nicht drankommt (*inf*); **don't let him ~ ~ the whisky** laß ihn nicht an den Whisky (ran); **let me ~ ~ him!** (*inf*) na, wenn ich den erwische! (*inf*); **the mice have been ~ting ~ the cheese again** die Mäuse waren wieder an Käse (*inf*); **woodworm/the damp had got ~ the furniture** der Holzwurm/die Feuchtigkeit war an die Möbel gekommen.

(b) (*discover, ascertain*) *sb's wishes, ideas, truth* herausbekommen *or* -finden; *facts* kommen an (+*acc*).

(c) (*inf: mean*) hinauswollen auf (+*acc*).

(d) **to ~ ~ sb** (*inf*) (*criticize*) an jdm etwas auszusetzen haben (*inf*); (*nag*) an jdm herumnörgeln (*inf*); **he had the feeling that he was being got ~** er hatte den Eindruck, daß ihm das galt *or* daß man ihm was am Zeug flicken wollte (*inf*); **are you trying to ~ ~ me?** hast du was an mir auszusetzen? (*inf*).

(e) (*inf: corrupt*) beeinflussen; (*by threats also*) unter Druck setzen (*inf*); (*by bribes also*) schmieren (*inf*).

(f) (*inf: start work on*) sich machen an (+*acc*).

◆ **get away 1** vi (*leave*) wegkommen; (*for holiday also*) fortkommen; (*prisoner, thief*) entkommen, entwischen (*from sb jdm, from prison* aus dem Gefängnis); (*sportsman: from start*) loskommen (*inf*). **I must ~ ~ from here** ich muß hier weg (*inf*); **could I ~ ~ early today?** könnte ich heute früher gehen *or* weg (*inf*)?; **I just can't ~ ~ from him/my work** ich kann ihm/der Arbeit einfach nicht entrinnen; **you can't ~ ~** *or* **being ~ting ~ from the fact that ...** man kommt nicht um die Tatsache herum, daß ...; **to ~ ~ from it all** ich will sich von allem frei- *or* losmachen; **~ ~ (with you)!** (*inf*) ach, hör auf! (*inf*).

2 vt always separate (a) (*remove*) wegbekommen; (*move* *physically*) *person* weg- or fortbringen; *objects* wegschaffen. ~ **her** ~ **from here/his influence** sehen Sie zu, daß sie hier/aus seinem Einflußbereich wegkommt; ~ **them** ~ **from danger** bringen Sie sie außer Gefahr; ~ **him** ~ **from the wall/propeller** sehen Sie zu, daß er von der Wand/dem Propeller weggeht; ~ **him/that dog** ~ **from me** schaff ihn mir/mir den Hund vom Leib; **the woman must be got** ~ **from the children** die Frau muß von den Kindern wegkommen; **to** ~ **sth** ~ **from sb** (*take away*) jdm etw weg- or abnehmen.

(b) (*post*) *letter* weg- or fortschicken.

♦ **get away with** *vi* +*prep obj* (a) (*abscond with*) entkommen mit.

(b) (*inf: escape punishment for*) **you'll/he'll** *etc* **never** ~ ~ ~ **that** das wird nicht gutgehen; **he** *etc* **got** ~ ~ **it** er ist ungestraft or ungeschoren (*inf*) davongekommen, es ist gutgegangen; **the things he** ~**s** ~ ~! was er sich (*dat*) alles erlauben kann!; **he** ~**s** ~ ~ **murder** er kann sich alles erlauben; **to let sb** ~ ~ ~ **sth** jdm etw durchgehen lassen.

(c) (*be let off with*) davonkommen mit.

♦ **get back 1** *vi* (a) (*return*) zurückkommen; zurückgehen. **to** ~ ~ (*home*) **to bed/to work** nach Hause kommen/wieder ins Bett gehen/wieder arbeiten; **I ought to be** ~**ting** ~ (**to the office/home**) ich sollte (ins Büro/nach Hause) zurück(gehen); **I must be** ~**ting** ~ (*home*) ich muß nach Hause; **to** ~ ~ **to the point** auf das Wesentliche zurückkommen.

(b) (*move backwards*) zurückgehen. ~ ~ ! zurück(treten)!

2 *vt sep* (a) (*recover*) *possessions, person* zurückbekommen; *good opinion, strength* zurückgewinnen. **now that I've got you/it** ~ jetzt, wo ich dich/es wiederhabe.

(b) (*bring back*) zurückbringen; (*put back in place*) zurücktun. **he took it out and can't** ~ **it** ~ er hat es herausgenommen und kriegt es nicht wieder hinein.

♦ **get back at** *vi* +*prep obj* (*inf*) sich rächen an (+*dat*). **to** ~ ~ **sb for sth** jdm etw heimzahlen (*inf*).

♦ **get back to** *vi* +*prep obj* (*esp Comm: recontact*) sich wieder in Verbindung setzen mit. **I'll** ~ ~ ~ **you on that** ich werde darauf zurückkommen.

♦ **get behind** *vi* (a) (+*prep obj*) *tree, person* sich stellen hinter (+*acc*).

(b) (*fig*) zurückbleiben; (*person*) ins Hintertreffen geraten; (+*prep obj*) zurückbleiben hinter (+*dat*); *schedule* in Rückstand kommen mit. **to** ~ ~ **with one's work/payments** mit seiner Arbeit/den Zahlungen in Rückstand kommen.

♦ **get by** *vi* (a) (*move past*) vorbeikommen (*prep obj* an +*dat*). **to let sb/a vehicle** ~ ~ jdn/ein Fahrzeug vorbeilassen.

(b) (*fig: pass unnoticed*) durchrutschen (*inf*). **how did that film** ~ ~ **the censors?** wie ist der Film nur durch die Zensur gekommen?; **how did that mistake** ~ ~ **the proofreader?** wie ist dieser Fehler dem Korrektor nur entgangen?

(c) (*inf: pass muster*) (*work, worker*) gerade noch annehmbar or passabel (*inf*) sein; (*knowledge*) gerade ausreichen. **do you think you/the car will** ~ ~ **with these tyres in the MOT?** meinst du, du kommst/das Auto kommt mit den Reifen durch den TÜV?; **she would just about** ~ ~ **with her German for the exam** mit ihren Deutschkenntnissen müßte sie die Prüfung gerade so schaffen (*inf*); **I haven't got a tie, do you think I'll** ~ ~ **with a cravat/without one?** ich habe keine Krawatte, meinst du ein Tuch reicht auch/meinst du, es geht auch ohne?

(d) (*inf: manage*) durchkommen (*inf*). **she** ~**s** ~ **on very little money** sie kommt mit sehr wenig Geld aus.

♦ **get down 1** *vi* (a) (*descend*) hinunter-/heruntersteigen (*prep obj, from* von); (*manage to* ~ ~, **in** *commands*) herunter-/hinunterkommen (*prep obj, from* acc); (*from horse, bicycle*) absteigen (*from* von); (*from bus*) aussteigen (*from* aus). **to** ~ ~ ! **the stairs** die Treppe hinuntergehen/herunterkommen; ~ ~ ! runter! (*inf*).

(b) (*leave table*) aufstehen.

(c) (*bend down*) sich bücken; (*to hide*) sich ducken. **to** ~ ~ **on one's knees** auf die Knie fallen; **to** ~ ~ **on all fours** sich auf alle viere begeben.

2 *vt sep* (a) (*take down*) herunternehmen; *trousers etc* herunterziehen; (*lift down*) herunterholen; (*carry down*) herunter-/hinunterbringen; (*manage to* ~) herunterbringen or -kriegen (*inf*). **to** ~ **sb** ~ **the stairs** jdn die Treppe hinunter-/herunterbringen.

(b) (*reduce*) (**to** auf +*acc*) beschränken; (*as regards length*) verkürzen; *temperature* herunterbekommen; *seller, price* herunterhandeln.

(c) (*swallow*) *food* hinunterbringen. ~ **this** ~ (**you**)! (*inf*) trink/iß das!

(d) (*make a note of*) aufschreiben, notieren.

(e) (*inf: depress*) fertigmachen (*inf*). **don't let it** ~ **you** ~ laß dich davon nicht unterkriegen (*inf*).

♦ **get down to** *vi* +*prep obj* sich machen an (+*acc*), in Angriff nehmen; (*find time to do*) kommen zu. **to** ~ ~ ~ **business** zur Sache kommen.

♦ **get in 1** *vi* (a) (*enter*) hinein-/hereinkommen (*prep obj, -to* in +*acc*); (*into car, train etc*) einsteigen (*prep obj, -to* in +*acc*); (*into bath*) hinein-/hereinsteigen; (*into bed*) sich hineinlegen. **to** ~ ~ (**to**) **the bath** in die Badewanne steigen; **to** ~ ~**to bed** sich ins Bett legen; **let the sun** ~ ~ laß die Sonne herein; **the water/smoke got** ~(**to**) **my eyes** ich habe Wasser/Rauch in die Augen bekommen or gekriegt (*inf*); **he can't** ~ ~ er kann (*inf*) nicht herein/hinein; **he got** ~ **between them** (*in car, bed etc*) er hat sich zwischen sie gesetzt/gelegt/gestellt.

(b) (*arrive: train, bus*) ankommen (*-to* in +*dat, -to station* am Bahnhof).

(c) (*be admitted*) hinein-/hereinkommen (*-to* in +*acc*); (*into school, profession*) ankommen, angenommen werden (*-to* in +*dat*).

(d) (*Pol: be elected*) gewählt werden (*-to* in +*acc*), es schaffen (*inf*).

(e) (*get home*) nach Hause kommen.

(f) (*inf*) **to** ~ ~ **with a request** ein Gesuch anbringen; **he got** ~ **first/before me/him** *etc* er ist mir/ihm *etc* zuvorgekommen.

2 *vt* (a) *sep* (*bring in*) hinein-/hereinbringen (*prep obj, -to* in +*acc*); *crops, harvest* einbringen; *taxes, debts* eintreiben; (*fetch*) herein-/hineinholen (*-to* in +*acc*); (*help enter*) hinein-/hereinhelfen (+*dat*) (*-to* in +*acc*). **I got the kids** ~(**to**) **bed** ich habe die Kinder ins Bett gebracht; **I got smoke/water** ~ **my eyes** ich habe Rauch/Wasser in die Augen bekommen or gekriegt (*inf*).

(b) *sep* (*receive*) *forms, homework etc* bekommen; (*submit*) *forms* einreichen; *homework* abgeben.

(c) *sep* (*plant*) (*prep obj, -to* in +*acc*) *bulbs etc* einpflanzen; *seeds also* säen.

(d) *always separate* (*get admitted to*) (*into club etc*) (*prep obj, -to* in +*acc*) (*as member*) zur Aufnahme verhelfen (+*dat*); (*as guest*) mitnehmen. **those exam results should** ~ **him** ~/~**to** **any university** mit den Zeugnissen müßte er angenommen werden or aufgenommen werden/an jeder Universität angenommen werden or ankommen; **his parents wanted to** ~ **him** ~**to a good school** seine Eltern wollten ihn auf eine gute Schule schicken; **how did his parents** ~ **him** ~(**to this school**)? wie haben es seine Eltern geschafft, daß er (in der Schule) angenommen wurde?

(e) *always separate* (*get elected*) *candidate* zu einem Sitz verhelfen (+*dat*) (*-to* in +*dat*); *party* zu einem Wahlsieg verhelfen (+*dat*). **that got the Liberals** ~**to Parliament** dadurch kamen die Liberalen ins Parlament.

(f) *sep* (*fit, insert into, find room for*) hineinbringen or -bekommen or -kriegen (*inf*) (*-to* in +*acc*); (*fig*) *blow, punch, request, words* anbringen. **he always tries to** ~ **it** ~**to the conversation that ...** er versucht immer, es in die Unterhaltung einfließen zu lassen, daß ...

(g) *sep* (*send for*) *groceries, coal* holen, ins Haus bringen. **to** ~ ~ **supplies** sich (*dat*) Vorräte zulegen.

(h) *sep* (*send for*) *doctor, tradesman* holen, kommen lassen; *specialist, consultant etc* zuziehen.

(i) *always separate* **to** ~ **one's eye/hand** ~ in Übung kommen.

♦ **get in on 1** *vi* +*prep obj* (*inf*) mitmachen bei (*inf*), sich beteiligen an (+*dat*). **to** ~ ~ ~ **the act** mitmachen (*inf*), mitmischen (*sl*). **2** *vt sep* +*prep obj* beteiligen an (+*dat*); (*let take part in*) mitmachen lassen bei; *specialist, consultant* zuziehen bei.

♦ **get into 1** *vi* +*prep obj see also* **get in 1** (a-d) *rage, panic, debt, situation, company etc* geraten in (+*acc*); *trouble, difficulties also* kommen in (+*acc*); (*inf: devil, something*) fahren in (+*acc*) (*inf*). **what's got** ~ **him?** (*inf*) was ist bloß in ihn gefahren? (*inf*).

(b) *bad habits* sich (*dat*) angewöhnen. **to** ~ ~ **the way of** (*doing*) **sth** sich an etw (*acc*) gewöhnen; **to** ~ ~ **the habit of doing sth** sich (*dat*) angewöhnen, etw zu tun; **it's easy once you've got** ~ **the swing or way of it** es ist leicht, wenn Sie erst mal ein bißchen Übung darin haben.

(c) (*get involved in*) *book* sich einlesen bei; *work* sich einarbeiten in (+*acc*). **once I've got** ~ **this job** or **it** wenn ich mich erst einmal eingearbeitet habe.

(d) (*put on*) anziehen, schlüpfen in (+*acc*); (*fit into*) hineinkommen or -passen in (+*acc*).

2 *vt* +*prep obj always separate see also* **get in 2** (a, c-f) (a) *rage, debt, situation etc* bringen in (+*acc*). **to** ~ **sb/oneself** ~ **trouble** jdn/sich in Schwierigkeiten (*acc*) bringen (*also euph*); **who got you** ~ **that?** wer hat dir das eingebracht? (*inf*).

(b) **to** ~ **sb** ~ **bad habits** jdm schlechte Angewohnheiten *pl* beibringen; **who/what got you** ~ **the habit of smoking?** wer/was ist daran schuld, daß Sie rauchen?; **who/what got you** ~ **the habit of getting up early?** wer hat Ihnen das angewöhnt/wieso haben Sie es sich angewöhnt, früh aufzustehen?

(c) **to** ~ **sb** ~ **a dress** jdm ein Kleid anziehen; (*manage to put on*) jdn in ein Kleid hineinbekommen or -kriegen (*inf*).

♦ **get in with** *vi* +*prep obj* (*associate with*) Anschluß finden an (+*acc*); *bad company* geraten in (+*acc*); (*ingratiate oneself with*) sich gut stellen mit.

♦ **get off 1** *vi* (a) (*descend*) (*from bus, train etc*) aussteigen (*prep obj* aus); (*from bicycle, horse*) absteigen (*prep obj* von). **to tell sb where to** ~ ~ (*inf*) **or where he** ~**s** ~ (*inf*) jdm gründlich die Meinung sagen (*inf*); **he knows where he can** ~ ~ ! (*inf*) der kann mich mal! (*inf*).

(b) (*remove oneself*) (*prep obj* von) (*from premises*) weggehen, verschwinden; (*from lawn, ladder, sb's toes, furniture*) heruntergehen; (*stand up: from chair*) aufstehen. ~ ~! (*let me go*) laß (mich) los!; **let's** ~ ~ **this subject/topic** lassen wir das Thema! (*inf*).

(c) (*leave*) weg- or loskommen; (*be sent away: letter etc*) wegkommen, abgeschickt werden. **it's time you got** ~ **to school** es ist Zeit, daß ihr in die Schule geht; **to** ~ **to an early start** früh wegkommen; **to** ~ ~ **to a good/bad start** (*Sport*) einen guten/schlechten Start haben; (*fig*) (*person*) einen guten/schlechten Anfang machen; (*campaign etc*) sich gut/schlecht anlassen.

(d) (*be excused*) *homework, task etc* nicht machen müssen. **to** ~ ~ **work/school** nicht zur Arbeit/Schule gehen müssen; **he got** ~ **tidying up his room** er kam darum herum, sein Zimmer aufräumen zu müssen (*inf*).

(e) (*fig: escape, be let off*) davonkommen (*inf*). **to** ~ ~ **lightly/with a reprimand/fine** billig/mit einem Verweis/einer Geldstrafe davonkommen.

(f) (*fall asleep*) **to** ~ ~ (**to sleep**) einschlafen.

(g) (*from work etc*) gehen können (*prep obj* in +*dat*). **I'll see if I can** ~ ~ (**work**) **early** ich werde mal sehen, ob ich früher (im Büro/von der Arbeit) wegkann (*inf*); **what time do you**

~ ~ **work?** wann hören Sie mit der Arbeit auf?

2 vt **(a)** sep (remove) wegbekommen or -bringen or -kriegen (inf) (prep obj von); clothes, shoes ausziehen; (manage to ~ ~) herunterbekommen or -kriegen (inf) (prep obj von); cover, lid heruntertun (prep obj von); (manage to ~ ~) abbekommen (prep obj aus); stains herausmachen (prep obj aus); (manage to ~ ~) herausbekommen or -bringen or -kriegen (inf) (prep obj aus); (take away from) abnehmen (prep obj dat); shipwrecked boat, stuck car etc freibekommen or -kriegen (inf). I want to ~ this ~ my desk ich möchte das vom Tisch kriegen (inf); ~ your dirty hands ~ that nimm deine schmutzigen Hände davon or da weg!; ~ your hat ~! nimm den Hut ab!; ~ him ~ me! schaff ihn mir vom Leib! (inf); ~ him ~ my property/chair/lawn! etc vertreiben Sie ihn von meinem Grundstück/Stuhl/Rasen! etc; can't you ~ him ~ that subject/ topic? können Sie ihn nicht von dem Thema abbringen?

(b) always separate (from bus etc) aussteigen lassen (prep obj aus); (manage to ~ ~) herausbekommen or -bringen (prep obj aus); (from boat, roof, ladder etc) herunterholen (prep obj von); (manage to ~ ~) herunterbringen or -bekommen or -kriegen (inf) (prep obj von).

(c) +prep obj always separate (inf: obtain) bekommen, kriegen (inf) (prep obj von). I got that idea/pencil ~ John ich habe die Idee/den Bleistift von John.

(d) sep (send away) mail, children losschicken. to ~ sb/sth ~ to a good start jdm/einer Sache zu einem guten Start verhelfen; to ~ sb/sth ~ to a bad start jdn/etw schon schlecht anfangen lassen; to ~ sb/oneself ~ to school jdn/sich für die Schule fertigmachen.

(e) always separate (let off) that got him ~ school for the afternoon/doing that dadurch mußte er am Nachmittag nicht in die Schule/dadurch ist er darum herumgekommen, es machen zu müssen.

(f) sep (save from punishment) accused (lawyer) freibekommen or -kriegen (inf); (evidence etc) entlasten. the child was going to be punished but I got him ~ das Kind sollte bestraft werden, ich konnte das aber verhindern; it was his good manners that got him ~ er ist nur wegen seines guten Benehmens davongekommen.

(g) always separate to ~ sb ~ (to sleep) jdn zum Schlafen bringen.

(h) sep (from work etc) day, afternoon freibekommen.

♦ **get off with** vi +prep obj (inf) **(a)** (start a relationship with) aufreißen (sl). **(b)** see **get away with (c)**.

♦ **get on 1** vi **(a)** (climb on) hinauf-/heraufsteigen; (+prep obj) (hinauf-/herauf)steigen auf (+acc); (on bus, train etc) einsteigen (prep obj, -to in +acc); (on bicycle, horse etc) aufsteigen (prep obj, -to auf +acc). to ~ ~ sth auf etw (acc) aufsteigen etc; ~ ~ the back and I'll give you a lift steigen Sie hinten auf, dann nehme ich Sie mit.

(b) (continue: with work etc) weitermachen; (manage to ~ ~) weiterkommen.

(c) (get late, old) time is ~ting ~ es wird langsam spät; he is ~ting ~ (in years) er wird langsam alt.

(d) see **get along 1 (a)**.

(e) (progress) vorankommen; (work also, patient, pupil) Fortschritte machen; (succeed) Erfolg haben. to ~ ~ in the world es zu etwas bringen.

(f) (fare, cope: in exam etc) zurechtkommen. how did you ~ ~ in the exam? wie ging's (dir) in der Prüfung?; how are you ~ting ~? wie geht's?; to ~ ~ without sb/sth ohne jdn/etw zurechtkommen.

(g) (have a good relationship) sich verstehen, auskommen (with mit). they don't ~ ~ (with each other) sie kommen nicht miteinander aus, sie verstehen sich nicht.

2 vt **(a)** sep (prep obj auf +acc) clothes, shoes anziehen; hat, kettle aufsetzen; lid, cover drauftun; load (onto cart etc) hinauftun; (manage to ~ ~) draufbekommen or -kriegen (inf).

(b) always separate (on train, bus etc) hineinsetzen; (+prep obj, -to) setzen in (+acc); (manage to ~ ~) hineinbekommen or -kriegen (inf) (prep obj, -to in +acc); (on bicycle, horse) hinaufsetzen; (prep obj, -to) setzen auf (+acc).

♦ **get on for** vi +prep obj (time, person in age) zugehen auf (+acc). he's ~ting ~ ~ 40 er geht auf 40 zu; there were/he had ~ting ~ ~ 60 es waren/er hatte fast 60.

♦ **get on to** vi +prep obj (inf) **(a)** (trace, get on track of) person auf die Spur or Schliche kommen (+dat) (inf); dubious activity, double-dealing aufdecken, herausfinden; whereabouts herausfinden. they got ~ ~ his trail/scent sie kamen ihm auf die Spur/sie haben seine Fährte aufgenommen.

(b) (move on to) next item, new subject übergehen zu.

(c) (contact) sich in Verbindung setzen mit. I'll ~ ~ ~ him about it ich werde ihn daraufhin ansprechen.

(d) (nag) herumhacken auf (+dat) (inf), herumnörgeln an (+dat) (inf).

♦ **get onto** vti +prep obj see **get on 1 (a)**, **2 (a, b)**.

♦ **get on with** vi +prep obj (continue) weitermachen mit; (manage to ~ ~ ~) weiterkommen mit. ~ ~ ~ it! nun mach schon! (inf); ~ ~ ~ what you're doing mach weiter; ~ ~ your meal, will you? nun iß schon!; to let sb ~ ~ ~ sth jdn etw machen lassen; to leave sb to ~ ~ ~ sth jdn einfach machen lassen; this will do to be ~ting ~ das tut's wohl für den Anfang (inf).

♦ **get out 1** vi **(a)** heraus-/hinauskommen (of aus); (walk out) hinaus-/herausgehen (of aus); (drive out) hinaus-/herausfahren (of aus); (of boat, train, car) aussteigen (of aus); (leave) weggehen (of aus); (fig) (of business, scheme, contact) aussteigen (inf) (of aus); (of job) wegkommen (of von). he has to ~ ~ of the country/town er muß das Land/die Stadt verlassen; let's ~ ~ (of here)! bloß weg hier! (inf); ~ ~! raus! (inf); ~ ~ of my house/

room! verlassen Sie mein Haus/Zimmer!, raus aus meinem Haus/Zimmer! (inf); ~ ~ of my life! ich will nichts mehr mit dir zu tun haben, verschwinde und laß dich nicht mehr blicken!; he couldn't ~ ~ (of the hole) er kam (aus dem Loch) nicht mehr heraus; I might need to ~ ~ in a hurry es kann sein, daß ich schnell raus- (inf) or hinausmuß; to ~ ~ of bed aufstehen; to ~ ~ while the going's good gehen or (of contract, affair etc) aussteigen (inf), solange man das noch kann.

(b) (go walking, shopping etc) weggehen. you ought to ~ ~ (of the house) more Sie müßten mehr rauskommen (inf); I'd like to ~ ~ into the countryside ich würde gern irgendwo ins Grüne kommen; to ~ ~ and about herumkommen.

(c) (lit, fig: escape, leak out) (of aus) herauskommen; (animal, prisoner also) entkommen; (poisonous liquid, gas also) entweichen; (news) an die Öffentlichkeit dringen.

2 vt sep **(a)** (remove) (of aus) cork, tooth, splinter, stain etc herausmachen; people hinaus-/herausbringen; (send out) hinausschicken; (manage to ~ ~) heraus-/hinausbekommen or -kriegen (inf). I couldn't ~ him/it ~ ich habe ihn/es nicht hinaus-/herausbekommen etc; ~ him ~ of my house/sight schaff mir ihn aus dem Haus/aus den Augen!; cold water will ~ the stain ~ mit kaltem Wasser bekommen etc Sie den Fleck heraus.

(b) (bring, take out) herausholen or -nehmen (of aus); car, boat, horse herausholen (of aus). he got his purse ~ of his pocket er holte or nahm den Geldbeutel aus der Tasche (heraus).

(c) (withdraw) money abheben (of von).

(d) (produce) words, apology herausbekommen or -bringen or -kriegen (inf).

(e) (publish, present) book, plans, list etc herausbringen.

(f) (borrow from library) ausleihen (of aus).

(g) (Sport) batsman ausschlagen.

(h) (derive) you only ~ ~ what you put in Sie bekommen nur das zurück, was Sie hineinstecken.

♦ **get out of 1** vi +prep obj see also **get out 1 (a, c)**. **(a)** (avoid, escape) duty, obligation, punishment herumkommen um; difficulty herauskommen aus. you can't ~ ~ ~ it now jetzt kannst du nicht mehr anders; there's no ~ting ~ ~ it man kommt nicht darum herum; I have signed the contract/promised it and now I can't ~ ~ ~ it ich habe den Vertrag unterschrieben/es versprochen, jetzt gibt es kein Zurück.

(b) (become unaccustomed to) I've got ~ ~ the way of playing tennis ich habe das Tennisspielen verlernt; I'll ~ ~ ~ practice ich verlerne es; to ~ ~ ~ the habit of doing sth exercises seine Übungen nicht mehr regelmäßig machen; it's hard to ~ ~ ~ that habit/the habit of waking up early es ist schwer, sich das abzugewöhnen/es sich abzugewöhnen, früh aufzuwachen.

2 vt +prep obj always separate see also **get out 2 (a-c)**. **(a)** (extract) words, confession, truth herausbekommen or -bringen or -kriegen (inf) aus. nothing could be got ~ ~ him aus ihm war nichts herauszubekommen etc.

(b) (gain from) profit machen bei; money herausholen aus; people profitieren von; benefit, knowledge, wisdom, much, little, nothing haben von; pleasure haben an (+dat); happiness etc finden in (+dat). there's nothing to ~ ~ ~ his lectures von seinen Vorlesungen hat man nichts; to ~ the best/most ~ ~ sth das Beste aus etw machen; what can we ~ ~ ~ them/ that? wie können wir von ihnen/davon profitieren?; what are you trying to ~ ~ ~ me? was willst du von mir (haben)?

(c) to ~ sb ~ ~ a habit/(the habit of) doing sth jdm eine Unsitte abgewöhnen/es jdm abgewöhnen, etw zu tun.

♦ **get over 1** vi **(a)** (cross) hinüber-/herüberkommen (über +acc); (climb over) hinüber-/herübersteigen or -klettern; (+prep obj) steigen or klettern über (+acc); (manage to ~ ~) hinüber-/herüberkommen; (+prep obj) kommen über (+acc). they got ~ to the other side sie kamen or gelangten auf die andere Seite.

(b) +prep obj (lit, fig: recover from) disappointment, loss, sb's cheek, fact, experience (hin)wegkommen über (+acc); shock, surprise, illness sich erholen von. I can't ~ ~ the fact that ... ich komme gar nicht darüber hinweg, daß ...; I can't ~ ~ it (inf) da komm ich nicht drüber weg (inf).

(c) +prep obj (overcome) problem, nervousness, handicap, obstacle überwinden.

(d) (communicate) (play, actor) ankommen (to bei); (speaker) sich verständlich machen (to dat).

2 vt **(a)** always separate (transport across) person, animal, vehicle hinüber-/herüberbringen (prep obj über +acc); (manage to ~ ~) hinüber-/herüberbekommen (prep obj über +acc); (send) hinüber-/herüberschicken; (fetch) holen; (help sb to cross, climb) hinüber-/herüberhelfen (sb jdm) (prep obj über +acc).

(b) sep (make comprehensible) information, ideas etc verständlich machen (to dat); (impress upon) klarmachen (to dat). the actor couldn't ~ these emotions ~ (to the audience) der Schauspieler konnte (dem Publikum) diese Gefühle nicht mitteilen; the actors got the scene ~ to the audience die Schauspieler kamen mit der Szene beim Publikum an or erreichten das Publikum mit dieser Szene; she ~s her songs ~ well sie kommt mit ihren Liedern gut an.

(c) see **get over with**.

♦ **get over with** vt always separate hinter sich bringen. let's ~ it ~ (~) bringen wir's hinter uns; to ~ sth ~ and done ~ etw ein für allemal erledigen or hinter sich bringen.

♦ **get past 1** vi see **get by (a, b)**. **2** vt sep vorbeibringen (prep obj an +dat).

♦ **get round 1** vi **(a)** (drive, walk etc round) herumkommen (prep obj um, the shops in den Geschäften).

(b) +prep obj (evade, circumvent) herumkommen um; diffi-

culty also, law, regulations umgehen.
(c) +prep obj (persuade) herumkriegen (inf).
(d) +prep obj to ~ ~ **the conference table** sich an einen Tisch setzen.
2 vt always separate **(a)** (restore to consciousness) zu Bewußtsein or zu sich bringen.
(b) (make agree) herumbringen or -kriegen (inf). **I'm sure I can ~ her** to my way of thinking ich bin sicher, daß ich sie überzeugen kann.
(c) +prep obj to ~ **one's tongue ~ a word** ein Wort aussprechen können; **I just can't ~ my tongue ~ that word** bei dem Wort breche ich mir fast die Zunge ab.
(d) +prep obj to ~ **people (together)** ~ **the conference table** Leute an einem Tisch zusammenbringen.
♦ **get round to** vi +prep obj (inf) to ~ ~ ~ **sth/doing sth** zu etw kommen/dazu kommen, etw zu tun.
♦ **get through 1** vi **(a)** (through gap, snow etc) durchkommen (prep obj durch). **why don't you ~ ~ there?** warum gehst/fährst/schlüpfst etc du nicht da durch?; **the news got ~ (to us)** die Nachricht kam (zu uns) durch.
(b) (be accepted, pass) durchkommen (prep obj bei). to ~ ~ **to the second round/final** in die zweite Runde/Endrunde kommen.
(c) (Telec) durchkommen (inf) (to sb zu jdm, to London/Germany nach London/Deutschland).
(d) (communicate, be understood) (person) durchdringen zu; (idea etc) klarwerden (to dat).
(e) +prep obj (finish) work fertigmachen, erledigen; (manage to ~ ~) schaffen (inf); book fertig- or auslesen. to ~ ~ **doing sth** etw fertigmachen; to ~ ~ **writing/reading/cleaning sth** etw fertigschreiben/-lesen/-putzen; **when I've got ~ this** wenn ich damit fertig bin.
(f) +prep obj (survive) days, time herumbekommen or -kriegen (inf).
(g) +prep obj (consume, use up) verbrauchen; clothes, shoes abnutzen; food aufessen, verputzen (inf); fortune durchbringen (inf).
2 vt always separate **(a)** person, vehicle, object durchbekommen or -bringen or -kriegen (inf) (prep obj durch). to ~ **a comb ~ one's hair** mit dem Kamm durchkommen.
(b) (cause to succeed) candidate, proposal, bill durchbekommen or -bringen (prep obj durch). to ~ **sb ~ an exam** (teacher) jdn durchs Examen bringen; **it was his English that got him ~** er hat das nur aufgrund seines Englisch geschafft (inf); **he got the team ~ to the finals** er hat die Mannschaft in die Endrunde gebracht.
(c) (send) message durchgeben (to dat); supplies durchbringen. **they couldn't ~ the ammunition/reinforcements ~ to the front/men** es ist ihnen nicht gelungen, Munition/Nachschub an die Front/zu den Leuten zu bringen; **we eventually got supplies/a message ~ to them** wir konnten ihnen schließlich Vorräte/eine Nachricht zukommen lassen.
(d) (make understand) to ~ **sth ~ (to sb)** jdm etw klarmachen.
♦ **get through with** vi +prep obj (inf: finish) hinter sich bringen; job also, formalities, subject erledigen; book auslesen (inf), durchbekommen (inf); person fertig werden mit. **once I've got ~ ~ him** wenn ich mit ihm fertig bin; **I'll never ~ ~ ~ that** ich werde das nie schaffen.
♦ **get to** vi +prep obj **(a)** (lit, fig: arrive at) kommen zu; hotel, town etc also ankommen in (+dat). **where have you got ~ in French/with that book?** wie weit seid ihr in Französisch/mit dem Buch?; to ~ **power/a high position** an die Macht/auf einen hohen Posten kommen or gelangen.
(b) he got ~ **screaming at everyone** er schrie alle nur noch an; **I got ~ thinking/wondering** ich hab mir überlegt/mich gefragt.
(c) (inf: annoy, upset) aufregen. **don't let them ~ ~ you with their sarcasm** laß dich von ihrem Sarkasmus nicht rausbringen (inf).
♦ **get together 1** vi zusammenkommen; (estranged couple) sich versöhnen; (combine forces) sich zusammenschließen. to ~ ~ **about sth** zusammenkommen or sich zusammensetzen und etw beraten; **let's ~ ~ and decide ...** wir sollten uns zusammensetzen und entscheiden ...; **why don't we ~ ~ later and have a drink?** warum treffen wir uns nicht später und trinken etwas?
2 vt sep people, parts, collection zusammenbringen; documents, papers zusammentun or -suchen; thoughts, ideas sammeln. to ~ **one's things ~** seine Sachen zusammenpacken; **once I've got my thoughts ~** wenn ich meine Gedanken beisammen habe (inf); to ~ **it ~ (sl)** es bringen (sl); **that's no good, come on, ~ it ~ (sl)** das taugt doch nichts, nun reiß dich mal am Riemen (sl).
♦ **get under 1** vi darunterkriechen; (under umbrella etc) daruntergehen/-kommen; (+prep obj) kriechen unter (+acc); kommen unter (+acc); (manage to ~ ~) darunterkommen; (+prep obj) kommen unter (+acc). **2** vt +prep obj always separate bringen unter (+acc).
♦ **get up 1** vi **(a)** (stand up, get out of bed) aufstehen.
(b) (climb up) hinauf-/heraufsteigen or -klettern (prep obj auf +acc); (on horse) aufsteigen (prep obj, on auf +acc); (manage to ~ ~) hinauf-/heraufkommen (prep obj, on auf +acc); (vehicle) hinauf-/heraufkommen (prep obj acc). to ~ ~ **behind sb** hinter jdm aufsitzen; ~**ting ~ is all right, coming down is much harder** hinauf or rauf (inf) kommt man leicht, nur hinunterzukommen ist schwieriger.
(c) (get stronger) (wind) aufkommen; (sea) stürmisch werden.
2 vt **(a)** always separate (get out of bed) aus dem Bett holen; (help to stand up) aufhelfen (+dat); (manage to ~ ~)

hochbringen. **he couldn't ~ it ~** (inf) er hat ihn nicht hochgekriegt (inf); **I'll ~ myself ~ in the morning** ich stehe morgen früh allein auf.
(b) always separate (carry up) hinauf-/heraufbringen (prep obj acc); (manage to ~ ~ also) hinauf-/heraufbekommen or -kriegen (inf) (prep obj acc); (help climb up) hinauf-/heraufhelfen (dat) (prep obj auf +acc); (fetch) hinauf-/heraufholen. to ~ **sb/sth ~ to the front** jdn/etw nach vorn or (Mil) an die Front bringen.
(c) sep (gather) steam aufbauen. to ~ ~ **speed** sich beschleunigen; to ~ **one's strength ~**, to ~ **one's strength** sich erholen, wieder neue Kräfte sammeln; to ~ ~ **an appetite/a thirst** (inf) Hunger/Durst bekommen or kriegen (inf).
(d) sep (organize) organisieren; play also auf die Beine stellen (inf); group also zusammenbringen, auf die Beine bringen (inf).
(e) always separate (dress up, make attractive) person, oneself zurechtmachen; article for sale aufmachen, herrichten. to ~ **oneself ~ as sb/sth** sich als jd/etw verkleiden; to ~ **sth ~ as sth** or **to look like sth** etw als etw aufmachen.
♦ **get up against** vi +prep obj (inf: come in conflict with) sich anlegen mit (inf).
♦ **get up to 1** vi +prep obj **(a)** (lit, fig: reach) erreichen; standard herankommen an (+acc), kommen auf (+acc); page kommen bis. **as soon as he got ~ ~ me** sobald er neben mir stand.
(b) (be involved in) anstellen (inf). to ~ ~ ~ **mischief** etwas anstellen; **what have you been ~ting ~ ~?** was hast du getrieben? (inf).
2 vt +prep obj always separate (bring up to) top of mountain hinauf-/heraufbringen auf (+acc); standard bringen auf (+acc).
get: ~**-at-able** [ˌget'ætəbl] adj (inf) leicht erreichbar or zu erreichen pred; house, person also zugänglich; **it's not very ~-at-able** es ist schwer zu erreichen; ~**away 1** n Flucht f; **to make one's/a quick ~away** sich davonmachen (inf)/schnell abhauen (inf); **2** adj attr car, plans Flucht-.
Gethsemane [geθ'semənɪ] n Gethsemane, Gethsemani no art.
get: ~**-together** n (inf) Treffen nt; **we have a ~-together once a year** wir treffen uns einmal im Jahr; ~**-up** n (inf) Aufzug m (inf), Aufmachung f (inf); **to buy a new ~-up** sich neu einkleiden or ausstaffieren (inf); **I want a new ~-up** ich möchte etwas Neues zum Anziehen; ~**-up-and-go** n (inf) Elan m.
geyser ['giːzəʳ] n **(a)** (Geol) Geiser, Geysir m. **(b)** (domestic ~) Durchlauferhitzer m.
G-force ['dʒiːfɔːs] n Andruck m.
Ghana ['gɑːnə] n Ghana nt.
Ghanaian [gɑː'neɪən] **1** adj ghanaisch. **2** n (person) Ghanaer(in f m).
ghastly ['gɑːstlɪ] adj **(a)** crime, injuries, accident entsetzlich, grauenerregend; mistake, tale schrecklich. **(b)** (inf: awful) gräßlich (inf), schauderhaft (inf), scheußlich (inf). **to look ~** gräßlich aussehen (inf); **I feel ~** mir geht's scheußlich (inf). **(c)** (pale, chalk-like) appearance, pallor gespenstisch.
Ghent [gent] n Gent nt.
gherkin ['gɜːkɪn] n Gewürz- or Essiggurke f.
ghetto ['getəʊ] n G(h)etto nt.
ghost [gəʊst] **1** n **(a)** (apparition) Geist m, Gespenst nt; (of sb) Geist m.
(b) (fig) **the ~ of a smile** der Anflug eines Lächelns; **she gave him the ~ of a smile** sie lächelte ihn zaghaft an; **to be a ~ of one's former self** nur noch ein Schatten seiner selbst sein; **I haven't the ~ of a chance** ich habe nicht die geringste Chance.
(c) **to give up the ~** (old) seinen Geist aufgeben (old); (inf) den Geist aufgeben (inf).
(d) (TV) Geisterbild nt.
(e) (writer) Ghostwriter m.
2 vi Ghostwriter sein (for sb jds).
3 vt **to be ~ed** von einem Ghostwriter geschrieben sein; **to get sth ~ed** sich (dat) etw von einem Ghostwriter schreiben lassen; **to ~ sb's books/speeches** für jdn Bücher/Reden (als Ghostwriter) schreiben.
ghosting ['gəʊstɪŋ] n (TV) Geisterbilder pl.
ghostly ['gəʊstlɪ] adj (+er) geisterhaft, gespenstisch. **a ~ presence** die Gegenwart eines Geistes.
ghost in cpds Geister-; ~ **story** n Geister- or Gespenstergeschichte f; ~ **town** n Geisterstadt f; ~**writer** n Ghostwriter m.
ghoul [guːl] n (evil spirit) Ghul m; (fig) Mensch m mit schaurigen Gelüsten.
ghoulish ['guːlɪʃ] adj makaber; laughter, interest schaurig.
ghoulishly ['guːlɪʃlɪ] adv write makaber; laugh schaurig. **he is ~ interested in ...** er hat ein schauriges Interesse an (+dat) ...
G.I. (US) abbr of **government issue 1** n GI, US-Soldat m. **2** adj attr uniform, bride GI-; haircut, kitbag, shoes (US-)Armee-.
giant ['dʒaɪənt] **1** n Riese m; (fig) (führende) Größe; (company) Gigant m. **a ~ of a man** ein Riese (von einem Mann); football ~ Fußballas nt, (führende) Größe im Fußball; **one of the ~s in that field** eine(r) der Großen auf dem Gebiet.
2 adj (huge) riesig, riesenhaft, Riesen-; hill enorm; (in animal names) Riesen-; combine, publisher etc Groß-, Riesen- (inf). ~ **(-size) packet** Riesenpackung f; ~ **strength** Riesenkräfte pl.
giantess ['dʒaɪəntɪs] n Riesin f.
giant: ~**-killer** n (fig) Goliathbezwinger m; ~ **panda** n Großer Panda, Bambusbär m.
Gib [dʒɪb] n abbr of **Gibraltar**.
gibber ['dʒɪbəʳ] vi (ape) schnattern; (foreigner also, idiot) brabbeln. **he ~ed at me** er schnatterte drauflos (inf); **to ~ with rage/fear** vor Wut/Angst stammeln.
gibberish ['dʒɪbərɪʃ] n Quatsch m (inf); (foreign language, baby's ~) Kauderwelsch nt.

gibbet ['dʒɪbɪt] n Galgen m.
gibbon ['gɪbən] n Gibbon m.
gibbous ['gɪbəs] adj moon Dreiviertel-.
gibe, jibe [dʒaɪb] 1 n Spöttelei, Sticheleí f. 2 vi spotten, sticheln. to ~ at sb/sth sich über jdn/etw lustig machen, spöttische Bemerkungen über jdn/etw machen.
giblets ['dʒɪblɪts] npl Geflügelinnereien pl.
Gibraltar [dʒɪˈbrɔːltəʳ] n Gibraltar nt.
giddily ['gɪdɪlɪ] adv (a) benommen. (b) climb etc schwindelerregend; spin in schwindelerregendem Tempo. the bit of wood tossing ~ at the bottom of the waterfall das Holzstückchen, das unten am Wasserfall herumgewirbelt wurde. (c) (fig) leichtfertig, unbesonnen.
giddiness ['gɪdɪnɪs] n (a) (dizziness) Schwindelgefühl nt. (b) (fig) Leichtfertigkeit, Unbesonnenheit f. the ~ of the life they lead der hektische Trubel ihres Lebens.
giddy ['gɪdɪ] adj (+er) (a) (lit: dizzy) schwind(e)lig; feeling Schwindel-. I feel ~ mir ist schwind(e)lig; it makes me feel ~ mir wird (davon) schwind(e)lig; heights always make me ~ ich bin nicht schwindelfrei.
(b) (causing dizziness) climb, speed schwindelerregend; heights also schwindelnd (also fig); spin rasend schnell.
(c) (fig: heedless, not serious) leichtfertig, flatterhaft. their life was one ~ round of pleasure ihr Leben bestand nur aus Jubel, Trubel, Heiterkeit; that's the ~ limit! (dated inf) das ist wirklich der Gipfel or die Höhe!
gift [gɪft] 1 n (a) (thing given) Geschenk nt (inf), Gabe f (liter); (donation to charity) Spende f; (Jur) Schenkung f. to make sb a ~ jdm ein Geschenk machen; to make a ~ of sth to sb jdm etw zum Geschenk machen (form); there is a free ~ with every purchase of ... bei jedem Kauf von ... erhalten Sie ein Geschenk; a free ~ of a tin of soup eine Dose Suppe umsonst; I wouldn't have it as a ~ ich möchte es nicht geschenkt haben; that exam/question/goal was a ~ (inf) die Prüfung/die Frage/das Tor war ja geschenkt (inf).
(b) (form: right to give) sth is in the ~ of sb jd kann etw vergeben.
(c) (talent) Gabe f. to have a ~ for sth ein Talent für etw haben; he has a ~ for languages/music etc er ist sprachbegabt/musikalisch etc begabt; see gab.
2 vt als Schenkung überlassen.
gifted ['gɪftɪd] adj begabt (in für). he is very ~ in languages/music etc er ist sehr sprachbegabt/musikalisch etc sehr begabt.
gift: ~ horse n: don't look a ~ horse in the mouth (prov) einem geschenkten Gaul schaut man nicht ins Maul (prov); ~ tax n Schenkungssteuer f; ~ token or voucher n Geschenkgutschein m; ~-wrap vt in or mit Geschenkpapier einwickeln; ~-wrapping n Geschenkpapier nt.
gig [gɪg] n (a) (carriage, boat) Gig nt. (b) (sl: concert) Konzert nt, Mucke f (sl).
gigantic [dʒaɪˈgæntɪk] adj riesig, riesengroß; building, man, task also gigantisch; appetite, mistake also gewaltig; amount riesenhaft, enorm, Riesen-; yawn kräftig, herzhaft; laugh dröhnend. it grew to ~ size es wurde riesengroß.
giggle ['gɪgl] 1 n Gekicher, Kichern nt no pl. she has such a silly ~ sie kichert so dumm; ..., he said with a ~ ..., sagte er kichernd; we had a good ~ about it (inf) wir haben uns darüber gekringelt (inf); it was a bit of a ~ (inf) es war ganz lustig. 2 vi kichern, gickeln (inf).
giggly ['gɪglɪ] adj (+er) albern, gickelig (inf).
gigolo ['ʒɪgələʊ] n Gigolo m.
gigot ['dʒɪgət] n (old) Hammelkeule f. ~ chop (Scot) Hammelkotelett nt mit Mark im Knochen.
gild [gɪld] pret ~ed, ptp ~ed or gilt vt vergolden. to ~ the lily des Guten zuviel tun.
gilder ['gɪldəʳ] n Vergolder m.
gilding ['gɪldɪŋ] n Vergoldung f.
gill¹ [gɪl] n (of fish) Kieme f. green about the ~s (inf) blaß um die Nase (inf).
gill² [dʒɪl] n (measure) Gill nt (0,148 l).
gillie ['gɪlɪ] n (Scot) Jagdaufseher m.
gilt [gɪlt] 1 ptp of gild. 2 n (material) Vergoldung f. a design in ~ ein vergoldetes Muster; to take the ~ off the gingerbread (fig) jdm die Freude verderben. 3 adj vergoldet.
gilt-edged [ˌgɪltˈedʒd] adj mit Goldrand, goldumrandet; (Fin) securities, stocks mündelsicher; (fig) solide.
gimcrack ['dʒɪmkræk] adj billig; furniture, toys also minderwertig; souvenirs, jewellery also Talmi- (geh).
gimlet ['gɪmlɪt] n Hand- or Vorbohrer m. to have eyes like ~s Augen wie ein Luchs haben; her eyes bored into him like ~s ihre Augen durchbohrten ihn; ~-eyed luchsäugig.
gimme ['gɪmɪ] (sl) = give me.
gimmick ['gɪmɪk] n Gag m (in film etc) effekthaschender Gag, Spielerei f; (gadget) Spielerei f. changing the name and not the product is just a (sales) ~ den Namen, aber nicht das Produkt zu ändern, ist nur ein (Verkaufs)trick.
gimmickry ['gɪmɪkrɪ] n Effekthascherei f; (in advertising, sales) Gags pl (gadgetry) Spielereien pl.
gimmicky ['gɪmɪkɪ] adj effekthascherisch.
gin¹ [dʒɪn] n (drink) Gin, Wacholder(schnaps) m. ~ and tonic Gin Tonic m; ~ and it Gin m und (italienischer) Wermut.
gin² n (a) (Hunt) Falle f; (snare) Schlinge f. (b) (Tex: cotton ~) (Baumwoll)entkernungsmaschine f.
ginger ['dʒɪndʒəʳ] 1 n (a) (Cook) Ingwer m. crystallized ~ kandierter Ingwer. (b) (pej inf: address for person) Rotkopf or -schopf m. 2 adj (a) (Cook) biscuit etc Ingwer-. (b) hair kupferrot; cat rötlichgelb.
♦ **ginger up** vt sep (inf) in Schwung or auf Vordermann (inf) bringen; person also aufmöbeln (inf); book, pudding würzen, anreichern.

ginger: ~-ale n Ginger Ale nt; ~ beer n Ingwerlimonade f; ~bread 1 n Leb- or Pfefferkuchen m mit Ingwergeschmack; 2 adj attr Lebkuchen-; ~ group n (Parl) Aktionsgruppe f.
gingerly ['dʒɪndʒəlɪ] adv vorsichtig, behutsam; (because sth is dirty) mit spitzen Fingern; (because sth is cold, hot etc) zaghaft.
ginger: ~-nut n Ingwerplätzchen nt; ~-snap n Ingwerwaffel f.
gingery ['dʒɪndʒərɪ] adj taste Ingwer-; hair rötlich.
gingham ['gɪŋəm] n Gingan, Gingham m.
gingivitis [ˌdʒɪndʒɪˈvaɪtɪs] n Zahnfleischentzündung f.
gin rummy n Rommé mit Zehn nt.
gippy tummy ['dʒɪpɪˈtʌmɪ] n (inf) Durchfall m.
gipsy, (esp US) gypsy ['dʒɪpsɪ] 1 n Zigeuner(in f) m. 2 adj attr Zigeuner-. ~ moth Schwammspinner m.
giraffe [dʒɪˈrɑːf] n Giraffe f.
gird [gɜːd] prep, ptp ~ed or (rare) girt vt (old) gürten (old); (fig) umgeben. he ~ed his waist with a cord er gürtete eine Schnur um seinen Leib (old); to ~ oneself sich gürten (with mit); (fig: prepare) sich wappnen.
♦ **gird up** vt sep (old) robe gürten. to ~ one's loins (esp Bibl) seine Lenden gürten (Bibl); to ~ oneself ~ (fig) sich wappnen; he ~ed himself ~ for action er machte sich bereit (zum Handeln).
girder ['gɜːdəʳ] n Träger m.
girdle¹ ['gɜːdl] 1 n (a) (belt, fig) Gürtel m. a ~ of hills eine Hügelkette. (b) (corset) Hüftgürtel or -halter m. 2 vt (lit) gürten; (fig) umgeben.
girdle² n (Scot) see griddle.
girl [gɜːl] n (a) Mädchen nt; (daughter also) Tochter f. an English ~ eine Engländerin; they are hoping for a little ~ sie wünschen sich (dat) ein Töchterchen; the Smith ~s die Smith-Mädchen, die Mädchen von den Smiths; my eldest ~ meine älteste Tochter, meine Älteste; the ~s (colleagues) die Damen; (friends) die/meine/ihre etc Freundinnen; thank you, ~s vielen Dank; the old ~ die Alte (inf) or alte Frau; (inf: wife, mother) meine/seine etc Alte (inf).
(b) (employee) Mädchen nt; (in shop also) Verkäuferin f; (in factory) Arbeiterin f.
girl: ~ Friday n Allround-Sekretärin f; ~friend n Freundin f; ~ guide n (Brit) Pfadfinderin f; ~hood n Mädchenzeit, Jugend f; during her ~hood in ihrer Jugend.
girlie ['gɜːlɪ] 1 n (inf) Mädchen nt. 2 adj attr magazine mit nackten Mädchen; photos von nackten Mädchen.
girlish ['gɜːlɪʃ] adj behaviour, appearance mädchenhaft; laugh, confidences also Mädchen-. she still looked ~ sie sah immer noch wie ein Mädchen aus.
girlishly ['gɜːlɪʃlɪ] adv mädchenhaft; dress also jugendlich.
girlishness ['gɜːlɪʃnɪs] n Mädchenhaftigkeit f.
girl scout n (US) Pfadfinderin f.
giro ['dʒaɪrəʊ] n (Brit) (bank ~) Giro(verkehr m) nt; (post-office ~) Postscheckverkehr or -dienst m. to pay a bill by ~ eine Rechnung durch Giro/mit Postscheck bezahlen.
girt [gɜːt] (rare) pret, ptp of gird.
girth [gɜːθ] n (a) (circumference) Umfang m. in ~ im Umfang; a man of ample ~ ein Mann mit beträchtlichem Umfang. (b) (harness) (Sattel)gurt m.
gismo n (US inf) see gizmo.
gist [dʒɪst] n, no pl (of report, conversation, argument) Wesentliche(s) nt. that was the ~ of what he said das war im wesentlichen, was er gesagt hat; to give sb the ~ of sth jdm sagen, worum es bei etw geht; to get the ~ of sth/the conversation im wesentlichen verstehen, worum es sich bei etw handelt/wovon geredet wird; I got the ~ of it das Wesentliche habe ich verstanden.
give [gɪv] (vb: pret gave, ptp given) 1 vt (a) geben (sb sth, sth to sb jdm etw); (as present) schenken (sb sth, sth to sb jdm etw); (donate also) spenden. it was ~n to me by my uncle, I was ~n it by my uncle ich habe es von meinem Onkel bekommen or (as present also) geschenkt bekommen; she was ~n a sedative sie hat ein Beruhigungsmittel bekommen, man hat ihr or ihr wurde ein Beruhigungsmittel gegeben; the teacher gave us three exercises der Lehrer hat uns drei Übungen gegeben or (as homework) aufgegeben; we were ~n three exercises wir haben drei Übungen bekommen or (as homework) aufbekommen; he gave me a present of a book or a book as a present er schenkte mir ein Buch, er machte mir ein Buch zum Geschenk; they gave us food and drink sie gaben uns zu essen und zu trinken; they gave us roast beef for lunch sie servierten uns Roastbeef zum (Mittag)essen; ~ me that bag to carry let mir die Tasche zum Tragen; to ~ sth for sth (sacrifice) etw für etw (her)geben; (exchange) etw gegen etw tauschen; what will you ~ me for it? was gibst du mir dafür?; what did you ~ for it? was hast du dafür bezahlt?; 11 o'clock, ~ or take a few minutes so gegen 11 Uhr; six foot, ~ or take a few inches ungefähr sechs Fuß; to ~ as good as one gets sich kräftig wehren; he gave everything he'd got (fig) er holte das Letzte aus sich heraus; to ~ sb one's cold (inf) jdn mit seiner Erkältung anstecken; I'd ~ a lot/the world/anything to know ... ich würde viel darum geben, wenn ich wüßte, ...
(b) (fig) geben; pleasure, joy machen, bereiten; pain bereiten; trouble machen; one's trust, attention schenken; hospitality erweisen; punishment erteilen; favour gewähren. this incident gave him the basic plot of or idea for the story durch dieses Ereignis bekam er die Grundidee zu seiner Geschichte; who/what gave you that idea or notion? wer hat dir denn auf die Idee gebracht/wie kommst du denn auf die Idee? I'll ~ you the choice between ... ich gebe or lasse Ihnen die Wahl zwischen ...; to ~ no choice die Wahl haben; I wasn't ~n the choice ich hatte keine (andere) Wahl; to ~ sb pain jdm weh tun (also fig), jdm Schmerzen bereiten; it ~s me great pleasure to ... es ist mir eine große Freude ...; he gave the

impression/appearance of being disturbed er machte einen verstörten Eindruck; to ~ sb help jdm helfen *or* Hilfe leisten; to ~ sb support jdn unterstützen; (God) ~ me strength to do it Gott gebe mir die Kraft, es zu tun!; ~ me strength/patience! großer Gott!, steh mir bei! (*dated*); he gave the child a spanking/100 lines er gab *or* verabreichte dem Kind eine Tracht Prügel/er gab dem Kind 100 Zeilen als Strafarbeit auf; to ~ sb five years jdn zu fünf Jahren verurteilen, jdm fünf Jahre aufbrummen (*inf*); he was ~n a spanking/five years er hat eine Tracht Prügel/fünf Jahre bekommen; to ~ sb to understand that ... jdm zu verstehen geben, daß ...; I was ~n to understand that ... mir wurde zu verstehen gegeben, daß ...; to ~ sb what for (*inf*), to ~ it to sb (*inf*) jdm Saures geben (*inf*), es jdm geben (*inf*); that will ~ you something to cry/think about da hast du Grund zum Weinen/etwas, worüber du nachdenken kannst; I'll ~ you something to cry about ich werde schon zusehen, daß du weißt, warum du weinst; ~ me Shakespeare/ Spain (every time)! (*inf*) es geht doch nichts über Shakespeare/Spanien; ~ me Renoir and Rembrandt, not these surrealist artists mir sind Renoir und Rembrandt viel lieber als diese Surrealisten; *see* thrill, idea.

  (c) (*allow*) *time* geben. they gave me a week to do it sie gaben or ließen mir eine Woche Zeit, um es zu machen; ~ yourself more time/half an hour lassen Sie sich mehr Zeit/rechnen Sie mit einer halben Stunde; I always ~ myself an extra hour in bed on Saturdays sonnabends genehmige ich mir eine Extrastunde im Bett; how long do you ~ that marriage? (*inf*) wie lange gibst du dieser Ehe? (*inf*); I'll ~ you that zugegeben; he's a good worker, I'll ~ him that eines muß man ihm lassen, er arbeitet gut.

  (d) (*report, tell, pass on*) *information, details, description, answer, advice* geben; *one's name, particulars* angeben; *suggestion* machen; (*let sb know by letter, phone etc*) *decision, opinion, results* mitteilen. the court hasn't ~n a decision yet das Gericht hat noch kein Urteil gefällt; he wouldn't ~ me his decision/opinion er wollte mir seine Meinung/Entscheidung nicht sagen; they interrupted the programme to ~ the football results sie unterbrachen das Programm, um die Fußballergebnisse zu bringen; ~ him my compliments *or* regards/thanks bestellen Sie ihm (schöne) Grüße/bestellen Sie ihm, daß ich ihm danke, richten Sie ihm (schöne) Grüße von mir/meinen Dank aus; to ~ the right/no answer richtig/nicht antworten; to ~ sb a warning jdn warnen; his letter gave us the latest news in seinem Brief stand das Neueste; she was ~n the news by John John hat ihr das mitgeteilt; he forgot to ~ us the date er hat vergessen, uns das Datum anzugeben *or* (*verbally also*) zu sagen *or* (*by letter, phone etc also*) mitzuteilen; who gave you that information? wer hat Ihnen das gesagt *or* die Auskunft gegeben *or* erteilt?; *see* message.

  (e) (*yield, produce*) *milk, warmth, light etc* geben; *results* (er)bringen; *answer* liefern. this TV ~s a very good picture dieser Fernseher hat ein sehr gutes Bild; this tree doesn't ~ much fruit dieser Baum trägt nicht gut.

  (f) (*hold, perform*) *party, dinner, play* geben; *speech* halten; *song* singen; *toast* ausbringen (*to sb* auf jdn). ~ us a song sing uns was vor; I ~ you Mary (*as toast*) auf Mary *or* Marys Wohl!; (*as speaker*) ich gebe Mary das Wort.

  (g) (*devote*) widmen (*to dat*). he has ~n himself entirely to medicine er hat sich ganz der Medizin verschrieben; he gave himself/his life to God er weihte sich/sein Leben Gott.

  (h) to ~ a cry/groan/laugh/sigh (auf)schreien/(auf)stöhnen/(auf)lachen/(auf)seufzen; the child gave a little jump of excitement das Kind machte vor Aufregung einen Luftsprung; he gave a shrug of his shoulders er zuckte mit den Schultern; to ~ sb a look/smile jdn ansehen/anlächeln; to ~ sb a blow jdn schlagen, jdm einen Schlag versetzen; to ~ sb a push/ kick jdm einen Stoß/Tritt geben, jdn stoßen/treten; to ~ sb's hand a squeeze jdm die Hand drücken; to ~ one's hair a brush/ wash sich (*dat*) die Haare bürsten/waschen.

  (i) in set phrases see under n to ~ birth gebären; to ~ chase die Verfolgung aufnehmen; to ~ evidence (*Jur*) aussagen; to ~ rise to sth Anlaß zu etw geben.

  2 vi (a) (*also* ~ way) (*lit, fig: collapse, yield*) (*strength, health, nerve, voice*) versagen; (*break: rope, cable*) reißen; (*cold weather*) nachlassen. my legs were giving at the knees *or* under me meine Knie gaben nach *or* wurden weich; when you're under as much strain as that, something is bound to ~ (*inf*) wenn man unter so viel Druck steht, muß es ja irgendwo aushaken (*inf*).

  (b) (*lit, fig: bend, be flexible*) nachgeben; (*bed*) federn; (*dress*) sich dehnen *or* weiten.

  (c) (~ *money etc*) geben, spenden. it is more blessed to ~ than to receive Geben ist seliger denn Nehmen; you have to be prepared to ~ and take in this world/in marriage (*fig*) man muß im Leben zu Kompromissen bereit sein *or* auch mal zurückstecken können/man muß in der Ehe geben und nehmen.

  (d) (*sl*) what ~s? was gibt's? (*inf*), was ist los? (*inf*); what ~s with him? was ist los mit ihm? (*inf*); what ~s in this town? was ist hier (in der Stadt) los?

  (e) (*US sl*) OK, now ~! also, raus mit der Sprache! (*inf*).

  3 n Nachgiebigkeit, Elastizität f; (*of floor, bed, chair*) Federung f. this elastic hasn't got much ~ left dieses Gummiband ist nicht mehr sehr elastisch; it has a lot of ~ es gibt sehr stark nach; he hasn't got enough ~ (*fig*) er ist nicht flexibel genug.

♦ **give away** *vt sep* (a) (*give without charge*) weggeben; (*as present*) verschenken. it isn't exactly ~n ~ at that price bei dem Preis ist es nicht gerade geschenkt; at £5 I'm practically giving it ~ ich will £ 5 dafür, das ist fast geschenkt.

  (b) *bride* (*als Brautvater etc*) zum Altar führen.

  (c) (*hand out*) *prizes etc* vergeben, verteilen.

  (d) (*fig: betray*) verraten (*to sb* an jdn). to ~ the game *or* show ~ (*inf*) alles verraten.

♦ **give back** *vt sep* zurück- *or* wiedergeben; *echo* widerhallen lassen, zurückgeben; (*mirror*) *image* reflektieren.

♦ **give in 1** *vi* (*surrender*) sich ergeben (*to sb* jdm); (*in guessing game etc*) aufgeben; (*accede, back down*) nachgeben (*to dat*). to ~ ~ to sb's views/the majority/blackmail sich jds Meinung/der Mehrheit beugen/auf Erpressung eingehen; to ~ ~ to temptation der Versuchung erliegen *or* nicht widerstehen.

  2 *vt sep* *document, essay* einreichen; *parcel* abgeben. to ~ ~ sb's/one's name jdn/sich anmelden.

♦ **give off** *vt insep* *heat, gas* abgeben; *smell* verbreiten, ausströmen; *rays* ausstrahlen.

♦ **give on to** *vi* + *prep obj* (*window*) hinausgehen auf (+ *acc*); (*door*) hinausführen auf (+ *acc*); *garden* hinausführen in (+ *acc*).

♦ **give out 1** *vi* (*supplies, patience, strength, road*) zu Ende gehen *or* (*in past tense*) sein; (*engine, feet*) versagen; (*inspiration*) versiegen. my memory gave ~ mein Gedächtnis ließ mich im Stich. **2** *vt sep* (a) (*distribute*) aus- *or* verteilen. (b) (*announce*) bekanntgeben. to ~ oneself ~ as sth *or* to be sth sich als etw ausgeben. **3** *vt insep see* give off.

♦ **give over 1** *vt sep* (a) (*hand over*) übergeben (*to dat*).

  (b) (*set aside, use for*) to be ~n ~ to sth für etw beansprucht werden.

  (c) to ~ oneself ~ to pleasure/despair *etc* sich ganz dem Vergnügen/der Verzweiflung *etc* hingeben; to be ~n ~ to pleasure (*person*) sich ganz dem Vergnügen hingegeben haben; (*life*) ganz dem Vergnügen gewidmet sein.

  2 *vti* (*dial inf*) aufhören. ~ ~! hör auf!; ~ ~ tickling me! hör auf, mich zu kitzeln!

♦ **give up 1** *vi* ~ ~ ich gebe auf, ich geb's auf (*inf*).

  2 *vt sep* (a) aufgeben; *claim also* verzichten auf (+ *acc*). to ~ ~ doing sth aufhören *or* es aufgeben, etw zu tun; I'm trying to ~ ~ smoking ich versuche, das Rauchen aufzugeben; to ~ ~ all thoughts of sth jeden Gedanken an etw (*acc*) aufgeben; I gave it/him ~ as a bad job ich/ihn habe ich abgeschrieben; to ~ sb/sth ~ as lost jdn/etw verloren geben; to ~ sb ~ as dead jdn für tot halten; *see* ghost.

  (b) (*surrender*) *land, territory* abgeben, abtreten (*to dat*); *authority* abgeben, abtreten (*to an* + *acc*); *keys of city etc* übergeben (*to dat*); *seat, place* freimachen (*to für*), abtreten (*to dat*); *ticket* abgeben (*to bei*).

  (c) (*hand over to authorities*) ausliefern (*to an* + *acc*), übergeben (*to dat*). to ~ oneself ~ sich stellen; (*after siege etc*) sich ergeben.

  (d) (*devote*) widmen. to ~ ~ one's life to music sein Leben der Musik widmen *or* verschreiben; he's ~n himself ~ to vice er ist dem Laster verfallen.

  (e) (*disclose, yield up*) *secret, treasure* enthüllen (*geh*).

♦ **give way** *vi* (a) (*lit*) *see* give 2 (a).

  (b) (*fig: yield*) nachgeben (*to dat*). to ~ ~ to intimidation sich einschüchtern lassen; don't ~ ~ to despair überlaß dich nicht der Verzweiflung; she gave ~ to tears sie ließ den Tränen freien Lauf.

  (c) (*be superseded*) to ~ ~ to sth von etw abgelöst werden; tears gave ~ to smiles die Tränen machten einem Lächeln Platz; radio has almost ~n ~ to television das Radio ist vom Fernsehen fast verdrängt worden.

  (d) (*Brit Mot*) ~ ~ to oncoming traffic der Gegenverkehr hat Vorfahrt, dem Gegenverkehr die Vorfahrt lassen; who has to ~ ~ here? wer hat hier Vorfahrt?; I was expecting him to ~ ~ ich nahm an, er würde mir die Vorfahrt lassen; "~ ~" „Vorfahrt (beachten)".

give: ~ and take n Entgegenkommen nt; (*in personal relationships*) Geben und Nehmen nt; ~-away n (a) the expression on her face was a ~-way ihr Gesichtsausdruck verriet alles; it was a real ~-away when he said ... er verriet sich, als er sagte ...; (b) (*inf*) that exam question was a ~-away diese Prüfungsfrage war geschenkt (*inf*); (c) (*US Comm: gift*) Geschenk nt; (d) (*US Rad, TV*) Preisraten nt; ~-away price n Schleuderpreis m.

given [ˈgɪvn] **1** ptp of give.

  2 adj (a) (*with indef art*) bestimmt; (*with def art*) angegeben. of a ~ size von einer bestimmten Größe; 500 bottles of the ~ size 500 Flaschen der angegebenen Größe.

  (b) ~ name (*esp US*) Vorname m.

  (c) (*having inclination*) to be ~ to sth zu etw neigen; I'm ~/not ~ to doing that ich tue das gern/es ist nicht meine Art, das zu tun; I'm not ~ to drinking on my own ich habe nicht die Angewohnheit, allein zu trinken.

  3 conj ~ sth (*with*) vorausgesetzt, man/er *etc* hat etw, wenn man/er *etc* etw hat; (*in view of*) angesichts einer Sache (*gen*); ~ that he ... (*in view of the fact*) angesichts der Tatsache, daß er ...; (*assuming*) vorausgesetzt *or* angenommen, (daß) er ...; ~ time, we can/could do it vorausgesetzt, wir haben/hätten genug Zeit *or* wenn wir genug Zeit haben/hätten, können/könnten wir es schaffen; ~ these circumstances/conditions unter diesen Umständen/Voraussetzungen; ~ these premises you can work out the answer anhand dieser Vorraussetzungen kannst du die Lösung finden; ~ the triangle ABC (*Math*) gegeben ist *or* sei das Dreieck ABC.

giver [ˈgɪvəʳ] n Geber(in f) m. he was a generous ~ to church funds er hat großzügig für die Kirche gespendet.

give-way sign [gɪvˈweɪˌsaɪn] n (*Brit*) Vorfahrtsschild nt.

gizmo [ˈgɪzməu] n (*US inf*) Ding nt (inf).

gizzard [ˈgɪzəd] n Muskelmagen m.

Gk abbr of Greek Griech.

glabrous [ˈglæbrəs] adj (*Zool*) unbehaart; (*liter*) *youth* bartlos.

glacé [ˈglæseɪ] adj *bun* mit Zuckerguß, glasiert; *fruit* kandiert; *leather* Glacé-. ~ icing Zuckerguß m.

glacial ['gleɪsɪəl] adj (a) (Geol) Gletscher-, glazial (spec). ~ epoch or era Eiszeit f, Glazial nt (form). (b) (cold) look, wind, temperature eisig.

glaciated ['gleɪsɪeɪtɪd] adj (covered with glaciers) gletscherbedeckt, vergletschert; (eroded by glaciers) durch Gletschertätigkeit entstanden.

glacier ['glæsɪəʳ] n Gletscher m.

glaciology [ˌgleɪsɪ'ɒlədʒɪ] n Gletscherkunde, Glaziologie (form) f.

glad [glæd] adj (+er) (a) (pleased) froh. to be ~ at or about sth sich über etw (acc) freuen; to be ~ of sth über etw (acc) froh sein; to be ~ that ... sich freuen, daß ...; (relieved) froh sein, daß ...; I'm ~ to see you ich freue mich, Sie zu sehen; (relieved) ich bin froh, Sie zu sehen; I'm so ~! das freut mich, da bin ich aber froh!; you'll be ~ to hear that ... es wird Sie freuen zu hören, daß ...; ..., you'll be ~ to hear ..., das wird Sie freuen, das werden Sie mit Freude vernehmen (geh); to feel/look ~ sich freuen/erfreut or froh aussehen; (relieved) froh sein/froh or erleichtert aussehen; we would be ~ of your help wir wären froh, wenn Sie helfen könnten; I'd be ~ of your opinion on this ich würde gerne Ihre Meinung dazu hören; you'll be ~ of it later du wirst später (noch) froh darüber sein; I'd be ~ to aber gern!

(b) (giving pleasure) froh; occasion, news also freudig; day also Freuden-. the ~ tidings die frohe Botschaft (old, hum).

gladden ['glædn] vt person, heart erfreuen.

glade [gleɪd] n Lichtung f.

glad: ~ eye n to give sb the ~ eye jdm schöne Augen machen (inf); ~ hand n (US) to give sb the ~ hand jdn überschwenglich begrüßen.

gladiator ['glædɪeɪtəʳ] n Gladiator m.

gladiatorial [ˌglædɪə'tɔːrɪəl] adj Gladiatoren-.

gladiolus [ˌglædɪ'əʊləs] n, pl **gladioli** [ˌglædɪ'əʊlaɪ] Gladiole f.

gladly ['glædlɪ] adv (a) (willingly) gern. (b) (joyfully) fröhlich.

gladness ['glædnɪs] n (a) (of person) Freude f; (relief) Erleichterung f; (of smile etc) Fröhlichkeit f. (b) (of occasion, news) Freudigkeit f.

gladrags ['glædˌrægz] npl (inf) Sonntagsstaat m (inf). to put/have one's ~ on (inf) sich in Schale werfen/in Schale sein (inf).

gladsome ['glædsəm] adj (old) freudenreich (liter).

glamor n (US) see glamour.

glamorize ['glæməraɪz] vt idealisieren, einen glamourösen Anstrich geben (+dat); job, life-style also einen besonderen Glanz or Reiz or eine besondere Faszination verleihen (+dat); author, war glorifizieren. to ~ one's image sein Image aufpolieren; to ~ oneself sich (dat) einen raffinierten or glamourösen Anstrich geben.

glamorous ['glæmərəs] adj bezaubernd, betörend; film star glamourös; job Traum-, glamourös; clothes flott; life glamourös; state occasion glanzvoll.

glamorously ['glæmərəslɪ] adv glamourös. a ~ exciting life ein fabelhaft aufregendes Leben.

glamour ['glæməʳ] n Glamour m; (of occasion, situation) Glanz m. she/the job doesn't have much ~ sie/dieser Beruf hat keinen besonderen Reiz; she has ~ as well as prettiness sie ist nicht nur hübsch, sondern besitzt auch noch einen besonderen Reiz.

glamour: ~ boy n (inf) Schönling m (inf); ~ girl n (inf) Glamourgirl nt.

glance [glɑːns] 1 n Blick m. at a ~ auf einen Blick; at first ~ auf den ersten Blick; she gave him an angry/amorous ~ sie warf ihm einen wütenden/verliebten Blick zu; to take or cast a quick ~ at sth einen kurzen Blick auf etw (acc) werfen; he cast or had a quick ~ round the room er sah sich kurz im Zimmer um.

2 vi sehen, blicken, schauen (esp S Ger). to ~ at sb/sth jdn/etw kurz ansehen, einen kurzen Blick auf etw (acc) werfen; to ~ at/through the newspaper a report einen kurzen Blick in die Zeitung/in einen Bericht werfen, die Zeitung/einen Bericht überfliegen or kurz durchsehen; to ~ over sth etw überfliegen; to ~ across to sb jdm einen Blick zuwerfen; to ~ down/in einen Blick hinunter-/hineinwerfen, kurz hinunter-/hineinsehen; to ~ up/aside aufsehen or -blicken (from von)/zur Seite sehen; to ~ round sich umblicken; he ~d round the room er sah sich im Zimmer um; the book merely ~s at the problem das Buch streift das Problem nur.

♦**glance off** vi (prep obj von) (bullet etc) abprallen; (sword) abgleiten; (light) reflektiert werden.

glancing ['glɑːnsɪŋ] adj to strike sth a ~ blow etw streifen; she struck him a ~ blow ihr Schlag streifte sein Gesicht; it was only a ~ blow ich/er etc wurde nur gestreift.

gland [glænd] n Drüse f; (lymph ~) Lymphdrüse f or -knoten m.

glandular ['glændjʊləʳ] adj Drüsen-. ~ fever Drüsenfieber nt.

glare [gleəʳ] 1 n (a) greller Schein; (from sun, bulb, lamp also) grelles Licht. the ~ of the sun das grelle Sonnenlicht; to avoid the ~ of publicity das grelle Licht der Öffentlichkeit scheuen.

(b) (stare) wütender or stechender Blick. a ~ of hatred/anger ein haßerfüllter/zorniger Blick; there was a ~ of anger in her eyes ihre Augen funkelten vor Zorn.

2 vi (a) (light, sun) grell scheinen; (headlights) grell leuchten; (bulb) grell brennen.

(b) (stare) (zornig) starren. to ~ at sb/sth jdn/etw zornig anstarren.

(c) (fig) that mistake really ~s at you dieser Fehler springt einem förmlich ins Gesicht.

3 vt (a) to ~ defiance/hatred at sb jdn trotzig or voller Trotz/haßerfüllt or voll von Haß anstarren.

(b) (fig) to ~ sb in the face jdm förmlich ins Gesicht springen.

glaring ['gleərɪŋ] adj (a) sun, colour grell. (b) her ~ eyes ihr stechender Blick. (c) (fig) omission eklatant; mistake

also grob; contrast kraß; injustice (himmel)schreiend.

glaringly ['gleərɪŋlɪ] adv (a) shine grell. ~ bright grell. (b) (fig) their words contrasted ~ with their deeds ihre Worte standen in krassem Gegensatz zu ihren Taten; it's ~ unjust/wrong es ist eine himmelschreiende Ungerechtigkeit/das ist ein eklatanter Fehler; it is ~ obvious that ... es liegt klar auf der Hand, daß ...

glass [glɑːs] 1 n (a) (substance) Glas nt. a pane of ~ eine Glasscheibe; to be grown under ~ (Hort) unter Glas gezogen werden.

(b) (object, vessel, contents, ~ware) Glas nt; (dated: mirror) Spiegel m. a ~ of wine ein Glas Wein; he gets quite cheerful when he's had a ~ (inf) er wird richtig fröhlich, wenn er ein Gläschen getrunken hat (inf).

(c) (pair of) ~es pl (spectacles) Brille f; he wears thick ~es er trägt eine starke Brille or starke Gläser.

(d) (instrument) (magnifying ~) (Vergrößerungs)glas nt, Lupe f; (telescope) Teleskop, Fernrohr nt; (barometer) Barometer nt. ~es pl (binoculars) (Fern)glas nt.

2 vt verglasen.

3 attr Glas-. people who live in ~ houses shouldn't throw stones (Prov) wer im Glashaus sitzt, soll nicht mit Steinen werfen (Prov).

glass in cpds Glas-; ~-blower n Glasbläser(in f) m; ~-cloth n Gläsertuch nt; ~-cutter n (tool) Glasschneider m; (person) Glasschleifer m; ~ eye n Glasauge nt; ~ fibre n Glasfaser f; ~ful n see glass 1 (b); ~house n (a) (Brit Hort) Gewächshaus nt; (b) (Mil sl) Bau, Bunker m (sl); ~-paper n Glaspapier nt; ~ware n Glaswaren pl; ~ wool n Glaswolle f; ~works npl Glashütte f.

glassy ['glɑːsɪ] adj (+er) surface, sea etc spiegelglatt; eye, look glasig. ~-eyed look glasig; to be ~-eyed einen glasigen Blick haben; to look at sb ~-eyed jdn mit glasigem Blick ansehen.

Glaswegian [glæs'wiːdʒɪən] 1 n (a) Glasgower(in f) m. (b) (dialect) Glasgower Dialekt m. 2 adj Glasgower, von Glasgow.

glaucoma [glɔː'kəʊmə] n grüner Star, Glaukom nt (form).

glaucous ['glɔːkəs] adj plums, grapes etc mit einer weißlichen Schicht überzogen. ~ blue/green gräulich-blau/gräulich-grün.

glaze [gleɪz] 1 n (on pottery, tiles, Cook) Glasur f; (on paper, fabric) Appretur f; (on painting) Lasur f.

2 vt (a) door, window verglasen.

(b) pottery, tiles glasieren; fabric, paper appretieren; painting lasieren. ~d tile Kachel f.

(c) (Cook) cake glasieren; meat also mit Gelee überziehen; fruit kandieren. a ~d ham Schinken in Aspik.

3 vi (eyes: also ~ over) glasig werden.

glazier ['gleɪzɪəʳ] n Glaser m.

glazing ['gleɪzɪŋ] n (a) (act) Verglasen nt; (glass) Verglasung f; (trade) Glaserei f. (b) see glaze 1.

GLC abbr of **Greater London Council.**

gleam [gliːm] n (a) Schein, Schimmer m; (of metal, water) Schimmer nt. a ~ of light/red ein Lichtschimmer m/ein roter Schimmer; the ~ from his torch der Schein seiner Taschenlampe; a few ~s of moonlight came through the curtains das Mondlicht schimmerte durch die Vorhänge.

(b) (fig) a ~ of hope ein Hoffnungsschimmer m; a ~ of humour/intelligence/sense ein Anflug m von Humor/Intelligenz/ein Hauch m von Vernunft; not a ~ of hope/humour/intelligence/sense kein Funke m Hoffnung/Humor/Intelligenz/Vernunft; he had a ~/a dangerous ~ in his eye seine Augen funkelten/funkelten gefährlich.

2 vi schimmern; (hair also) glänzen; (eyes) funkeln.

gleaming ['gliːmɪŋ] adj schimmernd; hair, silver, water also glänzend; eyes funkelnd.

glean [gliːn] vt (lit) corn, field nachlesen; (fig) facts, news herausbekommen, ausfindig machen, erkunden (geh). to ~ sth from sb/sth etw von jdm erfahren/etw einer Sache (dat) entnehmen.

gleaner ['gliːnəʳ] n Ährenleser(in f) m.

gleanings ['gliːnɪŋz] npl (lit) Nachlese f, aufgelesene Ähren pl. the ~ of twenty years of study die Ausbeute eines zwanzigjährigen Studiums; a few ~ from the press conference ein paar Informationen, die er/ich etc auf der Pressekonferenz in Erfahrung bringen konnte.

glebe [gliːb] n (Eccl) Pfarrland nt. ~ house pfarreieigenes Haus; (vicarage) Pfarrhaus nt.

glee [gliː] n (a) Freude f; (malicious) Schadenfreude f. he/they shouted in or with ~ er stieß einen Freudenschrei aus/sie brachen in (ein) Freudengeheul aus; he told the story with great ~ er erzählte die Geschichte mit großem Vergnügen; they were full of ~/malicious ~ sie waren (hell) begeistert/sie freuten sich hämisch or diebisch; his defeat caused great ~ among his enemies seine Feinde freuten sich diebisch or hämisch über seine Niederlage.

(b) (Mus) mehrstimmiges Lied. ~ club (esp US) Chor m.

gleeful ['gliːfʊl] adj fröhlich, vergnügt; (maliciously) hämisch, schadenfroh. they were all very ~ about his failure sie freuten sich alle diebisch über sein Versagen.

gleefully ['gliːfʊlɪ] adv see adj.

glen [glen] n (kleines) Tal.

glib [glɪb] adj (pej) gewandt; talker also zungenfertig; person glatt, zungenfertig, aalglatt (inf); reply, remark leichthin gemacht; speech, style glatt. I don't want to sound ~ ich möchte nicht den Eindruck erwecken, das so leichthin zu sagen; to have a ~ tongue zungenfertig sein, eine glatte Zunge haben; he gave a ~ reply/excuse er war mit einer Antwort/Entschuldigung schnell bei der Hand; he was always ready with a ~ explanation er war immer schnell mit einer Erklärung bei der Hand.

glibly ['glɪblɪ] adv (pej) speak gewandt; say, remark, reply leichthin; *lie geschickt*. he ~ produced a couple of excuses er war schnell ein paar Ausreden bei der Hand.

glibness ['glɪbnɪs] *n* (*pej*) (*of speech, excuses, lies*) Gewandtheit *f*; (*of person*) Zungenfertigkeit *f*. the ~ of his explanation/reply seine leichthin gegebene Erklärung/Antwort; the ~ of such a remark eine so leichthin gemachte Bemerkung.

glide [glaɪd] 1 *vi* (a) gleiten; (*through the air also*) schweben. to ~ into a room/in in ein Zimmer schweben/hereinschweben; to ~ off *or* away davongleiten; (*person, ghost*) davonschweben; the days ~d past die Tage glitten dahin.
(b) (*Aviat, bird*) gleiten; (*plane*) im Gleitflug fliegen; (*glider*) gleiten, schweben; (*fly in a glider*) segelfliegen. I would like to learn to ~ ich möchte Segelfliegen lernen; to ~ down to land zur Landung ansetzen.
2 *vt* gleiten lassen; *plane* im Gleitflug fliegen (lassen).
3 *n* (a) (*dancing*) Gleit- *or* Schleifschritt *m*.
(b) (*Mus*) Portamento *nt*; (*Phon*) Gleitlaut *m*.
(c) (*Aviat*) Gleitflug *m*.

glider ['glaɪdəʳ] *n* (*Aviat*) Segelflugzeug *nt*. ~ pilot Segelflieger(in *f*) *m*.

gliding ['glaɪdɪŋ] *n* (*Aviat*) Segelfliegen *nt*. ~ club Segelfliegerklub *m*.

glimmer ['glɪməʳ] 1 *n* (a) (*of light, candle etc*) Schimmer *m*; (*of fire*) Glimmen *nt*. the ~ of the distant river das Schimmern des Flusses in der Ferne; a few ~s from the dying fire ein Aufglimmen *nt* des verlöschenden Feuers.
(b) (*fig: also* ~ing) *see* gleam 1 (b).
2 *vi* (*light, water*) schimmern; (*flame, fire*) glimmen.

glimpse [glɪmps] 1 *n* Blick *m*. it was our last ~ of home das war der letzte Blick auf unser Zuhause; a ~ of life in 18th century London ein (Ein)blick *m* in das Leben im London des 18. Jahrhunderts; to catch a ~ of sb/sth einen flüchtigen Blick auf jdn/etw werfen können *or* von jdm/etw erhaschen; (*fig*) eine Ahnung von etw bekommen; I hope I'll catch a ~ of him before he goes abroad ich hoffe, daß ich ihn noch einmal zu Gesicht bekomme, bevor er ins Ausland geht.
2 *vt* kurz sehen, einen Blick erhaschen von.
3 *vi* to ~ at sth einen Blick auf etw (*acc*) werfen; to ~ through a book ein Buch überfliegen.

glint [glɪnt] 1 *n* (*of light, metal*) Glitzern, Blinken *nt no pl*; (*of cat's eyes*) Funkeln *nt no pl*. a ~ of light ein glitzernder Lichtstrahl; brown hair with golden ~s in it braunes Haar mit einem goldenen Schimmer; he has a wicked/merry ~ in his eyes seine Augen funkeln böse/lustig. 2 *vi* glitzern, blinken; (*eyes*) funkeln.

glissade [glɪ'seɪd] *n* (*in dancing*) Glissade *f*.

glisten ['glɪsn] 1 *vi* glänzen; (*dewdrops, eyes also, tears*) glitzern. 2 *n* Glänzen *nt*; Glitzern *nt*.

glister ['glɪstəʳ] *n, vi* (*old*) *see* glitter.

glitter ['glɪtəʳ] 1 *n* Glitzern *nt*; (*of eyes, diamonds*) Funkeln *nt*; (*for decoration*) Glitzerstaub *m*; (*fig*) Glanz, Prunk *m*. the ~ of life in London das glanzvolle Leben in London. 2 *vi* glitzern; (*eyes, diamonds*) funkeln. all that ~s is not gold (*Prov*) es ist nicht alles Gold, was glänzt (*Prov*).

glittering ['glɪtərɪŋ] *adj* glitzernd; *eyes, diamonds* funkelnd; *ceremony, occasion* glanzvoll; *career* glänzend; *prizes* verlockend.

glittery ['glɪtərɪ] *adj* (*inf*) glitzernd.

gloaming ['gləʊmɪŋ] *n* (*liter*) Dämmer- *or* Zwielicht *nt* (*geh*).

gloat [gləʊt] *vi* (*with pride at oneself*) sich großtun (*over, upon* mit); (*verbally also*) sich brüsten (*over, upon* mit); (*over sb's misfortune or failure*) sich hämisch freuen (*over, upon* über +*acc*). to ~ over one's possessions/sb's misfortune sich an seinen Reichtümern/jds Unglück weiden *or* ergötzen; to ~ over one's successes sich in seinen Erfolgen sonnen; there's no need to ~! das ist kein Grund zur Schadenfreude!

gloating ['gləʊtɪŋ] 1 *n* Selbstgefälligkeit *f*; (*over sb's misfortune or failure*) Schadenfreude *f*. his ~ over his possessions wie er sich genüßlich an seinem Besitz weidet; a look of ~ in his eyes ein selbstgefälliger/schadenfroher/genüßlicher Blick; it wasn't pleasant to listen to their ~ es war kein Vergnügen, ihren selbstgefälligen Reden/schadenfrohen Bemerkungen zuzuhören; their ~ over their own success ihre selbstgefällige Freude über ihren Erfolg; their premature ~(s) ihre voreilige Freude.
2 *adj* (*self-satisfied*) selbstgefällig; (*malicious*) hämisch, schadenfroh. the ~ miser der Geizhals, der sich genüßlich an seinen Schätzen weidet; with ~ eyes mit selbstgefälligem/hämischem/genüßlichem Blick; he cast a ~ look at the money er weidete sich genüßlich am Anblick des Geldes.

gloatingly ['gləʊtɪŋlɪ] *adv see adj*.

glob [glɒb] *n* (*inf*) Klacks *m* (*inf*); (*of mud*) Klümpchen *nt*.

global ['gləʊbl] *adj* global; *peace, war* Welt-. taking a ~ view of the matter ... global gesehen ...; a ~ figure of £2 million eine Gesamtsumme von £ 2 Millionen; the world is considered as a ~ village die Welt wird als Dorf angesehen.

globe [gləʊb] *n* (*sphere*) Kugel *f*; (*map*) Globus *m*; (*fish-bowl*) Glaskugel *f*. terrestrial/celestial ~ Erd-/Himmelskugel *f*; the ~ (*the world*) der Globus *or* Erdball *m*; all over the ~ auf der ganzen Erde *or* Welt.

globe: ~ artichoke *n* Artischocke *f*; ~-fish *n* Kugelfisch *m*; ~-trotter *n* Globetrotter, Welt(en)bummler *m*; ~-trotting 1 *n* Globetrotten *nt*; 2 *attr* Globetrotter-.

globular ['glɒbjʊləʳ] *adj* kugelförmig.

globule ['glɒbjuːl] *n* Klümpchen, Kügelchen *nt*; (*of oil, water*) Tröpfchen *nt*. ~s of grease floating on the soup Fettaugen *pl* auf der Suppe.

glockenspiel ['glɒkənʃpiːl] *n* Glockenspiel *nt*.

gloom [gluːm] *n* (a) (*darkness*) Düsterkeit *f*.
(b) (*sadness*) düstere *or* gedrückte Stimmung. an atmosphere of ~ eine düstere *or* gedrückte Atmosphäre; a look of ~

on his face seine düstere Miene; to cast a ~ over etw (*acc*) werfen; his future seemed to be filled with ~ seine Zukunft schien düster auszusehen; his speech was filled with ~ seine Rede war von düsteren Vorhersagen erfüllt.

gloomily ['gluːmɪlɪ] *adv* (*fig*) düster.

gloominess ['gluːmɪnɪs] *n see adj* Düsterkeit *f*; Finsterkeit *f*; Gedrücktheit *f*; Trübsinn *m*; Bedrückende(s) *nt*; Pessimismus *m*.

gloomy ['gluːmɪ] *adj* (+*er*) düster; *streets, forest also* finster; *atmosphere also* gedrückt; *thoughts also, character* trübsinnig; *news also* bedrückend; *outlook on life* pessimistisch. to take a ~ view of things schwarzsehen; to feel ~ niedergeschlagen *or* bedrückt sein; just thinking about the situation makes me feel ~ es bedrückt mich, wenn ich nur über die Lage nachdenke; he is very ~ about his chances of success er beurteilt seine Erfolgschancen sehr pessimistisch; to look ~ about sth wegen etw ins trübsinniges Gesicht machen.

glorification [ˌglɔːrɪfɪ'keɪʃən] *n* Verherrlichung *f*; (*of God also*) Lobpreis *m*; (*beautification*) Verschönerung *f*.

glorified ['glɔːrɪfaɪd] *adj* this restaurant is just a ~ snack-bar dieses Restaurant ist nur eine bessere Imbißstube.

glorify ['glɔːrɪfaɪ] *vt* verherrlichen; (*praise*) God lobpreisen. a service to ~ the memory of the war-dead ein Gottesdienst zur Ehrung der Gefallenen.

glorious ['glɔːrɪəs] *adj* (a) (*lit*) *saint, martyr etc* glorreich; *deed, victory also* ruhmreich. a ~ career of service to others ein segensreiches Leben im Dienst am Nächsten. (b) (*marvellous*) *weather, sky* herrlich, phantastisch. it was ~ fun das war herrlich; a ~ mess (*iro*) ein schönes *or* herrliches Durcheinander.

gloriously ['glɔːrɪəslɪ] *adv see adj*. he was ~ drunk (*inf*) er war herrlich betrunken (*inf*).

glory ['glɔːrɪ] 1 *n* (a) (*honour, fame*) Ruhm *m*. covered in ~ ruhmbedeckt.
(b) (*praise*) Ehre *f*. ~ to God in the highest Ehre sei Gott in der Höhe; ~ be! (*dated inf*) du lieber Himmel! (*inf*), du meine Güte! (*inf*).
(c) (*beauty, magnificence*) Herrlichkeit *f*. the rose in all its ~ die Rose in ihrer ganzen Pracht *or* Herrlichkeit; the glories of Nature die Schönheiten *pl* der Natur; Rome at the height of its ~ Rom in seiner Blütezeit.
(d) (*source of pride*) Stolz *m*.
(e) (*celestial bliss*) the saints in ~ die Heiligen in der himmlischen Herrlichkeit; Christ in ~ Christus in seiner Herrlichkeit; to go to ~ (*euph liter*) ins ewige Leben *or* in die Ewigkeit eingehen (*euph liter*).
2 *vi* to ~ in one's skill/strength/ability sich (*dat*) viel auf sein Geschick/seine Kraft/Fähigkeit zugute tun; to ~ in one's/sb's success sich in seinem/jds Erfolg sonnen; to ~ in the knowledge/fact that .../one's independence das Wissen/die Tatsache, daß .../seine Unabhängigkeit voll auskosten; they gloried in showing me my mistakes sie genossen es *or* kosteten es voll aus, mir meine Fehler zu zeigen; to ~ in the name/title of ... den stolzen Namen/Titel ... führen.

glory-hole ['glɔːrɪˌhəʊl] *n* (a) (*inf*) Rumpel- *or* Kramecke *f*; (*box*) Rumpelkiste *f*; (*drawer*) Kramschublade *f*. (b) (*Naut*) Logis *nt*.

gloss¹ [glɒs] *n* (*shine, lip* ~) Glanz *m*; (*fig: of respectability etc*) Schein *m*. paint with a high ~ Farbe mit Hochglanz; to take the ~ off sth (*lit*) etw stumpf werden lassen; (*fig*) einer Sache (*dat*) den Glanz nehmen; to lose its ~ (*lit, fig*) seinen Glanz verlieren; ~ finish (*Phot, on paper*) Glanz(beschichtung *f*) *m*; (*of paint*) Lackanstrich *m*; the photos had a ~ finish es waren Glanzabzüge.

◆ **gloss over** *vt sep* (*try to conceal*) vertuschen; (*make light of*) beschönigen. he ~ed the various points raised by the critics er hat die verschiedenen Punkte der Kritiker einfach vom Tisch gewischt.

gloss² *n* (*explanation*) Erläuterung *f*; (*note also*) Anmerkung, Glosse (*geh*) *f*. 2 *vt* erläutern.

glossary ['glɒsərɪ] *n* Glossar *nt*.

glossily ['glɒsɪlɪ] *adj* glänzend. ~ polished blankpoliert.

glossiness ['glɒsɪnɪs] *n* Glanz *m*.

gloss (paint) *n* Glanzlack(farbe *f*) *m*.

glossy ['glɒsɪ] 1 *adj* (+*er*) glänzend; *paper, paint* Glanz-; (*Phot*) *print* (Hoch)glanz-. to be ~ glänzen; ~ magazine (Hochglanz)-magazin *nt*. 2 *n* (*inf*) (Hochglanz)magazin *nt*.

glottal ['glɒtl] *adj* Stimmritzen-, glottal (*spec*). ~ stop (*Phon*) Knacklaut, Stimmritzenverschlußlaut *m*.

glottis ['glɒtɪs] *n* Stimmritze, Glottis (*spec*) *f*.

glove [glʌv] *n* (Finger)handschuh *m*; (*Sport*) Handschuh *m*. to fit (sb) like a ~ (jdm) wie angegossen passen; (*job*) wie für jdn geschaffen sein; with the ~s off (*fig*) schonungslos, ohne Rücksicht auf Verluste (*inf*); the ~s are off mit der Rücksichtnahme ist es vorbei, die Schonzeit ist vorbei.

glove box *n* (a) (*Tech*) Handschuh-Schutzkasten *m*. (b) (*also* glove compartment) (*Aut*) Handschuhfach *nt*.

gloved [glʌvd] *adj* behandschuht.

glove puppet *n* Handpuppe *f*.

glover ['glʌvəʳ] *n* Handschuhmacher(in *f*) *m*.

glow [gləʊ] 1 *vi* glühen; (*colour, hands of clock*) leuchten; (*lamp also, candle*) scheinen. she/her cheeks ~ed with health sie hatte ein blühendes Aussehen; to ~ with enthusiasm/pride/pleasure vor Begeisterung/Stolz glühen/vor Freude strahlen; she ~ed with love sie strahlte vor Liebe aus; her eyes ~ed with enthusiasm/anger/love ihre Augen leuchten vor Begeisterung/glühten vor Zorn/die Liebe leuchtete aus ihren Augen.
2 *n* Glühen *nt*; (*of colour, clock hands*) Leuchten *nt*; (*of lamp, candle*) Schein *m*; (*of fire, sunset, passion*) Glut *f*. her face had

a healthy ~, there was a ~ of health on her face ihr Gesicht hatte eine blühende Farbe; in a ~ of enthusiasm mit glühender Begeisterung; she felt a ~ of satisfaction/affection sie empfand eine tiefe Befriedigung/Zuneigung; radiant with the ~ of youth blühende Jugend ausstrahlend; there was a sort of ~ about her sie strahlte so.

glower ['glauə^r] 1 *vi* ein finsteres Gesicht machen. **to ~ at sb** jdn finster ansehen. 2 *n* finsterer Blick. **angry/infuriated ~** zorniger/wütender Blick; **there was a ~ on his face** ein finsterer Ausdruck lag auf seinem Gesicht.

glowering *adj*, **~ly** *adv* ['glauərıŋ, -lı] finster.

glowing ['glauıŋ] *adj* **(a)** glühend; *candle, colour, eyes* leuchtend; *cheeks, complexion* blühend.
(b) *(fig)* (enthusiastic) *account, description* begeistert; *words also* leidenschaftlich; *praise, report* überschwenglich; *pride, admiration, enthusiasm* glühend. **to paint sth in ~ colours** *(fig)* etw in glühenden Farben schildern.

glowingly ['glauıŋlı] *adv* *(fig)* begeistert; *describe* in glühenden Farben; *praise* überschwenglich.

glow-worm ['glau,wɜːm] *n* Glühwürmchen *nt*.

glucose ['gluːkəus] *n* Glucose *f*, Traubenzucker *m*.

glue [gluː] 1 *n* Klebstoff *m*; *(from bones etc)* Leim *m*. **to stick to sb/sth like ~** an jdm/etw kleben *(inf)*.
2 *vt* kleben; leimen. **to ~ sth together** etw zusammenkleben/ -leimen; **to ~ sth down/on** etw fest-/ankleben; **to ~ sth to sth** etw an etw *(acc)* kleben/leimen, etw an etw *(dat)* festkleben/ -leimen; **her ear was ~d to the keyhole** ihr Ohr klebte am Schlüsselloch; **to keep one's eyes ~d to sb/sth** jdn/etw nicht aus den Augen lassen; **always keep your eyes ~d to the road while you're driving** beim Autofahren müssen die Augen immer auf die Straße gerichtet sein; **his eyes were ~d to the screen/her cleavage** seine Augen hingen an der Leinwand/ihrem Ausschnitt; **he's ~d to the TV all evening** er hängt den ganzen Abend vorm Fernseher *(inf)*; **he stood there as if ~d to the spot** er stand wie angewurzelt da.

glue-pot ['gluː,pɒt] *n* Leimtopf *m*.

gluey ['gluːı] *adj* klebrig.

glum [glʌm] *adj* (+er) niedergeschlagen, bedrückt; *atmosphere* gedrückt; *thoughts* schwarz. **to feel ~** bedrückt sein.

glumly ['glʌmlı] *adv* niedergeschlagen, bedrückt.

glut [glʌt] 1 *vt* **(a)** *(Comm)* *market (manufacturer etc)* überschwemmen. **sugar is ~ting the world market** der Weltmarkt wird mit Zucker überschwemmt.
(b) **to ~ oneself** *(with food)* schlemmen; **they ~ted themselves with strawberries** sie haben sich an den Erbeeren gütlich getan; **that poor dog is ~ted with food** der arme Hund ist überfüttert; **they felt ~ted with pleasure** sie hatten der Genüsse genug und übergenug gehabt.
2 *n* Schwemme *f*; *(of manufactured goods also)* Überangebot *nt* (of an +dat). **a ~ of apples** eine Apfelschwemme.

gluteal ['gluːtıəl] *adj* Gesäß-.

gluten ['gluːtən] *n* Kleber *m*, Gluten *nt*.

glutinous ['gluːtınəs] *adj* klebrig.

glutton ['glʌtn] *n* Vielfraß *m* *(also Zool)*. **we ate like ~s** wir haben gegessen wie die Scheunendrescher *(inf)*; **to be a ~ for work/punishment** ein Arbeitstier *nt* *(inf)*/Masochist *m* sein.

gluttonous ['glʌtənəs] *adj* *(lit, fig)* unersättlich; *person* gefräßig.

gluttony ['glʌtənı] *n* Völlerei, Fresserei *(inf)* *f*.

glycerin(e) ['glısəriːn] *n* Glyzerin, Glycerin *(spec)* *nt*.

glycol ['glaıkɒl] *n* Glykol *nt*.

GM *(Brit)* *abbr of* **George Medal**.

gm *abbr of* **gram(s), gramme(s)** g.

G-man ['dʒiːmæn] *n, pl* **-men** [-men] *(US inf)* FBI-Mann *m*.

GMC *(Brit)* *abbr of* **General Medical Council**.

gms *abbr of* **gram(me)s** g.

GMT *abbr of* **Greenwich Mean Time** WEZ.

gnarled [nɑːld] *adj* *wood, tree* knorrig; *hand* knotig.

gnash [næʃ] *vt* **to ~ one's teeth** mit den Zähnen knirschen.

gnat [næt] *n* (Stech)mücke *f*; *see* **strain**[1].

gnaw [nɔː] 1 *vt* nagen an (+dat); *finger-nails also* kauen an (+dat); *(rust, disease)* fressen an (+dat); *hole* nagen; *(fig)* *conscience, sb* *(hunger, anxiety)* quälen; *(remorse)* verzehren. **to ~ sth off** etw abnagen; **the box had been ~ed by the rats** die Ratten hatten die Kiste angenagt. 2 *vi* nagen. **to ~ at sb/sth** an etw *(dat)* nagen; *(rust, disease)* sich durch etw fressen; *(fig)* jdn/etw quälen; **to ~ on sth** an etw *(dat)* nagen.

♦ **gnaw away** 1 *vi* nagen (at, on an +dat). 2 *vt sep* wegnagen.

gnawing ['nɔːıŋ] *adj* *(lit)* *sound* nagend; *(fig)* quälend; *feeling also* ungut.

gneiss [naıs] *n* Gneis *m*.

gnome [nəum] *n* Gnom *m*; *(in garden)* Gartenzwerg *m*. **the ~s of Zurich** die Zürcher Gnome *pl*.

GNP *abbr of* **gross national product**.

gnu [nuː] *n* Gnu *nt*.

go [gəu] *(vb: pret* **went**, *ptp* **gone**) 1 *vi* **(a)** *(proceed, move)* gehen; *(vehicle, by vehicle)* fahren; *(plane) also* fliegen; *(travel)* reisen; *(road)* führen. **to ~ to France/on holiday** nach Frankreich/in Urlaub gehen; **I have to ~ to the doctor/ London** ich muß zum Arzt (gehen)/nach London; **to ~ on a journey/course** verreisen, eine Reise/einen Kurs machen; **to ~ for a walk/swim** spazierengehen/schwimmen gehen; **to ~ fishing/shopping/shooting** angeln/einkaufen/auf die Jagd gehen; **the dog/the doll ~es everywhere with her** der Hund geht überall mit ihr mit/sie nimmt die Puppe überallhin mit; **we can talk as we ~** wir können uns unterwegs unterhalten; **where do we ~ from here?** *(lit)* wo gehen wir anschließend hin?; *(fig)* und was (wird) jetzt?; **you're ~ing too fast for me** *(lit, fig)* du bist mir zu schnell; **the favourite is ~ing well** der Favorit liegt gut im Rennen; **to ~ looking for sb/sth** nach jdm/etw suchen; **to ~ for a doctor/newspaper** einen Arzt/eine Zeitung holen

(gehen); **to ~ to sb for sth** *(ask sb)* jdn wegen etw fragen; *(fetch from sb)* bei jdm etw holen; **there he ~es!** da ist er ja!; **who ~es there?** *(guard)* wer da?; **you ~ first** geh du zuerst!; **you ~ next** du bist der nächste; **there you ~ again!** *(inf)* du fängst ja schon wieder an!; **here we ~ again!** *(inf)* jetzt geht das schon wieder los! *(inf)*; **to ~ to get sth, to ~ and get sth** etw holen gehen; ~ **and shut the door/tell him** mach mal die Tür zu/sag's ihm; **he's gone and lost his new watch** er hat seine neue Uhr verloren; **don't ~ telling him, don't ~ and tell him** geh jetzt bitte nicht hin und erzähl ihm das *(inf)*; **don't ~ doing that!, don't ~ and do that!** mach das bloß nicht!
(b) *(attend)* gehen. **to ~ to church/evening class** in die Kirche/in einen Abendkurs gehen, einen Abendkurs besuchen; **to ~ to work** zur Arbeit gehen; **he's ~ing as a pirate** er geht als Pirat; **what shall I ~ in?** was soll ich anziehen?
(c) *(depart)* gehen; *(vehicle, by vehicle also)* (ab)fahren; *(plane, by plane also)* (ab)fliegen. **has he gone yet?** ist er schon weg?; **I must ~ now** ich muß jetzt gehen or weg; **after I ~ or have gone or am gone** *(leave)* wenn ich weg bin; *(die)* wenn ich (einmal) nicht mehr (da) bin; **we must ~ or be ~ing or get ~ing** *(inf)* wir müssen gehen or uns langsam auf den Weg machen *(inf)*; **time I was gone** Zeit, daß ich gehe; **be gone!** *(old)* hinweg mit dir *(old)*; **~!** *(Sport)* los!; **here ~es!** jetzt geht's los! *(inf)*.
(d) *(disappear, vanish)* verschwinden; *(pain, spot, mark etc also)* weggehen; *(be used up)* aufgebraucht werden; *(time)* vergehen. **it has gone** *(disappeared)* es ist weg; *(used up, eaten etc)* es ist alle *(inf)*; **where has it gone?** wo ist es hin or geblieben?; **the trees have been gone for years** die Bäume sind schon seit Jahren nicht mehr da; **gone are the days when ...** die Zeiten sind vorbei, wo ...; **the money just ~es these days** das Geld zerrinnt einem heutzutage zwischen den Fingern; **I don't know where the money ~es** ich weiß nicht, wo all das Geld bleibt; **all his money ~es on records** er gibt sein ganzes Geld für Schallplatten aus, sein ganzes Geld geht für Schallplatten drauf *(inf)*; **£10 a week ~es in or on rent** £ 10 die Woche sind für die Miete *(weg)*; **the heat went out of the debate** die Debatte verlor an Hitzigkeit; **how is the time ~ing?** wie steht's mit der Zeit?; **it's just gone three** es ist gerade drei vorbei, es ist kurz nach drei; **two days to ~ till ...** noch zwei Tage bis ...; **only two more patients to ~** nur noch zwei Patienten; **two down and one to ~** zwei geschafft und noch eine(r, s) übrig; **there ~es another one!** und noch eine(r, s) weniger!
(e) *(be dismissed)* gehen; *(be got rid of)* verschwinden; *(be abolished)* abgeschafft werden. **that minister will have to ~** der Minister wird gehen müssen; **that old settee will have to ~** das alte Sofa muß weg; **once that table has gone** wenn der Tisch erst einmal weg ist; **apartheid must ~!** weg mit der Apartheid!
(f) *(be sold)* **the hats aren't ~ing very well** die Hüte gehen nicht sehr gut *(weg)*; **to ~ for nothing** umsonst sein; **to be ~ing cheap** billig sein; **it went for £5** es ging für £ 5 weg; **they are ~ing at 20p each** sie werden zu 20 Pence das Stück verkauft; **I won't let it ~ for less than that** billiger gebe ich es nicht her; **~ing, ~ing, gone!** zum ersten, zum zweiten, und zum dritten!
(g) *(have recourse to)* gehen. **to ~ to the country** *(Brit Parl)* Wahlen ausrufen; **to ~ to law/war** vor Gericht gehen/Krieg führen *(over* wegen*)*.
(h) *(prize, 1st place etc)* gehen *(to* an +acc*)*; *(inheritance)* zufallen *(to* sb jdm*)*.
(i) *(extend)* gehen. **the garden ~es down to the river** der Garten geht bis zum Fluß hinunter; **the difference between them ~es deep** der Unterschied zwischen ihnen geht tief; **I'll ~ to £100** ich gehe bis £ 100.
(j) *(run, function)* *(watch)* gehen; *(car, machine also)* laufen; *(workers)* arbeiten. **to ~ by steam** mit Dampf betrieben werden; **to ~ slow** *(workers)* im Bummelstreik sein; *(watch)* nachgehen; **to get ~ing** in Schwung or Fahrt kommen; **to get sth ~ing, to make sth ~** etw in Gang bringen; *party* etw in Fahrt bringen; *business* etw auf Vordermann bringen; **to get sb ~ing** jdn in Fahrt bringen; **to get ~ing on or with sth** etw in Angriff nehmen; **once you get ~ing on it** wenn man erst mal damit angefangen hat; **to keep ~ing** *(person)* weitermachen; *(machine, engine etc)* weiterlaufen; *(car)* weiterfahren; *(business)* weiter laufen; **keep ~ing!** weiter!; **to keep a factory ~ing** eine Fabrik in Betrieb halten; **to keep the fire ~ing** das Feuer anbehalten; **she needs these pills/his friendship to keep her ~ing** sie braucht diese Pillen/seine Freundschaft, um durchzuhalten; **this medicine/prospect kept her ~ing** dieses Medikament/diese Aussicht hat sie durchhalten lassen; **here's £50/some work to keep you ~ing** hier hast du erst mal £ 50/etwas Arbeit; **to keep sb ~ing in food/money** jdn mit Essen/Geld versorgen.
(k) *(happen, turn out)* *(project, things)* gehen; *(event, evening)* verlaufen; *(voting, election)* ausgehen. **I've forgotten how the words ~** ich habe den Text vergessen; **how does the story/tune ~?** wie war die Geschichte doch noch mal/wie geht die Melodie?; **how does his theory ~?** welche Theorie hat er?, was ist seine Theorie?; **the story or rumour ~es that ...** es geht das Gerücht, daß ...; **the election/decision went in his favour/against him** die Wahl/Entscheidung fiel zu seinen Gunsten/Ungunsten aus; **how's it ~ing?, how ~es it?** *(inf)* wie geht's (denn so)?; **how did it ~?** wie war's?; **how did the exam/your holiday ~?** wie ging's in der Prüfung/wie war der Urlaub?; **how's the essay ~ing?** was macht der Aufsatz?; **everything/the world is ~ing well (with us)** alles läuft gut, bei uns läuft alles gut/die Welt ist (für uns) in Ordnung; **if everything ~es well** wenn alles gutgeht; **all went well for him until ...** alles ging gut, bis ...; **we'll soon see how things ~** *(inf)* wir werden sehen, wie es läuft *(inf)* or geht; **you know the way things ~** Sie wissen ja, wie das so ist or geht; **the way things are ~ing** I'll ... so wie es aussieht, werde ich ...; **things have gone well/ badly for me** es ist gut/schlecht gelaufen; **as things ~ today**

that's not very expensive für heutige Verhältnisse ist das nicht teuer; she has a lot ~ing for her sie ist gut dran.

(l) (fail, break, wear out) (material, mechanism, bulb, zip etc) kaputtgehen; (through rust) (durch)rosten; (health, strength, eyesight etc) nachlassen; (brakes, steering) versagen; (button) abgehen; the jumper has gone at the elbows der Pullover ist an den Ärmeln durch (inf); his mind is ~ing er läßt geistig sehr nach; there ~es another bulb/button! schon wieder eine Birne kaputt/ein Knopf ab!

(m) (be permitted, accepted: behaviour, dress etc) gehen (inf). anything ~es! alles ist erlaubt; what I say ~es! was ich sage, gilt or wird gemacht!; that ~es for me too (that applies to me) das gilt auch für mich; (I agree with that) das meine ich auch.

(n) (be available) there are several houses/jobs ~ing es sind mehrere Häuser/Stellen zu haben; is there any tea ~ing? gibt es Tee?; I'll have whatever is ~ing ich nehme, was es gibt; what do you want? — anything that's ~ing was möchtest du? — was da ist or was du hast; the best beer ~ing das beste Bier, das es gibt; he's not bad as boys ~ verglichen mit anderen Jungen ist er nicht übel.

(o) (be, become) werden. to ~ deaf/mad/bad/grey taub/verrückt/schlecht/grau werden; to ~ hungry hungern; I went cold mir wurde kalt; to ~ in rags in Lumpen gehen; to ~ to sleep/ruin einschlafen/zerfallen; to ~ Japanese/ethnic auf japanisch/auf Folklore machen (inf); to ~ Labour Labour wählen.

(p) (be contained, fit) gehen, passen; (belong, be placed) hingehören; (in drawer, cupboard etc) (hin)kommen. it won't ~ in the box es geht or paßt nicht in die Kiste; the books ~ in that cupboard die Bücher kommen or gehören in den Schrank dort; 4 into 12 ~es 3 4 geht in 12 dreimal; 4 into 3 won't ~ 3 durch 4 geht nicht.

(q) (match) dazu passen. to ~ with sth zu etw passen.

(r) (contribute) the money ~es to help the poor das Geld soll den Armen helfen; the money will ~ towards a new car/the holiday das Geld für ein neues Auto/den Urlaub; the qualities that ~ to make a great man die Eigenschaften, die einen großen Mann ausmachen.

(s) (make a sound or movement) machen. to ~ bang/shh/ticktock peng/pst/ticktack machen; ~ like that (with your left foot) mach so (mit deinem linken Fuß); there ~es the bell es klingelt; as the bell went als es klingelte.

(t) (US) food to ~ Essen zum Mitnehmen.

2 aux vb (forming future tense) I'm/I was/I had been ~ing to do it ich werde/ich wollte es tun/ich habe es tun wollen; I wasn't ~ing to do it (anyway) ich hätte es sowieso nicht gemacht; it's ~ing to rain es wird wohl regnen; he knew that he wasn't ~ing to see her again er wußte, daß er sie nicht wiedersehen würde; there's ~ing to be trouble es wird Ärger geben.

3 vt (a) route, way gehen; (vehicle, by vehicle) fahren.
(b) (Cards etc) £5 gehen bis, mithalten bis.
(c) (inf) to ~ it (~fast) ein tolles Tempo draufhaben (inf); (live hard) es toll treiben (inf); (work hard) sich hineinknien (inf); to ~ it alone sich selbständig machen.
(d) my mind went a complete blank ich hatte ein Brett vor dem Kopf (inf).
(e) (inf) I could ~ a beer ich könnte ein Bier vertragen, ich könnte auf ein Bier (inf).

4 n, pl -es (a) (inf) (energy) Schwung m. to be full of ~ unternehmungslustig sein.
(b) to be on the ~ auf Trab sein (inf); to keep sb on the ~ jdn auf Trab halten; he's got two women/books on the ~ er hat zwei Frauen gleichzeitig/er liest zwei Bücher gleichzeitig; it's all ~ es ist immer was los (inf).
(c) (attempt) Versuch m. it's your ~ du bist dran (inf) or an der Reihe; you've had your ~ du warst schon dran (inf) or an der Reihe; miss one ~ einmal aussetzen; to have a ~ es versuchen, es probieren; let's have a ~! versuch's or probier's (inf) doch mal!; he's had several ~es at the exam er hat schon mehrere Anläufe auf das Examen genommen; to have a ~ at sb (criticize) jdn runterputzen (inf), (fight) es mit jdm aufnehmen; the public were warned not to have a ~ (at him) die Öffentlichkeit wurde gewarnt, nichts (gegen ihn) zu unternehmen; to have a ~ at doing sth versuchen or probieren, etw zu tun; at the first/second ~ auf Anhieb (inf)/beim zweiten Mal or Versuch; at or in one ~ auf einen Schlag (inf); (drink) in einem Zug (inf); she asked for a ~ on his bike sie wollte mal sein Fahrrad ausprobieren; can I have a ~? darf ich mal?
(d) (bout: of illness etc) Anfall m. I had a bad ~ of flu ich hatte eine üble Grippe (inf).
(e) (success) to make a ~ of sth in etw (dat) Erfolg haben; (it's) no ~ (inf) das ist nicht drin (inf), da ist nichts zu machen; it's all the ~ (inf) das ist der große Hit (inf) or große Mode.
(f) from the word ~ von Anfang an.

5 adj (esp Space) you are ~ for take-off/landing alles ist klar zum Start/zur Landung; all systems (are) ~ (es ist) alles klar.

♦ **go about 1 vi (a)** (move from place to place) herumgehen, herumlaufen (inf); (by vehicle) herumfahren; (in old clothes etc) herumlaufen. to ~ ~ in gangs in Banden durch die Gegend ziehen; to ~ ~ with sb mit jdm zusammensein or herumziehen (pej inf); she's ~ing ~ with John sie geht mit John (inf); you shouldn't ~ ~ doing that kind of thing solche Sachen solltest du nicht machen.
(b) (be current: rumour, flu etc) umgehen.
(c) (Naut: change direction) wenden.
2 vi +prep obj (a) (set to work at) task, problem anpacken. we must ~ ~ it carefully wir müssen vorsichtig vorgehen; how does one ~ ~ getting seats/finding a job? wie bekommt man Plätze/eine Stelle?
(b) (be occupied with) work, jobs erledigen. to ~ ~ one's

business or affairs sich um seine eigenen Geschäfte kümmern.

♦ **go across 1 vi +prep obj** überqueren; street etc also gehen über (+acc); river also fahren über (+acc). to ~ ~ the sea to Ireland übers Meer nach Irland fahren.
2 vi hinübergehen; (by vehicle) hinüberfahren; (by plane) hinüberfliegen; (to the enemy etc) überlaufen (to zu). to ~ ~ to the other side auf die andere Seite hinübergehen/hinüberfahren/zur anderen Seite überwechseln or übergehen; to ~ ~ to a neighbour/the pub zu Nachbars/in die Kneipe hinübergehen.

♦ **go after vi +prep obj (a)** (follow) nachgehen (+dat), nachlaufen (+dat); (in vehicle) nachfahren (+dat). the police went ~ the escaped criminal die Polizei hat den entkommenen Verbrecher gejagt.
(b) (try to win or obtain) anstreben, es abgesehen haben auf (+acc) (inf); job sich bemühen um, aussein auf (+acc) (inf); goal verfolgen, anstreben; (Sport) record einstellen wollen; personal best anstreben; girl sich bemühen um, nachstellen (+dat) (pej). when he decides what he wants he really ~es ~ it wenn er weiß, was er will, tut er alles, um es zu bekommen.

♦ **go against vi +prep obj (a)** (be unfavourable to) (luck) sein gegen; (events) ungünstig verlaufen für; (evidence, appearance) sprechen gegen.
(b) (be lost by) the verdict went ~ her das Urteil fiel zu ihren Ungunsten aus; the battle/first rounds went ~ him er hat die Schlacht/die ersten Runden verloren.
(c) (contradict, be contrary to) im Widerspruch stehen zu; principles, conscience gehen gegen; (oppose: person) handeln gegen, sich widersetzen (+dat).

♦ **go ahead vi (a)** (go in front) vorangehen; (in race) sich an die Spitze setzen; (go earlier) vorausgehen; (in vehicle) vorausfahren. to ~ ~ of sb vor jdm gehen; sich vor jdn setzen; jdm vorausgehen/-fahren.
(b) (proceed) (person) es machen; (work, project) vorangehen; he just went ~ and did it er hat es einfach gemacht; ~! nur zu!; to ~ ~ with sth etw durchführen.

♦ **go along vi (a)** (walk along) gehen, entlangspazieren (inf). as one ~es ~ unterwegs; (bit by bit) nach und nach; (at the same time) nebenbei, nebenher; ~ ~ with you! (inf) jetzt hör aber auf! (inf).
(b) (accompany) mitgehen, mitkommen (with mit). the furniture ~es ~ with the flat die Möbel gehören zur Wohnung.
(c) (agree) zustimmen (with dat); (not object) sich anschließen (with dat).

♦ **go around vi** see go about 1 (a, b), go round (f).

♦ **go at vi +prep obj** (inf: attack) person losgehen auf (+acc) (inf); task sich machen an (+acc). to ~ ~ it loslegen (inf).

♦ **go away vi** (weg)gehen; (for a holiday) wegfahren; (from wedding) abreisen, wegfahren. they went ~ together (illicitly) sie sind miteinander durchgebrannt (inf); "gone ~" (on letter) „verzogen"; the smell still hasn't gone ~ der Geruch ist immer noch nicht weg; ~ ~! dress Kleid, das die Braut trägt, wenn sie den Hochzeitsempfang verläßt.

♦ **go back vi (a)** (return) zurückgehen; (to a subject) zurückkommen (to auf +acc); (revert: to habits, methods etc) zurückkehren (to zu). they have to ~ ~ to Germany/school next week nächste Woche müssen sie wieder nach Deutschland zurück/wieder zur Schule; when do the schools ~ ~? wann fängt die Schule wieder an?; to ~ ~ to the beginning wieder von vorn anfangen; you can't ~ ~ now du kannst jetzt nicht zurück; there's no ~ing ~ now jetzt gibt es kein Zurück mehr; I'll ~ ~ there for a holiday da gehe ich noch mal in Urlaub hin; he went ~ for his hat er ging zurück, um seinen Hut zu holen.
(b) (be returned) (faulty goods) zurückgehen; (library books) zurückgebracht werden.
(c) (date back) zurückgehen, zurückreichen (to bis zu).
(d) (clock: be put back) zurückgestellt werden.
(e) (extend back: cave, garden etc) zurückgehen, zurückreichen (to bis zu).

♦ **go back on vi +prep obj** zurücknehmen; decision rückgängig machen; friend im Stich lassen. I never ~ ~ ~ my promises was ich versprochen habe, halte ich auch.

♦ **go before 1 vi** (live before) in früheren Zeiten leben; (happen before) vorangehen. those who have gone ~ (us) unsere Vorfahren; everything that had gone ~ alles Vorhergehende.
2 vi +prep obj to ~ ~ the court/headmaster/committee vor Gericht erscheinen/zum Rektor/vor den Ausschuß kommen.

♦ **go below vi** (Naut) unter Deck gehen.

♦ **go beyond vi +prep obj** (exceed) hinausgehen über (+acc); orders, instructions also überschreiten; hopes, expectations also übertreffen.

♦ **go by 1 vi** (person, opportunity) vorbeigehen (prep obj an +dat); (procession) vorbeiziehen (prep obj an +dat); (vehicle) vorbeifahren (prep obj an +dat); (time) vergehen. as time went ~ mit der Zeit; in days gone ~ in längst vergangenen Tagen.
2 vi +prep obj (a) (base judgement or decision on) gehen nach; (be guided by) compass, watch etc, sb's example sich richten nach; (stick to) rules sich halten an (+acc). if that's anything to ~ ~ wenn man danach gehen kann; ~ing ~ what he said nach dem, was er sagte; that's not much to ~ ~ das will nicht viel heißen.
(b) to ~ ~ the name of X X heißen.

♦ **go down vi (a)** hinuntergehen (prep obj acc); (by vehicle, lift) hinunterfahren (prep obj acc); (sun, moon: set) untergehen; (Theat: curtain) fallen; (fall) (boxer etc) zu Boden gehen; (horse) stürzen. to ~ ~ on one's knees hinknien; (to apologize, propose) auf die Knie fallen; this wine/cake ~es ~ rather well dieser Wein/der Kuchen schmeckt gut; it will help the tablet ~ ~ dann rutscht die Tablette besser (hinunter).
(b) (ship, person: sink) untergehen; (be defeated) geschlagen werden (to von); (fail examination) durchfallen; see fight 2.

(c) (*Brit Univ*) die Universität verlassen; (*for vacation*) in die Semesterferien gehen.

(d) (*inf: go to prison*) eingelocht werden (*inf*).

(e) (*be accepted, approved*) ankommen (*with* bei). **that won't ~ ~ well with him** das wird er nicht gut finden; **he went ~ big in the States** (*inf*) in den Staaten kam er ganz groß heraus (*inf*).

(f) (*be reduced, lessen*) (*floods, temperature, fever, supplies, swelling*) zurückgehen; (*taxes, value*) sich verringern, weniger werden; (*prices*) sinken, runtergehen (*inf*); (*barometer*) fallen; (*wind*) nachlassen; (*sea*) sich beruhigen; (*balloon, tyre*) Luft verlieren; (*deteriorate: neighbourhood*) herunterkommen. **he has gone ~ in my estimation** er ist in meiner Achtung gesunken; *see* **world**.

(g) (*go as far as*) gehen (*to* bis). **I'll ~ ~ to the bottom of the page** ich werde die Seite noch fertig machen.

(h) (*be noted, remembered*) vermerkt werden. **to ~ ~ to posterity/in history** der Nachwelt überliefert werden/in die Geschichte eingehen.

(i) (*Bridge*) den Kontrakt nicht erfüllen. **they went five ~** sie blieben fünf unter dem gebotenen Kontrakt.

(j) (*become ill*) **to ~ ~ with a cold** eine Erkältung bekommen.

(k) (*Mus inf: lower pitch*) heruntergehen (*inf*), tiefer singen/spielen.

♦ **go for** *vi* + *prep obj* **(a)** (*inf: attack*) *person* losgehen auf (+ *acc*) (*inf*); (*verbally*) herziehen über (+ *acc*). **these cigarettes went ~ my throat** ich habe die Zigaretten im Hals gespürt; **~ ~ him!** (*to dog*) faß!

(b) (*inf: admire, like*) gut finden, stehen auf (+ *acc*) (*inf*). **I could ~ ~ her/that** ich finde sie/das gut.

(c) (*aim at*) zielen auf (+ *acc*); (*fig*) aussein auf (+ *acc*) (*inf*); (*in claim etc*) fordern.

♦ **go forth** *vi* (*old, liter*) (*person*) hingehen; (*order*) ergehen (*liter*). **to ~ ~ into battle** in den Kampf ziehen.

♦ **go forward** *vi* **(a)** (*make progress: work etc*) vorangehen. **(b)** (*proceed, go ahead*) **to ~ ~ with sth** etw durchführen, etw in die Tat umsetzen. **(c)** (*be put forward: suggestion etc*) vorgelegt werden (*to dat*).

♦ **go in** *vi* **(a)** (*enter*) hineingehen; (*Cricket*) nach „innen" gehen. **I must ~ ~ now** ich muß jetzt hinein(gehen); **when does school/the theatre ~ ~?** wann fängt die Schule/das Theater an?; **~ ~ and win!** (*inf*) jetzt zeig's ihnen aber! (*inf*).

(b) (*sun, moon: go behind clouds*) weggehen, verschwinden.

(c) (*fit in*) hineingehen, hineinpassen.

(d) (*sink in, be assimilated*) jdm eingehen.

♦ **go in for** *vi* + *prep obj* **(a)** (*enter for*) teilnehmen an (+ *dat*). **(b)** (*approve of, be interested in, practise*) zu haben sein für; (*as career*) sich entschieden haben für, gewählt haben. **to ~ ~ sports/tennis** (*play oneself*) Sport treiben/Tennis spielen; (*be interested in*) sich für Sport/Tennis interessieren; **he's gone ~ growing vegetables/breeding rabbits** er hat sich auf Gemüse-/Kaninchenzucht etc verlegt; **he ~es ~ a very strange style of writing** er hat einen ziemlich eigenartigen Stil; **he ~es ~ ~ all these big words** all diese großartigen Wörter haben es ihm angetan.

♦ **go into** *vi* + *prep obj* **(a)** (*drawer, desk etc* kramen in (+ *dat*); *a house, hospital, politics, the grocery trade* gehen in (+ *acc*); *the army, navy etc* gehen zu. **to ~ ~ digs or lodgings** sich (*dat*) ein Zimmer nehmen; **to ~ ~ publishing** ins Verlagswesen gehen; **to ~ ~ teaching/parliament/the Church** Lehrer/Abgeordneter/Geistlicher werden; **it's ~ing ~ its second year** das geht jetzt schon ins zweite Jahr.

(b) (*crash into*) *car* (hinein)fahren in (+ *acc*); *wall* fahren gegen.

(c) (*embark on*) *explanation, description etc* von sich (*dat*) geben, vom Stapel lassen (*inf*); *routine* verfallen in (+ *acc*).

(d) *trance, coma* fallen in (+ *acc*); *convulsions, fit* bekommen. **to ~ ~ hysterics** hysterisch werden; **to ~ ~ peals of/a fit of laughter** laut loslachen/einen Lachanfall bekommen; **to ~ ~ mourning for sb** um jdn trauern.

(e) (*start to wear*) *long trousers, mourning* tragen.

(f) (*look into*) sich befassen mit; (*treat, explain at length*) abhandeln, auseinanderlegen. **I don't want to ~ ~ that now** darauf möchte ich jetzt nicht (näher) eingehen; **this matter is being gone ~** man befaßt sich im Moment mit dieser Angelegenheit.

♦ **go in with** *vi* + *prep obj* sich zusammentun *or* zusammenschließen mit.

♦ **go off** 1 *vi* **(a)** (*leave*) weggehen; (*by vehicle*) abfahren, wegfahren (*on* mit); (*Theat*) abgehen. **he went ~ to the States** er fuhr in die Staaten; **to ~ ~ with sb/sth** mit jdm/etw weggehen; (*illicitly*) mit jdm/etw auf und davon gehen (*inf*).

(b) (*stop operating*) (*light*) ausgehen; (*water, electricity, gas*) wegbleiben; (*telephones*) nicht funktionieren.

(c) (*gun, bomb, alarm*) losgehen; (*alarm clock*) klingeln.

(d) **to ~ ~ into fits of laughter** in schallendes Gelächter ausbrechen.

(e) (*go bad*) (*food*) schlecht werden; (*milk also*) sauer werden; (*butter also*) ranzig werden; (*fig*) (*person, work, performance*) nachlassen, sich verschlechtern; (*sportsman, writer, actor*) abbauen (*inf*), schlechter werden.

(f) (*inf*) (*go to sleep*) einschlafen; (*into trance*) in Trance verfallen.

(g) (*take place*) verlaufen. **to ~ ~ well/badly** gut/schlecht gehen.

2 *vi* + *prep obj* **(a)** (*lose liking for*) nicht mehr mögen; *hobby also* das Interesse verlieren an (+ *dat*). **I've gone ~ him/that** ich mache mir nichts mehr aus ihm/daraus, ich mag ihn/es nicht mehr; **it's funny how you ~ ~ people** so schnell kann einem jemand unsympathisch werden.

(b) **to ~ ~ the gold standard** vom Goldstandard abgehen.

♦ **go on** 1 *vi* **(a)** (*fit*) passen (*prep obj* auf + *acc*). **my shoes won't ~ ~** ich komme nicht in meine Schuhe.

(b) (*begin to operate*) (*light, power*) angehen.

(c) (*walk on etc*) weitergehen; (*by vehicle*) weiterfahren; (*ahead of others*) vorausgehen.

(d) (*carry on, continue*) (*talks, problems, war etc*) weitergehen; (*person*) weitermachen. **it ~es ~ and ~** es hört nicht mehr auf; **to ~ ~ with sth** etw fortsetzen, mit etw weitermachen; **to ~ ~ working/coughing/hoping/trying** weiterarbeiten/weiterhusten/weiter hoffen/es weiter(hin) versuchen; **~ ~ with your work** arbeite *or* mach weiter; **I want to ~ ~ being a teacher** ich möchte Lehrer etc bleiben; **to ~ ~ speaking** weitersprechen; (*after a pause*) fortfahren; **~ ~, tell me/try!** na, sag schon/na, versuch's doch!; **~ ~ (with you)!** (*iro inf*) na komm, komm! (*iro inf*); **to ~ ~ to have enough/something** to ~ ~ with *or* to be ~ing ~ with fürs erste genug/mal etwas haben; **to ~ ~ to another matter** zu einer anderen Sache übergehen; **he went ~ to say that ...** dann sagte er, daß ...; **I can't ~ ~** ich kann nicht mehr; (*I'm stuck*) ich weiß nicht mehr weiter.

(e) (*talk incessantly*) wie ein Buch (*inf*) *or* unaufhörlich reden; (*nag, harp on*) darauf herumhacken (*inf*). **she just ~es ~ and ~** sie redet und redet; **don't ~ ~ (about it)** nun hör aber auf; **you do ~ ~ a bit** du weißt manchmal nicht, wann du aufhören solltest; **to ~ ~ about sb/sth** (*talk a lot*) stundenlang von jdm/etw erzählen; (*complain*) dauernd über jdn/etw klagen; **to ~ ~ at sb** an jdm herumnörgeln, auf jdm herumhacken (*inf*).

(f) (*happen*) passieren, vor sich gehen; (*party, argument etc*) im Gange sein. **this has been ~ing ~ for a long time** das geht schon lange so; **what's ~ing ~ here?** was geht hier vor?

(g) (*time: pass*) vergehen. **as time ~es ~** im Laufe der Zeit.

(h) (*pej: behave*) sich aufführen. **what a way to ~ ~!** wie kann man sich nur so aufführen!

(i) (*Theat: appear*) auftreten; (*Sport*) dran sein (*inf*), an der Reihe sein.

2 *vi* + *prep obj* **(a)** (*ride on*) *bus, bike, roundabout etc* fahren mit; *horse, donkey etc* reiten auf (+ *dat*). **to ~ ~ the swings/slide** schaukeln/rutschen.

(b) (*be guided by*) gehen nach, sich verlassen auf (+ *acc*); *evidence* sich stützen auf (+ *acc*). **what have you to ~?** worauf stützt du dich dabei?, wovon gehst du dabei aus?

(c) **to ~ ~ short time/the dole** kurzarbeiten/stempeln gehen (*inf*); **to ~ ~ a diet/the pill** eine Schlankheitskur machen/die Pille nehmen.

(d) (*sl: like*) stehen auf (+ *acc*); *see* **gone**.

(e) (*approach*) *fifty etc* zugehen auf (+ *acc*).

♦ **go on for** *vi* + *prep obj* *fifty, one o'clock* zugehen auf (+ *acc*). **there were ~ing ~ ~ twenty people there** es waren fast zwanzig Leute da.

♦ **go out** *vi* **(a)** (*leave*) hinausgehen. **to ~ ~ of a room** aus einem Zimmer gehen.

(b) (*shopping etc*) weggehen; (*socially, to theatre etc*) ausgehen. **to ~ ~ riding** ausreiten; **to ~ ~ for a meal** essen gehen; **John has been ~ing ~ with Susan for months** John geht schon seit Monaten mit Susan aus.

(c) (*be extinguished: fire, light*) ausgehen.

(d) (*become unconscious*) das Bewußtsein verlieren, wegsein (*inf*); (*fall asleep*) einschlafen, wegsein (*inf*); (*euph: die*) sterben.

(e) (*become outmoded*) (*fashion*) unmodern werden; (*custom*) überholt sein.

(f) **to ~ ~ cleaning/to work** putzen/arbeiten gehen.

(g) (*Pol: leave office*) abgelöst werden.

(h) (*emigrate, go overseas*) **the family went ~ to Australia** die Familie ging nach Australien.

(i) (*strike*) streiken. **to ~ ~ on strike** in den Streik treten.

(j) (*tide*) zurückgehen.

(k) **my heart went ~ to him** ich fühlte mit ihm mit; **all our sympathy ~es ~ to you** wir teilen Ihr Leid.

(l) (*Sport: be defeated*) ausscheiden, herausfliegen (*inf*).

(m) (*strive*) **to ~ all ~** sich ins Zeug legen (*for* für).

(n) (*be issued*) (*pamphlet, circular*) (hinaus)gehen; (*Rad, TV: programme*) ausgestrahlt werden.

(o) (*year, month: end*) enden, zu Ende gehen.

(p) (*US: be a candidate for*) antreten für; (*Ftbl etc also*) spielen für.

♦ **go over** 1 *vi* **(a)** (*cross*) hinübergehen, rübergehen (*inf*); (*by vehicle*) hinüberfahren, rüberfahren (*inf*).

(b) (*change allegiance, habit, diet etc*) übergehen (*to* zu); (*to another party*) überwechseln (*to* zu). **to ~ ~ to the other side/to a pipe** zur anderen Seite überwechseln/zur Pfeife übergehen.

(c) (*TV, Rad: to news desk, another studio*) umschalten.

(d) (*vehicle etc: be overturned*) umkippen.

(e) (*be received: play, remarks etc*) ankommen.

2 *vi* + *prep obj* **(a)** (*examine, check over*) *accounts, report* durchgehen; *house, luggage* durchsuchen; *person, car* untersuchen; (*see over*) *house etc* sich (*dat*) ansehen, besichtigen.

(b) (*repeat, rehearse, review*) *lesson, role, facts* durchgehen. **to ~ ~ sth in one's mind** etw durchdenken *or* überdenken; **to ~ ~ the ground** es durchsprechen.

(c) (*wash, dust etc*) *windows, room* schnell saubermachen.

(d) (*redraw*) *outlines etc* nachzeichnen.

♦ **go past** *vi* vorbeigehen (*prep obj* an + *dat*); (*vehicle*) vorbeifahren (*prep obj* an + *dat*); (*procession*) vorbeiziehen (*prep obj* an + *dat*); (*time*) vergehen, verfließen.

♦ **go round** *vi* **(a)** (*turn, spin*) sich drehen. **my head is ~ing ~** mir dreht sich alles.

(b) (*make a detour*) außen herumgehen; (*by vehicle*) außen herumfahren. **to ~ ~ sth** um etw herumgehen/-fahren; **to ~ ~ the long way** ganz außen herumgehen/-fahren; **we went ~ by**

Winchester wir fuhren bei Winchester herum.
(c) (visit, call round) vorbeigehen (to bei).
(d) (tour: round museum etc) herumgehen (prep obj in + dat).
(e) (be sufficient) langen, (aus)reichen. there's enough food to ~ ~ (all these people) es ist (für alle diese Leute) genügend zu essen da; to make the money ~ ~ mit dem Geld auskommen.
(f) + prep obj (encircle, reach round) herumgehen um.
(g) see go about 1 (a, b).
♦ go through 1 vi (lit, fig) durchgehen; (business deal) abge-schlossen werden; (divorce) durchkommen.
2 vi + prep obj (a) hole, door, customs etc gehen durch.
(b) (suffer, endure) durchmachen.
(c) (examine, discuss, rehearse) list, subject, play, mail, lesson durchgehen.
(d) (search) pocket, suitcase durchsuchen.
(e) (use up) aufbrauchen; money ausgeben, durchbringen (inf); shoes durchlaufen (inf); food, ice-cream aufessen. he has gone ~ the seat of his trousers er hat seine Hose durch-gesessen; this book has already gone ~ 13 editions das Buch hat schon 13 Auflagen erlebt.
(f) formalities, apprenticeship, initiation durchmachen; course absolvieren; funeral, matriculation mitmachen. they went ~ the programme in two hours sie haben das Programm in zwei Stunden durchgezogen; to ~ ~ the marriage ceremony sich trauen lassen.
♦ go through with vi + prep obj plan, undertaking durch-ziehen (inf); crime ausführen. she realized that she had to ~ ~ ~ it sie sah, daß es kein Zurück gab or daß sich das nicht mehr vermeiden ließ; she couldn't ~ ~ ~ it sie brachte es nicht fertig.
♦ go to vi + prep obj (make an effort) to ~ ~ it sich ranhalten (inf); ~ ~ it! los, ran! (inf), auf geht's! (inf).
♦ go together vi (a) (harmonize: colours, ideas, people) zusammenpassen. (b) (go hand in hand: events, conditions) zusammen auftreten. (c) (go out together) miteinander gehen.
♦ go under 1 vi (sink: ship, person) untergehen; (fail) (businessman) scheitern (because of an + dat); (company) eingehen (inf). to ~ ~ to a disease einer Krankheit (dat) zum Opfer fallen; to ~ ~ to sb jdm unterliegen.
2 vi + prep obj (a) (pass under) durchgehen unter (+ dat); (fit under) gehen or passen unter (+ acc).
(b) to ~ ~ the name of X als X bekannt sein.
♦ go up vi (a) (rise: price, temperature etc) steigen. to ~ ~ (and up) in price (immer) teurer werden.
(b) (climb) (up stairs, hill) hinaufgehen, hinaufsteigen (prep obj acc); (up ladder) hinaufsteigen (prep obj acc); (up tree) hinaufklettern (prep obj auf + acc). to ~ ~ to bed nach oben gehen.
(c) (lift) hochfahren; (balloon) aufsteigen; (Theat: curtain) hochgehen; (be built: new flats etc) gebaut werden.
(d) (travel) (to the north) hinaufgehen; (to London) fahren. to ~ ~ to university (Brit) auf die Universität gehen.
(e) (explode, be destroyed) hochgehen (inf), in die Luft gehen. to ~ ~ in flames in Flammen aufgehen.
♦ go with vi + prep obj (a) sb gehen mit. (b) (go hand in hand with) Hand in Hand gehen mit. (c) (be included or sold with) gehören zu. (d) (harmonize with) passen zu.
♦ go without 1 vi + prep obj nicht haben. to ~ ~ food/breakfast nichts essen/nicht frühstücken; to have to ~ ~ sth ohne etw auskommen müssen, auf etw (acc) verzichten müssen; to manage to ~ ~ sth ohne etw auskommen; he doesn't like to ~ ~ the luxuries of life er verzichtet nicht gern auf den Luxus im Leben.
2 vi darauf verzichten.

goad [gəʊd] 1 n (stick) Stachelstock m; (fig) (spur) Ansporn m; (taunt) aufstachelnde Bemerkung. 2 vt (taunt) aufreizen. to ~ sb into sth jdn zu etw anstacheln or treiben.
♦ goad on vt sep cattle antreiben; (fig) anstacheln, aufstacheln.
go-ahead [ˈgəʊhed] 1 adj fortschrittlich, progressiv. 2 n to give sb/sth the ~ jdm/für etw grünes Licht or freie Fahrt geben.
goal [gəʊl] n (a) (Sport) Tor nt. to keep ~, to play in ~ im Tor stehen, im Tor spielen, das Tor hüten; to score/kick a ~ ein Tor erzielen/schießen. (b) (aim, objective) Ziel nt.
goal area n Torraum m.
goalie [ˈgəʊlɪ] n (inf) Tormann m.
goal: ~keeper n Torwart, Torhüter, Torsteher m; ~-kick n Abstoß m (vom Tor); ~-line n Torlinie f; ~mouth n unmittel-barer Torbereich; ~-post n Torpfosten m.
goanna [gəʊˈænə] n Waran m.
goat [gəʊt] n Ziege f; (inf) (silly person) (man) Esel m (inf); (woman) Ziege f (inf); (lecher) Bock m (inf). to act the (giddy) ~ (inf) herumalbern; to get sb's ~ jdn auf die Palme bringen (inf).
goatee (beard) [gəʊˈtiː(ˌbɪəd)] n Spitzbart m.
goat: ~herd n Ziegenhirte m; ~skin n Ziegenleder nt.
gob[1] [gɒb] n (lump) Klumpen m.
gob[2] n (Brit sl: mouth) Schnauze f (sl). shut your ~! halt die Schnauze! (sl).
gob[3] n (US sl: sailor) blauer Junge (inf), Blaujacke f (inf).
gobbet [ˈgɒbɪt] n Brocken m. ~s of cotton wool Wattebäusche pl.
gobble [ˈgɒbl] 1 vt verschlingen. 2 vi (a) (eat noisily) schmatzen. (b) (turkey) kollern. 3 n (of turkey) Kollern nt.
♦ gobble down vt sep hinunterschlingen.
♦ gobble up vt sep (lit, fig) verschlingen; (company) schlucken.
gobbledegook, **gobbledygook** [ˈgɒbldɪˌguːk] n (inf) Kauderwelsch nt.
gobbler [ˈgɒblər] n Truthahn m.
go-between [ˈgəʊbɪˌtwiːn] n, pl -s Vermittler(in f), Mittels-mann m.
Gobi Desert [ˈgəʊbɪˈdezət] n Wüste f Gobi.

goblet [ˈgɒblɪt] n Pokal m; (esp of glass) Kelchglas nt.
goblin [ˈgɒblɪn] n Kobold m.
gobstopper [ˈgɒbˌstɒpər] n (Brit) Riesenbonbon m or nt mit ver-schiedenen Farbschichten, ≈ Dauerlutscher m.
goby [ˈgəʊbɪ] n (fish) Meergrundel f.
GOC abbr of **General Officer Commanding**.
go: ~-by n (inf) to give sb the ~-by jdn schneiden, jdn links liegenlassen (inf); ~-cart n (child's cart) Seifenkiste f; (Sport: kart) Go-Kart m; (US: walker) Laufstuhl m; (US: pushchair) Sportwagen m.
god [gɒd] n (a) G~ Gott m; now he lies in G~'s (green) acre (euph) nun deckt ihn der grüne Rasen (euph); G~ willing so Gott will; G~ forbid (inf) Gott behüte or bewahre; would to G~ that (form) ich hoffe zu Gott, daß (geh); G~ (only) knows (inf) wer weiß; do you think he'll succeed? — G~ knows! glaubst du, daß er Erfolg haben wird? — das wissen die Götter!; (my) G~!, good G~!, G~ almighty! (all inf) O Gott! (inf), großer Gott! (inf); be quiet, for G~'s sake! sei still, verdammt noch mal (sl) or Herrgott noch mal! (inf); for G~'s sake! (inf) um Gottes or Himmels willen (inf); what in G~'s name ...? um Himmels willen, was ...?
(b) (non-Christian) Gott m. Mars, the ~ of war Mars, der Kriegsgott; to play ~ Gott or den Herrgott spielen; the com-mander was a ~ to his men der Kommandant wurde von seinen Leuten wie ein (Ab)gott verehrt; money is his ~ das Geld ist sein Gott or Götze.
(c) (Brit Theat inf) the ~s die Galerie, der Olymp (inf).
god: ~awful adj (US inf) beschissen (sl); ~child n Patenkind nt; ~dam(ned) adj (US inf) Scheiß- (sl), gottverdammt (inf); it's no ~dam use! (inf) es hat keinen Zweck, verdammt noch mal (sl); ~daughter n Patentochter f.
goddess [ˈgɒdɪs] n Göttin f.
god: ~father n Pate m; my ~father mein Patenonkel m; ~-fearing adj gottesfürchtig; ~forsaken adj (inf) gottverlassen; ~head n Gottheit f; the G~head Gott m; ~less adj gottlos; ~lessness n Gottlosigkeit f; ~like adj göttergleich; attitude gottähnlich; he looked ~like er sah aus wie ein junger Gott; his air of ~like superiority seine Art, sich wie (ein) Gott aufzu-spielen.
godliness [ˈgɒdlɪnɪs] n Frömmigkeit, Gottesfürchtigkeit f.
godly [ˈgɒdlɪ] adj (+er) fromm, gottesfürchtig.
god: ~mother n Patin f; my ~mother meine Patentante f; see fairy ~; ~parent n Pate m, Patin f; ~send n Geschenk nt des Himmels; ~son n Patensohn m; ~speed interj (old) behüt dich/euch Gott (old), geh/geht mit Gott (old); to wish sb ~speed jdn mit den besten Segenswünschen auf die Reise schicken.
goer [ˈgəʊər] n (a) (horse, runner) Geher m. to be a good/sweet ~ gut laufen. (b) (Austral inf: good idea) to be a ~ was taugen (inf).
-goer n suf -besucher(in f) m.
goes [gəʊz] 3rd pers sing present of **go**.
go-getter [ˈgəʊˌgetər] n (inf) Tatmensch, Ellbogentyp (pej inf) m.
goggle [ˈgɒgl] vi (person) staunen, starren, glotzen (pej inf); (eyes) starr or weit aufgerissen sein. to ~ at sb/sth jdn/etw anstarren or anglotzen (pej inf), auf jdn/etw starren or glotzen (pej inf).
goggle: ~-box n (Brit inf) Glotzkiste (inf), Glotze f (inf); ~-eyed adj mit Kulleraugen, kulleräugig; he stared at him/it ~-eyed er starrte or glotzte (pej inf) ihn/es an; a ~-eyed stare ein starrer Blick.
goggles [ˈgɒglz] npl Schutzbrille f; (inf: glasses) Brille f.
go-go [ˈgəʊgəʊ]: ~-dancer n Go-Go Tänzerin f, Go-Go-girl nt; ~-dancing n Go-Go nt.
going [ˈgəʊɪŋ] 1 n (a) (departure) Weggang m; (weg)gehen nt.
(b) (pace, conditions) it's slow ~ es geht nur langsam; that is good or fast ~ das ist ein flottes Tempo; the ~ is good/soft/hard (in racing) die Bahn ist gut/weich/hart; the road was heavy/rough ~ man kam auf der Straße nur schwer/mit Mühe voran; it's heavy ~ talking to him es ist sehr mühsam, sich mit ihm zu unterhalten; while the ~ is good solange es noch geht; to go while the ~ is good sich rechtzeitig absetzen.
2 adj attr (a) (viable) business gutgehend. to sell sth as a ~ concern etw als ein bestehendes Unternehmen verkaufen.
(b) (current) price, rate gängig.
going-over [ˌgəʊɪŋˈəʊvər] n (a) (examination) Untersuchung f. to give a contract/painting/patient/house a good ~ einen Ver-trag gründlich prüfen/ein Gemälde/einen Patienten untersuchen/ein Haus gründlich durchsuchen.
(b) (inf: beating-up) Abreibung f (inf). to give sb a good ~ jdm eine tüchtige Abreibung verpassen (inf).
goings-on [ˌgəʊɪŋˈzɒn] npl (inf: happenings) Dinge pl. there have been strange ~ da sind seltsame Dinge passiert; fine ~! schöne Geschichten!; the ~ at home was ~ zu Hause passiert.
goitre, (US) **goiter** [ˈgɔɪtər] n Kropf m.
go-kart [ˈgəʊkɑːt] n Go-Kart m.
gold [gəʊld] 1 n (a) Gold nt; (wealth) Geld nt; (inf: ~ medal) Goldmedaille f; see glitter. (b) (colour) Goldton m. 2 adj golden; (made of ~ also) Gold-.
gold: ~ braid n Goldtresse or -litze f; ~brick (US) 1 n (a) (inf) (gilded metal bar) falscher Goldbarren; (worthless object) schöner Schund; to sell sb a ~brick jdm etwas andrehen (inf); (b) (sl: shirker) Drückeberger m (inf); 2 vi (sl) sich drücken (inf); ~bricker n (US sl) see ~brick 1 (b); G~ Coast n Goldküste f; ~-coloured adj goldfarben; ~crest n Goldhähnchen nt; ~-digger n Goldgräber m; she's a real little ~-digger (inf) sie ist wirklich nur aufs Geld aus (inf); ~ dust n Goldstaub m.
golden [ˈgəʊldən] adj (lit, fig) golden; opportunity einmalig. ~ yellow/brown goldgelb/goldbraun; ~ boy/girl Goldjunge m/Goldmädchen nt; to follow the ~ mean die goldene Mitte wählen.

golden: ~ **age** n (Myth) Goldenes Zeitalter; (fig) Blütezeit f; the ~ **calf** n das Goldene Kalb; **G~ Delicious** n Golden Delicious m; ~ **eagle** n Steinadler m; **the G~ Fleece** n das Goldene Vlies; ~ **handshake** n (inf) Abstandssumme f; **the director got a ~ handshake of £500** der Direktor hat zum Abschied £ 500 bekommen; ~ **jubilee** n goldenes Jubiläum; ~ **labrador** n Goldener Labrador; ~ **oriole** n Pirol m; ~ **pheasant** n Goldfasan m; ~**rod** n Goldrute f; ~ **rule** n goldene Regel; ~ **syrup** n (Brit) (gelber) Sirup; ~ **wedding** (anniversary) n goldene Hochzeit.

gold: ~ **fever** n Goldfieber nt; ~**field** n Goldfeld nt; ~**finch** n (European) Stieglitz, Distelfink m; (US) Amerikanischer Fink; ~**fish** n Goldfisch m; ~**fish bowl** n Goldfischglas nt; **it's like living in a ~fish bowl** da ist man wie auf dem Präsentierteller; ~ **foil** n Goldfolie f; ~ **leaf** n Blattgold nt; ~ **medal** n Goldmedaille f; ~ **mine** n Goldbergwerk nt, Goldgrube f (also fig); ~ **plate** n (plating) Vergoldung f, Goldüberzug m; (plated articles) vergoldetes Gerät; (gold articles) goldenes Gerät; ~**plate** vt vergolden; ~ **reserves** npl Goldreserven pl; ~ **rush** n Goldrausch m; ~**smith** n Goldschmied m; ~ **standard** n Goldstandard m.

golf [gɒlf] **1** n Golf nt. **2** vi Golf spielen.

golf: ~ **bag** n Golftasche f; ~ **ball** n Golfball m; ~ **club** n (instrument) Golfschläger m; (association) Golfklub m; ~ **course** n, ~ **links** npl Golfplatz m.

golfer ['gɒlfəʳ] n Golfer(in f), Golfspieler(in f) m.

Goliath [gəʊ'laɪəθ] n (lit, fig) Goliath m.

golliwog ['gɒlɪwɒg] n Negerpuppe f. **to look like a ~** eine Negerkrause haben.

golly¹ ['gɒlɪ] n (Brit inf) see **golliwog.**

golly² interj (inf) Menschenskind (inf).

goloshes [gə'lɒʃəz] npl see **galoshes.**

Gomorrah, Gomorrha [gə'mɒrə] n Gomorr(h)a nt; see **Sodom.**

gonad ['gəʊnæd] n Gonade f.

gondola ['gɒndələ] n (a) (in Venice, of balloon, cable car etc) Gondel f. **(b)** (US Rail: also ~ car) offener Güterwagen.

gondolier [,gɒndə'lɪəʳ] n Gondoliere m.

gone [gɒn] **1** ptp of **go. 2** adj pred **(a)** (inf: enthusiastic) **to be ~ on sb/sth** von jdm/etw (ganz) weg sein (inf); **I'm not ~ on ...** ich bin nicht verrückt auf (+acc) ... (inf). **(b)** (inf: pregnant) **she was 6 months ~** sie war im 7. Monat. **(c)** see **far.**

goner ['gɒnəʳ] n (inf) **to be a ~** (car etc) kaputt sein (inf); (patient) es nicht mehr lange machen; (socially, professionally: person, company) weg vom Fenster sein (inf); **if you pull out the whole plan's a ~** wenn du nicht mitmachst, wird aus der ganzen Sache nichts.

gong [gɒŋ] n **(a)** Gong m. **(b)** (Brit sl: medal) Blech nt (inf). ~**s** Lametta nt (inf).

gonk [gɒŋk] n (toy) Stoffpuppe f.

gonorrhoea [,gɒnə'rɪə] n Gonorrhöe f, Tripper m.

goo [gu:] n (inf) (sticky stuff) Papp m (inf), Schmiere f (inf); (fig: sentimentality) Schmalz m (inf).

goober ['gu:bəʳ] n (US inf) Erdnuß f.

good [gʊd] **1** adj, comp **better,** superl **best (a)** gut. **that's a ~ one!** (joke) das ist gut!, das ist ein guter Witz (also iro); (excuse) wer's glaubt, wird selig! (inf); **you've done a ~ day's work** there da hast du gute Arbeit (für einen Tag) geleistet; **it's no ~ doing it** like that es hat keinen Sinn, das so zu machen; **that's no ~** das ist nichts; **a ~ fire was burning in the hearth** im Ofen brannte ein ordentliches or tüchtiges Feuer; **it's a ~ firm to work for** in der Firma läßt es sich gut arbeiten; **to be ~ at sport/languages** gut im Sport/in Sprachen sein; **to be ~ at sewing/typing** gut nähen/maschineschreiben können; **I'm not very ~ at that** das kann ich nicht besonders gut; **he's ~ at telling stories** er kann gut Geschichten erzählen; **he tells a ~ story** er erzählt gut; **to be ~ for sb** jdm guttun; (be healthy also) gesund sein; **to be ~ for toothache/one's health** gut gegen Zahnschmerzen/für die Gesundheit sein; **it's bound to be ~ for something** das muß doch zu or für etwas gut sein; **to drink more than is ~ for one** mehr trinken, als einem guttut; **it isn't ~ to eat unwashed fruit** es ist nicht gesund or gut, ungewaschenes Obst zu essen; **she looks ~ enough to eat** (hum) sie sieht zum Anbeißen aus (inf); **to be ~ with people** mit Menschen umgehen können; ~ **fortune** Glück nt; ~ **nature** Gutmütigkeit f; **you've never had it so ~!** es ist euch noch nie so gut gegangen, ihr habt es noch nie so gut gehabt; **it's too ~ to be true** es ist zu schön, um wahr zu sein; **to feel ~** sich wohl fühlen; **I don't feel too ~** mir ist nicht gut, ich fühle mich nicht wohl; **I don't feel too ~ about that/the company's future** mir ist nicht ganz wohl dabei/mir ist nicht ganz wohl, wenn ich an die Zukunft der Firma denke; **to come in a ~ third** einen guten dritten Platz belegen; **that's (not) ~ enough** das reicht (nicht); **is his work ~?** — **not ~ enough, I'm afraid/~ enough, I suppose** ist seine Arbeit gut? — leider nicht gut genug/es geht or reicht; **that's not ~ enough,** you'll have to do better than that das geht so nicht, du mußt dich schon etwas mehr anstrengen; **if he gives his word, that's ~ enough for me** wenn er sein Wort gibt, reicht mir das; **it's just not ~ enough!** so geht das nicht!; **his attitude/work/behaviour is just not ~ enough** er hat einfach nicht die richtige Einstellung/seine Arbeit ist einfach nicht gut genug/sein Benehmen ist nicht akzeptabel; **her parents thought he wasn't ~ enough for her** ihre Eltern meinten, er sei nicht gut genug für sie; **she felt he wasn't ~ enough for her** er war ihr nicht gut genug.

(b) (favourable, opportune) moment, chance, opportunity günstig, gut. **a ~ day for a picnic** ein guter Tag für ein Picknick; **it's a ~ thing or job I was there** (nur) gut, daß ich dort war.

(c) (enjoyable) holiday, evening schön. **the ~ life** das süße Leben; **to have a ~ time** sich gut amüsieren; **have a ~ time!** viel Spaß or Vergnügen!; **did you have a ~ day?** wie war's heute?, wie ging's (dir) heute?

(d) (kind) gut, lieb; Samaritan barmherzig. **to be ~ to sb** gut

or lieb zu jdm sein; **that's very ~ of you** das ist sehr lieb or nett von Ihnen; **(it was) ~ of you to come** nett, daß Sie gekommen sind; **that was really ~ of him** das war wirklich lieb von ihm; **would you be ~ enough to tell me ...** könnten Sie bitte sagen ..., wären Sie so nett, mir zu sagen ... (also iro); **she was ~ enough to help us** sie war so gut und hat uns geholfen; **he sends ~ wishes** er wünscht (euch) alles Gute; **with every ~ wish** mit den besten Wünschen; ~ **deed/works** gute Tat/Werke.

(e) (virtuous, honourable) name, manners, behaviour gut; (well-behaved, obedient) artig, brav (inf). **the G~ Book** das Buch der Bücher; **the G~ Shepherd** der Gute Hirte; **(as) ~ as gold** mustergültig; **be a ~ girl/boy** sei artig or lieb or brav (inf); **be a ~ girl/boy and ...** sei so lieb und ...; **all ~ men and true** alle wackeren und aufrechten Männer (old); **your ~ man/lady** (dated) Ihr werter Gemahl/Ihre werte Gemahlin (geh); **my ~ man** (dated) mein Guter (old), mein guter Mann (dated); ~ **man!** (dated) sehr löblich!; **gut gemacht!; ~ girl/boy!** das ist lieb!; (well done) gut!; ~ **old Charles!** der gute alte Charles!; **the ~ ship Santa Maria** die Santa Maria; **if you used to be ~,** be careful (hum) wenn du es schon tun mußt, sei wenigstens vorsichtig.

(f) (valid) advice, excuse gut; reason also triftig; ticket gültig; (Comm: sound) debt gedeckt; risk sicher. **is his credit ~?** ist er kreditfähig?; **what or how much is he ~ for?** (will he give us) mit wieviel kann man bei ihm rechnen?; (does he have) wieviel hat er?; (Comm) wieviel Kredit hat er?; **he's ~ for £10,000** bei ihm kannst du mit £ 10.000 rechnen/er hat gut und gern £ 10.000/er hat bis zu £ 10.000 Kredit; **he/the car is ~ for another few years** mit ihm kann man noch ein paar Jahre rechnen/das Auto hält or tut's (inf) noch ein paar Jahre; **I'm ~ for another 5 miles** (inf) ich schaffe noch 5 Meilen (inf).

(g) (handsome) looks, figure, features gut; legs also schön. **a ~ appearance** eine gute Erscheinung, ein gepflegtes Äußeres; **you look ~ in that** du siehst gut darin aus, das steht dir gut.

(h) (thorough) gut, gründlich, tüchtig (inf). **to give sb a ~ scolding** jdn gründlich or tüchtig ausschimpfen; **to give sth a ~ clean** etw gut or gründlich reinigen; **to have a ~ cry/laugh** sich ausweinen/ordentlich or so richtig lachen (inf); **to take a ~ look at sth** sich (dat) etw gut ansehen; **to have a ~ grounding in sth** gute Grundkenntnisse in etw (dat) haben.

(i) (considerable, not less than) hour, while gut; amount, distance, way also schön. **it's a ~ distance** es ist ein ganz schönes Stück (inf) or eine ganz schöne Strecke; **it's a ~ 8 km** es sind gute 8 km; **a ~ deal of effort/money** beträchtliche Mühe/ziemlich viel Geld; **he ate a ~ half of the chocolates at once** er hat gut und gern die Hälfte der Pralinen auf einmal gegessen; **a ~ many/few people** ziemlich viele/nicht gerade wenig Leute.

(j) **as ~ as** so gut wie; **as ~ as new/settled** so gut wie neu/abgemacht; **he was as ~ as his word** er hat sein Wort gehalten; **he as ~ as called me a liar/invited me to come** er nannte mich praktisch einen Lügner/er hat mich praktisch eingeladen.

(k) (in greetings) gut. ~ **morning/afternoon** guten Morgen/Tag.

(l) (in exclamations) gut, prima. **that's ~!** gut!, prima!; **(it's) ~ to see you/to be here** (es ist) schön, dich zu sehen/hier zu sein; ~**, I think that'll be all** gut or fein, ich glaube das reicht; ~ **enough!** (OK) schön!; ~ **heavens** or Lord or God! um Himmels willen! (inf); ~ **grief** or gracious! ach du liebe or meine Güte! (inf); **very ~, sir** jawohl or sehr wohl (old) (Herr); ~ **for** or **on** (Austral) **you/him** etc! gut!, prima!; (iro also) das ist ja toll!

2 adv **(a)** schön. **a ~ strong stick/old age** ein schön(er) starker Stock/ein schön(es) hohes Alter; ~ **and hard/proper/strong** (inf) ganz schön fest/ganz anständig/schön stark (inf).

(b) (incorrect for well) gut.

3 n **(a)** (what is morally right) Gute(s) nt. ~ **and evil** Gut(es) und Böse(s); **to do ~** Gutes tun; **there's some ~ in everybody** in jedem steckt etwas Gutes; **to be up to no ~** (inf) etwas im Schilde führen (inf), nichts Gutes im Schilde führen (inf).

(b) (advantage, benefit) Wohl nt. **the common ~** das Gemeinwohl; **for the ~ of the nation** zum Wohl(e) der Nation; **to stick to sb for ~** or ill jdm in guten wie in schlechten Zeiten beistehen; **it's done now, for ~** or **ill** es ist nun einmal geschehen; **I did it for your own ~** ich meine es nur gut mit dir, es war nur zu deinem Besten; **for the ~ of one's health** etc seiner Gesundheit etc zuliebe; **we were 5 glasses/£5 to the ~** wir hatten 5 Glas zuviel/£ 5 plus; **that's all to the ~** auch gut!; **he'll come to no ~** mit ihm wird es noch ein böses Ende nehmen.

(c) (use) what's the ~ of hurrying? wozu eigentlich die Eile?; **he's no ~ to us** er nützt uns (dat) nichts; **it's no ~ complaining** to me es ist sinnlos or es nützt nichts, sich bei mir zu beklagen; **it would be some ~** es wäre ganz nützlich; **if that is any ~ to you** wenn es dir hilft; **the applicant was no ~** der Bewerber war nicht gut; **he wasn't any ~ for the job** er eignete sich nicht für die Arbeit; **I'm no ~ at things like that** ich bin nicht gut in solchen Dingen.

(d) to do (some) ~ (etwas) helfen or nützen; **to do sb (some)** ~ jdm helfen; (rest, drink, medicine etc) jdm guttun; **what ~ will that do you?** was hast du davon?; **much ~ may it do you** (iro inf) na, dann viel Vergnügen! (iro inf); **that won't do much/any ~** das hilft auch nicht viel/nichts; **that won't do you much/any ~** das hilft dir auch nicht viel/nichts; (will be unhealthy etc) das ist nicht gut für dich; **a (fat) lot of ~ that will do!** (iro inf) als ob das viel helfen würde! (iro); **a (fat) lot of ~ that will do you!** (iro inf) und wie dir das guttun wird! (iro inf).

(e) (for ever) for ~ (and all) für immer (und ewig).

(f) (pl: people of virtue) the ~ die Guten pl.

good: ~**bye,** (US) ~**by 1** n Abschied m, Lebewohl nt (geh); **to say** ~**bye, to make one's** ~**byes** sich verabschieden, Lebewohl sagen (geh); **to wish sb** ~**bye, to say** ~**bye to sb** sich von jdm verabschieden, von jdm Abschied nehmen; **to say**

~bye to sth einer Sache (dat) Lebewohl sagen; **when all the** ~**byes were over** als das Abschiednehmen vorbei war; **2** interj auf Wiedersehen, lebe wohl (geh); **3** adj attr Abschieds-; ~**-for- nothing 1** n Nichtsnutz, Taugenichts m. **2** adj nichtsnutzig; his ~**-for-nothing brother** sein Nichtsnutz von Bruder; **G**~ **Friday** n Karfreitag m; ~**-hearted** adj gutherzig; ~**-humoured**, (US) ~**-humored** adj gut gelaunt; (good-natured) gutmütig.

goodish [ˈgʊdɪʃ] adj (quite good) ganz gut, anständig (inf); (considerable) ganz schön.

good: ~**-looker** n (inf) **to be a real** ~**-looker** wirklich gut or klasse (inf) aussehen; ~**-looking** adj gutaussehend.

goodly [ˈgʊdlɪ] adj ansehnlich, stattlich (geh).

good: ~**-natured** adj gutmütig; joke harmlos; ~**-naturedly** adv gutmütig.

goodness [ˈgʊdnɪs] n **(a)** Güte f; (of person also) Gütigkeit f; (of food also) Nährgehalt m. ~ **of heart** Herzensgüte f; **the** ~ **of the saint's life** das vorbildliche Leben des Heiligen; **would you have the** ~ **to ...** (form) hätten Sie bitte die Güte, zu ... (geh).
(b) (in exclamations etc) ~ **knows** weiß der Himmel (inf); **for** ~' **sake** um Himmels willen (inf); **I wish to** ~ **I had gone** wenn ich doch bloß gegangen wäre!; (my) ~! meine Güte! (inf); ~ **gracious** or **me!** ach du liebe or meine Güte! (inf).

goodnight [gʊdˈnaɪt] adj attr Gutenacht-.

goods [gʊdz] npl Güter pl (also Comm); (merchandise also) Waren pl; (possessions also) Gut nt (geh), Habe f (geh, liter). **leather-/knitted-/manufactured** ~ Leder-/Strick-/Fertig- waren pl; **canned** ~ Konserven pl; **stolen** ~ gestohlene Waren pl, Diebesgut nt; ~ **depot/train/wagon/yard** Güter- depot nt/-zug m/-wagen m/-bahnhof m; **one's** ~ **and chattels** sein Hab und Gut (also Jur), seine Siebensachen (inf); **to send sth (by)** ~ etw als Frachtgut schicken; **it's the** ~ (esp US inf) das ist große Klasse (inf); **to get/have the** ~ **on sb** (esp US inf) gegen jdn etwas in die Hand bekommen or in der Hand haben; **she's a nice bit** or **piece of** ~ (inf) sie ist 'ne nette Mieze (inf).

good: ~**-sized** adj ziemlich groß; building, room also geräumig; ~**-tempered** adj person verträglich; animal gutartig; smile, look gutmütig; ~**-time Charlie** n (US inf) Playboy m, Leichtfuß m; ~**-time girl** n Playgirl nt; (prostitute) Freudenmädchen nt; ~**will** n Wohlwollen nt; (between nations, Comm) Goodwill m; **a gesture of** ~**will** ein Zeichen seines/ihres etc guten Willens; **to gain sb's** ~**will** jds Gunst gewinnen; ~**will mission/tour** Goodwillreise f/-tour f.

goody [ˈgʊdɪ] (inf) **1** interj toll, prima. ~, ~ **gumdrops!** (hum) juchhei, juchhe! **2** n **(a)** (person) Gute(r) m. **(b)** (delicacy) gute Sache (inf), Leckerbissen m; (sweet) Süßigkeit f. **(c)** (inf: good joke etc) guter Witz/gute Geschichte etc. **that's a** ~! der/das ist gut!

goody-goody [ˈgʊdɪˌgʊdɪ] (inf) **1** n Tugendlamm, Musterkind (inf) nt. **2** adj tugendhaft, superbrav (pej inf); attitude, behaviour also musterhaft; (pretending) scheinheilig.

gooey [ˈguːɪ] adj (+er) (inf) **(a)** (sticky) klebrig; pudding pappig, matschig; toffees, centres of chocolates weich und klebrig; cake üppig. **(b)** (sentimental) schnulzig (inf), rührselig. **a** ~ **song** eine Schnulze.

goof [guːf] (inf) **1** n **(a)** (esp US: idiot) Dussel (inf), Doofie (inf) m.
(b) (mistake) Schnitzer m (inf), dicker Hund (sl).
2 vi **(a)** (blunder) sich (dat) etwas leisten (inf), danebenhauen (inf).
(b) (US: loiter) (also ~ **around**) (herum)trödeln, bummeln. **to** ~ **over/off** herüberschlendern or -zockeln (inf)/abzwitschern (inf).

♦**goof up** vt sep (inf) vermasseln (inf), vermurksen (inf).
goofball [ˈguːfbɔːl] n (esp US sl) Schnellmacher m (sl).
goofy [ˈguːfɪ] adj (+er) (inf) dämlich, doof (inf).
googly [ˈguːglɪ] n (Cricket) gedrehter Ball.
goon [guːn] n **(a)** (inf: idiot) Idiot, Dussel (inf) m. **(b)** (US sl: hired thug) Schlägertyp m (sl).
goose [guːs] n, pl geese (lit, inf) Gans f. **silly little** ~! (inf) dummes Gänschen! (inf); **all his geese are swans** bei ihm ist immer alles besser; **to kill the** ~ **that lays the golden eggs** das Huhn schlachten, das die goldenen Eier legt.
gooseberry [ˈgʊzbərɪ] n (plant, fruit) Stachelbeere f. ~ **bush** Stachelbeerstrauch m; **to play** ~ Anstandswauwau spielen (inf), das fünfte Rad am Wagen sein.
goose: ~**flesh** n see ~**pimples**; ~**neck lamp** n Bogenleuchte f; ~**pimples** npl Gänsehaut f; **to come out in** ~**pimples** eine Gän- sehaut bekommen; **that gives me** ~**pimples** da(bei) bekomme ich eine Gänsehaut; ~**-step 1** n Stechschritt m; **2** vi im Stechschritt marschieren.
GOP (US Pol) abbr of **Grand Old Party.**
gopher [ˈgəʊfər] n Taschenratte f; (squirrel) Ziesel m.
gorblimey [ˌgɔːˈblaɪmɪ] interj (Brit inf) ach du grüne Neune (inf), ich denk' mich laust der Affe (inf).
Gordian [ˈgɔːdɪən] adj gordisch. **to cut the** ~ **knot** den gordi- schen Knoten durchhauen.
gore[1] [gɔːʳ] n (liter: blood) Blut nt.
gore[2] vt aufspießen, durchbohren. ~**d to death by a bull** durch die Hörner eines Stiers tödlich verletzt.
gore[3] n (panel) Bahn f; (in sail) Gehren m.
gored [gɔːd] adj mit Bahnen. ~ **skirt** Bahnenrock m.
gorge [gɔːdʒ] **1** n **(a)** (Geog) Schlucht f.
(b) (old: gullet) Schlund m. **it stuck in my** ~ **to ...** (fig) es war mir zuwider, zu ...; **it makes my** ~ **rise, my** ~ **rises at it** (fig: make angry) dabei kommt mir die Galle hoch.
2 vr schlemmen, sich vollessen; (animal) gierig fressen, schlingen. **to** ~ **oneself on** or **with sth** etw in sich (acc) hineinschlingen, etw verschlingen.
3 vt **they were** ~**d** sie hatten sich reichlich gesättigt (with an +dat); (animals) sie hatten sich vollgefressen (with an +dat).

gorgeous [ˈgɔːdʒəs] adj herrlich, großartig, sagenhaft (inf); (beautiful also) woman hinreißend; (richly coloured) prächtig.
gorgeously [ˈgɔːdʒəslɪ] adv see adj. ~ **dressed** in silks is (farben)prächtigen Seidengewändern.
gorgeousness [ˈgɔːdʒəsnɪs] n Großartigkeit f, Pracht f; (beauty) hinreißende Schönheit; (colourfulness) (Farben)pracht f.
Gorgon [ˈgɔːgən] n (Myth) Gorgo f; (inf) Drachen m (inf).
gorgonzola [ˌgɔːgənˈzəʊlə] n Gorgonzola m.
gorilla [gəˈrɪlə] n Gorilla m.
gormless [ˈgɔːmlɪs] adj (Brit inf) doof (inf).
gorse [gɔːs] n Stechginster m. ~ **bush** Stechginsterstrauch m.
gory [ˈgɔːrɪ] adj (+er) battle etc blutig; person blutbesudelt. **all the** ~ **details** all die blutrünstigen Einzelheiten; (fig) die peinlichsten Einzelheiten.
gosh [gɒʃ] interj Mensch (inf), Mann (sl).
goshawk [ˈgɒshɔːk] n (Hühner)habicht m.
gosling [ˈgɒzlɪŋ] n junge Gans, Gänschen nt.
go-slow [ˈgəʊsləʊ] n Bummelstreik m.
gospel [ˈgɒspəl] n **(a)** (Bibl) Evangelium nt. **the G**~**s** das Evangelium, die Evangelien pl; **the G**~ **according to St John** das Evangelium nach Johannes; **St John's G**~ das Johan- nesevangelium; **the G**~ **for today** das heutige Evangelium.
(b) (fig: doctrine) Grundsätze, Prinzipien pl; (of ideology, religion) Lehre f. **to preach/spread the** ~ **of temperance** Abstinenz predigen/sich für Abstinenz einsetzen; **it's a matter of** ~ **to him** es ist für ihn das Evangelium; **she's a firm believer in the** ~ **of soap and water** sie ist eine überzeugte Anhängerin von Wasser und Seife; **to take sth for** or **as** ~ etw für bare Münze nehmen (inf); **what he said was always** ~ **to her** alles, was er sagte, war für sie (ein) Evangelium.
gospeller [ˈgɒspələʳ] n see hot ~.
gospel: ~ **song** n Gospel(lied) nt; ~ **truth** n (inf) reine Wahrheit.
gossamer [ˈgɒsəməʳ] **1** n **(a)** Spinnfäden, Marienfäden pl, Altweibersommer m. **(b)** (Tex) hauchdünne Gaze. **2** adj hauch- dünn.
gossip [ˈgɒsɪp] **1** n **(a)** Klatsch, Tratsch (inf) m; (chat) Schwatz m. **to have a** ~ **with sb** mit jdm schwatzen or plauschen (inf) or klönen (N Ger); **it started a lot of** ~ es gab Anlaß zu vielem Gerede or Klatsch or Tratsch (inf); **office** ~ Bürotratsch m (inf).
(b) (person) Klatschbase f.
2 vi schwatzen, plauschen (inf), klönen (N Ger); (maliciously) klatschen, tratschen (inf).
gossip: ~ **column** n Klatschkolumne or -spalte f; ~ **columnist** n Klatschkolumnist(in f) m.
gossiping [ˈgɒsɪpɪŋ] **1** adj geschwätzig, schwatzhaft; (mali- cious) klatschsüchtig. **to have a** ~ **tongue** ein Klatschmaul sein (inf); **her** ~ **tongue will get her into trouble** ihre Klatschsucht wird ihr noch einmal Unannehmlichkeiten einbringen.
2 n Geschwätz nt; (malicious) Geklatsche, Getratsche (inf) nt. **there's too much** ~ **and not enough work in this office** in diesem Büro wird zuviel geschwatzt und zuwenig gearbeitet.
gossip: ~**monger** n Klatschmaul nt (inf); ~**mongering** n Klatscherei, Tratscherei (inf) f.
gossipy [ˈgɒsɪpɪ] adj person geschwätzig; book, letter im Plauderton geschrieben. **a long** ~ **phone call** ein langer Schwatz or Tratsch am Telefon (inf); ~ **style** Plauderton m.
got [gɒt] pret, ptp of **get.**
Goth [gɒθ] n Gote m.
Gothic [ˈgɒθɪk] **1** n **(a)** people, language gotisch.
(b) architecture etc gotisch; (fig) vorsintflutlich. ~ **revival** Neugotik f; ~ **novel** (Liter) Schauerroman m.
(c) (Typ) gotisch; (US) grotesk.
2 n **(a)** (language) Gotisch nt.
(b) (type) Gotisch nt; (US) Grotesk f.
gotten [ˈgɒtn] (esp US) ptp of **get.**
gouache [gʊˈaːʃ] n Guasch, Gouache f.
gouge [gaʊdʒ] **1** n **(a)** (tool) Hohlmeißel or -beitel m; (groove) Rille, Furche f.
2 vt bohren. **the river** ~**d a channel in the mountainside** der Fluß grub sich (dat) sein Bett in den Berg.
♦**gouge out** vt sep herausbohren. **to** ~ **sb's eyes** ~ jdm die Augen ausstechen.
goulash [ˈguːlæʃ] n Gulasch nt.
gourd [gʊəd] n Flaschenkürbis m; (dried) Kürbisflasche f.
gourmand [ˈgʊəmənd] n Schlemmer, Gourmand m.
gourmet [ˈgʊəmeɪ] n Feinschmecker, Gourmet m.
gout [gaʊt] n (Med) Gicht f.
gouty [ˈgaʊtɪ] adj (+er) person gichtkrank; limb, joint also gich- tisch; symptoms Gicht-.
Gov abbr of **governor.**
govern [ˈgʌvən] **1** vt **(a)** (rule) country regieren; province, colony, school etc verwalten.
(b) (control) (rules, laws etc) bestimmen; (legislation) regeln; (determine, influence) choice, decision also, develop- ment, person, actions beeinflussen; life beherrschen. **regula- tions** ~**ing the sale of spirits** Bestimmungen pl über den Ver- kauf von Spirituosen; **to be** ~**ed by sb's wishes** sich nach jds Wünschen richten.
(c) (hold in check) passions etc beherrschen; (Mech) speed, engine regulieren. **to** ~ **one's temper** sich beherrschen.
(d) (Gram) case regieren. **the number of the verb is** ~**ed by the subject** das Verb richtet sich in der Zahl nach dem Subjekt; **the subjunctive mood is** ~**ed by the conditional** das Konditional erfordert einen Konjunktiv.
2 vi (Pol) regieren, an der Regierung sein.
governable [ˈgʌvnəbl] adj regierbar.
governess [ˈgʌvənɪs] n Gouvernante, Hauslehrerin f.
governing [ˈgʌvənɪŋ] adj (ruling) regierend. **the** ~ **party** die Regierungspartei; ~ **body** Vorstand m. **(b)** (guiding, controlling) beherrschend, entscheidend. ~ **principle**

government

Leitgedanke *m*; money was the ~ passion of his life die Geldgier beherrschte sein Leben.
government ['gʌvənmənt] *n* (a) (*action of governing, body of administrators*) Regierung *f*. strong ~ **is difficult in a democracy** es ist schwierig, in einer Demokratie mit fester Hand zu regieren; **to form a ~** eine Regierung bilden.
   (b) (*system*) Regierungsform *f*.
government in *cpds* Regierungs-, der Regierung; *agency* staatlich.
governmental [ˌgʌvən'mentl] *adj* Regierungs-. ~ **publication** Veröffentlichung *f* der Regierung.
government: ~ **department** *n* Ministerium *nt*; ~ **grant** *n* (staatliche) Subvention; **G~ House** *n* Gouverneursresidenz *f*; ~ **securities,** ~ **stocks** *npl* (*Fin*) Staatspapiere *or* -anleihen *pl*.
governor ['gʌvənə[r]] *n* (a) (*of colony, state etc*) Gouverneur *m*. ~**-general** (*Brit*) Generalgouverneur *m*.
   (b) (*esp Brit: of bank, prison*) Direktor *m*; (*of school*) ≈ Schulbeirat *m*. **the (board of) ~s** der Vorstand; (*of bank also*) das Direktorium; (*of school*) ≈ der Schulbeirat.
   (c) (*Brit inf*) (*boss*) Chef *m* (*inf*); (*father*) alter Herr (*inf*).
   (d) (*Mech*) Regler *m*.
governorship ['gʌvənəʃɪp] *n* (*office*) Gouverneursamt *nt*; (*period*) Amtszeit *f* als Gouverneur.
govt *abbr of* **government** Reg.
gown [gaʊn] **1** *n* (a) Kleid *nt*; (*evening* ~) Robe *f*, Abendkleid *nt*; (*dressing* ~) Morgenmantel *m*.
   (b) (*academic* ~) Robe *f*; (*of clergyman, judge*) Talar *m*; *see* **town**.
   2 *vt* kleiden. **to be ~ed by sb** von jdm eingekleidet werden.
GP (*Brit*) *abbr of* **general practitioner.**
GPO *abbr of* **General Post Office.**
gr 1 *n abbr of* **gross**[1] Gr. **2** *adj abbr of* **gross**[2] btto.
grab [græb] **1** *n* (a) Griff *m*. **to make a ~ at** *or* **for sth** nach etw greifen *or* schnappen (*inf*).
   (b) (*Mech*) Greifer *m*.
   (c) (*inf*) **the seat is up for ~s** es ist ein echtes Lotteriespiel, wer den Sitz bekommt (*inf*); **the business is up for ~s** das Geschäft geht an den Meistbietenden; ~ **bag** (*US*) Glücksbeutel, Krabbelsack *m*.
   2 *vt* (*seize*) packen; (*greedily also*) sich (*dat*) schnappen (*inf*); (*take, obtain*) wegschnappen (*inf*); *money* raffen; (*inf: catch*) *person* schnappen (*inf*); *chance* am Schopf packen (*inf*). **he ~bed my sleeve** *or* **packte mich am Ärmel; to snatch from under sb** jdm etw wegreißen; **the job was ~bed from under his nose** die Stelle wurde ihm vor der Nase weggeschnappt (*inf*); **how does that ~ you?** (*inf*) wie findest du das?, was meinst du dazu?
   3 *vi* (*hastig*) zugreifen *or* zupacken. **to ~ at** greifen *or* graps(ch)en (*inf*) nach, packen (+*acc*); **he ~bed at the chance of promotion** er ließ sich die Chance, befördert zu werden, nicht entgehen; **help yourselves, children, but don't ~** greift zu, Kinder, aber nicht so hastig.
grace [greɪs] **1** *n* (a) *no pl* (*gracefulness, graciousness*) Anmut *f*; (*of movement also*) Grazie *f*; (*of monarch etc*) Würde *f*. **written with ~ and charm** reizend und charmant geschrieben; **to do sth with good/bad ~** etw anstandslos/widerwillig *or* unwillig tun; **he bore his defeat with good/bad ~** er nahm seine Niederlage mit Fassung *or* anstandslos hin/man sah ihm seinen Ärger über die Niederlage an; **he took it with good/bad ~** er machte gute Miene zum bösen Spiel/er war sehr ungehalten darüber; **he had** *or* **did have/didn't even have the ~ to apologize** er war so anständig/brachte es nicht einmal fertig, sich zu entschuldigen.
   (b) (*pleasing quality*) (angenehme) Eigenschaft. **social ~s** (gesellschaftliche) Umgangsformen *pl*; **a young woman with many ~s** eine sehr kultivierte junge Dame.
   (c) (*favour*) **to be in sb's good/bad ~s** bei jdm gut/schlecht angeschrieben sein.
   (d) (*respite*) (*for payment*) Zahlungsfrist *f*. **a day's ~** ein Tag *m* Aufschub; **to give sb a few days' ~** jdm ein paar Tage Zeit lassen; **days of ~** (*Comm*) Respekttage *pl*.
   (e) (*prayer*) Tischgebet *nt*. **to say** ~ das Tischgebet sprechen.
   (f) (*mercy*) Gnade *f*. **act of ~** Gnadenakt *m*; **by the ~ of God** durch die Gnade Gottes; **by the ~ of God Queen ... Königin** ... von Gottes Gnaden; **in this year of ~ 1978** im Jahre des Heils 1978; **in a state of ~** (*Eccl*) im Zustand der Gnade; **to fall from ~** in Ungnade fallen.
   (g) (*title*) (*duke, duchess*) Hoheit *f*; (*archbishop*) Exzellenz *f*. **Your G~** Euer Gnaden.
   (h) (*Myth*) **the G~s** die Grazien *pl*.
   (i) (*Mus*) Verzierung, Manier *f*, Ornament *nt*. ~ **note** Verzierung *f*.
   2 *vt* (a) (*adorn*) zieren (*geh*).
   (b) (*honour*) beehren (*with mit*); *performance also, event etc* zieren (*geh*), sich (*dat*) die Ehre geben bei (+*dat*). **to ~ the occasion with one's presence** sich (*dat*) die Ehre geben.
graceful ['greɪsfʊl] *adj* anmutig; *outline, appearance also, behaviour* gefällig; *dancer also* graziös; *compliment* charmant, reizend; *letter* reizend. **with a ~ bow** mit einer eleganten *or* charmanten Verbeugung; **he made a ~ apology** er entschuldigte sich auf sehr charmante *or* nette Art; **(in order) to make the children more ~** damit sich die Kinder anmutiger bewegen lernen.
gracefully ['greɪsfəlɪ] *adv* see *adj*. **he gave in ~** er gab charmant nach; **we cannot ~ refuse** wir haben keine annehmbare Entschuldigung.
gracefulness ['greɪsfʊlnɪs] *n* Anmut(igkeit) *f*; (*of movement also*) Grazie *f*.
graceless ['greɪslɪs] *adj* (a) (*Eccl*) ruchlos, gottlos. (b) (*rude*) schroff; *person, behaviour also* ungehobelt; (*lacking charm*) *teenager* linkisch.

gracious

gracious ['greɪʃəs] **1** *adj* (*kind*) liebenswürdig; (*condescending*) huldvoll; (*lenient, merciful*) gütig, gnädig; *living, way of life, age* kultiviert. **our ~ Queen** unsere gnädige Königin; **by the ~ consent of** mit der gütigen Erlaubnis von; **Lord be ~ unto him** Herr sei ihm gnädig.
   2 *interj* (*good*) ~!, ~ **me!** du meine Güte!, lieber Himmel!
graciously ['greɪʃəslɪ] *adv* see *adj*.
graciousness ['greɪʃəsnɪs] *n* see *adj* Liebenswürdigkeit *f* (*towards* gegenüber +*dat*); huldvolle Art; Güte, Gnädigkeit *f*; Kultiviertheit *f*.
gradation [grə'deɪʃən] *n* (a) (*step, degree*) Abstufung *f*; (*mark on thermometer etc*) Gradeinteilung *f*. ~**s of madness** Stufen *or* Grade des Wahnsinns; **the ~s of public opinion ran from sympathy to anger** die Skala der öffentlichen Meinung reichte von Sympathie bis zu Zorn.
   (b) (*gradual change*) Abstufung *f*; (*increase in intensity*) Steigerung *f*.
grade [greɪd] **1** *n* (a) (*level, standard*) Niveau *nt*; (*of goods*) (Güte)klasse *f*. **high-/low-~ goods** hoch-/minderwertige Ware; **this is ~ A** (*inf*) das ist I a (*inf*); **to make the ~** (*fig*) es schaffen (*inf*).
   (b) (*job* ~) Position, Stellung *f*; (*Mil*) Rang, (Dienst)grad *m* (*auch von Beamten*); (*salary* ~) Klasse, Stufe *f*. **what ~ is your job?** welche Stellung *or* Position haben Sie in der Firma?/in welcher Gehaltsklasse *or* -stufe sind Sie?
   (c) (*Sch*) (*mark*) Note *f*; (*esp US: class*) Klasse *f*.
   (d) (*US*) see *gradient*.
   (e) (*US*) **at ~** auf gleicher Ebene; **an apartment at ~ (level)** eine Wohnung zu ebener Erde.
   2 *vt* (a) *wool, milk, animals* klassifizieren; *eggs, goods also* sortieren; *colours* abstufen; *students* einstufen.
   (b) (*Sch: mark*) benoten.
   (c) (*level*) *road, slope* ebnen.
♦ **grade down** *vt sep* (*put in lower grade*) niedriger einstufen; *exam paper* schlechter benoten.
♦ **grade up** *vt sep* höher einstufen; *exam paper* höher benoten.
grade: ~ **crossing** *n* (*US*) Bahnübergang *m*; ~ **school** *n* (*US*) ≈ Grundschule *f*.
gradient ['greɪdɪənt] *n* Neigung *f*; (*upward also*) Steigung *f*; (*downward also*) Gefälle *nt*. **a ~ of 1 in 10** eine Steigung/ein Gefälle von 10%; **what is the ~?** wie groß ist die Steigung/das Gefälle?; **what is the ~ of the hill?** welche Steigung/welches Gefälle hat der Berg?
gradual ['grædjʊəl] *adj* allmählich; *slope* sanft.
gradually ['grædjʊəlɪ] *adv* nach und nach, allmählich; *slope* sanft.
graduate[1] ['grædjʊət] *n* (*Univ*) (Hochschul)absolvent(in *f*) *m*; (*person with degree*) Akademiker(in *f*) *m*; (*US Sch*) Schulabgänger(in *f*) *m*. **high-school** ~ ≈ Abiturient(in *f*) *m*.
graduate[2] ['grædjʊeɪt] **1** *vt* (a) (*mark*) einteilen, graduieren (*form*).
   (b) *colours* abstufen.
   (c) (*US Sch*) als Absolventen haben; (*Univ also*) graduieren (*form*).
   2 *vi* (a) (*Univ*) graduieren; (*US Sch*) die Abschlußprüfung bestehen (*from an* +*dat*). **to ~ from a hard school** (*fig*) eine harte Lehre durchmachen.
   (b) (*change by degrees*) allmählich übergehen.
graduate ['grædjʊət] *in cpds* für Akademiker; *unemployment* unter den Akademikern; ~ **course** *n* Kurs *m* für Studenten mit abgeschlossenem Studium.
graduated ['grædjʊeɪtɪd] *adj* *markings, flask* Meß-; *scale* mit Meßeinteilung, graduiert (*form*); *salary scale, tax* abgestuft.
graduate student ['grædjʊət-] *n* *m* mit abgeschlossenem Studium, Jungakademiker(in *f*) *m*.
graduation [ˌgrædjʊ'eɪʃən] *n* (a) (*mark*) (Maß)einteilung *f*. (b) (*Univ, US Sch: ceremony*) (Ab)schlußfeier *f* (*mit feierlicher Überreichung der Zeugnisse*). **his ~ was delayed by illness** wegen Krankheit wurde ihm sein Zeugnis *or* seine Urkunde erst später überreicht.
graduation *in cpds* Abschluß-; ~ **day** *n* Tag *m* der Abschlußfeier (und Überreichung der Zeugnisse).
graffiti [grə'fiːtɪ] *npl* Wandschmiererein *pl*.
graft [grɑːft] **1** *n* (a) (*Bot*) (Pfropf)reis *nt*; (*Med*) Transplantat *nt*.
   (b) (*inf: corruption*) Mauschelei (*inf*), Schiebung (*inf*).
   (c) (*inf: hard work*) Schufterei (*inf*), Plackerei (*inf*) *f*.
   2 *vt* (*Bot*) (auf)pfropfen (*on auf* +*acc*); (*ein*)pfropfen (*in in* +*acc*); (*Med*) übertragen (*on auf* +*acc*), einpflanzen (*in in* +*acc*); (*fig: incorporate*) einbauen (*onto in* +*acc*); (*artificially*) aufpfropfen (*onto dat*).
   3 *vi* (*inf: work hard*) schuften (*at an* +*dat*) (*inf*), sich (ab)placken (*at mit*) (*inf*).
♦ **graft on** *vt sep see* **graft 2.**
grafter ['grɑːftə[r]] *n* (*inf*) (a) Gauner, Halunke *m*. (b) (*hard worker*) Arbeitstier *nt* (*inf*), Schaffer *m* (*dial*).
graham ['greɪəm] *adj* (*US*) Graham-, Weizenschrot-. ~ **flour** Weizenschrot(mehl) *nt*.
grail [greɪl] *n* Gral *m*.
grain [greɪn] **1** *n* (a) *no pl* Getreide, Korn *nt*.
   (b) (*of corn, salt, sand etc*) Korn *nt*; (*fig*) (*of sense, malice*) Spur *f*; (*of truth also*) Körnchen *nt*; (*of hope also*) Funke *m*. **that's a ~ of comfort** das ist wenigstens ein kleiner Trost.
   (c) (*of leather*) Narben *m*; (*of cloth*) Strich *m*; (*of meat*) Faser *f*; (*of wood, marble*) Maserung *f*; (*of stone*) Korn, Gefüge *nt*; (*Phot*) Korn *nt*. **it goes against the ~ (with sb)** (*fig*) es geht jdm gegen den Strich.
   (d) (*weight*) Gran *nt*.
   2 *vt* *wood* masern; *leather, paper* narben.
grain: ~ **alcohol** *n* Äthylalkohol *m*; ~ **elevator** *n* Getreideheber *m*.

grainy ['greɪnɪ] *adj* (+*er*) (a) (*granular*) *texture* körnig; *surface* gekörnt. (b) *leather* genarbt; *wood* maserig, gemasert.

gram, gramme [græm] *n* Gramm *nt*.

grammar ['græmə'] *n* (a) (*subject, book*) Grammatik, Sprachlehre *f*. your ~ is terrible in Grammatik bist du sehr schlecht; that is bad ~ das ist grammat(ikal)isch falsch. (b) (*inf*) *see* ~ school.

grammar book *n* Grammatik(buch *nt*) *f*, Sprachlehrbuch *nt*.

grammarian [grə'meərɪən] *n* Grammatiker(in *f*) *m*.

grammar school *n* (*Brit*) ≈ Gymnasium *nt*; (*US*) ≈ Mittelschule *f* (*Stufe f zwischen Grundschule und Höherer Schule*).

grammatical [grə'mætɪkəl] *adj* grammat(ikal)isch; *rules, mistakes also* Grammatik-. this is not ~ das ist grammatisch *or* grammatikalisch falsch; to speak ~ English grammat(ikal)isch richtiges Englisch sprechen.

grammatically [grə'mætɪkəlɪ] *adv* grammat(ikal)isch; *write, speak* grammat(ikal)isch richtig.

gramme *n see* gram.

gramophone ['græməfəʊn] *n* (*Brit old*) Grammophon *nt* (*dated*). ~ record Schallplatte *f*.

grampus ['græmpəs] *n* Rundkopf- *or* Rissosdelphin, Grampus (*spec*) *m*. to puff/snort like a ~ (*inf*) wie eine Lokomotive schnaufen (*inf*).

granary ['grænərɪ] *n* Kornkammer *f* (*also fig*), Kornspeicher *m*.

grand [grænd] **1** *adj* (+*er*) (a) (*magnificent, imposing*) großartig (*also pej*); *building, display* prachtvoll; (*lofty*) *idea* großartig, hochfliegend, verstiegen; (*dignified*) *air, person* feierlich, hoheitsvoll, würdevoll; (*posh*) *dinner party, person* vornehm, protzig (*pej*); (*important, great*) *person* groß, bedeutend. to live in ~ style in großem Stil *or* großartig leben; the ~ old man der große Alte; the G~ Old Party (*US Pol: abbr* GOP) die Republikanische Partei; *see* manner.
(b) (*main*) *question, room* groß; *staircase also* Haupt-.
(c) (*complete, final*) *total, result, design* Gesamt-.
(d) (*inf: splendid, fine*) fabelhaft, phantastisch (*inf*). to have a ~ time sich glänzend amüsieren.
(e) (*in titles*) Groß-. ~ master Großmeister *m*.

2 *n* (a) (*sl*) ≈ Riese *m* (*inf*) (*1000 Dollar/Pfund*). 50 ~ 50 Riesen (*inf*).
(b) (*piano*) Flügel *m*.

grand: G~ Canary *n* Gran Canaria *nt*; G~ Canyon *n* Grand Canyon *m*; ~child *n* Enkel(kind *nt*) *m*; ~(d)ad *n* (*inf*) Opa (*inf*) *m*; ~daughter *n* Enkelin *f*.

grandee [græn'di:] *n* (*of Spain*) Grande *m*; (*fig*) Fürst *m* (*inf*). the local ~s die lokalen Honoratioren *pl* (*hum inf*).

grandeur ['grændjə'] *n* (*of scenery, music also*) Größe *f*; (*of scenery, music also*) Erhabenheit *f*; (*of manner also*) Würde, Vornehmheit *f*; (*of position, event also*) Glanz *m*.

grand: ~father *n* Großvater *m*; ~father clock *n* Standuhr *f*; ~fatherly *adj* großväterlich; ~ finale *n* großes Finale.

grandiloquence [græn'dɪləkwəns] *n* (*of speech, style*) Schwülstigkeit *f*; (*of person*) gewählte *or* geschraube Ausdrucksweise.

grandiloquent *adj*, ~ly *adv* [græn'dɪləkwənt, -lɪ] hochtrabend.

grandiose ['grændɪəʊz] *adj* (*impressive*) *house, idea, speech* grandios (*also pej*), großartig; (*pej: pompous*) *person, style* schwülstig, bombastisch (*inf*); *idea* grandios, hochfliegend.

grandiosely [grændɪəʊzlɪ] *adv see adj*.

grand: ~ jury *n* (*US Jur*) Großes Geschworenengericht; ~ larceny *n* schwerer Diebstahl.

grandly ['grændlɪ] *adv* großartig; *decorated, built, situated* prachtvoll; (*with dignity*) feierlich, hoheitsvoll, würdevoll; (*in style*) vornehm. he had been thinking ~ of ... er hatte die großartige *or* hochfliegende Idee, zu ...

grand: ~ma *n* (*inf*) Oma (*inf*), Omi (*inf*) *f*; ~mother *n* Großmutter *f*; ~motherly *adj* großmütterlich; G~ National *n* Grand National *nt* (*bedeutendes Pferderennen in GB*).

grandness ['grændnɪs] *n see adj* (a) Großartigkeit *f*; Pracht *f*; Verstiegenheit *f*; Feierlichkeit, Würde *f*; Vornehmheit, Protzigkeit (*pej*) *f*; Größe, Bedeutung *f*.

grand: ~ opera *n* große Oper; ~pa *n* (*inf*) Opa (*inf*), Opi (*inf*) *m*; ~parent *n* Großelternteil *m* (*form*), Großvater *m*/-mutter *f*; ~parents *npl* Großeltern *pl*; ~ piano *n* Flügel *m*; G~ Prix *n* Grand Prix *m*; ~ slam *n* Großschlemm *m*; ~son *n* Enkel(sohn) *m*; ~stand *n* Haupttribüne *f*; a ~stand finish eine Entscheidung auf den letzten Metern; to have a ~stand view of sth (direkten) Blick auf etw (*acc*) haben; ~ tour *n* (*old*) Kavalierstour *f* (*old*).

grange [greɪndʒ] *n* Bauernhof *m*, (kleiner) Gutshof.

granite ['grænɪt] *n* Granit *m*.

granny, grannie ['grænɪ] *n* (a) (*inf*) Oma (*inf*), Omi (*inf*) *f*. (b) (*also* ~ knot) Altweiberknoten *m*.

grant [grɑ:nt] **1** *vt* (a) gewähren (*sb* jdm); *privilege also* zugestehen (*sb* jdm); *period of grace, prayer* erhören; *honour* erweisen (*sb* jdm); *permission* erteilen (*sb* jdm); *request* stattgeben (+*dat*) (*form*); *land, pension* zusprechen, bewilligen (*sb* jdm); *wish (give)* gewähren, freistellen (*sb* jdm); (*fulfil*) erfüllen. I beg your pardon — ~ed ich bitte (vielmals) um Entschuldigung — sie sei dir gewährt (*hum, form*).
(b) (*admit, agree*) zugeben, zugestehen. it must be ~ed that ... man muß zugeben, daß ...; ~ing *or* ~ed that this is true ... angenommen, das ist wahr ...; I ~ you that da gebe ich dir recht, das gebe ich zu; to take sb/sb's love/one's wealth for ~ed jdn/jds Liebe/seinen Reichtum als selbstverständlich hinnehmen; to take it for ~ed that ... es selbstverständlich finden *or* als selbstverständlich betrachten, daß ...; you take too much for ~ed für dich ist (zu) vieles (einfach) selbstverständlich.
2 *n* (*of money*) Subvention *f*; (*for studying etc*) Stipendium *nt*.

grant: ~-aided *adj* *student* gefördert; *theatre, school, programme* subventioniert; ~-in-aid *n* Zuschuß *m*, Beihilfe *f*.

granular ['grænjʊlə'] *adj* körnig, gekörnt, granular (*spec*).

---

leather genarbt, narbig. if the sugar becomes ~ wenn der Zucker auskristallisiert.

granulated sugar ['grænjʊleɪtɪd'ʃʊgə'] *n* Zuckerraffinade *f*.

granule ['grænju:l] *n* Körnchen *nt*.

grape [greɪp] *n* (Wein)traube, Weinbeere *f*. a pound of ~s ein Pfund (Wein)trauben; a bunch of ~s eine (ganze)Weintraube; the juice of the ~ (*liter*) der Rebensaft (*liter*).

grape: ~fruit *n* Grapefruit, Pampelmuse *f*; ~ harvest *n* Weinlese *f*; ~ hyacinth *n* Traubenhyazinthe *f*; ~ juice *n* Traubensaft *m*; ~-shot *n* (*Hist*) Kartätsche *f*; ~-sugar *n* Traubenzucker *m*; ~vine *n* Weinstock *m*; (*inf*) Nachrichtendienst *m* (*inf*). I heard it on the ~vine es ist mir zu Ohren gekommen.

graph [grɑ:f] *n* Diagramm, Schaubild *nt*; (*Math: of a function*) Graph *m*, Schaubild *nt*. ~ paper Millimeterpapier *nt*.

grapheme ['græfi:m] *n* Graphem *nt*.

graphic ['græfɪk] *adj* (a) grafisch, graphisch. ~ arts Grafik, Graphik *f*. (b) (*vivid*) *description* plastisch, anschaulich.

graphically ['græfɪkəlɪ] *adv see adj*.

graphics ['græfɪks] *n* (a) *sing* (*subject*) Zeichnen *nt*, zeichnerische *or* graphische Darstellung. (b) *pl* (*drawings*) Zeichnungen, (graphische) Darstellungen *pl*.

graphite ['græfaɪt] *n* Graphit *m*.

graphologist [græ'fɒlədʒɪst] *n* Graphologe *m*, Graphologin *f*.

graphology [græ'fɒlədʒɪ] *n* Graphologie, Handschriftendeutung *f*.

-graphy [-grəfɪ] *n suf* -graphie *f*.

grapnel ['græpnəl] *n* (a) (*anchor*) (Dregg)anker, Draggen (*spec*) *m*. (b) *see* grappling iron.

grapple ['græpl] **1** *n see* grappling iron.
2 *vi* (*lit*) ringen, kämpfen. to ~ with a problem/situation sich mit einem Problem/einer Situation herumschlagen; the wrestlers ~d with each other die Ringer hielten sich in enger Umklammerung.
3 *vt* festhaken; *enemy boat* die Enterhaken verwenden bei. the boats were ~d together die Boote waren durch Haken verbunden.

grappling ['græplɪŋ] *n* (*Sport inf*) Ringen *nt*.

grappling iron *n* Haken, Greifer *m*; (*Naut*) Enterhaken *m*.

grasp [grɑ:sp] **1** *n* (a) (*hold*) Griff *m*. he held my arm in a strong ~ er hielt meinen Arm mit festem Griff; just when safety/fame was within his ~ gerade als Sicherheit/Ruhm greifbar nahe war *or* in greifbare Nähe gerückt war.
(b) (*fig: understanding*) Verständnis *nt*. to have a good ~ of sth etw gut beherrschen; her ~ of the language/subject is not very good sie beherrscht die Sprache/das Gebiet nicht sehr gut; it is beyond/within his ~ das geht über seinen Verstand/das kann er verstehen *or* begreifen.
2 *vt* (a) (*catch hold of*) ergreifen, greifen nach; (*hold tightly*) festhalten. he ~ed the bundle in his arms er hielt das Bündel in den Armen; to ~ a chance/sb's hand eine Gelegenheit ergreifen/nach jds Hand greifen.
(b) (*fig: understand*) begreifen, erfassen.
3 *vi* to ~ at sth (*lit*) nach etw greifen; (*fig*) sich auf etw (*acc*) stürzen; to ~ at an excuse/an opportunity eine Entschuldigung begierig aufgreifen/eine Gelegenheit beim Schopfe packen.

grasping ['grɑ:spɪŋ] *adj* (*fig*) habgierig.

grass [grɑ:s] **1** *n* (a) (*plant*) Gras *nt*. wheat is a ~ der Weizen gehört zu den Gräsern; blade of ~ Grashalm *m*; to go to ~ verwildern, von Gras überwuchert werden; to let the ~ grow under one's feet etwas/die Sache auf die lange Bank schieben; you could almost hear the ~ growing man konnte fast das Gras wachsen hören; the ~ is always greener on the other side (*Prov*) auf des Nachbars Feld steht das Korn immer besser (*Prov*), die Kirschen in Nachbars Garten ... (*Prov*).
(b) *no pl* (*lawn*) Rasen *m*; (*pasture*) Weide(land *nt*) *f*. to play on ~ (*Sport*) auf (dem) Rasen spielen; the cattle are out at ~ das Vieh ist auf der Weide; to put *or* turn out to ~ cattle auf die Weide führen *or* treiben; *old horses* das Gnadenbrot geben (+*dat*); (*inf*) *employee* aufs Abstellgleis schieben (*inf*).
(c) (*sl: marijuana*) Gras *nt* (*sl*).
(d) (*Brit sl: informer*) Spitzel, Singvogel (*sl*) *m*.
2 *vt* (*also* ~ over) *ground* mit Gras bepflanzen.
3 *vi* (*Brit sl*) singen (*sl*) (*to* bei). to ~ on sb jdn verpfeifen (*inf*).

grass: ~-green *adj* grasgrün; ~hopper *n* Heuschrecke *f*, Grashüpfer *m* (*inf*); ~land *n* Grasland *nt*; ~-roots 1 *npl* Volk *nt*; (*of a party*) Basis *f*, Fußvolk *nt* (*hum inf*); 2 *adj attr* des kleinen Mannes, an der Basis; at ~-roots level an der Basis; a ~-roots movement to block planning permission eine Bürgerinitiative zur Verhinderung der Baugenehmigung; ~ seed *n* Grassamen *m*; ~ skirt *n* Bastrock *m*; ~ snake *n* Ringelnatter *f*; ~ widow *n* Strohwitwe *f*; (*US*) (*divorced*) geschiedene Frau; (*separated*) (von ihrem Mann) getrennt lebende Frau; ~ widower *n* Strohwitwer *m*; (*US*) (*divorced*) geschiedener Mann; (*separated*) (von seiner Frau) getrennt lebender Mann.

grassy ['grɑ:sɪ] *adj* (+*er*) grasig; *slope also* Gras-.

grate[1] [greɪt] *n* (*grid*) Gitter *nt*; (*in fire*) (Feuer)rost *m*; (*fireplace*) Kamin *m*.

grate[2] **1** *vt* (a) (*Cook*) reiben; *vegetables also* raspeln.
(b) (*bottom of car, boat etc: scrape*) streifen; (*person: make a grating noise with*) kratzen mit; *chalk also* quietschen mit; one's teeth knirschen mit.
2 *vi* (*scrape*) streifen (*against* acc); (*make a noise*) kratzen; (*chalk also, rusty door*) quietschen; (*feet on gravel*) knirschen; (*fig*) weh tun (*on sb* jdm), krank machen (*on sb* jdn). to ~ on sb's nerves/ears jdm auf die Nerven gehen, jds Nerven/Ohren angreifen.

grateful ['greɪtfʊl] *adj* (a) dankbar (*to sb* jdm). with ~ thanks mit tiefer *or* aufrichtiger Dankbarkeit. (b) (*liter: causing gratitude*) wohltuend, willkommen.

gratefully ['greɪtfəlɪ] *adv* dankbar.

grater ['greɪtə'] *n* Reibe *f*; (*for vegetable also*) Raspel *f*.

gratification [ˌgrætɪfɪ'keɪʃən] n (a) (pleasure) Genugtuung f. it is a source of great ~ to me ich empfinde große Genugtuung darüber. (b) (satisfying: of desires etc) Befriedigung f.

gratify ['grætɪfaɪ] vt (a) (give pleasure) erfreuen. to be gratified at or by or with sth über etw (acc) hoch erfreut sein; I was gratified to hear that ... ich habe mit Genugtuung gehört, daß ... (b) (satisfy) befriedigen, zufriedenstellen.

gratifying ['grætɪfaɪɪŋ] adj (sehr) erfreulich. it is ~ to learn that ... es ist erfreulich zu erfahren, daß ...

gratifyingly ['grætɪfaɪɪŋlɪ] adv erfreulich. he was ~ pleased es war erfreulich zu sehen, wie er sich freute.

grating[1] ['greɪtɪŋ] n Gitter nt.

grating[2] **1** adj kratzend; sound (squeaking) quietschend; (rasping) knirschend; (on nerves) auf die Nerven gehend; voice schrill. **2** n Kratzen nt; (of chalk also, of rusty door) Quietschen nt; (of teeth, feet on gravel) Knirschen nt.

gratis ['grætɪs] adj, adv gratis.

gratitude ['grætɪtjuːd] n Dankbarkeit f (to gegenüber).

gratuitous [grə'tjuːɪtəs] adj überflüssig, unnötig; (unasked-for) unerwünscht.

gratuitously [grə'tjuːɪtəslɪ] adv unnötig. quite ~ ohne ersichtlichen Grund.

gratuity [grə'tjuːɪtɪ] n Gratifikation, (Sonder)zuwendung f; (form: tip) Trinkgeld nt.

grave[1] [greɪv] n (lit, fig) Grab nt. silent as the ~ totenstill; the house was like a ~ es herrschte Totenstille im Haus; to turn in one's ~ sich im Grabe herumdrehen; from beyond the ~ aus dem Jenseits; to be brought to an early ~ einen frühen Tod finden; to rise from the ~ von den Toten auferstehen.

grave[2] adj (+er) (earnest, solemn) ernst; (serious, important) schwer; danger, risk groß; error ernst, gravierend; situation, matter ernst, bedenklich; symptoms bedenklich, ernstzunehmend; news schlimm.

grave[3] [grɑːv] **1** adj ~ accent Accent grave m; (in Greek) Gravis m; e ~, ~ e e Accent grave. **2** n Gravis m.

grave-digger ['greɪvˌdɪgəʳ] n Totengräber m.

gravel ['grævəl] **1** n (a) Kies m; (large chippings) Schotter m. (b) (Med) Nierensand or -grieß m; (in bladder) Harngrieß m. **2** adj attr Kies-. ~ path Kiesweg m; ~ pit Kiesgrube f. **3** vt path, lane mit Kies bestreuen; schottern.

gravelled, (US) **graveled** ['grævəld] adj path Kies-.

gravelly ['grævəlɪ] adj road kiesbedeckt; schotterbedeckt; soil steinig; (fig) voice rauh.

gravely ['greɪvlɪ] adv ernst; be mistaken schwer.

grave mound n Grabhügel m.

graven ['greɪvən] adj (old, liter) gehauen (on, in in +acc). ~ image Götzenbild nt; to be ~ on one's memory sich in jds Gedächtnis (acc) eingegraben haben (geh).

grave: ~ robber n Grabschänder m; ~side n at the ~side am Grabe; a ~side service ein Gottesdienst am Grabe; ~stone n Grabstein m; ~yard n Friedhof m; that ministry is a ~yard of political reputations in diesem Ministerium hat schon mancher sein politisches Ansehen zu Grabe getragen.

graving dock ['greɪvɪŋˌdɒk] n Trockendock nt.

gravitate ['grævɪteɪt] vi (lit) gravitieren (form) (to(wards) zu, auf +acc), angezogen werden (to(wards) von); (fig) hingezogen werden (to(wards) zu), angezogen werden (to(wards) von).

gravitation [ˌgrævɪ'teɪʃən] n (Phys) Gravitation, Schwerkraft f; (fig) Hinneigung f (to zu). the hippies' ~ to San Francisco die Anziehungskraft, die San Francisco auf die Hippies ausübt.

gravitational [ˌgrævɪ'teɪʃənl] adj Gravitations-. ~ field Gravitations- or Schwerefeld nt; ~ force Schwerkraft f; (Space) Andruck m; ~ pull Anziehungskraft f.

gravity ['grævɪtɪ] n (a) (Phys) Schwere, Schwerkraft f. the law of ~ das Gravitationsgesetz; centre of ~ Schwerpunkt m; force of ~ Schwerkraft f; ~ feed Fall- or Schwerkraftspeisung f; specific ~ spezifisches Gewicht. (b) (seriousness) see grave[2] Ernst m; Schwere f; Größe f; Ernst m; Ernst m, Bedenklichkeit f; Bedenklichkeit f. the ~ of the news die schlimmen Nachrichten; to preserve one's ~ ernst bleiben.

gravy ['greɪvɪ] n (a) (Cook) (juice) Fleisch- or Bratensaft m; (sauce) Soße f. ~ boat Sauciere, Soßenschüssel f. (b) (US inf) (perks) Spesen pl; (corrupt money) Schmiergelder pl (inf). to get on the ~ train auch ein Stück vom Kuchen abbekommen (inf).

gray n, adj, vti (esp US) see grey.

graze[1] [greɪz] **1** vi (cattle etc) grasen, weiden. **2** vt meadow, field abgrasen, abweiden; cattle weiden lassen.

graze[2] **1** vt (touch lightly) streifen; (scrape skin off) aufschürfen. to ~ one's knees/oneself sich (dat) die Knie aufschürfen/sich (dat) aufschürfen. **2** vi streifen. the car ~d against/along the wall das Auto hat die Mauer gestreift/ist an der Mauer entlanggestreift. **3** n Abschürfung, Schürfwunde f.

grazier ['greɪzɪəʳ] n (esp Brit) Viehzüchter m.

grazing ['greɪzɪŋ] n Weideland nt. this land offers good ~ dies ist gutes Weideland; ~ land Weideland nt; ~ rights Weiderechte pl.

grease [griːs] **1** n (a) Fett nt; (lubricant also) Schmierfett nt, Schmiere f. (b) (also ~ wool) Schweißwolle f. **2** vt fetten; skin einfetten, einschmieren (inf); (Aut, Tech) schmieren. to ~ back one's hair (inf) die Haare mit Pomade nach hinten frisieren; to ~ sb's palm (inf) jdm etwas zustecken (inf), jdn schmieren (inf); like ~d lightning (inf) wie ein geölter Blitz.

grease: ~gun n Fettspritze or -presse f; ~ mark n Fettfleck m; ~ monkey n (inf) Mechanikerlehrling m; ~paint n (Theat) (Fett)schminke f; ~proof adj fettdicht; ~proof paper Pergamentpapier nt.

greasiness ['griːsɪnɪs] n (a) Fettigkeit f; (of hands etc with car grease) Beschmiertheit, Schmierigkeit f; (slipperiness) Schlüpfrigkeit f. (b) (pej inf: of manner) Schmierigkeit f (pej inf).

greasy ['griːsɪ] adj (+er) (a) fettig; (containing grease) food fett; (smeared with car grease) machinery, axle ölig, schmierig; hands, clothes schmierig, ölbeschmiert; (slippery) road glitschig, schlüpfrig. ~ spoon (US sl) billiges Freßlokal (sl). (b) (fig pej) manner, person schmierig; speech salbungsvoll.

great [greɪt] **1** adj (+er) (a) groß. ~ big (inf) riesig, Mords- (inf); a ~ friend of ours ein guter Freund von uns; of no ~ importance unwichtig; a ~ deal of sehr viel; it annoyed her a ~ deal es hat sie sehr geärgert; a ~ number of, a ~ many eine große Anzahl, sehr viele; at a ~ pace sehr schnell, in or mit schnellem Tempo; he lived to a ~ age er erreichte ein hohes Alter; to be in ~ favour with sb bei jdm hoch angeschrieben sein; ~ good fortune großes Glück; with ~ good humour sehr gut gelaunt; in ~ detail ganz ausführlich; with ~ care ganz vorsichtig; to take a ~ interest in sich sehr interessieren für; she has a ~ heart sie hat ein gutes Herz; ~ with child (old) gesegneten Leibes (old, Bibl).

(b) (in achievement, character, importance) master, writer, statesman groß; mind genial. Frederick/Alexander the G~ Friedrich/Alexander der Große; he sat there thinking ~ thoughts er saß da und hatte geniale Gedanken; one of his ~est plays eines seiner bedeutendsten or größten Stücke; one of the ~ minds of our times einer der großen Geister unserer Zeit; the G~ Powers (Pol) die Großmächte; ~ landowner/industrialist Großgrundbesitzer m/Großindustrielle(r) m; to live in ~ style auf großem Fuß leben; the ~ thing is ... das Wichtigste ist ...; ~ minds think alike (inf) große Geister denken gleich.

(c) (inf: splendid, excellent) prima (inf), Klasse (inf), Spitze (sl). to be ~ at football/at singing/on jazz ein großer Fußballspieler/Sänger/Jazzkenner sein; he's a ~ one for criticizing others im Kritisieren anderer ist er (ganz) groß; G~ Scott! (old) großer Gott! (dated), lieber Himmel!

2 n (a) usu pl (~ person) Größe f.

(b) (Brit Univ) G~s ≃ Klassische Philologie.

great: ~-aunt n Großtante f; G~ Barrier Reef n Großes Barriereriff; G~ Bear n Großer Bär; G~ Britain n Großbritannien nt; ~coat n Überzieher, Paletot m; G~ Dane n Deutsche Dogge; G~ Divide n Rocky Mountains pl; (fig) Schwelle f des Todes (liter).

greater ['greɪtəʳ] adj, comp of great größer. to pay ~ attention besser aufpassen; of ~ importance is ... noch wichtiger ist ...; one of the ~ painters einer der bedeutenderen Maler; ~ and ~ immer größer; G~ London Groß-London nt.

greatest ['greɪtɪst] adj, superl of great größte(r, s). with the ~ (of) pleasure mit dem größten Vergnügen; he's the ~ (inf) er ist der Größte; it's the ~ (inf) das ist das Größte (sl), das ist einsame Klasse (sl).

great: ~-grandchild n Urenkel(kind nt) m; ~-grandparents npl Urgroßeltern pl; ~-great-grandchild n Ururenkel(kind nt) m; ~-great-grandparents npl Ururgroßeltern pl; ~-hearted adj (brave) beherzt; (generous) hochherzig; the G~ Lakes npl die Großen Seen pl.

greatly ['greɪtlɪ] adv außerordentlich, sehr; admired also stark; annoyed also höchst; improved bedeutend; superior bei weitem. it is ~ to be feared es ist stark zu befürchten.

great-nephew ['greɪtˌnefjuː] n Großneffe m.

greatness ['greɪtnɪs] n Größe f; (of size, height, degree etc also) Ausmaß nt; (importance also) Bedeutung f. ~ of heart Hochherzigkeit, Großmut f; ~ of mind Geistesgröße f.

great: ~ tit n Kohlmeise f; ~-uncle n Großonkel m; the G~ War n der erste Weltkrieg.

grebe [griːb] n (See)taucher m.

Grecian ['griːʃən] adj griechisch.

Greco- [grekəʊ-] pref Gräko-, gräko-.

Greece [griːs] n Griechenland nt.

greed [griːd] n Gier f (for nach +dat); (for material wealth also) Habsucht, Habgier f; (gluttony) Gefräßigkeit f. ~ for money/power Geldgier f/Machtgier f; the look of ~ in his eyes der gierige Blick in seinen Augen.

greedily ['griːdɪlɪ] adv gierig.

greediness ['griːdɪnɪs] n Gierigkeit f; (gluttony) Gefräßigkeit f.

greedy ['griːdɪ] adj (+er) gierig (for auf +acc, nach); (for material wealth also) habgierig; (gluttonous) gefräßig. ~ for power/money machtgierig/geldgierig; to be ~ for praise/love nach Lob/Liebe gieren; don't be so ~! sei nicht so unbescheiden.

Greek [griːk] **1** adj griechisch. ~ cross griechisches Kreuz; ~ Orthodox Church griechisch-orthodoxe Kirche.

2 n (a) Grieche m, Griechin f.

(b) (language) Griechisch nt. it's all ~ to me (inf) das ist Böhmisch für mich (inf).

green [griːn] **1** adj (+er) (a) (in colour) grün. ~ beans/peas/salad/vegetables grüne Bohnen pl/Erbsen pl/grüner Salat/Grüngemüse nt; to turn ~ (lit) grün werden; (fig: person) (ganz) grün im Gesicht werden; (with envy) blaß or grün or gelb vor Neid werden.

(b) (unripe) fruit, bacon, wood grün; meat nicht abgehangen; cheese jung, unreif. ~ corn frische Maiskolben pl.

(c) (fig) (inexperienced) grün; (gullible) naiv, dumm. I'm not as ~ as I look (inf) ich bin nicht so dumm, wie ich aussehe.

(d) (new, fresh) memory frisch.

2 n (a) (colour) Grün nt. dressed in ~ grün gekleidet; decorated in ~s and blues ganz in Grün und Blau gehalten.

(b) (piece of land) Rasen m, Grünfläche f; (Sport) Rasen, Platz m; (village ~) (Dorf)wiese f, Anger m (old).

(c) ~s pl (Cook) Grüngemüse nt; (US: greenery) Grün nt; (foliage) grüne Zweige pl.

green: ~back n (US sl) Lappen (sl), Geldschein m; ~ belt n Grüngürtel m.

greenery ['griːnərɪ] n Grün nt; (foliage) grünes Laub, grüne Zweige pl.

green: ~-eyed adj (lit) grünäugig; (fig) scheel(äugig), mißgünstig; the ~-eyed monster (fig) der blasse Neid; ~finch n Grünfink m; ~ fingers npl gärtnerisches Geschick; to have ~ fingers eine Hand für Pflanzen haben, einen grünen Finger haben (inf); ~fly n Blattlaus f; ~gage n Reneklode, Reineclaude f; ~grocer n (esp Brit) (Obst- und) Gemüsehändler m; at the ~grocer's (shop) im Gemüseladen; ~grocery n (esp Brit) (shop) Obst- und Gemüsehandlung f; (trade) Obst- und Gemüsehandel m; (articles) Obst und Gemüse nt; ~horn n (inf) (inexperienced) Grünhorn nt; (gullible) Einfaltspinsel m; ~house n Gewächshaus nt.

greenish ['griːnɪʃ] adj grünlich.

Greenland ['griːnlənd] n Grönland nt.

Greenlander ['griːnləndər] n Grönländer(in f) m.

green light n grünes Licht. to give sb the ~ jdm grünes Licht or freie Fahrt geben.

greenness ['griːnnɪs] n see adj (a) Grün nt. (b) Grünheit f; Unabgehangenheit f; Unreife f. (c) Grünheit f; Naivität, Dummheit f. (d) Frische f.

green: ~ pepper n (grüne) Paprikaschote; ~-room n (Theat) Garderobe f; ~stick fracture n Grünholzbruch m; ~ tea n grüner Tee; ~ thumb n (US) see ~ fingers.

Greenwich (Mean) Time ['grenɪdʒ'miːn,taɪm] n Greenwicher Zeit, Mittlere Zeit Greenwich (form).

greenwood ['griːnwʊd] n grüner Wald.

greet [griːt] vt (welcome) begrüßen; (receive, meet) empfangen; (say hallo to) grüßen; news, decision aufnehmen. a terrible sight ~ed his eyes/him ihm bot sich ein fürchterlicher Anblick; to ~ sb's ears an jds Ohr (acc) dringen.

greeting ['griːtɪŋ] n Gruß m; (act) (welcoming) Begrüßung f; (receiving, meeting) Empfang m. we had a friendly ~ from the crowd die Menge bereitete uns einen freundlichen Empfang; ~s Grüße pl; (congratulations also) Glückwünsche pl; ~s card/ telegram Grußkarte f/-telegramm nt, Glückwunschkarte f/ -telegramm nt; to send ~s to sb Grüße an jdn senden; (through sb else) jdn grüßen lassen; please give my ~s to them bitte grüße sie von mir.

gregarious [grɪ'geərɪəs] adj animal, instinct Herden-; person gesellig.

Gregorian [grɪ'gɔːrɪən] adj gregorianisch. ~ calendar/chant Gregorianischer Kalender/Choral or Gesang.

gremlin ['gremlɪn] n (hum) böser Geist, Maschinenteufel m (hum).

grenade [grɪ'neɪd] n Granate f.

grenadier [,grenə'dɪər] n Grenadier m.

grenadine [,grenə'diːn] n Grenadine f.

grew [gruː] pret of grow.

grey, (esp US) gray [greɪ] 1 adj (+er) (lit, fig) grau; day, outlook, prospect etc also trüb; (fig) jdn. to go or turn ~ grau werden, ergrauen (geh); little ~ cells (inf) kleine graue Zellen pl (inf); a ~ area (fig) eine Grauzone.

2 n (colour) Grau nt; (horse) Grauschimmel m.

3 vt grau werden lassen; hair, person also ergrauen lassen (geh).

4 vi grau werden; (hair, person also) ergrauen (geh). his ~ing hair sein angegrautes Haar.

grey: ~beard n Graubart m; G~ Friar n Franziskanermönch m; ~-haired adj grauhaarig; ~hound n Windhund m, Windspiel nt; ~hound racing n Windhundrennen nt.

greyish ['greɪɪʃ] adj gräulich.

grey: ~lag (goose) n Graugans, Wildgans f; ~ matter n (Med, inf) graue Masse or Substanz f.

greyness ['greɪnɪs] n (lit) Grau nt; (fig) Trübheit f; (of life) Öde f.

grey: ~parrot n Graupapagei m; ~ squirrel n Grauhörnchen nt.

grid [grɪd] n (a) (grating) Gitter nt; (in fireplace, on barbecue) Rost m. ~ system (in road-building) Rechteckschema nt.

(b) (on map) Gitter, Netz nt.

(c) (electricity, gas network) Verteilernetz nt. the (national) ~ (Elec) das Überland(leitungs)netz.

(d) (Motor-racing: starting ~) Start(platz) m; (US Ftbl) Spielfeld nt. they're on the ~ sie sind am Start or auf den Startplätzen.

(e) (Elec: electrode) Gitter nt.

(f) (Theat) Schnürboden m.

griddle ['grɪdl] n (Cook) gußeiserne Platte zum Pfannkuchenbacken. ~-cake kleiner Pfannkuchen.

gridiron ['grɪd,aɪən] n (a) (Cook) (Brat)rost m. (b) (US Ftbl) Spielfeld nt.

grief [griːf] n Leid nt, Kummer, Gram (geh) m; (because of loss) große Trauer, Schmerz, Gram (geh) m. to be a ~ to sb jdn zutiefst betrüben; (death, loss also) jdm großen Schmerz bereiten; (failure, sb's behaviour also) jdm großen Kummer bereiten; to come to ~ Schaden erleiden; (be hurt, damaged) zu Schaden kommen; (fail) scheitern.

grief-stricken ['griːf,strɪkən] adj untröstlich, tieftraurig; look, voice schmerzerfüllt, grambeugt (geh).

grievance ['griːvəns] n Klage f; (resentment) Groll m. ~ procedure Beschwerdeweg m; I've no ~s against him (no cause for complaint) ich habe an ihm nichts auszusetzen; (no resentment) ich nehme ihm nichts übel; to harbour a ~ against sb for sth jdm etw übelnehmen; to air one's ~s seine Beschwerden vorbringen, sich offen beschweren, sich beklagen.

grieve [griːv] 1 vt Kummer bereiten (+dat), betrüben. it ~s me to see that ... ich sehe mit Schmerz or Kummer, daß ...

2 vi sich grämen (geh), trauern (at, about über +acc). to ~ for sb/sth um jdn/etw trauern; to ~ for sb (sympathize with) zutiefst mit jdm mitfühlen, jds Schmerz teilen; my heart ~s for you mir blutet das Herz; to ~ over sb/sth sich über jdn/etw grämen (geh), über jdn/etw zutiefst bekümmert sein; she sat grieving over his body sie saß trauernd bei seinem Leichnam.

grievous ['griːvəs] adj (severe) injury, blow, crime schwer; fault, error also schwerwiegend; wrong also groß; (distressing) news betrüblich, schmerzlich; pain groß, schlimm; (sorrowful) cry etc schmerzlich, schmerzerfüllt. ~ bodily harm (Jur) schwere Körperverletzung.

grievously ['griːvəslɪ] adv schwer; distressed also ernstlich; cry schmerzlich. he was ~ at fault in ... er lud eine schwere Schuld auf sich (acc), als ...; he was ~ unaware that ... er war sich (dat) betrüblicherweise überhaupt nicht bewußt, daß ...

griffin ['grɪfɪn], **griffon**, **gryphon** n (Myth) (Vogel) Greif m.

griffon ['grɪfən] n (a) (bird) (Gänse)geier m. (b) (dog) Griffon, Affenpinscher m. (c) (Myth) see griffin.

grift [grɪft] (US sl) 1 n (money) ergaunertes or erschwindeltes Geld. to make money on the ~ auf die krumme Toure zu Geld kommen (sl). to make a small fortune out of ~ing er hat sich (dat) auf die krumme Toure ein kleines Vermögen verschafft (sl).

grifter ['grɪftər] n (US sl: swindler) Gauner, Schwindler m.

grig [grɪg] n: merry as a ~ lustig und fidel.

grill [grɪl] 1 n (a) (Cook) (on cooker etc) Grill m; (gridiron also) (Brat)rost m; (food) Grillgericht nt, Grillade f; (restaurant) Grill(room) m.

(b) see grille.

2 vt (a) (Cook) grillen.

(b) (inf: interrogate) in die Zange nehmen (inf). to ~ sb about sth jdn über etw (acc) ausquetschen (inf) or ins Verhör nehmen.

3 vi (a) (food) auf dem Grill liegen, gegrillt werden.

(b) (inf: in sun) schmoren (inf). the ~ing heat of the sun die sengende Sonne(nhitze).

grille [grɪl] n Gitter nt; (on window) Fenstergitter nt; (to speak through) Sprechgitter nt; (Aut) Kühlergrill m.

grilling ['grɪlɪŋ] n strenges Verhör. to give sb a ~/a ~ about sth jdn in die Zange or die Kur nehmen (inf)/jdn über etw (acc) ausquetschen (inf) or ins Verhör nehmen.

grillroom ['grɪlruːm] n Grillroom m.

grilse [grɪls] n junger Lachs.

grim [grɪm] adj (+er) (cruel, fierce) battle, struggle verbissen, erbittert, unerbittlich; warrior erbarmungslos, ingrimmig (old); (stern) face, smile, silence grimmig; master, teacher unerbittlich, hart; (fig) landscape, town, prospects trostlos; news, time, tale, task, job grauenhaft, grausig (inf); winter hart; weather erbarmungslos; times hart, schwer; determination, silence eisern; industriousness verbissen; necessity, truth hart, bitter. a ~ sense of humour Galgenhumor m, ein grimmiger Humor; to look ~ (person) ein grimmiges Gesicht machen; (things, prospects) schlimm or trostlos aussehen; one of the ~mest aspects of the present situation einer der schlimmsten Aspekte der momentanen Lage; to hold on (to sth) like ~ death sich verbissen (an etw dat) festhalten, sich verzweifelt (an etw dat) festklammern.

(b) (inf: unpleasant) grausig (inf), gräßlich.

grimace ['grɪməs] 1 n Grimasse f. to make a ~ eine Grimasse machen or schneiden; (with disgust, pain also) das Gesicht verziehen. 2 vi Grimassen machen or schneiden; (with disgust, pain etc also) das Gesicht verziehen.

grime [graɪm] n Ruß m.

grimly ['grɪmlɪ] adv fight, struggle, hold on verbissen; (sternly) mit grimmiger Miene; smile, silent grimmig; bleak, barren trostlos; depressing grauenhaft. ~ determined verbissen.

grimness ['grɪmnɪs] n see adj (a) Verbissenheit, Erbittertheit, Unerbittlichkeit f; Erbarmungslosigkeit f; Grimmigkeit f; Unerbittlichkeit, Härte f; Trostlosigkeit f; Grauenhaftigkeit f; Härte f; Erbarmungslosigkeit f; Härte f.

grimy ['graɪmɪ] adj (+er) rußig, schmutzig; buildings also verrußt.

grin [grɪn] 1 n see vi Lächeln, Strahlen nt; Grinsen nt.

2 vi (with pleasure) lächeln, strahlen; (in scorn, stupidly, cheekily) grinsen. to ~ and bear it gute Miene zum bösen Spiel machen; (tolerate pain) die Zähne zusammenbeißen; to ~ at sb jdn anlächeln/angrinsen; to ~ from ear to ear über das ganze Gesicht strahlen; to ~ like a Cheshire cat wie ein Honigkuchenpferd grinsen or strahlen.

grind [graɪnd] (vb: pret, ptp ground) 1 vt (a) (crush) zerkleinern, zermahlen; corn, coffee, pepper, flour mahlen; (in mortar) zerstoßen. to ~ sth to a powder etw fein zermahlen/zerstoßen; to ~ one's teeth mit den Zähnen knirschen.

(b) (polish, sharpen) gem, lens schleifen; knife also wetzen.

(c) (turn) handle, barrel organ drehen. to ~ one's cigarette butt/heel into the earth den Zigarettenstummel in die Erde treten/den Absatz in die Erde bohren.

(d) ground down by poverty von Armut (nieder)gedrückt; the tyrant ground the people into the dust der Tyrann hat das Volk zu Tode geschunden; to ~ the faces of the poor (liter) die Armen aussaugen (geh).

2 vi (a) (mill) mahlen; (brakes, teeth, gears) knirschen. the metal ground against the stone das Metall knirschte auf dem Stein; the ship ground against the rocks das Schiff lief knirschend auf die Felsen auf; to ~ to a halt or standstill (lit) quietschend zum Stehen kommen; (fig) stocken; (production etc) zum Erliegen kommen; (negotiations) sich festfahren; the process ~s slowly on das Verfahren schleppt sich hin.

(b) (inf: study) büffeln (inf). to ~ away at Latin Latein büffeln (inf).

3 *n* **(a)** *(sound)* Knirschen *nt; see* bump.
(b) *(fig inf: drudgery)* Schufterei *(inf) f; (US inf: swot)*
Streber(in *f*) *m (inf).* **the daily ~** der tägliche Trott; **it's a bit of a
~** das ist ganz schön mühsam *(inf).*
♦**grind down** *vt sep (lit) (mill) pepper etc* zermahlen; *(sea)
rocks* abschleifen; *(fig) people, resistance* zermürben.
♦**grind on** *vi (enemy, invasion)* unaufhaltsam vorrücken; *(fig:
bureaucracy etc)* unaufhaltsam sein. **to ~ ~ towards sth** einer
Sache *(dat)* unaufhaltsam entgegengehen.
♦**grind out** *vt sep article, essay* sich *(dat)* abquälen; *propaganda* ausspucken *(inf); tune* orgeln *(inf).*
grinder ['graɪndə'] *n* **(a)** *(meat~)* Fleischwolf *m; (coffee~)*
Kaffeemühle *f; (for sharpening)* Schleifmaschine *f; (stone)*
Schleifstein *m.* **(b)** *(person)* Messer-/Glasschleifer(in *f*) *m; see*
organ-grinder. **(c)** *(tooth)* Backenzahn *m; (of animals also)*
Mahlzahn *m.*
grinding ['graɪndɪŋ] *adj* knirschend; *poverty* drückend. **to come
to a ~** halt quietschend zum Stehen kommen.
grinding wheel *n* Schleifscheibe *f,* Schleifstein *m.*
grindstone ['graɪndstəʊn] *n:* **to keep one's/sb's nose to the ~**
hart arbeiten/jdn hart arbeiten lassen; **back to the ~** wieder in
die Tretmühle *(hum).*
gringo ['grɪŋgəʊ] *n (esp US)* Gringo *m.*
grip [grɪp] **1** *n* **(a)** *Griff m; (on rope also, on road)* Halt *m.* **to get a
~ on the road/rope** auf der Straße/am Seil Halt finden; **to get a
~ on oneself** *(inf)* sich zusammenreißen; **he had a good ~
on himself** er hatte sich gut im Griff *or* in der Gewalt; **to have a
good ~ of a subject/on an audience** ein Thema/ein Publikum
im Griff haben; **to let go** *or* **release one's ~** loslassen *(on sth
etw);* **to lose one's ~** *(lit)* den Halt verlieren; *(fig)* nachlassen;
the chairman is losing his ~ dem Vorsitzenden entgleiten die
Zügel; **I must be losing my ~** mit mir geht's bergab; **to lose
one's ~ on reality** den Bezug zur Wirklichkeit verlieren; **to lose
one's ~ on a situation** eine Situation nicht mehr im Griff haben;
to lose one's ~ on an audience ein Publikum aus dem Griff verlieren; **to have sb in one's ~** jdn in seiner Gewalt haben; **to be in
the ~ of rage/terror** *etc* von Wut/Angst *etc* erfaßt sein; **the
country is in the ~ of a general strike** das Land ist von einem
Generalstreik lahmgelegt; **the country is in the ~ of winter** der
Winter hat im Land seinen Einzug gehalten; **to get** *or* **come to
~s with sth** mit etw klarkommen *(inf),* etw in den Griff
bekommen; **to get** *or* **come to ~s with sb** jdm zu Leibe rücken,
zum Angriff gegen jdn übergehen.
(b) *(handle)* Griff *m.*
(c) *(hair~)* Klemmchen *nt.*
(d) *(travelling-bag)* Reisetasche *f.*
2 *vt* packen; *hand also, (fig: fear etc also)* ergreifen; *(film,
story etc also)* fesseln. **the car/tyre ~s the road well** der Wagen
liegt gut auf der Straße/der Reifen greift gut; **fear ~ped his
heart** Furcht ergriff *or* packte ihn.
3 *vi* greifen. **he ~ped at her wrist** er griff nach ihrem Handgelenk.
gripe [graɪp] **1** *n (US inf: annoy)* aufregen, fuchsen *(inf).*
2 *vi (inf: grumble)* meckern *(inf),* nörgeln. **to ~ at sb** jdn
anmeckern *(inf),* jdn anmotzen *(inf).*
3 *n* **(a)** *the* **~s** *pl* Kolik *f,* Bauchschmerzen *pl; ~* **water** Kolik-
mittel *nt.*
(b) *(inf: complaint)* Meckerei *f (inf).* **have you any more ~s?**
sonst hast du nichts zu meckern? *(inf).*
grippe [grɪp] *n (dated US)* Grippe *f.*
gripping ['grɪpɪŋ] *adj story* spannend, packend, fesselnd.
grisly ['grɪzlɪ] *adj (+er)* grausig, gräßlich.
grist [grɪst] *n* **it's all ~ to his/the mill** das kann er/man alles verwerten; *(for complaint)* das ist Wasser auf seine Mühle.
gristle ['grɪsl] *n* Knorpel *m.*
gristly ['grɪslɪ] *adj (+er)* knorpelig.
grit [grɪt] **1** *n* **(a)** *(dust, in eye)* Staub *m; (gravel)* Splitt *m;* feiner
Schotter; *(for roads in winter)* Streugut *nt.* **(b)** *(courage)* Mut,
Mumm *(inf) m.* **(c)** *(US)* **~s** *pl* Grütze *f.* **2** *vt* **(a)** *road etc*
streuen. **(b)** **to ~ one's teeth** die Zähne zusammenbeißen.
gritty ['grɪtɪ] *adj (+er)* **(a)** *Splitt-, Schotter-; path also* mit Splitt
or feinem Schotter bedeckt; *(like grit) coal, sweets* grobkörnig.
~ sandwiches sandige Sandwiches. **(b)** *(inf: brave)* tapfer;
person also mit Mumm *(inf).*
grizzle ['grɪzl] *vi (Brit inf)* quengeln.
grizzled ['grɪzld] *adj* hair ergraut; *person also* grauhaarig.
grizzly ['grɪzlɪ] *n (also ~ bear)* Grisly(bär), Grizzly(bär) *m.*
groan [grəʊn] **1** *n* Stöhnen *nt no pl; (of pain also, of gate, planks
etc)* Ächzen *nt no pl.* **to let out** *or* **give a ~** (auf)stöhnen.
2 *vi* stöhnen *(with vor +dat); (with pain also, gate, planks)*
ächzen *(with vor +dat).* **the table ~ed under** *or* **beneath the
weight** der Tisch ächzte unter der Last; **the country ~ed under**
or **beneath his rule** das Land ächzte unter seiner Herrschaft.
groat [grəʊt] *n (Brit Hist)* Silbermünze *f* im Wert von 4 alten
Pence. **I haven't a ~** ich habe keinen roten Heller.
groats [grəʊts] *npl* Schrot *nt or m; (porridge)* Grütze *f.*
grocer ['grəʊsə'] *n* Lebensmittelhändler, Kaufmann *m.* **at the
~'s** beim Lebensmittelhändler *or* Kaufmann.
grocery ['grəʊsərɪ] *n* **(a)** *(business, shop)* Lebensmittelgeschäft *nt.* **(b)** **groceries** *pl (goods)* Lebensmittel *pl.*
grog [grɒg] *n* Grog *m.*
groggily ['grɒgɪlɪ] *adv (inf)* groggy *(inf); shake one's head,
answer* schwach.
groggy ['grɒgɪ] *adj (+er) (inf)* groggy inv *(inf).*
groin [grɔɪn] *n* **(a)** *(Anat)* Leiste *f.* **to kick sb in the ~** jdn in den
Unterleib *or* die Leistengegend treten. **(b)** *(Archit)* Grat *m.* **(c)**
see groyne.
grommet ['grɒmɪt] *n* Öse *f; (Naut)* Taukranz *m.*
groom [gru:m] **1** *n* **(a)** *(in stables)* Stallbursche, Pferde- *or*
Reitknecht *m.*
(b) *(bride~)* Bräutigam *m.*

2 *vt* **(a)** *horse* striegeln, putzen. **to ~ oneself** *(birds, animals)*
sich putzen; *(people)* sich pflegen; **well/badly ~ed**
gepflegt/ungepflegt.
(b) *(prepare)* **he's being ~ed for the job of chairman/for the
Presidency** er wird als zukünftiger Vorsitzender/Präsi-
dentschaftskandidat aufgebaut; **to ~ sb for stardom** jdn als
Star lancieren; **he is ~ing him as his successor** er zieht sich
(dat) ihn als Nachfolger heran.
grooming ['gru:mɪŋ] *n* ein gepflegtes Äußeres.
groove [gru:v] **1** *n* Rille *f; (in rock also)* Rinne, Furche *f; (in
face)* Furche *f; (fig)* altes Gleis. **to be in the ~** *(dated sl)* in Stimmung sein *(inf);* **his thoughts run in the same old ~s** seine
Gedanken bewegen sich immer auf demselben alten Gleis.
2 *vt* Rillen machen in *(+acc),* rillen; *(water) stone* aushöhlen,
Rinnen *pl or* Furchen *pl* machen in *(+acc); face* furchen.
3 *vi (sl)* einen losmachen *(sl),* sich reinhängen *(sl).*
groover ['gru:və'] *n (sl) (man)* irrer *or* starker Typ *(sl);*
(woman) irre *or* starke Frau *(sl).*
groovy ['gru:vɪ] *adj (+er) (sl)* irr *(sl),* stark *(sl).*
grope [grəʊp] **1** *vi (also ~ around or about)* (herum)tasten *(for
nach); (for words)* suchen *(for nach).* **to be groping in the dark**
im dunkeln tappen; *(try things at random)* vor sich *(acc)* hin
wursteln *(inf);* **groping hands** tastende Hände *pl.*
2 *vt* tasten nach; *(inf) girlfriend* befummeln *(inf).* **to ~ one's
way** sich vorwärtstasten; **to ~ (one's way) in/out** sich hinein-/
hinaustasten; **they are groping their way towards a new theory**
sie machen tastende Versuche, eine neue Theorie zu entwik-
keln.
3 *n (inf)* **to have a ~** fummeln *(inf).*
gropingly ['grəʊpɪŋlɪ] *adv* tastend.
grosgrain ['grəʊgreɪn] *n* grob geripptes Seidentuch.
gross¹ [grəʊs] *n no pl* Gros *nt.*
gross² **1** *adj (+er) (a) (fat) person* dick, fett, plump.
(b) *(coarse, vulgar) person, language, joke, indecency* grob,
derb; *manners, tastes* roh; *food* grob; *eater, appetite* unmäßig.
(c) *(extreme, flagrant) kraß; crime, impertinence*
ungeheuerlich; *error, mistake also, negligence* grob.
(d) *(luxuriant) vegetation* üppig.
(e) *(total)* brutto; *income, weight* Brutto-. **he earns £ 250 ~** er
verdient brutto £ 250, er hat einen Bruttolohn von £ 250; **~
national product** Bruttosozialprodukt *nt;* **~ ton** Bruttoregister-
tonne *f.*
2 *vt* brutto verdienen; *(shop also)* brutto einnehmen.
grossly ['grəʊslɪ] *adv* **(a)** *(coarsely) behave, talk* derb, rüde. **to
eat ~** essen wie ein Schwein. **(b)** *(extremely) indecent, fat,
vulgar* ungeheuer, schrecklich; *exaggerated also* grob.
grossness ['grəʊsnɪs] *n see adj (a-d)* **(a)** Körperfülle, Dicke,
Fettheit *f.* **(b)** Grobheit, Derbheit *f;* Roheit *f;* Grobheit *f;*
Unmäßigkeit *f.* **(c)** Kraßheit *f;* Ungeheuerlichkeit *f; (of negligence)* ungeheures Ausmaß. **(d)** Üppigkeit *f.*
grotesque [grəʊ'tesk] **1** *adj* grotesk. **2** *n* **(a)** *(Art)* Groteske *f;
(figure)* groteske Figur. **(b)** *(Typ)* Groteske *f.*
grotesquely [grəʊ'tesklɪ] *adv see adj.* **~ enough he had ...**
groteskerweise hatte er ...; **he's ~ wrong** er irrt sich so
gewaltig, daß es schon grotesk ist.
grotesqueness [grəʊ'tesknɪs] *n* **the ~ of the shape/this ans-
wer/his appearance** diese groteske Form/Antwort/seine
groteske Erscheinung.
grotto ['grɒtəʊ] *n, pl* **-(e)s** Grotte, Höhle *f.* **fairy ~** Mär-
chenhöhle *f.*
grotty ['grɒtɪ] *adj (+er) (inf)* grausig *(inf); person, pub, town, job
also* mies *(inf).*
grouch [graʊtʃ] **1** *n* **(a)** *(complaint)* Klage *f.* **to have a ~**
(grumble) schimpfen *(about über +acc);* **to have a ~ against sb**
jdm grollen, auf jdn böse sein. **(b)** *(inf: person)* Miesepeter,
Muffel *m (inf).* **2** *vi* schimpfen, meckern *(inf).*
grouchiness ['graʊtʃɪnɪs] *n* schlechte Laune, Miesepetrigkeit
(inf) f.
grouchy ['graʊtʃɪ] *adj (+er)* griesgrämig, miesepetrig *(inf).*
ground¹ [graʊnd] **1** *n* **(a)** *(soil, terrain, fig)* Boden *m.* **snow on
high ~** Schnee in höheren Lagen; **hilly ~** hügeliges Gelände;
how much ~ do you own? wieviel Grund und Boden *or* wieviel
Land besitzen Sie?; **there is common ~ between us** uns verbindet einiges; **they found common ~ in the fact that ...** die
Tatsache, daß ..., verband sie; **to be on dangerous/firm** *or* **sure
~** *(fig)* sich auf gefährlichem Boden bewegen/festen *or*
sicheren Boden unter den Füßen haben; **to meet sb on his own
~** zu jdm kommen; **to be beaten on one's own ~** auf dem
eigenen Gebiet geschlagen werden; **to cut the ~ from under sb**
or **sb's feet** jdm den Boden unter den Füßen wegziehen; **to gain/
lose ~** Boden gewinnen/verlieren; *(disease, rumour)* um sich
greifen/im Schwinden begriffen sein; **to lose ~ to sb/sth**
gegenüber jdm/etw an Boden verlieren; **to give ~ to sb/sth** vor
jdm/etw zurückweichen; **to regain the ~ lost to sb** seine Position jdm gegenüber zurückerobern; **to break new** *or* **fresh ~**
(lit, fig) neue Gebiete erschließen; *(person)* sich auf ein neues
or unbekanntes Gebiet begeben; **to go over the ~** *(fig)* alles
durchgehen; **to cover the/a lot of ~** *(lit)* die Strecke/eine weite
Strecke zurücklegen; *(fig)* das Thema/eine Menge Dinge
behandeln; **that covers the ~** das umreißt das Thema; **to hold** *or*
keep *or* **stand one's ~** *(lit)* nicht von der Stelle weichen; *(fig)*
seinen Mann stehen, sich nicht unterkriegen lassen; **to shift
one's ~** *(fig)* seine Haltung ändern.
(b) *(surface)* Boden *m.* **above/below ~** über/unter der Erde;
(Min) über/unter Tage; *(fig)* unter den Lebenden/unter der
Erde; **to fall to the ~** *(lit)* zu Boden fallen; *(fig: plans)* ins
Wasser fallen, sich zerschlagen; **to sit on the ~** auf der Erde *or*
dem Boden sitzen; **our hopes were dashed to the ~** unsere
Hoffnungen wurden am Boden zerstört; **to burn/raze sth to the
~** etw niederbrennen/etw dem Erdboden gleichmachen; **it
suits me down to the ~** das ist ideal für mich; **to get off the ~**

(*plane etc*) abheben; (*plans, project etc*) sich realisieren; **to go to ~** (*fox*) im Bau verschwinden; (*person*) untertauchen (*inf*); **to run sb/sth to ~** jdn/etw aufstöbern, jdn/etw ausfindig machen; **to run sb/oneself into the ~** (*inf*) jdn/sich selbst fertigmachen (*inf*); **to run a car into the ~** (*inf*) ein Auto schrottreif fahren; **opinion on the ~ is turning against him** die Meinung der Masse wendet sich gegen ihn.

(**c**) (*pitch*) Feld *nt*, Platz *m*; (*parade ~, drill~*) Platz *m*. **recreation ~** Spiel- *or* Sportplatz *m*; **hunting ~s** Jagdgebiete *pl*; **fishing ~s** Fischgründe *pl*.

(**d**) **~s** *pl* (*premises, land*) Gelände *nt*; (*gardens*) Anlagen *pl*; **a house standing in its own ~s** ein von Anlagen umgebenes Haus.

(**e**) **~s** *pl* (*sediment*) Satz *m*; **let the ~s settle** warten Sie, bis sich der Kaffee/die Flüssigkeit *etc* gesetzt hat.

(**f**) (*background*) Grund *m*. **on a blue ~** auf blauem Grund.

(**g**) (*US Elec*) Erde *f*.

(**h**) (*sea-bed*) Grund *m*.

(**i**) (*reason*) Grund *m*. **to have ~(s) for sth** Grund zu etw haben; **to be ~(s) for sth** Grund für *or* zu etw sein; **to give sb ~(s) for sth** jdm Grund zu etw geben; **~(s) for divorce** Scheidungsgrund *m*; **~s for suspicion** Verdachtsmomente *pl*; **on the ~(s) of/that ...** aufgrund (+*gen*), auf Grund von/mit der Begründung, daß ...; **on health ~s** aus gesundheitlichen Gründen.

2 *vt* (**a**) *ship* auflaufen lassen, auf Grund setzen. **to be ~ed** aufgelaufen sein.

(**b**) (*Aviat*) *plane* (*for mechanical reasons*) aus dem Verkehr ziehen; *pilot* sperren, nicht fliegen lassen. **to be ~ed by bad weather/a strike** wegen schlechten Wetters/eines Streiks nicht starten *or* fliegen können.

(**c**) (*US Elec*) erden.

(**d**) (*base*) **to be ~ed on sth** sich auf etw (*acc*) gründen, auf etw (*dat*) basieren.

(**e**) **to ~ sb in a subject** jdm die Grundlagen eines Faches beibringen; **to be well ~ed in English** gute Grundkenntnisse im Englischen haben.

3 *vi* (*Naut*) auflaufen.

ground² **1** *pret, ptp of* **grind**. **2** *adj glass* matt; *coffee* gemahlen. **~ rice** Reismehl *nt*.

ground: **~ attack** *n* Bodenangriff *m*; **~bait** *n* Grundköder *m*; **~ bass** *n* Grundbaß *m*; **~ colour** *n* Untergrund *m*; (*undercoat*) Grundierfarbe *f*; **~ control** *n* (*Aviat*) Bodenkontrolle *f*; **~ cover** *n* (*Hort*) Bodenvegetation *f*; **~ crew** *n* Bodenpersonal *nt*.

grounder ['graʊndə^r] *n* (*US Sport*) Bodenball *m*.

ground: **~ floor** *n* Erdgeschoß *nt*; **to get in on the ~ floor** (*fig*) gleich zu Anfang einsteigen (*inf*); **~ frost** *n* Bodenfrost *m*; **~hog** *n* (*US*) Waldmurmeltier *nt*.

grounding ['graʊndɪŋ] *n* (**a**) (*basic knowledge*) Grundwissen *nt*. **to give sb a ~ in English** jdm die Grundlagen *pl* des Englischen beibringen.

(**b**) (*Aviat*) (*of plane*) Startverbot *nt* (*of* für); (*due to strike, bad weather*) Hinderung *f* am Start; (*of pilot*) Sperren *nt*.

ground: **~keeper** *n* (*US*) *see* **groundsman**; **~less** *adj* grundlos, unbegründet; **~ level** *n* Boden *m*; **below ~ level** unter dem Boden; **~nut** *n* Erdnuß *f*; **~ plan** *n* Grundriß *m*; **~ rent** *n* Grundrente *f*.

groundsel ['graʊnsl] *n* Kreuzkraut *nt*.

groundsheet ['graʊndʃiːt] *n* Zeltboden(plane *f*) *m*.

groundsman ['graʊndzmən] *n, pl* **-men** [-mən] (*esp Brit*) Platzwart *m*.

ground: **~ speed** *n* Bodengeschwindigkeit *f*; **~ staff** *n* Bodenpersonal *nt*; **~ stroke** *n* (*Tennis*) nicht aus der Luft gespielter Ball; **~swell** *n* Dünung *f*; (*fig*) Anschwellen *nt*, Zunahme *f*; **there was a growing ~swell of public opinion against him** die Öffentlichkeit wandte sich zunehmend gegen ihn; **~-to-air missile** *n* Boden-Luft-Rakete *f*; **~-to-~ missile** *n* Boden-Boden-Flugkörper *m*; **~wire** *n* (*US Elec*) Erdleitung *f*; **~work** *n* Vorarbeit *f*; **to do the ~work for sth** die Vorarbeit für etw leisten.

group [gruːp] **1** *n* Gruppe *f*; (*Comm also*) Konzern *m*; (*theatre ~ also*) Ensemble *nt*. **a ~ of people/houses/trees** eine Gruppe Menschen/eine Häusergruppe/eine Baumgruppe.

2 *attr* Gruppen-; *discussion, living, activities* in der Gruppe *or* Gemeinschaft.

3 *vt* gruppieren. **to ~ together** (*in one ~*) zusammentun; (*in several ~s*) in Gruppen einteilen *or* anordnen; **it's wrong to ~ all criminals together** es ist nicht richtig, alle Verbrecher über einen Kamm zu scheren *or* in einen Topf zu werfen (*inf*); **~ the blue ones with the red ones** ordnen Sie die blauen bei den roten ein, tun Sie die blauen mit den roten zusammen; **they ~ed themselves round him** sie stellten sich um ihn (herum) auf, sie gruppierten sich um ihn; **to ~ sth around sth** etw um etw herum anordnen; **the books were ~ed on the shelf according to subject** die Bücher standen nach Sachgruppen geordnet im Regal.

group: **~ captain** *n* (*Aviat*) Oberst *m*; **~ dynamics** *n* (**a**) *pl* (*relationships*) Gruppendynamik *f*; (**b**) *sing* (*subject*) Gruppendynamik *f*.

groupie ['gruːpɪ] *n* Groupie *nt* (*sl*).

grouping ['gruːpɪŋ] *n* Gruppierung *f*; (*group of things also*) Anordnung *f*.

group: **~ insurance** *n* Gruppenversicherung *f*; **~ practice** *n* Gemeinschaftspraxis *f*; **to be in a ~ practice** in einem Ärztekollektiv arbeiten; **~ therapy** *n* Gruppentherapie *f*.

grouse¹ [graʊs] *n, pl* **-** Waldhuhn, Rauhfußhuhn *nt*; (*red ~*) Schottisches Moor(schnee)huhn. **~ shooting** Moorhuhnjagd *f*; *see* **black ~**.

grouse² (*inf*) **1** *n* (*complaint*) Klage *f*. **to have a good ~** sich ausschimpfen (*inf*); **to be full of ~s** dauernd über etw (*acc*) schimpfen *or* meckern (*inf*). **2** *vi* schimpfen, meckern (*inf*) (*about* über +*acc*).

grouser ['graʊsə^r] *n* (*inf*) Meckerfritze *m*/-liese *f* (*inf*).

grout [graʊt] **1** *vt tiles* verfugen, verkitten; *bricks* mit Mörtel ausgießen. **2** *n* Vergußmaterial *nt*, Fugenkitt *m*; Mörtel *m*.

grove [grəʊv] *n* Hain *m*, Wäldchen *nt*.

grovel ['grɒvl] *vi* kriechen. **to ~ at sb's feet** (*person*) vor jdm kriechen; (*dog*) sich um jdn herumdrücken; **to ~ to or before sb** (*fig*) vor jdm kriechen; (*in apology*) vor jdm zu Kreuze kriechen.

groveller ['grɒvələ^r] *n* Kriecher (*inf*), Speichellecker (*inf*) *m*.

grovelling ['grɒvəlɪŋ] **1** *adj* kriecherisch (*inf*), unterwürfig. **2** *n* Kriecherei (*inf*), Speichelleckerei (*inf*) *f*.

grow [grəʊ] *pret* **grew**, *ptp* **grown** **1** *vt* (**a**) *plants* ziehen; (*commercially*) *potatoes, wheat, coffee etc* anbauen, anpflanzen; (*cultivate*) *flowers* züchten.

(**b**) **to ~ one's beard/hair** sich (*dat*) einen Bart/die Haare wachsen lassen.

2 *vi* (**a**) wachsen; (*person, baby also*) größer werden; (*hair also*) länger werden; (*in numbers*) zunehmen; (*in size also*) sich vergrößern; (*fig: become more mature*) sich weiterentwickeln. **to ~ in stature/wisdom/authority** an Ansehen/Weisheit/Autorität zunehmen; **to ~ in popularity** immer beliebter werden; **to ~ in beauty** schöner werden; **my, how you've ~n** du bist aber groß geworden!; **it'll ~ on you** das wird dir mit der Zeit gefallen, du wirst schon noch Geschmack daran finden; **the habit grew on him** es wurde ihm zur Gewohnheit.

(**b**) (*become*) werden. **to ~ to do/be sth** allmählich etw tun/sein; **to ~ to hate/love sb** jdn hassen/lieben lernen; **to ~ to enjoy sth** langsam Gefallen an etw (*dat*) finden; **I've ~n to expect him to be late** ich erwarte schon langsam, daß er zu spät kommt; **to ~ used to sth** sich an etw (*acc*) gewöhnen; **to ~ like sb** jdm immer ähnlicher werden.

♦**grow apart** *vi* (*fig*) sich auseinanderentwickeln.

♦**grow away** *vi* (*fig*) **to ~ ~ from sb** sich jdm entfremden.

♦**grow from** *vi* +*prep obj see* **grow out of** (**b**).

♦**grow in** *vi* (*hair*) nachwachsen; (*teeth*) kommen; (*toenail*) einwachsen.

♦**grow into** *vi* +*prep obj* (**a**) *clothes, job* hineinwachsen in (+*acc*).

(**b**) (*become*) sich entwickeln zu, werden zu. **to ~ ~ a man/woman** zum Mann/zur Frau heranwachsen; **to ~ ~ a scandal** sich zum Skandal auswachsen *or* entwickeln.

♦**grow out** *vi* (*perm, colour*) herauswachsen.

♦**grow out of** *vi* +*prep obj* (**a**) *clothes* herauswachsen aus. **to ~ ~ ~ a habit** eine Angewohnheit ablegen; **to ~ ~ ~ one's friends** seinen Freunden entwachsen (*geh*), sich von seinen Freunden entfernen. (**b**) (*arise from*) entstehen aus, erwachsen aus (*geh*).

♦**grow together** *vi* (*lit, fig*) zusammenwachsen.

♦**grow up** *vi* (*spend childhood*) aufwachsen; (*become adult*) erwachsen werden; (*fig*) (*custom, hatred*) aufkommen; (*city*) entstehen. **what are you going to do when you ~ ~?** was willst du mal werden, wenn du groß bist?; **to ~ ~ into a liar/beauty** sich zu einem Lügner/einer Schönheit entwickeln; **when are you going to ~ ~?** sei nicht kindisch!, werde endlich erwachsen!

grower ['grəʊə^r] *n* (**a**) (*plant*) **to be a fast/good ~** schnell/gut wachsen. (**b**) (*person*) (*of fruit, vegetables*) Anbauer *m*; (*of flowers*) Züchter *m*; (*of tobacco, coffee*) Pflanzer *m*.

growing ['grəʊɪŋ] **1** *adj* (*lit, fig*) wachsend; *child* heranwachsend, im Wachstum befindlich (*form*); *importance, interest, number etc also* zunehmend. **he's still a ~ boy** er steckt noch (*inf*) *or* befindet sich noch im Wachstum.

2 *n* Wachstum, Wachsen *nt*. **~ pains** (*Med*) Wachstumsschmerzen *pl*; (*fig*) Kinderkrankheiten, Anfangsschwierigkeiten *pl*; **~ season** Zeit *f* des Wachstums, Vegetationszeit *f* (*spec*).

growl [graʊl] **1** *n* Knurren *nt no pl*; (*of bear*) (böses) Brummen *no pl*. **2** *vi* knurren; (*bear*) böse brummen. **to ~ at sb** jdn anknurren/anbrummen. **3** *vt answer* knurren.

grown [grəʊn] **1** *ptp of* **grow**. **2** *adj* erwachsen. **fully ~** ausgewachsen; **they have a ~ family** sie haben schon erwachsene Kinder.

grown: **~ over** *adj* überwachsen; *garden also* überwuchert; **~-up 1** *adj* erwachsen; *clothes, shoes* Erwachsenen-, wie Erwachsene, wie Große (*inf*). **2** *n* Erwachsene(r) *mf*.

growth [grəʊθ] *n* (**a**) Wachstum *nt*; (*of person also*) Entwicklung *f*; (*of plant also*) Wuchs *m*; (*increase in quantity, fig: of love, interest etc*) Zunahme *f*, Anwachsen *nt*; (*increase in size also*) Vergrößerung *f*; (*of capital etc*) Zuwachs *m*; (*of business also*) Erweiterung *f*. **to reach full ~** seine/ihre volle Größe erreichen; **~ industry/stock** Wachstumsindustrie *f*/Wachstumsaktien *pl*; **rate of export ~** Wachstums- *or* Zuwachsrate *f* im Export.

(**b**) (*plants*) Vegetation *f*; (*of one plant*) Triebe *pl*. **covered with a thick ~ of weeds** von Unkraut überwuchert *or* überwachsen; **cut away the old ~** schneiden Sie die alten Blätter und Zweige aus; **a thick ~ of beard** dichter Bartwuchs; **with a two days' ~ on his face** mit zwei Tage alten Bartstoppeln.

(**c**) (*Med*) Gewächs *nt*, Wucherung *f*.

groyne [grɔɪn] *n* Buhne *f*.

grub [grʌb] **1** *n* (**a**) (*larva*) Larve *f*.

(**b**) (*inf: food*) Fressalien *pl* (*hum, inf*), Futterage *f* (*inf*). **~('s) up!** antreten zum Essenfassen (*inf*).

2 *vt* (*animal*) *ground, soil* aufwühlen, wühlen in (+*dat*).

3 *vi* (*also* **~ about** *or* **around**) (*pig*) wühlen (*in* in +*dat*); (*person*) (herum)kramen, (herum)wühlen (*in* in +*dat, for* nach).

♦**grub out** *vt sep* ausgraben.

♦**grub up** *vt sep weeds* jäten; *potatoes, bush etc* ausgraben; *soil* wühlen in (+*dat*); (*bird*) *worms* aus dem Boden ziehen; (*fig*) *information, people* auftreiben, zusammensammeln.

grubbily ['grʌbɪlɪ] *adv* schmuddelig (*inf*).

grubbiness ['grʌbɪnɪs] n Schmuddeligkeit f (inf).
grubby ['grʌbɪ] adj (+er) schmuddelig (inf); hands dreckig (inf).
grudge [grʌdʒ] **1** n Groll m (against gegen). **to bear sb a ~, to have a ~ against sb** jdm böse sein, jdm grollen, einen Groll gegen jdn hegen (geh); **I bear him no ~** ich trage ihm das nicht nach, ich nehme ihm das nicht übel; **to bear ~s nachtragend sein; to pay off a ~** eine alte Rechnung begleichen.
  2 vt **to ~ sb sth** jdm etw nicht gönnen, jdm etw neiden (geh); **I don't ~ you your success/these pleasures** ich gönne Ihnen Ihren Erfolg/das Vergnügen; **to ~ doing sth** etw äußerst ungern tun, etw mit Widerwillen tun; **I don't ~ doing it** es macht mir nichts aus, das zu tun; **I ~ spending money/time on it** es widerstrebt mir or es geht mir gegen den Strich (inf), dafür Geld auszugeben/Zeit aufzuwenden; **I don't ~ the money/time** es geht mir nichts ums Geld/um die Zeit; **I do ~ the money/time for things like that** das Geld/meine Zeit für solche Dinge tut mir leid.
grudging ['grʌdʒɪŋ] adj person, attitude unwirsch; contribution, gift widerwillig gegeben; admiration, praise, support widerwillig. **in a ~ tone of voice** widerwillig; **to ~ in one's support/praise for sth** etw nur widerwillig unterstützen/loben.
grudgingly ['grʌdʒɪŋlɪ] adv widerwillig.
gruel [gruəl] n Haferschleim m, Schleimsuppe f.
gruelling, (US) **grueling** ['gruəlɪŋ] adj task, day etc aufreibend, zermürbend; march, climb, race äußerst strapaziös, mörderisch (inf).
gruesome ['gruːsəm] adj grausig, schauerlich, schaurig; sense of humour schaurig, makaber.
gruesomely ['gruːsəmlɪ] adv schauerlich.
gruff [grʌf] adj (+er) voice, manner, reply barsch, schroff.
gruffly ['grʌflɪ] adv see adj.
gruffness ['grʌfnɪs] n Barschheit, Schroffheit f.
grumble ['grʌmbl] **1** n (complaint) Murren, Schimpfen nt no pl; (noise: of thunder, guns) Grollen nt. **his chief ~ is that ...** worüber er am meisten murrt or schimpft ist, daß ...; **all his ~s** sein ständiges Schimpfen or Gemecker (inf); **to do sth without a ~** ohne Murren or Widerspruch tun.
  2 vi murren, schimpfen (about, over über +acc); (thunder, gunfire) grollen. **to ~ at sb** jdm gegenüber schimpfen or klagen; **grumbling appendix** gereizter Blinddarm.
grumbler ['grʌmblə'] n Nörgler(in f) m, Brummbär m (inf).
grummet ['grʌmɪt] n see grommet.
grumpily ['grʌmpɪlɪ] adv see adj.
grumpy ['grʌmpɪ] adj (+er) brummig, mürrisch, grantig; child quengelig (inf), unleidlich.
grunt [grʌnt] **1** n (of pig, person) Grunzen nt no pl; (of pain, in exertion) Ächzen nt no pl, Ächzer m (inf). **to give a ~** grunzen (of vor +dat); ächzen (of vor +dat). **2** vi (animal, person) grunzen; (with pain, exertion) ächzen, aufseufzen; (in irritation also) knurren. **3** vt reply brummen, knurren.
gryphon ['grɪfən] n see griffin.
GS abbr of General Staff.
G-string ['dʒiːstrɪŋ] n (a) (Mus) G-Saite f. **Bach's Air on a ~** Bachs Air nt. (b) (clothing) Minislip m.
GT abbr of gran turismo GT.
guano ['gwaːnəʊ] n Guano m.
guarantee [ˌgærən'tiː] **1** n (a) (Comm) Garantie f; (~ slip also) Garantieschein m. **to have or carry a 6-month ~** 6 Monate Garantie haben; **there is a year's ~ on this watch** auf der Uhr ist ein Jahr Garantie; **while it is under ~** solange noch Garantie darauf ist; **to sell sth with a money-back ~** volles Rückgaberecht beim Verkauf von etw garantieren.
  (b) (promise) Garantie f (of für). **that's no ~ that ...** das heißt noch lange nicht, daß ...; **it will be sent today, I give you my ~ or you have my ~** es wird heute noch abgeschickt, das garantiere ich Ihnen.
  (c) (Jur) see guaranty.
  2 vt (a) (Comm) garantieren. **to be ~d for three months** drei Monate Garantie haben; **to ~ sth against theft/fire** etw gegen Diebstahl/Feuer absichern.
  (b) (promise, ensure) garantieren (sb sth jdm etw); (take responsibility for) garantieren für. **I can't ~ (that) he will be any good** ich kann nicht dafür garantieren, daß er gut ist; **I ~ to come tomorrow** ich komme garantiert or ganz bestimmt morgen.
  (c) (Jur) garantieren, gewährleisten; loan, debt bürgen für.
guaranteed [ˌgærən'tiːd] adj garantiert. **to be ~ pure gold/not to rust** garantiert echt Gold/nichtrostend sein; **~ price** Garantiepreis m; **that's a ~ success** das wird garantiert ein Erfolg.
guarantor [ˌgærən'tɔː'] n Garant m; (Jur also) Bürge m. **to stand ~ for sb** für jdn eine Bürgschaft übernehmen.
guaranty ['gærəntɪ] n (Jur) Garantie f; (pledge of obligation) Bürgschaft f; (security) Sicherheit f.
guard [gaːd] **1** n (a) (Mil) Wache f; (single soldier also) Wachtposten m; (on pl: squad also) Wachmannschaft f. die G~s (Brit) die Garde, das Garderegiment; **~ of honour** Ehrenwache f; **to change ~** Wachablösung machen.
  (b) (security ~) Sicherheitsbeamte(r) m, Sicherheitsbeamtin f; (at factory gates, in park etc) Wächter(in f) m; (esp US: prison ~) Gefängniswärter(in f); (Brit Rail) Schaffner(in f), Zugbegleiter(in f) m.
  (c) (watch, also Mil) Wache f. **under ~** unter Bewachung; **to be under ~** bewacht werden; (person also) unter Bewachung or Aufsicht stehen; **to keep sb/sth under ~** jdn/etw bewachen; **to be on ~, to stand or keep or mount ~** Wache halten or stehen; **to keep or stand or mount ~ over sth** etw bewachen; **to go on/off ~** die Wache übernehmen/übergeben; **to put a ~ on sb/sth** jdn/etw bewachen lassen.
  (d) (Boxing, Fencing) Deckung f. **on ~!** (Fencing) en garde!;

to take ~ in Verteidigungsstellung gehen; (Cricket) Schlagstellung gehen; **to drop or lower one's ~** (lit) seine Deckung vernachlässigen; (fig) seine Reserve aufgeben; **to have one's ~ down** (lit) nicht gedeckt sein; (fig) nicht auf der Hut sein; **he caught his opponent off his ~** er hat seinen Gegner mit einem Schlag erwischt, auf den er nicht vorbereitet or gefaßt war; **I was off my ~/he caught me off my ~** when he mentioned that ich war nicht darauf gefaßt or vorbereitet, als er das erwähnen würde/er hat mich völlig überrumpelt, als er das erwähnte; **to be on/off one's ~ (against sth)** (lit) gut/schlecht gedeckt sein; (fig) (vor etw dat) nicht auf der Hut sein, sich (vor etw dat) vorsehen/nicht vorsehen; **to put sb on his ~ (against sth)** (lit or fig) (vor etw dat) warnen; **to throw or put sb off his ~** (lit) jdn seine Deckung vernachlässigen lassen; (fig) jdn einlullen.
  (e) (safety device, for protection) Schutz m (against gegen); (on machinery also) Schutzvorrichtung f; (fire ~) Schutzgitter nt; (on foil) Glocke f; (on sword etc) Korb m.
  (f) (in basketball) Verteidigungsspieler m.
  2 vt prisoner, place, valuables bewachen; treasure also, secret, tongue hüten; machinery beaufsichtigen; luggage aufpassen auf (+acc); (protect) (lit) person, place schützen (from, against vor +dat), abschirmen (from, against from); one's life schützen; one's reputation achten auf (+acc); (fig) child etc behüten, beschützen (from, against vor +dat). **he wanted to ~ his family against illness** er wollte seine Familie vor Krankheit bewahren.
◆**guard against** vi +prep obj (take care to avoid) suspicion, being cheated, etc sich in acht nehmen vor (+dat); hasty reaction, bad habit, scandal also sich hüten vor (+dat); (take precautions against) illness, misunderstandings vorbeugen (+dat); accidents verhüten. **you must ~** catching cold/telling him too much Sie müssen aufpassen or sich in acht nehmen, daß Sie sich nicht erkälten/daß Sie ihm nicht zu viel sagen; **they shut the door to ~** being overheard sie machten die Tür zu, um nicht belauscht zu werden; **in order to ~ this** um (dem) vorzubeugen.
guard: **~ dog** n Wachhund m; **~ duty** n Wachdienst m; **to be on ~ duty** auf Wache sein, Wache haben (inf).
guarded ['gaːdɪd] adj (a) reply vorsichtig, zurückhaltend; smile zurückhaltend, reserviert; (under guard) prisoner bewacht; machinery geschützt, abgesichert. **to be ~ in one's remarks** sich sehr vorsichtig or zurückhaltend ausdrücken.
guardedly ['gaːdɪdlɪ] adv vorsichtig, zurückhaltend. **to be ~ optimistic** vorsichtigen Optimismus zeigen.
guardedness ['gaːdɪdnɪs] n Vorsichtigkeit f; (of smile) Reserviertheit f.
guardhouse ['gaːdhaʊs] n (Mil) (for soldiers) Wachlokal nt, Wachstube f; (for prisoners) Arrestlokal nt, Bunker m (sl).
guardian ['gaːdɪən] n Hüter, Wächter m; (Jur) Vormund m. **~ of law and order** Hüter m des Gesetzes; **~ angel** Schutzengel m.
guardianship ['gaːdɪənʃɪp] n Wachen nt (of über +acc); (Jur) Vormundschaft f (of über +acc).
guard-rail ['gaːdreɪl] n Schutzgeländer nt; (around machinery) Schutzleiste f; (Rail) Schutzschiene, Zwangsschiene f.
guardsman ['gaːdzmən] n, pl -men [-mən] Wache f, Wachtposten m; (member of guards regiment) Gardist m; (US: in National Guard) Nationalgardist m.
guard's van ['gaːdzvæn] n (Brit Rail) Schaffnerabteil nt, Dienstwagen m.
Guatemala [ˌgwaːtɪ'maːlə] n Guatemala nt.
Guatemalan [ˌgwaːtɪ'maːlən] **1** adj guatemaltekisch, aus Guatemala. **2** n Guatemalteke m, Guatemaltekin f.
guava ['gwaːvə] n Guave, Guajave f; (tree also) Guavenbaum, Guajavenbaum m.
gubbins ['gʌbɪnz] n (Brit dated inf) (things) Zeug nt (inf); (person) Dussel m (inf).
gubernatorial [ˌguːbənə'tɔːrɪəl] adj (esp US Pol) Gouverneurs-.
gudgeon ['gʌdʒən] n Gründling m.
guelder rose ['geldərəʊz] n (Bot) Schneeball m.
guer(r)illa [gə'rɪlə] **1** n Guerilla mf. **Palestinian ~s** palästinensische Freischärler or Guerillas pl. **2** attr Guerilla-. **~ war/warfare** Guerillakrieg m.
Guernsey ['gɜːnzɪ] n (a) Guernsey nt. (b) (sweater: also g~) dicker Pullover (von Fischern getragen).
guess [ges] **1** n Vermutung, Annahme f; (estimate) Schätzung f. **to have or make a ~ (at sth)** (etw) raten; (estimate) (etw) schätzen; **it was just a ~** ich habe nur geraten; **his ~ was nearly right** er hat es fast erraten; er hat es gut geschätzt; **it's a good ~** gut geraten or geschätzt or getippt; **it was just a lucky ~** das war nur gut geraten, das war ein Zufallstreffer m; **I'll give you three ~es** dreimal darfst du raten; **50 people, at a ~** schätzungsweise 50 Leute; **at a rough ~** grob geschätzt, über den Daumen gepeilt (inf); **my ~ is that ...** ich tippe darauf (inf) or schätze or vermute, daß ...; **your ~ is as good as mine!** (inf) da kann ich auch nur raten!; **it's anybody's ~** (inf) das wissen die Götter (inf).
  2 vi (a) raten. **how did you ~?** wie hast du das bloß erraten?; (iro) du merkst auch alles!; **to keep sb ~ing** jdn im ungewissen lassen; **he's only ~ing when he says they'll come** das ist eine reine Vermutung von ihm, daß sie kommen; **you'll never ~!** das wirst du nie erraten; **to ~ at sth** etw raten.
  (b) (esp US) **I ~ not** wohl nicht; **he's right, I ~** er hat wohl recht; **is he coming? — I ~ so** kommt er? — (ich) schätze ja (inf), ich glaube schon; **shall we go? — I ~ (so)** sollen wir gehen? — (ich) schätze ja (inf), na gut; **that's all, I ~** das ist wohl alles, (ich) schätze, das ist alles (inf).
  3 vt (a) (surmise) raten; (surmise correctly) erraten; (estimate) weight, numbers, amount schätzen. **I ~ed as much** das habe ich mir schon gedacht; **to ~ sb to be 20 years**

old/sth to be 10 lbs jdn auf 20/etw auf 10 Pfund schätzen; you'll never ~ who/what ... das errätst du nie, wer/was ...; ~ who! (inf) rat mal, wer!; ~ what! (inf) stell dir vor! (inf), denk nur! (inf).
(b) (esp US) schätzen (inf), vermuten, annehmen. I ~ we'll buy it wir werden es wohl or wahrscheinlich kaufen.

guessable ['gesəbl] adj answer erratbar, zu erraten pred; age also, number schätzbar, zu schätzen pred.

guessing game ['gesɪŋgeɪm] n Ratespiel nt; (fig) Raterei f no pl.

guesstimate ['gestɪmɪt] n grobe Schätzung.

guesswork ['geswɜːk] n (reine) Vermutung. there's too much ~ in historical essays in historischen Aufsätzen wird zuviel vermutet; it was pure or sheer ~ das war eine reine Vermutung; they did it all by ~ sie haben nur geraten; it's all ~ das sind doch nur Vermutungen, das ist doch alles nur geraten.

guest [gest] n Gast m. ~ of honour Ehrengast m; be my ~ (inf) nur zu! (inf).

guest in cpds Gast-; ~ appearance n Gastauftritt m; to make a ~ appearance als Gast auftreten; ~ artist n Gast(star), Gastkünstler(in f) m; (Theat) Gastspieler(in f) m; ~-house n Gästehaus nt; (boarding house) (Fremden)pension f; ~ list n Gästeliste f; ~-night n Gästeabend m; ~-room n Gästezimmer nt.

guff [gʌf] n (dated sl) Quark (dated sl), Käse (inf) m.

guffaw [gʌ'fɔː] 1 n schallendes Lachen no pl. ~s of laughter Lachsalven pl; to give a ~ schallend lachen. 2 vi schallend (los)lachen.

Guiana [gaɪ'ænə] n Guayana nt.

guidance ['gaɪdəns] n (direction) Führung, Leitung f; (counselling) Beratung f (on über +acc); (from superior, parents, teacher etc) Anleitung f. spiritual ~ geistiger Rat; for your ~ zu Ihrer Orientierung or Hilfe; to give sb ~ on sth jdn etw beraten; to pray for ~ um Erleuchtung bitten.

guidance: ~ system n (on rocket) Steuerungssystem nt; ~ teacher n (Scot) Verbindungslehrer(in f) m.

guide [gaɪd] 1 n (a) (person) Führer(in f) m; (fig: indication, pointer) Anhaltspunkt m (to für); (model) Leitbild nt. let reason/your conscience be your ~ lassen Sie sich von der Vernunft/Ihrem Gewissen leiten; they used the star as their ~ sie ließen sich von dem Stern leiten; he is my spiritual ~ er ist mein geistiger Berater.
(b) (Tech) Leitvorrichtung f.
(c) (Brit: girl ~) Pfadfinderin f.
(d) (instructions) Anleitung f; (manual) Leitfaden m, Handbuch nt (to gen); (travel ~) Führer m. take this dictionary/this piece of work as a ~, let this dictionary/this piece of work be your ~ orientieren Sie sich an diesem Wörterbuch/dieser Arbeit.
2 vt people, blind man etc führen; discussion also leiten; missile, rocket, sb's behaviour, studies, reading lenken. to ~ a plane in ein Flugzeug einweisen; to be ~d by sb/sth (person) sich von jdm/etw leiten lassen; his life was ~d by his father's example sein Leben war vom Vorbild seines Vaters bestimmt; to ~ sb on his way jdm den Weg zeigen or weisen.

guide-book ['gaɪdbʊk] n (Reise)führer m (to von).

guided missile [ˌgaɪdɪd'mɪsaɪl] n ferngelenktes Geschoß, Lenkflugkörper m (form).

guide-dog ['gaɪddɒg] n Blindenhund m.

guided tour [ˌgaɪdɪd'tʊər] n Führung f (of durch).

guide: ~line n Richtlinie, Richtschnur no pl f; (Typ, for writing) Leitlinie f; ~post n Wegweiser m.

guider ['gaɪdər] n (Brit) Pfadfinderinnenführerin f.

guide-rope ['gaɪdrəʊp] n Schlepptau nt.

guiding ['gaɪdɪŋ]: ~ hand n leitende Hand; ~ principle n Leitmotiv nt; ~ star n Leitstern m.

guild [gɪld] n (Hist) Zunft, Gilde f; (association) Verein m.

guilder ['gɪldər] n Gulden m.

guile [gaɪl] n Tücke, (Arg)list f. to have great ~ sehr tückisch or arglistig sein; to be without ~ ohne Arg or ohne Falsch sein (liter).

guileful ['gaɪlfʊl] adj hinterhältig, tückisch, arglistig.

guileless ['gaɪllɪs] adj arglos, harmlos, unschuldsvoll.

guillemot ['gɪlɪmɒt] n Lumme f.

guillotine [ˌgɪlə'tiːn] 1 n (a) Guillotine f, Fallbeil nt.
(b) (for paper) (Papier)schneidemaschine f.
(c) (Parl) Beschränkung f der Diskussionszeit. to put a ~ on a bill die Diskussionszeit für ein Gesetz einschränken.
2 vt (a) person mit der Guillotine or dem Fallbeil hinrichten.
(b) paper schneiden.
(c) (Parl) bill die Diskussionszeit einschränken für.

guilt [gɪlt] n Schuld f (for, of an +dat). to feel ~ about sth sich wegen etw schuldig fühlen, wegen etw Schuldgefühle haben; ~ complex Schuldkomplex m.

guiltily ['gɪltɪlɪ] adv schuldbewußt; act verdächtig.

guiltiness ['gɪltɪnɪs] n Schuld f; (feeling) Schuldbewußtsein m.

guiltless ['gɪltlɪs] adj schuldlos, unschuldig (of an +dat). he is ~ of any crime er ist keines Verbrechens schuldig.

guilty ['gɪltɪ] adj (+er) (a) schuldig (of gen). the ~ person/party der/die Schuldige/die schuldige Partei; verdict of ~ Schuldspruch m; to find sb ~/not ~ (of a crime) jdn (eines Verbrechens) für schuldig/nicht schuldig befinden; ~/not ~! (Jur) schuldig/nicht schuldig!; (fig) das war ich/das war ich nicht.
(b) look, voice schuldbewußt; conscience, thought schlecht; intent, thought böse.
(c) (inf: in phrases) we're all ~ of neglecting the problem uns trifft alle Schuld, daß das Problem vernachlässigt wurde; he was ~ of taking the book without permission er hat das Buch ohne Erlaubnis genommen; I've been ~ of that myself den Fehler habe ich auch schon begangen; I feel very ~ (about ...) ich habe ein sehr schlechtes Gewissen(, daß ...).

Guinea ['gɪnɪ] n Guinea nt.

guinea ['gɪnɪ] n (Brit old) Guinee, Guinea f (21 Shilling).

guinea: ~-fowl n Perlhuhn nt; ~-pig n Meerschweinchen nt; (fig) Versuchskaninchen nt.

guise [gaɪz] n (disguise) Gestalt f; (pretence) Vorwand m. in the ~ of a clown/swan als Clown verkleidet/in Gestalt eines Schwans; in human ~ in Menschengestalt; under the ~ of friendship unter dem Deckmantel der Freundschaft.

guitar [gɪ'taːr] n Gitarre f.

guitarist [gɪ'taːrɪst] n Gitarrist(in f) m.

gulch [gʌlʃ] n Schlucht f.

gulf [gʌlf] n (a) (bay) Golf, Meerbusen m. G~ Stream Golfstrom m; the G~ of Mexico/Bothnia der Golf von Mexico/der Bottnische Meerbusen; the (Persian) G~ der Persische Golf.
(b) (lit, fig: chasm) tiefe Kluft.

gull¹ [gʌl] n (sea~) Möwe f.

gull² (liter) 1 n Spielball m (of gen). 2 vt übertölpeln. to ~ sb out of his money jdm sein Geld ablisten; to be ~ed into doing sth durch eine üble List dazu gebracht werden, etw zu tun.

gullet ['gʌlɪt] n Speiseröhre, Kehle f. that really stuck in my ~ (fig) das ging mir sehr gegen den Strich (inf).

gullibility [ˌgʌlɪ'bɪlɪtɪ] n Leichtgläubigkeit f.

gullible adj, ~bly adv [ˈgʌlɪbl, -ɪ] leichtgläubig.

gully ['gʌlɪ] n (ravine) Schlucht f; (narrow channel) Rinne f.

gulp [gʌlp] 1 n Schluck m. at a/one ~ auf einen Schluck; ..., he said with a ~ ..., sagte er und schluckte.
2 vt (also ~ down) drink runterstürzen; food runterschlingen; medicine hinunterschlucken. to ~ back one's tears/a reply die Tränen/eine Antwort hinunterschlucken; what?, he ~ed was?, preßte er hervor.
3 vi (try to swallow) würgen; (eat fast) schlingen; (drink fast) hastig trinken; (from emotion) trocken schlucken. to drink with loud ~ing noises gluckernd trinken.

gum¹ [gʌm] n (Anat) Zahnfleisch nt no pl.

gum² 1 n (a) Gummi nt; (~-tree) Gummibaum m; (glue) Klebstoff m. (b) (chewing ~) Kaugummi m; (sweet) Weingummi m. (c) (US inf) see gum-shoe. 2 vt (stick together) kleben; (spread ~ on) gummieren.
♦ gum down vt sep label aufkleben; envelope zukleben.
♦ gum up vt sep verkleben. to ~ ~ the works (inf) alles verkleben; (fig) die Arbeit stoppen (inf); to get ~med up verkleben.

gum³ n (dated sl): by ~! Teufel noch mal! (dated sl).

gum arabic n Gummiarabikum nt.

gumbo ['gʌmbəʊ] n Gumbo m.

gum: ~boil n Zahnfleischabszeß m; ~boot n Gummistiefel m; ~drop n Weingummi m.

gummy ['gʌmɪ] adj (+er) gummiert; (sticky) klebrig.

gumption ['gʌmpʃən] n (inf) Grips m (inf). to have the ~ to do sth geistesgegenwärtig genug sein, etw zu tun.

gum: ~-shield n Zahnschutz m; ~-shoe (US) 1 n (a) (overshoe) Überschuh m, Galosche f; (gym shoe) Turnschuh m; (b) (sl: detective) Schnüffler m (inf); 2 vi (sl: move stealthily) schleichen; ~-tree n Gummibaum m; to be up a ~-tree (Brit inf) aufgeschmissen sein (inf).

gun [gʌn] 1 n (a) (cannon etc) Kanone f, Geschütz nt; (rifle) Gewehr nt; (pistol etc) Pistole f, Kanone f (sl), Schießeisen nt (sl). to carry a ~ (mit einer Schußwaffe) bewaffnet sein, eine Schußwaffe tragen (form); to draw a ~ on sb jdn mit einer Schußwaffe bedrohen; to fire a 21-~ salute 21 Salutschüsse abgeben; the big ~s die schweren Geschütze; big ~ (fig inf) hohes or großes Tier (inf) (in in +dat); to stick to one's ~s nicht nachgeben, festbleiben; to jump the ~ (Sport) Frühstart machen; (fig) voreilig sein or handeln; to be going great ~s wie geschmiert laufen (inf); (team, person etc) toll in Schwung or Fahrt sein (inf); (car) wie geschmiert laufen (inf); (business, economy) gut in Schuß sein (inf).
(b) (spray ~) Pistole f. grease ~ Schmierpresse, Fettpresse f.
(c) (person) Schütze m; (Hunt also) Jäger m; (inf esp US: ~man) Pistolenheld m (inf). he's the fastest ~ in the West (inf) er zieht am schnellsten im ganzen Westen (inf).
2 vt (kill: also ~ down) person erschießen, zusammenschießen; pilot, plane abschießen.
(b) (sl: rev) engine, car aufheulen lassen.
3 vi (a) (inf) to be ~ning for sb (lit) Jagd auf jdn machen; (fig) jdn auf dem Kieker haben (inf); for opponent jdn auf die Abschußliste gesetzt haben.
(b) (sl: speed) schießen (inf).

gun: ~ barrel n (on cannon) Kanonen- or Geschützrohr nt; (on rifle) Gewehrlauf m; (on pistol) Pistolenlauf m; ~boat n Kanonenboot nt; ~boat diplomacy Kanonenbootdiplomatie f; ~ carriage n Lafette f; ~-cotton n Schießbaumwolle f; ~ crew n Geschützbedienung f; ~ dog n Jagdhund m; ~-fight n Schießerei f; (Mil) Feuergefecht nt, Schußwechsel m; ~-fighter n Revolverheld m; ~fire n Schießerei f, Schüsse pl; (Mil) Geschützfeuer, Artilleriefeuer nt.

gunge [gʌndʒ] n (Brit inf) klebriges or schmieriges Zeug (inf).

gungy ['gʌndʒɪ] adj (+er) (inf) schmierig.

gunk [gʌŋk] n (US sl) see gunge.

gun: ~man n (mit einer Schußwaffe) Bewaffnete(r) m; they saw the ~man sie haben den Schützen gesehen; ~metal 1 n Geschützmetall nt, Geschützbronze f; (colour) metallisches Blaugrau; 2 adj attr aus Geschützmetall or -bronze; grey, colour metallisch.

gunnel ['gʌnəl] n see gunwale.

gunner ['gʌnər] n (Mil) Artillerist m; (title) Kanonier m; (Naut) Geschützführer m; (in plane) Bordschütze m. to be in the ~s (Mil) bei der Artillerie sein.

gunnery ['gʌnərɪ] n Schießkunst f. ~ officer Artillerieoffizier m.

gun: ~point n to hold sb at ~point jdn mit einer Pistole/einem Gewehr bedrohen; to force sb to do sth at ~point jdn mit vorgehaltener Pistole/vorgehaltenem Gewehr zwingen, etw zu tun; **to surrender at ~point** sich, von einer Pistole/einem Gewehr bedroht, ergeben; **~powder** n Schießpulver nt; **G~powder Plot** (Hist) Pulververschwörung f; **~room** n Waffenkammer f; (Naut) Kadettenmesse f; **~runner** n Waffenschmuggler or -schieber m; **~running** n Waffenschmuggel m, Waffenschieberei f (inf); **~shot** n Schuß m; (range) Schußweite f; **~shot wound** Schußwunde f; **~slinger** n (inf) Pistolenheld m (inf); **~smith** n Büchsenmacher m; **~turret** n Geschützturm m; **~wale** ['gʌnl] n Schandeck nt, Schandeckel m.

guppy ['gʌpɪ] n Guppy, Millionenfisch m.

gurgle ['gɜ:gl] 1 n (of liquid) Gluckern nt no pl; (of brook also) Plätschern, Glucksen nt no pl; (of baby) Glucksen nt no pl. **to give ~s of pleasure/laughter** vor Vergnügen/Lachen glucksen. 2 vi (liquid) gluckern; (brook also) plätschern, glucksen; (person) glucksen (with vor + dat).

guru ['guru:] n Guru m.

gush [gʌʃ] 1 n (a) (of liquid) Strahl, Schwall m; (of words) Schwall m; (of emotion) Ausbruch m.
(b) (inf: ~ing talk) Geschwärme nt (inf).
2 vi (a) (also ~ out) (water) heraussprudeln, herausprudeln; (smoke, blood, tears) hervorquellen; (flames) herausschlagen.
(b) (inf: talk) schwärmen (inf) (about, over von); (insincerely) sich ergeben (about, over über + acc).
3 vt (liter) (volcano) ausstoßen. **the wound ~ed blood** aus der Wunde schoß or quoll Blut; **her eyes ~ed tears** aus ihren Augen quollen die Tränen; **what a delightful hat, she ~ed** welch entzückender Hut, sagte sie überschwenglich.

gusher ['gʌʃəʳ] n (natürlich sprudelnde) Ölquelle; (inf: person) überschwengliche Person (inf).

gushing ['gʌʃɪŋ] adj (a) water herausspritzend, (heraus)schießend.
(b) (fig) überschwenglich; talk also schwärmerisch.

gushingly ['gʌʃɪŋlɪ] adv überschwenglich.

gusset ['gʌsɪt] n (in garment) Keil, Zwickel m.

gust [gʌst] 1 n (of wind) Stoß m, Bö(e) f; (of rain) Böe f; (fig) (of emotion) Welle f, Anfall m; (of anger) Ausbruch, Anfall m. **a ~ of smoke/flames** eine Rauchwolke/Stichflamme; **a ~ of laughter** eine Lachsalve; **a ~ of noise** plötzliches Getöse. 2 vi böig or stürmisch wehen.

gustily ['gʌstɪlɪ] adv böig, stürmisch.

gusto ['gʌstəʊ] n Begeisterung f. **to do sth with ~** etw mit Genuß tun.

gusty ['gʌstɪ] adj (+ er) wind, day, rain böig, stürmisch.

gut [gʌt] 1 n (a) (alimentary canal) Darm m; (stomach, paunch) Bauch m.
(b) usu pl (inf: stomach) Eingeweide nt; (fig) (essence: of problem, matter) Kern m; (contents) Substanz f. **to sweat or work one's ~s out** (inf) wie blöd schuften (inf); **to hate sb's ~s** (inf) jdn auf den Tod nicht ausstehen können (inf); **I'll have his ~s for garters!** (inf) den mache ich zur Minna (inf) or zur Schnecke (inf); **~ reaction** rein gefühlsmäßige Reaktion.
(c) (inf: courage) ~s pl Mumm (inf), Schneid (inf) m.
(d) (cat~) Darm m; (for racket, violin) Darmsaiten pl.
2 vt (a) animal, chicken, fish ausnehmen.
(b) (fire) ausbrennen; (remove contents) ausräumen. **it was completely ~ted by the fire** es war völlig ausgebrannt.

gutless ['gʌtlɪs] adj (fig inf) feige.

guts [gʌts] n (Brit inf) Freßsack m (inf).

gutsy ['gʌtsɪ] adj (+ er) (inf) (a) (greedy) verfressen (inf).

(b) (fig) prose, music, player rasant; resistance hart, mutig.

gutta-percha [ˌgʌtə'pɜːtʃə] n Guttapercha f or nt.

gutter ['gʌtəʳ] 1 n (on roof) Dachrinne f; (in street) Gosse f (also fig), Rinnstein m. **to be born in the ~** aus der Gosse kommen; **the language of the ~** die Gassensprache. 2 vi (candle, flame) flackern.

guttering ['gʌtərɪŋ] 1 n Regenrinnen pl. 2 adj flackernd.

gutter: **~press** n Boulevardpresse f; **~snipe** n Gassenkind nt.

guttural ['gʌtərəl] 1 n Guttural(laut), Kehllaut m. 2 adj guttural, kehlig.

guv [gʌv], **guv'nor** ['gʌvnəʳ] n (Brit inf) Chef m (inf).

guy¹ [gaɪ] 1 n (a) (inf: man) Typ (inf), Kerl (inf) m. **hey you ~s** he Leute (inf); **great ~s** die dufte Typen pl (inf); **I'll ask the ~ next door** ich werde (den Typ von) nebenan fragen (inf).
(b) (Brit: effigy) (Guy-Fawkes-)Puppe f; (inf: sight) Schießbudenfigur f (inf). **G~ Fawkes day** Jahrestag m der Pulververschwörung (5. November); **a penny for the ~** Geld nt für das (Guy Fawkes) Feuerwerk.
2 vt (ridicule) sich lustig machen über (+ acc).

guy² n (also ~-rope) Haltetau or -seil nt; (for tent) Zeltschnur f.

Guyana [gaɪˈænə] n Guyana (form), Guyana nt.

Guyanese [ˌgaɪəˈniːz] n Guyaner(in f) m.

guzzle ['gʌzl] vti (eat) futtern (inf); (drink) schlürfen.

gym [dʒɪm] n (gymnasium) Turnhalle f; (gymnastics) Turnen nt.

gymkhana [dʒɪmˈkɑːnə] n Reiterfest nt.

gymnasium [dʒɪmˈneɪzɪəm] n, pl **-s** or (form) **gymnasia** [dʒɪmˈneɪzɪə] Turnhalle f.

gymnast ['dʒɪmnæst] n Turner(in f) m.

gymnastic [dʒɪmˈnæstɪk] adj ability turnerisch; training, exercise also Turn-.

gymnastically [dʒɪmˈnæstɪkəlɪ] adv turnerisch.

gymnastics [dʒɪmˈnæstɪks] n (a) sing (discipline) Gymnastik f no pl; (with apparatus) Turnen nt no pl. (b) pl (exercises) Übungen pl. **mental ~** geistige Klimmzüge pl, Gehirnakrobatik f (inf); **verbal ~** Wortakrobatik f.

gym: **~ shoe** n (Brit) Turnschuh m; **~slip** n (Brit) Schulträgerrock m; **~ teacher** n Turnlehrer(in f) m.

gynaecological, (US) gynecological [ˌgaɪnɪkəˈlɒdʒɪkəl] adj gynäkologisch. **~ illness** Frauenleiden nt, gynäkologisches Leiden.

gynaecologist, (US) gynecologist [ˌgaɪnɪˈkɒlədʒɪst] n Gynäkologe m, Gynäkologin f, Frauenarzt m/-ärztin f.

gynaecology, (US) gynecology [ˌgaɪnɪˈkɒlədʒɪ] n Gynäkologie, Frauenheilkunde f.

gyp [dʒɪp] 1 n (a) (sl: swindle) Gaunerei f (inf). (b) (sl: swindler) Gauner m. (c) (Brit Univ inf) Putzfrau f. (d) (inf) **to give sb ~** jdn plagen (inf). 2 vt (sl) übers Ohr hauen (inf), reinlegen (inf). **to ~ sb out of sth** jdn um etw bringen (inf).

gypsum ['dʒɪpsəm] n Gips m.

gypsy n, adj attr (esp US) see **gipsy**.

gyrate [ˌdʒaɪəˈreɪt] vi (whirl) (herum)wirbeln; (rotate) sich drehen, kreisen; (dancer) sich drehen und winden.

gyration [ˌdʒaɪəˈreɪʃən] n see vi Wirbeln nt no pl; Drehung f, Kreisen nt no pl; Drehung und Windung f usu pl.

gyratory [ˌdʒaɪəˈreɪtərɪ] adj (whirling) wirbelnd; (revolving) kreisend.

gyrocompass ['dʒaɪərəʊˈkʌmpəs] n Kreisel-Magnetkompaß m.

gyroscope ['dʒaɪərəˌskəʊp] n Gyroskop nt.

H

H, h [eɪtʃ] n H, h nt; see **drop**.

H abbr of **hard** (on pencil) H.

h abbr of **hour(s)** h.

ha [hɑː] interj ha.

habeas corpus ['heɪbɪəs'kɔːpəs] n (Jur) Habeaskorpusakte f. **to issue a writ of ~** einen Vorführungsbefehl erteilen; **the lawyer applied for ~** der Rechtsanwalt verlangte, daß sein Klient einem Untersuchungsrichter vorgeführt wurde.

haberdasher ['hæbədæʃəʳ] n (Brit) Kurzwarenhändler(in f) m; (US) Herrenausstatter m.

haberdashery [ˌhæbəˈdæʃərɪ] n (Brit) (articles) Kurzwaren pl; (shop) Kurzwarengeschäft nt or -handlung f; (US) (articles) Herrenbekleidung f; Herrenartikel pl; (shop) Herrenmodengeschäft nt.

habiliments [həˈbɪlɪmənts] npl (form) Ornat nt (form).

habit ['hæbɪt] n (a) Gewohnheit f; (esp undesirable also) Angewohnheit f. **to be in the ~ of doing sth** die Angewohnheit haben, etw zu tun, etw gewöhnlich tun; **... as was his...** wie es seine Gewohnheit war; **it became a ~** es wurde zur Gewohnheit; **out of or by (sheer) ~** aus (reiner) Gewohnheit, (rein) gewohnheitsmäßig; **from (force of) ~** aus Gewohnheit; **I don't make a ~ of asking strangers in** (für) gewöhnlich bitte ich Fremde nicht herein; **don't make a ~ of it** lassen Sie (sich dat) das nicht zur Gewohnheit werden; **to get into/to get sb into the ~ of doing sth** sich/jdm angewöhnen or sich/jdn daran gewöhnen, etw zu tun; **I'd got into the ~ of seeing you in uniform** ich war gewöhnt, Sie in Uniform zu sehen; **to get or fall into bad ~s** schlechte Gewohnheiten annehmen; **to get out of/to get sb out of the ~ of doing sth** sich/jdm abgewöhnen, etw zu tun; **you must get out of the ~ of biting your nails** du mußt dir das Nägelkauen abgewöhnen; **to have a ~ of doing sth** die Angewohnheit haben, etw zu tun; **he has a strange ~ of staring at you** er hat die merkwürdige Art, einen anzustarren.
(b) (costume) Gewand nt; (monk's also) Habit nt or m. (riding) **~** Reitkleid nt.

habitable ['hæbɪtəbl] adj bewohnbar.

habitat ['hæbɪtæt] n Heimat f; (of animals also) Lebensraum m; (of plants also) Standort m.

habitation [ˌhæbɪˈteɪʃən] n (Be)wohnen nt; (place) Wohnstätte f, Behausung f. **to show signs of ~** bewohnt aussehen; **unfit for human ~** menschenunwürdig, für Wohnzwecke nicht geeignet.

habit-forming ['hæbɪtˌfɔːmɪŋ] adj **to be ~** zur Gewohnheit werden; **are those ~ drugs?** wird man davon abhängig?

habitual [həˈbɪtjuəl] *adj* gewohnt; *smoker, drinker, gambler* Gewohnheits-, gewohnheitsmäßig; *liar* gewohnheitsmäßig, notorisch. **his ~ courtesy/cheerfulness** *etc* die ihm eigene Höflichkeit/Heiterkeit *etc.*

habitually [həˈbɪtjuəlɪ] *adv* ständig.

habituate [həˈbɪtjueɪt] *vt* gewöhnen (*sb to sth* jdn an etw (*acc*), *sb to doing sth* jdn daran, etw zu tun). **you will have to ~ your-self to thinking more analytically** Sie werden (es) sich (*dat*) angewöhnen müssen, etwas analytischer zu denken.

habitué [həˈbɪtjueɪ] *n* regelmäßiger Besucher, regelmäßige Besucherin, Habitué (*geh, Aus*) *m*; (*in pubs etc*) Stammgast *m.*

hacienda [ˈhæsɪəndə] *n* Hazienda *f.*

hack¹ [hæk] **1** *n* (a) (*cut*) (Ein)schnitt *m*, Kerbe *f*; (*action*) Hieb *m.* **to take a ~ at sth** mit der Axt *etc* auf etw (*acc*) schlagen; (*in rage*) auf etw (*acc*) einhacken.
 (b) (*kick*) Tritt *m.* **he had a ~ at his opponent's ankle** er versetzte seinem Gegner einen Tritt gegen den Knöchel; **he got a ~ on the shin** er bekam einen Tritt gegen das Schienbein.
 (c) (*cough*) trockener Husten.
2 *vt* (a) (*cut*) schlagen, hacken. **don't ~ your meat, cut it** du mußt das Fleisch nicht hacken, sondern schneiden; **to hack sb/sth to pieces** (*lit*) jdn zerstückeln/etw (in Stücke) (zer)hacken *or* schlagen; (*fig*) jdn/etw zerfetzen; **to ~ sb to death** so lange auf jdn (mit einem Beil *etc*) einschlagen, bis er tot ist; **he was brutally ~ed to death** er ist brutal (mit einem Beil *etc*) erschlagen worden; **to ~ one's way out** sich einen Weg freischlagen; **to ~ one's way through (sth)** sich (*dat*) einen Weg (durch etw) schlagen, sich (durch etw) durchhauen.
 (b) (*Sport*) ball treten gegen, einen Tritt versetzen (+*dat*). **to ~ sb on the shin** jdn vors *or* gegen das Schienbein treten.
3 *vi* (a) (*chop*) hacken. **he ~ed at the branch with his axe** er schlug mit der Axt auf den Ast; **don't ~ at it** hack nicht daran herum.
 (b) (*cough*) trocken husten.
 (c) (*Sport*) **he was booked for ~ing** er wurde wegen Holzerei verwarnt.
♦**hack about** *vt sep* (*fig*) *text etc* zerstückeln.
♦**hack down** *vt sep* *bushes etc* abhacken; *people also* niedermetzeln; *tree* umhauen.
♦**hack off** *vt sep* abhacken, abschlagen. **to ~ sth ~ sth** etw von etw abhacken *or* abschlagen.
♦**hack out** *vt sep* *clearing* schlagen; *hole* herausmachen.
♦**hack up** *vt sep* zerhacken; *meat, wood, furniture also* kleinhacken; *bodies* zerstückeln.

hack² **1** *n* (a) (*hired horse*) Mietpferd *nt*; (*worn-out horse*) Gaul, Klepper *m.*
 (b) (*pej: literary ~*) Schreiberling *m*; (*of cheap novels also*) Schundliterat(in *f*) *m*; (*journalist also*) Schmierfink *m.* **the newspaper ~s** die Zeitungsschreiber *pl*; **paid ~** Soldschreiber *m.*
 (c) (*US: taxi*) Taxi *nt.*
2 *adj attr* (*pej*) writing stumpfsinnig. **~ writer** see **hack²** 1 (b).
3 *vi* einen Spazierritt machen. **to go ~ing** ausreiten.

hackie [ˈhækɪ] *n* (*US*) Taxifahrer(in *f*) *m.*

hacking [ˈhækɪŋ] *adj* (a) **~ cough** trockener Husten. **(b) ~ jacket** Sportsakko *m or nt*; (*for riding*) Reitjacke *f.*

hackle [ˈhækl] *n* (*Orn*) lange Nackenfeder; (*plumage also*) Nak-kengefieder *nt*; (*pl: of dog etc*) Fell *nt* im Nacken. **the dog's ~s rose** dem Hund sträubte sich das Fell; **his ~s rose at the very idea** bei dem bloßen Gedanken sträubte sich alles in ihm; **to get sb's ~s up** jdn reizen, jdn auf die Palme bringen (*inf*); **to have one's ~s up** auf (hundert)achtzig sein (*inf*).

hackney carriage [ˈhæknɪˌkærɪdʒ] *n* (*horse-drawn*) (Pferde)droschke *f*; (*form: taxi*) (Kraft)droschke *f* (*form*).

hackneyed [ˈhæknɪd] *adj* subject abgedroschen, abgegriffen; *metaphor, turn of phrase also* abgenutzt.

hacksaw [ˈhæksɔː] *n* Metallsäge *f.*

had [hæd] *pret, ptp of* **have.**

haddock [ˈhædək] *n* Schellfisch *m.*

Hades [ˈheɪdiːz] *n* (*Myth*) Hades *m.*

hadn't [ˈhædnt] *contr of* **had not.**

Hadrian [ˈheɪdrɪən] *n* Hadrian *m.* **~'s Wall** Hadrianswall *m.*

haematology, (*US*) **hematology** [ˌhiːməˈtɒlədʒɪ] *n* Hämatologie *f.*

haemoglobin, (*US*) **hemoglobin** [ˌhiːməˈɡləubɪn] *n* Hämo-globin *nt*, roter Blutfarbstoff.

haemophilia, (*US*) **hemophilia** [ˌhiːməˈfɪlɪə] *n* Bluterkrank-heit, Hämophilie (*spec*) *f.*

haemophiliac, (*US*) **hemophiliac** [ˌhiːməˈfɪlɪæk] *n* Bluter *m.*

haemorrhage, (*US*) **hemorrhage** [ˈhemərɪdʒ] **1** *n* Blutung, Hämorrhagie (*spec*) *f.* **2** *vi* bluten.

haemorrhoids, (*US*) **hemorrhoids** [ˈhemərɔɪdz] *npl* Hämor-rhoiden *pl.*

haft [hɑːft] *n* (*of knife*) Heft *nt*; (*of sword*) Griff *m.*

hag [hæg] *n* Hexe *f.*

haggard [ˈhæɡəd] *adj* ausgezehrt; (*from tiredness*) abgespannt; (*from worry*) abgehärmt, verhärmt. **he had a very ~ expres-sion throughout the trial** er wirkte während der ganzen Verhandlung sehr mitgenommen.

haggis [ˈhæɡɪs] *n* schottisches Gericht aus gehackten Schafsin-nereien und Haferschrot im Schafsmagen gekocht.

haggish [ˈhæɡɪʃ] *adj* zänkisch, garstig.

haggle [ˈhæɡl] *vi* (*bargain*) feilschen (*about or over* um); (*argue also*) sich (herum)streiten (*over* um *or* wegen). **let's stop haggling over who's going to pay** hören wir doch auf mit dem Hin und Her (darüber), wer nun bezahlt.

haggling [ˈhæɡlɪŋ] *n* Feilschen, Gefeilsche *nt*, Feilscherei *f.*

hagiographer [ˌhæɡɪˈɒɡrəfəʳ] *n* (*form*) Hagiograph *m* (*form*).

hagiography [ˌhæɡɪˈɒɡrəfɪ] *n* (*form*) Heiligengeschichte, Hagiographie (*spec*) *f.*

hagiology [ˌhæɡɪˈɒlədʒɪ] *n* (*form*) Hagiologie *f* (*spec*).

hag-ridden [ˈhæɡrɪdn] *adj* (*worried*) vergrämt, verhärmt; *atmosphere* drückend. **to be ~** (*hum: tormented by women*) unter Weiberherrschaft stehen.

Hague [heɪɡ] *n* **the ~** Den Haag *nt*; **in the ~** in Den Haag, im Haag (*geh*).

ha-ha [ˈhɑːˈhɑː] **1** *interj* ha-ha. **2** *n* (*fence*) versenkter Grenz-zaun.

hail¹ [heɪl] **1** *n* Hagel *m.* **a ~ of rocks/blows/curses** ein Steinhagel *m or* Hagel *m* von Steinen/Schlägen/Flüchen; **in a ~ of bullets** im Kugel- *or* Geschoßhagel. **2** *vi* hageln.
♦**hail down 1** *vi* (*stones etc*) niederprasseln, niederhageln (*on sb/sth* auf jdn/etw). **the blows ~ed ~ (on him)** es hagelte Schläge (auf ihn nieder). **2** *vt sep* blows niederprasseln lassen. **she ~ed ~ curses on him** sie überschüttete ihn mit einem Schwall von Flüchen.

hail² **1** *vt* (a) zujubeln (+*dat*), bejubeln. **he was ~ed (as) king by the crowd** die Menge jubelte ihm als König zu (*liter*).
 (b) (*call loudly*) zurufen (+*dat*); *ship* anrufen, preien (*Naut*); *taxi* (*by calling*) rufen; (*by making sign also*) anhalten, her-beiwinken, winken (+*dat*). **within ~ing distance** in Rufweite; **someone ~ed me from down in the valley** von unten aus dem Tal rief jemand zu mir herauf.
2 *vi* **a ship ~ing from London** ein Schiff *nt* mit (dem) Heimathafen London; **where does that boat ~ from?** was ist der Heimathafen dieses Schiffs?; **they ~ from all parts of the world** sie kommen *or* stammen aus allen Teilen der Welt; **where do you ~ from?** wo stammen Sie her?
3 *interj* (*obs, liter*) sei gegrüßt (*liter*) heil (+*dat*) (*liter*). **~ Caesar** heil dir Cäsar; **the H~ Mary** das Ave Maria.
4 *n* (Zu)ruf *m.* **within ~** in Rufweite.

hail-fellow-well-met [ˈheɪlfeləuˌwelˈmet] *adj* plump-vertraulich. **he tries to be ~ with everyone** er versucht, sich bei allen anzubiedern.

hail: ~stone *n* Hagelkorn *nt*; **~storm** *n* Hagel(schauer) *m.*

hair [heəʳ] **1** *n* (a) (*collective: on head*) Haare *pl*, Haar *nt.* **a fine head of ~** schönes volles Haar, schöne volle Haare; **to do one's ~** sich frisieren, sich (*dat*) die Haare (zurecht)machen (*inf*); **to have one's ~ cut/done** sich (*dat*) die Haare schneiden/ (zurecht)machen (*inf*) lassen; **her ~ is always very well done** sie ist immer sehr gut frisiert; **to let one's ~ down** (*lit*) sein Haar aufmachen *or* lösen (*geh*); (*fig*) aus sich (*dat*) herausgehen; **keep your ~ on!** (*inf*) ruhig Blut!; **to get in sb's ~** (*inf*) jdm auf den Wecker *or* auf die Nerven gehen (*inf*); **that film really made my ~ stand on end** bei dem Film lief es mir eiskalt die Rücken herunter.
 (b) (*single ~*) Haar *nt.* **not a ~ of his head was harmed** ihm wurde kein Haar gekrümmt; **not a ~ out of place** (*fig*) wie aus dem Ei gepellt; **to win/lose by a ~** ganz knapp gewinnen/ver-lieren; see **turn, split.**
 (c) (*on body*) Haar(e *pl*) *nt*; (*total body ~*) Behaarung *f.* **in comparison to the apes man shows little body ~** im Vergleich zum Affen weist der Mensch geringe Körperbehaarung auf.
 (d) (*of animal, plant*) Haar *nt*; (*of pig*) Borste *f.* **the best cure for a hangover is the ~ of the dog that bit you** einen Kater kuriert man am besten, wenn man mit dem anfängt, womit man aufgehört hat.
2 *attr* mattress, sofa Roßhaar-.

hair: ~ ball *n* Haarknäuel *nt*; **~-band** *n* Haarband *nt*; **~-breadth,** **~'s breadth** *n* Haaresbreite *f*; **by a ~'s breadth** um Haares-breite; **to be within a ~'s breadth of ruin** am Rande des Ruins stehen; **he was within a ~'s breadth of dying** er wäre um ein Haar gestorben; **to escape by a ~'s breadth** mit knapper Not entkommen; **~brush** *n* Haarbürste *f*; **~ clip** *n* Clip *m*; (*for pony-tail etc*) Haarspange *f*; **~-clippers** *npl* elektrische Haarschneidemaschine; **~ cream** *n* Haarcreme, Pomade *f*; **~ curler** *n* Lockenwickler *m*; **~cut** *n* Haarschnitt *m*; (*act also*) Haarschneiden *nt*; (*hairdo*) Frisur *f*; **to have or get a ~cut** sich (*dat*) die Haare schneiden lassen; **I need a ~cut** ich muß zum Friseur, ich muß mir die Haare schneiden lassen; **~do** *n* (*inf*) Frisur *f*; **~dresser** *n* Friseur *m*, Friseuse *f*; **the ~dresser's** der Friseur; **~dressing** *n* Frisieren *nt*; (*tonic*) Haarwasser *nt*; **~dressing salon** *n* Frisiersalon *m*; **~drier** *n* Haartrockner *m*; (*hand-held also*) Fön ® *m*; (*over head also*) Trockenhaube *f.*

-haired [ˈheəd] *adj suf* -haarig.

hair: ~ follicle *n* Haarfollikel *nt*, Haarbalg *m*; **~-grip** *n* Haar-klemme *f*, Klemmchen *nt.*

hairiness [ˈheərɪnɪs] *n* Behaartheit *f.* **is ~ a sign of virility?** ist starker Haarwuchs ein Zeichen von Männlichkeit?

hair: ~ lacquer *n* Haarspray *m or nt*, Haarlack *m* (*old*); **~less** *adj* unbehaart; *plant* haarlos; **~-line** *n* (a) Haaransatz *m*; (b) (*thin line*) haarfeine Linie; (*in telescope, on sight*) Faden *m*; (*Typ*) senkrechter Strich; **~-lines** Fadenkreuz *nt*; **~-line crack** *n* Haarriß *m*; **~net** *n* Haarnetz *nt*; **~ oil** *n* Haaröl *nt*; **~-piece** *n* Haarteil *nt*; (*for men*) Toupet *nt*; **~pin** *n* Haarnadel *f*; **~pin (bend)** *n* Haarnadelkurve *f*; **~-raiser** *n* (*inf*) (*experience*) haar-sträubendes *or* entsetzliches Erlebnis; (*film, story*) Horror- *or* Gruselfilm *m*/-geschichte *f*, Schocker *m* (*inf*); **~-raising** *adj* haarsträubend; **~ remover** *n* Haarentferner *m*, Haarentfer-nungsmittel *nt*; **~ restorer** *n* Haarwuchsmittel *nt*; **~ roller** *n* Lockenwickler *m*; **~'s breadth** *n see* **~-breadth**; **~ shirt** *n* härenes Gewand (*old, liter*); **~ slide** *n* Haarspange *f*; **~ space** *n* (*Typ*) Haarspatium *f*; **~-splitter** *n* Haarspalter *m*; **~-splitting 1** *n* Haarspalterei *f*; **2** *adj* haarspalterisch; **~spray** *n* Haarspray *m or nt*; **~-spring** *n* Spiralfeder *f*; **~-style** *n* Frisur *f*; **~stylist** *n* Coiffeur *m*, Coiffeuse *f*, Haarkünstler(in *f*) *m*; **~ trigger** *n* Stecher *m.*

hairy [ˈheərɪ] *adj* (+*er*) (a) stark behaart; *parts of body also, monster* haarig. **the cat makes everything all ~** die Katze hin-terläßt überall Haare; **some ~ freak** so ein behaarter Typ. **(b)** (*Bot*) behaart. **(c)** (*sl*) gefährlich; *bridge, corner, driving* kriminell (*sl*); *situation* brenzlig (*inf*).

Haiti ['heɪtɪ] n Haiti nt.
Haitian ['heɪʃɪən] **1** adj haitianisch, haitisch. **2** n (a) Haitianer(in f) m. (b) (language) Haitisch nt.
hake [heɪk] n See- or Meerhecht, Hechtdorsch m.
halberd ['hælbəd] n Hellebarde f.
halberdier [‚hælbə'dɪəʳ] n Hellebardier m.
halcyon ['hælsɪən] adj: ~ days glückliche Tage pl.
hale [heɪl] adj (+er) kräftig; old man rüstig. ~ and hearty gesund und munter.

half [hɑːf] **1** n, pl **halves** (a) Hälfte f. two halves make a whole zwei Halbe machen ein Ganzes; to cut in ~ halbieren; (with knife also) in zwei Hälften or Teile schneiden; journey time also um or auf die Hälfte verkürzen; salary etc um or auf die Hälfte kürzen; to break/tear sth in ~ etw durchbrechen/durchreißen; ~ of it/them die Hälfte davon/von ihnen; ~ the book/money/my life die Hälfte des Buches/Geldes/meines Lebens or das halbe Buch/Geld/mein halbes Leben; he gave me ~ er gab mir die Hälfte; ~ a cup/an hour/a lifetime eine halbe Tasse/Stunde/ein halbes Leben; he's only ~ a man er ist nur ein halber Mensch; ~ a second! (einen) Augenblick mal!; I'll be round in ~ a second (inf) ich komme gleich (mal) hin; to listen with ~ an ear nur mit halbem Ohr zuhören; to take ~ of sth die Hälfte von etw nehmen; to go halves (with sb on sth) (mit jdm mit etw) halbe-halbe machen (inf); that's only ~ the story das ist nur die halbe Geschichte; have ~ of my apple willst du einen halben Apfel von mir haben?; bigger by ~ anderthalbmal so groß; he is too clever by ~ (inf) das ist ein richtiger Schlaumeier; he's too cocky by ~ (inf) er hält sich für wer weiß was (inf); not ~ enough bei weitem nicht or längst nicht genug; one and a ~ eineinhalb, anderthalb; an hour and a ~ eineinhalb or anderthalb Stunden; not to do things by halves keine halben Sachen machen; ~ and ~ halb und halb; that's a hill and a ~! (inf) das ist vielleicht ein Berg!; that's not the ~ of it (inf), I haven't told you the ~ of it yet (inf) und das ist noch nicht einmal die Hälfte (inf).
(b) (Sport) (of match) (Spiel)hälfte f; (player) Läufer(in f) m.
(c) (of ticket) Abschnitt m der Fahrkarte; (travel, admission fee) halbe Karte (inf). return ~ Abschnitt m für die Rückfahrt; two adults and one ~, please zwei Erwachsene und ein Kind, bitte; two and a ~ (to London) zweieinhalb(mal London).
(d) (beer) kleines Bier, Halbe f (dial), Halbe(s), Kleine(s) nt; (Scot: whisky) einfacher Whisky.
2 adj halb. a ~ cup eine halbe Tasse; with ~ his usual strength nur mit halber Kraft; ~ one thing ~ another halb und halb, halb das eine und halb das andere; ~ man ~ beast halb Mensch, halb Tier; he's not ~ the man he used to be er ist längst nicht mehr das, was er einmal war; it's neither opera nor operetta but sort of ~ and ~ es ist so ein Zwischending nt zwischen Oper und Operette.
3 adv ~ halb. I ~ thought … ich hätte fast gedacht …; I was ~ afraid that … ich habe fast befürchtet, daß …; ~ melted halbgeschmolzen attr, halb geschmolzen pred; the work is only ~ done die Arbeit ist erst halb or zur Hälfte erledigt; that's ~ right das ist zur Hälfte richtig; ~ laughing, ~ crying halb lachend, halb weinend; ~ laughing, ~ crying he told me … mit einem lachenden und einem weinenden Auge erzählte er mir …; he ~ rose to his feet er erhob sich halb; I ~ think ich habe beinahe den Eindruck; he only ~ understands er begreift or versteht nur die Hälfte.
(b) (Brit inf) he's not ~ stupid/rich etc er ist vielleicht or unheimlich dumm/reich etc; it didn't ~ rain/he didn't ~ yell es hat vielleicht geregnet/er hat vielleicht gebrüllt; not ~ bad gar nicht schlecht; not ~! und wie! und ob!
(c) it's ~ past three or ~ three es ist halb vier.
(d) he is ~ as big as his sister er ist halb so groß wie seine Schwester; ~ as big again anderthalbmal so groß; he earns ~ as much as you er verdient halb so viel wie Sie; he earns ~ as much again as you er verdient die Hälfte mehr als du or anderthalbmal soviel wie du; give me ~ as much again gib mir noch die Hälfte dazu.

half-: ~-a-crown n see half-crown; ~-a-dozen n, adj see ~-dozen; ~ back n (Sport) Läufer(in f) m; ~-baked adj (fig) person, plan blödsinnig; ~-binding n (of book) Halbfranzband m; ~-bred adj Mischlings-; (esp Red Indian) Halbblut-; most ~-bred Americans die meisten amerikanischen Mischlinge; ~-breed **1** n (person) Mischling m; (esp Red Indian) Halbblut nt; (animal) Rassenmischung f; (horse) Halbblut nt, Halbblüter m; **2** adj animal gekreuzt; horse Halbblut-; a ~-breed dog eine Mischrasse, eine Rassenmischung; see also ~-bred; ~ brother n Halbbruder m; ~-caste **1** n Mischling m; (esp Red Indian) Halbblut nt; **2** adj Mischlings-; (esp Red Indian) Halbblut-; a ~-caste American ein amerikanischer Mischling; ~-circle n Halbkreis m; ~-cock n: to go off or at ~-cock (inf) ein Reinfall m sein (inf), ein Schuß m in den Ofen sein (sl); ~-cocked adj pistol in Vorderraststellung; ~-cooked adj halbgar attr, halb gar pred; ~-cracked adj (Brit sl: crazy) beknackt (sl), bescheuert (sl); ~-crown n (in old Brit system) Half Crown f, Zweieinhalbschillingstück nt; ~-cup brassière n Büstenhalter m mit Halbschalen; ~-cut adj (Brit sl: drunk) besoffen (sl); ~-day (holiday) n halber freier Tag; we've got a ~-day (holiday) wir haben einen halben Tag frei; ~-dead adj (lit, fig) halbtot (with vor +dat); ~-dollar n halber Dollar; ~-dozen n halbes Dutzend; ~-empty adj halbleer attr, halb leer pred; **2** vt zur Hälfte leeren or leermachen; ~-fare **1** n halber Fahrpreis; he still manages to get a ~-fare er kann immer noch zum halben Preis fahren; **2** adv zum halben Preis; ~-fill vt halb füllen; ~-frame camera n Halbformatkamera f; ~-full adj halbvoll attr, halb voll pred; ~-hearted adj halbherzig; attempt also lustlos; manner lustlos, lau; noises of approval also lau; he was rather ~-hearted about accepting er nahm ohne rechte

Lust an; he seems very ~-hearted about it er scheint sich dafür nicht so recht begeistern zu können; ~-heartedly adv agree halben Herzens, mit halbem Herzen; to do sth ~-heartedly etw ohne rechte Überzeugung or Lust tun; ~-heartedness n Halbherzigkeit, Lustlosigkeit f; the ~-heartedness of his attempts seine halbherzigen or lustlosen Versuche pl; ~-holiday n halber Urlaubstag/Feiertag; we've got a ~-holiday tomorrow morning wir haben morgen vormittag frei; ~-hour n halbe Stunde; ~-an-hour's or ~-hour interval eine halbstündige Pause, eine halbe Stunde Pause; it strikes on the ~-hour sie schlägt die halben Stunden; ~-hourly **1** adv jede or alle halbe Stunde, halbstündlich; **2** adj halbstündlich; ~-landing n Treppenabsatz m; ~-length adj ~-length portrait Brustbild nt; ~-life n (Phys) Halbwertszeit f; ~-light n Dämmerlicht, Halbdunkel nt; ~-mast n: at ~-mast (also hum) (auf) halbmast; with his trousers at ~-mast (not short) mit Hochwasserhosen; ~-measure n halbe Maßnahme; Stehenbleiben nt no pl auf halbem Weg; we don't do things by ~-measures wir machen keine halben Sachen, wir begnügen uns nicht mit Halbheiten; ~-moon n (a) Halbmond m; (b) (of fingernails) Mond m; ~-naked adj halbnackt attr, halb nackt pred; ~ nelson n (Wrestling) Halbnelson m; ~-note n (US Mus) halbe Note; ~-open **1** adj halboffen attr, halb offen pred; **2** vt halb öffnen or aufmachen; ~-pay n halber Lohn; halbes Gehalt; to be on ~-pay/to be put on ~-pay den halben Lohn etc bekommen/auf halben Lohn gesetzt werden; ~-pence n (a) (in old Brit system, also ha'pence) (value) halber Penny; (b) (in new Brit system) (value) halber Penny; (coin) Halbpennystück; ~-penny ['heɪpnɪ] **1** n halber Penny; **2** attr stamp Halbpenny-; increase um einen halben Penny; ~-pint n (a) = Viertelliter m or nt; (of beer also) kleines Bier; (b) (inf: person) halbe Portion (inf), Knirps m (inf); ~-price **1** n at ~-price zum halben Preis; reduced to ~-price auf den halben Preis heruntergesetzt; **2** adv zum halben Preis; ~-rest n (US Mus) halbe Pause; ~-seas over adj (dated inf) bezecht, leicht hinüber (inf); ~-sister n Halbschwester f; ~-size **1** n Zwischengröße f; **2** adj halb so groß; ~-size plate kleiner Teller; a ~-size model of sth ein Modell nt von etw in halber Größe; ~-term n (Brit) Ferien pl in der Mitte des Trimesters; we get three days for ~-term wir haben drei Tage Ferien in der Mitte des Trimesters; ~-timbered adj Fachwerk-; ~-timbering n Fachwerkbauweise f; ~-time **1** n (a) (Sport) Halbzeit f; at ~-time bei or zur Halbzeit; (b) (Ind) to be/to be put on ~-time auf Kurzarbeit sein/gesetzt werden; **2** attr whistle, score Halbzeit-, zur Halbzeit; **3** adv to work ~-time halbtags arbeiten or beschäftigt sein; ~-title n Schmutztitel m; ~-tone n (Art, Phot, US Mus) Halbton m; (Phot) (process) Halbtonverfahren nt; (picture) Halbtonbild nt; ~-tone screen n (Typ) Raster m; ~-track n (vehicle) Halbkettenfahrzeug nt; ~-truth n Halbwahrheit f; ~-volley (Tennis) **1** n Halfvolley, Halbflugball m; **2** vt ball als Halfvolley schlagen; **3** vi einen Halfvolley or Halbflugball schlagen.

halfway ['hɑːf'weɪ] **1** adj attr measures halb. at a ~ stage in einem Zwischenstadium; when we reached the ~ stage on our journey als wir die Hälfte der Reise hinter uns (dat) hatten; the project is at the ~ stage das Projekt ist zur Hälfte abgeschlossen; he was at the ~ stage of his musical career er befand sich in der Mitte seiner musikalischen Karriere; we're past the ~ stage wir haben die Hälfte geschafft; it is a sort of ~ stage between democracy and … das ist eine Art Zwischenstadium zwischen Demokratie und …; (temporal) it's almost eine Art Zwischenstellung zwischen Demokratie und … ein.
2 adv her hair reached ~ down her back die Haare gingen ihr bis weit über die Schultern; ~-way to auf halbem Weg nach; we drove ~ to London wir fuhren die halbe Strecke or den halben Weg nach London; ~ between two points (in der Mitte or genau) zwischen zwei Punkten; I live ~ up the hill ich wohne auf halber Höhe des Berges; we went ~ up the hill wir gingen den Berg halb hinauf; we were ~ down the hill when … wir waren den Berg schon halb hinunter, als …; ~ through a book halb durch ein Buch (durch); to go ~ (lit) die halbe Strecke or die Hälfte des Weges zurücklegen; this money will go ~ towards paying … diese Summe wird die Hälfte der Kosten für … decken; I don't accept the idea in toto but I am willing to go ~ with you ich stimme dieser Überlegung nicht in vollem Umfang zu, aber ich bin bereit, Ihnen (auf halbem Weg) entgegenzukommen; to meet sb ~ (lit, fig) jdm (auf halbem Weg) entgegenkommen.
3 attr ~ house n Gasthaus nt auf halbem Weg; (hostel) offene Anstalt; (fig) Zwischending nt; we could stop off at the King's Head, that's a ~ house wir können im „King's Head" einkehren, das liegt auf halbem Wege.
half-: ~-wit n Schwachsinnige(r) mf; (fig) Schwachkopf m; ~-witted ['hɑːf‚wɪtɪd] adj schwachsinnig; ~-year n Halbjahr nt; ~-yearly **1** adj halbjährlich; **2** adv halbjährlich, jedes halbe Jahr.
halibut ['hælɪbət] n Heilbutt m.
halitosis [‚hælɪ'təʊsɪs] n schlechter Mundgeruch.
hall [hɔːl] n (a) (entrance ~ of house) Diele f, Korridor m.
(b) (large building) Halle f; (large room) Saal m; (Brit: of college) Speisesaal m; (Brit: college mealtime) Essen nt; (dance-~) Tanzdiele f; (village ~) Gemeindehalle f, Gemeindehaus nt; (school assembly ~) Aula f. he will join the ~ of fame of … (fig) er wird in die Geschichte des … eingehen, er wird in die Ruhmeshalle des … aufgenommen (liter).
(c) (mansion) Herrensitz m, Herrenhaus nt; (students' residence: also ~ of residence) Studenten(wohn)heim nt. to live in ~ im Wohnheim wohnen; Ruskin ~ Haus Ruskin nt.
hallelujah [‚hælɪ'luːjə] **1** interj halleluja. **2** n Halleluja nt.
hallmark ['hɔːlmɑːk] **1** n (a) (on gold, silver) (Feingehalts)stempel m, Repunze f.
(b) (fig) Kennzeichen nt (of gen, für). a ~ of good quality ein

Gütesiegel *nt*; it bears *or* has all the ~s of an early Picasso es trägt *or* hat alle Kennzeichen eines frühen Picassos; this is the ~ of a true genius daran erkennt man das wahre Genie.
  2 *vt* gold, silver stempeln.

hallo [hə'ləʊ] *interj*, *n* see **hello**.

halloo [hə'luː] **1** *interj* hallo; (*Hunt*) horrido, hallo. **2** *n* Halloruf *m*; (*Hunt*) Horrido, Hallo *nt*. **3** *vi* (hallo) rufen; (*Hunt*) die Hunde hetzen.

hallow ['hæləʊ] *vt* heiligen; (*consecrate*) weihen. ~ed be Thy name (*Bibl*) geheiligt werde Dein Name.

Hallowe'en [ˌhæləʊ'iːn] *n* Tag *m* vor Allerheiligen.

hall: ~ **porter** *n* Portier *m*; ~**stand** *n* (Flur)garderobe *f*; (*tree-like*) Garderobenständer *m*.

hallucinate [hə'luːsɪneɪt] *vi* halluzinieren, Wahnvorstellungen haben.

hallucination [həˌluːsɪ'neɪʃən] *n* (a) Halluzination, Wahnvorstellung *f*. (b) (*inf: false idea*) Wahnvorstellung *f*.

hallucinatory [həˈluːsɪnətərɪ] *adj* halluzinatorisch; (*causing hallucinations*) Halluzinationen hervorrufend.

hallucinogenic [həˌluːsɪnə'dʒenɪk] *adj* Halluzinationen hervorrufend *attr*, halluzinogen (*spec*). LSD is ~ LSD ist ein Halluzinogen *nt*.

hallway ['hɔːlweɪ] *n* Flur, Korridor *m*.

halo ['heɪləʊ] **1** *n*, *pl* **-(e)s** (*of saint*) Heiligenschein *m*; (*fig iro*) Heiligen- *or* Glorienschein *m*; (*Astron*) Hof, Halo (*spec*) *m*. his ~ never slips nichts kann seinen Heiligenschein trüben. **2** *vt* (*fig*) umrahmen. his head, ~ed by the sun sein Haupt, umrahmt *or* umkränzt (*liter*) vom Sonnenlicht.

halogen ['heɪlə(ʊ)dʒɪn] *n* Halogen *nt*. ~ lamp Halogenlampe *f*; (*Aut*) Halogenscheinwerfer *m*.

halt[1] [hɔːlt] **1** *n* (a) (*stop*) Pause *f*; (*Mil*) Halt *m*; (*in production*) Stopp *m*. the officer ordered a ~ der Offizier befahl Halt; five minutes' ~ fünf Minuten Pause; to come to a ~ zum Stillstand kommen; to call a ~ to sth einer Sache (*dat*) ein Ende machen *or* bereiten; he called a ~ to the discussion er beendete die Diskussion; shall we call a ~ now, gentlemen? wollen wir jetzt Schluß machen, meine Herren?; ~ sign Stoppschild *nt*.
  (b) (*small station*) Haltepunkt *m*.
  2 *vi* zum Stillstand kommen; (*person*) anhalten, stehenbleiben; (*Mil*) halten. he was going to ... but then ~ed er wollte ..., aber hielt dann inne; we ~ed briefly before attempting the summit wir hielten kurz an *or* machten kurz halt, bevor wir den Gipfel in Angriff nahmen.
  3 *vt* anhalten; *production, vehicles, traffic also* zum Stehen *or* Stillstand bringen; *troops* halten lassen.
  4 *interj* halt; (*traffic sign*) stop.

halt[2] **1** *vi* (*obs*) hinken; (*in speech*) stockend sprechen. **2** *n* (*Bibl*) the ~ and the lame die Krummen und die Lahmen.

halter ['hɔːltəʳ] *n* (a) (*horse's*) Halfter *nt*. (b) (*for hanging*) Schlinge *f*.

halter-neck ['hɔːltənek] **1** *n* rückenfreies Kleid/Top *nt* mit Nackenband. **2** *adj* rückenfrei mit Nackenverschluß.

halting ['hɔːltɪŋ] *adj* walk unsicher; speech stockend; admission zögernd; verse holp(e)rig.

haltingly ['hɔːltɪŋlɪ] *adv* see *adj*.

halve [hɑːv] *vt* (a) (*separate in two*) halbieren; (*Math also*) durch zwei teilen. (b) (*reduce by one half*) auf die Hälfte reduzieren, halbieren.

halves [hɑːvz] *pl of* **half**.

halyard ['hæljəd] *n* (*Naut*) Fall *nt*; (*for flag*) Flaggleine *f*.

ham [hæm] **1** *n* (a) (*Cook*) Schinken *m*. ~ sandwich Schinkenbrot *nt*.
  (b) (*Anat*) ~s (hintere) Oberschenkel *pl*; (*of animal*) (Hinter)-keulen *pl*; to squat on one's ~s hocken, in der Hocke sitzen.
  (c) (*Theat*) Schmierenkomödiant(in *f*) *m*.
  (d) (*Rad inf*) Funkamateur *m*.
  2 *adj attr* acting übertrieben, zu dick aufgetragen.
  3 *vi* (*Theat*) übertrieben, übertrieben spielen.

♦ **ham up** *vt sep* (*inf*) übertreiben. to ~ it ~ zu dick auftragen.

hamburger ['hæmˌbɜːgəʳ] *n* (flache) Frikadelle *f*; (*with bread*) Hamburger *m*.

ham: ~**-fisted**, ~**-handed** *adj* ungeschickt; efforts, person *also* tolpatschig.

Hamitic [hæ'mɪtɪk] *adj* hamitisch.

hamlet ['hæmlɪt] *n* Weiler *m*, kleines Dorf.

hammer ['hæməʳ] **1** *n* (a) (*generally*) Hammer *m*; (*of gun*) Hahn *m*. to go at it ~ and tongs (*inf*) sich ins Zeug legen (*inf*), schwer rangehen (*sl*); (*work also*) schuften, daß die Fetzen fliegen (*inf*); (*quarrel*) sich in die Wolle kriegen (*inf*), sich streiten, daß die Fetzen fliegen; my heart was going like a ~ das Herz schlug mir bis zum Hals; to come under the ~ (*auction*) unter den Hammer kommen; throwing the ~ (*Sport*) Hammerwerfen *nt*; in the ~ (throwing) (*Sport*) im Hammerwurf.
  2 *vt* (a) nail, metal hämmern. to ~ a nail into a wall einen Nagel in die Wand schlagen; to ~ sth into shape metal etw zurechthämmern; (*fig*) plan, agreement etw ausarbeiten *or* austüfteln (*inf*); to ~ sth into sb *or* sb's head jdm etw einbleuen (*inf*).
  (b) (*inf: defeat badly*) eine Schlappe beibringen +*dat* (*inf*). Chelsea were ~ed 6–1 Chelsea mußte eine 6:1-Schlappe einstecken (*inf*).
  (c) (*St Ex sl*) stockbroker für zahlungsunfähig erklären.
  3 *vi* hämmern. to ~ at the door an die Tür hämmern.

♦ **hammer away** *vi* (darauflos)hämmern. to ~ ~ at a problem sich (*dat*) über ein Problem den Kopf zerbrechen; to ~ ~ at the door an die Tür hämmern; the boxer ~ed ~ at him der Boxer hämmerte auf ihn ein; his heart was ~ing ~ sein Herz hämmerte nur so; the pianist ~ed ~ at the keys der Pianist hämmerte auf die Tasten.

♦ **hammer down** *vt sep* festhämmern; nail einschlagen; bump flachhämmern.

♦ **hammer home** *vt sep* (a) nail festhineinschlagen. (b) argument, point etc Nachdruck verleihen (+*dat*), untermauern. he tried to ~ it ~ to the pupils that ... er versuchte, den Schülern einzubleuen (*inf*) *or* einzuhämmern, daß ...

♦ **hammer in** *vt sep* (a) nail etc einschlagen, einhämmern. (b) door einschlagen. (c) (*fig*) fact einhämmern, einbleuen (*inf*).

♦ **hammer out** *vt sep* (a) metal hämmern; nail, bricks (her)ausschlagen *or* -klopfen; dent ausbeulen. (b) (*fig*) plan, agreement, solution ausarbeiten, aushandeln; difficulties beseitigen, bereinigen; verse schmieden; tune hämmern.

hammer and sickle *n sing* Hammer und Sichel *pl*.

hammer: ~ **beam** *n* Stichbalken *m*; ~**head** *n* (*shark*) Hammerhai *m*; (*of hammer*) Hammerkopf *m*.

hammering ['hæmərɪŋ] *n* (a) Hämmern, Klopfen *nt*. (b) (*inf: defeat*) Schlappe *f* (*inf*). our team took a ~ unsere Mannschaft mußte eine Schlappe einstecken.

hammer toe *n* Hammerzehe *f or* -zeh *m*.

hammock ['hæmək] *n* Hängematte *f*.

hamper[1] ['hæmpəʳ] *n* (*basket*) Korb *m*; (*as present*) Geschenkkorb *m*.

hamper[2] *vt* behindern; movement *also* erschweren; person *also* Schwierigkeiten bereiten (+*dat*); to be ~ed gehindert werden; the police were ~ed in their search by the shortage of clues der Mangel an Hinweisen erschwerte der Polizei die Suche.

hamster ['hæmstəʳ] *n* Hamster *m*.

hamstring ['hæmstrɪŋ] (*vb: pret, ptp* **hamstrung** ['hæmstrʌŋ]) **1** *n* (*Anat*) Kniesehne *f*; (*of animal*) Achillessehne *f*.
  2 *vt* (a) (*lit*) person, animal die Kniesehne/Achillessehne durchschneiden (+*dat*).
  (b) (*fig*) attempt etc vereiteln, unterbinden; person handlungsunfähig machen. to be hamstrung ausgeschmissen sein (*inf*); (*project, undertaking*) lahmgelegt sein, lahmliegen.

hand [hænd] **1** *n* (a) Hand *f*; (*of clock*) Zeiger *m*. on ~s and knees auf allen vieren; he felt he held victory in his ~ (*fig*) er glaube, den Sieg schon in Händen zu haben; to take/lead sb by the ~ jdn an die *or* bei der Hand nehmen/an der Hand führen; ~s up! Hände hoch!; (*Sch*) meldet euch!; ~s up who knows the answer/who wants to go wer es weiß, meldet sich *or* hebt die Hand/Hand hoch, wer gehen will; ~s off (*inf*) Hände weg!; keep your ~s off my wife laß die Finger *or* Pfoten (*inf*) von meiner Frau!; done *or* made by ~ handgearbeitet; this sewing was done by ~ dies ist von Hand genäht worden; to send a letter by ~ einen Brief durch (einen) Boten schicken; "by ~" „durch Boten"; to raise an animal by ~ ein Tier von Hand *or* mit der Flasche aufziehen; pistol in ~ mit vorgehaltener Pistole, mit der Pistole in der Hand; to climb ~ over ~ Hand über Hand klettern; to live from ~ to mouth von der Hand in den Mund leben; I give you my ~ on it ich gebe dir die Hand darauf, ich verspreche es dir in die Hand; with a heavy/firm ~ (*fig*) mit harter/fester *or* starker Hand; see hold, shake.
  (b) (*side, direction, position*) Seite *f*. on the right ~ auf der rechten Seite, rechts, rechter Hand; on my right ~ rechts von mir, zu meiner Rechten (*geh*); on every ~, on all ~s auf allen Seiten, ringsum(her); surrounded on all ~s von allen Seiten umringt; on the one ~ ... on the other ~ ... einerseits *or* auf der einen Seite ..., andererseits *or* auf der anderen Seite ...
  (c) (*agency, possession etc*) it's the ~ of God/fate das ist die Hand Gottes/des Schicksals; your life is in your own ~s Sie haben Ihr Leben (selbst) in der Hand; it's in your own ~s what you do now Sie haben es selbst in der Hand, was Sie jetzt tun; to put sth into sb's ~s jdm etw in die Hand geben, etw in jds Hände legen; to leave sth in sb's ~s jdm etw in jds Obhut lassen/jdm etw überlassen; to put oneself in(to) sb's ~s sich jdm anvertrauen, sich in jds Hände begeben (*geh*); my life is in your ~s mein Leben ist *or* liegt in Ihren Händen; to fall into the ~s of jdm in die Hände fallen; to be in good ~s in guten Händen sein; I received some pretty rough treatment at her ~s ich bin von ihr ganz schön grob behandelt worden; he suffered terribly at the ~s of the enemy er machte in den Händen des Feindes Schreckliches durch; the treatment he experienced at the ~s of the enemy die Behandlung, die er von seiten des Feindes erfuhr; he has too much time on his ~s er hat zuviel Zeit zur Verfügung; he has this problem/a lot of work/five children on his ~s er hat ein Problem/viel Arbeit/fünf Kinder am Hals (*inf*); I've got enough on my ~s already ich habe schon genug um die Ohren (*inf*) *or* am Hals (*inf*); I like to have a lot on my ~s es macht mir Spaß, wenn ich viel zu tun *or* um die Ohren (*inf*) habe; to get sb/sth off one's ~s jdn/etw loswerden; to take sb/sth off sb's ~s jdm jdn/etw abnehmen; goods left on our ~s (*Comm*) nicht abgesetzte Waren; see die, change, free.
  (d) (*applause*) Applaus, Beifall *m*. they gave him a big ~ sie gaben ihm großen Applaus, sie klatschten ihm großen Beifall; let's give a big ~ to our guest und nun großen Beifall für unseren Gast.
  (e) (*worker*) Arbeitskraft *f*, Arbeiter *m*; (*Naut*) Besatzungsmitglied *nt*. to take on ~s Leute einstellen; (*Naut*) Leute anheuern; ~s Leute *pl*, Belegschaft *f*; (*ship's*) ~s Besatzung, Mannschaft *f*; all ~s on deck! alle Mann an Deck!; lost with all ~s mit der ganzen Besatzung untergegangen.
  (f) (*expert*) to be a good ~ at sth/doing sth (ein) Geschick *nt* für etw haben/ein Geschick dafür haben, etw zu tun; to be an old ~ (at sth) ein alter Hase (in etw dat) sein; see dab[3].
  (g) (*Measure: of horse*) = 10 cm.
  (h) (*handwriting*) Handschrift *f*. he writes a good ~ er hat eine gute (Hand)schrift.
  (i) (*Cards*) Blatt *nt*; (*person*) Mann *m*; (*game*) Runde *f*. 3 ~s (*people*) 3 Mann; a ~ of bridge eine Runde Bridge; to show one's ~ seine Karten sehen lassen *or* aufdecken; (*fig*) sich (*dat*) in die Karten sehen lassen.
  (j) summer/Christmas etc is (close) at ~ der Sommer/Weihnachten etc steht vor der Tür, es ist bald Sommer

Weihnachten *etc*; **at first/second ~** aus erster/zweiter Hand; **according to the information at** *or* **on ~** gemäß *or* laut der vorhandenen *or* vorliegenden Informationen; **we have little information at** *or* **on ~** wir haben kaum Informationen *pl* (zur Verfügung); **to keep sth at ~** etw in Reichweite haben; **it's quite close at ~** es ist ganz in der Nähe; **he had the situation well in ~** er hatte die Situation im Griff; **she took the child in ~** sie nahm die Erziehung des Kindes in die Hand; **to take sb in ~** (*discipline*) jdn in die Hand nehmen; (*look after*) jdn in Obhut nehmen, nach jdm sehen; **stock in ~** (*Comm*) Warenlager *nt*; **what stock have you in ~?** welche Waren haben Sie am Lager?; **he still had £600/a couple of hours in ~** er hatte £ 600 übrig/noch zwei Stunden Zeit; **the matter in ~** die vorliegende *or* (*in discussion*) zur Debatte stehende Angelegenheit; **work in ~** Arbeit, die zur Zeit erledigt wird; **we've got quite a lot of work in** *or* **on ~** wir haben sehr viel Arbeit anstehen *or* zu tun; **a matter/project** *etc* **is in ~** eine Sache/ein Projekt *nt etc* wird bearbeitet *or* ist in Bearbeitung; **to put sth in ~** zusehen, daß etw erledigt wird; **the children got out of ~** die Kinder waren nicht mehr zu bändigen *or* gerieten außer Rand und Band; **the party got out of ~** die Party ist ausgeartet; **the horse got out of ~** er hat/ich habe die Kontrolle über das Pferd verloren; **matters got out of ~** die Dinge sind außer Kontrolle geraten; **he has enough money to ~** ihm steht genügend Geld zur Verfügung; **I don't have the letter to ~** ich habe den Brief gerade nicht zur Hand; **your letter has come to ~** (*Comm*) wir haben Ihren Brief erhalten; **I don't know where it is right now but I'm sure it'll come to ~ before too long** ich weiß nicht, wo es im Augenblick ist, aber es wird sicherlich über kurz oder lang auftauchen; **he seized the first weapon to ~** er ergriff die erstbeste Waffe; see **palm²**, **cash**.

(k) (*phrases*) **to keep one's ~** in in Übung bleiben; **to eat out of sb's ~** (*lit, fig*) jdm aus der Hand fressen; **to force sb's ~** jdn zwingen, auf jdn Druck ausüben; **to wait on sb ~ and foot** jdn von vorne und hinten bedienen; **he never does a ~'s turn** er rührt keinen Finger, er macht keinen Finger krumm; **to have a ~ in sth** (*in decision*) an etw (*dat*) beteiligt sein; (*in crime*) die Hand bei etw im Spiel haben; **I had no ~ in it** ich hatte damit nichts zu tun; **to take a ~ in sth** an etw (*dat*) teilnehmen, sich an etw (+*dat*) beteiligen; **to lend** *or* **give sb a ~** jdm behilflich sein, jdm zur Hand gehen; **give me a ~!** hilf mir mal!; **to give sb a ~ up** jdm hochhelfen *or* auf die Beine helfen; (*push up*) jdn hochheben; (*pull up*) jdn hochziehen; **give me a ~ down** helfen Sie mir mal herunter/hinunter; **to be ~ in glove with sb** mit jdm unter einer Decke stecken, mit jdm gemeinsame Sache machen; **to have one's ~s full** with sth mit etw alle Hände voll zu tun haben; **to win ~s down** mühelos *or* spielend gewinnen; **to hold** *or* **stay one's ~** abwarten; **he is making money ~ over fist** er scheffelt das Geld nur so; **we're losing money/staff ~ over fist** wir verlieren massenweise Geld/Personal; **the inflation rate is rising ~ over fist** die Inflationsrate steigt rasend schnell; **to have the upper ~** die Oberhand behalten; **to get** *or* **gain the upper ~ (of sb)** (über jdn) die Oberhand gewinnen; **to ask for a lady's ~** (*in marriage*) um die Hand einer Dame anhalten.

2 *vt* **(a)** (*give*) reichen, geben (*sth to sb, sb sth* jdm etw). **you've got to ~ it to him** (*fig*) das muß man ihm lassen (*inf*).

(b) he ~ed the lady into/out of the carriage er half der Dame in die/aus der Kutsche.

♦**hand back** *vt sep* zurückgeben.

♦**hand down** *vt sep* **(a)** (*lit*) herunter-/hinunterreichen *or* -geben (*to sb* jdm).

(b) (*fig*) weitergeben; *tradition, belief also* überliefern; *heirloom etc* vererben (*to dat*); *clothes also* vererben (*inf*) (*to dat*); *story* (*from sb to sb*) überliefern (*to an* +*acc*), weitergeben (*to an* +*acc*). **all his clothes were ~ed ~ from his elder brothers** er mußte die Kleidung seiner älteren Brüder auftragen.

(c) (*Jur*) *sentence* fällen.

♦**hand in** *vt sep* abgeben; *forms, thesis also, resignation* einreichen.

♦**hand off** *vt sep* (*Rugby*) (mit der Hand) wegstoßen.

♦**hand on** *vt sep* weitergeben (*to an* +*acc*).

♦**hand out** *vt sep* austeilen, verteilen (*to sb* an jdn); *advice* geben, erteilen (*to sb* jdm); *heavy sentence* verhängen, austeilen. **the Spanish boxer was really ~ing it ~** *or* **~ing ~ the punishment** (*inf*) der spanische Boxer hat wirklich ganz schön zugeschlagen *or* ausgeteilt (*inf*).

♦**hand over 1** *vt sep* (*pass over*) (herüber-/hinüber)reichen (*to dat*); (*hand on*) weitergeben (*to an* +*acc*); (*give up*) (her)geben (*to dat*); (*to third party*) (ab)geben (*to dat*); *criminal, prisoner* übergeben (*to dat*); (*from one state to another*) ausliefern; *leadership, authority, powers* abgeben, abtreten (*to an* +*acc*); *the controls, property, business* übergeben (*to dat, an* +*acc*). **~ that gun!** Waffe her!; **I now ~ you ~ to our political correspondent** ich gebe nun weiter *or* übergebe nun an unseren (politischen) Korrespondenten.

2 *vi* **when the Conservatives ~ed ~ to Labour** als die Konservativen die Regierung an Labour abgaben; **when the chairman ~ed ~ to his successor** ... als der Vorsitzende das Amt an seinen Nachfolger abgab; **come on, ~ ~, I saw you take it** gib schon her, ich habe gesehen, wie du's genommen hast; **I now ~ ~ to our sports correspondent** ... ich übergebe nun an unseren Sportberichterstatter ...; **he ~ed ~ to the co-pilot** er übergab an den Kopiloten.

♦**hand round** *vt sep* herumreichen; *bottle also* herumgehen lassen; (*distribute*) *papers* austeilen, verteilen.

♦**hand up** *vt sep* hinauf-/heraufreichen.

hand: **~bag** *n* Handtasche *f*; **~ baggage** *n* Handgepäck *nt*; **~ball** **1** *n* (**a**) (*game*) Handball *m*; (**b**) (*Ftbl: foul*) Handspiel *nt*, Hand *f*; **2** *interj* (*Ftbl*) Hand!; **~barrow** *n* Schubkarre *f*; **~ basin** *n* Handwaschbecken *nt*; **~ bell** *n* Schelle *f*, Glocke *f* (mit Stiel);

~bill *n* Flugblatt *nt*, Handzettel *m*; **~book** *n* Handbuch *nt*; (*tourist's*) Reiseführer *m*; **~brake** *n* Handbremse *f*.

h & c *abbr of* **hot and cold (water)** k.u.w., kalt und warm.

hand: **~car** *n* (*Rail*) Draisine *f*; **~cart** *n* Handwagen *m*; **~clasp** *n* (*US*) Händedruck *m*; **~cuff** *vt* Handschellen anlegen (+*dat*); **he ~cuffed himself to the railings** er machte sich mit Handschellen am Geländer fest; **to be ~cuffed** Handschellen angelegt bekommen; **the accused was ~cuffed to a police officer** der Angeklagte war (mit Handschellen).an einen Polizisten gefesselt; **~cuffs** *npl* Handschellen *pl*.

handfeed ['hændˌfiːd] *pret, ptp* **handfed** ['hændˌfed] *vt animal* mit der Flasche aufziehen.

handful ['hændful] *n* **(a)** Handvoll *f*; (*of hair, fur*) Büschel *nt*. **a ~ of soil** eine Handvoll Erde; **by the ~, in ~s** händeweise; büschelweise.

(b) (*small number*) Handvoll *f*.

(c) (*fig*) **those children are a ~** die Kinder können einen ganz schön in Trab halten; **his new girl's quite a ~** (*hum*),an seiner neuen Freundin ist ganz hübsch was dran (*inf*).

hand: **~grenade** *n* Handgranate *f*; **~grip** *n* (Hand)griff *m*; (*handshake*) Händedruck *m*; **~gun** *n* Handfeuerwaffe *f*; **~-held** *adj* **taken with a ~-held camera** aus der (freien) Hand aufgenommen; **~hold** *n* Halt *m*.

handicap ['hændɪkæp] **1** *n* **(a)** (*Sport*) Handikap *nt*; (*in horse racing, golf also*) Vorgabe *f*; (*race*) Vorgaberennen *nt*. **a ~ of 5lbs** eine (Gewichts)vorgabe von 5 Pfund.

(b) (*disadvantage*) Handikap *nt*; (*for specific purpose also*) Nachteil *m*; (*physical, mental also*) Behinderung *f*. **to be under a great ~** sehr im Nachteil sein, stark gehandikapt sein.

2 *vt* ein Handikap *nt* darstellen für; (*for a specific purpose also*) benachteiligen; *chances* beeinträchtigen. **he has always been ~ped by his accent** sein Akzent war immer ein Nachteil *m* für ihn; **to be (physically/mentally) ~ped** (körperlich/geistig) behindert sein; **~ped children** behinderte Kinder *pl*.

handicraft ['hændɪkrɑːft] *n* **(a)** (*work*) Kunsthandwerk *nt*; (*needlework etc*) Handarbeit *f*; (*woodwork, modelling etc*) Werken *nt*, Bastelarbeit *f*. **(b)** (*skill*) Geschick *nt*, Handfertigkeit, Geschicklichkeit *f*.

handily ['hændɪlɪ] *adv* **a** *situated* günstig. **(b)** (*US: easily*) *win* mit Leichtigkeit.

handiness ['hændɪnɪs] *n* **(a)** (*skill: of person*) Geschick *nt*, Geschicklichkeit *f*.

(b) (*nearness, accessibility: of shops etc*) günstige Lage.

(c) (*convenience, usefulness: of tool, car etc*) Nützlichkeit *f*; (*easiness to handle*) Handlichkeit *f*. **the ~ of this tool makes it a must for every do-it-yourself man** dieses Werkzeug ist so praktisch, daß es jeder Heimwerker unbedingt haben muß.

hand-in-hand ['hændɪn'hænd] *adv* (*lit, fig*) Hand in Hand.

handiwork ['hændɪwɜːk] *n, no pl* **(a)** (*lit*) Arbeit *f*; (*Sch: subject*) Werken *nt*; (*needlework etc*) Handarbeit *f*. **examples of the children's ~** Werkarbeiten *pl*/Handarbeiten *pl* der Kinder; **to do ~** werken, handarbeiten; (*at home*) basteln.

(b) (*fig*) Werk *nt*; (*pej*) Machwerk *nt*. **that looks like the ~ of the Gillies gang** das sieht ganz nach der Gillies-Bande aus.

handkerchief ['hæŋkətʃɪf] *n* Taschentuch *nt*.

hand-knitted ['hænd,nɪtɪd] *adj* handgestrickt.

handle ['hændl] **1** *n* **(a)** Griff *m*; (*of knife also*) Heft *nt*, Knauf *m*; (*of door also*) Klinke *f*; (*esp of broom, comb, saucepan*) Stiel *m*; (*esp of basket, bucket, casserole, cup, jug etc*) Henkel *m*; (*of handbag etc*) Bügel *m*; (*of pump*) Schwengel *m*; (*of car: starting ~*) (Anlaß- *or* Start)kurbel *f*. **to fly off the ~** (*inf*) an die Decke gehen (*inf*).

(b) (*fig: pretext*) Handhabe *f*.

(c) (*inf*) Titel *m*. **to have a ~ to one's name** ein „von und zu" sein (*inf*).

2 *vt* **(a)** (*touch, use hands on*) anfassen, berühren; (*Ftbl*) *ball* mit der Hand berühren. **be careful how you ~** that gehen Sie vorsichtig damit um; **please do not ~ the goods** Waren bitte nicht berühren; **"~ with care"** „Vorsicht – zerbrechlich"; „Vorsicht Glas/Blumen/lebende Tiere etc".

(b) (*deal with*) *person, animal, plant, tool, weapon, machine etc* umgehen mit; *legal or financial matters* erledigen; *legal case* handhaben, bearbeiten; *applicant, matter, problem* sich befassen mit; *material for essay etc* bearbeiten, verarbeiten; (*tackle*) *problem, interview etc* anfassen, anpacken; (*succeed in coping with*) *child, drunk, situation, problem* fertigwerden mit; (*resolve*) *matter* erledigen; *vehicle, plane, ship* steuern. **how would you ~ the situation?** wie würden Sie sich in der Situation verhalten?; **you have to ~ that situation/your employees very carefully** in dieser Situation müssen Sie sehr behutsam vorgehen/Sie müssen Ihre Angestellten sehr vorsichtig behandeln; **a car that is easy to ~** ein Auto, das leicht zu fahren *or* zu steuern ist; **I can't ~ these fast balls** ich komme mit diesen schnellen Bällen nicht zurecht; **six children are too much for one woman to ~** mit sechs Kindern kann eine Frau allein nicht fertigwerden; **there's a salesman at the door — I'll ~ him** ein Vertreter ist an der Tür — ich werde ihn abfertigen; **you keep quiet, I'll ~ this** sei still, laß mich mal machen; **the accused decided to ~ his own defence** der Angeklagte beschloß, seine eigene Verteidigung zu übernehmen; **who's handling the publicity for this?** wer macht die Öffentlichkeitsarbeit dafür?; **could you ~ these interviews for me?** könnten Sie diese Interviews für mich machen?

(c) (*Comm*) *types of goods, items* handeln mit *or* in (+*dat*); *orders* bearbeiten; *prescriptions* ausführen; *shares, securities* handeln; *financial affairs* besorgen. **airport workers refused to ~ goods for Uganda** die Flughafenarbeiter weigerten sich, Waren nach Uganda abzufertigen; **we ~ tax problems for several big companies** wir bearbeiten die Steuerangelegenheiten mehrerer großer Firmen; **the millionaire has several secretaries to ~ his business** der Millionär hat mehrere Sekretäre, die seine Geschäfte für ihn führen; this department ~s all the export business diese Abteilung bearbeitet den gesamten Export.

3 *vi* (*ship, plane*) sich steuern lassen; (*car, motorbike*) sich fahren *or* lenken lassen; (*gun*) sich handhaben lassen.

4 *vr* he ~s himself well in a fight er kann sich in einer Schlägerei behaupten; if you live round here you have to know how to ~ yourself wer in dieser Gegend wohnt, muß seine Fäuste zu gebrauchen wissen.

handle: ~bar moustache *n* Schnauzbart, Schnauzer (*inf*) *m*; ~bar(s) *n(pl)* Lenkstange *f*.

handler ['hændlə^r] *n* (*dog*-~) Hundeführer *m*.

handling ['hændlɪŋ] *n* (a) (*touching*) Berühren *nt*.

(b) (*of plant, animal, matter, problem*) Behandlung *f*; (*of person, patient etc also, tool, weapon, machine, vehicle, plane, ship, drug, explosive*) Umgang *m* (*of* mit); (*of tool, weapon, machine*) Handhabung *f*; (*of writer's material*) Verarbeitung, Bearbeitung *f*; (*of legal or financial matters*) Erledigung *f*; (*official ~ of matters, of legal case*) Bearbeitung *f*. his skilful ~ of the class/troops/Senate seine geschickte Behandlung der Klasse/der Truppen/des Senats, seine geschickte Art, mit der Klasse/den Truppen/dem Senat umzugehen; the policeman's tactful ~ of the drunk/crowd/situation das taktvolle Verhalten des Polizisten gegenüber dem Betrunkenen/der Menge/in der Situation; his ~ of the matter/situation die Art, wie er die Angelegenheit/die Situation angefaßt *or* behandelt hat; his successful ~ of the difficulty/task seine Bewältigung der Schwierigkeit/der Aufgabe; the car/this parcel needs careful ~ man muß mit dem Auto vorsichtig umgehen/dieses Paket muß vorsichtig behandelt werden; these goods were damaged in ~ (*Comm*) diese Waren wurden beschädigt; his expert ~ of the deal sein Geschick beim Abschluß des Geschäfts.

(c) (*of vehicle*) what's its ~ like? wie fährt es sich?; a car not renowned for its easy ~ ein Auto, das sich nicht gerade durch leichte Lenkung auszeichnet.

hand: ~-loom *n* Handwebstuhl *m*; ~-loom carpet handgewebter Teppich; ~-loom weaving Handweben *nt*; ~-luggage *n* Handgepäck *nt*; ~-made *adj* handgearbeitet; this is ~-made das ist Handarbeit; ~maid *n* (*obs*) Zofe *f* (*old*); (*Bibl*) Magd *f*; ~-me-down *n* (*inf*) abgelegtes Kleidungsstück; ~-mirror *n* Handspiegel *m*; ~-off *n* (*Rugby*) Wegstoß (*en nt*) *m* (mit der Hand); ~-operated *adj* von Hand bedient *or* betätigt, handbedient, handbetrieben; ~out *n* (*inf: money*) Unterstützung, (Geld)zuwendung *f*; (*leaflet*) Flugblatt *nt*; (*with several pages*) Broschüre *f*; (*publicity* ~) Reklamezettel *m*; budget ~out Zuwendung *f or* Geschenk *nt* aus dem Etat; Christmas ~outs Weihnachtsgeld *nt*, Weihnachtsgratifikation *f*; ~-picked *adj* von Hand geerntet; (*specially selected, fig*) handverlesen; ~rail *n* (*of stairs etc*) Geländer *nt*; (*of ship*) Reling *f*; ~ saw *n* Handsäge *f*, Fuchsschwanz *m*; ~ set *n* 1 (*Telec*) Hörer *m*; 2 *vt* (*Typ*) (von Hand) setzen; ~shake *n* Händedruck *m*; ~shaking *n* Händeschütteln *nt*.

handsome ['hænsəm] *adj* (a) gutaussehend; *furniture* schön; *building* schön, ansehnlich. he is ~/he has a ~ face er sieht gut aus; she is a ~ woman for her age für ihr Alter sieht sie gut aus.

(b) (*noble, generous*) großzügig, nobel (*inf*); *conduct* großmütig, nobel (*inf*); *apology* anständig. ~ is as ~ does (*Prov*) edel ist, wer edel handelt.

(c) (*considerable*) *fortune, profit, price, inheritance etc* ansehnlich, stattlich, beträchtlich.

handsomely ['hænsəmlɪ] *adv* (a) (*elegantly*) elegant; *dressed also* gut. he grinned ~ at the camera er setzte für den Fotografen sein schönes Lächeln auf. (b) (*generously*) großzügig; *apologize* anständig. they were ~ rewarded for their patience ihre Geduld wurde reichlich belohnt.

handsomeness ['hænsəmnɪs] *n* (*of looks*) gutes Aussehen; (*generosity*) Großzügigkeit *f*.

hand: ~spring *n* (Handstand)überschlag *m*; ~-stand *n* Handstand *m*; to do a ~-stand (einen) Handstand machen; ~-stitched *adj* handgenäht; ~ to ~ 1 *adv* im Nahkampf, Mann gegen Mann; 2 *adj* ~-to-~ fight/fighting Nahkampf *m*; ~-to-mouth *adj existence* kümmerlich, armselig; to lead a ~-to-mouth existence von der Hand in den Mund leben; ~work *n* Handarbeit *f*; ~writing *n* Handschrift *f*; ~written *adj* handgeschrieben, von Hand geschrieben.

handy ['hændɪ] *adj* (+*er*) (a) *person* geschickt, praktisch. to be ~ at doing sth ein Geschick *nt* für etw haben; to be ~ with a gun gut mit einer Pistole umgehen können; he's pretty ~ with his fists er kann seine Fäuste gut gebrauchen.

(b) *pred* (*close at hand*) in der Nähe. to have *or* keep sth ~ etw griffbereit *or* zur Hand haben; my apartment is ~ for the shops meine Wohnung ist ganz in der Nähe der Geschäfte.

(c) (*convenient, useful*) praktisch; (*easy to handle also*) handlich. living here is handier for work es ist praktischer, hier in der Nähe des Arbeitsplatzes zu wohnen; that would come in ~ for ... das könnte man gut für ... gebrauchen; the new salary increase comes in ~ die neue Gehaltserhöhung kommt sehr gelegen; my experience as a teacher comes in ~ meine Lehrerfahrung erweist sich als nützlich *or* kommt mir zugute; he's a very ~ person to have around man kann ihn gut (ge)brauchen (*inf*); he's very ~ about the house er kann im Hause alles selbst erledigen.

handyman ['hændɪmæn] *n, pl* -men [-mən] (*servant*) Faktotum *nt*, Mädchen *nt* für alles (*inf*); (*do-it-yourself*) Bastler, Heimwerker *m*. I'm not much of a ~ myself ich bin kein großer Bastler, Basteln ist nicht gerade meine Stärke.

hang [hæŋ] (*vb: pret, ptp* hung) **1** *vt* (a) hängen; *painting* aufhängen; *door, gate* einhängen; (*Cook*) *game* abhängen lassen; *wallpaper* kleben. to ~ wallpaper tapezieren; to ~ sth from sth etw an etw (*dat*) aufhängen; to ~ sth on a hook etw an einen Haken hängen.

(b) the rooms of the castle were hung with: priceless pictures kostbare Gemälde hingen in den Räumen des Schlosses; the walls were hung with tapestries die Wände waren mit Gobelins behängt; they hung the windows/streets with bunting sie schmückten die Fenster/Straßen mit Fahnen.

(c) to ~ one's head den Kopf hängen lassen.

(d) to ~ fire (*lit: guns*) das Feuer einstellen; (*fig*) (*people*) zögern; I think we should ~ fire a little longer ich glaube, wir sollten noch etwas (zu)warten.

(e) *pret, ptp* hanged *criminal* hängen, aufhängen, henken (*form*). hung, drawn and quartered gehängt, gestreckt und geviertelt; to ~ oneself sich erhängen *or* aufhängen (*inf*).

(f) (*inf*) ~ him! zum Kuckuck mit ihm (*inf*); (I'm) ~ed if I will den Teufel werd' ich ... (*inf*); (I'm) ~ed if I know weiß der Henker (*inf*); ~ it! so ein Mist (*inf*), verflixt (noch mal) (*inf*).

2 *vi* (a) hängen (*on an* (+*dat*), *from* von); (*drapery, clothes, hair*) fallen; (*inelegantly*) (herunter)hängen; (*pheasant etc*) abhängen.

(b) (*gloom, fog etc*) hängen (*over* über +*dat*). to ~ in the air (*fig*) in der Schwebe sein; the hawk hung motionless in the sky der Falke stand bewegungslos in der Luft; time ~s heavy on my hands die Zeit wird mir sehr lang; she seemed to ~ motionless in the doorway for a second sie verharrte einen Augenblick lang regungslos in der Tür.

(c) (*criminal*) gehängt werden, aufgehängt werden (*inf*), hängen.

(d) it/he can go ~! (*inf*) es/er kann mir gestohlen bleiben (*inf*).

3 *n* (a) (*of drapery*) Fall *m*; (*of suit*) Sitz *m*.

(b) *no pl* (*inf*) to get the ~ of sth den (richtigen) Dreh (bei etw) herauskriegen *or* -finden (*inf*), auf den Dreh (von etw) kommen; to get the ~ of doing sth den Dreh herausbekommen, wie man etw macht (*inf*); do you get the ~ of what he's saying? kommst du bei dem mit? (*inf*), kapierst du, was er sagt? (*inf*).

(c) (*inf: damn*) I don't give *or* care a ~ es ist mir völlig egal *or* Wurst (*inf*).

♦**hang about** *or* **around 1** *vi* (a) (*inf*) (*wait*) warten; (*loiter*) sich herumtreiben (*inf*), herumlungern. to keep sb ~ing ~ jdn warten lassen; of course she wants to get married, you can't keep her ~ing ~ natürlich will sie heiraten, da kannst du sie doch nicht ewig hinhalten (*inf*).

(b) (*Brit sl: wait*) warten. ~ about, I'm just coming warte mal, ich komm ja schon; now ~ about, I didn't say that Moment mal (*inf*) *or* halt mal die Luft an (*sl*), das habe ich nicht gesagt.

(c) (*sl*) this car/he doesn't ~ ~ das Auto zieht ganz schön ab (*sl*)/er ist einer von der schnellen Truppe.

2 *vi +prep obj* to ~ ~ sb/a place um jdn herumstreichen/ sich an einem Ort herumtreiben (*inf*), an einem Ort herumlungern.

♦**hang back** *vi* (*lit*) sich zurückhalten; (*fig: hesitate*) zögern. one little boy was ~ing ~ at the edge of the group ein kleiner Junge hielt sich immer im Hintergrund; don't ~ ~, go and ask her worauf wartest du denn, frag sie doch; he hung ~ from suggesting that ... er zögerte *or* konnte sich nicht entschließen, den Vorschlag zu machen, daß ...; at the call of duty only cowards ~ ~ wenn die Pflicht ruft, zaudern nur Feiglinge.

♦**hang behind** *vi* zurückbleiben; (*dawdle*) (hinterher)bummeln *or* -trödeln.

♦**hang down 1** *vi* herunter-/hinunterhängen. his clothes hung ~ in rags seine Kleider hingen ihm in Fetzen vom Leib. **2** *vt sep* hinunter-/herunterhängen lassen.

♦**hang in** *vi* (*US sl*) just ~ ~ there! bleib am Ball (*inf*).

♦**hang on 1** *vi* (a) (*hold*) sich festhalten, sich festklammern (*to sth* an etw *dat*); (*wallpaper etc*) halten, kleben (bleiben).

(b) (*inf: wait*) warten. ~ ~ (a minute) wart mal, einen Augenblick (mal); ~ ~ tight, we're off! festhalten, es geht los!

2 *vi +prep obj* (a) to ~ ~ sb's arm an jds Arm (*dat*) hängen; to ~ ~ sb's words *or* lips an jds Lippen hängen; he ~s ~ her every word er hängt an ihren Lippen.

(b) (*depend on*) everything ~s ~ his decision/getting the cash alles hängt von seiner Entscheidung ab/alles hängt davon ab, ob man das Geld bekommt.

♦**hang on to** *vi +prep obj* (a) *hope* sich klammern an (+*acc*); *ideas* festhalten an (+*dat*). (b) (*keep*) behalten. could you ~ ~ ~ my seat until I get back? können Sie mir den Platz so lange freihalten, bis ich zurück bin?

♦**hang out 1** *vi* (a) (*tongue, shirt tails etc*) heraushängen. my tongue was ~ing ~ for a beer ich lechzte nach einem Bier.

(b) (*inf*) sich aufhalten; (*live also*) hausen, wohnen; (*be usually found also*) sich herumtreiben (*inf*), zu finden sein.

(c) (*resist, endure*) nicht aufgeben. they hung ~ for more pay sie hielten an ihrer Lohnforderung fest; the soldiers hung ~ for three more days die Soldaten hielten noch drei Tage durch.

(d) (*sl*) to let it all ~ ~ die Sau rauslassen (*sl*); come on now, let it all ~ ~ laß jucken (*sl*).

2 *vt sep* hinaushängen; *washing also* (draußen) aufhängen.

♦**hang over** *vi* (*continue*) andauern.

♦**hang together** *vi* (*people*) zusammenhalten; (*argument*) folgerichtig *or* zusammenhängend sein; (*alibi*) keinen Widerspruch aufweisen *or* enthalten; (*story, report etc*) gut verknüpft *or* zusammenhängend sein; (*statements*) zusammenpassen, keine Widersprüche *pl* aufweisen.

♦**hang up 1** *vi* (*Telec*) auflegen; aufhängen. he hung ~ on me er legte einfach auf. **2** *vt sep hat, picture* aufhängen; *telephone receiver* auflegen; aufhängen; *see* hung-up.

♦**hang upon** *vi +prep obj see* hang on 2 (b).

hangar ['hæŋə^r] *n* Hangar *m*, Flugzeughalle *f*.

hangdog ['hæŋdɒg] *adj look, expression* (*abject*) niedergeschlagen, trübsinnig; (*ashamed*) zerknirscht, Armsünder-.

hanger ['hæŋə^r] *n* (*for clothes*) (Kleider)bügel *m*; (*loop on garment*) Aufhänger *m*.

hanger-on [ˌhæŋər'ɒn] *n, pl* -s-on (*to celebrity*) Trabant, Satellit *m*. the film crew turned up with all its ~s-on die Filmmannschaft erschien mit ihrem ganzen Anhang; **the celebrity was accompanied by his usual crowd of** ~s-on die Berühmtheit kam mit dem üblichen Schwarm von Gefolgsleuten *or* zog den üblichen Kometenschweif von Gefolgsleuten hinter sich her.

hanging ['hæŋɪŋ] 1 n **(a)** (*of criminal*) Tod m durch den Strang, Erhängen nt; (*event*) Hinrichtung f (durch den Strang). **he deserves** ~ er sollte aufgehängt werden; **to bring back** ~ die Todesstrafe wiedereinführen.

(b) (*of wallpaper*) Anbringen, Kleben nt; (*of door*) Einhängen nt; (*of pictures*) (Auf)hängen nt. **the** ~ **of the wallpaper** das Tapezieren.

(c) (*curtains etc*) ~s pl Vorhänge pl; (*on wall*) Tapete f; (*tapestry*) Wandbehang m *or* -behänge pl; **bed** ~s Vorhänge pl des Himmelbetts.

2 attr **(a)** hängend; *bridge* Hänge-; *staircase* freischwebend; *sleeve* Flügel-. ~ **door** (*of garage*) Schwingtor nt; (*sliding*) Schiebetür f; **the** ~ **gardens of Babylon** die hängenden Gärten der Semiramis.

(b) ~ **judge** Richter, der (zu) leicht das Urteil zum Tode durch den Strang fällt; **it's a** ~ **matter** darauf steht der Galgen.

(c) ~ **committee** (*Art*) Hängekommission f.

hang: ~**man** n Henker m; (*game*) Galgen m; ~**nail** n Niednagel m; ~**-out** n (*inf*) (*place where one lives*) Bude f (*inf*); (*pub, café etc*) Stammlokal nt; (*of group*) Treff m (*inf*); **that disco is his favourite** ~**-out** er hängt mit Vorliebe in dieser Diskothek herum (*inf*); ~**over** n (*inf*) Kater (*inf*) m; Katzenjammer (*inf*) m; **(b)** (*sth left over*) Überbleibsel nt; ~**up** n (*inf*) Komplex m (*about* wegen); (*obsession*) Fimmel m (*inf*); **he has this** ~**up about people smoking** er stellt sich furchtbar an, wenn Leute rauchen (*inf*).

hank [hæŋk] n (*of wool etc*) Strang m; (*of hair, fur*) Büschel nt.

hanker ['hæŋkə'] vi sich sehnen, Verlangen haben (*for or after sth* nach etw). **to** ~ **after glory** ruhmsüchtig sein.

hankering ['hæŋkərɪŋ] n Verlangen nt, Sehnsucht f. **to have a** ~ **for sth** Verlangen *or* Sehnsucht nach etw haben; **she always had a** ~ **for the stage** es hat sie schon immer zur Bühne gezogen.

hankie, hanky ['hæŋkɪ] n (*inf*) Taschentuch nt.

hanky-panky ['hæŋkɪ'pæŋkɪ] n (*inf*) **(a)** (*dishonest dealings*) Mauscheleien pl (*inf*), Tricks pl (*inf*). **there's some** ~ **going on** hier ist was faul (*inf*); **there's quite a lot of** ~ **behind the scenes** hinter den Kulissen wird ziemlich gemauschelt (*inf*).

(b) (*love affair*) Techtelmechtel nt (*inf*).

(c) (*sexy behaviour*) Gefummel nt (*sl*), Knutscherei f (*inf*). **I'll come out with you but no** ~ ich komme mit, aber kein Gefummel (*sl*) *or* keine Fummelei (*sl*); **they were having a bit of** ~ **on the sofa** sie haben auf dem Sofa ein bißchen geknutscht (*inf*) *or* gefummelt (*sl*).

Hanover ['hænəuvə'] n Hannover nt.

Hanoverian [,hænəu'vɪərɪən] **1** adj hannover(i)sch. **the** ~ **dynasty** das Haus Hannover. **2** n Hannoveraner(in f) m.

Hansard ['hænsɑːd] n der Hansard, die britischen Parlamentsberichte.

Hanseatic [,hænzɪ'ætɪk] adj *towns* Hanse-. ~ **League** Hanse f, Hansebund m.

hansom ['hænsəm] n (zweirädriger) Einspänner, Hansom m.

Hants [hænts] abbr of Hampshire.

hap [hæp] vi (*obs*) see **happen**¹.

haphazard [,hæp'hæzəd] adj willkürlich, planlos. **the whole thing was very** ~ das Ganze war ziemlich zufällig *or* planlos; **the universe is neither ordered nor** ~ das Universum hat weder eine feste noch eine ganz zufällige *or* willkürliche Ordnung; **in a** ~ **way** planlos, wahllos; **to choose in a** ~ **way** aufs Geratewohl *or* auf gut Glück wählen; **at a** ~ **guess I should say ...** auf gut Glück geschätzt würde ich sagen ...

haphazardly [,hæp'hæzədlɪ] adv wahllos, (ganz) willkürlich, planlos. **decisions are made** ~ Entscheidungen werden willkürlich *or* aufs Geratewohl *or* auf gut Glück getroffen; **an** ~ **organized reception/company** eine völlig ungeplanter Empfang/eine völlig systemlos aufgebaute Firma.

hapless ['hæplɪs] adj glücklos. **yet another misfortune in this** ~ **man's life** noch ein Unglück im Leben dieses vom Pech verfolgten Menschen.

ha'p'orth ['heɪpəθ] n contr of **halfpennyworth**. **a** ~ **of sweets** Bonbons für einen halben Penny; **to spoil the ship for a** ~ **of tar** (*Prov*) am falschen Ende sparen.

happen¹ ['hæpən] vi **(a)** geschehen; (*somewhat special or important event also*) sich ereignen; (*esp unexpected, unintentional or unpleasant event also*) passieren; (*process also*) vor sich gehen. **it all** ~**ed like this ...** das Ganze geschah *or* war so ...; **nothing ever** ~**s here** hier ereignet sich *or* passiert (doch) überhaupt nie etwas; **the match/party/meeting never** ~**ed** das Spiel/die Party/das Treffen fand (gar) nicht statt; **it's all** ~**ing here today** heute ist hier ganz schön was los (*inf*); **where's it all** ~**ing tonight, where's the party?** wo ist denn heute abend etwas los, wo ist die Party?; **what's** ~**ing?** was läuft? (*inf*), was ist los?; **you can't just let things** ~ du kannst die Dinge nicht einfach laufen lassen; **it's broken, how did it** ~? es ist kaputt, wie ist denn das passiert?; **it just** ~**ed all by itself** es ist ganz von allein passiert *or* gekommen; **as if nothing had** ~**ed** als ob nichts geschehen *or* gewesen wäre; **worse things have** ~**ed** es ist schon Schlimmeres passiert *or* vorgekommen; **don't let it** ~ **again** daß das nicht noch mal vorkommt *or* passiert!; **these things** ~ so was kommt (schon mal) vor; **what has** ~**ed to him?** was ist ihm passiert *or* geschehen?; (*what have they done to him*) was ist mit ihm passiert?; (*what's wrong with him*) was ist mit ihm los?; (*what has become of him*) was ist aus ihm geworden?; **what's** ~**ed to your leg?** was ist mit deinem Bein los *or* passiert?; **if anything should** ~ **to me** wenn mir etwas zustoßen *or* passieren sollte; **accidents always** ~ **to other people** es sind immer die anderen, denen Unfälle passieren *or* zustoßen; **it all** ~**ed so quickly** es ging alles so schnell.

(b) (*chance*) **how does it** ~ **that ...?** (*cause*) wie kommt es, daß ...?; (*possibility*) wie ist es möglich, daß ...?; **it might** ~ **that you will be asked such a question** es könnte passieren *or* sein, daß Ihnen solch eine Frage gestellt wird; **how do you** ~ **to know?** wie kommt es, daß du das weißt?; **to** ~ **to do sth** zufällig(erweise) etw tun; **do you** ~ **to know whether ...?** wissen Sie vielleicht *or* zufällig, ob ...?; **I just** ~**ed to come along when ...** ich kam zufällig (gerade) vorbei, als ...; **he** ~**ed to see me just as I ...** muß er mich doch gerade in dem Augenblick sehen, als ich ...; **it so** ~**s** *or* **as it** ~**s I** (don't) like that kind of thing so etwas mag ich nun einmal (nicht); **as it** ~**s I've been there too** zufällig(erweise) bin ich auch dort gewesen; **as it** ~**s I'm going there today** zufällig(erweise) gehe ich heute dort(hin); **you don't want to come, do you?** — it so ~**s, I do** ich möchte doch sicher nicht kommen, oder? — doch, natürlich; **when he first** ~**ed into this world** als er das Licht der Welt erblickte (*geh*).

♦**happen along** vi zufällig (an)kommen.

♦**happen (up)on** vi +prep obj zufällig stoßen auf (+acc); *person* zufällig treffen *or* sehen.

happen² ['æpn] adv (*N Eng inf*: perhaps) vielleicht.

happening ['hæpnɪŋ] n **(a)** Ereignis nt; (*not planned*) Vorfall m. **some terrible** ~**s took place** schreckliche Dinge geschahen *or* ereigneten sich; **there have been some peculiar** ~**s in that house** in dem Haus sind sonderbare Dinge vorgegangen; **such** ~**s cannot be tolerated** so etwas kann nicht geduldet werden, man kann derartige Vorkommnisse nicht einfach hinnehmen.

(b) (*Theat*) Happening nt.

happenstance ['hæpənstæns] n (*US inf*) Zufall m.

happily ['hæpɪlɪ] adv **(a)** glücklich; (*cheerfully also*) fröhlich, vergnügt, heiter; (*contentedly also*) zufrieden. **they played** ~ **together** sie spielten vergnügt zusammen; **they lived** ~ **ever after** (in *fairy-tales*) und wenn sie nicht gestorben sind, dann leben sie heute noch; **his dream was to get married and live** ~ **ever after** sein Wunschtraum war, zu heiraten und dann glücklich und zufrieden zu leben.

(b) (*fortunately*) glücklicherweise, zum Glück.

(c) (*felicitously*) glücklich, treffend. **as it was** ~ **expressed** wie es sehr treffend formuliert war; **you could have worded the letter a little more** ~ Sie hätten den Brief etwas glücklicher formulieren können.

happiness ['hæpɪnɪs] n **(a)** Glück nt; (*feeling of contentment also*) Zufriedenheit f; (*disposition*) Heiterkeit, Fröhlichkeit f.

(b) (*of words*) glückliche Formulierung.

happy ['hæpɪ] adj (+er) **(a)** glücklich; (*cheerful also*) fröhlich, vergnügt, heiter; (*glad about sth*) froh; (*contented also*) zufrieden; (*causing joy*) *thought, scene etc* erfreulich, freudig (*geh*). **is she** ~? ist sie glücklich?; **did you have a** ~ **Christmas/birthday?** hast du schöne Weihnachten/einen schönen Geburtstag gehabt *or* verlebt?; **to celebrate the** ~ **birth of a son** die glückliche Geburt eines Sohnes feiern; **a** ~ **event** ein frohes *or* freudiges Ereignis; ~ **families** (*game*) Quartett nt; **that's all right,** ~ **to be of help, ich helfe (doch) gern**; **yes, I'd be** ~ **to** ja, sehr gern(e) *or* das würde mich freuen; **to be** ~ **to do sth** sich freuen, etw tun zu können *or* dürfen; **I am** ~ **to be here tonight** ich freue *or* es freut mich, heute abend hier zu sein; **(I'm)** ~ **to be of service** es freut *or* ich freue mich, helfen zu können; **I/the government would be only too** ~ **to do this, but ...** ich würde das ja zu gerne *or* liebend gerne tun/der Regierung wäre es eine Freude, aber ...; **not to be** ~ **with/about sth** mit etw nicht zufrieden sein/über etw (*acc*) nicht glücklich sein; **we are not entirely** ~ **with the plan** wir sind nicht so ganz glücklich über den Plan *or* zufrieden mit dem Plan; **the** ~ **few** die wenigen (Aus)erwählten; **she was so** ~ **to see her son again** sie war so glücklich/froh *or* sie freute sich so, ihren Sohn wiederzusehen.

(b) (*fortunate*) *solution* glücklich.

(c) (*felicitous*) *phrase, words* glücklich, gut getroffen; *gesture* geglückt.

(d) (*inf: slightly drunk*) angeheitert, beschwipst (*inf*).

(e) ~ **anniversary** herzlichen Glückwunsch zum Hochzeitstag; ~ **birthday!** herzlichen Glückwunsch *or* alles Gute zum Geburtstag!; ~ **Easter** fröhliche *or* frohe Ostern; ~ **New Year** ein glückliches *or* frohes neues Jahr.

-happy adj suf (*inf*) trigger-~/strike-~ schießfreudig/streikfreudig (*inf*); gold-~ goldgierig (*inf*).

happy-go-lucky ['hæpɪgəʊ'lʌkɪ] adj unbekümmert, sorglos. **to do sth in a** ~ **way** etw unbekümmert tun; **I wish you wouldn't be so** ~ **about things** ich wollte, du wärst nicht bei allem so sorglos *or* würdest nicht alles so lässig nehmen (*inf*); **the preparations were very** ~ die Vorbereitungen waren mehr oder weniger dem Zufall überlassen worden.

happy hunting ground n **(a)** (*Myth*) ewige Jagdgründe pl.

(b) (*fig*) Paradies nt.

harakiri [,hærə'kɪrɪ] n Harakiri nt.

harangue [hə'ræŋ] **1** n (*scolding*) (Straf)predigt f, Sermon m; (*lengthy also*) Tirade f; (*encouraging*) Appell m. **to give sb a** ~ jdm eine (Straf)predigt etc halten; einen Appell an jdn richten.

2 vt see n *person* eine (Straf)predigt *or* einen Sermon halten (+*dat*); eine Tirade loslassen auf (+*acc*) (*inf*); anfeuern, einen Appell richten an (+*acc*). **I don't like being** ~**d** ich kann es nicht leiden, wenn mir jemand lange Reden hält; **stop haranguing me about how lucky other men's wives are** hör auf, mir dauernd vorzuhalten *or* mir damit in den Ohren zu liegen (*inf*), wie gut es die Frauen anderer Männer haben.

harass ['hærəs] vt belästigen; (*mess around*) schikanieren; (*Mil*) *the enemy* Anschläge verüben auf (+*acc*), immer wieder überfallen. **to** ~ **sb with complaints** jdn mit Klagen belästigen; **don't** ~ **me** dräng *or* hetz (*inf*) mich doch nicht so!; **they eventually** ~**ed him into resigning** sie setzten ihm so lange zu, bis er schließlich zurücktrat, sie trieben ihn so weit, daß er zurücktrat; **constant** ~**ing of the goalie eventually made him lose his nerve** der Torwart wurde ständig so hart bedrängt, daß an schließlich die Nerven verlor; **the landlord was ~ing me about the rent** der Hauswirt belästigte mich ständig wegen der Miete; **a lot of these people are ~ed by the police** viele dieser Leute werden ständig von der Polizei schikaniert; **a salesman should never seem to ~ a potential customer** ein Vertreter sollte einem potentiellen Kunden gegenüber niemals auf- or zudringlich werden.

harassed ['hærəst] *adj* überspannt, angegriffen, mitgenommen; *(worried)* von Sorgen gequält. **a ~ family man** ein (viel)geplagter Familienvater; **she was very ~ that day** an dem Tag wußte sie nicht, wo ihr der Kopf stand; **he wiped his brow in a ~ manner** er wischte sich *(dat)* gequält die Stirn.

harassment ['hærəsmənt] *n (act)* Belästigung, Bedrängung *f*; *(messing around)* Schikanierung *f*; *(state)* Bedrängnis *f*; *(Mil)* Kleinkrieg *m*. **if we can't win him over by argument we'll defeat him by ~** wenn wir ihn nicht im Guten überreden können, müssen wir ihm eben so lange zusetzen, bis er aufgibt; **constant ~ of the enemy** ständiger Kleinkrieg gegen den Feind.

harbinger ['hɑːbɪndʒəʳ] *n (liter)* Herold *(liter)*, (Vor)bote *m*.

harbour, *(US)* **harbor** ['hɑːbəʳ] **1** *n* Hafen *m*.
2 *vt* **(a)** *criminal etc* beherbergen, Unterschlupf gewähren (+*dat*); *goods* (bei sich) aufbewahren.
(b) *suspicions, grudge* hegen.
(c) *(conceal, contain)* **its fur ~s a lot of fleas** in seinem Fell nisten die Flöhe in Scharen; **dirt ~s germs** Schmutz ist eine Brutstätte für Krankheitserreger; **these old tapestries ~ a lot of dirt** in diesen alten Gobelins hat sich viel Schmutz festgesetzt.

harbour: **~ bar** *n* Sandbank *f* vor dem Hafen; **~ dues** *npl* Hafengebühr(en *pl*) *f*; **~ master** *n* Hafenmeister *m*.

hard [hɑːd] **1** *adj* (+*er*) **(a)** *(generally)* hart; *see* **nail.**
(b) *(difficult)* schwer; *(complicated also)* schwierig; **(~ to endure)** hart. **~ of hearing** schwerhörig; **I find it ~ to believe that ...** es fällt mir schwer zu glauben *or* ich kann es kaum glauben, daß ...; **these conditions are ~ to accept** mit diesen Bedingungen kann man sich nur schwer abfinden; **it's ~ to accept that anyone would change so much** es ist kaum zu glauben, daß jemand sich so verändern kann; **I know it's ~ for or on you, but ...** ich weiß, es ist schwer *or* hart für Sie, aber ...; **he is ~ to get on with** es ist schwer *or* schwierig, mit ihm auszukommen; **learning Japanese is ~** going Japanisch zu lernen ist eine Schinderei *or* Plackerei; **this novel is ~ going** durch diesen Roman muß man sich mühsam durchbeißen; **chatting her up is ~** going es ist gar nicht so einfach, die anzumachen; **he had a ~ time of it** er hat es nicht leicht gehabt; *(in negotiations, boxing match etc)* es hat ihn einen harten Kampf gekostet; **she pulled through after the operation but she had a ~ time of it** sie erholte sich nur schwer von der Operation, aber es war eine schwere Zeit für sie; **~ luck!, ~ lines!** (so ein) Pech!; **it was ~ luck on that lines that ...** es war (ein) Pech, daß ...; *see* **cheese.**
(c) *(severe, harsh)* hart; *voice, tone also* schroff, barsch; *frost* streng. **a ~ man** ein harter Mann; *(esp ruthless)* ein knallharter Typ *(sl)*; **he thinks he's a ~ man** *(inf)* er kommt sich unheimlich hart vor *(inf)* **don't be ~ on the boy** sei nicht zu hart *or* streng zu dem Jungen; **he was (very) ~ on his staff** er war seinem Personal gegenüber sehr hart; **I'm all for speaking the truth but you were a bit ~ on her** ich bin dafür, die Wahrheit zu sagen, aber Sie sind ein bißchen zu hart mit ihr ins Gericht gegangen; **he's been getting ~ with them recently** in letzter Zeit ist er ziemlich *or* recht hart gegen sie geworden.
(d) *(strenuous)* *fight, match, worker, work* hart. **getting on with him is ~ work** *(inf)* es gehört schon etwas dazu, mit ihm auszukommen *(inf)*; **he's ~ work** *(inf)* er ist ziemlich anstrengend *(inf)*; *(difficult to know or persuade)* er ist ein harter Brocken *(inf)*; **it was ~ work for me not to swear at him** es hat mich große Mühe gekostet, ihn nicht zu beschimpfen.
(e) **to put the ~ word on sb** *(Austral sl)* jdn um etw anhauen.
2 *adv* (+*er*) **(a)** mit aller Kraft; *(with neg)* stark; *(violently)* heftig; *pull, push, hit also* kräftig; *hold also* fest; *drive* hart; *run* so schnell man kann; *breathe* schwer; *work* hart, schwer. **he worked ~ at clearing his name** er versuchte mit allen Mitteln, seinen Namen reinzuwaschen; **to listen ~** genau hinhören; **he stood outside the door listening ~** er stand vor der Tür und horchte angestrengt; **think ~** denk mal scharf *or* gut nach; **you're not thinking ~ enough** du denkst nicht angestrengt genug *or* richtig nach; **think ~er** denk mal ein bißchen besser nach; **he was obviously thinking ~** er dachte (offen)sichtlich scharf *or* angestrengt nach; **he has obviously thought ~ about this** er hat es sich *(dat)* offensichtlich gut *or* genau überlegt; **think ~ before you ...** überlegen Sie sich's gut, bevor Sie ...; **if you try ~ you can ...** wenn du dich richtig bemühst *or* anstrengst, kannst du ...; **try ~er to please her** gib dir doch ein bißchen mehr Mühe *or* bemühe dich doch etwas mehr, sie zufriedenzustellen; **you're not trying ~ enough** du strengst dich nicht genügend an; **he was really trying ~ to win** er bemühte sich wirklich ernsthaft zu gewinnen; **you're trying too ~** du bemühst dich zu sehr *or* zu krampfhaft; **he tried as ~ as he could** er hat sein Bestes getan *or* sich nach Kräften bemüht; **to look ~ at sb/sth** sich jdn/etw genau ansehen; *(critically)* jdn/etw scharf ansehen; **we'll have to look ~ at our budget for next year** wir müssen uns *(dat)* unser Budget fürs nächste Jahr genau ansehen; **to look ~ at** *(inf)* schwer am Werk *or* dabei sein *(inf)*; **~ a port!** *(Naut)* hart Backbord!; **he threw the wheel ~ over** er schlug das Steuerrad hart herum.
(b) *(in, with difficulty)* **to be ~ put to do** sth es sehr schwer finden *or* große Schwierigkeiten (damit) haben, etw zu tun; **I'd be ~ put to ...** es würde mir schwerfallen ...; **to be ~ up** *(inf)* knapp bei Kasse sein *(inf)*; **he's ~ up for ...** *(inf)* es fehlt ihm an (+*dat*) ...; **to be ~ up for something to fill one's day** *(inf)* nicht wissen, was man mit seiner Zeit anfangen soll; **it will go ~**

with him if he carries on this way er wird noch Schwierigkeiten kriegen, wenn er so weitermacht; **it'll go ~ with him if he's found out** es kann ihn teuer zu stehen kommen, wenn das herauskommt; **to be ~ done by** übel dran sein; **he reckons he's ~ done by having to work on Saturdays** er findet es hart, daß er samstags arbeiten muß; **he took it pretty ~** es ging ihm ziemlich nahe, es traf ihn schwer; **old traditions die ~** alte Traditionen sterben nur langsam.
(c) *rain, snow* stark. **it was freezing ~** es herrschte strenger Frost, es fror Stein und Bein.
(d) *(close)* **~ by the mill** ganz nahe bei *or* ganz in der Nähe der Mühle; **there's a mill ~ by** ganz in der Nähe ist eine Mühle.

hard: **~ and fast** *adj* fest; *rules also* bindend, verbindlich; **~ -back 1** *adj* (also **~backed**) *book* gebunden; **2** *n* gebundene Ausgabe; **~-bitten** *adj person* abgebrüht; *manager* knallhart *(inf)*; **~board** *n* Hartfaser- *or* Preßspanplatte *f*; **~-boiled** *adj* **(a)** *egg* hartgekocht; **(b)** *(fig: shrewd)* gerissen, ausgekocht *(inf)*, mit allen Wassern gewaschen *(inf)*; **(c)** *(fig: unsentimental)* abgebrüht *(inf)*, kaltschnäuzig *(inf)*; **(d)** *(fig: realistic)* *approach, appraisal etc* nüchtern, sachlich; **~ cash** *n* Bargeld, Bare(s) *(inf)* *nt*; **~ core 1** *n* **(a)** *(for road)* Schotter *m*; **(b)** *(fig)* harter Kern; *(pornography)* harter Porno *(inf)*; **2** *adj pornography* hart; **~-core magazine** hartes Pornoheft; **~ court** *n* Hartplatz *m*; **~ drink** *n* hartes Getränk; **~ drinker** *n* starker Trinker; **~ drug** *n* harte Droge; **~-earned** *adj wages* sauer verdient; *reward* redlich verdient; *victory* hart erkämpft.

harden ['hɑːdn] **1** *vt* *steel* härten; *body, muscles* kräftigen, stählen *(geh)*; *person (physically)* abhärten; *(emotionally)* verhärten *(pej)*, abstumpfen *(pej)*; *clay* hart werden lassen. **this ~ed his attitude** dadurch hat sich seine Haltung verhärtet; **to ~ oneself to sth** *(physically)* gegen etw abhärten; *(emotionally)* gegen etw unempfindlich werden; **to ~ one's mind against subversive propaganda** gegen subversive Propaganda immun *or* gefeit werden; **war had ~ed the soldiers to death and killing** der Krieg hatte die Soldaten gegen den Tod und das Töten abgestumpft; **to ~ one's heart to sb** sein Herz gegen jdn verhärten *(geh)*; *see* **hardened.**
2 *vi* *(substance)* hart werden; *(fig: attitude)* sich verhärten; *(St Ex)* *(cease to fluctuate)* sich festigen, sich stabilisieren; *(rise)* anziehen. **his voice ~ed** seine Stimme wurde hart *or* bekam einen harten Klang.
♦**harden off** *vt sep plants* widerstandsfähig machen.
♦**harden up 1** *vi (concrete, glue etc)* hart werden. **2** *vt sep (make hard)* härten, hart machen; *(fig: toughen)* abhärten.

hardened ['hɑːdnd] *adj* *steel* gehärtet; *criminal* Gewohnheits-; *troops* zäh, abgehärtet; *sinner* verstockt. **to be ~ to or against the cold/the climate/sb's insensitivity/life** gegen die Kälte/das Klima abgehärtet sein/an jds Gefühllosigkeit *(acc)* gewöhnt sein/vom Leben hart gemacht sein; **you become ~ to it after a while** daran gewöhnt man sich mit der Zeit; **he was ~ against suffering** er war gegen Leiden abgestumpft.

hardening ['hɑːdnɪŋ] *n (of steel)* (Er)härten *nt*, Härtung *f*; *(fig)* Verhärten *nt*, Verhärtung *f*; *(St Ex)* Versteifung, Festigung *f*; *(rise)* Anziehen *nt*. **I noticed a ~ of his attitude** ich habe bemerkt, daß sich seine Einstellung verhärtet; **~ of the arteries** Arterienverkalkung *f*.

hard: **~-featured** *adj person* mit harten Gesichtszügen; **~-fought** *adj battle* erbittert; *boxing match, competition, game* hart; **a ~-fought election** eine (erbitterte) Wahlschlacht; **~ hat** *n* Schutzhelm *m*; *(construction worker)* Bauarbeiter *m*; **~-headed** *adj* nüchtern; **~-hearted** *adj* hartherzig *(towards sb* jdm gegenüber*)*; **~-heartedness** *n* Hartherzigkeit *f*.

hardihood ['hɑːdɪhud] *n* Kühnheit *f*; *(courage also)* Mut *m*; *(audacity also)* Dreistigkeit *f*.

hardiness ['hɑːdɪnɪs] *n* **(a)** *(toughness)* Zähigkeit, Widerstandsfähigkeit *f*; *(Bot also)* Frostunempfindlichkeit *f*; *(of people also)* Ausdauer *f*. **(b)** *(courage)* Mut *m*.

hard: **~ labour** *n* Zwangsarbeit *f*; **~ line** *n* harte Haltung, harte Linie; **to take a ~ line** eine harte Haltung einnehmen, eine harte Linie verfolgen; **~-liner** *n* Vertreter *m* der harten Linie; **~ liquor** *n* Schnaps *m*.

hardly ['hɑːdlɪ] *adv* **(a)** *(scarcely)* kaum. **you've ~ eaten anything** du hast (ja) kaum etwas gegessen; **I need ~ tell you ich** muß Ihnen wohl kaum sagen; **I ~ know any French, I know ~ any French** ich kann kaum Französisch; **~ ever** kaum jemals, fast nie; **he had ~ gone or ~ had he gone when ...** er war kaum gegangen, als ...; **he would ~ have said that** das hat er wohl kaum gesagt; **~!** (wohl) kaum; **you don't agree, do you?** — Sie sind damit nicht einverstanden, oder? — nein, eigentlich nicht.
(b) *(rare: harshly)* hart, streng.

hardness ['hɑːdnɪs] *n* **(a)** *(generally)* Härte *f*; *(of winter also)* Strenge *f*. **(b)** *see adj* **(b)** Schwere *f*; Schwierigkeit *f*; Härte *f*; **~ of hearing** Schwerhörigkeit *f*. **(c)** *see adj* **(c)** Härte *f*; Schroffheit, Barschheit *f*; Strenge *f*. **the ~ of his heart** seine Hartherzigkeit. **(d)** *(St Ex)* Festigung *f*; *(rise)* Anziehen *nt*.

hard: **~-on** *n (sl)* Steife(r) *m (sl)*; **to have a ~-on** einen hoch *or* stehen haben *(sl)*; **~-packed** *adj snow* festgetreten; **~pad** *n (Vet)* Hartballenkrankheit *f*; **~pan** *n (Geol)* Ortgestein *nt*; **~-pressed** *adj troops etc* hart bedrängt; *(with work)* stark beansprucht; **to be ~-pressed** unter großem Druck stehen *or* sein, in harter Bedrängnis sein *(geh)*; **the ~-pressed minister attempted to answer his critics** in die Enge getrieben, versuchte der Minister, seinen Kritikern zu antworten; **to be ~-pressed for money** in Geldnot sein, knapp bei Kasse sein *(inf)*; **~ sell 1** *n* aggressive Verkaufstaktik, Hardsell *m*; **2** *attr* aggressiv, Hardsell-.

hardship ['hɑːdʃɪp] *n (condition)* Not *f*, Elend *nt*; *(instance)* Härte *f*; *(deprivation)* Entbehrung *f*. **a temporary ~** eine vorübergehende Notlage; **a little temporary ~** eine vorübergehende Unannehmlichkeit; **to suffer great ~s** große Not leiden; **the ~s of war** das Elend/die Entbehrungen des Kriegs;

is that such a great ~? ist das wirklich ein solches Unglück?; if it's not too much (of a) ~ for you ... wenn es dir nichts ausmacht *or* nicht zuviel Mühe macht ...; the ~(s) of living in the country die Entbehrungen *pl* des Landlebens.

hard: ~ **shoulder** *n* (*Brit*) Seitenstreifen *m*; ~**tack** *n* Schiffszwieback *m*; ~**top** *n* Hardtop *nt or m*; ~**ware** 1 *n* (a) Eisenwaren *pl*; (*household goods*) Haushaltswaren *pl*; (b) (*Computers*) Hardware *f*; (c) (*Mil*) (Wehr)material *nt*; (d) (*US sl: gun*) Schießeisen *nt* (*sl*), Kanone *f* (*sl*); 2 *attr* ~**ware dealer** *n* Eisenwarenhändler *m*; (*including household goods*) Haushalt- und Eisenwarenhändler *m*; ~**ware shop** *or* **store** *n* Eisenwarenhandlung *f*; (*including household goods*) Haushalt- und Eisenwarengeschäft *nt*; ~**-wearing** *adj* widerstandsfähig; *cloth, clothes* strapazierfähig; ~**-won** *adj battle, fight, victory* hart *or* schwer erkämpft; ~**wood** *n* Hartholz *nt*; ~**-working** *adj person* fleißig; *engine* leistungsfähig.

hardy ['hɑːdɪ] *adj* (+*er*) (a) (*tough*) zäh; *person also* abgehärtet; *plant* (frost)unempfindlich, winterhart; *tree* widerstandsfähig, kräftig. **that's pretty ~ of you not to wear a coat du mußt ganz schön abgehärtet sein, daß du keinen Mantel anziehst; ~ annual/perennial winterharte einjährige/mehrjährige Pflanze; ~ nationalization, that ~ annual of Labour congresses Verstaatlichung, ein Thema, das jedes Jahr beim Labour-Parteitag wieder auftaucht *or* akut wird.
  (b) (*bold*) *person* kühn, unerschrocken.

hare [heəʳ] 1 *n* (Feld)hase *m*. ~ **and hounds** (*game*) Schnitzeljagd *f*; **to run with the ~ and hunt with the hounds** (*prov*) auf beiden Schultern Wasser tragen (*prov*), es mit niemandem verderben wollen; **to start a ~** vom Thema ablenken; *see* mad. 2 *vi* (*inf*) sausen, flitzen (*inf*).

hare: ~**bell** *n* Glockenblume *f*; ~**-brained** *adj person, plan* verrückt, behämmert (*inf*); ~**lip** *n* Hasenscharte *f*.

harem [hɑːˈriːm] *n* Harem *m*.

haricot ['hærɪkəʊ] *n* ~ (**bean**) Gartenbohne *f*.

hark [hɑːk] *vi* **to** ~ **to sth** (*liter*) einer Sache (*dat*) lauschen (*liter*); ~! (*liter*) horch(t)! (*liter*), höret!; ~ **at him!** (*inf*) hör ihn dir nur an!, hör sich einer den an! (*inf*).
♦**hark back** *vi* zurückkommen (*to auf* +*acc*). **this custom ~s** ~ **to the days when ...** dieser Brauch geht auf die Zeit zurück, als ...; **he's always ~ing** ~ **to the good old days** er fängt immer wieder von der guten alten Zeit an; **the author is ~ing** ~ **to former times** der Autor geht auf vergangene Zeiten zurück.

Harlequin ['hɑːlɪkwɪn] 1 *n* (*Theat*) Harlekin, Hanswurst *m*. 2 *attr costume* Harlekin(s)-.

harlot ['hɑːlət] *n* (*old*) Metze (*old*), Hure *f*.

harm [hɑːm] 1 *n* (*bodily*) Verletzung *f*; (*material damage, to relations, psychological*) Schaden *m*. **to do** ~ **to sb** jdm eine Verletzung zufügen/jdm schaden *or* Schaden zufügen; **to do** ~ **to sth** einer Sache (*dat*) schaden; **you could do somebody/yourself** ~ **with** that axe mit der Axt können Sie jemanden/sich verletzen; **the blow didn't do him any** ~ der Schlag hat ihm nichts getan *or* ihn nicht verletzt; **he didn't do himself any** ~ **in the crash** er wurde bei dem Unfall nicht verletzt, er erlitt keinerlei Verletzungen bei dem Unfall; **leaving her husband did a lot of** ~ **to him** daß sie ihren Mann verlassen hat, hat ihn sehr mitgenommen; **he did himself quite a lot of** ~ *or* **he did quite a lot of** ~ **to himself with his TV broadcast** er hat sich (*dat*) (selbst) mit diesem Fernsehauftritt ziemlich geschadet; **you will come to no** ~ es wird Ihnen nichts geschehen; **it will do more** ~ **than good** es wird mehr schaden als nützen; **it will do you no/won't do you any** ~ es wird dir nicht schaden; **I see no** ~ **in the odd cigarette** ich finde nichts dabei, wenn man ab und zu eine Zigarette raucht; **to mean no** ~ es nicht böse meinen; **I don't mean him any** ~ ich meine es nicht böse mit ihm; (*bodily, not offend*) ich will ihm nicht weh tun; **there's no** ~ **in asking/trying** es kann nicht schaden, zu fragen/es zu versuchen; **there's no** ~ **in me putting a word in for him, is there?** es kann doch nichts schaden, wenn ich ein gutes Wort für ihn einlege, oder?; **where's** *or* **what's the** ~ **in that?** was kann denn das schaden?, **to keep** *or* **stay out of** ~**'s way** die Gefahr meiden, der Gefahr (*dat*) aus dem Weg gehen; **you stay here out of** ~**'s way** du bleibst schön hier, in Sicherheit; **I've put those tablets in the cupboard out of** ~**'s way** ich habe die Tabletten im Schrank in Sicherheit gebracht.
  2 *vt person* verletzen; *thing* schaden (+*dat*); *sb's interests, relations, reputation etc* schaden (+*dat*), abträglich sein (+*dat*). **don't** ~ **the children** tu den Kindern nichts (an); **it wouldn't** ~ **you to be a little more polite** es würde nicht(s) schaden, wenn du ein bißchen höflicher wärest.

harmful ['hɑːmfʊl] *adj* schädlich (*to für*); *remarks* verletzend. ~ **to one's health** gesundheitsschädlich.

harmless ['hɑːmlɪs] *adj* (a) harmlos; *animal, toy, weapon etc also* ungefährlich; *drugs also* unschädlich. **to make** *or* **render a bomb** ~ eine Bombe entschärfen. (b) (*innocent*) harmlos; *conversation, question also* unverfänglich.

harmlessly ['hɑːmlɪslɪ] *adv* harmlos, in aller Harmlosigkeit.

harmlessness ['hɑːmlɪsnɪs] *n* *see adj* Harmlosigkeit *f*; Ungefährlichkeit *f*; Unschädlichkeit *f*; Unverfänglichkeit *f*.

harmonic [hɑːˈmɒnɪk] 1 *n* (*Mus*) Oberton *m*. 2 *adj* (*Mus, Phys*) harmonisch.

harmonica [hɑːˈmɒnɪkə] *n* Harmonika *f*.

harmonics [hɑːˈmɒnɪks] *n sing* Harmonik *f*.

harmonious *adj*, ~**ly** *adv* [hɑːˈməʊnɪəs, -lɪ] (*Mus, fig*) harmonisch.

harmonium [hɑːˈməʊnɪəm] *n* Harmonium *nt*.

harmonize ['hɑːmənaɪz] 1 *vt* (*Mus*) harmonisieren; *ideas etc* miteinander in Einklang bringen; *plans, colours* aufeinander abstimmen (*sth with sth* etw auf etw *acc*). 2 *vi* (a) (*notes, colours, people etc*) harmonieren; (*facts*) übereinstimmen. (b) (*sing in harmony*) mehrstimmig singen.

harmony ['hɑːmənɪ] *n* Harmonie *f*; (*of colours also*) harmoni-

sches Zusammenspiel; (*fig: harmonious relations*) Eintracht *f*. **there is a certain lack of** ~ **in their relationship** ihrer Beziehung fehlt es an Harmonie; **to be in/out of** ~ **with** (*lit*) harmonisch *or* in Harmonie *or* in Eintracht mit jdm leben; **to be in/out of** ~ **with** (*fig also*) in Einklang/nicht in Einklang stehen *or* sein mit; **to sing in** ~ mehrstimmig singen; (*in tune*) rein singen; **his ideas are out of** ~ **with the age** seine Vorstellungen sind nicht zeitgemäß *or* passen nicht in die Zeit.

harness ['hɑːnɪs] 1 *n* (a) Geschirr *nt*. **to get back into** ~ (*fig*) sich wieder an die Arbeit machen, wieder in den täglichen Trott verfallen; **to be back in** ~ (*fig*) wieder bei der Arbeit *or* im gewohnten Trott sein; **to work in** ~ (*fig*) zusammenarbeiten; **to die in** ~ (*fig*) (*often hum*) in den Sielen sterben.
  (b) (*of parachute*) Gurtwerk *nt*; (*for baby*) Laufgurt *m*.
  2 *vt* (a) *horse* anschirren, aufzäumen. **a horse that has never been** ~**ed** ein Pferd, das nie im Geschirr gegangen ist; **to** ~ **a horse to a carriage** ein Pferd *or* einen Wagen spannen.
  (b) (*utilize*) *river etc* nutzbar machen; *resources* (aus)nutzen.

harp [hɑːp] 1 *n* Harfe *f*.
  2 *vi* **to** ~ **on sth** auf etw (*dat*) herumreiten; **he's always** ~**ing on about the need for** ... er spricht ständig von der Notwendigkeit +*gen* ...; **she's always** ~**ing on about her troubles** sie lamentiert ständig über ihre Probleme, sie jammert einem dauernd die Ohren voll mit ihren Problemen (*inf*); **she is always** ~**ing on the same string** es ist immer die alte Leier *or* das alte Lied bei ihr.

harpist ['hɑːpɪst] *n* Harfenspieler(in *f*), Harfenist(in *f*) *m*.

harpoon [hɑːˈpuːn] 1 *n* Harpune *f*. ~ **gun** Harpunenkanone *f*. 2 *vt* harpunieren.

harpsichord ['hɑːpsɪkɔːd] *n* Cembalo *nt*.

harpy ['hɑːpɪ] *n* Harpyie *f*; (*shrewish woman also*) Hexe *f*; (*grasping person also*) Hyäne *f*.

harpy eagle *n* Harpyie *f*.

harridan ['hærɪdən] *n* Vettel *f*, Drache *m*.

harrier ['hærɪəʳ] *n* (a) (*Sport*) Querfeldeinläufer(in *f*), Geländeläufer(in *f*) *m*. (b) (*Orn*) Weih *m*. (c) (*dog*) Hund *m* für die Hasenjagd.

harrow ['hærəʊ] 1 *n* Egge *f*. 2 *vt* (a) eggen. (b) (*fig: usu pass*) **to** ~ **sb** jdn quälen *or* peinigen (*geh*).

harrowed ['hærəʊd] *adj look* gequält.

harrowing ['hærəʊɪŋ] *adj story* entsetzlich, erschütternd, grauenhaft; *experience* qualvoll, grauenhaft.

Harry ['hærɪ] *n, dim of* Henry. **old** ~ (*Devil*) der Leibhaftige; **to play old** ~ **with sth** etw vollständig durcheinanderbringen; **with sb's lungs etc** etw kaputtmachen (*inf*).

harry ['hærɪ] *vt* (a) bedrängen, zusetzen (+*dat*). (b) (*old*) *country* plündern.

harsh [hɑːʃ] *adj* (+*er*) (a) *colour, contrast, light, sound* grell, hart; *taste* herb. **it was** ~ **to the touch/taste/ear** es fühlte sich rauh an/es schmeckte herb/es gellte in den Ohren.
  (b) (*severe*) hart; *words, tone of voice also* barsch, schroff; *treatment also* rauh; (*too strict*) streng. **fate dealt him a** ~ **blow** das Schicksal versetzte ihm einen harten *or* schweren Schlag; **to be** ~ **with** *or* **on sb** jdn hart anfassen; **don't be too** ~ **with him** sei nicht zu streng *or* hart mit ihm.

harshly ['hɑːʃlɪ] *adv see adj*.

harshness ['hɑːʃnɪs] *n see adj* (a) Rauheit *f*; Grelle, Härte *f*; Herbheit *f*. (b) Härte *f*; Barschheit, Schroffheit *f*; Rauheit *f*; Strenge *f*.

hart [hɑːt] *n* Hirsch *m*.

harum-scarum ['hɛərəmˈskɛərəm] 1 *adj* unbesonnen, unbedacht. 2 *n* unbedachter Tollkopf.

harvest ['hɑːvɪst] 1 *n* Ernte *f*; (*of wines, berries also*) Lese *f*; (*of hay also*) Mahd *f*; (*of the sea*) Ausbeute *f*, Ertrag *m*; (*fig*) Frucht *f*, Ertrag *m*. **the** ~ **of their efforts** die Früchte *pl* ihrer Arbeit *or* Anstrengungen; **a large** ~ **of apples** eine reiche Apfelernte.
  2 *vt* (*reap, also fig*) ernten; *vines also* lesen; (*bring in*) einbringen.
  3 *vi* ernten.

harvester ['hɑːvɪstəʳ] *n* (*person*) Erntearbeiter(in *f*) *m*; (*machine*) Mähmaschine *f*; (*cuts and binds*) Mähbinder, Binmäher *m*; (*combine* ~) Mähdrescher *m*.

harvest: ~ **festival** *n* Erntedankfest *nt*; ~ **home** *n* (*festival*) Erntefest *nt*; (*service*) Erntedankfest *nt*; ~ **moon** *n* Herbstmond *m*, heller Vollmond im September; ~ **time** *n* Erntezeit *f*.

has [hæz] 3rd pers sing present of **have**.

has-been ['hæzbiːn] *n* (*pej*) vergangene *or* vergessene Größe. **every comedian must dread finishing up a** ~ jeder Komiker muß befürchten, (im Alter) in Vergessenheit zu geraten.

hash [hæʃ] 1 *n* (a) (*Cook*) Haschee *nt*.
  (b) (*fig: mess*) Durcheinander *nt*, Kuddelmuddel *m* (*inf*); (*bad work*) Pfusch(erei *f*) *m* (*inf*). **to make a** ~ **of sth** etw verpfuschen *or* vermasseln (*inf*); **I'll soon settle his** ~ (*inf*) ich werde ihm (mal kurz) den Kopf zurechtsetzen *or* waschen (*inf*); **that settled his** ~ (*inf*) das hat ihn kuriert (*inf*).
  (c) (*inf: hashish*) Hasch *nt* (*inf*).
  2 *vt* (*Cook*) hacken.
♦**hash up** *vt sep* (a) (*Cook*) hacken, zerkleinern. (b) (*inf: mess up*) verpfuschen, vermasseln (*inf*).

hashish ['hæʃɪʃ] *n* Haschisch *nt*.

hash-up ['hæʃʌp] *n* (*inf*) (*mixture*) Mischmasch *m* (*pej inf*), Sammelsurium *nt* (*inf*); (*mess*) Kuddelmuddel *m* (*inf*), Durcheinander *nt* (*inf*); (*bad work*) Pfusch(erei *f*) *m* (*inf*). **a** ~ **of old ideas** olle Kamellen (*inf*); **to make a** ~ **of sth** etw verpfuschen (*inf*).

hasn't ['hæznt] *contr of* has not.

hasp [hɑːsp] *n* (*for chest, door etc*) Überfall *m*; (*for book covers*) (Verschluß)spange, Schließe *f*.

hassle ['hæsl] *n* (*inf*) Auseinandersetzung *f*; (*bother, trouble*) Mühe *f*, Theater *nt* (*inf*). **we had a real** ~ **getting these tickets for tonight** es war ein richtiges Theater (*inf*) *or* es hat uns (dat) viel Mühe gemacht, diese Karten für heute abend zu bekommen; **getting there is such a** ~ es ist so umständlich, dorthin zu kommen; **it's always such a** ~ getting him to do anything es ist immer ein solches Theater, ihn dazu zu bringen, etwas zu tun (inf); **it's too much** ~ **cooking for myself** es ist mir zu umständlich or mühsam, für mich allein zu kochen; **all this security** ~ dieser ganze Zirkus mit den Sicherheitsmaßnahmen (inf).

hassock ['hæsək] n Betkissen, Kniekissen nt.

hast [hæst] (obs) 2nd pers sing present of **have**.

haste [heist] n Eile f; (nervous) Hast f. **why the** ~? warum die Eile?, warum so eilig?; **to do sth in** ~ etw in Eile tun; **to be in** ~ **to do sth** sich beeilen, etw zu tun; **in great** ~ in großer Eile; **to make** ~ **to do sth** sich beeilen, etw zu tun; **make** ~! (old) spute dich (old); **more** ~ **less speed** (Prov) eile mit Weile (Prov).

hasten ['heisn] 1 vi sich beeilen. **he** ~**ed to add that** ... er fügte schnell hinzu, daß ..., er beeilte sich, hinzuzufügen, daß ...; **I** ~ **to add that** ... ich muß allerdings hinzufügen, daß ...; **she** ~ed **down the stairs** sie eilte or hastete die Treppe hinunter.

2 vt beschleunigen. **the strain of office** ~ed **his death** die Belastung seines Amtes trug zu seinem vorzeitigen Tod bei; **to** ~ **sb's departure** jdn zum Aufbruch drängen; **their departure from the country was** ~ed **by political unrest** politische Unruhen beschleunigten ihr Verlassen des Landes.

♦**hasten away** vi forteilen or -hasten, eilig weggehen.

♦**hasten back** vi eilig or schnell zurückkehren, zurückeilen.

♦**hasten off** vi weg- or forteilen.

hastily ['heistili] adv (a) (hurriedly) hastig, eilig. (b) (rashly) vorschnell.

hastiness ['heistinis] n (a) (hurriedness) Eile f. **his** ~ **in resorting to violence** daß er so schnell gewalttätig wird.
  (b) (rashness) Voreiligkeit, Unbesonnenheit f. **your** ~ **in making decisions** die Voreiligkeit, mit der Sie Ihre Entscheidungen fällen.
  (c) (dated: hot temper) Hitzigkeit (dated), Heftigkeit f.

hasty ['heisti] adj (+er) (a) (hurried) hastig, eilig. **they made a** ~ **exit** sie eilten or gingen eilig hinaus, sie machten, daß sie hinauskamen (inf); **the witness gave a** ~ **sketch of what he had seen** der Zeuge schilderte flüchtig, was er gesehen hatte; **don't be so** ~ nicht so hastig!; **I only had time for a** ~ **meal** ich hatte nur Zeit, hastig or eilig or schnell etwas zu essen.
  (b) (rash) vorschnell. **he's a bit** ~ **in his judgements** er urteilt etwas vorschnell.
  (c) (dated: hot-tempered) hitzig, heftig.

hasty pudding n (US) Maismehlbrei m.

hat [hæt] n (a) Hut m. **to put on one's** ~ den or seinen Hut aufsetzen; **to take one's** ~ off den Hut abnehmen; (for greeting also) den Hut ziehen (to sb vor jdm); ~**s off!** Hut ab!; **my** ~! (dated inf) daß ich nicht lache! (inf).
  (b) (fig phrases) **he's a bad** ~ (dated inf) er ist ein übler Patron (dated inf); **I'll eat my** ~ **if** ... ich fresse einen Besen, wenn ... (inf); **I take my** ~ **off to him** Hut ab vor ihm!; **to talk through one's** ~ (inf) dummes Zeug reden; **to keep sth under one's** ~ (inf) etw für sich behalten; **at the drop of a** ~ auf der Stelle, ohne weiteres; **to toss one's** ~ **in the ring** sich am politischen Reigen beteiligen; (non-political) sich einschalten; **that's old** ~ (inf) das ist ein alter Hut (inf); **they're all pretty old** ~ (inf) das sind doch alles olle Kamellen (inf); **to pass round the** ~ für sb für jdn sammeln or den Hut rumgehen lassen (inf).

hat: ~**band** n Hutband nt; ~**box** n Hutschachtel f.

hatch¹ [hætʃ] 1 vt (also ~ **out**) ausbrüten; (fig) plot, scheme also aushecken. 2 vi (also ~ **out**) (bird) ausschlüpfen. **when will the eggs** ~? wann schlüpfen die Jungen aus? 3 n (act of ~ing) Ausbrüten nt; (brood) Brut f.

hatch² n (a) (Naut) Luke f; (in floor, ceiling) Bodenluke f; (half-door) Halbtür, Niedertür f; (turret ~) Ausstiegsluke f (in Turm); see **batten down**. (b) (service) ~ Durchreiche f. (c) **down the** ~! (inf) hoch die Tassen! (inf).

hatch³ vt (Art) schraffieren.

hatchback ['hætʃbæk] n Hecktürmodell nt; (door) Hecktür f.

hatchery ['hætʃəri] n Brutplatz m or -stätte f.

hatchet ['hætʃit] n Beil nt; (tomahawk) Kriegsbeil nt. **to bury the** ~ das Kriegsbeil begraben.

hatchet: ~ **face** n scharfgeschnittenes Gesicht; (inf: person) Raubvogelgesicht nt; ~-**faced** adj mit scharfen Gesichtszügen; ~ **man** n (hired killer) gedungener Mörder; (fig) Vollstreckungsbeamte(r) m.

hatching ['hætʃɪŋ] n (Art) Schraffur, Schraffierung f.

hatchway ['hætʃwei] n see **hatch**² (a).

hate [heit] 1 vt hassen; (detest also) verabscheuen, nicht ausstehen können (inf); (dislike also) nicht leiden können. **to** ~ **the sound of sth** etw nicht hören können; **to** ~ **to do sth** or doing sth es hassen, etw zu tun; (weaker) etw äußerst ungern tun; **I** ~ **seeing her in pain** ich kann es nicht ertragen, sie leiden zu sehen; **I** ~ **the idea of leaving** der Gedanke, wegzumüssen, ist mir äußerst zuwider; **I** ~ **to bother you** es tut mir sehr unangenehm or es tut mir außerordentlich leid, daß ich Sie belästigen muß; **I** ~ **having to say it but** ... es ist mir sehr schwer or es ist mir sehr unangenehm, das sagen zu müssen, aber ...; **I** ~ **being late** ich hasse es, zu spät zu kommen, ich komme äußerst ungern zu spät; **you'll** ~ **yourself for not thinking of the answer** du wirst dich schwarz ärgern, daß du nicht auf die Antwort gekommen bist (inf); **you'll** ~ **me for this but** ... du wirst es mir vielleicht übelnehmen, aber ...; **don't** ~ **me for telling you the truth** nimm es mir nicht übel or sei mir nicht böse, daß ich dir einen Wein eingeschenkt habe; **I should** ~ **to keep you waiting** ich möchte Sie auf keinen Fall warten lassen.
  2 n (a) Haß m (for, of auf +acc).
  (b) (object of hatred) **one of his pet** ~**s is chrome furniture/having to queue up** Stahlmöbel sind/Schlangestehen ist ihm ein Greuel or gehören/gehört zu den Dingen, die er am

meisten haßt or verabscheut; **spiders are my pet** ~ ich kann Spinnen auf den Tod nicht ausstehen or leiden (inf).

hated ['heitid] adj verhaßt.

hateful ['heitful] adj abscheulich; remarks also häßlich; person unausstehlich. **sth is** ~ **to sb** jd findet etw abscheulich/etw ist jdm verhaßt; **it was** ~ **of you to do that** es war häßlich or abscheulich von dir, das zu tun.

hatefully ['heitfəli] adv see adj abscheulich; unausstehlich.

hat: ~**less** adj ohne Hut; ~**pin** n Hutnadel f; ~**rack** n Hutablage f.

hatred ['heitrid] n Haß m (for auf +acc); (of spinach, spiders etc) Abscheu m (of vor +acc).

hatter ['hætə'] n Hutmacher(in f) m; (seller) Hutverkäufer(in f) m; see **mad**.

hat-trick ['hættrɪk] n Hattrick, Hat-Trick m. **to get a** ~ einen Hattrick erzielen; **with two divorces already behind her this looks like making the** ~ nachdem sie nun schon zweimal geschieden ist, denkt sie wohl, aller guten Dinge sind drei.

haughtily ['hɔ:tili] adv see adj hochmütig, hochnäsig (inf), überblich. **she stalked** ~ **out of the room** stolz erhobenen Hauptes verließ sie das Zimmer.

haughtiness ['hɔ:tinis] n see adj Hochmut m, Hochnäsigkeit f (inf); Überheblichkeit f.

haughty ['hɔ:ti] adj (+er) hochmütig, hochnäsig (inf); (towards people) überheblich. **with a** ~ **toss of her head** mit hochmütig zurückgeworfenem Kopf.

haul [hɔ:l] 1 n (a) (hauling) **a truck gave us a** ~ ein Lastwagen schleppte uns ab or (out of mud etc) zog uns heraus; **they gave a good strong** ~ **at the rope** sie zogen mit aller Kraft am Seil.
  (b) (journey) Strecke f. **it's a long** ~ **to** es ist ein weiter Weg (bis) nach; **short/long/medium** ~ **aircraft** Kurz-/Lang-/Mittelstreckenflugzeug nt; **long-**~ **truck-driver** Fernfahrer m; **the project has been a long** ~ das Projekt hat sich lang hingezogen; **the long** ~ **through the courts** der lange Weg durch die Instanzen.
  (c) (Fishing) (Fisch)fang m; (fig: booty, from robbery) Beute f; (inf: of presents) Ausbeute f (inf). **our** ~ **on the last trawl was 500 kg of herring** bei unserer letzten Fahrt hatten wir eine Ausbeute von 500 kg Hering; **I got quite a** ~ **for Christmas** bei mir hat es zu Weihnachten ganz hübsch was gegeben (inf).
  2 vt (a) ziehen; heavy objects also schleppen; see **coal**.
  (b) (transport by lorry) befördern, transportieren.
  (c) (Naut) den Kurs (+gen) ändern. **to** ~ **a boat into the wind** an den Wind segeln.
  3 vi (Naut: also ~ **round**) den Kurs ändern. **the yacht** ~ed **into the wind** die Jacht segelte an den Wind.

♦**haul away** vi (pull) mit aller Kraft ziehen (at, on an +dat); (rowers) sich in die Riemen legen. ~ ~! hau ruck!

♦**haul down** vt sep (a) flag, sail ein- or niederholen. (b) (with effort) herunterschleppen; (pull down) herunterzerren.

♦**haul in** vt sep einholen; rope einziehen.

♦**haul off** vi (Naut) (ab)drehen, den Kurs ändern.

♦**haul round** vi (Naut) (ship) den Kurs ändern; (wind) drehen.

♦**haul up** vt sep (a) (carry) hinauf- or hochschleppen; (pull up) hochzerren, hochziehen; flag, sail hissen; (aboard ship) (an Bord) hieven, hochziehen; (onto beach) schleppen, ziehen. **the dinghies were lying** ~ed **on the beach for the winter** man hatte die Jollen für den Winter an Land gezogen.
  (b) (fig inf) **to** ~ **sb** ~ before the magistrate/headmaster/brigadier jdn vor den Kadi/Schulleiter/Brigadeführer schleppen (inf); **he's been** ~ed ~ on a drugs charge er wurde wegen einer Rauschgiftsache vor den Kadi gebracht.

haulage ['hɔ:lɪdʒ] n (a) (road transport) Transport m. ~ **business** (firm) Transport- or Fuhrunternehmen nt, Spedition(sfirma) f; (trade) Speditionsbranche f, Fuhrwesen nt; ~ **contractor** (firm) Transportunternehmen nt, Spedition(s-firma) f; (person) Transport- or Fuhrunternehmer, Spediteur m.
  (b) (transport charges) Speditions- or Transportkosten pl.

haulier ['hɔ:lɪə'] n Spediteur, Fuhrunternehmer m; (company) Spedition f. **firm of** ~**s** Spedition(sfirma) f, Transportunternehmen nt.

haulm [hɔ:m] n (single) Stengel m; (collectively) Stroh nt; (grain, grass also) Halm m.

haunch [hɔ:ntʃ] n (of person) Hüfte f; (hip area) Hüftpartie f; (of animal) (hindquarters) Hinterbacke f, (top of leg) Keule f; (Cook) Keule f, Lendenstück nt. ~**es** Gesäß nt; (of animal) Hinterbacken pl; **to go down on one's** ~**es** in die Hocke gehen; **the dog/he was sitting on his** ~**es** der Hund saß auf den Hinterbeinen/er saß in der Hocke; ~ **of venison** (Cook) Rehkeule f.

haunt [hɔ:nt] 1 vt (a) (ghost) house, place spuken in (+dat), umgehen in (+dat).
  (b) person verfolgen; (memory also) nicht loslassen; (fear also) quälen. **the nightmares which** ~ed **him** die Alpträume, die ihn heimsuchten.
  (c) (frequent) verkehren in (+dat), frequentieren, häufig besuchen; (animal) vorkommen, auftreten in.
  2 n (of person) (pub etc) Stammlokal nt; (favourite resort) Lieblingsort or -platz m; (of criminals) Treff(punkt) m; (of animal) Heimat f. **the riverbank is the** ~ **of a variety of animals** eine Vielzahl von Tieren lebt an Flußufern; **to revisit the** ~**s of one's youth** die Stätten seiner Jugend wieder aufsuchen; **a** ~ **of tax dodgers** ein Refugium nt für Steuerflüchtlinge; **an evil** ~ ein Ort m des Lasters (geh); **where are his** ~**s?** wo hält er sich vorwiegend or vorzugsweise auf?

haunted ['hɔ:ntid] adj (a) Spuk-. **a** ~ **house** ein Spukhaus nt, ein Haus nt, in dem es spukt; **this place is** ~ hier spukt es; **is it** ~? spukt es da?
  (b) look gehetzt, gequält; person ruhelos.

haunting ['hɔ:ntiŋ] adj doubt quälend, nagend; tune, visions, poetry eindringlich; music schwermütig. **these** ~ **final chords** diese Schlußakkorde, die einen nicht loslassen.

hauntingly [ˈhɔːntɪŋlɪ] adv eindringlich.
hauteur [ˈəʊtɜːʳ] n (liter) Hochmütigkeit f.
Havana [həˈvænə] n (a) Havanna nt. (b) Havanna(zigarre) f.
have [hæv] pret, ptp had, 3rd pers sing present has 1 aux vb (a) haben; (esp with vbs of motion) sein. to ~ been gewesen sein; to ~ seen/heard/eaten gesehen/gehört/gegessen haben; to ~ gone/run gegangen/gelaufen sein; I ~ /had been ich bin/war gewesen; I ~ /had seen ich habe/hatte gesehen; I ~ not/had not or I've not/I'd not or I ~n't/I hadn't seen ich habe/hatte ihn nicht gesehen; had I seen him, if I had seen him hätte ich ihn gesehen, wenn ich ihn gesehen hätte; having seen him (since) da or weil ich ihn gesehen habe/hatte; (after) als ich ihn gesehen hatte; after having said that he left nachdem or als er das gesagt hatte, ging er; I ~ lived or ~ been living here for 10 years/since January ich wohne or lebe schon 10 Jahre/seit Januar hier; you have grown du bist aber gewachsen.
   (b) (in tag questions etc) you've seen her, ~n't you? du hast sie gesehen, oder nicht?; you ~n't seen her, ~ you? du hast sie nicht gesehen, oder?; you ~n't seen her — yes, I ~ du hast sie nicht gesehen — doch or wohl (inf); you've made a mistake — no I ~n't du hast einen Fehler gemacht — nein(, hab' ich nicht inf); you've dropped your book — so I ~ dir ist dein Buch hingefallen — stimmt or tatsächlich or wahrhaftig; ~ you been there? if you ~/~n't ... sind Sie schon mal da gewesen? wenn ja/nein or nicht, ...; I ~ seen a ghost — ~ you? ich habe ein Gespenst gesehen — wahrhaftig or tatsächlich?; I've lost it — you ~n't (disbelieving) ich habe es verloren — nein!
   2 modal aux (+infin: to be obliged) I ~ to do it, I ~ got to do it (Brit) ich muß es tun or machen; I don't ~ to do it, I ~n't got to do it (Brit) ich muß es nicht tun, ich brauche es nicht zu tun; do you ~ to go now?, ~ you got to go now? (Brit) müssen Sie jetzt (wirklich) unbedingt gehen?; do you ~ to make such a noise? müssen Sie (unbedingt) so viel Lärm machen?; you didn't ~ to tell her das mußten Sie ihr nicht unbedingt sagen, das brauchten Sie ihr nicht unbedingt zu sagen, das hätten Sie ihr nicht unbedingt sagen müssen or brauchen; he doesn't ~ to work, he hasn't got to work (Brit) er braucht nicht zu arbeiten, er muß nicht arbeiten; she was having to get up at 6 each morning sie mußte jeden Morgen um 6 Uhr aufstehen; we've had to go and see her twice this week wir mußten diese Woche schon zweimal zu ihr (hin); we shall ~ to leave tomorrow morning müssen wir (unbedingt) gehen (inf) or abreisen; the letter will ~ to be written tomorrow der Brief muß morgen unbedingt geschrieben werden; it's got to be or it has to be the biggest scandal this year das ist todsicher der (größte) Skandal des Jahres; I'm afraid it has to be das muß leider sein.
   3 vt (a) (possess) haben. she has (got esp Brit) blue eyes sie hat blaue Augen; ~ you (got esp Brit) or do you ~ a suitcase? hast du einen Koffer?; I ~n't (got esp Brit) or I don't ~ a pen ich habe keinen Kugelschreiber; I must ~ more time ich brauche mehr Zeit; ~ you (got esp Brit) or do you have a cigarette? hast du (mal) eine Zigarette?; I ~ (got esp Brit) no German ich kann kein (Wort) Deutsch; he had her on the sofa er nahm sie auf dem Sofa; I ~ it! ich hab's!; what time do you ~? (US) wieviel Uhr hast du? (inf), wie spät hast du es?; judge Smith has it ... Kampfrichter Smith bewertet es mit ...
   (b) to ~ breakfast/lunch/dinner frühstücken/zu Mittag essen/zu Abend essen; to ~ tea with sb mit jdm (zusammen) Tee trinken; will you ~ tea or coffee/a drink/a cigarette? möchten Sie lieber Tee oder Kaffee/möchten Sie etwas zu trinken/eine Zigarette?, hätten Sie lieber Tee oder Kaffee/gern etwas zu trinken/gern eine Zigarette?; what will you ~? — I'll ~ the steak was möchten or hätten Sie gern(e)? — ich hätte or möchte gern das Steak; he had a cigarette/a drink/a steak er rauchte eine Zigarette/trank etwas/aß ein Steak; how do you ~ your eggs? wie hätten or möchten Sie die Eier gern(e)?; he had eggs for breakfast er aß Eier zum Frühstück; will you ~ some more? möchten Sie or hätten Sie gern(e) (noch etwas) mehr?; do you ~ coffee at breakfast? trinken Sie zum Frühstück Kaffee?; ~ another one nimm noch eine/einen/eines; trink noch einen; rauch noch eine; he likes to ~ his steak medium er hat sein Steak gern(e) halb durch(gebraten).
   (c) (receive, obtain, get) haben. to ~ news from sb von jdm hören; I ~ it from my sister that ... ich habe von meiner Schwester gehört or erfahren, daß ...; to let sb ~ sth jdm etw geben; I must ~ the money by this afternoon ich muß das Geld bis heute nachmittag haben; I must ~ something to eat at once ich brauche dringend etwas zu essen, ich muß dringend etwas zu essen haben; we had a lot of visitors wir hatten viel Besuch; there are no newspapers to be had es sind keine Zeitungen zu haben; it's nowhere to be had es ist nirgends zu haben or kriegen (inf); it's to be had at the chemist's es ist in der Apotheke erhältlich, man bekommt es in der Apotheke.
   (d) (maintain, insist) he will ~ it that Paul is guilty er besteht darauf, daß Paul schuldig ist; he won't ~ it that Paul is guilty er will nichts davon hören, daß Paul schuldig ist; as gossip has it dem Hörensagen nach, wie man so munkelt; as the Bible/Shakespeare has it wie es in der Bibel steht/wie Shakespeare sagt; as Professor James would ~ it (according to) laut Professor James; (as he would put it) um mit Professor James zu sprechen.
   (e) (neg: refuse to allow) I won't ~ this nonsense dieser Unsinn kommt (mir) nicht in Frage!; I won't ~ this sort of behaviour! diese Art (von) Benehmen lasse ich mir ganz einfach nicht bieten; I won't ~ it! das lasse ich mir nicht bieten!; I won't ~ him insulted ich lasse es nicht zu or dulde es nicht, daß man ihn beleidigt; I won't ~ him insult his mother ich lasse es nicht zu, daß er seine Mutter beleidigt; we won't ~ women in our club in unserem Klub sind Frauen nicht zugelassen; I'm not having any of that! (inf) mit mir nicht! (inf); but she wasn't having any (sl) aber sie wollte nichts davon wissen.

   (f) (hold) (gepackt) haben. he had (got) me by the throat/the hair er hatte or hielt mich am Hals/bei den Haaren gepackt; the dog had (got) him by the ankle der Hund hatte ihn am or beim Knöchel gepackt; I ~ (got) him where I want him ich habe ihn endlich soweit, ich habe ihn endlich (da), wo ich will; the champion had him now der Meister hatte ihn jetzt fest im Griff or in der Tasche (inf); he ought to ~ the fight by the third round er sollte den Kampf eigentlich bis zur dritten Rund im Griff or unter Kontrolle haben; I'll ~ you (inf) dich krieg ich (beim Kragen); you ~ me there da bin ich überfragt.
   (g) to ~ a child ein Kind bekommen; she is having a baby in April sie bekommt or kriegt (inf) im April ein Kind; she had twins sie hat Zwillinge bekommen or geboren or gekriegt (inf); our cat has had kittens unsere Katze hat Junge bekommen or gekriegt (inf).
   (h) (wish) mögen. which one will you ~? welche(n, s) möchten Sie haben or hätten Sie gern?; what more would you ~? was wollen Sie mehr?, was will man mehr?; as fate would ~ it, ... wie es das Schicksal so wollte, ...; what would you ~ me say? was soll ich dazu sagen?
   (i) (causative) to ~ sth done etw tun lassen; to ~ one's hair cut/a suit made sich (dat) die Haare schneiden lassen/einen Anzug machen lassen; I had my luggage brought up ich habe (mir) das Gepäck nach oben bringen lassen; ~ it mended geben Sie es in Reparatur, lassen Sie es reparieren; to ~ sb do sth jdn etw tun lassen; they had him shot sie ließen ihn erschießen; they ~ you understand ... Sie müssen nämlich wissen ...; she nearly had the table over sie hätte den Tisch beinahe umgekippt or zum Umkippen gebracht; I had him in such a state that ... er war in einer solchen Verfassung, daß ...; he had the audience in hysterics das Publikum kugelte sich vor Lachen; he had the police baffled die Polizei stand vor einem Rätsel.
   (j) (experience, suffer) he had his car stolen man hat ihm sein Auto gestohlen; he had his arm broken er hat/hatte einen gebrochenen Arm; I've had three windows broken (bei) mir sind drei Fenster eingeworfen worden; to ~ an operation sich einer Operation unterziehen (geh), operiert werden; I had my friends turn against me ich mußte es erleben, wie or daß sich meine Freunde gegen mich wandten.
   (k) (+n = vb identical with n) to ~ a walk einen Spaziergang machen, spazierengehen; to ~ a dream träumen.
   (l) party geben, machen; meeting abhalten. are you having a reception? gibt es einen Empfang?; we decided not to ~ a reception wir haben uns gegen einen Empfang entschieden.
   (m) (phrases) let him ~ it! gib's ihm! (inf); he/that coat has had it (inf) der ist weg vom Fenster (inf)/der Mantel ist im Eimer (inf); if I miss the last bus, I've had it (inf) wenn ich den letzten Bus verpasse, bin ich geliefert (inf) or ist der Ofen aus (inf); ~ it your own way machen Sie es or halten Sie es, wie Sie wollen; I didn't know he had it in him ich hätte ihn dazu nicht für fähig gehalten; to ~ a good time/a pleasant evening Spaß haben, sich amüsieren/einen netten Abend verbringen; ~ a good time! viel Spaß!; you've been had! (inf) da hat man dich übers Ohr gehauen (inf); I'll ~ the sofa in this room das Sofa möchte or werde ich in dieses Zimmer stellen; thanks for having me vielen Dank für Ihre Gastfreundschaft.

♦**have around** vt always separate (a) (bei sich) zu Besuch haben; (invite) einladen. (b) he's a useful man to ~ ~ es ist ganz praktisch, ihn zur Hand zu haben.
♦**have at** vi +prep obj (old) angreifen. she had ~ me with her umbrella sie ging mit ihrem Regenschirm auf mich los.
♦**have away** vt always separate: to ~ it ~ with sb (sl) es mit jdm treiben (inf).
♦**have back** vt sep zurückhaben.
♦**have down 1** vt sep people, guests (bei sich) zu Besuch haben.
   2 vt always separate (take down) scaffolding herunterhaben; (knock down) buildings abreißen; vase herunterwerfen; (take down) carpets verlegen.
♦**have in** vt always separate (a) im Haus haben. we've (got esp Brit) the decorators ~ all week wir haben die ganze Woche (über) die Anstreicher im Haus.
   (b) to ~ it ~ for sb (inf) jdn auf dem Kieker haben (inf).
   (c) (make come in) hereinrufen. can we ~ the next interviewee ~? können wir den nächsten Kandidaten haben?
   (d) (put in) he had the new engine ~ in a couple of hours er hatte den neuen Motor in ein paar Stunden drin (inf).
♦**have off** vt always separate (a) to ~ it ~ with sb (sl) es mit jdm treiben (inf). (b) (take off) he had the top ~ in a second er hatte den Deckel in Sekundenschnelle (he)runter; he had to ~ his arm ~ sein Arm mußte abgenommen werden.
♦**have on 1** vt sep (a) (wear) anhaben; radio anhaben.
   (b) (have sth arranged) vorhaben; (be busy with) zu tun haben. we've got a big job ~ wir haben ein großes Projekt in Arbeit.
   (c) (inf: deceive, trick) übers Ohr hauen (inf); (tease) auf den Arm nehmen (inf).
   2 vt always separate (a) to ~ nothing ~ sb gegen jdn nichts in der Hand haben; they've got nothing ~ me! mir kann keiner! (inf).
   (b) (put on) they had new tyres ~ in no time sie hatten die neuen Reifen im Nu drauf (inf); they still haven't got the roof ~ das Dach ist immer noch nicht drauf.
♦**have out** vt always separate (a) herausgenommen bekommen. he was having his tonsils ~ er bekam seine Mandeln herausgenommen. (b) (discuss) ausdiskutieren. to ~ it ~ with sb etw mit jdm ausdiskutieren; I'll ~ it ~ with him ich werde mit ihm reden, ich werde mich mit ihm aussprechen.
♦**have over or round** vt always separate (bei sich) zu Besuch haben; (invite) (zu sich) einladen.
♦**have up** vt always separate (a) (inf: cause to appear in court) drankriegen (inf). that's the second time he's been had ~ for

drunken driving jetzt haben sie ihn schon zum zweiten Mal wegen Trunkenheit am Steuer drangekriegt (*inf*); **he's been had ~ again** er war schon wieder vor dem Kadi (*inf*).
(b) (*put up*) **when we had the tent/shelves ~** als wir das Zelt aufgestellt/die Regale an der Wand hatten.

haves [hævz] *npl* (*inf*) **the ~** die Betuchten (*inf*), die Begüterten *pl*; **the ~ and the have-nots** die Betuchten und die Habenichtse.

havoc ['hævǝk] *n* verheerender Schaden; (*devastation also*) Verwüstung *f*; (*chaos*) Chaos *nt*. **to wreak ~ in or with sth, to play ~ with sth** bei etw verheerenden Schaden anrichten; (*physical damage also*) etw verwüsten, etw verheerend zurichten; (*with health, part of the body*) für etw üble *or* schlimme Folgen haben, sich übel auf etw (*acc*) auswirken; **the tornado wreaked ~ all along the coast** der Tornado richtete entlang der ganzen Küste große Verwüstungen an; **the sudden rise in oil prices wreaked ~ with India's five-year plan** der plötzliche Anstieg der Ölpreise hat Indiens Fünfjahresplan vollständig über den Haufen geworfen (*inf*); **the editor had wrought ~ with the original text** der Lektor hatte (mit dem Rotstift) im Originaltext gewütet; **his sense of guilt played ~ with his imagination** er stellte sich (*dat*) aufgrund seiner Schuldgefühle alles mögliche vor.

haw¹ [hɔː] *n* (*Bot*) Mehlfäßchen *nt*, Mehlbeere *f*.

haw² *see* **hum.**

Hawaii [hǝ'waiiː] *n* Hawaii *nt*; (*state also*) die Hawaii-Inseln *pl*.
Hawaiian [hǝ'waiǝn] **1** *adj* hawaiisch, Hawaii-. **~ guitar** Hawaiigitarre *f*. **2** *n* (**a**) Hawaiianer(in *f*) *m*. (**b**) (*language*) Hawaiisch *nt*.

hawk¹ [hɔːk] **1** *n* (**a**) (*Orn*) Habicht *m*; (*sparrow ~*) Sperber *m*; (*falcon*) Falke *m*. (**b**) (*fig: politician*) Falke *m*. **the ~s and the doves** die Falken und die Tauben. **2** *vi* mit Falken jagen.

hawk² *vi* (*with phlegm*) sich räuspern.

hawk³ *vt* hausieren (gehen) mit; (*in street*) verkaufen, feilhalten, feilbieten; (*by shouting out*) ausschreien.

◆**hawk about** *vi sep gossip etc* verbreiten, herumtratschen (*inf*).

◆**hawk up** *vt sep phlegm* aushusten.

hawker ['hɔːkǝʳ] *n* (**a**) (*hunter*) Falkner *m*. (**b**) (*pedlar*) (*door-to-door*) Hausierer(in *f*) *m*; (*in street*) Höker (*pej*), Straßenhändler(in *f*) *m*; (*at market*) Marktschreier(in *f*) *m*.

hawk-eyed ['hɔːkaɪd] *adj* scharfsichtig, adleräugig. **to be ~** Adleraugen haben.

hawking ['hɔːkɪŋ] *n* (Falken)beize, Falkenjagd *f*.

hawkmoth ['hɔːkmɒθ] *n* Schwärmer *m*.

hawser ['hɔːzǝʳ] *n* (*Naut*) Trosse *f*.

hawthorn ['hɔːθɔːn] *n* (*also ~ bush/tree*) Weiß- *or* Rot- *or* Hagedorn *m*. **~ hedge** Weiß- *or* Rotdornhecke *f*.

hay [heɪ] *n* Heu *nt*. **to make ~** Heu machen; **to hit the ~** (*inf*) sich in die Falle hauen (*sl*); **to make ~ while the sun shines** (*Prov*) das Eisen schmieden, solange es heiß ist (*Prov*).

hay: **~cock** *n* Heuhaufen *m*; **~ fever** *n* Heuschnupfen *m*; **~fork** *n* Heugabel *f*; (*motor-driven*) Heuwender *m*; **~loft** *n* Heuboden *m*; **~maker** *n* (**a**) Heumacher(in *f*) *m*; (**b**) (*Boxing inf*) knallharter Schlag, Schwinger *m*; **~making** *n* Heuen *nt*, Heuernte *f*; **~rack** *n* (*for fodder*) (Heu)raufe *f*; (*US: on wagon*) Heuwagenaufbau *m*; **~rick**, **~stack** *n* Heumiete *f*.

haywire ['heɪwaɪǝʳ] *adj pred* (*inf*) **to be (all) ~** (*vollständig*) durcheinander *or* ein Wirrwarr (*inf*); **her life's all ~ again** ihr Leben ist wieder ein einziges Kuddelmuddel (*inf*) *or* totales Chaos (*inf*); **to go ~** (*go crazy*) durchdrehen (*inf*); (*plans, arrangements*) durcheinandergeraten, über den Haufen geworfen werden (*inf*); (*machinery*) verrückt spielen (*inf*).

hazard ['hæzǝd] **1** *n* (**a**) (*danger*) Gefahr *f*; (*risk*) Risiko *nt*. **there is quite a large ~ involved** damit ist ein ziemliches Risiko verbunden; **a typical translating ~** eine typische Gefahr beim Übersetzen; **the ~s of war** die Gefahren des Krieges; **it's a fire ~** es ist feuergefährlich, es stellt eine Feuergefahr dar.
(b) (*chance*) **by ~** durch Zufall; **game of ~** Glücksspiel *nt*.
(c) (*Sport: Golf, Show-jumping*) Hindernis *nt*.
2 *vt* (**a**) (*risk*) *life, reputation* riskieren, aufs Spiel setzen.
(b) (*venture to make*) wagen, riskieren. **if I might ~ a remark/suggestion** wenn ich mir eine Bemerkung/einen Vorschlag erlauben darf; **to ~ a guess** (es) wagen, eine Vermutung anzustellen.

hazardous ['hæzǝdǝs] *adj* (*dangerous*) gefährlich, risikoreich, gefahrvoll; (*risky*) gewagt, riskant; (*exposed to risk*) unsicher.

haze [heɪz] *n* (**a**) Dunst *m*. **a ~ of exhaust fumes** ein Dunstschleier *m* von Abgasen.
(b) (*fig*) **I/his mind was in a ~** (*daze*) ich/er war wie im Tran; (*confusion of thought*) ich/er war vollkommen verwirrt; **I am in a ~ about what happened** ich kann mich nur verschwommen daran erinnern, was geschehen ist.

hazel ['heɪzl] **1** *n* (*Bot*) Haselnußstrauch, Haselbusch *m*. **2** *adj* (*colour*) haselnuß- *or* hellbraun.

hazelnut ['heɪzlnʌt] *n* Haselnuß *f*.

hazily ['heɪzɪlɪ] *adv* (**a**) **the island/hills loomed ~ through the mist** die Insel zeichnete/die Berge zeichneten sich verschwommen im Dunst ab. (**b**) (*vaguely*) *remember* vage.

haziness ['heɪzɪnɪs] *n* (**a**) **the ~ of the weather** das dunstige *or* diesige Wetter. (**b**) (*of ideas etc*) Verschwommenheit, Unklarheit *f*.

hazy ['heɪzɪ] *adj* (+*er*) (**a**) dunstig, diesig; *mountains* im Dunst (liegend). (**b**) (*unclear*) unklar, verschwommen; *ideas, statement also* vage. **I'm ~ about what happened** ich kann mich nur vage *or* verschwommen daran erinnern, was geschah; **he's still a bit ~** (*after anaesthetic etc*) er ist immer noch ein wenig benommen.

HB *adj* (*on pencil*) HB.

HE *abbr of* **His Excellency** S.E; **His Eminence** S.E.

he [hiː] **1** *pers pron* (**a**) er. **it is ~** (*form*) er ist es, es ist er; **if I were ~** (*form*) wenn ich er wäre; **~ didn't do it, I did it** nicht er

hat das getan, sondern ich, er hat das nicht getan, das war ich; **so ~'s the one** der (*inf*) *or* er ist es also!; **Harry Rigg? who's ~?** Harry Rigg? wer ist das denn?
(b) **~ who** (*liter*) *or* **that** (*liter*) ... derjenige, der ...; (*in proverbs*) wer ...
2 *n* (*of animal*) Männchen *nt*. **it's a ~** (*inf: of newborn baby*) es ist ein er.
3 *pref* männlich; (*of animals also*) -männchen *nt*.

head [hed] **1** *n* (**a**) (*Anat*) Kopf *m*, Haupt *nt* (*geh*). **from ~ to foot** von Kopf bis Fuß; **~ downwards** mit dem Kopf nach unten; **to stand on one's ~** auf dem Kopf stehen, einen Kopfstand machen; **to stand sth on its ~** etw auf den Kopf stellen; **you could do it standing on your ~** (*inf*) das kann man ja im Schlaf machen; **to stand or be ~ and shoulders above sb** (*lit*) jdn um Haupteslänge überragen; (*fig*) jdm haushoch überlegen sein; **he can hold his ~ (up) high** in any company er kann sich in jeder Gesellschaft sehen lassen; **the condemned man held his ~ high** as he went to the scaffold der Verurteilte ging erhobenen Hauptes zum Schafott; **to turn or go ~ over heels** einen Purzelbaum machen *or* schlagen; **to fall ~ over heels in love with sb** sich bis über beide Ohren in jdn verlieben; **to fall ~ over heels down the stairs** kopfüber die Treppe herunterfallen; **to keep one's ~ above water** (*lit*) den Kopf über Wasser halten; (*fig*) sich über Wasser halten; **to talk one's ~ off** (*inf*) reden wie ein Wasserfall (*inf*) *or* wie ein Buch (*inf*); **to laugh one's ~ off** (*inf*) sich fast totlachen; **to shout one's ~ off** (*inf*) sich (*dat*) die Lunge aus dem Leib schreien (*inf*); **to scream one's ~ off** (*inf*) aus vollem Halse schreien; **I've got some ~ this morning** (*inf*) ich habe einen ziemlichen Brummschädel heute morgen (*inf*); **to give a horse its ~** einem Pferd die Zügel schießen lassen; **to give sb his ~** jdn machen lassen; **on your (own) ~ be it** auf Ihre eigene Verantwortung *or* Kappe (*inf*); **you need a good ~ for heights** Sie müssen schwindelfrei sein; **she has no ~ for heights** sie ist nicht schwindelfrei; **he gave orders over my ~** er hat über meinen Kopf (hin)weg Anordnungen gegeben; **to go over sb's ~** etw über jds Kopf (*acc*) (hin)weg tun; **to be promoted over sb's ~** vor jdm bevorzugt befördert werden; **to go to one's ~** (*whisky, power*) einem in den *or* zu Kopf steigen; **I can't make ~ nor tail of it** daraus werde ich nicht schlau.
(b) (*measure of length*) Kopf *m*; (*Racing also*) Kopflänge *f*. **taller by a ~** (*um*) einen Kopf größer; **by a short ~** (*Horse-racing, fig*) um Nasenlänge.
(c) (*mind, intellect*) Kopf, Verstand *m*. **use your ~** streng deinen Kopf an; **to get sth into one's ~** etw begreifen; **he won't get it into his ~ that ...** es will ihm nicht in den Kopf, daß ...; **get this into your ~** schreib dir das hinter die Ohren; **I can't get it into his ~** ich kann ihm das nicht begreiflich machen; **to take it into one's ~ to do sth** sich (*dat*) in den Kopf setzen, etw zu tun; **it never entered his ~ that ...** es kam ihm nie in den Sinn, daß ...; **what put that idea into his ~?** wie kommt er denn darauf?; (*unrealistic wish also*) wer hat ihm denn den Floh ins Ohr gesetzt? (*inf*); **to put or get sth out of one's ~** sich (*dat*) etw aus dem Kopf schlagen; **don't put ideas into his ~** bring ihn bloß nicht auf dumme Gedanken!; (*unrealistic wish etc*) setz ihm bloß keinen Floh ins Ohr!; **he has a good ~ for mathematics** er ist mathematisch begabt; **he has a good business ~** er hat einen ausgeprägten Geschäftssinn; **he has a good ~ on his shoulders** er ist ein heller *or* kluger Kopf; **he has an old ~ on young shoulders** er ist sehr reif für sein Alter; **two ~s are better than one** (*prov*) besser zwei als einer allein; (*in spotting things*) vier Augen sehen mehr als zwei; **we put our ~s together** wir haben unsere Köpfe zusammengesteckt; **to be above or over sb's ~** über jds Horizont (*acc*) gehen; **he talked above or over their ~s** er hat über ihre Köpfe weg geredet; **to keep one's ~** den Kopf nicht verlieren; **to lose one's ~** den Kopf verlieren; **he is off his ~** (*inf*) er ist (ja) nicht (ganz) bei Trost (*inf*), er hat ja den Verstand verloren; **to be weak or soft in the ~** (*inf*) einen (kleinen) Dachschaden haben (*inf*).
(d) **twenty ~ of cattle** zwanzig Stück Vieh; **to pay 10 marks a ~ or per ~** 10 Mark pro Kopf bezahlen.
(e) (*of flower, lettuce, cabbage, asparagus, hammer, nail, page, pier*) Kopf *m*; (*of celery*) Staude *f*; (*of arrow, spear*) Spitze *f*; (*of bed*) Kopf(ende *nt*) *m*; (*on beer*) Blume *f*; (*of cane*) Knauf, Griff *m*; (*of corn*) Ähre *f*; (*Archit: of column*) Kapitell *nt*; (*of stream*) (*upper area*) Oberlauf *m*; (*source*) Ursprung *m*; (*Med: of abscess etc*) Eiterpfropf *m*. **~ of steam/water** (*pressure*) Dampf-/Wasserdruck *m*; **at the ~ of the lake** am Zufluß des Sees; **at the ~ of the page/stairs** oben auf der Seite/an der Treppe; **at the ~ of the list** oben auf der Liste; **at the ~ of the table** oben am Tisch, am Kopf(ende) des Tisches; **at the ~ of the queue/army** an der Spitze der Schlange/des Heeres.
(f) (*fig: crisis*) Krise *f*, Höhepunkt *m*. **the illness has come to a ~** die Krise (der Krankheit) ist eingetreten; **to bring matters to a ~** die Sache auf die Spitze treiben; **to (decision)** die Entscheidung herbeiführen; **if things come to a ~** wenn sich die Sache zuspitzt.
(g) (*of family*) Oberhaupt *nt*; (*of business, organization*) Chef, Boss (*inf*) *m*; (*of department also*) Leiter *m*; (*of office, sub-department also*) Vorsteher *m*; (*Sch inf*) Schulleiter *m*; (*of secondary school also*) Direx *m* (*sl*); (*of primary school also*) Rex *m* (*sl*). **~ of department** (*in business*) Abteilungsleiter *m*; (*Sch, Univ*) Fachbereichsleiter(in *f*) *m*. **~ of state** Staatsoberhaupt *nt*.
(h) (*~ing, division in essay etc*) Rubrik *f*. **listed under several main ~s** in verschiedenen Rubriken eingetragen; **they should be treated/examined under separate ~s** sie müssen in verschiedenen Abschnitten behandelt werden/unter verschiedenen Aspekten untersucht werden.
(i) (*of coin*) Wappenseite *f*. **~s or tails?** Wappen oder Zahl?; **~s I win** bei Wappen gewinne ich.

(j) (*Naut*) (*bow*) Bug *m*; (*of mast*) Topp *m*; (*toilet*) Pütz *f*.
(k) (*on tape-recorder*) Tonkopf *m*.
(l) (*sl*) Junkie *m* (*sl*).
2 *vt* **(a)** (*lead*) anführen; (*be in charge of also*) führen; *list, poll also* an oberster Stelle *or* an der Spitze stehen von.
(b) (*direct*) steuern, lenken (*towards, for* in Richtung).
(c) (*give a* ~*ing*) überschreiben, eine/die Überschrift geben (+*dat*). **in the chapter** ~**ed ...** in dem Kapitel mit der Überschrift ...; **he** ~**s each chapter with a quotation** er stellt jedem Kapitel ein Zitat voran; ~**ed writing paper** Schreibpapier mit Briefkopf.
(d) (*Ftbl*) köpfen.
3 *vi* gehen; fahren. **where are you** ~**ing** *or* ~**ed** (*inf*)? wo gehen *or* fahren Sie hin?; **are you** ~**ing my way?** gehen/fahren Sie in der gleichen Richtung wie ich?; **and the meteorite was** ~**ing my way** und der Meteorit kam auf mich zu.

♦ **head back** *vi* zurückgehen/-fahren. **to be** ~**ing** ~ auf dem Rückweg sein; **it's time we started** ~**ing** ~ now es ist Zeit, umzukehren *or* sich auf den Rückweg zu machen.

♦ **head for** *vi* +*prep obj* **(a)** *place, person* zugehen/zufahren auf (+*acc*); *town, country, direction* gehen/fahren in Richtung (+*gen*); (*with continuous tense also*) auf dem Weg sein zu/nach; *pub, bargain counter, prettiest girl also* zusteuern auf (+*acc*) (*inf*); (*ship also*) Kurs halten auf (+*acc*). **where are you** ~**ing** *or* ~**ed** ~? wo gehen/fahren *or* steuern (*inf*) *or* streben (*inf*) Sie hin?
(b) (*fig*) zusteuern auf (+*acc*), auf dem Weg sein zu. **you're** ~**ing** ~ **trouble** du bist auf dem besten Weg, Ärger zu bekommen; **he is** ~**ing** ~ **a fall** er rennt in sein Verderben.

♦ **head in 1** *vt sep ball* hineinköpfen. **to** ~ **the ball** ~ **to the net** den Ball ins Netz köpfen. **2** *vi* köpfen.

♦ **head off** *vt sep* **(a)** abfangen. **(b)** (*avert*) *quarrel, war, strike* abwenden; *person asking questions* ablenken; *questions* abbiegen.

♦ **head up** *vt sep committee, delegation* führen, leiten.

head *in cpds* (*top, senior*) Ober-; ~**ache** *n* Kopfweh *nt*, Kopfschmerzen *pl*; (*inf: problem*) Problem *nt*; **this is a bit of a** ~**ache** das macht mir/uns ziemliches Kopfzerbrechen; ~**band** *n* Stirnband *nt*; ~**board** *n* Kopfteil *nt*; ~ **boy** *n vom Schulleiter bestimmter Schulsprecher*; ~**cheese** *n* (*US*) Schweinskopfsülze *f*; ~ **clerk** *n* (*Comm*) Bürovorsteher(in *f*) *m*; (*Jur*) Kanzleivorsteher(in *f*) *m*; ~**count** *n* **to have a** ~**count** abzählen; ~**dress** *n* Kopfschmuck *m*.

-headed [-hedɪd] *adj suf* -köpfig. **a curly-**~ **child** ein lockiges Kind, ein Kind mit lockigen Haaren.

header ['hedə'] *n* **(a)** (*dive*) Kopfsprung, Köpfer (*inf*) *m*. **to take a** ~ **into the water** einen Kopfsprung ins Wasser machen; (*fall*) kopfüber ins Wasser fallen. **(b)** (*Ftbl*) Kopfstoß, Kopfball *m*. **he's a good** ~ **of the ball** er köpft gut.

head: ~**first** *adv* (*lit, fig*) kopfüber; ~**gate** *n* (*oberes*) Schleusentor; ~**gear** *n* Kopfbedeckung *f*; (*of horse: bridle*) Zaumzeug *nt*; ~ **girl** *n vom Schulleiter bestimmte Schulsprecherin*; ~**hunter** *n* (*lit, fig*) Kopfjäger *m*.

headiness ['hedɪnɪs] *n* **this wine is known for its** ~ dieser Wein ist dafür bekannt, daß er einem schnell zu Kopf(e) steigt; **the** ~ **of this intellectual atmosphere** diese geistesgeladene Atmosphäre.

heading ['hedɪŋ] *n* **(a)** Überschrift *f*; (*on letter, document*) Kopf *m*; (*in encyclopedia*) Stichwort *nt*. **under the** ~ **of anthropology** unter dem Stichwort Anthropologie. **(b)** (*Ftbl*) Köpfen *nt*.

head: ~**lamp, ~light** *n* Scheinwerfer *m*; ~**land** *n* Landspitze *f*; ~**less** *adj* ohne Kopf; (*fig, old*) kopflos; ~**line** *n* (*Press*) Schlagzeile *f*; **he is always in the** ~**lines** er macht immer Schlagzeilen; **to hit** *or* **make the** ~**lines** Schlagzeilen machen; **the news** ~**lines** *npl* Kurznachrichten *pl*, die Wichtigste in Kürze; ~**long** *adj, adv fall* mit dem Kopf voran; *rush* überstürzt, Hals über Kopf; ~**man** *n* (*of tribe*) Häuptling *m*, Stammesoberhaupt *nt*; ~**master** *n* Schulleiter *m*; (*of secondary school also*) Direktor *m*; (*of primary school also*) Rektor *m*; ~**mistress** *n* Schulleiterin *f*; (*of secondary school also*) Direktorin *f*; (*of primary school also*) Rektorin *f*; ~ **office** *n* Zentrale *f*; ~**-on 1** *adj collision* frontal; *confrontation* direkt; **2** *adv collide* frontal; **to tackle a problem** ~**-on** ein Problem geradewegs angehen; ~**phones** *npl* Kopfhörer *pl*; ~ **post office** *n* Hauptpostamt *nt*; ~**quarters** *n sing or pl* (*Mil*) Hauptquartier *nt*; (*of business*) Hauptstelle, Zentrale *f*; (*of political party*) Parteizentrale *f*, Hauptquartier *nt*; **police** ~**quarters** Polizeipräsidium *nt*; ~**race** *n* Gerinne *nt*; ~**rest** *n* Kopfstütze *f*; ~**restraint** *n* Kopfstütze *f*; ~**room** *n* lichte Höhe; (*in car*) Kopfraum *m*; **15 ft** ~**room** (lichte) Höhe 15 Fuß; ~**scarf** *n* Kopftuch *nt*; ~**set** *n* Kopfhörer *pl*; ~**ship** *n* Schulleiterstelle, Direktoren-/Rektorenstelle *f*; **under his** ~**ship** unter ihm als Schulleiter; ~**shrinker** *n* (*lit*) Schrumpfkopffindianer *m*; (*sl: psychiatrist*) Seelenmasseur *m* (*inf*); ~ **start** *n* Vorsprung *m* (*on sb* jdm gegenüber); ~**stone** *n* (*on grave*) Grabstein *m*; ~**strong** *adj* eigensinnig, dickköpfig; ~ **teacher** *n* (*Brit*) *see* ~**master**, ~**mistress**; ~ **waiter** *n* Oberkellner *m*; ~**waters** *npl* Quellflüsse *pl*; ~**way** *n* **to make** ~**way** (*lit, fig*) vorankommen; **did you make any** ~**way with the unions?** haben Sie bei den Gewerkschaften etwas erreicht?; ~**wind** *n* Gegenwind *m*; ~**word** *n* Anfangswort *nt*; (*in dictionary*) Stichwort *nt*.

heady ['hedɪ] *adj* (+*er*) *scent, wine,* (*fig*) *atmosphere* berauschend; *person* impulsiv, unbedacht (*pej*); *atmosphere* geistesgeladen. **in those** ~ **days** in jenen Tagen der Begeisterung.

heal [hi:l] **1** *vi* (*Med, fig*) heilen. **2** *vt* **(a)** (*Med*) heilen; *person also* gesund machen. **time** ~**s all wounds** (*prov*) die Zeit heilt alle Wunden (*Prov.*). **(b)** (*fig*) *differences etc* beilegen; (*third party*) schlichten.

♦ **heal over** *vi* zuheilen.

♦ **heal up 1** *vi* zuheilen. **2** *vt sep* zuheilen lassen.

healer ['hi:lə'] *n* Heiler(in *f*) *m* (*geh*); (*herb etc*) Heilmittel *nt*.

healing ['hi:lɪŋ] **1** *n* Heilung *f*; (*of wound*) (Zu)heilen *nt*. **2** *adj* (*Med*) Heil-, heilend, heilsam (*old*); (*fig*) besänftigend.

health [helθ] *n* **(a)** Gesundheit *f*; (*state of* ~) Gesundheitszustand *m*. **in good/poor** ~ gesund/nicht gesund, bei guter/schlechter Gesundheit; **state of** ~ Gesundheitszustand *m*, Befinden *nt*; **how is his** ~? wie geht es ihm gesundheitlich?; **to regain one's** ~ wieder gesund werden; **to enjoy good** ~/**to have poor** *or* **bad** ~ sich guter Gesundheit (*gen*) erfreuen/kränklich sein; **to be good/bad for one's** ~ gesund/ungesund *or* gesundheitsschädlich sein, der Gesundheit (*dat*) zuträglich/nicht zuträglich sein; **Ministry of H**~ Gesundheitsministerium *nt*; **I'm not just doing it for the good of my** ~ (*inf*) ich mache das doch nicht bloß aus Spaß (*inf*).
(b) (*fig*) Gesundheit *f*.
(c) to drink (to) sb's ~ auf jds Wohl (*acc*) *or* Gesundheit (*acc*) trinken; **your** ~!, **good** ~! zum Wohl!, auf Ihre Gesundheit!

health: ~ **centre** *n* Ärztezentrum *nt*; ~ **certificate** *n* Gesundheitszeugnis *nt*; ~ **club** *n* Keep-fit-Verein *m*; (*place also*) Fitness- *or* Fitneß-Center *nt*; ~ **education** *n* Hygiene *f*; ~ **food** *n* Reformkost *f*; ~ **food shop** (*Brit*) *or* **store** (*esp US*) *n* Reformhaus *nt*, Bioladen *m*.

healthful ['helθfʊl], **healthgiving** ['helθ,gɪvɪŋ] *adj* gesund.

health hazard *n* Gefahr *f* für die Gesundheit.

healthily ['helθɪlɪ] *adv* gesund. **we felt** ~ **tired** wir fühlten eine gesunde Müdigkeit.

healthiness ['helθɪnɪs] *n* Gesundheit *f*.

health: ~ **inspector** *n* Sozialarbeiter(in *f*) *m* (*in der Gesundheitsfürsorge*); ~ **insurance** *n* Krankenversicherung *f*; ~ **problem** *n* Gesundheitsgefährdung *f*; **he retired because of a** ~ **problem** er trat aus gesundheitlichen Gründen in den Ruhestand; ~ **resort** *n* Kurort *m*; (*spa also*) Kurbad, Heilbad *nt*; **the H**~ **Service** *n* (*Brit*) das Gesundheitswesen; **H**~ **Service doctor** Kassenarzt *m*/-ärztin *f*; ~ **visitor** *n* Sozialarbeiter(in *f*) *m* (*in der Gesundheitsfürsorge*).

healthy ['helθɪ] *adj* (+*er*) (*lit, fig*) gesund. **it's not** ~ **to mix with that sort of person** es ist nicht ratsam *or* es kann einem schlecht bekommen, mit so jemandem zu verkehren; **it's not a** ~ **relationship** es ist eine ungesunde Beziehung.

heap [hi:p] **1** *n* **(a)** Haufen *m*; (*inf: old car*) Klapperkiste *f* (*inf*). **(to be piled) in a** ~ auf einem Haufen (liegen); **the building was reduced to a** ~ **of rubble** das Haus sank in Schutt und Asche; **I was struck all of a** ~ (*inf*) ich war wie vom Donner gerührt (*inf*); **he fell in a** ~ **on the floor** er sackte zu Boden.
(b) ~**s of** (*inf*) ein(en) Haufen (*inf*); **it happens** ~**s of times** (*inf*) das kommt andauernd vor; **do you have any glasses?** — **yes,** ~**s** haben Sie Gläser? — (ja,) jede Menge (*inf*).
2 *adv* ~**s** (*inf*) (unheimlich) viel.
3 *vt* häufen. **he** ~**ed his clothes together** er warf seine Kleider auf einen Haufen; **to** ~ **praises on sb/sth** über jdn/etw voll des Lobes sein (*geh*), jdn/etw über den grünen Klee loben (*inf*); (*in addressing*) jdn mit Lob überhäufen (*inf*); **to** ~ **insults on sb** sich über jdn sehr beleidigend äußern; (*in addressing*) jdm Beleidigungen an den Kopf werfen; (*cursing*) jdn mit einer Flut von Schimpfwörtern überschütten; ~**ed spoonful** gehäufter Löffel.

♦ **heap up 1** *vt sep* aufhäufen. **he** ~**ed** ~ **the litter into piles/a pile** er machte aus dem Abfall Haufen/einen Haufen; (*by sweeping*) er kehrte den Abfall in Haufen zusammen/auf einen Haufen; **you'll only be** ~**ing** ~ **problems for yourself later on** Sie schaffen sich (*dat*) (so) nur für später eine Menge Probleme. **2** *vi* sich häufen.

hear [hɪə'] *pret, ptp* **heard 1** *vt* **(a)** (*also learn*) hören. **I** ~**d him say that ...** ich habe ihn sagen hören, daß ...; **I** ~**d somebody come in** ich habe jemanden (herein)kommen hören; **no sound was** ~**d** es war kein Laut zu hören, man hörte keinen Laut; **he was** ~**d to say that ...** man hat ihn sagen hören, daß ...; **to make oneself** ~**d** sich (*dat*) Gehör verschaffen; **you're not going, do you** ~ **me!** du gehst nicht, hörst du (mich)!; **now** ~ **this!** Achtung, Achtung!; **to** ~ **him speak you'd think ...** wenn man ihn so reden hört, könnte man meinen, ...; **I've often** ~**d say** *or* **it said that ...** ich habe oft gehört *or* sagen hören, daß ...; **you play chess, I** ~ ich höre, Sie spielen Schach; **have you** ~**d the one about ...?** (haben Sie) den schon gehört von ...?; **I** ~ **tell you're going away** ich höre, Sie gehen weg; **I've** ~**d tell of monsters in the lake** ich habe von Ungeheuern in dem See sagen hören *or* gehört; **I've been** ~**ing things about you** von dir hört man ja schöne Dinge, ich habe da ja schöne Dinge über dich gehört; **I must be** ~**ing things** ich glaube, ich höre nicht richtig.
(b) (*listen to*) *lecture, programme etc* hören. **to** ~ **a case** (*Jur*) einen Fall verhandeln; **Lord,** ~ **our prayer/us** Herr, (er)höre unser Gebet/wir bitten dich, erhöre uns; **let's** ~ **your prayers before you go to sleep** wir wollen beten, bevor du schläfst.
2 *vi* **(a)** hören. **he does not** *or* **cannot** ~ **very well** er hört nicht sehr gut. ~, ~! (sehr) richtig!; (*Parl*) hört!, hört!
(b) (*get news*) hören. **he's left his wife** — **yes, so I** ~ er hat seine Frau verlassen — ja, ich habe es gehört; **I** ~ **from my daughter every week** ich höre jede Woche von meiner Tochter; **you'll be** ~**ing from me!** (*threatening*) Sie werden noch von mir hören!; **to** ~ **about sth** von etw hören *or* erfahren; **have you** ~**d about John?** he's getting married haben Sie gehört? John heiratet; **I** ~ **of him retiring** ich höre, daß er in den Ruhestand treten will; **never** ~**d of him/I nie (von ihm/davon) gehört; **I've** ~**d of him** ich habe schon von ihm gehört; **he wasn't** ~**d of for a long time** man hat lange Zeit nichts von ihm gehört; **he was never** ~**d of again** man hat nie wieder etwas von ihm gehört; **I've never** ~**d of such a thing!** das ist ja unerhört!; **I** ~ **of nothing else but that!** ich höre dauernd nichts anderes mehr!

♦ **hear of** *vi* +*prep obj* (*fig: allow*) hören wollen von. **I won't** ~ ~ it ich will davon (gar) nichts hören.

♦ **hear out** *vt sep person* ausreden lassen; *story* zu Ende hören.

heard [hɜ:d] *pret, ptp of* **hear**.

hearer ['hɪərəʳ] n Hörer(in f) m.
hearing ['hɪərɪŋ] n (a) Gehör nt. **to have a keen sense of** ~ ein gutes Gehör haben.
  (b) **within/out of** ~ **(distance)** in/außer Hörweite; **he said that in/out of my** ~ ich war in Hörweite/nicht in Hörweite, als er das sagte.
  (c) (Pol) Hearing nt, Anhörung f; (Jur) Verhandlung f. **preliminary** ~ Voruntersuchung f; ~ **of witnesses** (Jur) Zeugenvernehmung f; **he was refused a** ~ er wurde nicht angehört; **he didn't get a fair** ~ man hörte ihn nicht richtig an; (Jur) er bekam keinen fairen Prozeß; **the Minister gave the petitioners a** ~ der Minister hörte die Überbringer der Petition an; **to condemn sb without a** ~ jdn verurteilen, ohne ihn (an)gehört zu haben; (Jur) jdn ohne Anhörung verurteilen.
hearing aid n Hörgerät nt, Hörhilfe f.
hearken ['hɑːkn] vi (old, liter) horchen (to auf +acc).
hearsay ['hɪəseɪ] n Gerüchte pl. **to have sth from** or **by** or **on** ~ etw vom Hörensagen wissen or haben.
hearsay: ~ **account** n Bericht m aus zweiter Hand; ~ **evidence** n Zeugenaussage, die auf Hörensagen beruht.
hearse [hɜːs] n Leichenwagen m.
heart [hɑːt] n (a) (Anat) Herz nt.
  (b) (fig: for emotion, courage etc) Herz nt. **to break sb's** ~ jdm das Herz brechen; **to break one's** ~ **over sth** sich über etw (acc) zu Tode grämen; **she thought her** ~ **would break** sie meinte, ihr würde das Herz brechen; **you're breaking my** ~ (iro) ich fang' gleich an zu weinen (iro); **after my own** ~ ganz nach meinem Herzen; **to have a change of** ~ sich anders besinnen, seine Meinung ändern; **to learn/know/recite sth by** ~ etw auswendig lernen/kennen/aufsagen; **to know sth by** ~ (through acquaintance) etw (in- und) auswendig wissen; **in my** ~ **of** ~**s** im Grunde meines Herzens; **with all my** ~ von ganzem Herzen; **from the bottom of one's** ~ aus tiefstem Herzen; ~ **and soul** mit Leib und Seele; **to put** ~ **and soul into sth** sich mit Leib und Seele einer Sache (dat) hingeben; **to take sth to** ~ sich (dat) etw zu Herzen nehmen; **we have your interests at** ~ Ihre Interessen liegen uns am Herzen; **to set one's** ~ **on sth** sein Herz an etw (acc) hängen (geh); **it did my** ~ **good** es wurde mir warm ums Herz; **to set sb's** ~ **at rest** jds Gemüt or jdn beruhigen; **to one's** ~'**s content** nach Herzenslust; **most men are boys at** ~ die meisten Männer sind im Grunde (ihres Herzens) noch richtige Kinder; **I couldn't find it in my** ~ **to say no** ich konnte es nicht übers Herz bringen, nein zu sagen; **if you could find it in your** ~ **to forgive me** wenn du's übers Herz brächtest, mir zu verzeihen; **his** ~ **isn't in his work/in it** er ist nicht mit dem Herzen bei der Sache/dabei; **he's putting/not putting his** ~ **into his work** er geht in seiner Arbeit völlig auf/er ist nur mit halbem Herzen bei seiner Arbeit; **to lose** ~ den Mut verlieren; **to lose one's** ~ **(to sb/sth)** sein Herz (an jdn/etw) verlieren; **to take** ~ Mut fassen; **he took** ~ **from his brother's example** das Beispiel seines Bruders machte ihm Mut; **they've taken him to their** ~**s** sie haben ihn ins Herz geschlossen; **to put new** ~ **into sb/sth** jdn mit neuem Mut erfüllen/etw mit neuem Leben füllen; **to be in good** ~ (liter) guten Mutes sein (geh); **be of good** ~ (liter) sei guten Mutes (geh); **to have one's** ~ **in the right place** (inf) das Herz auf dem rechten Fleck haben (inf); **to have a** ~ **of stone** ein Herz aus Stein haben; **to wear one's** ~ **on one's sleeve** (prov) das Herz auf der Zunge tragen (prov); **my** ~ **was in my mouth** (inf) mir schlug das Herz bis zum Hals; **his** ~ **was in his boots** (inf) ihm ist das Herz in die Hose(n) gerutscht (inf); **have a** ~! (inf) hab ein Einsehen!; **not to have the** ~ **to do sth** es nicht übers Herz bringen, etw zu tun; **she has a** ~ **of gold** sie hat ein goldenes Herz; **my** ~ **sank** (with apprehension) mir wurde bang ums Herz (liter), mir rutschte das Herz in die Hose(n) (inf); (with sadness) das Herz wurde mir schwer; **(I was discouraged)** mein Mut sank.
  (c) (centre: of town, country, cabbage etc) Herz nt. **in the** ~ **of winter** im tiefsten or mitten im Winter; **the** ~ **of the matter** der Kern der Sache; **in the** ~ **of the forest** mitten im Wald, im tiefsten Wald; **the** ~ **of the tree** das Mark des Baumes; **artichoke** ~ Artischockenboden m.
  (d) **yes, my** ~ (liter) ja, mein Herz (liter); **dear** ~ (old, liter) liebes Herz (liter).
  (e) (Cards) ~**s** pl Herz nt; **queen of** ~**s** Herzdame f.
heart: ~**ache** n Kummer m, Herzeleid (old liter), Herzweh (geh) nt; ~ **attack** n Herzanfall m; (thrombosis) Herzinfarkt m; **I nearly had a** ~ **attack** (fig inf) (shock) ich habe fast einen Herzschlag gekriegt (inf); (surprise also) da hat mich doch fast der Schlag getroffen (inf); ~**beat** n Herzschlag m; ~**break** n großer Kummer, Leid nt; **I've had my share of** ~**breaks** ich habe meinen Teil an Kummer gehabt; **it was a** ~**break for him** es brach ihm (beinahe) das Herz; ~**breaking** adj herzzerreißend; **it was** ~**breaking to see him with crutches** es brach einem das Herz, ihn an Krücken zu sehen; **it's a** ~**breaking job** es bricht einem das Herz; ~**broken** adj untröstlich; **she was** ~**broken about it** sie war darüber todunglücklich; (because of love, death etc also) es hat ihr das Herz gebrochen; **don't look so** ~**broken** schau (doch) nicht so unglücklich drein; ~**burn** n Sodbrennen nt; ~**-case** n Herzpatient(in f) m; ~ **complaint** n Herzbeschwerden pl; ~ **condition** n Herzleiden nt; **he has a** ~ **condition** er ist herzleidend, er hat's am Herzen (inf); ~ **disease** n Herzkrankheit f.
-hearted [-hɑːtɪd] adj suf -herzig.
hearten ['hɑːtn] vt ermutigen.
heartening ['hɑːtnɪŋ] adj news ermutigend.
heart: ~ **failure** n Herzversagen nt; ~**felt** adj von Herzen or tief empfunden; sympathy herzlichst.
hearth [hɑːθ] n Feuerstelle f; (whole fireplace) Kamin m; (fig: home) (häuslicher) Herd. **the kettle was keeping hot on the** ~ der Kessel wurde auf dem Herd warm gehalten; ~ **and home** Haus und Herd.

hearth: ~**brush** n Kaminbesen m; ~**rug** n Kaminvorleger m.
heartily ['hɑːtɪlɪ] adv (a) laugh, welcome herzlich; sing kräftig; eat herzhaft, kräftig. **I** ~ **agree** ich stimme von Herzen or voll und ganz zu. (b) (very) äußerst, herzlich.
heartland ['hɑːtlænd] n Herzland nt, Herz nt des Landes.
heart: ~**less** adj herzlos; (cruel also) grausam; ~**lessness** n see adj Herzlosigkeit f; Grausamkeit f; ~**-lung machine** n Herz-Lungen-Maschine f; ~ **murmur** n Herzgeräusch pl; ~**rending** adj herzzerreißend; **it was** ~**rending to see** es war ein herzzerreißender Anblick; ~**-searching** n Selbstprüfung, Gewissenserforschung f; ~**-shaped** adj herzförmig; ~**sick** adj (liter) **to be** ~**sick** Herzeleid haben (old liter); ~**strings** npl **to pull** or **tug at the sb's** ~**strings** einen/jdn zu Tränen rühren, auf die/bei jdm auf die Tränendrüsen drücken (inf); **to play on sb's** ~**strings** mit jds Gefühlen spielen; ~**throb** n (inf) Schwarm m (inf); ~**-to-** ~ **talk** offen; **to have a** ~**-to-** ~ sich mit jdm ganz offen aussprechen; **2** n offene Aussprache; **it's time we had a** ~**-to-** ~ es ist Zeit, daß wir uns einmal offen aussprechen; ~ **transplant** n Herztransplantation, Herzverpflanzung f; ~**-trouble** n Herzbeschwerden pl; ~**-warming** adj herzerfreuend.
hearty ['hɑːtɪ] **1** adj (+er) herzlich; kick, slap also, meal, appetite herzhaft, kräftig; dislike tief; person (robust) kernig; (cheerful) laut und herzlich, derb-herzlich. **he is a** ~ **eater** er hat einen gesunden Appetit, er langt kräftig zu (inf); see hale.
  2 n (a) (Naut inf) **me hearties!** Jungs! (inf), Leute!
  (b) (Brit Univ sl) Sportskamerad or -freund (inf) m.
heat [hiːt] **1** n (a) (also Phys) Hitze f; (pleasant, Phys) Wärme f; (of curry etc) Schärfe f; (~ing) Heizung f. **I don't mind the** ~ mir macht (die) Hitze nichts aus; **in the** ~ **of the day** wenn es heiß ist; **at (a) low** ~ bei schwacher Hitze; **to regulate the** ~ (in oven) die Hitze regulieren; (on fire) die Wärme regulieren.
  (b) (fig: of argument, discussion) Hitze f. **he spoke with great** ~ er redete sehr hitzig or leidenschaftlich; **in the** ~ **of the moment** in der Hitze des Gefechts; (when upset) in der Erregung; **the discussion generated quite a lot of** ~ die Diskussion erhitzte die Gemüter; **to take the** ~ **out of the situation/an argument** die Situation/Diskussion entschärfen.
  (c) (inf: pressure) Druck m. **to put the** ~ **on** Druck machen (inf); **to put the** ~ **on sb** jdn unter Druck setzen; **the** ~ **is off** der Druck ist weg (inf); (danger is past) die Gefahr ist vorbei.
  (d) (Sport) Vorlauf m; (Boxing etc) Vorkampf m. **final** ~ Ausscheidungskampf m.
  (e) (Zool) Brunst f; (Hunt) Brunft f; (of dogs, cats) Läufigkeit f. **on** ~ brünstig; brunftig; läufig, heiß; (inf: woman) heiß (inf).
  2 vt erhitzen; food also aufwärmen, heiß or warm machen; house, room heizen; pool beheizen; (provide with ~) house, town beheizen.
  3 vi (room etc) sich erwärmen, warm werden; (get very hot) sich erhitzen, heiß werden. **your dinner is** ~**ing in the oven** dein Essen steht (im Backofen) warm.
♦**heat up 1** vi sich erwärmen, warm werden; (get very hot) sich erhitzen; (engine also) heißlaufen. **your soup will soon** ~ ~ deine Suppe ist gleich warm. **2** vt sep erwärmen; food aufwärmen, warm or heiß machen; (fig) discussion anheizen.
heat death n Wärmetod m.
heated ['hiːtɪd] adj (a) (lit) geheizt; pool beheizt. (b) (fig) words, debate, discussion hitzig, erregt. **to get** ~ hitzig werden; **things got rather** ~ die Gemüter erhitzten sich sehr.
heatedly ['hiːtɪdlɪ] adv hitzig.
heater ['hiːtəʳ] n Ofen m; (electrical also) Heizgerät nt; (in car) Heizung f; (for fondue) Rechaud m; (US sl: gun) Knarre f (sl). **what sort of** ~**s do you have?** was für eine Heizung haben Sie?; **turn the** ~ **on** stell die Heizung an.
heat: ~ **exhaustion** n Hitzeschäden pl; ~ **flash** n Hitzeblitz m.
heath [hiːθ] n (a) (moorland) Heide f; (type of country also) Heideland nt. (b) (plant) Heidekraut nt, Erika f.
heat haze n Hitzeflimmern nt.
heathen ['hiːðən] **1** adj heidnisch, Heiden-; (fig) unkultiviert, unzivilisiert. **2** n Heide m, Heidin f; (fig) unkultivierter or unzivilisierter Mensch. **the** ~ (collectively) (lit) die Heiden; (fig) die Barbaren.
heathenish ['hiːðənɪʃ] adj heidnisch.
heathenism ['hiːðənɪzəm] n Heidentum nt.
heather ['heðəʳ] n Heidekraut nt, Erika, Heide f.
Heath Robinson [ˌhiːθ'rɒbɪnsən] adj (inf) gadget, machine phantastisch (inf).
heating ['hiːtɪŋ] n Heizung f; (act) (of room, house) (Be)heizen nt; (of substances) Erwärmen, Erhitzen nt. **what sort of** ~ **do you have?** was für eine Heizung haben Sie?
heating: ~ **apparatus** n Heizapparat m; ~ **element** n Heizelement nt; ~ **engineer** n Heizungsinstallateur m; ~ **system** n Heizungssystem nt; (apparatus) Heizungsanlage f.
heat: ~**proof** adj hitzebeständig; ~ **rash** n Hitzeausschlag m, Hitzepocken pl; ~**-resistant**, ~**-resisting** adj hitzebeständig; ~ **shield** n Hitzeschild m; ~ **spot** n Hitzebläschen nt; ~**stroke** n Hitzschlag m; ~ **treatment** n (Metal, Med) Wärmebehandlung f; ~**wave** n Hitzewelle f.
heave [hiːv] **1** vt (a) (lift) (hoch)hieven, (hoch)heben, wuchten (onto auf +acc); (drag) schleppen. **he** ~**d himself out of bed** er hievte sich aus dem Bett (inf); **to** ~ **coal** Kohlen schleppen.
  (b) (throw) werfen, schmeißen (inf).
  (c) sigh, sob ausstoßen.
  (d) (Naut) pret, ptp hove wenden. **to** ~ **anchor** den Anker lichten.
  2 vi (a) (pull) ziehen, hieven.
  (b) sich heben und senken; (sea, waves, bosom also) wogen (liter); (stomach) sich umdrehen; (body) sich krümmen. **whales heaving and wallowing in the waves** Wale, die sich in den Wogen auf und ab wälzen; **the earthquake made the ground** ~ bei dem Beben hob sich die Erde.

(c) *pret, ptp* **hove** (*Naut*) to ~ **in(to) sight** in Sicht kommen; to ~ **alongside** längsseits gehen.
3 *n* (*of sea, waves*) Auf und Ab, Wogen (*geh*) *nt*; (*of bosom, chest*) Wogen *nt*. **to lift/throw sth with a great** ~ etw mit großer Anstrengung hochhieven *or* hochwuchten/etw mit großer Wucht werfen.

♦**heave to** (*Naut*) **1** *vi* beidrehen. **2** *vt sep* **ship** stoppen.

♦**heave up 1** *vi* (*inf: vomit*) brechen. **2** *vt sep* **(a)** hochhieven, hochwuchten; (*push up also*) hochstemmen. **(b)** (*inf: vomit*) ausbrechen, von sich geben (*inf*).

heave ho *interj* hau ruck.

heaven *n* **(a)** (*lit, fig inf*) Himmel *m*. **in** ~ im Himmel; **to go to** ~ in den Himmel kommen; **he is in (his seventh)** ~ er ist im siebten Himmel; **to move** ~ **and earth** Himmel und Hölle in Bewegung setzen; **it was** ~ es war einfach himmlisch; **the ~s opened** der Himmel öffnete seine Schleusen.
(b) (*inf*) (*good*) ~s! (*du*) lieber Himmel! (*inf*), du liebe Zeit! (*inf*); **would you like to?** — (**good**) ~s **no!** möchten Sie? — um Gottes *or* Himmels willen, bloß nicht!; **did he say so?** — (**good**) ~ **no!** hat er das gesagt? — ach wo, um Gottes Willen!; ~ **knows what** ... weiß Gott *or* der Himmel, was ... (*inf*); ~ **forbid!** bloß nicht, um Himmels willen! (*inf*); ~ **forbid that I should end up the same** daß ich doch bloß nicht *or* um Himmels willen nicht auch so werde! (*inf*); **for** ~'s **sake!** um Himmels *or* Gottes willen!

heavenly ['hevnlɪ] *adj* **(a)** himmlisch, Himmels-. ~ **body** Himmelskörper *m*; ~ **host** himmlische Heerscharen *pl*. **(b)** (*inf: delightful*) himmlisch, traumhaft.

heaven-sent ['hevn,sent] *adj* **opportunity** ideal. **it was** ~ das kam wie gerufen.

heavenward(s) ['hevnwəd(z)] *adv* zum Himmel, gen Himmel (*liter*). **to raise one's eyes** ~ die Augen zum Himmel erheben.

heaves [hi:vz] *n sing* (*Vet*) Dämpfigkeit *f*. **to have the** ~ dämpfig sein.

heavily ['hevɪlɪ] *adv* **(a)** *loaded, weigh* (*also fig*), *fall, breathe* schwer; *move, walk* schwerfällig. ~ **built** kräftig gebaut; **time hung** ~ **on his hands** die Zeit verging ihm nur langsam.
(b) *rain, smoke, drink, concentrate, rely, wooded, populated, disguised, influenced, overdrawn, in debt* stark; *defeated* schwer; *underlined* dick, fett; *lose, tax* hoch; *sleep* tief; *buy in* großem Umfang. **to be** ~ **drugged** unter starkem Drogeneinfluß stehen; ~ **committed** stark engagiert; **too** ~ **fished** überfischt; **to be** ~ **subscribed** viele Abonnenten haben.

heaviness ['hevɪnɪs] *n see adj* **(a)** Schwere *f*; Grobheit *f*. ~ **of heart** schweres Herz; ~ **of spirit** gedrückte Stimmung, Niedergeschlagenheit *f*. **(b)** Schwere *f*; Stärke *f*; Höhe *f*; (*of buying*) Umfang *m*; Dicke *f*; Tiefe *f*; Reichheit *f*. **(c)** Schwerfälligkeit *f*. **(d)** Schwüle *f*; Bedecktheit *f*. **the** ~ **of the silence** die bedrückende Stille. **(e)** Schwere *f*. **(f)** Schwere *f*, Ernst *m*.

heavy ['hevɪ] **1** *adj* (+*er*) **(a)** (*of great weight, Phys, fig*) schwer; *features* grob. **with a** ~ **heart** schweren Herzens, mit schwerem Herzen; ~ **with young** (*Zool*) trächtig; ~ **with incense/pollen/scent** mit Weihrauch/Pollen geschwängert (*geh*)/duftgeschwängert (*geh*); ~ **with sleep** *person* schläfrig; *eyes also* schwer; ~ **with wine** voll des süßen Weines (*liter*); ~ **goods vehicle** Lastkraftwagen *m*; ~ **industry** Schwerindustrie *f*; ~ **artillery** (*Mil*) schwere Artillerie.
(b) *tread, blow, gunfire, casualties, fog, clouds, sea, odour, music, book, wine, meal, sarcasm* schwer; *rain, cold also, traffic, eater, drinker, smoker* stark; *defeat, losses also, expenses, taxes* hoch; *buying* groß; *line* dick; *sleep* tief; *crop* reich. ~ **buyer** Großabnehmer *m*; ~ **type** (*Typ*) Fettdruck *m*; **to be** ~ **on petrol** viel Benzin brauchen.
(c) (~-*handed*) *manner, style, sense of humour* schwerfällig.
(d) (*oppressive*) *silence* bedrückend; *weather, air* drückend, schwül; *sky* bedeckt.
(e) (*difficult*) *task, work, day* schwer. **the going was** ~ wir kamen nur schwer voran; **the conversation was** ~ **going** die Unterhaltung war mühsam; **this book is very** ~ **going** das Buch liest sich schwer.
(f) (*Theat*) *part* schwer, ernst.
(g) (*inf: strict*) streng (*on* mit). **to play the** ~ **father** den gestrengen Vater spielen.
(h) (*dated US sl*) prima (*inf*), dufte (*inf*).
2 *adv* schwer. **his guilt weights** *or* **lies** ~ **on him** seine Schuld lastet schwer auf ihm; **time hangs** ~ **on our hands** die Zeit vergeht nur langsam.
3 *n* **(a)** (*inf: thug*) Schlägertyp *m*.
(b) (*Theat: villain*) Schurke *m*.
(c) (*Scot: beer*) dunkleres, obergäriges Bier.

heavy-: ~-**duty** *adj clothes, tyres etc* strapazierfähig; *boots* Arbeits-; *machine* Hochleistungs-; ~-**footed** *adj* schwerfällig; ~-**handed** *adj* schwerfällig, ungeschickt; ~-**hearted** *adj* mit schwerem Herzen, bedrückt; ~-**laden** *adj* (*also Bibl*) schwer beladen; **the air was** ~-**laden with incense** die Luft war von Weihrauch geschwängert (*geh*); ~ **water** *n* schweres Wasser; ~**weight 1** *n* (*Boxing*) Schwergewicht *nt*; (*fig inf*) großes Tier (*inf*), Größe(r) *m*; **the literary** ~**weights** die literarischen Größen; **2** *adj attr* Schwergewichts-.

hebdomadal [heb'domədl] *adj* (*form*) wöchentlich.

Hebrew ['hi:bru:] **1** *adj* hebräisch. **2** *n* **(a)** Hebräer(in *f*) *m*. **(b)** (*language*) Hebräisch *nt*; *see also* **English**.

Hebridean [,hebrɪ'di:ən] *adj* Hebriden-, der Hebriden.

Hebrides ['hebrɪdi:z] *npl* Hebriden *pl*.

heck [hek] *interj* (*inf*) oh ~! zum Kuckuck! (*inf*); ah, what the ~! ach, was soll's! (*inf*); what the ~ **do you mean?** was zum Kuckuck soll das heißen? (*inf*); **I've a** ~ **of a lot to do** ich habe irrsinnig viel zu tun (*inf*).

heckle ['hekl] **1** *vt speaker* (durch Zwischenrufe) stören. **2** *vi* stören, Zwischenrufe machen.

heckler ['heklər] *n* Zwischenrufer, Störer (*pej*) *m*.

heckling ['heklɪŋ] *n* Zwischenrufe *pl*.

hectare ['hekta:ʳ] *n* Hektar *m or nt*.

hectic ['hektɪk] *adj* hektisch.

hectogramme, (*US*) **hectogram** ['hektəʊgræm] *n* Hektogramm *nt*.

hectolitre, (*US*) **hectoliter** ['hektəʊ,li:təʳ] *n* Hektoliter *m*.

hector ['hektəʳ] *vt* (*liter: bully*) tyrannisieren.

hectoring ['hektərɪŋ] *adj* herrisch, tyrannisch.

he'd [hi:d] *contr of* **he would**; **he had**.

hedge [hedʒ] **1** *n* Hecke *f*; (*fig: protection*) Schutz *m*. **2** *vi* Fragen ausweichen, kneifen (*inf*) (*at* bei). **stop hedging and say what you think** weich nicht immer aus, sag, was du denkst! **3** *vt* **(a)** *investment* absichern. **to** ~ **one's bets** (*lit, fig*) sich absichern, auf Nummer Sicher gehen (*inf*). **(b)** *field, garden* (mit einer Hecke) umgeben.

♦**hedge about** *or* **around** *vt sep* **(a)** (*with restrictions etc*) *life* einengen; *procedure* erschweren, behindern. **(b)** (*rare: field*) (mit einer Hecke) einfassen.

♦**hedge in** *or* **round** *vt sep* **(a)** *field* mit einer Hecke umgeben *or* einfassen. **(b)** (*fig*) *procedure* behindern, erschweren. **to** ~ **sb** ~ jdn in seiner Freiheit einengen *or* beschränken.

♦**hedge off** *vt sep* mit einer Hecke abgrenzen *or* abtrennen.

hedgehog ['hedʒhɒg] *n* Igel *m*.

hedge: ~**hop** *vi* tief fliegen; ~**row** *n* Hecke *f*, Knick *m* (*N Ger*); ~ **sparrow** *n* Heckenbraunelle *f*.

hedonism ['hi:dənɪzm] *n* Hedonismus *m*.

hedonist ['hi:dənɪst] **1** *n* Hedonist(in *f*) *m*. **2** *adj* hedonistisch.

hedonistic [,hi:dən'ɪstɪk] *adj* hedonistisch.

heebie-jeebies ['hi:bɪ'dʒi:bɪz] *npl* (*sl*) Gänsehaut *f* (*inf*). **it/he gives me the** ~ dabei/wenn ich ihn sehe, bekomm' ich eine Gänsehaut (*inf*).

heed [hi:d] **1** *n* Beachtung *f*. **to take** ~ achtgeben, aufpassen; **to give** *or* **pay** ~/**no** ~ **to sb/sth**, **to take** ~/**no** ~ **of sb/sth** jdn/etw beachten/nicht beachten, jdm/einer Sache Beachtung/keine Beachtung schenken; **to take** ~ **to do sth** darauf achten, etw zu tun.
2 *vt* beachten, Beachtung schenken (+*dat*). **just** ~ **what your father says** hör auf deinen Vater; **he never** ~**s my advice** er hört nie auf meinen Rat.

heedful ['hi:dfʊl] *adj* **to be** ~ **of sb's warning/advice** auf jds Warnung (*acc*)/Rat (*acc*) hören.

heedless ['hi:dlɪs] *adj* rücksichtslos; *extravagance* leichtsinnig. **to be** ~ **of sth** etw nicht beachten, auf etw (*acc*) nicht achten; ~ **of their complaints** ohne sich um ihre Beschwerden zu kümmern, ohne Rücksicht auf ihre Beschwerden.

heedlessly ['hi:dlɪslɪ] *adv* rücksichtslos. **he** ~ **ignored my warning** er schlug meine Warnung achtlos in den Wind.

heehaw ['hi:hɔ:] **1** *n* Iah *nt*. **2** *vi* iahen.

heel¹ [hi:l] **1** *n* **(a)** Ferse *f*; (*of shoe*) Absatz *m*. **with his dog/the children at his** ~**s** gefolgt von seinem Hund/den Kindern; **to be right on sb's** ~**s** jdm auf den Fersen folgen; (*fig: chase*) jdm auf den Fersen sein; **to follow hard upon sb's** ~**s** jdm dicht auf den Fersen sein, sich an jds Fersen (*acc*) heften (*geh*); **winter followed hard upon autumn's** ~**s** (*liter*) der Herbst mußte dem Winter weichen (*liter*); **panic buying came on the** ~**s of the government's announcement** Hamsterkäufe folgten der Erklärung der Regierung auf dem Fuße; **to be down at** ~ (*person*) abgerissen *or* heruntergekommen sein; (*shoes*) schiefe Absätze haben, abgelaufen sein; **to take to one's** ~**s** sich aus dem Staub(e) machen, Fersengeld geben (*dated, hum*); **to show sb a clean pair of** ~**s** (*escape*) vor jdm davonlaufen, jdm die Fersen zeigen (*geh*); (*leave behind*) jdm weit voraus sein, jdn weit hinter sich lassen; ~! (*to dog*) (bei) Fuß!; **he brought the dog to** ~ er befahl dem Hund, bei Fuß zu gehen; **to bring sb to** ~ jdn an die Kandare nehmen (*inf*); **to turn on one's** ~ auf dem Absatz kehrtmachen; **to cool** *or* **kick one's** ~**s** (*wait*) warten; (*do nothing*) Däumchen drehen; ~ **bar** Absatzbar *f*.
(b) (*of golf club*) Ferse *f*; (*of loaf*) Kanten *m*; (*of mast*) Fuß *m*.
(c) (*pej sl: person*) Schwein *nt* (*sl*), Scheißkerl *m* (*sl*).
2 *vt* **(a)** **to** ~ **shoes** auf Schuhe neue Absätze machen; **the shoes need** ~**ing** die Schuhe brauchen neue Absätze; **to be well** ~**ed** (*inf*) betucht sein (*inf*), sich gut stehen (*inf*).
(b) (*Rugby*) *ball* hakeln.

heel² (*Naut*) **1** *vi* (*ship: also* ~ **over**) krängen (*spec*), sich (auf die Seite) legen *or* neigen. **to** ~ **hard over** sich stark auf die Seite legen, stark krängen (*spec*).
2 *vt* krängen lassen (*spec*), sich seitlich überlegen lassen.
3 *n* (*seitliches*) Überlegen, Seitenneigung *f*.

heft [heft] **1** *vt* (*US inf: lift*) (hoch)heben; (*assess weight*) abwägen, das Gewicht (ab)schätzen von. **2** *n* Gewicht *nt*; (*strength*) (Muskel)kraft *f*.

hefty ['heftɪ] *adj* (+*er*) (*inf*) kräftig; *person also* gut beieinander (*inf*); *woman also* drall; *child also* stramm; *book* (*extensive*) dick; *object, workload* (*schön*) schwer; *stroke, blow also* saftig (*inf*); *sum of money, amount* saftig (*inf*), ganz schön (*inf*), *argument* (durch)schlagend.

Hegelian [heɪ'geɪlɪən] **1** *adj* Hegelsch; (*in* ~ *tradition*) hegelianisch. **2** *n* Hegelianer(in *f*) *m*.

hegemony [hɪ'gemənɪ] *n* Hegemonie *f*.

hegira [hɪ'dʒaɪərə] *n* Hedschra *f*.

Heidelberg man ['haɪdlbɜ:g'mæn] *n* Homo Heidelbergensis *m*.

heifer ['hefəʳ] *n* Färse *f*.

heigh [heɪ] *interj* ~-**ho!** nun ja!

height [haɪt] *n* **(a)** (*of building, mountain etc, altitude*) Höhe *f*; (*of person*) Größe *f*. **to be six feet in** ~ sechs Fuß groß *or* (*wall etc*) hoch sein; **what is your** ~? wie groß sind Sie?; **he pulled himself up to his full** ~ er richtete sich zu voller Größe auf; ~ **above sea-level** Höhe über dem Meeresspiegel; **you can raise the** ~ **of the saddle** du kannst den Sattel höher stellen.

(b) (*high place*) ~s pl Höhen pl; **to scale the** ~**s of Everest** den Mount Everest besteigen; **fear of** ~**s** Höhenangst f; **to be afraid of** ~**s** nicht schwindelfrei sein.
(c) (*fig*) Höhe f; (*of success, power, stupidity also*) Gipfel m. **at the** ~ **of his power** auf der Höhe seiner Macht; **that is the** ~ **of folly** das ist der Gipfel der Torheit; **the** ~ **of glory** der höchste Ruhm; **that is the** ~ **of ill-manners!** das ist doch die Höhe!, das ist der Gipfel der Unverschämtheit!; **it is the** ~ **of ill-manners to ... es** verstößt gegen jede Etikette, zu ...; **at the** ~ **of the season** in der Hauptsaison; **at the** ~ **of the storm** als das Gewitter am heftigsten war; **dressed in the** ~ **of fashion** nach der neuesten Mode gekleidet; **the** ~ **of fashion** der letzte Schrei, große Mode; **at the** ~ **of summer** im Hochsommer.

heighten ['haɪtn] **1** vt (*raise*) höher stellen or machen; (*emphasize*) colour etc hervorheben; (*Med*) fever steigen lassen, erhöhen; *intensity* steigern; colour, feelings, anger, love, ambition verstärken; passions, fear, fitness, effect also erhöhen. **with** ~**ed colour** mit (hoch)rotem Gesicht.
2 vi (*fig: increase*) wachsen, größer or stärker werden.
heinous ['heɪnəs] adj abscheulich, verabscheuungswürdig.
heinously ['heɪnəslɪ] adv auf abscheuliche Weise.
heinousness ['heɪnəsnɪs] n Abscheulichkeit f.
heir [ɛəʳ] n Erbe m (**to** gen). ~ **apparent** gesetzlicher Erbe; ~ **to the throne** Thronfolger m.
heiress ['ɛəres] n Erbin f.
heirloom ['ɛəluːm] n Erbstück nt.
heist [haɪst] (*esp US sl*) **1** n Raubüberfall m. **2** vt rauben.
held [held] pret, ptp of **hold**.
Helen ['helɪn]n Helene f; (*Myth*) Helena f. ~ **of Troy** die Schöne Helena.
helical ['helɪkəl] adj gear Schnecken-, Schrägverzahnungs-.
helicopter ['helɪkɒptəʳ] n Hubschrauber m.
Heligoland ['helɪgəʊlænd] n Helgoland nt.
heliocentric [ˌhiːliəʊ'sentrɪk] adj heliozentrisch.
heliograph ['hiːliəʊgrɑːf] **1** n Heliograph m. **2** vt heliographisch übermitteln.
heliotrope ['hiːliətrəʊp] **1** n (*Bot, colour*) Heliotrop nt. **2** adj heliotrop(isch).
heliotropic [ˌhiːliəʊ'trəʊpɪk] adj heliotrop(isch).
heliport ['helɪpɔːt] n Hubschrauberlandeplatz m.
helium ['hiːliəm] n Helium nt.
helix ['hiːlɪks] n (räumliche) Spirale, Helix f.
hell [hel] n (a) Hölle f. **to go to** ~ (*lit*) in die Hölle kommen, zur Hölle fahren (*liter*).
(b) (*fig uses*) **all** ~ **was let loose** die Hölle war los; **it's** ~ **working there** es ist die reine Hölle, dort zu arbeiten; **it was** ~ **in the trenches** es war die reine Hölle in den Schützengräben; **life was** ~ **on earth** das Leben dort war die reinste Hölle or die Hölle auf Erden; **life became** ~ das Leben wurde zur Hölle; **he made his life** ~ sie machte ihm das Leben zur Hölle; **to give sb** ~ (*inf*) (*a row*) jdm die Hölle heiß machen; (*make life unpleasant*) jdm das Leben zur Hölle machen; **you'll get** ~ **if he finds out** (*inf*) der macht dich zur Schnecke (*inf*) or Sau (*sl*), wenn er das erfährt; **there'll be** (**all**) ~ **when he finds out** wenn er das erfährt, ist der Teufel los (*inf*); **to play** ~ **with sth** etw total durcheinanderbringen; **I did it for the** ~ **of it** (*inf*) ich habe es nur zum Spaß or aus Jux gemacht; ~ **for leather** was das Zeug hält; (*run also*) was die Beine hergaben.
(c) (*inf: intensifier*) **a** ~ **of a noise** ein Höllen- or Heidenlärm (*inf*); **to work like** ~ arbeiten, was das Zeug hält, wie wild arbeiten (*inf*); **to run like** ~ laufen, was die Beine hergeben; **we had a** ~ **of a time** (*bad, difficult*) es war grauenhaft; (*good*) wir haben uns prima amüsiert (*inf*); **a** ~ **of a lot** verdammt viel (*inf*); **she's a** or **one** ~ **of a girl** die ist schwer in Ordnung (*inf*), das ist ein klasse Mädchen (*inf*); **that's one** or **a** ~ **of a problem/difference/bruise/climb** das ist ein verdammt (*inf*) or wahnsinnig (*inf*) schwieriges Problem/wahnsinnige (*inf*) Unterschied/Bluterguß/eine wahnsinnige (*inf*) Kletterei; **to** ~ **with you/him** hol dich/ihn der Teufel (*inf*), du kannst/der kann mich mal (*sl*); **to** ~ **with it!** verdammt noch mal! (*inf*); **to** ~ **with your problems!** deine Probleme können mir gestohlen bleiben (*inf*); **go to** ~**!** scher dich or geh zum Teufel! (*inf*); **what the** ~ **do you want?** was willst du denn, verdammt noch mal? (*inf*); **like** ~ **he will!** den Teufel wird er tun (*inf*); **pay that price for a meal?** **like** ~ **so viel für ein Essen bezahlen?** ich bin doch nicht verrückt!; **he knows the Queen? — like** ~ **!** er und die Königin kennen? — wer's glaubt!; ~**! so'n Mist!** (*inf*), verdammt noch mal! (*inf*); ~**'s bells!** (*euph*) or **teeth!** (*euph*) (*surprise*) heiliger Strohsack (*inf*) or Bimbam (*inf*)!; (*anger*) zum Kuckuck noch mal! (*inf*); **where the** ~ **is it?** wo ist es denn, verdammt noch mal? (*inf*).
he'll [hiːl] contr of **he shall, he will**.
hell: ~**-bent** adj versessen (**on** auf +acc); **to be** ~**-bent on vengeance** unerbittlich auf Rache sinnen; ~**-cat** n Giftziege f (*inf*).
Hellenic [he'liːnɪk] adj hellenisch. **a** ~ **cruise** eine Hellas-Kreuzfahrt.
hell: ~**-fire** n Höllenfeuer nt; (*punishment*) Höllenqualen pl; ~**hole** n gräßliches Loch; **the trenches were a real** ~**hole** die (Schützen)gräben waren die reine Hölle.
hellish ['helɪʃ] adj (*inf*) höllisch (*inf*). **the exams were** ~ die Prüfungen waren verteufelt schwer (*inf*); **it's** ~ **not having any money** es ist schrecklich, wenn man kein Geld hat.
hellishly ['helɪʃlɪ] adv (*inf*) verteufelt (*inf*), verdammt (*inf*).
hello [hə'ləʊ] **1** interj (*all senses*) hallo. **say** ~ **to your aunt** sag deiner Tante mal schön „guten Tag!"; **say** ~ **to your parents** (*from me*) grüß deine Eltern (von mir); ~, ~, ~**! what's going on here?** nanu or he! was ist denn hier los? **2** n Hallo nt.
hell's angels npl Hell's Angels pl.
helluva ['heləvə] adj, adv (*sl*) = **hell of a;** see **hell** (c).
helm [helm] n (a) (*Naut*) Ruder, Steuer nt. **to be at the** ~ (*lit, fig*) am Ruder sein. **(b)** (*obs: helmet*) Helm m.
helmet ['helmɪt] n Helm m; (*Fencing*) Maske f.

helmeted ['helmɪtɪd] adj behelmt.
helmsman ['helmzmən] n, pl -**men** [-mən] Steuermann m.
help [help] **1** n, no pl Hilfe f; (*person: with pl*) Hilfe f. **with his brother's** ~ mit (der) Hilfe seines Bruders; **with the** ~ **of a knife** mit Hilfe eines Messers; **we need all the** ~ **we can get** wir brauchen jede nur mögliche Hilfe; **he is beyond** ~**/beyond medical** ~ ihm ist nicht mehr zu helfen/ihm kann kein Arzt mehr helfen; **to give** ~ Hilfe leisten; **to go/come to sb's** ~ jdm zu Hilfe eilen/kommen; **to be of** ~ **to sb** jdm helfen; (*person also*) jdm behilflich sein; (*thing also*) jdm nützen; **can I be of any** ~ **to you?** kann ich Ihnen irgendwie helfen or behilflich sein?; **is that of any** ~ **to you?** hilft or nützt Ihnen das etwas?; **he isn't much** ~ **to me** er ist mir keine große Hilfe; **you're a great** ~**!** (*iro*) du bist mir eine schöne Hilfe!; **we are short of** ~ **in the shop** wir haben nicht genügend (Hilfs)kräfte im Geschäft; **there's no** ~ **for it** da ist nichts zu machen.
2 vt (a) helfen (+dat). **to** ~ **sb (to) do sth** jdm (dabei) helfen, etw zu tun; **to** ~ **sb with the washing-up/his bags** jdm beim Abwaschen/mit seinen Taschen helfen; ~**! Hilfe!**, **so** ~ **me God!** so wahr mir Gott helfe!; **can I** ~ **you?** kann ich (Ihnen) helfen or behilflich sein? (*in shop also*) womit kann ich dienen?; **that won't** ~ **you** das wird Ihnen nichts nützen; **his explanation didn't** ~ **me** seine Erklärung hat mir nicht geholfen or genützt; **this will** ~ **the pain/your headache** das wird gegen die Schmerzen/gegen Ihr Kopfweh helfen; **it will** ~ **the wound to heal** das wird die Heilung (der Wunde) fördern; **it will** ~ **the crops to grow** es wird das Wachstum des Getreides fördern; **God** ~**s those who** ~ **themselves** (*Prov*) hilf dir selbst, so hilft dir Gott (*Prov*); **a man is** ~**ing the police with their enquiries** (*form euph*) ein Mann wird zur Zeit von der Polizei vernommen.
(b) (*with particle*) **to** ~ **sb down** jdm hinunter-/herunterhelfen; **take some water to** ~ **the pill down** trinken Sie etwas Wasser, damit die Tablette besser rutscht; **to** ~ **sb off with his coat** jdm aus dem Mantel helfen; **he** ~**ed her out of the car/a jam** er half ihr aus dem Auto/einer Klemme; **to** ~ **sb over the street** jdm über die Straße helfen; **to** ~ **sb through a difficult time** (*belief, hope, pills etc*) jdm in einer schwierigen Zeit durchhelfen; (*person also*) jdm in einer schwierigen Zeit beistehen; **to** ~ **sb up** (*from floor, chair etc*) jdm aufhelfen or (*up stairs etc*) hinaufhelfen; **to** ~ **sb up with a suitcase** jdm helfen, den Koffer hochzuheben.
(c) **she** ~**ed me to potatoes/meat** sie gab mir Kartoffeln/legte mir Fleisch auf; **to** ~ **oneself to sth** sich mit etw bedienen; **to** ~ **oneself to vegetables** sich (dat) Gemüse nehmen; ~ **yourself!** nehmen Sie sich doch!; **I'll** ~ **the children first** (*inf*) ich gebe den Kindern zuerst.
(d) (*with can or cannot*) **he can't** ~ **it, he was born with it** er kann nichts dafür, das ist angeboren; **he can't** ~ **it!** (*hum inf: he's stupid*) (d)er ist nun mal so (doof); **I can't** ~ **being so clever** (*inf*); ich kann nichts dafür), ich bin nun mal ein Genie or so schlau (*inf*); **he can't** ~ **the way he is** das ist nun mal (so) seine Art; **don't say more than you can** ~ sagen Sie nicht mehr als unbedingt nötig; **not if I can** ~ **it** nicht, wenn ich etwas zu sagen habe, nicht, wenn es nach mir geht; **I couldn't** ~ **thinking/laughing** ich konnte mir nicht helfen, ich mußte (*einfach*) glauben/lachen, ich konnte nicht umhin zu glauben/lachen (*geh*); **I had to do it, I couldn't** ~ **it** or **myself** ich konnte mir nicht helfen, ich mußte es einfach tun; **one cannot** ~ **wondering whether ...** man muß sich wirklich fragen, ob ...; **it can't be** ~**ed** das läßt sich nicht ändern, das ist nun mal so; **I can't** ~ **it if he always comes late** ich kann nichts dafür, daß er immer zu spät kommt; **can I** ~ **it if it rains?** kann ich was dafür, daß es regnet?
3 vi helfen. **to** ~ **out** vi aushelfen (**with** bei). **2** vt sep helfen (+dat) (**with** mit); (*in crisis also*) aufhelfen (+dat) (**with** bei). **will £3** ~ **you** ~**?** reicht Ihnen £3 weiter?

♦ **help out 1** vi aushelfen (**with** bei). **2** vt sep helfen (+dat) (**with** mit); (*in crisis also*) aufhelfen (+dat) (**with** bei). **will £3** ~ **you** ~**?** reicht Ihnen £3 weiter?

helper ['helpəʳ] n Helfer(in f) m; (*assistant*) Gehilfe m, Gehilfin f.
helpful ['helpfʊl] adj person hilfsbereit, gefällig, hilfreich (*old*); (*useful*) gadget, remark, knowledge nützlich; advice nützlich, hilfreich. **you have been most** ~ **to me** Sie haben mir sehr geholfen; **you'll find these tablets most** ~ diese Tabletten werden Ihnen sehr helfen or guttun.
helpfully ['helpfʊlɪ] adv hilfreich. ~**, the instructions were written in three languages** es war eine große Hilfe, daß die Gebrauchsanweisung in drei Sprachen war; **the rear doors are** ~ **fitted with child-proof locks** es ist sehr nützlich or von Vorteil, daß die hinteren Türen kindersichere Schlösser haben.
helpfulness ['helpfʊlnɪs] n see adj Hilfsbereitschaft, Gefälligkeit f; Nützlichkeit f.
helping ['helpɪŋ] **1** n (*at table*) Portion f. **to take a second** ~ **of sth** sich (dat) noch einmal von etw nehmen; **he even had a third** ~ er nahm sich (dat) sogar noch eine dritte Portion. **2** adj attr **to give** or **lend a** ~ **hand to sb** jdm helfen, jdm behilflich sein; **if you want a** ~ **hand ...** wenn Sie Hilfe brauchen, ...
helpless ['helplɪs] adj hilflos. **are you** ~**?** bist du aber hilflos!; **I was** ~ **to avoid the collision** ich konnte nichts tun, um den Zusammenstoß zu verhindern; **she was** ~ **with laughter** sie konnte sich vor Lachen kaum halten.
helplessly ['helplɪslɪ] adv see adj.
helplessness ['helplɪsnɪs] n Hilflosigkeit f.
help: ~**mate** (*old*), ~**meet** (*obs*) n Gefährte m (*geh*), Gefährtin f (*geh*); (*helper*) Gehilfe m (*old*), Gehilfin f (*old*).
helter-skelter ['heltə'skeltə'] **1** adv Hals über Kopf (*inf*). **2** adj wirr, wild. **3** n (a) (*confusion*) Tohuwabohu nt, (wildes) Durcheinander. **(b)** (*Brit: on fairground*) Rutschbahn f.
hem¹ [hem] interj see **hum** 2 (c).
hem² **1** n Saum m. **2** vt säumen.

♦**hem about** or **around** vt sep umgeben. **(b)** (fig)
♦**hem in** vt sep **(a)** (troops etc) einschließen, umgeben. **(b)** (fig) einengen.

he-man ['hiːmæn] n, pl **-men** [-men] (inf) He-man m, sehr männlicher Typ, echter or richtiger Mann. **he fancies himself as a ~** er kommt sich unheimlich männlich vor (inf).

hematite ['hiːmətaɪt] n Hämatit m.

hematology n (US) see **haematology**.

hemidemisemiquaver [ˌhemɪˈdemɪˈsemɪˌkweɪvəʳ] n (Mus) Vierundsechzigstel(note f) nt.

hemiplegia [ˌhemɪˈpliːdʒɪə] n halbseitige Lähmung.

hemisphere ['hemɪsfɪəʳ] n Halbkugel, Hemisphäre f; (of brain) Hemisphäre, Gehirnhälfte f. **in the northern ~** auf der nördlichen Halbkugel, in der nördlichen Hemisphäre.

hemline ['hemlaɪn] n Saum m. **~s are lower this year** der Rocksaum ist dieses Jahr etwas tiefer gerutscht.

hemlock ['hemlɒk] n (Bot: poisonous plant) Schierling m; (tree) Schierlings- or Hemlocktanne f; (poison) Schierling(saft) m. **Socrates drank the ~** Sokrates trank den Schierlingsbecher.

hemo- in cpds (US) see **haemo-**.

hemp [hemp] n **(a)** (Bot) Hanf m. **~ seed** Hanfsamen pl. **(b)** (drug) Hanf m. **(c)** (fibre) Hanf(faser f) m.

hem-stitch ['hemstɪtʃ] **1** vt in Hohlsaum nähen. **2** n Hohlsaum m.

hen [hen] n **(a)** Huhn nt, Henne f. **(b)** (female bird, lobster) Weibchen nt. **(c)** (inf) (also mother ~) Glucke f (inf).

hen: **~bane** n Bilsenkraut nt; **~ bird** n (Vogel)weibchen nt.

hence [hens] adv **(a)** (for this reason) also. **~ the name** daher der Name. **(b)** (from now) **two years ~** in zwei Jahren. **(c)** (obs, liter: from here) von hier. **(get thee) ~!** hinweg (mit dir)! (liter); **get thee ~, Satan!** weiche, Satan! (liter); **I must ~** ich muß von hinnen scheiden (obs).

henceforth [ˌhensˈfɔːθ], **henceforward** [ˌhensˈfɔːwəd] adv (from that time on) von da an, fortan (liter); (from this time on) von nun an, künftig.

henchman ['hentʃmən] n, pl **-men** [-mən] (pej) Spießgeselle, Kumpan m.

hen-coop ['henkuːp] n Hühnerstall m.

hendecagon [henˈdekəgən] n Elfeck, Hendekagon nt.

henhouse ['henhaʊs] n Hühnerhaus m, Hühnerstall m.

henna ['henə] **1** n Henna f. **2** vt mit Henna färben.

hen: **~-party** n (inf) Damenkränzchen nt, = Kaffeeklatsch m (inf), reine Weibergesellschaft (pej, inf); (before wedding) für die Braut vor der Hochzeit arrangierte Damengesellschaft; **~peck** vt unterm Pantoffel haben (inf); **a ~pecked husband** ein Pantoffelheld m (inf); **he is ~pecked** er steht unterm Pantoffel (inf); **he's started to look ~pecked** es sieht langsam so aus, als ob er unterm Pantoffel steht (inf); **~-run** n Hühnerhof m.

Henry ['henrɪ] n Heinrich m.

hep [hep] adj (US sl) see **hip¹**.

hepatitis [ˌhepəˈtaɪtɪs] n Hepatitis f.

heptagon ['heptəgən] n Siebeneck, Heptagon nt.

her [hɜːʳ] **1** pers pron **(a)** (dir obj, with prep +acc) sie; (indir obj, with prep +dat) ihr; (when she is previously mentioned in clause) with her books about ~ mit ihren Büchern um sich. **(b)** (emph) sie. **it's ~ sie** ist's; **who, ~?** wer, sie? **2** poss adj ihr; see also **my**.

Heraclitean [ˌherəˈklaɪtɪən] adj Heraklitisch.

Heraclitus [ˌherəˈklaɪtəs] n Heraklit m.

herald ['herəld] **1** n **(a)** (Hist) Herold m; (in newspaper titles) Bote m. **(b)** (fig) (Vor)bote m (geh). **~ of spring** Frühlingsbote m. **(c)** (Her) **College of H~s** Heroldsamt nt. **2** vt arrival of summer ankündigen, Vorbote(in) sein für. **to ~ (in) a new age** den Beginn eines neuen Zeitalters ankündigen.

heraldic [heˈrældɪk] adj heraldisch, Wappen-. **~ arms** Wappen pl.

heraldry ['herəldrɪ] n **(a)** (science) Wappenkunde, Heraldik f. **(b)** (heraldic signs) Wappen pl. **(c)** (ceremonial) traditioneller höfischer Prunk.

herb [hɜːb] n Kraut nt. **~ garden** Kräutergarten m.

herbaceous [hɜːˈbeɪʃəs] adj krautig. **~ border** Staudenrabatte f.

herbage ['hɜːbɪdʒ] n Grünpflanzen pl; (leaves and stems) Grünzeug nt; (pasturage) Weide(land nt) f.

herbal ['hɜːbəl] **1** adj Kräuter-. **2** n Kräuterbuch nt.

herbalist ['hɜːbəlɪst] n Kräutersammler(in f) m; (healer) Naturheilkundige(r) mf.

herbarium [hɜːˈbɛərɪəm] n Herbarium nt.

herbivorous [hɜːˈbɪvərəs] adj (form) pflanzenfressend.

herculean [hɜːkjʊˈliːən] adj herkulisch; strength Bären-, Riesen-, herkulisch (liter); proportions riesenhaft; effort übermenschlich. **a ~ task** eine Herkulesarbeit.

Hercules ['hɜːkjuːliːz] n (lit, fig) Herkules m.

herd [hɜːd] **1** n (of cattle etc) Herde f; (of deer) Rudel nt; (fig pej: of people) Herde, Schar f. **the common ~** die breite Masse. **2** vt **(a)** (drive) cattle, prisoners treiben. **(b)** (tend) cattle hüten.

♦**herd together 1** vi sich zusammendrängen. **2** vt sep zusammentreiben.

herd: **~ instinct** n Herdentrieb m; **~sman** n Hirt, Hirte m.

here [hɪəʳ] **1** adv **(a)** hier; (with motion) hierher, hierhin. **~!** (at roll call) hier!; (to dog) hierher!; **~ I am** da or hier bin ich; **spring is ~** der Frühling ist da; **this man ~** dieser Mann (hier) ...; **John ~ reckons ...** John hier meint ...; **this notice** (incorrect) dieser Anschlag da (inf); **~ and now** auf der Stelle, jetzt sofort; **this one ~** der/die/das hier or da; **I won't be ~ for lunch** ich bin zum Mittagessen nicht da; **shall we wait till he gets ~?** sollen wir warten, bis er hier or da ist?; **~ and there** hier und da; **~, there and everywhere** überall; around/about **~** hier herum, hier in der Nähe; up/down to **~** bis ungefähr hier; near **~** (hier) in der Nähe; **it's in/over ~** es ist hier (drin)/hier drüben; **put it in/over ~** stellen Sie es hier herein/hierüber

or hier herüber or hierher; **come in/over ~** kommen Sie hier herein/hierüber or hier herüber or hierher; **from ~ on in** (esp US) von jetzt or nun an.
(b) (in phrases) **~ you are** (giving sb sth) hier (, bitte); (on finding sb) da bist du ja!, ach, hier bist du!; (on finding sth) da or hier ist es ja; **~ we are, home again** so, da wären wir also wieder zu Hause; **~ we are again**, confronted by yet another crisis so, da hätten wir also wieder eine neue Krise; **~ he comes** da kommt or ist er ja; **look out, ~ he comes** Vorsicht, er kommt!; **~ comes trouble** jetzt geht's los (inf); **~ goes!** (before attempting sth) dann mal los ~, try this one hier, versuch's mal damit; **~, let me do that** komm, laß mich das machen; **~!** he!; **~'s to you!** (in toasts) auf Ihr Wohl!; **~'s to the success of the venture!** auf den Erfolg des Vorhabens!; **it's neither ~ nor there** es spielt keine Rolle, tut nichts zur Sache.
2 n **the ~ and now** das Hier und Heute; (Rel, Philos) das Diesseits.

here: **~abouts** ['hɪərəbaʊts] adv hier herum, in dieser Gegend; **~after 1** adv (in books, contracts: following this) im folgenden; (in the future also) künftig, in Zukunft; (after death) im Jenseits; **during my lifetime and ~after** zu meinen Lebzeiten und danach; **2** n **the ~after** das Jenseits; **~by** adv (form) hiermit.

hereditable [həˈredɪtəbl] adj (Jur) vererbbar; (Med also) (ver)erblich.

hereditary [hɪˈredɪtərɪ] adj erblich, Erb-. **~ enemies** Erbfeinde pl; **~ disease** Erbkrankheit f; **to be ~** (also hum) erblich sein.

heredity [hɪˈredɪtɪ] n Vererbung f. **the title is his by ~** er hat den Titel geerbt/wird den Titel erben.

here: **~in** adv (form) hierin, darin; **~of** adv (form) hiervon (form); **the house and the inhabitants ~of** das Haus und die Bewohner desselben (form).

heresy ['herəsɪ] n Ketzerei, Häresie (spec) f. **heresies** Ketzereien, ketzerische Lehren pl.

heretic ['herətɪk] n Ketzer(in f), Häretiker(in f) (spec) m.

heretical [hɪˈretɪkəl] adj ketzerisch, häretisch (spec).

here: **~to** adv (form) **the documents attached ~to** die beigefügten Dokumente; **his reply ~to** seine Antwort darauf/hierauf; **he gave his signature ~to** er setzte seine Unterschrift hinzu; **~tofore** adv (form) (up to this time) bisher; (up to that time) bis dahin; **~unto** adv (form) see **hereto**; **~upon** adv daraufhin; **~with** adv (form) hiermit.

heritable ['herɪtəbl] adj **(a)** erblich. **(b)** (Jur) person erbfähig.

heritage ['herɪtɪdʒ] n (lit, fig) Erbe n, Erbschaft f.

hermaphrodite [hɜːˈmæfrədaɪt] **1** n Zwitter, Hermaphrodit (geh) m. **2** adj zwittrig, hermaphroditisch (geh); plants also gemischtgeschlechtig.

hermetic [hɜːˈmetɪk] adj hermetisch.

hermetically [hɜːˈmetɪkəlɪ] adv see adj. **~ sealed** hermetisch verschlossen or (fig) abgeriegelt.

hermit ['hɜːmɪt] n Einsiedler (also fig), Eremit m.

hermitage ['hɜːmɪtɪdʒ] n (lit, fig) Einsiedelei, Klause f.

hermit crab n Einsiedlerkrebs m.

hernia ['hɜːnɪə] n (Eingeweide)bruch m, Hernie f (spec).

hero ['hɪərəʊ] n, pl **-es** Held, Heros (geh) m; (fig: object of heroworship also) Idol nt; (Liter: of novel etc) Held m. **the ~ of the hour** der Held des Tages; **the ~ of the rescue** der mutige or beherzte Retter.

Herod ['herəd] n Herodes m.

heroic [hɪˈrəʊɪk] **1** adj mutig, heldenhaft, heldenmütig; behaviour, action, decision also heroisch; (daring) kühn; proportions, size mächtig, gewaltig; effort gewaltig; words heroisch. **~ age/deed** Heldenzeitalter nt/Heldentat f; **~ couplet** Heroic Couplet nt, Reimpaar nt aus fünffüßigen Jamben; **~ verse** heroischer Vers; **~ tenor** Heldentenor m.
2 n **~s** pl hochtrabende or große Worte pl; **the actor's ~s** das übertriebene Pathos des Schauspielers; **the goalkeeper's ~s** (inf) die Heldentaten des Torwarts (inf).

heroically [hɪˈrəʊɪkəlɪ] adv see adj mutig, heldenhaft, heldenmütig; heroisch; kühn; mächtig, gewaltig; gewaltig; heroisch. **a ~ worded speech** eine pathetische Rede.

heroin ['herəʊɪn] n Heroin nt. **~ addict** Heroinsüchtige(r) mf.

heroine ['herəʊɪn] n Heldin f; (Theat also) Heroine f.

heroism ['herəʊɪzm] n Heldentum nt; (heroic conduct) (Helden)mut, Heroismus m; (daring) Kühnheit f. **I'm not one for ~** ich bin kein Held.

heron ['herən] n Reiher m.

hero-worship ['hɪərəʊˌwɜːʃɪp] **1** n Verehrung f; (in ancient tribe etc) Heldenverehrung f; (of popstar etc) Schwärmerei f. **the ~ of a boy for his older brother** die blinde Bewunderung eines Jungen für seinen älteren Bruder. **2** vt anbeten, verehren; popstar etc schwärmen für.

herring ['herɪŋ] n Hering m. **~-gull** Silbermöwe f; **~-pond** (hum inf) großer Teich (hum); see **red ~**.

herringbone ['herɪŋbəʊn] **1** n **(a)** (pattern) Fischgrät m. **(b)** (Ski) Grätenschritt m. **2** adj attr **~ pattern** Fischgrät(en)-muster nt; **~ stitch** Hexenstich m; **~ suit** Anzug m mit Fischgrätmuster.

hers [hɜːz] poss pron ihre(r, s). **~ (on towels etc)** sie; see also **mine¹**.

herself [hɜːˈself] **1** pers pron **(a)** (dir and indir obj, with prep) sich; see also **myself**. **(b)** (emph) (sie) selbst. **2** n (Ir inf) **it was ~ who told me** sie selbst hat es mir gesagt.

Herts [hɑːts] abbr of Hertfordshire.

he's [hiːz] contr of he is; he has.

hesitancy ['hezɪtənsɪ] n Zögern, Zaudern (geh) nt.

hesitant ['hezɪtənt] adj answer, smile zögernd; person also unentschlossen, unschlüssig. **he was so ~ that ...** er war so unentschlossen or zögerte lange or war lange, bis ...; **he was very ~ to accept** er zögerte lange or war sich (dat) sehr unschlüssig, ob er annehmen sollte.

hesitantly ['hezɪtəntlɪ] adj accept zögernd, zaudernd (geh).

hesitate ['hezɪteɪt] vi zögern, zaudern (geh); (in speech) stocken.

if they don't stop hesitating we'll be lost wenn sie noch länger zögern, sind wir verloren; **he who ~s is lost** (*Prov*) dem Feigen kehrt das Glück den Rücken (*Prov*); **I ~ to ask him over ich bin** mir nicht schlüssig, ob ich ihn herüberbitten soll; **if he starts to ~ to agree** wenn er sich nicht entschließen kann zuzustimmen; **I'd ~ to take** *or* **at taking on such a task** ich würde es mir gut überlegen, ob ich so eine Aufgabe übernehmen würde; **I ~d at the expenditure/about having a child at my age** ich hatte Bedenken wegen der Ausgabe/ich hatte Bedenken, in meinem Alter ein Kind zu bekommen; **even he would ~ at murder** selbst er hätte bei einem Mord Bedenken; **he ~s at nothing er macht** vor nichts halt, **er schreckt vor nichts zurück; I am still hesitating about what I should do** ich bin mir immer noch nicht schlüssig, was ich tun soll; **I ~ to say it, but ...** es widerstrebt mir, das zu sagen, aber ...; **if I did think that, I wouldn't ~ to say** so wenn ich wirklich der Meinung (*gen*) wäre, hätte ich keine Hemmungen, es zu sagen; **don't ~ to ask me** fragen Sie ruhig; (*more formally*) zögern Sie nicht, mich zu fragen.

hesitation [ˌhezɪ'teɪʃən] *n* Zögern, Zaudern (*geh*) *nt*. **a moment's ~** ein Augenblick des Zögerns; **without the slightest ~** ohne auch nur einen Augenblick zu zögern; **I have no ~ in saying that ...** ich kann ohne weiteres sagen, daß ...

hessian ['hesɪən] **1** *n* Sackleinwand *f*, Rupfen *m*. **2** *attr* Rupfen-.

hetero ['hetərəʊ] *n* (*sl*) Heterosexuelle(r) *mf*. **he's a good straight ~** er ist sexuell total normal (*inf*) *or* einwandfrei hetero (*sl*).

heterodox ['hetərədɒks] *adj* heterodox, andersgläubig.

heterodoxy ['hetərədɒksɪ] *n* Heterodoxie, Andersgläubigkeit *f*.

heterogeneity [ˌhetərəʊdʒɪ'neɪɪtɪ] *n* Heterogenität *f*.

heterogeneous [ˌhetərəʊ'dʒiːnɪəs] *adj* heterogen.

heterosexual [ˌhetərəʊ'seksjʊəl] **1** *adj* heterosexuell. **2** *n* Heterosexuelle(r) *mf*.

heterosexuality [ˌhetərəʊˌseksjʊ'ælɪtɪ] *n* Heterosexualität *f*.

het up ['het'ʌp] *adj* (*inf*) aufgeregt. **to get ~ about/over sth** sich über etw (*acc*)/wegen einer Sache (*gen*) aufregen.

heuristic [hjʊə'rɪstɪk] **1** *adj* heuristisch. **2** *n* **~s** *sing* Heuristik *f*.

hew [hjuː] *pret* **~ed**, *ptp* **hewn** *or* **~ed** *vt* hauen; (*shape*) behauen. **to ~ into pieces/logs in Stücke hauen/zu Klötzen** hacken; **they ~ed their captives to pieces** sie zerstückelten ihre Gefangenen.
♦**hew down** *vt sep* **trees** fällen, umhauen; **persons** niederhauen; (*with machine gun also*) niedermähen.
♦**hew off** *vt sep* abhauen, abhacken, abschlagen.
♦**hew out** *vt sep* heraushauen, herausschlagen (*of* aus). **they ~ed their way ~ of the mine** sie schlugen sich (*dat*) einen Weg aus der Grube; **he's ~n ~ a career for himself** er hat sich (*dat*) seine Karriere erkämpft; **they ~ed ~ a formula for peace** sie schmiedeten eine Friedensformel.
♦**hew up** *vt sep* zerstückeln; **wood** zerhacken.

hewer ['hjuːəʳ] *n* (*Min*) Hauer *m*. **~s of wood** Holzhauer *pl*.

hex [heks] (*esp US inf*) **1** *n* Fluch *m*. **there must be a ~ on this project** dieses Unternehmen muß verhext sein (*inf*); (*more serious*) auf dem Unternehmen muß ein Fluch liegen (*inf*); **to put a ~ on sth** etw verhexen. **2** *vt* verhexen.

hexagon ['heksəgən] *n* Sechseck, Hexagon *nt*.

hexagonal [hek'sægənəl] *adj* sechseckig, hexagonal.

hexameter [hek'sæmɪtəʳ] *n* Hexameter *m*.

hey [heɪ] *interj* (*to attract attention*) he (*Sie/du*); (*in surprise*) he, Mensch (*inf*). **~ presto** Hokuspokus (Fidibus).

heyday ['heɪdeɪ] *n* Glanzzeit, Blütezeit *f*. **in the ~ of its power** auf dem Höhepunkt seiner Macht; **in his ~** in seiner Glanzzeit.

HGV (*Brit*) *abbr of* **heavy goods vehicle** LKW *m*.

HH *adj* (*on pencil*) HH, 2H.

hi [haɪ] *interj* hallo.

hiatus [haɪ'eɪtəs] *n* Lücke *f*; (*Gram, Poet*) Hiatus *m*.

hibernate ['haɪbəneɪt] *vi* Winterschlaf halten *or* machen.

hibernation [ˌhaɪbə'neɪʃən] *n* (*lit, fig*) Winterschlaf *m*.

Hibernian [haɪ'bɜːnɪən] *adj* (*Poet*) hibernisch.

hibiscus [haɪ'bɪskəs] *n* Hibiskus, Eibisch *m*.

hiccough, hiccup ['hɪkʌp] **1** *n* Schluckauf *m*. **to have the ~** den Schluckauf haben; **to let out/give a ~** hick machen (*inf*), hicksen (*dial*); **the computer had a slight ~** (*fig inf*) der Computer spielte leicht verrückt (*inf*). **2** *vi* hicksen (*dial*). **he started ~ing** er bekam den Schluckauf.

hick [hɪk] *n* (*US inf*) Hinterwäldler *m* (*inf*); (*female*) Land-pomeranze *f* (*inf*).

hickory ['hɪkərɪ] *n* (*tree*) Hickory(nußbaum *m*; (*wood*) Hik-kory(holz) *nt*.

hide¹ [haɪd] (*vb: pret* **hid**, *ptp* **hidden** ['hɪdn] *or* **hid**) **1** *vt* **face** (*from* vor +*dat*); **truth, tears, grief, feelings, face** verbergen (*from* vor +*dat*); (*obstruct from view*) **moon, rust** verdecken. **hidden from view** nicht zu sehen, dem Blick *or* den Blicken entzogen; **he's hiding something in his pocket** er hat etwas in seiner Tasche versteckt; **I have nothing to ~** ich habe nichts zu verbergen; **his words had a hidden meaning** seine Worte hatten eine verborgene *or* versteckte Bedeutung; **you're hiding something from me** (*truth etc*) Sie verheimlichen mir etwas, Sie verbergen etwas vor mir; **if the meaning of life is hidden from man** wenn der Sinn des Lebens dem Menschen verborgen ist.
2 *vi* sich verstecken, sich verbergen (*from sb* vor jdm). **quick! ~ in the cupboard** schnell, versteck dich im Schrank!; **he was hiding in the cupboard** er hielt sich im Schrank versteckt *or* verborgen; **he's just hiding behind his boss/his reputation** er versteckt sich bloß hinter seinem Chef/Ruf.
3 *n* Versteck *nt*.
♦**hide away 1** *vi* sich verstecken, sich verbergen. **2** *vt sep* verstecken.
♦**hide out** *or* (*US*) **up** *vi* sich verstecken; (*to be hiding also*) sich versteckt *or* verborgen halten.

hide² *n* (*of animal*) Haut *f*; (*on furry animal*) Fell *nt*; (*processed*) Leder *nt*; (*fig: of person*) Haut *f*, Fell *nt*. **to strip an animal of its ~** einem Tier die Haut/das Fell abziehen, ein Tier häuten; **the bags are made out of the finest ~** die Taschen sind aus feinstem Leder; **to save one's own ~** die eigene Haut retten; **I haven't seen ~ nor hair of him for weeks** (*inf*) den habe ich in den letzten Wochen nicht mal von weitem gesehen.

hide: **~-and-seek** *n* Versteckspiel *nt*; **to play ~-and-seek** Verstecken spielen; **~away** *n* Versteck *nt*; (*refuge*) Zufluchtsort *m*; **~bound** *adj* **person, views** engstirnig; **an officer of the old school, ~bound by convention** ein Offizier der alten Schule, der den Konventionen verhaftet ist.

hideous ['hɪdɪəs] *adj* grauenhaft, scheußlich; **day, colour, disappointment** schrecklich.

hideousness ['hɪdɪəsnɪs] *n see adj* Grauenhaftigkeit, Scheußlichkeit *f*; Schrecklichkeit *f*.

hideout ['haɪdaʊt] *n* Versteck *nt*.

hiding¹ ['haɪdɪŋ] *n* **to be in ~** sich versteckt halten; **to go into ~** untertauchen, sich verstecken; **he came out of ~** er tauchte wieder auf, er kam aus seinem Versteck; **~ place** Versteck *nt*.

hiding² *n* (**a**) (*beating*) Tracht *f* Prügel. **to give sb a good ~** jdm eine Tracht Prügel geben. (**b**) (*inf: defeat*) Schlappe *f* (*inf*). **the team got a real ~** die Mannschaft mußte eine schwere Schlappe einstecken (*inf*).

hie [haɪ] *vr* (*old, hum*) eilends laufen. **~ thee hence!** hebe dich hinweg (*old, hum*).

hierarchic(al) [ˌhaɪə'rɑːkɪk(əl)] *adj*, **hierarchically** [ˌhaɪə'rɑːkɪkəlɪ] *adv* hierarchisch.

hierarchy ['haɪərɑːkɪ] *n* Hierarchie *f*.

hieroglyph ['haɪərəglɪf] *n* Hieroglyphe *f*.

hieroglyphic [ˌhaɪərə'glɪfɪk] **1** *adj* hieroglyphisch. **2** *n* **~s** *pl* Hieroglyphen(schrift *f*) *pl*.

hi-fi ['haɪˌfaɪ] **1** *n* (**a**) Hi-Fi *nt*. (**b**) (*equipment*) Hi-Fi-Gerät *nt*; (*systems*) Hi-Fi-Anlage *f*. **2** *adj* Hi-Fi-.

higgledy-piggledy ['hɪgldɪ'pɪgldɪ] **1** *adv* durcheinander, wie Kraut und Rüben (*inf*). **2** *adj* durcheinander; (*confused*) wirr.

high [haɪ] **1** *adj* (+*er*) (**a**) *mountain, wall, forehead, building* hoch hohe(r, s) *attr*. **a building 80 metres ~** ein 80 Meter hohes Gebäude; **a ~ dive** ein Kopfsprung aus großer Höhe; **the ~er flats are more expensive** die oberen Wohnungen sind teurer; **on one of the ~er floors** in einem der oberen Stockwerke; **he lives on a ~er floor** er wohnt weiter oben; **the ~est flat/floor** die oberste Wohnung/Etage; **at ~ tide** *or* **water** bei Flut *or* Hochwasser (*spec*); **the river is quite ~** der Fluß führt ziemlich viel Wasser; **~ and dry** (*boat*) auf dem Trockenen; **he left her ~ and dry with four little children** er hat sie mit vier kleinen Kindern sitzen lassen; **to be left ~ and dry** auf dem Trockenen sitzen (*inf*); **I knew him when he was only so ~** ich kannte ihn, als er nur so groß war *or* noch so klein war.
(**b**) (*important, superior*) **hoch** hoch pred, hohe(r, s) *attr*. **~ office** hohes Amt; **on the ~est authority** von höchster Stelle; **to be** *or* **act ~ and mighty** erhaben tun; **to be on one's ~ horse** (*fig*) auf dem hohen Roß sitzen; **O Lord most ~** (*Bibl*) erhabener Gott.
(**c**) (*considerable, extreme, great*) **opinion, speed, tempera-ture, fever, pressure, salary, price, tax, density, sea** hoch pred, hohe(r, s) *attr*; **altitude** groß; **wind** stark; **complexion, colour** (hoch)rot. **in the ~ latitudes** in fernen Breiten; **to pay a ~ price for sth** (*lit, fig*) etw teuer bezahlen; **to set a ~ value on sth** etw hoch einschätzen; **the ~est common factor** der größte gemein-same Teiler; **in the ~est degree** in höchstem Grad *or* Maß; **in (very) ~ spirits** in Hochstimmung, in äußerst guter Laune; **to have a ~ old time** (*inf*) sich prächtig amüsieren, mächtig Spaß haben (*inf*); **it was ~ drama** es war hochdramatisch.
(**d**) (*good, admirable*) **ideals** hoch. **a ~ calling** ein Ruf zu Höherem; **a man of ~ character** ein Mann von Charakter.
(**e**) (*of time*) **~ noon** zwölf Uhr mittags; **it's ~ time you went home/understood** es ist *or* wird höchste Zeit, daß du nach Hause gehst/endlich begreifst.
(**f**) *sound, note* hoch; (*shrill*) schrill.
(**g**) (*sl*) (*on drugs*) high (*sl*); (*on drink*) blau (*sl*).
(**h**) *meat* angegangen; *game also* anbrüchig (*spec*).
(**i**) (*Cards*) hoch pred, hohe(r, s) *attr*. **aces ~** As ist die höchste (Stich)karte.
2 *adv* (+*er*) **up** hoch. **~ up** (*position*) hoch oben; (*motion*) hoch hinauf; **one floor ~er** ein Stockwerk höher.
(**b**) **to go as ~ as £200** bis zu £ 200 (hoch)gehen; **the sea is running ~** das Meer ist sehr stürmisch *or* bewegt; **feelings ran ~** die Gemüter erhitzten sich; **to search ~ and low** überall suchen.
3 *n* (**a**) **God on ~** Gott in der Höhe *or* im Himmel; **the orders have come from on ~** (*hum inf*) der Befehl kommt von oben.
(**b**) **unemployment has reached a new ~** die Arbeitslosenzif-fern haben einen neuen Höchststand erreicht.
(**c**) (*Met*) Hoch *nt*.
(**d**) (*sl: on drugs*) **he's still got his ~** er ist immer noch high.
(**e**) (*US Aut: top gear*) **in ~** im höchsten Gang; **he moved into ~** er schaltete hoch *or* in den vierten/fünften Gang.
(**f**) (*US inf: high school*) Penne *f* (*inf*).

high: **~ altar** *n* Hochaltar *m*; **~ball** *n* (*US*) Highball *m*; **~ beam** *n* (*Aut*) Fernlicht *nt*; **~born** *adj* von hoher Geburt, von edler Abkunft (*liter*); **~ boy** *n* (*US*) hohe Kommode; **~brow 1** *n* Intellektuelle(r) *mf*, Intelleller *m* (*hum*); **2** *adj* **interests** intellektuell, hochgestochen (*pej*); **tastes, music** an-spruchsvoll; **~chair** *n* Hochstuhl *m*; **H~ Church 1** *n* Hoch-kirche *f*; **2** *adj* der Hochkirche; **to be very H~ Church** streng hochkirchlich eingestellt sein; **H~ Churchman** *n* he is a H~ **Churchman** er gehört der Hochkirche an; **~-class** *adj* hochwertig; **~ comedy** *n* Gesellschaftskomödie *f*; **~ commis-sion** *n* Hochkommissariat *nt*; **~ commissioner** *n* Hochkom-missar *m*; **~ court** *n* oberstes *or* höchstes Gericht; (*institu-tion also*) oberster Gerichtshof; **~ court judge** *n*

Richter *m* am obersten Gerichtshof; ~ **diving** *n* Turmspringen *nt*.

higher ['haɪəʳ] *adj* (a) *comp of* **high**. (b) *mathematics, education* höher; *animals, life-forms* höher (entwickelt). **the ~ forms** *or* **classes** (*Sch*) die höheren *or* oberen Klassen.

higher-up ['haɪərʌp] *n* (*inf*) höheres Tier (*inf*).

high: ~ **explosive** *n* hochexplosiver Sprengstoff; ~ **-explosive shell** *n* Sprenggranate *f*, Brisanzgeschoß *nt*; ~ **-faluting**(**g**) *adj* (*inf*) *language* hochtrabend, geschwollen; *people* aufgeblasen, hochgestochen; ~-**fidelity** 1 *n* High-Fidelity, Tontreue *f*; 2 *adj* High-Fidelity-; ~ **flier** *n* (*inf*) (*successful person*) Senkrechtstarter *m*; (*ambitious*) Ehrgeizling *m* (*pej*); **he's a ~ flier er will hoch hinaus**; ~-**flown** *adj* *style, speech* hochtrabend, geschwollen; *ambitions* hochgesteckt; *ideas, plans* hochfliegend; ~ **frequency** 1 *n* Hochfrequenz *f*; 2 *adj* Hochfrequenz-; **H~ German** *n* Hochdeutsch *nt*; ~-**grade** *adj* hochwertig; *ore* gediegen; ~-**handed** *adj* eigenmächtig; *character* überheblich; ~-**hat** (*US inf*) 1 *adj* hochnäsig (*inf*); 2 *n* hochnäsiger Typ (*inf*); 3 *vt* herablassend behandeln, von oben herab behandeln; ~-**heeled** *adj* mit hohen Absätzen, hochhackig; ~ **heels** *npl* hohe Absätze; ~-**jack** *vt, n see* **hijack**; ~-**jacker** *n see* **hijacker**; ~-**jinks** *npl* (*inf*) **they were having ~ jinks** bei denen war Highlife (*inf*); ~ **jump** *n* (*Sport*) Hochsprung *m*; **to be for the ~ jump** (*fig inf*) dran sein (*inf*); ~-**land** *adj* Hochland-, hochländisch; **H~lander** *n* Bewohner(in *f*) *m* des schottischen Hochlands; **H~land fling** *n* schottischer Volkstanz; **H~land Games** *npl* schottisches Volksfest mit traditionellen Wettkämpfen; **H~lands** *npl* schottisches Hochland; (*generally*) Berg- *or* Hochland *nt*; ~-**level** *adj* *talks, discussion* auf höchster Ebene; *road* Hoch-; ~ **life** *n* Highlife *nt*, Leben *nt* in großem Stil; ~-**light** 1 *n* (a) (*Art, Phot*) Glanzlicht *nt*; (*in hair*) Strähne *f*; (b) (*fig*) Glanzstück *nt*; Höhepunkt *m*; 2 *vt* *need, problem* ein Schlaglicht werfen auf (+*acc*), hervorheben; *hair* Strähnen machen in (+*acc*); ~ **living** *n* flottes *or* (*pej*) ausschweifendes Leben.

highly ['haɪlɪ] *adv* hoch-. ~ **spiced** *dishes* stark *or* (*hot*) scharf gewürzte Gerichte; **to be ~ paid** hoch bezahlt werden; **to think ~ of sb** eine hohe Meinung von jdm haben, große Stücke auf jdn halten; **to speak ~ of sb** sich sehr positiv über jdn äußern.

highly: ~-**coloured** *adj* (*lit*) farbenfroh, sehr bunt; (*fig*) *report, description* (*one-sided*) stark gefärbt; (*detailed*) ausgeschmückt; ~-**strung** *adj* nervös.

high: **H~ Mass** *n* Hochamt *nt*; ~-**minded** *adj* hochgeistig; *ideals* hoch; ~-**necked** *adj* hochgeschlossen.

highness ['haɪnɪs] *n* (a) Höhe *f*. ~ **of ideals** hohe Ideale *pl*. (b) **Her/Your H~** Ihre/Eure Hoheit; yes, **Your H~** ja, Hoheit.

high: ~-**octane** *adj* mit einer hohen Oktanzahl; ~-**pitched** *adj* (a) *sound* hoch; (b) (*Archit*) *roof* steil; ~-**powered** *adj* (a) *car* starkmotorig, Hochleistungs-; (b) (*fig*) *businessman, politician* Vollblut-; *academic* Spitzen-; *conversation* sehr anspruchsvoll, hochintellektuell; **our new ~-powered professor** unser neuer Professor, der wirklich was auf dem Kasten hat (*inf*); ~-**pressure** *adj* (a) (*Tech, Met*) Hochdruck-; ~-**pressure area** *n* Hochdruckgebiet *nt*; **a ~-pressure area over the Atlantic** ein Hoch(druck)gebiet *nt* über dem Atlantik, ein atlantisches Hoch; (b) (*fig*) *salesman* aufdringlich; *sales technique* aggressiv; ~-**priced** *adj* teuer, **the more ~-priced range** die höhere Preisklasse; ~ **priest** *n* (*lit, fig*) Hohepriester *m*; **a ~ priest ein Hoherpriester** *m*; **of the ~ priest** des Hohenpriesters; ~-**ranking** *adj* hoch(rangig), von hohem Rang; ~ **relief** *n* Hochrelief *nt*; ~-**rise** *adj* *block* Hochhaus-; ~-**rise flats** *npl* (*Wohn*)hochhaus *nt*; ~ **road** *n* (*old*) Landstraße *f*; **the ~road to success** der sichere Weg zum Erfolg; ~ **school** *n* (*US*) Oberschule *f*; **the ~ seas** *npl* die Meere *pl*; **on the ~ seas** auf hoher See, auf offenem Meer; ~ **society** *n* High-Society *f*; ~-**sounding** *adj* klangvoll; ~-**speed** *adj* Schnell-; *drill* mit hoher Umdrehungszahl; ~-**speed lens** hochlichtstarkes Objektiv, lichtstarke Linse; ~-**speed film** hoch(licht)empfindlicher Film; ~-**spirited** *adj* temperamentvoll, lebhaft; ~ **spot** *n* Höhepunkt *m*; **to hit the ~ spots** (*inf*) auf den Putz hauen (*inf*); ~-**strung** *adj* (*US*) nervös; ~ **summer** *n* Hochsommer *m*; ~ **table** *n* (*Sch*) Lehrertisch *m*; (*Univ*) Tisch *m* für Professoren und Dozenten.

hightail ['haɪteɪl] *vi* (*US sl*) **to ~** (*it*) **out of a place** (aus einem Ort) abhauen (*sl*), (von *or* aus einem Ort) verduften (*sl*).

high: ~ **tea** *n* (frühes) Abendessen; ~-**tension** *adj* (*Elec*) Hochspannungs-; ~ **treason** *n* Hochverrat *m*; ~-**up** 1 *adj* *person* hochgestellt; 2 *n* (*inf*) hohes Tier (*inf*); ~-**water mark** *n* (*lit*) Hochwasserstandsmarke *f*; (*fig*) höchster Stand; ~**way** *n* Landstraße *f*; *public* ~**way** öffentliche Straße; **the ~ways and byways** Straßen und Wege; **he knows all the ~ways and byways of Dorset** er kennt Weg und Steg in Dorset; ~**way code** *n* Straßenverkehrsordnung *f*; ~**wayman** *n* Räuber, Wegelagerer, Strauchdieb *m*; ~**way robbery** *n* Straßenraub *m*; (*fig inf*) Nepp *m* (*inf*); **H~ways Department** *n* Tiefbauamt *nt*.

hijack ['haɪdʒæk] 1 *vt* entführen, (*rob*) lorry überfallen. 2 *n see vt* Entführung *f*; Überfall *m* (*of auf* +*acc*).

hijacker ['haɪdʒækəʳ] *n see vt* Entführer *m*; Räuber *m*.

hike [haɪk] 1 *vi* wandern. 2 *n* Wanderung *f*.

♦**hike up** *vt sep* hochziehen.

hiker ['haɪkəʳ] *n* Wanderer(in *f*) *m*, Wanderin *f*.

hiking ['haɪkɪŋ] *n* Wandern *nt*.

hilarious [hɪ'lɛərɪəs] *adj* sehr komisch *or* lustig, urkomisch (*inf*); (*loud and happy*) *mood* ausgelassen, übermütig.

hilariously [hɪ'lɛərɪəslɪ] *adv* ~ **funny** zum Schreien.

hilarity [hɪ'lærɪtɪ] *n* (*of person, party etc*) übermütige Ausgelassenheit, (*of film*) Komik *f*. **his statement caused some ~** seine Behauptung löste einige Heiterkeit aus.

Hilary ['hɪlərɪ] *n* (*Oxford Univ*) Frühjahrstrimester *nt*; (*Jur*) Frühjahrssitzungsperiode *f*.

hill [hɪl] *n* (a) Hügel *m*; (*higher*) Berg *m*; (*incline*) Hang *m*. **the castle stands on a ~** die Burg steht auf einem Berg; **the houses on the ~ beneath the castle** die Häuser am Burgberg; **these**

flats **are built on a ~** diese Wohnungen sind am Hang *or* Berg gebaut; **to park on a ~** am Berg parken; **up ~ and down dale** bergauf und bergab; **over ~ and dale** über Berg und Tal; **this car takes the ~s beautifully** dieses Auto nimmt Steigungen mühelos; **as old as the ~s** steinalt, uralt; **that joke's as old as the ~s** der Witz hat ja so einen langen Bart; **to take to the ~s** sich in die Berge flüchten; **to be over the ~** (*fig inf*) seine beste Zeit *or* die besten Jahre hinter sich (*dat*) haben.

(b) *see* **anthill, molehill** etc.

hillbilly ['hɪlbɪlɪ] (*US inf*) 1 *n* Hinterwäldler *m* (*pej*); (*female*) Landpomeranze *f* (*inf*). 2 *adj* hinterwäldlerisch (*pej*). ~ **music** Hillbilly no art, Hillbilly-Musik *f*.

hilliness ['hɪlɪnɪs] *n* Hügeligkeit *f*; (*higher*) Bergigkeit *f*. **the ~ of the terrain** das hügelige *or* (*higher*) bergige Gelände.

hillock ['hɪlək] *n* Hügel *m*, Anhöhe *f*.

hill: ~**side** *n* Hang *m*; ~**top** *n* Gipfel *m*.

hilly ['hɪlɪ] *adj* (+*er*) hüge(e)lig; (*higher*) bergig.

hilt [hɪlt] *n* Heft *nt*; (*of dagger*) Griff *m*. **up to the ~** (*fig*) voll und ganz; (*involved, in debt also*) bis über beide Ohren (*inf*); **I'll back you up to the ~** ich stehe voll und ganz hinter Ihnen.

him [hɪm] *pers pron* (a) (*dir obj, with prep* +*acc*) ihn; (*indir obj, with prep* +*dat*) ihm; (*when he is previously mentioned in clause*) sich. **with his things around ~** mit seinen Sachen um sich.

(b) (*emph*) er. **it's ~** er ist's; **who, ~?** wer, er?

Himalayan [ˌhɪmə'leɪən] *adj* Himalaya-; *mountains* des Himalaya.

Himalayas [ˌhɪmə'leɪəz] *npl* Himalaya *m*.

himself [hɪm'self] 1 *pers pron* (a) (*dir and indir obj, with prep*) sich; *see also* **myself**. (b) (*emph*) (er) selbst. 2 *n* (*Ir inf*) **it was ~ who told me** er selbst hat es mir gesagt.

hind[1] [haɪnd] *n* (*Zool*) Hirschkuh, Hindin (*poet*) *f*.

hind[2] *adj, superl* **hindmost** hintere(r, s). ~ **legs** Hinterbeine *pl*; **to get up on one's ~ legs** (*inf: speak in public*) den Mund aufmachen (*inf*); **she could talk the ~ legs off a donkey** (*inf*) sie redet wie ein Buch (*inf*).

hinder ['hɪndəʳ] *vt* (a) (*obstruct, impede*) behindern; (*delay*) *person* aufhalten; *arrival* verzögern. (b) (*stop, prevent from happening*) **to ~ sb from doing sth** jdn daran hindern *or* davon abhalten, etw zu tun.

Hindi ['hɪndɪ] *n* Hindi *nt*.

hind: ~**most** *adj superl of* **hind**[2] hinterste(r, s); ~**quarters** *npl* Hinterteil *nt*; (*of carcass*) Hinterviertel *nt*; (*of horse*) Hinterhand *f*.

hindrance ['hɪndrəns] *n* Behinderung *f*. **the rules/children are a ~** die Regeln/Kinder sind hinderlich; **it was a serious ~ to progress** es behinderte den Fortschritt sehr; **he/it is more of a ~ than a help** er/es hindert mehr, als daß er/es hilft; *see* **let**[1].

hindsight ['haɪndsaɪt] *n:* **now with the benefit/wisdom of ~** jetzt, hinterher *or* im nachhinein ist man ja immer schlauer; **with ~ it's easy to criticize** hinterher *or* im nachhinein ist es leicht zu kritisieren.

Hindu ['hɪnduː] 1 *adj* *customs, religion* hinduistisch, Hindu-. 2 *n* *people* Hindu(s) *pl*. 2 *n* Hindu *m*.

Hinduism ['hɪnduːɪzəm] *n* Hinduismus *m*.

Hindustan [ˌhɪndu'staːn] *n* Hindustan, Hindostan *nt*.

Hindustani [ˌhɪndu'staːnɪ] 1 *adj* hindustanisch. 2 *n* (a) Bewohner(in *f*) *m* Hindustans. (b) (*language*) Hindustani *nt*.

hinge [hɪndʒ] 1 *n* (a) (*of door*) Angel *f*; (*of box etc*) Scharnier *nt*; (*of limb, shell*) Gelenk *nt*; (*fig*) Angelpunkt *m*. **the door/lid hangs on its ~s** die Tür ist aus den Angeln/das Scharnier des Deckels ist ab; **take the door off its ~s** häng die Tür aus!

(b) (*also* **stamp ~**) (Klebe)falz *m*.

2 *vt* **to ~ sth** etw mit Angeln/einem Scharnier an etw (*dat*) befestigen; **to ~ sth** (**up**)**on sth** (*fig*) etw von etw abhängig machen.

3 *vi* (*fig*) abhängen (*of von*), ankommen (*of auf* +*acc*).

hinged [hɪndʒd] *adj* Scharnier-; *door* eingehängt; *lid also, box* mit einem Scharnier versehen.

hint [hɪnt] 1 *n* (a) (*intimation, suggestion*) Andeutung *f*, Hinweis *m*. **to give a/no ~ of sth** etw ahnen lassen *or* andeuten/nicht ahnen lassen *or* andeuten; **to give** *or* **drop sb a ~** jdm einen Wink geben, jdm gegenüber eine Andeutung machen; **he was given a gentle ~ about attention to detail** man hat ihm leise angedeutet *or* den leisen Wink gegeben, auf Details zu achten; **to throw out** *or* **let fall** *or* **drop a ~** eine Andeutung machen, eine Bemerkung fallenlassen; **to know how to take a ~** einen Wink verstehen; OK, **I can take a ~** schon recht, ich verstehe *or* habe den Wink mit dem Zaunpfahl verstanden (*inf*); **I've almost run out of this perfume,** ~, ~ ich habe fast nichts mehr von dem Parfüm, Nachtigall, hörst du mir trapsen? (*hum inf*).

(b) (*trace*) Spur *f*. **a ~ of garlic/irony** eine Spur *or* ein Hauch *m* von Knoblauch/Spott; **with a ~ of sadness in his smile** mit einem leichten Anflug von Traurigkeit in seinem Lächeln; **with the ~ of a smile** mit dem Anflug eines Lächelns.

(c) (*tip, piece of advice*) Tip *m*. ~**s for travellers** Reisetips *pl*.

2 *vt* andeuten (*to gegenüber*). **what are you ~ing?** was wollen Sie damit sagen *or* andeuten?

♦**hint at** *vi* +*prep obj* **he ~ed ~ changes in the cabinet** er deutete an, daß es Umbesetzungen im Kabinett geben würde; **he ~ed ~ my involvement in the affair** er spielte auf meine Rolle in der Affäre an.

hinterland ['hɪntəlænd] *n* Hinterland *nt*.

hip[1] [hɪp] *n* Hüfte *f*. **with one's hands on one's ~s** die Arme in die Hüften gestemmt.

hip[2] *n* (*Bot*) Hagebutte *f*.

hip[3] *interj* ~! ~!, **hurrah!** hipp hipp, hurra!

hip[4] *adj* (*sl*) **she is really ~** sie steigt voll durch (*sl*); **a ~ artist etc** sie ist wirklich *or* echt Spitze (*sl*); **to be ~ to sth in etw** (*dat*) voll durchsteigen (*sl*); **they played to some really ~ audiences** sie spielten vor wirklich Spitze Publikum (*sl*); **she really gets ~ to**

the Stones wenn sie die Stones hört, ist sie weg (*sl*).

hip *in cpds* Hüft-; ~ **bath** *n* Sitzbad *nt*; ~**bone** *n* (*Anat*) Hüftbein *nt*, Hüftknochen *m*; ~**-flask** *n* Taschenflasche *f*, Flachmann (*inf*), Plattmann (*dial*) *m*; ~ **joint** *n* (*Anat*) Hüftgelenk *nt*; ~ **measurement** *n* Hüftweite *f*, Hüftumfang *m*.

-hipped [-hɪpt] *adj suf* -hüftig. a **big-~ woman** eine Frau mit breiten Hüften, eine breithüftige Frau.

hippie *n see* **hippy.**

hippo [ˈhɪpəʊ] *n* (*inf*) Nilpferd *nt*.

hip pocket *n* Gesäßtasche *f*.

Hippocratic oath [ˌhɪpəˌkrætɪkˈəʊθ] *n* hippokratischer Eid, Eid *m* des Hippokrates.

hippodrome [ˈhɪpədrəʊm] *n* Hippodrom *nt* or *nt*; (*dated: music hall*) Varieté(theater) *nt*.

hippopotamus [ˌhɪpəˈpɒtəməs] *n*, *pl* **-es** or **hippopotami** [ˌhɪpəˈpɒtəmaɪ] Nilpferd, Flußpferd *nt*, Hippopotamus *m* (*spec*).

hippy, hippie [ˈhɪpɪ] *n* Hippie *m*.

hipster [ˈhɪpstəʳ] **1** *n* (**a**) (*sl: one who is hip*) Hipster *m* (*sl*). (**b**) ~**s** *pl* (*trousers*) Hüfthose(n *pl*) *f*. **2** *adj* Hüft-.

hire [haɪəʳ] **1** *n* (**a**) Mieten *nt*; (*of car also*, *suit*) Leihen *nt*; (*of servant*) Einstellen *nt*. **to have/get the ~ of sth** etw mieten/leihen; **to have sth for ~** etw vermieten/verleihen; **for ~** (*taxi*) frei; **you pay more for the ~ of a car in London** in London kostet ein Leih- or Mietwagen mehr; **it's on ~** es ist geliehen/gemietet; **to let sth (out) on ~** etw vermieten.
(**b**) (*wages*) Lohn *m*; (*of sailor*) Heuer *f*. **to be worth one's ~** sein Geld wert sein, seines Lohnes wert sein (*old*).
2 *vt* (**a**) mieten; *cars also*, *suits* leihen; *staff*, *person* einstellen. ~**d assassin** gedungener Mörder; ~**d car** Mietwagen, Leihwagen *m*; ~**d gun** gedungener Mörder, bezahlter Killer (*inf*); ~**d hand** Lohnarbeiter *m*.
(**b**) *see* **hire out.**

♦ **hire out 1** *vt sep* vermieten, verleihen. **2** *vi* (*US*) sich verdingen.

hireling [ˈhaɪəlɪŋ] *n* (*pej*) Mietling *m* (*old pej*).

hire purchase *n* (*Brit*) Ratenkauf, Teilzahlungskauf *m*. **on ~** auf Raten or Teilzahlung; ~ **agreement** Teilzahlungs-(kauf)vertrag *m*.

hirsute [ˈhɜːsjuːt] *adj* stark behaart.

his [hɪz] **1** *poss adj* sein; *see also* **my. 2** *poss pron* seine(r, s). ~ (*on towels etc*) er; *see also* **mine¹.**

Hispanic [hɪsˈpænɪk] *adj* hispanisch; *community* spanisch.

hiss [hɪs] **1** *vi* zischen; (*cat*) fauchen. **2** *vt actor*, *speaker* auszischen. **come here, he ~ed** komm her, zischte er. **3** *n* Zischen *nt*; (*of cat*) Fauchen *nt*.

histamine [ˈhɪstəmiːn] *n* (*Med*) Histamin *nt*.

histology [hɪsˈtɒlədʒɪ] *n* Histologie *f*.

historian [hɪsˈtɔːrɪən] *n* Historiker(in *f*) *m*; (*in ancient times*) Geschichtsschreiber(in *f*) *m*.

historic [hɪsˈtɒrɪk] *adj* (*also Gram*) historisch.

historical [hɪsˈtɒrɪkəl] *adj* historisch; *studies*, *investigation*, *method also* geschichtlich, Geschichts-. **from a ~ point of view** aus historischer Sicht; **places of ~ interest** historisch or geschichtlich interessante Stätten *pl*.

historicism [hɪsˈtɒrɪsɪzəm] *n* Historizismus *m*.

historicity [ˌhɪstəˈrɪsɪtɪ] *n* Geschichtlichkeit, Historizität *f*.

historiography [ˌhɪstɒrɪˈɒɡrəfɪ] *n* Geschichtsschreibung, Historiographie *f*.

history [ˈhɪstərɪ] *n* (**a**) Geschichte *f*; (*study of ~ also*) Geschichtswissenschaft *f*. ~ **will be our judge** die Geschichte wird ihr Urteil fällen; ~ **has taught us that ...** die Geschichte lehrt uns, daß ...; **to make ~** Geschichte machen.
(**b**) (*personal record*) Geschichte *f*. **he has a ~ of violence** er hat eine Vorgeschichte als Gewalttäter; **the family/he has a ~ of heart disease** Herzleiden liegen in der Familie/er hat schon lange ein Herzleiden.
(**c**) (*background*) Vorgeschichte *f*. **to know the inner ~ of an affair** die inneren Zusammenhänge einer Affäre kennen; **bring me the ~ on this from the files** bringen Sie mir die Akten dazu.

histrionic [ˌhɪstrɪˈɒnɪk] *adj* (**a**) (*overdone*, *affected*) theatralisch. (**b**) Schauspieler-; *art* Schauspiel-; *ability* schauspielerisch.

histrionics [ˌhɪstrɪˈɒnɪks] *npl* (**a**) theatralisches Getue. **to indulge in ~** sich theatralisch aufführen. (**b**) Schauspielkunst *f*.

hit [hɪt] (*vb: pret*, *ptp* ~) **1** *n* (**a**) (*blow*) Schlag *m*; (*on target*, *Fencing*) Treffer *m*; (*Baseball*) Schlag *m*; *see* **score.**
(**b**) (*success*, *also Theat*) Erfolg, Knüller (*inf*) *m*; (*song*) Schlager, Hit *m*. **to be or make a ~ with sb** bei jdm gut ankommen.
(**c**) (*of sarcasm etc*) Spitze *f*. **that's a ~ at me** das ist eine Spitze gegen mich; (*indirect also*) das ist auf mich gemünzt.
(**d**) (*sl: murder*) Mord *m*.
2 *vt* (**a**) (*strike*) schlagen. **to ~ sb a blow** jdm einen Schlag versetzen; **he ~ him a blow over the head** er gab ihm einen Schlag auf den Kopf; **to ~ one's head against sth** sich (*dat*) den Kopf an etw (*dat*) anschlagen, mit dem Kopf gegen etw schlagen; **he ~ his head on the pavement** er schlug mit dem Kopf auf dem Pflaster auf; **the car ~ a tree** das Auto fuhr gegen einen Baum; **he was ~ by a stone** er wurde von einem Stein getroffen, ihn traf ein Stein; **the house was ~ by a shell** das Haus wurde von einer Granate getroffen; **to ~ one's way out of trouble** sich freischlagen; (*Tennis*) sich freispielen; (*Boxing*) sich freiboxen; **we're going to ~ the enemy with everything we've got** wir werden mit allen verfügbaren Mitteln gegen den Feind vorgehen; **the commandos ~ the town** die Kommandos griffen die Stadt im Morgengrauen an; **if I catch them taking bribes I'm going to ~ them hard** wenn ich sie dabei erwische, daß sie Bestechungsgelder nehmen, werde ich ganz scharf durchgreifen; **it ~s you (in the eye)** (*fig*) das fällt or springt einem ins Auge.

(**b**) (*wound*) treffen. **he's been ~ in the leg** es hat ihn am Bein getroffen, er ist am Bein getroffen worden; **I've been ~!** ich bin getroffen worden, mich hat's erwischt (*inf*).
(**c**) *mark*, *target*, (*Fencing*) treffen. **that ~ home** (*fig*) das hat getroffen, das saß (*inf*); **now you've ~ it** (*fig*) du hast es getroffen.
(**d**) (*affect adversely*) betreffen. **the crops were ~ by the rain** der Regen hat der Ernte geschadet; **to be hard ~ by sth** von etw schwer getroffen werden; **how will this tax ~ the lower paid?** wie wird sich diese Steuer auf die schlechter Bezahlten auswirken?
(**e**) (*achieve*, *reach*) *likeness*, *top C* treffen; *speed*, *level*, *top form etc* erreichen.
(**f**) (*news*, *story*) **to ~ the papers** in die Zeitungen kommen; **the news ~ us/Wall Street like a bombshell** die Nachricht schlug bei uns/in Wall Street wie eine Bombe ein.
(**g**) (*occur to*) **to ~ sb** jdm aufgehen; **has it ever ~ you how alike they are?** ist es Ihnen schon mal aufgefallen, wie ähnlich sie sich sind?
(**h**) (*come to*, *arrive at*) *beaches etc* erreichen. **to ~ town** (*inf*) die Stadt erreichen; **we eventually ~ the right road** schließlich haben wir den richtigen Weg gefunden or erwischt (*inf*); **we're going to ~ the rush hour** wir geraten or kommen direkt in den Stoßverkehr; **the driver ~ a patch of ice** der Fahrer geriet auf eine vereiste Stelle; **to ~ trouble/a problem** in Schwierigkeiten/an ein Problem geraten, auf Schwierigkeiten/ein Problem stoßen.
(**i**) (*score*) schlagen. **to ~ a century** hundert Läufe machen.
(**j**) (*sl: murder*) killen (*sl*), umlegen (*sl*).
(**k**) (*US inf*) **to ~ sb for $50** jdn um $ 50 anhauen (*inf*).
(**l**) (*fig inf phrases*) **to ~ the bottle** zur Flasche greifen; **to ~ the ceiling** or **roof** an die Decke or in die Luft gehen (*inf*); **to ~ the deck** sich zu Boden werfen, sich hinwerfen; **the vase ~ the deck and shattered** die Vase schlug or knallte (*inf*) auf den Boden und zerschellte; **to ~ the road** or **trail** sich auf den Weg or die Socken (*inf*) machen.
3 *vi* (**a**) (*strike*) schlagen. **he ~s hard** er schlägt hart zu.
(**b**) (*collide*) zusammenstoßen.
(**c**) (*attack*, *go in*) losschlagen.

♦ **hit back 1** *vi* (*lit*, *fig*) zurückschlagen. **to ~ ~ at the enemy** zurückschlagen; **he ~ ~ at his critics** er gab seinen Kritikern Kontra. **2** *vt sep* zurückschlagen.

♦ **hit off** *vt sep* **to ~ a likeness** jdn/etw sehr gut treffen; **he ~ him ~ beautifully** er hat ihn ausgezeichnet getroffen.
(**b**) **to ~ it ~ with sb** (*inf*) sich gut mit jdm verstehen, prima mit jdm auskommen (*inf*); **they ~ it ~** sie haben sich von Anfang an gut verstanden.

♦ **hit out** *vi* (*lit*) einschlagen, losschlagen (*at sb* auf jdn); (*fig*) scharf angreifen, attackieren (*at* or *against sb* jdn).

♦ **hit (up)on** *vi* +*prep obj* stoßen auf (+*acc*), finden.

hit-and-run [ˈhɪtənˈrʌn] **1** *n* **there was a ~ here last night** hier hat heute nacht jemand einen Unfall gebaut und Fahrerflucht begangen.
2 *adj* ~ **raid** (*Mil*) Blitzüberfall *m*; ~ **accident/incident** Unfall *m* mit Fahrerflucht; ~ **cases** Fälle von Fahrerflucht; ~ **driver** unfallflüchtiger Fahrer, Fahrer, der Unfall- or Fahrerflucht begangen hat/begeht.

hitch [hɪtʃ] **1** *n* (**a**) (*snag*) Haken *m*; (*in plan*, *proceedings*, *programme*) Schwierigkeit *f*, Problem *nt*. **without a ~** reibungslos, ohne Schwierigkeiten; **but there's one ~** aber die Sache hat einen Haken; **there's been a ~** es haben sich Schwierigkeiten ergeben, da ist ein Problem aufgetaucht.
(**b**) (*quick pull*) Ruck *m*. **she gave it a quick ~** sie zog kurz daran.
(**c**) (*knot*) Knoten *m*; (*Naut*) Ste(e)k *m*.
(**d**) (*inf: lift*) **I got a ~ all the way to London** ich bin in einem Rutsch bis London (*durch*)getrampt (*inf*).
2 *vt* (**a**) (*fasten*) festmachen, anbinden (*sth to sth* etw an etw +*dat*). ~**ing post** Pfosten *m* (*zum Anbinden von Pferden*).
(**b**) (*inf*) **to get ~ed** heiraten, vor Anker gehen (*hum*); **why don't we get ~ed?** warum heiraten wir (*eigentlich*) nicht?
(**c**) **to ~ a lift** trampen, per Anhalter fahren; **she ~ed a lift from a lorry** ein Lastwagen nahm sie mit.
3 *vi* trampen, per Anhalter fahren; *see also* ~**-hike.**

♦ **hitch up** *vt sep* (**a**) *horses*, *oxen* anschirren, anspannen. **we ~ed ~ the horses to the wagon** wir spannten die Pferde vor den Wagen. (**b**) *trousers* hochziehen.

hitcher [ˈhɪtʃəʳ] *n* (*inf*) Anhalter(in *f*), Tramper(in *f*) *m*.

hitch: ~**-hike** *vi* per Anhalter fahren, trampen; **he's been away ~-hiking** er war per Anhalter unterwegs; ~**-hiker** *n* Anhalter(in *f*), Tramper(in *f*) *m*; ~**-hiking** *n* Trampen *nt*.

hither [ˈhɪðəʳ] *adv* (*obs*) hierher. ~ **and thither** (*liter*) hierhin und dorthin.

hitherto [ˌhɪðəˈtuː] *adv* bisher, bis jetzt.

hit: ~**man** *n* (*sl*) Killer *m* (*sl*); ~**-or-miss** *adj* auf gut Glück *pred*, aufs Geratewohl *pred*; *methods*, *planning* schlampig, schludrig (*inf*); **it was a rather ~-or-miss affair** das ging alles aufs Geratewohl; ~ **parade** *n* Hitparade, Schlagerparade *f*; ~ **record** *n* Schlagerplatte *f*; ~ **show** *n* erfolgreiche Show, Publikumserfolg *m*; ~ **song** *n* Schlager *m*; ~ **tune** *n* Schlagermelodie *f*.

hive [haɪv] **1** *n* (**a**) (*bee* ~) Bienenkorb, Bienenstock *m*; (*bees in a* ~) (Bienen)schwarm *m*, (Bienen)volk *nt*.
(**b**) (*fig*) **what a ~ of industry** das reinste Bienenhaus; **the office was a ~ of activity** das Büro glich einem Bienenhaus.
2 *vt bees*, *swarm* einfangen, in den Stock bringen.
3 *vi* (*swarm*) in den (Bienen)stock (ein)fliegen, den/einen Stock beziehen.

♦ **hive off 1** *vt sep department* ausgliedern, abspalten. **2** *vi* (**a**) (*branch out*) sich absetzen. (**b**) (*sl: slip away*) abschwirren (*sl*).

hives [haɪvz] *npl* (*Med*) Nesselausschlag *m*, Nesselsucht *f*.

HM *abbr of* His/Her Majesty S.M./I.M.

HMI (*Brit*) *abbr of* His/Her Majesty's Inspector.

HMSO (*Brit*) *abbr of* Her Majesty's Stationery Office.

HNC (*Brit*) *abbr of* Higher National Certificate.

HND (*Brit*) *abbr of* Higher National Diploma.

hoar [hɔːʳ] *n* Reif *m*.

hoard [hɔːd] **1** *n* Vorrat *m*; (*treasure*) Schatz, Hort *m*. a ~ of weapons ein Waffenlager *nt*; the miser's ~ der Schatz des Geizhalses; ~ of money Schatz *m*, gehortetes Geld.
2 *vt* (*also* ~ up) *food etc* hamstern; *money* horten. a squirrel ~s nuts for the winter ein Eichhörnchen hortet Nüsse für den Winter.

hoarding[1] [ˈhɔːdɪŋ] *n* (*of food etc*) Hamstern *nt*; (*of capital*) Anhäufen *nt*, Anhäufung *f*.

hoarding[2] *n* (*Brit*) (*fence, board*) Bretterzaun *m*; (*at building sites also*) Bauzaun *m*. **(advertisement)** ~ Plakatwand *f*.

hoarfrost [ˈhɔːˈfrɒst] *n* (*Rauh*)reif *m*.

hoarse [hɔːs] *adj* (+*er*) heiser. he shouted himself ~ er schrie sich heiser; you sound rather ~ deine Stimme klingt heiser.

hoarsely [ˈhɔːslɪ] *adv* mit heiserer Stimme.

hoarseness [ˈhɔːsnɪs] *n* (*of person*) Heiserkeit *f*. the ~ of his voice seine heisere Stimme.

hoary [ˈhɔːrɪ] *adj* (+*er*) **(a)** *hair* ergraut, (schloh)weiß; *old man etc* weißhaarig, ergraut.
(b) (*fig: old*) uralt, altehrwürdig. a ~ old joke ein alter Hut, ein Witz mit (einem langen) Bart.

hoax [həʊks] **1** *n* (*practical joke*) Streich *m*; (*trick etc*) Trick *m*; (*false alarm*) blinder Alarm. to play a ~ on sb jdm einen Streich spielen; ~ caller *see* hoaxer; ~ story Zeitungsente *f*.
2 *vt* anführen, hereinlegen (*inf*). to ~ sb into believing sth jdm etw weismachen; he ~ed him into paying money er hat ihm Geld abgeschwindelt *or* abgeluchst (*inf*); we were completely ~ed wir ließen uns anführen, wir fielen darauf herein.

hoaxer [ˈhəʊksəʳ] *n* (*in bomb scares etc*) jd, der einen blinden Alarm auslöst.

hob [hɒb] *n* Kamineinsatz (zum Warmhalten) *m*; (*on modern cooker*) Kochmulde *f*.

hobble [ˈhɒbl] **1** *vi* humpeln, hinken. to ~ in herein-/hineinhumpeln. **2** *vt* *horse* Fußfesseln anlegen (–*dat*), die Vorderbeine fesseln (–*dat*). **3** *n* (*for horses*) Fußfessel *f*.

hobbledehoy [ˈhɒbldɪˈhɔɪ] *n* (*old*) Tolpatsch *m*.

hobby [ˈhɒbɪ] *n* Hobby, Steckenpferd (*dated*) *nt*.

hobby-horse [ˈhɒbɪhɔːs] *n* (*lit, fig*) Steckenpferd *nt*; (*lit: rocking horse*) Schaukelpferd *nt*. to be on one's ~ (*fig*) bei seinem Lieblingsthema sein; don't get him on his ~ (*fig*) bring ihn (bloß) nicht auf sein Lieblingsthema.

hobgoblin [hɒbˈgɒblɪn] *n* Kobold, Butzemann *m*; (*bogey*) schwarzer Mann, Butzemann *m*.

hobnail [ˈhɒbneɪl] *n* Schuhnagel *m*, Schuhzwecke *f*.

hobnailed [ˈhɒbneɪld] *adj* genagelt. ~ boots genagelte Schuhe, Nagelschuhe *pl*.

hobnob [ˈhɒbnɒb] *vi* of course I'm not used to ~bing with the aristocracy ich stehe *or* bin natürlich nicht mit dem Adel auf du und du; she's been seen ~bing with some rather peculiar types sie ist mit ein paar ziemlich merkwürdigen Typen durch die Gegend gezogen (*inf*); he shouldn't still be ~bing with his bachelor friends er sollte nicht immer noch mit seinen Freunden aus der Junggesellenzeit zusammenstecken; who was that you were ~bing with last night? mit wem hast du da gestern zusammengesessen?

hobo [ˈhəʊbəʊ] *n* (*US*) **(a)** (*tramp*) Penner *m* (*inf*). **(b)** (*worker*) Wanderarbeiter *m*.

Hobson's choice [ˈhɒbsənsˈtʃɔɪs] *n* it's a case of ~ da habe ich (wohl) keine andere Wahl.

hock[1] [hɒk] *n* (*Anat: of animal*) Sprunggelenk *nt*.

hock[2] *n* (*wine*) weißer Rheinwein.

hock[3] (*sl*) **1** *vt* (*pawn*) versetzen, verpfänden. **2** *n* in ~ verpfändet, versetzt, im Leihhaus; to get sth out of ~ etw auslösen.

hockey [ˈhɒkɪ] *n* Hockey *nt*; (*US*) Eishockey *nt*. ~ pitch Hockeyfeld *nt*; ~ player Hockeyspieler(in *f*) *m*; (*US*) Eishockeyspieler *m*; ~ stick Hockeyschläger *m*.

hocus-pocus [ˈhəʊkəsˈpəʊkəs] *n* (a) (*inf: trickery*) faule Tricks *pl* (*inf*), Hokuspokus *m*. **(b)** (*formula*) Hokuspokus *m*.

hod [hɒd] *n* **(a)** (*for bricks, mortar etc*) Tragmulde *f*. **(b)** (*also coal* ~) Kohlenschütte(r *m*) *f*.

hodgepodge [ˈhɒdʒpɒdʒ] *n see* hotchpotch.

hoe [həʊ] **1** *n* Hacke *f*. **2** *vt* hacken.

hoedown [ˈhəʊdaʊn] *n* (*US*) Schwof *m* (*inf*).

hog [hɒg] **1** *n* **(a)** (*Mast*)schwein *nt*; (*US: pig*) Schwein *nt*.
(b) (*pej inf: person*) Schwein *nt* (*inf*); (*greedy*) Vielfraß *m* (*inf*); (*selfish*) Saukerl *m* (*sl*); (*dirty*) Sau *f* (*sl*), Ferkel *nt* (*inf*); *see* roadhog, whole ~.
2 *vt* (*inf*) sich (*dat*) aneignen, in Beschlag nehmen. he ~ged all the biscuits for himself er grapschte sich (*dat*) alle Kekse (*inf*); she ~ged his attention all evening sie belegte ihn den ganzen Abend lang mit Beschlag; a lot of drivers ~ the middle of the road viele Fahrer meinen, sie hätten die Straßenmitte gepachtet (*inf*).

Hogmanay [ˌhɒgməˈneɪ] *n* (*Scot*) Silvester *nt*, Silvesterabend *m*.

hogshead [ˈhɒgzhed] *n* großes Faß; (*measure*) Oxhoft *nt* (*obs*); *Flüssigkeitsmaß zwischen 200–250 l*.

hog: ~tie *vt* (*US*) an allen vieren fesseln; (*inf*) handlungsunfähig machen; we're ~tied uns (*dat*) sind Hände und Füße gebunden; ~wash *n* **(a)** (*swill*) Schweinefutter *nt*; **(b)** (*inf: nonsense*) Quatsch, Quark *m* (*inf*), blödes Zeug (*inf*).

hoi polloi [ˌhɔɪpəˈlɔɪ] *n* (*pej*) Volk *nt*, Pöbel, Plebs *m*.

hoist [hɔɪst] **1** *vt* hochheben, hieven (*inf*); (*pull up*) hochziehen, hieven (*inf*); *flag* hissen; *sails* aufziehen, hissen. to be ~ with one's own petard (*prov*) in die eigene Falle gehen.
2 *n* **(a)** Hebezeug *nt*, Hebevorrichtung *f*; (*in ships also*)

Hebewerk *nt*; (*lift*) (Lasten)aufzug *m*; (*block and tackle*) Flaschenzug *m*; (*winch*) Winde *f*; (*crane*) Kran *m*.
(b) (*act of* ~ing) to give sb a ~ (up) jdn hochheben; (*pull up*) jdm hinauf-/heraufhelfen.

hoity-toity [ˈhɔɪtɪˈtɔɪtɪ] (*inf*) **1** *adj* hochnäsig, eingebildet. she's gone all ~ sie markiert die feine Dame (*inf*); oh ~, are we? wohl zu fein für unsereins? **2** *interj* sieh mal einer an (*inf*).

hokum [ˈhəʊkəm] *n* (*US inf*) **(a)** (*nonsense*) Quatsch (*inf*), Mumpitz *m*. **(b)** (*cheap sentiment*) Gefühlsduselei *f* (*inf*).

hold [həʊld] (*vb: pret, ptp* held) **1** *n* **(a)** Griff *m*; (*fig*) Einfluß *m* (*over* auf + *acc*), Gewalt *f* (*over* über + *acc*). to seize *or* grab ~ of sb/sth (*lit*) jdn/etw fassen *or* packen; to get (a) ~ of sth sich an etw (*dat*) festhalten; get ~ of my hand faß mich bei der Hand; he lost his ~ on the rope er konnte sich nicht mehr am Seil festhalten; to have/catch ~ of sth (*lit*) etw festhalten/etw fassen *or* packen; to keep ~ of sth etw nicht loslassen; (*keep*) etw behalten; to get ~ of sb (*fig*) jdn finden *or* auftreiben (*inf*); (*on phone etc*) jdn erreichen; to get *or* lay ~ of sth (*fig*) etw finden *or* auftreiben (*inf*); where did you get ~ of that idea? wie kommst du denn auf die Idee?; to have a firm ~ on sb (*lit*) jdn festhalten; (*fig*) jdn fest im Griff haben; he hasn't got any ~ on *or* over me (*fig*) er kann mir nichts anhaben; to have a ~ over *or* on sb (*fig*) (großen) Einfluß auf jdn ausüben; *audience, followers* jdn in seiner Gewalt haben; he has such a ~ on *or* over her er hat sie so in seiner Gewalt; to get (a) ~ of oneself (*fig*) sich in den Griff bekommen; get (a) ~ of yourself! reiß dich zusammen!
(b) (*Mountaineering*) Halt *m* no *pl*. he lost his ~ and fell er verlor den Halt und stürzte ab; the face offers few ~s to climbers die Wand bietet dem Bergsteiger wenig Halt.
(c) (*Wrestling*) Griff *m*. no ~s barred (*lit*) alle Griffe (sind) erlaubt; when those two have a row, there are no ~s barred (*fig*) wenn die beiden sich streiten, dann kennen sie nichts mehr (*inf*) *or* kein Pardon (*inf*).
(d) (*Naut, Aviat*) Laderaum, Frachtraum *m*.
2 *vt* **(a)** (*grasp, grip*) halten. to ~ hands sich an der Hand halten, sich anfassen; (*lovers, children etc*) Händchen halten; to walk along ~ing hands angefaßt gehen; to ~ one's sides with laughter sich (*dat*) den Bauch vor Lachen halten; to ~ sb/sth tight jdn/etw (ganz) festhalten; the frightened children held each other tight die verängstigten Kinder klammerten sich aneinander; this car ~s the road well dieses Auto hat eine gute Straßenlage; he held the corner well er hat die Kurve gut genommen; to ~ sth in place etw (fest)halten.
(b) (*carry, maintain*) halten. to ~ oneself upright sich gerade *or* aufrecht halten; the corporal held himself upright der Unteroffizier stand stramm; to ~ oneself/sth ready *or* in readiness sich/etw bereithalten.
(c) (*contain*) enthalten; (*have capacity etc of: bottle, tank etc*) fassen; (*have room for: bus, plane, hall etc*) Platz haben für. this room ~s twenty people in diesem Raum haben zwanzig Personen Platz; the box will ~ all my books in der Kiste ist Platz für alle meine Bücher; this ~s the radar equipment dies enthält die Radarausrüstung; my head can't ~ so much information at one time soviel kann ich nicht auf einmal behalten; what does the future ~? was bringt *or* birgt (*geh*) die Zukunft?; life ~s no fears/mystery for them das Leben hat *or* birgt (*geh*) nichts Beängstigendes/Geheimnisvolles für sie.
(d) (*believe*) meinen; (*maintain also*) behaupten. to ~ sth to be true/false/immoral etc etw für wahr/falsch/unmoralisch etc halten; to ~ the belief that ... glauben, daß...; to ~ such a belief ... so etwas zu glauben ...; to ~ the view that ... die Meinung vertreten, daß ...
(e) (*consider*) she held her youngest grandchild dear ihr jüngstes Enkelkind bedeutete ihr sehr viel *or* war ihr teuer (*liter*); she held the memory of her late husband dear sie hielt das Andenken an ihren verstorbenen Mann hoch.
(f) (*restrain, retain, keep back*) *train* aufhalten; *one's breath* anhalten; *suspect, hostages etc* festhalten; *parcel, confiscated goods etc* zurückhalten; (*discontinue*) *fire* einstellen. ~ your fire! (*don't shoot*) nicht schießen!; to ~ sb (*prisoner*) jdn gefangenhalten; if she wants to leave you, you can't ~ her wenn sie dich verlassen will, kannst du sie nicht (zurück)halten; do you find it difficult to ~ staff? finden Sie es schwierig, das Personal zu halten?; there's no ~ing him er ist nicht zu bremsen (*inf*); ~ hard, ~ your horses (*inf*) immer mit der Ruhe, immer sachte mit dem jungen Pferden! (*inf*); ~ it! (*inf*) Momentchen (*inf*), Moment mal (*inf*); ~ everything! (*inf*) stop!; ~ it! (*when taking photograph*) so ist gut; ~ it right there, buster (*inf*) keine Bewegung, Freundchen (*inf*).
(g) (*possess, occupy*) *post, position* innehaben, bekleiden (*form*); *passport, permit* haben; (*Fin*) *shares* besitzen; (*Sport*) *record* halten; (*Mil*) *position* halten; (*against attack*) behaupten, halten; (*Eccl*) *living* innehaben. the family ~s most of the shares die meisten Aktien sind *or* befinden sich in den Händen *or* im Besitz der Familie; when Spain held vast territories in South America als Spanien riesige Besitzungen in Südamerika hatte; she ~s the key to the mystery sie hat den Schlüssel zu dem Geheimnis; this ~s the key to your success das ist der Schlüssel zum Erfolg; *see* stage.
(h) (*keep, not let go*) to ~ its value seinen Wert behalten; to ~ one's ground *or* own sich behaupten (können); to ~ course for (*Naut*) Kurs halten auf (+ *acc*); to ~ one's course die Richtung beibehalten; I'll ~ you to your promise *or* word *or* that! ich werde Sie beim Wort nehmen; to ~ a note (*Mus*) einen Ton halten.
(i) he can't ~ his whisky/liquor er verträgt keinen Whisky/nichts; she can ~ her drink sie verträgt was; a man can always ~ his water ein richtiger Mann kann sein Wasser halten.
(j) *meeting, session, debate* abhalten; (*Eccl*) *service*

(ab)halten. *services are held every Sunday at 11 am* Gottesdienst findet jeden Sonntag um 11 Uhr statt; *to ~ a check on sb/sth* jdn/etw kontrollieren; *to ~ a conversation* eine Unterhaltung führen *or* haben, sich unterhalten.

3 *vi* **(a)** *(rope, nail etc)* halten. *to ~ firm or fast* halten.
(b) *~ still!* halt (doch mal) still!; *~ tight!* festhalten!
(c) *(continue)* will the good weather ~? wird sich das gute Wetter wohl halten?; *if his luck ~s* wenn ihm das Glück treu bleibt.
(d) *(be valid, apply to)* gelten. *this rule ~s good for everybody* diese Regel gilt für alle; *his promise still ~s (good)* sein Versprechen gilt immer noch.

♦**hold against** *vt always separate* to ~ sth ~ sb jdm etw übelnehmen *or* verübeln; *criminal record, past failings* jdm etw anlasten *or* zur Last legen.

♦**hold back 1** *vi* *(stay back, hesitate, not perform fully)* sich zurückhalten; *(fail to act)* zögern. I think he's ~ing, he knows more *ich glaube, er weiß mehr und rückt nur nicht mit der Sprache heraus;* I held ~ from telling him just what I thought of him *ich unterließ es, ihm meine Meinung zu sagen.*
2 *vt sep* **(a)** zurückhalten; *river, floods* (auf)stauen; *crowd, mob also* aufhalten; *tears also* unterdrücken; *emotions* verbergen, unterdrücken. *to ~ sb ~ from doing sth* jdn daran hindern, etw zu tun.
(b) *(prevent from making progress)* daran hindern, vorankommen. *he would let nothing ~ him ~ from getting his way* nichts kann ihn daran hindern, seinen Willen durchzusetzen; *nothing can ~ him ~ now* jetzt ist er nicht mehr aufzuhalten.
(c) *(withhold)* verheimlichen, verbergen; *information, report* geheimhalten; *pay increase* verzögern. *he was ~ing something ~ from me* er verheimlichte *or* verbarg mir etwas.

♦**hold down** *vt sep* **(a)** *(keep on the ground)* niederhalten, unten halten; *(keep in its place)* (fest)halten; *(oppress) country, people* unterdrücken; *(keep in check)* unter Kontrolle haben; *(keep low) prices, costs, numbers, pressure* niedrig halten. *to ~ one's head* ~ den Kopf senken.
(b) *job* haben. *he can't ~ any job ~ for long* er kann sich in keiner Stellung lange halten.

♦**hold forth 1** *vi* sich ergehen *(geh)*, sich auslassen *(on über +acc)*. **2** *vt sep (form: offer)* bieten.

♦**hold in** *vt sep* *stomach* einziehen; *emotions* zurückhalten; *horse* zurückhalten, zügeln. *to ~ ~ one's temper* seinen Ärger unterdrücken; *to ~ oneself ~ (stomach)* den Bauch einziehen; *(emotionally)* sich beherrschen, an sich halten.

♦**hold off 1** *vi* **(a)** *(keep away)* sich fernhalten *(from dat)*; *(not act)* warten; *(enemy)* nicht angreifen. *they held ~ where they should have intervened* sie hätten eingreifen sollen, haben sich aber zurückgehalten; *she ~s ~ from all close friendships* sie vermeidet enge Freundschaften.
(b) *(rain, storm)* ausbleiben. *I hope the rain ~s ~* ich hoffe, daß es nicht regnet.
2 *vt sep (keep back, resist) enemy, attack* abwehren; *inflation* eindämmen. *how much longer can she go on ~ing him ~?* wie lange kann sie ihn wohl noch hinhalten?

♦**hold on 1** *vi* *(lit: maintain grip)* sich festhalten; *(endure, resist)* durchhalten, aushalten; *(wait)* warten. *~ ~! Moment!; (Telec)* einen Moment bitte. *now ~ ~ a minute!* Moment mal!
2 *vt sep (fest)*halten. *to be held ~ by sth* mit etw befestigt sein; *this sellotape won't ~ it ~* mit dem Tesafilm hält das nicht.

♦**hold on to** *vi + prep obj* **(a)** festhalten. *here, ~ ~ ~ this!* halt das mal (fest)!; *he was ~ing ~ ~ the ledge* er hielt *or* klammerte sich am Felsvorsprung fest; *they firmly held ~ ~ each other* sie klammerten sich aneinander.
(b) *(hope)* nicht aufgeben; *idea* festhalten an *(+dat)*.
(c) *(keep)* behalten; *position* beibehalten. *to ~ ~ ~ the lead* in Führung bleiben.

♦**hold out 1** *vi* **(a)** *(supplies etc)* reichen.
(b) *(endure, resist)* aushalten, durchhalten; *(refuse to yield)* nicht nachgeben. *to ~ ~ against sb/sth* sich gegen jdn/etw behaupten; *to ~ ~ for sth* auf etw *(dat)* bestehen.
2 *vt sep* **(a)** vorstrecken, ausstrecken. *to ~ ~ sth to sb* jdm etw hinhalten; *to ~ ~ one's hand* die Hand ausstrecken; *your hand* ~ halt die Hand auf; *she held ~ her arms* sie breitete die Arme aus.
(b) *(fig: offer) prospects* bieten; *offer* machen. I held ~ little hope of his still being alive *ich hatte nur noch wenig Hoffnung, daß er noch lebte;* his case ~s ~ little hope *in seinem Fall besteht wenig Hoffnung.*

♦**hold out on** *vi + prep obj (inf)* you've been ~ing ~ ~ me du verheimlichst mir doch was *(inf)*.

♦**hold over** *vt sep* *question, matter* vertagen; *meeting also, decision* verschieben *(until acc + acc)*.

♦**hold to** *vi + prep obj* festhalten an *(+dat)*; bleiben bei. I ~ ~ my belief that ... *ich bleibe dabei, daß ...;* you should ~ ~ the assurance you gave them *Sie sollten Ihr Wort ihnen gegenüber einhalten.*

♦**hold together** *vti* zusammenhalten.

♦**hold under** *vt sep country, race* unterdrücken, knechten.

♦**hold up 1** *vi* **(a)** *(stay up) (tent, wall etc)* stehen bleiben; *(light fitting, tile etc)* halten.
(b) *(belief)* standhalten; *(theory)* sich halten lassen.
2 *vt sep* **(a)** hochheben, hochhalten; *face* nach oben wenden. *~ ~ your hand* hebt die Hand; *to ~ sth ~ to the light* etw gegen das Licht halten.
(b) *(support) (from above)* halten; *(from the side)* stützen; *(from beneath)* tragen.
(c) *to ~ sb/sth ~ to ridicule/scorn* jdn/etw lächerlich/verächtlich machen; *to ~ sb ~ as an example* jdn als Beispiel hinstellen. I don't want to ~ him ~ as the perfect statesman/goalkeeper etc but ... *ich möchte ihn nicht als*

---

den perfekten Politiker/Torwart *etc* hinstellen, aber ...
(d) *(stop)* anhalten; *(delay) people* aufhalten; *traffic, production* ins Stocken bringen; *talks, delivery* verzögern. *my application was held ~ by the postal strike* durch den Poststreik hat sich meine Bewerbung verzögert.
(e) *(robbers) bank, person, vehicle* überfallen.

♦**hold with** *vi + prep obj (inf)* I don't ~ ~ that ich bin gegen so was *(inf)*.

holdall [ˈhəʊldɔːl] *n* Reisetasche *f*.

holder [ˈhəʊldəʳ] *n* **(a)** *(person)* Besitzer(in *f*), Inhaber(in *f*) *m*; *(of title, office, record, passport)* Inhaber(in *f*) *m*; *(of farm)* Pächter(in *f*) *m*. **(b)** *(object)* Halter *m*; *(cigarette-~)* Spitze *f*; *(flowerpot-~)* Übertopf *m*.

holding [ˈhəʊldɪŋ] *n* **(a)** *(Boxing)* Festhalten *nt*. **(b)** *(land)* Land *nt*; *(with buildings)* Gut *nt*. ~s *pl* (Grund- *or* Land)besitz *m*; Gutsbesitz *m*. **(c)** *(Fin)* ~s *pl* Anteile *pl*; *(stocks)* Aktienbesitz *m*; ~ **company** Dach- *or* Holdinggesellschaft *f*.

hold-up [ˈhəʊldʌp] *n* **(a)** *(delay, blockage)* Verzögerung *f*; *(of traffic)* Stockung *f*. *what's the ~?* warum dauert das so lange?; *the strike caused a two-week ~ in production* der Streik brachte die Produktion zwei Wochen lang ins Stocken; *there's been a (bit of a) ~ in our plans* unsere Pläne haben sich verzögert.
(b) *(armed robbery)* bewaffneter Raubüberfall. *this is a ~!* Hände hoch, das ist ein Überfall!

hole [həʊl] **1** *n* **(a)** Loch *nt*. *to make a ~ in sb's savings* ein Loch in jds Ersparnisse reißen; *the argument is full of ~s* Ihre Argumentation weist viele Mängel auf; *he's talking through a ~ in his head (inf)* er quatscht lauter Blödsinn *(inf)*.
(b) *(inf: awkward situation)* Klemme *(inf)*, Patsche *(inf) f*. *to be in a ~* in der Patsche *or* Klemme sitzen *(inf)*; *to get sb out of a ~* jdm aus der Patsche *or* Klemme helfen *(inf)*.
(c) *(rabbit's, fox's)* Bau *m*, Höhle *f*; *(mouse's)* Loch *nt*.
(d) *(pej inf)* Loch *nt (inf)*; *(town)* Kaff *(inf)*, Nest *(inf) nt*.
(e) *(Golf)* Loch *nt*. *an 18-~ course* ein 18-Löcher-Platz *m*; *~-in-one* Hole in One *nt*.
2 *vt* ein Loch machen in *(+acc)*. *to be ~d* ein Loch bekommen; *the ship was ~d by an iceberg* der Eisberg schlug das Schiff leck.
(b) *ball (Golf)* einlochen, versenken; *(Billiards)* versenken.
3 *vi* **(a)** *(socks etc)* Löcher bekommen.
(b) *(Golf)* einlochen.

♦**hole out** *vi (Golf)* das/ein Loch spielen. *to ~ ~ in one* ein Hole in One spielen.

♦**hole up** *vi (animal)* sich verkriechen; *(inf: gang etc) (hide)* sich verkriechen *(inf) or* verstecken; *(barricade themselves in)* sich verschanzen.

hole-and-corner [ˈhəʊlənˈkɔːnəʳ] *adj* obskur, zwielichtig.

holey [ˈhəʊlɪ] *adj (inf)* löchrig.

holiday [ˈhɒlədɪ] **1** *n* **(a)** *(day off)* freier Tag; *(public ~)* Feiertag *m*. *to take a ~* einen Tag frei nehmen.
(b) *(esp Brit: period)* often *pl* Urlaub *m (esp for working people)*, Ferien *pl*; *(Sch)* Ferien *pl*. *on ~* in den Ferien; auf *or* im Urlaub; *to go on ~* in Ferien/Urlaub machen; *where are you going for your ~?* wo fahren Sie in den Ferien/im Urlaub hin?, wo machen Sie Ferien/Urlaub?; *we're going to Germany for our ~s* wir fahren in den Ferien/im Urlaub nach Deutschland; *to take a ~* Urlaub nehmen *or* machen; *I need a ~* ich bin ferienreif; *to take a month's ~* einen Monat Urlaub nehmen; *~ with pay/paid ~s* bezahlter Urlaub; *it was no ~, I can tell you* ich kann dir sagen, das war alles andere als eine Erholung.
2 *vi (esp Brit)* Ferien *or* Urlaub machen.

holiday *in cpds* Ferien-; Urlaubs-; *~ camp* *n* Feriendorf *nt*; *~ clothes* *npl* Urlaubskleidung *f*; *~ feeling* *n* Urlaubs-/Ferienstimmung *f*; *~ guest* *n (esp Brit)* Feriengast *m*; *~maker* *n (esp Brit)* Urlauber(in *f*) *m*; *~ mood* *n* Urlaubs-/Ferienstimmung *f*; *~ resort* *n* Ferienort *m*; *~ spirit* *n* Urlaubs-/Ferienstimmung *f*.

holier-than-thou [ˈhəʊlɪəðənˈðaʊ] *adj attitude* selbstgerecht, selbstgefällig.

holiness [ˈhəʊlɪnɪs] *n* Heiligkeit *f*. *His/Your H~ (Eccl)* Seine/Eure Heiligkeit.

holism [ˈhəʊlɪzəm] *n* Holismus *m*.

holistic [həʊˈlɪstɪk] *adj* holistisch.

Holland [ˈhɒlənd] *n* Holland *nt*.

Hollander [ˈhɒləndəʳ] *n (Typ)* Holländer *m*.

holler [ˈhɒləʳ] *(inf)* **1** *n* Schrei *m*. **2** *vti (also ~ out)* brüllen.

hollow [ˈhɒləʊ] **1** *adj (+er)* **(a)** hohl. *I feel ~* ich habe ein Loch im Bauch *(inf)*; *(emotionally empty)* ich fühle mich ausgehöhlt *or* (innerlich) leer.
(b) *sound* hohl, dumpf; *voice* hohl, Grabes-.
(c) *(fig)* hohl; *laughter also* unecht; *person* innerlich hohl; *life* inhaltslos, leer; *sympathy, praise* unaufrichtig; *promise* leer; *victory* wertlos.
(d) *cheeks* hohl, eingefallen; *eyes* tiefliegend.
2 *adv sound* hohl. *they beat us ~ (inf)* sie haben uns haushoch geschlagen, sie haben uns fertiggemacht *(inf)*.
3 *n (of tree)* hohler Teil, Höhlung *f*; *(in ground)* Vertiefung, Mulde *f*; *(valley)* Senke *f*. *a wooded ~* eine bewaldete Niederung; *the ~ of one's hand* die hohle Hand; *the ~ of one's back* das Kreuz; *in the ~ between two waves* im Wellental.

♦**hollow out** *vt sep* aushöhlen.

hollow-eyed [ˈhɒləʊaɪd] *adj* hohläugig.

holly [ˈhɒlɪ] *n* **(a)** *(tree)* Stechpalme *f*, Ilex *m*. **(b)** *(foliage)* Stechpalme(nzweige *pl*) *f*.

hollyhock [ˈhɒlɪhɒk] *n* Malve *f*.

holm oak [ˈhəʊmˌəʊk] *n* Steineiche *f*.

holocaust [ˈhɒləkɔːst] *n* Inferno *nt*. *nuclear ~* Atominferno *nt*.

hologram [ˈhɒləgræm] *n* Hologramm *nt*.

holograph [ˈhɒləgrɑːf] **1** *n* handschriftliches Dokument. **2** *adj* eigenhändig geschrieben, holographisch *(form)*.

holography [hɒ'lɒgrəfɪ] n Holographie f.

hols [hɒlz] abbr of **holidays**.

holster ['həʊlstə'] n (Pistolen)halfter nt or f.

holy ['həʊlɪ] **1** adj (+er) **(a)** heilig; chastity, poverty gottgefällig; bread, ground geweiht. ~ **water** Weihwasser nt; **the H~ Bible** die Bibel; **the H~ City** die Heilige Stadt; **H~ Communion** Heilige Kommunion; **H~ Father** Heiliger Vater; **H~ Ghost or Spirit** Heiliger Geist; **H~ Land** Heiliges Land; **H~ Trinity** Heilige Dreieinigkeit; **H~ Oil** geweihtes Öl; **H~ Week** Karwoche, Passionswoche f; **H~ Scripture(s)** die Heilige Schrift; **H~ Saturday** Karsamstag m; **H~ Office** Inquisition f.

(b) (inf) ~ **smoke** or **cow or Moses!** heiliger Strohsack or Bimbam!, Kruzitürken! (all inf); **that child is a ~ terror** das Kind ist eine Nervensäge (inf) or eine Plage.

2 n **the H~ of Holies** (lit) das Allerheiligste; (fig) ein Heiligtum.

homage ['hɒmɪdʒ] n Huldigung f. **to pay** or **do ~ to sb** jdm huldigen; jdm seine Ehrerbietung erweisen; **to pay ~ to the dead king** um dem König die letzte Ehre zu erweisen; **they stood there in silent ~** sie standen in stummer Ehrerbietung da.

homburg ['hɒmbɜːg] n Homburg m.

home [həʊm] **1** n **(a)** (house) Heim nt; (country, area etc) Heimat f. **gifts for the ~** Geschenke pl für das Haus or Heim or die Wohnung; **a useful gadget to have in your ~** ein sehr praktisches Haushaltsgerät or Gerät für den Haushalt; **his ~ is in Brussels** er ist in Brüssel zu Hause; **Bournemouth is his second ~** Bournemouth ist seine zweite Heimat (geworden); **haven't you got a ~ to go to?** hast du kein Zuhause?; **he invited us round to his ~** er hat uns zu sich (nach Hause) eingeladen; **away from ~** von zu Hause weg; **a long way from ~** weit von zu Hause weg or entfernt; (in different country also) weit von der Heimat entfernt; **to live away from ~** nicht zu Hause wohnen; **he worked away from ~** er hat auswärts gearbeitet; **he has no ~** er hat kein Zuhause; **hasn't this hammer got a ~?** gehört der Hammer nicht irgendwohin?; **to have a ~ of one's own** ein eigenes Heim or Zuhause haben; **to find a ~ for sb/an animal/an object** ein Zuhause für jdn/ein Tier finden/einen Gegenstand irgendwo unterbringen; **I'll give that picture a ~** bei mir wird das Bild einen guten Platz finden or haben; **it's a ~ from ~** es ist wie zu Hause; **at ~** zu Hause; (Comm) im Inland; (Sport) auf eigenem Platz; **the next match will be at ~** das nächste Spiel ist ein Heimspiel; **Miss Hooper is not at ~ to anyone today** Frau Hooper or die gnädige Frau ist heute für niemanden zu Hause or zu sprechen; **Lady X will be at ~ on Friday** (form) Lady X gibt sich die Ehre, Sie für Freitag einzuladen (form); **to be or feel at ~ with sb** sich in jds Gegenwart (dat) wohl fühlen; **he doesn't feel at ~ in English** er fühlt sich im Englischen nicht sicher or zu Hause; **he is at ~ on anything to do with economics** er kennt sich bei allem aus, was mit Volkswirtschaft zu tun hat; **I don't feel at ~ with this new theory yet** ich komme mit dieser neuen Theorie noch nicht ganz zurecht; **to make oneself at ~** sich (dat) gemütlich or bequem machen; **to make sb feel at ~** es jdm gemütlich machen; **to leave ~** von zu Hause weggehen; **Scotland is the ~ of the haggis** Schottland ist die Heimat der Haggis, die Haggis sind in Schottland zu Hause; **there's no place like ~** (Prov) daheim ist daheim (prov), eigner Herd ist Goldes wert (Prov); **~ sweet ~** (Prov) trautes Heim, Glück allein (Prov).

(b) (institution) Heim nt; (for orphans also) Waisenhaus nt; (for blind also) Anstalt f; see **nursing ~**.

(c) (Zool, Bot) Heimat f.

(d) (Sport: base) Mal nt; (Racing) Ziel nt.

2 adv **(a)** (position) zu Hause, daheim; (with verb of motion) nach Hause, heim. **to go ~** (to house) nach Hause gehen/fahren, heimgehen/heimfahren; (to country) heimfahren; **I'll be ~ at 5 o'clock** ich bin um 5 Uhr zu Hause or daheim; **on the way ~** auf dem Heim- or Nachhauseweg; **the first runner ~ will .../was** Fred wer als erster durchs Ziel geht .../Fred ging als erster durchs Ziel; **to get ~** nach Hause kommen, heimkommen; (in race) durchs Ziel gehen; **I have to get ~ before ten** ich muß vor zehn zu Hause or daheim sein; **to return ~ from abroad** aus dem Ausland zurückkommen.

(b) (to the mark) **to drive a nail ~** einen Nagel einschlagen; **to bring or get sth ~ to sb** jdm etw klarmachen or beibringen; **it got ~ to him that ...** es wurde ihm klar, daß ...; **his words went ~** seine Worte hatten ihren Effekt; **to strike ~** ins Schwarze treffen, sitzen (inf); see **drive ~, hammer ~, hit, press, push.**

3 vi (pigeons) heimkehren.

♦**home in** vi (missiles) sich ausrichten (on sth auf etw acc). **the missile will ~** ~ das Geschoß findet sein Ziel; **to ~ ~ on a target** ein Ziel finden or selbständig ansteuern; **he immediately ~d ~ on the essential point** er hat sofort den wichtigsten Punkt herausgegriffen.

home: ~ **address** n Heimatadresse or -anschrift f; (as opposed to business address) Privatanschrift f; ~**-baked** adj selbstgebacken; ~ **base** n (Baseball) Heimbase nt; ~**-brew** n selbstgebrautes Bier, Selbstgebraute(s) nt, Marke Eigenbau (hum); ~**-brewed** adj selbstgebraut; ~ **comforts** npl häuslicher Komfort; ~**-coming** n Heimkehr f; ~ **cooking** n häusliche Küche, Hausmannskost f; **H~ Counties** npl Grafschaften, die an London angrenzen; ~**-cured** adj selbstgebeizt; ~ **economics** n sing Hauswirtschaft(slehre) f; ~ **front** n **on the ~ front** (Mil, Pol) im eigenen Land; (in business contexts) im eigenen Betrieb; (in personal, family contexts) zu Hause; ~ **game** n (Sport) Heimspiel nt; ~ **ground** n (Sport) eigener Platz; **to be on ~ ground** (fig) sich auf vertrautem Terrain bewegen; ~**-grown** adj vegetables selbstgezogen; (not imported) einheimisch; **H~ Guard** n Bürgerwehr f; ~ **help** n (Haushalts)hilfe f; ~ **improvement** n Hausverbesserung f; ~**land** n Heimat(land nt) f, Vaterland nt; ~**less** adj heimatlos;

tramp, vagrant etc obdachlos; ~**lessness** n see adj Heimatlosigkeit f; Obdachlosigkeit f; ~ **life** n Familienleben nt; ~**like** adj heimelig, wie daheim; ~**-loving** adj häuslich.

homely ['həʊmlɪ] adj (+er) **(a)** food Hausmacher-, bürgerlich; person (home-loving) häuslich, hausbacken (pej); atmosphere heimelig, gemütlich, behaglich; style anspruchslos, hausbacken (pej); advice einfach. **(b)** (US: plain) person unscheinbar; face reizlos.

home: ~**-made** adj selbstgemacht; ~**maker** n (US) (housewife) Hausfrau, Hausmutter f; (social worker) Familienfürsorger(in f) m; ~ **market** n Inlandsmarkt m, inländischer Markt; ~ **match** n (Sport) Heimspiel nt; ~ **news** n Meldungen pl aus dem Inland; **H~ Office** n (Brit) Innenministerium nt; (with relation to aliens) Einwanderungsbehörde f.

homeopath etc (US) see **homoeopath** etc.

home: ~ **plate** n (Baseball) Ausgangsbase nt; ~ **port** n Heimathafen m.

Homer ['həʊmə'] n Homer m.

Homeric [həʊ'merɪk] adj homerisch.

home: **H~ Rule** n Selbstbestimmung, Selbstverwaltung f; (in British contexts also) Homerule f; ~ **run** n (Baseball) Lauf m um alle vier Male; **H~ Secretary** n (Brit) Innenminister m; ~**sick** adj heimwehkrank; **to be ~sick** Heimweh haben (for nach); ~**sickness** n Heimweh nt (for nach); ~ **side** n (Sport) Gastgeber pl, Heimmannschaft f; ~**spun 1** adj **(a)** cloth selbst- or handgesponnen; (fig: simple) einfach; (pej) hausbacken; ~**spun remedies** Hausmittel pl; ~**spun philosophies** Lebensweisheiten pl; ~**spun advice** altbewährter Rat; **2** n (cloth) Homespun nt (grober, genoppter Wollstoff); ~**stead** n **(a)** Heimstätte f; **(b)** (US) Heimstätte f für Siedler; ~**steader** n **(a)** Heimstättenbesitzer m; **(b)** (US) Heimstättensiedler m; ~ **straight, ~ stretch** n (Sport) Zielgerade f; **we're on the ~ straight now** (fig inf) das Ende ist in Sicht; ~ **team** n (Sport) Gastgeber pl, Heimmannschaft f, Platzherren pl (inf); ~ **town** n Heimatort m, Vaterstadt f; ~ **truth** n bittere Wahrheit; **to tell sb some ~ truths** jdm den Star stechen (inf).

homeward ['həʊmwəd] adj journey, flight Heim-. **in a ~ direction** heim(wärts); (to country also) in Richtung Heimat; **we are ~-bound** es geht Richtung Heimat.

homeward(s) ['həʊmwəd(z)] adv nach Hause, heim; to country also) in Richtung Heimat.

home: ~ **waters** npl (Naut) heimatliche Gewässer pl; ~**work** n (Sch) Hausaufgaben, Schulaufgaben pl; **to give sb sth for ~work** jdm etw aufgeben; **what have you got for ~work?** was hast du auf?; **the minister had not done his ~work** (inf) der Minister hatte sich mit der Materie nicht vertraut gemacht.

homey ['həʊmɪ] adj (+er) (US inf) gemütlich; atmosphere also heimelig, behaglich; personality also warm.

homicidal [ˌhɒmɪ'saɪdl] adj gemeingefährlich; mood also Mord-. **in his ~ fury** in seinem Mordrausch.

homicide ['hɒmɪsaɪd] n **(a)** Totschlag m. culpable ~ Mord m; ~ **(squad)** Mordkommission f. **(b)** (person) Mörder(in f) m; Totschläger(in f) m.

homily ['hɒmɪlɪ] n Predigt f; (fig also) Sermon m (pej).

homing ['həʊmɪŋ] adj missile mit Zielsucheinrichtung. ~ **pigeon** Brieftaube f; ~ **instinct** Heimfindevermögen nt; ~ **device** Zielfluggerät nt, Zielsucheinrichtung f.

homo ['həʊməʊ] n (dated sl) Homo m (inf).

homoeopath, (US) **homeopath** ['həʊmɪəʊpæθ] n Homöopath m, Homöopathin f.

homoeopathic, (US) **homeopathic** [ˌhəʊmɪəʊ'pæθɪk] adj homöopathisch.

homoeopathy, (US) **homeopathy** [ˌhəʊmɪ'ɒpəθɪ] n Homöopathie f.

homogeneity [ˌhɒməʊdʒə'niːɪtɪ] n Homogenität f.

homogeneous [ˌhɒmə'dʒiːnɪəs] adj homogen.

homogenize [hə'mɒdʒənaɪz] vt milk homogenisieren.

homogenous [hə'mɒdʒɪnəs] adj homogen.

homograph ['hɒməʊgrɑːf] n Homograph nt.

homologous [hə'mɒləgəs] adj homolog.

homonym ['hɒmənɪm] n Homonym nt.

homonymous [hə'mɒnɪməs] adj homonym.

homophone ['hɒməfəʊn] n Homophon nt.

Homo sapiens [ˌhəʊməʊ'sæpɪəns] n Homo sapiens m.

homosexual [ˌhɒməʊ'seksjʊəl] **1** adj homosexuell. **2** n Homosexuelle(r) mf.

homosexuality [ˌhɒməʊseksjʊ'ælɪtɪ] n Homosexualität f.

homunculus [hɒ'mʌŋkjʊləs] n Homunkulus m.

homy adj (+er) (US inf) see **homey.**

Hon abbr of **(a)** honorary. **(b)** Honourable.

Honduran [hɒn'djʊərən] **1** adj honduranisch. **2** n Honduraner(in f) m.

Honduras [hɒn'djʊərəs] npl Honduras nt.

hone [həʊn] **1** n Schleifstein, Wetzstein m. **2** vt blade schleifen; (fig) schärfen.

♦**hone down** vt sep (fig) (zurecht)feilen (to auf +acc).

honest ['ɒnɪst] **1** adj **(a)** ehrlich; (respectable) redlich; (not cheating) businessman redlich; business, action also anständig; truth rein. **be ~ with yourself** sei ehrlich gegen dich selbst, mach dir nichts vor (inf); **to be ~ with you, this is not good enough** um ehrlich zu sein, das ist nicht gut genug; **they are good ~ people** sie sind gute, rechtschaffene Leute; ~ **to goodness or God!** (inf); **he made an ~ woman of her** (inf) er machte sie zu seinem angetrauten Weibe (hum).

(b) money, profit ehrlich or redlich erworben. **to earn an ~ penny** sein Geld ehrlich or redlich verdienen; **after an ~ day's work** nach einem ordentlichen Tagewerk; **he's never done an ~ day's work in his life** er ist in seinem ganzen Leben noch keiner ordentlichen Arbeit nachgegangen.

2 adv (inf) ehrlich (inf), Ehrenwort (inf).

honestly ['ɒnɪstlɪ] adv **(a)** answer ehrlich, aufrichtig; earn *money* ehrlich, auf ehrliche Weise. **(b)** *(inf: really)* ehrlich *(inf)*; *(in exasperation)* also ehrlich. ~, **I don't care** das ist mir ehrlich *(inf) or* wirklich ganz egal; ~, **it's terrible** das ist wirklich furchtbar.

honest-to-goodness [ˈɒnɪstəˈgʊdnɪs] *adj (inf: genuine)* echt; *person, expression* waschecht.

honesty [ˈɒnɪstɪ] *n* **(a)** *see adj* Ehrlichkeit *f;* Redlichkeit *f;* Anständigkeit *f.* **in all** ~ ganz ehrlich; **one must admit, in all** ~, **...** man muß ehrlicherweise zugeben, ...; ~ **is the best policy** *(Prov)* ehrlich währt am längsten *(Prov)*.
(b) *(Bot)* Mondviole *f,* Silberblatt *nt,* Judassilberling *m (inf)*.

honey [ˈhʌnɪ] *n* **(a)** Honig *m.* **(b)** *(inf: dear)* Schätzchen *nt.* **his little daughter is an absolute** ~ seine kleine Tochter ist einfach süß *(inf) or* ist ein süßer Spatz *(inf)*; **she's a** ~ sie ist ein (Gold)schatz *(inf)*.
honey: ~-**bee** *n* (Honig)biene *f;* ~**bunch** *n (inf)* Schätzchen *nt;* ~**comb** 1 *n* (Bienen)wabe *f;* *(filled with honey also)* Honigwabe *f.* 2 *vt usu pass* durchlöchern; **the mountain was** ~**combed with caves** der Berg war von Höhlen durchsetzt; ~**dew** *n* Honigtau *m;* ~**dew melon** Honigmelone *f.*
honeyed [ˈhʌnɪd] *adj words* honigsüß.
honeymoon [ˈhʌnɪmuːn] 1 *n* Flitterwochen *pl; (trip)* Hochzeitsreise *f.* **to be on one's** ~ in den Flitterwochen/auf Hochzeitsreise sein; **where did you go for your** ~? wo habt ihr eure Flitterwochen verbracht?; **wohin habt ihr eure Hochzeitsreise gemacht?; six months in the jungle was no** ~ sechs Monate im Dschungel war kein Zuckerlecken; **the** ~ **is over** *(fig inf)* jetzt werden andere Saiten aufgezogen *(inf)*, **die Schonzeit ist vorbei;** ~ **couple** Flitterwöchner *pl.*
2 *vi* seine Hochzeitsreise machen. **they are** ~**ing in Spain** sie sind in Spanien auf Hochzeitsreise.
honey: ~**mooner** [ˈhʌnɪˌmuːnəʳ] *n* Hochzeitsreisende(r) *mf; (man also)* Flitterwöchner *m (hum);* ~**suckle** *n* Geißblatt *nt.*
honk [hɒŋk] 1 *n (of car)* Hupen *nt; (of goose etc)* Schrei *m.* 2 *interj* ~ ~ tut-tut, tüt, tüt. 3 *vi* **(a)** *(car)* hupen, tuten. **(b)** *(geese)* schreien. 4 *vt* **horn** drücken auf (+*acc*).
honky [ˈhɒŋkɪ] *n (negro pej sl)* Weiße(r) *mf.*
honky-tonk [ˌhɒŋkɪˈtɒŋk] 1 *n (US sl: night-club)* Schuppen *m (sl).* 2 *adj music, piano* schräg.
Honolulu [ˌhɒnəˈluːluː] *n* Honolulu *nt.*
honor *etc (US) see* **honour** *etc.*
honorarium [ˌɒnəˈrɛərɪəm] *n, pl* **honoraria** [ˌɒnəˈrɛərɪə] Honorar *nt.*
honorary [ˈɒnərərɪ] *adj secretary* ehrenamtlich; *member, president* Ehren-. ~ **degree** *ehrenhalber verliehener akademischer Grad;* ~ **doctor** Ehrendoktor, Doktor h.c.
honour, *(US)* **honor** [ˈɒnəʳ] 1 *n* **(a)** Ehre *f.* **sense of** ~ Ehrgefühl *nt;* **he made it a point of** ~ er betrachtete es als Ehrensache; **he decided to make it a point of** ~ **never to ...** er schwor sich *(dat)*, nie zu ...; **there is** ~ **among thieves** es gibt so etwas wie Ganovenehre; ~ **where** ~ **is due** Ehre, wem Ehre gebührt; **on my** ~! *(old)* bei meiner Ehre *(old)*; **I promise on my** ~ ich gebe mein Ehrenwort; **you're on your** ~ Sie haben Ihr Ehrenwort gegeben; **to put sb on his** ~ jdm vertrauen; **he's put me on my** ~ **not to tell** ich habe ihm mein Ehrenwort gegeben, daß ich nichts sage; **man of** ~ Ehrenmann *m;* **to lose one's** ~ *(old)* seine Ehre verlieren *(old)*; **to do** ~ **to sb** *(at funeral)* jdm die letzte Ehre erweisen; *(action, thought etc)* jdm zur Ehre gereichen; **to do** ~ **to sth, to be an** ~ **to sth** eine Ehre für etw sein, einer Sache *(dat)* Ehre machen; **in** ~ **of sb/sth** zu jds Ehren, zu Ehren von jdm/etw; *(of dead person, past thing)* in ehrendem Andenken an jdn/etw; **may I have the** ~ **of accompanying you?** *(form)* ich bitte um die Ehre, Sie begleiten zu dürfen *(geh)*; **may I have the** ~ **(of the next dance)?** *(form)* darf ich (um den nächsten Tanz) bitten?; **if you would do me the** ~ **of accepting** *(form)* wenn Sie mir die Ehre erweisen würden anzunehmen *(geh)*; **to whom do I have the** ~ **of speaking?** *(form, hum)* mit wem habe ich die Ehre? *(geh, hum)*; **he is** ~ **bound to do** it es ist Ehrensache für ihn, das zu tun; **if you've promised, then you're** ~ **bound to ...** wenn du es versprochen hast, bist du auch (moralisch) verpflichtet, zu ...
(b) *(title)* **Your H**~ Hohes Gericht; **His H**~ das Gericht; **the case was up before His H**~ **Sir Charles** der Fall wurde unter dem Vorsitz des vorsitzenden Richters Sir Charles verhandelt.
(c) *(distinction, award)* ~**s** Ehren *pl,* Auszeichnung(en *pl*) *f;* **with full military** ~**s** mit militärischen Ehren; **New Year's H**~ Titelverleihung *f* am Neujahrstag.
(d) **to do the** ~**s** *(inf)* die Honneurs machen; *(on private occasions also)* den Gastgeber spielen.
(e) *(Univ)* ~**s** *(also* ~**s degree)* akademischer Grad mit Prüfung im Spezialfach; **to do/take** ~**s in English** Englisch belegen, um den „Honours Degree" zu erwerben; **to get first-class** ~**s** das Examen mit Auszeichnung *or* „sehr gut" bestehen.
(f) *(Golf)* **it's his** ~ er hat die Ehre.
(g) *(Cards)* eine der *(in bridge)* 5 *or (in whist)* 4 höchsten Trumpfkarten.
2 *vt* **(a)** *person* ehren. **to** ~ **sb with a title** jdm einen Titel verleihen; **I should be** ~**ed if you ...** ich würde mich geehrt fühlen, wenn Sie ...; **I am deeply** ~**ed** ich fühle mich zutiefst geehrt; **he** ~**ed me with his confidence** er zeichnete mich mit seinem Vertrauen aus; **we are** ~**ed by your visit** *(also iro)* wir fühlen uns durch Ihren Besuch geehrt; **he** ~**ed us with his presence** *(also iro)* er beehrte uns mit seiner Gegenwart; **it's Angelika, we are** ~**ed** *(iro)* es ist Angelika, welche Ehre.
(b) *cheque* annehmen, einlösen; *debt* begleichen; *bill of exchange* respektieren; *obligation* nachkommen (+*dat*); *commitment* stehen zu; *credit card* anerkennen.
honourable, *(US)* **honorable** [ˈɒnərəbl] *adj* **(a)** ehrenhaft; *person also* ehrenwert *(geh)*; *peace, discharge* ehrenvoll. **to receive** ~ **mention** rühmend *or* lobend erwähnt werden.
(b) *(Parl)* Anrede *f* von Abgeordneten innerhalb des Parla-

ments. the H~ **member for X** der (Herr) Abgeordnete für X; **the H**~ **member is wrong** der geschätzte *or* ehrenwerte *(iro)* (Herr) Kollege täuscht sich.
(c) *(title)* Titel *m* der jüngeren Söhne von Grafen und der Kinder von Freiherren und Baronen. **I didn't know he was an H**~ ich wußte nicht, daß er adelig *or* ein „von" *(inf)* ist; *see* **right.**
honourably, *(US)* **honorably** [ˈɒnərəblɪ] *adv* in Ehren; *behave* ehrenhaft, wie ein Ehrenmann; *settle* peace ehrenvoll; *mention* rühmend, lobend.
honours [ˈɒnəz-]: ~ **board** *n* Ehrentafel *f;* ~ **degree** *n see* honour 1 (e); ~ **list** *n* Liste *f* der Titel- und Rangverleihungen *(, die zweimal im Jahr veröffentlicht wird);* *(Univ)* Liste der Kandidaten, die den „Honours Degree" verliehen bekommen.
hooch [huːtʃ] *n (US sl)* Getränke *pl,* Stoff *m (sl).*
hood [hʊd] 1 *n* **(a)** Kapuze *f; (thief's)* Maske *f; (hawk's)* Kappe *f.* **(b)** *(Aut: roof)* Verdeck *nt; (US Aut)* (Motor)haube *f; (on fireplace etc)* Abzug *m; (on cooker)* Abzugshaube *f.* **(c)** *(of cobra)* Brillenzeichnung *f.* **(d)** *(esp US sl)* Gangster *(inf),* Ganove *(inf) m; (young ruffian)* Rowdy, Rüpel *m.*
2 *vt* eine Kapuze aufsetzen (+*dat*); *hawk* eine Kappe aufsetzen (+*dat*).
hooded [ˈhʊdɪd] *adj* **the** ~ **executioner/monk/robber** der Scharfrichter/Mönch mit seiner Kapuze/der maskierte Räuber; **their** ~ **heads** ihre Köpfe mit den Kapuzen; ~ **crow** Nebelkrähe *f;* ~ **eyes** Augen mit schweren Lidern.
hoodlum [ˈhuːdləm] *n* Rowdy *m; (member of gang)* Ganove *(inf),* Gangster *(inf) m.* **you young** ~ du Rowdy, du Rüpel.
hoodoo [ˈhuːduː] *n* Unglück *nt; (person, thing)* Unglücksbote *m.*
hoodwink [ˈhʊdwɪŋk] *vt (inf)* (he)reinlegen *(inf).* **to** ~ **sb into doing sth** jdn dazu verleiten, etw zu tun; **they** ~**ed him into signing the contract** er ließ sich von ihnen (dazu) verleiten, den Vertrag zu unterschreiben; **I was** ~**ed into buying an imitation** man hat mir eine Imitation angedreht *(inf).*
hooey [ˈhuːɪ] *n (US sl)* Gelabere *nt (sl),* Quatsch *m (inf).*
hoof [huːf] 1 *n, pl* ~**s** *or* **hooves** Huf *m.* **hooves** *(hum inf: feet)* Quadratlatschen *pl (sl);* **cattle on the** ~ Vieh *nt.* 2 *vi:* **to** ~ **it** *(inf) (go on foot)* latschen *(inf);* *(dance on stage)* tingeln *(inf).*
hoofbeat [ˈhuːfbiːt] *n* Hufschlag *m.*
hoofed [huːft] *adj* Huf-.
hook [hʊk] 1 *n* **(a)** Haken *m.*
(b) *(Boxing)* Haken *m; (Golf)* Kurvball *m (nach links).*
(c) *(Geog)* (gekrümmte) Landzunge.
(d) *(fig uses)* **he swallowed the story** ~, **line and sinker** er hat die Geschichte tatsächlich mit Stumpf und Stiel geschluckt *(inf);* **he fell for it/her** ~, **line and sinker** er ging dem auf den Leim/er war ihr mit Haut und Haaren verfallen; **by** ~ **or by crook** auf Biegen und Brechen; **to get sb off the** ~ *(inf)* jdn herausreißen *(inf); (out of trouble also)* jdn herauspauken *(inf);* **that gets him off the** ~ **every time** damit kommt er jedesmal wieder davon; **to get oneself off the** ~ sich aus der Schlinge ziehen; **that lets me off the** ~ *(inf)* damit bin ich aus dem Schneider *(inf);* **to leave the phone off the** ~ nicht auflegen.
2 *vt* **(a)** *(fasten with* ~*)* **he** ~**ed the door back/open** er hakte die Tür fest/er öffnete die Tür und hakte sie fest; **the old man** ~**s the rowing boats and pulls them in** der alte Mann zieht die Ruderboote mit einem Haken ans Ufer; **to** ~ **a trailer to a car** einen Anhänger an ein Auto hängen; **the bull had** ~**ed him on his horns** der Stier hatte ihn auf die Hörner genommen.
(b) **to** ~ **one's arm/feet around sth** seinen Arm/seine Füße um etw schlingen; **the trapeze artist** ~**s his legs over the bar** der Trapezkünstler hängt sich mit den Beinen an der Stange ein; **his car got its bumper** ~**ed around mine** sein Auto hat sich mit der Stoßstange in meiner verhakt.
(c) *(fish)* an die Angel bekommen; *husband* sich (*dat*) angeln. **to be** ~**ed** an der Angel hängen; **the helicopter** ~**ed him clean out of the water** der Hubschrauber zog *or* angelte *(inf)* ihn aus dem Wasser.
(d) *(Boxing)* einen Haken versetzen (+*dat*) *or* geben (+*dat*).
(e) **to be/get** ~**ed on sth** *(sl: addicted)* *(on drugs)* von etw abhängig sein/werden; *(on film, food, place etc)* auf etw *(acc)* stehen *(sl);* **he's** ~**ed on the idea** er ist von der Idee besessen; **don't get** ~**ed on the idea** versteif dich nicht zu sehr auf den Gedanken.
(f) *(Rugby)* hakeln.
(g) *(Sport)* *ball* einen Linksdrall geben (+*dat*).
(h) *(sl: clear off)* **to** ~ **it** Mücke machen *(sl).*
3 *vi (dress etc)* zugehakt werden.
♦ **hook on** 1 *vi* (an)gehakt werden *(to an* +*acc); (with tow-bar)* angekoppelt *or* angehängt werden *(to an* +*acc); (burrs etc)* sich festhaken *(to an* +*dat).* **this piece** ~**s** ~ **to this one** dieses Teil wird an das andere (an)gehakt; *(to make a solid object)* dieses Teil wird in das andere (ein)gehakt; **he** ~**ed** ~ **to him** *(fig)* er hängte *or* klammerte sich an ihn.
2 *vt sep* anhaken *(to an* +*acc),* mit Haken/einem Haken befestigen *(to an* +*dat); (with tow-bar)* ankoppeln, anhängen. **to** ~ **sth** ~ **to sth** etw an etw *(acc)* (an)haken; **the gliders were** ~**ed behind the tow-plane** die Segelflugzeuge waren hinten an das Schleppflugzeug angehängt *or* angekoppelt.
♦ **hook up** 1 *vi (dress)* Haken zugemacht werden.
(b) *(Rad, TV)* gemeinsam ausstrahlen. **to** ~ ~ **with sb** sich jdm anschließen.
2 *vt sep* **(a)** *dress etc* zuhaken. ~ **me** *or* **the dress** ~, **please** mach mir bitte die Haken zu, mach an dem Kleid bitte die Haken zu.
(b) *(Rad, TV)* anschließen *(with an* +*acc).*
(c) *trailer, caravan* ankoppeln, anhängen; *broken-down car* abschleppen; *(by recovery vehicle)* auf den Haken nehmen.
hookah [ˈhʊkɑ:] *n* Wasserpfeife, Huka *f.*
hook and eye *n* Haken und Öse *no art, pl vb.*

hooked [hʊkt] *adj* **(a)** *beak* Haken-, gebogen. ~ nose Haken-nase *f.* **(b)** (*equipped with hooks*) mit Haken versehen. these insects have ~ legs diese Insekten haben Beine mit Wider-haken *or* haben Widerhaken an den Beinen.

hooker[1] ['hʊkə[r]] *n* (*US inf*) Nutte *f* (*inf*).

hooker[2] *n* (*Rugby*) Hakler *m.*

hook: ~-nosed *adj* mit einer Hakennase, hakennasig; ~-up *n* (*Rad, TV*) gemeinsame Ausstrahlung; there will be a ~-up be-tween the major European networks die größeren europä-ischen Sender übertragen gemeinsam; ~worm *n* Hakenwurm *m*; (*disease*) Hakenwurmkrankheit *f.*

hooky ['hʊkɪ] *n* (*US inf*) Schuleschwänzen *nt* (*inf*). to play ~ (die) Schule schwänzen (*inf*).

hooligan ['huːlɪgən] *n* Rowdy *m.*

hooliganism ['huːlɪgənɪzəm] *n* Rowdytum *nt.*

hoop [huːp] **1** *n* Reifen *m*; (*in croquet*) Tor *nt*; (*on bird's plumage*) Kranz *m*; (*on animal*) Ring *m.* to go through the ~s (*fig inf*) durch die Mangel gedreht werden (*inf*); to put sb through the ~s (*fig inf*) jdn durch die Mangel drehen (*inf*).
2 *vt barrel* bereifen. ~(ed) *skirt* Reifrock *m.*

hoop-la ['huːplɑː] *n* Ringwerfen *nt.*

hoopoe ['huːpuː] *n* Wiedehopf *m.*

hooray [hʊ'reɪ] *interj see* **hurrah.**

hoosegow ['huːsgaʊ] *n* (*US sl: jail*) Knast *m* (*sl*).

hoot [huːt] **1** *n* **(a)** (*of owl*) Ruf, Schrei *m.* ~s of derision ver-ächtliches Gejohle; ~s of laughter johlendes Gelächter; I don't care a ~ *or* two ~s (*inf*) das ist mir piepegal (*inf*) *or* völlig schnuppe (*inf*); to be a ~ (*inf*) (*person, event etc*) zum Schreien (komisch) sein, zum Schießen sein (*inf*).
(b) (*Aut*) Hupen *nt no pl*; (*of train, hooter*) Pfeifen *nt no pl.*
2 *vi* **(a)** (*owl*) schreien, rufen; (*person: derisively*) johlen, buhen. to ~ with derision verächtlich johlen; to ~ with laughter in johlendes Gelächter ausbrechen.
(b) (*Aut*) hupen; (*train, factory hooter*) pfeifen.
3 *vt actor, speaker* auspfeifen, ausbuhen. he was ~ed off the stage er wurde mit Buhrufen von der Bühne verjagt.
♦ **hoot down** *vt sep* niederschreien.

hootchy-kootchy ['huːtʃɪ'kuːtʃɪ] *n* (*US sl*) Bauchtanz *m.*

hootenanny ['huːtənænɪ] *n* Hootenanny *f.*

hooter ['huːtə[r]] *n* **(a)** (*Aut*) Hupe *f*; (*at factory*) Sirene *f.* **(b)** (*Brit sl: nose*) Zinken *m* (*sl*).

hoover ® ['huːvə[r]] **1** *n* Staubsauger *m.* **2** *vt* (staub)saugen; *carpet also* (staub)saugen. **3** *vi* (staub)saugen.

hooves [huːvz] *pl of* **hoof.**

hop[1] [hɒp] **1** *n* **(a)** (*kleiner*) Sprung; (*of bird, insect also*) Hüpfer *m*; (*of deer, rabbit also*) Satz *m*; (*of person also*) Hüpfer, Hopser (*inf*) *m.* to catch sb on the ~ (*fig inf*) jdn überraschen *or* überrumpeln; to keep sb on the ~ (*fig inf*) jdn in Trab halten.
(b) (*inf: dance*) Tanz *m*, Hopserei *f* (*pej inf*).
(c) (*Aviat inf*) Sprung, Satz (*inf*) *m.* a short ~ ein kleiner Satz (*inf*), ein Katzensprung *m* (*inf*).
2 *vi* **(a)** (*animal*) hüpfen, springen; (*rabbit*) hoppeln; (*person*) (auf einem Bein) hüpfen, hopsen (*inf*). ~ in, said the driver steigen Sie ein, sagte der Fahrer; she'd ~ into bed with anyone die steigt mit jedem ins Bett (*inf*); to ~ off aussteigen (*from moving vehicle*) abspringen; to ~ off the train aus dem Zug aussteigen; (*while moving*) vom Zug abspringen; he ~ped off his bicycle er sprang vom Fahrrad; to ~ on aufsteigen; (*onto moving vehicle*) aufspringen; to ~ on a train in einen Zug ein-steigen; (*while moving*) auf einen Zug aufspringen; he ~ped on his bicycle er schwang sich auf sein Fahrrad; to ~ out heraushüpfen; he ~ped over the wall er sprang über die Mauer.
(b) (*inf*) ~ it! verschwinde, zieh Leine (*inf*); I ~ped it quick ich habe mich schnell aus dem Staub gemacht (*inf*).
3 *vt ditch* springen über (+*acc*); *train* schwarzfahren in (+*dat*) *or* mit.
♦ **hop off** *vi* (*inf*) sich verdrücken (*inf*), sich aus dem Staub machen (*inf*) (*with sth* mit etw).

hop[2] *n* (*Bot*) Hopfen *m.* ~ picker Hopfenpflücker(in *f*) *m*; ~ picking Hopfenernte *f*, Hopfenpflücken *nt*; ~-picking season Hopfenernte *f*; ~ garden Hopfengarten *m.*

hope [həʊp] **1** *n* (*also person*) Hoffnung *f.* past *or* beyond all ~ hoffnungslos, aussichtslos; the patient is beyond all ~ für den Patienten besteht keine Hoffnung mehr; to be full of ~ hoff-nungsvoll *or* voller Hoffnung sein; my ~ is that ... ich hoffe nur, daß ...; in the ~ of doing sth in der Hoffnung, etw zu tun; to have ~s of doing sth hoffen, etw zu tun; to live in ~ of sth in der Hoffnung auf etw (*acc*) leben; well, we live in ~ nun, wir hoffen eben (weiter); to place one's ~ in sb/sth seine Hoff-nungen in *or* auf jdn/etw setzen; there is no ~ of him having survived es besteht keine Hoffnung, daß er überlebt hat; we have some ~ of success es besteht die Hoffnung, daß wir Erfolg haben; there's no ~ of that da braucht man sich gar keine Hoffnungen zu machen; where there's life there's ~ es ist noch nicht aller Tage Abend; (*said of invalid*) solange er/sie sich noch regt, besteht auch noch Hoffnung; to lose ~ of doing sth die Hoffnung aufgeben, etw zu tun; what a ~! (*inf*), some ~(s)! (*inf*) schön wär's! (*inf*); ~ springs eternal (*prov*) wenn die Hoffnung nicht wäre!
2 *vi* hoffen (*for* auf +*acc*). to ~ for the best das Beste hoffen; you can't ~ for anything else from him man kann sich doch von ihm nichts anderes erhoffen; one might have ~d for something better man hätte (eigentlich) auf etwas Besseres hoffen dürfen, man hätte sich eigentlich Besseres erhoffen dürfen; I ~ so/not hoffentlich/hoffentlich nicht, ich hoffe es/(es) nicht; to ~ against ~ that ... trotz allem die Hoffnung nicht aufgeben, daß ..., wider alle Hoffnung hoffen, daß ...
3 *vt* hoffen. we ~ to go to Spain wir hoffen, nach Spanien fahren zu können; I ~ to see you hoffentlich sehe ich Sie, ich hoffe, daß ich Sie sehe; hoping to hear from you (*inf*), von

Ihnen zu hören, in der Hoffnung (*form*), von Ihnen zu hören.

hope chest *n* (*US*) Aussteuertruhe *f.*

hopeful ['həʊpfʊl] **1** *adj* **(a)** hoffnungsvoll. don't be too ~ machen Sie sich (*dat*) keine zu großen Hoffnungen; they weren't very ~ sie hatten keine große Hoffnung; they continue to be ~ sie hoffen weiter, sie geben die Hoffnung nicht auf; to be ~ that ... hoffen, daß ...; I'm ~ of a recovery ich hoffe auf Besserung; you think they'll agree? boy, you're ~ du glaubst, sie sind einverstanden? du bist vielleicht ein Optimist (*inf*).
(b) *situation, response, sign* vielversprechend, aussichts-reich. it looks ~ es sieht vielversprechend aus.
2 *n* (*inf*) a young ~ (*seems likely to succeed*) eine junge Hoff-nung; (*hopes to succeed*) ein hoffnungsvoller junger Mensch.

hopefully ['həʊpfəlɪ] *adv* **(a)** hoffnungsvoll. **(b)** hoffentlich. ~ it won't rain hoffentlich regnet es nicht.

hopeless ['həʊplɪs] *adj* **(a)** *person* hoffnungslos. **(b)** *situation, outlook* aussichtslos, hoffnungslos; *liar, weather, food* unmöglich (*inf*). you're ~ du bist ein hoffnungsloser Fall; he's ~ at maths/a ~ teacher in Mathematik/als Lehrer ist er ein hoffnungsloser Fall.

hopelessly ['həʊplɪslɪ] *adv* hoffnungslos. we were ~ lost wir hatten uns hoffnungslos verirrt; I'm ~ bad at maths in Mathematik bin ich ein hoffnungsloser Fall.

hopelessness ['həʊplɪsnɪs] *n* (*of situation*) Hoffnungslosigkeit *f*; (*of task*) Aussichtslosigkeit *f.*

hoplite ['hɒplaɪt] *n* Hoplit *m.*

hop-o'-my-thumb [ˌhɒpəmaɪ'θʌm] *n* Knirps, Stöpsel (*inf*) *m.*

hopper ['hɒpə[r]] *n* **(a)** (*Tech*) Einfülltrichter *m*; (*for coal also*) Speisetrichter *m.* **(b)** (*young locust*) junge Heuschrecke.

hopping mad ['hɒpɪŋ'mæd] *adj* (*inf*) fuchsteufelswild (*inf*).

hop: ~scotch *n* Himmel-und-Hölle(-Spiel) *nt*, Hopse *f* (*inf*); ~, step *or* skip and jump *n* Dreisprung *m.*

Horace ['hɒrɪs] *n* Horaz *m.*

Horatian [hɒ'reɪʃən] *adj* horazisch.

horde [hɔːd] *n* **(a)** (*of nomads, wild animals*) Horde *f*; (*of insects*) Schwarm *m.* **(b)** (*inf*) Masse *f*; (*of football fans, chil-dren etc*) Horde *f* (*pej*). ~s of books massenhaft Bücher (*inf*).

horizon [hɒ'raɪzn] *n* Horizont *m*; (*fig*) Horizont, Gesichtskreis *m no pl.* on the ~ am Horizont; the ship went over *or* beneath the ~ das Schiff verschwand am Horizont.

horizontal [ˌhɒrɪ'zɒntl] *adj* waag(e)recht, horizontal. ~ line Waag(e)rechte, Horizontale *f.*

horizontal: ~ bar *n* Reck *nt*; ~ hold *n* (*TV*) Zeilenfang, Bild-fang *m.*

horizontally [ˌhɒrɪ'zɒntəlɪ] *adv see adj.*

hormonal [hɔː'məʊnəl] *adj* hormonal, hormonell.

hormone [ˈhɔːməʊn] *n* Hormon *nt.*

horn [hɔːn] **1** *n* **(a)** (*of cattle, substance, container, Mus*) Horn *nt*; (*sl: trumpet, saxophone etc*) Kanne (*sl*), Tüte (*sl*) *f.* ~s *pl* (*of deer*) Geweih *nt*; (*fig: of cuckold*) Hörner *pl*; caught on the ~s of a dilemma in einer Zwickmühle; that is the other ~ of the dilemma das ist die andere Gefahr; ~ of plenty Füllhorn *nt*; to lock ~s (*lit*) beim Kampf die Geweihe verhaken; (*fig*) die Klingen kreuzen.
(b) (*Aut*) Hupe *f*; (*Naut*) (Signal)horn *nt.* to sound *or* blow the ~ (*Aut*) hupen, auf die Hupe drücken (*inf*); (*Naut*) tuten, das Horn ertönen lassen.
(c) (*of snail, insect*) Fühler *m.* to draw in one's ~s (*fig*) einen Rückzieher machen; (*spend less*) den Gürtel enger schnallen.
(d) (*of crescent moon*) Spitze *f* (der Mondsichel).
2 *vt* (*gore*) mit den Hörnern aufspießen; (*butt*) auf die Hörner nehmen.
♦ **horn in** *vi* (*sl*) (*interfere*) mitmischen (*on* bei); (*muscle in*) sich hineindrängen (*on* in +*acc*). dozens of entrepreneurs started ~ing ~ zig Unternehmer versuchten, auch ein Stück vom Kuchen zu bekommen (*inf*).

horn *in cpds* Horn-; ~beam *n* (*Bot*) Hain- *or* Weißbuche *f*; ~bill *n* (*Orn*) (Nas)hornvogel *m.*

horned [hɔːnd] *adj* gehörnt, mit Hörnern. ~ owl Ohreule *f*; ~ toad Krötenechse *f.*

hornet ['hɔːnɪt] *n* Hornisse *f.* to stir up a ~'s nest (*fig*) in ein Wespennest stechen.

hornless ['hɔːnlɪs] *adj* ohne Hörner, hornlos.

horn: ~pipe *n* englischer Seemannstanz; ~-rimmed *adj* specta-cles Horn-.

horny ['hɔːnɪ] *adj* (+*er*) **(a)** (*like horn*) hornartig; *hands etc* schwielig; *soles* hornig. **(b)** (*inf: randy*) scharf (*inf*), geil (*inf*).

horology [hɒ'rɒlədʒɪ] *n* (*measuring time*) Zeitmessung *f*; (*watchmaking*) Uhrmacherkunst *f.*

horoscope ['hɒrəskəʊp] *n* Horoskop *nt.*

horrendous [hɒ'rendəs] *adj* *crime* abscheulich, entsetzlich; *prices, lie* horrend.

horrendously [hɒ'rendəslɪ] *adv* abscheulich, entsetzlich; *expensive* horrend.

horrible ['hɒrɪbl] *adj* fürchterlich, schrecklich. don't be ~ to your sister sei nicht so gemein zu deiner Schwester (*inf*).

horribly ['hɒrɪblɪ] *adv see adj.*

horrid ['hɒrɪd] *adj* entsetzlich, fürchterlich, schrecklich. don't be so ~ sei nicht so gemein (*inf*).

horridly ['hɒrɪdlɪ] *adv see adj.*

horrific [hɒ'rɪfɪk] *adj* entsetzlich, schrecklich; *documentary* erschreckend; *price increase also* horrend.

horrify ['hɒrɪfaɪ] *vt* entsetzen. he was horrified by *or* at the suggestion er war über den Vorschlag entsetzt; it horrifies me to think what ... ich denke nur mit Entsetzen daran, was ...; he likes to ~ people er schockiert gern.

horrifying *adj*, ~ly *adv* ['hɒrɪfaɪŋ, -lɪ] schrecklich, fürchter-lich, entsetzlich.

horror ['hɒrə[r]] **1** *n* **(a)** Entsetzen, Grauen *nt*; (*strong dislike*) Horror *m* (*of vor* +*dat*). to have a ~ of doing sth einen Horror davor haben, etw zu tun; he has a ~ of growing old er hat eine panische Angst vor dem Altwerden, ihm graut vor dem Altwerden; **she shrank back in ~** sie fuhr entsetzt zurück; **a scene of ~** ein Bild des Grauens.

  (b) *usu pl (horrifying thing; of war etc)* Schrecken, Greuel *m.*

  (c) *(inf)* **to be a real ~** furchtbar sein *(inf);* **you little ~!** du kleines Ungeheuer! *(inf).*

  (d) *(inf usages)* **to have the ~s** *(in delirium tremens)* weiße Mäuse sehen *(inf);* **that gives me the ~s** da läuft's mir kalt den Rücken runter *(inf).*

  2 *attr books, comics, films* Horror-.

horror-stricken ['hɒrəstrɪkn], **horror-struck** ['hɒrəstrʌk] *adj* von Entsetzen or Grauen gepackt. **I was ~ when he told me** mir grauste es or ich war hell entsetzt, als er es mir erzählte.

hors de combat ['ɔːdə'kɒmbaː] *adj (lit, fig)* außer Gefecht gesetzt, kampfunfähig.

hors d'oeuvre [ɔː'dɜːv] *n* Hors d'oeuvre *nt,* Vorspeise *f.*

horse [hɔːs] *n* **(a)** Pferd, Roß *(liter, pej) nt.*

  (b) *(fig usages)* **wild ~s would not drag me there** keine zehn Pferde würden mich dahin bringen; **to eat like a ~** wie ein Scheunendrescher *m* essen or fressen *(inf);* **I could eat a ~** ich könnte ein ganzes Pferd essen; **to work like a ~** wie ein Pferd arbeiten; **straight from the ~'s mouth** aus berufenem Mund; **to back the wrong ~** aufs falsche Pferd setzen; **but that's a ~ of a different colour** aber das ist wieder was anderes.

  (c) *(Gymnastics)* Pferd *nt;* *(saw~)* Sägebock *m.*

  (d) *(Mil)* collective sing Reiterei, Kavallerie *f.* **light ~** leichte Kavallerie; **a thousand ~** tausend Reiter or Berittene.

♦ **horse about** or **around** *vi (inf)* herumblödeln *(inf),* herumalbern *(inf).*

horse: **~-artillery** *n* berittene Artillerie; **~back: on ~back** *adv* zu Pferd, zu Roß *(liter);* **to go/set off on ~back** reiten/wegreiten; **~-box** *n (van)* Pferdetransporter *m;* *(trailer)* Pferdetransportwagen *m;* *(in stable)* Box *f;* **~ brass** *n* Zaumzeugbeschlag *m;* **~-chestnut** *n (tree, fruit)* Roßkastanie *f;* **~-doctor** *n (inf)* Viehdoktor *m (inf);* **~-drawn** *adj* von Pferden gezogen; *hearse, milk-cart* pferdebespannt *attr;* **~-drawn cart** Pferdewagen *m;* **~-flesh** *n (meat of horse)* Pferdefleisch *nt;* *(horses collectively)* Pferde *pl;* **a good judge of ~flesh** ein guter Pferdekenner; **~-fly** *n (Pferde)*bremse *f;* **H~ Guards** *npl* berittene Garde, Gardekavallerie *f;* **~-hair** 1 *n* Roßhaar *nt;* 2 *adj attr* Roßhaar-; **~ latitudes** *npl* Roßbreiten *pl;* **~-laugh** *n* wieherndes Lachen or Gelächter; **~-less** *adj* ohne Pferd; **~less carriage** *n (old: motorcar)* selbstfahrender Wagen; **~-man** *n* Reiter *m;* **~manship** *n* Reitkunst *f;* **~-meat** *n* Pferdefleisch *nt;* **~-opera** *n (hum inf: Film)* Western *m;* **~-play** *n* Albernei, Balgerei *f;* **to have a bit of ~play with sb** mit jdm herumbalgen; **~-power** *n* Pferdestärke *f;* **a twenty ~power car** ein Auto mit zwanzig PS or Pferdestärken; **~-race** *n* Pferderennen *nt;* **~-racing** *n* Pferderennsport *m;* *(races)* Pferderennen *pl;* **~-radish** *n* Meerrettich *m;* **~-sense** *n* gesunder Menschenverstand; **~-shoe** 1 *u* Hufeisen *nt;* 2 *attr* hufeisenförmig, Hufeisen-; **~ show** *n* Pferdeschau *f;* **~-trading** *n (fig)* Kuhhandel *m;* **~-whip** 1 *n* Reitpeitsche *f;* 2 *vt* auspeitschen; **~-woman** *n* Reiterin *f.*

hors(e)y ['hɔːsɪ] *adj (+er) (fond of horses)* pferdenärrisch; *appearance* pferdeähnlich. **~ people** Pferdenarren *pl;* **~ face** Pferdegesicht *nt;* **she is going through a ~ stage** sie hat gerade einen Pferdefimmel *(inf).*

hortative ['hɔːtətɪv] *adj* anspornend.

horticultural [ˌhɔːtɪ'kʌltʃərəl] *adj* Garten(bau)-. **~ show** Gartenschau, Gartenbauausstellung *f.*

horticulture ['hɔːtɪkʌltʃəˡ] *n* Gartenbau(kunst *f) m.*

horticulturist [ˌhɔːtɪ'kʌltʃərɪst] *n* Gärtner(in *f) m.*

hosanna [həʊ'zænə] 1 *interj* hos(i)anna. 2 *n* Hos(i)anna *nt.*

hose¹ [həʊz] 1 *n (also ~pipe)* Schlauch *m.* 2 *vt (also ~ down)* abspritzen.

♦ **hose out** *vt sep* ausspritzen.

hose² *n, no pl* **(a)** *(Comm: stockings)* Strümpfe, Strumpfwaren *pl.* **(b)** *(Hist: for men)* (Knie)hose *f.*

hosier ['həʊʒəˡ] *n* Strumpfwarenhändler *m.*

hosiery ['həʊʒərɪ] *n* Strumpfwaren *pl.*

hospice ['hɒspɪs] *n* Hospiz *nt.*

hospitable *adj,* **~bly** *adv* [hɒs'pɪtəbl, -ɪ] gastfreundlich, gastlich.

hospital ['hɒspɪtl] *n* Krankenhaus *nt,* Klinik *f,* Hospital *nt (old, Sw).* **in or (US) in the ~** im Krankenhaus; **he's got to go to or (US) to the ~** er muß ins Krankenhaus (gehen).

hospital *in cpds* Krankenhaus-; **~ bed** Krankenhausbett *nt;* **~ case** *n* Fall, der im Krankenhaus behandelt werden muß; **~ facilities** *npl (equipment)* Krankenhauseinrichtung(en *pl) f;* *(hospitals)* Kranken(heil)anstalten *pl.*

hospitality [ˌhɒspɪ'tælɪtɪ] *n* Gastfreundschaft, Gastlichkeit *f.*

hospitalization [ˌhɒspɪtəlaɪ'zeɪʃən] *n* **(a)** Einweisung *f* ins Krankenhaus; *(stay in hospital)* Krankenhausaufenthalt *m.* **(b)** *(US:* ~ *insurance)* Versicherung *f* für Krankenhauspflege.

hospitalize ['hɒspɪtəlaɪz] *vt* ins Krankenhaus einweisen. **he was ~d for three months** or lag drei Monate lang im Krankenhaus.

hospital: **~ nurse** *n* Krankenschwester *f* (im Krankenhaus); **~ porter** *n* Pfleger(in *f) m;* *(doorman)* Pförtner(in *f) m* (im Krankenhaus); **~ ship** *n* Lazarett- or Krankenschiff *nt;* **~ train** *n* Lazarettzug *m.*

host¹ [həʊst] 1 *n* **(a)** Gastgeber *m;* *(in own home also)* Hausherr *m.* **to be ~ to sb** jds Gastgeber sein; *(in own home also)* jdn zu Besuch or Gast haben; **~ country** Gastland *nt.*

  (b) *(in hotel etc)* Wirt *m,* Herr *m* des Hauses *(form).* **your ~s are Mr and Mrs X** Ihre Wirtsleute sind Herr und Frau X; **mine ~** *(obs, hum)* der Herr Wirt.

  (c) *(Bot)* Wirt(spflanze *f) m;* *(Zool)* Wirt(stier *nt) m.*

  (d) *(on TV programme etc)* Gastgeber *m.*

  2 *vt TV programme, games* Gastgeber sein bei.

host² *n* **(a)** Menge, Masse *(inf) f.* **he has a ~ of friends** er hat massenweise *(inf)* or eine Menge Freunde; **a whole ~ of**

reasons eine ganze Menge or Anzahl von Gründen.

  (b) *(obs, liter)* Heerschar *f (obs, liter).* **a ~ of angels** eine Engelschar; **the Lord of H~s** der Herr der Heerscharen.

Host [həʊst] *n (Eccl)* Hostie *f.*

hostage ['hɒstɪdʒ] *n* Geisel *f.* **to take ~s** Geiseln nehmen.

hostel ['hɒstəl] 1 *n (for students, workers etc)* (Wohn)heim *nt.* **Youth H~** Jugendherberge *f.* 2 *vi:* **to go ~ling** in Jugendherbergen übernachten.

hosteller ['hɒstələˡ] *n* Heimbewohner(in *f) m;* *(in Youth Hostel)* Herbergsgast *m.*

hostelry ['hɒstəlrɪ] *n (obs)* Herberge *f (liter).*

hostess ['həʊstes] *n* **(a)** *(person)* Gastgeberin *f;* *(in own home also)* Hausherrin *f.* **to be ~ to sb** jds Gastgeberin sein; *(in own home also)* jdn zu Besuch or Gast haben.

  (b) *(in hotels also)* Wirtin *f.*

  (c) *(in night-club)* Hosteß *f.*

  (d) *(air-~)* Stewardeß *f;* *(at exhibition etc)* Hosteß *f.*

  (e) *(on TV programme etc)* Gastgeberin *f.*

hostile ['hɒstaɪl] *adj* **(a)** *(of an enemy)* feindlich. **(b)** *(showing enmity)* feindlich (gesinnt); *reception, looks* feindselig. **to be ~ to sb** sich jdm gegenüber feindselig verhalten; **to be ~ to sth** einer Sache *(dat)* feindlich gegenüberstehen.

hostility [hɒs'tɪlɪtɪ] *n* **(a)** Feindseligkeit *f; (between people)* Feindschaft *f.* **to show ~ to sb** sich jdm gegenüber feindselig verhalten; **to show ~ to sth** einer Sache *(dat)* feindlich gegenüberstehen; **feelings of ~** feindselige Gefühle *pl;* **he feels no ~ towards anybody** er ist niemandem feindlich gesinnt.

  (b) **hostilities** *pl (warfare)* Feindseligkeiten *pl.*

hostler ['ɒsləˡ] *n see* ostler.

hot [hɒt] 1 *adj (+er)* **(a)** heiß; *meal, tap, drink* warm. **I am or feel ~** mir ist (es) heiß; **with ~ and cold water** mit warm und kalt Wasser; **it was a ~ and tiring climb** der Aufstieg machte warm und müde; **the weather is ~** es ist heißes Wetter; **in the ~ weather** bei dem heißen Wetter, wenn es so heiß ist; **Africa is a ~ country** in Afrika ist es heiß; **to get ~** *(things)* heiß werden; **I'm getting ~** mir wird (es) warm; **you're getting ~** *(fig: when guessing)* jetzt wird's schon wärmer *(inf).*

  (b) *(to taste) curry, spices etc* scharf.

  (c) *(inf: radioactive material)* radioaktiv, heiß *(inf).*

  (d) *(sl) stolen goods* heiß *(inf).* **it's too ~ to sell** so heiße Ware läßt sich nicht verkaufen *(inf).*

  (e) *(inf: in demand) product* zugkräftig.

  (f) *(inf: good, competent)* stark *(inf); person also* fähig. **he/it isn't (all) that ~** so umwerfend ist er/das auch wieder nicht *(inf);* **he's pretty ~ at maths** in Mathe ist er ganz schön stark *(inf);* **I'm not feeling too ~** mir geht's nicht besonders *(inf).*

  (g) *(fig)* **to be (a) ~ favourite** hoch favorisiert sein, der große Favorit sein; **~ tip** heißer Tip; **~ jazz** Hot Jazz *m;* **~ news** das Neuste vom Neuen; **~ from the press** gerade erschienen; **the pace was so ~** das Tempo war so scharf; **she has a ~ temper** sie braust leicht auf, sie hat ein hitziges or leicht erregbares Wesen; **she's too ~ to handle** *(inf)* mit der wird keiner fertig *(inf);* **it's too ~ to handle** *(inf) (stolen goods)* das ist heiße Ware *(inf);* *(political issue, in journalism)* das ist ein heißes Eisen; **to get into ~ water** in Schwulitäten kommen *(inf),* in (des) Teufels Küche kommen *(inf);* **to be/get (all) ~ and bothered** *(inf)* ganz aufgeregt sein/werden *(about wegen);* **to look/feel ~ and bothered** *(inf)* ganz aufgeregt aussehen/ins Schwitzen kommen *(inf);* **to get ~ under the collar about sth** wegen etw in Rage geraten; *(embarrassed)* wegen etw verlegen werden; **I went ~ and cold all over** *(inf) (illness)* mir wurde abwechselnd heiß und kalt; *(emotion)* mir wurde es ganz anders *(inf);* **things started getting ~ in the tenth round** *(inf)* in der zehnten Runde wurde es langsam spannend or ging's los *(inf)/*bei der Diskussion ging's heiß her *(inf);* **to make a place or things too ~ for sb** *(inf)* jdm die Hölle heiß machen *(inf),* jdm einheizen *(inf);* **it's getting too ~ for me here** *(inf)* hier wird mir der Boden unter den Füßen zu heiß *(inf); see* trail 1 (b).

  2 *adv (+er)* **the engine's running ~** der Motor läuft heiß; **he keeps blowing ~ and cold** er sagt einmal hü und einmal hott.

  3 *n* **to have the ~s for sb** *(inf)* auf jdn scharf sein *(inf).*

♦ **hot up** *(inf)* 1 *vi* **the pace is ~ting ~** das Tempo wird schneller; **things are ~ting ~** in the Middle East die Lage im Nahen Osten spitzt sich zu or verschärft sich; **things are ~ting ~** es geht langsam los *(inf); (at a party also)* die Sache kommt in Schwung.

  2 *vt sep (fig) music* verpoppen *(inf); pace* steigern; *engine* frisieren.

hot: **~ air** *n (fig)* leeres Gerede, Gewäsch *nt;* **~-air** *adj attr* balloon Heißluft-; *(fig)* Blaba *nt;* **~ bed** Brutstätte *f,* Nährboden *m (*für*);* **(b)** *(Hort)* Mist- or Frühbeet *nt;* **~-blooded** *adj* heißblütig.

hotchpotch ['hɒtʃpɒtʃ] *n* Durcheinander *nt,* Mischmasch *m.*

hot: **~ cross bun** *n* Rosinenbrötchen *nt* mit kleinem Teigkreuz, *wird in der Karwoche gegessen;* **~ dog** *n* Hot dog *m* or *nt.*

hotel [həʊ'tel] *n* Hotel *nt.*

hotelier [həʊ'telɪəˡ] *n* Hotelier *m.*

hotel: **~ industry** *n* Hotelgewerbe *nt,* Hotellerie *f;* **~ keeper** *n* Hotelier, Hotelbesitzer *m;* **~ porter** *n* Haus- or Hoteldiener *m.*

hot: **~foot** 1 *adv* eilends *(geh);* 2 *vi (inf)* **he ~footed it back home/out of town** er ging schleunigst nach Hause/er verließ schleunigst die Stadt; **~ gospeller** *n* Erweckungsprediger *m;* **~head** *n* Hitzkopf *m;* **~headed** *adj* hitzköpfig, unbeherrscht; **~house** 1 *n (lit, fig)* Treibhaus *nt;* 2 *adj attr (lit) plant* Treibhaus-; *(fig) atmosphere* spannungsgeladen, angespannt; **~ line** *n (Pol)* heißer Draht; **to get on the ~ line** sich an den heißen Draht hängen *(inf).*

hotly ['hɒtlɪ] *adv* argue heiß; *say, argue, deny* heftig. **he was ~ pursued by two policemen** zwei Polizisten waren ihm dicht auf den Fersen; **she blushed ~** sie wurde über und über rot.

hot: **~ metal** *(Typ)* 1 *n* Blei *nt;* *(setting)* Bleisatz *m;* 2 *adj attr* *setting* Blei-; ~ **pants** *npl* heiße Höschen, Hot Pants *pl*; ~**plate** *n* **(a)** *(of stove)* Koch- *or* Heizplatte *f*; **(b)** *(plate-warmer)* Warmhalteplatte, Wärmplatte *f*; ~**pot** *n* *(esp Brit Cook)* Fleischeintopf *m* mit Kartoffeleinlage; ~ **potato** *n* *(fig inf)* heißes Eisen; ~ **pursuit** *n* *(Mil)* Nacheile *f*; **to set off/be in** ~ **pursuit of** *sb/sth* jdm/einer Sache nachjagen; **in** ~ **pursuit of the thief** in wilder Jagd auf den Dieb; ~**rod** *n* *(Aut)* hochfrisiertes Auto; ~ **seat** *n* Schleudersitz *m*; *(US sl: electric chair)* elektrischer Stuhl; **to be in the** ~ **seat** auf dem Schleudersitz sein; *(in quiz etc)* auf dem Armsünderbänkchen sitzen *(hum)*; **to take the** ~ **seat** auf den Schleudersitz kommen; *(in quiz)* sich auf das Armsünderbänkchen setzen *(hum)*; ~**shot** *(US sl)* **1** *n* Kanone *f* *(inf)*, As *nt* *(inf)*; **2** *adj attr* Spitzen- *(inf)*, erstklassig; ~ **spot** *n* *(Pol)* Krisenherd *m*; ~ **spring** *n* heiße Quelle, Thermalquelle *f*; ~ **stuff** *n* *(inf)* **it's** ~ **stuff** *(very good)* das ist große Klasse *(inf)*; *(provocative)* das ist Zündstoff; **she's/he's** ~ **stuff** *(very good)* sie/er ist große Klasse *(inf)* or eine Kanone *(inf)*; *(very sexy)* das ist eine Klassefrau *(inf)* or scharfe Frau *(sl)*/das ist ein scharfer Typ *(sl)*; ~**-tempered** *adj* leicht aufbrausend, jähzornig.

Hottentot [ˈhɒtəntɒt] **1** *n* **(a)** Hottentotte *m*, Hottentottin *f*. **(b)** *(language)* Hottentottisch *nt*. **2** *adj* hottentottisch.

hot-water bottle [ˌhɒtˈwɔːtəˌbɒtl] *n* Wärmflasche *f*.

hound [haʊnd] **1** *n* **(a)** *(Hunt)* (Jagd)hund *m*. **the** ~**s lost the scent** die Meute verlor die Spur; **to ride to** ~**s** *(person)* mit der Meute jagen. **(b)** *(any dog)* Hund *m*, Tier *nt*. **2** *vt* hetzen, jagen. **to be/feel** ~**ed** gehetzt sein/sich gehetzt fühlen.

♦**hound down** *vt sep* Jagd machen auf (+*acc*), niederhetzen *(form)*; *(criminal also)* zur Strecke bringen. **the lion was** ~**ed** ~ **and killed** nach einer unerbittlichen Jagd wurde der Löwe zur Strecke gebracht.

♦**hound out** *vt sep* verjagen, vertreiben *(of* aus).

hound's-tooth (check) [ˈhaʊndztuːθ(ˌtʃek)] *n* Hahnentritt- (muster *nt*) *m*.

hour [ˈaʊəʳ] *n* **(a)** Stunde *f*; *(time of day also)* Zeit *f*. **half an** ~, **a half** ~ eine halbe Stunde; **three-quarters/a quarter of an** ~ eine dreiviertel Stunde, dreiviertel Stunden/eine Viertelstunde; **an** ~ **and a half** anderthalb *or* eineinhalb Stunden; **it's two** ~**s' walk from here** von hier geht man zwei Stunden, von hier sind es zu Fuß zwei Stunden; **two** ~**s' walk from here there is ...** nach einem Weg von zwei Stunden kommt man an (+*acc*) *or* zu ...; **at 1500/1530** ~**s**, *(spoken)* **at fifteen hundred/fifteen thirty** ~ um 15⁰⁰/15³⁰ Uhr, *(gesprochen)* um fünfzehn Uhr/fünfzehn Uhr dreißig; ~ **by** ~ mit jeder Stunde, stündlich; **on the** ~ zur vollen Stunde; **every** ~ **on the** ~ jede volle Stunde; **20 minutes past the** ~ 20 Minuten nach; **at the** ~ **of his death** in der Stunde seines Todes, in seiner Todesstunde; **at an early/a late** ~ früh/spät, zu früher/später Stunde *(geh)*; **at all** ~**s (of the day and night)** zu jeder (Tages- und Nacht)zeit; **what! at this** ~ **of the night!** was! zu dieser nachtschlafenden Zeit!; **what is the** ~? *(old)* wieviel Uhr ist es?; **to walk/drive at 10 kilometres an** ~ zu Fuß 10 Kilometer in der Stunde zurücklegen/10 Kilometer in der Stunde *or* 10 Stundenkilometer fahren; **a 30 mile(s) an** *or* **per** ~ **limit** eine Geschwindigkeitsbegrenzung von 30 Meilen in der Stunde; **to be paid by the** ~ stundenweise bezahlt werden; **she is paid £3 an** ~ sie bekommt £ 3 pro Stunde *or* (für) die Stunde *or* in der Stunde.

(b) ~**s** *pl (inf: a long time)* Stunden *pl*; **for** ~**s** stundenlang; ~**s and** ~**s** Stunden und aber Stunden; **I/the train was** ~**s late** ich war sehr spät dran *(inf)*, ich hatte mich um Stunden verspätet/der Zug hatte Stunden Verspätung; **he took** ~**s to do it** er brauchte ewig lang *(inf)* or stundenlang dazu.

(c) ~**s** *pl (of banks, shops etc)* Geschäftszeit(en *pl*) *f*; *(of shops also, pubs, park etc)* Öffnungszeiten *pl*; *(of post office)* Schalterzeiten *pl*; *(office* ~*s)* Dienststunden *pl*; *(working* ~*s etc)* Arbeitszeit *f*; *(of doctor etc)* Sprechstunde *f*; **out of/after** ~**s** *(in pubs)* außerhalb der gesetzlich erlaubten Zeit/nach der Polizeistunde; *(in shops etc)* außerhalb der Geschäftszeit(en)/ nach Laden- *or* Geschäftsschluß; *(in office etc)* außerhalb der Arbeitszeit/nach Dienstschluß; *(of doctor etc)* außerhalb/nach der Sprechstunde; **what are your** ~**s?** *(shops, pubs etc)* wann haben Sie geöffnet *or* offen?; *(employee)* wie ist Ihre Arbeitszeit?; **to work long** ~**s** einen langen Arbeitstag haben, lange arbeiten; *(doctors, nurse, policeman etc)* lange Dienststunden haben.

(d) *(fig)* **his** ~ **has come** seine Stunde ist gekommen; *(death also)* sein (letztes) Stündchen hat geschlagen; **in the** ~ **of danger** in der Stunde der Gefahr; **the man of the** ~ der Mann der Stunde; **the problems of the** ~ die aktuellen Probleme.

hour: ~ **glass** 1 *n* Sanduhr *f*, Stundenglas *nt* *(old)*; **2** *adj figure* kurvenreich; ~ **hand** *n* Stundenzeiger *m*, kleiner Zeiger.

houri [ˈhuːrɪ] *n (Rel)* Huri *f*; *(fig)* orientalische Schönheit.

hourly [ˈaʊəlɪ] **1** *adj* stündlich. **at** ~ **intervals** jede Stunde, stündlich, ~ **rate/wage** Stundensatz/-lohn *m*. **2** *adv* stündlich, jede Stunde; *(hour by hour)* mit jeder Stunde.

house [haʊs] **1** *n*, *pl* **houses** [ˈhaʊzɪz] **(a)** Haus *nt*; *(household also)* Haushalt *m*. **at/to my** ~ bei mir (zu Hause)/zu mir (nach Hause); **to set up** ~ einen eigenen Hausstand gründen; *(in particular area)* sich niederlassen; **they set up** ~ **together** sie gründeten einen gemeinsamen Hausstand; **to put** *or* **set one's** ~ **in order** *(fig)* seine Angelegenheiten in Ordnung bringen; **he's getting on like a** ~ **on fire** *(inf)* (*in new job etc*) er macht sich prächtig *(inf)*; *(with building, project etc)* er kommt prima *or* prächtig voran *(inf)*; **he gets on with her like a** ~ **on fire** *(inf)* er kommt ausgezeichnet *or* prima *(inf)* mit ihr aus; **they get on like a** ~ **on fire** *(inf)* sie kommen ausgezeichnet miteinander aus; **as safe as** ~**s** *(Brit)* bombensicher *(inf)*; **H**~ **of God** *or* **the Lord** Haus Gottes, Gotteshaus *nt*; **a** ~ **of worship** ein Ort des Gebets, ein Haus der Andacht.

(b) *(Pol)* **the upper/lower** ~ das Ober-/Unterhaus; **H**~ **of Commons/Lords** *(Brit)* (britisches) Unter-/Oberhaus; **the**

H~ *(Brit inf)* das Parlament; *(as address also)* das Hohe Haus; **H**~ **of Representatives** *(US)* Repräsentantenhaus *nt*; **the H**~**s of Parliament** das Parlament(sgebäude).

(c) *(family, line)* Haus, Geschlecht *nt*. **the H**~ **of Bourbon** das Haus Bourbon, das Geschlecht der Bourbonen.

(d) *(firm)* Haus *nt*. **on the** ~ auf Kosten des Hauses; *(on the company)* auf Kosten der Firma; **he was given a drink on the** ~ er bekam ein Getränk auf Kosten des Hauses; **can I give you something for the phone call/meal?** — **oh no, it's on the** ~ kann ich dir etwas für das Telefon/Essen geben? — nein, nein, das geht auf Kosten des Hauses/das spendiere ich dir.

(e) *(Theat)* Haus *nt*; *(performance)* Vorstellung *f*. **to bring the** ~ **down** *(inf)* ein Bombenerfolg (beim Publikum) sein *(inf)*.

(f) *(in boarding school)* Gruppenhaus *nt*; *(in day school)* eine von mehreren Gruppen verschiedenaltriger Schüler, die z.B. in Wettkämpfen gegeneinander antreten.

(g) *(in debate)* **H**~ Versammlung *f*; **the motion before the H**~ das Diskussionsthema, das zur Debatte *or* Diskussion stehende Thema; **this H**~ **believes capital punishment should be reintroduced** wir stellen die Frage zur Diskussion, ob die Todesstrafe wieder eingeführt werden sollte; *(in conclusion)* die Anwesenden sind der Meinung, daß die Todesstrafe wieder eingeführt werden sollte.

(h) *full* ~ *(Cards)* Full House *nt*; *(bingo)* volle Karte.

(i) *(Astrol)* Haus *nt*.

2 [haʊz] *vt people, goods* unterbringen; *(Tech also)* einbauen. **this building** ~**s three offices/ten families** in diesem Gebäude sind drei Büros/zehn Familien untergebracht, dieses Gebäude beherbergt drei Büros/zehn Familien.

house *in cpds* Haus-; ~ **arrest** *n* Hausarrest *m*; ~**boat** *n* Hausboot *nt*; ~**bound** *adj* ans Haus gefesselt; ~**boy** *n* Boy *m*; ~**breaker** *n* Einbrecher *m*; ~**breaking** *n* Einbruch(sdiebstahl) *m*; ~ **captain** *n (Brit Sch)* *(in boarding school)* Haussprecher(in *f) m*, Hausälteste(r) *mf*; *(in day school)* Gruppensprecher(in *f) m*, Gruppenälteste(r) *mf*; ~**coat** *n* Morgenrock *or* -mantel *m*; ~**-dog** *n* Haushund *m*; ~**dress** *n* *(US)* Schürzenkleid *nt*; ~**fly** *n* Stubenfliege *f*; ~**guest** *n* (Haus)gast *m*.

household [ˈhaʊshəʊld] **1** *n* Haushalt *m*. **H**~ **Cavalry** Gardekavallerie *f*. **2** *attr* Haushalts-. ~ **chores** häusliche Pflichten *pl*, Hausarbeit *f*.

householder [ˈhaʊsˌhəʊldəʳ] *n* Haus-/Wohnungsinhaber(in *f) m*.

household: ~ **god** *n* Hausgott *m*; **the telly has become the** ~ **god in many homes** der Fernseher ist in vielen Familien zum Götzen geworden; ~ **linen** *n* Tisch- und Bettwäsche, Weißwäsche *(dated) f*; ~ **name** *n* **to be/become a** ~ **name** für jeden ein Begriff sein/zu einem Begriff werden; ~ **word** *n* Begriff *nt*; **to be/become a** ~ **word for sth** ein (In)begriff für etw sein/zu einem (In)begriff für etw werden.

house: ~**-hunt** *vi* auf Haussuche sein; **they have started** ~**-hunting** sie haben angefangen, nach einem Haus zu suchen; ~**-hunting** *n* Haussuche *f*; ~ **journal** *or* **magazine** *n* Hausnachrichten *pl*; ~**keeper** *n* Haushälterin, Wirtschafterin *f*; *(in institution also)* Wirtschaftsleiterin *f*; **his wife is a good** ~**keeper** seine Frau ist eine gute Hausfrau; ~**keeping** *n* **(a)** Haushalten *nt*; **(b)** *(also* ~**keeping money)** Haushalts- *or* Wirtschaftsgeld *nt*; ~**lights** *npl* Lichter *pl* im Saal; ~**maid** *n* Dienstmädchen *nt*; ~**maid's knee** *n* Schleimbeutelentzündung *f*, ~**man** *n (Brit)* Medizinalassistent *m*; ~ **martin** *n* Mehlschwalbe *f*; ~**master/-mistress** *n (Brit)* Erzieher(in *f) m*; *(on teaching staff)* Lehrer(in *f) m*, der/die für ein Gruppenhaus zuständig ist; ~ **parent** *n* Hausvater *m*/-mutter *f*; ~ **parents** *pl* Hauseltern *pl*; ~ **party** *n* mehrtägige Einladung; *(group invited)* Gesellschaft *f*; ~ **physician** *n* im (Kranken)haus wohnender Arzt; *(in private clinic etc)* Haus- *or* Anstaltsarzt *m*/-ärztin *f*; ~**-proud** *adj* **she is** ~**-proud** sie ist eine penible Hausfrau; ~**room** *n*: **I wouldn't give it** ~**room** *(inf)* das wollte ich nicht geschenkt haben; ~ **rule** *n* (Bestimmung der) Hausordnung *f*; ~ **style** *n* Stil *m* des Hauses; ~ **surgeon** *n* im (Kranken)haus wohnender Chirurg; *(in private clinic)* Haus- *or* Anstaltschirurg *m*; ~**-to-** *adj collection* Haus-; **a** ~**-to-** ~ **search** eine Suche *or* Fahndung von Haus zu Haus; **to conduct** ~**-to-** ~ **enquiries** von Haus zu Haus gehen und fragen; ~**top** *n* (Haus)dach *nt*; **to cry** *or* **proclaim** *or* **shout sth from the** ~**tops** etw an die große Glocke hängen; ~**-train** *vt* stubenrein machen; ~**-trained** *adj* stubenrein; ~ **warming (party)** *n* Einzugsparty *f*; **to give** *or* **hold** *or* **have a** ~ **warming (party)** Einzug feiern; ~**wife** *n* **(a)** *(person)* Hausfrau *f*; **(b)** [ˈhʌzɪf] *(dated: sewing case)* Nähetui, Nähzeug *nt*; ~**wifely** *adj* hausfraulich; **she has a very** ~**wifely outlook on life** sie betrachtet das Leben vom Hausfrauenstandpunkt aus; ~**work** *n* Hausarbeit *f*.

housey-housey [ˈhaʊsɪˈhaʊsɪ] *n (dated)* Lotto *nt*.

housing [ˈhaʊzɪŋ] *n* **(a)** *(act)* Unterbringung *f*. **(b)** *(houses)* Wohnungen *pl*; *(temporary)* Unterkunft *f*. **(c)** *(provision of houses)* Wohnungsbeschaffung *f*; *(building of houses)* Wohnungsbau *m*. **(d)** *(Tech)* Gehäuse *nt*.

housing *in cpds* Wohnungs-; ~ **association** *n* Wohnungsbaugesellschaft *f*; ~ **conditions** *npl* Wohnbedingungen *or* -verhältnisse *pl*; ~ **estate** *n* Wohnsiedlung *f*; ~ **programme** *n* Wohnungsbeschaffungsprogramm *nt*; ~ **scheme** *n* *(estate)* Siedlung *f*; *(project)* Siedlungsbauvorhaben *nt*.

hove [həʊv] *pret, ptp of* **heave 1 (d), 2 (c)**.

hovel [ˈhɒvəl] *n* armselige Hütte; *(fig pej)* Bruchbude *f*, Loch *nt* *(inf)*. **my humble** ~ *(hum)* meine bescheidene Hütte.

hover [ˈhɒvəʳ] *vi* **(a)** schweben; *(bird also)* stehen.

(b) *(fig)* **a smile** ~**ed on her lips** ein Lächeln lag auf ihren Lippen; ~**ed on the verge of tears/of a decision** sie war den Tränen nahe/sie schwankte in ihrer Entscheidung; **danger was** ~**ing all around them** ringsum lauerte Gefahr; **to** ~ **on the brink of disaster** am Rande des Ruins stehen; **he** ~**ed between two alternatives** er schwankte zwischen zwei Alternativen; **he**

was ~ing between life and death er schwebte zwischen Leben und Tod.

(c) (*fig: stand around*) herumstehen. **to ~ over sb** jdm nicht von der Seite weichen; **don't ~ over me** geh endlich weg; **he's always ~ing over me** ich habe ihn ständig auf der Pelle (*inf*); **a waiter ~ed at his elbow,** waiting to refill his glass ein Kellner schwebte herum und wartete nur darauf, nachzuschenken.

♦**hover about** *or* **around 1** *vi* (*persons*) herumlungern, herumhängen; (*helicopter, bird etc*) (in der Luft) kreisen. **he was ~ing ~,** waiting for us to ask him to join us er strich um uns herum und wartete offensichtlich darauf, daß wir ihn einluden.

2 *vi* **+prep obj to ~ ~ sb/sth** um jdn/etw herumschleichen *or* -streichen, sich um jdn/etw herumdrücken; **the hostess ~ed ~ her guests** die Gastgeberin umsorgte ihre Gäste mit (über-) großer Aufmerksamkeit.

hover: ~craft *n* Luftkissenfahrzeug, Hovercraft *nt*; **~port** *n* Anlegestelle *f* für Hovercrafts; **~train** *n* Schwebezug *m*.

how¹ [hau] *adv* **(a)** (*in what way*) wie. **~ will we ever survive?** wie sollen *or* können wir nur *or* bloß überleben?; **~ so?,** **~'s that?,** **~ come?** (*inf*) wieso (denn das)?, wie kommt (denn) das?; **~ is it that we** *or* **~ come** (*inf*) **we earn less?** wieso *or* warum verdienen wir denn weniger?; **~ can that be?** wie ist das möglich?; **~ is it that ...?** wie kommt es, daß ...?; **I see ~ it is** ich verstehe (schon); **~ do you know that?** woher wissen Sie das?; **to learn/know ~ to do sth** lernen/wissen, wie man etw macht; **I would like to learn ~ to ride/swim/drive etc** ich würde gerne reiten/schwimmen/Autofahren *etc* lernen.

(b) (*in degree, quantity etc*) wie. **~ much** (**+**n, adj, adv**) wieviel; (**+**vb**) wie sehr; (**+**vbs of physical action**) wieviel; **~ much do you visit them/go out?** wie oft besuchen Sie sie/gehen Sie aus?; **~ many** wieviel, wie viele.

(c) (*regarding health, general situation etc*) **~ do you do?** (*at introduction*) Guten Tag/Abend!, angenehm! (*form*); **~ are you?** wie geht es Ihnen?; **~'s work/the pound?** *etc* was macht die Arbeit/das Pfund? *etc* (*inf*); **~ are things at school/in the office?** *etc* wie geht's in der Schule/im Büro? *etc*

(d) **~ about ...** wie wäre es mit ...; **~ about it?** wie steht's?, na, was ist?; (*about suggestion*) wie wäre es damit?; **~ about going for a walk?** wie wär's mit einem Spaziergang?

(e) **and ~!** und ob *or* wie!; **~ he's grown!** er ist aber *or* vielleicht groß geworden; **look ~ he's grown!** sieh mal, wie groß er geworden ist.

(f) (*that*) daß. **she told me ~ she had seen him there** sie sagte mir, daß sie ihn dort gesehen hat.

how² *interj* (*Indian greeting*) hugh.

howdah ['haudə] *n* Sänfte *f* (auf Elefanten).

howdy ['haudɪ] *interj* (*esp US*) Tag (*inf*).

how-d'ye-do ['haudjə:du:] (*inf*) **1** *interj* Tag (*inf*), Tagchen (*inf*). **2** *n* (*palaver, fuss*) Theater *nt*; (*argument also*) Krach *m*. **a fine** *or* **pretty ~** eine schöne Bescherung (*inf*).

howe'er [hau'ɛəʳ] *conj, adv* (*poet*) *contr of* however.

however [hau'ɛvəʳ] **1** *conj* ~ jedoch, aber. ~, **we finally succeeded** wir haben es schließlich doch noch geschafft.

(b) (*inf: oh well*) na ja (*inf*), nun ja (*inf*).

2 *adv* **(a)** (*no matter how*) wie ... auch, egal wie (*inf*); (*in whatever way*) wie. **~ strong he is** wie stark er ist, egal wie stark er ist (*inf*); **~ you do it** wie immer du es machst, wie du es auch machst; **do it ~ you like** mach's, wie du willst; **buy it ~ expensive it is** kaufen Sie es, egal, was es kostet; **~ much you cry** und wenn du noch so weinst, wie sehr du auch weinst; **~ that may be** wie dem auch sei.

(b) (*in question*) wie ... bloß *or* nur. **~ did you manage it?** wie hast du das bloß *or* nur geschafft?

howitzer ['hauɪtsəʳ] *n* Haubitze *f*.

howl [haul] **1** *n* **(a)** Schrei *m*; (*of animal, wind*) Heulen *nt no pl.* **the dog let out a ~** der Hund heulte auf *or* jaulte; **a ~ of pain/fear** ein Schmerzens-/Angstschrei; **~s of excitement/approval/rage** aufgeregtes/zustimmendes/wütendes Geschrei *or* Gebrüll; **~s of laughter** brüllendes Gelächter; **~s** (of protest) Protestgeschrei *nt*.

(b) (*Elec*) (*from loudspeaker*) Pfeifen *nt no pl*, Rück(e)lung *f*.

2 *vi* **(a)** (*person*) brüllen, schreien; (*animal*) heulen, jaulen; (*wind*) heulen. **to ~ with laughter** in brüllendes Gelächter ausbrechen; **if you want anything just ~** (*inf*) wenn du etwas willst, brauchst du nur zu schreien (*inf*).

(b) (*weep noisily*) heulen; (*baby*) schreien, brüllen (*inf*).

(c) (*Elec: loudspeaker etc*) rückkoppeln, pfeifen.

3 *vt* hinausbrüllen, hinausschreien. **they ~ed their disapproval** sie äußerten ihr Mißfallen lautstark.

♦**howl down** *vt sep* niederbrüllen, niederschreien.

howler ['hauləʳ] *n* (*inf*) Hammer (*sl*), Schnitzer (*inf*) *m*. **he made a real ~** da hat er sich (*dat*) einen Hammer geleistet (*sl*).

howling ['haulɪŋ] **1** *n* (*of person*) Gebrüll, Geschrei *nt*; (*noisy crying, of animal*) Heulen, Geheul *nt*; (*of wind*) Heulen *nt*. **stop that child's ~!** bring das Kind zum Schweigen! **2** *adj* (*lit*) heulend. **(b)** (*inf: tremendous*) enorm; *success also* Riesen-.

howsoever [ˌhausəu'ɛvəʳ] *adv* (*old, form*) wie auch immer.

hoy [hɔɪ] *interj* he.

hoyden ['hɔɪdn] *n* wilde Range (*dated*), Wildfang *m* (*dated*).

hoydenish ['hɔɪdənɪʃ] *adj* rangenhaft (*dated*), wild, ungestüm.

HP, hp *abbr of* **hire purchase. (b) horse power** ≈ PS.

HQ *abbr of* **headquarters.**

HRH *abbr of* **His/Her Royal Highness** S.M./I.M.

ht *abbr of* **height.**

hub [hʌb] *n* **(a)** (*of wheel*) (Rad)nabe *f*. **(b)** (*fig*) Zentrum *nt*, Mittelpunkt *m*. **the ~ of the universe** der Nabel der Welt.

hubble-bubble ['hʌbl'bʌbl] *n* **(a)** (*pipe*) Wasserpfeife *f*. **(b)** (*noise*) Brodeln *nt*.

hubbub ['hʌbʌb] *n* Tumult *m*. **a ~ of** (*of noise*) ein Radau *m*; **a ~ of voices** ein Stimmengewirr *nt*.

hubby ['hʌbɪ] *n* (*inf*) Mann *m*.

hubcap ['hʌbkæp] *n* Radkappe *f*.

hubris ['hju:brɪs] *n* (*liter*) Anmaßung *f*; (*esp in Greek drama*) Hybris *f*.

huckleberry ['hʌklbərɪ] *n* amerikanische Heidelbeere.

huckster ['hʌkstəʳ] *n* **(a)** (*hawker*) Straßenhändler(in *f*) *m*. **(b)** (*US inf*) Reklamefritze *m* (*inf*).

huddle ['hʌdl] **1** *n* (*wirrer*) Haufen *m*; (*of people*) Gruppe *f*. **in a ~** dicht zusammengedrängt; **to go into a ~** (*inf*) die Köpfe zusammenstecken. **2** *vi* (*also* **to be ~d**) (sich) kauern.

♦**huddle down** *vi* sich kuscheln.

♦**huddle together** *vi* sich aneinanderkauern. **to be ~d ~** aneinanderkauern.

♦**huddle up** *vi* sich zusammenkauern. **to be ~d ~** zusammenkauern; **to ~ ~ against sb/sth** sich an jdn/etw kauern.

hue¹ [hju:] *n* (*colour*) Farbe *f*; (*shade*) Schattierung *f*; (*fig: political leaning*) Schattierung, Färbung, Couleur (*geh*) *f*.

hue² *n*: **~ and cry** Zeter und Mordio (*against gegen*); **to set up** *or* **raise a ~ and cry** Zeter und Mordio schreien.

huff [hʌf] **1** *n* **to be/go off in a ~** beleidigt *or* eingeschnappt sein/abziehen (*inf*); **to get into a ~** einschnappen (*inf*), den Beleidigten spielen; **~s never last long** er ist nie lange beleidigt. **2** *vi* **to ~ and puff** (*inf*) schnaufen und keuchen.

huffily ['hʌfɪlɪ] *adv* beleidigt.

huffiness ['hʌfɪnɪs] *n* Beleidigtsein *nt*; (*touchiness*) Empfindlichkeit *f*. **the ~ in his voice** sein beleidigter Ton.

huffy ['hʌfɪ] *adj* (**+**er) (*in a huff*) beleidigt; (*touchy*) empfindlich. **to get/be ~ about sth** wegen etw eingeschnappt (*inf*) *or* beleidigt sein; **he's a rather ~ kind of person** er ist leicht beleidigt *or* eingeschnappt (*inf*).

hug [hʌg] **1** *n* Umarmung *f*. **to give sb a ~** jdn umarmen. **2** *vt* **(a)** (*hold close*) umarmen; (*bear etc also*) umklammern; (*fig*) **hope, belief** sich klammern an (**+**acc). **to ~ sb/sth to oneself** jdn/etw an sich (*acc*) pressen *or* drücken. **(b)** (*keep close to*) sich dicht halten an (**+**acc); (*car, ship etc also*) dicht entlangfahren an (**+**dat). **3** *vr* **(a)** **to ~ oneself to keep warm** die Arme verschränken, damit einem warm ist. **(b)** **to ~ oneself over** *or* **about sth** (*fig*) sich zu etw beglückwünschen.

huge [hju:dʒ] *adj* (**+**er) riesig, gewaltig; **cheek, lie, mistake, appetite, thirst, town** also Riesen-.

hugely ['hju:dʒlɪ] *adv* ungeheuer; **enjoy, be pleased** also riesig.

hugeness ['hju:dʒnɪs] *n* Größe *f*, (*gewaltiges/riesiges*) Ausmaß.

Huguenot ['hju:gənəu] **1** *adj* hugenottisch, Hugenotten-. **2** *n* Hugenotte *m*, Hugenottin *f*.

huh [hʌ] *interj* was; (*derision*) haha.

hula ['hu:lə] *n* Hula(-Hula) *m or f*. **to do the ~** (**~**) Hula(-Hula) tanzen; **~ hoop** Hula-Hoop-Reifen *m*; **~ skirt** Bastrock *m*.

hulk [hʌlk] *n* **(a)** (*Naut: body of ship*) (Schiffs)rumpf *m*. **(b)** (*inf: person*) Klotz *m* (*inf*). **(c)** (*wrecked vehicle*) Wrack *nt*; (*building etc*) Ruine *f*.

hulking ['hʌlkɪŋ] *adj*: **~ great, great ~** massig; **a great ~ wardrobe** ein Ungetüm *nt* von einem Kleiderschrank; **a ~ great brute** (*of a man/dog*) ein grobschlächtiger, brutaler Kerl/ein scheußliches Ungetüm von einem Hund.

hull¹ [hʌl] *n* (*Naut*) Schiffskörper *m*; (*Aviat*) Rumpf *m*. **ship ~ down on the horizon** Schiff in Sicht am Horizont.

hull² **1** *n* Hülse *f*; (*of peas also*) Schote *f*; (*of barley, oats also*) Spelze *f*; (*of strawberries etc*) Blättchen *nt*. **2** *vt* schälen; **beans, peas** enthülsen, ausmachen (*inf*); **strawberries etc** entstielen.

hullabaloo [ˌhʌləbə'lu:] *n* (*inf*) Spektakel *m*; (*noise also*) Radau *m*.

hullo [hʌ'ləu] *interj see* hello.

hum [hʌm] **1** *n* **(a)** *see vi* **(a)** Summen *nt*; Brausen *nt*; Brummen *nt*; Surren *nt*; (*of voices*) Gemurmel *nt*. **(b)** (*inf: smell*) Gestank *m* (*inf*). **to give off a ~** stinken (*inf*). **2** *vi* **(a)** (*insect, person*) summen; (*traffic*) brausen; (*engine, electric tool, wireless, top etc*) brummen; (*small machine, camera etc*) surren. **the lines were/the office was ~ming with the news** (*fig*) die Drähte liefen heiß/im Büro sprach man von nichts anderem.

(b) (*fig inf: party, concert etc*) in Schwung kommen. **to make things/the party ~** die Sache/die Party in Schwung bringen, Leben in die Sache/Bude bringen (*inf*); **the headquarters was ~ming with activity** im Hauptquartier ging es zu wie in einem Bienenstock.

(c) **to ~ and haw** (*inf*) herumdrucksen (*inf*) (*over, about* um).

(d) (*inf: smell*) stinken (*inf*).

3 *vt* **music, tune** summen.

4 *interj* hm.

human ['hju:mən] **1** *adj* menschlich. **you can't do that, it's not ~** das kannst du nicht tun, das ist unmenschlich; **~ race** menschliche Rasse, Menschengeschlecht *nt* (*liter*); **these footprints certainly aren't ~** diese Fußspuren sind *or* stammen sicher nicht von Menschen; **she's only ~** sie ist auch nur ein Mensch; **that's only ~** das ist doch menschlich; **I would be less than ~ if ...** ich wäre ein Übermensch, wenn ...; **~ interest** die menschliche Seite; **a ~ interest story on the front page** eine Geschichte aus dem Leben auf der ersten Seite; **~ nature** die menschliche Natur; **that's (only) ~ nature** das liegt (nun einmal) in der Natur des Menschen; **~ sacrifice** Menschenopfer *nt*; **the ~ touch** die menschliche Wärme; **to lack the ~ touch** nichts Menschliches haben; (*person also*) es an der menschlichen Wärme fehlen lassen.

2 *n* (*also* **~ being**) Mensch *m*.

humane [hju:'meɪn] *adj* human, menschlich. **~ killer** Mittel *nt* zum schmerzlosen Töten; **~ society** Gesellschaft *f* zur Verhinderung von Grausamkeiten an Mensch und Tier.

humanely [hju:'meɪnlɪ] *adv see adj*. **the dog was put down very ~** der Hund wurde auf humane Weise getötet.

humanism ['hjuːmənɪzəm] n Humanismus m.
humanist ['hjuːmənɪst] **1** n Humanist m. **2** adj humanistisch.
humanistic [ˌhjuːmə'nɪstɪk] adj humanistisch.
humanitarian [hjuːˌmænɪ'teərɪən] **1** n Vertreter(in f) m des Humanitätsgedankens. **2** adj humanitär.
humanitarianism [ˌhjuːmænɪ'teərɪənɪzəm] n Humanitarismus m; (of individual) humanitäre Gesinnung.
humanity [hjuː'mænɪtɪ] n (a) (mankind) die Menschheit. (b) (human nature) Menschlichkeit, Menschenhaftigkeit f. (c) (humaneness) Humanität, Menschlichkeit f. to treat sb with ~ jdn human behandeln. (d) **humanities** pl Geisteswissenschaften pl; (Latin and Greek) Altphilologie f.
humanize ['hjuːmənaɪz] vt humanisieren.
humankind [ˌhjuːmən'kaɪnd] n die Menschheit.
humanly ['hjuːmənlɪ] adv menschlich. to do all that is ~ possible alles menschenmögliche tun.
humble ['hʌmbl] **1** adj (+er) (unassuming) bescheiden; (meek, submissive, Rel) demütig; apology also zerknirscht; (lowly) einfach, bescheiden. my ~ **apologies**! ich bitte inständig um Verzeihung!; of ~ **birth** or **origin** von niedriger Geburt or Herkunft; my ~ **self** meine Wenigkeit; in my ~ **opinion** meiner bescheidenen Meinung nach; to eat ~ **pie** klein beigeben, zu Kreuze kriechen (inf); see **servant**. **2** vt demütigen. to ~ **oneself** sich demütigen or erniedrigen.
humble-bee ['hʌmblˌbiː] n Hummel f.
humbleness ['hʌmblnɪs] n Bescheidenheit f; (lowliness also) Einfachheit f; (meekness, submissiveness) Demut f.
humbly ['hʌmblɪ] adv (unassumingly, with deference) demütig (esp Rel), bescheiden; (in a lowly way) einfach, bescheiden. I ~ **submit this little work** in aller Bescheidenheit überreiche ich diese kleine Arbeit; ~ **born** von niedriger Geburt; he ~ **apologized/agreed that he was wrong** er entschuldigte sich zerknirscht/er gab kleinlaut zu, daß er unrecht hatte.
humbug ['hʌmbʌg] n (a) (Brit: sweet) Pfefferminzbonbon m or nt. (b) (inf: talk) Humbug, Mumpitz m (inf). (c) (inf: person) Gauner, Halunke m.
humdinger ['hʌmdɪŋəʳ] n (sl: person, thing) to be a ~ **Spitze** or **große Klasse sein** (sl); a ~ **of a job/girl etc** ein klasse Job/Mädchen etc (sl); he hit him with a real ~ **of a left hook** er landete einen erstklassigen linken Haken bei ihm (inf).
humdrum ['hʌmdrʌm] adj stumpfsinnig.
humerus ['hjuːmərəs] n Oberarmknochen m.
humid ['hjuːmɪd] adj feucht.
humidifier [hjuː'mɪdɪfaɪəʳ] n Verdunster m; (humidification system) Luftbefeuchtungsanlage f.
humidify [hjuː'mɪdɪfaɪ] vt befeuchten.
humidity [hjuː'mɪdɪtɪ] n (Luft)feuchtigkeit f, Feuchtigkeitsgehalt m (der Luft).
humidor ['hjuːmɪdɔːʳ] n Feuchtraum m.
humiliate [hjuː'mɪlɪeɪt] vt see n demütigen, erniedrigen; beschämen.
humiliation [hjuːˌmɪlɪ'eɪʃən] n Demütigung, Erniedrigung f; (because of one's own actions) Beschämung f no pl. **much to my** ~ sehr zu meiner Schande or Beschämung; she couldn't hide her ~ sie konnte das Gefühl der Demütigung/Beschämung nicht verbergen; he brought about her complete ~ sie wurde zutiefst gedemütigt/sie war zutiefst beschämt.
humility [hjuː'mɪlɪtɪ] n Demut f; (unassumingness) Bescheidenheit f.
humming ['hʌmɪŋ] n see vi **2** (a) Summen nt; Brausen nt; Brummen nt; Surren nt; (of voices) Murmeln, Gemurmel nt.
humming: ~**bird** n Kolibri m; ~**-top** n Brummkreisel m.
hummock ['hʌmək] n (kleiner) Hügel m.
humor etc (US) see **humour** etc.
humorist ['hjuːmərɪst] n Humorist(in f) m.
humorous ['hjuːmərəs] adj person humorvoll; book, story etc also, situation lustig, komisch; speech also launig; idea, thought witzig; smile, programme lustig, heiter.
humorously ['hjuːmərəslɪ] adv humorvoll, witzig; reflect, smile heiter.
humour, (US) **humor** ['hjuːməʳ] **1** n (a) Humor m. a **sense of** ~ (Sinn m für) Humor m; a **story full of** ~ eine humorvolle Geschichte; **I don't see the** ~ **in that** ich finde das gar nicht komisch or lustig; **this is no time for** ~ jetzt ist nicht die Zeit für Witze.
(b) (mood) Stimmung, Laune f. to be in a good/in high ~ in guter/ausgezeichneter Stimmung sein, gute/glänzende or ausgezeichnete Laune haben; with good ~ gutgelaunt; to be out of ~ schlechte Laune haben, schlecht gelaunt sein.
(c) (old Med) Körpersaft m.
2 vt to ~ **sb** jdm seinen Willen lassen or tun; do it just to ~ **him** tu's doch, damit er seinen Willen hat; to ~ **sb's wishes** sich jds Wünschen fügen, jdm seinen Willen lassen; to ~ **sb's whims/demands** jds Launen/Forderungen (dat) nachgeben.
-humoured, (US) **-humored** ['hjuːməd] adj suf -gelaunt.
humourless, (US) **humorless** ['hjuːməlɪs] adj humorlos, ohne jeden Humor; speech, book etc also trocken.
humourlessly, (US) **humorlessly** ['hjuːməlɪslɪ] adv humorlos, ohne jeden Humor.
hump [hʌmp] **1** n (a) (Anat) Buckel m; (of camel) Höcker m. (b) (hillock) Hügel, Buckel (esp S Ger) m. **we're over the** ~ **now** (fig) wir sind jetzt über den Berg.
(c) (Brit inf) he's got the ~ er ist sauer (inf); he/that gives me the ~ er/das fällt mir auf den Wecker (inf).
2 vt (a) to ~ **one's back** einen Buckel machen.
(b) (inf: carry) schleppen; (on back, shoulders) auf dem Rücken or Schultern or schleppen. to ~ **sth onto one's back/shoulders** sich (dat) etw auf den Rücken or Buckel (inf)/auf die Schultern laden or wuchten (inf).
hump: ~**back** n (person) Buck(e)lige(r) mf; (back) Buckel m; ~**backed** adj person buck(e)lig; bridge gewölbt.

humph [mm] interj hm.
humpy ['hʌmpɪ] adj (+er) country hügelig, buckelig (esp S Ger).
humus ['hjuːməs] n Humus m.
Hun [hʌn] n (a) (Hist) Hunne m, Hunnin f. (b) (pej inf) Teutone m (pej), Teutonin f (pej), Boche m (pej).
hunch [hʌntʃ] **1** n (a) (hump on sb's back) Buckel m.
(b) (premonition) Gefühl nt, Ahnung f. **to have a** ~ **that ... den** (leisen inf) **Verdacht** or **das (leise) Gefühl haben, daß ...**
2 vt (also ~ **up**) back krümmen; shoulders hochziehen. to ~ (up) **one's back** einen Buckel machen, den Rücken krümmen; he was ~ed up over his desk er saß über seinen Schreibtisch gebeugt; ~ed up with pain vor Schmerzen gekrümmt.
hunch: ~**back** n (person) Buck(e)lige(r) mf; (back) Buckel m; **The H**~**back of Notre Dame** der Glöckner von Notre-Dame; ~**backed** adj buck(e)lig.
hundred ['hʌndrɪd] **1** adj hundert. a or one ~ **years** (ein)hundert Jahre; **two/several** ~ **years** zweihundert/mehrere hundert Jahre; a or one ~ **and one** (lit) (ein)hundert(und)eins; (fig) tausend; a or one ~ **and two** ten (ein)hundert(und)zwei/-zehn; (one) ~ **and first/second etc** hundert(und)erste(r, s)/-zweite(r, s) etc; a or one ~ **thousand** (ein)hunderttausend; a ~**-mile walk** ein Hundertmeilenmarsch; a or one ~ **per cent** hundert Prozent; a (one) ~ **per cent increase** eine hundertprozentige Erhöhung, eine Erhöhung von or um hundert Prozent; **I'm not a** or one ~ **per cent fit** ich bin nicht hundertprozentig fit; a or one ~ **per cent inflation** eine Inflationsrate von hundert Prozent; **the H**~ **Years' War** (Hist) der Hundertjährige Krieg; **never in a** ~ **years!** nie im Leben!
2 n hundert num; (written figure) Hundert f. ~**s** (lit, fig) Hunderte pl; (Math: figures in column) Hunderter pl; **to count in** ~**s/up to a** or one ~ in Hundertern/bis hundert zählen; the ~**s column** (Math) die Hunderterspalte; **one in a** ~ einer unter hundert; **eighty out of a** ~ achtzig von hundert; **an audience of** a or one/two ~ hundert/zweihundert Zuschauer; ~**s of times** hundertmal, Hunderte von Malen; ~**s and** ~**s** Hunderte und aber Hunderte; ~**s of thousands** Hunderttausende pl; ~**s and thousands** Hunderttausende pl; (Cook) Liebesperlen pl; **he earned nine** ~ **a year** er verdiente neunhundert im Jahr; **I'll lay (you) a** ~ **to one** ich wette hundert gegen eins; **to sell sth by the** ~ (lit, fig) etw im Hundert verkaufen; **it'll cost you a** ~ **das wird dich einen Hunderter kosten; to live to be a** ~ hundert Jahre alt werden; **they came in (their)** ~**s** or **by the** ~ sie kamen zu Hunderten.
hundredfold ['hʌndrɪdfəʊld] adj, adv hundertfach. **to increase a** ~ um das Hundertfache steigern.
hundredth ['hʌndrɪdθ] **1** adj (in series) hundertste(r, s); (of fraction) hundertstel. **2** n Hundertste(r, s) decl as adj; (fraction) Hundertstel nt; see also **sixth**.
hundredweight ['hʌndrɪdweɪt] n Zentner m; (Brit) 50,8 kg; (US) 45,4 kg.
hung [hʌŋ] pret, ptp of **hang**.
Hungarian [hʌŋ'geərɪən] **1** adj ungarisch. **2** n (a) (person) Ungar(in f) m. (b) (language) Ungarisch nt.
Hungary ['hʌŋgərɪ] n Ungarn nt.
hunger ['hʌŋgəʳ] **1** n (a) (lit) Hunger m. **to go on (a)** ~ **strike in (den) Hungerstreik treten; a** ~ **march** Hungermarsch m or -demonstration f. (b) (fig) Hunger m (for nach). ~ **for news** sehnsüchtiges Warten auf Nachricht. **2** vi (old, liter) hungern.
♦**hunger after** or **for** vi +prep obj (liter) hungern nach; news sehnsüchtig warten auf (+acc).
hungrily ['hʌŋgrɪlɪ] adv (lit, fig) hungrig.
hungry ['hʌŋgrɪ] adj (+er) (a) (lit) hungrig. **to be** or **feel/get** ~ Hunger haben/bekommen; **to go** ~ hungern.
(b) (fig) hungrig; soil mager, karg. ~ **for knowledge/love/power/adventure/success** bildungs-/liebes-/macht-/abenteuer-/erfolgshungrig; **to be** ~ **for news** sehnsüchtig auf Nachricht warten; **to be** ~ **for fame/riches/company** sich nach Ruhm/Reichtum/Gesellschaft sehnen.
hung-up [ˌhʌŋ'ʌp] adj (inf) **to be/get** ~ (about sth) (be neurotic) (wegen etw) einen Knacks weghaben (inf)/(wegen etw) durchdrehen (inf); (have complex) Komplexe (wegen etw) haben/kriegen; **he's really** ~ **about things like that** wenn es darum geht, hat er einen richtigen Knacks weg (inf); **to be** ~ **about being old/single etc** einen Komplex haben, weil man alt/nicht verheiratet etc ist; **he's** ~ **on drugs** (sl) er kommt von den Drogen nicht mehr los; **he's** ~ **on her** (sl) er steht auf sie (sl).
hunk [hʌŋk] n (a) Stück nt. (b) (fig inf: man) **a gorgeous** ~ (of a man) ein Mann! (inf).
hunky-dory ['hʌŋkɪ'dɔːrɪ] adj (inf) that's ~ das ist in Ordnung.
hunt [hʌnt] **1** n (a) Jagd f; (huntsmen) Jagd(gesellschaft) f; (fig: search) Suche f. tiger ~ Tigerjagd f; ~ **ball** Jagdball m; **the** ~ **is on** or **up** die Suche hat begonnen; **to have a** ~ **for sth** (inf) nach etw fahnden (inf), eine Suche nach etw veranstalten; **to be on the** ~ **for sth** (for animal) etw jagen, auf etw (acc) Jagd machen; (fig) auf der Suche or Jagd nach etw sein (inf).
2 vt (a) (Hunt) jagen; (search for) criminal also Jagd machen auf (+acc); missing article etc suchen; missing person suchen, fahnden nach. **to** ~ **the slipper/thimble** Pantoffel-/Fingerhutverstecken nt.
(b) **to** ~ **a horse/hounds** zu Pferd/mit Hunden jagen.
3 vi (a) (Hunt) jagen. **to go** ~**ing** jagen, auf die Jagd gehen. (b) (to search) suchen (for, after nach). **to** ~ **for an animal** auf ein Tier Jagd machen; **to** ~ **high and low** überall suchen (for nach), alles auf den Kopf stellen (for auf der Suche nach).
♦**hunt about** or **around** vi herumsuchen or -kramen (for nach).
♦**hunt down** vt sep animal, person (unerbittlich) Jagd machen auf (+acc); (capture) zur Strecke bringen.
♦**hunt out** vt sep heraussuchen, hervorkramen (inf); person, facts ausfindig machen, aufstöbern (inf).
♦**hunt up** vt sep history, origins Nachforschungen anstellen über (+acc), forschen nach (+dat); person also, facts

auftreiben (inf), ausfindig machen; old clothes, records etc kramen nach (+dat), hervorkramen. ~ him ~ for me, would you? sieh mal bitte nach, ob du ihn irgendwo auftreiben kannst.

hunter ['hʌntəʳ] n (a) (person) Jäger m; (horse) Jagdpferd nt; (dog) Jagdhund m. (b) (watch) Sprungdeckeluhr f. (c) (Astron) the H~ Orion m.

hunting ['hʌntɪŋ] n (a) (Sport) die Jagd, das Jagen; (also fox-~) (die) Fuchsjagd f. the horse has never been used for ~ das Pferd ist nie zur Jagd geritten worden; there's good ~ in these woods diese Wälder sind ein gutes Jagdgebiet. (b) (fig: search) Suche f (for nach). after months/a lot of ~ ... nach monatelanger/langer Suche ...

hunting in cpds Jagd-; ~ box Jagdhütte f; ~ lodge n Jagdhütte f; (larger) Jagdschloß nt; ~ pink n (colour) Rot nt (des Reitrockes); (clothes) roter (Jagd)rock.

huntress ['hʌntrɪs] n Jägerin f.

huntsman ['hʌntsmən] n, pl -men [-mən] Jagdreiter m.

huntswoman ['hʌntswʊmən] n, pl -women [-wɪmɪn] Jagdreiterin f.

hurdle ['hɜːdl] 1 n (a) (Sport) Hürde f. ~s sing (race) Hürdenlauf m; (Horseracing) Hürdenrennen nt; the 100m ~s (die) 100 m Hürden, (der) 100-m-Hürdenlauf. (b) (fig) Hürde f. to fall at the first ~ (schon) über die erste or bei der ersten Hürde stolpern.
2 vt fence nehmen.
3 vi Hürdenlauf machen. he isn't good at hurdling er ist nicht gut im Hürdenlauf.

hurdler ['hɜːdləʳ] n (Sport) Hürdenläufer(in f) m.

hurdy-gurdy ['hɜːdɪˌɡɜːdɪ] n Leierkasten m, Drehorgel f.

hurl [hɜːl] vt schleudern. to ~ oneself at sb/into the fray sich auf jdn/in das Getümmel stürzen; they ~ed back their attackers sie warfen ihre Angreifer zurück; to ~ abuse/insults at sb jdn wüst beschimpfen (inf)/jdm Beleidigungen ins Gesicht schleudern.

hurly-burly ['hɜːlɪ'bɜːlɪ] n Getümmel nt, Rummel m (inf). the ~ of politics der Rummel der Politik.

hurrah [hʊˈrɑː], **hurray** [hʊˈreɪ] interj Hurra. ~ for the king! ein Hoch dem König!

hurricane ['hʌrɪkən] n Orkan m; (tropical) Wirbelsturm m. ~ force Orkanstärke f; ~ lamp Sturmlaterne f.

hurried ['hʌrɪd] adj eilig; letter, essay eilig or hastig geschrieben; ceremony hastig durchgeführt, abgehaspelt (inf); work in Eile gemacht; (with little preparation) departure, wedding etc überstürzt. to eat a ~ meal hastig etwas essen.

hurriedly ['hʌrɪdlɪ] adv eilig.

hurry ['hʌrɪ] 1 n Eile f. it was rather a ~ (for us) to be ready es war eine ziemliche Hetze, bis wir fertig waren; in my ~ to get it finished ... vor lauter Eile, damit fertig zu werden ...; to do sth in a ~ etw schnell or (too fast) hastig tun; I need it in a ~ ich brauche es schnell or eilig or dringend; to be in a ~ es eilig haben, in Eile sein; I won't do that again in a ~ (inf) das mache ich so schnell nicht wieder!; what's the/your ~? was soll die Eile or Hast/warum (hast du's) so eilig?; is there any ~ for it? eilt es damit?; there's no ~ es eilt nicht, es hat Zeit.
2 vi sich beeilen; (run/go quickly) laufen, eilen (geh). there's no need to ~ kein Grund zur Eile; can't you make me ~? kannst du sie nicht zur Eile antreiben?; don't ~! laß dir Zeit!, immer mit der Ruhe! (inf); I must ~ back ich muß schnell zurück; don't ~ over it laß dir Zeit dabei.
3 vt person (make act quickly) (zur Eile) antreiben; (make move quickly) scheuchen (inf); (work etc) beschleunigen, schneller machen; (do too quickly) überstürzen. troops were hurried to the spot es wurden schleunigst Truppen dorthin gebracht; don't ~ me hetz mich nicht so!; don't ~ your meals schling das Essen nicht so runter!

♦**hurry along** 1 vi sich beeilen. ~ ~ there, please! schnell weitergehen, bitte!; she hurried ~ to her friend sie lief schnell zu ihrer Freundin; to ~ ~ the road die Straße entlanglaufen. 2 vt sep person weiterdrängen; (with work etc) zur Eile antreiben; things, work etc vorantreiben, beschleunigen.

♦**hurry away** or **off** 1 vi schnell weggehen, forteilen (geh). 2 vt sep schnell wegbringen. they hurried him ~ to the waiting car sie brachten ihn schnell zu dem wartenden Wagen.

♦**hurry on** 1 vi weiterlaufen; (verbally, with work) weitermachen. 2 vt sep person weitertreiben; (with work) antreiben.

♦**hurry out** 1 vi hinauslaufen or -eilen. 2 vt sep schnell hinausbringen or -treiben.

♦**hurry up** 1 vi sich beeilen. ~ ~! Beeilung!, beeil dich!; can't you make him ~ ~? kannst du nicht dafür sorgen, daß er sich beeilt? 2 vt sep person zur Eile antreiben; work etc vorantreiben, beschleunigen.

hurry-scurry ['hʌrɪ'skʌrɪ] 1 n Gewühl, Gewimmel nt. 2 vi (hin- and her)hasten, herumschwirren; (children, insects) wuseln.

hurt [hɜːt] (vb: pret, ptp ~) 1 vt (lit, fig) (cause pain) person, animal weh tun (+dat); (injure) verletzen. to ~ oneself sich (dat) weh tun; to ~ one's arm sich (dat) am Arm weh tun; (injure) sich (dat) den Arm verletzen; my arm is ~ing me mein Arm tut mir weh, mir tut der Arm weh; if you go on like that someone is bound to get ~ wenn ihr so weitermacht, verletzt sich bestimmt noch jemand or (fig) fühlt sich bestimmt noch jemand verletzt.
(b) (harm) schaden (+dat). it won't ~ him to wait es schadet ihm gar nicht(s), wenn er etwas wartet or warten muß; walking on the grass doesn't ~ it es schadet dem Gras nicht, wenn man darauf (herum)läuft; those most ~ by this measure die von dieser Maßnahme am stärksten Betroffenen.
2 vi (a) (be painful) weh tun; (fig also) verletzend sein. that ~s! (lit, fig) das tut weh!; nothing ~s like the truth nichts schmerzt mehr or tut mehr weh als die Wahrheit.
(b) (do harm) schaden. but surely a little drink won't ~ aber

---

ein kleines Gläschen kann doch wohl nicht schaden.
3 n Schmerz m; (baby-talk) Wehweh nt; (to feelings) Verletzung f (to gen); (to reputation etc) Schädigung f (to gen).
4 adj limb, feelings verletzt; tone, look gekränkt.

hurtful ['hɜːtfʊl] adj words, action verletzend. it was very ~ to him/his feelings es verletzte ihn/seine Gefühle sehr.

hurtfully ['hɜːtfəlɪ] adv see adj ... she said ~ ... sagte sie in verletzendem Ton.

hurtle ['hɜːtl] vi rasen. the car was hurtling along das Auto sauste or brauste dahin; it ~d against/into the wall es sauste gegen die Mauer; he came hurtling round the corner er kam um die Ecke gerast.

husband ['hʌzbənd] 1 n Ehemann m. my/her etc ~ mein/ihr etc Mann; give my best wishes to your ~ grüßen Sie Ihren Mann or Gatten (form) von mir. 2 vt strength, resources haushalten or sparsam umgehen mit.

husbandry ['hʌzbəndrɪ] n (a) (management) Haushalten, Wirtschaften nt. (b) (farming) Landwirtschaft f.

hush [hʌʃ] 1 vt person zum Schweigen bringen; (soothe) fears etc beschwichtigen. 2 vi still sein. 3 n Stille f. 4 interj pst.
♦**hush up** vt sep vertuschen.

hushed [hʌʃt] adj voices gedämpft; words leise. in ~ tones mit gedämpfter Stimme, im gedämpften Ton.

hush-hush ['hʌʃhʌʃ] adj (inf) streng geheim.

hush-money ['hʌʃˌmʌnɪ] n Schweigegeld nt.

husk [hʌsk] 1 n Schale f; (of wheat) Spelze f; (of maize) Hüllblatt nt; (of rice also) Hülse f. 2 vt schälen.

huskily ['hʌskɪlɪ] adv mit rauher Stimme; (hoarsely) heiser, mit heiserer Stimme.

huskiness ['hʌskɪnɪs] n Rauheit f; (hoarseness) Heiserkeit f.

husky[1] ['hʌskɪ] adj (+er) (a) rauh, belegt; singer's voice also rauchig; (hoarse) heiser. a voice made ~ with emotion eine vor Erregung heisere Stimme. (b) (sturdy) person stämmig.

husky[2] n (dog) Schlittenhund m.

hussar [hʊˈzɑːʳ] n Husar m.

hussy ['hʌsɪ] n (pert girl) Fratz m (inf), (freche) Göre (inf); (whorish woman) Flittchen nt (pej).

hustings ['hʌstɪŋz] npl (Brit) (campaign) Wahlkampf m; (meeting) Wahlveranstaltung f. on the ~ im Wahlkampf; (at election meeting) in or bei einer Wahlveranstaltung.

hustle ['hʌsl] 1 n (jostling) Gedränge nt; (hurry) Hetze, Eile f. the ~ (and bustle) of the city centre das geschäftige Treiben or das Gewühl (inf) in der Innenstadt.
2 vt (a) to ~ sb into a room etc/out of the building jdn schnell in einen Raum etc/aus einem Gebäude bringen or befördern (inf); she ~d her way through the crowd sie drängelte sich durch die Menge.
(b) (fig) drängen. I won't be ~d into a decision ich lasse mich nicht zu einer Entscheidung drängen; to ~ things (on or along) die Dinge vorantreiben or beschleunigen.
3 vi (a) hasten, eilen; (through crowd etc) sich (durch)-drängeln.
(b) (solicit) auf den Strich gehen (inf). to ~ for custom nach Freiern Ausschau halten (inf).
(c) (US inf: work quickly) sich ins Zeug legen (inf).

hustler ['hʌsləʳ] n (a) (prostitute) Straßenmädchen, Strichmädchen (inf) nt; (male) Strichjunge m (inf). (b) (US inf: hard worker) Arbeitstier nt (inf).

hustling ['hʌslɪŋ] n (Straßen)prostitution f, der Strich (inf).

hut [hʌt] n Hütte f; (Mil) Baracke f.

hutch [hʌtʃ] n Verschlag, Stall m.

hyacinth ['haɪəsɪnθ] n Hyazinthe f.

hyaena, hyena [haɪˈiːnə] n Hyäne f. to laugh like a ~ wiehernd lachen.

hybrid ['haɪbrɪd] 1 n (Ling) hybride Bildung or Form; (Bot, Zool) Kreuzung f, Hybride mf (form); (fig) Mischform f. 2 adj (Ling) hybrid (spec); (Bot, Zool) Misch-.

hybridism ['haɪbrɪdɪzəm] n (lit, fig) Hybridismus m.

hybridization [ˌhaɪbrɪdaɪˈzeɪʃən] n (Ling) Hybridisation f (spec); (Bot, Zool also) Kreuzung f; (fig) Mischung f, Zwitter m.

hybridize ['haɪbrɪdaɪz] vt (Ling) hybridisieren (spec); (Bot, Zool also) kreuzen; (fig) mischen, kreuzen.

hydra ['haɪdrə] n (Zool, Myth) Hydra f.

hydrangea [haɪˈdreɪndʒə] n Hortensie f.

hydrant ['haɪdrənt] n Hydrant m.

hydrate ['haɪdreɪt] 1 n Hydrat nt. 2 [haɪˈdreɪt] vt hydratisieren.

hydrated [haɪˈdreɪtɪd] adj wasserhaltig.

hydraulic [haɪˈdrɒlɪk] adj hydraulisch.

hydraulics [haɪˈdrɒlɪks] n sing Hydraulik f.

hydric ['haɪdrɪk] adj Wasserstoff-, wasserstoff-, Hydro-, hydro-.

hydride ['haɪdraɪd] n Hydrid nt.

hydro ['haɪdrəʊ] n Kurhotel nt (mit Hydrotherapie).

hydro- ['haɪdrəʊ-] pref (concerning water) Hydro-, hydro-, Wasser-, wasser-; (Chem) (+n) -wasserstoff m. ~carbon Kohlenwasserstoff m; ~cephalic [ˌhaɪdrəʊˈsefælɪk] wasserköpfig, mit einem Wasserkopf; ~cephalus [ˌhaɪdrəʊˈsefələs] Wasserkopf m; ~chloric acid Salzsäure f; ~dynamics Hydrodynamik f; ~electric hydroelektrisch; ~electric power durch Wasserkraft erzeugte Energie; ~electric power station Wasserkraftwerk nt; ~electricity durch Wasserkraft erzeugte Energie f; ~foil (boat) Tragflächen- or Tragflügelboot nt; (fin) Tragfläche f or -flügel m.

hydrogen ['haɪdrɪdʒən] n Wasserstoff m, Hydrogenium nt (spec). ~ bomb Wasserstoffbombe f; ~ bond Wasserstoffbrücke(nbindung) f; ~ sulphide (gas) Schwefelwasserstoff m.

hydrography [haɪˈdrɒɡrəfɪ] n Gewässerkunde f.

hydrology [haɪˈdrɒlədʒɪ] n Hydrologie f.

hydrolysis [haɪˈdrɒlɪsɪs] n Hydrolyse f.

hydrometer [haɪˈdrɒmɪtəʳ] n Hydrometer nt.

hydro-: ~**pathic** [,haɪdrəʊ'pæθɪk] *adj* hydrotherapeutisch; ~**phobia** *n* Hydrophobie (*spec*), Wasserscheu *f*; (*rabies*) Tollwut *f*; ~**plane** *n* (a) (*Aviat: aircraft*) Wasserflugzeug, Flugboot *nt*; (*float*) Schwimmer *m*; (b) (*Naut*) (*boat*) Gleitboot *nt*; (*of submarine*) Tiefenruder *nt*; ~**therapeutics** *n sing* Wasserheilkunde, Hydrotherapeutik (*spec*) *f*; ~**therapy** *n* Wasserbehandlung, Hydrotherapie (*spec*) *f*.

hydroxide [haɪ'drɒksaɪd] *n* Hydroxyd, Hydroxid *nt*.

hyena [haɪ'iːnə] *n see* **hyaena.**

hygiene ['haɪdʒiːn] *n* Hygiene *f*. **personal** ~ Körperpflege *f*.

hygienic *adj*, ~**ally** *adv* [haɪ'dʒiːnɪk, -əlɪ] hygienisch.

hygienics [haɪ'dʒiːnɪks] *n sing* Hygiene, Gesundheitslehre *f*.

hygro- [haɪgrəʊ-] *pref* Hygro-, hygro-, (Luft)feuchtigkeits-. ~**meter** ['haɪˈgrɒmɪtə'] Hygrometer *nt*.

hymen ['haɪmen] *n* Hymen (*spec*), Jungfernhäutchen *nt*.

hymenopterous [,haɪmə'nɒptərɪs] *adj* ~ **insect** Hautflügler *m*.

hymn [hɪm] **1** *n* Hymne *f*. **2** *vt* (*old*) besingen; (*Eccl*) (lob-)preisen.

hymnal ['hɪmnəl] *n* Gesangbuch *nt*.

hymnbook ['hɪmbʊk] *n* Gesangbuch *nt*.

hymn-singing ['hɪm,sɪŋɪŋ] *n* Singen *nt* (von Chorälen). **we had ~ once a week** wir hatten einmal in der Woche Choralsingen.

hyped up ['haɪpt'ʌp] *adj* (*sl*) **high** (*sl*), unter Strom (*sl*).

hyper- ['haɪpə'] *pref* Hyper-, hyper-, Über-, über-, Super-, super-. ~**acidity** Übersäuerung, Hyperazidität (*spec*) *f*; ~**active** sehr *or* äußerst aktiv; **a** ~**active thyroid** eine Überfunktion der Schilddrüse.

hyperbola [haɪ'pɜːbələ] *n* (*Math*) Hyperbel *f*.

hyperbole [haɪ'pɜːbəlɪ] *n* (*Liter*) Hyperbel *f*.

hyperbolic(al) [,haɪpə'bɒlɪk(əl)] *adj* (*Liter, Math*) hyperbolisch; (*Math also*) Hyperbel-.

hyper-: ~**critical** *adj* übertrieben kritisch; ~**market** *n* großer Supermarkt; ~**sensitive** *adj* überempfindlich; ~**tension** *n* Hypertonie *f*, erhöhter Blutdruck; ~**thyroidism** *n* Überfunktion *f* der Schilddrüse, ~**trophy** *n* Hypertrophie *f*.

hyphen ['haɪfən] *n* Bindestrich *m*; (*at end of line*) Trenn(ungs-)strich *m*; (*Typ*) Divis *nt*.

hyphenate ['haɪfəneɪt] *vt* mit Bindestrich schreiben; (*Typ*) koppeln (*spec*). ~**d word** Bindestrich- *or* (*Typ*) Koppelwort *nt*.

hypno- [hɪpnəʊ-] *pref* Hypno-, hypno-.

hypnosis [hɪp'nəʊsɪs] *n* Hypnose *f*. **under** ~ unter *or* in Hypnose, in hypnotisiertem Zustand.

hypnotic [hɪp'nɒtɪk] **1** *adj* hypnotisch; (*hypnotizing, fig*) hypnotisierend. **2** *n* (a) (*drug*) Hypnotikum (*spec*), Schlafmittel *nt*.

(b) (*person*) (*easily hypnotized*) leicht hypnotisierbarer Mensch; (*under hypnosis*) Hypnotisierte(r) *mf*.

hypnotism ['hɪpnətɪzəm] *n* Hypnotismus *m*; (*act*) Hypnotisierung *f*.

hypnotist ['hɪpnətɪst] *n* Hypnotiseur *m*, Hypnotiseuse *f*.

hypnotize ['hɪpnətaɪz] *vt* hypnotisieren.

hypo- [haɪpəʊ-] *pref* Hypo-, hypo. ~**chondria** *n* Hypochondrie *f*.

hypochondriac [,haɪpəʊ'kɒndriæk] **1** *n* Hypochonder *m*. **2** *adj* (*also* ~**al** [-əl]) hypochondrisch.

hypocrisy [hɪ'pɒkrɪsɪ] *n* (*hypocritical behaviour*) Heuchelei *f*; (*sanctimony*) Scheinheiligkeit *f*.

hypocrite ['hɪpəkrɪt] *n* Heuchler(in *f*) *m*; Scheinheilige(r) *mf*.

hypocritical *adj*, ~**ly** *adv* [,hɪpə'krɪtɪkəl, -ɪ] heuchlerisch, scheinheilig.

hypodermic [,haɪpə'dɜːmɪk] **1** *adj injection* subkutan. ~ **syringe/needle** Subkutanspritze *f*/-nadel *f*; (*loosely*) Spritze *f*/Nadel *f*. **2** *n* (a) (*syringe*) subkutane Spritze. (b) (*injection*) subkutane Injektion.

hypotenuse [haɪ'pɒtɪnjuːz] *n* Hypotenuse *f*. **the square on the** ~ das Quadrat über der Hypotenuse.

hypothermia [,haɪpəʊ'θɜːmɪə] *n* Unterkühlung *f*; Kältetod *m*.

hypothesis [haɪ'pɒθɪsɪs] *n*, *pl* **hypotheses** [haɪ'pɒθɪsiːz] Hypothese, Annahme *f*. **working** ~ Arbeitshypothese *f*.

hypothesize [haɪ'pɒθɪsaɪz] **1** *vi* Hypothesen/eine Hypothese aufstellen. **2** *vt* annehmen.

hypothetical [,haɪpəʊ'θetɪkəl] *adj* hypothetisch, angenommen. **purely** ~ reine Hypothese.

hypothetically [,haɪpəʊ'θetɪkəlɪ] *adv* hypothetisch.

hysterectomy [,hɪstə'rektəmɪ] *n* Hysterektomie (*spec*), Totaloperation *f*.

hysteria [hɪ'stɪərɪə] *n* Hysterie *f*. **mass** ~ Massenhysterie *f*.

hysterical [hɪ'sterɪkəl] *adj* hysterisch; (*inf: very funny*) wahnsinnig komisch (*inf*).

hysterically [hɪ'sterɪkəlɪ] *adv* hysterisch. **to laugh** ~ hysterisch lachen; (*fig*) vor Lachen brüllen; ~ **funny** (*inf*) irrsinnig komisch (*inf*).

hysterics [hɪ'sterɪks] *npl* Hysterie *f*, hysterischer Anfall. **to stop sb's** ~ jds Hysterie (*dat*) ein Ende machen; **to go into** ~ hysterisch werden, einen hysterischen Anfall bekommen; (*fig inf: laugh*) sich totlachen, sich nicht mehr halten können vor Lachen; **we were in** ~ **about it** (*inf*) wir haben uns darüber (halb) totgelacht (*inf*); **just looking at Charlie Chaplin was enough to give you** ~ schon beim bloßen Anblick von Charlie Chaplin konnte man sich (halb) totlachen (*inf*).

I

I¹, i [aɪ] *n* I, i *nt; see* **dot.**

I² *abbr of* **Island, Isle.**

I³ *pers pron* ich. **it is** ~ (*form*) ich bin es; **his conversation is full of "I's"** wenn er redet, hört man dauernd nur „ich".

iambic [aɪ'æmbɪk] **1** *adj* jambisch. ~ **pentameter** fünffüßiger Jambus. **2** *n* Jambus *m*.

IATA [aɪ'ɑːtə] *abbr of* **International Air Transport Association** IATA *f*.

IBA (*Brit*) *abbr of* **Independent Broadcasting Authority.**

Iberia [aɪ'bɪərɪə] *n* Iberien *nt*.

Iberian [aɪ'bɪərɪən] **1** *adj* iberisch. ~ **Peninsula** Iberische Halbinsel. **2** *n* (a) Iberer(in *f*) *m*. (b) (*language*) Iberisch *nt*.

ibex ['aɪbeks] *n* Steinbock *m*.

ib(id) *abbr of* **ibidem** ib., ibd.

ibis ['aɪbɪs] *n* Ibis *m*.

i/c, I/C *abbr of* **in charge** v.D., vom Dienst.

ice [aɪs] **1** *n* (a) Eis *nt*; (*on roads*) (Glatt)eis *nt*. **to be as cold as** ~ eiskalt sein; **my hands are like** ~ ich habe eiskalte Hände; **"Cinderella on I~"** „Aschenputtel auf dem Eis"; **to keep** *or* **put sth on** ~ (*lit*) etw kalt stellen; (*fig*) etw auf Eis legen; **to break the** ~ (*fig*) das Eis brechen; **to be** *or* **be treading** *or* **be skating on thin** ~ (*fig*) sich aufs Glatteis begeben/begeben haben; **you are (skating) on thin** ~ **there** da begibst du dich aufs Glatteis; **to cut no** ~ **with sb** (*inf*) auf jdn keinen Eindruck machen; **that cuts no** ~ **with me** (*inf*) das kommt bei mir nicht an.

(b) (*Brit*: ice-cream) (Speise)eis *nt*, Eiskrem *f*.

(c) **no** *pl* (*US sl: diamond*) Klunker *m* (*sl*).

2 *vt* (a) (*make cold*) (mit Eis) kühlen; (*freeze*) tiefkühlen. (b) *cake* glasieren, mit Zuckerguß überziehen.

♦**ice over** *vi* zufrieren; (*windscreen*) vereisen.

♦**ice up** *vi* (*aircraft wings, rail points, windscreen*) vereisen; (*pipes etc*) einfrieren.

ice in *cpds* Eis-. ~ **age** *n* Eiszeit *f*; ~ **axe** *n* Eispickel *m*; ~**berg** *n* (*lit, fig*) Eisberg *m*; ~**boat** *n* (a) (*Sport*) Segelschlitten *m*; (b) *see* ~**breaker**; ~**bound** *adj* port zugefroren, vereist; *ship* vom Eis eingeschlossen; *road* vereist; ~**box** *n* (*Brit: in refrigerator*) Eisfach *nt*; (*US*) Eisschrank *m*; (*insulated box*) Eisbox, Kühltasche

f; **this room is like an** ~**box** dieses Zimmer ist der reinste Eiskeller; ~**breaker** *n* Eisbrecher *m*; ~ **bucket** *n* Eiskühler *m*; ~**cap** *n* Eisdecke, Eisschicht *f*; (*polar*) Eiskappe *f*; ~-**cold** *adj* eiskalt; ~-**cream** *n* Eis *nt*, Eiskrem *f*; ~-**cream parlour** *n* Eisdiele *f*; ~-**cream soda** *n* Eisbecher *m* mit Sirup, Marmelade, Früchten, Milch und Ingwerbier; ~ **cube** *n* Eiswürfel *m*.

iced [aɪst] *adj* (a) (*cooled*) eisgekühlt; (*covered with ice*) vereist, mit Eis bedeckt. ~ **coffee** Eiskaffee *m*; ~ **water** Eiswasser *nt*. (b) *cake* glasiert, mit Zuckerguß überzogen.

ice: ~ **floe** *n* Eisscholle *f*; ~ **hockey** *n* Eishockey *nt*; ~**house** *n* Eiskeller *m*.

Iceland ['aɪslənd] *n* Island *nt*.

Icelander ['aɪsləndə'] *n* Isländer(in *f*) *m*.

Icelandic [aɪs'lændɪk] **1** *adj* isländisch. **2** *n* (*language*) Isländisch *nt*.

ice: ~ **lolly** *n* (*Brit*) Eis *nt* am Stiel; ~**man** *n* (*US*) Eisverkäufer *m*; ~ **pack** *n* Packeis *nt*; (*on head*) Eisbeutel *m*; ~ **pick** *n* Eispickel *m*; ~ **rink** *n* (Kunst)eisbahn, Schlittschuhbahn *f*; ~ **sheet** *n* Eisschicht *f*; ~-**skate** *vi* Schlittschuh laufen *or* fahren; ~**skate** *n* Schlittschuh *m*; ~-**skating** *n* Eislauf *m*, Schlittschuhlaufen *nt*; ~-**tray** *n* Eisschale *f*.

ichneumon fly [ɪk'njuːmən,flaɪ] *n* Schlupfwespe *f*.

ichthyology [,ɪkθɪ'ɒlədʒɪ] *n* Fischkunde, Ichthyologie *f*.

ICI *abbr of* **Imperial Chemical Industries** ICI *f*.

icicle ['aɪsɪkl] *n* Eiszapfen *m*.

icily ['aɪsɪlɪ] *adv* (*lit, fig*) eisig. **the wind blew** ~ es wehte ein eisiger Wind; **to look** ~ **at sb** jdm einen eisigen Blick zuwerfen.

iciness ['aɪsɪnɪs] *n* Eiseskälte *f*, eisige Kälte; (*of road etc*) Vereisung *f*.

icing ['aɪsɪŋ] *n* (a) (*Cook*) Zuckerguß *m*. ~ **sugar** (*Brit*) Puderzucker *m*. (b) (*on aircraft, rail points*) Eisbildung, Vereisung *f*.

icon ['aɪkɒn] *n* Ikone *f*.

iconoclasm [aɪ'kɒnəklæzəm] *n* (*lit, fig*) Bilderstürmerei *f*.

iconoclast [aɪ'kɒnəklæst] *n* (*lit, fig*) Bilderstürmer, Ikonoklast (*liter*) *m*.

iconoclastic [aɪ,kɒnə'klæstɪk] *adj* (*lit*) bilderstürmend; (*fig*) bilderstürmerisch.

iconographic [aɪˌkɒnə'græfɪk] adj ikonographisch.
icy ['aɪsɪ] adj (+er) (lit, fig) eisig; (covered with ice) road vereist; ground gefroren.
I'd [aɪd] contr of I would; I had.
id [ɪd] n (Psych) Es nt.
ID abbr of identification; identity.
idea [aɪ'dɪə] n (a) Idee f (also Philos); (sudden also) Einfall m. good ~! gute Idee!; that's not a bad ~ das ist keine schlechte Idee; what an ~! so eine or was für eine Idee!; who thought of that ~? wer hat sich (dat) denn das einfallen lassen?; he's our new ~s man (inf) er ist hier der Mann mit den neuen Ideen; history of ~s Geistesgeschichte f; man of ~s Denker m; the very ~! (nein), so was!; the very ~ of eating horsemeat revolts me der bloße Gedanke an Pferdefleisch ekelt mich; the ~ never entered my head! auf den Gedanken bin ich überhaupt nicht gekommen; he is full of (bright) ~s ihm fehlt es nie an (guten) Ideen; to hit upon the ~ of doing sth den plötzlichen Einfall haben, etw zu tun; that gives me an ~, we could ... da fällt mir ein, wir könnten ...; he got the ~ for his novel while he was having a bath die Idee zu seinem Roman kam ihm in der Badewanne; to lack ~s phantasielos or einfallslos sein; whose bright ~ was that? (iro) wer hat denn diese glänzende Idee gehabt?; he hasn't an ~ in his head er ist völlig ideenlos; he's somehow got the ~ into his head that ... er bildet sich (dat) irgendwie ein, daß ...; don't get ~s or don't you go getting ~s about promotion machen Sie sich (dat) nur keine falschen Hoffnungen auf eine Beförderung; don't get or go getting any ~s about that fur coat bilde dir das nicht ein, du würdest den Pelzmantel bekommen; to put ~s into sb's head jdm einen Floh ins Ohr setzen, jdn auf dumme Gedanken bringen.
(b) (purpose) the ~ was to meet at 6 wir wollten uns um 6 treffen; what's the ~ of keeping him waiting? was soll denn das, ihn warten zu lassen?; what's the big ~? (inf) was soll das denn?; the ~ is to ... es ist beabsichtigt, zu ...; that's the ~ so ist es richtig, genau (das ist's)!; you're getting the ~ Sie verstehen langsam, worum es geht.
(c) (opinion) Meinung, Ansicht f; (conception) Vorstellung f. if that's your ~ of fun wenn Sie das lustig finden, wenn das Ihre Vorstellung von Spaß ist; he has some very strange ~s er hat manchmal merkwürdige Vorstellungen; according to his ~ seiner Ansicht or Meinung nach; he has no ~ of right and wrong er kann Gut und Böse nicht auseinanderhalten; his ~ of a pleasant evening is ... seine Vorstellung von einem angenehmen Abend ist, ...
(d) (knowledge) Ahnung f. you've no ~ how worried I've been du kannst dir nicht vorstellen, welche Sorgen ich mir gemacht habe; to have some ~ of art ein bißchen von Kunst verstehen; (I've) no ~ (ich habe) keine Ahnung; I haven't the least or slightest or faintest ~ ich habe nicht die leiseste or geringste Ahnung; I have an ~ that ... ich habe so das Gefühl, daß ...; I had no ~ that ... ich hatte ja keine Ahnung, daß ...; just to give me an ~ of how long damit ich so ungefähr weiß, wie lange; could you give me an ~ of how long ...? könnten Sie mir ungefähr sagen, wie lange ...?; to give you an ~ of how difficult it is um Ihnen eine Vorstellung davon zu vermitteln, wie schwierig es ist.
ideal [aɪ'dɪəl] 1 adj ideal, vollkommen. 2 n Idealvorstellung f, Ideal nt (also Philos).
idealism [aɪ'dɪəlɪzəm] n Idealismus m.
idealist [aɪ'dɪəlɪst] n Idealist(in f) m.
idealistic [aɪˌdɪə'lɪstɪk] adj idealistisch.
idealize [aɪ'dɪəlaɪz] vt idealisieren.
ideally [aɪ'dɪəlɪ] adv ideal. they are ~ suited for each other sie passen ausgezeichnet zueinander; ~, the house should have four rooms idealerweise or im Idealfall sollte das Haus vier Zimmer haben.
identical [aɪ'dentɪkəl] adj (exactly alike) identisch, (völlig) gleich; (same) derselbe/dieselbe/dasselbe. can you be sure this is the ~ man you saw? sind Sie auch wirklich sicher, daß dies der Mann ist, den Sie gesehen haben?; ~ twins eineiige Zwillinge pl; we have ~ views wir haben die gleichen Ansichten.
identically [aɪ'dentɪkəlɪ] adv identisch, gleich.
identifiable [aɪˌdentɪ'faɪəbl] adj erkennbar; (esp in scientific contexts) identifizierbar. he is ~ by his red hair er ist an seinem roten Haar zu erkennen; that makes him/it ~ daran kann man ihn/es erkennen.
identification [aɪˌdentɪfɪ'keɪʃən] n (a) (of criminal, dead person etc) Identifizierung f, Feststellung f der Identität. a system of fingerprint ~ ein erkennungsdienstliches System auf der Basis von Fingerabdrücken.
(b) (papers) Ausweispapiere pl, Legitimation f. because he had no ~ (means of) ~ weil er sich nicht ausweisen konnte.
(c) (considering as identical, equation) Gleichsetzung, Identifizierung f.
(d) (association) Identifikation f. a politician who has any form of ~ with a criminal group ein Politiker, der irgendwie mit einer kriminellen Gruppe in Verbindung gebracht wird.
identification: ~ papers npl Ausweispapiere pl; ~ parade n Gegenüberstellung f (zur Identifikation des Täters); ~ tag n (US) Erkennungsmarke f.
identify [aɪ'dentɪfaɪ] 1 vt (a) (establish identity of) identifizieren, die Identität (+gen) feststellen; plant, species etc bestimmen; (mark identity of) kennzeichnen; (recognize, pick out) erkennen. to ~ sb/sth by sth jdn/etw an etw (dat) erkennen.
(b) (consider as the same) gleichsetzen (with mit), als identisch betrachten.
(c) (associate with) assoziieren.
2 vr (a) to ~ oneself sich ausweisen.
(b) to ~ oneself with sb/sth sich mit jdm/etw identifizieren.
3 vi (with film hero etc) sich identifizieren (with mit).
identikit [aɪ'dentɪkɪt] n: ~ (picture) Phantombild nt.
identity [aɪ'dentɪtɪ] n (a) Identität f. to prove one's ~ sich ausweisen; a driving licence will be accepted as proof of ~ ein Führerschein genügt, um sich auszuweisen; proof of ~ (permit) Legitimation f; see mistaken.
(b) (identicalness) Gleichheit, Übereinstimmung, Identität f. there is no ~ of interest between ... es gibt keine Interessengleichheit zwischen ...
identity: ~ bracelet n Identitätsarmband nt; ~ card n (Personal)ausweis m, Kennkarte f (dated); ~ crisis n Identitätskrise f; ~ disc n (Mil) Erkennungsmarke f; (for dogs) Hundemarke f; ~ papers npl Ausweispapiere pl.
ideogram ['ɪdɪəʊgræm], **ideograph** ['ɪdɪəʊgrɑːf] n Ideogramm nt.
ideological adj, ~ly adv [ˌaɪdɪə'lɒdʒɪkəl, -ɪ] weltanschaulich, ideologisch (often pej).
ideologist [ˌaɪdɪ'ɒlədʒɪst] n Ideologe m, Ideologin f.
ideology [ˌaɪdɪ'ɒlədʒɪ] n Weltanschauung, Ideologie f.
ides [aɪdz] npl Iden pl. the ~ of March die Iden pl des März.
idiocy ['ɪdɪəsɪ] n (a) no pl Idiotie f, Schwachsinn m. (b) (stupid act, words) Dummheit, Blödheit f.
idiolect ['ɪdɪəlekt] n Idiolekt m.
idiom ['ɪdɪəm] n (a) (special phrase, group of words) idiomatische Wendung, Redewendung f. (b) (language) Sprache f, Idiom nt; (of region) Mundart f, Dialekt m; (of author) Ausdrucksweise, Diktion f. ... to use the modern ~ ... um es modern auszudrücken.
idiomatic [ˌɪdɪə'mætɪk] adj idiomatisch. to speak ~ German idiomatisch richtiges Deutsch sprechen; an ~ expression eine Redensart, eine idiomatische Redewendung.
idiomatically [ˌɪdɪə'mætɪkəlɪ] adv see adj.
idiomaticity [ˌɪdɪəʊmə'tɪsɪtɪ] n Idiomatik f. his language lacked ~ er drückte sich nicht sehr idiomatisch aus.
idiosyncrasy [ˌɪdɪə'sɪŋkrəsɪ] n Eigenheit, Eigenart, Besonderheit f; (Ling, Med) Idiosynkrasie f.
idiosyncratic [ˌɪdɪəsɪŋ'krætɪk] adj eigenartig; (Ling, Med) idiosynkratisch. he has a very ~ way of ... er hat eine eigene Art zu ...
idiot ['ɪdɪət] n Idiot, Dummkopf, Schwachkopf m; (old Med) Idiot(in f) m, Schwachsinnige(r) mf. what an ~! so ein Idiot or Dummkopf!; you (stupid) ~! du Idiot!; where's that ~ waiter? wo ist dieser blöde Ober, wo ist dieser Idiot von Ober?; this ~ brother of mine dieser Schwachkopf or Dummkopf or Idiot von meinem Bruder; you're speaking like an ~ du redest völligen Blödsinn; what an ~ I am/was! ich Idiot!
idiot card n (TV) Neger m.
idiotic [ˌɪdɪ'ɒtɪk] adj blöd(sinnig), idiotisch. don't be ~ sei kein Idiot; what an ~ price to pay! idiotisch, so viel dafür zu bezahlen!
idiotically [ˌɪdɪ'ɒtɪkəlɪ] adv blödsinnig, idiotisch; expensive lachhaft, absurd; exaggerated lächerlich. ~, I had ... blödsinniger- or idiotischerweise hatte ich ...
idle ['aɪdl] 1 adj (a) (not working) person müßig, untätig. the ~ rich die reichen Müßiggänger; in my ~ moments in ruhigen or stillen Augenblicken; ~ life faules Leben; money lying ~ totes Kapital; we don't want to let the money lie ~ wir wollen das Geld nicht ungenutzt liegen lassen; his car was lying ~ most of the time sein Auto stand meistens unbenutzt herum.
(b) (lazy) faul, träge.
(c) (in industry) person unbeschäftigt; machine stillstehend attr, stillgelegt attr, außer Betrieb. 500 men have been made ~ by the strike durch den Streik mußten 500 Leute ihre Arbeit einstellen; the whole factory stood ~ die ganze Fabrik hatte die Arbeit eingestellt; the machine stood ~ die Maschine stand still or arbeitete nicht or war außer Betrieb.
(d) (promise, threat, words leer; (useless) nutzlos, vergeblich, eitel (old). it would be ~ to go on trying es wäre nutzlos or zwecklos, (es) weiter zu versuchen; ~ curiosity pure or bloße Neugier; ~ fear grundlose or unbegründete Angst; ~ wish Wunschtraum m; the ~ pleasures of this worldly life die eitlen Vergnügungen dieses Erdenlebens.
2 vi (a) (person) untätig sein, faulenzen, nichts tun. a day spent idling on the river ein Tag, den man untätig auf dem Wasser verbringt.
(b) (engine) leerlaufen. when the engine is idling wenn der Motor im Leerlauf ist.
♦ **idle about** or **around** vi herumtrödeln, bummeln; (loiter) herumlungern. we were idling ~ on the beach wir faulenzten am Strand; don't ~ ~ trödle nicht herum!, bummle nicht!
♦ **idle away** vt sep one's time etc vertrödeln, verbummeln.
idleness ['aɪdlnɪs] n (a) (state of not working) Untätigkeit f; (pleasurable) Muße f, Müßiggang (liter) m. to live in ~ ein untätiges Leben führen, ein Leben der Muße führen (liter); a life of blissful ~ ein Leben voller köstlicher Muße.
(b) (laziness) Faulheit, Trägheit f.
(c) see adj (d) Leere f; Müßigkeit f; Nutzlosigkeit, Vergeblichkeit, Eitelkeit f.
idler ['aɪdlər] n (person not working) Müßiggänger(in f) m; (lazy person) Faulenzer(in f) m, Faulpelz m. (b) (Tech) (wheel) Zwischenrad nt; (pulley) Spannrolle f.
idly ['aɪdlɪ] adv (a) (without working) untätig; (pleasurably) müßig. to stand ~ by untätig herumstehen. (b) (lazily) faul, träge. (c) (without thinking) say, suggest ohne sich/mir etc etwas dabei zu denken; (vainly) speculate müßig.
idol ['aɪdl] n (lit) Götze m, Götzenbild nt; (fig) Idol nt, Abgott m; (Film, TV etc) Idol nt.
idolater [aɪ'dɒlətər] n Götzendiener m.
idolatress [aɪ'dɒlətrɪs] n Götzendienerin f.
idolatrous [aɪ'dɒlətrəs] adj (lit) Götzen-; (fig) abgöttisch.
idolatry [aɪ'dɒlətrɪ] n (lit) Götzendienst m, Götzenverehrung f; (fig) Vergötterung f, abgöttische Verehrung.
idolize ['aɪdəlaɪz] vt abgöttisch lieben or verehren, vergöttern. to ~ wealth Reichtum anbeten.

I'd've ['aɪdəv] contr of **I would have**.

idyll ['ɪdɪl] n (a) (Liter) Idyll(e) f. (b) (fig) Idyll nt.

idyllic adj, **~ally** adv [ɪ'dɪlɪk, -lɪ] idyllisch.

i.e. abbr of id est i.e., d.h.

if [ɪf] **1** conj wenn; (in case also) falls, für den Fall, daß ...; (whether, in direct clause) ob. **I would be pleased ~ you could do it** wenn Sie das tun könnten, wäre ich sehr froh; **~ it rains tomorrow** wenn es or falls es morgen regnet; **I wonder ~ he'll come** ich bin gespannt, ob er kommt; **do you know ~ they have gone?** wissen Sie, ob sie gegangen sind?; **I'll let you know when or ~ I come to a decision** ich werde Ihnen mitteilen, ob und wenn ich mich entschieden habe; **where will you live when you get married? — ~ we get married!** wo wollt ihr wohnen, wenn ihr heiratet? — wenn wir überhaupt heiraten!; **~ I asked him he helped me er** half mir immer, wenn ich ihn darum bat; (even) ~ auch wenn; **it's a good film (even) ~ rather long** es ist ein guter Film, auch wenn er etwas lang ist; (even) **~ they are poor, at least they are happy** sie sind zwar arm, aber wenigstens glücklich; **~ only** wenn (doch) nur; **~ only I had known!** wenn ich das nur gewußt hätte!; **I would like to see him, ~ only for a few hours** ich würde ihn gerne sehen, wenn auch nur für ein paar Stunden; **as ~** als ob; **he acts as ~ he were or was (inf) rich** er tut so, als ob er reich wäre; **as ~ by chance** wie zufällig; **he stood there as ~ he were dumb** er stand wie stumm da; **~ necessary** falls nötig, im Bedarfsfall; **~ so** wenn ja; **~ not** falls nicht; **~ not, why not?** falls nicht, warum?; **~ I were you/him** wenn ich Sie/er wäre, an Ihrer/seiner Stelle; **~ anything this one is bigger** wenn überhaupt, dann ist dieses hier größer; **~ I know Pete, he'll ...** so wie ich Pete kenne, wird er ...; **well, ~ he didn't try to steal my bag!** (inf) wollte der doch tatsächlich meine Tasche klauen (inf); **well, ~ it isn't old Jim!** (inf) ich werd' verrückt, das ist doch der Jim (inf).

2 n Wenn nt. **it's a big ~** das ist noch sehr fraglich, das ist die große or noch sehr die Frage; **~s and buts** Wenn und Aber nt.

iffy ['ɪfɪ] adj (+er) (inf) strittig, fraglich, zweifelhaft.

igloo ['ɪgluː] n Iglu m or nt.

igneous ['ɪgnɪəs] adj (Geol) **~ rock** Eruptivgestein nt.

ignite [ɪg'naɪt] **1** vt entzünden, anzünden; (Aut) zünden. **2** vi sich entzünden, Feuer fangen; (Aut) zünden.

ignition [ɪg'nɪʃən] n (a) Entzünden, Anzünden nt. (b) (Aut) Zündung f. **we have ~** (of rocket) „Zündung".

ignition (Aut) in cpds Zünd-; **~ coil** n Zündspule f; **~ key** n Zündschlüssel m.

ignoble [ɪg'nəʊbl] adj schändlich, unwürdig, unehrenhaft. **~ peace** schmachvoller Frieden.

ignominious [‚ɪgnə'mɪnɪəs] adj schmachvoll, entwürdigend, schmählich; behaviour schändlich, unehrenhaft.

ignominiously [‚ɪgnə'mɪnɪəslɪ] adv see adj.

ignominy ['ɪgnəmɪnɪ] n Schmach, Schande f, Schimpf m (old).

ignoramus [‚ɪgnə'reɪməs] n Nichtswisser, Ignorant m.

ignorance ['ɪgnərəns] n (general lack of knowledge, education) Unwissenheit f, Mangel m an Bildung, Ignoranz f; (of particular subject, language, plan etc) Unkenntnis f. **to keep sb in ~ of sth** jdn in Unkenntnis über etw (acc) lassen, jdn etw nicht wissen lassen; **to be in ~ of sth** etw nicht wissen or kennen; **~ (of the law) is no excuse** Unkenntnis schützt vor Strafe nicht.

ignorant ['ɪgnərənt] adj (a) (generally uneducated) unwissend, ungebildet, ignorant; (of particular subject) unwissend; (of plan, requirements etc) nicht informiert (of über +acc). **to be ~ of geography** in Geographie nicht bewandert sein, sich in Geographie nicht auskennen; **I am not exactly ~ of what has been going on** es ist nicht so, als wüßte ich nicht, was los ist; **to be ~ of the facts** die Tatsachen nicht kennen; **they are ~ of or about what happened** sie wissen nicht, was geschehen ist.

(b) (ill-mannered) unhöflich, ungeschliffen, ungehobelt. **you ~ fool** du ungehobelter Patron.

ignorantly ['ɪgnərəntlɪ] adv unwissentlich; behave unhöflich, ungeschliffen, ungehobelt.

ignore [ɪg'nɔːʳ] vt ignorieren, (deliberately overlook also) hinwegsehen über (+acc); (pass over, pay no attention to) nicht beachten, unbeachtet lassen; remark also überhören, übergehen; person also übersehen, nicht beachten. **I'll ~ that** ich habe nichts gehört/gesehen; **but I can't ~ the fact that ...** aber ich kann mich der Tatsache nicht verschließen, daß ...

iguana [ɪ'gwɑːnə] n Leguan m.

ikon ['aɪkɒn] n Ikone f.

ilex ['aɪleks] n (a) (holm oak) Steineiche, Immergrüneiche f. (b) (holly) Ilex, Stechpalme f.

Iliad ['ɪlɪæd] n Ilias, Iliade f.

ilk [ɪlk] n **people of that ~** solche Leute; **all things of that ~** und lauter solche Dinge; **and others of that ~** und dergleichen, und ihresgleichen.

ill[1] abbr of illustrated; illustration Abb., Abbildung f.

ill[2] [ɪl] **1** adj (a) pred (sick) krank. **to fall or take (inf) or be taken ~** erkranken (with sth an etw dat), krank werden; **to feel ~** sich unwohl or krank fühlen; **I feel (terribly) ~** mir ist gar nicht gut; **he is ~ with fever/a cold** er hat Fieber/eine Erkältung; **~ with anxiety/jealousy** krank vor Angst/Eifersucht.

(b) comp **worse**, superl **worst** (bad) schlecht, schlimm, übel. **~ feeling** böses Blut; **no ~ feeling?** ist es wieder gut?; **no ~ feeling!** ist schon vergessen; **due to ~ health** aus Gesundheitsgründen; **~ humour** or (US) **humor** schlechte Laune; **~ luck** Pech nt; **as ~ luck would have it** wie es der Teufel so will; **~ nature** Übellaunigkeit f; **~ will** böses Blut; **I don't bear them any ~ will** ich trage ihnen nichts nach; **it's an ~ wind (that blows nobody any good)** (Prov) so hat alles seine guten Seiten.

2 n (a) **to think ~ of sb** schlecht or Schlechtes von jdm or über jdn denken; **to speak ~ of sb** Schlechtes über jdn sagen, schlecht über jdn reden.

(b) **~s** pl (misfortunes) Mißstände, Übel pl; (miseries) Mißge-

schicke pl. **to do ~** (old) Böses or Unrecht tun.

3 adv schlecht. **to take sth ~** (old) etw übelnehmen; **things went ~ with him** (liter) es erging ihm nicht gut, es ward ihm kein Glück beschieden (old); **he can ~ afford to refuse** er kann es sich (dat) schlecht leisten abzulehnen; **it ~ becomes you** (form) es steht Ihnen (dat) nicht an (form).

I'll [aɪl] contr of **I will; I shall**.

ill-: ~-advised adj person unklug; action also unratsam; **you would be ~-advised to trust her** Sie wären schlecht beraten, wenn Sie ihr trauten; **~-assorted** adj group, bunch schlecht zusammenpassend; **I always felt ~-at-ease in his presence** ich habe mich in seiner Gegenwart nie wohl gefühlt; **~-bred** adj ungezogen, schlecht erzogen; **~-breeding** n schlechte Erziehung, Unerzogenheit f; **it's a sign of ~-breeding to ...** es ist ein Zeichen für eine schlechte Kinderstube, wenn man ...; **~-considered** adj action, words unüberlegt, unbedacht; measure übereilt, unüberlegt; **~-disposed** adj **to be ~-disposed to(wards) sb/sth** jdm übel gesinnt sein, jdm nicht wohlgesinnt sein.

illegal [ɪ'liːgəl] adj unerlaubt; (against a specific law) gesetzwidrig; trade, immigration, possession etc illegal; (Sport) regelwidrig.

illegality [‚ɪlɪ'gælɪtɪ] n see adj Ungesetzlichkeit f; Gesetzwidrigkeit f; Illegalität f.

illegally [ɪ'liːgəlɪ] adv imported illegal eingeführt; **you're ~ parked** Sie parken hier unerlaubterweise; **to act ~** sich gesetzwidrig verhalten.

illegibility [ɪ‚ledʒɪ'bɪlɪtɪ] n Unleserlichkeit f.

illegible adj, **~bly** adv [ɪ'ledʒəbl, -blɪ] unleserlich.

illegitimacy [‚ɪlɪ'dʒɪtɪməsɪ] n see adj (a) Unehelichkeit f. (b) Unzulässigkeit f; Unrechtmäßigkeit f.

illegitimate [‚ɪlɪ'dʒɪtɪmɪt] adj (a) child unehelich.

(b) (contrary to law) unzulässig, unerlaubt; government unrechtmäßig. **~ use of the verb** regelwidriger Gebrauch des Verbs; **the ~ use of drugs** (der) Drogenmißbrauch.

(c) argument, conclusion, inference unzulässig, nicht folgerichtig, illegitim. **given your Marxist principles, such behaviour is surely ~** ein solches Benehmen ist doch wohl unvereinbar mit Ihren marxistischen Prinzipien.

illegitimately [‚ɪlɪ'dʒɪtɪmɪtlɪ] adv see adj (a) unehelich.

(b) unzulässig, unerlaubt; parked an verbotener Stelle; use unrechtmäßigerweise, unzulässigerweise.

(c) unzulässig, nicht folgerichtig. **he concluded ~ that ...** er kam zu dem unzulässigen or nicht folgerichtigen Schluß, daß ...

ill-: ~-fated adj (a) (unfortunate, unlucky) person vom Unglück verfolgt, unglücklich; (b) (doomed, destined to fail) unglückselig, verhängnisvoll; **the ~-fated Titanic** die unglückselige Titanic; **~-favoured** adj (liter: ugly) ungestalt (liter), häßlich, unschön; **~-founded** adj unbegründet, unerwiesen, fragwürdig; **~-gotten gains** npl unrechtmäßiger Gewinn, Sündengeld nt (hum); **~-humoured**, (US) **~-humored** adj schlecht or übel gelaunt, schlecht aufgelegt, verstimmt.

illiberal [ɪ'lɪbərəl] adj (a) (narrow-minded) engstirnig, intolerant, engherzig. (b) (niggardly) knauserig, geizig.

illicit [ɪ'lɪsɪt] adj verboten; (illegal also) illegal; spirits schwarz hergestellt or gebrannt. **~ trade or sale** Schwarzhandel m.

illicitly [ɪ'lɪsɪtlɪ] adv verbotenerweise, (illegally) illegal(erweise). **~ acquired** unrechtmäßig erworben.

illimitable [ɪ'lɪmɪtəbl] adj grenzenlos, unbegrenzt. **the ~ ocean** der unendliche Ozean.

ill-informed ['ɪlɪn‚fɔːmd] adj person schlecht informiert or unterrichtet; attack, criticism, speech wenig sachkundig.

illiteracy [ɪ'lɪtərəsɪ] n Analphabetentum nt. **~ rate** Analphabetismus m.

illiterate [ɪ'lɪtərət] **1** adj (a) des Schreibens und Lesens unkundig; (badly-educated, uncultured) person ungebildet, unwissend; (handwriting) ungeübt, krakelig (inf); letter voller Fehler. **he's ~** er ist Analphabet. **2** n Analphabet(in f) m.

ill-: ~-judged adj unklug, wenig bedacht; **~-mannered** adj ungezogen, ungehobelt, schlecht erzogen; **~-matched** adj nicht zusammenpassend; **I think they're ~-matched** ich glaube, die beiden passen nicht zueinander; **~-natured** adj, **~-naturedly** adv übellaunig.

illness ['ɪlnɪs] n Krankheit f.

illogical adj, **~ly** adv [ɪ'lɒdʒɪkəl, -ɪ] unlogisch.

illogicality [ɪ‚lɒdʒɪ'kælɪtɪ] n mangelnde Logik, Unlogik f. **the illogicalities in his argument** die logischen Fehler in seiner Argumentation.

ill-: ~-omened ['ɪl‚əʊmənd] adj unter einem unglücklichen Stern or unter einem Unstern stehend; **~-prepared** adj schlecht vorbereitet; **~-starred** adj person vom Unglück or Pech verfolgt; day, undertaking etc unter einem ungünstigen Stern (stehend), Unglücks-; **~-suited** adj (to one another) nicht zusammenpassend; (to sth) ungeeignet (to für); **they are clearly ~-suited** sie passen offensichtlich nicht zueinander; **~-tempered** adj (habitually) mißmutig, übellaunig; (on particular occasion) schlecht gelaunt pred; (violently) schlechtgelaunt attr; **~-timed** adj unangelegen, unpassend; intervention, move, speech zeitlich schlecht abgestimmt; **~-treat** vt schlecht behandeln, mißhandeln; **~ treatment** n Mißhandlung f, schlechte Behandlung.

illuminate [ɪ'luːmɪneɪt] vt (a) (light up) room, street, building erhellen, erleuchten, beleuchten; (spotlight etc) anstrahlen; (decorate with lights) festlich beleuchten, illuminieren. **~d sign** Leuchtzeichen nt.

(b) (Art) manuscript illuminieren. **~d letters** (verzierte) Initialen pl.

(c) (fig) question, subject erhellen, erläutern.

illuminating [ɪ'luːmɪneɪtɪŋ] adj (instructive) aufschlußreich.

illumination [ɪ‚luːmɪ'neɪʃən] n (a) (of street, room, building) Beleuchtung f. **source of ~** Lichtquelle f. (b) (decorative lights) ~s pl festliche Beleuchtung, Illumination f. (c) (Art: of manuscript) Illumination f; (subject also) Buchmalerei f. (d) (fig) Erläuterung f.

illuminator [ɪ'luːmɪneɪtə'] n (Art: of manuscript) Buchmaler, Illuminator m.

illumine [ɪ'luːmɪn] vt (liter) erleuchten, erhellen; (fig) erläutern, erhellen.

ill-use [,ɪl'juːz] vt schlecht behandeln, schlecht umgehen mit; (physically) mißhandeln.

illusion [ɪ'luːʒən] n Illusion f; (hope also) trügerische Hoffnung; (misperception) Täuschung f. to be under an ~ einer Täuschung (dat) unterliegen, sich (dat) Illusionen machen; to be under the ~ that ... sich (dat) einbilden, daß ...; to have or be under no ~s sich (dat) keine Illusionen machen, sich (dat) nichts vormachen (about sth über + acc); it gives the ~ of space es vermittelt die Illusion von räumlicher Weite; see optical.

illusionist [ɪ'luːʒənɪst] n Illusionist(in f) m.

illusive [ɪ'luːsɪv], **illusory** [ɪ'luːsərɪ] adj illusorisch, trügerisch.

illustrate ['ɪləstreɪt] vt (a) book, story illustrieren, bebildern. his lecture was ~d by coloured slides er veranschaulichte seinen Vortrag mit Farbdias; ~d (magazine) Illustrierte f. (b) (fig) erläutern, veranschaulichen, illustrieren.

illustration [,ɪləs'treɪʃən] n (a) (picture) Abbildung f, Bild nt, Illustration f. (b) (fig) (of problem, subject) Erklärung, Erläuterung f; (of rule) (act) Veranschaulichung f; (thing) Beispiel nt. by way of ~ als Beispiel.

illustrative ['ɪləstrətɪv] adj veranschaulichend, erläuternd, verdeutlichend. ~ of bezeichnend or beispielhaft für.

illustrator ['ɪləstreɪtə'] n Illustrator m.

illustrious [ɪ'lʌstrɪəs] adj vornehm, erlaucht; deeds berühmt.

ILO abbr of **International Labour Organization**.

I'm [aɪm] contr of **I am**.

image ['ɪmɪdʒ] n (a) (carved, sculpted figure) Standbild nt, Figur f; (of god also) Götterbild nt; (painted figure) Bild, Bildnis (geh) nt.
  (b) (likeness) Ebenbild, Abbild nt. he is the living or spitting ~ of his father (inf) er ist der lebende und leibt und lebt, er ist seinem Vater wie aus dem Gesicht geschnitten; God created man in his own ~ Gott (er)schuf den Menschen nach seinem Bilde.
  (c) (Opt) Bild nt. ~ converter (Elec) Bildwandler m.
  (d) (mental picture) Vorstellung f, Bild nt.
  (e) (public face) Image nt. brand ~ Markenimage nt.
  (f) (Liter) to speak in ~s in Bildern or Metaphern sprechen; a style full of ~s ein bilderreicher or metaphorischer Stil.

imagery ['ɪmɪdʒərɪ] n Metaphorik f. visual ~ Bildersymbolik f.

imaginable [ɪ'mædʒɪnəbl] adj vorstellbar, denkbar, erdenklich. the best thing ~ das denkbar Beste; the easiest/fastest way ~ der denkbar einfachste/schnellste Weg.

imaginary [ɪ'mædʒɪnərɪ] adj danger eingebildet, imaginär; characters frei ersonnen, erfunden. an ~ case ein konstruierter Fall; ~ number imaginäre Zahl.

imagination [ɪ,mædʒɪ'neɪʃən] n (creative) Phantasie, Vorstellungskraft f, Einbildungskraft f; (self-deceptive) Einbildung f. to have (a lively or vivid) ~ (eine lebhafte or rege) Phantasie haben; use your ~ lassen Sie Ihre Phantasie spielen; in order to encourage children to use their ~(s) um die Phantasie von Kindern anzuregen; to lack ~ phantasielos or einfallslos sein; he lives too much in his ~ er lebt zu sehr in einer Phantasiewelt; it's only (your) ~! das bilden Sie sich (dat) nur ein!; it's all in your ~ das ist alles Einbildung.

imaginative [ɪ'mædʒɪnətɪv] adj phantasiereich, phantasievoll; plan, idea also einfallsreich.

imaginatively [ɪ'mædʒɪnətɪvlɪ] adv phantasievoll; einfallsreich.

imaginativeness [ɪ'mædʒɪnətɪvnɪs] n see adj Phantasiereichtum m; Einfallsreichtum m; (of person also) Phantasie f.

imagine [ɪ'mædʒɪn] vt (a) (picture to oneself) sich (dat) vorstellen, sich (dat) denken. ~ yourself rich stellen Sie sich mal vor, Sie wären reich; I can't ~ what you mean ich kann mir nicht vorstellen, was Sie meinen; ~ a situation in which ... stellen Sie sich eine Situation vor, in der ...; you can ~ how I felt Sie können sich vorstellen or denken, wie mir zumute war; you can't ~ how ... Sie machen sich kein Bild or Sie können sich nicht vorstellen or denken, wie ...; just ~ my surprise stellen Sie sich nur meine Überraschung vor; you can't ~ it! Sie machen sich keine Vorstellungen!; as may (well) be ~d wie man sich (leicht) denken or vorstellen kann.
  (b) (be under the illusion that) sich (dat) einbilden. don't ~ that ... bilden Sie sich nur nicht ein, daß ..., denken Sie nur nicht, daß ...; he is always imagining things (inf) er leidet ständig an Einbildungen; you're (just) imagining things (inf) Sie bilden sich das alles nur ein.
  (c) (suppose, conjecture) annehmen, vermuten. are you tired? — well, what do you ...! bist du müde? — na, was glaubst du wohl?; is it time now? — I would ~ so ist es soweit? — ich denke schon; I would never have ~d he would have done that ich hätte nie gedacht, daß er das tun würde.

imbalance [ɪm'bæləns] n Unausgeglichenheit f.

imbecile ['ɪmbəsiːl] 1 adj (a) person beschränkt, schwachsinnig, geistig minderbemittelt (inf); laugh, trick, book schwachsinnig, dumm, blöd(e); idea, word dumm, töricht.
  (b) (Med) schwachsinnig, geistesschwach, imbezil (spec).
  2 n (a) Dummkopf, Idiot, Schwachkopf m. to behave like an ~ sich völlig blödsinnig or wie ein Idiot benehmen.
  (b) (Med) Schwachsinnige(r) mf.

imbecilic [,ɪmbə'sɪlɪk] adj see **imbecile 1 (a)**.

imbecility [,ɪmbə'sɪlɪtɪ] n (a) Beschränktheit, Idiotie f, Schwachsinn m. (b) (Med) Schwachsinn m.

imbibe [ɪm'baɪb] 1 vt (a) (form, hum) trinken, bechern (hum).

(b) (fig) ideas, information in sich (acc) aufnehmen. 2 vi (hum: drink) viel trinken. will you ~? ein Gläschen?; I don't ~ ich trinke nicht.

imbroglio [ɪm'brəʊlɪəʊ] n (liter) verwickelte Lage, Verwirrung f.

imbue [ɪm'bjuː] vt (fig) durchdringen, erfüllen. this ~d them with fresh courage das erfüllte sie mit neuem Mut.

IMF abbr of **International Monetary Fund** IWF m, Internationaler Währungsfonds.

imitable ['ɪmɪtəbl] adj nachahmbar, imitierbar.

imitate ['ɪmɪteɪt] vt (a) (copy) person, accent etc imitieren, nachmachen, nachahmen. children learn by imitating their parents Kinder lernen dadurch, daß sie ihre Eltern nachahmen. (b) (counterfeit) nachmachen, imitieren; signature also fälschen.

imitation [,ɪmɪ'teɪʃən] 1 n Imitation, Nachahmung f. to do an ~ of sb jdn imitieren or nachmachen or nachahmen. 2 adj unecht, künstlich, falsch. ~ gold/pearl/brick Gold-/Perlen-/Ziegelimitation f; ~ leather Lederimitation f, Kunstleder nt; ~ jewellery unechter Schmuck; ~ fur Webpelz m.

imitative ['ɪmɪtətɪv] adj nachahmend, imitierend. a style ~ of Cézanne ein Cézanne imitierender Stil; young children are naturally ~ kleine Kinder machen von Natur aus alles nach.

imitator ['ɪmɪteɪtə'] n Nachahmer, Imitator m.

immaculate [ɪ'mækjʊlɪt] adj (a) untadelig, tadellos, picobello inv (inf); behaviour tadellos, mustergültig; manuscript etc fehlerrei, einwandfrei. (b) (Eccl) the I ~ Conception die Unbefleckte Empfängnis.

immaculately [ɪ'mækjʊltlɪ] adv tadellos; behave also untadelig.

immanence ['ɪmənəns] n Immanenz f.

immanent ['ɪmənənt] adj (a) innewohnend, immanent. to be ~ in sth einer Sache (dat) eigen sein or innewohnen. (b) (Philos, Eccl) immanent.

immaterial [,ɪmə'tɪərɪəl] adj (a) (unimportant) objection, question nebensächlich, unwesentlich, bedeutungslos. it is quite ~ to me (whether) ... es ist für mich ohne Bedeutung or unwichtig, (ob) ...; ~ to the subject (under discussion) gegenstandslos or unwesentlich für das (diskutierte) Thema; that's (quite) ~ das spielt keine Rolle, das ist egal.
  (b) (Philos etc) immateriell. ghosts are ~ Gespenster sind körperlos.

immature [,ɪmə'tjʊə'] adj (lit, fig) unreif; wine nicht ausreichend gelagert; plans, ideas etc also unausgegoren. don't be so ~ sei nicht so kindisch!

immaturely [,ɪmə'tjʊəlɪ] adv react, behave unreif.

immaturity [,ɪmə'tjʊərɪtɪ] n Unreife f.

immeasurable [ɪ'meʒərəbl] adj unermeßlich, grenzenlos; amount, distances unermeßbar, riesig.

immeasurably [ɪ'meʒərəblɪ] adv unermeßlich, grenzenlos.

immediacy [ɪ'miːdɪəsɪ] n Unmittelbarkeit, Direktheit f; (urgency) Dringlichkeit f. while I do not doubt the ~ of your needs ... ich bezweifle die Dringlichkeit Ihrer Bedürfnisse nicht, aber ...

immediate [ɪ'miːdɪət] adj (a) successor, knowledge, future, object, need unmittelbar; cause, successor also direkt; neighbour, vicinity also nächste. only the ~ family were invited nur die engste Familie wurde eingeladen; our ~ plan is to go to France wir fahren zuerst einmal nach Frankreich.
  (b) (instant) reply, reaction sofortig, umgehend, prompt; thought, conclusion unmittelbar. to take ~ action sofort handeln; this had the ~ effect of ... das hatte prompt zur Folge, daß ...; for ~ delivery zur sofortigen Lieferung.

immediately [ɪ'miːdɪətlɪ] 1 adv (a) (at once) sofort, gleich; reply, return, depart also umgehend. ~ after/before unmittelbar danach/davor; that's not ~ obvious das ist nicht sofort or unmittelbar klar. 2 conj (directly) direkt, unmittelbar. (Brit) sobald, sofort, als ...

immemorial [,ɪmɪ'mɔːrɪəl] adj uralt, unvordenklich. from time ~ seit undenklichen Zeiten, seit Urzeiten.

immense [ɪ'mens] adj difficulty, fortune, sum of money, possibilities riesig, enorm, immens; problem, difference also, ocean, heat gewaltig; self-confidence, success ungeheuer, enorm; achievement großartig.

immensely [ɪ'menslɪ] adv unheimlich (inf), enorm. to enjoy oneself ~ sich ausgezeichnet or unheimlich (inf) or köstlich amüsieren; we are ~ grateful for your help wir sind Ihnen für Ihre Hilfe äußerst dankbar.

immensity [ɪ'mensɪtɪ] n ungeheure Größe, Unermeßlichkeit f. we do not underestimate the ~ of this task wir unterschätzen keineswegs das gewaltige Ausmaß dieser Aufgabe; the ~ of space die Unendlichkeit des (Welt)alls.

immerse [ɪ'mɜːs] vt (a) eintauchen (in in + acc). to ~ one's head in water den Kopf ins Wasser tauchen; to be ~d in water unter Wasser sein.
  (b) (fig) to ~ oneself in one's work sich in seine Arbeit vertiefen or stürzen (inf); to ~ oneself in a language sich vollkommen in eine Sprache vertiefen; to be ~d in one's work in seine Arbeit vertieft sein; to be ~d in one's reading in seine Lektüre versunken or vertieft sein.
  (c) (Eccl) untertauchen.

immersion [ɪ'mɜːʃən] n (a) Eintauchen, Untertauchen nt. after two hours' ~ in this solution nach zwei Stunden in dieser Flüssigkeit; ~ heater (Brit) Boiler, Heißwasserspeicher m; (for jug etc) Tauchsieder m.
  (b) (fig) Vertieftsein, Versunkensein nt.
  (c) (Eccl) Taufe f durch Untertauchen.

immigrant ['ɪmɪgrənt] 1 n Einwanderer m, Einwanderin f, Immigrant(in f) m.
  2 attr ~ labour/workers ausländische Arbeitnehmer pl; (esp in BRD) Gastarbeiter pl; (in Switzerland) Fremdarbeiter pl; ~

population die Einwanderer pl; ... **has an ~ population of 50,000** ... hat einen ausländischen Bevölkerungsanteil von 50.000; **~ schools** Schulen mit hohem Anteil an Ausländern.

immigrate ['ɪmɪgreɪt] vi einwandern, immigrieren (to in + dat).

immigration [,ɪmɪ'greɪʃən] n Einwanderung, Immigration f. **to restrict ~** die Einwanderung or die Immigration einschränken; **~ officer** Beamte(r) m der Einwanderungsbehörde; (at customs) Grenzbeamte(r) m.

imminence ['ɪmɪnəns] n nahes Bevorstehen. **he hadn't appreciated the ~ of the danger/of war** er war sich (dat) nicht bewußt, daß die Gefahr/der Krieg so unmittelbar bevorstand.

imminent ['ɪmɪnənt] adj nahe bevorstehend. **to be ~** nahe bevorstehen; **I think an announcement is ~** ich glaube, es steht eine Ankündigung bevor.

immobile [ɪ'məʊbaɪl] adj (not moving) unbeweglich; (not able to move) person (through injury etc) bewegungslos; (through lack of transport) unbeweglich, immobil. **the car was completely ~** das Auto rührte sich nicht (von der Stelle); **to make or render a car ~** ein Auto benutzungsunfähig machen; **in space the rocket looks as though it's ~** im Weltraum sieht die Rakete aus, als würde sie sich nicht bewegen.

immobility [,ɪmə'bɪlɪtɪ] n see adj Unbeweglichkeit f; Bewegungslosigkeit f; Immobilität f.

immobilize [ɪ'məʊbɪlaɪz] vt traffic lahmlegen, zum Erliegen bringen; car, broken limb stillegen; army tanks außer Gefecht setzen; (Fin) capital festlegen.

immoderate [ɪ'mɒdərɪt] adj desire, appetite übermäßig, unmäßig, maßlos; demands also überzogen, übertrieben; views übertrieben, übersteigert, extrem.

immoderately [ɪ'mɒdərɪtlɪ] adv see adj.

immodest [ɪ'mɒdɪst] adj unbescheiden; (indecent) unanständig.

immodestly [ɪ'mɒdɪstlɪ] adv see adj.

immodesty [ɪ'mɒdɪstɪ] n see adj Unbescheidenheit f; Unanständigkeit f.

immolate ['ɪməʊleɪt] vt (liter) opfern, zum Opfer bringen.

immoral [ɪ'mɒrəl] adj action unmoralisch; behaviour also unsittlich; person also sittenlos. **~ earnings** (Jur) Einkünfte pl aus gewerbsmäßiger Unzucht.

immorality [,ɪmə'rælɪtɪ] n Unmoral f; (of behaviour also) Unsittlichkeit f; (of person also) Sittenlosigkeit f; (immoral act) Unsittlichkeit f.

immorally [ɪ'mɒrəlɪ] adv see adj.

immortal [ɪ'mɔːtl] **1** adj person, God unsterblich; fame also unvergänglich, ewig; life ewig. **2** n Unsterbliche(r) mf.

immortality [,ɪmɔː'tælɪtɪ] n see adj Unsterblichkeit f; Unvergänglichkeit f, Ewigkeit f.

immortalize [ɪ'mɔːtəlaɪz] vt verewigen. **the film which ~d her** der Film, der sie unsterblich machte.

immovable [ɪ'muːvəbl] adj **(a)** (lit) unbeweglich; (fig) obstacle unüberwindlich, unbezwinglich. **(b)** (fig) person (steadfast) fest. **he remained ~** er ließ sich nicht bewegen, er blieb beharrlich or fest.

immune [ɪ'mjuːn] adj **(a)** (Med) immun (against, from, to gegen). **(b)** (fig) sicher (from vor + dat); (from temptation etc also) geschützt, gefeit (from gegen); (not susceptible: to criticism etc) unempfindlich, immun (to gegen). **nobody was ~ from his outbursts** keiner war vor seinen Wutanfällen sicher.

immunity [ɪ'mjuːnɪtɪ] n **(a)** (Med) Immunität f. **he developed a sort of ~ to her temper/sarcasm** er entwickelte eine Art Immunität gegen ihre Launen/ihren Sarkasmus. **(b)** (diplomatic) Immunität f. **(c)** (fig) see adj Sicherheit f; Geschütztheit, Gefeitheit f; Unempfindlichkeit, Immunität f.

immunization [,ɪmjʊnaɪ'zeɪʃən] n Immunisierung f.

immunize ['ɪmjʊnaɪz] vt immunisieren, immun machen.

immure [ɪ'mjʊə'] vt einkerkern. **he ~d himself in his study** er schloß sich in seinem Arbeitszimmer ein.

immutability [ɪ,mjuːtə'bɪlɪtɪ] n Unveränderlichkeit, Unwandelbarkeit f.

immutable [ɪ'mjuːtəbl] adj unveränderlich, unwandelbar.

imp [ɪmp] n Kobold m; (inf: child also) Racker m (inf).

impact ['ɪmpækt] n Aufprall m (on, against auf + acc); (of two moving objects) Zusammenprall m, Aufeinanderprallen nt; (of bomb) (on house, factory) Einschlag m (on in + acc); (on roof, ground) Aufschlag m (on auf + dat); (of light, rays) Auftreffen nt (on auf + acc); (force) Wucht f; (fig) (Aus)wirkung f (on auf + acc). **on ~** (with) beim Aufprall (auf + acc)/Zusammenprall (mit) etc; **he staggered under the ~ of the blow** er taumelte unter der Wucht des Schlages; **his speech had a great ~ on his audience** seine Rede machte großen Eindruck auf seine Zuhörer; **you can imagine the ~ of this on a four-year old** Sie können sich vorstellen, wie sich das auf einen Vierjährigen auswirkt.

impacted [ɪm'pæktɪd] adj eingeklemmt, eingekeilt; tooth also impaktiert (spec).

impair [ɪm'peə'] vt beeinträchtigen; hearing, sight also verschlechtern; relations also, health schaden (+ dat).

impala [ɪm'pɑːlə] n Impala f.

impale [ɪm'peɪl] vt aufspießen (on auf + dat).

impalpable [ɪm'pælpəbl] adj (lit) nicht fühlbar, (fig) nicht greifbar, vage.

impanel [ɪm'pænl] vt als Geschworenen einsetzen.

imparity [ɪm'pærɪtɪ] n Ungleichheit f.

impart [ɪm'pɑːt] vt **(a)** (make known) information, news mitteilen, übermitteln; knowledge vermitteln; secret preisgeben. **(b)** (bestow) verleihen, geben (to dat).

impartial [ɪm'pɑːʃəl] adj person, attitude unparteiisch, unvoreingenommen; decision, judgement also gerecht.

impartiality [ɪm,pɑːʃɪ'ælɪtɪ], **impartialness** [ɪm'pɑːʃəlnɪs] n

see adj Unparteilichkeit, Unvoreingenommenheit f; Gerechtigkeit f.

impartially [ɪm'pɑːʃəlɪ] adv see adj.

impassable [ɪm'pɑːsəbl] adj unpassierbar.

impasse [ɪm'pɑːs] n (fig) Sackgasse f. **to have reached an ~** sich festgefahren haben, einen toten Punkt erreicht haben.

impassioned [ɪm'pæʃnd] adj leidenschaftlich.

impassive adj, **~ly** adv [ɪm'pæsɪv, -lɪ] gelassen.

impassiveness [ɪm'pæsɪvnɪs], **impassivity** [ɪmpæ'sɪvɪtɪ] n Gelassenheit f.

impatience [ɪm'peɪʃəns] n Ungeduld f; (intolerance) Unduldsamkeit f.

impatient [ɪm'peɪʃənt] adj ungeduldig; (intolerant) unduldsam (of gegenüber). **to be ~ to do sth** unbedingt etw tun wollen.

impatiently [ɪm'peɪʃəntlɪ] adv see adj.

impeach [ɪm'piːtʃ] vt **(a)** (Jur: accuse) public official (eines Amtsvergehens) anklagen; (US) president also ein Impeachment einleiten gegen. **to ~ sb for or with sth/for doing sth** jdn wegen einer Sache anklagen/jdn anklagen, etw getan zu haben. **(b)** (challenge) sb's character, motives in Frage stellen, anzweifeln; witness's testimony also anfechten. **to ~ a witness** die Glaubwürdigkeit eines Zeugen anzweifeln or anfechten.

impeachable [ɪm'piːtʃəbl] adj person (eines Amtsvergehens) anzuklagen; action als Amtsvergehen verfolgbar.

impeachment [ɪm'piːtʃmənt] n see vt **(a)** (Jur) Anklage f (wegen eines Amtsvergehens); Impeachment nt. **(b)** Infragestellung f; Anfechtung f; Anfechtung f.

impeccable adj, **~bly** adv [ɪm'pekəbl, -ɪ] untadelig, tadellos.

impecunious [,ɪmpɪ'kjuːnɪəs] adj mittellos, unbemittelt.

impede [ɪm'piːd] vt person hindern; action, success behindern, erschweren; movement, traffic behindern.

impediment [ɪm'pedɪmənt] n **(a)** Hindernis nt. **(b)** (Med) Behinderung f. **speech ~** Sprachfehler m, Sprachstörung f.

impedimenta [ɪm,pedɪ'mentə] npl **(a)** (inf) (unnötiges) Gepäck. **(b)** (Mil) Troß m.

impel [ɪm'pel] vt **(a)** (force) nötigen. **to ~ sb to do sth** jdn (dazu) nötigen, etw zu tun. **(b)** (drive on) (voran)treiben.

impend [ɪm'pend] vi bevorstehen; (threaten) drohen.

impending [ɪm'pendɪŋ] adj bevorstehend; death also nahe; storm also heraufziehend; (threatening) drohend.

impenetrability [ɪm,penɪtrə'bɪlɪtɪ] n see adj Undurchdringlichkeit f; Uneinnehmbarkeit f; Undurchlässigkeit f; Unergründlichkeit f; Undurchschaubarkeit, Undurchsichtigkeit f.

impenetrable [ɪm'penɪtrəbl] adj undurchdringlich; fortress uneinnehmbar; enemy lines undurchlässig; mind, character also, mystery unergründlich; theory undurchschaubar, undurchsichtig.

impenitence [ɪm'penɪtəns] n Reuelosigkeit f.

impenitent [ɪm'penɪtənt] adj reuelos. **he remained quite ~** er zeigte keine Reue, er bereute es gar nicht; **to die ~** sterben, ohne bereut zu haben.

impenitently [ɪm'penɪtəntlɪ] adv ohne Reue.

imperative [ɪm'perətɪv] **1** adj **(a)** need, desire dringend. **to be ~** unbedingt nötig or erforderlich sein. **(b)** manner gebieterisch, befehlend, herrisch; order strikt. **(c)** (Gram) imperativisch, Imperativ-, befehlend, Befehls-. **2** n (Gram) Imperativ, Befehl m. **in the ~** im Imperativ, in der Befehlsform.

imperceptible [,ɪmpə'septəbl] adj nicht wahrnehmbar; difference, movement also unmerklich; sight also unsichtbar; sound also unhörbar.

imperceptibly [,ɪmpə'septəblɪ] adv see adj kaum wahrnehmbar; unmerklich; unsichtbar; unhörbar.

imperfect [ɪm'pɜːfɪkt] **1** adj **(a)** (faulty) unvollkommen, mangelhaft; (Comm) goods fehlerhaft. **(b)** (incomplete) unvollständig, unvollkommen. **(c)** (Gram) Imperfekt-, Vergangenheits-. **2** n (Gram) Imperfekt nt, (erste or unvollendete) Vergangenheit f.

imperfection [,ɪmpə'fekʃən] n **(a)** no pl see adj Unvollkommenheit, Mangelhaftigkeit f; Fehlerhaftigkeit f; Unvollständigkeit, Unvollkommenheit f. **(b)** (fault, defect) Mangel m.

imperfectly [ɪm'pɜːfɪktlɪ] adv see adj.

imperial [ɪm'pɪərɪəl] adj **(a)** (of empire) Reichs-; (of emperor) kaiserlich, Kaiser-. **~ Rome** das Rom der Kaiserzeit; **His I~ Highness** Seine Kaiserliche Majestät. **(b)** (of British Empire) Empire-, des Empire. **~ trade** Handel m im or des Empire. **(c)** (lordly, majestic) majestätisch, gebieterisch. **(d)** weights, measures englisch.

imperialism [ɪm'pɪərɪəlɪzəm] n Imperialismus m (often pej), Weltmachtpolitik f.

imperialist [ɪm'pɪərɪəlɪst] n Imperialist(in f) m.

imperialistic [ɪm,pɪərɪə'lɪstɪk] adj imperialistisch.

imperially [ɪm'pɪərɪəlɪ] adv majestätisch, gebieterisch.

imperil [ɪm'perɪl] vt gefährden, in Gefahr bringen.

imperious [ɪm'pɪərɪəs] adj (commanding) herrisch, gebieterisch.

imperiously [ɪm'pɪərɪəslɪ] adv see adj.

imperishable [ɪm'perɪʃəbl] adj (lit) unverderblich; (fig) unvergänglich.

impermanence [ɪm'pɜːmənəns] n Unbeständigkeit f.

impermanent [ɪm'pɜːmənənt] adj unbeständig.

impermeable [ɪm'pɜːmɪəbl] adj undurchlässig, impermeabel (spec).

impersonal [ɪm'pɜːsnl] adj unpersönlich (also Gram).

impersonality [ɪm,pɜːsə'nælɪtɪ] n Unpersönlichkeit f.

impersonate [ɪm'pɜːsəneɪt] vt **(a)** (pretend to be) sich ausgeben als (+ nom). **(b)** (take off) imitieren, nachahmen.

impersonation [ɪm,pɜːsə'neɪʃən] n see vt **(a)** Verkörperung f.

his ~ of an officer sein Auftreten nt als Offizier. **(b)** Imitation, Nachahmung f. he does ~s of politicians/females er imitiert Politiker/spielt Frauen.

impersonator [ɪmˈpɜːsəneɪtə^r] n (Theat) Imitator(in f) m.

impertinence [ɪmˈpɜːtɪnəns] n Unverschämtheit, Impertinenz (dated) f. what ~!, the ~ of it! so eine Unverschämtheit!

impertinent [ɪmˈpɜːtɪnənt] adj **(a)** (impudent) unverschämt (to zu, gegenüber), impertinent (dated) (to gegenüber). **(b)** (form: irrelevant) irrelevant.

impertinently [ɪmˈpɜːtɪnəntlɪ] adv see adj.

imperturbability [ˈɪmpə‚tɜːbəˈbɪlɪtɪ] n Unerschütterlichkeit f.

imperturbable [‚ɪmpəˈtɜːbəbl] adj unerschütterlich. he is completely ~ er ist durch nichts zu erschüttern.

impervious [ɪmˈpɜːvɪəs] adj **(a)** substance undurchlässig. ~ to rain/water regen-/wasserundurchlässig; coat, material regen-/wasserdicht.
(b) (fig) unzugänglich (to zu für); (to people's feelings also, criticism) unberührt (to von). he is ~ to reason ihm ist mit Verstand nicht beizukommen.

impetigo [‚ɪmpɪˈtaɪgəʊ] n (Med) Eiterflechte, Impetigo f.

impetuosity [ɪm‚petjuˈɒsɪtɪ] n **(a)** see adj Ungestüm nt; Impulsivität f; Stürmische(s) nt. **(b)** (impetuous behaviour) ungestümes Handeln.

impetuous [ɪmˈpetjʊəs] adj act, person ungestüm, stürmisch; decision impulsiv; (liter) attack, wind stürmisch.

impetuously [ɪmˈpetjʊəslɪ] adv see adj.

impetuousness [ɪmˈpetjʊəsnɪs] n see impetuosity.

impetus [ˈɪmpɪtəs] n (lit, fig) Impuls m; (force) Kraft f; (momentum) Schwung, Impetus (geh) m. the ~ behind this increase in activity die treibende Kraft hinter dieser zunehmenden Aktivität; to give an ~ to sth (fig) einer Sache (dat) Impulse geben.

impiety [ɪmˈpaɪətɪ] n **(a)** see impious Gottlosigkeit, Ungläubigkeit f; Pietätlosigkeit f; Ehrfurchtslosigkeit f; Respektlosigkeit f. **(b)** (act) Pietätlosigkeit f; Respektlosigkeit f; (remark also) Lästerung f.

impinge [ɪmˈpɪndʒ] vi **(a)** (have effect on sb's life, habits) sich auswirken (on auf +acc), beeinflussen (on acc); (infringe: on sb's rights etc also) einschränken (on acc). to ~ on sb/sb's consciousness or mind jdm zu Bewußtsein kommen. **(b)** (strike) (auf)treffen, fallen (on auf +acc).

impingement [ɪmˈpɪndʒmənt] n **(a)** Auswirkung f, Einfluß m (on auf +acc). the gradual ~ of this idea on his consciousness wie ihm die Idee langsam zu(m) Bewußtsein kam.
(b) (striking) Auftreffen nt (on auf +dat).

impious [ˈɪmpɪəs] adj (not pious) gottlos, ungläubig; (irreverent) pietätlos; (to God) ehrfurchtslos; (to superior also) respektlos.

impiously [ˈɪmpɪəslɪ] adv see adj.

impish [ˈɪmpɪʃ] adj remark schelmisch; smile, look also verschmitzt; child also lausbübisch.

impishly [ˈɪmpɪʃlɪ] adv see adj.

impishness [ˈɪmpɪʃnɪs] n see adj Schelmische(s) nt; Verschmitztheit f; Lausbubenhaftigkeit f.

implacable [ɪmˈplækəbl] adj opponent, enemy erbittert; hatred also unversöhnlich.

implacably [ɪmˈplækəblɪ] adv see adj. he was ~ opposed to capital punishment er war ein erbitterter Gegner der Todesstrafe.

implant [ɪmˈplɑːnt] 1 vt **(a)** einpflanzen (in sb jdm). to be deeply ~ed in sb (tief) in jdm verwurzelt sein. **(b)** (Med) implantieren, einpflanzen. 2 [ˈɪmplɑːnt] n Implantat nt.

implantation [‚ɪmplɑːnˈteɪʃən] n see vt Einpflanzung f; Implantation, Einpflanzung f.

implausibility [ɪm‚plɔːzəˈbɪlɪtɪ] n see adj mangelnde Plausibilität; Unglaubhaftigkeit, Unglaubwürdigkeit f; Ungeschicktheit f.

implausible [ɪmˈplɔːzəbl] adj nicht plausibel; story, tale, excuse also unglaubhaft, unglaubwürdig; lie wenig überzeugend, ungeschickt.

implement [ˈɪmplɪmənt] 1 n **(a)** Gerät nt; (tool also) Werkzeug nt. farm ~s landwirtschaftliche Geräte pl. **(b)** (fig: agent) Werkzeug nt. 2 [ˈɪmplɪˈment] vt law vollziehen; contract, promise erfüllen; (carry out, put into effect) plan etc durchführen, ausführen.

implementation [‚ɪmplɪmenˈteɪʃən] n see vt Vollzug m; Erfüllung f; Ausführung, Durchführung f.

implicate [ˈɪmplɪkeɪt] vt to ~ sb in sth jdn in etw verwickeln.

implication [‚ɪmplɪˈkeɪʃən] n **(a)** Implikation f; (of law, agreement etc also) Auswirkung f; (of events also) Bedeutung f no pl. the ~ of your statement is that ... Ihre Behauptung impliziert, daß ...; the possible ~s of his decision die ganze Tragweite seiner Entscheidung; by ~ implizit(e). **(b)** (in crime) Verwicklung f (in in +acc).

implicit [ɪmˈplɪsɪt] adj **(a)** (implied) implizit; threat also indirekt, unausgesprochen; agreement, recognition also stillschweigend. to be ~ in sth durch etw impliziert werden; (in contract etc) in etw (dat) impliziert sein; a threat was ~ in his action in seiner Handlungsweise lag eine indirekte Drohung.
(b) (unquestioning) belief, confidence absolut, unbedingt.

implicitly [ɪmˈplɪsɪtlɪ] adv see adj.

implied [ɪmˈplaɪd] adj impliziert; threat also indirekt.

implode [ɪmˈpləʊd] 1 vi implodieren. 2 vt (Ling) als Verschlußlaut or Explosivlaut sprechen.

implore [ɪmˈplɔː^r] vt person anflehen, inständig bitten; forgiveness etc erbitten, erflehen. do it, I ~ you! ich flehe Sie an, tun Sie es!

imploring adj, ~ly adv [ɪmˈplɔːrɪŋ, -lɪ] flehentlich, flehend; beg also inständig.

imply [ɪmˈplaɪ] vt **(a)** andeuten, implizieren. are you ~ing or do you mean to ~ that ...? wollen Sie damit vielleicht sagen or andeuten, daß ...? it implies that he has changed his mind das

deutet darauf hin, daß er es sich (dat) anders überlegt hat.
(b) (indicate, lead to conclusion) schließen lassen auf (+acc).
(c) (involve) bedeuten.

impolite adj, ~ly adv [‚ɪmpəˈlaɪt, -lɪ] unhöflich.

impoliteness [‚ɪmpəˈlaɪtnɪs] n Unhöflichkeit f.

impolitic [ɪmˈpɒlɪtɪk] adj unklug.

imponderable [ɪmˈpɒndərəbl] 1 adj unberechenbar, unwägbar. 2 n unberechenbare or unwägbare Größe. ~s Unwägbarkeiten, Imponderabilien (geh) pl.

import [ˈɪmpɔːt] 1 n **(a)** (Comm) Import m, Einfuhr f. **(b)** (of speech, document etc) (meaning) Bedeutung f; (significance also) Wichtigkeit f. 2 [ɪmˈpɔːt] vt **(a)** (Comm) goods einführen, importieren. **(b)** (mean, imply) bedeuten, beinhalten.

importable [ɪmˈpɔːtəbl] adj einführbar.

importance [ɪmˈpɔːtəns] n Wichtigkeit f; (significance also) Bedeutung f; (influence also) Einfluß m. I don't see the ~ of that ich verstehe nicht, warum das wichtig sein soll; to be of no (great) ~ nicht (besonders) wichtig sein; to be without ~ unwichtig sein; to attach the greatest ~ to sth einer Sache (dat) größten Wert or größte Wichtigkeit beimessen; a man of ~ ein wichtiger or einflußreicher Mann; to be full of one's own ~ ganz von seiner eigenen Wichtigkeit erfüllt sein.

important [ɪmˈpɔːtənt] adj wichtig; (significant also) bedeutend; (influential) einflußreich, bedeutend. that's not ~ das ist unwichtig; it's not ~ (doesn't matter) das macht nichts; to try to look ~ sich (dat) ein gewichtiges Aussehen geben.

importantly [ɪmˈpɔːtəntlɪ] adv **(a)** (usu pej) wichtigtuerisch (pej). **(b)** it is ~ different das ist entscheidend anders.

importation [‚ɪmpɔːˈteɪʃən] n (Comm) Einfuhr f, Import m.

import in cpds Einfuhr-, Import-; ~ duty n (Comm) Einfuhrzoll, Importzoll m.

imported [ɪmˈpɔːtɪd] adj importiert, eingeführt, Import-.

importer [ɪmˈpɔːtə^r] n Importeur(in f) m (of von); (country also) Importland nt (of für).

import: ~-export trade n Import-Export-Handel m, Ein- und Ausfuhr f; ~ licence n Einfuhrlizenz, Importlizenz f; ~ permit n Einfuhr- or Importerlaubnis f or -bewilligung f.

importunate [ɪmˈpɔːtjʊnɪt] adj aufdringlich; salesman also, creditor, demand hartnäckig, beharrlich.

importunately [ɪmˈpɔːtjʊnɪtlɪ] adv see adj.

importunateness [ɪmˈpɔːtjʊnɪtnɪs] n see adj Aufdringlichkeit f; Hartnäckigkeit, Beharrlichkeit f.

importune [‚ɪmpɔːˈtjuːn] vt belästigen; (creditor, with questions) zusetzen (+dat); (visitor) zur Last fallen (+dat).

importunity [‚ɪmpɔːˈtjuːnɪtɪ] n **(a)** see importunateness. **(b)** (demand, request) unverschämte Bitte; (of creditor) hartnäckige Forderung.

impose [ɪmˈpəʊz] 1 vt **(a)** task, conditions aufzwingen, auferlegen (on sb jdm); sanctions, fine, sentence verhängen (on gegen); tax einführen. to ~ a tax on sth etw mit einer Steuer belegen, etw besteuern.
(b) to ~ oneself or one's presence on sb jdm sich aufdrängen; he ~d himself on them for three months er ließ sich einfach drei Monate bei ihnen nieder.
2 vi zur Last fallen (on sb jdm). to ~ on sb's kindness/friendship jds Freundlichkeit/Freundschaft ausnützen or mißbrauchen or übermäßig in Anspruch nehmen; I don't wish to ~ ich möchte Ihnen nicht zur Last fallen.

imposing [ɪmˈpəʊzɪŋ] adj beeindruckend, imponierend; person, appearance, building also stattlich, imposant.

imposition [‚ɪmpəˈzɪʃən] n **(a)** no pl see vt **(a)** Aufzwingen nt, Auferlegung f; Verhängung f; Erhebung f.
(b) (tax) Steuer f (on für, auf +dat).
(c) (taking advantage) Zumutung f (on für). I'd love to stay if it's not too much of an ~ ich würde liebend gern bleiben, wenn ich Ihnen nicht zur Last falle; and other ~s on his generosity which they made und wie sie seine Großzügigkeit noch weiter ausnutzten.

impossibility [ɪm‚pɒsəˈbɪlɪtɪ] n Unmöglichkeit f. that's an ~ das ist unmöglich or ein Ding der Unmöglichkeit.

impossible [ɪmˈpɒsəbl] 1 adj (all senses) unmöglich. ~! ausgeschlossen!, unmöglich!; it is ~ for him to leave/do that er kann unmöglich gehen/das unmöglich tun.
2 n Unmögliche(s) nt. to ask for the ~ Unmögliches verlangen; to do the ~ (in general) Unmögliches tun; (in particular case) das Unmögliche tun.

impossibly [ɪmˈpɒsəblɪ] adv unmöglich.

impostor [ɪmˈpɒstə^r] n Betrüger(in f), Schwindler(in f) m; (assuming higher position also) Hochstapler(in f) m.

imposture [ɪmˈpɒstʃə^r] n see impostor Betrug m, Schwindelei f; Hochstapelei f.

impotence [ˈɪmpətəns] n see adj Schwäche, Kraftlosigkeit f; Impotenz f; Schwäche, Machtlosigkeit f; Ohnmacht f.

impotent [ˈɪmpətənt] adj (physically) schwach, kraftlos; (sexually) impotent; (fig) schwach, machtlos; grief, rage ohnmächtig.

impound [ɪmˈpaʊnd] vt **(a)** (seize) goods, contraband beschlagnahmen. **(b)** cattle einsperren; car abschleppen (lassen).

impoverish [ɪmˈpɒvərɪʃ] vt person, country in Armut bringen, verarmen lassen; soil auslaugen, erschöpfen; (fig) culture verkümmern or verarmen lassen.

impoverished [ɪmˈpɒvərɪʃt] adj arm; person, conditions also ärmlich; (having become poor) verarmt; soil ausgelaugt, erschöpft; supplies erschöpft; (fig) dürftig.

impoverishment [ɪmˈpɒvərɪʃmənt] n see vt Verarmung f; Auslaugung, Erschöpfung f; Verkümmerung f.

impracticability [ɪm‚præktɪkəˈbɪlɪtɪ] n see adj Impraktikabilität f; Unbrauchbarkeit f; schlechte Befahrbarkeit.

impracticable [ɪmˈpræktɪkəbl] adj impraktikabel; plan also in der Praxis nicht anwendbar, praktisch unmöglich; design, size unbrauchbar; road schwer befahrbar.

impractical [ɪm'præktɪkəl] *adj* unpraktisch; *scheme also* unbrauchbar.
impracticality [ɪm.præktɪ'kælɪtɪ] *n* (*of person*) unpraktische Art; (*of scheme, idea*) Unbrauchbarkeit *f*.
imprecation [.ɪmprɪ'keɪʃən] *n* Verwünschung *f*, Fluch *m*.
imprecise *adj*, **~ly** *adv* [.ɪmprɪ'saɪs, -lɪ] ungenau, unpräzis(e).
imprecision [.ɪmprɪ'sɪʒən] *n* Ungenauigkeit *f*.
impregnable [ɪm'pregnəbl] *adj* (*Mil*) *fortress, defences* uneinnehmbar; (*fig*) *position* unerschütterlich; *argument* unwiderlegbar, unumstößlich.
impregnate ['ɪmpregneɪt] *vt* (**a**) (*saturate*) tränken. (**b**) (*fig*) erfüllen; *person also* durchdringen. (**c**) (*Biol: fertilize*) befruchten; *humans also* schwängern.
impregnation [.ɪmpreg'neɪʃən] *n see vt* Tränkung *f*; Erfüllung *f*; Durchdringung *f*; Befruchtung *f*; Schwängerung *f*.
impresario [.ɪmpre'saːrɪəʊ] *n* Impresario *m*; Theater-/Operndirektor *m*.
impress [ɪm'pres] **1** *vt* (**a**) beeindrucken; (*favourably, memorably also*) Eindruck machen auf (+ *acc*); (*arouse admiration in*) imponieren (+ *dat*). how does it ~ you? wie finden Sie das?; he/it ~ed me favourably/unfavourably er/das hat einen/keinen guten *or* günstigen Eindruck auf mich gemacht; I am not ~ed das beeindruckt mich nicht, das imponiert mir gar nicht; he is not easily ~ed er läßt sich nicht so leicht beeindrucken.
(**b**) (*fix in mind of*) einschärfen (*on sb* jdm); *idea, danger, possibility* (deutlich) klarmachen (*on sb* jdm).
(**c**) (*press to make mark*) to ~ a pattern etc onto/into sth ein Muster *etc* auf etw (*acc*) aufdrücken *or* aufprägen/in etw (*acc*) eindrücken *or* einprägen; his parting words ~ed themselves on my mind seine Abschiedsworte haben sich mir eingeprägt.
2 *vi* Eindruck machen; (*person: deliberately*) Eindruck schinden (*inf*).
3 ['ɪmpres] *n* Abdruck *m*.
impression [ɪm'preʃən] *n* (**a**) Eindruck *m*. to make a good/bad ~ on sb einen guten/schlechten Eindruck auf jdn machen; his words made an ~ seine Worte machten Eindruck; he created an ~ of power er erweckte den Eindruck von Macht; first ~s are usually right der erste Eindruck ist gewöhnlich richtig; it's wrong to judge by first ~s es ist falsch, nach dem ersten Eindruck zu urteilen.
(**b**) (*vague idea*) Eindruck *m*; (*feeling*) Gefühl *nt*. to give sb the ~ that ... jdm den Eindruck vermitteln, daß ...; I was under the ~ that ... ich hatte den Eindruck, daß ...; that gives an ~ of light/warmth das vermittelt den Eindruck von Licht/ein Gefühl der Wärme; he had the ~ of falling er hatte das Gefühl, zu fallen.
(**c**) (*on wax etc*) Abdruck, Eindruck *m*; (*of engraving*) Prägung *f*.
(**d**) (*of book etc*) Nachdruck *m*. first ~ Erstdruck *m*.
(**e**) (*take-off*) Nachahmung, Imitation *f*. to do an ~ of sb jdn imitieren *or* nachahmen.
impressionable [ɪm'preʃnəbl] *adj* für Eindrücke empfänglich, leicht zu beeindrucken *pred* (*pej*). at an ~ age in einem Alter, in dem man für Eindrücke besonders empfänglich ist.
impressionism [ɪm'preʃənɪzəm] *n* Impressionismus *m*.
impressionist [ɪm'preʃənɪst] *n* Impressionist(in *f*) *m*.
impressionistic [ɪm.preʃə'nɪstɪk] *adj* impressionistisch; (*fig*) *story, account also* in groben Zügen (geschildert).
impressive [ɪm'presɪv] *adj* beeindruckend; *performance, speech, ceremony, personality also* eindrucksvoll; (*in size*) *building, person also* imposant.
impressively [ɪm'presɪvlɪ] *adv see adj*.
imprint [ɪm'prɪnt] **1** *vt* (**a**) (*mark*) *leather* prägen; *paper* bedrucken; *seal, paper etc* aufprägen (*on auf* + *acc*); (*on paper*) aufdrucken (*on auf* + *acc*). the document was ~ed with the seal of ... das Dokument trug das Siegel + *gen or* von ...
(**b**) (*fig*) einprägen (*on sb* jdm). to ~ itself on sb's mind/memory sich jdm/sich in jds Gedächtnis (*acc*) einprägen.
2 ['ɪmprɪnt] *n* (**a**) (*lit*) (*on leather, wax etc*) Abdruck *m*; (*on paper*) (Auf)druck *m*; (*fig*) Spuren, Zeichen *pl*, bleibender Eindruck. he left the ~ of his ideas on his followers seine Nachfolger waren noch von seinen Ideen geprägt.
(**b**) (*Typ*) Impressum *nt*. under the Collins ~ mit dem Collins-Impressum.
imprison [ɪm'prɪzn] *pret, ptp* ~ed *vt* (*lit*) inhaftieren, einsperren (*inf*); (*fig*) gefangenhalten. to be/keep ~ed (*lit, fig*) gefangen sein/gefangenhalten.
imprisonment [ɪm'prɪznmənt] *n* (*action*) Einsperren *nt* (*inf*), Inhaftierung *f*; (*state*) Gefangenschaft *f*. to sentence sb to one month's/life ~ jdn zu einem Monat Gefängnis *or* Freiheitsstrafe/zu lebenslänglicher Freiheitsstrafe verurteilen; to serve a sentence *or* term of ~ eine Freiheitsstrafe verbüßen.
improbability [ɪm.probə'bɪlɪtɪ] *n* Unwahrscheinlichkeit *f*.
improbable [ɪm'probəbl] *adj* unwahrscheinlich. it is ~ that it will happen es ist sehr unwahrscheinlich, daß das geschieht.
impromptu [ɪm'promptjuː] **1** *adj* improvisiert. **2** *adv* improvisiert; *perform* aus dem Stegreif. to speak/sing/act ~ improvisieren. **3** *n* (*Mus*) Impromptu *nt*.
improper [ɪm'propəʳ] *adj* (*unsuitable*) unpassend, unangebracht; (*unseemly*) unschicklich; (*indecent*) unanständig; (*wrong*) *diagnosis, interpretation* unzutreffend; *use* unsachgemäß; (*dishonest*) *practice* unlauter; (*not professional*) *conduct* unehrenhaft. it is ~ to do that es gehört sich nicht, das zu tun; ~ use of tools/drugs/one's position Zweckentfremdung *f* von Geräten/Drogen-/Amtsmißbrauch *m*.
improperly [ɪm'propəlɪ] *adv see adj*.
impropriety [.ɪmprə'praɪətɪ] *n* Unschicklichkeit *f*; (*of behaviour etc, language, remark*) Ungehörigkeit *f*; (*indecency: of jokes etc*) Unanständigkeit *f*. to behave with ~ sich ungehörig benehmen.
improve [ɪm'pruːv] **1** *vt* (**a**) verbessern; *area, appearance* ver-

schönern; *sauce, food etc also* verfeinern; *production, value also* erhöhen, steigern; *knowledge also* erweitern; *low salaries also* aufbessern. to ~ one's mind sich weiterbilden.
(**b**) to ~ the shining hour die Gelegenheit beim Schopfe packen.
2 *vi see vt* sich verbessern, sich bessern; schöner werden; sich erhöhen, steigen. he has ~d in maths er hat sich in Mathematik verbessert; to ~ with use mit Gebrauch besser werden; wine ~s with age je älter der Wein desto besser; the invalid is improving dem Kranken geht es besser; I'll try to ~ ich werde versuchen, mich zu bessern; things are improving es sieht schon besser aus, die Lage bessert sich langsam; this book ~s on re-reading das Buch gewinnt beim zweiten Lesen; his style has ~d in precision sein Stil hat an Genauigkeit gewonnen, sein Stil ist genauer geworden.
3 *vr* to ~ oneself an sich (*dat*) arbeiten.
♦**improve (up)on** *vi* + *prep obj* (**a**) übertreffen, besser machen. that can't be ~d ~ das kann man nicht übertreffen.
(**b**) (*Comm, Fin*) *offer* überbieten, gehen über (+ *acc*).
improved [ɪm'pruːvd] *adj* besser, verbessert; *offer also* höher.
improvement [ɪm'pruːvmənt] *n see vt* Verbesserung *f*, Besserung *f*; Verschönerung *f*; Verfeinerung *f*; Erhöhung, Steigerung *f*; Erweiterung *f*; Aufbesserung *f*; (*in health*) Besserung *f*; (*in studies also*) Fortschritte *pl*. an ~ in pay eine Gehaltsaufbesserung; ~ of one's mind Weiterbildung *f*; to be open to ~ verbesserungsfähig sein; an ~ on the previous one eine Verbesserung/Besserung *etc* gegenüber dem Früheren; to make ~s Verbesserungen machen *or* durchführen (*to an* + *dat*); to carry out ~s to a house Ausbesserungs- *or* (*to appearance*) Verschönerungsarbeiten an einem Haus vornehmen.
improvidence [ɪm'provɪdəns] *n* mangelnde Vorsorge (*of für*), Sorglosigkeit *f* (*of in bezug auf* + *acc*).
improvident [ɪm'provɪdənt] *adj* sorglos. he was ~ of the future er sorgte nicht für die Zukunft vor.
improvidently [ɪm'provɪdəntlɪ] *adv see adj*.
improving [ɪm'pruːvɪŋ] *adj* informativ, lehrreich; *book, also* bildend; (*morally ~*) erbaulich.
improvisation [.ɪmprovaɪ'zeɪʃən] *n* Improvisation, Improvisierung *f*; (*object improvised*) Provisorium *nt*.
improvise ['ɪmprovaɪz] *vti* improvisieren.
imprudence [ɪm'pruːdəns] *n* Unklugheit *f*.
imprudent *adj*, **~ly** *adv* [ɪm'pruːdənt, -lɪ] unklug.
impudence ['ɪmpjʊdəns] *n* Unverschämtheit, Frechheit *f*. what ~! so eine Unverschämtheit *or* Frechheit!; he had the ~ to ask me er hatte die Stirn *or* er besaß die Frechheit, mich zu fragen.
impudent *adj*, **~ly** *adv* ['ɪmpjʊdənt, -lɪ] unverschämt, dreist.
impugn [ɪm'pjuːn] *vt person* angreifen; *sb's behaviour etc also* scharfe Kritik üben an (+ *dat*); *sb's honesty, motives* in Zweifel ziehen, Zweifel hegen an (+ *dat*); *statement, evidence, veracity of witness* bestreiten, anfechten.
impulse ['ɪmpʌls] *n* Impuls *m*; (*driving force*) (Stoß- *or* Trieb)kraft *f*. nerve ~ nervöser Reiz *or* Impuls; to give an ~ to business dem Handel neue Impulse geben; creature/man of ~ impulsives Wesen/impulsiver Mensch; to yield to a sudden *or* rash ~ einem Impuls nachgeben *or* folgen; on ~ aus einem Impuls heraus, impulsiv; ~ buying impulsives *or* spontanes Kaufen; an ~ buy *or* purchase ein Impulsivkauf *m*; I had an ~ to hit him ich hatte den (unwiderstehlichen) Drang *or* das plötzliche Verlangen, ihn zu schlagen; he is ruled by his ~s er läßt sich von seinen spontanen Regungen leiten.
impulsion [ɪm'pʌlʃən] *n* (*lit: act of impelling*) Antrieb *m*; (*lit, fig: driving force also*) Antriebskraft *f*; (*fig*) (*impetus*) Impuls *m*; (*compulsion*) Trieb, Drang *m*.
impulsive [ɪm'pʌlsɪv] *adj* (**a**) impulsiv; *action, remark also* spontan. (**b**) (*Phys, Tech*) *force* Trieb-, (an)treibend.
impulsively [ɪm'pʌlsɪvlɪ] *adv see adj* (*a*).
impulsiveness [ɪm'pʌlsɪvnəs] *n see adj* (*a*) Impulsivität *f*; Spontaneität *f*.
impunity [ɪm'pjuːnɪtɪ] *n* Straflosigkeit *f*. with ~ ungestraft.
impure [ɪm'pjʊəʳ] *adj water, drugs* unrein; *food* verunreinigt; *thoughts, mind also, motives* unsauber; *style* nicht rein.
impurity [ɪm'pjʊərɪtɪ] *n see adj* Unreinheit *f*; Verunreinigung *f*; Unsauberkeit *f*; Unreinheit *f*. the impurities in the liquid die Verunreinigungen in der Flüssigkeit.
imputation [.ɪmpjʊ'teɪʃən] *n* (*of crime*) Bezichtigung *f*; (*of lie also*) Unterstellung *f*.
impute [ɪm'pjuːt] *vt* zuschreiben (*to sb/sth* jdm/einer Sache). to ~ a crime/lie to sb jdn eines Verbrechens bezichtigen/jdm eine Lüge unterstellen, jdn einer Lüge bezichtigen.
in [ɪn] **1** *prep* (**a**) (*position*) in (+ *dat*); (*with motion*) in (+ *acc*). it was ~ the pocket/car es war auf dem Lastwagen/in der Tasche/im Auto; he put it ~ the lorry/car/pocket er legte es auf den Lastwagen/ins Auto/steckte es in die Tasche; ~ here/there hierin/darin, hier/da drin (*inf*); (*with motion*) hier/da hinein/herein, hier/da rein (*inf*); go ~ that direction gehen Sie in diese *or* dieser Richtung; ~ the street auf der/die Straße; ~ Thompson Street in der Thompsonstraße; he lives ~ a little village er wohnt auf *or* in einem kleinen Dorf; sitting ~ the window am Fenster sitzend; a flag hung ~ the window eine Flagge hing im Fenster; ~ (the) church in der Kirche; to stay ~ the house im Haus *or* (*at home*) zu Hause bleiben; ~ bed/prison/town im Bett/Gefängnis/in der Stadt; ~ Germany/Iran/Switzerland/the United States in Deutschland/im Iran/in der Schweiz/in den Vereinigten Staaten; the best ~ the class der Beste der Klasse, der Klassenbeste.
(**b**) (*people, works*) bei. we find it ~ Dickens wir finden das bei Dickens *or* in Dickens' Werken; rare ~ a child of that age selten bei einem Kind in diesem Alter; you have a great leader ~ him in ihm habt ihr einen großen Führer.
(**c**) (*time: with dates etc, during*) in (+ *dat*). ~ 1974 (im Jahre) 1974; ~ the sixties in den sechziger Jahren; ~ the reign of

unter der Herrschaft von, in or während der Regierungszeit von; ~ June im Juni; ~ (the) spring im Frühling; ~ the morning(s) morgens, am Morgen, am Vormittag; ~ the afternoon nachmittags, am Nachmittag; ~ the daytime tagsüber, während des Tages; ~ the evening abends, am Abend; three o'clock ~ the afternoon drei Uhr nachmittags; ~ those days damals, zu jener Zeit; ~ the beginning am Anfang, anfangs; once ~ a lifetime (nur) einmal im Leben.

(d) (time: interval) in (+dat); (within) innerhalb von. ~ a moment or minute sofort, gleich; ~ a short time in kurzer Zeit; ~ a week('s time) in einer Woche; I haven't seen him ~ years ich habe ihn seit Jahren or jahrelang nicht mehr gesehen.

(e) (manner, state, condition) to speak ~ a loud/soft voice mit lauter/leiser Stimme sprechen, laut/leise sprechen; to speak ~ a whisper flüstern, flüsternd sprechen; to speak ~ German Deutsch or deutsch reden; the background is painted ~ red der Hintergrund ist rot (gemalt) or in Rot gehalten; to pay ~ dollars mit or in Dollar bezahlen; to stand ~ a row/~ groups in einer Reihe/in Gruppen or gruppenweise stehen; ~ this way so, auf diese Weise; packed ~ hundreds zu Hunderten abgepackt; to walk ~ twos zu zweit or zu zweien gehen; to count ~ fives in Fünfern zählen; ~ good/bad health gesund/krank, bei guter/schlechter Gesundheit (geh); she squealed ~ delight sie quietschte vor Vergnügen; ~ anger im Zorn; to be ~ a rage wütend or zornig sein; ~ a good state in gutem Zustand; to live ~ luxury/poverty im Luxus/in Armut leben.

(f) (dress) in (+dat). ~ one's best clothes in Sonntagskleidung; ~ his shirt/shirt sleeves/slippers im Hemd/in Hemdsärmeln, hemdsärmelig/in Hausschuhen; dressed ~ white weiß gekleidet; the lady ~ green die Dame in Grün.

(g) (substance, material) upholstered ~ silk mit Seide bezogen; she was dressed ~ silk sie war in Seide gekleidet; to paint ~ oils in Öl malen; to write ~ ink/pencil mit Tinte/Bleistift schreiben; ~ marble in Marmor, marmorn; a sculptor who works ~ marble ein Bildhauer, der mit Marmor arbeitet.

(h) (ratio) there are 12 inches ~ a foot ein Fuß hat 12 Zoll; one (man) ~ ten einer von zehn, jeder zehnte; one book/child ~ ten jedes zehnte Buch/Kind, ein Buch/Kind von zehn; fifteen pence ~ the pound discount fünfzehn Prozent Rabatt.

(i) (degree, extent) ~ large/small quantities in großen/kleinen Mengen; ~ some measure in gewisser Weise, zu einem gewissen Grad; ~ part teilweise, zum Teil; to die ~ hundreds zu Hunderten sterben.

(j) (in respect of) blind ~ the left eye auf dem linken Auge or links blind; weak or poor ~ maths in Mathematik schwach or schlecht; weak ~ character charakterschwach; a rise ~ prices ein Preisanstieg m, ein Anstieg m der Preise; ten feet ~ height by thirty ~ length zehn Fuß hoch auf dreißig Fuß lang; to be too long ~ the leg zu lange Beine haben; five ~ number fünf an der Zahl; the latest thing ~ hats der letzte Schrei bei Hüten.

(k) (occupation, activity) he is ~ the army er ist beim Militär; he is ~ banking/the motor business er ist im Bankwesen/in der Autobranche (tätig); he travels ~ ladies' underwear er reist in Damenunterwäsche.

(l) (+prp) ~ saying this, I ... wenn ich das sage, ... ich; ~ trying to escape beim Versuch zu fliehen, beim Fluchtversuch; but ~ saying this aber indem ich dies sage; ~ making a fortune im Streben nach Reichtum; he made a mistake ~ saying that es war ein Fehler von ihm, das zu sagen.

(m) ~ that insofern als.

2 adv (a) da; (at home also) zu Hause. there is nobody ~ es ist niemand da/zu Hause; the train is ~ der Zug ist da or angekommen; the harvest is ~ die Ernte ist eingebracht; our team is ~ (Cricket) unsere Mannschaft ist am Schlag; we were asked ~ wir wurden hereingebeten; see vbs.

(b) (fig) strawberries are now ~ es ist Erdbeerzeit; miniskirts are ~ Miniröcke sind in (inf) or in Mode; the Socialists are ~ die Sozialisten sind an der Regierung; the Communist candidate is ~ der kommunistische Kandidat ist gewählt or reingekommen (inf); the fire is still ~ das Feuer ist noch an or brennt noch.

(c) (phrases) we are ~ for trouble wir können uns auf was gefaßt machen (inf); we are ~ for rain/a cold spell uns (dat) steht Regen/eine Kältewelle bevor; he's ~ for it! der kann sich auf was gefaßt machen (inf), der kann sich freuen (iro); you don't know what you are ~ for/letting yourself ~ for Sie wissen nicht, was Ihnen bevorsteht/auf was Sie sich da einlassen; are you ~ for the race? machen Sie bei dem Rennen mit?; he is ~ for the post of manager er hat sich um die Stelle des Managers beworben; he hasn't got it ~ him er hat nicht das Zeug dazu; it's not ~ him to ... er hat einfach nicht das Zeug dazu, zu ...; to have it ~ for sb (inf) es auf jdn abgesehen haben (inf); to be ~ on sth an einer Sache beteiligt sein; (on secret etc) über etw (acc) Bescheid wissen; he likes to be ~ on things er mischt gern (überall) mit (inf); to be (well) ~ with sb sich gut mit jdm verstehen; my luck is ~ ich habe einen Glückstag.

3 adj attr (a) „~" door Eingangstür f; "~" tray Ablage f für Eingänge; see in-patient etc.

(b) (inf) in inv (inf). an ~ subject ein Modefach nt; the ~ thing to do ~ es ist in (inf) or zur Zeit Mode, zu ...

4 n (a) to know the ~s and outs of a matter von einer Sache genau Bescheid wissen.

(b) (US Pol) the ~s die Regierungspartei.

inability [ˌɪnəˈbɪlɪtɪ] n Unfähigkeit f, Unvermögen nt. ~ to pay Zahlungsunfähigkeit f.

inaccessibility [ˈɪnækˌsesəˈbɪlɪtɪ] n see adj Unzugänglichkeit f; Unerreichbarkeit f.

inaccessible [ˌɪnækˈsesəbl] adj information, person unzugänglich; place also unerreichbar.

inaccuracy [ɪnˈækjʊrəsɪ] n see adj Ungenauigkeit f; Unrichtigkeit f.

inaccurate [ɪnˈækjʊrɪt] adj (lacking accuracy) ungenau; (not correct) unrichtig. while it would be ~ to claim ... während es unrichtig wäre, zu behaupten, ...; she was ~ in her judgement of the situation ihre Beurteilung der Lage traf nicht zu.

inaccurately [ɪnˈækjʊrɪtlɪ] adv see adj.

inaction [ɪnˈækʃən] n Untätigkeit f, Tatenlosigkeit f.

inactive [ɪnˈæktɪv] adj untätig; person, life, hands also müßig (geh); mind träge, müßig (geh); volcano erloschen, untätig. don't have money lying ~ in the bank lassen Sie (Ihr) Geld nicht auf der Bank brachliegen.

inactivity [ˌɪnækˈtɪvɪtɪ] n Untätigkeit f; (of mind) Trägheit f; (Comm) Stille, Flaute f.

inadequacy [ɪnˈædɪkwəsɪ] n see adj Unzulänglichkeit f; Unangemessenheit f.

inadequate [ɪnˈædɪkwɪt] adj unzulänglich, inadäquat (geh); supplies, resources, punishment, reasons, proposals also unzureichend; measures unangemessen. he is ~ for such a job/responsibility er ist für eine solche Stelle nicht geeignet/er ist einer solchen Verantwortung nicht gewachsen; she makes him feel ~ sie gibt ihm das Gefühl der Unzulänglichkeit; Jones, your work is ~ Jones, Ihre Arbeit ist unzulänglich.

inadequately [ɪnˈædɪkwɪtlɪ] adv unzulänglich, inadäquat (geh); equipped, explained, documented also unzureichend.

inadmissibility [ˈɪnədˌmɪsəˈbɪlɪtɪ] n Unzulässigkeit f.

inadmissible [ˌɪnədˈmɪsəbl] adj unzulässig.

inadvertence [ˌɪnədˈvɜːtəns] n Ungewolltheit f. through ~ versehentlich, aus Versehen.

inadvertent [ˌɪnədˈvɜːtənt] adj unbeabsichtigt, ungewollt.

inadvertently [ˌɪnədˈvɜːtəntlɪ] adv versehentlich.

inadvisability [ˈɪnədˌvaɪzəˈbɪlɪtɪ] n Unratsamkeit f (of doing sth etw zu tun).

inadvisable [ˌɪnədˈvaɪzəbl] adj unratsam, nicht zu empfehlen pred, nicht zu empfehlen attr.

inalienable [ɪnˈeɪlɪənəbl] adj rights unveräußerlich.

inane [ɪˈneɪn] adj dumm; suggestion also hirnverbrannt.

inanely [ɪˈneɪnlɪ] adv dumm. he suggested ~ that ... er machte den hirnverbrannten Vorschlag, zu ...

inanimate [ɪnˈænɪmɪt] adj leblos, tot; nature unbelebt.

inanition [ˌɪnəˈnɪʃən] n Auszehrung f.

inanity [ɪˈnænɪtɪ] n see adj Dummheit f; Hirnverbranntheit f.

inappetency [ɪnˈæpɪtənsɪ] n (fig liter) Lustlosigkeit, Unlust f.

inapplicable [ɪnˈæplɪkəbl] adj answer unzutreffend; laws, rules nicht anwendbar (to sb auf jdn).

inapposite [ɪnˈæpəzɪt] adj unpassend, unangebracht; action also unangemessen.

inappropriate [ˌɪnəˈprəʊprɪɪt] adj unpassend, unangebracht; action also unangemessen; time unpassend, ungelegen, ungünstig. this translation/treatment is rather ~ das ist keine angemessene Übersetzung/Behandlung; you have come at a most ~ time Sie kommen sehr ungelegen.

inappropriately [ˌɪnəˈprəʊprɪɪtlɪ] adv see adj.

inappropriateness [ˌɪnəˈprəʊprɪɪtnɪs] n see adj Unpassende nt, Unangebrachtheit f; Unangemessenheit f; Ungünstigkeit f.

inapt [ɪnˈæpt] adj ungeschickt; remark also unpassend.

inaptitude [ɪnˈæptɪtjuːd] n (of person) Unfähigkeit f; (for work etc) Untauglichkeit f; (of remark) Ungeschicktheit f, Unangebrachtheit f.

inarticulate [ˌɪnɑːˈtɪkjʊlɪt] adj (a) essay schlecht or unklar ausgedrückt, inartikuliert (geh); speech also schwerfällig. she's very ~ sie kann sich kaum or nur schlecht ausdrücken; a brilliant but ~ scientist ein glänzender, aber wenig wortgewandter Wissenschaftler; he was too ~ to impress a student audience or war nicht wortgewandt genug, um eine Zuhörerschaft von Studenten zu beeindrucken; he was ~ about his real feelings er konnte seine wahren Gefühle nur schwer ausdrücken; ~ with rage sprachlos vor Zorn; just a string of ~ grunts nur eine Reihe unverständlicher Grunzlaute.

(b) (Zool) nicht gegliedert.

inartistic adj, ~ally adv [ˌɪnɑːˈtɪstɪk, -əlɪ] unkünstlerisch; work also kunstlos.

inasmuch [ˌɪnəzˈmʌtʃ] adv: ~ as da, weil; (to the extent that) insofern als.

inattention [ˌɪnəˈtenʃən] n Unaufmerksamkeit f. ~ to detail Ungenauigkeit f im Detail.

inattentive adj, ~ly adv [ˌɪnəˈtentɪv, -lɪ] unaufmerksam.

inattentiveness [ˌɪnəˈtentɪvnɪs] n Unaufmerksamkeit f.

inaudibility [ɪnˌɔːdəˈbɪlɪtɪ] n Unhörbarkeit f.

inaudible adj, **inaudibly** adv [ɪnˈɔːdəbl, -ɪ] unhörbar.

inaugural [ɪˈnɔːgjʊrəl] **1** adj lecture Antritts-; meeting, address, speech Eröffnungs-. **2** n (speech) Antritts-/Eröffnungsrede f.

inaugurate [ɪˈnɔːgjʊreɪt] vt (a) president, official (feierlich) in sein/ihr Amt einsetzen or einführen, inaugurieren (geh); pope, king, bishop also inthronisieren (geh).

(b) policy einführen; building einweihen; exhibition eröffnen; era einleiten.

inauguration [ɪˌnɔːgjʊˈreɪʃən] n see vt (a) Amtseinführung, Inauguration (geh) f; Inthronisierung f (geh). (b) Einführung f; Einweihung f; Eröffnung f; Beginn, Anbruch m.

inauspicious [ˌɪnɔːsˈpɪʃəs] adj unheilverheißend; circumstances, omen also unheilträchtig.

inauspiciously [ˌɪnɔːsˈpɪʃəslɪ] adv see adj.

in-between [ˌɪnbɪˈtwiːn] (inf) **1** n: the ~s wer/was dazwischenliegt or -kommt. **2** adj Mittel-, Zwischen-. it is sort of ~ es ist so ein Mittelding; ~ stage Zwischenstadium nt; ~ weather Übergangswetter nt; ~ the ~ ages zwischendurch, dazwischen.

inboard [ˈɪnbɔːd] (Naut) **1** adj Innenbord-. **2** adv innenbords. **3** n Innenbordmotor m.

inborn [ˈɪnˈbɔːn] adj angeboren.

inbred [ˈɪnˈbred] adj (a) they look very ~ sie sehen nach Inzucht aus; to stop them becoming ~ um die Inzucht bei ihnen aufzuhalten; **the royal family became very** ~ in der Königsfamilie herrschte Inzucht. **(b)** *quality* angeboren.

inbreeding ['ɪn'briːdɪŋ] *n* Inzucht *f.*

Inc (*US*) *abbr of* **Incorporated.**

Inca ['ɪŋkə] **1** *n* Inka *mf.* **2** *adj* (*also* ~n) Inka-, inkaisch.

incalculable [ɪn'kælkjʊləbl] *adj* **(a)** *amount* unschätzbar, unermeßlich; *damage, harm also, consequences* unabsehbar. **(b)** (*Math*) nicht berechenbar. **(c)** *character, mood* unberechenbar, unvorhersehbar.

incandescence [ˌɪnkæn'desns] *n* (Weiß)glühen *nt*, (Weiß)glut *f.*

incandescent [ˌɪnkæn'desnt] *adj* (*lit*) (weiß)glühend; (*fig liter*) hell leuchtend, strahlend. ~ **lamp** Glühlampe, Glühbirne *f.*

incantation [ˌɪnkæn'teɪʃən] *n* Zauber(spruch) *m*, Zauberformel *f*; (*act*) Beschwörung *f.*

incapability [ɪnˌkeɪpə'bɪlɪtɪ] *n* Unfähigkeit *f*, Unvermögen *nt* (*of doing sth* etw zu tun).

incapable [ɪn'keɪpəbl] *adj* **(a)** *person* unfähig; (*physically*) hilflos. **to be** ~ **of doing sth** unfähig *or* nicht imstande sein, etw zu tun, etw nicht tun können; **drunk and** ~ volltrunken; **he was completely** ~ (*because drunk*) er war volltrunken; ~ **of working** unfähig; ~ **of tenderness** zu Zärtlichkeit nicht fähig; **do it yourself, you're not** ~ (*inf*) mach es doch selbst, du bist nicht so hilflos.

(b) ~ **of proof** nicht beweisbar; ~ **of measurement** nicht meßbar; ~ **of improvement** nicht verbesserungsfähig.

incapacitate [ˌɪnkə'pæsɪteɪt] *vt* **(a)** unfähig machen (*for* für, *from doing sth* etw zu tun). **physically** ~d körperlich behindert; **somewhat** ~d **by his broken ankle** durch seinen gebrochenen Knöchel ziemlich behindert. **(b)** (*Jur*) entmündigen.

incapacity [ˌɪnkə'pæsɪtɪ] *n* **(a)** Unfähigkeit *f* (*for* für). ~ **for work** Arbeitsunfähigkeit *f.* **(b)** (*Jur*) mangelnde Berechtigung (*for* zu). ~ **to inherit** Erbunfähigkeit *f*; ~ **of a minor** Geschäftsunfähigkeit *f* eines Minderjährigen.

incarcerate [ɪn'kɑːsəreɪt] *vt* einkerkern.

incarnate [ɪn'kɑːnɪt] **1** *adj* (*Rel*) fleischgeworden, menschgeworden; (*personified*) leibhaftig *attr*, in Person. **to become** ~ Fleisch werden, Mensch werden; **the word I**~ das fleischgewordene Wort; **he's the devil** ~ er ist der leibhaftige Teufel *or* der Teufel in Person.

2 ['ɪnkɑːneɪt] *vt* (*make real*) Gestalt *or* Form geben (+ *dat*); (*be embodiment of*) verkörpern.

incarnation [ˌɪnkɑː'neɪʃən] *n* (*Rel*) Inkarnation (*geh*), Menschwerdung, Fleischwerdung *f*; (*fig*) Inbegriff *m*, Verkörperung, Inkarnation (*geh*) *f.*

incautious *adj*, ~**ly** *adv* [ɪn'kɔːʃəs, -lɪ] unvorsichtig, unbedacht.

incendiary [ɪn'sendɪərɪ] **1** *adj* **(a)** (*lit*) *bomb* Brand-. ~ **device** Brandsatz *m.* **(b)** (*fig*) *speech* aufwiegelnd, aufhetzend. **2** *n* **(a)** (*bomb*) Brandbombe *f.* **(b)** (*person*) (*lit*) Brandstifter(in *f*) *m*; (*fig*) Aufrührer(in *f*), Unruhestifter(in *f*) *m.*

incense¹ [ɪn'sens] *vt* wütend machen, erbosen, erzürnen. ~**d** wütend, erbost (*at, by* über + *acc*).

incense² ['ɪnsens] *n* (*Eccl*) Weihrauch *m*; (*fig*) Duft *m.*

incense: ~ **bearer** *n* Weihrauchschwenker *or* -träger *m*; ~ **burner** *n* Weihrauchschwenker *m*, Räucherpfanne *f.*

incentive [ɪn'sentɪv] *n* Anreiz *m.* **it'll give them a bit of** ~ das wird ihnen einen gewissen Anreiz *or* Ansporn geben; ~ **scheme** (*Ind*) leistungsabhängiges Schema.

inception [ɪn'sepʃən] *n* Beginn, Anfang *m.* **from/at its** ~ von Anbeginn an/zu Anbeginn.

incertitude [ɪn'sɜːtɪtjuːd] *n* Ungewißheit, Unsicherheit *f.*

incessant [ɪn'sesnt] *adj* unaufhörlich, unablässig; *complaints also* nicht abreißend; *noise* ununterbrochen.

incessantly [ɪn'sesntlɪ] *adv see adj.*

incest ['ɪnsest] *n* Inzest *m*, Blutschande *f.*

incestuous [ɪn'sestjʊəs] *adj* blutschänderisch, inzestuös (*geh*).

inch [ɪntʃ] **1** *n* Inch, ≈ Zoll *m.* **because of his lack of** ~es **weil er ein bißchen kleiner ist/war; she's gained a few** ~es **sie hat in der Taille ein paar Zentimeter zugenommen; she's grown a few** ~es **sie ist ein paar Zentimeter gewachsen; by** ~ **Zentimeter um Zentimeter; he came within an** ~ **of winning** victory er hätte um ein Haar *or* beinahe gewonnen; **he came within an** ~ **of being killed** er ist dem Tod um Haaresbreite entgangen; **he was within an** ~ **of death** sein Leben stand auf des Messers Schneide; **he missed being run over by** ~es **er wäre um ein Haar überfahren worden; the lorry missed me by** ~es **der Lastwagen hat mich um Haaresbreite verfehlt; he knows every** ~ **of the area** er kennt die Gegend wie seine Westentasche; **he is every** ~ **a soldier** er ist jeder Zoll ein Soldat; **we will not surrender one** ~ **of our territory** wir werden keinen Zentimeter unseres Gebiets abtreten; **they searched every** ~ **of the room** sie durchsuchten das Zimmer Zentimeter für Zentimeter; **we need every** ~ **of our office** wir brauchen jedes Fleckchen in unserem Büro; **he couldn't see an** ~ **in front of him** er konnte die Hand nicht vor den Augen sehen; **give him an** ~ **and he'll take a mile** (*prov*) wenn man ihm den kleinen Finger gibt, nimmt er die ganze Hand (*prov*).

2 *vi* **to** ~ **forward/out/in** sich millimeterweise *or* stückchenweise vorwärts-/hinaus-/heraus-/hinein-/hereinschieben; **because prices are** ~**ing up** weil die Preise allmählich ansteigen; **the Dutch swimmer is** ~**ing ahead** der holländische Schwimmer schiebt sich langsam an die Spitze.

3 *vt* langsam manövrieren. **he** ~**ed his way forward** er schob sich langsam vorwärts.

inchoate ['ɪnkəʊeɪt] *adj* (*liter*) unausgeformt.

incidence ['ɪnsɪdəns] *n* **(a)** (*Opt*) Einfall *m.* **angle of** ~ Einfallswinkel *m.* **(b)** (*of crime, disease*) Häufigkeit *f.* **a high** ~ **of crime** eine hohe Verbrechensquote; **the** ~ **of death from malaria** die Häufigkeit von Todesfällen durch Malaria.

incident ['ɪnsɪdənt] **1** *n* **(a)** (*event*) Ereignis *nt*, Begebenheit *f*, Vorfall *m.* **a life full of** ~s **ein ereignisreiches Leben; an** ~

from his childhood eine Episode aus seiner Kindheit. **(b)** (*diplomatic etc*) Zwischenfall *m*; (*disturbance in pub etc*) Vorfall *m.* **without** ~ ohne Zwischenfälle. **(c)** (*in book, play*) Episode *f.*

2 *adj* **(a)** ~ **to** (*form*) verbunden mit. **(b)** (*Opt*) *ray* einfallend.

incidental [ˌɪnsɪ'dentl] **1** *adj* **(a)** **dangers** ~ **to foreign travel** mit Auslandsreisen verbundene Gefahren; ~ **music** Begleitmusik *f*; ~ **expenses** Nebenkosten *pl.*

(b) (*unplanned*) *event* zufällig.

(c) (*secondary etc*) nebensächlich; *remark* beiläufig.

2 *n* Nebensächlichkeit, Nebensache *f.* ~s (*expenses*) Nebenausgaben *pl.*

incidentally [ˌɪnsɪ'dentəlɪ] *adv* übrigens. **it's only** ~ **important** das ist nur von nebensächlicher Bedeutung; **a few** ~ **made comments** ein paar Bemerkungen nebenbei.

incinerate [ɪn'sɪnəreɪt] *vt* verbrennen; (*cremate*) einäschern.

incineration [ɪnsɪnə'reɪʃən] *n see vt* Verbrennung *f*; Einäscherung *f.*

incinerator [ɪn'sɪnəreɪtəʳ] *n* (Müll)verbrennungsanlage *f*; (*garden* ~) Verbrennungsofen *m*; (*in crematorium*) Feuerbestattungsofen, Verbrennungsofen *m.*

incipience [ɪn'sɪpɪəns] *n* Anfang, Beginn *m.*

incipient [ɪn'sɪpɪənt] *adj* anfangend, beginnend; *disease, difficulties also* einsetzend.

incise [ɪn'saɪz] *vt* **(a)** (ein)schneiden (*into* in + *acc*). **(b)** (*Art*) (*in wood*) (ein)schnitzen; (*in metal, stone*) eingravieren, einritzen.

incision [ɪn'sɪʒən] *n* Schnitt *m*; (*Med*) Einschnitt *m.*

incisive [ɪn'saɪsɪv] *adj* *style, tone, words* prägnant; *criticism* treffend, scharfsinnig; *mind* scharf; *person* scharfsinnig.

incisively [ɪn'saɪsɪvlɪ] *adv* *speak, formulate, put* prägnant; *argue, criticize, reason* treffend, scharfsinnig.

incisiveness [ɪn'saɪsɪvnɪs] *n see adj* Prägnanz *f*; Treffende *nt*, Scharfsinnigkeit *f*; Schärfe *f*; Scharfsinnigkeit *f.*

incisor [ɪn'saɪzəʳ] *n* Schneidezahn *m.*

incite [ɪn'saɪt] *vt* aufwiegeln; *masses also* aufwiegeln; *racial hatred* aufhetzen zu. **to** ~ **the masses/sb to violence** die Massen/jdn zu Gewalttätigkeiten aufhetzen.

incitement [ɪn'saɪtmənt] *n* **(a)** *no pl see vt* Aufhetzung *f*; Aufwieg(e)lung *f.* **(b)** (*incentive*) Anreiz, Ansporn *m* (*to* zu).

incivility [ˌɪnsɪ'vɪlɪtɪ] *n* Unhöflichkeit *f.*

incl *abbr of* **inclusive(ly)** incl., inkl.; **including** incl., inkl.

inclemency [ɪn'klemənsɪ] *n see adj* Rauheit, Unfreundlichkeit *f*; Unbarmherzigkeit, Unerbittlichkeit *f.*

inclement [ɪn'klemənt] *adj* *weather, wind* rauh, unfreundlich; *judge, attitude* unbarmherzig, unerbittlich.

inclination [ˌɪnklɪ'neɪʃən] *n* **(a)** (*tendency, wish etc*) Neigung *f.* **he follows his (own)** ~s **er folgt seinen Neigungen; what are his natural** ~s? **welches sind seine Neigungen?; my (natural)** ~ **is to carry on** ich neige dazu, weiterzumachen; ~ **to stoutness** Anlage *or* Neigung *f* zu Korpulenz; **to have an** ~ **towards rudeness** zur Unhöflichkeit neigen; **I have no** ~ **to see him again** ich habe keinerlei Bedürfnis, ihn wiederzusehen; **my immediate** ~ **was to refuse** mein erster Gedanke war abzulehnen; **he showed no** ~ **to leave** er schien nicht gehen zu wollen.

(b) (*of head, body*) Neigung *f.*

(c) (*of hill, slope etc*) Neigung *f*, Gefälle, Abfallen *nt.*

incline [ɪn'klaɪn] **1** *vt* **(a)** *head, body, roof* neigen. **if you would** ~ **your ear** (*hum, liter*) wenn ich Sie um Ihr geneigtes Ohr bitten dürfte (*hum, geh*); **this** ~s **me to think that he must be lying** das läßt mich vermuten, daß er lügt.

(b) (*dispose*) veranlassen, bewegen. **the news** ~s **me to stay** aufgrund der Nachricht würde ich gern bleiben; *see* **inclined.**

2 *vi* **(a)** (*slope*) sich neigen; (*ground also*) abfallen.

(b) (*be disposed, tend towards*) neigen. **to** ~ **to a point of view** zu einer Ansicht neigen *or* tendieren; **he** ~s **to laziness** er neigt zur Faulheit; **he's beginning to** ~ **towards our point of view** er beginnt unserer Ansicht zuzuneigen.

3 ['ɪnklaɪn] *n* Neigung *f*; (*of hill*) Abhang *m*; (*gradient: Rail etc*) Gefälle *nt.*

inclined [ɪn'klaɪnd] *adj* **(a) to be** ~ **to do sth** (*feel that one wishes to*) Lust haben, etw zu tun, etw tun wollen; (*have tendency to*) dazu neigen, etw zu tun; **they are** ~ **to be late** sie kommen gern zu spät, sie neigen zum Zuspätkommen; **I am** ~ **to think that ...** ich neige zu der Ansicht, daß ...; **if you feel** ~ wenn Sie Lust haben *or* dazu aufgelegt sind; **to be well** ~ **towards sb** jdm geneigt *or* gewogen sein; **if you're** ~ **that way** wenn Ihnen so etwas liegt; **I'm** ~ **to disagree** ich möchte da doch widersprechen; **I am not** ~ **to approve of this** ich bin nicht geneigt, das gutzuheißen; **I'm** ~ **to believe you** ich möchte Ihnen gern glauben; **it's** ~ **to break** das bricht leicht.

(b) *plane* geneigt, schräg.

inclose [ɪn'kləʊz] *vt see* **enclose.**

include [ɪn'kluːd] *vt* einschließen, enthalten; (*on list, in group etc*) aufnehmen, einbeziehen. **your name is not** ~d **on the list** Ihr Name ist nicht auf der Liste; **the tip is not** ~d **in the bill** Trinkgeld ist in der Rechnung nicht inbegriffen; **all** ~d **alles** inklusive *or* inbegriffen; **the invitation** ~s **everybody** die Einladung betrifft alle; **they were all** ~d **in the accusation** die Anschuldigung bezog sich auf alle; **the children** ~d **mit(samt)** den Kindern, einschließlich der Kinder; **does that** ~ **me?** gilt das auch für mich?; **shut up! you** ~d **or that** ~s **you** Ruhe! Sie sind auch gemeint; **to** ~ **sb in one's prayers** jdn in sein Gebet einschließen; **in which category would you** ~ **this?** in welche Kategorie würden Sie das aufnehmen?; **I think we should** ~ **a chapter on ...** ich finde, wir sollten auch ein Kapitel über ... dazunehmen; **the book** ~s **two chapters on grammar** das Buch enthält auch zwei Grammatikkapitel.

♦**include out** *vt sep* (*hum inf*) auslassen. ~ **me** ~ ohne mich.

including [ɪn'kluːdɪŋ] *prep* inklusive, inbegriffen, mit. **that**

makes seven ~ you mit Ihnen sind das sieben; that comes to 200 marks ~ packing das kommt auf 200 DM inklusive or einschließlich Verpackung or Verpackung inbegriffen; there were six rooms ~ kitchen mit Küche waren es sechs Zimmer, es waren sechs Zimmer einschließlich Küche; ~ the service charge inklusive Bedienung, Bedienung (mit) inbegriffen; not ~ service exklusive Bedienung, Bedienung nicht inbegriffen or eingeschlossen; up to and ~ chapter V bis inklusive or einschließlich Kapitel V; up to and ~ March 4th bis einschließlich 4. März.

inclusion [ɪn'kluːʒən] n Aufnahme f. with the ~ of John that makes seven mit John macht das sieben.

inclusive [ɪn'kluːsɪv] adj inklusive, einschließlich; price Inklusiv-, Pauschal-. ~ sum Pauschale, Pauschalsumme f; ~ terms Pauschalpreis m; to be ~ of einschließlich (+gen) sein, einschließen (+acc); to the fifth page ~ bis einschließlich der fünften Seite, bis Seite fünf einschließlich; from 1st to 6th May ~ vom 1. bis einschließlich or inklusive 6. Mai, vom 1. bis 6. Mai inklusive.

inclusively [ɪn'kluːsɪvlɪ] adv inklusive, einschließlich. from 7 to 10 ~ von 7 bis einschließlich or inklusive 10.

incognito [ɪnkɒg'niːtəʊ] 1 adv inkognito. 2 n Inkognito nt. 3 adj traveller Inkognito-. to remain ~ inkognito bleiben.

incoherence [ɪnkəʊ'hɪərəns] n (of style, prose) Zusammenhanglosigkeit f, mangelnder Zusammenhang. with each further drink his ~ grew seine Worte wurden mit jedem Glas wirrer or zusammenhangloser.

incoherent [ɪnkəʊ'hɪərənt] adj style, argument zusammenhanglos, unzusammenhängend, inkohärent (geh); speech, conversation also wirr; person sich unklar or undeutlich ausdrückend; drunk etc schwer verständlich. he was ~ with rage seine wütenden Worte waren kaum zu verstehen.

incoherently [ɪnkəʊ'hɪərəntlɪ] adv talk, write zusammenhanglos, unzusammenhängend, wirr.

incombustible [ɪnkəm'bʌstəbl] adj unbrennbar.

income [ˈɪnkʌm] n Einkommen nt; (receipts) Einkünfte pl. to live within/beyond one's ~ seinen Verhältnissen entsprechend/über seine Verhältnisse leben.

income group n Einkommensklasse or -schicht f.

incomer [ˈɪnkʌmə] n (new arrival) Neuankömmling m; (successor) Nachfolger(in f) m.

income: ~s policy n Lohnpolitik f; ~ tax n Lohnsteuer f; (on private ~) Einkommensteuer f; ~ tax return n Steuererklärung f.

incoming [ˈɪnkʌmɪŋ] adj ankommend; train also einfahrend; ship also einlaufend; (succeeding) president etc nachfolgend, neu; mail, orders etc eingehend. ~ tide Flut f.

incomings [ˈɪnkʌmɪŋz] npl Einkünfte, Einnahmen pl.

incommensurable [ɪnkə'menʃərəbl] adj nicht zu vergleichen attr, nicht vergleichbar; (Math) inkommensurabel.

incommensurate [ɪnkə'menʃərɪt] adj (a) to be ~ with sth in keinem Verhältnis zu etw stehen. (b) (inadequate) unzureichend (to für).

incommode [ɪnkə'məʊd] vt (form) lästig sein (+dat). I don't wish to ~ you but could you/but could I ... ich möchte Sie nicht behelligen, aber könnten Sie vielleicht .../würde es Sie sehr stören, wenn ich ...

incommodious [ɪnkə'məʊdɪəs] adj (form) lästig, unbequem; (cramped) beengt.

incommunicado [ɪnkəmjunɪ'kɑːdəʊ] adj pred ohne jede Verbindung zur Außenwelt, abgesondert. he was held ~ er hatte keinerlei Verbindung zur Außenwelt; to be ~ (fig) für niemanden zu sprechen sein.

incomparable [ɪn'kɒmpərəbl] adj nicht vergleichbar (with mit); beauty, skill unvergleichlich.

incomparably [ɪn'kɒmpərəblɪ] adv unvergleichlich.

incompatibility [ˈɪnkəm,pætə'bɪlɪtɪ] n see adj Unvereinbarkeit f; Unverträglichkeit f. divorce on grounds of ~ Scheidung aufgrund der Unvereinbarkeit der Charaktere der Ehepartner.

incompatible [ɪnkəm'pætəbl] adj characters, ideas, propositions, temperaments unvereinbar; technical systems also nicht zueinander passend; drugs, blood groups, colours nicht miteinander verträglich. the drugs are ~ die Arzneimittel vertragen sich nicht miteinander; we are ~, she said wir passen überhaupt nicht zusammen or zueinander, sagte sie; the possession of great wealth is surely ~ with genuine Marxist beliefs der Besitz großer Reichtümer läßt sich wohl kaum mit echtem Marxismus vereinbaren.

incompetence [ˈɪnkɒmpɪtəns], **incompetency** [ˈɪnkɒmpɪtənsɪ] n (a) Unfähigkeit f; (for job) Untauglichkeit f. (b) (Jur) Unzuständigkeit f, Inkompetenz f.

incompetent [ɪn'kɒmpɪtənt] 1 adj (a) person unfähig; (for sth) untauglich; piece of work unzulänglich. to be ~ in business nicht geschäftstüchtig sein; to be ~ to teach music unfähig sein, Musik zu unterrichten, zum Musiklehrer untauglich sein. (b) (Jur) unzuständig, nicht zuständig, inkompetent. 2 n Nichtskönner m, Niete f (inf).

incompetently [ɪn'kɒmpɪtəntlɪ] adv schlecht, stümperhaft.

incomplete [ɪnkəm'pliːt] adj collection, series unvollkommen, unvollständig; (referring to numbers) unvollständig, nicht vollzählig; (not finished also) painting, novel unfertig. an ~ pack of cards ein nicht vollzähliges or vollständiges Kartenspiel.

incompletely [ɪnkəm'pliːtlɪ] adv see adj.

incompleteness [ɪnkəm'pliːtnɪs] n see adj Unvollkommenheit, Unvollständigkeit f; Unvollständigkeit f; Unfertigkeit f.

incomprehensible [ɪn,kɒmprɪ'hensəbl] adj unverständlich; act also unbegreiflich, unfaßbar. people like that are just ~ solche Leute kann ich einfach nicht begreifen.

incomprehensibly [ɪn,kɒmprɪ'hensəblɪ] adv see adj.

inconceivability [ˈɪnkən,siːvə'bɪlɪtɪ] n see adj Unvorstell-

barkeit f; Unfaßbarkeit, Unbegreiflichkeit f.

inconceivable [ɪnkən'siːvəbl] adj unvorstellbar, undenkbar; (hard to believe also) unfaßbar, unbegreiflich.

inconceivably [ɪnkən'siːvəblɪ] adv see adj.

inconclusive [ɪnkən'kluːsɪv] adj (not decisive) result unbestimmt, zu keiner Entscheidung führend; action, discussion, investigation ohne (schlüssiges) Ergebnis, ergebnislos; (not convincing) evidence, argument nicht überzeugend, nicht schlüssig, nicht zwingend.

inconclusively [ɪnkən'kluːsɪvlɪ] adv (without result) ergebnislos; argue nicht überzeugend, nicht schlüssig, nicht zwingend. his speech ended rather ~ seine Rede kam zu keinem überzeugenden Schluß.

incongruity [ɪnkɒŋ'gruːɪtɪ] n (a) no pl (of remark, sb's presence) Unpassende(s), Unangebrachtsein nt; (of dress) Unangemessenheit f, Mißverhältnis nt (of sth with sth zwischen etw dat und etw dat); (of juxtaposition, mixture) Mißklang m. such was the ~ of his remark/his presence seine Bemerkung war so unangebracht or unpassend/er war so fehl am Platz; the film relies on the ~ of these images der Film lebt von der inneren Widersprüchlichkeit dieser Bilder; he commented on the ~ of the Rolls parked in the slums er bemerkte, wie fehl am Platz sich der im Slum geparkte Rolls Royce ausmachte; because of the ~ of this Spanish-style villa in a Scottish setting weil diese Villa im spanischen Stil so gar nicht in die schottische Landschaft paßte/paßt. (b) (incongruous thing) Unstimmigkeit f.

incongruous [ɪn'kɒŋgruəs] adj couple, juxtaposition, mixture wenig zusammenpassend attr; thing to do, behaviour, remark unpassend; (out of place) fehl am Platz. he uses these ~ images er benutzt diese unstimmigen Bilder; a red jacket with a most ~ green shirt ein rote Jacke mit einem überhaupt nicht dazu passenden grünen Hemd; it seems ~ that ... es scheint abwegig or widersinnig, daß ...; how ~ that he should have been chosen! eigenartig, daß sie ausgerechnet ihn ausgewählt haben!

inconsequent [ɪn'kɒnsɪkwənt] adj unlogisch, nicht folgerichtig; remark nicht zur Sache gehörend attr, beziehungslos.

inconsequential [ɪn,kɒnsɪ'kwenʃəl] adj beziehungslos, irrelevant; (not logical) unlogisch, nicht folgerichtig; (unimportant) unbedeutend, unwichtig.

inconsequentially [ɪn,kɒnsɪ'kwenʃəlɪ] adv unlogisch.

inconsiderable [ɪnkən'sɪdərəbl] adj unbedeutend, unerheblich. a not ~ amount ein nicht unbedeutender Betrag.

inconsiderate [ɪnkən'sɪdərɪt] adj rücksichtslos; (in less critical sense, not thinking) unaufmerksam.

inconsiderately [ɪnkən'sɪdərɪtlɪ] adv see adj.

inconsistency [ɪnkən'sɪstənsɪ] n (a) (contradictoriness) Widersprüchlichkeit f, mangelnde Übereinstimmung, Ungereimtheit f. (b) (unevenness: of work, in quality etc) Unbeständigkeit f.

inconsistent [ɪnkən'sɪstənt] adj (a) (contradictory) action, speech widersprüchlich, ungereimt. to be ~ with sth zu etw im Widerspruch stehen, mit etw nicht übereinstimmen. (b) (uneven, irregular) work unbeständig, ungleich; person inkonsequent. but you're ~, sometimes you say ... aber da sind Sie nicht konsequent, manchmal sagen Sie ...

inconsistently [ɪnkən'sɪstəntlɪ] adv (a) argue widersprüchlich. he is behaving ~ with his beliefs sein Verhalten steht im Widerspruch zu seinen Auffassungen; he then maintains, ~ with his initial posit, that ... und dann behauptet er, im Widerspruch zu seiner anfänglichen Behauptung, daß ... (b) work, perform unbeständig, ungleichmäßig. if you apply the rules ~ wenn Sie die Regeln nicht immer gleich anwenden.

inconsolable [ɪnkən'səʊləbl] adj untröstlich.

inconspicuous [ɪnkən'spɪkjuəs] adj unauffällig. to make oneself ~ so wenig Aufsehen wie möglich erregen, sich klein machen (inf); an ~ little man ein unscheinbarer kleiner Mann.

inconspicuously [ɪnkən'spɪkjuəslɪ] adv unauffällig.

inconstancy [ɪn'kɒnstənsɪ] n see adj Unbeständigkeit f, Wankelmut m; Unstetigkeit f, Wankelmut m; Veränderlichkeit, Unbeständigkeit f.

inconstant [ɪn'kɒnstənt] adj person (in friendship) unbeständig, wankelmütig; (in love) unstet, wankelmütig; (variable) weather, quality veränderlich, unbeständig.

incontestable [ɪnkən'testəbl] adj unbestreitbar, unanfechtbar. it is ~ that ... es ist unbestritten, daß ...

incontestably [ɪnkən'testəblɪ] adv see adj.

incontinence [ɪn'kɒntɪnəns] n (Med) Inkontinenz f (spec), Unfähigkeit f, Stuhl und/oder Harn zurückzuhalten; (of desires) Zügellosigkeit, Hemmungslosigkeit f.

incontinent [ɪn'kɒntɪnənt] adj (Med) unfähig, Stuhl und/oder Harn zurückzuhalten; desires zügellos, hemmungslos.

incontrovertible [ɪn,kɒntrə'vɜːtəbl] adj unstreitig, unbestreitbar, unwiderlegbar.

inconvenience [ɪnkən'viːnɪəns] 1 n (a) Unannehmlichkeit f. there are ~s to living in the country das Leben auf dem Land hat lästige Nachteile or bringt Unannehmlichkeiten mit sich; it was something of an ~ not having a car es war eine ziemlich lästige or leidige Angelegenheit, kein Auto zu haben. (b) no pl Unannehmlichkeit(en pl) f (to sb für jdn). she complained about the ~ of having no shops nearby sie beklagte sich darüber, wie unbequem or beschwerlich es sei, keine Geschäfte in der Nähe zu haben; I don't want to cause you any ~ ich möchte Ihnen keine Umstände bereiten or machen; to put sb to great ~ jdm große Umstände bereiten; he went to a great deal of ~ to help er machte sich viele Unannehmlichkeiten, um zu helfen; at considerable personal ~ trotz beträchtlicher persönlicher Unannehmlichkeiten; because of the ~ of the time/date weil die Uhrzeit/der Termin ungelegen war. 2 vt Unannehmlichkeiten or Umstände bereiten (+dat); (with *reference to time*) ungelegen kommen (+*dat*). **don't ~ yourself** machen Sie keine Umstände.

inconvenient [ˌɪnkən'viːnɪənt] *adj time* ungelegen, ungünstig; *house, design* unbequem, unpraktisch; *location* ungünstig; *shops* ungünstig *or* ungeschickt gelegen; *journey* beschwerlich, lästig. **3 o'clock is very ~ for me** 3 Uhr kommt mir sehr ungelegen *or* ist sehr ungünstig für mich; **you couldn't have chosen a more ~ time** einen ungünstigeren Zeitpunkt hätten Sie kaum wählen können; **it's very ~ of you to come so early** es kommt mir wirklich sehr ungelegen, daß Sie so früh kommen; **it's very ~ of you to live so far out** es ist wenig rücksichtsvoll von Ihnen, so weit außerhalb zu wohnen.

inconveniently [ˌɪnkən'viːnɪəntlɪ] *adv see adj.*

inconvertibility ['ɪnkənˌvɜːtɪ'bɪlɪtɪ] *n* (*Fin*) Uneinlösbarkeit, Inkonvertibilität *f.*

inconvertible [ˌɪnkən'vɜːtəbl] *adj* uneinlösbar, inkonvertibel.

incorporate [ɪn'kɔːpəreɪt] *vt* (**a**) (*integrate*) aufnehmen, einbauen, integrieren (*into* in +*acc*). **the chemicals are ~d with** *or* **in the blood** die Chemikalien werden ins Blut aufgenommen; **Hannover was ~d into Prussia in 1886** Hannover wurde 1886 Preußen angegliedert *or* mit Preußen vereinigt.

(**b**) (*contain*) (in sich *dat*) vereinigen, enthalten. **the tax is ~d in the price** (die) Steuer ist im Preis enthalten; **a new James Bond film incorporating all the ingredients of ...** ein neuer James-Bond-Film, der alle Bestandteile von ... verbindet *or* in sich (*dat*) vereinigt; **all the tribes are now ~d in one state** alle Stämme sind jetzt zu einem Staat zusammengeschlossen.

(**c**) (*Jur, Comm*) gesellschaftlich organisieren; (*US*) (amtlich) als Aktiengesellschaft eintragen, registrieren. **to ~ a company** eine Gesellschaft gründen; **~d company** (*US*) (handelsgerichtlich) eingetragene Gesellschaft.

incorporation [ɪnˌkɔːpə'reɪʃən] *n see vt* (**a**) Aufnahme, Einfügung, Integration *f* (*into* in +*acc*). (**b**) Verbindung, Vereinigung *f.* (**c**) (*Jur, Comm*) Gründung, Errichtung *f.*

incorporeal [ˌɪnkɔː'pɔːrɪəl] *adj* nicht körperlich, körperlos.

incorrect [ˌɪnkə'rekt] *adj* (**a**) (*wrong*) falsch; *wording, calculation also* fehlerhaft; *statement, assessment also* unzutreffend, unrichtig, unwahr; *opinion also* irrig; *text* ungenau, fehlerhaft. **you are ~** Sie irren sich, Sie haben unrecht; **that is ~** das stimmt nicht, das ist nicht richtig *or* wahr; **it would be ~ to say that ...** es wäre unzutreffend, zu sagen, daß ...; **you are ~ in thinking that ...** Sie haben unrecht, wenn Sie denken, daß ...

(**b**) (*improper*) *behaviour* inkorrekt, nicht einwandfrei; *dress* inkorrekt, falsch. **it is ~ to ...** es ist nicht korrekt, zu ...

incorrectly [ˌɪnkə'rektlɪ] *adv see adj.* **I had ~ assumed that ...** ich hatte fälschlich(erweise) angenommen, daß ...

incorrigible [ɪn'kɒrɪdʒəbl] *adj* unverbesserlich.

incorruptible [ˌɪnkə'rʌptəbl] *adj* (**a**) *person* charakterstark; (*not bribable*) unbestechlich. **she's ~** man kann sie nicht verderben. (**b**) *material, substance* unzerstörbar.

increase [ɪn'kriːs] **1** *vi* zunehmen; (*taxes*) erhöht werden; (*pain also*) stärker werden; (*amount, number, noise, population also*) anwachsen; (*possessions, trade, riches also*) sich vermehren, (an)wachsen; (*pride also, strength, friendship*) wachsen; (*price, sales, demand*) steigen; (*supply, joy, rage*) sich vergrößern, größer werden; (*business firm, institution, town*) sich vergrößern, wachsen; (*rain, wind*) stärker werden. **to ~ in volume/weight** umfangreicher/schwerer werden, an Umfang/Gewicht zunehmen; **to ~ in width/size/number** sich erweitern/vergrößern/vermehren, weiter/größer/mehr werden; **to ~ in height** höher werden.

2 *vt* vergrößern; *rage, sorrow, joy, possessions, riches also* vermehren; *darkness, noise, love, resentment also, effort* verstärken; *trade, sales, business firm also* erweitern; *numbers, taxes, price, speed, demand* erhöhen. **he ~d his efforts** er strengte sich mehr an, er machte größere Anstrengungen; **then to ~ our difficulties** was die Dinge noch schwieriger machte; **~d demand** erhöhte *or* verstärkte Nachfrage; **~d standard of living** höherer Lebensstandard; **~d efficiency** Leistungssteigerung *f*; **we ~d output to ...** wir erhöhten den Ausstoß auf ...

3 *n* Zunahme, Erhöhung, Steigerung *f*; (*in size*) Vergrößerung, Erweiterung *f*; (*in number*) Vermehrung *f*, Zuwachs *m*, Zunahme *f*; (*in speed*) Erhöhung, Steigerung *f* (*in gen*); (*of business*) Erweiterung, Vergrößerung *f*; (*in sales*) Aufschwung *m*; (*in expenses*) Vermehrung, Steigerung *f* (*in gen*); (*of effort etc*) Vermehrung, Steigerung, Verstärkung *f*; (*of demand*) Verstärkung *f*, Steigen *nt*; (*of work*) Mehr *nt* (*of* +*dat*), Zunahme *f*; (*of violence*) Zunahme *f*, Anwachsen *nt*; (*of salary*) Gehaltserhöhung *or* -aufbesserung *f*; (*of noise*) Zunahme, Verstärkung *f*. **an ~ in the population of 10% per year** eine jährliche Bevölkerungszunahme *or* ein jährlicher Bevölkerungszuwachs von 10%; **to get an ~ of £5 per week** £ 5 pro Woche mehr bekommen, eine Lohnerhöhung von £ 5 pro Woche bekommen; **to be on the ~** ständig zunehmen; **~ in value** Wertzuwachs *m*, Wertsteigerung *f*; **rent ~** Mieterhöhung *f.*

increasing [ɪn'kriːsɪŋ] *adj* zunehmend, steigend, (an)wachsend. **an ~ number of people are changing to ...** mehr und mehr Leute steigen auf (+*acc*) ... um.

increasingly [ɪn'kriːsɪŋlɪ] *adv* zunehmend, immer mehr. **he became ~ angry** er wurde immer *or* zunehmend ärgerlicher; **~, people are finding that ...** man findet in zunehmendem Maße, daß ...; **this is ~ the case** dies ist immer häufiger der Fall.

incredible [ɪn'kredəbl] *adj* unglaublich; (*inf: amazing also*) unwahrscheinlich (*inf*). **this music is ~** diese Musik ist sagenhaft (*inf*); **you're ~** du bist wirklich unschlagbar.

incredibly [ɪn'kredəblɪ] *adv* unglaublich, unwahrscheinlich. **~, he wasn't there** unglaublicherweise war er nicht da.

incredulity [ˌɪnkrɪ'djuːlɪtɪ] *n* Ungläubigkeit, Skepsis *f.*

incredulous *adj*, **~ly** *adv* [ɪn'kredjʊləs, -lɪ] ungläubig, skeptisch; *look also* zweifelnd.

increment ['ɪnkrɪmənt] *n* (**a**) (*in salary*) Gehaltserhöhung *or* -zulage *f.* (**b**) Zuwachs *m*, Steigerung *f.*

incriminate [ɪn'krɪmɪneɪt] *vt* belasten.

incriminating [ɪn'krɪmɪneɪtɪŋ], **incriminatory** [ɪn'krɪmɪnətərɪ] *adj* belastend.

incrimination [ɪnˌkrɪmɪ'neɪʃən] *n* Belastung *f.*

incrust [ɪn'krʌst] *vt see* **encrust.**

incubate ['ɪnkjʊbeɪt] **1** *vt egg* ausbrüten; *bacteria* züchten; *plan, idea* ausbrüten (*inf*), ausreifen lassen. **2** *vi* (*lit*) ausgebrütet *or* bebrütet werden; (*fig*) (aus)reifen; sich formen.

incubation [ˌɪnkjʊ'beɪʃən] *n see vb* Ausbrüten *nt*; Züchten *nt*; Ausreifen *nt*. **~ period** (*Med*) Inkubationszeit *f.*

incubator ['ɪnkjʊbeɪtə'] *n* (*for babies*) Brutkasten, Inkubator *m*; (*for chickens*) Brutapparat *m*; (*for bacteria*) Brutschrank *m.*

incubus ['ɪnkjʊbəs] *n* (**a**) (*demon*) Alp *m.* (**b**) (*burden*) Alptraum *m*, drückende Last.

inculcate ['ɪnkʌlkeɪt] *vt* einimpfen, einprägen (*in sb* jdm).

inculcation [ˌɪnkʌl'keɪʃən] *n* Einimpfen *nt*, Einimpfung *f.*

incumbency [ɪn'kʌmbənsɪ] *n* (**a**) (*Eccl*) Pfründe *f.* (**b**) (*form: tenure of office*) Amtszeit *f.* (**c**) (*form: obligation*) Obliegenheit (*form*), Verpflichtung *f.*

incumbent [ɪn'kʌmbənt] (*form*) **1** *adj* (**a**) **to be ~ upon sb** jdm obliegen (*form*), jds Pflicht sein (*to do sth* etw zu tun). (**b**) **the ~ mayor** der amtshabende *or* amtierende Bürgermeister. **2** *n* Amtsinhaber *m*; (*Eccl*) Inhaber *m* einer Pfarrstelle.

incunabula [ˌɪnkjʊ'næbjʊlə] *npl* Inkunabeln, Wiegendrucke *pl.*

incur [ɪn'kɜː'] *vt* (**a**) *anger, injury, displeasure* sich (*dat*) zuziehen, auf sich (*acc*) ziehen; *risk* eingehen, laufen. **the disadvantages which you will ~** die Nachteile, die Ihnen erwachsen. (**b**) (*Fin*) *loss* erleiden; *debts, expenses* machen. **other expenses ~red** weitere Auslagen *or* Ausgaben *pl.*

incurable [ɪn'kjʊərəbl] **1** *adj* (*Med*) unheilbar; (*fig*) unverbesserlich. **2** *n* (*Med*) unheilbar Kranke(r) *or* Erkrankte(r) *mf.*

incurably [ɪn'kjʊərəblɪ] *adv see adj.*

incurious [ɪn'kjʊərɪəs] *adj* (*not curious*) nicht wißbegierig, nicht neugierig; (*uninterested*) gleichgültig, uninteressiert.

incursion [ɪn'kɜːʃən] *n* Einfall *m*, Eindringen *nt* (*into* in +*acc*); (*fig*) Ausflug *m* (*into* in +*acc*); (*of darkness*) Einbruch *m.*

indebted [ɪn'detɪd] *adj* (*fig*) verpflichtet. **to be ~ to sb for sth** jdm für etw (zu Dank) verpflichtet sein, für etw in jds Schuld (*dat*) stehen; **he's obviously greatly ~ to Matisse/Steinbeck** hat offensichtlich Matisse/Steinbeck viel zu verdanken; **thank you very much, I am most ~ to you** vielen Dank, ich stehe zutiefst in Ihrer Schuld (*geh*). (**b**) (*Fin*) verschuldet (*to sb* bei jdm).

indebtedness [ɪn'detɪdnɪs] *n* (*fig*) Dankesschuld (*to* bei), Verpflichtung (*to* gegenüber) *f*; (*Fin*) Verschuldung *f*. **we can see his obvious ~ to Matisse** wir können sehen, daß er Matisse viel zu verdanken hat.

indecency [ɪn'diːsnsɪ] *n* Unanständigkeit, Anstößigkeit *f.* **act of ~** (*Jur*) unsittliches Verhalten.

indecent [ɪn'diːsnt] *adj* unanständig, anstößig; (*Jur*) *act* unsittlich, unzüchtig; *joke* schmutzig, unanständig, zotig. **with ~ haste** mit ungebührlicher Eile *or* Hast; *see* **assault.**

indecently [ɪn'diːsntlɪ] *adv see adj.*

indecipherable [ˌɪndɪ'saɪfərəbl] *adj* nicht zu entziffern *pred*, nicht zu entziffernd *attr*; *handwriting* unleserlich.

indecision [ˌɪndɪ'sɪʒən] *n* Unentschlossenheit, Unschlüssigkeit *f.*

indecisive [ˌɪndɪ'saɪsɪv] *adj* (**a**) *person, manner* unschlüssig, unentschlossen. (**b**) *discussion* ergebnislos; *argument, battle* nicht(s) entscheidend *attr.*

indecisively [ˌɪndɪ'saɪsɪvlɪ] *adv see adj.*

indeclinable [ˌɪndɪ'klaɪnəbl] *adj* (*Gram*) nicht deklinierbar, unbeugbar, beugungsunfähig.

indecorous [ɪn'dekərəs, -lɪ] **~ly** *adv* (*really, in reality, in fact*) unziemlich, unschicklich, ungehörig.

indecorum [ˌɪndɪ'kɔːrəm] *n* Unziemlichkeit, Unschicklichkeit, Ungehörigkeit *f.*

indeed [ɪn'diːd] *adv* (**a**) (*really, in reality, in fact*) tatsächlich, wirklich, in der Tat. **~ I am tired** ich bin wirklich *or* tatsächlich *or* in der Tat müde; **I feel, ~ I know he is right** ich habe das Gefühl, ja ich weiß (sogar), daß er recht hat; **who else?** — **~, who else?** wer anders? — in der Tat *or* ganz recht, wer sonst?

(**b**) (*confirming*) **isn't that wrong?** — **~** ist das nicht falsch? — allerdings; **are you coming?** — **~ I am!** kommst du? — aber sicher *or* natürlich; **may I open the window?** — **you may ~/~** you may not darf ich das Fenster öffnen? — ja bitte, aber gern doch!/das dürfen Sie nicht; **are you pleased?** — **yes, ~ or ~, yes!** bist du zufrieden? — oh ja, das kann man wohl sagen!; **is that Charles?** — **~ it is** das Charles? — ganz recht.

(**c**) (*as intensifier*) wirklich. **very ... ~** wirklich sehr ...; **thank you very much** — **~** vielen herzlichen Dank.

(**d**) (*showing interest, irony, surprise*) wirklich, tatsächlich. **did you/is it ~?** nein wirklich?, tatsächlich?; **his wife, ~!** seine Frau ...!, daß ich nicht lache!; **who is she ~!** na, wer wohl *or* schon!; **what ~!** was wohl!; **~?** ach so?, ach wirklich?

(**e**) (*admittedly*) zwar. **there are ~ mistakes in it, but ...** sind zwar Fehler darin, aber ...

(**f**) (*expressing possibility*) **if ~ ... falls ...** wirklich; **if ~ he were wrong** falls er wirklich unrecht haben sollte; **I may ~ come** es kann gut sein, daß ich komme.

indefatigable *adj*, **~bly** *adv* [ˌɪndɪ'fætɪgəbl, -ɪ] unermüdlich, rastlos.

indefensible [ˌɪndɪ'fensəbl] *adj* (**a**) *behaviour, remark etc* unentschuldbar, nicht zu rechtfertigen *attr or* rechtfertigen *pred.* (**b**) *town etc* nicht zu verteidigen *attr or* verteidigen *pred*, unhaltbar. (**c**) *cause, theory* unhaltbar, unvertretbar.

indefinable [ˌɪndɪ'faɪnəbl] *adj word, colour, charm* unbestimmbar, undefinierbar; *feeling, impression also* unbestimmt. **she has a certain ~ something** sie hat das gewisse Etwas.

indefinite [ɪn'defɪnɪt] *adj* **(a)** *(with no fixed limit)* number, length unbestimmt. **~ leave** unbeschränkter *or* unbegrenzter Urlaub, Urlaub auf unbestimmte Zeit.
(b) *(Gram)* unbestimmt.
(c) *(vague)* unklar, undeutlich. **he was very ~ about it** er war sehr unbestimmt *or* vage in dieser Sache; **our plans are still ~** wir haben noch keine festen Pläne.

indefinitely [ɪn'defɪnɪtlɪ] *adv* **(a)** *wait etc* unbegrenzt (lange), unendlich lange, endlos; *postpone* auf unbestimmte Zeit. **we can't go on like this ~** wir können nicht endlos *or* immer so weitermachen. **(b)** *(vaguely)* unklar, undeutlich.

indelible [ɪn'delɪbl] *adj* stain nicht zu entfernen; *ink also* wasserunlöslich; *(fig)* impression unauslöschlich. **~ ink** Wäschetinte *f*; **~pencil** Kopierstift, Tintenstift *m*.

indelibly [ɪn'delɪblɪ] *adv* *(fig)* unauslöschlich.

indelicacy [ɪn'delɪkəsɪ] *n* Taktlosigkeit, Ungehörigkeit *f*; *(of person)* Mangel *m* an Feingefühl, Taktlosigkeit *f*; *(crudity)* Geschmacklosigkeit *f*.

indelicate [ɪn'delɪkət] *adj* person taktlos; *act, remark also* ungehörig; *(crude)* geschmacklos.

indelicately [ɪn'delɪkətlɪ] *adv see adj* taktlos; ungehörig; *(crudely)* geschmacklos.

indemnification [ɪnˌdemnɪfɪ'keɪʃən] *n* **(a)** *(compensation)* Schadensersatz *m*, Entschädigung *f* (*for* für); *(sum received)* Schadensersatz(summe *f*) *m*, Entschädigung(ssumme) *f*; *(for expenses)* Erstattung *f* (*for* gen). **(b)** *(for against* gegen) *(safeguard)* Absicherung *f*; *(insurance)* Versicherung *f*.

indemnify [ɪn'demnɪfaɪ] *vt* **(a)** *(compensate)* entschädigen, Schadensersatz *m* leisten (*for* für); *(for expenses)* erstatten (*for* acc). **(b)** *(safeguard)* absichern (*from, against* gegen); *(insure)* versichern (*against, from* gegen).

indemnity [ɪn'demnɪtɪ] *n* **(a)** *(compensation)* *(for damage, loss etc)* Schadensersatz *m*, Entschädigung, Abfindung *f*; *(after war)* Wiedergutmachung *f*. **(b)** *(insurance)* Versicherung(sschutz *m*) *f*. **deed of ~** *(Jur)* = Versicherungspolice *f*.

indent [ɪn'dent] **1** *vt* border, edge einkerben; *coast* zerklüften, einbuchten; *(Typ)* word, line einrücken, einziehen; *(leave dent in)* metal etc einbeulen.
2 *vi* **to ~ on sb for sth** *(Brit Comm)* etw bei jdm ordern.
3 ['ɪndent] *n* *(in border etc)* Einkerbung, Kerbe *f*; *(in coast)* Einbuchtung *f*; *(Typ: of line)* Einrückung *f*, Einzug *m*; *(dent: in metal etc)* Beule, Delle *f*.

indentation [ˌɪnden'teɪʃən] *n* **(a)** *no pl see vt* Einkerben *nt*; Zerklüften *nt*; Einrücken, Einziehen *nt*; Einbeulen *nt*.
(b) *(notch, dent)* *(in border, edge)* Kerbe *f*, Einschnitt *m*; *(in coast)* Einbuchtung *f*; *(Typ)* Einrückung *f*, Einzug *m*; *(in metal etc)* Delle, Vertiefung *f*.

indenture [ɪn'dentʃəᵣ] **1** *n* **(a)** **~s** *pl* *(of apprentice)* Ausbildungs- *or* Lehrvertrag *m*.
(b) *(Jur)* Vertrag *m* in zwei oder mehreren Ausführungen mit bestimmter Kanteneinkerbung zur Identifizierung.
2 *vt* apprentice in die Lehre nehmen, durch Lehrvertrag binden. **he was ~d with Hobson's** er ging bei Hobson in die Lehre.

independence [ˌɪndɪ'pendəns] *n* Unabhängigkeit *f* (*of* von); *(of person: in attitude, spirit also)* Selbständigkeit *f*. **to achieve ~** die Unabhängigkeit erlangen; **I~ Day** *(US)* der Unabhängigkeitstag.

independent [ˌɪndɪ'pendənt] **1** *adj* **(a)** unabhängig (*of* von) *(also Pol)*; *person in attitude, spirit also* selbständig; *school* frei, unabhängig (vom Staat); *income* eigen, privat. **he has a car, so he is ~ of buses** er hat ein Auto und ist nicht auf den Bus angewiesen; **she is a very ~ young lady** sie ist eine sehr selbständige junge Dame; **a man of ~ means** eine Person mit Privateinkommen, ein Privatier *m*.
(b) *(unconnected, unrelated to work of others)* reports, research, thinker etc unabhängig. **they reached the summit by ~ routes** sie erreichten den Gipfel auf getrennten *or* gesonderten Wegen; **the two explosions were ~** die beide Explosionen hatten nichts miteinander zu tun *or* hatten keine gemeinsame Ursache; **~ suspension** *(Aut)* Einzel(rad)aufhängung *f*.
(c) **~ clause** *(Gram)* übergeordneter Satz, Hauptsatz *m*.
2 *n* *(Pol)* Unabhängige(r) *mf*.

independently [ˌɪndɪ'pendəntlɪ] *adv* unabhängig; *(in attitude, spirit also)* selbständig; *(on own initiative also)* von allein(e). **quite ~** he offered to help er bot von sich aus seine Hilfe an; **they each came ~ to the same conclusion** sie kamen unabhängig voneinander zur gleichen Schlußfolgerung.

in-depth ['ɪndepθ] *adj* eingehend, gründlich.

indescribable [ˌɪndɪ'skraɪbəbl] *adj* unbeschreiblich; *(inf: terrible)* fürchterlich, schrecklich, unglaublich. **a certain ~ something** ein unbeschreibliches Etwas.

indescribably [ˌɪndɪ'skraɪbəblɪ] *adv see adj.*

indestructibility ['ɪndɪˌstrʌktə'bɪlɪtɪ] *n* Unzerstörbarkeit *f*.

indestructible *adj*, **~bly** *adv* [ˌɪndɪ'strʌktəbl, -ɪ] unzerstörbar.

indeterminable [ˌɪndɪ'tɜːmɪnəbl] *adj* unbestimmbar, nicht zu bestimmend *attr or* bestimmen *pred.*

indeterminate [ˌɪndɪ'tɜːmɪnɪt] *adj* amount, length unbestimmt; *duration also* ungewiß; *meaning, concept* unklar, vage. **of ~ sex** von unbestimmbarem *or* nicht bestimmbarem Geschlecht.

indeterminately [ˌɪndɪ'tɜːmɪnɪtlɪ] *adv see adj.* **it continued ~** es ging auf unbestimmte Zeit weiter.

indetermination ['ɪndɪˌtɜːmɪ'neɪʃən] *n* *(indecisiveness)* Entschlußlosigkeit, Unschlüssigkeit, Unentschiedenheit *f*.

index ['ɪndeks] **1** *n* **(a)** *pl* **-es** *(in book)* Register *nt*, Index *m*; *(of sources)* Quellenverzeichnis *nt*; *(in library)* *(of topics)* (Schlagwort)katalog *m*; *(of authors)* (Verfasser)katalog *m*; *(card ~)* Kartei *f*. **I~** *(Eccl)* Index *m*.

(b) *pl* **indices** *(pointer)* *(Typ)* Hinweiszeichen, Handzeichen *nt*; *(on scale)* *(An)*zeiger *m*, Zunge *f*. **this is a good ~ to** *or* **of his character** das zeigt deutlich seinen Charakter, das läßt deutlich auf seinen Charakter schließen; **to provide a useful ~ to** *or* **of the true state of affairs** nützlichen Aufschluß über den wahren Stand der Dinge geben.
(c) *pl* **-es** *or* **indices** *(number showing ratio)* Index *m*, Meßzahl, Indexziffer *f*. **cost-of-living ~** Lebenshaltungskosten-Index *m*.
(d) *pl* **indices** *(Math)* Index *m*; *(exponent)* Wurzelexponent *m*.
2 *vt* mit einem Register *or* Index versehen; *word* in das Register *or* in den Index aufnehmen. **the book is well ~ed** das Buch hat ein gutes Register *or* einen guten Index.

index-: **~ card** *n* Karteikarte *f*; **~ finger** *n* Zeigefinger *m*; **~-linked** *adj* rate, salaries der Inflationsrate (*dat*) angeglichen; *pensions* dynamisch.

India ['ɪndɪə] *n* Indien *nt*. **~ ink** *(US)* Tusche *f*; **~ man** Indienfahrer *m*.

Indian ['ɪndɪən] **1** *adj* **(a)** indisch. **(b)** *(American ~)* indianisch, Indianer-. **~ Ocean** Indischer Ozean. **2** *n* **(a)** Inder(in *f*) *m*. **(b)** *(American ~)* Indianer(in *f*) *m*.

Indian: **~ club** *n* Keule *f*; **~ corn** *n* Mais *m*; **~ file** *n* Gänsemarsch *m*; **in ~ file** im Gänsemarsch; **~ giver** *n* *(US inf)* jd, der etwas Geschenktes zurückfordert; **~ ink** *n* Tusche *f*; **~ summer** *n* Altweibersommer, Spät- *or* Nachsommer *m*; *(fig)* zweiter Frühling; **~ wrestling** *n* Armdrücken *nt*.

India: **~ paper** *n* Dünndruckpapier *nt*; **~ rubber** **1** *n* Gummi, Kautschuk *m*; *(eraser)* Radiergummi *m*; **2** *attr* Gummi-.

indicate ['ɪndɪkeɪt] **1** *vt* **(a)** *(point out, mark)* zeigen, bezeichnen, deuten auf (+*acc*). **to ~ a place on a map** einen Ort auf der Karte zeigen, auf einen Ort auf der Karte deuten *or* zeigen; **large towns are ~d in red** Großstädte sind rot eingezeichnet *or* gekennzeichnet.
(b) *(person: gesture, express)* andeuten, zeigen, zu verstehen geben. **to ~ one's feelings** seine Gefühle zeigen *or* zum Ausdruck bringen; **~ your intention to turn right** zeigen Sie Ihre Absicht an, nach rechts abzubiegen.
(c) *(be a sign of, suggest)* erkennen lassen, schließen lassen auf (+*acc*), (hin)deuten auf (+*acc*). **what does it ~ to you?** was erkennen Sie daraus, welche Schlüsse ziehen Sie daraus?
(d) *(register and display)* temperature, speed (an)zeigen.
(e) *(Med)* treatment indizieren; *illness* Anzeichen sein für, anzeigen.
2 *vi* *(Aut)* (Richtungswechsel) anzeigen *(form)*, blinken, den Blinker setzen. **to ~ right** rechts blinken, Richtungswechsel nach rechts anzeigen *(form)*.

indication [ˌɪndɪ'keɪʃən] *n* **(a)** *(sign)* (An)zeichen *nt* *(also Med)* *(of* für), Hinweis *m* *(of* auf + *acc*). **there is every/no ~ that he is right** alles/nichts weist darauf hin *or* läßt darauf schließen, daß er recht hat; **he gave a clear ~ of his intentions** er zeigte seine Absichten deutlich, er ließ seine Absichten deutlich erkennen; **what are the ~s that it will happen?** was deutet darauf hin *or* spricht dafür *or* welchen Hinweis gibt es dafür, daß es geschieht?; **we had no ~ that ...** es gab kein Anzeichen dafür, daß ...; **that is some ~ of what we can expect** das gibt uns einen Vorgeschmack auf das, was wir zu erwarten haben; **if you could give me a rough ~ of ...** wenn sie mir eine ungefähre Vorstellung davon geben könnten ...
(b) *(showing, marking)* *(by gesturing, facial expression)* Anzeigen, Erkennenlassen *nt*; *(by pointing, drawing)* Anzeigen, Bezeichnen *nt*. **~ of the boundaries on this map is very poor** die Grenzen sind auf dieser Karte sehr undeutlich bezeichnet.
(c) *(on gauge)* Anzeige *f*. **what is the ~ of the pressure ~?** wie ist die Druck- *or* Manometeranzeige?

indicative [ɪn'dɪkətɪv] **1** *adj* **(a)** bezeichnend *(of* für). **to be ~ of** sth auf etw *(acc)* schließen lassen, auf etw *(acc)* hindeuten; **sb's character** für etw bezeichnend sein.
(b) *(Gram)* indikativisch. **~ mood** Indikativ *m*, Wirklichkeitsform *f*.
2 *n* *(Gram)* Indikativ *m*, Wirklichkeitsform *f*. **in the ~** im Indikativ, in der Wirklichkeitsform.

indicator ['ɪndɪkeɪtəᵣ] *n* *(instrument, gauge)* Anzeiger *m*; *(needle)* Zeiger *m*; *(Aut)* Richtungsanzeiger *m* *(form)*; *(flashing)* Blinker *m*; *(Chem)* Indikator *m*; *(fig: of economic position etc)* Meßlatte *f*. **altitude/pressure ~** Höhen-/Druckmesser *m*; **(arrival/departure) ~ board** *(Rail, Aviat)* Ankunfts-/Abfahrts(anzeige)tafel *f*.

indices ['ɪndɪsiːz] *pl of* **index**.

indict [ɪn'daɪt] *vt* *(charge)* anklagen, beschuldigen *(on a charge of* sth einer Sache gen), unter Anklage stellen; *(US Jur)* Anklage erheben gegen *(for* wegen +*gen*). **to ~ sb as a murderer** jdn unter Mordanklage stellen, jdn des Mordes anklagen.

indictable [ɪn'daɪtəbl] *adj* person strafrechtlich verfolgbar; *offence* strafbar. **is the President ~?** kann der Präsident strafrechtlich verfolgt *or* belangt werden?

indictment [ɪn'daɪtmənt] *n* *(of person)* *(accusation)* Beschuldigung, Anschuldigung *f*; *(charge sheet)* Anklage *f* *(for, on a charge of* wegen); *(US: by grand jury)* Anklageerhebung *f*. **to bring an ~ against sb** gegen jdn Anklage erheben, jdn unter Anklage stellen; **to draw up a bill of ~** eine Anklageschrift verfassen; **to be an ~ of sth** *(fig)* ein Armutszeugnis für etw sein.

indifference [ɪn'dɪfrəns] *n see adj* **(a)** Gleichgültigkeit, Indifferenz (geh) *f* *(to, towards* gegenüber). **it's a matter of complete ~ to me** das ist mir völlig egal *or* gleichgültig. **(b)** Mittelmäßigkeit, Durchschnittlichkeit *f*.

indifferent [ɪn'dɪfrənt] *adj* **(a)** *(lacking interest)* gleichgültig, indifferent (geh) *(to, towards* gegenüber). **he is quite ~ about it/to her** es/sie ist ihm ziemlich gleichgültig; **~ to her despair** ungerührt von ihrer Verzweiflung. **(b)** *(mediocre)* mittelmäßig, durchschnittlich.

indifferently [ɪnˈdɪfrəntlɪ] *adv* (a) *see adj* (a). (b) *(mediocrely)* (mittel)mäßig (gut), nicht besonders (gut).

indigence [ˈɪndɪdʒəns] *n* Bedürftigkeit, Armut *f*.

indigenous [ɪnˈdɪdʒɪnəs] *adj* einheimisch (*to* in +*dat*); *customs* landeseigen; *language* Landes-. **plants ~ to Canada** in Kanada heimische *or* beheimatete Pflanzen; ~ **peoples of South America** die einheimischen *or* eingeborenen Völker Südamerikas.

indigent [ˈɪndɪdʒənt] *adj* bedürftig, arm, ärmlich.

indigestible [ˌɪndɪˈdʒestəbl] *adj* (*Med*) unverdaulich; (*fig*) schwer verdaulich, schwer zu ertragend *attr or* ertragen *pred*.

indigestion [ˌɪndɪˈdʒestʃən] *n* Magenverstimmung *f*.

indignant [ɪnˈdɪgnənt] *adj* entrüstet, indigniert (*dated, geh*) (*at, about* über +*acc*), unwillig (*at, about* wegen). **to be ~ with sb** mit jdm ungehalten sein; **to make sb ~** jds Unwillen *or* Entrüstung erregen; **it's no good getting ~** es hat keinen Zweck, sich zu entrüsten *or* sich aufzuregen.

indignantly [ɪnˈdɪgnəntlɪ] *adv see adj*.

indignation [ˌɪndɪgˈneɪʃən] *n* Entrüstung *f* (*at, about, with* über +*acc*), Unwillen *m* (*at, about* wegen).

indignity [ɪnˈdɪgnɪtɪ] *n* Demütigung, Schmach (*liter*) *f*. **oh, the ~ of it!** also, das ist doch der Gipfel!

indigo [ˈɪndɪgəʊ] **1** *n* Indigo *nt or m*. **2** *adj* indigofarben. ~ **blue** indigoblau.

indirect [ˌɪndɪˈrekt] *adj* (a) indirekt; *consequence, result etc also* mittelbar. **by ~ means** auf Umwegen; **by an ~ route/path/road** auf Umwegen *or* einem Umweg; **to make an ~ reference to sb/sth** auf jdn/etw anspielen *or* indirekt Bezug nehmen.
  (b) (*Gram*) indirekt. ~ **object** Dativobjekt *nt*; ~ **speech** *or* (*US*) **discourse** indirekte Rede.

indirectly [ˌɪndɪˈrektlɪ] *adv see adj* (a).

indirectness [ˌɪndɪˈrektnɪs] *n* Indirektheit *f*. **the ~ of his criticism** seine indirekte Kritik.

indiscernible [ˌɪndɪˈsɜːnəbl] *adj* nicht erkennbar *or* sichtbar; *improvement, change etc also* unmerklich; *noise* nicht wahrnehmbar. **to be almost ~** kaum zu erkennen sein; (*noise*) kaum wahrzunehmen sein.

indiscernibly [ˌɪndɪˈsɜːnɪblɪ] *adv see adj*.

indiscipline [ɪnˈdɪsɪplɪn] *n* Mangel *m* an Disziplin, Undiszipliniertheit, Disziplinlosigkeit *f*.

indiscreet [ˌɪndɪˈskriːt] *adj* indiskret; (*tactless*) taktlos, ohne Feingefühl. **he is too ~ ever to be a successful diplomat** wegen seiner Neigung zu Indiskretionen wird er nie ein erfolgreicher Diplomat werden.

indiscreetly [ˌɪndɪˈskriːtlɪ] *adv see adj*.

indiscreetness [ˌɪndɪˈskriːtnɪs] *n see* **indiscretion**.

indiscretion [ˌɪndɪˈskreʃən] *n see adj* Indiskretion *f*; Taktlosigkeit *f*, Mangel *m* an Feingefühl; (*affair*) Abenteuer *nt*, Affäre *f*. **his youthful ~s** seine jugendliche Unvernunft, sein jugendlicher Leichtsinn.

indiscriminate [ˌɪndɪˈskrɪmɪnɪt] *adj* wahllos; *spending also* unüberlegt; *reading also* kritiklos, unkritisch; *mixture also* kunterbunt; *choice* willkürlich; *reader, shopper* kritiklos, unkritisch; *tastes* unausgeprägt. **you shouldn't be so ~ in the friends you make** du solltest dir deine Freunde etwas sorgfältiger aussuchen; **he was completely ~ in whom he punished** er verteilte seine Strafen völlig wahllos *or* willkürlich.

indiscriminately [ˌɪndɪˈskrɪmɪnɪtlɪ] *adv see adj*.

indiscriminating [ˌɪndɪˈskrɪmɪneɪtɪŋ] *adj* unkritisch, kritiklos.

indispensability [ˈɪndɪˌspensəˈbɪlɪtɪ] *n* Unentbehrlichkeit *f*, unbedingte Notwendigkeit (*to* für).

indispensable [ˌɪndɪˈspensəbl] *adj* unentbehrlich, unbedingt notwendig *or* erforderlich (*to* für). ~ **to life** lebensnotwendig; **to make oneself ~** sich für jdn unentbehrlich machen.

indispensably [ˌɪndɪˈspensəblɪ] *adv* **it is ~ necessary to them** es ist unbedingt notwendig *or* erforderlich für sie; **that is necessarily and ~ a part of our system** das ist notwendiger und unverzichtbarer Bestandteil unseres Systems.

indisposed [ˌɪndɪˈspəʊzd] *adj* (a) (*unwell*) unwohl, indisponiert (*geh*), unpäßlich (*geh*). (b) (*disinclined*) **to be ~ to do sth** nicht gewillt *or* geneigt sein, etw zu tun.

indisposition [ˌɪndɪspəˈzɪʃən] *n see adj* (a) Unwohlsein *nt*, Indisposition (*geh*), Unpäßlichkeit (*geh*) *f*. (b) Unwilligkeit *f*. ~ **to work** Arbeitsunwilligkeit *f*, Mangel *m* an Arbeitswilligkeit.

indisputability [ˈɪndɪˌspjuːtəˈbɪlɪtɪ] *n* Unbestreitbarkeit, Unstrittigkeit *f*.

indisputable [ˌɪndɪˈspjuːtəbl] *adj* unbestreitbar, unstrittig, nicht zu bestreiten *attr or* bestreiten *pred*; *evidence* unanfechtbar.

indisputably [ˌɪndɪˈspjuːtəblɪ] *adv* unstrittig, unbestreitbar.

indissolubility [ˈɪndɪˌsɒljuˈbɪlɪtɪ] *n* (*Chem*) Unlöslichkeit, Unlösbarkeit *f*; (*fig*) Unauflöslichkeit, Unauflösbarkeit *f*.

indissoluble *adj*, ~ **bly** *adv* [ˌɪndɪˈsɒljʊbl, -ɪ] (*Chem*) unlöslich, unlösbar; (*fig*) unauflöslich, unauflösbar, unlöslich.

indistinct [ˌɪndɪˈstɪŋkt] *adj* *object, shape, words* verschwommen, unklar, undeutlich; *noise* schwach, unklar; *memory* undeutlich; *voice* undeutlich, unklar.

indistinctly [ˌɪndɪˈstɪŋktlɪ] *adv* **see** nicht deutlich, unscharf, verschwommen; *speak* undeutlich, unklar; *remember* schwach, unklar, dunkel.

indistinguishable [ˌɪndɪˈstɪŋgwɪʃəbl] *adj* (a) nicht unterscheidbar, nicht zu unterscheiden *attr or* unterscheiden *pred* (*from* von). **the twins are ~** (one from the other) man kann die Zwillinge nicht (voneinander) unterscheiden.
  (b) (*indiscernible*) nicht erkennbar *or* sichtbar; *improvement, change, difference etc also* unmerklich; *noise* nicht wahrnehmbar.

individual [ˌɪndɪˈvɪdjʊəl] **1** *adj* (a) (*separate*) einzeln. ~ **cases** Einzelfälle *pl*; **to give ~ help** jedem einzeln helfen, Einzelhilfe leisten; ~ **tastes differ** jeder hat einen eigenen *or* individuellen Geschmack, die Geschmäcker sind verschieden.

  (b) (*own*) eigen; (*for one person*) *portion etc* einzeln, Einzel-. **our own ~ plates** unsere eigenen Teller; ~ **portions cost 55p** eine Einzelportion kostet 55 Pence.
  (c) (*distinctive, characteristic*) eigen, individuell.
2 *n* Individuum *nt*, Einzelne(r) *mf*, Einzelperson *f*; (*inf*) Individuum *nt*, Mensch *m*, Person *f*. **the freedom of the ~** die Freiheit des einzelnen, die individuelle Freiheit; *see* **private**.

individualism [ˌɪndɪˈvɪdjʊəlɪzəm] *n* Individualismus *m*.

individualist [ˌɪndɪˈvɪdjʊəlɪst] *n* Individualist(in *f*) *m*.

individuality [ˈɪndɪˌvɪdjʊˈælɪtɪ] *n* Individualität *f*, (*eigene*) Persönlichkeit.

individualize [ˌɪndɪˈvɪdjʊəlaɪz] *vt* individualisieren; (*treat separately*) einzeln behandeln; (*give individuality to*) *book, author's style, performance* eine persönliche *or* individuelle *or* eigene Note verleihen (+*dat*).

individually [ˌɪndɪˈvɪdjʊəlɪ] *adv* individuell; (*separately*) einzeln. ~ **styled suit** Modellanzug *m*.

indivisible *adj*, ~ **bly** *adv* [ˌɪndɪˈvɪzəbl, -ɪ] unteilbar (*also Math*), untrennbar.

Indo- [ˈɪndəʊ-] *pref* Indo-. ~ **-China** *n* Indochina *nt*.

indoctrinate [ɪnˈdɒktrɪneɪt] *vt* indoktrinieren.

indoctrination [ɪnˌdɒktrɪˈneɪʃən] *n* Indoktrination *f*.

Indo- ~ **-European 1** *adj* indogermanisch, indoeuropäisch; **2** *n* (a) Indogermane *m*, Indogermanin *f*, Indoeuropäer(in *f*) *m*; (b) (*language*) Indogermanisch, Indoeuropäisch *nt*; ~ **-Germanic** (*old*) *adj, n see* ~ **-European 1, 2** (b).

indolence [ˈɪndələns] *n* Trägheit, Indolenz (*rare*) *f*.

indolent *adj*, ~ **ly** *adv* [ˈɪndələnt, -lɪ] träge, indolent (*rare*).

indomitable [ɪnˈdɒmɪtəbl] *adj* *person, courage* unbezähmbar, unbezwingbar; *will* unbeugsam, eisern, unerschütterlich. **his ~ pride** sein nicht zu brechender Stolz.

Indonesia [ˌɪndəʊˈniːzɪə] *n* Indonesien *nt*.

Indonesian [ˌɪndəʊˈniːzɪən] **1** *adj* indonesisch. **2** *n* (a) Indonesier(in *f*) *m*. (b) (*language*) Indonesisch *nt*.

indoor [ˈɪndɔːʳ] *adj* *aerial* Zimmer-, Innen-; *plant* Zimmer-, Haus-; *clothes* Haus-; *photography* Innen-; *sport* Hallen-; *swimming pool* Hallen-; (*private*) überdacht. ~ **work** Arbeit, die nicht im Freien ausgeführt wird; ~ **games** Spiele *pl* fürs Haus, Haus- *or* Zimmerspiele *pl*; (*Sport*) Hallenspiele *pl*.

indoors [ɪnˈdɔːz] *adv* drin(nen) (*inf*), innen; (*at home*) zu Hause. **what's the house like ~?** wie sieht das Haus innen aus?; **to stay ~** im Haus bleiben, drin bleiben (*inf*); **go and play ~** geh im Haus *or* drinnen spielen; **to go ~** ins Haus gehen, nach drinnen gehen; ~ **and outdoors** im und außer Haus, drinnen und draußen, im Haus und im Freien.

indubitable [ɪnˈdjuːbɪtəbl] *adj* zweifellos, unzweifelhaft.

indubitably [ɪnˈdjuːbɪtəblɪ] *adv* zweifellos, zweifelsohne.

induce [ɪnˈdjuːs] *vt* (a) (*persuade*) dazu bewegen *or* bringen *or* veranlassen.
  (b) *reaction, hypnosis* herbeiführen, bewirken, hervorrufen; *sleep* herbeiführen; *illness* verursachen, führen zu; *labour, birth* einleiten. **this drug ~s sleep** dieses Mittel hat eine einschläfernde Wirkung; **she had to be ~d** die Geburt mußte eingeleitet werden; (*artificially*) ~ **d sleep** künstlicher Schlaf.
  (c) (*Philos*) induktiv *or* durch Induktion erarbeiten.
  (d) (*Elec*) *current, magnetic effect* induzieren.

inducement [ɪnˈdjuːsmənt] *n* (a) (*no pl: persuasion*) Überredung *f*; (*motive, incentive*) Anreiz *m*, Ansporn *m no pl*. **he won't do that without a lot of ~** ohne viel Überredung wird er das nicht machen; **he can't work without ~s** er kann nicht arbeiten, ohne daß man ihn dazu anspornt; **as an added ~** besonderer Anreiz *or* Ansporn.
  (b) *see* **induction** (b).

induct [ɪnˈdʌkt] *vt* (a) *bishop, president etc* in sein Amt einsetzen *or* einführen. (b) (*US Mil*) einziehen, einberufen.

inductee [ɪndʌkˈtiː] *n* (*US Mil*) (zum Wehrdienst) Eingezogene(r) *or* Einberufene(r) *m*.

induction [ɪnˈdʌkʃən] *n* (a) (*of bishop, president etc*) Amtseinführung *f*; (*US Mil*) Einberufung, Einziehung *f*.
  (b) (*bringing about*) (*of sleep, reaction etc*) Herbeiführen *nt*; (*of labour, birth*) Einleitung *f*.
  (c) (*Philos, Math, Elec*) Induktion *f*. ~ **coil** *n* (*Elec*) Induktionsspule *f*.

inductive *adj*, ~ **ly** *adv* [ɪnˈdʌktɪv, -lɪ] (*all senses*) induktiv.

indulge [ɪnˈdʌldʒ] **1** *vt* (a) *appetite, desires etc* nachgeben (+*dat*); *person also* nachsichtig sein mit; (*over~*) *children* verwöhnen, verhätscheln; *one's imagination* frönen (+*dat*). **to ~ oneself in sth** sich (*dat*) etw gönnen, in etw schwelgen.
  (b) *debtor* Zahlungsaufschub gewähren (+*dat*).
2 *vi* **to ~ in sth** sich (*dat*) etw gönnen *or* genehmigen (*inf*); (*in vice, drink, daydreams*) einer Sache (*dat*) frönen, sich einer Sache (*dat*) hingeben; **he ~s in some very peculiar hobbies** er frönt einigen sehr eigenartigen Hobbies; **to ~ in sth to excess** etw bis zum Exzeß treiben; **dessert came, but I didn't ~** (*inf*) der Nachtisch kam, aber ich konnte mich beherrschen; **will you ~?** (*inf*) (*offering drink etc*) genehmigen Sie sich auch einen/eine etc? (*inf*); **I don't ~** ich trinke/rauche etc nicht.

indulgence [ɪnˈdʌldʒəns] *n* (a) Nachsicht *f*; (*of appetite etc*) Nachgiebigkeit *f* (*of* gegenüber); (*over~*) Verwöhnung, Verhätschelung *f*. **the ~ of his wishes** das Erfüllen seiner Wünsche; **too much ~ of your children's wishes is bad for their character** wenn man den Wünschen seiner Kinder zu oft nachgibt, ist das schlecht für ihre charakterliche Entwicklung.
  (b) (*in activity, drink etc*) ~ **in drink** übermäßiges Trinken; **he regards ~ in any unconventional sexual activity with horror** jede Art von unkonventioneller sexueller Betätigung ist ihm ein Graus; **excessive ~ in vice led to the collapse of the Roman Empire** die Lasterhaftigkeit der Römer führte zum Untergang ihres Reiches; **too much ~ in sport is bad for your studies** übermäßiges Sporttreiben wirkt sich schlecht auf das Lernen aus.
  (c) (*thing indulged in*) Luxus *m*; (*food, drink, pleasure*) Genuß

m. such are his little ~s das sind die kleinen Genüsse, die er sich (*dat*) gönnt; **I occasionally allow myself a little** ~ ab und zu gönne ich mir ein bißchen Luxus.
   (d) (*form: permission*) Einwilligung, Zustimmung *f.*
   (e) (*Eccl*) Ablaß *m.*

indulgent [ɪn'dʌldʒənt] *adj* (*to* gegenüber) nachsichtig; *mother etc also* nachgiebig; (*to one's own desires etc*) zu nachgiebig.

indulgently [ɪn'dʌldʒəntlɪ] *adv see adj.*

industrial [ɪn'dʌstrɪəl] *adj production, designer, diamond, worker, equipment, state, archeology* Industrie-; *production also, expansion* industriell; *research, training, medicine, experience, accident* Betriebs-; *medicine, psychology* Arbeits-. ~ **action** Arbeitskampfmaßnahmen *pl*; **to take** ~ **action** in den Ausstand treten; ~ **democracy** Demokratie *f* im Betrieb; ~ **dispute** Auseinandersetzungen *pl* zwischen Arbeitgebern und Arbeitnehmern; ~ **estate** (*Brit*) Industriegebiet *nt*; ~ **fabric** Industriefasern *pl*; ~ **injury** Arbeitsunfall *m*; ~ **insurance** Unfallversicherung *f*; ~ **relations** Beziehungen *pl* zwischen Arbeitgebern und Gewerkschaften; I~ **Revolution** Industrielle Revolution *f*; ~ **tribunal** Arbeitsgericht *nt*; ~ **trouble**, ~ **unrest** Arbeitsunruhen *pl.*

industrialism [ɪn'dʌstrɪəlɪzəm] *n* Industrie *f.*

industrialist [ɪn'dʌstrɪəlɪst] *n* Industrielle(r) *mf.*

industrialization [ɪn,dʌstrɪəlaɪ'zeɪʃən] *n* Industrialisierung *f.*

industrialize [ɪn'dʌstrɪəlaɪz] *vti* industrialisieren.

industrious *adj*, ~**ly** *adv* [ɪn'dʌstrɪəs, -lɪ] arbeitsam, fleißig, emsig.

industriousness [ɪn'dʌstrɪəsnɪs] *n* Arbeitsamkeit *f*, Fleiß *m*, Emsigkeit *f.*

industry ['ɪndəstrɪ] *n* (a) (*trade, branch of* ~) Industrie *f.* **heavy/light** ~ Schwer-/Leichtindustrie *f*; **hotel** ~ Hotelgewerbe *nt*; **tourist** ~ Touristik, Tourismusbranche *or* -industrie *f*; **in certain industries** in einigen Branchen. (b) (*industriousness*) Fleiß *m.*

inebriate [ɪ'niːbrɪɪt] **1** *n* (*form*) Trinker(in *f*) *m.* **2** *adj see* **inebriated** (a). **3** [ɪ'niːbrɪeɪt] *vt* (*lit*) betrunken machen; (*fig*) trunken machen; (*success, popularity etc*) berauschen. ~**d by** his own words berauscht *or* trunken von seinen eigenen Worten.

inebriated [ɪ'niːbrɪeɪtɪd] *adj* (a) (*form*) betrunken, unter Alkoholeinfluß (*form*). (b) (*fig*) berauscht, trunken (*liter*).

inebriation [ɪ,niːbrɪ'eɪʃən], **inebriety** [,ɪniː'braɪətɪ] *n* (*form*) betrunkener Zustand.

inedible [ɪn'edɪbl] *adj* nicht eßbar; (*unpleasant*) *meal etc* ungenießbar.

ineducable [ɪn'edjukəbl] *adj* bildungsunfähig.

ineffable *adj*, ~**bly** *adv* [ɪn'efəbl, -lɪ] unsäglich (*liter*), unsagbar, unaussprechlich.

ineffective [,ɪnɪ'fektɪv] *adj* unwirksam, wirkungslos, ineffektiv; *attempt also* fruchtlos, nutzlos; *reasoning also* unergiebig; *person* unfähig, untauglich.

ineffectively [,ɪnɪ'fektɪvlɪ] *adv see adj.*

ineffectiveness [,ɪnɪ'fektɪvnɪs] *n see adj* Unwirksamkeit, Wirkungslosigkeit, Ineffektivität *f*; Fruchtlosigkeit, Nutzlosigkeit *f*; Unergiebigkeit *f*; Unfähigkeit, Untauglichkeit *f.*

ineffectual [,ɪnɪ'fektjʊəl] *adj* ineffektiv.

inefficacious [,ɪnefɪ'keɪʃəs] *adj* unwirksam, wirkungslos, ohne Wirkung; *policy* erfolglos, fruchtlos.

inefficacy [ɪn'efɪkəsɪ] *n see adj* Unwirksamkeit, Wirkungslosigkeit *f*; Erfolglosigkeit, Fruchtlosigkeit *f.*

inefficiency [,ɪnɪ'fɪʃənsɪ] *n see adj* Unfähigkeit, Ineffizienz (*geh*) *f*; Inkompetenz *f*; Leistungsunfähigkeit *f*; Unproduktivität, Ineffizienz (*geh*) *f.*

inefficient [,ɪnɪ'fɪʃənt] *adj person* unfähig, ineffizient (*geh*); *worker, secretary also* inkompetent; *machine, engine, factory, company* leistungsunfähig; *method, organization* unrationell, unproduktiv, ineffizient (*geh*). **to be** ~ **at doing sth** etw schlecht machen; **the** ~ **working of a mechanism** das schlechte Funktionieren eines Mechanismus.

inefficiently [,ɪnɪ'fɪʃəntlɪ] *adv* schlecht. **he works very** ~ er ist ineffizient *or* inkompetent.

inelastic [,ɪnɪ'læstɪk] *adj* (*lit*) unelastisch; (*fig*) starr, nicht flexibel.

inelasticity [,ɪnɪlæs'tɪsɪtɪ] *n* (*lit*) Mangel *m* an Elastizität; (*fig*) Mangel *m* an Flexibilität, Starrheit *f.*

inelegance [ɪn'elɪgəns] *n see adj* Uneleganz *f*; Mangel *m* an Schick *or* Eleganz; Schwerfälligkeit, Unausgewogenheit *f*; Ungeschliffenheit, Plumpheit, Schwerfälligkeit *f*; Derbheit, Unschönheit *f.*

inelegant [ɪn'elɪgənt] *adj* unelegant; *clothes also* ohne Schick *or* Eleganz; *person also* ohne Eleganz; *style also* schwerfällig, unausgewogen; *prose, phrase also* ungeschliffen, plump, schwerfällig; *dialect* derb, unschön, schwerfällig.

inelegantly [ɪn'elɪgəntlɪ] *adv see adj.* **she walks very** ~ ihr Gang ist ohne Eleganz, sie hat einen wenig eleganten Gang.

ineligibility [ɪn,elɪdʒə'bɪlɪtɪ] *n see adj* Nichtberechtigtsein *nt*; Unwählbarkeit *f*; mangelnde Eignung, Untauglichkeit *f.*

ineligible [ɪn'elɪdʒəbl] *adj* (*for benefits, grant*) nicht berechtigt (*for zu* Leistungen + *gen*); (*for election*) nicht wählbar; (*for job, office, as husband*) ungeeignet, untauglich. ~ **for military service** wehruntauglich; **you are** ~ **for social security benefits** Sie sind nicht zu Leistungen der Sozialversicherung berechtigt; **to be** ~ **for a pension** nicht pensionsberechtigt sein.

ineloquent [ɪn'eləkwənt] *adj* nicht wortgewandt.

ineluctable [,ɪnɪ'lʌktəbl] *adj* (*liter*) unausweichlich, unabwendbar (*liter*).

inept [ɪ'nept] *adj behaviour* ungeschickt, linkisch, unbeholfen; *remark* unpassend, unangebracht, ungeschickt; *compliment, refusal, attempt* plump; *comparison* ungeeignet, unpassend; *person* (*clumsy*) ungeschickt, ungelehrig, unbeholfen; (*slow at learning*) begriffsstutzig, unverständig.

ineptitude [ɪ'neptɪtjuːd], **ineptness** [ɪ'neptnɪs] *n see adj* Ungeschicktheit, Unbeholfenheit *f*; Unangebrachtheit, Ungeschicktheit *f*; Plumpheit *f*; Ungeeignetheit *f*; Ungeschicktheit *nt*, Ungeschicktheit, Ungelehrigkeit, Unbeholfenheit *f*; Begriffsstutzigkeit *f.* **full of stylistic** ~**s** voller Stilbrüche.

inequality [,ɪnɪ'kwolɪtɪ] *n* (*lack of equality*) Ungleichheit *f*; (*instance of* ~) Unterschied *m.* **great inequalities in wealth** große Unterschiede *pl* in der Verteilung von Reichtum; ~ **of opportunity** Chancenungleichheit *f*; ~ **of opportunity in education** Ungleichheit *f* der Bildungschancen.

inequitable [ɪn'ekwɪtəbl] *adj* ungerecht.

inequity [ɪn'ekwɪtɪ] *n* Ungerechtigkeit *f.*

ineradicable [,ɪnɪ'rædɪkəbl] *adj mistake, failing* unabänderlich, unwiderruflich; *feeling of guilt, hatred* tiefsitzend, unauslöschlich; *disease, prejudice* unausrottbar.

inert [ɪ'nɜːt] *adj* unbeweglich; (*Phys*) *matter* träge; (*Chem*) *substance* inaktiv. ~ **gas** Edelgas *nt.*

inertia [ɪ'nɜːʃə] *n* (*lit, fig*) Trägheit *f.* ~**-reel seat belt** Automatikgurt *m.*

inescapable [,ɪnɪs'keɪpəbl] *adj* unvermeidlich; *consequence also* unausweichlich; *conclusion also* zwangsläufig; *necessity also* unentrinnbar.

inescapably [,ɪnɪs'keɪpəblɪ] *adv see adj.*

inessential [,ɪnɪ'senʃəl] **1** *adj* unwesentlich, unerheblich, unwichtig. **2** *n* Unwesentliche(s) *nt no pl*, Nebensächlichkeit *f.*

inestimable [ɪn'estɪməbl] *adj* unschätzbar.

inevitability [ɪn,evɪtə'bɪlɪtɪ] *n* Unvermeidlichkeit *f.*

inevitable [ɪn'evɪtəbl] *adj* unvermeidlich, unvermeidbar; *result also* zwangsläufig. **victory/defeat seemed** ~ der Sieg/die Niederlage schien unabwendbar; **a tourist with his** ~ **camera** ein Tourist mit dem unvermeidlichen Photoapparat.

inevitably [ɪn'evɪtəblɪ] *adv* **if it's** ~ **the case that ...** wenn es notgedrungenerweise *or* zwangsläufig so sein muß, daß ...; ~ **rising prices** zwangsläufig steigende Preise; ~, **he got drunk/was late** es konnte ja nicht ausbleiben, daß er sich betrank/zu spät kam; **as** ~ **happens on these occasions** wie es bei solchen Anlässen immer ist.

inexact *adj*, ~**ly** *adv* [,ɪnɪg'zækt, -lɪ] ungenau.

inexcusable *adj*, ~**bly** *adv* [,ɪnɪks'kjuːzəbl, -ɪ] unverzeihlich, unverzeihbar, unentschuldbar.

inexhaustible [,ɪnɪg'zɔːstəbl] *adj source, spring* nie versiegend, unerschöpflich; *supply, wealth, patience* unerschöpflich; *curiosity* unstillbar, unendlich; *person, talker* unermüdlich.

inexorable [ɪn'eksərəbl] *adj* (*relentless*) erbarmungslos, unerbittlich; (*not to be stopped*) unaufhaltsam; *truth, facts* unumstößlich.

inexorably [ɪn'eksərəblɪ] *adv see adj.*

inexpediency [,ɪnɪks'piːdɪənsɪ] *n see adj* Ungeeignetheit, Unzweckmäßigkeit *f*; Unratsamkeit, Unklugheit *f.*

inexpedient [,ɪnɪks'piːdɪənt] *adj plan, measures, action, decision* ungeeignet, unzweckmäßig; *policy* unratsam, unklug. **that was rather** ~ **of you** das war ziemlich unklug von Ihnen.

inexpensive [,ɪnɪks'pensɪv] *adj* billig, preisgünstig.

inexpensively [,ɪnɪks'pensɪvlɪ] *adv* billig; *live also* ohne große Kosten.

inexperience [,ɪnɪks'spɪərɪəns] *n* Unerfahrenheit *f*, Mangel *m* an Erfahrung. **his** ~ **with our techniques** seine mangelnde Vertrautheit mit unseren Methoden.

inexperienced [,ɪnɪks'spɪərɪənst] *adj* unerfahren; *woodworker, skier etc* ungeübt, nicht so versiert. **to be** ~ **in doing sth** wenig Erfahrung mit etw haben, in etw (*dat*) wenig geübt sein.

inexpert [ɪn'ekspɜːt] *adj* unfachmännisch, laienhaft; *treatment also* unsachgemäß; (*untrained*) ungeübt. **to be** ~ **in doing sth** ungeübt darin sein, etw zu tun.

inexpertly [ɪn'ekspɜːtlɪ] *adv see adj.*

inexpertness [ɪn'ekspɜːtnɪs] *n see adj* Laienhaftigkeit *f*; Unsachgemäßheit *f*; Ungeübtheit *f.*

inexplicability [,ɪnɪksplɪkə'bɪlɪtɪ] *n* Unerklärlichkeit, Unerklärbarkeit *f.*

inexplicable [,ɪnɪks'plɪkəbl] *adj* unerklärlich, unerklärbar.

inexplicably [,ɪnɪks'plɪkəblɪ] *adv* (+ *adj*) unerklärlich; (+ *vb*) unerklärlicherweise.

inexplicit [,ɪnɪks'splɪsɪt] *adj* unklar, ungenau.

inexpressible [,ɪnɪks'spresəbl] *adj thoughts, feelings* unbeschreiblich, unbeschreibbar; *pain, joy also* unsagbar.

inexpressive [,ɪnɪks'spresɪv] *adj face* ausdruckslos; *word* blaß, nichtssagend; *style* blaß, ohne Ausdruckskraft.

inextinguishable [,ɪnɪks'stɪŋgwɪʃəbl] *adj fire* unlöschbar; *love, hope* unerschütterlich, beständig; *passion* unbezwinglich.

inextricable [,ɪnɪks'strɪkəbl] *adj tangle* unentwirrbar; *confusion* unüberschaubar; *difficulties* verwickelt, unlösbar.

inextricably [,ɪnɪks'strɪkəblɪ] *adv entangled* unentwirrbar; *linked* untrennbar. **he has become** ~ **involved with her** er kommt nicht mehr von ihr los.

infallibility [ɪn,fælə'bɪlɪtɪ] *n* Unfehlbarkeit *f* (*also Eccl*).

infallible [ɪn'fæləbl] *adj* unfehlbar (*also Eccl*).

infallibly [ɪn'fæləblɪ] *adv* unfehlbar; *work* fehlerfrei; *argued* unanfechtbar, unwiderlegbar.

infamous ['ɪnfəməs] *adj* (*notorious*) berüchtigt, verrufen; (*shameful*) *person* niederträchtig, gemein, ruchlos (*old, liter*); *deed, conduct* niederträchtig, infam, schändlich (*geh*).

infamy ['ɪnfəmɪ] *n* (a) *see adj* Verrufenheit *f*; Niedertracht, Gemeinheit *f*; Niedertracht, Infamie, Schändlichkeit (*geh*) *f.* (b) (*public disgrace*) Schande *f.*

infancy ['ɪnfənsɪ] *n* frühe Kindheit, Kindesalter *nt*; (*Jur*) Minderjährigkeit *f*; (*fig*) Anfangsstadium *nt.* **data processing is no longer in its** ~ die Datenverarbeitung steckt nicht mehr in den Kinderschuhen *or* ist den Kinderschuhen entwachsen.

infant ['ɪnfənt] *n* (*baby*) Säugling *m*; (*young child*) Kleinkind *nt*; (*Jur*) Minderjährige(r) *mf.* ~ **class** (*Brit*) erste und zweite

Grundschulklasse; ~ **mortality** Säuglingssterblichkeit *f;* ~ **school** *(Brit) Grundschule f für die ersten beiden Jahrgänge;* **she teaches** ~**s** sie unterrichtet Grundschulkinder.

infanta [ɪnˈfæntə] *n* Infantin *f.*

infante [ɪnˈfæntɪ] *n* Infant *m.*

infanticide [ɪnˈfæntɪsaɪd] *n* Kindesmord *m,* Kindestötung *f;* *(person)* Kindesmörder(in *f) m.*

infantile [ˈɪnfəntaɪl] *adj* (a) *(childish)* kindisch, infantil. **(b)** *(Med)* Kinder-. ~ **paralysis** *(dated)* Kinderlähmung *f.*

infantry [ˈɪnfəntrɪ] *n (Mil)* Infanterie, Fußtruppe *(Hist) f.*

infantryman [ˈɪnfəntrɪmən] *n, pl* -**men** [-mən] Infanterist, Fußsoldat *(Hist) m.*

infarction [ɪnˈfɑːkʃən] *n* Infarkt *m.*

infatuated [ɪnˈfætjʊeɪtɪd] *adj* vernarrt, verknallt *(inf) (with* in +*acc).* **to become** ~ **with sb** sich in jdn vernarren; **he's** ~ **with his own importance** er hält sich für den Nabel der Welt.

infatuation [ɪnˌfætjuˈeɪʃən] *n* (a) *(state)* Vernarrtheit *f (with* in +*acc).* (object of ~) Angebetete(r) *mf.* **tidiness has become an** ~ **with her** Ordnung ist bei ihr zur Leidenschaft geworden.

infect [ɪnˈfekt] *vt* **a** *wound* infizieren; *(lit) person also* anstecken; *water* verseuchen, verunreinigen; *meat* verderben. **to be** ~**ed with** *or* **by an illness** sich mit einer Krankheit infiziert *or* angesteckt haben; **his wound became** ~**ed** seine Wunde entzündete sich; **her cold** ~**ed all her friends** sie steckte alle ihre Freunde mit ihrer Erkältung an. **(b)** *(fig) (with enthusiasm etc)* anstecken. **the whole village was** ~**ed by a spirit of patriotism** das ganze Dorf war von patriotischem Geist erfüllt.

infection [ɪnˈfekʃən] *n* (a) *(illness)* Infektion, Entzündung *f.* **(b)** *(act of infecting)* Infektion *f; (of person also)* Ansteckung *f; (of water)* Verseuchung, Verunreinigung *f.*

infectious [ɪnˈfekʃəs] *adj* (a) *(Med) disease* ansteckend, infektiös. **are you still** ~? besteht bei dir noch Ansteckungsgefahr? **(b)** *(fig) enthusiasm, laugh* ansteckend; *idea* zündend.

infectiousness [ɪnˈfekʃəsnɪs] *n* (a) *(Med)* **the** ~ **of this disease** die Ansteckungs- *or* Infektionsgefahr bei dieser Krankheit. **(b)** *(fig)* **the** ~ **of these views** das Ansteckende an diesen Anschauungen; **the** ~ **of his laughter/enthusiasm** sein ansteckendes Lachen/seine mitreißende Begeisterung.

infelicitous [ˌɪnfɪˈlɪsɪtəs] *adj* unglücklich; *remark etc* unangebracht, unpassend.

infelicity [ˌɪnfɪˈlɪsɪtɪ] *n (form)* **the** ~ **of the expression caused general embarrassment** der unglücklich *or* ungeschickt gewählte Ausdruck führte zu allgemeiner Verlegenheit; **several infelicities of style made the critics shudder** einige sehr ungeschickte Stilfehler ließen die Kritiker schaudern.

infer [ɪnˈfɜːʳ] *vt* (a) schließen, folgern *(from* aus). **nothing can be** ~**red from this** daraus kann man nichts schließen *or* folgern. **(b)** *(imply)* andeuten, zu verstehen geben.

inferable [ɪnˈfɜːrəbl] *adj* ableitbar, zu folgern *pred,* zu schließen *pred.*

inference [ˈɪnfərəns] *n* Schluß(folgerung *f) m.* **he was intelligent enough to realize by** ~ **from what I said that ...** er war intelligent genug, um aus dem, was ich sagte, den Schluß zu ziehen, daß ...; **by** ~ **he said that ...** implizit sagte er, daß ...

inferential [ˌɪnfəˈrenʃəl] *adj* schlußfolgernd; *proof* Indizien-.

inferior [ɪnˈfɪərɪəʳ] **1** *adj* (a) *(in quality)* minderwertig; *quality also* minder, geringer; *person* unterlegen; *(in rank)* untergeordnet, niedriger; *court* untergeordnet. **an** ~ **workman** ein weniger guter Handwerker; **to be** ~ **in quality** von minderer *or* geringerer Qualität sein als etw, gegen etw abfallen *or* nicht ankommen; **to be** ~ **to sb** jdm unterlegen sein; *(in rank)* jdm untergeordnet *or* nachgestellt sein; **he feels** ~ er kommt sich *(dat)* unterlegen *or* minderwertig vor. **(b)** *(Typ)* letter tiefstehender Buchstabe. **(c)** *(Biol) order, species* niedriger.

2 in one's ~**s** *(in social standing)* Leute *or* Personen *pl* aus einer niedrigeren Schicht; *(in rank)* seine Untergebenen *pl.*

inferiority [ɪnˌfɪərɪˈɒrɪtɪ] *n (in quality)* Minderwertigkeit *f; (of person)* Unterlegenheit *f (to* gegenüber); *(in rank)* untergeordnete Stellung, niedrigere Stellung, niedrigerer Rang *(to* als). ~ **complex** Minderwertigkeitskomplex *m.*

infernal [ɪnˈfɜːnl] *adj (lit)* Höllen-; *(fig) cruelty, scheme* teuflisch; *weather* gräßlich; *(inf) impudence, nuisance* verteufelt; *noise* höllisch.

infernally [ɪnˈfɜːnəlɪ] *adv (inf)* teuflisch, verdammt *(inf).*

inferno [ɪnˈfɜːnəʊ] *n (hell)* Hölle *f,* Inferno *nt; (blazing house etc)* Flammenmeer *nt.* **a blazing** ~ ein flammendes Inferno; **it's like an** ~ **in here** *(fig)* hier ist es wie in einem Brutofen.

infertile [ɪnˈfɜːtaɪl] *adj soil, womb* unfruchtbar; *mind* unergiebig, ideenlos.

infertility [ˌɪnfɜːˈtɪlɪtɪ] *n see adj* Unfruchtbarkeit *f;* Unergiebigkeit, Ideenlosigkeit *f.*

infest [ɪnˈfest] *vt (rats, lice)* herfallen über (+*acc); (plague also)* befallen; *(fig: unwanted people)* heimsuchen, verseuchen. **to be** ~**ed with rats/mice** von Ratten verseucht sein; **to be** ~**ed** *(with lice etc)* mit Ungeziefer verseucht sein.

infestation [ˌɪnfesˈteɪʃən] *n* Verseuchung *f.* **an** ~ **of rats** eine Rattenplage.

infidel [ˈɪnfɪdəl] *n (Hist, Rel)* Ungläubige(r) *mf.*

infidelity [ˌɪnfɪˈdelɪtɪ] *n* Untreue *f.*

in-fighting [ˈɪnfaɪtɪŋ] *n (Boxing)* Nahkampf *m; (fig)* interner Machtkampf.

infiltrate [ˈɪnfɪltreɪt] **1** *vt* (a) *troops* infiltrieren; *enemy lines also* eindringen in (+*acc); (Pol) organization also* unterwandern; *spies, informer* einschleusen. **(b)** *(liquid)* einsickern in (+*acc),* durchsickern in (+*acc),* durchdringen. **to** ~ **a liquid into a substance** eine Flüssigkeit in eine Substanz einsickern *or* eindringen lassen.

2 *vi* (a) *(Mil)* eindringen *(into* in +*acc); (spy, informer also)* sich einschleusen *(into* in +*acc),* unterwandern *(into acc); (fig:*

ideas) infiltrieren, eindringen *(into* in +*acc).* **(b)** *(liquid)* **to** ~ **into a substance** eine Substanz eindringen *or* einsickern; **to** ~ **through sth** durch etw durchsickern.

infiltration [ˌɪnfɪlˈtreɪʃən] *n* (a) *(Mil)* Infiltration *f; (Pol also)* Unterwanderung *f.* **the** ~ **of spies** das Einschleusen von Spionen; **by** ~ **of the enemy's lines** durch Eindringen in die feindlichen Linien, durch Infiltration der feindlichen Linien. **(b)** *(of liquid)* Eindringen, Durchsickern, Einsickern *nt.*

infiltrator [ˈɪnfɪlˌtreɪtəʳ] *n (Mil)* Eindringling *m; (Pol)* Unterwanderer *m; (Mil)* Sickertruppe *f.*

infinite [ˈɪnfɪnɪt] **1** *adj (lit)* unendlich; *(fig also) care, trouble, joy, pleasure* grenzenlos; *knowledge* grenzenlos, unendlich groß. **an** ~ **amount of time/money/space** unendlich viel Zeit/Geld/unbegrenzt *or* unbeschränkt viel Platz.

2 n: the ~ *(space)* das Unendliche; *(God)* der Unendliche.

infinitely [ˈɪnfɪnɪtlɪ] *adv* unendlich; *(fig also)* grenzenlos; *improved* ungeheuer; *better, worse* unendlich viel.

infinitesimal [ˌɪnfɪnɪˈtesɪməl] *adj* unendlich klein, winzig; *(Math)* infinitesimal, unendlich klein. ~ **calculus** Infinitesimalrechnung *f.*

infinitesimally [ˌɪnfɪnɪˈtesɪməlɪ] *adv smaller, better, different* nur ganz geringfügig; *small* zum Verschwinden.

infinitive [ɪnˈfɪnɪtɪv] *(Gram)* **1** *adj* Infinitiv-, infinitivisch. **2** *n* Infinitiv *m,* Grundform *f.* **in the** ~ im Infinitiv.

infinitude [ɪnˈfɪnɪtjuːd] *n (infinite number)* unbegrenztes Maß *(of an* +*dat); (of facts, possibilities etc)* unendliches Maß *(of an* +*dat); (of space)* unendliche Weite *(of gen).*

infinity [ɪnˈfɪnɪtɪ] *n (lit)* Unendlichkeit *f; (fig also)* Grenzenlosigkeit *f; (Math)* das Unendliche. **to** ~ *(bis)* ins Unendliche; **in** ~ in der Unendlichkeit/im Unendlichen; **to focus on** ~ *(Phot)* (auf) Unendlich einstellen; **I have an** ~ **of things to do** ich habe unendlich viel zu tun; **composed of an** ~ **of parts** aus unendlich vielen Teilen *or* einer Unzahl von Teilen zusammengesetzt.

infirm [ɪnˈfɜːm] *adj* gebrechlich, schwach. ~ **of purpose** *(liter)* willensschwach, wenig zielstrebig.

infirmary [ɪnˈfɜːmərɪ] *n (hospital)* Krankenhaus *nt; (in school etc)* Krankenzimmer *nt or* -stube *f; (in prison, barracks)* (Kranken)revier *nt,* Krankenstation *f.*

infirmity [ɪnˈfɜːmɪtɪ] *n* Gebrechlichkeit *f.* **the infirmities of old age** die Altersgebrechen *pl;* **his** ~ **of purpose** *(liter)* seine Willensschwäche, sein Mangel *m* an Zielstrebigkeit.

infix 1 [ɪnˈfɪks] *vt idea* einprägen; *(Ling)* einfügen. **the idea is** ~**ed in his mind** diese Idee hat sich bei ihm festgesetzt.

2 [ˈɪnfɪks] *n (Ling)* Infix *nt,* Einfügung *f.*

infixation [ˌɪnfɪkˈseɪʃən] *n (of idea)* Einprägen, Festsetzen *nt; (Ling)* Einfügung *f.*

in flagrante delicto [ˌɪnfləˈgræntɪdɪˈlɪktəʊ] *adv* in flagranti.

inflame [ɪnˈfleɪm] *vt* (a) *(Med)* entzünden. **her eyes were** ~**d with crying** ihre Augen waren vom Weinen gerötet; **to become** ~**d** *(wound, eyes etc)* sich entzünden.

(b) *person* erzürnen, aufbringen; *feelings* entflammen, entfachen; *anger* erregen, entfachen. **his speech** ~**d the people** seine Rede brachte die Menge in Harnisch *or* auf; **they were** ~**d by the news** die Nachricht brachte sie in Harnisch *or* auf; ~**d with rage** wutentbrannt; ~**d with passion/indignation** *etc,* **he ...** von glühender Leidenschaft/leidenschaftlicher Entrüstung *etc* erfaßt, ... er ...; **he was** ~**d with rage/indignation/desire** *etc* er glühte vor Zorn/Entrüstung/Begierde *etc.*

inflammable [ɪnˈflæməbl] **1** *adj (lit)* feuergefährlich, (leicht) entzündbar, inflammabel *(form); (fig) temperament* explosiv, leicht reizbar; *situation* brisant, gereizt. **"highly** ~", **"Vorsicht Feuergefahr", "feuergefährlich". 2** *n* feuergefährlicher *or* leicht brennbarer Stoff.

inflammation [ˌɪnfləˈmeɪʃən] *n* (a) *(Med)* Entzündung *f.* **(b)** *(fig: of passion, anger etc)* Aufstacheln *nt,* Aufstachelung *f.*

inflammatory [ɪnˈflæmətərɪ] *adj speech, pamphlet* aufrührerisch, aufwieglerisch, Hetz-.

inflatable [ɪnˈfleɪtəbl] **1** *adj* aufblasbar; *dinghy* Schlauch-. **2** *n (boat)* Gummiboot *nt.*

inflate [ɪnˈfleɪt] **1** *vt* (a) aufpumpen; *(by mouth)* aufblasen. **(b)** *(Econ) prices, bill* steigern, hochtreiben. **to** ~ **the currency** die Inflation anheizen, den Geldumlauf steigern. **(c)** *ego* steigern, erhöhen; *sb's ego etc also* aufblähen. **to** ~ **with pride** mit *or* vor Stolz geschwollen.

2 *vi* sich mit Luft füllen.

inflated [ɪnˈfleɪtɪd] *adj prices* überhöht, inflationär; *pride* übersteigert, übertrieben; *style, rhetoric* geschwollen, hochtrabend. **to have an** ~ **opinion of oneself** ein übertriebenes Selbstbewußtsein haben.

inflation [ɪnˈfleɪʃən] *n* (a) *(Econ)* Inflation *f.* **to fight** ~ die Inflation bekämpfen. **(b)** *(act of inflating) see vt* Aufpumpen *nt;* Aufblasen *nt;* Steigern, Hochtreiben *nt;* Steigern, Erhöhen *nt;* Aufblähen *nt.*

inflationary [ɪnˈfleɪʃənərɪ] *adj politics, demands* inflationär, inflationistisch *(pej);* spiral Inflations-.

inflationism [ɪnˈfleɪʃənɪzəm] *n* Inflationspolitik *f.*

inflect [ɪnˈflekt] **1** *vt* (a) *(Gram)* flektieren, beugen. **(b)** *voice* modulieren. **2** *vi (Gram)* flektierbar *or* veränderlich sein, gebeugt werden.

inflected [ɪnˈflektɪd] *adj word* flektiert, gebeugt; *language* flektierend.

inflection [ɪnˈflekʃən] *n see* **inflexion.**

inflexibility [ɪnˌfleksɪˈbɪlɪtɪ] *n (lit)* Unbiegbarkeit, Steifheit, Starrheit *f; (fig)* Unbeugsamkeit *f,* geringe Flexibilität, Sturheit *(pej) f.*

inflexible [ɪnˈfleksəbl] *adj (lit) substance, object* unbiegbar, steif, starr; *(fig) person, attitude, opinion* unbeugsam, wenig flexibel, stur *(pej).*

inflexion [ɪnˈflekʃən] *n* (a) *(Gram: of word, language)* Flexion, Beugung *f.* **(b)** *(of voice)* Tonfall *m.*

inflexional [ɪnˈflekʃənl] *adj (Gram)* ending Flexions-.

inflict [ɪnˈflɪkt] *vt punishment, fine* verhängen (*on, upon* gegen), auferlegen (*on or upon sb* jdm); *suffering* zufügen (*on or upon sb* jdm); *wound* zufügen, beibringen (*on or upon sb* jdm); *blow* versetzen (*on or upon sb* jdm). to ~ oneself *or* one's company on sb sich jdm aufdrängen; he always has to ~ all his troubles on us er muß uns immer mit seinen Problemen behelligen.

infliction [ɪnˈflɪkʃən] *n* (a) (*act*) *see vt* Verhängung (*on, upon* gegen), Auferlegung *f*; Zufügen *nt*; Beibringen *nt*; Versetzen *nt*. (b) (*misfortune*) Plage *f*, Kreuz *nt*. the ~s of the poor die Leiden *or* Nöte *pl* der Armen.

in-flight [ˈɪnflaɪt] *adj entertainment* während des Fluges.

inflorescence [ˌɪnfloːˈresns] *n* Blütenstand *m*.

inflow [ˈɪnfləʊ] *n* (a) (*of water, air*) (*action*) Zustrom *m*, Einfließen, Zufließen *nt*; (*quantity*) Zufluß(menge *f*), Einfluß(menge *f*) *m*; (*place*) Zufluß *m*. ~ pipe Zuflußrohr *nt*. (b) (*fig*) (*of foreign currency, goods*) Zustrom *m*; (*of people also*) Andrang *m*; (*of ideas etc*) Eindringen *nt*.

influence [ˈɪnfluəns] **1** *n* Einfluß *m* (*over* auf +*acc*). to have an ~ on sb/sth (*person*) Einfluß auf jdn/etw haben; (*fact, weather etc also*) Auswirkungen *pl* auf jdn/etw haben; the weather had a great ~ on the number of voters das Wetter beeinflußte die Zahl der Wähler stark; to have a great deal of ~ with sb großen Einfluß bei jdm haben; he was a great ~ in ... er war ein bedeutender Faktor bei ...; he's been a bad ~ on you er war ein schlechter Einfluß für Sie; she is a good ~ in the school *or* on the pupils sie hat einen guten Einfluß auf die Schüler; to bring ~ to bear on sb, to exert an ~ on sb Einfluß auf jdn ausüben; to use one's ~ *or* bring one's ~ to bear to get sth seinen Einfluß ausüben *or* geltend machen, um etwas zu bekommen; you have to have ~ to get a job here Sie müssen schon einigen Einfluß haben, wenn Sie hier eine Stelle haben wollen; a man of ~ eine einflußreiche Person; under the ~ of drink/drugs unter Alkohol-/Drogeneinfluß, unter Alkohol-/Drogeneinwirkung; under the ~ (*inf*) betrunken; the changes were due to American ~ die Veränderungen sind auf amerikanische Einflüsse zurückzuführen; one of my early ~s was Beckett einer der Schriftsteller, die mich schon früh beeinflußt haben, war Beckett.
2 *vt* beeinflussen. to be easily ~d leicht beeinflußbar *or* zu beeinflussen sein.

influential [ˌɪnfluˈenʃəl] *adj* einflußreich. these factors were ~ in my decision diese Faktoren haben meine Entscheidung beeinflußt.

influenza [ˌɪnfluˈenzə] *n* Grippe *f*.

influx [ˈɪnflʌks] *n* (a) (*of capital, shares, foreign goods*) Zufuhr *f*; (*of people*) Zustrom, Andrang *m*; (*of ideas etc*) Zufluß *m*. (b) *see* inflow (a).

info [ˈɪnfəʊ] *n* (*inf*) *see* information.

inform [ɪnˈfɔːm] **1** *vt* (a) *person* benachrichtigen, informieren (*about* über +*acc*); unterrichten. to ~ sb of sth jdn von etw unterrichten, jdn über etw informieren; I am pleased to ~ you that ... ich freue mich, Ihnen mitteilen zu können *or* Sie davon in Kenntnis setzen zu können (*form*), daß ...; to ~ the police die Polizei verständigen *or* benachrichtigen *or* informieren; to keep sb/oneself ~ed jdn/sich auf dem laufenden halten (*of* über +*acc*); to ~ oneself about sth sich über etw (*acc*) informieren; until we are better ~ed bis wir Näheres wissen *or* besser Bescheid wissen *or* genauer informiert sind; why was I not ~ed? warum wurde mir das nicht mitgeteilt?, warum wurde ich nicht (darüber) informiert?; I should like to be ~ed just as soon as he arrives unterrichten Sie mich bitte sofort von seiner Ankunft, informieren Sie mich bitte sofort über seine Ankunft. (b) (*liter*) durchdringen, erfüllen. love of nature ~ed his writings all seine Schriften waren von der Liebe zur Natur durchdrungen.
2 *vi* to ~ against *or* on sb jdn anzeigen *or* denunzieren (*pej*).

informal [ɪnˈfɔːməl] *adj* (*esp Pol: not official*) *meeting, talks* nicht formell, nicht förmlich; *visit* inoffiziell, nicht förmlich; *arrangement* inoffiziell; (*simple, without ceremony*) *meeting, gathering, party* zwanglos; *manner, tone also* leger; *language, speech* ungezwungen, informell; *restaurant* gemütlich. the ~ use of "du" die vertraute Anrede „du"; "dress ~", „zwanglose Kleidung"; he is rather ~ sein Stil ist eher leger.

informality [ˌɪnfɔːˈmælɪtɪ] *n see adj* nicht formeller *or* förmlicher Charakter; inoffizieller Charakter; Zwanglosigkeit, Ungezwungenheit *f*; Ungezwungenheit *f*, informeller Charakter *or* Ton; Gemütlichkeit *f*; legere Art. the ~ of his behaviour sein legeres Benehmen.

informally [ɪnˈfɔːməlɪ] *adv* (*unofficially*) inoffiziell; (*casually, without ceremony*) zwanglos, ungezwungen.

informant [ɪnˈfɔːmənt] *n* Informant, Gewährsmann *m*. according to my ~ the book is out of print wie man mir mitteilt *or* berichtet, ist das Buch vergriffen.

information [ˌɪnfəˈmeɪʃən] *n* (a) Auskunft *f*, Informationen *pl*. a piece of ~ eine Auskunft *or* Information; for your ~ zu Ihrer Information *or* Kenntnisnahme (*form*); (*indignantly*) damit Sie es wissen; his ~ on the subject is most extensive sein Wissen auf diesem Gebiet ist äußerst umfassend; to give sb ~ about *or* on sb/sth jdm Auskunft *or* Informationen über jdn/etw geben; to get ~ about *or* on sb/sth sich über jdn/etw informieren, über jdn/etw Erkundigungen einziehen; to ask for ~ on *or* about sb/sth um Auskunft *or* Informationen über jdn/etw bitten; "~" „Auskunft"; we have no ~ about that wir wissen darüber nicht Bescheid; until further ~ is available bevor wir nichts Näheres wissen; what ~ do we have on Kowalsky? welche Informationen besitzen wir über Kowalsky?; where did you get your ~? woher haben Sie diese Kenntnisse *or* Informationen?; detailed ~ Einzelheiten *pl*. (b) (*Computers, ~ content*) Information *f*.

information: ~ **bureau** *n* Auskunft(sbüro *nt*) *f*, Verkehrsbüro *nt*; ~ **content** *n* Informationsgehalt *m*; ~ **retrieval** *n*

Datenabruf *m*; ~ **sciences** *npl* Informatik *f*; ~ **storage** *n* Datenspeicherung *f*; ~ **theory** *n* Informationstheorie *f*.

informative [ɪnˈfɔːmətɪv] *adj* aufschlußreich, informativ (*geh*); *book, lecture also* lehrreich. he's not very ~ about his plans er ist nicht sehr mitteilsam, was seine Pläne betrifft.

informed [ɪnˈfɔːmd] *adj* (*having information*) *observers* informiert, (*gut*) unterrichtet; (*educated*) gebildet.

informer [ɪnˈfɔːməʳ] *n* Informant, Denunziant (*pej*) *m*. police ~ Polizeispitzel *m*; to turn ~ seine Mittäter verraten.

infra dig [ˌɪnfrəˈdɪg] *adj* (*inf*) unter meiner/seiner *etc* Würde.

infra-red [ˈɪnfrəˈred] *adj* infrarot.

infrastructure [ˈɪnfrəˌstrʌktʃəʳ] *n* Infrastruktur *f*.

infrequency [ɪnˈfriːkwənsɪ] *n* Seltenheit *f*.

infrequent [ɪnˈfriːkwənt] *adj* selten. at ~ intervals in großen Abständen; her mistakes are so ~ sie macht so selten Fehler.

infrequently [ɪnˈfriːkwəntlɪ] *adv see adj*.

infringe [ɪnˈfrɪndʒ] **1** *vt* verstoßen gegen; *law also* verletzen, übertreten; *copyright also* verletzen. **2** *vi* to ~ (up)on sb's rights/privacy in jds Rechte/Privatsphäre (*acc*) eingreifen, jds Rechte/Privatsphäre verletzen.

infringement [ɪnˈfrɪndʒmənt] *n* (a) an ~ (of a rule) ein Regelverstoß *m*; ~ of the law Gesetzesverletzung *or* -übertretung *f*; ~ of a patent/copyright Patentverletzung *f*/Verletzung *f* des Urheberrechts. (b) (*of privacy*) Eingriff *m* (*of* in +*acc*).

infuriate [ɪnˈfjʊərɪeɪt] *vt* wütend *or* rasend machen, zur Raserei bringen. to be/get ~d wütend *or* rasend sein/werden.

infuriating [ɪnˈfjʊərɪeɪtɪŋ] *adj* (äußerst) ärgerlich. an ~ habit eine Unsitte; an ~ person ein Mensch, der einen zur Raserei bringen kann *or* der einen rasend *or* wütend machen kann.

infuriatingly [ɪnˈfjʊərɪeɪtɪŋlɪ] *adv* aufreizend. she's ~ slow sie ist aufreizend *or* zum Verzweifeln langsam.

infuse [ɪnˈfjuːz] **1** *vt* (a) *courage, enthusiasm etc* einflößen, geben (*into sb* jdm). they were ~d with new hope sie waren von neuer Hoffnung erfüllt, sie hatten wieder frischen Mut geschöpft. (b) (*Cook*) *tea, herbs* aufbrühen, aufgießen. **2** *vi* ziehen.

infuser [ɪnˈfjuːzəʳ] *n* Tee-Ei *nt*.

infusion [ɪnˈfjuːʒən] *n* (a) (*of hope etc*) Einflößen *nt*. (b) (*Cook*) Aufguß *m*; (*tea-like*) Tee *m*. an ~ of rose-hip tea Hagebuttentee *m*. (c) (*Med*) Infusion *f*.

ingenious [ɪnˈdʒiːnɪəs] *adj* genial; *person also* erfinderisch, geschickt, findig; *idea, method also* glänzend, ingeniös (*geh*); *device, instrument also* raffiniert, geschickt.

ingeniously [ɪnˈdʒiːnɪəslɪ] *adv* genial, glänzend.

ingeniousness [ɪnˈdʒiːnɪəsnɪs] *n see* ingenuity.

ingénue [ˈænʒeɪnjuː] *n* naives Mädchen; (*Theat*) Naive *f*.

ingenuity [ˌɪndʒɪˈnjuːɪtɪ] *n* Genialität *f*; (*of person also*) Einfallsreichtum *m*, Findigkeit *f*; (*of idea, method also*) Brillanz *f*; (*of device, instrument also*) Raffiniertheit *f*.

ingenuous [ɪnˈdʒenjʊəs] *adj* (a) (*candid*) offen, aufrichtig, unbefangen. (b) (*naive*) naiv, unverdorben.

ingenuously [ɪnˈdʒenjʊəslɪ] *adv see adj*.

ingenuousness [ɪnˈdʒenjʊəsnɪs] *n see adj* (a) Offenheit, Aufrichtigkeit, Unbefangenheit *f*. (b) Naivität, Unverdorbenheit *f*.

ingest [ɪnˈdʒest] *vt* (*Biol*) zu sich nehmen, aufnehmen.

ingestion [ɪnˈdʒestʃən] *n* (*Biol*) Nahrungsaufnahme *f*.

inglenook [ˈɪŋglnʊk] *n* Kaminecke *f*.

inglorious [ɪnˈglɔːrɪəs] *adj* unrühmlich, unehrenhaft; *defeat* schmählich, ruhmlos.

ingoing [ˈɪngəʊɪŋ] *adj mail* eingehend, einlaufend. ~ tenant neuer Mieter, Nachmieter *m*.

ingot [ˈɪŋgət] *n* Barren *m*. steel ~ Stahlblock *m*.

ingrained [ˌɪnˈgreɪnd] *adj* (a) (*fig*) *habit* fest, eingefleischt; *prejudice* tief verwurzelt *or* eingewurzelt; *belief* fest verankert, unerschütterlich. to be ~ fest verwurzelt sein. (b) *dirt* tief eingedrungen, tiefsitzend (*attr*). the dirt was deeply ~ in the carpet der Schmutz hatte sich tief im Teppich festgesetzt; hands ~ with dirt Hände, bei denen sich der Schmutz in den Poren festgesetzt hat.

ingrate [ˈɪngreɪt] *n* undankbarer Mensch, Undankbarer *m* (*old, liter*), Undankbare *f* (*old, liter*).

ingratiate [ɪnˈgreɪʃɪeɪt] *vr* to ~ oneself with sb sich bei jdm einschmeicheln.

ingratiating [ɪnˈgreɪʃɪeɪtɪŋ] *adj person, speech* schmeichlerisch, schöntuerisch; *smile* schmeichlerisch süßlich.

ingratiatingly [ɪnˈgreɪʃɪeɪtɪŋlɪ] *adv see adj*.

ingratitude [ɪnˈgrætɪtjuːd] *n* Undank *m*. sb's ~ jds Undankbarkeit *f*.

ingredient [ɪnˈgriːdɪənt] *n* Bestandteil *m*, Ingredienz *f* (*spec*); (*for recipe*) Zutat *f*. all the ~s of success alles, was man zum Erfolg braucht; the ~s of a man's character alles, was den Charakter eines Menschen ausmacht.

ingress [ˈɪngres] *n* (*form*) Zutritt, Eintritt *m*. no right of ~ Zutritt verboten; to have free ~ Recht auf freien Zugang haben.

in-group [ˈɪngruːp] *n* maßgebliche Leute *pl*, Spitze *f*; (*Sociol*) In-Group *f*.

ingrowing [ˈɪngrəʊɪŋ] *adj* (*Med*) *toenail* eingewachsen.

inhabit [ɪnˈhæbɪt] *vt* bewohnen; (*animals*) leben in (+*dat*).

inhabitable [ɪnˈhæbɪtəbl] *adj* bewohnbar.

inhabitant [ɪnˈhæbɪtənt] *n* (*of house, burrow etc*) Bewohner(in *f*) *m*; (*of island, town also*) Einwohner(in *f*) *m*.

inhalation [ˌɪnhəˈleɪʃən] *n* (*Med*) Inhalation *f*.

inhalator [ˈɪnhəleɪtəʳ] *n* Inhalationsapparat *m*.

inhale [ɪnˈheɪl] **1** *vt* einatmen; (*Med*) inhalieren. **2** *vi* (*in smoking*) Lungenzüge machen, inhalieren.

inhaler [ɪnˈheɪləʳ] *n* Inhalationsapparat *m*.

inharmonious [ˌɪnhɑːˈməʊnɪəs] *adj* unharmonisch.

inhere [ɪnˈhɪəʳ] *vi* to ~ in sth einer Sache (*dat*) innewohnen *or* eignen.

inherent [in'hiərənt] *adj* innewohnend, eigen, inhärent (*esp Philos*) (*to, in dat*). **the ~ hardness of diamonds** die den Diamanten eigene Härte; **instincts ~ in all animals** allen Tieren inhärente *or* eigene Instinkte.

inherently [in'hiərəntli] *adv* von Natur aus.

inherit [in'herit] **1** *vt* (*lit, fig*) erben. **the problems which we ~ed from the last government** die Probleme, die uns die letzte Regierung hinterlassen *or* vererbt hat. **2** *vi* erben. **to ~ from sb** jdn beerben.

inheritable [in'heritəbl] *adj* (*lit, fig*) erblich; *goods, shares* vererbbar.

inheritance [in'heritəns] *n* Erbe *nt* (*also fig*), Erbschaft *f*. **he got it by ~** er hat es durch eine Erbschaft bekommen.

inherited [in'heritid] *adj* *qualities, disease* ererbt.

inhibit [in'hibit] *vt* hemmen (*also Psych, Sci*). **to ~ sb from doing sth** jdn daran hindern, etw zu tun; **don't let me ~ you** haben Sie meinetwegen keine Hemmungen; **don't let my presence ~ the discussion** lassen Sie sich durch meine Anwesenheit in Ihrer Diskussion nicht stören.

inhibited [in'hibitid] *adj* gehemmt. **to be ~** Hemmungen haben, gehemmt sein; **you're so ~!** du bist so gehemmt *or* voller Hemmungen *or* verklemmt (*inf*).

inhibition [,inhi'biʃən] *n* Hemmung *f* (*also Psych, Sci*). **a feeling of ~** Hemmungen *pl*; **he has no ~s about speaking French** er hat keine Hemmungen, Französisch zu sprechen.

inhibitory [in'hibitəri] *adj* (*Psych*) hemmend; (*Physiol also*) behindernd.

inhospitable [,inho'spitəbl] *adj* ungastlich; *climate, region* unwirtlich.

inhospitably [,inho'spitəbli] *adv* ungastlich.

inhospitality [,in,hospi'tæliti] *n* Ungastlichkeit *f*, mangelnde Gastfreundschaft; (*of climate*) Unwirtlichkeit *f*.

inhuman [in'hju:mən] *adj* (*lit*) *monster, shape* nicht menschlich; (*fig*) unmenschlich.

inhumane [,inhju:'mein] *adj* inhuman; (*to people also*) menschenunwürdig.

inhumaneness [,inhju:'meinnis] *n* see *adj* Inhumanität *f*; Menschenunwürdigkeit *f*.

inhumanity [,inhju:'mæniti] *n* Unmenschlichkeit *f*. **the ~ of man to man** die Unmenschlichkeit der Menschen untereinander.

inhumation [,inhju:'meiʃən] *n* (*form*) Beisetzung *f* (*form*).

inhume [in'hju:m] *vt* (*form*) beisetzen (*form*).

inimical [i'nimikəl] *adj* (*hostile*) feindselig (*to* gegen); (*injurious*) abträglich (*to* für).

inimitable [i'nimitəbl] *adj* unnachahmlich.

iniquitous [i'nikwitəs] *adj* ungeheuerlich.

iniquity [i'nikwiti] *n* (*no pl: wickedness*) Ungeheuerlichkeit *f*; (*sin*) Missetat *f*; (*crime*) Greueltat *f*; see **den**.

initial [i'niʃəl] **1** *adj* (**a**) anfänglich, Anfangs-. **my ~ reaction** meine anfängliche Reaktion; **in the ~ stages** im Anfangsstadium; **the ~ teaching alphabet** die Lautschrift für den Anfangsunterricht im Lesen.

(**b**) (*Ling*) Anlaut-, anlautend.

(**c**) (*Typ*) ~ **letter** Anfangsbuchstabe *m*, Initiale *f*.

2 *n* Initiale *f*; (*Typ also*) Anfangsbuchstabe *m*. **to sign a letter with one's ~s** seine Initialen *or* (*Pol*) Paraphe unter einen Brief setzen; (*Comm*) einen Brief abzeichnen *or* mit seinem Namenszeichen versehen.

3 *vt* *letter, document* mit seinen Initialen unterzeichnen; (*Comm*) abzeichnen; (*Pol*) paraphieren.

initially [i'niʃəli] *adv* anfangs, zu *or* am Anfang; (*Ling*) im Anlaut.

initiate [i'niʃieit] **1** *vt* **a** (*set in motion*) den Anstoß geben zu, initiieren; *negotiations also* einleiten. **to ~ proceedings against sb** (*Jur*) gegen jdn einen Prozeß anstrengen.

(**b**) (*formally admit: into club etc*) feierlich aufnehmen; (*in tribal society*) *adolescents* initiieren.

(**c**) (*instruct: in knowledge, skill*) einweihen.

2 *n* (*in club etc*) Neuaufgenommene(r) *mf*; (*in tribal society*) Initiierte(r) *mf*; (*in knowledge*) Eingeweihte(r) *mf*.

initiation [i,niʃi'eiʃən] *n* (**a**) (*of project, fashion etc*) Initiierung *f*; (*of negotiations also*) Einleitung *f*.

(**b**) (*into society*) Aufnahme *f*; (*as tribal member*) Initiation *f*. ~ **ceremony** Aufnahmezeremonie *f*; ~ **rite** *n* Initiationsritus *m*.

(**c**) (*into branch of knowledge*) Einweihung *f*.

initiative [i'niʃətiv] *n* Initiative *f*. **to take the ~** die Initiative ergreifen; **on one's own ~** aus eigener Initiative; **to have ~** Initiative haben.

initiator [i'niʃieitə*r*] *n* Initiator(in *f*) *m*.

inject [in'dʒekt] *vt* (ein)spritzen; (*fig*) *comment* einwerfen; *money into economy* pumpen. **to ~ sb with sth** (*Med*) jdm etw spritzen *or* injizieren; **to ~ sb with enthusiasm, to ~ enthusiasm into sb** jdn mit Begeisterung erfüllen; **he ~ed new life into the club** er brachte neues Leben in den Verein.

injection [in'dʒekʃən] *n* (*act*) Einspritzung *f*; (*of gas*) Einblasen *nt*; (*that injected*) Injektion, Spritze *f*. **to give sb an ~** jdm eine Injektion *or* Spritze geben; **the ~ of more money into the economy** eine größere Finanzspritze für die Wirtschaft; **the team needed an ~ of new life** die Mannschaft brauchte frisches Blut; ~ **moulding** Spritzguß *m*.

injector [in'dʒektə*r*] *n* Einspritzpumpe *f*.

injudicious [,indʒu:'diʃəs] *adj*, **~ly** *adv* [,indʒu:'diʃəs, -li] unklug.

injunction [in'dʒʌŋkʃən] *n* Anordnung *f*; (*Jur*) gerichtliche Verfügung *f*.

injure ['indʒə*r*] *vt* (**a**) (*lit*) verletzen. **to ~ one's leg** sich (*dat*) das Bein verletzen, sich (*acc*) am Bein verletzen; **the horse was ~d** das Pferd verletzte sich; **how many were ~d?, how many ~d were there?** wie viele Verletzte gab es?

(**b**) (*fig*) (*offend*) *sb, sb's feelings* verletzen, kränken;

(*damage*) *reputation* schaden (+*dat*). **his ~d reputation** sein geschädigter Ruf; **the ~d party** (*Jur*) der/die Geschädigte.

injurious [in'dʒuəriəs] *adj* schädlich. **to be ~ to sb/sth** jdm/einer Sache schaden *or* schädlich sein; ~ **to the health** gesundheitsschädigend *or* -schädlich.

injury ['indʒəri] *n* Verletzung *f* (*to gen*); (*fig also*) Kränkung *f* (*to gen*). **to do sb/oneself an ~** jdn/sich verletzen; **to play ~ time** (*Sport*) nachspielen, Nachspielzeit haben; **they are into ~ time** (*Sport*) das ist Nachspielzeit.

injustice [in'dʒʌstis] *n* (*unfairness, inequality*) Ungerechtigkeit *f*; (*violation of sb's rights*) Unrecht *nt* no *pl*. **the struggle against ~** der Kampf gegen (die) Ungerechtigkeit *or* das Unrecht; **to do sb an ~** jdm Unrecht tun; **if a real ~ has been done to you...** wenn Ihnen wirklich Unrecht geschehen ist ...

ink [iŋk] **1** *n* Tinte (*also Zool*) *f*; (*Art*) Tusche *f*; (*Typ*) Druckfarbe *f*; (*for newsprint*) Druckerschwärze *f*. **written in ~** mit Tinte geschrieben; **a sketch in ~** eine Tuschzeichnung. **2** *vt* mit Tinte beschmieren; (*Typ*) einfärben.

♦**ink in** *vt sep* *outline, writing* mit Tinte *or* (*Art*) Tusche ausziehen *or* nachziehen; (*fill in*) *shape* mit Tinte *or* (*Art*) Tusche ausmalen *or* ausfüllen.

♦**ink out** *vt sep* mit Tinte übermalen.

♦**ink over** *vt sep* mit Tinte *or* (*Art*) Tusche ausziehen *or* nachzeichnen.

ink *in cpds* Tinten-; (*Art*) Tusch-; ~ **bag** *n* (*Zool*) Tintenbeutel *m*; ~**-bottle** *n* Tintenfaß *nt*; ~ **eraser** *n* Tintenradiergummi, Tintenradierer (*inf*) *m*.

inkling ['iŋkliŋ] *n* (*vague idea*) dunkle Ahnung. **he hadn't an ~** er hatte nicht die leiseste Ahnung *or* keinen blassen Schimmer (*inf*); **to give sb an ~** jdm eine andeutungsweise Vorstellung geben; **there was no ~ of the disaster to come** nichts deutete auf die bevorstehende Katastrophe hin.

ink: ~ **pad** *n* Stempelkissen *nt*; ~**pot** *n* Tintenfaß *nt*; ~**stain** *n* Tintenfleck *m*; ~**stained** *adj* tintenbeschmiert; ~**stand** *n* Tintenfaß *nt* (*mit Halter für Federn etc*); ~**well** *n* (*in eine Tischplatte eingelassenes*) Tintenfaß *nt*.

inky ['iŋki] *adj* (+*er*) (**a**) (*lit*) tintenbeschmiert, voller Tinte, tintig; *fingers also* Tinten-. (**b**) (*fig*) *darkness* tintenschwarz; *blue, black* tintig.

inlaid [in'leid] **1** *ptp of* **inlay**. **2** *adj* eingelegt (*with* mit). ~ **table** Tisch mit Einlegearbeit; ~ **work** Einlegearbeit *f*.

inland ['inlænd] **1** *adj* (**a**) *waterway, navigation, sea* Binnen-. ~ **town** Stadt *f* im Landesinnern.

(**b**) (*domestic*) *mail* Inland(s)-; *trade* Binnen-. ~ **produce** inländisches Erzeugnis, inländische Erzeugnisse *pl*, Inlandserzeugnis(se *pl*) *nt*; **I~ Revenue** (*Brit*) ≈ Finanzamt *nt*.

2 *adv* landeinwärts.

inlaw ['inlɔ:] *n* angeheirateter Verwandter, angeheiratete Verwandte. ~**s** (*parents-in-law*) Schwiegereltern *pl*.

inlay [in'lei] (*vb: pret, ptp* **inlaid**) **1** *n* (*in table, box*) Einlegearbeit *f*, Intarsien *pl*; (*Dentistry*) Plombe, Füllung *f*; (*of gold etc*) Inlay *nt*. **2** *vt* einlegen (*with* mit).

inlet ['inlet] *n* (**a**) (*of sea*) Meeresarm *m*; (*of river*) Flußarm *m*. (**b**) (*Tech*) Zuleitung *f*; (*of ventilator*) Öffnung *f*.

inlet: ~ **pipe** *n* Zuleitung(srohr *nt*) *f*; ~ **valve** *n* Einlaßventil *nt*.

inmate ['inmeit] *n* Insasse *m*, Insassin *f*.

inmost ['inmoust] *adj* see **innermost**.

inn [in] *n* (**a**) Gasthaus *nt*; (*old: hotel*) Herberge *f* (*old*); (*old: tavern*) Schenke *f*. (**b**) (*Jur*) **the I~s of Court** die vier englischen Juristenverbände.

innards ['inədz] *npl* Innereien *pl* (*also fig*), Eingeweide *pl*.

innate [i'neit] *adj* angeboren. **man's ~ desire for happiness** das dem Menschen angeborene Streben nach Glück.

inner ['inə*r*] **1** *adj* (**a**) innere(r, s); *side, surface, door, court, city,* (*Anat*) *ear also* Innen-. ~ **harbour** Innenbecken *nt*.

(**b**) (*fig*) *emotions* innere(r, s); *meaning* verborgen; *life* Seelen-. **his ~ circle of friends** sein engster Freundeskreis; **he wasn't one of the ~ circle** er gehörte nicht zum engeren Kreise; **the ~ man** (*soul*) das Innere; **the needs of the ~ man** die inneren Bedürfnisse; **to satisfy the ~ man** für sein leibliches Wohl sorgen.

2 *n* (*Archery*) Schwarze(s) *nt*.

innermost ['inəmoust] *adj* innerst. ~ **in sb** zuinnerst in jdm; **in the ~ recesses of the mind** in den hintersten Winkeln des Gehirns; **in the ~ depths of the forest** im tiefsten Wald.

inner tube *n* Schlauch *m*.

inning ['iniŋ] *n* (*Baseball*) Inning *nt*.

innings ['iniŋz] *n* (*Cricket*) Innenrunde *f*. **to have one's ~** (*fig inf*) an der Reihe sein; **he has had a long or a good ~** (*fig inf*) er war lange an der Reihe; (*life*) er hatte ein langes, ausgefülltes Leben.

innkeeper ['in,ki:pə*r*] *n* (Gast)wirt *m*.

innocence ['inəsəns] *n* (**a**) Unschuld *f*. **to pretend ~** vorgeben, unschuldig zu sein, unschuldig tun; **in all ~** in aller Unschuld. (**b**) (*liter: ignorance*) Unkenntnis *f*.

innocent ['inəsənt] **1** *adj* (**a**) unschuldig; *mistake, misrepresentation* unabsichtlich. **she is ~ of the crime** sie ist an dem Verbrechen unschuldig; **to put on an ~ air** eine Unschuldsmiene aufsetzen; **as ~ as a newborn babe** unschuldig wie ein Lamm; **he is ~ about night life in a big city** er ist die reine Unschuld, was das Nachtleben in einer Großstadt angeht.

(**b**) ~ **of** (*liter: ignorant*) nicht vertraut mit; (*devoid of*) frei von, ohne.

2 *n* Unschuld *f*. **he's a bit of an ~** er ist eine rechte Unschuld; **massacre of the Holy I~s** der Kindermord zu Bethlehem; **Holy I~s' Day** das Fest der Unschuldigen Kinder.

innocently ['inəsəntli] *adv* unschuldig; (*in all innocence*) in aller Unschuld.

innocuous *adj*, ~**ly** *adv* [i'nɒkjuəs, -li] harmlos.

innovate ['inouveit] **1** *vt* neu einführen. **the new techniques**

which he ~d die neuen Techniken, die er einführte. **2** *vi* Neuerungen einführen.

innovation [ˌɪnəʊ'veɪʃən] *n* Innovation *f*; *(introduction also)* Neueinführung *f (of gen)*; *(thing introduced also)* Neuerung *f*.

innovative [ɪnə'veɪtɪv] *adj* auf Neuerungen aus, innovatorisch *(geh)*.

innovator ['ɪnəʊveɪtər] *n* Neuerer *m*; *(of reform)* Begründer *m*.

innuendo [ˌɪnjʊ'endəʊ] *n, pl* **-es** versteckte Andeutung. **to make ~es about sb** über jdn Andeutungen fallenlassen.

innumerable [ɪ'njuːmərəbl] *adj* unzählig.

innumeracy [ɪ'njuːmərəsɪ] *n* Nicht-Rechnen-Können *nt*.

innumerate [ɪ'njuːmərɪt] *adj* **to be ~** nicht rechnen können.

inoculate [ɪ'nɒkjʊleɪt] *vt person* impfen *(against gegen)*. **to ~ sb with a virus** jdm einen Virus einimpfen.

inoculation [ɪˌnɒkjʊ'leɪʃən] *n* Impfung *f*. **to give sb an ~ (against smallpox)** jdn (gegen Pocken) impfen.

inoffensive [ˌɪnə'fensɪv] *adj* harmlos.

inoperable [ɪn'ɒpərəbl] *adj disease, tumour* inoperabel, nicht operierbar; *policy* undurchführbar.

inoperative [ɪn'ɒpərətɪv] *adj* **(a)** *(ineffective) law, rule* außer Kraft, ungültig. **to become ~** außer Kraft treten, ungültig werden. **(b)** *(not working)* **to be ~** *(machine, radio)* nicht funktionieren; **to render sth ~** etw außer Betrieb setzen.

inopportune [ɪn'ɒpətjuːn] *adj* inopportun; *demand, visit, moment also* ungelegen; *words* unpassend, nicht angebracht. **to be ~** ungelegen *or* zur Unzeit kommen; **it's very ~ that ...** es kommt sehr ungelegen, daß ...

inopportunely [ɪn'ɒpətjuːnlɪ] *adv* zur Unzeit.

inordinate [ɪ'nɔːdɪnɪt] *adj* unmäßig; *number of people, size, sum of money* ungeheuer.

inordinately [ɪ'nɔːdɪnɪtlɪ] *adv* unmäßig; *large* ungeheuer.

inorganic [ˌɪnɔː'gænɪk] *adj* anorganisch; *(fig)* unorganisch.

in-patient ['ɪnpeɪʃnt] *n* stationär behandelter Patient/behandelte Patientin.

input ['ɪnpʊt] *n* **(a)** *(into computer)* Input *m or nt*; *(of capital)* Investition *f*; *(of manpower)* (Arbeits)aufwand *m*; *(power ~)* Energiezufuhr *f*. **(b)** *(point of ~, ~ terminal)* Eingang *m*.

inquest ['ɪnkwest] *n (into death)* gerichtliche Untersuchung der Todesursache; *(fig)* Manöverkritik *f*.

inquietude [ɪn'kwaɪətjuːd] *n (liter)* Unruhe *f*.

inquire [ɪn'kwaɪər] *etc (esp US) see* **enquire** *etc.*

inquisition [ˌɪnkwɪ'zɪʃən] *n* **(a)** *(Hist Eccl)* **the I~** die Inquisition. **(b)** *(Jur)* Untersuchung *f*. **(c)** *(fig)* Inquisition *f*, Verhör *nt*.

inquisitive [ɪn'kwɪzɪtɪv] *adj* neugierig; *(for knowledge)* wißbegierig. **he's very ~ about** my friends are will alles über meine Freunde wissen.

inquisitively [ɪn'kwɪzɪtɪvlɪ] *adv see adj.*

inquisitiveness [ɪn'kwɪzɪtɪvnɪs] *n (of person)* Neugier *f*; *(for knowledge)* Wißbegier(de) *f*. **the ~ of** her look/questions *etc* ihr neugieriger Blick/ihre neugierigen Fragen *etc.*

inquisitor [ɪn'kwɪzɪtər] *n (Hist Eccl, fig)* Inquisitor *m*.

inquisitorial [ɪnˌkwɪzɪ'tɔːrɪəl] *adj* inquisitorisch. **after an ~ session with the headmaster** nachdem ihn der Rektor streng verhört hatte *or ins* Verhör genommen hatte.

inroad ['ɪnrəʊd] *n* **(a)** *(Mil)* Einfall *m (into* in +*acc)*. **(b)** *(fig)* **to make ~s** upon *or* into sb's rights in jds Rechte *(acc)* eingreifen; **the Japanese are making ~s into the British market** die Japaner dringen in den britischen Markt ein; **these expenses are making heavy ~s into** my bank account diese Ausgaben greifen mein Bankkonto stark an *or* reißen ein großes Loch in mein Bankkonto; **extra work has made ~s (up)on** *or* into my spare time zusätzliche Arbeit hat meine Freizeit sehr eingeschränkt.

inrush ['ɪnrʌʃ] *n* Zustrom *m*; *(of water)* Einbruch *m*. **there was a sudden ~** of tourists die Touristen kamen plötzlich in Strömen.

ins *abbr of* **(a)** *insurance* Vers. **(b)** **inches.**

insalubrious [ˌɪnsə'luːbrɪəs] *adj* unzuträglich.

insane [ɪn'seɪn] **1** *adj* **(a)** geisteskrank, wahnsinnig; *(fig)* wahnsinnig, irrsinnig. **you must be ~!** du bist wohl geisteskrank *or* wahnsinnig!; **that's ~!** das ist Wahnsinn *or* Irrsinn! **(b)** *(esp US)* **~ asylum/ward** Anstalt *f*/Abteilung *f* für Geisteskranke. **2** *npl* **the ~** die Geisteskranken *pl*.

insanely [ɪn'seɪnlɪ] *adv* irr; *(fig)* verrückt; *jealous* irrsinnig.

insanitary [ɪn'sænɪtərɪ] *adj* unhygienisch.

insanity [ɪn'sænɪtɪ] *n* Geisteskrankheit *f*, Wahnsinn *m*; *(fig)* Irrsinn, Wahnsinn *m*.

insatiability [ɪnˌseɪʃə'bɪlɪtɪ] *n see adj* Unersättlichkeit *f*; Unstillbarkeit *f*.

insatiable [ɪn'seɪʃəbl], **insatiate** [ɪn'seɪʃɪt] *(liter) adj* unersättlich; *curiosity, desire also* unstillbar.

inscribe [ɪn'skraɪb] *vt* **a)** *words, symbols etc (engrave) (on ring etc)* eingravieren; *(on rock, stone, wood)* einmeißeln; *(on tree)* einritzen. **to ~ sth on sth** etw in etw *(acc)* eingravieren/einmeißeln/einritzen. **(b)** *book* eine Widmung schreiben in (+*acc)*. **(c)** **to ~ sth in sb's memory** etw in jds Gedächtnis *(dat)* verankern. **(d)** *(Math)* einbeschreiben *(in a circle etc* einem Kreis *etc)*. **(e)** *(Fin)* **~d stock** Namensaktien *pl*.

inscription [ɪn'skrɪpʃən] *n* **(a)** *(on monument etc)* Inschrift *f*; *(on coin)* Aufschrift *f*. **(b)** *(in book)* Widmung *f*.

inscrutability [ɪnˌskruːtə'bɪlɪtɪ] *n* Unergründlichkeit *f*.

inscrutable [ɪn'skruːtəbl] *adj* unergründlich. **~ face** undurchdringlicher Gesichtsausdruck; **don't pretend to be so ~** tu nicht so geheimnisvoll.

insect ['ɪnsekt] *n* Insekt, Kerbtier *nt*.

insect: **~ bite** *n* Insektenstich *m*; **~ eater** *n* Insektenfresser *m*; **~-eating plant** *n* fleischfressende Pflanze.

insecticide [ɪn'sektɪsaɪd] *n* Insektengift, Insektizid *(form) nt*.

insectivorous [ˌɪnsek'tɪvərəs] *adj* insektenfressend.

insect: **~-powder** *n* Insektenpulver *nt*; **~-repellent 1** *adj*

insektenvertreibend; **2** *n* Insektenbekämpfungsmittel *nt*.

insecure [ˌɪnsɪ'kjʊər] *adj* unsicher; *foundation also* nicht sicher. **if they feel ~ in their jobs** wenn sie sich in ihrem Arbeitsplatz nicht sicher fühlen.

insecurely [ˌɪnsɪ'kjʊəlɪ] *adv fastened* nicht sicher.

insecurity [ˌɪnsɪ'kjʊərɪtɪ] *n* Unsicherheit *f*.

inseminate [ɪn'semɪneɪt] *vt* inseminieren *(spec)*, befruchten; *cattle* besamen; *(fig) beliefs* einimpfen.

insemination [ɪnˌsemɪ'neɪʃən] *n see vt* Insemination *(spec)*, Befruchtung *f*; Besamung *f*; Einimpfung *f*; *(fig: of knowledge)* Vermittlung *f*.

insensate [ɪn'senseɪt] *adj (liter)* **(a)** *matter, stone* leblos, tot. **(b)** *(fig: unfeeling)* gefühllos. **she flew into an ~ fury** ein unmäßiger Zorn bemächtigte sich ihrer *(liter)*.

insensibility [ɪnˌsensə'bɪlɪtɪ] *n* **(a)** *(bodily)* Unempfindlichkeit *f (to* gegenüber); *(unconsciousness)* Bewußtlosigkeit *f*. **(b)** *(lack of feeling)* Gefühllosigkeit *f (to* gegenüber). **artistic ~** Unempfänglichkeit *f* für Künstlerisches.

insensible [ɪn'sensəbl] *adj* **(a)** *(bodily)* unempfindlich *(to* gegen); *(unconscious)* bewußtlos. **he seems to be ~ to the cold** er scheint kälteunempfindlich zu sein; **his hands became ~ to any feeling** seine Hände verloren jegliches Gefühl. **(b)** *(liter: of beauty, music)* unempfänglich *(of, to* für). **(c)** *(liter: unaware)* **~ of** *or* to sth einer Sache *(gen)* nicht bewußt. **(d)** *(form: imperceptible)* unmerklich, nicht wahrnehmbar.

insensitive [ɪn'sensɪtɪv] *adj* **(a)** *(emotionally)* gefühllos. **(b)** *(unappreciative)* unempfänglich. **~ to artistic form/the beauties of nature** *etc* für künstlerische Formen/Schönheiten der Natur *etc* unempfänglich sein. **(c)** *(physically)* unempfindlich. **~ to pain/light** schmerz-/lichtunempfindlich.

insensitivity [ɪnˌsensɪ'tɪvɪtɪ] *n* **(a)** *(emotional)* Gefühllosigkeit *f (towards* gegenüber). **(b)** *(unappreciative)* Unempfänglichkeit *f (to* für). **his ~ to the beauties of nature** seine Unempfänglichkeit für die Schönheiten der Natur; **his ~ towards the reasons behind the demands** seine Verständnislosigkeit *or* sein Unverständnis für die Gründe, die hinter den Forderungen stehen. **(c)** *(physical)* Unempfindlichkeit *f*.

inseparability [ɪnˌsepərə'bɪlɪtɪ] *n see adj* Untrennbarkeit *f*; Unzertrennlichkeit *f*.

inseparable [ɪn'sepərəbl] *adj* untrennbar; *friends* unzertrennlich. **these two questions are ~** diese beiden Fragen sind untrennbar miteinander verbunden.

inseparably [ɪn'sepərəblɪ] *adv* untrennbar.

insert [ɪn'sɜːt] **1** *vt (stick into)* hineinstecken; *(place in)* hineinlegen; *(place between)* einfügen; *zip, pocket* einsetzen; *thermometer, suppository, shell* einführen; *coin* einwerfen; *injection needle* einstechen. **to ~ sth in sth** etw in etw *(acc)* stecken; **to ~ an extra paragraph in a chapter** einen weiteren Absatz in ein Kapitel einfügen; **to ~ an advert in a paper** eine Anzeige in eine Zeitung setzen, in einer Zeitung inserieren; **he managed to ~ himself between two other students on the crowded benches** es gelang ihm, sich auf den überfüllten Bänken zwischen zwei andere Studenten zu zwängen. **2** ['ɪnsɜːt] *n (in book)* Einlage *f*; *(word)* Beifügung, Einfügung *f*; *(in magazine)* Beilage *f*; *(advertisement)* Inserat *nt*.

insertion [ɪn'sɜːʃən] *n* **(a)** *see vt* Hineinstecken *nt*; Hineinlegen *nt*; Einfügen *nt*; Einsetzen *nt*; Einführen *nt*; Einwerfen *nt*; Einstechen *nt*; *(of an advert)* Aufgeben *nt*; *(by printer)* Einrücken *nt*. **(b)** *see* **insert 2. (c)** *(Sew)* Einsatz *m*.

in-service ['ɪn,sɜːvɪs] *adj attr* **~ training** (berufsbegleitende) Fortbildung; *(in firm also)* innerbetriebliche Fortbildung; *(course also)* Fortbildungslehrgang *m*.

inset ['ɪnset] *(vb: pret, ptp ~)* **1** *vt map, illustration* einfügen; *(Sew)* einsetzen. **2** ['ɪnset] *n (pages)* Einlage, Beilage *f*; *(also ~ map)* Nebenkarte *f*; *(on diagram)* Nebenbild *m*. **(b)** *(Sew)* Einsatz *m*.

inshore [ɪn'ʃɔːr] **1** *adj* Küsten-. **~ fishing** Küstenfischerei *f*. **2** *adv fish, be in* Küstennähe; *blow, flow* auf die Küste zu.

inside ['ɪn'saɪd] **1** *n* **(a)** Innere(s) *nt*; *(of pavement)* Innenseite *f*. **keep to the ~ of the road** halte dich am Straßenrand; **the car overtook on the ~** das Auto überholte innen; **it's painted on the ~** es ist innen bemalt; **you'll have to ask someone on the ~** Sie müssen einen Insider *or* Eingeweihten fragen; **to know a company from the ~** interne Kenntnisse über eine Firma haben; **he's seen politics from the ~** er kennt die Politik von innen; **locked from** *or* on the ~ von innen verschlossen. **(b)** **the wind blew the umbrella ~ out** der Wind hat den Schirm umgestülpt; **your jumper's ~ out** du hast deinen Pullover links *or* verkehrt herum an; **to turn sth ~ out** etw umdrehen; *(fig) flat etc* etw auf den Kopf stellen; **to know sth ~ out** etw in- und auswendig kennen. **(c)** *(inf) (stomach: also ~s)* Eingeweide, Innere(s) *nt*. **to have pains in one's ~s** Bauch- *or* Leibschmerzen haben.

2 *adj* Innen-, innere(r, s). **~ information** Insider-Informationen *pl*, interne Informationen *pl*; **it is an ~ job** *(done in office etc)* das wird betriebsintern gemacht; **it looks like an ~ job** *(crime)* es sieht nach dem Werk von Insidern aus *(inf)*; **~ lane** *(Sport)* Innenbahn *f*; *(Aut)* Innenspur *f*; **~ leg measurement** innere Beinlänge; **~ pocket** Innentasche *f*; **~ seat** Platz *m* an der Wand/am Fenster, Fensterplatz *m*; **~ story** *(Press)* Inside-Story *f*; **~ track** Innenbahn *f*; **~ forward** Halbstürmer *m*; **~ left** Halblinke(r) *m*; **~ right** Halbrechte(r) *m*.

3 *adv* **(a)** innen; *(indoors)* drin(nen); *(direction)* nach innen, hinein/herein. **look ~** sehen Sie hinein; *(search)* sehen Sie innen nach; **come ~!** kommen Sie herein!; **let's go ~** gehen wir hinein; **he passed the ball ~** er spielte nach innen ab; **there is something ~** es ist etwas (innen) drin; **to be ~** *(inf) (in prison)* sitzen *(inf)*.

4 prep (also esp US: ~ of) (a) (place) innen in (+dat); (direction) in (+acc) ... (hinein). **don't let him come ~ the house** lassen Sie ihn nicht ins Haus (herein); **he was waiting ~ the house er wartete im Haus; once ~ the door he ...** wenn er erst einmal im Haus ist/war ...; **he went ~ the house** er ging ins Haus (hinein).

(b) (time) innerhalb. **he's well ~ a record time** er liegt noch gut unter der Rekordzeit; **he was 5 secs ~ the record** er ist 5 Sekunden unter dem Rekord geblieben.

insider [ɪnˈsaɪdəʳ] n Insider, Eingeweihte(r) m.

insidious adj, **~ly** adv [ɪnˈsɪdɪəs, -lɪ] heimtückisch.

insight [ˈɪnsaɪt] n (a) no pl Verständnis nt. **he lacks ~** ihm fehlt das Verständnis; **he has a great ~ into modern science** er versteht viel viel von den modernen Naturwissenschaften; **his ~ into my problems** sein Verständnis für meine Probleme; **~ into human nature** Menschenkenntnis f.

(b) Einblick m (into in +acc). **to gain an ~ into sth** in etw (einen) Einblick gewinnen or bekommen.

insignia [ɪnˈsɪgnɪə] npl Insignien pl.

insignificance [ˌɪnsɪgˈnɪfɪkəns] n see adj Belanglosigkeit f; Geringfügigkeit f; Unscheinbarkeit f.

insignificant [ˌɪnsɪgˈnɪfɪkənt] adj belanglos; sum, difference also unbedeutend, geringfügig; little man, person unscheinbar.

insincere [ˌɪnsɪnˈsɪəʳ] adj unaufrichtig; person, smile also falsch.

insincerely [ˌɪnsɪnˈsɪəlɪ] adv see adj.

insincerity [ˌɪnsɪnˈserɪtɪ] n see adj Unaufrichtigkeit f; Falschheit f.

insinuate [ɪnˈsɪnjʊeɪt] vt (a) (hint, suggest) andeuten (sth to sb etw jdm gegenüber). **what are you insinuating?** was wollen Sie damit sagen?; **are you insinuating that I am lying?** willst du damit sagen, daß ich lüge? **(b) to ~ oneself into sb's favour** sich bei jdm einschmeicheln.

insinuating [ɪnˈsɪnjʊeɪtɪŋ] adj remark anzüglich; article also voller Anzüglichkeiten; tone of voice spitz, bedeutungsvoll. **he said it in such an ~ way** er sagte es auf eine so anzügliche Art.

insinuation [ɪnˌsɪnjʊˈeɪʃən] n Anspielung f (about auf +acc). **he objected strongly to any ~ that ...** er wehrte sich heftig gegen jede Andeutung, daß ...; **he argued rather by ~** er argumentierte vielmehr mit Anspielungen.

insipid [ɪnˈsɪpɪd] adj fad; person, novel, lyrics also geistlos.

insipidity [ˌɪnsɪˈpɪdɪtɪ] n see adj Fadheit f; Geistlosigkeit f.

insist [ɪnˈsɪst] vti bestehen. **I ~!** ich bestehe darauf!; **I didn't want to but he ~ed** ich wollte nicht, aber er bestand darauf; **but he still ~ed that ...** aber er beharrte or bestand trotzdem darauf, daß ...; **if you ~** wenn Sie darauf bestehen; (if you like) wenn's unbedingt sein muß; **I must ~ that you stop** ich muß darauf bestehen, daß Sie aufhören; **I must ~ that I am right in** ich muß doch nachdrücklich betonen, daß ich recht habe; **he ~s on his innocence** or **that he is innocent** er behauptet beharrlich, unschuldig zu sein; **to ~ (up)on a point auf einem Punkt** beharren; **to ~ on silence** auf absoluter Ruhe bestehen; **I ~ on the best** ich bestehe auf bester Qualität; **he ~s on punctuality** er besteht auf Pünktlichkeit; **to ~ on doing sth/on sb doing sth** darauf bestehen, etw zu tun/daß jd etw tut; **he will ~ on calling her by the wrong name** er redet sie beharrlich beim falschen Namen an; **if you will ~ on smoking that foul tobacco** wenn Sie schon unbedingt diesen scheußlichen Tabak rauchen müssen.

insistence [ɪnˈsɪstəns] n Bestehen nt (on auf +dat). **the accused's ~ on his innocence** die Unschuldsbeteuerungen des Angeklagten; **in spite of his ~ that he was right** trotz seiner beharrlichen Behauptung, recht zu haben; **I did it at his ~** ich tat es auf sein Drängen, ich tat es, weil er darauf bestand; **I can't understand his ~ on the use of oil** ich kann nicht verstehen, warum er darauf besteht, daß Öl benutzt wird.

insistent [ɪnˈsɪstənt] adj (a) person beharrlich, hartnäckig; salesman etc aufdringlich. **I didn't want to but he was ~** ich wollte eigentlich nicht, aber er bestand or beharrte darauf; **he was most ~ that ...** er bestand hartnäckig darauf, daß ...; **he was most ~ about it** er beharrte or bestand hartnäckig darauf. **(b)** (urgent) demand, tone, singing, rhythm nachdrücklich, penetrant (pej).

insistently [ɪnˈsɪstəntlɪ] adv mit Nachdruck.

insofar [ˌɪnsəʊˈfɑːʳ] adv: **~ as** soweit.

insole [ˈɪnsəʊl] n Einlegesohle f; (part of shoe) Brandsohle f.

insolence [ˈɪnsələns] n Unverschämtheit, Frechheit f. **the ~ of it!** so eine Unverschämtheit or Frechheit!

insolent adj, **~ly** adv [ˈɪnsələnt, -lɪ] unverschämt, frech.

insolubility [ɪnˌsɒljʊˈbɪlɪtɪ] n see adj (a) Unlöslichkeit f. (b) Unlösbarkeit f.

insoluble [ɪnˈsɒljʊbl] adj (a) substance unlöslich. (b) problem unlösbar.

insolvency [ɪnˈsɒlvənsɪ] n Zahlungsunfähigkeit, Insolvenz (geh) f.

insolvent [ɪnˈsɒlvənt] adj zahlungsunfähig, insolvent (geh).

insomnia [ɪnˈsɒmnɪə] n Schlaflosigkeit f.

insomniac [ɪnˈsɒmnɪæk] n **to be an ~** an Schlaflosigkeit leiden.

insomuch [ˌɪnsəʊˈmʌtʃ] adv see **inasmuch**.

insouciance [ɪnˈsuːsɪəns] n (liter) Unbekümmertheit, Sorglosigkeit f.

inspect [ɪnˈspekt] vt (a) (examine) kontrollieren, prüfen. **to ~ sth for sth** etw auf etw (acc) (hin) prüfen or kontrollieren. **(b)** (Mil etc: review) inspizieren.

inspection [ɪnˈspekʃən] n (a) Kontrolle, Prüfung f; (medical) Untersuchung f; (of school) Inspektion f. **on ~** bei näherer Betrachtung or Prüfung; **customs ~** Zollkontrolle f; **for your ~** zur Prüfung or Einsicht; **~ copy** Ansichtsexemplar nt. **(b)** (Mil) Inspektion f.

inspector [ɪnˈspektəʳ] n (factory ~, on buses, trains) Kontrol-

leur(in f) m; (of schools) Schulrat m, Schulrätin f; (of police) Polizeiinspektor m; (higher) Kommissar m; (of taxes) Steuerinspektor m. **customs ~** Zollinspektor(in f) m.

inspectorate [ɪnˈspektərɪt] n Inspektion f.

inspiration [ˌɪnspəˈreɪʃən] n Inspiration (for zu or für), Eingebung (for zu) f. **he gets his ~ from ...** er läßt sich von ... inspirieren; **you give me ~** Sie inspirieren mich; **I haven't had any ~ for months** habe ich keine Inspirationen mehr; **that idea of yours was a real ~!** Ihre Idee war wirklich eine Inspiration; **to have a sudden ~** eine plötzliche Inspiration or Erleuchtung haben; **you are my ~** du inspirierst mich; **his courage has been an ~ to us** all sein Mut hat uns alle inspiriert.

inspire [ɪnˈspaɪəʳ] vt (a) respect, trust, awe einflößen (in sb jdm); hope, confidence etc (er)wecken (in in +dat); hate hervorrufen (in bei). **to ~ sb with hope/confidence/hate/respect** jdn mit Hoffnung/Vertrauen/Haß/Respekt erfüllen.

(b) (be inspiration to) person inspirieren. **to ~ sb with an idea** jdn zu einer Idee inspirieren; **I was ~d by his example/courage** sein Vorbild/Mut hat mich inspiriert; **whatever ~d you to change it?** (iro) was hat dich bloß dazu inspiriert, es zu ändern?

inspired [ɪnˈspaɪəd] adj genial; work also voller Inspiration; author also inspiriert. **in an ~ moment** in einem Augenblick der Inspiration; (iro) in einem lichten Moment; **it was an ~ guess** das war genial geraten.

inspiring [ɪnˈspaɪərɪŋ] adj speech inspirierend. **this subject/translation isn't particularly ~** (inf) dieses Thema/diese Übersetzung reißt einen nicht gerade vom Stuhl (inf).

Inst abbr of **Institute** Inst.

inst abbr of **instant** d.M.

instability [ˌɪnstəˈbɪlɪtɪ] n Instabilität f; (of character also) Labilität f.

install [ɪnˈstɔːl] vt installieren; telephone also anschließen; bathroom, fireplace einbauen; person also (in ein Amt) einsetzen or einführen; priest investieren. **to have electricity ~ed** ans Elektrizitätsnetz angeschlossen werden; **to ~ a new mayor** einen neuen Bürgermeister in sein Amt einsetzen or einführen; **when you've ~ed yourself in your new office** wenn Sie sich in Ihrem neuen Büro installiert or eingerichtet haben; **he ~ed himself in the best armchair** (inf) er pflanzte sich auf den besten Sessel (inf).

installation [ˌɪnstəˈleɪʃən] n (a) see vt Installation f; Anschluß m; Einbau m; Amtseinsetzung or -einführung f; Investitur f. **(b)** (machine etc) Anlage, Einrichtung f. **(c)** military ~ militärische Anlage.

instalment, (US) **installment** [ɪnˈstɔːlmənt] n (a) (of story, serial) Fortsetzung f; (Rad, TV) (Sende)folge f. **(b)** (Fin, Comm) Rate f. **monthly ~** Monatsrate f; **to pay in or by ~s** in Raten or ratenweise bezahlen.

installment plan n (US) Ratenzahlung(splan m) f. **to buy on the ~** auf Raten kaufen.

instance [ˈɪnstəns] **1** n (a) (example) Beispiel nt; (case) Fall m. **for ~** zum Beispiel; **as an ~ of** als (ein) Beispiel für; **let's take an actual ~** nehmen wir doch einen wirklichen Fall; **in many ~s** in vielen Fällen; **there have been many ~s of people refusing** es hat viele Fälle gegeben, in denen Leute abgelehnt haben; **in the first ~** zuerst or zunächst (einmal); **the appointment will be for two years in the first ~** die Anstellung ist zunächst auf zwei Jahre befristet; **this is a good ~ of the way ...** das ist ein gutes Beispiel dafür, wie ...

(b) at the ~ of (form) auf Ersuchen or Betreiben (+gen) (form), auf Veranlassung f.

(c) (Jur) court of first ~ erste Instanz.

2 vt (a) (exemplify) Beispiele anführen für.

(b) (cite) cost, example anführen.

instant [ˈɪnstənt] **1** adj (a) unmittelbar; relief, result, reply, success also sofortig attr. **~ replay** (TV) Wiederholung f.

(b) (Cook) Instant-. **~ coffee** Pulver- or Instantkaffee m; **~ milk** Trockenmilch f; **~ food** Sofortgerichte pl; **~ potatoes** fertiger Kartoffelbrei.

(c) (Comm) dieses Monats. **your letter of the 10th inst(ant)** Ihr Schreiben vom 10. dieses Monats.

2 n Augenblick m. **this (very) ~** sofort, auf der Stelle; **I'll be ready in an ~** ich bin sofort fertig; **he left the ~ he heard the news** sofort, als er die Nachricht hörte, ist er gegangen; **at that very ~ he appeared** genau in dem Augenblick tauchte er auf.

instantaneous [ˌɪnstənˈteɪnɪəs] adj unmittelbar. **death was ~** der Tod trat sofort or unmittelbar ein; **the reaction was almost ~** die Reaktion erfolgte fast sofort.

instantaneously [ˌɪnstənˈteɪnɪəslɪ] adv sofort, unverzüglich.

instanter [ɪnˈstæntəʳ] adv stante pede, stehenden Fußes (geh).

instantly [ˈɪnstəntlɪ] adv sofort.

instead [ɪnˈsted] **1** prep **~ of** statt (+gen or (inf) +dat), anstelle von. **~ of going to school** (an)statt zur Schule zu gehen; **~ of that** statt dessen; **his brother came ~ of him** sein Bruder kam an seiner Stelle or statt ihm (inf); **he accidentally hit Jim ~ of John** er traf aus Versehen Jim (an)statt John; **this is ~ of a Christmas present** das ist anstelle eines Weihnachtsgeschenks.

2 adv statt dessen, dafür. **if he doesn't want to go, I'll go ~** wenn er nicht gehen will, gehe ich statt dessen; **if he doesn't come here, I shall go there ~** wenn er nicht herkommt, gehe ich statt dessen hin; **I didn't go home, I went to the pictures ~** ich bin nicht nach Hause gegangen, sondern statt dessen ins Kino.

instep [ˈɪnstep] n (a) (Anat) Spann, Rist m. **to have high ~s** einen hohen Rist haben. **(b)** (of shoe) Blatt nt.

instigate [ˈɪnstɪgeɪt] vt anstiften; rebellion, strike also anzetteln; new idea, reform etc initiieren.

instigation [ˌɪnstɪˈgeɪʃən] n see vt Anstiftung f; Anzettelung f; Initiierung f. **at sb's ~** auf jds Betreiben or Veranlassung f.

instigator [ˈɪnstɪgeɪtəʳ] n (of crime etc) Anstifter(in f) m; (of *new idea, reform etc*) Initiator(in f) m.

instil [ɪnˈstɪl] vt einflößen, einprägen (*into sb* jdm); *knowledge, attitudes* beibringen (*into sb* jdm).

instinct [ˈɪnstɪŋkt] **1** n Instinkt m. **the sex/survival ~** der Geschlechtstrieb/Überlebenstrieb; **by** or **from ~** instinktiv; **to have an ~ for business, to have a good business ~** einen ausgeprägten Geschäftssinn or -instinkt haben.
2 [ɪnˈstɪŋkt] adj (*liter*) **~ with** erfüllt von.

instinctive [ɪnˈstɪŋktɪv] adj instinktiv; *behaviour also* Instinkt-, instinktgesteuert.

instinctively [ɪnˈstɪŋktɪvlɪ] adv instinktiv.

institute [ˈɪnstɪtjuːt] **1** vt **(a)** *new laws, custom, reforms* einführen; (*found*) *organization etc* einrichten; *search* einleiten. **a newly ~d post** eine neu eingerichtete Stelle.
(b) (*Jur*) *enquiry* einleiten; *an action* einleiten (*against sb* gegen jdn); *proceedings* anstrengen (*against* gegen). **to ~ divorce proceedings** die Scheidung einreichen.
2 n Institut nt; (*home*) Anstalt f. **I~ of Technology/Education** technische Hochschule/pädagogische Hochschule; **educational ~** pädagogische Einrichtung; **women's ~** Frauenverein m.

institution [ˌɪnstɪˈtjuːʃən] n *see vt* **(a)** Einführung f; Einrichtung f; Einleitung f.
(b) Einleitung f; Anstrengung f; Einreichung f.
(c) (*organization*) Institution, Einrichtung f.
(d) (*building, home etc*) Anstalt f.
(e) (*custom*) Institution f. **he's been here so long he's become an ~** er ist schon so lange hier, daß er zur Institution geworden ist.

institutional [ˌɪnstɪˈtjuːʃənl] adj **(a)** *life etc* Anstalts-. **~ care** in hospital/an old folk's home stationäre Versorgung or Pflege im Krankenhaus/in einem Altenheim. **(b)** (*US*) **~ advertising** Prestigewerbung f.

institutionalize [ˌɪnstɪˈtjuːʃənəlaɪz] vt (*all senses*) institutionalisieren.

instruct [ɪnˈstrʌkt] vt **(a)** (*teach*) *person* unterrichten. **to ~ sb in the use of a machine** jdn in der Handhabung einer Maschine unterweisen.
(b) (*tell, direct*) *person* anweisen; (*command*) die Anweisung erteilen (+*dat*); (*Brit Jur*) *solicitor* (*give information to*) unterrichten, instruieren; (*appoint*) *lawyer* beauftragen; *jury* instruieren, belehren. **I've been ~ed to report to you ich habe** (An)weisung, Ihnen Meldung zu erstatten; **what were you ~ed to do?** welche Instruktionen or Anweisungen haben Sie bekommen?
(c) (*form: inform*) in Kenntnis setzen.

instruction [ɪnˈstrʌkʃən] n **(a)** (*teaching*) Unterricht m. **course of ~** Lehrgang m; **to give sb ~ in fencing** jdm Fechtunterricht erteilen.
(b) (*order, command*) Anweisung, Instruktion f; (*of jury*) Belehrung, Instruktion f; (*for computers*) Befehl m. **what were your ~s?** welche Instruktionen or Anweisungen hatten Sie?; **on whose ~s did you do that?** auf wessen Anweisung or Anordnung haben Sie das getan?; **~s for use** Gebrauchsanweisung, Gebrauchsanleitung f; **~ book** (*Tech*) Bedienungsanleitung f.

instructive [ɪnˈstrʌktɪv] adj instruktiv, aufschlußreich; (*of educational value*) lehrreich.

instructor [ɪnˈstrʌktə^r] n (*also Sport*) Lehrer m; (*US*) Dozent m; (*Mil*) Ausbilder m.

instructress [ɪnˈstrʌktrɪs] n (*also Sport*) Lehrerin f; (*US*) Dozentin f; (*Mil*) Ausbilderin f.

instrument [ˈɪnstrʊmənt] **1** n **(a)** (*Mus, Med, Tech*) Instrument nt; (*domestic*) Gerät nt. **to fly an aircraft by** or **on ~s** ein Flugzeug nach den (Bord)instrumenten fliegen.
(b) (*person*) Werkzeug nt.
(c) (*Jur*) Urkunde f, Dokument nt.
2 [ˈɪnstrʊment] vt **(a)** (*Mus*) instrumentieren.
(b) (*put into effect*) durch- or ausführen.

instrumental [ˌɪnstrʊˈmentl] **1** adj **(a)** **he was ~ in getting her the job** er hat ihr zu dieser Stelle verholfen; **he was ~ in bringing about the downfall of the government** er war am Sturz der Regierung beteiligt.
(b) (*Mus*) *music, accompaniment* Instrumental-. **~ performer** Instrumentalist(in f) m.
2 n (*Mus*) Instrumentalstück nt.

instrumentalist [ˌɪnstrʊˈmentəlɪst] n Instrumentalist(in f) m.

instrumentality [ˌɪnstrʊmenˈtælɪtɪ] n **through** or **by the ~ of sb** durch jds Vermittlung or Eingreifen.

instrumentation [ˌɪnstrʊmenˈteɪʃən] n Instrumentation f.

instrument in *cpds* (*Aviat*) Instrumenten-; **~ panel** n (*Aviat, Aut*) Armaturenbrett nt.

insubordinate [ˌɪnsəˈbɔːdənɪt] adj aufsässig, widersetzlich.

insubordination [ˌɪnsəbɔːdɪˈneɪʃən] n Aufsässigkeit f, Widersetzlichkeit f; (*Mil*) Gehorsamsverweigerung, Insubordination f (*dated*) f.

insubstantial [ˌɪnsəbˈstænʃəl] adj wenig substantiell; *fear, hopes, accusation also* gegenstandslos; *dreams* immateriell; *ghost* nicht körperhaft or wesenhaft; *amount* gering(fügig); *meal, plot also* dürftig.

insufferable adj, **~bly** adv [ɪnˈsʌfərəbl, -ɪ] unerträglich.

insufficiency [ˌɪnsəˈfɪʃənsɪ] n (*of supplies*) Knappheit f, unzureichende Menge; (*of sb's work*) Unzulänglichkeit f.

insufficient [ˌɪnsəˈfɪʃnt] adj nicht genügend, ungenügend *pred*; *work, insulation also* unzulänglich.

insufficiently [ˌɪnsəˈfɪʃntlɪ] adv ungenügend, unzulänglich.

insular [ˈɪnsjʊlə^r] adj **(a)** (*narrow*) engstirnig. **(b)** *administration, climate* Insel-, insular.

insularity [ˌɪnsjʊˈlærɪtɪ] n *see adj* **(a)** Engstirnigkeit f. **(b)** insulare Lage, Insellage, Insularität f.

insulate [ˈɪnsjʊleɪt] vt **(a)** *room*, (*Elec*) isolieren. **in this anorak you're well ~d against the cold** in diesem Anorak sind Sie gut gegen Kälte geschützt; **~d pliers** Isolierzange f. **(b)** (*fig: from unpleasantness etc*) abschirmen (*from* gegen).

insulating [ˈɪnsjʊleɪtɪŋ]: **~ material** n Isoliermaterial nt; **~ tape** n Isolierband nt.

insulation [ˌɪnsjʊˈleɪʃən] n **(a)** Isolation f; (*material also*) Isoliermaterial nt. **(b)** (*fig*) Geschütztheit f (*from* gegen).

insulator [ˈɪnsjʊleɪtə^r] n (*Elec: device*) Isolator m; (*material also*) Isolierstoff m; (*for heat*) Wärmeschutzisolierung f.

insulin [ˈɪnsjʊlɪn] n Insulin nt.

insult [ɪnˈsʌlt] **1** vt beleidigen; (*by words also*) beschimpfen.
2 [ˈɪnsʌlt] n Beleidigung f; (*with words also*) Beschimpfung f. **an ~ to the profession** eine Beleidigung für den ganzen Berufsstand; **an ~ to common sense/my intelligence** eine Beleidigung des gesunden Menschenverstands/meiner Intelligenz; **that's not a salary, it's an ~!** das ist doch kein Gehalt, das ist blanker Hohn or eine Beleidigung; **to add ~ to injury** das Ganze noch schlimmer machen.

insulting [ɪnˈsʌltɪŋ] adj beleidigend; *question* unverschämt. **to use ~ language to sb** jdm gegenüber beleidigende Äußerungen machen, jdn beschimpfen; **he was very ~ to her** er hat sich ihr gegenüber sehr beleidigend geäußert.

insultingly [ɪnˈsʌltɪŋlɪ] adv beleidigend; *behave* in beleidigender or unverschämter Weise.

insuperable [ɪnˈsuːpərəbl] adj unüberwindlich.

insuperably [ɪnˈsuːpərəblɪ] adv **it was ~ difficult** es hat unüberwindliche Schwierigkeiten bereitet.

insupportable [ˌɪnsəˈpɔːtəbl] adj unerträglich.

insurable [ɪnˈʃʊərəbl] adj versicherbar.

insurance [ɪnˈʃʊərəns] n Versicherung f; (*amount paid out*) Versicherungssumme f or -betrag m. **to take out ~** eine Versicherung abschließen (*against* gegen); **he got £100 ~ when his car was damaged** er bekam £ 100 von der Versicherung, als sein Auto beschädigt wurde.

insurance: **~ agent** n Versicherungsvertreter(in f) m; **~ broker** n Versicherungsmakler m; **~ company** n Versicherungsgesellschaft f; **~ office** n Versicherungsanstalt f/ **-büro** nt; **~ policy** n Versicherungspolice f; (*fig*) Sicherheitsvorkehrung f; **to take out an ~ policy** eine Versicherung abschließen; (*fig*) Sicherheitsvorkehrungen treffen; **as an ~ policy** (*fig*) für alle Fälle, sicherheitshalber; **~ scheme** n Versicherung(smöglichkeit) f; **~ stamp** n (*Brit*) Versicherungsmarke f.

insure [ɪnˈʃʊə^r] vt *car, house* versichern (lassen). **to ~ oneself** or **one's life** eine Lebensversicherung abschließen; **to ~ oneself against poverty/failure etc** (*fig*) sich gegen Armut/einen Fehlschlag etc (ab)sichern.

insured [ɪnˈʃʊəd] **1** adj versichert. **2** n **the ~** (*party*) der/die Versicherungsnehmer(in), der/die Versicherte.

insurer [ɪnˈʃʊərə^r] n Versicherer, Versicherungsgeber m.

insurgent [ɪnˈsɜːdʒənt] **1** adj aufständisch. **2** n Aufständische(r) mf.

insurmountable [ˌɪnsəˈmaʊntəbl] adj unüberwindlich.

insurrection [ˌɪnsəˈrekʃən] n Aufstand m.

insurrectionary [ˌɪnsəˈrekʃənərɪ] **1** adj aufständisch. **2** n Aufständische(r) mf.

insurrectionist [ˌɪnsəˈrekʃənɪst] n Aufständische(r) mf.

intact [ɪnˈtækt] adj (*not damaged*) unversehrt, intakt; (*whole, in one piece*) intakt. **not one window was left ~** kein einziges Fenster blieb ganz or heil; **not many manuscripts emerge from the censor's office ~** nicht viele Manuskripte kommen von der Zensur unverändert zurück; **his confidence remained ~** sein Vertrauen blieb ungebrochen or unerschüttert.

intake [ˈɪnteɪk] n **(a)** (*act*) (*of water, electric current*) Aufnahme f; (*of steam*) Ansaugen nt; (*amount*) (*of water, electricity*) Aufnahme f, aufgenommene Menge; (*of steam*) angesaugte or einströmende Menge; (*pipe*) (*for water*) Zuflußrohr, Einführungsrohr nt; (*for steam*) Einströmungsrohr nt, Ansaugöffnung f, Einführungsrohr nt. **air ~** Luftzufuhr f; **food ~** Nahrungsaufnahme f.
(b) (*Sch*) Aufnahme f; (*Mil*) Rekrutierung f. **what is your yearly ~?** (*Sch*) wie viele neue Schüler nehmen Sie im Jahr auf?; (*Mil*) wie viele Männer rekrutieren Sie im Jahr?

intake: **~ class** n (*Sch*) Anfängerklasse f; **~ valve** n Ansaug-/ Einlaß-/Einströmventil nt.

intangible [ɪnˈtændʒəbl] adj **(a)** nicht greifbar. **(b)** *fears, longings* unbestimmbar. **(c)** (*Jur, Comm*) **~ property** unkörperliche (*spec*) or immaterielle Güter *pl*; **~ assets** immaterielle Werte *pl*.

integer [ˈɪntɪdʒə^r] n ganze Zahl.

integral [ˈɪntɪɡrəl] **1** adj **(a)** *part* wesentlich, integral (*geh*). **(b)** (*whole*) vollständig, vollkommen. **(c)** (*Math*) **calculus** Integral-. **2** n (*Math*) Integral nt.

integrate [ˈɪntɪɡreɪt] **1** vt (*all senses*) integrieren. **to ~ sth into sth** etw in etw (*acc*) integrieren; **to ~ sth with etw** auf etw (*acc*) abstimmen; **to ~ a school/college** (*US*) eine Schule/ein College auch für Schwarze etc zugänglich machen. **2** vi (*US: schools etc*) auch für Schwarze etc zugänglich werden.

integrated [ˈɪntɪɡreɪtɪd] adj *plan* einheitlich; *piece of work* einheitlich, ein organisches Ganzes bildend; *school, town* ohne Rassentrennung. **to become ~ into a group** in eine Gruppe integriert or eingegliedert werden; **a fully ~ personality** eine in sich ausgewogene Persönlichkeit; **~ circuit** integrierter Schaltkreis.

integration [ˌɪntɪˈɡreɪʃən] n (*all senses*) Integration f (*into* in +*acc*). (*racial*) **~** Rassenintegration f.

integrationist [ˌɪntɪˈɡreɪʃənɪst] n (*US*) Vertreter(in f) m der Rassenintegration.

integrity [ɪnˈteɡrɪtɪ] n **(a)** (*honesty*) Integrität f. **(b)** (*wholeness*) Einheit f.

integument [ɪnˈteɡjʊmənt] n Integument nt (*spec*).

intellect [ˈɪntɪlekt] n **(a)** Intellekt m. **a man of such ~** ein Mann mit einem solchen Intellekt; **his powers of** ~ seine intellektuellen Fähigkeiten. **(b)** (person) großer Geist.

intellectual [ɪntɪˈlektjʊəl] **1** adj intellektuell; **interests** also geistig. **something a little more** ~ etwas geistig Anspruchsvolleres. **2** n Intellektuelle(r) mf.

intellectualism [ɪntɪˈlektjʊəlɪzəm] n Intellektualismus m.

intellectualize [ɪntɪˈlektjʊəlaɪz] vt intellektualisieren.

intellectually [ɪntɪˈlektjʊəlɪ] adv intellektuell. **he always approaches emotional problems much too** ~ er geht an Gefühlsprobleme immer viel zu verstandesmäßig heran.

intelligence [ɪnˈtelɪdʒəns] n **(a)** Intelligenz f. **hedgehogs don't have much** ~ Igel haben keine große Intelligenz; **a man of little** ~ ein Mensch von geringer Intelligenz; **if he hasn't got the** ~ **to wear a coat** wenn er nicht gescheit genug ist, einen Mantel anzuziehen.
(b) (news, information) Informationen pl. **according to our latest** ~ unseren letzten Meldungen or Informationen zufolge; **shipping** ~ Meldungen pl für die Schiffahrt; **enemy shipping** ~ Informationen pl über Feindschiffe.
(c) (Mil etc) Geheim- or Nachrichtendienst m.

intelligence: ~ **corps** n (Mil) Geheim- or Nachrichtendienst m; ~ **officer** n (Mil) Nachrichtenoffizier m; ~ **quotient** n Intelligenzquotient m; ~ **service** n (Pol) Geheim- or Nachrichtendienst m; ~ **test** n Intelligenztest m.

intelligent [ɪnˈtelɪdʒənt] adj intelligent, klug. **are there** ~ **beings on Mars?** gibt es auf dem Mars vernunftbegabte or intelligente Lebewesen?

intelligently [ɪnˈtelɪdʒəntlɪ] adv intelligent.

intelligentsia [ɪnˌtelɪˈdʒentsɪə] n Intelligenz, Intelligenzija f.

intelligibility [ɪnˌtelɪdʒəˈbɪlɪtɪ] n Verständlichkeit f; (of handwriting) Leserlichkeit f.

intelligible [ɪnˈtelɪdʒəbl] adj zu verstehen pred, verständlich; handwriting leserlich (to sb für jdn).

intelligibly [ɪnˈtelɪdʒəblɪ] adv deutlich.

intemperance [ɪnˈtempərəns] n (lack of moderation) Maßlosigkeit, Unmäßigkeit f; (drunkenness) Trunksucht f.

intemperate [ɪnˈtempərɪt] adj **(a)** person (lacking moderation) unmäßig, maßlos; (addicted to drink) trunksüchtig. **(b)** climate extrem; wind heftig; zeal, haste übermäßig.

intend [ɪnˈtend] vt **(a)** (+n) beabsichtigen, wollen. **I** ~ **him to go with me** ich beabsichtige or habe vor, ihn mitzunehmen; (insist) er soll mit mir mitkommen; **I** ~**ed no harm es war** (von mir) nicht böse gemeint; (with action) ich hatte nichts Böses beabsichtigt; **did you** ~ **that?** hatten Sie das beabsichtigt?, war das Ihre Absicht?; **I didn't** ~ **it as an insult** das sollte keine Beleidigung sein; **it was** ~**ed as a compliment** das sollte ein Kompliment sein; **I wondered what he** ~**ed by that remark** ich fragte mich, was er mit dieser Bemerkung beabsichtigte; **the meaning which he** ~**ed was not the same as that which came across** er meinte das nicht so, wie es aufgefaßt wurde; **he is** ~**ed for the diplomatic service** er soll einmal in den diplomatischen Dienst; **this park is** ~**ed for the general public** dieser Park ist für die Öffentlichkeit gedacht or bestimmt; **that remark was** ~**ed for you** diese Bemerkung war auf Sie gemünzt, mit dieser Bemerkung waren Sie gemeint; **this water is not** ~**ed for drinking** dieses Wasser ist nicht zum Trinken (gedacht); **games** ~**ed for young children** Spiele, die für kleine Kinder gedacht sind; **this film was never** ~**ed for children** dieser Film war nie für Kinder bestimmt or gedacht.
(b) (+vb) beabsichtigen, fest vorhaben. **he** ~**s to win** er hat fest vor, zu gewinnen; **I** ~ **to leave next year** ich beabsichtige or habe vor, nächstes Jahr zu gehen; **if you don't change your mind then you should know that I** ~ **to leave you!** laß dir gesagt sein, wenn du es dir nicht anders überlegst, mache ich ernst und verlasse dich; **what do you** ~ **to do about it?** was beabsichtigen Sie, dagegen zu tun?; **I fully** ~ **to punish him** ich habe fest vor or bin fest entschlossen, ihn zu bestrafen; **you are** ~**ed to help me** Sie sollen mir helfen; **did you** ~ **that to happen?** hatten Sie das beabsichtigt?

intended [ɪnˈtendɪd] **1** adj **(a)** effect beabsichtigt, geplant. **what is the** ~ **meaning of that remark?** was ist mit dieser Bemerkung gemeint? **(b)** husband, wife zukünftig, in spe pred. **2** n my ~ (inf) mein Zukünftiger (inf)/meine Zukünftige (inf).

intense [ɪnˈtens] adj **(a)** intensiv; joy, anxiety, disappointment äußerst groß. **(b)** person ernsthaft; study, life intensiv. **he suddenly looked very** ~ er sah plötzlich ganz ernst aus.

intensely [ɪnˈtenslɪ] adv cold, hot, disappointed, angry, difficult äußerst; study intensiv, ernsthaft. **he spoke so** ~ **that none could doubt his sincerity** er sprach mit einer solchen Intensität, daß niemand an seiner Aufrichtigkeit zweifeln konnte.

intenseness [ɪnˈtensnɪs] n see intensity.

intensification [ɪnˌtensɪfɪˈkeɪʃən] n Intensivierung f; (Phot) Verstärkung f.

intensifier [ɪnˈtensɪfaɪəʳ] n (Gram) Verstärkungspartikel f. **image** ~ (Phys) Bildverstärker m.

intensify [ɪnˈtensɪfaɪ] **1** vt intensivieren; meaning verstärken. **2** vi zunehmen; (pain, heat also) stärker werden; (fighting also) sich verschärfen.

intensity [ɪnˈtensɪtɪ] n Intensität f; (of feeling, storm also) Heftigkeit f. ~ **of a negative** (Phot) Dichte f eines Negativs.

intensive [ɪnˈtensɪv] adj intensiv, Intensiv-. **to be in** ~ **care** (Med) auf der Intensivstation sein; ~ **care unit** Intensiv(pflege)station f; **they came under** ~ **fire** sie kamen unter heftigen Beschuß.

intensively [ɪnˈtensɪvlɪ] adv intensiv.

intent [ɪnˈtent] **1** n Absicht f. **with good** ~ in guter Absicht; **to all** ~**s and purposes** im Grunde; **with** ~ **to** (esp Jur) in der Absicht or mit dem Vorsatz zu; **to do sth with** ~ etw vorsätzlich tun; see loiter.
2 adj **(a)** look durchdringend, forschend.
(b) to be ~ **on achieving sth** fest entschlossen sein, etw zu

erreichen; **he was so** ~ **on catching the bus that he didn't notice the lorry coming** er war so darauf bedacht, den Bus zu kriegen, daß er den Lastwagen nicht kommen sah; **to be** ~ **on one's work** auf seine Arbeit konzentriert sein.

intention [ɪnˈtenʃən] n **(a)** Absicht, Intention f. **what was your** ~ **in saying that?** mit welcher Absicht haben Sie das gesagt?; **it is my** ~ **to punish you severely** ich beabsichtige, Sie streng zu bestrafen; **I have every** ~ **of doing that** ich habe die feste Absicht, das zu tun; **to have no** ~ **of doing sth** nicht die Absicht haben, etw zu tun; **I have no or haven't the least or the slightest** ~ **of staying!** ich habe nicht die geringste Absicht hierzubleiben, ich denke nicht daran hierzubleiben; **with good** ~s mit guten Vorsätzen; **with the best of** ~s in der besten Absicht; **with the** ~ **of ...** in der Absicht zu ..., mit dem Vorsatz zu ...; **his** ~s are good, but he seldom carries them out er hat immer gute Vorsätze pl, aber er führt sie selten aus.
(b) ~s (inf) (Heirats)absichten pl; **his** ~s are honourable er hat ehrliche Absichten pl.

intentional [ɪnˈtenʃənl] adj absichtlich, vorsätzlich (esp Jur). **it wasn't** ~ das war keine Absicht, es war unabsichtlich.

intentionally [ɪnˈtenʃnəlɪ] adv absichtlich.

intently [ɪnˈtentlɪ] adv listen, gaze konzentriert.

inter [ɪnˈtɜːʳ] vt (form) bestatten.

inter- [ˈɪntəʳ] pref zwischen-, Zwischen-.

interact [ˌɪntərˈækt] vi aufeinander wirken; (Phys) wechselwirken; (Psychol, Sociol) interagieren.

interaction [ˌɪntərˈækʃən] n see vi gegenseitige Einwirkung, Wechselwirkung f (also Phys); Interaktion f.

interbreed [ˈɪntəˈbriːd] **1** vt kreuzen. **2** vi (crossbreed) sich kreuzen; (inbred) sich untereinander vermehren.

intercede [ˌɪntəˈsiːd] vi sich einsetzen, sich verwenden (with bei, for on behalf of für); (in argument) vermitteln.

intercellular [ˌɪntəˈseljʊləʳ] adj interzellular.

intercept [ˌɪntəˈsept] vt message, person, plane, pass abfangen; (Math) abschneiden. **they** ~**ed the enemy** sie schnitten dem Feind den Weg ab.

interception [ˌɪntəˈsepʃən] n see vt Abfangen nt; Sektion f. **point of** ~ (Math) Schnittpunkt m.

interceptor [ˌɪntəˈseptəʳ] n (Aviat) Abfangjäger m.

intercession [ˌɪntəˈseʃən] n Fürsprache f; (in argument) Vermittlung f.

intercessor [ˌɪntəˈsesəʳ] n Fürsprecher(in f) m; (in argument) Vermittler(in f) m.

interchange [ˈɪntəˈtʃeɪndʒ] **1** n **(a)** (of roads) Kreuzung f; (of motorways) (Autobahn)kreuz nt. **(b)** (exchange) Austausch m.
2 [ˌɪntəˈtʃeɪndʒ] vt **(a)** (switch round) (miteinander) vertauschen, (aus)tauschen. **(b)** ideas etc austauschen (with mit).

interchangeable [ˌɪntəˈtʃeɪndʒəbl] adj austauschbar. **the front wheels are** ~ **with the back ones** Vorder- und Hinterräder sind austauschbar.

interchangeably [ˌɪntəˈtʃeɪndʒəblɪ] adv austauschbar. **they are used** ~ sie können ausgetauscht werden.

inter-city [ˌɪntəˈsɪtɪ] adj Intercity-. ~ **train** Intercityzug m; **to go** ~ den Intercity nehmen.

intercollegiate [ˈɪntəkəˈliːdʒɪɪt] adj zwischen Colleges.

intercom [ˈɪntəkɒm] n (Gegen)sprechanlage f; (in ship, plane) Bordverständigungsanlage f; (in schools etc) Lautsprecheranlage f.

intercommunicate [ˌɪntəkəˈmjuːnɪkeɪt] vi (departments, people) miteinander in Verbindung stehen; (rooms) miteinander verbunden sein.

intercommunication [ˈɪntəkəˌmjuːnɪˈkeɪʃən] n gegenseitige Verbindung, Verbindung f untereinander.

intercommunion [ˌɪntəkəˈmjuːnɪən] n Beziehungen pl.

interconnect [ˌɪntəkəˈnekt] **1** vt miteinander verbinden; parts schlüssig verbinden; loudspeakers, circuits also zusammenschalten. ~**ed facts/results/events** etc zueinander in Beziehung stehende Tatsachen pl/Ergebnisse pl/Ereignisse pl etc; **are these events** ~**ed in any way?** besteht irgendein Zusammenhang zwischen diesen Vorfällen?
2 vi (parts) sich schlüssig verbinden; (rooms) miteinander verbunden sein; (facts, events) in Zusammenhang stehen. ~**ing rooms** miteinander verbundene Zimmer pl.

interconnection [ˌɪntəkəˈnekʃən] n Verbindung f; (of parts) schlüssige Verbindung; (of circuits etc) Zusammenschaltung f; (of facts, events etc) Verbindung f, Zusammenhang m.

intercontinental [ˈɪntəˌkɒntɪˈnentl] adj interkontinental, Interkontinental-.

intercourse [ˈɪntəkɔːs] n **(a)** Verkehr m. **commercial** ~ Handelsbeziehungen pl; **human/social** ~ Verkehr m mit Menschen/gesellschaftlicher Verkehr; **he maintains that he has direct** ~ **with the Deity** er behauptet, er habe direkte Beziehungen zu der Gottheit.
(b) (sexual) ~ (Geschlechts)verkehr m; **did** ~ **take place?** hat (Geschlechts)verkehr or Beischlaf stattgefunden?

interdenominational [ˈɪntədɪˌnɒmɪˈneɪʃənl] adj interkonfessionell.

interdepartmental [ˈɪntədiːpɑːtˈmentl] adj relations, quarrel zwischen den Abteilungen; conference, projects mehrere Abteilungen betreffend.

interdependence [ˌɪntədɪˈpendəns] n wechselseitige Abhängigkeit, Interdependenz f (geh).

interdependent [ˌɪntədɪˈpendənt] adj wechselseitig voneinander abhängig, interdependent (geh).

interdict [ˈɪntədɪkt] **1** vt **(a)** (Jur) untersagen, verbieten. **(b)** (Eccl) person, place mit dem Interdikt belegen; priest suspendieren. **2** n **(a)** (Jur) Verbot nt. **(b)** (Eccl) Interdikt nt.

interdiction [ˌɪntəˈdɪkʃən] n (Jur) Verbot nt, Untersagung f; (Eccl) Interdikt nt.

interest [ˈɪntrɪst] **1** n **(a)** Interesse nt. **do you have any** ~ **in chess?** interessieren Sie sich für Schach?, haben Sie Interesse an Schach (dat)?; **to take/feel an ~ in** sb/sth sich für jdn/etw interessieren; **to take a sympathetic ~ in** sth an etw (dat) Anteil nehmen; **after that he took no further ~ in** us/it danach war er nicht mehr an uns (dat)/daran interessiert; **to show an ~ in** sb/sth Interesse für jdn/etw zeigen; **is it of any ~ to you?** (do you want it) sind Sie daran interessiert?; **just for ~** nur aus Interesse, nur interessehalber; **he has lost ~** er hat das Interesse verloren; **what are your ~s?** was sind Ihre Interessen(gebiete)?; **his ~s are ...** er interessiert sich für...

(b) (importance) Interesse nt (to für). **matters of vital ~ to the economy** Dinge pl von lebenswichtiger Bedeutung or lebenswichtigem Interesse für die Wirtschaft; **questions of public ~** Fragen pl von öffentlichem Interesse.

(c) (advantage, welfare) Interesse nt. **to act in sb's/one's own ~(s)** in jds/im eigenen Interesse handeln; **in the ~(s) of** sb/sth in jds Interesse (dat)/im Interesse einer Sache (gen); **the public ~** das öffentliche Wohl; **in the public ~** im öffentlichen Interesse.

(d) (Fin) Zinsen pl. **~ on an investment** Zinsen aus einer Kapitalanlage; **rate of ~, ~ rate** Zinssatz m; **to bear ~ at 4%** 4% Zinsen tragen, mit 4% verzinst sein; **loan with ~** verzinstes Darlehen; **to repay a loan with ~** ein Darlehen mit Zins und Zinseszins zurückzahlen; **to return sb's kindness with ~** (fig) jds Freundlichkeit vielfach erwidern; **I'll pay him back with ~** (fig) ich werde es ihm mit Zinsen heimzahlen.

(e) (Comm) (share, stake) Anteil m; (~ group) Kreise pl, Interessentengruppe f. **shipping/oil ~s** (shares) Reederei-/Ölanteile pl; (people) Reeder, Reedereikreise pl/Vertreter pl von Ölinteressen; **the landed ~(s)** die Landbesitzer pl, die Gutsbesitzer pl; **he has a financial ~ in the company** er ist finanziell an der Firma beteiligt; **British trading ~s** britische Handelsinteressen pl; **German ~s in Africa** deutsche Interessen pl in Afrika.

2 vt interessieren (in für, an +dat). **to ~ sb in doing sth** jdn dafür or daran interessieren, etw zu tun; **can I ~ you in a little drink?** kann ich Sie zu etwas Alkoholischem überreden?; **to ~ a pupil in maths** das Interesse eines Schülers an or für Mathematik wecken, einen Schüler für Mathematik interessieren; **to ~ oneself in** sb/sth sich für jdn/etw interessieren.

interested ['ɪntrɪstɪd] adj (a) interessiert (in an +dat). **I'm not ~** ich habe kein Interesse (daran), ich bin nicht (daran) interessiert; **... and I'm not ~ either ...** und es interessiert mich auch gar nicht; **to be ~ in** sb/sth sich für jdn/etw interessieren, an jdm/etw interessiert sein; **would you be ~ in a game of cards?** hätten Sie Interesse, Karten zu spielen?; **I'm going to the cinema, are you ~?** (in coming)? ich gehe ins Kino, haben Sie Interesse daran or Lust mitzukommen?; **I'm selling my car, are you ~?** ich verkaufe meinen Wagen, sind Sie interessiert?; **the company is ~ in expanding its sales force** die Firma hat Interesse daran or ist daran interessiert, ihren Absatz zu vergrößern; **I'd be ~ to know how ...** es würde mich ja schon interessieren, wie ...; **she was ~ to see what he would do** sie war gespannt, was er wohl tun würde; **I was ~ to hear that** es interessierte mich, das zu hören.

(b) (having personal or financial interest) befangen; (involved) beteiligt. **he is an ~ party** er ist befangen/daran beteiligt.

interesting ['ɪntrɪstɪŋ] adj interessant. **she's in an ~ condition** (euph) sie ist in anderen Umständen.

interestingly ['ɪntrɪstɪŋlɪ] adv see adj. **~ enough, I saw him yesterday** interessanterweise habe ich ihn gestern gesehen.

interface ['ɪntəfeɪs] 1 n Grenzfläche, Grenzschicht f; (Computers) Anpaßschaltung f, Interface nt. **there's a bigger ~ between these two fields than I thought** diese beiden Gebiete berühren sich in mehr Punkten or haben mehr Berührungspunkte, als ich gedacht hätte; **the man/machine ~ in society** die Interaktion von Mensch und Maschine in der Gesellschaft.

2 [ɪntəˈfeɪs] vt koppeln.

interfacing [ɪntəˈfeɪsɪŋ] n (Sew) Einlage f.

interfere [ɪntəˈfɪəʳ] vi (a) (meddle) (in argument, sb's affairs) sich einmischen (in in +acc); (with machinery, sb's property) sich zu schaffen machen (with an +dat); (euph: sexually) sich vergehen (with an +dat). **don't ~ with the machine** laß die Finger von der Maschine; **who's been interfering with my books?** wer war an meinen Büchern?; **the body has been ~d with** jemand hatte sich an der Leiche zu schaffen gemacht; (sexually) die Leiche zeigte Spuren eines Sittlichkeitsverbrechens.

(b) (thing, event: disrupt, obstruct) **to ~ with** etw stören (also Rad); **to ~ with sb's plans** jds Pläne durchkreuzen.

interference [ɪntəˈfɪərəns] n (a) (meddling) Einmischung f. **I don't want any ~ with my books/papers** ich will nicht, daß jemand an meine Bücher/Papiere geht. (b) (disruption, Rad, TV) Störung f (with gen).

interfering [ɪntəˈfɪərɪŋ] adj person sich ständig einmischend. **his ~ ways annoy me** es ärgert or stört mich, wie er sich immer einmischt; **don't be so ~** misch dich nicht immer ein.

intergalactic [ɪntəgəˈlæktɪk] adj intergalaktisch.

interim ['ɪntərɪm] 1 n Zwischenzeit f, Interim nt (geh). **in the ~** in der Zwischenzeit. 2 adj vorläufig; agreement, arrangements, solution also Übergangs-, Interims- (geh); report, payment Zwischen-; government Übergangs-, Interims- (geh). **~ dividend** (Fin) Abschlagsdividende f.

interior [ɪnˈtɪərɪəʳ] 1 adj (inside) Innen-; (inland) Binnen-; (domestic) Inlands-, Binnen-.

2 n (of country) Innere(s) nt; (Art) Interieur nt; (of house) Innenausstattung f, Interieur nt (geh); (Phot) Innenaufnahme f. **deep in the ~** tief im Landesinneren; **deep in the ~ of Africa** etc tief im Inneren or Herzen Afrikas etc; **Department of the I~** (US) Innenministerium nt; **the ~ of the house has been**

newly decorated das Haus ist innen neu gemacht.

interior: **~ angle** n Innenwinkel m; **~ decoration** n Innenausstattung f; (decor also) Interieur nt; **~ decorator** n Innenausstatter(in f) m; (decor also) Interieur nt; **~ design** n Innenarchitektur f; **~ designer** n Innenarchitekt(in f) m; **~ monologue** n innerer Monolog; **~-sprung** adj mattress Federkern-.

interject [ɪntəˈdʒekt] vt remark, question einwerfen. ..., he **~ed** ..., rief er dazwischen.

interjection [ɪntəˈdʒekʃən] n (exclamation) Ausruf m; (Ling also) Interjektion f; (remark) Einwurf m.

interlace [ɪntəˈleɪs] 1 vt threads etc verflechten; (in cloth also) verweben; cloth (with thread) durchwirken; fingers verschlingen; (fig) scenes, styles verflechten. 2 vi sich ineinander verflechten; (twigs) verschlungen sein.

interlacing [ɪntəˈleɪsɪŋ] 1 adj verflochten; branches also verschlungen. 2 n Flechtwerk nt.

interlard [ɪntəˈlɑːd] vt **to ~ a speech with facetious comments** witzige Kommentare in eine Rede einflechten; **a speech ~ed with jokes** eine mit Witzen gespickte Rede.

interleave [ɪntəˈliːv] vt (mit Zwischenblättern) durchschießen.

inter-library loan [ɪntəˈlaɪbrərɪˈləʊn] n Fernleihe f. **to have a book on ~** ein Buch über die Fernleihe (ausgeliehen) haben.

interline [ɪntəˈlaɪn] vt (a) (Typ) corrections, translation interlinear einfügen. (b) (Sew) mit einer Einlage versehen.

interlinear [ɪntəˈlɪnɪəʳ] adj Interlinear-, interlinear.

interlink [ɪntəˈlɪŋk] 1 vt ineinanderhängen; (fig) theories etc miteinander verknüpfen or verbinden. 2 vi ineinanderhängen; (fig: theories etc) zusammenhängen.

interlock [ɪntəˈlɒk] 1 vt (fest) zusammen- or ineinanderstecken. 2 vi ineinandergreifen; (one piece) fest stecken or sitzen (with in +dat); (antlers, chariot wheels etc) sich verfangen; (antlers) sich verhaken; (fig: destinies) verkettet sein.

interlocutor [ɪntəˈlɒkjʊtəʳ] n Gesprächspartner(in f) m; (asking questions) Fragesteller(in f) m.

interloper ['ɪntələʊpəʳ] n Eindringling m.

interlude ['ɪntəluːd] n Periode f; (Theat) (interval) Pause f; (performance) Zwischenspiel nt; (Mus) Interludium nt; (episode) Intermezzo nt, Episode f. **a brief ~ of peace** eine kurze Zeit or Periode des Friedens. **a peaceful ~ in his busy life** eine friedliche Unterbrechung seines geschäftigen Lebens.

intermarriage [ɪntəˈmærɪdʒ] n (between groups) Mischehen pl; (within the group) Heirat f untereinander.

intermarry [ɪntəˈmærɪ] vi (marry within the group) untereinander heiraten; (two groups: marry with each other) sich durch Heirat vermischen, Mischehen eingehen.

intermediary [ɪntəˈmiːdɪərɪ] 1 n (Ver)mittler(in f) m, Mittelsperson f, Mittelsmann m. 2 adj (intermediate) Zwischen-; (mediating) Vermittlungs-, vermittelnd.

intermediate [ɪntəˈmiːdɪət] adj Zwischen-; French, maths etc für fortgeschrittene Anfänger. **an ~ student** ein fortgeschrittener Anfänger; **A is ~ in size between B and C** A liegt größenmäßig or in der Größe zwischen B und C; **~-range missile** Mittelstreckenrakete f.

interment [ɪnˈtɜːmənt] n Beerdigung, Bestattung f.

intermezzo [ɪntəˈmetsəʊ] n Intermezzo nt.

interminable [ɪnˈtɜːmɪnəbl] adj endlos. **after what seemed an ~ journey** nach einer Reise, die nicht enden zu wollen schien.

interminably [ɪnˈtɜːmɪnəblɪ] adv endlos, ewig.

intermingle [ɪntəˈmɪŋgl] 1 vt vermischen. 2 vi sich mischen (with unter +acc). **people from many countries ~d at the conference** Menschen aus vielen Ländern bekamen bei der Konferenz Kontakt miteinander.

intermission [ɪntəˈmɪʃən] n (a) Unterbrechung, Pause f. (b) (Theat, Film) Pause f.

intermittent [ɪntəˈmɪtənt] adj periodisch auftretend; (Tech) intermittierend. **~ fever** Wechselfieber nt.

intermittently [ɪntəˈmɪtəntlɪ] adv periodisch; (Tech) intermittierend.

intermix [ɪntəˈmɪks] 1 vt vermischen. 2 vi sich vermischen.

intern[1] [ɪnˈtɜːn] vt person internieren; ship etc festhalten.

intern[2] ['ɪntɜːn] (US) 1 n Medizinalassistent(in f) m. 2 vi das Medizinalpraktikum absolvieren.

internal [ɪnˈtɜːnl] adj (inner) innere(r, s); (Math) angle, diameter Innen-; (within country also) trade etc Binnen-, im Inland, landesintern; (within organization) policy, mail examination, examiner intern; (within organization) telephone Haus-. **~ combustion engine** Verbrennungsmotor m; **~ evidence** (Liter) inhärenter Beweis (geh); **~ medicine** Innere Medizin; **~ rhyme** Binnenreim m; **I~ Revenue Service** (US) Steueramt, Finanzamt nt; **~ affairs** innere Angelegenheiten pl, Inneres nt.

internalize [ɪnˈtɜːnəlaɪz] vt verinnerlichen, internalisieren (spec).

internally [ɪnˈtɜːnəlɪ] adv innen, im Inneren; (in body) innerlich; (in country) landesintern; (in organization) intern. **he is bleeding ~** er hat innere Blutungen pl; **"not to be taken ~"** „nicht zur internen Anwendung", „nicht zum Einnehmen".

international [ɪntəˈnæʃnəl] 1 adj international. **~ law** Völkerrecht nt, internationales Recht; **~ reply coupon** internationaler Antwortschein; **~ date line** Datumsgrenze f; **I~ Monetary Fund** Internationaler Währungsfonds; **~ money order** Auslandsanweisung f.

2 n (a) (Sport) (match) Länderspiel nt; (player) Nationalspieler(in f) m.

(b) (Pol) I~ Internationale f.

Internationale [ɪntəˌnæʃəˈnɑːl] n Internationale f.

internationalism [ɪntəˈnæʃnəlɪzm] n Internationalismus m.

internationalist [ɪntəˈnæʃnəlɪst] n Internationalist(in f) m.

internationalize [ɪntəˈnæʃnəlaɪz] vt internationalisieren.

internationally [ɪntəˈnæʃnəlɪ] adv international.

interne n, vi see **intern**[2].

internecine [ɪntəˈniːsaɪn] adj (mutually destructive) für beide

Seiten verlustreich; (*bloody*) mörderisch. ~ war gegenseitiger Vernichtungskrieg; ~ strife innere Zerrissenheit.

internee [ˌɪntɜːˈniː] n Internierte(r) mf.

internist [ɪnˈtɜːnɪst] n (US) Internist(in f) m.

internment [ɪnˈtɜːnmənt] n Internierung f. ~ camp Internierungslager nt.

internship [ˈɪntɜːnʃɪp] n (US) Medizinalpraktikum nt.

internuncio [ˌɪntəˈnʌnsɪəʊ] n Internuntius m.

interplanetary [ˌɪntəˈplænɪtərɪ] adj interplanetar.

interplay [ˈɪntəpleɪ] n Zusammenspiel nt.

Interpol [ˈɪntəpɒl] n Interpol f.

interpolate [ɪnˈtɜːpəleɪt] vt remark einwerfen; matter into book etc interpolieren, einfügen; (Math) interpolieren.

interpolation [ɪnˌtɜːpəˈleɪʃən] n (of remark) Einwerfen nt; (remark made) Einwurf m; (in text) Interpolation, Einfügung f; (Math) Interpolation f.

interpose [ˌɪntəˈpəʊz] 1 vt (a) object dazwischenbringen or -stellen/-legen. to ~ sth between two things etw zwischen zwei Dinge bringen or stellen/legen; to be ~d between two things zwischen zwei Dingen stehen/liegen; to ~ oneself between two people sich zwischen zwei Leute stellen.
(b) (interject) remark, question einwerfen; objection vorbringen (into in +dat).
2 vi (intervene) eingreifen.

interpret [ɪnˈtɜːprɪt] 1 vt (a) (translate orally) dolmetschen.
(b) (explain, understand) auslegen, interpretieren, omen, dream deuten; (Theat, Mus) interpretieren. how would you ~ what he said? wie würden Sie seine Worte verstehen or auffassen? 2 vi dolmetschen.

interpretation [ɪnˌtɜːprɪˈteɪʃən] n see vt (b) Auslegung, Interpretation f; Deutung f; Interpretation f. what ~ do they put on his speech? wie legen sie seine Rede aus?, wie interpretieren sie seine Rede?; the speech can be given several ~s die Rede kann verschieden ausgelegt or interpretiert werden; an ~ of a poem eine Gedichtinterpretation.

interpretative [ɪnˈtɜːprɪtətɪv] adj interpretierend.

interpreter [ɪnˈtɜːprɪtəʳ] n Dolmetscher(in f) m; (Theat, Mus) Interpret(in f) m; (of dreams) Traumdeuter(in f) m.

interpretive [ɪnˈtɜːprɪtɪv] adj see interpretative.

interracial [ˌɪntəˈreɪʃəl] adj (between races) zwischen den or verschiedenen Rassen; (multiracial) gemischtrassig. ~ tensions Rassenspannungen pl.

interregnum [ˌɪntəˈregnəm] n, pl -s or interregna [ˌɪntəˈregnə] Interregnum nt.

interrelate [ˌɪntərɪˈleɪt] vt two things zueinander in Beziehung bringen, eine Beziehung herstellen zwischen (+dat). to ~ one thing with another eine Sache in Beziehung zu einer anderen bringen; to be ~d zueinander in Beziehung stehen, zusammenhängen; ~d facts zusammenhängende Tatsachen pl.

interrelation [ˌɪntərɪˈleɪʃən] n Beziehung f (between zwischen +dat).

interrogate [ɪnˈterəgeɪt] vt (police) verhören; (father, headmaster etc) regelrecht verhören.

interrogation [ɪnˌterəˈgeɪʃən] n Verhör nt. why should I submit to your ~? warum soll ich mich von dir verhören lassen?; ~ room Vernehmungsraum m or -zimmer nt.

interrogative [ˌɪntəˈrɒgətɪv] 1 adj look, tone fragend; (Gram) Frage-, Interrogativ-. ~ mood Interrogativ m. 2 n (Gram) (pronoun) Interrogativpronomen, Fragefürwort nt; (mood) Interrogativ m.

interrogatively [ˌɪntəˈrɒgətɪvlɪ] adv fragend; (Gram also) interrogativ.

interrogator [ɪnˈterəgeɪtəʳ] n Vernehmungsbeamte(r) mf (form). my/his ~s die, die mich/ihn verhörten/verhören.

interrogatory [ˌɪntəˈrɒgətərɪ] adj fragend.

interrupt [ˌɪntəˈrʌpt] 1 vt (break the continuity of) unterbrechen (also Elec); (in conversation: rudely also) ins Wort fallen (+dat); activity, work also stören; traffic flow also aufhalten, stören; (obstruct) view versperren.
2 vi (in conversation) unterbrechen; (~ sb's work etc) stören. stop ~ing! fall mir/ihm etc nicht dauernd ins Wort!

interrupter [ˌɪntəˈrʌptəʳ] n (Elec) Unterbrecher m.

interruption [ˌɪntəˈrʌpʃən] n Unterbrechung f; (of work, activity, traffic flow also) Störung f; (of view) Versperrung f. without ~ ohne Unterbrechung, ununterbrochen.

intersect [ˌɪntəˈsekt] 1 vt durchschneiden; (Geometry) schneiden. 2 vi sich kreuzen; (Geometry, in set theory) sich schneiden. ~ing sets Schnittmengen pl.

intersection [ˌɪntəˈsekʃən] n (crossroads) Kreuzung f; (Geometry) Schnittpunkt m. point of ~ Schnittpunkt m.

intersperse [ˌɪntəˈspɜːs] vt (scatter) verteilen. ~d with sth mit etw dazwischen; a speech ~d with quotations eine mit Zitaten gespickte Rede; boredom ~d with periods of ... Langweile und dazwischen or zwischendurch ...

interstate [ˌɪntəˈsteɪt] adj (US) zwischen den (US-Bundes)staaten, zwischenstaatlich. ~ highway Bundesautobahn f, Interstate Highway m.

interstellar [ˌɪntəˈsteləʳ] adj interstellar.

interstice [ɪnˈtɜːstɪs] n Zwischenraum m; (in wall etc also) Sprung, Riß m; (between panels also) Fuge f.

intertribal [ˌɪntəˈtraɪbl] adj zwischen den or verschiedenen Stämmen. ~ war Stammeskrieg m.

intertwine [ˌɪntəˈtwaɪn] 1 vt verschlingen; (fig) destinies also verknüpfen; stories verweben. 2 vi (branches, arms etc) sich ineinander verschlingen; (threads) verschlungen sein; (fig: destinies) sich verbinden.

interurban [ˌɪntəˈɜːbən] adj (US) railroad städteverbindend.

interval [ˈɪntəvəl] n (a) (space, time) Abstand m, Intervall nt (form). at ~s in Abständen; sunny ~s (Met) Aufheiterungen pl. (b) (Sch, Theat etc) Pause f. (c) (Mus) Intervall nt.

intervene [ˌɪntəˈviːn] vi (person) einschreiten (in bei), inter-

venieren; (event, fate) dazwischenkommen. if nothing ~s wenn nichts dazwischenkommt; twelve years ~ between these events zwölf Jahre liegen zwischen den Ereignissen.

intervening [ˌɪntəˈviːnɪŋ] adj period of time dazwischenliegend. in the ~ weeks in den Wochen dazwischen, in den dazwischenliegenden Wochen; the ~ meetings were less well attended die Versammlungen dazwischen or die dazwischen stattfindenden Versammlungen waren weniger gut besucht.

intervention [ˌɪntəˈvenʃən] n Eingreifen nt, Eingriff m, Intervention f.

interventionist [ˌɪntəˈvenʃənɪst] 1 n Interventionist(in f) m. 2 adj interventionistisch.

interview [ˈɪntəvjuː] 1 n (a) (for job) Vorstellungsgespräch nt; (with authorities, employer etc) Gespräch nt; (for grant) Auswahlgespräch nt.
(b) (Press, TV etc) Interview nt.
(c) (formal talk) Gespräch nt, Unterredung f.
2 vt (a) job applicant ein/das Vorstellungsgespräch führen mit; applicant for grant etc Fragen stellen (+dat). he is being ~ed on Monday for the job er hat am Montag sein Vorstellungsgespräch.
(b) (Press, TV etc) interviewen.
3 vi (a) das Vorstellungsgespräch/die Vorstellungsgespräche führen.
(b) (Press, TV etc) interviewen.

interviewee [ˌɪntəvjuːˈiː] n (for job) Kandidat(in f) m (für die Stelle); (Press, TV etc) Interviewte(r) mf.

interviewer [ˈɪntəvjuːəʳ] n (for job) Leiter(in f) m des Vorstellungsgesprächs; (Press, TV etc) Interviewer(in f) m.

interwar [ˈɪntəwɔːʳ] adj years zwischen den Weltkriegen.

interweave [ˌɪntəˈwiːv] 1 vt (lit, fig) verweben; branches, fingers verschlingen, ineinanderschlingen. 2 vi sich verweben; (branches) sich ineinanderschlingen.

intestate [ɪnˈtestɪt] adj (Jur) nicht testamentarisch vermacht. to die ~ sterben, ohne ein Testament zu hinterlassen, ohne Testament sterben.

intestinal [ɪnˈtestɪnl] adj Darm-, intestinal (form).

intestine [ɪnˈtestɪn] n Darm m. small/large ~ Dünn-/Dickdarm m.

intimacy [ˈɪntɪməsɪ] n Vertrautheit, Intimität f; (euph: sexual ~) Intimität f. in the ~ of the home in der Vertrautheit or vertrauten Atmosphäre seines Heims; acts of ~ Vertraulichkeiten pl; ~ took place (form euph) es kam zu Intimitäten.

intimate¹ [ˈɪntɪmɪt] 1 adj (a) friend eng, vertraut, intim (geh); (sexually) intim. we're friends but we are not ~ wir sind befreundet, stehen aber nicht auf so vertraulichem Fuß; to be on ~ terms with sb mit jdm auf vertraulichem Fuß stehen; he was a bit too ~ with my wife er war ein bißchen zu vertraulich mit meiner Frau; to be/become ~ with sb mit jdm vertraut sein/werden; (sexually) mit jdm intim sein/werden.
(b) (fig) intim (geh); feelings, thoughts also geheim; connection also eng; knowledge gründlich.
(c) freshness intim, im Intimbereich. ~ deodorant Intimspray m or nt.
2 n Vertraute(r) mf.

intimate² [ˈɪntɪmeɪt] vt andeuten. he ~d to them that they should stop er bedeutete ihnen aufzuhören.

intimately [ˈɪntɪmɪtlɪ] adv acquainted bestens; behave, speak vertraulich; related, connected eng; know genau, gründlich. we know each other but not ~ wir kennen uns, aber nicht besonders gut; he is ~ involved in local politics er ist tief in Lokalpolitik verwickelt.

intimation [ˌɪntɪˈmeɪʃən] n Andeutung f.

intimidate [ɪnˈtɪmɪdeɪt] vt einschüchtern. they ~d him into not telling the police sie schüchterten ihn so ein, daß er der Polizei nichts erzählte; we won't be ~d wir lassen uns nicht einschüchtern.

intimidation [ɪnˌtɪmɪˈdeɪʃən] n Einschüchterung f.

into [ˈɪntʊ] prep in (+acc); (against) crash, drive gegen. to translate sth ~ French etw ins Französische übersetzen; to divide 3 ~ 9 9 durch 3 teilen or dividieren, 3 ~ 9 goes 3 3 geht dreimal in 9; they worked far ~ the night sie arbeiteten bis tief in die Nacht hinein; it turned ~ a nice day es wurde ein schöner Tag; I'm not really ~ the job yet (inf) ich bin noch nicht ganz drin im Job (inf); I'm not ~ that (sl) darauf stehe ich nicht (sl); he's (heavily) ~ jazz (sl) er steht (schwer) auf Jazz (sl).

intolerable adj, **~bly** adv [ɪnˈtɒlərəbl, -ɪ] unerträglich.

intolerance [ɪnˈtɒlərəns] n (a) Intoleranz, Unduldsamkeit f (of gegenüber). (b) (esp Med) Überempfindlichkeit f (to, of gegen).

intolerant [ɪnˈtɒlərənt] adj intolerant, unduldsam (of gegenüber); (Med) überempfindlich (to, of gegen).

intolerantly [ɪnˈtɒlərəntlɪ] adv in meiner/seiner etc Intoleranz.

intonate [ˈɪntəʊneɪt] vt (Ling) intonieren.

intonation [ˌɪntəʊˈneɪʃən] n Intonation f; (Ling also) Satzmelodie f. ~ pattern Intonationsmuster nt.

intone [ɪnˈtəʊn] vt intonieren.

in toto [ɪnˈtəʊtəʊ] adv im ganzen, in toto (geh).

intoxicant [ɪnˈtɒksɪkənt] n Rauschmittel nt.

intoxicate [ɪnˈtɒksɪkeɪt] vt (lit, fig) berauschen.

intoxicated [ɪnˈtɒksɪkeɪtɪd] adj betrunken, berauscht (also fig), im Rausch (also fig). ~ by drugs/with success im Drogenrausch/vom Erfolg berauscht.

intoxication [ɪnˌtɒksɪˈkeɪʃən] n Rausch m (also fig), (Be)trunkenheit f; (Med: poisoning) Vergiftung f. in a state of ~ (form) in (be)trunkenem Zustand, im Rausch.

intra- [ˌɪntrə-] pref intra-.

intractable [ɪnˈtræktəbl] adj metal unnachgiebig; problem, illness hartnäckig; child, temper unlenksam.

intramural [ˌɪntrəˈmjʊərəl] adj (esp Univ) (course) innerhalb der Universität; activities studienspezifisch.

intransigence [ɪn'trænsɪdʒəns] n Unnachgiebigkeit, Intransigenz (geh) f.

intransigent [ɪn'trænsɪdʒənt] adj unnachgiebig, intransigent (geh).

intransitive [ɪn'trænsɪtɪv] **1** adj verb intransitiv, Intransitiv-. **2** n Intransitiv nt.

intrastate [ˌɪntrə'steɪt] adj (US) innerhalb des (Bundes)staates.

intra-uterine device [ˌɪntrə'juːtəraɪndɪˌvaɪs] n Intrauterinpessar nt.

intravenous [ˌɪntrə'viːnəs] adj intravenös.

intrepid adj, **~ly** adv [ɪn'trepɪd, -lɪ] unerschrocken, kühn.

intrepidity [ˌɪntrɪ'pɪdɪtɪ] n Unerschrockenheit, Kühnheit f.

intricacy ['ɪntrɪkəsɪ] n Kompliziertheit f; (intricate part: of law, chess etc) Feinheit f.

intricate ['ɪntrɪkɪt] adj kompliziert; (involved also) verwickelt.

intricately ['ɪntrɪkɪtlɪ] adv kompliziert.

intrigue 1 [ɪn'triːg] **1** vi intrigieren.
2 vt (arouse interest of) faszinieren; (arouse curiosity of) neugierig machen. **I would be ~d to know why ...** es würde mich schon interessieren, warum ...
3 ['ɪntriːg] n **(a)** (plot) Intrige f; (no pl: plotting) Intrigen(spiel nt) pl.
(b) (dated: love affair) Liaison, Liebschaft f.

intriguer [ɪn'triːgəʳ] n Intrigant(in f), Ränkeschmied m.

intriguing [ɪn'triːgɪŋ] **1** adj faszinierend, interessant. **2** n Intrigen(spiel nt) pl.

intriguingly [ɪn'triːgɪŋlɪ] adv auf faszinierende Weise.

intrinsic [ɪn'trɪnsɪk] adj merit, value immanent; (essential) wesenhaft, wesentlich. **is this form ~ to the poem?** ist dies eine dem Gedicht innewohnende Form? (geh).

intrinsically [ɪn'trɪnsɪkəlɪ] adv an sich.

intro ['ɪntrəʊ] n see **introduction**.

introduce [ˌɪntrə'djuːs] vt **(a)** (make acquainted) (to person) vorstellen (to sb jdm), bekannt machen (to mit); (butler) ankündigen; (to subject) einführen (to in +acc). **have you two been ~d?** hat man Sie bekannt gemacht?; **I don't think we've been ~d** ich glaube nicht, daß wir uns kennen; **to ~ oneself** sich vorstellen; **he was ~d to drink at an early age** er hat schon früh Bekanntschaft mit dem Alkohol gemacht; **who ~d him to heroin?** durch wen ist er ans Heroin geraten?; **he was ~d to flying by a friend** er ist durch einen Freund zum Fliegen gekommen; **to ~ sb/sth into sb's presence** jdn/etw vor jdn bringen.
(b) fashion, practice, reform, invention einführen; (Parl) bill einbringen; mood bringen (into in +acc); book, subject, era einleiten; (announce) speaker vorstellen, ankündigen; programme ankündigen.
(c) (insert) einführen (into in +acc).

introduction [ˌɪntrə'dʌkʃən] n **(a)** (to person) Vorstellung f. **since his ~ to Lord X** seit er Lord X vorgestellt worden ist; **to make or perform the ~s** die Vorstellung übernehmen; **letter of ~** Einführungsbrief m or -schreiben nt.
(b) (introductory part) (to book, music) Einleitung f (to zu).
(c) (elementary course, book) Einführung f. **an ~ to French** eine Einführung ins Französische.
(d) (introducing, being introduced) (to subject) Einführung f (to in +acc); (to habit, hobby) Bekanntschaft f (to mit); (of fashion, practice, reform etc) Einführung f; (of bill) Einbringen nt; (announcing) (of speaker) Vorstellung, Ankündigung f; (of programme) Ankündigung f; (bringing or carrying in) Einführung f (into in +dat); (insertion) Einführung f (into in +acc).

introductory [ˌɪntrə'dʌktərɪ] adj page, paragraph, chapter einleitend; words, remarks einführend; talk Einführungs-.

introit ['ɪntrɔɪt] n Introitus m.

introspection [ˌɪntrəʊ'spekʃən] n Selbstbeobachtung, Introspektion (geh) f.

introspective [ˌɪntrəʊ'spektɪv] adj person selbstbeobachtend, introspektiv (geh); novel, remarks introspektiv.

introspectiveness [ˌɪntrəʊ'spektɪvnɪs] n (of novel, remarks) introspektiver Charakter; (of person) Neigung f zur Selbstbeobachtung or Introspektion (geh).

introversion [ˌɪntrəʊ'vɜːʃən] n (Psych) Introversion f.

introvert ['ɪntrəʊvɜːt] **1** n (Psych) Introvertierte(r) mf. **to be an ~** introvertiert sein. **2** vt (Psych) nach innen wenden; (Biol) nach innen stülpen.

introverted ['ɪntrəʊvɜːtɪd] adj introvertiert, in sich gekehrt.

intrude [ɪn'truːd] **1** vi sich eindrängen. **to ~ in sb's affairs** sich in jds Angelegenheiten (acc) mischen; **am I intruding?** störe ich?; **to ~ on sb's privacy/grief** jds Privatsphäre verletzen/jdn in seinem Kummer stören; **to ~ on a conversation** sich in eine Unterhaltung (ein)mischen; **to ~ on sb's leisure time** jds Freizeit in Anspruch nehmen.
2 vt remark einwerfen. **the thought ~d itself into my mind** der Gedanke drängte sich mir auf; **to ~ oneself or one's presence/one's views upon sb** sich jdm/jdm seine Ansichten aufdrängen; **to ~ oneself into sb's affairs** sich in jds Angelegenheiten (acc) mischen.

intruder [ɪn'truːdəʳ] n Eindringling m.

intrusion [ɪn'truːʒən] n **(a)** Störung f; (on sb's privacy also) Verletzung f (on gen). **forgive the ~, I just wanted to ask ...** entschuldigen Sie, wenn ich hier so eindringe, ich wollte nur fragen ...; **the ~ of his work on his free time** daß seine Arbeit immer mehr von seiner Freizeit beanspruchte; **the sudden ~ of reality on his dreams** das plötzliche Eindringen der Wirklichkeit in seine Träume; **they regarded her advice as an ~** sie betrachteten ihren Rat als eine Einmischung.
(b) (forcing: of opinions, advice, one's presence) Aufdrängen nt. **this continual ~ of his views into every conversation ...** dadurch, daß er sich ständig mit seinen Ansichten in die Unterhaltung mischte, ...

intrusive [ɪn'truːsɪv] adj person aufdringlich; (Phon) intrusiv.

intuition [ˌɪntjuː'ɪʃən] n Intuition f; (of future events etc) (Vor)ahnung f (of von). **to know sth by ~** etw intuitiv wissen.

intuitive [ɪn'tjuːɪtɪv] adj intuitiv; guess, feeling, assessment instinktiv.

intuitively [ɪn'tjuːɪtɪvlɪ] adv intuitiv. **~ I'd say 50** ich hätte instinktiv 50 gesagt.

inundate ['ɪnʌndeɪt] vt (lit, fig) überschwemmen, überfluten; (with work) überhäufen. **have you a lot of work? — I'm ~d** haben Sie viel Arbeit? — ich ersticke darin.

inundation [ˌɪnʌn'deɪʃən] n (lit, fig) (with invitations, offers etc) Überschwemmung f; (with work) Überhäufung f. **an ~ of tourists/letters** eine Flut von Touristen/Briefen.

inure [ɪn'jʊəʳ] vt gewöhnen (to an +acc); (physically) abhärten (to gegen); (to danger) stählen (to gegen). **to become ~d to sth** sich an etw (acc) gewöhnen/sich gegen etw abhärten/stählen.

invade [ɪn'veɪd] vt (Mil) country einmarschieren in (+acc); (fig) überfallen, heimsuchen; privacy eindringen in (+acc), stören.

invader [ɪn'veɪdəʳ] n (Mil) Invasor m; (fig) Eindringling m (of in +acc); (of privacy) Eindringling (of in +acc), Störer m (of gen).

invading [ɪn'veɪdɪŋ] adj einmarschierend; Huns, Vikings etc einfallend; army, troops also Invasions-.

invalid [ˈɪnvəlɪd] **1** adj **(a)** krank; (disabled) invalide, körperbehindert.
(b) (for invalids) Kranken-; Invaliden-. **~ chair** Roll- or Krankenstuhl m; **~ car** Invaliden(kraft)fahrzeug nt.
2 n Kranke(r) mf; (disabled person) Invalide, Körperbehinderte(r) mf. **he's been an ~ all his life** er hat sein ganzes Leben lang ein körperliches Leiden gehabt.
♦**invalid out** vt sep dienstuntauglich or -unfähig schreiben or erklären. **to be ~ed ~ of the army** wegen Dienstuntauglichkeit aus dem Heer entlassen werden.

invalid² [ɪn'vælɪd] adj (esp Jur) ungültig; deduction, argument nicht schlüssig or stichhaltig; assumption nicht zulässig. **it makes the argument ~** es entkräftet das Argument.

invalidate [ɪn'vælɪdeɪt] vt ungültig machen; theory entkräften.

invalidation [ɪnˌvælɪ'deɪʃən] n (of document) Ungültigmachung f; (of theory) Entkräftung f.

invalidism ['ɪnvəlɪdɪzəm] n körperliches Leiden; (disability) Körperbehinderung, Invalidität f.

invalidity [ɪnvə'lɪdɪtɪ] n see **invalid²** Ungültigkeit f; mangelnde Schlüssigkeit or Stichhaltigkeit; Unzulässigkeit f.

invaluable [ɪn'væljʊəbl] adj unbezahlbar; service, role unschätzbar; jewel, treasure von unschätzbarem Wert. **to be ~ (to sb)** (für jdn) von unschätzbarem Wert sein.

invariable [ɪn'vɛərɪəbl] **1** adj (also Math) unveränderlich; bad luck konstant, ständig. **2** n (Math) Konstante f.

invariably [ɪn'vɛərɪəblɪ] adv ständig, unweigerlich; (not changing) unveränderlich. **do you trust his judgement? — ~!** trauen Sie seinem Urteil? — ausnahmslos!

invasion [ɪn'veɪʒən] n (lit, fig) Invasion f; (of privacy etc) Eingriff m (of in +acc). **the Viking ~** der Einfall der Wikinger; **the German ~ of Poland** der Einmarsch or Einfall (pej) der Deutschen in Polen.

invective [ɪn'vektɪv] n Beschimpfungen (against gen), Schmähungen (geh) (against gegen), Invektiven (liter) pl.

inveigh [ɪn'veɪ] vi **to ~ against sb/sth** (liter) jdn/etw schmähen (liter), sich in Schimpfreden gegen jdn/etw ergehen (geh).

inveigle [ɪn'viːgl] vt (liter) verleiten (into zu); (lure) locken. **to ~ sb into doing sth** jdn dazu verleiten or verlocken, etw zu tun.

invent [ɪn'vent] vt erfinden.

invention [ɪn'venʃən] n **(a)** Erfindung f. **of one's own ~** selbsterfunden. **(b)** (inventiveness) Phantasie f.

inventive [ɪn'ventɪv] adj (creative) powers, skills, mind schöpferisch; novel, design einfallsreich; (resourceful) erfinderisch. **games which encourage a child to be ~** Spiele, die die Phantasie des Kindes anregen.

inventiveness [ɪn'ventɪvnɪs] n Einfallsreichtum m.

inventor [ɪn'ventəʳ] n Erfinder(in f) m.

inventory ['ɪnvəntrɪ] n Inventar nt, Bestandsaufnahme f. **to make or take an ~ of sth** Inventar von etw or den Bestand einer Sache (gen) aufnehmen. **2** vt (Comm) inventarisieren.

inverse ['ɪn'vɜːs] **1** adj umgekehrt, entgegengesetzt. **in ~ order** in umgekehrter Reihenfolge; **to be in ~ proportion to ...** im umgekehrten Verhältnis zu ... stehen; (Math) umgekehrt proportional zu ... sein. **2** n Gegenteil nt.

inversion [ɪn'vɜːʃən] n Umkehrung f; (Mus also, Gram) Inversion f; (fig: of roles, values) Verkehrung, Umkehrung f.

invert [ɪn'vɜːt] vt umkehren; object also auf den Kopf stellen; order also umdrehen; (Gram) subject and object umstellen; word order umkehren. **~ed commas** (Brit) Anführungszeichen pl; **that's just ~ed snobbery** das ist auch eine Art Snobismus.

invertebrate [ɪn'vɜːtɪbrɪt] **1** n Wirbellose(r), Invertebrat (spec) m. **2** adj wirbellos.

invest [ɪn'vest] **1** vt **(a)** (Fin, fig) investieren (in in +acc or dat). (Fin also) anlegen (in in +dat).
(b) (form: with rank or authority) president etc einsetzen, investieren (old). **to ~ sb/sth with sth** jdm/einer Sache etw verleihen; **the event was ~ed with an air of mystery** das Ereignis war von etwas Geheimnisvollem umgeben.
(c) (Mil: besiege) belagern.
2 vi investieren, Geld anlegen (in in +acc or dat, with bei). **to ~ in shares** in Aktien investieren, sein Geld in Aktien anlegen; **to ~ in a new car** sich (dat) ein neues Auto anschaffen.

investigate [ɪn'vestɪgeɪt] **1** vt untersuchen; (doing scientific research etc) erforschen; sb's political beliefs, an insurance claim, business affairs überprüfen; complaint nachgehen (+dat); motive, reason erforschen; crime untersuchen; (by police also) Ermittlungen anstellen über (+acc). **to ~ a case** in einem Fall ermitteln or Ermittlungen anstellen.
2 vi nachforschen; (police) ermitteln, Ermittlungen anstellen.

investigation [ɪnˌvestɪ'geɪʃən] n (a) (to determine cause) Untersuchung f (into gen); (official enquiry also) Ermittlung f. on ~ it turned out that ... bei näherer Untersuchung stellte (es) sich heraus, daß ...
  (b) (looking for sth) Nachforschung f; (by police) Ermittlungen pl; (of affairs, applicants, political beliefs etc) Überprüfung f. despite his ~s he could not find the missing person trotz seiner Nachforschungen konnte er die vermißte Person nicht finden; to be under ~ überprüft werden; he is under ~ (by police) gegen ihn wird ermittelt; new methods of criminal ~ neue polizeiliche Ermittlungsmethoden; (private) ~ agency Detektei f, Detektivbüro nt.
  (c) (scientific research) (in field) Forschung f; (of bacteria, object etc) Erforschung f (into gen). his biochemical ~s seine biochemischen Forschungen; recent scientific ~s have shown ... die neuesten wissenschaftlichen Untersuchungen haben gezeigt ...; his ~s into the uses of this word seine Forschungen über den Gebrauch dieses Wortes.

investigative [ɪn'vestɪgətɪv] adj journalism Enthüllungs-; technique Forschungs-; mind Forscher-.

investigator [ɪn'vestɪgeɪtə^r] n Ermittler m; (private ~) (Privat)detektiv m; (insurance ~) (Schadens)ermittler(in f) m; (from government department) Untersuchungs- or Ermittlungsbeamte(r) m. a team of ~s ein Untersuchungsausschuß m, eine Untersuchungskommission.

investiture [ɪn'vestɪtʃə^r] n (of president etc) (feierliche) Einsetzung, Amtseinführung f; (of royalty) Investitur f; (of honour) Verleihung f; (occasion) Auszeichnungsfeier f. after his ~ with the VC, ... nachdem ihm das Viktoriakreuz verliehen worden war, ...

investment [ɪn'vestmənt] n (a) (Fin) Investition f; (act also) Anlage f. industry needs more ~ die Industrie braucht mehr Investitionen; to make an ~ investieren (of sth etw); oil/this company is a good ~ Öl/diese Firma ist eine gute (Kapital)anlage; learning languages is a good ~ es macht sich bezahlt, wenn man Sprachen lernt; ~ trust Investmentgesellschaft f.
  (b) (investiture) (as sth) (Amts)einsetzung f; (with sth) Verleihung f (+gen).
  (c) (Mil: blockade) Belagerung f.

investor [ɪn'vestə^r] n Kapitalanleger, Investor m. the small ~ die Kleinanleger pl.

inveterate [ɪn'vetərɪt] adj dislike, hatred tief verwurzelt, abgrundtief; opposition, prejudice hartnäckig; enemies, hatred unversöhnlich; criminal, smoker Gewohnheits-; liar, gambler unverbesserlich.

invidious [ɪn'vɪdɪəs] adj remark gehässig, boshaft; task, position unerfreulich, unangenehm; behaviour, conduct gemein; distinctions, comparison ungerecht. it would be ~ to ... es wäre ungerecht, zu ...

invigilate [ɪn'vɪdʒɪleɪt] (Brit) 1 vt exam Aufsicht führen bei. 2 vi Aufsicht führen.

invigilation [ɪnˌvɪdʒɪ'leɪʃən] n (Brit) Aufsicht f. to do the ~ Aufsicht führen.

invigilator [ɪn'vɪdʒɪleɪtə^r] n (Brit) Aufsicht f, Aufsichtführende(r) mf, Aufsichtsperson f.

invigorate [ɪn'vɪgəreɪt] vt beleben; (tonic, cure) kräftigen.

invigorating [ɪn'vɪgəreɪtɪŋ] adj climate gesund; sea air, shower erfrischend, belebend; tonic, cure kräftigend, stärkend; (fig) attitude, frankness (herz)erfrischend. he found the American business world very ~ die amerikanische Geschäftswelt stimulierte ihn.

invincibility [ɪnˌvɪnsɪ'bɪlɪtɪ] n Unbesiegbarkeit f.

invincible [ɪn'vɪnsəbl] adj army etc unbesiegbar, unschlagbar; courage, determination unerschütterlich.

inviolability [ɪnˌvaɪələ'bɪlɪtɪ] n see adj Unantastbarkeit f; Unverletzlichkeit f; Heiligkeit f.

inviolable [ɪn'vaɪələbl] adj unantastbar; frontiers also unverletzlich; law, oath heilig.

inviolate [ɪn'vaɪəlɪt] adj (form) honour unbeschadet; rights unangetastet. a virgin pure and ~ (liter) eine reine, unberührte Jungfrau.

invisibility [ɪnˌvɪzə'bɪlɪtɪ] n Unsichtbarkeit f.

invisible [ɪn'vɪzəbl] adj unsichtbar. ~ earnings/exports (Econ) unsichtbare Einkünfte/Exporte pl; ~ ink Geheimtinte f; ~ mending Kunststopfen nt; ~ thread Nylonfaden m; ~ to the naked eye mit dem bloßen Auge nicht erkennbar.

invisibly [ɪn'vɪzəblɪ] adv unsichtbar. you should have it ~ mended du solltest es kunststopfen lassen.

invitation [ɪnvɪ'teɪʃən] n Einladung f. by ~ (only) nur auf Einladung; at sb's ~ auf jds Aufforderung (acc) (hin); an ~ to burglars eine Aufforderung zum Diebstahl.

invite [ɪn'vaɪt] 1 vt (a) person einladen. to ~ sb to do sth jdn auffordern or bitten, etw zu tun; he ~d me to try for myself er bot mir an, es doch selbst zu versuchen.
  (b) (ask for, attract) suggestions, questions, a discussion bitten um; (behaviour) ridicule, contempt, trouble auslösen, führen zu. written in such a way as to ~ further discussion so geschrieben, daß es zu weiteren Diskussionen auffordert; it ~s comparison with another theory der Vergleich mit einer anderen Theorie drängt sich auf; you're inviting defeat/an accident by ... das muß ja zu einer Niederlage/einem Unglück führen, wenn du ...; you're inviting ridicule/criticism du machst dich lächerlich/setzt dich der Kritik aus; he just seems to ~ trouble wo er auftaucht, gibt es meistens Unannehmlichkeiten; there's no need to ~ trouble man muß es ja nicht auf Ärger anlegen.
  2 ['ɪnvaɪt] n (inf) Einladung f.
♦**invite in** vt sep hereinbitten, ins Haus bitten. could I ~ you ~ for (a) coffee? möchten Sie auf eine Tasse Kaffee hereinkommen?
♦**invite out** vt sep einladen. I ~d her ~ ich habe sie gefragt, ob

sie mit mir ausgehen möchte; to ~ sb ~ for a meal jdn in ein Restaurant einladen.
♦**invite round** vt sep (zu sich) einladen.
♦**invite up** vt sep heraufbitten.

inviting [ɪn'vaɪtɪŋ] adj einladend; prospect, idea, meal verlockend.

invitingly [ɪn'vaɪtɪŋlɪ] adv einladend; (temptingly) verlockend.

invocation [ˌɪnvəʊ'keɪʃən] n Beschwörung f; (Eccl) Invokation f. an ~ to the muses (Liter) eine Anrufung der Musen.

invoice ['ɪnvɔɪs] 1 n (bill) (Waren)rechnung, Faktura f; (list) Lieferschein m, Faktura f. 2 vt goods in Rechnung stellen, berechnen, fakturieren. to ~ sb for sth jdm für etw eine Rechnung ausstellen; has he been ~d for these yet? hat er dafür schon eine Rechnung bekommen?; ~ clerk Fakturist(in f) m.

invoke [ɪn'vəʊk] vt (a) (appeal to, call for) God, the law, muse anrufen; evil spirits beschwören. to ~ the name of Marx ins Feld führen; to ~ God's blessing/help from God Gottes Segen erbitten/Gott um Hilfe anflehen; to ~ vengeance on one's enemies Rache auf seine Feinde herabflehen or -rufen.
  (b) (call into operation) treaty etc sich berufen auf (+acc). to ~ sb's help an jds Hilfsbereitschaft (acc) appellieren.

involuntarily [ɪn'vɒləntərɪlɪ] adv unbeabsichtigt, unabsichtlich; (automatically) unwillkürlich. he found himself ~ involved er sah sich unfreiwilligerweise verwickelt.

involuntary [ɪn'vɒləntərɪ] adj unbeabsichtigt, ungewollt; muscle movement etc unwillkürlich. I found myself an ~ listener/agent of their plot ich wurde zum unfreiwilligen Zuhörer/Werkzeug ihres Komplotts.

involute ['ɪnvəluːt] adj (liter: complex) verwickelt.

involve [ɪn'vɒlv] vt (a) (entangle) verwickeln (sb in sth jdn in etw acc); (include) beteiligen (sb in sth jdn an etw dat); (concern) betreffen. to ~ sb in a quarrel jdn in einen Streit verwickeln or hineinziehen; don't ~ yourself in any unnecessary expense machen Sie sich keine unnötigen Ausgaben; to ~ sb in expense jdm Kosten verursachen; the book doesn't ~ the reader das Buch fesselt or packt den Leser nicht; I was watching TV but I wasn't really ~d in it ich habe ferngesehen, war aber gar nicht richtig dabei; it wouldn't ~ you at all du hättest damit gar nichts zu tun; to be ~d in sth etwas mit etw zu tun haben; (have part in also) an etw (dat) beteiligt sein; (in sth bad also) in etw (acc) verwickelt sein; to get ~d in sth in etw (acc) verwickelt werden; (in quarrel, crime etc also) in etw (acc) hineingezogen werden; I didn't want to get ~d ich wollte damit/mit ihm etc nichts zu tun haben; I didn't want to get too ~d ich wollte mich nicht zu sehr engagieren; a matter of principle is ~d es ist eine Frage des Prinzips, es geht ums Prinzip; the person ~d die betreffende Person; we are all ~d in the battle against inflation der Kampf gegen die Inflation geht uns alle an; to be/get ~d with sth etwas mit etw zu tun haben; (have part in) an etw (dat) beteiligt sein; (work etc) mit etw beschäftigt sein; are you ~d with the union? sind Sie gewerkschaftlich engagiert?; he got ~d with local politics er hat sich lokalpolitisch engagiert; to be ~d with sb mit jdm zu tun haben; (sexually) mit jdm ein Verhältnis haben; he's very ~d with her er hat sich bei ihr sehr stark engagiert; he's ~d with some shady characters er hat Umgang mit einigen zwielichtigen Gestalten; to get ~d with sb mit jdm Kontakt bekommen, sich mit jdm einlassen (pej). I don't want to get ~d with them ich will mit ihnen nichts zu tun haben; he got ~d with a girl er hat eine Beziehung mit einem Mädchen angefangen; she doesn't want to get ~d sie will sich nicht engagieren or enger binden.
  (b) (entail) mit sich bringen, zur Folge haben; (encompass) umfassen; (mean) bedeuten. what does your job ~? worin besteht Ihre Arbeit?; this problem ~s many separate issues dieses Problem umfaßt viele verschiedene Punkte or schließt viele verschiedene Punkte ein; to ~ considerable expense/a lot of hard work beträchtliche Kosten/viel Arbeit mit sich bringen or zur Folge haben; it's involving too much of my time es beansprucht zuviel Zeit, es kostet mich zuviel Zeit; he doesn't understand what's ~d in this sort of work er weiß nicht, worum es bei dieser Arbeit geht; do you realize what's ~d in raising a family? weißt du denn, was es bedeutet, eine Familie großzuziehen?; about £1,000 was ~d es ging dabei um etwa £1.000; the job ~d 50 workmen für die Arbeit wurden 50 Arbeiter gebraucht; it would ~ moving to Germany das würde bedeuten, nach Deutschland umzuziehen; finding the oil ~d the use of a special drill um das Öl zu finden, brauchte man einen Spezialbohrer; the planning ~d a new technique bei der Planung wurde eine neue Technik angewendet.

involved [ɪn'vɒlvd] adj kompliziert; regulations also verwirrend; story also verwickelt; style komplex, umständlich (pej). long ~ sentences umständliche Schachtelsätze pl.

involvement [ɪn'vɒlvmənt] n (being concerned with) Beteiligung f (in an + dat); (in quarrel, crime etc) Verwicklung f (in in +acc); (commitment) Engagement nt; (sexually) Verhältnis nt; (complexity) Kompliziertheit, Verworrenheit (pej) f. his ~ with shady characters sein Umgang m mit zwielichtigen Gestalten; the extent of his ~ with her/his work das Maß, in dem er sich bei ihr/bei seiner Arbeit engagiert hat; we don't know the extent of his ~ in the plot/plan wir wissen nicht, wie weit er an dem Komplott/Plan beteiligt ist/war; there is no ~ of the reader in the novel der Leser fühlt sich von dem Roman nicht angesprochen.

invulnerability [ɪnˌvʌlnərə'bɪlɪtɪ] n see adj Unverwundbarkeit, Unverletzbarkeit f; Uneinnehmbarkeit f; Unangreifbarkeit f.

invulnerable [ɪn'vʌlnərəbl] adj unverwundbar, unverletzbar; fortress uneinnehmbar; (lit, fig) position unangreifbar. ~ to attack unbezwingbar.

inward ['ɪnwəd] adj (a) (inner) innere(r, s); smile, life innerlich;

thoughts innerste(r, s). **(b)** *curve* nach innen gehend; *mail* eintreffend.

inward-looking ['ɪnwəd'lʊkɪŋ] *adj* in sich gekehrt, beschaulich.

inwardly ['ɪnwədlɪ] *adv* innerlich, im Inneren.

inwardness ['ɪnwədnɪs] *n* Innerlichkeit *f*.

inward(s) ['ɪnwəd(z)] *adv* nach innen. **his thoughts turned** ~ er versank in Selbstbetrachtung.

iodine ['aɪədiːn] *n* Jod *nt*.

ion ['aɪən] *n* Ion *nt*.

Ionic [aɪ'ɒnɪk] *adj* ionisch.

ionic [aɪ'ɒnɪk] *adj* Ionen-.

ionization [ˌaɪənaɪ'zeɪʃən] *n* Ionisierung *f*.

ionize ['aɪənaɪz] *vti* ionisieren.

ionosphere [aɪ'ɒnəsfɪəʳ] *n* Ionosphäre *f*.

iota [aɪ'əʊtə] *n* Jota *nt*. **not an** ~ **or one** ~ nicht ein Jota; **not an** ~ **of truth** kein Funke *m* or Körnchen *nt* Wahrheit.

IOU [ˌaɪəʊ'juː] *abbr of* **I owe you** Schuldschein *m*. **to give sb an** ~ jdm einen Schuldschein ausschreiben.

IPA *abbr of* **International Phonetic Association, International Phonetic Alphabet.**

ipso facto ['ɪpsəʊ'fæktəʊ] *adv* eo ipso.

IQ *abbr of* **intelligence quotient** IQ, Intelligenzquotient *m*. ~ **test** Intelligenztest, IQ-Test *m*.

IRA *abbr of* **Irish Republican Army** IRA *f*.

Iran [ɪ'rɑːn] *n* (der) Iran.

Iranian [ɪ'reɪnɪən] **1** *adj* iranisch. **2** *n* **(a)** Iraner(in *f*) *m*. **(b)** (*language*) Iranisch *nt*.

Iraq [ɪ'rɑːk] *n* der Irak.

Iraqi [ɪ'rɑːkɪ] **1** *adj* irakisch. **2** *n* **(a)** Iraker(in *f*) *m*. **(b)** (*dialect*) Irakisch *nt*.

irascibility [ɪˌræsɪ'bɪlɪtɪ] *n* Reizbarkeit *f*, Jähzorn *m*.

irascible [ɪ'ræsɪbl] *adj* reizbar, erregbar, jähzornig; *temperament also* jähzornig, heftig, aufbrausend.

irascibly [ɪ'ræsɪblɪ] *adv* gereizt.

irate [aɪ'reɪt] *adj* zornig; *crowd* wütend.

irately [aɪ'reɪtlɪ] *adv* zornig.

ire [aɪəʳ] *n* (*liter*) Zorn *m*.

Ireland ['aɪələnd] *n* Irland *nt*. **Northern** ~ Nordirland *nt*. **Republic of** ~ Republik *f* Irland.

iridescence [ˌɪrɪ'desəns] *n see adj* (*liter*) Irisieren *nt*; Schillern *nt*; Schimmern *nt*.

iridescent [ˌɪrɪ'desənt] *adj* (*liter*) irisierend; *plumage also, water* schillernd; *opals etc, silk* schimmernd.

iris [aɪərɪs] *n* **(a)** (*of eye*) Regenbogenhaut, Iris *f*. **(b)** (*Bot*) Iris, Schwertlilie *f*.

Irish ['aɪərɪʃ] **1** *adj* **(a)** irisch. ~ **coffee** Irish Coffee *m*; ~ **Free State** irischer Freistaat; ~ **joke** Irenwitz, Ostfriesenwitz *m*; ~**man** Ire, Irländer *m*; ~ **Republican Army** Irisch-Republikanische Armee; ~ **Sea** Irische See; ~ **setter** Irish Setter *m*; ~ **stew** Irish Stew *nt*; ~**woman** Irin, Irländerin *f*.
(b) (*hum inf: illogical*) unlogisch, blödsinnig.
2 *n* **(a)** *pl* **the** ~ die Iren, die Irländer *pl*.
(b) (*language*) Irisch *nt*, irisches Gälisch.

irk [ɜːk] *vt* verdrießen (*geh*), ärgern.

irksome ['ɜːksəm] *adj* lästig.

iron ['aɪən] **1** *n* **(a)** Eisen *nt*. **old** ~ Alteisen *nt*; ~ **tablets** *pl* Eisentabletten *pl*; **a man of** ~ ein stahlharter Mann; **a will of** ~ ein eiserner Wille; **to rule with a rod of** ~ mit eiserner Rute or Hand herrschen.
(b) (*electric* ~, *flat*~) Bügeleisen, Plätteisen (*dial*) *nt*. **to have more than one** ~ **in the fire** (*fig*) mehrere Eisen im Feuer haben; **he has too many** ~**s in the fire** er macht zuviel auf einmal; **to strike while the** ~ **is hot** (*Prov*) das Eisen schmieden, solange es heiß ist (*Prov*).
(c) (*Golf*) Eisen *nt*.
(d) (*fetters*) ~**s** *pl* Hand- und Fußschellen *pl*; **to put a man in** ~**s** jdn in Eisen legen.
2 *adj* **(a)** (*Chem*) Eisen-; (*made of* ~) Eisen-, eisern, aus Eisen. ~ **pyrites** Eisenkies, Pyrit *m*.
(b) (*fig*) *constitution, hand* eisern; *will* eisern, stählern; *rule* streng, unbarmherzig. **to rule with an** ~ **hand** mit eiserner Faust regieren; **the I**~ **Chancellor** der Eiserne Kanzler; **they soon discovered that here was an** ~ **fist in a velvet glove** es wurde ihnen bald klar, daß mit ihm *etc* nicht zu spaßen war, obwohl *etc* so sanft wirkte.
3 *vt clothes* bügeln, plätten (*dial*).
4 *vi* (*person*) bügeln; (*cloth*) sich bügeln lassen.

♦ **iron out** *vt sep* (*lit, fig*) ausbügeln; *differences also* ausgleichen; *problems, difficulties also* aus dem Weg räumen.

iron: I~ **Age** *n* Eisenzeit *f*; ~**clad 1** *adj* gepanzert; **2** *n* (*obs*) Panzerschiff *nt*; I~ **Curtain** *n* Eiserner Vorhang; **the** I~ **Curtain countries** die Länder hinter dem Eisernen Vorhang; ~**grey** *adj hair* eisgrau; ~ **horse** *n* (*old: train*) Dampfroß *nt* (*old hum*).

ironic(al) [aɪ'rɒnɪk(əl)] *adj* ironisch; *smile also* spöttisch; *position paradox*, witzig (*inf*). **it's really** ~ das ist wirklich witzig (*inf*); **it's really** ~ **that now he's got a car he's not allowed to drive** es ist doch paradox or wirklich witzig (*inf*), daß er jetzt, wo er ein Auto hat, nicht fahren darf.

ironically [aɪ'rɒnɪkəlɪ] *adv* ironisch. **and then,** ~ **enough, he turned up** komischerweise or witzigerweise (*inf*) or ulkigerweise (*inf*) tauchte er dann auf; **and then,** ~, **it was he himself who** ... und dann hat ausgerechnet er ...; und dann hat paradoxerweise er ...

ironing ['aɪənɪŋ] *n* (*process*) Bügeln, Plätten (*dial*) *nt*; (*clothes*) Bügelwäsche, Plättwäsche (*dial*) *f*. **to do the** ~ (die Wäsche) bügeln; ~ **board** Bügelbrett, Plättbrett (*dial*) *nt*.

iron: ~ **lung** *n* eiserne Lunge; ~**monger** *n* (*Brit*) Eisen(waren)händler(in *f*) *m*; ~**monger's (shop)** *n* (*Brit*) Eisenund Haushaltswarenhandlung *f*; ~**mongery** *n* (*Brit*) (*shop*)

Eisen- und Haushaltswarenhandlung *f*; (*goods*) Eisenwaren *pl*; ~ **ore** *n* Eisenerz *nt*; ~ **rations** *npl* eiserne Ration; ~**work** *n* Eisen *nt*; (*on chest, cart etc*) Eisenbeschläge *pl*; **to do** ~**work** Eisenarbeiten machen; *ornamental* ~**work** Eisenverzierungen *pl*; ~**works** *n sing or pl* Eisenhütte *f*.

irony ['aɪərənɪ] *n* Ironie *f no pl*. **the** ~ **of it is that** ... das Ironische daran ist, daß ..., die Ironie liegt darin, daß ...; **one of the ironies of fate** die Ironie des Schicksals; **life's ironies** die Ironie des Lebens.

irradiate [ɪ'reɪdɪeɪt] *vt* **(a)** (*emit*) *heat, light rays* ausstrahlen. **(b)** (*liter: illumine*) erhellen (*liter*). **(c)** (*treat by irradiating*) bestrahlen.

irrational [ɪ'ræʃənl] *adj* **(a)** (*illogical, Math*) irrational; *fear, belief also* unsinnig; (*not sensible*) unvernünftig. **his illness made him quite** ~ seine Krankheit ließ ihn völlig irrational werden; **if you maintain X, then it is** ~ **to deny Y** wenn Sie X behaupten, ist es widersinnig or unlogisch, Y zu leugnen. **(b)** (*not having reason*) *animal* vernunftlos.

irrationality [ɪˌræʃə'nælɪtɪ] *n see adj* Irrationalität *f*; Unsinnigkeit *f*; Unvernünftigkeit *f*.

irrationally [ɪ'ræʃnəlɪ] *adv* irrational; (*not sensibly*) unvernünftig. **quite** ~, **he believed** ... er glaubte gegen jede Vernunft or völlig unsinnigerweise ...

irreconcilable [ɪˌrekən'saɪləbl] *adj* **(a)** *enemy, hatred* unversöhnlich. **(b)** *belief, opinion, differences* unvereinbar.

irreconcilably [ɪˌrekən'saɪləblɪ] *adv see adj*.

irrecoverable [ˌɪrɪ'kʌvərəbl] *adj* endgültig or für immer verloren, unwiederbringlich verloren; *loss* unersetzlich, unersetzbar; *debt* nicht eintreibbar, uneinbringlich. **the thieves were caught, but the money was** ~ die Diebe wurden gefaßt, aber das Geld konnte nicht mehr sichergestellt werden; **the company's losses are** ~ die Verluste der Firma können nicht mehr wettgemacht werden.

irrecoverably [ˌɪrɪ'kʌvrəblɪ] *adv* ~ *lost* für immer verloren.

irredeemable [ˌɪrɪ'diːməbl] *adj* **(a)** *currency, pawned object* nicht einlösbar; *bonds* unkündbar, untilgbar; *pawned object, annuity, debt* nicht ablösbar.
(b) (*fig*) *sinner* (rettungslos) verloren; *loss* unwiederbringlich; *fault* unverbesserlich; *transgression* unverzeihlich. ~ *disaster* völlige Katastrophe; **a period of** ~ *gloom* eine Zeit völliger Hoffnungslosigkeit.

irredeemably [ˌɪrɪ'diːməblɪ] *adv* *lost* rettungslos; *confused* hoffnungslos. **he's an** ~ **wicked man** er ist ein von Grund auf böser or ein abgrundtief böser Mensch.

irreducible [ˌɪrɪ'djuːsəbl] *adj* (*Chem, Math*) nicht reduzierbar. **the** ~ **minimum** das Allermindeste.

irrefragable [ɪ'refrəgəbl] *adj* (*form*) unwiderlegbar.

irrefutability [ˌɪrɪfjuːtə'bɪlɪtɪ] *n* Unwiderlegbarkeit *f*.

irrefutable [ˌɪrɪ'fjuːtəbl] *adj* unwiderlegbar, unbestreitbar.

irrefutably [ˌɪrɪ'fjuːtɪblɪ] *adv* unwiderlegbar; *demonstrate also* eindeutig.

irregular [ɪ'regjʊləʳ] **1** *adj* **(a)** (*uneven*) unregelmäßig; *intervals, teeth also, shape, coastline* ungleichmäßig; *surface* uneben. **to be** ~ **in one's attendance** unregelmäßig erscheinen; **the windows are deliberately** ~ die Fenster sind bewußt uneinheitlich; **to keep** ~ **hours** ein ungeregeltes Leben führen, keine festen Zeiten haben; **he's been a bit** ~ **recently** (*inf*) er hat in letzter Zeit ziemlich unregelmäßigen Stuhlgang.
(b) (*not conforming*) unstatthaft; (*contrary to rules*) unvorschriftsmäßig; (*contrary to law*) ungesetzlich; *marriage* ungültig; *behaviour* ungebührlich, ungehörig. **well, it's a bit** ~, **but I'll** ... eigentlich dürfte ich das nicht tun, aber ich ...; **it's a most** ~ **request, but** ... das ist ein höchst unübliches Ersuchen, aber ...; **this is most** ~! das ist äußerst ungewöhnlich!; **because of** ~ **procedures, the contract was not valid** wegen einiger Formfehler war der Vertrag ungültig.
(c) (*Gram*) unregelmäßig.
(d) *troops* irregulär.
2 *n* (*Mil*) Irreguläre(r) *m*. **the** ~**s** die irreguläre Truppe.

irregularity [ɪˌregjʊ'lærɪtɪ] *n see adj* **(a)** Unregelmäßigkeit *f*; Ungleichmäßigkeit *f*; Unebenheit *f*; Uneinheitlichkeit *f*; Ungeregeltheit *f*.
(b) Unstatthaftigkeit *f*; Unvorschriftsmäßigkeit *f*; Ungesetzlichkeit *f*; (*of marriage*) unvorschriftsmäßige Durchführung; Ungebührlichkeit, Ungehörigkeit *f*. **a slight** ~ **in the proceedings** ein kleiner Formfehler; **a slight** ~ **with one of his pupils/the chambermaid** eine kleine Entgleisung mit einem seiner Schüler/dem Zimmermädchen; *behavioural* ~ normwidriges Verhalten.
(c) (*Gram*) Unregelmäßigkeit *f*.

irregularly [ɪ'regjʊləlɪ] *adv see adj* **(a)** unregelmäßig; ungleichmäßig; uneben. **(b)** unstatthaft; unvorschriftsmäßig; ungesetzlich; ungebührlich, ungehörig. **the business has been conducted rather** ~ es wurden ziemlich ungewöhnliche Geschäftsmethoden angewandt.

irrelevance [ɪ'reləvəns], **irrelevancy** [ɪ'reləvənsɪ] *n* Irrelevanz *f no pl*; (*of details also*) Unwesentlichkeit, Nebensächlichkeit *f*; (*of titles, individuals*) Bedeutungslosigkeit *f*. **the** ~ **of his contribution to the discussion** die Belanglosigkeit or Irrelevanz seiner Diskussionsbeiträge; **his speech was full of irrelevancies** vieles in seiner Rede war irrelevant or nebensächlich or unwesentlich.

irrelevant [ɪ'reləvənt] *adj* irrelevant; *details also, information* unwesentlich, nebensächlich; *titles etc* bedeutungslos. **it is** ~ **whether he agrees or not** es ist irrelevant or belanglos, ob er zustimmt; **it's** ~ **to the subject** das ist für das Thema irrelevant; **don't be** ~ (*in discussion*) bleib bei der Sache; (*in essay writing*) bleiben Sie beim Thema.

irrelevantly [ɪ'reləvəntlɪ] *adv* belanglos. ..., **he said** ~ ..., sagte er, obwohl das gar nicht zur Sache gehörte; **he rambled on** ~ er schwafelte irrelevantes or belangloses Zeug.

irreligious [ˌɪrɪ'lɪdʒəs] *adj* unreligiös, irreligiös; *youth, savages* gottlos; *(lacking respect)* pietätlos.

irremediable [ˌɪrɪ'miːdɪəbl] *adj character defects, errors* nicht behebbar; *situation* nicht mehr zu retten *pred or* rettend *attr*.

irremediably [ˌɪrɪ'miːdɪəblɪ] *adv* hoffnungslos.

irreparable [ɪ'repərəbl] *adj damage* irreparabel, nicht wiedergutzumachen *pred or* wiedergutzumachend *attr; loss* unersetzlich; *harm also* bleibend.

irreparably [ɪ'repərəblɪ] *adv* irreparabel. his reputation was ~ damaged sein Ruf war unwiderruflich zerstört.

irreplaceable [ˌɪrɪ'pleɪsəbl] *adj* unersetzlich.

irrepressible [ˌɪrɪ'presəbl] *adj urge, curiosity* unbezähmbar; *optimism* unerschütterlich, unverwüstlich; *person* nicht unter- *or* kleinzukriegen; *child* sonnig; *delight* unbändig. his ~ high spirits sein sonniges Gemüt; he has an ~ disposition er ist eine Frohnatur; you're ~ du bist nicht kleinzukriegen.

irreproachable [ˌɪrɪ'prəʊtʃəbl] *adj manners* tadellos, einwandfrei; *conduct also* untadelig.

irreproachably [ˌɪrɪ'prəʊtʃəblɪ] *adv* tadellos.

irresistible [ˌɪrɪ'zɪstəbl] *adj* unwiderstehlich.

irresistibly [ˌɪrɪ'zɪstəblɪ] *adv* unwiderstehlich. it's ~ funny es ist von unwiderstehlicher Komik.

irresolute [ɪ'rezəluːt] *adj* unentschlossen, unentschieden.

irresolutely [ɪ'rezəluːtlɪ] *adv* unentschlossen, unschlüssig.

irresoluteness [ɪ'rezəluːtnɪs], **irresolution** [ˌɪrezə'luːʃən] *n* Unentschiedenheit, Unentschlossenheit *f*.

irrespective [ˌɪrɪ'spektɪv] *adj:* ~ of ungeachtet (+*gen*), unabhängig von; candidates should be chosen ~ of sex bei der Auswahl der Kandidaten sollte das Geschlecht keine Rolle spielen; ~ of whether they want to or not egal *or* gleichgültig, ob sie wollen oder nicht.

irresponsibility [ˌɪrɪˌsponsə'bɪlɪtɪ] *n see adj* Unverantwortlichkeit *f*; Verantwortungslosigkeit *f*.

irresponsible [ˌɪrɪ'sponsəbl] *adj action, behaviour* unverantwortlich; *person* verantwortungslos.

irresponsibly [ˌɪrɪ'sponsəblɪ] *adv* unverantwortlich; *behave also* verantwortungslos.

irretrievable [ˌɪrɪ'triːvəbl] *adj* nicht mehr wiederzubekommen; *past, happiness etc* unwiederbringlich; *loss* unersetzlich. the erased information is ~ die gelöschte Information kann nicht mehr abgerufen werden; ~ breakdown of marriage (unheilbare) Zerrüttung der Ehe.

irretrievably [ˌɪrɪ'triːvəblɪ] *adv* ~ lost für immer verloren; ~ broken down (unheilbar) zerrüttet.

irreverence [ɪ'revərəns] *n see adj* Unehrerbietigkeit *f*; Respektlosigkeit, Despektierlichkeit *f*; Respektlosigkeit *f*; Pietätlosigkeit *f*.

irreverent [ɪ'revərənt] *adj behaviour* unehrerbietig; *remark* respektlos, despektierlich; *novel, author* respektlos; *(towards religion, the dead)* pietätlos.

irreverently [ɪ'revərəntlɪ] *adv see adj*.

irreversible [ˌɪrɪ'vɜːsəbl] *adj* nicht rückgängig zu machen; *judgment* unwiderruflich; *(Med, Phys, Chem)* irreversibel; *damage* bleibend; *decision* unumstößlich.

irrevocable [ɪ'revəkəbl] *adj* ~bly *adv* [ɪ'revəkəbl, -ɪ] unwiderruflich.

irrigate ['ɪrɪgeɪt] *vt* **(a)** *land, crop* bewässern. **(b)** *(Med)* spülen.

irrigation [ˌɪrɪ'geɪʃən] *n* **(a)** *(Agr)* Bewässerung *f*. ~ canal Bewässerungskanal *m*. **(b)** *(Med)* Spülung, Irrigation *f*.

irritability [ˌɪrɪtə'bɪlɪtɪ] *n* Reizbarkeit *f*; Gereiztheit *f*.

irritable ['ɪrɪtəbl] *adj (as characteristic)* reizbar; *(on occasion)* gereizt. don't be so ~ sei doch nicht so gereizt.

irritably ['ɪrɪtəblɪ] *adv* gereizt.

irritant ['ɪrɪtənt] *n (Med)* Reizerreger *m*; *(person)* Nervensäge *f (inf)*; *(noise etc)* Ärgernis *nt*.

irritate ['ɪrɪteɪt] *vt* **(a)** *(annoy)* ärgern, aufregen; *(deliberately)* reizen; *(get on nerves)* irritieren. to get ~d ärgerlich werden; she's easily ~d sie ist sehr reizbar *or* schnell verärgert; I get ~d at *or* with him er reizt *or* ärgert mich, er regt mich auf. **(b)** *(Med)* reizen.

irritating ['ɪrɪteɪtɪŋ] *adj* ärgerlich; *cough* lästig. I find his presence/jokes most ~ seine Anwesenheit regt/Witze regen mich wirklich auf; you really are the most ~ person du kannst einem wirklich auf die Nerven gehen; how ~ for you! wie ärgerlich!

irritatingly ['ɪrɪteɪtɪŋlɪ] *adv* ärgerlich. he very ~ changed his mind ärgerlicherweise hat er seine Meinung geändert.

irritation [ˌɪrɪ'teɪʃən] *n* **(a)** *(state)* Ärger *m*, Verärgerung *f*; *(act)* Ärgern *nt*; *(deliberate)* Reizen *nt*; *(thing that irritates)* Ärgernis *nt*, Unannehmlichkeit *f*. the noise is a source of ~ der Lärm irritiert einen; to avoid the ~ of a long delay um eine ärgerliche *or* lästige Verzögerung zu vermeiden. **(b)** *(Med)* Reizung *f*.

irrupt [ɪ'rʌpt] *vi* eindringen, hereinstürzen; *(water also)* hereinbrechen.

irruption [ɪ'rʌpʃən] *n* Eindringen, Hereinstürzen *nt*; *(of water also)* Hereinbrechen *nt*.

Is *abbr of* Island(s), Isle(s).

is [ɪz] *3rd person sing present of* be.

Isaiah [aɪ'zaɪə] *n* Jesaja *m*.

ISBN *abbr of* **International Standard Book Number** ISBN-Nummer *f*.

-ise [-aɪz] *vb suf* -isieren.

-ish [-ɪʃ] *adj suf* (+*adj*) -lich; (+*n*) -haft; *(esp Brit: approximately)* um ... herum, zirka. green~ grünlich; cold~ ziemlich kalt; boy~ jungenhaft; forty~ um vierzig herum, zirka vierzig.

isinglass ['aɪzɪŋglɑːs] *n* Fischleim *m*.

Islam ['ɪzlɑːm] *n (religion)* der Islam; *(Moslems collectively)* Mohammedaner *pl*.

Islamic [ɪz'læmɪk] *adj* islamisch.

island ['aɪlənd] *n (lit, fig)* Insel *f*.

---

islander ['aɪləndər] *n* Insulaner(in *f*), Inselbewohner(in *f*) *m*.

isle [aɪl] *n (poet)* Eiland *nt (poet)*. the I~ of Man die Insel Man.

islet ['aɪlɪt] *n* kleines Eiland *(poet)*, Inselchen *nt*.

ism ['ɪzəm] *n (inf)* Ismus *m (inf)*.

isn't ['ɪznt] *contr of* is not.

isobar ['aɪsəʊbɑːr] *n* Isobare *f*.

isolate ['aɪsəʊleɪt] *vt* **(a)** *(separate)* absondern, isolieren; *(Med, Chem)* isolieren. the causes of crime cannot be ~d from social conditions man kann die Gründe für kriminelles Verhalten nicht von den gesellschaftlichen Verhältnissen gesondert *or* isoliert betrachten; we have to ~ probable from possible causes wir müssen die wahrscheinlichen von den möglichen Ursachen trennen.

(b) *(cut off)* abschneiden, isolieren. to ~ oneself from other people sich (von anderen) abkapseln; to ~ oneself from the world sich isolieren, sich von der Welt zurückziehen.

(c) *(pinpoint)* herausfinden; *problem also, essential factor* herauskristallisieren.

isolated ['aɪsəʊleɪtɪd] *adj* **(a)** *(cut off)* abgeschnitten, isoliert; *(remote)* abgelegen; *existence* zurückgezogen; *(Med)* isoliert. **(b)** *(single)* einzeln. ~ instances Einzelfälle *pl*.

isolating ['aɪsəʊleɪtɪŋ] *adj:* ~ language isolierende Sprache.

isolation [ˌaɪsəʊ'leɪʃən] *n* **(a)** *(act)* *(separation, cutting-off)* Absonderung, Isolierung *(esp Med, Chem) f*; *(pinpointing)* Herausfinden *nt*; *(of problem also, of essential factor)* Herauskristallisierung *f*.

(b)~ *(state)* Isoliertheit, Abgeschnittenheit *f*; *(remoteness)* Abgelegenheit, Abgeschiedenheit *f*. his ~ from the world seine Abgeschiedenheit von der Welt; this deliberate and self-imposed social ~ diese absichtliche und selbstauferlegte gesellschaftliche Isolation; spiritual ~ geistige Isolation; he felt a sense of ~ er fühlte sich isoliert; Splendid I~ *(Hist)* Splendid Isolation *f*; he lived in splendid ~ in a bedsitter in the suburbs *(iro)* er wohnte, weitab vom Schuß *(inf) or* jenseits von Gut und Böse *(hum)*, in einem möblierten Zimmer am Stadtrand; to keep a patient in ~ einen Patienten isolieren; to live in ~ zurückgezogen leben; to consider sth in ~ etw gesondert *or* isoliert betrachten; it doesn't make much sense in ~ ohne Zusammenhang *or* isoliert ist es ziemlich unverständlich.

isolation hospital *n* Isolierspital *nt*.

isolationism [ˌaɪsəʊ'leɪʃənɪzəm] *n* Isolationismus *m*.

isolationist [ˌaɪsəʊ'leɪʃənɪst] **1** *adj* isolationistisch. **2** *n* Isolationist(in *f*) *m*.

isolation ward *n* Isolierstation *f or* -haus *nt*.

isomer ['aɪsəʊmər] *n (Chem)* Isomer(e) *nt*.

isomeric [ˌaɪsəʊ'merɪk] *adj (Chem)* isomer.

isometrics [ˌaɪsəʊ'metrɪks] *n sing* Isometrie *f*.

isomorphic [ˌaɪsəʊ'mɔːfɪk] *adj (form)* isomorph.

isosceles [aɪ'sɒsɪliːz] *adj:* ~ triangle gleichschenkliges Dreieck.

isotherm ['aɪsəʊθɜːm] *n (Met)* Isotherme *f*.

isotope ['aɪsəʊtəʊp] *n* Isotop *nt*.

Israel ['ɪzreɪl] *n* Israel *nt*.

Israeli [ɪz'reɪlɪ] **1** *adj* israelisch. **2** *n* Israeli *mf*.

Israelite ['ɪzrɪəlaɪt] *n (Bibl)* Israelit(in *f*) *m*.

issue ['ɪʃuː] **1** *vt* **(a)** *(give, send out)* *passport, documents, certificate, driving licence* ausstellen; *tickets, library books* ausgeben; *shares, banknotes* ausgeben, emittieren; *stamps* herausgeben; *coins* ausgeben; *order, warning* ergehen lassen (to an +*acc*), erteilen *(to dat); warning* aussprechen; *proclamation* erlassen; *details* bekanntgeben. the issuing authorities die ausstellende Behörde; to ~ sb with a visa, to ~ a visa to sb jdm ein Visum ausstellen; a warrant for his arrest was ~d gegen ihn wurde Haftbefehl erlassen; who ~s a warrant? wer stellt einen Haftbefehl aus?

(b) *(publish)* *book, newspaper* herausgeben.

(c) *(supply)* *rations, rifles, ammunition* ausgeben. to ~ sth to sb/to ~ sb with sth etw an jdn ausgeben; all troops are ~d with ... alle Truppen sind mit ... ausgerüstet.

2 *vi* *(liquid, gas)* austreten; *(smoke)* (heraus)quellen; *(sound)* *(hervor- or heraus)*dringen; *(people etc)* (heraus)strömen. his actions ~ from a desire to help seine Handlungen entspringen dem Wunsch zu helfen; the sewage/river ~s into the sea das Abwasser fließt/der Fluß mündet ins Meer.

3 *n* **(a)** *(question)* Frage *f*; *(matter also)* Angelegenheit *f*; *(problematic)* Problem *nt*. the factual ~s die Tatsachen *pl*; the ~ is whether ... es geht darum *or* die Frage ist, ob ...; the whole future of the country is at ~ es geht um die Zukunft des Landes; what is at ~? worum geht es?; that's not at ~ das steht nicht zur Debatte; to join ~ with sb over sth jdn in einer Sache aufgreifen; to take ~ with sb over sth jdm in etw *(dat)* widersprechen; this has become something of an ~ das ist zu einem Problem geworden; to make an ~ of sth etw aufbauschen; to evade the ~ ausweichen; do you want to make an ~ of it? *(inf)* du willst dich wohl mit mir anlegen?; to face the ~ den Tatsachen ins Auge sehen.

(b) *(outcome, result)* Ergebnis *nt*. that decided the ~ das war entscheidend *or* ausschlaggebend; to bring sth to an ~ eine Entscheidung in etw *(dat)* herbeiführen; to force the ~ eine Entscheidung erzwingen.

(c) *(giving out, that given out)* *(of banknotes, shares, coins, stamps etc)* Ausgabe *f*; *(of shares also)* Emission *f*. place of ~ *(of tickets)* Ausgabestelle *f*; *(of passports)* Ausstellungsort *m*; date of ~ *(of tickets)* Ausstellungsdatum *nt*; *(of stamps)* Ausgabetag *m*; ~ desk Ausgabe(schalter *m*) *f*.

(d) *(handing-out)* Ausgabe *f*; *(supplying, thing supplied)* Lieferung *f*. the ~ of blankets/guns to the troops die Versorgung der Truppen mit Decken/die Ausrüstung der Truppen mit Gewehren; this rifle is the latest ~ dieses Gewehr ist das neueste Modell; it's part of the clothing ~ es ist Teil der Ausstattung.

(e) (of book etc) Herausgabe f; (book etc) Ausgabe f.
(f) (of liquid, gas) Ausströmen nt. ~ of pus Eiterabsonderung f; an ~ of blood from the cut eine Blutung der Wunde.
(g) (Jur: offspring) Nachkommenschaft f.
Istanbul [,ɪstæn'buːl] n Istanbul nt.
isthmus ['ɪsməs] n Landenge f, Isthmus m.
it¹ [ɪt] 1 pron (a) (when replacing German noun) (subj) er/sie/es; (dir obj) ihn/sie/es; (indir obj) ihm/ihr/ihm. of ~ davon; behind/over/under etc ~ dahinter/darüber/darunter etc; who is ~? — ~'s me or I (form) wer ist da? — ich (bin's); who is ~? — ~'s the Browns! wer ist da? — die Browns!; what is ~? was ist es or das?; (matter) was ist los?; that's not ~ (not the trouble) das ist es (gar) nicht; (not the point) darum geht's gar nicht; the cheek of ~! so eine Frechheit!; the worst of ~ is that ... das Schlimmste daran ist, daß ...; do you believe ~? glaubst du das?
(b) (indef subject) es. ~'s raining es regnet; yes, ~ is a problem/pleasant change ja, das ist ein Problem/eine angenehme Abwechslung; ~ seems simple to me mir scheint das ganz einfach; if ~ hadn't been for her, we would have come wenn sie nicht gewesen wäre, wären wir gekommen; why is ~ always me who has to ...? warum bin ich immer derjenige etc, der etc ...?, warum muß (ausgerechnet) immer ich ...?; why is ~ always him who can't ...? warum ist es immer er, der nicht ... kann?; ~ wasn't me ich war's nicht; ~ was the Italians/10 miles es waren die Italiener/10 Meilen; I don't think ~ (is) wise of you ... ich halte es für unklug, wenn du ...; I've seen/known ~ happen ich habe es (schon) gesehen/erlebt.
(c) (emph) ~ was him or he (form) who asked her er hat sie gefragt; ~ was a cup that he dropped and not ... er hat eine Tasse fallen lassen und nicht ...; ~'s his appearance I object to ich habe nur etwas gegen sein Äußeres; ~ was for his sake that she lied nur um seinetwillen hat sie gelogen; ~'s the other one I like ich mag den anderen/das andere etc.
(d) (inf phrases) that's ~! (agreement) ja, genau!; (annoyed) jetzt reicht's mir!; that's ~ (then)! (achievement) ja, genau!; wär's!, geschafft!; (disappointment) ja, das war's dann wohl; this is ~! (before action) jetzt geht's los!; see at, in, with-it.
2 n (inf) (a) (in children's games) you're ~! du bist!
(b) this is really ~! das ist genau das richtige, das ist es; he really thinks he's ~ er bildet sich (dat) ein, er sei sonst wer.
(c) my cat's an ~ meine Katze ist ein Neutrum.
(d) (dated: sex appeal) Sex-Appeal m.
it² n (dated sl): gin and ~ Gin mit italienischem Wermut.
ITA (Brit) abbr of **Independent Television Authority.**
ita abbr of **initial teaching alphabet.**
Italian [ɪ'tæljən] 1 adj italienisch. 2 n (a) Italiener(in f) m. (b) (language) Italienisch nt.
Italianate [ɪ'tæljənət] adj nach italienischer Art. the ~ style of the church/painting der von der italienischen Schule beeinflußte Stil der Kirche/des Gemäldes.
italic [ɪ'tælɪk] 1 adj kursiv. ~ type Kursivdruck m; ~ script Kurrentschrift f. 2 n ~s pl Kursivschrift, Kursive f; in ~s kursiv (gedruckt); my ~s Hervorhebung von mir.
italicize [ɪ'tælɪsaɪz] vt kursiv schreiben/drucken.
Italy ['ɪtəlɪ] n Italien nt.
itch [ɪtʃ] 1 n (a) Jucken nt, Juckreiz m. I have an ~ mich juckt es, ich habe einen Juckreiz.
(b) (inf: urge) Lust f. I have an ~ to do sth/for sth es reizt or juckt (inf) mich, etw zu tun/etw reizt or juckt (inf) mich.
2 vi (a) jucken. my back ~es mein Rücken juckt (mich), mir or mich juckt der Rücken; that rash made me ~ all over der Ausschlag juckte am ganzen Körper.

(b) (inf) he is ~ing to ... es reizt or juckt (inf) ihn, zu ...; he's ~ing for a fight er ist auf Streit aus.
itching ['ɪtʃɪŋ] 1 adj juckend. to have an ~ palm (fig) gern die Hand aufhalten (inf). 2 n Jucken nt, Juckreiz m. ~ powder Juckpulver nt.
itchy ['ɪtʃɪ] adj (+er) (a) (itching) juckend. it is ~ es juckt; I've got ~ feet (inf) ich will hier weg (inf); (want to travel also) mich packt das Fernweh; he's got ~ fingers/an ~ palm (inf) er macht lange Finger/er hält gern die Hand auf (inf).
(b) (causing itching) cloth kratzig.
it'd ['ɪtəd] contr of **it would; it had.**
-ite [-aɪt] n suf (follower of) -anhänger(in f) m.
item ['aɪtəm] n (a) (in programme, on agenda etc) Punkt m; (Comm: in account book) (Rechnungs)posten m; (article) Stück, Ding nt, Gegenstand m; (in catalogue etc) Artikel m; (Brit: in variety show) Nummer f. ~s of furniture Möbelstücke pl; he went through the business ~ by ~ er ging die Sache Punkt für Punkt durch; petrol is one of the most expensive ~s I have to buy Benzin gehört zu den teuersten Dingen, die ich kaufe.
(b) (of news) Bericht m; (short, Rad, TV also) Meldung f. a short news ~ eine Zeitungsnotiz/eine Kurzmeldung.
itemization [,aɪtəmaɪ'zeɪʃən] n detaillierte Aufstellung, Einzelaufführung f.
itemize ['aɪtəmaɪz] vt spezifizieren, einzeln aufführen. ~d account spezifizierte Rechnung; to ~ a bill die Rechnungsposten einzeln aufführen, die Rechnung spezifizieren.
iterate ['ɪtəreɪt] vt (form) wiederholen.
iteration [ɪtə'reɪʃən] n (form) Wiederholung f.
iterative ['ɪtərətɪv] adj (Gram) iterativ.
itinerant [ɪ'tɪnərənt] adj umherziehend, wandernd, Wander-; preacher Wander-; minstrel fahrend; worker Saison-, Wander-; judge Reise-. ~ theatre group Wandertruppe f.
itinerary [aɪ'tɪnərərɪ] n (route) (Reise)route f; (map) Straßenkarte f, Wegeverzeichnis nt.
it'll ['ɪtl] contr of **it will; it shall.**
ITN (Brit) abbr of **Independent Television News.**
its [ɪts] poss adj sein(e)/ihr(e)/sein(e).
it's [ɪts] contr of **it is** (as aux).
itself [ɪt'self] pron (a) (reflexive) sich.
(b) (emph) selbst. and now we come to the text ~ und jetzt kommen wir zum Text selbst; the frame ~ is worth £1,000 der Rahmen allein or schon der Rahmen ist £ 1.000 wert; in ~, the actual amount is not important der Betrag an sich ist unwichtig; enthusiasm is not enough in ~ Begeisterung allein genügt nicht.
(c) by ~ (alone) allein; (automatically) von selbst, selbsttätig; seen by ~ einzeln betrachtet; the bomb went off by ~ die Bombe ging von selbst los.
ITV (Brit) abbr of **Independent Television.**
IUD abbr of **intra-uterine device.**
I've [aɪv] contr of **I have.**
ivied ['aɪvɪd] adj efeuumrankt.
ivory ['aɪvərɪ] 1 n (a) (also colour) Elfenbein nt. (b) (Art) Elfenbeinschnitzerei f. (c) (inf) ivories (piano keys) Tasten pl; (billiard balls) Billardkugeln pl; (dice) Würfel pl; (dated: teeth) Beißer pl (inf). 2 adj (a) elfenbeinern. (b) colour elfenbeinfarben.
Ivory Coast n Elfenbeinküste f.
ivory tower 1 n (fig) Elfenbeinturm m. 2 adj attr weltfremd.
ivy ['aɪvɪ] n Efeu m.
Ivy League n (US) Eliteuniversitäten der USA.
-ize [-aɪz] vb suf -isieren.

J

J, j [dʒeɪ] n J, j nt.
jab [dʒæb] 1 vt (a) (with stick, elbow etc) stoßen; (with knife also) stechen. he ~bed his elbow into my side er stieß mir den or mit dem Ellbogen in die Seite; she ~bed the jellyfish with a stick sie pik(s)te mit einem Stock in die Qualle (hinein) (inf); he ~bed his finger er stach sich (dat) in den Finger; he ~bed his finger at the map er tippte mit dem Finger auf die Karte; a sharp ~bing pain ein scharfer, stechender Schmerz.
(b) (inf: give injection to) eine Spritze geben or setzen or verpassen (inf) (+dat).
2 vi zustoßen (at sb with sth mit etw auf jdn); (Boxing) eine (kurze) Gerade schlagen (at auf +acc).
3 n (a) (with stick, elbow) Stoß m; (with needle, knife) Stich m. he gave the jellyfish a ~ with a stick er stieß or pik(s)te (inf) mit dem Stock in die Qualle (hinein); he got a nasty ~ in the eye when she opened her umbrella sie stach ihn ins Auge, als sie den Regenschirm öffnete.
(b) (inf: injection) Spritze f.

(c) (Boxing) (kurze) Gerade.
jabber ['dʒæbər] 1 vt (daher)plappern (inf); poem, prayers herunterrasseln, abhaspeln (inf). 2 vi (also ~ away) plappern, schwätzen, quasseln (inf). they sat there ~ing away in Spanish sie saßen da und quasselten (inf) Spanisch. 3 n Geplapper, Gequassel (inf), Geschnatter nt.
jabbering ['dʒæbərɪŋ] n Geplapper, Plappern, Geschnatter nt.
jacaranda [,dʒækə'rændə] n Jakaranda(baum) m; (wood) Jakarandaholz nt, Palisander(holz) nt) m.
Jack [dʒæk] n dim of **John** Hans m. I'm all right ~ das kann mich überhaupt nicht jucken (inf); his attitude of I'm all right ~ seine Einstellung „das kann mich überhaupt nicht jucken".
jack [dʒæk] n (a) Hebevorrichtung f; (Aut) Wagenheber m.
(b) (Cards) Bube m.
(c) (Naut: flag) Gösch, Bugflagge f; see Union J~.
(d) (Bowling) Zielkugel f.
(e) (boot~) Stiefelknecht m.
(f) every man ~ (of them) (inf) alle ohne Ausnahme, (alle)

geschlossen; **every man ~ of them voted against it** sie stimmten alle ohne Ausnahme *or* geschlossen dagegen.

♦ **jack in** *vt sep* (*sl*) *university, job etc* stecken (*sl*), aufgeben; *girlfriend* Schluß machen mit (*inf*). **~ it ~!** (*stop it*) hör auf damit!, steck's (*sl*).

♦ **jack up** *vt sep* (*a*) *car* aufbocken. (*b*) (*sl*) *prices, wages* (in die Höhe) treiben.

jackal ['dʒækɔːl] *n* Schakal *m*.

jackanapes ['dʒækəneips] *n, pl* - (*old*) (*man*) Fant *m* (*old*), (eingebildeter) Laffe (*old*); (*child*) Racker *m* (*old*).

jackass ['dʒækæs] *n* (*donkey*) Eselhengst *m*; (*inf: person*) Esel (*inf*), Dummkopf (*inf*) *m*.

jackboot ['dʒækbuːt] *n* Schaftstiefel *m*.

jackdaw ['dʒækdɔː] *n* Dohle *f*.

jacket ['dʒækit] *n* (*a*) (*garment*) Jacke *f*; (*man's tailored ~ also*) Jackett *nt*; (*life ~*) Schwimmweste *f*.
(*b*) (*of book*) Schutzumschlag *m*, Buchhülle *f*; (*US: of record*) Plattenhülle *f*.
(*c*) (*esp US: for papers etc*) Umschlag *m*.
(*d*) **~ potatoes, potatoes (baked) in their ~s** (in der Schale) gebackene Kartoffeln *pl*.
(*e*) (*Tech: of boiler etc*) Mantel *m*, Ummantelung *f*.

jack: **J~ Frost** *n* der Frost, der Reif (*personifiziert*); **J~ Frost has been, J~ Frost has painted the window** es sind Eisblumen am Fenster; **~-in-office** *n* Beamtenseele *f*; **~-in-the-box** *n* Schachtel- *or* Kastenteufel *m*; **he was up and down like a ~-in-the-box** er sprang immer wieder auf, der reinste Hampelmann.

jackknife ['dʒæknaif] **1** *n* (*a*) (*großes*) Taschenmesser. (*b*) (*also ~ dive*) gehechteter Sprung. **2** *vi* **the lorry ~d** der Auflieger *or* Anhänger hat sich quergestellt.

jack: **~-of-all-trades** *n* Alleskönner *m*; **to be a (~-of-all-trades (and master of none)** (*prov*) ein Handampf *m* in allen Gassen sein; **~-o'-lantern** *n* Kürbislaterne *f*; (*will-o'-the-wisp*) Irrlicht *nt*; **~ plane** *n* (*Tech*) Schropp- *or* Doppelhobel *m*.

jackpot ['dʒækpɔt] *n* Pott *m* (*inf*); (*Cards also*) Jackpot *m*; (*in lottery etc*) Hauptgewinn *m*. **the ~ this week stands at £200** diese Woche ist der Höchstgewinn £ 200; **to hit the ~** (*lit*) einen Treffer haben; (*in lottery*) den Hauptgewinn bekommen; (*fig*) das große Los ziehen.

jack: **~ rabbit** *n* Eselhase *m*; **J~ Robinson** [ˌdʒæk'rɔbinsən]: **before you could say J~ Robinson** (*inf*) im Nu, im Handumdrehen.

jacks [dʒæks] *n sing* (*game*) Kinderspiel *nt* mit kleinem Gummiball *und* Metallsternchen.

jackstraws ['dʒæk,strɔːz] *n sing*: dem Mikado ähnliches Spiel.

Jack Tar *n* (*Naut inf*) Seebär *m* (*inf*).

Jacob ['dʒeikəb] *n* Jakob *m*.

Jacobean [ˌdʒækə'biːən] *adj* aus der Zeit Jakobs I.

Jacobite ['dʒækəbait] *n* Jakobit *m*.

jade¹ [dʒeid] **1** *n* (*stone*) Jade *m or f*; (*colour*) Jadegrün *nt*. **2** *adj* Jade-; (*colour*) jadegrün. **~ green** Jadegrün *nt*.

jade² *n* (*old*) (*a*) (*horse*) Schindmähre *f* (*old*), Klepper *m* (*old*). (*b*) (*loose woman*) Weibsbild, Weibsstück *nt*; (*pert girl*) freches *or* keckes Weibsbild.

jaded ['dʒeidid] *adj* (*physically*) matt, abgespannt; (*permanently*) verbraucht, abgelebt; (*mentally dulled*) stumpfsinnig, abgestumpft; (*from overindulgence etc*) übersättigt; *appearance* verlebt, verbraucht; *palate* abgestumpft.

jag [dʒæg] *n* (*a*) (*of rock*) Zacke, Spitze *f*; (*of saw*) Zacke *f*. (*b*) **to go on a ~** (*sl*) einen draufmachen (*sl*).

jagged ['dʒægid] *adj* zackig; *edge, hole also* schartig, (aus)gezackt; *wound, tear* ausgefranst; *coastline* zerklüftet.

jaguar ['dʒægjuəʳ] *n* Jaguar *m*.

jail [dʒeil] **1** *n* Gefängnis *nt*. **in ~** im Gefängnis; **after 2 years ~** nach zwei Jahren Gefängnis, nach zweijähriger Haft; **to go to ~** eingesperrt werden, ins Gefängnis kommen. **2** *vt* einsperren, ins Gefängnis sperren.

jail: **~bird** *n* (*inf*) Knastbruder *m* (*inf*); **~break** *n* Ausbruch *m* (*aus dem Gefängnis*); **~breaker** *n* Ausbrecher *m*.

jailer ['dʒeiləʳ] *n* Gefängniswärter(in *f*) *or* -aufseher(in *f*) *m*.

jail house *n* (*US*) Gefängnis *nt*.

jalop(p)y [dʒə'lɔpi] *n* (*inf*) alte (Klapper)kiste *or* Mühle (*inf*).

jalousie ['ʒæluˌ(ː)ziː] *n* Jalousie *f*.

jam¹ [dʒæm] *n* Marmelade, Konfitüre *f*. **you want ~ on it too, do you?** (*Brit inf*) du kriegst wohl nie genug *or* den Hals voll (*inf*)?

jam² **1** *n* (*a*) (*crowd*) Gedränge, Gewühl *nt*.
(*b*) (*traffic ~*) (Verkehrs)stau *m*, Stauung *f*.
(*c*) (*blockage in machine, of logs etc*) Stockung, Stauung *f*. **there's a ~ in the pipe** das Rohr ist verstopft.
(*d*) (*inf: tight spot*) Klemme (*inf*), Patsche (*inf*) *f*. **to be in a ~** in der Klemme *or* Patsche sitzen (*inf*); **to get into a ~** ins Gedränge kommen (*inf*); **to get into a ~ with sb/sth** mit jdm/etw Schwierigkeiten haben; **to get sb out of a ~** jdm aus der Klemme helfen, jdn aus der Patsche ziehen (*inf*).
2 *vt* (*a*) (*make stick*) *window, drawer etc* verklemmen, verkanten; *gun, brakes etc* blockieren; (*wedge*) (*to stop rattles etc*) festklemmen; (*between two things*) einklemmen. **be careful not to ~ the lock** paß auf, daß sich das Schloß nicht verklemmt; **they had him ~med up against the wall** sie hatten ihn gegen die Wand gedrängt; **it's ~med es klemmt**; **the ship was ~med in the ice** das Schiff saß im Eis fest; **he got his finger ~med** *or* **he ~med his finger in the door** er hat sich (*dat*) den Finger in der Tür eingeklemmt.
(*b*) (*cram, squeeze*) (*into* in +*acc*) *things* stopfen, hineinzwängen, quetschen; *people* quetschen, pferchen. **to be ~med together** (*things*) zusammengezwängt sein; (*people*) zusammengedrängt sein; (*in train etc also*) zusammengepfercht sein; **why ~ all the facts into one article?** warum zwängen *or* quetschen (*inf*) Sie alle Fakten in einen Artikel?
(*c*) (*crowd, block*) *street, town etc* verstopfen, blockieren; (*people also*) sich drängen in (+*dat*). **a street ~med with cars**

eine verstopfte Straße; **the passage was ~med with people** Menschen verstopften *or* versperrten den Durchgang.
(*d*) (*move suddenly*) **to ~ one's foot on the brake** eine Vollbremsung machen, auf die Bremse steigen (*inf*) *or* latschen (*inf*); **he ~med his knees into the donkey's flanks** er preßte dem Esel die Knie in die Flanken; *see also* **~ on**.
(*e*) (*Rad*) *station, broadcast* stören.
3 *vi* (*a*) **the crowd ~med into the bus** die Menschenmenge zwängte sich in den Bus.
(*b*) (*become stuck*) (*brake*) sich verklemmen; (*gun*) Ladehemmung haben; (*door, window etc*) klemmen.

♦ **jam in** **1** *vt sep* (*a*) (*wedge in*) einkeilen. **he was ~med ~ by the crowd** er war in der Menge eingekeilt. (*b*) (*press in*) (*herein*)stopfen in (+*acc*). **2** *vi* (*crowd in*) sich herein-/hineindrängen.

♦ **jam on** **1** *vt sep* (*a*) **to ~ ~ the brakes** eine Vollbremsung machen, voll auf die Bremse latschen (*inf*). (*b*) **to ~ ~ one's hat** sich (*dat*) den Hut aufstülpen. **2** *vi* (*brakes*) klemmen.

♦ **jam up** *vt sep* (*a*) *see* **jam²** 2 (*a*). (*b*) (*block*) *roads, entrance etc* blockieren, versperren; *drain, pipe* verstopfen, blockieren.

Jamaica [dʒə'meikə] *n* Jamaika *nt*.

Jamaican [dʒə'meikən] **1** *adj* jamaikanisch, jamaikisch. **~ rum** Jamaikarum *m*. **2** *n* Jamaikaner(in *f*), Jamaiker(in *f*) *m*.

jamb [dʒæm] *n* (Tür-/Fenster)pfosten *m*.

jamboree [ˌdʒæmbə'riː] *n* (*Scouts'*) Jamboree, (Pfadfinder)treffen *nt*; (*dated: party*) Rummel *m* (*inf*). **village ~** Dorffest *nt*.

James [dʒeimz] *n* Jakob *m*.

jam: **~-full** *adj* *container* vollgestopft, gepfropft voll; *room, bus* überfüllt, knallvoll (*inf*), proppenvoll (*inf*); **~-full of people** vollgestopft mit Leuten; **~ jar** *n* Marmeladenglas *nt*.

jamming ['dʒæmiŋ] *n* (*Rad*) Störung *f*. **~ station** Störsender *m*.

jammy ['dʒæmi] *adj* (+*er*) (*Brit sl: lucky*) Glücks-. **a ~ shot** ein Glückstreffer *m*; **the ~ bugger won three in a row** der mit seinem Schweineglück *or* der verdammte Glückspilz hat dreimal nacheinander gewonnen (*inf*).

jam: **~-packed** *adj* überfüllt, proppenvoll (*inf*); **~-packed with tourists** voller Touristen; **~ pot** *n* Marmeladentöpfchen *nt*; **~ puff** *n* Blätterteigteilchen *nt* mit Marmelade; **~ roll** *n* Biskuitrolle *f*; **~ session** *n* Jam Session *f*.

Jan *abbr of* **January** Jan.

Jane [dʒein] *n* (*a*) *see* **plain**. (*b*) **j~** (*US sl: woman*) Weib *nt* (*inf*).

jangle ['dʒæŋgl] **1** *vi* *keys, money* klimpern (*inf*); (*bells*) bimmeln (*inf*); *chains, harness* klirren, rasseln. **2** *vt* *money* klimpern mit; *bell* bimmeln lassen; *keys also, chains* rasseln mit. **it ~d my nerves** das ist mir durch Mark und Bein gegangen. **3** *n* *see* **jangling** 2.

jangling ['dʒæŋgliŋ] **1** *adj* *keys, money* klimpernd; *bells* bimmelnd; *chains, harness* klirrend, rasselnd. **2** *n see vi* Klimpern *nt*, Geklimper (*inf*) *nt*; Bimmeln *nt*; Klirren, Rasseln *nt*.

janitor ['dʒænitəʳ] *n* Hausmeister *m*; (*of block of flats also*) Hauswart *m*.

janitress ['dʒænitris] *n* Hausmeisterin *f*.

January ['dʒænjuəri] *n* Januar *m*; *see also* **September**.

Janus ['dʒeinəs] *n* Janus *m*.

Jap [dʒæp] *n* (*pej inf*) Japs(e) *m* (*pej*).

japan [dʒə'pæn] **1** *n* schwarzer Lack, Japanlack *m*. **2** *vt* mit Japanlack überziehen.

Japan [dʒə'pæn] *n* Japan *nt*.

Japanese [ˌdʒæpə'niːz] **1** *adj* japanisch. **2** *n* (*a*) Japaner(in *f*) *m*. (*b*) (*language*) Japanisch *nt*.

jape [dʒeip] **1** *n* (*old*) Spaß, Scherz *m*; (*trick*) Streich *m*. **2** *vi* spaßen, scherzen.

japonica [dʒə'pɔnikə] *n* japanische Quitte.

jar¹ [dʒɑːʳ] *n* (*a*) (*for jam, marmalade etc*) Glas *nt*; (*without handle*) Topf *m*, Gefäß *nt*; (*with handle*) Krug *m*. (*b*) (*inf: drink*) Bierchen *nt* (*inf*). **fancy a ~?** kommst du (mit) auf ein Bierchen? (*inf*).

jar² **1** *n* (*a*) (*jolt*) Ruck *m*. **he/his neck got quite a ~ in the accident** er/sein Hals hat bei dem Autounfall einen schweren Stoß abbekommen.
(*b*) (*fig*) Schock *m*. **the news gave me a bit of a ~** die Nachricht hat mir einen ziemlichen Schock *or* Schlag versetzt.
2 *vi* (*a*) (*grate: metal etc*) kreischen, quietschen. **to ~ on** *or* **against sth** auf etw (*dat*) quietschen *or* kreischen.
(*b*) (*be out of harmony*) (*note*) schauerlich klingen; (*colours, patterns*) sich beißen (*inf*), nicht harmonieren (*with* mit); (*ideas, opinions*) sich nicht vertragen, nicht harmonieren (*with* mit). **this ~s stylistically** das fällt stilmäßig aus dem Rahmen.
3 *vt* *building* etc erschüttern; *back, knee* sich (*dat*) stauchen; (*jolt continuously*) durchrütteln; (*fig*) einen Schock versetzen (+*dat*). **he must have ~red the camera** er muß den Photoapparat gewackelt haben; **someone ~red my elbow** jemand hat mir an den *or* mich am Ellbogen gestoßen.

♦ **jar (up)on** *vi* +*prep obj* Schauer über den Rücken jagen (+*dat*). **this noise ~s ~ my nerves** dieser Lärm geht mir auf die Nerven; **her voice ~s ~ my ears** ihre Stimme geht mir durch und durch.

jardinière [ˌdʒɑːdɪnɪ'ɛəʳ] *n* Blumenbank *f*.

jargon ['dʒɑːgən] *n* Jargon *m* (*pej*), Fachsprache *f*.

jarring ['dʒɑːriŋ] *adj* *sound* gellend, kreischend; *accent* störend; *colour, pattern* sich beißend *attr* (*inf*), nicht zusammenpassend *attr*.

jasmin(e) ['dʒæzmin] *n* Jasmin *m*. **winter ~** gelber Jasmin.

Jason ['dʒeisən] *n* Jason *m*.

jasper ['dʒæspəʳ] *n* Jaspis *m*.

jaundice ['dʒɔːndis] *n* Gelbsucht *f*.

jaundiced ['dʒɔːndist] *adj* (*a*) (*lit*) gelbsüchtig. (*b*) *attitude* verbittert, zynisch. **to take a ~ view of sth** in bezug auf etw (*acc*) zynisch sein.

jaunt [dʒɔːnt] *n* Trip *m*, Spritztour *f*. **to go for** *or* **on a ~** einen

jauntily

Ausflug *or* eine Spritztour machen; **on his last ~ through Europe** auf seiner letzten Europatour, auf seinem letzten Trip durch Europa.

jauntily ['dʒɔːntɪlɪ] *adv* munter, fröhlich, unbeschwert; *walk also* schwungvoll. **with his hat perched ~ over one ear** den Hut keck aufgesetzt, den Hut keck auf einem Ohr.

jauntiness ['dʒɔːntɪnɪs] *n* Unbeschwertheit, Sorglosigkeit *f*; *(of singing)* Munterkeit, Fröhlichkeit, Heiterkeit *f*. **the ~ of his step** sein schwungvoller *or* munterer Gang.

jaunty ['dʒɔːntɪ] *adj (+er)* munter, fröhlich, unbeschwert; *tune also*, *hat* flott; *attitude* unbeschwert, sorglos, unbekümmert; *steps also* schwungvoll. **he wore his hat at a ~ angle** er hatte den Hut keck aufgesetzt.

Java ['dʒɑːvə] *n* Java *nt*.

Javanese [ˌdʒɑːvə'niːz] **1** *adj (also Javan)* javanisch. **2** *n* (a) Javaner(in *f*) *m*. **(b)** *(language)* Javanisch *nt*.

javelin ['dʒævlɪn] *n* Speer *m*. **in the ~** *(Sport)* beim Speerwerfen; **throwing the ~, ~ throwing** Speerwerfen *nt*; **~ thrower** Speerwerfer(in *f*) *m*.

jaw [dʒɔː] **1** *n* (a) Kiefer *m*, Kinnlade *f*. **the lion opened its ~s** der Löwe riß seinen Rachen auf; **with its prey between its ~s** mit der Beute im Maul.

(b) **~s** *pl (fig) (of valley etc)* Mündung, Öffnung *f*; **the ~s of death** die Klauen *pl* des Todes; **the company charged into the ~s of death** die Kompanie ging in den sicheren Tod; **snatched from the very ~s of death** den Klauen des Todes entrissen; **like walking into the ~s of death** wie ein Gang zum Schafott.

(c) *(of pincer, vice)* (Klemm)backe *f*.

(d) *(inf: chatting)* Gerede, Geschwätz *nt*; *(chat)* Schwatz *m*, Schwätzchen *nt*.

(e) *(inf: sermonizing)* (Moral)predigt *f (inf)*; *(sermon)* Moralpredigt *f (inf)*.

2 *vi* (a) *(inf: chat)* quatschen *(inf)*, quasseln *(inf)*.

(b) *(inf: moralize)* predigen *(inf)*.

jaw: **~bone** *n* Kieferknochen *m*, Kinnbacke *f*; **~breaker** *n (inf)* Zungenbrecher *m*.

jay [dʒeɪ] *n* Eichelhäher *m*.

jay: **~walk** *vi* sich als Fußgänger unachtsam verhalten; **~walker** *n* unachtsamer Fußgänger; **~walking** *n* Unachtsamkeit *f* (eines Fußgängers) im Straßenverkehr.

jazz [dʒæz] **1** *n* (a) *(Mus)* Jazz *m*.

(b) *(inf: talk)* Getön *(inf)*, Gewäsch *(pej)*. **he gave me a lot of ~ about his marvellous job** er schwärmte mir was von seinem tollen Job vor *(inf)*; **... and all that ~** ... und all so 'n Zeug *(inf)*, ... und das ganze Drum und Dran *(inf)*.

2 *attr* band, music Jazz-.

3 *vi (dated: play ~)* jazzen, Jazz machen.

♦**jazz up** *vt sep* aufmöbeln *(inf)*, aufpeppen *(inf)*. **to ~ ~ the classics** klassische Musik verjazzen.

jazzman ['dʒæzmæn] *n, pl* **-men** [-men] Jazzer *m*.

jazzy ['dʒæzɪ] *adj (+er)* colour knallig *(inf)*, auffallend, schreiend *(pej)*; pattern wild, stark gemustert, auffallend; dress, tie poppig *(inf)*, knallig *(inf)*.

JC *abbr of* **Jesus Christ** J. Chr.

jealous ['dʒeləs] *adj* (a) husband, lover, child etc eifersüchtig; *(envious: of sb's possessions, success etc)* neidisch, mißgünstig. **to be ~ of sb** auf jdn eifersüchtig sein/jdn beneiden; **I'm not at all ~ of his success** ich bin nicht neidisch auf seinen Erfolg, ich beneide ihn nicht um seinen Erfolg.

(b) *(watchful, careful)* sehr besorgt *(of um)*, bedacht *(of auf +acc)*. **guardian** strenger Wächter *or* Hüter; **to keep a ~ watch over** *or* **a ~ eye on sb** jdn mit Argusaugen bewachen.

(c) *(Bibl)* **a ~ God** ein eifersüchtiger Gott.

jealously ['dʒeləslɪ] *adv* (a) *see adj* (a). **(b)** *(carefully)* sorgsam, sorgfältig.

jealousy ['dʒeləsɪ] *n see adj (of auf +acc)* Eifersucht *f*; Neid *m*, Mißgunst *f*. **their small-minded, petty jealousies** ihre engstirnigen, kleinlichen Eifersüchteleien *pl*.

jeans [dʒiːnz] *npl* Jeans *pl*. **a pair of ~** (ein Paar) Jeans *pl*.

jeep [dʒiːp] *n* Jeep *m*.

jeepers (creepers) ['dʒiːpəz('kriːpəz)] *interj (US inf)* Mensch *(inf)*.

jeer [dʒɪər] **1** *n (remark)* höhnische Bemerkung, Spöttelei *f*; *(shout, boo)* Buhruf *m*, Johlen *nt no pl*; *(laughter)* Hohngelächter *nt*, schadenfrohes *or* hämisches Lachen *no pl*.

2 *vi see n* höhnische Bemerkungen machen, höhnen *(old, geh)*; johlen, buhen; höhnisch *or* hämisch *or* schadenfroh lachen. **to ~ at sb** jdn (laut) verhöhnen; **he's doing his best, don't ~** er versucht sein Bestes, also spotte nicht.

jeering ['dʒɪərɪŋ] *see jeer* **1 1** *adj* höhnisch; johlend; hämisch *or* höhnisch lachend. **2** *n* höhnische Bemerkungen *pl*; Johlen, Gejohle *nt*; Hohngelächter *nt*.

Jehovah [dʒɪ'həʊvə] *n* Jehova, Jahwe *m*. **~'s witness** Zeuge *m* Jehovas.

jejune [dʒɪ'dʒuːn] *adj (liter) (dull)* fade, langweilig; *(naive, simple)* simpel.

jell [dʒel] *vi see* **gel**.

jello ['dʒeləʊ] *n (US)* Wackelpeter *m (inf)*.

jelly ['dʒelɪ] **1** *n* (a) Gelee *nt*; *(esp Brit: dessert)* (rote) Grütze, Wackelpeter *m (inf)*; *(esp US: jam)* Marmelade *f*; *(round meat etc)* Aspik, Gallert(e) *f*. **it forms a kind of ~** es bildet eine gelee- *or* gallertartige Masse. **(b)** *(sl: gelignite)* Dynamit *nt*. **2** *vt* in Aspik einlegen. **jellied eels** Aal in Aspik, Sülzaale *pl*.

jelly: **~baby** *n (Brit)* Gummibärchen *nt*; **~bean** *n* Geleebonbon *m or nt*; **~fish** *n* Qualle *f*.

jemmy ['dʒemɪ], *(US)* **jimmy** *n* Brecheisen, Stemmeisen *nt*.

jenny ['dʒenɪ] *n (donkey)* Eselin *f*; *(mule)* weibliches Maultier; *(spinning ~)* (frühe) Feinspinnmaschine. **~ wren** Zaunkönigweibchen *nt (in children's stories)* Frau Zaunkönig.

jeopardize ['dʒepədaɪz] *vt* gefährden, in Gefahr bringen.

jeopardy ['dʒepədɪ] *n* Gefahr *f*. **in ~** in Gefahr, gefährdet; **to**

---

put sb/sth in ~ jdn/etw gefährden *or* in Gefahr bringen; **to be in ~ of one's life** in Lebensgefahr schweben *or* sein.

jerbil *n see* **gerbil**.

jeremiad [ˌdʒerɪ'maɪəd] *n (liter)* Jeremiade *f (liter)*, Klagelied *nt*.

Jeremiah [ˌdʒerɪ'maɪə] *n* Jeremia(s) *m*.

Jericho ['dʒerɪkəʊ] *n* Jericho *nt*.

jerk [dʒɜːk] **1** *n* (a) Ruck *m*; *(jump)* Satz *m*; *(spasm, twitch)* Zuckung *f*, Zucken *nt no pl*. **to give sth a ~** einer Sache *(dat)* einen Ruck geben; rope, fishing line an etw *(dat)* ruckartig ziehen; **to give a ~** *(car)* rucken, einen Satz machen; *(twitch)* *(person)* zusammenzucken; *(knee etc)* zucken; *(head)* zurückzucken; **the train stopped with a ~/a series of ~s** der Zug hielt mit einem Ruck/ruckweise an; **to move in a series of ~s** sich ruckartig bewegen.

(b) *see* **physical ~s**.

(c) *(sl: person)* Trottel *(inf)*, Dämlack *(inf) m*.

2 *vt* rucken *or* ruckeln *(inf)* an *(+dat)*. **the impact ~ed his head forward/back** beim Aufprall wurde sein Kopf nach vorn/hinten geschleudert; **he ~ed the fish out of the water** er zog den Fisch mit einem Ruck aus dem Wasser; **he ~ed his head back to avoid the punch** er riß den Kopf zurück, um dem Schlag auszuweichen; **to ~ up one's head** den Kopf hochreißen; **he ~ed the book away/out** er riß das Buch weg/er riß mir das Buch aus der Hand; **he ~ed himself free** er riß sich los; **to ~ out one's words** die Worte hervorstoßen.

3 *vi* *(rope, fishing line)* rucken; *(move jerkily)* ruckeln *(inf)*; *(body, muscle)* zucken, zusammenzucken; *(head)* zurückzucken. **he ~ed away from me** er sprang mit einem Satz von mir weg; **his head ~ed forward** sein Kopf wurde nach vorne geschleudert; **the car ~ed forward** der Wagen machte einen Satz *or* Ruck nach vorn; **the car ~ed to a stop** das Auto hielt ruckweise an; **to ~ out/open** heraus-/aufspringen.

♦**jerk off** *vi (sl: masturbate)* sich *(dat)* einen runterholen *(sl)*.

jerkily ['dʒɜːkɪlɪ] *adv* ruckartig; *(over cobbles etc)* holpernd, rüttelnd; write, speak holprig.

jerkin ['dʒɜːkɪn] *n* Jacke *f*; *(Hist)* (Leder)wams *nt*.

jerkwater ['dʒɜːkˌwɔːtəʳ] *adj attr (US inf)* Provinz-. **a ~ town** ein Kaff *(inf)*, ein (Provinz)nest *(inf) nt*.

jerky ['dʒɜːkɪ] *adj (+er)* (a) ruckartig; *way of speaking also* abgehackt; *style* sprunghaft, abgehackt. **a ~ ride over cobbles/in an old bus** eine holprige Fahrt über Kopfsteinpflaster/in einem alten Bus. **(b)** *(sl: foolish)* trottelig *(inf)*, blöd *(inf)*.

jeroboam [ˌdʒerɪ'bəʊəm] *n* Doppelmagnum(flasche) *f*.

Jerome [dʒə'rəʊm] *n* Hieronymus *m*.

jerry ['dʒerɪ] *n (Brit sl: chamberpot)* Pott *(inf)*, Thron *(inf) m*.

Jerry ['dʒerɪ] *n (esp Mil sl) (German soldier)* deutscher Soldat, Deutsche(r) *m*; *(the Germans)* die Deutschen *pl*.

jerry: **~-builder** *n* schlampiger *or* pfuschender Bauunternehmer; **~-building** *n* schlampige *or* gehudelte *(S Ger)* Bauweise; **~-built** *adj* schlampig gebaut; **~ can** *n* großer (Blech)kanister.

jersey ['dʒɜːzɪ] *n* (a) Pullover *m*; *(Cycling, Ftbl etc)* Trikot *nt*; *(cloth)* Jersey *m*. **~ wool** Wolljersey *m*.

Jersey ['dʒɜːzɪ] *n* (a) Jersey *nt*. **(b)** *(cow)* Jersey(rind) *nt*.

Jerusalem [dʒə'ruːsələm] *n* Jerusalem *nt*. **~ artichoke** Jerusalem- *or* Erdartischocke *f*, Topinambur *m*.

jessamine ['dʒesəmɪn] *n* Jasmin *m*.

jest [dʒest] **1** *n (no pl: fun)* Spaß *m*; *(joke also)* Scherz, Witz *m*. **in ~** im Spaß. **2** *vi* scherzen, spaßen. **you ~, sir!** *(old)* Sie belieben zu scherzen, mein Herr! *(old)*; **she's not a woman to ~ with** sie läßt nicht mit sich spaßen; **to ~ about sth** über etw *(acc)* Scherze *or* Witze machen.

jester ['dʒestəʳ] *n* (a) *(Hist)* Narr *m*. **the King's ~** der Hofnarr. **(b)** *(joker)* Spaßvogel, Witzbold *(inf) m*.

jesting ['dʒestɪŋ] **1** *adj* spaßend, scherzhaft. **it's no ~ matter** darüber macht man keine Späße *or* Witze. **2** *n* Spaßen, Scherzen *nt*.

jestingly ['dʒestɪŋlɪ] *adv* im Spaß, scherzhaft.

Jesuit ['dʒezjuːɪt] *n* Jesuit *m*.

Jesuitic(al) [ˌdʒezjuː'ɪtɪk(əl)] *adj* jesuitisch, Jesuiten-. *m*.

Jesuitism ['dʒezjuːtɪzəm], **Jesuitry** ['dʒezjuːtrɪ] *n* Jesuitismus *m*.

Jesus ['dʒiːzəs] **1** *n* Jesus *m*. **~ Christ** Jesus Christus. **2** *interj (sl)* Mensch *(inf)*. **~ Christ!** Herr Gott, (noch mal)! *(inf)*; *(surprised)* Menschenskind! *(inf)*.

jet¹ [dʒet] **1** *n* (a) *(of water, vapour)* Strahl *m*. **a thin ~ of water** ein dünner Wasserstrahl; **a ~ of gas** (aus einer Düse) austretendes Gas.

(b) *(nozzle)* Düse *f*.

(c) *(engine)* Düsentriebwerk, Strahltriebwerk *nt*; *(also ~ plane)* Düsenflugzeug *nt*, Jet *m (inf)*.

2 *vi* (a) *(water etc)* schießen.

(b) *(Aviat)* jetten *(inf)*.

3 *attr (Aviat)* Düsen-.

jet² *n (Miner)* Jett *m or nt*, Gagat *m*. **~ black** kohl(pech)rabenschwarz.

jet: **~ engine** *n* Düsentriebwerk, Strahltriebwerk *nt*; **~-engined** *adj* Düsen-, mit Düsenantrieb; **~ fighter** *n* Düsenjäger *m*; **~-lag** *n* Schwierigkeiten *pl* durch die Zeitumstellung; **he's suffering from ~-lag** er ist durch die Zeitumstellung völlig aus dem Rhythmus gekommen; **~ plane** *n* Düsenflugzeug *nt*; **~-powered, ~-propelled** *adj* mit Strahl- *or* Düsenantrieb, Düsen-; **~ propulsion** *n* Düsen- *or* Strahlantrieb *m*.

jetsam ['dʒetsəm] *n* über Bord geworfenes Gut; *(on beach)* Strandgut *nt*; *see* **flotsam**.

jet: **~ set** *n* Jet-set *m*; **~-setter** *n* he has become a real ~-setter der ist voll in den Jet-set eingestiegen *(inf)*; **~-setting** *n* Jet-set-Leben *nt*.

jettison ['dʒetɪsn] *vt* (a) *(Naut, Aviat)* (als Ballast) abwerfen *or* über Bord werfen. **(b)** *(fig)* plan über Bord werfen; person abhängen, aufgeben; *unwanted articles* wegwerfen.

jetty ['dʒetɪ] n (*breakwater*) Mole f, Hafendamm m; (*landing pier*) Landesteg, Pier m, Landungsbrücke f.

Jew [dʒuː] n (a) Jude m, Jüdin f. **~-baiting** Judenverfolgung, Judenhetze f. (b) (*pej inf*) Geizkragen, Geizhals (*inf*) m.

jewel ['dʒuːəl] n (a) (*of crane*) Edelstein m, Juwel nt (*geh*); (*piece of jewellery*) Schmuckstück nt. **~ box**, **~ case** Schmuckkästchen nt, Schmuckkasten m; **a case full of ~s** ein Koffer voll Juwelen or wertvoller Schmuckstücke. (b) (*of watch*) Stein m. (c) (*fig: person*) Juwel, Goldstück (*inf*) nt.

jewelled, (*US*) **jeweled** ['dʒuːəld] adj mit Juwelen (*geh*) or Edelsteinen besetzt; *watch* mit Steinen.

jeweller, (*US*) **jeweler** ['dʒuːələʳ] n Juwelier, Schmuckhändler m; (*making jewellery*) Goldschmied m. **at the ~'s (shop)** beim Juwelier, im Juwelierladen.

jewellery, (*US*) **jewelry** ['dʒuːəlrɪ] n Schmuck m no pl. **a piece of ~** ein Schmuckstück nt.

Jewess ['dʒuːɪs] n Jüdin f.

Jewish ['dʒuːɪʃ] adj jüdisch; (*pej inf: mean*) knickerig (*inf*).

Jewry ['dʒʊərɪ] n die Juden pl, das jüdische Volk.

jew's-harp ['dʒuːz'hɑːp] n Maultrommel f, Brummeisen nt.

Jezebel ['dʒezəbel] n (*Bibl*) Isebel f; (*fig*) verruchtes Weib.

jib [dʒɪb] n 1 n (a) (*of crane*) Ausleger, Dreharm m. (b) (*Naut*) Klüver m. **~-boom** Klüverbaum m. (c) (*dated inf*) until I see the cut of his ~ bis ich weiß, was für ein Mensch er ist; I don't like the cut of his ~ seine Nase gefällt mir nicht.
2 vi (*horse*) scheuen, bocken (*at vor + dat*). **to ~ at sth** (*person*) sich gegen etw sträuben.

jibe [dʒaɪb] n, vi see gibe.

jiffy ['dʒɪfɪ], **jiff** [dʒɪf] n (*inf*) Minütchen nt (*inf*). I won't be a ~ ich komme sofort or gleich; (*back soon*) ich bin sofort or gleich wieder da; half a ~/wait a ~! Augenblick(chen)! (*inf*); in a ~ sofort, gleich.

jig [dʒɪg] 1 n (a) (*dance*) lebhafter Volkstanz. she did a little ~ (*fig*) sie vollführte einen Freudentanz.
(b) (*Tech*) Spannvorrichtung f.
2 vi (*dance*) tanzen; (*fig: also ~ about*) herumhüpfen. **to ~ up and down** Sprünge machen, herumspringen.
3 vt he was ~ging his foot up and down er wippte mit dem Fuß; **to ~ a baby up and down on one's knees** ein Kind auf den Knien reiten lassen or schaukeln.

jigger ['dʒɪgəʳ] n (a) (*sieve*) Schüttelsieb nt. (b) (*US: measure*) Meßbecher m für Alkohol: 1¼ Unzen. (c) (*sandflea*) Sandfloh m.

jiggered ['dʒɪgəd] adj (*inf*) well, I'm ~! da bin ich aber platt (*inf*) or baff (*inf*); I'm ~ if I'll do it den Teufel werde ich tun (*inf*); **to be ~** (*tired*) kaputt sein (*inf*).

jiggery-pokery ['dʒɪgərɪ'pəʊkərɪ] n (*inf*) Schmu m (*inf*). I think there's been some ~ going on here ich glaube, hier geht es nicht ganz hasenrein zu (*inf*) or hier ist was faul (*inf*).

jiggle ['dʒɪgl] vt wackeln mit; *door handle* rütteln an (+ dat).

jigsaw ['dʒɪgsɔː] n (a) (*Tech*) Tischler-Bandsäge f. (b) (*also ~ puzzle*) Puzzle(spiel) nt.

jilt [dʒɪlt] vt *lover* den Laufpaß geben (+ dat); *girl* sitzenlassen. **~ed** verschmäht.

Jim [dʒɪm] n dim of **James**.

Jim Crow 1 n (*pej: negro*) Nigger (*pej*), Schwarze(r) m; (*discrimination*) Rassendiskriminierung f. 2 attr *law, policy* (*gegen Neger*) diskriminierend; *saloon etc* Neger-.

jim-dandy ['dʒɪm'dændɪ] adj (*US inf*) prima (*inf*), klasse (*inf*).

jiminy ['dʒɪmɪnɪ] interj (*US*) Menschenskind (*inf*).

jim-jams ['dʒɪmdʒæmz] n (*sl*) (a) (*nervousness*) Muffe f (*sl*), Muffensausen nt (*sl*). he has the ~ ihm geht die Muffe (*sl*), er hat Muffensausen (*sl*); it gives me the ~ da geht mir die Muffe (*sl*), da kriege ich Muffensausen (*sl*). (b) (*the creeps*) Gruseln, Grausen nt, Gänsehaut f. he gives me the ~ bei dem kriege ich das große Grausen (*inf*).

jimmy ['dʒɪmɪ] n (*US*) see **jemmy**.

Jimmy ['dʒɪmɪ] n dim of **James**.

jingle ['dʒɪŋgl] 1 n (a) (*of keys, coins etc*) Geklimper, Klimpern nt; (*of bells*) Bimmeln nt.
(b) (*catchy verse*) Spruch m, Verschen nt; (*for remembering*) Merkvers m. **advertising ~** Werbespruch m.
2 vi (*keys, coins etc*) klimpern; (*bells*) bimmeln.
3 vt *keys, coins* klimpern mit; *bells* bimmeln lassen.

jingly ['dʒɪŋglɪ] adj klingelnd, bimmelnd.

jingo ['dʒɪŋgəʊ] n, pl **-es** (a) Hurrapatriot, Chauvinist m. (b) (*dated inf*) by ~! Tod und Teufel! (*old*), Teufel, Teufel! (*inf*).

jingoism ['dʒɪŋgəʊɪzəm] n Hurrapatriotismus, Chauvinismus m.

jingoistic [ˌdʒɪŋgəʊ'ɪstɪk] adj hurrapatriotisch, chauvinistisch.

jinks [dʒɪŋks] npl (*inf*) see **high ~**.

jinn [dʒɪn] n Dschinn m.

jinx [dʒɪŋks] n there must be or there's a ~ on it das ist verhext; he's been a ~ on us er hat uns nur Unglück gebracht; **to put a ~ on sth** etw verhexen.

jitney ['dʒɪtnɪ] n (*US sl*) Fünfcentmünze f; (*bus*) billiger Bus.

jitterbug ['dʒɪtəbʌg] 1 n (a) (*dance*) Jitterbug m. (b) (*inf: panicky person*) Nervenbündel nt (*inf*). 2 vi Jitterbug tanzen.

jitters ['dʒɪtəz] npl (*inf*) the ~ das große Zittern (*inf*) or Bibbern (*inf*); his ~ sein Bammel m (*inf*); he had a bad case of) the ~ about the exam er hatte wegen der Prüfung das große Zittern (*inf*); **to give sb the ~** jdn ganz rappelig machen (*inf*).

jittery ['dʒɪtərɪ] adj (*inf*) nervös, rappelig (*inf*).

jiujitsu [dʒuː'dʒɪtsuː] n Jiu-Jitsu nt.

jive [dʒaɪv] 1 n (*dance*) Swing m. 2 vi swingen, Swing tanzen.

Joan [dʒəʊn] n Johanna f. **~ of Arc** Johanna von Orleans, Jeanne d'Arc.

Job [dʒəʊb] n (*Bibl*) Hiob, Job m. **the Book of ~** das Buch Hiob; he/that would try the patience of ~ bei ihm/da muß man eine Engelsgeduld haben; **~'s comforter** jemand, der durch seinen

---

Trost die Situation nur verschlimmert; you're a real ~'s comforter du bist vielleicht ein schöner or schwacher Trost.

job [dʒɒb] 1 n (a) (*piece of work*) Arbeit f. I have a ~ to do ich habe zu tun; I have several ~s to do ich habe verschiedene Sachen zu erledigen; I have a little ~ for you ich habe da eine kleine Arbeit or Aufgabe für Sie; it's quite a ~ to paint the house das ist vielleicht eine Arbeit or eine Heidenarbeit (*inf*), das Haus zu streichen; the car's in for a spray ~ (*inf*) der Wagen ist zum Lackieren in der Werkstatt; the plumbers have a lot of ~s on just now die Klempner haben zur Zeit viele Aufträge; **to be paid by the ~** für (die) geleistete Arbeit bezahlt werden, pro Auftrag bezahlt werden; he's on the ~ (*inf: at work*) er ist bei or an der Arbeit; (*sl: having sex*) er ist am Ball (*inf*) or zu Gange (*inf*); **to make a good/bad ~ of sth** etw gut or sauber (*inf*) hinkriegen/etw verpatzen or versauen (*inf*); he knows his ~ er versteht sein Handwerk, er versteht sich auf seine Arbeit; see **odd**.
(b) (*employment*) Stelle f, Job m (*inf*). the nice thing about a teaching ~ is ... das Schöne am Lehrberuf or an einer Anstellung als Lehrer ist ...; he had a vacation ~ or a ~ for the vacation er hatte eine Ferienarbeit or einen Ferienjob (*inf*); 500 ~s lost 500 Arbeitsplätze verlorengegangen; **to bring new ~s to a region** in einer Gegend neue Arbeitsplätze schaffen.
(c) (*duty*) Aufgabe f. that's not my ~ dafür bin ich nicht zuständig; it's not my ~ to tell him es ist nicht meine Aufgabe, ihm das zu sagen; I'll do my ~ and you do yours ich mache meine Arbeit, und Sie Ihre; it's your ~ to make the tea Sie haben sich um den Tee zu kümmern, es ist Ihre Aufgabe, den Tee zu machen; I had the ~ of breaking the news to her es fiel mir zu, ihr die Nachricht beizubringen; he's not doing his ~ er erfüllt seine Aufgabe(n) nicht; I'm only doing my ~ ich tue nur meine Pflicht.
(d) that's a good ~! so ein Glück; what a good ~ or it's a good ~ I brought my cheque book, I brought my cheque book and a good ~ too! nur gut, daß ich mein Scheckbuch mitgenommen habe; it's a bad ~ schlimme Sache (*inf*); **to give sb/sth up as a bad ~** jdn/etw aufgeben; that should do the ~ das müßte hinhauen (*inf*); this is just the ~ das ist goldrichtig or genau das richtige; a holiday in the sun would be just the ~ Ferien in der Sonne, das wäre jetzt genau das richtige; double whisky? — just the ~ einen doppelten Whisky? — prima Idee (*inf*).
(e) (*difficulty*) I had a ~ doing it or to do it das war gar nicht so einfach; you'll have a ~ das wird gar nicht so einfach sein; she has a ~ getting up the stairs es ist gar nicht einfach für sie, die Treppe raufzukommen; it was quite a ~ das war ganz schön schwer (*inf*) or schwierig.
(f) (*sl: crime*) Ding nt (*sl*). we're going to do a ~ next week wir drehen nächste Woche ein Ding (*sl*); remember that bank ~? erinnerst du dich an das große Ding in der Bank? (*sl*).
(g) (*inf: person, thing*) Ding nt. his new car's a lovely little ~ sein neues Auto ist wirklich große Klasse (*inf*) or eine Wucht (*inf*); that blonde's a gorgeous little ~ die Blondine (da) sieht wirklich klasse aus (*inf*).
(h) (*baby-talk*) **to do a (big/little) ~** ein (großes/kleines) Geschäft machen (*inf*), Aa/Pipi machen (*baby-talk*).
2 vi (a) (*do casual work*) Gelegenheitsarbeiten tun or verrichten, jobben (*sl*). a graphic designer who ~s for various advertising firms ein Graphiker, der für verschiedene Werbeagenturen Aufträge or Arbeiten ausführt.
(b) (*St Ex*) als Makler tätig sein, Maklergeschäfte betreiben.
(c) (*profit from public position*) sein Amt (zu privatem Nutzen) mißbrauchen.
3 vt (*also ~ out*) *work* in Auftrag geben, auf Kontrakt or auf feste Rechnung vergeben.

jobber ['dʒɒbəʳ] n (a) (*St Ex*) Makler, Börsenhändler, Effektenhändler m. (b) (*casual worker*) Gelegenheitsarbeiter m. (c) (*dishonest person*) Schieber m, jemand, der seine Stellung mißbraucht.

jobbery ['dʒɒbərɪ] n Amtsmißbrauch m, Schiebung f.

jobbing ['dʒɒbɪŋ] 1 adj *worker, gardener* Gelegenheits-; *printer* Akzidenz-. 2 n (a) (*casual work*) Gelegenheitsarbeit f. (b) see **jobbery**. (c) (*St Ex*) Börsen- or Effektenhandel m.

job: **~ description** n Tätigkeitsbeschreibung f; **~ evaluation** n Arbeitsplatzbewertung f; **~ holder** n Arbeitnehmer(in f) m; **~ hunter** n Arbeitsuchende(r) mf; **~ hunting** n Arbeitsuche, Stellensuche (*inf*) f; **to be ~ hunting** auf Arbeitssuche or Stellenjagd (*inf*) sein; **~less** 1 adj arbeitslos, stellungslos; 2 n the **~less** pl die Arbeitslosen pl; **~ lot** n (*Comm*) (Waren)posten m; **~ printer** n Akzidenzdrucker m.

Jock [dʒɒk] n (*inf*) Schotte m.

jockey ['dʒɒkɪ] 1 n Jockei, Jockey, Rennreiter(in f) m.
2 vi **to ~ for position** (*lit*) sich in eine gute Position zu drängeln versuchen, sich gut plazieren wollen; (*fig*) rangeln; they were all ~ing for office in the new government sie rangelten alle um ein Amt in der neuen Regierung; there was a lot of ~ing behind the scenes es gab ziemliche Rangeleien hinter den Kulissen.
3 vt (*force by crafty manoeuvres*) **to ~ sb into doing sth** jdn dazu bringen, etw zu tun; he felt he had been ~ed into it er hatte das Gefühl, daß man ihn da reingequetzt hatte (*inf*); **to ~ sb out of a job** jdn aus seiner Stellung hinausdrängeln (*inf*).

jockstrap ['dʒɒkstræp] n Suspensorium nt.

jocose [dʒə'kəʊs] adj scherzend, launig (*geh*).

jocular ['dʒɒkjʊləʳ] adj lustig, spaßig, witzig. **to be in a ~ mood** zu Scherzen or Späßen aufgelegt sein.

jocularity [ˌdʒɒkjʊ'lærɪtɪ] n Spaßigkeit, Witzigkeit, Scherzhaftigkeit f.

jocularly ['dʒɒkjʊləlɪ] adv scherzhaft; (*as a joke*) im Scherz.

jocund ['dʒɒkənd] adj heiter, fröhlich, frohsinnig (*geh*).

jodhpurs ['dʒɒdpəz] npl Reithose(n pl) f.

Joe [dʒəʊ] n dim of **Joseph** Sepp (*S Ger*), Jupp (*dial*) m.

joey ['dʒəʊɪ] n (Austral inf) junges Känguruh.
jog [dʒɒg] **1** vt stoßen an (+acc) or gegen; person anstoßen. he ~ged the child up and down on his knee er ließ das Kind auf seinem Knie reiten; he was being ~ged up and down on the horse das Pferd schüttelte ihn durch; to ~ sb's memory jds Gedächtnis (dat) nachhelfen or auf die Sprünge helfen.
  2 vi trotten, zuckeln (inf); (Sport) Dauerlauf machen, joggen. to ~ up and down auf und ab hüpfen.
  3 n (a) (push, nudge) Stoß, Schubs, Stups m. to give sb's memory a ~ jds Gedächtnis (dat) nachhelfen.
  (b) (run) trabender Lauf, Trott m; (Sport) Dauerlauf m. he broke into a ~ er fing an zu traben; he came back at a gentle ~ er kam langsam zurückgetrabt or zurückgetrottet; to go for a ~ (Sport) einen Dauerlauf machen, joggen (gehen).
♦**jog about** or **around 1** vi hin und her gerüttelt werden. **2** vt sep durchschütteln, durchrütteln.
♦**jog along** vi (a) (go along: person, vehicle) entlangzuckeln. (b) (fig) (person, worker, industry) vor sich (acc) hin wursteln (inf); (work) seinen Gang gehen.
jogging ['dʒɒgɪŋ] n Dauerlauf m, Joggen nt.
joggle ['dʒɒgl] **1** vt schütteln, rütteln. **2** n Schütteln, Rütteln nt.
jog-trot ['dʒɒgtrɒt] n Trott m.
John [dʒɒn] n Johannes m. ~ the Baptist Johannes der Täufer; ~ Barleycorn der Gerstensaft; ~ Bull ein typischer Engländer, John Bull m; (the English) die Engländer pl; ~ Doe (US) Otto Normalverbraucher m (inf).
john [dʒɒn] n (esp US inf) (toilet) Lokus m (inf), Klo nt (inf); (prostitute's customer) Freier m (inf).
Johnny ['dʒɒnɪ] n dim of **John** Hänschen nt, Hänsel m (old). j~ (Brit sl) (man) Typ m (inf); (condom) Pariser m (inf).
joie de vivre [,ʒwɑːdəˈviːvr] n Lebensfreude, Lebenslust f.
join [dʒɔɪn] **1** vt (a) (lit, fig: connect, unite) verbinden (to mit); (attach also) anfügen (to an +acc). to ~ two things together zwei Dinge (miteinander) verbinden; (attach also) zwei Dinge zusammenfügen or aneinanderfügen; to ~ battle (with the enemy) den Kampf mit dem Feind aufnehmen; to ~ hands (lit, fig) sich (dat) or einander die Hände reichen; ~ed in marriage durch das heilige Band der Ehe verbunden or vereinigt; to his genius he ~s a great humanity er verbindet or vereint Genie mit großer Menschlichkeit; we ~ our prayers to theirs wir stimmen in ihre Gebete ein.
  (b) (become member of) army gehen zu; one's regiment sich anschließen (+dat), sich begeben zu; political party, club beitreten (+dat), Mitglied werden von or bei or in (+dat), eintreten in (+dat); religious order eintreten in (+acc), beitreten (+dat); university (as student) anfangen an (+dat); (as staff) firm anfangen bei; group of people, procession sich anschließen (+dat). to ~ the queue sich in die Schlange stellen or einreihen; he has been ordered to ~ his ship at Liverpool er hat Order bekommen, sich in Liverpool auf seinem Schiff einzufinden or zu seinem Schiff zu begeben; Dr Morris will be ~ing us for a year as guest professor Dr Morris wird ein Jahr bei uns Gastprofessor sein.
  (c) he ~ed us in France er stieß in Frankreich zu uns; I ~ed him at the station wir trafen uns am Bahnhof, ich traf mich mit ihm am Bahnhof; I'll ~ you in five minutes ich bin in fünf Minuten bei Ihnen; (follow you) ich komme in fünf Minuten nach; may I ~ you? kann ich mich Ihnen anschließen?; (sit with you) darf ich Ihnen Gesellschaft leisten?, darf ich mich zu Ihnen setzen?; (in game, plan etc) kann ich mitmachen?; will you ~ us? machen Sie mit, sind Sie dabei?; (sit with us) wollen Sie sich nicht Gesellschaft leisten?, wollen Sie sich (nicht) zu uns setzen?; (come with us) kommen Sie mit?; do ~ us for lunch wollen Sie nicht mit uns essen?; will you ~ me in a drink? trinken Sie ein Glas mit mir?; Paul ~s me in wishing you ... Paul schließt sich meinen Wünschen für ... an; they ~ed us in singing ... sie sangen mit uns zusammen ...
  (d) (river) another river, the sea einmünden or fließen in (+acc); (road) another road (ein)münden in (+acc). his estates ~ ours seine Ländereien grenzen an unsere (an).
  2 vi (a) (also ~ together) (two parts) (be attached) (miteinander) verbunden sein; (be attachable) sich (miteinander) verbinden lassen; (grow together) zusammenwachsen; (meet, be adjacent) zusammenstoßen, zusammentreffen; (rivers) aneinander (an)grenzen; (rivers) zusammenfließen, sich vereinigen; (roads) sich treffen. let us all ~ together in the Lord's Prayer wir wollen alle zusammen das Vaterunser beten; he ~s with me in wishing you ... er schließt sich meinen Wünschen für ... an; to ~ together in doing sth etw zusammen or gemeinsam tun; the bones wouldn't ~ properly die Knochen wollten nicht richtig zusammenheilen; they all ~ed together to get her a present sie taten sich alle zusammen, um ihr ein Geschenk zu kaufen.
  (b) (club member) beitreten, Mitglied werden.
  3 n Naht(stelle) f; (in pipe, knitting) Verbindungsstelle f.
♦**join in** vi (in activity) mitmachen (prep obj bei); (in game also) mitspielen (prep obj bei); (in demonstration also, in protest) sich anschließen (prep obj +dat); (in conversation) sich beteiligen (prep obj an +dat). he doesn't ~ ~ much er beteiligt sich nicht sehr (stark); ~ ~, everybody! (in song etc) alle (mitmachen)!; they all ~ed ~ in singing the chorus sie sangen alle den Refrain mit; everybody ~ed ~ the chorus sie sangen alle zusammen den Refrain, alle fielen in den Refrain ein; he didn't want to ~ ~ the fun er wollte nicht mitmachen.
♦**join on 1** vi (be attachable) sich verbinden lassen (prep obj, -to mit), sich anfügen lassen (prep obj, -to an +acc); (be attached) verbunden sein (prep obj, -to mit); (people: in procession etc) sich anschließen (prep obj, -to +dat, an +acc). **2** vt sep verbinden (prep obj, -to mit); (extend with) ansetzen (prep obj, -to an +acc).
♦**join up 1** vi (a) (Mil) Soldat werden, zum Militär gehen. (b)

(meet: road etc) sich treffen, aufeinanderstoßen; (join forces) sich zusammenschließen, sich zusammentun (inf). **2** vt sep (miteinander) verbinden.
joiner ['dʒɔɪnər] n Tischler, Schreiner m.
joinery ['dʒɔɪnərɪ] n (trade) Tischlerei f, Tischlerhandwerk nt; (piece of ~) Tischlerarbeit f.
joint [dʒɔɪnt] **1** n (a) (Anat, tool, in armour etc) Gelenk nt. he's feeling a bit stiff in the ~s (inf) er fühlt sich ein bißchen steif in den Knochen; the times are out of ~ (fig liter) die Zeit or Welt ist aus den Fugen; see nose.
  (b) (join) (in woodwork) Fuge f; (in pipe etc) Verbindung(s-stelle) f; (welded etc) Naht(stelle) f; (junction piece) Verbindungsstück n.
  (c) (Cook) Braten m. a ~ of beef ein Rindsbraten m.
  (d) (sl: place) Laden (inf), m; (for gambling) Spielhölle f.
  (e) (sl: of marijuana) Joint m (sl).
  2 vt (a) (Cook) (in Stücke) zerlegen or zerteilen.
  (b) boards, pipes etc verbinden.
  3 adj attr gemeinsam; (in connection with possessions also) gemeinschaftlich; action, work, decision also Gemeinschafts-; (co-) ruler, owner etc Mit-; rulers, owners etc gemeinsam; (total, combined) influence, strength vereint. ~ account mehrerer Firmen mit einer Gewerkschaft; ~ agreement nt gemeinsamer or gemischter Ausschuß; it was a ~ effort das ist in Gemeinschaftsarbeit entstanden; it took the ~ efforts of six strong men to move it es waren die vereinten Anstrengungen or Kräfte von sechs starken Männern nötig, um es von der Stelle zu bewegen; ~ estate Gemeinschaftsbesitz m; ~ heir Miterbe m, Miterbin f; they were ~ heirs sie waren gemeinsame Erben; ~ life insurance wechselseitige (Über)lebensversicherung; ~ ownership Miteigentum nt, Mitbesitz m; ~ partner Teilhaber m; ~ plaintiff/plaintiffs Nebenkläger m/gemeinsame Kläger pl; ~ resolution (US Pol) gemeinsamer Beschluß (beider gesetzgebender Versammlungen); ~ stock Aktienkapital nt; ~ stock company/bank Aktiengesellschaft f/-bank f; ~ venture Gemeinschaftsunternehmen nt.
jointed ['dʒɔɪntɪd] adj (articulated) mit Gelenken versehen, gegliedert. a ~ doll eine Gliederpuppe; a ~ fishing rod eine zerlegbare Angel.
jointly ['dʒɔɪntlɪ] adv gemeinsam; decide, work, rule also zusammen, miteinander.
jointure ['dʒɔɪntʃər] n (Jur) Wittum nt.
joist [dʒɔɪst] n Balken m; (of metal, concrete) Träger m.
joke [dʒəʊk] **1** n Witz m; (hoax) Scherz m; (prank) Streich m; (inf: pathetic person or thing) Witz m; (laughing stock) Gespött, Gelächter nt. for a ~ zum Spaß, zum or aus Jux (inf); I don't see the ~ ich möchte wissen, was daran so lustig ist or sein soll; he treats the school rules as a big ~ für ihn sind die Schulregeln ein Witz; he can/can't take a ~ er versteht Spaß/keinen Spaß; what a ~! (inf), zum Totlachen! (inf), zum Schießen! (inf); it's no ~ das ist nicht witzig; the ~ is that ... das Witzige or Lustige daran ist, daß ...; it's beyond a ~ das ist kein Spaß or Witz mehr, das ist nicht mehr lustig; this is getting beyond a ~ das geht (langsam) zu weit; the ~ was on me der Spaß ging auf meine Kosten; why do you have to turn everything into a ~? warum müssen Sie über alles Ihre Witze machen or alles ins Lächerliche ziehen?; I'm not in the mood for ~s ich bin nicht zu(m) Scherzen aufgelegt; to play a ~ on sb jdm einen Streich spielen; to make a ~ about sb/sth einen Witz über jdn/etw machen or reißen (inf); to make ~s about sb/sth über jdn/etw lustig machen, über jdn/etw Witze machen or reißen (inf).
  2 vi Witze machen, scherzen (geh) (about über +acc); (pull sb's leg) Spaß machen. I'm not joking ich meine das ernst; you must be joking! das ist ja wohl nicht Ihr Ernst, das soll wohl ein Witz sein; you're joking! mach keine Sachen (inf) or Witze!; ..., he ~d ..., sagte er scherzhaft.
joker ['dʒəʊkər] n (a) (person) Witzbold, Spaßvogel m. (b) (sl) Typ (inf), Kerl (inf) m. (c) (Cards) Joker m.
jokey adj see joky.
jokily ['dʒəʊkɪlɪ] adv lustig; say scherzhaft, im Scherz.
joking ['dʒəʊkɪŋ] **1** adj tone scherzhaft, spaßend. I'm not in a ~ mood ich bin nicht zu Scherzen or Späßen aufgelegt, mir ist nicht nach Scherzen zumute. **2** n Witze pl. ~ apart or aside Spaß or Scherz beiseite.
jokingly ['dʒəʊkɪŋlɪ] adv im Spaß; say, call also scherzhaft.
joky ['dʒəʊkɪ] adj lustig.
jollification [,dʒɒlɪfɪˈkeɪʃən] n (hum) Festivität f (hum); (merrymaking: also ~s) Festlichkeiten pl.
jollity ['dʒɒlɪtɪ] n Fröhlichkeit, Ausgelassenheit f.
jolly ['dʒɒlɪ] **1** adj (+er) (a) (merry) fröhlich, vergnügt.
  (b) (inf: tipsy) angeheitert (inf).
  2 adv (Brit inf) ganz schön (inf), vielleicht (inf); nice, warm, happy, pleased mächtig (inf). you are ~ lucky Sie haben vielleicht Glück or ein Mordsglück (all inf); ~ good/well prima (inf), famos (dated inf); that's ~ kind of you das ist furchtbar or unheimlich nett von Ihnen; it's getting ~ late es wird langsam spät; you ~ well will go! und ob du gehst!; so you ~ well should be! das will ich schwer meinen! (inf); I should ~ well think so too! das will ich auch gemeint haben!
  3 vt to ~ sb into doing sth jdn bereden, etw zu tun; to ~ sb along jdm aufmunternd zureden; to ~ sb up jdn aufmuntern.
jolly: ~ boat n Beiboot nt; J~ Roger n Totenkopfflagge, Piratenflagge f.
jolt [dʒəʊlt] **1** vi (vehicle) holpern, rüttelnd fahren; (give one ~) einen Ruck machen. to ~ along rüttelnd entlangfahren; the cart ~ed off down the track der Karren fuhr rüttelnd or holpernd den Weg hinunter; to ~ to a halt ruckweise anhalten.
  2 vt (lit) (shake) durchschütteln, durchrütteln; (once) einen Ruck geben or versetzen (+dat); (fig) aufrütteln. to ~ sb out of his complacency jdn aus seiner Zufriedenheit aufrütteln or

reißen; it ~ed him into action das hat ihn aufgerüttelt.
3 *n* (a) (*jerk*) Ruck *m*.
(b) (*fig inf*) Schock *m*. he realized with a ~ ... mit einem Schlag wurde ihm klar, ...; it gave me a ~ das hat mir einen Schock versetzt.

jolting ['dʒəʊltɪŋ] *n* Rütteln, Schütteln, Holpern *nt*. we had a bit of a ~ on the way wir sind auf der Fahrt ziemlich durchgeschüttelt worden.

jolty ['dʒəʊltɪ] *adj* (+er) *cart etc* holp(e)rig, rüttelnd; *road* holp(e)rig, uneben.

Jonah ['dʒəʊnə] *n* Jona(s) *m*.

jonquil ['dʒɒŋkwɪl] *n* Jonquille *f* (*Art von Narzisse*).

Jordan ['dʒɔːdn] *n* (*country*) Jordanien *nt*; (*river*) Jordan *m*.

Joseph ['dʒəʊzɪf] *n* Joseph, Josef *m*.

Josephine ['dʒəʊzɪfiːn] *n* Josephine *f*.

josh [dʒɒʃ] (*US inf*) **1** *vt* aufziehen, veräppeln, verulken (*all inf*).
2 *vi* Spaß machen (*inf*). **3** *n* Neckerei, Hänselei *f*.

Joshua ['dʒɒʃjʊə] *n* Josua *m*.

joss stick ['dʒɒsstɪk] *n* Räucherstäbchen *nt*.

jostle ['dʒɒsl] **1** *vi* drängeln. he ~d against me er rempelte mich an; the people jostling round the stalls die Leute, die sich vor den Buden drängelten; *see* position.
2 *vt* anrempeln, schubsen. they ~d him out of the room sie drängten *or* schubsten ihn aus dem Zimmer; he was ~d along with the crowd die Menge schob ihn mit sich.
3 *n* Gedränge *nt*, Rempelei *f*.

jot [dʒɒt] *n* (*inf*) (*of truth, sense*) Funken *m*, Fünkchen, Körnchen *nt*. it won't do a ~ of good das nützt gar nichts *or* nicht das geringste bißchen; not one ~ or tittle (*inf*) aber auch nicht das kleinste bißchen (*inf*), keinen Deut.

♦ **jot down** *vt sep* sich (*dat*) notieren, sich (*dat*) eine Notiz machen von. to ~ ~ notes Notizen machen.

jotter ['dʒɒtə'] *n* (*note pad*) Notizblock *m*; (*notebook*) Notizheft(chen) *nt*.

jottings ['dʒɒtɪŋz] *npl* Notizen *pl*.

journal ['dʒɜːnl] *n* (a) (*magazine*) Zeitschrift *f*; (*newspaper*) Zeitung *f*. (b) (*diary*) Tagebuch *nt*. to keep a ~ Tagebuch führen. (c) (*Naut*) Logbuch, Bordbuch, Schiffsjournal *nt*; (*Comm*) Journal *nt*; (*daybook*) Tagebuch *nt*; (*Jur*) Gerichtsakten *pl*.

journalese [,dʒɜːnə'liːz] *n* Zeitungsstil, Journalistenjargon *m*.

journalism ['dʒɜːnəlɪzəm] *n* Journalismus *m*.

journalist ['dʒɜːnəlɪst] *n* Journalist(in *f*) *m*.

journalistic [,dʒɜːnə'lɪstɪk] *adj* journalistisch.

journalistically [,dʒɜːnə'lɪstɪkəlɪ] *adv* im Zeitungsstil, in journalistischem Stil.

journey ['dʒɜːnɪ] **1** *n* Reise *f*; (*by car, train etc also*) Fahrt *f*; (*of spaceship etc also*) Flug *m*. to go on a ~ eine Reise machen, verreisen; they have gone on a ~ sie sind verreist; to go on one's/a ~ abreisen/eine Reise antreten; it is a ~ of 50 miles *or* a 50 mile ~ es liegt 50 Meilen entfernt; from X to Y is a ~ of 50 miles/two hours es sind 50 Meilen/zwei Stunden (Fahrt) von X nach Y; a two day ~ eine Zwei-Tage-Reise; it's a two day ~ to get to ... from here man braucht zwei Tage, um von hier nach ... zu kommen; a bus/train ~ eine Bus-/Zugfahrt; the ~ home die Heimreise, die Heimfahrt; he has quite a ~ to get to work er muß ziemlich weit fahren, um zur Arbeit zu kommen; to reach one's ~'s end (*liter*) am Ziel der Reise angelangt sein; his ~ through life sein Lebensweg *m*.
2 *vi* reisen. to ~ on weiterreisen.

journeyman ['dʒɜːnɪmən] *n, pl* -men [-mən] Geselle *m*. ~ baker Bäckergeselle *m*.

joust [dʒaʊst] **1** *vi* im Turnier kämpfen, turnieren (*obs*). **2** *n* Zweikampf *m* im Turnier.

jousting ['dʒaʊstɪŋ] *n* Turnier(kämpfe *pl*) *nt*.

Jove [dʒəʊv] *n* Jupiter *m*. by ~! (*dated*) Donnerwetter!; have you/did he, by ~! tatsächlich!

jovial ['dʒəʊvɪəl] *adj* fröhlich, jovial (*esp pej*); *welcome* freundlich, herzlich.

joviality [,dʒəʊvɪ'ælɪtɪ] *n see adj* Fröhlichkeit, Jovialität (*esp pej*) *f*; Herzlichkeit *f*.

jovially ['dʒəʊvɪəlɪ] *adv see adj*.

jowl [dʒaʊl] *n* (*jaw*) (Unter)kiefer *m*; (*often pl*) (*cheek*) Backe *f*; (*fold of flesh*) Hängebacke *f*; *see* cheek.

joy [dʒɔɪ] *n* (a) Freude *f*. to my great ~ zu meiner großen Freude; she/the garden is a ~ to behold *or* to the eye sie/der Garten ist eine Augenweide; it's a ~ to hear him es ist eine wahre Freude *or* ein Genuß, ihn zu hören; to wish sb ~ jdm Glück und Zufriedenheit) wünschen; I wish you ~ (of it)! (*iro*) na dann viel Spaß *or* viel Vergnügen!; one of the ~s of this job is ... eine der erfreulichen Seiten dieses Berufs ist ...; that's the ~ of this system das ist das Schöne an diesem System; *see* jump.
(b) *no pl* (*Brit inf: success*) Erfolg *m*. I didn't get much/any ~ ich hatte nicht viel/keinen Erfolg; any ~? hat es geklappt? (*inf*); you won't get any ~ out of him bei ihm werden Sie keinen Erfolg haben.

joyful ['dʒɔɪfʊl] *adj* freudig, froh.

joyfully ['dʒɔɪfəlɪ] *adv* freudig.

joyfulness ['dʒɔɪfʊlnɪs] *n* Fröhlichkeit *f*; (*of person also*) Frohsinn *m*, Heiterkeit *f*.

joyless ['dʒɔɪlɪs] *adj* freudlos; *person also* griesgrämig.

joyous ['dʒɔɪəs] *adj* (*liter*) freudig, froh.

joy: ~-ride *n* Spritztour *f*, Vergnügungsfahrt *f* (*in einem gestohlenen Auto*); to go for a ~-ride (ein Auto stehlen und damit) eine Spritztour *or* Vergnügungsfahrt machen; ~-rider *n* Autodieb, der den Wagen nur für eine Spritztour will; ~-stick *n* (*Aviat*) Steuerknüppel *m*.

JP (*Brit*) *abbr of* Justice of the Peace.

Jr *abbr of* junior jr., jun.

jubilant ['dʒuːbɪlənt] *adj* überglücklich; (*expressing joy*) jubelnd *attr*; *voice* jubelnd *attr*, frohlockend *attr*; *face*

strahlend *attr*; (*at sb's failure etc*) triumphierend *attr*. they gave him a ~ welcome sie empfingen ihn mit Jubel; to be ~ überglücklich sein; jubeln; strahlen; triumphieren.

jubilation [,dʒuːbɪ'leɪʃən] *n* Jubel *m*. a cause for ~ ein Grund zum Jubel; a sense of ~ ein Gefühl von Triumph.

jubilee ['dʒuːbɪliː] *n* Jubiläum *nt*.

Judaea [dʒuː'diːə] *n* Judäa *nt*.

Judah ['dʒuːdə] *n* Juda *m*.

Judaic [dʒuː'deɪɪk] *adj* judaisch.

Judaism ['dʒuːdeɪɪzəm] *n* Judaismus *m*.

Judas ['dʒuːdəs] *n* (a) (*Bibl, fig*) Judas *m*. (b) j~ (*hole*) Guckloch *nt*.

judder ['dʒʌdə'] (*Brit*) **1** *n* Erschütterung *f*; (*in car etc*) Ruckeln *nt*. to give a ~ *see vi*. **2** *vi* erzittern; (*person*) zucken; (*car etc*) ruckeln. the train ~ed to a standstill der Zug kam ruckartig zum Stehen.

Judea *n see* Judaea.

judge [dʒʌdʒ] **1** *n* (a) (*Jur*) Richter(in *f*) *m*; (*of competition*) Preisrichter(in *f*) *m*; (*Sport*) Punktrichter(in *f*), Kampfrichter(in *f*) *m*. ~ of appeal Berufungsrichter *m*; ~-advocate (*Mil*) Beisitzer *m* bei einem Kriegsgericht, Kriegsgerichtsrat *m*.
(b) (*fig*) Kenner *m*. to be a good/bad ~ of character ein guter/schlechter Menschenkenner sein; to be a good/no ~ of wine/horses ein/kein Weinkenner/Pferdekenner sein; to be a good ~ of quality Qualität gut beurteilen können; I'll be the ~ of that das müssen Sie mich schon selbst beurteilen lassen.
(c) (*Bibl*) (the Book of) J~s (das Buch der) Richter.
2 *vt* (a) (*Jur*) *person* die Verhandlung führen über (+*acc*); *case* verhandeln; (*God*) richten.
(b) *competition* beurteilen, bewerten; (*Sport*) Punktrichter *or* Kampfrichter sein bei.
(c) (*fig: pass judgement on*) ein Urteil fällen über (+*acc*). you shouldn't ~ people by appearances Sie sollten Menschen nicht nach ihrem Äußeren beurteilen.
(d) (*consider, assess, deem*) halten für, erachten für (*geh*). this was ~d to be the best way dies wurde für die beste Methode gehalten *or* erachtet (*geh*); you can ~ for yourself which is better/how upset I was Sie können selbst beurteilen, was besser ist/Sie können sich (*dat*) denken, wie bestürzt ich war; I can't ~ whether he was right or wrong ich kann nicht beurteilen, ob er recht oder unrecht hatte; I ~d from his manner that he was guilty ich schloß aus seinem Verhalten, daß er schuldig war; how would you ~ him? wie würden Sie ihn beurteilen *or* einschätzen?
(e) (*estimate*) *speed, width, distance etc* einschätzen. he ~d the moment well er hat den richtigen Augenblick abgepaßt.
3 *vi* (a) (*Jur*) Richter sein; (*God*) richten; (*at competition*) Preisrichter sein; (*Sport*) Kampfrichter *or* Punktrichter sein.
(b) (*fig*) (*pass judgement*) ein Urteil fällen; (*form an opinion*) (be)urteilen. who am I to ~? ich kann mir dazu kein Urteil erlauben; as far as one can ~ soweit man (es) beurteilen kann; judging by *or* from sth nach etw zu urteilen; judging by appearances dem Aussehen nach; to ~ by appearances nach dem Äußeren urteilen; to ~ for yourself beurteilen Sie das selbst; he let me ~ for myself er überließ es meinem Urteil.

judg(e)ment ['dʒʌdʒmənt] *n* (a) (*Jur*) (Gerichts)urteil *nt*; (*Eccl*) Gericht *nt*; Richterspruch *m*; (*divine punishment*) Strafe *f* Gottes. to await ~ (*Jur*) auf sein *or* das Urteil warten; (*Eccl*) auf das Gericht *or* den Richterspruch (Gottes) warten; the Day of J~ der Tag des Jüngsten Gerichtes; to pass (*also fig*) *or* give *or* deliver ~ ein Urteil fällen, das Urteil sprechen (on über +*acc*); to sit in ~ on a case einen Fall verhandeln, Richter in einem Fall sein; to sit in ~ on sb über jdn zu Gericht sitzen *or* ziehen; (*Jur also*) die Verhandlung über jdn führen; I don't want to sit in ~ on you ich möchte mich nicht zu Ihrem Richter aufspielen; it's a ~ from above das ist die Strafe Gottes; it's a ~ on him for being so lazy das ist die Strafe Gottes dafür, daß er so faul war/ist.
(b) (*opinion*) Meinung, Ansicht *f*, Urteil *nt*; (*moral ~, value ~*) Werturteil *nt*; (*estimation: of distance, speed etc*) Einschätzung *f*. to give one's ~ on sth sein Urteil über etw (*acc*) abgeben, seine Meinung zu etw äußern; an error of ~ eine falsche Einschätzung, eine Fehleinschätzung; in my ~ meines Erachtens, meiner Meinung nach.
(c) (*discernment*) Urteilsvermögen *nt*. a man of ~ ein Mensch mit einem guten Urteilsvermögen; to show ~ ein gutes Urteilsvermögen beweisen *or* zeigen; it's all a question of ~ das ist eine Frage des Gefühls.

judg(e)ment: J~ Day *n* Tag *m* des Jüngsten Gerichts; ~ seat *n* Gottes Richterstuhl *m*.

judicature ['dʒuːdɪkətʃə'] *n* (*judges*) Richterstand *m*; (*judicial system*) Gerichtswesen *nt*, Gerichtsbarkeit *f*.

judicial [dʒuː'dɪʃl] *adj* (a) (*Jur*) gerichtlich, Justiz-; *power* richterlich; ~ function Richteramt *nt*; to take *or* bring ~ proceedings against sb ein Gerichtsverfahren *nt* gegen jdn anstrengen *or* einleiten; ~ murder Justizmord *m*; ~ separation Gerichtsbeschluß *m* zur Aufhebung der ehelichen Gemeinschaft.
(b) (*critical*) *mind* klar urteilend *attr*, kritisch.

judiciary [dʒuː'dɪʃɪərɪ] *n* (*branch of administration*) Gerichtsbehörden (*pl*); (*legal system*) Gerichtswesen *nt*; (*judges*) Richterstand *m*.

judicious [dʒuː'dɪʃəs] *adj*, **~ly** *adv* [dʒuː'dɪʃəs, -lɪ] klug, umsichtig.

judo ['dʒuːdəʊ] *n* Judo *nt*.

Judy ['dʒuːdɪ] *n abbr of* Judith; (*in Punch and ~*) Gretel *f*; *see* Punch.

jug[1] [dʒʌg] **1** *n* (a) (*for milk, coffee etc*) (*with lid*) Kanne *f*; (*without lid*) Krug *m*; (*small*) Kännchen *nt*.
(b) (*sl: prison*) Kittchen *nt* (*sl*), Knast *m* (*sl*). in ~ hinter schwedischen Gardinen (*inf*), im Kittchen (*sl*) *or* Knast (*sl*).
2 *vt* (*Cook*) schmoren. **~ged hare** ≈ Hasenpfeffer *m*.

jug² n (of nightingale) Flöten nt.
juggernaut ['dʒʌgənɔːt] n (a) (Brit: lorry) Schwerlaster m. (b) (Rel) J~ Dschagannath, Jagannath m. (c) (fig: destructive force) verheerende Gewalt. the ~ of war der Moloch des Krieges; Puritanism, like some huge ~, swept across the country der Puritanismus rollte mit unaufhaltsamer Gewalt über das Land.
juggins ['dʒʌgɪnz] n (Brit inf) Depp (S Ger), Trottel (inf) m.
juggle ['dʒʌgl] 1 vi jonglieren. to ~ with the facts/figures die Fakten/Zahlen so hindrehen, daß sie passen. 2 vt balls jonglieren (mit); facts, figures so hindrehen, daß sie passen.
juggler ['dʒʌglər] n (a) (lit) Jongleur m. (b) (fig: trickster) Schwindler m. ~ with words Wortverdreher m.
jugglery ['dʒʌgləri] n see juggling.
juggling ['dʒʌglɪŋ] n (a) (lit) Jonglieren nt. (b) (fig) Verdrehen nt (with von). ~ with words/figures Wort-/Zahlenakrobatik f; (falsification) Wortverdrehung f/Frisieren nt von Zahlen; there is a bit of ~ here das ist doch so hingedreht worden, daß es paßt, das ist doch nicht ganz hasenrein (inf).
Jugoslav ['juːgəʊˌslɑːv] 1 adj jugoslawisch. 2 n Jugoslawe m, Jugoslawin f.
Jugoslavia [ˌjuːgəʊˈslɑːvɪə] n Jugoslawien nt.
jugular ['dʒʌgjʊlər] adj: ~ vein Drosselvene, Jugularvene f.
juice [dʒuːs] n (a) (of fruit, meat) Saft m. (b) usu pl (of body) Körpersäfte pl. (c) (sl: electricity, petrol) Saft m (sl).
juiciness ['dʒuːsɪnɪs] n (lit) Saftigkeit f; (fig) Pikanterie, Schlüpfrigkeit f, gewisser Reiz; (of scandal) Saftigkeit f (inf).
juicy ['dʒuːsɪ] adj (+er) fruit saftig; (inf) profit saftig (inf); squelch schmatzend, quatschend; story pikant, schlüpfrig; scandal gepfeffert (inf), saftig (inf); (inf) girl knackig (inf). a big ~ kiss ein dicker Schmatz (inf).
jujitsu [dʒuːˈdʒɪtsuː] n Jiu-Jitsu nt.
jujube ['dʒuːdʒuːb] n (Bot) Jujube f; (berry also) Brustbeere f.
jukebox ['dʒuːkbɒks] n Musikbox f, Musikautomat m.
Jul abbr of July.
julep ['dʒuːlep] n (a) = Sirup, Saft m. (b) see mint².
Julian ['dʒuːlɪən] 1 n Julian m. 2 adj julianisch. ~ calendar Julianischer Kalender m.
Julius ['dʒuːlɪəs] n Julius m. ~ Caesar Julius Caesar m.
July [dʒuːˈlaɪ] n Juli m; see also September.
jumble ['dʒʌmbl] 1 vt (also ~ up) (a) (lit) durcheinanderwerfen, kunterbunt vermischen. ~d up durcheinander, kunterbunt vermischt; to ~ everything up alles durcheinanderbringen or in Unordnung bringen; his clothes are ~d together on his bed seine Kleider liegen in einem unordentlichen Haufen auf dem Bett.
(b) (fig) facts, details durcheinanderbringen, verwirren.
2 n (a) Durcheinander nt; (of ideas also) Wirrwarr m.
(b) no pl (for ~ sale) gebrauchte Sachen pl. ~ sale (Brit) = Flohmarkt m (von Vereinen veranstalteter Verkauf von gebrauchten Sachen); (for charity) Wohltätigkeitsbasar m.
jumbo ['dʒʌmbəʊ] n (a) (inf) Jumbo m (inf). (b) (~ jet) Jumbo (-Jet) m.
jump [dʒʌmp] 1 n (a) (lit) Sprung m; (of animal also) Satz m; (with parachute) Absprung m; (on race-course) Hindernis nt. a ~ of 5 feet ein Sprung von 5 Fuß; (in length also) ein 5 Fuß weiter Sprung; (in height also) ein 5 Fuß hoher Sprung; this horse is no good over the ~s dieses Pferd taugt bei den Hindernissen nichts.
(b) (fig) (of prices) (plötzlicher or sprunghafter) Anstieg; (in narrative) Sprung m, abrupter Übergang. to take a sudden ~ (prices, temperature) ruckartig or sprunghaft ansteigen, in die Höhe schnellen; the temperature took a sudden ~ up to 35° die Temperatur stieg sprunghaft auf 35° an; the movie is full of ~s der Film ist sprunghaft.
(c) (start) to give sb a ~ jdn erschrecken, jdn zusammenfahren or zusammenzucken lassen; you gave me such a ~ du hast mich aber erschreckt; it gave him a ~ er fuhr or zuckte zusammen.
(d) to have the ~ on sb (sl) jdm gegenüber im Vorteil sein.
2 vi (a) (leap) springen, einen Satz machen; (Sport) springen; (parachutist) (ab)springen. to ~ into a river in einen Fluß springen; this horse ~s well dieses Pferd springt gut or nimmt die Hindernisse gut; to ~ for joy Freudensprünge pl/einen Freudensprung machen; (heart) vor Freude hüpfen; to ~ up and down on the spot auf der Stelle hüpfen; they ~ed up and down on his stomach sie hüpften auf seinem Bauch herum; to ~ to conclusions vorschnelle Schlüsse ziehen.
(b) (typewriter) Buchstaben überspringen or auslassen.
(c) (fig) springen, unvermittelt übergehen; (prices, shares) in die Höhe schnellen, sprunghaft ansteigen. ~ to it! los schon!, mach schon!; the film suddenly ~s from the 18th into the 20th century die Film macht plötzlich einen Sprung vom 18. ins 20. Jahrhundert; if you keep ~ing from one thing to another wenn Sie nie an einer Sache bleiben; let's offer £200 and see which way they ~ (inf) machen wir ihnen doch (einfach) ein Angebot von £ 200 und sehen dann, wie sie darauf reagieren.
(d) (start) zusammenfahren, zusammenzucken. the shout made him ~ er zuckte or fuhr bei dem Schrei zusammen; you made me ~ du hast mich (aber) erschreckt; his heart ~ed when ... sein Herz machte einen Satz, als ...
3 vt (a) ditch etc überspringen, hinüberspringen über (+acc); (horses also) (hinüber)setzen über (+acc).
(b) horse springen lassen. he ~ed his horse over the fence er setzte mit seinem Pferd über den Zaun.
(c) (skip) überspringen, auslassen; pages also überblättern.
(d) (pick-up) groove überspringen. to ~ the rails (train) entgleisen; to ~ a man (Draughts) einen überspringen.
(e) (inf usages) (Jur) to ~ bail abhauen (inf) (während man auf Kaution freigelassen ist); to ~ a claim einen schon be-

stehenden Anspruch (auf Land or Rechte) übergehen; to ~ the lights bei Rot drüberfahren (inf) or über die Kreuzung fahren; to ~ the queue (Brit) sich vordrängeln; to ~ ship (Naut) (passenger) das Schiff vorzeitig verlassen; (sailor) heimlich abheuern; to ~ a train (get on) auf einen Zug aufspringen; (get off) von einem Zug abspringen; they ~ed a train to Acapulco sie fuhren schwarz nach Acapulco; to ~ sb jdn überfallen.
♦ **jump about** or **around** vi herumhüpfen or -springen.
♦ **jump at** vi +prep obj person (lit) anfahren; (fig) anfahren; object zuspringen auf (+acc); offer sofort zugreifen bei, sofort ergreifen; suggestion sofort aufgreifen; chance sofort beim Schopf ergreifen.
♦ **jump down** vi hinunter-/herunterhüpfen or -springen (from von). to ~ ~ sb's throat jdn anfahren, jdm dazwischenfahren (inf); ~ ~! spring or hüpf (runter)!
♦ **jump in** vi hineinspringen/hereinspringen. ~ ~! (to car) steig ein!; (at swimming pool etc) spring or hüpf (hinein/herein)!
♦ **jump off** vi herunterspringen (prep obj von); (from train, bus) aussteigen (prep obj aus); (when moving) abspringen (prep obj von); (from bicycle, horse) absteigen (prep obj von).
♦ **jump on** vi (lit) (onto vehicle) einsteigen (prep obj, -to in +acc); (onto moving train, bus) aufspringen (prep obj, -to auf +acc); (onto bicycle, horse) aufsteigen (prep obj, -to auf +acc). to ~ ~ (to) sb/sth auf jdn/etw springen; he ~ed ~(to) his bicycle er schwang sich auf sein Fahrrad.
2 vi +prep obj (inf) person anfahren; suggestion kritisieren, heruntermachen (inf).
♦ **jump out** vi hinaus-/herausspringen or -hüpfen; (from vehicle) aussteigen (of aus); (when moving) abspringen (of von). to ~ ~ of bed aus dem Bett springen or hüpfen; to ~ ~ of the window aus dem Fenster springen, zum Fenster hinausspringen.
♦ **jump up** vi hochspringen; (from sitting or lying position also) aufspringen; (onto sth) hinaufspringen (onto auf +acc).
jump ball n Schiedsrichterball m.
jumped-up ['dʒʌmpt'ʌp] adj (inf) this new ~ manageress dieser kleine Emporkömmling von einer Abteilungsleiterin.
jumper ['dʒʌmpər] n (a) (garment) (Brit) Pullover m; (US: dress) Trägerkleid nt. (b) (person, animal) Springer m.
jumpiness ['dʒʌmpɪnɪs] n see adj (inf) Nervosität f; Schreckhaftigkeit f.
jumping jack ['dʒʌmpɪŋ'dʒæk] n Hampelmann m.
jumping-off place ['dʒʌmpɪŋ'ɒfpleɪs] n (fig) (for negotiations) Ausgangsbasis f; (for job) Sprungbrett nt.
jump: ~ jet n Senkrechtstarter m; ~ leads npl (Brit Aut) Starthilfekabel pl; ~-off n (Show-jumping) Stechen nt; ~ seat n Notsitz, Klappsitz m; ~ suit n Overall m.
jumpy ['dʒʌmpɪ] adj (+er) (inf) person nervös; (easily startled) schreckhaft; market unsicher. (b) motion ruckartig.
Jun abbr of **June**; **junior** jr., jun.
junction ['dʒʌŋkʃən] n (a) (Rail) Gleisanschluß m; (of roads) Kreuzung f; (of rivers) Zusammenfluß m. a very sharp ~ eine sehr scharfe Abzweigung; Clapham J~ Claphamer Kreuz nt; Hamm is a big railway ~ Hamm ist ein großer Eisenbahnknotenpunkt.
(b) (Elec) Anschlußstelle f.
(c) (act) Verbindung f.
junction box n (Elec) Verteilerkasten, Kabelkasten m.
juncture ['dʒʌŋktʃər] n: at this ~ zu diesem Zeitpunkt.
June [dʒuːn] n Juni m; see also September.
jungle ['dʒʌŋgl] n Dschungel (also fig), Urwald m.
junior ['dʒuːnɪər] 1 adj (a) (younger) jünger. he is ~ to me er ist jünger als ich; Hiram Schwarz, ~ Hiram Schwarz junior; Smith, ~ (at school) Smith II, der kleine Smith; the ~ miss die kleine Dame; ~ classes (Sch) Unterstufe f; ~ school (Brit) Grundschule f; ~ college (US Univ) College, an dem man die ersten zwei Jahre eines 4-jährigen Studiums absolviert; ~ high (school) (US) = Mittelschule f.
(b) (subordinate) employee untergeordnet; officer rangniedriger. to be ~ to sb unter jdm stehen; ~ clerk zweiter Buchhalter; he's just some ~ clerk er ist bloß ein kleiner Angestellter; ~ Minister Staatssekretär m; ~ partner jüngerer Teilhaber; (in coalition) kleinerer (Koalitions)-partner.
(c) (Sport) Junioren-, der Junioren. ~ team Junioren-mannschaft f.
2 n (a) Jüngere(r) mf, Junior m. he is my ~ by two years, he is two years my ~ er ist zwei Jahre jünger als ich; where's ~? wo ist der Junior?
(b) (Brit Sch) (at primary school) Grundschüler(in f) m; (at secondary school) Unterstufenschüler(in f) m.
(c) (US Univ) Student(in f) m im vorletzten Studienjahr.
(d) (Sport) the ~s die Junioren pl.
juniper ['dʒuːnɪpər] n Wacholder m. ~ berry Wacholderbeere f.
junk¹ [dʒʌŋk] n (a) (discarded objects) Trödel m, altes Zeug, Gerümpel nt. (b) (inf: trash) Ramsch, Plunder, Schund m. (c) (sl: drugs) Stoff m (sl).
junk² n (boat) Dschunke f.
junket ['dʒʌŋkɪt] n (a) (Cook) Dickmilch f. (b) (old, hum: merrymaking) Gelage, Fest nt, Lustbarkeit f (old, hum). 2 vi (old, hum) ein Gelage abhalten.
junketing ['dʒʌŋkɪtɪŋ] n (a) (old, hum: merrymaking) Festivität(en pl) (esp hum), Lustbarkeit f (old, hum). (b) (US: trip at public expense) (Vergnügungs)reise f auf Staatskosten.
junkie ['dʒʌŋkɪ] n (sl) Fixer(in f) (sl), Junkie (sl) m.
junk: ~ room n Rumpelkammer f; ~ shop n Trödelladen m; ~ yard n (for metal) Schrottplatz m; (for discarded objects) Schuttabladeplatz m; (of rag and bone merchant) Trödellager(platz m) nt.
junta ['dʒʌntə] n Junta f.
Jupiter ['dʒuːpɪtər] n Jupiter m.

juridical [dʒʊəˈrɪdɪkəl] *adj* (*of law*) juristisch, Rechts-; (*of court*) gerichtlich.

jurisdiction [ˌdʒʊərɪsˈdɪkʃən] *n* Gerichtsbarkeit *f*; (*range of authority*) Zuständigkeit(sbereich *m*) *f*. **matters that do not fall under the ~ of this court** Fälle, für die dieses Gericht nicht zuständig ist; **this court has no ~ over him** er untersteht diesem Gericht nicht; **that's not (in) my ~** dafür bin ich nicht zuständig.

jurisprudence [ˌdʒʊərɪsˈpruːdəns] *n* Jura *nt*, Rechtswissenschaft, Jurisprudenz (*old*) *f*; *see* **medical**.

jurist [ˈdʒʊərɪst] *n* Jurist(in *f*), Rechtswissenschaftler(in *f*) *m*.

juror [ˈdʒʊərə*] *n* Schöffe *m*, Schöffin *f*; (*for capital crimes*) Geschworene(r) *mf*; (*in competition*) Preisrichter(in *f*) *m*, Jury-Mitglied *nt*.

jury [ˈdʒʊərɪ] *n* (a) (*Jur*) the ~ die Schöffen *pl*; (*for capital crimes*) die Geschworenen *pl*; **they don't have juries there** da gibt's keine Schöffengerichte *or* (*for capital crimes*) Schwurgerichte; **to sit on the ~** Schöffe/Geschworener sein; **Gentlemen of the J~** meine Herren Schöffen/Geschworenen; *see* **grand ~, coroner**.

(b) (*for examination*) Prüfungsausschuß *m*; (*for exhibition, competition*) Jury *f*, Preisgericht *nt*.

jury: ~ **box** *n* Schöffen-/Geschworenenbank *f*; ~ **man** *n* Schöffe *m*; Geschworene(r) *m*; ~ **rig** *n* (*Naut*) Hilfstakelage, Nottakelage *f*; ~ **service** *n* Schöffenamt *nt*; Amt *nt* des Geschworenen; **to do ~ service** Schöffe/Geschworener sein; **he's never been called for ~ service** er wurde nie als Schöffe/Geschworener berufen; ~ **system** *n* Schöffengerichte *pl or* (*for capital crimes*) Schwurgerichte *pl*.

just¹ [dʒʌst] *adv* (a) (*immediate past*) gerade, (so)eben. **they have ~ left** sie sind gerade *or* (so)eben gegangen; **she left ~ before I came** sie war, gerade *or* kurz bevor ich kam, weggegangen; **he's ~ been appointed** er ist gerade *or* eben erst ernannt worden; **I met him ~ after lunch** ich habe ihn direkt *or* gleich nach dem Mittagessen getroffen.

(b) (*at this/that very moment*) gerade. **hurry up, he's ~ going** beeilen Sie sich, er geht gerade; **he's ~ coming** er kommt gerade *or* eben; **I'm ~ coming** ich komme ja schon; **I was ~ going to ...** ich wollte gerade ...; ~ **as I was going** genau in dem Moment *or* gerade, als ich gehen wollte.

(c) (*barely, almost not*) gerade noch, mit knapper Not. **he ~ escaped being run over** er wäre um ein Haar überfahren worden; **it ~ missed** es hat fast *or* beinahe getroffen; **I only ~ caught the train** ich habe den Zug gerade noch *or* mit knapper Not erreicht; **I've got only ~ enough to live on** mir reicht es gerade so *or* so eben noch zum Leben; **I arrived ~ in time** ich bin gerade (noch) zurecht gekommen.

(d) (*exactly*) genau, gerade. **it is ~ five o'clock** es ist genau fünf Uhr; **that's ~ like you** das sieht dir ähnlich; **it's ~ on nine o'clock** es ist gerade neun Uhr; **it happened ~ as I expected** es passierte genau so, wie ich es erwartet hatte; **it's ~ because of that that he insists** gerade *or* eben deshalb besteht er darauf; **that's ~ it!** das ist's ja gerade *or* eben!; **that's ~ what I was going to say** genau das wollte ich (auch) sagen; ~ **what do you mean by that?** was wollen Sie damit sagen?; ~ **what does this symbol mean?** was bedeutet dieses Zeichen genau?; **it was ~ there** there genau das war es; ~ **at that moment** genau *or* gerade in dem Augenblick; ~ **so!** (*old*) genau, ganz recht; **everything has to be ~ so** es muß alles seine Ordnung haben.

(e) (*only, simply*) nur, bloß. **I can stay ~ a minute** ich kann nur *or* bloß eine Minute bleiben; ~ **you and me** nur wir beide, wir beide allein; **this is ~ to show you how it works** dies soll Ihnen lediglich zeigen, wie es funktioniert; **this is ~ to confirm ...** hiermit bestätigen wir, daß ...; **he's ~ a boy** er ist doch noch ein Junge; **why don't you want to/like it?** — **I ~ don't** warum willst du nicht/magst du es nicht? — ich will/mag's eben *or* halt (*inf*) nicht; ~ **like that** (ganz) einfach so; **I don't know, I ~ don't** ich weiß (es) nicht, beim besten Willen nicht; **you can't ~ assume ...** Sie können doch nicht einfach *or* doch nicht ohne weiteres annehmen ...; **it's ~ not good enough** es ist halt (*inf*) *or* einfach nicht gut genug; **I ~ prefer it this way** ich find's halt (*inf*) *or* eben *or* einfach besser so.

(f) (*a small distance, with position*) gleich. ~ **round the corner** gleich um die Ecke; ~ **above the trees** direkt über den Bäumen; **put it ~ over there** stell's mal da drüben hin; ~ **here** (genau) hier.

(g) (*absolutely*) einfach, wirklich. **it was ~ fantastic** es war einfach prima; **it's ~ terrible** das ist ja schrecklich!

(h) ~ **as** genauso, ebenso. **the blue hat is ~ as nice as the red one** der blaue Hut ist genauso hübsch wie der rote; **she didn't understand you — it's ~ as well!** sie hat Sie nicht verstanden — vielleicht auch besser *or* auch recht; **it's ~ as well you stayed at home, you didn't miss anything** es macht nichts, daß Sie zu Hause geblieben sind, Sie haben nichts verpaßt; **it's ~ as well you didn't go out** nur gut, daß Sie nicht weggegangen sind; **it would be ~ as well if you came** es wäre doch besser, wenn Sie kämen; **come ~ as you are** kommen Sie so, wie Sie sind; **it's ~ as you please** wie Sie wollen; ~ **as I thought!** ich habe es mir doch gedacht!

(i) ~ **about** in etwa, so etwa; **I am ~ about ready** ich bin so ziemlich fertig; **it's ~ about here** es ist (so) ungefähr hier; **did he make it in time?** — ~ **about** hat er's (rechtzeitig) geschafft?

— **so gerade; will this do** — ~ **about** ist das recht so? — so in etwa; **I am ~ about fed up with it!** (*inf*) so langsam aber sicher hängt es mir zum Hals raus (*inf*); **that's ~ about the limit!** das ist doch die Höhe!

(j) **im Moment.** ~ **now** (*in past*) soeben (erst), gerade erst; **not ~ now** im Moment nicht; ~ **now?** jetzt gleich?; **you can go, but not ~ now** Sie können gehen, aber nicht gerade jetzt.

(k) (*other uses*) ~ **think** denk bloß; ~ **listen** hör mal; ~ **try** versuch's doch mal; ~ **taste** this probier das mal; (*it's awful*) **probier bloß das mal**; ~ **let me try** lassen Sie's mich doch mal versuchen; ~ **shut up!** sei bloß still!; ~ **wait here a moment** warten Sie hier mal (für) einen Augenblick; ~ **a moment** *or* **minute!** Moment mal!; **I can ~ see him as a soldier** ich kann ihn mir gut als Soldat vorstellen; **I can ~ see you getting up so early** (*iro*) du – und so früh aufstehen!; **can I ~ finish this?** kann ich das mal eben *or* mal schnell fertigmachen?; **the possibilities ~ go on for ever** die Möglichkeiten sind ja unerschöpflich; **don't I ~!** und ob (ich ...); ~ **watch it** nimm dich bloß in acht; ~ **you dare** wehe, wenn du's wagst.

just² *adj* (+*er*) (a) *person, decision* gerecht (**to** gegenüber). (b) *punishment, reward* gerecht; *anger* berechtigt; *suspicion* gerechtfertigt, begründet. **a ~ cause** eine gerechte Sache; **I had ~ cause to be alarmed** ich hatte guten Grund, beunruhigt zu sein; **as (it) is only ~** wie es recht und billig ist.

justice [ˈdʒʌstɪs] *n* (a) (*Jur*) (*quality*) Gerechtigkeit *f*; (*system*) Gerichtsbarkeit, Justiz *f*. **British ~** britisches Recht; **is this the famous British ~?** ist das die berühmte britische Gerechtigkeit?; **to bring a thief to ~** einen Dieb vor Gericht bringen; **court of ~** Gerichtshof *m*, Gericht *nt*; **to administer ~** Recht sprechen; *see* **poetic**.

(b) (*fairness*) Gerechtigkeit *f*; (*of claims*) Rechtmäßigkeit *f*. **to do him ~** um ihm gegenüber gerecht zu sein, um mal fair zu sein (*inf*); **this photograph doesn't do me ~** auf diesem Foto bin ich nicht gut getroffen; **she never does herself ~** sie kommt nie richtig zur Geltung; **that's not true, you're not doing yourself ~** das stimmt nicht, Sie unterschätzen sich; **you didn't do yourself ~ in the exams** Sie haben im Examen nicht gezeigt, was Sie können; **to do sb ~** jdm gegenüber gerecht sein; **they did ~ to my dinner** sie wußten mein Essen zu würdigen; **he complained, with ~, that ...** er hat sich zu Recht beklagt, daß ...; **and with ~** und (zwar) zu Recht; **there's no ~, is there?** das ist doch nicht gerecht.

(c) (*judge*) Richter *m*. **Lord Chief J~** oberster Richter in Großbritannien; **J~ of the Peace** Friedensrichter *m*; **Mr J~ Plod** Richter Plod.

justifiable [ˌdʒʌstɪˈfaɪəbl] *adj* gerechtfertigt, zu rechtfertigen **pred**, berechtigt.

justifiably [ˌdʒʌstɪˈfaɪəblɪ] *adv* zu Recht, berechtigterweise.

justification [ˌdʒʌstɪfɪˈkeɪʃən] *n* (a) Rechtfertigung *f* (*of gen, for* für). **it can be said in his ~ that ...** zu seiner Verteidigung *or* Entschuldigung kann gesagt werden, daß ...; **as a ~ for his action** zur Rechtfertigung *or* Verteidigung seiner Handlungsweise; **he had no ~ for lying** er hatte keine Rechtfertigung *or* Entschuldigung für seine Lüge.

(b) (*Typ*) Justieren *nt*.

justify [ˈdʒʌstɪfaɪ] *vt* (a) (*show to be right*) rechtfertigen, verteidigen (*sth to sb* etw vor jdm *or* jdm gegenüber). **you don't need to ~ yourself** Sie brauchen sich nicht zu rechtfertigen *or* verteidigen; **don't try to ~ your action** versuchen Sie nicht, Ihre Tat zu entschuldigen *or* verteidigen; **am I justified in thinking that ...?** gehe ich recht in der Annahme, daß ...?

(b) (*be good reason for*) rechtfertigen, ein Grund sein für. **the future could hardly be said to ~ great optimism** die Zukunft berechtigt wohl kaum zu großem Optimismus; **this does not ~ his being late** das ist kein Grund für sein Zuspätkommen; **he was justified in doing that** es war gerechtfertigt, daß er das tat; **you're not justified in talking to her like that** Sie haben kein Recht, so mit ihr zu reden.

(c) (*Typ*) justieren.

justly [ˈdʒʌstlɪ] *adv* zu Recht, mit Recht; *treat, try* gerecht; *condemn* gerechterweise.

justness [ˈdʒʌstnɪs] *n* (*of cause*) Gerechtigkeit, Billigkeit (*liter*) *f*; (*of character*) Gerechtigkeit *f*.

jut [dʒʌt] *vi* (*also* ~ **out**) hervorstehen, hervorragen, herausragen. **he saw a gun ~ting (out) from behind the wall** er sah ein Gewehr hinter der Mauer (her)vorragen; **the cliff ~s out into the sea** die Klippen ragen ins Meer hinaus; **to ~ out over the street** über die Straße vorstehen *or* hinausragen.

jute [dʒuːt] *n* Jute *f*.

Jutland [ˈdʒʌtlənd] *n* Jütland *nt*.

juvenile [ˈdʒuːvənaɪl] *n* **1** (*Admin*) Jugendliche(r) *mf*. **2** *adj* (*youthful*) jugendlich; (*for young people*) Jugend-, für Jugendliche; (*pej*) kindisch, unreif.

juvenile: ~ **court** *n* Jugendgericht *nt*; ~ **delinquency** *n* Jugendkriminalität *f*, Kriminalität *f* bei Jugendlichen; ~ **delinquent** *n* jugendlicher Straftäter; ~ **lead** *n* (*Theat*) Rolle *f* des jugendlichen Hauptdarstellers; (*actor*) jugendlicher Hauptdarsteller.

juxtapose [ˈdʒʌkstəpəʊz] *vt* nebeneinanderstellen; *ideas also* gegeneinanderhalten; *colours* nebeneinandersetzen.

juxtaposition [ˌdʒʌkstəpəˈzɪʃən] *n* (*act*) Nebeneinanderstellung *f*. **in ~** (direkt) nebeneinander.

K

K, k [keɪ] n K, k nt.
Kaffir ['kæfə'] n Kaffer m.
kagul n see cagoule.
kale, kail [keɪl] n Grünkohl m.
kaleidoscope [kə'laɪdəskəup] n Kaleidoskop nt.
kaleidoscopic [kə,laɪdə'skɒpɪk] adj kaleidoskopisch.
kangaroo [,kæŋgə'ruː] n Känguruh nt. ~ **court** inoffizielles Gericht, Femegericht nt.
kaolin ['keɪəlɪn] n Kaolin m or nt, Porzellanerde f.
kapok ['keɪpɒk] n Kapok m.
kaput [kə'put] adj (sl) kaputt (inf).
karat ['kærət] n see carat.
karate [kə'rɑːtɪ] n Karate nt. ~ **chop** Karateschlag or -hieb m.
Kashmir [kæʃ'mɪə'] n Kaschmir nt.
Kate [keɪt] n dim of **Catherine** Käthe, Kathi f.
katydid ['keɪtɪdɪd] n Laubheuschrecke f.
kayak ['kaɪæk] n Kajak m or nt.
KC (Brit) abbr of **King's Counsel**.
kc abbr of **kilocycle**.
kedge [kedʒ] n (Naut) Warpanker m.
kedgeree [,kedʒə'riː] n Reisgericht nt mit Fisch und Eiern.
keel [kiːl] n (Naut) Kiel m. to be on an even ~ again (lit) sich wieder aufgerichtet haben; he put the business back on an even ~ er brachte das Geschäft wieder ins Lot or wieder auf die Beine (inf); when things are more on an even ~ wenn sich alles besser eingespielt hat.
♦ **keel over** vi (ship) kentern; (fig inf) umkippen. she ~ed ~ in a faint sie klappte zusammen (inf), sie kippte um (inf).
keelhaul ['kiːlhɔːl] vt kielholen.
keen¹ [kiːn] adj (+er) (a) (sharp) blade scharf; wind scharf, schneidend.
 (b) (acute, intense) appetite kräftig; interest groß, stark; pleasure stark, tief; desire, pain heftig, stark; sight, eye, hearing, ear gut, scharf; mind, wit scharf; (esp Brit) prices günstig; competition scharf. he has a ~ sense of history er hat ein ausgeprägtes Gefühl für Geschichte.
 (c) (enthusiastic) begeistert; football fan, golf player also, supporter leidenschaftlich; (eager, interested) applicant, learner stark interessiert; (hardworking) eifrig. ~ to learn/know lernbegierig/begierig zu wissen; try not to seem too ~ versuchen Sie, Ihr Interesse nicht zu sehr zu zeigen; if he's ~ we can teach him wenn er wirklich interessiert ist or Interesse hat, können wir es ihm beibringen; he is terribly ~ seine Begeisterung/sein Interesse/sein Eifer kennt kaum Grenzen; to be ~ on sb von jdm sehr angetan sein, scharf auf jdn sein (inf); on pop group, actor, author von jdm begeistert sein; to be ~ on sth etw sehr gern mögen; classical music, Italian cooking also, football sehr viel für etw übrig haben; to be ~ on doing sth (like to do) etw gern or mit Begeisterung tun; to be ~ to do sth (want to do) sehr darauf erpicht sein or darauf sein (inf), etw zu tun; to be ~ on mountaineering/ dancing begeisterter or leidenschaftlicher Bergsteiger/ Tänzer sein, leidenschaftlich gern bergsteigen/tanzen; he is very ~ on golf/tennis etc er ist ein Golf-/Tennis- etc-narr m; to become ~ on sb/sth sich für jdn/etw erwärmen; I'm not very ~ on him/that idea ich bin von ihm/dieser Idee nicht gerade begeistert; he's very ~ on getting the job finished ihm liegt sehr viel daran, daß die Arbeit fertig wird; he's not ~ on her coming er legt keinen (gesteigerten) Wert darauf, daß sie kommt; he's very ~ that we should go er legt sehr großen Wert darauf or ihm ist sehr daran gelegen, daß wir gehen.
 (d) (US sl: very good) Spitze (sl).
keen² (Ir) 1 n Totenklage f. 2 vi die Totenklage halten.
keenly ['kiːnlɪ] adv (a) (sharply) scharf, schneidend. (b) (intensely, acutely) feel leidenschaftlich, tief, stark; interested, wish, desire stark, sehr, leidenschaftlich. the competition was ~ contested im Wettbewerb wurde hart gekämpft. (c) (enthusiastically) mit Begeisterung.
keenness ['kiːnnɪs] n (a) (of blade, mind, wind, sight) Schärfe f. (b) see adj (c) Begeisterung f; Leidenschaftlichkeit f; starkes Interesse; Eifer m. his ~ to go is suspicious daß er so unbedingt gehen will, ist verdächtig; he doesn't show much ~ er legt nicht viel Begeisterung or Lust an den Tag.
keep [kiːp] (vb: pret, ptp **kept**) 1 vt (a) (retain) behalten. to ~ one's temper sich beherrschen; to ~ sb/sth in mind an jdn/etw denken; please ~ me in mind for the job bitte denken Sie an mich bei der Vergabe des Postens; to ~ a place for sb einen Platz für jdn freihalten; to ~ one's place in a book sich (dat) die Stelle im Buch markieren; I can't ~ that number in my head ich kann die Nummer nicht behalten or mir die Nummer nicht merken; to ~ a note of sth sich (dat) etw notieren; Onkel Jim wanted to ~ him another week Onkel Jim wollte ihn noch eine Woche bei sich behalten; they wanted to ~ me for dinner sie wollten, daß ich zum Essen bleibe; you can ~ it! (inf) das kannst du behalten or dir an den Hut stecken (inf).
 (b) shop, hotel, restaurant haben, unterhalten, führen; bees, pigs etc halten. who kept your dog while you were on holiday? wer hat Ihren Hund gehabt, während Sie in Urlaub waren?; to ~ house for sb jdm den Haushalt führen; to ~ ser-

vants/a car sich (dat) Diener/ein Auto halten.
 (c) (support) versorgen, unterhalten. I earn enough to ~ myself ich verdiene genug für mich (selbst) zum Leben; I have six children to ~ ich habe sechs Kinder zu versorgen or unterhalten; he ~s a mistress er hält sich (dat) eine Geliebte; to ~ sb in clothing (person) für jds Kleidung sorgen; I couldn't afford to ~ you ich könnte deine Getränke nicht bezahlen; what I earn wouldn't even ~ you in cigarettes was ich verdiene, wäre nicht einmal für die Zigaretten genug.
 (d) (maintain in a certain state or place or position) halten. to ~ one's dress clean sein Kleid nicht schmutzig machen; to ~ sb quiet zusehen or dafür sorgen, daß jd still ist; that'll ~ them quiet for a while das wird für eine Weile Ruhe schaffen; it kept her in bed for a week sie mußte deswegen eine Woche im Bett bleiben; he kept his hands in his pockets er hat die Hände in der Tasche gelassen; just to ~ her happy damit sie zufrieden ist; to ~ sb alive jdn am Leben halten; to ~ sb at work jdn bei der Arbeit halten; to ~ sb waiting jdn warten lassen; ~ her hoping lassen Sie ihr die Hoffnung; can't you ~ him talking? können Sie ihn nicht in ein Gespräch verwickeln?; to ~ sth tidy or in order etw sauber or in Ordnung halten; ~ your hands to yourself! nehmen Sie Ihre Hände weg!; the garden was well kept der Garten war (gut) gepflegt; to ~ the traffic moving den Verkehr in Fluß or am Fließen halten; to ~ a machine running eine Maschine laufen lassen; to ~ the conversation going das Gespräch in Gang halten.
 (e) (in a certain place, look after) aufbewahren; (put aside) aufheben. where does he ~ his money? wo bewahrt er sein Geld auf?; where do you ~ your spoons? wo sind die Löffel?; I've been ~ing it for you ich habe es für Sie aufgehoben.
 (f) (be faithful to, observe, fulfil) promise halten; law, rule einhalten, befolgen; treaty einhalten; obligations nachkommen (+dat), erfüllen; appointment einhalten. to ~ a vow einen Schwur halten, ein Gelübde erfüllen.
 (g) (celebrate) to ~ Lent/the Sabbath das Fasten/die Sonntagsruhe or den Sabbat (ein)halten.
 (h) (guard, protect) (be)hüten; sheep etc hüten, aufpassen auf (+acc). God ~ you! (old) Gott befohlen! (old); to ~ goal (Ftbl) im Tor sein or stehen, das Tor hüten; see ~ from 1 (b).
 (i) accounts, diary etc führen (of über +acc).
 (j) (Comm: stock) führen, (zu verkaufen) haben.
 (k) (detain) aufhalten, zurückhalten. I mustn't ~ you ich darf Sie nicht aufhalten; what kept you? wo waren Sie denn so lang?; what's ~ing him? wo bleibt er denn?; illness kept her at home Krankheit fesselte sie ans Haus; to ~ sb prisoner jdn gefangenhalten or festhalten; to ~ sb in prison jdn in Haft halten.
 (l) (not disclose) can you ~ this from your mother? können Sie das vor Ihrer Mutter geheimhalten or verbergen?; ~ it to yourself behalten Sie das für sich; see secret.
 (m) (US: continue to follow) road, path weitergehen or -fahren, folgen (+dat); direction einhalten. to ~ one's course (den) Kurs (ein)halten.
 (n) (esp US: remain in) to ~ one's bed/one's room im Bett/auf seinem Zimmer bleiben; to ~ one's seat sitzenbleiben.
 (o) to ~ late hours lange aufbleiben.
 2 vi (a) (continue in a specified direction) to ~ (to the) left/ right sich links/rechts halten; to ~ to the left (Aut) auf der linken Seite bleiben, links fahren; to ~ to the middle of the road immer in der Mitte der Straße fahren; ~ on this road bleiben Sie auf dieser Straße; ~ north gehen/fahren Sie immer Richtung Norden.
 (b) (continue) to ~ doing sth (not stop) etw weiter tun; (repeatedly) etw immer wieder tun; (constantly) etw dauernd tun; to ~ walking weitergehen; he kept lying to her er hat sie immer wieder belogen; if you ~ complaining wenn Sie sich weiter beschweren; she ~s talking about you all the time sie redet dauernd von Ihnen; ~ going machen Sie weiter; I ~ hoping she's still alive ich hoffe immer noch, daß sie noch lebt; I ~ thinking ... ich denke immer ...
 (c) (remain in a certain state, position) bleiben. to ~ quiet still sein; to ~ silent schweigen; to ~ calm ruhig bleiben, Ruhe bewahren; she kept indoors for three days sie blieb drei Tage im Haus.
 (d) (food etc) sich halten. apples that ~ all winter Äpfel, die sich den ganzen Winter halten; that meat won't ~ dieses Fleisch hält sich nicht or bleibt nicht gut.
 (e) (be in a certain state of health) how are you ~ing? und wie geht es Ihnen denn so?; to ~ well gesund bleiben; to ~ fit fit bleiben, sich in Form halten; he's ~ing better now es geht ihm wieder besser; to ~ in good health sich guter Gesundheit erfreuen; to ~ alive sich am Leben halten.
 (f) (wait) that business can ~ das kann warten; will it ~? kann das warten?
 (g) (dated Univ: reside) wohnen.
 3 n (a) (livelihood, food) Unterhalt m. I got £10 a week and my ~ ich bekam £ 10 pro Woche und freie Kost und Logis; he's not worth his ~ (inf) er ist sein Brot nicht wert, der bringt doch nichts (ein) (inf).

(b) (*in castle*) Bergfried *m*; (*as prison*) Burgverlies *nt*.

(c) for ~s (*inf*) für immer; he's playing for ~s ihm ist's ernst; it's yours for ~s das darfst du behalten.

♦**keep ahead** *vi* vorne bleiben. to ~ ~ of one's rivals seinen Konkurrenten vorausbleiben; to ~ one step ~ of the others den anderen einen Schritt voraus sein.

♦**keep at 1** *vi* +*prep obj* **(a)** (*continue with*) weitermachen mit. ~ ~ it machen Sie weiter so. **(b)** (*nag*) herumnörgeln an (+*dat*). ~ ~ him until he says yes laß ihm so lange keine Ruhe, bis er ja sagt. **2** *vt* +*prep obj* to ~ sb ~ **a task** jdn nicht mit einer Arbeit aufhören lassen; to ~ sb ~ it jdn hart hernehmen (*inf*), jdn an der Kandare haben.

♦**keep away 1** *vi* (*lit*) wegbleiben; (*not approach*) nicht näher herankommen (*from an* +*acc*). ~ ~! nicht näherkommen!; ~ ~ from that place gehen Sie da nicht hin; he just can't ~ ~ from the pub es zieht ihn immer wieder in die Wirtschaft; I just can't ~ ~ es zieht mich immer wieder hin; ~ ~ from him lassen Sie die Finger von ihm; he just can't ~ ~ from her/drink er kann einfach nicht von ihr/vom Alkohol lassen.

2 *vt always separate* person, children, pet *etc* fernhalten (*from* von). to ~ sth ~ from sth nicht an etw (*acc*) kommen lassen; ~ your hand ~ from the cutting edge kommen Sie mit Ihrer Hand nicht an die Schneide; ~ them ~ from each other halten Sie sie auseinander; business kept him ~ for three months er war aus geschäftlichen Gründen drei Monate weg; what's been ~ing you ~? wo waren Sie denn so lange?

♦**keep back 1** *vi* zurückbleiben, nicht näherkommen. ~ ~! bleiben Sie, wo Sie sind!, treten Sie zurück!; please ~ ~ from the edge bitte gehen Sie nicht zu nahe an den Rand.

2 *vt sep* **(a)** (*hold back*) person, hair, crowds, enemy zurückhalten; water stauen; tears unterdrücken. to ~ sb/sth ~ from sb jdn/etw von jdm abhalten.

(b) (*withhold*) money, taxes einbehalten; information, facts *etc* verschweigen (*from sb* jdm); (*from parent, husband etc*) verheimlichen, verschweigen (*from sb* jdm). I know you're ~ing something ~ ich weiß, daß du mir etwas verheimlichst or verschweigst; they are ~ing ~ the names of the victims die Namen der Opfer werden nicht bekanntgegeben.

(c) (*make late*) aufhalten; pupil dabehalten. I don't want to ~ you ~ ich möchte Sie nicht aufhalten.

(d) (*hold up, slow down*) behindern. being with the slower learners is ~ing him ~ weil er mit schwächeren Schülern zusammen ist, kommt er nicht so schnell voran; because she might ~ him ~ in his social progress weil sie ihn am gesellschaftlichen Aufstieg hindern könnte.

♦**keep down 1** *vi* unten bleiben. ~ ~! duck dich!, bleib unten!

2 *vt sep* **(a)** (*lit*) unten lassen; (*hold down*) unten halten; head ducken. ~ your voices ~ reden Sie leise or nicht so laut.

(b) people, revolt, one's anger unterdrücken; dog bändigen; rebellious person im Zaum or unter Kontrolle halten; rabbits, weeds *etc* in Grenzen or unter Kontrolle halten. you can't ~ a good man ~ der Tüchtige läßt sich nicht unterkriegen.

(c) taxes, rates, prices niedrig halten; spending einschränken. to ~ one's weight ~ nicht zunehmen.

(d) food *etc* bei sich behalten.

(e) (*Sch*) wiederholen lassen. he was kept ~ er mußte wiederholen.

♦**keep from 1** *vt* +*prep obj* **(a)** sb hindern an (+*dat*); (*from going, doing sth also*) abhalten von. I couldn't ~ him ~ doing it/going there ich konnte ihn nicht daran hindern or davon abhalten(, das zu tun), dort hinzugehen; to ~ sb ~ falling jdn am Fallen hindern; to ~ oneself ~ doing sth sich (*davor*) hüten, etw zu tun; the bells ~ me ~ sleeping die Glocken lassen mich nicht schlafen; to ~ sb ~ school jdn nicht in die Schule (gehen) lassen; ~ them ~ getting wet verhindern Sie es, daß sie naß werden; you should ~ your engine ~ overheating Sie sollten den Motor nicht zu heiß werden lassen; this will ~ the water ~ freezing das verhindert, daß das Wasser gefriert; you shouldn't ~ them ~ their work Sie sollten sie nicht von der Arbeit abhalten.

(b) (*protect*) to ~ sb ~ sth jdn vor etw (*dat*) bewahren.

(c) (*withhold*) to ~ sth ~ sb jdm etw verschweigen; piece of news *also* jdm etw vorenthalten.

2 *vi* +*prep obj* to ~ ~ doing sth etw nicht tun; (*avoid doing also*) es vermeiden, etw zu tun; in order to ~ ~ becoming overworked um sich nicht zu überarbeiten; she couldn't ~ ~ laughing sie mußte einfach lachen, sie konnte das Lachen nicht unterdrücken; to ~ ~ drink das Trinken unterlassen.

♦**keep in 1** *vt sep* **(a)** fire nicht ausgehen lassen; feelings zügeln.

(b) schoolboy nachsitzen lassen. I've been kept ~! ich mußte nachsitzen!; his mummy's kept him ~ seine Mutti hat ihn nicht weggelassen or gehen lassen.

(c) stomach einziehen. ~ your tummy ~! Bauch rein!

2 *vi* **(a)** (*fire*) anbleiben. it'll ~ ~ all night es brennt die ganze Nacht durch.

(b) (*stay indoors*) drinnen bleiben.

(c) (*with group, person*) he's just trying to ~ ~ er will sich lieb Kind machen.

♦**keep in with** *vi* +*prep obj* sich gut stellen mit.

♦**keep off 1** *vi* (*person*) wegbleiben. if the rain ~s ~ wenn es nicht regnet; "~ ~!" "Betreten verboten!"

2 *vt sep* **(a)** dog, person fernhalten (*prep obj* von); one's hands wegnehmen, weglassen (*prep obj* von). this weather will ~ the crowds ~ dieses Wetter wird einen Massenandrang verhindern; "~ ~ the grass" "Betreten des Rasens verboten"; ~ him ~ me halten Sie ihn mir vom Leib; ~ your hands ~ Hände weg!; ~ the dog ~ the couch lassen Sie den Hund nicht aufs Sofa.

(b) jacket *etc* abgehalten; hat abbehalten.

3 *vi* +*prep obj* vermeiden. ~ ~ the whisky lassen Sie das Whiskytrinken.

♦**keep on 1** *vi* **(a)** weitermachen, nicht aufhören. to ~ ~ doing sth etw weiter tun; (*repeatedly*) etw immer wieder tun; (*incessantly*) etw dauernd tun; he ~s ~ swearing er flucht dauernd; ~ ~ talking! reden Sie weiter!; if you ~ ~ like this wenn du so weitermachst; ~ ~ trying versuchen Sie es weiter; I ~ ~ telling you ich sage dir ja immer; the rain kept ~ all night es regnete die ganze Nacht durch; the child kept ~ crying the whole night das Kind hat die ganze Nacht unaufhörlich geweint.

(b) (*keep going*) weitergehen or -fahren. ~ ~ past the church fahren Sie immer weiter an der Kirche vorbei; ~ ~ straight ~ immer geradeaus.

(c) to ~ ~ at sb (*inf*) dauernd an jdm herummeckern (*inf*); they kept ~ at him until he agreed sie haben ihm so lange keine Ruhe gelassen, bis er zustimmte.

(d) to ~ ~ about sth (*inf*) unaufhörlich von etw reden; there's no need to ~ ~ so (*inf*) es ist wirklich nicht nötig, ewig darauf herumzuhacken (*inf*); don't ~ ~ so! (*inf*) hören Sie doch endlich auf damit!

2 *vt sep* **(a)** servant, employee weiterbeschäftigen, behalten.

(b) coat *etc* anbehalten; hat aufbehalten.

♦**keep out 1** *vi* (*of room, building*) draußen bleiben; (*of property, land, area*) etw nicht betreten. to ~ ~ of a room/bar/area ein Zimmer/eine Bar/eine Gegend nicht betreten; ~ ~ of my room! geh/komm nicht in mein Zimmer; "~ ~" "Zutritt verboten"; to ~ ~ of the rain/cold/sun nicht in den Regen/die Kälte/die Sonne gehen; to ~ ~ of sight sich nicht zeigen; (*hiding*) in Deckung bleiben; to ~ ~ of danger Gefahr meiden; to ~ ~ of debt keine Schulden machen; that child can never ~ ~ of mischief das Kind stellt dauernd etwas an; to ~ ~ of a quarrel sich nicht in einen Streit einmischen, sich aus einem Streit heraushalten; you ~ ~ of this! halten Sie sich da or hier raus!

2 *vt sep* **(a)** person nicht hereinlassen (*of* in +*acc*); light, cold, rain, enemy *etc* abhalten. this screen ~s the sun ~ of your eyes diese Blende schützt Ihre Augen vor Sonne; how can I ~ the rabbits ~ (of my garden)? was kann ich tun, daß die Kaninchen nicht hereinkommen/nicht in meinen Garten kommen?

(b) to ~ sb ~ of danger/harm jdn vor Gefahr/Gefahren schützen; to ~ sb ~ of a quarrel jdn nicht mit in einen Streit hereinziehen; I wanted to ~ him ~ of this ich wollte nicht, daß er da mit hereingezogen wurde; to ~ sb's name ~ of the papers jds Namen nicht in der Zeitung erwähnen; ~ the plants ~ of the sun/cold schützen Sie die Pflanzen vor Sonne/Kälte; ~ him ~ of my way halte ihn mir vom Leib; they kept him ~ of their plans sie haben ihn von ihren Plänen ausgeschlossen.

♦**keep to 1** *vi* +*prep obj* **(a)** to ~ ~ one's promise sein Versprechen halten, zu seinem Wort stehen; to ~ ~ one's bed/one's room im Bett/in seinem Zimmer bleiben; ~ ~ the main road bleiben Sie auf der Hauptstraße; to ~ ~ the schedule/plan den Zeitplan einhalten, sich an den Zeitplan/Plan halten; to ~ ~ the traditional way an der herkömmlichen Art festhalten; to ~ ~ the subject/point bei der Sache or beim Thema bleiben; to ~ ~ the text sich an den Text halten, am Text bleiben.

(b) to ~ ~ (oneself) ~ oneself nicht sehr gesellig sein, ein Einzelgänger sein; they ~ (themselves) ~ themselves (*as a group*) sie bleiben unter sich.

2 *vt* +*prep obj* to ~ sb ~ his word/promise jdn beim Wort nehmen; ~ them ~ the target sorgen Sie dafür, daß sie ihr Soll erfüllen; to ~ sth ~ a minimum etw auf ein Minimum beschränken.

♦**keep together 1** *vi* (*stay together*) zusammenbleiben; (*as friends etc*) zusammenhalten; (*singers, oarsmen etc*) im Einklang or Takt sein. **2** *vt sep* zusammen aufbewahren; (*fix together, unite*) things, people zusammenhalten; (*conductor*) orchestra im Takt halten.

♦**keep under 1** *vt sep* fire unter Kontrolle halten; anger, feelings unterdrücken, nicht hochkommen lassen; passions zügeln; people, race unterdrücken; subordinates streng behandeln, an der Kandare haben; (*keep under anaesthetic*) unter Narkose halten. you won't ~ him ~ der läßt sich nicht unterkriegen or kleinkriegen.

2 *vi* (*under water etc*) unter Wasser bleiben.

♦**keep up 1** *vi* **(a)** (*tent, pole*) stehen bleiben.

(b) (*rain*) (an)dauern; (*weather, hurricane etc*) anhalten; (*prices, output, standard*) gleich hoch bleiben; (*moral, strength, determination*) nicht nachlassen. their spirits ~ ~ sie verzagen nicht, sie bleiben guten Muts.

(c) to ~ ~ (with sb/sth) (*in race, work, with prices*) (mit jdm/etw) Schritt halten; (*with jdm/etw*) mithalten können (*inf*); (*in comprehension*) (jdm/einer Sache) folgen können; they bought it just to ~ ~ with the Joneses sie kauften es nur, um den Nachbarn nicht nachzustehen; to ~ ~ with the times mit der Zeit gehen; to ~ ~ with the news sich auf dem laufenden halten; I haven't kept ~ with my French ich bin mit meinem Französisch ganz aus der Übung gekommen.

(d) (*keep in touch with*) to ~ ~ with sb mit jdm in Kontakt bleiben; we haven't kept ~ at all since she went abroad wir haben nichts mehr voneinander gehört, seit sie im Ausland ist.

2 *vt sep* **(a)** pole, tent aufrecht halten. the lifebelt kept him ~ der Rettungsring hielt ihn über Wasser; to ~ his trousers ~ damit die Hose nicht herunterrutscht.

(b) (*not stop*) nicht aufhören mit; study *etc* fortsetzen, weitermachen; quality, prices, output, friendship aufrechterhalten; tradition, custom weiterpflegen, aufrechterhalten; subscription beibehalten; payments *etc* weiterzahlen; workrate, speed (*maintain*) halten; (*endure*) durchhalten. I try to ~ ~ my Latin ich versuche, mit meinem Latein nicht aus der Übung zu kommen; to ~ ~ a correspondence in Briefwechsel bleiben; to ~ ~ one's morale ~ den Mut nicht verlieren; he kept their morale ~ er hat ihnen Mut gemacht; to ~ it ~! (machen Sie) weiter so!; he couldn't ~ it ~ er

hat schlaff gemacht (*inf*); (*sexually*) er ist ihm weggeschlafft (*sl*).
 (c) (*maintain*) *house* unterhalten; *road* in Stand halten. **(d)** (*prevent from going to bed*) am Schlafengehen hindern. **that child kept me ~ all night** das Kind hat mich die ganze Nacht nicht schlafen lassen; **I was kept ~ pretty late last night** ich bin gestern abend ziemlich spät ins Bett gekommen.
keeper ['ki:pə'] *n* (*in asylum, zoo*) Wärter(in *f*), Betreuer(in *f*) *m*; (*of museum*) Kustos *m*; (*guard*) Wächter(in *f*), Aufseher(in *f*), Aufpasser(in *f*) *m*. **am I my brother's ~?** soll ich meines Bruders Hüter sein?
keeping ['ki:pɪŋ] *n* **(a)** (*care*) **to put sb in sb's ~** jdn in jds Obhut (*acc*) geben; **to put sth in sb's ~** jdm etw zur Aufbewahrung übergeben; *see* safe-keeping.
 (b) (*of rule*) Beachten, Einhalten *nt*.
 (c) **in ~ with** in Übereinstimmung *or* Einklang mit; **her behaviour was out of ~ with the dignity of the occasion** ihr Benehmen entsprach nicht der Feierlichkeit des Anlasses.
keg [keg] *n* **(a)** (*barrel*) kleines Faß, Fäßchen *nt*. **(b)** (*also ~ beer*) (Bier *nt*) vom Faß.
kelp [kelp] *n* Seetang *m*.
ken [ken] **1** *n* **it is beyond *or* outside my ~** das entzieht sich meiner Kenntnis. **2** *vti* (*Scot*) *see* know.
kennel ['kenl] *n* **(a)** Hundehütte *f*. **(b)** ~s (*cage*) Hundezwinger *m*; (*for breeding*) Hundezucht *f*; (*boarding*) (Hunde)heim, Tierheim *nt*; **to put a dog in ~s** einen Hund in Pflege geben.
Kenya ['kenjə] *n* Kenia *nt*.
Kenyan ['kenjən] **1** *n* Kenianer(in *f*) *m*. **2** *adj* kenianisch.
kepi ['keɪpɪ] *n* Käppi *nt*.
kept [kept] **1** *pret, ptp of* keep. **2** *adj* **~ woman** Mätresse *f*; **she's a ~ woman** sie läßt sich aushalten.
kerb [kɜ:b] *n* (*Brit*) Bordkante *f*, Randstein *m*.
kerb: **~ drill** *n* Verkehrserziehung *f*; **~stone** *n* Bordstein, Randstein *m*.
kerchief ['kɜ:tʃɪf] *n* (*old*) Hals- *or* Kopftuch *nt*.
kerfuffle [kə'fʌfl] *n* (*Brit inf*) (*noise*) Lärm *m*, Gedöns *nt* (*inf*); (*fight*) Balgerei *f* (*inf*); (*trouble*) Theater *nt* (*inf*).
kernel ['kɜ:nl] *n* (*lit, fig*) Kern *m*.
kerosene ['kerəsi:n] *n* Kerosin *nt*. **~ lamp** Petroleum- *or* Paraffinlampe *f*.
kestrel ['kestrəl] *n* Turmfalke *m*.
ketch [ketʃ] *n* Ketsch *f*.
ketchup ['ketʃəp] *n* Ketchup *nt or m*.
kettle ['ketl] *n* Kessel *m*. **I'll put the ~ on** ich stelle mal eben (Kaffee-/Tee)wasser auf; **the ~'s boiling** das Wasser kocht; **this is a pretty ~ of fish** (*inf*) das ist eine schöne Bescherung; **this is a different ~ of fish** (*inf*) das ist doch was ganz anderes.
kettledrum ['ketldrʌm] *n* (Kessel)pauke *f*.
key [ki:] **1** *n* **(a)** Schlüssel *m*.
 (b) (*fig: solution*) Schlüssel *m*. **education is the ~ to success** Bildung ist der Schlüssel zum Erfolg; **the ~ to the mystery der** Schlüssel zum Geheimnis, des Rätsels Lösung; **this was the ~ to the murderer's identity** das gab Aufschluß darüber *or* den Hinweis, wer der Mörder war.
 (c) (*answers*) Lösungen *pl*, Schlüssel *m*; (*Sch*) Schlüssel *m*, Lehrerheft *nt*; (*Math etc*) Lösungsheft *nt*; (*for maps etc*) Zeichenerklärung *f*.
 (d) (*of piano, typewriter etc*) Taste *f*.
 (e) (*Mus*) Tonart *f*. **to sing off ~** falsch singen; **change of ~** Tonartwechsel *m*, Modulation *f*; **in the ~ of C** in C-Dur/c-Moll.
 (f) (*Build*) Untergrund *m*.
 2 *adj attr* (*vital*) Schlüssel-, wichtigste(r, s). **~ industry** Schlüsselindustrie *f*; **~ man** Schlüsselfigur *f*; **~ sprin-gender Punkt; ~ position** Schlüsselposition *or* -stellung *f*; **~ question** Schlüsselfrage *f*; **~ role** Schlüsselrolle *f*.
 3 *vt speech etc* (*to or for one's audience*) (auf jdn) abstimmen *or* zuschneiden (*to, for auf* + *acc*), anpassen (*to, for dat*).
♦ **key up** *vt sep* **she was (all) ~ed ~ about the interview** sie war wegen des Interviews ganz aufgedreht (*inf*); **he was all ~ed ~ for the big race** er hatte sich schon ganz auf das große Rennen eingestellt; **to ~ the crowds ~ for the big speech** die Menge auf die große Rede einstimmen.
key: **~board** **1** *n* (*of piano*) Klaviatur, Tastatur *f*; (*of organ*) Manual *nt*; (*of typewriter*) Tastatur *f*; **~board operator** Maschinensetzer(in *f*) *m*; **a genius on the ~board** (*Mus*) ein Klaviergenie *n*; **2** *vt* (*Typ*) setzen; **~hole** *n* Schlüsselloch *nt*; **~ money** *n* Provision *f*, Schlüsselgeld *nt*; **~ note** *n* (*Mus*) Grundton *m*; (*of a speech*) Leitgedanke, Tenor *m*; **~note speech** (*Pol etc*) programmatische Rede; **~ ring** *n* Schlüsselring *m*; **~ signature** *n* (*Mus*) Tonartbezeichnung *f*; **~stone** *n* (*Archit*) Schlußstein *m*; (*fig*) Grundpfeiler *m*, Anschlag *m*.
KG (*Brit*) *abbr of* **Knight of the Garter**.
kg *abbr of* **kilogramme(s), kilogram(s)** kg.
KGB *n* KGB *m*.
khaki ['kɑ:kɪ] **1** *n* K(h)aki *nt*. **2** *adj* k(h)aki(braun *or* -farben).
kibbutz [kɪ'buts] *n, pl* **-im** Kibbuz *m*.
kibosh ['kaɪbɒʃ] *n* (*sl*): **to put the ~ on sth** etw vermasseln (*inf*).
kick [kɪk] **1** *n* **(a)** (*act of ~ing*) Tritt, Stoß, Kick (*inf*) *m*. **to take a ~ at sb/sth** nach jdm/etw treten; **he gave the ball a tremendous ~** er trat mit Wucht gegen den Ball; **a tremendous ~ by Beckenbauer** ein toller Schuß von Beckenbauer; **he hasn't much of a ~ with his left leg** links kann er nicht kräftig schießen *or* zutreten; **to give the door a ~** gegen die Tür treten; **give it a ~** tritt mal dagegen; **to get a ~ on the leg** einen Tritt ans Bein bekommen, gegen das *or* ans Bein getreten werden; **it's better than a ~ in the pants** (*inf*) das ist besser als ein Tritt in den Hintern (*inf*); **what he needs is a good ~ up the backside** (*inf*) er braucht mal einen kräftigen Tritt in den Hintern (*inf*).
 (b) (*inf: thrill*) **she gets a ~ out of it** es macht ihr eine Riesenspaß (*inf*); (*physically*) sie verspürt einen Kitzel dabei;

to do sth for ~s etw zum Spaß *or* Jux (*inf*) *or* Fez (*inf*) tun; **just for ~s** nur aus Jux und Tollerei (*inf*); **she just lives for ~s** sie lebt nur zu ihrem Vergnügen; **how do you get your ~s?** was machen Sie zu ihrem Vergnügen?
 (c) *no pl* (*power to stimulate*) Feuer *nt*, Pep *m* (*inf*). **this drink has plenty of ~** in it dieses Getränk hat es in sich; **this drink hasn't much ~ in it** dieses Getränk ist ziemlich zahm (*inf*).
 (d) (*of gun*) Rückstoß *m*.
 2 *vi* (*person*) treten; (*struggle*) um sich treten; (*baby, while sleeping*) strampeln; (*animal*) austreten, ausschlagen; (*dancer*) das Bein hochwerfen; (*gun*) zurückstoßen *or* -schlagen, Rückstoß haben; (*inf: engine*) stottern (*inf*). **he ~ed into third** (*sl*) er ging in den dritten (Gang).
 3 *vt* **(a)** (*person, horse*) *sb* treten, einen Tritt versetzen (+*dat*); *door, ball* treten gegen; *ball* kicken (*inf*); *object* einen Tritt versetzen (+*dat*), mit dem Fuß stoßen. **to ~ sb's behind** jdn in den Hintern treten; **to ~ a goal** ein Tor schießen; **to ~ the bucket** (*inf*) abkratzen (*inf*), ins Gras beißen (*inf*); **I could have ~ed myself** (*inf*) ich hätte mich ohrfeigen können, ich hätte mich selbst *or* mir in den Hintern treten können (*inf*).
 (b) (*sl: stop*) **to ~ heroin** vom Heroin runterkommen (*sl*); **to ~ a habit** es stecken (*sl*).
♦ **kick about** *or* **around** **1** *vi* (*sl*) (*person*) herumgammeln (*sl*), rumhängen (*sl*) (*prep obj* in +*dat*); (*thing*) rumliegen (*inf*) (*prep obj* in +*dat*).
 2 *vt sep* **to ~ a ball ~** (herum)bolzen (*inf*), den Ball herum-kicken (*inf*); **you shouldn't let them ~ you ~** Sie sollten sich nicht so herumstoßen lassen; **don't ~ that book ~** werfen Sie das Buch nicht so herum; **to ~ an idea ~** (*sl*) eine Idee durchdiskutieren.
♦ **kick against** *vi* +*prep obj* treten gegen. **to ~ ~ the pricks** sich widersetzen, wider *or* gegen den Stachel löcken (*geh*).
♦ **kick at** *vi* +*prep obj* treten nach.
♦ **kick away** *vt sep* wegstoßen; (*knock down*) niedertreten.
♦ **kick back** **1** *vi* **(a)** zurücktreten. **if you annoy him he'll ~ ~** (*fig*) wenn Sie ihn ärgern, gibt er es Ihnen zurück. **(b)** (*gun*) zurückstoßen, einen Rückstoß haben. **2** *vt sep* *blanket* weg-strampeln; *ball* zurückspielen *or* -schießen *or* -schlagen.
♦ **kick in** *vt sep* *door* eintreten. **to ~ sb's teeth ~** jdm die Zähne einschlagen.
♦ **kick off** **1** *vi* (*Ftbl*) anstoßen; (*player also*) den Anstoß ausführen (*inf also*); (*inf*) losgehen (*inf*), beginnen. **who's going to ~ ~?** (*fig inf*) wer fängt an? **2** *vt sep* wegtreten; *shoes* von sich schleudern.
♦ **kick out** **1** *vi* (*horse*) ausschlagen; (*person*) um sich treten. **to ~ ~ at sb** nach jdm treten. **2** *vt sep* hinauswerfen (*of aus*). **he was ~ed ~ of the club** er ist aus dem Verein hinausgeworfen worden *or* geflogen (*inf*).
♦ **kick over** *vi* +*prep obj*: **to ~ ~ the traces** über die Stränge schlagen.
♦ **kick up** *vt sep* **(a)** *dust* aufwirbeln. **(b)** (*fig inf*) **to ~ ~ a row or a din** Krach machen (*inf*); **to ~ ~ a fuss** Krach schlagen (*inf*).
kick: **~back** *n* (*inf*) (*reaction*) Auswirkung *f*; (*as bribe*) Provision *f*; (*perk*) Nebeneinnahme *f*; **~down** *n* Kickdown *m*.
kicker ['kɪkə'] *n* Spieler, der Strafstöße etc ausführt.
kick: **~-off** *n* **(a)** (*Sport*) Anpfiff, Anstoß *m*; **the ~-off is at 3 o'clock** Anpfiff ist um 3 Uhr; **(b)** (*sl: of ceremony etc*) Start, Anfang *m*; **the ~-off is at 3 o'clock** um 3 geht's los (*inf*); **~-start(er)** *n* Kickstarter *m*; **~turn** *n* (*Ski*) Kehre *f*.
kid [kɪd] **1** *n* **(a)** (*young goat*) Kitz, Zicklein (*liter*) *nt*.
 (b) (*leather*) Ziegen- *or* Glacéleder *nt*.
 (c) (*inf: child*) Kind *nt*. **when I was a ~** als ich klein war; **to get the ~s to bed** die Kleinen ins Bett bringen; **it's ~'s stuff** (*for children*) das ist was für kleine Kinder (*inf*); (*easy*) das ist doch ein Kinderspiel.
 (d) (*inf*) (*man*) Junge, Bursche (*inf*) *m*; (*woman*) Kleine *f* (*inf*). **listen ~, I didn't mean it** nun hör mir mal gut zu, ich hab's doch nicht so gemeint; **listen ~, you keep out of this** hör mal Kleiner, du hältst dich hier raus (*inf*); **come on ~s!** los Jungs! (*inf*); **she's some ~** die ist nicht ohne (*inf*); (*clever*) die ist ganz schön clever (*inf*); **he's done it already? some ~** was, er hat das schon gemacht? stark (*sl*) *or* tolle Leistung (*inf*).
 2 *adj attr* **~ brother** kleiner Bruder, Brüderchen *nt*; **~ gloves** Glacéhandschuhe *pl*; **to handle sb with ~ gloves** (*fig*) jdn mit Samthandschuhen *or* Glacéhandschuhen anfassen.
 3 *vt* (*inf*) **to ~ sb** (*on*) (*tease*) jdn aufziehen (*inf*); (*deceive*) ~ me mir kannst du doch nichts vormachen; **you can't ~ me** mir kannst du doch nichts vormachen; **don't ~ yourself!** machen Sie sich doch nichts vor!; **I ~ you not** das ist mein Ernst, ganz ehrlich (*inf*).
 4 *vi* (*inf*) Jux machen (*inf*). **no ~ding** im Ernst, ehrlich (*inf*).
♦ **kid on** *vt sep see* kid 3.
kiddo ['kɪdəʊ] *n* (*sl*) *see* kid 1 (d).
kiddy ['kɪdɪ] *n* (*inf*) Kleinchen (*inf*), Kindchen (*inf*) *nt*.
kidnap ['kɪdnæp] *vt* entführen, kidnappen.
kidnapper ['kɪdnæpə'] *n* Entführer(in *f*), Kidnapper(in *f*) *m*.
kidnapping ['kɪdnæpɪŋ] *n* Entführung *f*, Kidnapping *nt*.
kidney ['kɪdnɪ] *n* **(a)** (*Anat, Cook*) Niere *f*. **(b)** (*fig: type, temperament*) **of the same ~** vom gleichen Schlag *or* Typ.
kidney: **~ bean** *n* Gartenbohne *f*; **~ dish** *n* Nierenschale *f*; **~ machine** *n* künstliche Niere; **~-shaped** *adj* nierenförmig; **~ stone** *n* (*Med*) Nierenstein *m*.
kill [kɪl] **1** *vt* töten, umbringen; (*by beating*) totschlagen, erschlagen; (*by shooting*) erschießen, totschießen; (*by stab-bing*) erstechen, erdolchen; *animals* töten; (*Hunt*) erlegen; (*slaughter*) schlachten; (*shock*) umbringen; *pains* beseitigen; *weeds* vernichten. **to be ~ed in action/in battle/in the war** fallen/im Kampf fallen/im Krieg fallen; **too many people are being ~ed on the roads** zu viele Menschen sterben auf der Straße *or* kommen auf der Straße um; **last year's drought ~ed thousands of animals** bei der letztjährigen Trockenheit kamen

Tausende von Tieren um; **her brother was ~ed in a car accident** ihr Bruder ist bei einem Autounfall ums Leben gekommen; **how many were ~ed?** wieviel Todesopfer gab es?; **smoking will ~ you** das Rauchen wird Sie (noch) das Leben kosten; **the frost has ~ed my geraniums** meine Geranien sind erfroren; **she ~ed herself** sie brachte sich um, sie nahm sich (*dat*) das Leben; **he was ~ed with this weapon** dies ist die Mord- *or* Tatwaffe; **please, don't ~ me** bitte, lassen Sie mich leben; **he was ~ed by cancer** er starb an Krebs; **many people were ~ed by the plague** viele Menschen sind der Pest zum Opfer gefallen; **he was ~ed with poison/a knife/a hammer** er wurde vergiftet/(mit einem Messer) erstochen/(mit einem Hammer) erschlagen; **each man ~s the thing he loves** jeder zerstört das, was er liebt; **I'll ~ him!** (*also fig*) den bring' ich um (*inf*); **the bullet ~ed him** die Kugel traf ihn tödlich *or* tötete ihn.

(b) (*fig uses*) *feelings, love etc* töten, zerstören. **to ~ time** die Zeit totschlagen; **we have two hours to ~** wir haben noch zwei Stunden übrig; **to ~ two birds with one stone** (*Prov*) zwei Fliegen mit einer Klappe schlagen (*Prov*); **these stairs/the children are ~ing me** (*inf*) diese Treppe/die Kinder bringen mich (noch) mal) um (*inf*); **my girdle is ~ing me** (*inf*) mein Hüfthalter bringt mich um (*inf*); **she was ~ing herself (laughing)** (*inf*) sie hat sich totgelacht *or* kaputtgelacht (*inf*); **this one'll ~ you** (*inf*) da lachst du dich tot (*inf*); **this heat is ~ing me** (*inf*) ich vergehe vor Hitze; **my feet are ~ing me** (*inf*) mir brennen die Füße; **they're not exactly ~ing themselves** (*inf: overworking*) sie bringen sich nicht gerade um (*inf*), sie reißen sich (*dat*) kein Bein aus; **don't ~ yourself** (*iro*) übernehmen Sie sich nicht.

(c) (*spoil the effect of*) *taste, flavour, performance* verderben, überdecken; *hopes* vernichten, zunichte machen. **this red ~s the other colours** dieses Rot übertönt *or* erschlägt die anderen Farben.

(d) (*inf*) *parliamentary bill, proposal* zu Fall bringen.

(e) *sound* schlucken. **to ~ a ball** eine Bombe schlagen (*inf*); **~ that light!** (*inf*) Licht aus!

(f) (*Press etc*) *paragraph, story* streichen, abwürgen (*sl*).

(g) (*Tech*) *engine etc* abschalten, ausschalten; (*Elec*) *circuit* unterbrechen.

(h) (*inf*) *bottle* leermachen, auf den Kopf stellen (*inf*).

2 *vi* töten. **cigarettes can ~** Zigaretten können tödlich sein *or* tödliche Folgen haben; **he was dressed to ~** er hatte sich in Schale geworfen (*inf*).

3 *n* **(a)** (*Hunt*) Erlegen *nt*, Abschuß *m*; (*at bullfight*) Todesstoß *m*. **the wolves gathered round for the ~** die Wölfe kreisten die Beute ein, um sie zu erlegen; **the tiger has made a ~** der Tiger hat ein Opfer erlegt *or* geschlagen; **to be in at the ~** (*lit*) beim Abschuß dabei sein; (*fig*) am Ende dabei sein.

(b) (*Hunt etc: animals killed*) Beute *f no pl*.

♦**kill off** *vt sep* vernichten, töten; *whole race* ausrotten, vernichten; *cows, pigs, elephants* abschlachten; *weeds* vertilgen.

killer ['kɪlə'] *n* (*person*) Mörder(in *f*), Killer (*inf*) *m*. **this disease is a ~** diese Krankheit ist tödlich; *see* lady-killer, weed-killer.

killer: **the ~ instinct** *n* (*lit*) der Tötungsinstinkt; **a boxer with the ~ instinct** ein Boxer, in dem der Killer wach wird (*inf*); **a successful businessman needs the ~ instinct** ein erfolgreicher Geschäftsmann muß über Leichen gehen können; **~ whale** *n* Schwertwal, Mordwal *m*.

killing ['kɪlɪŋ] **1** *n* **(a)** (*of animals*) (*Hunt*) Erlegen *nt*; (*at abattoir*) (*Ab*)schlachten *nt*.

(b) (*of person*) Töten *nt*, Tötung *f*. **three more ~s in Belfast** drei weitere Morde *or* Todesopfer in Belfast.

(c) (*fig*) **to make a ~** einen Riesengewinn machen.

2 *adj* **(a)** *blow etc* tödlich.

(b) (*exhausting*) *work* mörderisch (*inf*).

(c) (*funny*) urkomisch (*inf*).

killingly ['kɪlɪŋlɪ] *adv*: **~ funny** zum Totlachen (*inf*).

killjoy ['kɪldʒɔɪ] *n* Spielverderber, Miesmacher *m*.

kiln [kɪln] *n* (*for baking, burning*) (Brenn)ofen *m*; (*for minerals*) Röst- *or* Kiesofen *m*; (*for drying bricks etc*) Trockenofen *m*; (*for hops etc*) Darre *f*, Darrofen *m*.

kilo ['kiːləʊ] *n* Kilo *nt*.

kilocycle ['kɪləʊˌsaɪkl] *n* Kilohertz *nt*.

kilogramme, (*US*) **kilogram** ['kɪləʊgræm] *n* Kilogramm *nt*.

kilohertz ['kɪləʊhɜːts] *n* Kilohertz *nt*.

kilolitre, (*US*) **kiloliter** ['kɪləʊˌliːtə'] *n* Kiloliter *m*.

kilometre, (*US*) **kilometer** ['kɪləʊˌmiːtə'] *n* Kilometer *m*.

kilowatt ['kɪləʊwɒt] *n* Kilowatt *nt*. **~ hour** Kilowattstunde *f*.

kilt [kɪlt] *n* Kilt, Schottenrock *m*.

kimono [kɪˈməʊnəʊ] *n* Kimono *m*.

kin [kɪn] **1** *n* Familie *f*, Verwandte *pl*, Verwandtschaft *f*. **has he any ~?** hat er Verwandte *or* Familie?; *see* kith, next of ~. **2** *adj* verwandt (*to* mit).

kind¹ [kaɪnd] *n* **(a)** (*class, variety, nature*) Art *f*; (*of coffee, sugar, paint etc*) Sorte *f*. **they differ in ~** sie sind verschiedenartig; **several ~s of flour** mehrere Mehlsorten; **this ~ of book** diese Art Buch; **what ~ of ...?** was für ein(e) ...?; **what ~ of people does he think we are?** für wen hält er uns denn?; **the only one of its ~** das einzige seiner Art; **this specimen is perfect of its ~** dieses Exemplar ist ein ausgezeichneter Vertreter seiner Art; **a funny ~ of person** ein komischer Mensch *or* Typ; **he is not the ~ of man to refuse** er ist nicht der Typ, der nein sagt; **he's not that ~ of person** so ist er nicht; **I'm not that ~ of girl** so eine bin ich nicht; **they're two of a ~** die beiden sind vom gleichen Typ *or* von der gleichen Art; (*people*) sie sind vom gleichen Schlag; **I know your ~** deinen Typ kenne ich; **your ~ never do any good** Leute Ihres Schlags *or* Leute wie Sie tun nie gut; **this ~ of thing** so etwas; **you know the ~ of thing I mean** Sie wissen, was ich meine; **... of all ~s** alle möglichen ...; **something of the ~** so etwas ähnliches; **nothing of the ~** nichts dergleichen; **you'll do nothing of the ~** du wirst dich schwer hüten, du wirst das schön bleiben lassen!; **it was beef of a ~** (*pej*) es war Rindfleisch oder

so was ähnliches (*inf*); **it's not my ~ of holiday** (*inf*) solche Ferien sind nicht mein Fall (*inf*) *or* nach meinem Geschmack; **she's my ~ of woman** (*inf*) sie ist mein Typ.

(b) **a ~ of ... eine Art ..., so ein(e) ...; a ~ of box** so (etwas wie) eine Schachtel, eine Art Schachtel; **in a ~ of way I'm sorry** (*inf*) irgendwie tut es mir leid; **he was ~ of worried-looking** (*inf*) *and* **he said** (*inf*) *and he did*) ich habe eigentlich gedacht, daß er ...; (*and he did*) ich habe es mir beinahe gedacht, daß er ...; **I was ~ of disappointed** (*a little*) ich war irgendwie enttäuscht; (*very*) ich war ziemlich enttäuscht; **I was ~ of frightened that ...** (*inf*) ich hatte schon Angst, daß ...; **are you nervous?** — **~ of** (*inf*) bist du nervös? — ja, schon (*inf*).

(c) (*goods, as opposed to money*) Naturalien *pl*, Ware *f*. **payment in ~** = Bezahlung in Naturalien; **I shall pay you in ~** (*fig*) ich werde es Ihnen in gleicher Münze zurückzahlen.

kind² *adj* (+ *er*) liebenswürdig, nett, freundlich (*to zu*). **he's ~ to animals** er ist gut zu Tieren; **would you be ~ enough to open the door** wären Sie (vielleicht) so nett *or* freundlich *or* lieb, die Tür zu öffnen; **he was so ~ as to show me the way** er war so nett *or* freundlich und zeigte mir den Weg; **it was very ~ of you to help me** es war wirklich nett *or* lieb von Ihnen, mir zu helfen.

kindergarten ['kɪndəˌgɑːtn] *n* Kindergarten *m*.

kind-hearted ['kaɪnd'hɑːtɪd] *adj* gutherzig, gütig.

kind-heartedness ['kaɪnd'hɑːtɪdnɪs] *n* Gutherzigkeit, Güte *f*.

kindle ['kɪndl] **1** *vt* *fire* entfachen, anzünden, entzünden; *passions, desire* entfachen, wecken. **2** *vi* (*fire, wood etc*) brennen; (*passions, enthusiasm etc*) entbrennen, aufflammen.

kindliness ['kaɪndlɪnɪs] *n* Freundlichkeit, Güte, Liebenswürdigkeit *f*.

kindling ['kɪndlɪŋ] *n* (*wood*) Anzündholz, Anmachholz *nt*.

kindly ['kaɪndlɪ] **1** *adv* **(a)** *speak, act* freundlich, nett; *treat* liebenswürdig, freundlich. **they ~ put me up for a night** sie nahmen mich freundlicherweise *or* liebenswürdigerweise für eine Nacht auf.

(b) **will you ~ do it now** tun Sie das sofort, wenn ich bitten darf; **~ shut the door** machen Sie doch bitte die Tür zu; **would you ~ shut up!** halten Sie doch endlich den Mund.

(c) **I don't take ~ to his smoking** sein Rauchen ist mir gar nicht angenehm; **he won't take at all ~ to that** das wird ihm gar nicht gefallen; **I don't take ~ to not being asked** es ärgert mich, wenn ich nicht gefragt werde; **she didn't take ~ to the idea of going abroad** sie konnte sich gar nicht mit dem Gedanken anfreunden, ins Ausland zu gehen; **she didn't take it ~ when I said ...** sie hat es nicht gut aufgenommen, als ich sagte ...

2 *adj* (+ *er*) *person* lieb, nett, freundlich; *advice* gut gemeint, freundlich; *voice* sanft, gütig.

kindness ['kaɪndnɪs] *n* **(a)** *no pl* Freundlichkeit, Liebenswürdigkeit *f* (*towards* gegenüber); (*goodness of heart*) Güte *f* (*towards* gegenüber). **thank you very much for all your ~** vielen Dank, daß Sie so freundlich *or* liebenswürdig waren; **to treat sb with ~, to show sb ~** freundlich *or* liebenswürdig zu jdm sein; **out of the ~ of one's heart** aus reiner Nächstenliebe; **would you have the ~ to ...?** hätten Sie die Freundlichkeit *or* Güte, zu ...?

(b) (*act of ~*) Gefälligkeit, Aufmerksamkeit *f*. **to do sb a ~** jdm eine Gefälligkeit erweisen; **it would be a ~ to tell him** man würde ihm einen Gefallen tun, wenn man es ihm sagen würde; **thank you for all your many ~es** vielen Dank für alles, was Sie für mich getan haben.

kindred ['kɪndrɪd] **1** *n, no pl* (*relatives*) Verwandtschaft *f*. **2** *adj* (*related*) verwandt. **~ spirit** Gleichgesinnte(r) *mf*.

kinetic [kɪˈnetɪk] *adj* kinetisch.

kinfolk ['kɪnfəʊk] *n see* **kinsfolk**.

king [kɪŋ] *n* **(a)** (*lit*) König *m*. **K ~'s Bench** (*Jur*) erste Kammer des Obersten Gerichts in Großbritannien; **K ~'s Counsel** (*Jur*) Kronanwalt *m* (*Staatsanwalt, der in höheren Strafsachen die Krone vertritt*); **the ~'s highway** (*old, form*) eine öffentliche Straße; **~'s messenger** (*Diplomacy*) königlicher Gesandter; **it must have cost a ~'s ransom** das muß eine stolze Summe *or* ein Vermögen gekostet haben.

(b) (*Zool*) König *m*. **an oil ~** ein Ölkönig *or* -magnat *m*.

(c) (*Chess, Cards*) König *m*; (*Draughts*) Dame *f*.

king: **~ bolt** *n* (*US*) *see* **~pin**; **~cup** (*buttercup*) Hahnenfuß *m*, Butterblume *f*; (*marsh marigold*) Sumpfdotterblume *f*.

kingdom ['kɪŋdəm] *n* **(a)** (*lit*) Königreich *nt*. **(b)** (*Rel*) **~ of heaven** Himmelreich *nt*; **to send sb to ~ come** (*inf*) jdn ins Jenseits befördern (*inf*); **you can go on doing that till ~ come** (*inf*) Sie können (so) bis in alle Ewigkeit weitermachen; **he's gone to ~ come** (*inf*) er hat das Zeitliche gesegnet (*hum inf*). **(c)** (*Zool, Bot*) Reich *nt*.

kingfisher ['kɪŋˌfɪʃə'] *n* Eisvogel *m*. **~-blue** eisblau, gletscherblau.

kingly ['kɪŋlɪ] *adj* königlich, majestätisch.

king: **~maker** *n* (*lit, fig*) Königsmacher *m*; **~pin** *n* (*Tech*) Königsbolzen, Drehzapfen *m*; (*Aut*) Achsschenkelbolzen *m*; (*fig: person*) Stütze *f*; **he's the ~pin of the whole organization** mit ihm steht und fällt die ganze Organisation; **~ship** *n* Königtum *nt*; **~-size(d)** *adj* (*inf*) in Großformat, großformatig; *cigarettes* King-size; *bed* extra groß; **I've got a ~-size(d) headache** (*hum*) ich hab' vielleicht einen Brummschädel (*inf*) *or* einen dicken Kopf (*inf*).

kink [kɪŋk] **1** *n* **(a)** (*in rope etc*) Knick *m*, Schlaufe *f*; (*in hair*) Welle *f*. **(b)** (*mental peculiarity*) Schrulle *f*, Tick *m* (*inf*); (*sexual*) abartige Veranlagung. **2** *vi* (*rope*) Schlaufen bilden, sich verdrehen; (*hair*) sich wellen.

kinky ['kɪŋkɪ] *adj* (+ *er*) **(a)** *hair* wellig. **(b)** (*inf*) *person, ideas, mind* verdreht (*inf*), schrullig, spleenig (*inf*); *boots, fashion* verrückt (*inf*), irr (*sl*); (*sexually*) abartig. **~! inf**, so was! (*inf*), ist ja irre! (*sl*), lustig, lustig! (*inf*).

kinsfolk ['kɪnzfəʊk] *n* Verwandtschaft *f*, Verwandte(n) *pl*.

kinship ['kɪnʃɪp] *n* Verwandtschaft *f*.

kinsman ['kınzmən] *n, pl* **-men** [-mən] Verwandte(r) *m*.

kinswoman ['kınzwʊmən] *n, pl* **-women** [-wımın] Verwandte *f*.

kiosk ['kiːɒsk] *n* **(a)** Kiosk, Verkaufsstand *m*, Bude *f*. **(b)** (*Brit Telec*) (Telephon)zelle *f*.

kip [kıp] (*Brit sl*) **1** *n* (*sleep*) Schläfchen *nt*, Ratzer(chen *nt*) *m* (*sl*). **I've got to get some ~** ich muß mal 'ne Runde pennen (*sl*); **I need a good ~** ich muß mal (wieder) richtig pennen (*sl*) *or* ratzen (*sl*). **2** *vi* (*also ~ **down***) pennen (*sl*).

kipper ['kıpə^r] *n* Räucherhering, Bückling *m*.

kirk [kɜːk] *n* (*Scot*) Kirche *f*. **the K~** *die Presbyterianische Kirche Schottlands.*

kiss [kıs] **1** *n* Kuß *m*. **~ of life** Mund-zu-Mund-Beatmung *f*; **~ of death** (*fig*) Todesstoß *m*; **that will be the ~ of death for them** das wird ihnen den Todesstoß versetzen; **~ curl** Schmachtlocke *f*; **she felt the ~ of the wind on her hair** sie fühlte, wie der Wind sanft über ihr Haar strich; *see* **blow**².

2 *vt* küssen; (*fig: touch gently*) sanft berühren. **to ~ sb's cheek** jdn auf die Wange küssen; **to ~ sb's hand** jdm die Hand küssen; (*woman's hand: in greeting*) jdm einen Handkuß geben; **they ~ed each other** sie gaben sich einen Kuß, sie küßten sich; **to ~ sb back** jds Kuß (*acc*) erwidern, jdn wieder-küssen; **to ~ sb good night/goodbye** jdm einen Gute-Nacht-Kuß/Abschiedskuß geben; **come here and I'll ~ it better** komm her, ich werde mal blasen, dann tut's nicht mehr weh.

3 *vi* küssen; (*~ each other*) sich küssen. **to ~ and make up** sich mit einem Kuß versöhnen.

♦**kiss away** *vt sep* **she ~ed ~ the child's tears** sie küßte dem Kind die Tränen fort.

kissable ['kısəbl] *adj* **mouth** zum Küssen einladend *attr*. **a ~ girl** ein Mädchen, das man küssen möchte.

kisser ['kısə^r] *n* (*sl*) Fresse (*sl*), Schnauze (*sl*) *f*.

kissing gate ['kısıŋgeıt] *n* Schwinggatter *nt* (*an Weidenzäunen und Hecken, das nur je eine Person durchläßt*).

kissproof ['kıspruːf] *adj* kußecht.

kit [kıt] *n* **(a)** (*equipment*) (*for fishing, photography etc*) Ausrüstung *f*; (*Mil also*) Montur *f* (*old*). **~ inspection** (*Mil*) Bekleidungs- *or* Ausrüstungsappell *m*.

(b) (*Sport: clothes*) Ausrüstung *f*, Zeug *nt* (*inf*), Sachen *pl* (*inf*). **gym ~** Sportzeug *nt*, Sportsachen *pl*.

(c) (*belongings, luggage etc*) Sachen *pl*; *see* **caboodle**.

(d) (*set of items*) (*tools*) Werkzeug *nt*; (*in box*) Werkzeug-kasten *m*; (*puncture repair ~*) Flickzeug *nt*; (*first-aid ~*) Erste-Hilfe-Ausrüstung *f*, Verbandszeug *nt*.

(e) (*for self-assembly*) Bastelsatz *m*.

♦**kit out** *or* **up** *vt sep* ausrüsten (*esp Mil*), ausstatten; (*clothe*) einkleiden. **he arrived ~ted ~ in oilskins** er erschien (ausge-stattet) in Ölzeug.

kitbag ['kıtbæg] *n* Seesack *m*.

kitchen ['kıtʃın] **1** *n* Küche *f*. **2** *attr* Küchen-; *scales also*, **soap** Haushalts-. **~ foil** Haushalts- *or* Alufolie *f*; **~ garden** Gemüsegarten, Küchengarten *m*; **~ range** Küchenherd *m*; **~ scissors** Küchenschere, Haushaltsschere *f*; **~ unit** Küchenschrank *m*.

kitchenette [,kıtʃı'net] *n* (*separate room*) kleine Küche; (*part of one room*) Kochnische *f*.

kitchen: **~maid** *n* Küchenmagd *f*; **~ sink** *n* Spüle *f*, Ausguß, Spülstein *m*; **I've packed everything but the ~ sink** (*inf*) ich habe den ganzen Hausrat eingepackt; **~-sink drama** *n* Alltagsdrama, Wohnküchendrama *nt*; **~ware** *n* Küchengeräte *pl*.

kite [kaıt] *n* **(a)** (*Orn*) Milan *m*. **(b)** (*toy*) Drachen *m*. **K~ mark** (*Brit*) dreieckiges Gütezeichen. **(c)** (*Aviat sl*) Vogel *m* (*sl*).

kith [kıθ] *n*: **~ and kin** Blutsverwandte *pl*; **we're ~ and kin with the British** wir sind mit den Briten blutsverwandt, die Briten sind unsere Blutsbrüder; **they came with ~ and kin** sie kamen mit Kind und Kegel.

kitsch [kıtʃ] *n* Kitsch *m*.

kitschy ['kıtʃı] *adj* (*+er*) kitschig.

kitten ['kıtn] *n* kleine Katze, Kätzchen *nt*. **to have ~s** (*inf*) Junge *or* Zustände kriegen (*inf*).

kittenish ['kıtənıʃ] *adj* verspielt; (*fig*) *woman* kokett.

kittiwake ['kıtıweık] *n* Dreizehenmöwe *f*.

kitty ['kıtı] *n* **(a)** (*shared money*) (gemeinsame) Kasse; (*Cards etc also*) Spielkasse *f*. **we'll have a ~ for the drinks** wir machen eine Umlage für die Getränke; **I've nothing left in the ~** die Kasse ist leer. **(b)** (*inf: cat*) Mieze *f*.

kiwi ['kiːwiː] *n* **(a)** Kiwi *m*. **(b)** (*also ~ fruit*) Kiwi(frucht) *f*.

KKK *abbr of* **Klu Klux Klan**.

klaxon ['klæksn] *n* Horn *nt*, Hupe *f*.

Kleenex ® ['kliːneks] *n* Tempo(taschentuch) ® *nt*.

kleptomania [,kleptəʊ'meınıə] *n* Kleptomanie *f*.

kleptomaniac [,kleptəʊ'meınıæk] **1** *n* Kleptomane *m*, Kleptomanin *f*. **2** *adj* kleptomanisch.

km *abbr of* **kilometre(s)** km.

kmph *abbr of* **kilometres per hour** km/h.

knack [næk] *n* Trick, Kniff *m*; (*talent*) Talent, Geschick *nt*. **there's a (special) ~ (to or in it)** da ist ein (gewisser) Trick *or* Kniff dabei; **there's a (special) ~ to opening it** da ist ein Trick *or* Kniff dabei, wie man das aufbekommt; **to learn or get the ~ of doing sth** es herausbekommen, wie man etw macht; **you'll soon get the ~ of it** Sie werden den Dreh bald rausbekommen *or* raushaben; **I've lost the ~** ich bekomme *or* kriege (*inf*) das nicht mehr hin *or* fertig; **she's got a ~ of saying the wrong thing** sie hat ein Geschick *or* Talent, immer das Falsche zu sagen; **he has the ~ of disappearing when he's needed** er hat ein beson-deres Talent dafür, immer gerade dann zu verschwinden, wenn man ihn braucht.

knacker ['nækə^r] *n* (*Brit*) (*of horses*) Abdecker, Schinder *m*; (*of boats, houses*) Abbruchunternehmer *m*. **to send a horse to the ~'s (yard)** ein Pferd zum Abdecker *or* auf den Schindanger (*old*) bringen.

knackered ['nækəd] *adj* (*Brit sl*) kaputt (*inf*), ausgebufft (*sl*).

knapsack ['næpsæk] *n* Proviantbeutel, Tornister (*esp Mil*), Knappsack (*old*) *m*.

knave [neıv] *n* **(a)** (*old*) Bube (*old*), Schurke *m*. **(b)** (*Cards*) Bube, Unter (*old*) *m*.

knavery ['neıvərı] *n* (*old*) Bubenstück *nt* (*old*), Büberei *f* (*old*).

knavish ['neıvıʃ] *adj* (*old*) bübisch (*old*), schurkisch.

knead [niːd] *vt* **wax etc** kneten; (*massage*) **muscles** massieren, durchkneten (*inf*).

knee [niː] **1** *n* Knie *nt*. **to be on one's ~s** (*lit, fig*) auf den Knien liegen; **on one's ~s, on bended ~(s)** (*liter, hum*) kniefällig; **to go (down) on one's ~s** (*lit*) niederknien, (sich) hinknien; (*fig*) sich auf die Knie werfen; **to go down on one's ~s to sb** (*lit, fig*) sich vor jdm auf die Knie werfen, vor jdm einen Kniefall machen; **to bow or bend the ~ (to sb)** (vor jdm) die Knie beugen; **to bring sb to his ~s** (*lit, fig*) jdn in die Knie zwingen; **he sank in up to or over his ~s** er sank knietief *or* bis zu den Knien ein; **at ~ level** in Kniehöhe; **~ jerk or reflex** (*Med*) Kniesehnenreflex, Patellar-reflex (*spec*) *m*; **I'll put you over my ~ in a minute** ich lege dich gleich übers Knie.

2 *vt* mit dem Knie stoßen. **he ~d his opponent in the chest** er hat seinem Gegner mit dem Knie eins gegen den Brustkasten gegeben (*inf*).

knee: **~ breeches** *npl* Kniehose, Bundhose *f*; **~cap** *n* Knie-scheibe *f*; **~-deep** *adj* knietief; **the water was ~-deep** das Wasser ging mir *etc* bis zum Knie *or* war knietief; **he was ~-deep in mud** er steckte knietief im Schlamm; **~-high** *adj* kniehoch, in Kniehöhe; **~ joint** *n* (*Med, Tech*) Kniegelenk *nt*.

kneel [niːl] *pret, ptp* **knelt** *or* **~ed** *vi* (*before* vor *+dat*) knien; (*also ~ **down***) niederknien, (sich) hinknien. **he had to ~ on his case to shut it** er mußte sich auf den Koffer knien, um ihn zu schließen.

knee-length ['niːleŋθ] *adj* **skirt** knielang; **boots** kniehoch.

kneeler ['niːlə^r] *n* Kniepolster *nt*; (*stool*) Kniebank *f*.

knee pad *n* Knieschützer *m*, Knieleder *nt*.

knell [nel] *n* Geläut *nt*, (Toten)glocke *f*. **to sound the ~** die (Toten)glocke läuten.

knelt [nelt] *pret, ptp of* **kneel**.

knew [njuː] *pret of* **know**.

knickerbockers ['nıkəbɒkəz] *npl* Knickerbocker *pl*.

knickers ['nıkəz] *npl* **(a)** Schlüpfer *m*. **to get one's ~ in a twist** (*sl*) sich (*dat*) ins Hemd machen (*sl*); **~!** (*sl*) (*rubbish*) Quatsch! (*inf*); (*bother*) Mist! (*inf*). **(b)** (*old*) *see* **knickerbockers**.

knick-knack ['nıknæk] *n* nette Kleinigkeit, Kinkerlitzchen *nt*. **~s** Krimskrams *m*; (*esp figurines*) Nippes, Nippsachen *pl*.

knife [naıf] **1** *n, pl* **knives** Messer *nt*. **~, fork and spoon** Besteck *nt*; **he's got his ~ into me** (*inf*) der hat es auf mich abgesehen (*inf*); **to be/go under the ~** (*Med inf*) unterm Messer sein (*inf*)/unters Messer kommen (*inf*); **to turn or twist the ~ (in the wound)** (*fig*) Salz in die Wunde streuen; **before you could say ~** (*inf*) eh' man sich's versah, im Nu; **it's war to the ~ between them** sie bekämpfen sich bis aufs Messer.

2 *vt* einstechen auf (*+acc*); (*fatally*) erstechen, erdolchen.

knife: **~ box** *n* Besteckkasten *m*; **~ edge** *n* (*lit*) (Mes-ser)schneide *f*; **to be balanced on a ~ edge** (*fig*) auf Messers Schneide stehen; **~ grinder** *n* (*person*) Scherenschleifer(in *f*) *m*; (*thing*) Schleifrad *nt* *or* -stein *m*; **~ pleat** *n* einfache Falte; **~ rest** *n* Messerbänkchen *nt*; **~ sharpener** *n* Messerschärfer *m*.

knifing ['naıfıŋ] *n* Messerstecherei *f*.

knight [naıt] **1** *n* (*title, Hist*) Ritter *m*; (*Chess*) Springer *m*, Pferd(chen), Rössel *nt*. **K~ of the Garter** Träger *m* des Hosenbandordens; **~ of the road** (*Brit hum*) Kapitän *m* der Landstraße (*hum*). **2** *vt* adeln, zum Ritter schlagen.

knight: **~ errant** *n, pl* **~s errant** fahrender Ritter; **~-errantry** [naıt'erəntrı] *n* fahrendes Rittertum; (*fig*) Ritterlichkeit *f*.

knighthood ['naıthʊd] *n* **(a)** (*knights collectively*) Ritterschaft *f*. **(b)** (*rank*) Ritterstand *m*. **to receive a ~** in den Ritterstand erhoben werden.

knightly ['naıtlı] *adj* (*+er*) ritterlich.

knit [nıt] *pret, ptp* **~ted** *or* **~** **1** *vt* **(a)** stricken. **the wool is then ~ted into ...** aus der Wolle wird dann ... gestrickt; **~ three, purl two** drei rechts, zwei links. **(b)** **to ~ one's brow** die Stirn run-zeln. **2** *vi* **(a)** stricken. **(b)** (*bones: also ~ together*, **~ up**) ver-wachsen, zusammenwachsen.

♦**knit together** **1** *vt sep* **(a)** **stitches** zusammenstricken. **(b)** (*unite*) **threads of story** (miteinander) verknüpfen; **people** eng verbinden. **2** *vi* **(a)** *see* **knit 2 (b)**. **(b)** (*unite*) miteinander ver-wachsen. **they ~ well** sie harmonieren gut; (*through experi-ence*) sie sind gut aufeinander eingespielt.

♦**knit up** **1** *vi* **(a)** (*wool*) sich stricken. **(b)** *see* **knit 2 (b)**. **2** *vt sep* **jersey** stricken.

knitted ['nıtıd] *adj* gestrickt; *cardigan, dress etc* Strick-. **~ goods** Strickwaren *or* -sachen *pl*.

knitter ['nıtə^r] *n* Stricker(in *f*) *m*.

knitting ['nıtıŋ] *n* **(a)** Stricken *nt*; (*material being knitted*) Strickzeug *nt*, Strickarbeit *f*; (*knitted goods*) Gestrickte(s) *nt*, Stricksachen *pl*. **this cardigan is a nice piece of ~** die Jacke ist schön gestrickt; **she was doing her ~** sie strickte. **(b)** (*of bones etc*) Verwachsen, Zusammenwachsen.

knitting: **~ machine** *n* Strickmaschine *f*; **~ needle** *n* Strick-nadel *f*; **~ wool** *n* (Strick)wolle *f*, Strickgarn *nt*.

knitwear ['nıtweə^r] *n* Strickwaren, Strick- *or* Wollsachen *pl*.

knives [naıvz] *pl of* **knife**.

knob [nɒb] *n* **(a)** (*on walking stick*) Knauf *m*; (*on door also*) Griff *m*; (*on instrument etc*) Knopf *m*. **and the same to you with (brass) ~s on** (*Brit sl*) das beruht auf Gegenseitigkeit. **(b)** (*small swelling*) Beule *f*, Knubbel *m* (*inf*); (*on tree*) Knoten, Auswuchs *m*. **(c)** (*small piece*) Stückchen *nt*.

knobbly ['nɒblı] *adj* (*+er*) **wood** knorrig, verwachsen; **surface** uneben, höckrig, knubbelig (*inf*). **~ knees** Knubbelknie *pl* (*inf*).

knobby ['nɒbı] *adj* (*+er*) **wood, trunk** knorrig.

knock [nɒk] **1** *n* **(a)** (*blow*) Stoß *m*; (*esp with hand, tool etc*) Schlag *m*. **to get a ~** einen Stoß/Schlag abbekommen; **my head got a ~, I got a ~ on the head** (*was hit*) ich habe einen Schlag auf den Kopf bekommen; (*hit myself*) ich habe mir den Kopf angeschlagen *or* angestoßen; **his knee got a ~** er hat sich (*dat*) das Knie angeschlagen; **he got a ~ from the swing** die Schaukel hat ihn getroffen; **he had a bit of a ~** er hat etwas abbekommen (*inf*); **the car got a few ~s** das Auto ist ein paarmal gerammt worden, mit dem Auto hat es ein paarmal gebumst (*inf*); **the gatepost got a ~ from the car** das Auto hat den Torpfosten gerammt; **the furniture has had a few ~s** die Möbel haben ein paar Schrammen abbekommen; **he gave himself a nasty ~** er hat sich böse angeschlagen *or* angestoßen; **he gave the car/lamppost a ~** er hat das Auto/den Laternenpfahl gerammt.

(b) (*noise*) Klopfen, Pochen (*liter*) *nt no pl*; (*in engine*) Klopfen *nt no pl*, Klopfgeräusch *nt*. **there was a ~ at the door** es hat (an der Tür) geklopft; **I heard a ~** ich habe es klopfen hören; **I'll give you a ~ at 7 o'clock** (*Brit*) ich klopfe um 7 Uhr (an deine Tür).

(c) (*fig: setback*) (Tief)schlag *m*. ~**s** (*inf: criticism*) Kritik *f*; **to (have to) take a lot of ~s** viele Tiefschläge einstecken (müssen); (*be criticized*) unter starkem Beschuß kommen; **to take a ~** (*self-confidence, pride etc*) erschüttert werden; (*person*) einen Tiefschlag erleben; **the company took a bit of a ~ as a result of the tax changes** die Steuerreform hat der Firma einen Schlag versetzt; **that was a hard ~ for him** das war ein harter Schlag für ihn.

2 *vt* **(a)** (*hit, strike*) stoßen; (*with hand, tool, racket etc*) schlagen; **one's knee, head etc** anschlagen, anstoßen (*on an +dat*); (*nudge, jolt*) stoßen gegen; (*collide with*) (*car, driver*) rammen. **to ~ one's head/elbow etc** sich (*dat*) den Kopf/Ellbogen *etc* anschlagen *or* anstoßen; **he ~ed his foot against a stone** er stieß mit dem Fuß gegen einen Stein; **to ~ sb on the head** jdn an *or* auf den Kopf schlagen; **that ~ed his plans on the head** (*inf*) das hat all seine Pläne über den Haufen geworfen (*inf*); **to ~ sb to the ground** jdn zu Boden werfen; **to ~ sb unconscious** jdn bewußtlos werden lassen; (*person*) jdn bewußtlos schlagen; **he ~ed some holes in the side of the box** er machte ein paar Löcher in die Seite der Kiste; **to ~ holes in an argument** ein Argument zerpflücken; **to ~ sb/sth out of the way** jdn/etw beiseite stoßen; **she ~ed the gun out of his hand** sie schlug ihm die Waffe aus der Hand; **he ~ed it as he went past** er ist beim Vorbeigehen dagegengestoßen; (*deliberately*) er hat ihm/ihr *etc* beim Vorbeigehen einen Stoß versetzt *or* gegeben; **she ~ed the glass to the ground** sie stieß gegen das Glas, und es fiel zu Boden; **don't ~ your glass off the table** werfen *or* stoßen Sie Ihr Glas nicht vom Tisch; **somebody ~ed the nose off the statue** jemand hat der Statue die Nase abgeschlagen; **to ~ the nonsense out of sb** jdm den Unsinn austreiben; **to ~ some sense into sb** *or* **sb's head** jdn zur Vernunft bringen.

(b) (*inf: criticize*) (he)runtermachen (*inf*). **if you don't know it, don't ~ it** verdamme doch nicht etwas, was du überhaupt nicht kennst.

3 *vi* **(a)** klopfen, pochen (*liter*); (*engine etc*) klopfen. **to ~ at the door/window** an die Tür klopfen, anklopfen/gegen das Fenster klopfen; ~ **before entering** bitte anklopfen; **he ~ed on the table** er schlug *or* klopfte auf den Tisch.

(b) (*bump, collide*) stoßen (*into, against* gegen). **he ~ed into** *or* **against the gatepost** er rammte den Türpfosten.

(c) **his knees were ~ing** ihm zitterten *or* schlotterten (*inf*) die Knie.

4 *interj* ~ ~! klopf, klopf.

◆**knock about** *or* **around 1** *vi* (*inf*) **(a)** (*person*) herumziehen (*prep obj in +dat*). **to ~ ~ the house** im Haus rumgammeln (*inf*); **he has ~ed ~ a bit** er ist schon (ganz schön) (he)rumgekommen (*inf*).

(b) (*object*) herumliegen (*prep obj in +dat*).

2 *vt sep* **(a)** (*ill-treat*) verprügeln, schlagen. **he was badly ~ed ~ in the crash** er ist beim Unfall ziemlich zugerichtet worden.

(b) (*damage*) ramponieren (*inf*), beschädigen. **the car/place was rather ~ed ~** das Auto/das Zimmer *etc* war ziemlich mitgenommen.

(c) **to ~ a ball ~** ein paar Bälle schlagen.

◆**knock back** *vt sep* (*inf*) **(a)** **he ~ed ~ his whisky** er kippte sich (*dat*) den Whisky hinter die Binde (*inf*); **come on, ~ it ~** nun trink schon (aus) (*inf*).

(b) (*cost*) **this watch ~ed me ~ £20** ich habe für die Uhr £ 20 hingelegt, die Uhr hat mich £ 20 gekostet; **what did they ~ you ~ for it?** was mußten Sie dafür hinlegen *or* blechen? (*inf*).

(c) (*shock*) schocken, erschüttern.

(d) (*reject*) zurückweisen.

◆**knock down** *vt sep* **(a)** *person, thing* umwerfen, zu Boden werfen; *opponent* (*by hitting*) niederschlagen; (*car, driver*) anfahren, umfahren; (*fatally*) überfahren; *building* abreißen, niederreißen; *tree* fällen, umhauen; *door* einschlagen; *obstacle, fence* niederreißen; (*car*) umfahren. **she was ~ed ~ and killed** sie wurde überfahren; **he ~ed him ~ with one blow** er schlug *or* streckte (*geh*) ihn mit einem Schlag zu Boden.

(b) *price* (*buyer*) herunterhandeln (*to* auf *+acc*); (*seller*) heruntergehen mit. **I managed to ~ a pound** ich konnte ein Pfund herunterhandeln; **I ~ed him ~ to £15** ich habe es auf £ 15 heruntergehandelt; **he ~ed the price ~ by £5 for me** er hat mir £ 5 nachgelassen.

(c) (*at auction*) zuschlagen (*to sb* jdm). **to be ~ed ~ at £1** für ein Pfund versteigert werden.

(d) *machine, furniture* zerlegen, auseinandernehmen.

◆**knock in** *vt sep* *nail* einschlagen.

◆**knock off 1** *vi* (*inf*) aufhören, Feierabend *or* Schluß machen (*inf*). **let's ~ ~ now** Schluß für heute (*inf*); **to ~ ~ for lunch** Mittag machen.

2 *vt sep* **(a)** (*lit*) *vase, cup, person etc* hinunterstoßen; *nose off statue etc* abschlagen; *insect* abschütteln; **high jump bar** reißen. **the branch ~ed the rider ~** (**his horse**) der Ast riß den Reiter (vom Pferd).

(b) (*inf: reduce price by*) nachlassen (*for sb* jdm), runtergehen (*inf*). **he ~ed £5 ~ the bill/price** er hat £ 5 von der Rechnung/vom Preis nachgelassen; **I got something ~ed ~** ich habe es billiger bekommen.

(c) (*inf: do quickly*) *essay, painting* hinhauen (*inf*); (*with good result*) aus dem Ärmel schütteln (*inf*).

(d) (*Brit sl: steal*) klauen (*inf*).

(e) (*sl: kill*) umlegen (*inf*).

(f) (*inf: stop*) aufhören mit; *smoking, criticizing* stecken (*sl*). **to ~ ~ work** Feierabend machen; ~ **it ~!** nun hör schon auf!

◆**knock out** *vt sep* **(a)** *tooth* ausschlagen; *nail* herausschlagen (*of* aus); *pipe* ausklopfen; *contents* herausklopfen (*of* aus).

(b) (*stun*) bewußtlos werden lassen; (*by hitting*) bewußtlos schlagen, k.o. schlagen. (*Boxing*) k.o. schlagen; (*drink*) umhauen (*inf*). **he was ~ed ~** er wurde bewußtlos; (*Boxing*) er wurde k.o. geschlagen; **ihn hat's umgehauen** (*inf*).

(c) (*from competition*) besiegen (*of* in *+dat*). **to be ~ed ~** ausscheiden, rausfliegen (*inf*) (*of* aus).

(d) (*inf: stun, shock*) (*good news*) umwerfen, umhauen (*inf*); (*bad news, sb's death etc*) schocken.

(e) (*sl: bowl over*) hinreißen (*inf*), umhauen (*inf*). **that music really ~s me ~** die Musik ist wirklich irre (*sl*) *or* umwerfend.

(f) (*inf: exhaust*) schaffen (*inf*), kaputtmachen (*inf*).

◆**knock over** *vt sep* umwerfen, umstoßen; (*car*) anfahren; (*fatally*) überfahren.

◆**knock together 1** *vi* **his knees were ~ing ~** seine Knie zitterten *or* schlotterten (*inf*). **2** *vt sep* **(a)** (*make hurriedly*) *shelter, object* zusammenzimmern; *meal, snack* auf die Beine stellen (*inf*). **(b)** (*lit*) aneinanderstoßen. **I'd like to ~ their heads ~** ich möchte die beiden schütteln.

◆**knock up 1** *vi* **(a)** (*Brit Sport*) sich einspielen, ein paar Bälle schlagen.

(b) (*US sl*) bumsen (*inf*).

2 *vt sep* **(a)** (*hit upwards*) hochschlagen.

(b) (*Brit: wake*) (auf)wecken.

(c) (*make hurriedly*) *meal* auf die Beine stellen (*inf*), herzaubern (*inf*); *building* hochziehen, hinstellen; *shelter* zusammenzimmern.

(d) (*Brit sl: exhaust*) kaputtmachen (*inf*), schaffen (*inf*); (*experience, shock*) schaffen (*inf*). **he was really ~ed ~** er war total kaputt (*inf*) *or* abgeschlafft (*inf*).

(e) (*sl*) (*make pregnant*) ein Kind anhängen (*+dat*) (*inf*), ein Kind machen (*+dat*) (*inf*); (*US: have sex with*) bumsen mit (*inf*). **she's ~ed ~** die hat 'nen dicken Bauch (*sl*).

(f) (*Cricket*) **to ~ ~ 20 runs** 20 Läufe machen.

(g) (*inf: do*) *mileage* fahren; *overtime* machen.

knock: ~**about 1** *adj* ~**about comedy** (*Theat*) Klamaukstück *nt*; ~**about clothes** gammelige Kleidung; **2** *n* (*Naut*) kleiner Einmaster; ~**down** *adj attr furniture etc* zerlegbar; ~**down price** Schleuderpreis *m*; (*at auction*) Mindestpreis *m*; ~**down blow** (*Boxing*) Niederschlag *m*; **to give sb a** ~**down blow** jdn niederschlagen.

knocker ['nɒkə'] *n* **(a)** (*door* ~) (Tür)klopfer *m*.

(b) (**pair of**) ~**s** (*Brit sl: breasts*) Vorbau *m* (*inf*); **what a pair of** ~**s!** toller Vorbau (*inf*), ganz schön Holz vor der Hütte (*sl*).

(c) (*inf: critic*) Kritikaster *m* (*inf*). **every good new idea is sure to have its** ~**s** bei jeder guten Idee gibt's jemanden, der was dran auszusetzen hat.

knocking ['nɒkɪŋ] *n* **(a)** Klopfen, Pochen (*liter*) *nt*; (*in engine*) Klopfen *nt*. **(b)** (*inf*) Kritik *f* (*of an +dat*). **he has taken** *or* **had a lot of ~** er ist ziemlich unter Beschuß gekommen.

knocking shop *n* (*Brit sl*) Puff *m* (*inf*), Knallhütte *f* (*sl*).

knock: ~**-kneed** [nɒk'niːd] *adj* X-beinig; **to be** ~**-kneed** X-Beine haben; ~**out 1** *n* (*Boxing*) Knockout, K.o. *m*; (*inf: person, thing*) Wucht *f* (*inf*); **2** *attr* **(a)** (*Boxing, fig*) ~**out blow** K.o.-Schlag *m*; **(b)** ~**out competition** Ausscheidungskampf *m*; ~**-up** *n* (*Brit Sport*) **to have a** ~**-up** ein paar Bälle schlagen.

knoll [nəʊl] *n* Hügel *m*, Kuppe *f*.

knot [nɒt] *n* **1 (a)** (*in string, tie, fig*) Knoten *m*; (*in muscle*) Verspannung *f*. **to tie/undo** *or* **untie a ~** einen Knoten machen/aufmachen *or* lösen; **marriage ~** Band *nt or* Bund *m* der Ehe (*geh*); **to tie the ~** (*fig*) den Bund fürs Leben schließen; **to tie oneself (up) in ~s** (*fig*) sich immer mehr verwickeln *or* tiefer verstricken; **his stomach was in a ~** sein Magen krampfte sich zusammen; **his muscles stood out in ~s** seine Muskeln traten *or* wölbten sich; **the whole matter is full of legal ~s** die ganze Sache ist rechtlich äußerst verwickelt.

(b) (*Naut: speed*) Knoten *m*. **to make 20 ~s** 20 Knoten machen; *see* **rate**[1] **1** (*a*).

(c) (*in wood*) Ast *m*, Verwachsung *f*.

(d) (*group*) Knäuel *m*. **a ~ of tourists** ein Touristenknäuel *m*.

2 *vt* einen Knoten machen in (*+acc*); (~ *together*) verknoten, verknüpfen. **to ~ sth to sth** etw mit etw verknoten; **get ~ted!** (*sl*) du kannst mich mal! (*inf*), rutsch mir den Buckel runter! (*inf*); **I told him to get ~ted** (*sl*) ich hab ihm gesagt, er kann mich mal (*inf*) *or* er kann mir den Buckel runterrutschen (*inf*).

3 *vi* sich verknoten, Knoten bilden.

◆**knot together** *vt sep* verknoten.

knotty ['nɒtɪ] *adj* (*+er*) *wood* astreich, knorrig; *veins, rope* knotig; *problem* verwickelt, verzwickt (*inf*).

knout [naʊt] *n* Knute *f*.

know [nəʊ] (*vb: pret* **knew**, *ptp* **known**) **1** *vti* **(a)** (*have knowledge about*) wissen; *answer, facts, dates, results etc* also kennen; *French, English etc* können. **to ~ how to do sth** (*in theory*) wissen, wie man etw macht; (*in practice*) etw tun können; **he ~s a thing or two** (*inf*) er weiß Bescheid, er weiß ganz schön viel (*inf*); **she ~s all the answers** sie weiß Bescheid, sie kennt sich aus; (*pej*) sie weiß immer alles besser; he thinks he ~s all the answers *or* everything er meint, er wüßte alles; do you ~ the difference between ...? wissen Sie, was der Unterschied zwischen ... ist?; to ~ that/why ... wissen, daß/warum ...; I ~ you are wrong ich weiß, daß Sie Unrecht haben; I ~ him to be honest/for a liar (*old*) ich weiß, daß er ehrlich/ein Lügner ist; he knew himself (to be) guilty er wußte, daß er schuldig war, er wußte sich schuldig (*liter*); to let sb ~ sth (*not keep back*) jdn etw wissen lassen; (*tell, inform*) jdm von etw Bescheid sagen *or* geben; he soon let me ~ what he thought of it er hat mich schnell wissen lassen, was er davon hielt; when can you let me ~? wann können Sie es mich wissen lassen?, wann können Sie mir Bescheid sagen?; let me ~ when/where *etc* sagen Sie mir (Bescheid), wann/wo *etc*; that's what I'd like to ~ (*too*) das möchte ich auch wissen; *that's* what I'd like to ~ das möchte ich wirklich wissen; that's worth ~ing das ist ja interessant; that might be worth ~ing es könnte interessant sein, das zu wissen; as far as I ~ soviel ich weiß, meines Wissens; he might even be dead for all I ~ vielleicht ist er sogar tot, was weiß ich; not that I ~ nicht daß ich wüßte; who ~s? wer weiß?, weiß ich's; there's no ~ing (*inf*) das kann keiner sagen, das weiß niemand; there's no ~ing what he'll do man weiß nie, was er noch tut; the channel was rough, as I well ~ *or* as well I ~! die Überfahrt war stürmisch, das kann ich dir sagen; I'd have you ~ that ... ich möchte doch sehr betonen, daß ...; to ~ what one is talking about wissen, wovon man redet; to ~ one's own mind wissen, was man will; before you ~ where you are the man kann's nicht versieht; I've been a fool and don't I ~ it! (*inf*) ich seh's ja ein, ich war doof (*inf*), ich war vielleicht doof (*inf*); she's angry! — don't I ~ it! (*inf*) sie ist wütend! — wem sagst du das! (*inf*); he just didn't want to ~ er wollte einfach nicht hören; afterwards they just didn't want to ~ nachher wollten sie einfach nichts mehr davon wissen; he didn't want to ~ me er wollte nichts mit mir zu tun haben; I ~! ich weiß!, weiß ich (doch)!; (*having a good idea*) ich weiß was!, ich habe eine Idee!; I don't ~ (*das*) weiß ich nicht; I don't ~ that that is a good idea ich weiß nicht, ob das eine gute Idee ist; I wouldn't ~ (*inf*) weiß ich (doch) nicht (*inf*); don't you ~? weißt du das denn nicht?; how should I ~ wie soll ich das wissen?; what do you ~! (*inf*) sieh mal einer an!; what do you ~! I've just seen her! (*inf*) stellen Sie sich vor, ich habe sie eben gesehen; you never ~ man kann nie wissen.

(b) you ~, we could/there is ... weißt du, wir könnten/da ist ...; he gave it away/he didn't come, you ~ er hat es nämlich weggegeben/er ist nämlich nicht gekommen; if you come back later, she might be back, you ~ (wissen Sie,) wenn Sie später noch einmal kommen, ist sie vielleicht da; you have to give me more time/details, you ~ (wissen Sie,) Sie müssen mir schon etwas mehr Zeit/genauere Einzelheiten geben; it's not so easy, you ~ (wissen Sie,) das ist gar nicht so einfach; it's raining, you ~ es regnet; then there was this man, you ~, and ... und da war dieser Mann, nicht (wahr), und ...; and then we'll go to your place, you ~, and ... und dann gehen wir zu dir, nicht (wahr), und ...; it's long and purple and, you ~, sort of crinkly es ist lang und lila und, na ja, so kraus; it's got those catches that work magnetically, you ~? das hat so eine Schließvorrichtung, die magnetisch ist, weißt du *or* verstehst du?

(c) (*be acquainted with*) people, places, book, author kennen; I ~ Bavaria well ich kenne Bayern gut, ich kenne mich gut in Bayern aus; to get to ~ sb/sth jdn/etw kennenlernen; do you ~ him to speak to? kennen Sie ihn näher?; if I ~ John, he'll already be there wie ich John kenne, ist er schon da; ~ thyself! erkenne dich selbst!; *see* name 1 (a), sight 1 (b).

(d) to get to ~ sb/a place jdn/einen Ort kennenlernen; to get to ~ sth methods, techniques, style, pronunciation *etc* etw lernen; habits, faults, shortcuts *etc* etw herausfinden.

(e) (*recognize*) erkennen. to ~ sb by his voice/walk jdn an der Stimme/am Gang *etc* erkennen; would you ~ him again? würden Sie ihn wiedererkennen?; he ~s a good thing when he sees it er weiß, was gut ist; he ~s a bargain/good manuscript when he sees one er weiß, was ein guter Kauf/ein gutes Manuskript ist; a sailor is ~n by his blue uniform man erkennt einen Matrosen an der blauen Uniform.

(f) (*be able to distinguish*) unterscheiden können. don't you ~ your right from your left? können Sie rechts und links nicht unterscheiden?; you wouldn't ~ him from his brother Sie könnten ihn nicht von seinem Bruder unterscheiden; to ~ the difference between right and wrong, to ~ right from wrong den Unterschied zwischen Gut und Böse kennen, Gut und Böse unterscheiden können; he wouldn't ~ the difference das merkt er nicht; he doesn't ~ one end of a horse/hammer from the other er hat keine Ahnung von Pferden/er hat keine Ahnung, was ein Hammer ist (*inf*).

(g) (*experience*) erleben. I've never ~n it to rain so heavily so einen starken Regen habe ich noch nie erlebt; I've never ~n him to smile to have ihn noch nie lächeln sehen, ich habe es noch nie erlebt, daß er lächelt; you have never ~n me to tell a lie Sie haben mich noch nie lügen hören; have you ever ~n such a thing to happen before? haben Sie je schon so etwas erlebt?, ist Ihnen so etwas schon einmal vorgekommen?

(h) (*in passive*) to be ~n (to sb) (jdm) bekannt sein; it is (well) ~n that ... es ist (allgemein) bekannt, daß ...; is he/that ~n here? ist er/das hier bekannt?, kennt man ihn/das hier?; he is ~n to have been here man weiß, daß er hier war; he ~s man X man kennt ihn als Herrn X; she wishes to be ~n as Mrs X sie möchte Frau X genannt werden; to make sb/sth ~n jdn/etw bekanntmachen; to make oneself ~n sich melden (*to sb* bei jdm); (*introduce oneself*) sich vorstellen (*to sb* jdm); (*become well-known*) sich (*dat*) einen Namen machen; to become ~n bekannt werden; (*famous*) berühmt werden; to make one's presence ~n sich melden (*to* bei).

(i) I ~ better than that ich bin ja nicht ganz dumm; I ~ better than to say something like that ich werde mich hüten, so etwas zu sagen; he ~s better than to eat into his capital er ist nicht so dumm, sein Kapital anzugreifen; he/you ought to have ~n better das war dumm (von ihm/dir); he ought to have *or* should have ~n better than to do that es war dumm von ihm, das zu tun; you ought to ~ better at your age in deinem Alter müßte man das aber (besser) wissen; they don't ~ any better sie kennen's nicht anders; he says he didn't do it, but I ~ better er sagt, er war es nicht, aber ich weiß, daß das nicht stimmt; mother always ~s best Mutter weiß es am besten; OK, you ~ best o.k., Sie müssen's wissen.

(j) (*obs, Bibl: sexually*) erkennen.

2 *n* (*inf*) to be in the ~ eingeweiht sein, im Bild sein (*inf*), Bescheid wissen (*inf*); the people in the ~ say ... Leute, die darüber Bescheid wissen, sagen ..., die Fachleute sagen ...

♦ **know about 1** *vi +prep obj* (*have factual knowledge, experience of*) history, maths, politics sich auskennen in (+*dat*); Africa Bescheid wissen über (+*acc*); women, cars, horses sich auskennen mit; (*be aware of, have been told about*) wissen von. I ~ ~ that das weiß ich; I didn't ~ ~ that das wußte ich nicht; I only knew ~ it yesterday ich habe erst gestern davon gehört; I'd rather not ~ ~ it das möchte ich lieber nicht wissen; did you ~ ~ Maggie? weißt du über Maggie Bescheid?; I ~ ~ John, but is anyone else absent? John, das weiß ich, aber fehlt sonst noch jemand?; to get to ~ ~ sb/sth von jdm/etw hören; I don't ~ ~ that davon weiß ich nichts; (*don't agree*) da bin ich aber nicht so sicher; that isn't ~n ~ davon weiß man nichts; she's very clever, isn't she? — I don't ~ ~ clever, but she certainly knows how to use people ist sie sehr klug, nicht wahr? — klug, na, ich weiß nicht, aber sie weiß Leute auszunützen.

2 *vt sep +prep obj* to ~ a lot/nothing/something ~ sth (*have factual knowledge*) viel/nichts/etwas über etw (*acc*) wissen; (*in history, maths etc*) in etw (*dat*) gut/nicht/etwas Bescheid wissen; (*about women, cars, horses etc*) sich gut/nicht/etwas mit etw auskennen, viel/nichts/etwas von etw verstehen; (*be aware of, have been told about*) viel/nichts/etwas von etw wissen; that was the first I knew ~ it davon hatte ich nichts gewußt; not much is ~n ~ that darüber weiß man nicht viel; I ~ all ~ that da kenne ich mich aus; (*I'm aware of that*) das weiß ich; (*I've been told about it*) ich weiß Bescheid; I ~ all ~ you ich weiß über Sie Bescheid; that's all you ~ ~ it! (*iro*) das meinst auch nur du!

♦ **know of** *vi +prep obj* café, better method of) sb, sb's death gehört haben von. I soon got to ~ ~ all the facts/all his hang-ups ich war bald über alle Fakten/all seine Komplexe informiert; not that I ~ ~ nicht, daß ich wüßte.

knowable ['nəʊəbl] *adj* der/die/das man wissen kann.

know: ~-all *n* Alleswisser, Allesbesserwisser *m*; ~-how *n* praktische Kenntnis, Know-how *nt*; he hasn't got the ~-how for the job er hat nicht die nötige Sachkenntnis für diese Arbeit.

knowing ['nəʊɪŋ] *adj* look, smile wissend; person verständnisvoll, wissend.

knowingly ['nəʊɪŋlɪ] *adv* (a) (*consciously*) bewußt, absichtlich, wissentlich. (b) look, smile wissend.

know-it-all ['nəʊɪtɔːl] *n* (*US*) *see* know-all.

knowledge ['nɒlɪdʒ] *n* (a) (*understanding, awareness*) Wissen *nt*, Kenntnis *f*. to have ~ of Kenntnis haben *or* besitzen von, wissen von; to have no ~ of keine Kenntnis haben von, nichts wissen von; to (the best of) my ~ soviel ich weiß, meines Wissens; to the best of my ~ and belief nach bestem Wissen und Gewissen; not to my ~ nicht, daß ich wüßte; without his ~ ohne sein Wissen; without the ~ of her mother ohne Wissen ihrer Mutter, ohne daß ihre Mutter es wußte/weiß; it has come to my ~ that ... ich habe erfahren, daß ..., es ist mir zu Ohren gekommen, daß ...

(b) (*learning, facts learnt*) Kenntnisse *pl*, Wissen *nt*. my ~ of English meine Englischkenntnisse *pl*; my ~ of D.H. Lawrence was ich von D.H. Lawrence kenne; I have a thorough ~ of this subject auf diesem Gebiet weiß ich gründlich Bescheid *or* besitze ich umfassende Kenntnisse; the police have no ~ of him/his activities die Polizei weiß nichts über ihn/seine Aktivitäten; his ~ will die with him sein Wissen wird mit ihm sterben; the advance of ~ der Fortschritt der Wissenschaft.

knowledgeable ['nɒlɪdʒəbl] *adj* person kenntnisreich, mit großem Wissen; report gut fundiert. to be ~ viel wissen (*about* über +*acc*).

known [nəʊn] **1** *ptp of* know. **2** *adj* bekannt; expert also anerkannt. it is a ~ fact that ... es ist (allgemein) bekannt, daß ..., es ist eine anerkannte Tatsache, daß ...

knuckle ['nʌkl] *n* (Finger)knöchel *m*; (*of meat*) Hachse, Haxe *f*; *see* near 2 (a), rap.

♦ **knuckle down** *vi* (*inf*) sich dahinterklemmen (*inf*), sich dranmachen (*inf*). to ~ ~ to work sich hinter die Arbeit klemmen (*inf*), sich an die Arbeit machen.

♦ **knuckle under** *vi* (*inf*) spuren (*inf*), sich fügen.

knuckle: ~bone *n* Knöchelbein *nt*; ~bones *npl see* jacks; ~duster *n* Schlagring *m*; ~head *n* (*inf*) Blödmann *m* (*inf*); ~joint *n* (Anat) Knöchel- *or* Fingergelenk *nt*; (Tech) Kardan- *or* Kreuzgelenk *nt*.

knurl [nɜːl] *n* Einkerbung, Riffelung *f*; (Tech) Rändelrad *nt*. **2** *vt* rändeln, kordieren.

KO 1 *n* K.o.(-Schlag) *m*. **2** *vt* (Boxing) k.o.-schlagen.

koala [kəʊˈɑːlə] *n* (also ~ bear) Koala(bär) *m*.

kookaburra ['kʊkəˌbʌrə] *n* Rieseneisvogel *m*, Lachender Hans.

kooky ['kʊkɪ] *adj* (+ er) (*US* inf) komisch (*inf*), verrückt (*inf*); person also versponnen.

Koran [kɒˈrɑːn] *n* Koran *m*.

Korea [kəˈrɪə] *n* Korea *nt*.

Korean [kəˈrɪən] **1** *adj* koreanisch. ~ war Koreakrieg *m*. **2** *n* (a) Koreaner(in *f*) *m*. (b) (*language*) Koreanisch *nt*.

kosher ['kəʊʃə^r] adj (a) koscher. (b) (inf) in Ordnung. to make everything ~ alles in Ordnung bringen; there's something not quite ~ about that deal an dem Geschäft ist etwas faul (inf).

kowtow ['kaʊtaʊ] vi einen Kotau machen, dienern. to ~ to sb vor jdm dienern or katzbuckeln (inf) or einen Kotau machen.

kph abbr of **kilometres per hour** kph.

kraal [krɑːl] n Kral m.

kraken ['krækən] n Krake m.

Kraut [kraʊt] n, adj als Schimpfwort gebrauchte Bezeichnung für Deutsche und Deutsches.

Kremlin ['kremlɪn] n: the ~ der Kreml.

kremlinologist [ˌkremlɪ'nɒlədʒɪst] n Kremlforscher(in f) m.

kremlinology [ˌkremlɪ'nɒlədʒɪ] n Kremlforschung f.

krypton ['krɪptɒn] n Krypton nt.

kudos ['kjuːdɒs] n Ansehen nt, Ehre f. he only did it for the ~ er tat es nur der Ehre wegen; he doesn't have much ~ with me von dem halte ich nicht viel.

Kurd [kɜːd] n Kurde m, Kurdin f.

Kurdish ['kɜːdɪʃ] 1 adj kurdisch. 2 n Kurdisch nt.

Kuwait [kʊ'weɪt] n Kuwait nt.

kw abbr of **kilowatt(s)** kW.

kWh, kwh abbr of **kilowatt hour(s)** kWh.

L

L, l [el] n L, l nt.

L abbr of (a) (Brit Mot) **Learner** L. (b) **Lake**. (c) **large**.

l abbr of (a) **litre(s)** l. (b) **left** l.

LA abbr of **Los Angeles**.

lab [læb] abbr of **laboratory**.

Lab (Pol) abbr of **Labour**.

label ['leɪbl] 1 n (a) Etikett nt; (showing contents, instructions etc) Aufschrift, Beschriftung f; (on specimen, cage) Schild nt; (tied on) Anhänger m; (adhesive) Aufkleber m, Aufklebeetikett nt; (on parcel) Paketadresse f; (of record company) Schallplattengesellschaft, Plattenfirma f. on the Pye ~ von Pye herausgegeben.
(b) (fig) Etikett nt (usu pej).
2 vt (a) etikettieren, mit einem Schild/Anhänger/Aufkleber versehen; (write on) beschriften. the bottle was ~led "poison" die Flasche trug die Aufschrift „Gift".
(b) (fig) ideas abstempeln. to ~ sb (as) sth jdn als etw abstempeln; he got himself ~led as a troublemaker er brachte sich (dat) den Ruf eines Unruhestifters ein.

labia ['leɪbɪə] pl of **labium**.

labial ['leɪbɪəl] 1 adj (Anat, Phon) labial, Lippen-. 2 n (Phon) Labial, Lippenlaut m.

labium ['leɪbɪəm] n, pl **labia** (Anat) Schamlippe f, Labium nt (spec).

labor etc (US) see **labour** etc. ~ **union** n (US) Gewerkschaft f.

laboratory [lə'brɒtərɪ, (US) 'læbrə,tɔːrɪ] n Labor(atorium) nt. ~ **assistant** Laborant(in f) m; the project was abandoned at the ~ **stage** das Projekt wurde im Versuchsstadium abgebrochen.

laborious [lə'bɔːrɪəs] adj task, undertaking mühsam, mühselig; style schwerfällig, umständlich.

laboriously [lə'bɔːrɪəslɪ] adv mühsam; speak umständlich.

labour, (US) **labor** ['leɪbə^r] 1 n (a) (work in general) Arbeit f; (toil) Anstrengung, Mühe f. after much ~ the job was at last completed nach langen Mühen war die Arbeit endlich vollendet; they succeeded by their own ~s sie haben es aus eigener Kraft geschafft.
(b) (task) Aufgabe f. it was a ~ of love ich/er etc tat es aus Liebe zur Sache; the ~s of Hercules die Arbeiten pl des Herkules; a ~ of Hercules eine Herkulesarbeit.
(c) (Jur) see **hard**.
(d) (persons) Arbeiter, Arbeitskräfte pl. to withdraw one's ~ die Arbeit verweigern; **organized** ~ die organisierte Arbeiterschaft.
(e) (Brit Pol) **L~** die Labour Party; this district is **L~** dies ist ein Labourbezirk m.
(f) (Med) Wehen pl. to be in ~ in den Wehen liegen, die Wehen haben; to go into ~ die Wehen bekommen.
2 vt point, subject auswalzen, breittreten (inf). I won't ~ the point ich will nicht darauf herumreiten, ich will mich unter darüber auslassen (inf).
3 vi (a) (in fields etc) arbeiten; (work hard) sich abmühen (at, with mit). they ~ed hard to get the house finished on time sie gaben sich die größte Mühe, das Haus rechtzeitig fertigzustellen; to ~ for or in a cause sich für eine Sache einsetzen; to ~ under a delusion/misapprehension sich einer Täuschung/Illusion (dat) hingeben; to ~ under difficulties mit Schwierigkeiten zu kämpfen haben.
(b) (move with effort or difficulty) sich quälen. the engine is ~ing der Motor hört sich gequält an; (in wrong gear) der Motor läuft untertourig; to ~ up a hill sich einen Hügel hinaufquälen, mühsam den Berg hochkriechen; the yacht ~ed into the harbour through heavy seas die Jacht kämpfte sich durch die aufgewühlte See in den Hafen; his breathing became ~ed er begann, schwer zu atmen.

labour: ~ **camp** n Arbeitslager nt; **L~ Day** n der Tag der Arbeit.

labourer, (US) **laborer** ['leɪbərə^r] n (Hilfs)arbeiter m; (farm ~) Landarbeiter m; (day-~) Tagelöhner m. a ~ in the cause of justice ein Kämpfer m für die Gerechtigkeit.

labour: **L~ Exchange** n (Brit) Arbeitsamt nt; ~ **force** n

Arbeiterschaft f; (of company) Belegschaft f.

labouring, (US) **laboring** ['leɪbərɪŋ] adj class Arbeiter-, arbeitend; job Aushilfs-.

labourite, (US) **laborite** ['leɪbəraɪt] n (pej) Labour-Anhänger m.

labour: ~-**market** n Arbeitsmarkt m; ~ **movement** n Arbeiterbewegung f; ~ **pains** npl Wehen pl; ~ **relations** npl die Beziehungen pl zwischen Unternehmern und Arbeitern or Gewerkschaften; ~-**saving** adj arbeitssparend; ~ **ward** n Kreißsaal m.

Labrador ['læbrədɔː^r] n Labradorhund m.

laburnum [lə'bɜːnəm] n Goldregen m.

labyrinth ['læbɪrɪnθ] n (lit, fig) Labyrinth nt.

labyrinthine [ˌlæbɪ'rɪnθaɪn] adj labyrinthisch (also fig), labyrinthähnlich.

lace [leɪs] 1 n (a) (fabric) Spitze f; (as trimming) Spitzenborte f or -besatz m; (of gold, silver) Tresse, Litze f.
(b) (of shoe) (Schuh)band nt, Schnürsenkel m. ~-**up** (shoe) Schnürschuh m.
2 vt (a) schnüren; shoe also zubinden; (fig) fingers ineinander verschlingen.
(b) to ~ a drink einen Schuß Alkohol in ein Getränk geben; ~d with brandy mit einem Schuß Weinbrand; a ~d drink ein Getränk mit Schuß.
3 vi (shoes etc) (zu)geschnürt werden. shoes that ~ Schuhe zum Schnüren.

◆**lace into** vi +prep obj to ~ ~ sb (verbally) jdm eine Standpauke halten, jdn anschnauzen (inf); (physically) auf jdn losgehen, jdn verprügeln.

◆**lace up** 1 vt sep (zu)schnüren. 2 vi geschnürt werden.

lacerate ['læsəreɪt] vt (a) verletzen; (by glass etc) zerschneiden; (by thorns) zerkratzen, aufreißen; (by claws, whip) zerfetzen; painting aufschlitzen. he ~d his arm er zog sich (dat) tiefe Wunden am Arm zu; she ~d her wrist with a razor-blade sie schlitzte sich (dat) die Pulsadern mit einer Rasierklinge auf; her knee was badly ~d sie hatte tiefe Wunden am Knie.
(b) (fig) feeling, pride zutiefst verletzen.

laceration [ˌlæsə'reɪʃən] n (a) Verletzung, Fleischwunde f; (tear) Rißwunde f; (from blow) Platzwunde f; (from whip) Striemen m; (from glass) Schnittwunde f; (from claws etc) Kratzwunde f.
(b) (fig: of feeling, pride) Verletzung f.

lachrymal ['lækrɪml] adj Tränen-.

lachrymose ['lækrɪməʊs] adj (liter) person weinerlich; story, film etc rührselig, ergreifend.

lacing ['leɪsɪŋ] n (of shoe) Schnürsenkel, Schuhbänder pl; (of corset) Schnürung f. uniforms with gold ~ goldbetreßte Uniformen pl; tea with a ~ of rum Tee m mit einem Schuß Rum.

lack [læk] 1 n Mangel m. for or through ~ of sth aus Mangel an etw (dat); they failed for or through ~ of support sie scheiterten, weil es ihnen an Unterstützung fehlte or mangelte; his absence was a real ~ er fehlte sehr; ~ of water/time Wasser-/Zeitmangel m; there is no ~ of money in that family in dieser Familie fehlt es nicht an Geld.
2 vt we ~ the necessary equipment/talent es fehlt ihnen an der notwendigen Ausrüstung/am richtigen Talent; we ~ time uns fehlt die nötige Zeit; we're ~ing three players to make up a team uns fehlen noch drei Spieler für ein Team; he ~s confidence ihm fehlt Selbstvertrauen.
3 vi (a) to be ~ing fehlen; his sense of humour is sadly ~ing mit seinem Sinn für Humor ist es nicht weit her.
(b) he is ~ing in confidence ihm fehlt es an Selbstvertrauen; he is completely ~ing in any sort of decency er besitzt überhaupt keinen Anstand.
(c) he ~ed for nothing es fehlte ihm an nichts.

lackadaisical [ˌlækə'deɪzɪkəl] adj (lacking energy) lustlos, desinteressiert; (careless) nachlässig, lasch.

lackey ['lækɪ] n (lit, fig) Lakai m.

lacking ['lækɪŋ] *adj* **(a)** to be found ~ sich nicht bewähren, der Sache (*dat*) nicht gewachsen sein; **they were not found** ~ sie haben ihren Mann gestanden, sie waren der Sache (*dat*) gewachsen.
  (b) (*inf*) geistig minderbemittelt (*inf*), beschränkt.
lacklustre ['læk,lʌstə^r] *adj surface* stumpf, glanzlos; *style* farblos, langweilig; *eyes also* trübe.
laconic [lə'kɒnɪk] *adj* lakonisch; *prose, style* knapp.
laconically [lə'kɒnɪkəlɪ] *adv* lakonisch; *write* knapp.
lacquer ['lækə^r] **1** *n* Lack *m*; (*hair* ~) Haarspray *nt*; (*nail* ~) Nagellack *m*. **2** *vt* lackieren; *hair* sprayen.
lacquered ['lækəd] *adj* lackiert; *hair* gesprayt; *wood* Lack-.
lacrimal, lacrymal *adj see* **lachrymal**.
lacrosse [lə'krɒs] *n* Lacrosse *nt*.
lactate ['lækteɪt] *vi* Milch absondern, laktieren (*spec*).
lactation [læk'teɪʃən] *n* Milchabsonderung, Laktation (*spec*) *f*; (*period*) Stillzeit, Laktationsperiode (*spec*) *f*.
lacteal ['læktɪəl] *adj* Milch-.
lactic ['læktɪk] *adj* ~ **acid** Milchsäure *f*.
lactose ['læktəʊs] *n* Milchzucker *m*, Laktose *f*.
lacuna [lə'kju:nə] *n, pl* **-e** [lə'kju:ni:] Lakune *f*.
lacy ['leɪsɪ] *adj* (+er) Spitzen-; (*like lace*) spitzenartig.
lad [læd] *n* Junge *m*; (*in stable etc*) Bursche *m*. **young** ~ junger Mann; **listen,** ~ hör mir mal zu, mein Junge!; **when I was a** ~ **als ich ein junger Bursche war; he's only a** ~ er ist (doch) noch jung, er ist (doch) noch ein Junge; **a simple country** ~ ein einfacher Bauernjunge, ein einfacher Junge vom Land; **all together,** ~**s, push!** alle Mann anschieben!, alle zusammen, Jungs, anschieben!; **he's a bit of a** ~ (*inf*) er ist ein ziemlicher Draufgänger; **he's a bit of a** ~ **with the girls** (*inf*) er ist ein ganz schöner Frauentyp (*inf*); **he likes a night out with the** ~**s** (*inf*) er geht gern mal mit seinen Kumpels weg (*inf*).
ladder ['lædə^r] **1** *n* **(a)** Leiter *f*.
  (b) (*fig*) (Stufen)leiter *f*. **social** ~ Leiter des gesellschaftlichen Erfolges; **the climb up the social** ~ der gesellschaftliche Aufstieg; **it's a first step up the** ~ das ist ein Anfang; **a big step up the** ~ ein großer Schritt nach vorn; *see* **top**.
  (c) (*Brit: in stocking*) Laufmasche *f*. ~**proof** maschenfest, laufmaschensicher.
  2 *vt* (*Brit*) *stocking* zerreißen. **I've** ~**ed my stocking** ich habe mir eine Laufmasche geholt.
  3 *vi* (*Brit: stocking*) Laufmaschen bekommen.
laddie ['lædɪ] *n* (*esp Scot*) Junge, Bub (*S Ger, Aus, Sw*) *m*.
lade [leɪd] *pret* ~ **d,** *ptp* **laden 1** *vt ship* beladen; *cargo* verladen. **2** *vi* Ladung übernehmen *or* an Bord nehmen.
laden ['leɪdn] *adj* (*lit, fig*) beladen (*with* mit). **bushes** ~ **with flowers** blütenschwere Büsche *pl*.
la-di-da ['lɑ:dɪ'dɑ:] *adj* (*inf*) affektiert, affig (*inf*).
lading ['leɪdɪŋ] *n* (*act*) Verladen *nt*; (*cargo*) Ladung *f*.
ladle ['leɪdl] **1** *n* (Schöpf- *or* Suppen)kelle *f*, Schöpflöffel *m*. **2** *vt* schöpfen. **he's ladling money into that business** er steckt *or* pumpt massenhaft Geld in das Geschäft.
◆**ladle out** *vt sep soup, praise* austeilen. **he** ~**s** ~ **praise to everyone** er überschüttet jeden mit Lob.
ladleful ['leɪdlfʊl] *n* one ~ eine Kelle (voll); **each pan holds ten** ~**s** in jeden Topf paßt der Inhalt von zehn Schöpfkellen.
lady ['leɪdɪ] *n* **(a)** Dame *f*. **"Ladies"** (*lavatory*) „Damen"; **where is the ladies or the ladies' room?** wo ist die Damentoilette?; **ladies and gentlemen!** sehr geehrte *or* meine (*sehr verehrten*) Damen und Herren!; **ladies, ...** meine Damen, ...; ~ **of the house** Dame des Hauses; **the minister and his** ~ der Minister und seine Gattin; **your good** ~ (*hum, form*) Ihre Frau Gemahlin (*hum, form*); **the old** ~ (*inf*) (*mother*) die alte Dame (*inf*); (*wife*) meine/deine/seine Alte (*inf*) *or* Olle (*N Ger inf*); **young** ~ junge Dame; (*scoldingly*) mein Fräulein; **his young** ~ seine Freundin; **she's no** ~ sie ist keine Dame; **ladies' man** Charmeur, Frauenheld *m*; **he's a bit of a ladies' man** er wirkt auf Frauen.
  (b) (*noble*) Adlige *f*. **L~** (*as a title*) Lady *f*; **dinner is served, my** ~ es ist angerichtet, Mylady *or* gnädige Frau; **the lords and ladies flocked to the party** der (ganze) Adel strömte zu der Gesellschaft; **to live like a** ~ wie eine große Dame leben.
  (c) **Our L~** die Jungfrau Maria, Unsere Liebe Frau; **Church of Our L~** Kirche (zu) Unserer Lieben Frau(en), (Lieb)frauenkirche *f*.
lady: ~**bird,** (*US*) ~**bug** *n* Marienkäfer *m*; **L~ chapel** *n* Marienkapelle *f*; **L~ Day** *n* Mariä Verkündigung *no art*; ~ **doctor** *n* Ärztin *f*; ~ **friend** *n* Dame *f*; ~**-in-waiting** *n* Ehrendame, Hofdame *f*; ~**-killer** *n* (*inf*) Herzensbrecher *m*; ~**like** *adj* damenhaft, vornehm; **a** ~**like woman** eine vornehme Dame; **it's not** ~**like** es ist nicht ladylike, es gehört sich nicht für eine Dame/ein Mädchen; ~**-love** *n* (*old*) Geliebte *f*, Feinsliebchen *nt* (*old*); ~ **mayoress** *n* Titel der Frau des Lord Mayor, Frau *f* (Ober)bürgermeister (*dated*); ~**ship** *n*: **Her/Your L~ship** Ihre Ladyschaft; **certainly, Your L~ship** gewiß, Euer Gnaden; ~**'s maid** *n* (Kammer)zofe *f*.
lag¹ [læg] **1** *n* (*time*~) Zeitabstand *m*, Zeitdifferenz *f*; (*delay*) Verzögerung *f*. **there is too much of a** ~ es vergeht zuviel Zeit; **after a** ~ **of 15 minutes** nach 15 Minuten, nachdem 15 Minuten vergangen *or* verstrichen waren; **there was a** ~ **of six months between buying the house and actually being able to move in** das Haus konnte erst sechs Monate nach dem Kauf bezogen werden; **there was a** ~ **in the conversation for a few minutes** die Unterhaltung stockte für ein paar Minuten; **the cultural** ~ **is very apparent** der kulturelle Rückstand ist offensichtlich.
  2 *vi* (*time*) langsam vergehen, dahinkriechen; (*in pace*) zurückbleiben.
◆**lag behind** *vi* zurückbleiben. **we** ~ ~ **in space exploration** in der Raumforschung liegen wir (weit) zurück *or* hinken wir hinterher (*inf*); **why don't you walk beside me instead of always**

~**ging** ~? warum läufst du nicht neben mir, anstatt immer hinterherzutrödeln?
lag² *vt boiler, pipe* umwickeln, isolieren.
lag³ *n* (*sl: also* old ~) (ehemaliger) Knacki (*sl*).
lager ['lɑ:gə^r] *n* helles Bier. **a glass of** ~ ein (Glas) Helles.
laggard ['lægəd] **1** *n* (*sb who has fallen behind*) Nachzügler(in *f*) *m*; (*idler*) Trödler *m*. **he is a** ~ **in love** (*liter, hum*) er ist nicht so stürmisch. **2** *adj student, worker* faul.
lagging ['lægɪŋ] *n* Isolierschicht *f*; (*material*) Isoliermaterial *nt*.
lagoon [lə'gu:n] *n* Lagune *f*.
laid [leɪd] *pret, ptp of* **lay⁴**.
lain [leɪn] *ptp of* **lie²**.
lair [lɛə^r] *n* Lager *nt*; (*cave*) Höhle *f*; (*den*) Bau *m*.
laird [lɛəd] *n* (*Scot*) Gutsherr *m*.
laissez-faire ['leɪseɪ'fɛə^r] **1** *n* Laisser-faire *nt*. **there's too much** ~ **here** hier geht es zu leger zu. **2** *adj* (*Econ*) Laisser-faire-; (*fig*) leger, lax.
laity ['leɪɪtɪ] *n* **(a)** (*laymen*) Laienstand *m*, Laien *pl*. **(b)** (*those outside a profession*) Laien *pl*.
lake¹ [leɪk] *n* See *m*.
lake² *n* (*colour*) Karm(es)inrot *nt*.
lake: **L~ District** *n* Lake District *m* (*Seengebiet nt im NW Englands*); ~**-dweller** *n* Pfahlbaubewohner *m*; ~**-dwelling** *n* Pfahlbau *m*; **L~ Poets** *npl* Dichter *pl* des Lake District: Wordsworth, Coleridge, Southey; ~**side 1** *n* Seeufer *nt*; **2** *attr* am See.
lam¹ [læm] (*sl*) **1** *vt* vermöbeln (*sl*). **2** *vi* **to** ~ **into sb** jdn zur Schnecke machen (*sl*); (*physically*) auf jdn eindreschen (*inf*).
lam² *n* (*US sl*) **he's on the** ~ hinter dem sind sie her (*sl*); **he took it on the** ~ er machte (die) Mücke (*sl*), er türmte (*inf*).
lama ['lɑ:mə] *n* Lama *m*.
lamb [læm] **1** *n* **(a)** (*young sheep*) Lamm *nt*.
  (b) (*meat*) Lamm(fleisch) *nt*.
  (c) (*person*) Engel *m*. **the little** ~**s** (*children*) die lieben Kleinen *pl*; **my poor** ~! mein armes Lämmchen!; **she took it like a** ~ sie ertrug es geduldig wie ein Lamm; **like a** ~ **to the slaughter** wie das Lamm zur Schlachtbank, wie ein Opferlamm.
  (d) **the L~ of God** das Lamm Gottes.
  2 *vi* lammen. **the** ~**ing season** die Lammungszeit.
lambast [læm'bæst], **lambaste** [læm'beɪst] *vt* fertigmachen (*inf*), es tüchtig geben (+*dat*) (*inf*); (*physically also*) verprügeln.
lamb: ~ **chop** *n* Lammkotelett *nt*; ~**skin** *n* Lammfell *nt*; ~**'s tail** *n* (*Bot*) Haselkätzchen *nt*; ~**swool** *n* Lammwolle *f*.
lame [leɪm] **1** *adj* (+er) **(a)** lahm; (*as result of stroke etc*) gelähmt. **to be** ~ **in one foot** einen lahmen Fuß haben; **to be** ~ **in one leg** auf einem Bein lahm sein; **the horse went** ~ das Pferd fing an zu lahmen.
  (b) (*fig*) *excuse* lahm, faul; *argument* schwach, wenig überzeugend; *metre* holprig. ~ **duck** Niete *f* (*inf*).
  2 *vt* lähmen; *horse* lahm machen.
lamé ['lɑ:meɪ] *n* Lamé *nt*.
lamely ['leɪmlɪ] *adv argue, say etc* lahm. **to walk** ~ hinken; (*of horse*) lahmen; **he limped** ~ **into the room** er humpelte ins Zimmer; ~ **he mumbled an excuse** er murmelte eine lahme Entschuldigung vor sich hin.
lameness ['leɪmnɪs] *n* **(a)** Lähmung *f* (*in, of* gen). **his** ~ sein Gelähmtsein *nt*. **(b)** (*fig*) *see adj* **(b)** Lahmheit *f*; Schwäche *f*; mangelnde Überzeugungskraft; Holprigkeit *f*.
lament [lə'ment] **1** *n* **(a)** (*expression of sorrow*) Klage(n *pl*), Wehklage *f*. **in** ~ (weh)klagend.
  (b) (*Liter, Mus*) Klagelied *nt*.
  2 *vt* beklagen, beweinen; *misfortune etc* bejammern, beklagen. **to** ~ **sb** jds Tod beklagen, um jdn trauern; **it is much to be** ~**ed that ...** es ist sehr zu beklagen, daß ...; **what will become of me now?, he** ~**ed** was soll nun aus mir werden?, klagte *or* jammerte er.
  3 *vi* (weh)klagen. **to** ~ **for sb** um jdn trauern; **to** ~ **over sth** über etw (*acc*) jammern, etw bejammern *or* beklagen; **she** ~**ed over his dead body** sie wehklagte über seinem Leichnam.
lamentable ['læməntəbl] *adj* beklagenswert; *piece of work* jämmerlich schlecht, erbärmlich.
lamentably ['læməntəblɪ] *adv* erbärmlich, beklagenswert. **he failed** ~ er scheiterte kläglich; ~, **this idea is not practicable** bedauerlicherweise läßt sich diese Idee nicht verwirklichen; **she was** ~ **ignorant of politics** es war traurig *or* zum Weinen, wie wenig sie von Politik wußte.
lamentation [,læmen'teɪʃən] *n* (Weh)klage *f*; (*act*) Klagen, Jammern *nt*; (*poem, song*) Klagelied *nt*. **he cried out in** ~ er brach in lautes Wehklagen aus.
laminated ['læmɪneɪtɪd] *adj* geschichtet; *windscreen* Verbundglas-; *book cover* laminiert. ~ **glass** Verbundglas *nt*; ~ **wood** Sperrholz *nt*; ~ **plastic** Resopal ® *nt*; ~ **working surfaces** Arbeitsflächen aus Resopal.
lamp [læmp] *n* Lampe *f*; (*in street*) Laterne *f*; (*Aut, Rail*) Scheinwerfer *m*; (*rear*~) Rücklicht *nt*; (*torch*) Taschenlampe *f*; (*sun*~) Höhensonne *f*; (*fig*) Licht *nt*.
lamp: ~**black** *n* Farbruß *m*; ~ **bracket** *n* Lampenhalterung *f*; ~ **chimney,** ~ **glass** *n* Zylinder *m*; ~**light** *n* Lampenlicht *nt*, Schein *m* der Lampe(n); (*in street*) Licht *nt* der Laterne(n); **by** ~**light** bei Lampenlicht; **in the** ~**light** im Schein der Lampe(n); ~**lighter** *n* Laternenanzünder *m*.
lampoon [læm'pu:n] **1** *n* Spott- *or* Schmähschrift *f*. **2** *vt* verspotten, verhöhnen.
lamppost ['læmppəʊst] *n* Laternenpfahl *m*.
lamprey ['læmprɪ] *n* Neunauge *nt*, Bricke *f*; (*sea* ~) Lamprete *f*.
lamp: ~**shade** *n* Lampenschirm *m*; ~**-standard** *n see* ~**post**.
lance [lɑ:ns] **1** *n* Lanze *f*. ~**-corporal** Obergefreite(r) *m*. **2** *vt* (*Med*) öffnen, aufschneiden.
lancer ['lɑ:nsə^r] *n* Lanzenreiter, Ulan *m*.

lancers ['lɑːnsəz] n sing (dance) Lancier m, Quadrille f.
lancet ['lɑːnsɪt] n (a) (Med) Lanzette f. (b) (Archit) ~ arch Spitzbogen m; ~ window Spitzbogenfenster nt.
Lancs [læŋks] abbr of **Lancashire**.
land [lænd] 1 n (a) (not sea) Land nt. by ~ auf dem Landweg; by ~ and by sea zu Land und zu Wasser; as they approached ~ als sie sich dem Land näherten; to see how the ~ lies (lit) das Gelände erkunden or auskundschaften; (fig) die Lage sondieren or peilen; the lay or lie of the ~ (lit) die Beschaffenheit des Geländes; until I've seen the lay or lie of the ~ (fig) bis ich die Lage sondiert habe; see **dry land**.
(b) (nation, region, fig) Land nt. to be in the ~ of the living unter den Lebenden sein.
(c) (as property) Grund und Boden m; (estates) Ländereien pl. to own ~ Land besitzen; get off my ~! verschwinden Sie von meinem Grundstück or Grund und Boden!
(d) (Agr) Land nt; (soil) Boden m. to return to the ~ zur Scholle zurückkehren; to work on the ~ das Land bebauen; the drift from the ~ die Landflucht; to live off the ~ (grow own food) sich vom Lande ernähren, von den Früchten des Landes leben (liter); (forage) sich aus der Natur ernähren.
2 vt (a) (Naut) passengers absetzen, von Bord gehen lassen; troops landen; goods an Land bringen, löschen; fish at port anlanden; boat an Land ziehen. he ~ed the boat on the beach er zog das Boot an den Strand.
(b) (Aviat) passengers absetzen, von Bord gehen lassen; troops landen; goods abladen. to ~ a plane (mit einem Flugzeug) landen; the helicopter ~ed a doctor on the ship der Hubschrauber setzte einen Arzt auf dem Schiff ab; the space-ship ~ed its cargo on the moon das Raumschiff landete seine Fracht auf dem Mond; scientists will ~ a space probe on the moon Wissenschaftler werden eine Raumsonde auf dem Mond landen.
(c) fish on hook an Land ziehen.
(d) (inf: obtain) kriegen (inf); contract sich (dat) verschaffen; prize (sich dat) holen (inf). she finally ~ed him sie hat sich (dat) ihn schließlich geangelt (inf).
(e) (inf) blow landen (inf). he ~ed him one or a punch on the jaw er versetzte ihm or landete (bei ihm) einen Kinnhaken.
(f) (inf: place) bringen. behaviour like that will ~ you in trouble/jail bei einem solchen Betragen wirst du noch mal Ärger bekommen/im Gefängnis landen; it ~ed me in a mess dadurch bin ich in einen ganz schönen Schlamassel (inf) geraten or gekommen; I've ~ed myself in a real mess ich bin (ganz schön) in die Klemme geraten (inf); I ~ed myself in an argument ich habe mich auf einen Streit eingelassen.
(g) (inf: lumber) to ~ sb with sth jdm etw aufhalsen (inf) or andrehen (inf); I got ~ed with the job man hat mir die Arbeit aufgehalst (inf); I got ~ed with him for two hours ich hatte ihn zwei Stunden lang auf dem Hals.
3 vi (a) (from ship) an Land gehen.
(b) (Aviat) landen; (bird, insect) landen, sich setzen. as it ~ed (Aviat) bei der Landung; we're coming in to ~ wir setzen zur Landung an.
(c) (fall, be placed, strike) landen. the bomb ~ed on the building die Bombe fiel auf das Gebäude; to ~ on one's feet (lit) auf den Füßen landen; (fig) auf die Füße fallen; to ~ on one's head auf den Kopf fallen; he ~ed awkwardly er ist ungeschickt aufgekommen or gelandet (inf).
♦**land up** vi (inf) landen (inf). you'll ~ ~ in trouble du wirst noch mal Ärger bekommen; I ~ed ~ with only £2 (had left) ich hatte noch ganze £ 2 in der Tasche (inf); (obtained only) ich habe nur £ 2 herausgeschlagen (inf); he ~ed ~ being sacked from the job after all er wurde schließlich doch entlassen.
land-agent [lænd,eɪdʒənt] n Gutsverwalter(in f) m.
landau ['lændɔ:] n Landauer m.
land: ~-breeze n Landwind m; ~ defences npl Landwehr f.
landed ['lændɪd] adj the ~ class die Großgrundbesitzer pl; ~ gentry Landadel m; ~ property Grundbesitz m.
land: ~fall n Sichten nt von Land; (land sighted) gesichtetes Land; to make ~fall Land sichten; ~ forces npl Landstreitkräfte pl; ~holder n (~-owner) Grundbesitzer m; (tenant) Pächter m.
landing ['lændɪŋ] n (a) (Naut) (of person) Landung f; (of ship also) Anlegen nt; (of goods) Löschen nt. (b) (Aviat) Landung f. (c) (on stairs) (inside house) Flur, Gang m; (outside flat door) Treppenabsatz m; (corridor outside flat doors) Gang, Etagenabsatz m.
landing: ~-card n Einreisekarte f; ~-craft n Landungsboot nt; ~-field n Landeplatz m; ~-gear n Fahrgestell nt; ~-net n Kescher m; ~-party n Landetrupp m; ~-place n (Naut) Anlegeplatz m; ~-stage n (Naut) Landesteg m, Landungsbrücke f; ~-strip n Landebahn f; ~ wheels npl (Lauf)räder pl.
land: ~lady n (Haus)wirtin f; (in pub) Wirtin f; ~ law n Bodenrecht nt; ~less adj landlos; ~locked adj von Land eingeschlossen; a ~locked country ein Land ohne Zugang zum Meer, ein Binnenstaat m; ~lord n (Haus)wirt m; (of land) Grundbesitzer m; (of flat etc) (Haus)wirt m; (of pub) Wirt m; ~lord! Herr Wirt!; ~lubber n Landratte f (inf); ~mark n (Naut) Landmarke f; (boundary mark) Grenzstein, Grenzpfahl m; (well-known thing) Wahrzeichen nt; (fig) Meilenstein, Markstein m; ~mine n Landmine f; ~owner n Grundbesitzer m; ~ reform n Boden(rechts)reform f; ~ route n Landweg m; by the ~ route auf dem Landweg; ~scape ['lændskeɪp] 1 n Landschaft f; 2 vt big area, natural park landschaftlich gestalten; garden, grounds gärtnerisch gestalten, anlegen; ~scape gardener n (for big areas etc) Landschaftsgärtner(in f) m; (for gardens etc) Gartengestalter(in f) m; ~scape gardening n Landschaftsgärtnerei or -gestaltung f; Gartengestaltung f; ~slide n (lit, fig) Erdrutsch m; a ~slide victory ein überwältigender Sieg; ~slip n Erdrutsch m; ~ tax n Grundsteuer f; ~ward adj view zum

(Fest)land; they were sailing in a ~ward direction sie fuhren in Richtung Land or auf das Land zu; on the ~ward side auf der Landseite, auf der dem Land zugekehrten Seite; ~ward(s) adv landwärts; to ~ward in Richtung Land.
lane [leɪn] n (in country) (for walking) (Feld)weg m; (for driving) Sträßchen nt; (in town) Gasse f, Weg m; (Sport) Bahn f; (motorway) Spur f; (shipping ~) Schiffahrtsweg m or -linie f; (air ~) (Flug)route, Luftstraße f. "get in ~" „bitte einordnen".
language ['læŋgwɪdʒ] n Sprache f. a book on ~ ein Buch über die Sprache; philosophy of ~ Sprachphilosophie f, the ~ of flowers die Blumensprache; to study ~s Philologie studieren; your ~ is disgusting deine Ausdrucksweise ist abscheulich, du drückst dich abscheulich aus; that's no ~ to use to your mother! so spricht man nicht mit seiner Mutter!; it's a bloody nuisance! — ~!verfluchter Mist! — na, so was sagt man doch nicht!; bad ~ Kraftausdrücke, unanständige Ausdrücke pl; strong ~ Schimpfwörter, derbe Ausdrücke pl; (forceful ~) starke Worte pl; he used strong ~, calling them fascist pigs er beschimpfte sie als Faschistenschweine; the request/complaint was couched in rather strong ~ die Aufforderung/Beschwerde hörte sich ziemlich kraß an; putting it into plain ~ ... (simply) einfach ausgedrückt ...; (bluntly) um es ganz direkt or ohne Umschweife zu sagen, ...; to talk sb's ~ jds Sprache sprechen; to talk the same ~ (as sb) die gleiche Sprache (wie jd) sprechen.
language: ~ course n Sprachkurs(us) m; ~ lab(oratory) n Sprachlabor nt; ~-learning 1 n Spracherlernung f; 2 adj Sprachlern-; ~ teacher n Sprachlehrer(in f) m.
languid ['læŋgwɪd] adj träge, matt; appearance, manner lässig, gelangweilt; walk lässig, schlendernd; voice müde.
languidly ['læŋgwɪdlɪ] adv träge, lässig. is that all? she said ~ ist das alles?, sagte sie gelangweilt; the model posed ~ against the sofa das Modell lehnte sich in einer lässigen Pose gegen das Sofa; ~ she waved to the crowd mit einer müden or matten Geste winkte sie der Menge zu; the chords build up slowly and ~ die Akkorde bauen sich langsam und schleppend auf.
languidness ['læŋgwɪdnɪs] n see adj Trägheit f, Mattigkeit f; Lässigkeit f. the ~ of his manner seine lässige or gelangweilte Art; the ~ of her voice ihre müde Stimme.
languish ['læŋgwɪʃ] vi schmachten; (flowers) dahinwelken; (pine) sich sehnen (for nach). he ~ed in hospital for months er war monatelang ans Krankenbett gefesselt (geh); the panda merely ~ed in its new home der Panda wurde in seiner neuen Heimat immer apathischer or stumpfer; the child ~ed during his mother's absence das Kind verzehrte sich nach seiner Mutter (geh); I ~ without you, he wrote ich verzehre mich vor Sehnsucht nach dir, schrieb er; I'm ~ing away in this boring town ich verkümmere in dieser langweiligen Stadt.
languishing ['læŋgwɪʃɪŋ] adj schmachtend; death langsam und qualvoll.
languor ['læŋgə'] n (indolence) Trägheit, Schläfrigkeit f; (weakness) Mattigkeit, Schlappheit f; (emotional) Stumpfheit, Apathie f. the ~ of the tropical days die schläfrige Schwüle der tropischen Tage.
languorous ['læŋgərəs] adj träge, schläfrig; heat schläfrig, wohlig; feeling wohlig; music schmelzend; rhythm, metre gleitend, getragen; tone, voice schläfrig. a ~ beauty eine schwüle Schönheit.
languorously ['læŋgərəslɪ] adv träge; speak mit schläfriger Stimme. the soft, ~ sentimental mood of the poem die weiche, schwül-sentimentale Stimmung des Gedichts; she stretched out ~ sie räkelte sich verführerisch.
lank [læŋk] adj person, body dürr, hager; hair strähnig, kraftlos; grass dürr, mager.
lanky ['læŋkɪ] 1 adj (+er) schlaksig. 2 n (inf) Lange(r) mf (inf).
lanolin(e) ['lænəʊlɪn] n Lanolin nt.
lantern ['læntən] n (also Archit) Laterne f; see Chinese.
lantern: ~-jawed adj hohlwangig; ~-slide n Glasdiapositiv, Lichtbild nt.
lanyard ['lænjəd] n (cord) Kordel f (an der Pfeife oder Messer getragen wird); (Naut) Taljereep nt.
Laos [laʊs] n Laos nt.
Laotian ['laʊʃən] 1 adj laotisch. 2 n Laote m, Laotin f.
lap¹ [læp] n Schoß m. on her ~ auf dem/ihrem Schoß; his opponent's mistake dropped victory into his ~ durch den Fehler seines Gegners fiel ihm der Sieg in den Schoß; it's in the ~ of the gods es liegt im Schoß der Götter; to live in the ~ of luxury ein Luxusleben führen; ~ and diagonal seat belt Dreipunkt(sicherheits)gurt m.
lap² (over~) 1 n Überlappung f. 2 vt überlappen. 3 vi sich überlappen. the meeting ~ped over into extra time die Versammlung ging über die vorgesehene Zeit hinaus.
lap³ vt (wrap) wickeln.
lap⁴ (Sport) 1 n (round) Runde f; (fig: stage) Etappe, Strecke f, Abschnitt m. his time for the first ~ seine Zeit in der ersten Runde; on the second ~ in der zweiten Runde; ~ of honour Ehrenrunde f; we're on the last ~ now (fig) wir haben es bald geschafft. 2 vt überrunden. 3 vi to ~ at 90 mph with one Geschwindigkeit von 90 Meilen pro Stunde seine Runden drehen; he's ~ping at 58 seconds (athlete) er läuft die Runde in einer Zeit von 58 Sekunden.
lap⁵ 1 n (lick) Schlecken, Lecken nt; (of waves) Klatschen, Schlagen, Plätschern nt. the cat took a cautious ~ at the milk die Katze leckte or schleckte vorsichtig an der Milch.
2 vt (a) (lick) lecken, schlecken.
(b) (water) the waves ~ped the shore die Wellen rollten an or plätscherten an or klatschten gegen das Ufer.
3 vi (waves, water) plätschern (against an +acc), schlagen, klatschen (against gegen). to ~ over sth schwappen über etw (acc).

♦**lap up** *vt sep* (a) *liquid* auflecken, aufschlecken, aufschlabbern (*inf*). the children hungrily ~ped ~ their soup die Kinder löffelten hungrig ihre Suppe.
 (b) *praise, compliments* genießen; *nonsense* schlucken. she ~ped it ~ das ging ihr runter wie Honig (*inf*); he ~ped ~ the compliments die Komplimente gingen ihm wie Honig runter.

lap-dog ['læpdɒg] *n* Schoßhund *m*.

lapel [lə'pel] *n* Aufschlag *m*, Revers *nt or m.*

lapidary ['læpɪdərɪ] **1** *adj* ~ art (Edel)steinschneidekunst *f*; ~ inscription in Stein gehauene Inschrift. **2** *n* Steinschneider *m.*

lapis lazuli ['læpɪs'læzjulaɪ] *n* Lapislazuli *m.*

Lapland ['læplænd] *n* Lappland *nt.*

Laplander ['læplændə*ʳ*], **Lapp** [læp] *n* Lappländer(in *f*) *m*, Lappe *m*, Lappin *f.*

Lapp [læp] *n* (a) *see* **Laplander**. (b) *see* **Lappish**.

lapping ['læpɪŋ] *n* (*of water*) Plätschern, Schlagen *nt.*

Lappish ['læpɪʃ] *n* Lappländisch, Lappisch *nt.*

lapse [læps] **1** *n* (a) (*error*) Fehler *m*; (*moral*) Fehltritt *m*, Verfehlung *f*. ~ of justice Justizirrtum *m*; he had a ~ of memory es ist ihm entfallen; to suffer from ~s of memory an Gedächtnisschwäche leiden; ~ of good taste Geschmacksverirrung *f.*
 (b) (*decline*) Absinken, Abgleiten *nt no pl*. a ~ in confidence ein Vertrauensschwund *m*; ~ in standards Niveauabfall *m.*
 (c) (*expiry*) Ablauf *m*; (*of claim*) Verfall *m*, Erlöschen *nt*; (*cessation*) Aussterben, Schwinden *nt.*
 (d) (*of time*) Zeitspanne *f*, Zeitraum *m*. after a ~ of 4 months nach (einem Zeitraum von) 4 Monaten; there was a ~ in the conversation es gab eine Gesprächspause.
 2 *vi* (a) (*make mistake*) einen Fehler begehen, etwas falsch machen; (*morally*) fehlen (*liter*), einen Fehltritt begehen, unrecht tun. to ~ from one's faith von seinem Glauben abfallen, seinem Glauben abtrünnig werden; to ~ from duty seine Pflicht vernachlässigen.
 (b) (*decline*) verfallen (*into* in +*acc*); abgleiten (*from sth into sth* von etw in etw *acc*). his taste must have ~d when he bought that picture er muß an Geschmacksverirrung gelitten haben, als er das Bild kaufte; to ~ into one's old ways wieder in seine alten Gewohnheiten verfallen; he ~d into the vernacular er verfiel (wieder) in seinen Dialekt; he ~d into silence er versank in Schweigen; he ~d into a coma er sank in ein Koma; he/his work is lapsing er/seine Arbeit läßt nach, mit ihm/seiner Arbeit geht es bergab.
 (c) (*expire*) ablaufen; (*claims*) verfallen, erlöschen; (*cease to exist*) aussterben; (*friendship, correspondence*) einschlafen. the plan ~d because of lack of support der Plan wurde mangels Unterstützung fallengelassen.

lapsed [læpst] *adj Catholic* abtrünnig, vom Glauben abgefallen; *insurance policy* abgelaufen, verfallen.

lapwing ['læpwɪŋ] *n* Kiebitz *m.*

larboard ['lɑːbəd] (*old*) **1** *adj* Backbord-. **2** *n* Backbord *nt.*

larceny ['lɑːsənɪ] *n* (*Jur*) Diebstahl *m.*

larch [lɑːtʃ] *n* (*also* ~ tree) Lärche *f*; (*wood*) Lärche(nholz *nt*) *f.*

lard [lɑːd] **1** *n* Schweineschmalz *nt.* **2** *vt* mit Schweineschmalz bestreichen; (*with strips of bacon, fig*) spicken.

larder ['lɑːdə*ʳ*] *n* (*room*) Speisekammer *f*; (*cupboard*) Speiseschrank *m.*

lardy-cake ['lɑːdɪˌkeɪk] *n* Schmalzkuchen *m* aus Brotteig mit Rosinen.

large [lɑːdʒ] **1** *adj* (+*er*) (a) (*big*) groß; *person* stark, korpulent; *meal* reichlich, groß; *list* lang. a ~ land-owner ein Großgrundbesitzer *m*; she looks as ~ as life in that photograph sie sieht auf dem Foto aus, wie sie leibt und lebt; there he/it was as ~ as life da war er/es in voller Lebensgröße.
 (b) (*extensive*) *interests, power* weitreichend, bedeutend. his interests were on a ~ scale er hatte weitreichende *or* breit gestreute Interessen; taking the ~ view global betrachtet.
 (c) (*old: generous, tolerant*) großzügig. a ~ understanding ein großes Verständnis.
 2 *adv* groß. guilt was written ~ all over his face die Schuld stand ihm deutlich im Gesicht geschrieben.
 3 *n* (a) (*in general*) at ~ im großen und ganzen, im allgemeinen; people *or* the world at ~ die Allgemeinheit; he wanted to tell his story to the world at ~ er wollte der ganzen Welt seine Geschichte erzählen.
 (b) to be at ~ (*free*) frei herumlaufen; the goats wander at ~ die Ziegen laufen frei herum.
 (c) at ~ (*in detail, at length*) ausführlich, lang und breit.
 (d) strewn at ~ (*at random*) kreuz und quer verstreut; scattering accusations at ~ mit Anschuldigungen um sich werfend.
 (e) ambassador at ~ Sonderbotschafter *m.*

large-hearted ['lɑːdʒˌhɑːtɪd] *adj* großherzig.

largely ['lɑːdʒlɪ] *adv* (a) (*mainly*) zum größten Teil. (b) (*old: generously*) großzügig.

large-minded ['lɑːdʒˌmaɪndɪd] *adj* aufgeschlossen.

largeness ['lɑːdʒnɪs] *n see adj* (a) Größe *f*; Umfang *m*; Reichlichkeit *f*; Länge *f.* (b) Bedeutung *f*, Umfang *m.* (c) Großzügigkeit *f.*

large: ~-scale *adj* groß angelegt; *reception, party* in großem Rahmen, ~-scale changes Veränderungen *pl* in großem Umfang *or* Rahmen; a ~-scale producer of food ein Großhersteller *m* von Nahrungsmitteln; ~-scale rioting Massenaufruhr *m*, Massenunruhen *pl*; a ~-scale map eine (Land)karte in großem Maßstab; ~-sized *adj* groß.

largesse [lɑː'ʒes] *n* Großzügigkeit, Freigebigkeit; (*gift*) (großzügige) Gabe.

largish ['lɑːdʒɪʃ] *adj* ziemlich groß.

largo ['lɑːgəʊ] *n* Largo *nt.*

lariat ['lærɪət] *n* Lasso *nt or m.*

lark[1] [lɑːk] *n* (*Orn*) Lerche *f*. to get up with the ~ mit den Hühnern aufstehen; as happy as a ~ quietschfidel.

lark[2] *n* (*inf*) (a) (*joke, fun, frolic*) Jux (*inf*), Spaß *m*. let's go to the party, it'll be a bit of a ~ gehen wir zur Party, das wird bestimmt lustig; that's the best ~ we've had for a long time! so viel Spaß haben wir schon lange nicht mehr gehabt!; what a ~! das ist (ja) zum Schreien *or* Schießen!; that was a ~, it was a good ~ das hat Spaß gemacht, das war ein richtiger Jux; to do sth for a ~ etw (nur) zum Spaß *or* aus Jux machen; to have a ~ with sb mit jdm zusammen Spaß haben.
 (b) (*business, affair*) this whole agency ~ is ... die ganze Geschichte mit der Agentur ist ... (*inf*); he's got involved in the used-car ~ er ist ins Gebrauchtwagengeschäft eingestiegen (*inf*); I wouldn't get involved in that ~ auf so was *or so* 'ne Sache würde ich mich nicht einlassen (*inf*); politics and all that ~ Politik und der ganze Kram (*inf*); this dinner-jacket ~ dieser Blödsinn mit dem Smoking (*inf*).

♦**lark about** *or* **around** *vi* (*inf*) herumblödeln, herumalbern. to ~ ~ with sth mit etw herumspielen.

larkspur ['lɑːkspɜː*ʳ*] *n* Rittersporn *m.*

larva ['lɑːvə] *n, pl* ~e ['lɑːvɪ] Larve *f.*

larval ['lɑːvəl] *adj* Larven-, larvenartig.

laryngeal [lə'rɪndʒəl] *adj* Kehlkopf-.

laryngitis [ˌlærɪn'dʒaɪtɪs] *n* Kehlkopfentzündung, Laryngitis (*spec*) *f.*

larynx ['lærɪŋks] *n* Kehlkopf, Larynx (*spec*) *m.*

lascivious [lə'sɪvɪəs] *adj* lasziv (*geh*); *movements, person, look, behaviour also* lüstern; *book* schlüpfrig.

lasciviously [lə'sɪvɪəslɪ] *adv* lüstern. the dancer moved ~ die Bewegungen der Tänzerin waren lasziv.

lasciviousness [lə'sɪvɪəsnɪs] *n see adj* Laszivität *f* (*geh*); Lüsternheit *f*; Schlüpfrigkeit *f.*

laser ['leɪzə*ʳ*] *n* Laser *m*. ~ beam Laserstrahl *m.*

lash[1] [læʃ] *n* (*eye*~) Wimper *f*. she fluttered her ~es at him sie machte ihm schöne Augen.

lash[2] **1** *n* (a) (*whip*) Peitsche *f*; (*thong*) Schnur *f.*
 (b) (*stroke, as punishment*) (Peitschen)schlag *m.*
 (c) (~ing) (*of tail*) Schlagen *nt*; (*of waves, rain also*) Peitschen *nt.*
 (d) (*fig*) Schärfe *f*. the ~ of her tongue ihre scharfe Zunge; the ~ of her criticism ihre beißende Kritik.
 2 *vt* (a) (*beat*) peitschen; (*as punishment*) auspeitschen; (*hail, rain, waves*) peitschen gegen; (*tail*) schlagen mit. the wind ~ed the sea into a fury wütend peitschte der Wind die See; the cow ~ed the flies with its tail die Kuh schlug mit ihrem Schwanz nach den Fliegen; to ~ the crowd into a fury die Menge aufpeitschen; he ~ed himself into a fury er steigerte sich in seine Wut hinein; his speech ~ed his audience into a passion of enthusiasm seine Rede riß die Zuhörer zu Begeisterungsstürmen hin.
 (b) (*fig: criticize*) heruntermachen (*inf*), abkanzeln.
 (c) (*tie*) festbinden (*to an* +*dat*). to ~ sth together etw zusammenbinden.
 3 *vi* ~ against peitschen gegen.

♦**lash about** *or* **around** *vi* (*wild*) um sich schlagen.

♦**lash along** *vt sep see* **lash on.**

♦**lash around** *vi see* **lash about.**

♦**lash back** *vt sep* festbinden.

♦**lash down 1** *vt sep* (*tie down*) festbinden *or* -zurren. **2** *vi* (*rain etc*) niederprasseln.

♦**lash into** *vi* ~ *prep obj* to ~ ~ sb (*physically*) auf jdn einschlagen; (*with words*) jdn anfahren *or* anbrüllen (*inf*).

♦**lash on** *or* **along** *vt sep* horse, slaves mit der Peitsche antreiben.

♦**lash out 1** *vi* (a) (*physically*) (wild) um sich schlagen *or* hauen; (*horse*) ausschlagen. to ~ ~ at sb auf jdn losgehen.
 (b) (*in words*) vom Leder ziehen (*inf*). to ~ ~ against *or* at sb/sth gegen jdn/etw wettern; "TUC boss ~es ~" „Gewerkschaftsboß holt zum Schlag aus".
 (c) (*inf: with money*) sich in Unkosten stürzen. to ~ ~ on sth sich (*dat*) etw was kosten lassen (*inf*); to ~ ~ on sb spendabel gegenüber jdm sein (*inf*); I'm going to ~ ~ on a new car ich werde mir ein neues Auto leisten (*inf*); now we can really ~ ~ jetzt können wir uns wirklich mal etwas leisten.
 2 *vt insep sum of money* springenlassen.

♦**lash up** *vt sep* verschnüren.

lashing ['læʃɪŋ] *n* (a) (*beating*) Prügel *pl*; (*punishment*) Auspeitschung *f*. she gave him a ~ with her tongue sie putzte ihn herunter (*inf*), sie machte ihn zur Schnecke (*inf*).
 (b) (*tie*) Verschnürung *f*; (*of prisoner*) Fesseln *pl*; (*Naut*) Tau *nt*, Zurring *m.*
 (c) ~s *pl* (*inf*) eine Unmenge (*inf*); ~s of money/cream eine Unmenge *or* massenhaft Geld/Schlagsahne (*inf*).

lass [læs] *n* (*junges*) Mädchen, Mädel *nt* (*dial*); (*country* ~) Mädchen *nt* vom Land; (*sweetheart*) Freundin *f*, Schatz *m.*

lassie ['læsɪ] *n* (*inf: esp Scot, N Engl*) *see* **lass.**

lassitude ['læsɪtjuːd] *n* Mattigkeit, Trägheit *f.*

lasso [læ'suː] **1** *n, pl* -(e)s Lasso *m or nt.* **2** *vt* mit dem Lasso einfangen.

last[1] [lɑːst] **1** *adj* (a) letzte(r, s). he was ~ to arrive er kam als letzter an; the ~ person der letzte; the ~ but one, the second ~ (one) der/die/das vorletzte; the third ~ house das drittletzte Haus; (the) ~ one there buys the drinks! der letzte *or* wer als letzter ankommt, zahlt die Getränke; ~ Monday, on Monday ~ letzten Montag; ~ year letztes Jahr, im vorigen Jahr; during the ~ 20 years, these ~ 20 years in den letzten 20 Jahren; to have the ~ laugh zum Schluß das Lachen haben; ~ but not least nicht zuletzt, last not least.
 (b) (*most unlikely, unsuitable etc*) that's the ~ thing I worry about das ist das letzte, worüber ich mir Sorgen machen würde; that was the ~ thing I expected damit hatte ich am wenigsten gerechnet; he was the ~ person I expected to see mit ihm habe ich am wenigsten gerechnet; that's the ~ thing I wanted to

happen das habe ich am wenigsten gewollt; he's the ~ person I want to see er ist der letzte, den ich sehen möchte; you're the ~ person to be entrusted with it du bist der letzte, dem man das anvertrauen kann.

2 n **(a)** (final one or part, one before) der/die/das letzte. he was the ~ of the visitors to leave er ging als letzter der Besucher; he withdrew the ~ of his money from the bank er hob sein letztes Geld von der Bank ab; each one is better than the ~ eins ist besser als das andere; this is the ~ of the cake das ist der Rest des Kuchens; that's the ~ of the trouble jetzt hat der Ärger ein Ende; I hope this is the ~ we'll hear about it ich hoffe, damit ist die Sache erledigt; that was the ~ we saw of him danach haben wir ihn nicht mehr gesehen; the ~ we heard of him was ... das letzte, was wir von ihm hörten, war ...; that was the ~ we heard of it/him seitdem haben wir nichts mehr darüber/von ihm gehört; that's the ~ I want to hear about it ich möchte davon nichts mehr hören; I shall be glad to see the ~ of this/him ich bin froh, wenn ich das hinter mir habe/wenn ich den los bin (inf) or nicht mehr sehe; we shall never hear the ~ of it das werden wir noch lange zu hören kriegen; to look one's ~ on sth den letzten Blick auf etw (acc) werfen; my ~ (Comm) mein letztes Schreiben.

(b) at ~ endlich; at long ~ schließlich und endlich; so you're ready at long ~! du bist also endlich fertig geworden!; to the ~ bis zum Schluß.

3 adv when did you ~ have a bath or have a bath ~? wann hast du das letztemal gebadet?; I ~ heard from him a month ago vor einem Monat habe ich das letztemal von ihm gehört; he spoke ~ er sprach als letzter; the horse came in ~ das Pferd ging als letztes durchs Ziel.

last² **1** vt it will ~ me/a careful user a lifetime das hält/bei vernünftiger Benutzung hält es ein Leben lang or ewig (inf); the car has ~ed me eight years das Auto hat acht Jahre (lang) gehalten; these cigarettes will ~ me a week diese Zigaretten reichen mir eine Woche.

2 vi (continue) dauern; (remain intact: cloth, flowers, marriage) halten. it can't ~ es hält nicht an; it won't ~ es wird nicht lange anhalten or so bleiben; it's too good to ~ das ist zu schön, um wahr zu sein; he'll stay as long as the beer ~s er bleibt, solange Bier da ist; will this material ~? ist dieses Material haltbar or dauerhaft?; none of his girlfriends ~s for long bei ihm hält sich keine Freundin lange; he won't ~ long in this job er wird in dieser Stelle nicht alt werden (inf); the previous boss ~ed only a week der letzte Chef blieb nur eine Woche.

♦**last out 1** vt sep ausreichen für; (people) durchhalten. **2** vi (money, resources) ausreichen; (person) durchhalten.

last³ n Leisten m. cobbler, stick to your ~! Schuster, bleib bei deinem Leisten!

last: the L~ Day n der Jüngste Tag; ~-ditch adj allerletzte(r, s); attempt etc in letzter Minute.

lasting ['lɑːstɪŋ] adj relationship dauerhaft; material also haltbar; shame etc anhaltend.

Last Judgement n the ~ das Jüngste or Letzte Gericht.

lastly ['lɑːstlɪ] adv schließlich, zum Schluß.

last: ~-minute adj in letzter Minute; ~ post n Zapfenstreich m; ~ rites npl Letzte Ölung; the L~ Supper n das (Letzte) Abendmahl; the ~ word n (in fashion) der letzte Schrei; to have the ~ word das letzte Wort haben; the ~ word on biochemistry/on this subject das maßgebende Werk über Biochemie/auf diesem Gebiet.

Lat abbr of **Latin** lat, Lat.

lat abbr of **latitude** Br.

latch [lætʃ] **1** n Riegel m. to be on the ~ nicht verschlossen sein, nur eingeklinkt sein; to leave the door on the ~ die Tür nur einklinken; to drop the ~ den Riegel vorschieben, die Tür verriegeln.

2 vt verriegeln.

♦**latch on** vi (inf) **(a)** (get hold) sich festhalten; (with teeth) sich festbeißen (to sth an etw dat). he ~ed ~ to the idea of coming with us er hat es sich (dat) in den Kopf gesetzt, mitzukommen.

(b) (attach oneself) sich anschließen (to dat). she ~ed ~ to me at the party sie hängte sich auf der Party an mich (inf).

(c) (understand) kapieren (inf).

latchkey ['lætʃˌkiː] n Haus-/Wohnungsschlüssel m. ~ child Schlüsselkind nt.

late [leɪt] **1** adj (+er) **(a)** spät. to be ~ (for sth) (zu etw) zu spät kommen; the trains tend to be ~ die Züge haben oft Verspätung; dinner will be ~ tonight wir essen heute abend später; (in hotels) es wird heute abend später serviert; I was ~ in getting up this morning ich bin heute morgen zu spät aufgestanden; he is ~ with his rent er hat seine Miete noch nicht bezahlt; he is always ~ with his rent er bezahlt seine Miete immer zu spät; I don't want to make you ~ ich möchte Sie nicht aufhalten; you'll make me ~ Ihretwegen werde ich mich verspäten or zu spät kommen; that made me ~ for work dadurch bin ich zu spät zur Arbeit gekommen; I don't want to make you ~ for work ich möchte nicht, daß du zu spät zur Arbeit kommst; that made the coach ~ dadurch hatte der Bus Verspätung; that made the harvest ~ dadurch verzögerte sich die Ernte; due to the ~ arrival of ... wegen der verspäteten Ankunft ... (+gen).

(b) it's ~ es ist spät; it's getting ~ es ist schon spät; is it as ~ as that? ist es schon so spät?

(c) hour späte; opening hours lang; bus, train Spät-. at this ~ hour zu so später Stunde, so spät; at a ~ hour zu später or vorgerückter Stunde; he keeps very ~ hours er geht sehr spät ins Bett; the night was cold and the hour ~ die Nacht war kalt, und es war sehr spät; they had a ~ dinner yesterday sie haben gestern spät zu Abend gegessen; there is no ~ delivery of post on Saturdays sonnabends gibt es keine zweite Zustellung; ~ night club Nachtbar f; ~ potato/summer/edition/programme

Spätkartoffel f/-sommer m/-ausgabe f/-programm nt; ~ entrants to the examination will be charged £1 extra für Nachmeldungen zur Prüfung wird eine Gebühr von £ 1 erhoben; this essay was a ~ entry for the competition dieser Aufsatz wurde verspätet für den Wettbewerb eingereicht; (last-minute) dieser Aufsatz wurde in letzter Minute eingereicht; it happened in the ~ eighties es geschah Ende der achtziger Jahre; a man in his ~ eighties ein Mann hoch in den Achtzigern, ein Endachtziger; in the ~ morning am späten Vormittag; a ~ 18th-century building ein Gebäude aus dem späten 18. Jahrhundert; he came in ~ June er kam Ende Juni; L~ Stone Age Jungsteinzeit f; L~ Latin Spätlatein nt; Easter is ~ this year Ostern liegt or ist dieses Jahr spät; spring is ~ this year wir haben dieses Jahr einen späten Frühling.

(d) attr (deceased) verstorben. the ~ John F. Kennedy John F. Kennedy.

(e) (former) the ~ Prime Minister der frühere or vorige Premierminister.

(f) (recent) jüngst. in the ~ war im letzten Krieg.

(g) ~ of No 13 White St ehemals or bis vor kurzem White St Nr. 13; ~ of the Diplomatic Service ehemals or bis vor kurzem im diplomatischen Dienst tätig.

2 adv spät. to come ~ zu spät kommen; I'll be home ~ today ich komme heute spät nach Hause, es wird heute spät; the train arrived eight minutes ~ der Zug hatte acht Minuten Verspätung; all trains are running ~ today alle Züge haben heute Verspätung; better ~ than never lieber or besser spät als gar nicht; to sit or stay up ~ lange aufbleiben; don't wait up ~ for me warte nicht zu lange auf mich; to work ~ at the office länger im Büro arbeiten; ~ at night spät abends; ~ in the night spät in der Nacht; ~ into the night bis spät in die Nacht; ~ in the afternoon am späten Nachmittag; ~ last century/in the year (gegen) Ende des letzten Jahrhunderts/Jahres; he took up the piano rather ~ in life er begann ziemlich spät mit dem Klavierspielen; Goethe was still active even ~ in life Goethe war auch im hohen Alter noch aktiv; of ~ in letzter Zeit; until as ~ as 1900 noch bis 1900; it was as ~ as 1900 before child labour was abolished erst 1900 wurde die Kinderarbeit abgeschafft; I saw him as ~ as yesterday ich habe ihn erst gestern (noch) gesehen.

latecomer ['leɪtkʌmə'] n Zuspätkommende(r) mf, Nachzügler(in f) m (inf). the firm is a ~ to the industry die Firma ist neu in der Industrie.

lateen sail [lə'tiːn'seɪl] n Lateinsegel nt.

late lamented adj kürzlich verstorben or verschieden (geh). my ~ boss (iro) mein heißgeliebter ehemaliger Chef (iro).

lately ['leɪtlɪ] adv in letzter Zeit. till ~ bis vor kurzem.

latency ['leɪtənsɪ] n Latenz f. the ~ of his artistic abilities seine verborgenen or latenten künstlerischen Fähigkeiten.

lateness ['leɪtnɪs] n (being late at work etc) Zuspätkommen nt; (of train, payments) Verspätung f; (of meal) späte Zeit; (of harvest, seasons) spätes Eintreten; of the ~ of the hour die so späte Stunde.

latent ['leɪtənt] adj latent; strength also verborgen; artistic talent, ability also verborgen, versteckt; heat also gebunden; energy ungenutzt; (Med) period Latenz-. the evil which is ~ in all men das in jedem Menschen latent vorhandene Böse.

later ['leɪtə'] **1** adj später. at a ~ hour, at a ~ time später, zu einer späteren Zeit; this version is ~ than that one diese Version ist neuer als die andere; in his ~ years in vorgerücktem Alter, in seinem späteren Leben.

2 adv später. Mr Smith, ~ to become Sir John; Mr Smith, der spätere Sir John; the weather cleared up ~ in the day das Wetter klärte sich im Laufe des Tages auf; ~ that night/week/day später, in der Nacht/Woche/an dem Tag; a moment ~ einen Augenblick später, im nächsten Augenblick; see you ~! bis nachher, bis später; I saw him no ~ than yesterday ich habe ihn (erst) gestern noch gesehen; come at 7 o'clock and no ~ komm um 7 Uhr und nicht um keine Minute später; don't come any ~ than 7 o'clock komme bis spätestens or nicht später als 7 Uhr; not ~ than 1980 spätestens 1980; ~ on nachher.

lateral ['lætərəl] adj seitlich; view, window Seiten-. ~ line (of fish) Seitenlinie f; ~ thinking spielerisches Denken.

laterally ['lætərəlɪ] adv seitlich.

latest ['leɪtɪst] **1** adj **(a)** späteste(r, s). what is the ~ date you can come? wann kannst du spätestens kommen?

(b) (most recent) fashion, version neu(e)ste(r, s). the ~ news das Neu(e)ste.

(c) people letzte(r, s). the ~ men to resign die letzten, die zurückgetreten sind; he was the ~ to arrive er kam als letzter.

2 adv am spätesten. he came ~ er kam zuletzt or als letzter.

3 n **(a)** what's the ~ (about John)? was gibt's Neues (über John)?; wait till you hear the ~! warte, bis du das Neueste gehört hast!; have you seen John's ~? (girl) hast du Johns Neu(e)ste schon gesehen?; have you heard John's ~? (joke) hast du Johns Neuesten schon gehört?

(b) at the (very) ~ spätestens.

latex ['leɪteks] n Latex (spec), Milchsaft m.

lath [læθ] n Latte f. ~s pl (structure) Lattenwerk nt.

lathe [leɪð] n Drehbank f. ~ operator Dreher m.

lather ['lɑːðə'] **1** n (Seifen)schaum m; (sweat) Schweiß m. work the soap into a rich ~ die Seife zum Schäumen bringen; the horse/athlete was in a ~ das Pferd/der Sportler war schweißnaß; to get into a ~ (about sth) (inf) sich (über etw acc) aufregen, (wegen etw dat) durchdrehen (inf).

2 vt einschäumen.

3 vi schäumen.

Latin ['lætɪn] **1** adj **(a)** (Roman) civilization, world römisch; poets, literature also lateinisch. ~ language lateinische Sprache; (of ancient Latium) latinische Sprache.

(b) (of Roman origin) romanisch; temperament, charm

südländisch. **~ Quarter** Quartier Latin *nt*.
  (c) *(Rel)* römisch-katholisch.
  2 *n* **(a)** *(inhabitant of ancient Latium)* Latiner(in *f*) *m*; *(Roman)* Römer(in *f*) *m*; *(a member of any Latin race)* Südländer(in *f*), Romane *m*, Romanin *f*.
  (b) *(language)* Latein(isch) *nt*.
Latin America *n* Lateinamerika *nt*.
Latin-American [ˈlætɪnəˈmerɪkən] **1** *adj* lateinamerikanisch. **2** *n* Lateinamerikaner(in *f*) *m*.
latinism [ˈlætɪnɪzəm] *n* Latinismus *m*.
latinist [ˈlætɪnɪst] *n* Latinist *m*.
latinity [ləˈtɪnɪtɪ] *n (rare)* Latinität *f*.
latinization [ˌlætɪnaɪˈzeɪʃən] *n* Latinisierung *f*.
latinize [ˈlætɪnaɪz] *vt* latinisieren.
latish [ˈleɪtɪʃ] **1** *adj* ziemlich spät; *applicant, letter* verspätet; *amendment* neuer, später. **2** *adv* ziemlich spät.
latitude [ˈlætɪtjuːd] *n* Breite *f*, Spielraum *m*.
latitudinal [ˌlætɪˈtjuːdɪnl] *adj* Breiten-. **~ lines** Breitengrade *pl*.
latrine [ləˈtriːn] *n* Latrine *f*.
latter [ˈlætəʳ] **1** *adj* **(a)** *(second of two)* letztere(r, s).
  (b) *(at the end)* **the ~ part of the book/story** is better gegen Ende wird das Buch/die Geschichte besser; **the ~ part/half of the week/year/century** die zweite Hälfte der Woche/des Jahres/des Jahrhunderts; **in the ~ years** in den letzten Jahren; **in his ~ years** in den späteren Jahren seines Lebens.
  2 *n* **the ~** der/die/das/letztere; die letzteren.
latter-day [ˈlætəˈdeɪ] *adj* modern. **the L~ Saints** die Heiligen der Letzten Tage.
latterly [ˈlætəlɪ] *adv* in letzter Zeit.
lattice [ˈlætɪs] *n* Gitter *nt*. **~-work** Gitterwerk *nt*.
latticed [ˈlætɪst] *adj* vergittert.
Latvia [ˈlætvɪə] *n* Lettland *nt*.
Latvian [ˈlætvɪən] **1** *adj* lettisch. **2** *n* **(a)** Lette *m*, Lettin *f*. **(b)** *(language)* Lettisch *nt*.
laud [lɔːd] *vt (old)* preisen *(geh)*.
laudable [ˈlɔːdəbl] *adj* lobenswert.
laudably [ˈlɔːdəblɪ] *adv* lobenswerterweise. **~ unselfish remarks** lobenswert selbstlose Worte *pl*.
laudanum [ˈlɔːdnəm] *n* Laudanum *nt*.
laudatory [ˈlɔːdətərɪ] *adj* lobend. **a ~ speech** eine Lobrede *or* Laudatio *(geh)*.
laugh [lɑːf] **1** *n* **(a)** Lachen *nt*. **no, she said, with a ~** nein, sagte sie lachend; **she let out** *or* **gave a loud ~** sie lachte laut auf; **that woman has a ~ like a hyena** die Frau gackert wie ein Huhn; **what a ~ (she's got)!** die hat vielleicht 'ne Lache! *(inf)*; **to have a good ~ over** *or* **about sth** sich köstlich über etw *(acc)* amüsieren; **you'll have a good ~ about it** one day eines Tages wirst du darüber lachen können; **give us a ~!** *(inf)* bring uns mal zum Lachen!; **it'll give us a ~** *(inf)* das wird lustig; **the ~ was on me** der Witz ging auf meine Kosten; **to have the last ~** *(over or on sb)* es jdm zeigen *(inf)*; **I'll have the last ~** ich werd's dir schon noch zeigen *(inf)*; **to play for ~s** Lacherfolge haben wollen; **he played Hamlet for ~s** er machte aus Hamlet eine komische Figur; **they played "Othello" for ~s** sie machten aus „Othello" eine Komödie.
  (b) *(inf: fun)* **what a ~** (das ist ja) zum Totlachen *or* zum Schreien *(inf)*!; **just for a ~** nur (so) aus Spaß; **it'll be a good ~** es wird bestimmt lustig; **we didn't achieve much, but we had a good ~** wir haben nicht viel geschafft, aber es war trotzdem lustig; **he's a ~** er ist urkomisch *or* zum Schreien *(inf)*; **to be good for a ~** ganz lustig sein.
  2 *vi* lachen *(about, at, over* über +*acc)*. **to ~ at sb** sich über jdn lustig machen; **to ~ up one's sleeve** sich *(dat)* ins Fäustchen lachen; **she's ~ing up her sleeve at us** sie macht sich heimlich über uns lustig; **it's nothing to ~ about** das ist nicht zum Lachen; **it's all very well for you to ~** du hast gut lachen; **you'll be ~ing on the other side of your face soon** dir wird das Lachen noch vergehen; **to ~ out loud** laut auflachen; **to ~ in sb's face** jdm ins Gesicht lachen; **he who ~s last ~s longest** *(Prov)* wer zuletzt lacht, lacht am besten *(Prov)*; **don't make me ~!** *(iro inf)* daß ich nicht lache! *(inf)*; **you've got your own house, you're ~ing** *(inf)* du hast ein eigenes Haus, du hast es gut.
  3 *vt* **to ~ oneself silly** sich tot- *or* kaputtlachen *(inf)*; **he was ~ed out of court** er wurde ausgelacht; **the idea was ~ed out of court** die Idee wurde verlacht.
♦**laugh away** **1** *vt sep* mit Humor tragen, sich lachend hinwegsetzen über (+*acc*). **my father ~ed ~ my fears** mein Vater nahm mir mit einem Lachen die Angst. **2** *vi* he sat there ~ing ~ er saß da und lachte und lachte.
♦**laugh down** *vt sep* auslachen, mit Gelächter übertönen. **the audience ~ed him/his reply ~** er/seine Antwort ging im Gelächter des Publikums unter.
♦**laugh off** *vt* **(a)** *always separate* **to ~ one's head ~** sich tot- *or* kaputtlachen *(inf)*. **(b)** *sep (dismiss)* lachen über (+*acc*), mit einem Lachen abtun.
laughable [ˈlɑːfəbl] *adj* lachhaft, lächerlich. **if it wasn't so serious, it would be almost ~** wenn es nicht so ernst wäre, könnte man fast darüber lachen.
laughably [ˈlɑːfəblɪ] *adv* lächerlich.
laughing [ˈlɑːfɪŋ] **1** *adj* lachend. **it's no ~ matter** das ist nicht zum Lachen, das ist gar nicht komisch. **2** *n* Lachen *nt*. **the sound of hysterical ~** der Klang hysterischen Gelächters.
laughing: **~ gas** *n* Lachgas *nt*; **~ hy(a)ena** *n* Tüpfel- *or* Fleckenhyäne *f*.
laughingly [ˈlɑːfɪŋlɪ] *adv see adj*.
laughing: **~ jackass** *n* Rieseneisvogel *m*; **~ stock** *n* Witzfigur *f*; **his visionary ideas made him a ~ stock** mit seinen phantastischen Ideen machte er sich lächerlich *or* zum allgemeinen Gespött.
laughter [ˈlɑːftəʳ] *n* Gelächter *nt*. **~ broke out among the audience** das Publikum brach in Gelächter aus; **children's ~**

Kinderlachen *nt*; **he shook with silent ~** er schüttelte sich vor Lachen; **at this there was ~** das rief Gelächter hervor.
launch [lɔːntʃ] **1** *n* **(a)** *(vessel)* Barkasse *f*.
  (b) *(~ing) (of ship)* Stapellauf *m*; *(of lifeboat)* Aussetzen *nt*; *(of rocket)* Abschuß *m*.
  (c) *(~ing) (of company)* Gründung, Eröffnung *f*; *(of new product)* Einführung *f*; *(with party, publicity: of film, play, book)* Lancierung *f*; *(bringing out) (of film, play)* Premiere *f*; *(of book)* Herausgabe *f*; *(of shares)* Emission *f*.
  2 *vt* **(a)** *new vessel* vom Stapel lassen; *(christen)* taufen; *lifeboat* zu Wasser lassen, aussetzen; *rocket* abschießen; *plane* katapultieren. **Lady X ~ed the new boat** der Stapellauf fand in Anwesenheit von Lady X statt; **she was ~ed in Belfast** sie wurde in Belfast vom Stapel gelassen; **the rocket was ~ed into space** die Rakete wurde in den Weltraum geschossen.
  (b) *company, newspaper* gründen; *new product* einführen, auf den Markt bringen; *(with party, publicity) film, play, book* lancieren; *(bring out) film* anlaufen lassen; *play* auf die Bühne bringen; *book* herausbringen; *plan* in die Wege leiten; *programme, scheme* einführen; *policy* in Angriff nehmen; *shares* emittieren, ausgeben. **to ~ an offensive** *or* **attack against the enemy** zum Angriff gegen den Feind übergehen; **the attack was ~ed at 15.00 hours** der Angriff fand um 15^{00} Uhr statt; **to ~ sb into society** jdn in die Gesellschaft einführen; **to ~ pupils into the world** Schüler ins Leben entlassen; **to ~ sb on his way** jdm einen guten Start geben; **he helped ~ his son into the City** er brachte seinen Sohn in Finanzkreisen unter; **once he is ~ed on this subject ...** wenn er einmal mit diesem Thema angefangen hat *or* bei diesem Thema gelandet ist, ...; **now that he's ~ed himself on this long description** da er jetzt mit dieser langen Beschreibung losgelegt hat *(inf)*.
  (c) *(hurl)* schleudern. **he ~ed himself into the crowd** er stürzte sich in die Menge.
♦**launch forth** *vi see* **launch out (a, d)**.
♦**launch into** *vi* +*prep obj (question, attack etc vigorously)* angreifen. **the author ~es straight ~ his main theme** der Autor kommt gleich zum Hauptthema *or* springt gleich ins Hauptthema.
♦**launch out** *vi* **(a)** *(also ~ forth)* **the astronauts ~ed ~ into the unknown** die Astronauten starteten ins Unbekannte.
  (b) *(diversify)* sich verlegen *(in auf* +*acc)*. **the company ~ed ~ in several new directions** die Firma stieg in einige neue Branchen ein.
  (c) *(inf: spend a lot)* **to ~ ~ (into extravagance)** sich in Unkosten stürzen; **now we can afford to ~ ~ a bit** jetzt können wir es uns leisten, etwas mehr auszugeben *(on für)*.
  (d) *(start: also ~ forth)* anfangen *(into sth* mit etw, etw *acc)*. **to ~ ~ into a new career** eine neue Karriere starten; **to ~ ~ into a violent speech** er ließ eine wütende Rede vom Stapel *(inf)*; **he ~ed ~ into a violent attack on the government** er ließ wütende Angriffe gegen die Regierung vom Stapel *(inf) or* losderung der/des ... los *(inf)*; **he ~ed ~ into a description of ...** er legte mit einer Schilderung der/des ... los *(inf)*.
launching [ˈlɔːntʃɪŋ] *n see* **launch 1 (b, c)**.
launching: **~ pad** *n* Start- *or* Abschußrampe *f*; *(fig)* Sprungbrett *nt*; **~ party** *n (of film, play)* Premierenfeier *f*; **~ site** *n* Abschußbasis *f*.
launder [ˈlɔːndəʳ] **1** *vt* waschen und bügeln. **2** *vi* waschen und bügeln. **modern fabrics ~ easily** moderne Gewebe lassen sich leicht reinigen *or* sind pflegeleicht.
launderette [ˌlɔːndəˈret] *n* Münzwäscherei *f*, Waschsalon *m*.
laundress [ˈlɔːndrɪs] *n* Waschfrau, Wäscherin *f*.
laundry [ˈlɔːndrɪ] *n (establishment)* Wäscherei *f*; *(clothes) (dirty)* schmutzige Wäsche; *(washed)* Wäsche *f*. **to do the ~** *(Wäsche)* waschen; **~man** Wäschemann *m (inf)*.
laureate [ˈlɔːrɪɪt] *n:* **poet ~** Hofdichter, Poeta laureatus *m*.
laurel [ˈlɒrəl] *n* Lorbeer *m*. **to look to one's ~s** sich behaupten (müssen); **to rest on one's ~s** sich auf seinen Lorbeeren ausruhen; **to win** *or* **gain one's ~s** Lorbeeren ernten.
lav [læv] *n (Brit inf)* Klo *nt (inf)*.
lava [ˈlɑːvə] *n* Lava *f*.
lavatory [ˈlævətrɪ] *n* Toilette *f*. **~ attendant** Toilettenfrau *f*/-mann *m*; **~ seat** Toilettensitz *m*, Brille *f (inf)*.
lavender [ˈlævɪndəʳ] **1** *n (flower)* Lavendel *m*; *(colour)* Lavendel *nt*. **2** *adj (colour)* lavendelfarben. **eyes of ~ blue** lavendelblaue Augen *pl*.
lavender: **~ bag** *n* Lavendelsäckchen *nt*; **~ water** *n* Lavendelwasser *nt*.
lavish [ˈlævɪʃ] **1** *adj* *gifts* großzügig, üppig; *praise* reich, überschwenglich; *affection* überschwenglich, überströmend; *banquet* üppig; *party* feudal; *(pej)* verschwenderisch; *expenditure* verschwenderisch. **to be ~ in** *or* *(form)* **of sth** mit etw verschwenderisch sein *or* umgehen; **he was ~ in his help to others** er half anderen großzügig; **he's ~ in giving money to good causes** für gute Zwecke spendet er großzügig Geld; **you were very ~ with the cream** du hast ja mit der Sahne nicht gespart; **the author is a little too ~ with the adjectives** der Autor geht mit den Adjektiven etwas zu verschwenderisch um; **to be ~ with one's money** das Geld mit vollen Händen ausgeben.
  2 *vt* **to ~ sth on sb** jdn mit etw überhäufen *or* überschütten; **she ~ed food and drink on them** sie bewirtete sie fürstlich; **to ~ care on sth** viel Sorgfalt auf etw *(acc)* verwenden.
lavishly [ˈlævɪʃlɪ] *adv give* großzügig; *praise* überschwenglich, put paint on, spread reichlich; *entertain* üppig, reichlich. **they entertain ~** sie geben feudale Feste; **~ furnished** luxuriös *or* aufwendig eingerichtet; **to spend (money) ~** das Geld mit vollen Händen ausgeben *(on für)*; **he is ~ extravagant in his hospitality** seine Gastfreundschaft kennt keine Grenzen.
lavishness [ˈlævɪʃnɪs] *n (of gifts)* Großzügigkeit, Üppigkeit *f*; *(of praise, affection)* Überschwenglichkeit *f*; *(of banquet)*

Üppigkeit f; (of person) Großzügigkeit f; (pej) Verschwendungssucht f. **the ~ of the party/his expenditure** die feudale Party/seine verschwenderischen Ausgaben.

law [lɔː] n **(a)** (rule, Jewish, Sci) Gesetz nt. **~ of nature** Naturgesetz nt; **it's the ~** das ist Gesetz; **his word is ~** sein Wort ist Gesetz; **to become ~** rechtskräftig werden; **is there a ~ against it?** ist das verboten?; **there is no ~ against asking, is there?** (inf) man darf doch wohl noch fragen, oder?, he/his **behaviour is a ~ unto himself/itself** er macht, was er will, er/sein Benehmen ist (recht) eigenwillig.
(b) (body of laws) Gesetz nt no pl; (system) Recht nt. **in or under French ~** nach französischem Recht; **he is above/outside the ~** er steht über dem Gesetz/außerhalb des Gesetzes; **what is the ~ on drugs?** wie sind die Drogengesetze?; **to keep within the ~** sich im Rahmen des Gesetzes bewegen; **in ~** vor dem Gesetz; **ignorance is no defence in ~** Unwissenheit schützt vor Strafe nicht; **by ~** gesetzlich; **the ~ as it relates to property** die gesetzlichen Bestimmungen über das Eigentum.
(c) (as study) Jura no art, Recht(swissenschaft f) nt.
(d) (Sport) Regel f; (Art) Gesetz nt. **the ~s of harmony** die Harmonielehre; **one of the basic ~s of harmony** eins der grundlegenden Prinzipien der Harmonielehre.
(e) (operation of ~) **to practise ~** eine Anwaltspraxis haben; **to go to ~** vor Gericht gehen, den Rechtsweg beschreiten; **to take sb to ~** vor Gericht gehen, jdn vor Gericht bringen; **to take a case against sb** to **~** in einer Sache gegen jdn gerichtlich vorgehen. **to take the ~ into one's own hands** das Recht selbst in die Hand nehmen; **~ and order** Ruhe or Recht und Ordnung, Law and Order; **the forces of ~ and order** die Ordnungskräfte pl.
(f) **the ~** (inf) die Polente (sl); **I'll have the ~ on you** ich hole die Polizei; **he got the ~ on to me** er hat mir die Polizei auf den Hals gehetzt (inf).

law: **~-abiding** adj gesetzestreu; **~breaker** n Rechtsbrecher m; **~ court** n Gerichtshof m, Gericht nt; **~ enforcement** n the duty of the police is **~ enforcement** Aufgabe der Polizei ist es, dem Gesetz Geltung zu verschaffen; **~ enforcement officer** n Polizeibeamte(r) m.

lawful [ˈlɔːful] adj rechtmäßig. **~ wedded wife** rechtmäßig angetraute Frau; **will you take this man to be your ~ wedded husband?** willst du mit diesem Mann den Bund der Ehe eingehen?

lawfully [ˈlɔːfəlɪ] adv see adj. **he was ~ entitled to compensation** er hat einen Rechtsanspruch or rechtmäßigen Anspruch auf Entschädigung; **he was careful to carry on his activities ~** er achtete darauf, daß seine Handlungen im Rahmen des Gesetzes blieben.

lawgiver [ˈlɔːgɪvəʳ] n Gesetzgeber m.

lawless [ˈlɔːlɪs] adj act gesetzwidrig; person gesetzlos; country ohne Gesetzgebung. **~ seizure of power** unrechtmäßige Machtergreifung.

lawlessness [ˈlɔːlɪsnɪs] n Gesetzwidrigkeit f. **~ among young people** gesetzwidriges Verhalten unter Jugendlichen; **after the coup, the country reverted to ~** nach dem Staatsstreich fiel das Land in einen Zustand der Gesetzlosigkeit zurück.

lawn¹ [lɔːn] n (grass) Rasen m no pl. **the ~s in front of the houses** der Rasen vor den Häusern.

lawn² n (Tex) Batist, Linon m.

lawn: **~mower** n Rasenmäher m; **~ tennis** n Rasentennis, Lawn-Tennis nt.

law: **~ reports** npl Entscheidungs- or Fallsammlung f; (journal) Gerichtszeitung f; **~ school** n (US) juristische Fakultät; **~ student** n Jurastudent(in f) m, Student(in f) m der Rechte (form); **~suit** n Prozeß m, Klage f; **he brought a ~suit for damages** er strengte eine Schadensersatzklage an.

lawyer [ˈlɔːjəʳ] n (Rechts)anwalt m, (Rechts)anwältin f.

lax [læks] adj (+er) **(a)** lax; discipline also lasch; morals also locker, lose. **she is rather ~ in her relations with men** sie hat ein recht lockeres Verhältnis zu Männern; **to be ~ about sth** etw vernachlässigen; **he's ~ about washing/imposing discipline** er nimmt's mit dem Waschen/der Disziplin nicht so genau; **they are too ~ about doing their homework** sie machen ihre Hausaufgaben zu nachlässig; **I've been rather ~ about replying to your letters** ich habe mir mit der Beantwortung Ihrer Briefe reichlich viel Zeit gelassen; **things are very ~ at the school** in der Schule geht es sehr lax or undiszipliniert zu.
(b) **~ bowels** dünner Stuhl(gang).

laxative [ˈlæksətɪv] **1** adj abführend, laxativ (spec). **2** n Abführmittel, Laxativ(um) (spec) nt.

laxity [ˈlæksɪtɪ], **laxness** [ˈlæksnɪs] n (lack of vigour, discipline) Laxheit f; (carelessness also) Nachlässigkeit f. **the ~ of his private life** sein lockeres Leben; **his moral ~** seine lockeren or laxen moralischen Einstellungen; **the sexual ~ of our times** die lockeren Sitten or sexuelle Freizügigkeit unserer Zeit.

lay¹ [leɪ] n (Liter, Mus) Ballade f, Lied nt.

lay² adj Laien-. **~ opinion** die öffentliche Meinung, die Öffentlichkeit; **a ~ opinion** die Meinung eines Laien.

lay³ pret of **lie**.

lay⁴ (vb: pret, ptp **laid**) **1** n **(a)** Lage f; see **land** 1(a).
(b) (sl) **she's an easy ~** sie läßt jeden ran (sl); **she's a good ~** sie ist gut im Bett (inf); **that's/she is the best ~ I ever had** das war die beste Nummer, die ich je gemacht habe (sl)/sie hat's bisher am besten gebracht (sl).
2 vt **(a)** (place, put) legen (sth on sth etw auf etw acc). **to ~ (one's) hands on** (get hold of) erwischen, fassen; (find) finden; **to ~ a hand on sb** jdm etwas tun, jdm an jdn legen (geh); **I never laid a hand on him** ich habe ihn überhaupt nicht angefaßt or ihm nichts getan; **he grabs all the money he can ~ his hands on** er rafft alles Geld an sich, das ihm unter die Finger kommt.
(b) bricks, foundations, track legen; concrete gießen; cable, mains, pipes verlegen; road bauen, anlegen; carpet,

lino (ver)legen. **to ~ a floor with carpets** einen Boden mit Teppichen auslegen.
(c) (prepare) fire herrichten; table decken; mines, ambush legen; trap aufstellen; plans schmieden. **to ~ breakfast/lunch** den Frühstücks-/Mittagstisch decken; **to ~ a trap for sb** jdm eine Falle stellen.
(d) (non-material things) burden auferlegen (on sb jdm). **to ~ the blame for sth on sb/sth** jdm/einer Sache die Schuld an etw (dat) geben; **to ~ responsibility for sth on sb** jdn für etw verantwortlich machen; **to ~ an injunction on sb** eine Verfügung gegen jdn erlassen; **to ~ a tax on sth** etw mit einer Steuer belegen; **to ~ an embargo on sth** ein Embargo über etw (acc) verhängen; **the scene of the novel is laid in Ancient Rome** der Roman spielt im alten Rom, der Schauplatz des Romans ist das alte Rom; **the importance which he ~s on it** die Bedeutung, die er dieser Sache (dat) beimißt; **the stress which he ~s on it** der Nachdruck, den er darauf legt.
(e) (bring forward) complaint vorbringen (before bei); accusation erheben. **the police laid a charge of murder against him** die Polizei erstattete gegen ihn Anzeige wegen Mordes; **the crime was laid to his charge** das Verbrechen wurde ihm zur Last gelegt; **he laid his case before them** er trug ihnen seinen Fall vor; **he laid information with the police about his accomplices** (form) er sagte bei der Polizei über seine Komplizen aus.
(f) dust binden; ghost austreiben; fear zerstreuen; doubts beseitigen. **he laid him sprawling** er schlug ihn nieder or zu Boden; **to ~ waste** verwüsten; see **low¹, open** etc.
(g) eggs (hen) legen; (fish, insects) ablegen.
(h) bet abschließen; money setzen. **to ~ a bet on sth** auf etw (acc) wetten; **I only ~ bets on certainties** ich wette nur, wenn die Sache ganz sicher ist; **I ~ you a fiver on it!** ich wette mit dir um 5 Pfund!; **I'll ~ you that …** ich wette mit dir, daß …; **I'll ~ you anything …** ich gehe mit dir jede Wette ein.
(i) (sl) **to ~ a woman** eine Frau aufs Kreuz legen (sl); **he just wants to get laid** er will nur bumsen (inf).
3 vi (hen) legen.

♦**lay about 1** vi um sich schlagen. **2** vt sep losschlagen gegen.

♦**lay aside** or **away** vt sep, **lay by** vt sep (keep in reserve, save) beiseite or auf die Seite legen; (cast away) ablegen; doubts aufgeben; plans etc auf Eis legen.

♦**lay back** vt sep ears anlegen; person zurücklegen.

♦**lay before** vt +prep obj **to ~ sth ~ sb** plan jdm etw vorlegen; ideas also jdm etw unterbreiten; claim, complaint etw bei jdm vorbringen.

♦**lay by** vt sep beiseite or auf die Seite legen.

♦**lay down** vt sep **(a)** book, pen etc hinlegen. **he laid his bag ~ on the table** er legte seine Tasche auf den Tisch; **she laid herself ~ to sleep** (liter) sie begab sich zur Ruhe.
(b) (give up) burden ablegen; office niederlegen; **to ~ one's arms** die Waffen niederlegen; **to ~ one's life** sein Leben geben or opfern.
(c) (impose, establish) condition festsetzen or -legen; policy festsetzen, bestimmen; rules aufstellen, festlegen; price festsetzen, vorschreiben. **it is laid ~ that** es wurde festgelegt, daß; **to ~ the law** (inf) Vorschriften machen (to sb jdm).
(d) (store) lagern.
(e) ship auf Stapel legen.
(f) deposit hinterlegen.

♦**lay in** vt sep food etc einlagern; supplies also anlegen. **they have laid ~ plenty of water** sie haben (sich dat) einen großen Wasservorrat angelegt.

♦**lay into** vi +prep obj **to ~ ~ sb** auf jdn losgehen; (verbally) jdn fertigmachen (inf) or runterputzen (inf).

♦**lay off 1** vi (inf: stop) aufhören (prep obj mit). **~ ~, will you?** hör (mal) auf, ja?; **~ ~ it!** hör auf damit!, laß das!; **you'll have to ~ ~ smoking** du wirst das Rauchen aufgeben müssen (inf); **I wish you'd ~ ~ coming here every day** ich wünschte, du würdest nicht mehr jeden Tag hierherkommen; **~ ~ my little brother, will you!** laß bloß meinen kleinen Bruder in Ruhe!
2 vt sep workers Feierschichten machen lassen. **to be laid ~** Feierschichten einlegen müssen.

♦**lay on** vt sep **(a)** (apply) paint auftragen; see **thick**.
(b) (prepare, offer) hospitality bieten (for sb jdm); (supply) entertainment sorgen für; excursion veranstalten; extra buses einsetzen; water, electricity anschließen. **if you ~ ~ the drinks I'll get the food** wenn du die Getränke stellst, besorge ich das Essen; **she had laid ~ a lot of food** sie hatte sehr viel zu essen aufgetischt; **an extra flight was laid ~** eine Sondermaschine wurde eingesetzt or bereitgestellt.
(c) (impose) **to ~ a tax ~ sth** etw mit einer Steuer belegen, etw besteuern.

♦**lay out** vt sep **(a)** ausbreiten. **the vast plain laid ~ before us** die weite Ebene, die sich vor uns ausbreitete.
(b) (prepare) clothes zurechtlegen; corpse (waschen und) aufbahren.
(c) (design, arrange) anlegen, planen; garden also gestalten; room aufteilen; rooms in house verteilen, anordnen; office aufteilen, anordnen; book gestalten; page umbrechen; (in magazines) das Layout (+gen) machen.
(d) money (spend) ausgeben; (invest) investieren.
(e) (knock out) **to ~ sb ~** jdn k.o. schlagen, jdn erledigen (inf); **three whiskies were enough to ~ him ~** nach drei Whiskys war er erledigt (inf); **he laid himself ~ cold when he fell downstairs** er verlor das Bewußtsein, als er die Treppe hinunterfiel.
2 vr (dated: take trouble) sich bemühen, sich (dat) Mühe geben. **to ~ oneself ~ to please** sich Mühe geben, zu gefallen.

♦**lay over** vi (US) Aufenthalt haben.

♦**lay to** vi (Naut) beidrehen.

♦**lay up** vt sep **(a)** (store) lagern; supply anlegen; (amass, save) anhäufen, ansammeln. **he's ~ing ~ trouble for himself** in

the future er wird später noch (viel) Ärger bekommen.
  (b) (*immobilize*) *ship* auflegen; *boat* aufbocken; *car* stilllegen, einmotten (*inf*). **to be laid ~ (in bed)** auf der Nase (*inf*) *or* im Bett liegen; **you'd better take it easy or you'll ~ yourself ~** Sie müssen etwas langsamer treten, sonst liegen Sie nachher flach *or* auf der Nase (*inf*).

lay: **~about** *n* Nichtstuer, Arbeitsscheue(r) *m*; **~ brother** *n* Laienbruder *m*; **~by** *n* (*Brit*) (*in town*) Parkbucht *f*; (*in country*) Parkplatz *m*; (*big*) Rastplatz *m*.

layer ['leɪəʳ] **1** *n* **(a)** Schicht *f* (*also Geol*), Lage *f*. **to arrange the meat in ~s** das Fleisch lagenweise anordnen; **we climbed through ~ upon ~ of cloud** wir stiegen durch eine Wolkenschicht nach der anderen auf; **the cake was covered with ~ upon ~ of chocolate** der Kuchen war mit vielen Schokoladenschichten überzogen; **~ cake** Schichttorte *f*.
  (b) (*Hort*) Ableger *m*.
  (c) (*hen*) Legehenne *f*.
  2 *vt* (*Hort*) absenken.

layette [leɪ'et] *n* Babyausstattung *f*.
lay figure *n* Gliederpuppe *f*; (*fig*) Marionette *f*.
laying ['leɪɪŋ] *n*: **~ on of hands** Handauflegen *nt*.
lay: **~man** *n* Laie *m*; **~-off** *n further* **~-offs were unavoidable** weitere Arbeiter mußten Feierschichten einlegen; **during the ~-off period** während der Feierschichten; **~out** *n* Anordnung, Anlage *f*; (*Typ*) Layout *nt*; **the standard ~out of German stations** wie deutsche Bahnhöfe normalerweise angelegt sind; **we have changed the ~out of this office** wir haben dieses Büro anders aufgeteilt; **our house has a different ~out** unser Haus hat eine andere Zimmerverteilung *or* ist anders angelegt; **~over** *n* (*US*) Aufenthalt *m*; **~reader** *n* Vorbeter, Hilfsdiakon *m*; **~ sister** *n* Laienschwester *f*; **~woman** *n* Laie *m*.
laze [leɪz] **1** *n* **to have a ~** faulenzen; **to have a long ~ in bed** lange faul im Bett (liegen) bleiben. **2** *vi* faulenzen.
♦ **laze about** *or* **around** *vi* faulenzen, auf der faulen Haut liegen. **stop lazing ~** steh/sitz *etc* nicht so faul herum!
♦ **laze away** *vt sep* verbummeln.
lazily ['leɪzɪlɪ] *adv* faul; (*languidly, unhurriedly*) träge.
laziness ['leɪzɪnɪs] *n* Faulheit *f*; (*languor*) Trägheit *f*.
lazy ['leɪzɪ] *adj* (+*er*) (*not inclined to work*) faul; (*slow-moving*) langsam, träge; (*lacking activity*) träge. **~ little streams** träge fließende kleine Bäche *pl*; **we had a ~ holiday** wir haben im Urlaub nur gefaulenzt; **I enjoy a ~ day at home** ich mache mir gerne einen faulen *or* gemütlichen Tag zu Hause.
lazybones ['leɪzɪbəʊnz] *n sing* (*inf*) Faulpelz *m*, Faultier *nt*.
lb *n* (*weight*) ≈ Pfd *nt*.
lbw *abbr of* **leg before wicket**.
LEA (*Brit*) *abbr of* **Local Education Authority**.
lea [liː] *n* (*poet*) Au(e) *f* (*poet*), Wiesengrund *m* (*liter*).
leach [liːtʃ] *vt* (durch)filtern; (*extract*) auslaugen.
lead¹ [led] **1** *n* **(a)** (*metal*) Blei *nt*. **they filled him full of ~** (*inf*) sie pumpten ihn mit Blei voll (*sl*). **(b)** (*in pencil*) Graphit *nt*; (*single ~*) Mine *f*. **(c)** (*Naut*) Lot *nt*. **(d)** **~s** *pl* (*on roof*) Bleiplatten *pl*; (*in window*) Bleifassung *f*. **2** *vt* (*weight with ~*) mit Blei beschweren.
lead² [liːd] (*vb: pret, ptp* **led**) **1** *n* **(a)** (*front position*) Spitzenposition *f*; (*leading position, Sport*) Führung, Spitze *f*; (*in league etc*) Tabellenspitze *f*. **to be in the ~** führend sein, in Führung liegen; (*Sport*) in Führung *or* vorn liegen, führen; **to take the ~, to move into the ~** in Führung gehen, die Führung übernehmen; (*in league*) Tabellenführer werden; **he took the ~ from the German runner** er ging vor dem deutschen Läufer in Führung; **Japan took the ~ from Germany in exports** Japan lief Deutschland auf dem Exportmarkt den Rang ab.
  (b) (*distance, time ahead*) Vorsprung *m*. **to have two minutes' ~ over sb** zwei Minuten Vorsprung vor jdm haben.
  (c) (*example*) Beispiel *nt*. **to give sb a ~** jdm etw vormachen; **to take the ~, to show a ~** mit gutem Beispiel vorangehen.
  (d) (*clue*) Indiz *nt*, Anhaltspunkt *m*; (*in guessing etc*) Hinweis, Tip *m*. **the police have a ~** die Polizei hat eine Spur; **it gave the police a ~** das brachte die Polizei auf die Spur.
  (e) (*Cards*) it's my **~** ich fange an.
  (f) (*Theat*) (*part*) Hauptrolle *f*; (*person*) Hauptdarsteller(in *f*) *m*. **to sing the ~** die Titelpartie *or* die tragende Partie singen.
  (g) (*leash*) Leine *f*. **on a ~** an der Leine.
  (h) (*Elec*) Leitung(skabel *nt*) *f*, Kabel *nt*; (*from separate source*) Zuleitung *f* (*form*).
  2 *vt* **(a)** (*conduct*) *person, animal* führen; *water* leiten. **that road will ~ you back to the station** auf dieser Straße kommen Sie zum Bahnhof zurück; **to ~ the way** (*lit, fig*) vorangehen; (*fig: be superior*) führend sein; **all this talk is ~ing us nowhere** dieses ganze Gerede bringt uns nicht weiter; **each crossreference led me to another** ich wurde immer weiter verwiesen; **the argument led us round in a circle** unsere Argumentation drehte sich im Kreis.
  (b) (*be the leader of, direct*) (an)führen; *expedition, team* leiten; *regiment* führen; *movement, revolution* anführen; *orchestra* (*conductor*) leiten; (*first violin*) führen. **to ~ a government** an der Spitze einer Regierung stehen, Regierungschef sein; **to ~ a party** Parteivorsitzender sein, den Parteivorsitz führen.
  (c) (*be first in*) anführen. **they led us by 30 seconds** sie lagen mit 30 Sekunden vor uns (*dat*); **Britain ~s the world in textiles** Großbritannien ist auf dem Gebiet der Textilproduktion führend in der Welt.
  (d) *card* ausspielen.
  (e) *life* führen. **to ~ a life of luxury/misery** in Luxus/im Elend leben, ein Luxusleben/elendes Leben führen; **to ~ sb a wretched life** jdm das Leben schwermachen.
  (f) (*influence*) **to ~ sb to do sth** jdn dazu bringen, etw zu tun; **what led him to change his mind?** wie kam er dazu, seine Meinung zu ändern?; **to ~ sb to believe that ...** jdm den Ein-

druck vermitteln, daß ...; **jdn glauben machen, daß ...** (*geh*); **I am led to believe that ...** ich habe Grund zu der Annahme, daß ...; **to ~ sb into error** jdn irreleiten *or* fehlleiten; **to ~ sb into trouble** jdn in Schwierigkeiten bringen; **he is easily led** er läßt sich leicht beeinflussen; (*deceive*) er läßt sich leicht täuschen *or* sich (*dat*) leicht etwas weismachen; **this led me to the conclusion that ...** daraus schloß ich, daß ...; **I am led to the conclusion that ...** ich komme zu dem Schluß, daß ...; **what ~s you to think that?** woraus schließen Sie das?
  (g) *wire, flex* legen, entlangführen.
  3 *vi* **(a)** (*go in front*) vorangehen; (*in race*) in Führung liegen. **to ~ by 10 metres** einen Vorsprung von 10 Metern haben, mit 10 Metern in Führung liegen; **he easily ~s** er liegt klar in Führung; **he always follows where his brother ~s** er macht alles nach, was sein Bruder macht; **the "Times" led with a story about the financial crisis** die "Times" berichtete auf der ersten Seite ausführlich über die Finanzkrise; **he always ~s with his right** (*Boxing*) er führt seine Schläge immer mit der Rechten aus.
  (b) (*be a leader, also in dancing*) führen. **he had shown the ability to ~** er hat gezeigt, daß er Führungsqualitäten besitzt.
  (c) (*Cards*) ausspielen (*with sth* etw). **who ~s?** wer spielt aus?, wer fängt an?
  (d) *street etc* führen, gehen. **it ~s into that room** es führt zu diesem Raum; **this road ~s nowhere** diese Straße führt nirgendwohin *or* geht nicht weiter.
  (e) (*result in, cause*) führen (*to* zu). **all this talk is ~ing nowhere** dieses ganze Gerede führt zu nichts; **remarks like that could ~ to trouble** solche Bemerkungen können unangenehme Folgen haben; **what will all these strikes ~ to?** wo sollen all diese Streiks hinführen?
♦ **lead along** *vt sep* führen. **he led him ~ the street** er führte ihn die Straße entlang.
♦ **lead aside** *vt sep* auf die Seite *or* beiseite nehmen.
♦ **lead away 1** *vt sep* wegführen *or* -bringen; *criminal, prisoner* abführen. **we must not allow this argument to ~ us ~ from the matter in hand** wir dürfen uns durch dieses Argument nicht vom eigentlichen Thema abbringen lassen. **2** *vi* **this is ~ing ~ from the subject** das führt vom Thema ab.
♦ **lead off 1** *vt sep* abführen. **a policeman led the drunk man ~ the pitch** ein Polizist führte den Betrunkenen vom Platz.
  2 *vi* **(a)** (*go off from*) abgehen. **several streets led ~ the square** mehrere Straßen gingen von dem Platz ab.
  (b) (*start*) beginnen. **my partner led ~ with the ten of hearts** mein Partner spielte die Herz Zehn aus.
♦ **lead on 1** *vi usu imper* **~ ~,** **sergeant!** führen Sie an, Oberfeldwebel!; **~ ~, John!** geh vor, John!
  2 *vt sep* (*deceive*) anführen (*inf*), hinters Licht führen; (*tease*) aufziehen, auf den Arm nehmen (*inf*). **he led us ~ to believe that we would get the money** er hat uns vorgemacht, wir würden das Geld bekommen; **she's just ~ing him ~** sie hält ihn nur zum Narren *or* führt ihn nur an der Nase herum.
♦ **lead out 1** *vt sep* hinausführen. **he led his wife ~ onto the dance floor** er führte seine Frau auf die Tanzfläche. **2** *vi* hinausgehen.
♦ **lead up 1** *vt sep* hinaufführen (*to* auf +*acc*); (*lead across*) führen (*to* zu). **to ~ sb ~ the garden path** (*fig*) jdm etwas vormachen, jdn an der Nase herumführen.
  2 *vi* **(a)** (*come before*) **the events/years that led ~ to the war** die Ereignisse/Jahre, die dem Krieg voran- *or* vorausgingen.
  (b) (*introduce*) **he was obviously ~ing ~ to an important announcement** er schickte sich offensichtlich an, etwas Wichtiges anzukündigen; **his speech was obviously ~ing ~ to an important announcement** seine Rede war offensichtlich die Einleitung zu einer wichtigen Ankündigung; **what are you ~ing ~ to?** worauf willst du hinaus?; **what's all this ~ing ~ to?** was soll das Ganze?
leaded ['ledɪd] *adj window* bleiverglast, Bleiglas-.
leaden ['ledn] *adj* **(a)** (*old: of lead*) bleiern (*geh*), Blei-. **(b)** *sky, colour* bleiern (*geh*); *heart, limbs* bleischwer.
leader ['liːdəʳ] *n* **(a)** Führer *m*; (*of union, party also*) Vorsitzende(r) *mf*; (*military also*) Befehlshaber *m*; (*of gang, rebels*) Anführer *m*; (*of expedition, project*) Leiter(in *f*) *m*; (*Sport*) (*in league*) Tabellenführer *m*; (*in race*) der/das Erste; (*Mus*) (*of orchestra*) Konzertmeister *m*; (*of choir*) Führer *m*; (*of band*) erster Bläser; (*of jazz band, pop group*) Leader *m*. **to be the ~** (*in race, competition*) in Führung liegen; **the ~s** (*in race, competition*) die Spitzengruppe; **~ of the opposition** Oppositionsführer(in *f*) *m*; **the ~s of fashion** die Modemacher *pl*; **the product is a ~ in its field** dieses Produkt ist ein Spitzenreiter *m or* ist auf diesem Gebiet führend; **we are still the ~s in biochemical research** wir sind auf dem Gebiet der biochemischen Forschung immer noch führend; **has he the qualities to be a ~ of men?** hat er Führungsqualitäten?
  (b) (*Brit Press*) Leitartikel *m*. **~ writer** Leitartikler *m*.
leaderless ['liːdəlɪs] *adj* führerlos, ohne Führer; *party, union* führungslos.
leadership ['liːdəʃɪp] *n* **(a)** Führung, Leitung *f*; (*office also*) Vorsitz *m*. **under the ~ of** unter (der) Führung von; **a crisis in the ~** eine Führungskrise. **(b)** (*quality*) Führungsqualitäten *pl*. **the country is looking for ~** das Land ruft nach einer straffen Führung.
lead-in ['liːdɪn] *n* Einführung, Einleitung *f* (*to* in +*acc*).
leading ['liːdɪŋ] *adj* **(a)** (*first*) vorderste(r, s); *runner, horse, car also* führend. **the ~ car in the procession** das die Kolonne anführende Auto.
  (b) (*most important*) *person, company* führend; *sportsman, product* Spitzen-; *issue* Haupt-, wichtigste(r, s); *part, rôle* (*Theat*) tragend, Haupt-; (*fig*) führend. **we are a ~ company in ...** unsere Firma ist führend auf dem Gebiet ... (+*gen*).
leading: **~ article** *n* Leitartikel *m*; **~ edge** *n* (*Aviat*)

(Flügel)vorderkante f; ~ **lady** n Hauptdarstellerin f; ~ **light** n Nummer eins f; (person also) großes Licht, Leuchte f; ~ **man** n Hauptdarsteller m; ~ **question** n Suggestivfrage f.

lead [led-]: ~ **pencil** n Bleistift m; ~**-poisoning** n Bleivergiftung f; ~ **shot** n Schrot m or nt.

lead story ['li:d-] n Hauptartikel m.

leaf [li:f] **1** n, pl **leaves** (a) Blatt nt. to be in ~ grün sein; to come into ~ grün werden, ausschlagen (poet); he swept the leaves into a pile er fegte das Laub auf einen Haufen.

(b) (of paper) Blatt nt. to take a ~ out of sb's book sich (dat) von jdm eine Scheibe abschneiden; to turn over a new ~ einen neuen Anfang machen; it's time you turned over a new ~, said the teacher es wird Zeit, daß du dich änderst, sagte der Lehrer.

(c) (of table) Ausziehplatte f. pull the leaves out zieh den Tisch aus!

(d) (of metal) Folie f. **gold/silver** ~ Blattgold/-silber nt.

2 vi to ~ **through a book** ein Buch durchblättern.

leaf: ~ **bud** n Blattknospe f; ~**less** adj blattlos, kahl.

leaflet ['li:flɪt] n (a) Prospekt m; (single page) Hand- or Reklamezettel m; (with instructions) Merkblatt nt; (handout) Flugblatt nt; (brochure for information) Broschüre f, Informationsblatt nt. (b) (young leaf) Blättchen nt.

leafy ['li:fɪ] adj branch, tree grün, belaubt; bower, lane grün.

league¹ [li:g] n (measure) Wegstunde f.

league² n (a) (treaty) Bündnis nt, Bund m; (organization) Verband m, Liga f. L~ **of Nations** Völkerbund m; to enter into a ~ ein Bündnis eingehen, einen Bund schließen; to be in ~ **with sb** mit jdm gemeinsame Sache machen; to be in ~ **with the devil** mit dem Teufel im Bunde sein; these two boys must be in ~ **with each other** diese beiden Jungen stecken sicher unter einer Decke (inf); to be in ~ **against sb** sich gegen jdn verbündet haben.

(b) (Sport) Liga f. the club is top of the ~ der Klub ist Tabellen- or Ligaführer; he was not in the same ~ (fig) er hatte nicht das gleiche Format; Peter's car is not in the same ~ as Wendy's Peters Auto ist eine Nummer kleiner als Wendys.

league: ~ **game** n Ligaspiel nt; ~ **leaders** npl Tabellenführer m; ~ **table** n Tabelle f.

leak [li:k] **1** n (a) (hole) undichte Stelle; (in container) Loch nt; (Naut) Leck nt. to have a ~ undicht sein; (bucket etc) laufen, lecken (N Ger); my Biro has a ~ mein Kugelschreiber läuft aus or ist nicht dicht; there's a ~ in the gas pipe die Gasleitung ist undicht; the rain is coming in through a ~ in the roof es regnet durchs Dach herein.

(b) (escape of liquid) Leck nt. a gas ~ eine undichte Stelle in der Gasleitung; the tunnel was flooded because of the ~s der Tunnel wurde vom eindringenden Wasser überflutet; a faulty joint caused a ~ of gas durch die fehlerhafte Verbindung strömte Gas aus.

(c) (fig) undichte Stelle. there was a ~ of information es sind Informationen durchgesickert; a security/news ~ eine undichte Stelle; the news ~ may have been the result of carelessness die Nachricht kann aufgrund einer Unachtsamkeit durchgesickert sein; a ~ to the press eine Indiskretion der Presse gegenüber; they wanted to break the news gently by a series of ~s to the press sie wollten die Nachricht langsam an die Presse durchsickern lassen.

(d) (sl) to go for or have a ~ pissen gehen (sl).

2 vt (a) durchlassen. that tank is ~ing acid aus diesem Tank läuft Säure aus.

(b) (fig) information, story, plans zuspielen (to sb jdm).

3 vi (a) (ship, receptacle, pipe) lecken; (roof) undicht or nicht dicht sein; (pen) auslaufen, undicht sein.

(b) (gas) ausströmen, entweichen; (liquid) auslaufen; (ooze out) tropfen (from aus). water is ~ing through the roof das Wasser tropft or sickert durch das Dach, es regnet durch (das Dach durch); to ~ away auslaufen.

◆**leak out** vi sep news zuspielen (to sb jdm). **2** vi (a) (liquid) auslaufen, durchsickern. (b) (news) durchsickern.

leakage ['li:kɪdʒ] n (a) (act) Auslaufen nt; (of body fluids) Austreten nt. there's a ~ of water into the oil da läuft or tropft Wasser ins Öl; there's still a slight ~ es ist immer noch etwas undicht; there's still a ~ in the pipe das Rohr ist immer noch undicht; the ground was polluted by a ~ of chemicals der Boden war durch auslaufende Chemikalien verunreinigt.

(b) (fig) a ~ of information (act) Durchsickern nt von Informationen, the government was worried by repeated security ~s die Regierung war besorgt, weil wiederholt Informationen durchgesickert waren.

leaky ['li:kɪ] adj (+er) undicht; boat also leck.

lean¹ [li:n] **1** adj (+er) (a) (thin) mager, dünn; face, person schmal; (through lack of food) hager; meat mager. to grow ~ schlank or schmal werden.

(b) (poor) year, harvest mager.

2 n mageres Fleisch.

lean² (vb: pret, ptp ~**ed** or **leant**) **1** n Neigung f.

2 vt (a) (put in sloping position) lehnen (against gegen, an +acc). to ~ one's head on sb's shoulder seinen Kopf an jds Schulter (acc) lehnen.

(b) (rest) aufstützen (on auf +dat or acc). to ~ one's elbow on sth sich mit dem Ellbogen auf etw (acc) stützen.

3 vi (a) (be off vertical) sich neigen (to nach); (trees) sich biegen. the box was ~ing dangerously on its side die Kiste neigte sich gefährlich auf die Seite; he ~t across the counter er beugte sich über den Ladentisch; a motorcyclist should ~ into the corner ein Motorradfahrer sollte sich in die Kurve legen.

(b) (rest) sich lehnen. to ~ against sth sich gegen etw lehnen; ~ing against the bar an die Bar gelehnt; she ~t on my arm sie stützte sich auf meinen Arm; he ~t on the edge of the

table er stützte sich auf die Tischkante; to ~ on one's elbow sich mit dem Ellbogen aufstützen.

(c) (tend in opinion etc) to ~ **towards the left/socialism** nach links/zum Sozialismus tendieren; to ~ **towards sb's opinion** zu jds Ansicht neigen or tendieren; **which way does he** ~? in welche Richtung tendiert er?; he started to ~ **away from the party line** er entfernte sich allmählich von der Parteilinie; at least they're ~ing in the direction of reform sie neigen immerhin Reformen (dat) zu.

◆**lean back** vi sich zurücklehnen.

◆**lean forward** vi sich vorbeugen.

◆**lean on** vi (a) (depend) to ~ ~ **sb** sich auf jdn verlassen. (b) (inf: put pressure on) to ~ ~ **sb** jdn bearbeiten (inf) or beknien (inf); **they** ~**t** ~ **him too hard** sie haben ihn zu sehr unter Druck gesetzt (inf).

◆**lean out** vi sich hinauslehnen (of aus).

◆**lean over** vi (a) (be off vertical) sich (vor)neigen.

(b) sich vorbeugen. **they** ~ ~ **the side of the bridge** sie beugten sich über das Brückengeländer; he ~**t** ~ **her shoulder** er beugte sich über ihre Schulter; see backwards.

leaning ['li:nɪŋ] **1** adj schräg, schief. the **L**~ **Tower of Pisa** der Schiefe Turm von Pisa.

2 n Hang m, Neigung f. he had a ~ **towards the left** er hatte einen Hang nach links; **what are his** ~**s?** was sind seine Neigungen?; **artistic** ~**s** künstlerische Neigungen pl.

leanness ['li:nnɪs] n Magerkeit f. the ~ of his face sein schmales Gesicht; (through lack of food) sein hageres Gesicht.

leant [lent] pret, ptp of **lean**.

lean-to ['li:ntu:] **1** n Anbau m; (shelter) Wetterschutz m or -schirm m. **2** adj angebaut.

leap [li:p] (vb: pret, ptp ~**ed** or **leapt**) **1** n Sprung, Satz (inf) m. in one ~, at a ~ mit einem Satz; to take a ~ at sth einen Satz (acc) machen, über etw (acc) setzen; a great ~ **forward** (fig) ein großer Sprung nach vorn; a ~ **in the dark** (fig) ein Sprung ins Ungewisse; by ~**s and bounds** (fig) sprunghaft.

2 vt springen or setzen über (+acc). he ~**t the horse across** the ditch er ließ das Pferd über den Graben springen.

3 vi springen. my heart ~**ed (with joy)** mein Herz hüpfte vor Freude (geh), mein Herz machte vor Freude einen Sprung; to ~ **about** herumspringen; to ~ **for joy** vor Freude hüpfen, Freudensprünge machen; **try to** ~ **over to the other side** versuch mal, auf die andere Seite zu springen or hinüberzuspringen; to ~ **to one's feet** aufspringen; he ~**t to her assistance** er sprang ihr zu Hilfe; **the house** ~**t into view** das Haus kam plötzlich in Sicht or tauchte plötzlich auf; see look.

◆**leap at** vt insep to ~ ~ **a chance** eine Gelegenheit beim Schopf packen, sofort zugreifen; to ~ ~ **an offer** sich (förmlich) auf ein Angebot stürzen.

◆**leap out** vi (a) (jump out) hinaus-/herausspringen (of aus +dat). he ~ ~ **of the car** er sprang aus dem Auto.

(b) (colours) ins Auge springen, hervorstechen. **the bright colours** ~ ~ **at you** die hellen Farben springen einem ins Auge.

◆**leap up** vi (person, animals) aufspringen; (flames) hochschlagen; (prices) sprunghaft ansteigen, emporschnellen. he ~**t** ~ **from behind the wall** er sprang hinter der Mauer hervor; to ~ ~ **into the air** in die Höhe springen.

leapfrog ['li:pfrɒg] **1** n Bockspringen nt. to play ~ Bockspringen spielen or machen (inf).

2 vi bockspringen. **the children** ~**ged over one another** die Kinder spielten or machten (inf) Bocksprünge.

3 vt he ~**ged him** er machte einen Bocksprung über ihn; he ~**ged his way to the top of the company** er machte in der Firma eine Blitzkarriere; he ~**ged his way to success** er machte eine Blitzkarriere.

leap year n Schaltjahr nt.

leapt [lept] pret, ptp of **leap**.

learn [lɜ:n] pret, ptp ~**ed** or **learnt 1** vt (a) (gain knowledge, skill etc) lernen; language also erlernen. **where did you** ~ **that habit?** wo hast du dir das angewöhnt?; I ~**t (how) to swim** ich habe schwimmen gelernt; **we** ~**t (how) to write business letters** wir lernten Geschäftsbriefe schreiben.

(b) (be informed) erfahren. I can't play the piano, but I'm hoping to ~ ich kann nicht Klavier spielen, aber ich hoffe, es zu lernen; **he'll never** ~! er lernt es nie!; some people never ~! manche lernen's nie!; to ~ **from experience** aus der or durch Erfahrung lernen.

2 vi (a) (gain knowledge etc) lernen. I can't play the piano, but I'm hoping to ~ ich kann nicht Klavier spielen, aber ich hoffe, es zu lernen; **he'll never** ~! er lernt es nie!; some people never ~! manche lernen's nie!; to ~ **from experience** aus der or durch Erfahrung lernen.

(b) (find out) hören, erfahren (about, of von).

◆**learn off** vt sep lernen.

◆**learn up** vt sep (learn by study) lernen, pauken (inf); (memorize) (auswendig) lernen.

learned ['lɜ:nɪd] adj gelehrt; book also, journal wissenschaftlich; society also, profession akademisch. a ~ **man** ein Gelehrter m; my ~ **colleague** mein geschätzter Kollege.

learnedly ['lɜ:nɪdlɪ] adv gelehrt.

learner ['lɜ:nəʳ] n Anfänger(in f) m; (student) Lernende(r) mf; (~ **driver**) Fahrschüler(in f) m. ~**s of languages** Sprachschüler or -studenten pl; **special classes for slow** ~**s** Sonderklassen pl für lernschwache Schüler.

learning ['lɜ:nɪŋ] n (a) (act) Lernen nt. difficulties encountered during the ~ of geometry/English Schwierigkeiten beim Erlernen der Geometrie/beim Englischlernen.

(b) (erudition) Gelehrsamkeit, Gelehrtheit f. a man of ~ ein Gelehrter m; the ~ **contained in these volumes** das in diesen Bänden enthaltene Wissen; **seat of** ~ Stätte f der Gelehrsamkeit.

learnt [lɜ:nt] pret, ptp of **learn**.

lease [li:s] **1** n (of land, farm, business premises etc) Pacht f; (contract) Pachtvertrag m; (of house, flat, office) Miete f; (contract) Mietvertrag m. the ~ **was prematurely terminated** die Pacht or das Pachtverhältnis/das Mietverhältnis wurde vorzeitig beendet; **to take a ~ on a house** ein Haus mieten; **to take a ~ on business premises** ein Geschäft(sgrundstück) *nt* pachten; **to occupy a house on a 99-year ~** ein Haus auf 99 Jahre pachten; **you can buy the ~ for a period of 99 years** Sie können einen Pachtvertrag für 99 Jahre abschließen; **we have the house/farm on a ~** wir haben das Haus gemietet/den Bauernhof gepachtet; **to let sth out on ~** etw in Pacht geben, etw verpachten/vermieten; **to give sb/sth a new ~ of life** jdm/einer Sache (neuen) Aufschwung geben.

2 *vt* (*take*) pachten (*from* von), in Pacht nehmen (*from* bei); mieten (*from* von); (*give: also ~ out*) verpachten (*to* an +*acc*), in Pacht geben (*to sb* jdm); vermieten (*to* an +*acc*).

lease: **~hold 1** *n* (*property*) Pachtbesitz *m*; (*land also*) Pachtgrundstück *nt*; (*building also*) gepachtetes Gebäude; (*contract, tenure*) Pachtvertrag *m*; **who has the ~hold on the property?** wer hat das Land/Gebäude gepachtet?; **we own the house on ~hold** wir haben das Haus langfristig gepachtet; **~hold reform** Mietrechtsreform *f*; **2** *adj* gepachtet, in Pacht; *property* Pacht-; **~holder** *n* Pächter *m*.

leash [li:ʃ] *n* Leine *f*. **on a ~** an der Leine; *see* **strain¹**.

least [li:st] **1** *adj* (**a**) (*slightest, smallest*) geringste(r, s). (**b**) (*with uncountable nouns*) wenigste(r, s). **he has the ~ money** er hat am wenigsten Geld.

2 *adv* (**a**) (+*vb*) am wenigsten. **~ of all would I wish to offend him** auf gar keinen Fall möchte ich ihn beleidigen.

(**b**) (+*adj*) **possible expenditure** möglichst geringe Kosten; **the ~ expensive car** das billigste *or* preiswerteste Auto; **the ~ difficult method** die einfachste Methode; **the ~ important matter** das Unwichtigste; **of all my ·worries that's the ~ important** das ist meine geringste Sorge; **the ~ talented player** der am wenigsten talentierte Spieler; **the ~ known** der/die/das Unbekannteste; **the ~ interesting** der/die/das Uninteressanteste; **he's the ~ aggressive of men** er ist nicht im mindesten aggressiv; **not the ~ bit drunk** kein bißchen *or* nicht im geringsten betrunken.

3 *n* **the ~** der/die/das Geringste *or* Wenigste; **that's the ~ of my worries** darüber mache ich mir die wenigsten Sorgen; **I have many worries, and money is the ~ of them** ich habe viele Sorgen, und Geld kümmert mich am wenigsten; **it's the ~ one can do** es ist das wenigste, was man tun kann; **you gave yourself the ~** du hast dir (selbst) am wenigsten gegeben; **at ~, I think so** ich glaube wenigstens; **at ~ it's not raining** wenigstens *or* zumindest regnet es nicht; **we can at ~ try** wir können es wenigstens versuchen; **there were eight at ~** es waren mindestens acht da; **we need at ~ three** wir brauchen wenigstens *or* mindestens drei; **we need three at the very ~** allermindestens brauchen wir drei; **there must have been twenty at the very ~** es waren mindestens zwanzig da; **at the very ~ you could apologize** du könntest dich wenigstens *or* zumindest entschuldigen; **and that's the ~ of it** und das ist noch das wenigste; **not in the ~!** nicht im geringsten!, ganz und gar nicht!; **he was not in the ~ upset** er war kein bißchen *or* nicht im geringsten verärgert; **to say the ~** um es milde zu sagen; **the ~ said, the better, ~ said, soonest mended** (*Prov*) je weniger man darüber spricht, desto besser.

leastways [ˈliːstweɪz] *adv* (*inf*) zumindest, wenigstens. **~ he didn't ...** er hat zumindest *or* wenigstens nicht ...

leather [ˈleðəʳ] **1** *n* Leder *nt*. **~neck** (*US sl*) Ledernacken *m*. **2** *adj* Leder-, ledern. **3** *vt* (*inf*) versohlen (*inf*), ein paar überziehen (+*dat*) (*inf*).

leathering [ˈleðərɪŋ] *n* (*inf*) Tracht *f* Prügel.

leathery [ˈleðərɪ] *adj* *material* lederartig; *smell* Leder-; *skin* ledern; *meat* zäh.

leave [li:v] (*vb: pret, ptp* **left**) **1** *n* (**a**) (*permission*) Erlaubnis *f*. **by your ~** (*form*) mit Ihrer (gütigen) Erlaubnis (*form*); **to ask sb's ~ to do sth** jdn um Erlaubnis bitten, etw zu tun; **he borrowed my car without so much as a by your ~** er hat sich (*dat*) so einfach *or* so mir nichts, dir nichts mein Auto geliehen.

(**b**) (*permission to be absent, Mil*) Urlaub *m*. **to be on ~** auf Urlaub haben; **to be on ~ from sth** von etw beurlaubt sein; **I've got ~ to attend the conference** ich habe freibekommen, um an der Konferenz teilzunehmen; **a two-day ~** zwei Tage Urlaub; **~ of absence** Beurlaubung *f*; **to be on ~ of absence** beurlaubt sein.

(**c**) **to take one's ~** sich verabschieden; **to take ~ of one's senses** den Verstand verlieren; **~-taking** Abschied *m*; (*act*) Abschiednehmen *nt*.

2 *vt* (**a**) (*depart from, quit*) *place, person* verlassen. **the train left the station** der Zug fuhr aus dem Bahnhof; **when the plane left Rome** als das Flugzeug von Rom abflog; **when he left Rome** als er von Rom wegging/wegfuhr/abflog *etc*; **you may ~ us** Sie können gehen; **please sir, may I ~ the room?** Herr X, darf ich mal raus?; **to ~ home** von zu Hause weggehen/wegfahren; (*permanently*) von zu Hause weggehen; **she left her parents' home** sie verließ ihr Elternhaus; **to ~ school** die Schule verlassen; (*prematurely also*) (von der Schule) abgehen; **to ~ the table** vom Tisch aufstehen; **to ~ one's job** seine Stelle aufgeben; **to ~ the road** (*crash*) von der Straße abkommen; (*turn off*) von der Straße abbiegen; **to ~ the rails** entgleisen; **the rocket left the ground** die Rakete hob (vom Boden) ab; **I'll ~ you at the station** am Bahnhof trennen wir uns dann, (*in car*) ich setze dich am Bahnhof ab.

(**b**) (*allow or cause to remain*) lassen; *bad taste, dirty mark, message, scar* hinterlassen. **I'll ~ my address with you** ich lasse Ihnen meine Adresse da; **I'll ~ the key with the neighbours** ich hinterlege *or* lasse den Schlüssel bei den Nachbarn; **to ~ one's supper** sein Abendessen stehenlassen; **the postman left three letters for you** der Briefträger hat drei Briefe für dich gebracht; **"to be left until called for"** „wird abgeholt"; (*in post office*) postlagernd; **to ~ a good impression with sb** einen guten Eindruck bei jdm hinterlassen.

(**c**) (~ *in a certain condition*) lassen. **who left the window open?** wer hat das Fenster offengelassen?; **to ~ two pages blank** zwei Seiten freilassen; **this ~s me free for the afternoon/free to go shopping** dadurch habe ich den Nachmittag frei/Zeit zum Einkaufen; **this new development ~s us with a problem** diese neue Entwicklung stellt uns vor ein Problem; **the death of her uncle left her with no financial worries** nach dem Tod ihres Onkels hatte sie keine finanziellen Probleme mehr; **~ the dog alone** laß den Hund in Ruhe; **~ me alone!** laß mich (in Ruhe)!; **to ~ well alone** die Finger davonlassen (*inf*); **to ~ sb to himself** jdn allein lassen; **to ~ go or hold of** loslassen; **let's ~ it at that** lassen wir es dabei (bewenden); **his rudeness left me speechless** seine Unverschämtheit verschlug mir die Sprache; **if we ~ it so that he'll contact us** wenn wir dabei verbleiben, daß er sich mit uns in Verbindung setzt; **how did he ~ things at the last meeting?** wobei hat er es beim letzten Treffen belassen?

(**d**) (*forget*) liegen- *or* stehenlassen.

(**e**) (*after death*) *person, money* hinterlassen. **he left his wife very badly off** er ließ seine Frau fast mittellos zurück.

(**f**) **to be left** (*remain, be over*) übrigbleiben; **all I have left** alles, was ich noch habe; **how many are there left?** wie viele sind noch da *or* übrig?; **3 from 10 ~s 7 10 minus 3 ist** *or* (*ist*) **gleich 7**; **what does that ~?** wieviel bleibt übrig?; (*Math*) wieviel gibt *or* ist das?; **nothing was left for me but to sell it** mir blieb nichts anderes übrig, als es zu verkaufen.

(**g**) (*entrust*) überlassen (*up to sb* jdm). **~ it to me** laß mich nur machen; **I ~ it to you to judge** es bleibt dir überlassen, zu urteilen; **to ~ sth to chance** etw dem Zufall überlassen.

(**h**) (*stop*) **let's ~ this now** lassen wir das jetzt mal.

3 *vi* (*weg*)gehen, abfahren, abfliegen; (*train, bus, ship*) abfahren; (*plane*) abfliegen. **we ~ for Sweden tomorrow** wir fahren morgen nach Schweden; **which flight did he ~ on?** welchen Flug hat er genommen?

♦**leave aside** *vt sep* beiseite lassen.

♦**leave behind** *vt sep* (**a**) *the car, the children* dalassen, zurücklassen. **we've left all that ~ us** das alles liegt hinter uns; **we've left all our worries ~ us** (*settled*) wir sind alle Sorgen los; (*forgotten*) wir haben all unsere Sorgen vergessen.

(**b**) (*outstrip*) hinter sich (*dat*) lassen. **he left all his fellow-students ~** er stellte alle seine Kommilitonen in den Schatten.

(**c**) (*forget*) liegen- *or* stehenlassen.

♦**leave in** *vt sep* *sentence, scene in play etc* lassen, nicht herausnehmen, drinlassen (*inf*). **don't ~ the dog ~ all day** lassen Sie den Hund nicht den ganzen Tag im Haus; **how long should the meat be left ~?** wie lange muß das Fleisch im Ofen bleiben *or* gelassen werden?

♦**leave off 1** *vt sep* *clothes* nicht anziehen; *lid* nicht darauftun, ablassen (*inf*); *radio, lights* auslassen; *umlaut* weglassen. **you can ~ your coat** du brauchst deinen Mantel nicht anzuziehen; **don't ~ the top ~ your pen** laß den Füllhalter nicht offen *or* ohne Kappe liegen; **you left her name ~ the list** Sie haben ihren Namen nicht in die Liste aufgenommen.

2 *vi* +*prep obj* (*inf*) aufhören. **we left ~ work after lunch** wir haben nach dem Mittagessen Feierabend gemacht; **~ ~ doing that, will you!** hör auf damit, ja?

3 *vi* (*inf*) aufhören. **~ ~!** laß das!

♦**leave on** *vt sep* *clothes* anbehalten, anlassen (*inf*); *lights, fire etc* anlassen. **we left the wall-paper ~ and painted over it** wir haben die Tapete drangelassen (*inf*) *or* nicht entfernt und sie überstrichen.

♦**leave out** *vt sep* (**a**) (*not bring in*) draußen lassen.

(**b**) (*omit*) auslassen; (*exclude*) *people* ausschließen (*of* von). **he was instructed to ~ ~ all references to politics** er bekam Anweisung, alle Hinweise auf Politik wegzulassen; **he had been left ~ in the restructuring** er wurde bei der Neugliederung nicht berücksichtigt; **you ~ my wife/politics ~ of this** lassen Sie meine Frau/die Politik aus dem Spiel; **he got left ~ of things at school** er wurde in der Schule immer ausgeschlossen *or* nie mit einbezogen.

(**c**) (*leave available*) dalassen. **I'll ~ the books ~ on my desk** ich lasse die Bücher auf meinem Schreibtisch; **will you ~ the tools ~ ready?** legen Sie bitte das Werkzeug zurecht.

(**d**) (*not put away*) nicht wegräumen, liegen lassen.

♦**leave over** *vt sep* (**a**) (*leave surplus*) übriglassen. **to be left ~** übrig(geblieben) sein. (**b**) (*postpone*) verschieben, vertagen.

leaven [ˈlevn] **1** *n* (*also* **~ing** [-ɪŋ]) Treibmittel *nt*; (*fermenting dough*) Sauerteig *m*; (*fig*) Auflockerung *f*. **even his most serious speeches had a ~ of humour** auch seine ernstesten Reden waren mit Humor gewürzt.

2 *vt* (*auf*)gehen lassen, treiben; (*fig*) auflockern.

leaves [li:vz] *pl of* **leaf**.

leaving [ˈliːvɪŋ] *n* Fortgang, Weggang *m*. **~ was very difficult (for him)** das Weggehen fiel ihm schwer, es war ein schwerer Abschied.

leaving: **~ certificate** *n* Abgangszeugnis *nt*; **~ day** *n* (*Sch*) Schuljahrsabschluß *m*, letzter Schultag; **~ -party** *n* Abschiedsfeier *or* -party *f*; **~ present** *n* Abschiedsgeschenk *nt*.

leavings [ˈliːvɪŋz] *npl* (*food*) (Über)reste *pl*; (*rubbish*) Abfälle *pl*.

Lebanese [ˌlebəˈniːz] **1** *adj* libanesisch. **2** *n* Libanese *m*, Libanesin *f*.

Lebanon [ˈlebənən] *n* **the ~** der Libanon.

lecher [ˈletʃəʳ] **1** *n* Lüstling, Wüstling *m*; (*hum*) Lustmolch *m*. **2** *vi* lüstern sein. **to ~ after sb** (*chase*) jdm nachstellen; (*in mind*) sich lüsterne Vorstellungen *pl* über jdn machen.

lecherous [ˈletʃərəs] *adj* lüstern; *man, behaviour also* geil.

lecherously [ˈletʃərəslɪ] *adv* lüstern.

lechery [ˈletʃərɪ] *n* Lüsternheit, Geilheit *f*. **his reputation for ~** sein Ruf *m* als Wüstling.

lectern [ˈlektɜːn] *n* Pult *nt*.

lecture [ˈlektʃəʳ] **1** *n* (**a**) Vortrag *m*; (*Univ*) Vorlesung *f*. **to give**

a ~ einen Vortrag/eine Vorlesung halten (*to* für, *on sth* über etw *acc*); **I asked for a short explanation and got a** ~ ich wollte nur eine kurze Erklärung und bekam einen Vortrag zu hören.

(b) (*scolding*) (Straf)predigt f. **to give sb a** ~ jdm eine Strafpredigt *or* Standpauke (*inf*) halten (*about* wegen).

2 *vt* **(a)** (*give a* ~) **to** ~ **sb on sth** jdm einen Vortrag/eine Vorlesung über etw (*acc*) halten; **he** ~**s us in French** wir hören bei ihm (Vorlesungen in) Französisch.

(b) (*scold*) tadeln, abkanzeln. **to** ~ **sb** jdm eine Strafpredigt halten (*on* wegen).

3 *vi* einen Vortrag halten; (*Univ*) (*give* ~) eine Vorlesung halten; (*give* ~ *course*) lesen, Vorlesungen halten (*on* über +*acc*). **he** ~**s in English** er ist Dozent für Anglistik; **he** ~**s on Victorian poetry** er liest über Viktorianische Dichtung; **have you ever heard him** ~? hast du schon mal eine Vorlesung bei ihm gehört?; **he** ~**s at Princeton** er lehrt in Princeton; **he** ~**s well** seine Vorlesungen sind gut.

lecture: ~ **course** *n* Vorlesungs-/Vortragsreihe f; ~ **notes** *npl* (*professor's*) Manuskript *nt*; (*student's*) Aufzeichnungen *pl*; (*handout*) Vorlesungsskript *nt*.

lecturer ['lɛktʃərə'] *n* Dozent *m*; (*speaker*) Redner(in f) *m*. **assistant** ~ ≈ Assistent *m*; **senior** ~ Dozent *m* in höherer Position.

lecture room *n* Hörsaal *m*.

lectureship ['lɛktʃəʃɪp] *n* Stelle f als Dozent, Lehrauftrag *m*. **to take up a university** ~ einen Lehrauftrag an einer Universität annehmen.

lecture tour *n* Vortragsreise f.

led [lɛd] *pret, ptp of* **lead²**.

ledge [lɛdʒ] *n* **(a)** Leiste, Kante f; (*along wall*) Leiste f; (*of window*) (*inside*) Fensterbrett *nt*; (*outside*) (Fenster)sims *nt or m*; (*shelf*) Ablage f, Bord *nt*; (*mountain* ~) (Fels)vorsprung *m*.

(b) (*ridge of rocks*) Riff *nt*.

ledger ['lɛdʒə'] *n* Hauptbuch *nt*. ~ **line** (*Mus*) Hilfslinie f.

lee [li:] **1** *adj* Lee-. **2** *n* **(a)** (*Naut*) Lee f. **(b)** (*shelter*) Schutz, Windschatten *m*.

leech [li:tʃ] *n* Blutegel *m*; (*fig*) Blutsauger *m*.

leek [li:k] *n* Porree, Lauch *m*.

leer [lɪə'] **1** *n* (*knowing, sexual*) anzügliches Grinsen; (*evil*) heimtückischer Blick. **2** *vi* anzüglich grinsen; einen heimtückischen *or* schrägen Blick haben. **he** ~**ed at the girl** er warf dem Mädchen lüsterne Blicke zu.

lees [li:z] *npl* Bodensatz *m*.

leeward ['li:wəd] **1** *adj* Lee-. **2** *adv* leewärts. **the ship was anchored** ~ **of the island** das Schiff ankerte an der Leeseite der Insel. **3** *n* Lee(seite) f. **to** ~ an der Leeseite; **steer to** ~ nach der Leeseite steuern, leewärts steuern.

Leeward Isles ['li:wəd,aɪlz] *npl* Leeward-Inseln *pl* (*nördlicher Teil der Inseln über dem Winde*).

leeway ['li:weɪ] *n* **(a)** (*Naut*) Abtrift f, Leeweg *m*.

(b) (*fig*) (*flexibility*) Spielraum *m*; (*time lost*) Zeitverlust *m*. **to make up** ~ den Zeitverlust aufholen; **there's a lot of** ~ **to make up** es gibt viel nachzuarbeiten, ein großer Rückstand muß aufgeholt werden.

left¹ [lɛft] *pret, ptp of* **leave**.

left² **1** *adj* (*also Pol*) linke(r, s). **his thinking is rather** ~ er hat ziemlich linke Ansichten *pl* (*inf*); **no** ~ **turn** Linksabbiegen verboten; **he's got two** ~ **hands** (*inf*) er hat zwei linke Hände (*inf*).

2 *adv* links (*of* von). **turn** ~ (*Aut*) links abbiegen; **keep** ~ links halten, links fahren; **move** ~ **a little** rücken Sie ein bißchen nach links; ~, **right**, ~, **right** links, rechts, links, rechts; ~ **turn!** (*Mil*) links um!

3 *n* **(a)** Linke(r, s). **on the** ~ links (*of* von), auf der linken Seite (*of* +*gen*); **on** *or* **to your** ~ links (*von Ihnen*), auf der linken Seite; **his wife sat on my** ~ seine Frau saß links von mir *or* zu meiner Linken (*form*); **to keep to the** ~ sich links halten, links fahren; **to fall to the** ~ nach links fallen.

(b) (*Pol*) Linke f. **to be on the** ~ links stehen; **he's further to the** ~ **than I am** er steht weiter links als ich; **to be on** *or* **to the** ~ **of the party** dem linken Flügel der Partei angehören.

(c) (*Boxing*) Linke f.

left: ~ **back** *n* linker Verteidiger; ~ **half** *n* linker Vorstopper; ~-**hand** *adj* ~-**hand drive** Linkssteuerung f; ~-**hand side** linke Seite; **he stood on the** ~-**hand side of the king** er stand zur Linken des Königs; ~-**hand turn** linke Abzweigung; **take the** ~-**hand turn** bieg links ab; ~-**handed** *adj* linkshändig; **tool für** ~-**handed** Linkshänder; (*fig*) *compliment* zweifelhaft; **both the children are** ~-**handed** beide Kinder sind Linkshänder; **a** ~-**handed blow** ein linker Treffer.

leftie ['lɛftɪ] *n* (*pej*) linker Typ (*pej*), Sozi *m* (*usu pej*).

leftish ['lɛftɪʃ] *adj* linksliberal, links angehaucht (*inf*). **his views are** ~ er ist links angehaucht (*inf*).

leftist ['lɛftɪst] **1** *adj* linke(r, s), linksgerichtet. **his views are** ~ er ist linksgerichtet, er steht links. **2** *n* Linke(r) *mf*.

left: ~-**luggage (office)** *n* Gepäckaufbewahrung f; **is there anywhere for** ~-**luggage in this station?** kann man auf diesem Bahnhof irgendwo sein Gepäck zur Aufbewahrung geben?; ~-**luggage locker** *n* Gepäckschließfach *nt*; ~-**over 1** *adj* übriggeblieben; **2** *n* ~-**overs** (Über)reste *pl*; ~-**wing 1** *adj* (*Pol*) linke(r, s); *politician also* linksgerichtet; **2** *n* ~-**wing** linker Flügel (*also Sport*); (*player*) (*Sport*) Linksaußen *m*; ~-**winger** *n* (*Pol*) Linke(r) *mf*; (*Sport*) Linksaußen *m*.

leg [lɛg] **1** *n* **(a)** (*also of trousers*) Bein *nt*. **to be all** ~**s** staksig sein; **the newly-born calf seemed to be all** ~**s** das neugeborene Kalb schien nur aus Beinen zu bestehen; **to be on one's last** ~**s** in den letzten Zügen liegen (*inf*); (*person*) auf dem letzten Loch pfeifen (*inf*); **this dress/carpet is on its last** ~**s** dieses Kleid/dieser Teppich hält *or* macht's (*inf*) nicht mehr lange; **he hasn't a** ~ **to stand on** (*fig*) (*no excuse*) er kann sich nicht herauslehnen; (*no proof*) das kann ich nicht belegen; **to walk one's** ~**s off** sich (*dat*) die Füße wund laufen; **to walk sb's** ~**s off** jdn (*ganz*

schön) scheuchen (*inf*), jdm davonlaufen; **you've walked my** ~**s off** du bist mir zu schnell gelaufen; **to run sb's** ~**s off** (*fig*) jdn herumscheuchen (*inf*); **he ran the other athletes'** ~**s off** rannte den anderen Läufern davon; **he ran the dog's** ~**s off** gab dem Hund Auslauf; **I'll take the children to the park and run their** ~**s off** ich gehe mit den Kindern in den Park, da können sie sich austoben; **to be out** ~ **before wicket** (*Cricket*) aus sein, weil seine Beine von einem Wurf getroffen wurden.

(b) (*as food*) Keule, Hachse f. ~ **of lamb** Lammkeule f.

(c) (*of furniture*) Bein *nt*; (*of bed also*) Fuß *m*.

(d) (*stage*) Etappe f.

2 *vt:* **to** ~ **it** (*inf*) laufen, zu Fuß gehen.

legacy ['lɛgəsɪ] *n* (*lit, fig*) Erbschaft f, Vermächtnis *nt*; (*fig also*) Erbe *nt*; (*fig pej*) Hinterlassenschaft f. **she bought a car with the** ~ sie kaufte sich (*dat*) ein Auto von dem geerbten Geld *or* von der Erbschaft; **our** ~ **to future generations must not be a polluted world** wir dürfen den zukünftigen Generationen keine verschmutzte Welt hinterlassen.

legal ['li:gl] *adj* **(a)** (*lawful*) legal, rechtlich zulässig; *claim* Rechts-, rechtmäßig; (*according to the law*) *tender*, *restrictions*, *obligation*, *limit* gesetzlich; (*allowed by law*) *fare*, *speed* zulässig; (*valid before law*) *will*, *purchase* rechtsgültig. **to become** ~ rechtskräftig werden; **to make sth** ~ etw legalisieren; **the** ~ **age for marriage** das gesetzliche Heiratsalter, die Ehemündigkeit; **it is not** ~ **to sell drink to children** es ist gesetzlich verboten, Alkohol an Kinder zu verkaufen; ~ **separation** gesetzliche Trennung, Trennung f von Tisch und Bett; ~ **rights** gesetzlich verankerte Rechte *pl*; **they don't know what their** ~ **rights are** sie kennen ihre eigenen Rechte nicht; **is it** ~ **to marry your cousin?** ist es rechtlich zulässig, seinen Vetter zu heiraten?; **the** ~ **custody of the children** das Sorgerecht für die Kinder; **women had no** ~ **status** Frauen waren nicht rechtsfähig; **he made** ~ **provision for his ex-wife** er hat die Versorgung seiner geschiedenen Frau rechtlich geregelt.

(b) (*relating to the law*) *matters*, *affairs* juristisch, rechtlich, Rechts-; *advice*, *journal*, *mind* juristisch; *fees*, *charges* Gerichts-; *dictionary*, *act*, *protection*, *adviser* Rechts-; *decision* richterlich, Gerichts-; *inquiry*, *investigation* gerichtlich. ~ **action** Klage f; **to take** ~ **action against sb** gegen jdn Klage erheben, jdn verklagen; **from a** ~ **point of view** aus juristischer Sicht, rechtlich gesehen; **what's his** ~ **position?** wie ist seine rechtliche Stellung?; ~ **aid** Rechtshilfe f; **to take** ~ **advice** juristischen Rat einholen; **there is no** ~ **defence against that** dagegen gibt es keinen rechtlichen Schutz; ~ **department** Rechtsabteilung f, juristische Abteilung; ~ **offence** strafbare Handlung; **drug-peddling is a** ~ **offence** der Handel mit Drogen ist strafbar; **the** ~ **profession** die Anwaltsstand, die Anwaltschaft; (*including judges*) die Juristenschaft; ~ **representative** gesetzlicher Vertreter; (*counsel*) (Rechts)anwalt, Verteidiger *m*.

legality [lɪ:'gælɪtɪ] *n* Legalität f; (*of claim*) Rechtmäßigkeit f; (*of tender*) Gesetzlichkeit f; (*of restrictions*, *obligation*) Gesetzmäßigkeit f; (*of fare*, *speed*) Zulässigkeit f; (*of contract also*, *of will*, *marriage*, *purchase*, *decision*, *limit*) rechtliche Gültigkeit, Rechtsgültigkeit f.

legalization [,li:gəlaɪ'zeɪʃən] *n* Legalisierung f.

legalize ['li:gəlaɪz] *vt* legalisieren.

legally ['li:gəlɪ] *adv* (*lawfully*) *transacted* legal; *married* rechtmäßig; *guaranteed*, *obliged*, *set down* gesetzlich; (*relating to the law*) *advise* juristisch; *indefensible* rechtlich. **what's the position** ~? wie ist die Lage rechtlich gesehen?; **there was no objection** rechtlich *or* juristisch gesehen gab es keine Einwände; ~ **speaking** vom rechtlichen Standpunkt aus, juristisch gesehen; **it's wrong** — ~ **or morally?** es ist nicht richtig — aus rechtlicher oder moralischer Sicht?; ~ **responsible** vor dem Gesetz verantwortlich; **to be** ~ **entitled to sth** einen Rechtsanspruch auf etw (*acc*) haben; ~ **binding** rechtsverbindlich; ~, **he can only stay for 3 months** legal(erweise) kann er nur 3 Monate bleiben; ~ **valid** rechtsgültig.

legate ['lɛgɪt] *n* Legat *m*.

legatee [,lɛgə'ti:] *n* Vermächtnisnehmer(in f) *m*.

legation [lɪ'geɪʃən] *n* (*diplomats*) Gesandtschaft, Vertretung f; (*building*) Gesandtschaftsgebäude *nt*.

legend ['lɛdʒənd] *n* **(a)** Legende f; (*fictitious*) Sage f. **heroes of Greek** ~ griechische Sagenhelden *pl*; **Robin Hood is a figure of** ~ **rather than of fact** die Figur Robin Hoods beruht eher auf Legenden als auf Tatsachen; **to become a** ~ **in one's lifetime** schon zu Lebzeiten zur Legende werden.

(b) (*inscription*, *caption*) Legende f.

legendary ['lɛdʒəndərɪ] *adj* **(a)** legendär; *person also* sagenumwoben. **(b)** (*famous*) berühmt.

legerdemain [,lɛdʒədə'meɪn] *n* Taschenspielerei f.

-**legged** [-'lɛgd, -'lɛgɪd] *adj suf* -beinig. **bare-**~ ohne Strümpfe.

leggings ['lɛgɪŋz] *npl* (hohe *or* lange) Gamaschen *pl*; (*fireman's*, *yachtsman's*) Beinlinge f; (*trousers*) Überhose f, (*baby's*) Gamaschenhose f.

leggy ['lɛgɪ] *adj* (+ *er*) langbeinig; (*gawky*) staksig.

Leghorn ['lɛghɔːn] *n* Livorno *nt*.

legibility [,lɛdʒɪ'bɪlɪtɪ] *n* Lesbarkeit f; Leserlichkeit f.

legible ['lɛdʒɪbl] *adj* lesbar; *handwriting also* leserlich.

legibly ['lɛdʒɪblɪ] *adv* lesbar; *write* leserlich.

legion ['li:dʒən] *n* **(a)** Armee f; (*Foreign L*~) Legion f.

(b) (*Roman*) Legion f.

(c) (*organization*) L~ Legion f; **American/British L~** American/British Legion f (*Verband m der Kriegsteilnehmer des 1. Weltkrieges*); **L~ of Honour** Ehrenlegion f.

(d) (*fig: large number*) Legion f. **they are** ~ ihre Zahl ist Legion; **his supporters are** ~ seine Anhänger sind Legion.

legionary ['li:dʒənərɪ] **1** *adj* Legions-. **2** *n* (*also* **legionnaire**) Legionär *m*.

legislate ['ledʒɪsleɪt] **1** vi (a) Gesetze/ein Gesetz erlassen. parliament's job is to ~ die Aufgabe des Parlaments ist die Gesetzgebung.
(b) (fig) to ~ for sth etw berücksichtigen; (give ruling on) für etw Regeln aufstellen.
2 vt to ~ sth out of existence etw durch Gesetz aus der Welt schaffen; attempts to ~ the trade unions into submission Versuche pl, die Gewerkschaften durch Gesetz zu unterwerfen.

legislation [ledʒɪs'leɪʃən] n (making laws) Gesetzgebung, Legislatur (geh) f; (laws) Gesetze pl.

legislative ['ledʒɪslətɪv] adj gesetzgebend, legislativ (geh). ~ reforms Gesetzesreformen pl.

legislator ['ledʒɪsleɪtər] n Gesetzgeber m.

legislature ['ledʒɪsleɪtʃər] n Legislative f.

legit [lɪ'dʒɪt] adj (sl) O.K. (inf).

legitimacy [lɪ'dʒɪtɪməsɪ] n Rechtmäßigkeit, Legitimität f; (of birth) Ehelichkeit f; (of conclusion) Berechtigung f. I don't doubt the ~ of your excuse/reason ich bezweifle nicht, daß Ihre Entschuldigung/Ihr Grund gerechtfertigt ist.

legitimate [lɪ'dʒɪtɪmət] adj (a) (lawful) rechtmäßig, legitim. how ~ is his claim? wie legitim ist sein Anspruch? (b) (reasonable) berechtigt; excuse begründet. his use of the company car was not ~ er war nicht berechtigt, den Firmenwagen zu benutzen. (c) (born in wedlock) ehelich.

legitimatize [lɪ'dʒɪtɪmətaɪz], **legitimize** [lɪ'dʒɪtɪmaɪz] vt legitimieren; children für ehelich erklären.

legitimately [lɪ'dʒɪtɪmətlɪ] adv (lawfully) legitim; (with reason) berechtigterweise, mit Recht. he argues, quite ~, that ... er führt das berechtigte Argument an, daß ...; it can ~ be expected of people that ... man kann mit Recht von den Leuten erwarten, daß ...

leg: ~less adj (without legs) ohne Beine; (sl: drunk) sternhagelvoll (sl); ~man n (US) kleiner Reporter, der Informationsquellen abklappert; (who runs errands) Laufbursche, Bote m; ~-pull n (inf) Scherz, Bluff (inf) m; what he said to us was only a ~-pull damit wollte er uns nur auf den Arm nehmen; ~room n Platz m für die Beine, Beinfreiheit f; ~-show n (inf) Revue f.

legume ['legjuːm] n (species) Hülsenfrüchtler m; (fruit) Hülsenfrucht f.

leguminous [le'gjuːmɪnəs] adj Hülsenfrucht-.

leg: ~ up n to give sb a ~ up jdm hochhelfen; to give sb a ~ up the social ladder jdm zum gesellschaftlichen Aufstieg verhelfen; ~work n Lauferei f.

Leics abbr of **Leicestershire**.

leisure ['leʒər] n Freizeit f. a gentleman of ~ ein Privatier m (dated); to be a lady of ~ nicht berufstätig sein; she decided to give up her job and become a lady of ~ sie entschloß sich, ihren Beruf aufzugeben und in Muße zu leben; to lead a life of ~ ein Leben in or der Muße führen (geh), sich dem (süßen) Nichtstun ergeben; the problem of what to do with one's ~ das Problem der Freizeitgestaltung; the Prime Minister is seldom at ~ der Premierminister hat selten Zeit für sich or hat selten freie Zeit; do it at your ~ (in own time) tun Sie es, wenn Sie Zeit or Ruhe dazu haben; (at own speed) lassen Sie sich (dat) Zeit damit; to have the ~ to do sth die Zeit or Muße haben, etw zu tun; ~ hours Freizeit f.

leisure: ~ activities npl Hobbys, Freizeitbeschäftigungen pl; ~ clothes npl Freizeitkleidung f.

leisured ['leʒəd] adj the ~ classes die feinen Leute.

leisurely ['leʒəlɪ] adj geruhsam. to walk at a ~ pace gemächlich or langsam gehen.

leisure: ~ time n Freizeit f; ~wear n Freizeitkleidung f.

lemming ['lemɪŋ] n Lemming m.

lemon ['lemən] n **1** (a) (tree) Zitrone f; (colour) Zitronengelb nt; (tree) Zitrone(nbaum m) f. **(b)** (inf: fool) Dussel m (inf). **2** adj Zitronen-. ~ paint zitronengelbe Farbe; ~ yellow Zitronengelb nt.

lemonade [lemə'neɪd] n Limonade f, (süßer) Sprudel; (with lemon flavour) Zitronensprudel m or -limonade f.

lemon: ~ cheese or curd n zähflüssiger Brotaufstrich mit Zitronengeschmack; ~ meringue pie n mit Baisermasse gedeckter Mürbeteig mit einer Zitronencremefüllung; ~ sole n Seezunge f; ~ squash n Zitronensaft m; (in bottle) Zitronensirup m; ~ squeezer n Zitronenpresse f; ~ tea n Zitronentee m.

lemur ['liːmər] n Lemur, Maki m.

lend [lend] pret, ptp **lent 1** vt (a) (loan) leihen (to sb jdm); (banks) money verleihen (to an +acc).
(b) (fig: give) verleihen (to dat); name geben. I am not going to ~ my name to this dafür gebe ich meinen (guten) Namen nicht her; to ~ a hand helfen, mit anfassen.
2 vr to ~ oneself to sth sich für etw hergeben; (be suitable) sich für etw eignen.

♦ **lend out** vt sep verleihen; books also ausleihen.

lender ['lendər] n (professional) Geldverleiher m. he returned the £100 to the ~ er gab die £100 an den zurück, der sie ihm geliehen hatte.

lending ['lendɪŋ] adj library Leih-. ~ rights Verleihrecht nt; (for author) Anspruch m auf Leihbücherei-Tantiemen.

lend-lease ['lend'liːs] n: ~ agreement Leih-Pacht-Abkommen nt.

length [leŋθ] n (a) Länge f. a journey of incredible ~ eine unglaublich lange or weite Reise; to be 4 metres in ~ 4 Meter lang sein; what ~ is it? wie lang ist es?; what ~ do you want it? wie lang hätten Sie es gerne?; of some ~ ziemlich lang; the river, for most of its ~, meanders through meadows der Fluß schlängelt sich in seinem Verlauf größtenteils durch Wiesen; along the whole ~ of the river/lane den ganzen Fluß/Weg entlang; the pipe, for most of its ~, ... fast das ganze Rohr ...; it turns in its own ~ es kann sich um die eigene Achse drehen; over all the ~ and breadth of England in ganz England; (travelling) kreuz und quer durch ganz England; the ~ of

skirts die Rocklänge; at full ~ in voller Länge.
(b) (section) (of cloth, rope, pipe) Stück nt; (of wallpaper) Bahn f; (of road) Abschnitt m; (of pool) Bahn, Länge f.
(c) (of time) Dauer f; (great ~) lange Dauer. of some ~ ziemlich lange, von einiger Dauer; we didn't stay any (great) ~ of time wir sind nicht lange geblieben; the ~ of time needed die Zeit, die man dazu braucht; in that ~ of time I could have ... in dieser Zeit hätte ich ...; for any ~ of time für längere Zeit; for what ~ of time? für wie lange?; ~ of life (of people) Lebenserwartung f; (of animals) Lebensalter nt; (of machine) Lebensdauer f; ~ of service with a company Betriebszugehörigkeit f; ~ of service with the army Dienstjahre pl bei der Armee; at ~ (finally) schließlich; (for a long time) lange, ausführlich, lang und breit (pej).
(d) (Phon, Poet, Sport) Länge f. ~ mark Längenzeichen nt; to win by half a ~ mit einer halben Länge siegen.
(e) to go to any ~s to do sth vor nichts zurückschrecken, um etw zu tun; to go to great ~s sich (dat) sehr viel Mühe geben, alles mögliche versuchen; to go to the ~ of ... so weit gehen, daß ...

lengthen ['leŋθən] **1** vt verlängern; clothes länger machen. **2** vi länger werden.

lengthily ['leŋθɪlɪ] adv ausführlich, langatmig (pej).

lengthways ['leŋθweɪz], **lengthwise** ['leŋθwaɪz] **1** adj Längen-, Längs-. ~ measurement Längenmessung f; ~ cut Längsschnitt m. **2** adv der Länge nach.

lengthy ['leŋθɪ] adj (+er) lange; (dragging on) langwierig; speech ausführlich, langatmig (pej).

lenience ['liːnɪəns], **leniency** ['liːnɪənsɪ] n see adj Nachsicht f; Milde f.

lenient ['liːnɪənt] adj nachsichtig (towards gegenüber); judge, attitude milde.

leniently ['liːnɪəntlɪ] adv nachsichtig; judge milde.

Leninism ['lenɪnɪzəm] n Leninismus m.

lens [lenz] n (Anat, Opt, Phot) Linse f; (in spectacles) Glas nt; (camera part containing ~) Objektiv nt; (eyeglass) Klemmlupe f; (for stamps etc) Vergrößerungsglas nt, Lupe f.

lent [lent] pret, ptp of **lend**.

Lent [lent] n Fastenzeit f.

Lenten ['lentən] adj Fasten-. ~ fast Fasten nt (zur Fastenzeit).

lentil ['lentl] n Linse f. ~ soup Linsensuppe f.

Leo ['liːəʊ] n (Astrol) Löwe m.

leonine ['liːənaɪn] adj Löwen-, löwenartig. the ~ bust of Karl Marx die Büste von Karl Marx mit seiner Löwenmähne.

leopard ['lepəd] n Leopard m. the ~ never changes its spots (prov) die Katze läßt das Mausen nicht (Prov).

leotard ['liːətɑːd] n Trikot nt; (gymnastics) Gymnastikanzug m.

leper ['lepər] n Leprakranke(r), Lepröse(r) (spec), Aussätzige(r) (old, fig) mf. ~ colony Leprasiedlung f, Lepradorf nt.

lepidoptera [lepɪ'dɒptərə] npl Falter, Lepidopteren (spec) pl.

leprechaun ['leprəkɔːn] n Gnom, Kobold m.

leprosy ['leprəsɪ] n Lepra f, Aussatz m (old).

leprous ['leprəs] adj leprös, Lepra-, aussätzig (old).

lesbian ['lezbɪən] **1** adj lesbisch. **2** n Lesbierin, Lesbe (inf) f.

lesbianism ['lezbɪənɪzəm] n (in general) lesbische Liebe; (of one person) Lesbiertum nt.

lèse-majesté, lese majesty ['leɪz'mæʒəsteɪ] n (high treason) Hochverrat m; (fig: to dignity) Majestätsbeleidigung f.

lesion ['liːʒən] n Verletzung f; (structural change) krankhafte Gewebsveränderung f. ~ in the brain Gehirnverletzungen pl.

Lesotho [lɪ'səʊtəʊ] n Lesotho nt.

less [les] **1** adj, adv, n weniger. of ~ importance von geringerer Bedeutung, weniger bedeutend; ~ noise, please! nicht so laut, bitte!; no ~ a person than the bishop kein Geringerer als der Bischof; that was told me by the minister, no ~ das hat mir kein Geringerer als der Minister gesagt; he needs ~ time er braucht weniger Zeit; he did it in ~ time er hat es in kürzerer Zeit or schneller getan; to grow ~ weniger werden; (grow at slow rate) langsamer wachsen; (decrease) abnehmen; his problem is ~ one of money than of enthusiasm sein Problem ist weniger das Geld als vielmehr mangelnde Begeisterung; ~ and ~ immer weniger; she saw him ~ and ~ (often) sie sah ihn immer seltener; a sum ~ than £1 eine Summe unter £ 1; it's nothing ~ than disgraceful/than a disaster es ist wirklich eine Schande/ein Unglück nt; this is nothing ~ than blackmail das ist ja direkt Erpressung; it was little ~ than blackmail das war schon fast or so gut wie Erpressung; he was ~ frightened than angry er war nicht so sehr ängstlich, sondern eher ärgerlich; ~ beautiful nicht so schön; ~ quickly nicht so schnell; he works ~ than I (do) er arbeitet weniger als ich; still or even ~ noch weniger; none the ~ trotzdem, nichtsdestoweniger; I didn't find the film any the ~ interesting ich fand den Film nicht weniger interessant; I don't love her any the ~ ich liebe sie nicht weniger; their apology did not make him any the ~ angry ihre Entschuldigung konnte seinen Ärger nicht besänftigen; we see ~ of her nowadays wir sehen sie jetzt nicht mehr so oft; can't you let me have it for ~? können Sie es mir nicht etwas billiger lassen?; I hope you won't think (any the) ~ of me ich hoffe, du denkst nicht schlecht von mir; ~ of that! komm mir nicht so!

2 prep weniger; (Comm) abzüglich. a year ~ 4 days ein Jahr weniger 4 Tage; 6 ~ 4 is 2 6 weniger or minus 4 ist 2.

-less [-lɪs] adj suf -los. hat~ ohne Hut; sun~ ohne Sonne.

lessee [le'siː] n Pächter m; (of house, flat) Mieter m.

lessen ['lesn] **1** vt (a) (make less) verringern; cost senken, vermindern; effect vermindern, abschwächen.
(b) (make seem less important etc) herabsetzen, herabwürdigen; a person's contribution, services also schmälern.
2 vi nachlassen; (danger, wind, enthusiasm, difficulty also) abnehmen; (value of money) sich verringern, abnehmen.

lessening ['lesnɪŋ] n Nachlassen nt (in sth +gen). ~ of value

Wertabnahme f; a ~ **in the rate of inflation** ein Rückgang m or eine Verringerung der Inflationsrate.

lesser ['lesəʳ] *adj* geringer; (*in names*) klein. to a ~ **extent** in geringerem Maße; a ~ **amount** ein kleinerer Betrag; the ~ **weight** das leichtere Gewicht; **which is the ~ crime?** welches Verbrechen ist weniger schlimm?; **he is a ~ man than his brother** (*less good*) er ist kein so guter Mensch wie sein Bruder; (*less great*) er ist weniger bedeutend als sein Bruder.

lesson ['lesn] *n* (a) (*Sch usw*) Stunde f; (*unit of study*) Lektion f. ~s Unterricht m; (*homework*) (Haus)aufgaben pl; **his ~s are boring** sein Unterricht ist or seine Stunden sind langweilig; ~s **begin at 9** der Unterricht or die Schule beginnt um 9; **he's not very good at his ~s** er ist kein besonders guter Schüler; **a French ~, a ~ in or on French** eine Französischstunde; **a driving ~** eine Fahrstunde; **to give or teach a ~** eine Stunde geben, unterrichten; **we're having a French ~ now** wir haben jetzt Französisch.

(b) (*fig*) Lehre f. **to be a ~ to sb** jdm eine Lehre sein; **he has learnt his ~** er hat seine Lektion gelernt; **to teach sb a ~** jdm eine Lektion erteilen; **what ~ can we learn from this story?** was können wir aus dieser Geschichte lernen?; **he had not learned the big ~ of life that ...** er hatte die goldene Lebensregel nicht begriffen, daß ...

(c) (*Eccl*) Lesung f. **to read the ~** die Lesung halten.

lessor [le'sɔːʳ] *n* (*form*) Verpächter m; (*of flat etc*) Vermieter m.

lest [lest] *conj* (*form*) (a) (*for fear that*) aus Furcht, daß; (*in order that ... not*) damit ... nicht; (*in case*) für den Fall, daß. **I didn't do it ~ somebody should want** ich habe es aus Furcht, daß jemand dagegen sein könnte, nicht getan; ~ **we forget** damit wir nicht vergessen; **we watched all night ~ they should return** wir blieben die ganze Nacht wach für den Fall, daß sie zurückkommen könnten.

(b) (*after fear, be afraid etc*) daß. **I was frightened ~ he should fall** ich hatte Angst, daß er fallen könnte.

let¹ [let] *n* (a) (*Tennis*) Netz(ball m) nt. (b) **without ~ or hindrance** (*Jur*) ungehindert.

let² *n* **they are looking for a ~ in this area** sie wollen eine Wohnung/ein Haus in dieser Gegend mieten; **I have this house on a long ~** ich habe dieses Haus für längere Zeit gemietet.

let³ *pret, ptp* ~ *vt* (a) (*permit*) lassen. **to ~ sb do sth** jdn etw tun lassen; **she ~ me borrow the car** sie lieh mir das Auto, ich durfte ihr Auto nehmen; **we can't ~ that happen** wir dürfen das nicht zulassen; **he wants to but I won't ~ him** er möchte gern, aber ich lasse ihn nicht or erlaube es ihm nicht; **the particle wants to escape but the magnetic force won't ~ it** das Teilchen möchte sich freimachen, aber die magnetische Kraft verhindert es; **oh please ~ me** bitte, bitte, laß mich doch (mal)!; ~ **me help you** darf ich Ihnen helfen or behilflich sein?; ~ **me know what you think** sagen Sie mir (Bescheid) or lassen Sie mich wissen, was Sie davon halten; **to ~ sb be** jdn (in Ruhe) lassen; **to ~ sb/sth go, to ~ go of sb/sth** jdn/etw loslassen; **to ~ sb go** (*depart*) jdn gehen lassen; ~ **me go!** lassen Sie mich los!, loslassen!; **to ~ oneself go** (*neglect oneself*) sich gehenlassen; (*relax*) aus sich herausgehen; **to ~ sth go** (*neglect*) etw vernachlässigen; **to ~ it go at that** es dabei bewenden lassen; **to ~ sb pass** jdn vorbeilassen; **we'll ~ it pass or go this once** (*disregard*) error wir wollen es mal durchgehen lassen; see **drop, fly², slip**.

(b) (*old: causative*) lassen. ~ **the bells be rung** lasset die Glocken ertönen (*liter*); ~ **it be known by all citizens, that ...** allen Bürgern sei kundgetan, daß ... (*old*); ~ **it be known, that ...** alle sollen wissen, daß ...

(c) **to ~ sb/sth alone** jdn/etw in Ruhe lassen; **we can't improve it any more, we'd better ~ it alone** wir können es nicht mehr verbessern, also lassen wir es lieber so; **we'd better ~ well alone** wir lassen besser die Finger davon; (*let sb/sth through*) jdn/etw durchlassen.

(d) ~ **alone** (*much less*) geschweige denn.

(e) ~**'s go home** komm, wir gehen nach Hause; ~**'s go!** gehen wir!; ~**'s get out of here** bloß weg von hier!; **yes,** ~**'s oh ja!**; **it's late, but yes** ~**'s** es ist spät, aber na ja, einverstanden; ~**'s not** lieber nicht; **don't** ~**'s or** ~**'s not fight** wir wollen uns doch nicht streiten; ~**'s be happy** laß uns glücklich sein; ~**'s be friends** wir wollen Freunde sein; ~**'s all be a bit more friendly** seien wir doch alle ein bißchen freundlicher; ~ **him try (it)!** das soll er nur or mal versuchen!; ~ **me think or see, where did I put it?** warte mal or Moment mal, wo habe ich das nur hingetan?; ~ **their need be never so great** mag ihre Not auch noch so groß sein; ~ **X be 60 X sei 60**; ~ **there be no mistake about it** lassen Sie sich (*dat*) das gesagt sein!; ~ **there be music** laßt Musik erklingen; ~ **there be peace** es soll Friede sein; ~ **there be light** es werde Licht; ~ **us pray** laßt uns beten; ~ **us suppose ...** nehmen wir (mal) an, daß ...

(f) (*esp Brit: hire out*) vermieten. **"to ~"** „zu vermieten"; **we can't find a house to ~** wir können kein Haus finden, das zu mieten ist.

(g) **to ~ blood** einen Aderlaß machen; **they ~ so much of his blood** sie nahmen ihm so viel Blut ab.

◆**let down** *vt sep* (a) (*lower*) rope, person hinunter-/herunterlassen; seat herunterklappen; hair, window herunterlassen. **to ~ sb ~ gently** (*fig*) jdm sehr/das schonend beibringen.

(b) (*lengthen*) dress länger machen.

(c) (*deflate*) **to ~ a tyre ~** die Luft aus einem Reifen lassen.

(d) (*fail to help*) **to ~ sb ~** jdn im Stich lassen (*over* mit); **the weather ~ us ~** das Wetter machte uns einen Strich durch die Rechnung; **to ~ the side ~** die anderen hängenlassen (*inf*) or im Stich lassen.

(e) (*disappoint*) enttäuschen. **to feel ~ ~** enttäuscht sein.

(f) **to ~ the school/oneself ~** die Schule/sich blamieren or in

Verruf bringen; **you'd be** ~**ting yourself** ~ **if you only got 5 out of 10** es wäre unter deinem Niveau, nur 5 von 10 Punkten zu bekommen.

◆**let in** 1 *vt sep* (a) water durchlassen.

(b) (*admit*) air, cat, visitor hereinlassen; (*to club etc*) zulassen (*to* zu). **he** ~ **himself** ~ **(with his key)** er schloß die Tür auf und ging hinein; **he** ~ **himself** ~**to the flat** er ging in die Wohnung hinein; **just** ~ **yourself** ~ geh einfach hinein; **I was just** ~**ting myself** ~ ich schloß gerade die Tür auf.

(c) (*involve in*) **to** ~ **sb** ~ **for a lot of work** jdm eine Menge Arbeit aufhalsen; **see what you've** ~ **me** ~ **for now** da hast du mir aber was eingebrockt! (*inf*); **to** ~ **oneself** ~ **for sth** sich auf etw (*acc*) einlassen; **to** ~ **oneself/sb** ~ **for trouble** sich/jdm Ärger einbringen or einhandeln; **I got** ~ ~ **for £5** ich bin £ 5 losgeworden (*inf*).

(d) (*allow to know*) **to** ~ **sb** ~ **on sth, to** ~ **sb** ~**to sth** jdn in etw (*acc*) einweihen; **she** ~ **me** ~ **on the secret** sie hat es mir verraten.

(e) (*Sew*) **to** ~ ~ **a panel** eine Bahn einsetzen.

2 *vi* (*shoes, tent*) Wasser durchlassen, undicht sein.

◆**let off** 1 *vt sep* (a) *also vt* (*fire*) arrow abschießen; gun, shot abfeuern.

(b) (*explode*) firework, bomb hochgehen lassen.

(c) (*emit*) vapour von sich geben; gases absondern; smell verbreiten. **to** ~ ~ **steam** (*lit*) Dampf ablassen; (*fig also*) sich abreagieren.

(d) (*forgive*) **to** ~ **sb** ~ jdm etw durchgehen lassen; **I'll** ~ **you** ~ **this time** diesmal drücke ich noch ein Auge zu; **OK, I'll** ~ **you** ~**, you're quite right** ich will dir mal ausnahmsweise recht geben; **to** ~ **sb** ~ **sth** jdm etw erlassen; **to** ~ **sb** ~ **with a warning/fine** jdn mit einer Verwarnung/Geldstrafe davonkommen lassen; **to** ~ **sb** ~ **lightly** mit jdm glimpflich verfahren; **to be** ~ ~ **lightly** glimpflich davonkommen; **he's been** ~ ~ **man** hat ihn laufenlassen.

(e) (*allow to go*) gehen lassen. **we were** ~ ~ **early** wir durften früher gehen.

(f) (*from car etc*) herauslassen (*inf*), aussteigen lassen.

2 *vi* (*fart*) einen fahren lassen (*inf*).

◆**let on** *vi* (a) *also vt* (*inf: tell, give away*) don't ~ ~ **you know** laß du bloß nicht anmerken, daß du das weißt; **he** ~ ~ **that he had known all the time** er kam damit heraus (*inf*), daß er es schon die ganze Zeit gewußt hatte; **don't** ~ ~ **about our meeting with John** sag nichts über unser Treffen mit John.

(b) (*pretend*) **to** ~ ~ **that ...** vorgeben, daß ...

◆**let out** *vt sep* (a) (*allow to go out*) cat, smell, air hinaus-/herauslassen; (*from car*) absetzen. **to** ~ **oneself** ~ sich (*dat*) die Tür aufmachen; **I'll** ~ **myself** ~ ich finde alleine hinaus.

(b) prisoner entlassen, rauslassen (*inf*); (*divulge*) news bekanntgeben or -machen; secret verraten, ausplaudern (*inf*).

(c) (*emit*) yell ausstoßen. **to** ~ ~ **a laugh** auflachen; **to** ~ ~ **a yawn** (*laut*) gähnen; **to** ~ ~ **a groan** (*auf*)stöhnen.

(d) (*make larger*) dress weiter machen, auslassen.

(e) fire ausgehen lassen.

(f) (*free from responsibility*) **that** ~**s me** ~ **(of it)** da komme ich (schon mal) nicht in Frage.

(g) (*rent*) vermieten.

◆**let up** *vi* (a) (*cease*) aufhören. **he never** ~**s** ~ **about his money** er redet unaufhörlich or pausenlos von seinem Geld.

(b) (*ease up*) nachlassen.

(c) **to** ~ ~ **on sb** jdn in Ruhe lassen; **the trainer didn't** ~ ~ **on them until they were perfect** der Trainer hat so lange nicht locker gelassen or sie so lange getriezt (*inf*), bis sie perfekt waren.

-let [-lɪt] *suf* -lein, -chen.

let-down ['letdaʊn] *n* (*inf: disappointment*) Enttäuschung f.

lethal ['liːθəl] *adj* tödlich. **a** ~**-looking knife** ein gefährlich aussehendes Messer.

lethargic [lɪ'θɑːdʒɪk] *adj* (a) appearance, person träge, lethargisch; atmosphere also schläfrig; animal träge; pace of music schleppend; (*uninterested*) lethargisch, teilnahmslos, lustlos. **a** ~**-looking child** ein teilnahmsloses aussehendes Kind.

(b) (*Med*) schlafsüchtig, lethargisch.

lethargically [lɪ'θɑːdʒɪkəlɪ] *adv see adj*.

lethargy ['leθədʒɪ] *n* (a) Lethargie, Trägheit f. **an atmosphere of** ~ eine schläfrige or träge Atmosphäre. (b) (*Med*) Schlafsucht, Lethargie f.

let's [lets] *contr of* **let us**.

Lett [let] *adj, n see* **Latvian**.

letter ['letəʳ] 1 *n* (a) (*of alphabet*) Buchstabe m. **the** ~ **of the law** der Buchstabe des Gesetzes; **to the** ~ buchstabengetreu, genau; **did he do it? — to the** ~ hat er es getan? — ganz nach Vorschrift.

(b) (*written message*) Brief m; (*Comm etc*) Schreiben nt (*form*) (*to an* +acc). **by** ~ schriftlich, brieflich; ~ **of credit** Kreditbrief m, Akkreditiv nt; ~**s patent** Patent(urkunde f) nt.

(c) (*Liter*) ~**s** Literatur f; **man of** ~**s** Belletrist m; (*writer*) Literat m.

(d) (*US: award*) als Auszeichnung verliehenes Schulabzeichen.

2 *vt* sign, label beschriften. **he** ~**ed the invitations in gold** er ließ die Einladungen in Gold(buchstaben) drucken.

letter: ~ **bomb** *n* Briefbombe f; ~ **box** *n* Briefkasten m; ~**-card** *n* Briefkarte f.

lettered ['letəd] *adj* (a) (*rare*) person gelehrt. (b) object beschriftet. ~ **in gold** in Goldschrift.

letterhead ['letəhed] *n* Briefkopf m; (*writing paper*) Geschäfts(brief)papier nt.

lettering ['letərɪŋ] *n* Beschriftung f.

letterpress ['letəpres] *n* Hochdruck m.

letting ['letɪŋ] *n* Vermieten nt. **he's in the** ~ **business** er ist in der Wohnungsbranche.

Lettish ['letɪʃ] *adj, n see* **Latvian.**

lettuce ['letɪs] *n* Kopfsalat *m*; (*genus*) Lattich *m*.

let-up ['letʌp] *n* (*inf*) Pause *f*; (*easing up*) Nachlassen *nt*. **if there is a ~ in the rain** wenn der Regen aufhört/nachläßt.

leucocyte, leukocyte ['luːkəʊsaɪt] *n* Leukozyt *m*.

leukaemia, leukemia [luːˈkiːmɪə] *n* Leukämie *f*.

Levant [lɪˈvænt] *n* Levante *f*.

Levantine ['levəntaɪn] **1** *adj* levantinisch. **2** *n* (*person*) Levantiner(in *f*) *m*.

levee[1] ['levɪ] *n* (*Hist*) (*on awakening*) Lever *nt*; (*at British court*) Nachmittagsempfang *m*.

levee[2] ['levɪ] *n* Damm, Deich *m*.

level ['levl] **1** *adj* (a) (*flat*) *ground, surface, floor* eben; *spoonful* gestrichen. **try to keep the boat ~** versuchen Sie, das Boot waagerecht zu halten; **the glider maintained a ~ course** das Segelflugzeug behielt die gleiche Flughöhe bei.

(b) (*at the same height*) auf gleicher Höhe (*with mit*); (*parallel*) parallel (*with zu*). **to be ~ with the ground** zu gleicher Höhe mit dem Boden sein; (*parallel*) parallel zum Boden sein; **the bedroom is ~ with the ground** das Schlafzimmer liegt ebenerdig *or* in einer Ebene; **to be ~ with the water** auf der gleichen Höhe wie der Wasserspiegel sein.

(c) (*equal*) *race* Kopf-an-Kopf-; (*fig*) gleich gut. **the two runners are absolutely ~ or dead ~** die beiden Läufer liegen *or* sind genau auf gleicher Höhe; **Jones was almost ~ with the winner** Jones kam fast auf gleiche Höhe mit dem Sieger; **the two teams are ~ in the league** die beiden Mannschaften haben den gleichen Tabellenstand.

(d) (*steady*) *tone of voice* ruhig; (*well-balanced*) ausgeglichen; *judgement* ab- *or* ausgewogen; *head* kühl. **to have/keep a ~ head** einen kühlen Kopf haben/bewahren.

(e) **I'll do my ~ best** ich werde mein möglichstes tun.

2 *adv* **~ with** in Höhe (*+gen*); **it should lie ~ with ...** es sollte gleich hoch sein wie ...; **the pipe runs ~ with the ground** das Rohr verläuft zu ebener Erde; (*parallel*) das Rohr verläuft parallel zum Boden; **they're running absolutely ~** sie laufen auf genau gleicher Höhe; **the value of the shares stayed ~ for some time** der Wert der Aktien blieb für einige Zeit gleich; **to draw ~ with sb** jdn einholen, mit jdm gleichziehen; (*in league etc*) punktegleich mit jdm sein; **the two runners drew ~ on the last lap** in der letzten Runde zogen die beiden Läufer gleich.

3 *n* (a) (*instrument*) Wasserwaage *f*.

(b) (*altitude*) Höhe *f*. **on a ~ (with)** auf gleicher Höhe (mit); **water always finds its own ~** Wasser kehrt immer in die Waagerechte zurück; **at eye ~** in Augenhöhe; **the trees were very tall, almost ~ with roof** die Bäume waren sehr hoch, sie reichten fast bis zum Dach; **to be on a ~ with the ground** in Bodenhöhe *or* zu ebener Erde sein *or* liegen.

(c) (*flat place*) ebene Fläche, ebenes Stück.

(d) (*storey*) Geschoß *nt*.

(e) (*position on scale*) Niveau *nt*, Ebene *f*. **they're on a different ~** sie haben ein unterschiedliches Niveau; **to descend or sink or come down to that ~** auf ein so tiefes Niveau absinken; **he expects everyone to come down to his ~** er erwartet von jedem, daß er sich auf sein Niveau herabbegibt; **she tried to go above her own natural ~** sie versuchte, ihre natürlichen Grenzen zu überschreiten; **to be on a ~ with** auf gleichem Niveau sein wie; **they are on a ~ as far as salaries are concerned** sie bekommen das gleiche Gehalt; **he tried to raise the ~ of the conversation** er versuchte, der Unterhaltung etwas mehr Niveau zu geben; **if profit keeps on the same ~** wenn sich der Gewinn auf dem gleichen Stand hält; **he maintains his high ~ of excellence** er hält sein äußerst hohes Niveau; **a high ~ of intelligence** ein hoher Intelligenzgrad; **the very high ~ of production** das hohe Produktionsniveau; **a low ~ of sales** ein sehr geringer Absatz; **a high ~ of civilization** eine hohe Kulturstufe; **the higher ~s of academic research** die höheren Stufen der wissenschaftlichen Forschung; **the talks were held at a very high ~** die Gespräche fanden auf hoher Ebene statt; **the varying ~s of abilities** die verschiedenen Fähigkeitsgrade; **to reduce sth to a more comprehensible ~** etw auf eine etwas verständlichere Ebene bringen; **he reduces everything to the commercial ~** er reduziert alles auf eine rein kommerzielle Basis; **on the moral ~** moralisch gesehen, aus moralischer Sicht; **on a purely personal ~** rein persönlich, auf rein persönlicher Ebene.

(f) (*amount, degree*) **a high ~ of hydrogen** ein hoher Wasserstoffanteil *or* Anteil an Wasserstoff; **the ~ of alcohol in the blood** der Alkoholspiegel im Blut; **what sort of ~ of mistakes can you tolerate?** welche Fehlerquote können Sie dulden?

(g) (*inf: straightforward, honest*) **it's on the ~** (*business*) es ist reell; (*proposition*) es ist ehrlich gemeint; **I guess you're on the ~** du bist wohl schon in Ordnung (*inf*); **is he on the ~?** meint er es ehrlich?; **are you telling me this on the ~?** meinst du das ehrlich?, ist das dein Ernst?; **to be on the ~ with sb** jdm gegenüber ehrlich *or* aufrichtig sein.

4 *vt* (a) *ground, site etc* einebnen, planieren; *building* abreißen; *town* dem Erdboden gleichmachen. **you can't ~ all men** man kann nicht alle Menschen gleichmachen; **to ~ sth to or with the ground** etw dem Erdboden gleichmachen.

(b) *blow* versetzen, verpassen (*inf*) (*at sb* jdm); *weapon* richten (*at auf* +*acc*); *accusation* erheben (*at gegen*); *remark* richten (*at gegen*). **to ~ a charge against sb** Anklage gegen jdn erheben, jdn anklagen; **he was ~ling his remarks at his mother** seine Bemerkungen richteten sich gegen seine Mutter.

5 *vi* (*sl*) **to ~ with sb** jdm keinen Quatsch *or* Scheiß erzählen (*sl*); **I'll ~ with you** ich werde ehrlich mit dir sein (*inf*).

♦**level down** *vt sep* (*lit*) einebnen; (*fig*) auf ein tieferes Niveau bringen *or* herabsetzen; *salaries* nach unten angleichen.

♦**level out 1** *vi* (*also ~ off*) (a) (*ground*) eben *or* flach werden; (b) (*Aviat*) (*pilot*) das

Flugzeug abfangen; (*plane*) sich fangen; (*after rising*) horizontal fliegen. **2** *vt sep* *site* planieren, einebnen; (*fig*) *differences* ausgleichen.

♦**level up** *vt sep* (*lit*) ausgleichen; *salaries* angleichen; (*fig*) auf ein höheres Niveau bringen. **they aim to ~ educational standards** ~ sie wollen das Bildungsniveau anheben; **you sit on the other side of the boat and that'll ~ it** ~ du setzt dich auf die andere Seite des Bootes, dann wird das Gleichgewicht (wieder) hergestellt.

level: **~ crossing** *n* (*Brit*) (höhengleicher) Bahnübergang *m*; **~-headed** *adj person* ausgeglichen; *attitude, reply, decision* ausgewogen; *reply, decision also* überlegt.

leveller ['levlər] *n* Gleichmacher *m*. **death is a great ~** der Tod macht alle (Menschen) gleich.

levelly ['levlɪ] *adv* (*calmly*) ruhig; *gaze* gerade.

level pegging *adj* punktgleich. **with 30 votes each they are ~** mit jeweils 30 Stimmen liegen sie auf gleicher Höhe; **it's ~ as they go round the final bend** sie liegen in der letzten Kurve auf gleicher Höhe.

lever ['liːvər, (*US*) 'levər] **1** *n* Hebel *m*; (*crowbar*) Brechstange *f*; (*fig*) Druckmittel *nt*. **that should give us a ~** das können wir als Druckmittel benutzen.

2 *vt* (hoch)stemmen, mit einem Hebel/einer Brechstange (an- *or* hoch)heben. **he ~ed the machine-part into place** er hob das Maschinenteil durch Hebelwirkung an seinen Platz; **he ~ed the box open** er stemmte die Kiste auf; **he ~ed himself onto the ledge** er hievte sich auf den Felsvorsprung (hoch); **he seems to have ~ed himself into a position of power** er scheint sich in eine Machtposition manövriert zu haben.

♦**lever out** *vt sep* herausstemmen *or* -brechen. **we'll never ~ him ~ of such a comfortable job** aus diesem bequemen Job werden wir ihn nie heraushöhlen *or* -lotsen können (*inf*); **he ~ed himself ~ of the armchair** er hievte sich aus dem Sessel (hoch).

♦**lever up** *vt sep* mit einem Hebel/einer Brechstange hochheben, aufstemmen.

leverage ['liːvərɪdʒ] *n* Hebelkraft *f*; (*fig*) Einfluß *m*. **this spanner can exert considerable ~** dieser Schraubenschlüssel kann eine beträchtliche Hebelwirkung ausüben; **to use sth as ~** (*fig*) etw als Druckmittel benutzen; (*to one's own advantage*) etw zu seinem Vorteil ausnützen; **knowing this should give us a bit of ~ in forcing our demands** diese Informationen werden uns helfen, unsere Forderungen durchzusetzen; **this gave us a bit of ~ with the authorities** dadurch konnten wir etwas Druck auf die Behörden ausüben; **his approval gives us a bit of ~ with them** seine Zustimmung verstärkt unsere Position ihnen gegenüber.

leveret ['levərɪt] *n* junger Hase, Häschen *nt*.

leviathan [lɪˈvaɪəθən] *n* Leviathan *m*, Meerungeheuer *nt*; (*fig*) Gigant *m*; (*state*) Leviathan *m*.

Levis, levis ® ['liːvaɪz] *npl* Levis ® *f*, Jeans *pl*.

levitate ['leviteit] **1** *vt* schweben lassen. **2** *vi* schweben.

levitation [ˌleviˈteɪʃən] *n* Levitation *f*, freies Schweben.

Levite ['liːvaɪt] *n* Levit(e) *m*.

levity ['leviti] *n* Leichtfertigkeit *f*. **sounds of ~** Gelächter *nt*.

levy ['levi] **1** *n* (*act*) (Steuer)einziehung *or* -eintreibung *f*; (*tax*) Steuer *f*, Abgaben *pl*; (*Mil*) Aushebung *f*; (*of supplies*) Einziehung, Beschlagnahme *f*. **there were 100 men in the first ~** 100 Männer wurden bei der ersten Aushebung eingezogen.

2 *vt* (a) (*raise*) *tax* einziehen, erheben; *fine* auferlegen (*on sb* jdm); (*Mil*) *army, troops* ausheben; *supplies* einziehen, beschlagnahmen. **to ~ a tax on beer** Bier mit einer Steuer belegen, Steuern *pl* auf Bier erheben.

(b) (*wage*) *war* führen (*against, on gegen*).

lewd [luːd] *adj* (+*er*) unanständig; (*lustful*) lüstern; *remark* anzüglich; *joke, song* unanständig, anstößig, anzüglich; *imagination* schmutzig. **don't be ~** werd nicht anzüglich.

lewdly ['luːdlɪ] *adv* anzüglich. **he spoke ~ about his amorous adventures** er erzählte lüstern *or* in anzüglicher Weise von seinen amourösen Abenteuern.

lewdness ['luːdnɪs] *n* (*being indecent*) Anstößigkeit, Unanständigkeit *f*; (*being lustful*) Lüsternheit *f*; (*of remark*) Anzüglichkeit *f*; (*of imagination*) Schmutzigkeit *f*.

lexical ['leksɪkəl] *adj* lexikalisch.

lexicographer [ˌleksɪˈkɒgrəfər] *n* Lexikograph(in *f*) *m*.

lexicographic(al) [ˌleksɪkəʊˈgræfɪk(əl)] *adj* lexikographisch.

lexicography [ˌleksɪˈkɒgrəfɪ] *n* Lexikographie *f*.

lexicon ['leksɪkən] *n* Wörterbuch, Lexikon *nt*; (*in linguistics*) Lexikon *nt*.

Leyden jar ['laɪdnˈdʒɑːr] *n* Leidener Flasche *f*.

l.h.d. *abbr of* **left hand drive.**

liability [ˌlaɪəˈbɪlɪtɪ] *n* (a) (*burden*) Belastung *f*.

(b) (*being subject to*) one's ~ **for tax** jds Steuerpflicht *f*; **he has a tax ~ of £1,000** er muß £ 1000 Steuern bezahlen; **~ for jury service** Pflicht zur Ausübung des Schöffen-/Geschworenenamtes; **~ to pay damages** Schadensersatzpflicht *f*.

(c) (*proneness*) Anfälligkeit *f* (*to für*). **our economy's ~ to inflation** die Inflationsanfälligkeit unserer Wirtschaft.

(d) (*responsibility*) Haftung *f*. **we accept no ~ for ...** wir übernehmen keine Haftung für ...; **his ~ for his wife's debts** seine Haftung *or* Haftbarkeit für die Schulden seiner Frau; **that is not my ~** dafür hafte ich nicht.

(e) (*Fin*) **liabilities** Verbindlichkeiten, Verpflichtungen *pl*.

liable ['laɪəbl] *adj* (a) (*subject to*) **to be ~** unterliegen (*for sth* einer Sache *dat*); **to be ~ for tax** (*things*) besteuert werden; (*person*) steuerpflichtig sein; **people earning over £X are ~ for surtax** wer mehr als £ X verdient, unterliegt einer Zusatzsteuer *or* ist zusatzsteuerpflichtig; **~ to penalty** strafbar; **you'll make yourself ~ to a heavy fine** Sie können zu einer hohen Geldstrafe verurteilt werden.

(b) (*prone to*) anfällig. **he's always been ~ to bronchitis** er war schon immer anfällig für Bronchitis; ~ **to inflation** inflationsanfällig.

    (c) (*responsible*) **to be** ~ haften, haftbar sein; **to be** ~ **for** haftbar sein or haften für, aufkommen müssen für.

    (d) (*likely to*) **we are** ~ **to get shot here** wir können hier leicht beschossen werden; **the pond is** ~ **to freeze** der Teich friert leicht zu; **is he** ~ **to come?** ist anzunehmen, daß er kommt?; **he's** ~ **to tell the police** es wäre ihm zuzutrauen, daß er es der Polizei meldet; **if you don't write it down I'm** ~ **to forget it** wenn Sie das nicht aufschreiben, kann es durchaus sein, daß ich es vergesse; **the computer is still** ~ **to make mistakes** der Computer kann durchaus noch Fehler machen; **at that temperature the metal is** ~ **to crack** bei dieser Temperatur kann das Metall leicht brechen; **the plan is** ~ **to changes** der Plan wird möglicherweise geändert; **I don't think it's** ~ **to happen tonight** ich halte es für nicht wahrscheinlich, daß es heute nacht passiert; **the car is** ~ **to run out of petrol any minute** dem Auto kann jede Minute das Benzin ausgehen; **if you tell him that, he's** ~ **to lose his temper** wenn Sie ihm das sagen, wird er bestimmt wütend.

liaise [lɪˈeɪz] *vi* als Verbindungsmann or V-Mann (*inf*) fungieren. **he has a sort of liaising job** er ist eine Art Verbindungsmann.

liaison [liːˈeɪzɒn] *n* **(a)** (*coordination*) Verbindung, Zusammenarbeit *f*; (*person*) Verbindungsmann, V-Mann (*inf*) *m*; (*Mil*) Verbindung *f*; (*person*) Verbindungsmann or -offizier *m*. **(b)** (*affair*) Liaison *f*.

liaison officer *n* Verbindungsmann *m*; (*Mil*) Verbindungsoffizier *m*. **the firm's** ~ der Firmensprecher.

liar [laɪəʳ] *n* Lügner(in *f*) *m*.

Lib (*Pol*) *abbr of* **Liberal.**

libation [laɪˈbeɪʃən] *n* **(a)** (*offering*) Trankopfer *nt*. **(b)** (*inf: drinking session*) ~**s** Trinkgelage, Saufgelage (*inf*) *nt*.

libel [ˈlaɪbəl] **1** *n* (schriftlich geäußerte) Verleumdung (*on gen*). **to utter/publish a** ~ **against sb** jdn verleumden; **it's a** ~ **on all of us** das ist eine Verleumdung, die uns alle trifft; **it's a** ~ **on the whole neighbourhood** es ist eine Verleumdung der gesamten Nachbarschaft.

    2 *vt* verleumden.

libellous, (*US*) **libelous** [ˈlaɪbələs] *adj* verleumderisch.

liberal [ˈlɪbərəl] **1** *adj* **(a)** (*generous*) *offer, supply* großzügig; *helping of food* reichlich.

    (b) (*broad-minded*) liberal.

    (c) ~ **education** Allgemeinbildung *f*; **the** ~ **arts** die geisteswissenschaftlichen Fächer.

    (d) (*Pol*) liberal.

    2 *n* (*Pol*: L~) Liberale(r) *mf*. **he's a** ~ **in social matters** er hat eine liberale Einstellung in sozialen Angelegenheiten.

liberalism [ˈlɪbərəlɪzəm] *n* Liberalität *f*; (*Pol*: L~) der Liberalismus.

liberality [ˌlɪbəˈrælɪtɪ] *n* **(a)** (*generosity*) Großzügigkeit *f*. **(b)** *see* **liberal-mindedness.**

liberalization [ˌlɪbərəlaɪˈzeɪʃən] *n* Liberalisierung *f*.

liberalize [ˈlɪbərəlaɪz] *vt* liberalisieren.

liberally [ˈlɪbərəlɪ] *adv* liberal; (*generously*) großzügig. **he applies the paint very** ~ er trägt die Farbe dick or reichlich auf.

liberal: ~**-minded** *adj* person liberal (eingestellt); *views* liberal; ~**-mindedness** *n* (*of person*) liberale Einstellung or Gesinnung; (*of views*) Liberalität *f*.

liberate [ˈlɪbəreɪt] *vt* **(a)** (*free*) *prisoner, country* befreien. **(b)** *gas etc* freisetzen. **the experiment** ~**d a poisonous gas** bei dem Experiment wurde ein giftiges Gas frei(gesetzt).

liberation [ˌlɪbəˈreɪʃən] *n* Befreiung *f*; (*of gases*) Freisetzung *f*.

liberator [ˈlɪbəreɪtəʳ] *n* Befreier *m*.

Liberia [laɪˈbɪərɪə] *n* Liberia *nt*.

Liberian [laɪˈbɪərɪən] **1** *adj* liberianisch, liberisch. **2** *n* Liberianer(in *f*), Liberier(in *f*) *m*.

libertine [ˈlɪbətiːn] *n* Wüstling, Libertin (*geh*) *m*.

liberty [ˈlɪbətɪ] *n* **(a)** Freiheit *f*. ~ **of conscience** Gewissensfreiheit *f*; **basic liberties** Grundrechte *pl*; **to restore sb to** ~ jdm die Freiheit wiedergeben; **to be at** ~ (*criminal etc*) frei herumlaufen; (*having time*) Zeit haben; **to be at** ~ **to do sth** (*permitted*) etw tun dürfen; **I am not at** ~ **to comment** es ist mir nicht gestattet, darüber zu sprechen; **you are at** ~ **to go** es steht Ihnen frei zu gehen; **is he at** ~ **to come?** darf er kommen?

    (b) (*presumptuous action, behaviour*) **I have taken the** ~ **of giving your name** ich habe mir erlaubt, Ihren Namen anzugeben; **to take liberties with a text** einen Text sehr frei bearbeiten; **to take liberties with sb** sich jdm gegenüber Freiheiten herausnehmen; **what a** ~! (*inf*) so eine Frechheit or Unverschämtheit!

libidinous [lɪˈbɪdɪnəs] *adj* lüstern; *person, behaviour also* triebhaft; (*Psych*) libidinös.

libido [lɪˈbiːdəʊ] *n* Libido *f*.

Libra [ˈliːbrə] *n* Waage *f*.

Libran [ˈliːbrən] *n* Waage(mensch *m*) *f*.

librarian [laɪˈbreərɪən] *n* Bibliothekar(in *f*) *m*.

librarianship [laɪˈbreərɪənʃɪp] *n* **(a)** (*subject*) Bibliothekswesen *nt* or -lehre *f*. **(b)** (*job*) Bibliothekarsstelle *f*.

library [ˈlaɪbrərɪ] *n* **(a)** (*public*) Bibliothek, Bücherei *f*. **(b)** (*private*) Bibliothek *f*. **(c)** (*collection of books/records*) (Bücher)sammlung/(Schallplatten)sammlung *f*. **(d)** (*series of books*) Buchreihe, Bibliothek *f*.

library: ~ **book** *n* Leihbuch *nt*; ~ **edition** *n* Leihbuchausgabe *f*; ~ **science** *n* Bibliothekswissenschaften *pl*; ~ **ticket** *n* Leserausweis *m*.

librettist [lɪˈbretɪst] *n* Librettist *m*.

libretto [lɪˈbretəʊ] *n* Libretto *nt*.

Libya [ˈlɪbɪə] *n* Libyen *nt*.

Libyan [ˈlɪbɪən] **1** *adj* libysch. **2** *n* Libyer(in *f*) *m*.

lice [laɪs] *pl of* **louse.**

licence, (*US*) **license** [ˈlaɪsəns] *n* **(a)** (*permit*) Genehmigung, Erlaubnis *f*; (*by authority*) behördliche Genehmigung, Konzession *f*; (*Comm*) Lizenz *f*; (*driving* ~) Führerschein *m*; (*gun* ~) Waffenschein *m*; (*hunting* ~) Jagdschein *m*; (*marriage* ~) Eheerlaubnis *f*; (*radio* ~, *television* ~) (Rundfunk-/Fernseh)genehmigung *f*; (*dog* ~) Hundemarke *f*. **he hasn't paid his (dog)** ~ er hat seine Hundesteuer nicht bezahlt; **you have to have a (television)** ~ man muß Fernsehgebühren bezahlen; **a** ~ **to practise medicine** die Approbation, die staatliche Zulassung als Arzt; **the restaurant has lost its** ~ (*to sell drinks*) das Restaurant hat seine Schankerlaubnis or Konzession verloren; **we'll get a late** ~ **for the reception** für den Empfang bekommen wir eine Genehmigung für verlängerte Ausschankzeiten; **a** ~ **to kill** ein Freibrief zum Töten; **to manufacture sth under** ~ etw in Lizenz herstellen.

    (b) (*freedom*) Freiheit *f*. **translated with a good deal of** ~ sehr frei übersetzt; **the editor altered the text with too great a degree of** ~ der Lektor erlaubte sich bei der Änderung des Textes zu große Freiheiten.

    (c) (*excessive freedom*) Zügellosigkeit *f*. **there is too much** ~ **in sexual matters/the cinema nowadays** in sexuellen Dingen/im Kino geht es heutzutage zu freizügig zu.

licence: ~ **number** *n* (*Aut*) Kraftfahrzeug- or Kfz-Kennzeichen *nt*; ~ **plate** *n* (*Aut*) Nummernschild *nt*.

license [ˈlaɪsəns] **1** *n* (*US*) *see* **licence. 2** *vt* eine Lizenz/Konzession vergeben an (+*acc*). **a car must be** ~**d every year** die Kfz-Steuer muß jedes Jahr bezahlt werden; **to** ~ **a pub** einer Gaststätte Schankerlaubnis or eine Schankkonzession erteilen; **to be** ~**d to do sth** die Genehmigung haben, etw zu tun; **he is** ~**d to practise medicine** er ist approbierter Arzt, er ist als Arzt zugelassen; **we're not** ~**d for dancing** wir haben keine Tanzgenehmigung; **we are not** ~**d to sell alcohol** wir haben keine Schankerlaubnis or Konzession; **secret agents are** ~**d to kill** Geheimagenten dürfen Leute totschießen.

licensed [ˈlaɪsənst] *adj* ~ **house/premises** Lokal *nt* mit Schankerlaubnis; **fully** ~ mit voller Schankkonzession or -erlaubnis; ~ **victualler** Lebensmittelhändler *m* mit einer Konzession für den Verkauf von Alkohol.

licensee [ˌlaɪsənˈsiː] *n* *see* **licence** Konzessions-/Lizenzinhaber(in *f*) *m*; Inhaber(in *f*) *m* eines Waffenscheins etc; (*of bar*) Inhaber(in *f*) *m* einer Schankerlaubnis. **the** ~ **of our local pub** der Wirt unserer Stammkneipe; **postage paid by** ~ Gebühr bezahlt Empfänger.

licensing [ˈlaɪsənsɪŋ] *adj* ~ **hours** Ausschankzeiten *pl*; **after** ~ **hours** über die Polizeistunde or Sperrzeit hinaus; ~ **laws** Schankgesetze *pl*, Gesetz *nt* über den Ausschank und Verkauf alkoholischer Getränke.

licentiate [laɪˈsenʃɪɪt] *n* Lizentiat *m*; (*degree*) Lizentiat *nt*.

licentious [laɪˈsenʃəs] *adj* ausschweifend, lasterhaft; *behaviour* unzüchtig; *book* sehr freizügig; *look* lüstern.

licentiously [laɪˈsenʃəslɪ] *adv see adj*.

licentiousness [laɪˈsenʃəsnɪs] *n* Unmoral, Lasterhaftigkeit, Unzüchtigkeit *f*; (*of book*) Freizügigkeit *f*; (*of look*) Lüsternheit *f*.

lichen [ˈlaɪkən] *n* Flechte *f*.

lichgate, lychgate [ˈlɪtʃgeɪt] *n* überdachter Kirchhofseingang.

licit [ˈlɪsɪt] *adj* erlaubt, gesetzlich.

lick [lɪk] **1** *n* **(a)** (*with tongue*) Lecken, Schlecken (*dial*) *nt*. **to give sth a** ~ an etw (*dat*) lecken.

    (b) (*salt* ~) (Salz)lecke *f*; (*artificial*) Leckstein *m*.

    (c) (*inf: small quantity*) **it's time we gave the kitchen a** ~ **of paint** die Küche könnte auch mal wieder etwas Farbe vertragen (*inf*); **to give oneself a** ~ **and a promise** Katzenwäsche machen.

    (d) (*inf: pace*) **the project is coming along at a good** ~ das Projekt geht ganz gut voran (*inf*); **to go/drive at a good** ~ einen (ganz schönen) Zahn draufhaben (*inf*); **he rushed to the station at full** ~ er raste mit Volldampf zum Bahnhof (*inf*).

    2 *vt* **(a)** (*with tongue*) lecken. **he** ~**ed the stamp** er leckte an der Briefmarke; **he** ~**ed the ice-cream** er leckte am Eis; **to** ~ **one's lips** sich (*dat*) die Lippen lecken; (*fig*) sich (*dat*) die Finger lecken; **to** ~ **one's wounds** (*fig*) seine Wunden lecken; **to** ~ **sb's boots** (*fig*) vor jdm kriechen (*inf*), jds Stiefel lecken; **to** ~ **sb into shape** (*fig*) jdn auf Zack or auf Vordermann bringen (*inf*).

    (b) (*waves*) plätschern an (+*acc*); (*flames*) züngeln an (+*dat*).

    (c) (*inf: beat, defeat*) in die Pfanne hauen (*sl*), einseifen (*inf*). **he'll get** ~**ed for breaking that window** er kriegt eine Tracht Prügel or den Hintern voll (*inf*) dafür, daß er die Fensterscheibe eingeworfen hat; **this** ~**s everything!** das haut dem Faß den Boden aus! (*inf*); **I think we've got it** ~**ed** ich glaube, wir haben die Sache jetzt im Griff.

    3 *vi* **to** ~ **at sth** an etw (*dat*) lecken; *flames* ~**ed round the building** Flammen züngelten am Gebäude empor.

◆**lick off** *vt sep* ablecken. **to** ~ **sth** ~ **sth** etw von etw ablecken or abschlecken (*dial*).

◆**lick up** *vt sep* auflecken.

lickety-split [ˈlɪkɪtɪˈsplɪt] *adv* (*US inf*) blitzschnell, mit Volldampf (*inf*).

licking [ˈlɪkɪŋ] *n* (*inf*) (*beating*) Tracht *f* Prügel; (*defeat*) Niederlage *f*. **to give sb a** ~ (*beating*) jdm eine Abreibung geben (*inf*); (*defeat*) jdn in die Pfanne hauen (*sl*) or einseifen (*inf*).

licorice *n see* **liquorice.**

lid [lɪd] *n* **(a)** Deckel *m*. **that puts the (tin)** ~ **on it** (*inf*) das ist doch die Höhe, das schlägt dem Faß den Boden aus; **a documentary that really takes the** ~ **off Hollywood** ein Dokumentarfilm, der das wahre Gesicht Hollywoods zeigt; **the press took the** ~ **off the whole plan** die Presse hat den Plan enthüllt or aufgedeckt.

    (b) (*eye*~) Lid *nt*.

(c) (*sl: hat*) Deckel *m* (*inf*).

lidless ['lɪdlɪs] *adj* **(a)** ohne Deckel. **(b)** *eyes* ohne Lider.

lido ['liːdəʊ] *n* Freibad *nt*.

lie[1] [laɪ] **1** *n* Lüge *f*. it's a ~! das ist eine Lüge!, das ist gelogen!; **to tell a** ~ lügen; **to give the** ~ **to sb** jdn der Lüge bezichtigen *or* beschuldigen; **to give the** ~ **to a report** die Unwahrheit eines Berichtes zeigen *or* beweisen, einen Bericht Lügen strafen (*geh*); ~ **detector** Lügendetektor *m*.
  2 *vi* lügen. **to** ~ **to sb** jdn belügen *or* anlügen.
  3 *vt* **to** ~ **one's way out of sth** sich aus etw herauslügen.

lie[2] (*vb: pret* **lay**, *ptp* **lain**) **1** *n* (*position*) Lage, Position *f*.
  2 *vi* **(a)** (*in horizontal or resting position*) liegen; (~ *down*) sich legen. he lay where he had fallen er blieb liegen, wo er hingefallen war; ~ **on your back** leg dich auf den Rücken; **obstacles** ~ **in the way of our success** unser Weg zum Erfolg ist mit Hindernissen verstellt; **the snow didn't** ~ der Schnee blieb nicht liegen; **to** ~ **with sb** (*Bibl, old*) bei jdm liegen (*Bibl, old*).
  (b) (*be buried*) ruhen. **to** ~ **at rest** zur letzten Ruhe gebettet sein (*geh*).
  (c) (*be situated*) liegen. **the runner who is lying third** der Läufer, der auf dem dritten Platz liegt; **the castle** ~**s to the north of the town** das Schloß liegt im Norden der Stadt; **Russia** ~**s to the north of India** Rußland liegt nördlich von Indien; **Uganda** ~**s far from the coast** Uganda liegt weit von der Küste ab *or* entfernt; **our road lay along the river** unsere Straße führte am Fluß entlang; **our futures** ~ **in quite different directions** unsere zukünftigen Wege führen in verschiedene Richtungen; **you are young and your life** ~**s before you** du bist jung, und das Leben liegt noch vor dir.
  (d) (*be, remain in a certain condition*) liegen. **to** ~ **asleep** (daliegen und) schlafen; **to** ~ **helpless** hilflos daliegen; **to** ~ **dying** im Sterben liegen; **he lay resting on the sofa** er ruhte sich auf dem Sofa aus; **to** ~ **still** still (da)liegen; **the snow lay deep** es lag tiefer Schnee; **the book lay unopened** das Buch lag ungeöffnet da; **to** ~ **low** untertauchen, sich nicht mehr sehen lassen; **how do things** ~? wie steht die Sache?; **to** ~ **heavy on the stomach** schwer im Magen liegen; **these duties** ~ **heavy on me** diese Pflichten lasten schwer auf mir; **to** ~ **heavy on the conscience** schwer auf dem Gewissen lasten.
  (e) (*immaterial things*) liegen. **where does the difficulty** ~? wo liegt die Schwierigkeit?; **it** ~**s with you to solve the problem** es liegt bei dir, das Problem zu lösen; **his interests** ~ **in music** seine Interessen liegen auf dem Gebiet der Musik *or* gelten der Musik; **he did everything that lay in his power to help us** er tat alles in seiner Macht stehende, um uns zu helfen; **that responsibility** ~**s with your department** dafür ist Ihre Abteilung verantwortlich.

♦**lie about** *or* **around** *vi* herumliegen.

♦**lie back** *vi* **(a)** (*recline*) sich zurücklehnen.
  (b) (*fig: take no action*) es sich gemütlich machen, sich ausruhen. **we can't afford to** ~ ~ **and relax until the job's finished** wir können uns (*dat*) keine Ruhe gönnen, bis die Arbeit erledigt ist.

♦**lie down** *vi* **(a)** sich hinlegen. **he lay** ~ **on the bed** er legte sich aufs Bett; ~ ~! (*to a dog*) leg dich!, hinlegen!
  (b) (*fig: accept, submit*) **don't expect me to** ~ ~ **and listen to your insults** erwarte nicht, daß ich mir deine Beleidigungen ruhig anhöre; **to** ~ ~ **under sth** sich (*dat*) etw gefallen *or* bieten lassen; **he won't take that lying** ~! das läßt er sich nicht gefallen *or* bieten!; **he didn't take defeat lying** ~ er nahm die Niederlage nicht tatenlos hin.

♦**lie in** *vi* **(a)** (*stay in bed*) im Bett bleiben. **(b)** (*old: childbirth*) im Wochenbett liegen.

♦**lie off** *vi* (*Naut: be anchored nearby*) vor Anker liegen. **the ship lay** ~ **Aberdeen** das Schiff lag vor Aberdeen vor Anker.

♦**lie over** *vi* vertagt *or* zurückgestellt werden.

♦**lie to** *vi* (*Naut*) **(a)** (*be anchored*) vor Anker liegen, ankern. **(b)** (*come into a position for anchoring*) beidrehen.

♦**lie up** *vi* **(a)** (*rest after illness etc*) im Bett bleiben.
  (b) (*hide*) untertauchen. **the robbers are lying** ~ die Räuber sind untergetaucht.
  (c) (*be out of use*) nicht benutzt werden, unbenutzt stehen; (*car*) abgestellt sein.

lie-abed ['laɪəbed] *n* Langschläfer(in *f*) *m*.

Liechtenstein ['liːxtən͵ʃtaɪn] *n* Liechtenstein *nt*.

lie-down ['laɪdaʊn] *n* (*inf*) Schläfchen (*inf*), Nickerchen (*inf*) *nt*. **to have a** ~ ein Schläfchen *or* Nickerchen machen (*inf*).

lief [liːf] *adv* (*old*) **I would as** ~ ich würde ebenso gern; **I would as** ~ ... as anything ich würde nichts lieber tun als ...

liege [liːdʒ] *n* (*old*) **(a)** (*also* ~ **lord**) Lehnsherr *m*. **my** ~ Euer Gnaden. **(b)** (*also* ~ **man**) Lehnsmann, Vasall *m*.

lie-in ['laɪɪn] *n* (*inf*) **to have a** ~ (sich) ausschlafen.

lien [lɪən] *n* Zurückbehaltungsrecht, Pfandrecht *nt*.

lieu [luː] *n* (*form*) **money in** ~ statt dessen Geld; **in** ~ **of X** an Stelle von X; **in** ~ **of that** statt dessen.

Lieut. (*Mil*) *abbr of* **lieutenant** Lt.

lieutenancy [lef'tenənsɪ, (*US*)luː'tenənsɪ] *n* Leutnantsrang *m*. **he gained his** ~ er ist zum Leutnant befördert worden.

lieutenant [lef'tenənt, (*US*) luː'tenənt] *n* **(a)** Leutnant *m*; (*Brit*) Oberleutnant *m*. **first** (*US*)/**second** ~ Oberleutnant/Leutnant. **(b)** (*governor*) Statthalter, Gouverneur *m*.

lieutenant: ~**-colonel** *n* Oberstleutnant *m*; ~**-commander** *n* Fregattenkapitän *m*; ~**-general** *n* Generalleutnant *m*; ~**-governor** *n* Vizegouverneur *m*.

life [laɪf] *n*, *pl* **lives** **(a)** Leben *nt*. **bird/plant** ~ die Vogel-/ Pflanzenwelt; **there is not much insect** ~ **here** hier gibt es nicht viele Insekten; **drawn from** ~ lebensnah; **to the** ~ lebensecht; **the battle resulted in great loss of** ~ bei der Schlacht kamen viele ums Leben; **this is a matter of** ~ **and death** hier geht es um Leben und Tod; **a** ~ **and death struggle** ein Kampf

auf Leben und Tod; ~ **begins at 40** das Leben fängt mit 40 (erst richtig) an; **to bring sb back to** ~ jdn wiederbeleben, jdn ins Leben zurückrufen; **his book brings history to** ~ sein Buch läßt die Geschichte lebendig werden; **to come to** ~ (*fig*) lebendig werden; **I'm the sort of person who comes to** ~ **in the evenings** ich bin ein Typ, der erst abends munter wird; **after half an hour the discussion came to** ~ nach einer halben Stunde kam Leben in die Diskussion; **to put new** ~ **into sb** jdm wieder Auftrieb geben; **for dear** ~ verzweifelt; **they swam for dear** ~ sie schwammen um ihr Leben; **they looked at him in the oxygen tent fighting for dear** ~ sie sahen, wie er im Sauerstoffzelt um sein Leben kämpfte; **at my time of** ~ in meinem Alter; **marriage should be for** ~ eine Ehe sollte fürs Leben geschlossen werden; **he's got a job for** ~ er hat eine Stelle auf Lebenszeit; **the murderer was imprisoned for** ~ der Mörder bekam „lebenslänglich" (*inf*) *or* wurde zu lebenslänglicher Freiheitsstrafe verurteilt; **he's doing** ~ (*inf*) er ist ein Lebenslänglicher (*inf*); **he got** ~ **for the murder** (*inf*) er hat „lebenslänglich" für den Mord gekriegt (*inf*).
  (b) (*individual life*) **how many lives were lost?** wie viele (Menschen) sind ums Leben gekommen?; **the lives of the prisoners** das Leben der Gefangenen; **to take sb's** ~ jdn umbringen; **to take one's own** ~ sich (*dat*) das Leben nehmen; **to save sb's** ~ (*lit*) jdm das Leben retten; (*fig*) jdn retten; **the suspected murderer is on trial for his** ~ für den Mordverdächtigen geht es bei dem Prozeß um Leben und Tod; **early/later in** ~, **in early/later** ~ in frühen Jahren/in späteren Jahren *or* später im Leben; **she began (her working)** ~ **as a teacher** sie begann ihr Berufsleben als Lehrerin; **all his** ~ sein ganzes Leben lang; **I've never been to London in my** ~ ich war in meinem ganzen Leben noch nicht in London; **run for your lives!** rennt um euer Leben!; **I can't for the** ~ **of me ...** (*inf*) ich kann beim besten Willen nicht ...; **never in my** ~ **have I heard such nonsense** ich habe mein Lebtag noch nicht *or* noch nie im Leben so einen Unsinn gehört; **not on your life!** (*inf*) ich bin doch nicht verrückt! (*inf*); **would you ever disobey him?** — **not on your** ~! (*inf*) würdest du je seine Befehle mißachten? — nie im Leben!; **a** ~ **for a** ~ Auge um Auge, Zahn um Zahn; **he is a good/bad** ~ (*Insur*) er ist ein hohes/niedriges Risiko.
  (c) (*the world, social activity*) **to see** ~ die Welt sehen; **there isn't much** ~ **here in the evenings** hier ist abends nicht viel Leben *or* nicht viel los.
  (d) (*liveliness*) Leben *nt*. **those children are full of** ~! diese Kinder stecken voller Leben *or* sind sehr lebhaft!; **the performance of the play was full of** ~ die Aufführung war sehr lebendig; **he's still got so much** ~ **in him** er ist noch so vital *or* steckt noch voller Leben; **there's** ~ **in the old girl yet** (*inf*) sie ist noch schwer aktiv (*inf*); (*of car*) die Kiste bringt's noch (*sl*); **he is the** ~ **and soul of every party** er bringt Leben in jede Party; **wherever John goes, he wants to be the** ~ **and soul of the party** John will überall im Mittelpunkt stehen.
  (e) (*way of life*) Leben *nt*. ~ **is hard in the arctic regions** das Leben in der Arktis ist hart; **village** ~ das Leben auf dem Dorf; **this is the** ~! ja, ist das ein Leben!; **what a** ~! was für ein Leben!; **such is** ~ so ist das Leben!; **to lead the** ~ **of Riley** wie Gott in Frankreich leben; **it's a good** ~ es ist ein schönes Leben; **the good** ~ das süße Leben.
  (f) (*useful or active life of sth*) Lebensdauer *f*. **during the** ~ **of the present Parliament** während der Legislaturperiode des gegenwärtigen Parlaments; **there's not much** ~ **left in the battery** die Batterie macht's nicht mehr lange (*inf*).
  (g) (*book*) (*biography*) Biographie *f*; (*of saint, king etc*) Lebensbeschreibung *f*.

life: ~ **annuity** *n* Leib- *or* Lebensrente *f*; ~ **assurance** *n* Lebensversicherung *f*; ~**belt** *n* Rettungsgürtel *m*; ~**blood** *n* Blut *nt*; (*fig*) Lebensnerv *m*; **to drain away sb's** ~**blood** (*fig*) jdn ausbluten lassen; ~**boat** *n* (*from shore*) Rettungsboot *nt*; (*from ship also*) Beiboot *nt*; ~**buoy** *n* Rettungsring *m*; ~ **cycle** *n* Lebenszyklus *m*; ~ **expectancy** *n* Lebenserwartung *f*; ~ **force** *n* Lebenskraft *f*; ~**-giving** *adj* lebenspendend; ~**-giving aid to poor countries** lebensnotwendige Hilfe für arme Länder; ~**guard** *n* **(a)** (*on beach*) Rettungsschwimmer *m*; (*in baths*) Bademeister *m*; **(b)** (*Mil*) Leibwache *f*; ~ **history** *n* Lebensgeschichte *f*; (*Biol*) Entwicklungsgeschichte *f*; ~ **imprisonment** *n* lebenslängliche Freiheitsstrafe; ~ **insurance** *n* *see* **assurance**; ~ **jacket** *n* Schwimmweste *f*.

lifeless ['laɪflɪs] *adj* **(a)** (*inanimate*) leblos, tot; *planet* unbelebt, ohne Leben. **(b)** (*dead, as if dead*) leblos. **(c)** (*fig*) (*listless, dull*) lahm (*inf*), langweilig; *people also* teilnahmslos.

lifelessly ['laɪflɪslɪ] *adv* leblos; (*fig*) teilnahmslos.

lifelessness ['laɪflɪsnɪs] *n* Leblosigkeit *f*; (*fig*) Teilnahmslosigkeit *f*.

life: ~**like** *adj* lebensecht; *imitation also* naturgetreu; ~**line** *n* **(a)** Rettungsleine *f*; (*of diver*) Signalleine *f*; (*fig*) Rettungsanker *m*; **the telephone is a** ~**line for many old people** das Telefon ist für viele alte Leute lebenswichtig; **in doing this they risked severing their financial** ~**line** dadurch haben sie riskiert, daß ihnen der Geldhahn zugedreht wird; **(b)** (*Palmistry*) Lebenslinie *f*; ~**long** *adj* lebenslang; **they are** ~**long friends** sie sind schon ihr Leben lang Freunde; **he's my** ~**long friend** er war schon immer mein Freund; **we became** ~**long friends** wir wurden Freunde fürs Leben; **his** ~**long devotion to the cause** die Sache, in deren Dienst er sein Leben gestellt hat; **her** ~**long fear of water** ihre angeborene Angst vor Wasser; ~ **peer** *n* Peer *m* auf Lebenszeit; ~ **preserver** *n* **(a)** (*Brit*) Totschläger *m*; **(b)** (*US*) Schwimmweste *f*.

lifer ['laɪfə[r]] *n* (*sl*) Lebenslängliche(r) *mf* (*inf*).

life: ~ **raft** *n* Rettungsfloß *nt*; ~**saver** *n* (a) Lebensretter(in *f*) *m*; (*lifeguard*) Rettungsschwimmer(in *f*) *m*; **(b)** (*fig*) Retter *m* in der Not; **it was a real** ~**saver!** das hat mich gerettet; ~**-saving 1** *n* Lebensrettung *f*; (*saving people from drowning*)

Rettungsschwimmen nt; **2** adj techniques, apparatus Rettungs-; phone call, drug lebensrettend; drop of whisky rettend; **~-saving certificate** Rettungsschwimmabzeichen nt; **~ sentence** n lebenslängliche Freiheitsstrafe; **~-size(d)** adj in Lebensgröße, lebensgroß; **~span** n (of people) Lebenserwartung f; (of animals, plants) Leben(sdauer f) nt; **~ support system** n Lebenserhaltungssystem nt; **~time** n (a) Lebenszeit f; (of battery, machine, animal) Lebensdauer f; once in a ~time einmal im Leben; during or in my ~time während meines Lebens; in his ~time there were no buses zu seiner Zeit gab es keine Busse; the chance of a ~time eine einmalige Chance, die Chance (inf); a ~time's devotion to charity ein Leben, das der Wohltätigkeit gewidmet ist; the work of a ~time ein Lebenswerk nt; (b) (fig) Ewigkeit f; **~work** n Lebenswerk nt.

lift [lɪft] **1** n (a) (~ing) Heben nt. he saluted us with a ~ of his hand er grüßte uns mit einer Handbewegung; he questioned the story with a ~ of the eyebrows er zog die Augenbrauen hoch, als er die Geschichte hörte; the haughty ~ of her head ihre hochmütige Kopfhaltung; give me a ~ up heb mich mal hoch; give me a ~ with this trunk hilf mir, den Koffer hochzuheben.

  (b) (Weightlifting) that was a good ~ das war eine gute Leistung; his next ~ is 100 kg beim nächsten Versuch will er 100 kg heben; different types of ~ mehrere verschiedene Hebearten pl.

  (c) (emotional uplift) to give sb a ~ jdn aufmuntern; (drug) jdn aufputschen; (prospect) jdm Auftrieb geben.

  (d) (in car etc) to give sb a ~ (take along) jdn mitnehmen; (as special journey) jdn fahren; to get a ~ from sb von jdm mitgenommen werden/von jdm gefahren werden; don't take ~s from strangers laß dich nicht von Fremden mitnehmen; want a ~? möchten Sie mitkommen/soll ich dich fahren?

  (e) (Brit: elevator) Fahrstuhl, Aufzug, Lift m; (for goods) Aufzug m. he took the ~ er fuhr mit dem Fahrstuhl etc.

  (f) (Aviat) Auftrieb m.

2 vt (a) (also ~ up) hochheben; window hochschieben; feet, head heben; eyes aufschlagen; hat lüften, ziehen; potatoes etc ernten; child etc hochnehmen. to ~ the baby out of his pram das Baby aus dem Kinderwagen heben; to ~ one's hand to sb die Hand gegen jdn erheben.

  (b) (fig also ~ up) heben; voice erheben. ~ (up) your hearts to God erhebt eure Herzen zu Gott; the news ~ed him out of his depression durch die Nachricht verflog seine Niedergeschlagenheit; his new job ~ed him far above his humble origins seine neue Stellung war für ihn ein Aufstieg aus seiner bescheidenen Herkunft; the excellence of his style ~s him far above his contemporaries sein ausgezeichneter Stil stellt ihn weit über seine Zeitgenossen.

  (c) (remove) restrictions etc aufheben.

  (d) (inf: steal) mitgehen lassen (inf), klauen (inf); (plagiarize) abschreiben, klauen (sl).

  (e) to have one's face ~ed sich (dat) das Gesicht straffen or liften lassen.

  (f) (sl: arrest) schnappen (inf).

3 vi (a) (be lifted) sich hochheben lassen. that chair is too heavy (for you) to ~ dieser Stuhl ist zu schwer zum Hochheben.

  (b) (mist) sich lichten.

  (c) (rocket, plane) abheben. it ~ed slowly into the sky es stieg langsam zum Himmel auf.

◆**lift down** vt sep herunterheben.

◆**lift off** vti sep abheben.

◆**lift up 1** vt sep see lift 2 (a, b). to ~ ~ one's head (fig) den Kopf hochhalten; I'll never ~ ~ ~ my head again ich kann niemandem mehr in die Augen blicken. **2** vi hochgeklappt werden.

lift: ~ **attendant** n (Brit), ~**man** n (Brit) Fahrstuhlführer m; ~**boy** n (Brit) Liftboy m; ~**-off** n (Space) Abheben nt, Start m; we have ~-off wir haben abgehoben; ~**shaft** n Aufzugsschacht m.

ligament ['lɪɡəmənt] n Band, Ligament nt. he's torn a ~ in his shoulder er hat einen Bänderriß in der Schulter.

ligature ['lɪɡətʃəʳ] n (Med, Mus, Typ) Ligatur f; (bandage) Binde f; (Med: thread or cord) Abbindungsschnur f/-draht m.

light¹ [laɪt] (vb: pret, ptp lit or ~ed) **1** n (a) (in general) Licht nt. ~ and shade Licht und Schatten; at first ~ bei Tagesanbruch; to read by the ~ of a candle bei Kerzenlicht lesen; hang the picture in a good ~ häng das Bild in ein richtiges Licht; to cast or shed or throw ~ on sth (lit) etw beleuchten; (fig also) Licht in etw (acc) bringen; the moon cast its silvery ~ on ... der Mond beleuchtete ... silbern or warf sein silbernes Licht auf (+acc) ...; to cast a new or fresh ~ on sth neues Licht auf etw (acc) werfen; to stand in sb's ~ (lit) jdm im Licht stehen; his clever brother always stood in his ~ (fig) er stand immer im Schatten seines klugen Bruders; in the cold ~ of day (fig) bei Licht besehen; this story shows his character in a bad ~ diese Geschichte wirft ein schlechtes Licht auf seinen Charakter; it revealed him in a different ~ es ließ ihn in einem anderen Licht erscheinen; I don't see things in that ~ ich sehe die Dinge anders or in einem anderen Licht; to see sth in a new ~ etw mit anderen Augen betrachten; in the ~ of angesichts (+gen); the theory, seen in the ~ of recent discoveries die Theorie im Licht(e) der neuesten Entdeckungen betrachtet; in the ~ of what you say in Anbetracht dessen, was Sie sagen; to bring to ~ ans Tageslicht bringen; to come to ~ ans Tageslicht kommen; to see the ~ (liter: be born) das Licht der Welt erblicken (liter); (liter: be made public) veröffentlicht werden; finally I saw the ~ (inf) endlich ging mir ein Licht auf (inf); (morally) endlich wurden mir die Augen geöffnet; to go out like a ~ sofort weg sein (inf).

  (b) Licht nt; (lamp) Lampe f; (fluorescent ~) Neonröhre f. put out the ~/~s before you go to bed mach das Licht aus, bevor du ins Bett gehst; all the ~s went out during the storm während des Sturms gingen alle Lichter aus; (traffic) ~s Ampel f; the ~s (of a car) die Beleuchtung; all ships must show a ~ while at sea alle Schiffe müssen auf See Lichter führen; ~s out (Mil) Zapfenstreich m; ~s out for the boys was at 8 pm um 20 Uhr mußten die Jungen das Licht ausmachen; ~s out! Licht aus(machen)!; to hide one's ~ under a bushel (prov) sein Licht unter den Scheffel stellen (prov).

  (c) (flame) have you a ~? haben Sie Feuer?; to put a ~ to sth, to set ~ to sth etw anzünden.

  (d) (Archit) (Dach)fenster nt; (skylight) Oberlicht nt. leaded ~s in Blei gefaßte Fensterscheiben.

  (e) (in eyes) Leuchten nt. the ~ went out of her eyes das Strahlen erlosch in ihren Augen.

  (f) (standards) according to his ~s nach bestem Wissen und Gewissen.

2 adj (+er) hell. a ~ green dress ein hellgrünes Kleid; it is ~ now es ist jetzt hell or Tag.

3 vt (a) (illuminate) beleuchten; lamp, light anmachen. electricity ~s the main streets die Hauptstraßen werden elektrisch beleuchtet; a smile lit her face ein Lächeln erhellte ihr Gesicht; to ~ the way for sb jdm leuchten; (fig) jdm den Weg weisen; his pioneering work lit the way for a whole generation of scholars seine Pionierarbeit war wegweisend für eine ganze Gelehrtengeneration.

  (b) anzünden; cigarette also anstecken; fire also anmachen.

4 vi (begin to burn) brennen. this fire won't ~ das Feuer geht nicht an.

◆**light up 1** vi (a) (be lit) aufleuchten. the shop signs ~ ~ after dark die Leuchtreklamen werden nach Einbruch der Dunkelheit eingeschaltet; the room/whole house suddenly lit ~ plötzlich ging das Licht im Zimmer an/plötzlich gingen die Lichter im Haus an.

  (b) (face) sich erhellen; (eyes) aufleuchten. his face lit ~ with joy sein Gesicht strahlte vor Freude.

  (c) (smoke) the men took out their pipes and lit ~ die Männer holten ihre Pfeifen hervor und zündeten sie an.

2 vt sep (a) (illuminate) beleuchten; (from inside also) erhellen; lights anmachen. a smile lit ~ his face ein Lächeln erhellte sein Gesicht; Piccadilly Circus was all lit ~ der Piccadilly Circus war hell erleuchtet.

  (b) cigarette etc anzünden.

  (c) (fig sl) to be lit ~ angesäuselt (inf) or beduselt (sl) sein.

◆**light (up)on** vi (inf) entdecken, stoßen auf (+acc).

light² **1** adj (+er) leicht; taxes niedrig; punishment milde. ~ lorry/railway Kleinlastwagen m/Kleinbahn f; to give sb ~ weight jdm zuwenig abwiegen; she has a very ~ touch on the piano sie hat einen sehr weichen Anschlag; she has a ~ touch or hand with pastry ihr gelingt der Teig immer schön locker; to be a ~ eater wenig essen, kein großer Esser sein; ~ comedy Lustspiel nt, Schwank m; ~ opera Operette f; ~ reading Unterhaltungslektüre f; a ~ and cheerful approach to life eine unbeschwerte, fröhliche Einstellung zum Leben; with a ~ heart leichten Herzens; as ~ as air or a feather federleicht; a bit ~ in the head (crazy) nicht ganz richtig im Kopf; (tipsy) angeheitert; (dizzy) benommen; to be ~ on one's feet sich leichtfüßig bewegen; to make ~ of one's difficulties seine Schwierigkeiten auf die leichte Schulter nehmen; you shouldn't make ~ of her problems du solltest dich über ihre Probleme nicht lustig machen; to make ~ work of spielend fertigwerden mit.

2 adv to travel ~ mit wenig or leichtem Gepäck reisen.

light³ vi pret, ptp ~ed or lit [lɪt] (liter) sich niederlassen.

light: ~**-armed** adj leichtbewaffnet; ~ **bulb** n Glühlampe or -birne f; ~**-coloured** adj, comp ~er-coloured, superl ~est-coloured hell.

lighten¹ ['laɪtn] **1** vt erhellen; colour, hair aufhellen; gloom aufheitern. **2** vi hell werden, sich aufhellen. to thunder and ~ (Met) donnern und blitzen.

lighten² **1** vt load leichter machen. to ~ a ship/a ship's cargo ein Schiff leichtern; to ~ sb's burden jds Lage erleichtern; to ~ sb's workload jdm etwas Arbeit abnehmen; the good news ~ed her cares/heart die gute Nachricht befreite sie von ihren Sorgen/machte ihr das Herz leichter.

2 vi (load) leichter werden. her heart ~ed ihr wurde leichter ums Herz.

lighter¹ ['laɪtəʳ] n Feuerzeug nt.

lighter² n (Naut) Leichter m.

light: ~**-fingered** [ˌlaɪt'fɪŋɡəd] adj, comp ~er-fingered, superl ~est-fingered langfingerig; ~ **fitting**, ~ **fixture** n (~bulb holder) Fassung f; (bracket) (Lampen)halterung f; ~**-footed** adj, comp ~er-footed, superl ~est-footed leichtfüßig; ~**-haired** adj, comp ~er-haired, superl ~est-haired hellhaarig; animals also mit hellem Fell; ~**-headed** adj, comp ~er-headed, superl ~est-headed benebelt (inf); (dizzy also) benommen; (tipsy also) angeheitert; (with fever) wirr (im Kopf); (frivolous) oberflächlich, leichtfertig; I felt quite ~-headed when I heard I'd passed the exam ich wurde ganz ausgelassen or übermütig, als ich hörte, daß ich die Prüfung bestanden hatte; wine makes me ~-headed Wein steigt mir in den Kopf; ~**-headedness** n see adj Benommenheit f; angeheiterter Zustand; Verwirrtsein nt; Oberflächlichkeit, Leichtfertigkeit f; Ausgelassenheit f, Übermut m; ~**-hearted** adj unbeschwert, unbekümmert; chat zwanglos; reply scherzhaft; book, film fröhlich, vergnüglich; look at life heiter, unbekümmert; comedy leicht; ~**-heartedly** adv unbekümmert, leichten Herzens; reply scherzhaft; ~**-heartedness** n see adj Unbeschwertheit, Unbekümmertheit f; Zwanglosigkeit f; Scherzhaftigkeit f; Fröhlichkeit, Vergnüglichkeit f; Heiterkeit f; ~**-heavyweight** n Halbschwergewicht f; (boxer) Halbschwergewichtler m; ~**house** n Leuchtturm m; ~**house keeper** n Leuchtturmwärter m.

lighting ['laɪtɪŋ] n Beleuchtung f. candles were used

for ~ the dining room das Eßzimmer war mit Kerzen beleuchtet.

lighting-up time [ˌlaɪtɪŋˈʌptaɪm] n Zeitpunkt m, zu dem Straßen- und Fahrzeugbeleuchtung eingeschaltet werden muß. **when is ~?** wann wird die Beleuchtung angemacht?

lightish [ˈlaɪtɪʃ] adj colour hell. **a ~ brown** ein helleres Braun.

lightless [ˈlaɪtlɪs] adj dunkel, lichtlos.

lightly [ˈlaɪtlɪ] adv **(a)** touch, rain, eat, wounded, stressed leicht; walk, tread leise. **to sleep ~** einen leichten Schlaf haben; **~ clad (in sth)** leicht (mit etw) bekleidet; **they are ~ taxed** sie haben niedrige Steuern; **to get off ~** glimpflich davonkommen; **to touch ~ on a subject** ein Thema nur berühren or streifen.

(b) (casually) say leichthin. **to speak ~ of sb/sth** sich abfällig or geringschätzig über jdn/etw äußern; **he spoke ~ of his illness** er nahm seine Krankheit auf die leichte Schulter; **don't take her problems so ~** nimm ihre Probleme etwas ernster; **to treat sth too ~** etw nicht ernst genug nehmen; **she referred ~ to the fact that ...** sie erwähnte leichthin, daß ...; **a responsibility not to be ~ undertaken** eine Verantwortung, die man nicht unüberlegt auf sich nehmen sollte; **it's not a job I'd ~ do again** die Arbeit würde ich so leicht nicht wieder tun.

light: ~ **meter** n Belichtungsmesser m; **~-minded** adj oberflächlich, leichtfertig.

lightness[1] [ˈlaɪtnɪs] n Helligkeit f.

lightness[2] n **(a)** geringes Gewicht, Leichtheit f; (of task, step, movements) Leichtigkeit f; (of taxes) Niedrigkeit f; (of punishment) Milde f; (of soil, cake) Lockerheit f. **the ~ of the breeze/wound/music** etc die leichte Brise/Verletzung/Musik etc; **a feeling of ~ came over him** ein Gefühl der Erleichterung überkam ihn; **there was a certain ~ in her attitude to life** ihre Einstellung zum Leben hatte etwas Unbeschwertes.

(b) (lack of seriousness) mangelnder Ernst. **a certain ~ in your attitude towards the authorities** eine gewisse Leichtfertigkeit den Behörden gegenüber.

lightning [ˈlaɪtnɪŋ] **1** n Blitz m. **a flash of ~** ein Blitz m; (doing damage) ein Blitzschlag m; **struck by ~** vom Blitz getroffen; **what causes ~?** wie entstehen Blitze?; **we had some ~ an hour ago** vor einer Stunde hat es geblitzt; **as quick as ~, like (greased) ~** wie der Blitz, wie ein geölter Blitz; **~ conductor** or (US) **rod** Blitzableiter m.

2 attr blitzschnell, Blitz-. **~ attack** Überraschungs- or Blitzangriff m; **~ strike** spontaner Streik, spontane Arbeitsniederlegung; **with ~ speed** blitzschnell, mit Blitzesschnelle.

lights [laɪts] npl (Anat) Tierlunge f.

light: **~ship** n Feuerschiff nt; **~-skinned** adj, comp **~er-skinned**, superl **~est-skinned** hellhäutig; **~ wave** n (Licht)welle f; **~weight 1** adj leicht; (boxer) Leichtgewichts-; (fig) schwach; **the ~weight boxing championship** die Boxmeisterschaft im Leichtgewicht; **2** n Leichtgewicht nt; (boxer) Leichtgewichtler m; (fig) Leichtgewicht nt; **he is regarded as a ~weight in academic circles** er wird in akademischen Kreisen nicht für voll genommen; **~-year** n Lichtjahr nt.

ligneous [ˈlɪgnɪəs] adj hölzern, holzartig.

lignite [ˈlɪgnaɪt] n Lignit m.

likable adj see **lik(e)able.**

like[1] [laɪk] **1** adj **(a)** (similar) ähnlich. **the two boys are very ~** die beiden Jungen sind sich (dat) sehr ähnlich.

(b) (same) of ~ origin gleicher Herkunft.

2 prep (similar to) ähnlich (+dat); (in comparisons) wie. **to be ~ sb** jdm ähnlich sein; **they are very ~ each other** sie sind sich sehr ähnlich; **he is rather ~ you** er ist dir ziemlich ähnlich; **who(m) is he ~?** wem sieht er ähnlich?, wem gleicht er?; **what's he ~?** wie ist er?; **what's your new coat ~?** wie sieht dein neuer Mantel aus?; **she was ~ a sister to me** sie war wie eine Schwester zu mir; **that's just ~ him!** das sieht ihm ähnlich!, das ist typisch!; **it's not ~ him** es ist nicht seine Art; **I never saw anything ~ it** so (et)was habe ich noch nie gesehen; **that's just ~ a woman!** typisch Frau!; **that's more ~ it!** so ist es schon besser!; **that that's nothing ~ as nice as this** one der Hut ist bei weitem nicht so hübsch wie dieser; **there's nothing ~ a nice cup of tea!** es geht nichts über eine schöne Tasse Tee!; **there's nothing ~ it** das ist einmalig; **is this what you had in mind?** — **it's something/nothing ~ it** hattest du dir so etwas vorgestellt? — ja, so ähnlich/nein, überhaupt nicht; **that's something ~ a steak!** das ist vielleicht ein Steak!, das nenne ich ein Steak!; **the Americans are ~ that** so sind die Amerikaner; **people ~ that** solche Leute; **a car ~ that** so ein Auto, ein solches Auto; **I found one ~ it** ich habe ein ähnliches gefunden; **one exactly ~ it** eines, das genau gleich ist; **eyes ~ stars** Augen wie Sterne; **it will cost something ~ £10** es wird etwa or so ungefähr £ 10 kosten; **I was thinking of something ~ a doll** ich habe an so etwas wie eine Puppe gedacht; **that sounds ~ a good idea** das hört sich gut an; **~ a man** wie ein Mann; **~ mad** (inf), **~ anything** (inf) wie verrückt (inf) or wild (inf); **~ that so; it wasn't ~ that at all** so war's doch gar nicht; **he thinks ~ us** er denkt wie wir; **A ~ B, thinks that ...** A wie (auch) B meinen, daß ...

3 adv (inf) **it's nothing ~** es ist nichts dergleichen; **as ~ as not, very ~, ~ enough** höchst wahrscheinlich, sehr wahrscheinlich; **I found this money, ~** (dial) ich hab da das Geld gefunden, nich (sl) or wa (dial) or gell (S Ger).

4 conj (strictly incorrect) **~ I said** wie ich schon sagte, wie gesagt; **it's just ~ I say** das sage ich ja immer; **~ we used to (do)** wie früher; **do it ~ I do** mach es so wie ich.

5 n (equal etc) **we shall not see his ~** wir werden einen Mann or so etwas (inf) wie ihn bekommen wir nicht wieder; **did you ever see the ~?** hast du so was schon gesehen?; **and the ~, and such ~** und dergleichen; **I've met the ~s of you before** solche wie dich kenne ich schon; **I've no time for the ~s of him** (inf) mit solchen Leuten gebe ich mich nicht ab (inf).

like[2] **1** n usu pl (taste) Geschmack m. **she tried to find out his ~s and dislikes** sie wollte herausbekommen, was er mochte und was nicht; **when it comes to food he has far too many ~s and dislikes** beim Essen ist er viel zu wählerisch.

2 vt **(a)** person mögen, gern haben. **don't you ~ me a little bit?** magst du mich nicht ein kleines bißchen?; **how do you ~ him?** wie gefällt er dir?; **I don't ~ him** ich kann ihn nicht leiden, ich mag ihn nicht; **he is well ~d here** er ist hier sehr beliebt.

(b) (find pleasure in) **I ~ black shoes** ich mag or mir gefallen schwarze Schuhe; **I ~ it** das gefällt mir; **I ~ chocolate** ich mag Schokolade, ich esse gern Schokolade; **I ~ football** (playing) ich spiele gerne Fußball; (watching) ich finde Fußball gut; **I ~ dancing** ich tanze gern; **I ~ this translation** ich finde diese Übersetzung gut; **we ~ it here** es gefällt uns hier; **I ~ wine but wine doesn't ~ me** (inf) ich trinke gern Wein, aber er bekommt mir nicht; **how do you ~ Cádiz?** wie gefällt Ihnen Cádiz?; **how would you ~ a walk?** was hältst du von einem Spaziergang?; **how would you ~ a black eye?** du willst dir wohl ein blaues Auge holen!; **your father won't ~ that!** (inf) deinem Vater wird das nicht gefallen!; **well, I ~ that!** (inf) na, wie finde ich denn das? (inf), **das ist ein starkes Stück!** (inf); **(well) how do you ~ that?** (inf) wie findest du denn das? (inf); **I ~ your nerve!** (inf) du hast Nerven! (inf).

(c) (wish, wish for) **I should ~ more time** ich würde mir gerne noch etwas Zeit lassen; **they should have ~d to come** sie wären gern gekommen; **I should ~ to know why** ich wüßte gerne, warum; **I should ~ you to do it** ich möchte, daß du es tust; **I ~ to be obeyed** ich erwarte Gehorsam; **whether he ~s it or not** ob es ihm paßt oder nicht, ob er will oder nicht; **I didn't ~ to disturb him** ich wollte ihn nicht stören; **what would you ~?** was hätten or möchten Sie gern?, was darf es sein?; **would you ~ a drink?** möchten Sie etwas trinken?; **how do you ~ your coffee?** wie trinken Sie Ihren Kaffee?; **would you ~ to go to Seville?** würden Sie gern nach Sevilla fahren?

3 vi **he is free to act as he ~s** es steht ihm frei, zu tun, was er will; **as you ~** wie Sie wollen; **if you ~** wenn Sie wollen.

-like adj suf -ähnlich, -artig.

lik(e)able [ˈlaɪkəbl] adj sympathisch, liebenswert.

lik(e)ableness [ˈlaɪkəblnɪs] n liebenswertes Wesen. **there's a certain ~ about him** er hat etwas Sympathisches or Liebenswertes an sich.

likelihood [ˈlaɪklɪhʊd] n Wahrscheinlichkeit f. **in all ~** aller Wahrscheinlichkeit nach; **there is no ~ of that** das ist nicht wahrscheinlich; **there is little ~ that ...** es ist kaum anzunehmen, daß ...; **is there any ~ of him coming?** besteht die Möglichkeit, daß er kommt?; **what's the ~ of their getting married?** wie wahrscheinlich ist es or wie groß ist die Wahrscheinlichkeit, daß die beiden heiraten?; **what's the ~ of you coming out with me tonight?** wie sind die Chancen, daß du heute abend mit mir ausgehst?

likely [ˈlaɪklɪ] **1** adj (+er) **(a)** (probable) wahrscheinlich. **he is not ~ to come** es ist unwahrscheinlich, daß er kommt; **is it ~ that I would do that?** trauen Sie mir das zu?; **the plan most ~ to succeed** der erfolgversprechendste Plan; **an incident ~ to cause trouble** ein Zwischenfall, der möglicherweise Ärger nach sich zieht; **a ~ explanation** eine mögliche or wahrscheinliche Erklärung; (iro) **wer's glaubt, wird selig!** (inf); **this is a ~ place for him to stay** es ist wahrscheinlich or gut möglich, daß er sich hier aufhält; **a ~ story!** (iro) das soll mal einer glauben!, vor allem das!

(b) (inf: suitable) **a ~ spot for a picnic** ein geeignetes or prima (inf) Plätzchen für ein Picknick; **he is a ~ person for the job** er kommt für die Stelle in Frage; **~ candidates** aussichtsreiche Kandidaten; **a ~ lad** ein vielversprechender junger Mann.

2 adv not **~!** (inf) wohl kaum (inf); **as ~ as not** höchstwahrscheinlich; **very ~ they've lost it** höchstwahrscheinlich haben sie es verloren; **they'll ~ be late** (dial) sie sind wahrscheinlich zu spät; **it's more ~ to be early than late** es wird eher früh als spät werden.

like-minded [ˈlaɪkˈmaɪndɪd] adj gleichgesinnt. **~ people** Gleichgesinnte pl.

liken [ˈlaɪkən] vt vergleichen (to mit).

likeness [ˈlaɪknɪs] n (resemblance) Ähnlichkeit f; (portrait) Bild(nis) nt. **the ghost appeared in the ~ of a monk** der Geist erschien in der Gestalt eines Mönchs; **the god took on the ~ of a bull** der Gott nahm die Form eines Stiers an.

likewise [ˈlaɪkwaɪz] adv ebenso, gleichermaßen. **~ it is true that ...** ebenso trifft es zu, daß ...; **he did ~** er machte es ebenso, er tat das gleiche; **have a nice weekend** — **~ schönes Wochenende!** — danke gleichfalls!; **I'm going to the cinema tonight — ~** ich gehe heute abend ins Kino — ich auch.

liking [ˈlaɪkɪŋ] n **(a)** (for particular person) Zuneigung f; (for types) Vorliebe f. **to have a ~ for sb** Zuneigung für jdn empfinden, jdn gern haben; **she took a ~ to him** sie mochte ihn (gut leiden), er war ihr sympathisch.

(b) (for thing) Vorliebe f. **to take a ~ to sth** eine Vorliebe für etw bekommen; **to be to sb's ~** nach jds Geschmack nt sein.

lilac [ˈlaɪlək] **1** n **(a)** (plant) Flieder m. **(b)** (colour) (Zart)lila nt. **2** adj fliederfarben, (zart)lila.

Lilliput [ˈlɪlɪpət] n Liliput nt.

Lilliputian [ˌlɪlɪˈpjuːʃɪən] **1** adj (lit) Liliputaner-; (fig) winzig, liliputanerhaft. **2** n (lit, fig) Liliputaner(in f) m.

lilo ® [ˈlaɪˌləʊ] n Luftmatratze f.

lilt [lɪlt] **1** n **(a)** (of song) munterer Rhythmus; (of voice) singender Tonfall. **the Irish have a ~ in their voices** die Iren sprechen mit einem singenden Tonfall; **she spoke with a Welsh ~** sie sprach mit dem singenden Tonfall der Waliser.

(b) (song) fröhliches or munteres Lied.

2 vt song trällern.

3 vi **I love the way her voice ~s** ich mag ihren singenden Tonfall; **her voice ~ed as she spoke** sie sprach mit einem sin-

genden Tonfall; **the tune ~s merrily along** die Melodie plätschert munter dahin.
lilting ['lıltıŋ] adj accent singend; ballad, tune, melody beschwingt, munter.
liltingly ['lıltıŋlı] adv see adj. **to speak ~** mit singendem Tonfall sprechen; **the tune continues ~** die Melodie geht munter or beschwingt weiter.
lily ['lılı] n Lilie f; (water ~) Seerose f. **~ of the valley** Maiglöckchen nt.
lily: ~-livered ['lılı͵lıvəd] adj feige; **~ pad** n Seerosenblatt nt; **~-white** adj schnee- or blütenweiß; (fig) tugendhaft.
limb [lım] n (a) (Anat) Glied nt. **~s** pl Glieder, Gliedmaßen pl; **the lower ~s** die unteren Gliedmaßen; **to rest one's tired ~s** seine müden Glieder or Knochen (inf) ausruhen; **to tear sb ~ from ~** jdn in Stücke reißen; **life and ~** Leib und Leben.
(b) (of tree) Ast m. **to be out on a ~** (fig) (ganz) allein (da)stehen; **those ideas of John's put him out on a ~** mit diesen Ideen steht John allein auf weiter Flur; **he had left himself out on a ~** er hatte sich in eine prekäre Lage gebracht.
(c) (of cross) Balken m; (of organization etc) Glied nt.
-limbed [-lımd] adj suf -glied(e)rig.
limber¹ ['lımbə^r] n (Mil) Protze f.
limber² adj beweglich, gelenkig.
♦limber up vi Lockerungsübungen machen; (fig) sich vorbereiten. **~ ~ with a few easy exercises** machen Sie sich mit ein paar einfachen Übungen warm; **he ~s (himself) ~ with exercises every morning** er bringt sich jeden Morgen mit Gymnastik in Schwung.
limbless ['lımlıs] adj tree astlos. **a ~ person** ein Versehrter; (with no limbs) ein Mensch ohne Gliedmaßen.
limbo ['lımbəu] n (a) (Rel) Vorhölle f, Limbus m (spec).
(b) (fig) Übergangs- or Zwischenstadium nt. **our expansion plans are in ~** because of lack of money unsere Erweiterungspläne sind wegen Geldmangels in der Schwebe; **a sort of ~ for retired politicians** eine Art Abstellgleis für zurückgetretene Politiker; **I'm in a sort of ~** ich hänge in der Luft (inf).
lime¹ [laım] 1 n (a) (Geol) Kalk m. (b) (bird~) (Vogel)leim m. 2 vt mit Kalk düngen.
lime² n (Bot: linden, also ~ tree) Linde(nbaum m) f.
lime³ n (Bot: citrus fruit) Limone(lle) f; (tree) Limonenbaum m. **~ juice** Limonensaft m.
lime kiln n Kalkofen m.
limelight ['laımlaıt] n Rampenlicht nt. **to be in the ~** im Rampenlicht or im Licht der Öffentlichkeit stehen; **he never sought the ~** er stand nie gern im Rampenlicht or im Licht der Öffentlichkeit.
limerick ['lımərık] n Limerick m.
limestone ['laımstəun] n Kalkstein m.
limey ['laımı] n (US sl) Engländer(in f) m.
limit ['lımıt] 1 n (a) Grenze f; (limitation) Beschränkung, Begrenzung f; (speed ~) Geschwindigkeitsbegrenzung f; (Comm) Limit nt. **the city ~s** die Stadtgrenzen pl; **a 40-mile ~** eine Vierzigmeilengrenze; (speed ~) eine Geschwindigkeitsbegrenzung von 40 Meilen pro Stunde; **is there any ~ on the size?** gibt es irgendwelche Größenbeschränkungen?; **is the Größe begrenzt or beschränkt?; to put a ~ on sth, to set a ~ to or on sth** etw begrenzen, etw beschränken; **within the spatially restricted ~s of the office** innerhalb der räumlich begrenzten Möglichkeiten des Büros; **that's beyond my financial ~s** das übersteigt meine finanziellen Möglichkeiten; **I am at the ~ of my patience** meine Geduld ist am Ende; **we're constantly working at the ~ of our abilities** unsere Arbeit bringt uns ständig an die Grenzen unserer Leistungsfähigkeit; **there's a ~!** alles hat seine Grenzen!; **there is a ~ to what one person can do** ein Mensch kann nur so viel tun und nicht mehr; **there's a ~ to the time you should spend** Sie sollten nicht allzuviel Zeit darauf verwenden; **there is no ~ to his stupidity** seine Dummheit kennt keine Grenzen; **there's a ~ to the amount of money we can spend** unseren Ausgaben sind Grenzen gesetzt, wir können nicht unbegrenzt Geld ausgeben; **it is true within ~s** es ist bis zu einem gewissen Grade richtig; **without ~s** unbegrenzt, unbeschränkt; **off ~s to military personnel** Zutritt für Militär verboten, für Militär gesperrt; **to go to the ~ to help sb** bis zum Äußersten gehen, um jdm zu helfen; **to know no ~s** keine Grenzen kennen; **40 mph is the ~** die Geschwindigkeit ist auf 40 Meilen pro Stunde beschränkt; **over the ~** zuviel; (in time) zu lange; **you are over your baggage is over the ~** Ihr Gepäck hat Übergewicht; **he was driving over the ~** er hat die Geschwindigkeitsbegrenzung überschritten; **he had more than the legal ~ (of alcohol) in his blood** er hatte mehr Promille als gesetzlich erlaubt; **top C is my ~** höher als bis zum hohen C komme ich nicht; **I'll offer £40, that's my ~** ich biete £ 40, das ist mein Limit or höher kann ich nicht gehen; **50 pages per week is my ~** 50 Seiten pro Woche sind mein Limit.
(b) (inf) **it's the (very) ~!** das ist die Höhe (inf) or das letzte (inf); **that child is the ~!** dieses Kind ist eine Zumutung! (inf); **he's the ~!, isn't he the ~?** das ist 'ne Type! (inf).
2 vt begrenzen, beschränken; freedom, spending, possibilities einschränken; imagination hemmen. **to ~ sth to sth** etw auf etw (acc) beschränken; **are you ~ed for time?** ist Ihre Zeit begrenzt?; **to ~ oneself to a few remarks** sich auf einige (wenige) Bemerkungen beschränken; **time is the ~ing factor** wir sind zeitlich gebunden; **what are the ~ing factors?** wodurch sind uns (dat) Grenzen gesetzt?
limitation [͵lımı'teıʃən] n Beschränkung f; (of freedom, spending) Einschränkung f. **poor education is a great ~** eine schlechte Schulbildung ist ein großes Handikap; **there is no ~ on exports of coal** es gibt keine Beschränkungen für den Kohleexport; **the ~s of a bilingual dictionary** die beschränkten Möglichkeiten eines zweisprachigen Wörterbuchs; **to have one's/it's ~s** seine Grenzen haben.

limited ['lımıtıd] adj improvement, knowledge begrenzt; edition, means also beschränkt; intelligence, knowledge also mäßig; person beschränkt. **in a more ~ sense** in engerem Sinn; **this is only true in a ~ sense** dies ist nur in gewissem Maße wahr; **~ liability company** (Brit) Gesellschaft f mit beschränkter Haftung.
limitless ['lımıtlıs] adj grenzenlos.
limousine ['lıməziːn] n Limousine f.
limp¹ [lımp] 1 n Hinken, Humpeln nt. **to walk with a ~** hinken, humpeln; **the accident left him with a ~** seit dem Unfall hinkt er; **he has a bad ~** er hinkt or humpelt sehr stark.
2 vi hinken, humpeln. **the ship managed to ~ into port** das Schiff kam gerade noch or mit Müh und Not in den Hafen.
limp² adj (+er) schlapp, schlaff; flowers welk; material, cloth weich; voice matt, müde; (of homosexual etc) süßlich. **he's a ~ sort of character** er hat einen schwachen Charakter; **let your body go ~** alle Muskeln entspannen, alles locker lassen.
limpet ['lımpıt] n Napfschnecke f. **to stick to sb like a ~** (inf) wie eine Klette an jdm hängen; **~ mine** Haftmine f.
limpid ['lımpıd] adj klar; liquid also durchsichtig.
limpidly ['lımpıdlı] adv klar. **her eyes gazed ~ at me** sie sah mich mit blanken Augen an.
limply ['lımplı] adv schlapp, schlaff. **~ bound in calfskin** in weiches Kalbsleder gebunden; **..., he said ~ ...,** sagte er mit matter Stimme; (of homosexual etc) **...,** flötete er (inf).
limpness ['lımpnıs] n see adj Schlaffheit, Schlappheit f; Welkheit f; Weichheit f; Mattigkeit f; Süßlichkeit f.
limy ['laımı] adj (+er) kalkhaltig.
linchpin ['lıntʃpın] n Achs(en)nagel m, Lünse f; (fig) Stütze f. **accurate timing is the ~ of the entire operation** das ganze Unternehmen steht und fällt mit genauer Zeiteinteilung.
linden ['lındən] n (also ~ tree) Linde(nbaum m) f.
line¹ [laın] 1 n (a) (rope etc, washing ~, fishing ~) Leine f.
(b) (Math etc, on tennis court etc, on paper, palm) Linie f; (on face) Falte f. **drawn in a few bold ~s** mit wenigen kühnen Strichen gezeichnet; **his drawings show great delicacy of ~** seine Zeichnungen weisen eine sehr feine Linienführung auf; **all along the ~** (fig) auf der ganzen Linie; see hard.
(c) (boundary, outline) **the ~** die Linie, der Äquator; **the state ~** die Staatsgrenze; **the ~ between right and wrong** die Grenze zwischen Recht und Unrecht; **the snow/tree ~** die Schnee-/Baumgrenze; **the ship's graceful ~s** die schnittigen Linien des Schiffes.
(d) (row) Reihe f; (of people, cars also) Schlange f; (of hills) Kette f; (Sport) Linie f. **in (a) ~** in einer Reihe; **in a straight ~** geradlinig; **the rocket goes in a curving ~** die Rakete fliegt eine gekrümmte Bahn; **a ~ of soldiers** eine Reihe Soldaten; **a ~ of traffic** eine Autoschlange; **a single ~ of traffic** einspuriger Verkehr; **John is next in ~ for promotion** John ist als nächster mit der Beförderung an der Reihe; **to be out of ~ with sb/sth** (fig) mit jdm/etw nicht übereinstimmen or in Einklang stehen; **to be in ~ (with)** (fig) in Einklang stehen (mit), übereinstimmen (mit); **to bring sb into ~ with sth** (fig) jdn auf die gleiche Linie wie etw (acc) bringen; **it's time these rebels were brought into ~** es wird Zeit, daß die Rebellen zurückgepfiffen werden; **to fall or get into ~** (abreast) sich in Reih und Glied aufstellen; (behind one another) sich hintereinander or in einer Reihe aufstellen; **the policemen fell into ~ six abreast** die Polizisten stellten sich in Sechserreihen auf; **he refused to fall into ~ with the new proposals** er weigerte sich, mit den neuen Vorschlägen konform zu gehen; **it's time these rebels fell into ~** es ist Zeit, daß sich diese Rebellen anpassen or daß diese Rebellen spuren (inf); **to keep the party in ~** die Einheit der Partei wahren; **to step out of ~** (lit) aus der Reihe treten; (fig) aus der Reihe tanzen; **he was stepping out of ~ telling the director what to do** es war anmaßend von ihm, dem Direktor zu sagen, was er zu tun hätte; **if he steps out of ~ again** wenn er sich noch einmal etwas zuschulden kommen läßt.
(e) (US: queue) Schlange f. **to stand in ~** Schlange stehen.
(f) (in factory) Band nt.
(g) (company: of aircraft, liners, buses) Gesellschaft, Linie f; (shipping company also) Reederei f.
(h) (of descent) **in the male ~** in der männlichen Linie; **he was descended from a long ~ of farmers** er stammte aus einem alten Bauerngeschlecht; **royal ~** königliche Familie; **in an unbroken ~** in ununterbrochener Folge; **who is fourth in ~ to the throne?** wer steht an vierter Stelle der Thronfolge?
(i) (Rail) (in general) Strecke, Bahnlinie f; (section of track) Strecke f. **~s** pl Gleise pl; **to reach the end of the ~** (fig) am Ende sein.
(j) (Telec: cable) Leitung f. **the firm has 52 ~s** die Firma hat 52 Anschlüsse; **this is a very bad ~** die Verbindung ist sehr schlecht; **his ~ is engaged** seine Leitung or sein Anschluß ist besetzt; **to be on the ~ to sb** mit jdm telefonieren; **get off the ~!** gehen Sie aus der Leitung!; **hold the ~** bleiben Sie am Apparat!; **can you get me a ~ to Chicago?** können Sie mir eine Verbindung nach Chicago geben?
(k) (written) Zeile f. **~s** (Sch) Strafarbeit f; **the teacher gave me 200 ~s** der Lehrer ließ mich 200mal ... schreiben; **~s** (Theat) Text m; **I don't get any good ~s in this part** der Text für diese Rolle or diese Partie ist sehr dürftig; **what a ~!** you don't expect me to say that! Sie können doch nicht erwarten, daß ich so einen Text spreche or so etwas sage!; **he gets all the funny ~s** er bekommt immer die lustigen Stellen; **this ~ has been changed so often** diese Textstelle ist so oft geändert worden; **the poem "~s to a skylark"** das Gedicht „An die Lerche"; **to drop sb a ~** jdm ein paar Zeilen or Worte schreiben; **to read between the ~s** zwischen den Zeilen lesen.
(l) (direction, course) **we tried a new ~ of approach to the problem** wir versuchten, an das Problem anders heranzugehen; **~ of argument** Argumentation f; **~ of attack**

(Mil) Angriffslinie *f*; *(fig)* Taktik *f*; **what's your ~ of attack?** wie wollen Sie an die Sache herangehen?; **the police refused to reveal their ~s of inquiry** die Polizei weigerte sich, zu sagen, in welcher Richtung sie ermittelte; **~ of thought** Denkrichtung *f*; **~ of vision** Blickrichtung *f*; **I can't see if you stand in my ~ of vision** ich kann nichts sehen, wenn du mir die Sicht versperrst; **to be on the right ~s** *(fig)* auf dem richtigen Weg sein, richtig liegen *(inf)*; **a possible ~ of development** eine mögliche Entwicklungsrichtung; **we must take a firm or strong ~ with these people** wir müssen diesen Leuten gegenüber sehr bestimmt auftreten; **the government will take a strong ~ over inflation** die Regierung wird gegen die Inflation energisch vorgehen; **he took a strong/moderate ~ in the discussion** er vertrat in der Diskussion einen festen/gemäßigten Standpunkt; **the ~ of least resistance** der Weg des geringsten Widerstandes; **he took the ~ that ...** er vertrat den Standpunkt, daß ...; **I've heard that ~ before** *(inf)* die Platte kenn' ich schon *(inf)*; **what sort of ~ do you think I should take when I see him?** wie meinen Sie, soll ich mich verhalten, wenn ich ihn sehe?; **what ~ is your thesis going to take?** in welcher Richtung wollen Sie in Ihrer Doktorarbeit argumentieren?; **to be along the ~s of** ungefähr so etwas wie ... sein; **to be on the same ~s as** in der gleichen Richtung liegen wie; **the essay is written along the ~s of the traditional theory of** der Aufsatz ist in Richtung der herkömmlichen Lehre verfaßt; **along rather general ~s** in ziemlich groben Zügen; **the story developed along these ~** die Geschichte hat sich so or folgendermaßen entwickelt; **along these ~s** ungefähr so; **something along these ~s** etwas in dieser Richtung or Art; **I was thinking along the same ~s** ich hatte etwas ähnliches gedacht; **on or along rather expressionistic ~s** auf ziemlich expressionistische Art; **it's all in the ~ of duty** das gehört zu meinen/seinen *etc* Pflichten; **things you do in the ~ of duty** dienstliche Pflichten *pl*.

(m) *(Mil)* **~ of battle** Kampflinie *f*; **to draw up the ~s of battle** *(fig)* (Kampf)stellung beziehen; **enemy ~s** feindliche Stellungen or Linien *pl*; **~s of communication** Verbindungswege *pl*; **~ of retreat** Rückzugslinie *f*; **to keep one's ~s of retreat open** *(dat)* den Rückzug offenhalten; *see* **fire.**

(n) *(fig: business)* Branche *f*. **what ~ is he in?, what's his ~?** was ist er von Beruf?, was macht er beruflich?; **that's not in my ~ of business** damit habe ich nichts zu tun; **we're in the same ~ of business** wir sind in der gleichen Berufssparte or Branche tätig; **that's not in my ~** das liegt mir nicht; **fishing's more in my ~** Angeln liegt mir mehr or gefällt mir besser.

(o) *(range of items)* **the best in its ~** das beste seiner Art; **we have a new ~ in spring hats** wir haben eine neue Kollektion Frühjahrshüte; **that ~ did not sell at all** dieses Modell ließ sich überhaupt nicht verkaufen; **he has a good ~ in patter** *(inf)* das ist eine gute Masche, wie er die Leute anquatscht *(inf)*.

(p) *(clue, information)* **to give sb a ~ on sth** jdm einen Hinweis auf etw *(acc)* geben; **can you give me a ~ on it?** können Sie mir darüber etwas sagen?; **the police eventually managed to get a ~ on him** die Polizei konnte ihm schließlich etwas nachweisen; **once a journalist has got a ~ on a story ...** wenn ein Journalist einer Geschichte erst einmal auf der Spur ist ...

(q) *(inf)* **to lay it on the ~** *(inf)* die Karten auf den Tisch legen *(inf)*; **they laid it on the ~ to the government, that ...** sie erklärten der Regierung klipp und klar, daß ... *(inf)*; **to lay it on the ~ to sb** jdm reinen Wein einschenken *(inf)*.

2 *vt* **(a)** *(cross with ~s)* linieren, liniieren. **worry had ~d his face** sein Gesicht war von Sorge gezeichnet.

(b) *streets* säumen. **an avenue ~d with trees** eine baumbestandene Allee; **the streets were ~d with cheering crowds** eine jubelnde Menge säumte die Straßen; **the crew ~d the sides of the ship** die Mannschaft hatte sich auf beiden Seiten des Schiffes aufgestellt; **portraits ~d the walls** an den Wänden hing ein Porträt neben dem andern.

♦ **line up 1** *vi* *(stand in line)* sich aufstellen, antreten; *(queue)* sich anstellen. **the teams ~d ~ like this** die Mannschaften hatten folgende Aufstellung; **the party ~d ~ behind their leader** (fig) die Partei stellte sich hinter ihren Vorsitzenden.

2 *vt sep* **(a)** *troops, pupils, prisoners* antreten lassen; *boxes, books etc* in einer Reihe or nebeneinander aufstellen. **the police ~d the gang ~ with their backs to the wall** die Polizei befahl den Bande, sich mit dem Rücken zur Wand aufzustellen; **they ~d the prisoners ~ along the wall** die Gefangenen mußten sich an der Wand entlang aufstellen.

(b) *(prepare, arrange)* *entertainment* sorgen für, auf die Beine stellen *(inf)*; *speakers* aufbieten, verpflichten; *support* mobilisieren. **what have you got ~d ~ for me today?** was haben Sie für mich geplant?; **have you anything special ~d ~ for this evening?** haben Sie für heute abend etwas Bestimmtes geplant?; **I've ~d ~ a meeting with the directors** ich habe ein Treffen mit den Direktoren arrangiert; **I've got a meeting with John ~d ~ for 10 o'clock** um 10 Uhr steht ein Treffen mit John auf dem Programm; **I've got a nice little date ~d ~ for this evening** ich habe für heute abend eine nette Verabredung arrangiert; **we've got a little surprise ~d ~ for you** wir haben eine kleine Überraschung für dich geplant.

line² *vt* *clothes* füttern; *pipe* auskleiden, innen beziehen; *floor of attic* auslegen. **~ the box with paper** den Karton mit Papier auskleiden or ausschlagen; **to ~ brakes** Bremsbeläge *pl* erneuern (lassen); **the membranes which ~ the stomach** die Schleimhäute, die den Magen auskleiden or innen überziehen; **to ~ one's own pockets** *(fig)* sich bereichern, in die eigene Tasche arbeiten or wirtschaften *(inf)*.

lineage ['lɪnɪɪdʒ] *n* *(descent)* Abstammung *f*; *(descendants)* Geschlecht *nt*.

lineal ['lɪnɪəl] *adj* *descent* direkt.

lineament ['lɪnɪəmənt] *n* *(form)* Lineament *nt* *(rare)*. **~s pl (of**

face) Gesichtszüge *pl*; **fear showed in every ~ (of his face)** ihm stand die Angst deutlich im Gesicht (geschrieben).

linear ['lɪnɪəʳ] *adj* *motion* linear, geradlinig; *design* Linien-; *measure* Längen-. **~ B** Linear B *f*.

lined [laɪnd] *adj* *face etc* *(of old people)* faltig; *(through worry, tiredness etc)* gezeichnet; *paper* liniert, liniiert. **to become ~ with age** Altersfalten bekommen.

line drawing *n* Zeichnung *f*.

linen ['lɪnɪn] **1** *n* Leinen *nt*; *(table ~)* Tischwäsche *f*; *(sheets, garments etc)* Wäsche *f*. **~ closet, ~ cupboard** Wäscheschrank *m*. **2** *adj* Leinen-.

line-out ['laɪnaut] *n* *(Rugby)* Gasse *f*.

liner ['laɪnəʳ] *n* *(ship)* Passagierschiff *nt*, Liniendampfer *m*; *(plane)* Verkehrsflugzeug *nt*.

linesman ['laɪnzmən], *(US also)* **lineman** ['laɪnmən] *n*, *pl* **-men** [-mən] *(Sport)* Linienrichter *m*; *(Rail)* Streckenwärter *m*; *(Elec, Telec)* Leitungsmann *m*; *(for faults)* Störungssucher *m*.

line-up ['laɪnʌp] *n* *(Sport)* Aufstellung *f*; *(cast)* Besetzung *f*; *(alignment)* Gruppierung *f*; *(US: queue)* Schlange *f*. **she picked the thief out of the ~** sie erkannte den Dieb bei der Gegenüberstellung.

ling¹ [lɪŋ] *n* *(Zool)* Leng(fisch) *m*.

ling² *n* *(Bot)* Heidekraut *nt*.

linger ['lɪŋgəʳ] *vi* **(a)** *(also ~ on)* (zurück)bleiben, verweilen *(liter)*; *(in dying)* zwischen Leben und Tod schweben; *(custom)* fortbestehen, sich halten; *(doubts, suspicions)* zurückbleiben; *(feeling, emotion, pain)* anhalten, bleiben; *(memory)* fortbestehen, bleiben; *(chords)* nachklingen; *(scent)* sich halten. **the party was over, but many of the guests ~ed in the hall** die Party war vorbei, aber viele Gäste standen noch im Flur herum; **it was incredible how Franco ~ed on** es war erstaunlich, wie fest Franco am Leben hielt.

(b) *(delay)* sich aufhalten, verweilen *(liter)*. **I mustn't ~ or I'll miss the bus** ich darf mich nicht lange aufhalten, sonst verpasse ich den Bus; **if you ~ too long at any one picture ...** wenn Sie sich bei jedem Bild zu lange aufhalten ...

(c) *(dwell)* **to ~ on a subject** bei einem Thema verweilen *(geh)* or bleiben; **I let my eyes ~ on the scene** ich ließ meinen Blick auf der Szene ruhen; **to ~ over a meal** sich *(dat)* bei einer Mahlzeit Zeit lassen, sich bei einer Mahlzeit lange aufhalten; **we ~ed over a glass of wine** wir tranken gemächlich ein Glas Wein; **to ~ over a task** sich (lange) mit einer Aufgabe aufhalten.

lingerie ['læŋʒəriː] *n* (Damen)unterwäsche *f*.

lingering ['lɪŋgərɪŋ] *adj* lang, ausgedehnt; *death* langsam; *illness* langwierig, schleppend; *doubt* zurückbleibend; *look* sehnsüchtig; *chords* lange (nach)klingend; *kiss* innig. **the lovers took a ~ farewell of each other** der Abschied der Liebenden wollte kein Ende nehmen; **I've still got one ~ doubt** es bleibt noch ein Zweifel (zurück); **the customs officer gave him a long ~ look** der Zollbeamte sah ihn lange prüfend an.

lingo ['lɪŋgəʊ] *n* *(inf)* Sprache *f*; *(specialist jargon)* Kauderwelsch *nt* *(inf)*.

lingua franca ['lɪŋgwə'fræŋkə] *n* Verkehrssprache, Lingua franca *f*; *(official language)* Amtssprache *f*.

lingual ['lɪŋgwəl] *adj* Zungen-.

linguist ['lɪŋgwɪst] *n* **(a)** *(speaker of languages)* Sprachkundige(r) *mf*. **he's a good ~** er ist sehr sprachbegabt; **I'm no ~** ich bin nicht sprachbegabt.

(b) *(specialist in linguistics)* Linguist(in *f*), Sprachforscher(in *f*) *m*.

linguistic [lɪŋ'gwɪstɪk] *adj* **(a)** *(concerning language)* sprachlich; *competence* Sprach-. **(b)** *(of science)* linguistisch, sprachwissenschaftlich.

linguistically [lɪŋ'gwɪstɪkəlɪ] *adv* *see adj* sprachlich; linguistisch. **~ aware** sprachbewußt.

linguistics [lɪŋ'gwɪstɪks] *n sing* Linguistik, Sprachwissenschaft *f*.

liniment ['lɪnɪmənt] *n* Einreibemittel, Liniment *(spec)* *nt*.

lining ['laɪnɪŋ] *n* *(of clothes etc)* Futter *nt*; *(~ material)* Futterstoff *m*; *(of brake)* (Brems)belag *m*; *(of pipe)* Auskleidung *f*; *(of attic floor)* Belag *m*. **the ~ of the stomach** die Magenschleimhaut.

link [lɪŋk] **1** *n* **(a)** *(of chain, fig)* Glied *nt*; *(person)* Verbindungsmann *m*, Bindeglied *nt*.

(b) *(cuff~)* Manschettenknopf *m*.

(c) *(connection)* Verbindung *f*. **a new rail ~ for the village** eine neue Zug- or Bahnverbindung zum Dorf; **photographs give you a ~ with the past** Fotos verbinden einen mit der Vergangenheit; **he broke all his ~s with his family** er brach alle Beziehungen or jede Verbindung mit seiner Familie ab; **cultural ~s** kulturelle Beziehungen *pl*; **this is the first cultural ~ between our two countries** das ist der Anfang der kulturellen Beziehungen zwischen unseren beiden Ländern; **the strong ~s between Britain and Australia** die starken Bindungen or engen Beziehungen zwischen Großbritannien und Australien; **the ~ of friendship** freundschaftliche Bande or Bindungen *pl*; **are there any ~s between the two phenomena?** besteht zwischen diesen beiden Phänomenen ein Zusammenhang or eine Beziehung or eine Verbindung?

(d) *(Measure)* Link *nt*.

2 *vt* verbinden; *spaceships also* aneinanderkoppeln. **to ~ arms** sich unterhaken (*with* bei); **the police ~d arms** die Polizisten bildeten einen Kordon; **we are ~ed by telephone to ...** wir sind telefonisch verbunden mit ...; **the two companies are now ~ed** die beiden Firmen haben sich zusammengeschlossen; **do you think these two murders are ~ed?** glauben Sie, daß zwischen den Morden eine Verbindung besteht?; **success in business is closely ~ed with self-confidence** Erfolg im Beruf hängt eng mit Selbstvertrauen zusammen; **his name is closely ~ed with several reforms** sein Name ist mit mehreren

Reformen eng verbunden.
3 *vi* to ~ **(together)** (*parts of story*) sich zusammenfügen lassen; (*parts of machine*) verbunden werden; (*railway lines*) sich vereinigen, zusammenlaufen.

♦ **link up 1** *vi* zusammenkommen; (*people*) sich zusammentun; (*facts*) übereinstimmen, zusammenpassen; (*companies*) sich zusammenschließen. **to ~ ~ in space** ein Kopplungsmanöver im Weltraum durchführen; **how does that ~ ~ with what Freud says?** wie hängt das mit dem zusammen, was Freud sagt? **2** *vt sep* miteinander verbinden; *bits of evidence* miteinander in Verbindung bringen; *spaceships* koppeln.

link man *n, pl* - **men** [-men] Verbindungsmann *m*; (*Rad, TV*) Moderator *m*.

links *npl* **(a)** Dünen *pl*. **(b)** (*golf course*) Golfplatz *m*.

link-up ['lɪŋkʌp] *n* (*Telec, general*) Verbindung *f*; (*of spaceships*) Kopplung(smanöver *nt*) *f*.

linnet ['lɪnɪt] *n* (*Blut*)hänfling *m*.

lino ['laɪnəʊ] *n* Linoleum *nt*. ~ **cut** Linolschnitt *m*.

linoleum [lɪ'nəʊlɪəm] *n* Linoleum *nt*.

linotype ® ['laɪnəʊtaɪp] *n* Linotype ®, Zeilengieß- *or* Setzmaschine *f*.

linseed ['lɪnsiːd] *n* Leinsamen *m*. ~ **oil** Leinöl *nt*.

lint [lɪnt] *n* Scharpie *f*, Mull *m*.

lintel ['lɪntl] *n* Sturz *m* (*Archit*).

lion ['laɪən] *n* Löwe *m*. **he was one of the literary** ~**s of his day** er war einer der bedeutendsten *or* größten Schriftsteller seiner Zeit; **social** ~ Salonlöwe *m*; **the** ~**'s share** der Löwenanteil.

lioness ['laɪənɪs] *n* Löwin *f*.

lionhearted ['laɪən'hɑːtɪd] *adj* unerschrocken, furchtlos.

lionize ['laɪənaɪz] *vt* to ~ **sb** jdn feiern, jdn zum Helden machen.

lip [lɪp] *n* **(a)** (*Anat*) Lippe *f*. **he wouldn't open his** ~**s** er wollte den Mund nicht aufmachen; **to hang on sb's** ~**s** an jds Lippen (*dat*) hängen; **to keep a stiff upper** ~ Haltung bewahren; **to lick** *or* **smack one's** ~**s** sich (*dat*) die Lippen lecken. **(b)** (*of jug*) Schnabel *m*; (*of cup, crater*) Rand *m*. **(c)** (*inf: cheek*) Frechheit(en *pl*) *f*. **to give sb a lot of** ~ jdm gegenüber eine (dicke *or* freche) Lippe riskieren (*inf*); **any more of your** ~ **and there'll be trouble** wenn du weiterhin so eine (dicke *or* freche) Lippe riskierst, gibt's Ärger (*inf*); **none of your** ~! sei nicht so frech.

-lipped [-lɪpt] *adj suf* -lippig.

lip: ~**read 1** *vt* **I could** ~**read what he said** ich konnte ihn von den Lippen *or* vom Mund ablesen, was er sagte; **2** *vi* von den Lippen *or* vom Mund ablesen; ~**reading** *n* **deaf people use/learn** ~**reading** Taube lesen vom Mund ab/lernen, vom Mund abzulesen; ~ **service** *n* **to pay** ~ **service to an idea** ein Lippenbekenntnis zu einer Idee ablegen; ~**stick** *n* Lippenstift *m*.

liquefaction [ˌlɪkwɪ'fækʃən] *n* Verflüssigung *f*.

liquefy ['lɪkwɪfaɪ] **1** *vt* verflüssigen. **2** *vi* sich verflüssigen.

liqueur [lɪ'kjʊəʳ] *n* Likör *m*.

liquid ['lɪkwɪd] **1** *adj* **(a)** flüssig; *measure* Flüssigkeits-; (*fig*) *eyes* blank, glänzend; (*fig*) *notes, song* perlend. **(b)** (*Comm*) *asset* (frei) verfügbar, flüssig. **(c)** (*Phon*) ~ **consonant** Liquida *f*, Fließlaut *m*. **2** *n* **(a)** Flüssigkeit *f*. **she can only take** ~**s** sie kann nur Flüssiges zu sich nehmen. **(b)** (*Phon*) Liquida *f*, Fließlaut *m*.

liquidate ['lɪkwɪdeɪt] *vt* **(a)** (*Comm*) liquidieren; *assets also* flüssig machen; *company also* auflösen. **to** ~ **a debt** eine Schuld/Schulden tilgen. **(b)** *enemy etc* liquidieren.

liquidation [ˌlɪkwɪ'deɪʃən] *n* **(a)** (*Comm*) Liquidation, Liquidierung *f*; (*of company also*) Auflösung *f*; (*of debts*) Tilgung *f*. **to go into** ~ in Liquidation gehen. **(b)** Liquidierung *f*.

liquidator ['lɪkwɪdeɪtəʳ] *n* Liquidator, Abwickler *m*.

liquidity [lɪ'kwɪdɪtɪ] *n* Liquidität *f*.

liquidize ['lɪkwɪdaɪz] *vt* (im Mixer) pürieren *or* zerkleinern.

liquidizer ['lɪkwɪdaɪzəʳ] *n* Mixgerät *nt*.

liquor ['lɪkəʳ] *n* **(a)** *whisky, brandy etc* Spirituosen *pl*; (*alcohol*) Alkohol *m*. **people who drink hard** ~ Leute, die scharfe Sachen trinken, Schnapstrinker *pl*; **a powerful** ~ ein hochprozentiges Getränk *nt*; **the local** ~ der am Ort hergestellte Schnaps; **he can't take his** ~ er verträgt nichts. **(b)** (*juice*) Flüssigkeit *f*. **potato** ~ Kartoffelwasser *nt*.

♦ **liquor up** *vt sep* (*US sl*) **to get** ~**ed** ~ sich besaufen (*sl*); **to be** ~**ed** ~ besoffen sein (*sl*).

liquorice, licorice ['lɪkərɪs] *n* (*plant*) Süßholz *nt*; (*root*) Süßholzwurzel *f*; (*flavouring, sweetmeat*) Lakritze *f*.

liquor store *n* (*US*) = Wein- und Spirituosengeschäft *nt*.

lira ['lɪərə] *n* Lira *f*. **10** ~**(s)** 10 Lire.

Lisbon ['lɪzbən] *n* Lissabon *nt*.

lisle [laɪl] *n* (*also* ~ **thread**) Florgarn *nt*. ~ **stockings** Baumwollstrümpfe *pl*.

lisp [lɪsp] **1** *n* Lispeln *nt*. **to speak with a** ~, **to have a** ~ lispeln. **2** *vti* lispeln.

lissom(e) ['lɪsəm] *adj* geschmeidig; *person also* gelenkig.

list¹ [lɪst] *n* **(a)** Liste *f*; (*shopping* ~) Einkaufszettel *m*. **it's not on the** ~ es steht nicht auf der Liste; ~ **of names** Namensliste *f*; (*esp in book*) Namensregister, Namensverzeichnis *nt*; ~ **of applicants** Bewerberliste *f*; **there's a long** ~ **of people waiting for houses** für Häuser besteht eine lange Warteliste; **it's on my** ~ **for tomorrow** es steht für morgen auf dem Programm. **(b)** (*publisher's* ~) Programm *nt*. **we'd like to start an educational** ~ wir würden gern Lehrbücher in unser Programm aufnehmen. **2** *vt* aufschreiben, notieren; *single item* in die Liste aufnehmen; (*verbally*) aufzählen. **it is not** ~**ed** es ist nicht aufgeführt.

list² (*Naut*) **1** *n* Schlagseite, Krängung (*spec*) *f*. **to have a bad** ~ schwere Schlagseite haben; **to have a** ~ **of 20°** sich um 20° auf die Seite neigen; **a** ~ **to port** Schlagseite nach Backbord. **2** *vi* Schlagseite haben, krängen (*spec*). **to** ~ **badly** schwere Schlagseite haben.

list³ *vi* (*obs*) lauschen (*old*).

list⁴ *vi* (*obs, poet*) **the wind bloweth where it** ~**eth** der Wind bläst, wo er will.

listen ['lɪsn] *vi* **(a)** (*hear*) hören (*to sth etw acc*). **to** ~ **to the radio** Radio hören; **if you** ~ **hard, you can hear the sea** wenn du genau horchst *or* hinhörst, kannst du das Meer hören; **she** ~**ed** carefully to everything he said sie hörte ihm genau zu; **to** ~ **for sth** auf etw (*acc*) horchen; **the boys are** ~**ing for the bell at the end of the lesson** die Jungen warten auf das Klingeln am Ende der Stunde; **to** ~ **for sb** horchen *or* hören, ob jd kommt. **(b)** (*heed*) zuhören. ~ **to me!** hör mir zu!; ~, **I know what we'll do** paß auf, ich weiß, was wir machen; ~, **I'm warning you** hör mal, ich warne dich!; **don't** ~ **to him** hör nicht auf ihn; **if he suggests anything, don't** ~ hör nicht darauf, wenn er etwas vorschlägt; **he wouldn't** ~ er wollte nicht hören.

♦ **listen in** *vi* (im Radio) hören (*to sth etw acc*); (*listen secretly*) mithören (*on sth etw acc*). **I'd like to** ~ ~ **on** *or* **to your discussion** ich möchte mir Ihre Diskussion mit anhören.

listener ['lɪsnəʳ] *n* Zuhörer(in *f*) *m*; (*Rad*) Hörer(in *f*) *m*. **to be a good** ~ gut zuhören können.

listening ['lɪsnɪŋ] *n* **good** ~! gute Unterhaltung!; **we don't do much** ~ **now we've got television** wir hören nicht mehr viel Radio, seit wir Fernsehen haben; ~ **post** (*Mil, fig*) Horchposten *m*.

listless ['lɪstlɪs] *adj* lustlos; *patient* teilnahmslos.

listlessly ['lɪstlɪslɪ] *adv see adj*.

listlessness ['lɪstlɪsnɪs] *n see adj* Lustlosigkeit *f*; Teilnahmslosigkeit *f*.

list price *n* Listenpreis *m*.

lists [lɪsts] *npl* (*Hist*) Schranken *pl*. **to enter the** ~ (*fig*) in die Schranken treten (*liter*), zum Kampf antreten; **he entered the** ~ **in defence of his friend** er trat für seinen Freund in die Schranken (*liter*), er ergriff Partei für seinen Freund; **he entered the** ~ **after the first ballot** er trat nach dem ersten Wahlgang in den Wahlkampf ein.

lit [lɪt] *pret, ptp of* **light¹, light³**.

litany ['lɪtənɪ] *n* Litanei *f*.

liter *n* (*US*) *see* **litre**.

literacy ['lɪtərəsɪ] *n* Fähigkeit *f*, lesen und schreiben zu können. ~ **campaign** Kampagne *f* gegen das Analphabetentum, Alphabetisierungskampagne *f*; **the** ~ **rate in Slobodia is only 30%** die Analphabetenquote in Slobodia beträgt 70%; ~ **is low in Slobodia** Slobodia hat eine hohe Analphabetenquote; ~ **test** Lese- und Schreibtest *m*.

literal ['lɪtərəl] **1** *adj* **(a)** (*esp Typ*) ~ **error** Schreib-/Tipp-/Druckfehler *m*. **(b)** *translation* wörtlich; *meaning, sense also* eigentlich. **(c)** (*real*) **that is the** ~ **truth** das ist die reine Wahrheit; **it was a** ~ **disaster** es war im wahrsten Sinne des Wortes eine Katastrophe; **the** ~ **impossibility of working there** die völlige *or* buchstäbliche Unmöglichkeit, dort zu arbeiten. **(d)** (*prosaic*) nüchtern, prosaisch. **he has a very** ~ **mind** *or* **is very** ~-**minded** er denkt sehr nüchtern, er ist sehr prosaisch. **2** *n* Schreib-/Tipp-/Druckfehler *m*.

literally ['lɪtərəlɪ] *adv* **(a)** (*word for word, exactly*) (wort)wörtlich. **to take sth** ~ etw wörtlich nehmen. **(b)** (*really*) buchstäblich, wirklich. **the best meal I've ever had,** ~ wirklich das Beste, was ich je gegessen habe; **it was** ~ **impossible to work there** es war wirklich *or* einfach unmöglich, dort zu arbeiten; **he was** ~ **a giant** er war im wahrsten Sinne des Wortes ein Riese.

literariness ['lɪtərərɪnɪs] *n* literarische Stilebene.

literary ['lɪtərərɪ] *adj* literarisch. **he has** ~ **tastes** er interessiert sich für Literatur; **a** ~ **man** ein Literaturmensch; (*author*) ein Literat *or* Autor *m*; ~ **historian** Literaturhistoriker(in *f*) *m*.

literate ['lɪtərɪt] *adj* **(a) to be** ~ lesen und schreiben können; **they aim to achieve a** ~ **population in one generation** sie wollen die Bevölkerung in einer Generation alphabetisieren. **(b)** (*well-educated*) gebildet. **his style is not very** ~ er schreibt einen ungeschliffenen Stil.

literati [ˌlɪtə'rɑːtiː] *npl* Literaten *pl*.

literature ['lɪtərɪtʃəʳ] *n* Literatur *f*; (*inf: brochures etc*) Informationsmaterial *nt*; (*specialist* ~) (Fach)literatur *f*.

lithe [laɪð] *adj* (+*er*) geschmeidig; *person, body also* gelenkig.

lithium ['lɪθɪəm] *n* Lithium *nt*.

litho ['laɪθəʊ] *n* (*inf*) Litho *nt*.

lithograph ['lɪθəʊɡrɑːf] **1** *n* Lithographie *f*, Steindruck *m*. **2** *vt* lithographieren.

lithographer [lɪ'θɒɡrəfəʳ] *n* Lithograph(in *f*) *m*.

lithographic [ˌlɪθəʊ'ɡræfɪk] *adj* lithographisch, Steindruck-.

lithography [lɪ'θɒɡrəfɪ] *n* Lithographie *f*, Steindruck(verfahren *nt*) *m*.

Lithuania [ˌlɪθjʊ'eɪnɪə] *n* Litauen *nt*.

Lithuanian [ˌlɪθjʊ'eɪnɪən] **1** *adj* litauisch. **2** *n* **(a)** Litauer(in *f*) *m*. **(b)** (*language*) Litauisch *nt*.

litigant ['lɪtɪɡənt] *n* prozeßführende Partei. **the** ~**s** die prozeßgegner *pl*, die prozeßführenden Parteien.

litigate ['lɪtɪɡeɪt] *vi* einen Prozeß führen *or* anstrengen.

litigation [ˌlɪtɪ'ɡeɪʃən] *n* Prozeß, Rechtsstreit *m*. **he threatened them with** ~ er drohte ihnen mit einem Prozeß.

litigious [lɪ'tɪdʒəs] *adj* prozeßsüchtig. **a** ~ **person** jd, der ständig Prozesse führt, ein Prozeßhansel *m* (*inf*).

litmus ['lɪtməs] *n* Lackmus *m or nt*. ~ **paper** Lackmuspapier *nt*.

litotes [laɪ'təʊtiːz] *n* Litotes *f*.

litre, (*US*) **liter** ['liːtəʳ] *n* Liter *m or nt*.

litter ['lɪtəʳ] **1** *n* **(a)** Abfälle *pl*; (*papers, wrappings*) Papier *nt*. **the park was strewn with** ~ der Park war mit Papier und Abfällen übersät; **a** ~ **of papers/books** ein Haufen *m* Papier/Bücher.

(b) (*Zool*) Wurf *m*.
(c) (*vehicle*) Sänfte *f*; (*Med*) Tragbahre, Trage *f*.
(d) (*bedding for animals*) Streu *f*, Stroh *nt*; (*for plants*) Stroh *nt*; (*cat* ~) Kies *m*.
  2 *vt* **(a)** to be ~ed with sth (*lit, fig*) mit etw übersät sein; old cans ~ed the countryside alte Dosen verschandelten die Landschaft; to ~ papers about a room, to ~ a room with papers Papier(e) im Zimmer verstreuen.
  (b) (*give birth to*) werfen.
  (c) *plant* abdecken; *animal* Streu geben (+*dat*).
  3 *vi* **(a)** (*have young*) werfen.
  (b) (*esp US*) Abfall wegwerfen.
litter: ~ basket *n* Abfallkorb *m*; ~ bin *n* Abfalleimer *m*; (*hooked on*) Abfallkorb *m*; (*bigger*) Abfalltonne *f*; ~ bug (*inf*), ~ lout (*inf*) *n* Dreckspatz (*inf*), Schmutzfink (*inf*) *m*.
little ['lɪtl] **1** *adj* klein. a ~ house ein Häuschen *nt*, ein kleines Haus; a funny ~ nose ein lustiges Näschen; the ~ ones die Kleinen *pl*; a nice ~ profit ein hübscher Gewinn; the ~ people *or* folk die Elfen; he will have his ~ joke er will auch einmal ein Witzchen machen; to worry about ~ things sich (*dat*) über Kleinigkeiten Gedanken machen; he has a ~ mind er ist ein Kleingeist; ~ things please ~ minds so kann man auch mit kleinen Sachen Kindern eine Freude machen; a L~ Englander Gegner *m* des Imperialismus im 19. Jahrhundert, Isolationist *m*; a ~ while ago vor kurzem, vor kurzer Zeit; it's only a ~ while till I ... es ist nicht mehr lange, bis ich ...; in a ~ while bald.
  2 *adv*, *n* **(a)** wenig. of ~ importance/interest von geringer Bedeutung/geringem Interesse; he knows ~ Latin and less Greek er kann (nur) wenig Latein und noch weniger Griechisch; ~ better than kaum besser als; ~ more than a month ago vor kaum einem Monat; ~ short of fast schon, beinahe; ~ did I think that ... ich hätte kaum gedacht, daß ...; ~ does he know that ... er hat keine Ahnung, daß ...; they ~ realize what will happen to them sie sind sich (*dat*) wohl kaum darüber im klaren, was mit ihnen geschehen wird; I walk as ~ as possible ich laufe so wenig wie möglich; to spend ~ or nothing so gut wie (gar) nichts ausgeben; every ~ helps Kleinvieh macht auch Mist (*Prov*); please donate, every ~ helps auch die kleinste Spende hilft; he had ~ to say er hatte nicht viel zu sagen; I see very ~ of her nowadays ich sehe sie in letzter Zeit sehr selten; there was ~ we could do wir konnten nicht viel tun; the ~ of that book that I have read das wenige *or* bißchen, was ich von seinem Buch gelesen habe; she did what ~ she could sie tat das Wenige, das sie tun konnte; ~ by ~ nach und nach; ~ by ~, he dragged himself across the room Stückchen für Stückchen schleppte er sich durch das Zimmer; to make ~ of sth etw herunterspielen *or* bagatellisieren; I could make ~ of this book ich konnte mit diesem Buch nicht viel anfangen.
  (b) a ~ ein wenig, ein bißchen; a ~ hot/better etwas *or* ein bißchen heiß/besser, ein wenig besser; with a ~ effort mit etwas Anstrengung; I'll give you a ~ advice ich gebe dir einen kleinen Tip; a ~ after five kurz nach fünf; we were not a ~ worried wir waren recht besorgt; I was not a ~ surprised ich war einigermaßen überrascht; we walked on for a ~ wir liefen noch ein bißchen *or* Stück *or* Weilchen weiter; after a ~ nach einer Weile; for a ~ für eine Weile.
littleness ['lɪtlnɪs] *n* Kleinheit *f*, geringe Größe; (*of contribution*) Geringfügigkeit *f*; (*of mind*) Beschränktheit, Begrenztheit *f*.
littoral ['lɪtərəl] (*form*) **1** *adj* litoral (*spec*), Litoral- (*spec*); (*of lake also*) Ufer-; (*of sea also*) Küsten-. **2** *n* Litorale *nt*; Uferland *nt*; Küstenstrich *m or* -region *f*.
liturgical [lɪ'tɜːdʒɪkəl] *adj* liturgisch.
liturgy ['lɪtədʒɪ] *n* Liturgie *f*.
livable, liveable ['lɪvəbl] *adj* life erträglich.
livable: ~-in *adj* (*inf*) the house is ~-in in dem Haus kann man *or* läßt es sich wohnen; ~-with *adj* (*inf*) John's too moody to be ~-with John ist zu launisch, mit ihm kann man nicht zusammen leben; arthritis can't be cured, but it can be made ~-with Arthritis ist unheilbar, kann aber erträglich gemacht werden.
live¹ [lɪv] **1** *vt* life führen. to ~ a part in einer Rolle aufgehen; he had been living a lie sein Leben war eine Lüge; to ~ one's own life sein eigenes Leben leben.
  2 *vi* **(a)** leben. there is no man living who can equal him es gibt niemanden, der es ihm gleichtun könnte; will he ~, doctor? wird er (über)leben, Herr Doktor?; don't worry, you'll ~, it's only a broken ankle reg dich nicht auf, du stirbst schon nicht, du hast nur einen gebrochenen Knöchel; long ~ Queen Anne! lang lebe Königin Anne! we ~ and learn man lernt nie aus; to ~ and let ~ leben und leben lassen; to ~ like a king *or* lord fürstlich *or* wie Gott in Frankreich leben; not many people ~ to be a hundred nicht viele Menschen werden hundert (Jahre alt); to ~ to a ripe old age ein hohes Alter erreichen; his spirit ~s sein Geist lebt weiter; his name will ~ for ever sein Ruhm wird nie vergehen; his poetry will ~ for ever seine Dichtung ist unvergänglich; we will ~ again after death wir werden nach dem Tode wiedergeboren werden; if the spirit of the Renaissance should ever ~ again wenn der Geist der Renaissance je wiedererwachen sollte; it was as though the father were living again in the son es war, als lebte der Vater im Sohn weiter; to ~ by one's wits sich (so) durchschlagen; to ~ by one's pen von seinen Büchern *or* vom Schreiben leben; he ~d through two wars er hat zwei Kriege miterlebt; to ~ through an experience eine Erfahrung durchmachen; the patient was not expected to ~ through the night man rechnete nicht damit, daß der Patient die Nacht überstehen *or* überleben würde; I would rather like to ~ to the end of the century ich möchte die Jahrhundertwende noch miterleben; to ~ within/beyond one's income nicht über/über seine Verhältnisse leben; you'll ~ to regret it das wirst du noch bereuen.
  (b) (*experience real living*) I want to ~ ich will leben *or* was erleben (*inf*); that's existing, not living das ist doch kein Leben; you've never skied? you haven't ~d! du bist noch nie Ski gefahren? du weißt gar nicht, was du versäumt hast!; you've never ~d until you've discovered Crete wer Kreta nicht kennt, hat noch nicht gelebt; before she met him she hadn't ~d sie begann erst zu leben, als sie ihn kennenlernte.
  (c) (*reside*) wohnen; (*in town, in country also, animals*) leben. he ~s at 19 Marktstraße er wohnt in der Marktstraße Nr.19; he ~s in Gardner St/on the High St er wohnt in der Gardner St/auf der *or* in der Hauptstraße; who ~s in that big house? wer bewohnt das große Haus?, wer wohnt in dem großen Haus?; to ~ in the country auf dem Land wohnen *or* leben; he ~s with his parents er wohnt bei seinen Eltern; a house not fit to ~ in ein unbewohnbares Haus, ein Haus, in dem man nicht wohnen kann; this house is not fit for a human being to ~ in dies ist eine menschenunwürdige Behausung.
  (d) (*inf: belong*) where does this jug ~? wo gehört der Krug hin?; the knives ~ in this drawer die Messer gehören in diese Schublade.
  (e) the other athletes couldn't ~ with him/the pace die anderen Läufer konnten mit ihm/mit dem Tempo nicht mithalten.
◆**live down** *vt sep scandal, humiliation* hinwegkommen über (+*acc*), verwinden; (*actively*) *scandal, mistake* Gras wachsen lassen über (+*acc*). he'll never ~ it ~ das wird man ihm nie vergessen.
◆**live in** *vi* im Haus/im Heim/auf dem Universitätsgelände *etc* wohnen, nicht außerhalb wohnen.
◆**live off** *vi* +*prep obj* to ~ ~ one's estates von seinem Besitz leben; to ~ ~ one's relations auf Kosten seiner Verwandten leben.
◆**live on** **1** *vi* (*continue to live*) weiterleben.
  2 *vi* +*prep obj* leben von, sich ernähren von. to ~ ~ eggs sich von Eiern ernähren, von Eiern leben; he doesn't earn enough to ~ ~ er verdient nicht genug, um davon zu leben; to ~ ~ hope (nur noch) von der Hoffnung leben; to ~ ~ one's reputation von seinem Ruf zehren.
◆**live out** **1** *vi* außerhalb (des Hauses/des Heims/des Universitätsgeländes *etc*) wohnen. **2** *vt sep life* verbringen; *winter* überleben. he ~d ~ a life of poverty in the country er lebte bis an sein Ende in Armut auf dem Land.
◆**live together** *vi* (*cohabit*) zusammenleben; (*share a room, flat etc*) zusammenwohnen.
◆**live up** *vt always separate:* to ~ it ~ (*inf*) die Puppen tanzen lassen (*inf*); (*extravagantly*) in Saus und Braus leben (*inf*); in my young days we really knew how to ~ it ~ in meiner Jugend wußten wir noch, wie man sich so richtig auslebt.
◆**live up to** *vi* +*prep obj* the holidays ~d ~ ~ expectations/the advertiser's claims der Urlaub hielt, was er *etc*/die Werbung versprochen hatte; to ~ ~ ~ standards/one's reputation den Anforderungen/seinem Ruf gerecht werden; the reality never ~s ~ ~ the anticipation die Wirklichkeit kommt nie an die Erwartungen heran; the holiday didn't ~ ~ ~ our hopes the days didn't ~ ~ ~ our hopes der Urlaub entsprach nicht dem, was wir uns (*dat*) erhofft hatten; he's got a lot to ~ ~ ~ in ihn werden große Erwartungen gesetzt; if he wants to emulate his father he's got a lot to ~ ~ ~ er hat sich (*dat*) ein hohes Ziel gesteckt, wenn er seinem Vater nacheifern will; you should ~ ~ ~ your father's principles du solltest die Grundsätze deines Vaters anstreben; I doubt whether he can ~ ~ ~ his brother ich bezweifle, daß er seinem Bruder das Wasser reichen kann.
live² [laɪv] **1** *adj* **(a)** (*alive*) lebend; *issue, question* aktuell. a real ~ duke ein waschechter Herzog; ~ births Lebendgeburten *pl*.
  (b) (*having power or energy*) *coal* glühend; *match* ungebraucht; *cartridge, shell* scharf; (*Elec*) geladen. "danger, ~ wires!" „Vorsicht Hochspannung!"; she's a real ~ wire (*fig*) sie ist ein richtiges Energiebündel.
  (c) (*Rad, TV*) live. a ~ programme eine Livesendung.
  2 *adv* (*Rad, TV*) live, direkt.
liveable ['lɪvəbl] *adj see* livable.
livelihood ['laɪvlɪhʊd] *n* Lebensunterhalt *m*. rice is their ~ sie verdienen ihren Lebensunterhalt mit Reis; to earn a ~ sich (*dat*) seinen Lebensunterhalt verdienen; they earned a ~ from farming sie lebten von der Landwirtschaft.
liveliness ['laɪvlɪnɪs] *n see adj* Lebhaftigkeit *f*; Lebendigkeit *f*; Dynamik *f*; Schnelligkeit *f*; Aufgewecktheit *f*.
livelong ['lɪvlɒŋ] *adj:* all the ~ day/night den lieben langen Tag, den ganzen Tag über/die ganze Nacht durch.
lively ['laɪvlɪ] *adj* (+*er*) lebhaft; *scene, account* lebendig; *campaign* dynamisch; *pace* flott; *mind* wach, aufgeweckt. things are getting ~ es geht hoch her (*inf*); things are getting ~ on the stock exchange die Börse wird lebhaft; at 8 things will start to get ~ um 8 wird es dann lebhafter; we had a ~ time es war viel los (*inf*); he's having a ~ time of it in his new job in seiner neuen Stelle kann er sich über Langeweile nicht beklagen.
liven up ['laɪvən'ʌp] **1** *vt sep* beleben, Leben bringen in (+*acc*) (*inf*). **2** *vi* in Schwung kommen; (*person*) aufleben.
liver¹ ['lɪvə'] *n* clean ~ solider Mensch; he's a fast ~ er führt ein flottes Leben (*inf*).
liver² *n* (*Anat, Cook*) Leber *f*. ~ sausage, ~ wurst Leberwurst *f*.
liveried ['lɪvərɪd] *adj* livriert.
liverish ['lɪvərɪʃ] *adj* **(a)** to be ~ etwas mit der Leber haben; I felt a bit ~ after the party mir ging es nach der Party ziemlich mies (*inf*). **(b)** (*bad-tempered*) mürrisch.
Liverpudlian [lɪvə'pʌdlɪən] **1** *n* Bewohner(in *f*) *m* von Liverpool. **2** *adj* von Liverpool.
liverwort ['lɪvəwɜːt] *n* (*Bot*) Lebermoos *nt*; (*hepatica*) Leberblümchen *nt*.
livery ['lɪvərɪ] *n* Livree *f*; (*fig liter*) Kleid *nt*.

livery: ~ **company** n Zunft f; ~ **stable** n Mietstall m.
lives [laɪvz] pl of **life**.
livestock ['laɪvstɒk] n Vieh nt; (number of animals) Viehbestand m.
livid ['lɪvɪd] adj (a) (inf) wütend, fuchsteufelswild (inf). to be ~ with rage wütend sein; he got ~ with us er hatte eine Stinkwut auf uns (inf). (b) blau. the sky was a ~ grey der Himmel war blaugrau.
living ['lɪvɪŋ] 1 adj lebend; example, faith lebendig. a ~ creature ein Lebewesen nt; not a ~ soul keine Menschenseele; (within) ~ memory seit Menschengedenken; he is ~ proof of ... er ist der lebende Beweis für ...; her existence was a ~ death ihr Leben war eine einzige Qual; ~ or dead tot oder lebendig; see **daylight**.
  2 n (a) the ~ pl die Lebenden pl.
  (b) (way of ~) the art of ~ Lebenskunst f; he is fond of good ~ er lebt gern gut; **gracious** ~ die vornehme Lebensart; **loose** ~ lockerer Lebenswandel; see **standard**.
  (c) (livelihood) Lebensunterhalt m. to earn or make a ~ sich (dat) seinen Lebensunterhalt verdienen; he sells brushes for a ~ er verkauft Bürsten, um sich (dat) seinen Lebensunterhalt zu verdienen; they made a bare ~ out of the soil sie hatten mit dem Ertrag des Bodens ihr Auskommen; to work for one's ~ arbeiten, um sich (dat) seinen Lebensunterhalt zu verdienen; some of us have to work for a ~ es gibt auch Leute, die arbeiten müssen.
  (d) (Eccl) Pfründe f.
living: ~ **conditions** npl Wohnverhältnisse pl; ~ **room** n Wohnzimmer nt; ~ **space** n (in house) Wohnraum m; (for a nation) Lebensraum m; ~ **wage** n ausreichender Lohn; £15 a week is not a ~ wage von £ 15 pro Woche kann man nicht leben.
Livy ['lɪvɪ] n Livius m.
lizard ['lɪzəd] n Eidechse f; (including larger forms also) Echse f.
ll abbr of **lines** z.
llama ['lɑːmə] n Lama m.
LlB abbr of **Bachelor of Laws**.
LLD abbr of **Doctor of Laws** Dr. jur.
lo [ləʊ] interj (old) siehe (old). ~ **and behold!** und siehe da.
loach [ləʊtʃ] n Schmerle f.
load [ləʊd] 1 n (a) (sth carried, burden) Last f; (cargo) Ladung f; (on girder, axle etc, fig) Belastung, Last f. what sort of ~ was the ship/lorry carrying? was hatte das Schiff/der Lastwagen geladen?; to put a ~ on sth etw belasten; to put too heavy a ~ on sth etw überlasten; the maximum ~ for that bridge is 10 tons die maximale Tragkraft or -fähigkeit dieser Brücke beträgt 10 Tonnen; an arm-~ of shopping ein Armvoll Einkäufe; a train-~ of passengers ein Zug voll Reisender; (work) ~ (Arbeits)pensum nt; he has a heavy teaching ~ this term er hat in diesem Semester eine hohe Stundenzahl; he carries a heavy ~ of responsibility er trägt eine schwere Verantwortung; that's a ~ off my mind! da fällt mir ein Stein vom Herzen!; to take a ~ off sb's mind jdm eine Last von der Seele nehmen.
  (b) (Elec) (supplied) Leistung f; (carried) Spannung f.
  (c) (inf usages) ~s of, a ~ of massenhaft (inf), jede Menge (inf); thanks, we have ~s danke, wir haben jede Menge (inf); it's a ~ of old rubbish das ist alles Blödsinn (inf) or Quatsch (inf); (film, book, translation) das ist alles Mist! (inf); to take on a ~ (ganz schön) einen heben (inf); get a ~ of this! (listen) hör dir das mal an!; (look) guck dir das mal an! (inf).
  2 vt (a) goods laden; lorry etc beladen. the ship was ~ed with bananas das Schiff hatte Bananen geladen.
  (b) (burden, weigh down) beladen. the branch was ~ed with pears der Ast war mit Birnen überladen.
  (c) (fig) überhäufen. to ~ sb with honours jdn mit Ehrungen überschütten or -häufen; the whole matter is ~ed with problems die Angelegenheit steckt voller Probleme; we're ~ed with debts wir stecken bis zum Hals in Schulden; they ~ed themselves with debts sie haben sich in Schulden gestürzt.
  (d) gun laden. to ~ a camera einen Film (in eine Fotoapparat) einlegen; is this camera ~ed? ist ein Film im Apparat?
  (e) dice fälschen, präparieren. to ~ the dice (fig) mit gezinkten Karten spielen; to ~ the dice against sb (fig) jdn übervorteilen; the dice had been ~ed against him (fig) es war Schiebung (inf) or ein abgekartetes Spiel.
  3 vi (a) laden. ~ing bay Ladeplatz m; "~ing and unloading" „Be- und Entladen".
  (b) (~ gun) laden; (~ camera) einen Film einlegen. ~! Gewehr(e) laden!; how does this gun/camera ~? wie lädt man dieses Gewehr?/wie legt man einen Film in diesen Apparat ein?
♦ **load down** vt sep (schwer) beladen; (fig) überladen. the poor animal was ~ed ~ by its burden das arme Tier wurde von seiner Last niedergedrückt; he is ~ed ~ with sorrows Sorgen lasten schwer auf ihm or drücken ihn.
♦ **load up** 1 vi aufladen. 2 vt sep lorry beladen; goods aufladen.
load: ~-**bearing** adj wall tragend; ~ **capacity** n (Elec) Belastung(sfähigkeit) f; (of lorry) maximale Nutzlast.
loaded ['ləʊdɪd] adj beladen; dice falsch, präpariert; camera mit eingelegtem Film; gun geladen. a ~ basket ein schwerer or schwer beladener Korb; he's ~ (inf: rich) er ist stink- or steinreich (inf), er schwimmt im Geld (inf); (sl: drunk) der hat schwer or ganz schön geladen (inf).
load: ~ **line** n Ladelinie f; ~**star** n see **lodestar**; ~**stone** n see **lodestone**.
loaf [ləʊf] n, pl **loaves** Brot nt; (unsliced) (Brot)laib m; (meat ~) Hackbraten m. a ~ of bread ein (Laib) Brot; a small white ~ ein kleines Weißbrot; **half a** ~ **is better than none** or **than no bread** (Prov) (wenig ist) besser als gar nichts; **use your** ~! (sl) streng deinen Grips an (inf); **use your** ~, **show some tact** (sl) denk mal ein bißchen, und sei etwas taktvoller (inf).
♦ **loaf about** or **around** vi (inf) faulenzen. he ~ed ~ the house

all day er hing den ganzen Tag zu Hause herum (inf).
loafer ['ləʊfər] n (a) (inf: idler) Faulenzer, Nichtstuer m. (b) (US: casual shoe) Halbschuh, Trotteur m.
loam [ləʊm] n Lehmerde f.
loamy ['ləʊmɪ] adj (+er) lehmig. ~ **soil** Lehmboden m.
loan [ləʊn] 1 n (a) (thing lent) Leihgabe f; (from bank etc) Darlehen nt; (public ~) Anleihe f. **my friend let me have the money as a** ~ mein Freund hat mir das Geld geliehen; **it's not a gift, it's a** ~ es ist nicht geschenkt, sondern nur geliehen; **government** ~s Regierungsdarlehen nt; (borrowings) Staatsanleihen pl.
  (b) **I asked for the** ~ **of the bicycle** ich bat darum, das Fahrrad ausleihen zu dürfen; **he gave me the** ~ **of his bicycle** er hat mir sein Fahrrad geliehen; **conditions governing the** ~ **of this book** Leihbedingungen pl für dieses Buch; **it's on** ~ es ist geliehen; (out on ~) es ist verliehen or ausgeliehen; **the machinery is on** ~ **from the American government** die Maschinen sind eine Leihgabe der amerikanischen Regierung; **to have sth on** ~ etw geliehen haben (from von).
  2 vt leihen (to sb jdm).
loan: ~ **collection** n Leihgaben pl; ~ **shark** n (inf) Kredithai m (inf); ~ **word** n Lehnwort nt.
loath, loth [ləʊθ] adj to be ~ to do sth etw ungern tun; ~ **as I am to leave** so ungern ich auch gehe; **he was** ~ **for us to go** er ließ uns ungern gehen; **nothing** ~ (old) bereitwillig(st).
loathe [ləʊð] vt thing, person verabscheuen; modern art, spinach, jazz etc nicht ausstehen können. **I** ~ **doing it** (in general) ich hasse es, das zu tun; (on particular occasion) es ist mir zuwider, das zu tun; **she** ~s **watching television** sie kann Fernsehen nicht ausstehen, sie haßt Fernsehen.
loathing ['ləʊðɪŋ] n Abscheu m.
loathsome ['ləʊðsəm] adj thing, person abscheulich, widerlich; task verhaßt; deformity abstoßend, abscheuerregend; wound ekelerregend.
loathsomeness ['ləʊðsəmnɪs] n see adj Abscheulichkeit, Widerlichkeit f; Verhaßtheit f; abstoßender Anblick.
loaves [ləʊvz] n, pl of **loaf**.
lob [lɒb] 1 n (Tennis) Lob m. 2 vt ball im Lob spielen, lobben. ~**bed the grenade over the wall** er warf die Granate im hohen Bogen über die Mauer; **to** ~ **sth over to sb** jdm etw zuwerfen; ~ **it over!** wirf es herüber! 3 vi (Tennis) lobben.
lobby ['lɒbɪ] 1 n (entrance hall) Vor- or Eingangshalle f; (of hotel, theatre) Foyer nt; (corridor) Flur, Korridor m; (anteroom, waiting room) Vorzimmer nt; (place in Parliament) Lobby f; (Pol) Lobby, Interessengruppe f or -verband m. **the** ~ **railway** ~ die Eisenbahnlobby.
  2 vt to ~ one's Member of Parliament auf seinen Abgeordneten Einfluß nehmen; to ~ a bill through parliament als Interessengruppe ein Gesetz durchs Parlament bringen.
  3 vi auf die Abgeordneten Einfluß nehmen, Lobbyist sein. **they are** ~**ing for this reform** die Lobbyisten versuchen, diese Reform durchzubringen; **the farmers are** ~**ing for higher subsidies** die Bauernlobby will höhere Subventionen durchsetzen.
lobbying ['lɒbɪɪŋ] n Beeinflussung f von Abgeordneten (durch Lobbies). **the Prime Minister refused to be influenced by** ~ der Premierminister wollte sich nicht von Lobbies or Interessenverbänden beeinflussen lassen.
lobbyist ['lɒbɪɪst] n Lobbyist m.
lobe [ləʊb] n (Anat) (of ear) Ohrläppchen nt; (of lungs, brain) Lappen, Lobus (spec) m; (of leaf) Ausbuchtung f.
lobed [ləʊbd] adj gelappt.
lobelia [ləʊˈbiːlɪə] n Lobelie f.
lobster ['lɒbstər] n Hummer m. ~ **pot** Hummer(fang)korb m.
local ['ləʊkəl] 1 adj of Orts-; (in this area) hiesig; (in that area) dortig; radio station lokal, Orts-; newspaper Lokal-, Orts-; train Nahverkehrs-; politician Kommunal-; anaesthetic lokal, örtlich. **all the** ~ **residents** alle Ortsansässigen pl; **he's a** ~ **man** er ist ein Ortsansässiger, er ist von hier (inf); ~ **authorities** städtische Behörden pl; (council) Gemeindeverwaltung f; Stadtverwaltung f; Stadt- und Kreisverwaltung f; ~ **government** Kommunal- or Gemeindeverwaltung f; Kreisverwaltung f; **he is in** ~ **government** er arbeitet bei der Stadtverwaltung, ist bei der Stadt (inf); **reform of** ~ **government** Gemeindereform f; ~ **opinion is against the change** die öffentliche Meinung am Ort ist gegen die Änderung; **the latest** ~ **gossip** der neueste Klatsch (hier/dort); ~ **bus** Stadtbus m; (serving the immediate locality) Nahverkehrsbus m; ~ **colour** Lokalkolorit nt; **go into your** ~ **branch** gehen Sie zu Ihrer Zweigstelle; **vote for your** ~ **candidate** wählen Sie den Kandidaten Ihres Wahlkreises; **accents with the usual** ~ **variations** Dialekte mit den üblichen regionalen Unterschieden; **one of our** ~ **sons** einer der Söhne unserer Gemeinde/Stadt; **we used the** ~ **shops when we were in Spain** wir haben in den Läden der Einheimischen eingekauft, als wir in Spanien waren; **our village hasn't got a** ~ **butcher** unser Dorf hat keinen eigenen Schlachter; **there are two** ~ **grocers** es gibt zwei Lebensmittelhändler am Ort; **the** ~ **shops aren't very good** die dortigen/hiesigen Geschäfte sind nicht sehr gut; **our** ~ **doctor back home in Canada** unser Doktor zu Hause in Kanada; **what are their main** ~ **products there?** was wird dort hauptsächlich erzeugt?; **our best** ~ **wine** der beste hiesige Wein; **the** ~ **wine over there will make you sick** von dem dortigen Wein wird es einem schlecht.
  2 n (a) (pub) **the** ~ (in village) der Dorfkrug, die Dorfkneipe (inf); (in community) das Stammlokal; **our** ~ unsere Stammkneipe (inf), unser Stammlokal nt.
  (b) (born in) Einheimische/r m/f; (living in) Einwohner(in f) m.
locale [ləʊˈkɑːl] n Schauplatz m.
locality [ləʊˈkælɪtɪ] n Gegend f. **in the** ~ **of the crime** am Ort des Verbrechens.
localize ['ləʊkəlaɪz] vt (a) (detect) lokalisieren. (b) this custom,

once widespread, has now become very ~d die einst weitverbreitete Sitte ist jetzt auf wenige Orte begrenzt.

locally ['ləʊkəlɪ] *adv* am Ort; *(Med)* örtlich. **houses are dear** ~ Häuser sind hier teuer; **I prefer to shop** ~ ich kaufe lieber im Ort ein; **the shops are situated** ~ die Geschäfte befinden sich in günstiger Lage; **do you live** ~? wohnen Sie am Ort?; **I work in Glasgow but I don't live** ~ ich arbeite in Glasgow, wohne aber nicht hier/da; **was she well-known** ~? war sie in dieser Gegend sehr bekannt?; **he's not approved of** ~ er wird hier am Ort/bei sich zu Hause nicht geschätzt; **if each district is** ~ **governed** wenn jeder Bezirk regional regiert wird; **the plant grows** ~ die Pflanze wächst in dieser Gegend.

locate [ləʊ'keɪt] *vt* **(a)** *(position)* legen; *headquarters* einrichten; *(including act of building)* bauen, errichten; *sportsground, playground* anlegen; *road* bauen, anlegen. **to be** ~d **at** or **in** sich befinden in (+*dat)*; **the hotel is centrally** ~d das Hotel liegt zentral; **where shall we** ~ **the new branch?** wohin sollen wir die neue Zweigstelle legen?
  (b) *(find)* ausfindig machen; *submarine, plane* orten.

location [ləʊ'keɪʃən] *n* **(a)** *(position, site)* Lage *f*; *(of building also)* Standort *m*; *(of road)* Führung *f*; *(of ship)* Position *f*. **this would be an ideal** ~ **for the road/airport** das wäre ein ideales Gelände für die Straße/den Flughafen; **they shifted the** ~ **of the factory** sie verlegten die Fabrik; **the precise** ~ **of the earthquake** wo das Erdbeben genau stattgefunden hat; **the doctors haven't determined the precise** ~ **of the tumour** die Ärzte haben den Tumor noch nicht genau lokalisiert; **that shop is in a good** ~ dieses Geschäft hat eine gute Lage.
  (b) *(positioning, siting)* *(of building, road)* Bau *m*; *(of park)* Anlage *f*; *(of headquarters)* *(removal)* Einrichtung *f*; *(building)* Errichtung *f*. **they discussed the** ~ **of the road/airport** sie diskutierten, wo die Straße/der Flughafen gebaut werden soll.
  (c) *(finding)* Auffinden *nt*; *(of tumour)* Lokalisierung *f*; *(of star, ship)* Ortung, Positionsbestimmung *f*. **the** ~ **of oil in the North Sea** die Entdeckung von Erdöl in der Nordsee.
  (d) *(Film)* Drehort *m*. **to be on** ~ **in Mexico** *(person)* bei Außenaufnahmen in Mexiko sein; **part of the film was done on** ~ **in Mexico** Außenaufnahmen für den Film wurden in Mexiko gedreht; **we had a lot of** ~ **work** wir mußten viele Außenaufnahmen machen.

locative ['lokətɪv] *n* Lokativ *m*.

loc cit ['lok'sɪt] *abbr of* **loco citato** l.c., a.a.O.

loch [lɒx] *n* *(Scot)* See *m*; *(sea* ~*)* fjordartiger Meeresarm.

loci ['ləʊkɪ] *pl of* **locus**.

lock¹ [lɒk] *n* *(of hair)* Locke *f*.

lock² *n* **(a)** *(on door, box, gun)* Schloß *nt*. **to put sb/sth under** ~ **and key** jdn hinter Schloß und Riegel bringen/etw wegschließen; **to keep money under** ~ **and key** Geld unter Verschluß halten; **he offered me the house** ~, **stock and barrel** er bot mir das Haus mit allem Drum und Dran an *(inf)*; **they destroyed it** ~, **stock and barrel** sie haben es total zerstört; **to condemn sth** ~, **stock and barrel** etw in Grund und Boden verdammen; **they rejected the idea** ~, **stock and barrel** sie lehnten die Idee in Bausch und Bogen ab; **he swallowed my story** ~, **stock and barrel** er hat mir die Geschichte voll und ganz abgenommen; **it is finished** ~, **stock and barrel** es ist ganz und gar fertig.
  (b) *(canal* ~*)* Schleuse *f*.
  (c) *(hold)* Fesselgriff *m*.
  (d) *(Aut)* Wendekreis *m*. **the steering wheel was on** or **at full** ~ das Lenkrad war voll eingeschlagen.
  2 *vt* *door* etc ab- or zuschließen; *steering wheel* sperren, arretieren; *wheel* blockieren. **to** ~ **sb in a room** jdn in einem Zimmer einschließen; **the armies were** ~ed **in combat** die Armeen waren in Kämpfe verwickelt; **they were** ~ed **in each other's arms** sie hielten sich fest umschlungen; **he** ~ed **my arm in a firm grip** er umklammerte meinen Arm mit festem Griff; **this bar** ~s **the wheel in position** diese Stange hält das Rad fest; **the chains were** ~ed **round his arms** die Ketten waren an seinen Armen festgemacht; *see* **stable²**.
  3 *vi* schließen; *(wheel)* blockieren. **a suitcase that** ~s ein verschließbarer Koffer, ein Koffer, der sich abschließen läßt; **his jaw had** ~ed **fast** er hatte Mundsperre; **the lion's jaws** ~ed **round his arm** der Kiefer des Löwen schloß sich fest um seinen Arm.

♦**lock away** *vt sep* wegschließen; *person* einsperren. **he** ~ed **the money** ~ **in his safe** er schloß das Geld in seinem Safe ein.

♦**lock in** *vt sep* einschließen. **to be** ~ed ~ eingesperrt sein.

♦**lock on** **1** *vi* *(spaceship etc)* gekoppelt werden *(to* mit). **the radio automatically** ~s ~**to a channel** das Radio hat automatische Feineinstellung; **the missile** ~s ~**to its target** das Geschoß richtet sich auf das Ziel; **his mind has** ~ed ~ **to one way of thinking** er hat sich auf eine Denkart festgefahren.
  2 *vt sep* *radio, scanner* einstellen *(to* auf +*acc)*. **with a padlock he** ~ed **the extra piece** ~ er befestigte das zusätzliche Stück mit einem Anhängeschloß.

♦**lock out** *vt sep* aussperren.

♦**lock together** **1** *vi* *(rockets)* (miteinander) gekoppelt werden; *(pieces of jigsaw)* sich zusammenstecken lassen.
  2 *vt sep* *rockets* (miteinander) koppeln; *pieces of jigsaw* zusammenstecken. ~ed ~ **in a passionate embrace** in einer leidenschaftlichen Umarmung fest umschlungen.

♦**lock up** **1** *vt sep* **(a)** *thing, house* abschließen; *person* einsperren. **to** ~ **sth** ~ **in sth** etw in etw *(dat)* einschließen; **he ought to be** ~ed ~! den müßte man einsperren! **(b)** *(Comm)* *capital* fest anlegen. **2** *vi* abschließen.

locker ['lokə'] *n* Schließfach *nt*; *(Naut, Mil)* Spind *m*. ~ **room** Umkleideraum *m*.

locket ['lokɪt] *n* Medaillon *nt*.

lock: ~ **gate** *n* Schleusentor *nt*; ~**jaw** *n* Wundstarrkrampf *m*; ~

keeper *n* Schleusenwärter *m*; ~**nut** *n* Gegenmutter *f*; ~**out** *n* Aussperrung *f*; ~**smith** *n* Schlosser(meister) *m*; ~**stitch** *n* Steppstich *m*; ~**up** *n* **(a)** *(shop)* Laden *m*, Geschäft *nt*; *(garage)* Garage *f*; **(b)** *(prison)* Gefängnis *nt*.

loco¹ *n* *(Rail inf)* Lok *f* *(inf)*.

loco² *adj* *(esp US sl)* bekloppt *(sl)*. **he's gone** ~ der spinnt *(inf)*.

loco citato [,ləʊkəʊsɪ'tɑːtəʊ] *see* **loc cit**.

locomotion [,ləʊkə'məʊʃən] *n* Fortbewegung *f*. **means of** ~ Fortbewegungsmittel *nt*.

locomotive [,ləʊkə'məʊtɪv] **1** *adj* Fortbewegungs-. ~ **power** Fortbewegungsfähigkeit *f*; ~ **engine** Lokomotive *f*. **2** *n* Lokomotive *f*.

locum (tenens) ['ləʊkəm('tenenz)] *n* Vertreter(in *f*) *m*.

locus ['lokəs] *n*, *pl* **loci** geometrischer Ort.

locust ['ləʊkəst] *n* Heuschrecke *f*. ~ **tree** Robinie *f*.

locution [lə'kjuːʃən] *n* Ausdrucksweise *f*; *(expression)* Ausdruck *m*. **a set** ~ eine feste or feststehende Redewendung.

lode [ləʊd] *n* Ader *f*.

lode: ~**star** *n* Leitstern *m*; Polarstern *m*; *(fig)* *(person)* Leitbild *nt*; *(principle)* Leitstern *m*; ~**stone** *n* Magnetit, Magneteisenstein *m*.

lodge [lodʒ] **1** *n* *(in grounds)* Pförtnerhaus *nt*; *(of Red Indian)* Wigwam *m*; *(shooting* ~, *skiing* ~ *etc)* Hütte *f*; *(porter's* ~*)* Pförtnerloge *f*; *(in school, Univ)* Pedellzimmer *nt*; *(masonic* ~*)* Loge *f*; *(of beaver)* Bau *m*.
  2 *vt* **(a)** *person* unterbringen.
  (b) *complaint* einlegen *(with* bei); *charge* einreichen.
  (c) *(insert)* *spear* stoßen. **to be** ~d *(fest)*stecken.
  (d) *jewellery, money* deponieren, hinterlegen.
  3 *vi* **(a)** *(live)* (zur or in Untermiete) wohnen *(with sb, at sb's* bei jdm*)*; *(at boarding house)* wohnen *(in in* +*dat)*.
  (b) *(object, bullet)* steckenbleiben.

lodger ['lodʒə'] *n* Untermieter(in *f*) *m*. **I was a** ~ **there** once ich habe dort einmal zur or in Untermiete gewohnt; **she takes** ~s sie vermietet (Zimmer), sie nimmt Untermieter auf.

lodging ['lodʒɪŋ] *n* **(a)** Unterkunft *f*. **they gave me a night's** ~ sie gaben mir Unterkunft or ein Zimmer für die Nacht.
  (b) ~s *pl* ein möbliertes Zimmer; möblierte Zimmer *pl*; **where are your** ~s? wo wohnen Sie?; **we took** ~s **with Mrs B** wir mieteten uns bei Frau B ein; ~ **house** Pension *f*.

loess ['ləʊɪs] *n* Löß *m*.

loft [loft] **1** *n* **(a)** Boden, Speicher *m*; *(hay*~*)* Heuboden *m*. **in the** ~ auf dem Boden or Speicher. **(b)** *(organ* ~, *choir* ~*)* Empore *f*.
  2 *vt* *(Sport)* hochschlagen. **he** ~ed **the ball over the fence** er schlug den Ball im hohen Bogen über den Zaun.

loftily ['loftɪlɪ] *adv* hoch; *say, speak* stolz, hochmütig. **to speak** ~ **of sth** in stolzen Worten über etw *(acc)* sprechen.

loftiness ['loftɪnɪs] *n* **(a)** *(of tree, mountain)* Höhe *f*. **(b)** *(of sentiments)* Erhabenheit *f*; *(of prose)* erlesener or gehobener or hochtrabender *(pej)* Stil. **the** ~ **of his ambitions/ideals** seine hochfliegenden Ambitionen/seine hohen or hochfliegenden Ideale. **(c)** *(haughtiness)* Hochmütigkeit *f*.

lofty ['loftɪ] **1** *adj* (+*er*) **(a)** *(high)* hoch. **(b)** *(noble)* *ideals* hoch(fliegend); *ambitions* hochfliegend; *sentiments* erhaben; *prose, style* erlesen, gehoben, hochtrabend *(pej)*. **(c)** *(haughty)* stolz, hochmütig. **2** *n (inf)* Lange(r) *mf (inf)*.

log¹ [log] *n* Baumstamm *m*; *(short length of tree trunk)* Block, Klotz *m*; *(for a fire)* Scheit *nt*. **to sleep like a** ~ schlafen wie ein Bär; *(exhausted)* schlafen wie ein Klotz; ~ **cabin** Blockhaus *nt* or -hütte *f*; ~ **rolling** *(Pol)* Kuhhandel *m (inf)*; *(Sport)* Wettkampf *m*, bei dem zwei Gegner auf einem im Wasser schwimmenden Baumstamm stehen und sich durch Drehen desselben zum Fallen bringen.

log² **1** *n* **(a)** *(Naut: apparatus)* Log *nt*. **(b)** *(record)* Aufzeichnungen *pl*; *(Naut)* Logbuch *nt*. **to make** or **keep a** ~ **of sth** über etw *(acc)* Buch führen. **2** *vt* **(a)** *(Naut)* (ins Logbuch) eintragen. **(b)** *(travel)* zurücklegen.

♦**log up** *vt sep (Naut)* (ins Logbuch) eintragen; *(clock up)* distance zurücklegen; *(fig)* successes einheimsen *(inf)*.

log³ *abbr of* **logarithm** log. ~ **tables** Logarithmentafel *f*.

loganberry ['ləʊgənbərɪ] *n* *(fruit)* Loganbeere *f*; *(bush)* Loganbeerbusch *m*.

logarithm ['logərɪðəm] *n* Logarithmus *m*.

logarithmic [,logə'rɪðmɪk] *adj* logarithmisch.

log book *n (Naut)* Logbuch *nt*; *(Aviat)* Bordbuch *nt*; *(of lorries)* Fahrtenbuch *nt*; *(Aut: registration book)* Kraftfahrzeug- or Kfz-Brief *m*; *(in hospitals, police stations etc)* Dienstbuch *nt*.

loggerheads ['logəhedz] *npl*: **to be at** ~ *(with sb)* Streit (mit jdm) haben, sich *(dat)* (mit jdm) in den Haaren liegen *(inf)*; **they were constantly at** ~ **with the authorities** sie standen mit den Behörden dauernd auf Kriegsfuß; **his views are at** ~ **with the traditional theory** seine Auffassungen vertragen sich überhaupt nicht mit der herkömmlichen Lehre.

loggia ['lodʒɪə] *n* Loggia *f*.

logging ['logɪŋ] *n* Holzfällen *nt*.

logic ['lodʒɪk] *n* Logik *f*.

logical ['lodʒɪkəl] *adj* logisch; *conclusion also* folgerichtig. **he has a** ~ **mind** er denkt logisch.

logically ['lodʒɪkəlɪ] *adv* *think, argue* logisch. ~, **he may be right** logisch gesehen könnte er recht haben.

logician [lo'dʒɪʃən] *n* Logiker(in *f*) *m*.

logistic [lo'dʒɪstɪk] *adj* logistisch.

logistics [lo'dʒɪstɪks] *n sing* Logistik *f*.

logo ['ləʊgəʊ] *n* Firmenzeichen *nt*.

loin [lɔɪn] *n* Lende *f*. ~ **cloth** Lendenschurz *m*; *see* **gird up**.

loiter ['lɔɪtə'] **1** *vt* **to** ~ **away the time** die Zeit verbummeln *(inf)*.
  2 *vi* **(a)** *(waste time)* trödeln, bummeln.
  (b) *(hang around suspiciously)* sich herumtreiben, herumlungern. "**no** ~**ing**" „unberechtigter Aufenthalt verboten"; **to** ~ **with intent** sich verdächtig machen, sich auffällig verhalten.

♦**loiter about** or **around** *vi* herumlungern.

loiterer ['lɔɪtərə'] n Herumtreiber(in f), Herumlungerer m; (straggler) Nachzügler(in f), Bummelant m (inf).

loll [lɒl] vi lümmeln. **stand up straight, don't ~** stell dich gerade hin, laß dich nicht so hängen (inf) or lümmle nicht so herum; **he was ~ing in an easy chair** er hing (inf) or räkelte sich im Sessel; **to ~ against sth** sich (lässig) gegen or an etw (acc) lehnen.

♦ **loll about** or **around** vi herumlümmeln, herumhängen (inf).

♦ **loll back** vi sich zurücklehnen.

♦ **loll out** vi heraushängen. **the dog's tongue was ~ing ~** dem Hund hing die Zunge heraus.

lollipop ['lɒlɪpɒp] n Lutscher m; (iced ~) Eis nt am Stiel. ~ **man/ woman** (Brit inf) ≈ Schülerlotse m.

lollop ['lɒləp] vi (also ~ **along**) (animal) trotten, zotteln; (puppy, rabbit) hoppeln; (person) zockeln. **he ran with a ~ing stride** er rannte in großen, schlaksigen Sätzen.

lolly ['lɒlɪ] n (a) (inf: lollipop) Lutscher m. **an ice(d) ~** ein Eis nt am Stiel. (b) (sl: money) Mäuse (sl), Piepen (sl) pl.

Lombard ['lɒmbɑːd] 1 adj lombardisch. 2 n Lombarde m, Lombardin f.

Lombardy ['lɒmbədɪ] n Lombardei f.

London ['lʌndən] 1 n London nt. 2 adj Londoner.

Londoner ['lʌndənə'] n Londoner(in f) m.

lone [ləun] adj einzeln, einsam; (only) einzig. **he prefers to play a ~ hand** er macht lieber alles im Alleingang; **he tracked down the criminal by playing a ~ hand** er spürte den Verbrecher im Alleingang auf; ~ **wolf** (fig) Einzelgänger m.

loneliness ['ləunlɪnɪs] n Einsamkeit f.

lonely ['ləunlɪ] adj (+er) einsam.

loner ['ləunə'] n Einzelgänger(in f) m.

lonesome ['ləunsəm] adj (esp US) einsam.

long¹ abbr of **longitude** L.

long² [lɒŋ] 1 adj (+er) (a) (in size) lang; glass hoch; journey weit. **it is 6 metres ~** es ist 6 Meter lang; **to be ~ in the leg** lange Beine haben; **to pull a ~ face** ein langes Gesicht machen; **it's a ~ way** das ist weit; **it's a ~ way to Hamburg** nach Hamburg ist es weit; **the odds against the government solving the problems are ~** die Chancen, daß die Regierung eine Lösung für die Probleme findet, stehen schlecht; **to have a ~ memory** ein gutes Gedächtnis haben; **to be ~ in the tooth** (inf) nicht mehr der/die Jüngste sein; **surely he is a bit ~ in the tooth to be climbing Everest** ist er nicht schon ein bißchen (zu) alt, um den Everest zu besteigen?

(b) (in time) lang; job langwierig. **it's a ~ time since I saw her** ich habe sie schon lange or seit längerer Zeit nicht mehr gesehen; **will you need it for a ~ time?** brauchen Sie es lange?; **he's been here (for) a ~ time** er ist schon lange hier; **she was abroad for a ~ time** sie war lange or (eine) lange Zeit im Ausland; **well hullo, it's been a ~ time** hallo, schon lange nicht mehr gesehen; ~ **time no see** (inf) sieht man dich auch mal wieder? (inf); **to take a ~ look at sth** etw lange or ausgiebig betrachten; **let's take a ~ look at the possibilities** wir müssen die Möglichkeiten eingehend or reiflich überdenken; **how ~ is the film?** wie lange dauert der Film?; **a year is 12 months** ~ ein Jahr hat 12 Monate; **how ~ are your holidays?** wie lange haben Sie Urlaub?; **to take the ~ view** etw auf lange Sicht betrachten; **the days are getting ~er** die Tage werden länger.

(c) (Poet, Phon) vowel, syllable lang.

(d) **a ~ drink** (mixed) ein Longdrink m; (beer) ein Bier nt; **a ~ gin** ein Gin mit Tonic und Eis etc; **I'd like something ~ and cool** ich möchte einen kühlen Longdrink.

2 adv (a) lang(e). **to be ~ in** or **about doing sth** lange zu etw brauchen; **don't be ~!** beeil dich!; **don't be too ~ about it** laß dir nicht zuviel Zeit, mach nicht zu lange (inf); **don't be too ~ about phoning me** ruf mich bald (mal) an; **I shan't be ~** (in finishing) ich bin gleich fertig; (in returning) ich bin gleich wieder da; **two months without you, it's been too ~** zwei Monate ohne dich, das war zu lang(e); **he drank ~ and deep** er nahm einen langen, tiefen Schluck; **all night ~** die ganze Nacht; **something he had ~ wished to happen** etwas, was er sich (dat) schon lange gewünscht hatte; ~ **ago** vor langer Zeit; **not ~ ago** vor kurzem; ~ **before** lange vorher; ~ **before now** viel früher; ~ **before they arrived** lange bevor sie ankamen; **not ~ before I met you** kurz bevor ich dich kennenlernte; **not ~ before that** kurz davor; **those days are ~ (since) past** diese Tage sind schon lange vorbei; **at the ~est** höchstens; **as ~ as long we are; we waited as ~ as we could** wir haben gewartet, solange wir konnten; **as ~ as, so ~ as** (provided that) solange; see also **ago, since.**

(b) (in comp) **how much ~er can you stay?** wie lange können Sie noch bleiben?; **I can't wait any ~er** (from then) länger kann ich nicht warten; (from now) ich kann nicht mehr länger warten; **if that noise goes on any ~er** wenn der Lärm weitergeht; **no ~er** (not any more) nicht mehr; **I'll wait no ~er** ich warte nicht länger; **I'll insist no ~er** ich werde nicht weiter darauf bestehen.

(c) **so ~!** (inf) tschüs! (inf), bis später!

3 n (a) **the ~ and the short of it is that ...** kurz gesagt ..., der langen Rede kurzer Sinn, ...; **that's the ~ and the short of it** und damit hat sich's (inf); **before ~** bald; **are you going for ~?** werden Sie länger weg sein?; **I won't stay for ~** ich bleibe nicht lange; **it won't take ~** das dauert nicht lange; **it won't take ~ before ...** es wird nicht lange dauern, bis ...; **I won't take ~** ich brauche nicht lange (dazu).

(b) (Poet) lange Silbe.

long³ vi sich sehnen (for nach); (less passionately) herbeisehnen, kaum erwarten können (for sth etw acc). ~**ed for his love to return** er wartete sehnsüchtig auf die Rückkehr seiner Liebsten; **I'm ~ing for him to resign** ich warte ungeduldig auf seinen Rücktritt; **the children were ~ing for the bell to ring** die Kinder warteten sehnsüchtig auf das Klingeln or

konnten das Klingeln kaum erwarten; **he is ~ing for me to make a mistake** er möchte zu gern, daß ich einen Fehler mache; **I'm ~ing to see my native hills** ich sehne mich danach, die heimatlichen Berge zu sehen; **I am ~ing to go abroad** ich brenne darauf, ins Ausland zu gehen; **he ~ed to know what was happening** er hätte zu gerne gewußt, was vorging; **I'm ~ing to see my cat again** ich möchte meine Katze so gern wiedersehen; **I'm ~ing to see that film** ich will den Film unbedingt sehen; **I'm ~ing to hear his reaction** ich bin sehr gespannt, wie er darauf reagiert, ich bin sehr auf seine Reaktion gespannt; **how I ~ for a cup of tea/a shower** wie ich mich nach einer Tasse Tee/einer Dusche sehne; ~**ed-for** ersehnt; **the much ~ed-for cup of tea** die heißersehnte Tasse Tee.

long: ~**boat** n großes Beiboot; (of Vikings) Wikingerboot nt; ~**bow** n (Lang)bogen m; ~**case clock** n Großvateruhr f; ~**distance 1** adj lorry, call Fern-; flight, race, runner also Langstrecken-; ~**distance bus** (Fern)reisebus, Überlandbus m; **2** adv **to call ~distance** ein Ferngespräch führen; ~ **division** n schriftliche Division; ~**drawn-out** adj speech, argument langatmig; meeting ausgedehnt, in die Länge gezogen.

longevity [lɒn'dʒevɪtɪ] n Langlebigkeit f.

long: ~**forgotten** adj längst vergessen; ~**haired** adj langhaarig; dog etc Langhaar-; ~**haired cow** Kuh f mit langhaarigem Fell; ~**hand** n Langschrift f; ~**headed** adj (fig) klug, weitblickend; ~**horn** n Longhorn nt.

longing ['lɒŋɪŋ] **1** adj look sehnsüchtig; eyes sehnsuchtsvoll. **2** n Sehnsucht f (for nach). **this sense of ~** diese Sehnsucht; **his great ~ in life** sein sehnsüchtigster Wunsch; **to have a ~ to do sth** sich danach sehnen, etw zu tun.

longingly ['lɒŋɪŋlɪ] adv sehnsüchtig.

longish ['lɒŋɪʃ] adj ziemlich lang.

longitude ['lɒŋgɪtjuːd] n Länge f. **lines of ~** Längengrade pl.

longitudinal [ˌlɒŋgɪ'tjuːdɪnl] adj Längen-; stripes, cut Längs-.

longitudinally [ˌlɒŋgɪ'tjuːdɪnəlɪ] adv der Länge nach.

long: ~ **johns** npl (inf) lange Unterhosen pl; ~ **jump** n Weitsprung m; ~ **jumper** n Weitspringer(in f) m; ~**legged** adj langbeinig; ~**limbed** adj langglied(e)rig; ~**lived** ['lɒŋlɪvd] adj langlebig; success dauerhaft, von Dauer; anger anhaltend, von Dauer; ~**lived trees** Bäume, die lange leben; **they are a ~lived family** in dieser Familie leben alle lang; ~**lost** adj person verloren geglaubt; ideals, enthusiasm etc verlorengegangen; ~**playing** adj Langspiel-; ~**range** adj gun weittragend; missile Fernkampf-; aircraft Langstrecken-; forecast, plane langfristig; ~**ship** n Wikingerboot nt; ~**shoreman** n (US) Hafenarbeiter m; ~ **shot** n (a) (Phot) Fernaufnahme f; (b) (inf) **it's a ~ shot, but it may pay off** es ist gewagt, aber es könnte sich auszahlen; **it was a ~ shot, but it proved to be true** die Vermutung war weit hergeholt, hat sich aber als wahr erwiesen; **that horse is a ~ shot** auf das Pferd zu setzen, ist gewagt; **to take a ~ shot** einen gewagten Versuch unternehmen; **not by a ~ shot** bei weitem nicht, noch lange nicht; ~**sight** n see ~**sightedness**; ~**sighted** adj (lit, fig) weitsichtig; ~**sightedness** n Weitsichtigkeit f; (fig) Weitsicht f; ~**standing 1** adj friendship also langjährig; interest, invitation schon lange bestehend; **2** n ~ **standing** see adj; ~**suffering** adj schwer geprüft; ~ **suit** n (Cards) lange Reihe; (fig) Trumpf m; ~**tailed** adj langschwänzig; ~**term 1** adj plans, investment langfristig; memory Langzeit-; **2** n **in the ~ term** langfristig gesehen; **to plan for the ~ term** auf lange Sicht planen; ~ **vacation** n (Univ) (Sommer)semesterferien pl; (Sch) große Ferien pl; ~**wave 1** adj Langwellen-; **2** n Langwelle f.

longways ['lɒŋweɪz] adv der Länge nach, längs.

long: ~**winded** adj umständlich; story langatmig; ~**windedly** adv langatmig; ~**windedness** n Langatmigkeit f.

loo [luː] n (Brit inf) Klo nt (inf). **to go to the ~** aufs Klo gehen (inf); **in the ~** auf dem Klo (inf).

loofah ['luːfə] n Luffa f; (as sponge) Luffa(schwamm) m.

look [lʊk] **1** n (a) (glance) Blick m. **she gave me a dirty ~, I put a dirty ~ from her** sie warf mir einen vernichtenden Blick zu; **she gave me a ~ of disbelief** sie sah mich ungläubig an; **he gave me such a ~!** er hat mir (vielleicht) einen Blick zugeworfen!; **we got some very odd ~s** wir wurden komisch angesehen; **to have** or **take a ~ at sth** sich (dat) etw ansehen; **he had a quick ~ at his watch** er sah kurz auf die Uhr; **can I have a ~?** darf ich mal sehen or gucken (inf)?; **have a ~ at this!** sieh or guck (inf) dir das mal an!; **is it in the dictionary? — have a ~** (and see) steht das im Wörterbuch? — sieh or guck (inf) mal nach; **let's have a ~** laß mal sehen, zeig mal her; **let's have a ~ at it/you** laß mal sehen, zeig mal/laß dich mal ansehen; **do you want a ~?** willst du mal sehen?; (at the paper) willst du mal hineinsehen or einen Blick hineinwerfen?; **to take a good ~ at sth** sich (dat) etw genau ansehen; **take** or **have a good ~** sehen or gucken (inf) Sie genau hin; **to have a ~ for sth** sich nach etw umsehen; **I can't find it — have another ~** ich finde es nicht — sieh or guck (inf) nochmal nach; **to have a ~ round** sich umsehen; **shall we have a ~ round the town?** sollen wir uns (dat) die Stadt ansehen?

(b) (air, appearances) Aussehen nt. **there was a ~ of despair in his eyes** ein verzweifelter Blick war in seinen Augen; **he put on a serious ~** er machte ein ernstes Gesicht; **he had the ~ of a sailor** er sah wie ein Seemann aus; **I don't like the ~ of him/this wound** er/die Wunde gefällt mir gar nicht; **by the ~ of him so, wie er aussieht; judging by the ~ of the sky** wenn man sich (dat) den Himmel ansieht, so, wie der Himmel aussieht; **to give sth a new ~** einer Sache (dat) ein neues Aussehen verleihen or Gesicht geben; **economic planning/the town has now taken on a new ~** die Wirtschaftsplanung/die Stadt hat ein neues Gesicht bekommen.

(c) ~**s** pl Aussehen nt; **good ~s** gutes Aussehen; ~**s aren't everything** auf das Aussehen allein kommt es nicht an; **you can't go by ~s alone** man kann nicht nur nach dem Aussehen or

Äußeren gehen; **a girl with your ~s shouldn't have any problems** bei deinem Aussehen solltest du doch keine Probleme haben; **she began to lose her ~s** sie verlor allmählich ihr gutes Aussehen.

2 *vt* **he is ~ing his age** man sieht ihm sein Alter an; **he's not ~ing himself these days** er sieht in letzter Zeit ganz verändert aus; **he's ~ing his old self again** er ist wieder ganz der alte; **to ~ one's best** sein vorteilhaft *or* attraktiv aussehen; **I want to ~ my best tonight** ich möchte heute abend besonders gut aussehen; **she ~s her best in red** Rot steht ihr am besten; **he ~ed death in the face** er sah dem Tod ins Angesicht (*geh*) *or* Auge; **~ what you've done!** sieh *or* guck (*inf*) dir mal an, was du da angestellt hast!; **~ what you've done, now she's offended** jetzt hast du's geschafft, nun ist sie beleidigt; **~ what you've made me do** (sieh *or* schau (*dial*) *or* guck (*inf*) mal), daran bist du schuld; **can't you ~ what you're doing!** kannst du nicht aufpassen, was du machst?; **~ where you're going!** paß auf, wo du hintrittst!; **just ~ where he's put the car!** sieh *or* schau (*dial*) *or* guck (*inf*) dir bloß mal an, wo er das Auto abgestellt hat!; **~ who's here!** guck (*inf*) *or* schau (*dial*) mal *or* sieh doch, wer da ist!

3 *vi* (a) (*see, glance*) gucken, schauen (*liter, dial*); (*with prep etc also*) sehen. **to ~ round** sich umsehen; **he ~ed in(to) the chest** er sah *or* schaute (*dial*) *or* guckte (*inf*) in die Kiste (hinein); **to ~ carefully** genau hinsehen *etc*; **to ~ and see** nachsehen *etc*; **~ here!** hör (mal) zu!; **now ~ here, it wasn't my fault** Moment mal, das war aber nicht meine Schuld; **~, I know you're tired, but ...** ich weiß ja, daß du müde bist, aber ...; **~, there's a much better solution** da gibt es doch eine wesentlich bessere Lösung; **just ~!** guck mal!; **to ~ over one's shoulder** über die Schulter sehen; **to ~ over sb's shoulder** jdm über die Schulter sehen; **~ before you leap** (*Prov*) erst wägen, dann wagen (*Prov*).

(b) (*search*) suchen, nachsehen.

(c) (*seem*) aussehen. **it ~s all right to me** es scheint mir in Ordnung zu sein; **it ~s suspicious to me** es kommt mir verdächtig vor, es sieht verdächtig aus; **how does it ~ to you?** was meinst du dazu?; **I think the cake is done, how does it ~ to you?** ich glaube, der Kuchen ist fertig, was meinst du?; **the car ~s about 10 years old** das Auto sieht so aus, als ob es 10 Jahre alt wäre; **it ~s well on you** es steht dir gut; **to ~ lively** schnell machen.

(d) **to ~ like** aussehen wie. **the picture doesn't ~ like him** das Bild sieht ihm nicht ähnlich; **it ~s like rain, it ~s as if it will rain** es sieht nach Regen aus; **it ~s like cheese to me** (ich finde,) das sieht wie Käse aus; **it ~s as if we'll be late** es sieht (so) aus, als würden wir zu spät kommen; **the festival ~s like being lively** auf dem Festival wird es wahrscheinlich hoch hergehen.

(e) (*face*) gehen nach. **this window ~s (towards the) north** dieses Fenster geht nach Norden; **the village ~s towards the forest** das Dorf liegt dem Wald zugewandt.

♦**look about** *vi* sich umsehen (*for sth* nach etw). **to ~ one** sich umsehen; **if we ~ we might find some more examples** wenn wir suchen, finden wir vielleicht noch ein paar Beispiele.

♦**look after** *vi* +*prep obj* (a) (*take care of*) sich kümmern um. **to ~ ~ oneself** (*cook etc*) für sich selbst sorgen, sich selbst versorgen; (*be capable, strong etc*) auf sich (*acc*) aufpassen; **he's only ~ing ~ his own interests** (*acc*) er handelt nur im eigenen Interesse. (b) (*temporarily*) sehen nach; **children also** aufpassen auf (+*acc*). (c) (*follow with eyes*) nachsehen (+*dat*).

♦**look ahead** *vi* (a) nach vorne sehen *or* gucken (*inf*). (b) (*fig*) vorausschauen. **when we ~ ~ to the next 30 years/ the future of this country** wenn wir die nächsten 30 Jahre/die Zukunft dieses Landes betrachten; **a good manager is one who can ~ ~** ein guter Manager muß Weitblick haben.

♦**look around** *vi* (a) sich umsehen. (b) (*in shop etc*) sich umsehen. (+*prep obj*) sich (*dat*) ansehen *or* angucken (*inf*).

♦**look at** *vi* +*prep obj* (a) ansehen, anschauen (*dial*), angucken (*inf*). **just ~ ~ him!** sieh etc dir den mal an!; **he ~ed ~ his watch** er sah etc auf die Uhr; **~ ~ the blackboard** schau(t) an *or* auf die Tafel; **don't ~ directly ~ the sun** sehen etc Sie nicht direkt in die Sonne; **I can't ~ ~ him without feeling ...** wenn ich ihn ansehe etc, habe ich immer das Gefühl, daß ...; **he/it isn't much to ~ ~** (*not attractive*) er/es sieht nicht besonders (gut) aus; (*nothing special*) er/es sieht nach nichts aus; **to ~ ~ him ...** wenn man ihn sieht ...

(b) (*examine*) sich (*dat*) ansehen *or* -schauen (*dial*) *or* -gucken (*inf*); *offer* prüfen. **we'll have to ~ ~ the financial aspect** wir müssen die finanzielle Seite betrachten; **has the manuscript been ~ed ~ yet?** ist das Manuskript schon durchgesehen worden?

(c) (*view*) betrachten, sehen. **they ~ ~ life in a different way** sie haben eine andere Einstellung zum Leben, sie sehen das Leben von einer anderen Warte aus; **to ~ ~ a problem in a new light** ein Problem in einem neuen *or* in neuem Licht sehen.

(d) (*consider*) *possibilities* sich (*dat*) überlegen; *suggestions, offer* in Betracht ziehen.

♦**look away** *vi* (a) wegsehen. (b) **the house ~s ~ from the sea** das Haus liegt vom Meer abgewendet.

♦**look back** *vi* sich umsehen; (*fig*) zurückblicken (*on sth, to sth* auf etw *acc*). **he's never ~ed ~** (*inf*) es ist ständig mit ihm bergauf gegangen.

♦**look down** *vi* hinunter-/heruntersehen *or* -schauen (*dial*) *or* -gucken (*inf*). **we ~ed ~ the hole** wir sahen *etc* ins Loch hinunter; **~ ~ on the valley beneath** sieh *etc* ins Tal hinunter.

♦**look down on** *vi* +*prep obj* herabsehen auf (+*acc*). **you shouldn't ~ ~ ~ his attempts to help** du solltest ihn nicht belächeln, wenn er versucht zu helfen.

♦**look for** *vi* +*prep obj* (a) (*seek*) suchen. **he's ~ing ~ trouble** er wird sich (*dat*) Ärger einhandeln; (*actively*) er sucht Streit. (b) (*expect*) erwarten.

♦**look forward to** *vi* +*prep obj* sich freuen auf (+*acc*). **I'm so ~ing ~ seeing you again** ich freue mich so darauf, dich wiederzusehen; **I ~ ~ ~ hearing from you** ich hoffe, bald von Ihnen zu hören.

♦**look in** *vi* (a) hinein-/hereinsehen *or* -schauen (*dial*) *or* -gucken (*inf*). (b) (*visit*) vorbeikommen (*on sb* bei jdm). **would you ~ ~ at Smith's and collect my dress?** kannst du bei Smith vorbeigehen und mein Kleid abholen? (c) (*watch TV*) fernsehen.

♦**look into** *vi* +*prep obj* untersuchen; *complaint etc* prüfen.

♦**look on** *vi* (a) (*watch*) zusehen, zugucken (*inf*). (b) **to ~ ~to** (*window*) (hinaus)gehen auf (+*acc*); (*building*) liegen an (+*dat*). (c) – *prep obj* (*also* **look upon**) betrachten, ansehen. **to ~ ~ sb as a friend** jdn als Freund betrachten; **I ~ ~ him as a good doctor** ich halte ihn für einen guten Arzt; **to ~ ~ sb with respect** Achtung *or* Respekt vor jdm haben.

♦**look out 1** *vi* (a) hinaus-/heraussehen *or* -schauen (*dial*) *or* -gucken (*inf*). **to ~ (of) the window** zum Fenster hinaussehen *etc*, aus dem Fenster sehen *etc*. (b) (*building etc*) **to ~ ~ on** *or* **over sth** einen Blick auf etw (*acc*) haben. (c) (*take care*) aufpassen.

2 *vt sep* heraussuchen.

♦**look out for** *vi* +*prep obj* (a) (*keep watch for*) **we'll ~ ~ ~ you at the station/after the meeting** wir werden auf dem Bahnhof/nach der Versammlung nach dir Ausschau halten; **~ ~ pickpockets/his left hook** nimm dich vor Taschendieben/ seinem linken Haken in acht, paß auf Taschendiebe/auf seinen linken Haken auf; **the bouncers were told to ~ ~ ~ troublemakers** die Rausschmeißer sollten auf Unruhestifter achten *or* achtgeben; **you must ~ ~ ~ spelling mistakes/snakes** Sie müssen auf Rechtschreibfehler/Schlangen achten. (b) (*seek*) *new job* sich umsehen nach; *new staff also, ideas* suchen.

♦**look over** *vt sep* *papers, notes etc* durchsehen; *house* sich (*dat*) ansehen.

♦**look round** *vi* see **look around**.

♦**look through 1** *vi* durchsehen *or* -schauen (*dial*) *or* -gucken (*inf*) (*prep obj* durch). **he stopped at the window and ~ed ~** er blieb am Fenster stehen und sah *etc* hinein/herein; **he ~ed ~ the window** er sah *etc* zum Fenster hinein/herein/hinaus/ heraus; **to ~ straight ~ sb** durch jdn hindurchgucken.

2 *vt sep* (*examine*) durchsehen.

♦**look to** *vi* +*prep obj* (a) (*look after*) sich kümmern um. **~ ~ it that ...** sieh zu, daß ...

(b) (*rely on*) sich verlassen auf (+*acc*). **they ~ed ~ him to solve the problem** sie verließen sich darauf, daß er das Problem lösen würde; **we ~ ~ you for support/to lead the country** wir rechnen auf Ihre *or* mit Ihrer Hilfe/wir rechnen damit *or* zählen darauf, daß Sie das Land führen; **there's no point in ~ing ~ him for help** es ist sinnlos, von ihm Hilfe zu erwarten; **we ~ ~ you for guidance** wir wenden uns an Sie um Rat.

♦**look up 1** *vi* (a) aufsehen *or* -blicken. **don't ~ ~** guck nicht hoch (*inf*). (b) (*improve*) besser werden; (*shares, prices*) steigen. **things are ~ing ~** es geht bergauf.

2 *vt sep* (a) **to ~ sb ~ and down** jdn von oben bis unten ansehen *or* mustern. (b) (*visit*) **to ~ sb ~** bei jdm vorbeischauen, jdn besuchen. (c) (*seek*) *word* nachschlagen.

♦**look upon** *vi* +*prep obj* see **look on** (c).

♦**look up to** *vi* +*prep obj* see **look on** (c). **he was always ~ed ~ ~** andere haben immer zu ihm aufgesehen.

look-around [ˈlʊkəraʊnd] *n* **to have** *or* **take a ~** sich umsehen; **I'd like a ~ in that shop sometime** in dem Geschäft würde ich mich gern einmal umsehen.

looked-for [ˈlʊktfɔːʳ] *adj* (*expected*) (lang)ersehnt.

looker [ˈlʊkəʳ] *n* (*inf*) **to be a (good) ~** klasse aussehen (*inf*).

looker-on [ˈlʊkəˈ(r)ɒn] *n* Zuschauer(in *f*) *m*, Schaulustige(r) *mf* (*pej*).

look-in [ˈlʊkɪn] *n* (*inf*) Chance *f*. **he didn't get a ~** er hatte keine Chance.

-looking [-ˈlʊkɪŋ] *adj suf* aussehend. **she/it is not bad-~** sie/es sieht nicht schlecht aus.

looking glass *n* Spiegel *m*.

look: **~-out** *n* (a) (*tower etc*) (*Mil*) Ausguck *m*; **~-out post/station/tower** Beobachtungsposten *m*/-station *f*/-turm *m*; (b) (*person*) (*Mil*) Wacht- *or* Beobachtungsposten *m*; **the thieves had a ~-out on the building** opposite einer der Diebe stand auf dem gegenüberliegenden Gebäude Wache *or* Schmiere (*inf*); **(c) to be on the ~-out for, to keep a ~-out for** see **look out for**; **(d)** (*prospect*) Aussichten *pl*; **it's a grim ~-out for us** es sieht schlecht *or* düster für uns; (e) (*inf: worry*) **that's his ~-out!** das ist sein Problem!; **~-see** *n* (*inf*) **to have a ~-see** nachgucken (*inf*) *or* -schauen (*dial*) *or* -sehen; **~-through** *n* (*inf*) Durchsicht *f*; **would you have a ~-through?** können Sie sich das mal durchsehen?; **to give sth a quick ~-through** etw kurz durchsehen.

loom¹ [luːm] *n* Webstuhl *m*.

loom² *vi* (*also* **~ ahead** *or* **up**) (*lit, fig*) sich abzeichnen; (*storm*) heraufziehen; (*disaster*) sich zusammenbrauen; (*danger*) drohen; (*difficulties*) sich auftürmen; (*exams*) bedrohlich näherrücken. **the ship ~ed (up) out of the mist** das Schiff tauchte undeutlich/bedrohlich aus dem Nebel (auf); **the threat of unemployment was ~ing on the horizon** Arbeitslosigkeit zeichnete sich drohend ab; **the fear of a sudden attack ~ed in their thoughts** sie schwebten in Angst vor einem plötzlichen Angriff; **to ~ large** eine große Rolle spielen; **the skyscraper ~s over the city** der Wolkenkratzer ragt über die Stadt.

loon¹ [luːn] *n* (*Orn*) Seetaucher *m*.

loon² *n* (*sl*) Blödmann *m* (*sl*).

loony ['lu:nı] (sl) **1** adj (+er) bekloppt (sl). **to drive sb** ~ jdn wahnsinnig machen (inf). **2** n Verrückte(r) (inf), Irre(r) mf. ~ **bin** Klapsmühle f (sl).

loop [lu:p] **1** n (a) (curved shape) Schlaufe f; (of wire) Schlinge f; (of river, Rail) Schleife f; (Med) Spirale f.
(b) (Aviat) Looping m. **to** ~ **the** ~ einen Looping machen.
2 vt rope etc schlingen (round um). **to** ~ **a rope through a ring** ein Seil durch einen Ring ziehen.
3 vi (rope etc) sich schlingen; (line, road etc) eine Schleife machen. **the road** ~s **round the fields** die Straße schlängelt sich um die Felder.
♦**loop back 1** vt sep ~ **the wire** ~ **around the lid** biegen Sie den Draht zurück um den Deckel. **2** vi (road) eine Schleife machen; (person) in einem Bogen zurückkehren. **this wire has to** ~ ~ dieser Draht muß zurückgebogen werden.
loop: ~**hole** n (Mil) Schießscharte f; (fig) Hintertürchen nt; a ~-hole in the law eine Lücke im Gesetz; ~**line** n (Rail) Schleife f.

loopy ['lu:pı] adj (+er) (sl) bekloppt (sl).

loose [lu:s] **1** adj (+er) (a) (not tight, movable) board, button lose; dress, collar weit; tooth, bandage, knot, screw, soil, weave locker; limbs beweglich, locker. ~ **change** Kleingeld nt; **he kept his change** ~ **in his pocket** er hatte sein Kleingeld lose in der Tasche; **a** ~ **connection** (Elec) ein Wackelkontakt m; **to come or work** ~ (screw, handle etc) sich lockern; (sole, cover etc) sich (los)lösen; (button) abgehen; **to hang** ~ lose herunterhängen; **her hair hung** ~ sie trug ihr Haar offen; **to have** ~ **bowels** Durchfall haben.
(b) (free) **to break or get** ~ (person, animal) sich losreißen; (from von); (ship) sich (von der Vertäuung) losreißen; (from group of players etc) sich trennen, sich lösen; (break out) ausbrechen; (from commitment, parental home etc) sich freimachen (from von); **to run** ~ frei herumlaufen; (of children) unbeaufsichtigt herumlaufen; **to be at a** ~ **end** (fig) nichts mit sich anzufangen wissen; **to turn or let or set** ~ frei herumlaufen lassen; prisoner freilassen; imagination freien Lauf lassen (+dat); **he let his imagination** ~ **on the possibilities** er malte sich (dat) die Möglichkeiten in allen Farben aus; **to tie up the** ~ **ends** (fig) ein paar offene or offenstehende Probleme lösen.
(c) (not exact, vague) translation frei; account, thinking, planning ungenau; connection lose.
(d) (too free, immoral) conduct lose; morals locker; person unmoralisch, lose. **a** ~ **life** ein lockerer Lebenswandel; **a** ~ **woman** eine Frau mit lockerem Lebenswandel; **in that bar you get** ~ **women** in der Bar findest du lose Mädchen; **do you think that's being** ~? meinst du, das ist unmoralisch?; **to have a** ~ **tongue** nichts für sich behalten können.
2 n (inf) **to be on the** ~ (prisoners, dangerous animals) frei herumlaufen; **he was on the** ~ **in Paris** er machte Paris unsicher; **the troops were on the** ~ **in the city** die Truppen wüteten in der Stadt; **oh dear, when these two are on the** ~ wehe, wenn sie losgelassen!
3 vt (a) (free) befreien.
(b) (untie) losmachen.
(c) (slacken) lockern.
♦**loose off 1** vt sep loslassen; shot, bullet abfeuern. **2** vi Feuer eröffnen (at auf +acc). **to** ~ ~ **at sb** (fig inf) eine Schimpfkanonade auf jdn loslassen (inf).
loose: ~**box** n Box f; ~ **covers** npl Überzüge pl; ~**-fitting** adj weit; ~**leaf book** n Ringbuch nt; ~**-leaf page** n Ringbucheinlage f; ~**-limbed** adj (lithe) gelenkig, beweglich; (gangling) schlaksig; ~**-living** adj verkommen, lose.

loosely ['lu:slı] adv (a) lose, locker. **in hot countries it's better to be** ~ **dressed** in warmen Ländern trägt man besser weitgeschnittene or lose hängende Kleider; **his hands dangled** ~ **from his wrists** er ließ seine Hände locker baumeln; **he held her hand** ~ **in his** er hielt ihre Hand locker in der seinen.
(b) ~ **speaking** grob gesagt; ~ **translated** frei übersetzt; **I was using the word rather** ~ ich habe das Wort ziemlich frei gebraucht; **a scientist cannot afford to use words** ~ ein Wissenschaftler kann es sich nicht erlauben, Begriffe vage zu gebrauchen; **they are** ~ **connected** sie hängen lose zusammen.
(c) (behave) unmoralisch. **he lives** ~ er führt ein loses or lockeres Leben.

loosen ['lu:sn] **1** vt (a) (free) befreien; tongue lösen. (b) (untie) losmachen, lösen. (c) (slacken) lockern; belt also weitermachen; soil auflockern; collar aufmachen. **2** vi sich lockern.
♦**loosen up 1** vt sep muscles lockern; soil auflockern. **2** vi (muscles) locker werden; (athlete) sich (auf)lockern; (relax) auftauen.

looseness ['lu:snıs] n Lockerheit f; (of clothes) Weite f; (of thinking) Ungenauigkeit f; (of translation) Freiheit f. ~ **of the bowels** zu rege Darmtätigkeit; **the** ~ **of her conduct** ihr loses or unmoralisches Benehmen; **the** ~ **of this way of life** ein solch lockerer Lebenswandel.

loot [lu:t] **1** n Beute f; (inf: money) Zaster m (sl). **2** vti plündern.

looter ['lu:təʳ] n Plünderer m.

lop [lop] vt (also ~ off) abhacken.

lope [ləup] vi in großen Sätzen springen; (hare) hoppeln. **he** ~**d along by her side** er lief mit großen Schritten neben ihr her; **to** ~ **off** davonspringen.

lop-eared ['lop,ıəd] adj mit Hängeohren.

lop ears npl Hänge- or Schlappohren (inf) pl.

lopsided ['lop'saıdıd] adj schief; (fig) einseitig. **the balance of the committee is definitely** ~ der Ausschuß ist sehr einseitig besetzt.

loquacious [lə'kweıʃəs] adj redselig.

loquacity [lə'kwæsıtı] n Redseligkeit f.

lord [lɔ:d] **1** n (a) (master, ruler) Herr m. ~ **and master** Herr und Meister m; (hum: husband) Herr und Gebieter m; tobacco ~s Tabakkönige pl.

(b) (Brit: nobleman) Lord m. **the (House of) L**~s das Oberhaus; **my** ~ (to bishop) Exzellenz; (to noble) (in English contexts) Mylord (to baron) Herr Baron; (to earl, viscount) Euer Erlaucht; (to judge) Euer Ehren.
(c) (Brit: important official) **First L**~ **of the Admiralty** Stabschef m der Marine; **L**~ **Chancellor** Lordsiegelbewahrer, Lordkanzler m; **L**~ **Mayor** = Oberbürgermeister m; **L**~ **Justice** Richter m an einem Berufungsgericht.
(d) (Rel) **L**~ Herr m; **the L**~ **(our) God** Gott, der Herr; **the L**~'s **day** der Tag des Herrn; **the L**~'s **prayer** das Vaterunser; **the L**~'s **supper** das (Heilige) Abendmahl; **(good) L**~! (inf) ach, du lieber Himmel! (inf), (ach,) du meine Güte! (inf); (annoyed) **mein Gott!** (inf); **L**~ **help him!** (inf) (dann) Gnade ihm Gott!; **L**~ **knows** (inf) wer weiß; **L**~ **knows I've tried often enough** ich hab's weiß Gott oft genug versucht.
2 vt **to** ~ **it** das Zepter schwingen; **to** ~ **it over sb** jdn herumkommandieren.

lordliness ['lɔ:dlınıs] n Vornehmheit f; (haughtiness) Überheblichkeit, Arroganz f.

lordly ['lɔ:dlı] adj (+er) (a) (magnificent) vornehm; house also (hoch)herrschaftlich. (b) (proud, haughty) hochmütig, arrogant; tone of voice herrisch, gebieterisch.

lordship ['lɔ:dʃıp] n (Brit: title) Lordschaft f. **his/your** ~ seine/Eure Lordschaft; (to bishop) seine/Eure Exzellenz; (to judge) seine/Eure Ehren or Gnaden.

lore [lɔ:ʳ] n Überlieferungen pl. **in local** ~ nach hiesiger Überlieferung; **gypsy** ~ Sagengut nt or Überlieferungen pl der Zigeuner; **plant** ~ Pflanzenkunde f.

lorgnette [lɔ:'njet] n Lorgnette f.

lorry ['lorı] n (Brit) Last(kraft)wagen, Lkw, Laster (inf) m. ~ **driver** Last(kraft)wagenfahrer, Lkw-Fahrer(in f) m.

lose [lu:z] pret, ptp lost **1** vt (a) verlieren; pursuer abschütteln; one's French vergessen, verlernen; prize nicht bekommen. **many men** ~ **their hair** vielen Männern gehen die Haare aus; **the cat has lost a lot of hair** die Katze hat viel Haar verloren; **the shares have lost 15% in a month** die Aktien sind in einem Monat um 15% gefallen; **you will** ~ **nothing by helping them** es kann dir nicht schaden, wenn du ihnen hilfst; **that mistake lost him his job/her friendship/the game** dieser Fehler kostete ihn die Stellung/ihre Freundschaft/den Sieg; **he lost himself in his work** er ging ganz in seiner Arbeit auf; **he likes to** ~ **himself in his memories** er verliert sich gern in Erinnerungen; **to** ~ **no time in doing sth** etw sofort tun.
(b) **my watch lost three hours** meine Uhr ist drei Stunden nachgegangen.
(c) **you've lost me now with all this abstract argument** bei dieser abstrakten Argumentation komme ich nicht mehr mit; **if a teacher goes too fast he will** ~ **his students** wenn ein Lehrer zu schnell macht, kommen seine Schüler nicht mehr mit or können ihm seine Schüler nicht mehr folgen.
(d) (not catch) train, opportunity verpassen; words nicht mitbekommen. **to** ~ **the post** die (Briefkasten)leerung verpassen.
(e) (passive usages) **to be lost** (things) verschwunden sein; (people) sich verlaufen haben; (fig) verloren sein; (words) untergehen; **I can't follow the reasoning, I'm lost** ich kann der Argumentation nicht folgen, ich verstehe nichts mehr; **he was soon lost in the crowd** er hatte sich bald in der Menge verloren; **to be lost at sea** auf See geblieben sein; (of ship) auf See vermißt sein; **the ship was lost with all hands** das Schiff war mit der ganzen Besatzung untergegangen; **all is lost!** alles verloren!; **to get lost** sich verlaufen; **I got lost after the second chapter** nach dem zweiten Kapitel kam ich nicht mehr mit; **get lost!** (inf) verschwinde! (inf); **to look lost** (ganz) verloren aussehen; (fig) ratlos or hilflos aussehen; **you look (as though you're) lost, can I help you?** haben Sie sich verlaufen or verirrt, kann ich Ihnen behilflich sein?; **to give sb/sth up for lost** jdn verloren geben/etw abschreiben; **the motion was lost** der Antrag wurde abgelehnt; **he was lost to science** er war für die Wissenschaft verloren; **he is lost to all finer feelings** er hat keinen Sinn für höhere Gefühle; **I'm lost without my watch** ohne meine Uhr bin ich verloren or aufgeschmissen (inf); classical music is lost on him er hat keinen Sinn für klassische Musik; **good wine is lost on him** er weiß guten Wein nicht zu schätzen; **the joke/remark was lost on her** der Witz/die Bemerkung kam bei ihr nicht an.
2 vi verlieren; (watch) nachgehen. **you can't** ~ du kannst nichts verlieren; **the novel** ~s **a lot in the film** der Roman verliert in der Verfilmung sehr; **you will not** ~ **by helping him** es kann dir nicht schaden, wenn du ihm hilfst.
♦**lose out** vi (inf) schlecht wegkommen (inf), den kürzeren ziehen (on bei).

loser ['lu:zəʳ] n Verlierer(in f) m. **he's a born** ~ er ist der geborene Verlierer.

losing ['lu:zıŋ] adj team Verlierer-; (causing to lose) die Niederlage entscheidend, verhängnisvoll. **a** ~ **battle** ein aussichtsloser Kampf; **to be on the** ~ **side** verlieren.

loss [lɒs] n (a) Verlust m. ~ **of memory** Gedächtnisverlust m; **progressive** ~ **of memory** Gedächtnisschwund m; **the** ~ **of the last three games upset the team** die letzten drei Niederlagen brachten die Mannschaft aus der Fassung; ~ **of speed/time** etc Geschwindigkeits-/Zeitverlust m etc; **he felt her** ~ **very deeply** ihr Tod war ein schwerer Verlust für ihn; **there was a heavy** ~ **of life** viele kamen ums Leben.
(b) (amount, sth lost) Verlust m. **how many** ~es **has the team had so far?** wieviele Spiele hat die Mannschaft bis jetzt verloren?; **the army suffered heavy** ~es die Armee erlitt schwere Verluste; **his business is running at a** ~ er arbeitet mit Verlust; **to sell sth at a** ~ etw mit Verlust verkaufen; **it's your** ~ es ist deine Sache; **he's no** ~ er ist kein (großer) Verlust; **a dead** ~ (inf) ein böser Reinfall (inf); (person) ein hoffnungsloser Fall (inf); **total** ~ Totalverlust m.

(c) to be at a ~ nicht mehr weiterwissen; we are at a ~ with this problem wir stehen dem Problem ratlos gegenüber; we are at a ~ what to do wir wissen nicht mehr aus noch ein; to be at a ~ to explain sth etw nicht erklären können; we are at a ~ to say why wir haben keine Ahnung, warum; to be at a ~ for words nicht wissen, was man sagen soll; he's never at a ~ for words/an excuse er ist nie um Worte/eine Ausrede verlegen.

lost [lɒst] **1** pret, ptp of lose.

2 adj verloren; art ausgestorben; cause aussichtslos; child verschwunden, vermißt; civilisation untergegangen, versunken; opportunity verpaßt. he is mourning his ~ wife er betrauert den Verlust seiner Frau; ~-and-found department (US), ~ property office Fundbüro nt.

lot¹ [lɒt] n **(a)** (for deciding) Los nt. by ~ durch Losentscheid, durch das Los; to cast or draw ~s losen, Lose ziehen; to cast or draw ~s for sth etw verlosen; to cast or draw ~s for a task eine Aufgabe auslosen; they drew ~s to see who would begin sie losten aus, wer anfangen sollte.

(b) (destiny) Los nt. failure was his ~ in life es war sein Los, immer zu versagen; it falls to my ~ to tell him mir fällt die Aufgabe zu, es ihm zu sagen; to throw in one's ~ with sb sich mit jdm zusammentun.

(c) (plot) Parzelle f; (Film) Filmgelände nt. building ~ Bauplatz m; parking ~ (US) Parkplatz m.

(d) (number of articles of same kind) Posten m; (at auction) Los nt.

(e) (group of things) where shall I put this ~? wo soll ich das hier or das Zeug (inf) hintun?; can you carry that ~ by yourself? kannst du das (alles) alleine tragen?; divide the books up into three ~s teile die Bücher in drei Teile or Stapel ein; we moved the furniture in two ~s wir haben die Möbel in zwei Fuhren befördert; I'd just finished marking the papers when he gave me another ~ ich war gerade mit dem Korrigieren fertig, da gab er mir einen neuen Packen or Stoß or noch eine Ladung (inf); we bought a new ~ of cutlery wir haben uns (ein) neues Besteck gekauft.

(f) he/she is a bad ~ (inf) er/sie taugt nichts, er/sie ist eine miese Type (sl); they are a bad ~ (inf) das sind ein übles Pack.

(g) (inf: group) Haufen m. that ~ in the next office die or die Typen (sl) vom Büro nebenan (inf); I'm fed up with you ~ ich hab' die Nase voll von euch allen (inf) or von euch Bande (inf); are you and your ~ coming to the pub? kommt ihr (alle) in die Kneipe?; bring your ~ with you bring die ganze Mannschaft mit.

(h) the ~ (inf) alle; alles; that's the ~ das ist alles, das wär's (inf); the whole ~ of them sie alle; (people also) die ganze Mannschaft (inf); he's eaten the ~ er hat alles aufgegessen; big ones, little ones, the ~! Große, Kleine, alle!

lot² **1** n a ~, ~s viel; a ~ of money viel or eine Menge Geld; a ~ of books, ~s of books viele or eine Menge Bücher; such a ~ so viel; what a ~! was für eine Menge!; what a ~ of time you take wie lange du nur brauchst!; what a ~ you've got du hast aber viel; how much has he got? — ~s or a ~ wieviel hat er? — jede Menge (inf) or viel; quite a ~ of books ziemlich viele or eine ganze Menge Bücher; such a ~ of books so viele Bücher; an awful ~ of things to do furchtbar viel zu tun; he made ~s and ~s of mistakes er hat eine Unmenge Fehler gemacht; I want ~s and ~s ich will jede Menge (inf); I read a ~ ich lese viel; we see a ~ of John these days wir sehen John in letzter Zeit sehr oft; I'd give a ~ to know ... ich würde viel drum geben, wenn ich wüßte ...

2 adv a ~, ~s viel; things have changed a ~ es hat sich vieles geändert; he disappointed me a ~ er hat mich sehr enttäuscht; I feel ~s or a ~ better es geht mir sehr viel besser; a ~ you care! dich interessiert das überhaupt nicht!

loth adj see loath.

lotion ['ləʊʃən] n Lotion f.

lottery ['lɒtərɪ] n Lotterie f. life is a ~ das Leben ist ein Glücksspiel.

lotus ['ləʊtəs] n Lotos m. ~-eater Lotophage, Lotosesser(in f) m; (fig) Müßiggänger m; ~ position Lotossitz m.

loud [laʊd] **1** adj (+er). **(a)** laut. he gave a ~ shout of laughter er lachte laut auf; he was ~ in his criticism of the government er übte heftige Kritik an der Regierung; he was ~ in his praise of the concert er lobte das Konzert überschwenglich; ~ and clear laut und deutlich.

(b) behaviour aufdringlich; colour grell, schreiend; (in bad taste) auffällig.

2 adv laut. to say sth out ~ etw laut sagen.

loudhailer [ˌlaʊd'heɪlə] n Megaphon nt, Flüstertüte f (inf); (not hand-held) Lautsprecher m.

loudly ['laʊdlɪ] adv see adj. he was ~ dressed in blue er war in ein grelles Blau gekleidet.

loud: ~-mouth n (inf) Großmaul nt (inf); ~-mouthed ['laʊdˌmaʊðd] adj (inf) großmäulig (inf).

loudness ['laʊdnɪs] n see adj Lautstärke f; Aufdringlichkeit f; Grellheit f; Auffälligkeit f. the ~ of his voice seine laute Stimme.

loudspeaker [ˌlaʊd'spiːkə] n Lautsprecher m; (of hi-fi also) Box f.

lounge [laʊndʒ] **1** n (in house) Wohnzimmer nt; (in hotel) Gesellschaftsraum m; (~ bar, on liner etc) Salon m; (at airport) Warteraum m. TV ~ Fernsehraum m.

2 vi faulenzen. to ~ about or around herumliegen/-sitzen/ -stehen; to ~ against a wall sich lässig gegen eine Mauer lehnen; to ~ back in a chair sich in einem Stuhl zurücklehnen; to ~ up to sb auf jdn zuschlendern.

lounge bar n Salon m (vornehmerer Teil einer Gaststätte).

lounger ['laʊndʒə] n Nichtstuer, Faulenzer m.

lounge: ~ lizard n Salonlöwe m; ~ suit n Straßenanzug m.

lour, lower ['laʊə] vi (person) ein finsteres Gesicht machen;

(clouds) sich türmen. **a threatening sky** ~ed above us der Himmel war drohlich dunkel or überzogen; to ~ at sb jdn finster or drohend ansehen.

louring ['laʊərɪŋ] adj finster.

louse [laʊs] **1** n, pl lice **(a)** (Zool) Laus f. **(b)** (sl) fieser Kerl (sl). he behaved like a real ~ to her er war richtig fies zu ihr (sl), er hat sich richtig fies benommen (sl). **2** vt (sl) to ~ sth up etw vermasseln (sl); friendship kaputtmachen (inf).

lousy ['laʊzɪ] adj **(a)** verlaust. he is ~ with money (sl) er hat Geld wie Dreck (sl).

(b) (sl: very bad) saumäßig (sl), beschissen (sl); trick etc fies (sl). I'm ~ at arithmetic in Mathe bin ich miserabel (inf) or saumäßig (sl); a ~ $3 popelige or lausige 3 Dollar (inf).

lout [laʊt] n Rüpel, Flegel m.

loutish ['laʊtɪʃ] adj rüpelhaft, flegelhaft.

louvre, louver ['luːvə] n Jalousie f. ~ door Jalousie- or Louvretür f.

louvred, louvered ['luːvəd] adj Jalousie-. ~ blinds Jalousie f.

lovable ['lʌvəbl] adj liebenswert.

love [lʌv] **1** n **(a)** (affection) Liebe f. ~ is ... die Liebe ist ...; the ~ he has for his wife die Liebe, die er für seine Frau empfindet; to have a ~ for or of sb/sth jdn/etw sehr lieben; he has a great ~ of swimming er schwimmt sehr gerne; ~ of learning Freude f am Lernen; ~ of adventure Abenteuerlust f; ~ of books Liebe f zu Büchern; the ~ of God for his creatures die Liebe Gottes zu seinen Geschöpfen; the ~ of God ruled his life die Liebe zu Gott bestimmte sein Leben; ~ of (one's) country Vaterlandsliebe f; for ~ aus Liebe; (free) umsonst; (without stakes) nur zum Vergnügen; for ~ nor money nicht für Geld und gute Worte; for the ~ of aus Liebe zu; for the ~ of God! um Himmels willen!; he studies history for the ~ of it er studiert Geschichte aus Liebe zur Sache; to be in ~ (with sb) (in jdn) verliebt sein; to fall in ~ (with sb) sich (in jdn) verlieben; there is no ~ lost between them sie können sich nicht ausstehen; to make ~ (dated: flirt) flirten (to sb mit jdm); (dated: court) den Hof machen (dated) (to sb jdm); (sexually) sich lieben, miteinander schlafen; to make ~ to sb (sexually) mit jdm schlafen; I've never made ~ ich habe noch mit keinem/keiner geschlafen; make ~ to me liebe mich; he's good at making ~ er ist gut in der Liebe; make ~ not war Liebe, nicht Krieg, make love not war.

(b) (greetings, in letters etc) with my ~ mit herzlichen Grüßen; give him my ~ grüß ihn von mir; to send one's ~ to sb jdn grüßen lassen; he sends his ~ er läßt grüßen.

(c) (sb/sth causing fondness) Liebe f. yes, (my) ~ ja, Liebling or Schatz; he sent some roses to his ~ (dated) er schickte seiner Liebsten (dated) ein paar Rosen; the child is a little ~ das Kind ist ein kleiner Schatz.

(d) (inf: form of address) mein Lieber/meine Liebe. I'm afraid the bus is full, ~ der Bus ist leider voll.

(e) (Tennis) null. fifteen ~ fünfzehn null; Rosewall lost 3 ~ games Rosewall verlor 3 Spiele zu null.

2 vt lieben; (like) thing gern mögen. I ~ tennis ich mag Tennis sehr gern; (to play) ich spiele sehr gern Tennis; he ~s swimming, he ~s to swim er schwimmt sehr or für sein Leben gern; don't be sad, you know we all ~ you sei nicht traurig, du weißt doch, daß wir dich alle sehr gern haben; I'd ~ to be with you all the time ich wäre so gerne die ganze Zeit mit dir zusammen; I'd ~ a cup of tea ich hätte (liebend) gern(e) eine Tasse Tee; I'd ~ to come ich würde sehr or liebend gerne kommen; I should ~ to! sehr or liebend gerne!; we'd all ~ you to come with us wir würden uns alle sehr freuen, wenn du mitkommen würdest.

3 vi lieben.

love: ~ affair n Liebschaft f, Verhältnis nt; ~bird n (Orn) Unzertrennliche(r) m; (fig inf) Turteltaube f; ~ child n (dated) Kind nt der Liebe (dated); ~ game n (Tennis) Zu-Null-Spiel nt; ~-hate relationship n Haßliebe f; they have a ~ relationship zwischen ihnen besteht eine Haßliebe; ~less adj ohne Liebe; home also lieblos; ~ letter n Liebesbrief m; ~ life n Liebesleben nt.

loveliness ['lʌvlɪnɪs] n Schönheit f; (of weather, view also) Herrlichkeit f.

lovelorn ['lʌvlɔːn] adj (liter) person liebeskrank (liter); song, poem liebesweh (liter).

lovely ['lʌvlɪ] **1** adj (+er) (beautiful) schön; object also hübsch; baby niedlich; (delightful) herrlich, wunderschön; joke herrlich; (charming, likeable) liebenswürdig, nett. we had a ~ time es war sehr schön; it's ~ and warm in this room es ist schön warm in diesem Zimmer; it's been ~ to see you es war schön, dich zu sehen; it's a ~ day for a picnic es ist ein herrlicher or idealer Tag für ein Picknick; how ~ of you to remember! wie nett or lieb, daß Sie daran gedacht haben; she has such a sweet and ~ character sie hat so ein liebes, nettes Wesen; what a ~ thing to say! wie nett, so was zu sagen!

2 n (inf: person) Schöne f. yes, my ~ ja, mein schönes Kind.

love: ~-making n (sexual) Liebe f; (dated: flirtation) Flirt m; (dated: courting) Liebeswerben nt (dated); oriental ~-making orientalische Liebeskunst; his expert ~-making sein gekonntes Liebesspiel; ~ match n Liebesheirat f; ~ nest n Liebesnest nt; ~ philtre (old), ~ potion n Liebestrank m.

lover ['lʌvə] n **(a)** Liebhaber, Geliebte(r) m; (old, liter) m, Geliebte f. the ~s die Liebenden pl, das Liebespaar; we were ~s for two years wir waren zwei Jahre lang eng or intim befreundet; Romeo and Juliet were ~s Romeo und Julia liebten sich; so she took a ~ da nahm sie sich (dat) einen Liebhaber.

(b) a ~ of books ein Bücherfreund m, ein Liebhaber m von Büchern; a ~ of good food ein Freund m or Liebhaber m von gutem Essen; music ~ Musikliebhaber or -freund m; football ~s Fußballanhänger or -begeisterte pl.

loverboy ['lʌvəbɔɪ] n (sl) unser Freund hier (inf); (boyfriend) Freund m. listen, ~ hör mal zu, mein Freund(chen) (inf).

love: ~ seat n S-förmiges Sofa, Tête-à-Tête nt; ~ set n (Tennis)

Zu-Null-Satz *m*; ~sick *adj* liebeskrank; to be ~sick Liebes-kummer *m* haben; ~song *n* Liebeslied *nt*; ~ story *n* Liebesge-schichte *f*.

loving ['lʌvɪŋ] *adj* liebend; *look, disposition* liebevoll. ~ kind-ness Herzensgüte *f*; *(of God)* Barmherzigkeit *f*; ~ cup Pokal *m*; your ~ son ... in Liebe Euer Sohn ...

lovingly ['lʌvɪŋlɪ] *adv* liebevoll.

low[1] [ləʊ] **1** *adj* (+*er*) **(a)** niedrig; *form of life, musical key* nieder; *bow, note* tief; *density, intelligence* gering; *food sup-plies* knapp, *pulse* schwach; *quality* gering; *(pej)* minderwertig *(pej)*; *light* gedämpft, schwach; *(Ling)* vowel offen; *(Math)* denominator klein. the lamp was ~ die Lampe brannte schwach; the sun was ~ in the sky die Sonne stand tief am Himmel; her dress was ~ at the neck ihr Kleid hatte einen tiefen Ausschnitt; ~ blow *or* punch Tiefschlag *m*; that punch was a bit ~ der Schlag war etwas tief; the river is ~ der Fluß hat *or* führt wenig Wasser; the barometer is ~ today der Barometerstand ist heute niedrig; a ridge of ~ pressure ein Tiefdruckkeil *m*; a ~-calorie diet eine kalorienarme Diät; ~ density housing aufgelockerte Bauweise; activity on the stock exchange is at its ~est die Börsentätigkeit hat ihren Tiefstand erreicht; to be ~ in funds knapp bei Kasse sein *(inf)*.

(b) *(not loud or shrill)* voice leise.

(c) *(socially inferior, vulgar)* birth nieder, niedrig; *rank, posi-tion also* untergeordnet; *tastes, manners* gewöhnlich, ordinär *(pej)*; *character, company* schlecht; *joke, song* geschmacklos; *trick* gemein. I really felt ~ having to tell him that ich kam mir richtig gemein vor, daß ich ihm das sagen mußte; how ~ can you get! wie kann man nur so tief sinken!; ~ life niederes Milieu; ~ cunning Gerissenheit *f*.

(d) *(weak in health or spirits)* resistance schwach, gering; morale schlecht. the patient is rather ~ today der Patient ist heute nicht auf der Höhe; to be in ~ health bei schlechter Gesundheit sein; to be in ~ spirits in gedrückter Stimmung sein, bedrückt *or* niedergeschlagen sein; to feel ~ sich nicht wohl *or* gut fühlen; *(emotionally)* niedergeschlagen sein; to make sb feel ~ *(events)* jdn mitnehmen, jdm zu schaffen machen; *(people)* jdn mitnehmen *or* bedrücken.

2 *adv* aim nach unten; *speak, sing* leise; *fly, bow* tief. the boxer swung ~ der Boxer holte zu einem tiefen Schwinger aus; they turned the lamps down ~ sie drehten die Lampen her-unter; a dress cut ~ in the back ein Kleid mit tiefem Rük-kenausschnitt; to fall ~ *(morally)* tief sinken; I would never sink so ~ as to ... so tief würde ich nie sinken, daß ich ...; share prices went so ~ that ... die Aktienkurse fielen so sehr, daß ...; to buy ~ and sell high billig kaufen und teuer verkaufen; to lay sb ~ *(punch)* jdn zu Boden strecken; *(disease)* befallen; he's been laid ~ with the flu er liegt mit Grippe im Bett; to play ~ *(Cards)* um einen niedrigen *or* geringen Einsatz spielen; to run or get ~ knapp werden; we are getting ~ on petrol uns *(dat)* geht das Benzin aus.

3 *n* **(a)** *(Met)* Tief *nt*; *(fig also)* Tiefpunkt, Tiefstand *m*. to reach a new ~ einen neuen Tiefstand erreichen; this repre-sents a new ~ in deceit das ist ein neuer Gipfel der Falschheit.

(b) *(Aut:* ~ *gear)* niedriger Gang.

low[2] **1** *n (of cow)* Muh *nt*. **2** *vi* muhen.

low: ~born *adj* von niedriger Geburt; ~boy *n (US)* niedrige Kommode; ~bred *adj* gewöhnlich, ordinär *(pej)*; ~brow **1** *adj* (geistig) anspruchslos; *person also* ungebildet; **2** *n* Kultur-banause *m (inf)*; L~ Church *n* reformierter, puritanischer Teil der Anglikanischen Kirche; ~ comedy *n* Schwank *m*, Klamotte *f (pej)*; ~cost *adj* preiswert; the L~ Countries *npl* die Nieder-lande *pl*; ~cut *adj* dress tief ausgeschnitten; ~down *(inf)* **1** *n* Informationen *pl*; what's the ~down on Kowalski? was wissen *or* haben *(inf)* wir über Kowalski?; he gave me the ~down on it er hat mich darüber aufgeklärt; to get the ~down on sth über etw *(acc)* aufgeklärt werden; **2** *adj (esp US)* gemein, fies *(sl)*.

lower[1] ['ləʊə*r*] **1** *adj* see low[1] niedriger; tiefer etc; *Austria, Saxony* Nieder-; *jaw, arm* Unter-; *limbs, storeys, latitudes* untere(r, s). the ~ school die unteren Klassen, die Unter- und Mittelstufe; the ~ reaches of the river der Unterlauf des Flusses; the ~ parts of the hill die tiefer gelegenen Teile des Berges; hemlines are ~ this year die Röcke sind dieses Jahr länger; the ~ classes die untere(n) Schicht(en), die Unterschicht *or* -klasse; the ~ deck das Unterdeck; *(men)* Unteroffiziere und Mannschaft.

2 *adv* tiefer; leiser. ~ down the mountain weiter unten am Berg; ~ down the scale/the list weiter unten auf der Skala/Liste; they live ~ down the skyscraper sie wohnen weiter unten im Wolkenkratzer.

3 *vt* **(a)** *(let down)* boat, injured man, load herunter-/hinunterlassen; *eyes, gun* senken; *mast* umlegen; *sail, flag* einholen; *bicycle saddle* niedriger machen. "~ the life-boats!" „Rettungsboote aussetzen!"; "~ away!" „holt ein!".

(b) *(reduce)* pressure verringern; *voice, price* senken; morale, resistance schwächen; *standard* herabsetzen. ~ your voice sprich leiser; that is no excuse for ~ing your standard of behaviour das ist keine Entschuldigung dafür, dich gehen-zulassen; his behaviour ~ed him in my opinion sein Benehmen ließ ihn in meiner Achtung sinken; don't ~ the tone of the conversation senke das Gesprächsniveau nicht; to ~ oneself sich hinunterlassen; he ~ed himself into an armchair/his sports car er ließ sich in einen Sessel nieder/stieg in seinen Sportwagen; he ~ed himself by associating with criminals durch den Umgang mit Kriminellen begab er sich unter sein Niveau; to ~ oneself to do sth sich herablassen, etw zu tun.

4 *vi* sinken, fallen.

lower[2] ['laʊə*r*] *vi* see lour.

lower: ~ case **1** *n* Kleinbuchstaben, Gemeine *(spec) pl*; **2** *adj* klein, gemein *(spec)*; L~ Chamber *n* Unterhaus *nt*, zweite Kammer; ~class *adj* Unterschicht-; *pub, habit, vocabulary*

der unteren *or* niederen Schichten; ~class people Leute der Unterschicht *or* unteren Schicht(en).

lowering ['laʊərɪŋ] *adj* see **louring**.

low: ~flying *adj* tieffliegend; ~flying plane Tiefflieger *m*; ~ frequency *n* Niederfrequenz *f*; L~ German *n* Platt(deutsch) *nt*; *(Ling)* Niederdeutsch *nt*; ~grade *adj* minderwertig; ~grade petrol *n* Benzin mit niedriger Oktanzahl; ~heeled *adj* shoes mit flachem *or* niedrigem Absatz.

lowing ['ləʊɪŋ] *n* Muhen *nt*.

low: ~key 1 *n* zurückhaltender Ton; 2 *adj* approach gelassen; handling besonnen; production, film's treatment einfach gehalten, unaufdringlich; reception reserviert; colours gedämpft; ~land 1 *n* Flachland *nt*; the L~lands of Scotland das schottische Tiefland; the ~lands of Northern Europe die Tiefebenen *pl* Mitteleuropas; 2 *adj* Flachland-; *(of Scotland)* Tiefland-; ~lander *n* Flachlandbewohner(in *f*) *m*; L~lander *n (in Scotland)* Bewohner(in *f*) *m* des schottischen Tieflandes; L~ Latin *n* nichtklassisches Latein.

lowliness ['ləʊlɪnɪs] *n* Bescheidenheit *f*; *(of position, birth also)* Niedrigkeit *f*.

lowly ['ləʊlɪ] *adj* (+*er*) *n* bescheiden; niedrig.

low: ~lying *adj* tiefgelegen; L~ Mass *n* (einfache) Messe; ~minded *adj* gemein; ~necked *adj* tief ausgeschnitten.

lowness ['ləʊnɪs] *n* see low[1] **(a)** Niedrigkeit *f*; Tiefe *f*; Knappheit *f*; Schwäche *f*; Minderwertigkeit *f*; Gedämpftheit, Schwäche *f*; *(of sun, shares)* niedriger Stand. ~ of density geringe Dichte; ~ of neckline tiefer Ausschnitt; ~ of a river niedriger Wasser-stand eines Flusses; ~ of intelligence geringer Grad an Intel-ligenz.

(b) the ~ of her voice ihre leise Stimme.

(c) Niedrigkeit *f*; Gewöhnlichkeit *f*; Schlechtheit, Schlechtig-keit *f*; Geschmacklosigkeit *f*; Gemeinheit *f*.

(d) Schwäche *f*. his present ~, the present ~ of his spirits seine gegenwärtige Niedergeschlagenheit.

low: ~pitched *adj* tief; ~pressure *adj (Tech)* Niederdruck-; *(Met)* Tiefdruck-; ~priced *adj* günstig; ~rise *adj* niedrig (gebaut); ~slung *adj* to have ~slung hips einen langen Ober-körper haben; ~spirited *adj*, ~spiritedly *adv* niederge-schlagen; ~tension *adj (Elec)* Niederspannungs-; ~ tide, ~ water *n* Niedrigwasser *nt*; ~water mark *n* Niedrigwasser-grenze *f*.

loyal ['lɔɪəl] *adj* (+*er*) **(a)** treu. he was very ~ to his friends er hielt (treu) zu seinen Freunden. **(b)** *(without emotional involvement)* loyal. he's too ~ to say anything against the party/his colleague er ist zu loyal, um etwas gegen seine Par-tei/seinen Kollegen zu sagen.

loyalist ['lɔɪəlɪst] **1** *n* Loyalist *m*. the ~s in the army die regierungstreuen Teile der Armee. **2** *adj* loyal; *army, troops* regierungstreu.

loyally ['lɔɪəlɪ] *adv* see adj **(a)** treu. **(b)** loyal. he ~ refused to give the names er war zu loyal, um die Namen zu verraten.

loyalty ['lɔɪəltɪ] *n* see adj **(a)** Treue *f*. conflicting loyalties nicht zu vereinbarende Treuepflichten; between ~ to X and ~ to Y hin- und hergerissen in der Treue zu X und der zu Y.

(b) Loyalität *f*. his changing political loyalties seine wech-selnden politischen Bekenntnisse.

lozenge ['lɒzɪndʒ] *n* **(a)** *(Med)* Pastille *f*. **(b)** *(shape)* Raute *f*, Rhombus *m*.

LP abbr of long player, long playing record LP *f*.

L-plate ['elpleɪt] *n* Schild *m* mit der Aufschrift „L" *(für Fahrschüler)*.

LRAM *(Brit)* abbr of Licentiate of the Royal Academy of Music.

LSD abbr of lysergic acid diethylamide LSD *nt*.

lsd *n (old Brit inf: money)* Geld *nt*, Pinke *f (inf)*.

LSE *(Brit)* abbr of London School of Economics.

Lt abbr of Lieutenant Lt.

LTA abbr of Lawn Tennis Association.

Ltd abbr of Limited GmbH.

lubricant ['luːbrɪkənt] **1** *adj* Schmier-; *(Med)* Gleit-. **2** *n* Schmiermittel *nt*; *(Med)* Gleitmittel *nt*.

lubricate ['luːbrɪkeɪt] *vt (lit, fig)* schmieren, ölen. ~d sheath Kondom *m* mit Gleitsubstanz; well-~d *(hum)* bezecht; to ~ the wheels of commerce den Handel reibungslos gestalten.

lubrication [luːbrɪ'keɪʃən] *n* Schmieren, Ölen *nt*; *(fig)* reibungslose Gestaltung.

lubricator ['luːbrɪkeɪtə*r*] *n* Schmiervorrichtung *f*.

lubricity [luː'brɪsɪtɪ] *n (liter: lewdness)* Schlüpfrigkeit *f*.

Lucerne [luː'sɜːn] *n* Luzern *nt*. Lake ~ Vierwaldstätter See *m*.

lucid ['luːsɪd] *adj* (+*er*) **(a)** *(clear)* klar; account, statement also präzise; explanation einleuchtend, anschaulich. **(b)** *(sane)* ~ intervals lichte Augenblicke; he was ~ for a few minutes ein paar Minuten lang war er bei klarem Verstand.

lucidity [luː'sɪdɪtɪ] *n* Klarheit *f*; *(of explanation)* Anschaulich-keit *f*.

lucidly ['luːsɪdlɪ] *adv* klar; explain einleuchtend, anschaulich; write verständlich.

Lucifer ['luːsɪfə*r*] *n* Luzifer *m*.

luck [lʌk] *n* Glück *nt*. his life was saved by ~ sein Leben wurde durch einen glücklichen Zufall gerettet; bad ~ Unglück, Pech *nt*; bad ~! so ein Pech!; bad ~, that's your own fault Pech (gehabt), da bist du selbst schuld; good ~ Glück *nt*; good ~! viel Glück!; good ~ to them! *(iro)*, and the best of (British) ~! *(iro)* na dann viel Glück!; it was his good ~ to be chosen er hatte das Glück, gewählt zu werden; here's ~! *(toast)* auf glückliche Zeiten!; no such ~! schön wär's! *(inf)*; just my ~! Pech (gehabt), wie immer!; it's just his ~ to miss the train es mußte ihm natürlich wieder passieren, daß er den Zug verpaßt hat; it's the ~ of the draw man muß es eben nehmen, wie's kommt; with any ~ mit etwas Glück; worse ~! leider, wie schade! better ~ next time! vielleicht klappt's beim nächsten Mal!;

to be in ~ Glück haben; **to be out of** ~ kein Glück haben; **he was a bit down on his** ~ er hatte eine Pechsträhne; **tramps and others who are down on their** ~ Landstreicher und andere, die kein Glück im Leben haben; **to bring sb bad** ~ jdm Unglück bringen; **as** ~ **would have it** wie es der Zufall wollte; **for** ~ als Glücksbringer *or* Talisman; **Bernstein kisses his cufflinks for** ~ Bernstein küßt seine Manschettenknöpfe, damit sie ihm Glück bringen; **to keep sth for** ~ etw als Glücksbringer aufheben; **one for** ~ und noch eine(n, s); **to try one's** ~ sein Glück versuchen.

luckily ['lʌkɪlɪ] *adv* glücklicherweise. ~ **for me** zu meinem Glück.

luckless ['lʌklɪs] *adj* glücklos; *attempt also* erfolglos.

lucky ['lʌkɪ] *adj* (+*er*) **(a)** *(having luck)* Glücks-. **a** ~ **shot** ein Glückstreffer *m*; **that was a** ~ **move** der Zug war Glück; **you** ~ **thing!**, ~ **you!** du Glückliche(r) *mf*; **who's the** ~ **man?** wer ist der Glückliche?; **to be** ~ Glück haben; **I was** ~ **enough to meet him** ich hatte das (große) Glück, ihn kennenzulernen; **you are** ~ **to be alive** du kannst von Glück sagen, daß du noch lebst; **you were** ~ **to catch him** du hast Glück gehabt, daß du ihn erwischt hast; **he's a** ~ **man to have a wife like that** mit dieser Frau hat er das große Los gezogen (*inf*); **you're a** ~ **man** du bist ein Glückspilz; **you'll be** ~ **to make it in time** wenn du das noch schaffst, hast du (aber) Glück; **I want another £500** — **you'll be** ~! ich will nochmal £ 500 haben — viel Glück!; **to be** ~ **at cards** Glück im Spiel haben; **to be born** ~ ein Glücks- *or* Sonntagskind sein; **to be** ~ **in that** ... Glück haben, daß ...

(b) *(bringing luck)* **star, day, number** Glücks-. ~ **charm** Glücksbringer, Talisman *m*; ~ **dip** = Glückstopf *m*; **it must be my** ~ **day** ich habe wohl heute meinen Glückstag.

(c) *(happening fortunately) coincidence* glücklich. **it was** ~ **I stopped him in time** ein Glück, daß ich ihn rechtzeitig aufgehalten habe, zum Glück habe ich ihn rechtzeitig aufgehalten; **it's** ~ **for you** that I remembered the number dein Glück, daß ich mich an die Nummer noch wußte; **that was very** ~ **for you** da hast du aber Glück gehabt; **they had a** ~ **escape from the fire** sie waren dem Feuer glücklich entkommen; **he had a** ~ **escape in the accident** bei dem Unfall ist er glücklich *or* noch einmal davongekommen; **that was a** ~ **escape** da habe ich/hast du *etc* nochmal Glück gehabt.

lucrative ['luːkrətɪv] *adj* einträglich, lukrativ.

lucrativeness ['luːkrətɪvnɪs] *n* Einträglichkeit *f*.

lucre ['luːkə'] *n* filthy ~ schnöder Mammon.

Lucretius [luːˈkriːʃəs] *n* Lukrez *m*.

lucubration [ˌluːkjuːˈbreɪʃən] *n* (*form*) geistige Arbeit.

ludicrous ['luːdɪkrəs] *adj* grotesk; *sight, words also* lächerlich; *suggestion also* haarsträubend; *prices, wages (low), speed (slow)* lächerlich, lachhaft; *prices, wages (high), speed (fast)* haarsträubend. **don't be** ~, **I can't do it that fast** das ist ja grotesk, so schnell kann ich das nicht (machen); **I've done the most** ~ **thing!** mir ist etwas Haarsträubendes passiert!

ludicrously ['luːdɪkrəslɪ] *adv see adj* grotesk; lächerlich; haarsträubend. **the old woman was** ~ **dressed in a miniskirt** die alte Frau hatte einen lächerlich *or* grotesk wirkenden Minirock an; **it takes me** ~ **long to ...** ich brauche lachhaft lange dazu, zu ...; ~ **expensive** absurd teuer; **prices are** ~ **high/low** die Preise sind haarsträubend *or* absurd hoch/lächerlich *or* grotesk niedrig.

ludicrousness ['luːdɪkrəsnɪs] *n see adj* Groteskheit *f*; Lächerlichkeit *f*; Lächerlichkeit, Lachhaftigkeit *f*; Absurdität *f*.

ludo ['luːdəʊ] *n* Mensch, ärgere dich nicht *nt*.

luff [lʌf] (*Naut*) **1** *n* Vorliek *nt*. **2** *vti* (an)luven.

lug¹ [lʌg] *n* **(a)** *(earflap)* Klappe *f*; (*Tech*) Haltevorrichtung *f*. **(b)** (*sl: ear*) Ohr *nt*. ~**-hole** (*sl*) Ohr *nt*, Löffel *pl* (*inf*).

lug² *n see* **lugsail**.

lug³ *vt* schleppen; *(towards one)* zerren. **to** ~ **sth about with one** etw mit sich herumschleppen; **to** ~ **sth along behind one** etw hinter sich (*dat*) herschleppen.

luggage ['lʌgɪdʒ] *n* (*Brit*) Gepäck *nt*.

luggage: ~ **carrier** *n* Gepäckträger *m*; ~ **rack** *n* (*Rail etc*) Gepäcknetz *nt or* -ablage *f*; (*Aut*) Gepäckträger *m*; ~ **trolley** *n* Kofferkuli *m*; ~ **van** *n* (*Rail*) Gepäckwagen *m*.

lugger ['lʌgə'] *n* Logger *m*.

lugsail ['lʌgsl] *n* Loggersegel *nt*.

lugubrious [luːˈguːbrɪəs] *adj person, song* schwermütig; *smile, tune* wehmütig; *face, expression* kummervoll.

lugubriously [luːˈguːbrɪəslɪ] *adv* traurig, kummervoll.

Luke [luːk] *n* Lukas *m*.

lukewarm ['luːkwɔːm] *adj* (*lit, fig*) lauwarm; *applause, support also* lau, mäßig; *friendship* lau, oberflächlich. **he's** ~ **on the idea** er ist von der Idee nur mäßig begeistert.

lull [lʌl] **1** *n* Pause *f*; (*Comm*) Flaute *f*. **a** ~ **in the wind** eine Windstille; **we heard the scream during a** ~ **in the storm** wir hörten den Schrei, als der Sturm für einen Augenblick nachließ; **a** ~ **in the conversation** eine Gesprächspause.

2 *vt baby* beruhigen; (*fig*) einlullen; *fears etc* zerstreuen, beseitigen. **to** ~ **a baby to sleep** ein Baby in den Schlaf wiegen; **he** ~**ed them into a sense of false security** er wiegte sie in trügerische Sicherheit.

lullaby ['lʌləbaɪ] *n* Schlaflied, Wiegenlied *nt*.

lumbago [lʌmˈbeɪgəʊ] *n* Hexenschuß *m*, Lumbago *f* (*spec*).

lumbar ['lʌmbə'] *adj* Lenden-, lumbal (*spec*).

lumber¹ ['lʌmbə'] **1** *n* **(a)** *(timber)* (Bau)holz *nt*. **(b)** *(junk)* Gerümpel *nt*.

2 *vt* (*a*) (*also* ~ **up**) *space, room* vollstopfen *or* -pfropfen. **(b)** (*Brit inf*) **to** ~ **sb with sth** jdm etw aufhalsen (*inf*); **he got** ~**ed with the job** man hat ihm die Arbeit aufgehalst (*inf*); **I got** ~**ed with her for the evening** ich hatte sie den ganzen Abend auf dem Hals (*inf*); **what a job! you've really been** ~**ed!** was für eine Arbeit! da hat man dir aber was aufgehalst! (*inf*).

(c) *(US) hillside, forest* abholzen.

3 *vi* Holz fällen, holzen.

lumber² *vi* *(cart)* rumpeln; *(tank)* walzen; *(elephant, person)* trampeln; *(bear)* tapsen. **a big fat man came** ~**ing into the room** ein dicker, fetter Mann kam ins Zimmer gewalzt; **she went** ~**ing about the room** sie trampelte im Zimmer herum.

lumbering¹ ['lʌmbərɪŋ] *adj see* **lumber²** rumpelnd; trampelnd; tapsig; *tank* schwer, klobig; *gait* schwerfällig.

lumbering² ['lʌmbərɪŋ] *n* Holzfällen *nt*, Holzfällerei *f*.

lumber: ~**jack**, ~**man** *n* Holzfäller *m*; ~ **jacket** *n* Lumberjack *m*; ~ **mill** *n* Sägemühle *f or* -werk *nt*; ~ **room** *n* Rumpelkammer *f*; ~**yard** *n* (*US*) Holzlager *nt*.

luminary ['luːmɪnərɪ] *n* (*a*) (*form*) Himmelskörper *m*, Gestirn *nt*. (*b*) (*fig*) Koryphäe, Leuchte (*inf*) *f*.

luminosity [ˌluːmɪˈnɒsɪtɪ] *n* (*form*) Helligkeit *f*; (*emission of light*) Leuchtkraft *f*; (*fig*) Brillanz *f*.

luminous ['luːmɪnəs] *adj* leuchtend; *paint, dial* Leucht-; (*fig liter*) *writings* brillant, luzid (*liter*).

lummox ['lʌməks] *n* (*US inf*) Trottel *m* (*inf*).

lummy, lumme ['lʌmɪ] *interj* (*Brit*) ach, du Schreck!

lump [lʌmp] **1** *n* **(a)** *(of coal)* Klumpen *m*; (*of sugar*) Stück *nt*.

(b) *(swelling)* Beule *f*; (*inside the body*) Geschwulst *f*; (*in breast*) Knoten *m*; (*on surface*) Huppel *m* (*inf*), kleine Erhebung. **with a** ~ **in one's throat** (*fig*) mit einem Kloß im Hals, mit zugeschnürter Kehle; **I get a** ~ **in my throat** mir ist die Kehle wie zugeschnürt, ich habe einen Kloß im Hals.

(c) (*inf: person*) Klotz *m*, Trampel *mf or nt* (*inf*). **a big or great fat** ~ (*of a man*) ein Fettkloß *m* (*inf*); **a great fat** ~ **of a dog** ein fetter Brocken (*inf*).

(d) **you can't judge them in the** ~ **like that** du kannst sie doch nicht so pauschal beurteilen *or* alle über einen Kamm scheren; **taken in the** ~, **they're not bad** alles in allem sind sie nicht schlecht; **to pay money in a** ~ (*at once*) auf einmal bezahlen; (*covering different items*) pauschal bezahlen.

2 *vt* (*inf: put up with*) **to** ~ **it** sich damit abfinden; **if he doesn't like it he can** ~ **it** wenn's ihm nicht paßt, hat er eben Pech gehabt (*inf*).

3 *vi* (*sauce, flour*) klumpen.

♦**lump together** *vt sep* (*a*) (*put together*) zusammentun; *books* zusammenstellen; *expenses, money* zusammenlegen. **(b)** (*judge together*) *persons, topics* in einen Topf werfen, über einen Kamm scheren. **he** ~**ed all the soldiers** ~ **as traitors** er urteilte all die Soldaten pauschal als Verräter ab.

lumpish ['lʌmpɪʃ] *adj person* klobig, plump.

lump: ~ **payment** *n* (*at once*) einmalige Bezahlung; (*covering different items*) Pauschalbezahlung *f*; ~ **sugar** *n* Würfelzucker *m*; ~ **sum** *n* Pauschalbetrag *m or* -summe *f*; **to pay sth in a** ~ **sum** etw pauschal bezahlen.

lumpy ['lʌmpɪ] *adj* (+*er*) *liquid etc, mattress, cushion* klumpig; *figure* pummelig, plump.

lunacy ['luːnəsɪ] *n* Wahnsinn *m*. **it's sheer** ~! das ist reiner Wahnsinn!; **lunacies** *pl* Verrücktheiten *pl*.

lunar ['luːnə'] *adj* Mond-, lunar (*spec*).

lunatic ['luːnətɪk] **1** *adj* verrückt, wahnsinnig. ~ **fringe** Extremisten *pl*, radikale *or* extremistische Randgruppe. **2** *n* Wahnsinnige(r), Irre(r) *mf*. ~ **asylum** Irrenanstalt *f*.

lunch [lʌntʃ] **1** *n* Mittagessen *nt*. **to have** *or* **take** ~ (zu) Mittag essen; **to give sb** ~ jdm zum Mittagessen einladen; **how long do you get for** ~? wie lange haben Sie Mittagspause?; **when do you have** ~ **in the office?** wann haben *or* machen Sie im Büro Mittag?; **he's at** ~ er ist beim Mittagessen; **to have** ~ **out** auswärts *or* im Restaurant (zu Mittag) essen.

2 *vt* zum Mittagessen einladen. **they** ~**ed me on caviar and steak** ich bekam Kaviar und Steak zum Mittagessen serviert.

3 *vi* zu Mittag essen. **we** ~**ed on a salad** zum (Mittag)essen gab es einen Salat.

♦**lunch out** *vi* auswärts *or* im Restaurant (zu) Mittag essen.

lunch break *n* Mittagspause *f*.

luncheon ['lʌntʃən] *n* (*form*) Lunch *nt or m*, Mittagessen *nt*.

luncheon: ~ **meat** *n* Frühstücksfleisch, Lunch(eon)meat *nt*; ~ **voucher** *n* Essen(s)bon *m or* -marke *f*.

lunch: ~ **hour** *n* Mittagsstunde *f*; (~ **break**) Mittagspause *f*; ~**room** *n* (*US*) Imbißstube *f*; (*canteen*) Kantine *f*; ~**time** *n* Mittagspause *f*; **they arrived at** ~**time** sie kamen um die Mittagszeit *or* gegen Mittag an.

lung [lʌŋ] *n* Lunge *f*; (*iron*) eiserne Lunge. **that baby has plenty of** ~ **power** das Baby hat eine kräftige Lunge; **he has weak** ~**s** er hat keine gute Lunge; ~ **cancer** Lungenkrebs *m*.

lunge [lʌndʒ] **1** *n* Satz *m* nach vorn; (*esp Fencing*) Ausfall *m*. **he made a** ~ **at his opponent** er stürzte sich auf seinen Gegner; (*Fencing*) er machte einen Ausfall.

2 *vi* (*sich*) stürzen; (*esp Fencing*) einen Ausfall machen. **to** ~ **at sb** sich auf jdn stürzen; **the exhausted boxer could only** ~ **at his opponent** der erschöpfte Boxer schlug nur noch wahllos nach seinem Gegner.

♦**lunge out** *vi* ausholen. **to** ~ ~ **at sb** sich auf jdn stürzen.

lupin, (*US*) **lupine** ['luːpɪn] *n* Lupine *f*.

lupine ['luːpaɪn] *adj* wölfisch.

lurch¹ [lɜːtʃ] *n*: **to leave sb in the** ~ (*inf*) jdn im Stich lassen, jdn hängenlassen (*inf*).

lurch² **1** *n* Ruck *m*; (*of boat*) Schlingern *nt*. **with a drunken** ~ **he started off down the road** betrunken taumelte *or* torkelte er die Straße hinunter; **to give a** ~ rucken, einen Ruck machen; (*boat*) schlingern.

2 *vi* **(a)** *see* **to give a** ~.

(b) (*move with* ~*es*) ruckeln, sich ruckartig bewegen; (*boat*) schlingern; (*person*) taumeln, torkeln. **the train** ~**ed to a standstill** der Zug kam mit einem Ruck zum Stehen; **to** ~ **about** hin und her schlingern/hin und her taumeln *or* torkeln; **the bus** ~**ed off down the bumpy track** der Bus ruckelte den holprigen Weg hinunter; **to** ~ **along** dahinruckeln/entlangtorkeln *or* -taumeln; **the economy still manages to** ~ **along** die Wirtschaft schlittert gerade soeben dahin.

lure [ljʊəʳ] **1** n (bait) Köder m; (person, for hawk) Lockvogel m; (general) Lockmittel nt; (fig: of city, sea etc) Verlockungen pl. the ~ of the wild der lockende Ruf der Wildnis; she used her beauty as a ~ sie benutzte ihre Schönheit als Lockmittel; he resisted all her ~s er widerstand all ihren Verführungskünsten.
   2 vt anlocken. to ~ sb away from sth jdn von etw weg- or fortlocken; to ~ sb/an animal into a trap jdn/ein Tier in eine Falle locken; to ~ sb on to destruction jdn ins Verderben stürzen; to ~ sb/an animal out jdn/ein Tier herauslocken.
♦**lure on** vt sep (inf) spielen mit.

lurid [ˈljʊərɪd] adj (+er) **(a)** colour, sky grell; dress grellfarben, in grellen Farben; posters also schreiend. a ~ sunset of pinks and oranges ein Sonnenuntergang in grellen Rosa- und Orangetönen; her taste in clothes is rather ~ sie mag Kleider in ziemlich grellen or schreienden Farben.
   (b) (fig) language reißerisch, blutrünstig; account reißerisch aufgemacht, sensationslüstern; detail blutig, grausig; (sordid) widerlich, peinlich. ~ tale Horrorgeschichte f; all the love scenes are presented in ~ detail die Liebesszenen werden bis in die allerletzten Einzelheiten dargestellt; ~ details of their quarrels peinliche Einzelheiten ihrer Streitereien.

luridly [ˈljʊərɪdlɪ] adv **(a)** grell. the sky glowed ~ der Himmel leuchtete in grellen Farben. **(b)** reißerisch.

luridness [ˈljʊərɪdnɪs] n see adj **(a)** Grellheit f.
   (b) (of account) reißerische or sensationslüsterne Aufmachung; (of details) grausige/peinliche Darstellung. the ~ of his language seine reißerische Sprache; the ~ of this tale diese blutrünstige or grausige Geschichte.

lurk [lɜːk] vi lauern. a nasty suspicion ~ed at the back of his mind er hegte einen fürchterlichen Verdacht; the fears which still ~ in the unconscious Ängste, die noch im Unterbewußtsein lauern; a doubt still ~ed in his mind ein Zweifel plagte ihn noch.
♦**lurk about** or **around** vi herumschleichen.

lurking [ˈlɜːkɪŋ] adj heimlich; doubt also nagend.

luscious [ˈlʌʃəs] adj köstlich, lecker; fruit also saftig; colour satt; girl zum Anbeißen (inf), knusprig (inf); figure (full) üppig; (pleasing) phantastisch.

lusciously [ˈlʌʃəslɪ] adv köstlich. ~ coated in thick cream mit einer köstlich dicken Sahneschicht; with custard poured ~ all over reichlich mit köstlicher Vanillesoße übergossen.

lusciousness [ˈlʌʃəsnɪs] n Köstlichkeit f; (of fruit also) Saftigkeit f; (of colour) Sattheit f; (of girl) knuspriges or appetitliches Aussehen (inf); (of figure) Üppigkeit f.

lush [lʌʃ] **1** adj grass, meadows saftig, satt; vegetation üppig. **2** n (US sl) Säufer(in f) m (inf).

lushness [ˈlʌʃnɪs] n see adj Saftigkeit f; Üppigkeit f.

lust [lʌst] **1** n (inner sensation) Wollust, Sinneslust f; (wanting to acquire) Begierde f (for nach); (greed) Gier f (for nach). rape is an act of ~ Vergewaltigungen entspringen triebhafter Gier; the ~s of the flesh die fleischlichen (Ge)lüste, die Fleischeslust; ~ for power Machtgier f; his uncontrollable ~ seine ungezügelte Gier/fleischliche Begierde.
   2 vi to ~ after, to ~ for (old, hum: sexually) begehren (+acc); (greedily) gieren nach.

luster n (US) see lustre.

lusterless n (US) see lustreless.

lustful adj, **~ly** adv [ˈlʌstfʊl, -fəlɪ] lüstern.

lustfulness [ˈlʌstfʊlnɪs] n Lüsternheit, Begierde f.

lustily [ˈlʌstɪlɪ] adv kräftig; work mit Schwung und Energie; eat herzhaft; sing aus voller Kehle; cry aus vollem Hals(e).

lustre [ˈlʌstəʳ] n **(a)** Schimmer m, schimmernder Glanz; (in eyes) Glanz m. **(b)** (fig) Glanz m, Ruhm m.

lustreless [ˈlʌstəlɪs] adj glanzlos; eyes, hair also stumpf.

lustrous [ˈlʌstrəs] adj schimmernd, glänzend.

lusty [ˈlʌstɪ] adj (+er) person gesund und munter, voller Leben; man also, life kernig, urwüchsig; appetite herzhaft, kräftig; cheer, cry laut, kräftig; push, kick etc kräftig, kraftvoll.

lute [luːt] n Laute f.

Luther [ˈluːθəʳ] n Luther m.

Lutheran [ˈluːθərən] **1** adj lutherisch. **2** n Lutheraner(in f) m.

Lutheranism [ˈluːθərənɪzəm] n Luthertum nt.

lux abbr of luxury.

Luxembourg [ˈlʌksəmbɜːg] n Luxemburg nt.

luxuriance [lʌgˈzjʊərɪəns] n Üppigkeit f; (of hair also) Fülle, Pracht f.

luxuriant adj, **~ly** adv [lʌgˈzjʊərɪənt, -lɪ] üppig.

luxuriate [lʌgˈzjʊərɪeɪt] vi to ~ in sth (people) sich in etw (dat) aalen; (plants) in etw (dat) prächtig gedeihen.

luxurious [lʌgˈzjʊərɪəs] adj luxuriös, Luxus-; carpet, seats, hotel also feudal; food üppig. he is a man of ~ habits/tastes er hat einen luxuriösen Lebensstil/einen Hang zum Luxus.

luxuriously [lʌgˈzjʊərɪəslɪ] adv luxuriös. to live ~ ein Luxusleben or ein Leben im Luxus führen; he sank back ~ into the cushions er ließ sich genüßlich in die Kissen sinken.

luxury [ˈlʌkʃərɪ] **1** n **(a)** (in general) Luxus m; (of car, house etc) luxuriöse or feudale Ausstattung, Komfort m. (to) to live a life of ~ ein Luxusleben or ein Leben im Luxus führen.
   (b) (article) Luxus m no pl. we can't allow ourselves many luxuries wir können uns (dat) nicht viel Luxus leisten; little luxuries Luxus m; (to eat) kleine Genüsse pl.
   2 adj (cruise, tax) Luxus-.

LV (Brit) abbr of luncheon voucher.

LW abbr of long wave LW.

lychgate n see lichgate.

lye [laɪ] n Lauge f.

lying [ˈlaɪɪŋ] **1** adj lügnerisch, verlogen. **2** n Lügen nt. that would be ~ das wäre gelogen.

lying-in [ˈlaɪɪŋˈɪn] n (old Med) Wochenbett nt (dated). during her ~ im Wochenbett (dated); ~ ward Wöchnerinnenstation f (dated).

lymph [lɪmf] n Lymphe, Gewebsflüssigkeit f. ~ node/gland Lymphknoten m/-drüse f.

lymphatic [lɪmˈfætɪk] **1** adj lymphatisch, Lymph-. **2** n Lymphgefäß nt.

lynch [lɪntʃ] vt lynchen.

lynching [ˈlɪntʃɪŋ] n Lynchen nt. there'll be a ~ soon er etc wird bestimmt gelyncht werden.

lynch law n Lynchjustiz f.

lynx [lɪŋks] n Luchs m.

lynx-eyed [ˈlɪŋks.aɪd] adj mit Luchsaugen. the ~ teacher der Lehrer, der Augen wie ein Luchs hatte.

lyre [laɪəʳ] n Leier, Lyra (geh) f. **~-bird** Leierschwanz m.

lyric [ˈlɪrɪk] **1** adj lyrisch. **2** n (poem) lyrisches Gedicht; (genre) Lyrik f; (often pl: words of pop song) Text m.

lyrical [ˈlɪrɪkəl] adj lyrisch; (fig) schwärmerisch. to get or wax ~ about sth über etw (acc) ins Schwärmen geraten.

lyrically [ˈlɪrɪkəlɪ] adv lyrisch; (fig) schwärmerisch; sing melodisch.

lyricism [ˈlɪrɪsɪzəm] n Lyrik f.

lysergic acid diethylamide [laɪˈsɜːdʒɪk.æsɪd.daɪəˈθɪləmaɪd] n Lysergsäurediäthylamid nt.

lysol [ˈlaɪsɒl] ® n Lysol ® nt.

M, m [em] n M, m nt.

M abbr of Medium.

m abbr of million(s) Mill., Mio.; metre(s) m; mile(s); minute(s) min; married verh.; masculine m.

MA abbr of Master of Arts.

ma [mɑː] n (inf) Mama (inf), Mutti (inf) f.

ma'am [mæm] n gnä' Frau f (form); see madam (a).

mac¹ [mæk] n (Brit inf) Regenmantel m.

mac² n (esp US inf) Kumpel m (inf).

macabre [məˈkɑːbrə] adj makaber.

macadam [məˈkædəm] n Schotter, Splitt m, Makadam m or nt. ~ road Schotterstraße f.

macadamize [məˈkædəmaɪz] vt schottern, makadamisieren (spec).

macaroni [ˌmækəˈrəʊnɪ] n Makkaroni pl. ~ cheese Käsemakkaroni pl.

macaronic [ˌmækəˈrɒnɪk] adj makkaronisch.

macaroon [ˌmækəˈruːn] n Makrone f.

macaw [məˈkɔː] n Ara m.

mace¹ [meɪs] n (weapon) Streitkolben m, Keule f; (mayor's) Amtsstab m. **~bearer** n Träger m des Amtsstabes.

mace² n (spice) Muskatblüte f, Mazis m.

Macedonia [ˌmæsɪˈdəʊnɪə] n Makedonien, Mazedonien nt.

Macedonian [ˌmæsɪˈdəʊnɪən] **1** n Makedonier(in f), Mazedonier(in f) m. **2** adj makedonisch, mazedonisch.

macerate [ˈmæsəreɪt] **1** vt aufweichen, einweichen. **2** vi aufweichen, weich werden.

Mach [mæk] n Mach nt. ~ number Mach-Zahl f; the jet was approaching ~ 2 das Flugzeug näherte sich (einer Geschwindigkeit von) 2 Mach.

machete [məˈtʃeɪtɪ] n Machete f, Buschmesser nt.

Machiavelli [ˌmækɪəˈvelɪ] n Machiavelli m.

Machiavellian [ˌmækɪəˈvelɪən] adj machiavellistisch.

machination [ˌmækɪˈneɪʃən] n usu pl Machenschaften pl.

machine [məˈʃiːn] **1** n Maschine f, Apparat m; (vending ~) Automat m; (car) Wagen m; (cycle, plane) Maschine f; (Pol) Partei-/Regierungsapparat m; (fig: person) Maschine f, Roboter m.

2 *vt* (*Tech*) maschinell herstellen; (*treat with machine*) maschinell bearbeiten; (*Sew*) mit der Maschine nähen.

machine: the ~ **age** *n* das Maschinenzeitalter; ~ **gun** **1** *n* Maschinengewehr *nt*; **2** *vt* mit dem Maschinengewehr beschießen/erschießen; ~ **gunner** *n* Soldat *m*/Polizist *m etc* mit Maschinengewehr; **~-made** *adj* maschinell hergestellt; ~ **operator** *n* Maschinenarbeiter *m*; (*skilled*) Maschinist *m*.

machinery [məˈʃiːnərɪ] *n* (*machines*) Maschinen *pl*, Maschinerie *f*; (*mechanism*) Mechanismus *m*; (*fig*) Maschinerie *f*. the ~ **of government** der Regierungsapparat.

machine: ~ **shop** *n* Maschinensaal *m*; ~ **tool** *n* Werkzeugmaschine *f*.

machinist [məˈʃiːnɪst] *n* (*Tech*) (*operator*) Maschinist *m*; (*constructor, repairer*) Maschinenschlosser *m*; (*Sew*) Näherin *f*.

mackerel [ˈmækərəl] *n* Makrele *f*.

mackintosh [ˈmækɪntɒʃ] *n* Regenmantel *m*.

macro- [ˈmækrəʊ-] *pref* makro-, Makro-.

macrobiotic [ˌmækrəʊbaɪˈɒtɪk] *adj* makrobiotisch.

macrocosm [ˈmækrəʊˌkɒzəm] *n* Makrokosmos *m*. the ~ **of Italian society** die italienische Gesellschaft als ganzes *or* in ihrer Gesamtheit.

mad [mæd] **1** *adj* (+*er*) (**a**) wahnsinnig, verrückt; *dog* tollwütig; *idea* verrückt. **to go** ~ verrückt *or* wahnsinnig werden; **to drive sb** ~ jdn wahnsinnig *or* verrückt machen; **it's enough to drive you** ~ es ist zum Verrücktwerden; **he has a** ~ **look in his eye** er hat einen irren Blick; **he's as** ~ **as a hatter** *or* **a March hare** (*prov*) er ist ein komischer Vogel *or* Kauz; **are you raving** ~? bist du total verrückt geworden?, du bist wohl völlig übergeschnappt!; **you must be** ~! du bist ja wahnsinnig!; **I must have been** ~ **to have believed him** ich war wohl von Sinnen, ihm zu glauben.

(**b**) (*inf: angry*) böse, sauer (*inf*). **to be** ~ **at sb** auf jdn böse *or* sauer (*inf*) sein; **to be** ~ **about** *or* **at sth** über etw (*acc*) wütend *or* sauer (*inf*) sein; **he makes me so** ~ er macht mich so wütend; **don't get** ~ **at** *or* **with me** sei nicht böse *or* sauer (*inf*) auf mich.

(**c**) (*stupid, rash*) verrückt. **you** ~ **fool!** du bist ja wahnsinnig *or* verrückt!; **it's a** ~ **hope** es ist verrückt, darauf zu hoffen; **that was a** ~ **thing to do** das war (völlig) idiotisch (*inf*), das war Wahnsinn (*inf*).

(**d**) (*inf: very keen*) **to be** ~ **about** *or* **on sth** auf etw (*acc*) verrückt sein; **I'm not exactly** ~ **about this job** ich bin nicht gerade versessen auf diesen Job; **I'm** (**just**) ~ **about you** ich bin (ganz) verrückt nach dir!

(**e**) (*wild*) wahnsinnig. **they made a** ~ **rush** *or* **dash for the door** sie stürzten zur Tür; **the prisoner made a** ~ **dash for freedom** der Gefangene unternahm einen verzweifelten Ausbruchsversuch; **to be** ~ **with joy** sich wahnsinnig freuen.

2 *adv* (*inf*) **to be** ~ **keen on sb/sth** ganz scharf auf jdn/etw sein (*inf*); **to be** ~ **keen to do sth** ganz versessen darauf sein, etw zu tun; **like** ~ wie verrückt, wahnsinnig; **he ran like** ~ er rannte wie wild.

Madagascan [ˌmædəˈgæskən] **1** *adj* madegassisch. **2** *n* Madegasse *m*, Madegassin *f*.

Madagascar [ˌmædəˈgæskɑː[r]] *n* Madagaskar *nt*.

madam [ˈmædəm] *n* (**a**) gnädige Frau (*old, form*). ~, **would you kindly desist!** würden Sie das bitte unterlassen! (*form*); **yes,** ~ sehr wohl, gnädige Frau (*old, form*), ja(wohl); **can I help you,** ~? kann ich Ihnen behilflich sein?; **dear** ~ sehr geehrte gnädige Frau.

(**b**) (*inf: girl*) kleine Prinzessin.

(**c**) (*of brothel*) Bordellwirtin, Puffmutter (*inf*) *f*.

madcap [ˈmædkæp] **1** *adj idea* versponnen; *youth* stürmisch; *tricks* toll. **2** *n* impulsiver Mensch.

madden [ˈmædn] *vt* (*make mad*) verrückt machen; (*make angry*) ärgern, fuchsen (*inf*). **it** ~**s me to think of the opportunity we missed** ich könnte mich schwarz ärgern (*inf*), wenn ich daran denke, was für eine Chance wir vertan haben.

maddening [ˈmædnɪŋ] *adj* unerträglich, zum Verrücktwerden; *delay* also lästig; *habit* aufreizend. **isn't it** ~? ist das nicht ärgerlich?; **this is** ~! das ist (ja) zum Verrücktwerden!

maddeningly [ˈmædnɪŋlɪ] *adv* unerträglich. **the train ride was** ~ **slow** es war zum Verrücktwerden, wie langsam der Zug fuhr.

madder [ˈmædə[r]] *n* (*plant*) Krapp *m*, Färberröte *f*; (*dye*) Krapprot *nt*, Krappfarbstoff *m*.

made [meɪd] *pret, ptp* of **make**.

Madeira [məˈdɪərə] *n* Madeira *nt*; (*wine*) Madeira *m*. ~ **cake** Sandkuchen *m*.

made-to-measure [ˈmeɪdtəˈmeʒə[r]] *adj* maßgeschneidert. ~ **suit** Maßanzug *m*; ~ **clothes** Maßkonfektion *f*.

made-up [ˈmeɪdʌp] *adj story* erfunden; *face* geschminkt.

madhouse [ˈmædhaʊs] *n* (*lit, fig*) Irrenhaus *nt*.

madly [ˈmædlɪ] *adv* (**a**) wie verrückt. **he worked** ~ **for weeks on end** er arbeitete wochenlang wie besessen *or* verrückt.

(**b**) (*inf: extremely*) wahnsinnig. **to be** ~ **in love (with sb)** bis über beide Ohren (in jdn) verliebt sein, total (in jdn) verschossen sein (*inf*); **I'm not** ~ **keen to go** ich bin nicht wahnsinnig scharf (*inf*) *or* erpicht darauf(, zu gehen).

madman [ˈmædmən] *n, pl* -**men** [-mən] Irrer, Verrückter *m*.

madness [ˈmædnɪs] *n* Wahnsinn *m*. **it's sheer** ~ **it's** either *or* reiner Wahnsinn!; **what** ~! das ist doch Wahnsinn!

Madonna [məˈdɒnə] *n* Madonna *f*; (*picture also*) Madonnenbild *nt*; (*statue also*) Madonnenfigur *f*.

Madrid [məˈdrɪd] *n* Madrid *nt*.

madrigal [ˈmædrɪgəl] *n* Madrigal *nt*.

Maecenas [miːˈsiːnəs] *n* Maecenas *m*; (*fig*) Mäzen *m*.

maelstrom [ˈmeɪlstrəʊm] *n* (*lit rare*) Malstrom *m*; (*fig*) Malstrom (*liter*), Sog *m*. **he returned to the** ~ **of public life** er kehrte in den Trubel des öffentlichen Lebens zurück.

maestro [ˈmaɪstrəʊ] *n* Maestro *m*.

Mae West [ˌmeɪˈwest] *n* (*hum*) Schwimmweste *f*.

Mafia [ˈmæfɪə] *n* Maf(f)ia *f*.

---

mag [mæg] *n* (*inf*) Magazin *nt*; (*glossy also*) Illustrierte *f*. **porn** ~ Pornoheft *nt*.

magazine [ˌmægəˈziːn] *n* (**a**) (*journal*) Zeitschrift *f*, Magazin *nt*. (**b**) (*in gun*) Magazin *nt*. (**c**) (*Mil: store*) Magazin (*Hist*), Depot *nt*.

magenta [məˈdʒentə] **1** *n* Fuchsin *nt*. **2** *adj* tiefrot.

maggot [ˈmægət] *n* Made *f*.

maggoty [ˈmægətɪ] *adj* madig. **the cheese has gone all** ~ der Käse wimmelt von Maden.

Magi [ˈmeɪdʒaɪ] *npl:* **the** ~ die Heiligen Drei Könige, die drei Weisen aus dem Morgenland.

magic [ˈmædʒɪk] **1** *n* (**a**) Magie, Zauberei, Zauberkunst *f*. **the witch doctor tried** ~ **to cure the woman** der Medizinmann versuchte, die Frau durch Magie zu heilen; **he entertained them with a display of** ~ er unterhielt sie mit ein paar Zauberkunststücken; **he made the spoon disappear by** ~ er zauberte den Löffel weg; **you don't expect the essay to write itself by** ~? glaubst du, daß der Aufsatz sich von alleine schreibt?; **as if by** ~ wie durch Zauberei, wie durch ein Wunder; **it worked like** ~ (*inf*) es klappte *or* lief wie am Schnürchen (*inf*).

(**b**) (*mysterious charm*) Zauber *m*.

2 *adj* Zauber-; *powers* magisch; *moment* zauberhaft. **the witch cast a** ~ **spell on her** die Hexe verzauberte sie; **the** ~ **word** (*having special effect*) das Stichwort; (*making sth possible*) das Zauberwort; **the** ~ **touch** ein geschicktes Händchen; **a pianist who really had the** ~ **touch** ein begnadeter Pianist; **he gave it his** ~ **touch and it worked** er hat es nur angefaßt, und schon funktionierte es.

magical [ˈmædʒɪkəl] *adj* magisch. **the effect was** ~ das wirkte (wahre) Wunder.

magically [ˈmædʒɪkəlɪ] *adv* wunderbar. ~ **transformed** auf wunderbare Weise verwandelt; **her headache disappeared** ~ ihre Kopfschmerzen waren auf einmal wie weggeblasen.

magic: ~ **carpet** *n* fliegender Teppich; ~ **circle** *n* Gilde *f* der Zauberkünstler; ~ **eye** *n* magisches Auge; **"The M**~ **Flute"** „Die Zauberflöte".

magician [məˈdʒɪʃən] *n* Magier, Zauberer *m*; (*conjuror*) Zauberkünstler *m*. **I'm not a** ~! ich kann doch nicht hexen!

magic: ~ **lantern** *n* Laterna magica *f*; ~ **wand** *n* Zauberstab *m*.

magisterial [ˌmædʒɪˈstɪərɪəl] *adj* (**a**) (*lit*) *powers, office, robes* eines Friedensrichters. (**b**) (*imperious*) gebieterisch.

magisterially [ˌmædʒɪˈstɪərɪəlɪ] *adv* gebieterisch.

magistracy [ˈmædʒɪstrəsɪ] *n* (*position*) Amt *nt* des Friedensrichters; (*judges*) Friedensrichter *pl*.

magistrate [ˈmædʒɪstreɪt] *n* Friedensrichter, Schiedsmann *m*. ~**s' court** Friedens- *or* Schiedsgericht *nt*.

magnanimity [ˌmægnəˈnɪmɪtɪ] *n* Großherzigkeit, Großmut *f*. **he acted with great** ~ er handelte sehr großherzig.

magnanimous *adj*, ~**ly** *adv* [mægˈnænɪməs, -lɪ] großmütig, großherzig.

magnate [ˈmægneɪt] *n* Magnat *m*.

magnesia [mægˈniːʃə] *n* Magnesia *f*.

magnesium [mægˈniːzɪəm] *n* Magnesium *nt*.

magnet [ˈmægnɪt] *n* (*lit, fig*) Magnet *m*.

magnetic [mægˈnetɪk] *adj* (*lit*) magnetisch; *charms* unwiderstehlich. **he has a** ~ **personality** er hat eine große Ausstrahlung *or* ein sehr anziehendes Wesen; **this perfume has a** ~ **effect on men** dieses Parfüm übt eine magnetische Wirkung auf Männer aus.

magnetically [mægˈnetɪkəlɪ] *adv* magnetisch.

magnetic: ~ **attraction** *n* magnetische Anziehungskraft; ~ **compass** *n* magnetischer Kompaß, Magnetkompaß *m*; ~ **field** *n* Magnetfeld *nt*; ~ **mine** *n* Magnetmine *f*; ~ **needle** *n* Magnetnadel *f*; ~ **north** *n* nördlicher Magnetpol; ~ **pole** *n* Magnetpol *m*; ~ **storm** *n* (erd)magnetischer Sturm; ~ **tape** *n* Magnetband *nt*.

magnetism [ˈmægnɪtɪzəm] *n* Magnetismus *m*; (*fig: of person*) Anziehungskraft, Ausstrahlung *f*.

magnetize [ˈmægnɪtaɪz] *vt* magnetisieren. **the audience was** ~**d by this incredible performance** das Publikum folgte dieser unglaublichen Darstellung wie gebannt.

magneto [mægˈniːtəʊ] *n* Magnetzünder *m*.

magnification [ˌmægnɪfɪˈkeɪʃən] *n* Vergrößerung *f*. **high/low** ~ starke/geringe Vergrößerung; **seen at 300** ~**s** in 300facher Vergrößerung, 300fach vergrößert.

magnificence [mægˈnɪfɪsəns] *n* (**a**) (*excellence*) Großartigkeit, Größe *f*. (**b**) (*splendid appearance*) Pracht *f*, Glanz *m*. (**c**) **his M**~ Seine Magnifizenz.

magnificent [mægˈnɪfɪsənt] *adj* (**a**) (*wonderful, excellent*) großartig; *food, meal* hervorragend, ausgezeichnet. (**b**) (*of splendid appearance*) prachtvoll, prächtig.

magnificently [mægˈnɪfɪsəntlɪ] *adv see adj* (**a**) großartig. **you did** ~ das hast du großartig gemacht; **a** ~ **rousing finale** ein glanzvolles (und) mitreißendes Finale. (**b**) prachtvoll, prächtig.

magnify [ˈmægnɪfaɪ] *vt* (**a**) vergrößern. **to** ~ **sth 7 times** etw 7fach vergrößern; ~**ing glass** Vergrößerungsglas *nt*, Lupe *f*.

(**b**) (*exaggerate*) aufbauschen.

(**c**) (*obs, liter: praise*) **the Lord** lobpreisen (*old, liter*).

magniloquence [mægˈnɪləkwəns] *n* (*liter*) Wortgewalt *f* (*liter*).

magniloquent [mægˈnɪləkwənt] *adj* (*liter*) wortgewaltig (*liter*).

magnitude [ˈmægnɪtjuːd] *n* (**a**) Ausmaß *nt*, Größe *f*; (*importance*) Bedeutung *f*. **I didn't appreciate the** ~ **of the task** ich war mir über den Umfang der Aufgabe nicht im klaren; **in operations of this** ~ bei Vorhaben dieser Größenordnung; **a matter of the first** ~ eine Angelegenheit von äußerster Wichtigkeit; **a fool of the first** ~ ein Narr erster Güte.

(**b**) (*Astron*) Größenklasse *f*.

magnolia [mægˈnəʊlɪə] *n* Magnolie *f*; (*also* ~ **tree**) Magnolienbaum *m*.

magnum ['mægnəm] n = Anderthalbliterflasche f (esp von Sekt). ~ **opus** Hauptwerk nt.

magpie ['mægpai] n Elster f.

Magyar ['mægjɑːʳ] 1 adj madjarisch, magyarisch. 2 n Madjar(in f), Magyar(in f) m.

maharajah [,mɑːhə'rɑːdʒə] n Maharadscha m.

maharani [,mɑːhə'rɑːniː] n Maharani f.

mahogany [mə'hogənı] 1 n Mahagoni nt; (tree) Mahagonibaum m. 2 adj Mahagoni-; (colour) mahagoni(farben).

Mahomet [mə'homɪt] n Mohammed, Mahomet (liter) m.

Mahometan [mə'homɪtən] 1 adj mohammedanisch. 2 n Mohammedaner(in f) m.

mahout [mə'haut] n Mahaut, Elefantenführer m.

maid [meɪd] n (a) (servant) (Dienst)mädchen nt, Hausangestellte f; (in hotel) Zimmermädchen nt; (lady's ~) Zofe f. (b) (old) (maiden) Jungfer (obs), Maid (old, poet) f; (young girl) Mägdelein nt (poet). the M~ of Orleans die Jungfrau von Orleans. (c) see old ~.

maiden ['meɪdn] 1 n (liter) Maid f (old, poet), Mädchen nt. 2 adj flight, voyage etc Jungfern-.

maiden: ~ aunt n unverheiratete, ältere Tante; ~hair n Frauenhaar nt; ~head n (Anat) Jungfernhäutchen nt; she lost her ~head (liter) sie hat ihre Unschuld verloren; ~hood n Jungfräulichkeit, Unschuld f; (time) Jungmädchenzeit f.

maidenly ['meɪdnlɪ] adj jungfräulich; (modest) mädchenhaft.

maiden: ~ name n Mädchenname m; ~ over n (Cricket) 6 Würfe ohne einen Lauf; ~ speech n Jungfernrede f.

maid: ~ of honour n Brautjungfer f; ~servant n Hausangestellte f, Hausmädchen nt.

mail¹ [meɪl] 1 n Post f. to send sth by ~ etw mit der Post versenden or schicken; is there any ~ for me? ist Post für mich da? 2 vt aufgeben; (put in letterbox) einwerfen; (send by ~) mit der Post schicken. ~ing list Anschriftenliste f.

mail² 1 n (Mil) Kettenpanzer m. 2 vt the ~ed fist of imperialism die gepanzerte Faust des Imperialismus.

mail: ~bag n Postsack m; ~boat n Postdampfer m; ~box n (US) Briefkasten m; ~car n (US Rail) Postwagen m; ~ coach n (Hist) Postkutsche f; (Rail) Postwagen m; ~ drop n (US) Briefeinwurf (form), Briefschlitz m; ~man n (US) Briefträger, Postbote m; ~-order catalogue n Versandhauskatalog m; ~-order firm, ~-order house n Versandhaus, Versandgeschäft nt; ~ train n Postzug m; ~ van n (on roads) Postauto nt; (Brit Rail) Postwagen m.

maim [meɪm] vt (mutilate) verstümmeln; (cripple) zum Krüppel machen. the wounded and the ~ed die Verletzten und Versehrten; he will be ~ed for life er wird sein Leben lang ein Krüppel bleiben; he was ~ed in the bomb attack der Bombenanschlag machte ihn zum Krüppel.

main [meɪn] 1 adj attr Haupt-. the ~ idea in this book der Haupt- or Leitgedanke in diesem Buch; what is the ~ thing in life? was ist die Hauptsache im Leben?; the ~ thing is to ... die Hauptsache ist, daß ...; the ~ thing is you're still alive Hauptsache, du lebst noch; see part.

2 n (a) (pipe) Hauptleitung f. the ~s (of town) das öffentliche Versorgungsnetz; (electricity also) das Stromnetz; (of house) der Haupthahn; (for electricity) der Hauptschalter; the machine is run directly off the ~s das Gerät wird direkt ans Stromnetz angeschlossen; ~s operated für Netzbetrieb, mit Netzanschluß; the water/gas/electricity was switched off at the ~s der Haupthahn/Hauptschalter für Wasser/Gas/Elektrizität wurde abgeschaltet.

(b) (poet) the ~ das offene Meer, die hohe See.

(c) in the ~ im großen und ganzen.

(d) see might².

main: ~brace n Großbrasse f; to splice the ~brace Rum an die Mannschaft ausgeben; ~ deck n Hauptdeck nt; ~ force n rohe Gewalt; ~land n Festland nt; on the ~land of Europe auf dem europäischen Festland; ~line 1 n Hauptstrecke f; ~line train Schnellzug m; 2 vi (sl) fixen (sl).

mainly ['meɪnlɪ] adv hauptsächlich, in erster Linie. the meetings are held ~ on Tuesdays die Besprechungen finden meistens dienstags statt; the climate is ~ wet das Klima ist vorwiegend or überwiegend feucht.

main: ~mast n Haupt- or Großmast m; ~ road n Hauptstraße f; ~sail n Haupt- or Großsegel nt; ~spring n (Mech) Triebfeder f; (fig) Triebfeder f, treibende Kraft; ~stay n (Naut) Haupt- or Großstag nt; (fig) Stütze f; ~stream n (a) Hauptrichtung f; to be in the ~stream of sth der Hauptrichtung (+ gen) angehören; (b) (Jazz) Mainstream m.

maintain [meɪn'teɪn] vt (a) (keep up) aufrechterhalten; law and order, peace etc also wahren; quality also, speed, attitude beibehalten; prices halten; life erhalten.

(b) (support) family unterhalten.

(c) (keep in good condition) machine warten; roads instand halten; building instand halten, unterhalten; car pflegen. this old car is too expensive to ~ dieses alte Auto ist im Unterhalt zu teuer or ist zu teuer zu unterhalten.

(d) (claim) behaupten. he still ~ed he was innocent er beteuerte immer noch seine Unschuld.

(e) (defend) theory vertreten; rights verteidigen.

maintenance ['meɪntɪnəns] n see vt (a) Aufrechterhaltung f; Wahrung f; Beibehaltung f; Aufrechterhaltung f; Erhaltung f.

(b) (of family) Unterhalt m; (social security) Unterstützung f. he has to pay ~ er ist unterhaltspflichtig; he's responsible for the ~ of his divorced wife er muß für den Unterhalt seiner geschiedenen Frau aufkommen.

(c) Wartung f; Instandhaltung f; Instandhaltung f, Unterhalt m; Pflege f; (cost) Unterhalt m. his hobby is car ~ er bastelt gern an Autos herum.

maintenance: ~ costs npl Unterhaltskosten pl; ~ crew n Wartungsmannschaft f.

---

maintop ['meɪntop] n Großmars m.

maisonette [,meɪzə'net] n (small flat) Appartement nt; (small house) Häuschen nt.

maize [meɪz] n Mais m.

Maj abbr of **major**.

majestic [mə'dʒestɪk] adj majestätisch; proportions stattlich; movement gemessen; music getragen; (not slow) grandios, erhaben.

majestically [mə'dʒestɪkəlɪ] adv move majestätisch. ~ proportioned buildings Gebäude von stattlichen Ausmaßen; the music ends ~ die Musik kommt zu einem erhabenen or grandiosen Schluß.

majesty ['mædʒɪstɪ] n (stateliness) Majestät f; (of movements etc) Würde f. the ~ of the mountains die Majestät or Erhabenheit der Bergwelt; music full of ~ and grace Musik voller Erhabenheit und Anmut; His/Her M~ Seine/Ihre Majestät; Your M~ Eure Majestät.

Maj Gen abbr of **major general**.

major ['meɪdʒəʳ] 1 adj (a) (of greater importance) bedeutend(er); (of greater extent) größer. a ~ road eine Hauptverkehrsstraße; a ~ poet ein bedeutender Dichter; matters of ~ interest Angelegenheiten pl von größerem Interesse; of ~ importance von größerer Bedeutung; ~ premise erste Prämisse, Obersatz m; a ~ operation eine größere Operation; a ~ work of art ein bedeutendes Kunstwerk.

(b) (Mus) key, scale Dur-. A/A flat/G sharp ~ A-/As-/Gis-Dur nt; ~ third große Terz.

(c) Jenkins M~ Jenkins der Ältere.

2 n (a) (Mil) Major m.

(b) (Mus) Dur nt. in the ~ in Dur.

(c) (Jur) to become a ~ volljährig or mündig werden.

(d) (US) (subject) Hauptfach nt. he's a psychology ~ Psychologie ist/war sein Hauptfach.

3 vi (US) to ~ in French Französisch als Hauptfach studieren, das Examen mit Französisch im Hauptfach ablegen.

Majorca [mə'jɔːkə] n Mallorca nt.

Majorcan [mə'jɔːkən] 1 adj mallorquinisch. 2 n Mallorquiner(in f) m.

major domo [,meɪdʒə'dəʊməʊ] n Haushofmeister, Majordomus m.

majorette [,meɪdʒə'ret] n Majorette f.

major general n Generalmajor m.

majority [mə'dʒorɪtɪ] n (a) Mehrheit f. the ~ of cases die Mehrheit or Mehrzahl der Fälle; to be in a ~ in der Mehrzahl sein; to be in a ~ of 3 eine Mehrheit von 3 Stimmen haben; to have/get a ~ die Mehrheit haben/bekommen; to have a ~ of 10 eine Mehrheit von 10 Stimmen haben; what was his ~? wie groß war seine Mehrheit?; a two-thirds ~ die Zweidrittelmehrheit; by a small ~ mit knapper Mehrheit.

(b) (Jur) Volljährigkeit, Mündigkeit f. to attain one's ~, to reach the age of ~ volljährig or mündig werden.

majority: ~ decision n Mehrheitsbeschluß m; ~ rule n Mehrheitsregierung f.

make [meɪk] (vb: pret, ptp **made**) 1 vt (a) (produce, prepare) machen; bread backen; cars herstellen; dress nähen; coffee kochen; house bauen; peace stiften; the world erschaffen. she made it into a suit sie machte einen Anzug daraus; it's made of gold es ist aus Gold; made in Germany in Deutschland hergestellt, made in Germany; to ~ enemies/an enemy of sb sich (dat) Feinde schaffen/sich (dat) jdn zum Feind machen; he's as clever as they ~ 'em (inf) der ist ein ganz gerissener Hund (inf); to show what one is made of zeigen, was in einem steckt; the job is made for him die Arbeit ist wie für ihn geschaffen; they're made for each other sie sind wie geschaffen füreinander; this car wasn't made to carry 8 people dieses Auto ist nicht dazu gedacht, 8 Leute zu transportieren; I'm not made for running ich bin nicht zum Laufen or zum Läufer geschaffen; see made-to-measure.

(b) (do, execute) bow, journey, mistake, attempt, plan, remarks, suggestions etc machen; speech halten; choice, arrangements treffen; decision fällen, treffen. to ~ an application/a guess sich bewerben/raten; I've made my last payment ich habe die letzte Rate bezahlt; to ~ sb a present of sth jdm etw schenken or zum Geschenk machen (geh).

(c) (cause to be or become) machen; (appoint) machen zu. to ~ sb happy/angry etc jdn glücklich/wütend etc machen; does that ~ you happy? bist du jetzt endlich zufrieden?; to ~ sb one's wife jdn zu seiner Frau machen; to ~ one's voice heard mit seiner Stimme durchdringen; he was made a judge man ernannte ihn zum Richter; they'll never ~ a soldier of him or out of him aus ihm wird nie ein Soldat; I'll ~ it easy for you ich mache es dir leicht or es leicht für dich; to ~ a success/a mess of a job etw glänzend erledigen/etw vermasseln (inf); he ~s Macbeth very evil er läßt Macbeth sehr böse erscheinen; it ~s the room look smaller es läßt den Raum kleiner wirken; to ~ good one's/sb's losses seine Verluste wettmachen/jdm seine Verluste ausgleichen or ersetzen; it ~s no difference to me es ist mir gleich; we decided to ~ a day/night of it wir beschlossen, den ganzen Tag dafür zu nehmen/(die Nacht) durchzumachen; let's ~ it Monday sagen wir Montag; do you want to ~ something of it? (inf) hast du was dagegen? (inf), stört's dich? (inf).

(d) (cause to do or happen) lassen, (dazu) bringen; (compel) zwingen. it all ~s me think that ... das alles läßt mich denken, daß ...; to ~ sb laugh jdn zum Lachen bringen; onions ~ your eyes water von Zwiebeln tränen einem die Augen; what ~s you say that? warum sagst du das?; I'll ~ him suffer for this dafür soll er mir büßen!; he ~s his heroine die er läßt seine Heldin sterben; to ~ sb do sth jdn dazu bringen or veranlassen (geh), etw zu tun; (force) jdn zwingen, etw zu tun; you can't ~ me! mich kann keiner zwingen!; ~ me! (challenging) versuch mal, mich zu zwingen!; **I'll ~ him** den zwing ich!; **to ~ sth do, to ~ do with sth** sich mit etw begnügen, mit etw zufrieden sein; **to ~ do with less money/on a small income** mit weniger Geld/einem niedrigen Gehalt auskommen; **you can't ~ things happen** man kann die Dinge nicht zwingen; **I wish I could ~ the rain stop** wenn ich nur machen (*inf*) *or* bewirken könnte, daß der Regen aufhört; **you can't ~ him agree** Sie können ihn nicht dazu bringen *or* (*force*) zwingen, zuzustimmen; **how can I ~ you understand?** wie kann ich es Ihnen verständlich machen?; **that made the cloth shrink** dadurch ging der Stoff ein; **what ~s the engine go?** was treibt den Motor an?, wie wird der Motor angetrieben?; **what made it explode?** was hat die Explosion bewirkt?; **that certainly made him think again** das hat ihm bestimmt zu denken gegeben; **what ~s you think you can do it?** was macht Sie glauben, daß Sie es schaffen können?; **the chemical ~s the plant grow faster** die Chemikalie bewirkt, daß die Pflanze schneller wächst; **that will ~ the pain go** dies wird den Schmerz vertreiben; **if I could ~ your doubts disappear** wenn ich (nur) Ihre Zweifel beseitigen könnte; **what made you come to this town?** was hat Sie dazu veranlaßt, in diese Stadt zu kommen?, was hat Sie in diese Stadt geführt?; **what will ~ you change your mind?** was wird Sie dazu bringen, Ihre Meinung zu ändern?; **what finally made me drop the idea was ...** was mich am Ende dazu veranlaßt hat, den Gedanken fallenzulassen, war ...

(e) (*earn*) *money* verdienen; *profit, loss, fortune* machen (*on* bei); *name, reputation* sich (*dat*) verschaffen; *name* sich (*dat*) machen. **how much do you stand to ~?** wieviel verdienst du (dabei)?, was bringt dir das ein? (*inf*).

(f) (*reach, achieve, also Sport*) schaffen (*inf*), erreichen; *train, plane etc also* erwischen (*inf*); *connection* schaffen; *summit, top, shore etc* es schaffen zu (*inf*); (*ship*) **20 knots** machen. **to ~ land/port** (*Naut*) anlegen/in den Hafen einlaufen; **we made good time** wir kamen schnell voran; **he just made it er** hat es gerade noch geschafft; **sorry I couldn't ~ your party last night** tut mir leid, ich habe es gestern abend einfach nicht zu deiner Party geschafft; **his first record didn't ~ the charts** seine erste Platte schaffte es nicht bis in die Hitparade; **to ~ it** *or* **~ good (as a writer)** es (als Schriftsteller) schaffen (*inf*) *or* zu etwas bringen; **we've made it!** wir haben es geschafft!; **he'll never ~ it through the winter** er wird den Winter nie überstehen; **we'll never ~ the airport in time** wir schaffen es garantiert nicht mehr zum Flughafen; **he made colonel one year** *or* brachte es in einem Jahr zum Obersten; **he was out to ~ the top** er wollte es ganz nach oben schaffen; **he made university/the first eleven** er schaffte es, an die Universität/in die erste Mannschaft zu kommen; **the story made the front page** die Geschichte kam auf die Titelseite.

(g) (*cause to succeed*) *stars etc* berühmt machen, zum Erfolg verhelfen (+*dat*). **this film made her** mit diesem Film schaffte sie es (*inf*) *or* den Durchbruch; **his performance ~s the play** das Stück lebt von seiner schauspielerischen Leistung; **you'll be made for life** Sie werden ausgesorgt haben; **he's got it made** (*inf*) er hat ausgesorgt; **he's a made man** er ist ein gemachter Mann; **but what really made the evening was ...** die eigentliche Krönung des Abends war ...; **that ~s my day!** das freut mich unheimlich!; (*iro*) das hat mir gerade noch gefehlt!; **the Queen made her day** sie war selig, als sie die Königin gesehen hatte; **you've made my day** ich könnte dir um den Hals fallen! (*inf*); **the weather will ~ or mar the parade** der Festzug steht und fällt mit dem Wetter; **he can ~ or break you** er hat dein Schicksal in der Hand.

(h) (*equal*) sein, (er)geben; (*constitute also*) machen, (ab)geben. **2 plus 2 ~s 4** 2 und 2 ist 4; **1760 yards ~ 1 mile** 1760 Yards sind eine Meile; **this ~s the fifth time** das ist nun das fünfte Mal; **that ~s £55 you owe me** Sie schulden mir damit (nun) £ 55; **how much does that ~ altogether?** was macht das insgesamt?; **to ~ a fourth at bridge** den vierten Mann beim Bridge machen; **it ~s good television/publicity** es ist sehr fernsehwirksam/werbewirksam; **he made a good father** er gab einen guten Vater ab; **he'll never ~ a soldier/an actor** aus dem wird nie ein Soldat/Schauspieler; **you'd ~ someone a good wife** Sie würden eine gute Ehefrau abgeben; **she made him a good wife** sie war ihm eine gute Frau; **he'd ~ a fantastic Hamlet/a good teacher** er wäre ein fantastischer Hamlet/guter Lehrer, er gäbe einen fantastischen Hamlet/guten Lehrer ab; **they ~ a good/an odd couple** sie sind ein gutes/ungleiches Paar; **it made a very strange sight** es war ein sehr merkwürdiger Anblick.

(i) (*estimate*) *distance, total* schätzen auf. **what time do you ~ it?, what do you ~ the time?** wie spät hast du es?, wie spät ist es bei dir?; **I ~ it 3.15** ich habe 3¹⁵, auf meiner Uhr ist es 3¹⁵; **I ~ the total 107** ich kriege insgesamt 107 heraus; **I ~ it 3 miles** nach meiner Rechnung haben wir 3 Meilen; **how many do you ~ it?** wie viele sind es nach deiner Zählung?; **things aren't as bad as he ~s them** es ist nicht so schlimm, wie er es hinstellt.

(j) (*Cards*) (*fulful*) *contract* erfüllen; (*win*) *trick* machen; (*shuffle*) *pack* mischen; *see* bid.

(k) (*Elec*) *circuit* schließen; *contact* herstellen.

(l) (*inf*) **to ~ a woman** mit einer Frau schlafen; **~ me, she** sighed nimm mich, seufzte sie; **to ~ it (with sb)** mit jdm schlafen; **they were making it all night** sie liebten sich die ganze Nacht.

(m) (*Naut: signal*) senden, funken. **~ (the following message) to HMS Victor** machen Sie die folgende Meldung an HMS Victor.

2 *vi* **(a)** (*go*) **to ~ towards a place** auf einen Ort zuhalten; (*ship*) Kurs auf einen Ort nehmen; **to ~ after sb** jdm nachsetzen; **he made at me with a knife** er ging mit einem Messer auf mich los; *see* **~ for, ~ off**.

(b) to ~ on a deal bei einem Geschäft verdienen.

(c) (*begin*) **to ~ as if to do sth** Anstalten machen, etw zu tun;

(*as deception*) so tun, als wolle man etw tun; **I made to run** ich machte Anstalten loszulaufen, ich wollte loslaufen.

(d) (*sl*) **to ~ like** so tun, als ob; **he made like he was dying** er tat so, als ob er am Sterben wäre, er markierte (*inf*) *or* spielte den Sterbenden; **he's started making like a big-shot** er hat angefangen, den starken Mann zu spielen *or* zu markieren (*inf*).

3 *vr* **(a) to ~ oneself useful** sich nützlich machen; **to ~ oneself comfortable** es sich (*dat*) bequem machen; **~ yourself small** mach dich klein; **you're deliberately making yourself heavy** du machst dich absichtlich schwer; **to ~ oneself conspicuous** auffallen; **you'll ~ yourself sick!** du machst dich damit krank!; **to ~ oneself an expert on ...** sich zum Experten für ... machen; (*pretend to be*) sich als Experte für ... ausgeben; **he made himself Emperor for life** er krönte *or* machte sich selbst zum Kaiser auf Lebenszeit; **to ~ oneself heard/understood** sich (*dat*) Gehör verschaffen/sich verständlich machen.

(b) to ~ oneself do sth sich dazu zwingen, etw zu tun.

4 *n* **(a)** (*brand*) Marke *f*, Fabrikat *nt*. **what ~ of car do you run?** welche (Auto)marke fahren Sie?; **it's a good ~** das ist eine gute Marke; **these are my own ~** die sind selbstgemacht *or* Eigenfabrikat (*hum*); **chocolates of their own/of Belgian ~** Pralinen eigener/belgischer Herstellung.

(b) (*pej inf*) **on the ~** (*for profit*) profitgierig (*inf*), auf Profit aus; (*ambitious*) karrieresüchtig (*inf*), auf Karriere aus; (*sexually*) sexhungrig (*inf*), auf sexuelle Abenteuer aus.

♦**make away** *vi see* **make off**.

♦**make away with** *vi* +*prep obj* **to ~ ~ ~ sb/oneself** jdn beseitigen, jdn/sich umbringen.

♦**make for** *vi* +*prep obj* **(a)** (*head for*) zuhalten auf (+*acc*); (*on foot also*) zustreben (+*dat*, auf +*acc*); (*crowd also*) zuströmen (+*dat*, auf +*acc*); (*attack*) losgehen auf (+*acc*); (*vehicle*) losfahren auf (+*acc*). **where are you making ~?** wo willst du hin?; **we are making ~ London** wir wollen nach London; (*by vehicle also*) wir fahren Richtung London; (*by ship also*) wir halten Kurs auf London.

(b) (*promote*) führen zu; *happy marriage, successful parties* den Grund legen für. **such tactics don't ~ ~ good industrial relations** solche Praktiken wirken sich nicht gerade günstig auf das Arbeitsklima aus; **the trade figures ~ ~ optimism** die Handelsziffern geben Anlaß zum Optimismus.

♦**make of** *vi* +*prep obj* halten von. **I didn't ~ much ~ it** ich konnte nicht viel dabei finden; **well, what do you ~ ~ that?** nun, was halten Sie davon?, was sagen Sie dazu?; **don't ~ too much ~ it** überbewerten Sie es nicht.

♦**make off** *vi* sich davonmachen (*with sth* mit etw).

♦**make out 1** *vt sep* **(a)** (*write out*) *cheque, receipt* ausstellen (*to* auf +*acc*); *list, bill* aufstellen, zusammenstellen; (*fill out*) *form* ausfüllen. **to ~ ~ a case for sth** für etw argumentieren.

(b) (*see, discern*) ausmachen; (*decipher*) entziffern; (*understand*) verstehen; *person, actions* schlau werden aus. **I can't ~ ~ what he wants** ich komme nicht dahinter, was er will; **how do you ~ that ~?** wie kommst du darauf?

(c) (*claim*) behaupten.

(d) (*imply*) **to ~ ~ that ...** es so hinstellen, als ob ...; **he made ~ that he was hurt** er tat, als sei er verletzt; **to ~ sb ~ to be clever/a genius** jdn als klug/Genie hinstellen; **she's not as rich as he ~s ~** sie ist nicht so reich, wie er es hinstellt; **he tried to ~ ~ it was my fault** er versuchte, es so hinzustellen, als wäre ich daran schuld; **Jesus is made ~ to be a Communist** Jesus wird zum Kommunisten gemacht.

2 *vi* **(a)** (*inf*) (*get on*) zurechtkommen; (*with people*) auskommen; (*succeed*) es schaffen. **he didn't ~ ~ with her** er ist bei ihr nicht gelandet (*inf*); **how did you ~ ~ at the interview?** wie sind Sie beim Interview zurechtgekommen?; **he eventually made ~** er hat es schließlich geschafft.

(b) (*US inf: pet*) knutschen (*inf*), fummeln (*inf*).

♦**make over** *vt sep* **(a)** (*assign*) überschreiben (*to sb dat*); (*bequeath*) *property, money* vermachen (*to sb dat*). **(b)** (*convert*) umändern, umarbeiten; *house* umbauen. **the gardens have been made ~ into a parking lot** man hat die Anlagen in einen Parkplatz umgewandelt.

♦**make up 1** *vt sep* **(a)** (*constitute*) bilden. **to be made ~ of** bestehen aus, sich zusammensetzen aus; **he made ~ the four at bridge** er war der vierte Mann zum *or* beim Bridge.

(b) (*put together*) *food, medicine, bed* zurechtmachen; *parcel also* zusammenpacken; *list, accounts* zusammenstellen, aufstellen; *team* zusammenstellen; (*Typ*) *page* umbrechen; (*design layout*) aufmachen. **to ~ material ~ into sth** Material zu etw verarbeiten; **they made the daffodils ~ into bunches** sie banden die Osterglocken zu Sträußen.

(c) *quarrel* beilegen, begraben. **to ~ it ~ (with sb)** sich (mit jdm) wieder vertragen, sich (mit jdm) aussöhnen; **come on, let's ~ it ~** komm, wir wollen uns wieder vertragen.

(d) *face, eyes* schminken. **the way she's made ~** wie sie geschminkt ist.

(e) to ~ one's mind (to do sth) sich (*dat*) entschließen (, etw zu tun); **~ your mind!** entschließ dich!; **my mind is quite made ~** mein Entschluß steht fest; **once his mind is made ~, that's it** wenn er einmal einen Entschluß gefaßt hat, bleibt es dabei; **I can't ~ ~ your mind for you** ich kann das nicht für dich entscheiden; **to ~ ~ one's mind about sb/sth** sich (*dat*) eine Meinung über jdn/etw bilden; **I can't ~ ~ my mind about him** ich weiß nicht, was ich von ihm halten soll.

(f) (*invent*) *story etc* (*dat*) ausdenken. **you're making that ~!** jetzt schwindelst du aber! (*inf*); **he ~s it ~ as he goes along** (*performer, storyteller*) er macht das aus dem Stegreif; (*child playing*) er macht das, wie es ihm gerade einfällt; (*making excuses, telling lies*) er saugt sich (*dat*) das nur so aus den Fingern; **it was all made ~** das war alles nur erfunden.

(g) (*complete*) *crew* vollständig *or* komplett (*inf*) machen. if you can raise £80 I'll ~ ~ the other £20 wenn Sie £ 80 aufbringen können, komme ich für die restlichen £ 20 auf; he made the gift ~ to £50 er rundete das Geschenk auf £ 50 auf; add water to ~ it ~ to one litre mit Wasser auf einen Liter auffüllen.

(h) (compensate for) loss ausgleichen; time einholen, aufholen; sleep nachholen. to ~ it ~ to sb (for sth) (compensate) jdn (für etw) entschädigen; (emotionally, return favour etc) jdm etw wiedergutmachen.

(i) fire (wieder) anschüren or anfachen.

2 vi (a) (after quarrelling) sich versöhnen, sich wieder vertragen. let's kiss and ~ ~ komm, gib mir einen Kuß und wir vertragen uns wieder.

(b) (material) this material will ~ ~ nicely/into a nice coat dieser Stoff wird sich gut verarbeiten lassen/wird sich als Mantel gut machen.

(c) (catch up) aufholen. to ~ ~ on sb jdn einholen, an jdn herankommen; you've a lot of making ~ to do du hast viel nachzuholen or aufzuarbeiten.

♦**make up for** vi +prep obj to ~ ~ ~ sth etw ausgleichen; to ~ ~ ~ lost time verlorene Zeit aufholen; to ~ ~ ~ the loss of sb/lack of sth jdn/etw ersetzen; that still doesn't ~ ~ ~ the fact that you were very rude das macht noch lange nicht ungeschehen, daß du sehr unhöflich warst.

♦**make up to** vi +prep obj (inf) sich heranmachen an (+acc).

♦**make with** vi +prep obj (esp US sl) he started making ~ his trumpet er legte mit seiner Trompete los (inf); OK, let's ~ ~ the paint brushes na dann, schnappen wir uns die Pinsel (inf); just ~ ~ the scissors mach schon los mit der Schere (inf); there she was on the dance-floor, making ~ her hips da war sie auf der Tanzfläche und schwang ihre or die Hüften.

make-believe ['meɪkbɪ,liːv] 1 adj attr Phantasie-, imaginär; world also Schein-. 2 n Phantasie f. a world of ~ eine Phantasiewelt; don't be afraid, it's only ~ hab keine Angst, das ist doch nur eine Geschichte. 3 vt sich (dat) vorstellen.

make-or-break ['meɪkɔː'breɪk] adj attr (inf) kritisch, entscheidend.

maker ['meɪkə'] n (manufacturer) Hersteller m. our M~ unser Schöpfer m; to go to meet one's M~ zum Herrn eingehen (geh).

-maker n suf (hat-~, clock-~) -macher(in f) m.

make: ~-ready n (Typ) Zurichtung f; ~shift 1 adj improvisiert; repairs Not-, behelfsmäßig; 2 n Übergangslösung f, Notbehelf m; see shift 1 (d); ~-up n (a) Make-up nt; (cosmetics also) Schminke f; (Theat also) Maske f; the star does his own ~-up der Star schminkt sich selbst/macht seine Maske selbst; she spends hours on her ~-up sie braucht Stunden zum Schminken; (b) (composition) (of team, party etc) Zusammenstellung f; (character) Veranlagung f; psychological ~-up Psyche f; loyalty is part of his ~-up er ist loyal veranlagt; it's part of their national ~-up das gehört zu ihrem Nationalcharakter; (c) (Typ) Umbruch m; (layout) Aufmachung f; ~-up girl n Maskenbildnerin f; ~-up kit n Schminkset nt; ~-up man n Maskenbildner m; ~-up mirror n Schminkspiegel m; ~weight n (a) (lit) he added a few more as ~weights er gab noch ein paar dazu, um das Gewicht vollzumachen; (b) (fig: person) Lückenbüßer m; to use sth as a ~weight etw in die Waagschale werfen.

making ['meɪkɪŋ] n (a) (production) Herstellung f; (of food) Zubereitung f. in the ~ im Werden, im Entstehen; his reputation was still in the ~ er war noch dabei, sich (dat) einen Ruf zu schaffen; here you can see history in the ~ hier hat man den Finger am Puls der Geschichte (liter); it's a civil war in the ~ hier ist ein Bürgerkrieg im Entstehen; the mistake was not of my ~ der Fehler war nicht mein Werk; it was the ~ of him das hat ihn zu dem gemacht, was er (heute) ist.

(b) ~s pl Voraussetzungen (of zu) pl; he has the ~s of an actor/a general etc er hat das Zeug zu einem Schauspieler/General etc; the situation has all the ~s of a strike die Situation bietet alle Voraussetzungen für einen Streik.

maladjusted [,mælə'dʒʌstɪd] adj (Psych, Sociol) verhaltensgestört. **pyschologically** ~ verhaltensgestört; **socially** ~ verhaltensgestört, umweltgestört; ~ youths fehlangepaßte or nicht angepaßte Jugendliche pl.

maladjustment [,mælə'dʒʌstmənt] n (Psych, Sociol) Verhaltensstörung f. her social ~ ihr soziales Fehlverhalten, ihre Verhaltensstörung.

maladministration ['mæləd,mɪnɪs'treɪʃən] n schlechte Verwaltung.

maladroit adj, ~ly adv [,mælə'drɔɪt, -lɪ] ungeschickt.

maladroitness [,mælə'drɔɪtnɪs] n Ungeschicklichkeit f.

malady ['mælədɪ] n Leiden nt, Krankheit f. social ~ gesellschaftliches Übel.

malaise [mæ'leɪz] n Unwohlsein nt; (fig) Unbehagen nt. I have a vague feeling of ~ about the future mich überkommt ein leises Unbehagen, wenn ich an die Zukunft denke.

malapropism ['mæləprɒpɪzəm] n Malapropismus m.

malaria [mə'lɛərɪə] n Malaria f.

malarial [mə'lɛərɪəl] adj Malaria-.

malarkey [mə'lɑːkɪ] n (sl) (messing about) Blödelei f (inf); (nonsense) Hokuspokus m (sl); (goings-on) faule Dinger pl (sl).

Malawi [mə'lɑːwɪ] n Malawi nt.

Malay [mə'leɪ] 1 adj malaiisch. 2 n (a) Malaie m, Malaiin f. (b) (language) Malaiisch nt.

Malaya [mə'leɪə] n Malaya nt.

Malayan [mə'leɪən] 1 adj malaiisch. 2 n Malaie m, Malaiin f.

Malaysia [mə'leɪzɪə] n Malaysia nt.

Malaysian [mə'leɪzɪən] 1 adj malaysisch. 2 n Malaysier(in f) m.

malcontent ['mælkən,tent] 1 adj unzufrieden. 2 n Unzufriedene(r) mf.

male [meɪl] 1 adj (a) männlich. ~ child Junge m; a ~ doctor ein Arzt m; ~ nurse Krankenpfleger m; ~ sparrow/crocodile

Spatzen-/Krokodilmännchen nt.

(b) choir, voice Männer-. an all-~ club ein reiner Männerverein; that's a typical ~ attitude das ist typisch männlich.

(c) (manly) männlich.

(d) (Mech) ~ screw Schraube f; ~ plug Stecker m.

2 n (animal) Männchen nt; (inf: man) Mann m, männliches Wesen. the ~ of the species das männliche Tier, das Männchen; that's typical of a ~ (inf) das ist typisch Mann (inf).

malediction [,mælɪ'dɪkʃən] n Fluch m, Verwünschung f.

malefactor ['mælɪfæktə'] n Übeltäter, Missetäter m.

malevolence [mə'levələns] n Boshaftigkeit f; (of action) Böswilligkeit f. to feel ~ towards sb einen Groll gegen jdn hegen, von Ranküne gegen jdn erfüllt sein (liter).

malevolent [mə'levələnt] adj boshaft; gods übelwollend; action böswillig.

malformation [,mælfɔː'meɪʃən] n Mißbildung f.

malformed [mæl'fɔːmd] adj mißgebildet.

malfunction [,mæl'fʌŋkʃən] 1 n (of liver etc) Funktionsstörung f; (of machine) Defekt m. a ~ of the carburettor ein Defekt im Vergaser, ein defekter Vergaser; a ~ in management ein Versagen nt der Betriebsleitung.

2 vi (liver etc) nicht richtig arbeiten; (machine etc) defekt sein, nicht richtig funktionieren; (system) versagen, nicht richtig funktionieren. the ~ing part das defekte Teil.

malice ['mælɪs] n (a) Bosheit, Bösartigkeit f; (of action) Böswilligkeit f. a look of ~ ein boshafter Blick; out of ~ aus Bosheit; to bear sb ~ einen Groll gegen jdn hegen; I bear him no ~ ich bin ihm nicht böse. (b) (Jur) with ~ aforethought in böswilliger Absicht, vorsätzlich.

malicious [mə'lɪʃəs] adj (a) person, words boshaft; behaviour bösartig, böswillig; crime gemein, arglistig; slander böswillig. (b) (Jur) damage mutwillig, böswillig.

maliciously [mə'lɪʃəslɪ] adv see adj.

malign [mə'laɪn] 1 adj (liter) intent böse; influence unheilvoll; see also malignant. 2 vt verleumden; (run down) schlecht machen. to ~ sb's character jdm Übles nachsagen; without wishing in any way to ~ her/her character ... ich will ihr ja nichts (Schlechtes) nachsagen, aber ...

malignancy [mə'lɪɡnənsɪ] n Bösartigkeit f; (Med also) Malignität f (form); (fig: evil thing) Übel nt.

malignant [mə'lɪɡnənt] adj bösartig; (Med also) maligne (spec). he took a ~ delight in our misfortunes unser Unglück bereitete ihm ein hämisches Vergnügen; a ~ growth (Med, fig) ein bösartiges Geschwür.

malignity [mə'lɪɡnɪtɪ] n Bösartigkeit f; (Med also) Malignität f (spec).

malinger [mə'lɪŋɡə'] vi simulieren, krank spielen.

malingerer [mə'lɪŋɡərə'] n Simulant m.

mallard ['mæləd] n Stockente f.

malleability [,mælɪə'bɪlɪtɪ] n Formbarkeit f; (of clay, wax also) Geschmeidigkeit f.

malleable ['mælɪəbl] adj formbar (also fig), weich; (of clay, wax also) geschmeidig. gold is much more ~ than iron Gold ist viel weicher or läßt sich viel leichter bearbeiten als Eisen.

mallet ['mælɪt] n Holzhammer m; (croquet) (Krocket)hammer m; (polo) (Polo)schläger m.

mallow ['mæləʊ] n Malve f.

malmsey ['mɑːmzɪ] n Malvasier(wein) m.

malnutrition [,mælnjʊ'trɪʃən] n Unterernährung f.

malodorous [mæl'əʊdərəs] adj (form) übelriechend.

malpractice [,mæl'præktɪs] n Berufsvergehen nt, Verstoß m gegen das Berufsethos, Amtsvergehen nt (eines Beamten). minor ~s common in the profession kleinere Unregelmäßigkeiten, wie sie in diesem Berufszweig häufig sind.

malt [mɔːlt] 1 n Malz nt. ~ extract Malzextrakt m; ~ loaf = Rosinenbrot nt; ~ whisky Malt Whisky m. 2 vt barley malzen, mälzen; drink etc mit Malz versetzen or mischen. ~ed milk Malzmilch f.

Malta ['mɔːltə] n Malta nt.

Maltese [,mɔːl'tiːz] 1 adj maltesisch. ~ cross Malteserkreuz nt. 2 n (a) Malteser(in f) m. (b) (language) Maltesisch nt.

maltreat [,mæl'triːt] vt schlecht behandeln; (using violence) mißhandeln.

maltreatment [,mæl'triːtmənt] n schlechte Behandlung; Mißhandlung f.

mamba ['mæmbə] n Mamba f.

mambo ['mæmbəʊ] n Mambo m.

mam(m)a [mə'mɑː] n (inf) Mama f (inf).

mammal ['mæml] n Säugetier nt, Säuger m.

mammalian [mæ'meɪlɪən] adj Säugetier-, der Säugetiere.

mammary ['mæmərɪ] adj Brust-. ~ gland Brustdrüse f.

mammon ['mæmən] n Mammon, Reichtum m. M~ der Mammon.

mammoth ['mæməθ] 1 n Mammut nt. 2 adj Mammut-; cost, enterprise kolossal.

mammy ['mæmɪ] n (inf) Mami f (inf); (US) (schwarze) Kinderfrau, Negermami (inf) f.

man [mæn] 1 n, pl men (a) (adult male) Mann m. be a ~! sei ein Mann!; to make a ~ out of sb einen Mann aus jdm machen; this incident made a ~ out of him dieses Ereignis hat ihn zum Mann gemacht; we'll never make a ~ out of him aus ihm wird nie ein Mann; he's only half a ~ er ist kein richtiger Mann; I'm only half a ~ without you ohne dich bin ich nur ein halber Mensch; he took it like a ~ er hat es wie ein Mann or mannhaft ertragen; that's just like a ~ das ist typisch Mann; her ~ (inf) ihr Mann; ~ and boy von Kindheit/Jugend an; they are ~ and wife sie sind Mann und Frau; the ~ in the street der Mann auf der Straße, der kleine Mann; ~ of God Mann m Gottes; ~ of letters (writer) Schriftsteller, Literat m; (scholar) Gelehrter m; ~ of property vermögender Mann; he's a ~ about town er kennt sich aus; a suit for the ~ about town ein Anzug für den feinen Herrn; a ~ of the world ein Mann *m* von Welt; well done, that ~! gut gemacht, alter Junge! (*inf*); old ~ (*dated*) alter Junge (*dated*) *or* Knabe (*dated*); *see* good.

(b) (*human race: also* M~) der Mensch; die Menschen.

(c) (*person*) man. no ~ keiner, niemand; any ~ jeder; any ~ who believes that ... wer das glaubt, ...; sometimes a ~ needs a change (*inf*) manchmal braucht man einfach etwas Abwechslung; men say that ... die Leute sagen, daß ...; that ~! dieser Mensch!; that ~ Jones dieser *or* der Jones!; the strong ~ of the government der starke Mann (in) der Regierung; as one ~ geschlossen, wie ein Mann; they are communists to a ~ sie sind allesamt Kommunisten.

(d) (*type*) the right/wrong ~ der Richtige/Falsche; you've come to the right ~ da sind or liegen (*inf*) Sie bei mir richtig; then I am your ~ dann bin ich genau der Richtige (für Sie), da sind Sie bei mir an der richtigen Adresse; he's not the ~ for the job er ist nicht der Richtige für diese Aufgabe; he's not the ~ to make a mistake like that so etwas würde ihm bestimmt nicht passieren; he's not a ~ to ... er ist nicht der Typ, der ...; he's not a ~ to meddle with mit ihm ist nicht gut Kirschen essen; he is a Cambridge ~ er hat in Cambridge studiert; medical ~ Mediziner *m*; family ~ Familienvater *m*; he's a family ~ (*home-loving*) er ist sehr häuslich; it's got to be a local ~ es muß jemand von hier *or* aus dieser Gegend sein; I'm not a drinking ~ ich bin kein großer Trinker; I'm a whisky ~ myself ich bin mehr für Whisky; I'm not a football ~ ich mache mir nicht viel aus Fußball; he's a 4-pint ~ mehr als 4 Halbe verträgt er nicht; unter 4 Halben tut er's nicht.

(e) (*sl: interj*) Mensch (*inf*), Mann (*inf*). you can't do that, ~ Mensch *or* Mann, das kannst du doch nicht machen! (*inf*); ~, was I surprised! Mann *or* Mensch, war ich vielleicht überrascht! (*sl*); fantastic, ~! dufte, Mann! (*sl*); see you, ~! bis später; are you coming with us, ~? du, kommst du noch mit?

(f) (*employee, soldier etc*) Mann *m*; (*servant also*) Bedienstete(r) *m*. she has a ~ to do the garden sie hat jemanden, der den Garten macht; officers and men Offiziere und Mannschaften; follow me, men! mir nach, Leute!

(g) (*Chess*) Figur *f*; (*in draughts*) Stein *m*.

2 *vt ship* bemannen; *fortress* besetzen; *power station, pump, gun* bedienen. the ship is ~ned by a crew of 30 das Schiff hat 30 Mann Besatzung; a fully ~ned ship ein vollbemanntes Schiff; he left 10 soldiers behind to ~ the fortress er ließ 10 Soldaten als Besatzung für die Festung zurück; ~ the guns/pumps! an die Geschütze/Pumpen!; the captain gave the signal to ~ the guns der Kapitän gab das Zeichen zur Besetzung der Geschütze; there's someone ~ning the telephone all day es ist den ganzen Tag über jemand da, der das Telefon bedient.

manacle ['mænəkl] 1 *n usu pl* Handfesseln, Ketten *pl*. 2 *vt person* in Ketten legen; *hands* (mit Ketten) fesseln. they were ~d together sie wurden/waren aneinandergekettet; he was ~d to the wall er war an die Wand gekettet.

manage ['mænɪdʒ] 1 *vt* (a) *company, organization* leiten; *property* verwalten; *affairs* in Ordnung halten, regeln; *football team, pop group* managen. he ~d the election er war Wahlleiter; the election was ~d (*pej*) die Wahl war manipuliert.

(b) (*handle, control*) *person, child, animal* zurechtkommen mit, fertigwerden mit; *car, ship* zurechtkommen mit, handhaben. the car is too big for her to ~ sie kommt mit dem Auto nicht zurecht, weil es zu groß ist; she can't ~ children sie kann nicht mit Kindern umgehen; I can ~ him mit dem werde ich schon fertig.

(c) *task* bewältigen, zurechtkommen mit; *another portion* bewältigen, schaffen (*inf*). £5 is the most I can ~ ich kann mir höchstens £ 5 leisten; I'll ~ it das werde ich schon schaffen; he ~d it very well er hat das sehr gut gemacht; you'll ~ it next time nächstes Mal schaffst du du's; I'll do that as soon as I can ~ it ich mache das so bald ich kann *or* so bald ich es schaffe; he should take some exercise as soon as he can ~ it er sollte sich so bald wie möglich Bewegung verschaffen; can you ~ the cases? kannst du die Koffer (allein) tragen?; thanks, I can ~ them danke, das geht schon; she can't ~ the stairs sie kommt die Treppe nicht hinauf/hinunter; can you ~ two more in the car? kriegst du noch zwei Leute in dein Auto? (*inf*); can you ~ 8 o'clock? 8 Uhr, ginge *or* geht das?; could you ~ (to be ready by) 8 o'clock? kannst du um 8 Uhr fertig sein?; can you ~ another cup? darf's noch eine Tasse sein?; could you ~ another whisky? schaffst du noch einen Whisky?; I could ~ another cake ich glaube, ich könnte noch ein Stück Kuchen vertragen; I couldn't ~ another thing ich könnte keinen Bissen mehr runterbringen.

(d) to ~ to do sth es schaffen, etw zu tun; we have ~d to reduce our costs es ist uns gelungen, die Kosten zu senken; do you think you'll ~ to do it? meinen Sie, Sie können *or* schaffen das?; I hope you'll ~ to come ich hoffe, Sie können kommen; how did you ~ to get a salary increase? wie hast du es geschafft *or* angestellt, eine Gehaltserhöhung zu bekommen?; he ~d to control himself es gelang ihm, sich zu beherrschen; he ~d not to get his feet wet es ist ihm gelungen, keine nassen Füße zu bekommen; how did you ~ to miss that? wie konnte Ihnen das nur entgehen?; how could you possibly ~ to do that? wie hast du denn das fertiggebracht?; how could anybody possibly ~ to be so stupid? wie kann ein Mensch nur so dumm sein?; could you possibly ~ to close the door? (*iro*) wäre es vielleicht möglich, die Tür zuzumachen?; could you possibly ~ to help me? könnten Sie mir vielleicht helfen?

2 *vi* zurechtkommen, es schaffen. can you ~? geht es?; thanks, I can ~ danke, es geht schon *or* ich komme schon zurecht; I thought I could cope with things, but I can't ~ ich dachte, ich käme zurecht, aber ich bringe es nicht fertig; she ~s well enough sie kommt ganz gut zurecht; how do you ~? wie schaffen *or* machen Sie das bloß?;

to ~ without sth ohne etw auskommen, sich (*dat*) ohne etw behelfen; we'll just have to ~ without dann müssen wir uns (*dat*) eben so behelfen, dann müssen wir eben so auskommen; to ~ without sb ohne jdn auskommen *or* zurechtkommen; I can ~ by myself ich komme (schon) allein zurecht; how do you ~ on only £20 a week? wie kommen Sie mit nur £ 20 pro Woche aus?

manageable ['mænɪdʒəbl] *adj child* folgsam, fügsam; *horse* fügsam; *amount, job* zu bewältigen; *hair* leicht frisierbar, geschmeidig; *number* überschaubar; *car* leicht zu handhaben. since the treatment he's been less violent, more ~ seit der Behandlung ist er nicht mehr so gewalttätig, man kann besser mit ihm umgehen *or* zurechtkommen; the children are no longer ~ for her sie wird mit den Kindern nicht mehr fertig; is that ~ for you? schaffen Sie das?; this company is just not ~ es ist unmöglich, dieses Unternehmen (erfolgreich) zu leiten; you should try and keep the book within ~ limits Sie sollten versuchen, das Buch in überschaubaren Grenzen zu halten; pieces of a more ~ size Stücke, die leichter zu handhaben sind, Stücke pl in handlicher Größe; a job of ~ size eine überschaubare Aufgabe; can you do that? — yes, that's ~ können Sie das tun? — ja, das läßt sich machen; the staircase isn't ~ for an old lady die Treppe ist für eine alte Dame zu beschwerlich.

management ['mænɪdʒmənt] *n* (a) (*act*) (*of company*) Leitung, Führung *f*, Management *nt*; (*of non-commercial organization*) Leitung *f*; (*of estate, assets, money*) Verwaltung *f*; (*of affairs*) Regelung *f*. losses due to bad ~ Verluste, die auf schlechtes Management zurückzuführen sind; crisis ~ Krisenmanagement *nt*; ~ course Managerkurs *m*; ~ studies Betriebswirtschaft *f*.

(b) (*persons*) Unternehmensleitung *f*; (*of single unit or smaller factory*) Betriebsleitung *f*; (*non-commercial*) Leitung *f*; (*Theat*) Intendanz *f*. "under new ~" „neuer Inhaber"; (*shop*) „neu eröffnet"; (*pub*) „unter neuer Bewirtschaftung".

manager ['mænɪdʒə⁻] *n* (*Comm etc*) Geschäftsführer, Manager *m*; (*of restaurant*) Geschäftsführer *m*; (*of smaller firm or factory*) Betriebsleiter *m*; (*of bank, chain store*) Filialleiter *m*; (*of department*) Abteilungsleiter *m*; (*of estate etc*) Verwalter *m*; (*Theat*) Intendant *m*; (*of private theatre*) Theaterdirektor *m*; (*of pop group, boxer etc*) Manager *m*; (*of team*) Trainer *m*. sales/publicity ~ Verkaufsleiter *m*/Werbeleiter *m*; business ~ (*for theatre*) Verwaltungsdirektor *m*.

manageress [,mænɪdʒə'res] *n* Geschäftsführerin *f*, Leiterin *f* eines Unternehmens/Hotels *etc*; (*of department*) Abteilungsleiterin *f*; (*of chain store*) Filialleiterin *f*.

managerial [,mænə'dʒɪərɪəl] *adj* geschäftlich; (*executive*) Management-; *post* leitend. he has no ~ skills er ist für leitende Funktionen ungeeignet.

managing director [,mænɪdʒɪŋdɪ'rektə⁻] *n* leitender Direktor.

man-at-arms [,mænət'ɑːmz] *n*, *pl* **men-at-arms** [,menət'ɑːmz] Soldat, Krieger (*old*) *m*.

manatee [,mænə'tiː] *n* (Rundschwanz)seekuh *f*.

Manchuria [mæn'tʃuərɪə] *n* die Mandschurei.

Manchurian [mæn'tʃuərɪən] 1 *adj* mandschurisch. 2 *n* (a) Mandschu *m*. (b) (*language*) Mandschu *nt*.

Mancunian [mæŋ'kjuːnɪən] 1 *n* Bewohner(in *f*) *m* Manchesters. he's a ~ er kommt *or* ist aus Manchester. 2 *adj* aus Manchester.

mandarin ['mændərɪn] *n* (a) (*Chinese official*) Mandarin *m*; (*official*) hoher Funktionär, Bonze *m* (*pej*). (b) (*language*) M~ Hochchinesisch *nt*. (c) (*fruit*) Mandarine *f*.

mandate ['mændeɪt] 1 *n* Auftrag *m*; (*Pol also*) Mandat *nt*; (*territory*) Mandat(sgebiet) *nt*. to give sb a ~ to do sth jdn den Auftrag geben *or* jdn damit beauftragen, etw zu tun; we have a clear ~ from the country to ... wir haben den eindeutigen Wählerauftrag, zu ...

2 *vt* to ~ a territory to sb ein Gebiet jds Verwaltung (*dat*) unterstellen *or* als Mandat an jdn vergeben.

mandated ['mændeɪtɪd] *adj territory* Mandats-.

mandatory ['mændətərɪ] *adj* obligatorisch; (*Pol*) mandatorisch. the ~ nature of this ruling der Zwangscharakter dieser Regelung; the Navy have ~ powers of arrest die Marine ist zur Festnahme befugt *or* ermächtigt; union membership is ~ Mitgliedschaft in der Gewerkschaft ist Pflicht.

man-day ['mændeɪ] *n* Manntag *m*.

mandible ['mændɪbl] *n* (*of vertebrates*) Unterkiefer(knochen) *m*, Mandibel *f* (*spec*). ~s (*of insects*) Mundwerkzeuge, Mundgliedmaßen *pl*, Mandibeln *pl* (*spec*); (*of birds*) Schnabel *m*.

mandolin(e) ['mændəlɪn] *n* Mandoline *f*.

mandrake ['mændreɪk] *n* Mandragora, Mandragore *f*. ~ root Alraune *f*.

mandrill ['mændrɪl] *n* Mandrill *m*.

mane [meɪn] *n* (*lit, fig*) Mähne *f*.

man: ~eater *n* Menschenfresser *m*; (*shark*) Menschenhai *m*; (*inf: woman*) männermordendes Weib (*inf*); ~-eating shark *n* Menschenhai *m*; ~-eating tiger *n* Menschenfresser *m*.

maneuver *n, vti* (*US*) *see* **manoeuvre.**

manful *adj*, ~ly *adv* ['mænfʊl, -fəlɪ] mannhaft (*geh*), mutig, beherzt.

manganese [,mæŋɡə'niːz] *n* Mangan *nt*.

mange [meɪndʒ] *n* Räude *f*; (*of man*) Krätze *f*.

mangel(-wurzel) ['mæŋɡl(,wɜːzl)] *n* Runkel- *or* Futterrübe *f*.

manger ['meɪndʒə⁻] *n* Krippe *f*.

mangle¹ ['mæŋɡl] 1 *n* Mangel *f*. 2 *vt clothes* mangeln.

mangle² *vt* (*also* ~ up) (übel) zurichten.

mango ['mæŋɡəʊ] *n* (*fruit*) Mango *f*; (*tree*) Mangobaum *m*.

mangold(-wurzel) ['mæŋɡəld(,wɜːzl)] *n* *see* **mangel (-wurzel).**

mangrove ['mæŋɡrəʊv] *n* Mangrove(n)baum *m*. ~ swamp Mangrove *f*.

mangy ['meɪndʒɪ] adj (+er) dog räudig; carpet schäbig; hotel schäbig, heruntergekommen.

man: ~-handle vt (a) grob or unsanft behandeln; he was ~-handled into the back of the van er wurde recht unsanft or gewaltsam in den Laderaum des Wagens verfrachtet; **(b)** piano etc hieven; ~hole n Kanal- or Straßenschacht m; (in boiler etc) Mannloch nt, Einsteigöffnung f.

manhood ['mænhʊd] n **(a)** (state) Mannesalter nt. **(b)** (manliness) Männlichkeit f. **(c)** (men) Männer pl.

man: ~-hour n Arbeitsstunde, Mannstunde f; ~hunt n Fahndung f; (for criminal also) Verbrecherjagd f; (hum: of woman) Männerfang m.

mania ['meɪnɪə] n **(a)** (madness) Manie f. persecution ~ Verfolgungswahn m.
(b) (inf: enthusiasm) Manie f, Tick (inf), Fimmel (inf) m. this ~ for nationalization diese Verstaatlichungsmanie; this current ~ for the 1920's die derzeitige Manie für die 20er Jahre; he has a ~ for collecting old matchboxes er hat den Tick or Fimmel, alte Streichholzschachteln zu sammeln (inf); he has this ~ for collecting stuff er hat einen Sammeltick (inf) or -fimmel (inf); ~ for cleanliness Sauberkeitstick (inf), Reinlichkeitsfimmel (inf) m; it has become a ~ with him das ist bei ihm zur Manie geworden.

maniac ['meɪnɪæk] **1** adj wahnsinnig. **2** n **(a)** Wahnsinnige(r), Irre(r) mf. **(b)** (fig) these sports ~s diese Sportfanatiker pl; you ~ du bist ja wahnsinnig!

maniacal [mə'naɪəkəl] adj wahnsinnig.

manic-depressive ['mænɪkdɪ'presɪv] **1** adj manisch-depressiv. **2** n Manisch-Depressive(r) mf. he is a ~ er ist manisch-depressiv.

manicure ['mænɪˌkjʊəʳ] **1** n Maniküre f. ~ set Nagelnecessaire, Nagel- or Maniküreetui nt. **2** vt maniküren. his well-~d hands seine gepflegten or sorgfältig manikürten Hände.

manicurist ['mænɪˌkjʊərɪst] n Handpflegerin f.

manifest ['mænɪfest] **1** adj offenkundig, offenbar; (definite also) eindeutig. I think it's ~ that ... es liegt doch wohl auf der Hand, daß ...; to make sth ~ etw klar or deutlich machen, etw manifestieren (geh); to make the truth ~ die Wahrheit offenbaren or manifestieren (geh); he made it ~ that ... er machte klar or deutlich, daß ...
2 n (Naut) Manifest nt.
3 vt zeigen, bekunden.
4 vr sich zeigen; (Sci, Psych etc) sich manifestieren; (ghost) erscheinen; (guilt etc) sich offenbaren, offenbar werden.

manifestation [ˌmænɪfe'steɪʃən] n (act of showing) Ausdruck m, Manifestierung, Bekundung f; (sign) Anzeichen nt, Manifestation f; (of spirit) Erscheinung f.

manifestly ['mænɪfestlɪ] adv eindeutig, offensichtlich. it's so ~ obvious es ist so völlig offensichtlich.

manifesto [ˌmænɪ'festəʊ] n, pl -(e)s Manifest nt.

manifold ['mænɪfəʊld] **1** adj mannigfaltig (geh), vielfältig. ~ uses vielseitige Anwendung; it's a ~ subject das ist ein sehr komplexes Thema; his ~ experience seine reichhaltigen Erfahrungen. **2** n (Aut) (inlet ~) Ansaugrohr nt; (exhaust ~) Auspuffrohr nt.

manikin ['mænɪkɪn] n (dwarf) Männchen, Knirps m; (Art) Modell nt, Gliederpuppe f.

manila, manilla [mə'nɪlə] n **(a)** (~ paper) Hartpapier nt. ~ envelopes braune Umschläge. **(b)** (~ hemp) Manilahanf m.

manioc ['mænɪɒk] n Maniok m.

manipulate [mə'nɪpjʊleɪt] vt **(a)** machine etc handhaben, bedienen; bones einrenken; (after fracture) zurechtdrücken. **(b)** public opinion, person, prices manipulieren; accounts, figures also frisieren (inf).

manipulation [məˌnɪpjʊ'leɪʃən] n Manipulation f.

manipulator [mə'nɪpjʊleɪtəʳ] n Manipulator, Manipulant m. he's a skilled ~ of public opinion er versteht es, die öffentliche Meinung geschickt zu manipulieren.

mankind [mæn'kaɪnd] n die Menschheit.

manlike ['mænlaɪk] adj menschlich; (like a male) männlich; robot menschenähnlich.

manliness ['mænlɪnɪs] n Männlichkeit f.

manly ['mænlɪ] adj (+er) männlich. to behave in a ~ fashion sich als Mann erweisen.

man-made ['mæn'meɪd] adj künstlich, Kunst-. ~ fibres Kunstfasern, synthetische Fasern pl.

manna ['mænə] n Manna nt.

manned [mænd] adj satellite etc bemannt.

mannequin ['mænɪkɪn] n (fashion) Mannequin nt; (Art) Modell nt; (dummy) Gliederpuppe f.

manner ['mænəʳ] n **(a)** (mode) Art, Weise, Art und Weise f. ~ of payment Zahlungsweise f; in or after this ~ auf diese Art und Weise; in or after the ~ of Petrarch im Stile Petrarcas; in the Spanish ~ im spanischen Stil; in like ~ (form) auf die gleiche Weise, ebenso; in such a ~ that ... so ..., daß ...; a painter in the grand ~ ein Maler der alten Schule; a ball in the grand ~ ein Ball alten Stils or im alten Stil; in a ~ of speaking sozusagen, gewissermaßen; in a ~ of speaking, the job's finished die Arbeit ist sozusagen or gewissermaßen fertig; it's just a ~ of speaking (of idiom) das ist nur so eine Redensart; I didn't mean to insult him, it was just a ~ of speaking das sollte keine Beleidigung sein, ich habe das nur so gesagt; as to the ~ born als sei er/sie dafür geschaffen; he writes dictionaries as to the ~ born er ist der geborene Lexikograph; a horseman as to the ~ born ein geborener Reiter.
(b) (behaviour etc) Art f. he has a very kind ~ er hat ein sehr freundliches Wesen; his ~ to his parents sein Verhalten gegenüber seinen Eltern, die Art, wie er mit seinen Eltern umgeht; I don't like his ~ ich mag seine Art nicht; there's something odd about his ~ er benimmt sich irgendwie komisch.

(c) ~s pl (good, bad etc) Manieren pl, Benehmen nt, Umgangsformen pl; road ~s Verhalten nt im Straßenverkehr; he hasn't got any road ~s er ist ein sehr unhöflicher or rücksichtsloser Fahrer; that's bad ~s das ist so etwas gebührt sich nicht, das ist unanständig; ~s! benimm dich!; it's bad ~s to ... es gehört sich nicht or es ist unanständig, zu ...; to have bad ~s schlechte Manieren haben; he has no ~s er hat keine Manieren, er kann sich nicht benehmen; have you forgotten your ~s? hast du denn deine Manieren gelassen?; now, don't forget your ~s! du weißt doch, was sich gehört!; to teach sb some ~s jdm Manieren beibringen.
(d) ~s pl (of society) Sitten (und Gebräuche) pl; a novel/ comedy of ~s ein Sittenroman m/eine Sittenkomödie.
(e) (class, type) Art f. all ~ of birds die verschiedensten Arten von Vögeln; we saw all ~ of interesting things wir sahen allerlei Interessantes or so manches Interessante; I've got all ~ of things to do yet ich habe noch allerlei or tausenderlei zu tun; by no ~ of means keineswegs, in keinster Weise (inf); what ~ of man is he? (Liter) was ist er für ein Mensch?

mannered ['mænəd] adj style manieriert; friendliness, subservience etc betont, prononciert (geh).

-mannered adj suf mit ... Manieren.

mannerism ['mænərɪzəm] n **(a)** (in behaviour, speech) Angewohnheit, Eigenheit f. **(b)** (of style) Manieriertheit f. his ~s seine Manierismen.

mannerliness ['mænəlɪnɪs] n Wohlerzogenheit f, gutes Benehmen.

mannerly ['mænəlɪ] adj wohlerzogen.

mannish ['mænɪʃ] adj woman männlich; clothes männlich wirkend.

manoeuvrability [məˌnuːvrə'bɪlɪtɪ] n Manövrierfähigkeit, Wendigkeit f.

manoeuvrable [mə'nuːvrəbl] adj manövrierfähig, wendig. easily ~ leicht zu manövrieren.

manoeuvre, (US) **maneuver** [mə'nuːvəʳ] **1** n **(a)** (Mil) Feldzug m. in a well-planned ~ durch einen geschickt geplanten Feldzug.
(b) (Mil) ~s Manöver nt or pl, Truppenübung f; the troops were out on ~s die Truppen befanden sich im Manöver.
(c) (clever plan) Manöver nt, Winkelzug, Schachzug m. rather an obvious ~ ein ziemlich auffälliges Manöver.
2 vt manövrieren. he ~d his troops out onto the plain er dirigierte or führte seine Truppen hinaus auf die Ebene; to ~ a gun into position ein Geschütz in Stellung bringen; to ~ sb into doing sth jdn dazu bringen, etw zu tun; he ~d his brother into a top job er manövrierte or lancierte seinen Bruder in eine Spitzenposition.
3 vi manövrieren; (Mil) ein Manöver durchführen. to ~ for position (lit, fig) sich in eine günstige Position manövrieren; the runners are still manoeuvring for position die Läufer sind immer noch dabei, sich in eine günstige Position zu manövrieren; room to ~ Spielraum m, Manövrierfähigkeit f.

man-of-war [ˌmænəv'wɔːʳ] n, pl **men-of-war** [ˌmenəv'wɔːʳ] (old) Portuguese.

manor ['mænəʳ] n Gut(shof m), Landgut nt. lord/lady of the ~ Gutsherr m/-herrin f; ~ house Herrenhaus nt.

manpower ['mæn,paʊəʳ] n Leistungs- or Arbeitspotential nt; (Mil) Stärke f. we haven't got the ~ wir haben dazu nicht genügend Personal or Arbeitskräfte pl.

manqué ['mɒŋkeɪ] adj pred (failed) gescheitert; (unfulfilled) verkannt. an artist ~ ein verkannter Künstler; he's a novelist ~ an ihm ist ein Schriftsteller verlorengegangen.

manse [mæns] n Pfarrhaus nt.

manservant ['mænsɜːvənt] n, pl **menservants** ['mensəːvənts] Diener m.

mansion ['mænʃən] n Villa f; (of ancient family) Herrenhaus nt.

man: ~-sized adj steak Riesen-; ~slaughter n Totschlag m.

manta (ray) ['mæntə(reɪ)] n Teufelsrochen, Manta m.

mantelpiece ['mæntlpiːs] n, **mantelshelf** ['mæntlʃelf] n, pl **-shelves** [-ʃelvz] (above fireplace) Kaminsims nt or m; (around fireplace) Kaminverkleidung or -einfassung f.

mantilla [mæn'tɪlə] n Mantille, Mantilla f.

mantis ['mæntɪs] n see **praying ~**.

mantle ['mæntl] **1** n **(a)** Umhang m; (fig) Deckmantel m. a ~ of snow eine Schneedecke. **(b)** (gas ~) Glühstrumpf m. **2** vt (liter) bedecken.

man: ~-to-~ adj, adv von Mann zu Mann; a ~-to-~ talk ein Gespräch von Mann zu Mann; ~trap n Fußangel f.

manual ['mænjʊəl] **1** adj manuell; control also von Hand; work also Hand-; labour körperlich. ~ labourer Schwerarbeiter m; ~ worker (manueller or Hand)arbeiter m; ~ skill Handwerk nt; he was trained in several ~ skills er hatte verschiedene Handwerksberufe pl erlernt; ~ gear change Schaltgetriebe nt, Schaltung f von Hand.
2 n **(a)** (book) Handbuch nt.
(b) (Mus) Manual nt.

manually ['mænjʊəlɪ] adv von Hand, manuell.

manufacture [ˌmænjʊ'fæktʃəʳ] **1** n (act) Herstellung f; (pl: products) Waren, Erzeugnisse pl. articles of foreign ~ ausländische Erzeugnisse pl.
2 vt **(a)** herstellen. ~d goods Fertigware f, Fertigerzeugnisse pl.
(b) (fig) excuse erfinden.
3 vi we started manufacturing ... wir begannen mit der Herstellung f.

manufacturer [ˌmænjʊ'fæktʃərəʳ] n Hersteller m. this country/firm has always been a big ~ of ... dieses Land/Unternehmen hat schon immer eine bedeutende Rolle bei der Herstellung von ... gespielt.

manufacturing [ˌmænjʊəlɪ] **1** adj techniques Herstellungs-; capacity Produktions-; industry verarbeitend.

2 *n* Erzeugung, Herstellung *f*.

manure [məˈnjʊəʳ] **1** *n* Dung, Mist *m*; (*esp artificial*) Dünger *m*. liquid ~ Jauche *f*; artificial ~ Kunstdünger *m*. **2** *vt* field düngen.

manuscript [ˈmænjʊskrɪpt] *n* Manuskript *nt*; (*ancient also*) Handschrift *f*. the novel is still in ~ der Roman ist noch in Manuskriptform; I read it first in ~ form ich habe es zuerst als Manuskript gelesen.

Manx [mæŋks] **1** *adj* der Insel Man. ~ cat Manx-Katze *f* (*stummelschwänzige Katze*). **2** *n* (*language*) Manx *nt*.

Manxman [ˈmæŋksmən] *n*, *pl* **-men** [-mən] Bewohner *m* der Insel Man, Manx *m*.

many [ˈmenɪ] **1** *adj* viele. ~ people viele (Menschen *or* Leute); there were as ~ as 20 es waren sogar 20 da; fifty went to France and as ~ to Germany fünfzig gingen nach Frankreich und ebenso viele nach Deutschland; as ~ again noch einmal so viele; so ~ cowards so viele Feiglinge *or* so mancher Feigling; there's one too ~ einer ist zuviel; he's had one too ~ er hat einen zuviel *or* einen über den Durst getrunken; they were too ~ for us sie waren zu viele *or* zu zahlreich für uns; he made one mistake too ~ er hat einen Fehler zuviel gemacht; a good soldier so mancher gute Soldat; ~ a time so manches Mal; she waited ~ a long year (*liter*) sie wartete gar manches lange Jahr (*liter*); ~'s the time I've heard that old story ich habe diese alte Geschichte so manches Mal gehört.

2 *n* eine ganze Menge *or* Reihe *or* Anzahl (von). a good/great ~ houses eine (ganze) Reihe *or* Anzahl Häuser; the ~ die (große) Masse.

many: ~-coloured *adj* bunt, vielfarbig; ~-sided *adj* vielseitig; figure also vieleckig; it's a ~-sided problem das Problem hat sehr viele verschiedene Aspekte.

Maoist [ˈmaʊɪst] *n* Maoist(in *f*) *m*.

Maori [ˈmaʊrɪ] **1** *adj* Maori-. **2** *n* (a) Maori *mf*. (b) (*language*) Maori *nt*.

map [mæp] **1** *n* (Land)karte *f*; (*of streets, town*) Stadtplan *m*; (*showing specific item*) Karte *f*. a ~ of the stars/rivers eine Stern-/Flußkarte; is it on the ~? ist das auf der Karte (eingezeichnet)?; this will put Cheam on the ~ (*fig*) das wird Cheam zu einem Namen verhelfen; it's right off the ~ (*fig*) das liegt (ja) am Ende der Welt *or* hinter dem Mond (*inf*); entire cities were wiped off the ~ ganze Städte wurden ausradiert.

2 *vt* (*measure*) vermessen; (*make a map of*) eine Karte anfertigen von. the history of her suffering was ~ped on her face ihr Gesicht war von Leid gezeichnet.

♦ **map out** *vt sep* (a) (*lit*) *see* **map 2**. (b) (*fig: plan*) entwerfen. the essay is well ~ped ~ der Aufsatz ist gut angelegt; our holiday schedule was all ~ped ~ in advance der Zeitplan für unsere Ferien war schon im voraus genau festgelegt; he has ~ped ~ what he will do er hat sich (*dat*) einen Plan zurechtgelegt, er hat bereits geplant, was er tun wird.

maple [ˈmeɪpl] *n* (*wood, tree*) Ahorn *m*.

maple: ~ leaf *n* Ahornblatt *nt*; ~ sugar *n* Ahornzucker *m*; ~ syrup *n* Ahornsirup *m*.

map: ~maker *n* Kartograph *m*; ~making *n* Kartographie *f*; ~reader *n* Kartenleser(in *f*) *m*; ~reading *n* Kartenlesen *nt*.

Mar *abbr of* **March**.

mar [mɑːʳ] *vt* verderben; *happiness* trüben; *beauty* mindern. he was determined to let nothing ~ his honeymoon er war fest entschlossen, sich (*dat*) seine Flitterwochen durch nichts verderben zu lassen; not a cloud to ~ the sky kein Wölkchen trübte den Himmel; his essay was ~red by careless mistakes durch seine Flüchtigkeitsfehler verdarb er (sich) den ganzen Aufsatz; *see* **make**.

marabou [ˈmærəbuː] *n* Marabu *m*.

maraca [məˈrækə] *n* Rassel, Maracá *f*.

maraschino [ˌmærəˈskiːnəʊ] *n* (*drink*) Maraschino *m*; (~ cherry) Maraschinokirsche *f*.

marathon [ˈmærəθən] **1** *n* (a) (*lit*) Marathon(lauf) *m*. (b) (*fig*) Marathon *nt*. this film is a real ~ das ist wirklich ein Marathonfilm *m*. **2** *adj* speech, film, meeting Marathon-.

maraud [məˈrɔːd] *vt* plündern. they went ~ing about the countryside sie zogen plündernd durch die Lande.

marauder [məˈrɔːdəʳ] *n* Plünderer *m*; (*animal*) Räuber *m*.

marauding [məˈrɔːdɪŋ] *adj* plündernd. the deer fled from the ~ wolf das Reh floh vor dem beutesuchenden Wolf.

marble [ˈmɑːbl] **1** *n* (a) Marmor *m*. (b) (*work in* ~) Marmorplastik *f*. (c) (*glass ball*) Murmel *f*, Klicker *m* (*inf*). he hasn't got all his ~s (*inf*) er hat nicht mehr alle Tassen im Schrank (*inf*). **2** *adj* Marmor-.

marbled [ˈmɑːbld] *adj* surface, pages marmoriert.

March [mɑːtʃ] *n* März *m*; *see also* September.

march¹ [mɑːtʃ] **1** *n* (a) (Mil, Mus) Marsch *m*; (*demonstration*) Demonstration *f*; (*fig: long walk*) Weg *m*. to move at a good stiff ~ mit strammen Schritten *or* stramm marschieren; we had been five days on the ~ wir waren fünf Tage lang marschiert; it's two days' ~ es ist ein Zwei-Tage-Marsch; he went for a good ~ across the moors er ist durchs Moorland marschiert. (b) (*of time, history, events*) Lauf *m*. (c) to steal a ~ on sb jdm zuvorkommen.

2 *vt* soldiers marschieren lassen; *distance* marschieren. to ~ sb off jdn abführen.

3 *vi* marschieren. forward ~! vorwärts(, marsch)!; quick ~! im Laufschritt, marsch!; to ~ in einmarschieren; she just ~ed into the room sie marschierte einfach (ins Zimmer) hinein; time ~es on die Zeit bleibt nicht stehen; to ~ out abmarschieren, ausrücken; to ~ past sb an jdm vorbeimarschieren; she ~ed straight up to him sie marschierte schnurstracks auf ihn zu.

march² *n* (Hist) Grenzmark *f*. the Welsh ~es das Grenzland zwischen England und Wales.

marcher [ˈmɑːtʃəʳ] *n* (*in demo*) Demonstrant(in *f*) *m*.

marching [ˈmɑːtʃɪŋ]: ~ orders *npl* (Mil) Marschbefehl *m*; (*inf*) Entlassung *f*; the new manager got his ~ orders der neue Manager ist gegangen worden (*inf*); she gave him his ~ orders sie hat ihm den Laufpaß gegeben; ~ song *n* Marschlied *nt*.

marchioness [ˈmɑːʃənɪs] *n* Marquise *f*.

march past *n* Vorbeimarsch, Aufmarsch *m*, Defilee *nt*.

Mardi gras [ˌmɑːdɪˈgrɑː] *n* Karneval *m*.

mare [mɛəʳ] *n* (*horse*) Stute *f*; (*donkey*) Eselin *f*.

mare's nest [ˈmɛəznest] *n* Windei *nt*, Reinfall *m*.

Margaret [ˈmɑːgərɪt] *n* Margarete *f*.

margarine [ˌmɑːdʒəˈriːn], **marge** [mɑːdʒ] (*inf*) *n* Margarine *f*.

margin [ˈmɑːdʒɪn] *n* (a) (*on page*) Rand *m*. a note (written) in the ~ eine Randbemerkung, eine Bemerkung am Rand. (b) (*extra amount*) Spielraum *m*. ~ of error Fehlerspielraum *m*; to allow for a ~ of error etwaige Fehler mit einkalkulieren; he left a safety ~ of one hour sicherheitshalber kalkulierte er einen Spielraum von einer Stunde ein; by a narrow ~ knapp; it's within the safety ~ das ist noch sicher. (c) (*Comm: also profit* ~) Gewinnspanne, Verdienstspanne *f*. (d) (*liter: edge*) Rand, Saum (*liter*) *m*. the grassy ~ of the lake das grüne Seeufer.

marginal [ˈmɑːdʒɪnl] *adj* (a) note Rand-. (b) improvement, difference geringfügig, unwesentlich; constituency unentschieden. this is a ~ constituency for the Tories die Tories haben in diesem Wahlkreis nur eine knappe Mehrheit.

marginally [ˈmɑːdʒɪnəlɪ] *adv* geringfügig, unwesentlich, nur wenig. is that better? — is that besser? — etwas, ein wenig; but only just ~ nur ganz knapp; it's only ~ useful es hat nur sehr begrenzte Anwendungsmöglichkeiten *pl*.

margin: ~ release *n* Randlöser *m*; ~ stop *n* Randsteller *m*.

marguerite [ˌmɑːgəˈriːt] *n* Margerite *f*.

marigold [ˈmærɪgəʊld] *n* (African *or* French ~) Tagetes, Studentenblume *f*; (*common or pot* ~) Ringelblume *f*.

marihuana, marijuana [ˌmærɪˈhwɑːnə] *n* Marihuana *nt*.

marina [məˈriːnə] *n* Yacht- *or* Jachthafen *m*.

marinade [ˌmærɪˈneɪd] *n* Marinade *f*.

marinate [ˈmærɪneɪt] *vt* marinieren.

marine [məˈriːn] **1** *adj* Meeres-, See-. ~ insurance Seeversicherung *f*; ~ life Meeresfauna und -flora *f*. **2** *n* (a) (*fleet*) Marine *f*. merchant ~ Handelsmarine *f*. (b) (*person*) Marineinfanterist *m*. the ~s die Marineinfanterie, die Marinetruppen *pl*; tell that to the ~s! (*inf*) das kannst du mir nicht weismachen, das kannst du deiner Großmutter erzählen! (*inf*).

mariner [ˈmærɪnəʳ] *n* Seefahrer, Seemann *m*.

marionette [ˌmærɪəˈnet] *n* Marionette *f*.

marital [ˈmærɪtl] *adj* ehelich. ~ status Familienstand *m*; ~ vows Ehegelübde *nt*; ~ bliss Eheglück *nt*; they lived together in ~ bliss sie genossen ein glückliches Eheleben.

maritime [ˈmærɪtaɪm] *adj* warfare, law See-. ~ regions Küstenregionen *pl*.

marjoram [ˈmɑːdʒərəm] *n* Majoran *m*.

Mark [mɑːk] *n* Markus *m*. ~ Antony Mark Anton.

mark¹ [mɑːk] *n* (Fin) Mark *f*.

mark² **1** *n* (a) (*stain, spot etc*) Fleck *m*; (*scratch*) Kratzer *m*, Schramme *f*. to make a ~ on sth einen Fleck auf etw (*acc*) machen/etw beschädigen; dirty ~s Schmutzflecken *pl*; with not a ~ on it in makellosem Zustand; will the operation leave a ~? wird die Operation Spuren *or* Narben hinterlassen?; the ~s of violence die Spuren der Gewalt; he left the ring without a ~ on him/his body er verließ den Ring, ohne auch nur eine Schramme abbekommen zu haben; the corpse didn't have a ~ on it die Leiche wies keine Verletzungen auf. (b) (~ing) (*on animal*) Fleck *m*; (*on person*) Mal *nt*; (*on plane, football pitch etc*) Markierung *f*; (*sign: on monument etc*) Zeichen *nt*. (c) (*in exam*) Note *f*. high *or* good ~s gute Noten *pl*; the ~s are out of 100 insgesamt kann/konnte man 100 Punkte erreichen; you get no ~s at all as a cook (*fig*) in puncto Kochen bist du ja nicht gerade eine Eins (*inf*); there are no ~s for guessing (*fig*) das ist ja wohl nicht schwer zu erraten; he gets full ~s for punctuality (*fig*) in Pünktlichkeit verdient er eine Eins. (d) (*sign, indication*) Zeichen *nt*. he had the ~s of old age er war vom Alter gezeichnet; it bears the ~s of genius das trägt geniale Züge; it's the ~ of a gentleman daran erkennt man den Gentleman. (e) (*instead of signature*) to make one's ~ drei Kreuze (als Unterschrift) machen. (f) (*level*) expenses have reached the £100 ~ die Ausgaben haben die 100-Pfund-Grenze erreicht; the temperature reached the 35° ~ die Temperatur stieg bis auf 35° an. (g) Cooper M~ II Cooper, II; the new secretary, a sort of Miss Jones M~ II die neue Sekretärin, eine zweite Ausführung von Fräulein Jones. (h) (*phrases*) to be quick off the ~ (Sport) einen guten Start haben; (*fig*) blitzschnell handeln *or* reagieren; you were quick off the ~ du warst aber fix!; he was quickest off the ~ er war der Schnellste; to be slow off the ~ (Sport) einen schlechten Start haben; (*fig*) nicht schnell genug schalten *or* reagieren; (*as characteristic*) eine lange Leitung haben (*inf*); to be up to the ~ den Anforderungen entsprechen; (*work also*) über dem Strich sein; his work is not up to the ~ seine Arbeit ist unter dem Strich; I'm not feeling quite up to the ~ ich bin *or* fühle mich nicht ganz auf dem Posten; to leave one's ~ (on sth) einer Sache (*dat*) seinen Stempel aufdrücken; to make one's ~ sich (*dat*) einen Namen machen; on your ~s! auf die Plätze!; to be wide of the ~ (*shooting*) danebentreffen, danebenschießen; (*fig: in guessing, calculating*) danebentippen, sich verhauen (*inf*); your calculations were wide of the ~ mit deiner Kalkulation

hast du dich ganz schön verhauen (inf); **to hit the ~** (lit, fig) ins Schwarze treffen.
  (i) (Rugby) Freifang m. "**~!**" „Marke!"
  2 vt **(a)** (adversely) beschädigen; (stain) schmutzig machen, Flecken machen auf (+acc); (scratch) zerkratzen. **the other boxer was not ~ed at all** der andere Boxer hatte nicht eine Schramme or überhaupt nichts abbekommen; **her face was ~ed for life** sie hat bleibende Narben im Gesicht zurückbehalten; **the experience ~ed him for life** das Erlebnis hat ihn für sein Leben gezeichnet.
  (b) (for recognition, identity) markieren, bezeichnen; (label) beschriften; (price) auszeichnen; playing cards zinken. **~ed with the name and age of the exhibitor** mit Namen und Alter des Ausstellers versehen; **the bottle was ~ed "poison"** die Flasche trug die Aufschrift „Gift"; **the chair is ~ed at £2** der Stuhl ist mit £ 2 ausgezeichnet; **the picture/cage isn't ~ed** das Bild ist ohne Angaben/der Käfig hat keine Aufschrift; **~ where you have stopped in your reading** machen Sie sich (dat) ein Zeichen, bis wohin Sie gelesen haben; **I can't stand people who ~ library books** ich kann es nicht ausstehen, wenn Leute in Bibliotheksbücher hineinschreiben; **to ~ sth with an asterisk** etw mit einem Sternchen versehen; **X ~s the spot** X markiert or bezeichnet die Stelle; **the teacher ~ed him absent** der Lehrer trug ihn als fehlend ein; **it's not ~ed on the map** es ist nicht auf der Karte eingezeichnet; **it's ~ed with a blue dot** es ist mit einem blauen Punkt gekennzeichnet; **~ your football boots so that they don't get mixed up** zeichnet eure Fußballstiefel, damit sie nicht verwechselt werden; **he ~ed his own books with a secret sign** er kennzeichnete seine eigenen Bücher mit einem Geheimzeichen.
  (c) (characterize) kennzeichnen. **a decade ~ed by violence** ein Jahrzehnt, das im Zeichen der Gewalt stand; **the new bill ~s a change of policy** das neue Gesetz deutet auf einen politischen Kurswechsel hin; **it ~ed the end of an era** damit ging eine Ära zu Ende; **it ~s him as a future star** daran zeigt sich, daß er eine große Karriere vor sich (dat) hat; **a month ~ed by inactivity** ein Monat, der sich durch Untätigkeit auszeichnete.
  (d) (usu pass) zeichnen. **~ed with grief** von Schmerz gezeichnet; **a beautifully ~ed bird** ein schön gezeichneter Vogel; **a bird ~ed with red** ein Vogel mit einer roten Zeichnung.
  (e) exam, paper korrigieren (und benoten). **to ~ a paper** A eine Arbeit mit (einer) Eins benoten; **to ~ a candidate** einem Kandidaten eine Note geben; **the candidate was ~ed ...** der Kandidate erhielt die Note ...; **we ~ed him A** wir haben ihm eine Eins gegeben; **to ~ sth wrong** etw anstreichen.
  (f) (heed) hören auf (+acc). **~ my words** eins kann ich dir sagen; (threatening, warning also) lassen Sie sich das gesagt sein!; **~ you, he may have been right** er könnte gar nicht so unrecht gehabt haben; **~ you, I didn't believe him** ich habe ihm natürlich nicht geglaubt.
  (g) (old: notice) bemerken. **did you ~ where it fell?** hast du dir gemerkt, wo es hingefallen ist?
  (h) (Sport) player, opponent decken.
  (i) **to ~ time** (Mil, fig) auf der Stelle treten.
  3 vi **(a)** (get dirty) schmutzen, schmutzig werden; (scratch) Kratzer bekommen.
  (b) **her skin ~s easily** sie bekommt leicht blaue Flecken.
  (c) (Sport) decken.

♦ **mark down** vt sep **(a)** (note down) (sich dat) notieren. **(b)** prices herab- or heruntersetzen.

♦ **mark off** vt sep kennzeichnen; boundary markieren; football pitch etc abgrenzen; danger area etc absperren. **these characteristics ~ him ~ from the others** durch diese Eigenschaften unterscheidet er sich von den anderen.

♦ **mark out** vt sep **(a)** tennis court etc abstecken.
  (b) (note) bestimmen (for für). **he's been ~ed ~ for promotion** er ist zur Beförderung vorgesehen; **the area has been ~ed ~ for special government grants** für das Gebiet sind besondere staatliche Zuschüsse vorgesehen.
  (c) (identify) his speeches have ~ed him **~ as a communist** aus seinen Reden geht hervor or kann man schließen, daß er Kommunist ist; **what ~s this example ~ as being different?** worin unterscheidet sich dieses Beispiel?

♦ **mark up** vt sep **(a)** (write up) notieren (on auf +dat). **(b)** price heraufsetzen, erhöhen.

marked [mɑːkt] adj **(a)** contrast merklich, deutlich; accent stark, deutlich; improvement spürbar, merklich. **it is becoming more ~** es wird immer deutlicher or tritt immer deutlicher zutage. **(b)** **he's a ~ man** er steht auf der schwarzen Liste.

markedly [ˈmɑːkɪdlɪ] adv merklich. **it is ~ better** es ist wesentlich or bedeutend besser; **not ~ so** nicht so, daß es auffallen würde; **they are not ~ different** es besteht kein besonderer or großer Unterschied zwischen ihnen.

marker [ˈmɑːkəʳ] n **(a)** Marke f; (to turn at) Wendemarke f, Wendepunkt m; (on road) Schild nt, Wegweiser m; (in book) Lesezeichen nt. **(b)** (for exams) Korrektor(in f) m; (scorekeeper in games) Punktezähler m. **will you be the ~?** schreibst du (die Punkte) auf? **(c)** (Ftbl) Beschatter m.

market [ˈmɑːkɪt] **1** n **(a)** Markt m. **when is the next ~?** wann ist wieder Markt(tag)?; **he took his sheep to ~** er brachte seine Schafe zum Markt; **at the ~** auf dem Markt; **to go to ~** auf den/zum Markt gehen.
  (b) (trade) Markt m. **world ~** Weltmarkt m; **open ~** offener Markt; **to be in the ~ for sth** an etw (dat) interessiert sein; **to be on the ~** auf dem Markt sein; **to come on(to) the ~** auf den Markt kommen; **to put on the ~** auf den Markt bringen; house zum Verkauf anbieten.
  (c) (area, demand) (Absatz)markt m; (area also) Absatzgebiet nt. **to create a ~** Nachfrage erzeugen; **to find a ready ~** guten Absatz finden.

(d) (stock-~) Börse f. **to play the ~** (an der Börse) spekulieren.
  2 vt vertreiben. **to ~ a (new) product** ein (neues) Produkt auf den Markt bringen; **it's a nice idea, but we can't ~** it das ist eine gute Idee, sie läßt sich nur nicht verkaufen or vermarkten; **the reason it didn't sell was simply that it wasn't properly ~ed** es fand wegen unzureichenden Marketings keinen Absatz.
  3 vi sich verkaufen, Absatz finden, gehen (inf).

marketable [ˈmɑːkɪtəbl] adj absetzbar, marktfähig or gängig.

market day n Markttag m.

marketeer [ˌmɑːkəˈtɪəʳ] n (Pol) (Common) M~ Anhänger or Befürworter m der EWG; **black ~** Schwarzhändler m.

market: **~ garden** n Gemüseanbaubetrieb m, Gärtnerei f; **~ gardener** n Gärtner(in f) m; **~ gardening** n (gewerbsmäßiger) Anbau von Gemüse.

marketing [ˈmɑːkɪtɪŋ] n Marketing nt.

market: **~place** n Marktplatz m; (world of trade) Markt m; **in/on the ~place** auf dem Markt(platz); **~ price** n Marktpreis m; **~ research** n Marktforschung f; **~ town** n Marktstädtchen nt; **~ value** n Marktwert m.

marking [ˈmɑːkɪŋ] n **(a)** Markierung f; (on aeroplane also) Kennzeichen nt; (on animal) Zeichnung f. **~ ink** Wäschetinte f. **(b)** (of exams) (correcting) Korrektur f; (grading) Benotung f. **(c)** (Sport) Decken nt, Deckung f.

marksman [ˈmɑːksmən] n, pl **-men** [-mən] Schütze m; (police etc) Scharfschütze m.

marksmanship [ˈmɑːksmənʃɪp] n Treffsicherheit f.

mark-up [ˈmɑːkʌp] n Handelsspanne f; (amount added) Preiserhöhung f or -aufschlag m. **~ price** Verkaufs- or Ladenpreis m.

marl [mɑːl] n Mergel m.

marlin [ˈmɑːlɪn] n Fächerfisch, Marlin m.

marlinspike [ˈmɑːlɪnspaɪk] n Marlspieker m, Spließeisen nt.

marmalade [ˈmɑːməleɪd] n Marmelade f aus Zitrusfrüchten. **(orange) ~** Orangenmarmelade f.

marmoreal [mɑːˈmɔːrɪəl] adj marmorn, aus Marmor; (resembling marble) marmorartig.

marmoset [ˈmɑːməʊzet] n Krallenaffe m, Pinseläffchen nt.

marmot [ˈmɑːmət] n Murmeltier nt.

maroon[1] [məˈruːn] **1** adj kastanienbraun, rötlichbraun. **2** n (colour) Kastanienbraun nt; (firework) Leuchtkugel f.

maroon[2] vt aussetzen. **~ed** von der Außenwelt abgeschnitten; **~ed by floods** vom Hochwasser eingeschlossen.

marquee [mɑːˈkiː] n Festzelt nt.

marquess [ˈmɑːkwɪs] n Marquis m.

marquetry [ˈmɑːkɪtrɪ] n Marketerie, Einlegearbeit f.

marquis [ˈmɑːkwɪs] n see **marquess**.

marram grass [ˈmærəmgrɑːs] n Strandhafer m, Dünengras nt.

marriage [ˈmærɪdʒ] n **(a)** (state) die Ehe; (wedding) Hochzeit, Heirat f; (~ ceremony) Trauung f. **civil ~** Zivilehe f/standesamtliche Trauung; **~ of convenience** Vernunftehe f; **relations by ~** angeheiratete Verwandte; **to be related by ~** (in-laws) miteinander verschwägert sein; (others) miteinander verwandt sein; **to give sb in ~ to sb** jdn jdm zur Frau geben; **to give sb in ~** jdn verheiraten; **an offer of ~** ein Heiratsantrag m.
  (b) (fig) Verbindung f. **a ~ of two minds** eine geistige Ehe.

marriageable [ˈmærɪdʒəbl] adj heiratsfähig. **of ~ age** im heiratsfähigen Alter.

marriage: **~-bed** n Ehebett nt; **~ ceremony** n Trauzeremonie f; **~ lines** npl (inf) Trauschein m; **~ portion** n (old) Mitgift f; **~ settlement** n Ehevertrag m; **~ vow** n Ehegelübde nt.

married [ˈmærɪd] adj life, state Ehe-; man, woman verheiratet. **~ couple** Ehepaar nt; **~ quarters** Unterkünfte für Eheleute; **he/she is a ~ man/woman** er/sie ist verheiratet.

marrow [ˈmærəʊ] n **(a)** (Anat) (Knochen)mark nt. **~bone** Markknochen m; **he's a Scot to the ~** er ist durch und durch Schotte; **to be frozen to the ~** völlig durchgefroren sein. **(b)** (fig: of statement etc) Kern m, Wesentliches nt. **(c)** (Bot) (also vegetable ~) Gartenkürbis m.

marry [ˈmærɪ] **1** vt **(a)** heiraten. **to ~ money** reich heiraten; **will you ~ me?** willst du mich heiraten?
  (b) (priest) trauen.
  (c) (father) verheiraten. **he married all his daughters into very rich families** er hat zugesehen, daß alle seine Töchter in reiche Familien einheirateten.
  2 vi (also get married) heiraten, sich verheiraten; (of couple) heiraten, sich vermählen (geh). **to ~ into a rich family** in eine reiche Familie einheiraten; **to ~ into money** reich heiraten; **he married into a small fortune** durch die Heirat ist er an ein kleines Vermögen gekommen; **he's not the ~ing kind** er ist nicht der Typ, der heiratet; **~ in haste, repent at leisure** (prov) Heiraten in Eile bereut man in Weile (prov).
  (b) (fig: of two pieces of wood etc) ineinanderpassen.

♦ **marry off** vt sep an den Mann/die Frau bringen (inf); girl also unter die Haube bringen (inf). **he has married ~ his daughter to a rich young lawyer** er hat dafür gesorgt, daß seine Tochter einen reichen jungen Anwalt heiratet.

Mars [mɑːz] n Mars m.

Marseillaise [ˌmɑːseɪˈleɪz] n: **the ~** die Marseillaise.

Marseilles [mɑːˈseɪlz] n Marseille nt.

marsh [mɑːʃ] n Sumpf m.

marshal [ˈmɑːʃəl] **1** n (Mil, of royal household) Marschall m; (at sports meeting etc) Platzwärter m; (at demo etc) Ordner m; (US) Bezirkspolizeichef m. **2** vt facts, arguments ordnen; soldiers antreten lassen; (lead) geleiten, führen.

marshalling yard [ˈmɑːʃəlɪŋˈjɑːd] n Rangier- or Verschiebebahnhof m.

marsh: **~ gas** n Methangas, Sumpf- or Grubengas nt; **~land** n Marschland nt; **~mallow** n (sweet) Marshmallow m; (Bot) Eibisch m; **~ marigold** n Sumpfdotterblume f.

marshy ['mɑːʃɪ] *adj* (+*er*) sumpfig. **a ~ district** ein Sumpfgebiet *nt*.

marsupial [mɑːˈsuːpɪəl] **1** *adj* **~ animal** Beuteltier *nt*. **2** *n* Beuteltier *nt*.

mart [mɑːt] *n* (*old*) Markt *m*. **property ~** (*in newspaper*) Immobilien(markt *m*) *pl*.

marten ['mɑːtɪn] *n* Marder *m*.

martial ['mɑːʃəl] *adj music* kriegerisch, Kampf-; *bearing* stramm, soldatisch. **the ~ arts** die Kampfkunst; **the ~ art of judo** der Kampfsport Judo; **~ law** Kriegsrecht *nt*; **the state was put under ~ law** über den Staat wurde (das) Kriegsrecht verhängt.

Martian ['mɑːʃɪən] **1** *adj atmosphere, exploration* des Mars; *invaders* vom Mars. **2** *n* Marsbewohner(in *f*), Marsmensch *m*.

martin ['mɑːtɪn] *n* Schwalbe *f*.

martinet [ˌmɑːtɪ'net] *n* (*stronger*) Zuchtmeister. **he's a real ~** er führt ein strenges Regiment.

martini [mɑːˈtiːnɪ] *n* Martini *m*.

Martinique [ˌmɑːtɪˈniːk] *n* Martinique *nt*.

Martinmas ['mɑːtɪnməs] *n* Martinstag *m*, Martini *nt*.

martyr ['mɑːtə'] **1** *n* Märtyrer(in *f*) *m*. **he was a ~ to the cause of civil rights** er wurde zum Märtyrer für die Sache der Bürgerrechtsbewegung; **to be a ~ to arthritis** entsetzlich unter Arthritis zu leiden haben; **there's no need to make a ~ of yourself** (*inf*) du brauchst dich nicht zu opfern (*inf*), du brauchst hier nicht den Märtyrer zu spielen (*inf*).

2 *vt* martern, (zu Tode) quälen. **thousands of Christians were ~ed** tausende von Christen starben den Märtyrertod.

martyrdom ['mɑːtədəm] *n* (*suffering*) Martyrium *nt*; (*death*) Märtyrertod *m*.

marvel ['mɑːvəl] **1** *n* Wunder *nt*. **the ~s of modern science** die Wunder der modernen Wissenschaft; **this medicine is a ~** diese Medizin wirkt Wunder; **if he ever gets there it will be a ~** (*inf*) wenn er jemals dort ankommt, ist das ein Wunder; **it's a ~ to me that he escaped unhurt** es kommt mir wie ein Wunder vor, daß er ohne Verletzungen davonkam; **it's a ~ how he does it** (*inf*) es ist mir einfach unerklärlich *or* schleierhaft, wie er das macht; **her desk is a ~ of tidiness** ihr Schreibtisch ist ein Muster an Ordnung; **you're a ~!** (*inf*) du bist ein Engel!; (*clever*) du bist ein Genie!

2 *vi* staunen (*at* über +*acc*). **to ~ at a sight** einen Anblick bestaunen; **they ~led at her beauty** (*liter*) sie bewunderten ihre Schönheit; **I ~ that she should stay** es verwundert mich, daß sie bleibt.

marvellous, (*US*) **marvelous** ['mɑːvələs] *adj* wunderbar, phantastisch, fabelhaft. **isn't it ~?** ist das nicht herrlich?; (*iro*) gut, nicht! (*iro*), das ist der Abschuß! (*inf*).

marvellously, (*US*) **marvelously** ['mɑːvələslɪ] *adv* (*with adj*) herrlich; (*with vb*) großartig, fabelhaft.

Marxian ['mɑːksɪən] *adj* Marxisch.

Marxism ['mɑːksɪzəm] *n* der Marxismus.

Marxist ['mɑːksɪst] **1** *adj* marxistisch. **2** *n* Marxist(in *f*) *m*.

Mary ['mɛərɪ] *n* Maria *f*.

marzipan [ˌmɑːzɪ'pæn] *n* Marzipan *nt or m*.

mascara [mæˈskɑːrə] **1** *n* Wimperntusche, Maskara *f*. **2** *vt* tuschen.

mascot ['mæskət] *n* Maskottchen *nt*.

masculine ['mæskjʊlɪn] **1** *adj* männlich; *woman* maskulin. **2** *n* (*Gram*) Maskulinum *nt*.

masculinity [ˌmæskjuˈlɪnɪtɪ] *n* Männlichkeit *f*.

mash [mæʃ] **1** *n* Brei *m*; (*for animals*) Futterbrei *m*, Schlempe *f*; (*potatoes*) Püree *nt*; (*in brewing*) Maische *f*. **2** *vt* zerstampfen.

mashed [mæʃt] *adj* **~ potatoes** Kartoffelbrei *m or* -püree *nt*.

masher ['mæʃə'] *n* Stampfer *m*; (*for potatoes*) Kartoffelstampfer *m*.

mask [mɑːsk] **1** *n* (*lit, fig*) Maske *f*. **the ~ slipped** (*fig*) er/sie *etc* ließ die Maske fallen; **surgeon's ~** Mundschutz *m*. **2** *vt* maskieren; (*clouds, trees etc*) verdecken; *feelings* verbergen; *intentions* maskieren.

masked [mɑːskt] *adj* maskiert. **~ ball** Maskenball *m*.

masochism ['mæsəʊkɪzəm] *n* Masochismus *m*.

masochist ['mæsəʊkɪst] *n* Masochist(in *f*) *m*.

masochistic [ˌmæsəʊˈkɪstɪk] *adj* masochistisch.

mason ['meɪsn] *n* (a) (*builder*) Steinmetz *m*; (*in quarry*) Steinhauer *m*; *see* **monumental**. (b) (*free~*) Freimaurer *m*.

masonic [məˈsɒnɪk] *adj* Freimaurer-. **~ lodge** Freimaurerloge *f*.

masonry ['meɪsnrɪ] *n* (a) (*stonework*) Mauerwerk *nt*. (b) (*free~*) Freimaurerei *f*, Freimaurertum *nt*.

masque [mɑːsk] *n* Maskenspiel *nt*.

masquerade [ˌmæskə'reɪd] **1** *n* Maskerade *f*. **that's just a ~,** **she's not really like that at all** (*fig*) das ist alles nur Theater, in Wirklichkeit ist sie gar nicht so.

2 *vi* **to ~ as** ... sich verkleiden als ...; (*fig*) sich ausgeben als ..., vorgeben, ... zu sein; **this cheap rubbish masquerading as literature** dieser Schund, der als Literatur ausgegeben wird.

mass[1] [mæs] *n* (*Eccl*) Messe *f*. **high ~** Hochamt *nt*; **to go to ~** zur Messe gehen; **to hear ~** die Messe feiern; **to say ~** die *or* eine Messe lesen.

mass[2] **1** *n* (a) (*general, Phys*) Masse *f*; (*of people*) Menge *f*. **a ~ of snow/rubble** eine Schneemasse/ein Schutthaufen *m*; **the ~ of rubble** der Haufen Schutt; **a ~ of cold air** eine kalte Luftmasse; **a ~ of red hair** ein Wust roter Haare; **a ~ of flames** ein einziges Flammenmeer; **this confused ~ of thoughts** dieser wirre Gedankenwust; **the essay is one great ~ of spelling mistakes** der Aufsatz wimmelt nur so von Schreibfehlern; **he's a ~ of bruises** er ist voller blauer Flecken; **the garden is a ~ of yellow/colour** der Garten ist ein Meer *nt* von Gelb/ein Farbenmeer *nt*; **the ~es** die Masse(n *pl*); **the great ~ of the population** die (breite) Masse der Bevölkerung; **the nation in the ~** die breite(n) Volksmasse(n); **people, in the ~, prefer** ...

die breite Masse (der Menschen) zieht es vor, ...

(b) (*bulk*) **the great ~ of the mountains** das riesige Bergmassiv; **the huge ~ of the ship loomed up out of the night** die riesige Form des Schiffes tauchte aus der Nacht auf.

(c) (*inf*) **~es** massenhaft, eine Masse (*inf*); **he has ~es of money/time** er hat massenhaft *or* massig (*inf*) *or* eine Masse (*inf*) Geld/Zeit; **the factory is producing ~es of cars** die Fabrik produziert Unmengen von Autos; **I've got ~es of things to do** ich habe noch massig (*inf*) zu tun.

2 *vt troops* massieren, zusammenziehen. **the ~ed bands of the Royal Navy** die vereinigten Militärkapellen der königlichen Marine.

3 *vi* (*Mil*) sich massieren; (*Red Indians etc*) sich versammeln; (*clouds*) sich (zusammen)ballen. **they're ~ing for an attack** sie sammeln sich zum Angriff.

mass *in cpds* Massen-.

massacre ['mæsəkə'] **1** *n* Massaker *nt*. **2** *vt* niedermetzeln, massakrieren. **last Saturday they ~d us 6-0** (*inf*) letzten Samstag haben sie uns mit 6:0 fertiggemacht (*inf*).

massage ['mæsɑːʒ] **1** *n* Massage *f*. **~ parlour** Massagesalon *m*. **2** *vt* massieren.

masseur [mæˈsɜː'] *n* Masseur *m*.

masseuse [mæ'sɜːz] *n* Masseuse *f*.

massif [mæ'siːf] *n* (*Geog*) (Gebirgs)massiv *nt*.

massive ['mæsɪv] *adj* riesig, enorm; *structure, wall* massiv, wuchtig; *forehead* breit, wuchtig; *boxer* wuchtig, massig; *task* gewaltig; *support, heart attack* massiv. **these ~ ponderous chords** diese wuchtigen, schweren Klänge; **the ship was designed on a ~ scale** das Schiff hatte riesenhafte Ausmaße; **the symphony is conceived on a ~ scale** die Symphonie ist ganz groß angelegt; **space research is planned and financed on a ~ scale** Raumforschung wird in ganz großem Rahmen geplant und finanziert.

massively ['mæsɪvlɪ] *adv* wuchtig. **a ~ built man** ein Schrank von einem Mann; **~ in debt** enorm verschuldet.

massiveness ['mæsɪvnɪs] *n* (*of expanse of land, plane, ship, hotel etc*) riesige *or* gewaltige Ausmaße *pl*; (*of fortune, expenditure, orchestra*) enorme Größe; (*of structure, wall*) Wuchtigkeit, Massivität *f*; (*of boxer, forehead*) Wuchtigkeit *f*. **the ~ of the task** die gewaltige Aufgabe.

mass: ~ media *npl* Massenmedien *pl*; **~ meeting** *n* Massenveranstaltung *f*; (*in company*) Betriebsversammlung *f*; (*of trade union*) Vollversammlung *f*; (*Pol*) Massenkundgebung *f*; **~ murderer** *n* Massenmörder *m*; **~ murders** *npl* Massenmord *m*; **~ number** *n* (*Phys*) Massenzahl *f*; **~-produce** *vt* in Massenproduktion *or* -fabrikation herstellen; *cars, engines etc* serienweise herstellen; **~-produced** *adj* **~-produced items** Massenartikel *pl*; **it looks as though it was ~-produced** das sieht sehr nach Massenware aus; **~ psychology** *n* Massenpsychologie *f*.

mast[1] [mɑːst] *n* (*Naut*) Mast(baum) *m*; (*Rad etc*) Sendeturm *m*. **10 years before the ~** 10 Jahre auf See.

mast[2] *n* (*Bot*) Mast *f*.

-masted [-mɑːstɪd] *adj suf* mastig. **a three-~ vessel** ein Dreimaster *m*.

master ['mɑːstə'] **1** *n* (a) (*of the house, dog, servants*) Herr *m*. **M~** (*Christ*) der Herr; (*in address*) Meister; **I am (the) ~ now** jetzt bin ich der Herr; **to be ~ in one's own house** (*also fig*) Herr im Hause sein; **to be one's own ~** sein eigener Herr sein.

(b) (*Naut*) Kapitän *m*. **~'s certificate** Kapitänspatent *nt*.

(c) (*musician, painter etc*) Meister *m*.

(d) (*teacher*) Lehrer *m*; (*of apprentice*) Meister *m*.

(e) **to be ~ of sth** etw beherrschen; **after years of practice he became a fluent ~ of Russian** nach jahrelanger Übung meisterte er die russische Sprache fließend; **to be ~ of the situation** Herr *m* der Lage sein; **to be the ~ of one's fate** sein Schicksal in der Hand haben; *see* **grand, past ~**.

(f) (*boy's title*) Master, Meister (*old*) *m*.

(g) (*of college*) Leiter, Rektor *m*.

(h) (*~ copy*) Original *nt*.

2 *vt* meistern; *one's emotions* unter Kontrolle bringen; *technique, method* beherrschen. **to ~ the violin** das Geigenspiel beherrschen; **to ~ one's temper** sich beherrschen, sein Temperament zügeln.

master *in cpds* (*with trades*) -meister *m*; **~-at-arms** *n* Bootsmann *m* mit Polizeibefugnis; **~ bedroom** *n* großes Schlafzimmer; **~ builder** *n* Baumeister *m*; **~ copy** *n* Original *nt*.

masterful ['mɑːstəfʊl] *adj* meisterhaft; *ball control* gekonnt; (*dominating*) *personality* gebieterisch. **he's got a ~, yet polite attitude** er hat eine bestimmte, aber trotzdem höfliche Art; **he said in a ~ tone** sagte er in bestimmtem Ton; **we were amazed at his ~ control of the meeting** wir staunten darüber, mit welcher Überlegenheit *or* wie überlegen *or* souverän *or* die Sitzung in der Hand hatte.

masterfully ['mɑːstəfʊlɪ] *adv* meisterhaft; *control* überlegen, souverän; *play, kick etc* gekonnt.

master key *n* Haupt- *or* Generalschlüssel *m*.

masterly ['mɑːstəlɪ] *adj* meisterhaft, gekonnt. **in a ~ fashion** meisterhaft, gekonnt.

master: ~ mariner *n* Kapitän *m*; **~ mason** *n* Steinmetzmeister *m*; **~-mind 1** *n* (*führender*) Kopf; **who's the ~mind who planned all these operations?** wer ist der Kopf, der hinter der Planung dieser Unternehmungen steckte?; **2** *vt* **who ~minded the robbery?** wer steckt hinter dem Raubüberfall?; **M~ of Arts/Science** *n* Magister *m* der philosophischen/naturwissenschaftlichen Fakultät; **~ of ceremonies** *n* (*at function*) Zeremonienmeister *m*; (*on stage*) Conférencier *m*; (*on TV*) Showmaster *m*; **~ of (fox)hounds** *n* Master *m*; **~piece** *n* Meisterwerk *nt*; **~ race** *n* Herrenvolk *nt*; **~ stroke** *n* Meister- *or* Glanzstück *nt*; **~ switch** *n* Hauptschalter *m*.

mastery ['mɑːstərɪ] *n* (*control: of language, technique*)

Meisterung f; (of instrument etc) Beherrschung f; (skill) Können nt; (over competitors etc) Oberhand f. ~ of the seas Herrschaft f über die Meere; the painter's ~ of colour and form des Malers meisterhafter Gebrauch von Form und Farbe; to gain the ~ of sth etw beherrschen.

masthead ['mɑːsthed] n (Naut) Mars, Mastkorb m; (US: in magazines etc) Impressum nt.

masticate ['mæstikeit] vti kauen; (for young) vorkauen.

mastication [,mæsti'keiʃən] n Kauen nt; Vorkauen nt.

mastiff ['mæstif] n Dogge f.

mastitis [mæ'staitis] n Brust(drüsen)entzündung, Mastitis f.

mastodon ['mæstədɒn] n Mastodon nt.

mastoid ['mæstɔid] 1 adj warzenförmig, mastoid (spec). 2 n Warzenfortsatz m, Mastoid nt (spec).

masturbate ['mæstəbeit] vi masturbieren, onanieren.

masturbation [,mæstə'beiʃən] n Masturbation, Onanie f.

mat¹ [mæt] 1 n Matte f; (door-) Fußmatte f or -abstreifer m; (on table) Untersetzer m; (of cloth) Deckchen nt; (of hair) Gewirr nt. place ~ Set nt. 2 vt the sea-water had ~ted his hair durch das Salzwasser waren seine Haare verfilzt geworden. 3 vi verfilzen.

mat² adj see matt.

matador ['mætədɔːʳ] n Matador m.

match¹ [mætʃ] n Streich- or Zündholz nt.

match² 1 n (a) (sb/sth similar, suitable etc) to be or make a good ~ gut zusammenpassen; the skirt is a good ~ for the jumper der Rock paßt gut zum Pullover; I want a ~ for this yellow paint ich möchte Farbe in diesem Gelbton; this chair is a ~ for that one dieser Stuhl ist das Gegenstück zu dem.
(b) (equal) to be a/no ~ for sb (be able to compete with) sich mit jdm messen/nicht messen können; (be able to handle) jdm gewachsen/nicht gewachsen sein; he's a ~ for anybody er kann es mit jedem aufnehmen; A was more than a ~ for B A war B weit überlegen; to meet one's ~ seinen Meister finden.
(c) (marriage) Heirat f. who thought up this ~? wer hat die beiden zusammengebracht?; she made a good ~ sie hat eine gute Partie gemacht; he's a good ~ er ist eine gute Partie.
(d) (Sport) (general) Wettkampf m; (team game) Spiel nt; (Tennis) Match nt, Partie f; (Boxing, Fencing) Kampf m; (quiz) Wettkampf, Wettbewerb m. athletics ~ Leichtathletikkampf m; I'll give you a ~ ich werde einmal gegen Sie spielen; we must have another ~ some time wir müssen wieder einmal gegeneinander spielen; that's ~ (Tennis) Match!, damit ist das Match entschieden.
2 vt (a) (pair off) they're well ~ed as man and wife die beiden passen gut zusammen; the two boxers were well ~ed die beiden Boxer waren einander ebenbürtig; the teams are well ~ed die Mannschaften sind gleichwertig; ~ each diagram with its counterpart ordnen Sie die Schaubilder einander zu; we had to ~ each noun with an adjective wir mußten zu jedem Substantiv ein passendes Adjektiv finden.
(b) (equal) gleichkommen (+dat) (in an +dat). A doesn't quite ~ B in originality A kann es an Originalität nicht mit B aufnehmen; nobody can ~ him in argument niemand kann so gut argumentieren wie er; a quality that has never been ~ed since eine Qualität, die bislang unerreicht ist or noch ihresgleichen sucht (geh); no knight could ~ him in battle kein Ritter konnte sich mit ihm messen; I can't ~ him in chess im Schach kann ich es mit ihm nicht aufnehmen; that sort of easy self-confidence which is not ~ed by any great degree of intelligence jene Selbstsicherheit, die nicht mit einem großen Maß an Intelligenz gepaart ist; ~ that if you can! das soll erst mal einer nachmachen, das macht so leicht keiner nach!; three kings! ~ that! drei Könige! kannst du da noch mithalten?; this climate/whisky can't be ~ed anywhere in the world so ein Klima/so einen Whisky gibt es nicht noch einmal.
(c) (correspond to) entsprechen (+dat). the results did not ~ our hopes die Ergebnisse entsprachen unseren Hoffnungen nicht.
(d) (clothes, colours) passen zu. she ~ed the carpet with some nice curtains sie fand nette, zum Teppich passende Vorhänge; can you ~ this fabric? haben Sie etwas, das zu diesem Stoff paßt?; to ~ colours and fabrics so that ... Farben und Stoffe so aufeinander abstimmen, daß ...; the colour of his face ~ed the red of his jumper sein Gesicht war so rot wie sein Pullover.
(e) (pit) he decided to ~ his team against or with the champions er beschloß, seine Mannschaft gegen die Meister antreten zu lassen; to be ~ed against sb gegen jdn antreten; to ~ one's wits/strength against sb sich geistig mit jdm messen/seine Kräfte mit jdm messen.
3 vi zusammenpassen. it doesn't ~ das paßt nicht (zusammen); with a skirt to ~ mit (dazu) passendem Rock.
♦**match up** 1 vi (a) (correspond) zusammenpassen. (b) (be equal) he ~ed ~ to the situation er war der Situation gewachsen. 2 vt sep colours aufeinander abstimmen. to ~ sth ~ with sth das Passende zu etw finden.

matchbox ['mætʃbɒks] n Streichholzschachtel f.

matching ['mætʃiŋ] adj (dazu) passend. they form a ~ pair sie passen or gehören zusammen; a ~ set of wine glasses ein Satz m Weingläser.

matchless ['mætʃlis] adj einzigartig, beispiellos, unvergleichlich.

match: ~lock n Luntenschloß nt; ~maker n Ehestifter(in f), Kuppler(in f) (pej) m; ~making n she loves ~making sie verkuppelt die Leute gern (inf); ~ point n (Tennis) Matchball m; ~stick n Streichholz nt; ~wood n Holz nt zur Herstellung von Streichhölzern; smashed to ~wood (fig) zu Kleinholz gemacht (inf).

mate¹ [meit] (Chess) 1 n Matt nt. 2 vt matt setzen. 3 vi white plays and ~s in two Weiß zieht und setzt den Gegner in zwei Zügen matt.

mate² 1 n (a) (fellow worker) Arbeitskollege, Kumpel m.
(b) (helper) Gehilfe, Geselle m.
(c) (Naut) Maat m.
(d) (of animal) (male) Männchen nt; (female) Weibchen nt. his ~ das Weibchen.
(e) (inf: friend) Freund(in f), Kamerad(in f) m. listen, ~ hör mal, Freund/chen! (inf); got a light, ~? hast du Feuer, Kumpel? (inf).
(f) (hum inf: husband, wife) Mann m/Frau f.
(g) (of pair) here's one sock, where's its ~? hier ist eine Socke, wo ist die andere or zweite?
2 vt animals paaren; female animal decken lassen; (fig hum) verkuppeln. they ~d their mare with our stallion sie haben ihre Stute von unserem Hengst decken lassen; they are well ~d (inf) sie passen gut zusammen.
3 vi (Zool) sich paaren.

mater ['meitəʳ] n (Brit inf) Mama f.

material [mə'tiəriəl] 1 adj (a) (of matter, things) materiell. ~ damage Sachschaden m.
(b) (of physical needs) needs, comforts materiell.
(c) (esp Jur: important) evidence wesentlich, erheblich; difference grundlegend, wesentlich. that's not ~ das ist nicht relevant.
2 n (a) Material nt; (for report, novel etc) Stoff m; (esp documents etc) Material nt. ~s Material nt; building ~s Baustoffe pl or -material nt; raw ~s Rohstoffe pl; writing ~s Schreibzeug nt; he's good editorial ~ er hat das Zeug zum Redakteur; this group would be good ~ for our show diese Band wäre für unsere Show ganz brauchbar.
(b) (cloth) Stoff m, Material nt.

materialism [mə'tiəriəlizəm] n der Materialismus.

materialist [mə'tiəriəlist] n Materialist(in f) m.

materialistic adj, ~ally adv [mə,tiəriə'listik, -əli] materialistisch.

materialize [mə'tiəriəlaiz] vi (a) (idea, plan) sich verwirklichen; (promises, hopes etc) wahr werden. this idea will never ~ aus dieser Idee wird nie etwas; the meeting never ~d das Treffen kam nie zustande; if this deal ever ~s wenn aus diesem Geschäft je etwas wird, wenn dieses Geschäft je zustande kommt; the money he'd promised me never ~d von dem Geld, das er mir versprochen hatte, habe ich nie etwas gesehen.
(b) (ghost) erscheinen; (indistinct object also) auftauchen.

materially [mə'tiəriəli] adv grundlegend, wesentlich. they are not ~ different sie unterscheiden sich nicht wesentlich.

matériel [mə,tiəri'el] n (US) Ausrüstung f.

maternal [mə'tɜːnl] adj mütterlich. ~ grandfather Großvater mütterlicherseits; ~ affection Mutterliebe f; ~ instincts Mutterinstinkte, mütterliche Instinkte pl.

maternity [mə'tɜːniti] n Mutterschaft f. the idea of ~ never appealed to her sie konnte sich nicht mit dem Gedanken befreunden, Mutter zu werden.

maternity: ~ benefit n Mutterschaftsgeld nt; ~ dress n Umstandskleid nt; ~ home, ~ hospital n Entbindungsheim nt; ~ unit n Entbindungs- or Wöchnerinnenstation f; ~ ward n Entbindungsstation f.

matey ['meiti] (Brit inf) 1 adj (+ er) person freundlich, kollegial; (pej) vertraulich; atmosphere freundschaftlich, kollegial, familiär; gathering vertraulich. careful what you say, he's ~ with the director sei vorsichtig mit dem, was du sagst, er steht mit dem Direktor auf du und du; he was getting just a bit too ~ with my wife er wurde ein wenig zu vertraulich mit meiner Frau.
2 n Kumpel m; (warningly) Freundchen nt (inf).

math [mæθ] n (US inf) Mathe f (inf).

mathematical adj, ~ly adv [,mæθə'mætikəl, -i] mathematisch.

mathematician [,mæθəmə'tiʃən] n Mathematiker(in f) m.

mathematics [,mæθə'mætiks] n (a) sing Mathematik f. (b) pl the ~ of this is complicated das ist mathematisch kompliziert.

maths [mæθs] n sing (Brit inf) Mathe f (inf).

matinée ['mætinei] n Matinee f; (in the afternoon also) Frühvorstellung f.

mating ['meitiŋ] n Paarung f.

mating: ~ call n Lockruf m; (of birds also) Balzlaut m; (of deer also) Brunstschrei m; ~ dance n Paarungstanz m; ~ season n Paarungszeit f.

matins ['mætinz] n sing (Catholic) Matutin f, Morgenlob nt; (Anglican) Morgenandacht f.

matriarch ['meitriɑːk] n Matriarchin f.

matriarchal [,meitri'ɑːkl] adj matriarchalisch.

matriarchy ['meitriɑːki] n Matriarchat nt.

matric [mə'trik] n (inf) see matriculation.

matrices ['meitrisiːz] pl of matrix.

matricide ['meitrisaid] n (act) Muttermord m; (person) Muttermörder(in f) m.

matriculate [mə'trikjuleit] 1 vi sich immatrikulieren. 2 vt immatrikulieren.

matriculation [mə,trikju'leiʃən] n Immatrikulation f; (ceremony) Immatrikulationsfeier f.

matrimonial [,mætri'məuniəl] adj vows, problems Ehe-.

matrimony ['mætriməni] n (form) Ehe f. to enter into holy ~ in den heiligen Stand der Ehe treten.

matrix ['meitriks] n, pl matrices or -es (a) (Biol) Gebärmutter f, Mutterleib m. (b) (mould) Matrize, Mater f. (c) (Geol, Math) Matrix f.

matron ['meitrən] n (a) (in hospital) Oberin, Oberschwester f; (in school) Schwester f. (b) (married woman) Matrone f.

matronly ['meitrənli] adj matronenhaft.

matt [mæt] adj matt, mattiert. a paint with a ~ finish ein Mattlack m.

matted ['mætid] adj verfilzt.

matter ['mætəʳ] **1** *n* **(a)** (*substance, not mind*) die Materie. **organic/inorganic** ~ organische/anorganische Stoffe *pl*.
(b) (*particular kind*) Stoff *m*. **advertising** ~ Reklame, Werbung *f*; **printed** ~ Drucksache(n *pl*) *f*; **colouring** ~ Farbstoff(e *pl*) *m*; **vegetable** ~ pflanzliche Stoffe *pl*.
(c) (*Med: pus*) Eiter *m*.
(d) (*Typ*) (*copy*) Manus(kript) *nt*; (*type set up*) Satz *m*.
(e) (*content*) Inhalt *m*. **the main** ~ **of his speech was** ... (der) Hauptgegenstand seiner Rede war ...
(f) (*question, affair*) Sache, Angelegenheit *f*; (*topic*) Thema *nt*, Stoff *m*. **can I talk to you on a** ~ **of great urgency?** kann ich Sie in einer äußerst dringenden Angelegenheit sprechen?; **this is a** ~ **I know little about** darüber weiß ich wenig; **in this** ~ in diesem Zusammenhang; **in the** ~ **of ... was** ... (+*acc*) anbelangt, hinsichtlich ... (+*gen*); **in the** ~ **of clothes** *etc* in puncto Kleidung *etc*; **there's the** ~ **of my expenses** da ist (noch) die Sache *or* Frage mit meinen Ausgaben; **it's no great** ~ das macht nichts, das ist nicht so wichtig; **that's quite another** ~ das ist etwas (ganz) anderes; **that's another** ~ altogether, that's a very **different** ~ das ist etwas völlig anderes; **it will be no easy** ~ (**to**) ... es wird nicht einfach sein, zu ...; **it's a serious** ~ das ist eine ernste Angelegenheit, die Sache ist ernst; **the** ~ **in hand** die vorliegende Angelegenheit; **that's not the** ~ **in hand** darum geht es gar nicht; **let's concentrate on the** ~ **in hand** wir sollten uns auf das eigentliche Thema konzentrieren; **the** ~ **is closed** die Sache *or* der Fall ist erledigt.
(g) ~s *pl* Angelegenheiten *pl*; **business** ~s geschäftliche Angelegenheiten *or* Dinge *pl*, Geschäftliche(s) *nt*; **money** ~s Geldangelegenheiten *or* -fragen *pl*; **as** ~s **stand** wie die Dinge liegen; **to make** ~s **worse** zu allem Unglück (noch).
(h) **for that** ~ eigentlich; **I haven't seen him for weeks, nor for that** ~ **has anybody else** ich habe ihn seit Wochen schon nicht mehr gesehen, und eigentlich hat ihn sonst auch niemand gesehen; **he wants to complain about it and for that** ~, **so do I** er will sich darüber beschweren und ich eigentlich auch; **questions concerning Glasgow, or for that** ~ **the whole of Scotland** Fragen, die Glasgow oder eigentlich ganz Schottland *or* oder ganz Schottland überhaupt betreffen.
(i) **a** ~ **of** eine Frage (+*gen*), eine Sache von; **it's a** ~ **of form/ time** das ist eine Formsache/Zeitfrage *or* Frage der Zeit; **it's a** ~ **of taste/opinion** das ist Geschmacks-/Ansichtssache; **it's a** ~ **of adjusting this part exactly** es geht darum, dieses Teil genau einzustellen; **it will be a** ~ **of a few weeks** es wird in ein paar Wochen dauern; **it's a** ~ **of 10 miles from** ... es sind 10 Meilen von ...; **it's a** ~ **of a couple of hours** das ist eine Sache von ein paar Stunden, das dauert ein paar Stunden; **if it's just a** ~ **of another 10 minutes, then I'll wait** wenn es sich nur noch um 10 Minuten handelt, dann warte ich so lange; **it can only be a** ~ **of a few days** es kann sich nur um ein paar Tage handeln, es ist nur eine Frage von ein paar Tagen; **in a** ~ **of minutes** innerhalb von Minuten; **it's a** ~ **of great concern to us** die Sache ist für uns von großer Bedeutung; **it's not just a** ~ **of increasing the money supply** es ist nicht damit getan, die Geldzufuhr zu erhöhen; **it's just a** ~ **of trying harder** man muß sich ganz einfach etwas mehr anstrengen; **as a** ~ **of course** selbstverständlich; **it's a** ~ **of course with us** für uns ist das eine Selbstverständlichkeit; **you should always take your passport with you as a** ~ **of course** es sollte für Sie eine Selbstverständlichkeit sein, stets Ihren Paß bei sich zu haben; **earthquakes happen as a** ~ **of course in that part of the world** Erdbeben sind in der Gegend an der Tagesordnung.
(j) **no** ~! macht nichts; **I've decided to leave tomorrow, no** ~ **what** ich gehe morgen, egal was passiert; **no** ~ **how/what/when/ where** *etc* ... egal, wie/was/wann/wo *etc* ...; **no** ~ **how you do it** wie du es auch machst, egal, wie du es machst; **no** ~ **how hot it was** auch *or* selbst bei der größten Hitze; **no** ~ **how hard he tried** so sehr er sich auch anstrengte.
(k) **sth is the** ~ **with sb/sth** etw ist mit jdm/etw los; (*ill*) etw fehlt jdm; **what's the** ~? was ist (denn) los?, was ist (denn)?; **what's the** ~ **with you this morning?** was ist denn heute morgen mit dir los?, was hast du denn heute morgen?; **what's the** ~ **with having a little fun?** was ist denn schon dabei, wenn man ein wenig vergnügt ist?; **what's the** ~ **with smoking?** was ist denn dabei, wenn man raucht?; **something's the** ~ **with the lights** mit dem Licht ist irgend etwas nicht in Ordnung; **what's the** ~ **with you?** — nothing's the ~ was ist denn mit dir los? — gar nichts; **as if nothing was the** ~ als ob nichts (los) wäre.
2 *vi* **it doesn't** ~ (es *or* das) macht nichts, ist schon gut; **what does it** ~? was macht das schon?; **I forgot it, does it** ~? — yes, it **does** ~ ich hab's vergessen, ist das schlimm? — ja, das ist schlimm; **does it** ~ **to you if I go?** macht es dir etwas aus, wenn ich gehe?; **doesn't it** ~ **to you at all if I leave you?** macht es dir denn gar nichts aus, wenn ich dich verlasse?; **why should it** ~ **to me?** warum sollte mir das etwas ausmachen?; **why should it** ~ **to me if people are starving?** was geht es mich an, wenn Menschen verhungern?; **it doesn't** ~ **to me what you do** es ist mir (ganz) egal, was du machst; **some things** ~ **more than others** es ist aber nicht alles gleich wichtig; **the things which** ~ **in life** was im Leben wichtig ist *or* zählt; **poverty** ~s Armut geht jeden etwas an.

matter-of-fact ['mætərəv'fækt] *adj* sachlich, nüchtern. **he was very** ~ **about it** er blieb sehr sachlich *or* nüchtern.
Matthew ['mæθju:] *n* Matthias *m*; (*Bibl*) Matthäus *m*.
matting ['mætɪŋ] *n* Matten *pl*; (*material*) Mattenmaterial *nt*.
mattock ['mætək] *n* Breithacke *f*.
mattress ['mætrɪs] *n* Matratze *f*.
maturation [,mætjʊ'reɪʃən] *n* Reifeprozeß *m*, Reifung *f*.
mature [mə'tjʊəʳ] **1** *adj* (+*er*) **(a)** person, mind reif; child verständig, vernünftig. **his mind is very** ~ geistig ist er schon sehr reif; **of** ~ **years** im reiferen *or* vorgerückten Alter.
(b) wine ausgereift; sherry, port, cheese reif; fruit reif, ausgereift; plant ausgewachsen; plans ausgereift. **after** ~ **deliberation** nach reiflicher Überlegung; **his** ~r **poems** seine reiferen Gedichte.
(c) (*Comm*) bill, debt fällig.
2 *vi* **(a)** (*person*) heranreifen (*geh*), reifer werden; (*animal*) auswachsen. **his character** ~d **during the war years** der Krieg ließ ihn reifer werden *or* machte ihn reifer.
(b) (*wine, cheese*) reifen, reif werden.
(c) (*Comm*) fällig werden.
3 *vt* **(a)** person reifer machen.
(b) wine, cheese reifen lassen.
maturely [mə'tjʊəlɪ] *adv* behave verständig, vernünftig. **a more** ~ **conceived novel** ein ausgereifterer Roman.
maturity [mə'tjʊərɪtɪ] *n* **(a)** Reife *f*. **to reach** ~ (*person*) erwachsen werden; (*legally*) volljährig werden; (*animal*) ausgewachsen sein; **poems of his** ~ Gedichte *pl* seiner reiferen Jahre; **he's somewhat lacking in** ~ ihm fehlt die nötige Reife.
(b) (*Comm*) Fälligkeit *f*; (*date*) Fälligkeitsdatum *nt*.
maudlin ['mɔːdlɪn] *adj* story rührselig; person sentimental, gefühlsselig.
maul [mɔːl] *vt* übel zurichten; (*fig*) writer, play *etc* verreißen.
Maundy ['mɔːndɪ] *n*: ~ money Almosen, die an Gründonnerstag verteilt werden; ~ **Thursday** Gründonnerstag *m*.
Mauritius [mə'rɪʃəs] *n* Mauritius *nt*.
mausoleum [,mɔːsə'lɪəm] *n* Mausoleum *nt*.
mauve [məʊv] **1** *adj* mauve, malvenfarben. **2** *n* Mauvein *nt*.
maverick ['mævərɪk] *n* **(a)** (*US Agr*) herrenloses Kalb/Rind *nt* ohne Brandzeichen.
(b) (*dissenter*) Abtrünnige(r) *m*.
(c) (*independent person*) Alleingänger, Einzelgänger *m*.
maw [mɔː] *n* **(a)** (*Anat*) Magen *m*; (*of cow*) (Lab)magen *m*; (*of bird*) Hals *m*. **(b)** (*liter*) Maul *nt*; (*fig*) Rachen, Schlund *m*.
mawkish ['mɔːkɪʃ] *adj* rührselig, kitschig; taste unangenehm *or* widerlich süß, süßlich.
mawkishness ['mɔːkɪʃnɪs] *n see adj* Rührseligkeit, Sentimentalität *f*; widerliche Süße.
max *abbr of* maximum max.
maxi ['mæksɪ] *n* (*dress*) Maxirock *m*/-kleid *nt*/-mantel *m*.
maxim ['mæksɪm] *n* Maxime *f*.
maximal ['mæksɪməl] *adj* maximal.
maximization [,mæksɪmaɪ'zeɪʃən] *n* Maximierung *f*.
maximize ['mæksɪmaɪz] *vt* maximieren.
maximum ['mæksɪməm] **1** *adj attr* Höchst-; size, height, costs, length maximal. **he scored** ~ **points** er hat die höchste Punktzahl erreicht; **the** ~ **salary in grade 6 is** ... das höchste Gehalt in Gehaltsstufe 6 ist ...; **a** ~ **speed of** ... eine Höchstgeschwindigkeit von ...; **we are producing at** ~ **speed** wir produzieren mit maximaler Geschwindigkeit; **5 is the** ~ **number allowed in a taxi** maximal *or* höchstens 5 Leute dürfen in ein Taxi.
2 *n, pl* -**s** *or* **maxima** ['mæksɪmə] Maximum *nt*. **up to a** ~ **of £8** bis zu maximal *or* höchstens £ 8; **temperatures reached a** ~ **of 34°** die Höchsttemperatur betrug 34°; **is that the** ~ **you can offer?** ist das Ihr höchstes Angebot?; **my salary is now at its** ~ ich bin jetzt in der höchsten *or* obersten Gehaltsstufe.
maxiskirt ['mæksɪ,skɜːt] *n* Maxirock *m*.
May [meɪ] **1** *n* Mai *m*. **2** *vi*: **to go m~ing** den Mai feiern.
may [meɪ] *vi pret* **might** (*see also* **might**[1]) **(a)** (*possibility: also* might) können. **it** ~ **rain** es könnte regnen, vielleicht regnet es; **it** ~ **be that** ... vielleicht ..., es könnte sein, daß ...; **although it** ~ **have been useful** obwohl es hätte nützlich sein können; **he** ~ **not be hungry** vielleicht hat er keinen Hunger; **I** ~ **have said so** es kann *or* könnte sein, daß ich das gesagt habe; **you** ~ **be right** (*doubting*) Sie könnten recht haben, Sie haben vielleicht recht; (*tentatively agreeing*) da können *or* könnten Sie recht haben; **you** ~**n't be so lucky next time** das nächste Mal haben Sie vielleicht nicht soviel Glück; **there** ~ **not be a next time** vielleicht gibt's gar kein nächstes Mal; **they** ~ **be brothers for all I know** es kann *or* könnte sein, daß sie Brüder sind; **yes, I** ~ **ja, das ist** möglich *or* das kann sein; **I** ~ **just do that** vielleicht tue ich das wirklich; **that's as** ~ **be** (*not might*) das mag ja sein, (aber ...); **one** ~ **well wonder why** ... die Frage wäre wohl berechtigt, warum ...; **you** ~ **well ask** das kann man wohl fragen.
(b) (*permission*) dürfen. ~ **I go now?** darf ich jetzt gehen?; **yes, you** ~ ja, Sie dürfen.
(c) **I hope he** ~ **succeed** ich hoffe, daß es ihm gelingt; **I had hoped he might succeed this time** ich hatte gehofft, es würde ihm diesmal gelingen; **such a policy as** ~ *or* **might bring peace** eine Politik, die zum Frieden führen könnte; **we** ~ *or* **might as well go** ich glaube, wir können (ruhig) gehen; **you** ~ *or* **might as well go now** du kannst jetzt ruhig gehen; **if they don't have it we** ~ *or* **might as well go to another firm** wenn sie es nicht haben, gehen wir am besten zu einer anderen Firma; **if they won't help we** ~ *or* **might just as well give up** wenn sie uns nicht helfen, können wir (ja) gleich aufgeben.
(d) (*in wishes*) ~ **you be successful!** (ich wünsche Ihnen) viel Erfolg!; ~ **your days be full of joy** mögen Ihnen glückliche Tage beschieden sein; ~ **you be very happy together** ich hoffe, ihr werdet glücklich miteinander; ~ **the Lord have mercy on your soul** der Herr sei deiner Seele gnädig; ~ **you be forgiven** (*inf*) so was tut man doch nicht!; ~ **I be struck dead if I lie!** ich will auf der Stelle tot umfallen, wenn das nicht stimmt.
(e) (*in questions*) **who** ~ *or* **might you be?** und wer sind Sie?, wer sind Sie denn?
Maya ['meɪə] *n* **(a)** Maya *mf*. **(b)** (*language*) Maya-sprache *f*.
Mayan ['meɪən] **1** *adj* Maya-. **2** *n* **(a)** Maya *mf*. **(b)** (*language*) Maya(sprache *f*) *nt*.
maybe ['meɪbi:] *adv* vielleicht, kann sein(, daß ...).
May: ~ **Day** *n* der 1. Mai, der Maifeiertag; ~**day** *n* (*distress call*) Maydaysignal *nt*, SOS-Ruf *m*; (*said*) Mayday.
mayest ['meɪəst] (*obs*), **mayst** (*obs*) *2nd pers sing of* **may**.

mayfly ['meɪflaɪ] n Eintagsfliege f.

mayhap ['meɪhæp] adv (old) vielleicht, möglicherweise.

mayhem ['meɪhem] n (a) (US Jur) (schwere) Körperverletzung. (b) (havoc) Chaos nt.

mayn't [meɪnt] contr of may not.

mayonnaise [ˌmeɪə'neɪz] n Mayonnaise f. salmon ~ Lachs m mit Mayonnaise.

mayor [meə'] n Bürgermeister(in f) m.

mayoral ['meərəl] adj des Bürgermeisters.

mayoralty ['meərəltɪ] n (office) Bürgermeisteramt nt, Amt nt des Bürgermeisters. during his ~ ... als er Bürgermeister war ..., während seiner Zeit als Bürgermeister ...

mayoress ['meəres] n Frau f Bürgermeister; Tochter f des Bürgermeisters; (lady mayor) Bürgermeisterin f.

may: ~pole n Maibaum m; M~ queen n Maikönigin f.

mayst [meɪst] (obs) see mayest.

maze [meɪz] n Irrgarten m; (puzzle) Labyrinth nt; (fig) Wirrwarr m, Gewirr nt. the ~ of streets das Gewirr der Straßen.

mazurka [mə'zɜ:kə] n Mazurka f.

MB abbr of **Bachelor of Medicine.**

MC abbr of (a) **Master of Ceremonies.** (b) **Military Cross.**

MCC abbr of **Marylebone Cricket Club.**

McCoy [mə'kɔɪ] n see real.

MD abbr of (a) **Doctor of Medicine** Dr. med. (b) **managing director.**

m.d. abbr of **mentally deficient.**

me [mi:] pron (a) (dir obj, with prep +acc) mich; (indir obj, with prep +dat) mir. with my books about ~ mit meinen Büchern um mich herum; he's older than ~ er ist älter als ich. (b) (emph) who, ~? wer, ich?; it's ~ ich bin's.

mead[1] [mi:d] n (drink) Met m.

mead[2] n (old, poet) Aue f.

meadow ['medəʊ] n Wiese, Weide f. in the ~ auf der Wiese etc.

meadow: ~land n Weideland nt; ~sweet n Mädesüß nt.

meagre, (US) **meager** ['mi:gə'] adj (a) spärlich; amount kläglich; meal dürftig, kärglich. (b) (liter: lean) hager.

meagrely, (US) **meagerly** ['mi:gəlɪ] adv spärlich; live kärglich.

meagreness, (US) **meagerness** ['mi:gənɪs] n see adj Spärlichkeit f; Kläglichkeit f; Dürftigkeit, Kärglichkeit f.

meal[1] [mi:l] n Schrot(mehl nt) m.

meal[2] n Mahlzeit f; (food) Essen nt. come round for a ~ komm zum Essen (zu uns); to go for a ~ essen gehen; to have a (good) ~ (gut) essen; hot ~s warme Mahlzeiten pl, warmes Essen; I haven't had a ~ for two days ich habe seit zwei Tagen nichts Richtiges mehr gegessen; don't make a ~ of it (inf) nun übertreib's mal nicht (inf); he really made a ~ of it (inf) er war nicht mehr zu bremsen (inf).

meal: ~ticket n (US: lit) Essensbon m or -marke f; that letter of introduction was his ~-ticket for the next few months dank des Empfehlungsschreibens konnte er sich die nächsten paar Monate über Wasser halten; a boyfriend is just a ~-ticket to a lot of girls viele Mädchen haben nur einen Freund, um ihn auszunützen or auszunehmen (inf); she's just his ~-ticket er hat bloß ein Bratkartoffelverhältnis mit ihr; ~time n Essenszeit f; you shouldn't smoke at ~times Sie sollten während des Essens nicht rauchen.

mealy ['mi:lɪ] adj mehlig.

mealy-mouthed ['mi:lɪ'maʊðd] adj unaufrichtig; politician schönfärberisch. let's not be ~ about it wir wollen doch mal nicht so um den heißen Brei herumreden.

mean[1] [mi:n] adj (+er) (a) (miserly) geizig, knauserig. don't be ~! sei doch nicht so geizig or knauserig!; you ~ thing! du Geizhals or Geizkragen!

(b) (unkind, spiteful) gemein. don't be ~! sei nicht so gemein or fies! (inf); you ~ thing! du gemeines or fieses (sl) Stück!, du Miststück! (sl); it made me feel ~ ich kam mir richtig schäbig or gemein vor.

(c) (base, inferior) birth, motives niedrig. the ~est citizen der Geringste unter den Bürgern (old).

(d) (shabby, unimpressive) shack, house schäbig, armselig.

(e) (vicious) bösartig; look gehässig, hinterhältig; criminal niederträchtig, abscheulich.

(f) he is no ~ player er ist ein beachtlicher Spieler; that's no ~ feat diese Aufgabe ist nicht zu unterschätzen or nicht von Pappe (inf); a sportsman/politician of no ~ ability ein sehr fähiger Sportler/Politiker.

mean[2] 1 n (middle term) Durchschnitt m; (Math) Durchschnitt, Mittelwert m, Mittel nt. the golden or happy ~ die goldene Mitte, der goldene Mittelweg. 2 adj mittlere(r, s). ~ sea level Normalnull nt.

mean[3] pret, ptp meant vt (a) bedeuten; (person: refer to, have in mind) meinen. what do you ~ by that? was willst du damit sagen?; the name ~s nothing to me der Name sagt mir nichts; it ~s a lot of expense for us das bedeutet eine Menge Ausgaben für uns; it ~s starting all over again das bedeutet or das heißt, daß wir wieder ganz von vorne anfangen müssen; this will ~ great changes dies wird bedeutende Veränderungen zur Folge haben; a pound ~s a lot to her für sie ist ein Pfund eine Menge Geld; your friendship/he ~s a lot to me deine Freundschaft/er bedeutet mir viel; you ~ everything to me du bist alles für mich.

(b) (intend) beabsichtigen. to ~ to do sth etw tun wollen; (do on purpose) etw absichtlich tun; to be ~t for sb/sth für jdn/etw bestimmt sein; to ~ sb to do sth wollen, daß jd etw tut; sth is ~t to be sth etw soll etw sein; what do you ~ to do? was wirst du tun?, was hast du vor?; I only ~t to help ich wollte nur helfen; of course it hurt, I ~t it to or it was ~t to natürlich tat das weh, das war Absicht; without ~ing to sound rude ich möchte nicht unverschämt klingen(, aber ...); I ~t it as a joke das sollte ein Witz sein; I ~t you to have it das solltest du haben; I was ~t to

do that ich hätte das tun sollen; you are ~t to be on time du solltest pünktlich sein; he wasn't ~t to be a leader er war nicht zum Führer bestimmt; I thought it was ~t to be hot in the south ich dachte immer, daß es im Süden so heiß sei; I ~ to be obeyed ich verlange, daß man mir gehorcht; this pad is ~t for drawing dieser Block ist zum Zeichnen gedacht or da (inf); if he ~s to be awkward ... wenn er vorhat, Schwierigkeiten zu machen, ...; this present was ~t for you dieses Geschenk sollte für dich sein or war für dich gedacht; you weren't ~t to see it du solltest das nicht zu sehen bekommen; see business, mischief.

(c) (be serious about) ernst meinen. I ~ it! das ist mein Ernst!, ich meine das ernst!; do you ~ to say you're not coming? willst du damit sagen or soll das heißen, daß du nicht kommst?; I ~ what I say ich sage das im Ernst, es ist mir Ernst damit; do you really ~ it this time? ist es dir diesmal Ernst damit?

(d) he ~s well/no harm er meint es gut/nicht böse; to ~ well by sb es gut mit jdm meinen; to ~ sb no harm es gut mit jdm meinen, jdm nichts Böses wollen; (physically) jdm nichts tun; (in past tense) jdm nichts tun wollen; I ~t no harm by what I said was ich da gesagt habe, war nicht böse gemeint; he ~t no offence er wollte niemanden beleidigen.

meander [mɪ'ændə'] vi (river) sich (dahin)schlängeln, mäandern; (person) wirr sein; (go off subject) (vom Thema) abschweifen; (walking) schlendern.

meanderings [mɪ'ændərɪŋz] npl see vi Windungen pl, Mäander m; Gefasel nt; Abschweifungen, Exkurse pl. it's hard to follow the ~ of his mind es ist schwer, seinen verworrenen Gedankengängen zu folgen.

meanie ['mi:nɪ] n (inf) (miserly person) Geizhals or -kragen m; (nasty person) Miststück nt (sl); (male also) Schuft m.

meaning ['mi:nɪŋ] 1 adj look etc vielsagend, bedeutsam.

2 n Bedeutung f; (sense: of words, poem etc also) Sinn m. a look full of ~ ein bedeutungsvoller or bedeutsamer Blick; what's the ~ of (the word) "hick"? was soll das Wort „hick" heißen or bedeuten?; to mistake sb's ~ jdn mißverstehen; do you get my ~? haben Sie mich (richtig) verstanden?; you don't know the ~ of love/hunger du weißt ja gar nicht, was Liebe/Hunger ist or bedeutet; what's the ~ of this? was hat denn das zu bedeuten?, was soll denn das (heißen)?

meaningful ['mi:nɪŋfʊl] adj (a) (semantically) word, symbol mit Bedeutung, sinntragend; (Ling) unit bedeutungstragend; poem, film bedeutungsvoll. to be ~ eine Bedeutung haben; the statistics only become ~ when ... die Zahlen ergeben nur dann einen Sinn, wenn ...

(b) (purposeful) job, negotiations sinnvoll.

meaningless ['mi:nɪŋlɪs] adj (a) (semantically) word, symbol etc ohne Bedeutung, bedeutungslos. to write "xybj" is ~ die Buchstaben „xybj" ergeben keinen Sinn or bedeuten nichts. (b) sinnlos. my life is ~ mein Leben hat keinen Sinn.

meanness ['mi:nnɪs] n see adj (a) Geiz m, Knauserigkeit f. (b) Gemeinheit f. (c) Niedrigkeit f. (d) Schäbigkeit, Armseligkeit f. (e) Bösartigkeit f; Gehässigkeit, Hinterhältigkeit f; Niederträcht f.

means [mi:nz] n (a) sing (method) Möglichkeit f; (instrument) Mittel nt. a ~ of transport ein Beförderungsmittel nt; a ~ of escape eine Fluchtmöglichkeit; a ~ to an end ein Mittel nt zum Zweck; have/there is no ~ of doing it es ist mir/es ist unmöglich, das zu tun?; there must be a ~ of doing it es muß doch irgendwie möglich sein, das zu tun?; there must be a ~ of doing it es muß doch irgendwie or auf irgendeine Art und Weise zu machen sein; we've no ~ of knowing wir können nicht wissen; he was the ~ of sending it man ließ es durch ihn überbringen; they used him as the ~ of getting the heroin across the border sie benutzten ihn, um das Heroin über die Grenze zu bringen; all known ~ have been tried man hat alles Mögliche versucht; by ~ of sth durch etw, mittels einer Sache (gen); by ~ of doing sth dadurch, daß man etw tut; by this ~ dadurch, auf diese Weise; by some ~ or other auf irgendeine Art und Weise, irgendwie.

(b) sing by all ~! (aber) selbstverständlich or natürlich!; by all ~ take one nehmen Sie sich ruhig (eins); by no ~, not by any ~ keineswegs, durchaus nicht; (under no circumstances) auf keinen Fall.

(c) pl (wherewithal) Mittel pl; (financial ~ also) Gelder pl. a man of ~ ein vermögender Mann; private ~ private Mittel; that is within/beyond my ~ das kann ich mir leisten/nicht leisten; to live beyond/within one's ~ über seine Verhältnisse leben/seinen Verhältnissen entsprechend leben; ~ test Einkommens- or Vermögensveranlagung f.

meant [ment] pret, ptp of mean[3].

meantime ['mi:ntaɪm] 1 adv inzwischen. 2 n for the ~ vorerst, im Augenblick, einstweilen; in the ~ in der Zwischenzeit, inzwischen.

meanwhile ['mi:nwaɪl] adv inzwischen.

measles ['mi:zlz] n sing Masern pl.

measly ['mi:zlɪ] adj (+er) (inf) mick(e)rig (inf), poplig (inf).

measurable ['meʒərəbl] adj (measurable) (perceptible) erkennbar.

measurably ['meʒərəblɪ] adv see adj meßbar; deutlich.

measure ['meʒə'] 1 n (a) (unit of measurement) Maß(einheit f) nt. a ~ of length ein Längenmaß nt; beyond ~ grenzenlos; her joy was beyond or knew no ~ ihre Freude kannte keine Grenzen; see weight.

(b) (object for measuring) Maß nt; (graduated for length) Maßstab m; (graduated for volume) Meßbecher m.

(c) (amount ~d) Menge f. a small ~ of flour ein wenig Mehl; wine is sold in ~s of 1/4 litre Wein wird in Vierteln ausgeschenkt; to give sb full/short ~ (barman) richtig/zuwenig ausschenken; (grocer) richtig/zu wenig abwiegen; in full ~ in höchstem Maße; for good ~ zur Sicherheit, sicherheitshalber; ... and another one for good ~ ... und noch eines obendrein.

(d) (fig: yardstick) Maßstab m (of für). can we regard this exam as a ~ of intelligence? kann diese Prüfung als Intelligenzmaßstab gelten?; what should we use as a ~ of inflation? woran sollte man die Inflation messen?; MacLeod's approval is the ~ of a good whisky MacLeods Urteil ist bezug auf Whisky ist (für mich) maßgebend or ausschlaggebend; please consider this as a ~ of my esteem for ...; bitte beurteilen Sie dies als Ausdruck meiner Anerkennung für ...; it gave us some ~ of the difficulty es gab uns einen Begriff von der Schwierigkeit; it's a ~ of his skill as a writer that ... seine schriftstellerischen Fähigkeiten lassen sich daran beurteilen, daß ...; words cannot always give the ~ of one's feelings Worte können Gefühle nicht immer angemessen ausdrücken.

(e) (extent) in some ~ in gewisser Hinsicht or Beziehung; some ~ of ein gewisses Maß an; to a or in large ~ in hohem Maße; to get the ~ of sb/sth jdn/etw (richtig) einschätzen.

(f) (step) Maßnahme f. to take ~s to do sth Maßnahmen ergreifen, um etw zu tun.

(g) (Poet) Versmaß nt.

(h) (US Mus) Takt m.

(i) (old: dance) Tanz m. to tread a ~ with sb mit jdm ein Tänzchen wagen.

2 vt messen; (length also abmessen; room also ausmessen; (take sb's measurements) Maß nehmen bei; (fig) beurteilen, abschätzen; words abwägen. a ~d mile genau eine Meile; to ~ one's length (fig) der Länge nach hinfallen.

3 vi messen. what does it ~? wieviel mißt es?, wie groß ist es?

♦ **measure off** vt sep area, length of cloth abmessen.

♦ **measure out** vt sep abmessen; weights also abwiegen.

♦ **measure up 1** vt sep (a) (take measurements of) wood, room etc abmessen; person for suit etc Maß nehmen bei.

(b) (fig: assess) situation abschätzen; person einschätzen.

2 vi (a) (be good enough, compare well) he didn't ~ ~ er hat enttäuscht; to ~ ~ to sth an etw (acc) herankommen; visually he ~d ~ (to the description) vom Aussehen her paßte er (auf die Beschreibung), it's a hard job, but he should ~ ~ das ist eine schwierige Aufgabe, aber er sollte ihr gewachsen sein.

(b) (take measurements) Maß nehmen, messen.

measured ['meʒəd] adj tread, pace gemessen (liter); tone, way of talking bedacht, bedächtig; statement, words wohlüberlegt, durchdacht. he walked with ~ steps er ging gemessenen Schrittes (liter).

measureless ['meʒəlis] adj unermeßlich.

measurement ['meʒəmənt] n (a) (act) Messung f. the metric system of ~ das metrische Maßsystem. (b) (measure) Maß nt; (figure) Meßwert m; (fig) Maßstab m. to take sb's ~s an or bei jdm Maß nehmen.

measuring ['meʒərɪŋ] n Messen nt. to take ~s of sth etw messen.

meat [miːt] n (a) Fleisch nt. cold ~ kalter Braten; (sausage) Wurst f; assorted cold ~s Aufschnitt m.

(b) (old: food) Essen nt, Speise f (liter). ~ and drink Speise und Trank; one man's ~ is another man's poison (Prov) des einen Freud, des andern Leid (Prov).

(c) (fig: of argument, book) Substanz f. a book with some ~ in it ein aussagestarkes Buch.

meat in cpds Fleisch-; ~ball n Fleischkloß m; ~ loaf n ≈ Fleischkäse m; ~ products npl Fleisch- und Wurstwaren pl; ~safe n Fliegenschrank m.

meaty ['miːtɪ] adj (+er) (a) taste Fleisch-. (b) (fig) book aussagestark.

Mecca ['mekə] n (lit, fig) Mekka nt.

mechanic [mɪ'kænɪk] n Mechaniker m.

mechanical [mɪ'kænɪkəl] adj (lit, fig) mechanisch; toy technisch. ~ engineer/engineering Maschinenbauer or -bauingenieur m/Maschinenbau m; a ~ device ein Mechanismus m; I don't understand all the ~ workings of this thing ich habe keine Ahnung, wie dieses Ding genau funktioniert.

mechanically [mɪ'kænɪkəlɪ] adv (lit, fig) mechanisch. ~-minded technisch begabt.

mechanics [mɪ'kænɪks] n (a) sing (subject) (engineering) Maschinenbau m; (Phys) Mechanik f. home ~ for the car-owner kleine Maschinenkunde für den Autobesitzer.

(b) pl (technical aspects) Mechanik f, Mechanismus m; (fig: of writing etc) Technik f. there is something wrong with the ~ of the car das Auto ist mechanisch nicht in Ordnung; I don't understand the ~ of parliamentary procedure ich verstehe den Mechanismus parlamentarischer Abläufe nicht.

mechanism ['mekənɪzəm] n Mechanismus m.

mechanistic adj, **~ally** adv [ˌmekə'nɪstɪk, -əlɪ] mechanistisch.

mechanization [ˌmekənaɪ'zeɪʃən] n Mechanisierung f.

mechanize ['mekənaɪz] vt mechanisieren.

med abbr of **medium**.

medal ['medl] n Medaille f; (decoration) Orden m.

medalist n (US) see **medallist**.

medallion [mɪ'dæljən] n Medaillon nt; (medal) Medaille f.

medallist, (US) medalist ['medəlɪst] n Medaillengewinner(in f) m.

meddle ['medl] vi (interfere) sich einmischen (in in +acc); (tamper) sich zu schaffen machen, herumfummeln (inf) (with an +dat). to ~ with sb sich mit jdm einlassen; he's not a man to ~ with mit ihm ist nicht gut Kirschen essen; he's always meddling er mischt sich in alles ein.

meddler ['medlər] n he's a terrible ~ er muß sich immer in anderer Leute Angelegenheiten or in alles einmischen.

meddlesome ['medlsəm] adj, **meddling** ['medlɪŋ] adj attr she's a ~ old busybody sie mischt sich dauernd in alles ein.

media ['miːdɪə] n, pl of **medium** Medien pl. he works in the ~ er ist im Mediensektor tätig or beschäftigt.

mediaeval adj see **medieval**.

mediaevalist n see **medievalist**.

medial ['miːdɪəl] adj (situated in the middle) mittlere(r, s). in (word) ~ position (Ling) im Inlaut.

median ['miːdɪən] 1 adj mittlere(r, s). ~ strip (US) Mittelstreifen m. 2 n (Math) Zentralwert m.

mediate[1] ['miːdɪət] adj (rare) mittelbar.

mediate[2] ['miːdɪeɪt] 1 vi vermitteln. 2 vt settlement aushandeln, herbeiführen.

mediation [ˌmiːdɪ'eɪʃən] n Vermittlung f.

mediator ['miːdɪeɪtər] n Vermittler, Mittelsmann m.

mediatory ['miːdɪətərɪ] adj vermittelnd, des Vermittlers. in a ~ capacity als Vermittler.

medic ['medɪk] n (inf) Mediziner m (inf).

medical ['medɪkəl] 1 adj medizinisch; (in military contexts) Sanitäts-; test, examination, treatment ärztlich; authority, board, inspector Gesundheits-; student Medizin-. ~ school ≈ medizinische Fakultät; the ~ world die Ärzteschaft; I'm not a ~ man ich bin kein Arzt or Doktor; her ~ history ihre Krankengeschichte; that made ~ history das hat in der Medizin Geschichte gemacht; ~ card (Brit) Krankenversicherungsschein m; ~ jurisprudence Gerichtsmedizin f; ~ ward Innere Abteilung.

2 n (ärztliche) Untersuchung. have you had your ~? bist du zur Untersuchung gewesen?, hast du dich untersuchen lassen?

medically ['medɪkəlɪ] adv medizinisch; examine ärztlich.

medicament [me'dɪkəmənt] n Medikament, Mittel nt.

Medicare ['medɪˌkɛər] n (US) staatliche Krankenversicherung und Gesundheitsfürsorge in den USA.

medicate ['medɪkeɪt] vt (medizinisch) behandeln. ~d medizinisch.

medication [ˌmedɪ'keɪʃən] n (act) (medizinische) Behandlung; (drugs etc) Verordnung f, Medikamente pl.

medicinal [me'dɪsɪnl] adj Heil-, heilend. for ~ purposes zu medizinischen Zwecken; the ~ properties of various herbs die Heilkraft verschiedener Kräuter.

medicinally [me'dɪsɪnəlɪ] adv use, take zu Heilzwecken, zu medizinischen Zwecken; valuable medizinisch.

medicine ['medsɪn, 'medɪsɪn] n (a) Arznei, Medizin (inf) f; (one particular preparation) Medikament nt. to take one's ~ (lit) seine Arznei einnehmen; (fig) die bittere Pille schlucken, in den sauren Apfel beißen; now we'll see how you like a taste of your own ~ jetzt werden wir sehen, wie es dir schmeckt, wenn dir das passiert; to give sb a taste of his own ~ (fig) es jdm mit gleicher Münze heim- or zurückzahlen.

(b) (science) Medizin f. to practise ~ den Arztberuf ausüben.

medicine: ~ ball n Medizinball m; ~ chest n Hausapotheke f, Arzneischränkchen nt; ~-man n Medizinmann m.

medico ['medɪkəʊ] n (dated inf) Medikus m (dated, hum).

medieval [ˌmedɪ'iːvəl] adj mittelalterlich.

medievalist [ˌmedɪ'iːvəlɪst] n Mediävist(in f) m.

mediocre [ˌmiːdɪ'əʊkər] adj mittelmäßig.

mediocrity [ˌmiːdɪ'ɒkrɪtɪ] n (a) (quality) Mittelmäßigkeit f. (b) (person) kleines Licht.

meditate ['medɪteɪt] 1 vt: to ~ revenge auf Rache sinnen (liter). 2 vi nachdenken (upon, on über +acc); (Rel, Philos) meditieren.

meditation [ˌmedɪ'teɪʃən] n Nachdenken nt; (Rel, Philos) Meditation f. "A M~ on Life" „Betrachtungen über das Leben".

meditative ['medɪtətɪv] adj nachdenklich; (Rel, Philos) Meditations-.

meditatively ['medɪtətɪvlɪ] adv see adj nachdenklich; meditierend.

Mediterranean [ˌmedɪtə'reɪnɪən] 1 n Mittelmeer nt. in the ~ (in sea) im Mittelmeer; (in region) am Mittelmeer, im Mittelmeerraum. 2 adj climate, nations Mittelmeer-; scenery, character, person südländisch. the ~ Sea das Mittelmeer; ~ fruit Südfrüchte pl; ~ types Südländer pl.

medium ['miːdɪəm] 1 adj quality, size etc mittlere(r s); steak halbdurch, medium; brown, sized etc mittel-. of ~ height/difficulty mittelgroß/-schwer.

2 n, pl media or -s (a) (means) Mittel nt; (TV, Rad, Press) Medium nt; (Art, Liter) Ausdrucksmittel nt. ~ of exchange Tauschmittel nt; the ~ of the press as opposed to TV das Medium Presse im Gegensatz zum Fernsehen; through the ~ of the press durch die Presse; advertising ~ Werbeträger m.

(b) (surrounding substance) (Phys) Medium nt; (environment) Umgebung f; (air, water etc) Element nt.

(c) (midpoint) Mitte f. happy ~ goldener Mittelweg.

(d) (spiritualist) Medium nt.

medium in cpds mittel-; ~ wave (Rad) Mittelwelle f. ~-rare adj rosa, englisch; ~-sized adj mittelgroß; ~ wave n Mittelwelle f.

medley ['medlɪ] n Gemisch nt; (Mus) Potpourri, Medley nt. ~ relay Staffellauf m, bei dem die einzelnen Teilnehmer über verschieden lange Strecken laufen, z.B. Schwedenstaffel, Olympische Staffel; (Swimming) Lagenstaffel f.

medulla [me'dʌlə] n Mark nt; (of spine) Rückenmark nt; (renal ~) Nierenmark nt.

meek [miːk] adj (+er) sanft(mütig), lammfromm (inf); (pej) duckmäuserisch; (uncomplaining) duldsam, geduldig. don't be so ~ and mild laß dir doch nicht (immer) alles gefallen!

meekly ['miːklɪ] adv sanft, lammfromm (inf); (pej) duckmäuserisch; agree widerspruchslos.

meekness ['miːknɪs] n see adj Sanftmut f; (pej) Duckmäuserei f; Duldsamkeit f.

meerschaum ['mɪəʃəm] n Meerschaum m; (pipe Meerschaumpfeife f.

meet[1] [miːt] adj (obs) geziemend (liter). it is ~ that ... es ist billig or (ge)ziemt sich (liter, old), daß ...; to be ~ for sich (ge)ziemen für (liter, old).

meet[2] (vb: pret, ptp met) 1 vt (a) (encounter) person treffen, begegnen (+dat); (by arrangement) treffen, sich treffen mit; *difficulty* stoßen auf (+*acc*); (*Sport*) treffen auf (+*acc*). **I'll ~ you outside** ich treffe euch draußen; **he met his guests at the door** er empfing seine Gäste an der Tür; **he met him in a duel** er duellierte sich mit ihm; **he met his death in 1800** im Jahre 1800 fand er den Tod; **to ~ death calmly** dem Tod gefaßt entgegentreten; **to arrange to ~ sb** sich mit jdm verabreden; **the last time Rangers met Celtic there was a riot** bei der letzten Begegnung zwischen Rangers und Celtic kam es zu heftigen Auseinandersetzungen; **his eyes** *or* **gaze met mine** unsere Blicke trafen sich; **she refused to ~ his eyes** *or* **gaze** sie wich seinem Blick aus; **I could not ~ his eye** ich konnte ihm nicht in die Augen sehen; **there's more to it than ~s the eye** da steckt mehr dahinter, als man auf den ersten Blick meint.

(b) (*get to know*) kennenlernen; (*be introduced to*) bekannt gemacht werden mit. **you don't know him? come and ~ him** du kennst ihn nicht? komm, ich mache euch miteinander bekannt *or* ich mache dich mit ihm bekannt; **pleased to ~ you!** guten Tag/Abend, sehr angenehm! (*form*).

(c) (*await arrival, collect*) abholen (*at an* +*dat*, *von*); (*connect with*) *train, boat etc* Anschluß haben an (+*acc*). **I'll ~ your train** ich hole dich vom Zug ab; **the car will ~ the train** der Wagen wartet am Bahnhof *or* steht am Bahnhof bereit.

(d) (*join, run into*) treffen *or* stoßen auf (+*acc*); (*converge with*) sich vereinigen mit; (*river*) münden *or* fließen in (+*acc*); (*intersect*) schneiden; (*touch*) berühren. **where East ~s West** (*fig*) wo Ost und West sich treffen.

(e) *expectations, target, obligations, deadline* erfüllen; *requirement, demand, wish* entsprechen (+*dat*), gerecht werden (+*dat*); *deficit, expenses, needs* decken; *debt* bezahlen, begleichen; *charge, objection, criticism* begegnen (+*dat*).

2 *vi* **(a)** (*encounter*) (*people*) sich begegnen; (*by arrangement*) sich treffen; (*society, committee etc*) zusammenkommen, tagen; (*Sport*) aufeinandertreffen; (*in duel*) sich duellieren. **keep it until we ~ again** behalten Sie es, bis wir uns mal wieder sehen; **until we ~ again!** bis zum nächsten Mal!; **to ~ halfway** einen Kompromiß schließen.

(b) (*become acquainted*) sich kennenlernen; (*be introduced*) bekannt gemacht werden. **we've met before** wir kennen uns bereits; **haven't we met before somewhere?** sind wir uns nicht schon mal begegnet?, kennen wir uns nicht irgendwoher?

(c) (*join etc*) *see vt* (d) sich treffen, aufeinanderstoßen; sich vereinigen; ineinanderfließen; sich schneiden; sich berühren. (*fig: come together*) sich treffen. **our eyes met** unsere Blicke trafen sich; **the skirt wouldn't ~ round her waist** der Rock ging an der Taille nicht zu.

3 *n* (*Hunt*) Jagd(veranstaltung) *f*; (*US Sport*) Sportfest *nt*. **swimming ~** Schwimmfest *nt*.

♦ **meet up** *vi* sich treffen.

♦ **meet with** *vi* +*prep obj* **(a)** (*encounter, experience*) *hostility, opposition, problems* stoßen auf (+*acc*); *success, accident* haben; *disaster, loss, shock* erleiden; *setback* erleben; *approval, disapproval, an untimely death* finden. **to ~ ~ praise/blame** gelobt/getadelt werden; **to ~ ~ kindness/a warm welcome** freundlich behandelt/herzlich empfangen werden.

(b) *person* treffen; (*esp US: have a meeting with*) (zu einer Unterredung) zusammenkommen mit.

meeting ['miːtɪŋ] *n* **(a)** Begegnung *f*, Zusammentreffen *nt*; (*arranged*) Treffen *nt*; (*business ~*) Besprechung, Konferenz *f*. **the minister had a ~ with the ambassador** der Minister traf zu Gesprächen *or* zu einer Unterredung mit dem Botschafter zusammen.

(b) (*of committee, board of directors, council*) Sitzung *f*; (*of members, employees, citizens*) Versammlung *f*, Meeting *nt*. **the last ~** bei der letzten Sitzung; **the committee has three ~s a year** der Ausschuß tagt dreimal im Jahr; **Mr Jones is at/in a ~** Herr Jones ist (gerade) in einer Sitzung; **~ of creditors** Gläubigerversammlung *f*.

(c) (*Sport*) Veranstaltung *f*; (*between teams, opponents*) Begegnung *f*, Treffen *nt*.

(d) (*of rivers*) Zusammenfluß *m*. **at the ~ of the X and the Y** wo X und Y zusammenfließen.

meeting: **~ house** *n* Gemeindehaus *nt* (der Quäker); **~ place** *n* Treffpunkt *m*; **~ point** *n* Treffpunkt *m*; (*of rivers*) Zusammenfluß *m*; (*of lines*) Schnitt-/Berührungspunkt *m*; **at the ~ point of the two roads/cultures** wo die beiden Straßen zusammentreffen/wo sich die beiden Kulturen treffen.

mega- ['mɛgə-] *pref* (*million*) Mega-.
megalith ['mɛgəlɪθ] *n* Megalith *m*.
megalithic [‚mɛgə'lɪθɪk] *adj* megalithisch.
megalomania [‚mɛgələʊ'meɪnɪə] *n* Größenwahn *m*, Megalomanie *f* (*spec*).
megalomaniac [‚mɛgələʊ'meɪnɪæk] *n* Größenwahnsinnige(r) *mf*. **he's a ~** er leidet an Größenwahn, er ist größenwahnsinnig.
megaphone ['mɛgəfəʊn] *n* Megaphon *nt*.
mega: **~volt** *n* Megavolt *nt*; **~watt** *n* Megawatt *nt*.
meiosis [maɪ'əʊsɪs] *n, pl* **-ses** [-siːz] (*Biol*) Meiose *f*.
melamine ['mɛləmiːn] *n* Melamin *nt*.
melancholia [‚mɛlən'kəʊlɪə] *n* Schwermut, Melancholie *f*.
melancholic [‚mɛlən'kɒlɪk] *adj* melancholisch, schwermütig.
melancholy ['mɛlənkəlɪ] **1** *adj* melancholisch, schwermütig; *duty, sight etc* traurig. **2** *n* Melancholie, Schwermut *f*.
Melba toast ['mɛlbə'təʊst] *n* dünner, harter Toast.
mêlée ['mɛleɪ] *n* (*confused struggle*) Gedränge, Gewühl *nt*; (*fighting*) Handgemenge *nt*.
mellifluous [mɛ'lɪfluəs] *adj* wohltönend *or* -klingend.
mellifluously [mɛ'lɪfluəslɪ] *adv* klangvoll. **..., he said ~ ...,** sagte er mit wohltönender *or* klangvoller Stimme.
mellow ['mɛləʊ] **1** *adj* (+*er*) *fruit* ausgereift, saftig; *wine* ausgereift, lieblich; *colour, light* warm; *sound* voll, rund, weich; *voice* weich, sanft. **a ~ instrument** ein Instrument mit einem vollen *or* weichen Klang.

(b) *person* abgeklärt, gesetzt; (*fig: slightly drunk*) heiter, angeheitert. **in the ~ later years** im gesetzteren Alter.
2 *vt* reifen, heranreifen lassen; (*relax*) heiter stimmen; *sounds, colours* dämpfen, abschwächen; *taste* mildern.
3 *vi* (*wine, fruit*) reif werden, (heran)reifen; (*colours, sounds*) weicher werden; (*person*) (*become gentler*) abgeklärter *or* gesetzter werden; (*relax*) umgänglicher werden.
mellowness ['mɛləʊnɪs] *n see adj* **(a)** Ausgereiftheit, Saftigkeit *f*; lieblicher Geschmack; Wärme *f*; Weichheit *f*; weicher *or* sanfter Klang. **(b)** Abgeklärtheit, Gesetztheit *f*; heitere *or* angeheiterte Stimmung.
melodic [mɪ'lɒdɪk] *adj* melodisch.
melodious [mɪ'ləʊdɪəs] *adj* melodiös, melodisch, wohlklingend. **a ~ tune** eine harmonische Melodie, eine melodische Weise (*liter*).
melodiously [mɪ'ləʊdɪəslɪ] *adv* melodiös, melodisch.
melodiousness [mə'ləʊdɪəsnɪs] *n* Wohlklang *m*, Melodik *f*.
melodrama ['mɛləʊ‚drɑːmə] *n* Melodrama *nt*.
melodramatic *adj*, **~ally** *adv* [‚mɛləʊdrə'mætɪk, -əlɪ] melodramatisch.
melody ['mɛlədɪ] *n* Melodie *f*; (*fig: of poetry etc*) Melodik *f*.
melon ['mɛlən] *n* Melone *f*.
melt [mɛlt] **1** *vt* **(a)** schmelzen; *snow also* zum Schmelzen bringen; *butter* zergehen lassen, zerlassen; *sugar, grease* auflösen.
(b) (*fig*) *heart etc* erweichen. **her tears ~ed my anger** beim Anblick ihrer Tränen verflog mein Zorn.
2 *vi* **(a)** schmelzen; (*butter also*) zergehen; (*sugar, grease*) sich (auf)lösen. **it just ~s in the mouth** es zergeht einem nur so auf der Zunge.
(b) (*fig*) (*person*) dahinschmelzen; (*anger*) verfliegen. **... and then his heart ~ed ...** und dann ließ er sich erweichen; **to ~ into tears** in Tränen zerfließen.
♦ **melt away** *vi* **(a)** (*lit*) (weg)schmelzen. **(b)** (*fig*) sich auflösen; (*person*) dahinschmelzen; (*anger, anxiety*) verfliegen; (*suspicion, money*) zerrinnen.
♦ **melt down** *vt sep* einschmelzen.
melting ['mɛltɪŋ-]: **~ point** *n* Schmelzpunkt *m*; **what is the ~ point of iron?** welchen Schmelzpunkt hat Eisen?; **~ pot** *n* (*lit, fig*) Schmelztiegel *m*; **to be in the ~ pot** in der Schwebe sein.
member ['mɛmbə'] *n* **(a)** Mitglied *nt*; (*of tribe, species*) Angehörige(r) *mf*. **"~s only"** „nur für Mitglieder"; **~ of the family** Familienmitglied *nt*; **if any ~ of the audience ...** falls einer der Zuschauer/Zuhörer ...; **you have to be a ~** Sie müssen Mitglied sein; **the ~ countries** die Mitgliedsstaaten *pl*.
(b) (*Parl*) Abgeordnete(r) *mf*. **~ of parliament** Parlamentsmitglied *nt*; (*in GB*) Abgeordnete(r) *mf* des Unterhauses; (*in BRD*) Bundestagsabgeordnete(r) *mf*; **the ~ for Woodford** der/die Abgeordnete für den Wahlkreis Woodford.
(c) (*Math, Logic*) Glied *nt*.
membership ['mɛmbəʃɪp] *n* Mitgliedschaft *f* (*of in* +*dat*); (*number of members*) Mitgliederzahl *f*. **when I applied for ~** of the club als ich mich um die Clubmitgliedschaft bewarb; **~ list** Mitgliederkartei *f*.
membrane ['mɛmbreɪn] *n* Membran(e) *f*.
membranous [mɛm'breɪnəs] *adj* membranartig.
memento [mə'mɛntəʊ] *n, pl* **-(e)s** Andenken *nt* (*of an* +*acc*).
memo ['mɛməʊ] *n abbr of* **memorandum (a)** Mitteilung *f*; (*reminder*) Notiz *f*. **~ pad** Notizblock *m*.
memoir ['mɛmwɑː'] *n* **(a)** Kurzbiographie *f*. **(b)** **~s** *pl* Memoiren *pl*.
memorable ['mɛmərəbl] *adj* unvergeßlich; (*important*) denkwürdig.
memorably ['mɛmərəblɪ] *adv* bemerkenswert.
memorandum [‚mɛmə'rændəm] *n, pl* **memoranda** [‚mɛmə'rændə] **(a)** (*in business*) Mitteilung *f*; (*personal reminder*) Notiz *f*, Vermerk *m*. **(b)** (*Pol*) Memorandum *nt*.
memorial [mɪ'mɔːrɪəl] **1** *adj* *plaque, service* Gedenk-. **2** *n* Denkmal *nt* (*to für*). **M~ Day** (*US*) ≈ Volkstrauertag *m*.
memorize ['mɛməraɪz] *vt* sich (*dat*) einprägen.
memory ['mɛmərɪ] *n* **(a)** Gedächtnis *nt*; (*faculty*) Erinnerungsvermögen *nt*. **from ~** aus dem Kopf; **to commit sth to ~** sich (*dat*) etw einprägen; *poem* etw auswendig lernen; **I have a bad ~ for faces/names** ich habe ein schlechtes Personengedächtnis/Namensgedächtnis; **if my ~ serves me right** wenn ich mich recht entsinne; **~ see living**.
(b) (*that remembered*) Erinnerung *f* (*of an* +*acc*). **I have no ~ of it** ich kann mich nicht daran erinnern; **to take a trip** *or* **to walk down ~ lane** in Erinnerungen schwelgen.
(c) (*Computers*) Speicher *m*. **~ bank** Datenbank *f*.
(d) **to honour sb's ~** jds Andenken ehren; **in ~ of** zur Erinnerung *or* zum Gedenken (*form*) an (+*acc*); *see* **blessed**.
men [mɛn] *pl of* **man**.
menace ['mɛnɪs] **1** *n* **(a)** Bedrohung *f* (*to gen*); (*issued by a person*) Drohung *f*; (*imminent danger*) drohende Gefahr *f*. **to demand money with ~s** unter Androhung von Gewalt Geld fordern. **(b)** (*inf: nuisance*) (Land)plage *f*. **she's a ~ on the roads** sie gefährdet den ganzen Verkehr.
2 *vt* bedrohen.
menacing ['mɛnɪsɪŋ] *adj* drohend.
menacingly ['mɛnɪsɪŋlɪ] *adv see adj*. **..., he said ~ ...,** sagte er mit drohender Stimme.
ménage [mɛ'nɑːʒ] *n* Haushalt *m*. **~ à trois** Dreiecksverhältnis *nt*.
menagerie [mɪ'nædʒərɪ] *n* Menagerie *f*.
mend [mɛnd] **1** *n* (*in shoe*) reparierte Stelle; (*in piece of metal, cloth etc also*) Flickstelle *f*; (*in roof, fence etc also*) ausgebesserte Stelle. **the ~ is almost invisible** man sieht kaum, daß es repariert/geflickt/ausgebessert worden ist; **to be on the ~** (*lit: person, fig*) sich (langsam) erholen, sich auf dem Wege der

Besserung befinden (form, hum); **the fracture is on the ~** der Bruch heilt schon wieder or ist am Verheilen (inf).

2 vt **(a)** (repair) reparieren; toy, machine also wieder ganz machen (inf); roof, fence also ausbessern; hole, clothes flicken. **my shoes need ~ing** ich muß meine Schuhe reparieren or machen (inf) lassen.

(b) (improve) **you'd better ~ your ways** das muß aber anders werden mit dir/Ihnen!; **to ~ one's ways** sich bessern; **to ~ matters** eine Angelegenheit bereinigen; **that won't ~ matters** das macht die Sache auch nicht besser.

3 vi (bone) (ver)heilen. **the patient is ~ing nicely** der Patient macht gute Fortschritte; **make do and ~** (prov) aus alt mach neu (prov).

mendacious [men'deɪʃəs] adj lügnerisch, verlogen; statement also unwahr.

mendaciously [men'deɪʃəslɪ] adv unwahrheitsgemäß.

mendacity [men'dæsɪtɪ] n Verlogenheit f; (of statement also) Unwahrheit f.

Mendelian [men'di:lɪən] adj Mendelsch.

mendicant ['mendɪkənt] **1** adj bettelnd; order, monk Bettel-. **2** n (beggar) Bettler(in f) m; (monk) Bettelmönch m.

mending ['mendɪŋ] n (articles to be mended) Flickarbeit f.

menfolk ['menfəʊk] npl Männer pl, Mannsvolk nt (old).

menial ['mi:nɪəl] **1** adj niedrig, untergeordnet. **she regards no task as too ~ for her** sie betrachtet keine Arbeit für unter ihrer Würde; **the ~ staff** die (unteren) Dienstboten, das Gesinde. **2** n (pej) Dienstbote m.

meningitis [ˌmenɪn'dʒaɪtɪs] n Hirnhautentzündung, Meningitis f.

meniscus [mɪ'nɪskəs] n, pl **menisci** [mɪ'nɪsaɪ] Meniskus m.

menopause ['menəʊpɔ:z] n Wechseljahre pl, Menopause f (spec).

menses ['mensi:z] npl (rare) Menses pl (dated).

menstrual ['menstrʊəl] adj Menstruations-, menstrual (spec). **~ bleeding** Monatsblutung f.

menstruate ['menstrʊeɪt] vi menstruieren (spec), die Menstruation haben.

menstruation [ˌmenstrʊ'eɪʃən] n die Menstruation or Periode.

mental ['mentl] adj **(a)** geistig; cruelty seelisch. **he has a ~ age of ten** er ist auf dem geistigen Entwicklungsstand eines Zehnjährigen; **to make a ~ note of sth** sich (dat) etw merken; **~ blackout** Bewußtseinsstörung f; **to have a ~ blackout** eine Bewußtseinsstörung haben, geistig weggetreten sein (inf); (due to alcohol) einen Filmriß haben (inf); (in exam) ein Brett vor dem Kopf haben (inf); **~ breakdown** Nervenzusammenbruch m; **~ arithmetic** Kopfrechnen nt; **~ health** Geisteszustand m; **~ home** (Nerven)heilanstalt f; **~ hospital** psychiatrische Klinik, Nervenklinik f; **~ illness** Geisteskrankheit f; **~ patient** Geisteskranke(r) mf; **~ process** geistiger or gedanklicher Prozeß, Denkvorgang m; **~ reservation** (stille) Bedenken, Vorbehalte pl; **the causes are ~ not physical** die Ursachen sind eher psychischer als physischer Natur; **he still shows great ~ agility** er ist geistig noch immer sehr rege.

(b) (sl: mad) übergeschnappt (sl).

mentality [men'tælɪtɪ] n Mentalität f. **they have a very aggressive ~** sie haben eine sehr aggressive Art; **how can we change this materialistic ~?** wie können wir diese materialistische Einstellung or Auffassung ändern?

mentally ['mentlɪ] adv **(a)** geistig. **~ handicapped/deficient** geistig behindert/geistesschwach; **he is ~ ill** er ist geisteskrank. **(b)** (in one's head) im Kopf.

menthol ['menθɒl] n Menthol nt. **~ cigarettes** Mentholzigaretten pl.

mentholated ['menθəleɪtɪd] adj Menthol-, mit Menthol.

mention ['menʃən] **1** n Erwähnung f. **to get or receive a ~** erwähnt werden; **he received a ~ for bravery** er erhielt eine Auszeichnung or Belobigung für seine Tapferkeit; **to give sth a ~** etw erwähnen; **there is a/no ~ of** it es wird erwähnt/nicht erwähnt; **I can't find any ~ of his name** ich kann seinen Namen nirgendwo finden; **there are several ~s of this tradition in earlier literature** diese Tradition wird verschiedentlich in früheren Quellen erwähnt; **his contribution certainly deserves ~** sein Beitrag verdient gewiß, erwähnt zu werden; **~ should also be made of ......** sollte Erwähnung finden (form); **it's hardly worth a ~** es ist kaum erwähnenswert, es lohnt sich kaum, das zu erwähnen; **at the ~ of his name/the police** als sein Name/das Wort Polizei fiel or erwähnt wurde ...

2 vt erwähnen (to sb jdm gegenüber). **he was ~ed in several dispatches** er wurde mehrfach lobend erwähnt; **not to ~ ...** nicht zu vergessen ...; (France and West Germany, not to ~ Holland Frankreich und die Bundesrepublik, von Holland ganz zu schweigen or ganz abgesehen von Holland; **too numerous to ~** zu zahlreich, um sie einzeln erwähnen zu können; **don't ~ it!** (das ist doch) nicht der Rede wert!, (bitte,) gern geschehen!; **if I may ~** it wenn ich das einmal sagen darf; **it hardly needs ~ing** that we're very grateful es versteht sich wohl von selbst, daß wir sehr dankbar sind; **the person we'd like to elect, ~ing no names, is ...** wen wir gerne wählen würden, ohne irgendwelche Namen nennen zu wollen, ist ...; **to ~ sb in one's will** jdn in seinem Testament berücksichtigen; **~ me to your parents!** empfehlen Sie mich Ihren Eltern! (form), viele Grüße an Ihre Eltern!

mentor ['mentɔ:r] n Mentor m.

menu ['menju:] n (bill of fare) Speisekarte f; (dishes served) Menü nt. **may we see the ~?** können or würden Sie uns bitte die Karte bringen?, können wir bitte die Karte sehen?; **what's on the ~?** was steht heute auf dem Speisezettel?, was gibt es heute (zu essen)?; **they have a very good ~** there man kann dort ausgezeichnet essen; **the typical British ~ consists of ...** ein typisches britisches Essen besteht aus ...

meow n, vi see miaow.

mercantile ['mɜ:kəntaɪl] adj Handels-; nation also handeltreibend. **the ~ marine** die Handelsmarine.

mercantilism ['mɜ:kəntɪlɪzəm] n Merkantilismus m.

mercenary ['mɜ:sɪnərɪ] **1** adj **(a)** person geldgierig. **his motives were purely ~** er tat es nur des Geldes wegen; **don't be so ~** sei doch nicht so hinter dem Geld her (inf); **he's got a rather ~ attitude** bei ihm spielt nur das Geld eine Rolle. **(b)** (Mil) troops Söldner-. **2** n Söldner m.

mercerized ['mɜ:səraɪzd] adj thread merzerisiert.

merchandise ['mɜ:tʃəndaɪz] n Ware f. **"please do not handle the ~"** „das Berühren der Ware(n) ist verboten".

merchant ['mɜ:tʃənt] n **(a)** Kaufmann m. corn/fruit/diamond ~ Getreide-/Obst-/Diamantenhändler m. **(b)** (Brit sl) Typ m (sl). **he's a real speed ~** der fährt wie der Henker (sl).

merchant in cpds Handels-; **~ bank** n Handelsbank f; **~man** n Handelsschiff nt; **~ navy** n Handelsmarine f; **~ prince** n reicher Kaufmann, Handelsboss (inf) m; **~ seaman** n Matrose m in der Handelsmarine; **~ ship** n Handelsschiff nt.

merciful ['mɜ:sɪfʊl] adj gnädig. o **~ Lord** gütiger Gott; **O Lord be ~!** Gott, sei uns (dat) gnädig!; **his death was a ~ release from pain** sein Tod war für ihn eine Erlösung; **~ heavens!** (dated) barmherziger Himmel! (dated).

mercifully ['mɜ:sɪfəlɪ] adv act barmherzig; treat sb gnädig; (fortunately) glücklicherweise. **his suffering was ~ short** es war eine Gnade, daß er nicht lange leiden mußte.

merciless ['mɜ:sɪlɪs] adj unbarmherzig, erbarmungslos; destruction schonungslos.

mercilessly ['mɜ:sɪlɪslɪ] adv erbarmungslos.

mercurial [mɜ:'kjʊərɪəl] adj (Chem) Quecksilber-; (containing mercury) quecksilberhaltig; (fig) (volatile) sprunghaft, wechselhaft; (lively) vif, quicklebendig.

Mercury ['mɜ:kjʊrɪ] n Merkur m.

mercury ['mɜ:kjʊrɪ] n Quecksilber nt.

mercy ['mɜ:sɪ] n **(a)** no pl (feeling of compassion) Erbarmen nt; (action, forbearance from punishment) Gnade f; (God's ~) Barmherzigkeit f. **to beg for ~** um Gnade bitten or flehen; **to have ~/no ~ on sb** mit jdm Erbarmen/kein Erbarmen haben; **have ~!** Gnade!, Erbarmen!; **Lord have ~ upon us** Herr, erbarme dich unser; **to show sb ~/no ~** Erbarmen/kein Erbarmen mit jdm haben; **to throw oneself on sb's ~** sich jdm auf Gnade und Ungnade ausliefern; **to be at the ~ of sb** jdm (auf Gedeih und Verderb) ausgeliefert sein; **to be at the ~ of** sth einer Sache (dat) ausgeliefert sein; **we're at your ~** wir sind in Ihrer Gewalt or Hand; **at the ~ of the elements** dem Spiel der Elemente preisgegeben; **a ~ mission**, a mission of ~ eine Hilfsaktion; **with a recommendation to ~** (Jur) mit einer Empfehlung auf Strafmilderung.

(b) (inf: blessing) Segen m, Glück nt. **it's a ~ nobody was hurt** man kann von Glück sagen, daß niemand verletzt wurde; **we must be thankful for small mercies** man muß schon mit wenigem zufrieden or für weniges dankbar sein.

mercy: **~ killing** n Euthanasie f, Töten nt aus Mitleid; **~ seat** n Gnadenthron or -stuhl m.

mere¹ [mɪər] n (poet) See m.

mere² adj bloß; formality also, nonsense rein. **he's a ~ clerk** er ist bloß ein kleiner Angestellter; **a ~ 3%/2 hours** bloß or lediglich 3%/2 Stunden; **a ~ nothing** eine (bloße) Lappalie; **but she's a ~ child** aber sie ist doch noch ein Kind!

merely ['mɪəlɪ] adv lediglich, bloß. **it's not ~ broken, it's ruined** es ist nicht bloß kaputt, es ist völlig ruiniert.

meretricious [ˌmerɪ'trɪʃəs] adj trügerisch.

merge [mɜ:dʒ] **1** vi **(a)** zusammenkommen; (colours) ineinander übergehen; (roads) zusammenlaufen or -führen. **to ~ with sth** mit etw verschmelzen, sich mit etw vereinen; (colour) in etw (acc) übergehen; (road) in etw (acc) einmünden; **to ~ (in) with/into the crowd** in der Menge untergehen/untertauchen; **to ~ into sth** in etw (acc) übergehen; **the bird ~d into or in with its background of leaves** der Vogel verschmolz mit dem Laubwerk im Hintergrund; **this question ~s into that bigger one** diese Frage geht in dem größeren Fragenkomplex auf; **"motorways ~"** „Autobahneinmündung".

(b) (Comm) fusionieren, sich zusammenschließen.

2 vt **(a)** miteinander vereinen or verbinden or verschmelzen; colours also ineinander übergehen lassen; metals legieren. **to ~ sth with sth** etw mit etw vereinen or verbinden or verschmelzen; etw in etw (acc) übergehen lassen.

(b) (Comm) zusammenschließen, fusionieren. **they were ~d into one company** sie wurden zu einer Firma zusammengeschlossen; **they were ~d with ...** sie haben mit ... fusioniert.

merger ['mɜ:dʒər] n (Comm) Fusion f.

meridian [mə'rɪdɪən] n (Astron, Geog) Meridian m; (fig) Höhepunkt, Gipfel m.

meringue [mə'ræŋ] n Meringe f, Baiser nt.

merino [mə'ri:nəʊ] n **(a)** (sheep) Merino(schaf nt) m. **(b)** (wool) Merinowolle f.

merit ['merɪt] **1** n (achievement) Leistung f, Verdienst nt; (advantage) Vorzug m. **to look or inquire into the ~s of sth** etw auf seine Vorteile or Vorzüge untersuchen; **men of ~** verdiente Leute pl; **a work of great literary ~** ein Werk von großem literarischem Wert; **what are the particular ~s of Greek drama?** wodurch zeichnet sich das griechische Drama besonders aus?; **she won the election on ~ alone** sie gewann die Wahl aufgrund persönlicher Fähigkeiten; **judged on ~ alone** ausschließlich nach Leistung(en) or ihren Verdiensten beurteilt; **I don't see any ~ in being rich** ich betrachte Reichtum als kein besonderes Verdienst; **there's no particular ~ in coming early** es ist keine besondere Leistung or kein besonderes Verdienst, früh zu kommen; **to treat a case on its ~s** einen Fall für sich selbst or gesondert behandeln; **to pass an exam with ~** ein Examen mit Auszeichnung bestehen.

2 *vt* verdienen. **it ~s your consideration** das ist es wert, daß Sie sich damit beschäftigen.

meritocracy [ˌmerɪ'tɒkrəsɪ] *n* Leistungsgesellschaft *f*.

meritorious *adj*, **~ly** *adv* [ˌmerɪ'tɔːrɪəs, -lɪ] lobenswert.

mermaid ['mɜːmeɪd] *n* Nixe, See- *or* Meerjungfrau *f*.

merman ['mɜːmæn] *n*, *pl* **-men** [-men] Nix, Wassergeist *m*.

merrily ['merɪlɪ] *adv* vergnügt.

merriment ['merɪmənt] *n* Heiterkeit, Fröhlichkeit *f*; (*laughter*) Gelächter *nt*. **at this there was much ~** das erregte allgemeine Heiterkeit, das rief großes Gelächter hervor.

merry ['merɪ] *adj* (+*er*) **(a)** (*cheerful*) fröhlich, vergnügt, lustig; *song, tune* fröhlich. **to make ~** lustig und vergnügt sein; **M~ Christmas!** Fröhliche *or* Frohe Weihnachten!; **M~ England** das gute alte England; **to give sb ~ hell** (*inf*) jdm einheizen (*inf*). **(b)** (*inf: tipsy*) beschwipst, angeheitert (*inf*). **to get ~** sich (*dat*) einen anpicheln (*inf*).

merry: ~-go-round *n* Karussell *nt*; **~maker** *n* Festgast *m*, Feiernde(r) *mf*; **~making** *n* Feiern *nt*, Belustigung, Lustbarkeit (*liter*) *f*; **after the ~making had finished** nach Beendigung des Festes *or* der Lustbarkeiten (*liter*).

mesa ['meɪsə] *n* Tafelberg *m*.

mescalin(e) ['meskəlɪn] *n* Meskalin *nt*.

mesh [meʃ] **1** *n* **(a)** (*hole*) Masche *f*; (*size of hole*) Maschenweite *f*. **caught in the fine ~ of the net** in den feinen Maschen des Netzes gefangen; **fine ~ stockings** feinmaschig-maschenfeste Strümpfe *pl*; **the broad ~ of this material makes it ideal** die Grobmaschigkeit dieses Materials ist ideal; **a 5mm ~ screen** ein 5 mm Maschendraht, ein Maschendraht mit 5 mm Maschenweite (*form*); **the ~ is big enough to see through** es ist großmaschig genug, um durchzusehen. **(b)** (*material*) (*wire ~*) Maschendraht *m*; (*network of wires*) Drahtgeflecht *nt*; (*Tex*) Gittergewebe *nt*. **(c)** (*Mech*) **out of/in ~** nicht im/im Eingriff; **the tight ~ of the cogwheels** die enge Verzahnung der Räder. **(d)** (*fig*) **to catch** *or* **entangle sb in one's ~es** jdn umgarnen, jdn in sein Netz locken; **to be caught in sb's ~es** jdm ins Netz gegangen sein; **he was entangled in the ~es of his own intrigues** er verfing sich im Netz seiner eigenen Intrigen. **2** *vi* **(a)** (*Mech*) eingreifen (*with +acc*). **the gears ~ (together)** die Zahnräder greifen ineinander. **(b)** (*fig: views, approach*) sich vereinen lassen. **he tried to make the departments ~ (together)** er versuchte, die einzelnen Abteilungen miteinander zu koordinieren. **3** *vt see* **enmesh**.

meshugge [mɪ'ʃʊɡə] *adj* (*sl*) meschugge (*inf*).

mesmeric [mez'merɪk] *adj* hypnotisch; *movement* hypnotisierend.

mesmerism ['mezmərɪzəm] *n* hypnotische Wirkung; (*old*) Mesmerismus *m*.

mesmerize ['mezməraɪz] *vt* hypnotisieren; (*fig*) faszinieren, fesseln. **the audience sat ~d** die Zuschauer saßen wie gebannt.

meson ['miːzɒn] *n* (*Phys*) Meson *nt*.

mess¹ [mes] **1** *n* **(a)** (*Durcheinander nt*; (*untidy also*) Unordnung *f*; (*dirty*) Schweinerei *f*. **to be (in) a ~** unordentlich sein, in einem fürchterlichen Zustand sein; (*disorganized*) ein einziges Durcheinander sein; (*fig: one's life, marriage, career etc*) verkorkst sein (*inf*); **to be a ~** (*piece of work*) eine Schweinerei sein; (*disorganized*) ein einziges *or* heilloses Durcheinander sein; (*person*) (*in appearance*) unordentlich aussehen; (*psychologically*) verkorkst sein (*inf*); **to look a ~** (*person*) unmöglich aussehen; (*untidy also*) schlampig *or* unordentlich aussehen; (*dirty also*) völlig verdreckt sein; (*room, piece of work*) unordentlich *or* schlimm aussehen; **to make a ~** (*be untidy*) Unordnung machen; (*be dirty*) eine Schweinerei machen; **to make a ~ of sth** (*make untidy*) etw in Unordnung bringen, etw durcheinanderbringen; (*make dirty*) etw verdrecken; (*bungle, botch*) etw verpfuschen, bei etw Mist bauen (*inf*); **one's life** etw verkorksen (*inf*) *or* verpfuschen; **I made a ~ of sewing it** ich habe beim Annähen Mist gebaut (*inf*); **you've really made a ~ of things** du hast alles total vermasselt (*inf*); **a fine ~ you've made of that** da hast du was Schönes angerichtet; **what a ~!** wie sieht das denn aus!, das sieht ja vielleicht aus!; (*fig*) ein schöner Schlamassel! (*inf*); **I'm not tidying up your ~** ich räume nicht für dich auf; **a ~ of beer cans/pots and pans** ein Haufen Bierdosen/Töpfe und Pfannen.
(b) (*awkward predicament*) Schwierigkeiten *pl*, Schlamassel *m* (*inf*). **cheating got him into a ~** durch seine Mogelei ist er in ziemliche Schwierigkeiten geraten; **he got into a ~ with the police** er hat Ärger mit der Polizei bekommen; **when he forgot his lines he panicked and got into a ~** als er seinen Text vergaß, geriet er in Panik und verhedderte sich völlig (*inf*).
(c) (*euph: excreta*) Dreck *m*. **the cat/baby has made a ~ on the carpet** die Katze/das Baby hat auf den Teppich gemacht.
2 *vi see* **mess about 2** (*c, d*).

♦ **mess about** *or* **around** (*inf*) **1** *vt sep* (*fiddle, tinker with*) herumpfuschen an (+*dat*) (*inf*); *plans* durcheinanderbringen; *person* an der Nase herumführen (*inf*); (*boss, person in authority*) herumschikanieren; (*by delaying decision*) hinhalten. **2** *vi* **(a)** (*play the fool*) herumalbern *or* -blödeln (*inf*). **(b)** (*do nothing in particular*) herumgammeln (*inf*). **he enjoys ~ing ~ on the river** er gondelt gern (im Boot) auf dem Fluß herum. **(c)** (*tinker, fiddle*) herumfummeln (*inf*) *or* -spielen (*with an +dat*); (*as hobby etc*) herumbasteln (*with an +dat*) (*inf*). **that'll teach you to ~ ~ with explosives** das soll dir eine Lehre sein, nicht mit Sprengkörpern herumzuspielen; **I don't like film directors ~ing ~ with my scripts** ich kann es nicht haben, wenn Regisseure an meinen Drehbüchern herumändern. **(d) to ~ ~ with sb** (*associate with*) sich mit jdm einlassen *or* abgeben; (*not take seriously*) jdn zum Narren haben.

♦ **mess up** *vt sep* durcheinanderbringen; (*make untidy also*)

unordentlich machen, in Unordnung bringen; (*make dirty*) verdrecken; (*botch, bungle*) verpfuschen, verhunzen (*inf*); *marriage* kaputtmachen (*inf*), ruinieren; *life, person* verkorksen (*inf*); *person* (*as regards looks*) übel zurichten. **missing the connection ~ed ~ the whole journey** dadurch, daß wir den Anschluß verpaßten, lief die ganze Reise schief; **her visit really ~ed me ~** (*inf*) ihr Besuch hat mir wirklich alles vermasselt (*inf*); **that's really ~ed things ~** das hat wirklich alles verdorben *or* vermasselt (*inf*).

mess² (*Mil*) **1** *n* Kasino *nt*; (*on ships*) Messe *f*; (*food*) Essen *nt*. **2** *vi* essen, das Essen einnehmen.

message ['mesɪdʒ] *n* **(a)** Mitteilung, Nachricht, Botschaft (*old, form*) *f*; (*radio ~*) Funkspruch *m* *or* -meldung *f*; (*report, police ~*) Meldung *f*. **a ~ from headquarters** eine Mitteilung vom Hauptquartier; **to take a ~ to sb** jdm eine Nachricht überbringen; **to give sb a ~** (*verbal*) jdm etwas ausrichten; (*written*) jdm eine Nachricht geben; **would you give John a ~ (for me)?** könnten Sie John etwas (von mir) ausrichten?; **I gave John a ~ for you** ich habe John gebeten, dir etwas auszurichten; **have you given him my ~ yet?** hast du es ihm schon ausgerichtet?; **to send a ~ to sb** jdm benachrichtigen; **to leave a ~ for sb** (*written*) jdm eine Nachricht hinterlassen; (*verbal*) jdm etwas ausrichten lassen; **can I take a ~ (for him)?** (*on telephone*) kann ich (ihm) etwas ausrichten?; **the Queen's ~ to the people** die (Fernseh)ansprache der Königin. **(b)** (*moral*) Botschaft *f*. **the ~ of the play is ...** die Aussage des Stückes ist ..., das Stück will folgendes sagen ...; **a pop song with a ~** ein Schlagertext, der einem etwas zu sagen hat. **(c) to get the ~** (*fig inf*) kapieren (*inf*); **I got the ~** ich habe schon verstanden *or* kapiert (*inf*). **(d)** (*Scot: errand*) Einkauf *m*. **to do** *or* **get one's ~s** einkaufen.

mess deck *n* Speisedeck *nt*.

messenger ['mesɪndʒəʳ] *n* Bote (*old, form*), Überbringer(in *f*) *m* (einer Nachricht); (*Mil*) Kurier *m*. **~ boy** Botenjunge, Laufbursche *m*; **bank/post office ~** Bank-/Postbote *m*.

mess hall *n* Kasino *nt*.

Messiah [mɪ'saɪə] *n* Messias *m*.

messianic [ˌmesɪ'ænɪk] *adj* messianisch.

mess: ~ jacket *n* Affenjäckchen *nt* (*inf*); **~ kit** *n* (*Brit*) Uniform *f* für gesellschaftliche Anlässe; (*US*) Eßgeschirr *nt*; **~ mate** *n* they were ~ mates sie waren Kameraden bei der Armee.

Messrs ['mesəz] *pl of* **Mr** *abbr of* **Messieurs** *not translated except on letters etc.* **to ~ ... an die Herren ...**

mess tin *n* Eß- *or* Kochgeschirr *nt*.

mess-up ['mesʌp] *n* Kuddelmuddel *nt* (*inf*). **there's been a bit of a ~** da ist etwas schiefgelaufen (*inf*).

messy ['mesɪ] *adj* (+*er*) (*dirty*) dreckig, schmutzig; (*untidy*) unordentlich; (*confused*) durcheinander; (*fig: unpleasant*) unschön. **~ writing** fürchterliche Klaue (*inf*); **he's a ~ eater** er kann nicht ordentlich essen, er ißt wie ein Schwein.

met¹ [met] *pret, ptp of* **meet²**.

met² *abbr of* **meteorological**.

meta- ['metə-] *pref* meta-, Meta-.

metabolic [ˌmetə'bɒlɪk] *adj* Stoffwechsel-, metabolisch.

metabolism [me'tæbəlɪzəm] *n* Stoffwechsel, Metabolismus *m*.

metacarpal [ˌmetə'kɑːpl] *n* Mittelhandknochen *m*.

metal ['metl] **1** *n* Metall *nt*; (*Brit: on road*) Asphalt *m*. **~s** *pl* (*Rail*) Schienen *pl*. **2** *vt road* asphaltieren; **~led road** Asphaltstraße *f*.

metallic [mɪ'tælɪk] *adj* metallisch.

metallurgic(al) [ˌmetə'lɜːdʒɪk(əl)] *adj* metallurgisch.

metallurgist [me'tælədʒɪst] *n* Metallurg(in *f*) *m*.

metallurgy [me'tælədʒɪ] *n* Hüttenkunde, Metallurgie *f*.

metal *in cpds* Metall-; **~ plating** *n* Metallschicht *f*; (*act*) Platierung *f*; **~ polish** *n* Metallpolitur *f*; **~work** *n* Metall *nt*; **we did ~work at school** wir haben in der Schule Metallarbeiten gemacht; **~worker** *n* Metallarbeiter *m*.

metamorphose [ˌmetə'mɔːfəʊz] **1** *vt* verwandeln; (*Sci*) umwandeln. **2** *vi* sich verwandeln; (*Sci*) sich umwandeln.

metamorphosis [ˌmetə'mɔːfəsɪs] *n*, *pl* **metamorphoses** [ˌmetə'mɔːfəsiːz] Metamorphose *f*; (*fig*) Verwandlung *f*.

metaphor ['metəfəʳ] *n* Metapher *f*.

metaphorical [ˌmetə'fɒrɪkəl] *adj* metaphorisch.

metaphorically [ˌmetə'fɒrɪkəlɪ] *adv see adj.* **~ speaking** metaphorisch ausgedrückt, bildlich gesprochen.

metaphysical *adj*, **~ly** *adv* [ˌmetə'fɪzɪkəl, -ɪ] metaphysisch.

metaphysician [ˌmetəfɪ'zɪʃn] *n* Metaphysiker(in *f*) *m*.

metaphysics [ˌmetə'fɪzɪks] *n sing* Metaphysik *f*.

metastasis [me'tæstəsɪs] *n*, *pl* **metastases** [mɪ'tæstəsiːz] Metastasenbildung, Metastasierung *f*.

metatarsal [ˌmetə'tɑːsl] *adj* Mittelfuß-, metatarsal (*spec*).

metathesis [me'tæθəsɪs] *n*, *pl* **metatheses** [me'tæθəsiːz] Metathese, Metathesis *f*.

metazoan [ˌmetə'zəʊən] **1** *n* Metazoon *nt* (*spec*), Vielzeller *m*. **2** *adj* vielzellig, metazoisch (*spec*).

mete [miːt] *vt:* **to ~ out** zuteil werden lassen (*to sb* jdm); *praise* austeilen; *rewards* verteilen; **to ~ out a punishment to sb** jdn bestrafen; **the function of the courts is to ~ out justice** es ist Aufgabe der Gerichte, zu richten; **justice was ~d out to them** es wurde über sie gerichtet *or* Gericht gesessen.

metempsychosis [ˌmetəmsaɪ'kəʊsɪs] *n*, *pl* **metempsychoses** [ˌmetəmsaɪ'kəʊsiːz] Metempsychose *f*.

meteor ['miːtɪəʳ] *n* Meteor *m*.

meteoric [ˌmiːtɪ'ɒrɪk] *adj* meteorisch; (*fig*) kometenhaft.

meteorite ['miːtɪəraɪt] *n* Meteorit *m*.

meteoroid ['miːtɪərɔɪd] *n* Sternschnuppe *f*.

meteorological [ˌmiːtɪərə'lɒdʒɪkəl] *adj* Wetter-, meteorologisch. **the M~ Office** (*Brit*) das Wetteramt.

meteorologist [ˌmiːtɪə'rɒlədʒɪst] *n* Meteorologe *m*, Meteorologin *f*.

meteorology [ˌmiːtɪə'rɒlədʒɪ] *n* Meteorologie, Wetterkunde *f*.

meter[1] ['miːtə[r]] **1** *n* Zähler *m*; (*gas* ~ *also*) Gasuhr *f*; (*water* ~) Wasseruhr *f*; (*parking* ~) Parkuhr *f*; (*exposure or light* ~) Belichtungsmesser *m*; (*slot* ~) Münzzähler *m*. the ~ has run out die Parkuhr ist abgelaufen/es ist kein Geld mehr im Zähler. **2** *vt* messen.

meter[2] *n* (*US*) see **metre**.

methane ['miːθeɪn] *n* Methan *nt*.

methinks [mɪ'θɪŋks] *pret* **methought** [mɪ'θɔːt] *vi impers* (*obs*) mich deucht (*obs*), mir or mich dünkt (*old*).

method ['meθəd] *n* Methode *f*; (*process*) Verfahren *nt*; (*Cook*) Zubereitung *f*; (*in experiment*) Vorgehens- or Verfahrensweise *f*. a man of ~ ein Mensch mit Methode; ~ of payment/application Zahlungs-/Anwendungsweise *f*; there's ~ in his madness seine Handlungsweise hat Methode; ~ acting Schauspielen *nt nach dem System Stanislawski*.

methodical *adj*, **~ly** *adv* [mɪ'θɒdɪkəl, -ɪ] methodisch.

Methodism ['meθədɪzəm] *n* Methodismus *m*.

Methodist ['meθədɪst] **1** *adj* methodistisch. **2** *n* Methodist(in *f*) *m*.

methodology [,meθə'dɒlədʒɪ] *n* Methodik, Methodologie *f*.

meths [meθs] *n sing abbr of* **methylated spirits** Spiritus *m*. ~ **drinker** ≈ Fuseltrinker *m*.

Methuselah [mə'θuːzələ] *n* Methusalem *m*. as old as ~ so alt wie Methusalem.

methyl alcohol ['miːθaɪl'ælkəhɒl] *n* Methylalkohol *m*.

methylated spirits ['meθɪleɪtɪd'spɪrɪts] *n sing* Äthylalkohol, (Brenn)spiritus *m*.

meticulous [mɪ'tɪkjʊləs] *adj* sorgfältig, (peinlich) genau, exakt. to be ~ about sth es mit etw sehr genau nehmen; with ~ attention to detail mit besonderer Sorgfalt für das Detail.

meticulously [mɪ'tɪkjʊləslɪ] *adv see adj*. ~ **clean** peinlich sauber.

métier ['meɪtɪeɪ] *n* Metier *nt*.

metonymy [mə'tɒnɪmɪ] *n* Metonymie *f*.

metre, (*US*) **meter** ['miːtə[r]] *n* (a) (*Measure*) Meter *m or nt*. (b) (*Poet*) Metrum *nt*.

metric ['metrɪk] *adj* metrisch. the ~ **system** das metrische Maßsystem; ~ **ton** Metertonne *f*; to go ~ auf das metrische Maßsystem umstellen.

metrical ['metrɪkəl] *adj* (*Poet*) metrisch.

metricate ['metrɪkeɪt] *vt* auf das metrische Maßsystem umstellen.

metrication [,metrɪ'keɪʃən] *n* Umstellung *f* auf das metrische Maßsystem.

metronome ['metrənəʊm] *n* Metronom *nt*.

metropolis [mɪ'trɒpəlɪs] *n* Metropole, Weltstadt *f*; (*capital*) Hauptstadt *f*.

metropolitan [,metrə'pɒlɪtən] **1** *adj* weltstädtisch, weltoffen; der Hauptstadt; (*Eccl*) Metropolitan-; *diocese* Erz-; *bishop* Diözesan-. a ~ **city** eine Weltstadt; **M~ Police** Londoner/New Yorker Polizei.
2 *n* Weltbürger(in *f*) *m*; (*citizen*) Großstädter(in *f*) *m*; Hauptstädter(in *f*) *m*; (*Eccl*) Metropolit *m*.

mettle ['metl] *n* (*spirit*) Courage *f*, Stehvermögen *nt*; (*of horse*) Zähigkeit *f*; (*temperament*) Feuer *nt*. a man of ~ ein Mann von echtem Schrot und Korn; to show one's ~ zeigen, was in einem steckt; to test sb's ~ herausfinden, was in jdm steckt; to be on one's ~ auf dem Posten sein; to put sb on his ~ jdn fordern.

mettlesome ['metlsəm] *adj person* couragiert, schneidig; *horse* feurig.

mew [mjuː] **1** *n* Miau(en) *nt*. **2** *vi* miauen.

mewl [mjuːl] *vi* (*cat*) maunzen, mauzen; (*baby*) wimmern.

mews [mjuːz] *n sing or pl* (*houses*) Siedlung *f ehemaliger zu modischen Wohnungen umgebauter Kutscherhäuschen*; (*street*) Gasse *f*; (*old: stables*) Stall(ungen *pl*) *m*. a ~ **cottage** ein ehemaliges Kutscherhäuschen.

Mexican ['meksɪkən] **1** *adj* mexikanisch. **2** *n* Mexikaner(in *f*) *m*.

Mexico ['meksɪkəʊ] *n* Mexiko *nt*.

mezzanine ['mezəniːn] *n* Mezzanin *nt*.

mezzo-soprano [,metsəʊsə'prɑːnəʊ] *n* Mezzosopran *m*.

mezzotint ['metsəʊtɪnt] *n* Mezzotint *nt*.

mfd *abbr of* **manufactured** hergestellt.

miaow [miː'aʊ] **1** *n* Miau(en) *nt*. **2** *vi* miauen.

miasma [mɪ'æzmə] *n*, *pl* **-ta** [mɪ'æzmətə] *or* **miasmas** [mɪ'æzməz] Miasma *nt*.

mica ['maɪkə] *n* Muskovit *m*.

mice [maɪs] *pl of* **mouse**.

Michaelmas ['mɪklməs] *n* Michaeli(s) *nt*. ~ **daisy** Herbstaster *f*; ~ **Day** Michaelis(tag) *nt*.

mickey ['mɪkɪ] *n* (*sl*): to take the ~ (out of sb) jdn auf den Arm or auf die Schippe nehmen (*inf*) or veräppeln (*inf*); are you taking the ~? du willst mich/ihn *etc* wohl veräppeln *etc* (*inf*).

Mickey Finn ['mɪkɪ'fɪn] *n* (*inf*) Betäubungsmittel *nt*; (*drink*) präparierter Drink. they slipped him a ~ sie haben ihm was in den Drink getan (*inf*).

micro- ['maɪkrəʊ-] *pref* mikro-, Mikro-.

microbe ['maɪkrəʊb] *n* Mikrobe *f*.

micro: ~**biology** *n* Mikrobiologie *f*; ~**chip** *n* Mikrochip *nt*; ~**cosm** *n* Mikrokosmos *m*; ~**dot** *n* Mikrobild *nt*; ~**fiche** *n* Mikrofiche *m or nt*, Mikrokarte *f*; ~**film** 1 *n* Mikrofilm *m*; 2 *vt* auf Mikrofilm aufnehmen.

micron ['maɪkrɒn] *n* Mikron, Mikrometer *nt*.

micro: ~**organism** *n* Mikroorganismus *m*; ~**phone** *n* Mikrophon *nt*; ~**processor** *n* Mikroprozessor *m*; ~**scope** *n* Mikroskop *nt*.

microscopic [,maɪkrə'skɒpɪk] *adj details, print* mikroskopisch. ~ **creature** mikroskopisch kleines Lebewesen.

microscopically [,maɪkrə'skɒpɪklɪ] *adv* mikroskopisch.

microwave ['maɪkrəʊ,weɪv] *n* Mikrowelle *f*. ~ **oven** Mikrowellenofen *m*.

mid [mɪd] **1** *prep* (*poet*) see **amid(st)**.

2 *adj* mittel-, Mittel-. in ~ **January/June** Mitte Januar/Juni; in the ~ **1950s** Mitte der fünfziger Jahre; in the ~ **20th century** Mitte des 20. Jahrhunderts; **temperatures in the** ~ **eighties** Temperaturen um 85° Fahrenheit; in ~ **morning/afternoon** am Vormittag/Nachmittag; a ~-**morning/-afternoon break** eine Frühstücks-/Nachmittagspause; a ~-**morning/-afternoon snack** ein zweites Frühstück/ein Imbiß *m* am Nachmittag; in ~ **channel** in der Mitte des Kanals; in ~ **ocean** mitten auf dem Meer; in ~ **air** in der Luft; ~-**flight course corrections** Kurskorrekturen während des Flugs; in ~ **course** mittendrin (*inf*).

MIDAS ['maɪdəs] *abbr of* **Missile Defence Alarm System**.

Midas ['maɪdəs] *n* Midas *m*. the ~ **touch** eine glückliche Hand, Glück *nt*; he has the ~ **touch** er macht aus Dreck Geld (*inf*).

midday ['mɪd'deɪ] **1** *n* Mittag *m*. at ~ mittags, gegen Mittag, um die Mittagszeit. **2** *adj attr* mittäglich. ~ **meal** Mittagessen *nt*; ~ **sun/heat** Mittagssonne/-hitze *f*.

midden ['mɪdn] *n* (*Archeol*) Muschelhaufen *m*; (*dial*) (*dustbin*) Mülleimer *m*; (*rubbish dump*) Müll *m*.

middle ['mɪdl] **1** *n* Mitte *f*; (*central section: of book, film etc*) Mittelteil *m*, mittlerer Teil; (*inside of fruit, nut etc*) Innere(s) *nt*; (*stomach*) Bauch, Leib, (*waist*) Taille *f*. in the ~ of the table mitten auf dem Tisch; (*in exact centre*) in der Mitte des Tisches; he passed the ball to the ~ of the field er spielte den Ball zur (Feld)mitte; in the ~ of the night/morning mitten in der Nacht/am Vormittag; in the ~ of the day mitten am Tag; (*around midday*) gegen Mittag; in the ~ of nowhere j.w.d. (*inf*), am Ende der Welt; in the ~ of summer/winter mitten im Sommer/Winter; (*height of summer season*) im Hochsommer; in or about the ~ of May Mitte Mai; in the ~ of the century um die Jahrhundertmitte, Mitte des Jahrhunderts; we were in the ~ of lunch wir waren mitten beim Essen; in the ~ of my back im Kreuz; to be in the ~ of doing sth mitten dabei sein, etw zu tun; I'm in the ~ of reading it ich bin mittendrin; down the ~ in der Mitte; he parts/she parted his hair down the ~ er hat einen Mittelscheitel/sie scheitelte sein Haar in der Mitte.

2 *adj* mittlere(r, s); *part, point, finger* Mittel-. the ~ **house** das mittlere Haus, das Haus in der Mitte.

middle *in cpds* Mittel-, mittel-; ~ **age** *n* mittleres Lebensalter; a **man of** ~ **age** ein Mann mittleren Alters or in den mittleren Jahren; ~-**aged** *adj* in den mittleren Jahren, mittleren Alters; *feeling, appearance* alt; *attitudes* spießig (*pej*), altmodisch; **M~ Ages** *npl* Mittelalter *nt*; ~**brow 1** *adj* für den (geistigen) Normalverbraucher; *tastes* Durchschnitts-, des Normalverbrauchers, Allgemein-; **2** *n* (geistiger) Normalverbraucher; ~ **C** *n* (eingestrichenes) C; ~-**class** *adj* bürgerlich, spießig (*pej*); (*Sociol*) Mittelstands-, mittelständisch; he's so typically ~-**class** er ist ein typischer Vertreter der Mittelklasse, er ist ein richtiger Spießer (*pej*); ~ **class(es)** *n* Mittelstand *m or* -klasse or -schicht *f*; ~ **distance** *n* mittlere Entfernung; (*Art*) Mittelgrund *m*; ~ **ear** *n* Mittelohr *nt*; **M~ East** *n* Naher Osten; **M~ English** *n* Mittelenglisch *nt*; **M~ High German** *n* Mittelhochdeutsch *nt*; **M~ Low German** *n* mittelniederdeutsche Sprache; ~**man** *n* Mittelsmann *m*; (*Comm*) Zwischenhändler *m*; ~ **name** *n* zweiter (Vor)name; **modesty is my** ~ **name** (*fig*) ich bin die Bescheidenheit in Person; ~-**of-the-road** *adj policy, politician* der gemäßigten Mitte; ~-**of-the-roader** *n* Vertreter(in *f*) *m* der gemäßigten Mitte; ~ **watch** *n* Mittelwache *f*; ~**weight** (*Sport*) **1** *n* Mittelgewicht *nt*; (*person also*) Mittelgewichtler *m*; **2** *adj* Mittelgewichts-; ~**weight champion** Meister *m* im Mittelgewicht.

middling ['mɪdlɪŋ] **1** *adj* mittelmäßig; (*of size*) mittlere(r, s). **how are you?** — ~ wie geht es dir? — einigermaßen; **what was the weather like?** — ~ wie war das Wetter? — so lala (*inf*) or durchwachsen.

2 *adv* (*inf: fairly*) ~ **good** mittelprächtig (*inf*).

Middx *abbr of* **Middlesex**.

midfield [,mɪd'fiːld] **1** *n* Mittelfeld *nt*. **2** *adj player* Mittelfeld-.

midge [mɪdʒ] *n* Mücke *f*.

midget ['mɪdʒɪt] **1** *n* kleiner Mensch, Liliputaner *m*; (*child*) Knirps *m*. **2** *adj* winzig; *submarine* Kleinst-.

mid: ~**land** 1 *adj attr* im Landesinneren (gelegen); 2 *n* Landesinnere(s) *nt*; the **M~lands** die Midlands; ~**night** 1 *n* Mitternacht *f*; at ~**night** um Mitternacht; 2 *adj attr* mitternächtlich; *walk also, feast, hour* Mitternachts-; the ~**night sun** die Mitternachtssonne; ~**point** *n* mittlerer Punkt; (*Geom*) Mittelpunkt *m*; to reach ~**point** die Hälfte hinter sich (*dat*) haben.

midriff ['mɪdrɪf] *n* Taille *f*. a punch to the ~ ein Schlag in die Magengegend or -grube; a ~ **bulge** (*hum*) Fettpölsterchen *nt* um die Taille.

mid: ~**shipman** *n* Fähnrich *m* zur See; ~**ships** *adv* mittschiffs.

midst [mɪdst] **1** *n* Mitte *f*. in the ~ of mitten in; in the ~ of her tears unter Tränen; in the ~ of our troubles Grandpa died und zu allem Unglück starb noch Großvater; you can't expect us to do that in the ~ of our troubles das können Sie doch nicht von uns erwarten, wo wir bis zum Hals in Problemen stecken; in our ~ unter uns, in unserer Mitte (*geh*).

2 *prep* (*old poet*) see **amid(st)**.

mid: ~**stream** *n* in ~**stream** (*lit*) in der Mitte des Flusses; (*fig*) auf halber Strecke, mittendrin; ~**summer** 1 *n* Hochsommer *m*; **M~summer's Day** Sommersonnenwende *f*, Johanni(stag *m*) *nt*; 2 *adj* ~ **days, nights** Hochsommer-; "A **M~summer Night's Dream**" "Ein Sommernachtstraum"; ~**summer madness** Sommerkoller *m* (*inf*); **that was** ~**summer madness** das war eine Schnapsidee (*inf*); ~**term** 1 *n* in ~**term** mitten im Trimester/Schulhalbjahr; by ~**term** bis zur Trimesterhälfte/bis zur Mitte des Schulhalbjahres; it was ~**term before ...** das halbe Trimester/Schulhalbjahr war schon vorbei, bevor ...;
2 *adj* ~**term elections** (*Pol*) Zwischenwahlen *pl*; ~**term examinations** Prüfungen in der Mitte eines Trimesters/Schulhalbjahres; ~**way** 1 *adv* auf halbem Weg;

~**way through** sth mitten in etw (dat); **we are now** ~**way die Hälfte haben wir hinter uns** (dat); **2** adj **X is the** ~**way point between A and B X liegt auf halbem Wege zwischen A und B; we've now reached the** ~**way point/stage in the project das Projekt ist jetzt zur Hälfte fertig;** ~**week 1** adv mitten in der Woche; **by** ~**week Mitte der Woche; 2** adj attr Mitte der Woche; **he booked a** ~**week flight er buchte einen Flug für Mitte der Woche; M**~**west** n Mittelwesten m; **M**~**western** adj mittelwestlich; songs, dialect etc also des Mittelwestens.

midwife ['mɪdwaɪf] n, pl -**wives** Hebamme f.
midwifery [,mɪd'wɪfərɪ] n Geburtshilfe f.
midwinter [,mɪd'wɪntəʳ] **1** n Mitte f des Winters, Wintermitte f.
2 adj um die Mitte des Winters, mittwinterlich.
midwives ['mɪdwaɪvz] pl of **midwife**.
mien [miːn] n (liter) Miene f.
miff [mɪf] (inf) **1** n **to get into a** ~ sich auf den Schlips getreten fühlen (about von) (inf), sich erhitzen (about über +acc). **2** vt **to be** ~**ed at sth** sich wegen etw auf den Schlips getreten fühlen (inf); **to get** ~**ed at sth** sich über etw (acc) erhitzen (inf).
MI5 ['emaɪ'faɪv] abbr of **Military Intelligence** (5).
might[1] [maɪt] pret of **may**. **they** ~ **be brothers, they look so alike** sie könnten Brüder sein, sie sehen sich so ähnlich; **as you** ~ **expect wie zu erwarten war; how old** ~ **he be? wie alt er wohl ist?;** ~ **I smoke?, do you think I** ~ **smoke?** dürfte ich wohl rauchen?, ob ich wohl rauchen darf?; **you** ~ **try Smith's Sie könnten es ja mal bei Smiths versuchen; can I help you?** — **you** ~ **lay the table** kann ich dir behilflich sein? — du könntest den Tisch decken; **he** ~ **at least have apologized** er hätte sich wenigstens entschuldigen können; **she was thinking of what** ~ **have been** sie dachte an das, was hätte sein können.
might[2] n Macht f. **with** ~ **and main** mit aller Macht; **with all one's** ~ mit aller Kraft; **superior** ~ Übermacht, Überlegenheit f; ~ **is right** (Prov) Macht geht vor Recht (Prov).
mightily ['maɪtɪlɪ] adv **(a)** mit aller Macht; (fig: majestically, imposingly) gewaltig.
(b) (inf: extremely) mächtig (inf). **a** ~ **improved team** eine stark verbesserte Mannschaft.
mightiness ['maɪtɪnɪs] n Macht f; (of wave, shout, scream) Gewalt f; (of warrior, noise, cheer) Stärke f; (of ship, tree etc) gewaltige Ausmaße pl.
mightn't ['maɪtnt] contr of **might not**.
mighty ['maɪtɪ] **1** adj (+er) gewaltig; (wielding power) mächtig; warrior stark. **2** adv (inf) mächtig (inf).
mignonette [,mɪnjə'net] n Reseda, Resede f.
migraine ['miːgreɪn] n Migräne f.
migrant ['maɪgrənt] **1** adj Wander-. ~ **bird** Zugvogel m; ~ **worker** Wanderarbeiter m; (esp in EEC) Gastarbeiter m. **2** n Zugvogel m; Wanderarbeiter m; Gastarbeiter m.
migrate [maɪ'greɪt] vi (animals, workers) (ab)wandern; (birds) nach Süden ziehen; (fig: townsfolk etc) ziehen. **do these birds** ~? sind das Zugvögel?; **whole families** ~**d south** ganze Familien zogen nach Süden or wanderten in den Süden ab.
migration [maɪ'greɪʃən] n **(a)** Wanderung f; (of birds also) (Vogel)zug m; (fig: of people) Abwanderung f; (seasonal) Zug m. **(b)** (number) Schwarm m.
migratory [maɪ'greɪtərɪ] adj life Wander-. ~ **birds** Zugvögel; ~ **instinct** Wandertrieb m; ~ **worker** Wanderarbeiter m; ~ **creatures** Tiere, die auf Wanderung gehen.
mike [maɪk] n (inf) Mikrophon nt.
Mike [maɪk] n dim of **Michael**. **for the love of** ~! (inf) um Himmels willen (inf).
milady [mɪ'leɪdɪ] n Mylady f, gnädige Frau.
milage n see **mileage**.
Milan [mɪ'læn] n Mailand nt.
mild [maɪld] **1** adj (+er) **(a)** (gentle) climate, weather, punishment, spring day mild; breeze, criticism, rebuke leicht, sanft; medicine leicht; person, character sanft. **a detergent which is** ~ **to your hands** ein Waschmittel, das Ihre Hände schont.
(b) (in flavour) taste, cigar, cheese mild; cigarettes also, whisky leicht. **this cheese has a very** ~ **taste** der Käse ist sehr mild (im Geschmack); ~ **ale** leichtes dunkles Bier.
(c) (slight) leicht.
2 n (beer) leichtes dunkles Bier.
mildew ['mɪldjuː] **1** n Schimmel m; (on plants) Mehltau m. **2** vi verschimmeln, Schimmel ansetzen; (plants) von Mehltau befallen sein. **they are all** ~**ed with age** sie sind im Laufe der Jahre ganz verschimmelt.
mildewy ['mɪldjuːɪ] adj schimmelig, verschimmelt; plants von Mehltau befallen. **to get** ~ schimmelig werden, verschimmeln.
mildly ['maɪldlɪ] adv leicht; scold, say sanft; scold, rebuke milde. **to put it** ~ gelinde gesagt; **... and that's putting it** ~ **... und das ist noch milde ausgedrückt; they seemed** ~ **interested sie machten einen leicht interessierten Eindruck.
mildness ['maɪldnɪs] n see adj **(a)** Milde f; Sanftheit f; Leichtigkeit f; Sanftheit, Sanftmütigkeit f. **(b)** milder Geschmack, Milde f; Leichtigkeit f.
mile [maɪl] n Meile f. **how many** ~**s per gallon does your car do?** wieviel verbraucht Ihr Auto?; **a fifty-**~ **journey** eine Fahrt von fünfzig Meilen; ~**s (and** ~**s)** (inf) meilenweit; ~ **upon** ~ **of yellow beaches** meilenweite or meilenlange Sandstrände pl; **they live** ~**s away** sie wohnen meilenweit weg; **you can tell it a** ~ **off/it stands or sticks out a** ~ **das sieht ja ein Blinder (mit Krückstock)** (inf); **it smelled for** ~**s around** das roch meilenweit im Umkreis or 10 Kilometer gegen den Wind (inf); **you were** ~**s off the target** du hast meilenweit danebengetroffen; **he's** ~**s better at tennis than she is** er spielt hundertmal besser Tennis als sie (inf); **not a hundred** ~**s from here** (fig) in nächster Nähe, gar nicht weit weg.
mileage ['maɪlɪdʒ] n Meilen pl; (on odometer) Meilenstand m, Meilenzahl f. **what's the** ~ **from here to London?** wieviele

Meilen sind es von hier nach London?; **what** ~ **did you do yesterday?** wieviele Meilen seid ihr gestern gefahren?; ~ **per gallon** Benzinverbrauch m; **you get a much better** ~ **(per gallon) from this car if ...** dieser Wagen ist viel sparsamer im Verbrauch, wenn ...; ~ **allowance** ≈ Kilometerpauschale f; ~ **recorder** Meilenzähler, ≈ Kilometerzähler m; **we got a lot of** ~ **out of it** (fig inf) das war uns (dat) sehr dienlich.
mileometer [maɪ'lɒmɪtəʳ] n Tacho(meter), Meilenzähler m.
milepost ['maɪlpəʊst] n Meilenanzeiger or -pfosten m.
miler ['maɪləʳ] n 1500-Meter-Läufer(in f) m.
milestone ['maɪlstəʊn] n (lit, fig) Meilenstein m.
milieu ['miːljɜː] n Milieu nt.
militant ['mɪlɪtənt] **1** adj militant. **2** n militantes Mitglied/militanter Student/Gewerkschaftler/Politiker. **the** ~**s among the trade unionists** die militanten Gewerkschaftler.
militarily ['mɪlɪtrɪlɪ] adv militärisch (gesehen), auf militärischem Gebiet.
militarism ['mɪlɪtərɪzəm] n Militarismus m.
militarist ['mɪlɪtərɪst] **1** adj militaristisch. **2** n Militarist m.
militaristic [,mɪlɪtə'rɪstɪk] adj militaristisch.
militarize ['mɪlɪtəraɪz] vt militarisieren. **fully** ~**d** hochmilitarisiert.
military ['mɪlɪtərɪ] **1** adj militärisch; government, band Militär-. ~ **police** Militärpolizei f; ~ **service** Militärdienst, Wehrdienst m; **to do one's** ~ **service** seinen Wehr- or Militärdienst ableisten or machen (inf); **he's doing his** ~ **service** er ist gerade beim Militär or (BRD inf) Bund; **the top** ~ **men** die führenden Militärs.
2 n: **the** ~ das Militär.
militate ['mɪlɪteɪt] vi **to** ~ **against/in favour of sth** für/gegen etw sprechen.
militia [mɪ'lɪʃə] n Miliz, Bürgerwehr f.
militiaman [mɪ'lɪʃəmən] n, pl -**men** [-mən] Milizsoldat m.
milk [mɪlk] **1** n Milch f. ~ **of magnesia** Magnesiamilch f; **the land of** or **flowing with** ~ **and honey** das Land, wo Milch und Honig fließt; **the** ~ **of human kindness** die Milch der frommen Denk(ungs)art (liter); **she was not exactly flowing over with the** ~ **of human kindness** sie strömte nicht gerade über vor Freundlichkeit; **it's** or **there's no use crying over spilt** ~ (prov) was passiert ist, ist passiert.
2 vt (lit, fig) melken. **the little old lady was** ~**ed dry by some absolutely heartless swindler** die alte Frau wurde von einem gewissenlosen Betrüger nach Strich und Faden ausgenommen (inf).
3 vi Milch geben, milchen (dial).
milk in cpds Milch-; ~**and-water** adj (fig) seicht, verwässert; ~**bar** n Milchbar f; ~ **chocolate** n Vollmilchschokolade f; ~ **churn** n Milchkanne f; ~ **float** n Milchauto nt.
milkiness ['mɪlkɪnɪs] n Milchigkeit f.
milking ['mɪlkɪŋ] n Melken nt. ~ **machine** Melkmaschine f; ~ **stool** Melkschemel m.
milk: ~**maid** n Milchmädchen nt; ~**man** n Milchmann m; ~ **pudding** n Milchspeise f; ~ **shake** n Milchmixgetränk nt, Milchshake m; ~**sop** n Milchbart m, Milchgesicht nt; ~ **tooth** n Milchzahn m; ~**weed** n (US) Schwalbenwurzgewächs nt; ~**white** adj milchig-weiß, milchweiß.
milky ['mɪlkɪ] adj (+er) milchig. ~ **coffee** Milchkaffee m; **rich** ~ **chocolate** sahnige Vollmilchschokolade.
Milky Way [,mɪlkɪ'weɪ] n Milchstraße f.
mill [mɪl] **1** n **(a)** (building) Mühle f. **the poor man really went through the** ~ (inf) der Arme hat wirklich viel durchmachen müssen; (was questioned hard) der Arme wurde wirklich durch die Mangel gedreht (inf); **in training you're really put through the** ~ (inf) im Training wird man ganz schön hart rangenommen (inf).
(c) (paper, steel ~ etc) Fabrik f; (cotton ~) (for thread) Spinnerei f; (for cloth) Weberei f. **saw** ~ Sägemühle f or -werk nt.
2 vt flour, coffee etc mahlen; metal, paper walzen; (with milling machine) metal fräsen; coin rändeln.
♦**mill about** or **around** vi umherlaufen. **people were** ~**ing in the office** es herrschte ein Kommen und Gehen im Büro; **the crowds** ~**ing** ~ **the stalls on the market place** die Menschenmenge, die sich zwischen den Marktständen einherschob.
milled [mɪld] adj grain gemahlen; coin, edge gerändelt.
millennial [mɪ'lenɪəl] adj tausendjährig.
millennium [mɪ'lenɪəm] n, pl -**s** or **millennia** [mɪ'lenɪə] (1,000 years) Jahrtausend, Millennium nt; (state of perfection) Tausendjähriges Reich, Millennium nt.
millepede ['mɪlɪpiːd] n see **millipede**.
miller ['mɪləʳ] n Müller m.
millet ['mɪlɪt] n Hirse f.
milli- ['mɪlɪ-] pref Milli-.
milliard ['mɪlɪɑːd] n (Brit) Milliarde f.
milli: ~**bar** n Millibar nt; ~**gram(me)** n Milligramm nt; ~**litre,** (US) ~**liter** n Milliliter m or nt.
milliner ['mɪlɪnəʳ] n Hutmacher m, Hut- or Putzmacherin, Modistin f. **at the** ~'**s (shop)** im Hutgeschäft or -laden.
millinery ['mɪlɪnərɪ] n (trade) Hut- or Putzmacherhandwerk nt; (articles) Hüte pl.
milling machine ['mɪlɪŋmə,ʃiːn] n (for coins) Rändel(eisen) nt; (for metal) Fräse, Fräsmaschine f.
million ['mɪljən] n Million f. **4** ~ **people** 4 Millionen Menschen; **for** ~**s and** ~**s of years** für Millionen und aber Millionen von Jahren; **the starving** ~**s** die Millionen, die Hunger leiden; **one in a** ~ (inf) so jemanden wie sie findet man sobald nicht wieder, sie ist einsame Klasse (sl); **it will sell a** ~ (inf) das wird ein Millionenerfolg; **I've done it** ~**s of times** (inf) das habe ich schon tausendmal gemacht; **to feel like a** ~ **dollars** (inf) sich pudelwohl fühlen.
millionaire [,mɪljə'nɛəʳ] n Millionär m.
millionairess [,mɪljə'nɛəres] n Millionärin f.

millionth ['mɪljənθ] **1** adj (fraction) millionstel; (in series) millionste(r, s). **2** n Millionstel nt.

millipede ['mɪlɪpiːd] n Tausendfüßler m.

mill: ~pond n Mühlteich m; ~race n Mühlbach or -graben m; ~stone n Mühlstein, Mahlstein m; she's/it's a ~stone round his neck sie ist für ihn ein Klotz am Bein; ~wheel n Mühlrad nt.

milord [mɪ'lɔːd] n (person) Mylord, Lord m; (as address) Mylord m. like some English ~ wie ein englischer Lord.

milt [mɪlt] n (Fishing) Milch f.

mime [maɪm] **1** n (acting) Pantomime f; (actor) Pantomime m; (ancient play, actor) Mimus m. the art of ~ die Pantomimik, die Kunst der Pantomime; to do a ~ eine Pantomime darstellen. **2** vt pantomimisch darstellen. **3** vi Pantomimen spielen.

mimeograph ['mɪmɪəgrɑːf] **1** n Vervielfältigungsapparat m. **2** vt vervielfältigen, abziehen (inf).

mimic ['mɪmɪk] **1** n Imitator m. he's a very good ~ er kann sehr gut Geräusche/andere Leute nachahmen or -machen. **2** vt nachahmen or -machen; (ridicule) nachäffen.

mimicry ['mɪmɪkrɪ] n Nachahmung f; (Biol) Mimikry f. protective ~ Schutzfärbung, Tarnfarbe f; his talent for ~ sein Talent dafür, andere nachzuahmen.

mimosa [mɪ'məʊzə] n Mimose f.

Min abbr of **Minister** Min; **Ministry** Min.

min abbr of **minute(s)** min; **minimum** min.

minaret [,mɪnə'ret] n Minarett nt.

mince [mɪns] **1** n (Brit) Hackfleisch, Gehackte(s) nt.
2 vt meat hacken, durch den Fleischwolf drehen. he doesn't ~ his words er nimmt kein Blatt vor den Mund; not to ~ matters ... um es mal ganz deutlich or brutal (inf) zu sagen ...
3 vi (walk) tänzeln, trippeln, scharwenzeln; (behave/speak) sich geziert benehmen/ausdrücken.

mince: ~meat n süße Gebäckfüllung aus Dörrobst und Sirup; to make ~meat of sb (inf) (physically) Hackfleisch aus jdm machen (inf); (verbally) jdn zur Schnecke machen (inf); to make ~meat of sth (inf) keinen guten Faden an etw (dat) lassen; ~ pie n mit Mincemeat gefülltes Gebäck.

mincer ['mɪnsəʳ] n Fleischwolf m.

mincing ['mɪnsɪŋ] adj geziert; steps tänzelnd, trippelnd.

mind [maɪnd] **1** n **(a)** (intellect) Geist (also Philos), Verstand m. things of the ~ Geistiges; a phenomenon of ~ over matter ein Phänomen des willentlichen Einflusses auf die Materie; it's a question of ~ over matter es ist eine Willenssache or -frage; a triumph of ~ over matter ein Triumph des Geistes or Willens über den Körper; the conscious and unconscious ~ das Bewußte und das Unbewußte; it's all in the ~ das ist alles Einbildung; in one's ~'s eye vor seinem geistigen Auge, im Geiste; to blow sb's ~ (sl) jdn umwerfen (inf); (drugs) jdn high machen (sl); see close¹, cross¹, improve, open, boggle.
(b) (person) Geist m. one of the finest ~s of our times einer der großen Geister unserer Zeit; see great, two.
(c) (type of ~) Geist, Kopf m; (way of thinking) Denkweise f. to have a good ~ ein heller Kopf sein; he has that kind of ~ er ist so veranlagt; to have a literary/logical etc ~ literarisch/logisch etc veranlagt sein; to the child's/Victorian ~ in der Denkweise des Kindes/der viktorianischen Zeit; the female ~ was im Kopf von Frauen vorgeht; the public ~ das Empfinden der Öffentlichkeit; state or frame of ~ (seelische) Verfassung, (Geistes)zustand m.
(d) (thoughts) Gedanken pl. to be clear in one's ~ about sth sich (dat) über etw im klaren sein; he had something on his ~ ihn beschäftigte etwas; the child's death was constantly on his ~ der Gedanke an den Tod des Kindes ließ ihn nicht los or beschäftigte ihn ständig; to put or set or give one's ~ to sth (try to do) sich anstrengen, etw zu tun; (think about sth) sich auf etw (acc) konzentrieren; if you put or set your ~ to it wenn du dich anstrengst; keep your ~ on the job bleib mit den Gedanken or dem Kopf bei der Arbeit; she couldn't get or put the song/him out of her ~ das Lied/er ging ihr nicht aus dem Kopf; you can put that idea out of your ~! den Gedanken kannst du dir aus dem Kopf schlagen!; to take sb's ~ off things jdn auf andere Gedanken bringen/jdn etw vergessen lassen; don't let your ~ dwell on the problem grüble nicht über dieses Problem nach; he can't keep his ~ off sex er denkt nur an Sex or an nichts anderes als Sex; the idea never entered my ~ daran hatte/hätte ich überhaupt nicht gedacht, das ist/wäre mir nicht in den Sinn gekommen; it's been going through my ~ es ging mir im Kopf herum.
(e) (memory) Gedächtnis nt. to bear or keep sth in ~ etw nicht vergessen; facts also, application etw im Auge behalten; to bear or keep sb in ~ an jdn denken; applicant also jdn im Auge behalten; it went right out of my ~ daran habe ich überhaupt nicht mehr gedacht; that quite put it out of my ~ dadurch habe ich es vergessen; to bring or call sth to ~ etw in Erinnerung rufen, an etw (acc) erinnern; it puts me in ~ of sb/sth es weckt in mir Erinnerungen an jdn/etw; see sight, slip.
(f) (inclination) Lust f; (intention) Sinn m, Absicht f. to have sb/sth in ~ an jdn/etw denken; to have in ~ to do sth vorhaben or im Sinn haben, etw zu tun; to have it in ~ to do sth beabsichtigen or sich (dat) vorgenommen haben, etw zu tun; I've half a ~/a good ~ to ... ich hätte Lust/große or gute Lust, zu ...; to be of a ~ to do sth geneigt sein, etw zu tun (geh); nothing was further from my ~ nichts lag mir ferner; his ~ is set on that or his (dat) das in den Kopf gesetzt; he guessed what was in my ~ er erriet meine Gedanken; see read¹.
(g) (opinion) Meinung, Ansicht f. to change one's ~ seine Meinung ändern (about über +acc), es sich (dat) anders überlegen; to be in two ~s about sth sich (dat) über etw (acc) nicht im klaren sein; to be of one or the same ~ eines Sinnes (geh) or gleicher Meinung sein; I'm of the same ~ as you ich denke wie du, ich bin deiner Meinung; with one ~ wie ein Mann; to my ~ he's wrong meiner Ansicht nach or nach

meiner Meinung irrt er sich; to have a ~ of one's own (person) (think for oneself) eine eigene Meinung haben; (not conform) seinen eigenen Kopf haben; (hum: machine etc) seine Mucken haben (inf); see know, make up, piece, speak.
(h) (sanity) Verstand m, Sinne pl. his ~ is wandering er ist nicht ganz klar im Kopf; to go out of or lose one's ~ verrückt werden, den Verstand verlieren; to drive sb out of his ~ jdn um den Verstand bringen, jdn wahnsinnig machen; to be out of one's ~ verrückt or nicht bei Verstand sein; (with worry etc) ganz or völlig aus den Häuschen sein (inf); nobody in his right ~ kein normaler Mensch; while the balance of his ~ was disturbed (Jur) wegen Verlusts des seelischen Gleichgewichts.

2 vt **(a)** (look after) aufpassen auf (+acc); sb's chair, seat freihalten. I'm ~ing the shop (fig) ich sehe nach dem Rechten.
(b) (be careful of) aufpassen (auf +acc); (pay attention to) achten auf (+acc); (act in accordance with) beachten. ~ what you're doing! paß (doch) auf!; ~ what you're doing with that car paß auf das Auto auf; ~ what I say! laß dir das gesagt sein; (do as I tell you) hör auf das, was ich dir sage; ~ your language! drück dich anständig aus!; ~ your temper! nimm dich zusammen!; ~ the step! Vorsicht Stufe!; ~ your head! Kopf einziehen (inf), Vorsicht!; niedrige Tür/Decke etc; ~ your feet! (when sitting) zieh die Füße ein!; (when moving) paß auf, wo du hintrittst!; ~ your own business kümmern Sie sich um Ihre eigenen Angelegenheiten!; ~ you do it! sieh zu, daß du das tust.
(c) (care, worry about) sich kümmern um; (object to) etwas haben gegen. she ~s/doesn't ~ it es macht ihr etwas/nichts aus; (is/is not bothered, annoyed by) es stört sie/stört sie nicht; (is not/is indifferent to) es ist ihr nicht egal/ist ihr egal; I don't ~ the cold die Kälte macht mir nichts aus; I don't ~ what he does es ist mir egal, was er macht; I don't ~ four but six is too many ich habe nichts gegen vier, aber sechs sind zuviel; do you ~ coming with me? würde es dir etwas ausmachen, mitzukommen?; would you ~ opening the door? wären Sie so freundlich, die Tür aufzumachen?; do you ~ my smoking? macht es Ihnen etwas aus or stört es Sie or haben Sie etwas dagegen, wenn ich rauche?; I hope you don't ~ my asking you/sitting here ich hoffe, Sie nehmen es mir nicht übel, wenn ich frage/ich hoffe, Sie haben nichts dagegen, daß ich hier sitze; never ~ the expense (es ist) egal, was es kostet; never ~ that now das ist jetzt nicht wichtig, laß das doch jetzt; never ~ him kümmere dich or achte nicht auf ihn; never ~ your back, I'm worried about ... den Rücken ist mir doch egal, ich mache mir Sorgen um ...; don't ~ me laß dich (durch mich) nicht stören; (iro) nimm auf mich keine Rücksicht; I wouldn't ~ a cup of tea ich hätte nichts gegen eine Tasse Tee.

3 vi **(a)** (be careful) aufpassen. ~ and see if ... sieh zu, ob ...; ~ you get that done sieh zu, daß du das fertigbekommst.
(b) ~ you allerdings; ~ you, I'd rather not go ich würde eigentlich or allerdings lieber nicht gehen; it was raining at the time, ~ you allerdings hat es da geregnet; ~ you, he did try/ask er hat es immerhin versucht/hat immerhin gefragt; he's quite good, ~ you er ist eigentlich ganz gut; I'm not saying I'll do it, ~ ich will damit aber nicht sagen, daß ich es tue; he's not a bad lad, ~, just ... er ist eigentlich kein schlechter Junge, nur ...; he didn't do it, ~ er hat es (ja) nicht getan.
(c) (care, worry) sich kümmern, sich (dat) etwas daraus machen; (object) etwas dagegen haben. he doesn't seem to ~ about anything ihn scheint nichts zu kümmern; I wish he ~ed a little so richtete, es würde ihm etwas ausmachen or ihn ein bißchen kümmern; nobody seemed to ~ es schien keinem etwas auszumachen, niemand schien etwas dagegen zu haben; do you ~? haben es Ihnen etwas aus; do you ~! (iro) na hör mal!, ich möchte doch sehr bitten!; do you ~ if I open or would you ~ if I opened the window? macht es Ihnen etwas aus, wenn ich das Fenster öffne?; I don't ~ if I do ich hätte nichts dagegen; never you ~! kümmere du dich mal nicht darum; (none of your business) das geht dich überhaupt nichts an!
(d) never ~ macht nichts, ist doch egal; (in exasperation) ist ja auch egal, schon gut; I broke your vase — never ~ ich habe deine Vase kaputtgemacht — macht nichts; never ~, you'll find another mach dir nichts draus, du findest bestimmt einen anderen; I've hurt my knee — never ~, I'll kiss it better ich habe mir das Knie weh getan — ist nicht so schlimm, ich werde blasen; oh, never ~, I'll do it myself ach, laß (es) or schon gut, ich mache es selbst; never ~ about that now! laß das doch jetzt!, das ist doch nicht wichtig; never ~ about what you said to him, what did he say to you? es ist doch egal or unwichtig, was du zu ihm gesagt hast, was hat er zu dir gesagt?; never ~ about that mistake mach dir nichts aus dem Fehler; never ~ about your back (in exasperation) dein Rücken ist mir doch egal, laß mich doch mit deinem Rücken in Frieden.

◆**mind out** vi aufpassen (for auf +acc). ~ ~! paß (doch) auf!

mind: ~-bending, ~-blowing adj (sl) irre (sl); ~-boggling adj (inf) irrsinnig (inf), verrückt (inf).

minded ['maɪndɪd] adj gesonnen (geh), gewillt. to be ~ to do sth gewillt or gesonnen (geh) or geneigt (geh) sein, etw zu tun; if you are so ~ wenn Ihnen der Sinn danach steht (geh).

-minded adj suf romantically-~ romantisch veranlagt; nasty-~ übel gesinnt; an industrially-~ nation ein auf Industrie ausgerichtetes Land; I'm not really opera-~ ich mache mir nichts aus Opern (inf).

mindful ['maɪndfʊl] adj to be ~ of sth etw berücksichtigen or bedenken; ever ~ of the risks, she ... weil sie sich (dat) der Risiken bewußt war, ... sie ...; ever ~ of her feelings immer an ihre Gefühle denkend.

mind: ~less adj (stupid) hirnlos, ohne Verstand; (senseless) destruction, crime sinnlos; occupation geistlos; the ~less fury of the waves (liter) die wilde Wut der Wellen; ~-reader n Gedankenleser(in f) m; I'm not a ~-reader ich bin doch kein Gedankenleser.

mine¹ [maɪn] **1** *poss pron* meine(r, s). **this car is ~** das ist *mein* Auto, dieses Auto gehört mir; **is this ~?** gehört das mir?, ist das meine(r, s)? **his friends and ~** seine und meine Freunde; **a friend of ~** ein Freund von mir; **will you be ~?** *(old)* willst du die Meine werden? *(old)*; **~ is a rather different job** meine Arbeit ist ziemlich anders; **that cook of ~!** dieser Koch!; **no advice of ~ could ...** keiner meiner Ratschläge konnte ...; **~ is not to reason why** es ist nicht an mir, nach dem Warum zu fragen; **a favourite expression of ~** einer meiner Lieblingsausdrücke.

2 *adj (obs)* mein(e).

mine² **1** *n* **(a)** *(Min)* Bergwerk *nt*; *(copper ~, gold~, silver-~ also)* Mine *f*; *(coal~ also)* Grube, Zeche *f*. **to work down the ~s** unter Tage arbeiten.

(b) *(Mil, Naut etc)* Mine *f*. **to lay ~s** Minen legen.

(c) *(fig)* **the book is a ~ of information** das Buch ist eine wahre Fundgrube; **he is a ~ of information** er ist ein wandelndes Lexikon *(inf)*; **he's a ~ of information about history** er besitzt ein schier unerschöpfliches Geschichtswissen.

2 *vt* **(a)** *coal, metal* fördern, abbauen; *area* Bergbau betreiben *or* Bodenschätze abbauen in (+*dat*).

(b) *(Mil, Naut) channel, road* verminen; *ship* eine Mine befestigen an (+*dat*); *(blow up)* (mit einer Mine) sprengen.

3 *vi* Bergbau betreiben. **to ~ for sth** nach etw graben; **they ~d deep down into the mountain** sie trieben einen Stollen bis tief in den Berg hinein.

mine: **~-detector** *n* Minensuchgerät *nt*; **~field** *n* Minenfeld *nt*; **~layer** *n* Minenleger *m*.

miner [ˈmaɪnə^r] *n* Bergarbeiter, Bergmann *m*. **~'s lamp** Grubenlampe *f*.

mineral [ˈmɪnərəl] **1** *n* Mineral *nt*. **2** *adj* mineralisch; *deposit, resources, kingdom* Mineral-. **~ ores** Erze *pl*.

mineralogical [ˌmɪnərəˈlɒdʒɪkəl] *adj* mineralogisch.

mineralogist [ˌmɪnəˈrælədʒɪst] *n* Mineraloge *m*, Mineralogin *f*.

mineralogy [ˌmɪnəˈrælədʒɪ] *n* Mineralogie *f*.

mineral: **~ oil** *n* Mineralöl *nt*; **~ water** *n* Mineralwasser *nt*.

mineshaft [ˈmaɪnʃɑːft] *n* Schacht *m*.

minestrone [ˌmɪnɪˈstrəʊnɪ] *n* Minestrone, Gemüsesuppe *f*.

mine: **~sweeper** *n* Minenräumboot *or* -suchboot *nt or* -sucher *m*; **~ workings** *npl* Stollen *pl*.

Ming [mɪŋ] *adj* Ming-.

mingle [ˈmɪŋgl] **1** *vi* sich vermischen; *(people, groups)* sich untereinander vermischen. **he ~d with people of all classes** er hatte Umgang mit Menschen aller gesellschaftlichen Schichten; **to ~ with the crowd** sich unters Volk mischen.

2 *vt* mischen (*with* mit); *(liter) waters* vermischen. **love ~d with hate** mit Haß ver- *or* gemischte Liebe.

mingy [ˈmɪndʒɪ] *adj* (+*er*) *(Brit inf)* knickerig *(inf)*; *amount* lumpig *(inf)*, mickerig *(inf)*.

mini- [ˈmɪnɪ-] *pref* Mini-.

miniature [ˈmɪnɪtʃə^r] **1** *n* Miniatur- *or* Kleinausgabe *f*; *(Art)* Miniatur *f*; *(bottle)* Miniflasche *f*. **in ~** en miniature, im kleinen; **he's got his father's face in ~** er hat das Gesicht seines Vaters in Kleinformat. **2** *adj attr* Miniatur-.

miniature: **~ camera** *n* Kleinbildkamera *f*; **~ golf** *n* Mini- *or* Kleingolf *nt*; **~ poodle** *n* Zwergpudel *m*; **~ railway** *n* Liliputbahn *f*; **~ submarine** *n* Kleinst-U-Boot *nt*.

miniaturist [ˈmɪnɪtʃərɪst] *n* Miniaturmaler(in *f*) *m*.

miniaturize [ˈmɪnɪtʃəraɪz] *vt* verkleinern.

mini: **~bus** *n* Kleinbus *m*; **~cab** *n* Minicar *m*, Kleintaxi *nt*.

minim [ˈmɪnɪm] *n* *(Brit Mus)* halbe Note.

minimal *adj*, **~ly** *adv* [ˈmɪnɪml, -lɪ] minimal.

minimize [ˈmɪnɪmaɪz] *vt* **(a)** *(reduce)* expenditure, time lost etc auf ein Minimum reduzieren, minimieren *(form)*. **(b)** *(belittle, underestimate)* schlechtmachen, herabsetzen.

minimum [ˈmɪnɪməm] **1** *n* Minimum *nt*. **the temperature reached a ~ of 5 degrees** die Tiefsttemperatur betrug 5 Grad; **with a ~ of inconvenience** mit einem Minimum an Unannehmlichkeiten; **what is the ~ you will accept?** was ist für Sie das Minimum *or* der Mindestbetrag?; **a ~ of 2 hours/£50/10 people** mindestens 2 Stunden/£ 50/10 Leute; **to reduce sth to a ~** etw auf ein Minimum *or* Mindestmaß reduzieren.

2 *adj attr* Mindest-. **to achieve maximum possible profits from ~ possible expenditure** möglich hohe Gewinne mit möglichst geringen Ausgaben erzielen; **the ~ expenditure** will be ... das wird mindestens ... kosten; **~ temperature** Tiefsttemperatur *f*; **~ wage** Mindestlohn *m*.

mining [ˈmaɪnɪŋ] *n* **(a)** *(Min)* Bergbau *m*; *(work at the face)* Arbeit *f* im Bergwerk. **(b)** *(Mil) (of area)* Verminen *nt*; *(of ship)* Befestigung *f* einer Mine *(of* an +*dat*); *(blowing-up)* Sprengung *f* (mit einer Mine).

mining: **~ area** *n* Bergbaugebiet, Revier *nt*; **~ disaster** *n* Grubenunglück *nt*; **~ engineer** *n* Berg(bau)ingenieur *m*; **~ industry** *n* Bergbau *m*; **~ town** *n* Bergarbeiterstadt *f*.

minion [ˈmɪnɪən] *n* *(old)* Günstling *m*; *(fig)* Trabant *m*.

miniskirt [ˈmɪnɪˌskɜːt] *n* Minirock *m*.

minister [ˈmɪnɪstə^r] **1** *n* **(a)** *(Pol)* Minister *m*. **(b)** *(Eccl)* Pfarrer, Pastor *m*, protestantischer Geistlicher. **good morning, ~** guten Morgen, Herr Pfarrer *or* Herr Pastor.

2 *vi* **to ~ to sb** sich um jdn kümmern; **to ~ to sb's needs/wants** jds Bedürfnisse/Wünsche (*acc*) befriedigen; **a ~ing angel** *(liter)* ein barmherziger Engel.

ministerial [ˌmɪnɪˈstɪərɪəl] *adj* *(Pol)* ministeriell, Minister-. **~ post** Ministerposten *m*; **his ~ duties** seine Pflichten als Minister; **those of ~ rank** diejenigen, die im Rang eines Ministers stehen *(form)* *or* die einen Ministerposten innehaben.

ministration [ˌmɪnɪˈstreɪʃən] *n usu pl* Pflege, Fürsorge *f*.

ministry [ˈmɪnɪstrɪ] *n* **(a)** *(Pol)* Ministerium *nt*. **~ of defence/agriculture** Verteidigungs-/Landwirtschaftsministerium; **during his ~** in *or* während seiner Amtszeit (als Minister); **during the ~ of X** als X Minister war.

(b) *(Eccl)* geistliches Amt. **to join** *or* **enter** *or* **go into the ~** Pfarrer *or* Geistlicher werden; **to train for the ~** Theologie studieren, um Geistlicher zu werden.

(c) *(ministering)* Sendungsbewußtsein *nt*. **her ~ to the sick** ihr Dienst an den Kranken; **Christ's ~ here on earth** das Wirken Christi auf Erden.

miniver [ˈmɪnɪvə^r] *n* Hermelin *m*.

mink [mɪŋk] *n* Nerz *m*. **~ coat** Nerzmantel *m*.

minnow [ˈmɪnəʊ] *n* Elritze *f*.

Minoan [mɪˈnəʊən] *adj* minoisch.

minor [ˈmaɪnə^r] **1** *adj* **(a)** *(of lesser extent)* kleiner; *(of lesser importance)* unbedeutend, unwichtig; *offence, operation, injuries* leicht; *interest, importance* geringer; *poet, position* unbedeutend; *prophet, planet* klein; *road* Neben-. **a ~ role** eine Nebenrolle, eine kleinere Rolle; **he only played a ~ role in the company** er spielte in der Firma nur eine untergeordnete *or* ganz kleine Rolle; **I have one or two ~ criticisms of the hotel** ich habe an dem Hotel nur ein paar Kleinigkeiten auszusetzen; **it's only a ~ industry in this area** das ist ein ziemlich unbedeutender *or* nur ein kleiner Industriezweig in dieser Gegend; **~ premise** Untersatz *m*.

(b) *(Mus) key, scale* Moll-. **G/E flat/C sharp ~** g-/es-/cis-Moll *nt*; **~ third** kleine Terz; **the novel ends in a ~ key** *or* **on a ~ note** der Roman endet mit einer traurigen Note.

(c) *(Sch sl)* **Smith ~** Smith der Jüngere.

2 *n* **(a)** *(Mus)* **the ~ Moll** *nt*; **the music shifts to the ~** die Musik wechselt nach Moll über *or* geht in die Molltonart über.

(b) *(Jur)* Minderjährige(r) *mf*.

(c) *(US Univ)* Nebenfach *nt*.

3 *vi* *(US Univ)* im Nebenfach studieren (*in* acc).

Minorca [mɪˈnɔːkə] *n* Menorca *nt*.

Minorcan [mɪˈnɔːkən] **1** *adj* menorkinisch. **2** *n* Menorkiner(in *f*) *m*.

minority [maɪˈnɒrɪtɪ] **1** *n* **(a)** Minderheit, Minorität *f*. **to be in a ~** in der Minderheit sein; **you are in a ~ of one** Sie stehen allein da.

(b) *(Jur)* Minderjährigkeit *f*.

2 *adj attr* Minderheits-. **~ group** Minderheit, Minorität *f*; **~ programme** *(Rad, TV)* Programm, das nur einen kleinen Hörerkreis/Zuschauerkreis anspricht.

Minotaur [ˈmaɪnətɔː^r] *n* Minotaur(us) *m*.

minster [ˈmɪnstə^r] *n* Münster *nt*.

minstrel [ˈmɪnstrəl] *n* *(medieval)* Spielmann *m*; *(wandering)* *(fahrender)* Sänger; *(ballad-singer)* Bänkelsänger *m*; *(singer of love songs)* Minnesänger *m*; *(esp US: modern)* weißer als Neger zurechtgeschminkter Sänger und Komiker.

mint¹ [mɪnt] **1** *n* Münzanstalt *or* -stätte, Münze *f*. **(Royal) M~** (Königlich-)Britische Münzanstalt; **to be worth a ~** Gold wert *or* unbezahlbar sein; **he earns a ~ (of money)** er verdient ein Heidengeld *(inf)*; **his father made a ~ by selling raincoats** mit dem Verkauf von Regenmänteln hat sein Vater einen Haufen Geld gemacht *(inf)*.

2 *adj stamp* ungestempelt. **in ~ condition** in tadellosem Zustand.

3 *vt* coin, phrase prägen.

mint² *n* *(Bot)* Minze *f*; *(sweet)* Pfefferminz *nt*. **~ julep** Whisky *m* mit Eis und frischer Minze; **~ sauce** Minzsoße *f*.

minuet [ˌmɪnjʊˈet] *n* Menuett *nt*.

minus [ˈmaɪnəs] **1** *prep* **(a)** minus, weniger. **£100 ~ taxes** £ 100 abzüglich (der) Steuern.

(b) *(without, deprived of)* ohne. **he returned from the war ~ an arm** er kam mit einem Arm weniger aus dem Krieg zurück.

2 *adj quantity, value* negativ; *sign* Minus-, Subtraktions-; *temperatures* Minus-, unter Null. **~ three degrees centigrade** drei Grad minus; **an alpha ~** (+) eine Eins minus.

3 *n* *(sign)* Minus(zeichen) *nt*. **2 ~es make a plus** minus mal minus gibt plus; **if the result is a ~ ...** wenn das Ergebnis negativ *or* eine negative Größe ist ...

minuscule [ˈmɪnɪskjuːl] *adj* winzig.

minute¹ [ˈmɪnɪt] **1** *n* **(a)** *(of time, degree)* Minute *f*. **in a ~** gleich, sofort; **this (very) ~!** auf der Stelle!; **at this very ~** gerade jetzt *or* in diesem Augenblick; **I shan't be a ~**, it won't take a ~ es dauert nicht lang; **any ~** jeden Augenblick; **tell me the ~ he comes** sag mir sofort Bescheid, wenn er kommt; **let me know the ~ it stops** sagen Sie mir Bescheid, sobald es aufhört; **the police arrived the ~ they were called for** die Polizei war im Nu *or* sofort zur Stelle; **at 6 o'clock to the ~** genau um 6 Uhr, um Punkt 6 Uhr, um 6 Uhr auf die Minute; **have you got a ~?** hast du mal eine Minute *or* einen Augenblick Zeit?; **it won't take 5 ~s/a ~** es dauert keine 5 Minuten/keine Minute; **I enjoyed every ~ of it** ich habe es von Anfang bis Ende genossen; **at the last ~** in letzter Minute.

(b) *(official note)* Notiz *f*. **~s** Protokoll *nt*; **to take the ~s** das Protokoll führen.

2 *vt meeting* protokollieren; *remark, fact* zu Protokoll nehmen.

minute² [maɪˈnjuːt] *adj (small)* winzig; *resemblance* ganz entfernt; *(detailed, exact)* minuziös; *detail* kleinste(r, s).

minute³ [ˈmɪnɪt]: **~ book** *n* Protokollbuch *nt*; **~ hand** *n* Minutenzeiger *m*.

minutely [maɪˈnjuːtlɪ] *adv (by a small amount)* ganz geringfügig; *(in detail)* genauestens. **anything ~ resembling a fish** alles, was auch nur annähernd nach Fisch aussieht; **a ~ detailed account** eine sehr detaillierte Schilderung.

minute-man [ˈmɪnɪtmæn] *n, pl* **-men** [-men] *(US) Freiwilliger im Unabhängigkeitskrieg, der auf Abruf bereitstand.*

minuteness [maɪˈnjuːtnɪs] *n (size)* Winzigkeit *f*; *(of account, description)* Ausführlichkeit *f*; *(of detail)* Genauigkeit *f*.

minute steak *n* dünnes, kurz gebratenes Steak.

minutiae [mɪˈnjuːʃɪiː] *npl* genaue Einzelheiten *pl*. **the ~ of one's day-to-day affairs** die tägliche Kleinarbeit.

minx [mɪŋks] n Biest nt (inf).

miracle [ˈmɪrəkəl] n Wunder nt. **to work** or **perform ~s** (lit) Wunder tun or wirken or vollbringen; **I can't work ~s** ich kann nicht hexen or zaubern; **by a ~, by some ~** (fig) wie durch ein Wunder; **it will be a ~ if** ... das wäre ein Wunder, wenn...; **it's a ~ he** ... es ist ein Wunder, daß er ...; **her recovery/his victory was a ~** es war ein Wunder, daß sie wieder gesund geworden ist/er gewonnen hat; **it'll take a ~ for us** or **we'll need a ~ to be finished on time** da müßte schon ein Wunder geschehen, wenn wir noch rechtzeitig fertig werden sollen.

miracle: **~ drug** n Wunderdroge f; **~ play** n Mirakelspiel nt, geistliches Drama; **~ worker** n Wundertäter m.

miraculous [mɪˈrækjʊləs] adj wunderbar, wundersam (liter); powers Wunder-. **there was a ~ change in her appearance** es war kaum zu fassen, wie sie sich verändert hatte; **that is nothing short of ~** das grenzt ans Wunderbare or an ein Wunder.

miraculously [mɪˈrækjʊləslɪ] adv (lit) auf wunderbare or wundersame (liter) Weise; (fig) wie durch ein Wunder. **she was somehow ~ changed** es war nicht zu fassen, wie verändert sie war.

mirage [ˈmɪrɑːʒ] n Fata Morgana, Luftspiegelung f; (fig) Trugbild nt, Illusion f.

mire [maɪə'] n Morast (also fig), Schlamm m. **the football pitch was an absolute ~** der Fußballplatz war ein einziges Schlammfeld; **to drag sb through the ~** (fig) jds Namen in den Schmutz ziehen.

mirror [ˈmɪrə'] **1** n Spiegel m. **a ~ of 19th century life** ein Spiegel(bild) des Lebens im 19. Jahrhundert; **to hold a ~ up to sb/sth** jdm den Spiegel vorhalten/etw widerspiegeln; **~ image** Spiegelbild nt; **~ writing** Spiegelschrift f.
2 vt widerspiegeln, spiegeln. **the trees ~ed in the lake** die Bäume, die sich im See (wider)spiegelten.

mirth [mɜːθ] n Freude f, Frohsinn m; (laughter) Heiterkeit f. **sounds of ~ coming from the classroom** frohes or fröhliches Lachen, das aus dem Klassenzimmer drang.

mirthful [ˈmɜːθfʊl] adj froh, heiter, fröhlich.

mirthless [ˈmɜːθlɪs] adj freudlos; laughter unfroh.

mirthlessly [ˈmɜːθlɪslɪ] adv unfroh.

miry [maɪərɪ] adj morastig, schlammig.

misadventure [ˌmɪsədˈventʃə'] n Mißgeschick nt. **death by ~** Tod m durch Unfall; **he's had a ~** ihm ist ein Mißgeschick passiert.

misalliance [ˌmɪsəˈlaɪəns] n Mesalliance f.

misanthrope [ˈmɪzənθrəʊp], **misanthropist** [mɪˈzænθrəpɪst] n Misanthrop, Menschenfeind m.

misanthropic [ˌmɪzənˈθrɒpɪk] adj misanthropisch, menschenfeindlich.

misanthropy [mɪˈzænθrəpɪ] n Misanthropie, Menschenfeindlichkeit f.

misapply [ˈmɪsəˈplaɪ] vt falsch anwenden; funds falsch verwenden; one's energy verschwenden.

misapprehend [ˈmɪsˌæprɪˈhend] vt mißverstehen.

misapprehension [ˈmɪsˌæprɪˈhenʃən] n Mißverständnis nt. **I think you are under a ~** ich glaube, bei Ihnen liegt (da) ein Mißverständnis vor; **he was under the ~ that ...** er hatte fälschlicherweise or irrtümlicherweise angenommen, daß ...; **he did it under the ~ that ...** er tat es, weil er irrtümlicherweise angenommen hatte, daß ...; **there seems to be some ~ as to the reasons/as to why I did it** es scheint ein Mißverständnis darüber vorzuliegen, warum ich das getan habe.

misappropriate [ˈmɪsəˈprəʊprɪeɪt] vt entwenden; money veruntreuen.

misappropriation [ˈmɪsəˌprəʊprɪˈeɪʃən] n see vt Entwendung f; Veruntreuung f.

misbegotten [ˈmɪsbɪˈɡɒtn] adj (liter: illegitimate) unehelich; (fig: ill-conceived) schlecht konzipiert.

misbehave [ˈmɪsbɪˈheɪv] vi sich schlecht or unanständig benehmen, sich ungebührlich betragen (form); (child also) ungezogen sein. **I saw him misbehaving with my wife** ich habe ihn in einer unmißverständlichen or eindeutigen Situation mit meiner Frau gesehen.

misbehaviour, (US) **misbehavior** [ˈmɪsbɪˈheɪvjə'] n schlechtes Benehmen; (of child also) Ungezogenheit f. **sexual ~** sexuelles Fehlverhalten.

misbelief [ˈmɪsbɪˈliːf] n irrige Annahme; (Rel) Irrglaube m.

miscalculate [ˈmɪsˈkælkjʊleɪt] **1** vt falsch berechnen; (misjudge) falsch einschätzen. **to ~ a distance/a jump** sich in der Entfernung/bei einem Sprung verschätzen.
2 vi sich verrechnen; (estimate wrongly) sich verkalkulieren. (misjudge) sich verschätzen.

miscalculation [ˈmɪsˌkælkjʊˈleɪʃən] n Rechenfehler m; (wrong estimation) Fehlkalkulation f; (misjudgement) Fehleinschätzung f. **to make a ~ in sth** bei etw einen Rechenfehler machen/etw falsch kalkulieren/etw falsch einschätzen.

miscall [ˈmɪsˈkɔːl] vt einen falschen Namen geben (+dat). **X, ~ed "the Beautiful"** X, fälschlich „der Schöne" genannt.

miscarriage [ˈmɪsˌkærɪdʒ] n (a) (Med) Fehlgeburt f. **(b) ~ of justice** Justizirrtum m. **(c)** (form: of letter) Fehlleitung f.

miscarry [ˈmɪsˈkærɪ] vi (a) (Med) eine Fehlgeburt haben. **(b)** (fail: plans) fehllaufen or -schlagen. **(c)** (form: letter, goods) fehlgeleitet werden.

miscast [ˈmɪsˈkɑːst] pret, ptp **~** vt play falsch or schlecht besetzen, fehlbesetzen. **the actor was clearly ~ in this role** mit diesem Schauspieler war die Rolle eindeutig fehlbesetzt.

miscegenation [ˌmɪsɪdʒɪˈneɪʃən] n Rassenmischung f.

miscellanea [ˌmɪsəˈleɪnɪə] npl Verschiedenes nt; (of literary compositions, objects) (bunte) Sammlung.

miscellaneous [ˌmɪsəˈleɪnɪəs] adj verschieden; poems vermischt, verschiedenerlei; collection, crowd bunt. **"~"** „Verschiedenes"; **a ~ section** Vermischtes.

miscellaneously [ˌmɪsɪˈleɪnɪəslɪ] adv verschieden; grouped, collected bunt, wahllos.

miscellany [mɪˈselənɪ] n (collection) (bunte) Sammlung, (buntes) Gemisch; (variety) Vielfalt f; (of writings) vermischte Schriften pl; (of poems, articles) Sammelband m, Auswahl f.

mischance [ˈmɪsˈtʃɑːns] n unglücklicher Zufall. **by some ~** durch einen unglücklichen Zufall.

mischief [ˈmɪstʃɪf] n (a) (roguery) Schalk m, Verschmitztheit f; (naughty, foolish behaviour) Unsinn, Unfug m. **she's full of ~** sie ist stets zu dummen Streichen aufgelegt, sie hat nur Unfug im Kopf; **he's up to some ~** er führt etwas im Schilde; **there's some ~ going on** irgend etwas geht hier vor; **he's always getting into ~** er stellt dauernd etwas an; **to keep sb out of ~** aufpassen, daß jd keine Dummheiten macht; **to keep out of ~** keine Dummheiten or keinen Unfug machen; **that'll keep you out of ~** dann kannst du wenigstens nichts anstellen or kommst du wenigstens auf keine dummen Gedanken.
(b) (trouble) **to mean/make ~** Unfrieden stiften wollen/stiften; **to make ~ for sb** jdm Unannehmlichkeiten bereiten, jdn in Schwierigkeiten bringen; **~-maker** Unruhestifter m.
(c) (damage, physical injury) Schaden m. **to do sb a ~** jdm Schaden zufügen; (physically) jdm etwas (an)tun, jdn verletzen; **to do ~ to sth** Schaden bei etw anrichten.
(d) (person) Schlawiner m; (child, puppy also) Racker m.

mischievous [ˈmɪstʃɪvəs] adj (a) (roguish, playful) expression, smile schelmisch, verschmitzt, spitzbübisch. **a ~ person/child** ein Schlawiner/Schlingel or Racker; **her son is really ~** ihr Sohn ist ein Schlingel or hat nur Unfug im Sinn; **what ~ pranks are you up to now?** welche üblen Streiche heckst du jetzt aus?; **a ~ elf** eine Elfe, die Schabernack treibt.
(b) (troublemaking) rumour bösartig; person boshaft; strike schädlich; (physically disabling) blow verletzend.

mischievously [ˈmɪstʃɪvəslɪ] adv see adj (a) smile, say schelmisch, verschmitzt, spitzbübisch. **to behave ~** Unfug anstellen, Schabernack treiben. **(b)** bösartig; boshaft.

mischievousness [ˈmɪstʃɪvəsnɪs] n (roguery) Verschmitztheit f.

miscible [ˈmɪsɪbl] adj (form) mischbar.

misconceive [ˈmɪskənˈsiːv] vt (understand wrongly) verkennen, eine falsche Vorstellung haben von; (base on false assumption) von einer falschen Voraussetzung ausgehen bei.

misconception [ˈmɪskənˈsepʃən] n fälschliche or irrtümliche Annahme; (no pl: misunderstanding) Verkennung f. **to be under a ~ about sth** etw verkennen, sich (dat) falsche Vorstellungen von etw machen.

misconduct [ˈmɪsˈkɒndʌkt] **1** n (a) (improper behaviour) schlechtes Benehmen; (professional) Berufsvergehen nt; Verfehlung f im Amt; (sexual) Fehltritt m.
(b) (mismanagement) schlechte Verwaltung.
2 [ˈmɪskənˈdʌkt] vt schlecht verwalten.
3 [ˈmɪskənˈdʌkt] vr **to ~ oneself** sich schlecht benehmen; (professionally) sich falsch verhalten.

misconstruction [ˈmɪskənˈstrʌkʃən] n falsche Auslegung, Fehlinterpretation, Mißdeutung f. **he put a deliberate ~ on my words** er hat meine Worte absichtlich mißverstanden.

misconstrue [ˈmɪskənˈstruː] vt mißverstehen, mißdeuten, falsch auslegen. **you have ~d my meaning** Sie haben mich falsch verstanden; **to ~ sth as sth** etw irrtümlicherweise für etw halten.

miscount [ˈmɪsˈkaʊnt] **1** n there was a **~** da hat sich jemand verzählt. **2** [ˈmɪsˈkaʊnt] vt falsch (aus)zählen. **3** vi sich verzählen.

miscreant [ˈmɪskrɪənt] n (old) Bösewicht (old), Schurke m.

misdate [ˈmɪsˈdeɪt] vt letter falsch datieren.

misdeal [ˈmɪsˈdiːl] pret, ptp **misdealt** [ˈmɪsˈdelt] **1** vt cards falsch (aus)geben. **2** vi sich vergeben, falsch geben.

misdeed [ˈmɪsˈdiːd] n Missetat f (old).

misdemeanour, (US) **misdemeanor** [ˌmɪsdɪˈmiːnə'] n schlechtes Betragen or Benehmen; (Jur) Vergehen nt, Übertretung f. **she was guilty of a slight ~ at the party** sie benahm sich auf der Party leicht daneben.

misdirect [ˈmɪsdɪˈrekt] vt (a) letter falsch adressieren; energies falsch einsetzen, vergeuden; person (send astray) in die falsche Richtung schicken; (misinform) falsch informieren, eine falsche Auskunft geben (+dat); (Jur) jury falsch belehren.
(b) campaign, operation schlecht durchführen.

misdirection [ˈmɪsdɪˈrekʃən] n see vt **(a)** falsche Adressierung; falscher Einsatz, Vergeudung f; falsche Richtungsweisung; falsche Information; falsche Unterrichtung. **(b)** schlechte Durchführung.

mise-en-scène [ˈmiːzɑːnˈseɪn] n (Theat, fig) Kulisse f.

miser [maɪzə'] n Geizhals or -kragen m.

miserable [ˈmɪzərəbl] adj (a) (unhappy) unglücklich; colour trist. **I feel ~ today** ich fühle mich heute elend or miserabel; **~ with hunger/cold** elend vor Hunger/Kälte; **to make sb ~** jdm Kummer machen or bereiten, jdn unglücklich machen; **to make life ~ for sb** jdm das Leben schwer machen.
(b) (wretched, causing distress) headache, cold, weather gräßlich, fürchterlich; existence, hovels, spectacle erbärmlich, elend, jämmerlich. **he died a ~ death** er ist elend or jämmerlich zugrunde gegangen.
(c) (contemptible) miserabel, jämmerlich, erbärmlich; person gemein, nichtswürdig, erbärmlich; treatment, behaviour schofel (inf), gemein; failure kläglich, jämmerlich. **a ~ £3** miese £ 3 (inf); **you ~ little wretch!** du mieses kleines Biest!, du Miststück! (inf).

miserably [ˈmɪzərəblɪ] adv (a) (unhappily) unglücklich; say also kläglich.
(b) (wretchedly, distressingly) hurt, ache, rain gräßlich, fürchterlich; live, die elend, jämmerlich; poor erbärmlich.
(c) (contemptibly) pay, feed miserabel; play also erbärmlich, jämmerlich; treat, behave schofel (inf), gemein.

misericord ['mɪzərɪkɔːd] n Miserikordie f.

miserliness ['maɪzəlɪnɪs] n Geiz m.

miserly ['maɪzəlɪ] adj geizig; hoarding kleinlich.

misery ['mɪzərɪ] n (a) (sadness) Kummer m, Trauer f. she looked the picture of ~ sie war ein Bild des Jammers.
(b) (suffering) Qualen pl; (wretchedness) Elend nt. the ~ of waiting for the letter das qualvolle Warten auf den Brief; the ~ caused by war das Elend des Krieges; a life of ~ ein erbärmliches or jämmerliches or elendes Leben; to make sb's life a ~ jdm das Leben zur Qual or zur Hölle machen; to put an animal out of its ~ ein Tier von seinen Qualen erlösen; to put sb out of his ~ (fig) jdn nicht länger auf die Folter spannen.
(c) (inf: person) Miesepeter m (inf). ~-guts (inf) Miesmacher m (inf).

misfire ['mɪs'faɪə'] vi (engine, rocket) fehlzünden, eine Fehlzündung haben; (plan) fehlschlagen; (joke, trick) danebengehen.

misfit ['mɪsfɪt] n (person) Außenseiter(in f) m; (social ~ also) Nichtangepaßte(r) mf. society's ~s die Außenseiter der Gesellschaft; he's a real ~ er ist ein sehr schwieriger Fall; he's always been a ~ here er hat nie richtig hierher gepaßt, er hat sich hier nie angepaßt; I felt a ~ ich fühlte mich fehl am Platze.

misfortune [mɪs'fɔːtʃuːn] n (ill fortune, affliction) (schweres) Schicksal or Los nt; (bad luck) Pech nt no pl; (unlucky incident) Mißgeschick nt. companion in ~ Leidensgenosse m/-genossin f; it was my ~ or I had the ~ to ... ich hatte das Pech, zu ...; a life of disaster and ~ ein von Katastrophen und Mißgeschick(en) begleitetes Leben; a victim of ~ ein Unglücksrabe or Pechvogel m; financial ~s finanzielle Fehlschläge pl.

misgiving [mɪs'gɪvɪŋ] n Bedenken pl. I had (certain) ~s about the scheme/about lending him the money mir war bei dem Vorhaben/dem Gedanken, ihm das Geld zu leihen, nicht ganz wohl.

misgovern ['mɪs'gʌvən] vt schlecht regieren, schlecht verwalten.

misgovernment ['mɪs'gʌvənmənt] n Mißwirtschaft f (of in + dat).

misguided ['mɪs'gaɪdɪd] adj töricht; decision also, opinions irrig; (misplaced) kindness, enthusiasm, solicitude unangebracht, fehl am Platz. I think it was ~ of you or you were ~ to accept his proposal meiner Ansicht nach waren Sie schlecht beraten or war es töricht, seinen Vorschlag anzunehmen.

misguidedly ['mɪs'gaɪdɪdlɪ] adv töricht; teach, believe irrigerweise.

mishandle ['mɪs'hændl] vt case falsch or schlecht handhaben.

mishap ['mɪshæp] n Mißgeschick nt. without (further) ~ ohne (weitere) Zwischenfälle; he's had a slight ~ ihm ist ein kleines Mißgeschick or Malheur passiert.

mishear ['mɪs'hɪə'] pret, ptp misheard ['mɪs'hɜːd] 1 vt falsch hören. 2 vi sich verhören.

mishmash ['mɪʃmæʃ] n Mischmasch m.

misinform ['mɪsɪn'fɔːm] vt falsch informieren or unterrichten. you've been ~ed man hat Sie or Sie sind falsch informiert; does the press ~ the public? verbreitet die Presse falsche Informationen?

misinterpret ['mɪsɪn'tɜːprɪt] vt falsch auslegen or deuten; play, novel fehlinterpretieren, falsch auslegen; (interpreter) falsch wiedergeben or verdolmetschen. it could easily be ~ed as implying ingratitude es könnte (mir/dir etc) leicht als Undankbarkeit ausgelegt werden; he ~ed her silence as agreement er deutete ihr Schweigen fälschlich als Zustimmung.

misinterpretation ['mɪsɪn,tɜːprɪ'teɪʃən] n Fehldeutung f, falsche Auslegung; (of play, novel) Fehlinterpretation f, falsche Auslegung; (by interpreter) falsche Wiedergabe.

misjudge ['mɪs'dʒʌdʒ] vt falsch einschätzen, sich verschätzen in (+dat); person also falsch beurteilen.

misjudgement [,mɪs'dʒʌdʒmənt] n Fehleinschätzung f; (of person also) falsche Beurteilung.

mislay [,mɪs'leɪ] pret, ptp mislaid [,mɪs'leɪd] vt verlegen.

mislead [,mɪs'liːd] pret, ptp misled vt (a) (give wrong idea) irreführen. I fear you have been misled ich fürchte, Sie irren or täuschen sich or Sie befinden sich im Irrtum (form); don't be misled by appearances lassen Sie sich nicht durch Äußerlichkeiten täuschen; your description misled me into thinking that ... aufgrund Ihrer Beschreibung nahm ich (irrtümlich) an, daß ...
(b) (lead into bad ways) verleiten (into zu).
(c) (in guiding) in die Irre or falsche Richtung führen.

misleading [,mɪs'liːdɪŋ] adj irreführend. the ~ simplicity of his style die täuschende Einfachheit seines Stils.

misleadingly [,mɪs'liːdɪŋlɪ] adv irreführenderweise.

misled [,mɪs'led] pret, ptp of mislead.

mismanage ['mɪs'mænɪdʒ] vt company, finances schlecht verwalten; affair, deal schlecht abwickeln or handhaben.

mismanagement ['mɪs'mænɪdʒmənt] n Mißwirtschaft f. his ~ of the matter seine schlechte Abwicklung der Angelegenheit.

misname ['mɪs'neɪm] vt unzutreffend benennen.

misnomer ['mɪs'nəʊmə'] n unzutreffender Name, Fehlbezeichnung f.

misogamist [mɪ'sɒgəmɪst] n Misogam m.

misogamy [mɪ'sɒgəmɪ] n Misogamie f.

misogynist [mɪ'sɒdʒɪnɪst] n Weiberfeind, Misogyn (geh) m.

misogyny [mɪ'sɒdʒɪnɪ] n Weiberhaß m, Misogynie f (geh).

misplace ['mɪs'pleɪs] vt (a) document, file etc falsch einordnen; (mislay) verlegen. (b) to be ~d (confidence, trust, affection) fehl am Platz or unangebracht sein; her ~d affection/trust ihre törichte Zuneigung/ihr törichtes Vertrauen.

misplay [,mɪs'pleɪ] vt verschießen.

misprint ['mɪsprɪnt] 1 n Druckfehler m. 2 [,mɪs'prɪnt] vt verdrucken.

mispronounce ['mɪsprə'naʊns] vt falsch aussprechen.

mispronunciation ['mɪsprə,nʌnsɪ'eɪʃən] n falsche or fehlerhafte Aussprache.

misquotation ['mɪskwəʊ'teɪʃən] n falsches Zitat. his constant ~ of Shakespeare daß er Shakespeare ständig falsch zitiert/zitiert hat.

misquote ['mɪs'kwəʊt] vt falsch zitieren. he was ~d as having said ... man unterstellte ihm, gesagt zu haben ...

misread ['mɪs'riːd] pret, ptp misread ['mɪs'red] vt falsch or nicht richtig lesen; (misinterpret) falsch verstehen.

misrepresent ['mɪs,reprɪ'zent] vt falsch darstellen, ein falsches Bild geben von; facts verdrehen, falsch darstellen; ideas verfälschen. he was ~ed in the papers seine Worte etc wurden von der Presse verfälscht or entstellt wiedergegeben; he was ~ed as being for the strike er wurde zu Unrecht als Befürworter des Streiks hingestellt; he was ~ed as having said ... ihm wurde unterstellt, gesagt zu haben ...

misrepresentation ['mɪs,reprɪzen'teɪʃən] n falsche Darstellung; (of facts also) Verdrehung f; (of theory) Verfälschung f.

misrule ['mɪs'ruːl] 1 n schlechte Regierung; (by government also) Mißwirtschaft f. 2 vt schlecht regieren.

miss¹ [mɪs] 1 n (a) (shot) Fehltreffer or -schuß m; (failure) Mißerfolg m, Pleite f (inf), Reinfall m (inf). his first shot was a ~ sein erster Schuß ging daneben; it was a near ~ das war eine knappe Sache; (shot) das war knapp daneben; it was a near ~ with that car das Auto haben wir um Haaresbreite verfehlt; the sales department voted it a ~ in der Verkaufsabteilung räumte man dem keine Chance ein; a ~ is as good as a mile (prov) fast getroffen ist auch daneben.
(b) to give sth a ~ (inf) sich (dat) etw schenken.
2 vt (a) (fail to hit, catch, reach, find, attend etc) (by accident) verpassen; chance, appointment, bus, concert also versäumen; (deliberately not attend) nicht gehen zu or in (+acc); (not hit, find) target, ball, way, step, vocation, place, house verfehlen; (shot, ball) verfehlen, vorbeigehen an (+dat). to ~ breakfast nicht frühstücken; (be too late for) das Frühstück verpassen; you haven't ~ed much! da hast du nichts or nicht viel verpaßt or versäumt!; they ~ed each other in the crowd sie verpaßten or verfehlten sich in der Menge; to ~ the boat or bus (fig) den Anschluß verpassen; he ~ed school for a week er hat eine Woche lang die Schule versäumt; ~ a turn einmal aussetzen; have I ~ed my turn? bin ich übergangen worden?; if you ~ a pill wenn Sie vergessen, eine Pille zu nehmen.
(b) (fail to experience) verpassen; (deliberately) sich (dat) entgehen lassen; (fail to hear or perceive also) nicht mitbekommen; (deliberately) überhören/-sehen. I ~ed that das ist mir entgangen; he doesn't ~ much (inf) ihm entgeht so schnell nichts; I wouldn't have ~ed it for anything das hätte ich mir nicht entgehen lassen wollen.
(c) (fail to achieve) prize nicht bekommen or schaffen (inf). he narrowly ~ed being first/becoming president er wäre beinahe auf den ersten Platz gekommen/Präsident geworden.
(d) (avoid) obstacle (noch) ausweichen können (+dat); (escape) entgehen (+dat). to ~ doing sth etw fast or um ein Haar tun; the car just ~ed the tree das Auto wäre um ein Haar gegen den Baum gefahren; we narrowly ~ed having an accident wir hätten um ein Haar einen Unfall gehabt.
(e) (leave out) auslassen; (overlook, fail to deal with) übersehen. my heart ~ed a beat mir stockte das Herz.
(f) (notice or regret absence of) (person) people, things vermissen. I ~ him/my old car er/mein altes Auto fehlt mir; won't be ~ed keiner wird ihn vermissen; he'll never ~ it er wird es nie merken(, daß es ihm fehlt).
3 vi (a) nicht treffen; (punching also) danebenschlagen; (shooting also) danebenschießen; (not catch) danebengreifen; (not be present, not attend) fehlen; (ball, shot, punch also) danebengehen; (Aut: engine) aussetzen.
(b) (inf: fail) you can't ~ da kann nichts schiefgehen; he never ~es er schafft es immer; they keep ~ing sie schaffen es einfach nicht.

♦**miss out 1** vt sep auslassen; (accidentally not see) übersehen; last line or paragraph etc weglassen. my name was ~ed ~ from the list mein Name fehlte auf der Liste.
2 vi (inf) zu kurz kommen. to ~ ~ on sth etw verpassen; (get less) bei etw zu kurz kommen; he's been ~ing ~ on life er ist im Leben zu kurz gekommen.

miss² n (a) M~ Fräulein nt, Frl. abbr; M~ Germany 1980 (die) Miß Germany von 1980.
(b) (girl) a proper little ~ ein richtiges Dämchen or kleines Fräulein; look here, you cheeky little ~! hör mal, mein (kleines) Fräulein!; these saucy young ~es diese frechen (jungen) Dinger.
(c) (term of address) mein Fräulein; (to waitress etc) Fräulein; (to teacher) Fräulein or Frau X.

missal ['mɪsəl] n Meßbuch, Missale nt.

misshapen ['mɪs'ʃeɪpən] adj mißgebildet; plant, tree also verwachsen; chocolates unförmig, mißraten.

missile ['mɪsaɪl] n (a) (stone, javelin etc) (Wurf)geschoß nt. (b) (rocket) Rakete f, Flugkörper m (form). ~ base or site Raketenbasis f; ~ launcher Abschuß- or Startrampe f; (vehicle) Raketenwerfer m.

missilry ['mɪsɪlrɪ] n (science) Raketentechnik f; (missiles) Raketen(waffen) pl.

missing ['mɪsɪŋ] adj (not able to be found) person, soldier, aircraft, boat vermißt; object verschwunden; (not there) fehlend. to be ~/to have gone ~ fehlen; (mountaineer, aircraft, boat etc) vermißt werden; the coat has two buttons ~ an dem Mantel fehlen zwei Knöpfe; we are £50 ~ uns (dat) fehlen £ 50; the ~ clue to his identity der Schlüssel zu seiner Identität; ~ in action vermißt; ~ person Vermißte(r) mf; ~ link fehlendes Glied; (Biol) Missing link nt, Übergangs- or Zwischenform f.

mission ['mɪʃən] n (a) (business, task) Auftrag m; (calling) Aufgabe, Berufung f; (Mil) Befehl m; (operation) Einsatz m.

what is their ~? welchen Auftrag haben sie?; wie lauten ihre Befehle?; **our** ~ **is to** ... wir sind damit beauftragt, zu ...; **the soldiers'** ~ **was to** ... die Soldaten hatten den Befehl erhalten, zu ...; **to send sb on a secret** ~ jdn mit einer geheimen Mission beauftragen; **he's on a secret** ~ er ist in geheimer Mission unterwegs; **sense of** ~ Sendungsbewußtsein *nt*.
   (b) (*journey*) Mission *f.* **trade** ~ Handelsreise *f*; ~ **of inquiry** Erkundungsreise *f*; **Henry Kissinger's** ~ **to the Middle East** Kissingers Nahostmission.
   (c) (*people on* ~) Gesandtschaft, Delegation *f*; (*Pol*) Mission *f.* **trade** ~ Handelsdelegation *f*.
   (d) (*Rel*) Mission *f.* ~ **hut** Mission(sstation) *f*.
missionary ['mɪʃənrɪ] **1** *n* Missionar(in *f*) *m*. **2** *adj* missionarisch. **in the** ~ **position** (*fig inf*) auf altdeutsch.
missis ['mɪsɪz] *n* (*Brit inf*) (*wife*) bessere Hälfte (*hum inf*), Alte (*pej inf*), Olle (*sl*) *f*; (*mistress of household*) Frau *f* des Hauses. **yes,** ~ **ja(wohl).**
Mississippi [mɪsɪ'sɪpɪ] *n* Mississippi *m*.
missive ['mɪsɪv] *n* (*form, old*) Schreiben *nt* (*form*).
Missouri [mɪ'zuːrɪ] *n* (*river*) Missouri *m*; (*state*) Missouri *nt*.
misspell ['mɪs'spel] *pret, ptp* ~**ed** or **misspelt** *vt* verkehrt or falsch schreiben.
misspelling ['mɪs'spelɪŋ] *n* (*act*) falsches Schreiben; (*spelling mistake*) Rechtschreib(e)fehler *m*.
misspelt ['mɪs'spelt] *pret, ptp* of **misspell**.
misspent [mɪs'spent] *adj* vergeudet, verschwendet. **I regret my** ~ **youth** ich bedaure es, in meiner Jugend so ein liederliches Leben geführt zu haben; (*wasted youth*) ich bedaure es, meine Jugend so vergeudet or vertan zu haben.
misstate ['mɪs'steɪt] *vt* falsch darlegen or darstellen.
misstatement ['mɪs'steɪtmənt] *n* falsche Darstellung.
missus ['mɪsɪz] *n* (*inf*) see **missis**.
missy ['mɪsɪ] *n* (*inf*) Fräuleinchen *nt* (*inf*), kleines Fräulein.
mist [mɪst] *n* (a) Nebel *m*; (*in liquid*) Trübung *f*; (*haze*) Dunst *m*; (*on glass etc*) Beschlag *m*.
   (b) (*fig*) **through a** ~ **of tears** durch einen Tränenschleier; **to wait for the** ~**s to clear** warten, bis man einen klaren Kopf hat; **it is lost in the** ~**s of time/antiquity** das liegt im Dunkel der Vergangenheit; **the** ~**s of confusion surrounding the affair** das undurchsichtige Dunkel, in das die Angelegenheit gehüllt ist.
♦ **mist over 1** *vi* (*become cloudy*) sich trüben; (*glass, mirror: also* **mist up**) (sich) beschlagen. **her eyes** ~**ed** ~ **with tears** Tränen verschleierten ihren Blick (*liter*).
   2 *vt sep* **the condensation is** ~**ing** ~ **the windows** durch den Dampf beschlagen die Fensterscheiben.
mistakable [mɪ'steɪkəbl] *adj* **the twins are easily** ~ man kann die Zwillinge leicht miteinander verwechseln; **his j's are easily** ~ **for g's** seine J's kann man leicht mit G's verwechseln.
mistake [mɪ'steɪk] **1** *n* Fehler *m*. **to make a** ~ (*in writing, calculating etc*) einen Fehler machen; (*be mistaken*) sich irren; **you're making a big** ~ **in marrying him** Sie machen or begehen (*form*) einen schweren Fehler, wenn Sie ihn heiraten; **to make the** ~ **of asking too much** den Fehler machen or begehen (*form*) und zu viele Fragen stellen; **what a** ~ **(to make)!** wie kann man nur (so einen Fehler machen)!; **by** ~ aus Versehen, versehentlich; **there must be some** ~ da muß ein Fehler or Irrtum vorliegen; **the** ~ **is mine der Fehler liegt bei mir; there's no** ~ **about it,** ... (es besteht) kein Zweifel, ...; **let there be no** ~ **about it, make no** ~ **(about it)** ein(e)s or das steht fest: ...; **make no** ~, **I mean what I say** damit wir uns nicht falsch verstehen: mir ist es Ernst; **it's freezing and no** ~! (*inf*) (ich kann dir sagen,) das ist vielleicht eine Kälte! (*inf*).
   2 *vt pret* **mistook,** *ptp* **mistaken** (a) *words, meaning, remarks etc* falsch auffassen or verstehen; *seriousness, cause* verkennen, nicht erkennen; *house, road, time of train* sich irren or vertun (*inf*) in (+*dat*). **to** ~ **sb's meaning** jdn falsch verstehen; **I mistook you** or **what you meant** ich habe Sie falsch or nicht richtig verstanden; **there's no mistaking the urgency of the situation** die Dringlichkeit der Situation steht außer Frage; **there's no mistaking her writing** ihre Schrift ist unverkennbar or nicht zu verkennen; **there's no mistaking what he meant** er hat sich unmißverständlich ausgedrückt; **there was no mistaking his anger** er war eindeutig wütend.
   (b) **to** ~ **A for B** A mit B verwechseln, A für B halten; **it cannot possibly be** ~**n for anything else** das ist doch unverkennbar!, das kann man doch gar nicht verwechseln!
   (c) **to be** ~**n** sich irren; **you are badly** ~**n there** da irren Sie sich aber gewaltig; **if I am not** ~**n** ... wenn mich nicht alles täuscht ..., wenn mich nicht irre ...
mistaken [mɪ'steɪkən] *adj* (*wrong*) *idea* falsch; (*misplaced*) *loyalty, kindness* unangebracht, fehl am Platz; *affection, trust* töricht. **a case of** ~ **identity** eine Verwechslung.
mistakenly [mɪ'steɪkənlɪ] *adv* fälschlicherweise, irrtümlicherweise; (*by accident*) versehentlich.
mister ['mɪstə'] *n* (a) (*abbr* **Mr**) Herr *m*; (*on envelope*) Herrn; (*with politicians' names etc*) not translated. (b) (*inf: sir*) not translated. **please,** ~, **can you tell me** ... können Sie mir bitte sagen ...?; **now listen here,** ~ hören Sie mal her.
mistime ['mɪs'taɪm] *vt* (a) (*act*) einen ungünstigen Zeitpunkt wählen für. **a badly** ~**d political announcement** eine politische Erklärung, die zu einem ungünstigen Zeitpunkt kommt. (b) *race* falsch or fehlerhaft stoppen.
mistle thrush ['mɪsl͵θrʌʃ] *n* Misteldrossel *f*.
mistletoe ['mɪsltəʊ] *n* Mistel *f*; (*sprig*) Mistelzweig *m*.
mistook [mɪ'stʊk] *pret* of **mistake**.
mistral [mɪ'straːl] *n* Mistral *m*.
mistranslate ['mɪstrænz'leɪt] *vt* falsch übersetzen.
mistranslation ['mɪstrænz'leɪʃən] *n* (*act*) falsche Übersetzung; (*error also*) Übersetzungsfehler *m*.
mistreat [͵mɪs'triːt] *vt* schlecht behandeln; (*violently*) mißhandeln.

mistreatment [͵mɪs'triːtmənt] *n* schlechte Behandlung; (*violent*) Mißhandlung *f*.
mistress ['mɪstrɪs] *n* (a) (*of house, horse, dog*) Herrin *f.* **she is now** ~ **of the situation** sie ist jetzt Herr der Lage. (b) (*lover*) Geliebte, Mätresse (*old*) *f*. (c) (*teacher*) Lehrerin *f*. (d) (*old: Mrs*) Frau *f*.
mistrial ['mɪs'traɪəl] *n* **it was declared a** ~ das Urteil wurde wegen Verfahrensmängeln aufgehoben.
mistrust ['mɪs'trʌst] **1** *n* Mißtrauen *nt* (*of* gegenüber). **2** *vt* mißtrauen (+*dat*).
mistrustful [͵mɪs'trʌstfʊl] *adj* mißtrauisch. **to be** ~ **of sb/sth** jdm/einer Sache mißtrauen or gegenüber mißtrauisch sein.
misty ['mɪstɪ] *adj* (+*er*) *day, morning* neblig; (*hazy*) dunstig; *mountain peaks* in Nebel/Dunst gehüllt; *colour* gedeckt. ~ **weather** Nebel(wetter *nt*) *m*; **a** ~ **view of the valley** ein Blick auf das (nebel)verhangene or dunstige Tal.
   (b) (*fig*) *memory* verschwommen. **her eyes grew** ~, **a** ~ **look came into her eyes** ihr Blick verschleierte sich; ~**-eyed** mit verschleiertem Blick.
   (c) *glasses* (*misted up*) beschlagen; (*opaque*) milchig; *liquid* trübe. **the window is getting** ~ das Fenster beschlägt.
misunderstand [mɪsʌndə'stænd] *pret, ptp* **misunderstood 1** *vt* falsch verstehen, mißverstehen. **don't** ~ **me** ... verstehen Sie mich nicht falsch ... **2** *vi* **I think you've misunderstood** ich glaube, Sie haben das mißverstanden or falsch verstanden.
misunderstanding ['mɪsʌndə'stændɪŋ] *n* (a) Mißverständnis *nt.* **there must be some** ~ da muß ein Mißverständnis sein, da muß ein Mißverständnis vorliegen; **so that no** ~ **is possible** um Mißverständnissen vorzubeugen; **let there be no** ~ **(about it)** ... damit keine Mißverständnisse aufkommen or entstehen: ..., damit wir uns nicht mißverstehen: ...
   (b) (*disagreement*) Meinungsverschiedenheit *f*.
misunderstood ['mɪsʌndə'stʊd] **1** *ptp* of **misunderstand. 2** *adj* unverstanden; *artist, playwright* verkannt.
misuse ['mɪs'juːs] **1** *n* Mißbrauch *m*; (*of words*) falscher Gebrauch; (*of funds*) Zweckentfremdung *f.* ~ **of power/authority** Macht-/Amtsmißbrauch *m*. **2** ['mɪs'juːz] *vt see* mißbrauchen; *falsch gebrauchen; zweckentfremden.
misword ['mɪs'wɜːd] *vt* *contract etc* falsch formulieren.
MIT (*US*) *abbr of* **Massachusetts Institute of Technology.**
mite¹ [maɪt] *n* (*Zool*) Milbe *f*.
mite² **1** *n* (a) (*Hist: coin*) Scherf, Heller *m*; (*as contribution*) Scherflein *nt.* **to contribute one's** ~ **to sth** sein Scherflein zu etw beitragen.
   (b) (*small amount*) bißchen *nt.* **well, just a** ~ **then** na gut, ein (ganz) kleines bißchen; **a** ~ **of consolation** ein winziger Trost.
   (c) (*child*) Würmchen *nt* (*inf*). **poor little** ~! armes Wurm!
   2 *adv* (*inf*) **a** ~ **surprised/disappointed/early** etwas or ein bißchen überrascht/enttäuscht/früh dran; **could you wait a** ~ **longer?** können Sie noch ein Momentchen warten? (*inf*).
miter *n* (*US*) *see* **mitre.**
mitigate ['mɪtɪgeɪt] *vt* *pain* lindern; *punishment* mildern. **mitigating circumstances** mildernde Umstände *pl*.
mitigation [͵mɪtɪ'geɪʃən] *n see vt* Linderung *f*; Milderung *f.* **to say a word in** ~ etwas zu jds/seiner Verteidigung anführen; **have you anything to say in** ~ **of this accusation?** haben Sie irgend etwas zu Ihrer Entlastung vorzubringen?
mitre, (*US*) **miter** ['maɪtə'] *n* (a) (*Eccl*) Mitra *f*. (b) (*Tech: also* ~**-joint**) Gehrung, Gehrfuge *f*. **2** *vt* (*Tech*) gehren.
mitt [mɪt] *n* (a) *see* **mitten (a).** (b) (*baseball glove*) Fang- or Baseballhandschuh *m*. (c) (*sl: hand*) Pfote *f* (*inf*).
mitten ['mɪtn] *n* (a) Fausthandschuh, Fäustling *m*; (*with bare fingers*) Handschuh *m* ohne Finger or mit halben Fingern. (b) ~**s** *pl* (*Boxing*) Boxhandschuhe *pl*.
mix [mɪks] **1** *n* Mischung *f.* **a good social** ~ **at the party** ein gutgemischtes Publikum; **cake** ~ Backmischung *f*.
   2 *vt* (a) (*ver*)mischen; *drinks* mischen, mixen; (*Cook*) *ingredients* verrühren; *dough* zubereiten; *salad* untermengen, wenden. **to** ~ **business with pleasure** das Angenehme mit dem Nützlichen verbinden; **you shouldn't** ~ **business with pleasure** Dienst ist Dienst und Schnaps ist Schnaps (*prov*); **to** ~ **sth into sth** etw unter etw (*acc*) mengen or mischen.
   (b) (*confuse*) durcheinanderbringen. **to** ~ **sb/sth with sb/sth** jdn/etw mit jdm/etw verwechseln.
   (c) **to** ~ **it** (*sl*) sich prügeln or kloppen (*sl*); **the gangs were really** ~**ing** **it** die Banden haben sich eine ganz schöne Schlägerei geliefert (*inf*).
   3 *vi* (a) sich mischen lassen; (*chemical substances, races*) sich vermischen.
   (b) (*go together*) zusammenpassen. **business and pleasure don't** ~ Arbeit und Vergnügen lassen sich nicht verbinden.
   (c) (*people*) (*get on*) miteinander auskommen; (*mingle*) sich vermischen; (*associate*) miteinander verkehren. **to** ~ **with sb** mit jdm auskommen; sich unter jdn mischen; mit jdm verkehren; **he finds it hard to** ~ er ist nicht sehr gesellig or kontaktfreudig; **to** ~ **well** kontaktfreudig or gesellig sein; **he's started** ~**ing in high society recently** neuerdings verkehrt er in den besseren Kreisen.
♦ **mix in** *vt sep* *egg, water* unterrühren.
♦ **mix up** *vt sep* (a) vermischen; *ingredients* verrühren; *medicine* mischen.
   (b) (*get in a muddle*) durcheinanderbringen; (*confuse with sb/sth else*) verwechseln.
   (c) (*involve*) **to** ~ **sb** ~ **in sth** jdn in etw (*acc*) hineinziehen; (*in crime etc also*) jdn in etw (*acc*) verwickeln; **to be** ~**ed** ~ **in sth** in etw (*acc*) verwickelt sein; **he's got himself** ~**ed** ~ **with the police/that bunch** er hat Scherereien mit der Polizei bekommen/sich mit der Bande eingelassen.
mixed [mɪkst] *adj* (a) (*assorted*) gemischt. ~ **nuts/biscuits** Nuß-/Keksmischung *f*.
   (b) (*both sexes*) *choir, bathing, school* gemischt.

(c) (*varied*) gemischt; (*both good and bad*) unterschiedlich. a ~ set of people eine bunt zusammengewürfelte Gruppe; **I have ~ feelings about him/it** ich habe ihm gegenüber zwiespältige Gefühle/ich betrachte die Sache mit gemischten Gefühlen.

mixed: ~ **blessing** n it's a ~ **blessing** das ist ein zweischneidiges Schwert; **children are a ~ blessing** Kinder sind kein reines Vergnügen; ~ **doubles** npl (*Sport*) gemischtes Doppel; ~ **farming** n Ackerbau und Viehzucht (+pl vb); ~ **grill** n Grillteller m; ~ **marriage** n Mischehe f; ~ **metaphor** n gemischte Metapher, Bildervermengung f; ~ **pickles** npl Mixed Pickles, Mixpickles pl; ~-**up** adj durcheinander pred; (*muddled*) person also, ideas konfus; **I'm all ~-up** ich bin völlig durcheinander; **she's just a crazy ~-up kid** sie ist total verdreht.

mixer ['mɪksə^r] n (a) (*food* ~) Mixer m, Mixgerät nt; (*cement* ~) Mischmaschine f.
(b) (*Rad*) (*person*) Tonmeister m; (*thing*) Mischpult nt.
(c) (*sociable person*) **to be a good ~** kontaktfreudig sein; **David's not much of a ~** David ist ziemlich kontaktarm or verschlossen.

mixture ['mɪkstʃə^r] n Mischung f; (*Med*) Mixtur f; (*Cook*) Gemisch nt; (*cake* ~, *dough*) Teig m. ~ **of tobaccos/teas** Tabak-/Teemischung f; ~ **of gases** Gasgemisch nt; **I've had quite a ~ of drinks tonight** ich habe heute abend ziemlich viel durcheinander getrunken; **a ~ of comedy and tragedy** eine Mischung aus Komödie und Tragödie.

mix-up ['mɪksʌp] n Durcheinander nt. **we got in a ~ with the trains** mit unseren Zugverbindungen ging alles schief or durcheinander; **there seemed to be some ~ about which train ...** es schien völlig unklar, welchen Zug ...; **there must have been a ~** da muß irgend etwas schiefgelaufen sein (inf).

MLR (*Brit*) abbr of **minimum lending rate.**

mm abbr of **millimetre(s) mm.**

mnemonic [nɪ'mɒnɪk] 1 adj Gedächtnis-. ~ **trick** or **device** Gedächtnisstütze f; ~ **rhyme** Eselsbrücke f (inf). 2 n Gedächtnisstütze or -hilfe, Eselsbrücke (inf) f.

MO abbr of (a) **money order.** (b) **medical officer.**

mo [məʊ] n (inf) abbr of **moment.**

moan [məʊn] 1 n (a) (*groan*) Stöhnen nt; (*of wind*) Seufzen, Raunen (geh) nt; (*of trees etc*) Raunen nt (geh).
(b) (*grumble*) Gestöhn(e) nt no pl (inf). **to have a ~ about sth** über etw (acc) jammern or schimpfen.
2 vi (a) (*groan*) stöhnen; (*wind, trees*) raunen (geh).
(b) (*grumble*) stöhnen, schimpfen (*about* über +acc). ~, ~, ~, **that's all she does** sie ist ständig am Maulen (inf).
3 vt ..., **he ~ed** ... stöhnte er; **he ~ed a sigh of relief** er stöhnte erleichtert auf; **he ~ed a confession** er brachte das Geständnis stöhnend or unter Stöhnen heraus.

moaner ['məʊnə^r] n (inf) Miesepeter m (inf); Mäkelliese f (inf).

moaning ['məʊnɪŋ] n (a) Stöhnen nt; (*of wind also*) Seufzen nt; (*of trees etc*) Raunen nt (geh). (b) (*grumbling*) Gestöhn(e) nt.

moat [məʊt] n Wassergraben m; (*of castle also*) Burggraben m.

moated ['məʊtɪd] adj von einem Wassergraben umgeben.

mob [mɒb] 1 n (a) (*crowd*) Horde, Schar f; (*riotous, violent*) Mob m no pl. **an undisciplined ~** ein undisziplinierter Haufen; ~**s gathered to burn the houses** der Mob lief zusammen, um die Häuser zu verbrennen; **the crowd became a ~** das Volk wurde zur wütenden Menge; **they went in a ~ to the town hall** sie stürmten zum Rathaus.
(b) (inf) (*criminal gang*) Bande f; (fig: *clique*) Haufen m, Bande f. **which ~ were you in?** (Mil) bei welchem Haufen warst du denn? (inf).
(c) **the ~** (pej: *the masses*) die Masse(n pl).
2 vt herfallen über (+acc), sich stürzen auf (+acc); actor, pop star also belagern. **the prisoner was ~bed** die Menge fiel über den Gefangenen her.

mobcap ['mɒbkæp] n (Hist) (Spitzen)haube f.

mobile ['məʊbaɪl] 1 adj (a) (*person*) beweglich, mobil; (*having means of transport*) beweglich, motorisiert; (*Sociol*) mobil. **a salesman has to be ~** ein Vertreter muß jederzeit abkömmlich sein/muß beweglich or motorisiert sein; **the patient is ~ already** der Patient kann schon aufstehen.
(b) X-ray unit etc fahrbar. ~ **canteen** Kantine f auf Rädern, mobile Küche; ~ **home** Wohnwagen m; ~ **library** Fahrbücherei f; ~ **walkway** (US) Rollsteg m.
(c) mind wendig, beweglich; face, expression, features lebhaft, beweglich.
2 n Mobile nt.

mobility [məʊ'bɪlɪtɪ] n (of person) Beweglichkeit f; (of work force, Sociol) Mobilität f; (of mind also) Wendigkeit f; (of features, face etc also) Lebhaftigkeit f. **a car gives you ~** ein Auto macht Sie beweglicher.

mobilization [ˌməʊbɪlaɪ'zeɪʃən] n Mobilisierung f; (Mil also) Mobilmachung f.

mobilize ['məʊbɪlaɪz] 1 vt mobilisieren; (Mil also) mobil machen. 2 vi mobil machen.

mobocracy [mɒb'ɒkrəsɪ] n Pöbelherrschaft f.

mob rule n Herrschaft f des Pöbels.

mobster ['mɒbstə^r] n (esp US) Gangster, Bandit m.

mob violence n Massenausschreitungen pl.

moccasin ['mɒkəsɪn] n Mokassin m.

mocha ['mɒkə] n Mokka m.

mock [mɒk] 1 n **to make a ~ of sth** etw ad absurdum führen; (put an end to) etw vereiteln or zunichte machen.
2 adj attr emotions gespielt; attack, battle, fight Schein-; crash, examination simuliert; Tudor, Elizabethan Pseudo-.
3 vt (a) (ridicule) sich lustig machen über (+acc), verspotten.
(b) (mimic) nachmachen or -äffen.
(c) (defy) trotzen (+dat); law sich hinwegsetzen über (+acc); (set at nought) plans, efforts vereiteln, zunichte machen.
4 vi **to ~ at sb/sth** sich über jdn/etw lustig machen or

mokieren; **don't ~ mokier dich nicht!, spotte nicht!** (geh).

mocker ['mɒkə^r] n (a) Spötter(in f) m, spöttischer Mensch. (b) **to put the ~s on sth** (Brit sl) etw vermasseln (inf).

mockery ['mɒkərɪ] n (a) (derision) Spott m.
(b) (object of ridicule) Gespött nt. **they made a ~ of him** sie machten ihn zum Gespött der Leute; **to make a ~ of sth** etw lächerlich machen; (prove its futility) etw ad absurdum führen; **inflation will make a ~ of our budget** durch die Inflation wird unser Haushaltsplan zur Farce.
(c) **this is a ~ of justice** Gespött nt. das spricht jeglicher Gerechtigkeit hohn; **it was a ~ of a trial** der Prozeß war eine einzige Farce; **what a ~ (this is)!** das ist doch glatter or der reinste Hohn!

mock: ~-**heroic** adj (Liter) heroisch-komisch; ~-**heroic poem** komisches Epos; ~-**heroics** npl (Liter) heroisch-komische Passage(n pl).

mocking ['mɒkɪŋ] 1 adj spöttisch. 2 n Spott m.

mockingbird ['mɒkɪŋˌbɜːd] n Spottdrossel f.

mockingly ['mɒkɪŋlɪ] adv spöttisch, voller Spott. **she ~ repeated his words** sie äffte seine Worte nach.

mock: ~ **orange** n falscher Jasmin, Pfeifenstrauch m; ~ **turtle soup** n Mockturtlesuppe f; ~-**up** n Modell nt in Originalgröße.

MOD (Brit) abbr of **Ministry of Defence.**

mod [mɒd] (dated sl) 1 adj modern, pop(p)ig (inf). 2 n modisch gekleideter Halbstarker in den 60er Jahren.

modal ['məʊdl] adj modal. ~ **verb** Modalverb nt.

modality [məʊ'dælɪtɪ] n Modalität f.

mod cons ['mɒd'kɒnz] abbr of **modern conveniences** mod. Komf., (moderner) Komfort.

mode [məʊd] n (a) (Gram) Modus m; (Mus) Tonart f; (Philos) Modalität f.
(b) (way) Art f (und Weise); (form) Form f. ~ **of transport** Transportmittel nt; ~ **of life** Lebensweise f; (Biol) Lebensform f.
(c) (Fashion) Mode f. **to be the ~** in Mode sein.

model ['mɒdl] 1 n (a) Modell nt. **to make sth on the ~ of sth** etw (acc) einer Sache (dat) nachbilden; **it is built on the ~ of the Doge's Palace** es ist eine Nachbildung des Dogenpalastes; **our democracy is based on the ~ of Greece** unsere Demokratie ist nach dem Vorbild Griechenlands aufgebaut.
(b) (perfect example) Muster nt (of an +dat). **this book is a ~ of clear expression** dieses Buch ist beispielhaft für klare Ausdrucksweise; **to hold sb up as a ~** jdn als Vorbild hinstellen.
(c) (artist's, photographer's) Modell nt; (fashion ~) Mannequin nt; (male ~) Dressman m.
(d) (of car, dress, machine etc) Modell nt.
2 adj (a) railway, town Modell-; house, home Muster-.
(b) (perfect) vorbildlich, Muster-, mustergültig.
3 vt (a) **to ~ X on Y** Y als Vorlage or Muster für X benützen; **X is ~led on Y** Y dient als Vorlage or Muster für X; **this building is ~led on the Parthenon** dieses Gebäude ist dem Parthenon nachgebildet; **the system was ~led on the American one** das System war nach amerikanischem Muster aufgebaut; **this poem is ~led on Shakespeare's sonnets** dieses Gedicht ist Shakespeares Sonetten nachempfunden, dieses Gedicht nimmt Shakespeares Sonette zum Vorbild; **it's not ~led on anything** es ist frei entstanden, dafür gibt es keine Vorlage; **students nowadays all seem to be ~led on one pattern** die heutigen Studenten scheinen alle einen Typ zu verkörpern; **to ~ oneself/one's life on sb** sich (dat) jdn zum Vorbild nehmen.
(b) (make a ~) modellieren, formen. **her delicately ~led features** (fig) ihre fein geschnittenen Gesichtszüge.
(c) dress etc vorführen.
4 vi (a) (make ~s) modellieren.
(b) (Art, Phot) als Modell arbeiten or beschäftigt sein; (fashion) als Mannequin/Dressman arbeiten. **to ~ for sb** jdm Modell stehen/jds Kreationen vorführen.

modelling, (US) **modeling** ['mɒdlɪŋ] n (a) (of statue etc) Modellieren nt; (fig: of features) Schnitt m. (b) **to do ~** (Phot, Art) als Modell arbeiten; (Fashion) als Mannequin/Dressman arbeiten.

moderate ['mɒdərɪt] 1 adj gemäßigt (also Pol); language also, appetite, enjoyment, lifestyle, speed mäßig; demands also, price vernünftig, angemessen; drinker, eater maßvoll; number, income, success (mittel)mäßig, bescheiden; punishment, winter mild. **a ~ amount** einigermaßen viel; ~-**sized, of ~ size** mittelgroß.
2 n (Pol) Gemäßigte(r) mf.
3 ['mɒdəreɪt] vt mäßigen. **the climate is ~d by the Gulf Stream** das Klima wird durch den Golfstrom gemäßigter; **to have a moderating influence on sb** mäßigend auf jdn wirken.
4 ['mɒdəreɪt] vi nachlassen, sich mäßigen; (wind etc) nachlassen, sich abschwächen; (demands) gemäßigter or maßvoller werden.

moderately ['mɒdərɪtlɪ] adv einigermaßen. **a ~ expensive suit** ein nicht allzu or übermäßig teurer Anzug; **the house was ~ large** das Haus war mäßig groß.

moderation [ˌmɒdə'reɪʃən] n Mäßigung f. **there has been a ~ of the climate** das Klima ist gemäßigter geworden; **in ~** mit Maß(en).

moderator ['mɒdəreɪtə^r] n (Eccl) Synodalpräsident m.

modern ['mɒdən] 1 adj modern (also Art, Liter); times, world also heutig; history neuste und neueste. ~ **languages** neuere Sprachen, moderne Fremdsprachen pl; (Univ) Neuphilologie f; **M~ Greek** etc Neugriechisch etc nt; ~ **studies** Gegenwartskunde und Kulturwissenschaft f; ~ **French studies** französische Sprache und Landeskunde.
2 n Anhänger(in f) m der Moderne.

modernism ['mɒdənɪzəm] n Modernismus m.

modernist ['mɒdənɪst] 1 adj modernistisch. 2 n Modernist m.

modernistic [ˌmɒdə'nɪstɪk] adj modernistisch.

modernity [mɒ'dɜːnɪtɪ] n Modernität f.

modernization [ˌmɔdənaɪˈzeɪʃən] n Modernisierung f.
modernize ['mɔdənaɪz] vt modernisieren.
modernly ['mɔdənlɪ] adv (fashionably) modern. **more ~ known as** ... in neuerer Zeit als ... bekannt.
modernness ['mɔdənnɪs] n see **modernity.**
modest ['mɔdɪst] adj (a) (unboastful) bescheiden. **to be ~ about one's successes** nicht mit seinen Erfolgen prahlen.
  (b) (moderate) bescheiden; way of life, person also genügsam, anspruchslos; requirements also gering; price mäßig. **a ~ crowd turned out for the occasion** die Veranstaltung war (nur) mäßig besucht.
  (c) (chaste, proper) schamhaft; (in one's behaviour) anständig, sittsam (geh), züchtig (old). **to be ~ in one's dress** sich unauffällig or dezent kleiden.
modestly ['mɔdɪstlɪ] adv (a) (unassumingly, moderately) bescheiden. (b) (chastely, properly) schamhaft; behave anständig, züchtig (old); dress unauffällig, dezent.
modesty ['mɔdɪstɪ] n see adj (a) Bescheidenheit f. **in all ~ bei** aller Bescheidenheit; **the ~ of the man!** (iro) der ist ja überhaupt nicht von sich eingenommen! (iro inf).
  (b) Bescheidenheit f; Genügsamkeit, Anspruchslosigkeit f; Mäßigkeit f.
  (c) Schamgefühl nt; Anstand m, Sittsamkeit (geh), Züchtigkeit (old) f; Unauffälligkeit, Dezentheit f.
modicum ['mɔdɪkəm] n ein wenig or bißchen. **with a ~ of luck** mit ein (klein) wenig or einem Quentchen Glück; **a ~ of** hope/decorum/confidence ein Funke (von) Hoffnung/Anstand/Vertrauen; **a ~ of truth** ein Körnchen Wahrheit.
modifiable ['mɔdɪfaɪəbl] adj modifizierbar.
modification [ˌmɔdɪfɪˈkeɪʃən] n (Ver)änderung f; (of design) Abänderung f; (of terms, contract, wording) Modifizierung, Modifikation f. **to make ~s to sth** (Ver)änderungen an etw (dat) vornehmen; etw abändern; etw modifizieren; **the suggested ~s to his design** die Änderungsvorschläge pl zu seinem Entwurf.
modifier ['mɔdɪfaɪə'] n (Gram) Bestimmungswort nt, nähere Bestimmung.
modify ['mɔdɪfaɪ] vt (a) (change) (ver)ändern; design abändern; terms, contract, wording modifizieren. (b) (moderate) mäßigen. (c) (Gram) näher bestimmen.
modish ['mɔdɪʃ] adj (fashionable) modisch; (stylish) schick. **it is very ~ to** ... es ist große Mode, zu ...; **the Beatles made long hair ~** die Beatles haben lange Haare in Mode gebracht.
modishly ['mɔdɪʃlɪ] adv see adj. **he ~ professed his solidarity with the working classes** er folgte dem herrschenden Trend und bekannte sich mit der Arbeiterklasse solidarisch.
modiste [məʊˈdiːst] n Modistin f.
modular ['mɔdjʊlə'] adj aus Elementen zusammengesetzt. **the ~ design of their furniture** ihre als Bauelemente konzipierten Möbel.
modulate ['mɔdjʊleɪt] vti (Mus, Rad) modulieren. **the key (was) ~d from major to minor** die Tonart wechselte von Dur nach Moll.
modulation [ˌmɔdjʊˈleɪʃən] n (Mus, Rad) Modulation f.
module ['mɔdjuːl] n (Bau)element nt; (Space) Raumkapsel f. **command ~** Kommandokapsel f; **lunar ~** Mondlandefähre f or -fahrzeug nt; **service ~** Antriebsgruppe f.
modus operandi ['məʊdəsˌɔpəˈrændɪ] n Modus operandi m.
modus vivendi ['məʊdəsˌvɪˈvendɪ] n Modus vivendi m; (way of life) Lebensstil m or -weise f.
mogul ['məʊgəl] n Mogul m.
MOH abbr of **Medical Officer of Health.**
mohair ['məʊheə'] n Mohair m.
Mohammed [məʊˈhæmed] n Mohammed m.
Mohammedan [məʊˈhæmɪdən] **1** adj mohammedanisch. **2** n Mohammedaner(in f) m.
Mohammedanism [məʊˈhæmədənɪzəm] n Islam m.
moiety ['mɔɪtɪ] n (Jur: half) Hälfte f; (liter) (small amount) Hauch m (geh) (of an +dat); (small share) Bruchteil m.
moist [mɔɪst] adj (+er) feucht (from, with +dat).
moisten ['mɔɪsn] **1** vt anfeuchten. **to ~ sth with sth** etw mit etw befeuchten. **2** vi feucht werden.
moistness ['mɔɪstnɪs] n Feuchtigkeit f.
moisture ['mɔɪstʃə'] n Feuchtigkeit f. **drops of ~** Wasser-/ Schweißtropfen pl.
moisturize ['mɔɪstʃəraɪz] vt skin mit einer Feuchtigkeitscreme behandeln; (cosmetic) geschmeidig machen, Feuchtigkeit verleihen (+dat); air befeuchten.
moisturizer ['mɔɪstʃəraɪzə'], **moisturizing cream** ['mɔɪstʃəraɪzɪŋ'kriːm] n Feuchtigkeitscreme f.
moke [məʊk] n (Brit sl) Esel m.
molar (tooth) ['məʊlə'(ˌtuː:θ)] n Backenzahn m.
molasses [məʊˈlæsɪz] n Melasse f.
mold etc (US) see **mould** etc.
molt n, vti (US) see **moult.**
mole¹ [məʊl] n (Anat) Pigmentmal nt (form), Leberfleck m.
mole² n (Zool) Maulwurf m; (inf: secret agent) Agent m.
mole³ n (Naut) Mole f.
molecular [məʊˈlekjʊlə'] adj molekular, Molekular-.
molecule ['mɔlɪkjuːl] n Molekül nt.
mole: ~hill n Maulwurfshaufen or -hügel m; ~skin n (fur) Maulwurfsfell nt; (garment) Mantel/Jacke etc aus Maulwurfsfell; (fabric) Moleskin m or nt.
molest [məʊˈlest] vt belästigen.
molestation [ˌməʊlesˈteɪʃən] n Belästigung f.
moll [mɔl] n (sl) Gangsterbraut f.
mollify ['mɔlɪfaɪ] vt besänftigen, beschwichtigen. **~ing remarks** begütigende or beschwichtigende Worte pl; **he was somewhat mollified by this** daraufhin beruhigte er sich etwas.
mollusc ['mɔləsk] n Molluske f (spec), Weichtier nt.
mollycoddle ['mɔlɪˌkɔdl] **1** vt verhätscheln, verpäppeln, verzärteln. **to ~ oneself** sich päppeln. **2** n Weichling m.

Moloch ['məʊlɔk] n Moloch m.
Molotov cocktail ['mɔlətɔf'kɔkteɪl] n Molotowcocktail m.
molten ['məʊltən] adj geschmolzen; glass, lava flüssig.
mom [mɔm] n (US inf) see **mum².**
moment ['məʊmənt] n (a) Augenblick, Moment m. **there were one or two ~s when I thought** ... ein paarmal dachte ich ...; **from ~ to ~** zusehends, von Minute zu Minute; **any ~ now, (at) any ~** jeden Augenblick; **at any ~** (any time) jederzeit; **at the ~** im Augenblick, momentan; **at the ~ when** ... zu dem Zeitpunkt, als ...; **not at the or this ~** im Augenblick or zur Zeit nicht; **at the ~ of impact** beim Aufprall, im Augenblick des Aufpralls; **at the last ~** im letzten Augenblick; **at this (particular) ~ in time** momentan, augenblicklich; **for the ~** im Augenblick, vorläufig; **for a ~** (für) einen Moment; **for one ~ it seemed to have** stopped einen Augenblick lang schien es aufgehört zu haben; **not for a or one ~** ... nie(mals) ...; **I didn't hesitate for a ~** ich habe keinen Augenblick gezögert; **in a ~** gleich; **in a ~ of madness** in einem Anflug von geistiger Umnachtung; **in that ~ of happiness** im Augenblick des Glückes; **it was all over in a ~ or a few ~s** das ganze dauerte nur wenige Augenblicke or war im Nu geschehen; **to leave things until the last ~** alles erst im letzten Moment erledigen or machen (inf); **half a ~/one ~!** Momentchen/einen Moment!; **just a ~!, wait a ~!** Moment mal!; **I shan't be a ~** ich bin gleich wieder da; (nearly ready) ich bin gleich soweit; **do it this very ~!** tu das auf der Stelle!; **I have just this ~ heard of it** ich habe es eben or gerade erst erfahren; **we haven't a ~ to lose** wir haben keine Minute zu verlieren; **not a ~ too soon** keine Minute zu früh, in letzter Minute; **not a ~'s peace or rest** keine ruhige Minute; **the ~ it happened** (in dem Augenblick), als es passierte; **the ~ I saw him I knew** ... als ich ihn sah, wußte ich sofort ...; **the ~ he arrives there's trouble** sobald er auftaucht, gibt es Ärger; **tell me the ~ he comes** sagen Sie mir sofort Bescheid, wenn er kommt; **the ~ of truth** die Stunde der Wahrheit; **he is the man of the ~** er ist der Mann des Tages.
  (b) (Phys) Moment nt. **~ of acceleration/inertia** Beschleunigungs-/Trägheitsmoment nt.
  (c) (importance) Bedeutung f. **of little ~** bedeutungslos, unwichtig; **matters of ~** wichtige Angelegenheiten pl, Angelegenheiten pl von Bedeutung.
momentarily ['məʊməntərɪlɪ] adv (a) (für) einen Augenblick or Moment. (b) (US) (very soon) jeden Augenblick or Moment; (from moment to moment) zusehends.
momentary ['məʊməntərɪ] adj (a) kurz; glimpse also flüchtig. **there was a ~ silence** einen Augenblick lang herrschte Stille.
  (b) **he was in ~ fear of being captured** er hatte Angst, jeden Augenblick gefangengenommen zu werden.
momentous [məʊˈmentəs] adj (memorable, important) bedeutsam, bedeutungsvoll; (of great consequence) von großer Tragweite. **of ~ significance** von entscheidender Bedeutung.
momentousness [məʊˈmentəsnɪs] n Bedeutsamkeit f; (of decision) Tragweite f.
momentum [məʊˈmentəm] n (of moving object) Schwung m; (at moment of impact) Wucht f; (Phys) Impuls m; (fig) Schwung m. **the rock's ~ carried it through the wall** der Felsbrocken hatte eine solche Wucht, daß er die Mauer durchschlug; **he let the car go under its own ~** er ließ das Auto von allein weiterrollen; **to gather or gain ~** (lit) sich beschleunigen, in Fahrt kommen (inf); (fig: idea, movement, plan) in Gang kommen; **that idea is now gathering or gaining ~** diese Idee gewinnt an Boden; **to keep going under its own ~** (lit) sich aus eigener Kraft weiterbewegen; (fig) eine Eigendynamik entwickelt haben; **to lose ~** (lit, fig) Schwung verlieren.
Mon abbr of **Monday** Mo.
Monaco ['mɔnəkəʊ] n Monaco nt.
monarch ['mɔnək] n Monarch(in f), Herrscher(in f) m; (fig) König m. **absolute ~** Alleinherrscher m.
monarchic(al) [mɔˈnɑːkɪk(əl)] adj monarchisch; (favouring monarchy) monarchistisch.
monarchism ['mɔnəkɪzəm] n (system) Monarchie f; (advocacy of monarchy) Monarchismus m.
monarchist ['mɔnəkɪst] **1** adj monarchistisch. **2** n Monarchist(in f) m, Anhänger(in f) m der Monarchie.
monarchy ['mɔnəkɪ] n Monarchie f.
monastery ['mɔnəstərɪ] n (Männer- or Mönchs)kloster nt.
monastic [məˈnæstɪk] adj mönchisch, klösterlich; architecture Kloster-; life Ordens-, Kloster-. **~ vows** Ordensgelübde nt; **he leads a ~ existence** (fig) er lebt wie ein Mönch.
monasticism [məˈnæstɪsɪzəm] n Mönch(s)tum nt.
Monday ['mʌndɪ] n Montag m; see also **Tuesday.**
monetary ['mʌnɪtərɪ] adj (a) (pertaining to finance or currency) währungspolitisch, monetär; talks, reform, system Währungs-; reserves, institutions Geld-; unit Geld-, Währungs-. (b) (pecuniary) Geld-; considerations geldlich.
money ['mʌnɪ] n Geld nt; (medium of exchange) Zahlungsmittel nt. **to make ~** (person) (viel) Geld verdienen; (business) etwas einbringen, sich rentieren; **to lose ~** (person) Geld verlieren; (business) Verluste machen or haben; **~ talks** (Pol) Währungsgespräche pl; **there's ~ in it** das ist sehr lukrativ; **if you help me, there's ~ in it** wenn du mir hilfst, springt für dich auch etwas dabei heraus (inf); **it's a bargain for the ~** das ist eine günstige Anschaffung; **what can you expect for the ~?** was kann man bei dem Preis schon verlangen?; **that's the one for my ~!** ich tippe auf ihn/sie etc; **it's ~ for jam** (inf) or old rope (inf) da wird einem das Geld ja nachgeworfen (inf); **to be in the ~** (inf) Geld wie Heu haben; **what's in this job?** wie wird der Job bezahlt?; **to earn good ~** gut verdienen; **to get one's ~'s worth** etwas für sein Geld bekommen; **I've really had my ~'s worth** or **~ out of that car** der Wagen hat sich wirklich bezahlt gemacht or war wirklich sein Geld wert; **to keep sb in ~** jdn (finanziell) unterstützen; **do you think I'm made of ~?** (inf)

ich bin doch kein Krösus!; **that's throwing good ~ after bad** das ist rausgeschmissenes Geld (*inf*); **your ~ or your life!** Geld oder Leben!; **to put one's ~ where one's mouth is** (*inf*) (nicht nur reden, sondern) Taten sprechen lassen; **~ talks** (*inf*) mit Geld geht alles; **~ isn't everything** (*prov*) Geld (allein) macht nicht glücklich (*prov*); **~ makes ~** (*prov*) Kapital vermehrt sich von selbst.

money: **~ bag** *n* Geldsack *m*; **~bags** *n sing* (*inf*) Geldsack *m*; **~box** *n* Sparbüchse *f*; **~changer** *n* (Geld)wechsler *m*.

moneyed ['mʌnɪd] *adj* begütert.

money: **~grubber** *n* Raffke *m* (*inf*); **~grubbing** **1** *adj* geld- or raffgierig; **2** *n* Geld- or Raffgier *f*; **~lender** *n* Geld(ver)leiher *m*; **~maker** *n* (*idea*) einträgliche Sache; (*product*) Verkaufserfolg *m*; (*company*) gewinnbringendes or gutgehendes Unternehmen; **~making** **1** *adj idea, plan* gewinnbringend, einträglich; **2** *n* Geldverdienen *nt*; **~ market** *n* Geldmarkt *m*; **~ matters** *npl* Geldangelegenheiten *or* -dinge *pl*; **~ order** *n* Post- or Zahlungsanweisung *f*; **~ prize** *n* Geldpreis *m*; **~spinner** *n* (*inf*) Verkaufsschlager (*inf*) *or* -hit (*inf*) *m*.

Mongol ['mɒŋgəl] **1** *adj* (a) mongolisch. (b) (*Med*) m~ mongoloid. **2** *n* (a) *see* **Mongolian 2.** (b) (*Med*) he's a m~ er ist mongoloid.

Mongolia [mɒŋˈgəʊlɪə] *n* Mongolei *f*.

Mongolian [mɒŋˈgəʊlɪən] **1** *adj* mongolisch; *features, appearance* mongolid. **2** *n* (a) (Mongole *m*, Mongolin *f*. (b) (*language*) Mongolisch *nt*.

mongolism ['mɒŋgəlɪzəm] *n* (*Med*) Mongolismus *m*.

Mongoloid ['mɒŋgəlɔɪd] *adj* (a) mongolid. (b) (*Med*) m~ mongoloid.

mongoose ['mɒŋguːs] *n*, *pl* **-s** Mungo *m*.

mongrel ['mʌŋgrəl] **1** *adj race* Misch-. **2** *n* (*also* **~ dog**) Promenadenmischung *f*; (*pej*) Köter *m*; (*pej: person*) Mischling *m*.

moni(c)ker ['mɒnɪkəʳ] *n* (*Brit sl: signature*) Name, (Friedrich) Wilhelm (*inf*) *m*.

monitor ['mɒnɪtəʳ] **1** *n* (a) (*Sch*) Schüler(in *f*) *m* mit besonderen Pflichten. **stationery/book ~** Schreibwaren-/Bücherwart *m*.
(b) (*TV, Tech: screen*) Monitor *m*.
(c) (*control, observer*) Überwacher *m*; (*of telephone conversations*) Abhörer *m*; (*Rad*) Mitarbeiter(in *f*) *m* am Monitor-Dienst.
(d) (*also* **~ lizard**) Waran(echse *f*) *m*.
2 *vt* (a) *foreign station, telephone conversation* abhören; *TV programme* mithören.
(b) (*control, check*) überwachen.

monk [mʌŋk] *n* Mönch *m*.

monkey ['mʌŋkɪ] **1** *n* Affe *m*; (*fig: child*) Strolch, Schlingel *m*. **to make a ~ out of sb** (*inf*) jdn verhohnepiepeln (*inf*); **well, I'll be a ~'s uncle** (*inf*) (ich glaub,) mich laust der Affe (*inf*).
2 *vi* **to ~ about** (*inf*) herumalbern; **to ~ about with sth** an etw (*dat*) herumspielen or -fummeln (*inf*).

monkey: **~ business** *n* (*inf*) no **~ business!** mach(t) mir keine Sachen! (*inf*); **there's some ~ business going on here** da ist doch irgend etwas faul (*inf*); **what ~ business have you been up to?** was hast du jetzt schon wieder angestellt?; **~ jacket** *n* Affenjäckchen *nt* (*inf*); **~-nut** *n* Erdnuß *f*; **~-puzzle (tree)** *n* Andentanne, Araukarie (*spec*) *f*; **~ suit** *n* (*inf: tails*) Frack *m*; **he was all done up in his ~ suit** er hatte sich in volle Montur or in Schale geworfen (*inf*); **~-tricks** *npl* Unfug *m*, dumme Streiche *pl*; **none of your ~-tricks!** mach(t) mir keinen Unfug!; **I bet he's up to some ~-tricks again!** der hat doch sicher wieder irgendwas ausgeheckt (*inf*); **~-wrench** *n* verstellbarer Schraubenschlüssel, Engländer, Franzose *m*.

monkish ['mʌŋkɪʃ] *adj* mönchisch; (*fig pej*) pastorenhaft. **he has a ~ attitude towards women** er verhält sich Frauen gegenüber wie der reinste Mönch.

mono ['mɒnəʊ] **1** *n* Mono *nt*. **2** *adj* mono- *attr; record also* in Mono pred.

mono- *pref* Mono-, mono-.

monochrome ['mɒnəkrəʊm] **1** *adj* monochrom, einfarbig; *television* schwarz-weiß. **2** *n* (*Art*) monochrome or in einer Farbe gehaltene Malerei; (*TV*) Schwarz-weiß *nt*.

monocle ['mɒnəkəl] *n* Monokel *nt*.

monogamous [mɒˈnɒgəməs] *adj* monogam.

monogamy [mɒˈnɒgəmɪ] *n* Monogamie *f*.

monogram ['mɒnəgræm] *n* Monogramm *nt*.

monogrammed ['mɒnəgræmd] *adj* mit Monogramm.

mono: **~graph** *n* Monographie *f*; **~lingual** *adj* einsprachig.

monolith ['mɒnəʊlɪθ] *n* Monolith *m*.

monolithic [,mɒnəʊˈlɪθɪk] *adj* (*lit*) monolithisch; (*fig*) gigantisch, riesig.

monologue ['mɒnəlɒg] *n* Monolog *m*.

mono: **~mania** *n* Monomanie *f*; **~plane** *n* Eindecker *m*.

monopolization [məˌnɒpəlaɪˈzeɪʃən] *n* (*lit*) Monopolisierung *f*; (*fig*) (*of bathroom, best seat etc*) Beschlagnahme *f*; (*of person, sb's time etc*) völlige Inanspruchnahme; (*of conversation etc*) Beherrschung *f*.

monopolize [məˈnɒpəlaɪz] *vt* (*lit*) *market* monopolisieren, beherrschen; (*fig*) *person, place, sb's time etc* mit Beschlag belegen, in Beschlag nehmen; *conversation, discussion* beherrschen, an sich (*acc*) reißen. **to ~ the supply/distribution of ...** eine Monopolstellung für die Lieferung/den Vertrieb von ... haben; **she wants to ~ his affections** sie möchte seine Zuneigung or ihn ganz für sich haben.

monopoly [məˈnɒpəlɪ] *n* (a) (*lit*) Monopol *nt*. **~ position** Monopolstellung *f*; **there's a government ~ on or of ...** der Staat hat das Monopol für ...; **coal is a government ~** der Staat hat das Kohlenmonopol or das Monopol für Kohle.
(b) (*fig*) **to have the or a ~ on or of sth** etw für sich gepachtet haben (*inf*); **you haven't got a ~ on me** ich bin doch nicht dein Eigentum.
(c) **M~** ® (*game*) Monopoli ® *nt*.

mono: **~rail** *n* Einschienenbahn *f*; **~syllabic** *adj* (*lit, fig*) einsilbig, monosyllabisch (*Ling*); **~syllable** *n* einsilbiges Wort, Einsilber *m*; **to speak/answer in ~syllables** einsilbig sein/antworten, einsilbige Antworten geben; **~theism** *n* Monotheismus *m*; **~theistic** *adj* monotheistisch.

monotone ['mɒnətəʊn] *n* monotoner Klang; (*voice*) monotone Stimme.

monotonous [məˈnɒtənəs] *adj* (*lit, fig*) eintönig, monoton. **her ~ complaints** ihre sich ständig wiederholenden Klagen; **it's getting ~** es wird allmählich langweilig.

monotony [məˈnɒtənɪ] *n* (*lit, fig*) Eintönigkeit, Monotonie *f*. **the sheer ~ of it!** dieses ewige Einerlei!; (*of work, routine etc also*) dieser Stumpfsinn.

monotype ® ['mɒnəʊtaɪp] *n* Monotype-Verfahren ® *nt*. **~ machine** Monotype ® *f*.

monoxide [mɒˈnɒksaɪd] *n* Monoxyd *nt*.

Monsignor [mɒnˈsiːnjəʳ] *n* Monsignore *m*.

monsoon [mɒnˈsuːn] *n* Monsun *m*. **the ~ rains** der Monsunregen; **in the ~s or the ~ season** in der Monsunzeit.

monster ['mɒnstəʳ] **1** *n* (a) (*big animal, thing*) Ungetüm, Monstrum *nt*; (*animal also*) Ungeheuer *nt*. **a real ~ of a fish** ein wahres Monstrum or Ungeheuer von (einem) Fisch; **a ~ of a book** ein richtiger Schinken (*inf*), ein Mammutwerk; **a ~ of greed** ein (hab)gieriges Monster.
(b) (*abnormal animal*) Ungeheuer, Monster, Monstrum *nt*; (*legendary animal*) (groteskes) Fabelwesen.
(c) (*cruel person*) Unmensch *m*, Ungeheuer *nt*.
2 *attr* (a) (*enormous*) Riesen-; *film* Mammut-.
(b) (*to do with ~s*) Monster-.

monstrance ['mɒnstrəns] *n* (*Eccl*) Monstranz *f*.

monstrosity [mɒnˈstrɒsɪtɪ] *n* (*quality*) Ungeheuerlichkeit, Monstrosität *f*; (*thing*) Monstrosität *f*; (*cruel deed*) Greueltat *f*. **it's a ~ that ...** es ist unmenschlich or schändlich, daß ...

monstrous ['mɒnstrəs] *adj* (a) (*huge*) ungeheuer (groß), riesig.
(b) (*shocking, horrible*) abscheulich; *crime, thought, colour also* gräßlich; *suggestion* ungeheuerlich. **it's ~ that ...** es ist einfach ungeheuerlich or schändlich, daß ...; **how ~ of him!** das war schändlich (von ihm)!

monstrously ['mɒnstrəslɪ] *adv* schrecklich, fürchterlich.

montage [mɒnˈtɑːʒ] *n* Montage *f*.

month [mʌnθ] *n* Monat *m*. **in the ~ of October** im Oktober; **six ~s** ein halbes Jahr, sechs Monate; **in or for ~s** seit langem; **it went on for ~s** es hat sich monatelang hingezogen; **in the early ~s of the war** in den ersten Kriegsmonaten; **one ~'s salary** ein Monatsgehalt; **paid by the ~** monatlich bezahlt.

monthly ['mʌnθlɪ] **1** *adj* monatlich; *magazine, ticket* Monats-. **they have ~ meetings** sie treffen sich einmal im Monat. **2** *adv* monatlich. **twice ~** zweimal im or pro Monat. **3** *n* Monats(zeit)schrift *f*.

monument ['mɒnjumənt] *n* Denkmal *nt*; (*big also*) Monument *nt*; (*small, on grave etc*) Gedenkstein *m*; (*fig*) Zeugnis *nt* (*to gen*). **a ~ to British literature** ein Denkmal britischer Literatur; **his great trilogy survives as a ~ to his talent** seine große Trilogie legt Zeugnis von seinem Talent ab.

monumental [,mɒnjʊˈmentl] *adj* (a) **~ inscription** Grabinschrift *f*; **~ mason** Steinmetz, Steinbildhauer *m*; **~ sculptures** Steinfiguren *pl*. (b) (*very great*) enorm, monumental (*geh*); *proportions, achievement* gewaltig; *ignorance, stupidity, error* kolossal, ungeheuer.

moo [muː] **1** *n* (a) Muhen *nt*. **the cow gave a ~** die Kuh muhte or machte „muh" (*inf*); **~cow** (*baby-talk*) Muhkuh *f* (*baby-talk*).
(b) (*sl: woman*) Kuh *f* (*inf*). **2** *vi* muhen, „muh" machen (*inf*).

mooch [muːtʃ] (*inf*) **1** *vi* tigern (*inf*). **I spent all day just ~ing about or around the house** ich habe den ganzen Tag zu Hause herumgegammelt (*inf*). **2** *vt* (*US inf*) abstauben (*inf*).

mood¹ [muːd] *n* (a) (*of party, town etc*) Stimmung *f*; (*of one person also*) Laune *f*. **he was in a good/bad/foul ~** er hatte gute/schlechte/eine fürchterliche Laune, er war gut/schlecht/fürchterlich gelaunt; **to be in a cheerful ~** gut aufgelegt sein; **to be in a festive/forgiving ~** feierlich/versöhnlich gestimmt sein, in festlicher/versöhnlicher Stimmung sein; **to be in a generous ~** in Geberlaune sein; **in one of his crazy or mad ~s** aus einer plötzlichen Laune heraus, in einer seiner Anwandlungen; **I'm in no laughing ~** or **in no ~ for laughing** mir ist nicht nach or zum Lachen zumute; **to be in the ~ for sth/to do sth** zu etw aufgelegt sein/dazu aufgelegt sein, etw zu tun; **I'm not in the ~ for work or to work/for chess** ich habe keine Lust zum Arbeiten/zum Schachspielen; **I'm not in the ~ for this type of music** ich bin nicht in der Stimmung für diese Musik; **I'm not in the ~** ich bin nicht dazu aufgelegt; (*to do sth also*) ich habe keine Lust; (*for music etc also*) ich bin nicht in der richtigen Stimmung; **~ music** stimmungsvolle Musik.
(b) (*bad ~*) schlechte Laune. **he's in one of his ~s** er hat mal wieder eine seiner Launen; **he's in a ~** er hat schlechte Laune; **he has ~s** er ist sehr launisch; **he is a man of ~s** er ist sehr starken Gemüts- or Stimmungsschwankungen unterworfen.

mood² *n* (*Gram*) Modus *m*. **indicative/imperative/subjunctive ~** Indikativ/Imperativ/Konjunktiv *m*.

moodily ['muːdɪlɪ] *adv see adj*.

moodiness ['muːdɪnɪs] *n see adj* Launenhaftigkeit *f*; schlechte Laune; Verdrossenheit *f*. **his ~, the ~ of his disposition** sein launisches Wesen.

moody ['muːdɪ] *adj* (+ *er*) launisch, launenhaft; (*bad-tempered*) schlechtgelaunt *attr*, schlecht gelaunt *pred*; *look, answer* verdrossen, übellaunig.

moon [muːn] **1** *n* Mond *m*. **is there a ~ tonight?** scheint heute der Mond?; **the man in the ~** der Mann im Mond; **you're asking for the ~!** du verlangst Unmögliches!; **to promise sb the ~** jdm das Blaue vom Himmel versprechen; **to be over the ~** (*inf*) überglücklich sein. **2** *vi* (vor sich *acc* hin) träumen.

♦**moon about** or **around** vi ziellos herumstreichen. **to ~ ~ (in) the house** durchs Haus streichen.

♦**moon away** vt sep time verträumen.

moon in cpds Mond-; **~beam** n Mondstrahl m; **~calf** n (dated) Schwachsinnige(r) mf; (inf) Mondkalb nt; **~-faced** ['mu:n,feɪst] adj mit einem Mondgesicht, mondgesichtig; **~less** adj night mondlos; **~light 1** n Mondlicht nt or -schein m; **it was ~light** der Mond schien; **a ~light walk** ein Mondscheinspaziergang m; see **flit; 2** vi (inf) nebenher arbeiten; **~lighter** n (inf) Nebenberufler(in f) m, = Schwarzarbeiter m; **~lit** adj object mondbeschienen; night, landscape, lawn mondhell; **~shine** n **(a)** (~light) Mondschein, Mondenschein (poet) m; **(b)** (inf: nonsense) Unsinn m; (a) (inf: illegal whisky) illegal gebrannter Whisky; **~shiner** n (inf) Schwarzbrenner m; **~shot** n Mondflug m; **~stone** n Mondstein m; **~struck** adj (mad) mondsüchtig; (fig) vernarrt.

moony ['mu:nɪ] adj (+er) (inf: dreamy) verträumt.

Moor [muə'] n Maure m; (old: black man) Moor m.

moor[1] [muə'] n (Hoch- or Heide)moor nt; (Brit: for game) Moorjagd f. **a walk on the ~s** ein Spaziergang übers Moor.

moor[2] **1** vt festmachen, vertäuen; (at permanent moorings) nuren. **2** vi festmachen, anlegen.

moorage ['muərɪdʒ] n (place) Anlegeplatz m; (charge) Anlegegebühren pl.

moorhen ['muəhen] n Teichhuhn nt.

mooring ['muərɪŋ] n (act of ~) Anlegen nt; (place) Anlegeplatz m. **~s** (ropes, fixtures) Verankerung, Muring f; **~ buoy** Muringsboje f.

Moorish ['muərɪʃ] adj maurisch; invasion der Mauren.

moorland ['muələnd] n Moor- or Heideland(schaft f) nt.

moose [mu:s] n Elch m.

moot [mu:t] **1** adj: **a ~ point** or **question** eine fragliche Sache, **it's a ~ point** or **question whether** ... es ist noch fraglich or die Frage (inf), ob ... **2** vt aufwerfen; suggestion vorbringen. **it has been ~ed whether** ... es wurde zur Debatte gestellt, ob ...

mop [mɒp] **1** n (floor ~) (Naß)mop m; (dish ~) Spülbürste f; (sponge ~) Schwammop m; (inf: hair) Mähne f, Zotteln pl (inf). **her ~ of hair/curls** ihre Mähne/ihr Wuschelkopf.

2 vt floor, kitchen wischen. **to ~ one's face** sich (dat) den Schweiß vom Gesicht wischen.

♦**mop down** vt sep walls abwischen; floor wischen.

♦**mop up 1** vt sep **(a)** aufwischen. **to ~ (what's left of)** the enemy ein Gebiet von feindlichen Truppen säubern (inf); **~ping-~ operations** Säuberungsaktion f; (hum) Aufräumungsarbeiten pl. **2** vi (auf)wischen.

mopboard ['mɒpbɔːd] n (US) Scheuerleiste f.

mope [məup] vi Trübsal blasen (inf).

♦**mope about** or **around** vi mit einer Jammermiene herumlaufen. **to ~ ~ the house** zu Hause hocken und Trübsal blasen (inf).

moped ['məuped] n Moped nt; (very small) Mofa nt.

mopes [məups] npl (inf) **to have (a fit of) the ~** seinen or den Moralischen haben (inf).

mopy ['məupɪ] adj (+er) (inf) trübselig. **I'm feeling a bit ~ today** ich bin heute etwas in Tiefstimmung (inf).

moraine [mɒ'reɪn] n Moräne f.

moral ['mɒrəl] **1** adj **(a)** moralisch, sittlich; principles, philosophy Moral-; support, victory, obligation moralisch. **~ values** sittliche Werte, Moralvorstellungen pl; **~ code** (of individual) Auffassung von Moral f, (of society) Sitten- or Moralkodex m; **~ standards** Moral f; **~ sense** Gefühl nt für Gut und Böse, moralisches Bewußtsein; **~ courage** Charakter m; **~ lecture** Moralpredigt f; **M~ Rearmament** Moralische Aufrüstung f.

(b) (virtuous) integer, moralisch einwandfrei; (sexually) tugendhaft; (moralizing) story, book moralisch.

(c) **it's a ~ certainty that** ... es ist mit Sicherheit anzunehmen, daß ...; **to have a ~ right to sth** jedes Recht auf etw (acc) haben.

2 n **(a)** (lesson) Moral f. **to draw a ~ from sth** eine Lehre aus etw ziehen.

(b) **~s** pl (principles) Moral f; **his ~s are different from mine** er hat ganz andere Moralvorstellungen als ich; **she's a girl of loose ~s** sie hat eine recht lockere Moral; **do your ~s allow you to do this?** kannst du das moralisch vertreten?

morale [mɒ'rɑːl] n Moral f. **to boost sb's ~** jdm (moralischen) Auftrieb geben; **to destroy sb's ~** jdn entmutigen.

moralist ['mɒrəlɪst] n (Philos, fig) Moralist m.

moralistic [,mɒrə'lɪstɪk] adj moralisierend; (Philos) moralistisch.

morality [mə'rælɪtɪ] n Moralität f; (moral system) Moral, Ethik f. **~ play** Moralität f.

moralize ['mɒrəlaɪz] vi moralisieren. **to ~ about** or **upon sb/sth** sich über jdn/etw moralisch entrüsten; **stop your moralizing!** hör mit deinen Moralpredigten auf!

morally ['mɒrəlɪ] adv (a) (ethically) moralisch. **(b)** (virtuously) integer, moralisch einwandfrei; (sexually) tugendhaft.

morass [mə'ræs] n Morast, Sumpf (also fig) m. **to sink or be sucked into the ~ (of vice)** sich immer tiefer (im Laster) verstricken; **a ~ of problems/figures** ein Gewirr nt or Wust m von Problemen/ein Zahlengewirr nt or -wust m.

moratorium [,mɒrə'tɔːrɪəm] n Stopp m; (Mil) Stillhalteabkommen nt; (on treaty etc) Moratorium nt; (Fin) Zahlungsaufschub m. **a ~ on nuclear armament** ein Atomwaffenstopp m; **to declare a ~ on sth** etw (vorläufig) mit einem Stopp belegen; **in der Frage einer Sache** (gen) ein Moratorium beschließen; **there's been a ~ on new transplant techniques** neue Transplantationstechniken wurden vorläufig gestoppt.

morbid ['mɔːbɪd] adj (a) idea, thought, jealousy etc krankhaft; interest, attitude also unnatürlich; imagination, mind also, sense of humour, talk etc makaber; (gloomy) outlook, thoughts düster; person trübsinnig; (pessimistic) schwarzseherisch; poet, novel, music etc morbid. **that's ~!**, **that's a ~ thought** or

idea! das ist ja makaber; **don't be so ~!** sieh doch nicht alles so schwarz!; **he's such a ~ little boy** er hat einen Hang zum Makaberen.

(b) (Med) morbid; growth krankhaft.

morbidity [mɔː'bɪdɪtɪ] n see adj **(a)** Krankhaftigkeit f; Unnatürlichkeit f; Düsterkeit f; Hang m zu düsteren Gedanken; Morbidität f. **the ~ of his jokes/the story put me off** ich fand seine makabren Witze/diese makabre Geschichte wirklich abstoßend; **the ~ of it!** das ist ja schon krankhaft!

(b) Morbidität f; Krankhaftigkeit f.

morbidly ['mɔːbɪdlɪ] adv **to talk/think ~** krankhafte or düstere or morbide (geh) Gedanken äußern/haben; **a ~ humorous story** eine Geschichte von makabrem Humor; **he's ~ interested in bad crashes** er hat ein krankhaftes or unnatürliches or morbides (geh) Interesse an schweren Unfällen; **staring ~ out of the window** trübsinnig or düster aus dem Fenster schauend; **maybe I'll be dead then, he said ~** vielleicht bin ich dann schon tot, sagte er düster; **he was ~ aware that death could come at any time** das Bewußtsein, sterben zu müssen, war bei ihm schon krankhaft.

mordacious [mɔː'deɪʃəs] adj see mordant.

mordacity [mɔː'dæsɪtɪ], **mordancy** ['mɔːdənsɪ] n beißender Humor. **the ~ of his sarcasm/wit** sein beißender Sarkasmus/Humor.

mordant ['mɔːdənt] adj beißend, ätzend.

more [mɔː'] **1** n, pron **(a)** (greater amount) mehr; (a further or additional amount) noch mehr; (of countable things) noch mehr or welche. **~ and ~** immer mehr; **I want a lot ~** ich will viel mehr; (in addition) ich will noch viel mehr; **three/a few ~** noch drei/noch ein paar; **a little ~** etwas mehr; (in addition) noch etwas mehr; **many/much ~** viel mehr; **not many/much ~** nicht mehr viele/viel; **no ~** nichts mehr; (countable) keine mehr; **some ~** noch etwas; (countable) noch welche; **any ~?** noch mehr or etwas?; (countable) noch mehr or welche?; **there isn't/aren't any ~** mehr gibt es nicht; (here, at the moment, left over) es ist nichts mehr da/es sind keine mehr da; **is/are there any ~?** gibt es noch mehr?; (left over) ist noch etwas da/sind noch welche da?; **even ~** noch mehr; **I shall have ~ to say about this** dazu habe ich noch etwas zu sagen; **let's say no ~ about it** reden wir nicht mehr darüber; **we shall hear/see ~ of you** wir werden öfter von dir hören/dich öfter sehen; **there's ~ to come** da kommt noch etwas, das ist noch nicht alles; **what ~ do you want?** was willst du denn noch?; **what ~ could one want?** mehr kann man sich doch nicht wünschen; **there's ~ to it** da steckt (noch) mehr dahinter; **there's ~ to bringing up children than just** ... zum Kindererziehen gehört mehr als nur ...; **and what's ~, he** ... und außerdem or obendrein hat er ... (noch) ...; **they are ~ ... than we are** sie sind in der Mehrzahl.

(b) **(all) the ~** um so mehr; **the ~ you give him, the ~ he wants** je mehr du ihm gibst, desto mehr verlangt er; **it makes me (all) the ~ ashamed** das beschämt mich um so mehr; **all the ~ so because** ... um so mehr, weil ...; **the ~ the merrier** je mehr desto or um so (inf) besser.

2 adj (in addition) noch mehr. **two/five ~ bottles** noch zwei/fünf Flaschen; **one ~ day, one day ~** noch ein Tag; **~ and ~ money/friends** immer mehr Geld/Freunde; **a lot/a little ~ money** viel/etwas mehr Geld; (in addition) noch viel/noch etwas mehr Geld; **a few ~ friends/weeks** noch ein paar Freunde/Wochen; **you won't have many ~ friends/much ~ money** left du hast nicht mehr viele Freunde/nicht mehr viel Geld übrig; **no ~ money/friends** kein Geld mehr/keine Freunde mehr; **no ~ singing/quarrelling!** Schluß mit der Singerei/mit dem Zanken!; **do you want some ~ tea/books?** möchten Sie noch etwas Tee/noch ein paar Bücher?; **I don't want any ~ money/friends** ich will nicht (noch) mehr Geld/Freunde; **is there any ~ wine in the bottle?** ist noch (etwas) Wein in der Flasche?; **there isn't any ~ wine** es ist kein Wein mehr da; **there aren't any ~ books** mehr Bücher gibt es nicht; (here, at the moment) es sind keine Bücher mehr da; **(the) ~ fool you!** dumm wie du bist; **the ~ fool you for giving him** or **to give him the money** daß du auch so dumm bist, und ihm das Geld gibst.

3 adv **(a)** mehr. **~ and ~** immer mehr; **it will weigh/grow a bit ~** es wird etwas mehr wiegen/noch etwas wachsen; **will it weigh/grow any ~?** wird es mehr wiegen/noch wachsen?; **it'll grow ~ if you** ... es wächst besser, wenn du ...; **to like/want sth ~** etw lieber mögen/wollen; **~ than** mehr als; **£5/2 hours ~ than I thought** £ 5 mehr/2 Stunden länger, als ich dachte; **he is ~ than happy/satisfied/stupid/generous** er ist überglücklich/mehr als zufrieden/(schon) mehr als dumm/überaus or mehr als großzügig; **the house is ~ than half built** das Haus ist schon mehr als zur Hälfte fertig; **it will ~ than meet the demand** das wird die Nachfrage mehr als genügend befriedigen; **he's ~ lazy than stupid** er ist eher faul als dumm; **no ~ than nicht mehr als**; **no ~ a duchess than I am** genausowenig eine Herzogin wie ich (eine bin); **nothing ~ than ignorance** reine Unkenntnis; **no ~ do I** ich auch nicht; **he has resigned — that's no ~ than I expected** er hat gekündigt — das habe ich ja erwartet.

(b) (again) once **~** noch einmal, nochmal (inf); never **~** nie mehr or wieder.

(c) (longer) mehr. **no ~**, **not any ~** nicht mehr; **to be no ~** (person) nicht mehr sein or leben; (thing) nicht mehr existieren; **I can't stand it any ~** ich kann es nicht mehr or länger ertragen; **if he comes here any ~** ... wenn er noch weiter or länger hierher kommt ...

(d) (to form comp of adj, adv) -er (than als). **~ beautiful/beautifully** schöner; **~ and ~ beautiful** immer schöner; **no ~ stupid than I am** (auch) nicht dümmer als ich.

(e) **~ or less** mehr oder weniger; **neither ~ nor less, no ~, no less** nicht mehr und nicht weniger.

morello [mɒ'reləu] n Sauerkirsche, Morelle f.

moreover [mɔː'rəʊvə^r] *adv* überdies, zudem, außerdem.
mores ['mɔːreɪz] *npl* Sittenkodex *m*.
morganatic [ˌmɔːgə'nætɪk] *adj* morganatisch.
morgue [mɔːg] *n* (a) (*mortuary*) Leichenschauhaus *nt*. to be like a ~ wie ausgestorben sein. (b) (*Press*) Archiv *nt*.
moribund ['mɒrɪband] *adj person* todgeweiht (*geh*), moribund (*spec*); *species* im Aussterben begriffen; (*fig*) *plan, policy* zum Scheitern verurteilt; *customs, way of life* zum Aussterben verurteilt. the empire was in a ~ state das Weltreich stand vor dem Untergang *or* ging seinem Untergang entgegen.
Mormon ['mɔːmən] 1 *adj* mormonisch, Mormonen-; *doctrine* der Mormonen. 2 *n* Mormone *m*, Mormonin *f*.
Mormonism ['mɔːmənɪzəm] *n* Mormonentum *nt*.
morn [mɔːn] *n* (*poet*) Morgen *m*.
mornay ['mɔːneɪ] *adj sauce* Käse-. **cauliflower/eggs** ~ Blumenkohl/hartgekochte Eier in Käsesoße.
morning ['mɔːnɪŋ] 1 *n* Morgen *m*; (*as opposed to afternoon also*) Vormittag *m*; (*fig*) (*of life*) Frühling *m* (*liter*); (*of an era*) Anfänge *pl*, Beginn *m*. ~ dawned der Morgen *or* es dämmerte; in the ~ morgens, am Morgen; vormittags, am Vormittag; (*tomorrow*) morgen früh; early in the ~ früh(morgens), in der Frühe, am frühen Morgen; (*tomorrow*) morgen früh; very early in the ~ in aller Frühe, ganz früh (am Morgen); (*tomorrow*) morgen ganz früh; late (on) in the ~ am späten Vormittag, gegen Mittag; (at) 7 in the ~ (um) 7 Uhr morgens *or* früh; (*tomorrow*) morgen (früh) um 7; this/yesterday/tomorrow ~ *adv* heute morgen/gestern morgen/morgen früh, heute/gestern/morgen vormittag; on the ~ of November 28th am Morgen des 28. November, am 28. November morgens; the ~ after am nächsten *or* anderen Tag *or* Morgen; the ~ after the night before, the ~-after feeling der Katzenjammer *or* die Katerstimmung am nächsten Morgen.
   2 *attr* Morgen-; (*regularly in the* ~) morgendlich; *train, service etc* Vormittags-; (*early* ~) *train, news* Früh-. what time is ~ coffee? (*at work*) wann ist morgens die Kaffeepause?; (*in café*) ab wann wird vormittags Kaffee serviert?; the secretary makes the ~ coffee die Sekretärin macht morgens den Kaffee.
morning: ~ **coat** *n* Cut(away) *m*; ~ **dress** *n, no pl* Cut(away) *m*; (*dark*) Stresemann *m*; ~ **glory** *n* Winde *f*; ~ **gown** *n* Hauskleid *nt*; M~ **Prayer** *n* Morgenandacht *f*, Frühgottesdienst *m*; ~ **room** *n* Frühstückszimmer *nt*; ~ **sickness** *n* (Schwangerschafts)übelkeit *f*; ~ **star** *n* Morgenstern *m*; ~ **suit** *n* Cut(away) *m*; (*dark*) Stresemann *m*.
Moroccan [mə'rɒkən] 1 *adj* marokkanisch. 2 *n* Marokkaner(in *f*) *m*.
Morocco [mə'rɒkəʊ] *n* Marokko *nt*.
morocco [mə'rɒkəʊ] *n* (*also* ~ **leather**) Maroquin *m*.
moron ['mɔːrɒn] *n* (*Med*) Geistesschwache(r), Debile(r) (*spec*) *mf*; (*inf*) Trottel (*inf*), Schwachkopf (*inf*) *m*.
moronic [mə'rɒnɪk] *adj* (*Med*) geistesschwach, debil (*spec*); (*inf*) idiotisch (*inf*).
morose *adj*, ~ly *adv* [mə'rəʊs, -lɪ] verdrießlich, mißmutig.
moroseness [mə'rəʊsnɪs] *n* Verdrießlichkeit *f*, Mißmut *m*.
morpheme ['mɔːfiːm] *n* Morphem *nt*.
morphia ['mɔːfɪə], **morphine** ['mɔːfiːn] *n* Morphium, Morphin (*spec*) *nt*.
morphological [ˌmɔːfə'lɒdʒɪkəl] *adj* morphologisch.
morphology [mɔː'fɒlədʒɪ] *n* Morphologie *f*.
morrow ['mɒrəʊ] *n* (*old*) the ~ der kommende *or* folgende Tag; on the ~ am folgenden Tag, tags darauf; good ~! (*old*) guten Morgen!
morse [mɔːs] *n* (*also* M~ **code**) Morsezeichen *pl*, Morseschrift *f*. ~ **alphabet** Morsealphabet *nt*; do you know ~ *or* (the) M~ **code**? können Sie morsen?
morsel ['mɔːsl] *n* (*of food*) Bissen, Happen *m*; (*fig*) bißchen *nt*; (*of information*) Brocken *m*. not a ~ of food kein Bissen zu essen; a ~ of comfort ein kleiner Trost.
mortal ['mɔːtl] 1 *adj* (a) (*liable to die*) sterblich; (*causing death*) *injury, combat* tödlich.
   (b) (*extreme*) *agony, fear* tödlich, Todes-; *sin, enemy* Tod-; (*inf*) *hurry* irrsinnig (*inf*).
   (c) (*inf: conceivable*) no ~ use überhaupt kein Nutzen.
   (d) (*inf: tedious*) *hours, boredom* tödlich (*inf*).
   2 *n* Sterbliche(r) *mf*.
mortality [mɔː'tælɪtɪ] *n* (a) (*mortal state*) Sterblichkeit *f*.
   (b) (*number of deaths*) Todesfälle *pl*; (*rate*) Sterblichkeit(s-ziffer), Mortalität (*form*) *f*. ~ **rate, rate of** ~ Sterbeziffer, Sterblichkeitsziffer, Mortalität (*form*) *f*.
mortally ['mɔːtəlɪ] *adv* (*fatally*) tödlich; (*fig: extremely*) *shocked etc* zu Tode; *wounded* zutiefst; *offended* tödlich.
mortar¹ ['mɔːtə^r] *n* (a) (*bowl*) Mörser *m*. (b) (*cannon*) Minenwerfer *m*.
mortar² 1 *n* (*cement*) Mörtel *m*. 2 *vt* mörteln.
mortarboard ['mɔːtəbɔːd] *n* (a) (*Univ*) Doktorhut *m*. (b) (*Build*) Mörtelbrett *nt*.
mortgage ['mɔːgɪdʒ] 1 *n* Hypothek *f* (*on auf* + *acc/dat*). a ~ for £5,000/that amount eine Hypothek über *or* von £ 5.000/über diesen Betrag. 2 *vt house, land* hypothekarisch belasten. to ~ one's future (*fig*) sich (*dat*) die *or* seine Zukunft verbauen.
mortgagee [ˌmɔːgə'dʒiː] *n* Hypothekar *m*.
mortgagor [ˌmɔːgə'dʒɔː^r] *n* Hypothekenschuldner *m*.
mortice *n, vt see* **mortise**.
mortician [ˌmɔː'tɪʃən] *n* (*US*) Bestattungsunternehmer *m*.
mortification [ˌmɔːtɪfɪ'keɪʃən] *n* (a) Beschämung *f*; (*embarrassment*) äußerste Verlegenheit; (*humiliation*) Demütigung *f*. much to his ~, she ... er empfand es als sehr beschämend, daß sie ...; (*embarrassment*) es war ihm äußerst peinlich, daß sie ...; (*humiliation*) er empfand es als eine Schmach, daß sie ...; to my ~ that I had made a mistake ich stellte zu meiner größten Verlegenheit fest, daß ich einen Fehler gemacht hatte; because of her ~ at what had

happened weil ihr das, was geschehen war, so überaus peinlich war; oh the ~ of it all! diese Schande!; he felt great ~ at being rejected er empfand es als eine Schmach *or* Schande, daß er nicht angenommen wurde; all the ~ he suffered all die Demütigungen, die er hinnehmen mußte.
   (b) (*Rel*) Kasteiung *f*.
   (c) (*Med*) Brand *m*.
mortify ['mɔːtɪfaɪ] 1 *vt usu pass* (a) beschämen; (*embarrass*) äußerst peinlich sein (+ *dat*). he was mortified er empfand das als beschämend; (*embarrassed*) es war ihm äußerst peinlich; embarrassed? I was mortified! peinlich?, ich wäre am liebsten im Boden versunken!; his younger brother's success mortified him er empfand den Erfolg seines jüngeren Bruders als eine Schmach; a mortified look ein äußerst betretener Gesichtsausdruck.
   (b) (*Rel*) kasteien.
   (c) (*Med*) absterben lassen. to be mortified abgestorben sein.
   2 *vi* (*Med*) absterben.
mortifying *adj*, ~ly *adv* ['mɔːtɪfaɪɪŋ, -lɪ] beschämend; (*embarrassing*) peinlich.
mortise, mortice ['mɔːtɪs] 1 *n* Zapfenloch *nt*. ~ **lock** (Ein)steckschloß *nt*. 2 *vt* verzapfen (*into mit*).
mortuary ['mɔːtjʊərɪ] *n* Leichenhalle *f*.
Mosaic [məʊ'zeɪɪk] *adj* mosaisch.
mosaic [məʊ'zeɪɪk] 1 *n* Mosaik *nt*. 2 *attr* Mosaik-.
Moscow ['mɒskəʊ] *n* Moskau *nt*.
Moselle [məʊ'zel] *n* Mosel *f*; (*also* ~ **wine**) Mosel(wein) *m*.
Moses ['məʊzɪz] *n* Mose(s) *m*. ~ **basket** Körbchen *nt*.
Moslem ['mɒzləm] 1 *adj* mohammedanisch. 2 *n* Moslem *m*.
mosque [mɒsk] *n* Moschee *f*.
mosquito [mɒ'skiːtəʊ] *n, pl* -**es** Stechmücke *f*; (*in tropics*) Moskito *m*. ~ **net** Moskitonetz *nt*.
moss [mɒs] *n* Moos *nt*.
mossy ['mɒsɪ] *adj* (+ *er*) (*moss-covered*) moosbedeckt, bemoost; *lawn* vermoost; (*mosslike*) moosig, moosartig.
most [məʊst] 1 *adj superl* meiste(r, s); (*greatest*) *satisfaction, pleasure etc* größte(r, s); (*highest*) *speed etc* höchste(r, s). who has the ~ money? wer hat am meisten *or* das meiste Geld?; that gave me (the) ~ pleasure das hat mir am meisten Freude *or* die größte Freude gemacht; for the ~ part größtenteils, zum größten Teil; (*by and large*) im großen und ganzen.
   (b) (*the majority of*) die meisten. ~ men/people die meisten (Menschen/Leute); he's better than ~ people er ist besser als die meisten anderen.
   2 *n, pron* (*uncountable*) die meiste; (*countable*) die meisten. ~ of it/them das meiste/die meisten; ~ of the winter/day fast den ganzen Winter/Tag über; ~ of the time die meisten *or* fast die ganze Zeit; (*usually*) meist(ens); do the ~ you can machen Sie soviel (wie) Sie können; at (the) ~/the very ~ höchstens/allerhöchstens; to make the ~ of sth (*make good use of*) etw nach Kräften *or* voll ausnützen; (*enjoy*) etw gründlich genießen; to make the ~ of a story/an affair soviel wie möglich aus einer Geschichte/Affäre machen; to make the ~ of one's looks *or* oneself das Beste aus sich machen; the girl with the ~ (*inf*) die Superfrau (*inf*); it's the ~! (*dated sl*) das ist dufte! (*dated sl*).
   3 *adv* (a) *superl* (+ *vbs*) am meisten; (+ *adj*) -ste(r, s); (+ *adv*) am -sten. the ~ beautiful/difficult *etc* der/die/das schönste/schwierigste *etc*; which one did it ~ easily? wem ist es am leichtesten gefallen?; what ~ displeased him, what displeased him ~ ... am meisten mißfiel ihm ...; ~ of all am allermeisten; ~ of all because ... vor allem, weil ...
   (b) (*very*) äußerst, überaus. ~ likely höchstwahrscheinlich; he added ~ unnecessarily ... er sagte noch völlig unnötigerweise ...; he had told you ~ explicitly er hat Ihnen doch ganz eindeutig gesagt ...
   (c) (*old, dial: almost*) fast, so ziemlich (*inf*), schier (*old, S Ger*).
most-favoured-nation clause [ˌməʊst'feɪvəd'neɪʃn,klɔːz] *n* (*Pol*) Meistbegünstigungsklausel *f*.
mostly ['məʊstlɪ] *adv* (*principally*) hauptsächlich; (*most of the time*) meistens; (*by and large*) zum größten Teil. they are ~ women/over fifty die meisten sind Frauen/über fünfzig, sie sind zum größten Teil Frauen/über fünfzig; ~ because ... hauptsächlich, weil ...; it's ~ finished es ist zum größten Teil fertig.
MOT (*Brit*) (a) *abbr of* **Ministry of Transport**. (b) ~ (**test**) der TÜV. it failed its ~ es ist nicht durch den TÜV gekommen.
mote [məʊt] *n* (*old*) Staubkorn, Stäubchen *nt*. to see the ~ in one's neighbour's eye (**and not the beam in one's own**) den Splitter im Auge des anderen (und nicht den Balken im eigenen Auge) sehen.
motel [məʊ'tel] *n* Motel *nt*.
motet [məʊ'tet] *n* Motette *f*.
moth [mɒθ] *n* Nachtfalter *m*; (*wool-eating*) Motte *f*. the clothes had got ~s in den Kleidern waren die Motten.
moth: ~**ball** *n* Mottenkugel *f*; to put in ~**balls** (*lit, fig*) einmotten; *ship* stillegen, außer Dienst stellen; ~**-eaten** *adj* (*lit*) mottenzerfressen; (*fig*) ausgedient, vermottet (*inf*).
mother ['mʌðə^r] 1 *n* (a) Mutter *f*; (*animal also*) Muttertier *nt*; (*address to elderly lady*) Mütterchen *nt*. M~ **of God** Muttergottes, Mutter Gottes *f*; M~'s **Day** Muttertag *m*; ~'s **help** Haus(halts)hilfe *f*; a ~'s love Mutterliebe *f*; to be (like) a ~ to sb wie eine Mutter zu jdm sein; I had the ~ and father of a headache (*inf*) ich hatte vielleicht Kopfschmerzen!
   (b) (*US vulg*) Saftsack *m* (*vulg*). a real ~ of a ... ein/eine Scheiß- ... (*sl*).
   2 *attr church, plant* Mutter-; *bear, bird etc* -mutter *f*. ~ **hen** Glucke *f*; ~ **plane** Flugzeugmutterschiff *nt*; ~ **figure** Mutterfigur *f*.

3 vt (care for) young auf- or großziehen; (give birth to) zur Welt bringen; (cosset) bemuttern.

mother: ~ **country** n (native country) Vaterland nt, Heimat f; (head of empire) Mutterland nt; ~**craft** n Kinderpflege f; ~**fucker** n (US vulg) Saftsack m (vulg), Arschloch nt (vulg); ~**fucking** adj (US vulg) Scheiß- (vulg); ~**hood** n Mutterschaft f.

Mothering Sunday ['mʌðərɪŋ'sʌndɪ] n Lätare nt.

mother: ~**in-law** n, pl ~**s-in-law** Schwiegermutter f; ~**land** n (native country) Vaterland nt, Heimat f; (ancestral country) Land der Väter or Vorfahren; ~**less** adj mutterlos; he was left ~**less at the age of 2** er verlor mit 2 Jahren seine Mutter; ~ **love** n Mutterliebe f.

motherly ['mʌðəlɪ] adj mütterlich.

mother: ~**of-pearl 1** n Perlmutt nt, Perlmutter f; **2** adj Perlmutt-; ~ **ship** n Mutterschiff nt; M~ **Superior** n Mutter Oberin f; ~**to-be** n, pl ~**s-to-be** werdende Mutter; ~ **tongue** n Muttersprache f; ~ **wit** n Mutterwitz m.

moth: ~**hole** n Mottenloch nt; ~**proof 1** adj mottenfest; **2** vt mottenfest machen.

motif [məʊ'ti:f] n (Art, Mus) Motiv nt; (Sew) Muster nt.

motion ['məʊʃən] **1** n (a) no pl (movement) Bewegung f. **to be in** ~ sich bewegen; (engine, machine etc) laufen; (train, bus etc) fahren; **to set** or **put sth in** ~ etw in Gang bringen or setzen.

(b) (gesture) Bewegung f. **to go through the** ~**s** (of doing sth) (because protocol, etiquette etc demands it) etw pro forma or der Form halber tun; (pretend) so tun, als ob (man etw täte), den Anschein erwecken(, etw zu tun); (do mechanically) etw völlig mechanisch tun.

(c) (proposal) Antrag m. **to propose** or **make** (US) a ~ einen Antrag stellen.

(d) (in debate) Thema nt.

(e) (bowel ~) Stuhlgang m; (faeces) Stuhl m. **to have a** ~ Stuhlgang haben.

2 vti to ~ **(to) sb to do sth** jdm bedeuten, etw zu tun (geh), jdm ein Zeichen geben, daß er etw tun solle; **he** ~**ed me to a chair** er wies mir einen Stuhl an; **he** ~**ed me in/away** er winkte mich herein/er gab mir ein Zeichen, wegzugehen.

motion: ~**less** adj unbeweglich, reg(ungs)los; ~ **picture** n Film m; ~**picture** attr Film-.

motivate ['məʊtɪveɪt] vt motivieren. **he's just not** ~**d enough** es fehlt ihm einfach die nötige Motivation.

motivation [ˌməʊtɪ'veɪʃən] n Motivation f.

motive ['məʊtɪv] **1** n (a) (incentive, reason) Motiv nt, Beweggrund m; (for crime) (Tat)motiv nt. **the profit** ~ Gewinnstreben nt; **my** ~**s were of the purest** ich hatte die besten Absichten. **(b)** see **motif. 2** adj power, force Antriebs-, Trieb-.

motiveless ['məʊtɪvlɪs] adj grundlos, ohne Motiv, unmotiviert.

mot juste ['məʊ'ʒu:st] n passender or treffender Ausdruck.

motley ['mɒtlɪ] **1** adj kunterbunt; (varied also) bunt(gemischt); (multicoloured also) bunt (gescheckt). **2** n Narrenkostüm or -kleid nt. **on with the** ~! lache, Bajazzo!

motocross ['məʊtəkrɒs] n Moto-Cross nt.

motor ['məʊtə'] **1** n (a) Motor m. **(b)** (inf: car) Auto nt.

2 vi (dated) (mit dem Auto) fahren.

3 attr (a) (Physiol) motorisch. **(b)** (~-driven) Motor-.

motor: ~**assisted** adj mit Hilfsmotor; ~**bike** n Motorrad nt; ~**boat** n Motorboot nt.

motorcade ['məʊtəkeɪd] n Fahrzeug- or Wagenkolonne f.

motor: ~**car** n (dated, form) Automobil (dated), Kraftfahrzeug (form) nt; ~ **coach** n (dated) Autobus m; ~**cycle** n Motorrad, Kraftrad (form) nt; ~**cycle combination** n Motorrad mit Beiwagen; ~**cycling** n Motorradfahren nt; (Sport) Motorradsport m; ~**cyclist** n Motorradfahrer(in f) m; ~**driven** adj Motor-, mit Motorantrieb.

-motored [-'məʊtəd] adj suf -motorig. **petrol-**~ mit Verbrennungsmotor.

motoring ['məʊtərɪŋ] **1** adj attr accident, offence Verkehrs-; news, correspondent Auto-. ~ **skills** Fahrkünste pl; **the** ~ **public** die Autofahrer pl. **2** n Autofahren nt. **school of** ~ Fahrschule f.

motorist ['məʊtərɪst] n Autofahrer(in f) m.

motorization [ˌməʊtəraɪ'zeɪʃən] n Motorisierung f.

motorize ['məʊtəraɪz] vt motorisieren. **to be** ~**d** motorisiert sein; (private person also) ein Auto haben.

motor: ~**man** n (of train) Zugführer m; (of tram) Straßenbahnfahrer m; ~ **mechanic** n Kraftfahrzeugmechaniker, Kfz-Mechaniker m; ~ **nerve** n motorischer Nerv; ~ **race** n (Auto)rennen nt; ~ **racing** n Rennsport m; **he did a lot of** ~ **racing** er hat an vielen Autorennen teilgenommen; ~ **road** n Fahrstraße f; ~ **scooter** n (form) Motorroller m; ~ **show** n Automobilausstellung f; ~ **sport** n Motorsport m; (with cars also) Automobilsport m; ~ **truck** n (US) Lastwagen m; ~ **vehicle** n (form) Kraftfahrzeug nt; ~**way** n (Brit) Autobahn f.

mottled ['mɒtld] adj gesprenkelt; complexion fleckig. ~ **brown and white** braun und weiß gesprenkelt.

motto ['mɒtəʊ] n, pl -es Motto nt, Wahlspruch m; (personal also) Devise f; (Her also) Sinnspruch m; (in cracker, on calendar) Spruch m. **the school** ~ das Motto der Schule.

mould¹, (US) **mold** [məʊld] **1** n (a) (hollow form) (Guß)form f; (Typ also) Mater f; (shape, Cook) Form f.

(b) (jelly, blancmange) Pudding, Wackelpeter (inf) m.

(c) (fig: character, style) **to be cast in the same/a different** ~ (people) vom gleichen/von einem anderen Schlag sein, aus dem gleichen/einem anderen Holz geschnitzt sein; (novel characters) nach demselben/einem anderen Muster geschaffen sein; **the two painters/novelists etc are cast in the same/a different/the Dutch** ~ die beiden Maler/Schriftsteller etc verbindet viel/wenig miteinander/viel mit den Niederländern; **people of that/a simple** ~ Menschen dieses Schlages/mit einer einfachen Wesensart; **his younger sister cast him in a heroic** ~

für sein jüngere Schwester verkörperte er den Type des Helden; **to fit sb/sth into a** ~ jdn/etw in ein Schema zwängen.

2 vt (a) (lit) (fashion) formen (into zu); (cast) gießen.

(b) (fig) character, person formen. **to** ~ **sb into sth** etw aus jdm machen; **it/the hero is** ~**ed on ...** es orientiert sich an (+dat)/der Held ist nach dem Vorbild (+gen) geschaffen.

3 vr **to** ~ **oneself on sb** sich (dat) jdn zum Vorbild nehmen; **to** ~ **oneself on an ideal** sich an einem Ideal orientieren.

mould², (US) **mold** n (fungus) Schimmel m.

mould³, (US) **mold** n (soil) Humus(boden m or -erde f) m.

moulder¹, (US) **molder** ['məʊldə'] n (Tech) Former, (Form)gießer m.

moulder², (US) **molder** vi (lit) vermodern; (leaves also) verrotten; (food) verderben; (carcass) verwesen; (fig) (mental faculties, building) zerfallen; (equipment) vermodern, vergammeln (inf); (person) verkümmern.

mouldiness, (US) **moldiness** ['məʊldɪnɪs] n Schimmel m (of auf +dat), Schimmligkeit f. **a smell of** ~ ein Modergeruch m.

moulding, (US) **molding** ['məʊldɪŋ] n (a) (act) Formen nt; (of metals) Gießen nt. **(b)** (cast) Abdruck m; (of metal) (Ab)guß m; (ceiling ~) Deckenfries or -stuck m. **(c)** (fig) Formen nt.

mouldy, (US) **moldy** ['məʊldɪ] adj (+er) (a) (covered with mould) verschimmelt, schimmelig; (musty) mod(e)rig. **(b)** (dated inf) (pathetic, contemptible) miserabel (inf); (mean) person schäbig; amount lumpig (inf).

moult, (US) **molt** [məʊlt] **1** n (of birds) Mauser f; (of mammals) Haarwechsel m; (of snakes) Häutung f. **2** vt hairs verlieren; feathers, skin abstreifen. **3** vi (bird) sich mausern; (mammals) sich haaren; (snake) sich häuten.

mound [maʊnd] n (a) (hill, burial ~) Hügel m; (earthwork) Wall m; (Baseball) Wurfmal nt. **(b)** (pile) Haufen m; (of books, letters) Stoß, Stapel m.

mount¹ [maʊnt] n (poet: mountain, hill) Berg m. **(b)** (in names) M~ Etna/Kilimanjaro etc der Ätna/Kilimandscharo etc; M~ Everest Mount Everest m; **on** M~ Sinai auf dem Berg(e) Sinai.

mount² **1** n (a) (horse etc) Reittier, Roß (old, liter) nt.

(b) (support, base) (of machine) Sockel, Untersatz m; (of colour slide) Rahmen m; (of microscope slide) Objektträger m; (of jewel) Fassung f; (of photo, picture) Passepartout nt; (backing) Unterlage f, Rücken m; (stamp ~) Falz m.

2 vt (a) (climb onto) besteigen, steigen auf (+acc).

(b) (place in/on ~) montieren; picture, photo mit einem Passepartout versehen; (on backing) aufziehen; colour slide rahmen; microscope slide, specimen, animal präparieren; jewel (ein)fassen; stamp aufkleben.

(c) (organize) play inszenieren; attack, expedition, exhibition organisieren, vorbereiten; army aufstellen.

(d) to ~ **a guard** eine Wache aufstellen (on vor +dat); **to** ~ **guard** Wache stehen or halten (on vor +dat).

(e) (mate with) bespringen; (birds, inf: person) besteigen.

(f) (provide with horse) mit Pferden/einem Pferd versorgen.

3 vi (a) (get on) aufsteigen; (on horse also) aufsitzen.

(b) (increase: also ~ up) sich häufen.

mountain ['maʊntɪn] n (lit, fig) Berg m. **in the** ~**s** im Gebirge, in den Bergen; **to make a** ~ **out of a molehill** aus einer Mücke einen Elefant(en) machen (inf).

mountain in cpds Berg-; (alpine, Himalayan etc) Gebirgs-; ~ **ash** n Eberesche f; ~ **chain** n Berg- or Gebirgskette f, Gebirgszug m; ~ **dew** n (inf) illegal gebrannter Whisky.

mountaineer [ˌmaʊntɪ'nɪə'] **1** n Bergsteiger(in f) m. **2** vi bergsteigen, klettern.

mountaineering [ˌmaʊntɪ'nɪərɪŋ] **1** n Bergsteigen, Klettern nt. **2** attr Bergsteiger-, Kletter-. ~ **skill** bergsteigerisches Können, Kletterkunst f; **learn** ~ **skills with ...** erlernen Sie das Bergsteigen mit ...; **in** ~ **circles** unter Bergsteigern.

mountain lion n Puma, Silberlöwe m.

mountainous ['maʊntɪnəs] adj bergig, gebirgig; (fig: huge) riesig.

mountain: ~ **range** n Gebirgszug m or -kette f; ~ **sheep** n Dickhornschaf nt; ~ **sickness** n Höhen- or Bergkrankheit f; ~**side** n (Berg)hang m.

mountebank ['maʊntɪbæŋk] n Quacksalber, Scharlatan m.

mounted ['maʊntɪd] adj (on horseback) beritten; (Mil: with motor vehicles) motorisiert.

Mountie ['maʊntɪ] n (inf) berittener kanadischer Polizist.

mounting ['maʊntɪŋ] n (a) see **mount²** **2** (b) Montage f; Versehen nt mit einem Passepartout; Aufziehen nt; Rahmen nt; Präparieren nt; (Ein)fassen nt; Aufkleben nt. **(b)** (frame etc) see **mount²** **1** (b). **engine** ~**s** Motoraufhängung f.

mourn [mɔ:n] **1** vt person trauern um, betrauern; sb's death beklagen, betrauern; (with wailing) beklagen; (fig) nachtrauern (+dat). **who is she** ~**ing?** um wen trauert sie?; (wear ~ing for) warum trägt sie Trauer?; **what is to become of us?, she** ~**ed** was soll aus uns werden?, klagte sie.

2 vi trauern; (wear ~ing) Trauer tragen, in Trauer gehen. **to** ~ **for** or **over sb/sth** um jdn trauern, jds Tod (acc) betrauern/einer Sache (dat) nachtrauern.

mourner ['mɔ:nə'] n Trauernde(r) mf; (non-relative at funeral) Trauergast m.

mournful ['mɔ:nfʊl] adj (sad) person, occasion, atmosphere traurig, trauervoll; person (as character trait), voice weinerlich; look also jammervoll, Jammer-; sigh, appearance kläglich, jämmerlich; sound, cry klagend.

mournfully ['mɔ:nfəlɪ] adv see adj.

mournfulness ['mɔ:nfʊlnɪs] n see adj Traurigkeit f; Weinerlichkeit f; Jämmerlichkeit f; klagender Laut.

mourning ['mɔ:nɪŋ] n (act) Trauer f, Trauern nt (of um); (with wailing) Wehklage f; (period etc) Trauerzeit f; (dress) Trauer(kleidung) f. **to be in** ~ **for** sb um jdn trauern; **to come out of** ~ die Trauer ablegen; **to go**

into ~ trauern; (wear ~) Trauer anlegen; **next Tuesday has been declared a day of national** ~ für den kommenden Dienstag wurde Staatstrauer angeordnet.
mouse [maʊs] **1** n, pl **mice (a)** Maus f. **(b)** (inf: person) (shy) schüchternes Mäuschen; (nondescript) graue Maus. **2** vi Mäuse fangen, mausen. **to go mousing** auf Mäusejagd gehen.
mouse in cpds Mause-; ~-**coloured** adj mausgrau.
mouser ['maʊsə^r] n Mäusefänger(in f) or -jäger(in f) m.
mousetrap ['maʊstræp] n Mausefalle f.
mousey adj see **mousy**.
mousse [mu:s] n Creme(speise) f.
moustache, (US) **mustache** [mə'stɑ:ʃ] n Schnurrbart m.
mousy, mousey ['maʊsɪ] adj (+er) (timid, shy) schüchtern; (nondescript) farblos, unscheinbar; colour, hair mausgrau.
mouth [maʊθ] **1** n (of person) Mund m; (of animal) Maul nt; (of bird) Rachen m; (of bottle, cave, vice etc) Öffnung f; (of river) Mündung f; (of harbour) Einfahrt f. **to be down in the** ~ (inf) deprimiert or niedergeschlagen sein; **to keep one's (big)** ~ **shut** (inf) den Mund or die Klappe (inf) halten; **to have a foul** ~ ein grobes or ungewaschenes Maul haben (inf); **he has three** ~**s to feed** er hat drei Mäuler zu ernähren or stopfen (inf); see **word**.
2 [maʊð] vt (say affectedly) (über)deutlich artikulieren; (articulate soundlessly) mit Lippensprache sagen.
mouthful ['maʊθfʊl] n (of drink) Schluck m; (of food) Bissen, Happen (inf) m; (fig: difficult word) Zungenbrecher m; (long word) Bandwurm m. **the diver gulped in great** ~**s of air** der Taucher machte ein paar tiefe Atemzüge; **I got a** ~ **of salt water** ich habe einen ganzen Schwall Salzwasser geschluckt.
mouth in cpds Mund-; ~-**organ** n Mundharmonika f; ~**piece** n Mundstück nt; (of telephone) Sprechmuschel f; (fig: spokesman, publication) Sprachrohr nt; ~-**to**-~ adj Mund-zu-Mund-; ~**wash** n Mundwasser nt; ~-**watering** adj lecker; that smells/looks really ~-**watering** da läuft einem ja das Wasser im Mund(e) zusammen!; ~-**wateringly** adv appetitlich.
movability [,mu:və'bɪlɪtɪ] n see adj Beweglichkeit f; Transportfähigkeit f.
movable ['mu:vəbl] **1** adj beweglich (auch Jur, Eccl); (transportable) transportierbar, transportfähig. **not easily** ~ schwer zu bewegen/transportieren. **2** n **(a)** (portable object) bewegliches Gut. ~**s** Mobiliar nt, Mobilien pl. **(b)** usu pl (Jur) bewegliches Vermögen, Mobiliarvermögen nt.
move [mu:v] **1** n **(a)** (in game) Zug m; (fig: step, action) Schritt m; (measure taken) Maßnahme f. **it's my** etc ~ (lit, fig) ich etc bin am Zug or dran (inf); **to have first/to make a** ~ (lit) den ersten Zug/einen Zug machen; **to make a/the first** ~ (fig) etwas or Schritte unternehmen/den ersten Schritt tun; **that was a false** or **bad/good/clever** ~ (lit) das war ein schlechter/guter/raffinierter Zug; (fig) das war taktisch falsch or unklug/das war ein guter/geschickter Schachzug; **he's up to every** ~ **in the game** (fig) dem kann man kein X für ein U vormachen (inf).
(b) (movement) Bewegung f. **to be on the** ~ (things, people) in Bewegung sein; (fig: things, developments) im Fluß sein; (person: in different places) unterwegs or auf Achse (inf) sein; (vehicle) fahren; (country, institutions etc) sich im Umbruch befinden; **to watch sb's every** ~ jdn nicht aus den Augen lassen; **to get a** ~ **on (with sth)** (inf) (hurry up) zumachen (inf) or sich beeilen (mit etw); (make quick progress) (mit etw) vorankommen; **get a** ~ **on!** nun mach schon! (inf), mach mal zu! (inf); **to make a** ~ **to do sth** (fig) Anstalten machen, etw zu tun; **nobody had made a** ~ **(towards going)** keiner hatte Anstalten gemacht zu gehen; **it's time we made a** ~ es wird Zeit, daß wir gehen or daß wir uns auf den Weg machen.
(c) (of house etc) Umzug m; (to different job) Stellenwechsel m; (to different department) Wechsel m.
2 vt **(a)** (make sth ~) leaves, pointer, part bewegen; wheel, windmill etc (an)treiben; (shift) objects, furniture woanders hinstellen; (~ away) wegstellen; (shift about) umstellen, umräumen; chest, chair rücken; vehicle (engine) von der Stelle bewegen; (driver) wegfahren; (transport) befördern; (remove) soil, dirt, rubble wegschaffen; obstacle aus dem Weg räumen; rock von der Stelle bewegen; chess piece etc ziehen mit, einen Zug machen mit; (out of the way) wegnehmen. **to** ~ **sth to a different place** etw an einen anderen Platz stellen; **to be unable to** ~ **sth** (lift) etw nicht von der Stelle or vom Fleck (inf) bringen; screw, nail etw nicht losbekommen; **I can't** ~ **this** lid/handle der Deckel/Griff läßt sich nicht bewegen; **you'll have to** ~ **these books/your car (out of the way)** Sie müssen diese Bücher wegräumen/Ihr Auto wegfahren; **can you** ~ **that chest over here?**; können Sie die Kommode hierher stellen?; **don't** ~ **anything, said the detective** verändern Sie nichts or lassen Sie alles so, wie es ist, sagte der Detektiv; **you must have** ~**d the camera** da haben Sie wahrscheinlich gewackelt; **recent events have** ~**d the share index upwards/downwards** infolge der jüngsten Ereignisse sind die Aktien gestiegen/gefallen; **to** ~ **the direction in which the company is going** der Firma eine andere Richtung geben.
(b) parts of body bewegen; (take away) arm wegnehmen; one's foot, hand wegziehen. **not to** ~ **a muscle** sich nicht rühren; **could you** ~ **your head a little to the side?** können Sie vielleicht Ihren Kopf ein wenig zur Seite drehen?; **he** ~**d his face a little closer** er ging mit dem Gesicht etwas näher heran; ~ **yourself, can't you?** können Sie nicht mal etwas Platz machen?; **to** ~ **the** or **one's bowels** (form) Stuhlgang haben; **this mixture will help to** ~ **the bowels** dieses Mittel regt die Verdauung an or ist verdauungsfördernd.
(c) (change location of) offices, troops, production verlegen. **to** ~ **house/office** umziehen/(in ein anderes Büro) umziehen; **the removal men are moving us on Friday** die Spediteure machen am Freitag unseren Umzug; **we've been** ~**d to a new office** wir mußten in ein anderes Büro umziehen.

(d) enemy, demonstrators vertreiben; patient bewegen; (transport) transportieren; (transfer) verlegen; refugees transportieren; (out of area) evakuieren; employee (to different department etc) versetzen; (upgrade) befördern (to zu); pupil (by authorities) versetzen. ~ **those people** schicken Sie die Leute da weg; **to** ~ **sb to a hospital** jdn ins Krankenhaus einliefern; **to** ~ **soldiers into the city** in der Stadt Soldaten einsetzen; **I'm going to** ~ **you to sales manager/goalkeeper** etc ich werde Sie jetzt als Verkaufsleiter/Torwart etc einsetzen; **his parents** ~**d him to another school** seine Eltern haben ihn in eine andere Schule getan or gegeben.
(e) (fig: sway) **to** ~ **sb from an opinion** etc jdn von einer Meinung etc abbringen; **to** ~ **sb to do sth** jdn veranlassen or bewegen (geh) or dazu bringen, etw zu tun; **I am not to be** ~**d, I shall not be** ~**d** ich bleibe hart, ich bleibe dabei.
(f) (cause emotion in) rühren, bewegen; (upset) erschüttern, ergreifen. **his speech really** ~**d them** sie waren von seiner Rede tief bewegt; **to be** ~**d** gerührt sein; erschüttert sein; **I'm not easily** ~**d, but ... ich** bin ja sonst nicht so schnell gerührt/leicht zu erschüttern, aber ...; **to** ~ **sb to tears/anger/pity** jdn zu Tränen rühren/jds Zorn/Mitleid erregen; **to** ~ **sb to action** jdn veranlassen, etwas zu unternehmen.
(g) (form: propose) beantragen. **she** ~**d an amendment to the motion** sie stellte einen Abänderungsantrag; **I** ~ **that we adjourn** ich beantrage eine Vertagung.
(h) (Comm: sell) absetzen. **to** ~ **stock** das Lager räumen.
3 vi **(a)** sich bewegen. **nothing/nobody** ~**d** nichts/niemand rührte sich; **the wheel/vehicle began to** ~ das Rad/Fahrzeug setzte sich in Bewegung; **how does a caterpillar** ~? wie bewegt sich eine Raupe fort?; **she** ~**s gracefully/like a cat** ihre Bewegungen sind anmutig/katzenhaft; **don't** ~! stillhalten!; **don't** ~ **or I'll shoot** keine Bewegung, oder ich schieße!
(b) (not be stationary) (vehicle, ship) fahren; (traffic) vorankommen. **to keep moving** nicht stehenbleiben; **to keep sb/sth moving** jdn/etw in Gang halten; **keep those people moving!** sorgen Sie dafür, daß die Leute weitergehen!; **things are moving at last** endlich kommen die Dinge in Gang or geschieht etwas; ~! na los, wird's bald! (inf).
(c) (~ house) umziehen. **we** ~**d to London/to a bigger house** wir sind nach London/in ein größeres Haus umgezogen; **they** ~**d from London** sie sind von London weggezogen.
(d) (change place) gehen; (in car etc) fahren. **let's** ~ **into the garden** gehen wir in den Garten; **he has** ~**d to room 52** er ist jetzt in Zimmer 52; **he has** ~**d to another department/a different company** er hat die Abteilung/Firma gewechselt; **he used to sit here, has he** ~**d?** das war doch sein Platz, sitzt er nicht mehr da?; **he has** ~**d to Brown's** er ist zu Brown gegangen; **have the troops** ~**d?** sind die Truppen abgezogen?; **the troops** ~**d to another base** die Truppen zogen zu einem anderen Stützpunkt weiter; ~! weitergehen!; **(go away)** verschwinden Sie!; **don't** ~ gehen Sie nicht weg; **I won't** ~ **from here** ich rühre mich nicht von der Stelle; **it's time we were moving** or **we** ~**d** es wird Zeit, daß wir gehen.
(e) (progress) **to** ~ **(away) from/closer to** or **towards sth** sich von etw entfernen/sich etw (dat) nähern; **which way are events/is civilization moving?** in welche Richtung entwickelt sich die Dinge/entwickelt sich unsere Zivilisation?; **scientific progress** ~**s at an ever faster rate** die Wissenschaft macht immer raschere Fortschritte; **to** ~ **with the times** mit der Zeit gehen.
(f) (inf) (go fast) einen Zahn or ein Tempo draufhaben (inf); (hurry up) zumachen (inf), einen Zahn zulegen (sl). **he can** ~ der ist unheimlich schnell (inf); **150? that's moving!** 150? das ist aber ein ganz schönes Tempo! (inf).
(g) **to** ~ **in high society/in yachting circles** etc in den besseren Kreisen/in Seglerkreisen etc verkehren.
(h) (in games) (make a ~) einen Zug machen, ziehen; (have one's turn) am Zug sein, ziehen. **white** ~**s, white to** ~ Weiß ist am Zug or zieht.
(i) (fig: act) etwas unternehmen, Maßnahmen ergreifen. **they must** ~ **first** sie müssen den ersten Schritt tun; **a general must** ~ **swiftly** ein General muß rasch handeln (können).
(j) (form: propose, request) **to** ~ **for sth** etw beantragen.
(k) (sell) sich absetzen lassen, gehen (inf).
♦**move about 1** vt sep (place in different positions) umarrangieren; furniture, ornaments etc umstellen, umräumen; parts of body (in und her) bewegen; (fiddle with) herumspielen mit; employee versetzen; (make travel) umher- or herumschicken. **the families of servicemen get** ~**d** ~ **a lot** die Familien von Militärpersonal müssen oft umziehen.
2 vi sich (hin und her) bewegen; (fidget) herumzappeln; (travel) unterwegs sein; (move house) umziehen. **I can hear him moving** ~ ich höre ihn herumlaufen; **the car/stick will help her to** ~ ~ mit dem Auto/Stock ist sie beweglicher.
♦**move along 1** vt sep weiterrücken; car vorfahren; bystanders etc zum Weitergehen veranlassen. **2** vi (along seat etc) auf or durchrücken; (along pavement, bus etc) weitergehen; (cars) weiterfahren. **I'd better be moving** ~ (inf) ich glaube, ich muß weiter or los (inf).
♦**move around** vti sep see **move about**.
♦**move aside 1** vt sep zur Seite or beiseite rücken or schieben; person beiseite drängen. **2** vi zur Seite gehen, Platz machen.
♦**move away 1** vt sep wegräumen; car wegfahren; person wegschicken; (to different town, job etc) versetzen; troops abziehen; pupil wegsetzen. **this decision** ~**d many people** ~ **from supporting the government** diese Entscheidung hat viele Leute dazu veranlaßt, sich von der Regierung zu distanzieren; **to** ~ **sb** ~ **from sb/sth** jdn von jdm/etw entfernen.
2 vi **(a)** (move aside) aus dem Weg gehen, weggehen; (leave) (people) weggehen; (vehicle) losfahren; (move house) fort- or wegziehen (from aus, von); (firm) wegziehen (from von aus, aus),

verziehen; *(person) (from department)* verlassen *(from acc)*; *(from job)* wechseln *(from acc)*.

  (b) *(fig)* abkommen *(from* von); *(from ideology also)* sich distanzieren *(from* von); *(from policy, aims etc also)* sich entfernen *(from* von).

♦**move back** 1 *vt sep* **(a)** *(to former place)* zurückstellen; *people* zurückbringen; *(into old house, town)* wieder unterbringen *(into* in +*dat*); *(to job)* zurückversetzen; *soldiers* zurückbeordern. **they'll** ~ **you** ~ **when the danger is past** Sie werden zurückgeschickt, wenn die Gefahr vorbei ist; **this experience** ~**d him** ~ **to socialism** nach dieser Erfahrung wandte er sich wieder dem Sozialismus zu.

  (b) *(to the rear) things* zurückschieben *or* -rücken; *car* zurückfahren; *chess piece* zurückziehen, zurückgehen mit; *people* zurückdrängen; *troops* zurückziehen.

  2 *vi* **(a)** *(to former place)* zurückkommen; *(into one's house)* wieder einziehen *(into* in +*acc*); *(into old job)* zurückgehen *(to* zu); *(fig: to theory, ideology)* zurückkehren *(to* zu).

  (b) *(to the rear)* zurückweichen; *(troops)* sich zurückziehen; *(car)* zurückfahren. ~ ~**, please!** bitte zurücktreten!

♦**move down** 1 *vt sep* **(a)** *(downwards)* (weiter) nach unten stellen; *(along)* (weiter) nach hinten stellen; *(Sch)* zurückstufen; *(Sport)* absteigen lassen. **that item further** ~ **the list** führen Sie diesen Punkt weiter unten auf der Liste auf; **to** ~ **sb** ~ **the line/the bus)** jdn weiter hinten hinstellen/jdn (im Bus) aufrücken lassen; **he** ~**d the cows/soldiers** ~ **to the plains** er trieb die Kühe/beorderte die Soldaten ins Flachland hinunter.

  2 *vi* **(downwards)** nach unten rücken *or* rutschen; *(along)* weiterrücken *or* -rutschen; *(in bus etc)* nach hinten aufrücken; *(Sch)* zurückgestuft werden; *(team etc)* absteigen, zurückfallen *(to* auf +*acc*). ~ **(right)** ~ **the bus, please!** rücken Sie bitte (ans hintere Ende des Busses) auf!; **to** ~ ~ **the social scale** gesellschaftlich absteigen; **he had to** ~ ~ **a year** *(Sch)* er mußte eine Klasse zurück; **when the nomads/cows** ~**d** ~ **to the plain** als die Nomaden/Kühe ins Flachland herunterkamen.

♦**move forward** 1 *vt sep* **(a)** *person* vorgehen lassen; *chair, table etc* vorziehen *or* -rücken; *chess piece* vorziehen, vorgehen mit; *car* vorfahren; *troops* vorrücken lassen.

  (b) *(fig: advance) event, date* vorverlegen. **to** ~ **the hands of a clock** ~ den Zeiger *or* die Uhr vorstellen.

  2 *vi (person)* vorrücken; *(crowd)* sich vorwärts bewegen; *(car)* vorwärtsfahren; *(troops)* vorrücken; *(hands of clock)* vor- *or* weiterrücken.

♦**move in** 1 *vt sep* **(a)** *police, troops, extra staff* einsetzen (-*to* in +*dat*); *(march/drive in)* einrücken lassen (-*to* in +*acc*); *(take inside)* luggage etc herein-/hineinstellen (-*to* in +*acc*); *car* hineinfahren (-*to* in +*acc*).

  (b) the council/removal firm hasn't ~**d us** ~ **(to the house) yet** die Stadt hat uns noch nicht im Haus untergebracht/die Spedition hat unseren Umzug noch nicht gemacht.

  2 *vi* **(a)** *(into accommodation)* einziehen (-*to* in +*acc*).

  (b) *(come closer)* sich nähern *(on* dat); näher herankommen *(on* an +*acc*); *(camera)* näher herangehen *(on* an +*acc*); *(police, troops)* anrücken; *(start operations) (workers)* (an)kommen, anfangen; *(hooligans, firms etc)* auf den Plan treten. **to** ~ ~ **on sb** *(police, troops)* gegen jdn vorrücken; *(guests)* jdm auf den Leib rücken; **the big concerns** ~**d** ~ **on the market/the casinos** die großen Konzerne etablierten sich auf dem Markt/im Kasinogeschäft; **the troops** ~**d** ~**to the town** die Truppen rückten in die Stadt ein.

♦**move off** 1 *vt sep* people wegschicken. ~ **her** ~**!** *(car, train etc) (inf)* fahr los!; **let's try to get** ~**d** ~ **by 8 o'clock** *(inf)* wir sollten zusehen, daß wir um 8 Uhr loskommen *(inf)*.

  2 *vi* **(a)** *(go away) (people)* weggehen; *(troops)* abziehen.

  (b) *(start moving)* sich in Bewegung setzen; *(train, car also)* los- *or* abfahren.

♦**move on** 1 *vt sep hands of clock* vorstellen. **the policeman** ~**d them** ~ der Polizist forderte sie auf, weiterzugehen/weiterzufahren; **he** ~**d the discussion** ~ **to the next point** er leitete die Diskussion zum nächsten Punkt über.

  2 *vi (people)* weitergehen; *(vehicles)* weiterfahren. **it's about time I was moving** ~ *(fig)* es wird Zeit, daß ich (mal) etwas anderes mache; **to** ~ ~ **to higher things** sich Höherem zuwenden; **to** ~ ~ **to a more responsible job** zu einem verantwortungsvolleren Posten aufsteigen; **I've got to be moving** ~ **or I'll miss my train** ich muß unbedingt weiter, sonst verpasse ich noch den Zug; **let us** ~ ~ **to more important matters** wenden wir uns wichtigeren Dingen zu; **they** ~**d** ~ **to discuss the future of the company** als nächstes besprachen sie die Zukunft der Firma; **let's** ~ ~ **to the next point** gehen wir zum nächsten Punkt über; **time is moving** ~ die Zeit vergeht.

♦**move out** 1 *vt sep* **(a)** *car* herausfahren *(of* aus). **we had to** ~ ~ **the furniture** wir mußten die Möbel hinausräumen *or* -stellen; ~ **the table** ~ **of the corner** stellen *or* rücken Sie den Tisch von der Ecke weg; **she** ~**d it** ~ **from under the bed** sie zog es unter dem Bett (her)vor.

  (b) *(withdraw) troops* abziehen. **they are being** ~**d** ~ **(of their house)** sie müssen (aus ihrem Haus) ausziehen; **the council** ~**s** ~ **all bad tenants** die Stadt zwingt alle schlechten Mieter, ihre Wohnung zu räumen; **they** ~**d everybody** ~ **of the danger zone** alle mußten die Gefahrenzone verlassen *or* räumen; **the removal men are moving us** ~ **tomorrow** die Spediteure machen morgen unseren Umzug.

  2 *vi* **(a)** *(leave accommodation)* ausziehen; *(withdraw: troops)* abziehen. **to** ~ ~ **of an area** ein Gebiet räumen.

  (b) *(leave: train etc)* abfahren.

♦**move over** 1 *vt sep* herüber-/hinüberschieben. ~ **your bottom** ~ rück *or* rutsch mal ein Stück zur Seite *(inf)*; **he** ~**d the car** ~ **to the side** er fuhr an die Seite heran.

  2 *vi* zur Seite rücken *or* rutschen. ~ ~**, we all want to sit down** rück *or* rutsch mal ein Stück, wir wollen uns auch hinsetzen

(inf); ~ ~ **to your side of the bed** leg dich in deine Hälfte des Betts; **he** ~**d** ~ **to his own side of the bed** er rückte herüber in seine Betthälfte.

♦**move up** 1 *vt sep* **(a)** *(weiter)* nach oben stellen; *(promote)* befördern; *(Sch)* versetzen; *(Sport)* aufsteigen lassen. ~ **that** ~ **to the top of the list** stellen Sie das ganz oben an die Liste, führen Sie das ganz oben auf; **they** ~**d him** ~ **two places** sie haben ihn zwei Plätze vorgerückt; **they** ~**d the cows** ~ **to the pastures** sie trieben die Kühe auf die Alm (hinauf); **the general** ~**d his men** ~ **onto the hill** der General beorderte seine Leute auf den Hügel hinauf; **to** ~ **sb** ~ **(the line/the bus)** jdn weiter nach vorne stellen/jdn (im Bus) aufrücken lassen.

  (b) *troops etc (into battle area)* aufmarschieren lassen; *(to front line)* vorrücken lassen; *guns, artillery* auffahren.

  2 *vi* **(a)** *(fig)* aufsteigen; *(shares, rates etc)* steigen; *(be promoted)* befördert werden; *(Sch)* versetzt werden. **the tribe** ~**d** ~ **to the hills for the summer** der Stamm zog den Sommer über in die Berge hinauf; **to** ~ ~ **the social scale** die gesellschaftliche Leiter hinaufklettern.

  (b) *(move along)* auf- *or* weiterrücken. ~ ~ **the bus!** rücken Sie auf *or* weiter!

moveable *adj, n see* **movable**.

movement ['muːvmənt] *n* **(a)** *(motion)* Bewegung *f*; *(fig: trend)* Trend *m (towards* zu); *(of events)* Entwicklung *f*; *(of prices/rates)* Preis-/Kursbewegung *f*; *(of troops etc)* Truppenbewegung *f*. **a slight downward/upward** ~ eine leichte Abwärts-/Aufwärtsbewegung; **the novel lacks** ~ dem Roman fehlt die Handlung; ~ **(of the bowels)** *(Med)* Stuhlgang *m*; **there was a** ~ **towards the door** alles drängte zur Tür; **a marked** ~ **to the right** ein merklicher *or* deutlicher Rechtsruck; **the jumpy/flowing** ~ **of the piece** *(Mus)* der hüpfende/fließende Rhythmus des Stückes.

  (b) *(political, artistic etc* ~) Bewegung *f*.

  (c) *(transport: of goods etc)* Beförderung *f*.

  (d) *(Mus)* Satz *m*.

  (e) *(mechanism)* Antrieb(smechanismus) *m*, Getriebe *nt*; *(of clock)* Uhrwerk *nt*.

mover ['muːvər] *n* **(a)** *(of proposition)* Antragsteller *m*. **(b)** *(remover)* Möbelpacker *m*. **(c)** *(walker, dancer etc)* **he is a good/poor** ~ seine Bewegungen sind schön/plump *etc*.

movie ['muːvɪ] *n (esp US)* Film *m*. **the** ~ **(the)** ~**s** der Film; **to go to the** ~**s** ins Kino gehen.

movie *in cpds* Film-; ~ **camera** *n* Filmkamera *f*; ~**goer** *n* Kinogänger(in *f*) *m*; ~**-house** *n* Kino, Filmtheater *nt*.

moving ['muːvɪŋ] *adj* **(a)** *(that moves)* beweglich. ~ **staircase** *or* **stairs** Rolltreppe *f*; ~ **pavement** *(esp Brit) or* **walk** *(US)* Rollsteg *m*. **(b)** *(Tech: motive) power etc* Antriebs-; *(fig: instigating) force* treibend. **(c)** *(causing emotion)* ergreifend; *movement also* bewegend; *tribute* rührend.

movingly ['muːvɪŋlɪ] *adv* ergreifend.

mow[1] [məu] *pret* ~**ed**, *ptp* **mown** *or* ~**ed** *vti* mähen.

♦**mow down** *vt sep* abmähen; *(fig: slaughter)* niedermähen.

mow[2] *n (US)* Heuhaufen *m*; *(storing place)* Heuboden *m*.

mower ['məuər] *n (person)* Mäher, Schnitter *(old) m; (machine) (on farm)* Mähmaschine *f; (lawn~)* Rasenmäher *m*.

mowing ['məuɪŋ] *n* Mähen *nt*. ~ **machine** Mähmaschine *f*.

mown [məun] *ptp of* **mow**[1].

Mozambique [ˌməuzæm'biːk] *n* Mozambique, Moçambique *nt*.

MP *abbr of* **(a)** **Member of Parliament**. **(b)** **Military Police**.

  (c) **Metropolitan Police**.

mpg *abbr of* **miles per gallon**.

mph *abbr of* **miles per hour**.

Mr ['mɪstər] *abbr of* **Mister** Herr *m*.

MRP *abbr of* **manufacturer's recommended price**.

Mrs ['mɪsɪz] *abbr of* **Mistress** Frau *f*.

Ms [mɪz] *n* Frau *f (auch für Unverheiratete)*.

ms *abbr of* **manuscript** MS, Mskr.

MSc *abbr of* **Master of Science**.

Msg *abbr of* **Monsignor** Msgr., Mgr.

Mt *abbr of* **Mount**.

much [mʌtʃ] **1** *adj, n* **(a)** viel *inv*. **how** ~ wieviel *inv*; **not** ~ nicht viel; **that** ~ so viel; **but that** ~ **I do know der** *das* weiß ich; ~ **of this is true** viel *or* vieles daran ist wahr; **we don't see** ~ **of each other** wir sehen uns nicht oft *or* nur selten; **he/it isn't up to** ~ *(inf)* er/es ist nicht gerade berühmt *(inf)*; **I'm not** ~ **of a musician/cook/player** ich bin nicht sehr musikalisch/keine große Köchin/kein *(besonders)* guter Spieler; **not** ~ **of a gain** kein großer Gewinn; **that wasn't** ~ **of a dinner/party** das Essen/die Party war nicht gerade besonders; **I find that a bit (too)** ~ **after all I've done for him** nach allem was ich für ihn getan habe, finde ich das ein ziemlich starkes Stück *(inf)*.

  (b) **too** ~ *(in quantity, money, etc, inf: more than one can take)* zuviel *inv*; *(with emphatic too)* zu viel; *(sl) (marvellous, hilarious)* Spitze *(sl); (ridiculous)* das Letzte *(inf)*; **to be too** ~ **for sb** *(in quantity)* zuviel für jdn sein; *(too expensive)* jdm zuviel *or* zu teuer sein; **that insult was too** ~ **for me** die Beleidigung ging mir zu weit; **that jazz concert/the sight of her face was too** ~ **for me** *(inf)* ich fand das Jazzkonzert Spitze *(sl)/*ihr Gesicht war zum Schreien *(inf)*; **these children are/this job is too** ~ **for me** ich bin den Kindern/der Arbeit nicht gewachsen; **he'd be too** ~ **for anybody** er wäre für jeden eine Zumutung; **he doesn't do too** ~ er tut nicht übermäßig viel; **far too** ~**, too** ~ **by half** viel zu viel.

  (c) *(just)* **as** ~ ebensoviel *inv*, genausoviel *inv*; **about/not as** ~ ungefähr/nicht soviel; **three times as** ~ dreimal soviel; **I have twice** *or* **three times as** ~ **as I can eat** das kann ich nie im Leben aufessen; **as** ~ **as you want/can** *etc* soviel du willst/kannst *etc*; **he spends as** ~ **as he earns** er gibt (genau)soviel aus, wie er verdient; **as** ~ **again** noch einmal soviel; **I feared/thought** *etc* **as** ~ *(genau)* das habe ich befürchtet/mir gedacht *etc*; **it's as** ~ **as I can do to stand up** es fällt mir schwer genug aufzustehen;

as ~ as to say ... was soviel heißt or bedeutet wie ...

(d) so ~ soviel *inv*; *(emph so, with following that)* so viel; **it's not so ~ a problem of modernization as** ... es ist nicht so sehr ein Problem der Modernisierung, als ...; **at so ~ a pound** zu soundsoviel Mark/Pfund *etc* pro Pfund; **you know so ~** du weißt so viel; *see also* so.

(e) to make ~ of sb/sth viel Wind um jdn/etw machen; **Glasgow makes ~ of its large number of parks** Glasgow rühmt sich seiner vielen Parks; **I couldn't make ~ of that chapter** mit dem Kapitel konnte ich nicht viel anfangen *(inf)*.

2 *adv* **(a)** *(with adj, adv)* viel; *(with vb)* sehr; *(with vb of physical action)* drive, sleep, think, talk, laugh *etc* viel; come, visit, go out *etc* oft, viel *(inf)*. **a ~-admired/-married woman** eine vielbewunderte/oft verheiratete Frau; **he was ~ dismayed/embarrassed** *etc* er war sehr bestürzt/verlegen *etc*; **so ~/too ~** soviel/zuviel; so sehr/zu sehr; **I like it very/so ~** es gefällt mir sehr gut/so gut or so sehr; **I don't like him/it too ~** ich kann ihn/es nicht besonders leiden; **thank you very/(ever) so ~** vielen Dank/ganz or vielen herzlichen Dank; **I don't ~ care** or **care ~** es ist mir ziemlich egal; **however ~ he tries** sosehr or wie sehr er sich auch bemüht; **~ to my astonishment** sehr zu meinem Erstaunen, zu meinem großen Erstaunen; **as ~ I should like to** so gern ich möchte; **~ as I like him** sosehr ich ihn mag; *see also* so.

(b) *(by far)* weitaus, bei weitem. **~ the biggest** weitaus or bei weitem der/die/das größte, der/die/das weitaus größte; **I would ~ prefer to** or **~ rather stay** ich würde viel lieber bleiben.

(c) *(almost)* beinahe. **they are ~ of an age** or **~ the same age** sie sind fast or beinahe gleichaltrig; **they're (fairly) ~ the same size** sie sind beinahe or so ziemlich gleich groß.

muchness ['mʌtʃnɪs] n **they're much of a ~** *(inf)* *(things)* das ist eins wie das andere; *(people)* sie sind einer wie der andere.

muck [mʌk] n **(a)** *(dirt)* Dreck *m*; *(euph: cat's/dog's ~)* Kot *m*; *(manure)* Dung, Mist *m*; *(liquid manure)* Jauche *f*. **where there's ~, there's brass** or **money** *(Prov)* Dreck und Geld liegen nahe beisammen *(prov)*.

(b) *(fig)* *(rubbish)* Mist *m*; *(obscenities)* Schund *m*; *(food etc)* Zeug *nt* *(inf)*. **Lord/Lady ~** Graf Rotz *(inf)*/die feine Dame.

♦**muck about** or **around** *(inf)* **1** *vt sep* **(a) to ~ sb ~** mit jdm machen, was man will, jdn verarschen *(sl)*; *(by not committing oneself)* jdn hinhalten; **that applicant/the travel agents really ~ed us ~** das war ein ewiges Hin und Her mit dem Bewerber/dem Reisebüro *(inf)*; **stop ~ing me ~!** sag mir endlich, woran ich bin or was los ist!; **I wouldn't let him ~ me ~** like that so ein Hin und Her würde ich mir nicht gefallen lassen; **to ~ sb's plans ~** jds Pläne über den Haufen werfen *(inf)*.

(b) *(fiddle around with, spoil)* herumpfuschen an *(+dat)* *(inf)*. **to ~ things ~** alles durcheinanderbringen.

2 *vi* **(a)** *(lark about)* herumalbern or -blödeln *(inf)*; *(do nothing in particular)* herumgammeln *(inf)*. **to ~ ~ in boats** sich mit Booten beschäftigen; **to ~ ~ at sth/(at) doing sth** Zeit mit etw vertrödeln *(inf)*/Zeit damit vertrödeln, etw zu tun.

(b) *(tinker with)* herumfummeln *(with an +dat)*.

(c) to ~ ~ with sb jdn an der Nase herumführen *(inf)*.

♦**muck in** *vi* *(inf)* mit anpacken *(inf)*.

♦**muck out** *vti sep* *(aus)*misten.

♦**muck up** *vt sep* *(inf)* **(a)** *(dirty)* dreckig machen *(inf)*. **you've really ~ed ~ this place** ihr habt hier ja eine (ganz) schöne Schweinerei angerichtet!

(b) *(spoil)* vermasseln *(inf)*; *person (emotionally)* verkorksen *(inf)*. **that's really ~ed me/my plans ~** das hat mir alles/meine Pläne vermasselt *(inf)*.

muckiness ['mʌkɪnɪs] n Schmutzigkeit *f*.

muck: ~**-rake** *vi* *(fig inf)* im Schmutz wühlen; ~**-raker** *n* *(fig inf)* Sensationsmache(r) *f* *(inf)*; ~**-raking 1** *n* *(fig inf)* Sensationsmache(rei) *f* *(inf)*; **2** *adj* *(fig inf)* person sensationslüstern; **a ~-raking newspaper** ein Skandalblatt *nt*; ~**-spread** *vi* Mist streuen or *(aus)*breiten; ~**-spreading** *n* Miststreuen, Mistbreiten *nt*; ~**-up** *n* *(inf)* Durcheinander *nt*; *(fiasco)* Katastrophe *f*; **there's been a ~-up with the invitations** bei den Einladungen hat jemand/habe ich *etc* Mist gemacht *(inf)*; **I made a real ~-up of that exam** die Prüfung habe ich versaut *(inf)*.

mucky ['mʌkɪ] *adj* *(+er)* dreckig *(inf)*, schmutzig; *soil etc* matschig. **to get oneself/sth all ~** sich/etw ganz dreckig *(inf)* or schmutzig machen; **you ~ thing** or **pup!** *(inf)* du Ferkel! *(inf)*.

mucous ['mju:kəs] *adj* schleimig; *deposits, secretions etc* Schleim-. ~ **membrane** Schleimhaut *f*.

mucus ['mju:kəs] n Schleim *m*.

mud [mʌd] n *(a)* Schlamm *m*; *(on roads etc)* Matsch *m*. **the car stuck in the ~** der Wagen blieb im Matsch or Schlamm stecken; **(here's) ~ in your eye!** *(dated)* zum Wohl!, prösterchen! *(hum)*.

(b) *(fig)* **his name is ~** *(inf)* er ist unten durch *(inf)*; **to drag sb/sb's name** or **reputation through the ~** jdn/jds guten Namen in den Schmutz zerren or ziehen; **to throw** or **sling ~** im Schmutz or Dreck *(inf)* wühlen; **to throw** or **sling ~ at sb/sth** jdn mit Schmutz bewerfen/etw in den Dreck *(inf)* or Schmutz ziehen; **some of the ~ has stuck/is bound to stick** etwas ist hängengeblieben/bleibt immer hängen.

mud: ~**-bath** *n* Schlammbad *nt*; *(Med)* Moorbad *nt*; ~**-coloured** *adj* schmutzig grau.

muddle ['mʌdl] **1** *n* Durcheinander *nt*. **to get in(to) a ~** *(things)* durcheinandergeraten; *(person)* konfus werden; **to get in(to) a ~ with sth** mit etw nicht klarkommen; **how did things get into such a ~?** wie ist denn dieses Durcheinander entstanden?; **to get sb/sth in(to) a ~** jdn/etw völlig durcheinanderbringen; **to be in a ~** völlig durcheinander sein; **this room is (in) a real ~** in diesem Zimmer herrscht ein einziges Durcheinander or liegt es aus wie Kraut und Rüben *(inf)*; **to make a ~ of/with/over sth** etw völlig durcheinanderbringen.

2 *vt* durcheinanderbringen; *two things* or *people also* verwechseln; *(make confused)* *person also* verwirren, konfus

machen. **to ~ A with** or **and B** A mit or und B verwechseln; **you're only muddling the issue** du machst die Sache nur verworrener.

♦**muddle along** or **on** *vi* vor sich *(acc)* hin wursteln *(inf)*.

♦**muddle through** *vi* durchkommen, sich (irgendwie) durchwursteln *(inf)* or durchschlagen.

♦**muddle up** *vt sep* *see* muddle 2.

muddled ['mʌdld] *adj* konfus; *person also* durcheinander *pred*; *thoughts, ideas also* verworren, wirr. **~ sounds** ein Gewirr or Wirrwarr von Geräuschen; **set out in a ~ way** ziemlich konfus angelegt; **he has/this is a rather ~ way of doing things** er macht alles/das ist ja ziemlich kompliziert; **in a ~ way it does make sense** es ist zwar verworren, ergibt aber doch einen Sinn.

muddle-headed ['mʌdl,hedɪd] *adj* *person* zerstreut; *ideas* konfus, verworren.

muddler ['mʌdləʳ] n *(person)* Tölpel, Dussel *(inf)* *m*.

muddy ['mʌdɪ] **1** *adj* *(+er)* *floor, shoes, hands etc* schmutzig, schlammbeschmiert; *road, ground etc* schlammig, matschig; *liquid* schlammig, trübe. **to get** or **make sb/oneself/sth ~** jdn/sich/etw schmutzig machen or mit Schlamm beschmieren.

(b) *(fig)* *complexion* gräulich schimmernd; *style* verworren.

2 *vt* schmutzig machen, mit Schlamm beschmieren. **his explanation only helped to ~ the waters** durch seine Erklärung ist die Sache nur noch verworrener geworden.

mud: ~**flap** *n* Schmutzfänger *m*; ~**flat** *n* Watt(enmeer) *nt no pl*; ~**guard** *n* *(on cycles)* Schutzblech *nt*; *(on cars)* Kotflügel *m*; ~**hut** *n* Lehmhütte *f*; ~**pack** *n* Schlammpackung *f*; ~**pie** *n* Kuchen *m* *(aus Sand, Erde etc)*; ~**-slinger** *n* Dreckschleuder *f* *(inf)*; ~**-slinging 1** *n* Schlechtmacherei *f*; **all that ~-slinging before every election** diese gegenseitige Verunglimpfung vor jeder Wahl; **we've had enough ~-slinging** es ist genug im Schmutz or Dreck *(inf)* gewühlt worden; **I'm not descending to this level of ~-slinging** ich werde nicht so tief sinken, daß ich andere mit Schmutz bewerfe; **2** *adj* **a ~-slinging politician/newspaper** ein Politiker, der/eine Zeitung, die andere mit Schmutz bewirft; **the election turned into a ~-slinging match** die Wahlen arteten zur reinsten Schlammschlacht aus.

muezzin [mu:'ezɪn] n Muezzin *m*.

muff¹ [mʌf] n Muff *m*.

muff² *(inf)* **1** *n* **to make a ~ of sth** *see* vt.

2 *vt* vermasseln *(inf)*, verpatzen *(inf)*; *exam also* verhauen *(inf)*; *question* danebenhauen or sich verhauen bei *(inf)*; *kick, shot, ball* danebensetzen *(inf)*; *lines, text, passage* verpatzen *(inf)*. **to ~ a catch** danebengreifen *(inf)*, schlecht fangen; **he got a few notes er hat ein paarmal gepatzt** *(inf)*.

muffin ['mʌfɪn] n *(Brit)* weiches, flaches Milchbrötchen, meist warm gegessen; *(US)* kleiner pfannkuchenartiger Fladen.

muffle ['mʌfl] *vt* **a** *(wrap warmly: also ~ up)* person einmummen, einmummeln *(inf)*. **(b)** *(deaden)* sound, shot etc dämpfen; *noise* abschwächen, abdämpfen; *shouts* ersticken; *bells, oars, drum* umwickeln.

muffled ['mʌfld] *adj* *sound* gedämpft; *shouts* erstickt; *drum, bells, oars* umwickelt.

muffler ['mʌfləʳ] n **(a)** *(scarf)* (dicker) Schal. **(b)** *(Tech)* Schalldämpfer *m*; *(US Aut)* Auspuff(topf) *m*.

mufti ['mʌftɪ] n *(clothing)* Zivil(kleidung *f*) *nt*; *(Sch)* normale Kleidung. **in ~** in Zivil; ohne Schuluniform, normal gekleidet.

mug [mʌg] **1** *n* **(a)** *(cup)* Becher *m*; *(for beer)* Krug *m*.

(b) *(inf: dupe)* Trottel *m*. **have you found some ~ to do that?** hast du einen Dummen dafür gefunden?; **I was left looking a real ~** ich stand dann blöd da *(inf)*; **don't be such a ~** sei doch nicht so blöd *(inf)*; **to take sb for a ~** jdn für blöd halten; **that's a ~'s game** das ist doch schwachsinnig.

(c) *(sl: face)* Visage *f* *(sl)*. ~ **shot** Verbrecherfoto *nt* *(inf)*.

2 *vt* **(a)** *(attack and rob)* überfallen und zusammenschlagen, herfallen über *(+acc)* und berauben.

(b) *(US sl: photograph)* fotografieren.

♦**mug up** *vt sep* *(also: ~ ~ on)* *(inf)* **to ~ sth/one's French ~, to ~ ~ on sth/one's French** etw/Französisch pauken *(inf)*.

mugger ['mʌgəʳ] n Straßenräuber *m*.

mugging ['mʌgɪŋ] n Straßenraub *m no pl*. **a lot of ~s** viele Überfälle auf offener Straße.

muggins ['mʌgɪnz] n *sing* *(Brit inf)* Blödmann *m* *(inf)*. **while ~ does all the work** und ich bin mal wieder der/die Dumme und kann die ganze Arbeit allein machen *(inf)*; **and ~ here forgot ...** und ich Blödmann vergesse *(inf)* ...; **he's a bit of a ~** er ist etwas bescheuert *(inf)*.

muggy ['mʌgɪ] *adj* *(+er)* schwül; *heat* drückend.

mugwump ['mʌgwʌmp] n *(US pol)* Unabhängige(r) *mf*.

mulatto [mju:'lætəʊ] **1** *adj* Mulatten-; *complexion, features* eines Mulatten/einer Mulattin. **~ people** Mulatten *pl*. **2** *n, pl* **-es** Mulatte *m*, Mulattin *f*.

mulberry ['mʌlbərɪ] n *(fruit)* Maulbeere *f*; *(tree)* Maulbeerbaum *m*; *(colour)* Aubergine *nt*, dunkles Violett.

mulch [mʌltʃ] *(Hort)* **1** n Krümelschicht *f*, Mulch *m* *(spec)*. **2** *vt* mulchen *(spec)*, abdecken.

mulct [mʌlkt] *vt* **a** *(fine)* mit einer Geldstrafe belegen *(form)*. **(b)** *(defraud)* **to ~ sb of sth** jdm etw abschwindeln.

mule¹ [mju:l] n **(a)** *(of donkey and mare)* Maultier *nt*; *(of stallion and donkey)* Maulesel *m*. **~ skinner** *(US inf)* Maultiertreiber *m*. **(b)** *(inf: person)* Maulesel *m*. **(as) stubborn as a ~** (so) störrisch wie ein Maulesel. **(c)** *(Tech)* Selfaktor *m*.

mule² *n* *(slipper)* Schlappen *m* *(dial)*, Pantoffel *m*.

muleteer [,mju:lɪ'tɪəʳ] n Maultiertreiber *m*.

mulish ['mju:lɪʃ] *adj* stur, starrsinnig; *person also* störrisch. **~ obstinacy** Starrsinn *m*, Sturheit *f*.

mulishly ['mju:lɪʃlɪ] *adv* stur, starrsinnig. **he remained ~ obdurate on that point** er beharrte stur auf diesem Punkt.

mulishness ['mju:lɪʃnɪs] n Starrsinn *m*, Sturheit *f*.

mull [mʌl] *vt* mit Zucker und Gewürzen ansetzen und erhitzen.

to ~ wine Glühwein zubereiten; ~ed wine Glühwein m.

♦**mull over** vt sep sich (dat) durch den Kopf gehen lassen.

mullet ['mʌlɪt] n Meeräsche f.

mulligatawny [,mʌlɪgə'tɔːnɪ] n Currysuppe f.

mullion ['mʌlɪən] n Längs- or Zwischenpfosten m. ~s (in Gothic Archit) Stabwerk nt.

mullioned ['mʌlɪənd] adj window längs unterteilt.

multi ['mʌltɪ] n (inf: company) Multi m (inf).

multi- pref mehr-, Mehr-; (with Latin stem in German) Multi-, multi-.

multi: ~-cellular adj viel- or mehrzellig; ~channel adj (TV) mehrkanalig, Mehrkanal-; ~coloured adj mehrfarbig; material also, lights, decorations bunt; bird buntgefiedert; fish buntschillernd; ~coloured pen Mehrfarbenstift m.

multifarious [,mʌltɪ'fɛərɪəs] adj vielfältig, mannigfaltig. the ~ tribal languages die Vielfalt der Stammessprachen.

multi: ~form adj vielgestaltig; ~grade adj oil Mehrbereichs-; ~lateral adj (Pol) multilateral; (Math) shopping centre etc terrassenartig angelegt; ~lingual adj mehrsprachig; ~media adj multimedial; ~millionaire n Multimillionär(in f) m; ~national 1 n multinationaler Konzern; 2 adj multinational.

multiple ['mʌltɪpl] **1** adj (a) (with sing n: of several parts) mehrfach. ~ birth Mehrlingsgeburt f; ~ choice Multiple Choice f; ~ cropping mehrfache Bebauung; ~ personality (Psych) alternierende Persönlichkeit, Persönlichkeitsspaltung f; ~ star Sternhaufen m; ~-unit (train) Triebwagen m; ~ voting mehrfache Stimmberechtigung.
(b) (with pl n: many) mehrere.
2 n (a) (Math) Vielfache(s) nt. **eggs are usually sold in ~s of** six Eier werden gewöhnlich in Einheiten zu je sechs verkauft.
(b) (Brit: also ~ store) Ladenkette f.

multiple sclerosis n multiple Sklerose.

multiplicand [,mʌltɪplɪ'kænd] n Multiplikand m.

multiplication [,mʌltɪplɪ'keɪʃən] n (a) (Math) Multiplikation f; (act also) Multiplizieren, Malnehmen (inf) nt. ~ table Multiplikationstafel f; **he knows all his ~ tables** er kann das Einmaleins. (b) (fig) Vervielfachung, Vermehrung f.

multiplicity [,mʌltɪ'plɪsɪtɪ] n Vielzahl, Fülle f. **for a ~ of reasons** aus vielerlei Gründen.

multiplier ['mʌltɪplaɪəʳ] n (Math) Multiplikator m.

multiply ['mʌltɪplaɪ] **1** vt (a) (Math) multiplizieren, malnehmen (inf). **to ~ 8 by 7** 8 mit 7 multiplizieren or malnehmen (inf); **4 multiplied by 6 is 24** 4 mal 6 ist 24.
(b) (fig) vervielfachen, vermehren.
2 vi (Math) (a) (person) multiplizieren; (numbers) sich multiplizieren lassen.
(b) (fig) zunehmen, sich vermehren or vervielfachen.
(c) (breed) sich vermehren.

multi: ~-purpose adj Mehrzweck-; ~racial adj multirassisch, gemischtrassig; ~racial policy Politik der Rassenintegration; ~racial school Schule ohne Rassentrennung; ~stage adj Mehrstufen-; ~stor(e)y adj mehrstöckig; ~stor(e)y flats (Wohn)hochhäuser pl; ~stor(e)y car-park Park(hoch)haus nt; ~track adj mehrspurig; ~track recording Mehrspuraufzeichnung f.

multitude ['mʌltɪtjuːd] n Menge f. a ~ of eine Vielzahl von, eine Menge; (of people also) eine Schar (von); **for a ~ of reasons** aus vielerlei Gründen; **they came in ~s** sie kamen scharenweise.

multitudinous [,mʌltɪ'tjuːdɪnəs] adj zahlreich.

mum[1] [mʌm] n, adj (inf) ~'s the word! nichts verraten! (inf); **to keep ~** den Mund halten (about über +acc) (inf).

mum[2] n (Brit inf: mother) Mutter f; (as address) Mutti f (inf).

mumble ['mʌmbl] **1** n Gemurmel, Murmeln nt. **there was a ~ of discontent** ein Murren erhob sich; **he spoke in a ~** er nuschelte.
2 vt murmeln. **he ~d the words** er nuschelte.
3 vi vor sich hin murmeln; (speak indistinctly) nuscheln. **don't ~ (into your beard)** murm(e)le doch nicht so in deinen Bart.

mumbler ['mʌmbləʳ] n **he's a real ~** er nuschelt so.

mumblingly ['mʌmblɪŋlɪ] adv undeutlich.

mumbo jumbo ['mʌmbəʊ 'dʒʌmbəʊ] n (empty ritual, superstition) Mumpitz, Hokuspokus m; (gibberish) Kauderwelsch nt; (idol) Wodugott m.

mummer ['mʌməʳ] n (old) Mime m (old).

mummery ['mʌmərɪ] n (old) Pantomimenspiel nt; (fig) Mummenschanz m.

mummification [,mʌmɪfɪ'keɪʃən] n Einbalsamierung, Mumifizierung f.

mummify ['mʌmɪfaɪ] **1** vt einbalsamieren, mumifizieren. **2** vi mumifizieren.

mummy[1] ['mʌmɪ] n (corpse) Mumie f.

mummy[2] n (Brit inf: mother) Mami, Mama f (inf).

mumps [mʌmps] n sing Mumps m or f (inf) no art.

munch [mʌntʃ] vti mampfen (inf).

♦**munch away** vi vor sich hin mampfen (inf). **he was ~ing ~ on** or **at an apple** er mampfte einen Apfel or an einem Apfel.

mundane [,mʌn'deɪn] adj (worldly) weltlich, irdisch; (fig) schlicht und einfach; (pej: humdrum) profan, banal.

mundanely [,mʌn'deɪnlɪ] adv weltlich; (in a down-to-earth way) remark, describe nüchtern; dressed schlicht und einfach; (pej) banal. **from the exotic to the ~** trivial vom Außergewöhnlichen zum Banal-Trivialen.

mundaneness [,mʌn'deɪnnɪs] n see adj Weltlichkeit f; Schlichtheit f; Banalität f.

Munich ['mjuːnɪk] n München nt.

municipal [mjuː'nɪsɪpəl] adj städtisch; baths also Stadt-; administration, council, elections etc Stadt-, Gemeinde-.

municipality [mjuːnɪsɪ'pælɪtɪ] n (place) Ort m, Gemeinde f; (council) Stadt, Gemeinde f.

municipalization [,mjuːnɪsɪpəlaɪ'zeɪʃən] n Übernahme f

durch die Stadt or durch die Gemeinde.

municipalize [,mjuː'nɪsɪpəlaɪz] vt bus service, baths etc unter städtische Verwaltung or Gemeindeverwaltung bringen.

municipally [mjuː'nɪsɪpəlɪ] adv von der Stadt or Gemeinde. ~-owned im Besitz der Stadt or Gemeinde.

munificence [mjuː'nɪfɪsns] n (form) Großzügigkeit, Generosität (geh) f.

munificent [mjuː'nɪfɪsnt] adj (form) großzügig; person also generös (geh).

munificently [mjuː'nɪfɪsntlɪ] adv (form) großzügig, generös (geh). ~ donated by ... großzügigerweise gespendet von ...

muniments ['mjuːnɪmənts] npl (Jur form) Urkunde f.

munition [mjuː'nɪʃən] n usu pl Kriegsmaterial nt no pl, Waffen pl und Munition f. ~s dump (Waffen- und) Munitionslager or -depot nt.

mural ['mjʊərəl] 1 n Wandgemälde nt. 2 adj Wand-.

murder ['mɜːdəʳ] **1** n (a) Mord m. the ~ of John F. Kennedy der Mord an John F. Kennedy, die Ermordung John F. Kennedys; **to stand accused of ~** unter Mordverdacht stehen.
(b) (fig inf) **it was ~** es war mörderisch; **it'll be ~** das wäre (ja) glatter Selbstmord! (inf); **to cry ~, to shout blue ~** Zeter und Mordio schreien, ein Mordsspektakel or -theater machen (inf); **to get away with ~** sich (dat) alles erlauben können.
2 vt (a) ermorden, umbringen (inf); (slaughter) morden; (inf) opponents haushoch schlagen.
(b) (inf: ruin) music, play etc verhunzen (inf).

murderer ['mɜːdərəʳ] n Mörder m.

murderess ['mɜːdərɪs] n Mörderin f.

murderous ['mɜːdərəs] adj villain, soldiers etc mordgierig, blutrünstig; deed, intent, plot Mord-; (fig) mörderisch. ~ attack Mordanschlag m; a ~ type ein brutaler Typ; **there was a ~ look about him** er hatte etwas Brutales an sich; **he gave me a ~ look** er erdolchte mich mit Blicken; **once he had started on this ~ course** als er erst einmal den Weg der Gewalt eingeschlagen hatte.

murderously ['mɜːdərəslɪ] adv mordgierig, blutdürstig; (fig) mörderisch. **the knife glinted ~** das Messer blitzte tödlich; a ~ cunning trap eine teuflische Falle.

murk [mɜːk] n Düsternis f; (in water) trübes Wasser.

murkily ['mɜːkɪlɪ] adv trübe. **the wreck could be seen ~ through the muddy water** das Wrack zeichnete sich undeutlich im schlammigen Wasser ab.

murkiness ['mɜːkɪnɪs] n see adj Trübheit, Unklarheit, Unschärfe f; Finsterkeit f; Dunkel nt.

murky ['mɜːkɪ] adj (+er) trübe; fog dicht; photo, outline etc unscharf, unklar; (shady) character, deed finster; past dunkel. **it's really ~ outside** draußen ist es so düster.

murmur ['mɜːməʳ] **1** n (soft speech) Murmeln, Raunen (liter) nt; (of discontent) Murren nt; (of water, wind, leaves, traffic) Rauschen nt. **there was a ~ of approval/disagreement** ein beifälliges/abfälliges Murmeln erhob sich; **a soft ~ of voices** gedämpftes Stimmengemurmel; ..., **she said in a ~** ..., murmelte sie; **not a ~** kein Laut; **without a ~** ohne zu murren.
2 vt murmeln; (with discontent) murren.
3 vi murmeln; (with discontent) murren (about, against über +acc); (fig) rauschen.

murmuring ['mɜːmərɪŋ] n see vi Murmeln nt no pl; Murren nt no pl; Rauschen nt no pl. ~s (of discontent) Unmutsäußerungen (from gen); **do I hear ~?** asked the chairman irgendwelche Unstimmigkeiten?, fragte der Vorsitzende.

muscadel(le) [,mʌskə'del] n see muscatel.

muscat ['mʌskæt] n (grape) Muskatellertraube f.

muscatel [,mʌskə'tel] n (wine) Muskateller m.

muscle ['mʌsl] n Muskel m; (fig: power) Macht f. **he's all ~** er besteht nur aus Muskeln or ist sehr muskulös (gebaut); **you really need ~ for this job** für diese Arbeit braucht man wirklich Kraft or ganz schöne Muskeln (inf); **to have financial/industrial ~** finanzstark or -kräftig/wirtschaftlich einflußreich sein; **he never moved a ~** er rührte sich nicht.

♦**muscle in** vi (sl) mitmischen (sl) (on bei). **to ~ ~ on sb's territory** jdm dazwischenfunken (inf).

muscle: ~-bound adj (fig: muscular) muskulös; **to be ~-bound** eine überentwickelte Muskulatur haben; ~man n Muskelmann or -protz (pej) m.

Muscovite ['mʌskəvaɪt] **1** adj moskowitisch. **2** n Moskowiter(in f) m.

Muscovy ['mʌskəvɪ] n (Hist) Moskauer Staat m.

muscular ['mʌskjʊləʳ] adj Muskel-, muskulär (form); (having strong muscles) muskulös. ~ dystrophy Muskeldystrophie f.

musculature ['mʌskjʊlətʃəʳ] n Muskulatur f.

Muse [mjuːz] n (Myth) Muse f.

muse [mjuːz] **1** vi nachgrübeln, nachsinnen (liter) (about, on über +acc). **2** vt grüblerisch or sinnierend (liter) sagen.

museum [mjuː'zɪəm] n Museum nt. ~ piece (lit, hum) Museumsstück nt.

mush [mʌʃ] n (a) Brei m; (of fruit also) Mus nt. **the snow became a soft ~** der Schnee wurde matschig. (b) (inf) Schmalz m. **he always sings such ~** er singt immer solche Schnulzen.

mushroom ['mʌʃrʊm] **1** n (eßbarer) Pilz; (button ~) Champignon m; (atomic ~) Pilz m. **a great ~ of smoke** ein großer Rauchpilz; **to grow like ~s** wie die Pilze aus dem Boden schießen.
2 attr (a) (~-shaped) pilzförmig. ~ cloud Atompilz m.
(b) (made of ~) Pilz-; Champignon-.
(c) (rapid and ephemeral) growth sprunghaft; fame, success über Nacht erlangt, schlagartig. ~ town Stadt, die aus dem Boden geschossen ist.
3 vi pl **to go ~ing** in die Pilze gehen, Pilze sammeln (gehen).
(b) (grow rapidly) wie die Pilze aus dem Boden schießen. **his fame/success ~ed** er wurde schlagartig berühmt/erfolgreich; **to ~ into sth** sich rasch zu etw entwickeln.

(c) (*become* ~-*shaped*) **the smoke ~ed in the still air der** Rauch breitete sich pilzförmig in der Luft aus.

mushy ['mʌʃɪ] *adj* (+*er*) (a) matschig; *liquid, consistency* breiig. ~ **snow** Schneematsch *m*; ~ **peas** Erbsenmus *nt*. (b) (*inf: maudlin*) schmalzig.

music ['mjuːzɪk] *n* Musik *f*; (*of voice*) Musikalität *f*; (*written score*) Noten *pl*. **do you use** ~? spielen/singen Sie nach Noten?; **to set** *or* **put sth to** ~ etw vertonen; **of the spheres** Sphärenmusik *f*; **it was (like)** ~ **to my ears** das war Musik für mich *or* in meinen Ohren; **to face the** ~ (*fig*) dafür gradestehen.

musical ['mjuːzɪkəl] **1** *adj* (a) (*of music*) musikalisch; *instrument, evening* Musik-. ~ **box** Spieluhr *or* -dose *f*; ~ **chairs** sing Reise *f* nach Jerusalem; *see* saw[3].
(b) (*tuneful*) melodisch. **the** ~ **sweetness of her voice** der Wohllaut *or* Schmelz ihrer Stimme (*poet*).
(c) (*musically-minded*) musikalisch.
2 *n* Musical *nt*.

musicality [,mjuːzɪ'kælɪtɪ] *n* Musikalität *f*.

musically ['mjuːzɪkəlɪ] *adv* (a) musikalisch. (b) (*tunefully*) melodisch. **her laughter rang** ~ **in his ears** ihr Lachen klang wie Musik in seinen Ohren.

music *in cpds* Musik-; ~ **box** *n* (*esp US*) Spieldose *or* -uhr *f*; ~ **centre** *n* Kompaktanlage *f*, Musik-Center *nt*; ~ **drama** *n* Musikdrama *nt*; ~ **hall** *n* Varieté *nt*.

musician [mjuː'zɪʃən] *n* Musiker(in *f*) *m*.

musicianship [mjuː'zɪʃənʃɪp] *n* musikalisches Können.

musicological [,mjuːzɪkə'lɒdʒɪkəl] *adj* musikwissenschaftlich.

musicologist [,mjuːzɪ'kɒlədʒɪst] *n* Musikwissenschaftler(in *f*) *m*.

musicology [,mjuːzɪ'kɒlədʒɪ] *n* Musikwissenschaft *f*.

music: ~-**paper** *n* Notenpapier *nt*; ~ **stand** *n* Notenständer *m*; ~-**stool** *n* Klavierstuhl *or* -hocker *m*.

musing ['mjuːzɪŋ] **1** *adj* grüblerisch, nachdenklich, sinnierend (*liter*); *philosopher, book, article* gedankenvoll. **2** *n* Überlegungen *pl* (*on* zu).

musingly ['mjuːzɪŋlɪ] *adv see adj*.

musk [mʌsk] *n* (a) (*secretion, smell*) Moschus *m*. (b) (*Bot*) Moschuskraut *nt*.

musk deer *n* Moschustier *nt*, Moschushirsch *m*.

musket ['mʌskɪt] *n* Muskete *f*.

musketeer [,mʌskɪ'tɪər] *n* Musketier *m*.

musketry ['mʌskɪtrɪ] *n* (*muskets*) Musketen *pl*; (*troops*) Musketiere *pl*.

musk: ~-**melon** *n* Zucker- *or* Gartenmelone *f*; ~-**ox** *n* Moschusochse *m*; ~-**rat** *n* Bisamratte *f*; ~-**rose** *n* Moschusrose *f*.

musky ['mʌskɪ] *adj* (+*er*) moschusartig; *smell* Moschus-; *aftershave etc* nach Moschus riechend.

Muslim ['mʊzlɪm] *adj, n see* Moslem.

muslin ['mʌzlɪn] **1** *n* Musselin *m*. **2** *adj* Musselin-, aus Musselin.

musquash ['mʌskwɒʃ] *n* Bisamratte *f*.

muss [mʌs] (*US inf*) **1** *n* Durcheinander *nt*. **to be in a** ~ durcheinander (*inf*) *or* unordentlich sein. **2** *vt* (*also* ~ **up**) in Unordnung bringen; *hair, room also* durcheinanderbringen (*inf*). **to get** ~**ed (up)** in Unordnung geraten.

mussel ['mʌsl] *n* (*Mies*)muschel *f*. ~ **bed** Muschelbank *f*.

Mussulman ['mʌslmən] *n, pl* -**mans** (*old*) Muselman *m*.

mussy ['mʌsɪ] *adj* (+*er*) (*US inf*) unordentlich, durcheinander *pred* (*inf*).

must[1] [mʌst] **1** *vb aux present tense only* (a) müssen. **you** ~ (**go and**) **see this church** Sie müssen sich (*dat*) diese Kirche unbedingt ansehen; **do it if you** ~ tu, was du nicht lassen kannst; (~ **you/I?** *etc* (*really?*) ja (wirklich)?; (*do you/I have to?*) muß das sein?; **we** ~ **away** (*old*) wir müssen fort.
(b) (*in neg sentences*) dürfen. **I** ~**n't forget that** ich darf das nicht vergessen.
(c) (*be certain to*) **he** ~ **be there by now** er ist wohl inzwischen da; (*is bound to*) er ist inzwischen bestimmt da, er muß (wohl) inzwischen da sein; **he** (*surely*) ~ **be there by now** er *muß* doch inzwischen da sein; **I** ~ **have lost it** ich habe es wohl verloren, ich muß es wohl verloren haben; (*with stress on* ~) ich muß es verloren haben; **you** ~ **have heard of him** Sie haben bestimmt schon von ihm gehört; (*with stress on* ~) Sie müssen doch schon von ihm gehört haben; **there** ~ **have been five of them** es müssen fünf gewesen sein; (*about five*) es waren wohl etwa fünf; (*at least five*) es waren bestimmt fünf; **he** ~ **be older than that** er muß älter sein; **there** ~ **be a reason for it es** gibt bestimmt eine Erklärung dafür; (*with stress on* ~) es muß doch eine Erklärung dafür geben; **there** ~ **be a reason why he didn't come** er hat bestimmt einen Grund *or* (*with stress on* ~) er muß doch einen Grund haben, weshalb er nicht gekommen ist; **it** ~ **be about 3 o'clock** es wird wohl (so) etwa 3 Uhr sein, es muß so gegen 3 Uhr sein; **I** ~ **have been dreaming** da habe ich wohl geträumt; **I** ~ **have been mad** ich muß (wohl) wahnsinnig gewesen sein; **you** ~ **be crazy!** du bist ja *or* wohl wahnsinnig!
(d) (*showing annoyance*) müssen. **he** ~ **come just then/now** natürlich mußte/muß er gerade da/jetzt kommen.
2 *n* (*inf*) Muß *nt*. **a sense of humour/an umbrella is a** ~ **man** braucht unbedingt Humor/einen Schirm, Humor/ein Schirm ist unerläßlich; **tighter security is a** ~ bessere Sicherheitskontrollen sind unerläßlich; **this novel/programme is a** ~ **for** everyone diesen Roman/dieses Programm muß man einfach *or* unbedingt gelesen/gesehen haben; **this is a** ~ **for lovers of** architecture wer sich für Architektur interessiert, sollte sich das unbedingt ansehen.

must[2] *n* (*mustiness*) Muffigkeit *f*.

mustache *n* (*US*) *see* moustache.

mustachio [mʌ'stæʃɪəʊ] *n, pl* -**s** Schnauzbart *m*.

mustachioed [mʌ'stæʃɪəʊd] *adj* schnauzbärtig.

mustang ['mʌstæŋ] *n* Mustang *m*.

mustard ['mʌstəd] **1** *n* Senf *m*; (*colour*) Senfgelb *nt*. **to be**

---

as keen as ~ Feuer und Flamme sein. **2** *attr flavour, smell* Senf-; (*yellow*) senffarben.

mustard *in cpds* Senf-; ~ **plaster** *n* Senfpackung *f*; ~ **yellow** **1** *n* Senfgelb *nt*; **2** *adj* senfgelb.

muster ['mʌstər] **1** *n* (*esp Mil: assembly*) Appell *m*; (*cattle* ~) Zusammentreiben *nt* der Herde. **to pass** ~ (*fig*) den Anforderungen genügen.
2 *vt* (a) (*summon*) versammeln, zusammenrufen; (*esp Mil*) antreten lassen; *cattle* zusammentreiben. **the men were** ~**ed at 14.00** die Leute mußten um 14⁰⁰ zum Appell antreten.
(b) (*manage to raise: also* ~ **up**) zusammenbekommen, aufbringen; (*fig*) *powers of deduction, intelligence, strength etc* aufbieten; *strength, courage* aufbringen; **all one's strength, courage** zusammennehmen.
3 *vi* sich versammeln; (*esp Mil*) (zum Appell) antreten.

♦ **muster in** *vt sep* (*US*) *troops, recruits* einziehen.

♦ **muster out** *vt sep* (*US*) *troops* entlassen.

mustiness ['mʌstɪnɪs] *n* Muffigkeit *f*.

mustn't ['mʌsnt] *contr of* must not.

musty ['mʌstɪ] *adj* (+*er*) *air* muffig; *books* moderig.

mutability [,mjuːtə'bɪlɪtɪ] *n* Wandlungsfähigkeit, Mutabilität (*spec*) *f*.

mutable ['mjuːtəbl] *adj* variabel, veränderlich; (*Biol*) mutabel.

mutant ['mjuːtənt] **1** *n* Mutante (*spec*), Mutation *f*. **2** *adj* Mutations-.

mutate [mjuː'teɪt] **1** *vi* sich verändern; (*Biol*) mutieren (*to* zu); (*Ling*) sich verwandeln (*to in* +*acc*). **2** *vt* wandeln; (*Biol*) zu einer Mutation führen bei.

mutation [mjuː'teɪʃən] *n* (*process*) Veränderung *f*; (*result*) Variante *f*; (*Biol*) Mutation *f*; (*Ling*) Wandel *m* (*to* zu).

mute [mjuːt] **1** *adj* stumm (*also Ling*); *amazement, rage* sprachlos. **he was** ~ **with rage** er brachte vor Wut kein Wort heraus. **2** *n* (a) (*dumb person*) Stumme(r) *mf*. (b) (*hired mourner*) Totenkläger *m*; (*woman*) Klageweib *nt*. (c) (*Mus*) Dämpfer *m*. **3** *vt* dämpfen.

muted ['mjuːtɪd] *adj* gedämpft; (*fig*) *criticism etc* leise, leicht.

mutilate ['mjuːtɪleɪt] *vt person, animal, story, play* verstümmeln; *painting, building etc* verschandeln (*inf*).

mutilation [,mjuːtɪ'leɪʃən] *n see vt* Verstümmelung *f*; Verschandelung *f* (*inf*).

mutineer [,mjuːtɪ'nɪər] *n* Meuterer *m*.

mutinous ['mjuːtɪnəs] *adj* (*Naut*) meuterisch, aufrührerisch; (*fig*) rebellisch.

mutiny ['mjuːtɪnɪ] (*Naut, fig*) **1** *n* Meuterei *f*. **2** *vi* meutern.

mutism ['mjuːtɪzəm] *n* (*Psych*) Mutismus *m*.

mutt [mʌt] *n* (*pej sl*) (*dog*) Köter *m*; (*idiot*) Dussel *m* (*inf*).

mutter ['mʌtər] **1** *n* Murmeln, Gemurmel *nt*; (*of discontent*) Murren *nt*. **a** ~ **of voices** ein Stimmengemurmel; **a** ~ **of discontent** ein unzufriedenes Murren; **one more** ~ **out of you, and ...** noch einen Mucks, und ... (*inf*).
2 *vt* murmeln, brummeln. **they** ~**ed their discontent** sie murrten unzufrieden; **are you** ~**ing insults/threats at me?** höre ich Sie Beleidigungen/Drohungen (gegen mich) brummeln?
3 *vi* murmeln; (*with discontent*) murren.

muttering ['mʌtərɪŋ] *n* (*act*) Gemurmel *nt*; (*with discontent*) Murren *nt*; (*remark*) Gemurmel *nt no pl*; Meckerei *f* (*inf*).

mutton ['mʌtn] *n* Hammel(fleisch *nt*) *m*. **as dead as** ~ mausetot (*inf*); **she's** ~ **dressed as lamb** (*inf*) sie macht auf jung (*inf*).

mutton: ~-**chops** *npl* (*whiskers*) Koteletten *pl*; ~-**head** *n* (*fig inf*) Schafskopf *m* (*inf*).

mutual ['mjuːtjʊəl] *adj* (*reciprocal*) *trust, respect, affection etc* gegenseitig; (*bilateral*) *troop withdrawals, efforts, détente, satisfaction* beiderseitig; (*shared, in common*) *friends, dislikes etc* gemeinsam. **it would be for our** ~ **benefit** es wäre für uns beide von Vorteil *or* zu unser beider Nutzen (*form*); **the feeling is** ~ das beruht (ganz) auf Gegenseitigkeit; **I hate you!** — **the feeling is** ~ ich hasse dich! — ganz meinerseits (*inf*); ~ **insurance** Versicherung *f* auf Gegenseitigkeit.

mutuality [,mjuːtjʊ'ælɪtɪ] *n* Gegenseitigkeit *f*. **the** ~ **of their affection** ihre gegenseitige Zuneigung.

mutually ['mjuːtjʊəlɪ] *adv* beide; (*reciprocally*) distrust gegenseitig; *satisfactory, beneficial* für beide Seiten; *agreed, rejected* von beiden Seiten. **a gentleman** ~ **known to us** ein Herr, den wir beide kennen.

muzak ® ['mjuːzæk] *n* Berieselungsmusik *f* (*inf*).

muzziness ['mʌzɪnɪs] *n see adj* Benommenheit *f*; Verschwommenheit *f*; Verzerrtheit *f*.

muzzle ['mʌzl] **1** *n* (a) (*snout, mouth*) Maul *nt*. (b) (*for dog etc*) Maulkorb *m*. (c) (*of gun*) Mündung *f*; (*barrel*) Lauf *m*. **2** *vt* *animal* einen Maulkorb um- *or* anlegen (+*dat*); (*fig*) *critics, the press* mundtot machen; *criticism, protest* ersticken.

muzzle: ~-**loader** *n* Vorderlader *m*; ~-**loading** *adj* *gun* mit Vorderladung; ~ **velocity** *n* Mündungs- *or* Auffangsgeschwindigkeit *f*.

muzzy ['mʌzɪ] *adj* (+*er*) (*dizzy, dazed*) benommen, benebelt; (*blurred*) *view, memory etc* verschwommen; *noise* verzerrt.

MW *abbr of* medium wave MW.

my [maɪ] **1** *poss adj* mein. **I've hurt** ~ **leg/arm** *etc* ich habe mir das Bein/den Arm *etc* verletzt; ~ **father and mother** mein Vater und meine Mutter; **in** ~ **country** bei uns, in meinem Land (*form*); **I've got a car/problems of** ~ **own** ich habe mein eigenes Auto/meine eigenen Probleme, ich habe selbst ein Auto/Probleme.
2 *interj* (*surprise*) (du) meine Güte, du liebe Zeit; (*delight*) ach, oh. ~, ~, **hasn't she grown!** nein so was, die ist vielleicht groß geworden.

myna(h) bird ['maɪnə,bɜːd] *n* Hirtenstar *m*.

myopia [maɪ'əʊpɪə] *n* Kurzsichtigkeit, Myopie (*spec*) *f*.

myopic [maɪ'ɒpɪk] *adj* kurzsichtig.

myriad ['mɪrɪəd] **1** *n* Myriade *f*. **a** ~ **of** Myriaden von. **2** *adj* (*innumerable*) unzählige.

myrrh [mɜːʳ] n Myrrhe f.

myrtle [ˈmɜːtl] n Myrte f. ~ **green** moosgrün.

myself [maɪˈself] pers pron (a) (dir obj, with prep +acc) mich; (indir obj, with prep +dat) mir. **I said to** ~ ich sagte mir; **singing to** ~ vor mich hin singend; **I wanted to see (it) for** ~ ich wollte es selbst or selber sehen; **I tried it out on** ~ ich habe es an mir selbst or selber ausprobiert; **I addressed the letter to** ~ ich habe den Brief an mich selbst adressiert.
  (b) (emph) (ich) selbst. **my wife and** ~ meine Frau und ich; **I did it** ~ ich habe es selbst gemacht; **I thought/said so** ~ das habe ich auch gedacht/gesagt; ... **if I say so or it** ~ ... auch wenn ich es selbst sage; **(all) by** ~ (ganz) allein(e); **I'll go there** ~ ich gehe selbst hin; **I** ~ **believe** or ~, **I believe that** ... ich persönlich or ich selbst bin der Ansicht, ...; ~, **I doubt it** ich persönlich or ich für meinen Teil bezweifle das.
  (c) (one's normal self) **I'm not (feeling)** ~ **today** mit mir ist heute etwas in Ordnung or irgend etwas los; (healthwise also) ich bin heute nicht ganz auf der Höhe; **I didn't look** ~ **in that dress** das Kleid paßte überhaupt nicht zu mir; **I tried to be just** ~ ich versuchte, mich ganz natürlich zu geben.

mysterious [mɪˈstɪərɪəs] adj (puzzling) rätselhaft, mysteriös; (secretive) geheimnisvoll; atmosphere, stranger geheimnisvoll. **she is being quite** ~ **about it/him** sie macht ein großes Geheimnis daraus/um ihn; **why are you being so** ~? warum tust du so geheimnisvoll?

mysteriously [mɪˈstɪərɪəslɪ] adv vague, unwilling, pleased sonderbar; (puzzlingly) vanish, change auf rätselhafte or geheimnisvolle or mysteriöse Weise; disappointed, missing unerklärlicherweise; (secretively) geheimnisvoll.

mystery [ˈmɪstərɪ] n (puzzle) Rätsel nt; (secret) Geheimnis nt. **to be shrouded** or **veiled** or **surrounded in** ~ von einem Geheimnis umwittert or umgeben sein; **there's no** ~ **about it** da ist überhaupt nichts Geheimnisvolles dabei; **it's a** ~ **to me**

das ist mir schleierhaft or ein Rätsel; **don't make a great** ~ **out of it!** mach doch kein so großes Geheimnis daraus!; **why all the** ~? was soll denn die Geheimnistuerei?

mystery: ~ **play** n Mysterienspiel nt; ~ **story** n Kriminalgeschichte f, Krimi m (inf); ~ **writer** n Kriminalschriftsteller(in f) m.

mystic [ˈmɪstɪk] **1** adj mystisch; writing, words, beauty also geheimnisvoll. **2** n Mystiker(in f) m.

mystical [ˈmɪstɪkəl] adj mystisch.

mysticism [ˈmɪstɪsɪzəm] n Mystizismus m; (of poetry etc) Mystik f, Mystische(s) nt.

mystification [ˌmɪstɪfɪˈkeɪʃən] n (bafflement) Verwunderung, Verblüffung f; (act of bewildering) Verwirrung f. **that added to the students'** ~ das gab den Studenten noch größere Rätsel auf; **he put an end to my** ~ **by explaining** ... das Rätsel löste sich für mich, als er mir erklärte ...

mystify [ˈmɪstɪfaɪ] vt vor ein Rätsel stellen. **his explanation mystified us** all seine Erklärung blieb uns allen ein Rätsel; **I was completely mystified by the whole business** die ganze Sache war mir ein völliges Rätsel or völlig schleierhaft (inf); **the conjurer's tricks mystified the audience** die Kunststücke des Zauberers verblüfften das Publikum; ~**ing** unerklärlich, rätselhaft.

mystique [mɪˈstiːk] n geheimnisvoller Nimbus. **modern women have little** ~, **there is little** ~ **about modern women** die moderne Frau hat wenig Geheimnisvolles an sich.

myth [mɪθ] n Mythos m; (fig) Märchen nt. **it's a** ~ (fig) das ist doch ein Gerücht or Märchen.

mythical [ˈmɪθɪkəl] adj mythisch, sagenhaft; (fig) erfunden. ~ **figure/character** Sagengestalt f; ~ **story** Mythos m, Sage f.

mythological [ˌmɪθəˈlɒdʒɪkəl] adj mythologisch.

mythology [mɪˈθɒlədʒɪ] n Mythologie f.

myxomatosis [ˌmɪksəʊməˈtəʊsɪs] n Myxomatose f.

N

N, n [en] n N, n nt.

N abbr of north N.

n (a) (Math) n. (b) **'n** (inf) = **and.** (c) (inf: many) x (inf). ~ **times** x-mal (inf).

n abbr of (a) **noun** Subst. (b) **neuter** nt.

NAACP (US) abbr of **National Association for the Advancement of Colored People.**

Naafi [ˈnæfɪ] abbr of **Navy, Army and Air Force Institutes** (shop) Laden m der Britischen Armee; (canteen) Kantine f der Britischen Armee.

nab [næb] vt (inf) (a) (catch) erwischen; (police also) schnappen (inf). **the police** ~**bed him when he** ... die Polizei hat ihn dabei erwischt, wie er ...; **you'd better** ~ **her before she leaves** versuch' sie zu erwischen, bevor sie geht.
  (b) (take for oneself) sich (dat) grapschen (inf). **somebody had** ~**bed my seat** mir hatte jemand den Platz geklaut (inf).

nabob [ˈneɪbɒb] n Nabob m; (fig also) Krösus m.

nacelle [næˈsel] n (a) (on aeroplane) (Flugzeug)rumpf m. (b) (gondola) (on airship) (Luftschiff)gondel f; (on balloon) (Ballon)korb m.

nacre [ˈneɪkəʳ] n Perlmutter f or nt, Perlmutt nt.

nacreous [ˈneɪkrɪəs] adj perlmutterartig, Perlmutt(er)-.

nadir [ˈneɪdɪəʳ] n (a) (Astron) Nadir, Fußpunkt m. (b) (fig) Tiefstpunkt m. **the** ~ **of despair** tiefste Verzweiflung.

nag[1] [næg] **1** vt (find fault with) herumnörgeln an (+dat); (pester) keine Ruhe lassen (+dat) (for wegen). **she's forever** ~**ging me** sie nörgelt immerzu an mir herum, sie hat dauernd etwas an mir auszusetzen; **don't** ~ **me** nun laß mich doch in Ruhe!; **to** ~ **sb to do sth** jdm schwer zusetzen or die Hölle heiß machen, damit er etwas tut; **she kept on** ~**ging him until he did it** sie hat ihm solange zugesetzt or keine Ruhe gelassen, bis er es machte; **these things that's been** ~**ging me for some time is** ... was mich schon seit einiger Zeit plagt or nicht in Ruhe läßt, ist ...
  2 vi (find fault) herumnörgeln, meckern (inf); (be insistent) keine Ruhe geben. **to** ~ **at sb** jdm herumnörgeln, jdm keine Ruhe lassen; **stop** ~**ging** hör auf zu meckern (inf).
  3 n (fault-finder) Nörgler(in f) m; (woman also) Meckerliese, Meckerziege f (inf); (man also) Meckerfritze m (inf); (pestering) Quälgeist m. **don't be a** ~ nun meckre nicht immer (inf).

nag[2] n (old horse) Klepper m, Mähre f; (inf: horse) Gaul m.

nagger [ˈnægəʳ] n see **nag**[1] 3.

nagging [ˈnægɪŋ] **1** adj (a) wife meckernd (inf), nörglerisch; (pestering) ewig drängend. (b) pain dumpf; worry, doubt quälend. **2** n (fault-finding) Meckern nt (inf), Nörgelei f; (pestering) ewiges Drängen.

naiad [ˈnaɪæd] n Najade, Wassernymphe f.

nail [neɪl] **1** n (a) (Anat) Nagel m.
  (b) (Tech) Nagel m. **as hard as** ~**s** knallhart (inf), (unheim-

lich) hart; (physically) zäh wie Leder; **on the** ~ (fig inf) auf der Stelle, sofort; **to hit the** ~ ~ **(right) on the head** (fig) den Nagel auf den Kopf treffen; **to drive a** ~ **into sb's coffin**, **to be a** ~ **in sb's coffin** (fig) ein Nagel zu jds Sarg sein.
  2 vt (a) (fix with ~s, put ~s into) nageln. **to** ~ **sth to the floor/door/wall** etw an den Boden/an die Tür/Wand nageln, etw auf den Boden/an der Tür/Wand nageln; ~ **this on here** nageln Sie das hier an or fest; **he** ~**ed his opponent to the canvas** er pinnte seinen Gegner auf die Matte (inf).
  (b) (fig) person festnageln. panic ~**ed him to his chair** Furcht fesselte ihn an den Stuhl; **to be** ~**ed to the spot** or **ground** wie auf der Stelle festgenagelt sein; **fear** ~**ed him to the spot** er war vor Furcht wie auf der Stelle festgenagelt; **they** ~**ed the contract** sie haben den Vertrag unter Dach und Fach gebracht.
  (c) (inf) **to** ~ **sb** sich (dat) jdn schnappen (inf); (charge sb) jdn drankriegen (inf).

♦**nail down** vt sep (a) (lit) box zunageln; carpet, lid festnageln. (b) (fig) person festnageln (to auf +acc). **I** ~**ed him** ~ **to coming at 6 o'clock** ich nagelte ihn auf 6 Uhr fest.

♦**nail up** vt sep picture etc annageln; door, window vernageln; box zunageln; goods in Kisten verpacken und vernageln.

nail in cpds Nagel-; ~-**biting 1** n Nägelkauen nt; **2** adj (inf) terror atemberaubend; suspense also atemlos; match spannungsgeladen; ~-**brush** n Nagelbürste f; ~-**clippers** npl Nagelzwicker m; ~-**file** n Nagelfeile f; ~ **polish** n Nagellack m; ~ **polish remover** n Nagellackentferner m; ~ **scissors** npl Nagelschere f; ~ **varnish** n (Brit) Nagellack m.

naïve [naɪˈiːv] adj (+er) naiv; person, remark also einfältig.

naïvely [naɪˈiːvlɪ] adv naiv. **he** ~ **believed me** er war so naiv, mir zu glauben, in seiner Einfalt glaubte er mir.

naïveté [naɪˈiːvteɪ], **naïvety** [naɪˈiːvɪtɪ] n Naivität f; (of person also) Einfalt f.

naked [ˈneɪkɪd] adj (a) person nackt, unbekleidet, bloß (liter). **to go** ~ nackt or nackend gehen; **I feel** ~ **without my wristwatch/make-up** ich fühle mich ohne meine Armbanduhr unangezogen/ohne Make-up nackt und bloß; (as) ~ **as nature intended** (hum) im Adams-/Evaskostüm (hum); (as) ~ **as the day (that) he was born** splitterfasernackt (hum).
  (b) branch nackt, kahl; countryside nackt; sword bloß, blank, nackt; flame, light ungeschützt; truth, facts nackt. **the** ~ **eye** das bloße or unbewaffnete Auge; **a room with one** ~ **light** ein Zimmer, in dem nur eine Glühbirne hing.

nakedness [ˈneɪkɪdnɪs] n Nacktheit, Blöße f (liter).

NALGO [ˈnælgəʊ] (Brit) abbr of **National Association of Local Government Officers.**

namby-pamby [ˈnæmbɪˈpæmbɪ] (inf) **1** n Mutterkind nt; (boy also) Muttersöhnchen nt. **2** adj person verweichlicht, verzärtelt (inf); (indecisive) unentschlossen.

name [neɪm] **1** n (a) Name m. what's your ~? wie heißen Sie?, wie ist Ihr Name? (form); my ~ is ... ich heiße ..., mein Name ist ... (form); this man, Smith by ~ dieser Mann namens Smith; a man by the ~ of Gunn ein Mann namens or mit Namen Gunn; I know him only by ~ ich kenne ihn nur dem Namen nach; he knows all his customers by ~ er kennt alle seine Kunden bei Namen; to refer to sb/sth by ~ jdn/etw namentlich or mit Namen nennen; in ~ alone or only nur dem Namen nach; a marriage in ~ only or in ~ alone eine nur auf dem Papier bestehende Ehe; I won't mention any ~s ich möchte keine Namen nennen; he writes under the ~ of X er schreibt unter dem Namen X; fill in your ~(s) and address(es) Namen und Adresse eintragen; they married to give the child a ~ sie haben geheiratet, damit das Kind einen Namen hatte; what ~ shall I say? wie ist Ihr Name, bitte?; (on telephone) wer ist am Apparat?; (before showing sb in) wen darf ich melden?; to have one's ~ taken (Ftbl, Police etc) aufgeschrieben werden; in the ~ of im Namen (+gen); stop in the ~ of the law halt, im Namen des Gesetzes; in the ~ of peace/justice im Namen des Friedens/der Gerechtigkeit; in the ~ of goodness/God um Himmels/Gottes willen; all the big ~s were there da waren die großen Namen da; I'll put my/your ~ down (on list, in register etc) ich trage mich/dich ein; (for school, class, excursion, competition etc) ich melde mich/dich an (for zu, for a school in einer Schule); (for tickets, goods etc) ich lasse mich/dich vormerken; (on waiting list) ich lasse mich or meinen Namen/dich or deinen Namen auf die Warteliste setzen; to put one's ~ down for a vacancy sich um or für eine Stelle bewerben; I'll put your ~ down, Sir/Madam ich werde Sie vormerken, mein Herr/meine Dame; to call sb ~s jdn beschimpfen; you can call me all the ~s you like ... du kannst mich nennen, was du willst ...; not to have a penny/cent to one's ~ völlig pleite sein (inf), keinen roten Heller haben (dated); what's in a ~? was ist or bedeutet schon ein Name?; Name ist Schall und Rauch (Prov); in all but ~ praktisch; that's the ~ of the game (inf) darum geht es; for these people survival is the ~ of the game diesen Leuten geht es ums Überleben; I'll do it or my ~'s not Bob Brown ich mache das, so wahr ich Bob Brown heiße; ~s cannot hurt me man kann mich nennen, was man will.

(b) (reputation) Name, Ruf m. to have a good/bad ~ einen guten/schlechten Ruf or Namen haben; to get a bad ~ in Verruf kommen; to give sb a bad ~ jdn in Verruf bringen; to protect one's good ~ seinen Ruf or guten Namen wahren; to make one's ~ as, to make a ~ for oneself sich (dat) einen Namen machen als; to make one's ~ berühmt werden; this book made his ~ mit diesem Buch machte er sich einen Namen; to have a ~ for sth für etw bekannt sein.

2 vt (a) (call by a ~, give a ~ to) person nennen; plant, new star etc benennen, einen Namen geben (+dat); ship taufen, einen Namen geben (+dat). I ~ this child/ship X ich taufe dieses Kind/Schiff auf den Namen X; a person ~d Smith jemand namens or mit Namen Smith; the child is ~d Peter das Kind hat den or hört auf den Namen Peter; to ~ a child after or (US) for sb ein Kind nach jdm nennen; to ~ sb as a witness jdn als Zeugen nennen; he was ~d as the thief/culprit/victim er wurde als der Dieb/der Schuldige/das Opfer genannt or bezeichnet; to ~ names Namen nennen.

(b) (appoint, nominate) ernennen. to ~ sb mayor/as leader jdn zum Bürgermeister/Führer ernennen; to ~ sb for the post of mayor jdn für das Amt des Bürgermeisters vorschlagen; he has been ~d as Nobel Prize winner ihm wurde der Nobelpreis verliehen; they ~d her as the winner of the award sie haben ihr den Preis verliehen; they ~d him (as) footballer of the year sie haben ihn zum Fußballer des Jahres gewählt or ernannt; to ~ sb as an heir jdn zu seinem Erben bestimmen.

(c) (describe, designate) to ~ sb (as) sth jdn als etw bezeichnen.

(d) (specify, list) nennen. ~ the main plays by Shakespeare nenne mir die Hauptwerke Shakespeares; ~ your price nennen Sie Ihren Preis; to ~ the day (inf) den Hochzeitstag festsetzen; ~ the date and I'll be there bestimmen Sie den Tag, und ich werde da sein; you ~ it, they have it/he's done it es gibt nichts, was sie nicht haben/was er noch nicht gemacht hat.

-named [-neɪmd] adj suf genannt. the first-/last-~ der erst-/letztgenannte, der zuerst/zuletzt genannte.

name: ~-day n Namenstag m; ~-drop vi (inf) berühmte Bekannte in die Unterhaltung einfließen lassen; she's always ~-dropping sie muß dauernd erwähnen, wen sie alles kennt; ~-dropper n (inf) he's a terrible ~-dropper er muß dauernd erwähnen, wen er alles kennt; ~-dropping n (inf) Angeberei f mit berühmten Bekannten; his constant ~-dropping is most tedious es ist nicht auszuhalten, wie er ständig mit berühmten Namen um sich wirft; ~less adj (a) (unknown) person unbekannt; author also namenlos; (b) (undesignated) namenlos; a person who shall be/remain ~less jemand, der nicht genannt werden soll/der ungenannt bleiben soll; (c) (undefined) sensation, emotion unbeschreiblich; longing, terror, suffering also namenlos; (d) (shocking) vice, crime unaussprechlich.

namely ['neɪmlɪ] adv nämlich.

name: ~-part n Titelrolle f; ~-plate n Namensschild nt; (on door also) Türschild nt; (on business premises) Firmenschild nt; ~sake n (man) Namensvetter m; (woman) Namensschwester f; ~-tape n Wäschezeichen nt.

Namibia [næ'mɪbɪə] n Namibia nt.

nana [nɑːnə] n (inf) Trottel m (inf).

nancy-boy ['nænsɪˌbɔɪ] n (dated Brit inf) Schwule(r) m.

nankeen [næn'kiːn] n, no pl (cloth) Nanking(stoff m) m or nt.

nanny ['nænɪ] n (a) Kindermädchen nt. (b) (inf: also nanna) Oma, Omi f (inf). (c) (also ~-goat) Geiß f, Ziege f.

nap¹ [næp] **1** n Schläfchen, Nickerchen nt. afternoon ~ Nachmittagsschläfchen nt; to have or take a ~ ein Schläfchen or ein Nickerchen machen; he always has or takes a 20/15 minute ~ after lunch nach dem Mittagessen legt er sich immer 20 Minuten/eine Viertelstunde aufs Ohr or hin.
2 vi to catch sb ~ping (fig) jdn überrumpeln.

nap² n (Tex) Flor m; (Sew) Strich m.

nap³ (Racing) **1** vt winner, horse setzen auf (+acc). **2** n Tip m. to select a ~ auf ein bestimmtes Pferd setzen.

napalm ['neɪpɑːm] **1** n Napalm nt. **2** vt mit Napalm bewerfen.

napalm: ~ bomb n Napalmbombe f; ~ bombing n Abwurf m von Napalmbomben.

nape [neɪp] n (usu. ~ of the/one's neck) Nacken m, Genick nt.

naphtha ['næfθə] n Naphtha nt or f.

naphthalene ['næfθəliːn] n Naphthalin nt.

napkin ['næpkɪn] n (a) (table ~) Serviette f, Mundtuch nt (old). ~ ring Serviettenring m. (b) (for baby) Windel f; (US: sanitary ~) (Damen)binde f.

Naples ['neɪplz] n Neapel nt.

Napoleon [nə'pəʊlɪən] n Napoleon m.

Napoleonic [nə͵pəʊlɪ'ɒnɪk] adj Napoleonisch.

nappy ['næpɪ] n (Brit) Windel f.

narcissi [nɑː'sɪsaɪ] pl of **narcissus** (a).

narcissism [nɑː'sɪsɪzəm] n Narzißmus m.

narcissistic [͵nɑːsɪ'sɪstɪk] adj narzißtisch.

narcissus [nɑː'sɪsəs] n (a) pl narcissi (Bot) Narzisse f. (b) (Myth) N~ Narziß m.

narcosis [nɑː'kəʊsɪs] n Narkose f.

narcotic [nɑː'kɒtɪk] **1** adj (a) ~ substance/drug Rauschgift nt; in a ~ stupor vom Rauschgift benommen. (b) (Med) narkotisch. **2** n (a) Rauschgift nt. the ~s squad das Rauschgiftdezernat. (b) (Med) Narkotikum nt.

nark [nɑːk] (Brit) **1** vt (inf) ärgern. to get/feel ~ed wütend werden/sich ärgern. **2** n (sl) Spitzel m.

narky ['nɑːkɪ] adj (+er) (Brit inf) gereizt.

narrate [nə'reɪt] vt erzählen; events, journey etc schildern.

narration [nə'reɪʃən] n Erzählung f; (of events, journey) Schilderung f.

narrative ['nærətɪv] **1** n (a) (story) Erzählung f; (account) Schilderung f; (text) Text m. writer of ~ erzählender Autor. (b) (act of narrating) Erzählen nt; (of events, journey) Schilderung f. **2** adj erzählend; ability etc erzählerisch. ~ poem Ballade f; (modern) Erzählgedicht nt.

narrator [nə'reɪtə'] n Erzähler(in f) m. a first-/third-person ~ ein Ich-/Er-Erzähler m.

narrow ['nærəʊ] **1** adj (+er) (a) eng; road, path, passage, valley also, shoulders, hips schmal. to become ~ eng werden; (road etc) sich verengen.
(b) (fig) person, attitudes, ideas engstirnig, beschränkt; views also, sense, meaning, interpretation eng; existence beschränkt; majority, victory knapp; scrutiny peinlich genau. to have a ~ mind engstirnig sein; to have a ~ escape mit knapper Not davonkommen, gerade noch einmal davonkommen; that was a ~ escape/squeak (inf) das war knapp, das wäre beinahe ins Auge gegangen (inf).
(c) (Ling) vowel geschlossen.
2 n ~s pl enge Stelle.
3 vt road etc enger machen, verengen. to ~ the field (fig) die Auswahl reduzieren (to auf +acc); with ~ed eyes mit zusammengekniffenen Augen.
4 vi enger werden, sich verengen. the field ~ed to two candidates die Auswahl war auf zwei Kandidaten zusammengeschrumpft.

♦ **narrow down** (to auf +acc) **1** vi sich beschränken; (be concentrated) sich konzentrieren. the question ~s ~ to this die Frage läuft darauf hinaus.
2 vt sep (limit) beschränken, einschränken; possibilities etc beschränken; (concentrate) konzentrieren. that ~s it ~ a bit dadurch wird die Auswahl kleiner.

narrow: ~ boat n Kahn m; ~-gauge adj schmalspurig, Schmalspur-.

narrowly ['nærəʊlɪ] adv (a) (by a small margin) escape mit knapper Not. he ~ escaped being knocked down er wäre um ein Haar or beinahe überfahren worden; you ~ missed (seeing) him du hast ihn gerade verpaßt.
(b) interpret eng; examine peinlich genau. she looks at things/life much too ~ sie sieht die Dinge/das Leben viel zu eng.

narrow: ~-minded adj, ~-mindedly adv engstirnig; ~-mindedness n Engstirnigkeit f; ~-shouldered adj schmalschult(e)rig.

narwhal ['nɑːwəl] n Narwal m.

nary ['neərɪ] adj (old) with ~ a word ohne ein Wort zu sagen; she gave ~ a thought to her family sie verschwendete keinen Gedanken an ihre Familie.

NASA ['næsə] abbr of National Aeronautics and Space Administration NASA f.

nasal ['neɪzəl] **1** adj (a) (Anat) Nasen-. ~ cavities Nasenhöhle f. (b) sound nasal, Nasal-; accent, voice, intonation näselnd. her voice is ~ sie hat eine näselnde Stimme; to speak in a ~ voice durch die Nase sprechen, näseln. **2** n (Ling) Nasal(laut) m.

nasalization [͵neɪzəlaɪ'zeɪʃən] n Nasalierung f.

nasalize ['neɪzəlaɪz] vt nasalieren.

nasally ['neɪzəlɪ] adv pronounce nasal; speak durch die Nase, näselnd.

nascent ['næsnt] adj (a) (liter) republic, world, culture werdend, im Entstehen begriffen; state Entwicklungs-; doubt, hope, pride aufkommend. (b) (Chem) naszierend.

nastily ['nɑːstɪlɪ] adv (a) (unpleasantly) scheußlich; speak, say gehässig, gemein; behave also gemein. to say sth so jdm gehässig sein, jdn angiften (inf). (b) (awkwardly, dangerously) fall, cut oneself böse, schlimm; skid, veer gefährlich. his arm was ~ broken er hat sich (dat) den Arm schlimm gebrochen.

nastiness ['nɑːstɪnɪs] *n, no pl* **(a)** *see adj* (a) Scheußlichkeit *f*; Ekelhaftigkeit *f*; Abscheulichkeit *f*; Schmutzigkeit *f*; Gefährlichkeit *f*.
(b) *(of behaviour etc)* Gemeinheit *f*; *(of person also)* Bosheit *f*; *(of remarks etc also)* Gehässigkeit *f*; *(behaviour)* gemeines *or* scheußliches Benehmen (*to* gegenüber); *(remarks)* Gehässigkeit(en *pl*) *f* (*to/wards*) gegenüber).
(c) *see adj* (c) Anstößigkeit *f*; Ekelhaftigkeit *f*. **the ~ of his mind** seine üble/schmutzige Phantasie.

nasturtium [nəs'tɜːʃəm] *n* (Kapuziner)kresse *f*, Kapuziner *m*.

nasty ['nɑːstɪ] *adj* (+*er*) **(a)** *(unpleasant)* scheußlich; *smell, taste also, medicine* ekelhaft, widerlich; *weather, habit also* abscheulich, übel; *surprise also* böse, unangenehm; *(serious) break, cough, wound also* böse, schlimm; *(objectionable) crime, behaviour, language, word, names* abscheulich; *(dirty)* schmutzig; *(dangerous) virus, disease* böse, gefährlich; *corner, bend, fog* böse, übel, gefährlich. **that's a ~-looking sky/cut** der Himmel/der Schnitt sieht böse aus; **she had a ~ fall** sie ist böse *or* schlimm gefallen; **he had a ~ time of it** es ging ihm sehr schlecht *or* ganz übel; **he has a ~ look** in his eyes sein Blick verheißt nichts Gutes; **don't touch that, that's ~** pfui, faß das nicht an; **they pulled all his teeth out — ~!** sie haben ihm alle Zähne gezogen — wie scheußlich *or* unangenehm!; **to turn ~** *(situation, person)* unangenehm werden; *(animal)* wild werden; *(weather)* schlecht werden, umschlagen; **events took a ~ turn** die Dinge nahmen eine Wendung zum Schlechten.
(b) *person, behaviour* gemein, garstig, *(dated)*, fies *(inf)*; *trick* gemein, übel; *(spiteful) remark, person also* gehässig; *rumour* gehässig, übel. **he has a ~ temper** mit ihm ist nicht gut Kirschen essen; **don't say that, that's ~** pfui, so was sagt man doch nicht; **that was a ~ thing to say/do** das war gemein *or* fies *(inf)*; **you ~ little boy (you)!** du böser Junge; **what a ~ man** was für ein ekelhafter Mensch; **he's a ~ bit** *or* **piece of work** *(inf)* er ist ein übler Kunde *(inf)* *or* Typ *(inf)*; **he looks a ~ bit** *or* **piece of work** er sieht fies aus *(inf)*.
(c) *(offensive)* anstößig; *film, book also* ekelhaft, schmutzig. **to have a ~ mind** eine üble Phantasie haben; *(obsessed with sex)* eine schmutzige Phantasie haben.

Nat *abbr of* **national.**

natal ['neɪtl] *adj* Geburts-.

natality [nə'tælɪtɪ] *n (esp US)* Geburtenziffer *f*.

nation ['neɪʃən] *n* Volk *nt*; *(people of one country)* Nation *f*. **people of all ~s** Menschen aller Nationen; **the voice of the ~** die Stimme des Volkes; **in the service of the ~** im Dienste des Volkes; **to address the ~** zum Volk sprechen; **the whole ~ watched him** do it das ganze Land sah ihm dabei zu; **the Sioux ~** die Siouxindianer *pl*, das Volk der Sioux(indianer).

national ['næʃənəl] **1** *adj* national; *concern, problem, affairs also* das (ganze) Land betreffend, des Landes, des Staates; *interest, debt, income* Staats-, öffentlich; *strike, scandal* landesweit; *economy, wealth* Volks-; *security* Staats-; *team, character* National-; *defence, language, church, religion* Landes-; *custom, monument* Volks-; *(not local) agreement, radio station etc* überregional; *(in names)* Staats-, staatlich. **the ~ papers** die überregionale Presse; **~ status** Landeszugehörigkeit *f*.
2 *n* **(a)** *(person)* Staatsbürger(in *f*) *m*. **foreign ~** Ausländer(in *f*) *m*; **Commonwealth ~s** Angehörige *pl* des Commonwealth.
(b) *(inf: newspaper)* überregionale Zeitung.
(c) *(Sport)* **the Grand N~.**

national: **~ anthem** *n* Nationalhymne *f*; **~ assistance** *n* Sozialhilfe *f*; **to be on ~ assistance** Sozialhilfe erhalten; **~ bank** *n* National- *or* Staatsbank *f*; **~ costume, ~ dress** *n* National- *or* Landestracht *f*; **~ flag** *n* National- *or* Landesflagge *f*; **N~ Guard** *n (esp US)* Nationalgarde *f*; **N~ Health** *adj attr* ≃ Kassen-; **N~ Health (Service)** *n (Brit)* Staatlicher Gesundheitsdienst *m*; **I got it on the N~ Health** ≃ das hat die Krankenkasse bezahlt; **~ holiday** *n* gesetzlicher *or* staatlicher Feiertag; **~ insurance** *n (Brit)* Sozialversicherung *f*; **~ insurance benefits** Arbeitslosen- und Krankengeld *nt*.

nationalism ['næʃnəlɪzəm] *n* Nationalismus *m*. **feeling of ~** Nationalgefühl *nt*.

nationalist ['næʃnəlɪst] **1** *adj* nationalistisch. **2** *n* Nationalist(in *f*) *m*.

nationalistic [ˌnæʃnə'lɪstɪk] *adj* nationalistisch.

nationality [ˌnæʃə'nælɪtɪ] *n* Staatsangehörigkeit, Nationalität *f*. **what ~ is he?** welche Staatsangehörigkeit hat er?; **she is of German ~** sie hat die deutsche Staatsangehörigkeit; **the many nationalities present** die Menschen verschiedener Nationalitäten, die anwesend sind/waren.

nationalization [ˌnæʃnəlaɪ'zeɪʃən] *n* Verstaatlichung *f*.

nationalize ['næʃnəlaɪz] *vt industries etc* verstaatlichen.

nationally ['næʃnəlɪ] *adv (as a nation)* als Nation; *(nation-wide)* im ganzen Land, landesweit.

national: **~ park** *n* Nationalpark *m*; **~ savings certificate** *n (Brit)* festverzinsliches öffentliches Sparpapier; **~ service** *n* Wehrdienst *m*; **N~ Socialism** *n* der Nationalsozialismus; **N~ Socialist 1** *n* Nationalsozialist(in *f*) *m*; **2** *adj* nationalsozialistisch.

nationhood ['neɪʃənhʊd] *n* nationale Einheit *or* Geschlossenheit.

nation-wide ['neɪʃənwaɪd] *adj, adv* landesweit. **the speech was broadcast ~** die Rede wurde im ganzen Land übertragen.

native ['neɪtɪv] **1** *adj* **(a)** *land, country, town* Heimat-; *language* Mutter-; *product, costume, customs, habits, plants* einheimisch; *(associated with natives) question, quarters, labour* Eingeborenen-. **the ~ inhabitants** die Einheimischen *pl*; *(in colonial context)* die Eingeborenen *pl*; *(original inhabitants)* die Ureinwohner *pl*; **the ~ habitat of the tiger** die Heimat des Tigers; **my ~ Germany** mein Heimatland *nt or* meine Heimat Deutschland; **his ~ Berlin** seine Heimatstadt *or* Vater-

stadt Berlin; **a ~ German** ein gebürtiger Deutscher, eine gebürtige Deutsche; **an animal/tree ~ to India** ein in Indien beheimatetes Tier/beheimateter Baum; **to go ~** wie die Eingeborenen leben; **~ speaker** Muttersprachler(in *f*) *m*; **I'm not a ~ speaker of English** Englisch ist nicht meine Muttersprache; **he speaks English like a ~ speaker** er spricht Englisch, als wäre es seine Muttersprache.
(b) *(inborn) wit, quality* angeboren.
(c) *metal* gediegen.
2 *n* **(a)** *(person)* Einheimische(r) *mf*; *(in colonial contexts)* Eingeborene(r) *mf*; *(original inhabitant)* Ureinwohner(in *f*) *m*. **a ~ of Britain/Germany** ein gebürtiger Brite/Deutscher, eine gebürtige Britin/Deutsche; **to speak German like a ~** Deutsch wie ein Deutscher sprechen.
(b) **to be a ~ of** ... *(plant, animal)* in ... beheimatet sein.

native: **~-born** *adj attr* gebürtig; **~ country** *n* Heimatland, Vaterland *nt*; **~ land** *n* Vaterland *nt*.

nativity [nə'tɪvɪtɪ] *n* Geburt *f*. **the N~** Christi Geburt *f*; *(picture)* die Geburt Christi; **~ play** Krippenspiel *nt*.

NATO ['neɪtəʊ] *abbr of* **North Atlantic Treaty Organization** NATO *f*.

natter ['nætə^r] *(Brit inf)* **1** *vi (gossip)* schwatzen *(inf)*; *(chatter also)* quasseln *(inf)*. **to ~ away in German** deutsch quasseln *(inf)*; **to ~ on about sth** über etw *(acc)* quasseln *(inf)*. **2** *n* Schwatz *m (inf)*. **to have a ~** einen Schwatz halten *(inf)*.

natty ['nætɪ] *adj* (+*er*) **(a)** *(neat) dress* schick, schmuck *(dated)*; *person also* adrett. **he's a ~ dresser** er zieht sich immer elegant *or* schmuck *(dated)* an. **(b)** *(handy) tool, gadget* handlich.

natural ['nætʃrəl] **1** *adj* **(a)** natürlich; *rights* naturgegeben, Natur-; *laws, forces, phenomena, religion, silk, sponge* Natur-. **it is ~ for you/him to think** ... es ist nur natürlich, daß Sie denken/er denkt ...; **~ resources** Naturschätze *pl*; **the ~ world** die Natur; **in its ~ state** im Naturzustand; **~ childbirth** natürliche Geburt; *(method)* die schmerzlose Geburt; **to die a ~ death** *or* **of ~ causes** eines natürlichen Todes sterben; **death from ~ causes** *(Jur)* Tod durch natürliche Ursachen; **to be imprisoned for the rest of one's ~ life** *(Jur)* eine lebenslängliche Gefängnisstrafe verbüßen; **a ~ son of Utah** in Utah geboren.
(b) *(inborn) gift, ability, quality* angeboren. **to have a ~ talent for sth** eine natürliche Begabung für etw haben; **he is a ~ artist/comedian** er ist der geborene Künstler/Komiker; **it is ~ for birds to fly** Vögel können von Natur aus fliegen; **sth comes ~ to sb** etw fällt jdm leicht.
(c) *(unaffected) manner* natürlich, ungekünstelt.
(d) *(Math) number* natürlich.
(e) *parents* natürlich; *(old) child* natürlich.
2 *n* **(a)** *(Mus) (sign)* Auflösungszeichen *nt*; *(note)* Note *f* ohne Vorzeichen; *(note with a ~ sign)* Note *f* mit Auflösungszeichen. **B ~/D ~** H, h/D, d; **you played F sharp instead of a ~** Sie haben fis statt f gespielt; *see also* **major, minor.**
(b) *(inf: person)* Naturtalent *nt*. **he's a ~ for this part** diese Rolle ist ihm wie auf den Leib geschrieben.
(c) *(inf: life)* Leben *nt*. **I've never heard the like in all my ~** ich habe so was mein Lebtag noch nicht gehört *(inf)*.
(d) *(old: idiot)* Einfaltspinsel *m*.

natural: **~ gas** *n* Erdgas *nt*; **~ history** *n* Naturkunde *f*; *(concerning evolution)* Naturgeschichte *f*.

naturalism ['nætʃrəlɪzəm] *n* Naturalismus *m*.

naturalist ['nætʃrəlɪst] *n* **(a)** Naturforscher(in *f*) *m*. **(b)** *(Art, Liter)* Naturalist(in *f*) *m*.

naturalistic [ˌnætʃrə'lɪstɪk] *adj (Art, Liter)* naturalistisch.

naturalization [ˌnætʃrəlaɪ'zeɪʃən] *n* Naturalisierung, Einbürgerung *f*. **~ papers** Einbürgerungsurkunde *f*.

naturalize ['nætʃrəlaɪz] *vt* **(a)** *person* einbürgern, naturalisieren. **to become ~d** eingebürgert werden. **(b)** *animal, plants* heimisch machen; *word* einbürgern. **to become ~d** heimisch werden/sich einbürgern.

naturally ['nætʃrəlɪ] *adv* **(a)** von Natur aus. **he is ~ artistic/lazy** er ist künstlerisch veranlagt/von Natur aus faul.
(b) *(not taught)* natürlich, instinktiv. **it comes ~ to him** das fällt ihm leicht.
(c) *(unaffectedly) behave, speak* natürlich, ungekünstelt.
(d) *(of course)* natürlich.

naturalness ['nætʃrəlnɪs] *n* Natürlichkeit *f*.

natural: **~ philosophy** *n* Naturwissenschaft, Naturlehre *(old) f*; **~ science** *n* Naturwissenschaft *f*; **the ~ sciences** die Naturwissenschaften *pl*; **~ selection** *n* natürliche Auslese; **~ wastage** *n* natürliche Personalreduzierung.

nature ['neɪtʃə^r] *n* **(a)** Natur *f*. **N~** die Natur; **laws of ~** Naturgesetze *pl*; **against ~** gegen die Natur; **in a state of ~** *(uncivilized, inf: naked)* im Naturzustand; **to return to ~** *(person)* zur Natur zurückkehren; *(garden)* in den Naturzustand zurückkehren; **to paint from ~** nach der Natur malen.
(b) *(of person)* Wesen(sart *f*) *nt*, Natur *f*. **to have a jealous/happy ~** eine eifersüchtige/fröhliche Natur haben, ein eifersüchtiges/fröhliches Wesen haben; **it is not in my ~ to say things like that** es entspricht nicht meiner Art *or* meinem Wesen, so etwas zu sagen; **cruel by ~** von Natur aus grausam.
(c) *(of object, material)* Beschaffenheit *f*. **it's in the ~ of things** das liegt in der Natur der Sache; **the ~ of the case is such** ... der Fall liegt so ...
(d) *(type, sort)* Art *f*. **things of this ~** derartiges; **something in the ~ of an apology** so etwas wie eine Entschuldigung; **... or something of that ~** ... oder etwas in der Art.

nature: **~ conservancy** *n* Umweltschutz *m*; **~ cure** *n* Naturheilverfahren *nt*.

-natured ['neɪtʃəd] *adj suf things, animals* -artig; *person mit* einem ... Wesen. **good-** gutmütig; **ill-** bösartig.

nature: **~-lover** *n* Naturfreund *m*; **~ poet** *n* Naturdichter(in *f*) *m*; **~ reserve** *n* Naturschutzgebiet *nt*; **~ study** *n* Naturkunde *f*; **~ trail** *n* Naturlehrpfad *m*; **~ worship** *n* Naturreligion *f*.

naturism ['neɪtʃərɪzəm] n Freikörperkultur f, FKK no art.

naturist ['neɪtʃərɪst] **1** n Anhänger(in f) m der Freikörperkultur, FKK-Anhänger(in f) m. **2** adj FKK-, Freikörperkultur-.

naught [nɔːt] n (old, form) see **nought (b)**.

naughtily ['nɔːtɪlɪ] adv frech, dreist; (esp of child) say, remark ungezogen, frech; behave unartig, ungezogen. I very ~ opened your letter ich war so frech und habe deinen Brief aufgemacht; but he very ~ did it all the same aber frecherweise hat er es trotzdem getan.

naughtiness ['nɔːtɪnɪs] n see adj (a) Frechheit, Dreistigkeit f; Unartigkeit, Ungezogenheit f; Unartigkeit f, Ungehorsam m. **(b)** Unanständigkeit f.

naughty ['nɔːtɪ] adj (+er) **(a)** frech, dreist; child unartig, ungezogen; dog unartig, ungehorsam. you ~ boy/dog! du böser or unartiger Junge/Hund!; it was ~ of him to break it das war aber gar nicht lieb von ihm, daß er das kaputtgemacht hat; I was ~ and ate a whole bar of chocolate ich habe schwer gesündigt und eine ganze Tafel Schokolade gegessen; ~, ~! aber, aber!; how ~ of me/him! das war ja gar nicht lieb!; the kitten's been ~ on the carpet (inf) das Kätzchen hat auf den Teppich gemacht.

(b) (shocking) joke, word, story unanständig. ~! nein, wie unanständig!; the ~ nineties die frechen neunziger Jahre.

nausea ['nɔːsɪə] n (Med) Übelkeit f; (fig) Ekel m. a feeling of ~ Übelkeit f; (fig) ein Gefühl nt des Ekels; the very thought fills me with ~ bei dem Gedanken allein wird mir schon übel.

nauseate ['nɔːsɪeɪt] vt to ~ sb (Med) (bei) jdm Übelkeit verursachen, in jdm Übelkeit erregen; (fig) jdn anwidern.

nauseating ['nɔːsɪeɪtɪŋ] adj sight, smell, violence, food ekelerregend; film, book, style gräßlich; overpoliteness widerlich; person ekelhaft, widerlich. to have a ~ effect (Med) Übelkeit verursachen (on sb (bei) jdm); that is a ~ attitude bei der Einstellung kann einem übel werden.

nauseatingly ['nɔːsɪeɪtɪŋlɪ] adv widerlich.

nauseous ['nɔːsɪəs] adj **(a)** (Med) that made me (feel) ~ dabei wurde mir übel. **(b)** (fig) widerlich.

nautical ['nɔːtɪkəl] adj nautisch; chart also See-; prowess, superiority zur See, seefahrerisch; distance zur See; stories von der Seefahrt; language, tradition, appearance seemännisch. a ~ nation eine Seefahrernation; he is interested in ~ matters, he's a very ~ person er interessiert sich für die Seefahrt; the music/play has a ~ flavour die Musik/das Stück beschwört die See herauf; ~ mile Seemeile f; ~ almanac nautisches Jahrbuch.

nautically ['nɔːtɪkəlɪ] adv superior zur See, was die Seefahrt betrifft.

nautilus ['nɔːtɪləs] n Nautilus m, Schiffsboot nt.

naval ['neɪvəl] adj Marine-; base, agreement, parade Flotten-; battle, forces See-. his interests are ~ not military er interessiert sich für die Marine und nicht für das Heer.

naval: ~ academy n Marineakademie f; ~ architect n Schiffsbauingenieur m; ~ architecture n Schiffsbau m; ~ aviation n Seeflugwesen nt; ~ power n Seemacht f; ~ warfare n Seekrieg m.

nave [neɪv] n (of church) Haupt- or Mittel- or Längsschiff nt.

navel ['neɪvəl] n (a) (Anat) Nabel m. **(b)** (also ~ orange) Navelorange f.

navigable ['nævɪgəbl] adj (a) schiffbar. in a ~ condition (ship) seetüchtig. **(b)** balloon, airship lenkbar.

navigate ['nævɪgeɪt] **1** vi (in plane, ship) navigieren; (in car) den Fahrer dirigieren; (in rally) der Beifahrer sein. who was navigating? (in plane, ship) wer war für die Navigation zuständig?; (in car) wer war der Beifahrer?; I don't know the route, you'll have to ~ ich kenne die Strecke nicht, du mußt mir sagen, wie ich fahren muß or du mußt mich dirigieren.

2 vt (a) aircraft, ship, spaceship navigieren. to ~ sth through sth etw durch etw (hindurch)navigieren; (fig) etw durch etw hindurchschleusen; he ~d his way through the crowd er bahnte sich (dat) einen Weg durch die Menge.

(b) (journey through) durchfahren; (plane, pilot) durchfliegen.

navigation [ˌnævɪˈgeɪʃən] n (a) (act of navigating) Navigation f. **(b)** (shipping) Schiffsverkehr m. **(c)** (skill) (in ship, plane) Navigation f. how's your ~? (in car) bist du als Beifahrer gut zu gebrauchen?; his ~ was lousy, we got lost (in car) er hat mich so schlecht dirigiert, daß wir uns verirrt haben.

navigation: ~ law n Schiffahrtsregelung f; ~ light n Positionslicht nt or -lampe f.

navigator ['nævɪgeɪtər] n (Naut) Navigationsoffizier m; (Aviat) Navigator m; (Mot) Beifahrer m.

navvy ['nævɪ] n (Brit) Bauarbeiter m; (on road also) Straßenarbeiter m.

navy ['neɪvɪ] **1** n (a) (Kriegs)marine f. to serve in the ~ in der Marine dienen; N~ Department (US) Marineministerium nt. **(b)** (also ~ blue) Marineblau nt. **2** adj (a) attr Marine-. **(b)** (also ~ blue) marineblau.

nawab [nəˈwɒb] n see nabob.

nay [neɪ] **1** adv (a) (obs, dial) nein. **(b)** (liter) surprised, ~ astonished überrascht, nein vielmehr verblüfft. **2** n Nein nt, Neinstimme f; see yea.

Nazarene ['næzəriːn] n Nazaräer m.

Nazi ['nɑːtsɪ] **1** n Nazi m; (fig pej) Faschist m. **2** adj Nazi-.

Nazism ['nɑːtsɪzəm] n Nazismus m.

NB abbr of nota bene NB.

NCB (Brit) abbr of National Coal Board.

NCO abbr of non-commissioned officer.

NE abbr of north-east NO.

Neanderthal [nɪˈændətɑːl] adj Neandertaler attr. ~ man der Neandertaler.

neap [niːp] n (also ~-tide) Nippflut, Nippzeit, Nipptide (N Ger) f.

Neapolitan [nɪəˈpɒlɪtən] **1** adj neapolitanisch. ~ ice-cream Fürst-Pückler-Eis nt. **2** n Neapolitaner(in f) m.

near [nɪər] (+er) **1** adv (a) (close in space and time) nahe. to be ~ (person, object) in der Nähe sein; (event, departure, festival etc) bevorstehen; (danger, end, help etc) nahe sein; to be very ~ ganz in der Nähe sein; (in time) nahe or unmittelbar bevorstehen; (danger etc) ganz nahe sein; to be ~er/~est näher/am nächsten sein; (event etc) zeitlich näher liegen/zeitlich am nächsten liegen; to be ~ at hand zur Hand sein; (shops) in der Nähe sein; (help) ganz nahe sein; (event) unmittelbar bevorstehen; when death is so ~ wenn man dem Tod nahe ist; he lives quite ~ er wohnt ganz in der Nähe; don't sit/stand so ~ setzen Sie sich/stehen Sie nicht so nahe (daran); you live ~er/~est du wohnst näher/am nächsten; to move/come ~er näherkommen; could you get or move ~er together? könnten Sie näher or enger or mehr zusammenrücken?; to draw ~/~er heranrücken/näher heranrücken; his answer came ~er than mine/~est seine Antwort traf eher zu als meine/traf die Sachlage am ehesten; that was the ~est I ever got to seeing him da hätte ich ihn fast gesehen; this is the ~est I can get to solving the problem besser kann ich das Problem nicht lösen; that's the ~est I ever got to being fired da hätte nicht viel gefehlt, und ich wäre rausgeworfen worden.

(b) (closely, exactly, accurately) genau. as ~ as I can judge soweit ich es beurteilen kann; they're the same length or as ~ as makes no difference sie sind so gut wie gleich lang; it's as ~ stopped as makes no difference es hat so gut wie aufgehört; you won't get any ~er than that genauer kann man es kaum treffen; (that's) ~ enough so geht's ungefähr, das haut so ungefähr hin (inf); ... no, but ~ enough ... nein, aber es war nicht weit davon entfernt; there were ~ enough 60 people at the party es waren knapp 60 Leute auf der Party; the same size as ~ as dammit (inf) fast genau die gleiche Größe; the more you look at this portrait, the ~er it resembles him (old) je öfter man sich dieses Porträt ansieht, desto ähnlicher wird es ihm.

(c) (almost) fast, beinahe; impossible also, dead nahezu.

(d) it's nowhere or not anywhere ~ enough/right das ist bei weitem nicht genug/das ist weit gefehlt; we're not any ~er (to)/nowhere ~ solving the problem wir sind der Lösung des Problems kein bißchen nähergekommen/wir haben das Problem bei weitem nicht or noch nicht einmal annähernd gelöst; we're nowhere or not anywhere ~ finishing the book wir haben das Buch noch lange nicht fertig; nowhere ~ as much lange or bei weitem nicht soviel; the train is nowhere ~ full der Zug ist bei weitem nicht voll; you are nowhere or not anywhere ~ the truth das ist weit gefehlt, du bist weit von der Wahrheit entfernt; he is nowhere or not anywhere ~ as clever as you er ist lange or bei weitem nicht so klug wie du.

2 prep (also adv: ~ to) (a) (close to) (position) nahe an (+dat), nahe (+dat); (with motion) nahe an (+acc); (in the vicinity of) in der Nähe von or +gen; (with motion) in die Nähe von or +gen. to be/get ~ (to) the church in der Nähe der Kirche sein/in die Nähe der Kirche kommen; he lives ~ (to) the border er wohnt in der Nähe der Grenze or nahe der Grenze; the hotel is very ~ (to) the station das Hotel liegt ganz in der Nähe des Bahnhofs; the chair is ~/~er (to) the table der Stuhl steht neben dem or nahe an/näher an dem Tisch; move the chair ~/~er (to) the table rücken Sie den Stuhl an den/näher an den Tisch; to come or get ~/~er (to) sb/sth nahe/näher an jdn/etw herankommen; to stand ~/~er (to) the table am or neben dem or nahe am/näher am Tisch stehen; he won't go ~ anything illegal mit Ungesetzlichem will er nichts zu tun haben; she stood too ~ (to) the stove sie stand zu nahe am Herd; when we got ~ (to) the house als wir an das Haus herankamen or in die Nähe des Hauses kamen; when we are ~er home wenn wir nicht mehr so weit von zu Hause weg sind; keep ~ me bleib in meiner Nähe; ~ here/there hier/dort in der Nähe; don't come ~ me komm mir nicht zu nahe; ~ (to) where I had seen him nahe der Stelle, wo ich ihn gesehen hatte; to be ~est to sth einer Sache (dat) am nächsten sein; take the chair ~est (to) you/the table nehmen Sie den Stuhl direkt neben Ihnen/dem Tisch; that's ~er it das trifft schon eher zu; the adaptation is very ~ (to) the original die Bearbeitung hält sich eng ans Original; to be ~ (to) sb's heart or sb jdm am Herzen liegen; to be ~ the knuckle or bone (inf) (joke) gewagt sein; (remark) hart an der Grenze sein.

(b) (close in time: with time stipulated) gegen. ~ (to) death/her confinement dem Tode/der Geburt nahe; she is ~ her time es ist bald so weit (bei ihr); ~ (to) the appointed time um die ausgemachte Zeit herum; phone again ~er (to) Christmas rufen Sie vor Weihnachten noch einmal an; come back ~er (to) 3 o'clock kommen Sie gegen 3 Uhr wieder; on the Wednesday ~est Easter am Mittwoch (direkt) vor Ostern; to be ~er/~est (to) sth einer Sache (dat) zeitlich näher liegen/am nächsten liegen; ~ (to) the end of my stay/the play/book gegen Ende meines Aufenthalts/des Stücks/des Buchs; I'm ~ (to) the end of the book/my stay ich habe das Buch fast zu Ende gelesen/mein Aufenthalt ist fast zu Ende or vorbei; her birthday is ~ (to) mine ihr und mein Geburtstag liegen nahe beieinander; the sun was ~ (to) setting die Sonne war am Untergehen; the evening was drawing ~ (to) its close (liter) der Abend ging zur Neige (liter); it is drawing ~ (to) Christmas es geht auf Weihnachten zu, Weihnachten steht vor der Tür; as it drew ~/~er (to) his departure als seine Abreise heranrückte/näher heranrückte.

(c) (on the point of) to be ~ (to) doing sth nahe daran sein, etw zu tun; to be ~ (to) tears/despair etc den Tränen/der Verzweiflung nahe sein; she was ~ (to) laughing out loud sie hätte beinahe laut gelacht; the project is ~/~er (to) completion das Projekt steht vor seinem Abschluß/ist dem Abschluß nähergekommen; he came ~ to ruining his chances er hätte sich seine Chancen beinahe verdorben, es hätte nicht viel gefehlt, und er hätte sich seine Chancen verdorben; we were ~ to being drowned wir waren dem Ertrinken nahe, wir wären beinahe ertrunken; **our hopes are ~ (to) fruition** unsere Hoffnungen werden bald in Erfüllung gehen.

(d) (*similar to*) ähnlich (+*dat*). **German is ~er (to) Dutch than English is** Deutsch ist dem Holländischen ähnlicher als Englisch; **it's the same thing or ~** it es ist so ziemlich das gleiche; **nobody comes anywhere ~ him at swimming** (*inf*) im Schwimmen kann es niemand mit ihm aufnehmen (*inf*).

3 *adj* **(a)** (*close in space*) nahe. **it looks very ~** es sieht so aus, als ob es ganz nah wäre; **our ~est neighbours are 5 miles away** unsere nächsten Nachbarn sind 5 Meilen entfernt; **to get a ~er view of the parade** um die Parade aus näherer Entfernung sehen zu können; **these glasses make things look ~er** diese Brille läßt alles näher erscheinen.

(b) (*close in time*) nahe. **these events are still very ~** diese Ereignisse liegen noch nicht lange zurück; **the hour is ~ (when ...)** (*old*) die Stunde ist nahe, (da ...) (*old*); **her hour was ~** (*old*) ihre Stunde war nahe (*old*).

(c) (*closely related, intimate*) *relation* nah; *friend* nah, vertraut. **my ~est and dearest** meine Lieben *pl*; **a ~ and dear friend** ein lieber und teurer Freund.

(d) *escape* knapp; *resemblance* groß, auffallend. **a ~ disaster/accident** beinahe ein Unglück *nt*/ein Unfall *m*; **a ~ race/contest** ein Rennen *nt*/Wettkampf *m* mit knappem Ausgang; **that was a ~ guess** Sie haben es beinahe erraten, das war nicht schlecht geraten; **to be in a state of ~ collapse/hysteria** am Rande eines Zusammenbruchs/der Hysterie sein; **round up the ~est pound** runden Sie die Zahl auf das nächste Pfund auf; **£50 or ~est offer** (*Comm*) Angebote *pl* um £ 50; **we'll sell it for £50, or ~est offer** wir verkaufen es für £ 50 oder das nächstbeste Angebot; **the ~est in line to the throne** der unmittelbare Thronfolger; **this is the ~est equivalent** das kommt dem am nächsten; **this is the ~est translation** you'll get to a compliment/an answer ein besseres Kompliment/eine bessere Antwort kannst du kaum erwarten.

4 *vt place* sich nähern (+*dat*). **he was ~ing his end** sein Leben neigte sich dem Ende zu; **to be ~ing sth** (*fig*) auf etw (*acc*) zugehen; **to ~ completion** kurz vor dem Abschluß stehen.

nearby ['nɪə'baɪ] **1** *adv* (*also* **near by**) in der Nähe. **2** *adj* nahe gelegen.

Near East *n* Naher Osten. **in the ~** im Nahen Osten.

nearly ['nɪəlɪ] *adv* **(a)** (*almost*) beinahe, fast. **I ~ laughed** ich hätte fast *or* beinahe gelacht; **she was ~ crying** *or* **in tears** sie war den Tränen nahe.

(b) **not ~** bei weitem nicht, nicht annähernd; **not ~ enough** bei weitem nicht genug.

nearness ['nɪənɪs] *n* Nähe *f*.

near: **~side 1** *adj* auf der Beifahrerseite, linke(r, s)/rechte(r, s); **2** *n* Beifahrerseite *f*; **~-sighted** *adj* kurzsichtig; **~-sightedness** *n* Kurzsichtigkeit *f*; **~ thing** *n* that was a ~ thing das war ein knapp.

neat [niːt] *adj* (+*er*) **(a)** (*tidy*) *person, house, hair-style* ordentlich; *worker, work, handwriting, sewing also* sauber; *hair, appearance also* gepflegt. **to make a ~ job** of sth etwas tadellos machen; **he made a very ~ job of repairing the window** er hat das Fenster tadellos repariert; *see* **pin**.

(b) (*pleasing*) nett; *clothes also* adrett; *person, figure also* hübsch; *ankles* schlank; *car, ship, house also* schmuck (*dated*). **she has a ~ figure** sie hat ein nettes Figürchen; **~ little suit** schmucker *or* netter Anzug.

(c) (*skilful*) *gadget, speech* gelungen; *style* gewandt; *solution* sauber, elegant; *trick* schlau. **that's very ~** das ist sehr schlau.

(d) (*undiluted*) *spirits* pur; *wines* unverdünnt. **to drink one's ~ whisky** ~ Whisky pur trinken.

(e) (*US inf: excellent*) prima (*inf*), klasse (*inf*).

neaten ['niːtn] *vt* (*also* **~ up**) in Ordnung bringen; *phrasing* glätten.

'neath [niːθ] *prep* (*poet*) unter (+*dat*), unterhalb (+*gen*); (*with motion*) unter (+*acc*).

neatly ['niːtlɪ] *adv see* **adj** (*a-c*) **(a)** ordentlich; sauber.

(b) nett; adrett; hübsch. **a ~ turned ankle** eine hübsche schlanke Fessel.

(c) gelungen; gewandt; sauber, elegant; schlau. **~ put** treffend ausgedrückt; **~ turned phrases** gewandt formulierte Sätze *pl*.

neatness ['niːtnɪs] *n see* **adj** (*a-c*) **(a)** Ordentlichkeit *f*; Sauberkeit *f*. **(b)** Nettheit *f*, nettes Aussehen; Adrettheit *f*; hübsches Aussehen; Schlankheit *f*. **(c)** Gelungenheit *f*; Gewandtheit *f*; Sauberkeit, Eleganz *f*; Schlauheit *f*.

nebula ['nebjʊlə] *n*, *pl* **-e** ['nebjuliː] **(a)** (*Astron*) Nebel *m*, Nebelfleck *m*. **(b)** (*Med*) Trübung *f*.

nebulous ['nebjʊləs] *adj* **(a)** (*Astron*) Nebel-. **(b)** (*fig*) unklar, verworren, nebulös.

necessarily ['nesɪsərɪlɪ] *adv* notwendigerweise (*also Logic*), unbedingt. **not ~** nicht unbedingt; **if that is true, then it is ~ the case that ...** wenn das wahr ist, dann folgt notwendigerweise daraus, daß ...; **we must ~ agree to these changes** wir müssen diesen Änderungen notgedrungen zustimmen.

necessary ['nesɪsərɪ] **1** *adj* **(a)** notwendig, nötig, erforderlich (*to, for* für). **it is ~ to ...** man muß ...; **is it ~ for me to come too?** muß ich auch kommen?; **it's not ~ for you to come** Sie brauchen nicht zu kommen; **it is ~ for him to be there** es ist nötig *or* notwendig, daß er da ist, er muß (unbedingt) da sein; **all the ~ qualifications** alle erforderlichen Qualifikationen; **~ condition** Voraussetzung *f*, (*Logic*) notwendige Voraussetzung; **to be/become ~ to sb** jdm unentbehrlich sein/werden; **to make it ~ for sb to do sth** es erforderlich machen, daß jd etw tut; **if ~** wenn nötig, nötigenfalls; **you were rude to him, was that ~?** du warst grob zu ihm, war das denn notwendig *or* nötig?; **to make the ~ arrangements** die erforderlichen *or* notwendigen Anord-

nungen treffen; **to do everything ~, to do what is ~** alles Nötige tun; **good food is ~ to health** gutes Essen ist für die Gesundheit notwendig; **to do no more than is ~** nicht mehr tun, als unbedingt notwendig *or* nötig ist.

(b) (*unavoidable*) *conclusion, change, result* unausweichlich. **we drew the ~ conclusions** wir haben die entsprechenden Schlüsse daraus gezogen; **a ~ evil** ein notwendiges Übel.

2 *n* **(a)** (*inf: what is needed*) **the ~** das Notwendige; **will you do the ~?** wirst du das Notwendige *or* Nötige erledigen?

(b) (*inf: money*) **the ~** das nötige Kleingeld.

(c) *usu pl* **the ~** *or* **necessaries** das Notwendige.

necessitate [nɪ'sesɪteɪt] *vt* notwendig *or* erforderlich machen, erfordern (*form*). **the heat ~d our staying indoors** die Hitze zwang uns, im Haus zu bleiben.

necessitous [nɪ'sesɪtəs] *adj* (*old, form*) dürftig, armselig.

necessity [nɪ'sesɪtɪ] *n* **(a)** *no pl* Notwendigkeit *f*. **from** *or* **out of ~** aus Not; **of ~** notgedrungen, notwendigerweise; **he did not realize the ~ for a quick decision** er hat nicht erkannt, wie wichtig *or* notwendig eine schnelle Entscheidung war; **the ~ for quick action** die Wichtigkeit schnellen Handelns, die Notwendigkeit für schnelles Handeln; **it is a case of absolute ~** es ist unbedingt notwendig; **there is no ~ for you to do that** es besteht nicht die geringste Notwendigkeit, daß Sie das tun; **in case of ~** im Notfall; **~ is the mother of invention** (*Prov*) Not macht erfinderisch (*Prov*).

(b) *no pl* (*poverty*) Not, Armut *f*. **to live in ~** Not leiden, in Armut leben.

(c) (*necessary thing*) Notwendigkeit *f*. **the bare necessities (of life)** das Notwendigste (zum Leben).

neck [nek] **1** *n* **(a)** Hals *m*. **to break one's ~** sich (*dat*) das Genick *or* den Hals brechen; **but don't break your ~** (*inf*) bring dich nicht um (*inf*); **to risk one's ~** Kopf und Kragen riskieren; **to save one's ~** seinen Hals aus der Schlinge ziehen; **a stiff ~** ein steifer Hals *or* Nacken; **to win by a ~** um eine Kopflänge gewinnen; **to have sb round one's ~** (*fig inf*) jdn auf dem *or* am Halse haben; **to be up to one's ~ in work** bis über den Hals *or* über die Ohren in der Arbeit stecken; **he's in it up to his ~** (*inf*) er steckt bis über den Hals drin; **to get it in the ~** (*inf*) eins aufs Dach bekommen (*inf*); **to stick one's ~ out** seinen Kopf riskieren; **it's ~ or nothing** (*inf*) alles oder nichts; **in this ~ of the woods** (*inf*) in diesen Breiten; *see* **breathe**.

(b) (*Cook*) **~ of lamb** Halsstück *nt* vom Lamm.

(c) (*of bottle, vase, violin, bone*) Hals *m*; (*of land*) Landenge *f*.

(d) (*of dress etc*) Ausschnitt *m*. **it has a high ~** es ist hochgeschlossen.

(e) (*also* **~ measurement**) Halsweite *f*.

2 *vi* (*inf*) knutschen (*inf*), schmusen (*inf*).

neck: **~ and ~** (*lit, fig*) Kopf-an-Kopf-; **2** *adv* Kopf an Kopf; **~band** *n* Besatz *m*; (*of shirt*) Kragensteg *m*; (*of pullover*) Halsbündchen *nt*; **~cloth** *n* (*obs*) Halstuch *nt*.

neckerchief ['nekətʃiːf] *n* Halstuch *nt*.

necklace ['neklɪs] *n* (Hals)kette *f*.

necklet ['neklɪt] *n* Kettchen *nt*.

neck: **~line** *n* Ausschnitt *m*; **~tie** *n* (*esp US*) Krawatte *f*, Binder, Schlips *m*.

necrology [ne'krɒlədʒɪ] *n* (*form*) Totenverzeichnis, Nekrologium *nt*; (*obituary*) Nachruf, Nekrolog *m*.

necromancer ['nekrəʊˌmænsəʳ] *n* Toten- *or* Geisterbeschwörer(in *f*), Nekromant *m*.

necromancy ['nekrəʊˌmænsɪ] *n* Toten- *or* Geisterbeschwörung, Nekromantie *f*.

necrophilia [ˌnekrəʊ'fɪlɪə] *n* Leichenschändung, Nekrophilie *f*.

necropolis [ne'krɒpəlɪs] *n* Totenstadt, Nekropole, Nekropolis *f*.

nectar ['nektəʳ] *n* (*lit, fig*) Nektar *m*.

nectarine ['nektərɪn] *n* (*fruit*) Nektarine *f*; (*tree*) Nektarine(n-baum *m*) *f*.

NEDC ['nedɪ] (*Brit*) *abbr of* **National Economic Development Council**.

née [neɪ] *adj* **Mrs Smith, ~ Jones** Frau Smith, geborene Jones.

need [niːd] **1** *n* **(a)** *no pl* (*necessity*) Notwendigkeit *f* (*for* gen). **if ~ be** nötigenfalls, wenn nötig; **in case of ~** notfalls, im Notfall; **(there is) no ~ for sth** etw ist nicht nötig; **(there is) no ~ to do sth** etw braucht nicht *or* muß nicht unbedingt getan werden; **there is no ~ for sb to do sth** jd braucht etw nicht zu tun; **there is no ~ for tears** du brauchst zu weinen; **there's no ~ to hurry/worry** es hat keine Eile, du brauchst dich nicht zu beeilen/dir keine Sorgen zu machen; **there was no ~ to send it registered mail** es war nicht nötig, es eingeschrieben zu schicken; **there's no ~ to get angry** du brauchst nicht gleich wütend zu werden; **to be (badly) in ~ of sth** (*person*) etw (dringend) brauchen; **those most in ~ of help** diejenigen, die Hilfe am nötigsten brauchen; **to be in ~ of repair/an overhaul** reparaturbedürftig sein/(dringend) überholt werden müssen; **this window is in ~ of a coat of paint** dieses Fenster könnte ein wenig Farbe gut gebrauchen, dieses Fenster müßte gestrichen werden; **to have no ~ of sth** etw nicht brauchen; **to have no ~ to do sth** etw nicht zu tun brauchen.

(b) *no pl* (*misfortune*) Not *f*. **in time(s) of ~** in schwierigen Zeiten, in Zeiten der Not; **do not fail me in my hour of ~** (*usu iro*) verlaß mich nicht in der Stunde der Not.

(c) *no pl* (*poverty*) Not *f*. **to be in great ~** große Not leiden; **those in ~** die Notleidenden *pl*.

(d) (*requirement*) Bedürfnis *nt*. **the body's ~ for oxygen** das Sauerstoffbedürfnis des Körpers; **my ~s are few** ich stelle nur geringe Ansprüche *pl*; **a list of all your ~s** eine Aufstellung all dessen, was Sie brauchen; **your ~ is greater than mine** Sie haben es nötiger als ich; **there is a great ~ for ...** es besteht ein großer Bedarf an (+*dat*) ...; **investment is one of the firm's greatest ~s** die Firma braucht dringend Investitionen.

2 *vt* **(a)** (*require*) brauchen. **he ~ed no second invitation** man mußte ihn nicht zweimal bitten; **to ~ no introduction** keine spezielle Einführung brauchen; **much** ~**ed** dringend notwendig; **what I** ~ **is a good drink** ich brauche etwas zu trinken; **just what I** ~**ed** genau das richtige; **that's/you're all I** ~**ed** (iro) das hat/du hast mir gerade noch gefehlt; **this situation** ~**s some explanation** diese Situation bedarf einer Erklärung (gen); **it** ~**s a service/a coat of paint/careful consideration** es muß gewartet/gestrichen/gründlich überlegt werden; **a visa is** ~**ed to enter the USA** man braucht für die Einreise in die USA ein Visum; **it** ~**ed a revolution to change that** es bedurfte einer Revolution or brauchte eine Revolution, um das zu ändern; **it** ~**ed an accident to make him drive carefully** er mußte erst einen Unfall haben, bevor er vernünftig fuhr.

 (b) (in verbal constructions) **sth** ~**s doing** or **to be done** etw muß gemacht werden; **the book** ~**s careful reading** or **to be read carefully** das Buch muß sorgfältig gelesen werden; **he** ~**s watching/cheering up** man muß ihn beobachten/aufheitern, er muß beobachtet/aufgeheitert werden; **to** ~ **to do sth** (have to) etw tun müssen; **not to** ~ **to do sth** etw nicht zu tun brauchen; **he doesn't** ~ **to be told** man braucht ihm nicht zu sagen; **you shouldn't** ~ **to be told** das müßte man dir nicht erst sagen müssen; **it doesn't** ~ **me to tell you** daß das brauche ich dir ja wohl nicht zu sagen; **she** ~**s to have everything explained to her** man muß ihr alles erklären.

 3 v aux (a) (indicating obligation) (in positive contexts) müssen. ~ **he go?** muß er gehen?; ~ **I say more?** mehr brauche ich ja wohl nicht zu sagen; **I** ~ **hardly say that ...** ich brauche wohl kaum zu erwähnen, daß ...; **no-one** ~ **go** or ~**s to go home yet** es braucht noch keiner nach Hause zu gehen; **you only** ~**ed (to) ask** du hättest nur (zu) fragen brauchen; **one** ~ **only look** ein Blick genügt.

 (b) (indicating obligation) (in negative contexts) brauchen. **you** ~**n't wait** du brauchst nicht (zu) warten; **we** ~**n't have come/gone** wir hätten gar nicht kommen/gehen brauchen; **I/you** ~**n't have bothered** das war nicht nötig.

 (c) (indicating logical necessity) ~ **that be true?** ist das notwendigerweise wahr?; **that** ~**n't be the case** das muß nicht unbedingt der Fall sein; **it** ~ **not follow that ...** daraus folgt nicht unbedingt, daß ...

needful ['ni:dful] 1 adj (old) notwendig, nötig (for, to für, zu). 2 n (inf) (what is necessary) **to do the** ~ das Nötige tun; **to supply the** ~ (money) das nötige Kleingeld zur Verfügung stellen.

neediness ['ni:dinis] n Armut, Bedürftigkeit f.

needle ['ni:dl] 1 n (all senses) Nadel f. **it's like looking for a** ~ **in a haystack** es ist, als ob man eine Stecknadel im Heuhaufen or Heuschober suchte; **to give sb the** ~ (inf) jdn reizen.

 2 vt (inf: goad) ärgern, piesacken (inf). **what's needling him?** was ist ihm über die Leber gelaufen? (inf).

 (b) (US inf) **to** ~ **a drink** einen Schuß Alkohol in ein Getränk geben.

needle: ~-**book** n Nadelheft nt; ~-**case** n Nadeletui nt; ~**craft** n handarbeitliches Geschick; ~ **match** n spannendes Spiel; ~-**sharp** adj (inf) clever (inf), schwer auf Zack (inf).

needless ['ni:dlis] adj unnötig; remark etc also überflüssig. ~ **to say** natürlich; ~ **to say, he didn't come** er kam natürlich nicht.

needlessly ['ni:dlisli] adv unnötig(erweise), überflüssig(erweise). **he was quite** ~ **rude** er war ganz unnötig grob.

needle: ~**woman** n Näherin f; ~**work** n Handarbeit f; **a piece of** ~**work** eine Handarbeit.

needs [ni:dz] adv (obs) **I must** ~ **away/obey** ich muß fort/notwendigerweise gehorchen; ~ **must as the devil drives** (prov) nolens volens.

needy ['ni:di] 1 adj (+er) ärmlich, bedürftig. **in** ~ **circumstances** in ärmlichen Umständen. 2 n **the** ~ die Bedürftigen pl.

ne'er [nɛər] adv (old, poet: never) nie, niemals.

ne'er-do-well ['nɛədu:ˌwel] 1 n Tunichtgut, Taugenichts (dated) m. 2 adj nichtsnutzig.

ne'ertheless [ˌnɛərðə'les] adv (old, poet) nichtsdestoweniger.

nefarious [ni'fɛəriəs] adj verrucht, ruchlos (liter).

negate [ni'geit] vt (nullify) zunichte machen; (deny) verneinen (also Gram), negieren (geh).

negation [ni'geiʃən] n Verneinung f; (of statement, negative form also) Negation f.

negative ['negətiv] 1 adj negativ; answer verneinend; (Gram) form verneint. ~ **sign** (Math) Minuszeichen nt, negatives Vorzeichen; ~ **ion** Anion nt; **I got a** ~ **reply to my request** ich habe auf meinen Antrag einen abschlägigen Bescheid bekommen.

 2 n (a) (also Gram) Verneinung f. **to answer in the** ~ eine verneinende Antwort geben; (say no) mit Nein antworten; (refuse) einen abschlägigen Bescheid geben; **his answer was a curt** ~ er antwortete mit einem knappen Nein; **put this sentence into the** ~ verneinen Sie diesen Satz.

 (b) (Gram: word) Verneinungswort nt, Negation f; (Math) negative Zahl. **two** ~**s make a positive** (Math) zweimal minus gibt plus.

 (c) (Phot) Negativ nt.

 (d) (Elec) negativer Pol.

 3 interj nein.

negatively ['negətivli] adv negativ; (in the negative) verneinend. **how do you express this statement** ~? wie drückt man diesen Satz verneint or in der Verneinungsform aus?

negativity [ˌnegə'tiviti] n negative Einstellung.

neglect [ni'glekt] 1 vt vernachlässigen; promise nicht einhalten; opportunity versäumen; advice nicht befolgen. **to** ~ **to do sth** es versäumen or unterlassen, etw zu tun.

 2 n see vt Vernachlässigung f; Nichteinhalten nt; Versäumen nt; Nichtbefolgung f; (negligence) Nachlässigkeit f. ~ **of one's duties** Pflichtvergessenheit f, Pflichtversäumnis nt; **to be in a state of** ~ verwahrlost sein, völlig vernachlässigt sein; **the fire started through (his)** ~ das Feuer ist durch seine Nachlässigkeit entstanden; **the garden suffered through (our)** ~ der

Garten hat darunter gelitten, daß wir ihn vernachlässigt haben.

neglected [ni'glektid] adj vernachlässigt; area, garden etc also verwahrlost. **to feel** ~ sich vernachlässigt fühlen.

neglectful [ni'glektful] adj vernachlässigend; father, government etc pflichtvergessen. **to be** ~ **of sb/sth** sich nicht um jdn/etw kümmern, jdn/etw vernachlässigen.

neglectfully [ni'glektfəli] adv see adj.

négligé(e) ['negliʒei] n Negligé nt.

negligence ['neglidʒəns] n (carelessness) Nachlässigkeit f; (causing danger, Jur) Fahrlässigkeit f.

negligent ['neglidʒənt] adj (a) (causing danger, damage) fahrlässig. **to be** ~ **of sb/sth** jdn/etw vernachlässigen; **to be** ~ **of one's duties** pflichtvergessen sein; **both drivers were** ~ beide Fahrer haben sich fahrlässig verhalten.

 (b) (off-hand) lässig.

negligently ['neglidʒəntli] adv see adj (a) nachlässig; fahrlässig. **he very** ~ **forgot** in seiner Nachlässigkeit vergaß er es, nachlässig, wie er war, vergaß er es.

 (b) lässig.

negligible ['neglidʒəbl] adj unwesentlich, unbedeutend; quantity, amount, sum also geringfügig, unerheblich. **the opposition in this race is** ~ in diesem Rennen gibt es keinen ernstzunehmenden Gegner.

negotiable [ni'gəuʃiəbl] adj (a) (Comm) (can be sold) verkäuflich, veräußerlich; (can be transferred) übertragbar. **not** ~ nicht verkäuflich/übertragbar.

 (b) **these terms are** ~ über diese Bedingungen kann verhandelt werden.

 (c) road befahrbar; river, mountain pass passierbar; obstacle, difficulty überwindbar.

negotiate [ni'gəuʃieit] 1 vt (a) (discuss) verhandeln über (+acc); (bring about) aushandeln. (b) bend in road, (horse) fence nehmen; river, mountain, rapids passieren; obstacle, difficulty überwinden. (c) (Comm) shares handeln mit; sale tätigen (form). 2 vi verhandeln (for über +acc).

negotiation [ni,gəuʃi'eiʃən] n (a) siehe vt (a) Verhandlung f; Aushandlung f. **the matter is still under** ~ über diese Sache wird noch verhandelt; **it's a matter for** ~ darüber muß erst verhandelt werden; **the price is a matter for** ~ über den Preis kann verhandelt werden; **by** ~ auf dem Verhandlungsweg.

 (b) usu pl (talks) Verhandlung f. **to begin** ~**s with sb** Verhandlungen pl mit jdm aufnehmen; **to be in** ~**(s) with sb** mit jdm in Verhandlungen stehen.

 (c) (of river, mountain, rapids) Passage f, Passieren nt; (of obstacle, difficulty) Überwindung f. ~ **of the bend proved difficult** es war schwierig, die Kurve zu nehmen.

negotiator [ni'gəuʃieitəᵣ] n Unterhändler(in f) m.

Negress ['ni:gres] n Negerin f.

Negro ['ni:grəu] 1 adj Neger-. 2 n Neger m.

Negroid ['ni:grɔid] adj negroid.

neigh [nei] 1 vi wiehern. 2 n Wiehern nt.

neighbour, (US) neighbor ['neibəᵣ] 1 n (a) Nachbar(in f) m; (at table) Tischnachbar(in f) m; see **next-door**.

 (b) (Bibl) Nächste(r) mf.

 2 vt (adjoin) country, river angrenzen an (+acc).

 3 vi (a) **to** ~ **on** (adjoin) (an)grenzen an (+acc); (approach) grenzen an (+acc).

 (b) (US inf) **to** ~ **with sb** gutnachbarliche Beziehungen pl zu jdm haben.

neighbourhood, (US) neighborhood ['neibəhud] n (district) Gegend f, Viertel nt; (people) Nachbarschaft f. **get to know your** ~ lernen Sie Ihre nähere Umgebung or (people also) Ihre Nachbarschaft kennen; **all the children from the** ~ all die Kinder aus der Nachbarschaft or der Gegend; **she is very popular with the whole** ~ sie ist bei allen Nachbarn or in der ganzen Nachbarschaft sehr beliebt; **in the** ~ **of sth** in der Nähe von etw; (fig: approximately) um etw herum.

neighbouring, (US) neighboring ['neibəriŋ] adj house(s), village benachbart, angrenzend, Nachbar-; fields, community angrenzend, Nachbar-.

neighbourly, (US) neighborly ['neibəli] adj person nachbarlich; action, relations gutnachbarlich. **they are** ~ **people** sie sind gute Nachbarn; **to behave in a** ~ **way** sich als guter Nachbar erweisen.

neighing ['neiiŋ] n Wiehern nt.

neither ['naiðəᵣ] 1 adv ~ ... **nor** weder ... noch; **he** ~ **knows nor cares** er weiß es nicht und will es auch nicht wissen, er weiß es nicht, noch will er es wissen.

 2 conj auch nicht. **if you don't go,** ~ **shall I** wenn du nicht gehst, gehe ich auch nicht; **I'm not going** — ~ **am I** ich gehe nicht — ich auch nicht; **he didn't do it (and)** ~ **did his sister** weder er noch seine Schwester haben es getan; **I can't go,** ~ **do I want to** ich kann und will auch nicht gehen.

 3 adj keine(r, s) (der beiden). ~ **one of them** keiner von beiden; **in** ~ **case** in keinem Fall, weder in dem einen noch in dem anderen Fall.

 4 pron keine(r, s). ~ **of them** keiner von beiden; **which will you take?** — ~ welches nehmen Sie? — keines (von beiden).

nelly ['neli] n: **not on your** ~ (Brit hum inf) nie im Leben.

nelson ['nelsən] n (Wrestling) **full** ~ Doppelnelson m, doppelter Nackenheber; **half** ~ Nelson m, einfacher Nackenheber; **to put a half/full** ~ **on sb** den Nelson/Doppelnelson bei jdm ansetzen.

nem con [ˌnem'kɒn] adv ohne Gegenstimme.

nemesis ['nemisis] n Nemesis f (liter), die gerechte Strafe.

neo- ['ni:əu-] pref neo-, Neo-. ~**classical** klassizistisch; ~**classicism** Klassizismus m; ~**colonial** neokolonialistisch; ~**colonialism** Neokolonialismus m; ~**fascism** Neofaschismus m; ~**fascist** 1 adj neofaschistisch; 2 n Neofaschist(in f) m.

neolithic [ˌni:əu'liθik] adj jungsteinzeitlich, neolithisch.

neologism [ni'plɒdʒizəm] n (Ling) (Wort)neubildung f, Neologismus m.

neon ['niːɒn] **1** *n* (*Chem*) Neon *nt.* **2** *adj attr* lamp, lighting, tube Neon-. ~ **sign** (*name*) Neon- *or* Leuchtschild *nt*; (*advertisement*) Neon- *or* Leuchtreklame *f no pl.*

neo-Nazi [ˌniːəʊˈnɑːtsɪ] **1** *n* Neonazi *m.* **2** *adj* neonazistisch.

neophyte ['niːəfaɪt] *n* Neubekehrte(r) *mf*, Neophyt(in *f*) *m* (*spec*); (*in RC church*) neugeweihter Priester.

Neo: ~-**Platonic** *adj* neuplatonisch; ~-**Platonism** *n* Neuplatonismus *m*; ~-**Platonist** *n* Neuplatoniker(in *f*) *m*.

Nepal [nɪˈpɔːl] *n* Nepal *nt.*

Nepalese [ˌnepəˈliːz], **Nepali** [nɪˈpɔːlɪ] **1** *adj* nepalesisch, nepalisch. **2** *n* (a) Nepalese *m*, Nepalesin *f.* (b) (*language*) Nepalesisch *nt.*

nephew ['nevjuː, 'nefjuː] *n* Neffe *m.*

nephritis [neˈfraɪtɪs] *n* Nierenentzündung, Nephritis (*spec*) *f.*

nepotism ['nepətɪzəm] *n* Vetternwirtschaft *f*, Nepotismus *m.*

Neptune ['neptjuːn] *n* (*Astron, Myth*) Neptun *m.*

nereid ['nɪərɪɪd] *n* (*Myth*) Nereide, Meerjungfrau *f.*

nerve [nɜːv] **1** *n* (a) (*Anat*) Nerv *m.* **to suffer from** ~s nervös sein; **to have an attack** *or* **fit of** ~s in Panik geraten, durchdrehen (*inf*); (*before exam also*) Prüfungsangst haben; **to be in a terrible state of** ~s mit den Nerven völlig fertig *or* herunter sein; **it's only** ~s das ist *etc* nur nervös; **to be all** ~s ein Nervenbündel sein; **his** ~s **are bad** er hat schlechte Nerven; **to get on sb's** ~s (*inf*) jdm auf die Nerven gehen *or* fallen; **he doesn't know what** ~s **are** er hat die Ruhe weg (*inf*); **to live on one's** ~s nervlich angespannt sein, völlig überreizt sein; **to have** ~s **of steel** Nerven wie Drahtseile haben.
(b) *no pl* (*courage*) Mut *m.* **to lose/keep one's** ~ die Nerven verlieren/nicht verlieren; **to regain one's** ~, **to get one's** ~ **back** seine Angst überwinden; **his** ~ **failed him** ihn verließ der Mut, er bekam Angst; **to have the** ~ **to do sth** sich trauen, etw zu tun; **a test of** ~ eine Nervenprobe.
(c) *no pl* (*inf*: *impudence*) Frechheit, Unverschämtheit *f.* **to have the** ~ **to do sth** die Frechheit besitzen, etw zu tun; **he's got a** ~! der hat Nerven! (*inf*); **what a** ~!, **the** ~ **of it!** so eine Frechheit!
(d) (*Bot*) Ader *f*, Nerv *m.*
2 *vtr* **to** ~ **oneself for sth/to do sth** sich seelisch und moralisch auf etw (*acc*) vorbereiten/darauf vorbereiten, etw zu tun; **I can't** ~ **myself to do it** ich bringe einfach den Mut nicht auf, das zu tun; **to** ~ **sb to do sth** jdm den Mut geben, etw zu tun.

nerve *in cpds* Nerven-; ~ **cell** *n* Nervenzelle *f*; ~ **centre** (*Brit*) *or* (*US*) **center** *n* (*Anat*) Nervenknoten *m*; (*fig*) Schaltzentrale *f*; ~ **ending** *n* Nervende *nt*; ~ **gas** *n* Nervengas *nt.*

nerveless ['nɜːvlɪs] *adj* (a) (*without nerves*) ohne Nerven; plant also ohne Adern, ungeädert. (b) (*confident*) person gelassen, seelenruhig.

nerve-racking ['nɜːvrækɪŋ] *adj* nervenaufreibend.

nervous ['nɜːvəs] *adj* (a) (*Anat*) structure Nerven-; (*related to the nerves*) problem, disorder also nervös (bedingt); **exhaustion, reflex** nervös. ~ **tension** Nervenanspannung *f.*
(b) (*apprehensive, timid*) nervös; (*overexcited, tense also*) aufgeregt. **to feel** ~ nervös sein; **I feel** ~ **in big hotels** große Hotels machen mich nervös; **you make me (feel)** ~, **I am** *or* **I feel** ~ **of you** du machst mich (noch) ganz nervös; **I am** ~ **about the exam/him** mir ist bange vor dem Examen/um ihn; **I was rather** ~ **about giving him the job** mir war nicht wohl bei dem Gedanken, ihm die Stelle zu geben; **I am rather** ~ **about diving** ich habe einen ziemlichen Bammel vor dem Tauchen (*inf*); **to be in a** ~ **state** nervös *or* aufgeregt sein.

nervous *in cpds* Nerven-; ~ **breakdown** *n* Nervenzusammenbruch *m*; ~ **energy** *n* Vitalität *f*; **after the exam I still had a lot of** ~ **energy** nach dem Examen war ich noch ganz aufgedreht.

nervously ['nɜːvəslɪ] *adv* nervös; (*excitedly, tensely also*) aufgeregt.

nervousness ['nɜːvəsnɪs] *n* Nervosität *f*; (*tension also*) Aufgeregtheit *f.* **his** ~ **about flying** seine Angst vor dem Fliegen.

nervous: ~ **system** *n* Nervensystem *nt*; ~ **wreck** *n* (*inf*) **to be/look/feel a** ~ **wreck** mit den Nerven völlig am Ende *or* fertig sein.

nervy ['nɜːvɪ] *adj* (+*er*) (a) (*Brit*: *tense*) nervös, unruhig. (b) (*US inf*: *cheeky*) frech, unverschämt.

nest [nest] **1** *n* (a) (*of birds, bees, ants*) Nest *nt.* **to leave the** ~ (*lit, fig*) das Nest verlassen.
(b) (*of boxes etc*) Satz *m.* **a** ~ **of tables** ein Satztisch *m.*
(c) (*fig*: *den*) Schlupfwinkel *m.* **a** ~ **of thieves/crime** ein Diebes-/Verbrechernest; **a** ~ **of machine-guns** eine Maschinengewehrstellung.
2 *vi* (a) (*bird*) nisten.
(b) **to go** ~**ing** Nester ausheben *or* ausnehmen.

nest-egg ['nesteg] *n* (*lit*) Nestei *nt*; (*fig*) Notgroschen *m.* **to have a nice little** ~ (*fig*) sich (*dat*) einen Notgroschen zurückgelegt haben.

nesting-box ['nestɪŋbɒks] *n* Nistkasten *m.*

nestle ['nesl] *vi* **to** ~ **down** in bed sich ins Bett kuscheln; **to** ~ **up to sb** sich an jdn schmiegen *or* kuscheln; **to** ~ **against sb's shoulder** sich an jds Schulter (*acc*) schmiegen; **the village nestling in the hills** das Dorf, das zwischen den Bergen eingebettet liegt; **a house nestling** *or* ~**d among the trees** ein von Bäumen eingerahmtes Haus.

nestling ['nestlɪŋ] *n* Nestling *m.*

net¹ [net] **1** *n* (a) (*lit, fig*) Netz *nt.* **to make** ~s Netze knüpfen; **to walk into the police** ~ (*fig*) der Polizei ins Netz *or* Garn gehen; **to be caught in the** ~ (*fig*) in die Falle gehen; **he felt the** ~ **closing round him** (*fig*) er fühlte, wie sich die Schlinge immer enger zog.
(b) (*Sport*) Netz *nt.* **to come up to the** ~ ans Netz gehen; **the ball's in the** ~ der Ball ist im Tor *or* Netz; **the** ~s (*Cricket*) *von* Netzen umspannter Übungsplatz.
(c) (*Tex*) Netzgewebe *nt*; (*for curtains, clothes etc*) Tüll *m.*

2 *vt* (a) fish, game, butterfly mit dem Netz fangen; (*fig*) criminal fangen. **the police have** ~**ted the criminal** der Verbrecher ist der Polizei ins Netz gegangen; **we haven't** ~**ted many fish today** wir haben heute nicht viele Fische gefangen, uns sind heute nicht viele Fische ins Netz gegangen.
(b) (*Sport*) ball ins Netz schlagen. **to** ~ **a goal** ein Tor schießen *or* erzielen.
(c) (*cover with* ~) mit Netzen überspannen.

net² **1** *adj* (a) price, income, weight netto, Netto-. ~ **profit** Reingewinn, Nettoertrag *m*; **it costs £15** ~ es kostet £15 netto.
(b) (*fig*) result End-, letzendlich.
2 *vt* netto einnehmen; (*in wages, salary*) netto verdienen; (*show, deal etc*) einbringen. **I** ~**ted a salary of £250 a month** ich bezog ein Gehalt von £250 netto im Monat, ich hatte ein monatliches Nettogehalt von £250.

net: ~ **bag** *n* (*Einkaufs*)netz *nt*; ~**ball** *n* (*Brit*) Korbball *m*; ~ **curtain** *n* Tüllgardine *f*, Store *m.*

nether ['neðə'] *adj* (*liter*) untere(r, s). ~ **regions** Unterwelt *f.*

Netherlands ['neðələndz] *npl* **the** ~ die Niederlande *pl.*

nethermost ['neðəməʊst] *adj* (*liter*) unterste(r, s). **in the** ~ **parts of the earth** in den tiefsten Tiefen der Erde (*liter*).

net: ~ **play** *n* (*Tennis*) Spiel *nt* am Netz; ~ **stocking** *n* Netzstrumpf *m.*

nett see **net².**

netting ['netɪŋ] *n* Netz *nt*; (*wire*) Maschendraht *m*; (*fabric*) Netzgewebe *nt*; (*for curtains etc*) Tüll *m.*

nettle ['netl] **1** *n* (*Bot*) Nessel *f.* **to grasp the** ~ (*fig*) in den sauren Apfel beißen. **2** *vt* (*fig inf*) person ärgern, wurmen (*inf*), fuchsen (*inf*). **I was** ~**d by her remarks** ihre Worte haben mich geärgert *or* gewurmt (*inf*) *or* gefuchst (*inf*).

nettle: ~ **rash** *n* Nesselausschlag *m*; ~ **sting** *n* Brennesselstich *m*; **her legs were covered in** ~ **stings** ihre Beine waren von den Brennesseln völlig zerstochen.

network ['netwɜːk] **1** *n* (a) (*lit, fig*) Netz *nt.* (b) (*Rad, TV*) Sendenetz *nt*; (*Elec*) Netzwerk *nt.* **2** *vt* (*inf*) programme im ganzen Netzbereich ausstrahlen.

neural ['njʊərəl] *adj* Nerven-.

neuralgia [njʊəˈrældʒə] *n* Neuralgie *f*, Nervenschmerzen *pl.*

neurasthenia [ˌnjʊərəsˈθiːnɪə] *n* Neurasthenie, Nervenschwäche *f.*

neurasthenic [ˌnjʊərəsˈθenɪk] **1** *n* Neurastheniker(in *f*) *m.* **2** *adj* neurasthenisch.

neuritis [njʊəˈraɪtɪs] *n* Neuritis, Nervenentzündung *f.*

neurological [ˌnjʊərəˈlɒdʒɪkəl] *adj* neurologisch.

neurologist [njʊəˈrɒlədʒɪst] *n* Neurologe *m*, Neurologin *f*, Nervenarzt *m*/-ärztin *f.*

neurology [njʊəˈrɒlədʒɪ] *n* Neurologie *f.*

neuron ['njʊərɒn] *n* Neuron *nt.*

neuropath ['njʊərəpæθ] *n* Nervenkranke(r) *mf.*

neuropathic [njʊərəˈpæθɪk] *adj* neuropathisch.

neuropathology [ˌnjʊərəʊpəˈθɒlədʒɪ] *n* Neuropathologie *f*, Lehre *f* von den Nervenkrankheiten.

neurosis [njʊəˈrəʊsɪs] *n*, *pl* **neuroses** [njʊəˈrəʊsiːz] Neurose *f.*

neurosurgeon ['njʊərəʊˌsɜːdʒən] *n* Neurochirurg(in *f*) *m.*

neurosurgery ['njʊərəʊˌsɜːdʒərɪ] *n* Neurochirurgie *f.*

neurotic [njʊəˈrɒtɪk] **1** *adj* neurotisch. **to be** ~ **about sth** (*inf*) in bezug auf etw (*acc*) neurotisch sein; **he's getting rather** ~ **about this problem** das Problem ist bei ihm schon zur Neurose geworden. **2** *n* Neurotiker(in *f*) *m.*

neurotically [njʊəˈrɒtɪkəlɪ] *adv* neurotisch.

neuter ['njuːtə'] **1** *adj* (a) (*Gram*) sächlich. **this word is** ~ dieses Wort ist sächlich *or* ein Neutrum.
(b) animal, person geschlechtslos; (*castrated*) kastriert; plant ungeschlechtlich.
2 *n* (a) (*Gram*) Neutrum *nt*; (*noun also*) sächliches Hauptwort. **in the** ~ in der sächlichen Form, im Neutrum.
(b) (*animal*) geschlechtsloses Wesen; (*castrated*) kastriertes Tier; (*plant*) ungeschlechtliche Pflanze.
3 *vt* cat, dog kastrieren; female sterilisieren.

neutral ['njuːtrəl] **1** *adj* (*all senses*) neutral. **to remain** ~ neutral bleiben.
2 *n* (a) (*person*) Neutrale(r) *mf*; (*country*) neutrales Land.
(b) (*Aut*) Leerlauf *m.* **to be in** ~ im Leerlauf sein; **to put the car/gears in** ~ den Gang herausnehmen.

neutralism ['njuːtrəlɪzəm] *n* Neutralismus *m.*

neutrality [njuːˈtrælɪtɪ] *n* Neutralität *f.*

neutralization [ˌnjuːtrəlaɪˈzeɪʃən] *n* Neutralisation *f*; (*fig*) Aufhebung *f.*

neutralize [njuːtrəlaɪz] *vt* neutralisieren; (*fig*) aufheben; **the force of an argument** die Spitze nehmen (+*dat*). **neutralizing agent** neutralisierender Wirkstoff.

neutrino [njuːˈtriːnəʊ] *n* Neutrino *nt.*

neutron ['njuːtrɒn] *n* Neutron *nt.*

neutron: ~ **bomb** *n* Neutronenbombe *f*; ~ **star** *n* Neutronenstern *m.*

never ['nevə'] *adv* (a) (*not ever*) nie, niemals (*geh*). **I** ~ **eat it** das esse ich nie; **I have** ~ **seen him** ich habe ihn (noch) nie gesehen; ~ **again** nie wieder; ~ **do that again** mach das bloß nie wieder *or* nicht noch einmal; **I'll** ~ **try that again** das werde ich nie wieder *or* nicht noch einmal versuchen; ~ **again will I see my own country** nimmermehr werde ich mein Heimatland sehen (*liter*), ich werde meine Heimat nie wiedersehen; ~ **before** noch nie; **I have** ~ **seen him before, I have** ~ **before seen him** ich habe ihn noch nie gesehen; **I had** ~ **seen him before today** ich hatte ihn (vor heute) noch nie gesehen; ~ **before have men climbed this peak** noch nie hatten *or* nie zuvor haben Menschen diesen Gipfel erklommen; ~ **before had there been such a disaster** eine solche Katastrophe hatte es noch nie (zuvor) gegeben; ~ **even** nicht einmal; ~ **ever** gar *or* absolut *or* garantiert nie; **I have** ~ **ever been so insulted** ich bin noch nie so beleidigt worden; ~ **(ever) in all my life have**

I been so insulted ich bin in meinem ganzen Leben noch nie *or* nicht so beleidigt worden; **I have ~ yet been able to find ...** ich habe ... bisher noch nicht finden können; **I ~ heard such a thing!** so etwas ist mir noch nie zu Ohren gekommen!

  (b) (*emph: not*) **that will ~ do!** das geht ganz und gar nicht!; **I ~ slept a wink** ich habe kein Auge zugetan; **he ~ so much as smiled** er hat nicht einmal gelächelt; **he said ~ a word** er hat kein einziges Wort gesagt; **you've ~ left it behind!** (*inf*) du hast es doch wohl nicht etwa liegenlassen! (*inf*); **you've ~ done that!** hast du das wirklich gemacht?; **would you do it again?** — ~! würdest du das noch einmal machen? — bestimmt nicht; **Spurs were beaten — ~!** (*inf*) Spurs sind geschlagen worden — das ist doch nicht möglich *or* nein! *or* nein wirklich? (*iro*); **well I ~ (did)!** (*inf*) nein, so was!; **~ fear** keine Angst.

never-: ~**-ending** *adj* endlos, unaufhörlich; *discussions, negotiations also* nicht enden wollend *attr*; **it seemed ~-ending** es schien kein Ende nehmen zu wollen; **a ~-ending job** eine Arbeit ohne Ende; ~**-failing** *adj method etc* unfehlbar; *source, spring etc* unversieglich; ~**more** *adv* (*liter*) nimmermehr (*liter*), niemals wieder; **he departed ~more to return** er ging und kehrte niemals wieder (*liter*); ~**-never** *n* (*Brit inf*) **on the ~-never** auf Pump (*inf*); ~**-never land** *n* Wunsch- *or* Traumwelt *f*.

nevertheless [ˌnevəðə'les] *adv* trotzdem, dennoch, nichtsdestoweniger (*geh*).

never-to-be-forgotten ['nevətəbiːfə'gɒtn] *adj attr* unvergeßlich.

new [njuː] *adj* (+*er*) **(a)** neu. **~ moon** Neumond *m*; **there's a ~ moon tonight** heute nacht ist Neumond; **the ~ people at number five** die Neuen in Nummer fünf; **that's nothing ~** das ist nichts Neues; **that's something ~** das ist wirklich ganz was Neues!; **what's ~?** (*inf*) was gibt's Neues? (*inf*); **dressed in ~ clothes** neu eingekleidet; **to make sth (look) like ~** etw wie neu machen; **as ~** wie neu; **this system is ~ to me** dieses System ist mir neu; **he is a ~ man** (*fig*) er ist ein neuer Mensch; **that's a ~ one on me** (*inf*) das ist mir ja ganz neu; (*joke*) den kenne ich noch nicht; **a ~ kind of engine** ein neuartiger Motor.

  (b) (*fresh*) *potatoes* neu; *wine* neu, jung; *bread* frisch.

  (c) (*modern, novel*) modern; *fashion, style* neu. **the ~ woman** die moderne Frau; **the ~ diplomacy** die neue Diplomatie; **the ~ look** (*Fashion*) der New Look.

  (d) (*lately arrived, inexperienced*) *person, pupil, recruit* neu. **the ~ boys/girls** die Neuen *pl*, die neuen Schüler; **the ~ rich** die Neureichen *pl*; **I'm quite ~ to this job/to the company** ich bin neu in dieser Stelle/Firma; **to be ~ to business** ein Neuling im Geschäftsleben sein; **are you ~ here?** sind Sie neu hier?; **I am ~ to this place** ich bin erst seit kurzem hier.

new: ~**-born** *adj* neugeboren; **the ~-born babies** die Neugeborenen; ~**comer** *n* (*who has just arrived*) Neuankömmling *m*; (*in job, subject etc*) Neuling *m* (*to* in +*dat*); **they are ~comers to this town** sie sind neu in dieser Stadt, sie sind Zuzügler; **he is a ~comer to this area of engineering** er ist auf diesem Gebiet der Technik ein Neuling; **for the ~comers I will recap** für diejenigen, die neu dazugekommen sind, fasse ich kurz zusammen.

newel ['njuːəl] *n* (*of spiral staircase*) Spindel *f*; (*supporting banister*) Pfosten *m*.

new: **N~ England** *n* Neuengland *nt*; ~**-fangled** *adj* neumodisch; ~**-fashioned** *adj* modisch, modern; ~**-found** *adj friend, happiness* neu(gefunden); *confidence, hope* neugeschöpft; **N~foundland** 1 *n* Neufundland *nt*; 2 *adj attr* Neufundländer-, neufundländisch; **N~foundland dog** Neufundländer *m*; **N~foundlander** *n* Neufundländer(in *f*) *m*; **N~ Guinea** *n* Neuguinea *nt*.

newish ['njuːɪʃ] *adj* ziemlich neu.

new: ~**-laid** *adj* frisch; ~**-look** *adj* (*inf*) neu.

newly ['njuːlɪ] *adv* frisch. **a ~-dug trench** ein frisch gezogener Graben; ~**-made** ganz neu; *bread, cake etc* ganz frisch; *road, gardens etc* neuangelegt; *grave* frisch.

newlywed ['njuːlɪwed] *n* (*inf*) Neu- *or* Frischvermählte(r) *mf*.

new: **N~ Mexico** *n* New Mexico *nt*; ~**-mown** *adj* frisch gemäht.

newness ['njuːnɪs] *n* Neuheit *f*; (*of bread, cheese etc*) Frische *f*. **his ~ to this job/the trade/this town** die Tatsache, daß er neu in dieser Arbeit ist/daß er Neuling ist/daß er erst seit kurzem in dieser Stadt ist.

new: **N~ Orleans** *n* New Orleans *nt*; **~ penny** *n* (*Brit*) neuer Penny (*in der Dezimalwährung*).

news [njuːz] *n, no pl* (*a*) (*report, information*) Nachricht *f*; (*recent development*) Neuigkeit(en *pl*) *f*. **a piece of ~** eine Neuigkeit; **I have ~/no ~ of him** ich habe von ihm gehört/nicht von ihm gehört, ich weiß Neues/nichts Neues von ihm; **there is no ~** es gibt nichts Neues zu berichten; **have you heard the ~?** haben Sie schon (das Neueste) gehört?; **have you heard the ~ about Fred?** haben Sie schon das Neueste über Fred gehört?; **tell us your ~** erzähl uns die Neuigkeiten *or* das Neueste; **let us have *or* send us some ~ of yourself** lassen Sie mal von sich hören, schreiben Sie mal, was es Neues gibt; **what's your ~?** was gibt's Neues?; **is there any ~?** gibt es etwas Neues?; **I have ~ for you** (*iro*) ich habe eine Überraschung für dich; **bad/sad/good ~** schlimme *or* schlechte/traurige/gute Nachricht; **that is good ~** das ist erfreulich zu hören, das sind ja gute Nachrichten; **when the ~/the ~ of his death broke** als es/sein Tod bekannt wurde; **who will break the ~ to him?** wer wird es ihm sagen *or* beibringen?; **that is ~/no ~ (to me)!** das ist (mir) ganz/nicht neu!; **that isn't exactly ~** das ist nichts Neues; **it will be ~ to him that ...** er wird staunen, daß ...; **~ travels fast** wie sich doch alles herumspricht; **bad ~ travels fast** schlechte Nachrichten verbreiten sich schnell; **no ~ is good ~** keine Nachricht ist gute Nachricht.

  (b) (*Press, Film, Rad, TV*) Nachrichten *pl*. **~ in brief** Kurznachrichten *pl*; **financial ~** Wirtschaftsbericht *m*; **sports ~** Sportnachrichten *pl*; **it was on the ~** das kam in den Nach-

richten; **to be in the ~** von sich reden machen; **to make ~** Schlagzeilen machen; **that's not ~** damit kann man keine Schlagzeilen machen.

news: **~ agency** *n* Nachrichtenagentur *f*, Nachrichtendienst *m*; ~**agent** *n* (*Brit*) Zeitungshändler *m*; ~**-boy** *n* (*US*) Zeitungsjunge *m*; ~ **bulletin** *n* Bulletin *nt*; ~**cast** *n* Nachrichtensendung *f*; ~**caster** *n* Nachrichtensprecher(in *f*) *m*; ~ **cinema** *n* Aktualitätenkino *nt*; ~ **editor** *n* Nachrichtenredakteur *m*; ~**flash** *n* Kurzmeldung *f*; ~**hawk, ~ hound** *n* (*inf*) Zeitungsmann (*inf*), Reporter *m*; ~**headlines** *npl* Kurznachrichten *pl*; (*recap*) Nachrichten *pl* in Kürze; **~ item** *n* Neuigkeit, Nachricht *f*; **the three main ~ items today** die drei Hauptpunkte der Nachrichten; **a short ~ item** (*in paper*) eine Pressenotiz, eine Zeitungsnotiz; ~**letter** *n* Rundschreiben, Mitteilungsblatt *nt*; ~**monger** *n* Klatschmaul *nt*; (*in paper*) Klatschspaltenschreiber *m*.

New South Wales *n* Neu-Süd-Wales *nt*.

newspaper ['njuːzˌpeɪpəʳ] *n* Zeitung *f*. **daily/weekly ~** Tageszeitung/Wochenzeitung; **he works on a ~** er ist bei einer Zeitung beschäftigt.

newspaper: **~ article** *n* Zeitungsartikel *m*; **~ boy** *n* Zeitungsjunge *m*; **~ cutting** *n* Zeitungsausschnitt *m*; **~ man** *n* Zeitungsverkäufer, Zeitungsmann *m*; (*journalist*) Journalist *m*; **~ office** *n* Redaktion *f*; **~ report** *n* Zeitungsbericht *m*.

news: ~**print** *n* Zeitungspapier *nt*; ~**reader** *n* Nachrichtensprecher(in *f*) *m*; ~**reel** *n* Wochenschau *f*; ~**room** *n* (*newspaper*) Nachrichtenredaktion *f*; (*TV, Rad*) Nachrichtenstudio *nt or* -zentrale *f*; ~ **sheet** *n* Informationsblatt *nt*; ~**stand** *n* Zeitungsstand *m*; ~ **story** *n* Bericht *m*; ~ **theatre** *n* Aktualitätenkino *nt*.

new-style ['njuːstaɪl] *adj* im neuen Stil. **calendar ~** Kalender neuen Stils *or* nach neuer Zeitrechnung.

news: ~ **vendor** *n* Zeitungsverkäufer(in *f*) *m*; ~**worthy** *adj* sensationell; **to be ~worthy** Neuigkeitswert haben.

newsy ['njuːzɪ] *adj* (+*er*) (*inf*) voller Neuigkeiten.

newt [njuːt] *n* Wassermolch *m*. **as drunk as a ~** voll wie eine Strandhaubitze.

new: **N~ Testament** 1 *n* **the N~ Testament** das Neue Testament; 2 *adj attr* des Neuen Testaments; ~ **wave** 1 *n* (*in films*) neue Welle; 2 *adj attr* der neuen Welle; **the N~ World** *n* die Neue Welt.

New Year *n* neues Jahr; (~'s *Day*) Neujahr *nt*. **to bring in *or* see in the ~** das neue Jahr begrüßen; **Happy ~!** (ein) glückliches *or* gutes neues Jahr!; **over/at ~** über/an Neujahr; **~'s Day**, (*US also*) **~'s Day** Neujahr *nt*, Neujahrstag *m*; **~'s Eve** Silvester, Sylvester *nt*; **~ resolution** (guter) Vorsatz für das neue Jahr.

New: **~ York** 1 *n* New York *nt*; 2 *adj attr* New Yorker; **~ Yorker** *n* New Yorker(in *f*) *m*; **~ Zealand** 1 *n* Neuseeland *nt*; 2 *adj attr* Neuseeländer *attr*, neuseeländisch; **~ Zealander** *n* Neuseeländer(in *f*) *m*.

next [nekst] **1** *adj* **(a)** (*in place*) nächste(r, s).

  (b) (*in time*) nächste(r, s). **come back ~ week/Tuesday** kommen Sie nächste Woche/nächsten Dienstag wieder; **he came back the ~ day/week** er kam am nächsten Tag/in der nächsten Woche wieder; **(the) ~ time I see him** wenn ich ihn das nächste Mal sehe; **the ~ time I saw him** als ich ihn das nächste Mal sah; **(the) ~ moment he was gone** im nächsten Moment war er weg; **from one moment to the ~** von einem Moment zum anderen; **this time ~ week** nächste Woche um diese Zeit; **the year/week after ~** übernächstes Jahr/übernächste Woche; **the ~ day but one** der übernächste Tag.

  (c) (*order*) nächste(r, s). **who's ~?** wer ist der nächste?; **you're ~** Sie sind dran (*inf*) *or* an der Reihe; **~ please!** der nächste bitte!; **I come ~ after you** ich bin nach Ihnen an der Reihe *or* dran (*inf*); **I knew I was the ~ person to speak** ich wußte, daß ich als nächster sprechen sollte; **I'll ask the very ~ person (I see)** ich frage den nächsten(, den ich sehe); **my name is ~ on the list** mein Name kommt als nächster auf der Liste; **the ~ but one/die/das übernächste; **the ~ thing to do is (to) polish** als nächstes poliert man (es); **the ~ size smaller/bigger** die nächstkleinere/nächstgrößere Größe; **the ~ best** der/die/das nächstbeste; **the ~ tallest/oldest boy** (*second in order*) der zweitgrößte/zweitälteste Junge; **she is my ~ best friend** sie ist meine zweitbeste Freundin.

  2 *adv* **(a)** (*the ~ time*) das nächste Mal; (*afterwards*) danach. **what shall we do ~?** und was sollen wir als nächstes machen?; **when shall we meet ~?** wann treffen wir uns wieder *or* das nächste Mal?; **a new dress! what ~?** ein neues Kleid? sonst noch was?; **whatever ~?** (*in surprise*) Sachen gibt's! (*inf*); (*despairingly*) wo soll das nur hinführen?

  (b) **~ to sb/sth** neben jdm/etw; (*with motion*) neben jdn/etw; **the ~ to last row** die vorletzte Reihe; **he was ~ to last** er war der vorletzte; **the ~ to bottom shelf** das vorletzte Brett, das zweitunterste Brett; **~ to the skin** (*direkt*) auf der Haut; **~ to nothing/nobody** so gut wie nichts/niemand; **~ to impossible** nahezu unmöglich; **the thing ~ to my heart** (*most important*) was mir am meisten am Herzen liegt; (*dearest*) das mir liebste.

  3 *n* nächste(r) *mf*; (*child*) nächste(s) *nt*.

  4 *prep* (*old*) neben (+*dat*).

next-door ['neksdɔːʳ] **1** *adv* nebenan. **they live ~ to us** sie wohnen (direkt) neben uns *or* (gleich) nebenan; **we live ~ to each other** wir wohnen Tür an Tür; **the boy ~** der Junge von nebenan; **it's ~ to madness** das grenzt an Wahnsinn; **if he isn't mad he's ~ to it** wenn er nicht so nicht verrückt ist, ist er jedenfalls nicht weit davon entfernt.

  2 *adj* **the ~ neighbour/house** der direkte Nachbar/das Nebenhaus; **we are ~ neighbours** wir wohnen Tür an Tür.

next of kin *n, pl* - nächster Verwandter, nächste Verwandte, nächste Verwandte *pl*.

nexus ['neksəs] *n* Verknüpfung, Verkettung *f*. **the ~ of ties between these countries** die Verflochtenheit dieser Länder.

NF (*Brit*) *abbr of* **National Front**.
NFU (*Brit*) *abbr of* **National Farmers' Union**.
NHS (*Brit*) *abbr of* **National Health Service**.
niacin ['naɪəsɪn] *n* Nikotinsäure *f*, Niacin *nt* (*spec*).
Niagara [naɪˈægrə] *n* Niagara *m*. **(the)** ~ **Falls** die Niagarafälle *pl*.
nib [nɪb] *n* Feder *f*; (*point of* ~) (Feder)spitze *f*.
nibble ['nɪbl] **1** *vt* knabbern; (*pick at*) *food* nur anessen, herumnagen an (+*dat*) (*inf*).
  2 *vi* (*at an* +*dat*) knabbern; (*pick at*) herumnagen an (+*dat*) (*inf*); (*fig*) sich interessiert zeigen; **to** ~ **at the bait/an offer** (*fig*) sich interessiert zeigen.
  3 *n* **I think I've got a** ~ ich glaube, bei mir beißt einer an; **I feel like a** ~ (*inf*) ich habe Appetit auf etwas, ich brauche etwas zwischen die Zähne (*hum inf*).
nibs [nɪbz] *n* (*hum inf*): **his** ~ der hohe Herr (*hum*), seine Herrlichkeit (*hum inf*).
Nicaragua [ˌnɪkəˈrægjʊə] *n* Nicaragua *nt*.
Nicaraguan [ˌnɪkəˈrægjʊən] **1** *adj* nicaraguanisch. **2** *n* Nicaraguaner(in *f*) *m*.
nice [naɪs] *adj* (+*er*) **(a)** *nett*; *person, ways, voice also* sympathisch; (~-*looking*) *girl, dress, looks etc also* hübsch; *weather* schön, gut; *taste, smell, meal, whisky* gut; *warmth, feeling, car* schön; *food* gut, lecker; (*skilful*) *workmanship, work* gut, schön, fein. **be** ~ **to him** sei nett zu ihm; **that's not** ~! das ist aber nicht nett; **be a** ~ **girl and ... sei lieb und ...**; **to have a** ~ **time** sich gut amüsieren; **I had a** ~ **rest** ich habe mich gut *or* schön ausgeruht; **it's** ~ **to be needed** es ist schön, gebraucht zu werden; **how** ~ **of you to ...** wie nett *or* lieb von Ihnen, zu ...; **that's a** ~ **one** der/die/das ist toll (*inf*) *or* prima (*inf*); **he has a** ~ **taste in ties** er hat einen guten Geschmack, was Krawatten angeht.
  (b) (*intensifier*) schön. **a** ~ **long holiday** schön lange Ferien; ~ **and warm/near/quickly** schön warm/nahe/schnell; ~ **and easy** ganz leicht; **take it** ~ **and easy** überanstrengen Sie sich nicht; ~ **and easy does it** immer schön sachte.
  (c) (*respectable*) *girl* nett; *district* fein; *words* schön; (*refined*) *manners* gut, fein. **not a** ~ **word/district/book** gar kein schönes Wort/Viertel/Buch; **our neighbours are not exactly very** ~ **people** unsere Nachbarn sind nicht gerade feine Leute.
  (d) (*iro*) nett, schön, sauber (*all iro*). **here's a** ~ **state of affairs!** das sind ja schöne *or* nette Zustände!; **you're in a** ~ **mess** du sitzt schön im Schlamassel (*inf*); **that's a** ~ **way to talk to your mother** das ist ja eine schöne Art, mit deiner Mutter zu sprechen, **wie sprichst du denn mit deiner Mutter?**
  (e) (*subtle*) *distinction, shade of meaning* fein, genau. **overly** ~ **distinctions** überfeine *or* subtile Unterscheidungen; **that was a** ~ **point** das war eine gute Bemerkung; **one** *or* **two** ~ **points** ein paar brauchbare *or* gute Gedanken.
  (f) (*hard to please*) *person* anspruchsvoll, pingelig (*inf*), heikel (*dial*). **to be** ~ **about one's food** in bezug aufs Essen wählerisch *or* pingelig (*inf*) *or* heikel (*dial*) sein.
nice-looking ['naɪs'lʊkɪŋ] *adj* gut aussehend; *girl also, face, dress etc* nett aussehend; *hotel, village, girl* hübsch. **to be** ~ gut aussehen.
nicely ['naɪslɪ] *adv* **(a)** (*pleasantly*) nett; (*well*) *go, speak, behave, placed* gut. **to go** ~ wie geschmiert laufen (*inf*); **she thanked me** ~ sie hat sich nett bei mir bedankt; **eat up/say thank you** ~! iß mal schön auf/sag mal schön danke!; **that will do** ~ das reicht vollauf; **how's it going?** — ~, **thank you** wie geht es so? — danke, ganz gut; **a** ~ **situated home** ein hübsch gelegenes Haus; **to be** ~ **spoken** sich gepflegt ausdrücken; **he's such a** ~ **spoken young man** es ist eine Freude, diesem jungen Mann zuzuhören; ~ **done** gut gemacht, prima (*inf*); **when it's** ~ **warmed up** wenn es schön warmgelaufen ist.
  (b) (*carefully*) *distinguish* genau, fein.
niceness ['naɪsnɪs] *n* **(a)** (*pleasantness*) (*of person, behaviour*) Nettigkeit *f*; (*nice appearance*) nettes *or* hübsches Aussehen; (*skilfulness*) Qualität, Feinheit *f*.
  (b) (*subtlety*) Feinheit, Genauigkeit *f*.
  (c) (*fastidiousness*) anspruchsvolle Art, Pingeligkeit (*inf*), Heikelkeit (*dial*) *f*.
nicety ['naɪsɪtɪ] *n* **(a)** (*subtlety*) Feinheit *f*; (*of judgement also*) Schärfe *f*; (*precision*) (peinliche) Genauigkeit. **to a** ~ äußerst *or* sehr genau; **a point/question of some** ~ ein feiner *or* subtiler Punkt/eine subtile Frage.
  (b) **niceties** *pl* Feinheiten, Details *pl*.
niche [niːʃ] *n* (*Archit*) Nische *f*; (*fig*) Plätzchen *nt*.
Nicholas ['nɪkələs] *n* Nikolaus *m*.
Nick [nɪk] *n abbr of* **Nicholas**. **Old** ~ (*inf*) der Böse, der Leibhaftige (*old*).
nick[1] [nɪk] **1** *n* **(a)** Kerbe *f*. **I got a little** ~ **on my chin** ich habe mich leicht am Kinn geschnitten.
  (b) **in the** ~ **of time** gerade noch (rechtzeitig).
  (c) (*Brit inf*: *condition*) **in good/bad** ~ gut/nicht gut in Schuß (*inf*).
  2 *vt* **(a)** *wood, stick* einkerben. **to** ~ **oneself** *or* **one's chin** (*inf*) sich (am Kinn) schneiden.
  (b) (*bullet*) *person, wall, arm* streifen.
nick[2] (*Brit*) **1** *vt* (*inf*) **(a)** (*arrest*) einsperren (*inf*), einlochen (*inf*); (*catch*) schnappen (*inf*). **he got** ~ed den haben sie sich (*dat*) gekascht (*sl*) *or* geschnappt (*inf*).
  (b) (*steal*) klauen (*inf*), mitgehen lassen (*inf*).
  2 *n* (*sl*) (*prison*) Kittchen *nt* (*inf*), Knast *m* (*sl*); (*police station*) Wache *f*, Revier *nt*.
nick[3] *vt* (*US sl*) **to** ~ **sb for sth** jdm etw abknöpfen (+*dat*) (*inf*).
nickel ['nɪkl] *n* **(a)** (*metal*) Nickel *nt*. **(b)** (*US*) Nickel *m*, Fünfcentstück *nt*.
nickelodeon [ˌnɪkəlˈəʊdɪən] *n* (*US dated*) **(a)** (Film-/ Varieté)theater *nt* (mit Eintrittspreisen von 5 Cent). **(b)** (*jukebox*) Musikbox *f*.

nickel-plated ['nɪkl͵pleɪtɪd] *adj* vernickelt.
nicker ['nɪkəʳ] *n, pl* - (*Brit sl*) Lappen *m* (*sl*).
nickname ['nɪkneɪm] **1** *n* Spitzname *m*. **2** *vt* *person* betiteln, taufen (*inf*). **they** ~**d him Baldy** sie gaben ihm den Spitznamen Glatzköpfchen.
nicotine ['nɪkətiːn] *n* Nikotin *nt*.
nicotine: ~ **poisoning** *n* Nikotinvergiftung *f*; ~**-stained** *adj* gelb von Nikotin; *fingers also* nikotingelb.
niece [niːs] *n* Nichte *f*.
niff [nɪf] *n* (*Brit inf*) Mief *m* (*inf*).
niffy ['nɪfɪ] *adj* (+*er*) (*Brit inf*) muffig (*inf*).
nifty ['nɪftɪ] *adj* (+*er*) (*smart*) flott (*inf*); *gadget, tool* schlau (*inf*); (*quick*) *person* flott (*inf*), fix (*inf*). **a** ~ **piece of work** gute *or* lockere (*sl*) Arbeit; **he's pretty** ~ **with a gun** er hat ein lockeres Händchen mit dem Schießeisen (*inf*); **you'd better be** ~ **about it!** und ein bißchen dalli (*inf*); **a** ~ **little car** ein netter kleiner Flitzer (*inf*).
Niger ['naɪdʒəʳ] *n* Niger *m*.
Nigeria [naɪˈdʒɪərɪə] *n* Nigeria *nt*.
Nigerian [naɪˈdʒɪərɪən] **1** *adj* nigerianisch. **2** *n* Nigerianer(in *f*) *m*.
niggardliness ['nɪgədlɪnɪs] *n* *see adj* Knaus(e)rigkeit *f*; Armseligkeit, Kümmerlichkeit *f*.
niggardly ['nɪgədlɪ] *adj* *person* knaus(e)rig; *amount, portion also* armselig, kümmerlich.
nigger ['nɪgəʳ] *n* (*pej*) Nigger *m* (*pej inf*). **so you're the** ~ **in the woodpile** Sie sind es also, der querschießt; **there's a** ~ **in the woodpile** irgend jemand schießt quer (*inf*); (*snag*) da ist ein Haken dran (*inf*).
niggle ['nɪgl] **1** *vi* (*complain*) (herum)kritteln (*inf*), herumkritisieren (*about an* +*dat*). **2** *vt* (*worry*) plagen, quälen, zu schaffen machen (+*dat*).
niggling ['nɪglɪŋ] **1** *adj* *person* kritt(e)lig (*inf*), überkritisch; *question, doubt, pain* bohrend, quälend; *detail* pingelig (*inf*); *feeling* ungut. **2** *n* Krittelei, Meckern (*inf*) *nt*.
nigh [naɪ] **1** *adj* (*old, liter*) nahe. **2** *adv* (*old, liter*) **to draw** ~ sich nahen (*old, geh*) (*to dat*). **(b)** ~ **on** nahezu (*geh*); **it is well** ~ **impossible** es ist nahezu unmöglich. **3** *prep* (*old, liter*) nahe (+*dat*).
night [naɪt] **1** *n* **(a)** Nacht *f*; (*evening*) Abend *m*. **I saw him last** ~ ich habe ihn gestern abend gesehen; **I'll see him tomorrow** ~ ich treffe ihn morgen abend; **I stayed with them last** ~ ich habe heute *or* letzte Nacht bei ihnen übernachtet; **to stay four** ~**s with sb** vier Nächte lang bei jdm bleiben; **I'll stay with them tomorrow** ~ ich übernachte morgen nacht bei ihnen; **on Friday** ~ Freitag abend/nacht; **on the** ~ **of (Saturday) the 11th** am (Samstag, dem) 11. nachts; **11/6 o'clock at** ~ 11 Uhr nachts/6 Uhr abends; **to travel/see Paris by** ~ nachts reisen/Paris bei Nacht sehen; **far into the** ~ bis spät in die Nacht, bis in die späte Nacht; **in/during the** ~ in/während der Nacht; **the** ~ **before** they were ... am Abend/die Nacht zuvor waren sie ...; **the** ~ **before last** they were ... vorgestern abend/vorletzte Nacht waren sie ...; **to spend the** ~ at a hotel in einem Hotel übernachten; **to have a good/bad** ~/~**'s sleep** gut/schlecht schlafen; (*patient also*) eine gute/schlechte Nacht haben; **I need a good** ~**'s sleep** ich muß mal wieder ordentlich schlafen; **night-night!** (*inf*) gut Nacht! (*inf*); ~ **after** ~ jede Nacht, Nacht um Nacht (*geh*); **all** ~ **(long)** die ganze Nacht; ~ **and day** (*lit, fig*) Tag und Nacht; **to have a** ~ **out** (abends) ausgehen; **a** ~ **out with the lads** ein Abend mit den Kumpeln; **to make a** ~ **of it** durchmachen (*inf*); **to have/get a late/an early** ~ spät/früh ins Bett kommen, spät/früh schlafen gehen; **too many late** ~**s!** zu wenig Schlaf!; **late** ~**s are not good for you** es ist nicht gut, wenn man so spät schlafen geht; **after your early** ~ nachdem du so früh schlafen gegangen bist; **to work** ~**s nachts** arbeiten; **to be on** ~**s** (*policeman, nurse etc*) Nachtdienst haben; (*shift worker*) Nachtschicht haben.
  (b) (*darkness*) Nacht *f*. ~ **is falling** die Nacht bricht herein; **the** ~ **of the soul** (*fig*) die Nacht der Seele.
  (c) (*Theat*) Abend *m*. **last three** ~**s of** ... die letzten drei Abende von ...; **a Mozart** ~ ein Mozartabend *m*; *see* **first** ~.
  2 *adv* ~**s** (*esp US*) nachts.
night *in cpds* Nacht-; ~**-bird** *n* Nachtvogel *m*; (*fig*) Nachteule *f* (*inf*), Nachtschwärmer *m*; ~**-blindness** *n* Nachtblindheit *f*; ~**cap** *n* (*garment*) Nachtmütze *f*; (*for woman*) Nachthaube *f*; **(b)** (*drink*) Schlummertrunk *m* (*inf*); ~**clothes** *npl* Nachtzeug *nt*, Nachtwäsche *f* (*esp Comm*); ~**club** *n* Nachtlokal *nt or* -klub *m*; ~**dress** *n* Nachthemd, Nachtgewand (*geh*) *nt*; ~ **editor** *n* Redakteur *m* vom Nachtdienst; ~**fall** *n* Einbruch *m* der Dunkelheit; **at** ~**fall** bei Einbruch der Dunkelheit; ~**fighter** *n* Nachtjäger *m*; ~ **flight** *n* Nachtflug *m*; ~**gown** *n* Nachthemd *nt*; ~**-hawk** *n* (*US*) (*lit*) Amerikanischer Ziegenmelker; (*fig*) Nachtschwärmer *m*.
nightie ['naɪtɪ] *n* (*inf*) Nachthemd *nt*.
nightingale ['naɪtɪŋgeɪl] *n* Nachtigall *f*.
night: ~**jar** *n* Ziegenmelker *m*, Nachtschwalbe *f*; ~ **letter** *n* (*US*) (*zu billigem Tarif gesandtes*) Nachttelegramm *nt*; ~**-life** *n* Nachtleben *nt*; ~**-light** *n* **(a)** (*for child etc*) Nachtlicht *nt*; **(b)** (*for teapot etc*) Teelicht *nt*; ~**long** *adj* sich über die ganze Nacht hinziehend; (*lasting several nights*) nächtelang; **after their** ~**long vigil/discussion** nachdem sie die ganze Nacht gewacht/diskutiert hatten.
nightly ['naɪtlɪ] **1** *adj* (*every night*) (all)nächtlich, Nacht-; (*every evening*) (all)abendlich, Abend-. ~ **performances** (*Theat*) allabendliche Vorstellung.
  2 *adv* (*every night*) jede Nacht/jeden Abend. **performances/ three performances** ~ jeden Abend Vorstellung/drei Vorstellungen; **twice** ~ zweimal pro Abend.
nightmare ['naɪtmɛəʳ] *n* (*lit, fig*) Alptraum *m*. **that was a** ~ **of a journey** die Reise war ein Alptraum.
nightmarish ['naɪtmɛərɪʃ] *adj* grauenhaft, alptraumhaft.

night: ~-**nurse** n Nachtschwester f; (man) Nachtpfleger m; ~**owl** n (inf) Nachteule f (inf); ~-**porter** n Nachtportier m; ~**safe** n Nachtsafe m; ~**school** n Abendschule f.

nightshade ['naɪtʃeɪd] n Nachtschatten m; see **deadly** ~.

night: ~-**shift** n Nachtschicht f; to be or work on ~-**shift** Nachtschicht haben or arbeiten; ~-**shirt** n (Herren)nachthemd nt; ~**sky** n nächtlicher Himmel; ~-**spot** n Nachtlokal nt; ~**stick** n (US) Schlagstock m; ~-**storage heater** n Nachtspeicherofen m; ~-**time** 1 n Nacht f; at ~-**time** nachts; in the ~-**time** während der Nacht, nachts; 2 adj attr nächtlich, Nacht-; ~-**watch** n Nachtwache f; ~-**watchman** n Nachtwächter m; ~**wear** n Nachtzeug nt, Nachtwäsche f (esp Comm).

nihilism ['naɪlɪzəm] n Nihilismus m.

nihilist ['naɪlɪst] n Nihilist(in f) m.

nihilistic [ˌnaɪ'lɪstɪk] adj nihilistisch.

nil [nɪl] n (zero) null (also Sport); (nothing) nichts. the score was one—es stand eins zu null; the response etc was ~ die Reaktion etc war gleich null.

Nile [naɪl] n Nil m.

nimble ['nɪmbl] adj (+ er) (quick) fingers, feet flink; person also behende (geh); (agile) gelenkig, wendig, beweglich; (skilful) geschickt; mind beweglich. as ~ as a goat leichtfüßig (wie eine Gemse); she is still ~ sie ist noch sehr rüstig.

nimble: ~-**fingered** adj fingerfertig; ~-**footed** adj leichtfüßig.

nimbleness ['nɪmblnɪs] n see adj Flinkheit f; Behendigkeit f (geh); Gelenkigkeit, Wendigkeit, Beweglichkeit f; Geschicklichkeit f, Geschick nt; Beweglichkeit f.

nimble-witted ['nɪmbl,wɪtɪd] adj schlagfertig.

nimbly ['nɪmblɪ] adv work, respond flink; dance leicht(füßig); jump, climb gelenkig, behende (geh). her fingers moved ~ ihre Finger bewegten sich leicht und flink.

nimbus ['nɪmbəs] n (a) (Liter: halo) Nimbus (geh), Heiligenschein m. (b) (Met) see **cumulonimbus**.

nincompoop ['nɪŋkəmpuːp] n (inf) Trottel m, Simpel (inf) m.

nine [naɪn] 1 adj neun. ~ **times out of ten** in neun Zehntel der Fälle, so gut wie immer; to have ~ **lives** ein zähes Leben haben; a ~ **days' wonder** eine Eintagsfliege (inf). 2 n Neun f. dressed up to the ~s in Schale (inf); the N~ (Pol) die Neun; see also **six**.

ninepins ['naɪnpɪnz] n (game) Kegeln nt. to go down like ~ (fig) wie die Fliegen umfallen (inf).

nineteen ['naɪn'tiːn] 1 adj neunzehn. 2 n Neunzehn f. she **talks** ~ **to the dozen** sie redet wie ein Wasserfall (inf); they were talking ~ **to the dozen** sie redeten, was das Zeug hielt (inf); see also **sixteen**.

nineteenth ['naɪn'tiːnθ] 1 adj (in series) neunzehnte(r, s); (as fraction) neunzehntel. the ~ (**hole**) (Golf inf) das neunzehnte Loch (Bar im Clubhaus). 2 n Neunzehnte(r, s); Neunzehntel nt; see also **sixteenth**.

ninetieth ['naɪntɪɪθ] 1 adj (in series) neunzigste(r, s); (as fraction) neunzigstel. 2 n Neunzigste(r, s); Neunzigstel nt.

ninety ['naɪntɪ] 1 adj neunzig. 2 n Neunzig f. the **temperature was up in the nineties** die Temperatur war über 90° Fahrenheit gestiegen; see also **sixty**.

ninny ['nɪnɪ] n (inf) Dussel m (inf).

ninth [naɪnθ] 1 adj (in series) neunte(r, s); (as fraction) neuntel. 2 n Neunte(r, s); Neuntel nt; (Mus) None f; see also **sixth**.

Nip [nɪp] n (pej) Japs(e) m (inf).

nip[1] [nɪp] 1 n (a) (pinch) Kniff m; (bite from animal etc) Biß m. to give sb a ~ in the arm jdn in den Arm zwicken or kneifen; (dog) jdn in den Arm zwicken; the dog gave him a ~ der Hund hat kurz zugeschnappt; it was ~ and tuck (esp US inf) das war eine knappe Sache; they came up to the finishing line ~ and tuck sie lagen vor dem Ziel praktisch auf gleicher Höhe.

(b) there's a ~ in the air today es ist ganz schön frisch heute.

2 vt (a) (bite) zwicken; (pinch also) kneifen. the dog ~ped his ankle der Hund hat ihm am Knöchel gezwickt; to ~ oneself/ one's finger in sth sich (dat) den Finger in etw (dat) klemmen.

(b) (Hort) bud, shoot abknipsen. to ~ sth in the bud (fig) etw im Keim ersticken.

(c) (cold, frost etc) plants angreifen. the cold air ~ped our faces die Kälte schnitt uns ins Gesicht; the plants had been ~ped by the frost, the frost had ~ped the plants die Pflanzen hatten Frost abbekommen.

3 vi (Brit inf) sausen (inf), flitzen (inf). to ~ up(stairs)/down(stairs) hoch-/runtersausen (inf) or -flitzen (inf); I'll just ~ down to the shops ich gehe mal kurz einkaufen (inf); I'll just ~ round to his place ich gehe mal kurz bei ihm vorbei (inf); I'll ~ on ahead ich gehe schon mal voraus (inf).

♦ **nip along** vi (Brit inf) entlangsausen (inf) or -flitzen (inf). ~ to Joan's house lauf or saus mal schnell zu Joan rüber (inf).

♦ **nip in** vi (Brit inf) hinein-/hereinsausen (inf); (call in) auf einen Sprung vorbeikommen/-gehen. I've just ~ped ~ for a minute ich bin nur für ein Minütchen vorbeigekommen (inf); he just ~ped ~ to the pub for a drink er ging auf einen Sprung or nur mal kurz in die Kneipe (inf); to ~ ~ and out of the traffic sich durch den Verkehr schlängeln; he ~ped ~ in front of the others er setzte sich - wutsch - vor die anderen (inf).

♦ **nip off** 1 vi (Brit inf) davonsausen (inf). 2 vt sep twig abknicken; (with clippers etc) abzwicken. he ~ped ~ the end of his finger er hat sich (dat) die Fingerspitze gekappt.

♦ **nip out** vi (Brit inf) hinaus-/heraussausen (inf); (out of house etc) kurz weggehen (inf).

nip[2] n (inf: drink) Schlückchen nt.

nipper ['nɪpə'] n (a) (Zool) Schere, Zange f. (b) (Brit inf: child) Steppke m (inf).

nipple ['nɪpl] n (a) (Anat) Brustwarze f; (US: on baby's bottle) Sauger, Schnuller (inf) m. (b) (Aut) Nippel m.

nippy ['nɪpɪ] adj (+ er) (a) (Brit inf) flink, flott; car, motor spritzig. be ~ about it ein bißchen zack zack (inf) or dalli dalli (inf). (b) (sharp, cold) weather frisch; wind also beißend.

Nirvana [nɪə'vɑːnə] n Nirwana nt.

nisi ['naɪsaɪ] conj see **decree**.

Nissen hut ['nɪsn,hʌt] n (Brit) Nissenhütte f.

nit [nɪt] n (a) (Zool) Nisse, Niß f. (b) (Brit inf) Dummkopf, Blödmann (inf) m.

niter n (US) see **nitre**.

nit-picking ['nɪtpɪkɪŋ] adj (inf) kleinlich, pingelig (inf).

nitrate ['naɪtreɪt] n Nitrat nt.

nitre, (US) **niter** ['naɪtə'] n Salpeter m or nt.

nitric ['naɪtrɪk] adj (of nitrogen) Stickstoff-; (of nitre) Salpeter-.

nitric: ~ **acid** n Salpetersäure f; ~ **oxide** n Stick(stoffmon)oxyd nt.

nitrogen ['naɪtrədʒən] n Stickstoff m.

nitrogen in cpds Stickstoff-.

nitroglycerin(e) ['naɪtrəʊ'glɪsəriːn] n Nitroglyzerin nt.

nitrous ['naɪtrəs] n: ~ **acid** n salpetrige Säure; ~ **oxide** n Distickstoffmonoxyd, Lachgas nt.

nitty-gritty ['nɪtɪ'grɪtɪ] n (inf) to get down to the ~ zur Sache kommen.

nitwit ['nɪtwɪt] n (inf) Dummkopf, Schwachkopf (inf) m.

nix [nɪks] n (sl) nix (inf).

NNE abbr of north-north-east NNO.

NNW abbr of north-north-west NNW.

No, no abbr of (a) north N. (b) number Nr.

no [nəʊ] 1 adv (a) (negative) nein. oh ~! o nein!; to answer ~ (to question) mit Nein antworten, verneinen; (to request) nein sagen; she can't say ~ sie kann nicht nein sagen; the answer is ~ da muß ich nein sagen; (as emphatic reply also) nein (und noch mal nein); I wouldn't do it for £10, ~ not for £100 ich würde es nicht für £ 10, nicht einmal für £ 100 tun.

(b) (not) nicht. whether he comes or ~ er kommt oder nicht; hungry or ~, you'll eat it ob du Hunger hast oder nicht, das wird gegessen (inf).

(c) (with comp) nicht. I can bear it ~ longer ich kann es nicht länger ertragen; I have ~ more money ich habe kein Geld mehr; he has ~ more than anyone else er hat auch nicht mehr als jeder andere; I'm ~ less tired than you are ich bin auch nicht weniger müde als du; ~ later than Monday spätestens Montag; ~ longer ago than last week erst letzte Woche.

2 adj (a) (not any: also with numerals and "other") kein. a person of ~ intelligence ein Mensch ohne jede Intelligenz; a person of ~ integrity ein unredlicher Mensch; ~ one person could do it keiner könnte das allein tun; ~ two men could be less alike zwei verschiedenere Menschen könnte es nicht geben; ~ other man kein anderer; it's of ~ interest/importance das ist belanglos/unwichtig; it's ~ use or good das hat keinen Zweck.

(b) (forbidding) ~ parking/smoking Parken/Rauchen verboten; ~ surrender! wir kapitulieren nicht!

(c) (with gerund) there's ~ saying or telling what he'll do next man kann nie wissen, was er als nächstes tun wird; there's ~ denying it es läßt sich nicht leugnen; there's ~ pleasing him ihm kann man es auch nie recht machen.

(d) (emph) she's ~ genius/beauty sie ist nicht gerade ein Genie/eine Schönheit; president or ~ president Präsident hin oder her, Präsident oder nicht; this is ~ place for children das ist hier nichts für Kinder; I'm ~ expert, but ... ich bin ja kein Fachmann, aber ...; in ~ time im Nu; it's ~ small matter das ist keine Kleinigkeit; ~ little difficulty was caused by her objections ihre Einwände bereiteten einige Schwierigkeiten; theirs is ~ easy task sie haben keine leichte Aufgabe; there is ~ such thing so etwas gibt es nicht; it was/we did ~ such thing bestimmt nicht, nichts dergleichen; I'll do ~ such thing ich werde mich hüten.

3 n, pl -es Nein nt; (~ vote) Neinstimme f. I won't take ~ for an answer ich bestehe darauf, ich lasse nicht locker; he's the type who won't take ~ for an answer er läßt sich nicht mit einem Nein abspeisen, er läßt nicht locker; the ~es have it die Mehrheit ist dagegen.

Noah ['nəʊə] n Noah m. ~'s ark die Arche Noah.

nob[1] [nɒb] n (inf) einer der besseren Leute (inf). all the ~s all die besseren Leute (inf), alles, was Rang und Namen hat; he thinks he's a real ~ er meint, er sei was besseres (inf).

nob[2] n (inf: head) Rübe f (inf).

no-ball [nəʊ'bɔːl] n (Cricket) wegen Übertreten ungültiger Ball.

nobble ['nɒbl] vt (Brit inf) (a) horse, dog lahmlegen (inf). (b) (catch) sich (dat) schnappen (inf). (c) (obtain dishonestly) votes etc (sich dat) kaufen; money einsacken (inf).

Nobel prize [ˈnəʊbel'praɪz] n Nobelpreis m. ~ **winner** Nobelpreisträger(in f) m.

nobility [nəʊ'bɪlɪtɪ] n, no pl (a) (people) (Hoch)adel m. she is one of the ~ sie ist eine Adlige.

(b) (quality) Adel m, Edle(s) nt. ~ **of mind/thought** geistiger Adel; ~ **of feelings/sentiment** edle Gefühle pl/edles Gefühl; ~ **of ideals** hohe Ideale pl.

noble ['nəʊbl] 1 adj (+ er) (a) (aristocratic) person, rank adlig. to be of ~ birth adlig sein, von edler or adliger Geburt sein.

(b) (fine) person, deed, thought etc edel, nobel; appearance vornehm; soul, mind also adlig; (brave) resistance heldenhaft, wacker. the ~ art of self-defence die edle Kunst der Selbstverteidigung; that was a ~ attempt das war ein löblicher Versuch.

(c) monument stattlich, prächtig; stag also kapital.

(d) (inf: selfless) edel, großmütig, edelmütig. how ~ of you! (iro) zu gütig.

(e) metal edel, Edel-.

2 n Adlige(r) mf, Edelmann m (Hist). the ~s die Adligen or Edelleute (Hist).

noble: ~**man** n Adlige(r), Edelmann (Hist) m; ~-**minded** adj edel gesinnt, vornehm.

nobleness ['nəʊblnɪs] n (a) (of person) Adligkeit f; (of birth, rank) Vornehmheit f.

(b) (of deed, thought) Vornehmheit f; (of person) edle or noble

Gesinnung; (of soul, mind also) Adel m; (braveness) Heldenhaftigkeit f.
(c) (impressiveness) Stattlichkeit f.
(d) (inf: selflessness) Großmütigkeit f; (of person also) Großmut, Edelmut m.
noblesse oblige [nəʊ'blesəʊ'bli:ʒ] Adel verpflichtet, noblesse oblige.
noblewoman ['nəʊblwʊmən] n, pl -women [-wɪmɪn] Adlige f; (married also) Edelfrau f (Hist); (unmarried also) Edelfräulein nt (Hist).
nobly ['nəʊblɪ] adv (a) (aristocratically) vornehm. ~ born von edler Geburt; to be ~ connected Beziehungen pl zum Adel haben.
(b) (finely) edel, vornehm; (bravely) wacker, heldenhaft. you've done ~ du hast dich wacker geschlagen (inf).
(c) (impressively) proportioned prächtig, prachtvoll.
(d) (inf: selflessly) nobel, edel(mütig), großmütig.
nobody ['nəʊbədɪ] 1 pron niemand, keiner. who saw him? — ~ wer hat ihn gesehen? — niemand; ~ knows better than I niemand or keiner weiß besser als ich; there was ~ else da war niemand anderes or sonst niemand; ~ else could have done it es kann niemand anders or kein anderer gewesen sein; ~ else but you can do it nur du kannst das, niemand or außer dir kann das niemand; ~ else offered to give them money sonst hat sich keiner or niemand angeboten, ihnen Geld zu geben; like ~'s business wie nichts; the speed he works at is ~'s business er arbeitet wie kein anderer, er arbeitet mit einem Affentempo (inf); he's ~'s fool er ist nicht auf den Kopf gefallen.
2 n Niemand m no pl, Nichts nt no pl, kleines unbedeutendes Würstchen (inf). he's a mere ~ er ist überhaupt nichts, er ist doch ein Niemand or Nichts; to marry a ~ jdn heiraten, der nichts ist und nichts hat; they are nobodies sie sind doch niemand, das sind doch Nullitäten; I worked with him when he was (a) ~ ich habe mit ihm gearbeitet, als er noch nichts war.
no-claim(s) bonus ['nəʊˌkleɪm(z)'bəʊnəs] n Schadenfreiheitsrabatt m.
nocturnal [nɒk'tɜ:nl] adj nächtlich; sound also der Nacht; animal, bird Nacht-. ~ flowers Nachtblüher pl.
nocturne ['nɒktɜ:n] n (Mus) Nokturne f.
nod [nɒd] 1 n (a) Nicken nt. he gave a quick ~ er nickte kurz; to give sb a ~ jdm zunicken; to answer with a ~ (zustimmend) nicken; a ~ is as good as a wink (to a blind man) (inf) schon verstanden; das wird er schon verstehen; to go through on the ~ (inf) ohne Einwände angenommen werden.
(b) (inf: sleep) the land of N~ das Land der Träume.
2 vi (a) (person, flowers) nicken; (plumes) wippen. to ~ to sb jdm zunicken; to ~ in agreement/welcome zustimmend/zur Begrüßung nicken; he ~ded to me to leave er gab mir durch ein Nicken zu verstehen, daß ich gehen solle.
(b) (doze) ein Nickerchen nt machen (inf). she was ~ding over a book sie war über einem Buch eingenickt (inf).
(c) even Homer ~s Irren ist menschlich (Prov).
3 vt (a) to ~ one's head mit dem Kopf nicken; to ~ one's agreement/approval zustimmend nicken; to ~ a greeting/welcome to sb jdm zum Gruß/zur Begrüßung zunicken.
(b) (Sport) ball köpfen.
♦**nod off** vi einnicken (inf).
nodal ['nəʊdl] adj knotenartig, Knoten-; (fig) point Knoten-.
nodding ['nɒdɪŋ] adj to have a ~ acquaintance with sb jdn flüchtig kennen.
noddle ['nɒdl] n (Brit inf: head) Dez (inf), Schädel (inf) m.
node [nəʊd] n (all senses) Knoten m.
nodular ['nɒdjʊlə'] adj knötchenartig, Knötchen-.
nodule ['nɒdju:l] n (Med, Bot) Knötchen nt; (Geol) Klümpchen nt.
noggin ['nɒgɪn] n (a) (inf: head) Birne f (inf). (b) (Measure) Becher m (≈ 0,15 litres). let's have a ~ (inf) wie war's mit 'nem Gläschen? (inf).
no-go area ['nəʊˌgəʊ'eərɪə] n Sperrgebiet nt.
no: ~-good 1 adj person nichtsnutzig; 2 n (person) Nichtsnutz m; ~-hoper n (inf) völlige Niete (inf), Nulpe f (dial inf); ~how adv (incorrect, now) not ~how wie nimmer not ~how sie und nimmer.
noise [nɔɪz] 1 n Geräusch nt; (loud, irritating sound) Lärm, Krach m; (Elec: interference) Rauschen nt. what was that ~? was war das für ein Geräusch?; a hammering ~ ein hämmerndes Geräusch; the ~ of (the) jet planes der Düsenlärm; the ~ of the traffic/bells der Straßenlärm/der Lärm der Glocken; the ~ of horses coming up the street Pferdegetrappel die Straße herauf; ~s in the ears (Med) Ohrensausen nt; the rain made a ~ on the roof der Regen prasselte aufs Dach; it made a lot of ~ es war sehr laut, es hat viel Krach gemacht; don't make a ~! sei leise!; stop making such a (loud) ~ hör auf, solchen Lärm or Krach zu machen; stop that ~ hör mit dem Krach or Lärm auf; she made ~s about leaving early sie wollte unbedingt früh gehen; he's always making ~s about resigning er redet dauernd davon, daß er zurücktreten will; to make a lot of ~ about sth (inf) viel Geschrei um etw machen; to make a ~ in the world Aufsehen erregen, von sich reden machen; a big ~ (fig inf) ein großes Tier (inf); ~ level Geräuschpegel m; ~ abatement Lärmbekämpfung f.
2 vt to ~ sth abroad or about (old, hum) etw verbreiten; was ~d about that ... es ging das Gerücht (um), daß ..., man erzählte sich, daß ...
noiseless ['nɔɪzlɪs] adj geräuschlos; tread, step also lautlos.
noiselessly ['nɔɪzlɪslɪ] adv geräuschlos; move also lautlos.
noisily ['nɔɪzɪlɪ] adv see adj.
noisiness ['nɔɪzɪnɪs] n Lärm m; (of person) laute Art; (of children) Krachmacherei f (inf); (of protest, welcome, debate) Lautstärke f. the ~ of these pupils/this car der Lärm or Krach, den diese Schüler machen/dieses Auto macht; the ~ of this office der Lärm or Krach in diesem Büro.

noisome ['nɔɪsəm] adj (a) smell widerlich, eklig. (b) (noxious) giftig, (gesundheits)schädlich.
noisy ['nɔɪzɪ] adj (+er) laut; traffic, child also lärmend; machine, behaviour, work also geräuschvoll; protest, welcome, debate lautstark. don't be so ~ sei nicht so laut, mach nicht so viel Lärm; this is a ~ house in dem Haus ist es laut.
nomad ['nəʊmæd] n Nomade m, Nomadin f.
nomadic [nəʊ'mædɪk] adj nomadisch, Nomaden-; tribe, race Nomaden-.
no-man's-land ['nəʊmænzlænd] n (lit, fig) Niemandsland nt.
nom de plume ['nɒmdə'plu:m] n Pseudonym nt.
nomenclature [nəʊ'menklətʃə'] n Nomenklatur f.
nominal ['nɒmɪnl] adj (a) (in name) nominell. ~ value (of shares) Nenn- or Nominalwert m; ~ shares Stamm- or Gründungsaktien pl. (b) (small) salary, fee, amount, rent nominell, symbolisch. (c) (Gram) Nominal-.
nominalism ['nɒmɪnəlɪzəm] n (Philos) Nominalismus m.
nominally ['nɒmɪnəlɪ] adv nominell.
nominate ['nɒmɪneɪt] vt (a) (appoint) ernennen. he was ~d chairman er wurde zum Vorsitzenden ernannt or bestellt (form). (b) (propose) nominieren, (als Kandidat) aufstellen. he was ~d for the presidency er wurde als Präsidentschaftskandidat aufgestellt.
nomination [ˌnɒmɪ'neɪʃən] n (a) (appointment) Ernennung, Bestellung (form) f. (b) (proposal) Nominierung f, Kandidatenvorschlag m.
nominative ['nɒmɪnətɪv] (Gram) 1 n Nominativ, Werfall m. 2 adj (the) ~ case der Nominativ, der Werfall.
nominee [ˌnɒmɪ'ni:] n Kandidat(in f) m.
non- [nɒn-] pref nicht-.
non: ~-absorbent adj nicht absorbierend; ~-acceptance n (Comm, Fin) Nichtannahme, Annahmeverweigerung f; ~-adjustable adj nichtverstellbar attr, nicht verstellbar pred, unverstellbar; ~-affiliated adj (to an + acc) business, industry nichtangeschlossen attr, nicht angeschlossen pred.
nonagenarian [ˌnɒnədʒɪ'neərɪən] 1 n Neunziger(in f) m. 2 adj in den Neunzigern.
non-aggression [nɒnə'greʃən] n Nichtangriff m. ~ pact Nichtangriffspakt m.
nonagon ['nɒnəgɒn] n Neuneck, Nonagon nt.
non: ~-alcoholic adj nichtalkoholisch, alkoholfrei; ~-aligned adj (Pol) blockfrei, bündnisfrei; ~-alignment n (Pol) Blockfreiheit, Bündnisfreiheit f; ~-alignment policy Neutralitätspolitik f; ~-appearance n Nichterscheinen nt; ~-arrival n Ausbleiben nt; (of train, plane, letter also) Nichteintreffen nt; ~-attendance n Nichtteilnahme f (at an + dat); ~-availability n see adj Unerhältlichkeit f; Unabkömmlichkeit f; ~-available adj nicht erhältlich; person unabkömmlich; ~-belligerent 1 n Kriegsunbeteiligte(r) m; to be a ~-belligerent nicht am Krieg teilnehmen; 2 adj nicht kriegführend, kriegsunbeteiligt; ~-breakable adj unzerbrechlich, nicht zerbrechlich.
nonce-word ['nɒnswɜ:d] n Ad-hoc-Bildung f.
nonchalance ['nɒnʃələns] n Lässigkeit, Nonchalance f.
nonchalant adj, ~ly adv ['nɒnʃələnt, -lɪ] lässig, nonchalant.
non: ~-Christian 1 n Nichtchrist(in f) m; 2 adj nichtchristlich; ~-collegiate adj university nicht aus Colleges bestehend; ~-com n (Mil inf) Uffz m (sl); ~-combatant 1 n Nichtkämpfer, Nonkombattant (spec) m; 2 adj nicht am Kampf beteiligt; ~-combustible 1 adj nicht brennbar; 2 n nicht brennbarer Stoff; ~-commissioned adj (Mil) ~-commissioned officer Unteroffizier m; ~-committal adj zurückhaltend; answer also unverbindlich; to be ~-committal about whether ... sich nicht festlegen, ob ...; he's so ~-committal er legt sich nie fest; ~-committally adv answer, say unverbindlich; ~-communicant n (Eccl) Nichtkommunikant(in f) m; ~-completion n Nichtbeendung f; (of work also, contract) Nichtabschluß m; ~-compliance n (with regulations etc) Nichteinhaltung, Nichterfüllung f (with gen); (with wishes, orders) Zuwiderhandlung f, Zuwiderhandeln nt (with gegen).
non compos mentis ['nɒnˌkɒmpəs'mentɪs] adj nicht zurechnungsfähig, unzurechnungsfähig. to look/be ~ (inf) etwas geistesabwesend aussehen/nicht ganz da sein (inf).
non: ~-conformism n Nonkonformismus m; his social ~-conformism seine mangelnde Anpassung an die Gesellschaft; the ~-conformism of his views seine nonkonformistischen Ansichten; ~-conformist 1 n Nonkonformist(in f) m; 2 adj nonkonformistisch; ~-conformity n (with rules) Nichteinhaltung f (with gen), Nichtkonformgehen nt (form) (with mit); ~-contagious adj nichtansteckend attr, nicht ansteckend pred; ~-contributory adj benefits, insurance, pension scheme ohne Eigenbeteiligung; member beitragsfrei; ~-controversial adj für alle annehmbar, nicht kontrovers; to be ~-controversial keinen Anlaß zu Kontroversen bieten; ~-cooperation n unkooperative Haltung; ~-delivery n Nichtlieferung f; ~-denominational adj bekenntnisfrei, konfessionslos; ~-departure n (of train/flight) Ausfall m des Zuges/Fluges.
nondescript ['nɒndɪskrɪpt] adj taste, colour unbestimmbar; person, appearance unauffällig, unscheinbar (pej).
non: ~-detachable adj handle, hood etc nicht abnehmbar, fest angebracht; lining nicht ausknöpfbar; (without zip) nicht ausreißbar; ~-discrimination n Nichtdiskriminierung f (against, towards gen); ~-discriminatory adj nichtdiskriminierend; ~-drinker n Nichttrinker(in f) m; she is a ~-drinker sie trinkt keinen Alkohol; ~-driver n Nichtfahrer(in f) m; ~-drivers do not appreciate ... wer selbst nicht (Auto) fährt, weiß ... nicht zu schätzen; ~-dutiable adj unverzollbar.
none [nʌn] 1 pron keine(r, s); keine; (on form) keine. ~ of them/us is coming von ihnen/uns kommt keiner; ~ of the boys/the chairs/them/the girls keiner der Jungen/Stühle/von ihnen/keines der Mädchen; ~ of this/the cake nichts davon/von

dem Kuchen; ~ of this is any good das ist alles nicht gut; ~ of this money is mine von dem Geld gehört mir nichts; do you have any bread/apples? — ~ (at all) haben Sie Brot/Äpfel? — nein, gar keines/keine; there is ~ left es ist nichts übrig; money have I ~ (liter) Geld hab' ich keines; ~ but he/the best nur er/nur das Beste; their guest was ~ other than ... ihr Gast war kein anderer als ...; there is ~ better than him at climbing niemand kann besser klettern als er; but ~ of your silly jokes aber laß bitte deine dummen Witze; I want ~ of your excuses und ich will keine Entschuldigungen hören; (we'll have) ~ of that! jetzt reicht's aber!; I want ~ of this/this nonsense ich will davon/von diesem Unsinn nichts hören; I'll have ~ of your cheek (inf) ich dulde diese Frechheit nicht; he would have ~ of it er wollte davon nichts wissen.

2 adv to be ~ the wiser auch nicht or um nichts schlauer sein; it's ~ too warm es ist nicht or keineswegs zu warm; ~ too sure/easy durchaus nicht sicher/einfach; and ~ too soon either und auch keineswegs zu früh.

nonentity [nɒˈnentɪtɪ] n (person) Nullität f, unbedeutende Figur.

non-essential [nɒnɪˈsenʃəl] 1 adj unnötig; workers nicht unbedingt nötig; services nicht lebenswichtig. 2 n ~s pl nicht (lebens)notwendige Dinge pl.

nonetheless [nʌnðəˈles] adv nichtsdestoweniger, trotzdem.

non: ~-event n (inf) Reinfall m (inf), Pleite f (inf), Schlag m ins Wasser (inf); ~-existence n Nichtvorhandensein nt; (Philos) Nicht-Existenz f; ~-existent adj nichtvorhanden attr, nicht vorhanden pred; (Philos) nicht existent; his accent is practically ~-existent er hat praktisch keinen Akzent; ~-fat adj diet fettlos; ~-fattening adj nicht dickmachend attr; fruit is ~-fattening Obst macht nicht dick; ~-ferrous adj nicht eisenhaltig; ~-fiction 1 n Sachbücher pl; 2 adj ~-fiction book/publication Sachbuch nt; ~-fiction department Sachbuchabteilung f; ~-flammable adj nichtentzündbar attr, nicht entzündbar pred; ~-flowering adj nichtblühend; ~-hereditary adj nichtvererbbar attr, nicht vererbbar pred; disease also nichtvererblich attr, nicht vererblich pred; ~-infectious adj nicht ansteckend, nicht infektiös (form); ~-inflammable adj nicht feuergefährlich; ~-interference n Nichteinmischung f (in in +acc); ~-intervention n (Pol etc) Nichteinmischung f, Nichteingreifen nt (in in +acc); ~-iron adj bügelfrei; ~-member n Nichtmitglied nt; (of society also) Nichtangehörige(r) mf; open to ~-members Gäste willkommen; ~-migratory adj ~-migratory bird Standvogel, Nichtzieher (spec) m; ~-milk adj; ~-milk fat(s) nichttierische Fette pl; ~-negotiable adj ticket nicht übertragbar; ~-obligatory adj freiwillig, nicht Pflicht pred, freigestellt pred; ~-observance n Nicht(be)achtung f.

no-nonsense [nəʊˌnɒnsəns] adj (kühl und) sachlich, nüchtern.

non: ~-pareil [nɒnpəˈreɪ] 1 adj (liter) unerreicht; 2 n (a) (liter) (thing) Non plus ultra nt; (person) unerreichter Meister; (b) (Typ) Nonpareille(schrift) f; ~-partisan adj unparteiisch; ~-payment n Nichtzahlung f; ~-perishable adj dauerhaft, haltbar.

nonplus [nɒnˈplʌs] vt verblüffen. utterly ~sed völlig verdutzt or verblüfft.

non: ~-poisonous adj nicht giftig, ungiftig; ~-porous adj nichtporös attr, nicht porös pred; ~-productive adj ~-productive industries Dienstleistungssektor m; ~-productive worker Angestellte(r) mf im Dienstleistungssektor; ~-profit (US), ~-profit-making adj keinen Gewinn anstrebend attr; charity etc also gemeinnützig; ~-proliferation n Nichtweitergabe f von Atomwaffen; ~-proliferation treaty Atomsperrvertrag m; ~-publication n Nichterscheinen nt; ~-radioactive adj substance nicht radioaktiv, strahlenfrei; ~-reader n Analphabet(in f) m; there are still five ~-readers in this class in dieser Klasse können fünf Schüler noch nicht lesen; ~-recognition n Nichtanerkennung f; ~-refillable adj Wegwerf-; ~-resident 1 adj nicht ansässig; (in hotel) nicht im Hause wohnend; 2 n Nicht(orts)ansässige(r) mf; (in hotel) nicht im Haus wohnender Gast; open to ~-residents auch für Nichthotelgäste; ~-returnable adj bottle Einweg-; ~-run adj laufmaschenfrei, maschenfest; ~-scheduled adj flight, train außerplanmäßig; ~-sectarian adj nichtkonfessionell; assembly nicht konfessionsgebunden.

nonsense [ˈnɒnsəns] n, no pl (also as interjection) Unsinn, Quatsch (inf), Nonsens (geh) m; (verbal also) dummes Zeug; (silly behaviour) Dummheiten pl. a piece of ~ ein Unsinn or Quatsch (inf) m; that's a lot of ~! das ist (ja) alles dummes Zeug!; I've had enough of this ~ jetzt reicht's mir aber; to make (a) ~ of sth etw ad absurdum führen, etw unsinnig or sinnlos machen; what's all this ~ about a salary reduction/about them not wanting to go? was soll all das Gerede or einer Gehaltskürzung/was soll all das Gerede, daß sie nicht mitgehen wollen?; no more of your ~! Schluß mit dem Unsinn!; and no ~ und keine Dummheiten; I will stand or have no ~ from you ich werde keinen Unsinn or keine Dummheiten dulden; he will stand no ~ from anybody er läßt nicht mit sich spaßen; he won't stand any ~ over that was das betrifft, verträgt er keinen Spaß; a man with no ~ about him ein nüchterner or kühler und sachlicher Mensch; see stuff.

nonsense verse n Nonsens-Vers, Unsinnsvers m; (genre) Nonsens-Verse, Unsinnsverse pl.

nonsensical [nɒnˈsensɪkəl] adj idea, action unsinnig. don't be ~ sei nicht albern.

nonsensically [nɒnˈsensɪkəlɪ] adv ohne Sinn und Verstand.

non sequitur [nɒnˈsekwɪtəʳ] n unlogische (Schluß)folgerung.

non: ~-shrink adj nichteinlaufend attr; to be ~-shrink nicht einlaufen; ~-skid adj rutschsicher; ~-slip adj rutschfest; ~-smoker n (a) (person) Nichtraucher(in f) m; (b) (Rail) Nichtraucher(abteil nt) m; ~-smoking adj area Nichtraucher-;

~-standard adj sizes nicht der Norm entsprechend; (of clothes, shoes) Sonder-; (not usually supplied) fittings nicht üblich, Sonder-; ~-standard use of language unüblicher or ungewöhnlicher Sprachgebrauch; ~-starter n (a) (in race) (person) Nichtstartende(r) mf; (horse) nichtstartendes Pferd; there were two ~-starters zwei traten nicht an; (b) (fig: person, idea) Blindgänger m; ~-stick adj pan, surface kunststoffbeschichtet, Teflon- ®; ~-stop 1 adj train durchgehend; journey ohne Unterbrechung; flight, performances Nonstop-; 2 adv talk ununterbrochen; fly nonstop; travel ohne Unterbrechung, nonstop; ~-survival n Aussterben nt; ~-swimmer n Nichtschwimmer(in f) m; ~-taxable adj nichtsteuerpflichtig; ~-technical adj language etc für den Laien verständlich; subject nichttechnisch; ~-toxic adj ungiftig; ~-U adj (Brit) charakteristisch für die Gewohnheiten, Sprechweise etc des Kleinbürgertums, nicht vornehm; ~-union adj worker, labour nichtorganisiert; ~-verbal adj communication nichtverbal, wortlos, ohne Worte; ~-violence n Gewaltlosigkeit f; ~-violent adj gewaltlos; ~-vocational adj subject, course nicht berufsorientiert; ~-voter n Nichtwähler(in f) m; ~-white 1 n Farbige(r) mf; 2 adj nicht weiß.

noodle [ˈnuːdl] n (a) (Cook) Nudel f. (b) (dated inf: fool) Dummerjan m (dated inf).

nook [nʊk] n (corner) Ecke f, Winkel m; (remote spot) Winkel m. a shady ~ ein schattiges Fleckchen; a cosy ~ ein gemütliches Eckchen; in every ~ and cranny in jedem Winkel.

noon [nuːn] 1 n Mittag m. at ~ um 12 Uhr mittags. 2 adj 12-Uhr-, Mittags- (inf).

noonday [ˈnuːndeɪ] adj attr Mittags-, mittäglich.

no-one [ˈnəʊwʌn] pron see nobody 1.

noon: ~time, ~tide (liter) n Mittagszeit, Mittagsstunde (geh) f; at ~time or ~tide um die Mittagsstunde (geh).

noose [nuːs] n Schlinge f. to put one's head in the ~ (prov) den Kopf in die Schlinge stecken.

nope [nəʊp] adv (inf) ne(e) (dial), nein.

nor [nɔːʳ] conj (a) noch. neither ... ~ weder ... noch.
(b) (and not) und ... auch nicht. I shan't go, ~ will you ich gehe nicht, und du auch nicht; I don't like him — ~ do I ich mag ihn nicht — ich auch nicht; ~ was this all und das war noch nicht alles; that's not probable, ~ do I believe it's possible das ist nicht wahrscheinlich, und ich glaube nicht einmal, daß es möglich ist.

Nordic [ˈnɔːdɪk] adj nordisch.

nor'-east [nɔːˈriːst] (Naut) see north-east.

norm [nɔːm] n Norm f. our ~ is ... in der Regel leisten wir ..., die Norm liegt bei ...

normal [ˈnɔːməl] 1 adj (a) person, situation, conditions normal; procedure, practice, routine also, customary üblich. it's a perfectly or quite a ~ thing das ist völlig normal; ~ working will resume later der normale Betrieb wird später wieder aufgenommen; ~ temperature/consumption/output Normaltemperatur f/-verbrauch m/-leistung f; he is not his ~ self today er ist heute so anders.
(b) (Math) senkrecht.
(c) (Chem) solution Normal-.
2 n, no pl (of temperature) Normalwert, Durchschnitt m; (Math) Senkrechte f; (to tangent) Normale f. temperatures below ~ Temperaturen unter dem Durchschnitt; her temperature is above/below ~ sie hat erhöhte Temperatur/sie hat Untertemperatur; when things/we are back to ~ wenn sich alles wieder normalisiert hat.

normalcy [ˈnɔːməlsɪ] n see normality.

normality [nɔːˈmælɪtɪ] n Normalität f. the return to ~ after war die Normalisierung (des Lebens) or die Wiederaufnahme eines normalen Lebens nach dem Krieg; to return to ~ sich wieder normalisieren; despite his apparent ~ obwohl er ganz normal zu sein scheint/schien.

normalization [ˌnɔːməlaɪˈzeɪʃən] n Normalisierung f.

normalize [ˈnɔːməlaɪz] vt normalisieren; relations wiederherstellen. to be ~d sich normalisiert haben.

normally [ˈnɔːməlɪ] adv (usually) normalerweise, gewöhnlich; (in normal way) normal.

normal school n (US old) Pädagogische Hochschule.

Norman [ˈnɔːmən] 1 adj normannisch. the ~ Conquest der normannische Eroberungszug. 2 n Normanne m, Normannin f.

Normandy [ˈnɔːməndɪ] n Normandie f.

normative [ˈnɔːmətɪv] adj normativ.

nor'-nor'-east [ˌnɔːnɔːˈriːst] (Naut) see north-north-east.

nor'-nor'-west [ˌnɔːnɔːˈwest] (Naut) see north-north-west.

Norse [nɔːs] 1 adj mythology altnordisch. 2 n (Ling) Old ~ Altnordisch nt.

Norseman [ˈnɔːsmən] n, pl -men [-mən] (Hist) Normanne, Wikinger m. Norsemen Nordleute pl.

north [nɔːθ] 1 n (a) Norden m. in/from the ~ im/aus dem Norden; to live in the ~ im Norden leben; to the ~ of nördlich von, im Norden von; to veer/go to the ~ in nördliche Richtung or nach Norden drehen/gehen; the wind is in the ~ es ist Nordwind; to face (the) ~ nach Norden liegen; the N~ (of Scotland/England) Nordschottland/Nordengland nt.
(b) (US Hist) the N~ der Norden, die Nordstaaten.
2 adj attr Nord-.
3 adv (towards N~) nach Norden, gen Norden (liter), nordwärts (liter, Naut); (Met) in nördliche Richtung. ~ of nördlich or im Norden von.

north in cpds Nord-; N~ Africa n Nordafrika nt; N~ African 1 adj nordafrikanisch; 2 n Nordafrikaner(in f) m; N~ America n Nordamerika nt; N~ American 1 adj nordamerikanisch; 2 n Nordamerikaner(in f) m.

Northants [nɔːˈθænts] abbr of Northamptonshire.

north: ~bound adj carriageway nach Norden (führend); traffic in Richtung Norden; ~ country n Nordengland nt;

~-country adj nordenglisch; **~-east 1** n Nordosten, Nordost (esp Naut) m; **in/from the ~-east** im Nordosten/von Nordost; **2** adj Nordost-, nordöstlich; **3** adv nach Nordosten; **~-east of** nordöstlich von; **~-easterly 1** adj nordöstlich; **2** n (wind) Nordostwind m; **~-eastern** adj provinces nordöstlich, im Nordosten; **~-eastwards** adv nordostwärts, nach Nordost(en).

northerly ['nɔːðəlɪ] **1** adj wind, direction, latitude nördlich. **2** adv nach Norden, nordwärts (liter, Naut). **3** n Nordwind m.

northern ['nɔːðən] adj hemisphere, counties nördlich; Germany, Italy etc Nord-. **the ~ lights** das Nordlicht; **N~ Ireland** Nordirland nt; **with a ~ outlook** mit Blick nach Norden.

northerner ['nɔːðənəʳ] n (a) Bewohner(in f) m des Nordens; Nordengländer(in f) m/-deutsche(r) mf etc. **he is a ~** er kommt aus dem Norden des Landes. (b) (US) Nordstaatler(in f) m.

northernmost ['nɔːðənməʊst] adj area nördlichste(r, s).

north: **N~ Korea** n Nordkorea nt; **N~ Korean 1** adj nordkoreanisch; **2** n Nordkoreaner(in f) m; **~-north-east 1** n Nordnordosten (esp Naut) m; **2** adj Nordnordost-, nordnordöstlich; **3** adv nach Nordnordost(en); **~-north-east of** nordnordöstlich von; **~-north-west 1** n Nordnordwesten, Nordnordwest (esp Naut) m; **2** adj Nordnordwest-, nordnordwestlich; **3** adv nach Nordnordwest(en); **~-north-west of** nordnordwestlich von; **N~ Sea** gas/oil Nordseegas nt/-öl nt; **N~ Star** n Nordstern m; **N~ Vietnam** n Nordvietnam nt; **N~ Vietnamese 1** adj nordvietnamesisch; **2** n Nordvietnamese m/-vietnamesin f; **~ward, ~wardly 1** adj nördlich; **in a ~wardly direction** nach Norden, (in) Richtung Norden; **2** adv (also **~wards**) nach Norden, nordwärts; **~-west 1** n Nordwesten, Nordwest (esp Naut) m; **2** adj Nordwest-, nordwestlich; **the N~-west Passage** die Nordwestliche Durchfahrt; **3** adv nach Nordwest(en); **~-west of** nordwestlich von; **~-westerly 1** adj nordwestlich; **2** n Nordwestwind m.

Norway ['nɔːweɪ] n Norwegen nt.

Norwegian [nɔː'wiːdʒən] **1** adj norwegisch. **2** n (a) Norweger(in f) m. (b) (language) Norwegisch nt.

nor'-west ['nɔː'west] (Naut) see **north-west**.

Nos., nos. abbr of **numbers** Nrn.

nose [nəʊz] **1** n (a) (of person, animal) Nase f. **to hold one's ~** sich (dat) die Nase zuhalten; **to speak through one's ~** durch die Nase sprechen; **the tip of one's ~** die Nasenspitze; **to bleed at the ~** aus der Nase bluten; **my ~ is bleeding** ich habe Nasenbluten; **follow your ~** immer der Nase nach; **she always has her ~ in a book** sie hat dauernd den Kopf in einem Buch (vergraben); **to find sth under sb's ~** praktisch mit der Nase auf etw (acc) stoßen; **it was right under his ~** all the time er hatte es die ganze Zeit direkt vor der Nase; **to lead sb by the ~** jdn an der Nase herumführen; **to poke or stick one's ~ into sth** (fig) seine Nase in etw (acc) stecken; **you keep your ~ out of this** (inf) halt du dich da raus (inf); **to cut off one's ~ to spite one's face** (prov) sich ins eigene Fleisch schneiden; **to look down one's ~ at sb/sth** auf jdn/etw herabblicken; **with one's ~ in the air** mit hocherhobenem Kopf, hochnäsig; **to pay through the ~** (inf) viel blechen (inf), sich dumm und dämlich zahlen (inf); **to win by a ~** (horse) um eine Nasenlänge gewinnen; **to put sb's ~ out of joint** jdn vor den Kopf stoßen; **his ~ is out of joint over this** er fühlt sich dadurch vor den Kopf gestoßen, das ist ihm in die Nase gefahren; **to keep one's ~ clean** (inf) sauber bleiben (inf), eine saubere Weste behalten (inf); **to pay on the ~** sofort bezahlen.
(b) (sense of smell) Nase f; (fig also) Riecher m (inf). **to have a ~ for sth** (fig) eine Nase or einen Riecher (inf) für etw haben. (c) (of wines) Blume f. (d) (of plane) Nase f; (of car) Schnauze f; (of boat also) Bug m; (of torpedo) Kopf m. **~ to tail** (cars) Stoßstange an Stoßstange.
2 vti **the car/ship ~d (its way) through the fog** das Auto/Schiff tastete sich durch den Nebel; **the car ~d (its way) into the stream of traffic** das Auto schob sich in den fließenden Verkehr vor; **to ~ into sb's affairs** (fig) seine Nase in jds Angelegenheiten (acc) stecken (inf).

◆**nose about** or **around** vi herumschnüffeln (inf); (person also) herumspionieren (inf).

◆**nose out 1** vt sep aufspüren; secret, scandal ausspionieren (inf), ausschnüffeln (inf). **2** vi (car) sich vorschieben.

nose: **~bag** n Futtersack m; **~band** n Nasenriemen m; **~bleed** n Nasenbluten nt; **to have a ~bleed** Nasenbluten haben; **~cone** n (Aviat) Raketenspitze f.

-nosed [-nəʊzd] adj suf -nasig.

nose: **~dive 1** n (Aviat) Sturzflug m; **to go into a ~dive** zum Sturzflug ansetzen; **the car/he took or made a ~dive into the sea** das Auto stürzte vornüber or stürzte kopfüber ins Meer; **the company's affairs took a ~dive** mit der Firma ging es rapide bergab; **2** vi (plane) im Sturzflug herabgehen; **to ~dive off sth** vornüber von etw stürzen; (person) kopfüber von etw stürzen; **the company's affairs ~dived** mit der Firma ging es rapide bergab; **~drops** npl Nasentropfen pl; **~-flute** n Nasenflöte f; **~gay** n (Biedermeier)sträußchen nt; **~ ring** n Nasenring m; **~-wheel** n Bugrad nt.

nosey adj see **nosy**.

nosey parker [ˌnəʊzɪ'pɑːkəʳ] n (inf) Schnüffler(in f), Topfgucker (inf) m. **I don't like ~s** ich mag Leute nicht, die ihre Nase in alles stecken (inf); **~!** sei doch nicht so neugierig!

nosh [nɒʃ] (Brit sl) **1** n (food) Futter nt (inf); (meal) Schmaus m. **to have some ~** es was or futtern (inf). **2** vi futtern (inf).

nosh-up ['nɒʃʌp] n (Brit sl) Schmaus m. Fressgelage nt (sl).

nostalgia [nɒ'stældʒɪə] n Nostalgie f (for nach). **to feel ~ for sth** sich nach etw zurücksehnen.

nostalgic [nɒ'stældʒɪk] adj nostalgisch, wehmütig. **to feel/be ~ for sth** sich nach etw zurücksehnen.

nostril ['nɒstrəl] n Nasenloch nt; (of horse, zebra etc) Nüster f.

nostrum ['nɒstrəm] n (old lit, fig) Patentrezept nt.

nosy ['nəʊzɪ] adj (+er) (inf) neugierig.

not [nɒt] adv (a) nicht. **he told me ~ to come**/to do that er sagte, ich solle nicht kommen/ich solle das nicht tun; **do ~ or don't come** kommen Sie nicht; **that's how ~ to do it** so sollte man es nicht machen; **he was wrong in ~ making a protest** es war falsch von ihm, nicht zu protestieren; **~ wanting to be heard, he ... da** er nicht gehört werden wollte, ... er...; **~ I!** ich nicht!; **fear ~!** (old) fürchte dich/fürchtet euch nicht!
(b) (emphatic) nicht. **~ a sound/word etc** kein Ton/Wort etc, nicht ein Ton/Wort etc; **~ a bit** kein bißchen; **~ a sign of ...** keine Spur von ...; **~ one of them** kein einziger, nicht einer; **~ a thing** überhaupt nichts; **~ any more** nicht mehr; **~ yet** noch nicht; **~ so** (as reply) nein; **say ~ so** (old) sag, daß es nicht wahr ist.
(c) (in tag or rhetorical questions) **it's hot, isn't it** or **is it ~?** (form) es ist heiß, nicht wahr or nicht?; **isn't it hot?** (es ist) heiß, nicht wahr?, ist das vielleicht heiß!; **isn't he cheeky!** ist er nicht frech?, (er ist) ganz schön frech, nicht! (inf); **you are ~ coming, aren't you** or **are you ~?** Sie kommen doch, oder?; **he's ~ coming, is he?** er kommt doch nicht etwa, oder?; **you have got it, haven't you?** Sie haben es doch, oder?; **Sie haben es, nicht wahr?; you like it, don't you** or **do you ~?** (form) das gefällt dir, nicht (wahr)?; **you are ~ angry, are you?** Sie sind nicht böse, oder?; **you are ~ angry - or are you?** Sie sind doch nicht etwa böse?
(d) (as substitute for clause) nicht. **is he coming? — I hope/I believe ~** kommt er? — ich hoffe/glaube nicht; **it would seem** or **appear ~** anscheinend nicht; **he's decided not to do it — I should think/hope ~** er hat sich entschlossen, es nicht zu tun — das möchte ich auch meinen/hoffen.
(e) (elliptically) **are you cold? — ~ at all** ist dir kalt? — überhaupt or gar nicht; **thank you very much — ~ at all** vielen Dank — keine Ursache or gern geschehen; **~ in the least** überhaupt or gar nicht, nicht im geringsten; **~ that I care** nicht, daß es mir etwas ausmacht(e); **~ that I know of** nicht, daß ich wüßte; **it's ~ that I don't believe him** ich glaube ihm ja, es ist ja nicht so, daß ich ihm nicht glaube.

notability [ˌnəʊtə'bɪlɪtɪ] n (a) (person) bedeutende Persönlichkeit. **the notabilities of the town** die Honoratioren pl der Stadt. (b) (eminence) Berühmtheit, Bedeutung f.

notable ['nəʊtəbl] **1** adj (eminent) person bedeutend; (worthy of note) success, fact, event also bemerkenswert, beachtenswert, denkwürdig; (big) difference, improvement beträchtlich, beachtlich; (conspicuous) auffallend. **he was ~ by his absence** er glänzte durch Abwesenheit. **2** n see **notability (a)**.

notably ['nəʊtəblɪ] adv (a) (strikingly) auffallend; improved, different beträchtlich. **to be ~ absent** durch Abwesenheit glänzen. (b) (in particular) hauptsächlich, vor allem.

notarial [nəʊ'tɛərɪəl] adj seal, deed, style notariell; fees Notar-.

notary (public) ['nəʊtərɪ('pʌblɪk)] n Notar m.

notation [nəʊ'teɪʃən] n (a) (system) Zeichensystem nt, Notation f (Sci); (symbols) Zeichen pl; (phonetic also) Schrift f; (Mus) Notenschrift, Notation f. (b) (note) Notiz, Anmerkung f.

notch [nɒtʃ] **1** n Kerbe f; (of handbrake, for adjustment etc) Raste f; (in belt) Loch nt; (on damaged blade etc) Scharte f; (US Geog) Schlucht f. **to cut a ~ into sth** eine Kerbe in etw (acc) machen; **our team is a ~ above theirs** unsere Mannschaft ist eine Klasse besser als ihre; see **top-notch**.
2 vt einkerben, einschneiden.

◆**notch up** vt sep score, points erzielen, einheimsen (inf); record erringen, verzeichnen; success verzeichnen können.

note [nəʊt] **1** n (a) Notiz, Anmerkung f; (foot~) Anmerkung, Fußnote f; (official: in file etc) Vermerk m; (diplomatic) Note f; (informal letter) Briefchen nt, paar Zeilen pl. **~s** (summary) Aufzeichnungen pl; (plan, draft) Konzept nt; **a few rough ~s** ein paar Stichworte pl; lecture **~s** (professor's) Manuskript nt; (student's) Aufzeichnungen pl; (handout) Vorlesungsskript nt; **to speak without ~s** frei sprechen, ohne Vorlage sprechen; **to speak from ~s** (von einer Vorlage) ablesen; **"Author's N~"** „Anmerkung des Verfassers"; **exchange of ~s** (Pol) Notenaustausch m; **to send sb a ~** jdm ein paar Zeilen schicken; **to write a hasty ~** schnell ein paar Zeilen schreiben; **to take or make ~s** Notizen machen; (in lecture also, in interrogation) mitschreiben; **to make ~s on a text** (sich dat) Notizen zu einem Text machen; **to take or make a ~ of sth** (sich dat) etw notieren.
(b) no pl (notice) **to take ~ of sth** von etw Notiz nehmen, etw zur Kenntnis nehmen; (heed) einer Sache (dat) Beachtung schenken; **take no ~ of what he says** nehmen Sie keine Notiz von dem, was er sagt, achten Sie nicht darauf, was er sagt; **take ~ of what I tell you** hören Sie auf das, was ich zu sagen habe; **worthy of ~** beachtenswert, erwähnenswert.
(c) no pl (importance) **a man of ~** ein bedeutender Mann; **nothing of ~** nichts Beachtens- or Erwähnenswertes.
(d) (Mus) (sign) Note f; (sound, on piano etc) Ton m; (song of bird etc) Lied nt, Gesang m. **to give the ~** den Ton angeben; **to play/sing the right/wrong ~** richtig/falsch spielen/singen; **to strike the right ~** (fig) den richtigen Ton treffen; **it struck a wrong** or **false ~** (fig) da hat er etc sich im Ton vergriffen; (wasn't genuine) es klang nicht echt.
(e) (quality, tone) Ton, Klang m. **his voice had a ~ of desperation** aus seiner Stimme klang Verzweiflung, seine Stimme hatte einen verzweifelten Klang; **a ~ of nostalgia** eine nostalgische Note; **to sound** or **strike a ~ of warning/caution** warnen/zur Vorsicht warnen; **there was a ~ of warning in his voice** seine Stimme hatte einen warnenden Unterton.
(f) (Fin) Note f, Schein m. **a £5 ~, a five-pound ~** eine Fünfpundnote, ein Fünfpfundschein m.
2 vt (a) bemerken; (take note of) zur Kenntnis nehmen; (pay attention to) beachten. (b) see **~ down**.

◆**note down** vt sep notieren, aufschreiben; (as reminder) sich (dat) notieren or aufschreiben.

note: ~book *n* Notizbuch *or* -heft *nt*; ~case *n* Brieftasche *f*.
noted ['nəʊtɪd] *adj* bekannt, berühmt (*for* für, wegen).
note: ~pad *n* Notizblock *m*; ~paper *n* Briefpapier *nt*.
noteworthy ['nəʊtwɜːðɪ] *adj* beachtenswert, erwähnenswert.
nothing ['nʌθɪŋ] **1** *n, pron, adv* (a) nichts. to eat ~ nichts essen; ~ pleases him nichts gefällt ihm, ihm gefällt nichts; ~ could be easier nichts wäre einfacher; it was reduced to ~ es war nichts übrig; she is five foot ~ (*inf*) sie ist genau fünf Fuß; £50 ~! (*inf*) 50 Pfund, das ist doch wohl nicht ernst gemeint.
(b) (*with vb*) nichts. she is *or* means ~ to him sie bedeutet ihm nichts; she is ~ (compared) to her sister sie ist nichts im Vergleich zu ihrer Schwester; that came to ~ da ist nichts draus geworden; I can make ~ of it das sagt mir nichts, ich werde daraus nicht schlau; he thinks ~ of doing that er findet nichts dabei(, das zu tun); think ~ of it keine Ursache!; will you come? — ~ doing! (*inf*) kommst du? — ausgeschlossen!, da ist nichts drin (*sl*), kein Gedanke (*inf*); there was ~ doing at the club (*inf*) im Club war nichts los; I tried, but there's ~ doing (*inf*) ich hab's versucht, aber da spielt sich nichts ab (*sl*) *or* aber da ist nichts drin (*sl*) *or* aber da ist nichts zu machen.
(c) (*with prep*) all his fame was as ~ (*liter*) *or* stood *or* counted for ~ sein Ruhm galt nichts; for ~ (*free, in vain*) umsonst; it's not for ~ that he's called X er heißt nicht umsonst *or* ohne Grund X; there's ~ (else) for it but to leave da bleibt einem nichts übrig als zu gehen; there's ~ (else) for it, we'll have to ... da hilft alles nichts, wir müssen ...; there was ~ in it for me das hat sich für mich nicht gelohnt, ich hatte nichts davon; (*financially also*) dabei sprang nichts für mich heraus (*inf*); there's ~ in the rumour das Gerücht ist völlig unfundiert *or* aus der Luft gegriffen, an dem Gerücht ist nichts (Wahres); that is ~ to you für dich ist das doch gar nichts; (*isn't important*) das kümmert *or* berührt dich nicht, das ist dir egal; there's ~ to it (*inf*) das ist kinderleicht (*inf*).
(d) (*with adj, adv*) ~ but nur; he does ~ but eat er ißt nur *or* ständig, er tut nichts anderes als essen; ~ else sonst nichts; ~ more sonst nichts; he was ~ more than a simple teacher er war nur ein einfacher Lehrer; I'd like ~ more than that ich möchte nichts lieber als das; I'd like ~ more than to go to Canada ich würde (nur) zu gern nach Kanada gehen; ~ much nicht viel; ~ less than nur; ~ if not polite äußerst *or* überaus höflich; ~ new nichts Neues; it was ~ like so big as we thought es war lange nicht so groß, wie wir dachten.
2 *n* (a) (*Math*) Null *f*.
(b) (*thing, person of no value*) Nichts *nt*. it's a mere ~ compared to what he spent last year im Vergleich zu dem, was er letztes Jahr ausgegeben hat, ist das gar nichts; it was a mere ~ das war doch nicht der Rede wert, das war doch nur eine winzige Kleinigkeit; don't apologize, it's ~ entschuldige dich nicht, es ist nicht der Rede wert; what's wrong with you? — it's ~ was ist mit dir los? — nichts; to whisper sweet ~s to sb jdm Zärtlichkeiten ins Ohr flüstern.
nothingness ['nʌθɪŋnɪs] *n* Nichts *nt*.
no through road *n* it's a ~ es ist keine Durchfahrt.
notice ['nəʊtɪs] **1** *n* (a) (*warning, communication*) Bescheid *m*, Benachrichtigung *f*; (*written notification*) Mitteilung *f*; (*of forthcoming event, film etc*) Ankündigung *f*. ~ to pay (*Comm*) Zahlungsaufforderung *f*, Zahlungsbefehl *m*; ~ of receipt (*Comm*) Empfangsbestätigung *or* -bescheinigung *f*; final ~ letzte Aufforderung; we need three weeks ~ wir müssen drei Wochen vorher Bescheid wissen; to give ~ of sth von etw Bescheid geben; (*of film, change etc*) etw ankündigen; (*of arrival etc*) etw melden; to give sb one week's ~ of sth jdn eine Woche vorher von etw benachrichtigen; jdm eine Woche vorher über etw (*acc*) Bescheid geben; to give sb ~ of sth jdn von etw benachrichtigen, jdm etw mitteilen; to give ~ of appeal (*Jur*) Berufung einlegen; we must give advance ~ of the meeting wir müssen das Treffen ankündigen; to give official ~ that ... öffentlich bekanntgeben, daß ...; (*referring to future event*) öffentlich ankündigen, daß ...; without ~ ohne Ankündigung, (*of arrival also*) unangemeldet; ~ is hereby given that ... hiermit wird bekanntgegeben, daß ...; he didn't give us much ~, he gave us rather short ~ er hat uns nicht viel Zeit gelassen *or* gegeben; to have ~ of sth von etw Kenntnis haben; I must have ~ *or* you must give me some ~ of what you intend to do ich muß Bescheid wissen *or* Kenntnis davon haben (*form*), was Sie vorhaben; to serve ~ on sb (*Jur: to appear in court*) jdn vorladen; at short ~ kurzfristig; at a moment's ~ jederzeit, sofort; at three days' ~ binnen drei Tagen, innerhalb von drei Tagen; until further ~ bis auf weiteres.
(b) (*public announcement*) (on ~-board etc) Bekanntmachung *f*, Anschlag *m*; (*poster also*) Plakat *nt*; (*sign*) Schild *nt*; (*in newspaper*) Mitteilung, Bekanntmachung *f*; (*short*) Notiz *f*; (*of birth, wedding, vacancy etc*) Anzeige *f*. the ~ says ... da steht ...; to post a ~ einen Anschlag machen, ein Plakat *nt* aufhängen; public ~ öffentliche Bekanntmachung; birth/marriage/death ~ Geburts-/Heirats-/Todesanzeige *f*; I saw a ~ in the paper about the concert ich habe das Konzert in der Zeitung angekündigt gesehen.
(c) (*prior to end of employment, residence etc*) Kündigung *f*. ~ to quit Kündigung *f*; to give sb ~ (*employer, landlord*) jdm kündigen; (*lodger, employee also*) bei jdm kündigen; to give in one's ~ kündigen; I am under ~ (to quit), I got my ~ mir ist gekündigt worden; a month's ~ eine einmonatige Kündigungsfrist; I have to give (my landlady) a week's ~ ich habe eine einwöchige Kündigungsfrist; she gave me *or* I was given a month's ~ mir wurde zum nächsten Monat gekündigt.
(d) (*review*) Kritik, Rezension *f*.
(e) (*attention*) to take ~ of sth von etw Notiz nehmen; (*heed*) etw beachten, einer Sache (*dat*) Beachtung schenken; I'm afraid I wasn't taking much ~ of what they were doing ich muß gestehen, ich habe nicht aufgepaßt, was sie machten; to take no

~ of sb/sth jdn/etw ignorieren, von jdm/etw keine Notiz nehmen, jdm/etw keine Beachtung schenken; take no ~! kümmern Sie sich nicht darum!; a lot of ~ he takes of me! als ob er mich beachten würde!; to attract ~ Aufmerksamkeit erregen; that has escaped his ~ das hat er nicht bemerkt; it might not have escaped your ~ that ... Sie haben vielleicht bemerkt, daß ...; to bring sth to sb's ~ jdn auf etw (*acc*) aufmerksam machen; (*in letter, form etc*) jdn von etw in Kenntnis setzen; it came to his ~ that ... er erfuhr, daß ..., es ist ihm zu Ohren gekommen, daß ...; that is beneath my ~ das nehme ich nicht zur Kenntnis, mit so etwas gebe ich mich nicht ab.
2 *vt* bemerken; (*feel, hear, touch also*) wahrnehmen; (*recognize, acknowledge existence of*) zur Kenntnis nehmen; (*difference also*) feststellen; (*realize also*) merken. ~ the beautiful details achten Sie auf die schönen Einzelheiten; without my noticing it ohne daß ich etwas gemerkt *or* bemerkt habe, von mir unbemerkt; did anybody ~ him leave? hat jemand sein Gehen bemerkt?; I ~d her hesitating ich bemerkte *or* merkte, daß sie zögerte; did he wave? — I never ~d haben Sie gewunken? — ich habe es nicht bemerkt *or* gesehen; I ~ you have a new dress ich stelle fest, du hast ein neues Kleid, wie ich sehe, hast du ein neues Kleid; to get oneself ~d Aufmerksamkeit erregen, auf sich (*acc*) aufmerksam machen; (*negatively*) auffallen.
noticeable ['nəʊtɪsəbl] *adj* erkennbar, wahrnehmbar; (*visible*) sichtbar; (*obvious, considerable*) deutlich; relief, pleasure, disgust etc) sichtlich, merklich. the stain is very ~ der Fleck fällt ziemlich auf; his incompetence was very ~ seine Unfähigkeit trat klar zum Vorschein *or* zeigte sich deutlich; the change was ~ man konnte eine Veränderung feststellen; it is hardly ~, it isn't really ~ man merkt es kaum, es fällt so gut wie nicht auf; (*visible also*) man sieht es kaum; it is ~ that ... man merkt, daß ...; she was ~ because of her large hat sie fiel durch ihren großen Hut auf.
noticeably ['nəʊtɪsəblɪ] *adv* deutlich, merklich; relieved, pleased, annoyed etc sichtlich.
notice-board ['nəʊtɪsbɔːd] *n* Anschlagbrett *nt*; (*in school etc also*) Schwarzes Brett; (*sign*) Schild *nt*, Tafel *f*.
notifiable ['nəʊtɪfaɪəbl] *adj* meldepflichtig.
notification [ˌnəʊtɪfɪ'keɪʃən] *n* Benachrichtigung, Mitteilung *f*; (*of disease, crime, loss, damage etc*) Meldung *f*; (*written ~: of birth etc*) Anzeige *f*. ~ of the authorities (die) Benachrichtigung der Behörden; to send written ~ of sth to sb jdm etw schriftlich mitteilen; you must send ~ of your decision Sie müssen Ihre Entscheidung mitteilen.
notify ['nəʊtɪfaɪ] *vt person, candidate* benachrichtigen, unterrichten (*form*); change of address, loss, disease etc melden. to ~ sb of sth jdn von etw benachrichtigen, jdm etw mitteilen; authorities, insurance company jdm etw melden; to be notified of sth über etw (*acc*) informiert werden, von etw benachrichtigt *or* unterrichtet (*form*) werden.
notion ['nəʊʃən] *n* (a) (*idea, thought*) Idee *f*; (*conception also*) Vorstellung *f*; (*vague knowledge also*) Ahnung *f*; (*opinion*) Meinung, Ansicht *f*. I have no ~ *or* not the foggiest (*inf*) *or* slightest ~ of what he means ich habe keine Ahnung *or* nicht die leiseste Ahnung, was er meint; I haven't the foggiest *or* slightest ~ (*inf*) ich habe keine Ahnung (*inf*) *or* nicht die leiseste Ahnung; I have no ~ of time ich habe überhaupt kein Zeitgefühl; to give sb ~s, to put ~s into sb's head jdn auf Gedanken *or* Ideen bringen; that gave me the ~ of inviting her das brachte mich auf die Idee *or* den Gedanken, sie einzuladen; do you have any ~ of where he went? haben Sie eine Ahnung, wo er hingegangen ist?; where did you get the ~ *or* what gave you the ~ that I ...? wie kommst du denn auf die Idee, daß ich ...?; he got the ~ (into his head) *or* he somehow got hold of the ~ that she wouldn't help him irgendwie hat er sich (*dat*) eingebildet, sie würde ihm nicht helfen; I have a ~ that ... ich habe den Verdacht, daß ...; that's not my ~ of fun unter Spaß stelle ich mir etwas anderes vor; we need a rough ~ of how many he wants wir müssen ungefähr wissen *or* wir müssen eine ungefähre Vorstellung davon haben, wie viele er will.
(b) (*whim*) Idee *f*. to get/have a ~ to do sth Lust bekommen/haben, etw zu tun; if he gets a ~ to do something, nothing can stop him wenn er sich (*dat*) etwas in den Kopf gesetzt hat, kann ihn keiner davon abhalten; she has some strange ~s sie kommt manchmal auf seltsame Ideen *or* Gedanken; I hit (up)on *or* suddenly had the ~ of going to see her mir kam plötzlich die Idee, sie zu besuchen.
(c) (*esp US inf*) ~s *pl* Kurzwaren *pl*.
notional ['nəʊʃənl] *adj* (a) (*hypothetical*) fiktiv, angenommen; (*nominal*) payment nominell. (b) (*esp US*) versponnen, verträumt. (c) (*Philos*) spekulativ.
notoriety [ˌnəʊtə'raɪətɪ] *n* traurige Berühmtheit.
notorious [nəʊ'tɔːrɪəs] *adj* person, fact berüchtigt, berühmtberüchtigt; place also verrufen, verschrieen; (*well-known*) gambler, criminal, liar notorisch. a ~ woman eine Frau von schlechtem Ruf; to be ~ for sth für etw berüchtigt sein; it is a ~ fact that ... es ist leider nur allzu bekannt, daß ...
notoriously [nəʊ'tɔːrɪəslɪ] *adv* notorisch. to be ~ inefficient/violent etc für seine Untüchtigkeit/Gewalttätigkeit berüchtigt *or* bekannt sein.
no-trump ['nəʊ'trʌmp] (*Cards*) **1** *adj* Ohne-Trumpf-. **2** *n* (also ~s) Ohne-Trumpf-Spiel *nt*.
Notts [nɒts] *abbr of* **Nottinghamshire**.
notwithstanding [ˌnɒtwɪθ'stændɪŋ] (*form*) **1** *prep* ungeachtet (+*gen*) (*form*), trotz (+*gen*). **2** *adv* dennoch, trotzdem, nichtsdestotrotz (*form*). **3** *conj* ~ that ... obwohl *or* obgleich ...
nougat ['nuːgɑː] *n* Nougat *m*.
nought [nɔːt] *n* (a) (*number*) Null *f*. ~s and crosses Kinderspiel *nt* mit Nullen und Kreuzen. (b) (*liter: nothing*) Nichts *nt*. to come to ~ sich zerschlagen; to bring to ~ zunichte machen; she thinks ~ of it sie zögert nicht, das zu tun.

noun [naʊn] *n* Substantiv(um), Hauptwort, Dingwort *nt*. **proper/common/abstract/collective** ~ Name *m*/Gattungsname *or* -begriff *m*/Abstraktum *nt*/Sammelbegriff *m*; ~ **phrase** Nominalphrase *f*.

nourish [ˈnʌrɪʃ] **1** *vt* **(a)** nähren; *person also* ernähren; *leather* pflegen. **a good diet** ~**ed her back to health** gute Ernährung brachte sie wieder zu Kräften. **(b)** *(fig)* **hopes etc** nähren, hegen. **literature to** ~ **their minds** Literatur als geistige Nahrung. **2** *vi* nahrhaft sein.

nourishing [ˈnʌrɪʃɪŋ] *adj food, diet, drink* nahrhaft.

nourishment [ˈnʌrɪʃmənt] *n (food)* Nahrung *f*. **you need some real** ~ du brauchst gutes Essen.

nous [naʊs] *n (inf)* Grips *m (inf)*.

nouveau riche [ˌnuːvəʊˈriːʃ] **1** *n*, *pl* -**x** -**s** [ˌnuːvəʊˈriːʃ] Neureiche(r) *mf*. **2** *adj* typisch neureich.

Nov *abbr of* **November** Nov.

nova [ˈnəʊvə] *n*, *pl* -**e** [ˈnəʊvi] *or* -**s** Nova *f*.

Nova Scotia [ˌnəʊvəˈskəʊʃə] *n* Neuschottland *nt*.

novel[1] [ˈnɒvəl] *n* Roman *m*.

novel[2] *adj* neu(artig).

novelette [ˌnɒvəˈlet] *n (pej)* Romänchen *nt*, Kitschroman *m*.

novelettish [ˌnɒvəˈletɪʃ] *adj (pej) situation* rührselig, kitschig.

novelist [ˈnɒvəlɪst] *n* Romanschriftsteller(in *f*), Romancier *m*.

novelistic [ˌnɒvəˈlɪstɪk] *adj* Roman-.

novella [nəˈvelə] *n* Novelle *f*.

novelty [ˈnɒvəltɪ] *n* **(a)** *(newness)* Neuheit *f*. **once the** ~ **has worn off** wenn der Reiz des Neuen *or* der Neuheit vorbei ist. **(b)** *(innovation)* Neuheit *f*, Novum *nt*. **it was quite a** ~ das war etwas ganz Neues, das war ein Novum *nt*. **(c)** *(Comm: trinket)* Krimskrams *m*.

November [nəʊˈvembə[r]] *n* November *m*; *see also* September.

novena [nəʊˈviːnə] *n* Novene *f*.

novice [ˈnɒvɪs] *n (Eccl)* Novize *m*, Novizin *f*; *(fig)* Neuling, Anfänger(in *f*) *m* (at bei, in +*dat*).

noviciate, novitiate [nəʊˈvɪʃɪt] *n (Eccl)* **(a)** *(state)* Noviziat *nt*. **(b)** *(place)* Novizenhaus *nt*.

novocaine ® [ˈnəʊvəʊkeɪn] *n* Novokain, Novocain ® *nt*.

now [naʊ] **1** *adv* **(a)** jetzt, nun; *(immediately)* jetzt, sofort, gleich; *(at this very moment)* gerade, (so)eben; *(nowadays)* heute, heutzutage. **she** ~ **realized why ...** nun *or* da erkannte sie, warum ...; **just** ~ gerade; *(immediately)* gleich, sofort; ~ **is the time to do it** jetzt ist der richtige Moment dafür; **I'll do it just** *or* **right** ~ ich mache es jetzt gleich *or* sofort; **do it (right)** ~ mach es jetzt (sofort); **it's** ~ **or never** jetzt oder nie; **even** ~ **it's not right es** ist immer noch nicht richtig; ~ **for it los!**; **what is it** ~? was ist denn jetzt *or* nun schon wieder?; **by** ~ *(present, past)* inzwischen, mittlerweile; **they have/had never met before** ~ sie haben sich bis jetzt/sie hatten sich bis dahin noch nie getroffen; **before** ~ **it was thought ...** früher dachte man, daß ...; **you should have thought of that/done that before** ~ das hättest du dir eher überlegen müssen/schon früher *or* eher tun müssen; **we'd have heard before** ~ das hätten wir (inzwischen) schon gehört; **I've been there before** ~ ich war schon (früher) da; **for** ~ (jetzt) erst einmal, im Moment, vorläufig; **even** ~ auch *or* selbst jetzt noch; **from** ~ **on(wards)** von nun an; **between** ~ **and the end of the week** bis zum Ende der Woche; **in three days from** ~ (heute) in drei Tagen; **from** ~ **until then** bis dahin; **up to** ~, **till** ~, **until** ~ bis jetzt.

(b) *(alternation)* ~ **...** ~ **bald ... bald**; **(every)** ~ **and then,** ~ **and again** ab und zu, von Zeit zu Zeit, gelegentlich.

2 *conj* **(a)** ~ **(that)** you've seen him jetzt, wo Sie ihn gesehen haben, nun, da Sie ihn gesehen haben *(geh)*.

(b) *(in explanation etc)* nun.

3 *interj also.* ~, ~**!** na, na!; **well** ~ also; ~ **then** also (jetzt); **stop that** ~**!** Schluß jetzt!; **come** ~, **don't exaggerate** nun übertreib mal nicht; ~, **why didn't I think of that?** warum habe ich bloß nicht daran gedacht?

nowadays [ˈnaʊədeɪz] *adv* heute, heutzutage. **heroes of** ~ Helden von heute.

no way [ˈnəʊˈweɪ] *adv see* way 1 (h).

nowhere [ˈnəʊweə[r]] *adv* nirgendwo, nirgends; *(with verbs of motion)* nirgendwohin. ~ **special** irgendwo; *(with motion)* irgendwohin; **it's** ~ **you know du** kennst den Ort nicht; **it's** ~ **you'll ever find it** es ist an einem Platz, wo du es bestimmt nicht findest; **to appear from** *or* **out of** ~ ganz plötzlich *or* aus heiterem Himmel auftauchen; **to come** ~ *(Sport)* unter „ferner liefen" kommen *or* enden; **to come from** ~ **and win** *(Sport)* überraschend siegen; **we're getting** ~ **(fast)** wir machen keine Fortschritte, wir kommen nicht weiter; **rudeness will get you** ~ Grobheit bringt dir gar nichts ein, mit Grobheit bringst du es auch nicht weiter; *see* near.

nowt [naʊt] *n, pron, adv (Brit dial)* nix *(inf)*, nischt *(dial, inf)*.

noxious [ˈnɒkʃəs] *adj* schädlich; *habit* übel; *influence also* verderblich.

nozzle [ˈnɒzl] *n* Düse *f*; *(of syringe)* Kanüle *f*.

nr *abbr of* **near** b, bei.

NSB *(Brit) abbr of* **National Savings Bank.**

NSPCC *(Brit) abbr of* **National Society for the Prevention of Cruelty to Children.**

NT *abbr of* **New Testament** NT *nt*.

nth [enθ] *adj* **the** ~ **power** *or* **degree** die n-te Potenz; **for the** ~ **time** zum x-ten Mal *(inf)*.

nuance [ˈnjuːɑːns] *n* Nuance *f*; *(of colour also)* Schattierung *f*.

nub [nʌb] *n* **(a)** *(piece)* Stückchen, Klümpchen *nt*. **(b)** *(fig)* **the** ~ **of the matter** *or* **the** springende Punkt, der Kernpunkt.

Nubia [ˈnjuːbɪə] *n* Nubien *nt*.

Nubian [ˈnjuːbɪən] **1** *adj* nubisch. **2** *n* Nubier(in *f*) *m*.

nubile [ˈnjuːbaɪl] *adj girl* heiratsfähig; *(attractive)* gut entwickelt.

nuclear [ˈnjuːklɪə[r]] *adj* Kern-, Atom- *(esp Mil)*; *fusion, fission, reaction, research* Kern-; *fuel* nuklear, atomar; *attack,* test, testing Kernwaffen-, Atomwaffen-; *propulsion* Atom-; *submarine, missile* atomgetrieben, Atom-.

nuclear: ~ **deterrent** *n* nukleares Abschreckungsmittel; ~ **energy** *n see* ~ **power**; ~ **family** *n* Klein- *or* Kernfamilie *f*; ~ **physicist** *n* Kernphysiker(in *f*) *m*; ~ **physics** *n* Kernphysik *f*; ~ **pile** *n* Atommeiler *m*; ~ **power** *n* Atomkraft, Kernenergie *f*; ~-**powered** *adj* atomgetrieben; ~ **power station** *n* Kern- *or* Atomkraftwerk *nt*; ~ **reactor** *n* Kern- *or* Atomreaktor *m*; ~ **war** *n* Atomkrieg *m*; ~ **warfare** *n* Atomkrieg *m*.

nuclei [ˈnjuːklɪaɪ] *pl of* **nucleus.**

nucleic acid [njuːˈkleɪɪkˈæsɪd] *n* Nukleinsäure *f*.

nucleus [ˈnjuːklɪəs] *n, pl* **nuclei** *(Phys, Astron, fig)* Kern *m*; *(Biol: of cell also)* Nukleus *m*. **atomic** ~ Atomkern *m*.

nuddy [ˈnʌdɪ] *n* **in the** ~ *(Brit inf)* nackig *(inf)*.

nude [njuːd] **1** *adj* nackt; *(Art)* Akt-. ~ **study** *(Art)* Akt(studie *f*) *m*; ~ **figure/portrait** Akt *m*. **2** *n (person)* Nackte(r) *mf*; *(Art) (painting, sculpture etc)* Akt *m*; *(model)* Aktmodell *nt*. **to paint from the** ~ einen Akt malen; **in the** ~ nackt.

nudge [nʌdʒ] **1** *vt* anstoßen, anstoßen. ~ **sb's memory** *(fig)* jds Gedächtnis *(dat)* (ein wenig) nachhelfen. **2** *n* Stups *m*, kleiner Stoß. **to give sb a** ~ jdm einen Stups geben, jdn stupsen.

nudie [ˈnjuːdɪ] *adj (inf) picture etc* Nackt-.

nudism [ˈnjuːdɪzəm] *n* Freikörperkultur *f*, Nudismus *m*.

nudist [ˈnjuːdɪst] *n* Anhänger(in *f*) *m* der Freikörperkultur, FKK-Anhänger(in *f*), Nudist(in *f*) *m*. ~ **colony/camp/beach** FKK-Kolonie *f*/-platz *m*/-strand *m*, Nudistenkolonie *f*/-platz *m*/Nacktbadestrand *m*.

nudity [ˈnjuːdɪtɪ] *n* Nacktheit *f*.

nugatory [ˈnjuːɡətərɪ] *adj (liter)* belanglos, nichtig *(geh)*.

nugget [ˈnʌɡɪt] *n (of gold etc)* Klumpen *m*; *(fig: of information, knowledge)* Brocken *m*, Bröckchen *nt*.

nuisance [ˈnjuːsns] *n* **(a)** *(person)* Plage *f*; *(esp pestering)* Nervensäge *f*; *(esp child)* Quälgeist *m*. **he can be a** ~ er kann einen aufregen, er kann einem auf die Nerven *or* den Geist *(inf)* gehen; **to make a** ~ **of oneself** lästig werden; ~ **value** Störfaktor *m*; **he's good** ~ **value** er sorgt für Umtrieb.

(b) *(thing, event)* **to be a** ~ lästig sein; *(annoying)* ärgerlich sein; **what a** ~, **having to do it again** wie ärgerlich *or* lästig, das noch einmal machen zu müssen; **what a** ~ wie ärgerlich; **to become a** ~ lästig werden; **this wind is a** ~ dieser Wind ist eine Plage; **the flies are a** ~ die Fliegen können einem auf die Nerven gehen.

(c) *(Jur)* **public** ~ öffentliches Ärgernis; **to commit a (public)** ~ (öffentliches) Ärgernis erregen.

NUJ *(Brit) abbr of* **National Union of Journalists.**

nuke [njuːk] *n (US sl)* Kern- *or* Atomkraftwerk *nt*.

null [nʌl] *adj (Jur) act, decree* (null und) nichtig, ungültig. **to render sth** ~ **and void** etw null und nichtig machen.

nullification [ˌnʌlɪfɪˈkeɪʃən] *n* **(a)** Annullierung, Nichtigerklärung, Aufhebung *f*. **(b)** *(US)* unterlassene Amts- *or* Rechtshilfe.

nullify [ˈnʌlɪfaɪ] *vt* annullieren, für (null und) nichtig erklären.

nullity [ˈnʌlɪtɪ] *n (Jur)* Ungültigkeit, Nichtigkeit *f*.

NUM *(Brit) abbr of* **National Union of Mineworkers.**

numb [nʌm] **1** *adj* (+*er*) taub, empfindungslos, gefühllos; *feeling* taub; *(emotionally)* benommen, wie betäubt. **hands** ~ **with cold** Hände, die vor Kälte taub *or* gefühllos sind; ~ **with grief** starr *or* wie betäubt vor Schmerz, in *or* with ~ **disbelief** fassungslos.

2 *vt (cold)* taub *or* gefühllos machen; *(injection, fig)* betäuben. ~**ed with fear/grief** starr vor Furcht/Schmerz, vor Furcht erstarrt/wie betäubt vor Schmerz.

number [ˈnʌmbə[r]] **1** *n* **(a)** *(Math)* Zahl *f*; *(numeral)* Ziffer *f*. **the** ~ **of votes cast** die abgegebenen Stimmen.

(b) *(quantity, amount)* Anzahl *f*. **a** ~ **of problems/applicants** eine (ganze) Anzahl von Problemen/Bewerbern; **large** ~**s of people/books** eine große Anzahl von Leuten, (sehr) viele Leute/eine ganze Menge Bücher; **on a** ~ **of occasions** des öfteren; **boys and girls in equal** ~**s** ebenso viele Jungen wie Mädchen, Jungen und Mädchen zu gleicher Zahl *(geh)*; **in a small** ~ **of cases** in wenigen Fällen; **ten in** ~ zehn an der Zahl; **they were few in** ~ es waren nur wenige; **to be found in large** ~**s** zahlreich vorhanden sein, häufig zu finden sein; **in small/ large** ~**s** in kleinen/großen Mengen; **many in** ~ zahlreich; **a fair** ~ **of people/problems** eine ziemlich große Anzahl von Leuten/ Problemen, ziemlich viele Leute/Probleme; **a fair** ~ **of times** ziemlich oft; **times without** ~ unzählige Male; **any** ~ **can play** beliebig viele Spieler können teilnehmen; **any** ~ **of cards etc** *(when choosing)* beliebig viele Karten etc; *(many)* sehr viele Karten etc; **I've told you any** ~ **of times** ich habe es dir zigmal *or* x-mal gesagt *(inf)*; **to win by force of** ~**s** aufgrund zahlenmäßiger Überlegenheit gewinnen; **they have the advantage of** ~**s** sie sind zahlenmäßig überlegen; **they were defeated by superior** ~**s** sie wurden von einer zahlenmäßigen Übermacht geschlagen.

(c) *(of house, room, phone)* Nummer *f*; *(of page)* Seitenzahl *f*; *(of car)* (Auto)nummer *f*; *(Mil: of soldier etc)* Kennummer *f*. **at 4 (in)** Nummer 4; **N~ Ten (Downing Street)** Nummer Zehn (Downing Street); **to take a car's/sb's** ~ die Nummer eines Autos/jds Nummer aufschreiben; **I dialled a wrong** ~ ich habe mich verwählt; **it was a wrong** ~ ich/er etc war falsch verbunden; **the** ~ **one pop star/footballer** *(inf)* der Popstar/ Fußballer Nummer Eins *(inf)*; **to take care of** *or* **look after** ~ **one** *(inf)* (vor allem) an sich *(acc)* selbst denken; **my** ~ **two** *(inf)* er ist mein Vize *(inf)* *or* Stellvertreter *m*; **I'm (the)** ~ **two in the department** ich bin der zweite Mann in der Abteilung; **his** ~**'s up** *(inf)* er ist dran *(inf)*; **to do** ~ **one/two** *(baby-talk)* klein/groß machen *(baby-talk)*; **to get sb's** ~ *(US inf)* jdn einschätzen *or* einordnen *or* durchschauen.

(d) *(song, act etc)* Nummer *f*; *(issue of magazine etc also)* Ausgabe *f*, Heft *nt*; *(dress)* Kreation *f*. **the June** ~ das Juniheft,

die Juniausgabe or -nummer; she's a nice little ~ das ist eine tolle Mieze (inf).
(e) (Gram) Numerus m.
(f) (Eccl) The Book of N~s das Vierte Buch Mose, Numeri pl.
(g) (company) one of their/our ~ eine(r) aus ihren/ unseren Reihen.
(h) ~s pl (arithmetic) Rechnen nt.
2 vt **(a)** (give a number to) numerieren.
(b) (include) zählen (among zu). to be ~ed with the saints zu den Heiligen gezählt werden or zählen.
(c) (amount to) zählen. the group ~ed 50 es waren 50 (Leute in der Gruppe); the library ~s 30,000 volumes die Bibliothek hat 30.000 Bände.
(d) (count) zählen. to be ~ed (limited) begrenzt sein; his days are ~ed seine Tage sind gezählt.
3 vi (Mil etc: also ~ off) abzählen.
numbering ['nʌmbərɪŋ] n (of houses etc) Numerierung f. ~ system Numeriersystem nt.
number: ~less adj zahllos, unzählig; ~-plate n (Brit) Nummernschild, Kennzeichen nt.
numbness ['nʌmnɪs] n (of limbs etc) Taubheit, Starre f; (fig: of mind, senses) Benommenheit, Betäubung f.
num(b)skull ['nʌmskʌl] n (inf) Holz- or Schafskopf (inf) m.
numeracy ['njuːmərəsɪ] n Rechnen nt. his ~ seine rechnerischen Fähigkeiten.
numeral ['njuːmərəl] n Ziffer f.
numerate ['njuːmərɪt] adj rechenkundig. to be (very) ~ (gut) rechnen können.
numeration [njuːmə'reɪʃən] n Numerierung f.
numerator ['njuːməreɪtəʳ] n (Mcth) Zähler, Dividend m.
numerical [njuː'merɪkəl] adj symbols, equation numerisch, Zahlen-; value Zahlen-; order, superiority zahlenmäßig.
numerically [njuː'merɪkəlɪ] adv zahlenmäßig.
numerous ['njuːmərəs] adj zahlreich; family kinderreich.
numismatic [njuːmɪz'mætɪk] adj numismatisch.
numismatics [njuːmɪz'mætɪks] n sing Münzkunde, Numismatik f.
numismatist [njuː'mɪzmətɪst] n Numismatiker(in f) m.
numskull n see num(b)skull.
nun [nʌn] n Nonne f.
nunciature ['nʌnʃɪətjuəʳ] n Nuntiatur f.
nuncio ['nʌnʃɪəʊ] n (Papal ~) Nuntius m.
nunnery ['nʌnərɪ] n (old) (Nonnen)kloster nt.
nuptial ['nʌpʃəl] **1** adj bliss ehelich, Ehe-; feast, celebration Hochzeits-; vow Ehe-. the ~ day (hum) der Hochzeitstag. **2** n the ~s pl (hum, liter) die Hochzeit f.
NUR (Brit) abbr of National Union of Railwaymen.
nurse [nɜːs] **1** n Schwester f; (as professional title) Krankenschwester f; (nanny) Kindermädchen nt, Kinderfrau f; (wet-~) Amme f. male ~ Krankenpfleger m.
2 vt **(a)** pflegen; plant also, (fig) plan hegen; hope, wrath etc hegen, nähren; fire bewachen; (treat carefully) schonen. to ~ sb back to health jdn gesundpflegen; to ~ sb through an illness jdn während or in einer Krankheit pflegen; to ~ a cold an einer Erkältung herumlaborieren (inf); he stood there nursing his bruised arm er stand da und hielt seinen verletzten Arm; to ~ a business ein Geschäft sorgsam verwalten or erhalten; to ~ a business through bad times ein Geschäft durch schlechte Zeiten bringen; to ~ the economy die Wirtschaft hegen und pflegen.
(b) (suckle) child stillen; (cradle) in den Armen wiegen.
nursemaid ['nɜːsmeɪd] n (nanny, hum: servant) Kindermädchen nt.
nursery ['nɜːsərɪ] n **(a)** (room) Kinderzimmer nt; (in hospital) Säuglingssaal m. **(b)** (institution) Kindergarten m; (all-day) Kindertagesstätte f, Hort m. **(c)** (Agr, Hort) (for plants) Gärtnerei f; (for trees) Baumschule f; (fig) Zuchtstätte f.
nursery: ~man n Gärtner m; ~ nurse n Kindermädchen nt, Kinderfrau f; ~ rhyme n Kinderreim m; ~ school n Kindergarten m; ~ school teacher n Kindergärtner(in f) m; ~ slope n (Ski) Idiotenhügel (hum), Anfängerhügel m.
nursing ['nɜːsɪŋ] **1** n **(a)** (care of invalids) Pflege f, Pflegen nt.

(b) (profession) Krankenpflege f. she's going in for ~ sie will in der Krankenpflege arbeiten.
(c) (feeding) Stillen nt.
2 adj attr staff Pflege-; abilities pflegerisch. the ~ profession Krankenpflege f; (nurses collectively) die pflegerischen Berufe.
nursing: ~ auxiliary n Schwesternhelferin f; ~ bottle n (US) Flasche f, Fläschchen nt; ~ care n Pflege f; ~ home n Privatklinik f; (Brit: maternity hospital) Entbindungsklinik f; (convalescent home) Pflegeheim nt; ~ mother n stillende Mutter.
nurture ['nɜːtʃəʳ] **1** n (nourishing) Hegen nt; (upbringing) Erziehung, Bildung f. **2** vt **(a)** (lit, fig) to ~ sb on sth jdn mit etw aufziehen. **(b)** (fig: train) hegen und pflegen.
NUS (Brit) abbr of National Union of Students.
NUT (Brit) abbr of National Union of Teachers.
nut [nʌt] n **(a)** (Bot) Nuß f; (of coal) kleines Stück. a packet of ~s and raisins eine Tüte Studentenfutter; a hard ~ to crack (fig) eine harte Nuß.
(b) (inf: head) Nuß (inf), Birne (inf) f. use your' ~! streng deinen Grips an! (inf); to be off one's ~ nicht ganz bei Trost sein (inf), spinnen (inf); to go off one's ~ durchdrehen (inf), anfangen zu spinnen (inf); to do one's ~ (Brit sl) durchdrehen (inf); see also nuts.
(c) (inf: person) Spinner(in f) m (inf). he's a tough ~ (inf) er ist ein harter or zäher Brocken (inf).
(d) (Mech) (Schrauben)mutter f; the ~s and bolts of a theory die Grundbestandteile einer Theorie.
(e) ~s pl (US sl: testicles) Eier pl (sl).
nut: ~-brown adj nußbraun; ~-case n (inf) Spinner(in f) m (inf); ~cracker(s pl) n Nußknacker m; ~hatch n Kleiber m; ~-house n (inf) (lit, fig) Irrenhaus nt (inf); (lit also) Klapsmühle f (inf); ~meg n (spice) Muskat(nuß f) m; (also ~meg tree) Muskatnußbaum m.
nutrient ['njuːtrɪənt] **1** adj substance nahrhaft; properties Nähr-. **2** n Nährstoff m.
nutriment ['njuːtrɪmənt] n (form) Nahrung f.
nutrition [njuː'trɪʃən] n (diet, science) Ernährung f.
nutritional [njuː'trɪʃənl] adj value, content Nähr-.
nutritious [njuː'trɪʃəs] adj nahrhaft.
nutritiousness [njuː'trɪʃəsnɪs] n Nahrhaftigkeit f.
nutritive ['njuːtrɪtɪv] adj nahrhaft.
nuts [nʌts] adj pred (inf) to be ~ spinnen (inf); to go ~ durchdrehen (inf), anfangen zu spinnen (inf); to be ~ about sb/sth von jdm/etw ganz weg sein (inf); (keen on) ganz wild auf jdn/etw sein (inf); he can't dance for ~ er kann nicht für fünf Pfennig tanzen (inf); ~! (US) Quatsch! (inf); (in annoyance) Mist (inf)!; ~ to him! (US) er kann mich mal (gern haben)! (inf).
nutshell ['nʌtʃel] n Nußschale f. in a ~ (fig) kurz gesagt, mit einem Wort; to put the matter in a ~ (fig) um es (ganz) kurz or kurz und bündig zu sagen.
nutter ['nʌtəʳ] n (Brit sl) Spinner(in f) m (inf); (dangerous) Verrückte(r) mf. he's a ~ er hat einen Stich (inf) or Vogel (inf).
nutty ['nʌtɪ] adj (+er) **(a)** flavour Nuß-; cake also mit Nüssen.
(b) (inf: crazy) plemplem, meschugge, bekloppt (all inf); idea bekloppt (inf). to be ~ about sb/sth von jdm/etw ganz weg sein (inf); (keen) ganz wild auf jdn/etw sein (inf).
nuzzle ['nʌzl] **1** vt (pig) aufwühlen; (dog) beschnüffeln, beschnuppern. **2** vi to ~ (up) against sb, to ~ up to sb (person, animal) sich an jdn schmiegen or drücken.
NW abbr of north-west NW.
NY abbr of New York.
Nyasaland [naɪ'æsəlænd] n Njassaland nt.
NYC abbr of New York City.
nylon ['naɪlon] **1** n **(a)** (Tex) Nylon nt. **(b)** ~s pl Nylonstrümpfe pl. **2** adj Nylon-, ~ material Nylon nt.
nymph [nɪmf] n **(a)** (Myth) Nymphe f. **(b)** (Zool) Nymphe f.
nymphet ['nɪmfet] n Nymphchen nt.
nympho ['nɪmfəʊ] n (inf) Nympho f (inf).
nymphomania [nɪmfəʊ'meɪnɪə] n Nymphomanie, Mannstollheit f.
nymphomaniac [nɪmfəʊ'meɪnɪæk] n Nymphomanin f.
NZ abbr of New Zealand.

O

O, o [əʊ] n **(a)** O, o nt. **(b)** [(Brit) əʊ, (US) zɪərəʊ] (Telec) Null f.
O interj **(a)** (Poet) o. ~ my people o du mein Volk!
(b) (expressing feeling) oh, ach. ~ how wrong he was wie hatte er sich (doch) da geirrt; ~ for a bit of fresh air! ach, wenn es doch nur ein bißchen frische Luft gäbe!; ~ to be in France (ach,) wäre ich nur in Frankreich!; see also oh.
o' [ə] prep abbr of of.
oaf [əʊf] n, pl -s, oaves Flegel, Lümmel m. you clumsy ~! du altes Trampel (inf).

oafish ['əʊfɪʃ] adj flegelhaft, lümmelhaft; (clumsy) stieselig (inf), tölpelhaft.
oak [əʊk] n Eiche f; (wood also) Eichenholz nt. he has a heart of ~ er hat ein unerschütterliches Gemüt; dark ~ (colour) (in) dunkel Eiche.
oak in cpds Eichen-; ~ apple n Gallapfel m.
oaken ['əʊkən] adj (liter) Eichen-, eichen.
oakum ['əʊkəm] n Werg nt.
OAP (Brit) abbr of old-age pensioner.

oar [ɔːʳ] *n* **(a)** Ruder *nt*, Riemen (*Rowing*) *m*. **to pull at the ~s** rudern; sich in die Riemen legen; **to be** *or* **pull a good ~** ein guter Ruderer/eine gute Ruderin *or* Rudrerin sein; **he always has to put his ~ in** (*fig inf*) er muß (aber auch) immer mitmischen (*inf*); **to rest on one's ~s** (*fig*) langsamer treten (*inf*). **(b)** (*person*) Ruderer *m*, Ruderin, Rudrerin *f*.

-oared [-ɔːd] *adj suf*-ruderig. **four-~ boat** Boot mit vier Rudern.
oar: **~lock** *n* (*US*) (Ruder)dolle *f*; **~sman** *n* Ruderer *m*; **~smanship** *n* Rudertechnik *or* -kunst *f*.
OAS *abbr of* **Organization of American States** OAS *f*.
oasis [əʊˈeɪsɪs] *n, pl* **oases** [əʊˈeɪsiːz] (*lit, fig*) Oase *f*.
oast [əʊst] *n* Darre *f*, Trockenboden *m*. **~-house** Trockenschuppen *m or* -haus *nt*.
oat [əʊt] *n usu pl* Hafer *m*. **~s** *pl* (*Cook*) Haferflocken *pl*; **to sow one's wild ~s** (*fig*) sich (*dat*) die Hörner abstoßen; **he's feeling his ~s** ihn sticht der Hafer; **to be off one's ~s** (*hum sl*) keinen Appetit haben; **he hasn't had his ~s for some time** (*hum sl*) der hat schon lange keine mehr vernascht (*hum sl*).
oatcake [ˈəʊtkeɪk] *n* Leckerli *nt* Haferkeks.
oath [əʊθ] *n* **(a)** Schwur *m*; (*Jur*) Eid *m*. **to take** *or* **make** *or* **swear an ~** schwören; (*Jur*) einen Eid ablegen *or* leisten; **to declare under ~** *or* **on ~** (*Jur*) unter Eid aussagen; **to be under ~** (*Jur*) unter Eid stehen; **to break one's ~** seinen Schwur brechen; **to put sb on ~** (*Jur*) jdn vereidigen; **he put them on ~ to tell the truth** er hat sie auf die Wahrheit vereidigt; **to release sb from his ~** jdn von seinem Eid entbinden; **to take the ~** (*Jur*) vereidigt werden; **he refused to take the ~** (*Jur*) er verweigerte den Eid; **he refused to take the ~ on the Bible** er lehnte es ab, auf die Bibel zu schwören; **on my ~!** (*obs*) bei meiner Seele! (*obs*).
(b) (*curse, profanity*) Fluch *m*.
oatmeal [ˈəʊtmiːl] **1** *n, no pl* Haferschrot *m*, Hafermehl *nt*. **2** *adj colour, dress* hellbeige.
OAU *abbr of* **Organization of African Unity** OAU *f*.
oaves [əʊvz] *pl of* **oaf**.
ob *abbr of* **obiit** *got*.
obbligato *n, adj see* **obligato**.
obduracy [ˈɒbdjʊrəsɪ] *n see adj* Hartnäckigkeit *f*; Verstocktheit, Halsstarrigkeit *f*; Unnachgiebigkeit *f*.
obdurate [ˈɒbdjʊrɪt] *adj* (*stubborn*) hartnäckig; *sinner* verstockt, halsstarrig; (*hardhearted*) unnachgiebig, unerbittlich.
OBE *abbr of* **Order of the British Empire**.
obedience [əˈbiːdɪəns] *n, no pl* Gehorsam *m*. **in ~ to the law** dem Gesetz entsprechend; **in ~ to your wishes** (*form*) Ihren Wünschen gemäß; **to teach sb ~** jdn gehorchen lehren.
obedient [əˈbiːdɪənt] *adj* gehorsam; *child, dog also* folgsam. **to be ~** gehorchen (*to dat*); (*child, dog also*) folgen (*to dat*); (*steering, controls, car also*) reagieren, ansprechen (*to auf + acc*).
obediently [əˈbiːdɪəntlɪ] *adv see adj*. **the car responded ~** das Auto reagierte prompt.
obeisance [əʊˈbeɪsəns] *n* **(a)** (*form: homage, respect*) Ehrerbietung, Reverenz (*geh*), Huldigung (*liter*) *f*. **to do** *or* **make** *or* **pay ~ (to sb)** (jdm) seine Huldigung darbringen *or* Ehrerbietung bezeugen, jdm huldigen. **(b)** (*obs: deep bow*) Verbeugung, Verneigung *f*.
obelisk [ˈɒbɪlɪsk] *n* **(a)** (*Archit*) Obelisk *m*. **(b)** (*Typ*) Kreuz *nt*.
obese [əʊˈbiːs] *adj* fettleibig (*form, Med*), feist (*pej*).
obeseness [əʊˈbiːsnɪs], **obesity** [əʊˈbiːsɪtɪ] *n* Fettleibigkeit (*form, Med*), Feistheit (*pej*) *f*.
obey [əˈbeɪ] **1** *vt* gehorchen (+*dat*); *conscience also*, (*child, dog also*) folgen (+*dat*); *law, rules* sich halten an (+*acc*); *order* befolgen; (*Jur*) *summons* nachkommen (+*dat*), Folge leisten (+*dat*); (*machine, vehicle*) *controls* reagieren *or* ansprechen auf (+*acc*); *driver* gehorchen (+*dat*). **to ~ sb implicitly** jdm absoluten Gehorsam leisten; **he makes** *or* **can make himself ~ed** (bei) ihm gehorcht man; **I like to be ~ed** ich bin (es) gewohnt, daß man meine Anordnungen befolgt.
2 *vi* gehorchen; (*child, dog also*) folgen; (*machine, vehicle also*) reagieren. **the troops refused to ~** die Truppen verweigerten den Gehorsam.
obfuscate [ˈɒbfʌskeɪt] *vt* (*liter*) *mind* verwirren, trüben; *issue* unklar *or* verworren machen, vernebeln.
obituary [əˈbɪtjʊərɪ] *n* Nachruf *m*. **~ notice** Todesanzeige *f*; **I saw his ~ notice today** ich habe seinen Namen heute im Sterberegister gelesen; **~ column** Sterberegister *nt*.
object¹ [ˈɒbdʒɪkt] *n* **(a)** (*thing*) Gegenstand *m*, Ding *nt*; (*Philos, abstract etc*) Objekt, Ding *nt*. **he treats her like an ~** er behandelt sie wie ein Ding *or* Objekt; **she became an ~ of pity** mit ihr mußte man Mitleid haben; **he was an ~ of scorn** er war die Zielscheibe der Verachtung; **the cat is the sole ~ of her love** ihre ganze Liebe gilt ihrer Katze.
(b) (*aim*) Ziel *nt*, Absicht *f*, Zweck *m*. **with this ~ in view** *or* **in mind** mit diesem Ziel vor Augen; **with the sole ~ of (doing)** mit dem einzigen Ziel *or* nur in der Absicht(, zu ...); **he has no ~ in life** er hat kein Ziel im Leben *or* kein Lebensziel; **what's the ~ (of staying here)?** wozu *or* zu welchem Zweck (bleiben wir hier)?; **the ~ of the exercise** der Zweck *or* (*fig also*) Sinn der Übung; **to defeat one's own ~** sich (*dat*) selber schaden, sich (*dat*) ins eigene Fleisch schneiden (*inf*); **that defeats the ~** das macht es sinnlos, das verfehlt seinen Sinn *or* Zweck; **to succeed in one's ~** seinen Zweck *or* sein Ziel erreichen; **he made it his ~ to ...** er setzte es sich (*dat*) zum Ziel, zu ...
(c) (*obstacle*) Hinderungsgrund *m*. **money/distance (is) no ~** Geld/Entfernung spielt keine Rolle *or* (ist) nebensächlich.
(d) (*Gram*) Objekt *nt*. **direct/indirect ~** direktes/indirektes Objekt, Akkusativ-/Dativobjekt.
(e) (*inf: odd thing*) Ding, Dings (*inf*) *nt*; (*odd person*) Subjekt *nt*, Vogel *m* (*inf*).
object² [əbˈdʒekt] **1** *vi* dagegen sein; (*make objection, protest*) protestieren; (*be against: in discussion etc*) Einwände haben (*to gegen*); (*raise objection*) Einwände erheben; (*disapprove*)

Anstoß nehmen (*to an +dat*), sich stören (*to an +dat*). **to ~ to sth** (*disapprove*) etw ablehnen *or* mißbilligen; **I don't ~ to that** ich habe nichts dagegen (einzuwenden); **if you don't ~ wenn es (Ihnen) recht ist, wenn Sie nichts dagegen haben**; **do you ~ to my smoking?** stört es (Sie), wenn ich rauche?, haben Sie etwas dagegen, wenn ich rauche?; **he ~s to my drinking** *or* nimmt daran Anstoß *or* er hat etwas dagegen, daß ich trinke; **I ~ to your tone/to people smoking in my living room** ich verbitte mir diesen Ton/ich verbitte mir, daß in meinem Wohnzimmer geraucht wird; **I ~ most strongly to his smoking** ich mißbillige es aufs äußerste, daß er raucht; **I ~ most strongly to what he says/to his argument** ich protestiere energisch gegen seine Behauptung/ich lehne seine Argumentation energisch ab; **I ~ to him bossing me around** ich wehre mich dagegen, daß er mich (so) herumkommandiert; **I don't mind your being late, but I do ~ to your not coming home at all** es stört mich nicht, wenn du spät nach Hause kommst, aber daß du überhaupt nicht erscheinst, das kommt (mir) nicht in Frage!; **I ~ to orange curtains with green wallpaper** Vorhänge in Orange mit grünen Tapeten, da protestiere ich!; **she ~s to all that noise** sie stört sich an dem vielen Lärm; **he doesn't ~ to the odd little drink** er hat nichts gegen ein kleines Gläschen ab und zu (einzuwenden); **I ~!** ich protestiere!, ich erhebe Einspruch (*form*); **to ~ to a witness** (*Jur*) einen Zeugen ablehnen.
2 *vt* einwenden.
object: **~ clause** *n* Objektsatz *m*; **~ deletion** *n* (*Gram*) Unterdrückung *f* des Objekts.
objection [əbˈdʒekʃən] *n* **(a)** (*reason against*) Einwand *m* (*to gegen*). **to make** *or* **raise an ~** einen Einwand machen *or* erheben (*geh*); **I have no ~ to his going away** ich habe nichts dagegen (einzuwenden), daß er weggeht; **are there any ~s?** irgendwelche Einwände?; **I see no ~ to it** ich sehe nichts, was dagegen spricht; **what are your ~s to it/him?** was haben Sie dagegen/gegen ihn (einzuwenden)?, welche Einwände haben Sie dagegen/gegen ihn?; **~!** (*Jur*) Einspruch!; **I have no ~ to him** (*as a witness etc*) ich erhebe keinen Einspruch gegen ihn.
(b) (*dislike*) Abneigung *f*; (*disapproval*) Einspruch, Widerspruch *m*. **I have a strong ~ to dogs** ich habe eine starke Abneigung gegen Hunde; **I have no ~ to him** (*as a person*) ich habe nichts gegen ihn; **that's bound to meet with your parents' ~** da erheben deine Eltern bestimmt Einspruch.
objectionable [əbˈdʒekʃənəbl] *adj* störend; *conduct* anstößig, nicht einwandfrei; *remark, language* anstößig, unanständig; *smell* unangenehm, übel. **the censor removed everything he found ~** der Zensor entfernte alle Stellen, die er für anstößig hielt; **he's a most ~ person** er ist unausstehlich *or* ekelhaft; **he became ~** er wurde unangenehm.
objectionably [əbˈdʒekʃənəblɪ] *adv* unangenehm.
objective [əbˈdʒektɪv] **1** *adj* **(a)** (*impartial*) *person, article* objektiv, sachlich. **(b)** (*real*) objektiv. **~ fact** Tatsache *f*; **it doesn't exist in the ~ world** das gibt es nicht tatsächlich *or* in der Realität.
2 *n* **(a)** (*aim*) Ziel *nt*; (*esp Comm*) Zielvorstellung *f*; (*Mil*) Angriffsziel *nt*. **in establishing our ~s** bei unserer Zielsetzung.
(b) (*Opt, Phot*) Objektiv *nt*.
objectively [əbˈdʒektɪvlɪ] *adv* **(a)** (*unemotionally*) objektiv, sachlich. **(b)** (*in real life etc*) tatsächlich, wirklich.
objectivism [əbˈdʒektɪvɪzəm] *n* Objektivismus *m*.
objectivity [ˌɒbdʒekˈtɪvɪtɪ] *n* Objektivität *f*.
object lesson *n* **(a)** (*fig*) Paradebeispiel, Musterbeispiel *nt* (*in, on für, gen*). **(b)** (*Sch*) Anschauungsunterricht *m*.
objector [əbˈdʒektəʳ] *n* Gegner (*in*) *m* (*to gen*).
objet d'art [ˌɒbʒeɪˈdɑː] *n* Kunstgegenstand *m*.
objurgate [ˈɒbdʒɜːgeɪt] *vt* (*form*) rügen (*geh*), tadeln.
objurgation [ˌɒbdʒɜːˈgeɪʃən] *n* (*form*) Tadel *m*, Rüge *f*.
oblate¹ [ˈɒbleɪt] *adj* (*Math*) abgeplattet.
oblate² *n* (*Eccl*) Oblate *m*.
oblation [əʊˈbleɪʃən] *n* (*Eccl*) Opfergabe *f*, Opfer *nt*.
obligate [ˈɒblɪgeɪt] *vt* verpflichten (*sb to do sth* jdn, etw zu tun).
obligation [ˌɒblɪˈgeɪʃən] *n* Verpflichtung, Pflicht *f*. **to be under an ~ to do sth** verpflichtet sein *or* die Pflicht haben, etw zu tun; **to be under an ~ to sb** jdm verpflichtet sein; **you have placed us all under a great ~** wir sind Ihnen alle sehr verpflichtet; **without ~** (*Comm*) unverbindlich, ohne Obligo (*form*); **with no ~ to buy** ohne Kaufzwang.
obligato [ˌɒblɪˈgɑːtəʊ] **1** *n* (*part*) Obligato *nt*. **2** *adj* obligato.
obligatory [ɒˈblɪgətərɪ] *adj* obligatorisch; *rule* verbindlich; *subject* biology **is ~** Biologie ist Pflicht; **attendance is ~** Anwesenheit ist vorgeschrieben; **it's ~ to pay taxes** jeder ist steuerpflichtig; **to make it ~ to do sth/for sb to do sth** vorschreiben, daß etw getan wird/daß jd etw tut; *identity cards* **were made ~** Personalausweise wurden Vorschrift; **with the ~ piper** mit dem obligaten Dudelsackpfeifer.
oblige [əˈblaɪdʒ] **1** *vt* **(a)** (*compel*) zwingen; (*because of duty*) verpflichten (*sb to do sth* jdn, etw zu tun); (*Jur*) vorschreiben (*sb to do sth* jdm, etw zu tun). **to feel ~d to do sth** sich etw verpflichtet fühlen, sich verpflichtet fühlen, etw zu tun; **I was ~d to go** ich sah mich gezwungen zu gehen; **the law ~s us to obey the Highway Code** man ist gesetzlich zur Befolgung der Straßenverkehrsordnung verpflichtet, die Befolgung der Straßenverkehrsordnung ist gesetzlich vorgeschrieben; **you are not ~d to do it** Sie sind nicht dazu verpflichtet, es zwingt Sie keiner dazu; **you are not ~d to answer this question** Sie brauchen diese Frage nicht zu beantworten.
(b) (*do a favour to*) einen Gefallen tun (+*dat*), gefällig sein (+*dat*). **could you ~ me with a light?** wären Sie so gut, mir Feuer zu geben?; **please ~ me by opening a window** würden Sie mir bitte den Gefallen tun und ein Fenster öffnen?; **he ~d us with a song** er gab uns ein Lied gesungen; **would you ~ me by not interrupting** hätten Sie die Güte, mich nicht zu unterbrechen; **you would ~ me by shutting up!** würden Sie gefälligst

Ruhe geben!; **anything to ~ a friend** was tut man nicht alles für einen Freund!

(c) much ~d! herzlichen Dank!; **I am much ~d to you for this!** ich bin Ihnen dafür sehr verbunden *or* dankbar.

2 *vi* **she is always ready to ~** sie ist immer sehr gefällig *or* hilfsbereit; *(hum)* she ist niemals abgeneigt; **they called for a song, but no-one ~d** sie verlangten nach einem Lied, aber niemand kam der Aufforderung nach; **anything to ~** stets zu Diensten!; **I've asked you twice, now would you please ~** ich habe Sie schon zweimal gebeten, würden Sie nun bitte gefälligst der Aufforderung nachkommen *or* Folge leisten; **a prompt reply would ~** *(Comm)* für eine baldige Antwort wären wir sehr dankbar, um baldige Antwort wird gebeten.

obliging [ə'blaɪdʒɪŋ] *adj* entgegenkommend, gefällig; *personality* zuvorkommend. **it was very ~ of them** es war sehr entgegenkommend von ihnen.

obligingly [ə'blaɪdʒɪŋlɪ] *adv* entgegenkommenderweise, freundlicherweise, liebenswürdigerweise.

oblique [ə'bli:k] **1** *adj* **(a)** *line* schief, schräg, geneigt; *angle* schief; *(Gram)* *case* abhängig. **~ stroke** Schrägstrich *m*.

(b) *(fig)* *look* schief, schräg; *course* schräg; *method, style, reply* indirekt; *hint, reference* indirekt, versteckt. **he achieved his goal by rather ~ means** er erreichte sein Ziel auf Umwegen *or (dishonestly)* auf krummen Wegen.

2 *n* Schrägstrich *m*. **and ~ or** und Strich oder.

obliquely [ə'bli:klɪ] *adv* **(a)** schief *or* schräg. **(b)** *(fig)* indirekt.

obliqueness [ə'bli:knɪs] *n* **(a)** Schiefe, Schräge, Neigung *f*. **(b)** *(fig: of means)* Indirektheit *f*.

obliterate [ə'blɪtəreɪt] *vt* *(erase, abolish)* auslöschen; *past, memory also* tilgen *(geh)*; *city also, (inf)* *opposite team etc* vernichten; *(hide from sight)* *sun, view* verdecken. **the coffee stain has ~d most of the design/text** der Kaffeefleck hat das Muster/den Text fast ganz unkenntlich/unleserlich gemacht; **a sculpture whose features were ~d by age** eine vom Alter unkenntlich gemachte Skulptur; **by the 19th century this disease had been completely ~d** im 19. Jahrhundert war dann diese Krankheit völlig ausgerottet.

obliteration [ə,blɪtə'reɪʃən] *n see vt* Auslöschen *nt*; Vernichtung *f*; Verdecken *nt*.

oblivion [ə'blɪvɪən] *n* **(a)** Vergessenheit *f*, Vergessen *nt*. **to sink** *or* **fall into ~** in Vergessenheit geraten, der Vergessenheit anheimfallen *(geh)*; **to rescue sb/sth from ~** jdn/etw wiederbeleben *or* wieder ins Bewußtsein *or* ins Tageslicht bringen; **he drank himself into ~** er trank bis zur Bewußtlosigkeit.

(b) *(unawareness) see* **obliviousness.**

oblivious [ə'blɪvɪəs] *adj* **to be ~ of sth** sich *(dat)* etw nicht bewußt machen, sich *(dat)* einer Sache *(gen)* nicht bewußt sein; **he was quite ~ of his surroundings** er bemerkte seine Umgebung gar nicht, er nahm seine Umgebung gar nicht wahr; **~ of his surroundings** ohne Notiz von seiner Umgebung zu nehmen; **they are ~ of** *or* **to the beauty of their surroundings** sie haben für die Schönheit ihrer Umgebung keinen Sinn; **he was totally ~ of what was going on in his marriage** er (be)merkte gar nicht *or* wurde gar nicht gewahr *(geh)*, was in seiner Ehe vor sich ging; **~ of the traffic lights** ohne die Ampel zu bemerken; **how can anyone remain so ~ to other people's feelings!** wie kann man bloß so wenig an die Gefühle anderer denken; **~ of the world** weltvergessen.

obliviously [ə'blɪvɪəslɪ] *adv* **to carry on ~** einfach (unbeirrt) weitermachen.

obliviousness [ə'blɪvɪəsnɪs] *n* **because of his ~ of the danger he was in** weil er sich *(dat)* der Gefahr bewußt war, in der er schwebte; **because of his ~ of what was happening** weil er sich *(dat)* nicht dessen bewußt war *or* weil er gar nicht bemerkte, was vorging; **a state of blissful ~ to the world** ein Zustand seliger Weltvergessenheit.

oblong ['ɒblɒŋ] **1** *adj* rechteckig. **2** *n* Rechteck *nt*.

obloquy ['ɒbləkwɪ] *n* *(liter)* **(a)** *(blame, abuse)* Schmähung *(liter)*, Beschimpfung *f*. **(b)** *(disgrace)* Schande, Schmach *f*.

obnoxious [əb'nɒkʃəs] *adj* widerlich, widerwärtig; *person also, behaviour* unausstehlich. **an ~ person** eine Ekel *nt (inf)*; **don't be so ~ to her** sei nicht so gemein *or* fies *(inf)* zu ihr.

obnoxiously [əb'nɒkʃəslɪ] *adv see adj.*

obnoxiousness [əb'nɒkʃəsnɪs] *n see adj* Widerlichkeit *f*, Widerwärtigkeit *f*; Unausstehlichkeit *f*.

oboe ['əʊbəʊ] *n* Oboe *f*.

oboist ['əʊbəʊɪst] *n* Oboist(in *f*) *m*.

obscene [əb'si:n] *adj* obszön; *word, picture, book also* unzüchtig; *language, joke also* zotig; *gesture, posture, thought also* schamlos, unzüchtig; *(non-sexually, repulsive)* ekelerregend. **this colour scheme is positively ~** diese Farbzusammenstellung widert mich an *or* ist widerlich.

obscenely [əb'si:nlɪ] *adv* obszön; *(repulsively)* ekelerregend.

obscenity [əb'senɪtɪ] *n* Obszönität *f*. **the ~ of these crimes** diese ekelerregenden Verbrechen; **he used an ~** er benutzte *or* gebrauchte einen ordinären Ausdruck.

obscurantism [,ɒbskjʊə'ræntɪzəm] *n* Obskurantismus *m*, Aufklärungsfeindlichkeit *f*.

obscurantist [,ɒbskjʊə'ræntɪst] *n* Obskurant *m*, Feind *m* der Aufklärung.

obscure [əb'skjʊə^r] **1** *adj* (+*er*) **(a)** *(hard to understand)* dunkel; *style* unklar, undurchsichtig; *argument* verworren; *book, poet, poem* schwer verständlich. **is the meaning still ~ to you?** ist Ihnen die Bedeutung (immer) noch nicht klar?

(b) *(indistinct)* *feeling, memory* dunkel, undeutlich, unklar. **for some ~ reason** aus einem unerfindlichen Grund.

(c) *(unknown, little known, humble)* obskur; *poet, village also* unbekannt; *beginnings (humble)* unbedeutend; *(not known also)* dunkel; *life* wenig beachtenswert. **of ~ birth** von unbekannter Herkunft; **he holds some ~ post in the Civil Service** er hat so ein obskures Pöstchen im Staatsdienst.

(d) *(rare: dark)* düster, finster.

2 *vt* **(a)** *(hide)* *sun, view* verdecken. **the tree ~d the bay from our view** der Baum nahm uns *(dat)* die Sicht auf die Bucht.

(b) *(confuse)* verworren *or* unklar machen; *mind* verwirren.

obscurely [əb'skjʊəlɪ] *adv* **(a)** *written, presented, argued, remember* undeutlich, unklar. **(b)** **a movement which began ~ in the depths of Russia** eine Bewegung mit obskuren Anfängen im tiefsten Rußland. **(c)** *lit* schwach.

obscurity [əb'skjʊərɪtɪ] *n* **(a)** *no pl (of a wood, night)* Dunkelheit, Finsternis *f*, Dunkel *nt*.

(b) *(of style, ideas, argument)* Unklarheit, Unverständlichkeit, Verworrenheit *f*. **to lapse into ~** verworren *or* unklar werden; **he threw some light on the obscurities of the text** er erhellte einige der unklaren Textstellen.

(c) *no pl (of birth, origins)* Dunkel *nt*. **to live in ~** zurückgezogen leben; **to rise from ~** aus dem Nichts auftauchen; **in spite of the ~ of his origins** trotz seiner unbekannten Herkunft; **to sink into ~** in Vergessenheit geraten.

obsequies ['ɒbsɪkwɪz] *npl (form)* Beerdigungsfeier *f*, Leichenbegängnis *nt (liter)*.

obsequious *adj*, **~ly** *adv* [əb'si:kwɪəs, -lɪ] unterwürfig, servil *(geh)* **(to(wards)** gegen, gegenüber).

obsequiousness [əb'si:kwɪəsnɪs] *n* Unterwürfigkeit, Servilität *(geh) f*.

observable [əb'zɜ:vəbl] *adj* sichtbar, erkennbar. **as is ~ in rabbits** wie bei Kaninchen zu beobachten ist *or* beobachtet wird; **a welcome improvement has recently become ~** in letzter Zeit zeichnet sich eine willkommene Verbesserung ab; **there has been no ~ change in his condition today** es wurde heute keine Veränderung seines Befindens beobachtet.

observance [əb'zɜ:vəns] *n* **(a)** *(of law)* Befolgung, Beachtung *f*, Beachten *nt*.

(b) *(Eccl)* *(keeping of rites etc)* Einhalten *nt*, Einhaltung *f*, Beachten *nt*; *(celebration)* Kirchenfest *nt*; *(in a convent etc)* *(Orden)*regel, Observanz *f*. **~ of the Sabbath** Einhaltung *f* des Sabbats *or (non-Jewish)* des Sonntagsgebots; **religious ~s** religiöse *or (Christian also)* kirchliche Feste.

observant [əb'zɜ:vənt] *adj* **(a)** *(watchful)* *person* aufmerksam, wach(sam), achtsam. **that's very ~ of you** das hast du aber gut bemerkt; **if you'd been a little more ~** wenn du etwas besser aufgepaßt hättest.

(b) *(strict in obeying rules)* **you should be a little more ~ of the law** Sie sollten sich ein bißchen an das Gesetz halten.

observantly [əb'zɜ:vəntlɪ] *adv* aufmerksam. **... which he very ~ spotted ...,** wie er sehr gut bemerkt hat.

observation [,ɒbzə'veɪʃən] *n* **(a)** Beobachtung *f*; *(act also)* Beobachten *nt*. **to keep sb/sth under ~** jdn/etw unter Beobachtung halten; *(by police)* jdn/etw überwachen *or* observieren *(form)*; **~ of nature** Naturbeobachtung *f*; **to take an ~** *(Naut)* das Besteck nehmen; **powers of ~** Beobachtungsgabe *f*; **he's in hospital for ~** er ist zur Beobachtung im Krankenhaus; **to escape sb's ~** *(von jdm)* unbemerkt bleiben, jdm entgehen.

(b) *(of rules, Sabbath)* Einhalten *nt*.

(c) *(remark)* Bemerkung, Äußerung *f*. **~s on Kant** Betrachtungen über *or* zu Kant; **his ~s on the experiment** seine Versuchserläuterungen.

observational [,ɒbzə'veɪʃənl] *adj* empirisch, auf Grund von Beobachtungen gewonnen.

observation: ~ car *n (US Rail)* Aussichtswagen, Panoramawagen *m*; **~ lounge** *n* Aussichtsrestaurant *nt*; **~ post** *n* Beobachtungsposten *m*; **~ ward** *n* Beobachtungsstation *f*.

observatory [əb'zɜ:vətrɪ] *n* Observatorium *nt*, Sternwarte *f*; *(Met)* Observatorium *nt*, Wetterwarte *f*.

observe [əb'zɜ:v] **1** *vt* **(a)** *(see, notice)* beobachten, bemerken; *difference, change also* wahrnehmen. **did you actually ~ him do it?** haben Sie ihn wirklich dabei beobachtet?; **the thief was ~d to ...** der Dieb wurde dabei beobachtet, wie er ...

(b) *(watch carefully, study)* beobachten; *(by police)* überwachen. **children learn by observing adults** Kinder lernen dadurch, daß sie die Erwachsenen beobachten.

(c) *(remark)* bemerken, feststellen, äußern.

(d) *(obey)* achten auf (+*acc*); *rule, custom, ceasefire, Sabbath* einhalten; *anniversary etc* begehen, feiern. **to ~ a minute's silence** eine Schweigeminute einlegen; **failure to ~ the law** ein Verstoß gegen das Gesetz.

2 *vi* **(a)** *(watch)* zusehen; *(act as an observer)* beobachten.

(b) *(remark)* bemerken, feststellen (*on* zu, über +*acc*). **you were about to ~ ...?** Sie wollten gerade sagen ...?

observer [əb'zɜ:və^r] *n (watcher)* Zuschauer(in *f*) *m*; *(Mil, Aviat, Pol)* Beobachter *m*.

obsess [əb'ses] *vt* **to be ~ed by** *or* **with sb/sth** von jdm/etw besessen sein; **sth ~es sb** jd ist von etw besessen; **his one ~ing thought** der ihn ständig verfolgende Gedanke; **don't become ~ed by it** laß das nicht zum Zwang *or* zur Manie werden.

obsession [əb'seʃən] *n* **(a)** *(fixed idea)* fixe Idee, Manie *f*; *(fear etc)* Zwangsvorstellung, Obsession *(spec) f*. **the cat was an ~ with her** die Katze war ihre ganze Leidenschaft; **it's an ~ with him** das ist eine fixe Idee von ihm; *(hobby etc)* er ist davon besessen; **watching TV is an ~ with him** Fernsehen ist bei ihm zur Sucht geworden.

(b) *(state)* Besessenheit (*with* von), Monomanie *f*. **this ~ with order/tidiness/accuracy** dieser Ordnungs-/Aufräumungs-/Genauigkeitswahn *m*; **an unnatural ~ with detail** eine (ganz) unnatürliche Detailbesessenheit; **because of his ~ with her** weil er ihr gänzlich verfallen ist/war.

obsessive [əb'sesɪv] *adj* zwanghaft, obsessiv *(spec)*. **to become ~** zum Zwang *or* zur Manie werden; **an ~ thought/memory** ein Gedanke, der/eine Erinnerung, die einen nicht losläßt; **an ~ desire for wealth** eine Sucht nach Reichtum; **he is an ~ reader** er liest wie besessen, er hat die Lesewut *(inf)*; **~ neurosis** *(Psych)* Zwangsneurose *f*.

obsessively [əb'sesɪvlɪ] *adv* wie besessen. **she is ~ preoccupied with cleanliness** sie huldigt einem Sauberkeitswahn.

obsolescence [ˌɒbsə'lesns] *n* Veralten *nt; see* **planned.**

obsolescent [ˌɒbsə'lesnt] *adj* allmählich außer Gebrauch kommend. **to be ~** anfangen zu veralten.

obsolete ['ɒbsəliːt] *adj* veraltet, überholt, obsolet (*geh*). **to become ~** veralten.

obstacle ['ɒbstəkl] *n (lit, fig)* Hindernis *nt.* **~ race** (*Sport, fig*) Hindernisrennen *nt;* **to be an ~ to sb/sth** jdm/einer Sache im Weg(e) stehen, jdn/etw (be)hindern; **if they put any ~ in the way of our plans** wenn man uns Steine in den Weg legt *or* unsere Pläne behindert; **that's no ~ to our doing it** das wird uns nicht daran hindern; **all the ~s to progress/peace** *etc* alles, was den Fortschritt/Frieden *etc* behindert.

obstetric(al) [ɒb'stetrɪk(əl)] *adj* (*Med*) *techniques etc* Geburtshilfe-. **~ ward** Entbindungs- *or* Wöchnerinnenstation *f;* **~ clinic** Entbindungsheim *nt*, Geburtsklinik *f.*

obstetrician [ˌɒbstə'trɪʃən] *n* Geburtshelfer(in *f*) *m.*

obstetrics [ɒb'stetrɪks] *n sing* Geburtshilfe, Obstetrik (*spec*) *f;* (*ward*) Wöchnerinnenstation *f.*

obstinacy ['ɒbstɪnəsɪ] *n* **(a)** (*of person*) Hartnäckigkeit *f*, Starrsinn *m*, Widerspenstigkeit *f.* **his ~ in doing sth** die Hartnäckigkeit, mit der er etw tut. **(b)** (*of illness*) Hartnäckigkeit *f;* (*of resistance also*) Verbissenheit *f.*

obstinate ['ɒbstɪnɪt] *adj* **(a)** hartnäckig, starrsinnig; *nail etc* widerspenstig. **to remain ~** stur bleiben; **he was ~ in insisting that ...** er bestand stur *or* hartnäckig darauf, daß ... **(b)** *resistance, illness* hartnäckig.

obstinately ['ɒbstɪnɪtlɪ] *adv* hartnäckig, stur.

obstreperous [əb'strepərəs] *adj* aufmüpfig; *child* aufsässig. **the drunk became ~** der Betrunkene fing an zu randalieren; **it's not a real complaint, he's just being ~** es ist keine echte Beschwerde, er will nur Schwierigkeiten machen.

obstreperously [əb'strepərəslɪ] *adv see adj.*

obstreperousness [əb'strepərəsnɪs] *n see adj* Aufmüpfigkeit *f;* Aufsässigkeit *f.*

obstruct [əb'strʌkt] **1** *vt* **(a)** (*block*) blockieren; *passage, road also, view* versperren; (*Med*) *artery, pipe also* verstopfen. **you're ~ing my view** Sie nehmen *or* versperren mir die Sicht. **(b)** (*hinder*) (be)hindern; *navigation* behindern; *traffic, progress also* aufhalten, hemmen; (*Sport*) behindern; (*in possession of ball*) sperren. **to ~ a bill** (*Parl*) einen Gesetzentwurf blockieren; **to ~ a policeman in the execution of his duty** einen Polizisten an der Amtsausübung hindern; **to ~ the course of justice** die Rechtsfindung behindern.
2 *vi* (*be obstructionist*) obstruieren, Obstruktion treiben; (*Sport*) sperren.

obstruction [əb'strʌkʃən] *n* **(a)** *see vt* **(a)** Blockierung *f;* (*of view*) Versperren *nt;* Verstopfung *f.*
(b) *see vt* **(b)** Behinderung *f;* Hemmung *f;* Behinderung *f;* Sperren *nt.* **to cause an ~** den Verkehr behindern.
(c) (*obstacle*) Hindernis, Hemmnis (*esp fig*) *nt.* **there is an ~ in the pipe** das Rohr ist blockiert *or* verstopft; **all ~s to progress** alles, was den Fortschritt aufhält *or* hemmt.
(d) (*Pol*) Obstruktion, Behinderung *f.*

obstructionism [əb'strʌkʃənɪzəm] *n* Obstruktionspolitik *f.*

obstructionist [əb'strʌkʃənɪst] *n* Obstruktionspolitiker *m.*

obstructive [əb'strʌktɪv] *adj* obstruktiv (*esp Pol*), behindernd. **~ politician** Obstruktionspolitiker(in *f*) *m;* **to be ~** (*person*) Schwierigkeiten machen, sich querstellen (*inf*); **to be ~ to progress** dem Fortschritt hinderlich sein.

obtain [əb'teɪn] **1** *vt* erhalten, bekommen; *result, votes also* erzielen; *information, goods also* beziehen; *knowledge* erwerben. **to ~ sth by hard work** etw durch harte Arbeit erreichen; *possession* sich (*dat*) etw mühsam erarbeiten; **can food be ~ed from seawater?** können aus Meer(es)wasser Nahrungsmittel gewonnen werden?; **to ~ sth for sb** jdm etw be- *or* verschaffen; **the novel which ~ed him such a reputation** der Roman, der ihm solch einen Ruf verschaffte.
2 *vi* (*form*) gelten; (*rules also*) in Kraft sein; (*customs*) bestehen, herrschen.

obtainable [əb'teɪnəbl] *adj* erhältlich.

obtrude [əb'truːd] **1** *vt* **(a)** **to ~ oneself (up)on others** sich anderen aufdrängen; **to ~ one's opinion(s) (up)on sb** jdm seine Meinung aufzwingen.
(b) (*push out*) hervorstrecken, hervorschieben.
2 *vi* **(a)** (*intrude*) sich aufdrängen. **to ~ upon sb's private grief** jdn nicht in seinem Schmerz belästigen.
(b) (*protrude*) (her)vorstehen; (*fig*) hervortreten.

obtrusion [əb'truːʒən] *n* **(a)** Aufdrängen *nt.* **because of this ~ of himself/his ideas upon others** weil er sich/seine Ideen anderen aufdrängen will. **(b)** (*pushing out*) Hervorstrecken *nt.* **(c)** (*sticking out*) Herausragen *nt.*

obtrusive [əb'truːsɪv] *adj person* aufdringlich; *smell also* penetrant; *building, furniture* zu auffällig.

obtrusiveness [əb'truːsɪvlɪ] *adv see adj.*

obtrusiveness [əb'truːsɪvnɪs] *n see adj* Aufdringlichkeit *f;* Penetranz *f;* Auffälligkeit *f.*

obtuse [əb'tjuːs] *adj* **(a)** (*Geometry*) stumpf. **(b)** *person* begriffsstutzig, beschränkt. **are you just being ~?** tust du nur so beschränkt?

obtuseness [əb'tjuːsnɪs] *n* Begriffsstutzigkeit, Beschränktheit *f.*

obverse ['ɒbvɜːs] **1** *adj side* Vorder-. **2** *n* **(a)** (*of coin*) Vorderseite *f*, Avers *m.* **(b)** (*of statement, truth*) andere Seite, Kehrseite *f.*

obviate ['ɒbvɪeɪt] *vt* vermeiden, umgehen; *objection, need* vorbeugen (+*dat*).

obvious ['ɒbvɪəs] *adj* offensichtlich, deutlich; (*visually also*) augenfällig; (*not subtle*) plump; *proof* klar, eindeutig; *difference, fact* eindeutig, offensichtlich, offenkundig; *statement*

naheliegend, selbstverständlich; *reason* (leicht) ersichtlich; *dislike, reluctance, surprise* sichtlich. **an ~ truth** eine offenkundige Tatsache; **because of the ~ truth of what he maintains** da es so eindeutig *or* offensichtlich wahr ist, was er sagt; **that's the ~ translation/solution** das ist die naheliegendste Übersetzung/Lösung; **he was the ~ choice** es lag nahe, ihn zu wählen; **it was ~ he didn't want to come** er wollte offensichtlich nicht kommen; **it's quite ~ he doesn't understand** man merkt doch (sofort) *or* es ist doch klar, daß er nicht versteht; **to make sth a little more ~** etw etwas deutlicher *or* eindeutiger machen; **there's no need to make it so ~** man braucht das (doch) nicht so deutlich zu zeigen *or* so deutlich werden zu lassen; **do I have to make it even more ~?** muß ich denn noch deutlicher werden?; **we must not be too ~ about it** wir dürfen es nicht zu auffällig machen; **I would have thought that was perfectly ~** das ist doch völlig klar *or* eindeutig, das liegt doch auf der Hand; (*noticeable*) das springt doch ins Auge; **with the ~ exception of ...** natürlich mit Ausnahme von ...; **subtle? he's the most ~ person I know** raffiniert? ich kenne niemanden, der einfacher zu durchschauen wäre!; **even if I am stating the ~** selbst wenn ich hier etwas längst Bekanntes sage; **he has a gift for stating the ~** der merkt aber auch alles! (*inf*); **don't just state the ~,** try to be original sagen/schreiben Sie nicht, was sich von selbst versteht, sondern bemühen Sie sich um Originalität; **what's the ~ thing to do?** was ist das Naheliegendste?, was bietet sich am ehesten an?

obviously ['ɒbvɪəslɪ] *adv* offensichtlich, offenbar; (*noticeably*) (offen)sichtlich. **he's ~ French** er ist eindeutig ein Franzose; **~! natürlich!,** selbstverständlich!; **is he there? — well, ~ not** ist er da? — offensichtlich nicht; **he's not going to like it** das wird ihm natürlich nicht gefallen; **he's ~ not going to get the job** er bekommt die Stelle nicht, das ist ja klar (*inf*).

obviousness ['ɒbvɪəsnɪs] *n* Offensichtlichkeit, Deutlichkeit *f.* **amused by the ~ of his approach** belustigt über die Eindeutigkeit *or* Plumpheit seines Annäherungsversuchs.

OC *n abbr of* **Officer Commanding** (*Mil*) Oberbefehlshaber *m.* **who's ~ paper supply in the office?** (*sl*) wer ist hier im Büro der Papier-UvD (*hum*) *or* Papierhengst? (*sl*).

ocarina [ˌɒkə'riːnə] *n* Okarina *f.*

Occam's razor ['ɒkəmz'reɪzəᵣ] *n* **to apply ~ (to sth)** etw komprimieren, etw auf das Wesentliche beschränken.

occasion [ə'keɪʒən] **1** *n* **(a)** (*point in time*) Gelegenheit *f*, Anlaß *m.* **on that ~** damals, bei *or* zu jener Gelegenheit *or* jenem Anlaß (*geh*); **on another ~** ein anderes Mal, bei einer anderen Gelegenheit *etc;* **on several ~s** mehrmals, bei *or* zu mehreren Gelegenheiten *etc;* **(on) the first ~** beim ersten Mal, das erste Mal; **on ~** gelegentlich; (*if need be*) wenn nötig; **it does not befit the ~** es ist unpassend für diesen *or* zu diesem Anlaß; **to rise to the ~** sich der Lage gewachsen zeigen.
(b) (*special time*) Ereignis *nt.* **~s of state** Staatsanlässe *pl;* **on the ~ of his birthday** anläßlich *or* aus Anlaß seines Geburtstages (*geh*); **one's 21st birthday should be something of an ~** ein 21. Geburtstag sollte schon ein besonderes Ereignis sein.
(c) (*opportunity*) Gelegenheit, Möglichkeit *f.* **I never had the ~ to congratulate him** es bot sich mir keine *or* nicht die Gelegenheit *or* ich hatte nicht die Möglichkeit, ihm zu gratulieren; **I would like to take this ~ to ...** (*form*) ich möchte diese Gelegenheit ergreifen, um ...
(d) (*reason*) Grund, Anlaß *m*, Veranlassung *f.* **should the ~ arise** sollte es nötig sein *or* werden; **to give ~ to sth** (*form*) zu etw Anlaß geben; **if you have ~ to ...** sollten Sie Veranlassung haben, zu ...; **not an ~ for merriment** kein Grund zur Freude.
2 *vt* (*form*) verursachen, Anlaß geben zu, zeitigen (*geh*). **to ~ sb to do sth** jdn veranlassen, etw zu tun.

occasional [ə'keɪʒənl] *adj* **(a)** **he likes an ~ cigar** er raucht hin und wieder ganz gerne *or* gelegentlich ganz gern eine Zigarre; **I have the ~ good idea** ich habe gelegentlich *or* hin und wieder einen guten Einfall.
(b) (*designed for special event*) *poem, music* zu der Gelegenheit *or* dem Anlaß verfaßt/komponiert. **~ table** kleiner Wohnzimmertisch.

occasionally [ə'keɪʒnəlɪ] *adv* gelegentlich, hin und wieder, zuweilen (*geh*). **very ~** sehr selten, nicht sehr oft.

occident ['ɒksɪdənt] *n* (*liter*) Abendland *nt*, Okzident *m* (*geh*). **the O~** (*Pol*) der Westen.

occidental [ˌɒksɪ'dentl] **1** *adj* (*liter*) abendländisch. **2** *n* (*rare*) Abendländer(in *f*) *m.*

occipital [ɒk'sɪpɪtl] *adj* (*spec*) des Hinterkopfs.

occiput ['ɒksɪpʌt] *n* (*spec*) Hinterkopf *m.*

occlude [ɒ'kluːd] (*spec*) **1** *vt* (*Anat, Med*) *pores, artery* verschließen, verstopfen, okkludieren (*spec*); (*Chem*) *gas* adsorbieren. **~d front** (*Met*) Okklusion *f.* **2** *vi* (*Dentistry*) eine normale Bißstellung haben.

occlusion [ɒ'kluːʒən] *n* (*spec*) (*Med: of artery*) Verschluß *m*, Okklusion *f* (*spec*); (*Dentistry*) Biß *m*, normale Bißstellung; (*Phon*) Verschluß *m;* (*Chem*) Adsorption *f;* (*Met*) Okklusion *f.*

occult [ɒ'kʌlt] **1** *adj* okkult; (*of occultism*) okkultistisch; (*secret*) geheimnisvoll. **2** *n* **Okkulte(s)** *nt.*

occultism ['ɒkʌltɪzəm] *n* Okkultismus *m.*

occultist ['ɒkʌltɪst] *n* Okkultist(in *f*) *m.*

occupancy ['ɒkjʊpənsɪ] *n* (*period*) Wohndauer *f.* **a change of ~** ein Besitzerwechsel *m;* (*of rented property*) ein Mieterwechsel *m;* **levels of hotel ~** Übernachtungsziffern *pl.*

occupant ['ɒkjʊpənt] *n* (*of house*) Bewohner(in *f*) *m;* (*of post*) Inhaber(in *f*) *m;* (*of car*) Insasse *m.*

occupation [ˌɒkjʊ'peɪʃən] **1** *n* **(a)** (*employment*) Beruf *m*, Tätigkeit *f.* **what is his ~?** was ist er von Beruf?, welchen Beruf hat er?, welche Tätigkeit übt er aus?; **he is a joiner by ~** er ist Tischler von Beruf.
(b) (*pastime*) Beschäftigung, Betätigung, Tätigkeit *f.*
(c) (*Mil*) Okkupation *f;* (*act also*) Besetzung *f* (*of von*); (*state*

also) Besatzung *f* (*of in + dat*). **army of** ~ Besatzungsheer *nt*.
(d) (*of house etc*) Besetzung *f*. **to be in** ~ **of a house** ein Haus bewohnen; **ready for** ~ bezugsfertig, schlüsselfertig; **we found them already in** ~ wir sahen, daß sie schon eingezogen waren.

2 *adj attr* **troops** Besatzungs-, Okkupations-.

occupational [ˌɒkjʊˈpeɪʃənl] *adj* Berufs-, beruflich. ~ **disease** Berufskrankheit *f*; ~ **hazard** *or* **risk** Berufsrisiko *nt*; ~ **therapy** Beschäftigungstherapie *f*; ~ **therapist** Beschäftigungstherapeut(in *f*) *m*.

occupier [ˈɒkjʊpaɪəʳ] *n* (*of house, land*) Bewohner(in *f*) *m*; (*of post*) Inhaber(in *f*) *m*.

occupy [ˈɒkjʊpaɪ] *vt* **(a)** *house* bewohnen; *seat, room* belegen, besetzen; *hotel room* belegen. **is this seat occupied?** ist dieser Platz belegt?; **you** ~ **a special place in my memories** du hast einen besonderen Platz in meinem Herzen (inne).
(b) (*Mil etc*) besetzen; *country also* okkupieren.
(c) *post, position* innehaben, bekleiden (*geh*).
(d) (*take up*) beanspruchen; *space also* einnehmen; *time also* in Anspruch nehmen; (*help pass*) ausfüllen; *attention also* in Anspruch nehmen. **can't you find some better way of** ~**ing your time?** kannst du mit deiner Zeit nicht etwas Besseres anfangen?
(e) (*busy*) beschäftigen. **to be occupied (with)** beschäftigt sein (mit); **to** ~ **oneself** sich beschäftigen; **to keep sb occupied** jdn beschäftigen; **that'll keep him occupied** dann hat er was zu tun *or* ist er beschäftigt; **occupied with the thought of ...** mit dem Gedanken an (+*acc*) ... beschäftigt; **he kept his mind occupied** er beschäftigte sich geistig; **a thought which has been** ~**ing my mind** ein Gedanke, der mich beschäftigt.

occur [əˈkɜːʳ] *vi* **(a)** (*take place*) (*event*) geschehen, sich ereignen, vorkommen; (*difficulty*) sich ergeben; (*change*) stattfinden. **that doesn't** ~ **very often** das kommt nicht oft vor, das gibt es nicht so oft; **don't let it** ~ **again** lassen Sie das nicht wieder vorkommen, daß das nicht wieder passiert!; **should the case** ~ sollte der Fall eintreten; **if the opportunity** ~**s** wenn sich die Gelegenheit bietet *or* ergibt.
(b) (*be found: disease*) vorkommen.
(c) (*come to mind*) einfallen, in den Sinn kommen (*geh*) (*to sb* jdm). **if it** ~**s to you that he is wrong** falls es Ihnen so vorkommt, als habe er sich geirrt; **it** ~**s to me that ...** ich habe den Eindruck, daß ...; **the idea just** ~**red to me** es ist mir gerade eingefallen; **it never** ~**red to me** darauf bin ich noch nie gekommen; **it didn't even** ~ **to him to ask** er kam erst gar nicht auf den Gedanken, zu fragen; **did it ever** ~ **to you to apologize?** hast du eigentlich je daran gedacht, dich zu entschuldigen?

occurrence [əˈkʌrəns] *n* **(a)** (*event*) Ereignis, Vorkommnis *nt*, Begebenheit *f*. ~**s that could not have been predicted** unvorhergesehene Ereignisse; **an everyday** ~ ein alltägliches Ereignis, eine alltägliche Begebenheit.
(b) (*presence, taking place*) Auftreten *nt*; (*of minerals*) Vorkommen *nt*. **the** ~ **of typhoons in Dorset is rare** Taifune kommen in Dorset selten vor, Taifune treten in Dorset selten auf; **further** ~**s of this nature must be avoided** weitere Vorkommnisse dieser Art müssen vermieden werden.

ocean [ˈəʊʃən] *n* **(a)** Ozean *m*, Meer *nt*. **(b)** **an** ~ **of flowers** ein Blumenmeer; ~**s of** (*inf*) **jede Menge** (*inf*), massenhaft.

ocean: ~ **bed** *n* Meeresboden *or* -grund *m*; ~ **chart** *n* Seekarte *f*; ~ **climate** *n* Meeresklima *nt*, maritimes Klima; ~**-going** *adj* hochseetauglich; ~**-going tug** Hochseeschlepper *m*.

Oceania [ˌəʊʃɪˈeɪnɪə] *n* Ozeanien *nt*.

Oceanian [ˌəʊʃɪˈeɪnɪən] **1** *adj* ozeanisch. **2** *n* Ozeanier(in *f*) *m*.

oceanic [ˌəʊʃɪˈænɪk] *adj* Meeres-; (*fig*) riesenhaft.

ocean liner *n* Ozeandampfer *m*.

oceanographer [ˌəʊʃəˈnɒɡrəfəʳ] *n* Ozeanograph(in *f*), Meereskundler(in *f*) *m*.

oceanography [ˌəʊʃəˈnɒɡrəfɪ] *n* Ozeanographie, Meereskunde *f*.

ocean voyage *n* Schiffsreise, Seereise *f*.

ocelot [ˈɒsɪlɒt] *n* Ozelot *m*.

och [ɒx] *interj* (*Scot*) ach was, ach wo. ~ **aye** ach ja.

ochre, (*US*) **ocher** [ˈəʊkəʳ] **1** *n* Ocker *m or nt*. **red** ~ roter *or* rotes Ocker; **yellow** ~ (*substance*) Ocker *m or nt*; (*colour*) Ocker(gelb *nt*) *m or nt*. **2** *adj* ockerfarben.

o'clock [əˈklɒk] *adv* **(a)** **at** 5 ~ um 5 Uhr; **it is** 5 ~ es ist 5 Uhr; **what** ~ **is it?** (*obs*) was ist die Uhr? **(b)** *aircraft approaching at* 5 ~ Flugzeug aus Südsüdost; **face north and the house is at about** 11 ~ das Haus liegt Nordnordwest.

OCR *abbr of* **optical character recognition**.

Oct *abbr of* **October** Okt.

octagon [ˈɒktəɡən] *n* Achteck, Oktagon, Oktagon *nt*.

octagonal [ɒkˈtæɡənl] *adj* achteckig, oktogonal.

octahedron [ˌɒktəˈhiːdrən] *n* Oktaeder, Achtflächner *m*.

octane [ˈɒkteɪn] *n* Oktan *nt*. **high-**~ **petrol** Benzin mit hoher Oktanzahl; ~ **number,** ~ **rating** Oktanzahl *f*.

octave [ˈɒktɪv] *n* **(a)** (*Mus*) Oktave *f*. **(b)** (*of sonnet*) Oktett *nt*.

octavo [ɒkˈteɪvəʊ] *n* Oktav(format) *nt*; (*also* ~ **volume**) Oktavband *m*.

octet [ɒkˈtet] *n* (*Mus, Poet*) Oktett *nt*.

October [ɒkˈtəʊbəʳ] *n* Oktober *m*. **the** ~ **Revolution** die Oktoberrevolution; *see also* **September**.

octogenarian [ˌɒktəʊdʒɪˈnɛərɪən] **1** *n* Achtziger(in *f*) *m*, Achtzigjährige(r) *mf*. **2** *adj* achtzigjährig.

octopus [ˈɒktəpəs] *n* Tintenfisch *m*, Krake *f*.

ocular [ˈɒkjʊləʳ] *adj* (*form*) Augen-.

oculist [ˈɒkjʊlɪst] *n* Augenspezialist(in *f*) *m*.

OD (*sl*) **1** *n* Überdosis *f*. **2** *vi* eine Überdosis nehmen.

odalisque [ˈəʊdəlɪsk] *n* Odaliske *f*.

odd [ɒd] *adj* (+*er*) **(a)** (*peculiar*) merkwürdig, seltsam, sonderbar; *person, thing, idea also* eigenartig, absonderlich. **how** ~ **that we should meet him** (wie) eigenartig *etc*, daß wir ihn

trafen; **the** ~ **thing about it is that ...** das Merkwürdige *etc* daran ist, daß ...; **he's got some** ~ **ways** er hat eine schrullige *or* verschrobene Art.
(b) *number* ungerade.
(c) (*one of a pair or a set*) *shoe, glove* einzeln. **he/she is (the)** ~ **man** *or* **one out** er/sie ist übrig *or* überzählig *or* das fünfte Rad am Wagen; (*in character*) er/sie steht (immer) abseits *or* ist ein Außenseiter/eine Außenseiterin; **in each group underline the word/picture which is the** ~ **man** *or* **one out** unterstreichen Sie in jeder Gruppe das nicht dazugehörige Wort/Bild.
(d) (*about*) 600 ~ **marks** so um die 600 Mark, ungefähr *or* etwa 600 Mark.
(e) (*surplus, extra*) übrig, restlich, überzählig. **the** ~ **one left over** der/die/das Überzählige.
(f) (*not regular or specific*) *moments, times* zeitweilig; (*Comm*) *size* ausgefallen. **any** ~ **piece of wood** irgendein Stück(chen) Holz; **at** ~ **moments** *or* **times** ab und zu; **at** ~ **moments during the day** zwischendurch; ~ **job** (gelegentlich) anfallende Arbeit; **he does all the** ~ **jobs** er macht alles, was an Arbeit anfällt; ~ **job man** Mädchen *nt* für alles.

oddball [ˈɒdbɔːl] (*inf*) **1** *n* komischer Kauz. **2** *adj* komisch, kauzig, verschroben.

oddity [ˈɒdɪtɪ] *n* **(a)** (*strangeness: of person*) Wunderlichkeit, Absonderlichkeit, Eigenartigkeit *f*; (*of thing*) Ausgefallenheit *f*. **(b)** (*odd person*) komischer Kauz *or* Vogel; (*who doesn't fit*) Kuriosität *f*; (*thing*) Kuriosität *f*.

oddly [ˈɒdlɪ] *adv* *speak, behave* eigenartig, sonderbar, merkwürdig. **I find her** ~ **attractive** ich finde sie auf (eine) seltsame Art *or* auf merkwürdige Weise anziehend; **they are** ~ **similar** sie sind sich seltsam *or* merkwürdig ähnlich; ~ **enough she was at home** merkwürdigerweise *or* eigenartigerweise *or* seltsamerweise war sie zu Hause; ~ **enough you are right** Sie werden überrascht sein, aber das stimmt.

oddment [ˈɒdmənt] *n usu pl* Restposten *m*; (*of cloth also*) Rest *m*; (*single piece also*) Einzelstück *nt*.

oddness [ˈɒdnɪs] *n* Merkwürdigkeit, Seltsamkeit *f*.

odds [ɒdz] *npl* **(a)** (*Betting*) Odds *pl*, Gewinnquote *f*; (*of bookmaker also*) (feste) Kurse *pl*. **the** ~ **are 6 to 1** die Chancen stehen 6:1; **long/short** ~ geringe/hohe Gewinnchancen; **he won at long** ~ er hat mit einer hohen Gewinnquote gewonnen; **fixed** ~ feste Kurse; **to lay** *or* **give** ~ **of 2 to 1** (*against/in favour of sb*) den Kurs mit 2:1 (gegen/für jdn) angeben; **I'll lay** ~ (**of 3 to 1**) **that ...** (*fig*) ich wette (3 gegen 1), daß ...
(b) (*chances for or against*) Chance(n *pl*) *f*. **the** ~ **were against us** alles sprach gegen uns; **in spite of the tremendous** ~ **against him ...** obwohl alles so völlig gegen ihn sprach *or* war ...; **the** ~ **were in our favour** alles sprach für uns; **against all the** ~ **he won** wider Erwarten *or* entgegen allen Erwartungen gewann er; **what are the** ~ **on/against ...?** wie sind *or* stehen die Chancen, daß .../daß ... nicht?; **what are the** ~ **of our winning?** wie sind *or* stehen unsere Gewinnchancen?; **to fight against heavy/overwhelming** ~ (*Mil*) gegen eine große/überwältigende gegnerische Übermacht ankämpfen; **to struggle against impossible** ~ so gut wie keine Aussicht auf Erfolg haben; **the** ~ **are that he will come** es sieht ganz so aus, als ob er käme *or* kommen würde.
(c) (*inf*) **to pay over the** ~ einiges mehr bezahlen; **foreign buyers who are prepared to pay over the** ~ Ausländer, die gewillt sind, Liebhaberpreise zu bezahlen.
(d) (*difference*) **what's the** ~? was macht das schon (aus)?; **it makes no** ~ es spielt keine Rolle; **it makes no** ~ **to me** es ist mir (völlig) einerlei; **does it really make any** ~ **if I don't come?** macht es etwas aus, wenn ich nicht komme?
(e) (*variance*) **to be at** ~ **with sb over sth** mit jdm in etw (*dat*) nicht einiggehen; **we are at** ~ **as to the best solution** wir gehen nicht darin einig, wie das am besten gelöst werden soll.

odds and ends *npl* Krimskrams, Kram *m*; (*of food*) Reste *pl*; (*of cloth*) Reste, Flicken *pl*. **bring all your** ~ bringen Sie Ihren ganzen Kram *or* Ihre Siebensachen (*inf*).

odds and sods *npl* (*hum inf*) Kleinkram *m*. **I've got a few** ~ **to tidy up** ich muß hier und da noch ein paar Sachen in Ordnung bringen; **a few** ~ (*people*) ein paar Hansel (*inf*).

odds-on [ˈɒdzɒn] **1** *adj* (*Betting*) **favourite mit „Odds auf"** (*der Kurs ist für ihn angegeben*). **he's** ~ **favourite for the post** er hat die größten Aussichten, die Stelle zu bekommen. **2** *adv* **it's** ~ **that he'll come** es ist so gut wie sicher, daß er kommt.

ode [əʊd] *n* Ode *f* (*to, on an +acc*).

odious [ˈəʊdɪəs] *adj* *person* abstoßend, ekelhaft; *action* abscheulich, verabscheuenswürdig. **an** ~ **person** ein Ekel *nt*; **what an** ~ **thing to say** wie abscheulich, so etwas zu sagen.

odium [ˈəʊdɪəm] *n* (*being hated*) Haß *m*; (*repugnance*) Abscheu *m*. **he incurred the** ~ **of the whole nation** er zog sich (*dat*) den Haß der gesamten Nation zu; **held in public** ~ der Öffentlichkeit (*dat*) verhaßt.

odometer [ɒˈdɒmɪtəʳ] *n* Kilometerzähler *m*.

odontologist [ˌɒdɒnˈtɒlədʒɪst] *n* Odontologe *m*, Odontologin *f*, Facharzt *m*/-ärztin *f* für Zahnheilkunde.

odontology [ˌɒdɒnˈtɒlədʒɪ] *n* Odontologie, Zahnheilkunde *f*.

odor *etc* (*US*) *see* **odour** *etc*.

odoriferous [ˌəʊdəˈrɪfərəs] *adj* (*form*) wohlriechend, duftend.

odorous [ˈəʊdərəs] *adj* (*esp poet*) duftend, wohlriechend.

odour, (*US*) **odor** [ˈəʊdəʳ] *n* **(a)** (*lit, fig*) Geruch *m*; (*sweet smell*) Duft, Wohlgeruch *m*; (*bad smell*) Gestank *m*. **(b) to be in good/bad** ~ **with sb** gut/schlecht bei jdm angeschrieben sein.

odourless, (*US*) **odorless** [ˈəʊdəlɪs] *adj* geruchlos.

Odyssey [ˈɒdɪsɪ] *n* (*Myth, fig*) Odyssee *f*.

oecumenical [ˌiːkjuːˈmenɪkəl] *adj see* **ecumenical**.

oedema, (*US*) **edema** [ɪˈdiːmə] *n* Ödem *nt*.

Oedipus [ˈiːdɪpəs] *n* Ödipus *m*. ~ **complex** Ödipuskomplex *m*.

o'er [ɔːʳ] *prep, adv* (*poet*) *contr of* **over**.

oesophagus, (*US*) **esophagus** [iːˈsɒfəɡəs] *n* Speiseröhre *f*.

of [ɒv,əv] *prep* **(a)** (*indicating possession or relation*) von (+ *dat*), use of gen. **the wife** ~ **the doctor** die Frau des Arztes, die Frau vom Arzt; **a friend** ~ **ours** ein Freund von uns; **a painting** ~ **the Queen** ein Gemälde der *or* von der Königin; **a painting** ~ **the Queen's** (*belonging to her*) ein Gemälde (im Besitz) der Königin; (*painted by her*) ein Gemälde (von) der Königin; ~ **it davon**; **the first** ~ **May** der erste Mai; **the first** ~ **the month** der Erste (des Monats), der Monatserste; **it is no business** ~ **theirs** es geht sie nichts an; **that damn dog** ~ **theirs** ihr verdammter Hund; **it is very kind** ~ **you** es ist sehr freundlich von Ihnen.
(b) (*indicating separation in space or time*) **south** ~ **Paris** südlich von Paris; **within a month** ~ **his death** einen Monat nach seinem Tod; **a quarter** ~ **six** (*US*) Viertel vor sechs.
(c) (*indicating cause*) **he died** ~ **poison/cancer** er starb an Gift/Krebs; **he died** ~ **hunger** er verhungerte, er starb Hungers (*geh*); **it did not happen** ~ **itself** (*liter*) das ist nicht von selbst *or* von allein geschehen; **it tastes** ~ **garlic** es schmeckt nach Knoblauch; **she is proud** ~ **him** sie ist stolz auf ihn; **I am ashamed** ~ **it** ich schäme mich dafür.
(d) (*indicating deprivation, riddance*) **he was cured** ~ **the illness** er wurde von der Krankheit geheilt; **trees bare** ~ **leaves** Bäume ohne Blätter; **free** ~ **charge** kostenlos; **loss** ~ **appetite** Appetitlosigkeit *f*.
(e) (*indicating material*) aus. **dress made** ~ **wool** Wollkleid *nt*, Kleid *nt* aus Wolle; **house** ~ **brick** Backsteinhaus *nt*, Haus *nt* aus Backstein.
(f) (*indicating quality, identity etc*) **house** ~ **ten rooms** Haus *nt* mit zehn Zimmern; **man** ~ **courage** mutiger Mensch, Mensch *m* mit Mut; **girl** ~ **ten** zehnjähriges Mädchen, Mädchen *nt* von zehn Jahren; **a question** ~ **no importance** eine Frage ohne Bedeutung; **the city** ~ **Paris** die Stadt Paris; **person** ~ **swarthy complexion** dunkelhäutige Person; **a town** ~ **narrow streets** eine Stadt mit engen Straßen; **where is that rascal** ~ **a boy?** wo ist dieser verflixte Bengel?; **that idiot** ~ **a waiter** dieser Idiot von Kellner.
(g) (*objective genitive*) **fear** ~ **God** Gottesfurcht *f*; **his love** ~ **his father** die Liebe zu seinem Vater; **he is a leader** ~ **men** er hat die Fähigkeit, Menschen zu führen; **great eaters** ~ **fruit** große Obstesser *pl*; **writer** ~ **legal articles** Verfasser von juristischen Artikeln; **love** ~ **money** Liebe zum Geld.
(h) (*subjective genitive*) **love** ~ **God for man** Liebe Gottes zu den Menschen; **affection** ~ **a mother** Mutterliebe *f*.
(i) (*partitive genitive*) **the whole** ~ **the house** das ganze Haus; **half** ~ **the house** das halbe Haus; **how many** ~ **them do you want?** wie viele möchten Sie (davon)?; **many** ~ **them came** viele (von ihnen) kamen; **there were six** ~ **us** wir waren zu sechst, wir waren sechs; **he is not one** ~ **us** er gehört nicht zu uns; **one** ~ **the best** einer der Besten; **he asked the six** ~ **us to lunch** er lud uns sechs zum Mittagessen ein; ~ **the ten only one was absent** von den zehn fehlte nur einer; **the book he wanted most** ~ **all** das Buch, das er am meisten wollte; **today** ~ **all days** ausgerechnet heute; **you** ~ **all people** ought to know gerade Sie sollten das wissen; **they are the best** ~ **friends** sie sind die besten Freunde; **the best** ~ **teachers** der (aller)beste Lehrer; **the bravest** ~ **the brave** der Mutigste der Mutigen; **he drank** ~ **the wine** (*liter*) er trank von dem Weine (*liter*).
(j) (*concerning*) **what do you think** ~ **him?** was halten Sie von ihm?; **what has become** ~ **him?** was ist aus ihm geworden?; **he warned us** ~ **the danger** er warnte uns vor der Gefahr; **doctor** ~ **medicine** Doktor der Medizin; **what** ~ **it?** ja und?
(k) (*obs, liter: by*) **forsaken** ~ **men** von allen verlassen; **beloved** ~ **all** von allen geliebt.
(l) (*in temporal phrases*) **he's become very quiet** ~ **late** er ist letzlich *or* seit neuestem so ruhig geworden; **they go out** ~ **an evening** (*inf*) sie gehen abends (schon mal) aus (*inf*); **he died** ~ **a Saturday morning** (*dial*) er starb an einem Samstagmorgen, er starb eines Samstagmorgens (*liter*).

off [ɒf] 1 *adv* **(a)** (*distance*) **the house is 5 km** ~ das Haus ist 5 km entfernt; **some way** ~ (**from here**) in einiger Entfernung (von hier); **it's a long way** ~ das ist weit weg; (*time*) **das liegt in weiter Ferne**; **August isn't/the exams aren't very far** ~ es ist nicht mehr lang bis August/bis zu den Prüfungen; **Christmas is only a week** ~ es ist nur noch eine Woche bis Weihnachten; **noises** ~ (*Theat*) Geräusche *pl* hinter den Kulissen.
(b) (*departure*) **to be/go** ~ gehen; **he's** ~ **to school** er ist zur Schule gegangen; (**be**) ~ **with you!** fort mit dir!; **noch, daß du wegkommst!**; ~ **with him!** fort *or* weg mit ihm!; **I must be** ~ ich muß (jetzt) gehen *or* weg (*inf*); **it's time I was** ~ es wird *or* ist (höchste) Zeit, daß ich gehe; **where are you** ~ **to?** wohin gehen Sie denn?, wohin geht's denn (*inf*)?; ~ **we go!** los!, auf los geht's los!, na denn man los! (*inf*); **he's** ~ **playing tennis** *or* **he goes** ~ **playing tennis every evening** er geht jeden Abend Tennis spielen; **they're** ~ (*Sport*) sie sind vom Start; **she's** ~ (*inf: complaining etc*) sie legt schon wieder los (*inf*); *see* **vbs.**
(c) (*removal*) **he had his coat** ~ er hatte den Mantel aus; **he had his coat** ~ **in two seconds** er hatte seinen Mantel in zwei Sekunden aus(gezogen); **he helped me** ~ **with my coat** er half mir aus dem Mantel; **with his trousers** ~ ohne Hose; **with those wet clothes!** raus aus den nassen Kleidern!; **the handle is** ~ *or* **has come** ~ der Griff ist ab (*inf*) *or* ist abgegangen; **there are two buttons** ~ es fehlen zwei Knöpfe, da sind zwei Knöpfe ab (*inf*); ~ **with his head!** herunter mit seinem Kopf!, Kopf ab!; **he had the back of the TV** ~ er hatte die Rückwand des Fernsehers abgenommen; **the lid is** ~ der Deckel ist nicht drauf.
(d) (*discount*) **3%** ~ (*Comm*) 3% Nachlaß *or* Abzug; **3%** ~ **for cash** (*Comm*) 3% Skonto, bei Barzahlung 3%; **to give sb £5/something** ~ jdm £ 5 Ermäßigung/eine Ermäßigung geben; **he let me have £5** ~ er gab es mir (um) £ 5 billiger.
(e) (*not at work*) **to have time** ~ **to do sth** (Zeit) freibekommen haben, um etw zu tun; **I've got a day** ~ ich habe einen Tag frei(bekommen); **she's nearly always** ~ **on Tuesdays**

dienstags hat sie fast immer frei.
(f) (*in phrases*) ~ **and on, on and** ~ ab und zu, ab und an; **it rained** ~ **and on** es regnete mit Unterbrechungen; **right** *or* **straight** ~ gleich; **3 days straight** ~ 3 Tage hintereinander.
2 *adj* **(a)** *attr* (*substandard*) **year, day etc** schlecht. **I'm having an** ~ **day** today ich bin heute nicht in Form.
(b) *pred* (*not fresh*) verdorben, schlecht; **milk** also sauer; **butter** also ranzig.
(c) *pred* (*cancelled*) **match, party, talks** abgesagt; (*not available: in restaurant*) **chops, fish** aus. **I'm afraid veal is** ~ **today/now** Kalbfleisch gibt es heute nicht/das Kalbfleisch ist aus; **the bet/agreement is** ~ die Wette/Abmachung gilt nicht (mehr); **their engagement is** ~ ihre Verlobung ist gelöst; **the play is** ~ (*cancelled*) das Stück wurde abgesagt; (*no longer running*) das Stück wurde abgesetzt.
(d) **TV, light, machine** aus(geschaltet); **tap** zu(gedreht). **the gas/electricity was** ~ das Gas/der Strom war abgeschaltet; **the handbrake was** ~ die Handbremse war gelöst.
(e) **they are badly** *or* **poorly/well** *or* **comfortably** ~ sie sind nicht gut/(ganz) gut gestellt, sie stehen sich schlecht/(ganz) gut; **I am badly** ~ **for money/time** mit Geld/Zeit sieht es bei mir nicht gut aus; **how are we** ~ **for time?** wie sieht es mit der Zeit aus?, wieviel Zeit haben wir noch?; **he is better/worse** ~ **staying in England** er ist in England besser/schlechter dran, er steht sich in England besser/schlechter.
(f) *pred* (*wide of the truth etc*) **you're** ~ **there** da irrst du gewaltig, da vertust du dich; **he was quite badly** ~ **in his calculations** er hatte sich in seinen Berechnungen ziemlich *or* schwer (*inf*) vertan; **the high notes were a bit** ~ die hohen Töne waren etwas schief (*inf*) *or* unsauber.
(g) *pred* (*inf*) **that's a bit** ~! das ist ein dicker Hund! (*inf*); **it's a bit** ~ **not letting me know** das ist ja nicht die feine Art, mir nicht Bescheid zu sagen; **his behaviour was rather** ~ er hat sich ziemlich danebenbenommen.
3 *prep* **(a)** (*indicating motion, removal etc*) von (+ *dat*). **he jumped** ~ **the roof** er sprang vom Dach; **once you are** ~ **the premises** sobald Sie vom Gelände (herunter) sind; **he borrowed money** ~ **his father** (*inf*) er lieh sich (*dat*) von seinem Vater Geld; **they dined** ~ **a chicken** sie verspeisten ein Hühnchen; **I'll take** *or* **knock** (*inf*) **something** ~ **the price for you** ich lasse Ihnen vom *or* im Preis etwas nach; **he got £2** ~ **the shirt** er bekam das Hemd £ 2 billiger; **the lid had been left** ~ **the tin** jemand hatte den Deckel nicht wieder auf die Büchse getan; **the coat has two buttons** ~ **it** am Mantel fehlen zwei Knöpfe; **which coat is that button** ~? von welchem Mantel ist dieser Knopf?; **a song** ~ **his latest LP** ein Lied von seiner neusten LP.
(b) (*distant from*) ab(gelegen) von (+ *dat*); (*in a sidestreet from*) in einer Nebenstraße von (+ *dat*); (*Naut*) vor (+ *dat*). **the house was** ~/**1 mile** ~ **the main road** das Haus lag von der Hauptstraße ab/lag eine Meile von der Hauptstraße weg *or* entfernt; **height** ~ **the ground** Höhe vom Boden (weg); **just** ~ **Piccadilly** in der Nähe von Piccadilly, gleich bei Piccadilly; **a road** ~ **Bank Street** eine Querstraße von *or* zu Bank Street.
(c) ~ **the map** nicht auf der Karte; **I'm** ~ **sausages** Wurst kann mich zur Zeit nicht reizen; **I just want it** ~ **my hands** ich möchte das nur loswerden; *see* **duty, food** etc.

offal [ˈɒfəl] *n, no pl* Innereien *pl*; (*fig*) Abfall, Ausschuß *m*.
off-: ~**beat 1** *adj* **(a)** (*unusual*) unkonventionell, ausgefallen, ungewöhnlich; **(b)** *jazz* synkopiert; **2** *n* unbetonte Taktzeit; ~**centre**, (*US*) ~**-center** *adj* (*lit*) nicht in der Mitte; *construction* asymmetrisch; **his translation/explanation was a bit** ~**centre** seine Übersetzung/Erklärung war schief *or* ging an der Sache vorbei; ~**chance** *n* **I just did it on the** ~**-chance** ich habe es auf gut Glück getan; **to do sth on the** ~**-chance that** ... etw auf den Verdacht hin *or* in der unbestimmten Hoffnung tun, daß ...; **he bought it on the** ~**-chance that it would come in useful** er kaufte es, weil es vielleicht irgendwann mal nützlich sein könnte; **I came on the** ~**-chance of seeing her** ich kam in der Hoffnung, sie vielleicht zu sehen; ~**colour**, (*US*) ~**-color** *adj* **(a)** (*unwell*) unwohl; **to feel/be** ~**-colour** sich nicht wohl fühlen, sich daneben fühlen (*inf*); **(b)** (*indecent*) schlüpfrig, gewagt.
offence, (*US*) **offense** [əˈfens] *n* **(a)** (*Jur: crime*) Straftat *f*, Delikt *nt*; (*minor also*) Vergehen *nt*. **to commit an** ~ sich strafbar machen; **it is an** ~ **to ... ...** (*ist*) bei Strafe verboten; **first** ~ erste Straftat, erstes Vergehen; **second** ~ Rückfall *m*; **an** ~ **against ...** ein Verstoß *m* gegen ...
(b) (*fig*) **an** ~ **against good taste** eine Beleidigung des guten Geschmacks; **an** ~ **against common decency** eine Erregung öffentlichen Ärgernisses; **it is an** ~ **to the eye** das beleidigt das Auge.
(c) *no pl* (*to sb's feelings*) Kränkung, Beleidigung *f*; (*to sense of decency, morality etc*) Anstoß *m*. **to cause** *or* **give** ~ **to sb** jdn kränken *or* beleidigen; **without giving** ~ ohne kränkend zu sein; **to take** ~ **at sth** wegen etw gekränkt *or* beleidigt sein; **she is quick to take** ~ sie ist leicht gekränkt *or* beleidigt; **I meant no** ~ ich habe es nicht böse gemeint; **no** ~ (**meant**) nichts für ungut; **no** ~ (**taken**) ich nehme dir das nicht übel.
(d) (*Eccl: sin*) Sünde *f*.
(e) [ˈɒfens] (*attack*) Angriff *m*. ~ **is the best defence** Angriff ist die beste Verteidigung.
offend [əˈfend] **1** *vt* **(a)** (*hurt feelings of*) kränken; (*be disagreeable to*) Anstoß erregen bei. **don't be** ~**ed** seien Sie (doch) nicht beleidigt, nehmen Sie mir *etc* das nicht übel; **he has** ~**ed his friend** er hat seinen Freund gekränkt; **this novel would** ~ **a lot of people** viele Leute würden an diesem Roman Anstoß nehmen, dieser Roman würde bei vielen Leuten Anstoß erregen.
(b) **ear, eye** beleidigen; **reason** verstoßen gegen; **sense of justice** gegen ..., verletzen.
2 *vi* **(a)** (*give offence*) beleidigend sein.
(b) (*do wrong*) Unrecht tun.

♦**offend against** vi +prep obj task, common sense verstoßen gegen; God sündigen gegen.

offender [əˈfendəʳ] n (law-breaker) Täter(in f) m; (against traffic laws) Verkehrssünder(in f) m. young ~ jugendlicher Straffälliger; home for young ~s Jugendstrafanstalt f; who left that here? — I'm afraid I was the ~ wer hat das da liegenlassen? — ich war der Übeltäter; see first ~.

offending [əˈfendɪŋ] adj remark kränkend, beleidigend. the ~ party (Jur) die schuldige Partei; (fig) der/die Schuldige; the ~ object der Stein des Anstoßes.

offense n (US) see offence.

offensive [əˈfensɪv] 1 adj (a) weapon (Jur) Angriffs-; (Mil also) Offensiv-. ~ play (Sport) Offensivspiel nt.
(b) (unpleasant) smell, sight übel, abstoßend, widerlich; language, film, book anstößig, Anstoß erregend; (insulting, abusive) remark, gesture, behaviour beleidigend, unverschämt. his language was ~ to his parents seine Ausdrucksweise erregte Anstoß bei seinen Eltern; to find sb/sth ~ jdn/etw abstoßend finden; behaviour, language Anstoß an etw (dat) nehmen; he was ~ to her er beleidigte sie; there's no need to get ~ kein Grund, ausfällig or ausfallend zu werden.
2 n (Mil, Sport) Angriff m, Offensive f. to take the ~ in die Offensive gehen; to go over to the ~ zum Angriff übergehen; on the ~ in der Offensive.

offensively [əˈfensɪvlɪ] adv (a) (unpleasantly) übel, widerlich; (in moral sense) anstößig; (abusively) beleidigend, unverschämt; (obscenely) unflätig. (b) (Mil, Sport) offensiv.

offensiveness [əˈfensɪvnɪs] n see adj (b) Widerlichkeit f; Anstößigkeit f; Unverschämtheit f.

offer [ˈɒfəʳ] 1 n Angebot nt; (also ~ of marriage) (Heirats)antrag m. the ~'s there das Angebot gilt or steht; did you have many ~s of help? haben Ihnen viele Leute ihre Hilfe angeboten?; any ~s? ist jemand interessiert?; to make an ~ of sth to sb jdm etw anbieten; he made me an ~ (of £50) er machte mir ein Angebot (von £ 50); an ~ I couldn't refuse ein Angebot, zu dem ich nicht nein sagen konnte; ~s over £15,000 Angebote nicht unter £ 15.000; on ~ (Comm) (on special ~) im Angebot; (for sale also) verkäuflich; see near 3 (d).
2 vt (a) anbieten; reward, prize aussetzen. to ~ to do sth anbieten, etw zu tun; (~ one's services) sich an(er)bieten, etw zu tun, sich bereit erklären, etw zu tun; he ~ed to give me £5 for it er bot mir dafür £ 5 an; he ~ed to help er bot seine Hilfe an; to ~ one's services sich anbieten; he was ~ed the job ihm wurde die Stelle angeboten; did he ~ to? hat er sich angeboten?; he's got nothing to ~ er hat nichts zu bieten.
(b) advice anbieten; plan, suggestion unterbreiten; remark beisteuern; excuse vorbringen; consolation spenden; condolences aussprechen. to ~ an opinion sich (dazu) äußern.
(c) (present in worship or sacrifice) prayers, homage, sacrifice darbringen; one's life opfern. nuns ~ their lives to God Nonnen stellen ihr Leben in den Dienst Gottes.
(d) (put up, attempt to inflict) resistance bieten. to ~ violence gewalttätig werden (to gegen); see battle.
(e) (afford, make available) bieten. the cottage ~s sleeping accommodation for 5 das Landhaus bietet Schlafmöglichkeit für 5 Personen; the bay ~ed a fine view von der Bucht bot sich eine schöne Aussicht.
(f) subject (for exam) machen.
3 vi whenever the opportunity ~s wenn immer sich die Gelegenheit bietet or ergibt; did he ~? hat er es angeboten?

♦**offer up** vt sep prayers, sacrifice darbringen (to sb jdm). to ~ oneself ~ to a life of public service sein Leben in den Dienst der Öffentlichkeit stellen.

offering [ˈɒfərɪŋ] n Gabe f; (Rel) (collection) Opfergabe f; (sacrifice) Opfer nt; (iro: essay, play etc) Vorstellung f.

offertory [ˈɒfətərɪ] n (Eccl) (part of service) Opferung f, Offertorium nt; (collection) Kollekte, Geldsammlung f. ~ hymn Lied nt während der Opferung; ~ box Opferstock m.

offhand [ˌɒfˈhænd] 1 adj (also off-handed) (casual remark) lässig; manner, behaviour, tone also wurstig (inf). to be ~ to sb zu jdm wurstig sein (inf); sich jdm gegenüber lässig benehmen; to be ~ about sth etw leichthin abtun.
2 adv so ohne weiteres, aus der Lamäng (inf), aus dem Stand (inf). I couldn't tell you ~ das könnte ich Ihnen auf Anhieb or so ohne weiteres nicht sagen.

offhandedly [ˌɒfˈhændɪdlɪ] adv lässig, leichthin.

offhandedness [ˌɒfˈhændɪdnɪs] n see adj Lässigkeit f; Wurstigkeit f (inf).

office [ˈɒfɪs] n (a) Büro nt; (of lawyer) Kanzlei f; (part of organization) Abteilung f; (branch also) Geschäftsstelle f. at the ~ im Büro; local government ~s örtliche Behörde, örtliches Amtsgebäude.
(b) (public position) Amt nt. to take ~ sein or das Amt antreten; (political party) die Regierung übernehmen, an die Regierung kommen; to be in or hold ~ im Amt sein; (party) an der Regierung sein; he holds the ~ of Minister of Education er bekleidet das Amt des Erziehungsministers; to be out of ~ nicht mehr an der Regierung sein; (person) nicht im Amt sein.
(c) (duty) Aufgabe, Pflicht f.
(d) usu pl (attention, help) through his good ~s durch seine guten Dienste; through the ~s of ... durch Vermittlung von ...
(e) (Eccl) Gottesdienst m. ~ for the dead Totenamt nt; (RC) Totenmesse f.
(f) (Comm) "usual ~s" „übliche Nebenräume".

office: ~ bearer n Amtsträger(in f), Amtsinhaber(in f) m; ~ block n Bürohaus or -gebäude nt; ~ boy n Laufjunge m; ~ furniture n Büromöbel pl; ~ hours npl Arbeitsstunden pl, Dienstzeit f; (on sign) Geschäfts- or Öffnungszeiten pl; to work ~ hours normale Arbeitszeiten haben; ~ job n Stelle f im Büro; ~ junior n Bürogehilfe m/-gehilfin f; ~ party n Büroparty f.

officer [ˈɒfɪsəʳ] n (a) (Mil, Naut, Aviat) Offizier m. ~ of the day

diensthabender Offizier, Offizier m vom Dienst; ~s' mess Offizierskasino nt.
(b) (official) Beamte(r) m, Beamtin f; (police ~) Polizeibeamte(r), Polizist m; (of club, society) Vorstandsmitglied nt, Funktionär m. medical ~ of health Amtsarzt m; (Mil) Stabsarzt m; yes, ~ jawohl, Herr Wachtmeister.

office: ~ supplies npl Büroartikel pl, Bürobedarf m; ~-worker n Büroangestellte(r) mf.

official [əˈfɪʃəl] 1 adj offiziell; report, duties, meeting also amtlich; robes, visit Amts-; uniform Dienst-; (formal) ceremony, style förmlich, formell. ~ statement amtliche Verlautbarung; is that ~? ist das amtlich?; (publicly announced) ist das offiziell?; ~ secret Dienstgeheimnis, Amtsgeheimnis nt; O~ Secrets Act Gesetz nt zur amtlichen Schweigepflicht; acting in one's ~ capacity in Ausübung seiner Amtsgewalt; ~ seal Dienstsiegel, Amtssiegel nt.
2 n (railway ~, post office ~ etc) Beamte(r) m, Beamtin f; (of club, at race-meeting) Funktionär, Offizielle(r) (inf) m.

officialdom [əˈfɪʃəldəm] n (pej) Bürokratie f, Beamtentum nt.

officialese [ə,fɪʃəˈliːz] n Beamtensprache, Amtssprache f, Beamtenchinesisch nt (pej).

officially [əˈfɪʃəlɪ] adv offiziell. ~ approved offiziell anerkannt.

officiate [əˈfɪʃɪeɪt] vt amtieren, fungieren (at bei). to ~ as president als Präsident fungieren, das Amt des Präsidenten ausüben; to ~ at a marriage eine Trauung vornehmen.

officious [əˈfɪʃəs] adj (dienst)beflissen, übereifrig. to be ~ sich vor (Dienst)eifer überschlagen.

officiousness [əˈfɪʃəsnɪs] n (Dienst)beflissenheit f, Übereifer m.

offing [ˈɒfɪŋ] n: in the ~ in Sicht.

off: ~-key adj (Mus) falsch; ~-licence n (Brit) (a) (shop) Wein- und Spirituosenhandlung f; (b) (permit) Lizenz f zum Alkoholvertrieb or -verkauf; ~-load vt goods ausladen, entladen; passengers aussteigen lassen; ~-peak adj ~-peak central heating Nacht(strom)speicheröfen pl; ~-peak electricity Strom m außerhalb der Hauptabnahmezeit, Nachtstrom m; ~-peak charges verbilligter Tarif; (Elec) ≈ Nachttarif m; during ~-peak hours außerhalb der Stoßzeiten; ~-peak ticket verbilligte Fahrkarte/Flugkarte außerhalb der Stoßzeit; (for buses also) = Hausfrauenkarte f; ~-print n Sonderabdruck m; ~-putting adj (Brit) smell, behaviour abstoßend; sight also, meal wenig einladend; thought, idea, story wenig ermutigend; (daunting) entmutigend; interviewer wenig entgegenkommend; job unsympathisch; it can be rather ~-putting to see how sausages are made es kann einem den Appetit verderben or die Lust am Essen nehmen, wenn man sieht, wie Wurst gemacht wird; ~ sales n (Brit) (a) pl Verkauf m aus dem Haus; (b) sing see ~-licence (a); ~-season 1 n (in tourism) Nebensaison f; in the ~-season außerhalb der Saison; 2 adj travel, prices außerhalb der Saison.

offset [ˈɒfset] (vb: pret, ptp ~) 1 vt (a) (financially, statistically etc) ausgleichen; (make up for) wettmachen, aufwiegen. price increases must be ~ by higher wages Preissteigerungen müssen durch höhere Löhne ausgeglichen werden.
(b) (place non-centrally) versetzen.
2 n (a) (Typ) Offsetdruck m. ~ (lithography) Offsetdruck m.
(b) (Hort) Ausläufer m.
(c) (fig: counterbalancing factor) Ausgleich m. as an ~ zum Ausgleich, als Ausgleich (to für).

off: ~-shoot n (a) (of plant) Ausläufer, Ableger m; (of tree) Schößling, Sproß m; (b) (fig) (of family) Nebenlinie f; (of organization) Nebenzweig m; (of discussion, action etc) Randergebnis nt; ~-shore 1 adj fisheries Küsten-; island küstennah; wind ablandig; rig, installations etc im Meer; 2 adv the wind blew ~-shore der Wind kam vom Land; the ship anchored ~-shore das Schiff ankerte vor der Küste; ~-side 1 adj (a) (Sport) im Abseits; to be ~-side im Abseits sein or stehen; (b) (Aut) auf der Fahrerseite, rechte(r, s)/linke(r, s); 2 n (Aut) Fahrerseite f; 3 adv (Sport) abseits, im Abseits; ~-spring n (a) sing Sprößling m, Kind nt, Abkömmling m; (of animal) Junge(s) nt; (b) pl (form, hum: of people) Nachwuchs m (hum), Nachkommen pl; (of animals) (die/ihre) Jungen pl; how are your ~-spring? (hum) wie geht's dem Nachwuchs? (hum); ~-stage adv hinter den Kulissen, hinter der Bühne; ~-street parking n there isn't much ~-street parking in this area in dieser Gegend gibt es wenige Parkhäuser und Parkplätze; ~-the-cuff adj remark, speech aus dem Stegreif; ~-the-peg attr, ~ the peg pred (Brit) dress, suit von der Stange, Konfektions-; ~-white 1 adj gebrochen weiß; 2 n gebrochenes Weiß.

oft [ɒft] adv (liter) oft. an ~-told story eine gar oft erzählte Geschichte (liter).

often [ˈɒfən] adv oft, häufig. he went there ~, he ~ went there er ging oft or häufig da hin; you have been there as ~ as I have Sie sind schon (eben)sooft wie ich dortgewesen; do you go there as ~ as twice a week? gehen Sie tatsächlich zweimal in der Woche da hin?; not as ~ as twice a week weniger als zweimal in der Woche; as ~ as I ask you ... jedesmal wenn or sooft ich Sie frage ...; more ~ than not, as ~ as not meistens; every so ~ öfters, von Zeit zu Zeit; he did it once too ~ er hat es einmal zu oft or zuviel getan; how ~? wie oft?; it is not ~ that ... es kommt selten vor, daß ..., es geschieht nicht oft, daß ...; oft(en) times (obs) oftmals, gar viele Male (old).

ogle [ˈəʊgl] vt kein Auge lassen or wenden von, beäugeln (pej); (flirtatiously) liebäugeln mit, schöne Augen machen (+dat); legs, girls schielen nach, beäuge(l)n (esp hum), beaugapfeln (hum); (hum) cream cakes etc schielen nach.

ogre [ˈəʊgəʳ] n Menschenfresser m; (fig) Unmensch m.

ogress [ˈəʊgrɪs] n (lit) menschenfressende Riesin; (fig) Ungeheuer nt, Unmensch m.

oh [əʊ] interj ach; (admiring, surprised, disappointed) oh; (questioning, disinterested, in confirmation) tatsächlich, wahrhaftig. ~ **good!** au or Mensch prima! (inf); ~ **well na ja!;** ~ **bother/damn! Mist!** (inf)/verdammt! (sl); ~ **dear!** o je!; ~ **yes?** (interested) ach ja?; (disbelieving) so, so; ~ **yes, that's right** ach ja, das stimmt; ~ **yes, of course there'll be room** o ja, klar haben wir Platz; ~ **my God!** o Gott!, ach du lieber Gott!

ohm [əʊm] n Ohm nt. O~'s **law** Ohmsches Gesetz.

OHMS abbr of **On His/Her Majesty's Service.**

oil [ɔɪl] **1** n (a) Öl nt. to pour ~ **on troubled waters** die Wogen glätten, Öl auf die Wogen gießen.
(b) (petroleum) (Erd)öl nt. to strike ~ (lit) auf Öl stoßen; (fig) einen guten Fund machen; (get rich) das große Los ziehen.
(c) (Art) (painting) Ölgemälde nt. to paint in ~s in Öl malen; a painting in ~s ein Ölgemälde nt; did you use ~s? haben Sie in Öl gemalt?, haben Sie Ölfarben benutzt?
(d) (sl: flattery) Schmeichelein pl.
2 vt ölen, schmieren; table, furniture einölen. to ~ **sb's palm** (fig) jdn schmieren (inf); to ~ **sb's tongue** (fig) jdm die Zunge ölen or schmieren; to ~ **the wheels** (fig) die Dinge erleichtern.

oil in cpds Öl-; ~**-based** adj auf Ölbasis; ~**-based paint** Ölfarbe f; ~**-burning** adj lamp, stove Öl-; ~**cake** n Ölkuchen m; ~**can** n Ölkanne f; (for lubricating also) Ölkännchen nt; ~ **change** n Ölwechsel m; to do an ~ **change** Öl wechseln, einen Ölwechsel machen or vornehmen; **I took the car in for an** ~ **change** ich habe den Wagen zum Ölwechsel(n) gebracht; ~**cloth** n Wachstuch nt; ~ **colours** npl Ölfarben pl.

oiled [ɔɪld] adj (a) ~ **silk** Ölhaut f. (b) (sl: drunk) **he's well-~** der ist ganz schön voll (inf), der hat ganz schön getankt (inf).

oil: ~**field** n Ölfeld nt; ~**-fired** adj Öl-, mit Öl befeuert.

oiliness ['ɔɪlɪnɪs] n (a) ölige Beschaffenheit; (of food) Fettigkeit f. (b) (fig) (of person) aalglattes Wesen. **the** ~ **of his voice/manners** seine aalglatte Stimme/sein aalglattes Benehmen.

oil: ~ **lamp** n Öllampe f; ~ **level** n Ölstand m; ~**man** n Öltyp (inf), Ölmensch (inf) m; (trader) Ölhändler m; ~ **paint** n Ölfarbe f; ~ **painting** n (picture) Ölgemälde nt; (art) Ölmalerei f; **she's no** ~ **painting** (inf) sie ist nicht gerade eine Schönheit; ~**pan** n Ölwanne f; ~**-producing** adj ölproduzierend; ~**-rich** adj ölreich; ~ **rig** n (Öl)bohrinsel f; ~ **sheik** n Ölscheich m; ~**skin** n (cloth) Öltuch nt; ~**skins** npl (clothing) Ölzeug nt; ~ **slick** n Schlick, Ölteppich m; ~**stone** n geölter Wetzstein; ~ **stove** n Ölofen m; ~ **tanker** n (ship) (Öl)tanker m, Tankschiff nt; (lorry) Tankwagen m; ~ **terminal** n Ölhafen m; ~ **well** n Ölquelle f.

oily ['ɔɪlɪ] adj (+ er) (a) skin; food fettig; clothes, fingers voller Öl. (b) (fig) aalglatt, schleimig, ölig.

ointment ['ɔɪntmənt] n Salbe f.

OK, okay ['əʊ'keɪ] (inf) **1** interj okay (inf); (agreed also) einverstanden, in Ordnung. ~, ~! ist ja gut! (inf), okay, okay! (inf); **I'll come too,** ~? ich komme auch, okay (inf) or einverstanden?
2 adj in Ordnung, okay (inf). **that's** ~ **with** or **by me** (that's convenient) das ist mir recht, mir ist's recht; (I don't mind that) von mir aus, mir soll's recht sein; **is it** ~ **with you if ...?** macht es (dir) was aus, wenn ...?; **how's your mother?** — **she's** ~ wie geht's deiner Mutter? — gut or (not too well) so so la la (inf), so einigermaßen; **to be** ~ **(for time/money etc)** (noch) genug (Zeit/Geld etc) haben; **is your car** ~? ist Ihr Auto in Ordnung?; **is that** ~? geht das?, ist das okay? (inf); **what do you think of him?** — **he's** ~ was halten Sie von ihm? — der ist in Ordnung (inf); **he's an** ~ **guy** (esp US) er ist ein prima Kerl (inf).
3 adv (well) gut; (not too badly) einigermaßen (gut); (for sure) schon. **can you mend/manage it** ~? kannst du das reparieren/kommst du damit klar?; **he'll come** ~ der kommt schon.
4 vt order, plan, suggestion gutheißen, billigen; document, proposed expenses genehmigen. **you have to get the boss to** ~ **it, you have to** ~ **it with the boss** das muß der Chef bewilligen.
5 n Zustimmung f. **to give sth one's** ~ seine Zustimmung zu etw geben; **if the boss gives his** ~ wenn der Chef das bewilligt.

okey-doke ['əʊkɪ'dəʊk], **okey-dokey** ['əʊkɪ'dəʊkɪ] interj (inf) okay (inf).

old [əʊld] **1** adj (+ er) (a) alt. ~ **people** or **folk(s)** alte Leute, die Alten pl; **if I live to be old** ~ wenn ich (je) so alt werde; ~ **Mr Smith,** ~ **man Smith** (esp US) der alte (Herr) Smith; **he is 40 years** ~ er ist 40 (Jahre alt); **two-year-~** Zweijährige(r) mf; **the** ~ **part of Ulm** die Ulmer Altstadt; **the** ~ **(part of) town** die Altstadt; **my** ~ **school** meine alte or ehemalige Schule.
(b) (inf: as intensifier) **she dresses any** ~ **how** die ist vielleicht immer angezogen (inf); **any** ~ **thing** irgendwas, irgendein Dings (inf); **any** ~ **bottle/blouse** etc irgendeine Flasche/Bluse etc (inf); ~ **Mike** der Michael (inf); **the same** ~ **excuse** die gleiche alte Entschuldigung; **we had a great** ~ **time** wir haben uns prächtig amüsiert; **funny** ~ **guy** komischer Typ (inf).
2 n days of ~ in alten or früheren Zeiten; **the men of** ~ die Menschen früherer Zeiten; **I know him of** ~ ich kenne ihn von früher; **as of** ~ wie in alten Zeiten.

old: ~ **age** n das Alter; **to reach** ~ **age** ein hohes Alter erreichen; **in one's** ~ **age** auf seine alten Tage (also hum); ~**-age pension** n (Alters)rente f; ~**-age pensioner** n Rentner(in f) m; ~ **boy** n (Brit Sch) ehemaliger Schüler, Ehemalige(r) m; **the** ~**-boy network** Beziehungen pl (von der Schule her), Vitamin B nt (sl); ~ **country** n Mutterland nt, alte Heimat.

olden ['əʊldən] adj (liter) alt. **in** ~ **times** or **days** früher, vordem (liter), in alten Zeiten; **city of** ~ **times** Stadt vergangener Zeiten.

old: O~ **English 1** n Altenglisch nt; 2 adj altenglisch; O~ **English sheepdog** n Bobtail m; ~**-established** adj family, firm alteingesessen; custom seit langem bestehend, alt.

olde-worlde ['əʊldɪ'wɜːldɪ] adj altertümlich; (pej) auf alt getrimmt (inf) or gemacht.

old: ~**-fashioned** ['əʊld'fæʃnd] adj altmodisch; ~ **girl** n (Brit Sch) Ehemalige f, ehemalige Schülerin; O~ **Glory** n (US) die Flagge der USA; ~ **gold** n Altgold nt; ~ **guard** n (fig) alte

Garde; O~ **High German** n Althochdeutsch nt.

oldie ['əʊldɪ] n (inf) (joke) alter Witz; (record) alte Platte.

oldish ['əʊldɪʃ] adj ältlich.

old: ~ **lady** n (inf) **the/my** ~ **lady** (wife) die/meine Alte (inf) or Olle (inf); (mother) die/meine alte Dame (inf), die/meine Regierung (sl); ~**-line** adj (following tradition) der alten Schule; (long-established) alteingesessen; ~ **maid** n alte Jungfer; ~**-maidish** adj altjüngferlich, altbacken; ~ **man** n (inf) **my/the** ~ **man** (husband) mein/dein etc Alter (inf) or Oller (inf); (father) mein Alter/der Alte (inf), mein alter/der alte Herr (inf); **the** ~ **man** (boss etc) der Alte; ~ **master** n alter Meister; ~ **people's home** n Altersheim nt; ~ **salt** n (alter) Seebär; ~ **school** n (fig) alte Schule; ~ **school tie** n (lit) Schulschlips m; (fig) Gehabe, das von Ehemaligen einer Public School erwartet wird; ~ **stager** n (inf) alter Hase (inf).

oldster ['əʊldstər] n (US inf) älterer Mann. **some of us** ~s einige von uns Alten.

old: ~**-style** adj im alten Stil; ~**-style calendar** Kalender m alten Stils or nach alter Zeitrechnung; O~ **Testament** n Altes Testament; ~**-timer** n Alteingediente(r), Veteran m; ~ **wives' tale** n Ammenmärchen nt; ~ **woman** n (a) see ~ **lady**; (b) **he's an** ~ **woman** er ist wie ein altes Weib; ~**-womanish** adj tuntig (inf); O~ **World** n alte Welt; ~**-world** adj (a) (quaint) politeness, manners altväterlich; cottage, atmosphere altehrwürdig, heimelig; (b) (esp US: European etc) zur alten Welt gehörend.

oleaginous [ˌəʊlɪˈædʒɪnəs] adj (form) consistency ölig, Öl-; (containing oil) ölhaltig.

oleander [ˌəʊlɪˈændər] n Oleander m.

oleo- ['əʊlɪəʊ-] pref Öl-. ~**margarine** (esp US) Margarine f.

O Level ['əʊlevl] n (Brit) Abschluß m der Sekundarstufe 1, = mittlere Reife. **to do an** ~s = die mittlere Reife machen; **to have English** ~ bis zur mittleren Reife Englisch gelernt haben; **he failed his English** ~ er fiel durch die O-Level-Prüfung in Englisch; 3 ~s die mittlere Reife in 3 Fächern.

olfactory [ɒlˈfæktərɪ] adj Geruchs-, olfaktorisch (spec).

oligarchic(al) [ˌɒlɪˈɡɑːkɪk(əl)] adj oligarchisch.

oligarchy ['ɒlɪɡɑːkɪ] n Oligarchie f.

olive ['ɒlɪv] **1** n (a) Olive f; (also ~ **tree**) Olivenbaum m; (also ~ **wood**) Olive(nholz nt) f. (b) (colour) Olive nt. **2** adj (also ~**-coloured**) olivgrün; complexion dunkel.

olive: ~ **branch** n (lit, fig) Ölzweig m; **to hold out the** ~ **branch to sb** (fig) jdm seinen Willen zum Frieden bekunden; ~**-green 1** adj cloth olivgrün; 2 n Olivgrün nt; ~ **grove** n Olivenhain m; ~ **oil** n Olivenöl nt.

Olympiad [əʊˈlɪmpɪæd] n (Hist) Olympiade f (Zeitraum zwischen olympischen Spielen).

Olympian [əʊˈlɪmpɪən] **1** adj olympisch. **2** n **the** ~s die Olympier pl.

Olympic [əʊˈlɪmpɪk] **1** adj games, stadium olympisch. ~ **champion** Olympiasieger(in f), Olympionike m, Olympionikin f; ~ **flame** or **torch** olympisches Feuer. **2** n **the** ~s pl die Olympiade, die olympischen Spiele.

Olympus [əʊˈlɪmpəs] n (also Mount ~) der Olymp.

OM abbr of **Order of Merit.**

omasum [əʊˈmɑːsəm] n Blättermagen m.

ombudsman ['ɒmbʊdzmən] n, pl -**men** [-mən] Ombudsmann m.

omega ['əʊmɪɡə] n Omega f.

omelette, (US) omelet ['ɒmlɪt] n Omelett(e) nt. **you can't make an** ~ **without breaking eggs** (Prov) wo gehobelt wird, da fallen Späne (Prov).

omen ['əʊmen] n Omen, Zeichen nt. **it is an** ~ **of success** das bedeutet Erfolg; **a bird of ill** ~ ein Unglücksvogel m.

ominous ['ɒmɪnəs] adj bedrohlich; event, appearance also drohend; look, voice also unheilverkündend, unheilschwanger; sign also verhängnisvoll. **that's** ~ das läßt nichts Gutes ahnen; **that sounds** ~ das verspricht nichts Gutes.

ominously ['ɒmɪnəslɪ] adv bedrohlich; say in einem unheilverkündenden Ton.

omission [əʊˈmɪʃən] n (omitting: of word, detail etc) Auslassen nt; (word, thing etc left out) Auslassung f; (failure to do sth) Unterlassung f. **the** ~ **of ...** unter Auslassung (+ gen) ...; **sin of** ~ (Eccl, fig) Unterlassungssünde f; **sins of** ~ **and commission** (Eccl) Unterlassungssünden und begangene Sünden.

omit [əʊˈmɪt] vt (a) (leave out) auslassen. **please** ~ **all reference to me** bitte erwähnen Sie mich nicht, bitte unterlassen Sie jeden Hinweis auf mich. (b) (fail) (to do sth etw zu tun) es unterlassen; (accidentally also) versäumen.

omnibus ['ɒmnɪbəs] **1** n (a) (form: bus) Omnibus, Autobus m. (b) (book) Sammelausgabe f, Sammelband m. **2** adj (esp US) allgemein, umfassend. ~ **bill** (Parl) Sammelgesetz nt.

omnidirectional [ˌɒmnɪdɪˈrekʃənl] adj Rundstrahl-.

omnipotence [ɒmˈnɪpətəns] n, no pl Allmacht, Omnipotenz f.

omnipotent [ɒmˈnɪpətənt] **1** adj allmächtig, omnipotent. **2** n **The** O~ der Allmächtige.

omnipresence ['ɒmnɪˈprezəns] n Allgegenwart f.

omnipresent ['ɒmnɪˈprezənt] adj allgegenwärtig.

omniscience [ɒmˈnɪsɪəns] n Allwissenheit f.

omniscient [ɒmˈnɪsɪənt] adj allwissend.

on [ɒn] **1** prep (a) (indicating place, position) auf (+ dat); (with vb of motion) auf (+ acc); (on vertical surface, part of body) an (+ dat/acc). **the book is** ~ **the table** das Buch ist auf dem Tisch; **he put the book** ~ **the table** er legte das Buch auf den Tisch; **it was** ~ **the blackboard** es stand an der Tafel; **he hung it** ~ **the wall/nail** er hängte es an die Wand/den Nagel; **a ring** ~ **his finger** ein Ring am Finger; **he hit his head** ~ **the table** er schlug sich (dat) den Kopf am Tisch/auf dem or am Boden angeschlagen; **they came** ~**(to) the stage** sie kamen auf die Bühne; **they advanced** ~ **the fort** sie rückten zum Fort vor; **they made an attack** ~ **us** sie griffen uns an; **he turned his back** ~ **us** er kehrte uns (dat) den Rücken zu; ~ **the right** rechts;

~ **my right** rechts von mir, zu meiner Rechten; ~ **TV/the radio** im Fernsehen/Radio; **who's** ~ **his show tonight?** wer ist heute in seiner Show?; **I have no money** ~ **me** ich habe kein Geld bei mir; **to count sth** ~ **one's fingers** etw an den Fingern abzählen; **we had something to eat** ~ **the train** wir haben im Zug etwas gegessen; **Southend-~-Sea** Southend am Meer; **a house** ~ **the coast/main road** ein Haus am Meer/an der Hauptstraße; **it's quicker (to go)** ~ **the main road** es geht auf der Hauptstraße schneller; ~ **the bank of the river** am Flußufer; *see also* onto.

　(b) (*indicating means of travel*) **we went** ~ **the train/bus** wir fuhren mit dem Zug/Bus; ~ **a bicycle** mit dem (Fahr)rad; ~ **foot/horseback** zu Fuß/Pferd.

　(c) (*indicating means*) **he lives** ~ **his income** er lebt von seinem Einkommen; **I could live** ~ **that** davon könnte ich leben; **they live** ~ **potatoes** sie ernähren sich von Kartoffeln; **the heating works** ~ **oil** die Heizung wird mit Öl betrieben.

　(d) (*about, concerning*) über (+acc). **a book** ~ **German grammar** ein Buch über deutsche Grammatik; **we read Stalin** ~ **Marx** wir lasen Stalins Ausführungen zu Marx; **tonight we have Lord X** ~ **pornography** heute abend spricht Lord X über Pornographie *or* zum Thema Pornographie; **have you heard him** ~ **that?** haben Sie ihn zu diesem Thema gehört?

　(e) (*in expression of time*) an (+dat). ~ **Sunday** (am) Sonntag; ~ **Sundays** sonntags; ~ **December the first** am ersten Dezember; **stars visible** ~ **clear nights** Sterne, die in klaren Nächten sichtbar sind; ~ **or about the twentieth** um den Zwanzigsten herum; ~ **and after the twentieth** am Zwanzigsten und danach; ~ **the minute** auf die Minute genau.

　(f) (*at the time of*) bei (+dat). ~ **my arrival** bei meiner Ankunft; ~ **examination** bei der Untersuchung; ~ **request** auf Wunsch; ~ **hearing this** he left als er das hörte, ging er; ~ **(receiving) my letter** nach Erhalt meines Briefes.

　(g) (*as a result of*) auf (+acc) ... hin. ~ **receiving my letter** auf meinen Brief hin.

　(h) (*indicating membership*) in (+dat). **he is** ~ **the committee/the board** er gehört dem Ausschuß/Vorstand an, er sitzt im Ausschuß/Vorstand; **he is** ~ **the "Evening News"** er ist bei der „Evening News"; **he is** ~ **the teaching staff** er gehört zum Lehrpersonal.

　(i) (*engaged upon*) **I am working** ~ **a new project** ich arbeite gerade an einem neuen Projekt; **he was away** ~ **an errand** er war auf einem Botengang unterwegs; **I am** ~ **overtime** ich mache Überstunden; **we're** ~ **the past tense** (*Sch*) wir sind bei der Vergangenheit; **we were** ~ **page 72** wir waren auf Seite 72.

　(j) (*at the expense of etc*) **this round is** ~ **me** diese Runde geht auf meine Kosten; **have it** ~ **me** das spendiere ich (dir/Ihnen), ich gebe (dir/Ihnen) das aus; *see* house.

　(k) (*as against*) im Vergleich zu. **prices are up** ~ **last year('s)** im Vergleich zum letzten Jahr sind die Preise gestiegen.

　(l) (*Mus*) **he played (it)** ~ **the violin/trumpet** er spielte (es) auf der Geige/Trompete; ~ **drums/piano** am Schlagzeug/Klavier; ~ **trumpet/tenor sax** Trompete/Tenorsaxophon.

　(m) (*according to*) nach (+dat). ~ **your theory** Ihrer Theorie nach *or* zufolge, nach Ihrer Theorie.

　(n) (*in phrases*) *see also* n, vb *etc* **he made mistake** ~ **mistake** er machte einen Fehler nach dem anderen, er machte Fehler über Fehler; **I'm** ~ **£8,000 a year** ich bekomme £ 8.000 im Jahr; **he retired** ~ **a good pension** er trat mit einer guten Rente in den Ruhestand; **to be** ~ **a course** (*Sch, Univ*) an einem Kurs teilnehmen; **to be** ~ **drugs/pills** Drogen/Pillen nehmen; **he has nothing** ~ **me** (*not as good as*) er kann mir nicht das Wasser reichen; (*no hold over*) er hat nichts gegen mich in der Hand, er kann mir nichts anhaben.

　2 *adv see also* vb + on **(a)** (*indicating idea of covering*) **he put his hat** ~ er setzte seinen Hut auf; **he put his coat** ~ er zog seinen Mantel an; **he screwed the lid** ~ er schraubte den Deckel drauf; **try it** ~ probieren Sie es an; **she had nothing** ~ sie hatte nichts an; **what did he have** ~? was hatte er an?; **he had his hat** ~ **crooked** er hatte den Hut schief auf.

　(b) (*indicating advancing movement*) **move** ~! gehen Sie weiter!, weitergehen!; ~! ~! weiter! weiter!; **to pass a message** ~ eine Nachricht weitergeben.

　(c) (*indicating time*) **from that day** ~ von diesem Tag an; **later** ~ später; **it was well** ~ **in the night** es war zu vorgerückter Stunde, es war spät in der Nacht; **well** ~ **in the morning/afternoon** später am Morgen/Nachmittag; **it was well** ~ **into September** es war spät im September; *see* get ~.

　(d) (*indicating continuation*) **to keep** ~ **talking** immer weiterreden, in einem fort reden; **go** ~ **with your work** machen Sie Ihre Arbeit weiter; **life still goes** ~ das Leben geht weiter; **they talked** ~ **and** ~ sie redeten und redeten, sie redeten unentwegt; **the noise went** ~ **and** ~ der Lärm hörte überhaupt nicht auf; **she went** ~ **and** ~ sie hörte gar nicht mehr auf; *see* and.

　(e) (*indicating position towards one*) **put it this way** ~ stellen/legen Sie es so herum (darauf); **lengthways** ~ längs.

　(f) (*in phrases*) **he's always** ~ **at me** er hackt dauernd auf mir herum, er meckert dauernd an mir herum (*inf*); **he's always (going)** ~ **at me to get my hair cut** er liegt mir dauernd in den Ohren, daß ich mir die Haare schneiden lassen soll; **he's been** ~ **at me about that** several times er ist mir ein paarmal damit gekommen; **she's always** ~ **about her experiences in Italy** sie kommt dauernd mit ihren Italienerfahrungen; **what's he** ~ **about?** wovon redet er nun schon wieder?

　3 *adj* (*switched on*) **lights, TV, radio** an; **brake** angezogen; **electricity, gas** an(gestellt). **the** ~ **switch** der Einschalter; **in the** ~ **position** auf „ein" gestellt; **to leave the engine** ~ **den Motor laufen lassen; it wasn't one of his** ~ **days** (*inf*) er war nicht gerade in Form.

　(b) *pred* (*in place*) **lid, cover** drauf. **his hat/tie was** ~ **crookedly** sein Hut saß/sein Schlips hing schief; **his hat/coat**

was already ~ er hatte den Hut schon auf/den Mantel schon an.

　(c) **to be** ~ (*being performed*) (*in theatre, cinema*) gegeben *or* gezeigt werden; (*on TV, radio*) gesendet *or* gezeigt werden; **who's** ~? (*Theat, Film*) wer spielt heute abend?, wer tritt heute abend auf?; (*TV*) wer kommt heute abend (im Fernsehen)?; **you're** ~ now (*Theat, Rad, TV*) Ihr Auftritt!, Sie sind (jetzt) dran (*inf*); **is that programme still** ~? läuft das Programm immer noch?; **the play is still** ~ (*running*) das Stück wird immer noch gegeben *or* gespielt; **what's** ~ **tonight?** was ist *or* steht heute abend auf dem Programm?; **tell me when the English team is** ~ sagen Sie mir, wenn die englische Mannschaft dran ist *or* drankommt; **I have nothing** ~ **tonight** ich habe heute abend nichts vor; **there's a tennis match** ~ **tomorrow** morgen findet ein Tennismatch statt; **there's a tennis match** ~ **at the moment** ein Tennismatch ist gerade im Gang; **what's** ~ **in London?** was ist los in London?; **there's never anything** ~ **in this town** in dieser Stadt ist nie was los.

　(d) (*valid*) **to be** ~ (*bet, agreement*) gelten; **you're** ~! abgemacht!, topp (*inf*); **you're/he's not** ~ (*inf*) das ist nicht drin (*inf*); **it's just not** ~ (*not acceptable*) das ist einfach nicht drin (*inf*), das gibt es einfach nicht; **his behaviour was really not** ~ sein Benehmen war unmöglich; **are you** ~? (*inf: are you with us*) bist du mit von der Partie? (*inf*), machst du mit?

onanism [ˈəʊnənɪzəm] *n* (*form*) Coitus interruptus *m*; (*masturbation*) Onanie, Masturbation *f*.

once [wʌns] 1 *adv* (a) (*on one occasion*) einmal. ~ **a week** einmal in der Woche, einmal pro Woche; ~ **only** nur einmal; ~ **again** *or* **more** noch einmal; ~ **again we find that ...** wir stellen wiederum *or* erneut fest, daß ...; ~ **or twice** (*lit*) ein- oder zweimal; (*fig*) nur ein paarmal; ~ **and for all** ein für allemal; (**every**) ~ **in a while,** ~ **in a way** ab und zu mal; **you can come this** ~ dieses eine Mal können Sie kommen; **for** ~ ausnahmsweise einmal; **I never** ~ **wondered where you were** ich habe mich kein einziges Mal gefragt, wo Sie wohl waren; **if** ~ **you begin to hesitate** wenn Sie erst einmal anfangen zu zögern; ~ **is enough** einmal reicht.

　(b) (*in past*) einmal. **he was** ~ **famous** er war früher einmal berühmt; ~ **upon a time there was ...** es war einmal ...; **he** ~ **lived in Paris** er hat (früher) einmal in Paris gelebt.

　(c) **at** ~ (*immediately*) sofort, auf der Stelle; (*at the same time*) auf einmal, gleichzeitig; **all at** ~ auf einmal; (*suddenly*) ganz plötzlich; **they came all at** ~ sie kamen alle zur gleichen Zeit *or* gleichzeitig; **don't spend it all at** ~ gib es nicht alles auf einmal aus.

　2 *conj* wenn; (*with past tense*) als. ~ **you understand,** it's easy wenn Sie es einmal verstehen, ist es einfach; ~ **learnt,** it isn't easily forgotten was man einmal gelernt hat, vergißt man nicht so leicht.

once-over [ˈwʌnsəʊvəʳ] *n* (*inf*) (*quick look*) flüchtige Überprüfung, kurze Untersuchung. **to give sb/sth the** *or* **a** ~ (*appraisal*) jdn/etw mal begucken (*inf*) *or* kurz überprüfen *or* inspizieren; (*clean*) jdn/etw kurz über etw (*acc*) gehen (*inf*); **to give sb the** *or* **a** ~ (*beat up*) jdn in die Mache nehmen (*inf*).

oncoming [ˈɒnkʌmɪŋ] 1 *adj* **car, traffic** entgegenkommend; **danger** nahend, drohend. **the** ~ **traffic** der Gegenverkehr. 2 *n* (*of winter etc*) Nahen, Kommen *nt*.

one [wʌn] 1 *adj* (a) (*number*) ein/eine/ein. ~ **man in a thousand** einer von tausend; **there was** ~ **person** too many da war einer zuviel; ~ **girl was pretty, the other was ugly** das eine Mädchen war hübsch, das andere häßlich; **she was in** ~ **room, he was in the other** sie war im einen Zimmer, er im anderen; **the baby is** ~ (*year old*) das Kind ist ein Jahr (alt); **it is** ~ (*o'clock*) es ist eins, es ist ein Uhr; ~ **hundred pounds** hundert Pfund; (*on cheque etc*) einhundert Pfund; **there is only** ~ **way of doing it** da gibt es nur (die) eine Möglichkeit, es zu tun; **that's** ~ **way of doing it so** kann man's (natürlich) auch machen.

　(b) (*indefinite*) ~ **morning/day** etc he realized ... eines Morgens/Tages bemerkte er ...; **you'll regret it** ~ **day** Sie werden das eines Tages bereuen; ~ **morning next week** nächste Woche einmal morgens; ~ **day next week/soon** nächste Woche einmal/bald einmal; ~ **sunny summer's day** an einem sonnigen Sommertag.

　(c) (*a certain*) ~ **Mr Smith** ein gewisser Herr Smith.

　(d) (*sole, only*) **he is the** ~ **man to tell you** er ist der einzige, der es Ihnen sagen kann; **no** ~ **man could do it** niemand konnte es allein (für sich) tun; **my** ~ (**and only**) **hope** meine einzige Hoffnung; **my** ~ **thought** was to get away mein einziger Gedanke war: nichts wie weg; **the** ~ **and only** Brigitte Bardot die unvergleichliche Brigitte Bardot.

　(e) (*same*) **they all came in the** ~ **car** sie kamen alle in dem einen Auto; **they are** ~ **and the same person** das ist ein und dieselbe Person; **it is** ~ **and the same thing** das ist ein und dasselbe; **it's all** ~ das ist einerlei.

　(f) (*united*) **God is** ~ Gott ist unteilbar; **are they** ~ **with us?** sind sie mit uns eins?; **we are** ~ **on the subject** wir sind uns über dieses Thema einig; **they were** ~ **in wanting that** sie waren sich darin einig, daß sie das wollten.

　2 *pron* (a) eine(r s). **the** ~ **who ...** der(jenige), der .../die(jenige), die .../das(jenige), das ...; **he/that was the** ~ das war's; **do you have** ~? haben Sie einen/eine/ein(e)s?; **the red/big** etc ~ der/die/das rote/große etc; **he has very fine** ~s er hat sehr schöne; **a bigger** ~ ein größerer/eine größere/ein größeres; **my/his** ~ (*inf*) meiner/meine/mein(e)s/seiner/seine/sein(e)s; **not (a single)** ~ **of them,** never ~ of them nicht eine(r, s) von ihnen, kein einziger/keine einzige/kein einziges; **no** ~ **of these people** keiner dieser Leute; **any** ~ irgendeine(r, s); **every** ~ jede(r, s); **this** ~ diese(r, s); **that** ~ der/die/das, jene(r, s) (*geh*); **which** ~? welche(r, s)?; **our dear** ~s unsere Lieben *pl*; **the little** ~s (*children*) die Kleinen *pl*; (*animals*) die Jungen *pl*; **my sweet** ~ mein Süßer, meine Süße; **that's a good** ~ (*inf*) der (Witz) ist gut; (*iro: excuse etc*) (das ist ein) guter Witz;

I'm not ~ to go out often ich bin nicht der Typ, der oft ausgeht; I'm not usually ~ to go out often, but today ... ich gehe sonst nicht oft aus, aber heute ...; I am not much of a ~ for cakes (*inf*) ich bin kein großer Freund von Kuchen (*inf*), Kuchen ist eigentlich nicht mein Fall (*inf*); she was never ~ to cry weinen war noch nie ihre Art; (*but she did*) sonst weinte sie nie; he's never ~ to say no er sagt nie nein; what a ~ he is for the girls! der ist vielleicht ein Schwerenöter! (*inf*); he's a great ~ for discipline/turning up late der ist ganz groß, wenn's um Disziplin/ums Zuspätkommen geht; ooh, you are a ~! (*inf*) oh, Sie sind mir vielleicht eine(r)! (*inf*); she is a teacher, and he/her sister wants to be ~ too sie ist Lehrerin, und er möchte auch gern Lehrer werden/ihre Schwester möchte auch gern eine werden; I, for ~, think otherwise ich, zum Beispiel, denke anders; they came ~ and all sie kamen alle (ohne Ausnahme); ~ by ~ einzeln; ~ after the other eine(r, s) nach dem/der/dem anderen; take ~ or the other nehmen Sie das eine oder das andere/den einen oder den anderen/die eine oder die andere; you can't have ~ without the other Sie können das eine nicht ohne das andere haben; ~ or other of them will do it der/die/das eine oder andere wird es tun; we must choose ~ or other of the available alternatives wir müssen eine der möglichen Alternativen wählen; he is ~ of the family er gehört zur Familie; he is ~ of us er ist einer von uns; ~ who knows the country jemand, der das Land kennt; in the manner of ~ who ... in der Art von jemandem, der ...; like ~ demented/possessed wie verrückt/besessen.

  (**b**) (*impers*) (*nom*) man; (*acc*) einen; (*dat*) einem. ~ must learn to keep quiet man muß lernen, still zu sein; to hurt ~'s foot sich (*dat*) den Fuß verletzen; to wash ~'s face/hair sich (*dat*) das Gesicht/die Haare waschen; ~ likes to see ~'s or his (*US*) friends happy man sieht seine Freunde gern glücklich.

  3 *n* (*written figure*) Eins *f*. Chapter ~ Kapitel eins; in ~s and twos in kleinen Gruppen; they became ~ sie wurden eins; they were made ~ sie wurden vereint; to be at ~ (*with sb*) sich (*dat*) (mit jdm) einig sein; he was at ~ with the world er war mit der Welt im Einklang; he is not at ~ with himself er ist mit sich selbst nicht im reinen; it was bedroom and sitting-room (all) in ~ es war Schlaf- und Wohnzimmer in einem; the goods are sold in ~s die Waren werden einzeln verkauft; jumper and trousers all in ~ Pullover und Hose in einem Stück; I landed him ~ (*inf*) dem habe ich eine(n) *or* eins verpaßt (*inf*); to be ~ up on sb (*inf*) (*know more*) jdm etwas voraussein; (*have more*) jdm etwas voraushaben; Rangers were ~ up after the first half Rangers hatten nach der ersten Halbzeit ein Tor Vorsprung.

one-acter [ˈwʌnˌæktəʳ], **one-act play** [ˈwʌnæktˈpleɪ] *n* Einakter *m*.

one another = **each other**; see **each** 2 (b).

one: ~-armed *adj* einarmig; ~-armed bandit *n* (*inf*) einarmiger Bandit; ~-eyed *adj* einäugig; ~-handed 1 *adj person* einhändig; 2 *adv* mit einer Hand; ~-horse *adj* (a) *vehicle* einspännig; (b) (*sl: inferior*) ~-horse town Kuhdorf *nt* (*inf*); ~-legged *adj person* einbeinig; a ~-legged table ein Tisch mit einem Bein; ~-line *adj message etc* einzeilig; ~-man *adj* (*fig inf*) Einmannbetrieb *m*; ~-man band Einmannkapelle *f*; ~-man Arbeit *f* für einen einzelnen; ~-man show (*Art*) Ausstellung *f* eines einzigen Künstlers; (*Theat etc*) Einmannshow *f*; Rover's a ~-man dog Rover (er)kennt nur einen Herrn (an); she's a ~-man woman ihr liegt nur an einem Mann etwas.

oneness [ˈwʌnnɪs] *n* Einheit *f*; (*of personality, thought*) Geschlossenheit *f*; (*concord: with nature, fellow men*) Einklang *m*.

one: ~-night stand *n* (*Theat*) einmalige Vorstellung; (*fig*) einmalige Angelegenheit; ~-off (*Brit inf*) 1 *adj* einmalig; 2 n a ~-off etwas Einmaliges; ~-one *adj* (*US*) see ~-to-one; ~-owner *adj* a ~-owner car ein Auto, das nur einen Besitzer hatte; ~-party *adj* (*Pol*) system Einparteien-; ~-piece 1 *adj* einteilig; 2 *n* (*bathing costume*) (einteiliger) Badeanzug, Einteiler *m*; ~-room *attr*, ~-roomed *adj* Einzimmer-.

onerous [ˈɒnərəs] *adj responsibility* schwer(wiegend); *task, duty* beschwerlich, schwer.

oneself [wʌnˈself] *pron* (a) (*dir and indir, with prep*) sich; (~ *personally*) sich selbst *or* selber. (b) (*emph*) (sich) selbst; ~ *also* myself.

one: ~-shot *adj, n* (*US*) see ~-off; ~-sided *adj* einseitig; *judgement, account also* parteiisch; ~-time *adj* ehemalig; ~-to-one *adj correspondence, correlation* sich Punkt für Punkt entsprechend, eins-zu-eins; ~-to-one teaching Einzelunterricht *m*; ~-track *adj* he's got a ~-track mind der hat immer nur das eine im Sinn *or* Kopf; ~-upmanship [ˈwʌnˈʌpmənʃɪp] *n* that's just a form of ~-upmanship damit will er *etc* den anderen nur um eine Nasenlänge voraussein; the art of ~-upmanship (*hum*) die Kunst, allen anderen um einen Schritt *or* eine Nasenlänge vorauszusein; ~-way *adj traffic, street* Einbahn-; ~-way ticket (*US Rail*) Einfachfahrkarte *f*.

ongoing [ˈɒngəʊɪŋ] *adj* (*in progress*) *research, project* im Gang befindlich, laufend; (*long-term, continuing*) *development, relationship* andauernd.

onion [ˈʌnjən] *n* Zwiebel *f*. he knows his ~s (*Brit inf*) er kennt seinen Kram (*inf*).

onion: ~ dome *n* Zwiebelturm *m*; ~ man *n* Zwiebelmann *m* (*Zwiebelverkäufer aus Frankreich*); ~ skin *n* Zwiebelschale *f*; (*paper*) Florpost *f*; ~ soup *n* Zwiebelsuppe *f*.

onlooker [ˈɒnlʊkəʳ] *n* Zuschauer(in *f*) *m*.

only [ˈəʊnlɪ] **1** *adj attr* einzige(r, s). he's an/my ~ child er ist ein Einzelkind *nt*/mein einziges Kind; the ~ one *or* person/ones *or* people der/die einzige/die einzigen; he was the ~ one to leave *or* who left er ist als einziger gegangen; the ~ thing das einzige; the ~ thing I could suggest would be to invite him too ich könnte höchstens vorschlagen, daß wir *etc* ihn auch einladen; that's the ~ thing for it/the ~ thing to do das ist die einzige Möglichkeit; the ~ thing I have against it is that ... ich habe nur eins dagegen einzuwenden, nämlich, daß ...; the ~ thing *or*

problem is ... nur ...; the ~ thing is (that) it's too late es ist bloß *or* nur schon zu spät; my ~ wish/regret das einzige, was ich mir wünsche/was ich bedaure; the ~ real problem das einzig wirkliche Problem; her ~ answer was a grin ihre Antwort bestand nur aus einem Grinsen; see **one** 1(d).

  2 *adv* it's ~ five o'clock es ist erst fünf Uhr; ~ yesterday/last week erst gestern/letzte Woche; I ~ wanted to be with you ich wollte nur mit dir zusammen sein; I wanted ~ to be with you ich wollte weiter nichts, als mit dir zusammen zu sein; one person ~ nur eine Person; "members ~" „(Zutritt) nur für Mitglieder"; ~ think of it! stellen Sie sich das nur (mal) vor!; ~ to think of it made him ill der bloße Gedanke *or* schon der Gedanke daran machte ihn krank.

  (**b**) (*in constructions*) ~ too true/easy *etc* nur (all)zu wahr/leicht *etc*; I'd be ~ too pleased to help ich würde nur zu gerne helfen; if ~ that hadn't happened wenn das bloß *or* nur nicht passiert wäre; we ~ just caught the train wir haben den Zug gerade noch gekriegt; he has ~ just arrived er ist gerade erst angekommen; I've ~ just got enough ich habe gerade genug; not ~ ... but also ... nicht nur ..., sondern auch ...

  3 *conj* bloß, nur. I would do it myself, ~ I haven't time ich würde es selbst machen, ich habe bloß *or* nur keine Zeit.

ono *abbr* **of** or **near(est) offer**.

onomatopoeia [ˌɒnəʊmætəˈpiːə] *n* Lautmalerei, Onomatopöie (*spec*) *f*.

onomatopoeic [ˌɒnəˌmætəʊˈpiːɪk] *adj*, **onomatopoetic** [ˌɒnəˌmætəpəʊˈetɪk] *adj* lautmalend, onomatopoetisch (*spec*).

onrush [ˈɒnrʌʃ] *n* (*of people*) Ansturm *m*; (*of water*) Schwall *m*.

onset [ˈɒnset] *n* (*beginning*) Beginn *m*; (*of cold weather also*) Einbruch *m*; (*of illness*) Ausbruch *m*. at the first ~ of winter weather bei Einbruch *or* Beginn des Winters; the ~ of this illness is quite gradual diese Krankheit kommt nur allmählich zum Ausbruch; with the ~ of old age he ... als er alt zu werden begann ...

onshore [ˈɒnʃɔːʳ] **1** *adj* Land-; *wind* See-, auflandig. to be ~ an Land sein. **2** [ɒnˈʃɔːʳ] *adv* (*also on shore*) an Land; *blow* landwärts, küstenwärts.

onside [ɒnˈsaɪd] *adv* nicht im Abseits. to stay ~ nicht ins Abseits laufen.

onslaught [ˈɒnslɔːt] *n* (*Mil*) (heftiger) Angriff (*on auf +acc*); (*fig also*) Attacke *f* (*on auf +acc*). to make an ~ on sb/sth (*fig*) (*verbally*) jdn/etw angreifen *or* attackieren; (*on work*) einer Sache (*dat*) zu Leibe rücken; the initial ~ of the storm das Losbrechen des Sturms.

onto [ˈɒntʊ] *prep* (a) (*upon, on top of*) auf (+*acc*); (*on sth vertical*) an (+*acc*). to clip sth ~ sth etw an etw (*acc*) anklemmen; to get ~ the committee in den Ausschuß kommen.

  (**b**) (*in verbal expressions*) see also vb + **on** to get/come ~ a subject auf ein Thema zu sprechen kommen; are you ~ the next chapter already? sind Sie schon beim nächsten Kapitel?; when will you get ~ the next chapter? wann kommen Sie zum nächsten Kapitel?; to be/get ~ *or* on to sb (*find sb out*) jdm auf die Schliche gekommen sein/kommen (*inf*); (*police*) jdm auf der Spur sein/jdm auf die Spur kommen.

ontological [ˌɒntəˈlɒdʒɪkəl] *adj* ontologisch.

ontology [ɒnˈtɒlədʒɪ] *n* Ontologie *f*.

onus [ˈəʊnəs] *n, no pl* Pflicht *f*; (*burden*) Last, Bürde (*geh*) *f*. to shift the ~ for sth onto sb jdm die Verantwortung für etw zuschieben; the ~ to do it is on *or* lies with him es liegt an ihm, das zu tun; the ~ of proof rests with the prosecution die Anklage trägt die Beweislast.

onward [ˈɒnwəd] **1** *adj* the ~ march of time/progress das Fortschreiten der Zeit/der Vormarsch des Fortschritts; the ~ path we must tread der Weg nach vorn, den wir beschreiten müssen; the ~ course of events die fortschreitende Entwicklung der Dinge.

  2 *adv* (*also* ~s) voran, vorwärts; *march* weiter. from today/this time ~ von heute/der Zeit an.

  3 *interj* (*also* ~s) voran, vorwärts.

onyx [ˈɒnɪks] **1** *n* Onyx *m*. **2** *adj* Onyx-.

oodles [ˈuːdlz] *npl* (*inf*) jede Menge (*inf*). ~ and ~ Unmengen *pl* (*inf*); ~ (and ~s) of money Geld wie Heu (*inf*); ~ (and ~) of time massenhaft Zeit (*inf*).

ooh [uː] *interj* oh.

oomph [ʊmf] *n* (*sl*) (a) (*energy*) Pep (*inf*), Schwung *m*. (b) (*sex appeal*) Sex *m* (*inf*). to have ~ sexy sein (*inf*).

ooze [uːz] **1** *n* (a) (*sluggish flow*) (*of mud, glue, resin*) Quellen *nt*; (*of water, blood*) Sickern, Triefen *nt*.

  (**b**) (*mud*) Schlamm *m*.

  2 *vi* (a) triefen; (*water, blood also*) sickern; (*wound*) nässen; (*resin, mud, glue*) (heraus)quellen.

  (**b**) (*fig*) to ~ with sth see **3** (b); he stood there, sweat/charm oozing out of *or* from every pore er stand da, förmlich triefend vor Schweiß/Liebenswürdigkeit.

  3 *vt* (a) (aus)schwitzen, absondern. my shoes were oozing water das Wasser quoll mir aus den Schuhen.

  (**b**) (*fig*) *kindness, charm, culture* triefen von (*pej*), verströmen; *vanity, pride* strotzen von; *money, wealth* stinken vor (+*dat*) (*inf*). the house ~s money *or* wealth/culture das Haus verströmt eine Atmosphäre von Reichtum/Kultur.

♦**ooze away** *vi* wegsickern; (*into ground*) versickern; (*fig*) (*courage, pride, affection etc*) schwinden; (*strength*) versiegen, schwinden.

♦**ooze out** *vi* herausquellen; (*water, blood etc*) heraussickern.

op[1] *abbr* **of opus** op.

op[2] [ɒp] *n* (*inf*) see **operation**.

opacity [əʊˈpæsɪtɪ] *n* (a) Undurchsichtigkeit, Lichtundurchlässigkeit *f*; (*of paint*) Deckkraft *f*. (b) (*fig: of essay, meaning etc*) Undurchsichtigkeit *f*.

opal [ˈəʊpəl] **1** *n* (*stone*) Opal *m*; (*colour*) beige-graue Farbe. **2** *adj* Opal-; (*in colour*) opalen (*liter*), beige-grau-schimmernd.

opalescence [ˌəʊpəˈlesns] n Schimmern nt, Opaleszenz f.

opalescent [ˌəʊpəˈlesnt] adj schimmernd, opaleszierend.

opaline [ˈəʊpəliːn] adj opalen (liter).

opaque [əʊˈpeɪk] adj **(a)** opak; glass also, liquid trüb; paper undurchsichtig. **(b)** (fig) essay, prose undurchsichtig, unklar.

op art [ˈɒpˈɑːt] n Op-art f.

op cit [ɒpˈsɪt] abbr of opere citato op. cit.

OPEC [ˈəʊpek] abbr of **Organization of Petroleum Exporting Countries** OPEC f.

open [ˈəʊpən] **1** adj **(a)** door, bottle, book, eye, flower etc offen, auf pred, geöffnet; circuit offen; lines of communication frei; wound etc offen. to keep/hold the door ~ die Tür offen- or auflassen/offenhalten; to fling or throw the door ~ die Tür aufstoßen or aufwerfen; I can't keep my eyes ~ ich kann die Augen nicht offen- or aufhalten; the window flew ~ das Fenster flog auf; to lay sb's head ~ (surgeon) jds Schädel freilegen; the thugs laid his head ~ die Schläger brachten ihm eine klaffende Wunde am Kopf bei; his head was laid ~ when he fell er schlug sich beim Fallen schwer den Kopf auf; ~ door policy Politik f der offenen Tür; a shirt ~ at the neck ein am Hals offenes Hemd.
 (b) (~ for business: shop, bank etc) geöffnet. the baker/baker's shop is ~ der Bäcker hat/der Bäckerladen ist or hat geöffnet or hat auf (inf) or hat offen (inf).
 (c) (not enclosed) offen; country, ground also, view frei; carriage, car also ohne Verdeck. ~ sandwich belegtes Brot; in the ~ air im Freien; on ~ ground auf offenem or freiem Gelände; (waste ground) auf unbebautem Gelände.
 (d) pred (not blocked, Ling) offen; road, canal, pores also frei (to für), geöffnet; rail track, river frei (to für); (Mus) string leer; pipe offen. ~ note Grundton m; have you had your bowels ~ today? (Med form) haben Sie heute Stuhlgang gehabt?; ~ to traffic/shipping den Verkehr/die Schiffahrt freigegeben; "road ~ to traffic" „Durchfahrt frei"; ~ cheque (Brit) Barscheck m.
 (e) (officially in use) building eingeweiht; road, bridge also (offiziell) freigegeben; exhibition eröffnet. to declare sth ~ etw einweihen/freigeben/für eröffnet erklären.
 (f) (not restricted, accessible) letter, scholarship offen; market, competition also frei; (public) meeting, trial öffentlich. to be ~ to sb (competition, membership) jdm offenstehen; (admission) jdm freistehen; (place) für jdn geöffnet sein; (park) jdm zur Verfügung stehen; my house is always ~ to you mein Haus steht dir immer offen; two possibilities were ~ to him zwei Möglichkeiten standen ihm offen; ~ day Tag m der offenen Tür; in ~ court (Jur) in öffentlicher Verhandlung; ~ to the public der Öffentlichkeit zugänglich; park ~ to the public öffentlicher Park; ~ shop (Ind) Open Shop m; we have an ~ shop wir haben keinen Gewerkschaftszwang; ~ forum öffentliches Forum.
 (g) to be ~ to advice/suggestions/ideas Ratschlägen/Vorschlägen/Ideen zugänglich sein or gegenüber offen sein; I'm ~ to persuasion/correction ich lasse mich gern überreden/verbessern; I'm ~ to offers ich lasse gern mit mir handeln or reden; ~ to bribes Bestechungen zugänglich.
 (h) (not filled) evening, time frei; job, post also offen.
 (i) (not concealed) campaign, secret, resistance offen; hostility also unverhohlen, unverhüllt.
 (j) (not decided or settled) question offen, ungeklärt, ungelöst. they left the matter ~ sie ließen die Angelegenheit offen or ungeklärt; to keep an arrangement ~ es offen lassen; to keep an ~ mind alles offen lassen; (judge, jury) unvoreingenommen sein; to have an ~ mind on sth einer Sache (dat) aufgeschlossen gegenüberstehen; keep your mind ~ to new suggestions verschließen Sie sich neuen Vorschlägen nicht.
 (k) (exposed, not protected) (Mil) town offen; coast also ungeschützt. a position ~ to attack eine exponierte or leicht angreifbare Position; ~ to the elements Wind und Wetter ausgesetzt; to be ~/lay oneself ~ to criticism/attack der Kritik/Angriffen ausgesetzt sein/sich der Kritik/Angriffen aussetzen; a theory ~ to criticism eine anfechtbare Theorie.
 (l) weave locker; fabric, pattern durchbrochen.
 (m) (frank) character, face, person offen, aufrichtig. he was ~ with us er war ganz offen mit uns.
 2 n **(a)** the ~ (outside) im Freien; (on ~ ground) auf freiem Feld; it's all out in the ~ nun ist alles heraus (inf), nun ist es alles zur Sprache gekommen; to bring sth out into the ~ mit etw nicht länger hinterm Berg halten; to come out into the ~ (fig) (person) Farbe bekennen, sich erklären; (affair) herauskommen; he eventually came out into the ~ about what he meant to do er rückte endlich mit der Sprache heraus (inf), was er tun wollte; to force sb out into the ~ jdn zwingen, sich zu stellen; (fig) jdn zwingen, Farbe zu bekennen; to force sth out into the ~ etw zur Sprache bringen.
 3 vt **(a)** door, mouth, bottle, letter etc öffnen, aufmachen (inf); book also, newspaper aufschlagen; throttle, circuit öffnen. he didn't ~ his mouth once er hat kein einziges Mal den Mund aufgemacht; to ~ ranks (Mil) weg- or abtreten.
 (b) (officially) exhibition eröffnen; building einweihen; motorway (für den Verkehr) freigeben.
 (c) region erschließen. they ~ed a road through the mountains durch die Berge wurde eine Straße gebaut.
 (d) (reveal, unfold) öffnen. to ~ one's heart to sb sich jdm eröffnen (geh), jdm sein Herz aufschließen (geh); ~ your mind to new possibilities öffnen Sie sich (dat) den Blick für neue Möglichkeiten; it had ~ed new horizons for him dadurch erschlossen sich ihm neue Horizonte.
 (e) (start) case, trial eröffnen; account also einrichten; debate, conversation etc also beginnen.
 (f) (set up) shop eröffnen, aufmachen (inf); school einrichten.

 (g) (Med) pores öffnen. to ~ the bowels (person) Stuhlgang haben; (medicine) abführen.
 (h) to ~ fire (Mil) das Feuer eröffnen (on auf +acc).
 4 vi **(a)** aufgehen; (door, flower, book, wound, eyes also) sich öffnen. I couldn't get the bonnet/bottle to ~ ich habe die Motorhaube/Flasche nicht aufbekommen; it won't ~ es geht nicht auf; (door, box etc also) es etc läßt sich nicht aufmachen or öffnen.
 (b) (shop, museum) öffnen, aufmachen.
 (c) (afford access: door) führen (into in +acc). the two rooms ~ into one another diese zwei Zimmer sind durch eine Tür verbunden; see also ~ on to.
 (d) (start) beginnen (with mit); (Cards, Chess) eröffnen. the play ~s next week das Stück wird ab nächster Woche gegeben; when we the play ~ed in Hull bei unserer ersten Vorstellung in Hull/als das Stück nach Hull kam.

♦**open on to** vi +prep obj (window) gehen auf (+acc); (door also) führen auf (+acc).

♦**open out** vi **1** **(a)** (become wider: river, street) sich verbreitern (into zu); (valley also, view) sich weiten, sich öffnen.
 (b) (flower) sich öffnen, aufgehen.
 (c) (map) sich ausfalten lassen.
 (d) (fig: develop, unfold) (person) aus sich herausgehen; (business) sich ausdehnen (into auf +acc); (new horizons) sich auftun.
 2 vt sep **(a)** (unfold) map, newspaper etc auseinanderfalten, aufmachen (inf).
 (b) (make wider) hole etc erweitern, vergrößern.
 (c) (fig: make expansive) person aus der Reserve locken; (develop) business ausdehnen, erweitern.

♦**open up** **1** vi **(a)** (flower) sich öffnen, aufgehen; (fig) (prospects) sich eröffnen, sich ergeben, sich erschließen; (field, new horizons) sich auftun, sich erschließen.
 (b) (become expansive) gesprächiger werden. to get sb to ~ jdn zum Reden bringen; to ~ ~ about sth über etw (acc) sprechen or reden.
 (c) (inf: accelerate) aufdrehen (inf).
 (d) (unlock doors: of house, shop etc) aufschließen, aufmachen. ~ ~! aufmachen!
 (e) (start up: new shop) aufmachen.
 (f) (start firing: guns, enemy) das Feuer eröffnen.
 (g) (Sport: game) sich auseinanderziehen.
 2 vt sep **(a)** (make accessible) territory, mine, prospects erschließen; new horizons, field of research etc also auftun; (unblock) disused tunnel etc freimachen. to ~ ~ a country to trade ein Land für den Handel erschließen.
 (b) (cut, make) passage bauen; gap schaffen; hole machen; (make wider) hole größer or weiter machen, vergrößern.
 (c) (unlock) house, shop, car etc aufschließen, aufmachen.
 (d) (start) business eröffnen; shop also aufmachen.

open: ~-air adj im Freien; ~ air swimming pool n Freibad nt; ~-air theatre n Freilichtbühne f, Freilichttheater nt; ~-and-shut adj simpel; it's an ~-and-shut case es ist ein glasklarer Fall; ~-cast adj coal-mine Tage-; ~-cast mining Tagebau m; ~-ended adj (fig) contract offen, zeitlich nicht begrenzt; offer unbegrenzt; commitment Blanko-; discussion alles offen lassend attr; subject, category endlos, uferlos; this question/subject is ~-ended über diese Frage/dieses Thema kann man endlos weiterdiskutieren.

opener [ˈəʊpnə] n Öffner m.

open: ~-eyed adj mit weit offenen Augen; he stood in ~-eyed amazement er stand da und staunte nur; ~-handed adj freigebig, großzügig; ~-handedness n Freigebigkeit, Großzügigkeit f; ~-hearth adj (Tech) Herdofen-; process (Siemens-)Martin-; ~-heart surgery n Herzeingriff m am offenen Herzen; ~ house n it's ~ house there das ist ein gastfreundliches Haus, das ist ein Haus der offenen Tür; to keep ~ house ein offenes Haus führen.

opening [ˈəʊpnɪŋ] **1** n **(a)** Öffnung f; (in hedge, branches, clouds, wall etc also) Loch m; (cleft also) Spalt m; (in traffic stream) Lücke f; (esp US: forest clearing) Lichtung f; (fig: in conversation) Anknüpfungspunkt m.
 (b) (beginning, initial stages) Anfang m; (of debate, speech, trial also, Chess, Cards) Eröffnung f.
 (c) (official ~) (of exhibition, stores) Eröffnung f; (of building also) Einweihung f; (of motorway) Freigabe f (für den Verkehr). O~ of Parliament Parlamentseröffnung f.
 (d) (action) (of door, mouth, bottle, letter etc) Öffnen nt; (of sb also) Öffnung f; (of shop, pub etc also) Aufmachen nt; (of flower also) Aufgehen nt; (of account) Eröffnung f; (setting up: of shop, school etc) Eröffnen, Aufmachen nt. hours of ~ Öffnungszeiten pl.
 (e) (opportunity) Möglichkeit, Chance f; (for career also) Start m; (job vacancy) (freie) Stelle. he gave his adversary an ~ er bot seinem Gegner eine Blöße; leave an ~ for negotiations lassen Sie die Möglichkeit für Verhandlungen offen.
 2 attr (initial, first) erste(r, s); speech, move, gambit also Eröffnungs-; remarks einführend.

opening: ~ ceremony n Eröffnungsfeierlichkeiten pl; ~ night n Eröffnungsvorstellung f (am Abend); ~ price n (St Ex) Eröffnungs- or Anfangskurs m; ~ time n Öffnungszeit f; what are the bank's ~ times? wann hat die Bank geöffnet?; when is ~ time on Sundays? wann machen am Sonntag die Lokale auf?

openly [ˈəʊpənlɪ] adv (without concealment) offen; speak also freiheraus; (publicly) öffentlich.

open: ~-minded adj aufgeschlossen; ~-mindedness n Aufgeschlossenheit f; ~-mouthed [ˌəʊpnˈmaʊðd] adj (in surprise or stupidity) mit offenem Mund, baff pred (inf); she stood in ~-mouthed amazement sie sperrte (vor Staunen) Mund und Nase auf; ~-necked adj shirt mit offenem Kragen.

openness [ˈəʊpnɪs] n **(a)** (frankness) Offenheit, Aufrichtigkeit f; (publicness) Öffentlichkeit, Offenheit f. **(b)** (fig: of mind) Aufgeschlossenheit f (to für). **(c)** (of countryside, coast) Offenheit f. **(d)** (looseness: of weave) Lockerheit f.

open: ~-plan adj office Großraum-; stairs Frei-, frei angelegt; flat etc offen angelegt; ~ **prison** n offenes Gefängnis; ~ **season** n (Hunt) Jagdzeit f; **O~ University** n (Brit) Fernuniversität f; ~**work 1** n (Sew) Durchbrucharbeit f; (Archit) Durchbruchmauerwerk nt; **2** adj durchbrochen.

opera ['ɒprə] n Oper f. **to go to the** ~ in die Oper gehen.

operable ['ɒprəbl] adj **(a)** (Med) operierbar, operabel. **(b)** (practicable) durchführbar, praktikabel.

opera in cpds Opern-; ~ **glasses** npl Opernglas nt; ~ **hat** n Chapeau claque m; ~ **house** n Opernhaus nt; ~ **singer** n Opernsänger(in f) m.

operate ['ɒpəreɪt] **1** vi **(a)** (machine, mechanism) funktionieren; (be powered) betrieben werden (by, on mit); (be in operation) laufen, in Betrieb sein; (fig: worker) arbeiten. **how does it** ~? wie funktioniert es?; **to** ~ **at maximum efficiency** (lit, fig) Höchstleistung bringen.
  (b) (theory, plan, law) sich auswirken; (causes, factors also) hinwirken (on, for auf +acc); (organization, system) arbeiten; (medicine) wirken. **that law/plan is not operating properly** dieses Gesetz greift nicht richtig/der Plan funktioniert nicht richtig; **I don't understand how his mind** ~s ich verstehe seine Gedankengänge nicht; **to** ~ **against/in favour of sb/sth** gegen jdn/etw/zugunsten von jdm/etw wirken.
  (c) (carry on one's business) operieren; (detective, spy also) agieren; (company also) Geschäfte tätigen; (airport, station) in Betrieb sein; (buses, planes) verkehren. **I don't like the way he** ~s ich mag seine Methoden nicht; **that firm** ~s **by defrauding its customers** es gehört zu den (Geschäfts)methoden der Firma, die Kunden zu betrügen.
  (d) (Mil) operieren.
  (e) (Med) operieren (on sb/sth jdn/etw). **to be** ~**d on** operiert werden; **he** ~**d on him for appendicitis/a cataract** er operierte ihn am Blinddarm/auf grauen Star.
  2 vt **(a)** (person) machine, switchboard etc bedienen; (set in operation) in Betrieb setzen; small mechanism, brakes etc also betätigen; (lever, button etc) betätigen; small mechanism etc betätigen, auslösen; (electricity, batteries etc) betreiben.
  (b) (manage) business betreiben, führen.
  (c) (put into practice) system, law anwenden, arbeiten nach; policy also betreiben.
  (d) (airline etc) route bedienen; bus etc service unterhalten; holiday, tours veranstalten.

operatic [ˌɒpəˈrætɪk] adj singer, music Opern-.

operatics [ˌɒpəˈrætɪks] n sing: (amateur) ~ Amateuropern pl.

operating ['ɒpəreɪtɪŋ] adj attr **(a)** (Tech, Comm) altitude, pressure, cost Betriebs-. **(b)** (Med) Operations-. ~ **theatre** (Brit) or **room** Operationssaal, OP m.

operation [ˌɒpəˈreɪʃən] n **(a)** (act of operating vi) (of machine, mechanism, system) Funktionieren nt; (of machine also) Gang, Lauf m; (of plan) Durchführung f; (of theory) Anwendung f; (method of functioning) (of machine, organization) Arbeitsweise f; (of system, organ) Funktionsweise f; (of law) Wirkungsweise f. **to be in** ~ (machine) in Betrieb sein; (law) in Kraft sein; (plan) durchgeführt werden; **to be out of** ~ außer Betrieb sein; (fig: person) nicht einsatzfähig sein; **to come into** ~ (machine) in Gang kommen; (law) in Kraft treten; (plan) zur Anwendung gelangen; **to bring or put a law into** ~ ein Gesetz in Kraft setzen.
  (b) (act of operating vt) (of machine etc) Bedienung, Handhabung f; (of small mechanism) Betätigung f; (of business) Betreiben, Führen nt; (of system, policy) Anwendung f; (of plan, law) Durchführung f; (of route) Bedienung f; (of bus service etc) Unterhaltung f; (of tours) Veranstaltung f.
  (c) (Med) Operation f (on an +dat). **to have an** ~ operiert werden. **to have a serious/heart** ~ sich einer schweren Operation/Herzoperation unterziehen; **to have an** ~ **for a hernia** wegen eines Bruchs operiert werden.
  (d) (enterprise) Unternehmen nt, Unternehmung, Operation f; (task, stage in undertaking) Arbeitsgang m; (Math) Rechenvorgang m, Operation f. **(business)** ~s Geschäfte pl; **to cease/resume** ~s den Geschäftsverkehr einstellen/wieder aufnehmen; **mental** ~s Denkvorgänge pl.
  (e) (esp Mil: campaign) Operation f, Einsatz m, Unternehmen nt; (in police force etc) Einsatz m. ~ **s room** Hauptquartier nt; **O~ Cynthia** Operation Cynthia.

operational [ˌɒpəˈreɪʃənl] adj attr **(a)** (ready for use or action) machine, vehicle betriebsbereit or -fähig; army unit, aeroplane, tank etc, (fig) worker etc einsatzfähig; (in use or action) machine, vehicle etc in Betrieb, in or im Gebrauch; airport in Betrieb; army unit etc im Einsatz.
  (b) (Tech, Comm) altitude, fault, costs Betriebs-. **the** ~ **range of radar/an aircraft** der Einflußbereich von Radar/der Flugbereich eines Flugzeugs.
  (c) (Mil) patrol, flight Einsatz-; base Operations-. **these submarines have never seen** ~ **service** diese U-Boote sind nie eingesetzt worden or kamen nie zum Einsatz.

operative ['ɒpərətɪv] **1** adj **(a)** (producing an effect) measure, laws wirksam; clause maßgeblich, entscheidend; (in effect) law rechtgültig, geltend. **"if" being the** ~ **word** wobei ich „wenn" betone; **to become** ~ (law) in Kraft treten; (system etc) verbindlich eingeführt werden.
  (b) (Med) treatment operativ.
  (c) (manual) skills maschinentechnisch; class Arbeiter-.
  2 n (of machinery) Maschinenarbeiter(in f) m; (detective) Detektiv m; (spy) Agent(in f) m.

operator ['ɒpəreɪtə] n **(a)** (Telec) ≈ Vermittlung f, Dame f/Herr m von der Vermittlung. **a call through the** ~ ein handvermitteltes Gespräch.

  (b) (of machinery) (Maschinen)arbeiter(in f) m; (of vehicle, lift) Führer(in f) m; (of electrical equipment) Bediener m; (of computer etc) Operator(in f) m. **lathe etc** ~ Arbeiter(in f) m an der Drehbank etc.
  (c) (private company, company owner) Unternehmer m; (Fin) (Börsen)makler m; (tour ~) Veranstalter m.
  (d) (inf) (raffinierter) Kerl, Typ (inf) m; (criminal) Gauner m. **to be a smooth/clever** ~ raffiniert vorgehen.

operetta [ˌɒpəˈretə] n Operette f.

ophthalmic [ɒfˈθælmɪk] adj Augen-. ~ **optician** approbierter Augenoptiker, der berechtigt ist, Sehhilfen zu verschreiben.

ophthalmologist [ˌɒfθælˈmɒlədʒɪst] n Ophthalmologe m, Ophthalmologin f.

ophthalmology [ˌɒfθælˈmɒlədʒɪ] n Augenheilkunde, Ophthalmologie (spec) f.

ophthalmoscope [ɒfˈθælməskəʊp] n Augenspiegel m.

opiate ['əʊpɪɪt] **1** n Opiat nt; (fig) Beruhigungsmittel nt. **2** adj opiumhaltig.

opine [əʊˈpaɪn] vt (liter) dafürhalten (geh), meinen.

opinion [əˈpɪnjən] n **(a)** (belief, view) Meinung, Ansicht f (about, on zu); (political, religious) Anschauung f. **in my** ~ meiner Meinung or Ansicht nach, meines Erachtens; **in the** ~ **of certain experts** nach Ansicht gewisser Experten; **to be of the** ~ **that ...** der Meinung or Ansicht sein, daß ...; **to express or put forward an** ~ seine Meinung äußern or vorbringen; **to ask sb's** ~ jdn nach seiner Meinung fragen; **it is a matter of** ~ das ist Ansichtssache; **I have no** ~ **about it** or **on the matter** dazu habe ich keine Meinung.
  (b) no pl (estimation) Meinung f. **to have a good** or **high/low or poor** ~ **of sb/sth** eine gute or hohe/keine gute or eine schlechte Meinung von jdm/etw haben; **to form an** ~ **of sb/sth** sich (dat) eine Meinung über jdn/etw bilden.
  (c) (professional advice) Gutachten nt; (esp Med) Befund m. **it is the** ~ **of the court that ...** das Gericht ist zu der Auffassung or Ansicht gekommen, daß ...; **to seek or get a second** ~ (esp Med) ein zweites Gutachten or einen zweiten Befund einholen.

opinionated [əˈpɪnjəneɪtɪd] adj selbstherrlich, rechthaberisch.

opinion poll n Meinungsumfrage f.

opium ['əʊpɪəm] n (lit, fig) Opium nt. **the** ~ **of the masses** Opium nt für das Volk.

opium in cpds Opium-; ~ **den** n Opiumhöhle f; ~ **fiend** n Opiumsüchtige(r) mf; ~ **poppy** n Schlafmohn m.

opossum [əˈpɒsəm] n Opossum nt.

opp abbr of **opposite** Gegent.

opponent [əˈpəʊnənt] n Gegner(in f) m; (in debate, battle of wits etc also) Opponent m.

opportune ['ɒpətjuːn] adj time gelegen, günstig; remark an passender Stelle; action, event rechtzeitig, opportun (geh). **that remark was hardly** ~ das war wohl kaum der richtige Augenblick für diese Bemerkung.

opportunely ['ɒpətjuːnlɪ] adv gelegen, günstig, opportun (geh); remark an passender Stelle.

opportunism [ˌɒpəˈtjuːnɪzəm] n Opportunismus m.

opportunist [ˌɒpəˈtjuːnɪst] **1** n Opportunist m. **2** adj opportunistisch.

opportunity [ˌɒpəˈtjuːnɪtɪ] n **(a)** Gelegenheit f. **at the first or earliest** ~ bei der erstbesten Gelegenheit; **I have little/no** ~ **for listening** or **to listen to music** ich habe wenig/nie Gelegenheit, Musik zu hören; **to take/seize the** ~ **to do sth** or **of doing sth** die Gelegenheit nutzen/ergreifen, etw zu tun; **as soon as I get the** ~ sobald sich die Gelegenheit ergibt; ~ **makes the thief** (Prov) Gelegenheit macht Diebe (Prov).
  (b) (chance to better oneself) Chance, Möglichkeit f. **opportunities for promotion** Aufstiegsmöglichkeiten or -chancen pl; **equality of** ~ Chancengleichheit f.

oppose [əˈpəʊz] vt **(a)** (be against) ablehnen; (fight against) sich entgegenstellen or entgegensetzen (+dat), opponieren gegen (form); leadership, orders, plans, decisions, sb's wishes sich widersetzen (+dat); government sich stellen gegen. **if you think he is the best I won't** ~ you wenn Sie meinen, daß er der beste ist, werde ich mich nicht dagegen stellen; **he** ~s **our coming** er ist absolut dagegen, daß wir kommen.
  (b) (stand in opposition: candidate) kandidieren gegen.
  (c) (form) (against, to dat) (set up in opposition) entgegensetzen, entgegenstellen; (contrast) gegenüberstellen.

opposed [əˈpəʊzd] adj **(a)** pred (hostile) dagegen. **to be** ~ **to sb/sth** gegen jdn/etw sein; **I am** ~ **to your going away** ich bin dagegen, daß Sie gehen. **(b)** (opposite, contrasted) entgegengesetzt, gegensätzlich. **to** ~ **all reason** entgegen aller Vernunft.
  (c) as ~ to im Gegensatz zu.

opposing [əˈpəʊzɪŋ] adj team gegnerisch; army feindlich; characters entgegengesetzt, gegensätzlich; minority opponierend. ~ **party** (Jur) Gegenpartei f; ~ **counsel** (Jur) Anwalt m der Gegenpartei.

opposite ['ɒpəzɪt] **1** adj **(a)** (in place) entgegengesetzt; (facing) gegenüberliegend attr, gegenüber pred. **to be** ~ gegenüber liegen/stehen/sitzen etc; **on the** ~ **page** auf der Seite gegenüber, auf der gegenüberliegenden or anderen Seite.
  (b) (contrary) entgegengesetzt (to, from dat, zu). **the** ~ **sex** das andere Geschlecht; ~ **number** Pendant nt; ~ **poles** (Geog) entgegengesetzte Pole pl; (Elec also) Gegenpole pl; (fig) zwei Extreme; **they've got quite** ~ **characters** sie sind ganz gegensätzliche Charaktere.
  2 n (opposite, to; contrast: of pair) Gegensatz m. **black and white are** ~s Schwarz und Weiß sind Gegensätze; **quite the** ~! ganz im Gegenteil!; **she's quite the** ~ **of her husband** sie ist genau das Gegenteil von ihrem Mann.
  3 adv gegenüber, auf der anderen or gegenüberliegenden Seite. **they sat** ~ sie saßen uns/ihnen/sich etc gegenüber.
  4 prep gegenüber (+dat). ~ **one another** sich gegenüber; **they live** ~ **us** sie wohnen uns gegenüber, sie wohnen

gegenüber von uns; **to play ~ sb** (*Theat*) jds Gegenspieler sein, die Gegenrolle zu jdm spielen.

opposition [‚ɒpə'zɪʃən] *n* **(a)** (*resistance*) Widerstand *m*, Opposition *f*; (*people resisting*) Opposition *f*. **to offer ~ to sb/sth** jdm die Stirn bieten (*geh*), jdm/einer Sache Widerstand entgegensetzen; **to act in ~ to sth** einer Sache (*dat*) zuwiderhandeln; **to start up a business in ~ to sb** ein Konkurrenzunternehmen zu jdm aufmachen; **without ~** widerstandslos.
  (b) (*contrast*) Gegensatz *m*. **to be in ~ to sb** im Gegensatz zu etw stehen; **he found himself in ~ to** the general opinion er sah sich im Widerspruch zur allgemeinen Meinung.
  (c) (*Astron*) Opposition *f*, Gegenschein *m*. **planet in ~** Planet *m* in Opposition or im Gegenschein.
  (d) (*esp Brit Parl*) **O~** Opposition(spartei) *f*; **the O~**, Her Majesty's **O~** die Opposition; **leader of the O~** Oppositionsführer(in *f*) *m*; **O~ benches** Oppositionsbank *f*.

oppress [ə'pres] *vt* **(a)** (*tyrannize*) unterdrücken. **(b)** (*weigh down*) bedrücken, lasten auf (+*dat*); (*heat*) lasten auf (+*dat*). **the climate ~es me** das Klima macht mir schwer zu schaffen; **I feel ~ed by the heat** die Hitze lastet schwer auf mir.

oppression [ə'preʃən] *n* **(a)** (*tyranny*) Unterdrückung *f*. **(b)** (*fig*) (*depression*) Bedrängnis, Bedrücktheit *f*; (*due to heat, climate*) bedrückende Atmosphäre. **the ~ of his spirits** seine Bedrängtheit.

oppressive [ə'presɪv] *adj* **(a)** (*tyrannical*) *regime, laws* repressiv; *taxes* (er)drückend. **(b)** (*fig*) drückend; *thought* bedrückend; *heat also* schwül.

oppressively [ə'presɪvlɪ] *adv* **(a)** *rule* repressiv. **to tax ~** drückende Steuern *pl* erheben. **(b)** (*fig*) drückend.

oppressiveness [ə'presɪvnɪs] *n* **(a)** Unterdrückung *f* (*of* durch); (*of taxes*) (er)drückende Last. **(b)** (*fig*) bedrückende Atmosphäre; (*of thought*) schwere Last; (*of heat, climate*) Schwüle *f*.

oppressor [ə'presə^r] *n* Unterdrücker *m*.

opprobrious [ə'prəʊbrɪəs] *adj* *invective, remark* verächtlich, schmähend; *conduct* schändlich, schandhaft, schimpflich.

opprobrium [ə'prəʊbrɪəm] *n* (*disgrace*) Schande, Schmach *f*; (*scorn, reproach*) Schmähung *f*. **a term of ~** ein Schmähwort *nt*.

opt [ɒpt] *vi* **to ~ for sth/to do sth** sich für etw entscheiden/sich entscheiden, etw zu tun; **to ~ to belong to Britain** für Großbritannien optieren.

♦**opt out** *vi* sich anders entscheiden; (*of awkward situation also*) absprengen (*of* bei); (*of responsibility, invitation*) ablehnen (*of acc*); (*give up membership, Rad, TV*) austreten (*of aus*); (*of insurance scheme*) kündigen (*of acc*). **he ~ed ~ of going to the party** er entschied sich, doch nicht zur Party zu gehen.

optative ['ɒptətɪv] **1** *n* Optativ *m*, Wunschform *f*. **2** *adj* optativ.

optic ['ɒptɪk] *adj* *nerve, centre* Seh-.

optical ['ɒptɪkəl] *adj* optisch. **~ illusion** optische Täuschung.

optician [ɒp'tɪʃən] *n* Optiker(in *f*) *m*.

optics ['ɒptɪks] *n sing* Optik *f*.

optima ['ɒptɪmə] *pl of* **optimum**.

optimal ['ɒptɪml] *adj* optimal.

optimism ['ɒptɪmɪzəm] *n* Optimismus *m*.

optimist ['ɒptɪmɪst] *n* Optimist *m*.

optimistic [‚ɒptɪ'mɪstɪk] *adj* optimistisch, zuversichtlich. **to be ~ about sth** in bezug auf etw (*acc*) optimistisch sein; **I'm not very ~ about it** ich bin nicht sehr optimistisch.

optimistically [‚ɒptɪ'mɪstɪkəlɪ] *adv see adj*.

optimize ['ɒptɪmaɪz] *vt* optimieren.

optimum ['ɒptɪməm] **1** *adj* optimal; *conditions also* bestmöglich. **2** *n*, *pl* **optima** or **-s** Optimum *nt*. **at an ~** optimal.

option ['ɒpʃən] *n* **(a)** (*choice*) Wahl *f no pl*; (*possible course of action also*) Möglichkeit *f*. **since you've got the ~ of leaving or staying** da Sie die Wahl haben, ob Sie gehen oder bleiben wollen; **I have little/no ~** mir bleibt kaum eine/keine andere Wahl; **he had no ~ but to come** ihm blieb nichts anderes übrig, als zu kommen; **you have only two ~s (open to you)** es stehen Ihnen nur zwei Möglichkeiten zur Wahl; **that leaves us no ~** das läßt uns keine andere Wahl; **to leave one's ~s open** sich (*dat*) alle Möglichkeiten offenlassen; **imprisonment without the ~ of a fine** (*Jur*) Gefängnisstrafe *f* ohne Zulassung einer ersatzweisen Geldstrafe.
  (b) (*Comm*) Option *f* (*on auf* +*acc*); (*on house, goods etc also*) Vorkaufsrecht *nt* (*on an* +*dat*); (*on shares*) Bezugsrecht *nt* (*on für*). **with an ~ to buy** mit einer Kaufoption or (*on shares*) Bezugsoption; (*on approval*) zur Ansicht; **to have a 20-day ~** eine Option mit einer Frist von 20 Tagen haben.
  (c) (*Univ, Sch*) Wahlfach *nt*.

optional ['ɒpʃənl] *adj* (*not compulsory*) freiwillig; (*Sch, Univ*) *subject* Wahl-, wahlfrei, fakultativ; (*not basic*) *trim, mirror etc* auf Wunsch erhältlich. **"evening dress ~"** „Abendkleidung nicht Vorschrift"; **~ extras** Extras *pl*; **the cigar lighter is an ~ extra** der Zigarettenanzünder wird auf Wunsch eingebaut.

optometrist [ɒp'tɒmətrɪst] *n* (*US: optician*) Optiker(in *f*) *m*.

opulence ['ɒpjʊləns] *n*, *no pl see adj* Reichtum *m*; Wohlhabenheit *f*; Prunk *m*, Stattlichkeit *f*; Üppigkeit *f*; Üppigkeit, Fülligkeit *f*. **to live in ~** im Überfluß leben.

opulent ['ɒpjʊlənt] *adj* reich; *appearance* (*of person*) *also* wohlhabend; *clothes, building, room* prunkvoll, stattlich; *car, chairs, carpets* feudal; *décor also, lifestyle, vegetation* üppig; *figure* üppig, füllig.

opus ['əʊpəs] *n*, *pl* **opera** ['ɒpərə] *n* (*Mus*) Opus *nt*.

or¹ [ɔː^r] *n* (*Her*) Gold *nt*.

or² *conj* **(a)** oder; (*with neg*) noch. **he could not read ~ write** er konnte weder lesen noch schreiben; **without tears ~ sighs** ohne Tränen oder Seufzer; **speak ~ (else)** go out sprechen Sie oder gehen Sie hinaus; **you'd better go ~ (else)** you'll be late gehen Sie jetzt besser, sonst kommen Sie zu spät; **you'd better do it ~**

else! tu das lieber, sonst ...!; **in a day/month ~ two** in ein bis or oder zwei Tagen/Monaten.
  (b) (*that is*) (oder) auch. **the Lacedaemonians, ~ Spartans** die Lazedämonier, (oder) auch Spartaner; **the Congo, ~ rather, Zaire** der Kongo, beziehungsweise Zaire.

oracle ['ɒrəkl] *n* Orakel *nt*; (*person*) Seher(in *f*) *m*; (*fig*) Alleswisser *m*. **Delphic ~** delphisches Orakel, Orakel zu Delphi.

oracular [ɒ'rækjʊlə^r] *adj* *inscriptions, utterances* orakelhaft; *powers* seherisch; (*fig*) weise.

oral ['ɔːrəl] **1** *adj* **(a)** *consonant, phase etc* oral; *medicine also* Oral-; (*spec*), zum Einnehmen; *cavity, hygiene, sex also* Mund-. **(b)** (*verbal*) mündlich. **to improve one's ~ skills in a language** eine Sprache besser sprechen lernen. **2** *n* Mündliche(s) *nt*.

orally ['ɔːrəlɪ] *adv* **(a)** oral. **(b)** (*verbally*) mündlich.

orange ['ɒrɪndʒ] **1** *n* **(a)** (*fruit, tree*) Orange, Apfelsine *f*; (*drink*) Orangensaft *m*. **(b)** (*colour*) Orange *nt*. **2** *adj* **(a)** Orangen-. (*in colour*) orange *inv*, orange(n)farben or -farbig.

orangeade ['ɒrɪndʒeɪd] *n* Orangeade, Orangenlimonade *f*.

orange: **~-blossom** *n* Orangenblüte *f* wird von Bräuten zur Hochzeit getragen; **~ box** *n* Obst- or Apfelsinenkiste *f*; **~-coloured** *adj* orange(n)farben or -farbig; **~ grove** *n* Orangenhain *m*; **~ juice** *n* Orangensaft *m*; **O~man** *n* Anhänger *m* der Orange Order; **O~ March** *n* Demonstration *f* der Orange Order; **O~ Order** *n* protestantische Vereinigung, die den Namen Wilhelms von Oranien trägt; **~ peel** *n* Orangen- or Apfelsinenschale *f*; **~ stick** *n* Maniküstäbchen *nt*.

orang-outang, orang-utan [ɔː‚ræŋu'tæn] *n* Orang-Utan *m*.

orate [ɒ'reɪt] *vi* Reden/eine Rede halten (*to vor* +*dat*).

oration [ɒ'reɪʃən] *n* Ansprache *f*. *funeral* **~** Grabrede *f*.

orator ['ɒrətə^r] *n* Redner(in *f*), Orator (*rare, Hist*) *m*.

oratorical [‚ɒrə'tɒrɪkəl] *adj* oratorisch; *contest also* Redner-.

oratorio [‚ɒrə'tɔːrɪəʊ] *n* (*Mus*) Oratorium *nt*.

oratory¹ ['ɒrətərɪ] *n* (*art of making speeches*) Redekunst *f*. **to go off into a flight of ~** sich in großen Reden ergehen.

oratory² [‚ɒrətərɪ] *n* (*Eccl*) Oratorium *nt*.

orb [ɔːb] *n* **(a)** (*poet*) Ball *m*; (*star*) Gestirn *nt* (*geh*); (*eye*) Auge *nt*. **(b)** (*of sovereignty*) Reichsapfel *m*.

orbit ['ɔːbɪt] **1** *n* **(a)** (*Astron, Space*) (*path*) Umlaufbahn, Kreisbahn *f*, Orbit *m* (*spec*); (*single circuit*) Umkreisung *f*, Umlauf *m*. **to be in/go into ~** (*round the earth/moon*) in der (Erd-/Mond)umlaufbahn sein/in die (Erd-/Mond)umlaufbahn eintreten; **to put a satellite into ~** einen Satelliten in die Umlaufbahn schießen.
  (b) (*fig*) Kreis *m*; (*sphere of influence*) (Macht)bereich *m*, Einflußsphäre *f*.
  2 *vt* umkreisen.
  3 *vi* kreisen.

orbital ['ɔːbɪtl] *adj* orbital; *velocity* Umlauf-.

orchard ['ɔːtʃəd] *n* Obstgarten *m*; (*commercial*) Obstplantage *f*. **apple/cherry ~** Obstgarten *m* mit Apfel-/Kirschbäumen; (*commercial*) Apfel-/Kirschplantage *f*.

orchestra ['ɔːkɪstrə] *n* Orchester *nt*.

orchestral [ɔː'kestrəl] *adj* Orchester-, orchestral.

orchestrally [ɔː'kestrəlɪ] *adv* orchestral.

orchestra: ~ pit *n* Orchestergraben *m*; **~ stalls** *npl* Orchestersitze *pl*; **a seat in the ~ stalls** ein Orchestersitz *m*.

orchestrate ['ɔːkɪstreɪt] *vt* orchestrieren.

orchestration [‚ɔːkɪs'treɪʃən] *n* Orchestrierung, Orchesterbearbeitung *f*.

orchid ['ɔːkɪd] *n* Orchidee *f*.

ordain [ɔː'deɪn] *vt* **(a)** *sb* ordinieren; (*Eccl*) *a priest* weihen. **to be ~ed priest/to the ministry** ordiniert werden; (*Catholic also*) zum Priester geweiht werden.
  (b) (*destine: God, fate*) wollen, bestimmen. **God has ~ed that man should die** Gott hat es gewollt or hat bestimmt, daß der Mensch sterbe; **fate ~ed him to die** or **that he should die, it was ~ed that he should die** das Schicksal hat es so gefügt or es war ihm vom Schicksal bestimmt, daß er sterben sollte.
  (c) (*decree*) (*law*) bestimmen; (*ruler also*) verfügen.

ordeal [ɔː'diːl] *n* **(a)** Tortur *f*; (*stronger, long-lasting*) Martyrium *nt*; (*torment, emotional ~*) Qual *f*. **(b)** (*Hist: trial*) Gottesurteil *nt*. **~ by fire/water** Feuer-/Wasserprobe *f*.

order ['ɔːdə^r] **1** *n* **(a)** (*sequence*) (Reihen)folge, (An)ordnung *f*. **word ~** Wortstellung, Wortfolge *f*; **are they in ~/in the right ~?** sind sie geordnet/sind sie in der richtigen Reihenfolge?; **in ~ of preference/merit** *etc* in der bevorzugten/in der ihren Auszeichnungen entsprechenden Reihenfolge; **to put sth in (the right) ~** etw ordnen; **to be in the wrong ~** or **out of ~** durcheinander sein; (*one item*) nicht am richtigen Platz sein; **to get out of ~** durcheinandergeraten; (*one item*) an eine falsche Stelle kommen.
  (b) (*system*) Ordnung *f*. **there's no ~ in his work** seiner Arbeit fehlt die Systematik; **he has no sense of ~** er hat kein Gefühl für Systematik or Methode; **the ~ of the world** die Weltordnung; **it is in the ~ of things** es liegt in der Natur der Dinge.
  (c) (*tidy or satisfactory state*) Ordnung *f*. **his passport was in ~** sein Paß war in Ordnung; **to put** or **set one's life/affairs in ~** Ordnung in sein Leben/seine Angelegenheiten bringen.
  (d) (*discipline*) (*in society*) Ordnung *f*; (*in school, team also*) Disziplin *f*. **to keep ~** die Ordnung wahren; **die Disziplin aufrechterhalten; to keep the children in ~** die Kinder unter Kontrolle halten; **~ in court** (*Brit*) or **the courtroom!** (*US*) Ruhe im Gerichtssaal!; **~, ~!** Ruhe!
  (e) (*working condition*) Zustand *m*. **to be in good/bad ~** in gutem/schlechtem Zustand sein; (*work well/badly also*) in Ordnung/nicht in Ordnung sein; **to be out of/in ~** (*car, radio, telephone*) nicht funktionieren/funktionieren; (*machine, lift also*) außer/in Betrieb sein.
  (f) (*command*) Befehl *m*, Order *f* (*old, hum*). **by ~ of the court** laut gerichtlicher Anweisung; **~s are ~s** Befehl ist Befehl; **"no parking/smoking by ~"** „Parken/Rauchen verboten!"; **"no**

parking – by ~ of the Town Council" „Parken verboten – die Stadtverwaltung"; by ~ of the minister auf Anordnung des Ministers; I don't take ~s from anyone ich lasse mir von niemandem befehlen; to be under ~s to do sth Instruktionen haben, etw zu tun; until further ~s bis auf weiteren Befehl.

(g) (in restaurant etc, Comm) Bestellung f; (contract to manufacture) Auftrag m. made to ~ auf Bestellung (gemacht or hergestellt); to give an ~ to or place an ~ with sb eine Bestellung bei jdm aufgeben or machen; jdm einen Auftrag geben; to put sth on ~ etw in Bestellung/Auftrag geben.

(h) (Fin) cheque to ~ Orderscheck, Namensscheck m; pay to the ~ of zahlbar an (+acc) ...; pay X or O~ (zahlbar) an X oder dessen Order.

(i) in ~ to do sth um etw zu tun; in ~ that damit.

(j) (correct procedure at meeting, Parl etc) a point of ~ eine Verfahrensfrage; to be out of ~ gegen die Verfahrensordnung verstoßen; (Jur: evidence) unzulässig sein; (fig) aus dem Rahmen fallen; to call sb/the meeting to ~ jdn ermahnen, sich an die Verfahrensordnung zu halten; die Versammlung zur Ordnung rufen; an explanation/a drink would seem to be in ~ eine Erklärung/ein Drink wäre angebracht; is it in ~ for me to go to Paris? ist es in Ordnung, wenn ich nach Paris fahre?; his demand is quite in ~ seine Forderung ist völlig berechtigt; to be the ~ of the day der Tagesordnung (also fig) or der Tagesordnung stehen; (Mil) der Tagesbefehl sein; what's the ~ of the day? was steht auf dem Programm (also fig) or der Tagesordnung?; (Mil) wie lautet der Tagesbefehl?

(k) (Archit) Säulenordnung f; (Biol) Ordnung f; (fig: class, degree) Art f. intelligence of a high or the first ~ hochgradige Intelligenz; something in the ~ of ten per cent in der Größenordnung von zehn Prozent; something in the ~ of one in ten applicants etwa einer von zehn Bewerbern.

(l) (Mil: formation) Ordnung f.

(m) (social rank) Schicht f. the higher/lower ~s die oberen/unteren Schichten; the ~ of baronets der Freiherrnstand.

(n) (Eccl: of monks etc) Orden m. Benedictine ~ Benediktinerorden m.

(o) (Eccl) (holy) ~s pl Weihe(n pl) f; (of priesthood) Priesterweihe f; to take (holy) ~s die Weihen empfangen; he is in (holy) ~s er gehört dem geistlichen Stand an.

(p) (honour, society of knights) Orden m.

2 vt **(a)** (command, decree) sth befehlen, anordnen; (prescribe: doctor) verordnen (for sb jdm). to ~ sb to do sth jdn etw tun heißen (geh), jdm befehlen or (doctor) verordnen, etw zu tun; (esp Mil) jdn dazu beordern, etw zu tun; he was ~ed to be quiet man befahl ihm, still zu sein; (in public) er wurde zur Ruhe gerufen; the army was ~ed to retreat dem Heer wurde der Rückzug befohlen; he ~ed his gun to be brought (to him) er ließ sich (dat) sein Gewehr bringen; to ~ sb out/home (call in etc) jdn heraus-/heimbeordern (form, hum) or -rufen; (send in etc) jdn hinaus-/heimbeordern (form, hum) or -schicken.

(b) (direct, arrange) one's affairs, life ordnen. to ~ arms (Mil) das Gewehr abnehmen.

(c) (Comm etc) goods, dinner, taxi bestellen; (to be manufactured) ship, suit, machinery etc in Auftrag geben.

3 vi bestellen.

♦**order about** or **around** vt sep herumkommandieren.

order: ~ **book** n (Comm) Auftragsbuch nt; ~ **cheque** n Orderscheck, Namensscheck m; ~ **form** n Bestellformular nt, Bestellschein m.

orderliness ['ɔːdəlɪnɪs] n **(a)** Ordentlichkeit f. the ~ of his life sein geregeltes Leben. **(b)** (of group, demonstration) Friedlichkeit f, Gesittetheit f.

orderly ['ɔːdəlɪ] **1** adj **(a)** (tidy, methodical) ordentlich, geordnet; life also geregelt; person, mind ordentlich, methodisch. **(b)** (disciplined) group, demonstration ruhig, friedlich, gesittet.

2 n **(a)** (Mil) (attached to officer) Bursche m (dated). **(b)** (medical) ~ Pfleger(in f) m; (Mil) Sanitäter m.

orderly: ~ **officer** n diensthabender Offizier, Offizier m vom Dienst; ~ **room** n Schreibstube f.

order paper n (esp Parl) Tagesordnung f.

ordinal ['ɔːdɪnl] (Math) **1** adj Ordnungs-, Ordinal-. **2** n Ordnungs- or Ordinalzahl, Ordinale (spec) f.

ordinance ['ɔːdɪnəns] n **(a)** (order) (of government) Verordnung f; (Jur) Anordnung f; (of fate) Fügung f (geh). **(b)** (Eccl) (sacrament) Sakrament nt; (rite also) Ritus m.

ordinarily ['ɔːdnrɪlɪ] adv normalerweise, gewöhnlich; (+adj) normal, wie gewöhnlich. more than ~ stupid/intelligent außergewöhnlich dumm/intelligent.

ordinary ['ɔːdnrɪ] **1** adj **(a)** (usual) gewöhnlich, normal. to do sth in the ~ way etw auf die normale or gewöhnliche Art und Weise tun; in the ~ way I would ... normalerweise or gewöhnlich würde ich ...; ~ use normaler Gebrauch; my ~ doctor der Arzt, zu dem ich normalerweise gehe.

(b) (average) normal, durchschnittlich; (nothing special, commonplace) gewöhnlich; alltäglich. the ~ Englishman der normale Engländer; a very ~ kind of person ein ganz gewöhnlicher Mensch; this is no ~ car dies ist kein gewöhnliches Auto.

2 n **(a)** out of the ~ außergewöhnlich, außerordentlich; nothing/something out of the ~ nichts/etwas Außergewöhnliches or Ungewöhnliches; intelligence above the ~ überdurchschnittliche or außergewöhnliche Intelligenz.

(b) (form) physician/painter in ~ to the king Leibarzt m des Königs/königlicher Hofmaler.

ordinary: O~ Level n see O Level; ~ seaman n Maat m; ~ share n (Fin) Stammaktie f.

ordination [ɔːdɪ'neɪʃən] n Ordination f.

ordnance ['ɔːdnəns] n **(a)** (Mil) (artillery) (Wehr)material nt. **(b)** (supply) Material nt, Versorgung f; (corps) Technische

Truppe; (in times of war) Nachschub m.

ordnance: ~ **factory** n Munitionsfabrik f; O~ **Survey** n (Brit) = Landesvermessungsamt nt (BRD), Abteilung f Vermessung (im Ministerium des Innern) (DDR); O~ **Survey map** n (Brit) amtliche topographische Karte (form), Meßtischblatt nt.

ordure ['ɔːdjʊəʳ] n (liter) (excrement) Kot m; (rubbish) Unrat, Unflat (geh) m; (fig) Schmutz m no pl.

ore [ɔːʳ] n Erz nt.

oregano [ˌɒrɪ'gɑːnəʊ] n Origano, Oregano m.

organ ['ɔːgən] n **(a)** (Anat) Organ nt; (penis) Geschlecht nt. ~ of speech Sprechorgan. **(b)** (Mus) Orgel f. to be at the ~ die Orgel spielen; ~ loft n Orgelempore, Orgelbühne f. **(c)** (mouthpiece of opinion) Sprachrohr nt; (newspaper) Organ nt. **(d)** (means of action) Organ nt.

organdie, (US) **organdy** ['ɔːgəndɪ] **1** n Organdy m. **2** attr Organdy-.

organ-grinder ['ɔːgənˌgraɪndəʳ] n Drehorgel-Spieler, Leierkastenmann m.

organic [ɔː'gænɪk] adj **(a)** (Sci) organisch; vegetables, farming biodynamisch. **(b)** (fig) whole, unity organisch; part of whole substantiell; fault immanent.

organically [ɔː'gænɪkəlɪ] adv **(a)** (Sci) organisch; farm, grow biodynamisch. **(b)** (fig) integrated, connected etc organisch.

organism ['ɔːgənɪzəm] n (Biol, fig) Organismus m.

organist ['ɔːgənɪst] n Organist(in f) m.

organization [ˌɔːgənaɪ'zeɪʃən] n **(a)** (act) Organisation f (also Pol); (of time) Einteilung f; (of work also) Einteilung f. **(b)** (arrangement) see vt **(a)** Ordnung f; Organisation f; Einteilung f; Organisation, Einteilung f; Aufbau m; Planung f. **(c)** (institution) Organisation f; (Comm) Unternehmen nt.

organize ['ɔːgənaɪz] **1** vt **(a)** (give structure to, systematize) ordnen; facts also organisieren; time einteilen; work organisieren, einteilen; essay aufbauen; one's/sb's life planen. to get (oneself) ~d (get ready) alles vorbereiten; (to go out) sich fertigmachen; (for term, holiday etc) sich vorbereiten; (sort things out) seine Sachen in Ordnung bringen; (sort out one's life) ein geregeltes Leben anfangen; I'll have to get better ~d ich muß das alles besser organisieren; I'll come as soon as I've got (myself) ~d ich komme, sobald ich so weit bin; to get (oneself) ~d with a job/equipment etc sich (dat) einen Job/eine Ausrüstung besorgen; I've only just taken over the shop, but as soon as I've got ~d I'll contact you ich habe den Laden gerade erst übernommen, aber sobald alles (richtig) läuft, melde ich mich bei Ihnen; it took us quite a while to get ~d in our new house wir haben eine ganze Zeit gebraucht, uns in unserem neuen Haus (richtig) einzurichten.

(b) (arrange) party, meeting etc organisieren; food, music for party etc sorgen für; sports event also ausrichten; (into teams, groups) einteilen. to ~ things so that ... es so einrichten, daß ...; **organizing committee** Organisationskomitee nt.

(c) (Pol: unionize) organisieren.

2 vi (Pol) sich organisieren.

organized ['ɔːgənaɪzd] adj **(a)** (Sci) organisch. **(b)** (structured, systematized) organisiert; life geregelt. ~ **crime** organisiertes Verbrechen; he isn't very ~ (inf) bei ihm geht alles drunter und drüber (inf); you have to be ~ du mußt planvoll or systematisch or mit System vorgehen; as far as his work/social life is concerned, he's well ~ was seine Arbeit/sein gesellschaftliches Leben angeht, so läuft bei ihm alles sehr geregelt ab; he's well ~ (in new flat etc) er ist bestens eingerichtet; (well-prepared) er ist gut vorbereitet. **(c)** (Pol: unionized) organisiert.

organizer ['ɔːgənaɪzəʳ] n Organisator, Veranstalter m; (of sports event) Ausrichter m.

orgasm ['ɔːgæzəm] n (lit, fig) Orgasmus m. to go into ~s (fig sl) einen Orgasmus nach dem anderen kriegen (inf); to be in ~s (fig sl) ganz außer sich sein.

orgasmic [ɔː'gæzmɪk] adj orgasmisch.

orgiastic [ˌɔːdʒɪ'æstɪk] adj orgiastisch.

orgy ['ɔːdʒɪ] n (lit, fig) Orgie f. drunken ~ Sauforgie f; an ~ of killing eine Blutorgie; ~ of spending Kauforgie f; an ~ of colour eine orgiastische Farbenpracht.

oriel (window) ['ɔːrɪəl('wɪndəʊ)] n Erker(fenster nt) m.

orient ['ɔːrɪənt] **1** n (also O~) Orient m; (poet also) Morgenland nt. **2** adj (poet) sun, moon aufgehend. **3** vt see orientate.

oriental [ˌɔːrɪ'entl] **1** adj orientalisch; languages also östlich; (Univ) orientalistisch; rug Orient-. ~ **studies** pl Orientalistik f. **2** n (person) O~ Orientale m, Orientalin f.

orientate ['ɔːrɪənteɪt] **1** vr (lit) sich orientieren (by an +dat, by the map nach der Karte); (fig also) sich zurechtfinden. to ~ oneself to a new situation sich in einer neuen Situation zurechtfinden.

2 vt ausrichten (towards auf +acc); new employees etc einführen. you should ~ your thinking towards a more liberal attitude Sie sollten Ihr Denken an einer liberaleren Haltung orientieren; money-~d materiell ausgerichtet.

orientation [ˌɔːrɪən'teɪʃən] n **(a)** (getting one's bearing) Orientierung f; (fig also) Ausrichtung f; (of new employees etc) Einführung f. the first day was free for ~ der erste Tag stand zur Orientierung zur Verfügung.

(b) (position, direction) (lit: of boat, spaceship etc) Kurs m; (fig) Orientierung f; (attitude) Einstellung f (towards zu); (leaning) Ausrichtung f (towards auf +acc).

orienteering [ˌɔːrɪən'tɪərɪŋ] n Orientierungslauf m.

orifice ['ɒrɪfɪs] n Öffnung f.

origami [ˌɒrɪ'gɑːmɪ] n Origami nt.

origin ['ɒrɪdʒɪn] n **(a)** Ursprung m, Herkunft f; (of person, family) Herkunft, Abstammung f; (of world) Ursprung m; (of river) Ursprung m (geh). to have its ~ in sth auf etw (acc) zurückgehen; (river) in etw (dat) entspringen; his family had its ~ in France seine Familie ist französischer Herkunft;

country of ~ Herkunftsland *nt*; nobody knew the ~ of that rumour niemand wußte, wie das Gerücht entstanden war; what are his ~s? was für eine Herkunft hat er?; the ~s of the new state die Anfänge des neuen Staates; the ~(s) of the play die Herkunft des Stückes.
  (b) *(Math)* Ursprung *m*.
original [ə'rɪdʒɪnl] **1** *adj* **(a)** *(first, earliest)* ursprünglich. ~ sin die Erbsünde; ~ inhabitants of a country Ureinwohner *pl* eines Landes; ~ text/version Urtext *m*/Urfassung *f*; ~ edition Originalausgabe *f*.
  (b) *(not imitative)* painting original; *idea, writer, play* originell. ~ research eigene Forschung; ~ document *(Jur)* Originaldokument *nt*.
  (c) *(unconventional, eccentric)* character, person originell.
  2 *n* **(a)** Original *nt*; *(of model)* Vorlage *f*.
  (b) *(eccentric person)* Original *nt*.
originality [ə,rɪdʒɪ'nælɪtɪ] *n* Originalität *f*.
originally [ə'rɪdʒənəlɪ] *adv* **(a)** ursprünglich. **(b)** *(in an original way)* originell.
originate [ə'rɪdʒɪneɪt] **1** *vt* hervorbringen; *policy, company* ins Leben rufen; *product* erfinden. who ~d the idea? von wem stammt die Idee?
  2 *vi* **(a)** entstehen. the legend ~d in ... die Legende ist in *(+dat)* ... entstanden *or* hat ihren Ursprung in *(+dat)* ...; to ~ from a country aus einem Land stammen; to ~ with jdm stammen; the company ~d as a family concern die Firma war ursprünglich *or* anfänglich ein Familienbetrieb.
  (b) *(US: bus, train etc)* ausgehen (in von).
originator [ə'rɪdʒɪneɪtər] *n* *(of plan, idea)* Urheber(in *f*) *m*; *(of company)* Gründer(in *f*) *m*; *(of product)* Erfinder(in *f*) *m*.
oriole ['ɔ:rɪəʊl] *n* Pirol *m*.
Orkney Islands ['ɔ:knɪ'aɪləndz], **Orkneys** ['ɔ:knɪz] *npl* Orkneyinseln *pl*.
orlon ® ['ɔ:lɒn] *n* Orlon ® *nt*.
ormolu ['ɔ:məʊlu:] **1** *n* *(alloy)* Messing *nt*; *(decoration)* Messingverzierungen *pl*; *(mountings)* Messingbeschläge *pl*. **2** *adj* Messing-.
ornament ['ɔ:nəmənt] **1** *n* **(a)** *(decorative object)* Schmuck(gegenstand) *m no pl*, Verzierung *f*, Ziergegenstand *m*; *(on mantelpiece etc)* Ziergegenstand *m*; *(fig)* Zierde *f* (*to* gen). his secretary is just an ~ seine Sekretärin ist nur zur Verzierung *or* Dekoration da; she has the house full of ~s sie hat das Haus voller Nippes *(pej)* or Ziergegenstände; altar ~s *(Eccl)* Altarschmuck *m*.
  (b) *(no pl: ornamentation)* Ornamente *pl*; *(decorative articles, on clothes etc)* Verzierungen *pl*, Zierat *m* *(geh)*. by way of ~, for ~ zur Verzierung; the interior of the palace was rich in ~ das Innere des Palastes war prunkvoll ausgeschmückt.
  (c) *(Mus)* Verzierung *f*, Ornament *nt*.
  2 [ɔ:nə'ment] *vt* verzieren; *room* ausschmücken.
ornamental [,ɔ:nə'mentl] *adj* dekorativ; *object, garden, plant etc also* Zier-; *(decorative)* ausschmückend, zierend. to be purely ~ zur Verzierung *or* Zierde (da) sein; ~ lake Zierteich *m*; ~ object *or* piece Zier- *or* Schmuckgegenstand, Zierat *(geh) m*.
ornamentation [,ɔ:nəmen'teɪʃən] *n* **(a)** *(ornamenting)* Verzieren *nt*, Verzierung *f*; *(of room)* Ausschmücken *nt*, Ausschmückung *f*. **(b)** *(ornamental detail)* Verzierungen *pl*, Zierat *m* *(geh)*; *(Art, Archit)* Ornamentik *f*; *(ornaments: in room etc)* Schmuck *m*.
ornate [ɔ:'neɪt] *adj* kunstvoll; *(of larger objects)* prunkvoll; *decoration also* aufwendig; *music* ornamentreich; *description* reich ausgeschmückt, umständlich *(pej)*; *language, style* umständlich *(pej)*, überladen *(pej)*, reich.
ornately [ɔ:'neɪtlɪ] *adv* kunstvoll; *describe* mit beredten Worten, umständlich *(pej)*; *written* in reicher Sprache.
ornateness [ɔ:'neɪtnɪs] *n* Verzierungen *f*; *(of baroque church, palace etc also)* Prunk *m*, Prachtentfaltung *f*; *(of music also)* ornamentaler Reichtum; *(of style)* Reichtum *m*; *(of description)* Wortreichtum *m*, Umständlichkeit *f* *(pej)*; *(of decoration)* Reichtum *m*, Aufwendigkeit *f*.
ornithological [,ɔ:nɪθə'lɒdʒɪkəl] *adj* ornithologisch, vogelkundlich.
ornithologist [,ɔ:nɪ'θɒlədʒɪst] *n* Ornithologe *m*, Ornithologin *f*, Vogelkundler(in *f*) *m*.
ornithology [,ɔ:nɪ'θɒlədʒɪ] *n* Ornithologie, Vogelkunde *f*.
orphan ['ɔ:fən] **1** *n* Waise *f*, Waisenkind *nt*. the accident made *or* left him an ~ der Unfall machte ihn zur Waise *or* zum Waisenkind; like ~ Annie *(inf)* wie bestellt und nicht abgeholt.
  2 *adj child* Waisen-.
  3 *vt* zur Waise machen. to be ~ed zur Waise werden; he was ~ed by the war er ist *(eine)* Kriegswaise; ~ed since the age of three verwaist *or* eine Waise seit dem dritten Lebensjahr.
orphanage ['ɔ:fənɪdʒ] *n* Waisenhaus *nt*.
Orpheus ['ɔ:fju:s] *n* *(Myth)* Orpheus *m*.
orthodontic [,ɔ:θəʊ'dɒntɪk] *adj* kieferorthopädisch.
orthodontics [,ɔ:θəʊ'dɒntɪks] *n sing* Kieferorthopädie *f*.
orthodox ['ɔ:θədɒks] *adj* **(a)** *(Rel)* orthodox. **(b)** *(fig)* konventionell; *view, method, approach etc also* orthodox.
orthodoxy ['ɔ:θədɒksɪ] *n* **(a)** Orthodoxie *f*. **(b)** *see adj (b)* Konventionalität *f*; Orthodoxie *f*. **(c)** *(orthodox belief, practice etc)* orthodoxe Konvention.
orthographic(al) [,ɔ:θə'græfɪk(əl)] *adj* orthographisch, Rechtschreib(ungs)-.
orthography [ɔ:'θɒgrəfɪ] *n* Rechtschreibung, Orthographie *f*.
orthopaedic, *(US)* **orthopedic** [,ɔ:θəʊ'pi:dɪk] *adj* orthopädisch.
orthopaedics, *(US)* **orthopedics** [,ɔ:θəʊ'pi:dɪks] *n sing* Orthopädie *f*.
orthopaedist, *(US)* **orthopedist** [,ɔ:θəʊ'pi:dɪst] *n* Orthopäde *m*, Orthopädin *f*.
orthopaedy, *(US)* **orthopedy** ['ɔ:θəʊpi:dɪ] *n* Orthopädie *f*.

OS *abbr of* **(a)** ordinary seaman. **(b)** Ordnance Survey. **(c)** outsize.
Oscar ['ɒskər] *n* *(Film)* Oscar *m*.
oscillate ['ɒsɪleɪt] *vi* *(Phys)* oszillieren, schwingen; *(compass needle etc)* schwanken; *(rapidly)* zittern; *(fig)* schwanken. the needle ~d violently die Nadel schlug stark aus.
oscillating ['ɒsɪleɪtɪŋ] *adj* **(a)** *(Phys)* Schwing-, schwingend; *circuit* Schwing(ungs)-; *needle* ausschlagend; *(rapidly)* zitternd. **(b)** *(fig)* schwankend.
oscillation [,ɒsɪ'leɪʃən] *n see vi* Oszillation, Schwingung *f*; Schwanken *nt*; Zittern *nt*; Schwanken *nt*; *(individual movement etc)* Schwankung *f*.
oscillator ['ɒsɪleɪtər] *n* Oszillator *m*.
oscillograph [ə'sɪləgræf] *n* Oszillograph, Schwingungsschreiber *m*.
oscilloscope [ə'sɪləskəʊp] *n* Oszilloskop *nt*, Schwingungsmesser *m*.
osier ['əʊʒər] **1** *n* Korbweide *f*; *(twig)* Weidenrute *or* -gerte *f*. **2** *attr basket, branch etc* Weiden-; *chair etc* Korb-.
osmosis [ɒz'məʊsɪs] *n* Osmose *f*.
osmotic [ɒz'mɒtɪk] *adj* osmotisch.
osprey ['ɒspreɪ] *n* Fischadler *m*.
osseous ['ɒsɪəs] *adj* Knochen-, knöchern.
ossification [,ɒsɪfɪ'keɪʃən] *n* Verknöcherung, Ossifikation *(spec) f*.
ossify ['ɒsɪfaɪ] **1** *vt* *(lit)* verknöchern lassen; *(fig)* erstarren lassen; *(mind)* unbeweglich machen. to be/become ossified *(lit)* verknöchert sein/verknöchern; *(fig)* erstarrt sein/erstarren; unbeweglich sein/werden *(by durch)*. **2** *vi* *(lit)* verknöchern; *(fig)* erstarren; *(mind)* unbeweglich werden.
ossuary ['ɒsjʊərɪ] *n* Ossarium *nt*; *(building also)* Beinhaus *nt*.
Ostend [ɒ'stend] *n* Ostende *nt*.
ostensible *adj*, **~bly** *adv* [ɒ'stensəbl, -ɪ] vorgeblich; *(alleged)* angeblich.
ostentation [,ɒsten'teɪʃən] *n* **(a)** *(pretentious display)* *(of wealth etc)* Pomp *m*; *(of skills etc)* Großtuerei *f*. his ~ seine Großspurigkeit. **(b)** *(obviousness)* aufdringliche *or* penetrante Deutlichkeit. with ~ demonstrativ, ostentativ; with great ~ betont auffällig.
ostentatious [,ɒsten'teɪʃəs] *adj* **(a)** *(pretentious)* pompös, protzig *(inf)*. he is so ~ about his wealth er stellt seinen Reichtum so aufdringlich zur Schau, er protzt so mit seinem Geld *(inf)*. **(b)** *(conspicuous)* ostentativ, betont auffällig.
ostentatiously [,ɒsten'teɪʃəslɪ] *adv see adj* **(a)** pompös, protzig *(inf)*; *live* pompös, in Pomp, auf großem Fuße. **(b)** ostentativ, betont auffällig.
ostentatiousness [,ɒsten'teɪʃəsnɪs] *n see* **ostentation**.
osteoarthritis ['ɒstɪəʊɑ:'θraɪtɪs] *n* Arthrose *f*.
osteopath ['ɒstɪəpæθ] *n* Osteopath(in *f*) *m*.
osteopathy [,ɒstɪ'ɒpəθɪ] *n* Osteopathologie *f*.
ostler ['ɒslər] *n* *(Hist)* Stallknecht *m*.
ostracism ['ɒstrəsɪzəm] *n* Ächtung *f*.
ostracize ['ɒstrəsaɪz] *vt* ächten; *(Hist)* verbannen.
ostrich ['ɒstrɪtʃ] *n* Strauß *m*. ~ policy Vogel-Strauß-Politik *f*.
OT *abbr of* Old Testament AT.
OTC *abbr of* Officers' Training Corps.
other ['ʌðər] **1** *adj* **(a)** andere(r, s). ~ people andere (Leute); some ~ people will come later später kommen noch ein paar; there were 6 ~ people there as well es waren auch noch 6 andere (Leute) da; do you have any ~ questions? haben Sie sonst noch Fragen?; he had no ~ questions er hatte sonst keine Fragen; he could be no ~ than strict er konnte nicht anders als streng sein, er konnte nur streng sein; every ~ man was ill *(all the ~s)* alle anderen waren krank, sonst waren alle krank; the ~ day neulich; the ~ world das Jenseits, jene andere Welt *(liter)*; some ~ time *(in future)* ein andermal; *(in past)* ein anderes Mal; ~ people's property fremdes Eigentum; to see how the ~ half lives sehen, wie andere leben.
  (b) every ~ *(alternate)* jede(r, s) zweite.
  (c) ~ than *(except)* außer *(+dat)*; *(different to)* anders als.
  (d) some time *or* ~ irgendwann (einmal); some writer/house etc *or* ~ irgend so ein *or* irgendein Schriftsteller *m*/Haus *nt* etc.
  2 *pron* andere(r, s). he doesn't like hurting ~s er mag niemanden verletzen, er mag niemandem weh tun; there are 6 ~s da sind noch 6 (andere); are there any ~s there? sind noch andere *or* sonst noch welche da?; there were no ~s there es waren sonst keine da; something/someone *or* ~ irgend etwas/jemand; one *or* ~ of them will come einer (von ihnen) wird kommen; can you tell one from the ~? kannst du sie auseinanderhalten?; he fancied a bit of the ~ *(inf)* ihm war nach ein bißchen - na ja, du weißt schon *(inf)*; *see* each, one.
  3 *adv* he could do no ~ *(than come)* er konnte nicht anders (als kommen), er konnte nichts anderes tun (als kommen); I've never seen her ~ than with her husband ich habe sie immer nur mit ihrem Mann gesehen; somehow *or* ~ irgendwie, auf die eine oder andere Weise; somewhere *or* ~ irgendwo; he couldn't do it ~ than well/superficially er konnte es nur gut/oberflächlich machen.
other-directed ['ʌðədaɪ'rektɪd] *adj* fremdbestimmt.
otherness ['ʌðənɪs] *n* Andersein *nt*, Andersartigkeit *f*.
otherwise ['ʌðəwaɪz] **1** *adv* **(a)** *(in a different way)* anders. I could not do ~ than speak ich konnte nicht anders als (zu) reden; I am ~ engaged *(form)* ich bin anderweitig beschäftigt; except where ~ stated *(form)* sofern nicht anders angegeben; Richard I, ~ (known as) the Lionheart Richard I., auch bekannt als Löwenherz, Richard I. oder auch Löwenherz; you seem to think ~ Sie scheinen anderer Meinung zu sein.
  (b) *(in other respects)* sonst, ansonsten *(inf)*, im übrigen.
  2 *conj* *(or else)* sonst, andernfalls.
  3 *adj pred* anders. poems tragic and ~ tragische und andere Gedichte.

other: ~-**worldliness** n see adj Weltferne f; Entrücktheit f; ~-
worldly adj attitude weltfern; person also nicht von dieser
Welt; smile, expression entrückt.
otiose ['əʊʃɪəʊs] adj (liter) müßig (geh).
otter ['ɒtər] n Otter m.
Ottoman ['ɒtəmən] **1** adj osmanisch, ottomanisch (rare). **2** n
Osmane m, Osmanin f, Ottomane m (rare), Ottomanin f (rare).
ottoman ['ɒtəmən] n Polstertruhe f.
ouch [aʊtʃ] interj autsch.
ought¹ [ɔːt] v aux **(a)** (indicating moral obligation) I ~ to do it
ich sollte or müßte es tun; he ~ to have come er hätte kommen
sollen or müssen; this ~ to have been done das hätte man tun
sollen or müssen; ~ I to go too? — yes, you ~ (to)/no, you ~n't
(to) sollte or müßte ich auch (hin)gehen? — ja doch/nein, das
sollen Sie nicht; he thought he ~ to tell you/you ~ to know er
meinte, er sollte Ihnen das sagen/Sie sollten das wissen; **people
have come who** ~ not to have done es sind Leute gekommen, die
nicht hätten kommen sollen; ~/~n't you to have left by now?
hätten Sie schon/hätten Sie nicht schon gehen müssen?; **cars
are parked where they** ~ not to be Autos sind an Stellen
geparkt, wo sie nicht hingehören; he **behaved just as he** ~ (was
well-behaved) er hat sich völlig korrekt benommen; (did the
right thing) er hat sich völlig richtig verhalten.
(b) (indicating what is right, advisable, desirable) you ~ to
see that film den Film sollten Sie sehen; you ~ to have seen his
face sein Gesicht hätten Sie sehen müssen; she ~ to have been
a teacher sie hätte Lehrerin werden sollen.
(c) (indicating probability) he ~ to win the race er müßte
(eigentlich) das Rennen gewinnen; come at six, that ~ to be
early enough komm (mal) um sechs, das sollte or müßte früh
genug sein; one ~ to think so das sollte man meinen; that ~ to
do das dürfte wohl or müßte reichen; he ~ to be here soon er
müßte bald hier sein; he ~ to have left by now er müßte inzwischen gegangen or abgefahren sein; ... and I ~ to know! ... und
ich muß es doch wissen!
ought² n see aught.
ouija (board) ['wiːdʒə('bɔːd)] n Buchstabenbrett nt für spiritistische Sitzungen.
ounce [aʊns] n Unze f. **there's not an** ~ **of truth in it** daran ist
kein Fünkchen Wahrheit; **if he had an** ~ **of sense** wenn er nur
einen Funken or für fünf Pfennig (inf) Verstand hätte.
our ['aʊər] poss adj unser. **these are** ~ **own make** die stellen wir
selbst her; O~ **Father** (in prayer) Vater unser; **the** O~ **Father**
das Vaterunser or Unservater (Sw); see also my 1.
ours ['aʊəz] poss pron unsere(r, s). ~ **not to reason why**(, ~ **but to
do or die)** (prov) das wissen die Götter (inf), es ist nicht an uns,
nach dem Warum zu fragen; see also mine¹.
ourself [,aʊə'self] pers pron (form) (wir) selbst.
ourselves [,aʊə'selvz] pers pron (dir, indir obj +prep) uns;
(emph) selbst; see also myself.
oust [aʊst] vt (get, drive out) herausbekommen; sth stuck also
freibekommen; government absetzen; politician, colleague etc
ausbooten (inf), absägen (inf); heckler, anglicisms entfernen;
rivals ausschalten. **to** ~ **sb from**
office/his post jdn aus seinem Amt/seiner Stellung entfernen or
(by intrigue) hinausmanövrieren; **he managed to** ~ **all his
rivals from the board** es ist ihm gelungen, all seine Rivalen im
Vorstand auszuschalten or auszubooten (inf); **to** ~ **sb from the
market** jdn vom Markt verdrängen.
out [aʊt] **1** adv **(a)** (not in container, car etc) außen; (not in
building, room) draußen; (indicating motion) (seen from
inside) hinaus, raus (inf); (seen from ~side) heraus, raus (inf).
to be ~ weg sein; (when visitors come) nicht da sein; **they're** ~
in the garden/~ **playing** sie sind draußen im Garten/sie spielen
draußen; **they are** ~ **fishing/shopping** sie sind zum
Fischen/Einkaufen (gegangen), sie sind fischen/einkaufen;
he's ~ **in his car** er ist mit dem Auto unterwegs; **she was** ~ **all
night** sie war die ganze Nacht weg; **it's cold** ~ **here**/there es ist
kalt hier/da or dort draußen; ~ **you go!** hinaus or raus (inf) mit
dir!; ~! **raus (hier)!;** ~ **with him!** hinaus or raus (inf) mit ihm!;
~ **it goes!** hinaus damit, raus damit (inf); **everybody** ~! alle
Mann or alles raus!; he **likes to be** ~ **and about** er ist gern unterwegs; **at weekends I like to be** ~ **and about** an den
Wochenenden will ich (immer) raus; **we had a day** ~ **at the
beach/in London** wir haben einen Tag am Meer/in London verbracht; **we had a day** ~ **at the shops** wir haben einen Einkaufsbummel gemacht; **the journey** ~ die Hinreise; (seen from
destination) die Herfahrt; **the goods were damaged on the
journey** ~ die Waren sind auf dem Transport beschädigt
worden; **the book is** ~ (from library) das Buch ist ausgeliehen
or unterwegs (inf); **the Socialists are** ~ die Sozialisten sind
nicht mehr an der Regierung; **the workers are** ~ (on strike) die
Arbeiter streiken or sind im Ausstand; **school is** ~ die Schule
ist aus; **the tide is** ~ es ist Ebbe; **the chicks should be** ~
tomorrow die Küken sollten bis morgen heraus sein.
(b) (indicating distance) **when he was** ~ **in Persia** als er in
Persien war; **to go** ~ **to China** nach China fahren; ~ **in the Far
East** im Fernen Osten; ~ **here in Australia** hier in Australien;
Wilton Street? isn't that ~ **your way?** Wilton Street? ist das
nicht da (hinten) bei euch in der Gegend?; **the boat was ten
miles** ~ das Schiff war zehn Meilen weit draußen; **five days** ~
from Liverpool (Naut) fünf Tage nach dem Auslaufen in/vor
Liverpool; **five miles** ~ **from harbour** fünf Meilen vom Hafen
weg, fünf Meilen vor dem Hafen.
(c) **to be** ~ (sun) (he)raus or draußen sein; (stars, moon) am
Himmel stehen (geh), dasein; (flowers) blühen.
(d) (in existence) **the worst newspaper/best car** ~ die
schlechteste Zeitung/das beste Auto, die/das es zur Zeit gibt,
die schlechteste Zeitung/das beste Auto überhaupt; **to be** ~ (be
published) herausgekommen sein; **when will it be** ~? wann
kommt es heraus?; **there's a warrant** ~ **for him** es besteht Haftbefehl gegen ihn; **the warrant is not** ~ **yet** der Haftbefehl ist
noch nicht (he)raus.
(e) (not in prison) **to be** ~ draußen sein; (seen from ~side
also) (he)raus sein; **to come** ~ (he)rauskommen.
(f) (in the open, known) **their secret was** ~ ihr Geheimnis war
bekannt geworden or herausgekommen; **it's** ~ **now** jetzt ist es
heraus; **the results are** ~ die Ergebnisse sind (he)raus; **the
news will** ~ die Neuigkeit wird heraus; ~ **with it!** heraus damit!,
heraus mit der Sprache!
(g) (to or at an end) **before the day/month is/was** ~ vor Ende
des Tages/Monats, noch am selben Tag/im selben Monat.
(h) (light, fire) aus.
(i) (not in fashion) aus der Mode, passé, out (sl).
(j) (Sport) (ball) aus; (player) aus(geschlagen), out.
(k) (~ of the question, not permissible) ausgeschlossen, nicht
drin (inf).
(l) (worn ~) **the jacket is** ~ **at the elbows** die Jacke ist an den
Ellbogen durch.
(m) (indicating error) **he was** ~ **in his calculations, his
calculations were** ~ er lag mit seinen Berechnungen daneben
(inf) or falsch (inf), er hatte sich in seinen Berechnungen
geirrt; **not far** ~! beinah(e) (richtig)!; **you're not far** ~ Sie
haben es fast (getroffen); **you're far or way** ~! weit gefehlt!
(geh), da hast du dich völlig vertan (inf); **you're a little bit** ~
there das stimmt nicht ganz; **we were £5/20%** ~ wir hatten uns
um £ 5/20% verrechnet or vertan (inf); **that's £5/20%** ~ das
stimmt um £ 5/20% nicht; **the perspective is just a little bit** ~
die Perspektive stimmt nicht ganz; **the post isn't quite vertical
yet, it's still a bit** ~ der Pfahl ist noch nicht ganz senkrecht, er
ist noch etwas schief; **my clock is 20 minutes** ~ meine Uhr geht
20 Minuten falsch or verkehrt.
(n) (indicating loudness, clearness) **speak** ~ **loud** sprechen
Sie laut/lauter; **they shouted** ~ **(loud)** sie riefen laut (und
vernehmlich); **please speak** ~ bitte sprechen Sie laut.
(o) (indicating purpose) **to be** ~ **for sth** auf etw (acc) aussein;
to be ~ **for a good time** sich amüsieren wollen; **to be** ~ **for
trouble** Streit suchen; **she was** ~ **to pass the exam** sie war (fest)
entschlossen, die Prüfung zu bestehen; **he's** ~ **for all he can get**
er will haben, was er nur bekommen kann; **he's** ~ **to get her** er
ist hinter ihr her; **he's just** ~ **to make money** er ist nur auf Geld
aus, ihm geht es nur um Geld; **he was always** ~ **to make money**
er wollte immer das große Geld machen; **she's** ~ **to find a husband** sie ist auf der Suche nach einem Mann.
(p) (unconscious) **to be** ~ bewußtlos or weg (inf) sein; (drunk)
weg or hinüber sein (inf); (asleep) weg (inf) or eingeschlafen
sein; **she went straight** ~ sie war sofort weg (inf).
(q) (dirt, stain etc) (he)raus.
(r) ~ **and away** weitaus, mit Abstand.
2 n (a) see in. **(b)** (esp US inf: way ~) Hintertür f.
3 prep aus (+dat). **to go** ~ **the** door/window zur Tür/zum
Fenster hinausgehen; **from** ~ **the wood** (poet) aus dem Walde
heraus; see also out of.
out- pref with vbs **to** ~-**dance** etc **sb** jdn im Tanzen etc übertreffen, besser als jd tanzen etc.
outact [,aʊt'ækt] vt an die Wand spielen.
out-and-out ['aʊtən'aʊt] adj liar Erz-, ausgemacht; fool vollkommen, ausgemacht; defeat völlig, total. **he is an** ~ **revolutionary** er ist ein Revolutionär durch und durch; **it's an** ~ **disgrace** das ist eine bodenlose Schande.
outargue [,aʊt'ɑːgjuː] vt in der Diskussion überlegen sein
(+dat), argumentativ überlegen sein (+dat) (geh).
outback ['aʊtbæk] (in Australia) **1** n: **the** ~ das Hinterland. **2**
attr an ~ **farm** eine Farm im Hinterland.
out: ~**bid** pret, ptp ~**bid** vt überbieten; ~**board 1** adj motor
Außenbord-; ~**board motorboat** Außenborder m (inf), Motorboot nt mit Außenbordmotor; **2** n Außenborder m (inf); ~**bound**
adj ship auslaufend, ausfahrend; ~**box** vt sb besser boxen als;
for once he was completely ~**boxed** zum ersten Mal ließ ihn
seine Technik völlig im Stich; **he was** ~**boxed by the younger
man** der jüngere Boxer war ihm (technisch) überlegen.
outbreak ['aʊtbreɪk] n (of war, hostility, disease) Ausbruch m. **a
recent** ~ **of fire caused** ... ein Brand verursachte kürzlich ...; **if
there should be an** ~ **of fire** wenn ein Brand or Feuer ausbricht;
~ **of feeling/anger** Gefühls-/Zornesausbruch m; **at the** ~ **of
war** bei Kriegsausbruch.
outbuilding ['aʊtbɪldɪŋ] n Nebengebäude nt.
outburst ['aʊtbɜːst] n (of joy, anger) Ausbruch m. ~ **of temper
or anger** etc/**feeling** Wutanfall m/(Gefühls)ausbruch m; **and to
what do we owe that little** ~? und warum dieser kleine
Gefühlsausbruch, wenn ich mal fragen darf?
outcast ['aʊtkɑːst] **1** n Ausgestoßene(r) mf, Geächtete(r) mf;
(animal) Ausgestoßene(r) mf, Outcast m. **social** ~ Außenseiter
m der Gesellschaft; **he was treated as an** ~ er wurde zum
Außenseiter gestempelt; **one of the party's** ~s einer der von
der Partei Verstoßenen, einer, den die Partei verstoßen hat.
2 adj ausgestoßen, verstoßen.
outclass [,aʊt'klɑːs] vt voraus or überlegen sein (+dat), in den
Schatten stellen.
outcome ['aʊtkʌm] n Ergebnis, Resultat nt. **what was the** ~ **of
your meeting?** was ist bei eurem Treffen herausgekommen?;
what was the ~? was ist dabei herausgekommen?; **I don't know
whether there'll be any immediate** ~ ich weiß nicht, ob es
unmittelbar zu einem Ergebnis führen wird.
outcrop ['aʊtkrɒp] n (a) (Geol) **an** ~ (of rock) eine Felsnase. **(b)**
(fig) (of riots etc) (plötzlicher) Ausbruch; (undesirable
consequence) Auswuchs m.
outcry ['aʊtkraɪ] n Aufschrei m der Empörung (against über
+acc); (public protest) Protestwelle f (against gegen). **to raise
an** ~ **against sb/sth** gegen jdn/etw (lautstarken) Protest
erheben; **there was a general** ~ **about the increase in taxes** eine
Welle des Protests erhob sich wegen der Steuererhöhung;

there was a great ~ **in the press** eine Welle des Protestes *or* ein Aufschrei der Empörung ging durch die Presse.

out: ~**dated** *adj idea, theory* überholt; *machine, word, style, custom* veraltet; ~**did** *pret of* ~**do**; ~**distance** *vt* hinter sich *(dat)* lassen, abhängen *(inf)*; Y was ~**distanced by X** Y fiel hinter X *(dat)* zurück, Y wurde von X abgehängt *(inf)*.

outdo [ˌaʊtˈduː] *pret* **outdid** [ˌaʊtˈdɪd], *ptp* **outdone** [ˌaʊtˈdʌn] *vt* übertreffen, überragen, überbieten *(sb in sth jdn in etw dat)*. **he can ~ him in every sport** er ist ihm in jeder Sportart überlegen; **but Jimmy was not to be outdone** aber Jimmy wollte da nicht zurückstehen.

outdoor [ˈaʊtdɔː] *adj* ~ **games** Freiluftspiele *pl*, Spiele *pl* für draußen *or* im Freien; ~ **shoes** Straßenschuhe *pl*; ~ **clothes** wärmere Kleidung; ~ **type** sportlicher Typ; **the ~ life** das Leben im Freien; **to lead an ~ life** viel im Freien sein; ~ **swimming pool** Freibad *nt*; ~ **shot** *(Film)* Außenaufnahme *f*.

outdoors [ˈaʊtdɔːz] **1** *adv live, play, sleep* draußen, im Freien. **to go ~** nach draußen gehen, rausgehen *(inf)*; **and play** geh draußen spielen. **2** *n* **the great ~** *(hum)* die freie Natur.

outer [ˈaʊtə] *adj attr* äußere(r, s); *door etc also* Außen-. ~ **garments** Oberbekleidung, Überkleidung *f*; ~ **harbour** Außen- *or* Vorhafen *m*; ~ **man** *(appearance)* äußere Erscheinung, Äußere(s) *nt*; ~ **space** der äußere Weltraum.

Outer Hebrides [ˌaʊtəˈhebrɪdiːz] *npl* Äußere Hebriden *pl*.

outermost [ˈaʊtəməʊst] *adj* äußerste(r, s).

out: ~**fall** **1** *n (of drain, sewer)* Ausfluß *m*; **2** *attr sewer, pipe* Ausfluß-; ~**field** *n (Sport) (place)* Außenfeld *nt*; *(people)* Außenfeldspieler *pl*; ~**fielder** *n* Außenfeldspieler *m*; ~**fight** *pret, ptp* ~**fought** *vt* besser kämpfen als; *(defeat)* bezwingen.

outfit [ˈaʊtfɪt] *n* **(a)** *(clothes)* Kleidung *f*, Kleider *pl*; *(Fashion)* Ensemble *nt*; *(fancy dress)* Kostüm *nt*; *(uniform)* Uniform *f*; *(of scout)* Kluft *f*. **is that a new ~ you're wearing?** hast du dich neu eingekleidet?; **she has so many ~s** sie hat so viel anzuziehen; **her ~s range from ...** ihre Garderobe reicht von ...

(b) *(equipment)* Ausrüstung *f*.

(c) *(inf) (organization)* Laden *(inf)*, Verein *(inf) m*; *(Mil)* Einheit, Truppe *f*.

outfitter [ˈaʊtfɪtə] *n (of ships)* Ausrüster *m*. **gentlemen's ~'s** Herrenausstatter *m*, Herrenbekleidungsgeschäft *nt*; **sports ~'s** Sport(artikel)geschäft *nt*.

out: ~**flank** *vt* **(a)** *(Mil) enemy* umfassen, von der Flanke/den Flanken angreifen; ~**flanking movement** Umfassungsangriff *m or* -bewegung *f*; **(b)** *(fig: outwit)* überlisten, aufs Kreuz legen *(sl)*; ~**flow** *n (of gutter)* Ausfluß, Abfluß *m*; *(of water etc) (act)* Abfließen, Ausfließen *nt*, Abfluß, Ausfluß *m*; *(amount)* Ausfluß(menge *f) m*; *(of lava)* Ausfließen *nt*; Ausfluß, Auswurf *m*; *(of gas)* Ausströmen *nt*; Ausströmungsmenge *f*; *(of money)* Abfließen *nt*, Abfluß *m*; ~**fly** *pret* ~**flew**, *ptp* ~**flown** *vt (fliegerisch)* überlegen sein *(sb/sth jdm/etw)*; *(pilot also)* ein besserer Flieger sein als; ~**fought** *pret, ptp of* ~**fight**; ~**fox** *vt* überlisten, austricksen *(inf)*; ~**general** *vt* taktisch überlegen sein *(+dat)*; ~**go** *n (US)* Ausgabe(n *pl) f*.

outgoing [ˈaʊtgəʊɪŋ] **1** *adj* **(a)** *tenant* ausziehend; *office-holder* scheidend; *train, boat* hinausfahrend; *flight, plane* hinausgehend; *pipe, cable* wegführend, hinausführend; ~ **tide** ablaufendes Wasser, Ebbe *f*; **the ~ flight for New York** der Flug nach New York.

(b) *personality* aus sich herausgehend, kontaktfreudig.

2 *npl* ~**s** Ausgaben *pl*.

outgrow [ˌaʊtˈgrəʊ] *pret* **outgrew** [ˌaʊtˈgruː], *ptp* **outgrown** [ˌaʊtˈgrəʊn] *vt* **(a)** *clothes* herauswachsen aus.

(b) *habit* entwachsen *(+dat)*, hinauswachsen über *(+acc)*; *opinion* sich hinausentwickeln über *(+acc)*. **he has ~n such childish pastimes** über solche Kindereien ist er hinaus.

(c) *(grow taller than) (tree)* hinauswachsen über *(+acc)*; *(person)* über den Kopf wachsen *(+dat)*.

outgrowth [ˈaʊtgrəʊθ] *n (offshoot)* Auswuchs *m*; *(fig)* Folge *f*.

out: ~-**Herod** *vt*: **to ~-Herod Herod** dem Teufel Konkurrenz machen; ~**house** *n* Seitengebäude *nt*.

outing [ˈaʊtɪŋ] *n* Ausflug *m*. **school/firm's ~** Schul-/Betriebsausflug *m*; **to go for an ~ in the car** eine Fahrt mit dem Auto machen; **to go on an ~** einen Ausflug machen.

outlandish [ˌaʊtˈlændɪʃ] *adj* absonderlich, sonderbar; *behaviour also* befremdend, befremdlich; *idea etc also* verschroben *(pej)*, wunderlich; *prose etc* eigenwillig; *name* ausgefallen, extravagant; *wallpaper, colour-combination etc* ausgefallen, eigenwillig; *prices* haarsträubend. **such ~ nonsense** solch unglaublicher Unsinn.

outlandishly [ˌaʊtˈlændɪʃlɪ] *adv* sonderbar, absonderlich; *decorated, portrayed* eigenwillig; *expensive* haarsträubend.

outlandishness [ˌaʊtˈlændɪʃnɪs] *n see adj* Absonderlichkeit, Sonderbarkeit *f*; Befremdlichkeit *f*; Verschrobenheit *(pej)*, Wunderlichkeit *f*; Eigenwilligkeit *f*; Ausgefallenheit *f*; Extravaganz *f*; Ausgefallenheit, Eigenwilligkeit *f*.

outlast [ˌaʊtˈlɑːst] *vt (person) (live longer)* überleben; *(endure longer)* länger aus- *or* durchhalten als; *(thing)* länger halten als; *(idea etc)* überdauern, sich länger halten als.

outlaw [ˈaʊtlɔː] **1** *n* Geächtete(r), Vogelfreie(r) *mf*; *(in western etc)* Bandit *m*. **to declare sb an ~** jdn ächten, jdn (für) vogelfrei erklären. **2** *vt war* ächten; *person also* (für) vogelfrei erklären; *newspaper, action etc* für ungesetzlich erklären, verbieten.

outlawry [ˈaʊtlɔːrɪ] *n* Ächtung *f*; *(defiance)* Gesetzlosigkeit *f*.

outlay [ˈaʊtleɪ] *n* (Kosten)aufwand *m*; *(recurring, continuous)* Kosten *pl*. **the initial ~** die anfänglichen Aufwendungen; **capital ~** Kapitalaufwand *m*; **to recover one's ~** seine Auslagen wieder hereinholen *or* -bekommen; *(business)* die Unkosten wieder hereinwirtschaften.

outlet [ˈaʊtlet] **1** *n* **(a)** *(for water etc)* Abfluß, Auslaß *m*; *(for steam etc)* Abzug *m*; *(of river)* Ausfluß *m*.

(b) *(Comm)* Absatzmöglichkeit *f or* -markt *m*; *(merchant)* Abnehmer *m*; *(shop)* Verkaufsstelle *f*.

(c) *(fig) (for talents etc)* Betätigungsmöglichkeit *f*; *(for emotion)* Ventil *nt*.

2 *attr (Tech) drain, pipe* Auslaß-, Abfluß-; *(for steam etc)* Abzugs-; *valve* Auslaß-.

outline [ˈaʊtlaɪn] **1** *n* **(a)** *(of objects)* Umriß *m*; *(line itself)* Umrißlinie *f*; *(silhouette)* Silhouette *f*; *(of face)* Züge *pl*. **he drew the ~ of a head** er zeichnete einen Kopf im Umriß; **to draw sth in ~** etw im Umriß *or* in Umrissen zeichnen; ~ **drawing** Umrißzeichnung *f*.

(b) *(fig: summary)* Grundriß, Abriß *m*. **in (broad)** ~ in großen *or* groben Zügen; **just give (me) the broad ~s** umreißen *or* skizzieren Sie es (mir) grob; ~**s of botany** Abriß *or* Grundriß *m or* Grundzüge *pl* der Botanik.

(c) *(Shorthand)* Kürzel, Sigel, Sigle *nt*.

2 *attr drawing, map* Umriß-.

3 *vt* **(a)** *(draw outer edge of)* umreißen, den Umriß *or* die Umrisse zeichnen *(+gen)*. **the mountain was ~d against the sky** die Umrisse des Berges zeichneten sich gegen den Himmel ab; **she stood there ~d against the sunset** ihre Silhouette zeichnete sich gegen die untergehende Sonne ab.

(b) *(give summary of)* umreißen, skizzieren.

outlive [ˌaʊtˈlɪv] *vt* **(a)** *(live longer than) person* überleben; *century* überdauern. **to have ~d one's day** nicht mehr der/die sein, der/die man einmal war; **to have ~d one's usefulness** ausgedient haben; *(method, system)* sich überlebt haben.

(b) *(come safely through) storm etc* überstehen; *disgrace etc* sich reinigen (können) von *(geh)*, frei werden von.

outlook [ˈaʊtlʊk] *n* **(a)** *(view)* (Aus)blick *m*, Aussicht *f (over* über *+acc, on* to auf *+acc)*.

(b) *(prospects)* (Zukunfts)aussichten *pl*; *(Met)* Aussichten *pl*. **what's the ~ for the mining industry?** wie sind die (Zukunfts)aussichten im Bergbau?

(c) *(mental attitude)* Einstellung *f*. **his ~ (up)on life** seine Lebensauffassung *or* Einstellung zum Leben; **what's his ~ on the matter?** wie steht er zu der Sache?; **his breadth of ~** sein weiter Horizont; **narrow ~** beschränkter Horizont, (geistige) Beschränktheit; **if you adopt such a narrow ~** wenn Sie die Dinge so eng sehen.

out: ~**lying** *adj (distant)* entlegen, abgelegen; *(outside the town boundary)* umliegend; *district (of town)* Außen-, äußere(r, s); ~**lying suburbs** Außenbezirke, äußere Vororte *pl*; ~**manoeuvre**, *(US)* ~**maneuver** *vt (Mil, fig)* ausmanövrieren; *(in rivalry)* ausstechen; ~**match** *vt* übertreffen, überlegen sein *(+dat)*. Y was ~**matched by X** Y konnte gegen X nichts ausrichten, Y **can't ~match X** X kann gegen X nichts ausrichten; ~**moded** *adj* unzeitgemäß, altmodisch; *literary style etc also* verstaubt; *ideas etc also* überholt, verstaubt; *design etc also* antiquiert; *technology etc also* überholt, veraltet; ~**most** **1** *adj* äußerste(r, s); *regions etc also* entlegenste(r, s); **2** *n*: **at the ~most** äußerstenfalls, im äußersten Falle.

outnumber [ˌaʊtˈnʌmbə] *vt* in der Mehrzahl *or* Überzahl sein gegenüber *(in fight etc also)* zahlenmäßig überlegen sein *(+dat)*; *(in survey, poll etc also)* in der Mehrheit sein gegenüber. **we were ~ed (by them)** wir waren (ihnen) gegenüber) in der Minderzahl; wir waren (ihnen) zahlenmäßig unterlegen; wir waren (ihnen gegenüber) in der Minderheit; **we were ~ed five to one** sie waren fünfmal so viele wie wir; wir waren (ihnen) zahlenmäßig fünffach unterlegen; wir waren im Verhältnis fünf zu eins in der Minderheit.

out of *prep* **(a)** *(outside, away from) (position)* nicht in *(+dat)*, außerhalb *(+gen)*; *(motion)* aus *(+dat)*; *(fig)* außer *(+dat)*. **I'll be ~ town all week** ich werde die ganze Woche (über) nicht in der Stadt sein; **to go/be ~ the country** außer Landes gehen/sein; **he was ~ the room at the time** er war zu dem Zeitpunkt nicht im Zimmer; **he walked ~ the room** er ging aus dem Zimmer *(hinaus)*; **he went ~ the door** er ging zur Tür hinaus; **as soon as he was ~ the door** sobald er draußen war *or* zur Tür hinaus war; **to look ~ the window** aus dem Fenster sehen, zum Fenster hinaus-/herausgucken; **I saw him ~ the window** ich sah ihn durchs Fenster; ~ **danger/sight** außer Gefahr/Sicht; **get ~ my sight!** geh mir aus den Augen!; **he's ~ the tournament** er ist aus dem Turnier ausgeschieden; **he feels ~ it** *(inf)* er kommt sich *(dat)* ausgeschlossen vor, er fühlt sich ausgeschlossen; **he was a bit ~ it** *(inf)* er war etwas ausgeschlossen; **they were 150 miles ~ Hamburg** *(Naut)* sie waren 150 Meilen von Hamburg weg *or* vor Hamburg; **three days ~ Hamburg** vor drei Tage nach dem Auslaufen aus dem Hafen/vor dem Einlaufen in den Hafen; **he lives 10 miles ~ London** er wohnt 10 Meilen außerhalb Londons; **you're well ~ it** so ist es auch besser für dich.

(b) *(cause, motive)* aus *(+dat)*. ~ **curiosity** aus Neugier.

(c) *(indicating origins or source)* aus *(+dat)*. **to drink ~ a glass** aus einem Glas trinken; **made ~ silver** aus Silber (gemacht); **a filly ~ the same mare** ein Fohlen *nt* von derselben Stute; **a scene ~ a play** eine Szene aus einem Stück; **it's like something ~ a nightmare** es ist wie in einem Alptraum.

(d) *(from among)* von *(+dat)*. **in seven cases ~ ten** in sieben von zehn Fällen; **one ~ every four smokers** einer von vier Rauchern; **he picked one ~ the pile** er nahm einen aus dem Stapel *(heraus)*.

(e) *(without)* ~ **breath** außer Atem; **we are ~ money/petrol/bread** wir haben kein Geld/Benzin/Brot mehr, das Geld/Benzin/Brot ist alle *(inf)*; *see other nouns*.

out: ~**-of-date** *adj, pred* ~ **of date** *methods, technology, ideas* überholt, veraltet; *clothes, records* altmodisch, unmodern; *customs* veraltet; **you're ~ of date** Sie sind nicht auf dem laufenden; ~**-of-doors** *adv see* **outdoors** 1; ~**-of-pocket** *adj*, ~ **of pocket** *pred* ~**-of-pocket expenses** Barauslagen *pl*; **to be ~ of pocket** draufgeben, draufzahlen; **I was £5 ~ of pocket** ich habe £ 5 aus eigener Tasche bezahlt; **I'm still £2 ~ of pocket** ich habe immer noch £ 2 zuwenig; ~**-of-the-way** *adj, pred* ~ **of the way** *(remote) spot* abgelegen, aus der Welt; *(unusual) theory* ungewöhnlich; (*not commonly known*) facts wenig bekannt; ~**patient** *n* ambulanter Patient, ambulante Patientin; ~**patients' (department)** Ambulanz *f*; ~**patients' hospital** *or* **clinic** Poliklinik *f*; ~**play** *vt* (*Sport*) besser spielen als, überlegen sein (+*dat*); **we were completely** ~**played (by them)** wir konnten (gegen sie) absolut nichts ausrichten, sie waren uns haushoch überlegen; ~**point** *vt* auspunkten; ~**post** *n* (*Mil*, *fig*) Vorposten *m*; ~**pouring** *n* often *pl* Erguß *m* (*fig*).

output ['aʊtpʊt] *n* (*of machine, factory, person*) (*act*) Produktion *f*; (*quantity also*) Ausstoß *m*, Output *m* or *nt*; (*rate of* ~ *also*) (Produktions)leistung *f*, Output *m* or *nt*; (*quantity in agriculture also*) Ertrag *m*; (*Elec*) Leistung *f*; (~ *terminal*) Ausgang *m*; (*capacity of amplifier*) (Ausgangs)leistung *f*; (*of mine*) Förderung *f*; (*quantity*) Fördermenge, Förderung *f*; (*rate of* ~) Förderleistung, Förderung *f*; (*of computer*) Ausgangsinformation, Ausgabe *f*, Output *m* or *nt*. **effective** ~ **of a machine** Nutzleistung *f* einer Maschine; **this factory has an** ~ **of 600 radios a day** diese Fabrik produziert täglich 600 Radios.

outrage ['aʊtreɪdʒ] **1** *n* (**a**) (*wicked, violent deed*) Schandtat, Untat (*geh*) *f*; (*cruel also*) Greueltat *f*; (*by police, demonstrators etc*) Ausschreitung *f*. **bomb** ~ verbrecherischer Bombenanschlag; **an** ~ **against the State** ein schändliches or ruchloses (*liter*) Verbrechen gegen den Staat.
(**b**) (*indecency, injustice*) Skandal *m*. **it's an** ~ **to waste food** es ist ein Skandal or Frevel, Essen umkommen zu lassen; **an** ~ **against humanity** ein Verbrechen or gegen die Menschlichkeit; **an** ~ **against common decency** eine empörende Verletzung or eine Verhöhnung des allgemeinen Anstandsgefühls; **an** ~ **against public morality** ein empörender Verstoß gegen die guten Sitten or die öffentliche Moral; **an** ~ **against good taste** eine unerhörte Geschmacklosigkeit, eine Geschmacklosigkeit sondergleichen; **a linguistic** ~ ein Verbrechen *nt* or Frevel *m* an der Sprache.
(**c**) (*sense of* ~) Empörung, Entrüstung *f* (*at* über +*acc*). **he reacted with (a sense of)** ~ er war empört or entrüstet.
2 [aʊt'reɪdʒ] *vt* **morals, conventions** ins Gesicht schlagen (+*dat*), hohnsprechen (+*dat*) (*geh*); **sense of decency** beleidigen; **ideals** mit Füßen treten; **person** empören, entrüsten. **public opinion was** ~**d by this cruelty/injustice** die öffentliche Meinung war über diese Grausamkeit/Ungerechtigkeit empört; **he deliberately set out to** ~ **his critics** er hatte es darauf angelegt, seine Kritiker zu schockieren.

outrageous [aʊt'reɪdʒəs] *adj* (**a**) (*cruel, violent*) greulich, verabscheuungswürdig. **murder, rape, and other** ~ **deeds** Mord, Vergewaltigung und andere Untaten.
(**b**) unerhört, empörend; **demand, insolence, arrogance etc** *also* unglaublich, unverschämt; **conduct, exaggeration, nonsense** *also* haarsträubend, hanebüchen; **language** entsetzlich, unflätig; **lie** unerhört, unverschämt; **charge, defamation etc** ungeheuerlich; **clothes, make-up etc** ausgefallen, unmöglich (*inf*); (*indecent*) geschmacklos; **complexity, selfishness** unglaublich, unerhört. ~ **colour** Schockfarbe *f*.

outrageously [aʊt'reɪdʒəslɪ] *adv* fürchterlich; **lie** schamlos; **exaggerate** *also* maßlos, haarsträubend; **swear** *also* entsetzlich, unflätig; **made-up** *also*, **dressed** haarsträubend, unmöglich (*inf*); **selfish** *also* unglaublich, haarsträubend. **he suggested/demanded quite** ~ **that ...** er machte den unerhörten Vorschlag/stellte die unerhörte Forderung, daß ...; **an** ~ **low neckline** ein übertrieben tiefer Ausschnitt.

out: ~**ran** *pret of* ~**run**; ~**range** *vt* eine größere Reichweite haben als; **we were** ~**ranged** die anderen hatten/der Feind *etc* hatte eine größere Reichweite; ~**rank** *vt* (*Mil*) rangmäßig stehen über (+*dat*); **he was** ~**ranked** er war rangniedriger.

outré [u:treɪ] *adj* überspannt, extravagant.

out: ~**ride** *pret* ~**rode**, *ptp* ~**ridden** *vt* besser reiten als; (*on bike*) besser fahren als; (*outdistance*) davonreiten (+*dat*)/-fahren (+*dat*); **he was completely** ~**ridden** er konnte absolut nicht mithalten; **he can't be** ~**ridden** mit ihm kann keiner mithalten; ~**rider** *n* (*on motorcycle*) Kradbegleiter *m*; ~**rigger** *n* (*Naut*) Ausleger *m*; (*boat*) Auslegerboot *nt*.

outright [aʊt'raɪt] **1** *adv* (**a**) (*entirely*) **to buy sth** ~ etw ganz kaufen; (*on HP*) den ganzen Preis für etw sofort bezahlen.
(**b**) (*at once*) **kill** sofort, auf der Stelle, gleich. **he felled him** ~ er streckte ihn mit einem einzigen Schlag zu Boden.
(**c**) (*openly*) geradeheraus, unumwunden, ohne Umschweife.
2 [aʊtraɪt] *adj* (**a**) (*complete*) ausgemacht; **deception, lie** *also* rein, glatt (*inf*); **nonsense** *also* total, absolut; **disaster, loss** völlig, vollkommen, total; **refusal, denial** total, absolut, glatt (*inf*); **defeat, error** gründlich, ausgesprochen, absolut. **that's** ~ **arrogance/impertinence/deception/selfishness** das ist reine Arroganz/Unverschämtheit/das ist reiner or glatter (*inf*) Betrug/reiner Egoismus; ~ **sale** (*Comm*) Verkauf *m* gegen sofortige Zahlung der Gesamtsumme.
(**b**) (*open*) **person** offen.

out: ~**rode** *pret of* ~**ride**; ~**run** *pret* ~**ran**, *ptp* ~**run** *vt* schneller laufen als; (*outdistance*) davonlaufen (+*dat*); (*in race also*) schlagen; (*fig*) übersteigen; **the white horse** ~**ran the rest of the field** der Schimmel ließ das übrige Feld hinter sich (*dat*); ~**set** *n* Beginn, Anfang *m*; **at the** ~**set** zu or am Anfang; **from the** ~**set** von Anfang an, von Anbeginn (*geh*); **let me make it quite clear at the** ~**set that ...** lassen Sie mich von vornherein klarstellen, daß ...; ~**shine** *pret*, *ptp* ~**shone** *vt* überstrahlen (*geh*), heller sein als; (*fig*) in den Schatten stellen.

outside [aʊt'saɪd] **1** *n* (**a**) (*of house, car, object*) Außenseite *f*. **the** ~ **of the car is green** das Auto ist (von) außen grün; **to open the door from the** ~ die Tür von außen öffnen; **to stay on the** ~ **of a group** sich in einer Gruppe im Hintergrund halten; **people on the** ~ (*of society*) Menschen außerhalb der Gesellschaft; **to overtake on the** ~ außen überholen; **he sees it from the** ~ (*fig*) er sieht es von außen or als Außenstehender; **judging from the** ~ (*fig*) wenn man es als Außenstehender beurteilt.

(**b**) (*extreme limit*) **at the (very)** ~ im äußersten Falle, äußerstenfalls.
2 *adj* (**a**) (*external*) Außen-, äußere(r, s). ~ **aerial** Außenantenne *f*; **an** ~ **broadcast** eine nicht im Studio produzierte Sendung; **an** ~ **broadcast from Wimbledon** eine Sendung aus Wimbledon; **to get some** ~ **help** Hilfe von außen holen; ~ **influences** äußere Einflüsse, Einflüsse von außen; **the** ~ **lane** die äußere Spur, die Überholspur; ~ **seat** (*in a row*) Außensitz *m*; **Platz** *m* **am Gang**; ~ **toilet** Außentoilette *f*; ~ **work** Außendienst *m*; **I'm doing** ~ **work on the dictionary** ich arbeite freiberuflich am Wörterbuch mit; ~ **world** Außenwelt *f*.
(**b**) **price** äußerste(r, s). **at an** ~ **estimate** maximal.
(**c**) (*very unlikely*) **an** ~ **chance** eine kleine Chance.
3 *adv* (*on the outer side*) außen; (*of house, room, vehicle*) draußen. **to be/go** ~ draußen sein/nach draußen gehen; **seen from** ~ von außen gesehen; **put the cat** ~ bring die Katze raus (*inf*) or nach draußen; **I feel** ~ **it all** ich komme mir so ausgeschlossen vor.
4 *prep* (*also* ~ *of*) (**a**) (*on the outer side of*) außerhalb (+*gen*). **to be/go** ~ **the house** außerhalb einer Sache sein/aus etw gehen; **he went** ~ **the house** er ging aus dem/vors/hinters Haus, er ging nach draußen; **he is waiting** ~ **the door** er wartet vor der Tür; **the car** ~ **the house** das Auto vorm Haus.
(**b**) (*beyond limits of*) außerhalb (+*gen*). **it is** ~ **our agreement** es geht über unsere Vereinbarung hinaus; ~ **the Festival** außerhalb der Festspiele; **this falls** ~ **the scope of ...** das geht über den Rahmen (+*gen*) ... hinaus.
(**c**) (*apart from*) außer (+*dat*), abgesehen von (+*dat*).

outside: ~ **half** *n* (*Rugby*) äußerer Halb(spieler); ~ **left** *n* (*Ftbl*, *Hockey*) Linksaußen(spieler) *m*.

outsider [aʊt'saɪdə'] *n* Außenseiter(in *f*), Outsider *m*.

outside right *n* (*Ftbl*, *Hockey*) Rechtsaußen(spieler) *m*.

out: ~**size** *adj* (**a**) übergroß; ~**size clothes** Kleidung *f* in Übergröße, Übergrößen *pl*; **the** ~**size department** die Abteilung für Übergrößen; (**b**) (*inf: enormous*) riesig; ~**skirts** *npl* (*of town*) Außen- or Randgebiete *pl*, Stadtrand *m*; (*of wood*) Rand *m*; ~**smart** *vt* (*inf*) überlisten, austricksen (*inf*).

outspoken [aʊt'spəʊkən] *adj* **person, criticism, speech, book** freimütig; **remark** direkt; **answer** *also* unverblümt. **he is** ~ er nimmt kein Blatt vor den Mund; **there was no need for you to be so** ~ so deutlich hättest du nicht zu sein brauchen.

outspokenly [aʊt'spəʊkənlɪ] *adv* geradeheraus, unverblümt; **answer, write** *also* freimütig; **remark** *also* direkt.

outspokenness [aʊt'spəʊkənnɪs] *n see adj* Freimütigkeit *f*; Direktheit *f*; Unverblümtheit *f*.

outspread ['aʊtspred] (*vb: pret, ptp* ~) **1** *adj* ausgebreitet. **2** *vt* ausbreiten.

outstanding [aʊt'stændɪŋ] *adj* (**a**) (*exceptional*) hervorragend; **talent, beauty, brilliance** außerordentlich, überragend. **of** ~ **ability** hervorragend or außerordentlich begabt; **a bridge player of** ~ **skill** ein außerordentlich geschickter Bridgespieler; **work of** ~ **excellence** ganz ausgezeichnete Arbeit; **of** ~ **importance** von höchster Bedeutung.
(**b**) (*prominent, conspicuous*) **event** bemerkenswert; **detail** auffallend; **feature** hervorstechend, auffallend.
(**c**) (*Comm, Fin*) **business** unerledigt; **account, bill, interest** ausstehend. **a lot of work is still** ~ viel Arbeit ist noch unerledigt; **are there any problems still** ~? gibt es noch irgendwelche ungeklärten Probleme?; ~ **debts** Außenstände *pl*.

outstandingly [aʊt'stændɪŋlɪ] *adv* hervorragend.

out: ~**station** *n* Vorposten *m*; ~**stay** *vt* länger bleiben als; **I don't want to** ~**stay my welcome** ich will eure Gastfreundschaft nicht überbeanspruchen or nicht zu lange in Anspruch nehmen; ~**stretched** *adj* **body** ausgestreckt; **arms** *also* ausgebreitet; **with his legs** ~**stretched**, **with** ~**stretched legs** mit ausgestreckten Beinen; **to welcome sb with** ~**stretched arms** jdn mit offenen Armen empfangen; ~**strip** *vt* (**a**) überholen, (**b**) (*fig*) übertreffen (**in** an +*dat*); ~**swim** *pret* ~**swam**, *ptp* ~**swum** *vt* **to** ~**swim sb** jdm davonschwimmen; ~**tray** *n* Korb *m* für Ausgänge; ~**vote** *vt* überstimmen.

outward ['aʊtwəd] **1** *adj* (**a**) (*of or on the outside*) **appearance, form** äußere(r, s); **beauty** äußerlich. **that's only his** ~ **self** so erscheint er nur nach außen hin; **he spoke with an** ~ **show of confidence** er gab sich den Anstrich von Selbstsicherheit.
(**b**) (*going out*) **movement** nach außen führend or gehend; **freight** ausgehend; **journey, voyage** Hin-. **the** ~ **flow of traffic** der Verkehr(sstrom) aus der Stadt heraus.
2 *adv* nach außen. **the door opens** ~ die Tür geht nach außen auf; ~ **bound** (*ship*) auslaufend (*from* von, *for* mit Bestimmung, mit Kurs auf +*acc*); **O**~ **Bound course** Abenteuerkurs *m*.

outwardly ['aʊtwədlɪ] *adv* nach außen hin.

outwards ['aʊtwədz] *adv* nach außen.

out: ~**wear** *pret* ~**wore**, *ptp* ~**worn** (**a**) (*last longer than*) überdauern, länger halten als; (**b**) (*wear out*) **clothes** abtragen; *see also* ~**worn**; ~**weigh** *vt* (*argument*) überwiegen, mehr Gewicht haben als; **the advantages** ~**weigh the disadvantages** die Vorteile überwiegen die Nachteile; ~**wit** *vt* überlisten; (*in card games also*) austricksen (*inf*); ~**work** *n* (*Mil*) Außenwerk *nt*; ~**worn** *adj* **idea, subject, expression** abgedroschen, abgenutzt; **custom, doctrine** veraltet.

ouzo ['u:zəʊ] *n* Ouzo *m*.

ova ['əʊvə] *pl of* **ovum**.

oval ['əʊvəl] **1** *adj* oval. ~**-shaped** oval. **2** *n* Oval *nt*.

ovary ['əʊvərɪ] *n* (*Anat*) Eierstock *m*; (*Bot*) Fruchtknoten *m*.

ovation [əʊ'veɪʃən] *n* Ovation *f*, stürmischer Beifall. **to give sb an** ~ jdm eine Ovation darbringen, jdm stürmischen Beifall zollen; **to get an** ~ stürmischen Beifall ernten; *see* **standing**.

oven ['ʌvn] *n* (*Cook*) (Back)ofen *m*; (*Tech*) (for drying) Trocken)ofen *m*; (*for baking pottery etc*) (Brenn)ofen *m*. **to put sth in the** ~ etw in den Ofen tun or stecken; **put it in the** ~ **for two hours** backen Sie es zwei Stunden; **pottery** brennen Sie es zwei

Stunden; **to cook in a hot** or **quick/moderate/slow** ~ bei starker/mittlerer/schwacher Hitze backen; **it's like an** ~ **in here** hier ist ja der reinste Backofen.

oven: ~-**cloth** n Topflappen m; ~ **door** n Ofentür, Ofenklappe f; ~-**glove** n (Brit) Topfhandschuh m; ~**proof** adj dish feuerfest, hitzebeständig; ~-**ready** adj bratfertig; ~-**to-table-ware** n feuerfestes Geschirr; ~**ware** n feuerfeste Formen pl.

over ['əʊvəʳ] **1** prep **(a)** (indicating motion) über (+acc). **he spread the blanket** ~ **the bed** er breitete die Decke über das Bett; **he spilled coffee** ~ **it** er goß Kaffee darüber, er vergoß Kaffee darauf; **to hit sb** ~ **the head** jdm auf den Kopf schlagen; **to hit sb** ~ **the head with sth** jdm (mit) etw über den Kopf schlagen; (fig) jdm etw um die Ohren hauen.

(b) (indicating position: above, on top of) über (+dat). **if you hang the picture** ~ **the desk** wenn du das Bild über dem Schreibtisch aufhängst or über den Schreibtisch hängst; **with his hat** ~ **one ear** mit dem Hut über einem Ohr; **bent** ~ **one's books** über die Bücher gebeugt.

(c) (on the other side of) über (+dat); (to the other side of) über (+acc). **to look** ~ **the wall** über die Mauer schauen; **the noise came from** ~ **the wall** der Lärm kam von der anderen Seite der Mauer; **it's** ~ **the page** es ist auf der nächsten Seite; **he looked** ~ **my shoulder** er sah mir über die Schulter; **the house** ~ **the way** das Haus gegenüber; **the family from** ~ **the way** die Familie von gegenüber; **it's just** ~ **the road from us** das ist von uns (aus) nur über die Straße; **the bridge** ~ **the river** die Brücke über den Fluß; **we're** ~ **the main obstacles now** wir haben jetzt die größten Hindernisse hinter uns (dat); **when they were** ~ **the river** als sie über den Fluß hinüber/herüber waren; **they're all safely** ~ **the first fence** sie sind alle sicher über die erste Hürde gekommen.

(d) (in or across every part of) in (+dat). **it was raining** ~ **London** es regnete in (ganz) London; **they came from all** ~ **England** sie kamen aus allen Teilen Englands or aus ganz England; **I'll show you** ~ **the house** ich zeige Ihnen das Haus; **you've got ink all** ~ **you/your hands** Ihre Hände sind ganz voller Tinte; **a blush spread** ~ **her face** sie errötete über und über; **to be all** ~ **sb** (inf) ein Mordstheater um jdn machen (inf).

(e) (superior to) über (+dat). **Mr X is** ~ **me in the business** Herr X steht im Geschäft über mir; **to have jurisdiction/authority/command** ~ **sb** gesetzgebende Gewalt/Autorität/Befehlsgewalt über jdn haben; **he has no control** ~ **his urges/his staff** er hat seine Triebe nicht in der Gewalt/seine Angestellten nicht unter Kontrolle; **he was promoted** ~ **me** er wurde über mich befördert; **we were all** ~ **them** (inf) wir waren ihnen haushoch überlegen.

(f) (more than, longer than) über (+acc). ~ **and above that** darüber hinaus; ~ **and above the expenses** über die Ausgaben hinaus; **that was well** ~ **a year ago** das ist gut ein Jahr her, das war vor gut einem Jahr; **she will not live** ~ **the winter** sie wird den Winter nicht überleben.

(g) (in expressions of time) über (+acc); (during) während (+gen), in (+dat). **can we stay** ~ **the weekend?** können wir übers Wochenende bleiben?; ~ **the summer/Christmas** den Sommer über/über Weihnachten; ~ **the summer we have been trying ...** während des Sommers haben wir versucht ...; ~ **the (past) years I've come to realize ...** im Laufe der (letzten) Jahre ist mir klar geworden ...; **he has mellowed** ~ **the years** er ist mit den Jahren milder geworden; **the visits were spread** ~ **several months** die Besuche verteilten sich über mehrere Monate.

(h) they talked ~ **a cup of coffee** sie unterhielten sich bei einer Tasse Kaffee; **the speeches were made** ~ **coffee** die Reden wurden beim Kaffee gehalten; **let's discuss that** ~ **dinner/a beer** besprechen wir das beim Essen/bei einem Bier; **they'll be a long time** ~ **it** sie werden dazu lange brauchen; **to pause** ~ **a difficulty** bei or über einer Schwierigkeit verharren; **he dozed off** ~ **his work** er nickte über seiner Arbeit ein; **to get stuck** ~ **a difficulty** bei einer Schwierigkeit stecken bleiben.

(i) he told me ~ **the phone** er hat am Telefon gesagt; **I heard it** ~ **the radio** ich habe es im Radio gehört; **a voice came** ~ **the intercom** eine Stimme kam über die Sprechanlage.

(j) (about) über (+acc). **it's not worth arguing** ~ es lohnt (sich) nicht, darüber zu streiten; **that's nothing for you to get upset** ~ darüber braucht du dich nicht aufzuregen.

(k) what is 7 ~ **3?** wieviel ist 7 geteilt durch 3 or 7 durch 3?; **blood pressure of 150** ~ **120** Blutdruck m von 150 zu or über 120.

2 adv **(a)** (across) (away from speaker) hinüber (towards speaker) herüber; (on the other side) drüben. **they swam** ~ **to us** sie schwammen zu uns herüber; **he took the fruit** ~ **to his mother** er brachte das Obst zu seiner Mutter hinüber; **when the first man is** ~ **the second starts to climb/to swim** wenn der erste drüben angekommen ist, klettert/schwimmt der zweite los; **he swam** ~ **to the other side** er schwamm auf die andere or zur anderen Seite hinüber; **the ball went** ~ **into the field** der Ball flog ins Feld hinüber; **come** ~ **tonight** kommen Sie heute abend vorbei; **I just thought I'd come** ~ ich dachte, ich komme mal rüber (inf); **he is** ~ **here/there** er ist hier/dort drüben; ~ **to you!** Sie sind daran; **and now** ~ **to our reporter in Belfast** und nun schalten wir zu unserem Reporter in Belfast um; **and now** ~ **to Paris where ...** und nun (schalten wir um) nach Paris, wo ...; **he has gone** ~ **to America** er ist nach Amerika gefahren; **he drove us** ~ **to the other side of town** er fuhr uns ans andere Ende der Stadt; **he went** ~ **to the enemy** er lief zum Feind über.

(b) he searched the house ~ er durchsuchte das (ganze) Haus; **famous the world** ~ in der ganzen Welt berühmt; **I've been looking for it all** ~ ich habe überall danach gesucht; **I am aching all** ~ mir tut alles weh; **you've got dirt all** ~ Sie sind voller Schmutz, Sie sind ganz schmutzig; **he was shaking all** ~ er zitterte am ganzen Leib; **I'm wet all** ~ ich bin völlig naß; **he**

was black all ~ er war von oben bis unten schwarz; **the dog licked him all** ~ der Hund leckte ihn von oben bis unten ab; **that's him/Fred all** ~ das ist typisch für ihn/Fred, typisch Fred; **it happens all** ~ das gibt es überall.

(c) (indicating movement from one side to another, from upright position) to turn an object ~ (and ~) einen Gegenstand (immer wieder) herumdrehen; **he hit her and** ~ **she went** er schlug sie, und sie fiel um.

(d) (ended) (film, first act, operation, fight etc) zu Ende; (romance, summer also) vorbei; (romance also) aus. **the rain is** ~ der Regen hat aufgehört; **the pain will soon be** ~ der Schmerz wird bald vorbei sein; **the danger was** ~ die Gefahr war vorüber, es bestand keine Gefahr mehr; **when all this is** ~ wenn das alles vorbei ist; **it's all** ~ **with him** es ist Schluß or aus mit ihm; **it's all** ~ **between us** es ist aus zwischen uns.

(e) (indicating repetition) **he counted them** ~ **again** er zählte sie noch einmal; **to start (all)** ~ **again** noch einmal (ganz) von vorn anfangen; ~ **and** ~ **(again)** immer (und immer) wieder, wieder und wieder; **he did it five times** ~ er hat es fünfmal wiederholt; **must I say everything twice** ~! muß ich denn immer alles zweimal sagen!

(f) (excessively) übermäßig, allzu. **he has not done it** ~ **well** er hat es nicht gerade übermäßig gut gemacht; **he is not** ~ **healthy** er ist nicht allzu gesund; **there's not** ~ **much left** es ist nicht allzuviel übrig.

(g) (remaining) übrig. **there was no/a lot of meat (left)** ~ war kein Fleisch mehr übrig/viel Fleisch übrig; **there were two cakes each and one** ~ es waren zwei Kuchen für jeden, und einer war übrig; **7 into 22 goes 3 and 1** ~ 22 durch 7 ist 3, Rest 1; **6 metres and a little** ~ 6 Meter und ein bißchen; **after doing the books I was a few pounds** ~ (inf) nach der Abrechnung war ich ein paar Pfund im Plus.

(h) (more) **children of 8 and** ~ Kinder über or ab 8; **all results of 5.3 and** ~ alle Ergebnisse ab 5,3 or von 5,3 und darüber; **if it takes three hours or** ~ wenn es drei oder mehr Stunden dauert.

(i) (Telec) **come in, please,** ~ bitte kommen, over; ~ **and out** Ende der Durchsage; (Aviat) over and out.

3 n (Cricket) 6 aufeinanderfolgende Würfe.

over- pref über-.

over: ~**abundance** n Überfülle f (of von); ~**abundant** adj überreichlich, sehr reichlich; **to have an** ~**abundant supply of sth** überreichlich mit etw versorgt sein; ~**achieve** vi leistungsorientiert sein; **a society which encourages people to** ~**achieve** ein Gesellschaftssystem, das vom Menschen immer größere Leistungen fordert; ~**achiever** n leistungsorientierter Mensch; **a chronic** ~**achiever** ein typischer Erfolgsmensch; ~**act** (Theat) **1** vt role übertreiben, übertrieben gestalten; **2** vi übertreiben (also fig), chargieren; ~**active** adj zu or übertrieben aktiv, hyperaktiv (spec); ~**active thyroid** (Med) Schilddrüsenüberfunktion f; ~-**age** adj zu alt.

overage ['əʊvərɪdʒ] n (US Comm) Überschuß m.

overall¹ [ˌəʊvər'ɔːl] **1** adj **(a)** width, length, total gesamt, Gesamt-. ~ **dimensions** (Aut) Außenmaße pl; ~ **majority** absolute Mehrheit.

(b) (general) allgemein. **there's been an** ~ **improvement recently in his work/health** sein Gesundheitszustand hat sich/seine Leistungen haben sich in letzter Zeit allgemein verbessert; **the** ~ **effect of this was to ...** dies hatte das Endergebnis, daß ...

2 adv **(a)** insgesamt. **what does it measure** ~? wie sind die Gesamtmaße?

(b) (in general, on the whole) im großen und ganzen.

overall² ['əʊvərɔːl] n (Brit) Kittel m; (for women also) Kittelschürze f; (for children) Kittelchen nt.

overalls ['əʊvərɔːlz] npl Overall, Arbeitsanzug m.

over: ~**ambitious** adj übertrieben or zu ehrgeizig; ~**anxiety** n übersteigerte Angst; ~**anxious** adj übertrieben besorgt; (on particular occasion) übermäßig aufgeregt, übermäßig nervös; **he was** ~**anxious to start and caused two false starts** er konnte den Start kaum abwarten or erwarten und verursachte so zwei Fehlstarts; **he's** ~**anxious to please** er überschlägt sich, um zu gefallen; **I'm not exactly** ~**anxious to go** ich bin nicht gerade scharf darauf zu gehen; ~**arm** adj, adv (Sport) throw mit gestrecktem (erhobenem) Arm; serve über Kopf; ~**ate** pret of ~**eat**; ~**awe** vt (intimidate) einschüchtern; (impress) überwältigen, tief beeindrucken; ~**balance 1** vi (person, object) aus dem Gleichgewicht kommen, Übergewicht bekommen, das Gleichgewicht verlieren; **2** vt object umwerfen, umstoßen; boat kippen; person aus dem Gleichgewicht bringen.

overbearing [ˌəʊvə'bɛərɪŋ] adj herrisch; arrogance anmaßend.

overbearingly [ˌəʊvə'bɛərɪŋlɪ] adv herrisch. so ~ **arrogant** von einer derartig anmaßenden Arroganz.

over: ~**bid** pret, ptp ~**bid 1** vt **(a)** (at auction) überbieten; **(b)** (Cards) überreizen; **to** ~**bid one's hand** zu hoch reizen; **2** vi **(a)** (at auction) mehr bieten, ein höheres Angebot machen; **(b)** (Cards) überreizen, überrufen; ~**blouse** n Überbluse f; ~**blow** pret ~**blew**, ptp ~**blown** vt (Mus) überblasen; ~**blown** adj **(a)** flower verblühend; **(b)** prose, rhetoric geschwollen, schwülstig, hochtrabend; **(c)** (Mus) note überblasen.

overboard ['əʊvəbɔːd] adv **(a)** (Naut) über Bord. **to fall** ~ über Bord gehen or fallen; **man** ~! Mann über Bord!; **to throw sb/sth** ~ jdn/etw über Bord werfen; (fig) etw verwerfen.

(b) (fig inf) **to go** ~ übers Ziel hinausschießen, zu weit gehen, es übertreiben; **to go** ~ **for sb** von jdm ganz hingerissen sein, Feuer und Flamme für jdn sein (inf); **there's no need to go** ~ **(about it)** übertreib es nicht, kein Grund zum Übertreiben.

over: ~**bold** adj person, action verwegen; ~**burden** vt (lit) überladen, (fig) überlasten; ~**buy** pret, ptp ~**bought** vi zuviel kaufen, über Bedarf einkaufen; ~**call** (Cards) **1** vt überbieten; **2** n höheres Gebot; ~**came** pret of ~**come**; ~**careful** adj übervorsichtig; ~**cast** adj **(a)** weather bedeckt; sky also bewölkt; it's getting rather ~cast es zieht sich zu; (b) (Sew) stitch Überwendlings-; ~cast seam überwendliche Naht; ~cautious adj übervorsichtig, übertrieben vorsichtig; ~cautiousness n übertriebene Vorsicht.

overcharge [ˌəʊvəˈtʃɑːdʒ] **1** vt (a) person zuviel berechnen (+dat) or abverlangen (+dat) (for für). you've been ~d man hat dir zuviel berechnet; they ~d me by £2 sie haben mir £2 zuviel berechnet. (b) electric circuit überlasten. (c) (with detail, emotion) painting, style überladen. **2** vi zuviel verlangen (for für). to ~ on a bill zuviel berechnen or anrechnen.

overcoat [ˈəʊvəkəʊt] n Mantel, Überzieher m.

overcome [ˌəʊvəˈkʌm] pret overcame [ˌəʊvəˈkeɪm], ptp ~ **1** vt enemy überwältigen, bezwingen; bad habit sich (dat) abgewöhnen; shyness, nerves etc überwinden; temptation widerstehen (+dat), bezwingen; difficulty, obstacle überwinden, meistern; anger bezwingen, überwinden; disappointment hinwegkommen über (+acc); ~ by the fumes die giftigen Gase machten ihn bewußtlos or betäubten ihn; ~ by the cold von der Kälte betäubt; sleep overcame him der Schlaf übermannte ihn; he was ~ by the temptation er erlag der Versuchung; he was quite ~ by the song er war sehr gerührt von dem Lied; he was ~ by grief/by emotion Schmerz/Rührung übermannte ihn; he was ~ by remorse/a feeling of despair Reue/ein Gefühl der Verzweiflung überkam ihn; ~ with fear von Furcht ergriffen or übermannt; ~ with emotion ergriffen, gerührt; I don't know what to say, I'm quite ~ ich weiß gar nicht, was ich sagen soll, ich bin ganz ergriffen or gerührt. **2** vi siegen, siegreich sein. we shall ~ wir werden siegen.

over: ~compensate vi to ~compensate for sth etw überkompensieren; ~compensation n Überkompensation f; ~confidence n see adj (a) übersteigertes Selbstvertrauen or Selbstbewußtsein; (b) zu großer Optimismus; (c) blindes Vertrauen (in in +acc); ~confident adj (a) (extremely self-assured) übertrieben selbstsicher or selbstbewußt; (b) (too optimistic) zu optimistisch; he was ~confident of success er war sich (dat) seines Erfolges zu sicher; (c) (excessively trustful) blind vertrauend (in auf +acc); you are ~confident in him Sie haben zu großes Vertrauen in ihn; he was ~confident in the ability of this new method to ... er hatte zuviel Vertrauen in die Fähigkeit dieser neuen Methode, zu ...; ~consumption n zu großer Verbrauch (of an +dat); ~cook vt verbraten; (boil) verkochen; ~correct **1** vt überkorrigieren; **2** adj überkorrekt; ~critical adj zu kritisch; ~crowd vt überladen; bus etc also, room (with people) überfüllen; ~crowded adj (with things) überfüllt; town also übervölkert; (overpopulated) überbevölkert; (with things) überladen; ~crowding n (of bus, room, flat, class-room) Überfüllung f; (of town) Überbevölkerung f; ~dependent adj zu abhängig (on von); ~developed adj überentwickelt.

overdo [ˌəʊvəˈduː] pret overdid [ˌəʊvəˈdɪd], ptp overdone [ˌəʊvəˈdʌn] vt (a) (exaggerate) übertreiben. you are ~ing it or things (going too far) Sie übertreiben, Sie gehen zu weit; (tiring yourself) Sie übernehmen or überlasten sich; you've overdone the blue paint Sie haben es mit der blauen Farbe übertrieben; don't ~ the smoking/sympathy übertreibe das Rauchen nicht/übertreibe es nicht mit dem Mitleid; she rather overdid the loving wife sie hat die liebevolle Ehefrau etwas zu dick aufgetragen; gin? — please, but don't ~ the tonic Gin? — ja bitte, aber nicht zu viel Tonic; I'm afraid you've rather overdone the garlic ich fürchte, du hast es mit dem Knoblauch etwas zu gut gemeint.
(b) (cook too long) verbraten; (boil) verkochen.

over: ~done adj (a) (exaggerated) übertrieben; (b) see vt (b) verbraten; verkocht; ~dose **1** n (lit) Überdosis f; (fig) Zuviel nt (of an +dat); he died of an ~dose of sleeping pills er starb an einer Überdosis Schlaftabletten; **2** vt überdosieren, eine Überdosis geben (+dat); ~draft n Konto-Überziehung f; my bank manager wouldn't let me have a bigger ~draft der Direktor meiner Bank wollte mir kein weiteres Überziehen meines Kontos nicht gestatten; to have an ~draft of £10 sein Konto um £10 überzogen haben; I've still got an ~draft mein Konto ist immer noch überzogen; ~draw pret ~drew, ptp ~drawn vt one's account überziehen; I'm always ~drawn at the end of the month mein Konto ist am Ende des Monats immer überzogen; ~dress **1** [ˌəʊvəˈdres] vti (sich) übertrieben or zu viel kleiden; do you think I'm ~dressed? was meinst du, ist das zu angezogen (inf) or bin ich zu elegant angezogen?; **2** [ˈəʊvədres] n Überkleid nt; ~drive n (Aut) Schnellgang(getriebe nt), Schongang(getriebe nt) m; ~due adj überfällig; long ~due er müßte schon lange da sein; ~due interest Zinsrückstände pl; he is ~due er müßte schon lange da sein; ~eager adj übereifrig; he was ~eager to impress er war (zu) sehr darauf aus, Eindruck zu machen; he was ~eager to start er konnte den Start kaum abwarten; they're not exactly ~eager to learn sie sind nicht gerade übermäßig lernbegierig; ~eagerness n Übereifer m; ~eat pret ~ate, ptp ~eaten vi zuviel essen, sich überessen; ~eating n Überessen nt; ~elaborate adj design manieriert, gekünstelt; style verkünstelt; excuse, plan, scheme (viel zu) umständlich, zu ausgeklügelt; hairstyle, dress überladen; ~emphasis n Überbetonung f; to put an ~emphasis on sth etw überbetonen; an ~emphasis on money eine Überbewertung des Geldes; ~emphasize vt überbetonen, überbewerten; hips, cheekbones überbetonen; one cannot ~emphasize the importance of this man kann nicht genug betonen, wie wichtig das ist; ~employed adj (beruflich) überfordert; ~enthusiastic adj übertrieben begeistert; not exactly ~enthusiastic nicht gerade hingerissen; ~estimate **1** [ˌəʊvəˈrestɪmeɪt] vt price zu hoch einschätzen or ansetzen; importance überschätzen, überbewerten; chances, strength, danger, own importance überschätzen; **2** [ˌəʊvəˈrestɪmɪt] n (of price) Überbewertung f, zu hohe Schätzung f; ~excite vt zu sehr aufregen; ~excited adj

person überreizt, zu aufgeregt; children aufgedreht, zu aufgeregt; ~excitement n Überreiztheit f, zu starke Aufregung f; (of children) Aufgedrehtheit f; ~exercise **1** vt übertrainieren; **2** vi übermäßig viel trainieren; the dangers of ~exercising die Gefahren übermäßigen Trainings; ~exert vt überanstrengen; ~exertion n Überanstrengung f; ~expose vt (Phot) überbelichten; ~exposure n (Phot) Überbelichtung f; (in media etc: of topic) Überbehandlung f; the President's image is suffering from ~exposure (in the media) das Image des Präsidenten leidet darunter, daß er zu oft in den Medien erscheint; ~familiar adj to be ~familiar with sb etwas zu vertraulich or intim mit jdm sein; (too pally also) plumpvertraulich mit jdm sein; I'm not ~familiar with their methods ich bin nicht allzu vertraut mit ihren Methoden; ~feed pret, ptp ~fed vt überfüttern; ~fly pret ~flew pret of ~fly.

overflow [ˈəʊvəfləʊ] **1** n (a) (act) Überlaufen nt.
(b) (amount) Übergelaufene(s), Übergeflossene(s) nt.
(c) (outlet) Überlauf m.
(d) (excess: of people, population) Überschuß m (of an +dat).
2 [ˌəʊvəˈfləʊ] vt area überschwemmen; container, tank überlaufen lassen. the river has ~ed its banks der Fluß ist über die Ufer getreten.
3 [ˌəʊvəˈfləʊ] vi (a) (liquid, river etc) überlaufen, überfließen; (container) überlaufen; (room, vehicle) zum Platzen gefüllt sein, überfüllt sein (with mit). full to ~ing (bowl, cup) bis oben hin voll, zum Überlaufen voll; (room) überfüllt, zu voll; the crowd at the meeting ~ed into the street die Leute bei der Versammlung standen bis auf die Straße; you'll have to open the doors and let the crowd ~ into the grounds man wird die Türen öffnen müssen, damit die Leute in die Gartenanlagen ausweichen können.
(b) (fig: be full of) überfließen (with von). his heart was ~ing with love sein Herz lief or floß über vor Liebe; he's not exactly ~ing with generosity/ideas er überschlägt sich nicht gerade vor Großzügigkeit/er sprudelt nicht gerade über vor Ideen.

over: ~flow meeting n Parallelversammlung f; ~flow pipe n Überlaufrohr nt or -leitung f; ~fly pret ~flew, ptp ~flown vt (a) (fly over) town überfliegen; (b) (fly beyond) runway, airport hinausfliegen über (+acc); ~fond adj to be ~fond of sth/of doing sth etw nur zu gern haben/tun; he's ~fond of criticizing others er kritisiert andere nur zu gern; I'm not exactly ~fond of ... ich bin nicht gerade begeistert von ...; ~full adj übervoll (with von, mit); ~generous adj zu or übertrieben großzügig; she was ~generous in her praise sie geizte nicht mit Lob, sie spendete überreichliches Lob; he gave me an ~generous helping er überhäufte meinen Teller; ~grow pret ~grew, ptp ~grown vt path, garden, wall überwachsen, überwuchern; ~grown adj (a) überwachsen, überwuchert (with von); (b) child aufgeschossen, zu groß; he's just an ~grown schoolboy er ist ein großes Kind; you're just an ~grown baby du bist der reinste Säugling; ~hand adj, adv (a) (Sport) see ~arm; (b) (Naut) ~hand knot einfacher Knoten; ~hang (vb: pret, ptp ~hung) **1** vt hängen über (+acc); (project over: rocks, balcony) hinausragen über (+acc), vorstehen über (+acc); **2** n (of rock, building) Überhang m; (Archit) Überkragung f; ~hanging adj cliff, wall überhängend; balcony vorstehend; ~hasty adj voreilig, übereilt; don't do anything ~hasty übereilen Sie nichts, überstürzen Sie nichts; am I being ~hasty? bin ich da zu voreilig?; ~haul **1** n Überholung f, Generalüberholung f; (inf: of patient) Generalüberholung f (inf); the machine needs an ~haul die Maschine muß überholt werden; **2** vt (a) engine überholen; (b) (pass) überholen; (inf) patient gründlich untersuchen; (b) (pass) überholen; (catch up) einholen.

overhead[1] [ˌəʊvəˈhed] **1** adv oben; (in the sky: position) am Himmel, in der Luft. the people ~ (above us) die Leute über uns; (above them) die Leute darüber; a plane flew ~ ein Flugzeug flog über uns etc (acc) (hinweg).
2 [ˈəʊvəhed] adj cables, wires Frei-, ~cable Überlandleitung f; (high voltage) Hochspannungsleitung f; (Rail) Oberleitung f; ~ railway Hochbahn f; ~ cam(shaft) obenliegende Nockenwelle; ~ lighting Deckenbeleuchtung f; ~ travelling crane Laufkran m; ~valve engine obengesteuerter Motor; ~ valves obengesteuerte Ventile pl; ~ volley (Sport) Hochball m.
overhead[2] [ˈəʊvəhed] (Comm) **1** adj ~ charges or costs or expenses allgemeine Unkosten pl. **2** n ~s (Brit), ~ (US) allgemeine Unkosten pl; company ~s allgemeine Geschäftskosten or Betriebsunkosten pl.

overhear [ˌəʊvəˈhɪə] pret, ptp overheard [ˌəʊvəˈhɜːd] vt zufällig mit anhören, zufällig mitbekommen. we don't want him to ~ us wir wollen nicht, daß er uns zuhören kann or daß er mitbekommt, was wir sagen; I ~d them plotting ich hörte zufällig, wie sie etwas ausheckten; things you ~ in bars Dinge, die man in Bars so mit anhört or mitbekommt; the other day he was ~d to say that ... neulich hat ihn jemand sagen hören, daß ...; he was being ~d jemand hörte mit.

over: ~heat **1** vt engine überhitzen; room überheizen; **2** vi (engine) heißlaufen; ~heated adj heißgelaufen; room überheizt; discussion erhitzt; ~hung pret, ptp of ~hang.

overindulge [ˌəʊvərɪnˈdʌldʒ] **1** vt (a) person zu nachsichtig sein mit, zuviel durchgehen lassen (+dat).
(b) fantasies etc allzu freien Lauf lassen (+dat); passion, sexual appetite also zügellos frönen (+dat). I somewhat ~d myself last night ich habe mich gestern nacht etwas überessen lassen; a writer who ~s himself/his fantasies ein Schriftsteller, der seiner Phantasie allzu freien Lauf läßt.
2 vi zuviel genießen; (as regards eating also) Völlerei betreiben. I ~d at the party ich habe auf der Party ein bißchen zuviel des Guten gehabt; to ~ in wine zuviel Wein trinken.

overindulgence [ˌəʊvərɪnˈdʌldʒəns] n (a) allzu große Nachsicht or Nachgiebigkeit (of sb jdm gegenüber).
(b) (as regards eating) Völlerei f. ~ in wine übermäßiger

Weingenuß; ~ **in cigarettes** zu starkes Rauchen; **this constant** ~ **of his sexual appetite** sein zügelloses Sexualleben; **the author's regrettable** ~ **in the use of metaphor/in poor jokes** die bedauerlicherweise ungezügelte Vorliebe dieses Autors für Metaphern/für schlechte Witze; **health ruined by** ~ **in ... durch** übermäßigen Genuß von ... geschädigte Gesundheit.

overindulgent [ˈəʊvərɪnˈdʌldʒənt] adj parent zu nachsichtig, zu gütmütig (to(wards) sb jdm gegenüber, mit jdm). **should I have another or would that be** ~? soll ich mir noch einen nehmen, oder wäre das des Guten zuviel or Völlerei?; **the editor was** ~ **towards his own preferences** der Herausgeber ließ seinen eigenen Vorlieben zu sehr freien Lauf.

overjoyed [ˌəʊvəˈdʒɔɪd] adj überglücklich, äußerst erfreut (at, by über +acc). **he wasn't exactly** ~ er war nicht gerade erfreut.

over: ~**kill** n (Mil) Overkill m; (fig) Rundumschlag, Kahlschlag m; ~**laden** adj (lit, fig) überladen (with mit); lorry, circuit also überlastet; ~**laid** pret, ptp of ~**lay**; ~**land** 1 adj journey auf dem Landweg; ~**land route** Route f auf dem Landweg; 2 adv travel etc über Land, auf dem Landweg.

overlap [ˈəʊvəˈlæp] 1 n Überschneidung f; (spatial also) Überlappung f, Überlapp m; (of concepts) teilweise Entsprechung or Deckung. **3 inches'** ~ 3 Inches Überlapp(ung); **there's quite a lot of** ~ **between the work done by the various departments** die Arbeitsbereiche der verschiedenen Abteilungen überschneiden sich in vielen Punkten; **there is an** ~ **of two days between our holidays** unsere Ferien überschneiden sich um zwei Tage.

2 [ˌəʊvəˈlæp] vi (a) (tiles, boards) einander überdecken, überlappen; (teeth) übereinanderstehen. **made of** ~**ping planks** aus (einander) überlappenden Brettern.

(b) (visits, dates, responsibilities) sich überschneiden; (ideas, concepts, plans, work areas) sich teilweise decken.

3 [ˌəʊvəˈlæp] vt (a) part gehen über (+acc); liegen über (+dat); (person) überlappen. **the tiles** ~ **each other** die Dachziegel überlappen sich or liegen übereinander.

(b) holiday, visit etc sich überschneiden mit; idea etc sich teilweise decken mit.

4 adj attr joint Überlappungs-.

over: ~**lay** (vb: pret, ptp ~**laid**) 1 [ˌəʊvəˈleɪ] vt überziehen; (with metal) belegen; wall verkleiden; 2 [ˈəʊvəleɪ] n Überzug m; (metal) Auflage f; (on map) Auflegemaske f; (Typ) Zurichtung f, Zurichtebogen m; ~**leaf** adv umseitig; **the illustration** ~**leaf** die umseitige Abbildung; **see** ~**leaf** siehe umseitig; ~**load** 1 n Übergewicht nt, zu große Last, Überbelastung f; (Elec) Überlast f; 2 vt überladen; car, lorry, animal also, (Elec, Mech) überlasten; ~**long** 1 adj überlang; 2 adv zu lang.

overlook [ˌəʊvəˈlʊk] vt (a) (have view onto) überblicken. **we had a room** ~**ing the park** wir hatten ein Zimmer mit Blick auf den Park; **the castle** ~**s the whole town** vom Schloß aus hat man Aussicht auf die ganze Stadt; **the garden is not** ~**ed** niemand kann in den Garten hineinsehen.

(b) (fail to notice) detail übersehen, nicht bemerken. **a small point which it is easy to** ~ eine Kleinigkeit, die man leicht übersehen kann or übersieht.

(c) (ignore) mistake hinwegsehen über (+acc), durchgehen lassen. **I am prepared to** ~ **it this time** diesmal will ich noch ein Auge zudrücken.

over: ~**lord** n (Hist) Oberherr m; ~**lordship** n (Hist) Oberherrschaft f.

overly [ˈəʊvəlɪ] adv übermäßig, allzu.

over: ~**manned** adj **to be** ~**manned** eine zu große Belegschaft haben; ~**manning** n zu große Belegschaft(en pl); **we must not permit** ~**manning to occur** wir dürfen nicht zulassen, daß die unsere Belegschaft zu groß wird or (generally) daß die Belegschaften zu groß werden; ~**mantel** n (Archit) Kaminaufsatz or -mantel m; ~**much** 1 adv zuviel, übermäßig; **they're not paid** ~**much** sie bekommen nicht übermäßig viel bezahlt; 2 adj zuviel; ~**nice** adj distinction spitzfindig, zu genau.

overnight [ˈəʊvəˈnaɪt] 1 adv (a) über Nacht. **we drove** ~ wir sind die Nacht durchgefahren; **to stay** ~ **(with sb)** bei jdm übernachten, (bei jdm) über Nacht bleiben.

(b) (fig) von heute auf morgen, über Nacht. **the place had changed** ~ der Ort hatte sich über Nacht verändert.

2 adj (a) journey Nacht-. ~ **stay** Übernachtung f; ~ **bag** Reisetasche f.

(b) (fig: sudden) ganz plötzlich. **you can't expect an** ~ **change in her personality** Sie können nicht erwarten, daß sich ihre Persönlichkeit von heute auf morgen ändert; **an** ~ **success** ein Blitzerfolg m; **the play was an** ~ **success** das Stück wurde über Nacht ein Erfolg.

over: ~**part** pret, ptp of ~**pay**; ~**particular** adj zu genau, pingelig (inf); **he's not** ~**particular about what he eats** er ist nicht wählerisch or pingelig (inf), was (das) Essen angeht; **he wasn't** ~**particular about filling in his expenses form correctly** er nahm es mit dem Ausfüllen seines Spesenantrages nicht zu or so genau; ~**pass** n Überführung f; ~**pay** pret, ptp ~**paid** vt überbezahlen, zuviel bezahlen (+dat); **he's been** ~**paid by about £5** man hat ihm etwa £ 5 zuviel bezahlt; ~**payment** n(act) Überzahlung f; (amount) zuviel bezahlter Betrag; ~**play** vt (overact) übertrieben darstellen or spielen; **to** ~**play one's hand** (fig) es übertreiben, den Bogen überspannen; ~**plus** n (esp US) Überschuß m, Mehr nt (of an +dat); ~**populated** adj überbevölkert; ~**population** n Überbevölkerung f.

overpower [ˌəʊvəˈpaʊəʳ] vt (a) (physically: emotion, heat) überwältigen, übermannen. **he was** ~**ed by the drug** die Droge tat ihre Wirkung (bei ihm). (b) (Mech) **to be** ~**ed** übermotorisiert sein.

overpowering [ˌəʊvəˈpaʊərɪŋ] adj überwältigend; smell penetrant; perfume aufdringlich; heat glühend. **I felt an** ~ **desire ...** ich fühlte den unwiderstehlichen Drang, ...; **he's a bit** ~ **at times** seine Art kann einen manchmal zuviel werden.

over: ~**praise** vt übertrieben or zu sehr loben; ~**price** vt einen zu hohen Preis verlangen für; **if the public will pay for it then it's not** ~**priced, he said** wenn es die Leute bezahlen, dann ist der Preis nicht zu hoch angesetzt; **at £50 it's** ~**priced** £ 50 ist zuviel dafür; ~**print** 1 vt (a) stamp, text überdrucken; (Phot) überkopieren; (b) (print too many copies of) in zu großer Auflage drucken; 2 n (on stamp) Überdruck m; ~**produce** vi überproduzieren, zuviel produzieren; ~**production** n Überproduktion f; ~**protect** vt child überbehüten, zu sehr behüten; ~**protective** adj parent überängstlich; ~**ran** pret of ~**run**; ~**rate** vt überschätzen; person also zu hoch einschätzen; book, play, system etc also überbewerten; ~**reach** vr sich übernehmen; ~**react** vi übertrieben reagieren (to auf +acc); ~**reaction** n übertriebene Reaktion (to auf +acc).

override [ˌəʊvəˈraɪd] pret **overrode** [ˌəʊvəˈrəʊd], ptp **overridden** [ˌəʊvəˈrɪdn] vt (a) (disregard) sich hinwegsetzen über (+acc); opinion, claims also nicht berücksichtigen.

(b) (prevail over, cancel out) order, decision, ruling aufheben, außer Kraft setzen; objection ablehnen. **I'm afraid I'll have to** ~ **you there, said the chairman** dazu muß ich leider nein sagen, sagte der Vorsitzende; **to** ~ **sb's authority** sich über jds Autorität (acc) hinwegsetzen.

(c) horse müde reiten.

(d) (teeth) gehen über (+acc).

overriding [ˌəʊvəˈraɪdɪŋ] adj principle vorrangig, wichtigste(r, s); priority vordringlich; desire dringendst(e, r, s); (Jur) act, clause Aufhebungs-. **matters of** ~ **importance** äußerst bedeutende Angelegenheiten; **my** ~ **ambition is to ...** mein allergrößter Ehrgeiz ist es, zu ...

over: ~**ripe** adj überreif; ~**rode** pret of ~**ride**.

overrule [ˌəʊvəˈruːl] vt ablehnen; claim also nicht anerkennen; objection also zurückweisen; verdict, decision aufheben. **his objection was** ~**d** sein Einspruch wurde abgewiesen; **I wanted to insist on a complete revision but I was** ~**d** ich wollte auf einer völligen Überarbeitung bestehen, aber mein Vorschlag wurde abgewiesen; **we were** ~**d** unser Vorschlag/Einspruch wurde abgelehnt; **he was** ~**d by the majority** er wurde überstimmt.

overrun [ˌəʊvəˈrʌn] pret **overran** [ˌəʊvəˈræn], ptp ~ 1 vt (a) (weeds) überwuchern, überwachsen. **the town was** ~ **with tourists/mice** die Stadt war von Touristen/Mäusen überlaufen.

(b) (troops etc: invade) country, district einfallen in (+dat), herfallen über (+acc); enemy position überrennen.

(c) (go past) mark hinauslaufen über (+acc); (Rail) signal überfahren; (train) platform hinausfahren über (+acc); (plane) runway hinausrollen über (+acc).

(d) (go beyond) time überziehen, überschreiten. **the TV programme overran its time** das Fernsehprogramm überzog.

(e) (overflow) banks überfluten.

2 vi (in time: speaker, concert etc) überziehen. **you're** ~**ning** Sie überziehen (Ihre Zeit); **his speech overran by ten minutes** seine Rede dauerte zehn Minuten zu lang.

oversaw [ˌəʊvəˈsɔː] pret of **oversee**.

overseas [ˈəʊvəˈsiːz] 1 adj country überseeisch, in Übersee; market, trade Übersee-; telegram nach/aus Übersee; (in Europe) europäisch; telegram nach/aus Europa. **our** ~ **office** unsere Zweigstelle in Übersee/Europa; ~ **aid** Entwicklungshilfe f; **an** ~ **visitor** ein Besucher aus Übersee/Europa; ~ **service** (Mil) Militärdienst m in Übersee/Europa.

2 adv in Übersee/Europa leben; **to go** ~ nach Übersee/Europa gehen; **to be sent** ~ nach Übersee/Europa geschickt werden; **from** ~ aus Übersee/Europa.

over: ~**see** pret ~**saw**, ptp ~**seen** vt (supervise) person, work beaufsichtigen, überwachen; ~**seer** n Aufseher(in f) m; (foreman) Vorarbeiter(in f) m; (in coal-mine) Steiger m; ~**sell** pret, ptp ~**sold** vti (a) (sell too many) **to** ~**sell (sth)** (von etw) mehr verkaufen, als geliefert werden kann; concert, match etc zuviel Karten verkaufen für; (b) (promote too much) zuviel Reklame machen für; ~**sensitive** adj überempfindlich; ~**sew** pret ~**sewed**, ptp ~**sewed** or ~**sewn** vt umnähen; ~**sexed** adj **to be** ~**sexed** einen übermäßig starken Sexualtrieb haben; **don't leave me alone with that** ~**sexed brother of yours** laß mich bloß mit deinem Lustmolch von Bruder nicht allein (inf); **you're** ~**sexed!** du bist unersättlich!; ~**shadow** vt (lit, fig) überschatten; ~**shoe** n Überschuh m.

overshoot [ˌəʊvəˈʃuːt] pret, ptp **overshot** [ˌəʊvəˈʃɒt] 1 vt target, runway hinausschießen über (+acc). **the golfer overshot the green** der Golfer schlug (den Ball) über das Grün hinaus; **to** ~ **the mark** (lit, fig) übers Ziel hinausschießen; **the factory has actually overshot its output estimate** die Fabrik hat die veranschlagte Produktion tatsächlich übertroffen.

2 vi (plane) durchstarten.

oversight [ˈəʊvəsaɪt] n (a) Versehen nt. **by or through an** ~ aus Versehen; **whether by** ~ **or intention** ob absichtlich oder aus Versehen. (b) (supervision) Aufsicht, Beaufsichtigung f.

over: ~**simplification** n (zu) grobe Vereinfachung; ~**simplify** vt grob or zu sehr vereinfachen, zu einfach darstellen; ~**size(d)** adj übergroß; objects also überdimensional; ~**size(d) families** zu kinderreiche Familien pl; ~**sleep** pret, ptp ~**slept** vi verschlafen; ~**sold** pret, ptp of ~**sell**; ~**spend** pret, ptp ~**spent** 1 vi zuviel ausgeben; **we've** ~**spent** wir haben £ 10 zuviel ausgegeben; 2 vt überschreiten; ~**spill** (Brit) 1 [ˈəʊvəˌspɪl] n Bevölkerungsüberschuß m; ~**spill town** Trabantenstadt f; 2 [ˌəʊvəˈspɪl] vi see ~**flow** 3 (a); ~**staffed** adj übersetzt; **this office is** ~**staffed** dieses Büro hat zuviel Personal; ~**staffing** n zuviel Personal; ~**staffing has never been a problem here** wir hatten hier nie das Problem von zuviel Personal; ~**state** vt facts, case übertreiben, übertrieben darstellen; ~**statement** n Übertreibung f, übertriebene Darstellung; ~**stay** vt see out-stay; ~**steer** 1 n Übersteuern nt; 2 vi übersteuern; ~**step** vt überschreiten; **to** ~**step the mark** zu weit gehen.

overstock [ˌəʊvəˈstɒk] 1 vt farm, pond zu hoch bestücken. the farm/pond is ~ed der Hof/der Teich hat einen zu großen Vieh-/Fischbestand; to ~ a shop in einem Geschäft das Lager überfüllen; the shop is ~ed der Laden hat zu große Bestände.
2 vi (shop) zu große (Lager)bestände haben, zuviel lagern; (farm) zu große (Vieh)bestände haben.

overstrain [ˌəʊvəˈstreɪn] vt horse, person überanstrengen, überfordern; metal überbelasten; resources, strength, theory überbeanspruchen. to ~ oneself sich übernehmen, sich überanstrengen; don't ~ yourself (iro) übernimm dich bloß nicht; to ~ one's heart sein Herz überlasten.

over: ~strung adj (a) person überspannt; (b) piano kreuzsaitig; ~subscribe vt (Fin) überzeichnen; the zoo outing was ~subscribed zu viele (Leute) hatten sich für den Ausflug in den Zoo angemeldet; ~supply 1 vt überbeliefern; 2 n Überangebot nt (of an +dat), Überversorgung f (of mit).

overt [əʊˈvɜːt] adj offen; hostility unverhohlen.

overtake [ˌəʊvəˈteɪk] pret **overtook** [ˌəʊvəˈtʊk], ptp **overtaken** [ˌəʊvəˈteɪkən] 1 vt (a) einholen; (pass) runner etc, (Brit) car überholen. (b) (take by surprise) storm, night) überraschen; (fate) ereilen (geh). ~n by fear von Furcht befallen; we were ~n by events, events have ~n us wir waren auf die Entwicklung der Dinge nicht gefaßt. 2 vi (Brit) überholen.

overtaking [ˌəʊvəˈteɪkɪŋ] n (Brit) Überholen nt.

over: ~tax vt (a) (fig) person, heart überlasten, überfordern; patience überfordern; to ~tax one's strength sich übernehmen; don't ~tax my patience stelle meine Geduld nicht auf die Probe; (b) (lit: tax too heavily) übermäßig besteuern; ~technical adj zu fachspezifisch; (regarding technology) zu technisch; ~-the-counter adj drugs nicht rezeptpflichtig; sale offen; ~throw (vb: pret ~threw, ptp ~thrown) 1 [ˌəʊvəˈθrəʊ] n (a) Sieg m (of über +acc); (being ~thrown) Niederlage f; (b) (Cricket) zu weiter Wurf; 2 [ˌəʊvəˈθrəʊ] vt (defeat) enemy besiegen; government, dictator, general stürzen, zu Fall bringen; plans umstoßen; country erobern.

overtime [ˈəʊvətaɪm] 1 n (a) Überstunden pl. I am on ~ or doing ~ ich mache Überstunden; he did four hours' ~ er hat vier (Stunden) Überstunden gemacht. (b) (US Sport) Verlängerung f. we had to play ~ es gab eine Verlängerung.
2 adv to work ~ Überstunden machen; his conscience was working ~ (fig inf) sein Gewissen ließ ihm keine Ruhe; my imagination was working ~ meine Phantasie lief auf Hochtouren (inf); his liver's been working ~ to keep up with all this alcohol (inf) seine Leber mußte ganz schön ranhalten (inf) or lief auf Hochtouren (inf), um all den Alkohol zu verkraften; we shall have to work ~ to regain the advantage we have lost (fig) wir müssen uns mächtig ranhalten, wenn wir den verlorenen Vorsprung wieder wettmachen wollen (inf).
3 [ˌəʊvəˈtaɪm] vt (Phot) photo überbelichten. the programme planners ~d the symphony die Programmgestalter hatten zuviel Zeit für die Symphonie eingeplant.
4 adj attr ~ ban Überstundenstopp m; ~ pay Überstundenlohn m; ~ rates Überstundentarif m.

overtired [ˌəʊvəˈtaɪəd] adj übermüdet.

overtly [əʊˈvɜːtlɪ] adv offen.

overtone [ˈəʊvətəʊn] n (a) (Mus) Oberton m. (b) (fig) Unterton m. unmistakable ~s of jealousy ein unverkennbarer Unterton von Eifersucht; political ~s politische Untertöne pl; what are the precise ~s of this speech/word? was genau ist der Unterton dieser Rede/was klingt bei diesem Wort alles mit?

over: ~took pret of ~take; ~top vt übertragen; ~train vti zuviel or zu hart trainieren; ~trick n (Cards) überzähliger Stich; ~trump vt übertrumpfen.

overture [ˈəʊvətjʊəʳ] n (a) (Mus) Ouvertüre f. (b) usu pl (approach) Annäherungsversuch m. to make ~s to sb Annäherungsversuche bei jdm machen; (to woman also) jdm Avancen machen; peace ~s Friedensannäherungen pl.

overturn [ˌəʊvəˈtɜːn] 1 vt (a) umkippen, umwerfen; (capsize) boat also zum Kentern bringen. the ship rocked violently ~ing chairs and tables das Schiff schwankte so heftig, daß Tische und Stühle umkippten.
(b) regime stürzen; philosophy, world view umstürzen.
2 vi (chair) umkippen; (boat also) kentern.
3 [ˈəʊvətɜːn] n (of government) Sturz, Umsturz m; (of world view etc) Umsturz m.

over: ~use 1 [ˌəʊvəˈjuːs] n übermäßiger or zu häufiger Gebrauch; 2 [ˌəʊvəˈjuːz] vt übermäßig oft or zu häufig gebrauchen; ~value vt goods zu hoch schätzen; object überbewerten; person zu hoch einschätzen, überbewerten; ~view n Überblick m (of über +acc).

overweening [ˌəʊvəˈwiːnɪŋ] adj überheblich, anmaßend; arrogance, pride, ambition maßlos.

overweight [ˈəʊvəweɪt] 1 adj thing zu schwer; person also übergewichtig. this box is 5 kilos ~ diese Schachtel hat 5 Kilo Übergewicht; luggage Gepäck mit Übergewicht; you're ~ Sie haben Übergewicht. 2 n Übergewicht nt.

overwhelm [ˌəʊvəˈwelm] vt (a) (overpower: strong feelings) überwältigen. he was ~ed when they gave him the present er war zutiefst gerührt, als sie ihm das Geschenk gaben; Venice ~ed me ich fand Venedig überwältigend; you ~ me! (iro) da bin ich aber sprachlos!
(b) (ruin, crush) enemy überwältigen; country besiegen; (Sport) defence überrennen.
(c) (submerge: water) überschwemmen, überfluten; (earth, lava) verschütten, begraben.
(d) (fig) (with favours, praise) überschütten, überhäufen; (with questions) bestürmen; (with work) überhäufen.

overwhelming [ˌəʊvəˈwelmɪŋ] adj überwältigend; desire, power unwiderstehlich; misfortune erschütternd.

overwhelmingly [ˌəʊvəˈwelmɪŋlɪ] adv see adj. he was quite ~ friendly er war umwerfend freundlich; they voted ~ for it sie haben mit überwältigender Mehrheit dafür gestimmt.

over: ~wind pret, ptp ~wound vt watch überdrehen; ~work 1 n Überarbeitung, Arbeitsüberlastung f; he is ill from ~work er hat sich krank gearbeitet; 2 vt horse etc überanstrengen; person überanstrengen; image, idea, theme etc überstrapazieren; to ~work oneself sich überarbeiten; 3 vi sich überarbeiten; ~written adj (too flowery etc) zu blumig (geschrieben); (too strong) zu stark formuliert; (too rhetorical) zu schwülstig.

overwrought [ˌəʊvəˈrɔːt] adj (a) person überreizt. (b) (too elaborate) style überfeinert, verkünstelt.

overzealous [ˌəʊvəˈzeləs] adj übereifrig.

Ovid [ˈɒvɪd] n Ovid m.

oviduct [ˈəʊvɪdʌkt] n Eileiter m.

oviform [ˈəʊvɪfɔːm] adj (form) eiförmig.

oviparous [əʊˈvɪpərəs] adj eierlegend, ovipar (spec).

ovipositor [ˌəʊvɪˈpɒzɪtəʳ] n Legebohrer, Legestachel m.

ovoid [ˈəʊvɔɪd] adj eiförmig, ovoid.

ovulation [ˌɒvjʊˈleɪʃən] n Eisprung m, Ovulation f.

ovule [ˈɒvjuːl] n (Zool) Ovulum, Ei nt; (Bot) Samenanlage f.

ovum [ˈəʊvəm] n, pl **ova** Eizelle f, Ovum nt.

owe [əʊ] 1 vt (a) money schulden, schuldig sein (sb sth, sth to sb jdm etw). can I ~ you the rest? kann ich dir den Rest schuldig bleiben?; I surely ~ you more than that ich schulde dir doch sicher mehr; I ~ him a meal ich bin ihm noch ein Essen schuldig, ich schulde ihm noch ein Essen; how much do I ~ you? (in shop etc) was bin ich schuldig?
(b) reverence, obedience, loyalty schulden, schuldig sein (to sb jdm); allegiance schulden (to sb jdm).
(c) (be under an obligation for) verdanken (sth to sb jdm etw). I ~ my life to him ich verdanke ihm mein Leben; to what do I ~ the honour of your visit? (iro) und was verschafft mir die Ehre Ihres Besuches?; we ~ it to them that we are alive today wir haben es ihnen zu verdanken, daß wir heute noch leben; he ~s it to himself to make a success of it er ist es sich (dat) (selber) schuldig, daraus einen Erfolg zu machen; you ~ it to yourself to keep fit du bist es dir schuldig, fit zu bleiben; he ~s his failure to himself er hat sich sein Versagen selbst zuzuschreiben; we ~ nothing to him, we ~ him nothing wir sind ihm (gar) nichts schuldig; you ~ it to her to tell the truth Sie sind es ihr schuldig, die Wahrheit zu sagen; I think you ~ me an explanation ich glaube, du bist mir eine Erklärung schuldig.
2 vi to ~ sb for sth jdm Geld für etw schulden; can I ~ you for the rest? kann ich Ihnen den Rest schuldig bleiben?; I still ~ him for the meal ich muß ihm das Essen noch bezahlen.

owing [ˈəʊɪŋ] 1 adj unbezahlt. the amount ~ on the house die Schulden, die auf dem Haus liegen; how much is still ~? wieviel steht noch aus?; a lot of money is ~ to me man schuldet mir viel Geld; the money still ~ to us (Comm) Außenstände pl; to pay what is ~ den ausstehenden Betrag bezahlen.
2 prep ~ to wegen (+gen or (inf) +dat), infolge (+gen); ~ to the circumstances umständehalber; ~ to his being foreign weil er Ausländer ist/war; and it's all ~ to him that we succeeded und unser Erfolg ist ihm allein zuzuschreiben.

owl [aʊl] n Eule f. wise ol ~ weise Eule.

owlish [ˈaʊlɪʃ] adj the glasses gave him a somewhat ~ look die Brille ließ ihn ein wenig eulenhaft erscheinen; his ~ face sein Eulengesicht nt; to look ~ wie eine Eule aussehen.

owlishly [ˈaʊlɪʃlɪ] adv look, stare wie eine Eule.

own¹ [əʊn] 1 vt (a) (possess) besitzen, haben. who ~s that? wem gehört das?; we used to rent the flat, now we ~ it wir hatten die Wohnung vorher gemietet, jetzt gehört sie uns; he looks as if he ~s the place er sieht so aus, als wäre er hier zu Hause; the tourists behaved as if they ~ed the hotel die Touristen benahmen sich, als gehöre das Hotel ihnen; you don't ~ me, she said ich bin nicht dein Privateigentum, sagte sie; if you're going to behave like that, I don't ~ you (inf) wenn du dich so benimmst, gehörst du nicht zu mir.
(b) (admit) zugeben, zugestehen; (recognize) anerkennen. he ~ed that the claim was reasonable er erkannte die Forderung als gerechtfertigt an, er gab zu, daß die Forderung gerechtfertigt war; he ~ed himself defeated er gab sich geschlagen; I ~ that I was wrong ich gestehe zu or gebe zu, daß ich unrecht hatte; to ~ a child (Jur) ein Kind (als seines) anerkennen.
2 vi to ~ to sth etw anerkennen; to ~ to having done it es gestand, es getan zu haben; he didn't ~ to having done it er hat nicht zugegeben, daß er es getan hat.

♦**own up** vi es zugeben. come on, ~ ~ (nun) gib schon zu; to ~ ~ to sth etw zugeben; he ~ed ~ to stealing the money er gab zu or er gestand, das Geld gestohlen zu haben.

own² 1 adj attr eigen. his ~ car sein eigenes Auto; one's ~ car ein eigenes Auto; he's his ~ man er geht seinen eigenen Weg; he likes beauty for its ~ sake er liebt Schönheit um ihrer selbst willen; he does (all) his ~ cooking er kocht für sich selbst; thank you, I'm quite capable of finding my ~ way out danke, ich finde sehr gut alleine hinaus; my ~ one is smaller meine(r, s) ist kleiner; my ~ one mein Einziger, meine Einzige.
2 pron (a) that's my ~ das ist mein eigenes; those are my ~ die gehören mir; my ~ is bigger meine(r, s) ist größer; my time is my ~ ich kann mit meiner Zeit machen, was ich will; I can scarcely call my time my ~ ich kann kaum sagen, daß ich über meine Zeit frei verfügen kann; his ideas were his ~ die Ideen stammten von ihm selbst; I'd like a little house to call my ~ ich würde gern ein kleines Häuschen mein eigen nennen; a house of one's ~ ein eigenes Haus; I have money of my ~ ich habe selbst Geld; it has a beauty all its ~ or of its ~ es hat eine ganz eigene or eigenartige Schönheit; for reasons of his ~ aus irgendwelchen Gründen; he gave me one of his ~ er gab mir eins von seinen (eigenen).
(b) (in phrases) can I have it for my (very) ~? darf ich das

ganz für mich allein behalten?; **to get one's ~ back (on sb)** es jdm heimzahlen; **he was determined to get his ~ back** er war entschlossen, sich zu revanchieren *or* es ihnen heimzuzahlen; **(all) on one's ~** (ganz) allein; *(without help also)* selbst; **on its ~** von selbst, von allein; **if I can get him on his ~** wenn ich ihn allein erwische.

owner ['əʊnəʳ] *n* Besitzer(in *f*), Eigentümer(in *f*) *m*; *(of shop, factory, firm etc)* Inhaber(in *f*) *m*; *(of house, car etc also)* Eigner *m (form)*; *(of dogs, car, slaves)* Halter *m*. **who's the ~ of this umbrella?** wem gehört dieser Schirm?; **at ~'s risk** auf eigene Gefahr.

owner: **~-driver** *n Fahrzeughalter, der sein eigenes Auto fährt;* **~-editor** *n* Redakteur *m* im eigenen Hause; **~-less** *adj* herrenlos; **~-occupied** *adj house* vom Besitzer bewohnt; **~-occupier** *n* Bewohner *m* im eigenen Haus.

ownership ['əʊnəʃɪp] *n* Besitz *m*. **to establish the ~ of sth** den Besitzer einer Sache *(gen)* feststellen; **there are doubts as to the ~ of the property** es ist nicht klar, wer der Eigentümer dieses Grundstücks ist; **under his ~ the business flourished** das Geschäft blühte in der Zeit, als es sich in seinem Besitz befand; **under new ~** unter neuer Leitung; **since we've been under new ~** seit der Eigentümer gewechselt hat; **this certifies your ~ of ...** das weist Sie als Eigentümer von ... aus; **responsibilities entailed by the ~ of property** Verantwortungen, die der Besitz von Grundstücken mit sich bringt.

ownsome ['əʊnsəm] *n*: **on one's ~** *(inf)* mutterseelenallein.

owt [aʊt] *pron (N Engl) see* **anything 1.**

ox [ɒks] *n, pl* **-en** Ochse *m*. **as strong as an ~** bärenstark.

oxalic [ɒk'sælɪk] *adj acid* Oxal-.

ox-bow lake ['ɒksbəʊ'leɪk] *n* toter Flußarm.

Oxbridge ['ɒksbrɪdʒ] **1** *n* Oxford und/oder Cambridge. **2** *adj accent* wie in Oxford oder Cambridge; *people* der Universität *(gen)* Oxford oder Cambridge.

ox cart *n* Ochsenkarren *m*.

oxen ['ɒksən] *pl of* **ox.**

oxford ['ɒksfəd] *n see* **Oxford shoe.**

Oxford: **~ bags** *npl* sehr weite Hosen *pl*; **~ blue** *n Mitglied eines Oxforder Studentensportclubs, das für die Universität angetreten ist;* **~ English** *n* Oxford-Englisch *nt*; **~ shoe** *n* geschnürter Halbschuh.

oxidation [ˌɒksɪ'deɪʃən] *n (Chem)* Oxydation, Oxidation *f*.

oxide ['ɒksaɪd] *n (Chem)* Oxyd, Oxid *nt*.

oxidize ['ɒksɪdaɪz] *vti* oxydieren, oxidieren.

oxlip ['ɒkslɪp] *n (Bot)* hohe *or* weiße Schlüsselblume.

Oxon ['ɒksən] *abbr of* **Oxfordshire; Oxoniensis.**

Oxonian [ɒk'səʊnɪən] **1** *n* Oxfordstudent(in *f*) *m*. **2** *adj* der Oxforder Universität angehörend.

ox: **~tail** *n* Ochsenschwanz *m*; **~tail soup** *n* Ochsenschwanzsuppe *f*.

oxyacetylene [ˌɒksɪə'setɪliːn] *adj* Azetylensauerstoff-. **~ burner** *or* **lamp** *or* **torch** Schweißbrenner *m*; **~ welding** Autogenschweißen *nt*.

oxygen ['ɒksɪdʒən] *n* Sauerstoff *m*.

oxygenate [ɒk'sɪdʒəneɪt] *vt* oxygenieren, mit Sauerstoff behandeln *or* anreichern.

oxygenation [ˌɒksɪdʒə'neɪʃən] *n* Oxygenierung *f*, Anreicherung *or* Behandlung *f* mit Sauerstoff.

oxygen: **~ bottle, ~ cylinder** *n* Sauerstoffflasche *f*; **~ mask** *n* Sauerstoff- *or* Atemmaske *f*; **~ tank** *n* Sauerstoffbehälter *m*; **~ tent** *n* Sauerstoffzelt *nt*.

oxymoron [ˌɒksɪ'mɔːrɒn] *n* Oxymoron *nt*.

oyez ['əʊjez] *interj (old)* Achtung, Achtung.

oyster ['ɔɪstəʳ] *n* Auster *f*. **the world's his ~** die Welt steht ihm offen *or* liegt ihm zu Füßen; **to shut up** *or* **clam up like an ~** kein Wort mehr sagen.

oyster: **~ bank, ~ bed** *n* Austernbank *f*; **~-breeding** *n* Austernzucht *f*; **~catcher** *n (Orn)* Austernfischer *m*; **~ farm** *n* Austernpark *m*; **~ shell** *n* Austernschale *f*.

oz *abbr of* **ounce(s).**

ozone ['əʊzəʊn] *n* Ozon *nt*. **~ layer** Ozonschicht *f*.

P

P, p [piː] *n* P, p *nt*. **to mind one's P's and Q's** *(inf)* sich anständig benehmen.

p *abbr of* **(a) page** S. **(b) penny, pence.**

PA *abbr of* **(a) Press Association. (b) personal assistant. (c) public address (system).**

p.a. *abbr of* **per annum.**

pa [pɑː] *n (inf)* Papa, Papi, Vati *m (all inf)*.

pace¹ ['peɪsɪ] *prep* ohne *(dat)* nahetreten zu wollen.

pace² [peɪs] **1** *n* **(a)** *(step)* Schritt *m*; *(lifting both legs on same side)* Paßgang *m*. **twelve ~s off** zwölf Schritt(e) entfernt; **to put a horse through its ~s** ein Pferd alle Gangarten machen lassen; **to put sb/a new car through his/its ~s** *(fig)* jdn/ein neues Auto auf Herz und Nieren prüfen.

(b) *(speed)* Tempo *nt*. **the more leisurely ~ of life in those days** das geruhsamere Leben damals; **those who fall victim to the ~ of modern city life** wer der Hektik des modernen Großstadtlebens zum Opfer fällt; **at a good** *or* **smart ~** recht schnell; **at an incredible ~** unglaublich schnell, mit *or* in unglaublichem Tempo; **at a slow ~** langsam; **we kept up a good ~ with the work** wir kamen mit der Arbeit gut voran; **how long will he keep this ~ up?** wie lange wird er das Tempo durchhalten?; **the present ~ of development** die momentane Entwicklungsrate; **to keep ~** Schritt halten; *(in discussing)* mitkommen; **I can't keep ~ with events** ich komme mit den Ereignissen nicht mehr mit; **to make** *or* **set the ~** das Tempo angeben; **to quicken one's ~** seinen Schritt beschleunigen; *(working)* sein Tempo beschleunigen; **I'm getting old, I can't stand the ~ any more** *(inf)* ich werde alt, ich kann nicht mehr mithalten; **the change of ~ between the third and fourth acts** der Tempowechsel zwischen dem dritten und vierten Akt; **~maker** *(in race, business, Med)* Schrittmacher *m*.

2 *vt* **(a)** *(measure)* floor, room mit Schritten ausmessen.

(b) *(in anxiety etc)* auf und ab gehen *or* schreiten in *(+dat)*.

(c) *competitor* das Tempo angeben *(+dat)*.

(d) *horse* im Paßgang gehen lassen.

3 *vi* **(a)** **to ~ around** hin und her laufen; **to ~ up and down** auf und ab gehen *or* schreiten.

(b) *(horse)* im Paßgang gehen.

♦ **pace off** *or* **out** *vt sep distance* ausschreiten, mit Schritten ausmessen *or* abmessen.

pacer ['peɪsəʳ], **pace-setter** ['peɪssetəʳ] *n (Sport)* Schrittmacher *m*.

pachyderm ['pækɪdɜːm] *n* Dickhäuter *m*.

Pacific [pə'sɪfɪk] *n* **the ~ (Ocean)** der Pazifische *or* Stille Ozean, der Pazifik; **~ time** Pazifische Zeit; **the ~ islands** die Pazifischen Inseln; **a ~ island** eine Insel im Pazifik.

pacific [pə'sɪfɪk] *adj people, nation* friedliebend, friedfertig.

pacifically [pə'sɪfɪkəlɪ] *adv* live in Frieden.

pacification [ˌpæsɪfɪ'keɪʃən] *n* Versöhnung *f*; *(of area)* Befriedung *f*. **attempts at ~** Friedensbemühungen *pl*.

pacifier ['pæsɪfaɪəʳ] *n* **(a)** *(peacemaker)* Friedensstifter(in *f*) *m*. **(b)** *(US: dummy)* Schnuller *m*.

pacifism ['pæsɪfɪzəm] *n* Pazifismus *m*.

pacifist ['pæsɪfɪst] **1** *adj* pazifistisch. **2** *n* Pazifist(in *f*) *m*.

pacify ['pæsɪfaɪ] *vt baby* beruhigen; *angry person also* besänftigen, beschwichtigen; *warring countries* Frieden herbeiführen in (+*dat*), miteinander aussöhnen; *area* befrieden. **just to ~ the unions** nur damit die Gewerkschaften stillhalten.

pack [pæk] **1** *n* **(a)** *(bundle)* Bündel *nt*; *(on animal)* Last *f*; *(rucksack)* Rucksack *m*; *(Mil)* Gepäck *nt no pl*, Tornister *m (dated)*.

(b) *(packet)* *(for cereal, washing powder, frozen food)* Paket *nt*; *(US: of cigarettes)* Packung, Schachtel *f*. **towels/books sold in ~s of six** Handtücher/Bücher im Sechserpack.

(c) *(Hunt)* Meute *f*.

(d) *(of wolves, boy scouts)* Rudel *nt*; *(of submarines)* Gruppe *f*.

(e) *(pej: group)* Horde, Meute *f*. **a ~ of thieves** eine Diebesbande; **he told us a ~ of lies** er tischte uns einen Sack voll Lügen auf; **it's all a ~ of lies** es ist alles erlogen; **you ~ of louts!** ihr Rabauken!

(f) *(of cards)* (Karten)spiel *nt*. **52 cards make a ~** ein Blatt *nt* besteht aus 52 Karten.

(g) *(Rugby)* Stürmer *pl*.

(h) *(Med, cosmetic)* Packung *f*.

(i) *(of ice)* Scholle *f*.

2 *vt* **(a)** *crate, container etc* vollpacken; *fish, meat in tin etc* abpacken. **~ed in dozens** im Dutzend abgepackt.

(b) *case, trunk* packen; *things in case, clothes etc* einpacken.

(c) *(wrap, put into parcel)* einpacken. **it comes ~ed in polythene** es ist in Cellophan verpackt.

(d) *(crowd, cram)* packen; *container also* vollstopfen; *articles also* stopfen, pfropfen. **the box was ~ed full of explosives** die Kiste war voll mit Sprengstoff; **the crowds that ~ed the stadium** die Menschenmassen, die sich im Stadium drängten; **the comedy was playing to ~ed houses** die Komödie lief vor ausverkauften Häusern; **to be ~ed** *(full)* gerammelt voll sein *(inf)*; **all this information is ~ed into one chapter** all diese Informationen sind in einem Kapitel zusammengedrängt; **a holiday ~ed with excitement** Ferien voller aufregender Erlebnisse; **a speech ~ed with jokes** eine mit Witzen gespickte Rede; **a thrill-~ed film** ein packender Film; **the coast is ~ed with tourists** an der Küste wimmelt es von Touristen.

(e) *(make firm)* soil etc festdrücken.

(f) *jury* mit den eigenen Leuten besetzen.

(g) *(US inf: carry)* gun tragen, dabei haben. **to ~ one's lunch** sich *(dat)* sein Mittagessen mitnehmen.

(h) *(inf)* **to ~ a (heavy) punch** kräftig zuschlagen; **he ~s a nasty left** er hat *or* schlägt eine ganz gemeine Linke *(inf)*.

(i) *leak, pipe* (zu)stopfen.

3 *vi* **(a)** *(items)* passen; *(person)* packen. **that won't all ~ into one suitcase** das paßt *or* geht nicht alles in einen Koffer; **it ~s** **(in)** nicely es läßt sich gut verpacken; **the boxes are designed to ~ into this container** die Kästen sind so gemacht, daß sie in diesen Behälter hineingehen; **I'm still ~ing** ich bin noch beim Packen.

(b) *(crowd)* **the crowds ~ed into the stadium** die Menge drängte sich in das Stadion; **we can't all ~ into one Mini** wir können uns nicht alle in einen Mini zwängen; **they ~ed round the president** sie belagerten *or* umringten den Präsidenten.

(c) *(become firm)* fest werden. **the snow had ~ed round the wheels** an den Rädern klebte eine feste Schneeschicht.

(d) *(inf)* **to send sb ~ing** jdn kurz abfertigen; **what would you do with a drunken husband like mine? — I'd send him ~ing** was würden Sie mit einem Trunkenbold wie meinem Mann machen? — ich würde ihn abservieren *(inf)*; **she sent him ~ing without any supper** sie setzte ihn ohne Abendessen vor die Tür.

♦**pack away 1** *vt sep* **(a)** *clothes, boxes etc* wegpacken. **~ your toys** **~ before you go out** räum deine Spielsachen weg, bevor du rausgehst; **I've ~ed all your books ~** in the attic ich habe alle deine Bücher auf den Boden geräumt; **he ~ed the deckchairs ~ for the winter** er räumte die Liegestühle für den Winter weg.

(b) *(inf)* **food he can really ~ it ~** er kann ganz schön was verdrücken *(inf)* *or* verputzen *(inf)*.

2 *vi* **the bed ~s ~ into a wall-cupboard** man kann das Bett in einem Wandschrank verschwinden lassen.

♦**pack down** *vi (Rugby)* eine Gedränge *nt* bilden.

♦**pack in 1** *vt sep* **(a)** *clothes etc* einpacken.

(b) *people* hineinpferchen in (+*acc*). **we can't ~ any more ~ here** *(people)* hier geht *or* paßt keiner mehr rein; *(things)* hier geht *or* paßt nichts mehr rein; **can you ~ one more ~ your car?** geht *or* paßt noch einer bei dir in den Wagen?

(c) *(play, actor etc)* in Scharen anziehen. **this film is really ~ing them ~** *(inf)* dieser Film zieht die Leute in Scharen an.

(d) *(Brit inf)* *(give up)* job hinschmeißen *(inf)*; *girlfriend* sausen lassen *(inf)*; *(stop)* noise aufhören mit; *work, activity* Schluß *or* Feierabend *(inf)* machen mit. **a footballer should know when it's time to ~ it ~** ein Fußballspieler sollte wissen, wann es Zeit ist, Schluß zu machen *or* aufzuhören; **~ it ~!** hör auf!, laß es gut sein!; *(job)* schmeiß die Sache hin!

2 *vi* **(a)** *(crowd in)* sich hineindrängen. **we all ~ed ~ to his car** wir zwängten uns alle in sein Auto.

(b) *(inf: stop working)* *(engine)* seinen Geist aufgeben *(hum)*; *(person)* zusammenpacken, Feierabend machen *(inf)*.

♦**pack off** *vt sep* **she ~ed them ~ to bed/school** sie verfrachtete sie ins Bett/schickte sie in die Schule.

♦**pack out** *vt sep usu pass* **to be ~ed ~** *(hall, theatre etc)* gerammelt voll sein *(inf)*, überfüllt sein.

♦**pack up 1** *vt sep* clothes etc zusammenpacken. **2** *vi* **(a)** *(prepare luggage)* packen. **he just ~ed ~ and left** er packte seine Sachen und ging. **(b)** *(inf: stop working)* *(engine)* seinen Geist aufgeben *(hum)*; *(person)* Feierabend machen *(inf)*. **(c)** **the tent ~s ~ easily** das Zelt läßt sich gut verpacken.

package ['pækɪdʒ] **1** *n* **(a)** *(parcel, esp US: packet)* Paket *nt*; *(of cardboard)* Schachtel *f*. **(b)** *(esp Comm: group, set)* Paket, Bündel *nt*. **2** *vt* **(a)** verpacken. **(b)** *(in order to enhance sales)* präsentieren.

package: **~ deal** *n* Pauschalangebot *nt*; **~ holiday** *n* Pauschalreise *f*; **~ store** *n* *(US)* Spirituosenhandlung *f*; **~ tour** *n* see **~ holiday**.

packaging ['pækɪdʒɪŋ] *n see* **vt (a)** Verpackung *f*. **this is where they do the ~** hier werden die Sachen verpackt. **(b)** *(Präsentation f.* the public don't buy the product, they buy the ~ die Leute kaufen nicht das Produkt, sondern die Verpackung.

pack: **~ animal** *n* Packtier, Lasttier *nt*; **~ drill** *n* Strafexerzieren *nt* in gefechtsmäßiger Ausrüstung.

packer ['pækə^r] *n* Packer(in *f*) *m*. **he's a very untidy ~** er packt sehr unordentlich.

packet ['pækɪt] *n* **(a)** Paket *nt*; *(of cigarettes)* Päckchen *nt*, Schachtel, Packung *f*; *(small box)* Schachtel *f*. **(b)** *(Naut)* Paketboot *nt*. **(c)** *(Brit sl: lot of money)* **to make a ~** ein Schweinegeld *nt* verdienen *(sl)*; **that must have cost a ~** das muß ein Heidengeld *nt* gekostet haben *(inf)*.

packet boat *n* Paketboot *nt*.

pack: **~horse** *n* Packpferd *nt*; **I'm not your ~horse!** ich bin nicht dein Packesel!; **~ice** *n* Packeis *nt*.

packing ['pækɪŋ] *n* **(a)** *(act)* *(in suitcases)* Packen *nt*; *(in factories etc)* Verpackung *f*. **to do one's ~** packen. **(b)** *(material)* Verpackung *f*; *(for leak)* Dichtung *f*.

packing: **~ case** *n* Kiste *f*; **~ house**, **~ plant** *n (US)* Abpackbetrieb *m*.

pack: **~ rat** *n* Buschschwanzratte *f*; **~sack** *n (US)* Rucksack *m*; **~-saddle** *n* Packsattel *m*; **~-thread** *n* Zwirn *m*; **~ train** *n* Tragtierkolonne *f*.

pact [pækt] *n* Pakt *m*. **to make a ~ with sb** mit jdm einen Pakt schließen.

pad¹ [pæd] *vi* **to ~ about** umhertapsen; **to ~ along** entlangtrotten; **the panther ~ded up and down der Panther** trottete auf und ab; **the tiger ~ded off into the bushes** der Tiger trottete ins Gebüsch.

pad² **1** *n* **(a)** *(stuffing)* *(for comfort etc)* Polster *nt*; *(for protection)* Schützer *m*; *(in bra)* Einlage *f*; *(brake ~ etc)* Belag *m*. **(b)** *(of paper)* Block *m*; *(of blotting paper)* Schreibunterlage *f*. **(c)** *(for inking)* Stempelkissen *nt*.

(d) *(of animal's foot)* Ballen *m*.

(e) *(launching ~)* (Abschuß)rampe *f*.

(f) *(inf: room, home)* Bude *f (inf)*.

2 *vt shoulders etc* polstern.

♦**pad out** *vt sep* **(a)** *shoulders* polstern. **(b)** *article, essay etc* auffüllen; *speech* ausdehnen, strecken.

padded ['pædɪd] *adj shoulders, armour, bra* wattiert; *dashboard* gepolstert. **~ cell** Gummizelle *f*.

padding ['pædɪŋ] *n* **(a)** *(material)* Polsterung *f*. **(b)** *(fig: in essay etc)* Füllwerk *nt*, Füllsel *pl*.

paddle ['pædl] **1** *n* **(a)** *(oar)* Paddel *nt*.

(b) *(blade of wheel)* Schaufel *f*; *(wheel)* Schaufelrad *nt*.

(c) *(for mixing)* Rührschaufel *f*.

(d) **Grandpa still enjoys a ~** Opa planscht noch gern durchs Wasser; **to go for a ~**, **to have a ~** durchs Wasser waten.

2 *vt* **(a)** *boat* paddeln.

(b) **to ~ one's feet in the water** mit den Füßen im Wasser planschen; **~ your feet and you'll stay afloat** du mußt mit den Füßen paddeln, dann gehst du nicht unter.

(c) *(US: spank)* verhauen, versohlen *(inf)*.

3 *vi* **(a)** *(in boat)* paddeln.

(b) *(with feet, swimming)* paddeln.

(c) *(walk in shallow water)* waten. **he ~d around for half an hour** er watete eine halbe Stunde im Wasser herum.

paddle: **~ boat** *n* Raddampfer *m*; *(small, on pond)* Paddelboot *nt*; **~ box** *n* Radkasten *m*; **~ steamer** *n* Raddampfer *m*; **~ wheel** *n* Schaufelrad *nt*.

paddling pool ['pædlɪŋ,pu:l] *n* Planschbecken *nt*.

paddock ['pædək] *n* *(field)* Koppel *f*; *(of racecourse)* Sattelplatz *m*; *(motor racing)* Fahrerlager *nt*.

Paddy ['pædɪ] *n (inf)* Paddy, Spitzname der Iren.

paddy¹ ['pædɪ] *n* **(a)** *(rice)* ungeschälter Reis. **(b)** *(also ~ field)* Reisfeld *nt*.

paddy² *n* *(Brit inf)* Koller *m (inf)*. **to get into a ~** einen Koller kriegen *(inf)*; **to be in a ~** einen Koller haben *(inf)*.

paddy wagon *n (US inf)* grüne Minna *(inf)*.

paddywhack ['pædɪwæk] *n (inf)* **(a)** *see* **paddy²**. **(b)** *(spank)* Klaps *m*.

padlock ['pædlɒk] **1** *n* Vorhängeschloß *nt*. **2** *vt* (mit einem Vorhängeschloß) verschließen.

padre ['pɑ:drɪ] *n* *(Mil)* Feldkaplan, Feldgeistliche(r) *m*. **yes, ~ ja**, Herr Kaplan.

paean ['pi:ən] *n* Lobrede *f*. **~ of praise** *(Rel)* Lobpreisung *f*; **he addressed a ~ of praise to the retiring vice-chancellor** er hielt eine Lobrede auf den scheidenden Rektor.

paediatric, *(US)* **pediatric** [,pi:dɪ'ætrɪk] *adj* Kinder-, pädiatrisch *(spec)*.

paediatrician, *(US)* **pediatrician** [,pi:dɪə'trɪʃən] *n* Kinderarzt *m*/-ärztin *f*, Pädiater *m (spec)*.

paediatrics, *(US)* **pediatrics** [,pi:dɪ'ætrɪks] *n* Kinderheilkunde, Pädiatrie *(spec) f*.

pagan ['peɪgən] **1** *adj* heidnisch. **2** *n* Heide *m*, Heidin *f*.

paganism ['peɪgənɪzəm] *n* Heidentum *nt*.

page¹ [peɪdʒ] **1** *n* *(also ~-boy)* Page *m*; *(of knight)* Page, Edelknabe *m*. **2** *vt* **to ~ sb** jdn ausrufen lassen; **paging Mr Cousin** Herr Cousin, bitte!

page² **1** *n* **(a)** Seite *f*. **on ~ 14** auf Seite 14; **write on both sides of the ~** beschreiben Sie beide Seiten.

(b) **a glorious ~ of English history** ein Ruhmesblatt *nt* in der Geschichte Englands; **in the ~s of history** in den Annalen der Geschichte; **to go down in the ~s of history** in die Geschichte *or* die Annalen der Geschichte eingehen.

2 *vt* *(Typ)* paginieren, mit Seitenzahlen versehen.

pageant ['pædʒənt] *n* *(show)* historische Aufführung, Historienspiel *nt*. **Christmas ~** Weihnachtsspiel *nt*; *(procession)* Festzug *m*; **a ~ of Elizabethan times** *(series of theatrical tableaux etc)* eine historische Darstellung der Elisabethanischen Zeitalters; *(procession)* ein Festzug *m or* festlicher Umzug im Stil des Elisabethanischen Zeitalters; **the whole ~ of life** die breite Fülle des Lebens.

pageantry ['pædʒəntrɪ] *n* Prunk *m*, Gepränge *nt*. **all the ~ of history** die ganze Pracht der Geschichte; **the coronation was celebrated with great ~** die Krönung wurde sehr prunkvoll *or* mit großem Prunk *or* Gepränge gefeiert.

page: **~-boy** *n* **(a)** Page *m*; **(b)** *(hairstyle)* Pagenkopf *m*; **~ make-up** *n (Typ)* Umbruch *m*; **~ number** *n* Seitenzahl *f*; **~ proof** *n* Korrekturfahne *f*.

paginate ['pædʒɪneɪt] *vt* paginieren.

pagination [,pædʒɪ'neɪʃən] *n* Paginierung *f*.

pagoda [pə'gəʊdə] *n* Pagode *f*.

pah [pɑ:] *interj* pah, bah.

paid [peɪd] **1** *pret*, *ptp of* **pay**.

2 *adj official, work* bezahlt. **to put ~ to sth** etw zunichte machen; **that's put ~ to my holiday** damit ist mein Urlaub geplatzt *or* gestorben *(inf)*; **that's put ~ to him** damit ist für ihn der Ofen aus *(inf)*, das war's dann wohl für ihn *(inf)*.

paid-up ['peɪdʌp] *adj share* eingezahlt. **a ~ membership of 500** 500 zahlende Mitglieder; **fully ~ member** Mitglied ohne Beitragsrückstände; **is he fully ~?** hat er alle Beiträge bezahlt?

pail [peɪl] *n* Eimer *m*; *(child's)* Eimerchen *nt*.

pailful ['peɪlful] *n* Eimer(voll) *m*.

paillasse ['pælɪæs] *n* Strohsack *m*.

pain [peɪn] **1** *n* **(a)** **~** Schmerz *m*. **is the ~ still there?** hast du noch Schmerzen?; **where is the ~ exactly?** wo tut es denn genau weh?; **this will help the ~** das ist gut gegen die Schmerzen; **is ~ to be regarded as a punishment?** ist Schmerz *m* als Strafe aufzufassen?; **to be in ~** Schmerzen haben; **you can't just leave him in ~** du kannst ihn nicht einfach leiden lassen; **he screamed in ~** er schrie vor Schmerzen; **do insects feel ~?** können Insekten Schmerz empfinden?; **a sharp ~** ein stechender Schmerz; **cucumber gives me a ~ in the stomach**

von Gurken bekomme ich Magenschmerzen *pl*; **my ankle has been giving** *or* **causing me a lot of** ~ mein Knöchel tut mir sehr weh; **I have a** ~ **in my leg** mein Bein tut mir weh, ich habe Schmerzen im Bein; **to put sb out of his** ~ jdn von seinen Schmerzen erlösen.

(b) *(mental)* Qualen *pl.* **the** ~ **of parting** der Abschiedsschmerz; **Werther: a soul in** ~ Werther: eine gequälte Seele; **being so totally ignored like that was a source of great** ~ **to her** so vollkommen ignoriert zu werden, war für sie sehr schmerzlich; **he suffered great mental** ~ er litt Seelenqualen; **the decision caused me a lot of** ~ die Entscheidung war sehr schmerzlich für mich; **a look of** ~ **came over his face** sein Gesicht nahm einen schmerzlichen Ausdruck an.

(c) ~s *pl (efforts)* Mühe *f*; **to be at (great)** ~s **to do sth** sich *(dat)* **(große)** Mühe geben, etw zu tun; **to take** ~s **over sth/to do sth** sich *(dat)* Mühe mit etw geben/sich *(dat)* Mühe geben, etw zu tun; **great** ~s **have been taken to ...** besondere Mühe wurde darauf verwendet ...; **she takes great** ~s **over her appearance** sie verwendet sehr viel Sorgfalt auf ihr Äußeres; **all he got for his** ~s **was a curt refusal** zum Dank für seine Mühe wurde er schroff abgewiesen; **see what you get for your** ~s! das hast du nun für deine Mühe!

(d) *(penalty)* **on** ~ **of death** bei Todesstrafe, bei Strafe des Todes *(old)*, unter Androhung der Todesstrafe; **with all the** ~s **and penalties of fame** mit allen Schattenseiten des Ruhmes.

(e) *(inf: also* ~ **in the neck** *or* **arse** *sl)* **to be a (real)** ~ einem auf den Wecker *(inf)* or Geist *(inf)* gehen; **this job is getting to be a** ~ dieser Job geht mir langsam auf den Wecker *(inf)*.

2 *vt* **(a)** *(mentally)* schmerzen. **it** ~s **me to see their ignorance** ihre Unwissenheit tut schon weh; **his behaviour** ~ed **his parents** mit seinem Benehmen bereitete er seinen Eltern *(dat)* großen Kummer; **it** ~s **me to have to tell you this but ...** es schmerzt mich, Ihnen dies mitteilen zu müssen, aber ...

(b) *(rare: physically)* **his arm was still** ~ing **him** sein Arm schmerzte noch immer.

pained [peɪnd] *adj expression, voice* schmerzerfüllt.

painful ['peɪnfʊl] *adj* **(a)** *(physically)* schmerzhaft. **is it** ~? tut es weh?; **it's** ~ **to the touch** es tut weh, wenn man es berührt; **my arm was becoming** ~ mein Arm fing an zu schmerzen.

(b) *(unpleasant) experience, memory* unangenehm. **it is my** ~ **duty to tell you that ...** ich habe die traurige Pflicht, Ihnen mitteilen zu müssen, daß ...; ~ **to behold** ein qualvoller Anblick.

(c) *(inf: terrible)* peinlich. ~, **isn't it?** das tut weh, was?; **I went to the party but it was really** ~ *(boring)* ich war auf der Party, aber es war zum Sterben langweilig; *(embarrassing)* ich war auf der Party, eine äußerst peinliche Angelegenheit; **she gave a** ~ **performance** ihre Vorführung war mehr als peinlich.

painfully ['peɪnfəlɪ] *adv* **(a)** *(physically)* schmerzhaft. **he dragged himself** ~ **along** er quälte sich mühsam weiter.

(b) *(inf: very)* schrecklich. **it was** ~ **obvious** es war nicht zu übersehen; **he was being** ~ **overpolite** es war peinlich, wie betont höflich er sich benahm; **he became** ~ **aware that ...** ihm wurde schmerzlich bewußt, daß ...

pain: ~killer *n* schmerzstillendes Mittel; ~killing *adj drug* schmerzstillend.

painless ['peɪnlɪs] *adj* schmerzlos. **I promise you the interview will be quite** ~ *(inf)* ich versichere Ihnen, daß das Interview kurz und schmerzlos wird *(inf)*; **a procedure which makes paying completely** ~ *(inf)* ein Verfahren, bei dem Sie von der Bezahlung überhaupt nichts merken; **don't worry, it's quite** ~ *(inf)* keine Angst, es tut gar nicht weh.

painlessly ['peɪnlɪslɪ] *adv see* **adj**.

painstaking ['peɪnz,teɪkɪŋ] *adj person, piece of work* sorgfältig. **with** ~ **accuracy** mit peinlicher Genauigkeit.

painstakingly ['peɪnz,teɪkɪŋlɪ] *adv* sorgfältig, gewissenhaft. **one has to be so** ~ **precise** man muß äußerst genau sein.

paint [peɪnt] **1** *n* **(a)** Farbe *f*; *(on car, furniture also)* Lack *m*; *(make-up)* Schminke *f*. **there's too much** ~ **on your face** du hast zu viel Farbe im Gesicht, du bist zu stark angemalt *(inf)*.

(b) ~s *pl* Farben *pl*; **box of** ~s Farb- *or* Malkasten *m*.

(c) *(US: piebald horse)* Schecke *m*.

2 *vt* **(a)** streichen; *car* lackieren; *door also* lackieren. **to** ~ **one's face** sich anmalen *(inf)*; *(Theat)* sich schminken; **to** ~ **the town red** *(inf)* die Stadt unsicher machen *(inf)*.

(b) *picture, person* malen. **he** ~ed **a very convincing picture of life on the moon** er zeichnete ein sehr überzeugendes Bild vom Leben auf dem Mond; *see* **black**.

3 *vi* malen; *(decorate)* (an)streichen.

♦ **paint in** *vt sep (add)* dazumalen; *(fill in)* ausmalen.

♦ **paint on** *vt sep* aufmalen.

♦ **paint out** *or* **over** *vt sep* übermalen; *(on wall)* überstreichen.

♦ **paint up** *vt sep building* neu *or* frisch anstreichen; *face* anmalen. **she gets all** ~ed ~ **on a Friday night** freitags abends legt sie immer ihre Kriegsbemalung an *(inf)*.

paint: ~box *n* Farb- *or* Malkasten *m*; ~brush *n* Pinsel *m*.

painted woman *n* ['peɪntɪd'wʊmən] *n* Flittchen *nt (inf)*.

painter[1] ['peɪntə'] *n (Art)* Maler(in *f*) *m*; *(decorator also)* Anstreicher(in *f*) *m*.

painter[2] *n (Naut)* Fangleine *f*.

painting ['peɪntɪŋ] *n* **(a)** *(picture)* Bild, Gemälde *nt*. **(b)** *no pl (Art)* Malerei *f*. **(c)** *no pl (of flat etc)* Anstreichen *nt*.

paint: ~ **pot** *n* Farbtopf *m*; ~ **roller** *n* Rolle *f*; ~ **shop** *n (Ind)* Lackiererei *f*; ~ **spray(er)** *n* Spritzpistole *f*; ~**work** *n* on car *etc*) Lack *m*; *(on wall, furniture)* Anstrich *m*.

pair [peə'] **1** *n* **(a)** *(of gloves, shoes, people)* Paar *nt*; *(of animals)* Pärchen *nt*; *(of cards)* Pärchen *nt*; *(hum sl: breasts)* Vorbau *(inf)* *m*, Dinger *pl (sl)*, Teile *pl (sl)*. **I've lost the** ~ **to this glove** ich habe den anderen *or* zweiten Handschuh verloren; **a** ~ **of trousers** eine Hose; **six** ~s **of trousers** sechs Hosen; **a new** ~ *(of trousers)* eine neue (Hose); *(of shoes)* (ein Paar) neue; **I've lost my scissors, could I borrow your** ~? ich habe meine Schere

verloren, kannst du mir deine leihen?; **he has a useful** ~ **of hands** *(Boxer)* er ist ein guter Boxer; **a huge** ~ **of eyes** ein riesiges Augenpaar; **in** ~s paarweise; **hunt, arrive, go out** zu zweit; *seated* in Zweiergruppen; **they're a** ~ **of rascals** das sind vielleicht zwei Lausejungen; **what a** ~ **of fools we are!** wir (beide) sind vielleicht dumm!; **you're a fine** ~ **you are!** *(iro)* ihr seid mir (vielleicht) ein sauberes Pärchen *(iro)*; *see* **carriage**.

(b) **the** ~s *sing or pl (Skating)* Paarlauf *m*; *(Rowing)* Zweier *m*; **in the** ~s im Paarlauf/Zweier.

2 *vi* **in Paaren** *or* **paarweise anordnen. I was** ~ed **with Bob for the next round** in der nächsten Runde mußte ich mit Bob ein Paar bilden.

3 *vi (Parl)* **mit einem Abgeordneten einer anderen Partei ein Abkommen für eine Wahl treffen.**

♦ **pair off 1** *vt sep* in Zweiergruppen einteilen. **to** ~ **sb** ~ **with sb** *(find boyfriend etc for)* jdn mit jdm zusammenbringen *or* verkuppeln *(inf)*; **she was** ~ed ~ **with Jean in the tournament** sie wurde beim Turnier mit Jean zusammengebracht; ~ ~ **each word with its opposite** ordnen Sie jedem Wort den jeweiligen Gegensatz zu.

2 *vi* Paare bilden. **all the people at the party had** ~ed ~ bei der Party hatten alle Pärchen gebildet.

pairing ['peərɪŋ] *n* Paarung *f*.

pair-skating ['peə,skeɪtɪŋ] *n* Paarlaufen *nt*.

paisley ['peɪzlɪ] **1** *n* türkisches Muster. **2** *adj pattern* türkisch; *shirt* türkisch gemustert.

pajamas [pə'dʒɑːməz] *npl (US) see* **pyjamas**.

Pakistan [,pɑːkɪs'tɑːn] *n* Pakistan *nt*.

Pakistani [,pɑːkɪs'tɑːnɪ] **1** *adj* pakistanisch. **2** *n* Pakistani *mf*, Pakistaner(in *f*) *m*.

pal [pæl] *n (inf)* Kumpel *m (inf)*. **OK, let's be** ~s **again** na gut, vertragen wir uns wieder!; **be a** ~! sei so nett!; **help me with this, there's a** ~ sei doch so nett und hilf mir dabei; **you've always been a** ~ **to me** du warst immer ein guter Kumpel *(inf)*.

♦ **pal up** *vi (inf)* sich anfreunden *(with* mit).

palace ['pælɪs] *n (lit, fig)* Palast *m*. **bishop's** ~ bischöfliches Palais, bischöfliche Residenz; **royal** ~ (Königs)schloß *nt*; **the PM was summoned to the** ~ der Premierminister wurde zur Königin/zum König bestellt.

palace: ~ **grounds** *npl* Schloßgelände *nt*; ~ **guard** *n* Schloßwache *f*; ~ **revolution** *n (lit, fig)* Palastrevolution *f*; ~ **wall** *n* Schloßmauer *f*.

paladin ['pælədɪn] *n* Paladin *m*.

palaeo- ['pælɪəʊ-] *pref see* **paleo-**.

palanquin [,pælən'kiːn] *n* Sänfte *f*.

palatability [,pælətə'bɪlɪtɪ] *n* **(a)** Schmackhaftigkeit *f*. **(b)** *(fig)* Attraktivität *f*.

palatable ['pælətəbl] *adj* genießbar; *food also* schmackhaft *(to* für)*; (fig)* attraktiv. **to some the truth is not always** ~ manchen Leuten schmeckt die Wahrheit nicht immer.

palatably ['pælətəblɪ] *adv* schmackhaft; *(fig also)* attraktiv.

palatal ['pælətl] **1** *adj* Gaumen-; *(Phon)* palatal. **2** *n (Phon)* Palatal(laut) *m*.

palatalize ['pælətəlaɪz] *vti (Phon)* den Palatallaut bilden. **the "t" is** ~d das „t" wird im vorderen Gaumen gebildet.

palate ['pælɪt] *n (lit)* Gaumen *m*. **hard** ~ harter Gaumen, Vordergaumen *m*; **soft** ~ weicher Gaumen, Gaumensegel *nt*; **to have a delicate** ~ einen empfindlichen Gaumen haben; **to have no** ~ **for sth** *(fig)* keinen Sinn für etw haben.

palatial [pə'leɪʃəl] *adj (spacious)* palastartig; *(luxurious)* luxuriös, prunkvoll, feudal *(hum inf)*.

palatially [pə'leɪʃəlɪ] *adv* luxuriös, prunkvoll, feudal *(hum inf)*.

palatinate [pə'lætɪnɪt] *n* Pfalz *f*.

palatine ['pælətaɪn] *n (also count* ~) Pfalzgraf *m*.

palaver [pə'lɑːvə'] *n (inf)* **(a)** *(fuss and bother)* Umstand *m*, Theater *nt (inf)*. **(b)** *(conference)* Palaver *nt*.

pale[1] [peɪl] **1** *adj (+er) colour, complexion, face* blaß; *light also, face (implying unhealthy etc)* bleich, fahl. **she has** ~ **gold hair** sie hat rötlichblondes Haar; ~ **green/orange etc** blaß- *or* zartgrün/blaß- *or* zartorange *etc*; **to go** *or* **turn** ~ **with fear/anger** vor Schreck/Wut bleich *or* blaß werden; **but a** ~ **imitation of the real thing** nur ein Abklatsch *m* des Originals.

2 *vi (person)* erbleichen, blaß *or* bleich werden; *(paper etc)* verblassen. **but X** ~s **beside Y** neben Y verblaßt X direkt; **to** ~ **into insignificance** vor Bedeutungslosigkeit herabsinken.

pale[2] *n (stake)* Pfahl *m*. **those last few remarks were quite beyond the** ~ diese letzten Bemerkungen haben eindeutig die Grenzen überschritten; **such things are beyond the** ~ **of rational enquiry** diese Dinge entziehen sich dem verstandesmäßigen Zugriff; **he is now regarded as beyond the** ~ man betrachtet ihn jetzt als indiskutabel.

pale: ~ **ale** *n (Brit)* helles Dunkelbier; ~**face** *n* Bleichgesicht *nt*.

palely ['peɪllɪ] *adv shine, lit* schwach, matt.

paleness ['peɪlnɪs] *n* Blässe *f*.

paleo- ['pælɪəʊ-] *pref* paläo-, Paläo-.

paleography [,pælɪ'ɒɡrəfɪ] *n* Paläographie *f*.

paleolithic [,pælɪəʊ'lɪθɪk] *adj* paläolithisch, altsteinzeitlich.

paleontology [,pælɪɒn'tɒlədʒɪ] *n* Paläontologie *f*.

paleozoic [,pælɪəʊ'zəʊɪk] *adj* paläozoisch.

Palestine ['pælɪstaɪn] *n* Palästina *nt*.

Palestinian [,pælə'stɪnɪən] **1** *adj* palästinensisch. **2** *n* Palästinenser(in *f*) *m*.

palette ['pælɪt] *n* Palette *f*. ~ **knife** Palettenmesser *nt*.

palfrey ['pɔːlfrɪ] *n* Zelter *m*.

palimpsest ['pælɪmpsest] *n* Palimpsest *m*.

palindrome ['pælɪndrəʊm] *n* Palindrom *nt*.

paling ['peɪlɪŋ] *n (stake)* Zaunpfahl *m*; *(fence)* Lattenzaun *m*; *(bigger)* Palisadenzaun *m*.

palisade [,pælɪ'seɪd] **1** *n* **(a)** Palisade *f*. **(b)** ~s *pl (US)* Steilufer *nt*. **2** *vt* einpfählen.

pall[1] [pɔːl] *n* **(a)** *(over coffin)* Bahrtuch, Sargtuch *nt*. **a** ~ **of**

smoke (fig) (covering) eine Dunstglocke; (rising in air) eine Rauchwolke. **(b)** (Eccl) Pallium nt.

pall² vi an Reiz verlieren; (book, film etc also) langweilig werden (on sb für jdn).

pall-bearer ['pɔːl,bɛərəʳ] n Sargträger m.

pallet ['pælɪt] n (bed) Pritsche f; (for storage) Palette f.

palliasse ['pæliæs] n Strohsack m.

palliate ['pælieɪt] vt (form) **(a)** disease lindern. **(b)** offence, seriousness of situation (make less serious) mildern; (make seem less serious) beschönigen.

palliative ['pælɪətɪv] (form) **1** adj drug, remedy lindernd, Linderungs-; explanation beschönigend. **2** n Linderungsmittel, Palliativ(um) nt.

pallid ['pælɪd] adj blaß, fahl; (unhealthy looking) bleich, fahl.

pallor ['pæləʳ] n Blässe, Fahlheit f.

pally ['pælɪ] adj (+er) (inf) he's a ~ sort er ist ein freundlicher Bursche; they're very ~ sie sind dicke Freunde (inf); to be ~ with sb mit jdm gut Freund sein; to get ~ with sb sich mit jdm anfreunden; he immediately tried to get ~ with the boss er versuchte sofort, sich beim Chef anzubiedern.

palm¹ [pɑːm] n (Bot) Palme f; (as carried at Easter) Palmzweig m. to carry off or bear the ~ die Siegespalme erringen, siegen.

palm² **1** n (Anat) Handteller m, Handfläche f; (of glove) Innenfläche f. the magician had concealed the ball in the ~ of his hand der Zauberkünstler hielt den Ball in der hohlen Hand versteckt; to grease sb's ~ jdn schmieren (inf); to read sb's ~ jdm aus der Hand lesen; see itching.

2 vt **(a)** card im Ärmel verstecken.

(b) the goalie just managed to ~ the ball over the crossbar der Torwart schaffte es gerade noch, den Ball mit der Handfläche über die Querlatte zu lenken.

♦**palm off** vt sep (inf) rubbish, goods andrehen (on(to) sb jdm) (inf); sb (with explanation) abspeisen (inf).

palmetto [pæl'metəʊ] n Palmetto f.

palmist ['pɑːmɪst] n Handliniendeuter(in f), Handleser(in f) m.

palmistry ['pɑːmɪstrɪ] n Handliniendeutung, Handlesekunst f.

palm: ~ leaf n Palmwedel m; ~ oil n Palmöl nt; P~ Sunday n Palmsonntag m; ~ tree n Palme f; ~ wine n Palmwein m.

palmy ['pɑːmɪ] adj (+er) days glücklich, unbeschwert.

palomino [ˌpæləˈmiːnəʊ] n Palomino nt.

palpable ['pælpəbl] adj **(a)** greifbar; (Med) tastbar, palpabel (spec). **(b)** (clear) lie, error offensichtlich.

palpably ['pælpəblɪ] adv (clearly) eindeutig.

palpate [pæl'peɪt] vt (Med) palpieren.

palpitate ['pælpɪteɪt] vi (heart) heftig klopfen; (tremble) zittern.

palpitation [ˌpælpɪ'teɪʃən] n (of heart) Herzklopfen nt; (trembling) Zittern nt. to have ~s Herzklopfen haben.

palsied ['pɔːlzɪd] adj gelähmt.

palsy ['pɔːlzɪ] n Lähmung f. cerebral ~ zerebrale Lähmung; sick of the ~ (hum inf) krank; (Bibl) gelähmt.

palsy-walsy ['pælzɪ'wælzɪ] adj (hum inf) they are all ~ again sie sind wieder ein Herz und eine Seele; see also pally.

paltriness ['pɔːltrɪnɪs] n Armseligkeit, Schäbigkeit f; (of reason) Unbedeutendheit, Geringfügigkeit f.

paltry ['pɔːltrɪ] adj armselig, schäbig. for a few ~ pounds für ein paar lumpige or armselige Pfund; for some ~ reason aus irgend einem unbedeutenden or geringfügigen Grund.

pampas ['pæmpəs] npl Pampas pl. ~ grass Pampasgras nt.

pamper ['pæmpəʳ] vt verwöhnen; child also verhätscheln, verzärteln; why don't you ~ yourself and buy the de-luxe edition? warum gönnst du dir nicht mal etwas und kaufst die Luxusausgabe?

pamphlet ['pæmflɪt] n (informative brochure) Broschüre f; (literary) Druckschrift f; (political, handed out in street) Flugblatt nt, Flugschrift f.

pamphleteer [ˌpæmflɪ'tɪəʳ] n Verfasser(in f) m von Druckschriften/Flugblättern.

pan¹ [pæn] **1** n **(a)** (Cook) Pfanne f; (sauce~) Topf m. **(b)** (of scales) Waagschale f; (for gold etc) Goldpfanne f; (of lavatory) Becken nt. **(c)** (in ground) Mulde f. **2** vt gold waschen. **(b)** (US) fish braten. **(c)** (US inf: slate) new play etc verreißen. **3** vi to ~ for gold Gold waschen.

♦**pan out** vi (inf) sich entwickeln. to ~ ~ well klappen (inf); if it ~s ~ as we hope wenn's so wird, wie wir es uns erhoffen.

pan² (Film) **1** n (Kamera)schwenk m.

2 vi panoramieren. a ~ning shot ein Schwenk m; the shot ~ned along the wall die Kamera fuhr langsam die Mauer ab; they ~ned the camera across the whole width of the scene sie fuhren mit der Kamera die ganze Szene ab; ~ this shot across to the left schwenke bei dieser Einstellung nach links hinüber; the camera ~ned in to the group in the centre die Kamera schwenkte auf die Gruppe in der Mitte ein; as the shot ~s slowly away während die Kamera langsam abschwenkt.

pan- pref pan-, Pan-. P~-African panafrikanisch.

panacea [ˌpænə'sɪə] n Allheilmittel nt. there's no universal ~ for ... es gibt kein Allheilmittel für ...

panache [pə'næʃ] n Schwung, Elan m. she dresses with ~ sie kleidet sich sehr extravagant.

Panama [ˌpænə'mɑː] n Panama nt. ~ Canal Panamakanal m.

panama (hat) n Panamahut m.

Panamanian [ˌpænə'meɪnɪən] **1** adj panamaisch. **2** n Panamaer(in f) m, Panamese m, Panamesin f.

Pan-American ['pænə'merɪkən] adj panamerikanisch.

Pan-Americanism ['pænə'merɪkənɪzəm] n Panamerikanismus m.

panatella [ˌpænə'telə] n (dünne, lange) Zigarre f.

pancake ['pænkeɪk] **1** n Pfannkuchen m. P~ Day Fastnachtsdienstag m; ~ landing Bauchlandung f. **2** vi (aeroplane) eine Bauchlandung machen.

panchromatic [ˌpænkrəʊ'mætɪk] adj panchromatisch.

pancreas ['pæŋkrɪəs] n Bauchspeicheldrüse f, Pankreas nt.

pancreatic [ˌpæŋkrɪ'ætɪk] adj Bauchspeicheldrüsen-.

panda ['pændə] n Panda, Katzenbär m.

panda car n (Brit) (Funk)streifenwagen m.

pandemonium [ˌpændɪ'məʊnɪəm] n Chaos nt. at this there was ~ daraufhin brach im Chaos aus or die Hölle los; judging by the ~ coming from the classroom dem Höllenlärm in der Klasse nach zu urteilen.

pander ['pændəʳ] **1** n (rare) Kuppler m. **2** vi nachgeben (to dat). to ~ to sb's desires jds Bedürfnisse (acc) befriedigen wollen; this is ~ing to the public's basest instincts damit wird an die niedrigsten Instinkte der Öffentlichkeit appelliert; to ~ to sb's ego jdm um den Bart gehen.

Pandora's box [pæn'dɔːrəz'bɒks] n Büchse f der Pandora.

p and p abbr of post(age) and packing.

pane [peɪn] n Glasscheibe f.

panegyric [ˌpænɪ'dʒɪrɪk] n Lobrede f, Panegyrikus m (Liter).

panel ['pænl] **1** n **(a)** (piece of wood) Platte, Tafel f; (in wainscoting, ceiling, door) Feld nt; (Sew) Streifen, Einsatz m; (Art) Tafel f; (painting) Tafelbild nt; (part of a plane's wing, fuselage) Verschalungs(bau)teil nt; (part of bodywork of a car) Karosserieteil nt. door/wing ~ (on car) Tür-/Kotflügelblech nt. **(b)** (of instruments, switches) Schalttafel f. **instrument** ~ Armaturenbrett nt; (on machine) Kontrolltafel f. **(c)** (Jur) (list of names) Geschworenenliste f; (Brit Med) ~ Liste f der Kassenärzte. **(d)** (of interviewers etc) Gremium nt; (in discussion) Diskussionsrunde f; (in quiz) Rateteam nt. a ~ of experts ein Sachverständigengremium nt; on the ~ tonight we have ... als Teilnehmer der Diskussionsrunde/des Rateteams begrüßen wir heute abend ...; a ~ of judges eine Jury.

2 vt wall, ceiling täfeln, paneelieren.

panel: ~ beater n Autoschlosser m; ~ discussion n Podiumsdiskussion f; ~ game n Ratespiel nt.

panel lighting n indirekte Beleuchtung.

panelling, (US) paneling ['pænlɪŋ] n Täfelung f, Paneel nt; (to conceal radiator etc, of plane) Verschalung f.

panellist, (US) panelist ['pænlɪst] n Diskussionsteilnehmer(in f) m.

panel: ~-pin n Stift m; ~ truck n (US) Lieferwagen m.

pang [pæŋ] n ~ of conscience Gewissensbisse pl; I felt a ~ of conscience ich hatte Gewissensbisse; ~s of hunger quälender Hunger; ~s of childbirth (old) Geburtswehen pl.

pan: ~handle ['pæn] n Pfannenstiel m; (shape of land) Zipfel m; **2** vi (US inf) die Leute anhauen (inf); ~handler n (US inf) Bettler, Schnorrer (inf) m.

panic ['pænɪk] **1** n Panik f. ~ on the stock exchange Börsenpanik f; to flee in ~ panikartig die Flucht ergreifen; a ~ reaction eine Kurzschlußreaktion; the country was thrown into a (state of) ~ das Land wurde von Panik erfaßt; a feeling of ~ in the bowels eine panische Angst.

2 vi in Panik geraten. don't ~ nur keine Panik!

3 vt Panik auslösen unter (+dat). to ~ sb into doing sth jdn veranlassen, etw überstürzt zu tun.

panicky ['pænɪkɪ] adj person überängstlich; act, measure etc Kurzschluß-. I get this ~ feeling whenever ... ich werde immer nervös or gerate immer in Panik, wenn ...; to get ~ in Panik geraten; don't get ~! keine Panik!, dreh bloß nicht durch! (inf).

panic-stricken ['pænɪk,strɪkən] adj von panischem Schrecken ergriffen; look panisch.

pannier ['pænɪəʳ] n Korb m; (on motor-cycle etc) Satteltasche f; (for mule etc) Tragkorb m.

panoplied ['pænəplɪd] adj knight in Rüstung. in its ~ splendour in seinem vollen Glanz.

panoply ['pænəplɪ] n (armour) Rüstung f; (covering) Baldachin m; (fig liter) Dach nt; (array) Palette f, Spektrum nt. beneath the oak's ~ of leaves unter den Blätterdach der Eiche; the ~ of the sky/of stars das Himmels-/Sternenzelt (liter).

panorama [ˌpænə'rɑːmə] n (view, also fig: of life etc) Panorama nt (of gen); (survey) Übersicht f (of über +acc). ~ window (Aut, Rail) Panoramafenster nt.

panoramic [ˌpænə'ræmɪk] adj view Panorama-. ~ shot (Phot) Panoramaaufnahme f; a ~ view of the hills ein Blick m auf das Bergpanorama; a ~ view of social development ein umfassender Überblick über die gesellschaftliche Entwicklung; ~ sight (Mil) Rundblickzielfernrohr nt.

pan-pipes ['pænpaɪps] npl Panflöte f.

pansy ['pænzɪ] n **(a)** (Bot) Stiefmütterchen nt. **(b)** (sl: homosexual) Schwule(r) (inf), Süße(r) (sl) m.

pant [pænt] **1** n Atemstoß m. he was breathing in short ~s er atmete stoßartig.

2 vi **(a)** keuchen; (dog) hecheln; (train) schnaufen. to be ~ing for a drink nach etwas zu trinken lechzen; he was ~ing for breath er schnappte nach Luft (inf), er rang nach Atem. **(b)** (inf: desire) lechzen (for nach). to be ~ing to do sth danach lechzen or darauf brennen, etw zu tun.

3 vt (also ~ out) message hervorstoßen.

pantaloon [ˌpæntə'luːn] n (Theat) Hanswurst m.

pantaloons [ˌpæntə'luːnz] npl (Hist) Pantalons pl.

pantechnicon [pæn'teknɪkən] n (Brit) Möbelwagen m.

pantheism ['pænθiːɪzəm] n Pantheismus m.

pantheist ['pænθiːɪst] n Pantheist(in f) m.

pantheistic [ˌpænθiː'ɪstɪk] adj pantheistisch.

pantheon ['pænθɪən] n Pantheon nt.

panther ['pænθəʳ] n Panther m.

panties ['pæntɪz] npl (for children) Höschen nt; (for women also) (Damen)slip m. a pair of ~ ein Höschen nt/ein Slip m.

pantile ['pæntaɪl] n Dachpfanne f.

panto ['pæntəʊ] n (Brit inf) = pantomime (a).

pantograph ['pæntəgrɑːf] n Pantograph m.

pantomime ['pæntəmaɪm] n **(a)** (in GB) Weihnachtsmärchen *nt.* **what a ~!** (*inf*) was für ein Theater! (*inf*). **(b)** (*mime*) Pantomime *f*.

pantry ['pæntri] *n* Speisekammer *f*.

pants [pænts] *npl* (*trousers*) Hose *f*; (*Brit: under~*) Unterhose *f*. **a pair of ~** eine Hose/Unterhose; **to wear the ~** (*US fig*) die Hosen anhaben (*inf*).

pantsuit ['pæntsu:t] *n* (*US*) Hosenanzug *m*.

panty: **~-girdle** *n* Miederhöschen *nt*; **~-hose** *n* Strumpfhose *f*; **~waist** *n* (*US sl*) Schwächling *m*, Memme *f* (*inf*).

pap [pæp] *n* (*food*) Brei *m*.

papa [pə'pɑ:] *n* (*dated inf*) Papa *m*.

papacy ['peɪpəsɪ] *n* Papsttum *nt*. **during the ~ of** ... während der Amtszeit des Papstes ..., unter Papst ...

papal ['peɪpəl] *adj* päpstlich.

papaya [pə'paɪə] *n* Papaye *f*; (*fruit*) Papaya *f*.

paper ['peɪpə[r]] **1** *n* (a) (*material*) Papier *nt*. **a piece of ~** ein Stück *nt* Papier; **a sheet of ~** ein Blatt *nt* Papier; **a writer who finds it hard to commit himself to ~** ein Schriftsteller, der nur zögernd etwas zu Papier bringt; **to get or put sth down on ~** etw schriftlich festhalten; **can we get your acceptance down on ~?** können wir Ihre Einwilligung schriftlich haben?; **it looks good on ~ but** ... auf dem Papier sieht es gut aus, aber ...; **on ~ they're the best firm** auf dem Papier ist das die beste Firma; **it's not worth the ~ it's written on** das ist schade ums Papier, auf dem es steht; **the walls are like ~** die Wände sind wie Pappe.

(b) (*newspaper*) Zeitung *f*. **to write for the ~s** für Zeitungen schreiben; **to write to the ~s about sth** Leserbriefe/einen Leserbrief schreiben; **a world-famous ~** eine weltbekannte Zeitung, ein weltbekanntes Blatt; **he's/his name is always in the ~s** er/sein Name steht ständig in der Zeitung.

(c) **~s** *pl* (*identity ~s*) Papiere *pl*.

(d) **~s** *pl* (*writings, documents*) Papiere *pl*; **private ~s** private Unterlagen *pl*.

(e) (*set of questions in exam*) Testbogen *m*; (*exam*) (*Univ*) Klausur *f*; (*Sch*) Arbeit *f*. **to do a good ~ in maths** eine gute Mathematikklausur/-arbeit schreiben.

(f) (*academic*) Referat, Paper (*sl*) *nt*. **he's going to read a ~ to the society** er wird vor der Gesellschaft ein Referat halten.

(g) (*wall~*) Tapete *f*.

(h) (*Parl*) **a white ~** ein Weißbuch *nt*.

(i) (*packet*) **a ~ of pins** ein Päckchen *nt* Stecknadeln.

2 *vt wall, room* tapezieren.

♦ **paper over** *vt sep* überkleben; (*fig*) *cracks* übertünchen.

paper *in cpds* Papier-; **~back** *n* Taschenbuch, Paperback (*sl*) *nt*; **~backed** *adj* Taschenbuch-; **~ bag** *n* Tüte *f*; **~boy** *n* Zeitungsjunge *m*; **~ chain** *n* Girlande *f*; **~ chase** *n* Schnitzeljagd *f*; **~ clip** *n* Büroklammer *f*; **~ handkerchief** *n* Tempo(taschen)tuch ®, Papiertaschentuch *nt*; **~-hanger** *n* Tapezierer *m*; **~-hanging** *n* Tapezieren *nt*; **~ knife** *n* Brieföffner *m*; **~ lantern** *n* Lampion *m*; **~ mill** *n* Papierfabrik, Papiermühle *f*; **~ money** *n* Papiergeld *nt*; **~ tape** *n* Lochstreifen *m*; **~-thin** *adj walls* hauchdünn; **~ tiger** *n* Papiertiger *m*; **~weight** *n* Briefbeschwerer *m*; **~work** *n* Schreibarbeit *f*.

papery ['peɪpərɪ] *adj plaster, pastry* bröckelig, krümelig.

papier mâché ['pæpɪeɪ'mæʃeɪ] **1** *n* Papiermaché, Pappmaché *nt*. **2** *adj* aus Papiermaché or Pappmaché.

papism ['peɪpɪzəm] *n* (*pej*) Papismus *m*.

papist ['peɪpɪst] *n* (*pej*) Papist(in *f*) *m*.

papistry ['peɪpɪstrɪ] *n* (*pej*) Papismus *m*.

papoose [pə'pu:s] *n* Indianerbaby *nt*; (*carrier for Indian baby*) Winkelbrettwiege *f*; (*carrier for baby*) Tragegestell *nt*.

pappy ['pæpɪ] *n* (*US inf*) Papi *m* (*inf*).

paprika ['pæprɪkə] *n* Paprika *m*.

Pap test ['pæptest] *n* Abstrich *m*.

Papua ['pæpjuə] *n* Papua *nt*.

Papuan ['pæpjuən] **1** *adj* papuanisch. **2** *n* (a) Papua *mf*. **(b)** (*language*) Papuasprache *f*.

papyrus [pə'paɪrəs] *n, pl* **papyri** [pə'paɪraɪ] (*plant*) Papyrus(staude *f*) *m*; (*paper*) Papyrus *m*; (*scroll*) Papyrus(rolle *f*) *m*.

par [pɑ:[r]] *n* (a) (*Fin*) Pari, Nennwert *m*. **to be above/below ~** über/unter pari or dem Nennwert stehen; **at ~** zum Nennwert, al pari.

(b) **to be on a ~ with sb/sth** sich mit jdm/etw messen können; **this objection is on a ~ with Harry's** dieser Einwand liegt auf der gleichen Ebene wie Harrys; **he's nowhere near on a ~ with her** er kann ihr nicht das Wasser reichen; **culturally, the two countries are on or can be put on a ~** in kultureller Hinsicht sind die beiden Länder miteinander vergleichbar; **an above-~ performance** eine überdurchschnittliche Leistung.

(c) **below ~** (*fig*) unter Niveau; **I'm feeling physically/mentally below ~** ich fühle mich körperlich/seelisch nicht auf der Höhe; **I'm not feeling quite up to ~ today** ich bin heute nicht ganz auf dem Damm (*inf*) or Posten (*inf*).

(d) (*Golf*) Par *m*. **to go round in six below/above ~** sechs Schläge unter/über dem Par spielen.

par, para ['pærə] *abbr of* **paragraph** Abschn.

parable ['pærəbl] *n* Parabel *f*, Gleichnis *nt*.

parabola [pə'ræbələ] *n* (*Math*) Parabel *f*.

parabolic [ˌpærə'bɒlɪk] *adj* (a) Parabol-; *curve* parabelförmig. **(b)** (*Liter*) gleichnishaft.

parachute ['pærəʃu:t] **1** *n* Fallschirm *m*. **by ~** mit dem Fallschirm.

2 *vt troops* mit dem Fallschirm absetzen; *supplies* abwerfen. **to ~ food to sb** für jdn Lebensmittel abwerfen.

3 *vi* (*also ~ down*) (mit dem Fallschirm) abspringen. **they ~d into the wrong zone** sie sprangen über dem falschen Gebiet ab; **to ~ to safety** sich mit dem Fallschirm retten.

♦ **parachute in 1** *vt sep troops* mit dem Fallschirm absetzen; *supplies* abwerfen. **2** *vi* (mit dem Fallschirm) abspringen.

parachute: **~ brake** *n* Bremsfallschirm *m*; **~ drop** *n* (*by person*) (Fallschirm)absprung *m*; (*of supplies*) (Fallschirm)ab-

wurf *m*; **there was a ~ drop of ten men** zehn Leute sprangen (mit dem Fallschirm) ab; **they got a ~ drop of medical supplies** medizinische Versorgungsmittel wurden (mit dem Fallschirm) für sie abgeworfen; **~ jump** *n* Absprung *m* (mit dem Fallschirm); **~ training** *n* Übung *f* im Fallschirmspringen.

parachutist ['pærəʃu:tɪst] *n* Fallschirmspringer(in *f*) *m*.

parade [pə'reɪd] **1** *n* (a) (*procession*) Umzug *m*; (*Mil, of boy scouts, circus*) Parade *f*; (*political*) Demonstration *f*. **church ~** Prozession *f*; **to be on ~** (*Mil*) eine Parade abhalten; **the regiment on ~** das Regiment bei der Parade; **in the school procession you'll be on ~** in front of the public bei der Schulparade sieht dich alle Welt; **and all the new hats will be out on ~** und dann werden alle neuen Hüte spazierengeführt.

(b) (*public walk*) Promenade *f*.

(c) (*fashion ~*) Modenschau *f*.

(d) (*display*) Parade *f*; (*of wealth etc*) Zurschaustellung *f*.

(e) (*US mil*) (*review*) Truppeninspektion *f*; (*ground*) Truppenübungsplatz, Exerzierplatz *m*.

(f) (*shopping ~*) Reihe *f* von Geschäften.

2 *vt* (a) *troops* auf- or vorbeimarschieren lassen; *military might* demonstrieren; *placards* vor sich her tragen.

(b) (*show off*) zur Schau stellen; *new clothes, new camera etc* also spazierentragen.

3 *vi* (*Mil*) auf- or vorbeimarschieren; (*political party*) eine Demonstration veranstalten. **the strikers ~d through the town** die Streikenden zogen durch die Stadt; **she ~d up and down with the hat on** sie stolzierte mit ihrem Hut auf und ab.

parade ground *n* Truppenübungsplatz, Exerzierplatz *m*.

paradigm ['pærədaɪm] *n* Musterbeispiel *nt*; (*Gram*) Paradigma *nt*.

paradigmatic [ˌpærədɪg'mætɪk] *adj* beispielhaft, paradigmatisch.

paradise ['pærədaɪs] *n* (*lit, fig*) Paradies *nt*. **a shopper's ~** ein Einkaufsparadies *nt*; **an architect's ~** ein Paradies *nt* für Architekten; **living there must be ~** compared with this place dort zu leben muß geradezu paradiesisch sein verglichen mit hier; **~, she sighed** himmlisch, seufzte sie; **an earthly ~** ein Paradies auf Erden; **~!** wie im Paradies!, paradiesisch!

paradisiac(al) [ˌpærə'dɪzɪək(əl)] *adj* paradiesisch.

paradox ['pærədɒks] *n* Paradox, Paradoxon (*liter*) *nt*. **life/he is full of ~es** das Leben/er steckt voller Widersprüche.

paradoxical [ˌpærə'dɒksɪkəl] *adj* paradox; *person* widersprüchlich.

paradoxically [ˌpærə'dɒksɪkəlɪ] *adv* paradoxerweise; *worded* paradox.

paraffin ['pærəfɪn] *n* (*Brit: oil*) Paraffin(öl) *nt*; (*US: wax*) Paraffin *nt*.

paraffin: **~ lamp** *n* Paraffinlampe *f*; **~ oil** *n* (*Brit*) Paraffinöl *nt*; **~ stove** *n* (*Brit*) Paraffinofen *m*; **~ wax** *n* Paraffin *nt*.

paragon ['pærəgən] *n* Muster *nt*. **a ~ of virtue** ein Muster *nt* an Tugendhaftigkeit, ein Ausbund *m* an Tugend (*hum*).

paragraph ['pærəgrɑ:f] **1** *n* (a) Absatz, Abschnitt *m*. **"new ~"** „(neuer) Absatz". **(b)** (*brief article*) Notiz *f*. **2** *vt* (in Abschnitte) gliedern, aufgliedern.

Paraguay ['pærəgwaɪ] *n* Paraguay *nt*.

Paraguayan [ˌpærə'gwaɪən] **1** *adj* paraguayisch. **2** *n* Paraguayer(in *f*) *m*.

parakeet ['pærəki:t] *n* Sittich *m*.

paraldehyde [pə'rældɪhaɪd] *n* Paraldehyd *nt*.

parallax ['pærəlæks] *n* Parallaxe *f*.

parallel ['pærəlel] **1** *adj* (a) *lines, streets* parallel. **at this point the road and river are ~** an dieser Stelle verlaufen Straße und Fluß parallel (zueinander); **~ bars** Barren *m*; **~ connection** (*Elec*) Parallelschaltung *f*; **in a ~ direction** parallel.

(b) (*fig*) *case, career, development* vergleichbar; *career, development also* parallel verlaufend. **a ~ case** ein Parallelfall *m*; **the two systems developed along ~ lines** die Entwicklung der beiden Systeme verlief vergleichbar; **he argues along ~ lines to me** er argumentiert ähnlich wie ich.

2 *adv* **to run ~** (*roads, careers*) parallel verlaufen.

3 *n* (a) (*Geometry*) Parallele *f*.

(b) (*Geog*) Breitenkreis *m*. **the 49th ~** der 49. Breitengrad.

(c) (*Elec*) **connected in ~** parallel geschaltet.

(d) (*fig*) Parallele *f*. **without ~** ohne Parallele; **it has no ~** es gibt dazu keine Parallele; **to draw a ~ between X and Y** eine Parallele zwischen X und Y ziehen.

4 *vt* (*fig*) gleichen (+*dat*). **a case ~led only by** ... ein Fall, zu dem es nur eine einzige Parallele gibt, nämlich ...; **it is ~led by** ... es ist vergleichbar mit ...

parallelism ['pærəlelɪzəm] *n* (*of lines*) Parallelität *f*; (*of cases also*) Ähnlichkeit *f*. **don't try to exaggerate the ~** versuche nicht, zu viele Parallelen zu ziehen.

parallelogram [ˌpærə'leləgræm] *n* Parallelogramm *nt*.

paralysis [pə'ræləsɪs] *n, pl* **paralyses** [pə'rælɪsi:z] Lähmung, Paralyse *f*; (*of industry etc*) Lahmlegung *f*. **creeping ~** progressive Paralyse; **infantile ~** Kinderlähmung *f*.

paralytic [ˌpærə'lɪtɪk] **1** *adj* (a) paralytisch, Lähmungs-. **(b)** (*Brit sl: very drunk*) total blau (*inf*), stockvoll (*sl*). **2** *n* Paralytiker(in *f*) *m*, Gelähmte(r) *mf*.

paralyze ['pærəlaɪz] *vt* (a) lähmen, paralysieren (*spec*). **to be ~d in both legs** mit beiden Beinen gelähmt sein; **to be ~d with fright** vor Schreck wie gelähmt sein. **(b)** *industry, economy* lahmlegen; *traffic also* zum Erliegen bringen.

parameter [pə'ræmɪtə[r]] *n* (*Math*) Parameter *m*. **(b)** **~s** *pl* (*framework, limits*) Rahmen *m*.

paramilitary [ˌpærə'mɪlɪtərɪ] *adj* paramilitärisch.

paramount ['pærəmaʊnt] *adj* Haupt-. **of ~ importance** von größter or höchster Wichtigkeit; **solvency must be ~** der Zahlungsfähigkeit muß Priorität eingeräumt werden.

paramour ['pærəmʊə[r]] *n* (*old*) Liebhaber *m*, Buhle *mf* (*old*); (*hum*) (*man*) Hausfreund *m* (*hum*); (*woman*) Geliebte *f* (*hum*).

paranoia [ˌpærəˈnɔɪə] n Paranoia f; (inf) Verfolgungswahn m. this ~ which stops nations trusting each other dieses krankhafte Mißtrauen, das die Völker voneinander trennt.

paranoiac [ˌpærəˈnɔɪɪk] 1 n Paranoiker(in f) m. 2 adj paranoisch.

paranoid ['pærənɔɪd] adj paranoid. or am I just being ~? oder bilde ich mir das nur ein?; she's getting ~ about what other people think of her die Angst vor dem, was andere von ihr denken, wird bei ihr langsam zur Manie; aren't you being rather ~? du scheinst unter Verfolgungswahn zu leiden.

paranormal [ˌpærəˈnɔːməl] adj paranormal.

parapet ['pærəpɪt] n (on rampart) (of bridge) Brüstung f; (of well) (Brunnen)wand f.

paraphernalia ['pærəfəˈneɪlɪə] npl Brimborium, Drum und Dran nt.

paraphrase ['pærəfreɪz] 1 n Umschreibung, Paraphrase (geh) f. 2 vt umschreiben, paraphrasieren (geh).

paraplegia [ˌpærəˈpliːdʒə] n doppelseitige Lähmung.

paraplegic [ˌpærəˈpliːdʒɪk] 1 adj doppelseitig gelähmt, paraplegisch (spec). 2 n Paraplegiker(in f) m (spec).

parapsychology [ˌpærəsaɪˈkɒlədʒɪ] n Parapsychologie f.

paras ['pærəz] npl (inf) Fallschirmjäger pl.

parasite ['pærəsaɪt] n (lit, fig) Parasit, Schmarotzer m.

parasitic(al) [ˌpærəˈsɪtɪk(əl)] adj animal, plant Schmarotzer-, parasitisch, parasitär (also fig). a ~ worm ein Schmarotzer m; to be ~ (up)on sth von etw schmarotzen.

parasitology [ˌpærəsɪˈtɒlədʒɪ] n Parasitologie f.

parasol ['pærəsɒl] n Sonnenschirm, Parasol (dated) m.

parataxis ['pærətæksɪs] n Parataxe f.

paratrooper ['pærətruːpəʳ] n Fallschirmjäger m.

paratroops ['pærətruːps] npl (soldiers) Fallschirmjäger pl; (division also) Fallschirmjägertruppe f.

paratyphoid ['pærəˈtaɪfɔɪd] n Paratyphus m.

parboil ['pɑːbɔɪl] vt vorkochen, halbgar kochen.

parcel ['pɑːsl] n (a) Paket nt. to do sth up in a ~ etw als Paket packen; ~ post Paketpost f; to send sth (by) ~ post etw als Paket schicken. (b) a ~ of land ein Stück nt Land; see part.

♦**parcel out** vt sep land, inheritance aufteilen.

♦**parcel up** vt sep als Paket verpacken.

parcel(s) office n (Rail) Paketstelle f.

parch [pɑːtʃ] vt ausdörren, austrocknen.

parched [pɑːtʃt] adj lips, throat ausgetrocknet; land also verdorrt. to be ~ (with thirst) (vor Durst) verschmachten; I'm ~ ich habe furchtbaren Durst.

parchment ['pɑːtʃmənt] n Pergament nt.

pard [pɑːd] n (obs: leopard) Leopard m.

pardon ['pɑːdn] 1 n (a) (Jur) Begnadigung f. he got a ~ er ist begnadigt worden; there will be no ~ for deserters für Fahnenflüchtige gibt es keinen Pardon; to grant sb a ~ jdn begnadigen; general ~ Amnestie f.

(b) I beg your ~, but could you ...? verzeihen or entschuldigen Sie bitte, könnten Sie ...?; I beg your ~! erlauben Sie mal!, ich muß doch sehr bitten!; (beg) ~? (Brit), I beg your ~? (Brit) bitte?, wie bitte?; to beg sb's ~ jdn um Verzeihung bitten; I beg your ~, beg ~ (apology) verzeihen or entschuldigen Sie, Verzeihung, Entschuldigung; a thousand ~s! ich bitte tausendmal um Verzeihung or Entschuldigung!; we beg the reader's ~ for ... wir bitten den Leser für ... um Nachsicht.

2 vt (a) (Jur) begnadigen.

(b) (forgive) verzeihen, vergeben (sb jdm, sth etw). to ~ sb sth jdm etw verzeihen or vergeben; ~ me, but could you ...? entschuldigen or verzeihen Sie bitte, könnten Sie ...?; ~ me! Entschuldigung!, Verzeihung!; ~ me? (US) bitte?, wie bitte?; ~ my mentioning it entschuldigen or verzeihen Sie bitte, daß ich das erwähne; ~ me for asking! (iro) entschuldige bitte, daß ich es gewagt habe zu fragen! (iro).

pardonable ['pɑːdnəbl] adj offence entschuldbar; weakness, mistake also verzeihlich.

pardonably ['pɑːdnəblɪ] adv he was ~ angry sein Ärger war verständlich; and ~ so und das war verständlich.

pare [pɛəʳ] vt nails schneiden; fruit, stick schälen. she ~d the skin off the apple sie schälte den Apfel.

♦**pare down** vt sep (fig) expenses einschränken; personnel einsparen. to ~ sth ~ to the minimum etw auf ein Minimum beschränken.

parent ['pɛərənt] 1 n (a) Elternteil m. ~s Eltern pl; the duties of a ~ die elterlichen Pflichten; his father was his favourite ~ von seinen Eltern hatte er seinen Vater am liebsten.

(b) (fig) Vorläufer m. the Copernican theory is the ~ of modern astronomy die moderne Astronomie geht auf die Lehren des Kopernikus zurück.

2 attr ~ birds Vogeleltern pl; ~ company Muttergesellschaft f; ~ plant Mutterpflanze f; ~ ship (Space) Mutterschiff nt.

parentage ['pɛərəntɪdʒ] n Herkunft f. of humble/unknown ~ (von) einfacher/unbekannter Herkunft.

parental [pəˈrentl] adj care etc elterlich attr.

parenthesis [pəˈrenθɪsɪs] n, pl **parentheses** [pəˈrenθɪsiːz] Klammer(zeichen nt) f, Parenthese f; (words, statement) Einschub m, Parenthese f. I just added that as a ~ das habe ich nur nebenbei or in Klammern hinzugefügt; in ~ in Klammern; could I just comment in ~ that ... darf ich vielleicht einflechten, daß ...

parenthetic(al) [ˌpærənˈθetɪk(əl)] adj beiläufig. could I make one ~ comment? darf ich eine Bemerkung einflechten?

parenthetically [ˌpærənˈθetɪkəlɪ] adv nebenbei, beiläufig.

parenthood ['pɛərənthʊd] n Elternschaft f. the joys of ~ die Vater-/Mutterfreuden pl; the idea of ~ frightened her sie schrak zurück vor dem Gedanken, Mutter zu sein.

parer ['pɛərəʳ] n (apple-/fruit-~) Schälmesser nt.

par excellence [pɑːrˈeksəlɑ̃ːns] adv par excellence.

parhelion [pɑːˈhiːlɪən] n (Astron) Nebensonne f.

pariah ['pærɪə] n (lit, fig) Paria m; (fig also) Ausgestoßene(r) mf.

parietal [pəˈraɪtl] adj (Anat) parietal. ~ bone Scheitelbein nt.

pari mutuel ['pærɪˈmjuːtuəl] n Wettsystem, bei dem der gesamte Einsatz abzüglich der Verwaltungskosten prozentual an die Gewinner verteilt wird.

parings ['pɛərɪŋz] npl (of nails) abgeschnittene Fingernägel pl; (of apple) Schalen pl.

pari passu ['pærɪˈpæsuː] adv gleichlaufend, synchron.

Paris ['pærɪs] n Paris nt.

parish ['pærɪʃ] n Gemeinde f; (district also) Pfarrbezirk m, Pfarre, Pfarrei f.

parish: ~ church n Pfarrkirche f; ~ clerk n Verwaltungsangestellte(r) mf des Gemeinderates; ~ council n Gemeinderat m.

parishioner [pəˈrɪʃənəʳ] n Gemeinde(mit)glied nt.

parish: ~ priest n Pfarrer m; ~-pump politics n Kirchturmpolitik f; ~ register n Kirchenbuch, Kirchenregister nt.

Parisian [pəˈrɪzɪən] 1 adj Pariser inv. 2 n Pariser(in f) m.

parity ['pærɪtɪ] n (a) (equality) Gleichstellung f; (as regards pay etc also, of opportunities) Gleichheit f. ~ of treatment Gleichstellung f; ~ of pay Lohngleichheit f.

(b) (equivalence) Übereinstimmung f. by ~ of reasoning mit den gleichen Argumenten.

(c) (Fin, Sci) Parität f. the ~ of the dollar die Dollarparität.

(d) (US Agr) Preisparität f.

park [pɑːk] 1 n (a) Park m. national ~ Nationalpark m.

(b) (Sport) (Sport)platz m.

(c) (US: car ~) Parkplatz m.

(d) (Mil) Arsenal nt.

(e) (Aut) to put/leave a car in ~ das Getriebe in Parkstellung bringen/lassen.

2 vt (a) car parken; (for longer period also) abstellen; bicycle abstellen. a ~ed car ein parkendes Auto; there's been a car ~ed outside for days draußen parkt schon seit Tagen ein Auto; he was very badly ~ed er hatte miserabel geparkt.

(b) (inf: put) luggage etc abstellen. he ~ed himself right in front of the fire er pflanzte sich direkt vor den Kamin (inf); we ~ed the children with the neighbours wir haben die Kinder bei den Nachbarn abgegeben or gelassen; find somewhere to ~ your bum (hum) such dir was, wo du platzen kannst (hum).

3 vi parken. there was nowhere to ~ es gab nirgendwo einen Parkplatz; to find a place to ~ einen Parkplatz finden; (in line of cars) eine Parklücke finden.

parka ['pɑːkə] n Parka m.

parking ['pɑːkɪŋ] n Parken nt. women are usually good at ~ Frauen sind gewöhnlich gut im Einparken; there's no ~ in this street in dieser Straße ist Parken verboten or ist Parkverbot; "no ~" „Parken verboten"; "good ~ facilities" „gute Parkmöglichkeiten"; "~ for 50 cars" „50 (Park)plätze".

parking: ~ attendant n Parkplatzwächter m; ~ fine n Geldbuße f (für Parkvergehen); ~ lights npl Parklicht nt, Parkleuchte f; ~ lot n (US) Parkplatz m; ~ meter n Parkuhr f; ~ orbit n (Space) Parkbahn f; ~ place n Parkplatz m; ~ ticket n Strafzettel m, Knöllchen nt (dial inf).

park: ~keeper n Parkwächter m; ~way n (US) Allee f.

parky ['pɑːkɪ] adj (+er) (Brit sl) kühl, frisch. (it's a bit) ~ today ganz schön kühl heute.

parlance ['pɑːləns] n in common ~ im allgemeinen Sprachgebrauch; in technical/legal ~ in der Fachsprache/Rechtssprache; in modern ~ im modernen Sprachgebrauch.

parley ['pɑːlɪ] 1 n Verhandlungen pl. 2 vi verhandeln.

parliament ['pɑːləmənt] n Parlament nt. to get into ~ ins Parlament kommen; ~ reconvenes in the early autumn das Parlament tritt Anfang Herbst wieder zusammen; the West German/East German ~ das west-/ostdeutsche Parlament, der Bundestag/die Volkskammer; the Austrian/Swiss ~ die Bundesversammlung.

parliamentarian [ˌpɑːləmənˈtɛərɪən] n Parlamentarier m.

parliamentarianism [ˌpɑːləmənˈtɛərɪənɪzəm] n Parlamentarismus m.

parliamentary [ˌpɑːləˈmentərɪ] adj parlamentarisch. ~ debates Parlamentsdebatten pl; the ~ Labour Party die Parlamentsfraktion der Labour Party; ~ private secretary (Brit) Abgeordnete(r), der/die einem Minister zuarbeitet.

parlor car n (US) Salonwagen m.

parlour, (US) **parlor** ['pɑːləʳ] n (a) (in house) Salon m. (b) (beauty ~, massage ~ etc) Salon m. ice-cream ~ Eisdiele f.

parlour: ~ game n Gesellschaftsspiel nt; ~maid n (Brit) Dienstmädchen nt.

parlous ['pɑːləs] adj (old, liter) to be in a ~ state sich in einem prekären Zustand befinden.

Parmesan [ˌpɑːmɪˈzæn] n Parmesan m.

Parnassus [pɑːˈnæsəs] n Mount ~ der Parnaß.

parochial [pəˈrəʊkɪəl] adj (a) (Eccl) Pfarr-, Gemeinde-. the ~ duties of a priest die Aufgaben eines Gemeindepfarrers; the ~ boundaries die Grenzen des Pfarrbezirks; ~ school (US) Konfessionsschule f.

(b) (fig) attitude, person engstirnig; mind, ideas beschränkt. English philosophers are often accused of being ~ in their interests den englischen Philosophen wird oft vorgeworfen, einen beschränkten Horizont zu haben; he's so ~ in his outlook er hat einen sehr beschränkten Gesichtskreis.

parochialism [pəˈrəʊkɪəlɪzəm] n (fig) Engstirnigkeit f.

parodist ['pærədɪst] n Parodist(in f) m.

parody ['pærədɪ] 1 n (a) Parodie f (of auf +acc). (b) (travesty) Abklatsch m. a ~ of justice eine Parodie auf die Gerechtigkeit. 2 vt parodieren.

parole [pəˈrəʊl] 1 n (a) (Jur) Bewährung f; (temporary release) Strafunterbrechung f, Kurzurlaub m. to put sb or let sb out on ~ jdn auf Bewährung entlassen; (temporarily) jdm Strafunterbrechung or Kurzurlaub gewähren; to be on ~ unter Bewährung stehen; (temporarily) auf Kurzurlaub sein; he's on

six months' ~ er hat sechs Monate Bewährung(sfrist); **to break one's ~** den Kurzurlaub zur Flucht benutzen.
  (b) (*Mil*) Parole f.
  2 vt prisoner auf Bewährung entlassen; (*temporarily*) Strafunterbrechung or Kurzurlaub gewähren (+dat).

paroxysm ['pærəksɪzəm] n Anfall m. ~ **of** grief Verzweiflungsanfall m; **to be seized by a ~ of rage** einen Wutanfall bekommen; **~s of laughter** ein Lachkrampf m.

parquet ['pɑːkeɪ] n **(a)** Parkett nt. **(b)** (*US Theat*) Parkett nt. **~ circle** Parkett nt.

parquetry ['pɑːkɪtrɪ] n Mosaikparkett nt.

parricide ['pærɪsaɪd] n (*act*) Vater-/Muttermord m; (*person*) Vater-/Muttermörder(in f) m.

parrot ['pærət] **1** n Papagei m. **2** vt (wie ein Papagei) nachplappern (sb jdm).

parrot: **~-fashion** adv to repeat sth **~-fashion** etw wie ein Papagei nachplappern; **he learnt the poem ~-fashion** er lernte das Gedicht stur auswendig; **~ fever** n Papageienkrankheit f; **~-fish** n Papageifisch m; **~-like** adj papageienhaft; this **~-like way of learning** dies sture Auswendiglernen.

parry ['pærɪ] **1** n (*Fencing, fig*) Parade f; (*Boxing*) Abwehr f. **2** vti (*Fencing, fig*) parieren; (*Boxing*) blow abwehren. **well parried!** gut pariert!; gut abgewehrt!

parse [pɑːz] **1** vt grammatisch analysieren. **2** vi analysieren. **this sentence doesn't ~ very easily** die Struktur dieses Satzes ist nicht leicht zu analysieren.

parsimonious [ˌpɑːsɪˈməʊnɪəs] adj geizig.

parsimoniously [ˌpɑːsɪˈməʊnɪəslɪ] adv see adj. **he ~ refused to** lend me any money at all er war zu geizig, mir auch nur einen einzigen Pfennig zu leihen.

parsimony ['pɑːsɪmənɪ] n Geiz m.

parsley ['pɑːslɪ] n Petersilie f.

parsnip ['pɑːsnɪp] n Pastinak m, Pastinake f.

parson ['pɑːsn] n Pfarrer, Pastor, Pfaffe (pej) m. **~'s nose** Bürzel, Sterz m.

parsonage ['pɑːsənɪdʒ] n Pfarrhaus nt.

part [pɑːt] **1** n **(a)** (*portion, fragment*) Teil m. **the stupid ~ of it is that ...** das Dumme daran ist, daß ...; **you haven't heard the best ~ yet** ihr habt ja das Beste noch gar nicht gehört; **~ and parcel** fester Bestandteil; **it is ~ and parcel of the job** das gehört zu der Arbeit dazu; **are transport costs included?** — yes, they're all **~ and parcel of the scheme** sind die Transportkosten enthalten? — ja, es ist alles inbegriffen; **the book is good in ~s** teilweise or streckenweise ist das Buch gut; **in ~ teilweise, zum Teil; the greater ~ of it/of the work is done** der größte Teil davon/der Arbeit ist fertig; **it is in large ~ finished/true** das ist zum großen Teil erledigt/wahr; **a ~ of the country/city I don't know** eine Gegend, die ich nicht kenne; **this is in great ~ due to ...** das liegt größtenteils or vor allem an (+dat) ...; **the darkest ~ of the night is ...** es ist am dunkelsten ...; **during the darkest ~ of the night in** tiefster Nacht; **they chose the darkest ~ of the night** sie haben sich die dunkelsten Stunden der Nacht ausgesucht; **I kept ~ of it for myself** ich habe einen Teil davon für mich behalten; **I lost ~ of the manuscript** ich habe einen Teil des Manuskripts verloren; **that's ~ of the truth** das ist ein Teil der Wahrheit; **for the main or most ~ hauptsächlich**, in erster Linie; **her performance was for the main or most ~ well controlled** ihre Darstellung war im großen und ganzen ausgewogen; **the house is built for the main or most ~ of wood** das Haus ist zum größten Teil aus Holz (gebaut); **in the latter ~ of the year** gegen Ende des Jahres; **the remaining ~ of our holidays** der Rest unseres Urlaubs; **she's become a ~ of me** sie ist ein Teil von mir geworden; **5 ~s of sand to 1 of cement** 5 Teile Sand auf ein(en) Teil Zement; **it's 3 ~s gone** drei Viertel sind schon weg.
  (b) (*Mech, of kit etc*) Teil nt. **spare ~** Ersatzteil nt.
  (c) (*Gram*) **~ of speech** Wortart f; **principal ~s of a verb** Stammformen pl.
  (d) (*of series*) Folge f; (*of serial*) Fortsetzung f; (*of encyclopaedia etc*) Lieferung f. **end of ~ one** (TV) Ende des ersten Teils.
  (e) (*share, role*) (An)teil m, Rolle f; (*Theat*) Rolle f, Part m (geh). **to play one's ~** (*fig*) seinen Beitrag leisten; **to take ~ in sth** an etw (dat) teilnehmen, bei etw (dat) mitmachen, sich an etw (dat) beteiligen; **who is taking ~?** wer macht mit?, wer ist dabei?; **he's taking ~ in the play** er spielt in dem Stück mit; **in the ~ of Lear** in der Rolle des Lear; **he looks the ~** (*Theat*) die Rolle paßt zu ihm; (*fig*) so sieht (d)er auch aus; **to play a ~** (*Theat, fig*) eine Rolle spielen; **to play no ~ in sth** nicht an etw (dat) beteiligt sein; **he's just playing a ~** (*fig*) der tut nur so.
  (f) (*Mus*) Stimme f, Part m. **the soprano ~** der Sopranpart, die Sopranstimme; **the piano ~** der Klavierpart, die Klavierstimme; **to sing in ~s** mehrstimmig singen.
  (g) **~s** pl (*region*) Gegend f; **from all ~s** überallher, von überall her; **in or around these ~s** hier in der Gegend, in dieser Gegend; **in foreign ~s** in der Fremde, in fremden Ländern; **what ~ are you from?** aus welcher Gegend sind Sie?; **he's not from these ~s** er ist nicht aus dieser Gegend or von hier.
  (h) (*side*) Seite f. **to take sb's ~** sich auf jds Seite (acc) stellen, für jdn Partei ergreifen; **for my ~ was mich betrifft, meinerseits; a miscalculation on my ~** eine Fehlkalkulation meinerseits; **on the ~ of** von seiten (+gen); seitens (+gen).
  (i) **to take sth in good/bad ~** etw nicht übelnehmen/etw übelnehmen.
  (j) **a man of ~s** ein Universalgenie nt; **a man of many ~s** ein vielseitiger Mensch.
  (k) (*US: in hair*) Scheitel m.
  (l) **~s** pl (*male genitals*) Geschlechtsteile pl.
  2 adv teils, teilweise. **is it X or Y?** — **~ one and ~ the other** ist es X oder Y? — teils (das eine), teils (das andere); **it is ~ iron and ~ copper** es teils aus Eisen, teils aus Kupfer; **brass is ~**

copper, **~ zinc** Messing ist eine Kupfer-Zink-Legierung; **it was ~ eaten** es war halb aufgegessen; **he's ~ French, ~ Scottish and ~ Latvian** er ist teils Franzose, teils Schotte und teils Lette.
  3 vt **(a)** (*divide*) teilen; hair scheiteln; curtain zur Seite schieben. **the police tried to ~ the crowd** die Polizei versuchte, eine Gasse durch die Menge zu bahnen.
  (b) (*separate*) trennen. **to ~ sb from sb/sth** jdn von jdm/etw trennen; **till death us do ~** bis daß der Tod uns scheidet; **she's not easily ~ed from her money** sie trennt sich nicht gern von ihrem Geld; **to ~ company with sb/sth** sich von jdm/etw trennen; (*in opinion*) mit jdm nicht gleicher Meinung sein; **on that issue, I must ~ company with you** in dem Punkt gehen unsere Meinungen auseinander; **to ~ company** sich trennen; **at this point the two theories ~ company** an diesem Punkt gehen die beiden Theorien auseinander; **the blouse had ~ed company with the skirt** (hum) die Bluse war aus dem Rock gerutscht.
  4 vi **(a)** (*divide*) sich teilen; (*curtains*) sich öffnen. **her lips ~ed in a smile** ihre Lippen öffneten sich zu einem Lächeln.
  (b) (*separate*) (*person*) sich trennen; (*temporarily also*) auseinandergehen, scheiden (geh); (*things*) sich lösen, abgehen. **to ~ from or with sb** sich von jdm trennen; **we ~ed friends** wir gingen als Freunde auseinander, wir schieden als Freunde (geh); **to ~ with sth** sich von etw trennen; **to ~ with money** Geld ausgeben or locker machen (inf); **to ~ from this life** (liter) aus diesem Leben scheiden (geh).

partake [pɑːˈteɪk] pret partook, ptp partaken [pɑːˈteɪkn] vi (form) **(a)** **to ~ of** food, drink zu sich (dat) nehmen; **will you ~ of a glass of sherry?** darf ich Ihnen ein Glas Sherry anbieten?; **will or do you ~?** (form, hum) darf or kann ich Ihnen etwas anbieten?; **no thank you, I don't ~** (form, hum) nein danke, für mich nicht.
  (b) (*share in*) **to ~ of sb's triumph etc** an jds Triumph (dat) etc teilhaben, jds Triumph (acc) etc teilen.
  (c) **to ~ of a quality** eine Eigenschaft an sich (dat) haben; **to a certain extent he ~s of his father's arrogance** er hat etwas von der Arroganz seines Vaters.
  (d) **to ~ in** (*an activity*) an etw (dat) teilnehmen.

parterre [pɑːˈteəʳ] n (*US*) Parterre nt.

part exchange n **to offer/take sth in ~** etw in Zahlung geben/nehmen.

parthenogenesis [ˌpɑːθɪnəʊˈdʒenɪsɪs] n Parthenogenese, Jungfernzeugung f.

Parthian shot [ˌpɑːθɪənˈʃɒt] n zum Abschied fallengelassene Spitze.

partial ['pɑːʃəl] adj **(a)** (*not complete*) Teil-, partiell (geh), teilweise; paralysis, eclipse teilweise, partiell. **~ payment** Anzahlung f; **to reach a ~ agreement** teilweise Übereinstimmung erzielen.
  (b) (*biased*) voreingenommen; judgement parteiisch.
  (c) **to be ~ to sth** eine Schwäche für etw haben; **after a while I became rather ~ to it** nach einiger Zeit hatte ich eine ziemliche Vorliebe dafür entwickelt.

partiality [ˌpɑːʃɪˈælɪtɪ] n **(a)** see adj **(b)** (*bias*) Voreingenommenheit f; Parteilichkeit f. **without ~** unvoreingenommen, unparteiisch. **(b)** (*liking*) Vorliebe, Schwäche f (for für).

partially ['pɑːʃəlɪ] adv **(a)** (*partly*) zum Teil, teilweise. **(b)** (*with bias*) parteiisch.

participant [pɑːˈtɪsɪpənt] n Teilnehmer(in f) m (in gen, an +dat); (in scuffle etc) Beteiligte(r) mf (in gen, an +dat). **the bank will not be a ~ in this project** die Bank wird sich nicht an diesem Vorhaben beteiligen.

participate [pɑːˈtɪsɪpeɪt] vi **(a)** (*take part*) sich beteiligen, teilnehmen (in an +dat). **the council was accused of participating in a housing swindle** man beschuldigte die Stadtverwaltung der Beteiligung an einem Bauschwindel; **it's no good complaining of being lonely if you don't ~** es hat keinen Sinn, über deine Einsamkeit zu klagen, wenn du nirgends mitmachst; **he actively ~d in the success of the scheme** er hat aktiv zum Erfolg des Projekts beigetragen.
  (b) (*share*) beteiligt sein (in an +dat). **to ~ in sb's sorrow** an jds Kummer (dat) Anteil nehmen.

participation [pɑːˌtɪsɪˈpeɪʃən] n Beteiligung f; (in competition etc) Teilnahme f; (worker ~) Mitbestimmung f. **~ in the profits** Gewinnbeteiligung f.

participator [pɑːˈtɪsɪpeɪtəʳ] n Teilnehmer(in f) m.

participatory [ˌpɑːtɪsɪˈpeɪtərɪ] adj teilnehmend; (Ind) Mitbestimmungs-.

participial [ˌpɑːtɪˈsɪpɪəl] adj Partizipial-, partizipial.

participle ['pɑːtɪsɪpl] n Partizip nt; see present, past.

particle ['pɑːtɪkl] n **(a)** (*of sand etc*) Teilchen, Körnchen nt; (*Phys*) Teilchen nt. **~ of dust** Stäubchen, Staubkörnchen nt; (fig) Körnchen nt; **there's not a ~ of truth in it** darin steckt kein Körnchen Wahrheit; **~ accelerator** Teilchenbeschleuniger m.
  (b) (*Gram*) Partikel f.

parti-coloured, (*US*) **parti-colored** ['pɑːtɪˌkʌləd] adj bunt, vielfarbig.

particular [pəˈtɪkjʊləʳ] **1** adj **(a)** (*as against others*) this **~ house is very nice** dies (eine) Haus ist sehr hübsch; **it varies according to the ~ case** das ist von Fall zu Fall verschieden; **in this ~ instance** in diesem besonderen Fall; **in certain ~ cases** in einigen besonderen Fällen; **there's a ~ France where ...** in Frankreich gibt es eine Stadt, wo ...; **is there any one ~ colour you prefer?** bevorzugen Sie eine bestimmte Farbe?; **your ~ duty is to ...** Ihre besondere Aufgabe besteht darin, zu ...
  (b) (*special*) besondere(r, s). **in ~** besonders, vor allem; **the wine in ~ was excellent** vor allem der Wein war hervorragend; **nothing in ~** nichts Besonderes or Bestimmtes; **is there anything in ~ you'd like?** haben Sie einen besonderen Wunsch?; **he's a ~ friend of mine** er ist ein guter Freund von mir; **for no ~ reason** aus keinem besonderen or bestimmten Grund; **to take ~ care to ...** besonders darauf achten, daß ...

(c) *(fussy, fastidious)* eigen; *(choosy)* wählerisch. he is very ~ about cleanliness/his children's education er nimmt es mit der Sauberkeit/der Erziehung seiner Kinder sehr genau; he's ~ about his car er ist sehr eigen *or* pingelig *(inf)* mit seinem Auto; I'm ~ about my friends ich suche mir meine Freunde genau aus; you can't be too ~ man kann gar nicht wählerisch genug sein; I'm not too ~ *(about it)* es kommt mir nicht so darauf an, mir ist es gleich; she was most ~ about it *(was definite)* sie bestand darauf.

2 n ~s pl Einzelheiten pl; *(about person)* Personalien pl; in this ~ in diesem Punkt; correct in every ~ in jedem Punkt richtig; for further ~s apply to the personnel manager weitere Auskünfte erteilt der Personalchef; to give ~s Angaben machen; please give full ~s bitte genaue Angaben machen; the ~ and the general das Besondere und das Allgemeine.

particularity [pəˌtɪkjuˈlærɪtɪ] n (a) *(individuality)* Besonderheit f. (b) *(detailedness)* Ausführlichkeit f. (c) *(fastidiousness)* Eigenheit f. she did not reveal an excessive degree of ~ in her choice of friends sie war nicht gerade wählerisch in der Auswahl ihrer Freunde.

particularize [pəˈtɪkjʊləraɪz] 1 vt spezifizieren, genau angeben. 2 vi in Detail *or* einzelne gehen. he did not ~ er nannte keine Einzelheiten.

particularly [pəˈtɪkjʊləlɪ] adv besonders, vor allem. everybody, but ~ Smith alle, aber vor allem *or* ganz besonders Smith; he said most ~ not to do it er hat ausdrücklich gesagt, daß man das nicht tun soll; do you want it ~ for tomorrow? brauchen Sie es unbedingt morgen?; we are ~ pleased to have with us today ... wir freuen uns besonders, heute ... bei uns zu haben; he was not ~ pleased er war nicht besonders erfreut; not ~ nicht besonders; it's important, ~ since time is getting short es ist wichtig, zumal die Zeit *or* vor allem, weil die Zeit knapp wird.

parting [ˈpɑːtɪŋ] 1 n (a) Abschied m. ~ is such sweet sorrow *(prov)* o süßer Abschiedsschmerz!; after the ~ of the ways nachdem sich ihre Wege getrennt hatten; is this the ~ of the ways then? das ist also das Ende (unserer Beziehung)?; this meeting was the ~ of the ways for the Leninists and the Trotskyites seit dieser Tagung sind die Leninisten und Trotzkisten getrennte Wege gegangen.

(b) *(Brit: in hair)* Scheitel m.

2 adj Abschieds-, abschließend. a ~ present ein Abschiedsgeschenk nt; Charles knows all about it already, was her ~ shot Charles weiß schon alles, schleuderte sie ihm nach; he made a ~ threat zum Abschied stieß er eine Drohung aus; his ~ words seine Abschiedsworte pl.

partisan [ˌpɑːtɪˈzæn] 1 adj (a) parteiisch *(esp pej)*, parteilich. ~ spirit Partei- *or* Vereinsgeist m. (b) *(Mil)* Partisanen-. ~ warfare Partisanenkrieg m. 2 n (a) Parteigänger m. (b) *(Mil)* Partisan(in f) m, Freischärler m.

partisanship [ˌpɑːtɪˈzænʃɪp] n Parteilichkeit f.

partition [pɑːˈtɪʃən] 1 n (a) Teilung f. (b) *(wall)* Trennwand f. (c) *(section)* Abteilung f. 2 vt country teilen, spalten; room aufteilen.

♦**partition off** vt sep abteilen, abtrennen.

partitive [ˈpɑːtɪtɪv] adj *(Gram)* partitiv.

partly [ˈpɑːtlɪ] adv zum Teil, teilweise, teils.

partner [ˈpɑːtnəʳ] 1 n Partner(in f) m; *(in limited company also)* Gesellschafter(in f) m; *(in crime)* Komplize m, Komplizin f. they were/became ~s in crime sie waren/wurden Komplizen; junior ~ Juniorpartner m; senior ~ Seniorpartner m.

2 vt to ~ sb jds Partner sein; to be ~ed by sb jdn zum Partner haben.

partnership [ˈpɑːtnəʃɪp] n (a) Partnerschaft, Gemeinschaft f; *(in sport, dancing etc)* Paar nt. we're *or* we make a pretty good ~ wir sind ein ziemlich gutes Paar; a relationship based on ~ eine partnerschaftliche Beziehung; to do sth in ~ with sb etw mit jdm gemeinsam *or* in Zusammenarbeit machen.

(b) *(Comm)* Personengesellschaft f. to enter into a ~ in eine Gesellschaft eintreten; to take sb into ~ jdn als Partner aufnehmen; general ~ offene Handelsgesellschaft; he left the ~ er ist aus der Gesellschaft ausgeschieden.

partook [pɑːˈtʊk] pret of **partake**.

part: ~ owner n Mitbesitzer(in f), Mitinhaber(in f) m; ~ payment n Teilzahlung f.

partridge [ˈpɑːtrɪdʒ] n Rebhuhn nt.

part: ~ song n *(individual)* mehrstimmiges Lied; *(genre)* mehrstimmiger Gesang; ~-time 1 adj job, teacher, employee Teilzeit-; I'm just ~-time ich arbeite nur Teilzeit; 2 adv can I do the job ~-time? kann ich (auf) Teilzeit arbeiten?; she only teaches ~-time sie unterrichtet nur stundenweise.

parturition [ˌpɑːtjʊəˈrɪʃən] n *(form)* Entbindung f.

party [ˈpɑːtɪ] n (a) *(Pol)* Partei f. to be a member of the ~ Parteimitglied sein, in der Partei sein *(inf)*.

(b) *(group)* Gruppe, Gesellschaft f; *(Mil)* Kommando nt, Trupp m. a ~ of tourists eine Reisegesellschaft; we were a ~ of five wir waren zu fünft; I was one of the ~ ich war dabei; to join sb's ~ sich jdm anschließen.

(c) *(celebration)* Fest nt, Party, Fête *(inf)* f; *(more formal)* Gesellschaft f. to have *or* give *or* throw *(inf)* a ~ eine Party geben *or* machen *or* schmeißen *(inf)*; eine Gesellschaft geben; at the ~ auf dem Fest *or* der Party; bei der Gesellschaft; let's keep the ~ clean *(fig inf)* wir wollen doch lieber im Rahmen bleiben.

(d) *(Jur, fig)* Partei f. a/the third ~ ein Dritter m/der Dritte; the parties to a dispute die streitenden Parteien; to be a ~ to an agreement einer Übereinkunft *(dat)* zustimmen; to be a ~ to a crime an einem Verbrechen beteiligt sein; were you a ~ to this? waren Sie daran beteiligt?; I will not be a ~ to any violence ich will mit Gewaltanwendung nichts zu tun haben.

(e) *(inf: person)* a ~ by the name of Johnson ein gewisser Johnson.

party: ~ dress n Partykleid nt; ~ line n (a) *(Pol)* Parteilinie f; (b) *(Telec)* Gemeinschaftsanschluß m; ~ man n Gefolgsmann m; ~ politics npl Parteipolitik f; ~ pooper n *(esp US inf)* Partymuffel m *(inf)*; ~ spirit n *(Pol)* Parteigeist m *or* -gesinnung f.

parvenu [ˈpɑːvənuː] n Emporkömmling, Parvenü m.

paschal [ˈpæskəl] adj Passah-, Oster-.

pas de deux [ˌpɑːdəˈdɜː] n Pas de deux m.

pasha [ˈpæʃə] n Pascha m.

paso doble [ˌpæsəʊˈdəʊbleɪ] n Paso doble m.

pass [pɑːs] 1 n (a) *(permit)* Ausweis m; *(Mil etc)* Passierschein m. a free ~ eine Freikarte; *(permanent)* ein Sonderausweis m.

(b) *(Brit Univ)* Bestehen nt einer Prüfung. to get a ~ in German seine Deutschprüfung bestehen; *(lowest level)* seine Deutschprüfung mit „ausreichend" bestehen; I need a ~ in physics ich muß noch einen Abschluß in Physik machen.

(c) *(Geog, Sport)* Paß m; *(Ftbl: for shot at goal)* Vorlage f.

(d) *(Fencing)* Ausfall m.

(e) *(movement)* *(by conjurer, hypnotist)* Bewegung, Geste f. the conjurer made a few quick ~es with his hand over the top of the hat der Zauberer fuhr mit der Hand ein paarmal schnell über dem Hut hin und her; the hypnotist made several slow ~es with a watch chain der Hypnotiseur ließ die Uhrkette ein paarmal hin- und herpendeln; the paint-sprayer makes two ~es over the metal der Lackierer spritzt das Metall zweimal.

(f) things have come to a pretty ~ when ... so weit ist es schon gekommen, daß ...; things had come to such a ~ that ... die Lage hatte sich so zugespitzt, daß ...; this is a fine ~ to be in, here's a pretty ~! *(dated)* das ist ja eine schöne Bescherung!

(g) to make a ~ at sb bei jdm Annäherungsversuche machen.

(h) *(Aviat)* the jet made three ~es over the ship der Düsenjäger flog dreimal über das Schiff; on its fourth ~ the plane was almost hit beim vierten Vorbeifliegen wurde das Flugzeug fast getroffen; the pilot made two ~es over the landing strip before deciding to come down der Pilot passierte die Landebahn zweimal, ehe er sich zur Landung entschloß.

2 vt (a) *(move past)* vorbeigehen an (+dat); vorbeifahren an (+dat); vorbeifliegen an (+dat). he ~ed me without even saying hello er ging ohne zu grüßen an mir vorbei; the ship ~ed the estuary das Schiff passierte die Flußmündung; when the rocket ~es Venus wenn die Rakete an der Venus vorbeifliegt.

(b) *(overtake)* athlete, car überholen. he's ~ed all the other candidates er hat alle anderen Kandidaten überflügelt.

(c) *(cross)* frontier etc überschreiten, überqueren, passieren. not a word ~ed her lips kein Wort kam über ihre Lippen.

(d) *(reach, hand)* reichen. they ~ed the photograph around sie reichten *or* gaben das Foto herum; ~ (me) the salt, please reich mir doch bitte das Salz!; he ~ed the hammer up er reichte den Hammer hinauf; the characteristics which he ~ed to his son die Eigenschaften, die er an seinen Sohn weitergab.

(e) it ~es belief es ist kaum zu fassen; it ~es my comprehension that ... es geht über meinen Verstand *or* meine Fassungskraft, daß ...; love which ~es all understanding Liebe, die jenseits allen Verstehens liegt.

(f) *(Univ etc)* exam bestehen; candidate bestehen lassen.

(g) this film will never ~ the censors dieser Film kommt nie und nimmer durch die Zensur; the play won't ~ the critics easily das Stück wird es mit den Kritikern nicht leicht haben.

(h) *(approve)* motion annehmen; plan gutheißen, genehmigen; *(Parl)* verabschieden. the motion was ~ed by 10 votes to 5 der Antrag wurde mit 10:5 Stimmen angenommen; the censors will never ~ this film die Zensur gibt diesen Film bestimmt nicht frei.

(i) ball etc to ~ the ball to sb jdm den Ball zuspielen; you should learn to ~ the ball and not hang on to it du solltest lernen abzuspielen, statt am Ball zu kleben.

(j) forged bank notes weitergeben.

(k) to ~ a cloth over sth mit einem Tuch über etw (acc) wischen; he ~ed his hand across his forehead er fuhr sich (dat) mit der Hand über die Stirn; ~ the thread through the hole führen Sie den Faden durch die Öffnung; he ~ed a chain around the front axle er legte eine Kette um die Vorderachse.

(l) *(spend)* time verbringen. he did it just to ~ the time er tat das nur, um sich (dat) die Zeit zu vertreiben.

(m) remark von sich geben; opinion abgeben; *(Jur)* sentence verhängen; judgement fällen.

(n) *(discharge)* excrement, blood absondern, ausscheiden. to ~ water Wasser *or* Harn lassen.

(o) *(omit)* I'll ~ this round ich lasse diese Runde aus.

3 vi (a) *(move past)* vorbeigehen, vorbeifahren. the street was too narrow for the cars to ~ die Straße war so eng, daß die Wagen nicht aneinander vorbeikamen; we ~ed in the corridor wir gingen im Korridor aneinander vorbei; there isn't room for him to ~ es ist so eng, daß er nicht vorbeikommt.

(b) *(overtake)* überholen.

(c) *(move, go)* ~ along the car please! bitte weiter durchgehen!; a stream of letters ~ed between them sie tauschten eine Flut von Briefen aus; words ~ed between them es gab einige Meinungsverschiedenheiten; the cars ~ down the assembly line die Autos kommen das Fließband herunter; as we ~ from feudalism to more open societies/youth to old age beim Übergang vom Feudalismus zu offeneren Gesellschaftsformen/mit zunehmendem Alter; the colours ~ from red to orange die Farbtöne gehen von Rot nach Orange; people were ~ing in and out of the building die Leute gingen in dem Gebäude ein und aus; to ~ into a tunnel in einen Tunnel fahren; to ~ into oblivion/a coma in Vergessenheit geraten/in ein Koma fallen; expressions which have ~ed into/out of the language Redensarten, die in die Sprache eingegangen sind/ aus der Sprache verschwunden sind; to ~ out of sight außer Sichtweite geraten; the firm has ~ed out of existence die Firma hat aufgehört zu bestehen; he ~ed out of our lives er ist aus unserem Leben verschwunden; **everything he said just ~ed over my head** was er sagte, war mir alles zu hoch; **when we ~ed over the frontier** als wir die Grenze passierten; **we're now ~ing over Paris** wir fliegen jetzt über Paris; **I'll just ~ quickly over the main points again** ich werde jetzt die Hauptpunkte noch einmal kurz durchgehen; **he's ~ing through a difficult period** er macht gerade eine schwere Zeit durch; **the manuscript has ~ed through a lot of hands** das Manuskript ist durch viele Hände gegangen; **the thread ~es through this hole** der Faden geht durch diese Öffnung; **the book has ~ed through several editions** das Buch ist mehrmals aufgelegt worden; **shall we ~ to the second subject on the agenda?** wollen wir zum zweiten Punkt der Tagesordnung übergehen?; **the crown always ~es to the eldest son** die Krone geht immer auf den ältesten Sohn über; **the area then ~ed under Roman rule** das Gebiet geriet dann unter römische Herrschaft; **he ~ed under the archway** er ging/fuhr durch das Tor.

(d) (*time*) (*also ~ by*) vergehen.

(e) (*disappear, end: anger, hope, era etc*) vorübergehen, vorbeigehen; (*storm*) (*go over*) vorüberziehen; (*abate*) sich legen; (*rain*) vorbeigehen. **it'll ~** das geht vorüber!

(f) (*be acceptable*) gehen. **to let sth ~** etw durchgehen lassen; **we can't let that ~!** das können wir nicht durchgehen lassen!; **let it ~!** vergiß es!, vergessen wir's!; **what ~es in New York may not be good enough here** was in New York geht, muß hier noch lange nicht gut genug sein; **it'll ~** das geht.

(g) (*be considered, be accepted*) angesehen werden (*for or as sth* als etw). **this little café ~es for a restaurant** dieses kleine Café dient als Restaurant; **in her day she ~ed for a great beauty** zu ihrer Zeit galt sie als große Schönheit; **she could easily ~ for 25** sie könnte leicht für 25 durchgehen; **or what ~es nowadays for a hat** oder was heute so als Hut betrachtet wird; **a coward often ~es as a hero** ein Feigling wird oft als Held angesehen.

(h) (*in exam*) bestehen. **I ~ed!** ich habe bestanden!; **did you ~ in chemistry?** bist du in Chemie durchgekommen?, hast du deine Chemieprüfung bestanden?

(i) (*Sport*) abspielen. **to ~ to sb** jdm zuspielen, an jdn abgeben.

(j) (*Cards*) passen. **(I) ~!** (ich) passe!; **~** (*in quiz etc*) passe!

(k) (*old: happen*) **to come to ~** sich begeben; **and it came to ~ in those days ...** und es begab sich zu jener Zeit ...; **to bring sth to ~ etw** bewirken.

♦**pass away** *vi* **(a)** (*end*) zu Ende gehen. **the days of our youth have ~ed ~ for ever** die Tage unserer Jugend sind für immer dahin. **(b)** (*euph: die*) entschlafen, hinscheiden. 2 *vt sep* **hours** sich (*dat*) vertreiben.

♦**pass between** *vi +prep obj* (*words*) fallen zwischen. **what has ~ed ~ us** was sich zwischen uns zugetragen hat.

♦**pass by 1** *vi* (*go past*) vorbeigehen; (*car etc*) vorbeifahren; (*time, months etc*) vergehen. **he just ~ed ~** er ging/fuhr einfach vorbei; **there was no room for the lorry to ~ ~** der Lastwagen kam nicht vorbei; **I can't let that ~ ~ without comment** ich kann das nicht kommentarlos durchgehen lassen; **to ~ ~ on the other side** (*fig*) achtlos vorbeigehen.

2 *vi +prep obj* **if you ~ ~ the grocer's ...** wenn du beim Kaufmann vorbeikommst, ...; **we ~ed ~ a line of hotels** wir kamen an einer Reihe Hotels vorbei.

3 *vt sep* (*ignore*) *problems* übergehen. **life has ~ed her ~** das Leben ist an ihr vorübergegangen.

♦**pass down** *vt sep* **(a)** *traditions* weitergeben (*to an +acc*), überliefern (*to dat*); *characteristics* weitergeben (*to an +acc*). **~ed ~ by word of mouth** mündlich überliefert. **(b)** (*transmit*) **the story was ~ed ~ through the ranks** die Sache sprach sich (bis) zu den Soldaten durch.

♦**pass off 1** *vi* **(a)** (*take place*) ablaufen, vonstatten gehen. **(b)** (*end*) vorüber- *or* vorbeigehen. **(c)** (*be taken as*) durchgehen (*as als*). **she could easily ~ ~ as an Italian** sie würde ohne weiteres als Italienerin durchgehen; **it ~ed ~ as a genuine Dali** es ging als echter Dali durch.

2 *vt sep* **to ~ oneself/sb/sth ~ as sth** sich/jdn/etw als *or* für etw ausgeben.

♦**pass on 1** *vi* **(a)** (*euph: die*) entschlafen, verscheiden. **(b)** (*proceed*) übergehen (*to zu*). **right gentlemen, shall we ~ ~?** gut, meine Herren, wollen wir nun zum nächsten Punkt übergehen?

2 *vt sep* *news, information* weitergeben; *disease* übertragen. **the financial benefits will be ~ed ~ to the public** die Erträge werden an die Öffentlichkeit weitergegeben; **~ it ~!** weitersagen!

♦**pass out 1** *vi* **(a)** (*become unconscious*) in Ohnmacht fallen, umkippen (*inf*). **he drank till he ~ed ~** er trank bis zum Umfallen. **(b)** (*new officer*) ernannt werden, sein Patent bekommen (*dated*). 2 *vt sep* *leaflets* austeilen, verteilen.

♦**pass over 1** *vt sep* übergehen. **he's been ~ed ~ again** er ist schon wieder übergangen worden. 2 *vi* (*euph: die*) entschlafen.

♦**pass through** *vi* **I'm only ~ing ~** ich bin nur auf der Durchreise; **you have to ~ ~ Berlin** du mußt über Berlin fahren.

♦**pass up** *vt sep* *chance* vorübergehen lassen.

passable ['pɑːsəbl] *adj* **(a)** *road etc also* befahrbar. **(b)** (*tolerable*) leidlich, passabel.

passably ['pɑːsəblɪ] *adv* leidlich, einigermaßen.

passage ['pæsɪdʒ] *n* **(a)** (*transition: from youth to manhood etc*) Übergang *m*. **the ~ of time** der Verlauf *or* Strom (*geh*) der Zeit; **in** *or* **with the ~ of time** mit der Zeit.

(b) (*through country*) Durchfahrt, Durchreise *f*; (*right of ~*) Durchreise *f*, Transit *m*, Durchreise- *or* Transitgenehmigung *f*. **to grant sb ~ through an area** jdm die Durchreise durch ein Gebiet genehmigen, jdm Durchreise- *or* Transitgenehmigung für ein Gebiet erteilen.

(c) (*voyage*) Überfahrt, Schiffsreise *f*; (*fare*) Überfahrt, Passage *f*; *see* **work**.

(d) (*Parl: process*) parlamentarische Behandlung; (*final*) Annahme, Verabschiedung *f*.

(e) (*corridor*) Gang *m*. **the ~ narrow** ~ **between Denmark and Sweden** die schmale Durchfahrt zwischen Dänemark und Schweden; **secret ~** Geheimgang *m*; **he forced a ~ through the crowd** er bahnte sich (*dat*) einen Weg durch die Menge.

(f) (*in book*) Passage *f*; (*Mus also*) Passage *f*. **selected ~s from Caesar** ausgewählte Passagen aus Cäsar; **a ~ from Shakespeare/the Bible** eine Shakespeare-/Bibelstelle.

passageway ['pæsɪdʒweɪ] *n* Durchgang *m*.

pass: **~ book** *n* Sparbuch *nt*; **~ degree** *n* niedrigster Grad an britischen Universitäten, „Bestanden".

passé ['pæseɪ] *adj* überholt, passé (*inf*).

passenger ['pæsɪndʒəʳ] *n* **(a)** (*on bus, in taxi*) Fahrgast *m*; (*on train*) Reisende(r) *mf*; (*on ship*) Passagier *m*; (*on plane*) Fluggast, Passagier *m*; (*in car*) Mitfahrer(in *f*), Beifahrer(in *f*) *m*; (*on motorcycle*) Beifahrer(in *f*) *m*.

(b) (*inf: ineffective member*) **we can't afford to carry any ~s** (*no incompetent people*) wir können es uns nicht leisten, Leute mit durchzuschleppen; (*no idle people*) wir können uns keine Drückeberger leisten; **he's just a ~ in the team** er wird von den anderen mit durchgeschleppt.

passenger: **~ aircraft** *n* Passagierflugzeug *nt*; **~ liner** *n* Passagierschiff *nt*; **~ list** *n* Passagierliste *f*; **~ mile** *n* (*Aviat*) Flugkilometer *m* je Fluggast; (*Rail*) Bahnkilometer *m* je Reisender; **~ train** *n* Zug *m* im Personenverkehr.

passe-partout ['pæspɑːtuː] *n* Passepartout *nt*.

passer-by ['pɑːsə'baɪ] *n, pl* **passers-by** Passant(in *f*) *m*, Vorübergehende(r) *mf*.

passim ['pæsɪm] *adv* passim, verstreut.

passing ['pɑːsɪŋ] **1** *n* **(a)** Vorübergehen *nt*. **with the ~ of time/the years** im Lauf(e) der Zeit/der Jahre; **I would like to mention in ~ that ...** ich möchte beiläufig noch erwähnen, daß ... **(b)** (*disappearance*) Niedergang *m*; (*euph: death*) Heimgang *m*. **the ~ of the old year** der Ausklang des alten Jahres. **(c)** (*Parl: of bill*) *see* **passage (d)**.

2 *adj* *car* vorbeifahrend; *clouds* vorüberziehend; *years* vergehend; *glance etc, thought* flüchtig; *comments, reference* beiläufig; *fancy* flüchtig, vorübergehend.

3 *adv* (*old: very*) gar (*old*), überaus (*liter*).

passing note *n* Durchgangston *m*.

passing-out (ceremony) [ˌpɑːsɪŋ'aʊt(ˌserɪmənɪ)] *n* (*Mil*) Abschlußfeier *f*.

passion ['pæʃən] *n* **(a)** Leidenschaft *f*; (*fervour*) Leidenschaftlichkeit *f*; (*enthusiasm also*) Begeisterung *f*. **to have a ~ for sth** eine Passion für etw haben; **with his ~ for accuracy/oysters/all things Greek** mit seinem Drang nach Genauigkeit/seiner Passion *or* ausgeprägten Vorliebe für Austern/alles Griechische; **~s were running high** die Erregung schlug hohe Wellen; **political ~s** politische Leidenschaften *pl*; **his ~ for the cause** sein leidenschaftliches Engagement für die Sache; **music is a ~ with him** die Musik ist bei ihm eine Leidenschaft; **his ~ is Mozart** Mozart ist seine Passion; **yes, my ~, what is it?** (*hum*) ja, du Traum meiner schlaflosen Nächte, was gibt's? (*hum*); **to be in a ~** erregt sein; **to fly into a ~** in Erregung geraten, sich erregen.

(b) (*Rel, Art, Mus*) Passion *f*; (*Bibl: account of ~ also*) Leidensgeschichte *f*. **The St Matthew P~** Die Matthäuspassion.

passionate ['pæʃənɪt] *adj* leidenschaftlich.

passionately ['pæʃənɪtlɪ] *adv* leidenschaftlich. **oh yes, she said ~** o ja, sagte sie voller Leidenschaft; **she wept ~** sie weinte heiße Tränen.

passion: **~ flower** *n* Passionsblume *f*; (*hum inf: as address*) Schatz *m*, Schätzchen *nt*; **~ fruit** *n* Passionsfrucht *f*; **~less** *adj* leidenschaftslos; **~ play** *n* Passionsspiel *nt*; **P~ Sunday** *n* Passionssonntag *m*; **P~ Week** *n* Karwoche *f*.

passive ['pæsɪv] **1** *adj* **(a)** passiv; *acceptance* widerspruchslos, widerstandslos. **~ resistance** passiver Widerstand; **~ vocabulary** passiver Wortschatz.

(b) (*Gram*) passivisch, passiv (*rare*), Passiv-.

2 *n* (*Gram*) Passiv *nt*, Leideform *f*. **in the ~** im Passiv.

passively ['pæsɪvlɪ] *adv* passiv; *accept* widerstandslos, widerspruchslos; *watch etc* tatenlos.

passiveness ['pæsɪvnɪs], **passivity** [pə'sɪvɪtɪ] *n* Passivität *f*.

pass key *n* Hauptschlüssel *m*.

Passover ['pɑːsəʊvəʳ] *n* Passah *nt*.

passport ['pɑːspɔːt] *n* Reisepaß, Paß (*inf*) *m*; (*fig*) Schlüssel *m* (*to* für, zu).

password ['pɑːswɜːd] *n* Losungs- *or* Kennwort *nt*, Parole *f*.

past [pɑːst] **1** *adj* **(a)** frühe(r, s) *attr*, vergangene(r, s) *attr*. **for some time ~** seit einiger Zeit; **in times ~** in früheren *or* vergangenen Zeiten; **it's ~ history now** das gehört jetzt der Vergangenheit an; **all that is now ~** das ist jetzt alles vorüber *or* vorbei; **what's ~ is ~** was vorbei ist, ist vorbei; **in the ~ week** letzte *or* vorige *or* vergangene Woche, in der letzten *or* vergangenen Woche; **~ president** früherer Präsident.

(b) (*Gram*) **~ tense** Vergangenheit, Vergangenheitsform *f*; **~ participle** Partizip Perfekt, zweites Partizip; **~ perfect** Plusquamperfekt *nt*, Vorvergangenheit *f*.

2 *n* (*also Gram*) Vergangenheit *f*. **in the ~** in der Vergangenheit (*also Gram*), früher; **to live in the ~** in der Vergangenheit leben; **the verb is in the ~** das Verb steht in der Vergangenheit; **to be a thing of the ~** der Vergangenheit (*dat*) angehören; **a town/woman with a ~** eine Stadt/Frau mit Vergangenheit; **he was believed to have a "~"** man nahm an, daß er kein unbeschriebenes Blatt sei.

3 *prep* **(a)** (*motion*) an (+*dat*) ... vorbei *or* vorüber; (*position: beyond*) hinter (+*dat*). **just ~ the library** kurz nach *or* hinter der Bücherei; **to run ~ sb** an jdm vorbeilaufen.

(b) (*time*) nach (+*dat*). **ten (minutes) ~ three** zehn (Minuten) nach drei; **half ~ four** halb fünf; **a quarter ~ nine** Viertel nach neun, Viertel zehn; it's ~ 12 es ist schon nach 12 or 12 vorbei; the trains run at a quarter ~ the hour die Züge gehen jeweils um Viertel nach; it's (well) ~ your bedtime du solltest schon längst im Bett liegen.

(c) *(beyond)* über *(+acc)*. ~ **forty** über vierzig; **his stupidity is ~ belief** seine Dummheit ist unglaublich, er ist unglaublich dumm; **the patient is ~ saving** der Patient ist nicht mehr zu retten; **we're ~ caring** es kümmert uns nicht mehr; **to be ~ sth** für etw zu alt sein; **he's ~ heavy work** schwere Arbeit kann er nicht mehr leisten; **my car is getting ~ it** *(inf)* mein Auto tut's allmählich nicht mehr or bringt's nicht mehr *(inf)*; **he's ~ it** *(inf)* er ist zu alt, er ist ein bißchen alt *(dated)*, er bringt's nicht mehr *(sl)*; **she's getting a bit ~ it** *(inf)* sie wird allmählich alt; **I wouldn't put it ~ him** *(inf)* ich würde es ihm schon zutrauen.

4 *adv* vorbei, vorüber. **to walk/run ~** vorüber- or vorbeigehen/vorbeirennen.

pasta ['pæstə] *n* Teigwaren, Nudeln *pl*.

paste [peɪst] **1** *n* **(a)** *(for sticking)* Kleister *m*.
(b) **mix to a smooth/firm ~** *(glue etc)* zu einem lockeren/festen Brei anrühren; *(cake mixture etc)* zu einem glatten/festen Teig anrühren.
(c) *(spread)* Brotaufstrich *m*; *(tomato ~)* Mark *nt*.
(d) *(jewellery)* Similistein, Straß *m*.
2 *vt* **(a)** *(apply ~ to)* **wallpaper etc** einkleistern, mit Kleister bestreichen; *(affix)* kleben. **to ~ pictures into a book** Bilder in ein Buch (ein)kleben; **to ~ sth to sth** etw an etw *(acc)* kleben.
(b) *(sl)* **opponent** eine Packung verabreichen *(+dat)* *(inf)*; *(Boxing)* die Hucke vollhauen *(+dat)* *(inf)*; **new play etc** zerreißen. **to ~ sb (one)** *(lit)* jdm eins vor den Latz knallen *(sl)*; **to ~ sb** *(defeat)* jdn in die Pfanne hauen *(inf)*; **to ~ sth** *(fig)* etw verhackstücken *(inf)*.

♦**paste up** *vt sep* aufkleben, ankleben; *(in publishing)* einen Klebeumbruch machen von.

pasteboard ['peɪstbɔːd] *n* Karton *m*, Pappe *f*.

pastel ['pæstl] **1** *n* *(crayon)* Pastellstift *m*, Pastellkreide *f*; *(drawing)* Pastellzeichnung *f*, Pastell *nt*; *(colour)* Pastellton *m*. **2** *adj attr* Pastell-, pastellen, pastellfarben. ~ **colour** Pastellfarbe *f*, Pastellton *m*; ~ **drawing** Pastellzeichnung *f*.

paste-up ['peɪstʌp] *n* Klebeumbruch *m*. **to do a ~** einen Klebeumbruch herstellen or machen.

pasteurization [,pæstəraɪ'zeɪʃən] *n* Pasteurisierung, Pasteurisation *f*.

pasteurize ['pæstəraɪz] *vt* pasteurisieren, keimfrei machen.

pastiche [pæ'stiːʃ] *n* Pastiche *m*; *(satirical writing)* Persiflage *f*.

pastille ['pæstɪl] *n* Pastille *f*.

pastime ['pɑːstaɪm] *n* Zeitvertreib *m*.

pastiness ['peɪstɪnɪs] *n* **the ~ of her complexion** ihr bläßliches or käsiges *(inf)* or kränkliches Aussehen.

pasting ['peɪstɪŋ] *n* *(sl)* **to get a ~** *(from sb* von jdm) fertiggemacht werden *(inf)*; *(Sport, from critic also)* in die Pfanne gehauen werden *(inf)*; **to give sb a ~** jdn fertigmachen *(inf)*; *(Sport, as critic also)* jdn in die Pfanne hauen *(inf)*.

past master *n* Experte *m*, Expertin *f*; *(Art, Sport also)* Altmeister(in *f)* *m*. **to be a ~ at doing sth** ein Experte darin sein, etw zu tun.

pastor ['pɑːstə^r] *n* Pfarrer *m*.

pastoral ['pɑːstərəl] **1** *adj* **(a)** *(Art, Liter, Mus)* pastoral. **Beethoven's P~ Symphony** Beethovens Pastorale *f*; ~ **poem** Schäfer- or Hirtengedicht *nt*; ~ **picture** Pastorale *f or nt*.
(b) *(Eccl)* pastoral, pfarramtlich; **duties also** seelsorgerisch; **responsibility** seelsorgerlich. ~ **care** Seelsorge *f*; ~ **staff** Bischofsstab *m*; ~ **letter** Hirtenbrief *m*.
2 *n* **(a)** *(Liter, Art, Mus)* Pastorale *f or nt*.
(b) *(Eccl)* Hirtenbrief *m*.

pastorale [,pæstə'rɑːl] *n* *(Mus)* Pastorale *f*.

pastry ['peɪstrɪ] *n* Teig *m*; *(cake also)* Stückchen *nt*. **pastries** *pl* Gebäck *nt*; **you've got a piece of ~ on your chin** du hast einen Krümel am Kinn; **see Danish**.

pastry-cook ['peɪstrɪkʊk] *n* Konditor(in *f)* *m*.

pasturage ['pɑːstjʊrɪdʒ] *n* **(a)** *(grass)* Weide *f*. **(b)** *(right of pasture)* Weiderecht *nt*.

pasture ['pɑːstʃə^r] **1** *n* **(a)** *(field)* Weide *f*. **to put out to ~** auf die Weide treiben; **to move on to ~s new** *(fig)* sich *(dat)* etwas Neues suchen, sich nach neuen Weidegründen *(geh)* umsehen.
(b) *no pl (also ~ land)* Weideland *nt*.
(c) *no pl (food)* Futter *nt*.
2 *vt* **animals** weiden lassen.
3 *vi* grasen.

pasty[1] ['peɪstɪ] *adj* **(a)** **consistency** zähflüssig; **material** klebrig.
(b) **colour, look** bläßlich, käsig *(inf)*, kränklich.

pasty[2] ['pæstɪ] *n* *(esp Brit)* Pastete *f*.

pasty-faced ['peɪstɪ'feɪst] *adj* blaß- or bleichgesichtig.

Pat [pæt] *n* *(sl)* Ire *m*.

pat[1] [pæt] *n* *(of butter)* Portion *f*. **cow ~** Kuhfladen *m*.

pat[2] **1** *adv* **to know or have sth off ~** etw wie am Schnürchen *(inf)* or wie aus dem Effeff *(inf)* können; **he knows the rules off ~** er kennt die Regeln in- und auswendig or aus dem Effeff *(inf)*; **to learn sth off ~** etw in- und auswendig lernen; **he's always got an answer ~** er hat immer eine Antwort parat; **to stand ~** keinen Zollbreit nachgeben.
2 *adj* **answer, explanation** glatt. **somehow his excuses seem a bit ~** to me er ist mir immer ein bißchen zu schnell mit Ausreden bei der Hand.

pat[3] **1** *n* Klaps *m*. **he gave his nephew a ~ on the head** er tätschelte seinem Neffen den Kopf; **he gave him a ~ on the shoulder in order to attract his attention** er tippte ihm auf die Schulter, um ihn auf sich aufmerksam zu machen; **excellent work, said the teacher, giving her a ~ on the shoulder** hervorragende Arbeit, sagte der Lehrer und klopfte ihr auf die Schulter; **he gave her knee an affectionate ~** er tätschelte ihr liebevoll das Knie; **to give one's horse/the dog a ~** sein Pferd/

seinen Hund tätscheln; *(once)* seinem Pferd or Hund einen Klaps geben; **to give sb/oneself a ~ on the back** *(fig)* jdm/sich selbst auf die Schulter klopfen; **that's a ~ on the back for you** das ist ein Kompliment für dich.
2 *vt* *(touch lightly)* tätscheln; *(hit gently)* **ball** leicht schlagen; **sand** festklopfen; **face** abtupfen. **to ~ sb/the dog on the head** jdm/dem Hund den Kopf tätscheln; **to ~ sth/one's face dry** etw/sein Gesicht trockentupfen; **she ~ted a few loose curls into place** sie drückte ein paar Locken an, die sich gelöst hatten; **the sculptor ~ted the plaster into shape** der Bildhauer klopfte den Gips in die richtige Form; **he ~ted aftershave onto his chin** er betupfte sein Kinn mit Rasierwasser; **to ~ sb on the back** *(lit)* jdm auf den Rücken klopfen; **to ~ sb/oneself on the back** *(fig)* jdm/sich selbst auf die Schulter klopfen.

♦**pat down** *vt sep* festklopfen; **hair** festdrücken, andrücken.

pat[4] *abbr of* **patent**.

Patagonia [,pætə'gəʊnɪə] *n* Patagonien *nt*.

Patagonian [,pætə'gəʊnɪən] **1** *adj* patagonisch. **2** *n* Patagonier(in *f)* *m*.

patch [pætʃ] **1** *n* **(a)** *(for mending)* Flicken *m*; *(on new garments)* Flecken *m*; *(eye ~)* Augenklappe *f*.
(b) **it's/he's not a ~ on ...** *(inf)* das/er ist gar nichts gegen ...
(c) *(small area, stain)* Fleck *m*; *(piece of land)* Stück *nt*; *(subdivision of garden)* Beet *nt*; *(part, section)* Stelle *f*; *(of time)* Phase *f*; *(inf: of policeman, prostitute)* Revier *nt*. **a ~ of blue sky** ein Stückchen *nt* blauer Himmel; **purple ~es** dotted the landscape die Landschaft war übersät mit violetten Farbtupfern; **~es of colour** Farbtupfer *pl*; **a ~ of oil** ein Ölfleck *m*; **~es of sunlight** dappled the floor of the forest (die) Sonnenstrahlen tanzten auf dem Waldboden; **then we hit a bad ~ of road** dann kamen wir auf ein schlechtes Stück Straße; **the cabbage ~** das Kohlbeet; **we drove through a few ~es of rain on our way here** wir hatten auf dem Weg stellenweise Regen; **there were sunny ~es during the day** hin und wieder schien die Sonne; **~es of depression** depressive Phasen *pl*; **he's going through a bad ~ at the moment** ihm geht's im Augenblick nicht sonderlich gut.
(d) *(cosmetic beauty spot)* Schönheitspflästerchen *nt*.
2 *vt* flicken. **this piece of cloth will just ~ that hole nicely** dieses Stück Stoff ist gerade richtig für das Loch.

♦**patch up** *vt sep* zusammenflicken; **quarrel** beilegen. **to ~ things ~ temporarily** die Dinge notdürftig zusammenflicken; **they managed to ~ ~ their relationship** sie haben sich schließlich wieder ausgesöhnt; **I want to ~ things ~ between us** ich möchte unsere Beziehung wieder ins Lot bringen.

patchiness ['pætʃɪnɪs] *n* *(of work)* Unregelmäßigkeit *f*; *(of knowledge)* Lückenhaftigkeit *f*; *(of film, book, essay etc)* unterschiedliche Qualität.

patch: ~ **pocket** *n* aufgesetzte Tasche; **~-up** *n* *(inf)* Flickwerk *nt no art*; **~work** *n* Patchwork *nt*; **~work quilt** Patchwork- or Flickendecke *f*; *(fig)* a **~work** of fields ein bunter Teppich von Feldern; a **~work** of songs eine bunte Folge von Liedern.

patchy ['pætʃɪ] *adj (+er)* **(a)** **work** ungleichmäßig, unterschiedlich; **knowledge, memory** lückenhaft. **what was the performance like? — ~** wie war die Aufführung? — gemischt; **his second novel however was much patchier** sein zweiter Roman war wesentlicher unausgeglichener; **this is the patchiest production I've seen** them do for a long time eine derart ungleichmäßige Inszenierung habe ich von ihnen lange nicht mehr gesehen; **what's his work like? — ~** wie ist seine Arbeit? — unterschiedlich.
(b) *(lit)* **material** gefleckt; **pattern** Flecken-. **the ~ appearance of the half rebuilt city** der Eindruck von Flickwerk, den die zur Hälfte neu aufgebaute Stadt vermittelt/vermittelte.

pate [peɪt] *n* Rübe *(inf)*, Birne *(sl)* *f*. **bald ~** Platte *(inf)*, Glatze *f*.

pâté ['pæteɪ] *n* Pastete *f*.

-pated [-peɪtɪd] *adj suf* -köpfig.

patella [pə'telə] *n* *(Anat)* Patella *(spec)*, Kniescheibe *f*.

paten ['pætən] *n* *(Eccl)* Patene *f*, Hostienteller *m*.

patent[1] ['peɪtənt] *adj* **(a)** *(obvious)* offensichtlich. **(b)** *(~ed)* **invention** patentiert. **he's got his own ~ method for doing that** *(fig)* dafür hat er seine Spezialmethode; **his ~ remedy for hangovers** *(fig)* sein Patent- or Spezialrezept gegen Kater.

patent[2] **1** *n* Patent *nt*. **~ applied for or pending** Patent angemeldet; **to take out a ~ (on sth)** ein Patent (auf etw *acc*) erhalten; **see letter**. **2** *vt* patentieren lassen. **is it ~ed?** ist das patentrechtlich geschützt?

patentee [,peɪtən'tiː] *n* Patentinhaber(in *f)* *m*.

patent leather *n* Lackleder *nt*. **~ shoes** Lackschuhe *pl*.

patently ['peɪtəntlɪ] *adv* offenkundig, offensichtlich. **~ obvious/clear** ganz offensichtlich/klar; **I would have thought that was ~ obvious** ich würde meinen, das liegt doch auf der Hand.

patent: ~ **medicine** *n* patentrechtlich geschütztes Arzneimittel; **P~ Office** *n* Patentamt *nt*.

pater ['peɪtə^r] *n* *(dated Brit inf)* Herr Vater *(dated)*.

paterfamilias [,peɪtəfə'mɪlɪəs] *n* Familienvater, Paterfamilias *(geh)* *m*.

paternal [pə'tɜːnl] *adj* väterlich. **my ~ uncle/grandmother etc** mein Onkel *m*/meine Großmutter etc väterlicherseits.

paternalism [pə'tɜːnəlɪzəm] *n* Bevormundung *f*.

paternalist [pə'tɜːnəlɪst] *n* Patriarch *m*.

paternalist(ic) [pə'tɜːnəlɪst, pə,tɜːnə'lɪstɪk] *adj*, **paternalistically** [pə'tɜːnə'lɪstɪkəlɪ] *adv* patriarchalisch.

paternally [pə'tɜːnəlɪ] *adv* **see adj**.

paternity [pə'tɜːnɪtɪ] *n* Vaterschaft *f*. ~ **suit** Vaterschaftsprozeß *m*; **the mother had her doubts about the baby's ~** die Mutter war sich nicht sicher, wer der Vater des Kindes war; **he denied ~ of the child** er bestritt die Vaterschaft an dem Kind.

paternoster ['pætə'nɒstə^r] *n* *(prayer)* Paternoster *nt*; *(~ bead)* Vaterunser-Perle *f*; *(lift)* Paternoster *m*.

path [pɑ:θ] n (a) (lit) (trodden) Weg, Pfad m; (surfaced) Weg m; (in field) Feldweg m. **we took a ~ across the fields** wir nahmen den Weg über das Feld.
 (b) (trajectory, route) Bahn f; (of hurricane) Weg m.
 (c) (fig) Weg m. **the Christian ~** der Weg des Christentums; **the ~ of or to salvation** der Weg des Heils; **the ~ of virtue** der Pfad der Tugend.

pathetic [pə'θetɪk] adj (a) (piteous) mitleiderregend. **the exhausted refugees made a ~ sight** die erschöpften Flüchtlinge boten ein Bild des Jammers; **it was ~ to see** es war ein Bild des Jammers; **a look of ~ helplessness in the eyes** ein Ausdruck vollkommener Hilflosigkeit in den Augen; **after three weeks the victim of the disease is reduced to the most ~ condition** nach drei Wochen bietet das Opfer der Krankheit ein Bild des Jammers or ist das Opfer der Krankheit in einem erbarmungswürdigen Zustand.
 (b) (poor) erbärmlich, jämmerlich. **it's ~** es ist zum Weinen or Heulen (inf); **what a ~ bunch they are!** oh, was ist das für ein jämmerlicher Haufen!; **honestly you're ~, can't you even boil an egg?** ehrlich, dich kann man zu nichts brauchen, kannst du nicht einmal ein Ei kochen?
 (c) **the ~ fallacy** die Vermenschlichung der Natur.

pathetically [pə'θetɪkəlɪ] adv (a) (piteously) mitleiderregend. **he limped along ~** es war ein mitleiderregender Anblick, wie er umherhumpelte; **~ thin/weak** erschreckend dünn/schwach.
 (b) slow, stupid, inefficient erbärmlich. **we have done ~ this year** wir haben dieses Jahr erbärmlich or miserabel abgeschnitten; **a ~ inadequate answer** eine äußerst dürftige Antwort; **a ~ weak attempt** ein kläglicher Versuch; **~ incapable** absolut unfähig; **the goalie dived ~ late/the trains are ~ late** es war zum Weinen or ein Jammer, wie unpünktlich die Züge sind; **it had become ~ obvious that she was ignoring him** es war schon peinlich zu sehen, wie sie ihn ignorierte.

path: **~finder** n (lit) Führer m; (fig: innovator) Wegbereiter(in f) m; **~less** adj weglos.
pathogen [ˈpæθədʒɪn] n (Med) Krankheitserreger m.
pathogenic [ˌpæθəˈdʒenɪk] adj pathogen, krankheitserregend.
pathological [ˌpæθəˈlɒdʒɪkəl] adj (lit, fig) pathologisch, krankhaft; studies etc pathologisch, Pathologie-. **an almost ~ concern for cleanliness** ein fast schon pathologischer or krankhafter Drang nach Sauberkeit.
pathologist [pəˈθɒlədʒɪst] n Pathologe m, Pathologin f.
pathology [pəˈθɒlədʒɪ] n (science) Pathologie f. **the ~ of a disease** das Krankheitsbild.
pathos [ˈpeɪθɒs] n Pathos nt.
pathway [ˈpɑːθweɪ] n see **path (a)**.
patience [ˈpeɪʃəns] n (a) Geduld f. **to have ~/no ~ (with sb/sth)** Geduld/keine Geduld haben (mit jdm/etw); **to have no ~ with sb/sth** (fig inf: dislike) für jdn/etw nichts übrig haben; **to lose (one's) ~ (with sb/sth)** (mit jdm/etw) die Geduld verlieren; **~ is a virtue** (prov) Geduld ist eine Tugend; **~, ~!** nur Geduld!, immer mit der Ruhe!; see **possess**.
 (b) (Brit Cards) Patience f. **to play ~** eine Patience legen.
patient [ˈpeɪʃənt] 1 adj geduldig. **a ~ piece of work** eine mit sehr viel Geduld angefertigte Arbeit; **~ endurance** zähe Geduld; **to be ~ with sb/sth** mit jdm/etw geduldig sein; **you must be very ~ about it** du mußt sehr viel Geduld haben or sehr geduldig sein; **we have been ~ long enough!** unsere Geduld ist erschöpft!
 2 n Patient(in f) m.
patiently [ˈpeɪʃəntlɪ] adv see adj. **a very ~ reconstructed picture of Babylonian life** ein mit Akribie rekonstruiertes Bild babylonischer Lebensweise.
patina [ˈpætɪnə] n Patina f.
patio [ˈpætɪəʊ] n Veranda, Terrasse f; (inner court) Innenhof, Patio m. **~ door** Terrassentür f.
patois [ˈpætwɑː] n Mundart f.
patriarch [ˈpeɪtrɪɑːk] n Patriarch m.
patriarchal [ˌpeɪtrɪˈɑːkəl] adj patriarchalisch.
patriarchy [ˌpeɪtrɪˈɑːkɪ] n Patriarchat nt.
patrician [pəˈtrɪʃən] 1 adj patrizisch. **the ~ classes** das Patriziertum; **the old ~ houses** die alten Patrizierhäuser. 2 n Patrizier(in f) m.
patricide [ˈpætrɪsaɪd] n Vatermord m; (murderer) Vatermörder(in f) m.
patrimony [ˈpætrɪmənɪ] n Patrimonium nt.
patriot [ˈpeɪtrɪət] n Patriot(in f) m.
patriotic [ˌpætrɪˈɒtɪk] adj patriotisch. **your ~ duty** deine Pflicht gegenüber dem Vaterland.
patriotically [ˌpætrɪˈɒtɪkəlɪ] adv see adj.
patriotism [ˈpætrɪətɪzəm] n Patriotismus m, Vaterlandsliebe f.
patrol [pəˈtrəʊl] 1 n (a) (patrolling) (by police) Streife f; (by aircraft, ship) Patrouille f; (by watchman etc) Runde f, Rundgang m. **the army made hourly ~s of the desert** jede Stunde patrouillierten Soldaten in der Wüste; **the army/navy carry out or make weekly ~s of the area** das Heer/die Marine patrouilliert das Gebiet wöchentlich; **the army/navy maintain a constant ~** das Heer/die Marine führt ständige Patrouillen durch; **on ~** (Mil) auf Patrouille; (police) auf Streife; (guard dogs, squad car, detectives) im Einsatz; **the watchman was on his ~ when the burglars broke in** der Wächter machte gerade seine Runde, als die Einbrecher kamen.
 (b) (~ unit, Mil) Patrouille f; (police ~) (Polizei)streife f; (of boy scouts) Fähnlein nt; (of girl guides) Gilde f.
 2 vt (Mil) district, waters, sky, streets patrouillieren, patrouillieren in (+dat); frontier, coast patrouillieren, patrouillieren vor (+dat); (policeman, watchman) seine Runden machen in (+dat); (police car) Streife fahren in (+dat); (guard dogs, gamewarden) einen Rund- or Streifengang or eine Runde machen in (+dat). **the frontier is not ~led** die Grenze wird nicht bewacht or ist unbewacht.

3 vi (soldiers, ships, planes) patrouillieren; (planes also) Patrouille fliegen; (policemen) eine Streife/Streifen machen; (watchman, store detective etc) seine Runden machen. **to ~ up and down** auf und ab gehen.
patrol: **~ boat** n Patrouillenboot nt; **~ car** n Streifenwagen m; **~ leader** n (of scouts) Fähnleinführer m; (of girl guides) Gildenführerin f; **~man** n Wächter m; (US: policeman) Polizist m; **~ wagon** n (US) grüne Minna (inf), Gefangenenwagen m; **~woman** n (US: policewoman) Polizistin f.
patron [ˈpeɪtrən] n (customer of shop) Kunde m, Kundin f; (customer of restaurant, hotel) Gast m; (of society) Schirmherr(in f) m; (of artist) Förderer, Gönner(in f) m; (~ saint) Schutzpatron(in f) m. **~s only** nur für Kunden/Gäste; **a ~ of the arts** ein Mäzen m; **our ~s** (of shop) unsere Kundschaft.
patronage [ˈpætrənɪdʒ] n (a) (support) Schirmherrschaft f. **under the ~ of** unter der Schirmherrschaft des/der; **his lifelong ~ of the arts** sein lebenslanges Mäzenatentum; **having secured the ~ of the Duke his election was a certainty** nachdem er sich die Unterstützung des Herzogs verschafft hatte, war seine Wahl sicher.
 (b) (form: of a shop etc) **we enjoy the ~ of ...** unseren Kunden zählen ...; **we thank you for your ~** wir danken Ihnen für Ihr Vertrauen; **the attitude of the new sales assistant caused her to withdraw her ~** das Benehmen des neuen Verkäufers veranlaßte sie, dort nicht mehr einzukaufen.
 (c) (right to appoint to government jobs) Patronat nt. **under (the) ~ of** unter der Schirmherrschaft von.
 (d) (rare: condescension) **an air of ~** eine gönnerhafte Miene.
patronize [ˈpætrənaɪz] vt (a) pub, cinema etc besuchen; the railway benutzen. **I hope you will continue to ~ our store** ich hoffe, daß Sie uns weiterhin beehren; **it's not a shop I ~** in dem Geschäft kaufe ich nicht; **the shop is well ~d** das Geschäft hat viel Kundschaft.
 (b) (treat condescendingly) gönnerhaft or herablassend behandeln, von oben herab behandeln.
 (c) (support) the arts etc unterstützen, fördern.
patronizing [ˈpætrənaɪzɪŋ] adj gönnerhaft, herablassend. **to be ~ to or towards sb** jdn herablassend or von oben herab behandeln; **there's no need to be so ~** du brauchst gar nicht so herablassend or von oben herab zu tun.
patronizingly [ˈpætrənaɪzɪŋlɪ] adv see adj. **a ~ tolerant attitude** herablassende Nachsicht.
patronymic [ˌpætrəˈnɪmɪk] 1 adj patronymisch. 2 n Patronymikon nt, Vatersname m.
patsy [ˈpætsɪ] n (US sl) (scapegoat) Sündenbock m; (easy victim) Leichtgläubige(r) mf; (weak man) Schlappschwanz (inf), Schwächling m.
patten [ˈpætən] n Stelzenschuh m.
patter [ˈpætə] 1 n (a) (of feet) Getrippel nt; (of rain) Plätschern nt. **the ~ of tiny feet** (fig) fröhliches Kinderlachen nt.
 (b) (of salesman, comedian, conjurer, disc jockey) Sprüche pl (inf). **to start one's ~** seine Sprüche loslassen; **you'll never pick up a girl unless you're good with the ~** du wirst nie eine Freundin aufreißen, wenn du nicht gut quatschen kannst (inf); **to have a good line in ~** (of comedian, disc jockey etc) gute Sprüche drauf or auf Lager haben (inf); **sales ~** Vertretersprüche pl; **the comedian delivered his ~ very rapidly/cleverly** der Komiker ließ am laufenden Band/sehr geschickt seine Sprüche los (inf).
 (c) (inf: jargon) Fachjargon m (inf).
 2 vi (person, feet) trippeln; (rain: also ~ down) plätschern.
patter-merchant [ˈpætəˌmɜːtʃənt] n (inf) Schönredner, Sprücheklopfer (inf) m.
pattern [ˈpætən] 1 n (a) Muster nt. **to make a ~** ein Muster bilden.
 (b) (Sew) Schnitt m, Schnittmuster nt; (Knitting) Strickanleitung f.
 (c) (fig: model) Vorbild nt. **according to a ~** nach einem (festen) Schema; **on the ~ of Albania, on the Albanian ~** nach albanischem Vorbild or Muster; **to set a or the ~ for sth** ein Muster or Vorbild für etw sein.
 (d) (fig: in events, behaviour etc) Muster nt; (set) Schema nt; (recurrent) Regelmäßigkeit f. **there's a distinct ~/no ~ to these crimes** in diesen Verbrechen steckt ein bestimmtes/kein Schema; **what ~ can we find in these events?** was verbindet diese Ereignisse?; **the ~ of events leading up to the war** der Ablauf der Ereignisse, die zum Krieg geführt haben; **a certain ~ emerged** es ließ sich ein gewisses Schema or Muster erkennen; **to follow the usual ~** nach dem üblichen Schema verlaufen; **behaviour ~s** Verhaltensmuster pl; **her behaviour follows a predictable ~/shows no obvious ~** ihr Verhalten folgt einem voraussagbaren/keinem erkennbaren Muster; **the natural ~ of life in the wild** die natürlichen Lebensvorgänge in der Wildnis; **the day-by-day ~ of his existence** die tägliche Routine seines Lebens; **the town's new buildings follow the usual ~ of concrete and glass** die Neubauten der Stadt entsprechen dem üblichen Baustil aus Beton und Glas; **it's the usual ~, the rich get richer and the poor get poorer** es läuft immer nach demselben Muster ab – die Reichen werden reicher und die Armen ärmer.
 (e) (verb ~, sentence ~ etc) Struktur f.
 2 vt (a) (model) machen (on nach). **this design is ~ed on one I saw in a magazine** die Idee für dieses Muster habe ich aus einer Illustrierten; **many countries ~ their laws on the Roman system** viele Länder orientieren sich bei ihrer Gesetzgebung an dem römischen Vorbild; **to be ~ed on sth** einer Sache (dat) nachgebildet sein; (music, poem, style etc) einer Sache (dat) nachempfunden sein; **to ~ oneself on sb** sich (dat) jdn zum Vorbild nehmen; **he ~ed his lifestyle on that of a country squire** er ahmte den Lebensstil eines Landadligen nach.

(b) (put ~s on) mit einen Muster versehen; *see* **patterned.**
pattern book *n* Musterbuch *nt*.
patterned ['pætənd] *adj* gemustert.
patty ['pætɪ] *n* Pastetchen *nt*.
paucity ['pɔːsɪtɪ] *n* (*liter*) Mangel *m* (*of an* + *dat*).
Pauline ['pɔːlaɪn] *adj* paulinisch.
paunch [pɔːntʃ] *n* Bauch, Wanst *m*; (*of cow etc*) Pansen *m*.
paunchy ['pɔːntʃɪ] *adj* (+ *er*) dick. **to be getting** ~ einen (dicken)
Bauch kriegen.
pauper ['pɔːpə'] *n* Arme(r) *mf*; (*supported by charity*)
Almosenempfänger(in *f*) *m*. ~'s **grave** Armengrab *nt*; **we may**
be materially better off, but we are spiritual ~s materiell geht
es uns zwar besser, geistig aber sind wir verarmt.
pauperism ['pɔːpərɪzəm] *n* (*lit, fig*) Armut *f*.
pauperization [‚pɔːpəraɪ'zeɪʃən] *n* Verarmung *f*; (*fig also*)
Verkümmerung *f*.
pauperize ['pɔːpəraɪz] *vt* arm machen; (*fig*) verkümmern
lassen.
pause [pɔːz] **1** *n* Pause *f*. **a hesitant** ~ ein kurzes Zögern; **an**
anxious/a pregnant ~ ein ängstliches/vielsagendes Schweigen;
there was a ~ **while** ... es entstand eine Pause, während ...; **to**
have a ~ (eine) Pause machen; **without (a)** ~ ohne Unterbrechung, pausenlos, ununterbrochen; **to give sb** ~ (*esp liter*)
jdm zu denken geben, jdn nachdenklich stimmen.
2 *vi* **(a)** stehenbleiben, stoppen; (*inf*); (*speaker*) innehalten.
can't we ~ **for a bit, I'm exhausted** können wir nicht eine kurze
Pause machen, ich bin erschöpft; **the shooting** ~**d while they**
negotiated das Feuer ruhte während der Verhandlungen; **he**
~**d dramatically er legte eine Kunstpause ein;** ~ **before you act**
überlege erst mal, bevor du etwas tust; **he** ~**d for breath/a**
drink er machte eine Pause, um Luft zu holen/etwas zu trinken;
he spoke for thirty minutes without once pausing er sprach
eine halbe Stunde ohne eine einzige Pause; **let's** ~ **here** machen
wir hier Pause; **it made him** ~ das machte ihn nachdenklich.
(b) (*dwell on*) **to** ~ **(up)on sth** auf etw (*acc*) näher eingehen.
pave [peɪv] *vt* befestigen (*in, with* mit); *road, path* (*with stones*
also) pflastern; *floor* (*with tiles*) fliesen, mit Fliesen auslegen.
to ~ **the way for sb/sth** (*fig*) jdm/für etw den Weg ebnen; **where**
the streets are ~**d with gold** wo die Straßen mit Gold gepflastert sind, wo das Geld auf der Straße liegt; **the path to hell is**
~**d with good intentions** (*prov*) der Weg zur Hölle ist mit guten
Vorsätzen gepflastert (*prov*); **the paths are** ~**d in or with purest**
marble die Wege sind mit feinstem Marmor ausgelegt; (*with*
slabs) mit Platten auslegen.
◆**pave over** *vt sep* betonieren; (*with slabs*) mit Platten
auslegen.
paved [peɪvd] *adj* befestigt (*in, with* mit).
pavement ['peɪvmənt] *n* (*Brit*) Gehsteig, Bürgersteig *m*, Trottoir *nt*; (*US: paved road*) Straße *f*; (*material*) Bodenbelag *m*. **to**
leave the ~ (*US Aut*) von der Straße abkommen; ~ **artist**
Pflastermaler(in *f*) *m*.
pavilion [pə'vɪliən] *n* Pavillon *m*; (*old: tent*) Zelt *nt*; (*Sport*)
(*changing* ~) Umkleideräume *pl*; (*clubhouse*) Klubhaus *nt*.
paving ['peɪvɪŋ] *n* Belag *m*; (*US: of road*) Decke *f*; (*material*)
Belag *m*; (*action*) Pflastern *nt*. ~ **stone** Platte *f*.
paw[1] [pɔː] **1** *n* (*of animal*) Pfote *f*; (*of lion, bear*) Pranke, Tatze *f*;
(*pej inf: hand*) Pfote *f* (*inf*). **keep your** ~**s off!** Pfoten weg! (*inf*).
2 *vt* **(a)** tätscheln; (*lion etc*) mit der Pfote *or* Tatze berühren.
to ~ **the ground** (*lit*) scharren; (*fig: be impatient*) ungeduldig *or*
kribbelig (*inf*) werden.
(b) (*pej inf: handle*) betatschen (*inf*).
3 *vi* **to** ~ **at sb/sth** jdn/etw betätscheln *or* betatschen (*inf*).
paw[2] *n* (*US dial inf*) Pa *m* (*inf*).
pawl [pɔːl] *n* Sperrklinke *f*.
pawn[1] [pɔːn] *n* (*Chess*) Bauer *m*; (*fig*) Schachfigur *f*.
pawn[2] **1** *n* (*security*) Pfand *nt*. **in** ~ verpfändet, versetzt; **to**
leave *or* **put sth in** ~ etw versetzen *or* auf die Pfandleihe *or* ins
Leihhaus bringen; **the company is in** ~ **to foreigners** das Unternehmen ist an ausländische Kapitalgeber verpfändet.
2 *vt* verpfänden, versetzen. **he had** ~**ed his soul to the devil** er
hatte seine Seele dem Teufel verpfändet.
pawn: ~**broker** *n* Pfandleiher *m*; ~**broker's (shop),** ~**shop** *n*
Pfandhaus, Leihhaus *nt*; ~ **ticket** *n* Pfandschein, Leihschein *m*.
pax [pæks] *interj* (*Brit*) Friede.
pay [peɪ] (*vb: pret, ptp* **paid**) **1** *n* Lohn *m*; (*of salaried employee*)
Gehalt *nt*; (*Mil*) Sold *m*; (*of civil servant*) Gehalt *nt*, Bezüge *pl*,
Besoldung *f*. **what's the** ~ **like?** wie ist die Bezahlung?; **it comes**
out of my ~ es wird mir vom Gehalt/Lohn abgezogen; **a low-**~
country ein Land mit niedrigen Löhnen, ein Niedriglohnland;
the discussions were about ~ in den Diskussionen ging es um
die Löhne; **to be in sb's** ~ für jdn arbeiten.
2 *vt* **(a)** *money, a sum, person, bill, duty, debt, charge,*
account, fee bezahlen; *interest, a sum, duty, charge also* zahlen;
dividend ausschütten, zahlen. **to** ~ **sb £10** jdm £ 10 zahlen; **to** ~
shareholders Dividenden ausschütten *or* zahlen; **how much is**
there to ~? was macht das?; **to be** *or* **get paid** (*in regular job*)
seinen Lohn/sein Gehalt bekommen; **when do I get paid for**
doing that? wann bekomme ich mein Geld dafür?, **wann werde**
ich dafür bezahlt?; **we don't** ~ **you for sitting around** wir
bezahlen Sie nicht fürs Herumsitzen; **savings accounts that** ~
5% Sparkonten, die 5% Zinsen bringen; I ~ **you to prevent such**
mistakes Sie werden schließlich dafür bezahlt, daß solche
Fehler nicht vorkommen; **"paid"** (*on bill*) „bezahlt"; *see* **paid.**
(b) (*lit, fig: be profitable to*) sich lohnen; (*honesty*) sich
auszahlen. **it doesn't** ~ **them to work more** wenn es sich für
sie nicht lohnt, mehr zu arbeiten; **in future it would** ~ **you to ask**
in Zukunft solltest du besser vorher fragen; **it doesn't** ~ **you to**
be kind nowadays es lohnt sich heutzutage nicht, freundlich zu sein; **but it paid him in the long run** aber auf die Dauer
hat es sich doch ausgezahlt.
(c) to ~ **(sb/a place) a visit** *or* **call, to** ~ **a visit to** *or* **a call on**

sb/a place jdn/einen Ort besuchen; (*more formal*) jdm/
einem Ort einen Besuch abstatten; **to** ~ **a visit to the doctor** den
Arzt aufsuchen; *see* **attention, compliment, respect.**
3 *vi* **(a)** zahlen. **to** ~ **on account** auf Rechnung zahlen; **they** ~
well for this sort of work diese Arbeit wird gut bezahlt; **no, no,**
I'm ~**ing** nein, nein, ich (be)zahle; **I'd like to know what I'm**
~**ing for** ich wüßte gern, für was ich eigentlich mein Geld
ausgebe; **to** ~ **for sth etw bezahlen; it's already paid for** es ist
schon bezahlt; **how much did you** ~ **for it?** wieviel hast du dafür
bezahlt?; **to** ~ **for sth jdn zahlen; I'll** ~ **for you this time**
dieses Mal zahle ich; **they paid for her to go to America** sie
zahlten ihr die Reise nach Amerika.
(b) (*be profitable*) sich lohnen. **it's a business that** ~s es ist
ein rentables Geschäft; **it's** ~**ing at last** es zahlt sich schließlich
doch aus; **crime doesn't** ~ (*prov*) Verbrechen lohnt sich nicht.
(c) (*fig: to suffer*) **to** ~ **for sth (with sth)** für etw (mit etw)
bezahlen; **you'll** ~ **for that!** dafür wirst du (mir) büßen; **to make**
sb ~ **(for sth)** jdn für etw büßen lassen; **I'll make you** ~ **for this!**
das wirst du mir büßen, das werde ich dir heimzahlen!
◆**pay back** *vt sep* (a) *money* zurückzahlen. **when do you want**
me to ~ **you** ~? wann willst du das Geld wiederhaben?; ~ **me** ~
when you like zahl's *or* gib's mir zurück, wenn du willst.
(b) *compliment, visit* erwidern; *insult, trick* sich revanchieren für. **to** ~ **sb** ~ es jdm heimzahlen.
◆**pay in 1** *vt sep* einzahlen. **to** ~ **money** ~**to an account** Geld auf
ein Konto einzahlen. **2** *vi* einzahlen.
◆**pay off 1** *vt sep* *workmen* auszahlen; *seamen* abmustern;
debt abbezahlen, tilgen; *HP* ab(be)zahlen; *mortgage* ablösen;
creditor befriedigen. **if this happens again we'll have to** ~ **him**
~ wenn das noch einmal vorkommt, müssen wir ihn entlassen;
see **score.** **2** *vi* sich auszahlen.
◆**pay out 1** *vt sep* **(a)** *money* (*spend*) ausgeben; (*count out*)
auszahlen. **(b)** *rope* ablaufen lassen. **2** *vi* bezahlen.
◆**pay over** *vt sep* aushändigen.
◆**pay up 1** *vt sep* *what one owes* zurückzahlen; *subscription*
bezahlen. **his account/he is paid** ~ er hat alles bezahlt; *see* **paid-**
up. 2 *vi* zahlen. **come on,** ~ ~**, I want my money** los, zahlen, ich
will mein Geld.
payable ['peɪəbl] *adj* zahlbar; (*due*) fällig. ~ **to bearer** zahlbar
an Überbringer; ~ **to order** zahlbar an Order; ~ **immediately**
zahlbar sofort; **to make a cheque** ~ **to sb** einen Scheck auf jdn
ausstellen.
pay: ~**-as-you-earn** *attr* ~**-as-you-earn tax system** *Steuer-*
system nt, bei dem die Lohnsteuer direkt einbehalten wird; ~
award *n* Gehalts-/Lohnerhöhung *f*; ~**-bed** *n* Privatbett *nt*; ~
cheque *n* Lohn-/Gehaltsüberweisung *f*; ~**-claim** *n* Lohn-/
Gehaltsforderung *f*; ~**-day** *n* Zahltag *m*; ~ **dirt** *n* abbauwür-
diges Erzlager.
PAYE (*Brit*) *abbr of* **pay-as-you-earn.**
payee [peɪ'iː] *n* Zahlungsempfänger *m*.
payer ['peɪə'] *n* Zahler *m*. **slow** ~ säumiger Zahler.
pay: ~ **freeze** *n* Lohnstopp *m*; ~ **increase** *n* Lohn-/
Gehaltserhöhung *f*.
paying ['peɪɪŋ] *adj* **(a)** (*profitable*) rentabel. **(b)** ~ **guest**
zahlender Gast; ~ **patient** Privatpatient(in *f*) *m*.
paying-in slip [‚peɪɪŋ'ɪn‚slɪp] *n* Einzahlungsschein *m*.
pay: ~**load** *n* Nutzlast *f*; (*of bomber*) Bombenlast *f*; ~**master** *n*
Zahlmeister *m*; **P**~**master General** für Lohn- und
Gehaltszahlungen im öffentlichen Dienst zuständiges
Kabinettsmitglied.
payment ['peɪmənt] *n* (*paying*) (*of person*) Bezahlung,
Entlohnung *f*; (*of bill, instalment etc*) Bezahlung, Begleichung
f; (*of debt, mortgage*) Abtragung, Rückzahlung *f*; (*of interest,*
bank charge etc) Zahlung *f*; (*sum paid*) Zahlung *f*; (*fig: reward*)
Belohnung *f*. **three monthly** ~s drei Monatsraten; **as or in** ~ **of**
a debt/bill in Begleichung einer Schuld/Rechnung; **as or in** ~
for goods/his services als Bezahlung für *or* von Waren/für
seine Dienste; **to accept sth as or in** ~ **(for ...)** etw in
Begleichung/als Bezahlung (für ...) annehmen; **on** ~ **of** bei Be-
gleichung/Bezahlung von; **without** ~ (*free*) umsonst; **to make a**
~ **eine Zahlung leisten; to make a** ~ **on sth eine Rate für etw**
zahlen; **to present sth for** ~ etw zur Zahlung vorlegen; **to stop**
~s die Zahlungen *pl* einstellen; **to stop** ~ **of a cheque** einen
Scheck sperren.
pay: ~ **negotiations** *npl see* ~ **talks;** ~**-off** *n* (*inf: bribe*) Bestechungsgeld *nt*; (*final outcome, climax*) Quittung *f*; (*of joke*)
Pointe *f*.
payola [peɪ'əʊlə] *n* (*esp US*) (*bribery*) Bestechung *f*; (*bribe*)
Schmiergeld *nt*.
pay: ~ **packet** *n* Lohntüte *f*; ~ **phone** *n* Münzfernsprecher *m*; ~
rise *n* Lohn-/Gehaltserhöhung *f*; ~**roll** **in they have 500 people**
on the ~**roll** sie haben eine Belegschaft von 500, sie haben 500
Beschäftigte; **a monthly** ~**roll of £75,000** eine monatliche
Lohn- und Gehaltssumme von £ 75.000; ~**slip** *n* Lohn-/
Gehaltsstreifen *m*; ~ **station** *n* (*US*) öffentlicher Fernsprecher; ~ **talks** *npl* Lohnverhandlungen *pl*; (*for profession,*
area of industry) Tarifverhandlungen *pl*; ~ **tone** *n* bei öffentlichen Fernsprechern: Ton, der anzeigt, daß Münzen eingeworfen werden müssen; ~ **TV** *n* Münzfernseher *m*.
PC (*Brit*) *abbr of* **(a) Police Constable. (b) Privy Council. (c)**
Privy Councillor.
pc *abbr of* **(a) post card. (b) per cent.**
pd *abbr of* **paid** bez.
PDQ (*inf*) *abbr of* **pretty damned quick** verdammt schnell
(*inf*).
PE *abbr of* **physical education.**
pea [piː] *n* Erbse *f*. **they are as like as two** ~s **(in a pod)** sie
gleichen sich (*dat*) wie ein Ei dem anderen.
peace [piːs] *n* **(a)** (*freedom from war*) Frieden, Friede (*geh*) *m*.
the Versailles *etc* ~ der Friede von Versailles *etc*; **a man of** ~
ein friedfertiger *or* friedliebender Mensch; **to be at** ~ **with**

sb/sth mit jdm/etw in Frieden leben; **the two countries are now at ~** zwischen den beiden Ländern herrscht jetzt Frieden; **to be at ~ with oneself** mit sich (dat) selbst in Frieden leben; **he is at ~** (euph: dead) er ruht in Frieden; **to hold one's ~** schweigen; **to make (one's) ~ (with sb)** sich (mit jdm) versöhnen or aussöhnen; **to make (one's) ~ with oneself** mit sich (dat) selbst ins reine kommen; **to make ~ between ...** Frieden stiften zwischen (+dat) ...; **to make one's ~ with the world** seinen Frieden mit der Welt schließen.
  (b) (Jur) öffentliche (Ruhe und) Ordnung. **the (King's/Queen's) ~** (Jur) die öffentliche Ordnung; **to keep the ~** (Jur) (demonstrator, citizen) die öffentliche Ordnung wahren; (policeman) die öffentliche Ordnung aufrechterhalten; (fig) Frieden bewahren.
  (c) (tranquillity, quiet) Ruhe f. **~ of mind** innere Ruhe, Seelenfrieden m; **the P~ of God** der Friede Gottes, Gottes Friede; **~ and quiet** Ruhe und Frieden; **to give sb some ~** jdn in Ruhe or Frieden lassen; **to give sb no ~** jdm keine Ruhe lassen; **to get some/no ~** zur Ruhe/nicht zur Ruhe kommen.
peaceable ['piːsəbl] adj settlement, discussion friedlich; person, nature also friedfertig, friedliebend.
peaceably ['piːsəblɪ] adv see adj.
peace: **~ conference** n Friedenskonferenz f; **P~ Corps** n (US) Friedenskorps nt.
peaceful ['piːsful] adj friedlich; (peaceable) nation, person etc friedfertig, friedliebend; (calm, undisturbed) holiday, sleep etc ruhig; death sanft; use of nuclear power für friedliche Zwecke. **a ~ transition to independence** die Erlangung der Unabhängigkeit auf friedlichem Wege; **he had a ~ reign** während seiner Regierungszeit herrschte Frieden; **I didn't get a ~ moment all day long** ich bin den ganzen Tag keine Sekunde zur Ruhe gekommen.
peacefully ['piːsfəlɪ] adv friedlich. **to die ~ (in one's sleep)** ohne Schmerzen sterben, sanft entschlafen (liter).
peacefulness ['piːsfulnɪs] n see adj Friedlichkeit f; Friedfertigkeit, Friedensliebe f; Ruhe f; Sanftheit f. **the ~ of the takeover/the demonstration** der friedliche Charakter des Machtwechsels/der Demonstration; **the ~ of a summer's evening** die friedliche Atmosphäre eines Sommerabends.
peace: **~keeper** n Friedenswächter m; **~keeping** 1 n Friedenssicherung f; **2** adj Friedens-; **UN troops have a purely ~keeping role** die UN-Truppen sind eine reine Friedenstruppe; **a ~keeping operation** Maßnahmen pl zur Sicherung des Friedens; **~loving** adj friedliebend; **~maker** n Friedensstifter(in f) m; **~ offensive** n Friedensoffensive f; **~offering** n Friedensangebot nt; (fig) Versöhnungsgeschenk nt; **~pipe** n Friedenspfeife f; **~ talks** npl Friedensverhandlungen, Friedensgespräche pl; **~time** 1 n Friedenszeiten pl; **2** adj in Friedenszeiten.
peach [piːtʃ] 1 n (a) (fruit) Pfirsich m; (tree) Pfirsichbaum m. **~ Melba** Pfirsich Melba m; **her complexion is like ~es and cream, she has a ~es-and-cream complexion** sie hat eine Haut wie ein Pfirsich, sie hat eine Pfirsichhaut.
  (b) (inf) **she's a ~** sie ist klasse (inf); **it's a ~** das ist prima or klasse or Spitze (all inf); **a ~ of a girl/dress/film etc** ein klasse Mädchen/Kleid/Film etc (all inf).
  (c) (colour) Pfirsichton m.
  2 adj pfirsichfarben.
pea: **~cock** n Pfau m; (fig: man) Geck m; **to strut like a ~cock** wie ein Pfau einherstolzieren; **~cock blue** adj pfauenblau; **~green** adj erbsengrün; **~hen** n Pfauenhenne f; **~-jacket** n (esp US) Pijacke f.
peak [piːk] 1 n (a) (of mountain) Gipfel m; (of roof) First m; (sharp point) Spitze f.
  (b) (of cap) Schirm m.
  (c) (maximum) Höhepunkt m; (on graph) Scheitelpunkt m. **he is at the ~ of fitness** er ist in Höchstform or Topform (inf); **when the empire was at its ~** als das Reich auf dem Höhepunkt seiner Macht stand; **when demand is at its ~** wenn die Nachfrage ihren Höhepunkt erreicht hat or am stärksten ist.
  2 adj attr value, voltage Spitzen-; production, power, pressure Höchst-. **a ~ year for new car sales** ein Rekordjahr nt für den Neuwagenabsatz.
  3 vi den Höchststand erreichen.
♦**peak off** vi zurückgehen.
peaked [piːkt] adj (a) cap, helmet etc spitz. **(b)** person, complexion etc verhärmt, abgehärmt.
peak: **~-hour** adj **~-hour consumption** Verbrauch m in der Hauptbelastungszeit; **~-hour travel costs more** in der Hauptverkehrszeit sind die öffentlichen Verkehrsmittel teurer; **measures to reduce ~-hour traffic** Maßnahmen zur Reduzierung der Belastung in der Hauptverkehrszeit; **~ hours** npl (of traffic) Hauptbelastungszeit, Stoßzeit f; (Telec, Elec) Hauptbelastungszeit f; **~ season** n Hochsaison f; **~ times** npl Hauptbelastungszeit f.
peaky ['piːkɪ] adj (+er) (Brit inf) complexion blaß; face verhärmt, abgehärmt; look, child kränklich. **to look ~** nicht gut aussehen, angeschlagen aussehen (inf).
peal [piːl] 1 n **~ of bells** (sound) Glockengeläut(e), Glockenläuten nt; (set) Glockenspiel nt; **~s of laughter** schallendes Gelächter; **~ of mad laughter** echoed ... ein irres Gelächter hallte ...; **~ of thunder** Donnerrollen nt, Donnerschlag m. **2** vt läuten. **3** vi (bell) läuten; (thunder) dröhnen.
♦**peal out** vi verhallen. **the bells ~ed ~ over the fields** das Geläut der Glocken verhallte über den Feldern.
peanut ['piːnʌt] n Erdnuß f. **~s** (inf: not much money) ein Apfel und ein Ei (inf) (to sb für jdn); **the pay is ~s** die Bezahlung ist miserabel or lächerlich (inf); **but we got ~s** wir haben kaum was gekriegt; **£2,000? that's ~s these days** £ 2.000? das ist doch ein Klacks heutzutage (inf); **~ butter** Erdnußbutter f; **~ gallery** (US inf) Olymp m (inf).

peapod ['piːpɒd] n Erbsenschote f.
pear [peə'] n Birne f; (tree) Birnbaum m.
pear: **~drop** n (pendant) tropfenförmiger Anhänger m; (sweet) hartes Bonbon in Birnenform; **~-drop** adj earring etc tropfenförmig.
pearl[1] [pɜːl] n, vt, vi see purl.
pearl[2] 1 n (lit, fig) Perle f; (mother-of-~) Perlmutt nt; (of sweat etc) Perle f, Tropfen m; (colour) Grauweiß nt. **~ of wisdom** weiser Spruch; **to cast ~s before swine** (prov) Perlen pl vor die Säue werfen (prov). **2** adj Perlen-; (~-coloured) grauweiß.
pearl: **~ barley** n Perlgraupen pl; **~ blue** adj silberblau; **~ fisher** n Perlenfischer(in f) m; **~ fishing** n Perlenfischerei f; **~ grey** adj silbergrau; **~-handled** adj perlmuttbesetzt; **~ oyster** n Perlenauster f.
pearly ['pɜːlɪ] adj (+er) (in colour) perlmuttfarben. **~ white** perlweiß; **~ buttons** Perlmuttknöpfe pl; **a ~ costume** ein Kostüm nt mit Perlmuttknöpfen; **~ king/queen** Straßenverkäufer(in) in London, der/die ein mit Perlmuttknöpfen und bunten Perlen besticktes Kostüm trägt; **P~ Gates** Himmelstür f.
pear-shaped ['peəʃeɪpt] adj birnenförmig.
peasant ['pezənt] 1 n (lit) (armer) Bauer; (pej inf) (ignoramus) Banause m; (lout) Bauer m; (pleb) Prolet m. **2** adj attr bäuerlich. **~ farmer** (armer) Bauer; **~ labour** Landarbeiterschaft f, landwirtschaftliche Arbeitskräfte pl; **~ woman** (arme) Bäuerin.
peasantry ['pezntrɪ] n Bauernschaft f; (class, status) Bauerntum nt.
pease-pudding ['piːz'pudɪŋ] n Erbspüree nt.
pea: **~shooter** n Pusterohr nt; **~ soup** n Erbsensuppe f; **~-souper** [piː'suːpə'] n Waschküche (inf), Suppe (inf) f.
peat [piːt] n Torf m; (piece) Stück nt Torf. **~bog** Torfmoor nt.
peaty ['piːtɪ] adj (+er) torfig; taste nach Torf.
pebble ['pebl] n Kiesel, Kieselstein m; (rock crystal) Bergkristall m; (after polishing) Kieselglas nt. **he/she is not the only ~ on the beach** (inf) es gibt noch andere.
pebble: **~-dash** n (Brit) (Kiesel)rauhputz m; **~ glasses** npl Brille f mit Gläsern aus Kieselglas; **~ lens** n Linse f aus Kieselglas.
pebbly ['peblɪ] adj steinig.
pecan [pɪ'kæn] n (nut) Pecannuß f; (tree) Hickory m.
peccadillo [,pekə'dɪləʊ] n, pl -(e)s kleine Sünde; (of youth) Jugendsünde f.
peccary ['pekərɪ] n Pekari, Nabelschwein nt.
peck[1] [pek] n (dry measure) Viertelscheffel m.
peck[2] 1 n (a) (inf: kiss) flüchtiger Kuß m, Küßchen nt. **(b)** the hen gave him a ~ die Henne hackte nach ihm. **2** vt (a) (bird) picken. **(b)** (inf) ~ed in Küßchen nt geben (+dat). **3** vi picken (at nach). **he just ~ed at his food** er stocherte nur in seinem Essen herum.
♦**peck out** vt sep aushacken.
pecker ['pekə'] n (a) (Brit inf) **keep your ~ up!** halt die Ohren steif! (inf). **(b)** (US sl: penis) Schwanz m (sl).
pecking order ['pekɪŋ,ɔːdə'] n (lit, fig) Hackordnung f.
peckish ['pekɪʃ] adj (Brit inf: hungry) **I'm (feeling) a bit ~** ich könnte was zwischen die Zähne gebrauchen (inf).
pectic ['pektɪk] adj Pektin-.
pectin ['pektɪn] n Pektin nt.
pectoral ['pektərəl] adj pektoral; fin, cross, ornament Brust-.
peculiar [pɪ'kjuːlɪə'] adj (a) (strange) seltsam, eigenartig. **(b)** (exclusive, special) eigentümlich (to für +acc). **an animal ~ to Africa** ein Tier, das nur in Afrika vorkommt; **his own ~ style** der ihm eigene Stil.
peculiarity [pɪ,kjuːlɪ'ærɪtɪ] n (a) (strangeness) Seltsamkeit f, Eigenartigkeit f.
  (b) (unusual feature) Eigentümlichkeit, Eigenheit, Besonderheit f. **"special peculiarities"** (on passport etc) „besondere Kennzeichen"; **there is some ~ which I cannot quite define** da ist so etwas Eigentümliches, das ich nicht beschreiben kann.
peculiarly [pɪ'kjuːlɪəlɪ] adv (a) (strangely) seltsam, eigenartig. **(b)** (exceptionally) besonders.
pecuniary [pɪ'kjuːnɪərɪ] adj (form) penalties, affairs Geld-; gain, advantage, problem finanziell; difficulties, problem also finanziell, pekuniär (geh).
pedagogic(al) [,pedə'dʒɪk(əl)] adj (form) pädagogisch.
pedagogue ['pedəgɒg] n (pedant) Schulmeister m; (form: teacher) Pädagoge m, Pädagogin f.
pedagogy ['pedəgɒgɪ] n (form) Pädagogik f.
pedal ['pedl] 1 n Pedal nt; (on waste bin etc) Trethebel m. **2** vt **he ~led the bicycle up the hill** er strampelte mit dem Fahrrad den Berg hinauf (inf); **he ~led the organ** er trat das Pedal der Orgel.
  3 vi (on bicycle) treten; (on organ) das Pedal treten. **he ~led for all he was worth** er trat in die Pedale, er strampelte (inf), sosehr er konnte; **to ~ off** (mit dem Rad) wegfahren.
pedal: **~bin** n Treteimer m; **~boat** n Tretboot nt; **~car** n Tretauto nt.
pedal(l)o ['pedələʊ] n Tretboot nt.
pedal-pushers ['pedəlpuʃəz] npl dreiviertellange Damen-/Mädchenhose.
pedant ['pedənt] n Pedant(in f), Kleinigkeitskrämer(in f) m.
pedantic adj, **~ally** adv [pɪ'dæntɪk, -əlɪ] pedantisch.
pedantry ['pedəntrɪ] n Pedanterie f.
peddle ['pedl] vt feilbieten, verkaufen; (fig) gossip etc verbreiten. **to ~ drugs** mit Drogen handeln.
peddler ['pedlə'] n (esp US) see pedlar.
pederast ['pedəræst] n Päderast m.
pederasty ['pedəræstɪ] n Päderastie f.
pedestal ['pedɪstl] n Sockel m. **to put or set sb (up) on a ~** (fig) jdn in den Himmel heben; **to knock sb off his ~** (fig) jdn von seinem Sockel stoßen.
pedestrian [pɪ'destrɪən] 1 n Fußgänger(in f) m. **2** adj (a) attr

(of pedestrians) Fußgänger-. ~ **controlled traffic lights** Fußgängerampeln pl; ~ **crossing** (Brit) Fußgängerüberweg m; ~ **precinct** Fußgängerzone f. **(b)** (prosaic) schwunglos.

pedestrianize [pɪ'destrɪənaɪz] vt street in eine Fußgängerzone umwandeln.

pediatric [ˌpiːdɪ'ætrɪk] etc (esp US) see **paediatric** etc.

pedicure ['pedɪkjʊər] n Pediküre f.

pedigree ['pedɪgriː] **1** n (lit, fig) Stammbaum m; (document) Ahnentafel f; (fig) Geschichte f. **2** attr reinrassig.

pedigreed ['pedɪgriːd] adj reinrassig.

pediment ['pedɪmənt] n Giebeldreieck nt.

pedlar ['pedlər] n Hausierer(in f) m; (of drugs) Drogenhändler(in f), Pusher(in f) (sl) m.

pedometer [pɪ'dɒmɪtər] n Pedometer nt, Schrittzähler m.

pee [piː] (inf) **1** n (urine) Urin m, Pipi (baby-talk) nt. **to need/have a ~** pinkeln müssen/pinkeln; **I'm just off for a ~** ich geh' mal eben pinkeln (inf). **2** vi (a) pinkeln (inf). **(b)** (also ~ **down**) (hum: rain) pinkeln (inf).

peek [piːk] **1** n kurzer Blick; (furtive, from under blindfold etc) verstohlener Blick. **to take or have a ~** kurz/verstohlen gucken (at nach); **may I just have a ~?** darf ich mal eben or kurz sehen or gucken?; **to get a ~ at sb/sth** jdn/etw kurz zu sehen bekommen. **2** vi gucken (at nach).

peekaboo [piːkə'buː] **1** n Guck-Guck-Spiel nt. **to play ~** guck-guck spielen. **2** interj guck-guck.

peel [piːl] **1** n Schale f. **2** vt schälen; see eye. **3** vi (wallpaper) sich lösen; (paint) abblättern; (skin, person) sich schälen or pellen (inf). **the paper was ~ing off the wall** die Tapete löste sich or kam von der Wand.

♦ **peel away 1** vt sep wallpaper, paint abziehen, ablösen (from von); wrapper abstreifen (from von); bark abschälen (from von). **2** vi (lit, fig) sich lösen (from von).

♦ **peel back** vt sep cover, wrapping abziehen.

♦ **peel off 1** vt sep (+ prep obj von) sticky tape, wallpaper, paint abziehen, ablösen; tree bark abschälen; wrapper, dress, glove etc abstreifen. **2** vi (a) see **peel away 2. (b)** (leave formation) ausscheren; (Aviat also) abdrehen.

peeler[1] ['piːlər] n (old Brit inf) Gendarm m (old).

peeler[2] n (potato ~) Schälmesser nt, Schäler m.

peeling ['piːlɪŋ] n (a) Abschälen nt. **(b)** ~s pl Schalen pl.

peep[1] [piːp] **1** n (sound) (of bird etc) Piep m; (of horn, whistle, inf: of person) Ton m. **to give a ~** (bird) einen Piep von sich geben; (horn, whistle) einen Ton von sich geben; not **to give a ~** keinen Pieps von sich geben (inf); **one ~ out of you and ...** (inf) noch einen Mucks (inf) or Pieps (inf) und ...; ~! ~! (of horn) tut! tut!; (of whistle) tüt! tüt!

2 vi (bird etc) piepen; (horn, car) tuten; (whistle) pfeifen; (person) (on horn) tuten; (on whistle) pfeifen.

3 vt I ~ed my horn at him, I ~ed him (inf) ich habe ihn angehupt (inf).

peep[2] **1** n (look) kurzer Blick; (furtive, when forbidden etc) verstohlener Blick. **to get a ~ at sth** etw kurz zu sehen bekommen; **to take or have a ~** (at sth) kurz/verstohlen (nach) gucken. **2** vt she ~ed her head out sie streckte ihren Kopf hervor.

3 vi gucken (at nach). **to ~ from behind sth** hinter etw (dat) hervorschauen; **to ~ over sth** über etw (acc) gucken; **to ~ through sth** durch etw gucken or lugen; **no ~ing!, don't ~ !** (aber) nicht gucken!

♦ **peep out** vi herausgucken. **the sun ~ed ~ from behind the clouds** die Sonne sah or kam hinter den Wolken hervor.

peepers ['piːpəz] npl (inf) Gucker pl (inf).

peephole ['piːphəʊl] n Guckloch nt; (in door also) Spion m.

peeping Tom ['piːpɪŋ'tɒm] n Spanner (inf), Voyeur m.

peep: ~ **show** n Peepshow f; ~**-toe 1** adj offen; **2** n (shoe) offener Schuh.

peer[1] [pɪər] n (a) (noble) Peer m. ~ **of the realm** Peer m. **(b)** (equal) Peer m (spec). **he was well-liked by his ~s** er war bei seinesgleichen beliebt; **to be tried by one's ~s** von seinesgleichen gerichtet werden; **as a musician he has or knows no ~ or is without ~** als Musiker sucht er seinesgleichen.

peer[2] vi starren; (short-sightedly, inquiringly) schielen. **to ~ (hard) at sb/sth** jdn/etw anstarren, jdn anschielen/auf etw (acc) schielen; **the driver ~ed through the fog** der Fahrer versuchte angestrengt, im Nebel etwas zu erkennen; **if you ~ through the mist you can just see ...** wenn es dir gelingt, im Nebel etwas zu erkennen, kannst du gerade noch sehen ...; ~**ing through the murky water, the diver ...** der Taucher, der in dem trüben Wasser kaum etwas erkennen konnte, ...

peerage ['pɪərɪdʒ] n (peers) Adelsstand m; (in GB) Peers pl; (rank also) Adelswürde f; (in GB) Peerage, Peerswürde f; (book) das britische Adelsverzeichnis. **to raise or elevate sb to the ~** jdn in den Adelsstand erheben; **to give sb a ~** jdm einen Adelstitel verleihen, jdn adeln; **to get a ~** geadelt werden, einen Adelstitel verliehen bekommen.

peeress ['pɪərɪs] n Peereß f.

peer group n Peer Group, Alterskohorte f.

peerless adj, ~**ly** adv ['pɪəlɪs, -lɪ] einzigartig, unvergleichlich.

peeve [piːv] vt (inf) ärgern, reizen, fuchsen (inf).

peeved [piːvd] adj (inf) eingeschnappt, ärgerlich, verärgert; look ärgerlich, verärgert.

peevish ['piːvɪʃ] adj (irritated) gereizt, mürrisch, brummig; (irritable) reizbar.

peevishly ['piːvɪʃlɪ] adv gereizt.

peevishness ['piːvɪʃnɪs] n (irritation) Gereiztheit, Brummigkeit f; (irritability) Reizbarkeit f.

peewit ['piːwɪt] n Kiebitz m.

peg [peg] **1** n (stake) Pflock m; (tent ~ also) Hering m; (for ~board, wood joints, in games) Stift m; (of musical instrument) Wirbel m; (Brit: clothes ~) (Wäsche)klammer f; (hook, for mountaineering) Haken m; (in barrel) Zapfen, Spund m. **off the ~** von der Stange; **a ~ of rum** etc ein Gläschen nt Rum etc; **to**

take or bring sb down a ~ or two (inf) jdm einen Dämpfer geben; **a (convenient) ~ on which to hang one's prejudices** etc ein guter Aufhänger für seine Vorurteile etc.

2 vt (a) (fasten) (with stake) anpflocken; (with clothes ~) anklammern; (to ~ board) anheften; (with tent ~) festpflocken.

(b) (mark out) area abstecken.

(c) (fig) prices, wages festsetzen.

♦ **peg away** vi (inf) nicht locker lassen (at mit).

♦ **peg down** vt sep tent etc festpflocken.

♦ **peg out 1** vt sep (a) washing aufhängen; skins ausspannen. **(b)** (mark out) area abstecken. **2** vi (sl) (die) abkratzen (sl), den Löffel abgeben (sl); (stop: machine) verrecken (sl).

♦ **peg up** vt sep washing aufhängen; notice heften (on an + acc).

Pegasus ['pegəsəs] n Pegasus m.

pegboard ['pegbɔːd] n Lochbrett nt.

peg-leg ['pegleg] n (inf) (person) Stelzfuß m; (leg also) Holzbein nt.

peignoir ['peɪnwɑː] n Négligé nt.

pejorative adj, ~**ly** adv [pɪ'dʒɒrɪtɪv, -lɪ] pejorativ, abwertend, abschätzig.

peke [piːk] n (inf) see **pekin(g)ese 1** etc.

Pekin(g) [piː'kɪŋ] n Peking nt. ~ **man** Pekingmensch m.

pekin(g)ese [ˌpiːkɪ'niːz] **1** n, pl - (a) (dog) Pekinese m. **(b)** P~ Einwohner(in f) m von Peking. **(c)** P~ (language) Dialekt m von Peking. **2** adj P~ Pekinger-.

pelerine ['pelərɪn] n (old) Pelerine f, Umhang m.

pelican ['pelɪkən] n Pelikan m. ~ **crossing** Ampelübergang m.

pelisse [pə'liːs] n (old) pelzbesetztes Kleid.

pellet ['pelɪt] n Kügelchen nt; (for gun) Schrot m or nt; (Biol: regurgitated ~) Gewölle nt.

pellicle ['pelɪkəl] n Film m; (Zool: membrane) Pellicula f.

pell-mell ['pel'mel] adv durcheinander, wie Kraut und Rüben (inf); (with vbs of motion) in heillosem Durcheinander.

pellucid [pe'luːsɪd] adj liquid, meaning klar; argument also einleuchtend.

pelmet ['pelmɪt] n Blende f; (of fabric) Falbel f, Querbehang m.

pelt[1] [pelt] n Pelz m, Fell nt.

pelt[2] **1** vt (a) (throw) schleudern (at nach). **to ~ sb/sth (with sth)** jdn/etw (mit etw) bewerfen.

(b) (beat hard) verprügeln.

2 vi (inf) (a) (go fast) pesen (inf).

(b) it ~**ed (with rain)** es hat nur so geschüttet (inf); **the rain/hail ~ed against the windows** der Regen/Hagel prasselte an or schlug gegen die Fensterscheiben.

3 n (inf) (a) (speed) at full/a fair or quite a ~ volle Pulle (inf).

(b) (blow) Schlag m. **she gave her one good ~ round the ear** sie gab ihr eine kräftige Ohrfeige.

♦ **pelt along** vi (inf) entlangrasen.

♦ **pelt down** vi it or the rain really ~ed ~ der Regen prasselte nur so herunter; **it's ~ing ~** es regnet in Strömen.

pelvic ['pelvɪk] adj Becken-; complaint, pains in der Beckengegend. ~ **girdle** Beckengürtel m; ~ **fin** Bauchflosse f.

pelvis ['pelvɪs] n Becken nt.

pen[1] [pen] **1** n (dip ~) Feder f; (fountain ~) Füllfederhalter, Füller m; (ball-point ~) Kugelschreiber, Kuli (inf) m. **to set or put ~ to paper** zur Feder greifen; **to wield a cutting/powerful** etc ~ eine spitze/gewandte etc Feder führen; **the ~ is mightier than the sword** (prov) die Feder ist mächtiger als das Schwert.

2 vt niederschreiben; poem etc also verfassen.

pen[2] **1** n (a) (for cattle) Pferch m; (for sheep) Hürde f; (for pigs) Koben m; (play ~) Laufstall m, Ställchen, Laufgitter nt. **(b)** (US inf: prison) Bau (inf), Knast (inf) m. **(c)** (for submarines) Bunker m. **2** vt einsperren.

♦ **pen in** vt sep einsperren; (fig) car etc einklemmen, einkeilen.

♦ **pen up** vt sep einsperren.

pen[3] n (swan) weiblicher Schwan.

penal ['piːnl] adj law, colony etc Straf-. ~ **code** Strafgesetzbuch nt; ~ **system** Strafrecht nt; ~ **reform** Strafrechtsreform f; ~ **offence** Straftat f, strafbares Vergehen; ~ **servitude** Zwangsarbeit f.

penalization [ˌpiːnəlaɪ'zeɪʃən] n (a) (punishment) Bestrafung f; (fig) Benachteiligung f. **(b)** (making punishable) Unter-Strafe-Stellen nt.

penalize ['piːnəlaɪz] vt (a) (punish) bestrafen. **(b)** (Sport) player einen Strafstoß etc verhängen gegen; (fig) benachteiligen. **we are ~d by not having a car** wir sind im Nachteil or benachteiligt, weil wir kein Auto haben. **(c)** (make punishable) unter Strafe stellen.

penalty ['penltɪ] n (a) (punishment) Strafe f; (fig: disadvantage) Nachteil m. **the ~ (for this) is death** darauf steht die Todesstrafe; **you know the ~** Sie wissen, welche Strafe darauf steht; "~ **£5**", bei Zuwiderhandlung wird eine Geldstrafe von £ 5 erhoben"; **on ~ of death/£5/imprisonment** bei Todesstrafe/bei einer Geldstrafe von £ 5/bei Gefängnisstrafe; **on ~ of excommunication** unter Androhung der Exkommunizierung; **to pay the ~** dafür büßen; **that's the ~ you pay for ...** das ist die Strafe dafür, daß ...

(b) (Sport) Strafstoß m; (Soccer) Elfmeter m; (Golf, Bridge) Strafpunkt m.

penalty: ~ **area** n Strafraum m; ~ **box** n (Ftbl) Strafraum m; (Ice Hockey) Strafbank f; ~ **clause** n Vertragsstrafe f; ~ **goal** n (Rugby) Straftor nt; ~ **kick** n Strafstoß m; ~ **line** n Strafraumgrenze f; ~ **spot** n Elfmeterpunkt m.

penance ['penəns] n (Rel) Buße f; (fig) Strafe f. **to do ~** Buße tun; (fig) büßen; **as a ~** (Rel) als Buße; (fig) zur or als Strafe; **it's a ~ for ...** (fig) das ist die Strafe für ...

pen-and-ink ['penənd'ɪŋk] adj Feder-.

pence [pens] n (a) Pence m. **(b)** pl of **penny.**

penchant ['pãːʃãː] n Schwäche, Vorliebe f (for für).

pencil ['pensl] **1** n Bleistift m; (eyebrow ~) Augenbrauenstift m; (Math, Phys: of lines, rays etc) Büschel nt. **2** vt (also ~ **in)**

mit Bleistift schreiben/zeichnen *etc.* ~**led eyebrows** nachgezogene Augenbrauen *pl.* **3** *attr drawing etc* Bleistift-; *line also* mit Bleistift gezogen.

pencil: ~ **box** *n* Federkasten *m*; ~ **case** *n* Federmäppchen *nt*; ~ **sharpener** *n* (Bleistift)spitzer *m*.

pendant ['pendənt] *n* Anhänger *m*.

pendent ['pendənt] *adj* herabhängend; *lamps also* Hänge-.

pending ['pendɪŋ] **1** *adj* anstehend; *lawsuit* anhängig. "~" „unerledigt"; **to be** ~ (*decision etc*) noch anstehen; (*trial*) noch anhängig sein; **when he died he left a number of matters** ~ bei seinem Tod waren verschiedene Dinge unerledigt.
2 *prep* ~ **his arrival/return** bis zu seiner Ankunft/Rückkehr; ~ **a decision** bis eine Entscheidung getroffen worden ist.

pendulous ['pendjʊləs] *adj* herabhängend. ~ **breasts** *or* **bosom** Hängebrüste *pl*, Hängebusen *m*.

pendulum ['pendjʊləm] *n* Pendel *nt*. **the** ~ **has swung back in the opposite direction** das Pendel ist in die entgegengesetzte Richtung ausgeschlagen (*lit, fig*); **the** ~ **has swung back in favour of** *or* **towards** ... die Tendenz geht wieder in Richtung (+*gen*) ...; **the swing of the** ~ die Tendenzwende.

penetrable ['penɪtrəbl] *adj* zu durchdringen. **the scarcely** ~ **jungle** der fast undurchdringliche Dschungel.

penetrate ['penɪtreɪt] **1** *vt* eindringen in (+*acc*); (*go right through*) *walls etc* durchdringen; (*Mil*) *enemy lines* durchbrechen; (*Med*) *vein* durchstechen; (*infiltrate*) *party* infiltrieren. **is there anything that will** ~ **that thick skull of yours?** geht denn auch überhaupt nichts in deinen Schädel rein!; **to** ~ **sb's disguise** hinter jds Maske (*acc*) schauen.
2 *vi* eindringen; (*go right through*) durchdringen. **the idea just didn't** ~ (*fig*) das ist mir/ihm *etc* nicht klar geworden; **has that** ~**d?** hast du/habt ihr das endlich kapiert?

penetrating ['penɪtreɪtɪŋ] *adj* durchdringend; *mind also* scharf; *insight* scharfsinnig; *light* grell; *pain* stechend.

penetratingly ['penɪtreɪtɪŋlɪ] *adv* durchdringend; *comment, analyze* scharfsinnig; *shine* grell. **a** ~ **accurate analysis** eine messerscharfe Analyse; **a** ~ **bright light** ein grelles Licht; **a** ~ **sharp pain** ein stechender Schmerz.

penetration [ˌpenɪ'treɪʃən] *n see vt* Eindringen *nt* (*into in* +*acc*); Durchdringen *nt* (*of gen*); Durchbrechen *nt*, Durchbrechung *f*; Durchstechen *nt*; Infiltration *f*. **the** ~ **of his gaze** sein durchdringender Blick; **the** ~ **of the noise** der durchdringende Lärm; **the** ~ **of the light** das grelle Licht; **the** ~ **of the needle** was 3 mm die Nadel war 3 mm tief eingedrungen; **the** ~ **of his mind/his powers of** ~ sein Scharfsinn *m*.

penetrative ['penɪtrətɪv] *adj see* **penetrating**.

penfriend ['penfrend] *n* Brieffreund(in *f*) *m*.

penguin ['peŋgwɪn] *n* Pinguin *m*. ~ **suit** (*hum*) Schwalbenschwanz *m* (*hum*).

penholder ['pen,həʊldə^r] *n* Federhalter *m*.

penicillin [ˌpenɪ'sɪlɪn] *n* Penizillin *nt*.

peninsula [pɪ'nɪnsjʊlə] *n* Halbinsel *f*.

peninsular [pɪ'nɪnsjʊlə^r] *adj* Halbinsel-. **the P~ War** der Krieg auf der Pyrenäenhalbinsel.

penis ['piːnɪs] *n* Penis *m*. ~ **envy** Penisneid *m*.

penitence ['penɪtəns] *n* Reue *f* (*also Eccl*), Zerknirschtheit *f*.

penitent ['penɪtənt] **1** *adj* reuig (*also Eccl*), zerknirscht. **2** *n* Büßer(in *f*) *m*; (*Eccl*) reuiger Sünder, reuige Sünderin.

penitential [ˌpenɪ'tenʃəl] *adj* reuevoll, reumütig, reuig; (*Eccl*) Buß-. **a** ~ **act** eine Bußtat.

penitentiary [ˌpenɪ'tenʃərɪ] *n* (*esp US: prison*) Strafanstalt *f*, Gefängnis *nt*.

pen: ~**knife** *n* Taschenmesser *nt*; ~ **name** *n* Pseudonym *nt*, Schriftstellername *m*.

pennant ['penənt] *n* Wimpel *m*.

pen nib *n* Feder *f*.

penniless ['penɪlɪs] *adj* mittellos. **to be** ~ keinen Pfennig Geld haben; **her husband died, leaving her** ~ ihr Mann starb, und sie stand völlig mittellos *or* ohne einen Pfennig Geld da.

pennon ['penən] *n see* **pennant**.

penn'orth ['penəθ] *n see* **pennyworth**.

Pennsylvania [ˌpensɪl'veɪnɪə] *n* Pennsylvanien *nt*.

Pennsylvania-Dutch [ˌpensɪl'veɪnɪə'dʌtʃ] **1** *n* (a) Pennsylvania-Deutsch *nt*. (b) *pl* (*people*) Pennsylvania-Deutsche *pl*. **2** *adj* pennsylvania-deutsch.

Pennsylvanian [ˌpensɪl'veɪnɪən] *adj* pennsylvanisch.

penny ['penɪ] *n, pl* (*coins*) **pennies,** (*sum*) **pence** Penny *m*; (*US*) Centstück *nt*. **in for a** ~, **in for a pound** (*prov*) wennschon, dennschon (*inf*); (*morally*) wer A sagt, muß auch B sagen (*prov*); **I'm not a** ~ **the wiser** ich bin genauso klug wie zuvor; **take care of the pennies and the pounds will take care of themselves** (*Prov*) spare im kleinen, dann hast du im großen; **a** ~ **for your thoughts** woran denkst du gerade?; **he hasn't got a** ~ (*inf*) der hat keinen Pfennig (*inf*); **to spend a** ~ (*inf*) austreten, mal eben verschwinden (*inf*); **the** ~ **dropped** (*inf*) der Groschen ist gefallen (*inf*); *see* **pretty, honest.**

penny: ~ **arcade** *n* Spielhalle *f*; ~ **dreadful** *n* (*Brit*) Groschenroman *m*; ~**-farthing** *n* Hochrad *nt*; ~**-pinch** *vi* jeden Pfennig umdrehen; ~**-pincher** *n* Pfennigfuchser *m*; ~**-pinching** *adj* knauserig (*inf*); ~**-weight** *n* Pennygewicht *nt*; ~ **whistle** *n* Kinderflöte *f*; ~ **wise** *adj* **to be** ~ **wise and pound foolish** immer am falschen Ende sparen; ~**-worth** *n* **a** ~**worth of liquorice/common-sense** für einen Penny Lakritz/für fünf Pfennig gesunden Menschenverstand.

penologist [piː'nɒlədʒɪst] *n* Kriminalpädagoge *m*, Kriminalpädagogin *f*.

penology [piː'nɒlədʒɪ] *n* Kriminalpädagogik *f*.

pen: ~**pal** *n* (*inf*) Brieffreund(in *f*) *m*; ~**pusher** *n* Schreiberling *m*; ~**pushing 1** *n* Schreiberei *f*, Schreibkram *m*; **2** *adj* *job* Schreib-; ~**pushing clerk** Bürohengst *m* (*inf*).

pension ['penʃən] *n* (a) (*money*) Rente *f*; (*for former salaried staff also*) Pension *f*; (*for civil servants also*) Ruhegehalt *nt*

(*form*). **company** ~ betriebliche Altersversorgung; **to be entitled to a** ~ Anspruch auf eine Rente *etc* haben, rentenberechtigt/pensionsberechtigt sein; **to be living on a** ~ von der Rente *etc* leben.
(b) (*board*) **full/half** ~ Voll-/Halbpension *f*.

♦**pension off** *vt sep* (*inf*) vorzeitig pensionieren.

pensionable ['penʃənəbl] *adj* **this position is** ~ diese Stellung berechtigt zu einer Pension/einem Ruhegehalt; **of** ~ **age** im Renten-/Pensionsalter.

pension book *n* Rentenausweis *m*.

pensioner ['penʃənə^r] *n see* **pension** Rentner(in *f*) *m*; Pensionär(in *f*) *m*; Ruhegehaltsempfänger(in *f*) *m* (*form*).

pension: ~ **fund** *n* Rentenfonds *m*; ~ **rights** *npl* Rentenanspruch *m*; ~ **scheme** *n* Rentenversicherung *f*.

pensive *adj*, ~**ly** *adv* ['pensɪv, -lɪ] nachdenklich; (*sadly serious*) schwermütig.

pensiveness ['pensɪvnɪs] *n see adj* Nachdenklichkeit *f*; Schwermütigkeit *f*.

pentagon ['pentəgən] *n* Fünfeck, Pentagon *nt*. **the P~** das Pentagon.

pentagonal [pen'tægənl] *adj* fünfeckig.

pentagram ['pentəgræm] *n* Drudenfuß *m*, Pentagramm *nt*.

pentahedron [ˌpentə'hiːdrən] *n* Fünfflächner *m*, Pentaeder *nt*.

pentameter [pen'tæmɪtə^r] *n* Pentameter *m*; *see* **iambic.**

Pentateuch ['pentətjuːk] *n* die fünf Bücher *pl* Mose, Pentateuch *m*.

pentathlete [pen'tæθliːt] *n* Fünfkämpfer(in *f*) *m*.

pentathlon [pen'tæθlən] *n* Fünfkampf *m*.

pentatonic [ˌpentə'tɒnɪk] *adj* pentatonisch. ~ **scale** fünfstufige Tonleiter.

Pentecost ['pentɪkɒst] *n* (*Jewish*) Erntefest *nt*; (*Christian*) Pfingsten *nt*.

pentecostal [ˌpentɪ'kɒstl] *adj* Pfingst-; *sect, service, revival* der Pfingstbewegung.

penthouse ['penthaʊs] *n* (*apartment*) Penthouse *nt*, Dachterrassenwohnung *f*; (*roof*) Überdachung *f*.

pent-up ['pent'ʌp] *adj* *person* (*with frustration, anger*) geladen *pred*; (*after traumatic experience*) aufgewühlt; (*nervous, excited*) innerlich angespannt; *emotions, passion, excitement* aufgestaut; *atmosphere* angespannt, geladen. **to get** ~ (*about sth*) sich (über etw *acc*) erregen, sich (in etw *acc*) hineinsteigern; **she had been very** ~ **about it** es hatte sich alles in ihr gestaut; ~ **feelings** ein Emotionsstau *m*, angestaute Gefühle *pl*.

penultimate [pe'nʌltɪmɪt] *adj* vorletzte(r, s).

penumbra [pɪ'nʌmbrə] *n, pl* **-e** [-briː] *or* **-s** Halbschatten *m*.

penurious [pɪ'njʊərɪəs] *adj* (*liter*) (*poor*) arm, armselig; *existence also* karg, dürftig; (*mean*) geizig, knauserig.

penuriously [pɪ'njʊərɪəslɪ] *adv see adj.*

penury ['penjʊrɪ] *n* Armut, Not *f*. **the company's present state of** ~ die gegenwärtigen Finanzschwierigkeiten der Firma.

penwiper ['pen,waɪpə^r] *n* Federwischer *m*.

peony ['piːənɪ] *n* Pfingstrose, Päonie (*spec*) *f*.

people ['piːpl] **1** *npl* (a) Menschen *pl*; (*not in formal context*) Leute *pl*. **we're concerned with** ~ uns geht es um die Menschen; **French** ~ **are very fond of their food** die Franzosen lieben ihre gute Küche; **that's typical of Edinburgh** ~ das ist typisch für (die) Leute aus Edinburgh; **a job where you meet** ~ eine Arbeit, wo man mit Menschen *or* Leuten zusammenkommt; ~ **who need** ~ Menschen, die andere Menschen brauchen; **the world is full of** ~ **like him** die Welt ist voll von Menschen *or* Leuten wie ihm; **all the** ~ **in the world** alle Menschen auf der Welt; **all** ~ **with red hair** alle Rothaarigen; **some** ~ **don't like it** manche Leute mögen es nicht; **most** ~ **in show business** die meisten Leute im Showgeschäft; **aren't** ~ **funny?** was gibt es doch für seltsame Menschen *or* Leute!; **the** ~ **you meet!** Menschen *or* Leute gibt's!; **why me of all** ~? warum ausgerechnet ich/mich?; **I met Harry of all** ~! ausgerechnet Harry habe ich getroffen!; **of all** ~ **who do you think I should meet!** stell dir mal vor, wen ich getroffen habe?; **what do you** ~ **think?** was haltet ihr denn davon?; **poor/blind/disabled** ~ arme Leute *or* Arme/Blinde/Behinderte; **middle-aged** ~ Menschen mittleren Alters; **city** ~ Stadtmenschen *pl*; **country** ~ Menschen *pl* vom Land, Landleute *pl* (*dated*); **some** ~! Leute gibt's!; **some** ~ **have all the luck** manche Leute haben einfach Glück.
(b) (*inhabitants*) Bevölkerung *f*. **the** ~ **of Rome/Egypt** *etc* die Bevölkerung von Rom/Ägypten *etc*; **Madrid has over 5 million** ~ Madrid hat über 5 Millionen Einwohner.
(c) (*one, they*) man; (~ *in general, the neighbours*) die Leute. ~ **say that** ... man sagt, daß ...; **what will** ~ **think!** was sollen die Leute denken!; ~ **in general tend to say** ... im allgemeinen neigt man zu der Behauptung ...
(d) (*nation, masses, subjects*) Volk *nt*. **the common** ~ das einfache Volk, die breite Masse; **a man of the** ~ ein Mann *m* des Volkes; **government by the** ~ (**of the** ~) eine Regierung des Volkes; **the Belgian** ~ die Belgier *pl*, das belgische Volk; **P~'s police/Republic** *etc* Volkspolizei *f*/-republik *f etc*.
2 *vt* besiedeln. **the world seems to be** ~**d with idiots** die Welt scheint von Idioten bevölkert zu sein.

pep [pep] *n* (*inf*) Schwung, Elan, Pep (*inf*) *m*.

♦**pep up** *vt sep* (*inf*) Schwung bringen in (+*acc*); *food, drink* pikanter machen; *person* munter machen. **pills to** ~ **you** ~ Aufputschmittel *pl*.

pepper ['pepə^r] **1** *n* Pfeffer *m*; (*green, red* ~) Paprika *m*; (*plant*) Pfefferstrauch *m*. **two** ~**s** zwei Paprikaschoten. **2** *vt* (a) pfeffern. (b) (*fig*) **to** ~ **a work with quotations** eine Arbeit mit Zitaten spicken; **to** ~ **sb with shot** jdn mit Kugeln durchlöchern.

pepper: ~**-and-salt** *adj* Pfeffer-und-Salz-; *hair* meliert; ~**corn** *n* Pfefferkorn *nt*; ~**mill** *n* Pfeffermühle *f*; ~**mint** *n* Pfefferminz *nt*; (*Bot*) Pfefferminze *f*; ~ **pot** *n* Pfefferstreuer *m*.

peppery ['pepərɪ] adj gepfeffert; (fig) old man etc hitzig, hitzköpfig. it tastes rather ~ es schmeckt stark nach Pfeffer.

pep pill n Aufputschpille, Peppille f.

peppy ['pepɪ] adj (+er) (sl) forsch, schwungvoll, zackig (inf); performance, music etc fetzig (sl).

pepsin ['pepsɪn] n Pepsin nt.

pep talk n (inf) aufmunternde Worte pl. to give sb a ~ jdm ein paar aufmunternde Worte sagen.

peptic ['peptɪk] adj peptisch. ~ ulcer Magengeschwür nt.

per [pɜː] prep pro. £20 ~ annum £ 20 im or pro Jahr; 60 ~ hour 60 Stundenkilometer, 60 km pro Stunde or in der Stunde; $2 ~ dozen das Dutzend für $ 2, $ 2 das Dutzend; £5 ~ copy £ 5 pro or je Exemplar, £ 5 für jedes Exemplar; as ~ gemäß (+dat); ~ se an sich, per se (geh); see usual.

peradventure [,pərəd'ventʃəʳ] adv (old: perhaps) vielleicht. if/lest ~ falls.

perambulate [pə'ræmbjuleɪt] (form) 1 vt sich ergehen in (+dat) (geh). 2 vi sich ergehen (liter).

perambulation [pə,ræmbju'leɪʃən] n (form) Spaziergang m.

perambulator ['præmbjuleɪtəʳ] n (Brit form) Kinderwagen m.

perceivable [pə'siːvəbl] adj erkennbar. scarcely ~ kaum auszumachen or zu erkennen.

perceive [pə'siːv] vt wahrnehmen; (understand, realize, recognize) erkennen. do you ~ anything strange? fällt Ihnen irgend etwas Ungewöhnliches auf?; ..., which we ~ to be the case (form) ..., was wir als zutreffend erkennen.

per cent, (US) **percent** [pə'sent] n Prozent nt. what ~? wieviel Prozent?; 20 ~ 20 Prozent; a 10 ~ discount 10 Prozent Rabatt.

percentage [pə'sentɪdʒ] 1 n (a) Prozentsatz m; (commission, payment) Anteil m; (proportion) Teil m. a small ~ of the population ein geringer Teil der Bevölkerung; expressed as a ~ prozentual or in Prozenten ausgedrückt; what ~? wieviel Prozent?; to get a ~ on all sales prozentual am Umsatz beteiligt sein.
(b) (inf: advantage) there's no ~ in it das bringt nichts (inf). 2 attr prozentual. on a ~ basis prozentual, auf Prozentbasis; the statistics are on a ~ basis die Statistiken werden in Prozenten angegeben; ~ sign Prozentzeichen nt.

perceptible [pə'septəbl] adj wahrnehmbar; improvement, trend, increase etc spürbar, deutlich. his unhappiness was ~ only to his close friends nur seine engsten Freunde spürten or merkten, daß er unglücklich war.

perceptibly [pə'septəblɪ] adv merklich, spürbar; (to the eye) wahrnehmbar, sichtbar. he blanched ~ er wurde sichtbar blaß; he is ~ older er ist sichtbar gealtert.

perception [pə'sepʃən] n (a) no pl Wahrnehmung f. his colour ~ is impaired seine Farbwahrnehmung ist beeinträchtigt.
(b) (mental image, conception) Auffassung f (of von). he seems to have a clear ~ of the dilemma I face er scheint meine schwierige Lage vollauf zu erkennen; one's ~ of the situation die eigene Einschätzung der Lage.
(c) (no pl: perceptiveness) Einsicht f; (perceptive remark, observation) Beobachtung f.
(d) no pl (act of perceiving) (of object, visible difference) Wahrnehmung f; (of difficulties, meaning, illogicality etc) Erkennen nt. his quick ~ of the danger saved us all from death weil er die Gefahr blitzschnell erkannte, rettete er uns allen das Leben; his ~ of the truth began when ... er fing an, die Wahrheit zu erkennen, als ...

perceptive [pə'septɪv] adj (a) faculties Wahrnehmungs-.
(b) (sensitive) person einfühlsam; (penetrating) analysis, speech, study erkenntnisreich, scharfsinnig; book, remark einsichtig. he has the ~ mind of a true artist er hat das Einfühlungsvermögen eines wahren Künstlers; very ~ of you sehr aufmerksam, gut beobachtet (iro).

perceptively [pə'septɪvlɪ] adv see adj.

perceptiveness [pə'septɪvnɪs] n see adj (b) Einfühlsamkeit f; Erkenntnisreichtum m, Scharfsinnigkeit f; Einsichtigkeit f; Aufmerksamkeit f.

perch¹ [pɜːtʃ] n (fish) Flußbarsch m.

perch² 1 n (a) (of bird) Stange f; (in tree) Ast m; (hen-roost) Hühnerstange f; (fig: for person etc) (hochliegender) Sitzplatz.
(b) (Measure) Längenmaß (5.029 m).
2 vt to ~ sth on sth etw auf etw (acc) setzen or (upright) stellen; to be ~ed on sth auf etw (dat) sitzen; (birds also) auf etw (dat) hocken; with his glasses ~ed on the end of his nose mit der Brille auf der Nasenspitze; Britain is ~ed on the edge of Europe Großbritannien liegt (ganz) am Rande Europas; a castle ~ed on the rock eine auf dem Felsen thronende Burg.
3 vi (bird, fig: person) hocken; (alight) sich niederlassen.

perchance [pə'tʃɑːns] adv (old) vielleicht.

percipient [pə'sɪpɪənt] adj see **perceptive**.

percolate ['pɜːkəleɪt] 1 vt filtrieren; coffee (in einer Kaffeemaschine) zubereiten. 2 vi (lit, fig) durchsickern. the coffee is just percolating der Kaffee läuft gerade durch.

percolator ['pɜːkəleɪtəʳ] n Kaffeemaschine f.

percuss [pə'kʌs] vt (Med) perkutieren (spec), abklopfen.

percussion [pə'kʌʃən] n (a) Perkussion f (also Med). ~ cap Zündhütchen nt. (b) (Mus) Schlagzeug nt. ~ instrument Schlaginstrument nt; ~ section Schlagzeug nt.

percussionist [pə'kʌʃənɪst] n Schlagzeuger(in f) m.

percussive [pə'kʌsɪv] adj perkussorisch (spec).

perdition [pə'dɪʃən] n ewige Verdammnis.

peregrination [,perɪgrɪ'neɪʃən] n (liter) Fahrt f. his literary ~s seine literarischen Exkurse.

peregrine (falcon) ['perɪgrɪn('fɔːlkən)] n Wanderfalke m.

peremptorily [pə'remptərɪlɪ] adv see adj.

peremptory [pə'remptərɪ] adj command, instruction kategorisch; voice gebieterisch; person herrisch.

perennial [pə'renɪəl] 1 adj plant mehrjährig, perennierend; (perpetual, constant) immerwährend, ewig; (regularly recurring) immer wiederkehrend. buying Christmas presents is a ~ problem der Kauf von Weihnachtsgeschenken ist ein alljährlich wiederkehrendes or sich neu stellendes Problem.
2 n (Bot) perennierende or mehrjährige Pflanze.

perennially [pə'renɪəlɪ] adv (perpetually, constantly) ständig; (recurrently) immer wieder.

perfect ['pɜːfɪkt] 1 adj (a) perfekt; wife, teacher, host, relationship also vorbildlich; harmony, balance, symmetry also vollkommen; meal, work of art, pronunciation, English also vollendet; weather, day, holiday also ideal; (Comm: not damaged) einwandfrei. it was the ~ moment es war genau der richtige Augenblick; that's the ~ hairstyle/woman for you das ist genau die richtige Frisur/Frau für dich; ~ number (Math) vollkommene Zahl; ~ rhyme rührender Reim; his Spanish is far from ~ sein Spanisch ist bei weitem nicht perfekt; with ~ self-confidence mit absolutem Selbstvertrauen; nobody is or can be ~ niemand ist perfekt or vollkommen.
(b) (absolute, utter) völlig; fool, nonsense also ausgemacht. she's a ~ terror/bore sie ist einfach schrecklich/sie ist ausgesprochen langweilig; ~ strangers wildfremde Leute pl; a ~ stranger ein Wildfremder m, eine Wildfremde; he's a ~ stranger to me er ist mir völlig fremd; it's a ~ disgrace es ist wirklich eine Schande.
(c) (Gram) ~ tense Perfekt nt; ~ ending Endung f im Perfekt; ~ form Vergangenheitsform f.
(d) (Mus) fourth rein; cadence authentisch; see pitch².
2 n (Gram) Perfekt nt. in the ~ im Perfekt.
3 [pə'fekt] vt vervollkommnen; technique, technology, process also perfektionieren.

perfectibility [pə,fektɪ'bɪlɪtɪ] n see adj Vervollkommnungsfähigkeit f; Perfektionierbarkeit f.

perfectible [pə'fektɪbl] adj vervollkommnungsfähig; technique, technology, process perfektionierbar.

perfection [pə'fekʃən] n Vollkommenheit, Perfektion f. to do sth to ~ etw perfekt tun.

perfectionism [pə'fekʃənɪzm] n Perfektionismus m.

perfectionist [pə'fekʃənɪst] n Perfektionist m.

perfective [pə'fektɪv] adj perfektiv.

perfectly ['pɜːfɪktlɪ] adv (a) (flawlessly, completely) perfekt; translated, drawn, cooked, matched also vollendet. he timed his entry ~ er hat seinen Eintritt genau abgepaßt; a ~ finished piece of work eine wirklich vollendete Arbeit; I understand you ~ ich weiß genau, was Sie meinen.
(b) (absolutely, utterly) absolut, vollkommen. we're ~ happy about it wir sind damit völlig zufrieden; a ~ lovely day ein wirklich herrlicher Tag.

perfidious adj, ~ly adv [pɜː'fɪdɪəs, -lɪ] (liter) perfid(e) (liter).

perfidiousness [pɜː'fɪdɪəsnɪs], **perfidy** ['pɜːfɪdɪ] n (liter) Perfidie f (liter).

perforate ['pɜːfəreɪt] 1 vt (with row of holes) perforieren; (pierce once) durchstechen, lochen; (Med) perforieren. 2 vi (ulcer) durchbrechen.

perforation [,pɜːfə'reɪʃən] n (act) Perforieren nt; (row of holes, Med) Perforation f.

perforce [pə'fɔːs] adv (old, liter) notgedrungen.

perform [pə'fɔːm] 1 vt play, concerto aufführen; solo, duet vortragen; part spielen; trick vorführen; miracle vollbringen; task verrichten, erfüllen; duty, function erfüllen; operation durchführen; ritual, ceremony vollziehen.
2 vi (a) (appear: orchestra, circus act etc) auftreten. to ~ on the violin Geige spielen.
(b) (car, machine, football team etc) leisten; (examination candidate etc) abschneiden. the 2 litre version ~s better die Zweiliterversion leistet mehr; the car ~ed excellently in the speed trials in den Geschwindigkeitsversuchen brachte der Wagen ausgezeichnete Ergebnisse; the choir ~ed very well der Chor war sehr gut or hat sehr gut gesungen; this car ~s best between 50 and 60 kmph dieser Wagen bringt seine optimale Leistung zwischen 50 und 60 Stundenkilometern; how did he ~? (actor, musician) wie war er?; how did the car ~? wie ist der Wagen gelaufen?; he ~ed brilliantly as Hamlet er spielte die Rolle des Hamlet brillant; the car is not ~ing properly der Wagen läuft nicht richtig; how does the metal ~ under pressure? wie verhält sich das Metall unter Druck?; he couldn't ~ (euph: sexually) er konnte nicht.
(c) (euph: excrete) sein Geschäft verrichten.

performance [pə'fɔːməns] n (a) (esp Theat: of play, opera etc) Aufführung f; (cinema) Vorstellung f; (by actor) Leistung f; (of a part) Darstellung f. the late ~ die Spätvorstellung; her ~ as Mother Courage was outstanding ihre Darstellung der Mutter Courage war hervorragend; he gave a splendid ~ er hat eine ausgezeichnete Leistung geboten, er hat ausgezeichnet gespielt/gesungen etc; it has not had a ~ since 1950 es ist seit 1950 nicht mehr aufgeführt worden; we are going to hear a ~ of Beethoven's 5th wir werden Beethovens 5. Sinfonie hören.
(b) (carrying out) see vt Aufführung f; Vortrag m; (of part) Darstellung f; Vorführung f; Vollbringung f; Verrichtung f, Erfüllung f; Erfüllung f; Durchführung f; Vollzug m. in the ~ of his duties in Ausübung seiner Pflicht; he died in the ~ of his duty er starb in Erfüllung seiner Pflicht.
(c) (effectiveness) (of machine, vehicle, sportsman etc) Leistung f; (of examination candidate etc) Abschneiden nt. he put up a good ~ er hat sich gut geschlagen (inf); 10 pages a week is not a very good ~ 10 Seiten in der Woche sind keine großartige Leistung; what was his ~ like in the test? wie hat er in der Prüfung abgeschnitten?; the team gave a poor ~ die Mannschaft hat eine schlechte Leistung gezeigt.
(d) (inf) (to-do, palaver) Umstand m; (bad behaviour) Benehmen nt. what a ~! was für ein Umstand!; welch ein Benehmen!; what a ~ to put on in front of all the guests sich so vor den Gästen zu benehmen!

performer [pəˈfɔːməʳ] n Künstler(in f) m.

performing [pəˈfɔːmɪŋ] adj animal dressiert. **the ~ arts** die darstellenden Künste; **~ rights** Aufführungsrechte pl.

perfume [ˈpɜːfjuːm] **1** n (substance) Parfüm nt; (smell) Duft m. **2** [pəˈfjuːm] vt parfümieren. **the flowers ~d** the air der Duft der Blumen erfüllte die Luft.

perfumer [pɜːˈfjuːməʳ] n (maker) Parfümeur m; (seller) Parfümhändler(in f) m; (device) Parfümzerstäuber m.

perfumery [pɜːˈfjuːmərɪ] n (making perfume) Parfümherstellung f; (perfume factory) Parfümerie f; (perfumes) Parfüm nt.

perfunctorily [pəˈfʌŋktərɪlɪ] adv see adj.

perfunctory [pəˈfʌŋktərɪ] adj flüchtig, der Form halber. **he said some ~ words of congratulation** er gratulierte mit ein paar flüchtig hingeworfenen Worten.

pergola [ˈpɜːgələ] n Pergola, Laube f.

perhaps [pəˈhæps, præps] adv vielleicht. **~ the greatest exponent of the art** der möglicherweise bedeutendste Vertreter dieser Kunst; **~ so** das kann or mag sein.

pericarp [ˈperɪkɑːp] n Perikarp nt.

peril [ˈperɪl] n Gefahr f. **to be in ~ of one's life** in Lebensgefahr sein; **do it at your (own) ~** auf Ihre eigene Gefahr.

perilous [ˈperɪləs] adj gefährlich; situation also bedrohlich.

perilously [ˈperɪləslɪ] adv gefährlich. **he was clinging ~ to an outcrop of rock** er hing lebensgefährlich an einem Felsvorsprung; **we came ~ close to bankruptcy/the precipice** wir waren dem Bankrott/Abgrund gefährlich nahe; **she came ~ close to falling** sie wäre um ein Haar heruntergefallen.

perimeter [pəˈrɪmɪtəʳ] n (Math) Umfang, Perimeter m; (Med) Perimeter m; (of grounds) Grenze f. **~ fence** Umzäunung f; **to walk round the ~** um das Gelände herumgehen.

period [ˈpɪərɪəd] n (a) (length of time) Zeit f; (age, epoch) Zeitalter nt, Epoche f; (Geol) Periode f. **Picasso's blue ~** Picassos blaue Periode; **for a ~ of eight weeks/two hours** für eine (Zeit)dauer or einen Zeitraum von acht Wochen/zwei Stunden; **within a three-month ~** innerhalb von drei Monaten; **for a three-month ~** drei Monate lang; **at that ~ (of my life)** zu diesem Zeitpunkt (in meinem Leben); **a ~ of cold weather** eine Kaltwetterperiode; **glacial ~** Eiszeit f; **the costume etc of the ~** die Kleidung etc der damaligen Zeit; **a writer of the ~** ein zeitgenössischer Schriftsteller.
  (b) (Sch) (Schul)stunde f. **double ~** Doppelstunde f.
  (c) (form: sentence) Periode f; (esp US: full stop) Punkt m.
  (d) (menstruation) Periode, Monatsblutung f, Tage pl (inf). **she missed a ~** sie bekam ihre Periode etc nicht.
  (e) (Chem) Periode f.

period: **~ costume, ~ dress** n zeitgenössische Kostüme pl; **~ furniture** n antike Möbel pl.

periodic [ˌpɪərɪˈɒdɪk] adj (intermittent) periodisch; (regular also) regelmäßig. **~ system/table** (Chem) Periodensystem nt.

periodical [ˌpɪərɪˈɒdɪkl] **1** adj see periodic. **2** n Zeitschrift f; (academic also) Periodikum nt.

periodically [ˌpɪərɪˈɒdɪkəlɪ] adv see periodic.

periodicity [ˌpɪərɪəˈdɪsɪtɪ] n (Chem) Periodizität f.

periodontitis [ˌperɪəʊdɒnˈtaɪtɪs] n Wurzelhautentzündung f.

period: **~ pains** npl Menstruationsschmerzen pl; **~ piece** n (a) antikes Stück; (painting, music etc) zeitgeschichtliches Dokument; **(b)** (also ~ play) Zeitstück nt.

peripatetic [ˌperɪpəˈtetɪk] adj umherreisend; existence rastlos; teacher an mehreren Schulen unterrichtend attr.

peripheral [pəˈrɪfərəl] adj Rand-; (Anat) peripher; (fig) nebensächlich, peripher.

periphery [pəˈrɪfərɪ] n Peripherie f. **young people on the ~ of society** junge Menschen am Rande der Gesellschaft.

periphrasis [pəˈrɪfrəsɪs] n, pl **periphrases** [pəˈrɪfrəsiːz] Periphrase f.

periphrastic [ˌperɪˈfræstɪk] adj periphrastisch.

periscope [ˈperɪskəʊp] n Periskop nt.

perish [ˈperɪʃ] **1** vi (a) (liter) (die) umkommen, sterben; (be destroyed: cities, civilization) untergehen. **we shall do it or ~ in the attempt** wir werden es machen, koste es, was es wolle; **he ~ed at sea** er fand den Tod auf See.
  (b) (rubber, leather etc) verschleißen, brüchig werden; (form: food) verderben, schlecht werden.
  2 vt (a) rubber, leather zerstören, brüchig werden lassen.
  (b) (inf) **~ the thought!** Gott behüte or bewahre!

perishable [ˈperɪʃəbl] **1** adj food verderblich. **"~"** „leicht verderblich". **2** npl **~s** leicht verderbliche Ware(n).

perished [ˈperɪʃt] adj (inf: with cold) durchfroren.

perisher [ˈperɪʃəʳ] n (Brit inf) Teufelsbraten m (inf).

perishing [ˈperɪʃɪŋ] adj (inf) (a) (very cold) room, weather eisig kalt. **I'm ~** ich geh' fast ein vor Kälte (inf). **(b)** (Brit inf: objectionable) verdammt (inf).

peristalsis [ˌperɪˈstælsɪs] n Peristaltik f.

peristyle [ˈperɪstaɪl] n Peristyl nt.

peritoneum [ˌperɪtəʊˈniːəm] n Bauchfell, Peritoneum (spec) nt.

peritonitis [ˌperɪtəʊˈnaɪtɪs] n Bauchfellentzündung f.

periwig [ˈperɪwɪg] n (Hist) Perücke f.

periwinkle [ˈperɪˌwɪŋkl] n (Bot) Immergrün nt; (Zool) Strandschnecke f.

perjure [ˈpɜːdʒəʳ] vr einen Meineid leisten.

perjured [ˈpɜːdʒəd] adj evidence, witness meineidig.

perjury [ˈpɜːdʒərɪ] n Meineid m. **to commit ~** einen Meineid leisten.

perk [pɜːk] n (esp Brit: benefit) Vergünstigung f.

♦**perk up 1** vt sep (a) (lift) head heben. **he ~ed ~ his ears** (dog, person) er spitzte die Ohren.
  (b) to ~ sb ~ (make lively: coffee etc) jdn aufmöbeln (inf) or munter machen; (make cheerful: visit, idea etc) jdn aufheitern; **to ~ ~ a room/party** ein Zimmer verschönern/eine Party in Schwung bringen.

2 vi (liven up: person, party) munter werden; (cheer up) aufleben; (become interested) hellhörig werden. **I hope this book ~s ~ soon** ich hoffe, das Buch wird bald interessanter.

perkily [ˈpɜːkɪlɪ] adv see adj.

perky [ˈpɜːkɪ] adj (+er) (cheerful, bright) munter; (cheeky, pert) keß, keck.

perm[1] [pɜːm] abbr of **permanent wave 1** n Dauerwelle f. **to give sb a ~** jdm eine Dauerwelle machen.
  2 vt **to ~ sb's hair** jdm eine Dauerwelle machen; **she only had the ends ~ed** sie ließ sich (dat) nur an den Enden eine Dauerwelle machen.
  3 vi **my hair doesn't ~ very easily** Dauerwelle hält bei mir sehr schlecht.

perm[2] n (for football pools) abbr of **permutation**.

permafrost [ˈpɜːməfrɒst] n Dauerfrostboden m.

permanence [ˈpɜːmənəns], **permanency** [ˈpɜːmənənsɪ] n Dauerhaftigkeit, Permanenz f; (of relationship, marriage also) Beständigkeit f; (of arrangement also, of job) Beständigkeit f. **having bought a flat, she began to feel some degree of ~** nachdem sie sich (dat) eine Wohnung gekauft hatte, entwickelte sie ein gewisses Gefühl der Bodenständigkeit; **children need a feeling of ~ and stability** Kinder brauchen ein Gefühl von Beständigkeit und Stabilität; **only art of high quality can achieve such ~** nur wirkliche Kunst kann eine solche Beständigkeit erreichen; **is there such a thing as ~?** ist überhaupt etwas beständig auf der Welt?

permanent [ˈpɜːmənənt] **1** adj ständig, permanent; arrangement, position, building fest; job, relationship, dye dauerhaft; agreement unbefristet. **the ~ revolution** die permanente Revolution; **I hope this is not going to become ~** ich hoffe, das wird kein Dauerzustand; **a ~ employee** ein Festangestellter m; **I'm not ~ here** ich bin hier nicht fest angestellt; **~ assets** Anlagevermögen nt; **~ capital** Anlagekapital nt; **~ fixture** (lit) festinstallierte Einrichtung; **he is a ~ fixture here** er gehört schon mit zum Inventar; **~ magnet** Permanentmagnet m; **~ pleats** Dauerfalten pl; **~ residence/address** ständiger or fester Wohnsitz; **one's ~ teeth** die zweiten Zähne; **~ way** (Brit) Bahnkörper m; **~ wave** see perm[1] 1.
  2 n (US) see perm[1] 1.

permanently [ˈpɜːmənəntlɪ] adv permanent, ständig; fixed fest. **a ~ depressing effect** eine anhaltend deprimierende Wirkung; **~ employed** festangestellt attr, fest angestellt pred; **~ glued together** dauerhaft verbunden; **~ pleated skirt** Rock mit Dauerfalten; **are you living ~ in Frankfurt?** ist Frankfurt Ihr fester or ständiger Wohnsitz?

permanganate [pɜːˈmæŋgənɪt] n Permanganat nt.

permeability [ˌpɜːmɪəˈbɪlɪtɪ] n Durchlässigkeit, Permeabilität (geh, Sci) f.

permeable [ˈpɜːmɪəbl] adj durchlässig, permeabel (geh, Sci).

permeate [ˈpɜːmɪeɪt] **1** vt (lit, fig) durchdringen. **2** vi dringen (into in +acc, through durch). **the smell ~d throughout the house** der Geruch durchdrang das ganze Haus.

permissible [pəˈmɪsɪbl] adj erlaubt (for sb jdm).

permission [pəˈmɪʃən] n Erlaubnis f. **with your ~** mit Ihrer Erlaubnis, wenn Sie gestatten; **without ~ from sb** ohne jds Erlaubnis; **to do sth with/by sb's ~** etw mit jds Erlaubnis tun; **to get ~/sb's ~** eine/jds Erlaubnis erhalten; **to give ~ (for sth)** etw erlauben, die Erlaubnis (für etw) erteilen; **to give sb ~ (to do sth)** jdm die Erlaubnis geben or jdm erlauben(, etw zu tun); **no ~ is needed** eine Erlaubnis ist nicht erforderlich; **to ask sb's ~, to ask ~ of sb** jdn um Erlaubnis bitten; **"by (kind) ~ of ..."** „mit (freundlicher) Genehmigung (+gen) ...".

permissive [pəˈmɪsɪv] adj nachgiebig, permissiv (geh); (sexually) freizügig. **it encourages youngsters to be ~** es führt zu allzu großer Freizügigkeit unter Jugendlichen; **the ~ society** die permissive Gesellschaft.

permissiveness [pəˈmɪsɪvnɪs] n Nachgiebigkeit, Permissivität (geh) f; (sexually) Freizügigkeit f.

permit [pəˈmɪt] **1** vt sth erlauben, gestatten. **to ~ sb to do sth** jdm erlauben, etw zu tun; **is it/am I ~ted to smoke?** darf man/ich rauchen?; **visitors are not ~ted after 10 o'clock** nach 10 Uhr sind keine Besucher mehr erlaubt; **~ me!** gestatten Sie bitte!; **I'll pay — no, ~ me!** ich zahle! — nein, gestatten Sie, daß ich das erledige.
  2 vi (a) if you (will) **~ wenn Sie gestatten or erlauben; if the weather ~s, weather ~ting** wenn es das Wetter erlaubt or gestattet or zuläßt; **time/space does not ~** die Zeit/der Platzmangel erlaubt or gestattet es nicht or läßt es nicht zu.
  (b) (form) **to ~ of sth** etw zulassen.
  3 [ˈpɜːmɪt] n Genehmigung f.

permutation [ˌpɜːmjʊˈteɪʃən] n Permutation f.

permute [pəˈmjuːt] vt permutieren.

pernicious [pɜːˈnɪʃəs] adj schädlich; (Med) perniziös, bösartig.

pernickety [pəˈnɪkɪtɪ] adj (inf) pingelig (inf).

peroration [ˌperəˈreɪʃən] n (liter) (concluding part) Resümee nt, Zusammenfassung f; (lengthy speech) endlose Rede.

peroxide [pəˈrɒksaɪd] n Peroxyd nt. **a ~ blonde** (pej) eine Wasserstoffblondine; **~ blonde hair** wasserstoffblonde Haare.

perpendicular [ˌpɜːpənˈdɪkjʊləʳ] **1** adj (a) senkrecht (to zu). **the wall is not quite ~ to the ceiling** die Mauer steht nicht ganz lotrecht zur Decke; **a ~ cliff** eine senkrecht abfallende Klippe.
  (b) (Archit) perpendikular.
  2 n Senkrechte f. **to drop a ~** ein Lot fällen; **to be out of ~** nicht im Lot sein.

perpendicularly [ˌpɜːpənˈdɪkjʊləlɪ] adv senkrecht.

perpetrate [ˈpɜːpɪtreɪt] vt begehen; crime also verüben. **this is the worst film he has ever ~d** (hum) das ist der schlimmste Film, den er je verbrochen hat (hum inf).

perpetration [ˌpɜːpɪˈtreɪʃən] n Begehen nt, Begehung f; (of crime also) Verübung f.

perpetrator [ˈpɜːpɪtreɪtəʳ] n Übeltäter m. **the ~ of this crime**

derjenige, der dieses Verbrechen begangen hat.

perpetual [pə'petjʊəl] adj ständig, fortwährend, immerwährend; joy stet; ice, snow ewig. you're a ~ source of amazement to me ich muß mich immer wieder über dich wundern; ~ motion/motion machine Perpetuum mobile nt.

perpetually [pə'petjʊəlɪ] adv ständig.

perpetuate [pə'petjʊeɪt] vt aufrechterhalten; memory bewahren. the old language of the area has been ~d in the place names die alte Sprache der Gegend lebt in den Ortsnamen fort.

perpetuation [pə,petjʊ'eɪʃən] n Aufrechterhaltung f; (of memory) Bewahrung f; (of old names etc) Beibehaltung f.

perpetuity [,pɜːpɪ'tjuːɪtɪ] n (form) Ewigkeit f. in ~ auf ewig; (Jur) lebenslänglich.

perplex [pə'pleks] vt verblüffen, verdutzen.

perplexed adj, ~ly adv [pə'plekst, -sɪdlɪ] verblüfft, verdutzt, perplex.

perplexing [pə'pleksɪŋ] adj verblüffend.

perplexingly [pə'pleksɪŋlɪ] adv verwirrend. a ~ difficult problem ein schwieriges or verwirrendes Problem.

perplexity [pə'pleksɪtɪ] n Verblüffung f. to be in some ~ etwas verblüfft or verdutzt or perplex sein.

perquisite [pɜː'kwɪzɪt] n (form) Vergünstigung f.

perry ['perɪ] n Birnenmost m.

per se ['pɜː'seɪ] adv an sich, per se (geh).

persecute ['pɜːsɪkjuːt] vt verfolgen.

persecution [,pɜːsɪ'kjuːʃən] n Verfolgung f (of von). his ~ by the press seine Verfolgung durch die Presse; to have a ~ complex an Verfolgungswahn leiden.

persecutor ['pɜːsɪkjuːtə'] n Verfolger(in f) m.

perseverance [,pɜːsɪ'vɪərəns] n Ausdauer (with mit), Beharrlichkeit (with bei) f.

persevere [,pɜːsɪ'vɪə'] vi nicht aufgeben. to ~ in one's studies mit seinem Studium weitermachen; he ~d with German er machte mit Deutsch weiter; to ~ in or with one's attempts/efforts to do sth unermüdlich weiter versuchen, etw zu tun.

persevering adj, ~ly adv [,pɜːsɪ'vɪərɪŋ, -lɪ] ausdauernd, beharrlich.

Persia ['pɜːʃə] n Persien nt.

Persian ['pɜːʃən] **1** adj persisch. ~ carpet Perser(teppich) m; ~ cat Perserkatze f; ~ lamb (animal) Karakulschaf nt; (skin, coat) Persianer m.
2 n (a) Perser(in f) m.
(b) (language) Persisch nt.

persiflage [,pɜːsɪ'flɑːʒ] n Persiflage f.

persimmon [pɜː'sɪmən] n Persimone f; (wood) Persimmon nt.

persist [pə'sɪst] vi (persevere) nicht lockerlassen, unbeirrt fortfahren (with mit); (be tenacious: in belief, demand etc) beharren, bestehen (in auf + dat); (last, continue: fog, pain etc) anhalten, fortdauern. if you ~ in misbehaving/coming late wenn du dich weiterhin so schlecht benimmst/wenn du weiterhin zu spät kommst; if the greenfly still ~ wenn das die Blattläuse nicht beseitigt; if you ~ in these statements I shall sue wenn Sie weiterhin solche Behauptungen aufstellen, werde ich Sie verklagen; we shall ~ in our efforts wir werden in unseren Bemühungen nicht nachlassen.

persistence [pə'sɪstəns], **persistency** [pə'sɪstənsɪ] n (tenacity) Beharrlichkeit, Hartnäckigkeit f; (perseverance) Ausdauer f; (of disease) Hartnäckigkeit f; (of fog, pain etc) Anhalten, Fortdauern nt. ~ of his questioning brought results sein beharrliches Fragen hat schließlich doch zu etwas geführt; the ~ of a high temperature anhaltend hohes Fieber.

persistent [pə'sɪstənt] adj (tenacious) demands, questions beharrlich; person hartnäckig; attempts, efforts ausdauernd; (repeated, constant) offender, drinking, drinker gewohnheitsmäßig, nagging, lateness, threats ständig; cheerfulness gleichbleibend; (continuing) rain, illness, pain, noise anhaltend. despite our ~ warnings ... obwohl wir sie/ihn etc immer wieder gewarnt haben ...

persistently [pə'sɪstəntlɪ] adv see adj.

person ['pɜːsn] n (a) pl people or (form) -s (human being) Mensch m; (in official contexts) Person f. no ~ kein Mensch, niemand; I know no such ~ so jemanden kenne ich nicht; any ~ jeder; a certain ~ ein gewisser Jemand; ~ to ~ call Gespräch nt mit Voranmeldung; 30 p per ~ 30 Pence pro Person; the murder was committed by ~ or ~s unknown der Mord wurde von einem oder mehreren unbekannten Tätern verübt.
(b) pl -s (Gram, Jur: legal ~) Person f. first ~ singular/plural erste Person Singular/Plural.
(c) pl -s (body, physical presence) Körper m; (appearance) Äußere(s) nt. in ~ persönlich; in the ~ of in Gestalt (+ gen); crime against the ~ Vergehen gegen die Person; on or about one's ~ bei sich.

persona [pɜː'səʊnə] n, pl -e (Psych) Persona f. ~ grata (Jur) Persona grata f; ~ non grata (Jur, fig) Persona non grata f.

personable ['pɜːsnəbl] adj von angenehmem or sympathischem Äußeren.

personae [pɜː'səʊniː] pl of **persona**.

personage ['pɜːsənɪdʒ] n Persönlichkeit f.

personal ['pɜːsnl] adj (a) persönlich. he gave several ~ performances to promote his new record er trat mehrmals persönlich auf, um für seine neue Platte zu werben; ~ freshness or cleanliness/hygiene Körperfrische f/-pflege f; it's nothing ~, I just don't think you're the right person nicht, daß ich was gegen Sie persönlich hätte, Sie sind nur nicht der/die Richtige; don't be ~ nun werden Sie mal nicht persönlich; I have no ~ knowledge of it mir ist's (persönlich) nichts davon bekannt; "~" (on letter) „privat"; ~ column Familienanzeigen pl; ~ property persönliches Eigentum, Privateigentum nt; ~ stationery Briefpapier nt mit persönlichem Briefkopf; ~ call Gespräch nt mit Voranmeldung; (private call) Privatgespräch nt; ~ matter persönliche or private Angelegenheit f.

(b) (Gram) ~ pronoun Personalpronomen nt, persönliches Fürwort.

personality [,pɜːsə'nælɪtɪ] n (a) (character, person) Persönlichkeit f. ~ cult Personenkult m; ~ disorder Persönlichkeitsstörung f; ~ development Persönlichkeitsentfaltung f.
(b) (personal remark) let's keep personalities out of this lassen wir persönliche Dinge aus dem Spiel; let's not descend to personalities wir wollen nicht persönlich werden.

personally ['pɜːsnəlɪ] adv persönlich. ~, I think that ... ich persönlich bin der Meinung, daß ...

personalty ['pɜːsnltɪ] n (Jur) bewegliches Vermögen.

personification [pɜː,sɒnɪfɪ'keɪʃən] n Personifizierung f. he is the ~ of good taste er ist der personifizierte gute Geschmack.

personify [pɜː'sɒnɪfaɪ] vt personifizieren; (be the personification of also) verkörpern. he is greed personified er ist der personifizierte Geiz or der Geiz in Person.

personnel [,pɜːsə'nel] **1** n sing or pl (a) Personal nt; (on plane) Besatzung f; (on ship) Besatzung, Mannschaft f; (Mil) Leute pl. this firm employs 800 ~ diese Firma beschäftigt 800 Leute or hat eine Belegschaft von 800 Leuten; with a larger ~ mit mehr Personal.
(b) (~ department) die Personalabteilung; (~ work) Personalarbeit f.
2 attr Personal-. ~ carrier (Mil) Mannschaftstransportwagen m/-transportflugzeug nt; ~ management Personalführung f; ~ manager/officer Personalchef m/-leiter m.

perspective [pə'spektɪv] n (lit) Perspektive f; (fig also) Blickwinkel m. to get a different ~ on a problem ein Problem aus einer anderen Perspektive or aus einem anderen Blickwinkel sehen; in ~ (Art) perspektivisch; the foreground isn't in ~ der Vordergrund ist perspektivisch nicht richtig; try to keep/get things in ~ versuchen Sie, nüchtern und sachlich zu bleiben/das nüchtern und sachlich zu sehen; to get sth out of ~ (lit: artist etc) etw perspektivisch verzerren; (fig) etw verzerrt sehen; in historical ~ aus historischer Sicht; to see things in their proper or true ~ die Dinge so sehen, wie sie sind.

Perspex® ['pɜːspeks] n Acrylglas nt.

perspicacious [,pɜːspɪ'keɪʃəs] adj person, remark etc scharfsinnig; decision weitsichtig.

perspicacity [,pɜːspɪ'kæsɪtɪ] n Scharfsinn, Scharfblick m; (of decision) Weitsicht f.

perspicuity [,pɜːspɪ'kjuːɪtɪ] n Klarheit f; (clearness: of expression, statement also) Verständlichkeit f.

perspicuous [,pɜː'spɪkjuːəs] adj einleuchtend; (clear) expression, statement klar, verständlich.

perspiration [,pɜːspɪ'reɪʃən] n (perspiring) Schwitzen nt, Transpiration f (geh); (sweat) Schweiß m. the ~ was dripping off him, he was dripping with ~ ihm lief der Schweiß in Strömen herunter; beads of ~ Schweißperlen pl.

perspire [pə'spaɪə'] vi schwitzen, transpirieren (geh).

persuadable [pə'sweɪdəbl] adj he may be ~ (amenable) vielleicht läßt er sich or ist er zu überreden; (convincible) vielleicht läßt er sich or ist er zu überzeugen.

persuade [pə'sweɪd] vt überreden; (convince) überzeugen. to ~ sb to do sth jdn überreden, etw zu tun; to ~ sb into doing sth jdn dazu überreden, etw zu tun; to ~ sb out of sth/doing sth jdm etw ausreden/jdn dazu überreden, etw nicht zu tun; to ~ sb of sth jdn von etw überzeugen; to ~ sb that ... jdn davon überzeugen, daß ...; I am ~d that ... ich bin überzeugt, daß ...; she is easily ~d sie ist leicht zu überreden/überzeugen; he doesn't take much persuading ihn braucht man nicht lange zu überreden.

persuader [pə'sweɪdə'] n Überredungskünstler(in f) m. the hidden ~s die heimlichen Verführer.

persuasible [pə'sweɪzəbl] adj see **persuadable**.

persuasion [pə'sweɪʒən] n (a) (persuading) Überredung f. advertising uses many subtle means of ~ die Werbung arbeitet mit vielen subtilen Überzeugungsmechanismen; her powers of ~ ihre Überredungskünste; she tried every possible means of ~ to get him to agree sie setzte ihre ganze Überredungskunst ein, um seine Zustimmung zu erlangen; I don't need much ~ to stop working man braucht mich nicht lange zu überreden, damit ich aufhöre zu arbeiten; it didn't take much ~ man brauchte dich/ihn etc nicht lange zu überreden.
(b) (persuasiveness) Überzeugungskraft f.
(c) (belief) Überzeugung f; (sect, denomination) Glaube(nsrichtung f) m. I am not of that ~ (don't believe that) davon bin ich nicht überzeugt; (don't belong to that sect) ich gehöre nicht diesem Glauben an; and others of that ~ und andere, die dieser Überzeugung anhängen; to be of left-wing ~, to have left-wing ~s linke Ansichten haben.

persuasive [pə'sweɪsɪv] adj salesman, voice beredsam; arguments etc überzeugend. he can be very ~ er kann einen gut überreden; (convincing) er kann einen leicht überzeugen; I had to be very ~ ich mußte meine ganze Überredungskunst aufwenden.

persuasively [pə'sweɪsɪvlɪ] adv argue etc überzeugend. ..., he said ~ ..., versuchte er sie/ihn etc zu überreden.

persuasiveness [pə'sweɪsɪvnɪs] n (of person, salesman etc) Überredungskunst, Beredsamkeit f; (of argument etc) Überzeugungskraft f.

pert [pɜːt] adj (+ er) keck, keß; (impudent) keck. a ~ little smile ein kesses or freches Lächeln.

pertain [pə'teɪn] vi to ~ to sth etw betreffen; (belong to: land etc) zu etw gehören; all documents ~ing to the case alle den Fall betreffenden Dokumente; the mansion and the lands ~ing to it das Gutshaus und die dazugehörigen Ländereien; and other matters ~ing to it und andere damit verbundene Fragen; of or ~ing to sth etw betreffend.

pertinacious [,pɜːtɪ'neɪʃəs] adj (persevering) beharrlich, ausdauernd; (tenacious, stubborn) hartnäckig.

pertinacity [ˌpɜːtɪˈnæsɪtɪ] n see adj Beharrlichkeit, Ausdauer f; Hartnäckigkeit f.

pertinence [ˈpɜːtɪnəns] n Relevanz f (to für); (of information) Sachdienlichkeit f.

pertinent [ˈpɜːtɪnənt] adj relevant (to für); information sachdienlich.

pertinently [ˈpɜːtɪnəntlɪ] adv passend, völlig richtig. he asked very ~ whether ... er stellte die relevante Frage, ob ...

pertly [ˈpɜːtlɪ] adv see adj.

pertness [ˈpɜːtnɪs] n Keckheit, Keßheit f; (impudence) Keckheit f.

perturb [pəˈtɜːb] vt beunruhigen.

perturbation [ˌpɜːtɜːˈbeɪʃən] n (state) Unruhe f; (act) Beunruhigung f. to be in (a state of) some ~ ziemlich in Unruhe sein.

perturbing adj, ~ly adv [pəˈtɜːbɪŋ, -lɪ] beunruhigend.

Peru [pəˈruː] n Peru nt.

perusal [pəˈruːzəl] n Lektüre f; (careful) sorgfältige Durchsicht, Prüfung f. after a brief ~ of the newspaper he ... nachdem er kurz einen Blick in die Zeitung geworfen hatte ...

peruse [pəˈruːz] vt (durch)lesen; (carefully) sorgfältig durchsehen, prüfen.

Peruvian [pəˈruːvɪən] 1 adj peruanisch. 2 n Peruaner(in f) m.

pervade [pɜːˈveɪd] vt erfüllen; (smell also) durchziehen; (light) durchfluten. his writing is ~d with dialect expressions seine Bücher sind voller Dialektausdrücke; the universities are ~d with subversive elements/propaganda die Universitäten sind mit subversiven Elementen durchsetzt/von subversiver Propaganda durchdrungen.

pervasive [pɜːˈveɪsɪv] adj smell etc durchdringend; influence, feeling, ideas um sich greifend.

pervasively [pɜːˈveɪsɪvlɪ] adv durchdringend. to spread ~ (smell etc) sich überall ausbreiten (through in +dat); (ideas, mood etc also) um sich greifen (through in +dat).

pervasiveness [pɜːˈveɪsɪvnɪs] n see adj durchdringender Charakter; um sich greifender Charakter.

perverse [pəˈvɜːs] adj (contrary) querköpfig, verstockt; (perverted) pervers, widernatürlich.

perversely [pəˈvɜːslɪ] adv see adj. do you have to be so ~ different? mußt du denn immer um jeden Preis anders sein?; he is really ~ old-fashioned er ist wirklich hoffnungslos altmodisch; the translation still sounds ~ French die Übersetzung klingt noch immer penetrant französisch.

perverseness [pəˈvɜːsnɪs] n see adj Querköpfigkeit, Verstocktheit f; Perversität, Widernatürlichkeit f.

perversion [pəˈvɜːʃən] n (esp sexual, Psych) Perversion f; (no pl: act of perverting) Pervertierung f; (Rel) Fehlglaube m; (no pl: act) Irreleitung f; (distortion: of truth etc) Verzerrung f.

perversity [pəˈvɜːsɪtɪ] n see perverseness.

pervert [pəˈvɜːt] 1 vt (deprave) person, mind verderben, pervertieren; (Rel) believer irreleiten; (change, distort) truth, sb's words verzerren. to ~ the course of justice (Jur) die Rechtsfindung behindern; (by official) das Recht beugen.
2 [ˈpɜːvɜːt] n perverser Mensch.

pervious [ˈpɜːvɪəs] adj (lit) durchlässig; (fig) zugänglich (to für). chalk is ~ (to water) Kalk ist wasserdurchlässig.

peseta [pəˈseɪtə] n Peseta f.

pesky [ˈpeskɪ] adj (+er) (esp US inf) nervtötend (inf).

pessary [ˈpesərɪ] n (contraceptive) Pessar nt; (suppository) Zäpfchen, Suppositorium (spec) nt.

pessimism [ˈpesɪmɪzəm] n Pessimismus m, Schwarzseherei f.

pessimist [ˈpesɪmɪst] n Pessimist(in f), Schwarzseher(in f) m.

pessimistic [ˌpesɪˈmɪstɪk] adj pessimistisch, schwarzseherisch. I'm rather ~ about it da bin ich ziemlich pessimistisch, da sehe ich ziemlich schwarz; I'm ~ about our chances of success ich bin pessimistisch, was unsere Erfolgschancen angeht, ich sehe schwarz für unsere Erfolgschancen.

pessimistically [ˌpesɪˈmɪstɪkəlɪ] adv pessimistisch.

pest [pest] n (a) (Zool) Schädling m. ~ control Schädlingsbekämpfung f. (b) (fig) (person) Nervensäge f; (thing) Plage f. (c) (obs: plague) Pest, Pestilenz (old) f.

pester [ˈpestəʳ] vt belästigen; (keep on at: with requests etc) plagen. to ~ the life out of sb jdm keine Ruhe lassen; she ~ed me for the book sie ließ mir keine Ruhe wegen des Buches, sie plagte mich wegen des Buches; to ~ sb to do sth jdn bedrängen, etw zu tun, jdn plagen, daß er etw tut.

pesticide [ˈpestɪsaɪd] n Schädlingsbekämpfungsmittel, Pestizid (spec) nt.

pestiferous [peˈstɪfərəs] adj verpestet; (inf: annoying) lästig.

pestilence [ˈpestɪləns] n (old, liter) Pest, Pestilenz (old) f.

pestilent [ˈpestɪlənt], **pestilential** [ˌpestɪˈlenʃəl] adj pesterfüllt; (fig: pernicious) schädlich, verderblich; (inf: loathsome) ekelhaft. a ~ disease eine Seuche.

pestle [ˈpesl] n Stößel m.

pet [pet] 1 adj attr animal Haus-; (favourite) pupil, idea etc Lieblings-. a ~ lion ein zahmer Löwe; her two ~ dogs ihre beiden Hunde; a ~ name ein Kosename m; see hate.
2 n (a) (animal) Haustier nt.
(b) (favourite) Liebling m. teacher's ~ Lehrers Liebling m or Schätzchen nt (inf); (as derogatory name) Streber m.
(c) (inf: dear) Schatz m. yes, (my) ~ ja, (mein) Schatz; he's rather a ~ er ist wirklich lieb or ein Schatz.
(d) (caress) he wants a ~ er möchte gestreichelt werden.
3 vt animal streicheln; child also liebkosen; (fig: spoil) (ver-)hätscheln.
4 vi (sexually) Petting machen.

pet[2] n (dated inf: huff) Verstimmung f. to be in/get into a ~ verstimmt or gekränkt sein/werden.

petal [ˈpetl] n Blütenblatt nt.

petard [peˈtɑːd] n Petarde f; see hoist.

Pete [piːt] n for ~'s or p~'s sake (inf) um Himmels willen.

Peter [ˈpiːtəʳ] n Peter m; (apostle) Petrus m. Saint ~ Sankt

Peter, der Heilige Petrus; to rob ~ to pay Paul ein Loch mit dem anderen zustopfen; he is a real ~ Pan er will einfach nicht erwachsen werden; ~ Pan collar Bubikragen m.

♦**peter out** vi langsam zu Ende gehen; (mineral vein) versiegen; (river) versickern; (song, noise) verhallen; (interest) sich verlieren, sich totlaufen; (excitement) sich legen; (plan) im Sande verlaufen.

peterman [ˈpiːtəmən] n, pl -men [-mən] (sl) Schränker (sl), Panzerknacker (inf) m.

petersham [ˈpiːtəʃəm] n (ribbon) Seidenripsband nt.

petiole [ˈpetɪəʊl] n Stengel m.

petit bourgeois [ˈpetɪˈbʊəʒwɑː] 1 n Kleinbürger(in f) m. 2 adj kleinbürgerlich.

petite [pəˈtiːt] adj woman, girl zierlich.

petite bourgeoisie [ˈpetɪˌbʊəʒwɑːˈziː] n Kleinbürgertum nt.

petit four [ˈpetɪˈfɔː] n, pl -s -s Petit four nt.

petition [pəˈtɪʃən] 1 n (a) (list of signatures) Unterschriftenliste f. to get up a ~ for/against sth Unterschriften für/gegen etw sammeln.
(b) (request) Gesuch nt, Bittschrift, Petition f. ~ for mercy Gnadengesuch nt.
(c) (Jur) ~ for divorce Scheidungsantrag m.
2 vt person, authorities (request, entreat) ersuchen (for um); (hand ~ to) eine Unterschriftenliste vorlegen (+dat).
3 vi (a) (hand in ~) eine Unterschriftenliste einreichen.
(b) (Jur) to ~ for divorce die Scheidung einreichen.

petitioner [pəˈtɪʃənəʳ] n Bittsteller(in f) m; (Jur) Kläger(in f) m.

petit [ˈpetɪ-]: ~ jury n see petty jury; ~ point n Petit point nt.

petits pois [ˌpetɪˈpwɑː] npl (form) Petits pois pl.

Petrarch [ˈpetrɑːk] n Petrarca m.

petrel [ˈpetrəl] n Sturmvogel m.

petri dish [ˈpetrɪˌdɪʃ] n Petrischale f.

petrifaction [ˌpetrɪˈfækʃən] n Versteinerung, Petrifikation f.

petrified [ˈpetrɪfaɪd] adj (a) (lit) versteinert. as though ~ wie erstarrt. (b) (fig) I was ~ (with fear) ich war starr vor Schrecken; she is ~ of spiders/of doing that sie hat panische Angst vor Spinnen/davor, das zu tun.

petrify [ˈpetrɪfaɪ] 1 vt (a) (lit) versteinern. (b) (frighten) he really petrifies me er jagt mir schreckliche Angst ein; a ~ing experience ein schreckliches Erlebnis; to be petrified by sth sich panisch vor etw fürchten. 2 vi versteinern.

petrochemical [ˈpetrəʊˈkemɪkəl] 1 n petrochemisches Erzeugnis. 2 adj petrochemisch.

petrol [ˈpetrəl] n (esp Brit) Benzin nt.

petrol in cpds Benzin-; ~ can n Reservekanister m.

petroleum [pɪˈtrəʊlɪəm] n Petroleum nt. ~ ether Petroläther m; ~ jelly Vaselin nt, Vaseline f.

petrol gauge n Benzinuhr f.

petrology [pɪˈtrɒlədʒɪ] n Gesteinskunde, Petrologie f.

petrol: ~ pump n (in engine) Benzinpumpe f; (at garage) Zapfsäule f; ~ station n Tankstelle f; ~ tank n Benzintank m; ~ tanker n (Benzin)tankwagen m.

petticoat [ˈpetɪkəʊt] n Unterrock m; (stiffened) Petticoat m. ~ government Weiberherrschaft f, Weiberregiment nt.

pettifogging [ˈpetɪfɒgɪŋ] adj objections kleinlich; details belanglos; person pedantisch.

pettiness [ˈpetɪnɪs] n see adj (a) Unbedeutendheit, Belanglosigkeit, Unwichtigkeit f; Billigkeit f; Geringfügigkeit f. (b) Kleinlichkeit f; spitzer Charakter.

petting [ˈpetɪŋ] n Petting nt.

pettish adj, ~ly adv [ˈpetɪʃ, -lɪ] bockig (inf).

pettishness [ˈpetɪʃnɪs] n bockige Art (inf).

petty [ˈpetɪ] adj (+er) (a) (trivial) unbedeutend, belanglos, unwichtig; excuse billig; crime geringfügig.
(b) (small-minded) kleinlich; (spiteful) remark spitz. you're being very ~ about it du bist so kleinlich.
(c) (minor) chieftain etc untergeordnet; (pej) official also unbedeutend, unwichtig. the ~ wars of the time die Kleinkriege jener Zeit.

petty: ~ bourgeois n, adj see petit bourgeois; ~ bourgeoisie n see petite bourgeoisie; ~ cash n Portokasse f; ~ jury n = Geschworene pl; ~ larceny n leichter Diebstahl; ~ officer n Fähnrich m zur See; ~ sessions npl see magistrate's court.

petulance [ˈpetjʊləns], **petulancy** [ˈpetjʊlənsɪ] n leicht pikierte Art; (of child) bockige Art (inf).

petulant [ˈpetjʊlənt] adj pikiert; child bockig (inf).

petulantly [ˈpetjʊləntlɪ] adv see adj.

petunia [pɪˈtjuːnɪə] n Petunie f.

pew [pjuː] n (Eccl) (Kirchen)bank f; (hum: chair) Platz m. have or take a ~! (hum) laß dich nieder! (hum).

pewit n see peewit.

pewter [ˈpjuːtəʳ] n (alloy) Zinn nt; (vessel) Zinnbecher m; (articles also) Zinngeschirr nt.

PF abbr of Patriotic Front.

phalanx [ˈfælæŋks] n, pl -es or phalanges [fæˈlændʒiːz] (a) (Anat) Finger-/Zehenglied nt, Phalanx f (spec). (b) (body of people, troops) Phalanx f.

phalli [ˈfælaɪ] pl of phallus.

phallic [ˈfælɪk] adj Phallus-, phallisch; symbol Phallus-.

phallus [ˈfæləs] n, pl -es or phalli Phallus m.

phantasm [ˈfæntæzəm], **phantasma** [fænˈtæzmə] n, pl phantasmata Phantasma nt.

phantasmagoria [ˌfæntæzməˈgɔːrɪə] n Phantasmagorie f.

phantasmagoric(al) [ˌfæntæzməˈgɒrɪk(əl)] adj phantasmagorisch.

phantasmal [fænˈtæzməl] adj imaginär.

phantasmata [fænˈtæzmətə] pl of phantasm, phantasma.

phantasy n see fantasy.

phantom [ˈfæntəm] 1 n Phantom nt; (ghost: esp of particular person) Geist m. ~s of the mind Phantasiegebilde pl. 2 adj attr Geister-; (mysterious) Phantom-. a ~ child/knight etc der

Geist eines Kindes/Ritters *etc*; ~ **limb pains** Phantomschmerzen *pl*; ~ **pregnancy** eingebildete Schwangerschaft.
Pharaoh ['fɛərəʊ] *n* Pharao *m*. **the tombs of the** ~**s** die Pharaonengräber *pl*.
Pharisaic(al) [.færɪ'seɪɪk(əl)] *adj* (a) pharisäisch. (b) p~ (*fig*) pharisäerhaft.
Pharisee ['færɪsɪ] *n* (*fig: also* p~) Pharisäer *m*.
pharmaceutic(al) [.fɑ:mə'sju:tɪk(əl)] *adj* pharmazeutisch.
pharmaceutics [.fɑ:mə'sju:tɪks] *n sing see* **pharmacy (a)**.
pharmacist ['fɑ:məsɪst] *n* Apotheker(in *f*) *m*; (*in research*) Pharmazeut(in *f*) *m*.
pharmacological [.fɑ:məkə'lɒdʒɪkəl] *adj* pharmakologisch.
pharmacologist [.fɑ:mə'kɒlədʒɪst] *n* Pharmakologe *m*, Pharmakologin *f*.
pharmacology [.fɑ:mə'kɒlədʒɪ] *n* Pharmakologie *f*.
pharmacopoeia [.fɑ:məkə'pi:ə] *n* Pharmakopöe *f* (*spec*), amtliches Arzneibuch.
pharmacy ['fɑ:məsɪ] *n* (a) (*science*) Pharmazie *f*. (b) (*shop*) Apotheke *f*.
pharyngeal [fə'rɪndʒɪəl], **pharyngal** [fə'rɪŋgəl] *adj* Rachen-.
pharyngitis [.færɪn'dʒaɪtɪs] *n* Rachenkatarrh *m*, Pharyngitis *f* (*spec*).
pharynx ['færɪŋks] *n* Rachen *m*, Pharynx *f* (*spec*).
phase [feɪz] **1** *n* (*all senses*) Phase *f*; (*of construction, project, history also*) Abschnitt *m*; (*of illness*) Stadium *nt*. **out of/in** ~ (*Tech, Elec*) phasenverschoben/phasengleich, in Phase; (*fig*) unkoordiniert/koordiniert; ~ **modulation** (*Elec*) Phasenmodulation *f*; **he's just going through a** ~ das geht wieder vorbei; **he's out of** ~ **with the times** er ist nicht im Gleichklang mit seiner Zeit.
2 *vt* (*introduce gradually*) plan, change-over, withdrawal schrittweise durchführen; (*coordinate, fit to one another*) starting times, production stages, traffic lights aufeinander abstimmen; machines *etc* gleichschalten, synchronisieren. **the traffic lights are not** ~**d here** hier gibt es keine grüne Welle; **a** ~**d withdrawal of troops** ein schrittweiser Truppenabzug.
♦**phase in** *vt sep* allmählich einführen.
♦**phase out** *vt sep* auslaufen lassen.
phasing ['feɪzɪŋ] *n* Synchronisierung, Gleichschaltung *f*.
PhD *n* Doktor *m*, Dr. ~ **thesis** Doktorarbeit *f*; **to do/get one's** ~ seinen Doktor machen *or* promovieren/den Doktor bekommen; **he has a** ~ **in English** er hat einen Doktor in Anglistik, er ist Doktor der Anglistik.
pheasant ['feznt] *n* Fasan *m*.
phenix *n* (*US*) *see* **phoenix**.
phenobarbitone [.fi:nəʊ'bɑ:bɪtəʊn], **phenobarbital** [.fi:nəʊ'bɑ:bɪtəl] *n* Phenobarbital *nt*.
phenol ['fi:nɒl] *n* Phenol *nt*.
phenomena [fɪ'nɒmɪnə] *pl of* **phenomenon**.
phenomenal [fɪ'nɒmɪnl] *adj* phänomenal, sagenhaft (*inf*); person, beauty, figure fabelhaft; boredom, heat unglaublich.
phenomenalism [fɪ'nɒmɪnəlɪzəm] *n* Phänomenalismus *m*.
phenomenally [fɪ'nɒmɪnəlɪ] *adv* außerordentlich; bad, boring *etc* unglaublich.
phenomenology [fɪ.nɒmɪ'nɒlədʒɪ] *n* Phänomenologie *f*.
phenomenon [fɪ'nɒmɪnən] *n, pl* **phenomena** Phänomen *nt*.
phenotype ['fi:nəʊtaɪp] *n* Phänotyp(us) *m*.
phew [fju:] *interj* Mensch, puh.
phial ['faɪəl] *n* Fläschchen *nt*; (*for serum*) Ampulle *f*.
Phi Beta Kappa ['faɪ'bi:tə'kæpə] *n* (*US*) Vereinigung *f* hervorragender Akademiker oder Mitglied dieser Vereinigung.
philander [fɪ'lændər] *vi* tändeln (*liter*).
philanderer [fɪ'lændərər] *n* Schwerenöter *m*.
philandering [fɪ'lændərɪŋ] *n* Liebeleien *pl*.
philanthropic(al) [.fɪlən'θrɒpɪk(əl)] *adj* menschenfreundlich; person also, organization philanthropisch (*geh*).
philanthropically [.fɪlən'θrɒpɪkəlɪ] *adv* menschenfreundlich.
philanthropist [fɪ'lænθrəpɪst] *n* Menschenfreund, Philanthrop (*geh*) *m*.
philanthropy [fɪ'lænθrəpɪ] *n* Menschenfreundlichkeit, Philanthropie (*geh*) *f*.
philatelic [.fɪlə'telɪk] *adj* philatelistisch.
philatelist [fɪ'lætəlɪst] *n* Philatelist(in *f*), Briefmarkensammler(in *f*) *m*.
philately [fɪ'lætəlɪ] *n* Philatelie, Briefmarkenkunde *f*.
-phile [-faɪl] *suf* **1** ~-phile, -freund *m*. **Anglo**~ Anglophile, Englandfreund *m*. **2** *adj* -phil, -freundlich. **Franco**~ frankophil, frankreichfreundlich.
philharmonic [.fɪlɑ:'mɒnɪk] **1** *adj* philharmonisch. ~ **hall/ society** Philharmonie *f*. **2** *n* P~ Philharmonie *f*.
Philip ['fɪlɪp] *n* Philipp *m*; (*Bibl*) Philippus *m*.
Philippians [fɪ'lɪpɪənz] *n sing* (*Bibl*) Philipper *pl*.
philippic [fɪ'lɪpɪk] *n* (*lit, fig*) Philippika *f*.
Philippine ['fɪlɪpi:n] *adj* philippinisch.
Philippines ['fɪlɪpi:nz] *npl* Philippinen *pl*.
Philistine ['fɪlɪstaɪn] **1** *n* (a) (*lit*) Philister-. (b) (*fig*) p~ kulturlos; **tell that** p~ **friend of yours ...** sag deinem Freund, diesem Banausen ... **2** *n* (a) (*lit*) Philister *m*. (b) (*fig*) p~ Banause *m*.
philistinism ['fɪlɪstɪnɪzəm] *n* Banausentum *nt*.
Phillips ® ['fɪlɪps]: ~ **screw** *n* Kreuzschlitzschraube *f*; ~ **screwdriver** *n* Kreuzschlitzschraubendreher *m*.
philological [.fɪlə'lɒdʒɪkəl] *adj* philologisch.
philologist [fɪ'lɒlədʒɪst] *n* Philologe *m*, Philologin *f*.
philology [fɪ'lɒlədʒɪ] *n* Philologie *f*.
philosopher [fɪ'lɒsəfər] *n* Philosoph *m*, Philosophin *f*. ~**'s stone** Stein *m* der Weisen.
philosophic(al) [.fɪlə'sɒfɪk(əl)] *adj* philosophisch; (*fig also*) gelassen.
philosophically [.fɪlə'sɒfɪkəlɪ] *adv see adj*. **his ideas are** ~ **naive** philosophisch betrachtet sind seine Gedanken naiv.

philosophize [fɪ'lɒsəfaɪz] *vi* philosophieren (*about, on* über +*acc*).
philosophy [fɪ'lɒsəfɪ] *n* Philosophie *f*. ~ **of life** Lebensphilosophie *f*; **that's my** ~ das ist meine Philosophie *or* Einstellung; ~ **of education** Erziehungsphilosophie *f*.
philtre, (*US*) **philter** ['fɪltər] *n* Zaubertrank *m*; (*love* ~) Liebestrank *m*.
phiz [fɪz] *n* (*dated sl*) Visage *f* (*sl*).
phlebitis [flɪ'baɪtɪs] *n* Venenentzündung, Phlebitis (*spec*) *f*.
phlegm [flem] *n* (*mucus*) Schleim *m*; (*obs: humour*) Phlegma *nt*; (*fig*) (*coolness*) Gemütsruhe *f*, stoische Ruhe; (*stolidness*) Trägheit, Schwerfälligkeit *f*, Phlegma *nt*.
phlegmatic [fleg'mætɪk] *adj* (*cool*) seelenruhig, stoisch; (*stolid*) träge, schwerfällig, phlegmatisch.
phlox [flɒks] *n* Phlox *m*.
-phobe [-fəʊb] *n suf* -phobe, -feind *m*. **Anglo**~ Anglophobe, Englandfeind *m*.
phobia ['fəʊbɪə] *n* Phobie *f*. **she has a** ~ **about it** sie hat krankhafte Angst davor.
-phobic [-'fəʊbɪk] *adj suf* -phob, -feindlich.
Phoenicia [fə'ni:ʃə] *n* Phönizien *nt*.
Phoenician [fə'ni:ʃən] **1** *adj* phönizisch. **2** *n* Phönizier(in *f*) *m*.
phoenix, (*US*) **phenix** ['fi:nɪks] *n* (*Myth*) Phönix *m*. **like a** ~ **from the ashes** wie der Phönix aus der Asche.
phone[1] [fəʊn] **1** *n* Telefon *nt*. **to pick up/put down the** ~ (den Hörer) abnehmen/auflegen; **I'll give you a** ~ (*inf*) ich ruf' dich an. **2** *vt* person anrufen; message telefonisch übermitteln. **3** *vi* anrufen, telefonieren; *see also* **telephone**.
♦**phone back** *vti* (*vt: always separate*) zurückrufen.
♦**phone in** **1** *vi* anrufen. **2** *vt sep* telefonisch übermitteln.
phone[2] *n* (*Ling*) Phon *nt*.
phone-in ['fəʊnɪn] *n* Rundfunkprogramm *nt*, an dem sich Hörer per Telefon beteiligen können, Phone-in *nt*.
phoneme ['fəʊni:m] *n* Phonem *nt*.
phonemic [fəʊ'ni:mɪk] *adj* phonemisch.
phonetic *adj*, ~**ally** *adv* [fəʊ'netɪk, -əlɪ] phonetisch.
phonetician [fəʊnɪ'tɪʃən] *n* Phonetiker(in *f*) *m*.
phonetics [fəʊ'netɪks] *n* (a) *sing* (*subject*) Phonetik *f*. (b) *pl* (*phonetic script*) Lautschrift *f*, phonetische Umschrift.
phon(e)y ['fəʊnɪ] (*inf*) **1** *adj* (*fake, pretentious*) unecht; excuse, deal, peace faul (*inf*); name falsch; passport, money gefälscht; story, report erfunden; company Schwindel-. **a** ~ **doctor** ein Scharlatan *m*; **a** ~ **businessman** ein Roßtäuscher *m*; **he's so** ~ der ist doch nicht echt (*inf*); **there's something** ~ **about it** da ist was faul dran (*inf*).
2 *n* (*thing*) Fälschung *f*; (*banknote also*) Blüte *f* (*inf*); (*bogus policeman etc*) Schwindler(in *f*) *m*; (*doctor*) Scharlatan *m*; (*pretentious person*) Angeber(in *f*) *m*.
phonic ['fɒnɪk] *adj* phonisch.
phonograph ['fəʊnəgrɑ:f] *n* (*old, US*) Phonograph *m*.
phonological [.fəʊnə'lɒdʒɪkəl] *adj* phonologisch.
phonology [fəʊ'nɒlədʒɪ] *n* (*science*) Phonologie *f*; (*system*) Lautsystem *nt*.
phony *adj, n see* **phon(e)y**.
phooey ['fu:ɪ] *interj* (*scorn*) pah, bah; (*disgust*) pfui.
phosphate ['fɒsfeɪt] *n* (*Chem*) Phosphat *nt*; (*Agr: fertilizer*) Phosphatdünger *m*.
phosphor ['fɒsfər] *n* Phosphor *m*.
phosphoresce [.fɒsfə'res] *vi* phosphoreszieren.
phosphorescence [.fɒsfə'resns] *n* Phosphoreszenz *f*.
phosphorescent [.fɒsfə'resnt] *adj* phosphoreszierend.
phosphoric [fɒs'fɒrɪk] *adj* phosphorig.
phosphorous ['fɒsfərəs] *adj* phosphorsauer.
phosphorus ['fɒsfərəs] *n* Phosphor *m*.
photo ['fəʊtəʊ] *n* Foto, Photo *nt*, Aufnahme *f*; *see also* **photograph**.
photo: ~**cell** *n* Photozelle *f*; ~**composition** *n* (*Typ*) Lichtsatz, Filmsatz *m*; ~**copier** *n* (Foto)kopiergerät *nt*; ~**copy** **1** *n* Fotokopie, Photokopie *f*; **2** *vt* fotokopieren, photokopieren; **3** *vi* **this won't** ~**copy** das läßt sich nicht fotokopieren; ~**electric** *adj* photoelektrisch; ~**electric cell** Photozelle *f*; ~**engraving** *n* (*process*) Klischieren *nt*; (*plate*) Klischee *nt*; ~**finish** *n* Fotofinish *nt*; ~**flash** *n* Blitzlicht *nt*; ~**flash lamp** Blitzgerät *nt*; ~**flood** (*lamp*) *n* Jupiterlampe *f*.
photogenic [.fəʊtəʊ'dʒenɪk] *adj* fotogen, photogen.
photograph ['fəʊtəgræf] **1** *n* Fotografie, Photographie, Aufnahme *f*. **to take a** ~ (*of sb/sth*) (jdn/etw) fotografieren *or* photographieren, eine Aufnahme *or* ein Bild (von jdm/etw) machen; **she takes a good** ~ (*is photogenic*) sie ist photogen; **this camera takes good** ~**s** diese Kamera macht gute Aufnahmen *or* Bilder *or* Fotos; ~ **album** Fotoalbum *nt*.
2 *vt* fotografieren, photographieren, knipsen (*inf*). "~**ed by** John Mayne" „Fotos: John Mayne".
3 *vi* **to** ~ **well/badly** sich gut/schlecht fotografieren lassen.
photographer [fə'tɒgrəfər] *n* Fotograf(in *f*), Photograph(in *f*) *m*.
photographic [.fəʊtə'græfɪk] *adj* fotografisch, photographisch; equipment, magazine, club Foto-, Photo-; style of painting, art naturgetreu. ~ **memory** fotografisches Gedächtnis.
photographically [.fəʊtə'græfɪkəlɪ] *adv* fotografisch, photographisch. **to record sth** ~ etw im Bild festhalten.
photography [fə'tɒgrəfɪ] *n* Fotografie, Photographie *f*; (*in film, book etc*) Fotografien, Photographien, Aufnahmen, Bilder *pl*. **his** ~ **is marvellous** seine Fotografien *etc* sind hervorragend.
photogravure [.fəʊtəʊgrə'vjʊər] *n* Photogravüre, Heliogravüre *f*.
photometer [fəʊ'tɒmɪtər] *n* Photometer *nt*.
photomontage [.fəʊtəʊmɒn'tɑ:ʒ] *n* Fotomontage, Photomontage *f*.
photon ['fəʊtɒn] *n* Photon *nt*.

photo: ~**sensitive** adj lichtempfindlich; ~**sensitize** vt lichtempfindlich machen; ~**set** vt (Typ) im Lichtsatz herstellen; ~**setting** n Lichtsatz m; ~**stat** ® n, vti see ~**copy**; ~**synthesis** n Photosynthese f; ~**telegraphy** n Bildtelegraphie f; ~**tropic** adj phototrop(isch); ~**tropism** n Phototropismus m.

phrasal ['freɪzəl] adj Satz-. ~ **verb** Verb nt mit Präposition.

phrase [freɪz] **1** n **(a)** (Gram) Phrase f, Satzglied nt or -teil m; (in spoken language) Phrase f. **noun/verb** ~ Nominal-/Verbalphrase f.
  (b) (mode of expression) Ausdruck m; (set expression) Redewendung f. in a ~ kurz gesagt; see set, turn.
  (c) (Mus) Phrase f.
  2 vt **(a)** formulieren; criticism, suggestion also ausdrücken.
  (b) (Mus) phrasieren.

phrase: ~**book** n Sprachführer m; ~ **marker** n (Ling) P-Marker, Formationsmarker m; ~**monger** n (pej) Phrasendrescher m.

phraseology [,freɪzɪ'ɒlədʒɪ] n Ausdrucksweise f; (of letter etc) Diktion f; (jargon) Jargon m.

phrase structure n Phrasenstruktur f.

phrasing ['freɪzɪŋ] n (act) Formulierung f; (style) Ausdrucksweise f, Stil m; (Mus) Phrasierung f.

phrenetic adj see frenetic.

phrenologist [frɪ'nɒlədʒɪst] n Phrenologe m, Phrenologin f.

phrenology [frɪ'nɒlədʒɪ] n Phrenologie f.

phthisis ['θaɪsɪs] n Schwindsucht, (Lungen)tuberkulose f.

phut [fʌt] (inf) **1** n Puff m. **2** adv: to go ~ (make noise) puff machen; (break down) kaputtgehen (inf), hops gehen (inf); (plans etc) platzen (inf).

phylum ['faɪləm] n, pl **phyla** ['faɪlə] (Biol) Stamm m; (Ling) Sprachstamm m.

physic ['fɪzɪk] (obs) **1** n Arznei f; (cathartic) Purgativ nt. **2** vt medikamentös behandeln.

physical ['fɪzɪkəl] **1** adj **(a)** (of the body) körperlich; (not psychological also) physisch; check-up ärztlich. you don't take/get enough ~ **exercise** Sie bewegen sich nicht genug; he's very ~ (inf) er ist sehr sinnlich; play got too ~ (Sport inf) das Spiel wurde zu ruppig or rabiat (inf); the ~ **force of the impact** die Wucht des Aufpralls; we don't actually need your ~ **presence** Ihre Anwesenheit ist nicht unbedingt nötig.
  (b) (material) physisch, körperlich; world faßbar.
  (c) (of physics) laws, properties physikalisch. it's a ~ **impossibility** es ist technisch unmöglich.
  2 n ärztliche Untersuchung; (Mil) Musterung f.

physical: ~ **chemistry** n physikalische Chemie; ~ **education** n (abbr PE) Sport m, Leibesübungen pl (form); ~ **education college** n Sporthochschule, Sportakademie f; ~ **education teacher** n Sportlehrer(in f) m; ~ **geography** n physikalische Geographie, Physiogeographie f; ~ **jerks** npl (inf) Gymnastik f.

physically ['fɪzɪklɪ] adv körperlich, physisch; (Sci) physikalisch. ~ **impossible** technisch unmöglich; the substance changed ~ die Substanz ging in einen anderen Zustand über; the journey is ~ **dangerous** die Reise ist gefährlich für Leib und Leben; they removed him ~ **from the meeting** sie haben ihn mit Gewalt aus der Versammlung entfernt.

physical: ~ **science** n Naturwissenschaft f; ~ **training** n (abbr PT) see ~ **education**.

physician [fɪ'zɪʃən] n Arzt m, Ärztin f, Humanmediziner(in f) m (form).

physicist ['fɪzɪsɪst] n Physiker(in f) m.

physics ['fɪzɪks] n (sing: subject) Physik f. the ~ **of this are quite complex** die physikalischen Zusammenhänge sind hierbei ziemlich komplex.

physiognomy [,fɪzɪ'ɒnəmɪ] n (face) Physiognomie f; (study) Physiognomik f; (fig) äußere Erscheinung, Aussehen nt. the ~ **of the Labour Party** das Gesicht der Labour Partei.

physiological [,fɪzɪə'lɒdʒɪkəl] adj physiologisch.

physiologist [,fɪzɪ'ɒlədʒɪst] n Physiologe m, Physiologin f.

physiology [,fɪzɪ'ɒlədʒɪ] n Physiologie f.

physiotherapist [,fɪzɪə'θerəpɪst] n Physiotherapeut(in f) m.

physiotherapy [,fɪzɪə'θerəpɪ] n Physiotherapie f, physikalische Therapie.

physique [fɪ'ziːk] n Körperbau m, Statur f.

pi [paɪ] n (Math) Pi nt.

pianist ['pɪənɪst] n Klavierspieler(in f) m; (concert ~) Pianist(in f) m.

piano ['pjænəʊ] n (upright) Klavier, Piano (geh, old) nt; (grand) Flügel m. who was at or on the ~? wer war am Klavier?

piano: ~-**accordion** n Pianoakkordeon nt; ~**forte** ['pjænəʊ'fɔːtɪ] n (form) Pianoforte nt.

pianola ® [pɪə'nəʊlə] n Pianola nt.

piano: ~ **lesson** n Klavierstunde f; ~ **music** n Klaviermusik f; ~-**player** n Klavierspieler(in f) m; ~ **stool** n Klavierhocker m; ~ **tuner** n Klavierstimmer(in f) m.

piazza [pɪ'ætsə] n Piazza f, (Markt)platz m; (US: veranda) (überdachte) Veranda.

picaresque [,pɪkə'resk] adj pikaresk, pikarisch; novel also Schelmen-.

picayune [,pɪkə'juːn] adj (US) (paltry) gering, minimal; (petty) kleinlich.

piccalilli ['pɪkə,lɪlɪ] n Piccalilli pl.

piccaninny [,pɪkə'nɪnɪ] n Negerkind nt.

piccolo ['pɪkələʊ] n Pikkoloflöte f.

pick [pɪk] **1** n **(a)** (~**axe**) Spitzhacke, Picke f, Pickel m; (Mountaineering) Eispickel m; (tooth~) Zahnstocher m.
  (b) (esp US: plectrum) Plektron, Plektrum nt.
  (c) (choice) he was our ~ wir hatten ihn (aus)gewählt; to have first ~ die erste Wahl haben; take your ~! such dir etwas/einen etc aus!
  (d) (best) Beste(s) nt; see bunch.
  2 vt **(a)** (choose) (aus)wählen. to ~ **a team** eine Mannschaft aufstellen; he has been ~ed for England er ist für England aufgestellt worden; to ~ **sides** wählen; to ~ **a winner** (lit) den Sieger erraten; (fig) das Große Los ziehen; **a handful of** ~ed **men** (Mil) ein paar ausgewählte Soldaten; to ~ **one's words** seine Worte mit Bedacht wählen; to ~ **one's time** den richtigen Zeitpunkt wählen; you really ~ **your times, don't you?** (iro) du suchst dir aber auch immer den günstigsten Augenblick aus! (iro); to ~ **one's way** seinen Weg suchen; to ~ **one's way through sth** seinen Weg durch etw finden; he knows how to ~ '**em** (inf) er hat den richtigen Riecher (inf); you do ~ '**em** (inf) du gerätst auch immer an den Falschen.
  (b) (pull bits off, make holes in) jumper, blanket etc zupfen an (+dat); spot, scab kratzen an (+dat); hole (with fingers, instrument) bohren; (with beak) picken, hacken. to ~ **one's nose** sich (dat) in der Nase bohren; to ~ **one's teeth** sich (dat) in den Zähnen herumstochern; to ~ **a lock** ein Schloß knacken or mit einem Dietrich öffnen; to ~ **a bone** (with fingers) abzupfen; (with teeth, beak) abnagen; to ~ **sth to pieces** (lit) etw zerzupfen; (fig) kein gutes Haar an etw (dat) lassen, etw verreißen; to ~ **holes in sth** (fig) etw bemäkeln; in argument, theory etw in ein paar Punkten widerlegen; to ~ **a fight** or **quarrel (with sb)** (mit jdm) einen Streit vom Zaun brechen; to ~ **pockets** sich als Taschendieb betätigen; he's **very good at** ~**ing pockets** er ist ein sehr geschickter Taschendieb; to ~ **sb's pocket** jdm die Geldbörse/Brieftasche stehlen; to ~ **sb's brains** sich von jdm inspirieren lassen; see bone.
  (c) (~ **out and remove**) fleas, splinter etc entfernen (from von); (pluck) flowers, fruit pflücken.
  (d) (esp US: pluck) chicken etc rupfen.
  (e) (esp US) strings zupfen, anreißen; banjo zupfen.
  (f) (peck up) corn etc picken.
  3 vi **(a)** (choose) wählen, aussuchen. to ~ **and choose** wählerisch sein.
  (b) (esp US: on guitar etc) zupfen.

♦**pick at** vi +prep obj **(a)** to ~ ~ **one's food** im Essen herumstochern, am Essen herumpicken. **(b)** (inf: criticize) to ~ ~ **sb/sth** auf jdm/etw herumhacken, an jdm/etw herummäkeln.

♦**pick off** vt sep **(a)** (remove) fluff etc wegzupfen; (pluck) fruit pflücken; nail polish abschütteln. **the crew were** ~ed ~ **by helicopter** die Mannschaft wurde von einem Hubschrauber aufgenommen. **(b)** (shoot) abschießen, abknallen (inf).

♦**pick on** vi +prep obj (choose) aussuchen; (victimize) herumhacken auf (+dat). **why** ~ ~ **me?** (inf) warum gerade ich?; ~ ~ **somebody your own size!** (inf) leg dich doch mit einem Gleichstarken an! (inf); **stop** ~**ing** ~ **me!** hack nicht ständig auf mir herum!

♦**pick out** vt sep **(a)** (choose) aussuchen, auswählen. to ~ ~ **a few examples** um ein paar Beispiele herauszugreifen.
  (b) (remove) bad apples etc heraussuchen, auslesen.
  (c) (see, distinguish) person, familiar face ausmachen, entdecken. **the spotlight** ~ed ~ **the leading dancer** der Scheinwerfer wurde auf den Haupttänzer gerichtet.
  (d) (highlight) hervorheben (in, with durch).
  (e) (Mus) to ~ ~ **a tune (on the piano)** eine Melodie (auf dem Klavier) improvisieren; **he** ~ed ~ **a few notes** er spielte ein paar Takte.

♦**pick over** or **through** vi +prep obj durchsehen, untersuchen.

♦**pick up 1** vt sep **(a)** (take up) aufheben; (lift momentarily) hochheben; stitch aufnehmen. to ~ ~ **a child in one's arms** ein Kind auf den Arm nehmen; ~ ~ **your feet when you walk!** heb deine Füsse (beim Gehen)!; to ~ **oneself** ~ aufstehen; **as soon as he** ~s ~ **a book** sobald er ein Buch in die Hand nimmt; **it's the sort of book you can** ~ ~ **when you have a free minute** das ist so ein Buch, das man mal zwischendurch lesen kann; to ~ ~ **the phone** den Hörer abnehmen; you just have to ~ ~ **the phone** du brauchst nur anzurufen; to ~ ~ **the bill** (fig) die Rechnung bezahlen; to ~ ~ **a story** mit einer Geschichte fortfahren; to ~ ~ **the pieces** (lit, fig) die Scherben aufsammeln or zusammensuchen; to ~ ~ **the thread of a lecture** den Faden (eines Vortrags) wiederfinden; **the interviewer** ~ed ~ **this reference and** ... der Interviewer nahm diese Bemerkung auf or knüpfte an diese Bemerkung an und ...
  (b) (get) holen; (buy) bekommen; (acquire) habit sich (dat) angewöhnen; news, gossip aufschnappen; illness sich (dat) holen or zuziehen; (earn) verdienen. to ~ **sth** ~ **at a sale** etw im Ausverkauf erwischen; to ~ ~ **speed** schneller werden; you never know what you'll ~ ~ (what illness etc) man weiß nie, was man sich (dat) da holen or zuziehen kann; **I must have** ~ed ~ **a flea** ich muß mir einen Floh geholt or gefangen haben; he ~ed ~ **a few extra points** er hat ein paar Extrapunkte gemacht.
  (c) (learn) skill etc sich (dat) aneignen; language also lernen; accent, word aufschnappen; information, tips etc herausbekommen. you'll soon ~ **it** ~ du wirst das schnell lernen.
  (d) (collect) person, goods abholen. **I'll come and** ~ **you** ~ ich hole dich ab, ich komme dich abholen.
  (e) (bus etc) passengers aufnehmen; (in car) mitnehmen.
  (f) (rescue) helicopter, lifeboat bergen.
  (g) (arrest, catch) wanted man, criminal schnappen (inf). **they** ~ed **him** ~ **for questioning** sie haben ihn geholt, um ihn zu vernehmen.
  (h) (inf) girl aufreißen (inf), sich (dat) anlachen (inf). **she got** ~ed ~ **at a party** die ist auf einer Party (von einem) abgeschleppt or aufgegabelt worden (inf).
  (i) (find) road finden. to ~ ~ **the trail** (Hunt, fig) die Fährte or Spur aufnehmen.
  (j) (Rad) station hereinbekommen, (rein)kriegen (inf); message empfangen, auffangen; (see) beacon etc ausmachen, sichten; (on radar) ausmachen; (record stylus) sound aufnehmen. **the surface was clearly** ~ed ~ **by the satellite's cameras** das Bild der Oberfläche wurde von den Satellitenkameras deutlich übermittelt; **we** ~ed ~ **a rabbit in the car headlights** wir sahen ein Kaninchen im Scheinwerferlicht.

(k) *(correct, put right)* korrigieren. he ~ed me ~ for mispronouncing it er hat meine falsche Aussprache korrigiert.
(l) *(restore to health)* wieder auf die Beine stellen.
(m) *(spot, identify)* mistakes finden.
(n) *(US inf: tidy)* room auf Vordermann bringen *(inf)*.
2 vi **(a)** *(improve)* besser werden; *(appetite also)* zunehmen; *(currency)* sich erholen; *(business)* florieren; *(after slump)* sich erholen; *(engine)* rund laufen; *(accelerate)* schneller werden.
(b) *(continue)* weitermachen. to ~ ~ where one left off da weitermachen, wo man aufgehört hat.
(c) *(inf)* to ~ ~ with sb *(get to know)* jds Bekanntschaft machen; he has ~ed ~ with a rather strange crowd er hat mit merkwürdigen Leuten Umgang.
pickaback ['pɪkəbæk] **1** n to give sb a ~ jdn huckepack nehmen; the little girl wanted a ~ das kleine Mädchen wollte huckepack getragen werden. **2** adv huckepack.
pickaninny n *(US)* see **piccaninny**.
pickaxe, *(US)* **pickax** ['pɪkæks] n Spitzhacke, Picke f, Pickel m.
picker ['pɪkə^r] n *(of fruit etc)* Pflücker(in f) m.
picket ['pɪkɪt] **1** n **(a)** *(of strikers)* Streikposten m. to mount a ~ *(at or on a gate)* (an or bei einem Tor) Streikposten aufstellen.
(b) *(Mil)* Feldposten, Vorposten m.
(c) *(stake)* Pfahl m. ~ fence Palisade f, Palisadenzaun m.
2 vt factory Streikposten aufstellen vor (+dat); *(demonstrators etc)* demonstrieren vor (+dat).
3 vi Streikposten aufstellen. he is ~ing at the front entrance er ist Streikposten am Vordereingang.
picket duty n Streikpostendienst m. to be on ~ Streikposten sein.
picketing ['pɪkɪtɪŋ] n Aufstellen nt von Streikposten. there was no ~ es wurden keine Streikposten aufgestellt; the ~ of the factory gates went on for six months es standen sechs Monate lang Streikposten vor dem Betrieb.
picket line n Streikpostenkette f. to cross a ~ eine Streikpostenkette durchbrechen.
picking ['pɪkɪŋ] n **(a)** *(amount of fruit picked)* Ernte f.
(b) ~s pl Ausbeute f; *(stolen goods)* Beute f; the kitchen staff are entitled to such ~s as leftover food das Küchenpersonal darf übriggebliebenes Essen mitnehmen; most office workers regard pens as legitimate ~s die meisten Büroangestellten sehen es als ihr Recht an, Kulis mitgehen zu lassen *(inf)* or einzustecken; she went along to see if there were any ~s sie ging hin, um zu sehen, ob es für sie was zu holen gab; the ~s are good es lohnt sich, die Ausbeute ist gut.
pickle ['pɪkl] **1** n **(a)** *(food)* Pickles pl.
(b) *(solution)* *(brine)* Salzlake f, Pökel m; *(vinegar)* Essigsoße f; *(for leather, wood)* Beize f; *(Med, Sci)* Naßpräparat nt.
(c) *(inf: predicament)* Klemme f *(inf)*. he was in a bit of a ~/a sorry ~ er steckte in einer Klemme *(inf)*, er saß in der Tinte *(inf)*; to get into a ~ in ein Kuddelmuddel geraten *(inf)*; what a ~! so eine verzwickte Lage!
2 vt *(in vinegar)* einlegen; *(in brine also)* pökeln; *(Med, Sci)* konservieren.
pickled ['pɪkld] adj **(a)** eingelegt. **(b)** pred *(inf: drunk)* besoffen *(inf)*, alkoholisiert *(inf)*.
pick: ~lock n *(tool)* Dietrich m; *(thief)* Einbrecher(in f) m; ~me-up n *(drink)* Muntermacher m, Stärkung f; *(holiday etc)* Erholung f; we stopped off at the pub for a ~-me-up wir sind auf ein Gläschen or einen Schluck in die Kneipe gegangen; hearing that was a real ~-me-up das hat mir richtig Auftrieb gegeben; ~pocket n Taschendieb(in f) m.
pick-up ['pɪkʌp] n **(a)** *(also ~ arm)* Tonabnehmer m.
(b) *(also ~ truck)* Kleinlieferwagen, Kleintransporter m.
(c) *(inf: acquaintance)* Bekanntschaft f. with his latest ~ mit seiner neusten Errungenschaft; he's just looking for a ~ er will nur eine aufreißen *(inf)*.
(d) *(collection)* Abholen nt. he was late for the ~ er kam zu spät zum Treffpunkt; the mail van makes 3 ~s a day der Postwagen kommt dreimal täglich (um die Post abzuholen); the bus makes four ~s der Bus hält viermal (, um Leute aufzunehmen); ~ point *(for excursion)* Sammelstelle f, Treffpunkt m; *(on regular basis)* Haltestelle f.
(e) *(improvement)* Verbesserung f; *(increase)* Ansteigen nt.
(f) *(acceleration)* Beschleunigung f.
picky ['pɪkɪ] adj (+er) *(inf)* pingelig *(inf)*; eater also wählerisch.
picnic ['pɪknɪk] **1** n Picknick nt. to have a ~ picknicken; to go for or on a ~ ein Picknick veranstalten or machen; a ~ lunch ein Picknick nt; it was no ~ *(fig inf)* es war kein Honiglecken.
2 vi picknicken, ein Picknick machen. we went ~king every Sunday wir machten jeden Sonntag ein Picknick.
picnic basket or **hamper** n Picknickkorb m.
picnicker ['pɪknɪkə^r] n jd, der ein Picknick macht or der picknickt. the ~s left all their rubbish behind them die Ausflügler ließen ihre Abfälle liegen.
picnic: ~ site n Rastplatz m; ~ table n Campingtisch m.
pics [pɪks] npl abbr of **pictures** *(Brit inf)* see **picture 1 (c)**.
Pict [pɪkt] n Pikte m, Piktin f.
Pictish ['pɪktɪʃ] **1** adj piktisch. **2** n Piktisch nt.
pictogram ['pɪktəgræm] n Piktogramm nt.
pictorial [pɪk'tɔːrɪəl] **1** adj calendar bebildert; magazine also illustriert; dictionary Bild-; impact bildlich; language, description bildhaft. a ~ masterpiece ein meisterliches Bild; to keep a ~ record of sth etw im Bild festhalten.
2 n *(magazine)* Illustrierte f; *(stamp)* Sondermarke f.
pictorially [pɪk'tɔːrɪəlɪ] adv *(in pictures)* in Bildern, bildlich; impressive vom Bild her; describe bildhaft.
picture ['pɪktʃə^r] **1** n **(a)** Bild nt; *(Art)* *(painting also)* Gemälde nt; *(drawing also)* Zeichnung f. ~s in the fire Phantasiegebilde pl im Kaminfeuer; (as) pretty as a ~ bildschön.
(b) *(TV)* Bild nt.

(c) *(Film)* Film m. the ~s *(Brit)* das Kino; to go to the ~s *(Brit)* ins Kino gehen; what's on at the ~s? *(Brit)* was gibt's im Kino?
(d) *(mental image)* Vorstellung f, Bild nt. I have no clear ~ of it ich kann mir davon kein klares Bild machen; these figures give the general ~ diese Zahlen geben ein allgemeines Bild; have you got the general ~? wissen Sie jetzt ungefähr Bescheid?; to give you a ~ of what life is like here damit Sie sich *(dat)* ein Bild vom Leben hier machen können; the other side of the ~ die Kehrseite der Medaille; to be in the ~ im Bilde sein; to put sb in the ~ jdn ins Bild setzen; I get the ~ *(inf)* ich hab's begriffen or kapiert *(inf)*; I'm beginning to get the ~ ich fange an zu begreifen or kapieren *(inf)*; he/that no longer comes into the ~ er/das spielt keine Rolle mehr.
(e) *(sight)* Bild nt; *(beautiful sight)* *(person also)* Traum m; *(thing also)* Gedicht nt, Traum m. his face was a ~ sein Gesicht war ein Bild für die Götter *(inf)*; she looked a ~ sie war bildschön; the garden is a ~ der Garten ist eine Pracht.
(f) *(embodiment)* Bild nt, Verkörperung f; *(spitting image)* Abbild, Ebenbild nt. she looked or was the ~ of happiness/ health sie sah wie das Glück/die Gesundheit in Person aus; she looked or was the ~ of misery sie war ein Bild des Elends.
2 vt **(a)** *(imagine)* sich *(dat)* vorstellen. to ~ sth to oneself sich *(dat)* etw vorstellen.
(b) *(describe)* beschreiben, darstellen.
(c) *(by drawing, painting)* darstellen; *(in book)* abbilden.
picture: ~ book n Bildband m; *(for children)* Bilderbuch nt; ~ card n Bild(karte f) nt; ~ frame n Bilderrahmen m; ~ gallery n Gemäldegalerie f; ~-goer n *(Brit)* Kinogänger(in f) or -besucher(in f) m; ~ hat n Florentiner(hut) m; ~ house *(dated Brit)*, ~ palace *(dated Brit)* n Lichtspielhaus *(old)*, Lichtspieltheater nt; ~ paper n *(Brit)* Illustrierte f; ~ postcard n Ansichts(post)karte f; ~ rail n Bilderleiste f.
picturesque [ˌpɪktʃə'resk] adj malerisch, pittoresk *(geh)*; *(fig)* description anschaulich, bildhaft.
picturesquely [ˌpɪktʃə'reskli] adv see adj.
picturesqueness [ˌpɪktʃə'resknɪs] n Malerische(s) nt; *(fig: of account, language)* Bildhaftigkeit, Anschaulichkeit f.
picture: ~ tube n Bildröhre f; ~ window n Aussichtsfenster nt; ~ writing n Bilderschrift f.
piddle ['pɪdl] *(inf)* **1** n Pipi nt *(inf)*. **2** vi **(a)** pinkeln *(inf)*; *(esp child)* Pipi machen *(inf)*. **(b)** to ~ around herummachen.
piddling ['pɪdlɪŋ] adj *(inf)* lächerlich.
pidgin ['pɪdʒɪn] n Mischsprache f. ~ English Pidgin-English nt.
pie [paɪ] n Pastete f; *(of meat, fish also)* Pirogge f; *(sweet)* Obstkuchen m; *(individual)* Törtelett nt. that's all ~ *(inf)* das sind nur verrückte Ideen; as nice/sweet as ~ *(inf)* superfreundlich *(inf)*; as easy as ~ *(inf)* kinderleicht.
piebald ['paɪbɔːld] **1** adj scheckig. **2** n Schecke mf.
piece [piːs] n **(a)** Stück nt; *(part, member of a set)* Teil nt; *(component part)* Einzelteil nt; *(fragment: of glass, pottery etc also)* Scherbe f; *(counter)* *(in draughts etc)* Stein m; *(in chess)* Figur f; *(Press: article)* Artikel m; *(Mil)* Geschütz nt; *(firearm)* Waffe f; *(coin)* Münze f. a 50p ~ ein 50-Pence-Stück, eine 50-Pence-Münze; a ~ of cake/land/paper ein Stück nt Kuchen/Land/Papier; a ~ of furniture/luggage/clothing ein Möbel-/Gepäck-/Kleidungsstück nt; a ten-~ band/coffee set eine zehnköpfige Band/ein zehnteiliges Kaffeeservice; a ~ of news/information/luck eine Nachricht/eine Information/ein Glücksfall m; a ~ of good luck glücklicherweise; a ~ of work eine Arbeit; ~ by ~ Stück für Stück; to take sth to ~s etw in seine Einzelteile zerlegen; to come to ~s *(collapsible furniture etc)* sich auseinandernehmen or zerlegen lassen; to come or fall to ~s *(broken chair, old book etc)* auseinanderfallen, sich in Wohlgefallen auflösen *(hum)*; *(glass, pottery)* zerbrechen; to be in ~s *(taken apart)* in Einzelteile zerlegt sein; *(broken: vase etc)* in Scherben sein, zerbrochen sein; to smash sth to ~s etw kaputtschlagen; he tore the letter (in)to ~s er zerriß den Brief (in Stücke or Fetzen); to put or fix together the ~s of a mystery die einzelnen Teile eines Rätsels zusammenfügen; to be paid by the ~ *(Ind)* Stücklohn or Akkordlohn erhalten; he said his ~ very nicely *(poem etc)* er hat das sehr nett vorgetragen; to recite a ~ etwas aufsagen; down the road a ~ *(US inf)* ein Stückchen die Straße runter *(inf)*.
(b) *(phrases)* to go to ~s *(crack up)* durchdrehen *(inf)*; *(lose grip)* die Kontrolle verlieren; *(sportsman, team)* abbauen *(inf)*; he's going to ~s mit ihm geht's bergab; all in one ~ *(intact)* heil, unversehrt; it's all of a ~ with his usual behaviour so benimmt er sich immer; his behaviour is all of a ~ sein Verhalten ist konsequent; to give sb a ~ of one's mind jdm gehörig or ordentlich die Meinung sagen; he got a ~ of my mind ich habe ihm meine Meinung gesagt, ich habe ihm Bescheid gestoßen *(inf)*; to say one's ~ seine Meinung sagen.
(c) *(sl: woman)* Weib nt *(sl)*.
♦**piece together** vt sep *(lit)* zusammenstückeln; *(fig)* sich *(dat)* zusammenreimen; evidence zusammenfügen. to ~ ~ a mystery die einzelnen Teile eines Rätsels zusammenfügen.
pièce de résistance [ˌpjesdə'reɪzɪ̃ˌstɑ̃s] n Krönung f. and now the or my ~ und nun die Krönung!
piece: ~meal **1** adv Stück für Stück, stückweise; *(haphazardly)* kunterbunt durcheinander; **2** adj stückweise; *(haphazard)* wenig systematisch; ~work n Akkordarbeit f; to be on ~work im Akkord arbeiten; ~worker n Akkordarbeiter(in f) m.
pie: ~ chart n Kreisdiagramm nt; ~crust n Teigdecke f.
pied [paɪd] adj gescheckt, gefleckt. the P~ Piper of Hamelin der Rattenfänger von Hameln.
pied-à-terre [ˌpjeɪdɑː'teə^r] n Zweitwohnung f.
pie dish n Pastetenform f.
pied wagtail n Trauerbachstelze f.
pie-eyed ['paɪ'aɪd] adj *(sl)* blau (wie ein Veilchen) *(inf)*.
pier [pɪə^r] n **(a)** Pier m or f; *(landing-place also)* Anlegestelle f, Anleger m. **(b)** *(of bridge etc)* Pfeiler m.

pierce [pɪəs] vt durchstechen; (knife, spear) durchstoßen, durchbohren; (bullet) durchbohren; (fig: sound, coldness etc) durchdringen. **to ~ a hole in sth** etw durchstechen; **to have one's ears ~d** sich (dat) die Ohrläppchen durchstechen lassen; **to ~ sth through and through** (lit, fig) etw durchbohren; **the news ~d him to the heart** die Nachricht traf ihn bis ins Herz.

piercing ['pɪəsɪŋ] adj durchdringend; cold, wind, voice also schneidend; yell also gellend; eyes also stechend; cold, sarcasm beißend; wit scharf.

piercingly ['pɪəsɪŋlɪ] adv see adj.

pierrot ['pɪərəʊ] n Pierrot m.

pietà [ˌpɪeˈtɑː] n Pietà f.

pietism ['paɪətɪzəm] n (a) P~ Pietismus m. (b) (piety) Pietät, Frömmigkeit f; (pej) Frömmelei f.

pietist ['paɪətɪst] n see pietism Pietist(in f) m; frommer Mensch; Frömmler(in f) m.

pietistic [ˌpaɪəˈtɪstɪk] adj (pej) frömmelnd.

piety ['paɪətɪ] n Pietät, Frömmigkeit f. **filial ~** Respekt m gegenüber den Eltern.

piffle ['pɪfl] n (inf) Quatsch (inf), Schnickschnack (inf) m.

piffling ['pɪflɪŋ] adj (inf) lächerlich.

pig [pɪg] **1** n (a) Schwein nt. **to buy a ~ in a poke** (prov) die Katze im Sack kaufen; **~ in the middle** Ball übern Kopf, einer in der Mitte; **~s might fly** (prov) wer's glaubt, wird selig; **they were living like ~s** sie haben wie die Schweine gehaust.
(b) (inf: person) (dirty, nasty) Schwein nt, Sau f (inf); (greedy) Vielfraß m (inf). **to make a ~ of oneself** sich (dat) den Bauch vollschlagen (inf), kräftig zulangen.
(c) (inf: awkward thing) fieses Ding (inf).
(d) (sl: policeman) Bulle m (sl).
(e) (Metal) (ingot) Massel f; (mould) Kokille f.
2 vt **to ~ it** (inf) hausen.

pigeon ['pɪdʒən] n (a) Taube f. (b) (inf) that's not my ~ das ist nicht mein Bier (inf).

pigeon: ~ **breast** n (Med) Hühnerbrust f; ~-**breasted** adj (Med) hühnerbrüstig; ~ **fancier** n Taubenzüchter(in f) m; ~**hole 1** n (in desk etc) Fach nt; **to put people in ~holes** (fig) Menschen (in Kategorien) einordnen, Leute abstempeln; **2** vt (in Fächer) einordnen; (fig: categorize) einordnen, ein- or aufteilen; ~ **house**, ~ **loft** n Taubenschlag m; ~-**toed** adj, adv mit einwärts gerichteten Fußspitzen; **he is/walks ~-toed** er geht über den großen Onkel (inf).

piggery ['pɪgərɪ] n (a) Schweinefarm, Schweinemästerei f.
(b) (inf: gluttony) Völlerei f.

piggish ['pɪgɪʃ] adj (a) eyes, face Schweins-. (b) (greedy) gefräßig; person also verfressen (inf); appetite unmäßig, kannibalisch; (dirty) saumäßig (inf); (nasty) fies (inf), schweinisch (inf); (stubborn) fies (inf).

piggishly ['pɪgɪʃlɪ] adv see adj (b).

piggishness ['pɪgɪʃnɪs] n see adj (a) Schweineartigkeit, Schweineähnlichkeit f. (b) Gefräßigkeit f; Verfressenheit f (inf); Unmäßigkeit f; Saumäßigkeit f (inf); Gemeinheit, Fiesheit (inf) f; Fiesheit f (inf).

piggy ['pɪgɪ] **1** n (baby-talk) Schweinchen nt. **2** adj (+er) (a) attr eyes, face Schweins-. (b) (inf: greedy) verfressen (inf).

piggyback ['pɪgɪbæk] n, adv see pickaback.

piggy bank n Sparschwein nt.

pigheaded ['pɪg'hedɪd] adj stur. **that was a ~ thing to do** so was von stur (inf).

pigheadedly ['pɪg'hedɪdlɪ] adv stur.

pigheadedness ['pɪg'hedɪdnɪs] n Sturheit f.

pig: ~ **iron** n Roheisen nt; ~ **Latin** n kindliche Geheimsprache durch Anfügen von Silben.

piglet ['pɪglɪt] n Ferkel nt.

pigman ['pɪgmən] n, pl -**men** [-mən] Schweinehirt(e) m.

pigment ['pɪgmənt] n Pigment nt.

pigmentation [ˌpɪgmənˈteɪʃən] n Pigmentierung f.

pigmy n see pygmy.

pig: ~**pen** n (US) see ~**sty**; ~'**s ear** n **to make a ~'s ear of sth** (Brit sl) etw vermasseln (inf); ~**skin** n (a) Schweinsleder nt; (b) (US inf: football) Pille f (inf), Leder nt (inf); ~**sty** n Schweinestall m; (fig also) Saustall m (inf); ~**swill** n Schweinefutter nt; (fig: coffee, soup etc) Spülwasser nt (inf); (porridge etc) Schweinefraß m; ~**tail** n Zopf m.

pike[1] [paɪk] n (weapon) Pike f, Spieß m.

pike[2] n (fish) Hecht m.

pike[3] n (US inf) (toll-road) Mautstraße f; (barrier) Mautschranke f.

pikestaff ['paɪkstɑːf] n: **as plain as a ~** sonnenklar.

pilaster [pɪˈlæstə'] n Pilaster, Halbpfeiler m.

pilchard ['pɪltʃəd] n Sardine f.

pile[1] [paɪl] **1** n (a) (heap) Stapel, Stoß m. **to put things in a ~** etw (auf)stapeln; **her things lay** or **were in a ~** ihre Sachen lagen auf einem Haufen; **he made a ~ of the books** er stapelte die Bücher aufeinander.
(b) (inf: large amount) Haufen m, Menge, Masse f. **a great ~ of work** eine Menge or Masse an Arbeit; **~s of money/trouble/food** eine or jede Menge (inf) Geld/Ärger/Essen; **a ~ of things to do** massenhaft zu tun (inf).
(c) (inf: fortune) Vermögen nt. **to make a/one's ~** einen Haufen Geld/sein Vermögen verdienen.
(d) (funeral ~) Scheiterhaufen m.
(e) (liter, hum: building) ehrwürdiges Gebäude.
(f) (atomic ~) Atommeiler m.
2 vt stapeln. **a table ~d high with books** ein Tisch mit Stapeln von Büchern; **the sideboard was ~d high with presents** auf der Anrichte stapelten sich die Geschenke.

♦**pile in 1** vi (inf) (-to in +acc) hinein-/hereindrängen; (get in) einsteigen. **~ ~! immer herein! 2** vt sep einladen (-to in +acc).

♦**pile off** vi (inf) hinaus-/herausdrängen (prep obj aus).

♦**pile on 1** vi (inf) hinein-/hereindrängen (-to in +acc).

2 vt sep (lit) aufhäufen (-to auf +acc). **she ~d rice ~(to) my plate** sie häufte Reis auf meinen Teller; **to ~ coal ~(to) the fire** Kohlen aufs Feuer häufen; **he's piling work ~(to) his staff** er überhäuft seine Leute mit Arbeit; **the teachers really ~ ~ the work before the exams** die Lehrer überhäufen uns/die Schüler etc vor den Prüfungen wirklich mit Arbeit; **they are really piling ~ the pressure** sie setzen uns/euch etc ganz gehörig unter Druck; **to ~ ~ the agony** (inf) dick auftragen (inf); **to ~ it ~** (inf) dick auftragen (inf).

♦**pile out** vi (inf) hinaus-/herausdrängen (of aus).

♦**pile up 1** vi (a) (lit, fig) sich (an)sammeln or anhäufen; (traffic, cars also) sich stauen; (snow, work also) sich (auf)türmen; (reasons) sich häufen; (evidence) sich verdichten. **he let the work ~ ~** die Arbeit türmte sich auf.
(b) (crash) aufeinander auffahren.
2 vt sep (a) (auf)stapeln; money horten; (fig) debts anhäufen; evidence sammeln. **her hair was ~d ~ on top of her head** sie trug ihre Haare hoch aufgetürmt; **to ~ the fire ~ (with logs/coal)** (Holz/Kohle) nachlegen; **he's piling ~ trouble for himself** er handelt sich (dat) Ärger ein.
(b) (inf: crash) car kaputtfahren.

pile[2] n Pfahl m.

pile[3] n (of carpet, cloth) Flor m.

pile: ~-**driver** n Ramme f; ~ **dwelling** n Pfahlbau m.

piles [paɪlz] npl Hämorrhoiden pl.

pile-up ['paɪlʌp] n (car crash) (Massen)karambolage f, Massenzusammenstoß m.

pilfer ['pɪlfə'] vti stehlen, klauen (inf). **there's a lot of ~ing in the office** im Büro wird viel geklaut (inf).

pilferer ['pɪlfərə'] n Dieb(in f), Langfinger (inf) m.

pilgrim ['pɪlgrɪm] n Pilger(in f) m. **the P~ Fathers** die Pilgerväter pl.

pilgrimage ['pɪlgrɪmɪdʒ] n Wallfahrt, Pilgerfahrt f. **to go on** or **make a ~** pilgern, wallfahren, eine Pilger- or Wallfahrt machen; **in our ~ through this life** (liter) auf unserem langen Weg or unserer langen Reise durch dieses Leben.

pill [pɪl] n (a) Tablette f. **the ~** die Pille; **to be/go on the ~** die Pille nehmen; see birth. (b) (sl: ball) Ball m.

pillage ['pɪlɪdʒ] **1** n (act) Plünderung f. (booty) Beute f. **2** vti plündern.

pillar ['pɪlə'] n Säule f. ~ **of salt** Salzsäule f; ~ **of water** Wassersäule f; **the P~s of Hercules** die Säulen pl des Herkules; **a ~ of society** eine Säule or Stütze der Gesellschaft; **from ~ to post** von Pontius zu Pilatus.

pillar-box ['pɪləbɒks] n (Brit) Briefkasten m. ~ **red** knallrot.

pillbox ['pɪlbɒks] n (a) (Med) Pillenschachtel, Pillendose f. (b) (Mil) Bunker m. (c) (also ~ hat) Pagenkäppi nt; (for women) Pillbox f.

pillion ['pɪljən] **1** n (a) (on motor-bike) Soziussitz, Soziussattel m. ~ **passenger** Sozius, Beifahrer(in f) m. (b) (Hist) Damensattel m. **2** adv **to ride ~** auf dem Sozius(sitz) or Beifahrersitz mitfahren.

pillory ['pɪlərɪ] **1** n (Hist) Pranger m. **to be in the ~** am Pranger stehen. **2** vt (fig) anprangern.

pillow ['pɪləʊ] n (Kopf)kissen nt. **2** vt betten. **her arms ~ed the sleeping child** das schlafende Kind war in ihre Arme gebettet.

pillow: ~**case** n (Kopf)kissenbezug m; ~ **fight** n Kissenschlacht f; ~**slip** n see ~**case**; ~ **talk** n Bettgeflüster nt.

pilot ['paɪlət] **1** n (a) (Aviat) Pilot(in f), Flugzeugführer(in f) m. ~'**s licence** Flugschein m, Flugzeugführererlaubnis f (form).
(b) (Naut) Lotse m.
(c) (~ light) Zündflamme f.
(d) (US: on train) Schienenräumer m.
2 vt plane führen, fliegen; ship lotsen; (fig) führen, leiten. **to ~ a bill through the House** eine Gesetzesvorlage durch das Parlament bringen.

pilot: ~ **boat** n Lotsenboot nt; ~ **fish** n Lotsen- or Piloten- or Leitfisch m; ~ **flag** n Lotsenrufflagge f; ~ **house** n Ruderhaus, Steuerhaus nt; ~ **lamp** n Kontrollampe f; ~**less** adj führerlos; ~ **light** n Zündflamme f; **P~ Officer** n (Brit Aviat) Leutnant m; ~ **plant** n Versuchs- or Pilotanlage f, Versuchs- or Pilotbetrieb m; ~ **scheme** n Versuchsprojekt nt; ~ **study** n Musterstudie f.

pimento [pɪˈmentəʊ] n (a) Paprikaschote f. (b) (allspice) Piment m or nt, Nelkenpfeffer m; (tree) Pimentbaum m.

pimp [pɪmp] **1** n Zuhälter, Lude (pej) m. **2** vi Zuhälter sein. **to ~ for sb** für jdn den Zuhälter machen, jds Lude sein (pej).

pimpernel ['pɪmpənel] n (Bot: also scarlet ~) (Acker)gauchheil m.

pimple ['pɪmpl] n Pickel m, Pustel f. **she/her face comes out in ~s** sie bekommt Pickel/sie bekommt Pickel im Gesicht.

pimply ['pɪmplɪ] adj (+er) pickelig.

pin [pɪn] **1** n (Sew) Stecknadel f; (tie ~, hat~, on brooch, hair~) Nadel f; (Mech) Bolzen, Stift m; (small nail) Stift m; (in grenade) Sicherungsstift m; (on guitar) Wirbel m; (Med) Stift, Nagel m; (Elec: of plug) Pol m. **a two-~ plug** ein zweipoliger Stecker; **I've got ~s and needles in my foot** mir ist der Fuß eingeschlafen; **~s and needles** sing or pl ein Kribbeln nt; **like a new ~** blitzsauber, funkelnagelneu; **neat as a (new) ~** wie aus dem Ei gepellt; **for two ~s I'd pack up and go** (inf) es fehlt nicht mehr viel, dann gehe ich; **I don't care a ~** (dated inf) es ist mir völlig egal or schnuppe (inf); **you could have heard a ~ drop** man hätte eine Stecknadel fallen hören können.
(b) (esp US) (brooch) Brosche, Schmucknadel f; (badge: also lapel ~, fraternity ~) Anstecknadel f, Abzeichen nt.
(c) (Golf) Flaggenstock m; (Bowling) Kegel m.
(d) ~s pl (inf: legs) Gestell nt (inf); **he wasn't very steady on his ~s** er war etwas wackelig auf den Beinen; **to be quick on one's ~s** gut zu Fuß sein.
2 vt (a) dress stecken. **to ~ sth to sth** etw an etw (acc) heften; **to ~ papers together** Blätter zusammenheften; **the bone had to be ~ned in place** der Knochen mußte genagelt werden.

(b) (fig) to ~ sb to the ground/against a wall jdn am Boden/an einer Wand festnageln; to ~ sb's arms to his side jdm die Arme an den Körper pressen; to ~ sb's arm behind his back jdm den Arm auf den Rücken drehen; to ~ one's hopes/faith on sb/sth seine Hoffnungen/sein Vertrauen auf jdn/etw setzen; you shouldn't ~ everything on one chance Sie sollten nicht alles auf eine Karte setzen; to ~ back one's ears die Ohren spitzen (inf).

(c) (inf: accuse of) to ~ sth on sb jdm etw anhängen.

(d) (US inf) to be/get ~ned verlobt sein/sich verloben.

♦**pin down** vt sep **(a)** (fix down) (with pins) an- or festheften; (hold, weight down) beschweren, niederhalten; (trap: rockfall etc) einklemmen. he ~ned him ~ on the canvas er drückte ihn auf die Matte; two of the gang ~ned him ~ zwei aus der Bande drückten ihn zu Boden; our troops were ~ned ~ by heavy artillery fire unsere Truppen wurden durch heftiges Artilleriefeuer festgehalten.

(b) (fig) to ~ sb ~ jdn festnageln or festlegen; he wouldn't be ~ned ~ to any particular date er ließ sich nicht auf ein bestimmtes Datum festnageln or festlegen; he's a difficult man to ~ ~ man kann ihn nur schwer dazu bringen, sich festzulegen; I've seen him/it somewhere before but I can't ~ him/it ~ ich habe ihn/es schon mal irgendwo gesehen, kann ihn/es aber nicht einordnen; we can't ~ ~ the source of the rumours wir können die Quelle der Gerüchte nicht lokalisieren; it's difficult to ~ the meaning of this word ~ es ist schwierig, die Bedeutung dieses Wortes zu präzisieren or genau zu umreißen; if you try to ~ his ideas ~ wenn Sie versuchen, seine Ideen genau zu umreißen; it's not easy to ~ ~ the precise cause of this es ist nicht leicht, die genaue Ursache dafür festzustellen; there's something odd here, but I can't ~ it ~ irgend etwas ist hier merkwürdig, aber ich kann nicht genau sagen was.

♦**pin up** vt sep notice anheften; hair aufstecken, hochstecken; hem, dress, sleeves stecken.

pinafore ['pɪnəfɔː^r] n (overall: for children) Kinderkittel m; (apron) Schürze f, Kittel m. ~ dress (Brit) Trägerkleid nt.

pinball ['pɪnbɔːl] n Flipper m. to have a game of ~ Flipper spielen, flippern; ~ machine Flipper(automat) m.

pince-nez ['pɪnsneɪ] n Kneifer m, Pincenez m (old).

pincer movement ['pɪnsə-] n (Mil fig) Zangenbewegung f.

pincers ['pɪnsəz] npl **(a)** Kneifzange, Beißzange f. a pair of ~ eine Kneifzange, eine Beißzange. **(b)** (Zool) Schere, Zange f.

pinch [pɪntʃ] **1** n **(a)** (with fingers) Kneifen, Zwicken nt no pl. to give sb a ~ on the arm jdn in den Arm kneifen or zwicken.

(b) (small quantity) Quentchen nt; (Cook) Prise f. a ~ of snuff eine Prise Schnupftabak.

(c) (pressure) I'm rather feeling the ~ at the moment ich bin im Augenblick ziemlich knapp bei Kasse (inf); to feel the ~ die schlechte Lage zu spüren bekommen; if it comes to the ~ wenn es zum Schlimmsten or Äußersten kommt; at a ~ zur Not.

2 vt **(a)** (with fingers) kneifen, zwicken; (with implement: squeeze) end of wire etc zusammendrücken, zusammenklemmen; (shoe) drücken. to ~ sb's bottom jdn in den Hintern kneifen; to ~ oneself sich kneifen; to ~ one's finger in the door sich (dat) den Finger in der Tür (ein)klemmen.

(b) (inf: steal) klauen, stibitzen, mopsen (all inf). don't let anyone ~ my seat paß auf, daß mir niemand den Platz wegnimmt; he ~ed Johnny's girl er hat Johnny (dat) die Freundin ausgespannt (inf); he ~ed that idea from Shaw die Idee hat er bei Shaw geklaut (inf); I had my car ~ed mein Auto ist geklaut worden (inf).

(c) (inf: arrest) schnappen (inf), erwischen.

3 vi **(a)** (shoe, also fig) drücken.

(b) to ~ and scrape sich einschränken.

♦**pinch back** or **off** vt sep bud abknipsen.

pinchbeck ['pɪntʃbek] **1** n (lit, fig) Talmi nt. **2** adj jewels aus Talmi.

pinched ['pɪntʃt] adj **(a)** verhärmt; (from cold) verfroren; (from fatigue) erschöpft. to be/look ~ with cold/hunger verfroren/verhungert sein/aussehen. **(b)** (inf: short) to be ~ for money/time knapp bei Kasse sein (inf)/keine Zeit haben; we're a bit ~ for space in here wir sind hier ein wenig beengt.

pinch-hit ['pɪntʃhɪt] vi (US) Ersatzspieler sein; (fig) einspringen.

pinch-hitter ['pɪntʃ,hɪtə^r] n (US) Ersatz(spieler) m; (fig) Ersatz m.

pinchpenny ['pɪntʃ,penɪ] adj knauserig, pfennigfuchserisch.

pin: ~ **curl** n Löckchen nt; ~**cushion** n Nadelkissen nt.

pine¹ [paɪn] n Kiefer f.

pine² vi **(a)** to ~ for sb/sth sich nach jdm/etw sehnen or verzehren. **(b)** (~ away, be sad) vor Gram vergehen, sich vor Kummer verzehren.

♦**pine away** vi (from grief) sich (vor Kummer) verzehren, vor Gram vergehen; (from disease) (dahin)siechen; (of animal, plant) eingehen. she ~d ~ and died sie starb an gebrochenem Herzen; the dog just ~d ~ and died der Hund ging langsam ein.

pineal gland ['pɪnɪəl-] n Zirbeldrüse, Epiphyse (spec) f.

pineapple ['paɪn,æpl] n Ananas f. ~ chunks Ananasstücke pl; ~ juice Ananassaft m.

pine: ~ **cone** n Kiefernzapfen m; ~ **forest** n Kiefernwald m; ~ **marten** n Baummarder m; ~ **needle** n Kiefernadel f; ~ **tree** n Kiefer f; ~ **wood** n Kiefernwald m; (material) Kiefernholz nt.

ping [pɪŋ] **1** n (of bell) Klingeln nt; (of bullet) Peng, Deng nt. to give or make a ~ (sonar, lift bell etc) klingeln; the stone made a ~ as it hit the glass der Stein machte klick, als er auf das Glas traf. **2** vi (bell) klingeln; (bullet) peng or deng machen.

ping-pong ['pɪŋpɒŋ] n Pingpong nt. ~ **ball** Pingpongball m.

pin: ~**head** n (Steck)nadelkopf m; (inf: stupid person) Holzkopf (inf), Strohkopf (inf) m; ~ **holder** n Blumenigel m; ~**hole** n Loch nt; ~**hole camera** n Lochkamera, Camera obscura f.

pinion ['pɪnjən] **1** n **(a)** (Mech) Ritzel m, Treibrad nt. **(b)** (poet: wing) Fittich m (poet), Schwinge f (poet). **(c)** (Orn) Flügel-

---

spitze f. **2** vt to ~ sb to the ground/against the wall jdn zu Boden/gegen eine Wand drücken.

pink¹ [pɪŋk] **1** n **(a)** (colour) Rosa nt; (hunting ~) Rot nt.

(b) (plant) Gartennelke f.

(c) to be in the ~ vor Gesundheit strotzen; I'm in the ~ mir geht's prächtig; to feel in the ~ sich bestens fühlen; in the ~ of condition in Top- or Hochform.

2 adj **(a)** (colour) rosa inv, rosafarben; cheeks, face rosig. ~ **gin** Pink Gin m; to turn ~ erröten; to see ~ elephants (inf) or mice (inf) weiße Mäuse sehen (inf).

(b) (Pol inf) rot angehaucht.

pink² vt **(a)** (Sew) mit der Zickzackschere schneiden. **(b)** (nick) streifen.

pink³ vi (Aut) klopfen.

pink-eye ['pɪŋkaɪ] n (inf) Bindehautentzündung f.

pinkie ['pɪŋkɪ] n (Scot inf, US inf) kleiner Finger.

pinking shears ['pɪŋkɪŋ,ʃɪəz] npl Zickzackschere f.

pinkish ['pɪŋkɪʃ] adj rötlich. ~ **white** blaßrosa.

pinko ['pɪŋkəʊ] n (Pol pej inf) roter Bruder m, rote Schwester (inf).

pin money n Nadelgeld nt.

pinnace ['pɪnɪs] n Pinasse f.

pinnacle ['pɪnəkl] n (Archit) Fiale f; (of rock, mountain) Gipfel m, Spitze f; (fig) Gipfel, Höhepunkt m.

pinnate ['pɪneɪt] adj (Bot) gefiedert.

pinny ['pɪnɪ] n (inf) Schürze f.

pinoc(h)le ['piːnʌkəl] n (Cards) Binokel nt.

pin: ~**point 1** n Punkt m; **the buildings were mere ~points on the horizon** die Gebäude zeichneten sich wie Stecknadelköpfe am Horizont ab; a ~**point of light** ein Lichtpunkt m; ~**point bombing** Punktzielbombardement nt; **2** vt (locate) genau an- or aufzeigen; (define, identify) genau feststellen or -legen; ~**prick** n Nadelstich m; (fig) Kleinigkeit f; ~**stripe** n (stripe) Nadelstreifen m; (cloth) Tuch nt mit Nadelstreifen; (~stripe suit) Nadelstreifenanzug m.

pint [paɪnt] n **(a)** (measure) Pint nt; see appendix. **(b)** (esp Brit: quantity) (of milk) Tüte f; (bottle) Flasche f; (of beer) Halbe f, Glas nt Bier. to have a ~ ein Bier nt trinken; fancy a quick ~? wie wär's mit einem Bier auf die Schnelle? (inf); he likes his ~ er hebt ganz gern mal einen (inf); a good ~ ein gutes Bier.

pinta ['paɪntə] n (Brit inf) halber Liter Milch.

pin table n Flipper(automat) m.

pint-mug ['paɪntmʌg] n Humpen m(, der ein Pint faßt).

pinto ['pɪntəʊ] n (US) Schecke mf.

pint-size(d) ['paɪntsaɪz(d)] adj (inf) stöpselig (inf), knirpsig (inf). a ~ boxer ein kleiner or feiner Boxer.

pin: ~ **tuck** n Biese f; ~**-up** n (picture) Pin-up-Foto nt; (person) (girl) Pin-up-girl nt; (man) Idol nt; ~**-up girl** n Pin-up-girl nt; ~**wheel** n (firework) Feuerrad nt; (US: toy) Windrädchen nt.

pioneer [,paɪə'nɪə^r] **1** n (also Mil) Pionier m; (fig also) Bahnbrecher, Wegbereiter m.

2 adj attr see **pioneering**.

3 vt way vorbereiten, bahnen; (fig) Pionierarbeit f leisten für. he ~ed a whole new area of research er leistete Pionierarbeit für ein ganz neues Forschungsgebiet; the firm which ~ed its technical development die Firma, die die technische Pionierarbeit dafür geleistet hat.

4 vi Pionierarbeit or Vorarbeit leisten, den Weg bahnen.

pioneering [,paɪə'nɪərɪŋ] adj attr Pionier-. the pride they take in their ~ ancestors der Stolz auf ihre Vorfahren, die Pioniere.

pious ['paɪəs] adj fromm; (pej also) frömmlerisch. a ~ hope ein frommer Wunsch.

piously ['paɪəslɪ] adv fromm.

piousness ['paɪəsnɪs] n Frömmigkeit f; (pej also) Frömmelei f.

pip¹ [pɪp] n **(a)** (Bot) Kern m.

(b) (on card, dice) Auge nt; (Brit Mil inf) Stern m; (on radar screen) Pip m, Echozeichen nt.

(c) (Rad, Telec) the ~s das Zeitzeichen; (in public telephone) das Tut-tut-tut; at the third ~ it will be ... beim dritten Ton des Zeitzeichens ist es ...; put more money in when you hear the ~s bitte Geld nachwerfen, sobald das Zeichen ertönt.

pip² n (Vet) Pips m. to give sb the ~ (Brit inf) jdn aufregen (inf).

pip³ vt (Brit inf) knapp besiegen or schlagen. to ~ sb at the post (in race) jdn um Haaresbreite schlagen, jdn im Ziel abfangen; (fig) jdm um Haaresbreite zuvorkommen; (in getting papers etc) jdm etw vor der Nase wegschnappen; there I was, ~ped at the post again da war mir wieder jemand zuvorgekommen.

pipe [paɪp] **1** n **(a)** (tube) (for water, gas, sewage) Rohr nt, Leitung f; (fuel ~, for steam) Leitung f; (in body) Röhre f.

(b) (Mus) Flöte f; (fife, of organ, bagpipe's) Pfeife f. ~**s** (bag~s) Dudelsack m; ~**s of Pan** Panflöte f.

(c) (for smoking) Pfeife f. ~ of peace Friedenspfeife; to smoke a ~ Pfeife rauchen; to smoke or have a ~ together zusammen ein Pfeifchen rauchen; put that in your ~ and smoke it! (inf) steck dir das hinter den Spiegel (inf).

2 vt **(a)** water, oil etc in Rohren leiten; music, broadcast ausstrahlen. water has to be ~d in from the next state Wasser muß in Rohrleitungen aus dem Nachbarstaat herangeschafft werden; ~d music (pej) Musikberieselung f (inf).

(b) (Mus) tune flöten, pfeifen; (sing in high voice) krähen; (speak in high voice) piepsen; (Naut) pfeifen. to ~ sb aboard jdn mit Pfeifensignal an Bord begrüßen or empfangen; he was even ~d to the gallows selbst zum Galgen wurde er mit Dudelsackmusik geleitet.

(c) (Cook) spritzen; cake mit Spritzguß verzieren; (Sew) paspelieren, paspeln.

3 vi **(a)** (Mus) flöten, (die) Flöte spielen; (bird) pfeifen; (young bird, anxiously) piep(s)en.

♦**pipe down** vi (inf) (be less noisy) die Luft anhalten (inf), ruhig sein; (become less confident) (ganz) klein werden.

pipe up vi (inf) (person) den Mund aufmachen, sich melden. **suddenly a little voice ~d ~** plötzlich machte sich ein Stimmchen bemerkbar; **then he ~d ~ with another objection** dann brachte er noch einen Einwand vor.

pipe: **~ band** n Dudelsackkapelle f; **~ clay** n (for making pipes) Pfeifenton m; **~ cleaner** n Pfeifenreiniger m; **~ dream** n Hirngespinst nt; that's just a **~ dream** das ist ja wohl nur ein frommer Wunsch; **~-layer** n Rohrleitungs(ver)leger(in f), Rohrleitungsmonteur(in f) m; **~-laying** n Verlegen nt von Rohrleitungen; **~line** n (Rohr)leitung f; (for oil, gas also) Pipeline f; **to be in the ~line** (fig) in Vorbereitung sein; **the pay rise hasn't come through yet but it's in the ~line** die Lohnerhöhung ist noch nicht durch, steht aber kurz bevor; **they say there are a few organizational changes in the ~line** es heißt, einige organisatorische Änderungen stünden bevor.

piper ['paɪpə] n Flötenspieler(in f) m; (on fife) Pfeifer m; (on bagpipes) Dudelsackpfeifer m. **to pay the ~** die Kosten tragen, für die Kosten aufkommen; **he who pays the ~ calls the tune** (Prov) wer bezahlt, darf auch bestimmen.

pipe: **~ rack** n Pfeifenständer m; **~ smoker** n Pfeifenraucher(in f) m; **~ tobacco** n Pfeifentabak m.

pipette [pɪ'pet] n Pipette f, Saugröhrchen nt.

piping ['paɪpɪŋ] **1** n (a) (pipework) Rohrleitungssystem nt; (pipe) Rohrleitung f. **(b)** (Sew) Paspelierung f; (on furniture) Kordel f; (Cook) Spritzgußverzierung f. **(c)** (Mus) Flötenspiel nt; (on bagpipes) Dudelsackpfeifen nt. **2** adj voice piepsend. **3** adv: **~ hot** kochendheiß.

piping bag n Spritzbeutel m.

pipistrelle [ˌpɪpɪ'strel] n Zwergfledermaus f.

pipit ['pɪpɪt] n Pieper m.

pippin ['pɪpɪn] n Cox m.

pipsqueak ['pɪpskwiːk] n (inf) Winzling m (inf).

piquancy ['piːkənsɪ] n Pikantheit, Würze f; (fig) Pikanterie f.

piquant ['piːkənt] adj (lit, fig) pikant.

pique [piːk] **1** n Groll m, Vergrämtheit f. **he resigned in a fit of ~** er kündigte, weil er vergrämt war; **you don't have to go straight into a fit of ~ just because ...** du brauchst nicht gleich pikiert or beleidigt zu sein, nur weil ...; **to be in a ~ with sb** (old) gegen jdn einen Groll hegen.

2 vt (offend, wound) kränken, verletzen. **to be ~d at sb/sth** über jdn/etw (acc) ungehalten or pikiert sein.

3 vr **to ~ oneself on sth** sich (dat) viel auf etw (acc) einbilden.

piqué ['piːkeɪ] n Pikee, Piqué m.

piracy ['paɪərəsɪ] n Seeräuberei, Piraterie f; (of book etc) Raubdruck m; (of record) Raubpressung f. **an act of ~** Seeräuberei, Piraterie f.

piranha (fish) [pɪ'rɑːnjə(ˌfɪʃ)] n Piranha m.

pirate ['paɪərɪt] **1** n Seeräuber, Pirat m; (~ ship) Seeräuberschiff, Piratenschiff nt; (also ~ cab) nicht konzessioniertes Taxi. **~ radio** Piratensender m.

2 vt book einen Raubdruck herstellen von; invention, idea stehlen. **a ~d version of the record** eine Raubpressung; **~d edition** Raubdruck m.

piratical [paɪ'rætɪkəl] adj seeräuberisch, piratenhaft.

pirouette [ˌpɪru'et] **1** n Pirouette f. **2** vi Pirouetten drehen, pirouettieren.

Pisces ['paɪsiːz] npl (Astron) Fische pl; (Astrol) Fisch m. **I'm (a) ~** ich bin Fisch.

piss [pɪs] (vulg) **1** n (act) Piß m (sl); (urine) Pisse f (sl). **to have a/go for a ~** pissen (sl)/pissen gehen (sl). **2** vti pissen (sl).

♦**piss about** or **around** vi herummachen (inf).

♦**piss off** (esp Brit sl) **1** n abhauen (inf). **~ ~!** (go away) verpiß dich! (sl). **(don't be stupid)** du kannst mich mal (inf). **2** vt ankotzen (sl). **to be ~ed ~ with sb/sth** von jdm/etw die Schnauze voll haben (inf).

pissed [pɪst] adj (sl) (Brit: drunk) sturz- or stockbesoffen (inf); (US: angry) stocksauer (inf).

pistachio [pɪ'stɑːʃɪəʊ] n Pistazie f; (colour) pistazienfarben.

pistil ['pɪstɪl] n Stempel m, Pistill nt (spec).

pistol ['pɪstl] n Pistole f. **~-shot** Pistolenschuß m; (person) Pistolenschütze m/-schützin f; **to hold a ~ to sb's head** (fig) jdm die Pistole auf die Brust setzen; **~ grip camera** Kamera f mit Handgriff.

pistol-whip ['pɪstlwɪp] vt (US) mit einer Pistole ein paar überziehen (+dat) (inf).

piston ['pɪstən] n Kolben m. **~ engine** Kolbenmotor m; **~ ring** Kolbenring m; **~ rod** Pleuel- or Kolbenstange f; **~ stroke** Kolbenhub m.

pit[1] [pɪt] **1** n (a) (hole) Grube f; (coalmine also) Zeche f; (quarry also) Steinbruch m; (trap) Fallgrube f; (in zoo etc) Grube f; (for cock-fighting) (Kampf)arena f; (of stomach) Magengrube f. **to have a sinking feeling in the ~ of one's stomach** ein ungutes Gefühl in der Magengegend haben; **to go down the ~** Bergmann or Bergarbeiter werden; **the ~(s) er** arbeitet unter Tage; **the ~** (hell) die Hölle; see bottomless.

(b) (Aut) (in garage) Grube f; (motor-racing) Box f; (Sport) (for long jump) Sprunggrube f; (for high jump) Sprunghügel m. **to make a ~ stop** einen Boxenstop machen.

(c) (Theat) (usu pl Brit: for audience) Parkett nt; (orchestra ~) Orchesterraum m or -versenkung f or -graben m.

(d) (US St Ex) Börsensaal m.

(e) (scar, on ceramics) Vertiefung f; (on skin also) Narbe f.

2 vt (a) **the surface of the moon is ~ted with small craters** die Mondoberfläche ist mit kleinen Kratern übersät; **where the meteorites have ~ted the surface** wo die Meteoriten Einschläge hinterlassen haben; **his face was ~ted with smallpox scars** sein Gesicht war voller Pockennarben; **the skin of an orange is ~ted with small dents** die Schale einer Apfelsine ist narbig; **the underside of the car was ~ted with rustholes** die Unterseite des Wagens war mit Rostlöchern übersät.

(b) to ~ one's strength/wits against sb/sth seine Kraft/seinen

Verstand an jdm/etw messen; **in the next round A is ~ted against B** in der nächsten Runde stehen sich A und B gegenüber; **they are clearly ~ting their new model against ours** mit ihrem neuen Modell nehmen sie offensichtlich den Kampf gegen uns auf; **to ~ oneself against the forces of nature** sich gegen die Elemente aufnehmen.

pit[2] (US) **1** n Stein m. **2** vt entsteinen.

pitapat ['pɪtə'pæt] **1** adv (of heart) poch poch, klopf klopf; (of feet) tapp tapp. **to go ~** (heart) pochen, klopfen. **2** n (of rain, heart) Klopfen nt; (of feet) Getrappel, Getrippel nt.

pitch[1] [pɪtʃ] n Pech nt. **as black as ~** pechschwarz.

pitch[2] **1** n (a) (throw) Wurf m. **he threw the ball back full ~** er schleuderte den Ball in hohem Bogen zurück.

(b) (Naut) Stampfen nt.

(c) (esp Brit Sport) Platz m, Feld nt.

(d) (Brit) (for doing one's business: in market, outside theatre etc) Stand m; (fig: usual place: on beach etc) Platz m. **keep off my ~!** (fig) komm mir nicht ins Gehege!; see queer.

(e) (inf: sales ~) (long talk) Sermon m (inf); (technique) Verkaufstaktik, Masche (inf) f. **if you changed your ~, you might sell more** mit einer anderen Verkaufsmasche könnten Sie vielleicht mehr verkaufen; **he gave us his ~ about the need to change our policy** er hielt uns (wieder einmal) einen Vortrag über die Notwendigkeit, unsere Politik zu ändern.

(f) (Phon, of note) Tonhöhe f; (of instrument) Tonlage f; (of voice) Stimmlage f. **to have perfect ~** das absolute Gehör haben; **their speaking voices are similar in ~** ihre Stimmlagen sind ähnlich; **a comedian has to find the right ~ for each audience** ein Komiker muß bei jedem Publikum aufs neue versuchen, den richtigen Ton zu treffen.

(g) (angle, slope: of roof) Schräge, Neigung f; (of propeller) Steigung f. **the roofs have a high ~** die Dächer sind sehr steil; **the floor was sloping at a precarious ~** der Boden neigte sich gefährlich.

(h) (fig: degree) **he roused the mob to such a ~ that ...** er brachte die Massen so sehr auf, daß ...; **the crowd/music had reached such a frenzied ~ that ...** die Menge/Musik hatte einen solchen Grad rasender Erregung erreicht, daß ...; **at its highest ~ auf dem Höhepunkt** or Gipfel; **a hitherto unknown ~ of excitement** ein bisher unbekannter Grad der Erregung; **we can't keep on working at this ~ much longer** wir können dieses Arbeitstempo nicht mehr lange durchhalten; **their frustration had reached such a ~ that ...** ihre Frustration hatte einen derartigen Grad erreicht, daß ...; **matters had reached such a ~ that ...** die Sache hatte sich derart zugespitzt, daß ...; see fever. **... die Sache hatte sich derart zugespitzt, daß ...**; see fever.

(i) (US sl) **what's the ~?** wie sieht's aus?, was liegt an? (inf).

2 vt (a) (throw) hay gabeln; ball werfen. **he was ~ed from** or **off his horse** er wurde vom Pferd geworfen; **he was ~ed through the windscreen** er wurde durch die Windschutzscheibe geschleudert; **as soon as he got the job he was ~ed into a departmental battle** kaum hatte er die Stelle, war er schon in einen Abteilungskrieg verwickelt; **sorry we have to ~ you straight in at the deep end** es tut mir leid, daß wir Sie gleich ins kalte Wasser werfen müssen.

(b) (Mus) song anstimmen; note (give) angeben; (hit) treffen; instrument stimmen. **she ~ed her voice higher** sie sprach mit einer höheren Stimme.

(c) (fig) **to ~ one's aspirations too high** seine Erwartungen or Hoffnungen zu hoch stecken; **his speech was ~ed in rather high-flown terms** seine Rede war ziemlich hochgestochen; **the production must be ~ed at the right level for London audiences** das Stück muß auf das Niveau des Londoner Publikums abgestimmt werden; **that's ~ing it rather strong** or **a bit high** das ist ein bißchen übertrieben; **to ~ sb a story** or **line** (inf) jdm eine Geschichte or ein Märchen auftischen (inf).

(d) (put up) camp aufschlagen; tent also, stand aufstellen.

(e) (Baseball) **he ~ed the first two innings** er spielte or machte in den ersten beiden Runden den Werfer.

3 vi (a) (fall) fallen, stürzen. **to ~ forward** vornüberfallen; **he ~ed off his horse** er fiel kopfüber vom Pferd; **he ~ed forward as the bus braked** er fiel nach vorn, als der Bus bremste.

(b) (Naut) stampfen; (Aviat) absacken. **the ship ~ed and tossed** das Schiff stampfte und rollte.

(c) (Baseball) werfen. **he's in there ~ing** (US fig inf) er schuftet wie ein Ochse (inf).

♦**pitch in 1** vt sep hineinwerfen or -schleudern. **2** vi (inf) einspringen. **if we all ~ ~ and help** wenn wir alle einspringen; **so we all ~ed ~ together** also packten wir alle mit an.

♦**pitch into** vi +prep obj (attack) herfallen über (+acc); food also, work sich hermachen über (+acc).

♦**pitch on** vi +prep obj (inf: choose) herauspicken (inf).

♦**pitch out** vt sep (lit, fig) hinauswerfen; (get rid of) wegwerfen. **he was ~ed ~ when the car crashed** beim Unfall wurde er aus dem Wagen geschleudert.

pitch: **~ black** adj pechschwarz; **~blende** n Pechblende f; **~ dark 1** adj pechschwarz; **2** n (tiefe) Finsternis.

pitched [pɪtʃt] adj (a) roof Sattel-, Giebel-. **(b)** battle offen.

pitcher[1] ['pɪtʃə[r]] n Krug m; (two-handled) Henkelkrug m.

pitcher[2] n (Baseball) Werfer m.

pitch: **~fork 1** n Heugabel f; (for manure) Mistgabel f; **2** vt gabeln; (fig) hineinwerfen; **~ pine** n Pechkiefer f.

piteous ['pɪtɪəs] adj mitleiderregend; sounds kläglich.

piteously ['pɪtɪəslɪ] adv mitleiderregend; cry etc also kläglich.

pitfall ['pɪtfɔːl] n (fig) Falle f, Fallstrick m. **"P~s of English"** „Hauptschwierigkeiten der englischen Sprache".

pith [pɪθ] n (Bot) Mark nt; (of orange, lemon etc) weiße Haut; (fig: core) Kern m, Wesentliche(s) nt. **remarks etc of great ~ (and moment)** bedeutungsschwere Äußerungen.

pithead ['pɪthed] n Übertageanlagen pl. **at the ~** über Tage; **~ ballot** Abstimmung f der Bergarbeiter.

pith hat, pith helmet n Tropenhelm m.

pithily ['pɪθɪlɪ] adv prägnant, kernig, markig.

pithiness ['pɪθɪnɪs] n (fig) Prägnanz, Markigkeit f.

pithy ['pɪθɪ] adj (+er) (Bot) reich an Mark; oranges etc dickschalig; (fig) prägnant, markig. ~ **remarks** Kernsprüche pl.

pitiable ['pɪtɪəbl] adj mitleiderregend, bemitleidenswert.

pitiful ['pɪtɪfʊl] adj (a) (moving to pity) sight, story mitleiderregend; person bemitleidenswert, bedauernswert; cry, whimper also jämmerlich.

(b) (poor, wretched) erbärmlich, jämmerlich, kläglich. **what a ~ little wretch you are** was bist du doch für ein erbärmlicher kleiner Schuft; **just a ~ stump** nur ein kläglicher Stumpf; **he had only a few ~ hairs on his upper lip** er hatte nur ein paar kümmerliche Haare auf der Oberlippe.

pitifully ['pɪtɪfəlɪ] adv see adj. **it was ~ obvious that ...** es war schon qualvoll offensichtlich, daß ...

pitiless ['pɪtɪlɪs] adj mitleidlos; person also, sun, glare unbarmherzig; cruelty also gnadenlos, erbarmungslos.

pitilessly ['pɪtɪlɪslɪ] adv see adj.

pit: ~ pony n Grubenpony nt; **~ prop** n Grubenstempel, Abbaustempel m.

pittance ['pɪtəns] n Hungerlohn m. **I can hardly live on the ~** they pay me ich kann von dem Hungerlohn, den or den paar Pfennigen, die sie mir zahlen, kaum leben.

pitter-patter ['pɪtə'pætə'] **1** n (of rain) Klatschen nt; (of feet) Getrappel, Getrippel nt. **2** adv run tapp tapp, tipp tapp. **her heart went ~** ihr Herz klopfte or pochte. **3** vi (rain) platschen, klatschen; (run) trappeln, trippeln.

pituitary (gland) [pɪ'tjʊətrɪ(.glænd)] n Hirnanhangdrüse f.

pit worker n Grubenarbeiter m.

pity ['pɪtɪ] **1** n **(a)** Mitleid, Mitgefühl, Erbarmen nt. **for ~'s sake!** Erbarmen!; (less seriously) um Himmels willen!; **to have or take ~ on sb, to feel ~ for sb** mit jdm Mitleid haben; **but the king took ~ on him and spared his life** aber der König hatte Erbarmen mit ihm und schonte sein Leben; **have you no ~?** hast du kein Mitleid?; **to do sth out of ~ (for sb)** etw aus Mitleid (mit jdm) tun; **to feel no ~** kein Mitgefühl etc haben, kein Mitleid fühlen; **to move sb to ~** jds Mitleid (acc) erregen.

(b) (cause of regret) (what a) ~! (wie) schade!; **what a ~ he can't come** (wie) schade, daß er nicht kommen kann; **more's the ~!** leider; **and I won't be able to attend, more's the ~** und ich kann leider nicht teilnehmen; **it is a ~ that ...** es ist schade, daß ...; **the ~ of it was that ...** das Traurige daran war, daß ...; **it's a great ~** es ist sehr schade, es ist jammerschade; (more formally) es ist sehr bedauerlich; **it is a thousand pities that ...** es ist ein Jammer, daß ...

2 vt bemitleiden, bedauern; (contemptuously) bedauern. **all I can say is that I ~ you** ich kann nur sagen, du tust mir leid.

pitying adj, **~ly** adv ['pɪtɪɪŋ, -lɪ] mitleidig; glance also bedauernd; (with contempt) verächtlich.

pivot ['pɪvət] (vb: pret, ptp ~ed) **1** n Lagerzapfen, Drehzapfen m; (Mil) Flügelmann m; (fig) Dreh- und Angelpunkt m. **~ bearing** Zapfenlager nt. **2** vt drehbar lagern. **he ~ed it on his hand** er ließ es auf seiner Hand kreiseln. **3** vi (switch. **to ~ on sth** (fig) sich um etw drehen.

pivotal ['pɪvətl] adj (fig) zentral.

pixie, pixy ['pɪksɪ] n Kobold, Elf m. **~ hat or hood** Rotkäppchenmütze f.

pixilated ['pɪksɪleɪtɪd] adj (hum sl) (crazy, eccentric) überspannt, überkandidelt (inf); (drunk) angeheitert (inf).

pizza ['pi:tsə] n Pizza f.

pizzeria [,pi:tsə'ri:ə] n Pizzeria f.

pizzle ['pɪzl] n Ochsenziemer m.

Pl abbr of **Place** Pl.

placard ['plækɑ:d] **1** n Plakat nt; (at demonstrations also) Transparent nt. **2** vt plakatieren. **to ~ a wall with slogans/posters** etc eine Wand mit Werbesprüchen/Plakaten bekleben; **the new beer is ~ed all over town** für das neue Bier wird in der ganzen Stadt Plakatwerbung gemacht.

placate [plə'keɪt] vt besänftigen, beschwichtigen.

placatory [plə'keɪtərɪ] adj beschwichtigend, besänftigend; gesture also versöhnlich.

place [pleɪs] **1** n **(a)** (in general) Platz m, Stelle f. **this is just the ~ for a picnic** das ist genau der richtige Platz or die richtige Stelle für ein Picknick; **this is the ~ where he was ...** hier or an dieser Stelle wurde er ...; **from ~ to ~** von einem Ort zum anderen; **in another ~** woanders; **some/any ~** irgendwo; **a poor man with no ~ to go** ein armer Mann, der nicht weiß wohin; **this is no ~ for you/children** das ist nichts or kein Platz für dich/für Kinder; **bed is the best ~ for him** im Bett ist er am besten aufgehoben; **we found a good ~ to watch the procession from** wir fanden einen Platz, von dem wir den Umzug gut sehen konnten; **there is no ~ for the unsuccessful in our society** für Erfolglose ist in unserer Gesellschaft kein Platz; **all over the ~** überall; **I can't be in two ~s at once!** ich kann doch nicht an zwei Stellen gleichzeitig sein; **it was the last ~ I expected to find him** da hätte ich ihn zuletzt or am wenigsten vermutet; **to laugh in the right ~s** an den richtigen Stellen lachen; **to go ~s** (travel) Ausflüge machen, herumreisen; **he's going ~s** (fig inf) er bringt's zu was (inf).

(b) (specific ~) Stätte f, Ort m. **~ of amusement** Vergnügungsstätte f; **~ of birth/residence** Geburtsort m/Wohnort m; **~ of business or work** Arbeitsstelle f.

(c) (on surface) Stelle f. **water is coming through in several ~s** an mehreren Stellen kommt Wasser durch.

(d) (district etc) Gegend f; (country) Land nt; (building) Gebäude nt; (town) Ort m. **there's nothing to do in the evenings in this ~** hier kann man abends nichts unternehmen; **this ~ is no longer big enough for the company** das Gebäude bietet für die Firma nicht mehr genügend Platz; **they're building a modern ~ out in the suburbs** sie bauen ein neues Gebäude am Stadtrand; **Sweden's a great ~** Schweden ist ein tolles Land.

(e) (house, home) Haus nt. **country ~** Gutshaus nt, Landsitz m; **a little ~ at the seaside** ein Häuschen nt am Meer; **come round to my ~ some time** besuch mich mal, komm doch mal vorbei; **let's go back to my ~** laß uns zu mir gehen; **I've never been to his ~** ich bin noch nie bei ihm gewesen; **where's your ~?** wo wohnst du?; **at Peter's ~** bei Peter; **your ~ or my ~?** (hum inf) gehen wir zu dir oder zu mir?

(f) (in street names) Platz m.

(g) (proper or natural ~) Platz m. **do the spoons have a special ~?** haben die Löffel einen bestimmten Platz?; **make sure the wire/screw is properly in ~** achten Sie darauf, daß der Draht/die Schraube richtig sitzt; **to be out of ~** in Unordnung sein; (one object) nicht an der richtigen Stelle; (fig) (remark) unangebracht or deplaziert sein; (person) fehl am Platze or deplaziert sein; **to look out of ~** fehl am Platz or deplaziert wirken; **to feel out of ~** sich fehl am Platz or deplaziert fühlen; **not a hair out of ~** tipptopp frisiert (inf); **she likes to have a ~ for everything and everything in its ~** sie hält sehr auf Ordnung und achtet darauf, daß alles an seinem Platz liegt; **everything in her drawing-room must be in its proper ~** in ihrem Wohnzimmer muß alles an seinem Platz sein; **your ~ is by his side** dein Platz ist an seiner Seite; **everything was in ~** alles war an seiner Stelle; **she still had each hair on her head perfectly in ~** jedes einzelne Haar auf ihrem Kopf war immer noch genau an der richtigen Stelle; **in the right/wrong ~** an der richtigen/falschen Stelle.

(h) (in book etc) Stelle f. **to find/keep one's ~** die richtige Stelle finden/sich (dat) die richtige Stelle markieren; **to lose one's ~** die Seite verblättern; (on page) die Zeile verlieren.

(i) (seat, at table, in team, school, hospital etc) Platz m; (in hospital also) Bettplatz m; (university ~) Studienplatz m; (job) Stelle f. **to lay an extra ~ for sb** ein zusätzliches Gedeck für jdn auflegen; **to take one's ~ (at table)** Platz nehmen; **take your ~s for a square dance!** Aufstellung zur Quadrille, bitte!; **~s for 500 workers** 500 Arbeitsplätze; **to give up/lose one's ~** (in a queue) jdm den Vortritt lassen/sich wieder hinten anstellen müssen.

(j) (social position etc) Rang m, Stelle f. **people in high ~s** Leute in hohen Positionen; **to know one's ~** wissen, was sich (für jdn) gehört; **of course I'm not criticizing your work, I know my ~!** (hum) ich kritisiere dich selbstverständlich nicht, das steht mir gar nicht zu; **it's not my ~ to comment/tell him what to do** es steht mir nicht zu, einen Kommentar abzugeben/ihm zu sagen, was er tun soll; **to keep or put sb in his ~** jdn in seine Schranken weisen; **that put him in his ~!** das hat ihn erst mal zum Schweigen gebracht, da hab' ich's ihm gezeigt (inf).

(k) (in exam, Sport etc) Platz m, Stelle f; (Math) Stelle f. **to work sth out to three decimal ~s** etw auf drei Stellen nach dem Komma berechnen; **P won, with Q in second ~** P hat gewonnen, an zweiter Stelle or auf dem zweiten Platz lag Q; **to win first ~** erste(r, s) sein.

(l) (Horseracing) Plazierung f. **to get a ~** eine Plazierung erreichen, einen der ersten drei Plätze belegen; **to back a horse for a ~** auf Platz wetten, eine Platzwette abschließen.

(m) in **~ of** statt (+gen); **if I were in your ~** (wenn ich) an Ihrer Stelle (wäre); **put yourself in my ~** versetzen Sie sich in meine Lage; **to give ~ to sth** einer Sache (dat) Platz machen; **to take ~** stattfinden; **to take the ~ of sb/sth** jdn/etw ersetzen, jds Platz or den Platz von jdm/etw einnehmen.

(n) in the **first/second/third ~** erstens/zweitens/drittens; **in the next ~** weiterhin, auch.

2 vt **(a)** (put) setzen, stellen, legen; person at table etc setzen; guards aufstellen; shot (with gun) anbringen; (Ftbl, Tennis) plazieren; troops in Stellung bringen; announcement (in paper) inserieren, plazieren; advertisement plazieren. **the magician ~d one hand over the other** der Zauberer legte eine Hand über die andere; **the dancer slowly ~d one foot forward** der Tänzer setzte langsam einen Fuß vor; **he ~d the cue-ball right behind the black** er setzte den Spielball direkt hinter den schwarzen Ball; **he ~d a knife at my throat** er setzte mir ein Messer an die Kehle; **she ~d a finger on her lips** sie legte den Finger auf die Lippen; **to ~ a matter before sb** jdm eine Angelegenheit vorlegen; **I shall ~ the matter in the hands of a lawyer** ich werde die Angelegenheit einem Rechtsanwalt übergeben; **to ~ a strain on sth** etw belasten; **to ~ too much emphasis on sth** auf etw (acc) zuviel Nachdruck legen; **that should be ~d first** das sollte an erster Stelle stehen; **where do you ~ love in your list of priorities?** an welcher Stelle steht die Liebe für dich?; **to ~ confidence/trust** etc in sb/sth Vertrauen in jdn/etw setzen; **historians ~ the book in the 5th century AD** Historiker datieren das Buch auf das 5. Jahrhundert; **in which school would you ~ this painting?** welcher Schule würden Sie dieses Gemälde zuordnen?; **I don't know, it's very difficult to ~** ich weiß es nicht, es ist sehr schwer einzuordnen.

(b) **to be ~d** (shop, town, house etc) liegen; **we are well ~d for the shops** was Einkaufsmöglichkeiten angeht, wohnen wir günstig; **the vase was dangerously ~d** die Vase stand an einer gefährlichen Stelle; **how are you ~d for time/money?** wie sieht es mit deiner Zeit/deinem Geld aus?; **it's six o'clock, how are you ~d?, can you stay on?** es ist sechs Uhr, wie sieht's mit deiner Zeit aus? kannst du noch bleiben?; **Liverpool are well ~d in the league** Liverpool liegt gut in der Tabelle; **they were well ~d to observe the whole battle** sie hatten einen günstigen Platz, von dem sie die ganze Schlacht verfolgen konnten; **we are well ~d now to finish the job** by next year wir stehen jetzt so gut da, daß wir die Arbeit im nächsten Jahr fertigstellen können; **with the extra staff we are better ~d now than we were last month** mit dem zusätzlichen Personal stehen wir jetzt besser da als vor einem Monat; **he is well ~d** (to get hold of things) er sitzt an der Quelle; **he is well ~d to get information** er kommt leicht an Informationen, er sitzt an der Quelle.

(c) *order* erteilen (*with sb* jdm); *contract* abschließen (*with sb* mit jdm); *phone call* anmelden; *money* deponieren; (*Comm*) *goods* absetzen. who did you ~ the computer type-setting with? wem haben Sie den Auftrag für den Computersatz erteilt?; this is the last time we ~ any work with you das ist das letzte Mal, daß wir Ihnen einen Auftrag erteilt haben; to ~ a book with a publisher's ein Buch bei einem Verleger unterbringen; to ~ money at sb's credit jdm eine Geldsumme gutschreiben; to ~ money at interest Geld zinsbringend anlegen; goods that are difficult to ~ (*Comm*) kaum absatzfähige Waren *pl*.

(d) (*in job etc*) unterbringen (*with* bei).

(e) (*in race, competition etc*) the German runner was ~d third der deutsche Läufer belegte den dritten Platz *or* wurde dritter; to be ~d (*in horse-race*) (*Brit*) sich plazieren, unter den ersten drei sein; (*US*) zweiter sein.

(f) (*remember, identify*) einordnen. I can't quite ~ him/his accent ich kann ihn/seinen Akzent nicht einordnen.

placebo [pləˈsiːbəʊ] *n* (*Med*) Placebo *nt*.

place: ~ card *n* Tischkarte *f*; ~ kick *n* Platztritt *m*; ~ mat *n* Set *nt*; ~-name *n* Ortsname *m*; ~-names (*as study*) Ortsnamenkunde, Toponymik (*spec*) *f*.

placenta [pləˈsentə] *n* Plazenta *f*.

placid [ˈplæsɪd] *adj* ruhig; *person also* gelassen; *disposition* friedfertig; *smile* still; *scene* beschaulich, friedvoll.

placidity [pləˈsɪdɪtɪ] *n see adj* Ruhe *f*; Gelassenheit *f*; Friedfertigkeit *f*; Stille *f*; Beschaulichkeit *f*.

placidly [ˈplæsɪdlɪ] *adv* ruhig, friedlich; *speak* bedächtig.

placket [ˈplækɪt] *n* Schlitz *m*.

plagiarism [ˈpleɪdʒərɪzəm] *n* Plagiat *nt*.

plagiarist [ˈpleɪdʒərɪst] *n* Plagiator(in *f*) *m*.

plagiarize [ˈpleɪdʒəraɪz] *vt book, idea* plagieren.

plague [pleɪg] **1** *n* (*Med*) Seuche *f*; (*Bibl, fig*) Plage *f*. the ~ die Pest; to avoid sb/sth like the ~ jdn/etw wie die Pest meiden; a ~ of reporters descended on the town eine Horde von Reportern suchte die Stadt heim; a ~ on him! (*old*) die Pest möge über ihn kommen (*old*)!

2 *vt* plagen. to ~ the life out of sb jdn (bis aufs Blut) quälen, jdm das Leben schwermachen; to be ~d by doubts von Zweifeln geplagt werden.

plaice [pleɪs] *n, no pl* Scholle *f*.

plaid [plæd] *n* Plaid *nt*. ~ *skirt* karierter Rock.

plain [pleɪn] **1** *adj* (+*er*) **(a)** klar; (*obvious also*) offensichtlich; *tracks, differences* deutlich. ~ to see offensichtlich; it's as ~ as the nose on your face (*inf*) das sieht doch ein Blinder (mit Krückstock) (*inf*); to make sth ~ to sb jdm etw klarmachen *or* klar zu verstehen geben; the reason is ~ to see der Grund ist leicht einzusehen; I'd like to make it quite ~ that ... ich möchte gern klarstellen, daß ...; do I/did I make myself *or* my meaning ~? ist das klar/habe ich mich klar ausgedrückt?; to make one's view *etc* ~ seine Meinung klar zum Ausdruck bringen.

(b) (*frank, straightforward*) *question, answer* klar; *truth* schlicht. ~ dealing Redlichkeit *f*; to be ~ with sb jdm gegenüber offen *or* direkt sein; in ~ language *or* English unmißverständlich, auf gut Deutsch; in ~ language *or* English, the answer is no um es klar *or* auf gut Deutsch zu sagen: die Antwort ist nein; it was ~ sailing es ging glatt (über die Bühne) (*inf*); it won't all be ~ sailing es wird gar nicht so einfach sein; from now on it'll be ~ sailing von jetzt an geht es ganz einfach.

(c) (*simple, with nothing added*) einfach; *dress, design also* schlicht; *living also* schlicht, bescheiden; *cooking, food also* (gut)bürgerlich; *cook* gutbürgerlich; *water* klar; *chocolate* bitter; *paper* unliniert; *colour* einheitlich. in a ~ colour einfarbig, uni *pred*; he's a ~ Mr er ist einfach Herr Sowieso; he used to be ~ Mr früher war er einfach *or* schlicht Herr X.

(d) (*sheer*) rein; *greed also* nackt; *nonsense etc also* völlig, blank (*inf*). it's just ~ commonsense das ist einfach gesunder Menschenverstand.

(e) (*not beautiful*) *person, appearance* nicht gerade ansprechend; *face also* alltäglich. she really is so ~ sie ist recht unansehnlich; ~ Jane unansehnliches Mädchen; she's a real ~ Jane sie ist nicht gerade hübsch *or* eine Schönheit.

2 *adv* **(a)** (*inf: simply, completely*) (ganz) einfach.

(b) I can't put it ~er than that deutlicher kann ich es nicht machen.

3 *n* **(a)** (*Geog*) Ebene *f*, Flachland *nt*. the ~s das Flachland, die Ebene; (*in North America*) die Prärie.

(b) (*Knitting*) rechte Masche.

plain clothes *npl* in ~ in Zivil.

plainclothesman [ˈpleɪnˌkləʊðzmən] *n, pl* -men [-mən] Polizist *m* in Zivil, Zivile(r) *m* (*inf*).

plainly [ˈpleɪnlɪ] *adv* **(a)** (*clearly*) eindeutig; *explain, remember, visible* klar, deutlich. **(b)** (*frankly*) offen, direkt. **(c)** (*simply, unsophisticatedly*) einfach.

plainness [ˈpleɪnnɪs] *n* **(a)** (*frankness, straightforwardness*) Direktheit, Offenheit *f*. **(b)** (*simplicity*) Einfachheit *f*. **(c)** (*lack of beauty*) Unansehnlichkeit *f*.

plainsman [ˈpleɪnzmən] *n, pl* -men [-mən] Flachländer *m*.

plain: ~song *n* Cantus planus *m*, Gregorianischer Gesang; ~ speaking *n* Offenheit *f*; some/a bit of ~ speaking ein paar offene Worte; ~-spoken *adj* offen, direkt; *criticism also* unverhohlen; to be ~-spoken sagen, was man denkt.

plaint [pleɪnt] *n* (*Poet*) (Weh)klage *f*.

plaintiff [ˈpleɪntɪf] *n* Kläger(in *f*) *m*.

plaintive [ˈpleɪntɪv] *adj* klagend; *voice etc also* wehleidig (*pej*); *song etc also* schwermütig, elegisch (*geh*); *look etc* leidend.

plaintively [ˈpleɪntɪvlɪ] *adv see adj*.

plait [plæt] **1** *n* Zopf *m*. she wears her hair in ~s sie trägt Zöpfe. **2** *vt* flechten.

plan [plæn] **1** *n* **(a)** (*scheme*) Plan *m*; (*Pol, Econ also*) Programm *nt*. ~ of action (*Mil, fig*) Aktionsprogramm *nt*; ~ of campaign (*Mil*) Strategie *f*; the ~ is to ... es ist geplant, zu ...; so, what's the

~? was ist also geplant?; the best ~ is to tell him first am besten sagt man es ihm zuerst; to make ~s (for sth) Pläne (für etw) machen, (etw) planen; to have great ~s for sb mit jdm Großes vorhaben, große Pläne mit jdm haben; have you any ~s for tonight? hast du (für) heute abend (schon) etwas vor?; according to ~ planmäßig, wie vorgesehen, programmgemäß.

(b) (*diagram*) Plan *m*; (*for novel etc also*) Entwurf *m*; (*for essay, speech*) Konzept *nt*; (*town* ~) Stadtplan *m*.

2 *vt* **(a)** (*arrange*) planen; *programme etc* erstellen, zusammenstellen, ausarbeiten.

(b) (*intend*) vorhaben. we weren't ~ning to wir hatten es nicht vor; this development was not ~ned diese Entwicklung war nicht eingeplant; it wasn't ~ned to happen that way so war das nicht geplant (gewesen).

(c) (*design*) planen; *buildings etc also* entwerfen.

3 *vi* planen. to ~ for sth sich etwas einplanen (+*acc*), rechnen mit; to ~ months ahead (auf) Monate vorausplanen; to ~ on sth mit etw rechnen; I'm not ~ning on staying ich wollte nicht bleiben, ich habe nicht vor zu bleiben.

♦ **plan out** *vt sep* in Einzelheiten planen.

plane¹ [pleɪn] *n* (*also* ~ tree) Platane *f*.

plane² **1** *adj* eben (*also* Math); *surface also* plan. **2** *n* **(a)** (*Math*) Ebene *f*. **(b)** (*fig*) Ebene *f*; (*intellectual also*) Niveau *nt*; (*social* ~) Stufe *f*. he lives on a different ~ er lebt in anderen Sphären. **(c)** (*tool*) Hobel *m*. **(d)** (*aeroplane*) Flugzeug *nt*. to go by ~/take a ~ fliegen. **3** *vt* hobeln. to ~ sth down etw abhobeln, etw glatt hobeln. **4** *vi* (*bird, glider, speedboat*) gleiten.

planeload [ˈpleɪnləʊd] *n* Flugzeugladung *f*.

planet [ˈplænɪt] *n* Planet *m*.

planetarium [ˌplænɪˈtɛərɪəm] *n* Planetarium *nt*.

planetary [ˈplænɪtərɪ] *adj* planetarisch, Planeten-; *travel* zu anderen Planeten.

plangent [ˈplændʒənt] *adj* (*liter*) getragen, klagend.

plank [plæŋk] **1** *n* (**a**) Brett *nt*; (*Naut*) Planke *f*; *see* **walk.** (**b**) (*Pol*) Schwerpunkt *m*. he stood for Parliament on a ~ of ... bei seiner Kandidatur fürs Parlament war ... sein Schwerpunkt *or* profilierte er sich besonders als ... **2** *vtr* (*inf*) *see* **plonk¹.**

planking [ˈplæŋkɪŋ] *n* Beplankung *f*, Planken *pl*.

plankton [ˈplæŋktən] *n* Plankton *nt*.

planned [plænd] *adj* geplant. ~ economy Planwirtschaft *f*; ~ obsolescence geplanter Verschleiß.

planner [ˈplænə] *n* Planer(in *f*) *m*.

planning [ˈplænɪŋ] *n* Planung *f*.

planning *in cpds* Planungs-; ~ permission Baugenehmigung *f*.

plant [plɑːnt] **1** *n* **(a)** (*Bot*) Pflanze *f*. rare/tropical ~s seltene/tropische Gewächse *pl*.

(b) (*no pl: equipment*) Anlagen *pl*; (*equipment and buildings*) Produktionsanlage *f*; (*no pl: US: of school, bank etc*) Einrichtungen *pl*; (*factory*) Werk *nt*. ~-hire Baumaschinenvermietung *f*; "heavy ~ crossing" „Baustellenverkehr".

(c) (*inf*) eingeschmuggelter Gegenstand *etc*, der jdn kompromittieren soll; (*frame-up*) Komplott *nt*.

2 *attr* Pflanzen-. ~ life Pflanzenwelt *f*.

3 *vt* **(a)** *plants, trees* pflanzen, ein- *or* anpflanzen; *field* bepflanzen. to ~ a field with turnips/wheat auf einem Feld Rüben anbauen *or* anpflanzen/Weizen anbauen *or* säen.

(b) (*place in position*) setzen; *bomb* legen; *kiss* drücken; *fist* pflanzen (*inf*); (*in the ground*) stick stecken; *flag* pflanzen. to ~ sth in sb's mind jdm etw in den Kopf setzen, jdn auf etw (*acc*) bringen; a policeman was ~ed at each entrance an jedem Eingang wurde ein Polizist aufgestellt *or* postiert; he ~ed himself right in the doorway er postierte sich genau im Eingang; he ~ed himself right in front of the fire (*inf*) er pflanzte sich genau vor dem Kamin auf (*inf*); she ~ed the children in the hall sie stellte die Kinder im Flur ab (*inf*); to ~ a punch on sb's chin (*inf*) jdm einen Kinnhaken geben.

(c) (*inf*) *incriminating evidence, stolen goods etc* manipulieren, praktizieren; (*in sb's car, home*) schmuggeln; *informer, spy etc* (ein)schleusen. to ~ sth on sb (*inf*) jdm etw unterjubeln (*inf*), jdm etw in die Tasche praktizieren.

♦ **plant out** *vt sep* auspflanzen.

plantain [ˈplæntɪn] *n* (*Bot*) **(a)** Plantainbanane *f*. **(b)** (*weed*) Wegerich *m*.

plantation [plænˈteɪʃən] *n* Plantage, Pflanzung *f*; (*of trees*) Schonung, Anpflanzung *f*.

planter [ˈplɑːntə] *n* Pflanzer(in *f*) *m*; (*plantation owner also*) Plantagenbesitzer(in *f*) *m*; (*machine*) Pflanzmaschine *f*; (*seed* ~) Sämaschine *f*; (*plantpot*) Übertopf *m*.

plaque [plæk] *n* **(a)** Plakette *f*; (*on building etc*) Tafel *f*. **(b)** (*Med*) Belag *m*; (*on teeth*) (Zahn)belag *m*.

plash [plæʃ] (*liter*) **1** *n* (*of water, rain*) Plätschern *nt*; (*of oars*) Platschen *nt*. **2** *vi* (*water, rain*) plätschern; (*oars*) platschen.

plasm [ˈplæzəm], **plasma** [ˈplæzmə] *n* Plasma *nt*.

plaster [ˈplɑːstə] **1** *n* **(a)** (*Build*) (Ver)putz *m*.

(b) (*Art, Med: also* ~ of Paris) Gips *m*; (*Med:* ~ cast) Gipsverband *m*. to have one's leg in ~ das Bein in Gips haben. **(c)** (*Brit: sticking* ~) Pflaster *nt*.

2 *vt* **(a)** (*Build*) *wall* verputzen. to ~ over a hole ein Loch zu- *or* vergipsen.

(b) (*inf: cover*) vollkleistern. to ~ a wall with posters, to ~ posters on a wall eine Wand mit Plakaten vollkleistern *or* bepflastern (*inf*); ~ed with mud schlammbedeckt; he ~ed down his wet hair with his hands er klatschte sich das nasse Haar mit den Händen an.

plaster: ~board *n* Gipskarton(platten *pl*) *m*; a sheet of ~board eine Gipskartonplatte; ~ cast *n* (*model, statue*) Gipsform *f*; (*footprint etc*) Gipsabdruck *m*; (*Med*) Gipsverband *m*.

plastered [ˈplɑːstəd] *adj pred* (*sl*) voll (*sl*). to get ~ sich volllaufen lassen (*sl*).

plasterer ['plɑ:stərəʳ] n Gipser, Stukkateur m.
plastic ['plæstɪk] **1** n Plastik nt or f, Plast m (esp DDR), Plaste f (DDR inf). ~s Kunststoffe, Plaste (esp DDR) pl.
  2 adj **(a)** (made of ~) Plastik-, aus Plastik, Plast- (esp DDR), aus Plast (esp DDR); (pej inf) food, person synthetisch; pub steril (fig), Plastik- (inf).
  (b) (flexible) formbar (also fig), modellierbar (also fig), plastisch. the ~ arts die gestaltenden Künste.
  (c) (Med) plastisch.
plastic: ~ **bag** n Plastiktüte f; ~ **bomb** n Plastikbombe f; ~ **explosive** n Plastiksprengstoff m.
plasticine ® ['plæstɪsi:n] n Plastilin nt.
plasticity [plæ'stɪsɪtɪ] n Formbarkeit, Modellierbarkeit f.
plastic: ~ **money** n (inf) Plastikgeld nt; ~s **industry** n Kunststoffindustrie f; ~ **surgeon** n plastischer Chirurg; ~ **surgery** n plastische Chirurgie; he had to have ~ surgery er mußte sich einer Gesichtsoperation unterziehen; she decided to have ~ surgery on her nose sie entschloß sich, eine Schönheitsoperation an ihrer Nase vornehmen zu lassen.
plate [pleɪt] **1** n **(a)** (flat dish, ~ful, collection ~) Teller m; (warming ~) Platte f. ~ **supper** (US) Tellergericht nt; a dinner at $1.00 a ~ (US) ein Essen für or zu $ 1.00 pro Person; cold ~ kalte Platte; to have sth handed to one on a ~ (fig inf) etw auf einem Tablett serviert bekommen (inf); to have a lot on one's ~ (fig inf) viel am Hals haben (inf).
  (b) (gold, silver) Silber und Gold nt; Tafelsilber nt; Tafelgold nt; (~d metal) vergoldetes/versilbertes Metall; (~d articles) (jewellery) Doublé nt, plattierte Ware, Doublee nt. a piece of ~ ein Stück or Gegenstand aus Gold/Silber etc; (~d article) ein vergoldeter/versilberter etc Gegenstand; it's only ~ es ist bloß or nur vergoldet/versilbert etc.
  (c) (Tech, Phot, Typ) Platte f; (name~, number ~) Schild nt.
  (d) (Racing) Cup, Pokal m; (race) Cup- or Pokalrennen nt.
  (e) (illustration) Tafel f.
  (f) (dental ~) (Gaumen)platte f.
  (g) (Baseball: home ~) Gummiplatte f.
  2 vt ship beplanken; (with armour-plating) panzern. **to** ~ (with gold/silver/nickel) vergolden/-silbern/-nickeln.
plateau ['plætəʊ] n, pl -s or -x (Geog) Plateau nt, Hochebene f. the rising prices have reached a ~ die Preise steigen nicht mehr und haben sich eingependelt.
plateful ['pleɪtfʊl] n Teller m. two ~s of salad zwei Teller (voll) Salat.
plate: ~ **glass** n Tafelglas nt; ~**holder** n (Phot) Plattenkassette f; ~**layer** n (Brit Rail) Streckenarbeiter m.
platelet ['pleɪtlɪt] n (Physiol) Plättchen nt.
plate rack n (Brit) Geschirrständer m.
platform ['plætfɔ:m] n **(a)** Plattform f; (stage) Podium nt, Bühne f. **(b)** (Rail) Bahnsteig m. **(c)** (Pol) Plattform f. **(d)** (inf: ~ shoe) Plateauschuh m.
platform: ~ **party** n Podiumsgäste pl; ~ **shoe** n Plateauschuh m; ~ **sole** n Plateausohle f; ~ **ticket** n Bahnsteigkarte f.
plating ['pleɪtɪŋ] n (act) Vergolden nt, Vergoldung f; Versilbern nt, Versilberung f; (material) Auflage f; (of copper also) Verkupferung f; (of nickel also) Vernickelung f; (on ship) Beplankung, Außenhaut f; (armour-~) Panzerung f.
platinum ['plætɪnəm] n Platin nt. a ~ **blonde** eine Platinblonde.
platitude ['plætɪtju:d] n Platitüde, Plattheit f.
platitudinous [ˌplætɪ'tju:dɪnəs] adj banal; speech also platt.
Platonic [plə'tɒnɪk] adj philosophy Platonisch. **p~** love, friend-ship platonisch.
platoon [plə'tu:n] n (Mil) Zug m.
platter ['plætəʳ] n Teller m; (wooden ~ also) Brett nt; (serving dish) Platte f; (sl: record) Platte f. to have sth handed to one on a silver ~ etw auf einem Tablett serviert bekommen (inf).
platypus ['plætɪpəs] n Schnabeltier nt.
plaudit ['plɔ:dɪt] n usu pl (liter) Ovation (usu pl), Huldigung f (geh). the headmaster's ~s made him blush die Lobeshymnen des Direktors ließen ihn erröten.
plausibility [ˌplɔ:zə'bɪlɪtɪ] n see adj Plausibilität f; Glaubwürdigkeit f; Geschicktheit f; überzeugende Art.
plausible ['plɔ:zəbl] adj plausibel; argument also einleuchtend; story also glaubhaft, glaubwürdig; excuse also glaubwürdig, glaubhaft; liar gut, geschickt; manner, person überzeugend.
plausibly ['plɔ:zəblɪ] adv plausibel; argue also einleuchtend; lie, present one's excuses geschickt; tell a story, act a part auf überzeugende Art, überzeugend.
play [pleɪ] **1** n **(a)** (amusement, gambling) Spiel nt. to be at ~ beim Spielen sein; to do/say sth in ~ etw aus Spaß tun/sagen; ~ on words Wortspiel nt; children at ~ spielende Kinder; children learn through ~ Kinder lernen beim Spiel; it's your ~ (turn) du bist dran; he lost £800 in a few hours' ~ er hat beim Spiel innerhalb von ein paar Stunden £ 800 verloren.
  (b) (Sport) Spiel nt. to abandon ~ das Spiel abbrechen; because of bad weather ~ was impossible es konnte wegen schlechten Wetters nicht gespielt werden; in a clever piece of ~, in a clever ~ (US) in einem klugen Schachzug; there was some exciting ~ towards the end gegen Ende gab es einige spannende (Spiel)szenen; to be in/out of ~ (ball) im Spiel/aus sein; to kick the ball out of ~ den Ball aus or ins Aus schießen.
  (c) (Tech, Mech) Spiel nt. 1 mm (of) ~ 1 mm Spiel.
  (d) (Theat) (Theater)stück nt; (Rad) Hörspiel nt; (TV) Fernsehspiel nt. the ~s of Shakespeare Shakespeares Dramen.
  (e) (fig: moving patterns) Spiel nt.
  (f) (fig phrases) to come into ~ ins Spiel kommen; to give full ~ to one's imagination seiner Phantasie (dat) freien Lauf lassen; the game allows the child's imagination full ~ das Spiel gestattet die freie Entfaltung der kindlichen Phantasie; to bring or call sth into ~ etw aufbieten or einsetzen; the ~ of opposing forces das Widerspiel der Kräfte; to make great ~ of sth viel Aufhebens or Trara (inf) um etw machen; to make a ~

for sb/sth sich um jdn bemühen/es auf etw (acc) abgesehen haben.
  2 vt **(a)** game, card, ball, position spielen; player aufstellen, einsetzen. to ~ sb (at a game) gegen jdn (ein Spiel) spielen; to ~ ball (with sb) (mit jdm) mitspielen; to ~ shop (Kauf-manns)laden spielen, Kaufmann spielen; to ~ a joke on sb jdm einen Streich spielen; to ~ a mean/dirty trick on sb jdn auf gemeine/schmutzige Art hereinlegen; to ~ the company game sich in der Firma profilieren wollen; they're all ~ing the game die machen doch alle mit; see card¹, game¹, market, hell etc.
  (b) (Theat, fig) part, play spielen; (perform in) town spielen in (+dat). to ~ the fool den Clown spielen, herumblödeln (inf).
  (c) instrument, record, tune spielen. to ~ the piano Klavier spielen; to ~ sth through/over etw durchspielen.
  (d) (direct) lights, jet of water richten.
  (e) (Fishing) drillen.
  3 vi **(a)** spielen. to go out to ~ rausgehen und spielen; run away and ~! geh spielen!; can Johnny come out to ~? darf Johnny zum Spielen rauskommen?; to ~ with oneself (euph) an sich (dat) herumspielen (euph); to ~ with the idea of doing sth mit dem Gedanken spielen, etw zu tun; we don't have much time/money to ~ with wir haben zeitlich/finanziell nicht viel Spielraum; we don't have that many alternatives to ~ with so viele Alternativen haben wir nicht zur Verfügung; he wouldn't ~ (fig inf) er wollte nicht mitspielen (inf).
  (b) (Sport, at game, gamble) spielen. to ~ at mothers and fathers/cowboys and Indians Vater und Mutter/Cowboy und Indianer spielen; to ~ at being a fireman Feuerwehrmann spielen; he was ~ing at being angry/the jealous lover seine Wut war gespielt/er spielte den eifersüchtigen Liebhaber; ~! An-spiel!; he's just ~ing at it er tut nur so; what are you ~ing at? (inf) was soll (denn) das? (inf); to ~ for money um Geld spielen; to ~ for time (fig) Zeit gewinnen wollen; to ~ into sb's hands (fig) jdm in die Hände spielen.
  (c) (Mus) spielen. to ~ to sb jdm vorspielen.
  (d) (move about, form patterns: sun, light, water) spielen; (fountain) tanzen. a smile ~ed on his lips ein Lächeln spielte um seine Lippen; the firemen's hoses ~ed on the flames die Schläuche der Feuerwehrmänner waren auf die Flammen gerichtet; the searchlights ~ed over the roofs die Suchschein-werfer strichen über die Dächer.
  (e) (Theat) (act) spielen; (be performed) gespielt werden.
  (f) (Sport: ground, pitch) sich bespielen lassen. the pitch ~s well/badly auf dem Platz spielt es sich gut/schlecht.
♦**play about** or **around** vi spielen. I wish he'd stop ~ing ~ and settle down to a steady job ich wollte, er würde mit dem stän-digen Hin und Her aufhören und sich eine feste Arbeit suchen; to ~ ~ with sth/an idea mit etw (herum)spielen/mit einer Idee spielen; to ~ ~ with sb/sb's feelings mit jdm/jds Gefühlen spielen.
♦**play along 1** vi mitspielen. he ~ed ~ with the system er arrangierte sich mit dem System; to ~ ~ with a suggestion auf einen Vorschlag eingehen/scheinbar eingehen.
  2 vt sep hinters Licht führen, ein falsches Spiel spielen mit; (in order to gain time) hinhalten.
♦**play back** vt sep tape recording abspielen. the conversation was ~ed ~ to us man spielte uns (dat) das Gespräch vor.
♦**play down** vt sep runterspielen (inf).
♦**play in** vt sep (dead inf) musikalisch begrüßen.
♦**play off 1** vt sep to ~ X ~ against Y X gegen Y ausspielen; he was ~ing them ~ against each other er spielte sie gegeneinander aus. **2** vi (Sport) um die Entscheidung spielen.
♦**play on 1** vi weiterspielen.
  2 vi +prep obj (also ~ upon) (exploit) sb's fears, feelings, good nature geschickt ausnutzen; (emphasize) difficulties, similarities herausstreichen. the hours of waiting ~ed ~ my nerves das stundenlange Warten zermürbte mich; the author is ~ing ~ words der Autor macht Wortspiele/ein Wortspiel.
♦**play out** vt sep **(a)** (Theat) scene (enact) darstellen; (finish acting) zu Ende spielen (also fig). their romance was ~ed ~ against a background of civil war ihre Romanze spielte sich vor dem Hintergrund des Bürgerkrieges ab.
  (b) (esp pass: use up) mine ausbeuten. to ~ ~ (the) time die Zeit herumbringen; (Sport also) auf Zeit spielen, Zeit schinden (pej); a ~ed-~ joke (inf) ein abgedroschener Witz; a ~ed-~ theory (inf) eine überstrapazierte Theorie; his talent is pretty well ~ed ~ (inf) sein Talent ist einigermaßen or ganz schön (inf) verbraucht; I was completely ~ed ~ after the game (inf) nach dem Spiel war ich völlig geschafft (inf).
  (c) (Mus: accompany) mit Musik hinausgeleiten. the organ ~ed the congregation ~ das Spiel der Orgel geleitete die Gemeinde hinaus.
♦**play through** vi +prep obj a few bars etw durchspielen.
♦**play up 1** vi **(a)** (play louder) lauter spielen.
  (b) (Sport inf: play better) aufdrehen (inf), (richtig) loslegen (inf), aufspielen (Sport sl). ~ ~! vor!, ran!
  (c) (Brit inf: cause trouble: car, injury, child) Schwierig-keiten machen, verrückt spielen (inf).
  2 vt sep (inf) **(a)** (cause trouble to) to ~ sb ~ jdm Schwierig-keiten machen; (child, injury also) jdn piesacken (inf).
  (b) (exaggerate) hochspielen.
♦**play upon** vi +prep obj see **play on 2**.
playable ['pleɪəbl] adj pitch bespielbar; ball zu spielen pred.
play: ~**-act** vi (fig inf) schauspielern; (fig also) Theater spielen; ~**-acting** n (dated Theat) Schauspielerei f; (fig also) Theater(spiel) nt; ~**-actor** n (dated Theat) Mime (old, geh), Schauspieler (also fig) m; ~**back** n (switch, recording) Wieder-gabe f; (playing-back also) Abspielen nt; the producer asked for a ~back der Produzent bat um eine Wiedergabe or ein Playback; they listened to the ~back of their conversation

sie hörten sich (*dat*) die Aufnahme ihres Gespräches an; ~**bill** *n* (*poster*) Theaterplakat *nt*; (*US: programme*) Theaterprogramm *nt*; ~**boy** *n* Playboy *m*.

player ['pleɪə'] *n* (*Sport, Mus*) Spieler(in *f*) *m*; (*Theat*) Schauspieler(in *f*) *m*; (*record* ~) Plattenspieler *m*.

player-piano ['pleɪə'pjɑːnəʊ] *n* automatisches Klavier.

playfellow ['pleɪfeləʊ] *n* Spielkamerad(in *f*) *m*.

playful ['pleɪfʊl] *adj* neckisch; *remark, smile, look also* schelmisch; *child, animal* verspielt, munter. **the dog is in a** ~ **mood/just being** ~ der Hund will spielen/spielt nur; **the boss is in a** ~ **mood today** der Chef ist heute zu Späßen aufgelegt; **to do sth in a** ~ **way** etw zum Scherz or aus Spaß tun.

playfully ['pleɪfəlɪ] *adv* neckisch; *remark, smile, look also* schelmisch. **to do/say sth** ~ etw zum Scherz tun/sagen.

playfulness ['pleɪfʊlnɪs] *n* (*of child, animal*) Verspieltheit *f*; (*of adult*) Ausgelassenheit, Lustigkeit *f*. **there was a touch of** ~ **in his manner as he replied** in der Art, wie er antwortete, lag etwas leicht Neckisches or Schelmisches.

play: ~**goer** *n* Theaterbesucher(in *f*) *m*; ~**ground** *n* Spielplatz *m*; (*Sch*) (Schul)hof *m*; (*fig*) Tummelplatz *m*, Spielwiese *f*; ~**group** *n* Spielgruppe *f*; ~**house** *n* (a) (*children's house*) Spielhaus *nt*; (*US: doll's house*) Puppenstube *f*; (b) (*Theat*) Schaubühne *f* (*dated*), Schauspielhaus *nt*.

playing ['pleɪɪŋ]: ~ **card** *n* Spielkarte *f*; ~ **field** *n* Sportplatz *m*; **the school** ~ **fields** der Schulsportplatz.

playlet ['pleɪlɪt] *n* Spiel, Stück *nt*.

play: ~**mate** *n see* ~**fellow**; ~**off** *n* Entscheidungsspiel *nt*; (*extra time*) Verlängerung *f*; ~**pen** *n* Laufstall *m*, Laufgitter *nt*; ~**room** *n* Spielzimmer *nt*; ~ **school** *n* Kindergarten *m*; ~**thing** *n* (*lit, fig*) Spielzeug *nt*; ~**things** *pl* Spielzeug *nt*, Spielsachen *pl*; ~**time** *n* Zeit *f* zum Spielen; (*Sch*) große Pause.

playwright ['pleɪraɪt] *n* Dramatiker(in *f*) *m*; (*contemporary also*) Stückeschreiber(in *f*) *m*.

plaza ['plɑːzə] *n* Piazza *f*; (*US: shopping complex*) Einkaufszentrum or -center *nt*.

plea [pliː] *n* (a) Bitte *f*; (*general appeal*) Appell *m*. **to make a** ~ **for sth** zu etw aufrufen; **to make a** ~ **for mercy/leniency** um Gnade/Milde bitten.
  (b) (*excuse*) Begründung *f*. **on the** ~ **of illness/ill health** aus Krankheitsgründen/aus gesundheitlichen Gründen.
  (c) (*Jur*) Plädoyer *nt*. **to enter a** ~ **of guilty/not guilty** ein Geständnis ablegen/seine Unschuld erklären; **to enter a** ~ **of insanity** Zurechnungsunfähigkeit geltend machen; **he put forward** or **made a** ~ **of self-defence** er machte Notwehr geltend, er berief sich auf Notwehr.

plead [pliːd] *pret, ptp* ~**ed** or (*Scot, US*) **pled** 1 *vt* (a) (*argue*) vertreten; **to** ~ **sb's case, to** ~ **the case for sb** (*Jur*) jdn vertreten; **to** ~ **the case for the defence** (*Jur*) die Verteidigung vertreten; **to** ~ **the case for sth** (*fig*) sich für etw einsetzen; **to** ~ **sb's cause** (*fig*) jds Sache vertreten, für jds Sache eintreten.
  (b) (*as excuse*) *ignorance, insanity* sich berufen auf (+*acc*).
  2 *vi* (a) (*beg*) bitten, nachsuchen (*for* um). **to** ~ **with sb to do sth** jdn bitten or ersuchen (*geh*), etw zu tun; **to** ~ **with sb for sth** (*beg*) jdn um etw bitten or ersuchen (*geh*).
  (b) (*Jur*) (*counsel*) das Plädoyer halten. **to** ~ **guilty/not guilty** sich schuldig/nicht schuldig bekennen; **how do you** ~? bekennen Sie sich schuldig?; **to** ~ **for sth** (*fig*) für etw plädieren.

pleading ['pliːdɪŋ] 1 *n* Bitten *nt*; (*Jur*) Plädoyer *nt*. 2 *adj look, voice* flehend.

pleadingly ['pliːdɪŋlɪ] *adv* flehend.

pleasant ['pleznt] *adj* angenehm; *surprise also, news* erfreulich; *person also, face* nett; *manner also, smile* freundlich. **to make oneself** ~ **to sb** jdn ein wenig unterhalten.

pleasantly ['plezntlɪ] *adv* angenehm; *smile, greet, speak etc* freundlich. ~ **decorated** nett or hübsch eingerichtet.

pleasantness ['plezntnɪs] *n* Freundlichkeit *f*; (*of news, surprise*) Erfreulichkeit *f*. **the** ~ **of her manner/face** ihre freundliche Art/ihr nettes Gesicht.

pleasantry ['plezntrɪ] *n* (*joking remark*) Scherz *m*; (*polite remark*) Höflichkeit, Nettigkeit *f*.

pleasa(u)nce ['plezəns] *n* (*old*) Lustgarten *m* (*old*).

please [pliːz] 1 *interj* bitte. (**yes,**) ~ (*acceptance*) (ja,) bitte; (*enthusiastic*) oh ja, gerne; ~ **pass the salt, pass the salt,** ~ würden Sie mir bitte das Salz reichen?; **may I?** — ~ **do!** darf ich? — aber bitte or bitte sehr!
  2 *vi* (a) **if you** ~ (*form: in request*) wenn ich darum bitten darf; **do it now, if you** ~ (*angrily*) aber sofort, wenn es recht ist or wenn ich bitten darf!; **and then, if you** ~**, he tried** ... und dann, stell dir vor, versuchte er ...; (**just**) **as you** ~ ganz wie du willst, wie es Ihnen beliebt (*form*); **to do as one** ~**s** machen or tun, was man will, machen or tun, was einem gefällt.
  (b) (*cause satisfaction*) gefallen. **anxious** or **eager to** ~ darum bemüht, alles richtig zu machen; (*girls*) darum bemüht, jeden Wunsch zu erfüllen; **a gift that is sure to** ~ ein Geschenk, das sicher gefällt or ankommt; **we aim to** ~ wir wollen, daß Sie zufrieden sind.
  3 *vt* (a) (*give pleasure to*) eine Freude machen (+*dat*); (*satisfy*) zufriedenstellen; (*do as sb wants*) gefallen (+*dat*), gefällig sein (+*dat*). **just to** ~ **you** nur dir zuliebe; **it** ~**s me to see him so happy** es freut mich, daß er so glücklich ist; **well do it then if it** ~**s you** tu's doch, wenn es dir Spaß macht; **music that** ~**s the ear** Musik, die das Ohr erfreut; **you can't** ~ **everybody** man kann es nicht allen recht machen; **there's no pleasing him** er ist nie zufrieden; **he is easily** ~**d** or **easy to** ~ er ist leicht zufriedenzustellen; (*iro*) er ist ein bescheidener Mensch; **to be hard to** ~ schwer zufriedenzustellen sein; **the joke** ~**d him** der Witz hat ihm gefallen; **I was only too** ~**d to help** es war mir wirklich eine Freude zu helfen; *see* **pleased**.
  (b) (*iro, form: be the will of*) belieben (+*dat*) (*iro, form*). **it** ~**d him to order that** ... er beliebte anzuordnen, daß ... (*form*); **may**

it ~ **Your Honour** (*Jur*) mit Erlaubnis des Herrn Vorsitzenden; **if it** ~**s God** wenn es Gott gefällt; ~ **God he will recover** gebe Gott, daß er wieder gesund wird; **he will return safely,** ~ **God!** er wird wohlbehalten zurückkehren, das gebe Gott!
  4 *vr* **to** ~ **oneself** tun, was einem gefällt; ~ **yourself!** wie Sie wollen!; **you can** ~ **yourself about where you sit** es ist Ihnen überlassen, wo Sie sitzen; **he has only himself to** ~ er braucht auf keinen Menschen irgendwelche Rücksichten zu nehmen.
  5 *n* **Bitte** *nt*. **without so much as a** ~ ohne auch nur „bitte" zu sagen.

pleased [pliːzd] *adj* (*happy*) erfreut; (*satisfied*) zufrieden. **to be** ~ (**about sth**) sich (über etw *acc*) freuen; **I'm** ~ **to hear that** ... es freut mich zu hören, daß ...; ~ **to meet you** angenehm (*form*), freut mich; **I'm** ~ **to be able to announce that** ... ich freue mich, mitteilen zu können, daß ...; **to be** ~ **at sth** über etw (*acc*) erfreut sein; **to be** ~ **with sb/sth** mit jdm/etw zufrieden sein; ~ **with oneself** mit sich selbst zufrieden, selbstgefällig (*pej*); **that's nothing to be** ~ **about** das ist aber gar nicht gut.

pleasing ['pliːzɪŋ] *adj* angenehm. **to be** ~ **to the eye/ear** ein recht netter Anblick sein/sich recht angenehm anhören.

pleasingly ['pliːzɪŋlɪ] *adv* angenehm. **a** ~ **laid-out garden** ein hübsch angelegter Garten.

pleasurable ['pleʒərəbl] *adj* angenehm; *anticipation* freudig.

pleasure ['pleʒə'] *n* (a) (*satisfaction, happiness*) Freude *f*. **it's a** ~, (**my**) ~ gern (geschehen)!; **with** ~ sehr gerne, mit Vergnügen (*form*); **the** ~ **is mine** (*form*) es war mir ein Vergnügen (*form*); **it gives me great** ~ **to be here** (*form*) es ist mir eine große Freude, hierzusein; **I have much** ~ **in informing you that** ... ich freue mich (sehr), Ihnen mitteilen zu können, daß ...; **it would give me great** ~ **to** ... es wäre mir ein Vergnügen, zu ...; **if it gives you** ~ wenn es dir Vergnügen bereitet; **to have the** ~ **of doing sth** das Vergnügen haben, etw zu tun; **he finds** ~ **in books** er hat Freude an Büchern; **he gets a lot of** ~ **out of his hobby** er hat viel Freude *or* Spaß an seinem Hobby; **he seems to take** ~ **in annoying me** es scheint ihm Vergnügen zu bereiten, mich zu ärgern; **but don't think I'll take** ~ **in it** aber glaub nicht, daß mir das Spaß macht; **may I have the** ~? (*form*) darf ich (um den nächsten Tanz) bitten? (*form*); **will you do me the** ~ **of dining with me?** (*form*) machen Sie mir das Vergnügen, mit mir zu speisen? (*form*); **Mrs X requests the** ~ **of Mr Y's company** (*form*) Frau X gibt sich die Ehre, Herrn Y einzuladen (*form*); **Mr Y has great** ~ **in accepting** ... (*form*) Herr Y nimmt ... mit dem größten Vergnügen an (*form*).
  (b) (*amusement*) Vergnügen *nt*. **is it business or** ~? (ist es) geschäftlich oder zum Vergnügen?
  (c) (*source of* ~) Vergnügen *nt*. **he's a** ~ **to teach** es ist ein Vergnügen, ihn zu unterrichten; **the** ~**s of country life** die Freuden des Landlebens; **all the** ~**s of London** alle Vergnügungen Londons.
  (d) (*iro, form: will*) Wunsch *m*. **at** (**one's**) ~ nach Belieben, nach Gutdünken; **to await sb's** ~ abwarten, was jd zu tun geruht; **during Her Majesty's** ~ (*Jur*) auf unbestimmte Zeit.

pleasure *in cpds* Vergnügungs-; ~ **boat** *n* (a) (*steamer*) Vergnügungsdampfer *m* or -schiff *nt*, Ausflugsdampfer *m* or -schiff *nt*; (b) (*yacht etc*) Hobbyboot *nt*; ~**craft** *n* Hobbyboot *nt*; ~**cruise** *n* Vergnügungsfahrt, Kreuzfahrt *f*; ~ **ground** *n* Parkanlage *f*; (*fairground*) Vergnügungspark *m*; ~**loving** *adj* lebenslustig, leichtlebig (*pej*); ~ **principle** *n* (*Psych*) Lustprinzip *nt*; ~**seeking** *adj* vergnügungssüchtig; ~**trip** *n* Vergnügungsausflug *m*, Vergnügungsreise, Lustfahrt (*dated*) *f*.

pleat [pliːt] 1 *n* Falte *f*. 2 *vt* fälteln.

pleated ['pliːtɪd] *adj* gefältelt, Falten-. ~ **skirt** Faltenrock *m*.

pleb [pleb] *n* (*pej inf*) Plebejer(in *f*) (*pej*), Prolet(in *f*) (*pej inf*) *m*. **the** ~**s** die Proleten *pl* (*pej inf*), der Plebs (*pej*).

plebby ['plebɪ] *adj* (*pej inf*) primitiv.

plebeian [plɪ'biːən] 1 *adj* plebejisch. 2 *n* Plebejer(in *f*) *m*.

plebiscite ['plebɪsɪt] *n* Plebiszit *nt*, Volksentscheid *m*.

plectrum ['plektrəm] *n* Plektron, Plektrum *nt*.

pled [pled] (*US, Scot*) *pret, ptp of* **plead**.

pledge [pledʒ] 1 *n* (a) (*in pawnshop, of love*) Pfand *nt*; (*promise*) Versprechen *nt*, Zusicherung *f*. **I give you my** ~ ich gebe dir mein Wort; **we have given them a** ~ **of aid** wir haben versprochen, ihnen zu helfen; **as a** ~ **of** als Zeichen (+*gen*); **under** (**the**) ~ **of secrecy** unter dem Siegel der Verschwiegenheit; **election** ~**s** Wahlversprechen *pl*; **to sign** or **take the** ~ (*lit*) sich schriftlich zur Abstinenz verpflichten; (*hum inf*) dem Alkohol abschwören (*usu hum*).
  (b) (*form: toast*) Toast (*form*), Trinkspruch *m*. **to drink a** ~ **to sb/sth** einen Toast *etc* auf jdn/etw ausbringen.
  2 *vt* (a) (*give as security, pawn*) verpfänden.
  (b) (*promise*) versprechen, zusichern. **to** ~ **one's word** sein Wort geben or verpfänden; **to** ~ **support for sb/sth** jdm/einer Sache seine Unterstützung zusichern; **I am** ~**d to secrecy** ich bin zum Schweigen verpflichtet; **he** ~**d me to secrecy** er verpflichtete mich zum Schweigen; **to** ~ (**one's**) **allegiance to sb/sth** jdm/einer Sache Treue schwören or geloben.
  (c) (*form: toast*) einen Toast (*form*) or Trinkspruch ausbringen auf (+*acc*).
  3 *vr* **to** ~ **oneself to do sth** geloben or sich verpflichten, etw zu tun.

Pleiades ['plaɪədiːz] *npl* Plejaden *pl*.

Pleistocene ['plaɪstəʊsiːn] 1 *n* Pleistozän *nt*. 2 *adj* pleistozän, Pleistozän-.

plenary ['pliːnərɪ] *adj* Plenar-, Voll-. ~ **session** Plenarsitzung, Vollversammlung *f*; ~ **powers** unbeschränkte Vollmachten *pl*.

plenipotentiary [ˌplenɪpə'tenʃərɪ] 1 *n* (General)bevollmächtigte(r) *mf*. 2 *adj* *ambassador* (general)bevollmächtigt. ~ **powers** Generalvollmachten *pl*.

plenitude ['plenɪtjuːd] *n* (*liter*) Fülle *f*.

plenteous ['plentɪəs] *adj* (*liter*) *see* **plentiful**.

plentiful ['plentɪful] adj reichlich; *commodities, gold, minerals etc* reichlich or im Überfluß vorhanden; *hair* voll. **eggs are now ~** Eier sind jetzt reichlich or im Überfluß zu haben; **to be in ~ supply** reichlich or im Überfluß vorhanden sein.

plentifully ['plentɪfəlɪ] adv reichlich.

plenty ['plentɪ] **1** n (a) eine Menge. **land of ~** Land des Überflusses; **times of ~** Zeiten des Überflusses, fette Jahre (*Bibl pl*; **in ~** im Überfluß; **three kilos will be ~** drei Kilo sind reichlich; **there's ~ here for six** es gibt mehr als genug für sechs; **that's ~, thanks!** danke, das ist reichlich; **you've already had ~** du hast schon reichlich gehabt; **I met him once, and that was ~!** ich habe ihn nur einmal getroffen, und das hat mir gereicht!; **have I got problems?** I've got ~ ob ich Probleme habe? mehr als genug!; **there's ~ more where that came from** davon gibt es genug; **take ~** nimm dir or bedien dich reichlich; **there are still ~ left** es sind immer noch eine ganze Menge da.

(b) ~ of viel, eine Menge; ~ of time/milk/eggs/reasons viel or eine Menge Zeit/Milch/viele or eine Menge Eier/Gründe; **there is no longer ~ of oil** Öl ist nicht mehr im Überfluß vorhanden; **he's certainly got ~ of nerve** der hat vielleicht Nerven! (*inf*); **a country with ~ of natural resources** ein Land mit umfangreichen Bodenschätzen; **has everyone got ~ of potatoes?** hat jeder reichlich Kartoffeln?; **there will be ~ of things to drink** es gibt dort ausreichend zu trinken; **he had been given ~ of warning** er ist genügend oft gewarnt worden; **we arrived in ~ of time to get a good seat** wir kamen so rechtzeitig, daß wir einen guten Platz kriegten; **don't worry, there's ~ of time** keine Angst, es ist noch genug or viel Zeit; **take ~ of exercise** Sie müssen viel Sport treiben.

2 adj (*US inf*) reichlich. ~ **bananas** reichlich Bananen.

3 adv (*esp US inf*) ~ **big (enough)** groß genug; **he's ~ mean** er ist ziemlich brutal; **she was ~ rude to her** er war ziemlich grob zu ihr; **it rained ~** es hat viel geregnet; **sure, I like it ~** sicher, ich mag das sehr.

plenum ['pliːnəm] n Plenum nt, Vollversammlung f.

pleonasm ['pliːənæzəm] n Pleonasmus m.

pleonastic [pliːə'næstɪk] adj pleonastisch.

plethora ['pleθərə] n (*form*) Fülle f.

pleurisy ['plʊərɪsɪ] n Brustfellentzündung, Pleuritis (*spec*) f.

plexus ['pleksəs] n Plexus m; (*of nerves also*) Nervengeflecht nt; (*of blood vessels also*) Gefäßgeflecht nt.

pliability [plaɪə'bɪlɪtɪ] n see adj Biegsamkeit f; Geschmeidigkeit f; Formbarkeit f; Fügsamkeit f.

pliable ['plaɪəbl], **pliant** ['plaɪənt] adj biegsam; *leather* geschmeidig; *character, mind, person* formbar; (*docile*) fügsam.

plied [plaɪd] pret, ptp of ply².

pliers ['plaɪəz] npl (also pair of ~) (Kombi)zange f.

plight¹ [plaɪt] vt (*liter*) **to ~ one's word** sein (Ehren)wort geben; **to ~ one's troth (to sb)** (*old, hum*) (jdm) die Ehe versprechen.

plight² n Not f, Elend nt; (*of currency, economy etc*) Verfall m. **to be in a sad or sorry ~** in einem traurigen Zustand sein; **the country's economic ~** die wirtschaftliche Misere des Landes.

plimsoll ['plɪmsəl] n (*Brit*) Turnschuh m.

Plimsoll line or **mark** n Höchstlademarke f.

plinth [plɪnθ] n Sockel m, Fußplatte, Plinthe (*spec*) f.

Pliocene ['plaɪəʊsiːn] **1** n Pliozän nt. **2** adj pliozän.

PLO abbr of **Palestinian Liberation Organization** PLO f.

plod [plɒd] **1** n Trott, Zockeltrab (*inf*) m. **a steady ~** ein gleichmäßiger Trott; **it's a long ~ to the village** es ist ein langer beschwerlicher Weg bis zum Dorf.

2 vi (a) trotten, zockeln (*inf*). **to ~ up a hill** einen Hügel hinaufstapfen; **to ~ along or on** weiterstapfen.

(b) (*fig*: in *work etc*) sich abplagen or abplagen or herumquälen. **to ~ away at sth** sich mit etw abmühen *etc*; **to ~ on** sich weiterkämpfen, sich durchquälen.

plodder ['plɒdə'] n zäher Arbeiter, zähe Arbeiterin.

plodding ['plɒdɪŋ] adj *walk* schwerfällig, mühsam; *student, worker* hart arbeitend attr; *research* langwierig, mühsam.

plonk¹ [plɒŋk] **1** n Bums m. **it fell with a ~ to the floor** es fiel mit einem Bums or einem dumpfen Geräusch auf den Boden.

2 adv fall, land bums, peng. ~ **in the middle** genau in die/in der Mitte.

3 vt (*inf: also* ~ **down**) (*drop, put down*) hinwerfen, hinschmeißen (*inf*); (*bang down*) hinknallen (*inf*), hinhauen (*inf*). **he ~ed a kiss on her cheek** er drückte ihr einen Kuß auf die Wange; **to ~ oneself (down)** sich hinwerfen, sich hinschmeißen (*inf*); **he ~ed himself down in a chair** er warf sich in einen Sessel, er ließ sich in einen Sessel fallen; **just ~ yourself down somewhere** hau dich einfach irgendwo hin (*inf*).

plonk² n (*Brit inf: wine*) (billiger) Wein, Gesöff nt (*hum, pej*).

plop [plɒp] **1** n Plumps m; (*in water*) Platsch m.

2 vi **it fell** or **went ~ into the water** es fiel mit einem Platsch ins Wasser.

3 vi (a) (*make a plopping sound*) platschen.

(b) (*inf: fall*) plumpsen (*inf*). **she ~ped into a chair** sie ließ sich in einen Sessel plumpsen (*inf*) or fallen.

4 vt (*inf*) hinwerfen, hinschmeißen (*inf*), fallen lassen.

plosive ['pləʊsɪv] **1** adj Verschluß-, explosiv. **2** n Verschlußlaut, Explosivlaut m, Explosivum nt (*spec*).

plot [plɒt] **1** n (a) (*Agr*) Stück nt Land; (*bed: in garden*) Beet nt; (*building* ~) Grundstück nt; (*allotment*) Parzelle f; (*in graveyard*) Grabstelle f. **a ~ of land** ein Stück nt Land; **a ~ of lettuces** ein Salatbeet nt; (*larger*) ein Salatfeld nt.

(b) (*US: diagram, chart*) (*of estate*) Plan m; (*of building*) Grundriß m.

(c) (*conspiracy*) Verschwörung f, Komplott nt; see **thicken**.

(d) (*Liter, Theat*) Handlung f, Plot m (*spec*).

2 vt (a) (*plan*) planen, aushecken (*inf*). **what are you ~ting now?** was heckst du nun schon wieder aus?; **they ~ted to kill him** sie schmiedeten ein Mordkomplott gegen ihn.

(b) *position, course* feststellen; (*draw on map*) einzeichnen; (*Math, Med*) *curve* aufzeichnen.

3 vi sich verschwören. **to ~ against sb** sich gegen jdn verschwören, gegen jdn ein Komplott schmieden.

plotter ['plɒtə'] n Verschwörer(in f) m.

plotting ['plɒtɪŋ] n Verschwörertum nt.

plough, (US) plow [plaʊ] **1** n Pflug m. **the P~** (*Astron*) der Wagen; **under the ~** unter den Pflug; **to put one's hand to the ~** (*fig*) sich in die Riemen legen.

2 vt (a) pflügen, umpflügen. **to ~ a lonely furrow** (*fig*) allein auf weiter Flur pflügen.

(b) (*Brit Univ dated sl*) reinreißen (*inf*), durchfallen lassen.

3 vi (a) pflügen.

(b) (*Brit Univ dated sl*) durchrasseln (*inf*).

♦ **plough back** vt sep (*Agr*) unterpflügen; (*Comm*) *profits* wieder (hinein)stecken, reinvestieren (*into* + *acc*).

♦ **plough in** vt sep *manure, crop etc* unterpflügen.

♦ **plough through** vti + prep obj (a) **the ship ~ed (its way) ~ the heavy seas** das Schiff pflügte sich durch die schwere See; **we had to ~ (our way) ~ knee-deep snow** wir mußten uns durch knietiefen Schnee kämpfen; **the car ~ed straight ~ our garden fence** der Wagen brach geradewegs durch unseren Gartenzaun.

(b) (*inf*) **to ~ (one's way) ~ a novel** *etc* sich durch einen Roman *etc* durcharbeiten (*inf*) or hindurchquälen.

♦ **plough up** vt sep *field* umpflügen; (*uncover*) beim Pflügen zu Tage bringen; (*uproot*) *tree* roden. **the heavy lorries had completely ~ed** the village green die schweren Lastwagen hatten den Dorfanger vollkommen zerpflügt; **the train ~ed** the track for 40 metres der Zug riß 40 Meter Schienen aus ihrer Verankerung.

plough, (US) plow: ~**boy** n Pflüger m; ~ **horse** n Ackergaul m.

ploughing, (US) plowing ['plaʊɪŋ] n Pflügen nt. **the ~ back of profits into the company** die Reinvestierung von Gewinnen in die Firma.

plough, (US) plow: ~**land** n Ackerland nt; ~**man** n Pflüger m; ~**man's lunch** Käse und Brot als Imbiß; ~**share** n Pflugschar f.

plover ['plʌvə'] n Regenpfeifer m; (*lapwing*) Kiebitz m.

plow etc (*US*) see **plough** etc.

ploy [plɔɪ] n (*stratagem*) Trick m.

pluck [plʌk] **1** n (a) (*courage*) Schneid (*inf*), Mut m.

(b) (*of animal*) Innereien pl.

2 vt (a) *fruit, flower* pflücken; *chicken* rupfen; *guitar, eyebrows* zupfen. **to ~ (at) sb's sleeve** jdn am Ärmel zupfen; **he ~ed a stray hair off his coat** er zupfte sich ein Haar von seinem Mantel; **his rescuers had ~ed him from the jaws of death** seine Retter hatten ihn den Klauen des Todes entrissen; **to ~ up (one's) courage** all seinen Mut zusammennehmen.

(b) (*also ~ out*) *hair, feather* auszupfen. **if thy right eye offend thee ~ it out** (*Bibl*) wenn dir dein rechtes Auge zum Ärgernis wird, so reiß es aus.

3 vi **to ~ at an etw (dat)** (herum)zupfen.

pluckily ['plʌkɪlɪ] adv tapfer, mutig.

pluckiness ['plʌkɪnɪs] n Unerschrockenheit f, Schneid (*inf*) m.

plucky ['plʌkɪ] adj (+er) *person, smile* tapfer; *little pony, action, person* mutig.

plug [plʌɡ] **1** n (a) (*stopper*) Stöpsel m; (*for stopping a leak*) Propfen m; (*in barrel*) Spund m. **a ~ of cotton wool** ein Wattebausch m; **to pull the ~ (in lavatory)** die Spülung ziehen.

(b) (*Elec*) Stecker m; (*incorrect: socket*) Steckdose f; (*Aut: spark* ~) (Zünd)kerze f.

(c) (*inf: piece of publicity*) Schleichwerbung f no pl. **to give sb/sth a ~, to put in a ~ for sb/sth** für jdn/etw Schleichwerbung machen.

(d) (*of tobacco*) Scheibe f; (*for chewing*) Priem m.

(e) (*Geol*) Vulkanstotzen m.

(f) (*US: fire~*) Hydrant m.

(g) (*sl: punch*) **to take a ~ at sb** jdm eine verplätten (*sl*).

2 vt (a) (*stop*) *hole, gap, crevice, leak* verstopfen, zustopfen; *barrel* (ver)spunden; *tooth* plombieren. **the doctor ~ged the wound with cotton wool** der Arzt stillte die Blutung mit Watte; **to ~ one's ears** (*dat*) (*with cotton wool etc*) sich (*dat*) etwas in die Ohren stopfen; **to ~ the drain on the gold reserves** den Abfluß der Goldreserven stoppen; **to ~ the gaps in the tax laws** die Lücken im Steuergesetz schließen.

(b) (*insert*) stecken. ~ **the TV into the socket, please** steck bitte den Stecker vom Fernseher in die Steckdose; **an old rag had been ~ged into the hole** man hatte einen alten Lappen in das Loch gestopft.

(c) (*inf: publicize*) Schleichwerbung machen für (*inf*).

(d) (*inf: push, put forward*) *idea* hausieren gehen mit.

(e) (*inf: shoot*) **to ~ sb in the head/stomach** *etc* jdm ein Loch in den Kopf/Bauch *etc* schießen; **they ~ged him full of lead** sie pumpten ihn mit Blei voll (*sl*).

(f) (*sl: punch*) eine verplätten (· *dat*) (*sl*).

♦ **plug away** vi (*inf*) ackern (*inf*). **to ~ at sth** sich mit etw abrackern or herumschlagen (*inf*).

♦ **plug in 1** vt sep *TV, heater etc* hineinstecken, einstöpseln, anschließen. **to be ~ged ~** angeschlossen sein. **2** vi **where does the TV ~ ~?** wo wird der Fernseher angeschlossen?; ~ ~, **then switch on** schließen Sie das Gerät an und schalten Sie es dann ein.

♦ **plug up** vt sep *gap, hole, leak etc* verstopfen, zustopfen; *crack* zuspachteln, verspachteln.

plug: ~ **hat** n (*old US sl*) Angströhre f (*dated hum*); ~**hole** n Abfluß(loch nt) m; ~ **tobacco** n Kautabak m; ~**ugly** (*inf*) **1** n Schlägertyp (*inf*), Rabauke (*inf*) m; **2** adj potthäßlich (*inf*).

plum [plʌm] **1** n (a) (*fruit, tree*) Pflaume f; (*Victoria ~, dark blue*) Zwetschge f. **to speak with a ~ in one's mouth** (*fig inf*) sprechen, als hätte man eine heiße Kartoffel im Mund.

(b) (*colour*) Pflaumenblau nt.

(c) *(fig inf: good job)* a real ~ *(of a job)* eine Bomben- or Mordsstelle *(inf)*.
2 *adj attr (inf)* job, position Bomben- *(inf)*, Mords- *(inf)*.

plumage ['plu:mɪdʒ] *n* Gefieder, Federkleid *(liter) nt*.

plumb [plʌm] **1** *n* (~-line) Lot, Senkblei *nt.* **out of** ~ nicht im Lot.
2 *adv* **(a)** lotrecht, senkrecht.
(b) *(inf) (completely)* total *(inf)*, komplett *(inf)*; *(exactly)* genau. ~ **crazy** vollkommen or total *(inf)* or komplett *(inf)* verrückt; ~ **in the middle** (mard)genau in der Mitte; **it hit him** ~ **on the nose** es traf ihn genau or mitten auf die Nase.
3 *vt* **(a)** *ocean, depth* (aus)loten.
(b) *(fig) mystery etc* ergründen. **to** ~ **the depths of despair** die tiefste Verzweiflung erleben; **a look that** ~ed **his very soul** ein Blick, der in die Tiefen seiner Seele drang.

plumbago [plʌm'beɪgəʊ] *n* Graphit *m*.

plumb bob *n* Lot, Senkblei *nt*.

plumber ['plʌmə^r] *n* Installateur, Klempner *m*.

plumbic ['plʌmbɪk] *adj* Bleidi-, Blei(IV)- *(spec)*.

plumbiferous [plʌm'bɪfərəs] *adj* bleihaltig, bleiführend.

plumbing ['plʌmɪŋ] *n* **(a)** *(work)* Installieren *nt.* **he decided to learn** ~ er beschloß, Installateur or Klempner zu werden; **he does all his own** ~ er macht alle Installations- or Klempnerarbeiten selbst.
(b) *(fittings)* Rohre, Leitungen, Installationen *pl*; *(bathroom fittings)* sanitäre Anlagen *pl.* **the** ~ **makes an awful noise** die Rohre machen einen furchtbaren Krach; **to inspect the** ~ *(hum)* die Lokalitäten aufsuchen *(hum)*.

plumb: ~-**line** *n* Lot, Senkblei *nt*; *(Naut also)* (Blei)lot *nt*; ~-**rule** *n* Lotwaage *f*.

plumbous ['plʌmbəs] *adj* Blei-, Blei(II)- *(spec)*.

plum duff ['plʌm'dʌf] *n* Plumpudding *m*.

plume [plu:m] **1** *n* Feder *f*; *(on helmet)* Federbusch *m.* ~ **of smoke** Rauchwolke, Rauchfahne *f*; **in borrowed** ~s mit fremden Federn geschmückt. **2** *vr* **(a)** *(bird)* sich putzen. **(b) to** ~ **oneself on sth** auf etw *(acc)* stolz sein wie ein Pfau.

plumed [plu:md] *adj helmet etc* federgeschmückt, mit Federschmuck. **the peacock with its magnificently** ~ **tail** der Pfau mit seinem prächtigen Schwanzgefieder.

plummet ['plʌmɪt] **1** *n* **(a)** *(weight)* Senkblei *nt*; *(Fishing)* Grundsucher *m*.
(b) *(falling)* *(Econ)* Sturz *m*; *(of bird, plane)* Sturzflug *m*.
2 *vi* *(bird, plane etc)* hinunter-/herunterstürzen; *(Econ) (sales figures etc)* stark zurückgehen; *(currency, shares etc)* fallen, absacken. **the £ has** ~ted **to DM 3.50** das £ ist auf DM 3,50 gefallen or abgesackt; **he has** ~ted **again to the depths of despair** er ist wieder in tiefster Verzweiflung.

plummy ['plʌmɪ] *adj* (+er) *(inf) job* Bomben- *(inf)*, Mords- *(inf)*; *voice* sonor.

plump [plʌmp] **1** *adj* (+er) **(a)** rundlich, mollig, pummelig; *legs etc* stämmig; *face* rundlich, pausbäckig, voll; *chicken etc* gut genährt, fleischig.
(b) *phrasing, reply* direkt, unverblümt.
2 *adv* **up fall** ~ **onto sth** mit einem Plumps auf etw *(acc)* fallen.
3 *vt* *(drop)* fallen lassen; *(throw)* werfen; *(angrily, noisily)* knallen *(inf)*. **to** ~ **sth down** etw hinfallen lassen/hinwerfen/hinknallen *(inf)*; **she** ~ed **herself down in the armchair** sie ließ sich in den Sessel fallen; **he had** ~ed **himself in the best chair** er hatte sich im besten Sessel breitgemacht *(inf)*.
4 *vi* *(fall)* fallen. **to** ~ **down onto a chair** auf einen Stuhl fallen or plumpsen *(inf)*.

♦ **plump for** *vi* +prep obj sich entscheiden für.

♦ **plump out** *vi (person)* (Gewicht) ansetzen.

♦ **plump up** *vt sep pillow* aufschütteln; *chicken* mästen.

plumpness ['plʌmpnɪs] *n see adj* Rundlichkeit, Molligkeit, Pummeligkeit *f*; Stämmigkeit *f*; Rundlichkeit, Pausbäckigkeit *f*; Wohlgenährtheit *f.* **the** ~ **of her cheeks** ihre Pausbäckigkeit.

plum: ~ **pudding** *n* Plumpudding *m*; ~ **tree** *n* Pflaumenbaum *m*; *(Victoria* ~) Zwetsch(g)enbaum *m*.

plunder ['plʌndə^r] **1** *n* **(a)** *(act) (of place)* Plünderung *f*; *(of things)* Raub *m*. **(b)** *(loot)* Beute *f*. **2** *vt place* plündern *(also hum)*; *(completely)* ausplündern; *people* ausplündern; *thing* rauben.

plunderer ['plʌndərə^r] *n* Plünderer *m*.

plundering ['plʌndərɪŋ] *n (of place)* Plünderung *f*, Plündern *nt*; *(of things)* Raub *m*.

plunge [plʌndʒ] **1** *vt* **(a)** *(thrust)* stecken; *(into water etc)* tauchen. **he** ~d **his knife into his victim's back** er jagte seinem Opfer das Messer in den Rücken; **he** ~d **his hand into the hole/his pocket** er steckte seine Hand tief in das Loch/in die Tasche; **he** ~d **his hands into his pockets** er vergrub seine Hände in den Taschen; **he** ~d **his head under the cold water** er steckte seinen Kopf in das kalte Wasser.
(b) *(fig)* **to** ~ **the country into war/debt** das Land in einen Krieg/in Schulden stürzen; **the room was/we were** ~d **into darkness** das Zimmer war in Dunkelheit getaucht/tiefe Dunkelheit umfing uns; **he was** ~d **into despair by the news** die Nachricht stürzte ihn in tiefe Verzweiflung.
2 *vi* **(a)** *(dive)* tauchen; *(goalkeeper)* sich werfen, hechten.
(b) *(rush, esp downward)* stürzen. **to** ~ **down the stairs** die Treppe hinunterstürzen; **to** ~ **to one's death** zu Tode stürzen; **the fireman** ~d **into the flames** der Feuerwehrmann stürzte sich in die Flammen; **the road** ~d **down the hill** die Straße fiel steil ab; **the path** ~d **over the brow of the hill** der Weg führte über den Kamm des Berges und fiel dann steil ab.
(c) *(share prices, currency etc)* stürzen, stark fallen.
(d) *(fig: into debate, studies, preparations etc)* sich stürzen *(into* in +*acc)*.
(e) *(dip) (horse)* bocken; *(ship)* stampfen.
(f) *(neckline)* fallen. **her deeply plunging neckline** der tiefe Ausschnitt ihres Kleides; **the dress** ~s **at the back** das Kleid ist hinten tief ausgeschnitten.

(g) *(speculate rashly)* sich verspekulieren.
3 *vr (into studies, job etc)* sich stürzen *(into* in +*acc)*.
4 *n* **(a)** *(dive)* (Kopf)sprung, Köpper *(inf) m*; *(of goalkeeper)* Hechtsprung *m.* **he takes/enjoys a quick** ~ **before breakfast** vor dem Frühstück schwimmt er/schwimmt er gern eine Runde; **to take the** ~ *(fig inf)* den Sprung or Schritt wagen.
(b) *(downward movement)* Sturz *m*.
(c) *(fig: into debt, despair etc, of shares, £ etc)* Sturz *m.* **his** ~ **into debt began when his business collapsed** nach dem Bankrott seines Geschäftes stürzte er sich in Schulden; **shares took a** ~ **after the government's announcement** nach der Ankündigung der Regierung kam es zu einem Kurssturz.
(d) *(rash investment)* Fehlspekulation *f*.

♦ **plunge in 1** *vt sep knife* hineinjagen; *hand* hineinstecken; *(into water)* hineintauchen. **he was** ~d **straight** ~ **(at the deep end)** *(fig)* er mußte gleich richtig ran *(inf)*, er mußte gleich voll einsteigen *(inf)*. **2** *vi (dive)* hineinspringen.

plunger ['plʌndʒə^r] *n* **(a)** *(piston)* Tauchkolben *m*. *(for clearing drain)* Sauger *m.* **(b)** ~ *(speculator)* Spekulant(in *f) m*.

plunging ['plʌndʒɪŋ] *adj neckline, back* tief ausgeschnitten.

plunk[1] [plʌŋk] *vt banjo* zupfen.

plunk[2] *n, adv, vt see* plonk[1].

pluperfect ['plu:'pɜ:fɪkt] **1** *n* Vorvergangenheit *f*, Plusquamperfekt *nt.* **2** *adj* in der Vorvergangenheit, im Plusquamperfekt. ~ **tense** Vorvergangenheit *f*, Plusquamperfekt *nt*.

plural ['pluərəl] **1** *adj* **(a)** *(Gram)* Mehrzahl-, Plural-. **(b)** ~ **voting** Pluralwahlrecht, Mehrstimmenwahlrecht *nt.* **2** *n* Mehrzahl *f*, Plural *m.* **in the** ~ im Plural, in der Mehrzahl.

pluralism ['pluərəlɪzəm] *n* Pluralismus *m*.

pluralistic [,pluərə'lɪstɪk] *adj* pluralistisch.

plurality [,pluə'rælɪti] *n* **(a)** Vielfalt, Mannigfaltigkeit *f*; *(Sociol)* Pluralität *f.* **(b)** *(US Pol)* (Stimmen)vorsprung *m*.

plus [plʌs] **1** *prep (added to, increased by)* plus (+*dat)*; *(together with)* und *(außerdem)*. **the day's takings were** ~ **£100** die Tageseinnahmen lagen um £ 100 höher.
2 *adj (Math, Elec, fig)* ~ **sign** Pluszeichen *nt*; **a** ~ **quantity** eine positive Menge; **the** ~ **terminal** der Pluspol; **a** ~ **factor/item** ein Pluspunkt *m*; **on the** ~ **side** auf der Habenseite.
(b) *(more than)* **he scored beta** ~ **in the exam** = er hat in der Prüfung eine Zwei plus bekommen; **50 pages/hours** ~ **a week** mehr als or über 50 Seiten/Stunden pro Woche; **she has personality** ~ sie hat ein gewinnendes Wesen.
3 *n (sign)* Pluszeichen *nt*; *(positive factor)* Pluspunkt *m*; *(extra)* Plus *nt.* **if after all the deductions you still finish up with a** ~ wenn dir nach allen Abzügen noch etwas übrigbleibt.

plus fours ['plʌs'fɔ:z] *npl* Knickerbocker *pl*.

plush [plʌʃ] **1** *n* Plüsch *m.* **2** *adj* (+er) **(a)** Plüsch-. **(b)** *(inf: luxurious)* feudal *(inf)*; *hotel, restaurant also* Nobel-; *furnishing also* elegant, vornehm.

plushy ['plʌʃɪ] *adj* (+er) *(inf) see* plush 2 (b).

Plutarch ['plu:tɑ:k] *n* Plutarch *m*.

Pluto ['plu:təʊ] *n (Myth)* Pluto, Pluton *m*; *(Astron)* Pluto *m*.

plutocracy [plu:'tɒkrəsɪ] *n* Plutokratie *f*.

plutocrat ['plu:təʊkræt] *n* Plutokrat(in *f) m*.

plutocratic [,plu:təʊ'krætɪk] *adj* plutokratisch.

plutonium [plu:'təʊnɪəm] *n* Plutonium *nt*.

pluvial ['plu:vɪəl] *adj (form)* Regen-. ~ **erosion** Erosion *f* durch Regen.

pluviometer [,plu:vɪ'ɒmɪtə^r] *n* Regen- or Niederschlagsmesser *m*, Pluviometer *nt*.

ply[1] [plaɪ] *n* **three-**~ *wood* dreischichtig; *wool* Dreifach-, dreifädig; *tissues* dreilagig; **what** ~ **is this wool?** wievielfach ist diese Wolle?, wie viele Fäden hat diese Wolle?

ply[2] **1** *vt* **(a)** *(work with, use) tool, brush etc* gebrauchen, umgehen mit, führen; *needle* gebrauchen; *oars* einsetzen; *(work busily with) tool, brush etc* fleißig führen or umgehen mit; *needle* tanzen lassen *(geh)*; *oars* kräftig einsetzen.
(b) *(work at) trade* ausüben, betreiben, nachgehen (+*dat)*.
(c) *(ships) sea, river, route* befahren; *seas also* durchfahren.
(d) to ~ **sb with questions** jdn mit Fragen überhäufen; **to** ~ **sb with drink(s)** jdm immer wieder zum Trinken auffordern; **she kept her guests well plied with drinks** sie sorgte dafür, daß ihren Gästen die Getränke nicht ausgingen; **to** ~ **sb for information** jdn um Informationen angehen.
2 *vi (ship)* **to** ~ **between** verkehren zwischen; **to** ~ **for hire** seine Dienste anbieten.

plywood ['plaɪwʊd] *n* Sperrholz *nt*.

PM *abbr of* **Prime Minister.**

pm *abbr of* **post meridiem** p.m.

pneumatic [nju:'mætɪk] *adj* **(a)** Luft-. **(b)** *(inf) young lady* vollbusig *(inf)*; *breasts* prall.

pneumatically [nju:'mætɪkəlɪ] *adv* mit or durch Druck- or Preßluft. **a** ~ **operated drill** ein preßluftbetriebener Bohrer.

pneumatic: ~ **brake** *n* Druckluftbremse *f*; ~ **drill** *n* Preßluftbohrer *m*; ~ **tyre** *n* Luftreifen *m*.

pneumonia [nju:'məʊnɪə] *n* Lungenentzündung *f*.

PO *abbr of* **post office** PA; **postal order.**

po [pəʊ] *n (inf)* (Nacht)topf, Pott *(inf) m*.

poach[1] [pəʊtʃ] *vt egg* pochieren; *fish* (blau) dünsten. ~ed **egg** pochiertes or verlorenes Ei; *(in poacher)* = Ei *nt* im Glas.

poach[2] **1** *vt* unerlaubt or schwarz *(inf)* fangen; *deer, rabbits etc also* unerlaubt or schwarz *(inf)* schießen.
2 *vi* **(a)** wildern *(for* auf +*acc)*. **to** ~ **for salmon** Lachs ohne Berechtigung or schwarz *(inf)* fangen.
(b) *(fig)* **to** ~ **(on sb's territory)** *(in sport)* jdm ins Gehege or in die Quere kommen; *(in work also)* jdm ins Handwerk pfuschen; **stop** ~ing, **that was my ball!** komm mir nicht ins Gehege or in die Quere, das war mein Ball.

poacher[1] ['pəʊtʃə^r] *n* Wilderer *m*; *(of game also)* Wilddieb *m*.

poacher[2] *n (for eggs)* Pochierpfanne *f*.

poaching ['pəʊtʃɪŋ] *n* Wildern *nt*, Wilderei *f*.

pock [pɒk] n (pustule) Pocke, Blatter f; (mark) Pocken- or Blatternarbe f.

pocket ['pɒkɪt] **1** n **(a)** (in garment) Tasche f. **to have sb/sth in one's ~** (fig) jdn/etw in der Tasche haben (inf); **take your hands out of your ~s!** nimm die Hände aus der Tasche!

(b) (receptacle: in suitcase, file etc) Fach nt; (in book cover: for map etc) Tasche f; (Baseball) Tasche f; (Billiards) Loch nt.

(c) (resources) Geldbeutel m. **to be a drain on one's ~** jds Geldbeutel strapazieren (inf); **that emptied his ~s/hit his ~** das hat seinen Geldbeutel ganz schön strapaziert (inf); **to be in ~** auf sein Geld kommen (inf); **I was £100 in ~ after the sale** nach dem Verkauf war ich um £ 100 reicher; **to put one's hand in one's ~** tief in die Tasche greifen; **with a car like that you'll always be putting your hand in your ~** bei so einem Wagen muß man ständig tief in die Tasche greifen; see **out-of-pocket**.

(d) (restricted area, space) Gebiet nt; (smaller) Einsprengsel nt. **~ of resistance** Widerstandsnest nt; **~ of unemployment** Gebiet nt mit hoher Arbeitslosigkeit; **~ of infection** Anstekkungsgebiet nt; **a ~ of ore** ein Einschluß m von Erz.

(e) (Aviat: air ~) Luftloch nt.

2 adj (for the pocket) comb, edition, dictionary Taschen-. **~ lens** Lupe f im Taschenformat.

3 vt **(a)** (put in one's pocket) einstecken. **to ~ one's pride** seinen Stolz überwinden; **to ~ an insult** eine Beleidigung einstecken (inf) or hinnehmen.

(b) (gain) kassieren; (misappropriate) einstecken (inf), einsacken (inf). **the treasurer ~ed the club funds** der Schatzmeister hat die Vereinsgelder in die eigene Tasche gesteckt.

(c) (Billiards) ins Loch bringen, einlochen.

(d) (US Pol) durch Veto aufschieben.

pocket: ~ battleship n Westentaschenkreuzer m; **~ billiards** n sing (a) (US) Poolbillard nt; (b) (hum sl) Knickern (sl), Taschenbillard (sl) nt; **~book** n (a) (notebook) Notizbuch nt; (b) (wallet) Brieftasche f; (c) (US: handbag) Handtasche f; **~ borough** n (Brit Hist) vor 1832 ein Wahlkreis, der sich praktisch in den Händen einer Person oder Familie befand; see **calculator** n Taschenrechner m.

pocketful ['pɒkɪtfʊl] n **a ~** eine Tasche voll.

pocket: ~ handkerchief n Taschentuch nt; **a ~ handkerchief(-sized) garden** ein Garten m im Westentaschenformat; **~-knife** n Taschenmesser nt; **~-money** n Taschengeld nt; **~-size(d)** adj book im Taschenformat; camera Miniatur-; person winzig; garden, dictator im Westentaschenformat; **~ veto** n (US Pol) Verzögerung f der Gesetzesverabschiedung durch aufschiebendes Veto des Präsidenten.

pock: ~mark n Pocken- or Blatternarbe f; **~-marked** adj face pockennarbig; surface narbig; **the ~-marked surface of the moon** die mit Kratern übersäte Oberfläche des Mondes; **~-marked with bullet holes** mit Einschüssen übersät.

pod [pɒd] **1** n (Bot) Hülse f; (of peas also) Schote f; (Aviat) (for missiles etc) Magazin nt; (for jet engine) Gehäuse nt. **2** vt peas ent- or aushülsen, auslösen.

podgy ['pɒdʒɪ] adj (+er) rundlich, pummelig; face schwammig. **~ fingers** Wurstfinger pl.

podiatrist [pɒ'diːətrɪst] n (US) Fußspezialist(in f) m.

podiatry [pɒ'diːətrɪ] n (US) Lehre f von den Fußkrankheiten; (treatment) Fußpflege f.

podium ['pəʊdɪəm] n Podest nt.

poem ['pəʊɪm] n Gedicht nt. **epic ~** Epos nt.

poesy ['pəʊɪzɪ] n (form: poetry) Lyrik, Poesie (old) f.

poet ['pəʊɪt] n Dichter, Poet (old) m; see **laureate**.

poetaster [ˌpəʊɪ'tæstə] n (pej) Poetaster, Dichterling m.

poetess ['pəʊɪtes] n Dichterin, Poetin (old) f.

poetic [pəʊ'etɪk] adj poetisch; talent, ability also dichterisch; place, charm stimmungsvoll, malerisch. **~ beauty** (visual) malerische Schönheit; (of thought, scene in play etc) poetische Schönheit; **he's not at all ~** er hat überhaupt keinen Sinn für Poesie; **he grew** or **became ~** er wurde poetisch or lyrisch; **what's ~ about this sculpture?** was ist an dieser Skulptur künstlerisch?; **~ justice** poetische Gerechtigkeit; **~ licence** dichterische Freiheit.

poetical [pəʊ'etɪkəl] adj see **poetic**.

poetically [pəʊ'etɪkəlɪ] adv see adj. **we analyse poems ~ not linguistically** wir untersuchen Gedichte vom dichterischen und nicht vom linguistischen Standpunkt her.

poetics [pəʊ'etɪks] n sing Poetik f.

poetry ['pəʊɪtrɪ] n **(a)** Dichtung f; (not epic also) Lyrik f. **to write ~** Gedichte schreiben, dichten; **the rules of ~** die Regeln der Versdichtung; **~ reading** Dichterlesung f.

(b) (fig) Poesie f. **there's no ~ in him** er ist völlig poesielos; **the dancing was ~ in motion** der Tanz war in Bewegung umgesetzte Poesie; **the sunset was sheer ~** der Sonnenuntergang war reinste Poesie; **her soufflés are/that dress is sheer ~** ihre Soufflés sind/dieses Kleid ist wirklich ein Gedicht.

po-faced ['pəʊfeɪst] adj (sl) (disapproving) grimmig, mürrisch. **a ~ woman** (ugly) eine Schrulle (inf).

pogo stick ['pəʊgəʊˌstɪk] n Springstock m.

pogrom ['pɒgrəm] n Pogrom nt.

poignancy ['pɔɪnjənsɪ] n see adj Ergreifende(s) nt; Wehmut f; Schmerzlichkeit f; Schärfe f. **the ~ of his words/look** die Wehmut, die in seinen Worten/seinem Blick lag; **he writes with great ~** er schreibt sehr ergreifend.

poignant ['pɔɪnjənt] adj ergreifend; memories, look wehmütig; distress, regret schmerzlich; wit scharf.

poignantly ['pɔɪnjəntlɪ] adv see adj. **old memories stirred ~ within her** alte Erinnerungen rührten sich wehmütig in ihr.

poinsettia [pɔɪn'setɪə] n Weihnachtsstern m, Poinsettia f (spec).

point [pɔɪnt] **1** n **(a)** (dot, punctuation mark, Typ, Geometry) Punkt m; (in Hebrew texts) Vokalzeichen nt. **(nought) ~ seven (0.7)** null Komma sieben (0,7).

(b) (unit on scale, on compass) Punkt m; (on thermometer)

Grad m. **from all ~s (of the compass)** aus allen (Himmels)richtungen; **the bag is full to bursting ~** die Tüte ist zum Bersten voll; **up to a ~** bis zu einem gewissen Grad or Punkt.

(c) (sharp end, of chin) Spitze f; (of a star) Zacke f; (of antler) (Geweih)ende nt, (Geweih)spitze f. **at the ~ of a gun/sword** mit vorgehaltener Pistole/gezücktem Schwert; **things look different at the ~ of a gun** alles sieht ein bißchen anders aus, wenn einem jemand die Pistole auf die Brust setzt; **not to put too fine a ~ on it** (fig) um ganz offen zu sein, ehrlich gesagt.

(d) (place) Punkt m, Stelle f. **the train stops at Slough and all ~s east** der Zug hält in Slough und allen Orten östlich davon; **~ of departure** (lit, fig) Ausgangspunkt m; **~ of entry** (over border) Ort m der Einreise; (of space capsule) Ort m des Wiedereintritts; **here at the northernmost ~ of Scotland** hier, am nördlichsten Punkt Schottlands; **~ of view** Stand- or Gesichtspunkt m; **from my ~ of view** von meinem Standpunkt aus, aus meiner Perspektive or Sicht; **from the ~ of view of productivity** von der Produktivität her gesehen; **at this ~** (spatially) an dieser Stelle, an diesem Punkt; (in time) (then) in diesem Augenblick; (now) jetzt; **from that ~ on they were friends** von da an waren sie Freunde; **at what ~ ...?** an welcher Stelle ...?; **at no ~** nie; **at no ~ in the book** nirgends in dem Buch, an keiner Stelle des Buches; **to be (up)on the ~ of doing sth** im Begriff sein, etw zu tun; **he was on the ~ of telling me the story when ...** er wollte mir gerade die Geschichte erzählen, als ...; **he had reached the ~ of resigning** er war nahe daran zu resignieren; **to reach the ~ of no return** (fig) den Punkt erreichen, von dem aus es kein Zurück gibt; **to be at the ~ of death** am Rande or an der Schwelle des Todes stehen; **they provoked him to the ~ where he lost his temper** sie reizten ihn so lange, bis er die Geduld verlor; **severe to the ~ of cruelty** streng bis an die Grenze der Grausamkeit; **she was indulgent to the ~ of spoiling the child** sie war nachgiebig in einem Maße, das schon in Verwöhnung des Kindes umschlug; **when it comes to the ~** wenn es darauf ankommt.

(e) (Sport, in test, St Ex etc) Punkt m. **~s for/against** Pluspunkte pl/Minuspunkte pl; **~s decision** Entscheidung f nach Punkten; **~s win** Punktsieg m, Sieg m nach Punkten; **to win on ~s** nach Punkten gewinnen; **the cost of living has gone up two ~s** die Lebenshaltungskosten sind um zwei Punkte gestiegen.

(f) (purpose) Zweck, Sinn m. **there's no ~ in staying** es hat keinen Zweck or Sinn zu bleiben; **I don't see the ~ of carrying on/changing our system now** ich sehe keinen Sinn darin, weiterzumachen/unser System jetzt zu ändern; **what's the ~?** was soll's?; **I just don't see the ~ of it** or **any ~ in it** das sehe ich überhaupt nicht ein, ich sehe überhaupt keinen Sinn darin; **the ~ of this is ...** Sinn und Zweck ist ...; **what's the ~ of trying?** wozu versuchen?; **he doesn't understand the ~ of doing this** er versteht nicht, weswegen wir/sie etc das machen; **do you see the ~ of what I'm saying?** weißt du, worauf ich hinauswill?; **the ~ is that ...** es ist nämlich so ..., die Sache ist die, daß ...; **that's the whole ~** (of doing it this way) deswegen machen wir das so; **the ~ of the joke/story** die Pointe; **his remarks lack ~** seine Bemerkungen besagen nichts or sagen nichts aus; **the news gave ~ to his arguments** die Nachrichten verliehen seinen Argumenten Nachdruck or Gewicht; **life has lost all ~** das Leben hat jeden or all seinen Sinn verloren.

(g) (detail, argument) Punkt m. **the ~ at issue** der strittige Punkt; **a 12-~ plan** ein Zwölfpunkte-Plan m; **a ~ of interest** ein interessanter Punkt; **on this ~ we are agreed** in diesem Punkt stimmen wir überein; **his arguments were off the ~** seine Argumente trafen den Kern der Sache nicht; **I'm afraid that's off the ~** das ist nicht relevant or gehört nicht hierher; **to come to the ~** zur Sache kommen; **to keep** or **stick to the ~** beim Thema bleiben; **beside the ~** unerheblich, irrelevant; **to the ~** zur Sache, zum Thema; **his remarks are very much to the ~** seine Bemerkungen sind sehr sachbezogen; **this is an important ~** das ist ein wichtiger Punkt or ein Punkt von Bedeutung; **a useful ~** ein nützlicher Hinweis; **~ by ~** Punkt für Punkt; **a ~ by ~ answer** eine Antwort Punkt für Punkt; **my ~ was ...** ich sagen wollte, war ...; **to make a ~** ein Argument nt anbringen; **he made the ~ that ...** er betonte, daß ...; **you've made your ~!** wissen wir ja schon!, das hast du ja schon gesagt!; **the chairman gave him just 30 seconds to make his ~** der Vorsitzende gab ihm nur 30 Sekunden, um sein Argument zu erläutern; **you have a ~ there** da ist etwas dran (inf); **if I may make another ~** wenn ich noch auf einen weiteren Punkt aufmerksam machen darf; **he took a long time to make his ~** er hat sehr lange gebraucht, um sich verständlich zu machen; **he makes his ~s very clear** er bringt seine Argumente sehr klar; **I take your ~, ~ taken** ich habe schon begriffen; **do you take my ~?** verstehst du mich?; **he may have a ~ you know** da kann er recht haben, weißt du; **no, wait a minute, I think the boy's got a ~** nein, warte mal, ich glaube der Junge hat gar nicht so unrecht; **can I put that same ~ another way?** kann ich das noch einmal anders formulieren?; **would you put that ~ more succinctly?** können Sie das etwas knapper fassen?; **to gain** or **carry one's ~** sich durchsetzen; **to get** or **see the ~** verstehen, worum es geht; **to miss the ~** nicht verstehen, worum es geht; **he missed the ~ of what I was saying** er hat nicht begriffen, worauf ich hinauswollte; **that's not the ~** darum geht es nicht; **that's the whole ~** das ist es ja gerade, das ist ja der Witz (daran) (inf); **but the pound has been devalued — that's the whole ~, your mark is worth more!** aber das Pfund wurde doch abgewertet — genau! deshalb ist die Mark jetzt mehr wert; **a case in ~** ein einschlägiger Fall; **the case in ~** der zur Debatte stehende Punkt; **to make a ~ of sth** auf etw (dat) bestehen, auf etw (acc) Wert legen; **he made a special ~ of being early** er legte besonderen Wert darauf, früh dazusein; **we make a ~ of stressing ordinary usage** wir legen besonderen Nachdruck auf den normalen Sprachgebrauch.

(h) *(matter)* a ~ of principle eine grundsätzliche Frage; a ~ of law eine Rechtsfrage; a ~ of order eine Frage der Geschäftsordnung; a ~ of detail eine Einzelfrage; *see* honour.

(i) *(characteristic) good/bad* ~s gute/schlechte Seiten *pl*; he has his ~s er hat auch seine Vorzüge *or* guten Seiten; the ~s to look for when buying a new car die Punkte *or* Dinge, auf die man beim Kauf eines neuen Wagens achten muß.

(j) ~s *pl (Brit Rail)* Weichen *pl*.

(k) *(Ballet: usu pl)* Spitze *f*. to dance on ~s Spitzentanz machen, auf den Spitzen tanzen.

(l) *(Aut: usu pl)* Unterbrecherkontakte *pl*.

(m) *(Brit Elec)* Steckdose *f*.

2 *vt* **(a)** *(aim, direct) gun, telescope etc* richten *(at auf +acc)*. he ~ed his stick in the direction of the house er zeigte *or* wies mit dem Stock auf das Haus; I asked him to ~ me on my way ich bat ihn, mir den Weg zu zeigen; he ~ed his boat upstream er drehte sein Boot stromaufwärts; he ~s his feet outwards when he walks er dreht seine Fußspitzen beim Gehen nach außen; they ~ed the drunk off in the right direction sie schickten den Betrunkenen in die richtige Richtung.

(b) *(mark, show)* zeigen. to ~ the way *(lit, fig)* den Weg weisen; that really ~ed the moral das bewies, wie recht wir/sie *etc* hatten; he used the decline in the company's profits to ~ the moral that ... er nahm das Absinken der Gewinne zum Anlaß zu betonen, daß ...

(c) *(sharpen) pencil, stick* (an)spitzen.

(d) *(Build) wall, brickwork* verfugen, ausfugen.

(e) *(punctuate) text* interpunktieren; *Hebrew* vokalisieren; *psalm* mit Deklarationszeichen versehen.

(f) *(Hunt) game* anzeigen.

3 *vi* **(a)** *(with finger etc)* zeigen, deuten *(at, to auf +acc)*. it's rude to ~ (at strangers) es ist unhöflich, mit dem Finger (auf Fremde) zu zeigen; don't ~! zeig nicht mit dem Finger!; he ~ed in the direction of the house/towards the house/back towards the house er zeigte *or* deutete in die Richtung des Hauses/zum Haus/zurück zum Haus; the compass needle ~s (to the) north die Kompaßnadel zeigt *or* weist nach Norden.

(b) *(indicate) (facts, events)* hinweisen, hindeuten *(to auf +acc)*; *(person: point out)* hinweisen. everything ~s that way alles weist in diese Richtung; the problems which you have ~ed to in your paper die Probleme, auf die du in deinem Aufsatz hingewiesen hast *or* die du in deinem Aufsatz aufgezeigt hast; the poet doesn't state, he ~s in certain directions der Dichter trifft keine Feststellungen, er deutet bestimmte Richtungen an; all the signs ~ to success alle Zeichen stehen auf Erfolg; all the signs ~ to economic recovery alles deutet *or* weist auf eine Erholung der Wirtschaft hin.

(c) *(face, be situated: building, valley etc)* liegen; *(be aimed: gun, vehicle etc)* gerichtet sein. with his gun ~ed *or* ~ing right at me, he said ... die Pistole direkt auf mich gerichtet, sagte er ...; the wheels aren't ~ing in the same direction die Räder zeigen nicht in dieselbe Richtung; in which direction is it ~ing? in welche Richtung zeigt es?

(d) *(Hunt)* (vor)stehen.

♦**point out** *vt sep* zeigen auf (+*acc*). to ~ sth ~ to sb jdn auf etw hinweisen *or* aufmerksam machen; could you ~ him ~ to me? kannst du mir zeigen, wer er ist?; I'll ~ him ~ to you ich zeige ihn dir; he ~ed ~ the house where Goethe lived er zeigte auf das Haus, in dem Goethe gelebt hatte; the guide ~ed ~ the most interesting paintings der Führer machte auf die interessantesten Gemälde aufmerksam.

(b) *(mention)* to ~ sth ~ (to sb) (jdn) auf etw (*acc*) aufmerksam machen, (jdn) auf etw (*acc*) hinweisen; may I ~ ~ that ...? darf ich darauf aufmerksam machen *or* darauf hinweisen, daß ...?; thank you for ~ing that ~ to me vielen Dank, daß Sie mich darauf aufmerksam gemacht haben.

♦**point up** *vt sep (emphasize)* unterstreichen, betonen; *(make clear)* veranschaulichen, verdeutlichen.

point-blank ['pɔɪnt'blæŋk] **1** *adj direct; refusal* glatt. at ~ range aus kürzester Entfernung *or* Distanz; a ~ shot ein Schuß aus kürzester Distanz *or* Entfernung.

2 *adv fire* aus kürzester Distanz *or* Entfernung; *ask* rundheraus. he refused to ~ help er weigerte sich rundweg *or* lehnte es rundheraus *or* schlankweg ab zu helfen.

pointed ['pɔɪntɪd] *adj* **(a)** *(sharp) stick, roof, chin, nose* spitz; *window, arch* spitzbogig. a stick with a sharply ~ end ein Stock mit sehr spitzem Ende; the ~ windows in the old church die Spitzbogenfenster in der alten Kirche.

(b) *(incisive) wit* scharf.

(c) *(obvious in intention) remark, comment* scharf, spitz; *reference* unverblümt; *absence, gesture, departure* ostentativ. her ~ lack of interest in my problems ihr ostentatives *or* betontes Desinteresse an meinen Problemen; that was rather ~ das war ziemlich deutlich.

pointedly ['pɔɪntɪdlɪ] *adv speak, comment* spitz; *refer* unverblümt; *leave, stay away etc* ostentativ.

pointer ['pɔɪntə^r] *n* **(a)** *(indicator)* Zeiger *m*.

(b) *(stick)* Zeigestock *m*.

(c) *(dog)* Pointer, Vorstehhund *m*.

(d) *(fig: hint)* Hinweis, Fingerzeig, Tip *m*. he gave me some ~s on how to behave er gab mir ein paar Hinweise, wie ich mich benehmen sollte.

(e) *(fig: indication)* Anzeichen *nt*, Hinweis *m*. the Government is looking for ~s on how the situation will develop die Regierung sucht nach Anzeichen für die weitere Entwicklung der Lage; a ~ to a possible solution ein Hinweis auf eine mögliche Lösung.

pointillism ['pwæntɪlɪzəm] *n* Pointillismus *m*.

pointillist ['pwæntɪlɪst] **1** *n* Pointillist *m*. **2** *adj* pointillistisch.

pointing ['pɔɪntɪŋ] *n (Build) (act)* Ausfugung *f*; *(material)* Fugenmörtel *m*. the ~ on these old buildings needs to be

restored das Mauerwerk dieser alten Gebäude muß neu ver- *or* ausgefugt werden.

pointless *adj*, **~ly** *adv* ['pɔɪntlɪs, -lɪ] sinnlos.

pointlessness ['pɔɪntlɪsnɪs] *n* Sinnlosigkeit *f*.

point(s) duty *n* Verkehrsdienst *m*.

pointsman ['pɔɪntsmən] *n, pl* **-men** [-mən] *(Brit Rail)* Weichensteller *m*.

point-to-point *n (also* ~ **race)** Geländejagdrennen *nt*.

poise [pɔɪz] **1** *n* **(a)** *(carriage of head, body)* Haltung *f*; *(grace)* Grazie *f*. the ~ of her head/body ihre Kopfhaltung/Körperhaltung; the graceful ~ of the dancer's body die Grazie *or* graziöse Haltung der Tänzerin/des Tänzers.

(b) *(composure, self-possession)* Gelassenheit, Selbstsicherheit *f*. a woman of great ~ and charm eine Frau voller Selbstsicherheit und Charme; her ~ as a hostess ihre Sicherheit als Gastgeberin; to lose/recover one's ~ seine Gelassenheit *or* Selbstsicherheit verlieren/wiedergewinnen.

2 *vt* **(a)** *(balance, hold balanced)* balancieren. he ~d the knife ready to strike er hielt das Messer so, daß er jederzeit zustechen konnte; she ~d her pen over her notebook sie hielt den Kugelschreiber schreibbereit über ihrem Notizblock; the diver ~d himself for the leap der Taucher machte sich sprungbereit *or* bereit zum Sprung; the tiger ~d itself to spring der Tiger machte sich sprungbereit; he ~d himself on his toes, ready to jump er verlagerte sein Körpergewicht auf die Zehenspitzen, bereit zum Sprung.

(b) *(in passive)* to be/hang ~d *(bird, rock, sword)* schweben; the diver was ~d on the edge of the pool der Taucher stand sprungbereit auf dem Beckenrand; the tiger was ~d ready to spring der Tiger lauerte sprungbereit; we sat ~d on the edge of our chairs wir balancierten auf den Stuhlkanten; women with water-jars ~d on their heads Frauen, die Wasserkrüge auf dem Kopf balancierten/balancierten.

(c) *(fig)* the enemy are ~d to attack der Feind steht angriffsbereit; they sat in the hall, ~d for departure sie saßen abfahrtbereit in der Halle; to be ~d on the brink/on the brink of sth dicht davor/dicht vor etw *(dat) or* am Rande von etw stehen *or* sein; a bright young man ~d on the brink of success ein intelligenter junger Mann an der Schwelle zum Erfolg.

3 *vi* (für einen Moment) unbeweglich bleiben; *(bird, helicopter)* schweben. he ~d for a second on the edge of the pool er verharrte einen Augenblick am Beckenrand.

poised [pɔɪzd] *adj (self-possessed)* gelassen, selbstsicher.

poison ['pɔɪzn] **1** *n (lit, fig)* Gift *nt*. what's your ~? *(inf)*, name your ~ *(inf)* was willst du trinken?; to hate sb like ~ jdn glühend *or* wie die Pest *(inf)* hassen; *see* meat.

2 *vt* **(a)** vergiften; *atmosphere, rivers* verpesten. it won't ~ you *(inf)* das wird dich nicht umbringen *(inf)*.

(b) *(fig)* vergiften; *marriage* zerrütten. to ~ sb's mind against sb/sth jdn gegen jdn/etw aufstacheln.

poisoner ['pɔɪznə^r] *n* Giftmörder(in *f*) *m*.

poison gas *n* Giftgas *nt*.

poisoning ['pɔɪznɪŋ] *n (lit, fig)* Vergiftung *f*. the gradual ~ of the atmosphere by ... die zunehmende Luftverpestung durch ...; to die of ~ an einer Vergiftung sterben.

poison ivy *n* kletternder Giftsumach, Giftefeu *m*.

poisonous ['pɔɪznəs] *adj* **(a)** *snake, plants etc* giftig, Gift-; *substance, fumes etc* giftig. whisky on top of beer, that's absolutely ~ *(inf)* Whisky auf Bier, das ist tödlich *(inf)*.

(b) *(fig) literature, doctrine* zersetzend; *remark etc* giftig; *propaganda* also Hetz-. she has a ~ tongue sie hat eine giftige Zunge; he's a ~ individual er ist ein richtiger Giftzwerg.

poison: ~**pen letter** *n* anonymer Brief; ~ **sumach** *n (US)* Giftsumach *m*.

poke¹ [pəʊk] *n (dial, Scot)* Beutel, Sack *(dial) m*; *(plastic, paper)* Tüte *f*; *see* pig.

poke² **1** *n* **(a)** *(jab)* Stoß, Schubs *(inf) m*. to give sb/sth a ~ *see vt* (a); I got a ~ in the eye from his umbrella er stieß mir den Regenschirm ins Auge.

(b) *(US inf: punch)* Schlag *m*. ~ on the nose Nasenstüber *m*.

(c) *(Brit vulg: act of intercourse)* Vögeln *nt (sl)*. to have a ~ vögeln *(sl)*, ficken *(vulg)*, einen wegstecken *(sl)*.

2 *vt* **(a)** *(jab with stick)* stoßen; *(with finger)* stupsen. to ~ the fire das Feuer schüren, im Feuer stochern; he ~d the ground with his stick er stieß mit seinem Stock auf den Boden; he accidentally ~d me in the eye er hat mir aus Versehen ins Auge gestoßen.

(b) *(US inf: punch)* hauen *(inf)*. to ~ sb on the nose jdm auf die Nase hauen *or* schlagen.

(c) *(thrust)* to ~ one's head/finger/a stick etc into sth seinen Kopf/Finger/einen Stock etc in etw *(acc)* stecken; he ~d his head round the door/out of the window er streckte seinen Kopf durch die Tür/aus dem Fenster.

(d) *(Brit vulg: have sex with)* vögeln *(sl)*, ficken *(vulg)*.

(e) *(make by poking)* hole bohren.

3 *vi* his elbows were poking through his sleeves an seinen Ärmeln kamen schon die Ellenbogen durch; to ~ at sth *(testing)* etw prüfen; *(searching)* in etw *(dat)* stochern; he ~d at me with his fist er schlug mit der Faust nach mir; he ~d at me with his finger *(touching)* er stupste mich; *(not touching)* er stieß mit dem Finger nach mir; the doctor ~d at his ribs der Arzt tastete seine Rippen ab; well, if you will go poking into things that don't concern you ... na ja, wenn du deine Nase ständig in Dinge steckst, die dich nichts angehen ...

♦**poke about** *or* **around** *vi (prod)* herumstochern. **(b)** *(inf: nose about)* stöbern, schnüffeln *(inf)*. **(c)** +*prep obj (inf: wander about)* (herum)bummeln. we spent a pleasant day poking ~ the shops wir haben einen netten Tag mit Geschäftebummeln verbracht.

♦**poke in** *vt sep* hinein-/hereinstecken *or* -strecken. he ~d his head ~ **through the window** er streckte seinen Kopf zum Fenster hinein/herein; **I'll just ~ my head ~ and say hello** (*inf*) ich will nur schnell vorbeischauen und Guten Tag sagen.

♦ **poke out 1** *vi* vorstehen. **he walked along with his stomach poking** ~ er ging mit vorgestrecktem Bauch; **the tortoise had its head poking** ~ **of its shell** die Schildkröte hatte ihren Kopf aus dem Panzer gestreckt; **that dress ~s** ~ **a bit at the waist** dies Kleid bauscht sich etwas an der Taille; **a handkerchief was poking** ~ **of his top pocket** ein Taschentuch schaute *or* guckte aus seiner Brusttasche hervor.

2 *vt sep* **(a)** (*extend*) heraus-/hinausstrecken.

(b) (*remove by poking*) **he ~d the dirt ~ with his fingers** er puhlte (*inf*) *or* kratzte den Schmutz mit den Fingern heraus; **to ~ sb's eye** ~ jdm das Auge ausstoßen.

♦ **poke up** *vt sep fire* schüren. **he ~d his finger ~ his nose** er bohrte mit dem Finger in der Nase.

poke bonnet *n* Kiepenhut *m*, Schute *f*.

poker[1] ['pəʊkə[r]] *n* (*for fire*) Schürhaken, Feuerhaken *m*.

poker[2] *n* (*Cards*) Poker *nt*.

poker-: ~ face *n* Pokerface, Pokerface *nt*; **~-faced** ['pəʊkə‚feɪst] *adj* mit einem Pokergesicht *or* Pokerface; (*bored*) mit unbewegter Miene.

pokeweed ['pəʊkwiːd] *n* (*US*) Kermesbeere *f*.

poky ['pəʊkɪ] *adj* (+*er*) (*pej*) *room, house* winzig. **it's so ~ in here** es ist so eng hier.

Polack ['pəʊlæk] *n* (*pej*) Polack(e) *m* (*pej*), Polackin *f* (*pej*).

Poland ['pəʊlənd] *n* Polen *nt*.

polar ['pəʊlə[r]] *adj* **(a)** Polar-, polar. **~ bear** Polar- *or* Eisbär *m*; **~ circle** Polarkreis *m*. **(b)** (*opposite*) polar.

polarity [pəʊ'lærɪtɪ] *n* (*Phys, fig*) Polarität *f*.

polarization [‚pəʊləraɪ'zeɪʃən] *n* (*Phys*) Polarisation *f*; (*fig*) Polarisierung *f*.

polarize ['pəʊləraɪz] **1** *vt* polarisieren. **2** *vi* sich polarisieren.

Pole [pəʊl] *n* Pole *m*, Polin *f*.

pole[1] [pəʊl] **1** *n* **(a)** Stange *f*; (*flag~, telegraph ~ also*) Mast *m*; (*of cart*) Deichsel *f*; (*ski-~*) Stock *m*; (*for vaulting*) Stab *m*; (*for punting*) Stange, Stake (*spec*) *f*. **to be up the ~** (*Brit inf*) eine Schraube locker haben (*inf*); **to drive sb up the ~** (*inf*) jdn die Wände hoch treiben (*inf*).

(b) (*Measure: old*) Rute *f* (*old*).

2 *vt punt* staken.

pole[2] *n* (*Geog, Astron, Elec*) Pol *m*. **they are ~s apart** sie (*acc*) trennen Welten, Welten liegen zwischen ihnen.

pole-: ~axe, (*US*) **~ax 1** *n* **(a)** (*Mil*) Streitaxt *f*; **(b)** (*for slaughtering*) Schlachtbeil *nt*; **2** *vt* **(a)** (*mit der Streitaxt*) niederschlagen *or* umhauen; **(b)** (*mit dem Schlachtbeil*) töten; **~cat** *n* Iltis *m*; (*US*) Skunk *m*, Stinktier *nt*.

polemic [pɒ'lemɪk] **1** *adj* polemisch. **2** *n* Polemik *f*; (*act also*) Polemisieren *nt*.

polemical [pɒ'lemɪkəl] *adj* polemisch.

polemicist [pɒ'lemɪsɪst] *n* Polemiker(in *f*) *m*.

polemics [pɒ'lemɪks] *n sing* Polemik *f*.

pole-: ~ position *n* (*Sport*) Innenbahn *f*; **in ~ position** auf der Innenbahn; **~ star** *n* Polarstern *m*; **~ vault 1** *n* Stabhochsprung *m*; (*one jump*) Sprung *m* mit dem Stab; **he did a ~ vault over the fence** er setzte *or* sprang mit einem Stab über den Zaun; **2** *vi* mit dem Stab springen; **~ vaulter** *n* Stabhochspringer(in *f*) *m*; **~ vaulting** *n* Stabhochspringen *nt*, Stabhochsprung *m*.

police [pə'liːs] **1** *n* (+*sing vb: institution, +pl vb: policemen*) Polizei *f*. **to join the ~** zur Polizei gehen; **he is in** *or* **a member of the ~** er ist bei der Polizei; **all ~ leave was cancelled** allen Polizisten wurde der Urlaub gesperrt; **hundreds of ~** hunderte von Polizisten; **extra ~ were called in** es wurden zusätzliche Polizeikräfte angefordert; **three ~ were injured** drei Polizeibeamte *or* Polizisten wurden verletzt.

2 *vt road, frontier, territory, agreement* kontrollieren; *road, agreement, pop-concert also* überwachen. **a heavily ~d area** ein Gebiet mit hoher Polizeidichte.

police-: ~ car *n* Polizeiwagen *m*; **~ constable** *n* (*Brit*) Polizist, Wachtmeister (*inf*) *m*; **~ court** *n* ≈ Polizeigericht *nt*; **~ dog** *n* Polizeihund *m*; **~ escort** *n* Polizei-Eskorte *f*; **~ force** *n* Polizei *f*; **one of the best-equipped ~ forces in the world** eine der bestausgestatteten Polizeitruppen der Welt; **~man** *n* Polizist *m*; **~ officer** *n* Polizeibeamter *m*; **~ protection** *n* Polizeischutz *m*; **~ record** *n* Vorstrafen *pl*; **to have a ~ record** vorbestraft sein; **~ state** *n* Polizeistaat *m*; **~ station** *n* (Polizei)wache *f or* -revier *nt*; **~woman** *n* Polizistin *f*.

policy[1] ['pɒlɪsɪ] *n* Politik *f no pl*; (*of business also*) Geschäfts- *or* Firmenpolitik *f* (*on bei*), Praktiken *pl* (*pej*) (*on in bezug auf* +*acc*); (*of government, newspaper also*) Linie *f*; (*of political party also*) Programm *nt*; (*of team, football manager: tactics*) Taktik *f*; (*principle*) Grundsatz *m*. **social and economic ~** Wirtschafts- und Sozialpolitik *f*; **our ~ on immigration/recruitment** unsere Einwanderungs-/Einstellungspolitik; **what is company ~ on this matter?** wie sieht die Geschäfts- *or* Firmenpolitik in diesem Falle aus?; **the newspaper followed a ~ of attacking the church** die Zeitung verfolgte eine kirchenfeindliche Linie *or* Politik; **a ~ of restricting immigration** eine Politik zur Einschränkung der Einwanderung; **the government was urged to pursue its policies vigorously** man drängte die Regierung, ihre Linie *or* Politik energisch weiterzuverfolgen; **a matter of ~** eine Grundsatzfrage; **~ decision** Grundsatzentscheidung *f*; **~ statement** Grundsatzerklärung *f*; **~-maker** Parteiideologe *m*; **your ~ should always be to give people a second chance** du solltest es dir zum Grundsatz machen, Menschen eine zweite Chance zu geben; **my ~ is to wait and see** meine Devise heißt abwarten; **it's our ~ to cater for the mid-twenties** wir wenden uns mit unserer Firmenpolitik an die Mittzwanziger; **our ~ is one of expansion** wir verfolgen eine expansionsorientierte Geschäftspolitik.

(b) (*prudence, a prudent procedure*) Taktik *f*. **it would not be**

~ **to refuse** es wäre unklug, abzulehnen; **~ demands that the government compromise** die Regierung muß aus taktischen Gründen Kompromisse eingehen; **it was good/bad ~** das war (taktisch) klug/unklug.

policy[2] *n* (*also* **insurance ~**) (Versicherungs)police *f*, Versicherungsschein *m*. **to take out a ~** eine Versicherung abschließen; **~ holder** Versicherungsnehmer *m*.

polio ['pəʊlɪəʊ] *n* Polio, Kinderlähmung *f*. **~ injection** (Spritz)impfung *f* gegen Kinderlähmung; **~ victim** Opfer *nt* der Kinderlähmung, Polioopfer *nt*.

poliomyelitis ['pəʊlɪəʊmaɪə'laɪtɪs] *n* (*form*) Poliomyelitis (*spec*), Kinderlähmung *f*.

Polish ['pəʊlɪʃ] **1** *adj* polnisch. **~ corridor** Polnischer Korridor. **2** *n* (*language*) Polnisch *nt*.

polish ['pɒlɪʃ] **1** *n* **(a)** (*material*) (*shoe ~*) Creme *f*; (*floor ~*) (flüssiges) Wachs; (*furniture ~*) Politur *f*; (*metal ~*) Poliermittel *nt*; (*nail ~*) Lack *m*.

(b) (*act*) **to give sth a ~** etw polieren; *shoes, silver also* etw putzen; *floor* etw bohnern; **my shoes need a ~** meine Schuhe müssen geputzt werden.

(c) (*~ed state, shine*) Glanz *m*; (*of furniture*) Politur *f*. **high ~** Hochglanz *m*, starker Glanz; **there was a high ~ on the floor** der Fußboden war stark gebohnert; **to put a ~ on sth** etw zum Glänzen bringen, Glanz auf etw (*acc*) bringen; **water will take the ~ off** Wasser nimmt den Glanz/greift die Politur an.

(d) (*fig: refinement*) (*of person, style, manners*) Schliff *m*; (*of performance*) Brillanz *f*. **to acquire ~** Schliff bekommen; (*performance*) brillant werden; **he lacks ~** ihm fehlt der Schliff/die Brillanz; **his style lacks ~** an seinem Stil muß noch gearbeitet werden; **he is still a simple lad underneath his ~** unter seiner glänzenden Oberfläche ist er immer noch ein einfacher Bursche.

2 *vt* **(a)** polieren; *silver, shoes also* putzen; *floor* bohnern. **(b)** (*fig*) *person, performance* den letzten Schliff geben (+*dat*); *manner, style also* polieren (*inf*), verfeinern.

♦ **polish off** *vt sep* (*inf*) *food* verdrücken (*inf*), verputzen (*inf*); *drink* wegputzen (*inf*); *work* wegschaffen (*inf*), erledigen; *opponent, competitor* abfertigen, abservieren (*inf*).

♦ **polish up 1** *vt sep* **(a)** *shoes, floor, silver etc* polieren, auf Hochglanz bringen. **(b)** (*fig: improve*) *style* aufpolieren, verfeinern; *work* überarbeiten; **one's French etc** aufpolieren (*inf*). **you'd better ~ ~ your ideas** (*inf*) du solltest dich besser auf den Hosenboden setzen (*inf*). **2** *vi* sich polieren lassen.

polished ['pɒlɪʃt] *adj* **(a)** *surface, furniture* poliert, glänzend; *floor* gebohnert; *stone, glass* geschliffen. **his highly ~ shoes** seine blankgeputzten Schuhe. **(b)** *style etc* verfeinert; *performance, performer* brillant. **(c)** *manners* geschliffen.

polisher ['pɒlɪʃə[r]] *n* (*person*) Schleifer(in *f*) *m*; (*machine*) Schleif-/Polier-/Bohnermaschine *f*.

polite [pə'laɪt] *adj* (+*er*) höflich. **it wouldn't be ~** es wäre unhöflich; **be ~ about her cooking** mach ein paar höfliche Bemerkungen über ihre Kochkunst; **when I said it was good I was just being ~** als ich sagte, es sei gut, wollte ich nur höflich sein; **there's no need to be ~ about it if you don't like it** du kannst es ruhig sagen, wenn es dir nicht gefällt; **~ conversation** höfliche Konversation; **we sat around making ~ conversation** wir saßen zusammen und machten Konversation; **what's a ~ way to end a letter?** was kann man als höfliche Schlußformel unter einen Brief schreiben?

(b) *society* fein.

politely [pə'laɪtlɪ] *adv* höflich.

politeness [pə'laɪtnɪs] *n* Höflichkeit *f*.

politic ['pɒlɪtɪk] *adj* **(a)** klug. **it would be ~ to apologize** es wäre diplomatisch *or* (taktisch) klug, sich zu entschuldigen; **he tended to do what was ~ rather than that which was proper** er machte eher (das), was klug *or* günstig war, als das, was recht gewesen wäre.

(b) **the body ~** das Staatswesen, das staatliche Gemeinwesen.

political [pə'lɪtɪkəl] *adj* politisch. **~ asylum** politisches Asyl; **~ economy** Volkswirtschaft *f*; **~ prisoner** politischer Gefangener, politische Gefangene; **~ science** Politologie *f*.

politically [pə'lɪtɪkəlɪ] *adv* politisch.

politician [‚pɒlɪ'tɪʃən] *n* Politiker(in *f*) *m*.

politicize [pə'lɪtɪsaɪz] *vt* politisieren.

politicking [pə'lɪtɪkɪŋ] *n* (*pej*) politische Aktivitäten *pl*.

politico [pə'lɪtɪkəʊ] *n* (*US pej*) Politiker(in *f*) *m*.

politico- *pref* politisch-.

politics ['pɒlɪtɪks] *n* **(a)** (+*pl vb*) Politik *f*; (*views*) politische Ansichten *pl*. **what are his ~?** welche politischen Ansichten hat er? **(b)** (+*sing or pl vb*) Politik *f*. **to go into ~** in die Politik gehen; **to talk ~** politisieren; **interested in ~** politisch interessiert; **to play ~** (*pej*) große Politik spielen (*pej*).

polity ['pɒlɪtɪ] *n* (*form of government*) politische Ordnung, Staats- *or* Regierungsform *f*; (*politically organized society*) Staat(swesen *nt*) *m*, Gemeinwesen *nt*; (*management of public affairs*) Staatsverwaltung *f*.

polka ['pɒlkə] *n* Polka *f*.

polka dot 1 *n* Tupfen *m*. **2** *adj* getupft, gepunktet.

poll [pəʊl] **1** *n* **(a)** (*Pol: voting*) Abstimmung *f*; (*election*) Wahl *f*. **to take a ~** abstimmen lassen, eine Abstimmung durchführen; **a ~ was taken among the villagers** unter den Dorfbewohnern wurde abgestimmt; **to head the ~** bei der Wahl führen.

(b) (*total of votes cast*) Wahlbeteiligung *f*; (*for individual candidate*) Stimmenanteil *m*. **there was an 84% ~** die Wahlbeteiligung betrug 84%.

(c) **~s** (*voting place*) Wahllokale *pl*; (*election*) Wahl *f*; **to go to the ~s** wählen *or* zur Wahl gehen, an die Urnen gehen; **a crushing defeat at the ~s** eine vernichtende Niederlage bei den Wahlen, eine vernichtende Wahlniederlage; **a photograph of Trudeau at the ~s** ein Foto von Trudeau bei der Stimmabgabe.

(d) (opinion ~) Umfrage f.
(e) (old: head, esp back of head) Schädel m.
2 vt **(a)** votes erhalten, auf sich (acc) vereinigen.
(b) (in opinion ~) befragen. **40% of those ~ed supported the Government** 40% der Befragten waren für die Regierung.
(c) horns stutzen; trees also zurückschneiden. **~ed cattle** Rinder mit gestutzten Hörnern.
3 vi **he ~ed badly in the election** er erhielt bei der Wahl wenige Stimmen, er schnitt bei der Wahl schlecht ab.
pollard ['pɒləd] 1 n (tree) gekappter Baum. 2 vt kappen.
pollen ['pɒlən] n Blütenstaub, Pollen m. **~ basket** Höschen nt, Hose f; **~ count** Pollenzahl f.
pollinate ['pɒlɪneɪt] vt bestäuben.
pollination [,pɒlɪ'neɪʃən] n Bestäubung f.
polling ['pəʊlɪŋ] n Stimmabgabe, Wahl f. **~ will be on Thursday** die Wahl ist am Donnerstag; **~ has been heavy** die Wahlbeteiligung war (sehr) hoch or stark.
polling: **~ booth** n Wahlkabine, Wahlzelle f; **~ card** n Wahlausweis m; **~ day** n Wahltag m; **~ station** n Wahllokal nt.
polliwog ['pɒlɪwɒg] n (US) Kaulquappe f.
pollster ['pəʊlstə'] n Meinungsforscher(in f) m.
pollutant [pə'luːtənt] n Schadstoff m.
pollute [pə'luːt] vt environment verschmutzen; river, atmosphere etc also verunreinigen; atmosphere also verpesten (pej); (fig) mind, morals verderben, korrumpieren.
pollution [pə'luːʃən] n **(a)** Umweltverschmutzung f. **the fight against ~** der Kampf gegen die Umweltverschmutzung. **(b)** see vt Verschmutzung f; Verunreinigung f; Verpestung (pej) f; (fig) Korrumpierung f.
pollywog n see **polliwog**.
polo ['pəʊləʊ] n Polo nt.
polonaise [,pɒlə'neɪz] n Polonaise, Polonäse f.
polo neck n **(a)** n Rollkragen m; (sweater) Rollkragenpulli or -pullover m. 2 adj Rollkragen-.
poltergeist ['pɒltəgaɪst] n Poltergeist, Klopfgeist m.
poltroon [pɒl'truːn] n (liter) feiger Wicht, Memme f.
poly (Brit) abbr of **polytechnic**.
polyandrous [,pɒlɪ'ændrəs] adj Vielmännerei betreibend, polyandrisch (spec); (Bot) polyadelphisch.
polyandry ['pɒlɪændrɪ] n Vielmännerei, Polyandrie (form) f.
polyanthus [,pɒlɪ'ænθəs] n (primrose) Gartenprimel f; (narcissus) Tazette f.
polychromatic [,pɒlɪkrəʊ'mætɪk] adj polychrom.
polyclinic ['pɒlɪklɪnɪk] n Poliklinik f.
polyester [,pɒlɪ'estə'] n Polyester m.
polyethylene [,pɒlɪ'eθəliːn] n Polyäthylen nt.
polygamist [pə'lɪgəmɪst] n Polygamist m.
polygamous [pə'lɪgəməs] adj polygam.
polygamy [pə'lɪgəmɪ] n Polygamie, Vielehe, Vielweiberei f.
polyglot ['pɒlɪglɒt] 1 adj polyglott, vielsprachig. 2 n (person) Polyglotte(r) mf.
polygon ['pɒlɪgən] n Polygon, Vieleck nt.
polygonal [pə'lɪgənl] adj polygonal, vieleckig.
polyhedron [,pɒlɪ'hiːdrən] n Polyeder nt, Vielflächner m.
polymath ['pɒlɪmæθ] n Mensch m mit vielseitigem Wissen.
polymer ['pɒlɪmə'] n Polymer nt.
polymeric [,pɒlɪ'merɪk] adj polymer.
polymerization [,pɒlɪməraɪ'zeɪʃən] n Polymerisation f.
polymorphic [,pɒlɪ'mɔːfɪk] adj polymorph, vielgestaltig.
polymorphism [,pɒlɪ'mɔːfɪzəm] n Polymorphismus m.
Polynesia [,pɒlɪ'niːzɪə] n Polynesien nt.
Polynesian [,pɒlɪ'niːzɪən] 1 adj polynesisch. 2 n **(a)** Polynesier(in f) m. **(b)** (language) Polynesisch nt.
polynomial [,pɒlɪ'nəʊmɪəl] 1 adj polynomisch. 2 n Polynom nt.
polyp ['pɒlɪp] n Polyp m.
polyphonic [,pɒlɪ'fɒnɪk] adj polyphon.
polyphony [pə'lɪfənɪ] n Polyphonie f.
polypropylene [,pɒlɪ'prɒpɪliːn] n Polyprophelyn nt.
polypus ['pɒlɪpəs] n Polyp m.
polysemous [pə'lɪsəməs] adj polysem.
polystyrene [,pɒlɪ'staɪriːn] n Polystyrol nt; (extended also) Styropor nt.
polysyllabic [,pɒlɪsɪ'læbɪk] adj viel- or mehrsilbig.
polysyllable ['pɒlɪ,sɪləbl] n Polysyllabum nt (spec), vielsilbiges Wort.
polytechnic [,pɒlɪ'teknɪk] n (Brit) = Polytechnikum nt; (degree-awarding) Technische Hochschule, TH f.
polytheism ['pɒlɪθiːɪzəm] n Polytheismus m.
polytheistic [,pɒlɪθiː'ɪstɪk] adj polytheistisch.
polythene ['pɒlɪθiːn] n (Brit) Polyäthylen nt; (in everyday language) Plastik nt. **~ bag** Plastiktüte f.
polyunsaturated fats [,pɒlɪʌn'sætʃəreɪtɪd'fæts] npl mehrfach ungesättigte Fettsäuren pl.
polyurethane [,pɒlɪ'jʊərɪθeɪn] n Polyurethan m.
polyvalent [pə'lɪvələnt] adj mehrwertig, polyvalent.
pom¹ [pɒm] n (Austral sl) Engländer(in f), Tommy (dated inf) m.
pom² n (inf) see **Pomeranian 2**.
pomade [pə'mɑːd] 1 n Pomade f. 2 vt mit Pomade einreiben.
pomander [pəʊ'mændə'] n Duftkugel f.
pomegranate ['pɒmə,grænɪt] n Granatapfel m; (tree) Granatapfelbaum, Granatbaum m.
Pomerania [,pɒmə'reɪnɪə] n Pommern nt.
Pomeranian [,pɒmə'reɪnɪən] 1 adj pommer(i)sch. 2 n Pommer(in f) m; (dog) Spitz m.
pommel ['pʌml] 1 n (on sword) Knauf m; (on saddle) Knopf m. 2 vt see **pummel**.
pommy ['pɒmɪ] n (Austral sl) Engländer(in f), Tommy (dated inf) m. **~ bastard** Scheißtommy m (sl).
pomp [pɒmp] n Pomp, Prunk m, Gepränge nt. **~ and circumstance** Pomp und Prunk.
pompadour ['pɒmpədʊə'] n (Hist) Pompadourfrisur f.

Pompeian [pɒm'peɪən] 1 adj pompej(an)isch. 2 n Pompej(an)er(in f) m.
Pompeii [pɒm'peɪiː] n Pompe(j)i nt.
Pompey ['pɒmpɪ] n Pompejus m.
pompom ['pɒmpɒm] n **(a)** (gun) automatische Flugzeugabwehrkanone f. **(b)** (on hat etc) Troddel, Bommel (dial) f.
pomposity [pɒm'pɒsɪtɪ] n see adj Aufgeblasenheit, Wichtigtuerei f; Gespreiztheit f; Schwülstigkeit f, Bombast m.
pompous ['pɒmpəs] adj person aufgeblasen, wichtigtuerisch; attitude, behaviour also, phrase gespreizt; language, letter, remark schwülstig, bombastisch. **don't be so ~** tu nicht so aufgeblasen, sei nicht so wichtigtuerisch.
pompously ['pɒmpəslɪ] adv write, speak schwülstig, bombastisch; behave aufgeblasen, wichtigtuerisch.
'pon [pɒn] prep (old, poet) contr of **upon**.
ponce [pɒns] (Brit sl) 1 n (pimp) Zuhälter, Loddel (inf), Lude (sl) m; (homosexual) Warme(r) (sl), Schwule(r) (inf) m. 2 vi **to ~ for sb** jds Zuhälter sein.
♦ **ponce about** or **around** vi (Brit sl) herumtänzeln.
poncho ['pɒntʃəʊ] n Poncho m.
poncy ['pɒnsɪ] adj (+er) (Brit sl) (homosexual) warm (sl), schwul (inf); pink sweater, walk, actor tuntig (sl).
pond [pɒnd] n Teich m. **the ~** (inf: Atlantic) der große Teich (hum); **~ life** Pflanzen- und Tierleben in Teichen.
ponder ['pɒndə'] 1 vt nachdenken über (+acc); possibilities, consequences etc erwägen, bedenken. 2 vi nachdenken (on, over über +acc).
ponderous ['pɒndərəs] adj schwerfällig; (heavy) massiv.
ponderously ['pɒndərəslɪ] adv schwerfällig.
ponderousness ['pɒndərəsnɪs] n Schwerfälligkeit f; (heaviness) Schwere, Gewichtigkeit f.
pondweed ['pɒndwiːd] n Laichkrautgewächs nt.
pone [pəʊn] n (US) Maisbrot nt.
pong [pɒŋ] (Brit sl) 1 n Gestank, Mief (inf) m. **there's a bit of a ~ in here** hier stinkt's or mieft's (inf). 2 vi stinken, miefen (inf).
poniard ['pɒnjəd] n (liter, old) Dolch m.
pontiff ['pɒntɪf] n Pontifex m; (pope also) Papst m.
pontifical [pɒn'tɪfɪkl] adj **(a)** (lit) pontifikal; (papal) päpstlich. **~ robes** Pontifikalien pl/päpstliche Gewänder pl; **~ duties** Pontifikalien pl/päpstliche Pflichten pl; **P~ Mass** Pontifikalamt nt; **~ office** Pontifikat nt. **(b)** (fig) päpstlich. **his ~ pronouncements** seine feierlichen Verkündigungen.
pontifically [pɒn'tɪfɪklɪ] adv (fig) päpstlich.
pontificate [pɒn'tɪfɪkɪt] 1 n Pontifikat nt. 2 [pɒn'tɪfɪkeɪt] vi (fig) dozieren. **I wish you wouldn't ~ to me** ich wünschte, du würdest nicht in diesem belehrenden Ton mit mir reden.
Pontius Pilate ['pɒnʃəs'paɪlət] n Pontius Pilatus m.
pontoon¹ [pɒn'tuːn] n Ponton m; (on flying boat) Schwimmer m. **~ bridge** Pontonbrücke f.
pontoon² n (Brit Cards) 17 und 4 nt.
pony ['pəʊnɪ] n **(a)** Pony nt. **(b)** (Brit sl) 25 Pfund. **(c)** (US sl: crib) Pons m (Sch sl), Klatsche f (Sch sl). **(d)** (US inf: small glass) Gläschen nt.
pony: **~ express** n Ponyexpress m; **~tail** n Pferdeschwanz m; **she was wearing her hair in a ~tail** sie trug einen Pferdeschwanz; **~ trekking** n Ponyreiten nt; **a ~ trekking holiday** ein Ponyreiturlaub m.
pooch [puːtʃ] n (inf) Hündchen nt.
poodle ['puːdl] n Pudel m.
poof(ter) ['pʊf(tə')] n (Brit sl) Warme(r) (sl), Schwule(r) (inf) m.
poofy ['pʊfɪ] adj (+er) (Brit sl) warm (sl), schwul (inf); clothes, colour, actor tuntig (sl), tuntenhaft (inf).
pooh [puː] interj (bad smell) puh, pfui; (disdain) pah, bah.
pooh-pooh ['puː'puː] vt verächtlich abtun.
pool¹ [puːl] n **(a)** Teich, Tümpel m; (underground) Teich m. **(b)** (of rain) Pfütze f; (of spilt liquid) Lache f. **a ~ of blood** eine Blutlache; **~s of sunlight/shade** sonnige/schattige Stellen. **(c)** (in river) Loch nt. **(d)** (artificial) Teich m; (swimming ~) (Schwimm)becken nt; (in private garden, hotel also) Swimming Pool m; (swimming baths) Schwimmbad nt. **to go to the (swimming) ~** ins Schwimmbad gehen; **an olympic ~ should measure ...** ein olympisches Wettkampfbecken muß ... groß sein; **in the kiddies' ~** im Kinderbecken; **we spent every afternoon down at the ~** wir verbrachten jeden Nachmittag im Schwimmbad; **she was sitting at the edge of the ~** sie saß am Beckenrand.
pool² 1 n **(a)** (common fund) (gemeinsame) Kasse f. **each player put £10 in the ~** jeder Spieler gab £ 10 in die Kasse; **the ~ was £40** es waren £ 40 in der Kasse. **(b)** (supply, source) (typing ~) Schreibzentrale f; (car ~) Fahrzeugpark m; (car-sharing) Fahrgemeinschaft f. **a ~ of labour** ein Bestand m an Arbeitskräften; **eine Arbeitskraftreserve**; **the Prime Minister's ~ of advisers** der Beraterstab des Premierministers; **among them they have a great ~ of experience/ideas** zusammen verfügen sie über eine Menge Erfahrung/Ideen; **there is a great ~ of untapped ability** es gibt große, noch ungenutzte Begabungsreserven. **(c)** **the ~s** pl (football ~) Toto m or nt; **to do the ~s** Toto spielen; **to win the ~s** im Toto gewinnen; **he won £1000 on the ~s** er hat £ 1000 im Toto gewonnen. **(d)** (US: form of snooker) Poolbillard nt. **(e)** (Comm) Interessengemeinschaft f; (US: monopoly, trust) Pool m, Kartell nt. 2 vt resources, savings zusammenlegen; efforts vereinigen (geh). **if we ~ our efforts we'll get the work done sooner** mit vereinten Kräften werden wir schneller mit der Arbeit fertig (werden); **the two scientists ~ed their results** die beiden Wissenschaftler kombinierten ihre Ergebnisse.
pool: **~ hall**, **~ room** n Billardzimmer nt; **~ table** n Billardtisch m.

poop¹ [puːp] n Hütte, Poop f. ~ **deck** Hütten- or Poopdeck nt.
poop² vt (sl: exhaust) schlauchen (sl). **to be ~ed (out)** geschlaucht (sl) or fertig (inf) sein.
poor [puə'] **1** adj (+er) **(a)** arm. ~ **whites** arme weiße Bevölkerung im Süden der USA; a country ~ in natural resources ein an Bodenschätzen armes Land; it's the ~ man's Mercedes/Monte Carlo (inf) das ist der Mercedes/das Monte Carlo des kleinen Mannes (inf); ~ **relation** (fig) armer Verwandter, arme Verwandte.
(b) (not good) schlecht; (lacking quality also, meagre) mangelhaft; health, effort, performance, excuse also, sense of responsibility, leadership schwach; soil also mager, unergiebig; quality also minderwertig. **a ~ chance of success** schlechte Erfolgsaussichten pl; **we had a ~ time of it last night** gestern Abend lief auch alles schief (inf); **a ~ joke** (weak) ein schwacher Witz; (in bad taste) ein geschmackloser Witz; **only £55? that's pretty ~, isn't it?** nur £ 55? das ist aber ziemlich wenig!; **he is a ~ traveller/flier** er verträgt Reisen/Flugreisen nicht gut; **a ~ friend you are!** du bist mir ein schöner Freund!; **that's ~ consolation** das ist ein schwacher Trost; **it's a ~ thing for Britain if ...** es wäre schlecht für Großbritannien, wenn ...; **it will be a ~ day for the world when ...** es wird ein schwarzer Tag für die Welt sein, wenn ...; **this is a pretty ~ state of affairs** das sieht aber gar nicht gut aus; **it's very ~ of them not to have replied** es ist sehr unhöflich, daß sie uns etc (dat) nicht geantwortet haben; **he has a very ~ grasp of the subject** er beherrscht das Fach sehr schlecht; **he showed a ~ grasp of the facts** er zeigte wenig Verständnis für die Fakten; **he is a ~ hand at public speaking** in der Öffentlichkeit zu sprechen liegt ihm nicht; **she was always ~ at languages** sie war immer schlecht or schwach in Sprachen.
(c) (pitiful, pitiable) arm. **you ~ (old) chap** (inf) or **thing** (inf) du armer Tropf (inf); **~ you!** du Ärmste(r)!; **she's all alone, ~ woman** sie ist ganz allein, die arme Frau; **~ things, they look cold** die Ärmsten, ihnen scheint kalt zu sein; **~ miserable creature that he is ...** armseliger Kerl or Tropf (inf), der er ist ...; **in my ~ opinion** (iro) meiner bescheidenen or unmaßgeblichen Meinung nach (iro); **it fell to my ~ self to ...** es blieb meiner Wenigkeit (dat) überlassen, zu ... (iro).
2 npl **the ~** die Armen pl.
poor: ~ **box** n Armen- or Almosenbüchse f; **~house** n (old) Armenhaus nt (old); ~ **laws** npl (Hist) Armengesetze pl.
poorly ['puəlɪ] **1** adv **(a)** arm; dressed, furnished ärmlich. ~ **off** arm dran (inf); **her husband left her very ~ off** ihr Mann ließ sie in sehr ärmlichen Verhältnissen zurück.
(b) (badly) schlecht. ~ **lit** schlecht or schwach beleuchtet; **to do ~ (at sth)** (in some dat) schwach or schlecht abschneiden; **we're rather ~ off for staff/new ideas** wir haben einen ziemlichen Mangel an Personal/neuen Ideen.
2 adj pred (ill) schlecht, krank, elend. **to be ~** sich schlecht etc fühlen.
poorness ['puənɪs] n **(a)** (lack of money) Armut f.
(b) (lack of quality) Dürftigkeit, Mangelhaftigkeit f; (of soil) Magerkeit, Unergiebigkeit f; (of effort, excuse, harvest, performance) Dürftigkeit f; (of quality) Minderwertigkeit f; (of weather, memory, health, eyesight) Unzulänglichkeit f; (of leadership) Schwäche f.
poor-spirited ['puə'spɪrɪtɪd] adj person ängstlich.
poove [puːv] n see **poof(ter)**.
pop¹ abbr of **population**.
pop² [pɒp] n (esp US inf) (father) Pa(pa) m (inf); (elderly man) Opa m (hum inf).
pop³ n (~ music) Popmusik f, Pop m.
pop⁴ n **(a)** (sound) Knall m. **the toy gun went off with a ~** peng, ging die Spielzeugpistole los.
(b) (inf: shot) Schuß m. **to have or take a ~ at sth** auf etw (acc) ballern (inf).
(c) (fizzy drink) Brause, Limo (inf) f.
(d) (dated inf: pawn) **in ~** verpfändet, versetzt.
2 adv **to go ~** (cork) knallen, hochgehen (inf); (balloon) platzen; (ears) mit einem Knacken aufgehen or (when going down) zugehen; **~!** peng!
3 vt **(a)** balloon, corn zum Platzen bringen. **to ~ corn** Popcorn machen.
(b) (inf: put) stecken. **to ~ a letter into the postbox** einen Brief einwerfen or einschmeißen (inf); **he ~ped his head round the door** er streckte den Kopf durch die Tür; **to ~ a jacket/hat on** sich (dat) ein Jackett überziehen/sich (dat) einen Hut aufsetzen; **to ~ the question** einen (Heirats)antrag machen.
(c) (dated inf: pawn) versetzen.
(d) (inf) pills einwerfen (sl), schlucken (inf).
4 vi **(a)** (inf: go ~, burst) (cork) knallen; (balloon) platzen; (seed-pods, buttons, popcorn) aufplatzen; (ears) mit einem Knacken aufgehen or (when going down) zugehen. **his eyes were ~ping out of his head** ihm gingen die Augen über, ihm fielen fast die Augen aus dem Kopf (inf); **suddenly her blouse ~ped open** plötzlich platzte or sprang ihre Bluse auf.
(b) (inf: go quickly or suddenly) **to ~ along/down to the baker's** schnell zum Bäcker laufen; **I'll just ~ upstairs** ich laufe mal eben nach oben; **~ across/over/round and see me sometime** komm doch mal auf einen Sprung bei mir vorbei (inf); **I thought I'd just ~ down to London for the weekend** ich dachte, ich fahr mal eben für ein Wochenende nach London; **the rabbit ~ped into its burrow/through the hedge** das Kaninchen sauste in seinen Bau/durch die Hecke.
◆ **pop at** vi +prep obj (inf: shoot at) ballern auf (+acc) (inf).
◆ **pop back** (inf) **1** vt sep (schnell) zurücktun (inf). ~ **the lid ~ on the box** klapp den Deckel wieder auf der Schachtel; ~ **it ~ into the box** tu es wieder in die Schachtel. **2** vi schnell zurücklaufen. **she ~ped ~ for her book** sie lief zurück, um ihr Buch zu holen.

◆ **pop in** (inf) **1** vt sep hineintun. **to ~ sth ~to sth** etw in etw (acc) stecken or werfen (inf).
2 vi schnell hereinkommen/hereingehen; (visit) auf einen Sprung vorbeikommen (inf). **to ~ for a short chat** auf einen kleinen Schwatz hereinschauen (inf); **she kept ~ping ~ and out** sie lief dauernd rein und raus; **we just ~ped ~to the pub for a quickie** wir gingen kurz in die Kneipe, um einen zu heben (inf); **just ~ ~ any time you're passing** komm doch mal vorbei, wenn du in der Gegend bist (inf).
◆ **pop off** (inf) vi **(a)** (die suddenly) den Geist aufgeben (hum), den Löffel abgeben (sl). **(b)** (inf: go off) verschwinden (inf) (to nach). **do you fancy ~ping ~ to Spain for a week?** wie wär's, wollen wir für eine Woche nach Spanien verschwinden?
◆ **pop out** (inf) vi **(a)** (go out) (schnell) rausgehen (inf)/rauskommen (inf); (spring, rabbit) herausspringen (of aus). **he has just ~ped ~ for a beer** er ist schnell auf ein Bierchen gegangen (inf); **he has just ~ped ~ to buy a paper/to the shops** er ist schnell eine Zeitung kaufen gegangen/er ist schnell zum Einkaufen gegangen.
(b) (eyes) vorquellen. **his eyes were ~ping ~ with amazement** vor Staunen bekam er Stielaugen or fielen ihm fast die Augen aus dem Kopf (inf).
◆ **pop up (a)** (put up) head hochstrecken.
(b) (bring up) schnell raufbringen (inf).
(c) (sl: liven up) old film, musical etc aufmotzen (inf).
2 vt **(a)** (appear suddenly) auftauchen; (head, toast) hochschießen (inf); (figures in illustrations) sich aufstellen.
(b) (come up) (mal eben) raufkommen (inf)/raufgehen (inf); (go up) (mal eben) raufgehen (inf). **do you feel like ~ping ~ to my place?** hast du Lust, mal eben zu mir raufzukommen? (inf).
pop: ~ **art** n Pop-art f; ~ **concert** n Popkonzert nt; **~corn** n Popcorn nt.
Pope [pəʊp] n Papst m.
popery ['pəʊpərɪ] n (pej) Pfaffentum nt. **no ~!** Pfaffen raus!
pop: ~ **eyed** adj person glotzäugig; (fig) mit Glotzaugen; ~ **festival** n Popfestival nt; ~ **group** n Popgruppe f; ~ **gun** n Spielzeugpistole f.
popinjay ['pɒpɪndʒeɪ] n (old) Geck, Laffe m.
popish ['pəʊpɪʃ] adj (pej) papistisch, ultramontan (geh).
poplar ['pɒplə'] n Pappel f.
poplin ['pɒplɪn] n Popeline f. ~ **dress** Popelinekleid nt.
pop: ~ **music** n Popmusik f; **~over** n (US) stark aufgehender hefiger Eierkuchen.
poppa ['pɒpə] n (US inf) Paps m (inf).
popper ['pɒpə'] n (Brit inf: press-stud) Druckknopf m.
poppet ['pɒpɪt] n (inf) Schatz m; (term of address also) Schätzchen nt. **hullo, ~!** grüß dich, Schätzchen or mein Schatz.
poppy ['pɒpɪ] n Mohn m.
poppycock ['pɒpɪkɒk] n (dated inf) Unsinn, Blödsinn (inf) m.
poppy: **P~ Day** (Brit) ≈ Volkstrauertag m (BRD); **~-seed** n Mohn m; **~-seed cake** Mohnkuchen m.
pops ['pɒps] n (esp US inf) Paps m (inf).
pop: ~ **shop** n (dated inf) Pfandhaus nt; ~ **singer** n Schlagersänger(in f) m; ~ **song** n Popsong m; (hit) Schlager m; ~ **star** n Popstar, Schlagerstar m.
popsy ['pɒpsɪ] n (dated sl) Biene (inf), Puppe (inf) f.
populace ['pɒpjʊlɪs] n breite Masse, breite Öffentlichkeit f. **the ~ of Rome** das Volk von Rom, die Bürger von Rom.
popular ['pɒpjʊlə'] adj **(a)** (well-liked) beliebt (with bei); (with the public also) populär (with bei); decision, measure populär. **I know I won't be ~ if I decide that, but ...** ich weiß, daß ich mich nicht gerade beliebt mache, wenn ich so entscheide, aber ...; **he's not the most ~ of men at the moment** er ist im Augenblick nicht gerade einer der Beliebtesten or (with the public also) Populärsten; **he was a very ~ choice** seine Wahl fand großen Anklang; **a ~ part of town to live in** ein als Wohngegend sehr beliebter or populärer Stadtteil.
(b) (suitable for the general public) populär; music leicht; prices erschwinglich; science Populär-; edition Volks-; lectures, journal populärwissenschaftlich. **a series of ~ concerts** eine Reihe volkstümlicher Konzerte.
(c) (widespread) belief, fallacy, conviction, discontent weitverbreitet; (of or for the people) government, approval, consent, support des Volkes. ~ **front** Volksfront f; ~ **remedy** Hausmittel nt; **it's ~ to despise politicians these days** es gehört heutzutage zum guten Ton, sich über Politiker abfällig zu äußern; **he's ~ idea of a great leader** er entspricht nicht gerade der gängigen Vorstellung von einem großen Führer; **to rule by ~ consent** mit Zustimmung der Allgemeinheit regieren; **by ~ request** auf allgemeinen Wunsch.
popularity [ˌpɒpjʊ'lærɪtɪ] n Beliebtheit f; (with the public also) Popularität f (with bei). **he'd do anything to win ~** er würde alles tun, um sich beliebt zu machen; **he'd never win a ~ contest!** er ist nicht gerade beliebt; **the sport is growing/declining in ~** dieser Sport wird immer populärer/verliert immer mehr an Popularität.
popularization [ˌpɒpjʊləraɪ'zeɪʃən] n **(a)** (act) Popularisierung f, allgemeine Einführung or Verbreitung.
(b) (popularized work) Popularisierung f. **his new book is a mere ~ of his previous work** sein neues Buch ist nur eine Popularfassung seines früheren Werkes; **a ~ of Hamlet** eine Volksfassung von Hamlet.
popularize ['pɒpjʊlaraɪz] vt **(a)** (make well-liked) populär machen, zum Durchbruch verhelfen (+dat). **(b)** (make understandable) science popularisieren, unter das Volk bringen (inf); ideas also zum Durchbruch verhelfen (+dat).
popularizer ['pɒpjʊləraɪzə'] n **he is a great ~ of political/scientific ideas** er macht politische/wissenschaftliche Ideen auch der breiten Masse zugänglich.
popularly ['pɒpjʊləlɪ] adv allgemein. **he is ~ believed to be a rich man** nach allgemeiner Ansicht ist er ein reicher Mann.

populate ['pɒpjʊleɪt] *vt* (*inhabit*) bevölkern; (*colonize*) besiedeln. this area is ~d mainly by immigrants in diesem Stadtteil leben *or* wohnen hauptsächlich Einwanderer; densely ~d areas/cities dichtbesiedelte Gebiete *pl*/dichtbevölkerte Städte *pl*.

population [ˌpɒpjʊˈleɪʃən] *n* (*of region, country*) Bevölkerung *f*; (*of village, town*) Bewohner, Einwohner *pl*; (*colonization*) Besiedlung *f*; (*number of inhabitants*) Bevölkerungszahl *f*. the ~ explosion die Bevölkerungsexplosion; the growing Negro ~ of London die wachsende Zahl von Schwarzen in London.

populous ['pɒpjʊləs] *adj country* dicht besiedelt; *town, area also* mit vielen Einwohnern, einwohnerstark.

pop-up ['pɒpʌp] *adj toaster* automatisch; *book, picture* Hochklapp- (*inf*).

porage *n see* porridge.

porcelain ['pɔːsəlɪn] **1** *n* Porzellan *nt*. **2** *adj* Porzellan-.

porch [pɔːtʃ] *n* (*of house*) Vorbau *m*, Vordach *nt*; (*US*) Veranda *f*; (*of church*) Vorhalle *f*, Portal *nt*.

porcine ['pɔːsaɪn] *adj* (*pig-like*) schweineartig; (*of pigs*) Schweine-. ... are members of the ~ family ... gehören zur Familie der Schweine *or* zu den Schweineartigen.

porcupine ['pɔːkjʊpaɪn] *n* Stachelschwein *nt*.

pore [pɔːʳ] *n* Pore *f*.

♦**pore over** *vi + prep obj* (*scrutinize*) genau studieren; (*meditate*) nachdenken *or* nachgrübeln über (+*acc*). to ~ one's books über seinen Büchern hocken.

pork [pɔːk] *n* (**a**) Schweinefleisch *nt*. (**b**) (*US sl*) von der Regierung aus politischen Gründen gewährte finanzielle Vergünstigungen *oder* Stellen.

pork: ~ barrel *n* (*US inf*) Geldzuwendungen *pl* der Regierung an örtliche Verwaltungsstellen, um deren Unterstützung zu gewinnen; ~ butcher *n* Schweinemetzger *m*; ~ chop *n* Schweine- *or* Schweinskotelett *nt*.

porker ['pɔːkəʳ] *n* Mastschwein *nt*.

pork: ~ pie *n* Schweinepastete *f*; ~ pie hat *n* runder, niedriger Filzhut; ~ sausage *n* Schweinewurst *f*.

porky ['pɔːkɪ] *adj* (+*er*) (**a**) Schweinefleisch-. (**b**) (*inf: fat*) fett.

porn [pɔːn], (*esp US*) **porno** ['pɔːnəʊ] *n* (*inf*) Porno *m* (*inf*). **hard/soft** ~ harter/zahmer Porno; ~-shop Pornoladen *m* (*inf*).

pornographic *adj*, ~ally *adv* [ˌpɔːnəˈɡræfɪk, -əlɪ] pornographisch.

pornography [pɔːˈnɒɡrəfɪ] *n* Pornographie *f*.

porosity [pɔːˈrɒsɪtɪ] *n* (*of rocks, of substance*) Porosität *f*; (*of skin*) Porigkeit *f*.

porous ['pɔːrəs] *adj rock, substance* porös; *skin* porig.

porousness ['pɔːrəsnɪs] *n see* porosity.

porphyry ['pɔːfɪrɪ] *n* Porphyr *m*.

porpoise ['pɔːpəs] *n* Tümmler *m*.

porridge ['pɒrɪdʒ] *n* Porridge, Haferbrei *m*. ~ oats Haferflocken *pl*.

porringer ['pɒrɪndʒəʳ] *n* Porridgetopf *m*.

port[1] [pɔːt] *n* (**a**) (*harbour*) Hafen *m*. naval ~ Kriegshafen *m*; to come/put into ~ in den Hafen einlaufen; ~ authority Hafenamt *nt*, Hafenbehörde *f*; ~ dues Hafengelder *pl*; any ~ in a storm (*prov*) in der Not frißt der Teufel Fliegen (*Prov*).

(**b**) (*city or town with a* ~) Hafen *m*, Hafenstadt *f*.

port[2] *n* (**a**) (*Naut, Aviat: ~hole*) Bullauge *nt*. (**b**) (*Naut: for cargo*) (Lade)luke *f*. (**c**) (*Tech*) Durchlaß(öffnung *f*) *m*.

port[3] **1** *n* (*Naut, Aviat: left side*) Backbord *m*. land to ~! Land an Backbord! **2** *adj side* Backbord-; *cabin, deck also* auf der Backbordseite. on the ~ bow Backbord voraus. **3** *vt* (*Naut*): to ~ the helm nach Backbord drehen.

port[4] *n* (*also* ~ wine) Portwein *m*.

port[5] (*Mil*) **1** *n* to hold the rifle at ~ das Gewehr (schräg nach links) vor dem Körper halten. **2** *vt arms* schräg nach links vor dem Körper halten. ~ arms! = präsentiert das Gewehr!

portable ['pɔːtəbl] *adj* tragbar; *radio, typewriter also* Koffer-. easily ~ leicht zu tragen; a ~ television ein Portable *nt*, ein tragbarer Fernseher *m*.

portage ['pɔːtɪdʒ] *n* (*Comm*) (*act*) Transport *m*, Beförderung *f*; (*cost*) Rollgeld *nt*, Transportkosten *pl*, Beförderungsentgelt *nt*.

portal ['pɔːtl] *n* (*liter*) Portal *nt*, Pforte *f* (*geh*), Tor *nt*. the ~s of heaven die Pforten *pl* des Himmels (*geh*).

portal vein *n* Pfortader *f*.

portcullis [pɔːtˈkʌlɪs] *n* Fallgitter, Fallgatter *nt*.

porte-cochère [ˌpɔːtkɒˈʃɛəʳ] *n* Wagenauffahrt *f*.

portend [pɔːˈtend] *vt* (*form*) bedeuten, hindeuten auf (+*acc*). what does this ~? was hat das zu bedeuten?

portent ['pɔːtent] *n* Zeichen, Omen (*geh*) *nt* (*of* für). a matter of great ~ for us all eine Angelegenheit (*von*) großer Tragweite für uns alle; a ~ of doom ein böses Omen; to be a ~ of sth etw ahnen lassen.

portentous [pɔːˈtentəs] *adj* (*ominous*) unheilschwanger; (*marvellous*) gewaltig; (*grave*) gewichtig; (*pompous*) bombastisch.

porter[1] ['pɔːtəʳ] *n* (*of office etc*) Pförtner, Portier *m*; (*hospital* ~) Pfleger *m*; (*at hotel*) Portier *m*; (*Rail, at airport*) Gepäckträger *m*; (*Sherpa etc*) (Lasten)träger *m*; (*US Rail*) Schlafwagenschaffner *m*. ~'s lodge Pförtnerloge *f*.

porter[2] *n* (*beer*) Porter *m or nt*.

porterage ['pɔːtərɪdʒ] *n* (*charge*) Trägerlohn *m*.

porterhouse steak ['pɔːtəhaʊsˈsteɪk] *n* Porterhouse Steak *nt*.

portfolio [pɔːtˈfəʊlɪəʊ] *n* (**a**) (*Akten*)mappe *f*. (**b**) (*Pol: office*) Portefeuille (*form*) *nt*, Geschäftsbereich *m*. **minister without** ~ Minister ohne Portefeuille (*form*) *or* Geschäftsbereich. (**c**) (*Fin*) Portefeuille *nt*. (**d**) (*of artist, designer*) Kollektion *f*.

porthole ['pɔːthəʊl] *n* Bullauge *nt*.

portico ['pɔːtɪkəʊ] *n* Portikus *m*.

portion ['pɔːʃən] *n* (**a**) (*piece, part*) Teil *m*; (*of ticket*) Abschnitt *m*. your/my ~ dein/mein Anteil *m*. (**b**) (*of food*) Portion *f*. (**c**) (*old, form: marriage* ~) Mitgift *f*, Heiratsgut *nt* (*old*). (**d**) (*liter: fate*) Los, Schicksal *nt*.

♦**portion out** *vt sep* aufteilen, verteilen (*among* unter +*acc*).

portliness ['pɔːtlɪnɪs] *n* Beleibtheit, Korpulenz *f*.

portly ['pɔːtlɪ] *adj* (+*er*) beleibt, korpulent.

portmanteau [pɔːtˈmæntəʊ] *n, pl* -s *or* -x Handkoffer *m*. ~ word Portmanteau-Wort *nt*.

Porto Rico ['pɔːtəʊˈriːkəʊ] *etc see* **Puerto Rico** *etc*.

portrait ['pɔːtrɪt] *n* (*also in words*) Porträt *nt*. to have one's ~ painted sich malen lassen; to sit for one's ~ für sein Porträt sitzen; to paint a ~ of sb jdn porträtieren; (*verbally also*) ein Porträt *or* Bild *nt* von jdm zeichnen.

portraitist ['pɔːtrɪtɪst] *n* Porträtist(in *f*) *m*.

portrait painter *n* Porträtmaler(in *f*) *m*.

portraiture ['pɔːtrɪtʃəʳ] *n* (*portrait*) Porträt *nt*; (*portraits collectively*) Porträts *pl*; (*art of* ~) (*painting*) Porträtmalerei *f*; (*Phot*) Porträtfotografie *f*.

portray [pɔːˈtreɪ] *vt* darstellen; (*paint also*) malen; (*describe also*) schildern.

portrayal [pɔːˈtreɪəl] *n* Darstellung *f*; (*description also*) Schilderung *f*.

Portugal ['pɔːtjʊɡəl] *n* Portugal *nt*.

Portuguese [ˌpɔːtjʊˈɡiːz] **1** *adj* portugiesisch. ~ man-of-war Staats- *or* Röhrenqualle, Portugiesische Galeere *f*. **2** *n* Portugiese *m*, Portugiesin *f*; (*language*) Portugiesisch *nt*.

pose [pəʊz] **1** *n* (**a**) (*position, attitude*) Haltung *f*; (*of model, pej also*) Pose *f*. to take up a ~ (*model*) eine Pose *or* Haltung einnehmen; to hold a ~ eine Pose *or* Haltung beibehalten; to strike a (*dramatic*) ~ sich (dramatisch) in Positur werfen; she's always striking ~s sie benimmt sich immer so theatralisch.

(**b**) (*affectation*) Pose *f*. it's only a ~ das ist nur Pose.

2 *vt* (**a**) (*position*) *model* aufstellen.

(**b**) (*put forward*) *question, problem* vortragen. the question ~d by his speech die in seiner Rede aufgeworfene Frage.

(**c**) (*formulate*) *question, problem* formulieren.

(**d**) (*constitute, present*) *difficulties, problem* aufwerfen; *threat* darstellen.

3 *vi* (**a**) (*model*) posieren; (*sitting also*) (Modell) sitzen; (*standing also*) Modell stehen. to ~ in the nude für einen Akt posieren *or* Modell sitzen/stehen.

(**b**) (*attitudinize*) posieren, sich in Pose werfen.

(**c**) (*present oneself as*) to ~ as sich ausgeben als.

Poseidon [pəˈsaɪdn] *n* Poseidon *m*.

poser ['pəʊzəʳ] *n* (**a**) (*person*) Wichtigtuer, Aufschneider *m*. **Tartuffe, the** ~ Tartuffe, der Heuchler. (**b**) (*inf: difficult problem or question*) harte Nuß (*inf*).

posh [pɒʃ] (*inf*) **1** *adj* (+*er*) piekfein (*inf*), vornehm; *neighbourhood, hotel, wedding also* nobel; *friends* vornehm, fein.

2 *adv* (+*er*) **to talk** ~ mit vornehmem Akzent sprechen.

3 *vt* **to** ~ **sth up** (*inf*) etw verschönern (*inf*).

poshly ['pɒʃlɪ] *adj* piekfein (*inf*), vornehm; *talk* vornehm.

poshness ['pɒʃnɪs] *n* Feinheit, Vornehmheit *f*; (*of accent*) Vornehmheit *f*, Distinguierte(s) *nt*.

posit ['pɒzɪt] **1** *n* (*claim*) Postulat *nt*, Grundannahme *f*. **2** *vt* (**a**) (*rare: put down*) absetzen. (**b**) (*claim*) postulieren; *hypothesis* aufstellen.

position [pəˈzɪʃən] **1** *n* (**a**) (*location, place where sb/sth is*) (*of person*) Platz *m*; (*of object also*) Stelle *f*; (*of microphone, statue, wardrobe, plant etc*) Standort *m*; (*of spotlight, table, in picture, painting*) Anordnung *f*; (*of town, house etc*) Lage *f*; (*of plane, ship, Sport: starting* ~, *Ftbl etc*) Position *f*; (*Mil: strategic site*) Stellung *f*. to be in/out of ~ an der richtigen/falschen Stelle sein; the actors were in ~ on the stage die Schauspieler hatten ihre Plätze auf der Bühne eingenommen; to jockey *or* jostle for ~ (*lit*) um eine gute Ausgangsposition kämpfen; (*fig*) um eine gute Position rangeln; the ~ of the picture/fireplace isn't very good das Bild hängt nicht sehr günstig/der Kamin hat keinen sehr günstigen Platz; what ~ do you play? auf *or* in welcher Position spielst du?; his ~ is full-back/goalkeeper er spielt Außenverteidiger/Torwart.

(**b**) (*posture, way of standing, sitting etc*) Haltung *f*; (*in lovemaking, Art: of model*) Stellung *f*; (*Ballet*) Position *f*. in a reclining ~ zurückgelehnt.

(**c**) (*in class, league etc*) Platz *m*. after the third lap he was in fourth ~ nach der dritten Runde lag er auf dem vierten Platz *or* war er Vierter; to finish in third ~ Dritter werden, auf dem dritten Platz landen (*inf*).

(**d**) (*social, professional standing*) Stellung, Position *f*. a man of ~ eine hochgestellte Persönlichkeit.

(**e**) (*job*) Stelle *f*. he has a high ~ in the Ministry of Defence er bekleidet eine hohe Stellung *or* Position im Verteidigungsministerium; a ~ of trust eine Vertrauensstellung.

(**f**) (*fig: situation, circumstance*) Lage *f*. to be in a ~ to do sth in der Lage sein, etw zu tun; what is the ~ regarding ...? wie sieht es mit ... aus?; I'm not in a ~ to say anything about that ich kann dazu nichts sagen; my ~ is that I don't have the qualifications/money mir geht es so, daß mir die Qualifikation/das Geld fehlt.

(**g**) (*fig: point of view, attitude*) Standpunkt *m*, Haltung, Einstellung *f*. what is the government's ~ on ...? welchen Standpunkt vertritt die Regierung zu ...?

2 *vt* (*place in* ~) *microphone, ladder, guards* aufstellen; *soldiers, policemen* postieren; (*artist, photographer etc*) plazieren. he ~ed himself where he could see her er stellte *or* (*seated*) setzte sich so, daß er sie sehen konnte.

positive ['pɒzɪtɪv] **1** *adj* (**a**) (*Math, Phot, Elec, Gram*) positiv; *pole* Plus-. the ~ degree (*Gram*) der Positiv.

(**b**) (*affirmative, constructive*) *result, answer* positiv; *attitude also* bejahend; *criticism, suggestion* konstruktiv. he is a very ~ person er hat eine sehr positive Einstellung zum Leben.

(**c**) (*definite*) *person, tone of voice* bestimmt; *instructions* streng; *evidence, answer* definitiv, eindeutig; *rule* fest. that is

~ **proof** or **proof** ~ das ist der sichere or eindeutige Beweis; **to my** ~ **knowledge** ... ich bin mir völlig sicher or weiß definitiv ...; **to be** ~ **that** ... sicher sein, daß ..., definitiv wissen, daß ...; **to be** ~ **about** or **of sth** sich (dat) einer Sache (gen) absolut sicher sein.

(d) (real, downright) **this is a** ~ **miracle/crime/disgrace** das ist wirklich ein Wunder/Verbrechen/eine Schande, das ist ein wahres Wunder/geradezu ein Verbrechen/eine Schande; **he's a** ~ **genius/menace** er ist wirklich ein Genie/Ärgernis, er ist ein wahres Genie/wirkliches Ärgernis.

2 n (Phot) Positiv nt; (Gram) Positiv m; (Elec) Pluspol m.

positively ['pozıtıvlı] adv (a) (affirmatively, constructively, Sci) positiv. (b) (decisively) bestimmt; (definitely, indisputably) prove definitiv, eindeutig. (c) (really, absolutely) wirklich, echt (inf).

positiveness ['pozıtıvnıs] n (a) (constructiveness) Positive(s) nt. I was reassured by the ~ of his attitude ich wurde durch seine positive Haltung bestärkt.
(b) (certainty) Überzeugung f; (of voice also) Bestimmtheit f; (of evidence) Überzeugungskraft f. her ~ about his innocence die Überzeugung, mit der sie an seine Unschuld glaubte.

positivism ['pozıtıvızəm] n Positivismus m.

positivist ['pozıtıvıst] 1 adj positivistisch. 2 n Positivist m.

positivistic adj, ~**ally** adv [pozıtı'vıstık, -əlı] positivistisch.

positron ['pozıtron] n Positron nt.

poss [pos] abbr of **possible, possibly** mögl.

posse ['posı] n (US: sheriff's ~) Aufgebot nt; (fig) Gruppe, Schar f. ~ **of searchers** Suchtrupp m.

possess [pə'zes] vt besitzen; (form) foreign language, facts verfügen über (+acc). **to** ~ **oneself of sth** (form) sich in den Besitz von etw bringen (form), etw (acc) an sich nehmen; **to be** ~**ed of sth** (form) über etw (acc) verfügen; **it** ~**s many advantages** es hat viele Vorteile; **to be** ~**ed by demons/by an idea** von Dämonen/einer Idee besessen sein; **to be** ~**ed by or with rage** voll von or voller Wut sein; **to fight like one** ~**ed** wie ein Besessener kämpfen; **whatever** ~**ed you to do that?** was ist bloß in Sie gefahren, so etwas zu tun?; **to** ~ **oneself** or **one's soul in patience** (form) sich in Geduld fassen.

possession [pə'zeʃən] n (a) (ownership) Besitz m; (Sport: of ball) Ballbesitz m; (fig: control: of feelings, oneself) Kontrolle f. **to have sth in one's** ~ etw in seinem Besitz haben; **to have/take** ~ **of sth** etw in Besitz haben/nehmen; **to come into/get** ~ **of sth** in den Besitz von etw gelangen/kommen; **to get/have** ~ **of the ball** in Ballbesitz gelangen/sein; **to be in** ~ **of sth** im Besitz von etw sein; **to be in** ~ **of a high income** über ein hohes Einkommen verfügen; **I'm in full** ~ **of the facts** ich verfüge über alle Tatsachen; **he put me in** ~ **of the information I required** er lieferte or verschaffte mir die Informationen, die ich benötigte; **according to the information in my** ~ nach den mir zur Verfügung stehenden Informationen; **to be in** ~ **of a house** ein Haus in Besitz haben; **to take** ~ **of a house** ein Haus in Besitz nehmen; ~ **is nine points of the law** (prov) das Recht steht auf der Seite des Besitzenden.
(b) (by demons) Besessenheit f.
(c) (thing possessed) Besitz m no pl; (territory) Besitzung f. **all his** ~**s** sein gesamter Besitz, seine gesamten Besitztümer.

possessive [pə'zesıv] 1 adj (a) (towards belongings) eigen; mother, boyfriend, love etc besitzergreifend. **to be** ~ **about sth** seine Besitzansprüche auf etw (acc) betonen; **to be** ~ **towards sb** an jdn Besitzansprüche stellen.
(b) (Gram) ~ **pronoun/adjective** besitzanzeigendes Fürwort, Possessivpronomen nt; ~ **case** Genitiv m, zweiter Fall.
2 n (Gram) (pronoun, adjective) Possessiv(um) nt; (case) Genitiv m, zweiter Fall.

possessively [pə'zesıvlı] adv (about things) eigen; (towards people) besitzergreifend.

possessiveness [pə'zesıvnıs] n eigene Art (about mit); (towards people) besitzergreifende Art (towards gegenüber).

possessor [pə'zesə'] n Besitzer(in f) m. **to be the proud** ~ **of sth** der stolze Besitzer von etw sein.

posset ['posıt] n heiße Milch mit Bier oder Wein und Gewürzen.

possibility [posə'bılıtı] n Möglichkeit f. **there's not much** ~ **of success/of his** or **him being successful** die Aussichten auf Erfolg/darauf, daß er Erfolg hat, sind nicht sehr groß; **within the bounds of** ~ im Bereich des Möglichen; **do you by any** ~ **happen to know** ...? wissen Sie zufällig ...?; **the** ~ **of doing sth** die Möglichkeit or Chance, etw zu tun; **it's a distinct** ~ **that** ... es besteht eindeutig die Möglichkeit, daß ...; **he is a** ~ **for the job** er kommt für die Stelle in Frage or Betracht; **a third world war is always a grim** ~ ein dritter Weltkrieg muß als düstere Möglichkeit immer in Betracht gezogen werden; **there is some** ~ or a ~ **that** ... es besteht die Möglichkeit, daß ...; **a job with real possibilities** eine Stelle mit echten Möglichkeiten or Chancen; **he/that has possibilities** in ihm/darin stecken Möglichkeiten.

possible ['posəbl] 1 adj möglich. **anything is** ~ möglich ist alles; **to make sth** ~ etw ermöglichen, etw möglich machen; **as soon/often/far as** ~ so bald/oft/weit wie möglich; **the best/worst/quickest** ~ ... der/die/das bestmögliche/schlechtestmögliche/schnellstmögliche ...; **if (at all)** ~ falls (irgend) möglich; **it's just** ~ **that I'll see you before then** eventuell sehe ich dich vorher noch; **it's just** ~, **I suppose** es ist unwahrscheinlich, aber möglich; **there is no** ~ **excuse for his behaviour** für sein Verhalten gibt es absolut keine Entschuldigung; **the only** ~ **choice, the only choice** ~ die einzig mögliche Wahl; **it will be** ~ **for you to return the same day** es besteht or Sie haben die Möglichkeit, am selben Tag zurückzukommen.
2 n Möglichkeit f. **a long list of** ~**s for the job** eine lange Liste möglicher Kandidaten für die Stelle; **the** ~**s played the probables** (Sport) die möglichen Kandidaten spielten gegen die wahrscheinlichen (Kandidaten); **he is a** ~ **for the English team** er kommt für die englische Mannschaft in Frage.

possibly ['posəblı] adv (a) not ~ unmöglich; **that can't** ~ **be true** das kann unmöglich wahr sein; **can that** ~ **be true?** kann das (vielleicht doch) stimmen?; **how could I** ~ **have come?** wie hätte ich denn kommen können?; **how could he** ~ **have known that?** wie konnte er das nur wissen?; **he did all he** ~ **could** er tat, was er nur konnte; **if I** ~ **can** wenn ich irgend kann.
(b) (perhaps) vielleicht, möglicherweise.

possum ['posəm] n Opossum nt, Beutelratte f. **to play** ~ (sleeping) sich schlafend stellen; (dead) sich tot stellen.

post[1] [pəust] 1 n (pole, door ~ etc) Pfosten m; (lamp ~) Pfahl m; (telegraph ~) Mast m. **a wooden/metal** ~ ein Holzpfosten or -pfahl m/ein Metallpfosten m; **starting/winning** or **finishing** ~ Start-/Zielpfosten m; **the horses were at the** ~ die Pferde standen am Start; **he was left at the** ~ sie ließen ihn stehen; **to be beaten at the** ~ (lit) im Ziel abgefangen werden; see **deaf**.
2 vt (a) (display) (also ~ **up**) anschlagen. "~ **no bills**" „Plakate ankleben verboten"; **to** ~ **a wall with advertisements** eine Wand plakatieren or mit Werbeplakaten bekleben.
(b) (announce) concert etc durch Anschlag bekanntmachen. **to** ~ **a reward** eine Belohnung ausschreiben; **to** ~ **(as) missing** als vermißt melden.

post[2] 1 n (a) (job) Stelle f, Posten m. **to look for/take up a** ~ eine Stelle suchen/antreten.
(b) (esp Mil: place of duty) Posten m. **at one's** ~ auf seinem Posten; **to die at one's** ~ im Dienst sterben.
(c) (Mil: camp, station) Posten m. **a frontier** ~ ein Grenzposten m; **a chain of** ~**s along the border** eine Postenkette entlang der Grenze; ~ **exchange** (abbr PX) (US) von der Regierung betriebener Vorzugsladen für Truppenangehörige; **to return to/leave the** ~ zur Garnison zurückkehren/die Garnison verlassen; **most of the officers live on the** ~ die meisten Offiziere leben in der Garnison; **the whole** ~ **fell sick** die ganze Garnison wurde krank.
(d) (Brit Mil: bugle-call) **first** ~ Wecksignal nt; **last** ~ Zapfenstreich m.
(e) (trading ~) Handelsniederlassung f.
2 vt (a) (position) postieren; sentry, guard also aufstellen.
(b) (send, assign) versetzen; (Mil also) abkommandieren. **to be** ~**ed to a batallion/an embassy/a ship** zu einem Bataillon/an eine Botschaft/auf ein Schiff versetzt or (Mil) abkommandiert werden; **he has been** ~**ed away** er ist versetzt or (Mil) abkommandiert worden.

post[3] 1 n (a) (esp Brit: mail) Post f. **by** ~ mit der Post, auf dem Postweg (form); **it's in the** ~ es ist unterwegs or in der Post; **to drop sth in the** ~ etw in (den Briefkasten) einwerfen; (in post office) etw zur Post bringen; **to catch/miss the** ~ (letter) noch/nicht mehr mit der Post mitkommen; (person) rechtzeitig zur Leerung kommen/die Leerung verpassen; **there is no** ~ **today** (no delivery) heute kommt keine Post, heute wird keine Post ausgetragen; (no letters) heute ist keine Post (für uns) gekommen; **has the** ~ **been?** war die Post schon da?
(b) (Hist) Post f. **to travel** ~ mit der Post(kutsche) reisen.
2 vt (a) (put in ~) aufgeben; (in letter-box) einwerfen, einstecken; (send by ~ also) mit der Post schicken. **I** ~**ed it to you on Monday** ich habe es am Montag an Sie abgeschickt.
(b) (inform) **to keep sb** ~**ed** jdn auf dem laufenden halten.
(c) (enter in ledger: also ~ **up**) eintragen (to in +acc). **all transactions must be** ~**ed (up) weekly** alle Geschäftsvorgänge müssen wöchentlich verbucht werden.
3 vi (old: travel by ~) mit der Post(kutsche) reisen.

♦**post off** vt sep abschicken.

post- [pəust-] pref nach-; (esp with foreign words) post-.

postage ['pəustıdʒ] n Porto nt, Postgebühr f (form). ~ **and packing** (abbr p&p) Porto und Verpackung; **what is the** ~ **to Germany?** wie hoch ist das Porto nach Deutschland?

postage: ~ **meter** n (US) Frankiermaschine f; ~ **paid** 1 adj portofrei; envelope frankiert, freigemacht, Frei-; 2 adv portofrei; ~ **rate** n Porto nt no pl, Postgebühr f; ~ **stamp** n Briefmarke f.

postal ['pəustl] 1 adj Post-, postalisch (form). 2 n (US inf) see ~ **card**.

postal: ~ **card** n (US) (letter card) Postkarte f mit aufgedruckter Briefmarke für offizielle Zwecke; (postcard) Postkarte f; (with picture) Ansichtskarte f; ~ **code** n (Brit) Postleitzahl f; ~ **district** n (of main sorting office) ~ Postort m (form); (of local sorting office) ~ Postzustellbereich m (form); ~ **order** n (Brit) Geldanweisung, die bei der Post gekauft und eingelöst wird; ~ **tuition** n Fernunterricht m; ~ **vote** n to have a ~ **vote** per Briefwahl wählen.

post: ~**bag** n (Brit) Postsack m; ~**box** n (Brit) Briefkasten m; ~**card** n Postkarte f; (picture) ~**card** n Ansichtskarte f; ~**chaise** n (Hist) Postkutsche f; ~**classical** adj nachklassisch; ~ **code** n (Brit) Postleitzahl f; ~**date** vt (a) cheque etc vordatieren; (b) (be later than) später datieren als (+nom); ~**doctoral** adj nach der or im Anschluß an die Promotion.

poster ['pəustə'] n (advertising) Plakat nt; (for decoration also) Poster nt. ~ **colour** or **paint** Plakatfarbe, Plakafarbe ® f.

poste restante ['pəust'resta:nt] (Brit) 1 n Aufbewahrungsstelle f für postlagernde Sendungen. 2 adv postlagernd.

posterior [po'stıərıə'] 1 adj (form) hinter; (in time) später. **to be** ~ **to sth** hinter etw (dat) liegen; nach etw (dat) kommen, auf etw (acc) folgen. 2 n (hum) Allerwertester m (hum).

posterity [po'sterıtı] n die Nachwelt.

postern ['pəustə:n] n (old) Seitenpforte, Nebenpforte f.

post: ~**free** adj, adv portofrei, gebührenfrei; ~**glacial** adj postglazial, nacheiszeitlich; ~**graduate** 1 n jd, der seine Studien nach dem ersten akademischen Grad weiterführt; 2 adj ~**graduate course** Anschlußkurs m; ~**haste** adv schnellstens, auf dem schnellsten Wege; ~**horn** n Posthorn nt; ~ **house** n (Hist) Posthalterei f.

posthumous ['postjuməs] adj post(h)um; child also nachgeboren.

posthumously ['pɒstjʊməslɪ] *adv* post(h)um.
postil(l)ion [pə'stɪlɪən] *n* Reiter *m* des Sattelpferdes, Fahrer *m* vom Sattel (*form*).
post-impressionism ['pəʊstɪm'preʃnɪzəm] *n* Nachimpressionismus *m*.
post-impressionist ['pəʊstɪm'preʃnɪst] **1** *adj* nachimpressionistisch. **2** *n* Nachimpressionist(in *f*) *m*.
posting ['pəʊstɪŋ] *n* (*transfer, assignment*) Versetzung *f*; (*Mil also*) Abkommandierung *f*. he's got a new ~ er ist wieder versetzt/abkommandiert worden.
postlude ['pəʊstluːd] *n* Nachspiel *nt*.
post: ~**man** *n* Briefträger, Postbote *m*; ~**man's knock** *n* Kinderspiel, bei dem für einen Brief mit einem Kuß bezahlt wird; ~**mark** *n* **1** *n* Poststempel *m*; date as ~**mark** Datum des Poststempels; **2** *vt* (ab)stempeln; the letter is ~**marked** "Birmingham" der Brief ist in Birmingham abgestempelt; ~**master** *n* Postmeister *m*; ~**master general** *n, pl* ~**masters general** ≈ Postminister *m*; ~**meridian** *adj* (*form*) nachmittäglich, Nachmittags-; ~ **meridiem** *adv* (*form*) nachmittags; ~**mistress** *n* Postmeisterin *f*; ~-**mortem** [pəʊst'mɔːtəm] *n* (a) (*also* ~-**mortem examination**) Obduktion, Autopsie, Leichenöffnung *f*; (b) (*fig*) nachträgliche Erörterung; to hold or have a ~-**mortem** on sth etw hinterher erörtern; ~-**natal** *adj* nach der Geburt, postnatal (*spec*); ~ office Postamt *nt*; the P~ Office (*institution*) die Post; ~ office box (*abbr* PO Box) Postfach *nt*; ~ office worker Postarbeiter(in *f*) *m*; he has £100 in ~ office savings or the P~ Office Savings Bank (*Brit*) er hat £ 100 auf dem Postsparbuch; ~-**operative** post operativ; ~-**paid 1** *adj* portofrei; *envelope* frankiert, freigemacht, Frei-; **2** *adv* portofrei; to reply ~-**paid** mit freigemachter Postkarte/ freigemachtem Briefumschlag antworten.
postpone [pəʊst'pəʊn] *vt* (a) aufschieben, hinausschieben; (*for specified period*) verschieben. it has been ~d till Tuesday es ist auf Dienstag verschoben worden; you mustn't ~ answering a day longer Sie dürfen die Antwort keinen Tag länger hinausschieben. (b) (*Gram form*) nachstellen.
postponement [pəʊst'pəʊnmənt] *n* (*act*) Verschiebung *f*; (*result*) Aufschub *m*.
post: ~**position** *n* (*Gram*) Nachstellung *f*; (*part of speech*) Postposition *f*; ~**prandial** [,pəʊst'prændɪəl] *adj* (*hum*) nach dem Essen; *walk* Verdauungs-; ~ **road** *n* (*Hist*) Poststraße *f*; ~**script(um)** *n* (*abbr* PS: *to letter*) Postskriptum *nt*; (*to book, article etc*) Nachwort *nt*; (*fig: to after-dinner speech*) Nachspiel *nt*; he added a ~**script** (*fig: in speech*) er fügte noch eine Bemerkung hinzu.
postulant ['pɒstjʊlənt] *n* (*Rel*) Postulant *m*.
postulate ['pɒstjʊlɪt] **1** *n* Postulat *nt*. **2** ['pɒstjʊleɪt] *vt* postulieren; *theory* aufstellen.
postulation [,pɒstjʊ'leɪʃən] *n* (*act*) Postulieren *nt*; (*theory*) Postulat *nt*.
posture ['pɒstʃəʳ] **1** *n* (*lit, fig*) Haltung *f*; (*pej*) Pose *f*. she has very poor ~ sie hat eine sehr schlechte Haltung. **2** *vi* sich in Positur or Pose werfen. is he merely posturing (because of the election)? ist das nur eine (Wahl)pose seinerseits?
postwar ['pəʊst'wɔːʳ] *adj* Nachkriegs-. ~ London das London der Nachkriegszeit.
posy ['pəʊzɪ] *n* Sträußchen *nt*.
pot [pɒt] **1** *n* (a) Topf *m*; (*tea-~, coffee-~*) Kanne *f*; (*dated: tankard*) Krug *m*; (*lobster ~*) Korb *m*; (*chimney ~*) Kaminaufsatz *m*. ~**s and pans** Töpfe und Pfannen; a pint ~ ≈ ein Humpen *m*; to keep the ~ boiling (*earn living*) dafür sorgen, daß der Schornstein raucht (*inf*); (*keep sth going*) den Betrieb aufrechterhalten; that's (a case of) the ~ calling the kettle black (*prov*) ein Esel schimpft den anderen Langohr (*prov*); to go to ~ (*inf*) (*person, business*) auf den Hund kommen (*inf*); (*plan, arrangement*) ins Wasser fallen (*inf*). (b) (*inf: large amount*) Haufen *m* (*inf*), Menge *f*. a ~ of money ein Haufen (*inf*) or eine Menge Geld; to have ~**s of money/time** massenhaft (*inf*) or jede Menge (*inf*) Geld/Zeit haben. (c) (*inf: important person*) a big ~ ein hohes Tier (*inf*). (d) (*sl: marijuana*) Gras *nt* (*sl*). (e) (*Cards: pool*) Topf *m*. (f) (*inf: prize, cup*) Topf *m* (*inf*). (g) (~-*shot*) Schuß *m* aufs Geratewohl. (h) (*inf:* ~-*belly*) Spitzbauch, Spitzkühler (*hum*) *m*. **2** *vt* (a) *meat* einmachen, einkochen; *jam* einfüllen. (b) *plant* eintopfen. (c) (*shoot*) *game* schießen. (d) (*Billiards*) *ball* einlochen. (e) (*inf*) *baby* auf den Topf setzen. **3** *vi* (a) to ~ at schießen auf (+*acc*); to ~ away wahllos schießen (*at* auf +*acc*). (b) (*inf: make pottery*) töpfern (*inf*).
potable ['pəʊtəbl] *adj* (*form*) trinkbar.
potash ['pɒtæʃ] *n* Pottasche *f*, Kaliumkarbonat *nt*.
potassium [pə'tæsɪəm] *n* Kalium *nt*. ~ **cyanide** Kaliumzyanid, Zyankali *nt*; ~ **nitrate** Kaliumnitrat *nt*, Kalisalpeter *m*.
potations [pəʊ'teɪʃənz] *npl* (*liter*) Zecherei *f*.
potato [pə'teɪtəʊ] *n, pl* -**es** Kartoffel *f*; *see* **hot** ~.
potato: ~ **beetle**, ~ **bug** (*esp US*) *n* Kartoffelkäfer *m*; ~ **chip** (*esp US*), ~ **crisp** (*Brit*) *n* Kartoffelchip *nt*; ~ **salad** *n* Kartoffelsalat *m*.
pot: ~**bellied** ['pɒt'belɪd] *adj* *person* spitzbäuchig; (*through hunger*) blähbäuchig; *stove* Kanonen-; ~**belly** *n* (*stomach*) (*from overeating*) Spitzbauch *m*; (*from malnutrition*) Blähbauch *m*; (*stove*) Kanonenofen *m*; ~**boiler** *n* rein kommerzielles Werk; ~**bound** *adj* *plant* eingewachsen.
poteen [pɒ'tiːn, pɒ'tʃiːn] *n* illegal destillierter irischer Whisky.
potency ['pəʊtənsɪ] *n see adj* Stärke *f*; Durchschlagskraft *f*; Potenz *f*; Macht *f*.
potent ['pəʊtənt] *adj* *drink, drug, charm, motive etc* stark; *argument, reason etc* durchschlagend; *man* potent; *ruler* mächtig.

potentate ['pəʊtənteɪt] *n* Potentat *m*.
potential [pəʊ'tenʃəl] **1** *adj* potentiell. **2** *n* Potential *nt* (*also Elec, Math, Phys*). the ~ **for growth** das Wachstumspotential; to have ~ ausbaufähig sein (*inf*).
potentiality [pəʊ,tenʃɪ'ælɪtɪ] *n* Möglichkeit *f*.
potentially [pəʊ'tenʃəlɪ] *adv* potentiell.
potful ['pɒtfʊl] *n* Topf *m*; (*of coffee, tea*) Kanne *f*.
pothead ['pɒthed] *n* (*sl*) Kiffer(in *f*) *m* (*sl*).
pother ['pɒðəʳ] *n* (*old*) Aufruhr, Wirbel *m*. to make a ~ about sth wegen etw (ein) Theater machen.
pot: ~**herb** *n* Küchenkraut *nt*; ~**hole** *n* (a) (*in road*) Schlagloch *nt*; (b) (*Geol*) Höhle *f*; ~**holer** *n* Höhlenforscher(in *f*) *m*; ~**holing** *n* Höhlenforschung *f*; ~**hook** *n* (a) (*for pot*) Kesselhaken *m*; (b) (*in writing*) Krakel *m*; ~**hunter** *n* (a) (*Sport*) unwaidmännischer Jäger; (b) (*for prizes*) Pokalsammler(in *f*) *m*.
potion ['pəʊʃən] *n* Trank *m*.
pot: ~**luck** *n*: to take ~**luck** nehmen, was es gerade gibt; ~**pie** *n* (*US*) in einer Auflaufform gebackene Pastete; ~**pourri** [,pəʊpʊ'riː] *n* (a) (*lit*) Duftmischung *f*; (b) (*fig: mixture, medley*) (kunter)bunte Mischung; (*of music*) Potpourri *nt*; ~ **roast** *n* Schmorbraten *m*; ~**sherd** *n* (*Archeol*) Scherbe *f*; ~**shot** *n* Schuß *m* aufs Geratewohl; to take a ~**shot** at sth aufs Geratewohl auf etw (*acc*) schießen.
potted ['pɒtɪd] *adj* (a) *meat* eingemacht; *fish* eingelegt. (b) *plant* Topf-. (c) (*shortened*) *history, biography* gekürzt, zusammengefaßt. he gave me a ~ version of the film er erzählte mir in kurzen Worten, wovon der Film handelte.
potter¹ ['pɒtəʳ] *n* Töpfer(in *f*) *m*. ~**'s clay** Töpferton *m*; ~**'s wheel** Töpferscheibe *f*.
potter², (*US also*) **putter** ['pʌtəʳ] *vi* (*do little jobs*) herumwerkeln; (*wander aimlessly*) herumschlendern. she ~s away in the kitchen for hours sie hantiert stundenlang in der Küche herum; to ~ round the house im Haus herumwerkeln; to ~ round the shops einen Geschäftsbummel machen; to ~ along the road (*car, driver*) dahinzuckeln; we ~ along quite happily wir leben recht zufrieden vor uns hin; you'd be on time if you didn't ~ about or around so much in the morning du könntest pünktlich sein, wenn du morgens nicht so lange trödeln würdest.
potterer ['pɒtərəʳ] *n* Trödelheini *m*, Trödelsuse *f*.
pottery ['pɒtərɪ] *n* (*workshop, craft*) Töpferei *f*; (*pots*) Töpferwaren, Tonwaren *pl*; (*glazed*) Keramik *f*; (*archaeological remains*) Tonscherben *m*.
potting: ~ **compost** *n* Pflanzerde *f*; ~ **shed** *n* Schuppen *m*.
potty¹ ['pɒtɪ] *n* (*esp Brit*) Töpfchen *nt*. ~-**trained** sauber.
potty² *adj* (+*er*) (*Brit inf: mad*) verrückt. to drive sb ~ jdn zum Wahnsinn treiben; he's ~ about her er ist verrückt nach ihr.
pouch [paʊtʃ] *n* Beutel *m*; (*under eyes*) (Tränen)sack *m*; (*of pelican, hamster*) Tasche *f*; (*Mil*) (Patronen)tasche *f*; (*Hist: for gunpowder*) (Pulver)beutel *m*; (*esp US: mail* ~) Postsack *m*.
pouf(fe) [puːf] *n* (a) (*seat*) Puff *m*. (b) (*Brit inf*) *see* **poof(ter)**.
poulterer ['pəʊltərəʳ] *n* (*Brit*) Geflügelhändler(in *f*) *m*. ~**'s (shop)** Geflügelhandlung *f*.
poultice ['pəʊltɪs] **1** *n* Umschlag, Wickel *m*; (*for boil*) Zugpflaster *nt*. **2** *vt* einen Umschlag or Wickel machen um; ein Zugpflaster kleben auf (+*acc*).
poultry ['pəʊltrɪ] *n* Geflügel *nt*. ~ **farm** Geflügelfarm *f*; ~ **farmer** Geflügelzüchter *m*; ~ **house** Hühnerhaus *nt*; ~**man** (*esp US*) (*farmer*) Geflügelzüchter(in *f*) *m*; (*dealer*) Geflügelhändler(in *f*) *m*.
pounce [paʊns] **1** *n* Sprung, Satz *m*; (*swoop by bird*) Angriff *m*; (*by police*) Zugriff *m*. **2** *vi* (*cat, lion etc*) einen Satz machen; (*bird*) niederstoßen; (*fig*) zuschlagen. to ~ on sb/sth (*lit, fig*) sich auf jdn/etw stürzen; (*bird*) auf etw (*acc*) niederstoßen; (*police*) sich (*dat*) jdn greifen/in etw (*dat*) eine Razzia machen.
pound¹ [paʊnd] *n* (a) (*weight*) ≈ Pfund *nt*. two ~s of apples zwei Pfund Äpfel; by the ~ pfundweise; he is making sure he gets his ~ of flesh er sorgt dafür, daß er bekommt, was ihm zusteht. (b) (*money*) Pfund *nt*. one ~ sterling ein Pfund Sterling; five ~s fünf Pfund; a one-/five-~ note eine Ein-/Fünfpfundnote, ein Ein-/Fünfpfundschein *m*; *see* **penny**.
pound² **1** *vt* (a) (*hammer, strike*) hämmern; *earth, paving slabs* feststampfen; *meat* klopfen; *dough* kneten; *piano, typewriter* hämmern auf (+*dat*); *table* hämmern auf (+*acc*); *door, wall* hämmern gegen; (*waves, sea*) *ship* schlagen gegen; (*guns, shells, bombs*) ununterbrochen beschießen; (*troops, artillery*) unter Beschuß haben. the boxer ~ed his opponent with his fists der Boxer hämmerte mit den Fäusten auf seinen Gegner ein; the ship was ~ed by the waves die Wellen schlugen gegen das Schiff; the old-style policeman ~ing his beat der Polizist alten Stils, der seine Runde abmarschiert; I tried to ~ some sense into his head (*inf*) ich versuchte, ihm etwas Vernunft einzuhämmern. (b) (*pulverize*) *corn etc* (zer)stampfen; *drugs, spices* zerstoßen. to ~ sth to pieces etw kleinstampfen; the guns ~ed the walls to pieces die Kanonen zertrümmerten die Mauern; the bombs ~ed the city to rubble die Bomben verwandelten die Stadt in ein Trümmerfeld; the waves ~ed the boat to pieces die Wellen zertrümmerten das Boot. **2** *vi* (a) (*beat*) hämmern; (*heart*) (wild) pochen; (*waves, sea*) schlagen (*on, against* gegen); (*drums*) dröhnen; (*engine, steamer, hooves*) stampfen. he ~ed at or on the door/on the table e hämmerte an or gegen die Tür/auf den Tisch. (b) (*run heavily*) stampfen; (*walk heavily, stamp*) stapfen. the sound of ~ing feet das Geräusch stampfender Füße; the messenger ~ed up and handed me a telegram der Bote stampfte auf mich zu und übergab mir ein Telegramm.
◆**pound away** *vi* hämmern; (*music, drums, guns*) dröhnen. our guns were ~ing ~ at the enemy position wir hatten die feindliche Stellung unter anhaltendem Beschuß; he was ~ing ~ at the typewriter er hämmerte auf der Schreibmaschine herum.

◆**pound down** vt sep earth, rocks feststampfen. to ~ sth ~ to a powder etw pulverisieren.

◆**pound out** vt sep to ~ ~ a tune/letter eine Melodie/einen Brief herunterhämmern.

pound³ n (for stray dogs) städtischer Hundezwinger; (for cars) Abstellplatz m (für amtlich abgeschleppte Fahrzeuge).

poundage ['paʊndɪdʒ] n (a) auf Pfundbasis berechnete Gebühr oder Abgabe. (b) (weight) Gewicht nt (in Pfund).

pound-cake ['paʊndkeɪk] n (US) reichhaltiger Früchtekuchen.

-pounder [-'paʊndəʳ] n suf -pfünder m (also Mil).

pound foolish adj see penny wise.

pounding ['paʊndɪŋ] n (a) Hämmern nt; (of heart) Pochen nt; (of music, drums) Dröhnen nt; (of waves, sea) Schlagen nt; (of engine, steamer, pile-driver, hooves, feet etc) Stampfen nt; (of guns, shells, bombs) Bombardement nt. the ship took a ~ from the waves das Schiff wurde von den Wellen gebeutelt; the city took a ~ last night gestern Nacht wurde die Stadt schwer bombardiert; his theory took a ~ from the critics seine Theorie wurde von den Kritikern scharf angegriffen; our team took quite a ~ on Saturday unsere Mannschaft hat am Samstag eine ziemliche Schlappe einstecken müssen (inf).
(b) (of corn etc) Zerstampfen nt; (of drugs) Zerstoßen nt.

pour [pɔːʳ] 1 vt liquid gießen; large amount also, sugar, rice etc schütten; drink eingießen, einschenken. to ~ sth for sb jdm etw eingießen or einschenken; to ~ the water off the potatoes die Kartoffeln abgießen; she looks as if she's been ~ed into that dress! (inf) das Kleid sitzt wie angegossen (inf); to ~ money into a project/men into a war Geld in ein Projekt/Männer in einen Krieg pumpen (inf); he ~ed all his ideas into one book alle seine Gedanken flossen in ein Buch.
2 vi (a) (lit, fig) strömen; (smoke also) hervorquellen. the sweat ~ed off him der Schweiß floß in Strömen an ihm herunter; books are ~ing off the presses Bücher werden in Massen ausgestoßen; cars ~ed along the road Autokolonnen rollten die Straße entlang.
(b) (rain) it's ~ing (with rain) es gießt (in Strömen), es schüttet (inf); the rain ~ed down es regnete or goß in Strömen; see rain.
(c) (~ out tea, coffee etc) eingießen, einschenken; (US: act as hostess) als Gastgeberin fungieren.
(d) this jug doesn't ~ well dieser Krug gießt nicht gut.

◆**pour away** vt sep weggießen.

◆**pour forth** vt sep see pour out 1, 2 (b, c).

◆**pour in** 1 vi hinein-/hereinström; (donations, protests) in Strömen eintreffen. 2 vt sep money, men hineinpumpen (inf).

◆**pour out** 1 vi hinaus-/herausströmen (of aus); (smoke also) hervorquellen (of aus); (words) heraussprudeln (of aus).
2 vt sep (a) liquid ausgießen; (in large quantities) sugar, rice etc ausschütten; drink eingießen, einschenken.
(b) (factories, schools) car, students ausstoßen. the underground stations ~ ~ thousands of workers die U-Bahn-stationen spucken Tausende von Arbeitern aus.
(c) (fig) feelings, troubles, story sich (dat) von der Seele reden. to ~ ~ one's thanks sich überströmend bedanken; to ~ one's heart to sb jdm sein Herz ausschütten.

pouring ['pɔːrɪŋ] adj ~ rain strömender Regen; a ~ wet day ein völlig verregneter Tag; ~ custard Vanillesoße f.

pout [paʊt] 1 n (a) (facial expression) Schmollmund m; (because upset also) Flunsch m (inf), Schnute f (inf).
(b) (sulking fit) Schmollen nt. to have a ~ schmollen.
2 vi (a) (with lips) einen Schmollmund machen; einen Flunsch or eine Schnute ziehen (inf).
(b) (sulk) schmollen.
3 vt lips schürzen; (sulkingly) zu einem Schmollmund or Schmollen verziehen.

poverty ['pɒvətɪ] n Armut f. ~ of ideas gedankliche Armut; ~-stricken notleidend; conditions kümmerlich; to be ~-stricken (hum inf) am Hungertuch nagen (hum).

PoW abbr of prisoner of war.

powder ['paʊdəʳ] 1 n Pulver nt; (face, talcum ~ etc) Puder m; (dust) Staub m. to grind sth to ~ etw pulverig or zu Pulver mahlen; to reduce sth to ~ etw zu Pulver machen.
2 vt (a) milk pulverisieren; sugar stoßen; chalk zermahlen.
(b) (apply ~ to) face, body, oneself pudern. to ~ one's nose (lit) sich (dat) die Nase pudern; (euph) kurz verschwinden (euph); the trees were ~ed with snow die Bäume waren mit Schnee überzuckert.
3 vti (crumble) (zu Staub) zerfallen. it ~s easily es zerfällt leicht; the cement had ~ed away der Mörtel war zu Staub zerfallen.

powder: ~ blue 1 adj taubenblau; 2 n Taubenblau nt; ~ compact n Puderdose f.

powdered ['paʊdəd] adj milk, eggs, chalk -pulver nt. ~ sugar (US) Puderzucker, Staubzucker (Aus) m.

powder-horn ['paʊdə,hɔːn] n Pulverhorn nt.

powdering ['paʊdərɪŋ] n (liter) there was a light ~ of snow on the grass das Gras war leicht mit Schnee überzuckert; the delicate ~ of snow on the hillsides die zart von Schnee überzukkerten Berghänge.

powder: ~ keg n (lit, fig) Pulverfaß nt; ~ magazine n Pulvermagazin nt, Pulverkammer f; ~-monkey n (Mil Hist) Pulverjunge m; (explosives man) Sprengmeister m; ~ puff n Puderquaste f; ~ room n Damentoilette f; ~ snow n Pulverschnee m.

powdery ['paʊdərɪ] adj (a) (like powder) pulvrig. (b) (crumbly) bröckelig; bones morsch. (c) (covered with powder) gepudert.

power ['paʊəʳ] 1 n (a) no pl (physical strength) Kraft f; (force: of blow, explosion etc) Stärke, Gewalt, Wucht f; (fig: of argument etc) Überzeugungskraft f. more ~ to your elbow! (inf) jetzt setzt euch durch!; the ~ of love/logic/tradition die Macht der Liebe/Logik/Tradition.
(b) (faculty, ability) (of hearing, imagination) Vermögen nt

no pl. her ~s of persuasion ihre Überredungskünste pl; his ~s of hearing sein Hörvermögen nt; mental/hypnotic ~s geistige/hypnotische Kräfte pl; to reduce or weaken their ~(s) of resistance um ihre Widerstandskraft zu schwächen.
(c) (capacity, ability to help etc) Macht f. he did all in his ~ to help them er tat (alles), was in seiner Macht or in seinen Kräften stand, um ihnen zu helfen; it's beyond my or not within my ~ to ... es steht nicht in meiner Macht, zu ...
(d) (no pl: sphere or strength of influence, authority) Macht f; (Jur, parental) Gewalt f; (usu pl: thing one has authority to do) Befugnis f. he has the ~ to act er ist handlungsberechtigt; the ~ of the police/of the law die Macht der Polizei/des Gesetzes; to be in sb's ~ in jds Gewalt sein (dat) sein; that does not fall within my ~(s)/that is beyond or outside my ~(s) das fällt nicht in meinen Machtbereich/das überschreitet meine Befugnisse; ~ of attorney (Jur) (Handlungs)vollmacht f; the party now in ~ die Partei, die im Augenblick an der Macht ist; to fall from ~ abgesetzt werden; to come into ~ an die Macht kommen; they have no ~ over economic matters in Wirtschaftsfragen haben sie keine Befugnisse; I have no ~ over her ich habe keine Gewalt über sie; he has been given full ~(s) to make all decisions man hat ihm volle Entscheidungsgewalt übertragen; that man has no ~ over his destiny daß der Mensch keine Gewalt über sein Schicksal hat; "student/worker ~" „Macht den Studenten/Arbeitern".
(e) (person or institution having authority) Autorität f, Machtfaktor m. to be the ~ behind the scenes/throne die graue Eminenz sein; the ~s that be (inf) die da oben (inf); the ~s of darkness/evil die Mächte der Finsternis/des Bösen.
(f) (nation) Macht f. a four-~ conference eine Viermächtekonferenz; a naval ~ eine Seemacht.
(g) (source of energy: nuclear, electric ~ etc) Energie f; (of water, steam also) Kraft f. the ship made port under her own ~ das Schiff lief mit eigener Kraft in den Hafen ein; they cut off the ~ (electricity) sie haben den Strom abgestellt.
(h) (of engine, machine, loudspeakers, transmitter) Leistung f; (of microscope, lens, sun's rays, drug, chemical) Stärke f. the ~ of suggestion die Wirkung or Wirkkraft des Unterschwelligen; a low-~ microscope ein schwaches Mikroskop; a 10-~ magnification eine 10-fache Vergrößerung.
(i) (Math) Potenz f. to the ~ (of) 2 hoch 2, in der 2. Potenz.
(j) (inf: a lot of) a ~ of help eine wertvolle or große Hilfe; that did me a ~ of good das hat mir unheimlich gut getan (inf).
2 vt (engine) antreiben; (fuel) betreiben. ~ed by electricity/by jet engines mit Elektro-/Düsenantrieb; as he ~s his way down the straight wie er die Gerade entlangbraust.

power: ~boat n Rennboot nt; ~ brakes npl Servobremsen pl; ~ cable n Stromkabel nt; ~ cut n Stromsperre f; (accidental) Stromausfall m; ~ dive (Aviat) 1 n (Vollgas)sturzflug m; 2 vi einen Sturzflug machen; ~ drill n Bohrmaschine f; ~-driven adj tool Motor-.

powerful ['paʊəfʊl] adj (a) (influential) government, person mächtig, einflußreich.
(b) (strong) boxer, engine, magnet, drug, emotions stark; stroke, punch, detergent kraftvoll; build, arm kräftig.
(c) (fig) speaker, actor mitreißend; music, film, performance also ausdrucksvoll; argument durchschlagend, massiv (inf); salesman überzeugend.
(d) a ~ lot of (dial) ganz schön viel (inf), gehörig viel (inf).

powerfully ['paʊəfəlɪ] adv (a) kraftvoll. ~ built kräftig gebaut. (b) (fig) speak kraftvoll; describe, act also mitreißend; argue massiv (inf). I was ~ affected by the book das Buch hat mich mächtig (inf) or stark beeindruckt.

powerhouse ['paʊəhaʊs] n (a) (lit) see power station. (b) (fig) treibende Kraft (behind hinter +dat). he's a real ~/an intellectual ~ er ist ein äußerst dynamischer Mensch/er hat eine erstaunliche intellektuelle Kapazität; he's a ~ of new ideas er hat einen unerschöpflichen Vorrat an neuen Ideen.

power: ~less (physically) punch, body kraftlos; (as regards ability to act) committee, person machtlos; to be ~less to resist nicht die Kraft haben, zu widerstehen; the government is ~less to deal with inflation die Regierung steht der Inflation machtlos gegenüber; we are ~less to help you es steht nicht in unserer Macht, Ihnen zu helfen, wir sind machtlos; ~ loom n Webmaschine f; ~mower n Motor-Rasenmäher m; (electric) Elektrorasenmäher m; ~ pack n (Elec) Netzteil nt; ~ plant n see ~ station; ~ point n (Elec) Steckdose f; ~ politics npl Machtpolitik f; ~ saw n Motorsäge f; (electric) Elektrosäge f; ~ station n Kraftwerk nt; ~ steering n (Aut) Servolenkung f; ~ tool n Elektrowerkzeug nt; ~ worker n Elektrizitätsarbeiter m.

powwow ['paʊwaʊ] n (of Red Indians) Versammlung f; (with Red Indians) indianische Verhandlungen pl; (inf) Besprechung f; (to solve problem) Kriegsrat m (hum). a family ~ ein Familienrat m.

pox [pɒks] n (old) (small~) Pocken, Blattern pl; (syphilis) Syphilis f. a ~ on ...! (old) zur Hölle mit ...!

pp abbr of (a) pages ff. (b) per procurationem = on behalf of.

PPE abbr of Philosophy, Politics and Economics.

PPS abbr of post-postscriptum PPS.

PR abbr of proportional representation; public relations.

pr abbr of pair.

practicability [,præktɪkə'bɪlɪtɪ] n see adj Durchführbarkeit, Praktikabilität (rare) f; Befahrbarkeit f.

practicable ['præktɪkəbl] adj durchführbar, praktikabel; road befahrbar.

practically ['præktɪkəblɪ] adv if it can ~ be done falls (es) durchführbar (ist).

practical ['præktɪkəl] adj praktisch; person praktisch (veranlagt). to have a ~mind praktisch denken; his ideas have no ~

application/value seine Ideen sind praktisch nicht anwend-
bar/haben keinen praktischen Wert.

practicality [ˌpræktɪˈkælɪtɪ] n (a) no pl (of person) praktische
Veranlagung. a person of great ~ ein sehr praktisch veranlagter Mensch.
  (b) no pl (of scheme etc) Durchführbarkeit f. your solution
shows/lacks ~ Ihre Lösung ist praxisnah/-fremd.
  (c) (practical detail) praktische Einzelheit.

practical: ~ joke n Streich m; ~ joker n Witzbold m (inf).

practically [ˈpræktɪkəlɪ] adv (all senses) praktisch.

practical nurse n (US) ≈ Hilfsschwester f.

practice [ˈpræktɪs] 1 n (a) (habit, custom) (of individual)
Gewohnheit, Angewohnheit f; (of group, in country) Brauch m,
Sitte f; (bad habit) Unsitte f; (in business) Verfahrensweise,
Praktik f. he opposes the ~ of pubs being open on Sundays er ist
dagegen, daß Lokale am Sonntag geöffnet sind; this is
normal business ~ das ist im Geschäftsleben so üblich; as is
my (usual) ~ wie es meine Gewohnheit ist; to make a ~ of
doing sth, to make it a ~ to do sth es sich (dat) zur Gewohnheit
machen, etw zu tun; Christian ~ dictates ... das christliche
Brauchtum verlangt ...; it is the ~ of this Court to ... es ist an
diesem Gericht üblich, zu ...; that's common ~ das ist allgemeine Praxis or allgemein üblich.
  (b) (exercise, training) Übung f; (rehearsal, trial run) Probe f;
(Sport) Training nt; (~ game) Trainingsspiel nt. ~ makes perfect (Prov) Übung macht den Meister (Prov); Niki Lauda had
the fastest time in ~ Niki Lauda fuhr im Training die schnellste
Zeit; this piece of music needs a lot of ~ für dieses (Musik-)
stück muß man viel üben; you should do 10 minutes' ~ each day
du solltest täglich 10 Minuten (lang) üben; to be out of/in ~ aus
der/in Übung sein; that was just a ~ run das war nur mal zur
Probe; to have a ~ session üben/Probe haben; trainieren; the
first ~ session die erste Übung/Probe/das erste Training.
  (c) (doing, as opposed to theory) Praxis f. in ~ in der Praxis;
that won't work in ~ das läßt sich praktisch nicht durchführen;
to put one's ideas into ~ seine Ideen in die Praxis umsetzen.
  (d) (of doctor, lawyer etc) Praxis f. he took up the ~ of law/
medicine er praktizierte als Rechtsanwalt/Arzt; to go into or
set up in ~ eine Praxis aufmachen or eröffnen, sich als
Arzt/Rechtsanwalt etc niederlassen; not to be in ~ any more
nicht mehr praktizieren; to retire from ~ sich aus der Praxis
zurückziehen; a large legal ~ eine große Rechtsanwaltspraxis.
  2 vti (US) see practise.

practise, (US) practice [ˈpræktɪs] 1 vt (a) thrift, patience etc
üben; self-denial, Christian charity praktizieren. to ~ what one
preaches (prov) seine Lehren in die Tat umsetzen.
  (b) (in order to acquire skill) üben; song, chorus proben. to ~
the violin Geige üben; to ~ the high jump/one's golf swing
Hochsprung/seinen Schlag im Golf üben or trainieren; to ~
doing sth etw üben; I'm practising my German on him ich probiere mein Deutsch an ihm aus.
  (c) (follow, exercise) profession, religion ausüben, praktizieren. to ~ law/medicine als Anwalt/Arzt praktizieren; all a
writer wants is peace to ~ his art alles, was ein Schriftsteller
braucht, ist Ruhe, um sich seiner Kunst widmen zu können.
  2 vi (a) (in order to acquire skill) üben.
  (b) (lawyer, doctor etc) praktizieren. to ~ at the bar als
Anwalt bei Gericht praktizieren.

practised, (US) practiced [ˈpræktɪst] adj geübt; marksman,
liar also erfahren. with a ~ eye/hand mit geübtem Auge/
geübter Hand; he's ~ in getting his own way er hat Übung
darin, seinen Willen durchzusetzen; with ~ skill gekonnt.

practising, (US) practicing [ˈpræktɪsɪŋ] adj lawyer, doctor,
homosexual praktizierend; Christian also, socialist aktiv.

practitioner [prækˈtɪʃənəʳ] n (of method) Benutzer, Anwender
m; (medical ~) praktischer Arzt, praktische Ärztin; (dental ~)
Zahnarzt m/-ärztin f; (legal ~) Rechtsanwalt m/-anwältin f. ~s
of this profession diejenigen, die diesen Beruf ausüben; a ~ of
Zen Buddhism/Christianity ein Anhänger des Zen Buddhis-
mus/ein praktizierender Christ; see general ~.

praesidium [prɪˈsɪdɪəm] n see presidium.

praetor [ˈpriːtəʳ] n Prätor m.

Praetorian Guard [prɪˈtɔːrɪənˈgɑːd] n (body) Prätorianer pl.

pragmatic adj, ~ally adv [prægˈmætɪk, -əlɪ] pragmatisch.

pragmatism [ˈprægmətɪzəm] n Pragmatismus m.

pragmatist [ˈprægmətɪst] n Pragmatiker(in f) m.

Prague [prɑːg] n Prag nt.

prairie [ˈprɛərɪ] n Grassteppe f; (in North America) Prärie f.

prairie: ~ chicken n (US) Präriehuhn nt; ~ dog n Präriehund m;
~ oyster n Prairie Oyster f; ~ schooner n Planwagen m; ~ wolf
n Präriewolf m.

praise [preɪz] 1 vt loben; (to others, worshipfully also) preisen
(geh), rühmen (geh). to ~ sb for having done sth jdn dafür
loben, etw getan zu haben.
  2 n Lob nt no pl. a hymn of ~ eine Lobeshymne; a poem in ~ of
beer ein Lobliled nt auf das Bier; he spoke/held a speech in ~ of
their efforts er sprach lobend von ihren Bemühungen/hielt
eine Lobrede auf ihre Bemühungen; to win ~ (person) Lob
ernten; (efforts) Lob einbringen; to be loud or warm in one's ~
(of sth) voll des Lobes (für etw) sein; I have nothing but ~ for
him ich kann ihn nur loben; he's beyond ~ er ist über jedes or
alles Lob erhaben; all ~ to him with all the Achtung!; ~ indeed! (also
iro) ein hohes Lob; ~ from him is ~ indeed Lob aus seinem
Mund will etwas heißen; ~ be to God! (in church) gelobt sei der
Herr!; ~(s) be! Gott sei Dank!; see sing.

praiseworthiness [ˈpreɪzˌwɜːðɪnɪs] n (of attempt, effort)
Löblichkeit f. I don't doubt his ~/the ~ of his motives ich
zweifle nicht an seinen lobenswerten Absichten/daran, daß
seine Motive lobenswert sind.

praiseworthy [ˈpreɪzˌwɜːðɪ] adj lobenswert; attempt, effort
also löblich.

---

praline [ˈprɑːliːn] n Praline f mit Nuß-Karamellfüllung.

pram [præm] n (Brit) Kinderwagen m; (dolls') Puppenwagen m.

prance [prɑːns] vi (horse) tänzeln; (person) (jump around)
herumhüpfen or -tanzen; (walk gaily, mince) tänzeln. she was
prancing about with nothing on sie lief nackt durch die Gegend;
to ~ in/out (person) herein-/hinausspazieren.

prang [præŋ] (esp Brit inf) 1 n (crash) Bums m (inf); (of plane)
Bruchlandung f. 2 interj krach. 3 vt (a) (crash) car ramponieren (inf), lädieren; plane eine Bruchlandung machen. (b)
(bomb) zerbomben, zusammenbomben (inf).

prank [præŋk] n Streich m; (harmless also) Ulk m. to play a ~ on
sb jdm einen Streich spielen; einen Ulk mit jdm machen.

prankish [ˈpræŋkɪʃ] adj person zu Streichen aufgelegt or bereit;
behaviour, act schelmisch.

prankster [ˈpræŋkstəʳ] n Schelm m.

prat [præt] n (Brit sl: idiot) Trottel m (inf).

prate [preɪt] vi faseln, schwafeln.

prating [ˈpreɪtɪŋ] 1 n Gefasel, Geschwafel nt. 2 adj faselnd,
schwafelnd.

prattle [ˈprætl] 1 n Geplapper nt. 2 vi plappern.

prawn [prɔːn] n Garnele f; ~ cocktail Krabbencocktail m.

pray [preɪ] 1 vi (a) (say prayers) beten. let us ~ lasset uns beten;
to ~ for sb/sth für jdn/um etw beten; to ~ for sth (want it badly)
stark auf etw (acc) hoffen; he's past ~ing for! (inf) bei ihm ist
alles zu spät (inf), er ist nicht mehr zu retten (inf).
  (b) (old, liter) ~ take a seat bitte, nehmen Sie doch Platz,
wollen Sie bitte Platz nehmen?; what good is that, ~ (tell)? was
hilft das, wenn ich mir die Frage gestatten darf?
  2 vt (old, liter) inständig bitten, ersuchen (geh). I ~ you tell
me (old) bitte, erzählen Sie mir doch; (stronger) ich bitte Sie
inständig, erzählen Sie mir doch; and what is that, I ~ you? und
was ist das, wenn ich mir die Frage gestatten darf?; they ~ed
the king for mercy sie flehten den König um Gnade an (geh).

prayer [prɛəʳ] n Gebet nt; (service, ~ meeting) Andacht f. to say
one's ~s beten, seine Gebete verrichten (geh); to be at ~ beim
Gebet sein; a ~ for peace ein Gebet für den Frieden; a life of ~
ein Leben im Gebet; Evening P~ Abendandacht f; we attended
Morning P~ wir besuchten die Morgenandacht; we have ~s
every morning wir haben jeden Morgen eine Andacht; family
~s Hausandacht f; the Book of Common P~ das Gebetbuch der
anglikanischen Kirche.

prayer: ~ book n Gebetbuch nt; ~ mat n Gebetsteppich m; ~
meeting n Gebetsstunde f; ~ rug n see ~ mat; ~ shawl n
Gebetsmantel m; ~ wheel n Gebetsmühle f.

praying mantis [ˈpreɪɪŋˈmæntɪs] n Gottesanbeterin f.

pre- [priː-] pref vor-; (esp with Latinate words in German) prä-.

preach [priːtʃ] 1 vt predigen; (fig) advantages etc propagieren.
to ~ a sermon (lit, fig) eine Predigt halten; to ~ the gospel das
Evangelium verkünden.
  2 vi (give a sermon, be moralistic) predigen. who is ~ing
today? wer predigt heute, wer hält heute die Predigt?; to ~
to/at sb jdm eine Predigt halten; to ~ to the converted (prov)
offene Türen einrennen.

preacher [ˈpriːtʃəʳ] n Prediger m; (fig: moraliser) Moral-
prediger(in f) m. all these ~s of détente alle diese Entspan-
nungsprediger.

preachify [ˈpriːtʃɪfaɪ] vi (pej inf) predigen, moralisieren.

preaching [ˈpriːtʃɪŋ] n (lit, fig) (act) Predigen nt; (sermon) Predigt f.

preachy [ˈpriːtʃɪ] adj (inf) moralisierend.

preadolescent [ˌpriːædəˈlesənt] adj vorpubertär.

preamble [priːˈæmbl] n Einleitung f; (of book) Vorwort nt; (Jur)
Präambel f.

preamplifier [priːˈæmplɪˌfaɪəʳ], **preamp** (inf) [priːˈæmp] n
Vorverstärker m.

prearrange [ˌpriːəˈreɪndʒ] vt vorher vereinbaren, vorher
abmachen.

prebend [ˈprebənd] n (form) (stipend) Pfründe, Präbende f;
(person) Pfründer, Pfründeninhaber, Präbendar(ius) m.

prebendary [ˈprebəndərɪ] n Pfründner, Pfründeninhaber,
Präbendar(ius) m.

Pre-Cambrian [priːˈkæmbrɪən] adj präkambrisch.

precarious [prɪˈkɛərɪəs] adj unsicher; situation also, relationship prekär; theory, assertion anfechtbar. that cup/that shelf
looks somewhat ~ die Tasse/das Regal sieht ziemlich gefährlich aus.

precariously [prɪˈkɛərɪəslɪ] adv to be ~ balanced (lit, fig) auf
der Kippe stehen; he lived rather ~ from his work as a photographer er verdiente einen ziemlich unsicheren Lebensunterhalt als Photograph; ~ perched on the edge of the table
gefährlich nahe am Tischrand; with a cup ~ balanced on the
end of his nose eine Tasse auf der Nase balancierend.

precast [priːˈkɑːst] (vb: pret, ptp ~) 1 vt vorfertigen. 2 adj concrete Fertigteil-, vorgefertigt.

precaution [prɪˈkɔːʃən] n Sicherheitsmaßnahme,
(Sicherheits)vorkehrung, Vorsichtsmaßnahme f. do you take
~s? (euph: use contraception) nimmst or machst du (irgend)
etwas?; to take the ~ of doing sth vorsichtshalber or
sicherheitshalber etw tun.

precautionary [prɪˈkɔːʃənərɪ] adj Vorsichts-, Sicherheits-,
vorbeugend. it's purely ~ es ist eine reine or nur eine Vorsichtsmaßnahme.

precede [prɪˈsiːd] vt (in order, time) vorangehen (+dat); (in
importance) gehen vor (+dat); (in rank) stehen über (+dat).
for a month preceding this den (ganzen) Monat davor; to ~ a
lecture with a joke einem Vortrag einen Witz vorausschicken.

precedence [ˈpresɪdəns] n (of person) vorrangige Stellung
(over gegenüber); (of problem etc) Vorrang m (over vor +dat).
to take/have ~ over sb/sth jdm/etw gegenüber eine
Vorrangstellung einnehmen/vor jdm/etw Vorrang haben; to
give ~ to sb/sth jdm/einer Sache Vorrang geben; the guests

entered the hall in order of ~ die Gäste betraten die Halle in der Reihenfolge ihres (gesellschaftlichen) Rangs; **dukes have ~ over barons** Herzöge stehen im Rang höher als Barone.

precedent ['presɪdənt] n Präzedenzfall m; (Jur also) Präjudiz nt. **according to ~** nach den bisherigen Fällen; **against all the ~s** entgegen allen früheren Fällen; **without ~** noch nie dagewesen; **to establish or create or set a ~** einen Präzedenzfall schaffen; **is there any ~ for this?** ist der Fall schon einmal dagewesen?; **there is no ~ for this decision** diese Entscheidung kann sich nicht an einem vergleichbaren Fall ausrichten.

preceding [prɪ'siːdɪŋ] adj time, month etc vorangegangen; page, example also vorhergehend.

precentor [prɪ'sentə'] n Vorsänger, Präzentor (spec) m.

precept ['priːsept] n Grundsatz m, Prinzip nt.

preceptor [prɪ'septə'] n (old, form) Lehrer, Präzeptor (old) m.

pre-Christian [priː'krɪstɪən] adj vorchristlich.

precinct ['priːsɪŋkt] n (pedestrian ~) Fußgängerzone f; (shopping ~) Geschäfts- or Einkaufsviertel nt; (US: police ~) Revier nt; (US: voting ~) Bezirk m. ~s pl (grounds, premises) Gelände, Areal nt; (environs) Umgebung f; (of cathedral) Domfreiheit f.

preciosity [ˌpresɪ'ɒsɪtɪ] n Preziosität f.

precious ['preʃəs] **1** adj **(a)** (costly) wertvoll, kostbar. **~ stone/metal** Edelstein m/Edelmetall nt. **(b)** (treasured) wertvoll; (iro) hochverehrt, heißgeliebt. **my ~ (one)!** mein Schatz!; **I have very ~ memories of that time/of him** ich habe wertvolle Erinnerungen an diese Zeit/an ihn, die mir sehr wertvoll or teuer (geh) sind. **(c)** language, humour etc preziös.

2 adv (inf) **~ little/few** herzlich wenig/wenige (inf); **I had ~ little choice** ich hatte keine große Wahl.

precipice ['presɪpɪs] n Steilabfall m; (lit liter, fig) Abgrund m.

precipitance [prɪ'sɪpɪtəns], **precipitancy** [prɪ'sɪpɪtənsɪ] n (hastiness) Hast, Eile f; (overhastiness) Voreiligkeit, Überstürztheit, Überstürzung f.

precipitant [prɪ'sɪpɪtənt] **1** n (Aus)fällungsmittel nt. **2** adj see precipitate 2.

precipitate [prɪ'sɪpɪteɪt] **1** n (Met) Niederschlag m; (Chem also) Präzipitat nt (spec).

2 [prə'sɪpɪtɪt] adj (hasty) hastig, eilig; (overhasty) übereilt, voreilig, überstürzt.

3 vt **(a)** (hurl) schleudern; (downwards) hinunter- or hinabschleudern; (fig) stürzen. **(b)** (hasten) beschleunigen. **(c)** (Chem) (aus)fällen; (Met) niederschlagen.

4 vi (Chem) ausfallen; (Met) sich niederschlagen.

precipitately [prɪ'sɪpɪtɪtlɪ] adv see adj.

precipitation [prɪˌsɪpɪ'teɪʃən] n **(a)** see vt Schleudern nt; Hinunter- or Hinabschleudern nt; Sturz m; Beschleunigung f; Ausfällen nt, (Aus)fällung f; Niederschlag m. **(b)** (haste) Hast, Eile f; (over-hastiness) Übereile, Übereiltheit, Überstürztheit f. **(c)** (Met) Niederschlag m.

precipitous [prɪ'sɪpɪtəs] adj steil; (hasty) überstürzt.

precipitously [prɪ'sɪpɪtəslɪ] adv see adj. **to fall away ~** (ground etc) senkrecht or jäh abfallen.

précis ['preɪsiː] n Zusammenfassung f; (Sch) Inhaltsangabe f.

precise [prɪ'saɪs] adj genau; answer, description etc, worker also präzis. **at that ~ moment** genau in dem Augenblick; **this was the ~ amount I needed** das war genau or exakt der Betrag, den ich brauchte; **please be more ~** drücken Sie sich bitte etwas genauer or deutlicher aus; **but was it this ~ colour?** aber war es genau diese Farbe?; **let's be ~ about this** da sollten wir genau sein; **18, to be ~** 18, um genau zu sein; **in that ~ voice of hers** genau or exakt, wie sie nun einmal spricht; **these ~ British accents** die akzentuierte Aussprache der Briten.

precisely [prɪ'saɪslɪ] adv genau; answer, describe, work also präzis; use instrument exakt. **at ~ 7 o'clock, at 7 o'clock ~** Punkt 7 Uhr, genau um 7 Uhr; **what ~ do you mean/want?** was meinen/wollen Sie genau (inf)?; **but it is ~ because the money supply is ...** aber gerade deshalb, weil das Kapital ... ist; **that is ~ why I don't want it** genau deshalb will ich es nicht; **it is 10 o'clock ~** es ist genau 10 Uhr; **~ nothing** gar nichts.

preciseness [prɪ'saɪsnɪs] n Genauigkeit, Exaktheit f.

precision [prɪ'sɪʒən] n Genauigkeit f; (of work, movement also) Präzision f.

precision: ~ **bombing** n gezielter Bombenabwurf m; ~ **instrument** n Präzisionsinstrument nt; ~ **tool** n Präzisionswerkzeug nt; ~ **work** n Präzisionsarbeit f.

preclassical [priː'klæsɪkəl] adj vorklassisch.

preclude [prɪ'kluːd] vt possibility, misunderstanding ausschließen. **to ~ sb from doing sth** jdn daran hindern, etw zu tun.

precocious [prɪ'kəʊʃəs] adj interest, teenager, behaviour frühreif; statement, way of speaking altklug.

precociously [prɪ'kəʊʃəslɪ] adv frühreif; talk altklug. ~ **dressed** auf „alt" angezogen (inf).

precociousness [prɪ'kəʊʃəsnɪs], **precocity** [prɪ'kɒsɪtɪ] n see adj Frühreife f; Altklugheit f.

precognition [ˌpriːkɒɡ'nɪʃən] n (Psych) Präkognition f; (knowledge) vorherige Kenntnis, vorheriges Wissen.

preconceived [ˌpriːkən'siːvd] adj opinion, idea vorgefaßt.

preconception [ˌpriːkən'sepʃən] n vorgefaßte Meinung.

precondition [ˌpriːkən'dɪʃən] n (Vor)bedingung, Voraussetzung f.

precook [priː'kuk] vt vorkochen.

precursor [prɪ'kɜːsə'] n Vorläufer m; (herald: of event etc) Vorbote m; (in office) (Amts)vorgänger(in f) m.

predate [ˌpriː'deɪt] vt (precede) zeitlich vorangehen (+dat); cheque, letter zurückdatieren.

predator ['predətə'] n (animal) Raubtier nt; (person) Plünderer m. **the main ~s of the gazelle** die Hauptfeinde der Gazelle.

predatory ['predətərɪ] adj animal Raub-; attack also, tribe räuberisch. **he has a ~ attitude towards all the girls in**

the office er betrachtet alle Mädchen im Büro als Freiwild.

predecease [ˌpriːdɪ'siːs] vt **to ~ sb** vor jdm sterben.

predecessor [ˈpriːdɪsesə'] n (person) Vorgänger(in f) m; (thing) Vorläufer m. **our ~s** (ancestors) unsere Ahnen or Vorfahren pl; **his latest book is certainly better than its ~s** sein neuestes Buch ist zweifellos besser als seine vorherigen.

predestination [priːˌdestɪ'neɪʃən] n Vorherbestimmung, Prädestination f.

predestine [priː'destɪn] vt vorherbestimmen, prädestinieren; person prädestinieren.

predetermination [ˈpriːdɪˌtɜːmɪ'neɪʃən] n see vt Vorherbestimmung f; Prädetermination f; vorherige Festlegung or Festsetzung; vorherige Ermittlung; Voraussicht f.

predetermine [ˈpriːdɪ'tɜːmɪn] vt course of events, sb's future etc vorherbestimmen; (Philos) prädeterminieren; (fix in advance) price, date etc vorher or im voraus festlegen or festsetzen; (ascertain in advance) costs vorher ermitteln; problems voraussehen.

predicable ['predɪkəbl] adj **to be ~ of sth** von etw ausgesagt or behauptet werden können.

predicament [prɪ'dɪkəmənt] n Zwangslage f, Dilemma nt. **to be in a ~** in einem Dilemma or in einer Zwangslage sein.

predicate ['predɪkɪt] **1** n (Gram) Prädikat nt, Satzaussage f; (Logic) Aussage f. ~ **noun** prädikatives Substantiv, Prädikativ(um) nt.

2 ['predɪkeɪt] vt (imply, connote) aussagen; (assert, state) behaupten. **to ~ sth on sth** (base) etw auf etw (dat) gründen; **to ~ sth of sth** (assert as quality of) etw von etw behaupten.

predicative adj, ~**ly** adv [prɪ'dɪkətɪv, -lɪ] prädikativ.

predict [prɪ'dɪkt] vt vorher- or voraussagen, prophezeien.

predictability [prəˌdɪktə'bɪlɪtɪ] n Vorhersagbarkeit f.

predictable [prɪ'dɪktəbl] adj vorher- or voraussagbar. **to be ~** vorher- or voraussagbar sein, vorher- or vorauszusagen sein; **you're so ~** man weiß doch genau, wie Sie reagieren.

predictably [prɪ'dɪktəblɪ] adv react vorher- or voraussagbar. **~, he was late** wie vorauszusehen kam er zu spät.

prediction [prɪ'dɪkʃən] n Prophezeiung, Voraussage f.

predigest [ˌpriːdaɪ'dʒest] vt vorverdauen; (artificially, chemically) aufschließen; (fig) vorkauen.

predilection [ˌpriːdɪ'lekʃən] n Vorliebe f, Faible nt (for für).

predispose [ˈpriːdɪs'pəʊz] vt geneigt machen; (Med) prädisponieren, anfällig machen. **to ~ sb in favour of sb/sth** jdn für jdn/etw einnehmen; **that people are ~d to behave in certain ways** daß die Menschen so veranlagt sind, sich auf eine bestimmte Weise zu verhalten; **that ~d her to this** das nahm sie für ihn ein; **it ~s me to think that ...** das führt mich zu der Annahme, daß ...; **I'm not ~d to help him** ich bin nicht geneigt, ihm zu helfen.

predisposition [ˈpriːdɪspə'zɪʃən] n (tendency, inclination) Neigung f (to zu); (Med) Prädisposition, Anfälligkeit f (to zu). **that children have a natural ~ to use language** daß Kinder eine natürliche Veranlagung haben, Sprache zu gebrauchen.

predominance [prɪ'dɒmɪnəns] n (control) Vorherrschaft, Vormachtstellung f; (prevalence) Überwiegen nt. **the ~ of women in the office** die weibliche Überzahl im Büro.

predominant [prɪ'dɒmɪnənt] adj (most prevalent) idea, theory vorherrschend; (dominating) person, animal beherrschend. **those things which are ~ in your life** die Dinge, die in ihrem Leben von größter Bedeutung sind; **he was the ~ member of the group** er war in der Gruppe tonangebend.

predominantly [prɪ'dɒmɪnəntlɪ] adv überwiegend, hauptsächlich.

predominate [prɪ'dɒmɪneɪt] vi **(a)** vorherrschen. **(b)** (in influence etc) überwiegen. **Good will always ~ over Evil** das Gute wird immer über das Böse siegen; **if you allow any one individual to ~** (over the others) wenn man einem einzigen gestattet, die anderen zu beherrschen.

pre-election [ˌpriːɪ'lekʃən] adj attr measure, atmosphere Wahlkampf-. ~ **promise** Wahlversprechen nt.

pre-eminence [priː'emɪnəns] n überragende Bedeutung.

pre-eminent [priː'emɪnənt] adj herausragend, überragend.

pre-eminently [priː'emɪnəntlɪ] adv hauptsächlich, vor allem, in erster Linie; (excellently) hervorragend.

pre-empt [priː'empt] vt zuvorkommen (+dat); (Bridge) seinen Gegenspielern durch eine nicht mehr zu überbietende Ansage zuvorkommen. **his decision to leave was ~ed by his dismissal** die Entlassung kam seinem Entschluß wegzugehen zuvor.

pre-emption [priː'empʃən] n Zuvorkommen nt.

pre-emptive [priː'emptɪv] adj präventiv, Präventiv-. ~ **bid** (Bridge) Ansage, die durch ihre Höhe weitere Ansagen ausschließt.

preen [priːn] **1** vt feathers putzen. **2** vr **to ~ oneself** (bird) sich putzen; (person) (be smug) sich brüsten (on mit); (dress up) sich herausputzen, sich aufputzen.

pre-exist [ˌpriːɪɡ'zɪst] vi (exist beforehand) vorher existieren, vorher vorhanden sein; (exist in previous life) präexistieren.

pre-existence [ˌpriːɪɡ'zɪstəns] n (no pl: existing before) vorherige Existenz, vorheriges Vorhandensein; (previous life) früheres Leben or Dasein, Präexistenz f.

pre-existent [ˌpriːɪɡ'zɪstənt] adj (existing before) vorher vorhanden or existent; (of an earlier life) präexistent.

prefab ['priːfæb] n Fertig(teil)haus nt.

prefabricate [ˈpriː'fæbrɪkeɪt] vt vorfertigen.

prefabricated [ˈpriː'fæbrɪkeɪtɪd] adj vorgefertigt, Fertig-; building Fertig(teil)-.

prefabrication [ˈpriːfæbrɪ'keɪʃən] n Vorfertigung f.

preface ['prefɪs] **1** n Vorwort nt; (of speech) Vorrede f. **2** vt einleiten; book mit einem Vorwort versehen.

prefatory ['prefətərɪ] adj einleitend.

prefect ['priːfekt] n Präfekt m; (Brit Sch) Aufsichtsschüler(in f) m. **form ~** (Sch) ≈ Klassensprecher(in f) m.

prefecture ['pri:fektjʊəʳ] n Präfektur f.

prefer [prɪ'fɜ:ʳ] vt **(a)** (like better) vorziehen (to dat), lieber mögen (to als); **drink, food, music** also lieber trinken/essen/hören (to als); **applicant, solution** vorziehen, bevorzugen; (be more fond of als) **person** lieber haben (to als). **he ~s blondes/hot countries** er bevorzugt Blondinen/warme Länder; **I ~ it that way** es ist mir lieber so; **which (of them) do you ~?** (of people) wen ziehen Sie vor?; (emotionally) wen mögen or haben Sie lieber?; (of things) welche(n, s) ziehen Sie vor or finden Sie besser?; (find more pleasing) welche(r, s) gefällt Ihnen besser?; **I'd ~ something less ornate** ich hätte lieber etwas Schlichteres; **to ~ to do sth** etw lieber tun, es vorziehen, etw zu tun; **I ~ to resign rather than ...** eher kündige ich, als daß ...; **I ~ walking/flying** ich gehe lieber zu Fuß/fliege lieber; **I ~ not to say** ich sage es lieber nicht; **I would ~ you to do it today** mir wäre es lieber, wenn Sie es heute täten.

(b) (Jur) **to ~ a charge/charges (against sb)** (gegen jdn) klagen, Klage (gegen jdn) einreichen or erheben.

(c) (esp Eccl: promote) befördern. **the bishop was ~red to the archbishopric of York** dem Bischof wurde die Würde eines Erzbischofs von York verliehen.

(d) (treat preferentially) bevorzugen (to vor +dat).

preferable ['prefərəbl] adj **X is ~ to Y X** ist Y (dat) vorzuziehen; **death is ~ to dishonour** lieber tot als ehrlos; **it would be ~ to do it that way** es wäre besser, es so zu machen; **he feels that resignation is a ~ course** er findet, daß es besser ist zu kündigen.

preferably ['prefərəblɪ] adv am liebsten. **tea or coffee? — coffee, ~** Tee oder Kaffee? — lieber Kaffee; **but ~ not Tuesday** aber, wenn möglich, nicht Dienstag.

preference ['prefərəns] n **(a)** (greater liking) Vorliebe f. **for ~** lieber; **to have a ~ for sth** eine Vorliebe für etw haben, etw bevorzugen; **my ~ is for country life** ich ziehe das Leben auf dem Land vor; **I drink coffee in ~ to tea** ich trinke lieber Kaffee als Tee; **he chose to stay at home in ~ to going abroad** er beschloß, lieber in der Heimat zu bleiben, als ins Ausland zu gehen, er zog es vor, in der Heimat zu bleiben, statt ins Ausland zu gehen; see order 1 **(a)**.

(b) (thing preferred) **what is your ~?** was wäre Ihnen am liebsten?; **just state your ~** nennen Sie einfach Ihre Wünsche; **I have no ~** mir ist das eigentlich gleich; **he didn't consult my ~s in the matter** mich hat er dabei nicht nach meinen Wünschen gefragt; **what are your ~s in the matter of food?** was essen Sie am liebsten?

(c) (greater favour) Vorzug m. **to show ~ to sb** jdn bevorzugen; **to give ~ to sb/sth** jdn/etw bevorzugen, jdm/etw den Vorzug geben (over gegenüber); **Commonwealth ~** (Comm) Commonwealth-Präferenz f; **to give certain imports ~** Vorzugs- or Präferenzzölle auf bestimmte Einfuhrartikel gewähren; **~ shares or stock** (Brit Fin) Vorzugsaktien pl.

preferential [prefə'renʃəl] adj **treatment** Vorzugs-; **terms** bevorzugt, Sonder-. **to give sb ~ treatment** jdn bevorzugt behandeln, jdm eine Vorzugsbehandlung zuteil werden lassen (form); **~ trade** (Comm) Präferenz- or Vorzugshandel m; **~ tariff** (Comm) Präferenz- or Vorzugszoll m; **~ ballot** (Pol) Präferenzwahl f; **~ voting** (Pol) Präferenzwahlsystem nt.

preferentially [prefə'renʃəlɪ] adv treat etc bevorzugt.

preferment [prɪ'fɜ:mənt] n **(a)** (esp Eccl: promotion) Beförderung f. **(b)** (Jur) **~ of charges** Klageerhebung f.

preferred [prɪ'fɜ:d] adj **creditor** bevorrechtigt. **~ stock** (US Fin) Vorzugsaktien pl.

prefigure [pri:'fɪgəʳ] vt (indicate) anzeigen, ankündigen; (imagine beforehand) sich (dat) ausmalen.

prefix ['pri:fɪks] **1** n (Gram) Vorsilbe f, Präfix nt; (title) Namensvorsatz m; (in code) Vorsatz m; (Telec) Vorwahl f.

2 [pri:'fɪks] vt (Gram) mit einer Vorsilbe or einem Präfix versehen; **name** mit einem Namensvorsatz versehen; **code** with (acc) voranstellen (+dat), voransetzen (+dat). **words ~ed by "un"** Wörter mit der Vorsilbe or dem Präfix „un".

preflight [pri:'flaɪt] adj attr **~ checks/instructions** Kontrollen pl/Anweisungen pl vor dem Flug.

preform [pri:'fɔ:m] vt vorformen.

prefrontal [pri:'frʌntl] adj des Stirnbeins, Stirnbein-.

preggers ['pregəz] adj pred (esp Brit inf) schwanger.

pregnancy ['pregnənsɪ] n Schwangerschaft f; (of animal) Trächtigkeit f; (fig) (of remarks etc) Bedeutungsgehalt m; (of silence, pause) Bedeutungsschwere, Bedeutungsgeladenheit f. **~ test** Schwangerschaftsuntersuchung f or -test m.

pregnant ['pregnənt] adj **(a)** woman schwanger; animal trächtig, tragend. **(b)** (fig) remark, silence, pause bedeutungsvoll or -schwer or -geladen. **~ with meaning/consequences** bedeutungsvoll or -geladen/folgenschwer.

preheat [pri:'hi:t] vt vorheizen.

prehensile [prɪ'hensaɪl] adj Greif-.

prehistoric [pri:hɪ'stɒrɪk] adj prähistorisch, vorgeschichtlich.

prehistory [pri:'hɪstərɪ] n Vorgeschichte f.

pre-ignition [pri:ɪg'nɪʃən] n Frühzündung f.

pre-industrial [pri:ɪn'dʌstrɪəl] adj vorindustriell.

prejudge [pri:'dʒʌdʒ] vt case, issue im vorhinein verurteilen; person im voraus verurteilen.

prejudice ['predʒʊdɪs] **1** n **(a)** (biased opinion) Vorurteil nt. **his ~ against ...** seine Voreingenommenheit gegen ...; **that's pure ~** das ist reine Voreingenommenheit; **there's a lot of ~ about ...** es gibt eine Menge Vorurteile hinsichtlich ...; **the newspaper report was full of ~ against ...** der Zeitungsbericht steckte voller Vorurteile gegen ...; **to have a ~ against sb/sth** ein Vorurteil nt gegen jdn/etw haben, gegen jdn/etw voreingenommen sein; **racial ~** Rassenvorurteile pl; **colour ~** Vorurteile pl gegen (Anders)farbige or aufgrund der Hautfarbe.

(b) (esp Jur: detriment, injury) Schaden m. **to the ~ of sb/sth** (form) zum Nachteil or Schaden von jdm (form)/unter

Beeinträchtigung von etw; **without ~ to one's own chances** ohne sich (dat) selbst zu schaden; **without ~** (Jur) ohne Verbindlichkeit or Obligo; **without ~ to any claim** (Jur) ohne Beeinträchtigung or unbeschadet irgendwelcher Ansprüche.

2 vt **(a)** (bias) einnehmen, beeinflussen; see also prejudiced.

(b) (injure) gefährden; chances also beeinträchtigen.

prejudiced ['predʒʊdɪst] adj person voreingenommen (against gegen); opinion vorgefaßt; judge befangen.

prejudicial [predʒʊ'dɪʃəl] adj abträglich (to sth einer Sache dat). **to be ~ to a cause/sb's chances** einer Sache (dat) schaden/jds Chancen gefährden.

prelacy ['preləsɪ] n (office) Prälatur f; (bishops) geistliche Würdenträger pl; (system) Kirchenhierarchie f.

prelate ['prelɪt] n Prälat m.

preliminary [prɪ'lɪmɪnərɪ] **1** adj talks, negotiations, enquiry, investigation, stage Vor-; remarks also, chapter einleitend; steps, measures vorbereitend.

2 n Einleitung f (to zu); (preparatory measure) Vorbereitung f, vorbereitende Maßnahme; (Sport) Vorspiel nt. **preliminaries** Präliminarien pl (geh, Jur); (for speech) einführende or einleitende Worte; (Sport) Vorrunde f; **the preliminaries are complete, now the actual work can begin** die Vorarbeit ist getan, jetzt kann die eigentliche Arbeit anfangen; **all the preliminaries to sth** alles, was einer Sache (dat) vorausgeht; **as a necessary ~ to the actual application of the paint** als notwendige Maßnahme vor dem Auftragen der Farbe; **let's dispense with the preliminaries** kommen wir gleich zur Sache.

prelims ['pri:lɪmz] npl **(a)** (Univ) Vorprüfung f. **(b)** (in book) Vorbemerkungen pl.

prelude ['prelju:d] n **1** n Vorspiel nt; (introduction to fugue) Präludium nt; (fig) Auftakt m. **2** vt einleiten, den Auftakt (+gen) bilden.

premarital [pri:'mærɪtl] adj vorehelich.

premature ['premətʃʊəʳ] adj baldness, birth, arrival vorzeitig; decision, action verfrüht. **you were a little ~** da waren Sie ein wenig voreilig; **the baby was three weeks ~** das Baby wurde drei Wochen zu früh geboren; **~ baby** Frühgeburt f.

prematurely ['premətʃʊəlɪ] adv bald vorzeitig; decide verfrüht; act voreilig. **he was born ~** er war eine Frühgeburt.

premed [pri:'med] n (inf) **(a)** see premedication. **(b)** (US) Medizinstudent, der einen auf das Medizinstudium vorbereitenden Einführungskurs besucht; dieser Kurs selbst.

premedical [pri:'medɪkl] adj (US) auf das Medizinstudium vorbereitend attr.

premedication [pri:medɪ'keɪʃən] n Beruhigungsspritze f (vor Anästhesie).

premeditate [pri:'medɪteɪt] vt vorsätzlich planen.

premeditated [pri:'medɪteɪtɪd] adj vorsätzlich.

premeditation [pri:medɪ'teɪʃən] n Vorsatz m.

premenstrual [pri:'menstrʊəl] adj prämenstruell, vor der Menstruation auftretend.

premier ['premɪəʳ] **1** adj führend. **of ~ importance** von äußerster Wichtigkeit. **2** n Premier(minister) m.

première ['premɪɛəʳ] **1** n Première f; (first ever also) Uraufführung f; (in particular place also) Erstaufführung f. **2** vt uraufführen; erstaufführen.

premiership ['premɪəʃɪp] n (period) Amtsperiode or -zeit f als Premier(minister); (office) Amt nt des Premier(minister)s.

premise ['premɪs] n **(a)** (esp Logic) Prämisse (spec), Voraussetzung f.

(b) **~s** pl (of school, factory) Gelände nt; (building) Gebäude nt; (shop) Räumlichkeiten pl; (form: house) Besitz m, Anwesen nt; **licensed ~s** Schankort m; **business ~s** Geschäftsräume pl; **to use as business ~s** geschäftlich nutzen; **drinking is not allowed in or on these ~s** es ist nicht erlaubt, hier Alkohol zu trinken; **will you escort him off the ~s?** würden Sie ihn bitte hinausbegleiten?; **get off my ~s** verlassen Sie sofort mein Land or Grundstück!

premiss n see premise **(a)**.

premium ['pri:mɪəm] n (bonus, additional sum) Bonus m, Prämie f; (surcharge) Zuschlag m; (insurance ~) Prämie f; (St Ex) Aufgeld, Agio nt. **~ bond** (Brit) Prämien- or Lotterieaktie f; **to sell sth at a ~** etw über seinem Wert verkaufen; **to be at a ~** (St Ex) über Pari stehen; (fig) hoch im Kurs stehen; **to put a ~ on sth** (fig) etw hoch einschätzen or bewerten.

premolar [pri:'məʊləʳ] n vorderer Backenzahn.

premonition [pri:mə'nɪʃən] n (presentiment) (böse or schlechte) Vorahnung, (böses or schlechtes) Vorgefühl; (forewarning) Vorwarnung f.

premonitory [prɪ'mɒnɪtərɪ] adj warnend.

prenatal [pri:'neɪtl] adj pränatal, vor der Geburt.

prenuptial [pri:'nʌpʃəl] adj vor der Hochzeit.

preoccupation [pri:ɒkjʊ'peɪʃən] n his face had a look of ~ seinem Gesicht sah man an, daß ihn etwas beschäftigte; **her ~ with her appearance** ihre ständige Sorge um ihr Äußeres; **her ~ with making money** was such that ... sie war so sehr mit dem Geldverdienen beschäftigt, daß ...; **that was his main ~** das war sein Hauptanliegen.

preoccupied [pri:'ɒkjʊpaɪd] adj look, tone of voice, smile gedankenverloren. **to be ~ with sth** nur an etw (acc) denken, sich ganz auf etw (acc) konzentrieren; **he has been (looking) rather ~ recently** er sieht in letzter Zeit so aus, als beschäftige ihn etwas; **he was too ~ to notice her** er war zu sehr mit anderen Dingen beschäftigt, um sie zu bemerken.

preoccupy [pri:'ɒkjʊpaɪ] vt (stark) beschäftigen.

preordain [pri:ɔ:'deɪn] vt vorherbestimmen.

prep [prep] (inf) n see preparation **(d)**.

prepackaged [pri:'pækɪdʒd], **prepacked** [pri:'pækt] adj abgepackt.

prepaid [pri:'peɪd] **1** ptp of prepay. **2** adj postage, goods vorausbezahlt; envelope vorfrankiert, freigemacht.

preparation [‚prepə'reɪʃən] n **(a)** (preparing) Vorbereitung f; (of meal, medicine etc) Zubereitung f. in ~ for sth als Vorbereitung für etw; to be in ~ in Vorbereitung sein.
(b) (preparatory measure) Vorbereitung f. ~s for war/a journey Kriegs-/Reisevorbereitungen pl; to make ~s Vorbereitungen treffen.
(c) (prepared substance) (Med, Sci) Präparat nt. beauty ~s Schönheitspräparate pl; a ~ of herbs (Med) ein Kräuterpräparat nt; (Cook) eine Kräutermischung.
(d) (Brit Sch) (homework) Hausaufgaben pl, Hausarbeit f; (homework period) Lernstunde f. we have a lot of French ~ wir haben eine Menge Französischaufgaben zu machen.

preparatory [prɪ'pærətərɪ] adj **(a)** step, measure vorbereitend; plan, work also Vorbereitungs-. the ~ arrangements die Vorbereitungen pl.
(b) (Sch) ~ education Erziehung or Ausbildung f in Vorbereitungsschulen; ~ school (Brit) private Vorbereitungsschule für die Public School; (US) private Vorbereitungsschule für die Hochschule; ~ student (US) Schüler einer privaten Vorbereitungsschule für die Hochschule.
(c) talks were held ~ to the summit conference es wurden Gespräche geführt, um die Gipfelkonferenz vorzubereiten; he paid all his bills ~ to going on holiday er bezahlte alle seine Rechnungen, bevor er in Urlaub fuhr.

prepare [prɪ'pɛəʳ] **1** vt vorbereiten (sb for sth jdn auf etw acc, sth for sth etw für or auf etw acc); plan, speech also ausarbeiten; meal, medicine zubereiten; guest-room zurecht- or fertigmachen; (Sci) präparieren; data aufbereiten. to ~ yourself for a shock! mach dich auf einen Schock gefaßt!; we ~d ourselves for a long wait wir stellten uns auf eine lange Wartezeit ein, wir machten uns auf eine lange Wartezeit gefaßt.
2 vi to ~ for sth sich auf etw (acc) vorbereiten, Vorbereitungen für etw treffen; to ~ for an exam sich auf eine Prüfung vorbereiten; the country is preparing for war das Land trifft Kriegsvorbereitungen, das Land rüstet zum Krieg; to ~ to do sth Anstalten machen, etw zu tun.

prepared [prɪ'pɛəd] adj **(a)** (also ready ~) vorbereitet; speech also ausgearbeitet, abgefaßt; food Fertig-.
(b) (in a state of readiness) vorbereitet (for auf +acc). I wasn't ~ for that! darauf war ich nicht vorbereitet or gefaßt; I wasn't ~ for him to do that ich war nicht darauf vorbereitet, daß er das tut; the country is ~ for war das Land ist kriegsbereit or zum Krieg gerüstet; are you ~ for your journey? sind Sie reisefertig?; "be ~" "allzeit bereit".
(c) (willing) to be ~ to do sth bereit sein, etw zu tun.

preparedness [prɪ'pɛərɪdnɪs] n (readiness) Vorbereitetsein nt (for auf +acc); (for untoward events) Gefaßtsein nt (for auf +acc); (willingness) Bereitschaft f. lack of ~ mangelnde Vorbereitung (for auf +acc); ~ for war Kriegsbereitschaft f; (of army) Einsatzbereitschaft f.

prepay [priː'peɪ] pret, ptp **prepaid** vt im voraus bezahlen.
prepayment [priː'peɪmənt] n Vorauszahlung f.
preponderance [prɪ'pɒndərəns] n Übergewicht nt; (in number also) Überwiegen nt.
preponderant [prɪ'pɒndərənt] adj überwiegend.
preponderate [prɪ'pɒndəreɪt] vi überwiegen.
preposition [‚prepə'zɪʃən] n Präposition f, Verhältniswort nt.
prepositional [‚prepə'zɪʃənl] adj präpositional; phrase Präpositional-, Verhältnis-.
prepossess [‚priːpə'zes] vt einnehmen (in sb's favour für jdn).
prepossessing [‚priːpə'zesɪŋ] adj einnehmend, anziehend.
preposterous [prɪ'pɒstərəs] adj grotesk, absurd. you're being ~ das ist ja grotesk.
preposterously [prɪ'pɒstərəslɪ] adv grotesk. he suggested, quite ~ ... er machte den grotesken or absurden Vorschlag ...; it took a ~ long time es dauerte absurd lange.
preposterousness [prɪ'pɒstərəsnɪs] n Absurdität, Groteskheit f.
prep school n see **preparatory (b)**.
prepublication [‚priːpʌblɪ'keɪʃən] adj attr vor der Veröffentlichung.
prepuce ['priːpjuːs] n Vorhaut f, Präputium nt (spec).
pre-Raphaelite [priː'ræfəlaɪt] **1** adj präraffaelitisch. **2** n Präraffaelit m.
prerecord [‚priːrɪ'kɔːd] vt vorher aufzeichnen. ~ed cassette bespielte Kassette.
prerequisite [‚priː'rekwɪzɪt] **1** n (Grund)voraussetzung, Vorbedingung f. **2** adj erforderlich, notwendig.
prerogative [prɪ'rɒgətɪv] n Vorrecht, Prärogativ (geh) nt. that's a woman's ~ das ist das Vorrecht einer Frau.
Pres abbr of **president** Präs.
presage ['presɪdʒ] **1** n (omen) Vorzeichen, Anzeichen nt, Vorbote m; (feeling) Vorahnung f. **2** vt ankündig(ig)en, andeuten.
Presbyterian [‚prezbɪ'tɪərɪən] **1** adj presbyterianisch. **2** n Presbyterianer(in f) m.
presbytery ['prezbɪtərɪ] n (priest's house) (katholisches) Pfarrhaus; (part of church) Presbyterium nt.
preschool ['priː'skuːl] adj attr vorschulisch. a child of ~ age ein Vorschulkind nt; ~ years Vorschuljahre pl.
preschooling ['priː'skuːlɪŋ] n Vorschulerziehung f.
prescience ['presɪəns] n vorheriges Wissen, vorherige Kenntnis, Vorherwissen nt.
prescribe [prɪ'skraɪb] **1** vt **(a)** (order, lay down) vorschreiben. **(b)** (Med, fig) verschreiben, verordnen (sth for sb jdm etw). **2** vi **(a)** (lay down rules) Vorschriften machen. **(b)** (Med) to ~ for sth für or gegen etw verschreiben.
prescription [prɪ'skrɪpʃən] n **(a)** (Med) Rezept nt. to make up or fill (US) a ~ eine Medizin zubereiten; ~ charge Rezeptgebühr f; only available on ~ rezeptpflichtig, nur auf Rezept erhältlich.
(b) (regulation) Vorschrift f.

prescriptive [prɪ'skrɪptɪv] adj normativ. to be ~ Vorschriften machen.
presealed ['priː'siːld] adj versiegelt; containers etc plombiert.
preseason ['priː'siːzn] adj (Sport) match, training vor der Saison; (in tourism) rates, weekend Vorsaison-.
preselect [‚priːsɪ'lekt] vt vorher auswählen; gear vorwählen.
presence ['prezns] n **(a)** Gegenwart, Anwesenheit f. in sb's ~, in the ~ of sb in jds (dat) Gegenwart or Anwesenheit, in Gegenwart or im Beisein von jdm; he was admitted to the king's ~ er wurde zum König vorgelassen; your ~ is requested/required Sie sind eingeladen/Ihre Anwesenheit ist erforderlich; to make one's ~ felt sich bemerkbar machen; in the ~ of danger im Angesicht der Gefahr.
(b) a military/police ~ Militär-/Polizeipräsenz f.
(c) (bearing, dignity) Auftreten nt, Haltung f; (of actor: also stage ~) Ausstrahlung f.
(d) (invisible spirit) they felt a ghostly/an invisible ~ sie spürten, daß etwas Geisterhaftes/Unsichtbares anwesend war.
presence of mind n Geistesgegenwart f.
present[1] ['preznt] adj **(a)** (in attendance) anwesend. to be ~ anwesend sein, da or dort/hier sein; he was ever ~ in her thoughts er war in ihren Gedanken immer gegenwärtig; to be ~ at sth bei etw (anwesend) sein; ~ company excepted Anwesende ausgenommen; all those ~ alle Anwesenden; as one of those ~ als einer der Anwesenden.
(b) (existing in sth) vorhanden. gases ~ in the atmosphere in der Atmosphäre vorhandene Gase; carbon is ~ in organic matter Kohlenstoff ist in organischen Stoffen enthalten; a quality ~ in all great men eine Eigenschaft, die man bei allen großen Männern findet.
(c) (at the ~ time) moment, state of affairs, world record etc gegenwärtig, derzeitig, augenblicklich; problems, manager, husband etc also jetzig; year, season etc laufend. at the ~ moment zum gegenwärtigen or derzeitigen or jetzigen Zeitpunkt; in the ~ circumstances unter den gegenwärtigen or gegebenen Umständen; in the ~ case im vorliegenden Fall; the ~ writer (form) der Autor des hier vorliegenden Werkes.
(d) (Gram) in the ~ tense in der Gegenwart, im Präsens; ~ participle Partizip nt Präsens, Mittelwort nt der Gegenwart; ~ perfect (tense) zweite Vergangenheit, Perfekt nt.
2 n Gegenwart f; (Gram also) Präsens nt. at ~ zur Zeit, im Moment or Augenblick, derzeit; up to the ~ bislang, bis jetzt; there's no time like the ~ (prov) was du heute kannst besorgen, das verschiebe nicht auf morgen (Prov); that will be all for the ~ das ist vorläufig or einstweilen alles.

present[2] **1** n (gift) Geschenk nt. a birthday ~ ein Geburtstagsgeschenk nt; to make sb a ~ of sth jdm etw schenken (also fig), jdm etw zum Geschenk machen (form); I got it or was given it as a ~ das habe ich geschenkt bekommen.
2 [prɪ'zent] vt **(a)** (hand over formally) medal, prize etc übergeben, überreichen; (give as a gift) art collection, book etc schenken, zum Geschenk machen (form). to ~ sb with sth, to ~ sth to sb jdm etw übergeben or überreichen; (as a gift) jdm etw schenken or zum Geschenk machen (form); they ~ed us with a hefty bill sie präsentierten or überreichten uns (dat) eine gesalzene Rechnung; he was ~ed with a gold watch ihm wurde eine goldene Uhr geschenkt or zum Geschenk gemacht (form); she ~ed him with a son sie schenkte ihm einen Sohn.
(b) (put forward) cheque (for payment) präsentieren; proof also erbringen (of sth für etw); proposal also unterbreiten. she asked me to ~ her apologies/compliments (form) sie bat mich, ihre Entschuldigung/Komplimente weiterzuleiten; please ~ my compliments to the chef (form) richten Sie dem Koch/der Köchin meine Komplimente aus; please ~ my apologies to your mother (form) bitte entschuldigen Sie mich bei Ihrer Mutter; his report ~s the matter in another light sein Bericht zeigt die Angelegenheit in anderem Licht or stellt die Angelegenheit in anderem Licht dar.
(c) (offer, provide) target, view, opportunity bieten. to ~ a brave face to the world sich (dat) nichts anmerken lassen; his action ~ed us with a problem seine Tat stellte uns vor ein Problem; he ~ed the appearance of normality nach außen hin wirkte er ganz normal.
(d) (Rad, TV) präsentieren; (Theat also) zeigen, aufführen; (commentator) moderieren. ~ing Nina Calcott as ... (Film) und erstmals Nina Calcott als ...; ~ing, in the blue corner ... in der blauen Ecke des Rings ~.
(e) (introduce) vorstellen. to ~ Mr X to Miss Y Herrn X Fräulein Y (dat) vorstellen; may I ~ Mr X? (form) erlauben Sie mir, Herrn X vorzustellen? (form), darf ich Ihnen Herrn X vorstellen?; to be ~ed at Court bei Hof eingeführt werden.
(f) (point) gun etc richten, zielen (at auf +acc). he ~ed the pistol at his head er richtete die Pistole auf seinen Kopf; ~ arms! (Mil) präsentiert das Gewehr!
3 [prɪ'zent] vr (opportunity, problem etc) sich ergeben. to ~ oneself as a candidate sich aufstellen lassen; to ~ oneself for an exam sich zu einer Prüfung anmelden; he was asked to ~ himself for interview er wurde gebeten, zu einem Gespräch zu erscheinen; to ~ oneself at an ideal moment im idealen Augenblick erscheinen.

presentable [prɪ'zentəbl] adj to be ~ sich sehen lassen können; it's not very ~ damit kann man sich nicht gut sehen lassen; to make sth ~ etw so herrichten, daß man es zeigen kann; to make oneself ~ sich zurechtmachen; a ~ person jemand, mit dem man sich sehen lassen kann; a ~ coat/skirt ein Mantel/Rock, in or mit dem man sich sehen lassen kann.
presentably [prɪ'zentəblɪ] adv annehmbar, akzeptabel. you have to be ~ dressed to get into that bar man muß angemessen angezogen sein, wenn man in diese Bar will.
presentation [‚prezən'teɪʃən] n **(a)** (of gift etc) Überreichung f; (of prize, medal also) Verleihung f; (ceremony) Ver-

leihung(szeremonie) f; (gift) Geschenk nt. to make the ~ die Preise/Auszeichnungen etc verleihen; to make sb a ~ jdm ein Geschenk überreichen; ~ **copy** Dedikationsexemplar nt.
  (b) (act of presenting) n (a) (of report, voucher, cheque etc) Vorlage, Präsentation f; (of petition) Überreichung f; (Jur: of case, evidence) Darlegung f. on ~ gegen Vorlage.
  (c) (manner of presenting) Darbietung, Präsentation f. the ~ is poor die Darbietung or Präsentation ist schlecht.
  (d) (Theat) Inszenierung f; (TV also, Rad) Produktion f; (announcing, commentary) Moderation f.
  (e) (Med: at birth) Lage f.
present-day ['preznt'deɪ] adj attr morality, problems, fashions unserer Zeit. ~ **Britain** das heutige Großbritannien.
presenter [prɪ'zentər] n (a) (of cheque) Überbringer(in f) m. the ~ of the petition was a child die Petition wurde von einem Kind überreicht; he was the ~ of the report der Bericht wurde von ihm vorgelegt. (b) (TV, Rad) Moderator(in f) m.
presentiment [prɪ'zentɪmənt] n (Vor)ahnung f, Vorgefühl nt. to have a ~ about sth ein ungutes Gefühl in bezug auf etw haben; to have a ~ that ... das Gefühl haben, daß ...
presently ['prezntlɪ] adv (a) (soon) bald. ~ we reached a farmhouse bald darauf kamen wir an ein Bauernhaus. (b) (at present) zur Zeit, derzeit, gegenwärtig.
preservation [prezə'veɪʃən] n see vt (a) Erhaltung f; Wahrung f; Aufrechterhaltung f; Bewahrung f. (b) Konservierung f (also of leather, wood); Präservierung f. to be in a good state of ~ gut erhalten sein. (c) Einmachen, Einkochen nt; Einwecken nt; Einlegen nt. (d) Bewahrung f.
preservative [prɪ'zɜ:vətɪv] 1 adj substance Konservierungs-. 2 n Konservierungsmittel nt.
preserve [prɪ'zɜ:v] 1 vt (a) (keep intact, maintain) customs, building, position, eyesight, manuscript erhalten; peace also, dignity, appearances wahren; memory, reputation aufrechterhalten, wahren; sense of humour, silence bewahren.
  (b) (keep from decay) konservieren; specimens etc präservieren; leather, wood konservieren. well ~d gut erhalten.
  (c) (Cook) einmachen, einkochen; (bottle also) einwecken; (pickle) einlegen. preserving jar Weck- or Einmachglas nt.
  (d) (keep from harm, save) bewahren. may God ~ you! Gott steh dir bei!; to ~ sb from sth jdn vor etw (dat) schützen or bewahren; heaven or the saints ~ me from that! (iro) der Himmel möge mich damit verschonen or mir das ersparen!
  (e) (Hunt) game, fish schützen, hegen. ~d fishing/river/wood unter Schutz stehende Fische/stehender Fluß/Wald.
  2 n (a) (Cook) ~s pl Eingemachtes nt; (bottled fruit also) Eingewecktes nt; peach ~(s) eingeweckte Pfirsiche pl; (Brit: jam) Pfirsichmarmelade f.
  (b) (special domain) Ressort nt. to poach on sb's ~(s) jdm ins Handwerk pfuschen; game ~ (Hunt) Jagd f, Jagdrevier nt.
preserver [prɪ'zɜ:vər] n Retter(in f) m.
preset [pri:'set] pret, ptp ~ vt vorher einstellen.
preshrink [pri:'ʃrɪŋk] pret **preshrank** [pri:'ʃræŋk], ptp **preshrunk** [pri:'ʃrʌŋk] vt vorwaschen.
preside [prɪ'zaɪd] vi (at meeting etc) den Vorsitz haben or führen (at bei); (at meal) den Vorsitz haben (at bei). to ~ over an organization etc eine Organisation etc leiten; Mrs Jones ~d at the piano am Klavier saß Frau Jones.
presidency ['prezɪdənsɪ] n Präsidentschaft f; (esp US: of company) Aufsichtsratsvorsitz m; (US Univ) Rektorat nt.
president ['prezɪdənt] n Präsident(in f) m; (esp US: of company) Aufsichtsratsvorsitzende(r) mf; (US Univ) Rektor(in f) m.
presidential [ˌprezɪ'denʃəl] adj (Pol) Präsidenten-; election also Präsidentschafts-. ~ **primary** Vorwahl f für die Präsidentschaft; his ~ **duties** seine Pflichten als Präsident.
presidium [prɪ'sɪdɪəm] n (Partei)präsidium nt.
press [pres] 1 n (a) (machine, trouser ~, flower ~) Presse f; (racket ~) Spanner m.
  (b) (Typ) (Drucker)presse f; (publishing firm) Verlag m. to go to ~ in Druck gehen; to be in the ~ im Druck sein.
  (c) (newspapers) Presse f. the daily/sporting ~ die Tages-/ Sportpresse; the weekly ~ die Wochenzeitungen pl; to get a good/bad ~ eine gute/schlechte Presse bekommen.
  (d) (squeeze, push) Druck m. to give sth a ~ etw drücken; dress etc etw bügeln; to take a suit for a ~ einen Anzug zum Bügeln bringen; your shirt could do with a ~ dein Hemd müßte mal gebügelt werden.
  (e) (dial, US: cupboard) Wandschrank m.
  (f) (crush) Gedränge nt. a ~ of people eine Menschenmenge; in the ~ of the battle im Schlachtgetümmel.
  (g) (Weight-lifting) Drücken nt.
  2 vt (a) (push, squeeze) drücken (to an + acc); button, doorbell, knob also, brake pedal drücken auf (+ acc); clutch, piano pedal treten; grapes, fruit (aus)pressen; flowers pressen. to ~ the accelerator Gas geben; to ~ the trigger (of a gun) abdrücken, den Abzug betätigen; the shoe ~es my foot here der Schuh drückt (mich) hier.
  (b) (iron) clothes bügeln.
  (c) (urge, persuade) drängen; (harass, importune) bedrängen, unter Druck setzen; (insist on) claim, argument bestehen auf (+ dat). to ~ sb hard jdm (hart) zusetzen; he didn't need much ~ing man brauchte ihn nicht lange zu drängen; to ~ home the point darauf beharren or herumreiten (inf); to ~ home an advantage einen Vorteil ausnutzen, sich (dat) einen Vorteil zunutze machen; to ~ home an attack einen Angriff energisch vortragen; to ~ money/one's views on sb jdm Geld/seine Ansichten aufdrängen; to be ~ed (for money/time) knapp dran sein (inf); in Geldnot sein/unter Zeitdruck stehen, in Zeitnot sein; to ~ sb/sth into service jdn/etw einspannen.
  (d) machine part, record etc pressen. ~ed steel gepreßter Stahl, Preßstahl m; ~ed pork gepreßtes Schweinefleisch.
  3 vi (a) (lit, fig: bear down, exert pressure) drücken. to ~

down on sb (debts, troubles) schwer auf jdm lasten.
  (b) (urge, agitate) drängen; (be insistent also) drängeln (inf). to ~ for sth auf etw (acc) drängen; time ~es die Zeit drängt.
  (c) (move, push) sich drängen. to ~ **ahead** or **forward** (with sth) (fig) (mit etw) weitermachen; (with plans) etw weiterführen.
♦**press on** vi weitermachen; (with journey) weiterfahren.
♦**press out** vt sep juice auspressen; pop-out models etc herausdrücken.
press: ~ **agency** n Presseagentur f; ~ **agent** n Presseagent m; ~ **baron** n Pressezar m; ~ **box** n Pressetribüne f; ~ **button** n see **push-button**; ~ **campaign** n Pressekampagne f or -feldzug m; ~ **card** n Presseausweis m; ~ **clipping** n Zeitungsausschnitt m; ~ **conference** n Pressekonferenz f; ~ **cutting** n (esp Brit) Zeitungsausschnitt m; ~ **gallery** n (esp Jur, Parl) Pressetribüne f; ~**gang** 1 n (Hist) (for navy) Preßpatrouille f; (for army) Werber pl; 2 vt (inf) dazu drängen; to ~**gang** sb into (doing) sth jdn drängen, etw zu tun.
pressing ['presɪŋ] 1 adj (a) (urgent) dringend.
  (b) (insistent) requests nachdrücklich. he was very ~ in his invitation er drängte mir etc seine Einladung richtig auf.
  2 n (records issued at one time) Auflage f; (copy of record) Pressung f.
press: ~ **lord** n see ~ **baron**; ~**man** n (a) (esp Brit: reporter) Zeitungsmann, Pressemann m; (b) (Typ) Drucker m; ~**mark** n Signatur f; ~ **office** n Pressestelle f; ~ **officer** n Pressesprecher(in f) m; ~ **photographer** n Pressefotograf(in f) m; ~ **release** n Presseverlautbarung f; ~ **report** n Pressebericht m; ~ **room** n Druckerei f, (Druck)maschinensaal m; ~ **stud** n (Brit) Druckknopf m; ~**up** n Liegestütz m.
pressure ['preʃər] 1 n (a) Druck m (also Phys, Met). at high/full ~ (lit, fig) unter Hochdruck.
  (b) (compulsion, influence) Druck, Zwang m. parental ~ Druck von seiten der Eltern; social ~s gesellschaftliche Zwänge pl; to do sth under ~ etw unter Druck or Zwang tun; to be under ~ to do sth unter dem Druck stehen, etw zu tun; to be under ~ from sb to do sth von jdm gedrängt werden(, etw zu tun); to put ~ on sb jdn unter Druck setzen; to put the ~ on (inf) Druck dahintermachen (inf), Dampf machen (inf).
  (c) (urgent demands, stress) Druck, Streß m no pl. ~ of work prevents me Arbeitsüberlastung hindert mich daran; the ~ of events der Druck der Ereignisse; business ~s geschäftliche Belastungen pl; the ~s of modern life die Belastungen pl or der Streß des modernen Lebens; he works better under ~ er arbeitet besser unter Druck; to be subjected to ~, to be under ~ unter Druck stehen or sein; he's been under a bit of ~ recently er war in letzter Zeit großen Belastungen ausgesetzt.
  2 vt see **pressurize (b).**
pressure: ~ **cabin** n (Aviat) Überdruckkabine f; ~**-cook** vt mit Dampf kochen; ~ **cooker** n Druck- or Dampf- or Schnellkochtopf m; ~ **gauge** n Manometer nt, Druckmesser m; ~ **group** n Pressure-group f; ~ **point** n (Anat) Druckpunkt m; ~ **suit** n (Aviat) Druckanzug m.
pressurization [ˌpreʃəraɪ'zeɪʃən] n (Aviat etc) Druckausgleich m. before ~ high altitude flying was impossible als es die Möglichkeit des Druckausgleichs noch nicht gab, war Fliegen in großer Höhe unmöglich.
pressurize ['preʃəraɪz] vt (a) cabin, spacesuit auf Normaldruck halten. the cabin is only ~d when ... der Druckausgleich in der Kabine wird erst hergestellt, wenn ...
  (b) unter Druck setzen. to ~ sb into doing sth jdn so unter Druck setzen, daß er schließlich etw tut; I refuse to be ~d into agreeing/going ich lasse mir meine Zustimmung nicht abpressen/ich lasse mich nicht zwingen zu gehen.
prestidigitation ['prestɪˌdɪdʒɪ'teɪʃən] n (form) Fingerfertigkeit, Geschicklichkeit f.
prestidigitator [ˌprestɪ'dɪdʒɪteɪtər] n (form) Taschenspieler m.
prestige [pre'sti:ʒ] n Prestige nt. ~ **value** Prestigewert m.
prestigious [pre'stɪdʒəs] adj Prestige-. to be (very) ~ (einen hohen) Prestigewert haben.
presto ['prestəʊ] adv see **hey.**
prestressed ['pri:strest] adj vorgespannt; concrete also Spann-.
presumable [prɪ'zju:məbl] adj vermutlich.
presumably [prɪ'zju:məblɪ] adv see adj. ~ he is very rich, is he? ich nehme an, er ist sehr reich, oder?; ~ he'll come later er wird voraussichtlich später kommen.
presume [prɪ'zju:m] 1 vt (a) (suppose) annehmen, vermuten; sb's death unterstellen (form). ~d dead mutmaßlich verstorben; to be ~d innocent als unschuldig gelten.
  (b) (venture) ~ to do sth sich (dat) erlauben or sich (dat) herausnehmen or sich erdreisten, etw zu tun.
  2 vi (a) (suppose) annehmen, vermuten. Dr Livingstone, I ~ Dr. Livingstone, wie ich annehme; it was his decision, I ~ ich nehme an or vermute, das war seine Entscheidung.
  (b) (take liberties, be presumptuous) I didn't want to ~ ich wollte nicht aufdringlich sein; I hope I'm not presuming ich hoffe, man hält mich nicht für aufdringlich; you ~ too much Sie sind wirklich vermessen; to ~ on or upon sth etw überbeanspruchen.
presumption [prɪ'zʌmpʃən] n (a) (assumption) Annahme, Vermutung f. the ~ is that ... es wird angenommen or man vermutet, daß ...; there is a strong ~ that ... es wird stark angenommen, daß ...; ~ of death/innocence Todes-/Unschuldvermutung f.
  (b) (boldness, arrogance) Unverschämtheit, Dreistigkeit f; (in connection with one's abilities) Überheblichkeit, Anmaßung, Vermessenheit (geh) f.
presumptive [prɪ'zʌmptɪv] adj (a) (Jur) ~ **evidence** Indizien(beweis m) pl; ~ **case** Indizienprozeß m. (b) (likely) ~ **heir**, **heir** ~ mutmaßlicher Erbe.

presumptuous adj, ~ly adv [prɪˈzʌmptjʊəs, -lɪ] unverschämt, dreist; (in connection with one's abilities) überheblich, anmaßend, vermessen (geh).

presumptuousness [prɪˈzʌmptjʊəsnɪs] n see adj Unverschämtheit, Dreistigkeit f; Überheblichkeit, Anmaßung, Vermessenheit (geh) f.

presuppose [ˌpriːsəˈpəʊz] vt voraussetzen; (require also) zur Voraussetzung haben.

presupposition [ˌpriːsʌpəˈzɪʃən] n Voraussetzung f.

pre-tax [priːˈtæks] adj unversteuert, vor Besteuerung.

pre-teen [ˈpriːˈtiːn] adj Kinder- (bezogen auf die Zeit etwa zwischen dem zehnten und zwölften Lebensjahr).

pretence, (US) **pretense** [prɪˈtens] n (a) (make-believe story) erfundene Geschichte; (make-believe person) erfundene Gestalt. he didn't really shoot me, it was just ~ er hat nicht auf mich geschossen, er hat nur so getan; the story of Red Riding Hood is only ~ Rotkäppchen ist nur eine erfundene Geschichte; to make a ~ of being sth so tun, als ob man etw sei or als sei man etw; we soon saw through his ~ of being a foreigner wir durchschauten bald, daß er nur vorspiegelte or vorgab, Ausländer zu sein; he made not even the slightest ~ of being interested er gab sich (dat) nicht einmal den Anschein des Interesses; this constant ~ that all is well die ständige Vorspiegelung, daß alles in Ordnung ist; to maintain a ~ of democracy den (An)schein einer Demokratie wahren; it's all a ~ das ist alles nur gespielt or Mache (inf).
(b) (feigning, insincerity) Heuchelei, Verstellung f. his coolness is just a (a) ~ seine Kühle ist nur gespielt; his ~ of innocence/friendship seine gespielte Unschuld/Freundschaft; he made a ~ of friendship er heuchelte Freundschaft, er gab Freundschaft vor; let's stop all this ~ hören wir mit der Heuchelei auf, hören wir auf, uns (dat) etwas vorzumachen; he is incapable of ~ er kann sich nicht verstellen.
(c) (affectation) Unnatürlichkeit, Geziertheit f. there is not a scrap of ~ in or about her sie ist durch und durch natürlich.
(d) to make no ~ to sth keinen Anspruch auf etw (acc) erheben.
(e) (pretext, excuse) Vorwand m. on or under the ~ of doing sth unter dem Vorwand, etw zu tun.

pretend [prɪˈtend] 1 vt (a) (make believe) so tun, als ob; (feign also) vortäuschen, vorgeben. to ~ to be interested so tun, als ob man interessiert wäre; to ~ to be sick/have a cold eine Krankheit/Erkältung vortäuschen or vorschützen; to ~ to be asleep sich schlafend stellen; he ~ed sympathy/ignorance of the rules er täuschte Mitgefühl/Unkenntnis der Regeln vor, er gab vor, Mitgefühl zu haben/die Regeln nicht zu kennen.
(b) (claim) I don't ~ to ... ich behaupte nicht, daß ich ...
2 vi (a) so tun, als ob; (keep up facade) sich verstellen. he is only ~ing er tut nur so (als ob); let's stop ~ing hören wir auf, uns (dat) etwas vorzumachen.
(b) (lay claim) to ~ to sth auf etw (acc) Anspruch erheben.
3 adj (inf: child language) jewellery, money, gun etc Spiel-. it's just ~ (story etc) das ist nur Spaß (inf).

pretender [prɪˈtendəʳ] n (to throne) Prätendent m (to auf +acc).

pretense n (US) see pretence.

pretension [prɪˈtenʃən] n (a) (claim) Anspruch m; (social, cultural) Ambition f. he makes no ~(s) to originality er beansprucht keineswegs, originell zu sein. (b) (ostentation) Prahlerei, Protzerei (pej inf) f; (affectation) Anmaßung f.

pretentious [prɪˈtenʃəs] adj (pretending to be important) anmaßend; speech, style, book hochtrabend, hochgestochen; (ostentatious) angeberisch, protzig (inf), großkotzig (inf); house, restaurant, décor pompös, bombastisch.

pretentiously [prɪˈtenʃəslɪ] adv see adj.

pretentiousness [prɪˈtenʃəsnɪs] n see adj Anmaßung f; Hochgestochenheit f; Angeberei, Protzigkeit (inf), Großkotzigkeit (inf) f; Pomp, Bombast m.

preter- [ˈpriːtəʳ-] pref über-.

preterite [ˈpretərɪt] 1 adj verb im Imperfekt; (in English) im Präteritum; form Imperfekt-; Präteritums-. the ~ tense das Präteritum, das Imperfekt. 2 n Imperfekt nt; Präteritum nt. in the ~ im Imperfekt/Präteritum.

preternatural [ˌpriːtəˈnætʃrəl] adj (a) (supernatural) übernatürlich. (b) (abnormal, exceptional) außergewöhnlich.

pretext [ˈpriːtekst] n Vorwand m. on or under the ~ of doing sth unter dem Vorwand, etw zu tun.

prettify [ˈprɪtɪfaɪ] vt verschönern.

prettily [ˈprɪtɪlɪ] adv nett; behave, thank, compliment also artig, lieb; dress also hübsch.

prettiness [ˈprɪtɪnɪs] n (pretty appearance) hübsches Aussehen; (of manners, compliment etc) Artigkeit f. the ~ of her hair/face ihr hübsches Haar/Gesicht.

pretty [ˈprɪtɪ] 1 adj (+er) girl, child, hübsch, nett; manners, compliment, speech artig. to make oneself ~ sich hübsch machen; I'm/she's not just a ~ face! (inf) ich bin gar nicht so dumm (wie ich aussehe) (inf)/sie hat auch Köpfchen; ~ Polly! (to parrot) Lora, Lora!; it wasn't ~/a ~ sight das war alles andere als schön/das war kein schöner Anblick; ~-pretty (inf) niedlich.
(b) (inf) hübsch, schön (inf); price, sum also stolz. it'll cost a ~ penny das wird eine schöne Stange Geld kosten (inf); a ~ state of affairs/kettle of fish eine schöne Geschichte/ein schöner Schlamassel; a ~ mess we're in! da sitzen wir ganz schön in der Tinte!; say ~ please sag mal schön bitte.
2 adv (rather) ziemlich; good also ganz; (very also) ganz schön (inf), ganz hübsch (inf). ~ nearly or well finished so gut wie or so ziemlich fertig (inf); how's your job/the patient? — much the same was macht die Arbeit/der Patient? — so ziemlich wie immer/immer noch so ziemlich gleich.
3 n my ~ mein Sternchen.
4 vt (inf) to ~ up schönmachen, verschönern; sb, oneself also hübsch machen.

pretzel [ˈpretsl] n Brezel f.

prevail [prɪˈveɪl] vi (a) (gain mastery) siegen (over, against über +acc), sich durchsetzen (over, against gegenüber). (b) (conditions, wind etc) vorherrschen; (be widespread: customs) weit verbreitet sein. (c) (persuade) to ~ (up)on sb to do sth jdn dazu bewegen or bringen, etw zu tun.

prevailing [prɪˈveɪlɪŋ] adj (a) (current) fashion, conditions derzeitig, derzeit herrschend, aktuell; opinion aktuell; (vor)herrschend. the ~ fashion is long skirts zur Zeit sind lange Röcke in Mode. (b) wind vorherrschend.

prevalence [ˈprevələns] n (widespread occurrence) Vorherrschen nt, weite Verbreitung; (of crime, disease) Häufigkeit f; (of fashion, style) Beliebtheit f.

prevalent [ˈprevələnt] adj (widespread) vorherrschend, weit verbreitet; opinion, attitude geläufig, weit verbreitet; custom, disease häufig anzutreffen pred, häufig anzutreffend attr, weit verbreitet; conditions, situation herrschend; fashions, style beliebt. that sort of thing is very ~ these days das ist heutzutage sehr geläufig or häufig anzutreffen.

prevaricate [prɪˈværɪkeɪt] vi Ausflüchte machen.

prevarication [prɪˌværɪˈkeɪʃən] n Ausflucht f; (prevaricating) Ausflüchte, Ausweichmanöver pl.

prevaricator [prɪˈværɪkeɪtəʳ] n Ausweichtaktiker(in f) m.

prevent [prɪˈvent] vt sth verhindern, verhüten; (through preventive measures) vorbeugen (+dat). to ~ sb (from) doing sth jdn daran hindern or davon abhalten, etw zu tun; the gate is there to ~ them from falling down the stairs das Gitter ist dazu da, daß sie nicht die Treppe hinunterfallen; to ~ sb from coming jdn am Kommen hindern; there is nothing to ~ me nichts kann mich daran hindern or davon abhalten; nothing could have ~ed him (from) falling nichts hätte seinen Sturz verhindern or verhüten können; to ~ sth (from) happening verhindern, daß etw geschieht.

preventable [prɪˈventəbl] adj vermeidbar, verhütbar.

prevention [prɪˈvenʃən] n Verhinderung, Verhütung f; (through preventive measures) Vorbeugung f (of gegen). ~ is better than cure vorbeugen ist besser als heilen; ~ is better for the ~ of cruelty to animals/children Tierschutzverein than crime vorbeugen Sie dem Verbrechen keine Chance; society m/Kinderschutzbund m; fire ~ Feuerschutz m.

preventive [prɪˈventɪv] 1 adj (a) Vorbeugungs-, Präventiv-. to be ~ zur Vorbeugung dienen; ~ medicine vorbeugende Medizin, Präventivmedizin f; ~ detention (Brit Jur) Vorbeugehaft f; (of habitual criminal) Sicherungsverwahrung f; ~ war Präventivkrieg m.
2 n (~ measure) Präventivmaßnahme f; (Med) vorbeugendes Mittel, Präventiv nt. as a ~ als Vorbeugung.

preview [ˈpriːvjuː] 1 n (a) (of play, film) Probeaufführung f; (of exhibition) Vorbesichtigung f. to give sb a ~ of sth (fig) jdm eine Vorschau auf etw (acc) geben.
(b) (Film: trailer, TV) Vorschau f (of auf +acc).
2 vt (view beforehand) vorher ansehen; (show beforehand) film vorher aufführen; paintings, fashions vorher zeigen.

previous [ˈpriːvɪəs] adj (a) (immediately preceding) vorherig; page, day vorhergehend; year vorangegangen; (with indef art) früher. the ~ page/day/year die Seite/der Tag/das Jahr davor; the/a ~ holder of the title der vorherige/ein früherer Titelträger; in ~ years in früheren Jahren, früher; have you made any ~ applications? haben Sie sich davor or früher schon einmal beworben?; on a ~ occasion zuvor, bei einer früheren Gelegenheit; I have a ~ engagement ich habe schon einen Termin; ~ experience necessary Vorkenntnisse (sind) nicht erforderlich; ~ conviction (Jur) Vorstrafe f; to have a ~ conviction vorbestraft sein; ~ owner Vorbesitzer(in f) m.
(b) (hasty) voreilig. you were rather ~ in assuming that I would agree es war ziemlich voreilig von Ihnen anzunehmen, daß ich zustimmen würde.
(c) ~ to vor (+dat); ~ to doing sth bevor man etw tut/tat.

previously [ˈpriːvɪəslɪ] adv vorher, früher. he'd arrived three hours ~ er war drei Stunden zuvor angekommen.

pre-war [ˈpriːˈwɔːʳ] adj Vorkriegs-.

prey [preɪ] 1 n (lit, fig) Beute f; (animal also) Beutetier nt. beast/bird of ~ Raubtier nt/Raubvogel m; to be/fall ~ to sb/sth (lit) eine Beute von jdm/etw werden; (fig) ein Opfer von jdm/etw werden; she was a ~ to anxiety/depression/suspicion sie verfiel in Angst/Depressionen/Argwohn.
2 vi to ~ (up)on (animals) Beute machen auf (+acc); (pirates, thieves) (aus)plündern; (swindler etc) als Opfer aussuchen; (doubts) nagen an (+dat); (anxiety) quälen. it ~ed (up)on his mind es ließ ihn nicht los, der Gedanke daran quälte ihn.

price [praɪs] 1 n (a) Preis m. the ~ of coffee/cars die Kaffee-/Autopreise pl; ~s and incomes policy Lohn-Preis-Politik f; to go up or rise/to go down or fall in ~ teurer/billiger werden, im Preis steigen/fallen; what is the ~ of that? was kostet das?; at a ~ of ... zum Preis(e) von ...; at a ~ zum entsprechenden Preis, wenn man genug dafür hinlegt (inf); at a reduced ~ verbilligt, zu herabgesetztem or reduziertem Preis (form); if the ~ is right wenn der Preis stimmt; ask him for a ~ for the job frag ihn (mal), was das kostet.
(b) (fig) Preis m. everybody has his ~ jeder hat seinen Preis; the ~ of victory/freedom/fame der Preis für den Sieg/die Freiheit/den Ruhm; but at what a ~! aber zu welchem Preis!; at any/not at any ~ um jeden/keinen Preis; at the ~ of losing his health and his family auf Kosten seiner Gesundheit und seiner Familie; it's too big a ~ to pay das ist ein zu hoher Preis; but what ~ honour? wie kann man Ehre bezahlen?
(c) (value, valuation) a diamond of great ~ ein sehr wertvoller Diamant; to put a ~ on sth einen Preis für etw nennen; but what ~ do you put on freedom? aber wie ließe sich die Freiheit mit Gold aufwiegen?; to be beyond/without ~ nicht mit Geld zu bezahlen or mit Gold aufzuwiegen sein.

(d) (*reward*) Preis m. to put a ~ on sb's head eine Belohnung auf jds Kopf (*acc*) aussetzen; to have a ~ on one's head steckbrieflich gesucht werden.

(e) (*Betting: odds*) Quote f. what ~ are they giving on that horse? wie stehen die Wetten für das Pferd?; the horse had a starting ~ of 3 to 1 das Pferd wurde vor dem Start mit 3:1 gewettet; what ~ our being able to ...? (*inf*) wetten, daß wir ... können?; what ~ freedom/workers' solidarity now? (*inf*) wie steht es jetzt mit der Freiheit/der Solidarität der Arbeiter?

2 *vt* (*fix — of*) den Preis festsetzen von; (*put — label on*) auszeichnen (*at mit*); (*ask — of*) nach dem Preis fragen von; (*fig: estimate value of*) schätzen. it was ~d at £5 (*marked £5*) es war mit £ 5 ausgezeichnet; (*cost £5*) es kostete £ 5; reasonably ~d angemessen im Preis; ~d too high/low zu teuer/billig; to ~ one's goods/oneself/sb out of the market seine Waren/sich selbst durch zu hohe Preise konkurrenzunfähig machen/jdn durch niedrigere Preise vom Markt verdrängen.

price: ~ bracket n see ~ range; ~ control n Preiskontrolle f; ~ cut n Preissenkung f; ~ cutting n Preissenkungen pl; ~ fixing n Preisfestlegung f; ~ freeze n Preisstopp m; ~ index n Preisindex m.

priceless ['praɪslɪs] *adj* unschätzbar, von unschätzbarem Wert; (*inf: amusing*) joke, film köstlich; person unbezahlbar.

price: ~ limit n Preisgrenze f; ~ list n Preisliste f; ~ range n Preisklasse f; ~ ring n Preiskartell nt; ~ rise n Preiserhöhung f; ~ support n (US) Subvention, Preisstützung f; ~ tag, ~ ticket n Preisschild nt; ~ war n Preiskrieg m.

pricey ['praɪsɪ] *adj* (*Brit inf*) kostspielig. that's a bit ~! das ist ein bißchen happig (*inf*).

prick [prɪk] **1** n **(a)** (*puncture, pricking sensation*) Stich m. to give sb/oneself a ~ jdn/sich stechen; ~s of conscience Gewissensbisse pl; see kick against.

(b) (*vulg: penis*) Schwanz m (*vulg*).

(c) (*vulg: person*) Arsch(loch nt) m (*vulg*).

2 *vt* **(a)** (*puncture*) oneself, sb stechen; balloon durchstechen; blister aufstechen; outline (durch Löcher) markieren. to ~ one's finger (with/on sth) sich (*dat*) (mit etw) in den Finger stechen/sich (*dat*) (an etw *dat*) den Finger stechen; like a ~ed balloon wie ein Ballon, aus dem die Luft heraus ist; his conscience ~ed him er bekam or hatte Gewissensbisse; it/she ~ed his conscience es/sie bereitete ihm Gewissensbisse.

(b) see ~ up 2.

3 *vi* **(a)** (*thorn, injection etc*) stechen; (*eyes*) brennen. the smoke makes my eyes ~ der Rauch brennt mir in den Augen.

(b) see ~ up 1.

♦ **prick out** *vt sep* **(a)** (*seedlings*) pflanzen, setzen, pikieren (*spec*). **(b)** (*mark*) pattern, shape, design punktieren; (*with marking wheel*) ausradeln.

♦ **prick up 1** *vi* her/its ears ~ed ~ sie/es spitzte die Ohren. **2** *vt sep* to ~ ~ its/one's ears (*lit, fig*) die Ohren spitzen.

pricking ['prɪkɪŋ] n (*sensation*) Stechen nt. ~s of conscience Gewissensbisse pl.

prickle ['prɪkl] **1** n **(a)** (*sharp point*) Stachel m; (*on plants also*) Dorn m. **(b)** (*sensation*) Stechen nt; (*caused by wool, beard etc*) Kratzen nt; (*tingle, fig*) Prickeln nt. **2** *vi* stechen; (*wool, beard*) kratzen; (*tingle, fig*) prickeln.

prickly ['prɪklɪ] *adj* (+ *er*) **(a)** plant, fish, animal stach(e)lig; beard, material kratzig; sensation stechend; (*tingling*) prickeln (*also fig*). **(b)** (*fig*) person bissig; girl also kratzbürstig (*inf*). as ~ as a hedgehog stachelig wie ein Igel.

prickly: ~ heat n Hitzepocken pl; ~ pear n (*plant*) Feigenkaktus m; (*fruit*) Kaktusfeige f.

pride [praɪd] **1** n **(a)** (*arrogance*) Hochmut m. to have too much ~ to do sth zu stolz sein, um etw zu tun; to take (a) ~ in sth/in one's appearance auf etw (*acc*) stolz sein/Wert auf sein Äußeres legen; to be a (great) source of ~ to sb jdn mit (großem) Stolz erfüllen; her ~ and joy ihr ganzer Stolz; the ~ of the army/our young men der Stolz der Armee/die Blüte unserer jungen Männer (*geh*); to have or take ~ of place den Ehrenplatz einnehmen; ~ comes before a fall (*Prov*) Hochmut kommt vor dem Fall (*Prov*).

(b) (*of lions*) Rudel nt.

2 *vr* to ~ oneself on sth sich einer Sache (*gen*) rühmen können; I ~ myself on being something of an expert in this field ich darf wohl behaupten, mich auf diesem Gebiet auszukennen; he ~s himself on the preciseness of his prose er legt großen Wert auf präzise Formulierung.

prie-dieu ['priːdjɜː] n Betpult nt.

priest [priːst] n Priester, Geistliche(r) m.

priestess ['priːstɪs] n Priesterin f.

priest: ~ hole n verborgener Winkel (*in dem verfolgte Priester versteckt wurden*); ~hood n Priestertum nt; (*priests collectively*) Priesterschaft f; to enter the ~hood Priester werden.

priestly ['priːstlɪ] *adj* priesterlich; robes, office also Priester-.

priest-ridden ['priːst,rɪdn] *adj* klerikalistisch.

prig [prɪg] n (*goody-goody*) Tugendbold m (*inf*); (*boy also*) Musterknabe m; (*snob*) Schnösel m (*inf*). don't be such a ~ tu doch nicht so.

priggish ['prɪgɪʃ] *adj* tugendhaft; (*snobbish*) hochnäsig.

priggishness ['prɪgɪʃnɪs] n see adj tugendhaftes Getue, Tugendhaftigkeit f; Hochnäsigkeit f.

prim [prɪm] *adj* (+ *er*) (*also* ~ and proper) etepetete *inv* (*inf*); (*demure*) person, dress sittsam, züchtig; (*prudish*) prüde.

prima ballerina ['priːmə,bælə'riːnə] n Primaballerina f.

primacy ['praɪməsɪ] n **(a)** (*supremacy*) Vorrang m; (*position*) Vorrangstellung f. **(b)** (*Eccl*) Primat nt or m.

prima donna ['priːmə'dɒnə] n (*lit, fig*) Primadonna f.

primaeval *adj* see primeval.

prima facie ['praɪmə'feɪʃɪ] **1** *adv* allem Anschein nach. **2** *adj* there are ~ reasons why ... es gibt klar erkennbare Gründe, warum ...; ~ evidence glaubhafter Beweis; the police have a ~

case die Polizei hat genügend Beweise.

primal ['praɪməl] *adj* ursprünglich, Ur-.

primarily ['praɪmərɪlɪ] *adv* hauptsächlich, in erster Linie.

primary ['praɪmərɪ] **1** *adj* (*chief, main*) Haupt-, wesentlich, primär (*form*). that is our ~ concern das ist unser Hauptanliegen or unsere Hauptsorge; of ~ importance von größter Bedeutung, von äußerster Wichtigkeit; the ~ meaning of a word die Grundbedeutung eines Wortes.

2 n **(a)** (*colour*) Grundfarbe f.

(b) (*US: election*) (innerparteiliche) Vorwahl.

primary: ~ accent n Hauptakzent m; ~ cell n Primärzelle f; ~ colour n Grundfarbe f; ~ education n Grundschul(aus)bildung f; ~ election n (US) (innerparteiliche) Vorwahl; ~ feather n Handschwinge f; ~ industry n Grund(stoff)industrie f; (*agriculture etc*) Urindustrie f, primäre Industrie (*form*); (*main industry*) Hauptindustrie f; ~ institution n Ureinrichtung f; ~ product n Primärprodukt nt; (*main product*) Hauptprodukt nt; ~ rocks npl Primärgestein nt; ~ school n Grundschule f; ~ stress n Haupton m; ~ teacher n Grundschullehrer(in f) m; ~ winding n Primärwindung f.

primate ['praɪmɪt] n **(a)** (*Zool*) Primat m. **(b)** (*Eccl*) Primas m. P~ of England/all England Erzbischof von York/Canterbury.

prime [praɪm] **1** *adj* **(a)** (*major, chief*) Haupt-, wesentlich. of ~ importance von größter Bedeutung, von äußerster Wichtigkeit; my ~ concern mein Hauptanliegen nt; she was a ~ favourite sie war ein hoher Favorit.

(b) (*excellent*) erstklassig, beste(r, s); example erstklassig. in ~ condition (*meat, fruit etc*) von hervorragender Qualität; (*athlete, car etc*) in erstklassiger or hervorragender Verfassung; ~ cut Stück nt bester Qualität.

(c) (*Math*) number, factor Prim-.

2 n **(a)** (*full vigour*) in the ~ of life/youth in der Blüte seiner Jahre/der Jugend; he is in/past his ~ er ist im besten Alter or in den besten Jahren/er ist über sein bestes Alter or seine besten Jahre hinaus; (*singer, artist*) er ist an seinem Höhepunkt angelangt/er hat seine beste Zeit hinter sich; this chop/chair is past its ~ dieses Kotelett ist auch nicht mehr das jüngste/der Stuhl hat auch schon bessere Zeiten gesehen.

(b) (*Math*) Primzahl f.

(c) (*Eccl: also* P~) Prim f.

3 *vt* **(a)** gun schußfertig machen; bomb scharf machen; pump vorpumpen; carburettor Anlaßkraftstoff einspritzen.

(b) surface for painting grundieren.

(c) (*with advice, information*) instruieren. to be well ~d for the interview/game für das Interview/Spiel gut gerüstet sein.

(d) person (*with drink*) alkoholisieren, unter Alkohol setzen. well ~d (*with drink*) gut gestärkt (*inf*).

prime: ~ costs npl (*Comm*) Selbstkosten, Gestehungskosten pl; ~ meridian n Nullmeridian m; ~ minister n Minister-präsident(in f), Premierminister(in f) m; ~ mover n (*Phys, Tech*) Zugmaschine f; (*Philos*) bewegende Kraft, Triebfeder f; (*fig: person*) treibende Kraft; ~ number n Primzahl f.

primer ['praɪmə'] n **(a)** (*paint*) Grundierfarbe, Grundierung f; (*coat*) Grundierung f, Grundieranstrich m. **(b)** (*book*) Fibel f. **(c)** (*explosive*) Zündhütchen nt, Treibladungszünder m.

prime: ~ ribs npl Hochrippen pl; ~ time n (US) Haupteinschaltzeit f.

primeval [praɪ'miːvəl] *adj* urzeitlich; forest Ur-. ~ soup or slime Urschleim m.

primitive ['primitiv] **1** *adj* primitiv; (*Art*) naiv. **2** n (*Art*) (*artist*) Naive(r) mf; (*work*) naives Werk.

primitivism ['primitivizəm] n (*Art*) naive Kunst.

primly ['primlɪ] *adv* (*demurely*) sittsam, züchtig; überkorrekt; (*prudishly*) prüde. sitting ~ sipping tea steif und vornehm an ihrem etc Tee nippend.

primness ['primnɪs] n etepetete Art f (*inf*); (*demureness*) Sittsamkeit, Züchtigkeit f; (*prudishness*) Prüderie f.

primogenitor [,praɪməʊ'dʒenɪtə'] n (*ancestor*) Ahn(e), Vorfahr m; (*first ancestor*) Urahn(e), Stammvater m.

primogeniture [,praɪməʊ'dʒenɪtʃə'] n Erstgeburt f. right of ~ Erstgeburtsrecht nt.

primordial [praɪ'mɔːdɪəl] *adj* primordial (*spec*), ursprünglich; matter Ur-.

primp [primp] **1** *vt* zurechtmachen; hair richten. to ~ oneself (up) sich feinmachen or schniegeln. **2** *vi* sich zurechtmachen.

primrose ['primrəʊz] **1** n (*Bot*) Erd-Schlüsselblume f; (*colour*) Blaßgelb n. **2** *adj* blaßgelb. the ~ path (*fig*) der Rosenpfad.

primula ['primjələ] n Primel f.

primus (stove) ® ['praɪməs(,stəʊv)] n Primuskocher m.

prince [prins] n (*king's son*) Prinz m; (*ruler*) Fürst m. P~ Charming (*in fairy story*) der Königsohn; (*fig*) Märchenprinz m; ~ consort/regent Prinzgemahl m/-regent m; the P~ of Darkness/Peace der Fürst der Finsternis/der Friedensfürst; a ~ among men eine herausragende Erscheinung.

princedom ['prinsdəm] n (*old*) Fürstentum nt.

princeling ['prinslɪŋ] n (*old, liter*) Prinzchen nt.

princely ['prinslɪ] *adj* (*lit, fig*) fürstlich.

princess [prin'ses] n Prinzessin f; (*wife of ruler*) Fürstin f. ~ line (*fashion*) Prinzeßform f.

principal ['prinsipəl] **1** *adj* Haupt-, hauptsächlich. the ~ cities of China die wichtigsten Städte Chinas; my ~ concern mein Hauptanliegen nt; ~ teacher m Rektor m; ~ horn in the Philharmonic Orchestra erster Hornist/erste Hornistin der Philharmoniker; ~ boy (*Theat*) jugendliche Hauptrolle in britischen Weihnachtsrevuen, die traditionsgemäß von einem Mädchen gespielt wird; ~ clause (*Gram*) Hauptsatz m; ~ parts (*Gram: of verb*) Stammformen pl.

2 n **(a)** (*of school, college*) Rektor m; (*in play*) Hauptperson f; (*in duel*) Duellant m.

(b) (*Fin*) (*of investment*) Kapital(summe f) nt; (*of debt*) Kreditsumme f.

  (c) *(esp Jur: client)* Klient(in *f*), Mandant(in *f*) *m*.

principality [ˌprɪnsɪˈpælɪtɪ] *n* Fürstentum *nt*.

principally [ˈprɪnsɪpəlɪ] *adv* vornehmlich, in erster Linie.

principle [ˈprɪnsɪpl] *n* **(a)** Prinzip *nt*. to go back to first ~s zu den Grundlagen zurückgehen.

  (b) *(moral precept)* Prinzip *nt*, Grundsatz *m*; *(no pl: integrity)* Prinzipien, Grundsätze *pl*. in/on ~ im/aus Prinzip, prinzipiell; a man of ~(s) ein Mensch mit *or* von Prinzipien *or* Grundsätzen; it's against my ~s es geht gegen meine Prinzipien; it's a matter of ~, it's the ~ of the thing es geht dabei ums Prinzip; I'm doing it for reasons of ~ ich tue das aus Prinzip *or* um des Prinzips willen.

  (c) *(basic element)* Element *nt*. the bitter ~ of quinine das bittere Element *or* das Bittere bei Chinin.

principled [ˈprɪnsɪpld] *adj* man, statesman mit Prinzipien *or* Grundsätzen, prinzipientreu. high-~ mit hohen Prinzipien *or* Grundsätzen; low-~ ohne Prinzipien *or* Grundsätze.

prink [prɪŋk] *vti see* primp.

print [prɪnt] **1** *n* **(a)** *(typeface, characters)* Schrift *f*; *(~ed matter)* Gedruckte(s) *nt*. out of/in ~ vergriffen/gedruckt; to be in ~ again wieder erhältlich sein; to see sth in cold ~ etw schwarz auf weiß sehen; he'll never get into ~ er wird nie etwas veröffentlichen; don't let that get into ~ das darf nicht erscheinen; in big ~ groß gedruckt; *see* small ~.

  (b) *(picture)* Druck *m*.

  (c) *(Phot)* Abzug *m*, Kopie *f*.

  (d) *(fabric)* bedruckter Stoff; *(cotton ~)* Kattun *m*; *(dress)* bedrucktes Kleid; *(of cotton)* Kattunkleid *nt*.

  (e) *(impression: of foot, hand etc)* Abdruck *m*. to take sb's ~s *(police)* von jdm Fingerabdrücke machen *or* nehmen.

  2 *vt* **(a)** book, design drucken; fabric bedrucken. it is ~ed on his memory das hat sich in sein Gedächtnis eingegraben.

  (b) *(publish)* story veröffentlichen.

  (c) *(write in block letters)* in Druckschrift schreiben. to ~ sth in large letters etw in Großbuchstaben schreiben.

  (d) *(Phot)* abziehen.

  (e) hoof marks ~ed in the sand Hufabdrücke *or* Hufspuren *pl* im Sand.

  3 *vi* **(a)** *(printer, printing machine)* drucken. ready to ~ *(book)* druckfertig; *(machine)* druckbereit; the book is ~ing now das Buch ist gerade im Druck; the photos didn't ~ well die Bilder kamen nicht gut heraus.

  (b) *(write in block letters)* in Druckschrift schreiben.

♦**print off** *vt sep (Typ)* drucken; *(Phot)* abziehen.

♦**print out** *vt sep (Computers)* ausdrucken. ~ ~ the results, please würden Sie bitte die Ergebnisse ausdrucken lassen.

printable [ˈprɪntəbl] *adj* druckfähig; photograph abzugsfähig, reproduzierbar.

printed [ˈprɪntɪd] *adj* Druck-, gedruckt; *(written in capitals)* in Großbuchstaben; fabric bedruckt. ~ matter/papers Drucksache *f*; the ~ word das gedruckte Wort; ~ circuit gedruckte Schaltung.

printer [ˈprɪntə^r] *n* Drucker *m*. the text has gone to the ~ der Text ist in Druck gegangen; ~'s devil Setzerjunge *m*; ~'s error Druckfehler *m*; ~'s ink Druckerschwärze *f*.

printery [ˈprɪntərɪ] *n* Druckerei *f*.

printing [ˈprɪntɪŋ] *n* **(a)** *(process)* Drucken *nt*. **(b)** *(unjoined writing)* Druckschrift *f*; *(characters, print)* Schrift *f*. **(c)** *(quantity printed)* Auflage *f*.

printing: ~ frame *n* Kopierrahmen *m*; ~-ink *n* Druckerschwärze *f*; ~ press *n* Druckerpresse *f*; ~ works *n sing or pl* Druckerei *f*.

print: ~-maker *n (artist)* Graphiker *m*; *(manufacturer)* Druckhersteller *m*; ~-out *n (Computers)* Ausdruck *m*; ~ run *n* Auflage *f*; ~-seller *n* Graphikhändler(in *f*) *m*; ~-shop *n* Graphikhandlung *f*; *(in printing works)* Druckmaschinensaal *m*.

prior¹ [ˈpraɪə^r] *adj* **(a)** knowledge, warning, agreement vorherig; *(of earlier origin)* claim, engagement früher. **(b)** ~ to sth vor etw *(dat)*; ~ to doing sth bevor man etw tut/tat.

prior² *n (Eccl)* Prior *m*.

prioress [ˈpraɪərɪs] *n* Priorin *f*.

priority [praɪˈɒrɪtɪ] *n* Vorrang *m*, Priorität *f*; *(thing having precedence)* vordringliche Sache *or* Angelegenheit. a top ~ eine Sache *or* Angelegenheit *(von)* äußerster Dringlichkeit *or* höchster Priorität; what is your top ~? was steht bei Ihnen an erster Stelle?; it must be given top ~ das muß vorrangig behandelt werden; to have ~ Vorrang *or* Priorität haben; to give ~ to sth etw vorrangig behandeln, einer Sache *(dat)* den Vorrang geben *or* einräumen, einer Sache *(dat)* Priorität geben; in strict order of ~ ganz nach Dringlichkeit; we must get our priorities right wir müssen unsere Prioritäten richtig setzen; you've got your priorities all wrong du weißt ja nicht, was wirklich wichtig ist; you should get your priorities right du solltest deine Prioritäten finden; high/low on the list of priorities *or* the ~ list oben/unten auf der Prioritätenliste.

priory [ˈpraɪərɪ] *n* Priorat *nt*; *(in church names)* ~ Münster *nt*.

prise, *(US)* **prize** [praɪz] *vt* to ~ sth open etw aufbrechen; to ~ the lid up/off den Deckel auf-/herunterbringen *or* -kriegen *(inf)*; to ~ sth out *(of sth)* etw aus etw herausbekommen; to ~ a secret out of sb jdm ein Geheimnis entlocken; to ~ sb out of his post jdn von seinem Posten verdrängen.

prism [ˈprɪzəm] *n* Prisma *nt*.

prismatic [prɪzˈmætɪk] *adj* prismatisch; colour Spektral-; *(multi-coloured)* in den Farben des Spektrums.

prison [ˈprɪzn] *n* **1** *(lit, fig)* Gefängnis *nt*. to be in ~ im Gefängnis sein *or* sitzen; to go to ~ for 5 years für *or* auf 5 Jahre ins Gefängnis gehen *or* wandern *(inf)*; to send sb to ~ jdn ins Gefängnis schicken, jdn zu einer Freiheitsstrafe verurteilen. **2** *attr* Gefängnis-; system, facilities Strafvollzugs-. ~ camp Gefangenenlager *nt*; ~ life das Leben im Gefängnis.

prisoner [ˈprɪznə^r] *n* Gefangene(r) *mf (also Mil, fig)*; *(Jur)*

  (under arrest) Festgenommene(r) *mf*; *(facing charge, at the bar)* Angeklagte(r) *mf*; *(convicted also)* Häftling, Sträfling *m*. to hold *or* keep sb ~ jdn gefangenhalten; to take sb ~ jdn gefangennehmen; ~ of war Kriegsgefangene(r) *m*; ~ of war camp (Kriegs)gefangenenlager *nt*.

prissy [ˈprɪsɪ] *adj (pej)* zimperlich; dress, hairstyle brav.

pristine [ˈprɪstaɪn] *adj* **(a)** *in unspoilt state)* beauty unberührt, ursprünglich; condition tadellos, makellos; *(original)* urtümlich, ursprünglich.

prithee [ˈprɪðiː] *interj (obs)* bitte.

privacy [ˈprɪvəsɪ, ˈpraɪvəsɪ] *n* Privatleben *nt*. there is no ~ in these flats in diesen Mietwohnungen kann man kein Privatleben führen; in the ~ of one's home im eigenen Heim; in an open-plan office one has no ~ in einem Großraumbüro hat man keinen privaten Bereich; he told me this in the strictest ~ er sagte mir das unter dem Siegel der Verschwiegenheit; in the strictest ~ *(meeting, preparations)* unter äußerster Geheimhaltung.

private [ˈpraɪvɪt] **1** *adj* **(a)** privat, Privat-; *(personal also)* letter, reasons persönlich; *(confidential also)* matter, affair vertraulich; *(secluded)* place abgelegen; dining room separat; *(not public)* funeral, wedding im engsten Kreis; hearing, sitting nichtöffentlich *attr*. they were sharing a ~ joke sie fanden irgend etwas lustig; it's just a ~ joke between us das ist ein Privatwitz von uns; no ~ jokes! laß uns mitlachen!; ~ and confidential streng vertraulich; ~ property Privateigentum *nt*; he acted in a ~ capacity er handelte als Privatperson; they wanted to be ~ sie wollten allein *or* für sich sein; to keep sth ~ etw für sich behalten; his ~ life sein Privatleben *nt*; in his ~ thoughts in seinen ganz persönlichen Gedanken.

  (b) ~ car Privatwagen *m*; ~ citizen Privatmann *m*; ~ company Privatgesellschaft *f*; ~ detective Privatdetektiv *m*; ~ enterprise Privatunternehmen *nt*; *(free enterprise)* freies Unternehmertum; ~ eye *(inf)* Privatdetektiv, Schnüffler *(pej inf)* *m*; ~ individual Einzelne(r) *mf*; ~ law Privatrecht *nt*; ~ means Privatvermögen *nt*; ~ member Abgeordnete(r) *mf*; ~ member's bill Gesetzesinitiative *f* eines Abgeordneten; ~ parts *(genitals)* Geschlechtsteile *pl*; ~ *(medical)* practice *(Brit)* Privatpraxis *f*; he is in ~ practice er hat Privatpatienten; ~ pupil Privatschüler(in *f*) *m*; ~ secretary Privatsekretär(in *f*) *m*; ~ school Privatschule *f*; ~ sector Privatbereich *m*, privater Sektor; ~ soldier *(Mil)* gemeiner *or* einfacher Soldat; ~ tuition Privatunterricht *m*; ~ tutor Privatlehrer(in *f*) *m*; ~ view Vorabbesichtigung *f*; ~ ward Privatabteilung *or* -station *f*.

  2 *n* **(a)** *(Mil)* Gefreite(r) *mf*. P~ X der Gefreite X; *(in address)* Gefreiter X; ~ first class *(US)* Obergefreite(r) *mf*.

  (b) ~s *pl (genitals)* Geschlechtsteile *pl*.

  (c) in ~ privat; *(Jur)* unter Ausschluß der Öffentlichkeit; we must talk in ~ wir müssen das unter vier Augen besprechen.

privateer [ˌpraɪvəˈtɪə^r] *n (ship)* Freibeuter *m*, Kaperschiff *nt*; *(crew member)* Freibeuter, Kaperer *m*.

privately [ˈpraɪvɪtlɪ] *adv* **(a)** *(not publicly)* privat, vertraulich. the meeting was held ~ das Treffen wurde in kleinem Kreis *or* Rahmen abgehalten; a ~ owned company eine Gesellschaft in Privatbesitz; he is being ~ educated er wird privat erzogen; I bought it ~ ich habe es privat gekauft.

  (b) *(secretly, personally, unofficially)* persönlich. I have been told ~ that ... mir wurde vertraulich mitgeteilt, daß ...; so he spoke ~ to me deshalb sprach er mit mir unter vier Augen; ~ I think that ... ich persönlich glaube, daß ...; but ~ he was very upset doch innerlich war er sehr aufgebracht.

privation [praɪˈveɪʃən] *n* **(a)** *(state)* Armut, Not *f*. a life of ~ ein Leben in Armut *or* Not. **(b)** *(hardship)* Entbehrung, Einschränkung *f*. to suffer many ~s viele Entbehrungen erleiden; wartime ~s die Entbehrungen *pl* der Kriegszeit.

privet [ˈprɪvɪt] *n (gemeiner)* Liguster. ~ hedge Ligusterhecke *f*.

privilege [ˈprɪvɪlɪdʒ] **1** *n (prerogative)* Privileg, Sonderrecht *nt*; *(honour)* Ehre *f*; *(Parl)* Immunität *f*. it's a lady's ~ es ist das Vorrecht einer Dame; to abolish all ~ alle Privilegien *or* Sonderrechte abschaffen.

  2 *vt* privilegieren, bevorrechtigen. I was ~d to meet him ich hatte das Privileg *or* die Ehre, ihm vorgestellt zu werden.

privileged [ˈprɪvɪlɪdʒd] *adj* person, classes privilegiert; *(Parl)* speech *or* Immunität unterliegend *attr*; claim, debt bevorrechtigt. for a ~ few für wenige Privilegierte, für eine kleine Gruppe von Privilegierten; ~ communication *(Jur)* vertrauliche Mitteilung; ~ stock Vorzugsaktie *f*.

privily [ˈprɪvɪlɪ] *adv (old)* insgeheim, im geheimen.

privy [ˈprɪvɪ] **1** *adj* **(a)** to be ~ to sth in etw *(acc)* eingeweiht sein. **(b)** P~ geheim; P~ Council, P~ Councillor Geheimer Rat; P~ Purse Privatschatulle *f*. **2** *n* Abort, Abtritt *m*.

prize¹ [praɪz] *n* **1** *n* **(a)** Preis *m*; *(in lottery also)* Gewinn *m*. the glittering ~s of the pop world der Flimmerglanz der Popwelt; there are no ~s for guessing *(inf)* dreimal darfst du raten.

  (b) *(Naut: captured ship)* Prise *f (old)*.

  2 *adj* **(a)** *(awarded a ~)* entry, essay, sheep preisgekrönt. ~ idiot *(inf)* Erzidiot *m*.

  (b) *(awarded as a ~)* trophy Sieges-. ~ cup (Sieger)pokal *m*; ~ medal Medaille *f*.

  (c) *(offering a ~)* competition Preis-. ~ draw Lotterie, Tombola *f*.

  3 *vt* (hoch)schätzen. to ~ sth highly etw sehr *or* hoch schätzen; to ~ sth above sth etw über *or* vor etw *(acc)* stellen; ~d possession wertvollster Besitz, wertvolles Stück; *(of museum etc)* Glanzstück, Paradestück *nt*.

prize² *vt (US) see* prise.

prize: ~ day *n (Sch)* (Tag *m* der) Preisverleihung *f*; ~-fight *n* Profi- *or* Berufsboxkampf *m*; ~-fighter *n* Profi- *or* Berufsboxer *m*; ~-fighting *n* Profi- *or* Berufsboxkampf *m*; ~-giving *n (Sch)* Preisverleihung *or* -verteilung *f*; ~-list *n (in lottery, competition)* Gewinnerliste *f*; ~ money *n* **(a)** *(cash ~)* Geld- *or*

Barpreis *m*; (*Boxing*) (Sieges)prämie *f*; (*in competition*) Gewinn *m*; **(b)** (*old Naut*) Prisengeld *nt*; **~-ring** *n* (*Boxing*) Ring *m*; **~winner** *n* (Preis)gewinner(in *f*) *m*; **~winning** *adj* entry, novel preisgekrönt; ticket Gewinn-.

PRO *abbr of* **public relations officer.**

pro¹ [prəʊ] *n* (*inf*) Profi *m*.

pro² *n* (*inf: prostitute*) Nutte *f* (*inf*), Profi *m* (*inf*).

pro³ 1 *prep* (*in favour of*) für. **2** *n* the **~s** and the cons das Für und Wider, das Pro und Kontra.

pro- pref (a) (*in favour of*) pro-. **~-Soviet** prosowjetisch. **(b)** (*acting for*) Pro-.

probability [ˌprɒbəˈbɪlɪtɪ] *n* Wahrscheinlichkeit *f*. **in all ~** aller Wahrscheinlichkeit nach, höchstwahrscheinlich; **what's the ~** *or* **what are the probabilities of that happening?** wie groß ist die Wahrscheinlichkeit, daß das geschieht?; **the ~ is that he will leave** wahrscheinlich wird er weggehen.

probable [ˈprɒbəbl] *adj* wahrscheinlich.

probably [ˈprɒbəblɪ] *adv see adj.* very **~**, but ... durchaus möglich, aber ...; **more ~ than not** höchstwahrscheinlich.

probate [ˈprəʊbɪt] *n* (*examination*) gerichtliche Testamentsbestätigung *f*; (*will*) beglaubigte Testamentsabschrift. **~ court** Nachlaßgericht *nt*; **to grant sb ~** jdm aufgrund der Testamentseröffnung einen Erbschein ausstellen.

probation [prəʊˈbeɪʃən] *n* **(a)** (*Jur*) Bewährung *f*. **to put sb on ~** (*for a year*) jdm (ein Jahr) Bewährung geben; **to be on ~** auf Bewährung sein, Bewährung haben; **~ officer** Bewährungshelfer(in *f*) *m*. **(b)** (*of employee*) Probe *f*; (**~ period**) Probezeit *f*; (*Rel*) Noviziat *nt*.

probationary [prəʊˈbeɪʃnərɪ] *adj* (*Jur*) Probe-. **~ period** Probezeit *f*; **his ~ 6 months** seine 6 Monate Probezeit. **(b)** (*Jur*) Bewährungs-.

probationer [prəʊˈbeɪʃnəʳ] *n* (*Jur*) auf Bewährung Freigelassene(r) *mf*; (*Med*) Lernschwester *f*; (*Rel*) Novize *m*, Novizin *f*.

probe [prəʊb] 1 *n* **(a)** (*device*) Sonde *f*. **(b)** (*investigation*) Untersuchung *f* (*into gen*). **a police ~ revealed ...** Nachforschungen der Polizei ergaben ... 2 *vt* untersuchen, sondieren; space, sb's past, subconscious, private life erforschen; mystery ergründen, erforschen. 3 *vi* suchen, forschen (*for* nach); (*Med*) untersuchen (*for auf* +*acc*); (*inquire*) forschen, bohren (*for* nach). **to ~ into a wound/sb's private life/sb's past** eine Wunde mit der Sonde untersuchen/in jds Privatleben (*dat*) herumschnüffeln/in jds Vergangenheit (*dat*) bohren.

probing [ˈprəʊbɪŋ] 1 *n* Untersuchung *f*; (*with device also*) Sondierung *f*, Sondieren *nt*. **all this ~ into people's private affairs** dieses Herumschnüffeln in den privaten Angelegenheiten der Leute. 2 *adj* question, study, fingers prüfend.

probity [ˈprəʊbɪtɪ] *n* (*form*) Redlichkeit, Integrität (*geh*) *f*.

problem [ˈprɒbləm] *n* Problem *nt*; (*Math: as school exercise*) Aufgabe *f*; (*problematic area*) Problematik *f*. **what's the ~?** wo fehlt's?; **he's got a drinking ~** er trinkt (zuviel); **I had no ~ in getting the money** ich habe das Geld ohne Schwierigkeiten bekommen; **no ~!** (*inf*) kein Problem!; **the whole ~ of modernization** die ganze Modernisierungsproblematik; **~ area** Problembereich *m*.

problematic(al) [ˌprɒbləˈmætɪk(əl)] *adj* problematisch.

problem: ~ child *n* Problemkind *nt*; **~ family** *n* Problemfamilie *f*; **~ page** *n* Problemseite *f*; **~ play** *n* Problemstück *nt*.

proboscis [prəʊˈbɒsɪs] *n* (*Zool, hum inf*) Rüssel *m*.

procedural [prəˈsiːdjʊrəl] *adj* verfahrenstechnisch; (*Jur*) verfahrensrechtlich.

procedure [prəˈsiːdʒəʳ] *n* Verfahren *nt*. **parliamentary/legal ~(s)** parlamentarisches/gerichtliches Verfahren; **what would be the correct ~ in such a case?** wie geht man in einem solchen Falle vor?, wie verfährt man in einem solchen Falle?; **business ~** geschäftliche Verfahrensweise; **rules of ~** Vorschriften *pl*; **questions of ~** verfahrenstechnische *or* (*Jur*) verfahrensrechtliche Fragen *pl*.

proceed [prəˈsiːd] 1 *vi* **(a)** (*form: go*) vehicles must **~** with caution vorsichtig fahren!; **I was ~ing along the High Street** ich ging die High Street entlang; **please ~ to gate 3** begeben Sie sich zum Flugsteig 3. **(b)** (*form: go on*) (*person*) weitergehen; (*vehicle, by vehicle*) weiterfahren. **we then ~ed to London** wir fuhren dann nach London weiter, wir begaben uns dann nach London (*geh*); **to ~ on one's way** seinen Weg fortsetzen. **(c)** (*carry on, continue*) fortfahren; (*as instruction in margin*) klar. **can we now ~ to the next item on the agenda?** können wir jetzt zum nächsten Punkt der Tagesordnung übergehen?; **they ~ed with their plan** sie führten ihren Plan weiter; (*start*) sie führten ihren Plan durch; **to ~ about one's business** (*form*) seinen Geschäften (*dat*) nachgehen (*geh*); **~ with your work** fahren Sie mit Ihrer Arbeit fort; **the text ~s as follows** der Text lautet dann wie folgt; **everything the plan is ~ing satisfactorily** alles läuft bestens/alles verläuft nach Plan; **negotiations are ~ing well** die Verhandlungen kommen gut voran; **you may ~ (speak)** Sie haben das Wort; **I would like to make a statement — ~** ich möchte eine Aussage machen — bitte! **(d)** (*set about sth*) vorgehen. **I wasn't sure how to ~** ich wußte nicht genau, wie ich vorgehen sollte; **how does one ~ in such cases?** wie verfährt man in solchen Fällen?, wie geht man in solchen Fällen vor?; **if you had ~ed according to the rules** wenn Sie vorschriftsmäßig vorgegangen wären; **to ~ on the assumption that ...** von der Voraussetzung ausgehen, daß ... **(e)** (*originate*) **to ~ from** kommen von; (*fig*) herrühren von; **all life ~s from the sea** alles Leben kommt aus dem Meer. **(f)** (*Jur*) **to ~ against sb** gegen jdn gerichtlich vorgehen; **to ~ with a case** einen Prozeß anstrengen. 2 *vt* now, he **~ed** nun, fuhr er fort; **to ~ to do sth** (dann) etw tun.

proceeding [prəˈsiːdɪŋ] *n* **(a)** (*action, course of action*) Vor-

gehen *nt*. **our best/safest way of ~** would be to ask him am besten/sichersten wäre es, wenn wir ihn fragten; **there were some odd ~s** merkwürdige Dinge gingen vor. **(b)** **~s** *pl* (*function*) Veranstaltung *f*. **(c)** **~s** *pl* (*esp Jur*) Verfahren *nt*; court **~s** Gerichtsverhandlung *f*; **to take/start ~s against sb** gegen jdn gerichtlich vorgehen; **to take legal/ divorce ~s** ein Gerichtsverfahren *or* einen Prozeß anstrengen/die Scheidung einreichen. **(d)** **~s** *pl* (*record*) (*written minutes etc*) Protokoll *nt*; (*published report*) Tätigkeitsbericht *m*.

proceeds [ˈprəʊsiːdz] *npl* (*yield*) Ertrag *m*; (*from sale, bazaar, raffle*) Erlös *m*; (*takings*) Einnahmen *pl*.

process¹ [ˈprəʊses] 1 *n* **(a)** Prozeß *m*. **the ~es of the law** der Gesetzesweg; **the ~ of time** will ... die Zeit wird ...; **in the ~ of time** im Laufe der Zeit, mit der Zeit; **in the ~ of doing sth/being made** dabei sein, etw zu tun/gerade gemacht werden. **(b)** (*specific method, technique*) Verfahren *nt*; (*Ind also*) Prozeß *m*. **~ engineering** Prozeß- *or* Verfahrenstechnik *f*. **(c)** (*Jur*) Prozeß *m*, Verfahren *nt*. **to serve a ~ on sb** jdn vorladen; **~-server** Zustellungsbeamte(r) *m*. **(d)** (*Biol*) vorstehender Teil. **a ~ of a bone/of the jaw** ein Knochen-/Kiefernvorsprung *m*. 2 *vt* (*treat*) raw materials, data, information, waste verarbeiten; food konservieren; milk sterilisieren; application, loan, wood bearbeiten; film entwickeln; (*deal with*) applicants, people abfertigen. **~ed cheese**, (*US*) **~ cheese** Schmelzkäse *m*.

process² [prəˈses] *vi* (*Brit: go in procession*) ziehen, schreiten.

processing [ˈprəʊsesɪŋ] *n see vt* Verarbeitung *f*; Konservieren *nt*; Sterilisierung *f*; Bearbeitung *f*; Entwicklung *f*; Abfertigung *f*.

procession [prəˈseʃən] *n* (*organized*) Umzug *m*; (*solemn*) Prozession *f*; (*line of people, cars etc*) Reihe, Schlange *f*. **funeral/carnival ~** Trauer-/Karnevalszug *m*; **to go or walk in ~** einen Umzug/eine Prozession machen.

processional [prəˈseʃənl] (*Eccl*) 1 *n* (*hymn*) Prozessionshymne *f*, Prozessionslied *nt*; (*book*) Prozessionsbuch *nt*. 2 *adj* Prozessions-; pace also gemessen.

proclaim [prəˈkleɪm] 1 *vt* **(a)** erklären. **to ~ sb king** jdn zum König erklären *or* ausrufen *or* proklamieren; **the day had been ~ed a holiday** der Tag war zum Feiertag erklärt worden. **(b)** (*reveal*) verraten, beweisen. 2 *vr* sich erklären. **to ~ oneself king** sich zum König erklären.

proclamation [ˌprɒkləˈmeɪʃən] *n* **(a)** (*act*) (*of war*) Erklärung *f*; (*of laws, measures*) Verkündung *f*; (*of state of emergency*) Ausrufung *f*. **after his ~ as Emperor** nach seiner Proklamation zum Kaiser. **(b)** (*that proclaimed*) Erklärung, Proklamation *f*.

proclivity [prəˈklɪvɪtɪ] *n* Schwäche, Vorliebe *f* (*for* für).

proconsul [ˌprəʊˈkɒnsəl] *n* Prokonsul *m*.

procrastinate [prəʊˈkræstɪneɪt] *vi* zögern, zaudern. **he always ~s** er schiebt die Dinge immer vor sich (*dat*) her.

procrastination [prəʊˌkræstɪˈneɪʃən] *n* Zögern, Zaudern *nt*. **won't solve your problems** durch Aufschieben lösen sich Ihre Probleme nicht.

procrastinator [prəʊˈkræstɪneɪtəʳ] *n* Zögerer, Zauderer *m*.

procreate [ˈprəʊkrɪeɪt] 1 *vi* zeugen, sich fortpflanzen. 2 *vt* zeugen, hervorbringen.

procreation [ˌprəʊkrɪˈeɪʃən] *n* Zeugung *f*, Fortpflanzung *f*.

Procrustean [prəʊˈkrʌstɪən] *adj* unnachgiebig, starr. **~ bed** Prokrustesbett *n*.

proctor [ˈprɒktəʳ] *n* (*Jur*) Prokurator *m*; (*Univ*) Proktor *m*; (*US: supervisor*) (Prüfungs)aufsicht *f*.

procurable [prəˈkjʊərəbl] *adj* erhältlich, zu beschaffen *pred*.

procurator [ˈprɒkjʊreɪtəʳ] *n* (*Hist*) Prokurator *m*; (*Jur: agent also*) Bevollmächtigte(r) *m*. **~ fiscal** (*Scot*) = Staatsanwalt *m*.

procure [prəˈkjʊəʳ] 1 *vt* **(a)** (*obtain*) beschaffen, sich (*dat*) veror beschaffen, besorgen; (*bring about*) bewirken, herbeiführen. **to ~ sth for sb/oneself** jdm/sich etw beschaffen *or* besorgen, etw für jdn/sich beschaffen *or* besorgen. **to ~ sb's release** jds Freilassung bewirken *or* erreichen. **(b)** (*for prostitution*) woman beschaffen (*for sb* jdm). 2 *vi* Kuppelei betreiben. **procuring** Kuppelei *f*.

procurement [prəˈkjʊəmənt] *n* Beschaffung *f*; (*of release*) Bewirkung *f*; (*of prostitutes*) Verkupplung *f*.

procurer [prəˈkjʊərəʳ] *n* (*pimp*) Zuhälter, Kuppler *m*.

procuress [prəˈkjʊərɪs] *n* Kupplerin *f*.

prod [prɒd] 1 *n* **(a)** Stoß, Knuff (*inf*) *m*. **to give sb a ~** jdm einen Stoß etc versetzen; **a ~ in the ribs** ein Rippenstoß *m*. **(b)** (*fig*) Ansporn, Anstoß, Schubs (*inf*) *m*. **to give sb a ~** jdm einen Stoß *or* Schubs (*inf*) geben. 2 *vt* **(a)** stoßen, knuffen (*inf*), puffen (*inf*). **he ~ded the donkey (on) with his stick** er trieb den Esel mit seinem Stock vorwärts; **he ~ded the hay with his stick** er stach mit seinem Stock ins Heu; **..., he said, ~ding the map with his finger ...,** sagte er und stieß mit dem Finger auf die Karte. **(b)** (*fig*) ansporn, anstacheln (*to do sth, into sth* zu etw). **to ~ sb into action** jdm einen Stoß geben. 3 *vi* stoßen. **he ~ded at the picture with his finger** er stieß mit dem Finger auf das Bild; **he ~ded at the cows with his stick** er trieb die Kühe mit seinem Stock an; **he doesn't need any ~ding** man braucht ihn nicht anzuspornen.

prodigal [ˈprɒdɪgəl] 1 *adj* verschwenderisch. **to be ~ with or of sth** verschwenderisch mit etw umgehen; **the ~ son** (*Bibl, fig*) der verlorene Sohn. 2 *n* Verschwender(in *f*) *m*.

prodigality [ˌprɒdɪˈgælɪtɪ] *n* (*liter*) Verschwendungssucht *f*; (*lavishness*) Fülle, Üppigkeit *f*.

prodigious [prəˈdɪdʒəs] *adj* (*vast*) ungeheuer, außerordentlich; (*marvellous*) erstaunlich, wunderbar.

prodigiously [prəˈdɪdʒəslɪ] *adv see adj.*

prodigy [ˈprɒdɪdʒɪ] *n* Wunder *nt*. **a ~ of nature** ein Naturwunder *nt*; **child or infant ~** Wunderkind *nt*.

produce ['prɒdjuːs] **1** n, no pl (Agr) Produkt(e pl), Erzeugnis nt. Italian ~, ~ of Italy italienisches Erzeugnis; **the low level of ~ this year** der geringe diesjährige Ertrag; **the ~ of the soil** die Bodenprodukte or -erzeugnisse pl.

2 [prə'djuːs] vt **(a)** (manufacture) produzieren; cars, steel, paper etc also herstellen; agricultural products also, electricity, energy, heat erzeugen; crop abwerfen; coal fördern; (create) book, article, essay schreiben; painting, sculpture anfertigen; ideas also, masterpiece hervorbringen; interest, return on capital bringen, abwerfen; meal machen, herstellen. **this is exactly the sort of environment that ~s criminal types** das ist genau das Milieu, das Kriminelle hervorbringt; **to ~ offspring** Junge bekommen; (hum: people) Nachwuchs bekommen; **to be well ~d** gut gemacht sein; (goods also) gut gearbeitet sein; (magazine also) gut in der Herstellung sein; **an artist who actually ~d very little** ein Künstler, der eigentlich sehr wenig hervorgebracht or zustande gebracht hat.

(b) (bring forward, show) gift, wallet etc hervorholen (from, out of aus); pistol ziehen (from, out of aus); proof, evidence liefern, beibringen; witness beibringen; ticket, documents vorzeigen. **she managed to ~ something special for dinner** es gelang ihr, zum Abendessen etwas Besonderes auf den Tisch zu bringen; **I can't ~ it out of thin air** ich kann es doch nicht aus dem Nichts hervorzaubern or aus dem Ärmel schütteln (inf); **where on earth does he ~ all these girlfriends from?** wo bekommt or kriegt (inf) er nur immer seine Freundinnen her?; **if we don't ~ results soon** wenn wir nicht bald Ergebnisse vorweisen können; **he ~d an incredible backhand** ihm gelang ein unglaublicher Rückhandschlag; **he ~d a sudden burst of energy** er hatte einen plötzlichen Energieausbruch.

(c) play inszenieren; film produzieren. **he ~d us in "The Dumb Waiter"** wir haben unter seiner Regie in „Der stumme Diener" gespielt; **who's producing you?** wer ist Ihr Regisseur?

(d) (cause) famine, bitterness, impression hervorrufen; interest, feeling of pleasure also, spark erzeugen. **this news ~d a sensation** diese Nachricht hat Sensation gemacht.

(e) (Math) line verlängern.

3 [prə'djuːs] vi **(a)** (Theat) das/ein Stück inszenieren; (Film) den/einen Film produzieren.

(b) (factory, mine) produzieren; (land) Ertrag bringen; (tree) tragen. **this cow hasn't ~d for years** diese Kuh hat jahrelang nicht mehr gekalbt; diese Kuh hat jahrelang keine Milch mehr gegeben; **when is she going to ~?** (hum) wann ist es denn so weit?; **it's about time that you ~d** (hum) es wird bald Zeit, daß ihr mal an Nachwuchs denkt.

producer [prə'djuːsə^r] n Hersteller, Produzent m; (Agr) Produzent, Erzeuger m; (Theat) Regisseur m; (Film, TV) Produzent m; (Rad) Spielleiter m. **~ goods** Produktionsgüter pl.

-producing [-prə'djuːsɪŋ] adj suf erzeugend, produzierend. **coal-~ countries** Kohleförderländer pl.

product ['prɒdʌkt] n Produkt, Erzeugnis nt; (fig: result, Math, Chem) Produkt nt. **food ~s** Nahrungsmittel pl.

production [prə'dʌkʃən] n **(a)** see vt **(a)** Produktion f; Herstellung f; Erzeugung f; Förderung f; Schreiben nt; Anfertigung f; Hervorbringung f. **to put sth into ~** die Herstellung or Produktion von etw aufnehmen; **when the new factory goes into ~** wenn die neue Fabrik ihre Produktion aufnimmt; **when the new car goes into ~** wenn der neue Wagen in die Produktion or Herstellung geht; **when we go into ~ (with this new model)** wenn wir (mit diesem neuen Modell) in die Produktion or Herstellung gehen; **is it still in ~?** wird das noch hergestellt?; **to take sth out of ~** etw aus der Produktion nehmen.

(b) (output) Produktion f.

(c) see vt **(b)** Hervorholen nt; Ziehen nt; Lieferung, Beibringung f; Vorweisen, Vorzeigen nt. **on ~ of this ticket** gegen Vorlage dieser Eintrittskarte.

(d) (of play) Inszenierung f; (of film) Produktion f. **there's no need to make a ~ out of it** (inf) es ist nicht notwendig, daraus eine Staatsaffäre zu machen (inf).

production: **~ capacity** n Produktionskapazität f; **~ costs** npl Produktions- or Herstellungskosten pl; **~ engineer** n Betriebsingenieur m; **~ line** n Fließband nt, Fertigungsstraße f; **~ manager** n Produktions- or Betriebsleiter m; **~ method** n Produktions- or Herstellungsmethode f; **~ model** n (car) Serienmodell nt.

productive [prə'dʌktɪv] adj produktiv; land ertragreich, fruchtbar; mind also schöpferisch, fruchtbar; well, mine ergiebig, ertragreich; business, shop rentabel. **to be ~ of sth** zu etw führen, etw einbringen; **I don't think it would be very ~ to argue with him** ich halte es nicht für sehr lohnend or lohnenswert or sich glaube, es bringt nichts, mit ihm zu streiten (inf).

productively [prə'dʌktɪvlɪ] adv produktiv.

productivity [‚prɒdʌk'tɪvɪtɪ] n see adj Produktivität f; Fruchtbarkeit f; schöpferische Kraft; Ergiebigkeit f; Rentabilität f.

productivity: **~ agreement** n Produktivitätsvereinbarung f; **~ bonus** n Leistungszulage f; **~ incentive** n Leistungsanreiz m.

proem ['prəʊem] n Einleitung f.

prof [prɒf] n (inf) Prof m (inf).

profanation [‚prɒfə'neɪʃən] n Entweihung, Profanierung f.

profane [prə'feɪn] **1** adj **(a)** (secular) weltlich, profan. **(b)** (irreverent, sacrilegious) (gottes)lästerlich. **don't be ~** lästere nicht; **to use ~ language** gotteslästerlich fluchen, lästern; **a ~ expression** eine Gotteslästerung. **2** vt entweihen, profanieren.

profanity [prə'fænɪtɪ] n see adj **(a)** Weltlichkeit, Profanität f. **(b)** Gotteslästerlichkeit f. **(c)** (act, utterance) (Gottes)lästerung f.

profess [prə'fes] **1** vt **(a)** faith, belief etc sich bekennen zu. **(b)** (claim to have) interest, enthusiasm, distaste bekunden; belief, disbelief kundtun; weakness, ignorance zugeben. **she ~es to be 25/a good driver** sie behauptet, 25/eine gute Fahrerin

zu sein; **I don't ~ to ...** ich behaupte nicht, ...

2 vr **to ~ oneself satisfied** seine Zufriedenheit bekunden (with über +acc); **the judge ~ed himself satisfied that this was so** der Richter fand den Sachverhalt als hinlänglich erwiesen; **to ~ oneself unable/willing to do sth** sich außerstande sehen/bereit erklären, etw zu tun.

professed [prə'fest] adj erklärt; (pej: purported) angeblich. **a ~ nun/monk** (Eccl) eine Nonne, die/ein Mönch, der die Gelübde abgelegt hat; **to be a ~ Christian** sich zum christlichen Glauben bekennen; **he is a ~ coward** er gibt zu, ein Feigling zu sein.

professedly [prə'fesɪdlɪ] adv zugegebenermaßen; (pej: purportedly) angeblich.

profession [prə'feʃən] n **(a)** (occupation) Beruf m. **the medical/teaching ~** der Arzt-/Lehrberuf; **the medical/architectural ~** (members of the ~) die Ärzteschaft/die Architekten pl; **the whole ~ was outraged** der gesamte Berufsstand war empört; **by ~** von Beruf; **the ~s** die gehobenen Berufe; **the oldest ~ in the world** das älteste Gewerbe der Welt.

(b) (declaration) (Eccl) Gelübde nt. **~ of faith** Glaubensbekenntnis nt; **a ~ of love** eine Liebeserklärung; **a ~ of contempt** eine Mißfallensäußerung; **a ~ of loyalty** ein Treuegelöbnis nt; **the ~ of Christianity** das Bekenntnis zum Christentum; **he is, by his own ~, ...** nach eigenem Bekunden ist er ...

professional [prə'feʃənl] **1** adj **~** Berufs-, beruflich; army, soldier, tennis player Berufs-; opinion fachmännisch, fachlich. **their ~ ability** ihre beruflichen Fähigkeiten; **his ~ life** sein Berufsleben; **our relationship is purely ~** unsere Beziehung ist rein geschäftlich(er Natur); **a ~ thief** ein professioneller Dieb; **we need your ~ help** here hier brauchen wir Ihre fachmännische Hilfe; **he's now doing it on a ~ basis** er macht das jetzt hauptberuflich; **in his ~ capacity as a doctor** in seiner Eigenschaft als Arzt; **to be a ~ singer/author etc** von Beruf Sänger/Schriftsteller etc sein; **"flat to let to quiet ~ gentleman"** „Wohnung zu vermieten an ruhigen gutsituierten Herrn"; **the pub is used mainly by ~ men** das Lokal wird hauptsächlich von Angehörigen der gehobenen Berufe besucht; **the ~ classes** die gehobenen Berufe, die höheren Berufsstände (dated); **to take ~ advice** fachmännischen Rat einholen; **it's not our ~ practice** es gehört nicht zu unseren geschäftlichen Gepflogenheiten; **to turn or go ~** Profi werden.

(b) (skilled, competent) piece of work etc fachmännisch, fachgemäß, fachgerecht; worker, person gewissenhaft; company, approach professionell. **he didn't make a very ~ job of that** er hat das nicht sehr fachmännisch erledigt; **he handled the matter in a very ~ manner** er hat die Angelegenheit in sehr kompetenter Weise gehandhabt; **that's not a very ~ attitude to your work** das ist doch nicht die richtige Einstellung (zu Ihrem Beruf); **it's not up to ~ standards** es entspricht nicht fachlichen Normen; **a typed letter looks more ~** ein maschinengeschriebener Brief sieht professioneller aus.

(c) (inf) worrier, moaner notorisch, gewohnheitsmäßig.

2 n Profi m.

professionalism [prə'feʃnəlɪzəm] n Professionalismus m; (of job, piece of work) Perfektion f; (Sport) Berufssportlertum, Profitum nt.

professionally [prə'feʃnəlɪ] adv beruflich; (in accomplished manner) fachmännisch. **he used to be an amateur but now he plays ~** früher war er Amateur, jetzt ist er Berufsspieler or Profi; **he is ~ recognized as the best ...** er ist in Fachkreisen als der beste ... bekannt; **X, ~ known as Y** (of artist, musician etc) X, unter dem Künstlernamen Y bekannt; (of writer) X, unter dem Pseudonym Y bekannt; **they acted most ~ in refusing to ...** daß sie ... ablehnten, zeugte von hohem Berufsethos; **have you ever considered playing football ~?** haben Sie je daran gedacht, Berufsfußballer or Fußballprofi zu werden?

professor [prə'fesə^r] n **(a)** Professor(in f) m; (US also) Dozent(in f) m. **the ~s** die Professorenschaft. **(b)** (of a faith) Bekenner(in f) m.

professorial [‚prɒfə'sɔːrɪəl] adj (of a professor) eines Professors; (professorlike) wie ein Professor, professoral (pej).

professorship [prə'fesəʃɪp] n Professur f, Lehrstuhl m. **to be appointed to a ~** eine Professur or einen Lehrstuhl bekommen.

proffer ['prɒfə^r] vt arm, gift, drink anbieten; apologies, thanks etc aussprechen; remark machen; suggestion vorbringen.

proficiency [prə'fɪʃənsɪ] n level or standard of ~ Leistungsstand m; her ~ at teaching/as a secretary ihre Tüchtigkeit als Lehrerin/Sekretärin; his ~ in English/translating/accountancy seine Englischkenntnisse/sein Können als Übersetzer/Buchhalter; his ~ with figures sein Können im Umgang mit Zahlen; **~ test** Leistungstest m.

proficient [prə'fɪʃənt] adj tüchtig, fähig. **he is just about ~ in German** seine Deutschkenntnisse reichen gerade aus; **how long would it take to become ~ in Japanese?** wie lange würde es dauern, bis man Japanisch beherrscht?

profile ['prəʊfaɪl] **1** n **(a)** Profil nt; (picture, photograph) Profilbild nt, Seitenansicht f; (biographical ~) Porträt nt; (Tech: section) (vertical) Längsschnitt m; (horizontal) Querschnitt m. **in ~** (person, head) im Profil; **to keep a low ~** sich zurückhalten.

2 vt (draw a ~ of) (pictorially) im Profil darstellen; (biographically) porträtieren; (Tech) im Längs- or Querschnitt zeichnen or darstellen.

profit ['prɒfɪt] n **(a)** (Comm) Gewinn, Profit m. **these ~s are not much (of a) ~ in this business** dieses Geschäft wirft kaum Gewinn or Profit ab; **~ and loss account** Gewinn-und-Verlustrechnung f; **to make a ~ (out of or on sth)** (mit etw) einen Profit or Gewinn machen, (an etw dat) verdienen, (mit etw) ein Geschäft machen; **to show or yield a ~** einen Gewinn or Profit verzeichnen; **to sell sth at a ~** etw mit Gewinn verkaufen; **the business is now running at a ~** das Geschäft wirft jetzt Gewinn or Profit ab, das Geschäft rentiert sich jetzt; **I'm not doing it for ~** ich tue das nicht, um damit Geld zu

verdienen; **a with-~s policy** (*Insur*) eine Police mit Gewinn-beteiligung; **the role of ~ in the economy** die Rolle, die der Profit in der Wirtschaft spielt.
    (b) (*fig*) Nutzen, Vorteil *m*. **to turn sth to ~** Nutzen aus etw ziehen; **you might well learn something to your ~** Sie können etwas lernen, was Ihnen von Nutzen *or* Vorteil ist.
    2 *vt* (*liter*) nutzen, nützen (*sb* jdm), von Nutzen sein (*sb* für jdn). **what does it ~ a man if ...** was nützt es dem Menschen, wenn ...
    3 *vi* (*gain*) profitieren (*by, from* von), Nutzen *or* Gewinn ziehen (*by, from* aus).
profitability [ˌprɒfɪtəˈbɪlɪti] *n* Rentabilität, Einträglichkeit *f*. **~ study** Rentabilitäts- *or* Wirtschaftlichkeitsstudie *f*.
profitable [ˈprɒfɪtəbl] *adj* (*Comm*) gewinn- *or* profitbringend, rentabel, profitabel; (*fig: beneficial*) nützlich, vorteilhaft. **could you not find a more ~ way of spending your time?** kannst du nichts Besseres mit deiner Zeit anfangen?
profitably [ˈprɒfɪtəblɪ] *adv see adj.* **you could ~ spend a couple of hours reading a book** es käme dir sehr zugute, wenn du ein paar Stunden mit Lesen verbringen würdest.
profiteer [ˌprɒfɪˈtɪəʳ] **1** *n* Profitmacher, Profitjäger, Profitgeier *m*. **war ~** Kriegsgewinnler *m*. **2** *vi* sich bereichern.
profiteering [ˌprɒfɪˈtɪərɪŋ] *n* Geldschneiderei *f*, Wucher *m*.
profitless [ˈprɒfɪtlɪs] *adj* **(a)** (*Comm*) unrentabel. **(b)** *discussion, exercise* zwecklos.
profitlessly [ˈprɒfɪtlɪslɪ] *adv* **(a)** (*Comm*) ohne Gewinn. **(b)** *argue* zwecklos.
profit: ~-making *adj organization* rentabel; **(~-orientated)** auf Gewinn gerichtet; **~ margin** *n* Gewinnspanne *f*; **~ motive** *n* Gewinnstreben *nt*; **~-sharing 1** *adj scheme* Gewinnbeteiligungs-; **2** *n* Gewinnbeteiligung *f*.
profligacy [ˈprɒflɪgəsɪ] *n* (*dissoluteness*) Lasterhaftigkeit, Verworfenheit *f*; (*extravagance*) Verschwendungssucht *f*; (*an extravagance*) Verschwendung *f*.
profligate [ˈprɒflɪgɪt] **1** *adj* (*dissolute*) lasterhaft, verworfen; (*extravagant*) verschwenderisch, verschwendungssüchtig (*pej*). **2** *n* (*roué*) Windhund, Leichtfuß, Liederjan (*inf*) *m*; (*prodigal*) Verschwender(in *f*) *m*.
pro forma invoice [ˌprəʊˈfɔːməˈɪnvɔɪs] *n* Pro-forma-Rechnung *f*.
profound [prəˈfaʊnd] *adj sleep, sigh, sorrow, love* tief; *thought* tiefsinnig, tiefschürfend, tiefgründig; *book* gehaltvoll, profund (*geh*); *thinker, knowledge* profund (*geh*), tiefgehend *attr*; *regret* tiefgehend *attr*; *hatred, mistrust* tiefsitzend *attr*; *indifference* vollkommen, völlig; *interest* stark; *changes* tiefgreifend *attr*. **you're very ~ today** (*also iro*) du bist heute sehr tiefsinnig; **that's very ~** (*also iro*) das ist sehr tiefsinnig.
profoundly [prəˈfaʊndlɪ] *adv* zutiefst. **~ sad** tieftraurig; **~ significant** äußerst bedeutsam; **~ indifferent** völlig *or* vollkommen gleichgültig; **..., he said ~ ...,** sagte er tiefsinnig; **to be ~ ignorant of sth** überhaupt keine Ahnung von etw haben.
profundity [prəˈfʌndɪtɪ] *n* **(a)** *no pl* Tiefe *f*; (*of thought, thinker, book etc*) Tiefgründigkeit, Tiefsinnigkeit *f*; (*of knowledge*) Gründlichkeit *f*. **(b)** (*profound remark*) Tiefsinnigkeit *f*.
profuse [prəˈfjuːs] *adj vegetation* üppig; *bleeding* stark; *thanks, praise* überschwenglich; *apologies* überreichlich. **to be ~ in one's thanks/apologies** sich überschwenglich bedanken/sich vielmals entschuldigen; **he was ~ in his praise** er geizte nicht mit seinem Lob; **where flowers grow in ~ abundance** wo Blumen in üppiger *or* verschwenderischer Fülle wachsen.
profusely [prəˈfjuːslɪ] *adv grow* üppig; *bleed* stark; *thank, praise* überschwenglich; *sweat* heftig, stark. **he apologized ~** er entschuldigte sich vielmals, er bat vielmals um Entschuldigung; **~ illustrated** reich illustriert.
profusion [prəˈfjuːʒən] *n* Überfülle *f*, verschwenderische Fülle. *trees/ice-cream* **in ~** Bäume/Eis in Hülle und Fülle; **his painting was a wild ~ of reds and blues** sein Gemälde war eine Orgie in Rot und Blau.
progenitor [prəʊˈdʒenɪtəʳ] *n* (*form*) Vorfahr, Ahn *m*; (*fig*) Vorläufer *m*.
progenitrix [prəʊˈdʒenɪtrɪks] *n* (*form*) Vorfahrin, Ahne *f*.
progeny [ˈprɒdʒɪnɪ] *n* Nachkommen *pl*, Nachkommenschaft *f*.
progesterone [prəʊˈdʒestərəʊn] *n* Progesteron, Gelbkörperhormon *nt*.
prognosis [prɒgˈnəʊsɪs] *n, pl* **prognoses** [prɒgˈnəʊsiːz] Prognose, Vorhersage, Voraussage *f*.
prognostic [prɒgˈnɒstɪk] *adj* (*form*) prognostisch.
prognosticate [prɒgˈnɒstɪkeɪt] **1** *vi* (*often hum*) Prognosen stellen, Vorhersagen machen. **2** *vt* prognostizieren.
prognostication [prɒgˌnɒstɪˈkeɪʃən] *n* Prognose, Vorhersage, Voraussage *f*.
program [ˈprəʊgræm] **1** *n* **(a)** (*Computers*) Programm *nt*. **(b)** (*US*) *see* **programme 1**. **2** *vt* **(a)** *computer* programmieren. **(b)** (*US*) *see* **programme 2**.
programme, (*US*) **program** [ˈprəʊgræm] **1** *n* (*all senses*) Programm *nt*; (*Rad, TV also*) Sendung *f*. **we've got a very heavy ~ of meetings** wir haben sehr viele Besprechungen auf unserem Programm; **what's the ~ for tomorrow?** was steht für morgen auf dem Programm?; **what's on the other ~?** was gibt es *or* läuft im anderen Programm?; **our ~s for this evening** das Programm des heutigen Abends.
    2 *vt computer* programmieren; (*fig*) *person* vorprogrammieren; **~d course/learning** programmierter Unterricht/programmiertes Lernen; **that's ~d for tomorrow** das steht für morgen auf dem Programm.
programme: ~ music *n* Programmusik *f*; **~ notes** *npl* Programmhinweise *pl*; **~ planner** *n* (*TV*) Programmplaner *m*.
programmer [ˈprəʊgræməʳ] *n* Programmierer(in *f*) *m*.
programming [ˈprəʊgræmɪŋ] *n* Programmieren *nt*. **~ language** Programmiersprache *f*.
progress [ˈprəʊgres] **1** *n* **(a)** *no pl* (*movement forwards*)

Fortschreiten, Vorwärtskommen *nt*; (*Mil*) Vorrücken, Vordringen *nt*. **we made slow ~ through the mud** wir kamen im Schlamm nur langsam vorwärts; **they made good ~ across the open country** sie kamen im offenen Gelände gut vorwärts.
    (b) *no pl* (*advance*) Fortschritt *m*. **the ~ of events** der Gang der Ereignisse; **to make (good/slow) ~** (*gute/langsame*) Fortschritte machen; **have you made any ~ in the negotiations/your search for a solution?** haben Sie bei den Verhandlungen/Ihrer Suche nach einer Lösung irgendwelche Fortschritte erzielt?, sind Sie bei den Verhandlungen/Ihrer Suche nach einer Lösung weitergekommen?; **I want to see some ~!** ich möchte Fortschritte sehen!; **~ report** Fortschrittsbericht *m*.
    (c) in ~ im Gange; **in full ~** in vollem Gange; **"silence please, meeting in ~"** „Sitzung! Ruhe bitte"; **the work still in ~** die noch zu erledigende Arbeit.
    (d) (*obs: journey*) Reise *f*.
    2 [prəˈgres] *vi* **(a)** (*move, go forward*) sich vorwärts bewegen, vorwärtsschreiten. **we ~ed slowly across the ice** wir bewegten uns langsam über das Eis vorwärts; **by the third day the enemy/expedition had ~ed as far as ...** am dritten Tag war der Feind bis ... vorgerückt *or* vorgedrungen/die Expedition bis ... vorgedrungen *or* gekommen.
    (b) (*in time*) **as the work ~es** mit dem Fortschreiten der Arbeit; **as the game ~ed** im Laufe des Spiels; **while negotiations were actually ~ing** während die Verhandlungen im Gange waren.
    (c) (*improve, make progress*) (*student, patient*) Fortschritte machen. **how far have you ~ed since our last meeting?** wie weit sind Sie seit unserer letzten Sitzung gekommen?; **investigations are ~ing well** die Untersuchungen kommen gut voran *or* machen gute Fortschritte; **we are, in fact, ~ing towards a solution** wir nähern uns jetzt einer Lösung; **that civilization is constantly ~ing** (*towards a state of perfection*) daß sich die Zivilisation ständig (auf einen Zustand der Perfektion hin) weiterentwickelt; **that mankind is ~ing towards some goal** daß sich die Menschheit auf ein Ziel zubewegt.
    (d) (*through hierarchy etc*) **as you ~ through the orders of mammals** wenn man die Entwicklungsreihe der Säugetiere durchgeht; **the employee ~es upwards through the company hierarchy** der Angestellte macht seinen Weg durch die Firmenhierarchie.
progression [prəˈgreʃən] *n* Folge *f*; (*Math*) Reihe, Progression *f*; (*Mus*) Sequenz *f*; (*development*) Entwicklung *f*; (*in taxation*) Progression *f*; (*discount rates etc*) Staffelung *f*. **sales have shown a continuous ~** im Absatz wurde eine stete Aufwärtsentwicklung verzeichnet; **his ~ from a junior clerk to managing director** sein Aufstieg vom kleinen Angestellten zum Direktor; **is there a natural ~ from marijuana to heroin?** ist das Umsteigen von Marihuana auf Heroin zwangsläufig?
progressive [prəˈgresɪv] **1** *adj* **(a)** (*increasing*) zunehmend; *disease etc* fortschreitend; *paralysis* progressiv; *taxation* progressiv. **~ form/tense** (*Gram*) Verlaufsform *f*.
    (b) (*favouring progress*) progressiv, fortschrittlich; (*Mus*) progressiv. **~ jazz** progressiver Jazz; **~ party** (*Pol*) fortschrittliche Partei, Fortschrittspartei *f*.
    2 *n* (*person*) Progressive(r) *mf*.
progressively [prəˈgresɪvlɪ] *adv* zunehmend. **he is becoming ~ more addicted** er wird zunehmend *or* immer abhängiger.
progressiveness [prəˈgresɪvnɪs] *n* Fortschrittlichkeit, Progressivität *f*.
prohibit [prəˈhɪbɪt] *vt* **(a)** verbieten, untersagen. **to ~ sb from doing sth** jdm etw verbieten *or* untersagen; **his health ~s him from swimming** sein Gesundheitszustand verbietet (es) ihm zu schwimmen; **"smoking ~ed"** „Rauchen verboten".
    (b) (*prevent*) verhindern. **to ~ sth being done** verhindern, daß etw geschieht; **to ~ sb from doing sth** jdn daran hindern, etw zu tun.
prohibition [ˌprəʊɪˈbɪʃən] **1** *n* Verbot *nt*. **(the) P~** (*Hist*) die Prohibition; **the ~ of smoking** das Rauchverbot. **2** *attr* (*in US*) *laws, party* Prohibitions-.
prohibitionism [ˌprəʊɪˈbɪʃənɪzəm] *n* Prohibition *f*.
prohibitionist [ˌprəʊɪˈbɪʃənɪst] **1** *adj* Prohibitions-. **2** *n* Prohibitionist(in *f*) *m*.
prohibitive [prəˈhɪbɪtɪv] *adj* **(a)** *tax* Prohibitiv-; *duty* Sperr-. **~ laws** Verbotsgesetze *pl*; **~ signs** Verbotsschilder *pl*; **~ rules** Verbote *pl*. **(b)** *price, cost* unerschwinglich. **the costs of producing this model have become ~** die Kosten für die Herstellung dieses Modells sind untragbar geworden.
prohibitory [prəˈhɪbɪtərɪ] *adj see* **prohibitive (a)**.
project[1] [ˈprɒdʒekt] *n* Projekt *nt*; (*scheme*) Unternehmen, Vorhaben *nt*; (*Sch, Univ*) Referat *nt*; (*in primary school*) Arbeit *f*. **~ engineer** Projektingenieur *m*.
project[2] [prəˈdʒekt] **1** *vt* **(a)** *film, map, figures* projizieren. **to ~ oneself/one's personality** sich selbst/seine eigene Person zur Geltung bringen; **to ~ one's neuroses/guilt onto somebody else** seine Neurosen/Schuldgefühle auf einen anderen projizieren; **to ~ one's voice** seine Stimme zum Tragen bringen; **to ~ one's voice to the back of the hall** seine Stimme so erheben, daß sie auch im hinteren Teil des Saals zu hören ist; **in order to ~ an adequate picture of our country** um ein angemessenes Bild unseres Landes zu vermitteln.
    (b) (*plan*) (*voraus*)planen; *costs* überschlagen.
    (c) (*Math*) *line* verlängern; *solid* projizieren.
    (d) (*propel*) abschießen. **to ~ a missile into space** eine Rakete in den Weltraum schießen.
    (e) (*cause to jut*) *part of building etc* vorspringen lassen.
    2 *vi* **(a)** (*plan*) planen.
    (b) (*jut out*) hervorragen, hervorspringen (*from* aus). **the upper storey ~s over the road** das obere Stockwerk ragt über die Straße.
    (c) (*Psych*) projizieren, von sich auf andere schließen.

(d) *(with one's voice: actor, singer)* you'll have to ~ more than that, we can't hear you at the back Sie müssen lauter singen/sprechen, wir können Sie hier hinten nicht hören.

projectile [prə'dʒektaɪl] n *(Wurf)*geschoß nt; *(Mil)* Geschoß, Projektil *(spec)* nt.

projection [prə'dʒekʃən] n **(a)** *(of films, guilt feelings, figures, map)* Projektion f. ~ **booth** or **room** Vorführraum m. **(b)** *(protrusion, overhang, ledge etc)* Vorsprung, Überhang m. **(c)** *(extension: of line)* Verlängerung f. **(d)** *(prediction, estimate)* (Voraus)planung f; *(of cost)* Überschlagung f.

projectionist [prə'dʒekʃnɪst] n Filmvorführer m.

projective [prə'dʒektɪv] adj geometry Projektions-; *(Psych)* projizierend.

projector [prə'dʒektə'] n *(Film)* Projektor m, Vorführgerät nt.

prolapse ['prəʊlæps] n *(Med)* Vorfall, Prolaps *(spec)* m.

prole [prəʊl] n *(esp Brit pej inf)* Prolet(in f) m *(inf).*

proletarian [,prəʊlə'teərɪən] **1** adj proletarisch. **2** n Proletarier(in f) m.

proletariat [,prəʊlə'teərɪət] n Proletariat nt.

proliferate [prə'lɪfəreɪt] vi *(number)* sich stark erhöhen; *(ideas)* um sich greifen; *(insects, animals)* sich stark vermehren; *(weeds, cells)* wuchern, sich rasch ausbreiten.

proliferation [prə,lɪfə'reɪʃən] n *(in numbers)* starke Erhöhung; *(of animals)* zahlreiche Vermehrung; *(of nuclear weapons)* Weitergabe f; *(of ideas)* Ausbreitung f, Umsichgreifen nt; *(of sects)* Umsichgreifen, Wuchern nt; *(of weeds)* Wuchern nt.

prolific [prə'lɪfɪk] adj fruchtbar; *writer* also sehr produktiv.

prolix ['prəʊlɪks] adj weitschweifig.

prolixity [prəʊ'lɪksɪtɪ] n Weitschweifigkeit f.

prologue, *(US)* **prolog** ['prəʊlɒg] n Prolog m; *(of book)* Vorwort nt; *(fig)* Vorspiel nt.

prolong [prə'lɒŋ] vt verlängern; *(pej)* process, pain hinauszögern; *(Fin)* draft prolongieren.

prolongation [,prəʊlɒŋ'geɪʃən] n see vt Verlängerung f; Hinauszögern nt; Prolongation, Prolongierung f.

prom [prɒm] n *(inf)* *(Brit: promenade)* (Strand)promenade f; *(Brit: concert)* Konzert nt *(in gelockertem Rahmen)*; *(US: ball)* Studenten-/Schülerball m.

promenade [,prɒmɪ'nɑːd] **1** n *(stroll, in dancing)* Promenade f; *(esp Brit: esplanade)* (Strand)promenade f; *(US: ball)* Studenten-/Schülerball m. ~ **concert** Konzert nt *(in gelokkertem Rahmen)*; ~ **deck** Promenadendeck nt. **2** vt *(stroll through)* promenieren in *(+dat)*; avenue entlangpromenieren; *(stroll with)* spazierenführen; *(in dance)* eine Promenade machen mit. **3** vi *(stroll)* promenieren; *(in dance)* eine Promenade machen.

Promethean [prə'miːθɪən] adj *(liter)* prometheisch *(liter).*

Prometheus [prə'miːθjuːs] n Prometheus m.

prominence ['prɒmɪnəns] n **(a)** no pl the ~ of his forehead seine ausgeprägte Stirn; because of the ~ of the castle on a rock in the middle of the city wegen der exponierten Lage des Schlosses auf einem Felsen inmitten der Stadt. **(b)** *(of ideas, beliefs)* Beliebtheit f; *(of writer, politician etc)* Bekanntheit f. the undisputed ~ of his position as ... seine unbestritten führende Position als ...; if you give too much ~ to any one particular aspect wenn Sie einen bestimmten Aspekt zu sehr in den Vordergrund stellen; to bring sb/sth into ~ *(attract attention to)* jdn/etw herausstellen or in den Vordergrund rücken; *(make famous)* jdn/etw berühmt machen; he came or rose to ~ in the Cuba affair er wurde durch die Kuba-Affäre bekannt; that aspect is coming into ~ dieser Aspekt rückt in den Vordergrund. **(c)** *(prominent part)* Vorsprung m.

prominent ['prɒmɪnənt] adj **(a)** *(jutting out)* cheek-bones, teeth vorstehend attr; crag vorspringend attr. to be ~ vorstehen; vorspringen. **(b)** *(conspicuous)* markings auffällig; feature, characteristic hervorstechend, auffallend. put it in a ~ position stellen Sie es deutlich sichtbar hin; the castle occupies a ~ position on the hill das Schloß hat eine exponierte Lage auf dem Hügel. **(c)** *(leading)* role führend; *(large, significant)* wichtig; position also einflußreich. he occupies a ~ position in the development of modern literature er nimmt eine bedeutende Stellung in der Entwicklung der modernen Literatur ein. **(d)** *(well-known, in the public eye)* personality, publisher prominent. she is ~ in London society sie ist ein bekanntes Mitglied der Londoner Gesellschaft.

prominently ['prɒmɪnəntlɪ] adv display, place deutlich sichtbar. he figured ~ in the case er spielte in dem Fall eine bedeutende Rolle.

promiscuity [,prɒmɪ'skjuːɪtɪ] n **(a)** Promiskuität f, häufiger Partnerwechsel m. **(b)** *(liter: confusion)* Wirrwarr m.

promiscuous [prə'mɪskjʊəs] adj **(a)** *(sexually)* promiskuitiv *(spec).* to be ~ häufig den Partner wechseln; *(behaviour)* häufigen Partnerwechsel zeigen; a ~ girl ein Mädchen, das häufig den Partner wechselt. **(b)** *(liter)* wirr.

promiscuously [prə'mɪskjʊəslɪ] adv see adj.

promise ['prɒmɪs] **1** n **(a)** *(pledge)* Versprechen nt. remember your ~ to me denken Sie an Ihr Versprechen; their ~ of help ihr Versprechen zu helfen; ~ of marriage Eheversprechen nt; under ~ of *(form)* mit dem Versprechen *(+gen)*; under a ~ of secrecy unter dem Siegel der Verschwiegenheit; is that a ~? ganz bestimmt?; to make sb a ~ jdm ein Versprechen geben or machen; make me one ~ versprich mir eins; I'm not making any ~s versprechen kann ich nichts; to hold or keep sb to his ~ jdn an sein Versprechen binden; ~s, ~s! Versprechen, nichts als Versprechen! **(b)** *(hope, prospect)* Hoffnung, Aussicht f. a young man of ~ ein vielversprechender junger Mann; to hold out a or the ~ of sth jdm Hoffnungen auf etw *(acc)* machen; to show ~ zu den

besten Hoffnungen berechtigen; she had a ~ of passion in her eyes ihre Augen verrieten Leidenschaft.

2 vt *(pledge)* versprechen; *(forecast, augur)* hindeuten auf *(+acc).* to ~ (sb) to do sth *(jdm)* versprechen, etw zu tun; to ~ sb sth, to ~ sth to sb jdm etw versprechen; ~ me one thing versprich mir eins; to be ~d to sb *(dated)* jdm versprochen sein *(old)*; I'm not promising anything but ... ich will nichts versprechen, aber ...; I won't do it again, I ~ you ich werde es nie wieder tun, das verspreche ich Ihnen; I ~ you I didn't mean to do it ehrlich, das habe ich nicht gewollt; you'll regret this, I ~ you ich verspreche dir, das wirst du bereuen; this ~s trouble das sieht nach Ärger aus; this ~s better things to come das läßt auf Besseres hoffen; that sky ~s rain der Himmel sieht nach Regen aus; the P~d Land *(Bibl, fig)* das Gelobte Land.

3 vi versprechen. (do you) ~? versprichst du es?; ~! *(will you~)* versprich's mir, ehrlich?; *(I~)* ehrlich!; I'll try, but I'm not promising ich werde es versuchen, aber ich kann nichts versprechen; but you ~d! aber du hast es doch versprochen! **(b)** to ~ well vielversprechend sein; this doesn't exactly ~ well das ist nicht gerade vielversprechend.

4 vr to ~ oneself sth sich *(dat)* etw versprechen; I've ~d myself never to do it again ich habe mir geschworen, daß ich das nicht noch einmal mache.

promising adj, ~ly adv ['prɒmɪsɪŋ, -lɪ] vielversprechend.

promissory note ['prɒmɪsərɪ'nəʊt] n Schuldschein m.

promontory ['prɒməntrɪ] n Vorgebirge, Kap nt.

promote [prə'məʊt] vt **(a)** *(in rank)* befördern. he has been ~d (to) colonel or to the rank of colonel er ist zum Obersten befördert worden; our team was ~d *(Ftbl)* unsere Mannschaft ist aufgestiegen. **(b)** *(foster)* fördern; *(Parl)* bill sich einsetzen für. **(c)** *(organize, put on)* conference, race-meeting, boxing match etc veranstalten. **(d)** *(advertise)* werben für; *(put on the market)* auf den Markt bringen. the new model has been widely ~d in the media für das neue Modell ist in den Medien intensiv geworben worden or Werbung gemacht worden.

promoter [prə'məʊtə'] n *(Sport, of beauty contest etc)* Promoter, Veranstalter m; *(of company)* Mitbegründer m. sales ~ Verkaufsleiter, Salespromoter *(Comm)* m.

promotion [prə'məʊʃən] n **(a)** *(in rank)* Beförderung f. to get or win ~ befördert werden; *(football team)* aufsteigen. **(b)** *(fostering)* Förderung f; *(Parl: of bill)* Einsatz m *(of für).* **(c)** *(organization: of conference etc)* Veranstaltung f. **(d)** *(advertising)* Werbung f *(of für)*; *(advertising campaign)* Werbekampagne f; *(marketing)* Einführung f auf dem Markt. we've got a special ~ by the Rochas people in the store this week wir haben diese Woche einen Rochas-Werbestand.

prompt [prɒmpt] **1** adj *(+er)* prompt; action unverzüglich, sofortig. he is always very ~ with or about such things solche Dinge erledigt er immer prompt or sofort; he is always very ~ *(on time)* er ist immer sehr pünktlich. **2** adv at 6 o'clock ~ pünktlich um 6 Uhr, Punkt 6 Uhr. **3** vt **(a)** *(motivate)* veranlassen *(to zu).* to ~ sb to do sth jdn *(dazu)* veranlassen, etw zu tun; what ~ed you to do it? was hat Sie dazu veranlaßt?; he was ~ed purely by a desire to help sein Beweggrund war einzig und allein der Wunsch zu helfen; in the hope that this might ~ a discussion in der Hoffnung, daß das eine Diskussion in Gang setzen wird; he didn't need any ~ing to ask her man brauchte ihn nicht darum zu bitten, sie zu fragen; he's a bit lazy, he needs a little ~ing er ist ein bißchen faul, man muß ihm manchmal auf die Sprünge helfen. **(b)** *(evoke)* memories, feelings wecken; conclusion nahelegen. it ~s the thought that ... es drängt einem den Gedanken auf, daß ...; I'll do it myself, I don't need you to ~ me ich mache das schon selbst, du brauchst mich nicht erst zu ermahnen; he doesn't need any ~ing, he's cheeky enough as it is er braucht keine Ermunterung, er ist auch so schon frech genug. **(c)** *(help with speech)* vorsagen *(sb jdm)*; *(Theat)* soufflieren *(sb jdm).* he recited the whole poem without any ~ing er sagte das ganze Gedicht auf, ohne daß ihm jemand (etwas) vorsagen mußte; the teacher had to keep ~ing him der Lehrer mußte ihm immer wieder Hilfestellung geben; he forgot his speech and had to be ~ed er hatte seine Rede vergessen, so daß man ihm mit Stichworten auf die Sprünge helfen mußte. **4** vi *(Theat)* soufflieren. **5** n **(a)** *(Theat)* he needed a ~ ihm mußte souffliert werden; he couldn't hear the ~ er hörte die Souffleuse nicht; to give sb a ~ jdm weiterhelfen; *(Theat)* soufflieren. **(b)** *(reminder, encouragement)* to give sb a ~ jdm einen Schubs geben *(inf)*, jdn anstoßen; we have to give our debtors the occasional ~ wir müssen uns bei unseren Schuldnern hin und wieder in Erinnerung bringen.

prompt: ~ **box** n Souffleurkasten m; ~ **copy** n Rollenheft nt.

prompter ['prɒmptə'] n Souffleur m, Souffleuse f; *(tele-~)* Neger m.

prompting ['prɒmptɪŋ] n **(a)** *(Theat)* Souffleren nt. **(b)** the ~s of conscience/the heart die Stimme des Gewissens/Herzens.

promptitude ['prɒmptɪtjuːd] n see promptness.

promptly ['prɒmptlɪ] adv prompt. they left ~ at 6 sie gingen pünktlich um 6 Uhr or Punkt 6 Uhr; of course he ~ forgot it all er hat natürlich prompt alles vergessen.

promptness ['prɒmptnɪs] n Promptheit f. the fire brigade's ~ der prompte Einsatz der Feuerwehr.

prompt note n *(Comm)* Ermahnung f.

promulgate ['prɒmʌlgeɪt] vt verbreiten; law verkünden.

promulgation [,prɒmʌl'geɪʃən] n see vt Verbreitung f; Verkündung f.

prone [prəʊn] adj **(a)** *(lying)* to be or lie ~ auf dem Bauch liegen; in a ~ position in Bauchlage. **(b)** *(liable)* to be ~ to sth/to do sth zu etw neigen/dazu neigen, etw zu tun.

proneness ['prəʊnnɪs] n Neigung f (to zu).

prong [prɒŋ] 1 n (a) (of fork) Zacke, Zinke f; (of antler) Sprosse f, Ende nt. (b) (fig) (of argument) Punkt m; (of attack) (Angriffs)spitze f. 2 vt aufspießen.

-pronged [-prɒŋd] adj suf (of fork) -zackig, -zinkig. a three-~ attack ein Angriff mit drei Spitzen; a three-~ argument ein dreigleisiges Argument.

pronominal [prəʊ'nɒmɪnl] adj Pronominal-.

pronoun ['prəʊnaʊn] n Fürwort, Pronomen nt.

pronounce [prə'naʊns] 1 vt (a) word etc aussprechen. I find Russian hard to ~ ich finde die russische Aussprache schwierig; the "p" isn't ~d das „p" wird nicht ausgesprochen.
(b) (declare) erklären für. the doctors ~d him unfit for work die Ärzte erklärten ihn für arbeitsunfähig; to ~ oneself for/against sth sich für/gegen etw aussprechen; to ~ sentence das Urteil verkünden; to ~ the benediction den Segen sprechen.
2 vi (a) to ~ in favour of/against sth sich für/gegen etw aussprechen; to ~ on sth zu etw Stellung nehmen.
(b) he ~s badly er hat eine schlechte Aussprache.

pronounced [prə'naʊnst] adj (marked) ausgesprochen; hip-bones ausgeprägt; improvement, deterioration deutlich; views prononciert. he has a ~ limp er hinkt sehr stark.

pronouncement [prə'naʊnsmənt] n Erklärung f; (Jur: of sentence) Verkündung f. to make a ~ eine Erklärung abgeben.

pronto ['prɒntəʊ] adv (inf) fix (inf). do it ~ aber dalli! (inf).

pronunciation [prə,nʌnsɪ'eɪʃən] n Aussprache f. what is the ~? wie lautet die Aussprache?

proof [pruːf] 1 n (a) Beweis m (of für). you'll need more ~ than that die Beweise reichen nicht aus; as or in ~ of als or zum Beweis für; to put sth to the ~ etw auf die Probe stellen; (Tech) etw erproben; that is ~ that ... das ist der Beweis dafür, daß ...; isn't that ~ enough? ist das nicht Beweis genug?; to give or show ~ of sth etw nachweisen, den Nachweis für etw liefern; can you give us any ~ of that? können Sie (uns) dafür Beweise liefern?; show me your ~ beweisen Sie (mir) das; but I've got ~ aber ich habe Beweise; what ~ is there that he meant it? und was beweist, daß er es ernst gemeint hat?
(b) (test, trial) Probe f. withstanding these conditions is the ~ of a good paint es ist der Beweis für die Qualität einer Farbe, wenn sie solchen Bedingungen standhält; the ~ of the pudding is in the eating (Prov) Probieren geht über Studieren (Prov).
(c) (Typ) (Korrektur)fahne f. (Phot) Probeabzug m.
(d) (of alcohol) Alkoholgehalt m. 70 ~ ≈ 40° Vol.
2 adj (resistant) to be ~ against fire/water/moisture/bullets feuersicher/wasserdicht/feuchtigkeitsundurchlässig/kugelsicher sein; to be ~ against temptation/her insults gegen Versuchungen/ihre Beleidigungen gefeit or unempfindlich sein; ~ against inflation inflationssicher.
3 vt (a) (against water) imprägnieren.
(b) (Typ) (make ~) einen Korrekturabzug herstellen; (read ~) Korrektur lesen.

proof: ~-read vti Korrektur lesen; ~-reader n Korrektor(in f) m; ~-reading n Korrekturlesen nt; at the ~-reading stage im Korrekturstadium.

prop¹ [prɒp] 1 n (lit) Stütze f; (fig also) Halt m. 2 vt to ~ the door open die Tür offenhalten; to ~ oneself/sth against sth sich/etw gegen etw lehnen; see ~ up.

♦prop up vt sep (a) (rest, lean) to ~ oneself/sth ~ against sth sich/etw gegen etw lehnen. (b) (support) tunnel, wall abstützen; engine aufbocken; (fig) régime, company, the pound stützen; organization unterstützen. to ~ oneself ~ on sth sich auf etw (acc) stützen; he spends most of his time ~ping ~ the bar (inf) er hängt die meiste Zeit an der Bar.

prop² n (inf: propeller) Propeller m.

prop³ n (inf) see property (d).

prop⁴ abbr of proprietor.

propaedeutic [,prəʊpiː'djuːtɪk] n (form) Propädeutik f.

propaganda [,prɒpə'gændə] n Propaganda f. ~ machine Propagandamaschinerie f.

propagandist [,prɒpə'gændɪst] 1 n Propagandist(in f) m. a tireless ~ for penal reform ein unermüdlicher Verfechter der Strafrechtsreform. 2 adj propagandistisch.

propagate ['prɒpəgeɪt] 1 vt (a) (disseminate). (b) (disseminate) verbreiten; views also propagieren. (c) (Phys) sound, waves fortpflanzen. (d) (Hort) plant vermehren. 2 vi sich fortpflanzen or vermehren; (views) sich aus- or verbreiten.

propagation [,prɒpə'geɪʃən] n (reproduction) Fortpflanzung f; (Hort: of plants) Vermehrung f; (dissemination) Verbreitung f; (of views) Verbreitung f, Propagierung f.

propane ['prəʊpeɪn] n Propan nt.

propel [prə'pel] vt antreiben; (fuel) betreiben. ~led along by the wind vom Wind getrieben; ~led by an unrelenting greed von unersättlicher Habgier getrieben; he was ~led through the window er wurde aus dem Fenster geworfen.

propellant, propellent [prə'pelənt] 1 n Treibstoff m; (in spray can) Treibgas nt. 2 adj treibend.

propeller [prə'pelə^r] n Propeller m. ~ shaft Antriebswelle f; (Aut) Kardanwelle f; (Naut) Schraubenwelle f.

propelling: ~ force n (lit, fig) Triebkraft f; ~ pencil n (Brit) Drehbleistift m.

propensity [prə'pensɪtɪ] n Hang m, Neigung f (to zu). to have a ~ to do sth/for doing sth dazu neigen, etw zu tun, die Neigung or den Hang haben, etw zu tun.

proper ['prɒpə^r] 1 adj (a) (peculiar, characteristic) eigen. ~ to the species der Art eigen, arteigen.
(b) (actual) eigentlich. physics ~ die eigentliche Physik; in the ~ sense of the word in der eigentlichen Bedeutung des Wortes; is that a ~ policeman's helmet? ist das ein richtiger Polizeihelm?; he's not a ~ electrician er ist kein richtiger Elektriker; not in Berlin ~ nicht in Berlin selbst.

(c) (inf: real) fool etc richtig; (thorough) beating gehörig, anständig (inf), tüchtig (inf). we got a ~ beating (team etc) wir sind ganz schön geschlagen worden (inf); we are in a ~ mess wir sitzen ganz schön in der Patsche (inf).
(d) (fitting, suitable) richtig. in ~ condition in ordnungsgemäßem Zustand; the ~ time die richtige Zeit; in the ~ way richtig; as you think ~ wie Sie es für richtig halten; to do the ~ thing by sb das tun, was sich gehört; the ~ thing to do would be to apologize es gehört sich eigentlich, daß man sich entschuldigt; don't touch the injured man unless you know the ~ thing to do lassen Sie den Verletzten liegen, solange Sie nicht genau wissen, was man machen muß; it wasn't really the ~ thing to say es war ziemlich unpassend, das zu sagen; in a manner ~ to his position wie es sich für jemanden in seiner Position gehört or (ge)ziemt (geh); we considered or thought it only ~ to ... wir dachten, es gehört sich einfach zu ...
(e) (seemly) anständig. what is ~ was sich gehört; it is not ~ for you to ... es gehört sich nicht, daß Sie ...
(f) (prim and ~) korrekt.
2 adv (a) (dial) cruel, poorly richtig (inf).
(b) (incorrect usage) behave anständig; talk richtig.

proper fraction n echter Bruch.

properly ['prɒpəlɪ] adv (a) (correctly) richtig. this word, although ~ a plural ... dieses Wort, das eigentlich or genaugenommen Plural ist; ~ speaking genaugenommen, strenggenommen; Holland, more ~ called the Netherlands Holland, eigentlich or richtiger die Niederlande; Yugoslav is ~ called Serbo-Croat Jugoslawisch heißt korrekt Serbo-kroatisch; not ~ dressed for walking nicht richtig angezogen zum Wandern.
(b) (in seemly fashion) anständig. to conduct oneself ~ sich korrekt verhalten; she very ~ refused sie hat sich zu Recht geweigert.
(c) (justifiably) zu Recht.
(d) (inf: really, thoroughly) ganz schön (inf).

proper name, proper noun n Eigenname m.

propertied ['prɒpətɪd] adj besitzend; person begütert. the ~ classes die besitzenden Schichten, das Besitzbürgertum.

property ['prɒpətɪ] n (a) (characteristic, Philos) Eigenschaft f. it has healing properties es besitzt heilende Kräfte.
(b) (thing owned) Eigentum nt. government/company ~ Eigentum nt der Regierung/Firma, Regierungs-/Firmeneigentum nt; that's my ~ das gehört mir; common ~ (lit) gemeinsames Eigentum; (fig) Gemeingut nt; ~ is theft Eigentum ist Diebstahl; to become the ~ of sb in jds Eigentum (acc) übergehen; a man of ~ ein begüterter Mann.
(c) (building) Haus nt; Wohnung f; (office) Gebäude nt; (land) Besitztum nt; (estate) Besitz m. this house is a very valuable ~ dieses Haus ist ein sehr wertvoller Besitz; put your money in ~ legen Sie Ihr Geld in Immobilien an; ~ in London is dearer die Preise auf dem Londoner Immobilienmarkt sind höher.
(d) (Theat) Requisit nt.

property: ~ developer n Häusermakler m; ~ man, ~ manager n (Theat) Requisiteur m; ~ market n Immobilienmarkt m; ~ owner n Haus- und Grundbesitzer m; ~ speculation n Immobilienspekulation f; ~ speculator n Immobilienspekulant m; ~ tax n Vermögenssteuer f.

prophecy ['prɒfɪsɪ] n Prophezeiung f. one skilled in the ~ of future events jemand, der zukünftige Ereignisse vorhersagen kann or der die Gabe der Prophetie hat.

prophesy ['prɒfɪsaɪ] 1 vt prophezeien. 2 vi Prophezeiungen machen. the king was enraged by his ~ing der König war über seine Prophezeiungen erzürnt.

prophet ['prɒfɪt] n Prophet m.

prophetess ['prɒfɪtɪs] n Prophetin f.

prophetic adj, ~ally adv [prə'fetɪk, -əlɪ] prophetisch.

prophylactic [,prɒfɪ'læktɪk] 1 adj prophylaktisch, vorbeugend. 2 n Prophylaktikum nt; (contraceptive) Präservativ nt.

prophylaxis [,prɒfɪ'læksɪs] n Prophylaxe f.

propinquity [prə'pɪŋkwɪtɪ] n (form) Nähe f (to zu); (in time) zeitliche Nähe (to zu); (of relationship) nahe Verwandtschaft (to mit).

propitiate [prə'pɪʃɪeɪt] vt (liter) (in favour of) günstig or versöhnlich stimmen; (appease) besänftigen.

propitiation [prə,pɪʃɪ'eɪʃən] n (liter) see vt Versöhnung f; Besänftigung f. as ~ for, in ~ of als Sühne für.

propitiatory [prə'pɪʃɪətərɪ] adj see vt versöhnend; besänftigend; mood versöhnlich.

propitious adj, ~ly adv [prə'pɪʃəs, -lɪ] günstig (to, for für).

prop-jet ['prɒpdʒet] n see turboprop.

proponent [prə'pəʊnənt] n Befürworter(in f) m.

proportion [prə'pɔːʃən] 1 n (a) (ratio, relationship in number) Verhältnis nt (of x to y zwischen x und y); (relationship in size, Art) Proportionen pl. ~s (size) Ausmaß nt; (of building) Ausmaße pl; (relative to one another: Art, of building etc) Proportionen pl; to be in/out of ~ (in one another) (in number) im richtigen/nicht im richtigen Verhältnis zueinander stehen; (in size, Art) in den Proportionen stimmen/nicht stimmen; (in time, effort etc) im richtigen/in keinem Verhältnis zueinander stehen; to be in/out of ~ to or with sth im Verhältnis/in keinem Verhältnis zu etw stehen; (in size, Art) in den Proportionen zu etw passen/nicht passen; in ~ to or with what she earns her contributions are very small im Verhältnis zu dem, was sie verdient, ist ihr Beitrag äußerst bescheiden; you should try to draw the face more in ~ to the body Sie sollten versuchen, das Gesicht proportional richtiger zum Körper zu zeichnen; to get sth in ~ (Art) etw proportional richtig darstellen; (fig) etw objektiv betrachten; he has got the arms out of ~ er hat die Arme proportional falsch dargestellt; he has let it all get out of ~ (fig) er hat den Blick für die Proportionen verloren; it's out of all ~! das steht doch in keinem Verhältnis!; sense of ~ (lit, *fig*) Sinn *m* für Proportionen; **in ~ as** in dem Maße wie; **a man of huge** ~s ein Koloß von einem Mann; **he admired her ample** ~s er bewunderte ihre üppigen Formen; **a room of good** ~s ein Zimmer mit guter Raumaufteilung.

(**b**) (*part, amount*) Teil *m*. **a certain ~ of** the population ein bestimmter Teil der Bevölkerung; **the ~ of drinkers in our society is** rising constantly der Anteil der Trinker in unserer Gesellschaft nimmt ständig zu; **what ~ of the industry is in private hands?** wie groß ist der Anteil der Industrie, der sich in Privathand befindet?; **a ~ of the industry is in private hands** ein Teil der Industrie befindet sich in Privathand.

2 *vt* you haven't ~ed the head properly Sie haben den Kopf proportional falsch dargestellt; **he ~ed the building beautifully** er hat das Gebäude wunderbar ausgewogen gestaltet; **an accurately/roughly ~ed model** ein maßstabgetreues/ungefähres Modell; **a nicely ~ed woman/building** eine wohlproportionierte Frau/ein wohlausgewogenes Gebäude.

proportional [prəˈpɔːʃənl] *adj* proportional (*to* zu); *share, distribution also* anteilmäßig (*to* zu). **~ representation/voting** Verhältnis- *or* Proportionalwahl *f*; **the West German system is partly ~** das Wahlsystem der Bundesrepublik Deutschland basiert zum Teil auf der Verhältniswahl *or* Proportionalwahl.

proportionally [prəˈpɔːʃnəlɪ] *adv* proportional; *share, distribute also* anteilmäßig; *more, less* entsprechend. **in Holland, MP's are elected ~** in Holland werden die Abgeordneten des Parlaments durch Verhältnis- *or* Proportionalwahl gewählt.

proportionate [prəˈpɔːʃnɪt] *adj* proportional. **to be/not to be ~ to sth** im Verhältnis/in keinem Verhältnis zu etw stehen.

proportionately [prəˈpɔːʃnɪtlɪ] *adv see adj.*

proposal [prəˈpəʊzl] *n* (**a**) Vorschlag *m* (*on, about* zu); (~ of marriage) (Heirats)antrag *m*. **to make sb a ~** jdm einen Vorschlag/(Heirats)antrag machen.

(**b**) (*act of proposing*) (*of toast*) Ausbringen *nt*; (*of motion*) Einbringen *nt*. **his ~ of this plan surprised his colleagues** daß er den Vorschlag zu diesem Plan machte, überraschte seine Kollegen; **his ~ of John as chairman was expected** daß er John zum Vorsitzenden vorschlägt, war erwartet worden.

propose [prəˈpəʊz] **1** *vt* (**a**) vorschlagen; *motion* stellen, einbringen. **to ~ marriage to sb** jdm einen (Heirats)antrag machen; **I ~ leaving now** *or* **that we leave now** ich schlage vor, wir gehen jetzt *or* daß wir jetzt gehen; **to ~ sb's health** einen Toast auf jdn ausbringen; *see* toast².

(**b**) (*have in mind*) beabsichtigen, vorhaben. **I don't ~ having any more to do with it/him** ich will nichts mehr damit/mit ihm zu tun haben; **but I don't ~ to** ich habe aber nicht die Absicht; **how do you ~ to pay for it?** wie wollen Sie das bezahlen?; **and just how do you ~ we pay for all that?** können Sie uns denn auch verraten, wie wir das alles bezahlen sollen?

2 *vi* (**a**) (*marriage*) einen (Heirats)antrag machen (*to* an). (**b**) **man ~s, God disposes** (*Prov*) der Mensch denkt, Gott lenkt (*Prov*).

proposer [prəˈpəʊzəʳ] *n* (*in debate*) Antragsteller(in *f*) *m*. **if you want to stand for the committee you'll have to find a ~** wenn Sie sich in den Ausschuß wählen lassen wollen, müssen Sie jemanden finden, der Sie vorschlägt.

proposition [ˌprɒpəˈzɪʃən] *n* (**a**) (*statement*) Aussage *f*; (*Philos, Logic*) Satz *m*; (*Math*) (Lehr)satz *m*. (**b**) (*proposal*) Vorschlag *m*; (*argument*) These *f*. **a paying ~** ein lohnendes Geschäft. (**c**) (*person or thing to be dealt with*) (*objective*) Unternehmen *nt*; (*opponent*) Fall *m*; (*prospect*) Aussicht *f*. (**d**) (*pej: improper ~*) unsittlicher Antrag.

propound [prəˈpaʊnd] *vt* darlegen.

proprietary [prəˈpraɪətərɪ] *adj class* besitzend; *rights* Besitz-; *attitude, manner* besitzergreifend; *medicine, article, brand* Marken-. **the author has rather strong ~ feelings about his work** der Autor sieht sein Werk als persönlichen Besitz an.

proprietor [prəˈpraɪətəʳ] *n* (*of pub, hotel, patent*) Inhaber(in *f*) *m*; (*of house, newspaper*) Besitzer(in *f*) *m*.

proprietorship [prəˈpraɪətəʃɪp] *n see* proprietor. **under his ~** während er der Inhaber/Besitzer war.

proprietress [prəˈpraɪətrɪs] *n* (*of pub, hotel*) Inhaberin *f*; (*of newspaper*) Besitzerin *f*.

propriety [prəˈpraɪətɪ] *n* (*correctness*) Korrektheit, Richtigkeit *f*; (*decency*) Anstand *m*; (*of clothing*) Gesellschaftsfähigkeit, Züchtigkeit (*liter*) *f*. **some countries still have doubts about the ~ of bikinis** in manchen Ländern werden Bikinis noch als anstößig betrachtet; **breach of ~** Verstoß *m* gegen die guten Sitten; **the proprieties** die Regeln *pl* des Anstands.

props [prɒps] *npl* (*Theat*) Requisiten *pl.*

propulsion [prəˈpʌlʃən] *n* Antrieb *m.*

pro rata [ˈprəʊˈrɑːtə] *adj, adv* anteilmäßig.

prorate [ˈprəʊreɪt] *vt* (*US*) anteilmäßig aufteilen *or* verteilen.

prorogation [ˌprəʊrəˈgeɪʃən] *n* Vertagung *f.*

prorogue [prəˈrəʊg] **1** *vt* vertagen. **2** *vi* sich vertagen.

prosaic [prəʊˈzeɪɪk] *adj* prosaisch; (*down-to-earth*) nüchtern; *life, joke* alltäglich.

prosaically [prəʊˈzeɪɪkəlɪ] *adv see adj.*

proscenium [prəʊˈsiːnɪəm] *n, pl* **proscenia** [prəʊˈsiːnɪə] (*also* **~ arch**) Proszenium *nt*. **~ stage** Bühne *f* mit Vorbühne.

proscribe [prəʊˈskraɪb] *vt* (*forbid*) verbieten; (*outlaw*) ächten; (*banish, exile*) verbannen.

proscription [prəʊˈskrɪpʃən] *n see vt* Verbot *nt*; Ächtung *f*; Verbannung *f.*

prose [prəʊz] *n* Prosa *f*; (*writing, style*) Stil *m*; (*Sch: translation text*) Übersetzung *f* in die Fremdsprache, Hinübersetzung *f.*
prose *in cpds* Prosa-; **~ composition** *n* Prosa *f.*

prosecutable [ˈprɒsɪkjuːtəbl] *adj* strafbar.

prosecute [ˈprɒsɪkjuːt] **1** *vt* (**a**) *person* strafrechtlich verfolgen *or* belangen (*for* wegen). **prosecuting counsel** Staatsanwalt *m*/-anwältin *f*. (**b**) (*form: carry on*) *inquiry, campaign etc* durchführen; *claim* weiterverfolgen.

2 *vi* Anzeige erstatten, gerichtlich vorgehen. **"shoplifting — we always ~"** „jeder Ladendiebstahl wird angezeigt *or* strafrechtlich verfolgt"; **Mr Jones, prosecuting, said ...** Herr Jones, der Vertreter der Anklage, sagte ...

prosecution [ˌprɒsɪˈkjuːʃən] *n* (**a**) (*Jur*) (*act of prosecuting*) strafrechtliche Verfolgung; (*in court: case, side*) Anklage *f* (*for* wegen). (**the**) **counsel for the ~** die Anklage(vertretung), der Vertreter/die Vertreterin der Anklage; **witness for the ~** Zeuge *m*/Zeugin *f* der Anklage, Belastungszeuge *m*/-zeugin *f*. (**b**) (*form*) *see vt(b)* Durchführung *f*; Weiterverfolgung *f.*

prosecutor [ˈprɒsɪkjuːtəʳ] *n* Ankläger(in *f*) *m.*

proselyte [ˈprɒsɪlaɪt] *n* Neubekehrte(r) *mf*, Proselyt(in *f*) *m.*

proselytize [ˈprɒsɪlɪtaɪz] **1** *vt* bekehren. **2** *vi* Leute bekehren.

prose: **~ style** *n* Stil *m*; **~ writer** *n* Prosaschriftsteller(in *f*) *m*; **~ writing** *n* Prosadichtung *f.*

prosodic [prəˈsɒdɪk] *adj* prosodisch.

prosody [ˈprɒsədɪ] *n* Verslehre *f.*

prospect [ˈprɒspekt] *n* (**a**) (*outlook, chance*) Aussicht *f* (*of* auf +*acc*). **what a ~!** (*iro*) das sind ja schöne Aussichten!; **he has no ~s** er hat keine Zukunft; **a job with no ~s** eine Stelle ohne Zukunft; **to hold out the ~ of sth** etw in Aussicht stellen; **to have sth in ~** etw in Aussicht haben.

(**b**) (*person, thing*) **he's not much of a ~ for her** er hat ihr nicht viel zu bieten; **I think this product would be a good ~** ich glaube, dieses Produkt ist sehr aussichtsreich; **Manchester is a good ~ for the cup** Manchester ist ein aussichtsreicher Kandidat für den Pokal; **a likely ~ as a customer/candidate/husband** ein aussichtsreicher Kunde/Kandidat/ein Mann, der als Ehemann in Frage kommt; **he's a good ~ for the team** (*could benefit it*) mit ihm hat die Mannschaft gute Aussichten.

(**c**) (*old, form*) (*view*) Aussicht *f* (*of* auf +*acc*); (*painting*) Ansicht *f* (*of* von).

(**d**) (*Min*) Schürfstelle *f.*

2 [prəˈspekt] *vt* (*Min*) nach Bodenschätzen suchen in (+*dat*).

3 [prəˈspekt] *vi* (*Min*) nach Bodenschätzen suchen.

prospecting [prəˈspektɪŋ] *n* (*Min*) Suche *f* nach Bodenschätzen.

prospective [prəˈspektɪv] *adj attr* (*likely to happen*) *journey, return* voraussichtlich; (*future*) *son-in-law, owner* zukünftig; *buyer* interessiert. **~ candidate** Kandidat *m*; **all the ~ cases** alle in Frage kommenden Fälle.

prospector [prəˈspektəʳ] *n* Prospektor, Gold-/Erz-/Ölsucher *m.*

prospectus [prəˈspektəs] *n* Verzeichnis *nt*; (*for holidays etc*) Prospekt *m.*

prosper [ˈprɒspəʳ] *vi* (*town, country, crime*) gedeihen, blühen; (*financially*) florieren, blühen; (*plan*) erfolgreich sein. **Britain would ~ under a coalition** unter einer Koalitionsregierung würde Großbritannien blühen und gedeihen; **how's he ~ing these days?** wie geht es ihm?

prosperity [prɒsˈperɪtɪ] *n* Wohlstand, Reichtum *m*; (*of business*) Prosperität *f.*

prosperous [ˈprɒspərəs] *adj* wohlhabend, reich; *business* gutgehend, florierend; *economy* florierend, blühend. **those were ~ times/years** das waren Zeiten/Jahre des Wohlstands; **he had a ~ look** about him er sah wohlhabend aus.

prosperously [ˈprɒspərəslɪ] *adv* **to live ~** im Wohlstand leben; **she was ~ dressed** ihre Kleidung verriet Wohlstand.

prostate (gland) [ˈprɒsteɪt(ˌglænd)] *n* Prostata, Vorsteherdrüse *f.*

prosthesis [prɒsˈθiːsɪs] *n* (*spec*) Prothese *f.*

prostitute [ˈprɒstɪtjuːt] **1** *n* Prostituierte *f*. **he is a male ~** er ist Strichjunge; **~s** männliche Prostituierte (*form*), Strichjungen *pl*. **2** *vt* (*lit*) prostituieren; *one's talents, honour, ideals* verkaufen. **3** *vr* sich prostituieren; (*fig also*) sich verkaufen.

prostitution [ˌprɒstɪˈtjuːʃən] *n* (*lit, fig*) Prostitution *f*; (*of one's talents, honour, ideals*) Verkaufen *nt.*

prostrate [ˈprɒstreɪt] **1** *adj* ausgestreckt. **he was found ~ on the floor** man fand ihn ausgestreckt am Boden liegend; **the servants lay ~ at their master's feet** die Diener lagen demütig *or* unterwürfig zu Füßen ihres Herrn; **she was ~ with grief/exhaustion** sie war vor Gram gebrochen/sie brach fast zusammen vor Erschöpfung.

2 [prɒˈstreɪt] *vt usu pass* (*lit*) zu Boden werfen; (*fig*) (*with fatigue*) erschöpfen, mitnehmen; (*with shock*) zusammenbrechen lassen, niederschmettern. **to be ~d by an illness** einer Krankheit (*dat*) zum Opfer gefallen sein; **to be ~d by or with grief** vor Gram gebrochen sein; **to be ~d by or with exhaustion** vor Erschöpfung fast zusammenbrechen; **he was almost ~d by the heat** die Hitze ließ ihn fast zusammenbrechen.

3 [prɒˈstreɪt] *vr* sich niederwerfen (*before* vor +*dat*).

prostration [prɒˈstreɪʃən] *n* (*lit*) Fußfall *m*; (*fig: exhaustion*) Erschöpfung *f.*

prosy [ˈprəʊzɪ] *adj* (+*er*) (*boring*) redselig; (*over-literary*) schwülstig.

Prot *abbr of* **Protestant** ev.

protagonist [prəʊˈtægənɪst] *n* Protagonist(in *f*) *m.*

protean [ˈprəʊtɪən] *adj* (*liter*) proteisch (*liter*).

protect [prəˈtekt] **1** *vt* schützen (*against* gegen, *from* vor +*dat*); (*person, animal*) *sb, young* beschützen (*against* gegen, *from* vor +*dat*); *one's interests, rights also* wahren. **don't try to ~ the culprit** versuchen Sie nicht, den Schuldigen zu decken.

2 *vi* schützen (*against* vor +*dat*).

protection [prəˈtekʃən] *n* (**a**) Schutz *m* (*against* gegen, *from* vor +*dat*); (*of interests, rights*) Wahrung *f*. **to be under sb's ~** unter jds Schutz (*dat*) stehen. (**b**) (*also* **~ money**) Schutzgeld *nt*. **~ racket** organisierte Erpresserunternehmen.

protectionism [prəˈtekʃənɪzəm] *n* Protektionismus *m.*

protectionist [prəˈtekʃənɪst] **1** *adj* protektionistisch. **2** *n* Protektionist *m.*

protective [prəˈtektɪv] *adj* Schutz-; *attitude, gesture* beschützend. **~ custody** Schutzhaft *f*; **~ colouring** Tarnfarbe,

Schutzfarbe *f*; ~ **instinct** Beschützerinstinkt *m*; **the mother is very** ~ **towards her children** die Mutter ist sehr fürsorglich ihren Kindern gegenüber; **some parents can be too** ~ manche Eltern sind übermäßig besorgt.

protectively [prəˈtektɪvlɪ] *adv* schützend; (*with regard to people*) beschützend. **don't be frightened, he said** ~ hab keine Angst, sagte er in beschützendem Ton.

protector [prəˈtektəʳ] *n* (a) (*defender*) Beschützer *m*. (b) (*protective wear*) Schutz *m*.

protectorate [prəˈtektərɪt] *n* Protektorat *nt*.

protectress [prəˈtektrɪs] *n* Beschützerin *f*.

protégé, protégée [ˈprɒtəʒeɪ] *n* Protegé, Schützling *m*.

protein [ˈprəʊtiːn] *n* Eiweiß, Protein *nt*. a **high-**~ **diet** eine eiweißreiche or stark proteinhaltige Kost.

pro tem [ˈprəʊˈtem] *abbr of* **pro tempore** zur Zeit, z.Zt.

protest [ˈprəʊtest] **1** *n* Protest *m*; (*demonstration*) Protestkundgebung *f*. **under** ~ unter Protest; **in** ~ aus Protest; **he did it without the slightest** ~ er tat es ohne den geringsten Protest or Widerspruch; **to make a/one's** ~ Protest or Widerspruch erheben; **letter of** ~, ~ **letter** Protestschreiben *nt*; ~ **march** Protestmarsch *m*.

2 [prəʊˈtest] *vi* (*against, about* gegen) protestieren; (*demonstrate*) demonstrieren. **the** ~**ing scream of the brakes** das gequälte Aufkreischen der Bremsen.

3 [prəʊˈtest] *vt* (a) *innocence, loyalty* beteuern. **but it's mine, he** ~**ed** das gehört aber mir, protestierte er.

(b) (*dispute*) *decision* protestieren gegen, Protest or Einspruch erheben gegen.

Protestant [ˈprɒtɪstənt] **1** *adj* protestantisch; (*esp in Germany*) evangelisch. **2** *n* Protestant(in *f*) *m*; Evangelische(r) *mf*.

Protestantism [ˈprɒtɪstəntɪzəm] *n* Protestantismus *m*.

protestation [ˌprɒteˈsteɪʃən] *n* (a) (*of love, loyalty etc*) Beteuerung *f*. (b) (*protest*) Protest *m*.

protester [prəˈtestəʳ] *n* Protestierende(r) *mf*; (*in demonstration*) Demonstrant(in *f*) *m*.

proto- [ˈprəʊtəʊ-] *pref* (*Chem*) proto-, Proto-; (*Ling*) ur-, Ur-.

protocol [ˈprəʊtəkɒl] *n* Protokoll *nt*.

protohistory [ˌprəʊtəʊˈhɪstərɪ] *n* Urgeschichte *f*.

proton [ˈprəʊtɒn] *n* Proton *nt*.

protoplasm [ˈprəʊtəʊplæzəm] *n* Protoplasma *nt*.

prototype [ˈprəʊtəʊtaɪp] *n* Prototyp *m*.

protozoan [ˌprəʊtəʊˈzəʊən] **1** *adj* einzellig. **2** *n* Protozoan (*spec*), Urtierchen *nt*.

protozoic [ˌprəʊtəʊˈzəʊɪk] *adj* einzellig.

protract [prəˈtrækt] *vt* hinausziehen, in die Länge ziehen; *illness* verlängern; *decision* hinauszögern.

protracted [prəˈtræktɪd] *adj illness* langwierig; *discussion, debate, negotiations also* sich hinziehend *attr*; *description* langgezogen; *absence, dispute* längere(r, s).

protraction [prəˈtrækʃən] *n* **that can only lead to the** ~ **of the discussion/illness** das kann nur dazu führen, daß sich die Diskussion/Krankheit hinzieht.

protractor [prəˈtræktəʳ] *n* (*Math*) Winkelmesser *m*.

protrude [prəˈtruːd] **1** *vi* (*out of, from* aus) vorstehen; (*eyes*) vortreten. **2** *vt* hervorstrecken, herausstrecken. **he** ~**d his gun slightly through the window** er schob sein Gewehr ein Stück durch die Fensteröffnung.

protruding [prəˈtruːdɪŋ] *adj* vorstehend; *rock, ledge, cliff also* herausragend; *eyes* vortretend; *forehead, chin* vorspringend.

protrusion [prəˈtruːʒən] *n* (a) (*protruding object*) Vorsprung *m*. (b) (*protruding*) (*of rock, buttress, teeth etc*) Vorstehen *nt*; (*of forehead, chin*) Vorspringen *nt*; (*of eyes*) Vortreten *nt*.

protrusive [prəˈtruːsɪv] *adj see* **protruding**.

protuberance [prəˈtjuːbərəns] *n* (*bulge*) Beule *f*; (*of stomach*) Vorstehen *nt*; (*of eyes*) Vortreten *nt*.

protuberant [prəˈtjuːbərənt] *adj* vorstehend; *eyes* vortretend.

proud [praʊd] **1** *adj* (a) *stolz* (*of auf +acc*). **it made his parents feel very** ~ das erfüllte seine Eltern mit Stolz; **to be** ~ **that ...** stolz (darauf) sein, daß ...; **to be** ~ **to do sth** stolz darauf sein, etw zu tun; **I hope you're** ~ **of yourself** (*iro*) ich hoffe, du bist stolz auf dich; **that's nothing to be** ~ **of** das ist nichts, worauf man stolz sein kann.

(b) (*projecting*) **to be** ~ (*nail etc*) heraus- or hervorragen; (*Typ: character*) erhaben sein; ~ **flesh** wildes Fleisch.

2 *adv* **to do sb/oneself** ~ jdn/sich verwöhnen.

proudly [ˈpraʊdlɪ] *adv* stolz.

provable [ˈpruːvəbl] *adj hypothesis, story* beweisbar; *guilt, innocence also* nachweisbar.

prove [pruːv] *pret* ~**d**, *ptp* ~**d** *or* **proven 1** *vt* (a) (*verify*) beweisen; *will* beglaubigen. **he** ~**d that she did it** er bewies or er wies nach, daß sie das getan hat; **to** ~ **sb innocent** or **sb's innocence** jds Unschuld beweisen or nachweisen; **to** ~ **something against sb** jdm etwas nachweisen; **this theory remains to be** ~**d** diese Theorie muß erst noch bewiesen werden; **whether his judgement was right remains to be** ~**d** es muß sich erst noch erweisen, ob seine Beurteilung zutrifft; **it all goes to** ~ **that ...** das beweist mal wieder, daß ...; **he was** ~**d right in the end** er hat schließlich doch recht behalten.

(b) (*test out, put to the proof*) *rifle, aircraft etc* erproben; *one's worth, courage* unter Beweis stellen, beweisen.

(c) (*Cook*) *dough* gehen lassen.

(d) *also vi* (*turn out*) **to** ~ (**to be**) **hot/useful etc** sich als heiß/nützlich *etc* erweisen; **if it** ~**s otherwise** wenn sich das Gegenteil herausstellt.

2 *vi* (a) (*Cook: dough*) gehen. (b) *see vt* (d).

3 *vr* (a) (*show one's value, courage etc*) sich bewähren.

(b) **to** ~ **oneself innocent/indispensable** *etc* sich als unschuldig/unentbehrlich *etc* erweisen; **to** ~ **oneself as sth** or **to be sth** sich als etw erweisen.

proven [ˈpruːvən] **1** *ptp of* **prove**. **2** [ˈprəʊvən] *adj* bewährt. **not** ~ (*Scot Jur*) unbewiesen.

provenance [ˈprɒvɪnəns] *n* Herkunft *f*, Ursprung *m*. **country of** ~ Herkunfts- *or* Ursprungsland *nt*.

provender [ˈprɒvɪndəʳ] *n* Futter *nt*.

proverb [ˈprɒvɜːb] *n* Sprichwort *nt*. (**the Book of**) **P**~**s** die Sprüche *pl*.

proverbial [prəˈvɜːbɪəl] *adj* (*lit, fig*) sprichwörtlich.

proverbially [prəˈvɜːbɪəlɪ] *adv* (*lit*) *express* in Form eines Sprichworts; (*fig*) sprichwörtlich.

provide [prəˈvaɪd] **1** *vt* (a) (*make available*) zur Verfügung stellen; *personnel* (*agency*) vermitteln; *money* bereitstellen; (*lay on, as part of service*) *chairs, materials, food etc* (zur Verfügung) stellen; (*see to, bring along*) *food, records etc* sorgen für; (*produce, give*) *ideas, specialist knowledge, electricity* liefern; *light, shade* spenden, geben; *privacy* sorgen für, schaffen; *topic of conversation* sorgen für, liefern. **X** ~**d the money and Y** (~**d**) **the expertise** X stellte das Geld bereit und Y lieferte das Fachwissen; **a local band** ~**d the music** eine örtliche Kapelle sorgte für die Musik; **candidates must** ~ **their own pens** die Kandidaten müssen ihr Schreibgerät selbst stellen.

(b) **to** ~ **sth for sb** etw für jdn stellen; (*make available*) jdm etw zur Verfügung stellen; (*find, supply: agency etc*) jdm etw besorgen; **to** ~ **food and clothes for one's family** für Nahrung und Kleidung seiner Familie sorgen; **I can't** ~ **enough chairs/food for everyone** ich kann nicht genug Stühle/Nahrung für alle stellen; **it** ~**s a certain amount of privacy/shade for the inhabitants** es schafft für die Bewohner eine gewisse Abgeschlossenheit/es spendet den Bewohnern etwas Schatten; **they** ~ **a restroom/bus for the use of their workers** sie stellen einen Ruheraum/Bus für ihre Arbeiter.

(c) **to** ~ **sb with sth** (*with food, clothing etc*) jdn mit etw versorgen; (*equip*) jdn mit etw versehen or ausstatten; (*with excuse, idea, answer*) jdm etw geben or liefern; (*with opportunity, information*) jdm etw verschaffen or geben or liefern; **the house was** ~**d with a garden/with running water** das Haus hatte einen Garten/fließendes Wasser; **the car was** ~**d with a radio** der Wagen war mit einem Radio ausgestattet; **this job** ~**d him with enough money/with the necessary overseas experience** die Stelle verschaffte ihm genug Geld/die nötige Auslandserfahrung; **this** ~**d the school with enough money to build a gymnasium** dadurch hatte die Schule genügend Geld zur Verfügung, um eine Turnhalle zu bauen.

(d) (*stipulate: clause, agreement*) vorsehen. **unless otherwise** ~**d** sofern nichts Gegenteiliges bestimmt ist; *see* **provided (that), providing (that)**.

2 *vi* **the Lord will** ~ (*prov*) der Herr wird's schon geben; **a husband who** ~**s well** ein Ehemann, der gut für seine Familie/Frau sorgt.

3 *vr* **to** ~ **oneself with sth** sich mit etw ausstatten; **to** ~ **oneself with a good excuse** sich (*dat*) eine gute Entschuldigung zurechtlegen.

♦**provide against** *vi* +*prep obj* vorsorgen für, Vorsorge or Vorkehrungen treffen für. **the law** ~**s** ~ **such abuses** das Gesetz schützt vor solchem Mißbrauch.

♦**provide for** *vi* +*prep obj* (a) *family etc* versorgen, sorgen für, Sorge tragen für. **he made sure that his family would be well** ~**d** ~ er stellte sicher, daß seine Familie gut versorgt war or daß für seine Familie gut gesorgt war.

(b) **the law/treaty** ~**s** ~ **penalties against abuses** bei Mißbrauch sieht das Gesetz/der Vertrag Strafe vor; **as** ~**d** ~ **in the 1970 contract** wie in dem Vertrag von 1970 vorgesehen; **we** ~**d** ~ **all emergencies** wir haben für alle Notfälle vorgesorgt; **we have** ~**d** ~ **an increase in costs of 25%** wir haben eine Kostensteigerung von 25% einkalkuliert; **the design of the house** ~**s** ~ **the later addition of a garage** im Entwurf des Hauses ist der spätere Anbau einer Garage vorgesehen.

provided (that) [prəˈvaɪdɪd(ˈðæt)] *conj* vorausgesetzt, gesetzt den Fall(, daß).

providence [ˈprɒvɪdəns] *n* (a) (*fate*) die Vorsehung. (b) (*dated: prudent thriftiness*) Vorsorge *f*. **his** ~ **in saving for his old age** sein vorsorgendes Sparen für das Alter.

provident [ˈprɒvɪdənt] *adj* vorsorglich, vorsorgend, vorausschauend. **his** ~ **care for the future** seine Vorsorge für die Zukunft; ~ **fund** Unterstützungskasse *f*; ~ **society** *private* Altersversicherung.

providential [ˌprɒvɪˈdenʃəl] *adj* (a) **God's** ~ **care** die göttliche Vorsehung. (b) (*lucky*) glücklich. **to be** ~ (**ein**) **Glück sein.

providentially [ˌprɒvɪˈdenʃəlɪ] *adv* (*luckily*) glücklicherweise. **it happened almost** ~ das war gleichsam die Fügung (des Schicksals).

providently [ˈprɒvɪdəntlɪ] *adv see* **provident**.

provider [prəˈvaɪdəʳ] *n* (*of family*) Ernährer(in *f*) *m*.

providing (that) [prəˈvaɪdɪŋ(ˈðæt)] *conj* vorausgesetzt(, daß), gesetzt den Fall(, daß).

province [ˈprɒvɪns] *n* (a) Provinz *f*.

(b) **the** ~**s** *pl* die Provinz.

(c) (*fig: area of knowledge, activity etc*) Gebiet *nt*, Bereich *m*. **it's not within my** ~ das fällt nicht in meinen Bereich or mein Gebiet; **it's outside the** ~ **of science** es liegt außerhalb des wissenschaftlichen Gebiets or Bereichs; **that is outside my** ~ das ist nicht mein Gebiet.

(d) (*area of authority*) Kompetenzbereich *m*. **that's not my** ~ dafür bin ich nicht zuständig.

provincial [prəˈvɪnʃəl] **1** *adj* Provinz-; *custom, accent* ländlich; (*pej*) provinzlerisch. ~ **narrowness** Engstirnigkeit *f*. **2** *n* Provinzbewohner(in *f*) *m*; (*pej*) Provinzler(in *f*) *m*.

provincialism [prəˈvɪnʃəlɪzəm] *n* Provinzialismus *m*.

proving ground [ˈpruːvɪŋˌgraʊnd] *n* (*for theory*) Versuchsfeld *nt*; (*situation: for sb, sb's abilities*) Bewährungsprobe *f*. **Belfast was his** ~ Belfast war für ihn die Bewährungsprobe.

provision [prəˈvɪʒən] **1** *n* (a) (*act of supplying*) (*for others*)

Bereitstellung f; (for one's own team, expedition etc) Beschaffung f; (of food, gas, water etc) Versorgung f (of mit, to sb jds).

(b) (supply) Vorrat m (of an +dat). **we had an ample ~ of reference books/houses** etc uns (dat) standen genügend Nachschlagewerke/Häuser etc zur Verfügung.

(c) ~s (food) Lebensmittel pl; (Mil, for journey, expedition) Verpflegung f, Proviant m; ~s ship Versorgungsschiff nt.

(d) (allowance) Berücksichtigung f; (arrangement) Vorkehrung f; (stipulation) Bestimmung f. **with the ~ that ...** mit dem Vorbehalt or der Bedingung, daß ...; **is there no ~ for such cases in the legislation?** sind solche Fälle im Gesetz nicht berücksichtigt or vorgesehen?; **there's no ~ for later additions** spätere Erweiterungen sind nicht vorgesehen; **to make ~ for sb/one's family/the future** für jdn/für seine Familie/für die Zukunft Vorsorge or Vorkehrungen treffen; **to make ~ for sth** etw vorsehen; (in legislation, rules also) etw berücksichtigen; **for margin of error etc** etw einkalkulieren; **our figures make ~ for a 5% error** in unseren Zahlen ist eine Fehlerquote von 5% einkalkuliert; **the council made ~ for recreation** die Stadt hat Freizeiteinrichtungen geschaffen; **to make ~ against sth** gegen etw Vorkehrungen treffen.

2 vt die Verpflegung liefern für; expedition verproviantieren; troops (mit Proviant) beliefern or versorgen.

provisional [prə'vɪʒənl] **1** adj provisorisch; measures, solution also, offer, acceptance, decision, legislation vorläufig. **~ driving licence** (Brit) vorläufige Fahrerlaubnis für Fahrschüler; **the ~ IRA** see n. **2** n (Ir Pol) **the P~s** Mitglieder pl der provisorischen irisch-republikanischen Armee.

provisionally [prə'vɪʒnəlɪ] adv vorläufig; appoint also provisorisch.

proviso [prə'vaɪzəʊ] n (condition) Vorbehalt m, Bedingung f; (clause) Vorbehaltsklausel f. **he made several ~s** er hat mehrere Bedingungen gestellt.

provisory [prə'vaɪzərɪ] adj (a) (with a proviso) vorbehaltlich. a **~ clause** eine Vorbehaltsklausel. (b) see provisional 1.

Provo [prəʊvəʊ] n (Ir Pol) see provisional 2.

provocation [ˌprɒvə'keɪʃən] n Provokation, Herausforderung f. **what ~ was there for you to hit him?** was hat dich dazu provoziert, ihn zu schlagen?; **he acted under ~** er wurde dazu provoziert or herausgefordert; **his deliberate ~ of a quarrel** seine bewußte Herbeiführung eines Streits; **to suffer great ~** sehr stark provoziert werden; **at the slightest ~** bei der geringsten Provokation or Herausforderung; **he hit me without any ~** er hat mich geschlagen, ohne daß ich ihn dazu provoziert hätte.

provocative [prə'vɒkətɪv] adj provozierend, provokatorisch; remark, behaviour also herausfordernd; dress provozierend. **he's just trying to be ~** er versucht nur zu provozieren.

provocatively [prə'vɒkətɪvlɪ] adv see adj.

provoke [prə'vəʊk] vt sb provozieren, reizen, herausfordern; animal reizen; reaction, anger, criticism, dismay, smile hervorrufen; lust, pity erwecken, erregen; reply, dispute provozieren; discussion, revolt, showdown herbeiführen, auslösen. **to ~ a quarrel or an argument** (person) Streit suchen; (action) zu einem Streit führen; **to ~ sb into doing sth or to do sth** jdn dazu bringen, etw zu tun; (taunt) jdn dazu treiben or so provozieren, daß er etw tut; **it ~d us to action** das hat uns zum Handeln veranlaßt.

provoking [prə'vəʊkɪŋ] adj provozierend; (annoying) fact, circumstance ärgerlich. a **~ child** ein Kind, das einen reizt; **how very ~!** wie ärgerlich!

provokingly [prə'vəʊkɪŋlɪ] adv provozierend. **most ~, it was cancelled** ärgerlicherweise wurde es abgesagt.

provost ['prɒvəst] n (a) (Scot) Bürgermeister m. (b) (Univ) = Dekan m. (c) (Eccl) Propst m.

provost marshal [prə'vəʊst'mɑːʃəl] n Kommandeur m der Militärpolizei.

prow [praʊ] n Bug m.

prowess ['praʊɪs] n (skill) Fähigkeiten pl, Können nt; (courage) Tapferkeit f. **his** (sexual) **~** seine Potenz, seine Manneskraft.

prowl [praʊl] **1** n Streifzug m. **to be on the ~** (cat, lion, burglar) auf Streifzug sein; (headmaster, boss) herumschleichen; (police car) auf Streife sein; (inf: for pick-up) auf Frauen-/Männerjagd sein.

2 vt durchstreifen.

3 vi (also ~ about or around) herumstreichen; (of boss, headmaster) herumschleichen. **he's always ~ing round the clubs** er streicht immer um die Klubs herum.

prowl car n (US) Streifenwagen m.

prowler ['praʊləʳ] n Herumtreiber(in f) m; (peeping Tom) Spanner m (inf). **he heard a ~ outside** er hörte, wie draußen jemand herumschlich.

prox [prɒks] abbr of proximo.

proximity [prɒk'sɪmɪtɪ] n Nähe f. **in ~/in close ~ to** in der Nähe (+gen)/in unmittelbarer Nähe (+gen); **~ in age** geringer Altersunterschied; **the ~ of their relationship** ihre enge Verwandtschaft.

proximo ['prɒksɪməʊ] adv (Comm) (des) nächsten Monats.

proxy ['prɒksɪ] n (power, document) (Handlungs)vollmacht f; (person) Stellvertreter(in f) m. **by ~** durch einen Stellvertreter; **to be married by ~** ferngetraut werden; **~ vote** stellvertretend abgegebene Stimme.

prude [pruːd] n **to be a ~** prüde sein; **only ~s would object to that** nur prüde Leute würden sich daran stoßen.

prudence ['pruːdəns] n see adj Umsicht f; Klugheit f; Überlegtheit f. **simple ~ should have made you stop** der gesunde Menschenverstand hätte Sie davon abbringen müssen.

prudent ['pruːdənt] adj person umsichtig; measure, action, decision klug; answer wohlüberlegt. **I thought it ~ to change the subject** ich hielt es für klüger, das Thema zu wechseln; **how ~!** sehr klug or weise!

prudently ['pruːdəntlɪ] adv wohlweislich; act umsichtig; answer überlegt.

prudery ['pruːdərɪ] n Prüderie f.

prudish ['pruːdɪʃ] adj prüde; clothes sittsam, züchtig.

prudishly ['pruːdɪʃlɪ] adv see adj. **they ~ cut out all the swearwords** prüde wie sie sind, haben sie alle Schimpfwörter gestrichen.

prudishness ['pruːdɪʃnɪs] n (prudish behaviour) Prüderie f; (prudish nature) prüde Art; (of clothes) Sittsamkeit f.

prune[1] [pruːn] n Backpflaume f; (inf: person) Muffel m (inf).

prune[2] vt (also ~ down) beschneiden, stutzen; hedge schneiden, zurechtstutzen; (fig) expenditure kürzen; workforce reduzieren; firm schrumpfen lassen; book, essay zusammenstreichen, kürzen. **to ~ away** ab- or wegschneiden; unnecessary details, verbiage etc wegstreichen; **to ~ an essay of** superfluous matter einen Aufsatz straffen.

pruners ['pruːnəz] npl Gartenschere, Rebschere f.

pruning ['pruːnɪŋ] n see vt Beschneiden, Stutzen nt; Schneiden, Zurechtstutzen nt; Kürzung f; Reduzierung f; Schrumpfung f; Zusammenstreichen nt. **the tree needs ~** der Baum muß beschnitten or gestutzt werden.

pruning: **~ hook** n Rebmesser nt; **~ knife** n Gartenmesser nt, Hippe f; **~ shears** npl Gartenschere, Rebschere f.

prurience ['prʊərɪəns] n see adj Anzüglichkeit, Schlüpfrigkeit f; Schwüle f (geh); Lüsternheit, Geilheit f.

prurient ['prʊərɪənt] adj anzüglich, schlüpfrig; imagination also schwül (geh); person lüstern, geil.

Prussia ['prʌʃə] n Preußen nt.

Prussian ['prʌʃən] **1** adj preußisch. **~ blue** preußischblau. **2** n (a) Preuße m, Preußin f. (b) (language) Preußisch nt. **Old ~** Altpreußisch nt.

prussic acid ['prʌsɪk'æsɪd] n Blausäure f.

pry[1] [praɪ] vi neugierig sein; (in drawers etc) (herum)schnüffeln (in in +dat). **I don't mean to ~, but ...** es geht mich ja nichts an, aber ...; **to ~ into sb's affairs** seine Nase in jds Angelegenheiten (acc) stecken; **to ~ into sb's secrets** jds Geheimnisse ausspionieren wollen; **to ~ about** herumschnüffeln.

pry[2] vt (US) see prise.

prying ['praɪɪŋ] adj neugierig.

PS abbr of postscript PS.

psalm [sɑːm] n Psalm m. **(the Book of) P~s** der Psalter; **~ book** Psalmenbuch nt.

psalmist ['sɑːmɪst] n Psalmist m.

psalmody ['sælmədɪ] n Psalmodie f.

psalter ['sɔːltəʳ] n Psalter m.

psaltery ['sɔːltərɪ] n Psalterium nt.

psephology [se'fɒlədʒɪ] n Wahlanalytik f.

pseud [sjuːd] (inf) **1** n Möchtegern m (inf). **you ~!** du Angeber(in)!

2 adj book, film auf intellektuell gemacht (inf), gewollt; views, ideas hochgestochen; décor, pub etc auf schick gemacht (inf); person affektiert; pseudointellektuell. **it's all so terribly ~** das ist alles so gewollt, das ist doch alles auf Schau gemacht (inf); **some of his friends are a bit ~** einige seiner Freunde machen wirklich nur auf Schau (inf).

pseudo ['sjuːdəʊ] (inf) **1** adj (a) (pretentious) see pseud 2. (b) (pretended) unecht; affection, simplicity aufgesetzt; revolutionary, intellectual etc Möchtegern- (inf), Pseudo-. **2** n see pseud 1.

pseudo- pref Pseudo-, pseudo.

pseudonym ['sjuːdənɪm] n Pseudonym nt.

pseudy ['sjuːdɪ] adj (+er) (inf) see pseud 2.

pshaw [pʃɔː] interj (dated) pah.

psittacosis [ˌpsɪtə'kəʊsɪs] n Papageienkrankheit, Psittakose (spec) f.

psoriasis [sɒ'raɪəsɪs] n Schuppenflechte, Psoriasis (spec) f.

PST abbr of Pacific Standard Time.

psych(e) [saɪk] (sl) **1** vt (a) (psychoanalyst) analysieren. (b) (understand, get taped) **to ~ sb** (out), to get sb ~ed (out) jdn durchschauen. (c) **to ~ oneself up**, to get oneself ~ed up sich hochputschen; **he was all ~ed up for the match** er hatte sich für das Spiel so richtig hochgeputscht. **2** vi **to ~ out** ausflippen (inf).

Psyche ['saɪkɪ] n (Myth) Psyche f.

psyche ['saɪkɪ] n Psyche f.

psychedelic [ˌsaɪkɪ'delɪk] adj psychedelisch; drugs also bewußtseinserweiternd.

psychiatric [ˌsaɪkɪ'ætrɪk] adj psychiatrisch; illness psychisch.

psychiatrist [saɪ'kaɪətrɪst] n Psychiater(in f) m.

psychiatry [saɪ'kaɪətrɪ] n Psychiatrie f.

psychic ['saɪkɪk] **1** adj übersinnlich; powers übernatürlich. **~ research** Parapsychologie f; **she is ~** sie besitzt übernatürliche Kräfte or übersinnliche Wahrnehmung; **you must be ~!** Sie müssen hellsehen können! **2** n Mensch m mit übernatürlichen Kräften or übersinnlicher Wahrnehmung.

psychical ['saɪkɪkl] adj see psychic 1.

psycho ['saɪkəʊ] n (US inf) Verrückte(r) mf.

psychoanalyse, (US) psychoanalyze [ˌsaɪkəʊ'ænəlaɪz] vt psychoanalytisch behandeln, psychoanalysieren.

psychoanalysis [ˌsaɪkəʊə'nælɪsɪs] n Psychoanalyse f.

psychoanalyst [ˌsaɪkəʊ'ænəlɪst] n Psychoanalytiker(in f) m.

psycholinguistic [ˌsaɪkəʊlɪŋ'gwɪstɪk] adj psycholinguistisch.

psycholinguistics [ˌsaɪkəʊlɪŋ'gwɪstɪks] n sing Psycholinguistik f.

psychological [ˌsaɪkə'lɒdʒɪkəl] adj (mental) psychisch; (concerning psychology) psychologisch. **~ moment** der psychologisch günstige Augenblick; **~ warfare** psychologische Kriegsführung; **he's not really ill, it's all ~** er ist nicht wirklich krank, das ist alles nur Einbildung; **it's all ~, you get further that way** das ist Psychologie, damit erreicht man mehr.

psychologically [ˌsaɪkə'lɒdʒɪkəlɪ] adv see adj. he is ~ unstable er ist psychisch sehr unausgeglichen.

psychologist [saɪ'kɒlədʒɪst] n Psychologe m, Psychologin f.

psychology [saɪ'kɒlədʒɪ] n (science) Psychologie f; (make-up) Psyche f. it's all a matter of ~ (inf) das ist alles eine Frage der Psychologie.

psychometrics [ˌsaɪkəʊ'metrɪks] n sing, **psychometry** [saɪ'kɒmɪtrɪ] n Psychometrie f.

psychopath ['saɪkəʊpæθ] n Psychopath(in f) m.

psychopathic [ˌsaɪkəʊ'pæθɪk] adj psychopathisch.

psychopharmacology [ˌsaɪkəʊˌfɑːmə'kɒlədʒɪ] n Psychopharmakologie, Pharmakopsychologie f.

psychophysics [ˌsaɪkəʊ'fɪzɪks] n sing Psychophysik f.

psychophysiology [ˌsaɪkəʊˌfɪzɪ'ɒlədʒɪ] n Psychophysiologie f.

psychosexual [ˌsaɪkəʊ'seksjʊəl] adj psychosexuell.

psychosis [saɪ'kəʊsɪs] n, pl **psychoses** [saɪ'kəʊsiːz] Psychose f.

psychosocial [ˌsaɪkəʊ'səʊʃəl] adj psychosozial.

psychosociological [ˌsaɪkəʊˌsəʊsɪə'lɒdʒɪkəl] adj psychosoziologisch.

psychosomatic [ˌsaɪkəʊsəʊ'mætɪk] adj psychosomatisch. ~ medicine Psychosomatik f, psychosomatische Medizin.

psychosurgery [ˌsaɪkəʊ'sɜːdʒərɪ] n Gehirnchirurgie f.

psychotherapist [ˌsaɪkəʊ'θerəpɪst] n Psychotherapeut(in f) m.

psychotherapy [ˌsaɪkəʊ'θerəpɪ] n Psychotherapie f.

psychotic [saɪ'kɒtɪk] 1 adj psychotisch. ~ illness Psychose f. 2 n Psychotiker(in f) m.

PT abbr of **physical training**.

pt abbr of **part; pint; payment; point** Pkt.

PTA abbr of **parent-teacher association** Lehrer-Eltern-Ausschuß m.

ptarmigan ['tɑːmɪgən] n Schneehuhn nt.

Pte (Mil) abbr of **Private**.

pterodactyl [ˌterəʊ'dæktɪl] n Pterodactylus m.

pto abbr of **please turn over** bitte wenden, b.w.

Ptolemaic [ˌtɒlə'meɪɪk] adj ptolemäisch. ~ system ptolemäisches Weltbild or (Welt)system.

Ptolemy ['tɒləmɪ] n (astronomer) Ptolemäus m; (king) Ptolemaois m; (dynasty) Ptolemäer pl.

ptomaine ['təʊmeɪn] n Leichengift, Ptomain (spec) nt. ~ poisoning Leichenvergiftung f.

pub [pʌb] n (Brit) Kneipe (inf), Wirtschaft f, Lokal nt; (in the country) Gasthaus, Wirtshaus nt. let's go to the ~ komm, wir gehen einen trinken or wir gehen in die Kneipe (inf); ~ grub/lunch in Trinkgaststätten servierter Imbiß.

pub-crawl ['pʌbkrɔːl] n (inf) Kneipenbummel m (inf). to go on a ~ einen Kneipenbummel machen (inf), einen Zug durch die Gemeinde machen (hum inf).

puberty ['pjuːbətɪ] n die Pubertät. to reach the age of ~ ins Pubertätsalter or in die Pubertät kommen.

pubes ['pjuːbiːz] pl of **pubis**.

pubescence [pjuː'besəns] n die Pubertät.

pubescent [pjuː'besənt] adj pubertierend.

pubic ['pjuːbɪk] adj Scham-.

pubis ['pjuːbɪs] n, pl **pubes** Schambein nt.

public ['pʌblɪk] 1 adj öffentlich; health, library also Volks-; spending, debts der öffentlichen Hand, Staats-. to be ~ knowledge ein öffentliches Geheimnis sein; to become ~ publik werden; at the ~ expense aus öffentlichen Mitteln; it's rather ~ here es ist nicht gerade privat hier; he is a ~ figure or person er ist eine Persönlichkeit des öffentlichen Lebens; in the ~ eye im Blickpunkt der Öffentlichkeit; to make sth ~ etw bekanntgeben, etw publik machen; (officially) etw öffentlich bekanntmachen; to go ~ (Comm) in eine Aktiengesellschaft umgewandelt werden.

2 n sing or pl Öffentlichkeit f. in ~ in der Öffentlichkeit; speak also, agree, admit öffentlich; our/their etc ~ unser/ihr etc Publikum; the reading/sporting/theatre-going ~ die lesende/sportinteressierte/theaterinteressierte Öffentlichkeit; the racing ~ die Freunde pl des Rennsports; the great American/British ~ (iro) die breite amerikanische/britische Öffentlichkeit.

public address system n Lautsprecheranlage f.

publican ['pʌblɪkən] n (a) (Brit) Gastwirt(in f) m. (b) (old: tax-collector) Zöllner m.

public assistance n (US) staatliche Fürsorge.

publication [ˌpʌblɪ'keɪʃən] n Veröffentlichung, Publikation (geh) f. ~ date Erscheinungsdatum nt, Datum nt der Veröffentlichung; when's ~? wann erscheint das Buch?

public: ~ **bar** n = Ausschank m, Schenke f, Schwemme f (inf); ~ **building** n öffentliches Gebäude; ~ **company** n Aktiengesellschaft f; ~ **convenience** n öffentliche Bedürfnisanstalt (form); ~ **debt** n (esp US) Verschuldung f der öffentlichen Hand; (national debt) Staatsverschuldung f; ~ **defender** n (US) Pflichtverteidiger(in f) m; ~ **domain** n (US) (a) (land) Domäne f; (b) (unpatented status) this book/invention will soon become ~ domain das Copyright für dieses Buch/das Patent für diese Erfindung läuft bald ab; ~ **enemy** n Staatsfeind m; ~ **enemy number one** Staatsfeind Nr. 1; ~ **holiday** n gesetzlicher Feiertag; ~ **house** n (Brit form) Gaststätte f.

publicist ['pʌblɪsɪst] n Publizist(in f) m.

publicity [pʌb'lɪsɪtɪ] n (a) Publicity f. (b) (Comm: advertising, advertisements) Werbung, Reklame f. a whole sheaf of ~ ein ganzer Stoß Reklame; we must get out some more ~ for this product wir müssen mehr Werbung für dieses Produkt treiben.

publicity: ~ **agent** n Publicitymanager m; ~ **campaign** n Publicitykampagne f; (Comm) Werbekampagne f; ~ **material** n Publicitymaterial nt; (Comm) Werbematerial nt.

publicize ['pʌblɪsaɪz] vt (a) (make public) bekanntmachen, an die Öffentlichkeit bringen. I don't want this ~d ich möchte nicht, daß das publik wird; I don't ~ the fact ich will das nicht an die große Glocke hängen (inf).

(b) (get publicity for) film, author Publicity machen für; new product also Werbung treiben or Reklame machen für. it has been well ~d es hat viel Publicity bekommen; dafür ist viel Werbung getrieben or Reklame gemacht worden.

public law n öffentliches Recht.

publicly ['pʌblɪklɪ] adv öffentlich. this factory is ~ owned diese Fabrik ist Gemeineigentum.

public: ~ **money** n öffentliche Gelder pl; ~ **opinion** n die öffentliche Meinung; ~ **opinion poll** n Meinungsumfrage f; ~ **ownership** n öffentlicher Besitz; under ~ ownership in öffentlichem Besitz; ~ **prosecutor** n Staatsanwalt m/-anwältin f; ~ **purse** n Staatskasse f, Staatssäckel m (inf); **P~ Record(s) Office** n (Brit) Nationalarchiv nt; Bundeszentralarchiv nt (BRD); ~ **relations** n pl Public Relations pl; (b) sing (area of work also) Öffentlichkeitsarbeit f; ~ **relations officer** n Pressesprecher(in f) m; ~ **school** n (Brit) Privatschule, Public School f; (US) staatliche Schule; ~ **schoolboy** n (Brit) Schüler m einer Privatschule; ~ **schoolgirl** n (Brit) Schülerin f einer Privatschule; ~ **sector** n öffentlicher Sektor; ~ **servant** n Arbeitnehmer(in f) m im öffentlichen Dienst; ~ **service** n (Civil Service) öffentlicher Dienst; (facility: water, transport etc) öffentlicher Dienstleistungsbetrieb; (benefit) Dienst m an der Allgemeinheit; ~ **service vehicle** n öffentliches Verkehrsmittel; ~ **speaker** n Redner(in f) m; ~ **speaking** n Redenhalten nt; a course in ~ speaking ein Rednerlehrgang m; I'm no good at ~ speaking ich kann nicht in der Öffentlichkeit reden; ~ **spirit** n Gemeinsinn m; ~**-spirited** adj act, attitude gemeinsinnig (geh), die von Gemeinschaftssinn zeugt; it's not very ~-**spirited** of them to ... es spricht nicht gerade für ihren Gemeinschaftssinn, daß sie ...; ~ **transport** n öffentliche Verkehrsmittel pl; ~ **utility** n öffentlicher Versorgungsbetrieb; ~ **works** npl staatliche Bauvorhaben pl.

publish ['pʌblɪʃ] 1 vt (a) (issue) veröffentlichen; book, magazine etc also herausbringen; research, thesis also publizieren. ~ed by Collins bei Collins or im Verlag Collins erschienen; "~ed monthly", "erscheint monatlich"; "just ~ed" "neu erschienen"; "to be ~ed shortly" "erscheint in Kürze"; who ~es that book? in welchem Verlag ist das Buch erschienen?; they ~ novels sie verlegen Romane.

(b) (make public) news, banns veröffentlichen, bekanntgeben; decree herausgeben; will eröffnen. to ~ sth abroad etw überall herumerzählen.

2 vi the magazine ~es on Tuesdays das Magazin erscheint dienstags; when are we going to ~? (book) wann bringen wir das Buch heraus?; (research) wann veröffentlichen or publizieren wir die Arbeit?; he used to ~ with Collins er hat seine Bücher früher bei Collins herausgebracht or veröffentlicht.

publisher ['pʌblɪʃə] n (person) Verleger(in f) m; (firm: also ~s) Verlag m. who are your ~s? wer ist Ihr Verleger?

publishing ['pʌblɪʃɪŋ] n (trade) das Verlagswesen. ~ company Verlagshaus nt; the decline of children's book ~ der Rückgang bei den Kinderbüchern.

puce [pjuːs] 1 n Braunrot nt. 2 adj braunrot; (fig: with rage, shame) rot.

puck¹ [pʌk] n (goblin) Kobold, Puck m.

puck² n (Sport) Puck m.

pucker ['pʌkə] 1 n (in cloth) Fältchen nt.

2 vt (also ~ up) one's lips, mouth verziehen; (for kissing) spitzen; one's brow runzeln; material Falten machen in (+acc).

3 vi (also ~ up) (lips) sich verziehen; (to be kissed) spitzen; (brow) sich runzeln; (material) Falten werfen.

puckish adj, ~**ly** adv ['pʌkɪʃ, -lɪ] koboldhaft.

pud [pʊd] n (inf) see **pudding**.

pudding ['pʊdɪŋ] n (a) (dessert) Nachspeise f; (crème caramel, instant whip etc) Pudding m. what's for ~? was gibt es als Nachspeise or Nachtisch? (b) (savoury: meat in suet) = (Fleisch)pastete f. black ~ = Blutwurst f; white ~ = Preßsack m. (c) (inf) (idiot) Knallkopp m (inf); (fatty) Dickerchen nt.

pudding: ~ **basin** n Puddingform f; ~**-basin haircut** n (Koch-)topfschnitt m (inf); ~ **club** n to be in the ~ club (sl) einen dicken Bauch haben (inf); ~**-face** n (inf) Vollmondgesicht nt (inf); ~**-head** n (inf) Knallkopp m (inf); ~ **stone** n Puddingstein m.

puddle ['pʌdl] n Pfütze f (also euph).

pudendum [pjuː'dendəm] n, pl **pudenda** [pjuː'dendə] (a) (of woman) Vulva f. (b) **pudenda** pl (of either sex) primäre Geschlechtsmerkmale pl, Scham f (geh).

pudgy ['pʌdʒɪ] adj (+er) see **podgy**.

puerile ['pjʊəraɪl] adj infantil.

puerility [pjʊə'rɪlɪtɪ] n Infantilität f.

puerperal fever [pjuː'ɜːpərəl'fiːvə] n Kindbettfieber, Puerperalfieber (spec) nt.

Puerto Rican ['pwɜːtəʊ'riːkən] 1 adj puertoricanisch, portorikanisch. 2 n (person) Puertoricaner(in f), Portorikaner(in f) m.

Puerto Rico ['pwɜːtəʊ'riːkəʊ] n Puerto Rico, Porto Rico nt.

puff [pʌf] 1 n (a) (of breathing, of engine) Schnaufen nt no pl; (of horse) Schnauben nt no pl; (inf: breath) Puste f (inf); (on cigarette etc) Zug m (at, of an +dat). a ~ of air/wind ein Luft-/Windstoß m; a ~ of air from the bellows ein wenig Luft aus dem Blasebalg; a ~ of smoke eine Rauchwolke; our hopes vanished in a ~ of smoke unsere Hoffnungen lösten sich in nichts auf; he blew out the candles with or in one ~ er blies die Kerzen auf einmal aus; to be out of ~ (inf) außer Puste sein (inf).

(b) (powder ~) Quaste f.

(c) (Cook) cream ~ Windbeutel m; jam ~ Blätterteigteilchen nt mit Marmelade; ~ pastry, (US) ~ paste Blätterteig m.

(d) (inf: advertisement) Schmus m (inf). to give sb/sth a ~ jdn/etw hochjubeln (inf).

2 vt (a) smoke ausstoßen; cigarette, cigar paffen (inf). to ~ sth away/down etw wegblasen/umblasen; stop ~ing smoke in my face blas mir nicht dauernd den Rauch ins Gesicht.

(b) (praise) hochjubeln (inf).

(c) (*Sew*) bauschen. ~ed sleeves Puffärmel *pl*.
(d) (*Cook*) to ~ rice Puffreis herstellen.
3 *vi* (*person, train*) schnaufen; (*horse*) schnauben; (*wind*) blasen; (*chimney, smoke*) qualmen. he was ~ing and panting er pustete und schnaufte; the train ~ed into the station der Zug fuhr schnaufend in den Bahnhof ein; to ~ (away) at *or* on a cigar an einer Zigarre paffen.

♦**puff out** *vt sep* **(a)** (*expand*) chest herausstrecken, herausdrücken; cheeks aufblasen; feathers (auf)plustern; sail blähen. **(b)** (*emit*) air, smoke ausstoßen; words hervorstoßen. **(c)** (*blow out*) auspusten. **(d)** (*inf*) always separate (make out of breath) außer Puste bringen (*inf*).

♦**puff up 1** *vt sep* **(a)** feathers (auf)plustern; (*blow up*) aufblasen. **(b)** (*fig*) to get/be ~ed ~ sich aufblasen; to be ~ed ~ with pride ganz aufgeblasen sein. **2** *vi* **(a)** (*swell: eyes, face etc*) anschwellen. **(b)** he came ~ing ~ to me er kam angeschnauft.

puff: ~-adder *n* Puffotter *f*; ~-ball *n* (*Bot*) Bovist *m*.
puffed [pʌft] *adj* (*inf*) außer Puste (*inf*).
puffer ['pʌfə^r] *n* (*baby-talk: train*) Puffpuff *f* (*baby-talk*).
puffin ['pʌfɪn] *n* Papageientaucher, Lund *m*.
puffiness ['pʌfɪnɪs] *n* Verschwollenheit *f*.
puff: ~-puff *n* (*baby-talk*) (*train*) Puffpuff *f* (*baby-talk*); (*sound*) Puffpuff *nt*; ~ sleeve *n* Puffärmel *m*.
puffy ['pʌfɪ] *adj* (+*er*) (*swollen*) geschwollen; face, eyes also verschwollen; (*from crying*) verquollen.
pug [pʌg] *n* (*also* ~ dog) Mops *m*.
pugilism ['pjuːdʒɪlɪzəm] *n* (*form*) Faustkampf *m*.
pugilist ['pjuːdʒɪlɪst] *n* (*form*) Faustkämpfer *m*.
pugnacious [pʌgˈneɪʃəs] *adj* kampfeslustig; (*verbally*) streitsüchtig; expression, remark also herausfordernd; support, defence hartnäckig; dog, campaign aggressiv.
pugnaciously [pʌgˈneɪʃəslɪ] *adv* see adj.
pugnacity [pʌgˈnæsɪtɪ] *n* see adj Kampfeslust *f*; Streitsüchtigkeit *f*; Herausforderung *f* (*of in* +*dat*); Hartnäckigkeit *f*; Aggressivität *f*. the ~ of his remarks die aus seinen Bemerkungen klingende Streitsucht.
pug: ~ nose *n* Knollennase *f*; ~-nosed *adj* knollennasig.
puke [pjuːk] *vti* (*sl*) kotzen (*sl*), spucken (*inf*). to ~ all over sth (*sl*) etw vollkotzen; he makes me ~ er kotzt mich an (*sl*).
pukey ['pjuːkɪ] *adj* (*sl*) colour Kack- (*sl*), eklig (*inf*).
pukka, pucka ['pʌkə] *adj* (*inf*) (*genuine*) echt; Original-; (*proper*) anständig (*inf*); (*excellent*) eine *a* (*inf*), erstklassig; (*posh, upper-class*) vornehm. ~ sahib Gentleman *m*.
pulchritude ['pʌlkrɪtjuːd] *n* (*liter*) Schönheit *f*.
pull [pʊl] **1** *n* **(a)** (*tug*) Ziehen *nt*; (*short*) Ruck *m*; (*lit, fig: attraction*) Anziehungskraft *f*; (*of current*) Sog *m*. he gave her/the rope a ~ er zog sie/am Seil; he gave her hair a ~ er zog sie an den Haaren; I felt a ~ at my sleeve ich spürte, wie mich jemand am Ärmel zog; the ~ of family ties brought him home again familiäre Bande zogen ihn wieder nach Hause; shall I take a ~ (at the oars)? soll ich mal rudern?)
(b) (*uphill journey*) Anstieg *m*.
(c) (*inf: influence*) Beziehungen *pl* (*with* zu). she has ~ with the manager sie kann beim Chef was erreichen (*inf*); he has ~ in the right places er hat an den richtigen Stellen seine Leute sitzen.
(d) (*at pipe, beer*) Zug *m*. he took a ~ at his pipe/glass er zog an seiner Pfeife/nahm einen Schluck aus seinem Glas.
(e) bell ~ Klingelzug *m*; beer ~ Bierpumpengriff *m*.
(f) (*Typ: proof*) Abzug *m*.
2 *vt* **(a)** (*draw, drag*) ziehen. he ~ed the dog behind him er zog den Hund hinter sich (*dat*) her; to ~ a door shut eine Tür zuziehen; he ~ed her towards him er zog sie an sich (*acc*).
(b) (*tug*) handle, rope, bell ziehen an (+*dat*); boat rudern. he ~ed her hair er zog sie an den Haaren; to ~ sth to pieces (*lit*) etw zerreißen, etw in Stücke reißen; (*fig: criticize*) etw verreißen; to ~ sb's leg (*inf*) jdn auf den Arm nehmen (*inf*); ~ the other one (, it's got bells on) (*inf*) das glaubst du ja selber nicht!, das kannst du deiner Großmutter erzählen! (*inf*); she was the one ~ing the strings or wires sie ließ alle nach ihrer Pfeife tanzen; to ~ rank (on sb) (jdm gegenüber) den Vorgesetzten herauskehren; to ~ one's punches (*Boxing*) verhalten schlagen; (*fig*) sich zurückhalten; when it came to criticizing other people he didn't ~ his *or* any punches wenn es darum ging, andere zu kritisieren, zog er ganz schön vom Leder (*inf*).
(c) (*extract, draw out*) tooth, cork (heraus)ziehen; gun, knife ziehen; weeds, lettuce herausziehen; beer zapfen (*Cook*) chicken ausnehmen. to ~ a gun on sb die Pistole ziehen, jdn mit der Pistole bedrohen.
(d) (*strain*) muscle sich (*dat*) zerren; (*tear*) thread ziehen.
(e) (*attract*) crowd anziehen. a sports car always ~s the girls (*inf*) mit einem Sportwagen kommt man leichter an die Mädchen ran (*inf*).
(f) (*inf: carry out, do*) deal durchziehen (*inf*); (*criminal job*) drehen (*inf*). what are you trying to ~? (*inf*) was heckst du wieder aus? (*inf*).
(g) (*Typ*) to ~ a proof einen Abzug machen.
(h) (*Golf, Cricket, Baseball*) verziehen, auf die der Schlaghand entgegengesetzte Seite schlagen.
3 *vi* **(a)** ziehen (*on, at* an +*dat*). to ~ to the left/right (*car, brakes*) nach links/rechts ziehen; the car/engine isn't ~ing very well der Wagen/Motor zieht nicht richtig; to ~ on *or* at one's cigarette an seiner Zigarette ziehen; to ~ for sb/sth (*US inf*) jdn/etw unterstützen.
(b) (*move: train, car etc*) fahren. the car ~ed into the driveway der Wagen fuhr in die Einfahrt; he ~ed across to the left-hand lane er wechselte auf die linke Spur über; to ~ alongside seitlich heranfahren; (*Naut*) längsseits kommen; at the last moment he ~ed clear of the obstacle im letzten Moment zog er an dem Hindernis vorbei; the oarsmen ~ed for *or* towards the shore die Ruderer hielten auf das Ufer zu; to ~

ahead (of sb) (*car, runner*) (an jdm) vorbeiziehen; (*fig: rival etc*) jdn hinter sich (*dat*) lassen.
♦**pull about** *vt sep* (*handle roughly*) toy etc herumzerren; person herumzerren an (+*dat*).
♦**pull apart 1** *vt sep* **(a)** (*separate*) auseinanderziehen; sheets of paper also, fighting people trennen; radio etc auseinandernehmen. **(b)** (*fig inf*) (*search thoroughly*) auseinandernehmen (*inf*); (*criticize also*) verreißen. **2** *vi* (*through design*) sich auseinandernehmen lassen; (*break*) auseinandergehen.
♦**pull away 1** *vt sep* wegziehen. she ~ed it ~ from him sie zog es von ihm weg; (*from his hands*) sie zog es ihm aus den Händen. **2** *vi* (*move off*) wegfahren; (*ship*) ablegen. the car/runner ~ed ~ from the others der Wagen/Läufer setzte sich (von den anderen) ab.
♦**pull back 1** *vt sep* zurückziehen. **2** *vi* (*lit*) sich zurückziehen. to ~ ~ (from doing sth) (*fig*) einen Rückzieher machen (und etw nicht tun) (*inf*); he ~ed ~ from his offer/promise er zog sein Angebot/Versprechen zurück.
♦**pull down 1** *vt sep* **(a)** herunterziehen. he ~ed his hat ~ over his eyes er zog sich (*dat*) den Hut über die Augen. **(b)** (*demolish*) buildings abreißen. **(c)** (*weaken, make worse*) (*illness*) person mitnehmen; (*exam, question*) marks herunterdrücken; (*failure, adverse conditions*) company etc mitnehmen; profits, results herunterdrücken. this bad mark ~ed you ~ diese schlechte Zensur hat deinen Notenschnitt (herunter)gedrückt. **(d)** (*US inf: earn*) reinholen (*inf*), machen (*inf*). **2** *vi* (*blind etc*) sich herunterziehen lassen.
♦**pull in 1** *vt sep* **(a)** claws, rope, stomach etc einziehen; (*into room, swimming-pool etc*) hineinziehen. to ~ sb/sth ~(to) sth jdn/etw in etw (*acc*) ziehen. **(b)** (*rein in*) horse zügeln. **(c)** (*attract*) crowds anziehen. **(d)** (*inf: earn*) kassieren (*inf*). **(e)** (*inf: take into custody*) einkassieren (*inf*). **2** *vi* **(a)** (*claws*) sich einziehen lassen. **(b)** (*into station, harbour, pier*) einfahren, einlaufen (*into in* +*acc*); (*into garage, driveway*) hineinfahren (*into in* +*acc*); (*stop, park*) anhalten. he ~ed ~to the next lay-by er fuhr auf den nächsten Halteplatz; he ~ed ~ to the kerb/the side of the road er fuhr an den Bordstein heran/an die Straßenrand.
♦**pull off** *vt sep* **(a)** wrapping paper abziehen; cover also abnehmen; (*violently*) abreißen; clothes, pullover, shoes ausziehen; gloves, tights ausziehen, abstreifen. to ~ one's hat ~ sich (*dat*) den Hut vom Kopf reißen; he ~ed his clothes ~ and jumped into the water er riß sich (*dat*) die Kleider vom Leib und sprang ins Wasser; he quickly ~ed his/her coat ~ er zog sich/ihr schnell den Mantel aus. **(b)** (*inf: succeed in*) schaffen (*inf*); deal, coup also zuwege bringen (*inf*); order an Land ziehen (*inf*); bank job, burglary drehen (*inf*).
♦**pull on** *vt sep* coat etc sich (*dat*) überziehen; hat aufsetzen.
♦**pull out 1** *vt sep* **(a)** (*extract*) tooth ziehen; (*of aus*) page herausziehen; tooth herausreißen, heraustrennen. **(b)** (*elongate*) table, dough ausziehen. **(c)** (*withdraw*) zurückziehen; troops abziehen. **2** *vi* **(a)** (*come out*) sich herausziehen lassen; pages sich heraustrennen lassen. **(b)** (*elongate*) sich ausziehen lassen. **(c)** (*withdraw*) aussteigen (*of aus*) (*inf*); (*troops*) abziehen. **(d)** (*leave: train etc*) herausfahren (*of aus*). **(e)** (*move on*) herausfahren. the car/driver ~ed ~ from behind the lorry der Wagen/Fahrer scherte hinter dem Lastwagen aus; the boat ~ed ~ into midstream das Boot fuhr in die Flußmitte hinaus.
♦**pull over 1** *vt sep* **(a)** hinüber-/herüberziehen (*prep obj* über +*acc*). **(b)** (*topple*) umreißen. he ~ed the whole bookcase ~ on top of him er hat das ganze Bücherregal mit sich gerissen. **2** *vi* (*car, driver*) zur Seite fahren.
♦**pull round 1** *vt sep* **(a)** (*turn round*) herumdrehen. **(b)** (*bring back to consciousness*) wieder zu sich bringen; (*help recover*) durchbringen. **2** *vi* (*regain consciousness*) wieder zu sich kommen; (*recover*) durchkommen.
♦**pull through 1** *vt sep* (*lit*) durchziehen; (*fig: help recover, help succeed*) durchbringen. to ~ sb/sth ~ sth (*lit*) jdn/etw durch etw ziehen; to ~ sb ~ a difficult period jdm helfen, eine schwierige Zeit zu überstehen. **2** *vi* (*fig: recover*) durchkommen. to ~ ~ sth (*lit*) sich durch etw ziehen lassen; (*fig*) etw überstehen.
♦**pull together 1** *vi* (*lit*) gemeinsam ziehen; (*row jointly*) im gleichen Takt rudern; (*fig: cooperate*) an einem *or* am gleichen Strang ziehen. **2** *vt sep* (*fig*) political party, members of family etc zusammenschweißen; novel etc in einen Zusammenhang bringen. **3** *vr* sich zusammenreißen.
♦**pull under** *vt sep* swimmer nach unten ziehen.
♦**pull up 1** *vt sep* **(a)** (*raise by pulling*) hochziehen; (*up slope, upstairs also*) nach oben ziehen; see sock[1]. **(b)** (*uproot*) herausreißen. to ~ ~ one's roots, to ~ ~ stakes (*esp US*) alles aufgeben. **(c)** (*stop*) anhalten. **(d)** (*reprimand*) (*for behaviour*) zurechtweisen; (*for pronunciation, grammar*) korrigieren. he ~ed me ~ about *or* on that er hat mich deswegen zurechtgewiesen/korrigiert. **(e)** (*improve*) marks verbessern. that good mark ~ed you ~ a bit durch diese gute Note hast du ein wenig aufgeholt. **2** *vi* **(a)** (*stop*) anhalten. **(b)** (*improve one's position*) aufholen. to ~ ~ ~ with sb/sth jdn/etw einholen, mit jdm/etw gleichziehen (*inf*).
pullet ['pʊlɪt] *n* junges Huhn, Hühnchen *nt*.
pulley ['pʊlɪ] *n* (*wheel*) Rolle *f*; (*winch*) Flaschenzug *m*; (*hospital apparatus*) Streckapparat *m*.

pull-in ['pulin] n (Brit) (lay-by) Halteplatz m; (café) Raststätte f.
Pullman ® ['pulmən] n (~ car) Pullmanwagen ® m; (~ train) Pullman ® m.
pull: ~-out 1 n (a) (withdrawal) Abzug m; (b) (supplement) heraustrennbarer Teil; 2 attr supplement heraustrennbar; table leaf, seat ausziehbar; ~over n Pullover m; ~-up n (Sport) Klimmzug m.
pulmonary ['pʌlmənərɪ] adj Lungen-.
pulp [pʌlp] 1 n (a) (soft mass, paper ~, wood ~) Brei m. to reduce sth to a ~ etw in Brei auflösen; wood etc (for paper) etw zu einem Brei verarbeiten; to beat sb to a ~ (inf) jdn zu Brei schlagen (sl); crushed to (a) ~ zu Brei zerquetscht.
(b) (of plant stem) Mark nt; (of fruit, vegetable) Fruchtfleisch nt; (of tooth) Zahnmark nt, Pulpa f (spec).
(c) (also ~ magazine) (pej) Schundmagazin nt.
2 vt fruit, vegetables zerdrücken; paper, book einstampfen; wood zu Brei verarbeiten.
pulpit ['pulpɪt] n Kanzel f.
pulpy ['pʌlpɪ] adj (+er) breiig.
pulsar ['pʌlsɑːᵊ] n Pulsar m.
pulsate [pʌl'seɪt] vi (lit, fig) pulsieren, (head, heart) klopfen, pochen, (voice, building) beben, (music) rhythmisch klingen. the whole school ~d with excitement die ganze Schule fieberte vor Aufregung; the whole town was pulsating with life die ganze Stadt war von pulsierendem Leben erfüllt.
pulsation [pʌl'seɪʃən] n (pulsating) Pulsieren nt; (of head, heart) Klopfen, Pochen nt; (one beat) Schwingung f; (of heart, in artery) Schlag m.
pulse¹ [pʌls] 1 n (Anat) Puls m; (Phys) Impuls m; (fig: of drums, music) Rhythmus m. ~ beat Pulsschlag m; ~ rate Puls(zahl f) m; to feel or take sb's ~ jdm den Puls fühlen; he felt the ~ of life in his veins er spürte, wie das Leben in seinen Adern pulsierte; he still keeps his finger on the ~ of economic affairs (fig) er hat in Wirtschaftsfragen immer noch den Finger am Puls der Zeit.
2 vi pulsieren; (machines) stampfen. the town ~d with life in der Stadt pulsierte das Leben; the music ~d through the whole building das ganze Haus vibrierte im Rhythmus der Musik.
pulse² n (Bot, Cook) Hülsenfrucht f.
pulverization [ˌpʌlvəraɪ'zeɪʃən] n Pulverisierung f.
pulverize ['pʌlvəraɪz] vt pulverisieren; (fig inf) (beat up) Kleinholz machen aus (inf); (defeat) fertigmachen (inf).
puma ['pjuːmə] n Puma m.
pumice (stone) ['pʌmɪs(ˌstəʊn)] n Bimsstein m.
pummel ['pʌml] vt eintrommeln auf (+acc).
pump¹ [pʌmp] 1 n Pumpe f.
2 vt pumpen; stomach auspumpen; pedal mehrmals treten. to ~ sth dry etw leerpumpen; to ~ sb dry (fig) jdn aussaugen; to ~ bullets/ten bullets into sb jdm mit Blei vollpumpen (sl)/jdm zehn Kugeln in den Körper jagen (inf); he ~ed my arm up and down er riß meinen Arm wie einen Pumpenschwengel auf und ab; to ~ money into sth Geld in etw (acc) hineinpumpen; to ~ sb (for information) jdn aushorchen or ausfragen; to ~ information out of sb Informationen aus jdm herausholen.
3 vi pumpen; (water, blood) herausschießen. the piston ~ed up and down der Kolben ging auf und ab.
♦**pump in** vt sep (lit, fig) hineinpumpen.
♦**pump out** vt sep liquid, air herauspumpen; boat, cellar auspumpen, leerpumpen; stomach auspumpen.
♦**pump up** vt sep (a) (inflate) tyre etc aufpumpen. (b) liquid hochpumpen; (from below ground also) heraufpumpen.
pump² n (dancing shoe) Lackschuh m; (ballet shoe) Ballettschuh m; (gym shoe) Turnschuh m; (US: court shoe) Pumps m.
pumpernickel ['pʌmpənɪkl] n Pumpernickel m.
pumping station ['pʌmpɪŋˌsteɪʃən] n Pumpwerk nt, Pumpstation f; (on a pipeline) Förderpumpe f.
pumpkin ['pʌmpkɪn] n Kürbis m.
pump-room ['pʌmpruːm] n Trinkhalle f, Brunnenhaus nt.
pun [pʌn] 1 n Wortspiel nt. 2 vi Wortspiele machen.
Punch [pʌntʃ] n Kasper m, Kasperle nt. ~-and-Judy show Kasper(le)theater nt; to be (as) pleased as ~ (inf) sich wie ein Schneekönig freuen (inf).
punch¹ [pʌntʃ] 1 n (a) (blow) Schlag m. (b) no pl (fig: vigour) Pfeffer (inf) m. 2 vti boxen. I wanted to ~ his face when he said that als er das sagte, hätte ich ihn or ihm am liebsten ins Gesicht geschlagen; see pack, pull.
punch² 1 n (for ~ing holes) Locher m; (in tickets) Lochzange f; (in leather) Lochstanzer m; (for stamping metal, leather etc) Prägestempel m; (for knocking out rivets etc) Punze f.
2 vt ticket etc lochen; leather, metal stanzen; holes stechen, stanzen; (stamp) metal, pattern prägen; (US) cattle hüten. to ~ the time clock/card die Uhr stechen/Karte stempeln.
♦**punch in** vt sep (a) I'll ~ your face ~ (inf) ich hau' dir auf die Schnauze (sl). (b) (Computers) data tasten, tippen (inf).
♦**punch out** vt sep ausstechen, ausstanzen; pattern etc prägen.
punch³ n (drink) Bowle f; (hot) Punsch m.
punch: ~ bag n Sandsack m; ~ ball n Birnball m; (round) Lederball m; ~ bowl n Bowle f; ~ card n Lochkarte f; ~-drunk adj (Boxing) benommen; (fig) durcheinander pred.
Punchinello [ˌpʌntʃɪ'neləʊ] n Pulcinella f; (clown) Hanswurst m.
punching bag ['pʌntʃɪŋˌbæg] n (US) see punch bag.
punch: ~-line n Pointe f; ~ tape n Lochstreifen m; ~-up n (Brit inf) Schlägerei f.
punchy ['pʌntʃɪ] adj (+er) (inf) flott (inf).
punctilious [pʌŋk'tɪlɪəs] adj (regarding etiquette) korrekt; (scrupulous, fastidious) sehr or peinlich genau. he is always ~ about arriving in time/writing to thank his host er nimmt es mit der Pünktlichkeit sehr genau/er achtet immer darauf, daß er sich bei seinem Gastgeber schriftlich bedankt.
punctiliously [pʌŋk'tɪlɪəslɪ] adv korrekt; (scrupulously,

fastidiously) peinlich genau; (+adj) peinlich; correct höchst. he was ~ polite to his mother-in-law er war äußerst korrekt gegenüber seiner Schwiegermutter.
punctual ['pʌŋktjʊəl] adj pünktlich. to be ~ pünktlich kommen.
punctuality [ˌpʌŋktjʊ'ælɪtɪ] n Pünktlichkeit f.
punctually ['pʌŋktjʊəlɪ] adv pünktlich.
punctuate ['pʌŋktjʊeɪt] 1 vt (a) (Gram) mit Satzzeichen versehen, interpunktieren.
(b) (intersperse) unterbrechen. he ~d his talk with jokes seine Rede war mit Witzen durchsetzt; he ~d his remarks with gestures er unterstrich seine Bemerkungen mit Gesten; a long happy life, ~d with or by short spells of sadness ein langes glückliches Leben, das zeitweise von traurigen Augenblicken überschattet war.
(c) (emphasize) betonen.
2 vi Satzzeichen setzen.
punctuation [ˌpʌŋktjʊ'eɪʃən] n Zeichensetzung, Interpunktion f. ~ mark Satzzeichen, Interpunktionszeichen nt.
puncture ['pʌŋktʃəᵊ] 1 n (in tyre, balloon etc) Loch nt; (in skin) (Ein)stich m; (flat tyre) Reifenpanne f, Platte(r) m (inf). lumbar ~ Lumbalpunktion f.
2 vt stechen in (+acc); membrane durchstechen; blister aufstechen; tyre, balloon Löcher/ein Loch machen in (+acc); pride einen Stich versetzen (+dat). a ~d lung eine perforierte Lunge.
3 vi (tyre) einen Platten haben (inf); (balloon) platzen. my front tyre ~d ich hatte einen Platten am Vorderrad.
pundit ['pʌndɪt] n (lit) Pandit m; (fig) Experte m, Expertin f.
pungency ['pʌndʒənsɪ] n (lit, fig) Schärfe f.
pungent ['pʌndʒənt] adj (lit, fig) scharf; smell also stechend, durchdringend. to have a ~ style of writing eine spitze or scharfe Feder führen.
pungently ['pʌndʒəntlɪ] adv see adj.
Punic ['pjuːnɪk] adj punisch. the ~ Wars die Punischen Kriege.
puniness ['pjuːnɪnɪs] n Schwächlichkeit, Mickerigkeit (pej) f.
punish ['pʌnɪʃ] vt (a) person bestrafen, strafen (geh); offence bestrafen. he was ~ed by a fine er wurde mit einer Geldstrafe belegt; he has been ~ed enough er ist genug bestraft worden; (has suffered enough) er ist gestraft genug; our team was ~ed for making that mistake unsere Mannschaft mußte für diesen Fehler büßen; the other team ~ed us for that mistake die andere Mannschaft ließ uns für diesen Fehler büßen.
(b) (fig inf: drive hard, treat roughly) strapazieren; horses, oneself schinden; opponent rannehmen (inf), vorführen (inf), zusetzen (+dat). he really ~ed his opponent in the fourth round in der vierten Runde hat er seinen Gegner vorgeführt (inf).
punishable ['pʌnɪʃəbl] adj strafbar. this offence is ~ by 2 years' imprisonment dieses Verbrechen wird mit 2 Jahren Gefängnis bestraft; it is a ~ offence es ist strafbar.
punishing ['pʌnɪʃɪŋ] 1 adj blow hart. to get or take some ~ treatment (cars, furniture) strapaziert werden; (Sport) vorgeführt werden (inf), eins aufs Dach bekommen (inf).
2 n to take a ~ (inf) (car, furniture etc) strapaziert werden; (team, boxer etc) vorgeführt werden (inf); he got a real ~ from his opponent (inf) er wurde von seinem Gegner regelrecht vorgeführt (inf); his self-confidence took a ~ sein Selbstbewußtsein litt darunter or bekam einen Knacks (inf).
punishment ['pʌnɪʃmənt] n (a) (penalty) Strafe f; (punishing) Bestrafung f. you know the ~ for such offences Sie wissen, welche Strafe darauf steht; to take one's ~ eine Strafe akzeptieren. (b) (fig inf) to take a lot of ~ (car, furniture etc) stark strapaziert werden; (Sport) vorgeführt werden (inf).
punitive ['pjuːnɪtɪv] adj Straf-; taxation, fines etc extrem (hoch).
Punjab [pʌndʒɑːb] n the ~ der or das Pandschab, das Fünfstromland (geh).
Punjabi [pʌn'dʒɑːbɪ] 1 adj Pandschab-. 2 n (a) Pandschabi mf. (b) (language) Pandschabi nt.
punk [pʌŋk] 1 n (a) (person: also ~ rocker) Punker, Punkrocker m; (music: also ~ rock) Punk-Rock m; (culture) Punk m. (b) (US sl: hoodlum) Ganove m (inf). (c) (dated inf: nonsense) Stuß m (inf). 2 adj (sl) music, party etc Punk-. ~ rock Punk-Rock m.
punnet ['pʌnɪt] n (Brit) Körbchen nt.
punster ['pʌnstəᵊ] n he is a brilliant ~ er versteht es hervorragend, Wortspiele zu machen.
punt¹ [pʌnt] 1 n (boat) Stechkahn, Stocherkahn m. 2 vti staken, stochern; (go or take by ~) im Stechkahn fahren.
punt² n Schuß m (aus der Hand). he gave the ball a ~ er schoß den Ball aus der Hand. 2 vti to ~ (the ball) (den Ball) aus der Hand schießen; he ~ed the ball back er schoß den Ball zurück.
punt³ 1 n (bet) Wette f; (gamble) Spiel nt. 2 vi wetten; spielen.
punter¹ ['pʌntəᵊ] n (boater) Stechkahnfahrer(in f), Stocherer m.
punter² n (a) (better) Wetter m; (gambler) Spieler(in f) m. (b) (sl) (customer etc) Macker m (sl); (of prostitute) Freier m (sl). the average ~ Otto Normalverbraucher.
puny ['pjuːnɪ] adj (+er) (weak) person schwächlich, mick(e)rig (pej); effort kläglich.
pup [pʌp] 1 n (a) Junge(s) nt. in ~ (bitch) trächtig; she's still a ~ sie ist noch jung or klein. (b) (pej: youth) see puppy (b). 2 vi werfen.
pupa ['pjuːpə] n, pl -e ['pjuːpiː] Puppe f.
pupate ['pjuːpeɪt] vi sich verpuppen.
pupil¹ ['pjuːpl] n (Sch, fig) Schüler(in f) m.
pupil² n (Anat) Pupille f.
puppet ['pʌpɪt] n Puppe f; (glove ~) Handpuppe f; (string ~, fig) Marionette f.
puppeteer [pʌpɪ'tɪəᵊ] n Puppenspieler(in f) m.
puppet: ~ government n Marionettenregierung f; ~ régime n Marionettenregime nt.
puppetry ['pʌpɪtrɪ] n das Puppenspiel.
puppet: ~-show n Puppenspiel nt; (with string ~s also) Marionettentheater nt; ~ state n Marionettenstaat m.

puppy ['pʌpɪ] n (a) (young dog) junger or kleiner Hund, Hündchen nt. **when he was still a ~** als er noch jung or klein war. (b) (pej dated: youth) Schnösel m (inf).

puppy: ~ **dog** n Hündchen nt; ~ **fat** n Babyspeck m; ~ **love** n Schwärmerei f.

purblind ['pɜːblaɪnd] adj (liter) (lit) halbblind attr, halb blind pred; (fig) blind.

purchasable ['pɜːtʃəsəbl] adj käuflich (zu erwerben geh).

purchase ['pɜːtʃɪs] 1 n (a) Kauf m; (of furniture, machine, flat, car also) Anschaffung f. **to make a ~** einen Kauf tätigen; eine Anschaffung machen.

(b) (grip) Halt m. **he couldn't get a ~ on the wet rope** er konnte an dem nassen Seil keinen Halt finden.

2 vt (buy) kaufen, erwerben (form), erstehen (form); (fig) success, victory erkaufen. **the pound now ~s much less than it used to** die Kaufkraft des Pfundes ist jetzt wesentlich geringer als früher; **purchasing power** Kaufkraft f.

purchase: ~-**money** n Kaufgeld nt; ~ **price** n Kaufpreis m.

purchaser ['pɜːtʃɪsəʳ] n Käufer(in f) m.

purchase tax n (Brit) nach dem Großhandelspreis berechnete Kaufsteuer.

purdah ['pɜːdə] n Vorhang m vor den Frauengemächern im Islam. **a woman in** ~ (lit) eine Frau, die von (fremden) Männern ferngehalten wird; **he keeps his wife (like a woman) in** ~ er hält seine Frau von allem fern.

pure [pjʊəʳ] adj (+er) rein; motive ehrlich, lauter (geh); (utter) madness, nonsense etc also reinste(r, s). **she stared at him in** ~ **disbelief** sie starrte ihn ganz ungläubig an; **malice** ~ **and simple** reine Bosheit; **a** ~ **wool dress** ein Kleid aus reiner Wolle, ein reinwollenes Kleid; **his motives were of the** ~**st** er hatte die lautersten Motive; **blessed are the** ~ **in heart** (Bibl) selig, die reinen Herzens sind.

purebred ['pjʊəbred] 1 adj reinrassig. 2 n reinrassiges Pferd etc.

purée ['pjʊəreɪ] 1 n Püree nt, Brei m. **tomato** ~ Tomatenmark nt. 2 vt pürieren.

purely ['pjʊəlɪ] adv rein.

pure-minded ['pjʊə'maɪndɪd] adj unverdorben.

pureness ['pjʊənɪs] n = purity.

purgation [pɜː'geɪʃən] n (liter) Reinigung f; (of sin, guilt) Buße f; (form: of bowels also) Entleerung f.

purgative ['pɜːgətɪv] 1 adj (Med) abführend, purgativ (spec); (fig liter) läuternd (geh). 2 n Abführmittel, Purgativ (spec) nt.

purgatorial [,pɜːgə'tɔːrɪəl] adj (Rel) Fegefeuer-; (fig) höllisch. ~ **fire** Fegefeuer nt.

purgatory ['pɜːgətərɪ] n (Rel) das Fegefeuer; (fig: state) die Hölle.

purge [pɜːdʒ] 1 n (a) (Med) (starkes) Abführmittel. (b) (Pol etc) Säuberung(saktion) f. **a** ~ **of all radical elements in the party** eine Säuberung der Partei von allen radikalen Elementen.

2 vt reinigen; body entschlacken; guilt, offence, sin büßen; (Pol etc) party, organization säubern (of von); traitor, member eliminieren (from aus). **to** ~ **the bowels** den Darm entleeren.

purification [,pjʊərɪfɪ'keɪʃən] n Reinigung f.

purifier ['pjʊərɪfaɪəʳ] n Reinigungsanlage f; (air-freshener) Luftreiniger m.

purify ['pjʊərɪfaɪ] vt reinigen.

purism ['pjʊərɪzəm] n Purismus m.

purist ['pjʊərɪst] n Purist(in f) m.

puritan ['pjʊərɪtən] (Rel: **P~**) 1 adj puritanisch. 2 n Puritaner(in f) m.

puritanical [,pjʊərɪ'tænɪkəl] adj puritanisch.

puritanism ['pjʊərɪtənɪzəm] (Rel: **P~**) n Puritanismus m.

purity ['pjʊərɪtɪ] n Reinheit f; (of motives) Lauterkeit (geh), Ehrlichkeit f.

purl [pɜːl] 1 n linke Masche. **is the next row (in)** ~? ist die nächste Reihe links? 2 vti links stricken. ~ **two** zwei links.

purlieus ['pɜːljuːz] npl (liter) Umgebung f.

purloin [pɜː'lɔɪn] vt (form, hum) entwenden (form, hum).

purple ['pɜːpl] 1 adj violett, lila; face dunkelrot, hochrot; (pej) prose, passage hochgestochen, hochtrabend. **a** ~ **bruise** ein blau-roter Fleck; **to go** ~ **(in the face)** hochrot or dunkelrot werden or anlaufen (inf).

2 n (a) (colour) Violett, Lila nt. (b) (fig) **the** ~ (nobility) der Adel; (bishops) der Kardinalsstand; **to be born in the** ~ von königlichem Geblüt sein; **to be raised to the** ~ den Kardinalspurpur anlegen.

purple heart n (a) (Brit) Amphetamintablette f. (b) (US) **P~ H~** Purpurherz nt, Verwundetenabzeichen nt.

purplish ['pɜːplɪʃ] adj leicht violett or lila.

purport ['pɜːpət] 1 n Tenor m.

2 [pɜː'pɔːt] vt (a) (convey, mean) hindeuten auf (+acc).

(b) (profess, claim) **to** ~ **to be/do sth** (person) vorgeben, etw zu sein/tun; (object) etw sein/tun sollen; **he is** ~**ed to be a spy** es wird behauptet, er sei ein Spion; **the law is** ~**ed to be in the public interest** das Gesetz soll dem Interesse der Öffentlichkeit dienen; **a message** ~**ing to come from the general** eine Nachricht, die vom General stammen soll.

purpose ['pɜːpəs] n (a) (intention) Absicht f; (result aimed at, set goal) Zweck m. **on** ~ mit Absicht, absichtlich; **what was your** ~ **in doing this?** was haben Sie damit beabsichtigt?, was war Ihre Absicht dabei?; **he did it for or with the** ~ **of improving his image** er tat es der Absicht or mit dem Ziel, sein Image zu verbessern; **he's a man with a** ~ **in life** er ist ein Mensch mit einem Lebensziel; **a novel with a** ~ ein Roman, der einen Zweck erfüllen soll; **to answer or serve sb's** ~**(s)** jds Zweck(en) entsprechen or dienen; **his activities seem to lack** ~ seine Aktivitäten scheinen nicht zweckgerichtet zu sein; **for our** ~**s** für unsere Zwecke; **for the** ~**s of this meeting** zum Zweck dieser Konferenz; **for all practical** ~**s** in der Praxis; **to the** ~

relevant; **to some/good/little** ~ mit einigem/gutem/wenig Erfolg; **to no** ~ ohne Erfolg.

(b) no pl (resolution, determination) Entschlossenheit f. **weakness of** ~ Mangel m an Entschlossenheit, Entschlußlosigkeit f; **strength of** ~ Zielbewußtsein nt, Entschlußkraft, Entschlossenheit f; **sense of** ~ Zielbewußtsein nt; (of nation) Ziel nt, Zielvorstellungen pl; **to have a/no sense of** ~ zielbewußt sein/kein Zielbewußtsein haben, ein/kein Ziel haben.

2 vt (liter) beabsichtigen. **to** ~ **to do sth** etw zu tun gedenken.

purpose-built ['pɜːpəs'bɪlt] adj spezial angefertigt, Spezial-; building speziell gebaut, Spezial-.

purposeful adj, ~**ly** adv ['pɜːpəsfʊl, -fəlɪ] entschlossen.

purposefulness ['pɜːpəsfʊlnɪs] n Entschlossenheit f.

purposeless ['pɜːpəslɪs] adj sinnlos; person ziellos.

purposely ['pɜːpəslɪ] adv bewußt, absichtlich.

purposive ['pɜːpəsɪv] adj remark, statement, behaviour gezielt. **to be** ~ einen Zweck verfolgen.

purr [pɜːʳ] 1 vi (cat, fig: person) schnurren; (engine) surren. 2 vt (say) säuseln. 3 n Schnurren nt no pl; Surren nt no pl.

purse [pɜːs] 1 n (a) (for money) Portemonnaie nt, Geldbeutel m (dial), Geldbörse f (form). **to hold the** ~ **strings** (fig) über die Finanzen bestimmen, die Finanzen in der Hand haben; **she decided to loosen/tighten the** ~ **strings** sie beschloß, ihm/ihr mehr Geld zu geben/sie beschloß, ihm/ihr das Geld kurzzuhalten; **the government has tightened the** ~ **strings on public spending** die Regierung hat den Geldhahn zugedreht (inf).

(b) (US: handbag) Handtasche f.

(c) (funds) Gelder pl. **that's beyond my** ~ das übersteigt meine Finanzen (inf); see public ~.

(d) (sum of money) (as prize) Preisgeld nt; (as gift) (to widow, refugee etc) (Geld)spende f; (on retirement) Geldgeschenk nt.

2 vt **to** ~ **one's lips/mouth (up)** einen Schmollmund machen.

purser ['pɜːsəʳ] n Zahlmeister m.

pursuance [pə'sjuːəns] n (form) (of plan) Verfolgung f; (of instruction) Durchführung, Ausführung f; (of duties) Ausübung, Erfüllung f.

pursuant [pə'sjuːənt] adj (form) ~ **to** gemäß (+dat), entsprechend (+dat); ~ **to our agreement** unserem Abkommen gemäß or entsprechend.

pursue [pə'sjuː] vt (a) verfolgen; girl, film star etc also, success nachlaufen (+dat); pleasure, success nachjagen (+dat), aus sein auf (+acc); happiness streben nach. **bad luck seems to** ~ **him** er scheint vom Pech verfolgt zu sein.

(b) (carry on) train of thought, course of action, idea verfolgen; inquiry durchführen; profession also, studies nachgehen (+dat); subject weiterführen.

pursuer [pə'sjuːəʳ] n Verfolger(in f) m.

pursuit [pə'sjuːt] n (a) (act of pursuing) (of person) Verfolgung (of gen), Jagd f (of auf +acc) f; (of knowledge) Streben, Trachten nt (of nach); (of pleasure) Jagd f (of nach); (of happiness) Streben nt (of nach). **he set off in** ~ (of her) er rannte/fuhr (ihr) hinterher; **to go in** ~ **of sb/sth** sich auf die Jagd nach jdm/etw machen; **in (the)** ~ **of his goal** in Verfolgung seines Ziels; **Kissinger's** ~ **of peace** Kissingers Friedensbemühungen pl.

(b) (occupation) Beschäftigung f; (hobby, pastime) Freizeitbeschäftigung f, Zeitvertreib m. **his literary** ~**s** seine Beschäftigung mit der Literatur.

pursuit plane n Jagdflugzeug nt.

purulence ['pjʊərʊləns], **purulency** ['pjʊərʊlənsɪ] n Eitern nt; (pus) Eiter m.

purulent ['pjʊərʊlənt] adj eitrig. **to become** ~ eitern.

purvey [pɜː'veɪ] vt (form) (sell) verkaufen. **to** ~ **sth to sb** (supply) jdm etw liefern; food also jdn mit etw beliefern; information also jdn mit etw versorgen; **he obtained a contract to** ~ **food to the Navy** er erhielt einen Vertrag für die Lieferung von Lebensmitteln an die Marine.

purveyance [pɜː'veɪəns] n (form: sale) Verkauf m. **the** ~ **of food to the Navy** die Lieferung von Lebensmitteln an die Marine.

purveyor [pɜː'veɪəʳ] n (form) (seller) Händler m; (supplier) Lieferant m.

purview ['pɜːvjuː] n (form) Rahmen m; (of department) Aufgabenbereich m, Ressort nt. **to come within/lie outside the** ~ **of an inquiry** noch/nicht mehr im Rahmen einer Untersuchung liegen.

pus [pʌs] n Eiter m.

push [pʊʃ] 1 n (a) Schubs m (inf); (short) Stoß m; (in childbirth) Drücken nt no pl. **to give sb/sth a** ~ jdn/etw schieben; jdm/etw einen Stoß versetzen; **to give a car a** ~ einen Wagen anschieben; **he needs a little** ~ **now and then** (fig) den muß man mal ab und zu in die Rippen stoßen (inf); **to get the** ~ (Brit inf) (employee) (raus)fliegen (inf) (from aus); (boyfriend) den Laufpaß kriegen (inf); **to give sb the** ~ (Brit inf) employee jdn rausschmeißen (inf); boyfriend jdm den Laufpaß geben (inf).

(b) (effort) Anstrengung f; (sales ~) Kampagne, Aktion f; (Mil: offensive) Offensive f. **to make a** ~ sich ranhalten (inf), Dampf machen (inf); (Mil) eine Offensive starten; **let's make a** ~ **to get it finished** halten wir uns ran (inf), damit wir fertig werden; **to have a** ~ **on sales** eine Verkaufskampagne führen.

(c) (drive, aggression) Durchsetzungsvermögen nt.

(d) (inf) **at a** ~ notfalls, im Notfall; **if/when it comes to the** ~ wenn es darauf ankommt.

2 vt (a) (shove, move by ~ing) schieben; (quickly, violently) stoßen, schubsen (inf); button, controls drücken. **to** ~ **a door open/shut** eine Tür auf-/zuschieben; (quickly, violently) eine Tür auf-/zustoßen; **he** ~**ed the book into my hand** er drückte mir das Buch in die Hand; **to** ~ **a car to get it started** einen Wagen anschieben; **he** ~**ed his way through the crowd** drängte sich durch die Menge; **he** ~**ed the thought to the back of his mind** er schob den Gedanken beiseite; **he** ~**ed the ball over the bar** (Sport) er hat den Ball über die Latte gestoßen.

(b) *(fig)* *views, claims, interests* durchzusetzen versuchen; *candidate* die Werbetrommel rühren für; *export side* intensiv fördern; *product* propagieren, massiv Werbung machen für; *drugs* schieben. **to ~** home an attack/one's advantage einen Angriff forcieren/seinen Vorteil ausnützen; the speaker ~ed home his points der Sprecher machte nachdrücklich seinen Standpunkt klar; don't ~ your luck treib's nicht zu weit! he's ~ing his luck trying to do that er legt es wirklich darauf an, wenn er das versucht; he must be ~ing 70 *(inf)* er muß auf die 70 zugehen.

(c) *(fig: put pressure on)* drängen, drängeln *(inf)*; *athlete, pupil, employee* antreiben. **to ~** sb into doing sth jdn dazu treiben, etw zu tun; **to ~** sb to do sth jdn dazu drängen, etw zu tun; **to ~** sb for payment jdn zum Zahlen drängen; don't ~ him so hard to make a decision drängen *or* drängeln *(inf)* Sie ihn nicht zu sehr zu einer Entscheidung; you shouldn't ~ your children so hard Sie sollten Ihre Kinder nicht so sehr antreiben; they ~ed him to the limits sie trieben ihn bis an seine Grenzen; that's ~ing it a bit *(inf)* das ist ein bißchen übertrieben; to be ~ed for time/money *(inf)* mit der Zeit/mit Geld knapp dransein, unter Zeitdruck stehen/knapp bei Kasse sein *(inf)*; I'm a bit ~ed just now *(inf) (for time)* ich habe momentan wenig Zeit; *(for money)* ich bin momentan ein bißchen knapp dran *(inf)*; I was ~ed to find the money/an answer ich hatte Probleme *or* Schwierigkeiten, das Geld zusammenzubringen/eine Antwort zu finden; **to ~** oneself hard sich schinden.

3 *vi* **(a)** *(shove)* schieben; *(quickly, violently)* stoßen; *(press, in childbirth)* drücken; *(in a crowd)* drängen, drängeln *(inf)*, *(press onward)* nach vorn(e) drängen; *(fig)* *(be ambitious)* assert oneself) kämpfen; *(apply pressure)* drängen, drängeln *(inf)*. "~" *(on door)* „drücken"; *(on bell)* „klingeln"; ~ harder! fester schieben/stoßen/drücken!; he ~es too much *(fig)* er ist zu aggressiv.

(b) this door ~es *(open)* bei dieser Tür muß man drücken.

◆**push about** *vt sep see* **push around**.

◆**push across** *vt sep see* **push over** *(a)*.

◆**push ahead** *vi* sich ranhalten *(inf)*, voranmachen *(inf)*. **to ~** with one's plans seine Pläne vorantreiben.

◆**push along** **1** *vt sep wheelbarrow etc* vor sich *(dat)* her schieben; *(fig: speed up)* *work etc* voranbringen, vorantreiben. **2** *vi* *(inf)* sich auf den Weg *or* auf die Socken machen *(inf)*.

◆**push around** *vt sep* **(a)** *(lit)* herumschieben; *(quickly, violently)* herumstoßen. **(b)** *(fig inf: bully)* *child* herumschubsen; *adult* herumkommandieren.

◆**push aside** *vt sep* zur Seite *or* beiseite schieben; *(quickly, violently)* zur Seite *or* beiseite stoßen; *(fig)* *problems, suggestions* einfach abtun; *rival* zur Seite drängen.

◆**push away** *vt sep* wegschieben; *(quickly)* wegstoßen.

◆**push back** *vt sep* *people* zurückdrängen; *(with one push)* zurückstoßen; *curtains, cover, lock of hair* zurückschieben.

◆**push by** *vi see* **push past**.

◆**push down** **1** *vt sep* **(a)** *(press down)* nach unten drücken. **(b)** *(knock over)* umstoßen; *fence* umreißen. **2** *vi* *(press down)* hinunterdrücken, nach unten drücken; *(in childbirth)* drücken.

◆**push for** *vi* +*prep obj* drängen auf (+*acc*).

◆**push forward** **1** *vi* **(a)** *(Mil)* vorwärts drängen. **(b)** *see* **push ahead**. **2** *vt sep* *(lit)* nach vorn schieben; *(fig)* *claim* geltend machen; *ideas* hervorheben, herausstellen; *sb, oneself* in den Vordergrund schieben.

◆**push in** **1** *vt sep* **(a)** hineinschieben; *(quickly, violently)* hineinstoßen. **to ~** sb/sth ~(to) sth jdn/etw in etw *(acc)* schieben/stoßen; **to ~** one's way ~ sich hineindrängen; **(b)** *(break)* *window, sides of box* eindrücken. **2** *vi* *(lit: in queue, into room etc)* sich hineindrängen *or* -drängeln *(inf)*; *(fig: interfere)* sich dazwischen drängen, sich reindrängen *(inf)*. he ~ed ~to the queue er drängelte sich (in der Schlange) vor.

◆**push off** **1** *vt sep* **(a)** hinunterschieben; *(quickly, violently)* hinunterstoßen; *lid, cap* wegdrücken. **to ~** sb ~ sth jdn von etw schieben/stoßen; **to ~** sth with sth etw von etw schieben/stoßen/drücken; I was ~ed ~ the pavement ich wurde vom Bürgersteig gedrängt. **(b)** *boat* abstoßen. **2** *vi* **(a)** *(in boat)* abstoßen. **(b)** *(inf: leave)* abhauen *(inf)*, abzwitschern *(inf)*. ~~! mach 'ne Fliege! *(sl)*, hau *or* zieh ab! *(inf)*. **(c)** the top just ~es ~ es der Deckel läßt sich einfach wegdrücken.

◆**push on** **1** *vi* **(a)** *(with journey)* weiterfahren; *(walking)* weitergehen; *(with job)* weitermachen. **2** *vt sep* **(a)** *top, lid* festdrücken. he ~ed the lid ~(to) the jar er drückte den Deckel auf das Glas. **(b)** *(fig)* *(urge on)* antreiben; *(incite)* anstacheln.

◆**push out** **1** *vt sep* **(a)** hinausschieben; *(quickly, violently)* hinausstoßen. **to ~** sb/sth ~ of sth jdn/etw aus etw schieben/stoßen; **to ~** one's way ~ (of sth) sich (aus etw) hinausdrängen. **(b)** *(fig)* *employee, government, member of group* hinausdrängen. **to ~** sb ~ of sth jdn aus etw drängen. **(c)** *(Bot)* *root, shoots* treiben. **2** *vi* *(Bot: roots, shoots)* treiben.

◆**push over** *vt sep* **(a)** *(pass over, move over)* hinüber-/herüberschieben; *(quickly, violently)* hinüber-/herüberstoßen. **to ~** sb/sth ~ sth jdn/etw über etw *(acc)* schieben/stoßen. **(b)** *(knock over)* umwerfen.

◆**push past** *vi* sich vorbeischieben *(prep obj* an +*dat)*; *(move violently)* sich vorbeidrängen *(prep obj* an +*dat)*.

◆**push through** **1** *vt sep* **(a)** *(shove through)* durchschieben; *(quickly, violently)* durchstoßen. **to ~** sb/sth ~ sth jdn/etw durch etw schieben/stoßen; **to ~** one's way ~/~ the crowd sich durchdrängen/sich durch die Menge drängen; **to ~** sb ~ an exam jdn durch eine Prüfung bringen *(inf)*. **(b)** *(get done quickly)* *bill, decision* durchpeitschen; *business* durchziehen *(inf)*. **2** *vi* *(through crowd)* sich durchschieben; *(more violently)*

sich durchdrängen; *(new shoots)* sich herausschieben. he ~ed ~ the crowd er schob/drängte sich durch die Menge.

◆**push up** **1** *vt sep* **(a)** *(lit)* hinaufschieben; *(quickly, violently)* hinaufstoßen; *window* hochschieben/-stoßen; *see* **daisy. (b)** *(fig)* *(raise, increase)* hochtreiben, hochdrücken.

push: ~**ball** *n* Pushball *m*; ~**bar** *n* Riegel *m*; ~-**bike** *n (Brit)* Fahrrad *nt*; ~-**button** *n* Drucktaste *f*, Druckknopf *m*; ~-**button controls** Druckknopfsteuerung *f*; ~-**button radio** Radio *nt* mit Drucktasten; ~-**button warfare** Krieg *m* auf Knopfdruck; ~-**cart** *n* (Hand)karren *m*; ~-**chair** *n (Brit)* Sportwagen *m*.

pusher ['pʊʃə^r] *n* **(a)** *(of drugs)* Pusher(in *f*) *m (inf)*; *(small-time)* Dealer(in *f*) *m (inf)*. **(b)** *(ambitious person)* he's a ~ er setzt sich durch.

pushiness ['pʊʃɪnɪs] *n (inf)* penetrante Art *(pej)*.

pushing ['pʊʃɪŋ], **pushy** *(inf) adj* penetrant *(pej)*.

push: ~-**over** *n (inf)* *(job etc)* Kinderspiel *nt*; *(match also)* Geschenk *nt (inf)*; *(person)* leichtes Opfer; he's a ~-over for a pretty face bei einem hübschen Gesicht wird er schwach; ~-**pull** *adj* circuit etc Gegentakt-; ~-**start 1** *vt car* anschieben; **2** *n* to give sb a ~-**start** jdn anschieben; ~-**up** *n* Liegestütz *m*.

pushy ['pʊʃɪ] *adj* (+*er*) *(inf) see* **pushing**.

pusillanimity [ˌpjuːsɪləˈnɪmɪtɪ] *n (liter)* Unbeherztheit, Feigheit *f*.

pusillanimous [ˌpjuːsɪˈlænɪməs] *adj (liter)* unbeherzt, feige.

puss [pʊs] *n (inf)* Mieze *(inf)*, Muschi *(inf) f.* ~, ~! Miez, Miez!; **P~ in Boots** der Gestiefelte Kater; she's a sly ~ *(inf)* sie ist ein schlaues Ding *(inf)*.

pussy ['pʊsɪ] *n* **(a)** *(cat)* Mieze *(inf)*, Muschi *(inf) f.* **(b)** *(sl: female genitals)* Kätzchen *nt (sl)*, Muschi *f (inf)*.

pussy: ~-**cat** *n (baby-talk)* Miezekatze *f (baby-talk)*; ~**foot** *vi (inf)* **(a)** *(move cautiously)* auf Zehenspitzen tappen, auf Samtpfoten schleichen; **(b)** *(act cautiously)* to ~**foot** *(about or over sth)* (um etw) wie die Katze um den heißen Brei schleichen *(inf)*; ~**footing** *(inf)* **1** *adj* überängstlich; **2** *n* I'm fed up with his ~**footing** ich habe es satt, wie er immer wie die Katze um den heißen Brei schleicht; ~ **willow** *n* Salweide *f*.

pustule ['pʌstjuːl] *n* Pustel *f*, Eiterpickel *m*.

put¹ [pʊt] *(vb: pret, ptp* ~) **1** *n (Sport)* Stoß *m.* **2** *vt* to ~ the shot kugelstoßen; ~**ting the shot** Kugelstoßen *nt*.

put² *pret, ptp* ~ **1** *vt* **(a)** *(place)* tun; *(~ down, position)* stellen, setzen; *(lay down)* legen; *(push in)* stecken. **to ~** sth in its place etw an seinen Platz tun/stellen *or* setzen; ~ the lid on the box tu *or* mach den Deckel auf die Schachtel; **to ~** sth in a drawer etw in eine Schublade tun *or* legen; he ~ his hand in his pocket er steckte die Hand in die Tasche; you've ~ the picture too high up du hast das Bild zu hoch (auf)gehängt; he ~ the corpse down the well er warf die Leiche in den Brunnen; they ~ a plank across the stream sie legten ein Brett über den Bach; he ~ his rucksack over the fence er setzte seinen Rucksack über den Zaun; he ~ some more coal on the fire und legte Kohle nach; ~ the dog in the kitchen tu *or* steck den Hund in die Küche; to ~ milk/sugar in one's coffee Milch/Zucker in den Kaffee tun *or* geben; he ~ his hat on his head er setzte sich *(dat)* den Hut auf; **to ~** the ball in the net *(Ftbl)* den Ball ins Netz setzen; *(Tennis)* den Ball ins Netz schlagen; he ~ the ball over the wall er schoß den Ball über die Mauer; her aunt ~ her on the train ihre Tante setzte sie in den Zug; to ~ sb across a river jdn über einen Fluß setzen; to ~ men on the moon Menschen auf den Mond bringen; to ~ a bullet through sb's head jdm eine Kugel durch den Kopf schießen; he ~ his toe in the water er steckte seinen Zeh ins Wasser; he ~ his hand/head on my shoulder er legte seine Hand auf/seinen Kopf an meine Schulter; he ~ his lips to my ear and whispered ... er kam ganz dicht und flüsterte mir ins Ohr ...; to ~ a glass to one's lips ein Glas zum Mund(e) führen; she ~ the shell to her ear sie hielt *(sich)* die Muschel ans Ohr; to ~ a heifer to a bull die Kuh mit dem Stier zusammenbringen *or* -führen; to ~ a horse to a fence mit einem Pferd ein Hindernis angehen *or* anreiten; to ~ one's hand over sb's mouth jdm/jds die Hand vor den Mund halten; ~ it there! *(concluding deal)* abgemacht!; *(congratulatory)* gratuliere!; *(conciliatory)* schon gut; I didn't know where to ~ myself ich wußte gar nicht, wo ich hingucken sollte.

(b) *(thrust)* stecken. he ~ his head round the door er steckte den Kopf zur Tür herein; to ~ one's fist through a window mit der Faust ein Fenster einschlagen; to ~ a knife into sb jdm einen Messerstich versetzen.

(c) *(fit, fix)* machen *(on* an +*acc)*, anbringen *(on* an +*dat)*. ~ a patch on sth einen Flicken auf etw *(acc)* setzen.

(d) to stay ~ liegen-/stehen-/hängen- etc bleiben; *(hair)* halten; *(person)* *(not move)* bleiben; *(not stand up)* sitzenbleiben; just stay ~! bleib, wo du bist!

(e) setzen. to ~ a child in a home ein Kind in ein Heim stecken; he was ~ under the care of a nurse er wurde in die Obhut einer Krankenschwester gegeben; to ~ money into sth *(sein)* Geld in etw *(acc)* stecken; he ~ £10/money on Red Rum er setzte £ 10/setzte auf Red Rum; I'm ~ting my money on him ich setze auf ihn; I'm ~ting my money on him to get the job ich gehe jede Wette ein, daß er die Stelle bekommt; we'll each ~ £5 towards the cost of it jeder von uns gibt £ 5 (zum Betrag) dazu; to ~ *(acc)* stecken; to ~ a lot of effort into one's work sich *(dat)* bei seiner Arbeit viel Mühe geben, viel Mühe in seine Arbeit stecken; he ~s all his energy into his work er steckt seine ganze Energie in die Arbeit; she has ~ a lot into her marriage sie hat eine Menge in ihre Ehe gesteckt *or* investiert; I would ~ complete confidence in him ich würde mein volles Vertrauen auf ihn *or* in ihn setzen; to ~ sb in possession of the facts jdn über den Stand der Dinge unterrichten; *see also* **nouns**.

(f) *(cause to be, do etc)* to ~ sb in a good/bad mood jdn fröhlich/mißmutig stimmen; that ~s him in another category das stuft ihn in eine andere Klasse ein; I ~ the children on their

best behaviour ich habe den Kindern eingeschärft, sich ja gut zu benehmen; **to ~ sb to do** or **doing sth** jdn abordnen, etw zu tun; **he ~ four men on the job** er setzte (für diese Arbeit) vier Leute ein; **they ~ someone over/under him in the office** sie haben jemanden über ihn gesetzt/ihm jemanden unterstellt; **he ~ his watch 5 minutes fast** er stellte seine Uhr 5 Minuten vor; **to ~ sb to great expense** jdm große Ausgaben verursachen; **I don't want to be ~ to a lot of expense** ich möchte nicht, daß mir damit große Ausgaben entstehen; **to be ~ to a lot of inconvenience over sth** mit etw viele Unannehmlichkeiten haben.

(g) (write) schreiben; comma, line machen; (draw) zeichnen, malen. **to ~ one's signature to a document** seine Unterschrift unter ein Schriftstück setzen; **~ your name here** schreiben or setzen Sie Ihren Namen hierhin; **to ~ a cross/tick against sb's name** jds Namen ankreuzen/abhaken; **he ~ it in his next novel** er brachte das in seinem nächsten Roman.

(h) (~ forward) case, question, proposal vorbringen. **to ~ a matter before a committee** eine Angelegenheit vor einen Ausschuß bringen; **to ~ the arguments for and against sth** das Für und Wider von etw (dat) aufzählen; **to ~ sth on the agenda** etw auf die Tagesordnung setzen; **you might ~ it to him that a contribution would be welcome** du könntest ihm nahelegen, daß ein Beitrag erwünscht wäre; **to ~ a question/suggestion to sb** jdm eine Frage stellen/einen Vorschlag unterbreiten; **I ~ it to you that** ... ich möchte Ihnen vorhalten, daß ...; **it was ~ to me that** ... es wurde mir nahegelegt, daß ...; **I ~ it to him that this might not fit in with his theory** ich gab ihm zu bedenken, daß dies vielleicht nicht in seine Theorie passen würde.

(i) (express) ausdrücken, sagen. **that's one way of ~ting it** so kann man's auch sagen; **as he would ~ it** wie er sich ausdrücken würde; **as Shakespeare ~s it** wie Shakespeare es ausdrückt; **~ it so as not to offend her** formulieren Sie es so, daß Sie sie nicht beleidigen; **how shall I ~ it?** wie soll ich (es) sagen?; **how will you ~ it to him?** wie wirst du es ihm beibringen?; **if I may ~ it so** wenn ich das so sagen darf, wenn ich mich (mal) so ausdrücken darf; **the compliment was gracefully ~** das Kompliment war elegant formuliert.

(j) to ~ **a text into Greek** einen Text ins Griechische übersetzen; **to ~ a verb into the past tense** ein Verb in die Vergangenheit setzen; **to ~ a poem to music** ein Gedicht vertonen.

(k) (rate) schätzen (at auf +acc). **he ~s money before his family's happiness** er stellt Geld über das Glück seiner Familie; **I ~ him above Tennyson** ich schätze ihn höher ein als Tennyson; **I wouldn't ~ him amongst the greatest poets** ich würde ihn nicht zu den größten Dichtern zählen; **to ~ a value of £10 on sth** den Wert einer Sache (gen) auf £ 10 schätzen.

2 vi (Naut) **to ~ to sea** in See stechen.

♦ **put about 1** vt sep (a) (circulate) news, rumour verbreiten, in Umlauf bringen. **he ~ it ~ that** ... er verbreitete (das Gerücht), daß ... **(b)** (Naut) **to ~ a ship** ~ den Kurs (eines Schiffes) ändern. **2** vi (Naut) den Kurs ändern.

♦ **put across** vt sep (a) (communicate) ideas verständlich machen (to sb jdm), klar zum Ausdruck bringen; knowledge vermitteln (to sb jdm); (promote) an den Mann bringen (inf). **to ~ a product ~ to the public** ein Produkt an den Mann bringen; **to ~ oneself** ~ den richtigen Eindruck von sich geben. **(b)** (inf: play a trick) **to ~ it** or **one ~ sb** jdn drankriegen (inf), jdn anführen; **he's just trying to ~ one ~ (you)** er will dich nur drankriegen (inf) or anführen.

♦ **put aside** vt sep (a) book, knitting etc beiseite legen. **(b)** (save for later use) beiseite or auf die Seite legen, zurücklegen; (in shop) zurücklegen. **(c)** (fig: forget, abandon) ablegen, über Bord werfen (inf); anger, grief, animosity begraben; thought aufgeben; differences vergessen.

♦ **put away** vt sep (a) (in usual place) einräumen; toys also aufräumen; (tidy away) wegräumen. **~ that money ~ in your bag** steck das Geld in deine Tasche; **~ that money ~!** steck das Geld weg!; **to ~ the car** ~ das Auto einstellen. **(b)** (save) zurücklegen. **(c)** (inf: consume) schaffen (inf); food also verdrücken (inf), verputzen (inf); drink also schlucken (inf). **he can certainly ~ it ~!** das kann was verdrücken/schlucken! **(d)** (lock up: in prison, mental home) einsperren. **(e)** (put to sleep) pet einschläfern.

♦ **put back 1** vt sep (a) (replace) see put zurücktun/-stellen or -setzen/-legen/-stecken. **(b)** (postpone) meeting, date verschieben; (set back) plans, production zurückwerfen; (readjust) watch etc zurückstellen. **to be ~ ~ a class** (Sch) eine Klasse zurückgestuft werden; see clock. **2** vi (Naut: go back) zurückkehren (to nach).

♦ **put by** vt sep zurücklegen, auf die hohe Kante legen. **I've got a few pounds ~ ~** ich habe ein paar Pfund auf der hohen Kante.

♦ **put down 1** vt sep (a) (set down) object see put wegtun/ -setzen or -stellen/weglegen; surface verlegen. **the punch ~ him ~ for the count of 8** der Schlag hat ihn bis 8 auf die Bretter geschickt (inf); **~ it ~ on the floor** stellen or setzen Sie es auf den Boden; **I simply couldn't ~ that book ~** ich konnte das Buch einfach nicht aus der Hand legen; see foot 1 (b). **(b)** (lower) umbrella zumachen, zuklappen; aerial einschieben; car roof zurückklappen; lid zuklappen. **(c)** passenger absetzen. **(d)** (land) landen. **(e)** (crush) rebellion niederschlagen; rebels niederwerfen; crime besiegen; prostitution, gambling, drinking unterdrücken; rumour zum Verstummen bringen; critic, heckler zum Schweigen bringen; (reject, humiliate) ducken. **(f)** (pay) anzahlen; deposit machen. **(g)** (store) einlagern; wine also als (dat) in den Keller legen. **(h)** (destroy) rats, vermin vernichten; pets einschläfern; injured horse etc den Gnadenschuß geben (+dat).

(i) (write down) niederschreiben, aufschreiben; (on form, in register) angeben; (Parl) motion, resolution vorlegen, einbringen. **to ~ one's son ~ for Eton** seinen Sohn für Eton anmelden; **you can ~ me ~ for £10** für mich können Sie £ 10 eintragen; **~ it ~ to** or **on my account/my husband's account** schreiben Sie es (mir)/meinem Mann an; **~ it ~ under sundries/on expenses** schreiben Sie es unter Verschiedenes auf/als Spesen an; see paper 1 (a), name.

(j) (classify) halten (as für). **I should ~ her ~ as about 30** ich würde sie auf etwa 30 schätzen.

(k) (attribute) zurückführen (to auf +acc), zuschreiben (to dat).

2 vi (Aviat) landen, niedergehen.

♦ **put forth** vt insep (liter) buds, shoots hervorbringen.

♦ **put forward** vt sep (a) (propose) idea, suggestion, plan vorbringen; person (for job etc) vorschlagen; (as candidate) aufstellen; (nominate) vorschlagen. **he ~ himself/his name ~ for the job** er hat sich für den Posten angeboten. **(b)** (advance) date, meeting vorverlegen (to auf +acc); schedule voranbringen, weiterbringen (by um); watch etc vorstellen.

♦ **put in 1** vt sep (a) (place in) see put hineintun/-setzen or -stellen/-legen/-stecken; (pack) einpacken. **he opened the drawer and ~ his hand** ~ er öffnete die Schublade und fuhr or griff mit der Hand hinein; **I'll just ~ the car** ~ ich stelle eben den Wagen weg. **(b)** (insert in book, speech etc) einsetzen, einfügen; (add) hinzufügen, dazusagen. **(c)** (interpose) remark einfügen. **(d)** (enter) application, protest einreichen; claim also stellen. **to ~ a plea of not guilty** (Jur) auf „nicht schuldig" plädieren; **to ~ one's name** ~ für sich um etw bewerben; for evening classes, exam sich für etw anmelden; **to ~ sb ~ for an exam/a race/an award** jdn für or zu einer Prüfung/für ein Rennen anmelden/für eine Ehrung vorschlagen; **to ~ the car** ~ for a service das Auto zur Wartung (in die Werkstatt) bringen. **(e)** (install) central heating, car radio einbauen. **(f)** (employ) night-watchman einsetzen; (elect) political party an die Regierung bringen, ranbringen (inf). **(g)** (Sport: send in) player hereinnehmen; team to bat (als Innenmannschaft) hereinschicken. **(h)** (devote, expend) time zubringen, verbringen (with mit), verwenden (with auf). **we have a couple of hours to ~ ~ at Heathrow** wir müssen uns in Heathrow ein paar Stunden die Zeit vertreiben; **to ~ ~ an hour at the piano/an hour's painting** eine Stunde Klavier spielen/eine Stunde lang malen; **could you ~ ~ a few hours' work at the weekend?** könnten Sie am Wochenende ein paar Stunden Arbeit einschieben?; **he ~ ~ a lot of hard work on the project** er hat eine Menge harter Arbeit in das Projekt gesteckt; **he always ~s ~ a good day's work** er schafft jeden Tag ein ordentliches Arbeitspensum.

2 vi (a) **to ~ ~ for sth for job** sich um etw bewerben; for leave, rise, house also etw beantragen. **(b)** (Naut: enter port) **to ~ ~ at a port** in einen Hafen einlaufen; (call at) einen Hafen anlaufen; **to ~ ~ to Bremen/harbour** in Bremen/in den Hafen einlaufen; **to ~ ~ for supplies** einen Hafen anlaufen, um die Vorräte aufzufüllen.

♦ **put inside** vt sep (inf: in prison) einsperren (inf).

♦ **put off** vt sep (a) (set down) passengers aussteigen lassen (prep obj aus); (forcibly) hinauswerfen (prep obj aus). **the conductor ~ us** ~ **at the theatre** der Schaffner sagte uns (dat) am Theater Bescheid, daß wir aussteigen müßten; **we asked to be ~ ~ at the theatre** wir baten darum, uns (dat) am Theater Bescheid zu sagen. **(b)** (lay aside) uniform ablegen, ausziehen; responsibilities, worries ablegen. **(c)** (postpone, delay) match, appointment etc verschieben; decision aufschieben; sth unpleasant hinauszögern. **it's too late to ~ our visitors** ~ es ist zu spät, die Besucher (wieder) auszuladen; **to ~ sth ~ till later** etw auf später verschieben; **to ~ sth ~ for 10 days/until January** etw um 10 Tage herausschieben or aufschieben/auf Januar verschieben. **(d)** (make excuses to, be evasive with) questioner, boyfriend, creditor hinhalten. **he's not easily ~ ~** er läßt sich nicht so leicht beirren; **I won't be ~ ~ any longer** ich lasse mich nicht länger hinhalten. **(e)** (discourage from doing sth) **to ~ sb ~ doing sth** jdn davon abbringen or (person also) es jdm ausreden, etw zu tun. **(f)** (repel) die Lust nehmen or verderben (+dat). **to ~ sb ~ sth** jdm etw verleiden, jdm die Lust an etw (dat) nehmen; **don't let his rudeness ~ you** ~ störe dich nicht an seiner Flegelhaftigkeit; **are you trying to ~ me ~?** versuchst du, mir das mieszumachen (inf) or zu verleiden?; **I've been ~ ~ the idea** diese Idee ist mir verleidet worden. **(g)** (distract) ablenken (prep obj von). **to ~ sb ~ the track** jdn von der Fährte abbringen; **he is easily ~ ~ his game** er läßt sich leicht vom Spiel ablenken; **I'd like to watch you if it won't ~ you** ~ ich würde dir gern zusehen, wenn es dich nicht stört. **(h)** (switch off) light, TV, heater ausmachen, ausschalten; power, motor abstellen.

♦ **put on** vt sep (a) coat, shoes etc anziehen; hat (sich dat) aufsetzen; make-up auftragen, auflegen; (fig: assume) accent, manners annehmen; facade, front aufsetzen, vortäuschen. **to ~ one's make-up** sich schminken; **to ~ ~ an air of innocence** eine unschuldige Miene aufsetzen; **his sorrow is all ~ ~** sein Kummer ist bloß Schau (inf); **to ~ it ~** (inf) so tun(, als ob); **to ~ sb ~** (inf) jdn verkohlen (inf); **she's just ~ting it ~ when she talks about her aristocratic relations** sie will nur angeben, wenn sie von ihren adligen Verwandten spricht; see front. **(b)** (increase, add) **to ~ ~ weight/a few pounds** zunehmen/ein paar Pfund zunehmen; **to ~ ~ speed** schneller fahren, beschleunigen; **he ~ ~ fifty runs** (Cricket) er erhöhte (das

Gesamtergebnis) um fünfzig Punkte; **10p was ~ ~ the price of a gallon of petrol** der Benzinpreis wurde um 10 Pence pro Gallone erhöht; **he saw I wanted it and promptly ~ another £10 ~** (the price) er sah, daß ich es haben wollte, und hat gleich noch einmal £ 10 aufgeschlagen; **he's been ~ting it ~ a bit** er hat ganz schön zugenommen.

(c) *play* aufführen; *party* geben; *exhibition* veranstalten; *film* vorführen; *train, bus* einsetzen; *food (on menu)* auf die Speisekarte setzen; *(fig) act, show* abziehen *(inf).* **Sobers was ~ to bowl Sobers** wurde als Werfer eingesetzt; **he ~ ~ quite a show of being angry** er tat so, als wäre er wütend; **she ~ ~ a display of temper** sie inszenierte einen Wutanfall.

(d) *(on telephone)* **to ~ sb ~ to sb** jdn mit jdm verbinden; **would you ~ him ~?** könnten Sie ihn mir geben?

(e) *(switch on) light, TV* anmachen, einschalten. **to ~ the kettle/dinner ~** das Wasser/das Essen aufsetzen *or* aufstellen.

(f) *watch etc* vorstellen; *see* **clock.**

(g) to ~ sb ~ to sth *(inform about)* jdm etw vermitteln; **to ~ sb ~ to a plumber/garage** *etc* jdm einen Installateur/eine Reparaturwerkstatt *etc* empfehlen; **he ~ me ~ to a first-rate dentist** durch ihn bin ich an einen erstklassigen Zahnarzt gekommen; **what ~ you ~ to it?** was hat dich darauf gebracht?; **to ~ the police ~ to sb** die Polizei auf jds Spur bringen; **to ~ sb ~ to a winner/good thing** jdm einen heißen *(inf) or* todsicheren Tip geben.

♦ **put out 1** *vt sep* **(a)** *(place outside) rubbish etc* hinausbringen; *cat, drunk* vor die Tür setzen. **to ~ the washing ~** (to dry) die Wäsche (zum Trocknen) raushängen; **to be ~ ~** *(asked to leave)* vor die Tür gesetzt werden; **to be ~ ~ of the Union** aus der Gewerkschaft ausgeschlossen werden; **to be ~ ~ of a restaurant** aus einem Restaurant hinausgeworfen werden; **to ~ sb ~ of business** jdn aus dem Markt drängen; **she could not ~ him ~ of her thoughts** er ging ihr nicht aus dem Sinn; **to ~ sb's eyes ~** jdm die Augen ausstechen; *see* **grass.**

(b) *(stretch out, push out) hand, foot* ausstrecken; *tongue, head* herausstrecken. **to ~ one's head ~ of the window** den Kopf zum Fenster hinausstrecken; *see* **feeler.**

(c) *(sprout) leaves, roots* hervorbringen, treiben.

(d) *cards, dishes, cutlery* auflegen; *chessmen etc* aufstellen.

(e) *(farm out) work* weggeben, vergeben *(to an +acc).*

(f) *(bring out, circulate) pamphlet, book* herausbringen; *propaganda* machen; *rumour* verbreiten; *regulations* erlassen; *statement* abgeben; *message, appeal* durchgeben; *description* bekanntgeben; *(on TV, radio) programme* bringen, senden.

(g) *(generate) kilowatts etc* abgeben; *horsepower* leisten.

(h) *(extinguish) fire, light, candle* ausmachen, löschen.

(i) *(make unconscious)* bewußtlos machen, betäuben; *(boxer)* k.o. schlagen.

(j) *(discontent, vex)* **to be ~ ~** (by sth) (über etw acc) verärgert *or* ungehalten sein; **nothing seems to ~ her ~** sie scheint sich über nichts zu ärgern; **she looked rather ~ ~** sie sah ziemlich verärgert *or* ungehalten aus.

(k) *(inconvenience)* **to ~ sb ~** jdm Umstände bereiten *or* machen; **to ~ oneself ~** (for sb) sich *(dat)* (wegen jdm) Umstände machen.

(l) *(dislocate) knee, shoulder* ausrenken; *(more severely)* auskugeln; *back* verrenken; *see* **nose.**

(m) *(make inaccurate) (fig) calculations, figures* verfälschen; *instruments* ungenau machen.

(n) *(lend at interest) money* verleihen *(to an +acc).* **to ~ money ~ at interest/at 12%** Geld für Zinsen/zu 12% (Zinsen) verleihen.

2 *vi (Naut: set sail)* auslaufen. **to ~ ~ to sea** in See stechen; **to ~ ~ of port/from Bremen** aus dem Hafen/von Bremen auslaufen.

♦ **put over** *vt sep* **(a)** *see* **put across. (b)** *(esp US: postpone)* verschieben *(to, until* auf *+acc).*

♦ **put through** *vt sep* **(a)** *plan, reform, proposal, bill* durchbringen; *(+prep obj)* bringen durch; *claim* weiterleiten; *job* durchführen, durchziehen *(inf); deal* tätigen.

(b) *+prep obj (cause to undergo)* durchmachen lassen. **to ~ sb ~ a test/an exam** jdn einem Test/einer Prüfung unterziehen; **he has ~ his family ~ a lot of suffering** seine Familie hat seinetwegen viel durchgemacht; **he was ~ ~ a lot of pain** er hat viel Schmerzen durchmachen müssen; **his guilty conscience ~ him ~ hell** sein schlechtes Gewissen machte ihm das Leben zur Hölle; **to ~ sb ~ university** jdn durch die Universität bringen; **they really ~ him ~ it!** *(inf)* den haben sie vielleicht durch die Mangel gedreht! *(inf); see* **mill, pace² 1 (a).**

(c) *(connect by telephone) person* verbinden *(to* mit*); call* durchstellen *(to* zu*).* **to ~ a call ~ to Beirut** ein Gespräch nach Beirut vermitteln *or* (caller) anmelden.

♦ **put together** *vt sep* **(a)** *(put in same room, cage etc)* zusammentun; *(seat together)* zusammensetzen. **he's better than all the others ~ ~** er ist besser als alle anderen zusammen; **we don't want to ~ two men ~ at the table** wir wollen nicht zwei Herren am Tisch nebeneinandersetzen; *see* **head 1 (c).**

(b) *(assemble)* zusammensetzen; *furniture, machine also* zusammenbauen; *book, essay, menu* zusammenstellen; *meal* auf die Beine stellen *(inf); collection, evidence, facts* zusammentragen; *case* aufstellen; *see* **two.**

♦ **put under** *vt sep (doctor)* betäuben.

♦ **put up 1** *vt sep* **(a)** *(raise, lift up) hand* hochheben; *car window* zumachen; *sash window* hochschieben; *umbrella* aufspannen; *hair* hochstecken; *collar* hochschlagen, hochklappen. **~ 'em ~!** *(inf) (hands in surrender)* Hände hoch!; *(fists to fight)* na, mach schon!; *see* **back 1 (a), foot 1 (a), wind¹ 1 (a).**

(b) *(hoist) flag, sail* hissen, aufziehen.

(c) *(fasten up) picture, decorations, curtains* aufhängen; *poster also* anmachen *(inf); notice also* anschlagen.

(d) *(erect) building, fence, barrier, memorial* errichten;

ladder, scaffolding aufstellen; *tent* aufschlagen.

(e) *(send up) missile, flare* hochschießen; *space probe also* hochschicken.

(f) *(increase) numbers, sales, demands* erhöhen; *rent also* heraufsetzen; *prices (company)* erhöhen; *(rising costs)* hochtreiben; *sb's temperature, blood pressure* hochtreiben.

(g) *see* **put forward (a).**

(h) *(offer)* **to ~ sth ~ for sale/auction** etw zum Verkauf anbieten/zur Versteigerung geben; **to ~ ~ resistance (to sb)** (jdm) Widerstand leisten, sich (gegen jdn) wehren; *see* **fight 1** (a), **struggle, performance.**

(i) *(feign) façade* vortäuschen.

(j) *(give accommodation to)* unterbringen.

(k) *(provide) capital* bereitstellen; *reward* aussetzen.

(l) **to ~ sb ~ to sth** jdn zu etw anstiften.

2 *vi* **(a)** *(stay)* wohnen; *(for one night)* übernachten.

(b) **~ ~ or shut up!** Geld her oder Maul halten! *(inf).*

♦ **put upon** *vi +prep obj (impose on)* ausnutzen. **I won't be ~ ~** any longer ich lasse mich nicht länger ausnutzen.

♦ **put up with** *vi +prep obj* sich abfinden mit. **I won't ~ ~ ~ that** das lasse ich mir nicht gefallen.

putative ['pju:tətıv] *adj (form)* vermutlich; *father, culprit* mutmaßlich. **the creatures which are our ~** ancestors die Lebewesen, die vermutlich unsere Vorfahren sind; **a ~ source of oil** eine vermutete Ölquelle.

put: **~-down** *n (snub)* Abfuhr *m;* **~-off** *n (inf)* faule Ausrede *(inf);* **~-on** *(inf)* **1** *adj* unecht, vorgetäuscht, aufgesetzt; *smile also* falsch; **2** *n* Bluff *m,* Schau *f (inf);* **it's just a ~-on** das ist nur Schau *or* (ein) Bluff.

put-put ['pʌtpʌt] **1** *n (sound)* Tuckern *nt.* **2** *vi* tuckern.

putrefaction [,pju:trı'fækʃən] *n* Verwesung *f.*

putrefy ['pju:trıfaı] *vi* verwesen.

putrescent [pju:'tresnt] *adj (form)* verwesend.

putrid ['pju:trıd] *adj* verfault; *smell* faulig; *(fig: corrupt)* zersetzt; *(inf: horrible)* gräßlich, ekelhaft. **the rubbish had become ~** der Abfall war verfault.

putsch [putʃ] *n* Putsch *m.*

putt [pʌt] **1** *n* Schlag *m (mit dem man einlocht).* **he needed a long ~ at the 5th hole** am 5. Loch mußte er aus großem Abstand einlochen. **2** *vti* putten, einlochen.

puttee, putty ['pʌtı] *n* (Wickel)gamasche *f.*

putter¹ ['pʌtə'] *n (golf-club)* Putter *m.* **he's a good ~** er kann gut einlochen.

putter² *(US) vi see* **potter.**

putting ['pʌtıŋ] *n* Putten, Einlochen *nt; (as game)* Putten *nt.* **~ green** kleiner Golfplatz nur zum Putten; *(green)* Grün *nt.*

putty¹ ['pʌtı] **1** *n* Kitt *m.* **~ knife** Spachtel *m;* **he was ~ in her hands** er war Wachs in ihren Händen. **2** *vt* kitten.

putty² *n see* **puttee.**

put: **~-up** *adj (inf)* **a ~-up job** ein abgekartetes Spiel; **~-upon** *adj (inf)* ausgenutzt; **she had a rather ~-upon air** sie guckte so, als fiele ihr ein Zacken aus der Krone; **~-you-up** *n (Brit inf)* Schlafcouch *f.*

puzzle ['pʌzl] **1** *n* **(a)** *(wordgame etc)* Rätsel *nt; (toy)* Geduldsspiel *nt; (jigsaw)* Puzzle(spiel) *nt.* **books of ~s** *or* **~ books for children** Rätselbücher *pl* für Kinder.

(b) *(mystery)* Rätsel *nt.* **it's a ~ to me** es ist mir ein Rätsel. **2** *vt* **(a)** verblüffen. **to be ~d about sth** sich über etw *(acc)* im unklaren sein; **the authorities are ~d** die Behörden stehen vor einem Rätsel. **(b)** **to ~ sth out** etw (her)austüfteln.

3 *vi* **to ~ about** *or* **over sth** sich *(dat)* über etw *(acc)* den Kopf zerbrechen.

puzzled ['pʌzld] *adj look, frown* verdutzt, verblüfft.

puzzlement ['pʌzlmənt] *n* Verblüffung, Verwirrung *f.* **the look of ~ on her face** die Verwirrung in ihrem Gesicht.

puzzler ['pʌzlə'] *n (problem)* harter Brocken *(inf).*

puzzling ['pʌzlıŋ] *adj* rätselhaft; *story, mechanism, attitude, question* verwirrend.

PVC *abbr of* **polyvinyl chloride** PVC *nt.*

Pvt *(US Mil) abbr of* **Private.**

PX *(US) abbr of* **Post Exchange.**

pygmy, pigmy ['pıgmı] **1** *n* **(a)** **P~** Pygmäe *m.* **(b)** *(small person, fig)* Zwerg *m.* **2** *adj* **(a)** **P~** Pygmäen-. **(b)** Zwerg-.

pyjama, (US) pajama [pə'dʒɑːmə] *adj attr jacket, trousers* Schlafanzug-, Pyjama-; *party* Pyjama-.

pyjamas, (US) pajamas [pə'dʒɑːməz] *npl* Schlafanzug, Pyjama *m.*

pylon ['paılən] *n* Mast *m.*

pylorus [paı'lɔ:rəs] *n* Pförtner, Pylorus *(spec) m.*

pyorrhoea, (US) pyorrhea [paıə'rıə] *n* Parodontitis *f (spec).*

pyramid ['pırəmıd] *n* Pyramide *f.* **~ selling** ≈ Schneeballsystem *nt.*

pyramidal [pı'ræmıdl] *adj* pyramidenförmig, Pyramiden-.

pyre ['paıə'] *n* Scheiterhaufen *m (zum Verbrennen von Leichen).*

Pyrenean [pırə'nıːən] *adj* pyrenäisch. **~ mountain dog** Pyrenäenhund *m.*

Pyrenees [pırə'niːz] *npl* Pyrenäen *pl.*

Pyrex ® ['paıreks] *n* Hartglas, Jenaer Glas ® *nt.*

pyrite(s) ['paıraıt(s)] *n* Eisen- *or* Schwefelkies, Pyrit *m.*

pyromania [,paıərəʊ'meınıə] *n* Pyromanie *f.*

pyromaniac [,paıərəʊ'meınıæk] *n* Pyromane *m,* Pyromanin *f.*

pyrotechnic [,paıərəʊ'teknık] *adj (lit)* pyrotechnisch; *(fig)* brillant.

pyrotechnics [,paıərəʊ'teknıks] *n (sing)* Pyrotechnik *f; (pl: display)* Feuerwerk *nt.* **a display of ~** *(lit, fig)* ein Feuerwerk *nt.*

Pyrrhic ['pırık] *adj:* **~ victory** Pyrrhussieg *m.*

Pythagoras [paı'θægərəs] *n* Pythagoras *m.* **~' theorem** der Satz des Pythagoras.

Pythagorean [paı,θægə'rıən] *adj* pythagoräisch.

python ['paıθən] *n* Python(schlange *f) m.*

pyx [pıks] *n* Hostienkelch *m; (for sick communion)* Bursa *f.*

Q

Q, q [kjuː] n Q, q nt; see P.
Q abbr of **Queen.**
QC abbr of **Queen's Counsel.**
QED abbr of **quod erat demonstrandum** q.e.d.
qt abbr of **quart.**
q.t. [ˌkjuːˈtiː] n: **on the ~** (inf) heimlich.
qtr abbr of **quarter.**
qua [kwɑː] adv als.
quack¹ [kwæk] **1** n Schnattern, Quaken nt no pl. **~-quack** (baby-talk) Entchen nt. **2** vi (duck) schnattern, quaken, quak machen (inf). **what? she ~ed** was?, quakte sie.
quack² **1** n (also ~ **doctor**) Quacksalber, Kurpfuscher m; (hum: doctor) Doktor, Medizinmann (hum) m. **2** adj attr methods Kurpfuscher-. **~ remedy/medicine** Mittelchen nt.
quackery [ˈkwækərɪ] n Quacksalberei, Kurpfuscherei f.
quad [kwɒd] n abbr of **(a) quadrangle** Hof m. **(b) quadruplet** Vierling m. **(c)** (Typ) **quadrat** Quadrat nt, Blockade f. **em/en ~** Geviert/Halbgeviert nt.
Quadragesima [ˌkwɒdrəˈdʒesɪmə] n Quadragesima f.
quadrangle [ˈkwɒdrængl] n **(a)** (Math) Viereck nt. **(b)** (Archit) (viereckiger) (Innen)hof.
quadrangular [kwɒˈdrængjʊləʳ] adj viereckig.
quadrant [ˈkwɒdrənt] n (all senses) Quadrant m.
quadrat [ˈkwɒdrət] n (Typ) see **quad (c).**
quadratic [kwɒˈdrætɪk] adj (Math) quadratisch.
quadrature [ˈkwɒdrətʃəʳ] n (Math, Astron) Quadratur f.
quadrilateral [ˌkwɒdrɪˈlætərəl] **1** adj (Math) vierseitig. **2** n Viereck nt.
quadrille [kwəˈdrɪl] n Quadrille f.
quadripartite [ˈkwɒdrɪˈpɑːtaɪt] adj (Pol form) Vierer-. **~ agreement** Viermächteabkommen nt; **the ~ division of Berlin** die Teilung Berlins in vier Sektoren.
quadroon [kwɒˈdruːn] n Viertelneger(in f) m, Terzerone m (spec), Terzeronin f (spec).
quadrophonic [ˌkwɒdrəˈfɒnɪk] adj quadrophonisch.
quadruped [ˈkwɒdrʊped] **1** n Vierfüß(l)er m. **2** adj vierfüßig.
quadruple [ˈkwɒdrʊpl] **1** adj vierfach; (Mus, Pol) Vierer-. **~ time** (Mus) Vierertakt m. **2** n Vierfache(s) nt. **3** vt vervierfachen. **4** vi sich vervierfachen.
quadruplet [kwɒˈdruːplɪt] n (child) Vierling m.
quadruplicate [kwɒˈdruːplɪkɪt] adj vierfach. **2** n: **in ~** in vierfacher Ausfertigung.
quaff [kwɒf] (old, hum) **1** vt trinken, schlürfen (hum). **2** vi zechen (old, hum); (take a swig) schlucken. **he ~ed long and deep** er nahm einen langen, kräftigen Schluck.
quagmire [ˈkwægmaɪəʳ] n Sumpf, Morast m; (fig: of vice etc) Morast m; (difficult situation) Schlamassel m (inf). **the paths were reduced to a ~** die Wege waren völlig aufgeweicht or matschig; **he was bogged down in a ~ of tiny details** er hatte sich in einem Wust von kleinen Einzelheiten festgebissen; **he was stuck in a ~ of indecision** er konnte sich zu keinem Entschluß durchringen; **in the ~ of his marriage** in seiner Ehemisere; **a ~ of sin** ein Sündenpfuhl m.
quail¹ [kweɪl] vi (vor Angst) zittern or beben (before vor +dat).
quail² n (Orn) Wachtel f.
quaint [kweɪnt] adj (+er) **(a)** (picturesque) cottage, village, scene malerisch, idyllisch; (charmingly old-fashioned) pub, custom, expression urig, reizend (used esp by women).
(b) (pleasantly odd) idea kurios, schnurrig, putzig (used esp by women); nickname originell; old lady, way of speaking drollig. **a ~ little dog/dress** ein putziges Hündchen/Kleidchen; **how ~ to live in such an old house** das ist ja urig, in so einem alten Haus zu wohnen; **what a thought, my dear, how ~!** nein so was, meine Liebe, wie originell!
quaintly [ˈkweɪntlɪ] adv **(a)** (picturesquely) malerisch, idyllisch; decorated, finished malerisch, urig.
(b) written schnurrig; dressed putzig; nicknamed originell. **their little daughter got up and danced so ~ that ...** ihr Töchterchen ist aufgestanden und hat so drollig getanzt, daß ...
quaintness [ˈkweɪntnɪs] n see adj **(a)** malerischer or idyllischer Anblick; Urigkeit f. **(b)** Kuriosität, Schnurrigkeit, Putzigkeit f; Originalität f; Drolligkeit f.
quake [kweɪk] **1** vi zittern, beben (with vor +dat); (earth, rafters etc) beben, erzittern. **he ~d at the knees** ihm zitterten or schlotterten (inf) die Knie. **2** n (inf: earth) (Erd)beben nt. **(b)** (of rafters etc) Beben nt.
Quaker [ˈkweɪkəʳ] n Quäker(in f) m.
Quakerism [ˈkweɪkərɪzəm] n Quäkertum nt.
qualification [ˌkwɒlɪfɪˈkeɪʃən] n **(a)** (on paper) Qualifikation f; (document itself) Zeugnis nt; (skill, ability, suitable quality) Voraussetzung f. **what ~s do you have for this job?** welche Qualifikationen haben Sie für diese Stelle?; **his only ~ was his keenness** seine einzige Qualifikation war sein starkes Interesse; **English ~s are not recognized by Scottish schools** englische Zeugnisse werden von schottischen Schulen nicht anerkannt; **the only ~ needed is patience/is a knowledge of French** die einzige Voraussetzung ist Geduld/sind Französischkenntnisse.
(b) (act of qualifying) Abschluß m von jds Ausbildung. **after**

his ~ **as a doctor/an insurance broker** nachdem er seine Ausbildung als Arzt/Versicherungsagent abgeschlossen hatte; **prior to his ~** vor Abschluß seines Studiums.
(c) (Sport) Qualifikation f.
(d) (prerequisite) Voraussetzung f.
(e) (limitation) Einschränkung f, Vorbehalt m; (modification) Modifikation f. **no amount of ~ can make me agree with your suggestion** wenn Sie Ihren Vorschlag auch noch so sehr modifizieren, ich kann doch nicht zustimmen; **to accept a plan with/without ~(s)** einen Plan unter Vorbehalt/vorbehaltlos billigen.
(f) (Gram) nähere Bestimmung.
qualified [ˈkwɒlɪfaɪd] adj **(a)** (having training) ausgebildet; engineer graduiert; (with university degree) Diplom-. **highly ~** hochqualifiziert; **to be ~ to do sth** qualifiziert sein, etw zu tun; **~ to practice doctor, lawyer** zugelassen; **he is/is not ~ to teach** er besitzt die/keine Lehrbefähigung; **he was not ~ for the job** ihm fehlte die Qualifikation für die Stelle; **he is fully ~** er ist voll ausgebildet; **now that you are ~** nachdem Sie nun Ihre Ausbildung abgeschlossen haben.
(b) (able, entitled) berechtigt. **to be ~ to vote** wahlberechtigt sein; **I'm not ~ to speak for her** ich bin nicht kompetent, in ihrem Namen zu sprechen; **what makes you think you're ~ to judge her?** mit welchem Recht meinen Sie, sie beurteilen zu können?
(c) (limited) praise, approval bedingt, nicht uneingeschränkt. **we're only prepared to make a ~ statement about ...** wir können uns nur bedingt or mit Einschränkungen zu ... äußern; **his theory is so ~ as to be ...** seine Theorie hat so viele Einschränkungen, daß sie ...; **in a ~ sense** mit Einschränkungen; **a ~ success** kein voller Erfolg; **~ acceptance** (Comm) bedingte Annahme.
qualifier [ˈkwɒlɪfaɪəʳ] n (Gram) Ausdruck m des Grades.
qualify [ˈkwɒlɪfaɪ] **1** vt **(a)** (make competent) qualifizieren; (make legally entitled) berechtigen, das Recht geben (+dat). **to ~ sb to do sth** (entitle) jdn berechtigen, etw zu tun; **his experience qualifies him to make these decisions** aufgrund seiner Erfahrung ist er qualifiziert or kompetent, diese Entscheidungen zu treffen; **this qualifies him for promotion** dadurch kommt er für eine Beförderung in Betracht.
(b) (limit) statement, criticism einschränken; (change slightly) opinion, remark modifizieren, relativieren. **this clause qualifies the meaning of the statement** dieser Satz modifiziert die Bedeutung der Aussage.
(c) (Gram) charakterisieren, näher bestimmen. **the adjective qualifies the noun** das Adjektiv bestimmt das Substantiv näher or ist eine nähere Bestimmung zum Substantiv.
(d) (describe) beschreiben, klassifizieren.
2 vi **(a)** (acquire degree etc) seine Ausbildung abschließen, sich qualifizieren. **to ~ as a lawyer/doctor/teacher** sein juristisches/medizinisches Staatsexamen machen/die Lehrbefähigung erhalten; **to ~ as an officer** das Offizierspatent erwerben; **if your salary increases when you ~** Sie bekommen nach bestandener Prüfung ein höheres Gehalt.
(b) (Sport, in competition) sich qualifizieren (for für). **those who pass the first round of tests ~ for the final interviews** diejenigen, die die erste Testreihe erfolgreich bearbeiten, kommen in die engere und letzte Auswahl.
(c) (fulfil required conditions) in Frage kommen (for für). **does he ~ for admission to the club?** erfüllt er die Bedingungen für die Aufnahme in den Klub?; **he hardly qualifies as a poet** er kann kaum als Dichter angesehen werden.
qualifying [ˈkwɒlɪfaɪɪŋ] adj adjective erläuternd; round, heat Qualifikations-. **~ examination** Auswahlprüfung f.
qualitative adj, **~ly** adv [ˈkwɒlɪtətɪv, -lɪ] qualitativ.
quality [ˈkwɒlɪtɪ] **1** n **(a)** (degree of goodness) Qualität f; (Comm: categorized also) Güteklasse f; (of justice, education etc) (hoher) Stand. **of the best ~** von bester Qualität; **of good/poor ~** von guter/schlechter Qualität, qualitativ gut/schlecht; **~ matters more than quantity** Qualität geht vor Quantität; **they vary in ~** sie sind qualitativ verschieden; **this wine has ~** dieser Wein hat Qualität; **he's got ~** er hat Format; **the excellent ~ of her mind** ihr hervorragender Verstand.
(b) (characteristics) (of person, thing) Eigenschaft f; (desirable also) Qualität f. **the ~ of patience/selflessness etc** Geduld f/Selbstlosigkeit f etc.
(c) (nature) Art f. **because of the special ~ of the relationship** da es eine Beziehung besonderer Art war; **the ~ of my love for him is such that ...** meine Liebe zu ihm ist dergestalt, daß ...; (geh); **the sad ~ of the song** die traurige Stimmung des Liedes.
(d) (of voice, sound) Klangfarbe f; (Ling) Qualität f; (of colour) Farbqualität f.
(e) (old, hum: high rank) vornehmer Stand. **the ~** die Oberschicht, die vornehme Welt; **people of ~** Leute von Rang und Namen; **a lady of ~** eine vornehme Dame.
2 attr **(a)** goods etc Qualitäts-; rating also, mark Güte-.
(b) (inf: good) erstklassig (inf); newspaper angesehen.
quality control n Qualitätskontrolle f.
qualm [kwɑːm] n **(a)** (doubt, scruple) Skrupel m, Bedenken nt. **I**

would feel no ~s about killing that dog ich würde keine Bedenken or Skrupel haben, den Hund zu töten; **without the slightest** ~ ohne die geringsten Skrupel or Bedenken; **without a** ~ ohne jeden Skrupel; **~s of conscience** Gewissensbisse *pl*; **he suddenly had** ~s **about it** ihn überkamen plötzlich Skrupel or Bedenken; **don't tell me you've got** ~s **about taking the money** sag bloß, daß du Skrupel hast, das Geld zu nehmen.

(b) (*misgiving*) Bedenken *nt*. **I had some** ~s **about his future** ich hatte mancherlei Bedenken wegen seiner Zukunft.

(c) (*old: nausea*) Übelkeit *f*.

quandary ['kwɒndərɪ] *n* Verlegenheit *f*, Dilemma *nt*. **what a** ~ **he was in!** was für ein Dilemma!; **he was in a** ~ **as to** or **about what to do** er wußte nicht, was er tun sollte; **to put sb in a** ~ jdn in Verlegenheit or eine mißliche Lage bringen.

quanta ['kwɒntə] *pl of* **quantum**.

quantification [ˌkwɒntɪfɪ'keɪʃən] *n* Quantifizierung *f*.

quantifier ['kwɒntɪfaɪəʳ] *n* (*Logic*) Quantor *m*.

quantify ['kwɒntɪfaɪ] *vt* quantifizieren (*form*), in Zahlen ausdrücken.

quantitative *adj*, **~ly** *adv* ['kwɒntɪtətɪv, -lɪ] quantitativ.

quantity ['kwɒntɪtɪ] *n* **(a)** (*amount*) Menge *f*; (*proportion*) Anteil *m* (*of an* + *dat*), Quantum *nt*. **to prefer** ~ **to quality** Quantität der Qualität vorziehen; **in** ~, **in large quantities** in großen Mengen; **how big was the** ~ **you ordered?** welche Menge haben Sie bestellt?; **a tiny** ~ **of poison** eine kleine Menge/eine kleine Dosis Gift; **what** ~ **of yeast was used?** wieviel Hefe wurde benutzt?; **the** ~ **of meat in these sausages is very small** der Fleischanteil in diesen Würsten ist sehr klein; **in equal quantities** zu gleichen Mengen or Teilen.

(b) *often pl* (*large amount or number of*) Unmenge *f*. **quantities of books/beer** Unmengen von Büchern/Bier.

(c) (*Math, Phys, fig*) Größe *f*.

(d) (*Poet, Phon*) Quantität *f*.

quantity: ~ **mark** *n* Quantitätszeichen *nt*; ~ **surveyor** *n* Baukostenkalkulator *m*.

quantum ['kwɒntəm] *n, pl* **quanta** (*Phys*) Quant *nt*. **the quality of life cannot be measured as a** ~ Lebensqualität kann nicht in Zahlen ausgedrückt werden; **the** ~ **of satisfaction** das (Aus)maß an Befriedigung.

quantum: ~ **mechanics** *n sing* Quantenmechanik *f*; ~ **number** *n* Quantenzahl *f*; ~ **physics** *n sing* Quantenphysik *f*; ~ **theory** *n* Quantentheorie *f*.

quarantine ['kwɒrəntiːn] **1** *n* Quarantäne *f*. **to be in** ~ in Quarantäne sein; (*ship*) unter Quarantäne liegen; **to put sb in** ~ jdn unter Quarantäne stellen. **2** *attr* Quarantäne-. **3** *vt person, ship* unter Quarantäne stellen.

quark [kwɑːk] *n* (*Phys*) Quark *nt*.

quarrel¹ ['kwɒrəl] *n* (*in window*) rautenförmiges Fensterglas.

quarrel² **1** *n* **(a)** Streit *m*; (*dispute*) Auseinandersetzung *f*. **they have had a** ~ sie haben Streit gehabt, sie haben sich gestritten; **let's not have a** ~ **about it** wir wollen uns nicht darüber streiten; **to start** or **pick a** ~ einen Streit anfangen (*with* mit).

(b) (*cause for complaint*) Einwand *m* (*with* gegen). **I have no** ~ **with him** ich habe nichts gegen ihn.

2 *vi* **(a)** (*have a dispute*) sich streiten (*with* mit, *about, over* über + *acc*, *over inheritance/girl* wegen or um Erbe/Mädchen); (*more trivially also*) sich zanken. **to** ~ **with fate** (*liter*) mit seinem Schicksal hadern (*liter*).

(b) (*find fault*) etwas auszusetzen haben (*with an* + *dat*). **you can't** ~ **with that** daran kann man doch nichts aussetzen.

quarrelling, (*US*) **quarreling** ['kwɒrəlɪŋ] *n* Streiterei *f*.

quarrelsome ['kwɒrəlsəm] *adj* streitsüchtig, händelsüchtig; *woman also* zänkisch.

quarrelsomeness ['kwɒrəlsəmnɪs] *n* Streitsucht, Händelsucht *f*.

quarry¹ ['kwɒrɪ] **1** *n* **(a)** Steinbruch *m*. **sandstone/slate** *etc* ~ Sandstein-/Schieferbruch *etc*. **(b)** (*fig*) Fundgrube *f*. **2** *vt* brechen, hauen. **3** *vi* Steine brechen or hauen. **to** ~ **for sth** etw hauen or brechen; (*fig*) nach etw suchen.

♦ **quarry out** *vt sep block* heraushauen or -brechen.

quarry² *n* **(a)** Beute *f*. **(b)** (*fig*) (*thing*) Ziel *nt*; (*person*) Opfer *nt*.

quarryman ['kwɒrɪmən] *n, pl* **-men** [-mən] Steinbrucharbeiter, Steinhauer *m*.

quart¹ [kwɔːt] *n* (*Measure*) Quart *nt*. **to try to put a** ~ **into a pint pot** Unmögliches versuchen.

quart² *n* **(a)** (*Fencing*) Quart *f*. **(b)** (*Cards*) Vierersequenz, Quart *f*. ~ **major** Quartmajor *f*.

quarter ['kwɔːtəʳ] **1** *n* **(a)** (*fourth part*) Viertel *nt*. **to divide sth into** ~s etw in vier Teile teilen; **the bottle was a** ~/**three-~s full** die Flasche war zu einem Viertel/drei Vierteln gefüllt or viertel/dreiviertel voll; **a** ~ (**of a pound**) **of tea** ein Viertel-(pfund) Tee; **a mile and a** ~ eineinviertel Meilen; **a** ~ **of a mile** eine Viertelmeile; **it was a** ~ **as big as the other one** es war ein Viertel so groß wie das andere; **for a** ~ (**of**) **the price, for ~ the price** zu einem Viertel des Preises.

(b) (*in expressions of time*) Viertel *nt*. **a** ~ **of an hour** eine Viertelstunde; **a** ~ **to seven** (*Brit*), **a** ~ **of seven** (*US*) (ein) Viertel vor sieben, dreiviertel sieben (*dial*); **a** ~ **past six** (*Brit*), **a** ~ **after six** (*esp US*) (ein) Viertel nach sechs, viertel sieben (*dial*); **it's just on the** ~ es ist gerade Viertel; **the clock strikes the** ~s die Uhr schlägt alle Viertelstunde; **the clock has just struck the** ~ die Uhr hat eben Viertel or die Viertelstunde geschlagen; **an hour and a** ~ eineinviertel Stunden, fünf viertel Stunden.

(c) (*fourth of year*) Vierteljahr, Quartal *nt*. **paid by the** ~ vierteljährlich bezahlt; **a** ~**'s rent** die Miete für ein Quartal.

(d) (*US*) Vierteldollar *m*, 25-Centstück *nt*.

(e) (*district in town*) Viertel *nt*.

(f) (*area*) **he has travelled in all** ~s **of the globe** er ist schon kreuz und quer durch die Welt gereist; **they came from all** ~s **of the earth** sie kamen aus allen Teilen der Welt; **in these** ~s in dieser Gegend.

(g) (*direction*) (Himmels)richtung *f*. **they came from all** ~s sie kamen aus allen Himmelsrichtungen.

(h) (*Naut: direction of wind*) Richtung *f*. **what** ~ **is the wind in?** aus welcher Richtung kommt der Wind?

(i) (*side*) Seite *f*; (*place*) Stelle *f*. **he won't get help from that** ~ von dieser Seite wird er keine Hilfe bekommen; **in high** ~s höheren Orts; **in various** ~s an verschiedenen Stellen.

(j) ~s *pl* (*lodgings*) Quartier *nt* (*also Mil*), Unterkunft *f*; **winter** ~s Winterquartier *nt*; **to take up one's** ~s (*Mil*) sein Quartier beziehen; **to be confined to** ~s (*Mil*) Stubenarrest haben.

(k) (*Naut: for battle*) Posten *m*. **to take up one's** ~s Posten beziehen.

(l) (*Naut: part of ship*) Achterschiff *nt*. **on the port/starboard** ~ backbord/steuerbord.

(m) (*mercy in battle*) Schonung *f*, Pardon *m*. **to give** ~ Schonung or Pardon gewähren; **to ask** or **cry for** ~ um Schonung bitten; **he showed no** ~ er kannte kein Pardon; **no** ~ **was asked for and none given** es wurde auf beiden Seiten schonungslos gekämpft.

(n) (*Her*) Wappenfeld *nt*.

(o) (*of moon*) Viertel *nt*.

(p) (*Sport: of match*) (Spiel)viertel *nt*.

(q) (*Measure*) = Viertelzentner *m*.

2 *adj pound, mile* Viertel-. **the/a** ~ **part** das/ein Viertel.

3 *vt* **(a)** vierteln; (*divide into four also*) in vier Teile teilen; *beef, horse* (in vier Teile) zerlegen; *traitor's body* vierteilen.

(b) (*lodge*) unterbringen, einquartieren (*also Mil*) (*on* bei).

quarter: ~**-back** *n* (*US Ftbl*) Quarterback *m*; ~**-day** *n* Quartalstag *m*; ~**deck** *n* (*Naut*) Achterdeck, Quarterdeck *nt*; ~**-final** *n* Viertelfinalspiel *nt*; ~**-finalist** *n* Teilnehmer(in *f*) *m* am Viertelfinale; ~**-finals** *npl* Viertelfinale *nt*.

quartering ['kwɔːtərɪŋ] *n* **(a)** *see vt* **(a)** Vierteln *nt*; Teilung *f* in vier Teile; Zerlegen *nt*; Vierteilen *nt*. **(b)** (*Mil*) Einquartierung *f*. **(c)** (*Her*) Einteilung *f* in vier Felder.

quarterlight ['kwɔːtəlaɪt] *n* (*Brit*) Dreieckfenster *nt*; (*openable*) Ausstellfenster *nt*.

quarterly ['kwɔːtəlɪ] **1** *adj* vierteljährlich. **2** *n* Vierteljahresschrift *f*. **3** *adv* vierteljährlich, alle Vierteljahre.

quartermaster ['kwɔːtəˌmɑːstəʳ] *n* **(a)** (*Mil*) Quartiermeister *m*. **(b)** (*Navy*) Steuermannsmaat *m*. ~**'s store** Versorgungslager *nt*.

Quartermaster General *n* Generalquartiermeister *m*.

quarter: ~**-note** *n* (*US Mus*) Viertel(note *f*) *nt*; ~**-note rest** Viertelpause *f*; ~ **sessions** *npl* vierteljährliche Gerichtssitzungen *pl*; ~**staff** *n* (*Hist*) Schlagstock *m*; ~**-tone** *n* Vierteltonintervall *nt*.

quartet(te) [kwɔː'tet] *n* (*Mus, foursome*) Quartett *nt*.

quarto ['kwɔːtəʊ] **1** *n* (*Typ*) Quart(format) *nt*. **2** *attr paper, volume* in Quart.

quartz ['kwɔːts] *n* Quarz *m*. ~ **clock** Quarzuhr *f*; ~ **crystal** Quarzkristall *m*; ~ (**iodine**) **lamp** Quarzlampe *f*.

quartzite ['kwɔːtsaɪt] *n* Quarzfels *m*.

quasar ['kweɪzɑːʳ] *n* Quasar *m*.

quash [kwɒʃ] *vt* **(a)** (*Jur*) *verdict* aufheben, annullieren. **(b)** *rebellion* unterdrücken; *suggestion, objection* ablehnen.

quasi- ['kwɑːzɪ] *pref* quasi-, quasi. **acting in a** ~**-managerial function** quasi als Manager handelnd.

quatercentenary [ˌkwɔːtəsen'tiːnərɪ] *n* (*also* ~ **celebrations**) Vierhundertjahrfeier *f*; (*anniversary*) vierhundertster Jahrestag.

quaternary [kwə'tɜːnərɪ] **1** *adj* (*Geol*) quartär; (*Chem*) quaternär, aus vier Teilen bestehend. **2** *n* (*Geol*) Quartär *nt*.

quatrain ['kwɒtreɪn] *n* Vierzeiler *m*.

quaver ['kweɪvəʳ] **1** *n* **(a)** (*esp Brit Mus*) Achtel(note *f*) *nt*. ~ **rest** Achtelpause *f*. **(b)** (*in voice*) Beben, Zittern *nt*. **with a** ~ **in her voice** mit bebender or zitternder Stimme. **2** *vi* (*voice*) beben, zittern; (*Mus*) tremolieren. **3** *vt* mit bebender or zitternder Stimme sagen.

quavering ['kweɪvərɪŋ], **quavery** ['kweɪvərɪ] *adj voice* bebend, zitternd; *notes* tremolierend.

quay [kiː] *n* Kai *m*. **alongside the** ~ am Kai.

quayside ['kiːsaɪd] *n* Kai *m*. **the** ~ **bars** die Hafenkneipen *pl*.

queasiness ['kwiːzɪnɪs] *n* Übelkeit *f*. **he feels on board ship** das Gefühl der Übelkeit, das er auf einem Schiff bekommt.

queasy ['kwiːzɪ] *adj* (+*er*) **I feel** ~ mir ist (leicht) übel; **it makes me** ~ da wird mir übel; **a** ~ **feeling** ein Gefühl *nt* der Übelkeit, ein Übelkeitsgefühl *nt*; **don't do it if you feel** ~ **about it** wenn dir nicht wohl dabei ist, dann tu's doch nicht.

queen [kwiːn] **1** *n* **(a)** (*also fig*) Königin *f*. **she was** ~ **to George V** sie war die Gemahlin von Georg V; ~ **of the May** Maikönigin *f*.

(b) (*bee, ant etc*) Königin *f*.

(c) (*Cards*) Dame *f*. ~ **of spades** Pik Dame.

(d) (*Chess*) Dame *f*. ~**'s bishop/pawn** Damenläufer/-bauer *m*.

(e) (*sl: homosexual*) Schwule(r) *m* (*inf*), Tunte *f* (*sl*).

(f) (*sl: rocker*) ~ Braut *f* (*sl*).

2 *vt* **(a)** (*Chess*) in eine Dame ver- or umwandeln.

(b) (*inf*) **to** ~ **it** die große Dame spielen or heraushängen (*inf*); **to** ~ **it over sb** jdn herumkommandieren (*inf*).

3 *vi* (*Chess*) sich in eine Dame verwandeln.

queen: ~ **bee** *n* Bienenkönigin *f*; ~ **consort** *n* Königin *f*, Gemahlin *f* des Königs; ~ **dowager** *n* Königinwitwe *f*.

queenly ['kwiːnlɪ] *adj* königlich; *bearing, dignity also* einer Königin; *duties, rule also* der Königin.

queen: ~ **mother** *n* Königinmutter *f*; **Q**~**'s Bench** *n* Oberster Gerichtshof.

Queensberry rules ['kwiːnzbərɪ'ruːlz] *npl* Queensberry-Regeln *pl*.

queen's: **Q**~ **Counsel** *n* Kronanwalt *m*, Anwalt *m* der Krone, = Staatsanwalt *m*; (*as title*) Justizrat *m*; ~ **English** *n* englische

Hochsprache; don't you understand the ~ English? verstehst du denn kein Englisch?; ~ **evidence** *n*: **to turn ~ evidence** als Kronzeuge auftreten; Q~ **Guide** *n* Pfadfinderin *f* mit den höchsten Auszeichnungen; ~ **peace** *n* **to keep the ~ peace** sich ordnungsgemäß verhalten; **a breach of the ~ peace** öffentliche Ruhestörung; Q~ **Scout** *n* Pfadfinder *m* mit den höchsten Auszeichnungen; ~ **shilling** *n* **to take the ~ shilling** (*old*) des Königs Rock anziehen (*obs*); Q~ **Speech** *n* Thronrede *f*.

queer [kwɪəʳ] **1** *adj* (*+er*) (a) (*strange*) eigenartig, seltsam, komisch; (*eccentric*) komisch, kauzig. **a ~-sounding name** ein komischer Name; **he's a bit ~ in the head** (*inf*) er ist nicht ganz richtig (im Kopf) (*inf*); **doesn't it feel ~ being the only woman?** kommst du dir nicht komisch vor als einzige Frau?
  (b) (*causing suspicion*) verdächtig, nicht ganz hasenrein. **there's something ~ about it** da ist etwas faul dran (*inf*).
  (c) (*inf*) (*unwell*) unwohl; (*peculiar*) *feeling* komisch. **I feel ~** mir ist nicht gut/mir ist ganz komisch (*inf*); **I came over all ~** mir wurde ganz anders (*inf*) or komisch (*inf*); **he was looking a bit ~** er sah ein bißchen angeknackst aus (*inf*).
  (d) (*inf: homosexual*) schwul (*inf*).
  2 *n* (*inf: homosexual*) Schwule(r) *mf* (*inf*).
  3 *vt* (*sl: spoil*) versauen (*sl*), vermasseln (*sl*). **to ~ sb's pitch** (*inf*) jdm einen Strich durch die Rechnung machen.

queer-bashing [ˈkwɪəbæʃɪŋ] *n* Verprügeln *nt* von Schwulen.

queerly [ˈkwɪəlɪ] *adv* eigenartig, seltsam, komisch.

queerness [ˈkwɪənɪs] *n* (a) Eigenartigkeit, Merkwürdigkeit, Seltsamkeit *f*. (b) (*inf: homosexuality*) Schwulheit *f* (*inf*).

Queer Street *n* (*Brit sl*) **to be in ~** pleite or blank sein (*inf*). **we'll really be in ~** if that happens wenn das passiert, sind wir wirklich in Schwulitäten (*inf*); **I spent most of my life in ~** ich pfeife schon immer auf dem letzten Loch (*inf*).

quell [kwel] *vt fear* bezwingen; *passion* bändigen, zügeln; *riot* unterdrücken, niederschlagen; *anxieties* überwinden.

quench [kwentʃ] *vt flames, fire* löschen; *thirst also,* (*liter*) *desire* stillen; *enthusiasm* dämpfen.

quenchless [ˈkwentʃlɪs] *adj* (*liter*) *flames* unlöschbar.

quern [kwɜːn] *n* Hand- or Drehmühle *f*; (*Archeol*) Mahlstein *m*.

querulous [ˈkwerʊləs] *adj* nörglerisch, mißmutig. **a ~ person** ein Querulant *m*.

querulously [ˈkwerʊləslɪ] *adv see adj*.

query [ˈkwɪərɪ] **1** *n* (a) (*question*) Frage *f*. **there was a note of ~ in his voice** seine Stimme hatte einen fragenden Unterton; **that raises a ~ as to whether/about** ... das wirft die Frage auf, ob .../das wirft die Frage (*+gen*) ... auf.
  (b) (*Typ*) Fragezeichen *nt*.
  2 *vt* (a) (*express doubt about*) bezweifeln; *statement, motives* in Frage stellen; *bill, item, invoice* reklamieren. **I'm not ~ing your right to do that but** ... ich bezweifle ja nicht, daß Sie dazu berechtigt sind, aber ...; **I'd ~ that das würde ich bezweifeln; £500! I'd ~ that** if I were you £ 500! da würde ich an Ihrer Stelle reklamieren; **to ~ whether** ... ich bezweifle, ob ...
  (b) (*check*) **to ~ sth with sb** etw mit jdm abklären.
  (c) (*with a question mark*) mit einem Fragezeichen versehen.

quest [kwest] **1** *n* (*search*) Suche *f*; (*for knowledge, happiness etc*) Streben *nt* (*for* nach). **to go in ~ of sth** (*old, liter*) sich auf die Suche nach etw machen.
  2 *vi* (a) (*old, liter: seek*) suchen (*for* nach). **to ~ for riches/truth** nach Reichtümern/der Wahrheit streben.
  (b) (*Hunt*) die Beute aufspüren.

question [ˈkwestʃən] **1** *n* (a) (*Gram etc*) Frage *f* (*to an +acc*); (*Parl also*) Anfrage *f* (*to an +acc*). **to ask sb a ~** jdm eine Frage stellen; **don't ask so many ~s** frag nicht so viel; **they'll buy anything, no ~s asked** sie kaufen alles und stellen keine dummen Fragen; **what a ~ (to ask)!** was für eine Frage!; **let me put the ~ another way** ich werde die Frage anders formulieren.
  (b) *no pl* (*doubt*) Zweifel *m*, Frage *f*. **beyond (all) or without ~** ohne Frage, ohne (jeden) Zweifel; **without ~ he is** ... er ist zweifellos or ohne Frage or ohne Zweifel ...; **his honesty is beyond ~** seine Ehrlichkeit steht außer Zweifel or Frage, an seiner Ehrlichkeit besteht kein Zweifel; **there is no ~ but that he has gone** (*form*) es besteht kein Zweifel darüber, er ist fort; **your sincerity is not in ~** niemand zweifelt an Ihrer Aufrichtigkeit; **to call sth into ~** etw in Frage stellen.
  (c) (*matter*) Frage *f*. **that's another ~** altogether das ist etwas völlig anderes; **that's not the ~** darum geht es nicht; **the German ~** die deutsche Frage; **success is a ~ of time** Erfolg ist eine Frage der Zeit; **it's not just a ~ of money** es ist nicht nur eine Geldfrage or Frage des Geldes; **if it's only a ~ of whether** ... wenn es nur darum geht (*inf*) or sich darum handelt, ob ...
  (d) *no pl* (*possibility, likelihood*) Rede *f*. **there's no ~ of him resigning** es ist die Rede von einer Wiedervereinigung/davon, daß er zurücktreten will, eine Wiedervereinigung/sein Rücktritt ist im Gespräch; **there's no ~ of that happening/of a strike** es steht außer Diskussion or es kann keine Rede davon sein, daß das passiert/von einem Streik kann keine Rede sein; **that's out of the ~** das kommt nicht in Frage; **the person/matter in ~** die fragliche or in Frage or in Rede (*form*) stehende Person/Angelegenheit.
  2 *vt* (a) (*ask ~s of*) fragen (*about* nach); (*police etc*) vernehmen, verhören (*about* zu); (*examiner*) prüfen (*on* über *+acc*). **my father started ~ing me** about where I'd been mein Vater fing an, mich auszufragen, wo ich gewesen war; **they were ~ed** by the immigration authorities viele Fragen von der Einwanderungsbehörde viele Fragen gestellt; **I don't like being ~ed**, she said ich mag diese Verhöre nicht, sagte sie.
  (b) (*express doubt about*) bezweifeln, zweifeln an (*+dat*); (*dispute, challenge*) in Frage stellen. **I ~ whether it's worth it** ich bezweifle, daß es der Mühe wert ist; **but I'm not ~ing that!** das bezweifle or bestreite ich ja nicht; **I don't ~ your good intentions** ich zweifle nicht an Ihrer guten Absicht; **he ~ed her inclusion on the committee** er äußerte Bedenken gegen ihre

Aufnahme in den Ausschuß.

questionable [ˈkwestʃənəbl] *adj* (a) (*suspect*) fragwürdig. **of ~ honesty** von zweifelhaftem Ruf; **in ~ taste** geschmacklos.
  (b) (*open to doubt*) *statement, figures* fraglich; *value, advantage also* zweifelhaft.

questioner [ˈkwestʃənəʳ] *n* Fragesteller(in *f*), Frager *m*.

questioning [ˈkwestʃənɪŋ] **1** *adj look* fragend.
  2 *n* (*by parents, husband*) Verhör *nt*; (*by police also*) Vernehmung *f*; (*of candidate*) Befragung *f*. **after hours of ~ by the immigration authorities** nach stundenlanger Befragung durch die Einwanderungsbehörde; **they brought him in for ~** sie holten ihn, um ihn zu vernehmen.

questioningly [ˈkwestʃənɪŋlɪ] *adv* fragend.

question: ~ **mark** *n* Fragezeichen *nt*; ~**-master** *n* Quizmaster *m*.

questionnaire [ˌkwestʃəˈneəʳ] *n* Fragebogen *m*.

question time *n* Zeit *f* für Fragen; (*Parl*) Fragestunde *f*.

queue [kjuː] **1** *n* (a) (*Brit: of people, cars*) Schlange *f*. **to form a ~** eine Schlange bilden; **to stand in a ~** Schlange stehen, anstehen; **to join the ~** sich (hinten) anstellen; **a ~ of cars** eine Autoschlange; **a long ~ of people** eine lange Schlange.
  (b) (*Hist: pigtail*) Zopf *m*.
  2 *vi* (*Brit: also ~ up*) Schlange stehen; (*people also*) anstehen; (*form a ~*) eine Schlange bilden; (*people*) sich anstellen. **they were queuing outside the cinema** sie standen vor dem Kino Schlange; **we ~d for an hour** wir haben eine Stunde angestanden; **they were queuing for the bus** sie standen an der Bushaltestelle Schlange; **they were queuing for bread** sie standen nach Brot an.

queue: ~**-jumper** *n* (*Brit*) jd, der sich vordräng(el)t; **the ~-jumpers were booed** die, die sich vordräng(el)ten, wurden ausgebuht; ~**-jumping** *n* (*Brit*) Vordräng(el)n *nt*; **hey you, no ~-jumping!** he, Vordräng(el)n gibt's nicht! (*inf*).

quibble [ˈkwɪbl] **1** *vi* (*be petty-minded*) kleinlich sein (*over, about* wegen); (*argue with sb*) sich herumstreiten (*over, about* wegen). **to ~ over details** auf Einzelheiten herumreiten; **he ~d about the design** er krittelte am Design herum; **they weren't arguing, just quibbling** sie diskutierten nicht, sondern stritten sich nur über Spitzfindigkeiten.
  2 *n* **these aren't really serious criticisms at all, just ~s** das ist doch keine ernsthafte Kritik, das sind doch nur Spitzfindigkeiten or Haarspaltereien; **let's try to avoid unnecessary ~s over details** wir wollen doch nicht unnötig auf Einzelheiten herumreiten; **I've got a few ~s about her work/the design** ich habe ein paar Kleinigkeiten an ihrer Arbeit/am Design auszusetzen; **I hope you don't think this is a ~, but** ... ich hoffe, Sie halten mich nicht für kleinlich, aber ...

quibbler [ˈkwɪbləʳ] *n* (*petty critic*) Krittler, Kritikaster (*pej*) *m*; (*hair-splitter*) Wortklauber, Haarspalter *m*.

quibbling [ˈkwɪblɪŋ] **1** *adj* (*petty*) *person* kleinlich; (*hair-splitting*) *person, details, argument* spitzfindig. **2** *n* kleinliches Getue (*inf*); (*hair criticism*) Krittelei *f*; (*hair-splitting*) Haarspalterei, Wortklauberei *f*. **all this ~ about details** dieses Herumreiten auf Einzelheiten.

quiche [kiːʃ] *n* Quiche *f*.

quick [kwɪk] **1** *adj* (*+er*) (a) (*rapid*) schnell; *answer also* prompt. **be ~!** mach schnell!; (*on telephone etc*) faß dich kurz!; **come on, ~, ~!** komm, schnell, schnell or zack, zack (*inf*)!; **and be ~ about it** aber ein bißchen dalli (*inf*); **you were/he was ~** das ist ja schnell gegangen, das war ja schnell; **he was the ~est to be promoted** er wurde am schnellsten befördert; **he was too ~ for me** in speech) das ging mir zu schnell; (*in escaping*) er war zu schnell für mich; ~ **march!** (*Mil*) im Eilschritt, marsch!; **it's ~er by train** mit dem Zug geht es schneller; **to be ~ to do sth** etw ganz schnell tun; **he is ~ to criticize other people** er ist mit seiner Kritik schnell bei der Hand; **he is ~ to anger** er wird leicht zornig; **the ~est way to the station** der schnellste Weg zum Bahnhof; **what's the ~est way to the station?** wie komme ich am schnellsten zum Bahnhof?; **what's the ~est way to finish it?** wie werde ich am schnellsten damit fertig?
  (b) (*short, ~ly done*) *kiss* flüchtig; *speech, synopsis* kurz; *rest* klein, kurz. **let me have a ~ look** laß mich mal schnell or kurz sehen; **we had a ~ meal** wir haben schnell etwas gegessen; **let's go for a ~ drive** komm, wir machen eine kleine Spritztour; **he took a ~ swig of whisky** er trank schnell einen Schluck Whisky; **could I have a ~ word?** könnte ich Sie mal kurz sprechen?; **could I have a ~ try?** darf ich mal schnell or kurz versuchen?; **I'll just write him a ~ note** ich schreibe ihm schnell mal or mal kurz; **I grabbed a ~ sleep** ich legte mich kurz hin; **time for a ~ beer** genügend Zeit, um schnell ein Bierchen zu trinken; **a ~ one** eine(r, s) auf die Schnelle (*inf*); (*question*) eine kurze Frage.
  (c) (*lively, ~ to understand*) *mind* wach; *person* schnell von Begriff (*inf*); *child* aufgeweckt; *temper* hitzig, heftig; *eye, ear* scharf. **the ~er children soon get bored** die Kinder, die schneller begreifen or eine schnellere Auffassungsgabe haben, langweilen sich bald; **he is ~ at figures** er kann schnell rechnen; **he's very ~** er begreift or kapiert (*inf*) schnell; **he's too ~ for me** mit ihm komme ich nicht mit; ~, **isn't he?** (*in repartee*) der ist aber schlagfertig.
  2 *n* (a) (*Anat*) empfindliches Fleisch (*besonders unter den Fingernägeln*). **to bite one's nails to the ~** die Nägel bis zum Fleisch abkauen; **to be cut to the ~** tief getroffen sein.
  (b) *pl* (*liter*) **the ~ and the dead** die Lebenden und die Toten.
  3 *adv* (*+er*) schnell.

quick: ~**-acting** *adj medicine* schnell wirkend *attr*; ~**-change artist** *n* (*Theat*) Verwandlungskünstler(in *f*) *m*.

quicken [ˈkwɪkən] **1** *vt* (a) (*also ~ up*) beschleunigen.
  (b) (*liter: make more lively*) *feelings* erhöhen; *appetite* anregen; *imagination* beflügeln (*geh*), anregen.
  2 *vi* (a) (*also ~ up*) schneller werden, sich beschleunigen.
  (b) (*liter*) (*hope, interest*) wachsen; (*foetus*) sich bewegen.

quick: ~-**fire questions** npl Fragen pl wie aus der Maschinenpistole; ~-**firing** adj (Mil) Schnellfeuer-; ~-**freeze** vt food einfrieren. einfrosten; ~-**frozen** adj Gefrier-, tiefgekühlt.

quickie ['kwɪkɪ] n (inf) eine(r, s) auf die Schnelle (inf); (question) kurze Frage. **the meeting has to be a** ~ **mit der Besprechung müssen wir's kurz machen** (inf).

quicklime ['kwɪklaɪm] n ungelöschter Kalk.

quickly ['kwɪklɪ] adv schnell.

quickness ['kwɪknɪs] n (a) (speed) Schnelligkeit f. **his** ~ **to appreciate the problem** die Schnelligkeit, mit der er das Problem erfaßt hat. **(b)** (intelligence) schnelle Auffassungsgabe. ~ **of mind** Fähigkeit, schnell zu denken; ~ **of temper** heftiges or aufbrausendes Temperament.

quick: ~**sand** n Treibsand m; ~**set hedge** n Hecke f; (hawthorn) Weißdornhecke f; ~-**setting** adj glue etc schnell trocknend attr; cement schnell bindend attr; ~**silver** 1 n Quecksilber nt; 2 adj attr (fig liter) quecksilbrig, lebhaft; ~**step** n Quickstep m; ~-**tempered** adj hitzig, leicht erregbar; **to be** ~-**tempered** leicht aufbrausen; ~-**witted** adj geistesgegenwärtig; answer schlagfertig; **the more** ~-**witted candidates** die Kandidaten mit einer schnelleren Auffassungsgabe; ~-**wittedness** n Geistesgegenwart f; Schlagfertigkeit f; schnelle Auffassungsgabe.

quid[1] [kwɪd] n, pl - (inf) Pfund nt. **20** ~ **20 Eier** (sl); **to be** ~**s in auf sein Geld kommen** (inf).

quid[2] n (tobacco) Priem m.

quiddity ['kwɪdɪtɪ] n (a) (Philos) Quiddität f (spec), Wesen nt. **(b)** (liter: quibble) Spitzfindigkeit f.

quid pro quo ['kwɪdprəʊ'kwəʊ] n Gegenleistung f.

quiescence ['kwɪ'esns] n Ruhe, Stille f.

quiescent [kwɪ'esnt] adj ruhig, still.

quiet ['kwaɪət] 1 adj (+er) (a) (silent) still; neighbours, person also, engine ruhig; footsteps, music, car, voice leise. **at night when the office is** ~ nachts, wenn im Büro alles still ist; **double-glazing makes the house** ~ er durch Doppelfenster wird das Haus ruhiger; **he's very** ~ er ist sehr still; **(be)** ~! Ruhe!, ruhig!; **to keep** ~ (not speak) still sein; (not make noise) leise sein; **keep** ~! sei/seid still!; **can't you keep your dog** ~! können Sie nicht zusehen, daß Ihr Hund still ist?; **to keep** ~ **about sth** über etw (acc) nichts sagen; **you've kept very** ~ **about it** du hast ja nicht viel darüber verlauten lassen; **to go** ~ still werden; (music etc) leise werden; **you've gone very** ~ du bist ja so still geworden; **could you make the class** ~ **for a minute?** könnten Sie die Klasse für eine Minute zur Ruhe bringen?; **turn the volume down** ~ dreh die Lautstärke zurück; **I can't make the radio any** ~**er** ich kann das Radio nicht (noch) leiser stellen. **(b)** (peaceful) ruhig; evening also geruhsam; conscience also gut; smile leise. **things are very** ~ **at the moment** im Augenblick ist nicht viel los; **business is** ~ das Geschäft ist ruhig; **to have a** ~ **mind** beruhigt sein; **he had a** ~ **sleep** er hat ruhig geschlafen; **yesterday everything was** ~ **on the Syrian border** gestern herrschte Ruhe or war alles ruhig an der syrischen Grenze; **I was just sitting there having a** ~ **drink** ich saß da und habe in aller Ruhe mein Bier etc getrunken.

(c) (gentle) face, character sanft; child ruhig; horse brav, gutwillig; irony leise.

(d) (unpretentious, simple) dress, tie dezent; colour also ruhig; style einfach, schlicht; elegance schlicht; wedding, dinner klein, im kleinen Rahmen.

(e) (not overt) hatred, envy still; resentment heimlich. **I'll have a** ~ **word with him** ich werde mal ein Wörtchen (im Vertrauen) mit ihm reden; **could we have a** ~ **word together some time?** könnten wir uns mal unter vier Augen unterhalten?; **I caught him having a** ~ **drink** ich habe ihn dabei erwischt, wie er heimlich getrunken hat; **they had a** ~ **laugh over it** sie haben im stillen darüber gelacht; **he kept the matter** ~ er behielt die Sache für sich; **keep it** ~ behalte es für dich.

2 n Ruhe f. **in the** ~ **of the night** in der Stille der Nacht; **the sudden** ~ **after the bombing** die plötzliche Stille or Ruhe nach dem Bombenangriff; **on the** ~ heimlich; **he left on the** ~ er ist still und heimlich weggegangen; see peace.

3 vt see **quieten**.

quieten ['kwaɪətn] vt (a) sb zum Schweigen bringen; noisy class, dog zur Ruhe bringen; crying baby beruhigen; engine ruhiger machen. **(b)** (make calm) person, conscience beruhigen; suspicion, fear zerstreuen; pain lindern.

♦ **quieten down** 1 vi (become silent) leiser werden; (become calm) sich beruhigen; (after wild youth) ruhiger werden. ~ ~, **boys!** ein bißchen ruhiger, Jungens!; **things have** ~**ed** ~ **a lot** es ist viel ruhiger geworden.

2 vt sep person beruhigen; engine ruhiger machen.

quietism ['kwaɪətɪzəm] n Quietismus m.

quietist ['kwaɪtɪst] 1 n Quietist(in f) m. 2 adj quietistisch.

quietly ['kwaɪətlɪ] adv (making little noise) leise; (peacefully, making little fuss) ruhig; (secretly) still und heimlich. **he's very** ~ **spoken** er spricht sehr leise; **a very** ~ **spoken man** ein sehr ruhiger junger Mann; **to be** ~ **confident** insgeheim sehr sicher sein; **I was sitting here** ~ **sipping my wine** ich saß da und trank in aller Ruhe meinen Wein; **he sat down and** ~ **died** er setzte sich hin und starb in aller Stille; **he was very** ~ **dressed** er war sehr dezent gekleidet; **they got married very** ~ sie haben im kleinen Rahmen geheiratet; **and all the time he was** ~ **writing a novel about all of us** und die ganze Zeit hat er still und heimlich einen Roman über uns geschrieben.

quietness ['kwaɪətnɪs] n (a) (lack of noise) Stille f; (of engine, car) Geräuscharmut f; (of footsteps etc) Geräuschlosigkeit f; (of person) stille Art. **the** ~ **of her voice** ihre leise Stimme; **then with the sudden** ~ **of the music** ... und dann, als die Musik plötzlich leise wurde ...

(b) (peacefulness) Ruhe f.

(c) (of tie, colour) Dezentheit f; (of style) Schlichtheit f.

quietude ['kwaɪətjuːd] n (liter) Ruhe f, Friede(n) m.

quietus [kwaɪ'iːtəs] n (old, liter) Todesstoß m. **to give sb his/sth its** ~ jdm/einer Sache den Todesstoß versetzen; **he found his** ~ er schied von ihnen (liter).

quiff [kwɪf] n (esp Brit) Stirnlocke, Tolle f.

quill [kwɪl] n (a) (feather) Feder f; (feather stem) Federkiel m. **(b)** (also ~-**pen**) Feder(kiel m) f. **(c)** (of porcupine) Stachel m.

quilt [kwɪlt] 1 n (continental ~) Steppdecke f; (unstitched) Federbett nt; (bedspread) Bettdecke f. 2 vt absteppen; (with padding) wattieren.

quilting ['kwɪltɪŋ] n (a) (process) (Ab)steppen nt; Wattieren nt. **(b)** (material) Steppstoff m.

quin [kwɪn] n (Brit) abbr of **quintuplet** Fünfling m.

quince [kwɪns] n (fruit, tree) Quitte f. ~ **jelly** Quittengelee nt.

quincentenary [ˌkwɪnsen'tiːnərɪ] n fünfhundertster Jahrestag; (also ~ **celebrations**) Fünfhundertjahrfeier f.

quinine ['kwɪniːn] n Chinin nt.

Quinquagesima [ˌkwɪŋkwə'dʒesɪmə] n Quinquagesima f.

quinquennia [kwɪn'kwenɪə] pl of **quinquennium**.

quinquennial [kwɪn'kwenɪəl] adj alle fünf Jahre (stattfindend); (lasting five years) fünfjährig.

quinquennium [kwɪn'kwenɪəm] n, pl **quinquennia** (form) Jahrfünft nt.

quinsy ['kwɪnzɪ] n (old) Mandelentzündung f.

quint [kwɪnt] n (US) abbr of **quintuplet** Fünfling m.

quintessence [kwɪn'tesns] n (Philos, fig) Quintessenz f; (embodiment) Inbegriff m.

quintessential [ˌkwɪntɪ'senʃəl] adj (liter) fundamental (geh). **the** ~ **English gentleman** der Inbegriff des englischen Gentleman; **an instance of his** ~ **bad taste** ein Beispiel für seinen von Grund auf schlechten Geschmack; **the** ~ **Catholicism of his whole attitude** seine fundamental (geh) or durch und durch katholische Haltung.

quintessentially [ˌkwɪntɪ'senʃəlɪ] adv (liter) durch und durch. **they are** ~ **different** sie sind fundamental (geh) or von Grund auf verschieden; **this is** ~ **Bach** das ist Bach reinsten Wassers.

quintet(te) [kwɪn'tet] n (Mus, group of five) Quintett nt.

quintuple ['kwɪntjupl] 1 adj fünffach. 2 n Fünffache(s) nt. 3 vt verfünffachen. 4 vi sich verfünffachen.

quintuplet [kwɪn'tjuːplɪt] n Fünfling m.

quip [kwɪp] 1 n witzige or geistreiche Bemerkung. 2 vti witzeln.

quipster ['kwɪpstər] n Spaßvogel m.

quire[1] ['kwaɪər] n (a) (24 sheets) 24 Bogen Papier. **(b)** (folded, unbound sheets) Bogen m.

quire[2] n (obs) see **choir**.

quirk [kwɜːk] n Schrulle, Marotte f; (of nature, fate) Laune f. by **a strange** ~ **of fate** durch eine Laune des Schicksals.

quirkiness ['kwɜːkɪnɪs] n Schrulligkeit f.

quirky ['kwɜːkɪ] adj (+er) person, character schrullig.

quirt [kwɜːt] n (US) geflochtene Reitpeitsche.

quisling ['kwɪzlɪŋ] n Quisling m.

quit [kwɪt] (vb: pret, ptp ~**ted** or ~) 1 vt (a) (leave) town, army verlassen; this life scheiden aus; (give up) job aufgeben, kündigen. **I've given her/I've had notice to** ~ **the flat** (form) ich habe ihr die Wohnung gekündigt/mir ist (die Wohnung) gekündigt worden; **the dog would not** ~ **his prey** (liter) der Hund wollte nicht von seiner Beute ablassen (liter).

(b) (inf: stop) aufhören mit. **to** ~ **doing sth** aufhören, etw zu tun; ~ **it!** hör (damit) auf!; **to** ~ **work** mit der Arbeit aufhören.

2 vi (a) (leave one's job) kündigen.

(b) (go away) weg- or fortgehen. **notice to** ~ Kündigung f; **they gave me notice to** ~ sie haben mir gekündigt.

(c) (accept defeat) aufgeben.

3 adj ~ **of** los or frei von, ledig (+gen) (geh); **we are** ~ **of him** wir sind ihn los.

quite [kwaɪt] adv (a) (entirely) ganz; (emph) völlig. ~ **unnecessary/wrong/unthinkable** völlig unnötig/falsch/undenkbar; **I am** ~ **happy where I am** ich bin eigentlich da, wo ich bin, ganz zufrieden; **I was** ~ **happy until you came along bevor du kamst, war ich völlig zufrieden; **it's** ~ **impossible to do that** das ist völlig or gänzlich unmöglich; **you're being** ~ **impossible** du bist einfach unmöglich; **are you** ~ **finished?** bist du jetzt fertig?; **when you're** ~ **ready** ... (iro) wenn du dann fertig bist ...; **he's** ~ **grown up now** er ist jetzt schon richtig erwachsen; **the cloth** ~ **covers it** das Tuch verdeckt es ganz; **I** ~ **agree with** you ich stimme völlig mit Ihnen überein; **he** ~ **understands that he must go** er sieht es durchaus or völlig ein, daß er gehen muß; **he has** ~ **recovered** er ist völlig or ganz wiederhergestellt; **that's** ~ **another matter** das ist doch etwas ganz anderes; **he said it in** ~ **another tone** er sagte es in einem ganz anderen Ton; **that's** ~ **enough for me** das reicht wirklich; **that's** ~ **enough of that** das reicht jetzt aber; **it was** ~ **four days ago** (es war) vor mindestens vier Tagen; **not** ~ nicht ganz; **you weren't** ~ **early/tall enough** Sie waren ein bißchen zu spät dran/zu klein; **he's not** ~ **rich enough to qualify** er ist noch nicht ganz reich genug, um in Frage zu kommen; **I don't** ~ **see what he means** ich verstehe nicht ganz, was er meint; **you don't** ~ **understand** Sie verstehen mich anscheinend nicht richtig; **that's not** ~ **your colour** das ist nicht ganz die richtige Farbe für Sie; **he's not** ~ **the James Bond type** er ist nicht gerade der James-Bond-Typ; **it was not** ~ **midnight** es war noch nicht ganz Mitternacht; **sorry!** — **that's** ~ **all right** entschuldige! — das macht nichts; **I'm** ~ **all right, thanks** danke, mir geht's gut; **thank you** — **that's** ~ **right** danke — bitte schön; **that's** ~ **all right, thank you, I can manage alone** das geht schon, danke, ich komme alleine zurecht; ~ **(so)! genau!, sehr richtig!, ganz recht!; ~ **the thing** (inf) ganz große Mode.

(b) (to some degree) ziemlich. ~ **likely/unlikely** sehr wahrscheinlich/unwahrscheinlich; **he's had** ~ **a lot to drink** er hat ziemlich viel or ganz schön viel (inf) getrunken; ~ **a few**

people ziemlich viele Leute; **he is ~ a good singer** er ist ein ziemlich guter Sänger; **I ~ like this painting** dieses Bild gefällt mir ganz gut; **yes, I'd ~ like to** ja, eigentlich ganz gern.

(c) (*really, truly*) wirklich. **she was ~ a beauty** sie war wirklich eine Schönheit; **she's ~ a girl/cook** *etc* sie ist ein tolles Mädchen/eine tolle Köchin *etc*; **it's ~ delightful** es ist entzückend, es ist einfach wunderbar; **it was ~ a shock/disappointment/change** es war ein ziemlicher *or* ganz schöner (*inf*) Schock/eine ziemliche *or* ganz schöne (*inf*) Enttäuschung/Veränderung; **it was ~ a job getting the piano upstairs** es war ganz schön schwierig *or* das war vielleicht schwierig, das Klavier nach oben zu bringen (*inf*); **that's ~ some bruise/bill/car** (*inf*) das ist vielleicht ein blauer Fleck/ eine Rechnung/ein Auto (*inf*); **it was ~ a party!** (*inf*) leicht eine Party! (*inf*); **he's ~ the gentleman now** er ist jetzt ganz der feine Herr; **he's ~ a hero now** jetzt ist er ein richtiger Held; **the little party-goer, aren't we?** (*inf*) du bist wohl so eine richtige kleine Partynudel, wie? (*inf*); **he's ~ a comedian, isn't he?** er ist ja sehr komisch.

quits [kwɪts] *adj* quitt. **to be/get ~ with sb** mit jdm quitt sein/ werden; **to cry ~** aufgeben, klein beigeben; **shall we call it ~?** lassen wir's?; *see* **double.**

quittance [ˈkwɪtəns] *n* Schuldenerlaß *m*.

quitter [ˈkwɪtəʳ] *n* (*inf*) **he's a ~** er gibt immer gleich auf.

quiver¹ [ˈkwɪvəʳ] **1** *vi* zittern; (*person also*) beben (*with* vor +*dat*); (*wings*) flattern; (*lips, eyelids, heart*) zucken; (*flesh*) wabbeln. **2** *n* Zittern *nt*; Beben *nt*; Flattern *nt*; Zucken *nt*; Wabbeln *nt*.

quiver² *n* Köcher *m*.

quiverful [ˈkwɪvəfʊl] *n* (*of arrows*) Köchervoll *m*; (*liter: of children*) Schar *f*.

qui vive [ˌkiːˈviːv] *n*: **on the ~** auf dem Quivive (*dated*), auf der Hut.

quixotic [kwɪkˈsɒtɪk] *adj* *behaviour, gesture etc* edelmütig, ritterlich; *ideals* schwärmerisch, idealistisch. **a foolish ~ act** eine Donquichotterie; **an idealist, a strange ~ character** ein Idealist, ein eigenartiger, an Don Quichotte erinnernder Mensch; **don't you find that a little ~?** finden Sie das nicht etwas versponnen?

quixotically [kwɪkˈsɒtɪkəlɪ] *adv see* **adj.**

quiz [kwɪz] **1** *n* **(a)** Quiz *nt*. **(b)** (*US Sch inf*) Prüfung *f*. **2** *vt* **(a)** (*question closely*) ausfragen (*about* über +*acc*). **(b)** (*US Sch inf*) abfragen, prüfen. **(c)** (*obs: stare at impudently*) mustern, beäugen. **(d)** (*obs: mock*) necken (*geh*).

quiz-: **~master** *n* Quizmaster *m*; **~ programme,** (*US*) **~ program** *n* Quizsendung *f*; **~ show** *n* Quiz *nt*.

quizzical [ˈkwɪzɪkəl] *adj* (*a*) *air, look* fragend; *smile* zweifelnd. **(b)** (*odd*) eigenartig, drollig.

quizzically [ˈkwɪzɪkəlɪ] *adv* *look* fragend, zweifelnd.

quoin [kwɔɪn] *n* (*a*) (*outer corner of wall*) Ecke *f*; (*cornerstone*) Eckstein *m*. **(b)** (*Typ*) Schließzeug *nt*.

quoit [kwɔɪt] *n* Wurfring *m*.

quoits [kwɔɪts] *n sing* Wurfringspiel *nt*. **to play ~** Wurfring spielen.

quondam [ˈkwɒndæm] *adj* (*liter*) ehemalig, früher. **his ~ wife** weiland seine Gattin (*obs*).

Quonset (hut) ® [ˈkwɒnsɪt(ˈhʌt)] *n* (*US*) Nissenhütte *f*.

quorum [ˈkwɔːrəm] *n* Quorum *nt*.

quota [ˈkwəʊtə] *n* **(a)** (*of work*) Pensum *nt*. **(b)** (*permitted amount*) Quantum *nt*; (*share allotted*) Anteil *m*; (*of goods*) Kontingent *nt*. **the ~ of immigrants allowed into the country** die zugelassene Einwanderungsquote; **import ~** Einfuhrkontingent *nt*.

quotability [ˌkwəʊtəˈbɪlɪtɪ] *n* Zitierbarkeit *f*. **something with a little more ~ for the headlines** ein Zitat, das sich besser als Schlagzeile eignet; **phrases which he valued for their ~** Aussprüche, die ihm als Zitate geeignet und wertvoll erschienen.

quotable [ˈkwəʊtəbl] *adj* zitierbar, zitierfähig. **a highly ~ author** ein gern zitierter Autor; **~ quips from his speech** geistreiche Bemerkungen aus seiner Rede, die sich als Zitate eignen.

quotation [kwəʊˈteɪʃən] *n* **(a)** (*passage cited*) Zitat *nt*; (*act*) Zitieren *nt*. **dictionary of ~s** Zitatenlexikon *nt*; **a ~ from the Bible/Shakespeare** ein Bibelzitat/Shakespeare-Zitat; **a two-bar ~ from Bach** zwei Takte, die von Bach übernommen sind. **(b)** (*Fin: statement of price*) (Börsen- *or* Kurs)notierung *f*. **(c)** (*Comm: estimate*) Kosten(vor)anschlag *m*.

quotation marks *npl* Anführungszeichen, Anführungsstriche *pl*. **open/close ~** Anführungsstriche unten/oben; **to put a word in ~** ein Wort in Anführungszeichen *or* -striche setzen.

quote [kwəʊt] **1** *vt* **(a)** *author, text* zitieren. **you can ~ me (on that)** Sie können das ruhig wörtlich wiedergeben; **please don't ~ me on this, but ...** (*this isn't authoritative*) ich kann mich nicht hundertprozentig dafür verbürgen, aber ...; (*don't repeat it*) bitte wiederholen Sie nicht, was ich jetzt sage, aber ...; **he was ~d as saying** man hat ihn mit den ~s zitiert *or* er soll gesagt haben, daß ...; **~ ... end ~** *or* **un~** Zitat Anfang ... Zitat Ende; **and the ~ liberals** und die Liberalen in Anführungszeichen. **(b)** (*cite*) anführen. **to ~ sb/sth as an example** jdn/etw als Beispiel anführen. **(c)** (*Comm*) *price* nennen; *reference number* angeben. **(d)** (*St Ex*) notieren. **the shares are ~d at £2** die Aktien werden mit £2 notiert. **2** *vi* zitieren. **to ~ from an author** einen Schriftsteller zitieren, aus dem Werk eines Schriftstellers zitieren; **... and I ~** ... und ich zitiere. **3** *n* **(a)** (*from author, politician*) Zitat *nt*. **a two-bar ~ from Bach** zwei von Bach übernommene Takte. **(b)** **~s** *pl* (*inf*) Anführungszeichen, Gänsefüßchen (*inf*) *pl*; **in ~s** in Anführungszeichen. **(c)** (*Comm inf*) Kosten(vor)anschlag *m*.

quoth [kwəʊθ] *defective vb* (*obs, hum*) sagte, sprach (*liter*).

quotidian [kwəʊˈtɪdɪən] *adj* (*form*) täglich.

quotient [ˈkwəʊʃənt] *n* (*Math*) Quotient *m*.

R

R, r [ɑːʳ] *n* R, r *nt*. **the three Rs** Lesen, Schreiben und Rechnen (*with sing or pl vb*).

R *abbr of* **(a)** Rex, Regina. **(b) river** Fl. **(c)** (*US Film*) **restricted** für Jugendliche nicht geeignet.

r *abbr of* **right** r.

RA *abbr of* **Royal Academy.**

rabbet [ˈræbɪt] *n* (*notch*) Nut *f*; (*joint*) Nutnaht *f*.

rabbi [ˈræbaɪ] *n* Rabbiner *m*; (*as title*) Rabbi *m*.

rabbinical [rəˈbɪnɪkəl] *adj* rabbinisch.

rabbit [ˈræbɪt] **1** *n* Kaninchen *nt*; (*fur also*) Kanin *nt* (*spec*). **2** *vi* **(a)** **to go ~ing** Kaninchen jagen, auf Kaninchenjagd gehen. **(b)** (*Brit inf: also* **~ on**) quasseln, schwafeln, sülzen (*all inf*).

rabbit *in cpds* Kaninchen-; **~ burrow** *or* **hole** *n* Kaninchenbau *m*; **~ hutch** *n* Kaninchenstall *m*; **~ punch** *n* Nacken- *or* Genickschlag *m*; **~ skin** *n* Kaninchenfell *nt*; (*material*) Kanin *nt* (*spec*); **~ warren** *n* **(a)** Gänge *pl* des Kaninchenbaus; **(b)** (*fig: maze*) Labyrinth *nt*.

rabble [ˈræbl] *n* (*disorderly crowd*) lärmende Menge, lärmender Haufen (*inf*); (*pej: lower classes*) Pöbel *m*.

rabble-: **~-rouser** *n* Hetzer, Volksverhetzer *m*; **~-rousing 1** *n* Hetze, Volksverhetzung *f*; **2** *adj* (auf)hetzerisch.

Rabelaisian [ˌræbəˈleɪzɪən] *adj* **(a)** (*of Rabelais*) des Rabelais. **(b)** (*like Rabelais*) im Stile Rabelais'.

rabid [ˈræbɪd] *adj* **(a)** (*Vet*) toll(wütig). **(b)** (*fanatical*) fanatisch; *reformer also* wild; *hatred also* rasend, wild.

rabidness [ˈræbɪdnɪs] *n see* **adj (b)** Fanatismus *m*; Wildheit *f*.

rabies [ˈreɪbiːz] *n* Tollwut *f*.

RAC *abbr of* **Royal Automobile Club.**

raccoon *n see* **racoon.**

race¹ [reɪs] **1** *n* **(a)** Rennen *nt*; (*on foot also*) (Wett)lauf *m*; (*swimming*) Wettschwimmen *nt*. **100 metres ~** 100-m-Lauf *m*; **to run a ~ (with *or* against sb)** (mit jdm um die Wette *or* gegen jdn) laufen; **to go to the ~s** zum Pferderennen gehen; **a day at the ~s** ein Tag auf der Pferderennbahn; **we were at the ~s yesterday** wir waren gestern beim Pferderennen; **the ~ for the Democratic nomination** das Rennen um die Nominierung des demokratischen Kandidaten; **it was a ~ to get the work finished** es war eine Hetze, die Arbeit fertigzumachen; **a ~ against time** ein Rennen *nt* gegen die Uhr; **his ~ is run** (*fig*) er ist erledigt (*inf*). **(b)** (*swift current*) Strömung *f*; (*mill ~*) Gerinne *nt*. **(c)** (*liter: of sun, moon*) Lauf *m*. **2** *vt* **(a)** (*compete with*) um die Wette laufen/reiten/fahren/ schwimmen *etc* mit; (*Sport*) laufen/reiten/fahren/schwimmen *etc* gegen. **I'll ~ you to school** ich mache mit dir ein Wettrennen bis zur Schule; **bet you can't ~ me to the beach** wetten, du bist nicht vor mir am Strand; **the car was racing the train** das Auto fuhr mit dem Zug um die Wette. **(b)** *engine* hochjagen; *car* rasen *or* jagen mit. **he ~d me off to the station** er raste *or* jagte mit mir zum Bahnhof. **(c)** (*Sport*) *car* ins Rennen schicken; *horse also* laufen *or* rennen lassen. **3** *vi* **(a)** (*compete*) laufen/reiten/fahren/schwimmen *etc*. **to ~ with *or* against sb** gegen jdn laufen *etc*, mit jdm um die Wette laufen *etc*; **to ~ against time** (*Sport*) gegen die Uhr laufen *etc*; **we're racing against time (to get this finished)** wir arbeiten gegen die Uhr(, um fertigzuwerden); **he ~s at Newmarket** er läßt seine Pferde in Newmarket laufen.

(b) *(rush)* rasen, jagen; *(on foot also)* rennen, hetzen; *(with work)* hetzen. **to ~ about** herumrasen/-rennen *etc*; **to ~ after sb/sth** hinter jdm/etw herhetzen *or* herjagen; **to ~ to get sth finished** Dampf machen, um etw fertigzubekommen *(inf)*; **to ~ ahead with one's plans/work** *etc* seine Pläne/Arbeit *etc* vorantreiben; **the project is racing ahead** die Arbeit am Projekt geht mit Riesenschritten voran; **clouds ~d across the sky** Wolken jagten über den Himmel.

(c) *(engine)* durchdrehen; *(pulse)* jagen, fliegen.

race² n **(a)** *(ethnic group, species)* Rasse f. **of mixed ~** gemischtrassig; **of noble ~** *(person)* edler Herkunft *or* Abstammung; *(horse)* (von) edler Rasse; **~ is causing a problem in this town** es gibt Rassenprobleme in dieser Stadt.

(b) *(fig: of authors, poets etc)* Kaste f.

race: **~ card** n Rennprogramm nt; **~course** n Rennbahn f; **~-goer** n Rennbesucher(in f) m; **~ hatred** n Rassenhaß m; **~horse** n Rennpferd nt; **~ meeting** n Rennveranstaltung f.

racer ['reɪsə'] n Rennfahrer(in f) m; *(car)* Rennwagen m; *(bicycle)* Rennrad nt; *(yacht)* Rennjacht f; *(horse)* Rennpferd nt.

race: **~ relations** n **(a)** pl Beziehungen pl zwischen den Rassen; **(b)** sing *(subject)* Rassenintegration f; **R~ Relations Board** n *(Brit)* Amt nt für Rassenfragen; **~ riot** n Rassenkrawall m; **~track** n Rennbahn f.

rachitic [ræ'kɪtɪk] adj rachitisch.

Rachmanism ['rækmænɪzəm] n *(Brit)* Mietwucher m.

racial ['reɪʃəl] adj rassisch, Rassen-. **~ discrimination** Rassendiskriminierung f; **~ equality** Rassengleichheit f.

racialism ['reɪʃəlɪzəm] n Rassismus m.

racialist ['reɪʃəlɪst] **1** n Rassist(in f) m. **2** adj rassistisch.

racial: **~ minority** n rassische Minderheit; **~ prejudice** n Rassenvorurteil nt.

racily ['reɪsɪlɪ] adv see adj.

raciness ['reɪsɪnɪs] n see adj **(a)** Schwung m, Feuer nt; Gewagtheit f. **(b)** Rassigkeit, Feurigkeit f. **(c)** Rasanz f.

racing ['reɪsɪŋ] n *(horse-~)* Pferderennsport m, Pferderennen nt; *(motor ~)* Motorrennen nt. **he often goes ~** er geht oft zu Pferderennen/Motorrennen.

racing in cpds Renn-; **~ bicycle** n Rennrad nt; **~ car** n Rennwagen m; **~ colours** npl Rennfarben pl; **~ cyclist** n Radrennfahrer(in f) m; **~ driver** n Rennfahrer(in f) m; **~ man** n Anhänger m des Pferderennsports; **~ stable** n Rennstall m; **~ tyres** npl Rennreifen pl; **~ world** n Welt f des Pferderennsports/Motorrennens; **~ yacht** n Rennjacht f.

racism ['reɪsɪzəm] n see racialism.

racist ['reɪsɪst] n, adj see racialist.

rack¹ [ræk] **1** n **(a)** *(for hats, toast, pipes etc)* Ständer m; *(for bottles, plates also)* Gestell nt; *(shelves)* Regal nt; *(luggage ~)* Gepäcknetz nt; *(on car, bicycle)* Gepäckträger m; *(for bombs)* Bombenträger m; *(for fodder)* Raufe f; *(Tech)* Zahnstange f.

(b) *(US Billiards)* see frame.

(c) *(Hist)* Folter(bank) f. **to put sb on the ~** *(lit, fig)* jdn auf die Folter spannen; **to be on the ~** *(lit)* auf der Folterbank sein; *(fig)* Folterqualen leiden.

2 vt **(a)** *(pain)* quälen, plagen. **~ed by** or **with pain/remorse** von Schmerz/Gewissensbissen gequält or geplagt.

(b) **to ~ one's brains** sich *(dat)* den Kopf zerbrechen, sich *(dat)* den Kopf or das Hirn zermartern *(inf)*.

(c) *(Hist)* auf die Folter spannen, auf der Folter strecken.

rack² n: **to go to ~ and ruin** *(person)* verkommen, vor die Hunde gehen *(inf)*; *(country, economy)* abwirtschaften, vor die Hunde gehen *(inf)*; *(building)* verfallen, in Schutt und Asche zerfallen.

rack³ vt wine, beer abfüllen.

rack-and-pinion steering ['rækən'pɪnjən,stɪ:rɪŋ] n *(Aut)* Zahnstangenlenkung f.

racket¹ ['rækɪt] n *(Sport)* Schläger m. **~ press** Spanner m.

racket² n **(a)** *(uproar)* Krach, Lärm, Krawall *(inf)*. **to make a ~** Krach *etc* machen.

(b) *(dishonest business)* Schwindelgeschäft nt *(inf)*, Gaunerei f *(inf)*; *(making excessive profit)* Wucher m. **the drugs ~** das Drogengeschäft; **that package tour was a dreadful ~** diese Pauschalreise war ein fürchterlicher Schwindel *(inf)*; **to be in on a ~** bei einer Gaunerei mitmischen *(inf)*.

(c) *(sl: business, job)* Job m *(inf)*. **what's his ~?** was macht er? *(inf)*; **what ~ are you in?** was ist Ihr Job? *(inf)*.

racketeer [,rækɪ'tɪə'] n Gauner m *(inf)*; *(making excessive profit)* Halsabschneider m *(inf)*.

racketeering [,rækɪ'tɪərɪŋ] n Gaunereien pl *(inf)*; *(excessive profit-making)* Beutelschneiderei f *(inf)*.

racking ['rækɪŋ] adj attr pain rasend, entsetzlich; cough fürchterlich, quälend.

rack: **~ railway** n Zahnradbahn f; **~ rent** n Wuchermiete f.

raconteur [,rækɒn'tɜ:'] n Erzähler(in f) m von Anekdoten.

racoon, raccoon [rə'ku:n] n Waschbär m.

racquet ['rækɪt] n see racket¹.

racy ['reɪsɪ] adj (+er) **(a)** speech, style, play schwungvoll, feurig; *(risqué)* gewagt. **(b)** wine feurig. **(c)** *(inf)* car rasant.

RADA ['rɑ:də] abbr of **Royal Academy of Dramatic Art.**

radar ['reɪdɑ:'] n Radar nt or m.

radar in cpds Radar-; **~ beacon** n Radarbake f, Radarfunkfeuer nt; **~ operator** n Bediener(in f) m eines/des Radargeräts; **~ scanner** n Rundsuchradargerät nt; **~ sensor** n Radarsensor m; **~ station** n Radarstation f; **~ trap** n Radarfalle f.

raddle ['rædl] **1** n Rötel, Roteisenstein m. **2** vt sheep (mit Rötel) zeichnen. **her ~d face** ihr rouge-geschminktes Gesicht.

radial ['reɪdɪəl] **1** adj *(Tech)* radial; beams, bars, lines also strahlenförmig, strahlig; *(Anat)* Speichen-. **~ engine** Sternmotor m; **~(-ply) tyre** Gürtelreifen m. **2** n Gürtelreifen m.

radiance ['reɪdɪəns] n see radiant Strahlen nt; Leuchten nt.

radiant ['reɪdɪənt] **1** adj **(a)** sun strahlend; colours also leuchtend; *(fig)* person, beauty, smile strahlend (with vor +dat); face leuchtend, strahlend. **to be ~ with health/joy** vor Gesundheit strotzen/vor Freude strahlen.

(b) *(Phys)* Strahlungs-. **~ heat** Strahlungswärme f; **~ heater** or **fire** Heizstrahler m; **~ heating** Flächenheizung f.

2 n **(a)** *(on electric fire etc)* Heizfläche f.

(b) *(Astron)* Radiant m.

radiantly ['reɪdɪəntlɪ] adv strahlend.

radiate ['reɪdɪeɪt] **1** vi **(a)** Strahlen aussenden; *(emit heat)* Wärme ausstrahlen; *(heat)* ausgestrahlt werden.

(b) *(lines, roads)* strahlenförmig or sternförmig ausgehen *(from von)*.

2 vt heat, light ausstrahlen; electric waves also abstrahlen; *(fig)* happiness, health, love *(förmlich)* ausstrahlen.

3 ['reɪdɪɪt] adj shape strahlenförmig, sternförmig.

radiation [,reɪdɪ'eɪʃən] n *(of heat etc)* (Aus)strahlung f; *(rays)* radioaktive Strahlung. **contaminated with ~** strahlenverseucht; **~ sickness** Strahlenkrankheit f; **~ therapy** or **treatment** Strahlenbehandlung f.

radiator ['reɪdɪeɪtə'] n *(for heating)* Heizkörper, Radiator m; *(Aut)* Kühler m. **~ cap** Kühlerverschlußdeckel m; **~ grill** Kühlergitter nt.

radical ['rædɪkəl] **1** adj **(a)** *(basic)* fundamental, Grund-; *(extreme)* change, reform radikal, grundlegend; rethinking, re-examination total; *(Pol)* radikal. **to effect a ~ cure** eine Radikalkur machen; **~ surgery** Radikalchirurgie f.

(b) *(Math)* sign Wurzel-. **a ~ expression** eine Wurzel.

(c) *(Bot)* Wurzel-; leaves bodenständig.

2 n *(Pol)* Radikale(r) mf; *(Math, Gram)* Wurzel f; *(in Chinese)* Radikal m; *(Chem)* Radikal nt.

radicalism ['rædɪkəlɪzəm] n *(Pol)* Radikalismus m.

radically ['rædɪkəlɪ] adv see adj. **there's something ~ wrong with this** hier stimmt etwas ganz und gar nicht.

radices ['reɪdɪsi:z] pl of radix.

radicle ['rædɪkl] n *(Bot)* Keimwurzel f; *(small root)* Würzelchen nt; *(Chem)* Radikal nt.

radii ['reɪdɪaɪ] pl of radius.

radio ['reɪdɪəʊ] **1** n **(a)** Rundfunk m; *(also ~ set)* Radio(apparat m), Rundfunkgerät nt. **to listen to the ~** Radio hören; **to hear sth on the ~** etw im Radio hören; **the programmes on the ~** die Programme pl im Radio, die Rundfunkprogramme pl; **he was on the ~ yesterday** er kam gestern im Rundfunk or Radio.

(b) no pl *(telegraphy)* Funk m. **over the/by ~** über or per Funk; **to talk over the ~** über Funk sprechen.

2 vt person per or über Funk verständigen; message, one's position funken, durchgeben. **to ~ that all is well** funken or über Funk durchgeben, daß alles in Ordnung ist.

3 vi **to ~ for help** per Funk einen Hilferuf durchgeben.

radio: **~active** adj radioaktiv; **~active waste** radioaktiver Müll; **~activity** n Radioaktivität f; **~ announcer** n Rundfunkansager(in f), Rundfunksprecher(in f) m; **~ astronomy** n Radioastronomie f; **~ beacon** n *(Aviat, Naut)* Funkfeuer nt, Funkbake f; **~ beam** n Funkleitstrahl m; **~ broadcast** n Rundfunksendung, Rundfunkübertragung f; **~carbon dating** n Radiokarbonmethode, Kohlenstoffdatierung f; **~ communication** n Funkverbindung f; **~ compass** n Radiokompaß f; **~ contact** n Funkkontakt m; **~ control** n Funksteuerung f; **~controlled** adj ferngesteuert, ferngelenkt; **~ direction finding** n Funkpeilung f; **~ engineer** n Rundfunktechniker(in f) m; **~ frequency** n Radiofrequenz f.

radiogram ['reɪdɪəʊgræm] n **(a)** *(apparatus)* Musiktruhe f. **(b)** *(message)* Funkspruch m. **(c)** see radiograph.

radiograph ['reɪdɪəʊgrɑ:f] n Radiogramm nt; *(X-ray also)* Röntgenogramm, Röntgenbild nt.

radiographer [,reɪdɪ'ɒgrəfə'] n Röntgenassistent(in f) m.

radiography [,reɪdɪ'ɒgrəfɪ] n Röntgenographie f.

radio: **~ isotope** n Radioisotop nt; **~ link** n Funkverbindung f.

radiologist [,reɪdɪ'ɒlədʒɪst] n Röntgenologe m, Röntgenologin f.

radiology [,reɪdɪ'ɒlədʒɪ] n Radiologie f; *(X-ray also)* Röntgenologie f.

radio: **~ mast** n Funkmast m; **~ programme** n Radio- or Rundfunkprogramm nt.

radioscopy [,reɪdɪ'ɒskəpɪ] n Radioskopie f; *(Med)* Röntgenuntersuchung f.

radio: **~ set** n Radioapparat m, Rundfunkgerät nt, Rundfunkempfänger m; **~ station** n Rundfunkstation f; **~ taxi** n Funktaxi nt; **~ telephone** n Funksprechgerät nt; **~ telephony** n Sprechfunk m; **~ telescope** n Radioteleskop nt; **~therapy** n Strahlen- or Röntgentherapie f; **~ van** n Funk- or Übertragungswagen m; **~ wave** n Radiowelle f.

radish ['rædɪʃ] n *(small red variety)* Radieschen nt; *(all other varieties)* Rettich m.

radium ['reɪdɪəm] n Radium nt. **~ treatment** *(Med)* Radiumtherapie f.

radius ['reɪdɪəs] n, pl radii **(a)** *(Math)* Radius, Halbmesser m; *(of ship, aircraft)* Aktionsradius, Wirkungsbereich m. **within a 6 km ~** *(of Hamburg)* in einem Umkreis von 6 km (von Hamburg). **(b)** *(Anat)* Speiche f.

radix ['reɪdɪks] n, pl radices *(Math)* Grundzahl f.

RAF abbr of **Royal Air Force** königliche (britische) Luftwaffe.

raffia ['ræfɪə] n *(plant)* Raphia(palme) f; *(fibre)* Raphia(bast m), Raffia(bast m) f; *(for handicraft, garden)* Bast m. **~ work** Bastarbeit f; **~ table-mat** Bastuntersetzer m.

raffish ['ræfɪʃ] adj appearance flott, verwegen.

raffle ['ræfl] **1** n Tombola, Verlosung f. **~ ticket** Los nt. **2** vt *(also ~ off)* verlosen.

raft [rɑ:ft] n Floß nt.

rafter ['rɑ:ftə'] n *(Dach)*sparren m.

rag¹ [ræg] n **(a)** Lumpen, Fetzen m; *(for cleaning)* Lappen, Lumpen m; *(for paper)* Lumpen, Hadern pl; *(inf: shirt, dress)* Fetzen m *(inf)*. **~s** Lumpen pl; *(inf: clothes)* Klamotten pl *(inf)*; **in ~s** zerlumpt, abgerissen; **~s and tatters** abgerissene

Lumpen *pl*; in ~s and tatters zerlumpt und abgerissen; to go from ~s to riches (*by luck*) vom armen Schlucker zum reichen Mann/zur reichen Frau werden; (*by work*) vom Tellerwäscher zum Millionär werden; to feel like a wet ~ (*inf*) total ausgelaugt sein (*inf*); see red ~.

(b) (*pej inf*: *newspaper*) Käseblatt *nt*.

rag² **1** *n* (*Brit inf*) (*joke*) Jux *m* (*inf*); (*Univ*) karnevalistische Veranstaltung der Studenten zu Wohltätigkeitszwecken. for a ~ aus Jux (*inf*); ~ week (*Univ*) Woche, in der Studenten durch Aufführungen Geld für Wohltätigkeitszwecke sammeln.

2 *vt* (a) (*tease*) aufziehen, foppen.

(b) (*Brit*: *play a trick on*) to ~ sb jdm einen Streich spielen, einen Jux mit jdm machen (*inf*).

ragamuffin ['rægəmʌfɪn] *n* Vogelscheuche *f* (*inf*); (*boy*) Bengel *m*; (*girl*) Göre *f*. you little ~ du kleiner Fratz.

rag: ~-and-bone man *n* Lumpenhändler, Lumpensammler *m*; ~bag *n* Lumpensack *m*; (*woman*) Schlampe *f*; (*fig*) Sammelsurium *nt* (*inf*); ~ doll *n* Flickenpuppe *f*.

rage [reɪdʒ] **1** *n* Wut *f*, Zorn *m*; (*liter*) (*of sea*) Toben *nt*; (*of storm*) Toben, Rasen *nt*. to be in a ~ wütend sein, toben; to fly into a ~ einen Wutanfall bekommen; fit of ~ Wutanfall *m*; to put sb into a ~ jdn wütend *or* (*stronger*) rasend machen; to be (all) the ~ (*inf*) der letzte Schrei sein (*inf*).

2 *vi* toben, rasen; (*sea*) toben. to ~ against sb/sth gegen jdn/etw wettern.

ragged ['rægɪd] *adj* person, clothes zerlumpt, abgerissen; beard, hair zottig, strähnig; coastline, rocks zerklüftet; wound schartig, zerfetzt; edge, cuff ausgefranst; (*fig*) performance, singing stümperhaft.

ragged robin *n* Kuckuck-Lichtnelke, Kuckucksnelke *f*.

raging ['reɪdʒɪŋ] **1** *adj* person wütend; fever heftig, sehr hoch; thirst brennend; pain, toothache rasend; storm, sea, wind tobend. he was ~ er tobte; to be in a ~ temper eine fürchterliche Laune haben; to be ~ mad (*inf*) eine Stinkwut haben (*inf*).

2 *n* (*of person, storm*) Toben, Rasen *nt*; (*of sea*) Toben *nt*.

raglan ['ræglən] **1** *adj* Raglan-. **2** *n* (*coat*) Mantel *m* mit Raglanärmeln.

rag man *n* see **rag-and-bone man**.

ragout ['rægu:] *n* (*Cook*) Ragout *nt*.

rag: ~, tag and bobtail *n* Hinz und Kunz (+*pl or sing vb*); the ~, tag and bobtail of society Krethi und Plethi (+*pl or sing vb*); ~time *n* Ragtime *m*; ~ trade *n* (*sl*) Kleiderbranche *f*; ~wort *n* Jakobskraut *nt*.

raid [reɪd] **1** *n* Überfall *m*; (*Mil also*) Angriff *m*; (*air* ~) Luftangriff *m*; (*police* ~) Razzia *f*; (*by thieves*) Einbruch *m*. **2** *vt* (a) überfallen; (*police*) eine Razzia durchführen in (+*dat*); (*thieves*) einbrechen in (+*acc*). (b) (*fig hum*) plündern.

raider ['reɪdə'] *n* (*bandit*) Gangster *m*; (*thief*) Einbrecher *m*; (*in bank*) Bankräuber *m*; (*ship*) Kaperschiff *nt*; (*plane*) Überfallflugzeug *nt*.

rail¹ [reɪl] **1** *n* (a) (*on bridge, stairs etc*) Geländer *nt*; (*Naut*) Reling *f*; (*curtain* ~) Schiene *f*; (*towel-*~) Handtuchhalter *m*; (*altar-*~) Kommunionbank *f*. ~s (*fence*) Umzäunung *f*.

(b) (*for train, tram*) Schiene *f*, Gleis *nt*. to go off the ~s (*lit*) entgleisen; (*fig*) (*morally*) auf die schiefe Bahn geraten (*mentally*) zu spinnen anfangen (*inf*).

(c) (~ travel, ~way) die (Eisen)bahn. to travel by ~ mit der Bahn fahren.

2 *vt* goods per *or* mit der Bahn verschicken *or* senden.

♦**rail in** *vt sep* einzäunen.

♦**rail off** *vt sep* abzäunen. ~ed ~ from the road gegen die Straße abgezäunt.

rail² *vi* to ~ at/against sb jdn beschimpfen/über jdn schimpfen; to ~ at fate mit dem Schicksal hadern.

rail *in cpds* Bahn-; ~head *n* Endbahnhof *m*; (*end of track*) Gleisende *nt*.

railing ['reɪlɪŋ] *n* (*rail*) Geländer *nt*; (*Naut*) Reling *f*; (*fence: also* ~s) Zaun *m*.

raillery ['reɪlərɪ] *n* Spott *m*, Spöttelei *f*.

railroad ['reɪlrəʊd] **1** *n* (*US*) (Eisen)bahn *f*. **2** *vt* (a) (*US*) goods per *or* mit der Bahn befördern. (b) (*esp US inf*) to ~ a bill eine Gesetzesvorlage durchpeitschen; to ~ sb into doing sth jdn dazu hetzen, etw zu tun.

rail: ~ strike *n* Bahnstreik *m*; ~ traffic *n* Bahnverkehr *m*.

railway ['reɪlweɪ] *n* (*esp Brit*) (Eisen)bahn *f*; (*track*) Gleis *nt*.

railway: ~ carriage *n* (*Brit*) Eisenbahnwagen *m*; ~ crossing *n* Bahnübergang *m*; ~ engine *n* Lokomotive *f*; ~ engineering *n* Bahntechnik *f*, Eisenbahntechnik *f*; ~ guide *n* Kursbuch *nt*; ~ line *n* (Eisen)bahnlinie *f*; (*track*) Gleis *nt*; ~ man *n* Eisenbahner *m*; ~ network *n* Bahnnetz *nt*; ~ porter *n* Gepäckträger *m*; ~ station *n* Bahnhof *m*.

raiment ['reɪmənt] *n* (*liter*) Gewand *nt* (*liter*).

rain [reɪn] **1** *n* (a) Regen *m*. in the ~ im Regen; ~ or shine, come ~ or come shine (*lit*) ob es regnet oder schneit; (*fig*) was auch geschieht; the ~s die Regenzeit; see right.

(b) (*fig: of arrows, bullets, blows*) Hagel *m*.

2 *vti impers* (*lit, fig*) regnen. it is ~ing es regnet; it never ~s but it pours (*prov*) ein Unglück kommt selten allein (*prov*); it's ~ing buckets (*inf*) *or* cats and dogs (*inf*) es gießt wie aus Kübeln, es schüttet nur so (*inf*).

3 *vt* to ~ blows on sb einen Hagel von Schlägen auf jdn niedergehen lassen; to ~ abuse on sb einen Hagel von Schimpfwörtern auf jdn niedergehen lassen, jdn mit Schimpfwörtern überschütten.

♦**rain down** *vi* (*blows etc*) niedergehen (*upon* +*acc*).

♦**rain off, (***US***) rain out** *vt sep* to be ~ed ~ wegen Regen nicht stattfinden; (*abandoned*) wegen Regen abgebrochen werden.

rain *in cpds* Regen-; ~ belt *n* Regenzone *f*.

rainbow ['reɪnbəʊ] *n* Regenbogen *m*. a dress (in) all the colours of the ~ ein Kleid in allen Regenbogenfarben; ~ trout Regenbogenforelle *f*.

rain: ~-check *n* (*US*) to take a ~-check (*fig inf*) die Sache auf ein andermal verschieben; ~ cloud *n* Regenwolke *f*; ~coat *n* Regenmantel *m*; ~drop *n* Regentropfen *m*; ~fall *n* Niederschlag *m*; ~ forest *n* Regenwald *m*; ~ gauge *n* Regenmesser *m*.

raininess ['reɪnɪnɪs] *n* regnerisches Wetter, Regenwetter *nt*; (*of season, area*) Neigung *f* zu regnerischem Wetter.

rain: ~less *adj* niederschlagsfrei (*Met*), ohne Regen, regenfrei; ~proof **1** *adj* wasserfest, wasserdicht; **2** *vt* imprägnieren; ~storm *n* schwere Regenfälle *pl*; ~water *n* Regenwasser *nt*.

rainy ['reɪnɪ] *adj* (+*er*) regnerisch, Regen-; area also regenreich. ~ season Regenzeit *f*; to keep sth for a ~ day (*fig*) etw für schlechte Zeiten zurücklegen *or* aufheben.

raise [reɪz] **1** *vt* (a) (*lift*) object, arm, head heben; blinds, eyebrow, (*Theat*) curtain hochziehen; (*Naut*) anchor lichten; sunken ship heben; (*Med*) blister bilden. to ~ one's hat (*lit, fig*) den Hut vor jdm ziehen *or* lüften; to ~ one's glass to sb jdm zutrinken; to ~ one's fist to sb jdm mit der Faust drohen; to ~ one's hand against sb die Hand gegen jdn erheben; to ~ one's eyes to heaven die Augen zum Himmel erheben; to ~ the pitch (*Mus*) eine höhere Tonlage wählen; to ~ sb from the dead von den Toten erwecken; to ~ one's voice lauter sprechen; (*get angry*) laut werden; not a voice was ~d in protest nicht eine Stimme des Protests wurde laut; to ~ sb's/one's hopes jdm/sich Hoffnung machen; to ~ the people to revolt das Volk zur Revolution aufhetzen; to ~ the roof (*fig*) (*with noise*) das Haus zum Beben bringen; (*with approval*) in Begeisterungsstürme ausbrechen; (*with anger*) fürchterlich toben; the Opposition ~d the roof at the Government's proposals die Opposition buhte gewaltig, als sie die Vorschläge der Regierung hörte.

(b) (*in height*) (*by um*) wall, ceiling erhöhen; level anheben.

(c) (*increase*) (to *auf* +*acc*) salary erhöhen, anheben; price also, limit, standard, temperature heraufsetzen; temperature erhöhen. to ~ the tone das Niveau heben.

(d) (*promote*) (er)heben (*to* in +*acc*); see peerage.

(e) (*build, erect*) statue, building errichten.

(f) (*create, evoke*) problem, difficulty schaffen, aufwerfen; question aufwerfen, vorbringen; objection erheben; suspicion, hope (er)wecken; spirits, ghosts (herauf)beschwören; mutiny anzetteln. to ~ a cheer/laugh/smile (*in others*) Beifall ernten/Gelächter ernten/ein Lächeln hervorrufen; (*oneself*) Beifall spenden/lachen/lächeln; to ~ a protest protestieren; to ~ hell (*inf*) einen Höllenspektakel machen (*inf*).

(g) (*grow, breed*) children aufziehen, großziehen; animals aufziehen; crops anbauen. to ~ a family Kinder großziehen.

(h) (*get together*) army auf die Beine stellen, aufstellen; taxes erheben; funds, money aufbringen, auftreiben; loan, mortgage aufnehmen. to ~ a loan on a life-insurance policy ein Darlehen auf eine Lebensversicherung aufnehmen.

(i) (*end*) siege, embargo aufheben, beenden.

(j) (*Cards*) erhöhen. I'll ~ you 6 (*Poker*) ich erhöhe um 6.

(k) (*Telec: contact*) Funkverbindung *or* Funkkontakt aufnehmen mit.

(l) (*Math*) to ~ a number to the power of 2/3 etc eine Zahl in die zweite/dritte etc Potenz erheben.

2 *n* (a) (*in salary*) Gehaltserhöhung *or* -aufbesserung *f*; (*in wages*) Lohnerhöhung *or* -aufbesserung *f*.

(b) (*Cards*) Erhöhung *f*.

♦**raise up** *vt sep* heben. he ~d himself ~ on his elbow er stützte sich auf den Ellbogen.

raised [reɪzd] *adj* arm angehoben; voice erhoben, laut. ~ type (*Typ*) erhabener Druck; see eyebrow.

raisin ['reɪzən] *n* Rosine *f*.

raj [rɑːdʒ] *n* Herrschaft *f* eines Radscha. the British R~ die britische Oberherrschaft in Indien.

rajah ['rɑːdʒə] *n* Radscha *m*.

rake¹ [reɪk] **1** *n* (*garden* ~, croupier's ~) Harke *f*, Rechen *m* (*dial*); (*for grate*) Kaminrechen *m*; (*for furnace*) Ofenkrücke *f*.

2 *vt* (a) garden, hay, leaves harken, rechen (*dial*); grate säubern; fire ausräumen.

(b) (*machine gun, searchlight*) bestreichen.

3 *vi* (*search*) to ~ around *or* about (herum)wühlen *or* (herum)stöbern; to ~ among *or* through old papers in alten Papieren wühlen *or* stöbern; to ~ around in one's memory sich (*dat*) den Kopf zermartern.

♦**rake in** *vt sep* (*inf*) money kassieren (*inf*). he's raking it ~, he's raking ~ the shekels er scheffelt das Geld nur so.

♦**rake out** *vt sep* fire ausräumen; (*inf*) information auskundschaften, herausfinden.

♦**rake over** *vt sep* earth, plot harken; (*fig*) past begraben.

♦**rake up** *vt sep* (a) leaves zusammenharken. (b) (*fig*) people, things auftreiben (*inf*); money also zusammenkratzen (*inf*). (c) fire schüren; (*fig*) quarrel schüren; memories, grievance aufwärmen, auffrischen. to ~ ~ the past in Vergangenheit wühlen, Vergangenes wieder hervorholen.

rake² *n* (*person*) Lebemann, Schwerenöter *m*.

rake³ *n* (*Naut: of mast*) schiefe Stellung, Neigung *f*; (*of stage, seating*) Neigung *f*; (*Aviat: of wing*) Anstellwinkel *m*; (*Aut: of seat*) verstellbare Rückenlehne. **2** *vi* (*Naut*) sich neigen; (*Theat*) ansteigen.

rake-off ['reɪkɒf] *n* (*inf*) (Gewinn)anteil *m*, Prozente *pl* (*inf*).

rakish¹ ['reɪkɪʃ] *adj* person, appearance flott, verwegen. to wear one's hat at a ~ angle den Hut verwegen aufgesetzt haben.

rakish² *adj* (*Naut*) schnittig.

rakishly ['reɪkɪʃlɪ] *adv* flott, verwegen. ..., he said ~ ..., sagte er verwegen.

rally¹ ['rælɪ] **1** *n* (a) (*gathering*) (Massen)versammlung *f*, (Massen)treffen *nt*; (*of troops*) (Ver)sammlung *f*; (*Aut*) Rallye *f*. electoral ~ Wahlversammlung *f*; peace ~ Friedenskundgebung *f*; youth ~ Jugendtreffen *nt*.

(b) (*in health, spirits*) Erholung *f*.

(c) (*Tennis*) Ballwechsel *m*. **(b)** (*St Ex*) Erholung *f*.
2 *vt troops, supporters* (ver)sammeln, zusammenrufen. **to ~ one's strength** all seine Kräfte sammeln *or* zusammennehmen.
3 *vi* (*sick person*) Fortschritte machen; (*St Ex*) sich erholen.
  (b) (*troops, people*) sich sammeln, sich versammeln. **~ing point** Sammelplatz *m*; **to ~ to the support of sb** (*fig*) jdm in Scharen zu Hilfe eilen.
  (c) (*Aut*) **to go ~ing** Rallyes/eine Rallye fahren *or* machen; **to enjoy ~ing** gern Rallyes fahren.
♦**rally round 1** *vt+prep obj leader* sich scharen um; *person in distress* sich annehmen (+*gen*). **2** *vi* sich seiner/ihrer *etc* annehmen.

rally² *vt* (*obs*) (*tease*) necken, hänseln.

ram [ræm] **1** *n* **(a)** (*animal*) Widder, Schafbock *m*. **the R~** (*Astrol*) der Widder.
  (b) (*Tech*) Ramme *f*, Rammbär, Rammbock *m*; (*of hydraulic press*) Stoßheber *m*, hydraulischer Widder.
  (c) (*Mil*) see **battering ~**.
  (d) (*sl: man*) Rammler *m* (*sl*).
2 *vt* **(a)** (*push*) *stick, post, umbrella* stoßen; (*with great force*) rammen; (*pack*) zwängen; (*Tech*) *pile* rammen. **to ~ cotton wool in(to) one's ears** sich (*dat*) Watte in die Ohren stopfen; **to ~ a charge home** (*Mil*) laden; (*Min*) eine Sprengladung anbringen; **to ~ home an argument** ein Argument durchsetzen; **to ~ sth down sb's throat** (*inf*) jdm etw eintrichtern (*inf*); **to ~ sth into sb's head** (*inf*) jdm etw einbleuen (*inf*).
  (b) (*crash into*) *ship, car* rammen. **the car ~med a lamppost** das Auto prallte gegen einen Laternenpfahl.
♦**ram down** *vt sep earth* feststampfen; *pile* einrammen. **his hat was ~med ~ over his ears** sein Hut war fest über beide Ohren gezogen.
♦**ram in** *vt sep* hineinstoßen; (*with great force*) hineinrammen.

Ramadan [ˌræmə'dæn] *n* der Ramadan.

ramble ['ræmbl] **1** *n* Wanderung *f*. **to go for** *or* **on a ~** einen Streifzug/eine Wanderung machen.
2 *vi* **(a)** (*wander about*) Streifzüge/einen Streifzug machen; (*go on hike*) wandern.
  (b) (*in speech*) (*old person*) unzusammenhängendes Zeug reden, faseln (*inf*); (*pej: also ~ on*) schwafeln (*inf*), vom Hundertsten ins Tausendste kommen.
  (c) (*Hort*) ranken, klettern.

rambler ['ræmbləʳ] *n* **(a)** (*person*) Spaziergänger(in *f*) *m*; (*member of club*) Wanderer(in *f*), Wanderfreund *m*. **(b)** (*also ~ rose*) Kletterrose *f*.

rambling ['ræmblɪŋ] **1** *adj* **(a)** *speech, writing* weitschweifig, umständlich; *old person* faselnd (*inf*), schwafelnd (*inf*); *building, town* weitläufig.
  (b) *plant* rankend, **~ rose** Kletterrose *f*.
  (c) **~ club/society** Wanderklub *m*/-verein *m*.
2 *n* **(a)** (*wandering about*) Streifzüge *pl*; (*hiking*) Wandern *nt*.
  (b) (*in speech: also ~s*) Gefasel (*inf*), Geschwafel (*inf*) *nt*.

ramekin ['ræmɪkɪn] *n* (*Cook*) **(a)** kleiner Käseauflauf. **(b)** (*also ~ dish*) Auflaufförmchen *nt*.

ramification [ˌræmɪfɪ'keɪʃən] *n* (*lit*) Verzweigung *f*; (*smaller*) Verästelung *f*; (*of arteries*) Verästelung *f*, Geäst *nt*. **the ~s of this matter are several** (*form*) dies ist eine sehr verzweigte Angelegenheit; **the race question and its many ~s** die Rassenfrage und die damit verbundenen Probleme.

ramified ['ræmɪfaɪd] *adj* (*lit, fig*) verzweigt; (*more intricate*) verästelt.

ramify ['ræmɪfaɪ] *vi* (*lit, fig*) sich verzweigen. **the problem ramifies into several areas** das Problem greift in verschiedene Bereiche über.

ramjet (engine) ['ræmdʒet('endʒɪn)] *n* Staustrahltriebwerk, Ram-Jet *nt*.

rammer ['ræməʳ] *n* Ramme *f*.

ramp [ræmp] *n* Rampe *f*; (*hydraulic ~*) Hebebühne *f*; (*Aviat: also* **approach** *or* **boarding ~**) Gangway *f*. **"(beware of caution) ~"** (*on road sign*) „Vorsicht Rampe *or* unebene Fahrbahn".

rampage [ræm'peɪdʒ] **1** *n* **to be/go on the ~** randalieren; (*be angry*) (herum)toben/einen Wutanfall bekommen; (*looting*) auf Raubzug sein/gehen. **2** *vi* (*also ~ about* or *around*) herumwüten; (*angrily*) herumtoben.

rampancy ['ræmpənsɪ] *n see adj* **(a)** Üppigkeit *f*, Wuchern *nt*; wilde(s) Wuchern.

rampant ['ræmpənt] *adj* **(a)** (*unrestrained*) *plants, growth* üppig, wuchernd *attr*; *heresy, evil, social injustice etc* wild wuchernd *attr*. **the ~ growth of das** Wuchern (+*gen*); **to be ~** (*wild*) wuchern. **(b)** (*Her*) (*drohend*) aufgerichtet. **lion ~** aufgerichteter Löwe.

rampart ['ræmpɑːt] *n* Wall *m*; (*fig: defence*) Schutzwall *m*.

ramrod ['ræmrɒd] *n* Ladestock *m*. **he's sitting there as stiff as a ~** er sitzt da, als hätte er einen Besen *or* Ladestock verschluckt.

ramshackle ['ræmˌʃækl] *adj building* morsch, baufällig; *car* klapprig, altersschwach.

ran [ræn] *pret, ptp of* **run**.

ranch [rɑːntʃ] **1** *n* Ranch, Viehfarm *f*. **~-hand** Farmhelfer *m*; **~-house** (*on ~*) Farmhaus *nt*; **~(-style) house** Bungalow *m*. **2** *vi* Viehwirtschaft treiben.

rancher ['rɑːntʃəʳ] *n* (*owner, manager*) Rancher, Viehzüchter *m*; (*employee*) Farmarbeiter *m*.

rancid ['rænsɪd] *adj* ranzig.

rancidity [ræn'sɪdɪtɪ], **rancidness** ['rænsɪdnɪs] *n* Ranzigkeit *f*.

rancor *n* (*US*) see **rancour**.

rancorous ['ræŋkərəs] *adj tone* bitter; *attack* bösartig.

rancour, (*US*) **rancor** ['ræŋkəʳ] *n see adj* Bitterkeit *f*, Verbitterung *f*; Boshaftigkeit *f*.

rand [rænd] *n* (*monetary unit*) Rand *m*.

randiness ['rændɪnɪs] *n* (*Brit*) Geilheit *f*.

random ['rændəm] **1** *n* **at ~** *speak, walk, drive* aufs Geratewohl;

shoot, drop bombs ziellos; *take* wahllos; **to hit out at ~** ziellos um sich schlagen; **to talk at ~** ins Blaue hineinreden; **a few examples chosen** *or* **taken at ~** ein paar willkürlich gewählte Beispiele; **he just said anything at ~** er hat einfach irgend etwas gesagt, er hat einfach drauflosgeredet; **I (just) chose one at ~** ich wählte einfach irgendeine (beliebige).
2 *adj selection* willkürlich, Zufalls-. **killed by a ~ bullet** von einer verirrten Kugel getötet; **to give a ~ shot** einen Schuß ins Blaue abgeben; **to make a ~ guess** auf gut Glück raten; **~ sample** Stichprobe *f*; **~ sampling** Stichproben *pl*.

randy ['rændɪ] *adj* (+*er*) (*Brit*) scharf (*inf*), geil. **you ~ old devil** du alter Lustmolch (*inf*).

rang [ræŋ] *pret, ptp of* **ring²**.

range [reɪndʒ] **1** *n* **(a)** (*scope, distance covered*) Aktionsradius *m*; (*of missile, telescope also*) Reichweite *f*; (*of gun also*) Reichweite, Schußweite *f*; (*of vehicle also*) Fahrbereich *m*; (*of plane also*) Flugbereich *m*. **at a ~ of** auf eine Entfernung von; **at close** *or* **short/long ~** auf kurze/große Entfernung; **to find the ~** (*Mil*) das Visier einstellen; **to be out of ~** außer Reichweite sein; (*of telescope*) außer Sichtweite sein; (*of gun*) außer Schußweite sein; **within shouting ~** in Hörweite; **within (firing) ~** in Schußweite, im Schuß- *or* Feuerbereich; **~ of vision** Gesichtsfeld *nt*.
  (b) (*spread, selection*) Reihe *f*; (*of goods also*) Sortiment *nt*; (*of colours also*) Skala *f*; (*of patterns, sizes, models*) Angebot *nt*, Auswahl *f* (*of an* +*dat*). **a wide ~** eine große Auswahl; **I met a (whole) ~ of interesting people on holiday** ich traf eine ganze Reihe interessanter Leute im Urlaub; **in this price/temperature ~** in dieser Preisklasse *or* Preislage/in diesem Temperaturbereich; **out of/within my price ~** außerhalb/innerhalb meiner (finanziellen) Möglichkeiten *or* meiner Preisklasse; **what sort of price ~ were you thinking of?** an welche Preislage haben Sie gedacht?; **a ~ of prices/temperatures/clients** unterschiedliche Preise *pl*/Temperaturen *pl*/Klienten *pl*; **models available in a whole ~ of prices** Modelle in unterschiedlichen Preislagen erhältlich; **a whole ~ of patterns/sizes/subjects** eine ganze Reihe verschiedener Muster/Größen/Themen; **we have the whole ~ of models/prices** wir führen sämtliche Modelle/Waren in allen Preislagen; **we cater for the whole ~ of customers** wir sind auf alle Kundenkreise eingestellt; **his ~ of knowledge is very limited** sein Wissen ist sehr beschränkt.
  (c) (*Mus*) (*of instruments*) (Ton)umfang *m*; (*of voice also*) (Stimm)umfang *m*.
  (d) (*domain, sphere*) Kompetenz *f*; (*of influence*) (Einfluß)bereich *m*. **this ~ is outside the ~ of the department/committee/this official** dies liegt außerhalb der Kompetenz dieser Abteilung/dieses Komitees/dieses Beamten.
  (e) (*also* **shooting ~**) (*Mil*) Schießplatz *m*; (*rifle ~*) Schießstand *m*; (*at fair*) Schießbude *f*.
  (f) (*cooking stove*) Herd *m*. **cooking ~** Koch- *or* Küchenherd *m*.
  (g) (*row*) Reihe *f*; (*mountain ~*) Kette *f*.
  (h) (*US: grazing land*) Freiland, Weideland *nt*. **~ cattle** Freilandvieh *nt*.
2 *vt* **(a)** (*place in a row*) aufstellen; *objects also* anordnen. **they ~d themselves along the pavement** sie stellten sich am Bürgersteig entlang auf; **to ~ oneself with sb** *or* **on sb's side** (*fig*) sich auf jds Seite (*acc*) stellen.
  (b) (*classify*) *person* zählen (*among, with* zu).
  (c) (*roam over*) durchstreifen, durchziehen. **to ~ the seas** die Meere befahren; **he ~d the whole country looking for ...** er suchte das ganze Land nach ... ab.
  (d) (*direct*) *gun, telescope* ausrichten (*on* auf +*acc*).
  (e) (*US*) *cattle* grasen lassen.
3 *vi* **(a)** (*extend*) (*from ... to*) gehen (*zwischen ... und*). **the discussion ~d from the president to the hot-water system** die Diskussion umfaßte alles, vom Präsidenten bis zum Heißwassersystem; **his interests ~ from skiing to chess** seine Interessen reichen vom Skifahren zum Schachspielen; **the conversation ~d over a number of subjects** die Unterhaltung kreiste um eine ganze Menge von Themen; **his knowledge ~s over a wide field** er hat ein sehr umfangreiches Wissen; **the search ~d over the whole country** die Suche erstreckte sich auf das ganze Land.
  (b) (*roam*) streifen. **to ~ over the area** im Gebiet umherstreifen.
  (c) **to ~ over** (*animals, plants*) verbreitet sein in (+*dat*); (*guns, missiles, shells*) seine Reichweite haben von.

range-finder ['reɪndʒˌfaɪndəʳ] *n* Entfernungsmesser *m*.

ranger ['reɪndʒəʳ] *n* **(a)** (*of forest etc*) Förster, Aufseher *m*. **(b)** (*US: mounted patrolman*) Ranger *m*; (*commando*) Überfallkommando *nt*. **(c)** (*Brit*) **~ (scout)/(guide)** Ranger *m*.

Rangoon [ræŋ'guːn] *n* Rangun *nt*.

rangy ['reɪndʒɪ] *adj* (+*er*) langglied(e)rig.

rani ['rɑːnɪ] *n* Rani *f*.

rank¹ [ræŋk] **1** *n* **(a)** (*Mil: grade*) Rang *m*. **officer of high ~** hoher Offizier; **to reach the ~ of general** den Rang eines Generals erlangen; see **pull**.
  (b) (*class, status*) Stand *m*, Schicht *f*. **people of all ~s** Leute *pl* aller Stände; **a person of ~** eine hochgestellte Persönlichkeit; **a singer of the first ~** ein erstklassiger Sänger; **a second-~ painter** ein zweitklassiger Maler.
  (c) (*row*) Reihe *f*; (*taxi ~*) Taxistand *m*. **the taxi at the head of the ~** das erste Taxi in der Reihe.
  (d) (*Mil: formation*) Glied *nt*. **to break ~(s)** aus dem Glied treten; **to keep ~(s)** in Reih und Glied stehen; **to serve in the ~s** gemeiner Soldat sein; **the ~s, other ~s** (*Brit*) die Mannschaften und die Unteroffiziere; **the ~ and file** (*Mil*) die Mannschaft; **the ~ and file of the party/union** die Basis der Partei/Gewerkschaft, die einfachen Partei-/Gewerkschaftsmitglieder; **the ~ and file workers** die einfachen Arbeiter;

to rise from the ~s aus dem Mannschaftsstand zum Offizier aufsteigen; (*fig*) sich hocharbeiten; **to reduce sb to the ~s** jdn degradieren; *see* **close**².

   (e) (*Mus*) Register *nt*.

   2 *vt* (*class, consider*) **to ~ sb among the best/great** *etc* jdn zu den Besten/Großen *etc* zählen; **where would you ~ Napoleon among the world's statesmen?** wie würden Sie Napoleon als Weltpolitiker einordnen *or* einstufen?

   3 *vi* **to ~ among** zählen zu; **to ~ above/below sb** bedeutender/weniger bedeutend als jd sein; (*athlete*) leistungsmäßig über/unter jdm liegen; (*officer*) rangmäßig über/unter jdm liegen; **to ~ high among the world's statesmen** einer der großen Staatsmänner sein; **he ~s high among her friends** er hat eine Sonderstellung unter ihren Freunden; **he ~s as a great composer** er gilt als großer Komponist.

rank² *adj* (+*er*) **(a)** *plants* üppig; *grass* verwildert; *soil* überwuchert. **~ with weeds** von Unkraut überwuchert; **to grow ~** wuchern.

   (b) (*offensive*) *smell* übel; *dustbin, drain* stinkend *attr*; *fat* ranzig; *person* derb, vulgär.

   (c) *attr* (*utter*) *disgrace, injustice* wahr; *poison, nonsense, insolence* rein; *traitor, liar* übel; *stupidity* ausgesprochen.

ranker ['ræŋkə'] *n* (*Mil*) (*soldier*) einfacher *or* gemeiner Soldat; (*officer*) aus dem Mannschaftsstand aufgestiegener Offizier.

ranking officer ['ræŋkɪŋ'ɒfɪsə'] *n* ranghöchster/ranghöherer Offizier.

rankle ['ræŋkl] *vi* **to ~ (with sb)** jdn wurmen.

rankness ['ræŋknɪs] *n see adj* **(a)** Üppigkeit *f*; Verwildertheit *f*; Überwucherung *f*. **(b)** Übelkeit *f*; Gestank *m*, Stinken *nt*; Ranzigkeit *f*; Derbheit, Vulgarität *f*.

ransack ['rænsæk] *vt* (*search*) *room, cupboards* durchwühlen; (*pillage*) *house* plündern; *town, region* herfallen über (+*acc*).

ransom ['rænsəm] **1** *n* (*rescue*) Auslösung *f*; (*release*) Freilassung *f*; (*Rel*) Erlösung *f*. **to hold sb to ~** (*lit*) jdn als Geisel halten; (*fig*) jdn erpressen; *see* **king**.

   2 *vt* (*buy free*) auslösen, Lösegeld bezahlen für; (*set free*) gegen Lösegeld freilassen; (*Rel*) erlösen.

rant [rænt] *vi* (*emotionally, angrily*) Tiraden loslassen; (*talk nonsense*) irres Zeug reden (*inf*). **to ~ (and rave)** (*be angry*) herumschimpfen; **to ~ (and rave) at sb** mit jdm schimpfen; **what's he ~ing (on) about?** worüber läßt er sich denn da aus? (*inf*).

ranting ['ræntɪŋ] **1** *n see vi* Tiraden *pl*; irres Zeug; Geschimpfe *nt*. **2** *adj* pathetisch.

ranunculus [rə'nʌŋkjʊləs] *n* (*garden flower*) Ranunkel *f*.

rap [ræp] **1** *n* (*noise, blow*) Klopfen *nt no pl*. **there was a ~ at the door** es hat geklopft; **to give sb a ~ on the knuckles** (*lit, fig*) jdm auf die Finger klopfen; **he got a ~ on the knuckles for that** (*lit, fig*) dafür hat er eins auf die Finger bekommen (*inf*); **to take the ~** (*inf*) die Schuld zugeschoben kriegen (*inf*); **I don't care a ~** (*inf*) das ist mir piepe (*inf*).

   2 *vt table* klopfen auf (+*acc*); *window* klopfen an (+*acc*). **to ~ sb's knuckles, to ~ sb over the knuckles** (*lit, fig*) jdm auf die Finger klopfen.

   3 *vi* klopfen. **to ~ at the door/window** kurz (an die Tür)/ans Fenster klopfen.

   ♦**rap out** *vt sep* **(a)** (*say curtly*) *oath, order* ausstoßen. **(b)** (*Spiritualism*) *message* klopfen.

rapacious *adj*, **~ly** *adv* [rə'peɪʃəs, -lɪ] habgierig.

rapacity [rə'pæsɪtɪ] *n* Habgier *f*.

rape¹ [reɪp] **1** *n* Vergewaltigung, Notzucht (*Jur*) *f*; (*obs: abduction*) Raub *m*. **2** *vt* vergewaltigen, notzüchtigen (*Jur*).

rape² *n* (*plant*) Raps *m*. **~ oil/seed** Rapsöl *nt*/Rapssamen *m*.

rape³ *n* (*grape pulp*) Trester *pl*.

rapid ['ræpɪd] **1** *adj* schnell; *action, movement also* rasch; *improvement, change, spread also* rapide; *decline, rise* rapide, steil; *smile also* kurz; *heartbeat, pulse also* flink; *loss of heat* plötzlich; *river, waterfall* reißend; *slope, descent* steil. **~ fire/firing** (*Mil*) Schnellfeuer *nt*; **~ fire of questions** Feuerwerk *nt* von Fragen; **~ eye movement sleep** REM-Schlaf *m*.

   2 *n* **~s** *pl* (*Geog*) Stromschnellen *pl*.

rapidity [rə'pɪdɪtɪ] *n see adj* Schnelligkeit *f*; Raschheit *f*; Rapidheit *f*; Rapidheit, Steilheit *f*; Kürze *f*; Flinkheit *f*; Plötzlichkeit *f*; reißende Strömung, Reißende *nt*; Steilheit *f*.

rapidly ['ræpɪdlɪ] *adv see adj*.

rapier ['reɪpɪə'] *n* Rapier *nt*. **~ thrust** (*lit*) Stoß *m* mit dem Rapier; (*fig*) (*remark*) Hieb *m*; (*retort*) Parade *f*.

rapine ['ræpaɪn] *n* (*liter*) Plünderung *f*.

rapist ['reɪpɪst] *n* Vergewaltiger, Frauenschänder (*geh*) *m*.

rapping ['ræpɪŋ] *n see vi*.

rapport [ræ'pɔː'] *n* **the ~ I have with my father** das enge Verhältnis zwischen mir und meinem Vater; **I envied them the obvious ~ that they had** *or* **that was between them** ich beneidete sie um ihr offensichtlich enges Verhältnis zueinander; **in ~ with** in Harmonie mit; **they are in ~ with each other** sie harmonieren gut (miteinander).

rapprochement [ræ'prɒʃmɑːŋ] *n* Annäherung *f*.

rapscallion [ræp'skæljən] *n* (*old*) Halunke, Gauner *m*.

rapt [ræpt] *adj* **(a)** *interest* gespannt; *attention* atemlos, höchste(r, s). **~ in contemplation/in thought** in Betrachtungen/Gedanken versunken. **(b)** *look, smile* verzückt.

rapture ['ræptʃə'] *n* (*delight*) Entzücken *nt*; (*ecstasy*) Verzükkung *f*. **to be in ~s** entzückt sein (*over* über +*acc, about* von); **they were in ~s over their new baby** sie waren ganz entzückt über ihr neues Baby; **she was in ~s when she heard he was returning** sie war außer sich vor Freude, als sie hörte, daß er zurückkommt; **to go into ~s** in Entzücken geraten; **to send sb into ~s** jdn in Entzücken versetzen.

rapturous ['ræptʃərəs] *adj* *applause, reception* stürmisch, begeistert; *exclamation* entzückt; *look* verzückt, hingerissen.

rapturously ['ræptʃərəslɪ] *adv see adj*.

rare [rɛə'] *adj* (+*er*) **(a)** (*uncommon*) selten, rar; *occurrence*

selten. **with very ~ exceptions** mit sehr wenigen Ausnahmen; **it's ~ for her to come** sie kommt nur selten.

   (b) *atmosphere* dünn; *gas* Edel-; *earths* selten.

   (c) *meat* roh; *steak also* blutig, englisch.

   (d) (*inf: great*) irrsinnig (*inf*). **a person of ~ kindness** ein selten freundlicher Mensch (*inf*); **kind to a ~ degree** selten freundlich.

rarebit ['rɛəbɪt] *n see* **Welsh ~**.

rarefaction [ˌrɛərɪ'fækʃən] *n* Dünne *f*; (*fig*) Exklusivität *f*.

rarefied ['rɛərɪfaɪd] *adj* *atmosphere, air* dünn; (*fig*) exklusiv.

rarefy ['rɛərɪfaɪ] **1** *vt air, atmosphere* verdünnen, dünn werden lassen; (*fig*) exklusiv machen. **2** *vi* (*air*) dünn werden.

rarely ['rɛəlɪ] *adv* selten.

rareness ['rɛənɪs] *n see adj* **(a)** Seltenheit, Rarheit *f*; (*of occurrence*) Rarheit *f*. **(b)** Dünne *f*. **(c)** Roheit *f*.

raring ['rɛərɪŋ] *adj*: **to be ~ to go** (*inf*) es kaum erwarten können, bis es losgeht (*inf*).

rarity ['rɛərɪtɪ] *n* Seltenheit *f*; (*rare occurrence also*) Rarität *f*.

rascal ['rɑːskəl] *n* Gauner *m*; (*child*) Schlingel, Frechdachs *m*; (*old: scoundrel*) Schurke *m*.

rascally ['rɑːskəlɪ] *adj* (*old, liter*) *trick* schändlich, schimpflich (*old, liter*); *person* schurkisch. **a ~ fellow** ein Schurke *m*.

rash¹ [ræʃ] *n* (*Med*) Ausschlag *m*. **to come out** *or* **break out in a ~** einen Ausschlag bekommen.

rash² *adj* (+*er*) *person* unbesonnen; *act also* voreilig, überstürzt; *thoughts* voreilig; *promise, words, decision* voreilig, vorschnell. **it was ~ of him to promise that** es war etwas voreilig von ihm, das zu versprechen.

rasher ['ræʃə'] *n* Streifen *m*. **~ of bacon** Speckstreifen *m*.

rashly ['ræʃlɪ] *adv see adj*.

rashness ['ræʃnɪs] *n see adj* Unbesonnenheit *f*; Voreiligkeit, Überstürztheit *f*; Voreiligkeit *f*.

rasp [rɑːsp] **1** *n* (*tool*) Raspel *f*; (*noise*) Kratzen *nt no pl*; (*of cough*) Keuchen *nt no pl*; (*when breathing*) Rasseln, Keuchen *nt no pl*; (*inf: raspberry*) Himbeere *f*.

   2 *vt* **(a)** (*Tech*) raspeln, feilen. **to ~ sth away** *or* **off** etw wegor abraspeln *or* -feilen.

   (b) (*say: also ~ out*) *insults* krächzen; *orders* schnarren.

   3 *vi* kratzen; (*breath*) rasseln; *see also* **rasping**.

raspberry ['rɑːzbərɪ] **1** *n* Himbeere *f*; (*plant: also ~ bush or cane*) Himbeerstrauch *m*. **to blow a ~** (*inf*) verächtlich schnauben; **to get a ~ (from sb)** (*inf*) (von jdm) nur ein verächtliches Schnauben ernten. **2** *adj* *ice-cream, jam, flavour* Himbeer-; *colour, dress* himbeerrot.

rasping ['rɑːspɪŋ] **1** *adj* *sound* kratzend; *voice* kratzig (*inf*), krächzend; *cough* keuchend; *breath* rasselnd, keuchend. **2** *n* (*sound*) Kratzen *nt*; (*of voice*) Krächzen, Gekrächze *nt*.

raster ['ræstə'] *n* Raster *m or nt*.

rat [ræt] **1** *n* (*Zool*) Ratte *f*; (*pej inf: person*) elender Verräter (*inf*). **he's a dirty ~** (*inf*) er ist ein dreckiges *or* gemeines Schwein (*inf*); **you ~!** du Hund! (*inf*); **~s!** (*inf*) (*annoyance*) Mist! (*inf*); (*rejection*) Quatsch! (*inf*); *see* **smell**.

   2 *vi* **(a)** **to ~ on sb** (*inf*) (*desert*) jdn sitzenlassen (*inf*); (*inform on*) jdn verpfeifen (*inf*).

   (b) **to go ~ting** auf Rattenfang gehen.

ratable *adj see* **rateable**.

rat *in cpds* Ratten-; **~bag** *n* (*pej inf*) Schrulle *f* (*inf*); **~-catcher** *n* Rattenfänger *m*; **~-catching** *n* Rattenfang *m*.

ratchet ['rætʃɪt] *n* Ratsche *f*. **~ wheel** Sperrad *nt*.

rate¹ [reɪt] **1** *n* **(a)** (*ratio, proportion, frequency*) Rate *f*; (*speed*) Tempo *nt*. **the failure ~ on this course/for this exam** die Durchfallrate *or* -quote bei diesem Kurs/Examen; **at the** *or* **a ~ of 100 litres an hour/14 feet per minute** (in einem Tempo von) 100 Liter pro Stunde/14 Fuß pro Minute; **~ of climb** (*Aviat*) Steigleistung *f*; **~ of consumption** Verbrauch *m*; **~ of flow** (*of water, electricity*) Fluß *m*; **pulse ~** Puls *m*; **at a great** *or* **terrific ~** (*inf*) ~, at a ~ (*inf*) in irrsinnigem Tempo (*inf*); (*move also*) mit hundert Sachen (*inf*); **if you continue at this ~** (*lit, fig*) wenn du so *or* in diesem Tempo weitermachst; **at his ~ of working** bei seinem Arbeitstempo; **at the ~ you're going you'll be dead before long** wenn du so weitermachst, bist du bald unter der Erde; **at any ~** auf jeden Fall; **at that ~ I suppose I'll have to agree** wenn das so ist, muß ich wohl zustimmen.

   (b) (*Comm, Fin*) Satz *m*; (*St Ex*) Kurs *m*. **~ of exchange** Wechselkurs *m*; **what's the ~ at the moment?** wie steht der Kurs momentan?; **what's the ~ of pay?** wie hoch ist der Satz (für die Bezahlung)?; **~ of interest** Zinssatz *m*; **~ of pay for overtime** Satz *m* für Überstunden; **postage/advertising/insurance ~s** Post-/Werbe-/Versicherungsgebühren *pl*; **there is a reduced ~ for children** Kinderermäßigung wird gewährt; **basic salary ~** Grundgehaltssatz *m*; **to pay sb at the ~ of £10 per hour** jdm einen Stundenlohn von £ 10 bezahlen.

   (c) **~s** *pl* (*Brit: municipal tax*) Gemeindesteuern, Kommunalsteuern *pl*; **~s and taxes** Kommunal- und Staatssteuern *pl*; **~(s) office** Gemeindesteueramt *nt*; *see* **water-~**.

   2 *vt* **(a)** (*estimate value or worth of*) (ein)schätzen. **to ~ sb/sth among ...** jdn/etw zu ... zählen *or* rechnen; **how do you ~ this effort/these results?** was halten Sie von dieser Leistung/diesen Ergebnissen?; **to ~ sb/sth as sth** jdn/etw für etw halten; **he is generally ~d as a great statesman** er gilt allgemein als großer Staatsmann; **I ~ him as fairly intelligent** ich halte ihn für ziemlich intelligent; **how does he ~ that film?** was hält er von dem Film?; **to ~ sb/sth highly** jdn/etw hoch einschätzen.

   (b) (*Brit: Local Government*) veranlagen. **a house ~d at £100 per annum** ein Haus, dessen steuerbarer Wert £ 100 ist.

   (c) (*deserve*) verdienen. **does this hotel ~ 3 stars?** verdient dieses Hotel 3 Sterne?; **I think he ~s a pass (mark)** ich finde, das kann man mit „ausreichend" oder besser bewerten.

   (d) (*sl: think highly of*) gut finden (*inf*).

   3 *vi* (*be classed*) **to ~ as/among ...** gelten als .../zählen zu ..., rangieren unter ... (+*dat*).

rate² vt (liter) see **berate**.

rateable, ratable ['reɪtəbl] adj (Brit) property steuerpflichtig, steuerbar. ~ **value** steuerbarer Wert.

ratepayer ['reɪtˌpeɪəʳ] n (Brit) Steuerzahler m (von Kommunal-steuern).

rather ['rɑːðəʳ] adv **(a)** (for preference) lieber. ~ **than wait, he** went away bevor er wartete, ging er (lieber), er ging lieber, als daß er wartete; **I would ~ have the blue dress ich hätte** lieber das blaue Kleid; **I would ~ be happy than rich ich wäre** lieber glücklich als reich; **I would ~ you came yourself mir** wäre es lieber, Sie kämen selbst; **I'd ~ not leben; I'd ~** not go ich würde lieber nicht gehen; **I'd ~ die!** eher sterbe ich!; **he expected me to phone ~ than (to) write er erwartete eher** einen Anruf als einen Brief von mir; **it would be better to phone ~ than (to) write** es wäre besser zu telefonieren, als zu schreiben.

(b) (more accurately) vielmehr. **he is, or ~ was, a soldier er** ist, beziehungsweise or vielmehr war, Soldat; **a car, or ~ an old** banger ein Auto, genauer gesagt eine alte Kiste.

(c) (to a considerable degree) ziemlich; (somewhat, slightly) etwas. **he's a ~ clever person or ~ a clever person er ist ziem-** lich klug; **he felt ~ better er fühlte sich bedeutend wohler; it's ~ more difficult than you think es ist um einiges schwieriger,** als du denkst; **it's ~ too difficult for me es ist etwas zu** schwierig für mich; **she's ~ an idiot/a killjoy sie ist reichlich** doof/ein richtiger Spielverderber; **I ~ think he's wrong ich** glaube fast, er hat Unrecht; **I've ~ got the impression ... ich** habe ganz den Eindruck, ...; ~! (inf) und ob! (inf), klar! (inf).

ratification [ˌrætɪfɪˈkeɪʃən] n Ratifizierung f.

ratify ['rætɪfaɪ] vt ratifizieren.

rating¹ ['reɪtɪŋ] n **(a)** (assessment) (Ein)schätzung f; (Brit: of house) Veranlagung f. **what's your ~ of his abilities?** wie schätzen Sie seine Fähigkeiten ein?

(b) (class, category) (Sport: of yacht, car) Klasse f; (Fin: also credit ~) Kreditfähigkeit f; (Elec) Leistung f; (of petrol: also octane ~) Oktanzahl f. **what's his ~?** wie wird er eingestuft?; **he has attained world-class ~** er hat Weltklasse(format) erreicht; **the popularity ~ of a TV programme die Zuschauer-** zahlen eines Fernsehprogramms; **security ~** Sicherheitsein-stufung f; **voltage ~** Grenzspannung f.

(c) (Naut) (rank) Rang m; (sailor) Matrose m.

rating² n (scolding) Schelte f.

ratio ['reɪʃɪəʊ] n Verhältnis nt. **the ~ of men to women das Ver-** hältnis von Männern zu Frauen; **in the or a ~ of 100 to 1** (written 100:1) im Verhältnis 100 zu 1; **in inverse ~** (Math) umgekehrt proportional; **inverse or indirect ~** umgekehrtes Verhältnis.

ratiocinate [ˌrætɪˈɒsɪneɪt] vi (form) reflektieren.

ration ['ræʃən] **1** n Ration f; (fig) Quantum nt. **~s** (food) Rationen pl; **to put sb on short ~s** jdn auf halbe Ration setzen; ~ **book/** card Bezug(s)scheinbuch nt/Bezug(s)schein m; (for food) = Lebensmittelkarte f/Lebensmittelmarke f.

2 vt goods, food rationieren; (state, government also) bewirtschaften. **he was ~ed to 1 kg ihm wurde nur 1 kg erlaubt;** **sugar is short, so housewives are being ~ed Zucker ist knapp** und wird daher für die Hausfrau rationiert; **I'm going to ~ you** **to one apple a day ich werde dich kurzhalten, du bekommst nur** einen Apfel pro Tag; **he ~ed himself to five cigarettes a day er** erlaubte sich (dat) nur fünf Zigaretten pro Tag.

♦**ration out** vt sep zuteilen.

rational ['ræʃənl] adj **(a)** (having reason) creature, person ver-nunftbegabt, rational.

(b) (sensible, reasonable) person, action, thinking ver-nünftig, rational; activity, solution vernünftig, sinnvoll; (Med: lucid, sane) person bei klarem Verstand. **it was the only ~ thing** to do es war das einzig Vernünftige.

(c) (Math) rational.

rationale [ˌræʃəˈnɑːl] n Gründe pl, Gedankengänge pl. **there** doesn't seem to be any ~ das scheint jeglicher Begründung zu entbehren.

rationalism ['ræʃnəlɪzəm] n Rationalismus m.

rationalist ['ræʃnəlɪst] n Rationalist m.

rationalistic [ˌræʃnəˈlɪstɪk] adj rationalistisch.

rationality [ˌræʃəˈnælɪtɪ] n see adj (b) Vernünftigkeit, Rationalität f; Vernünftigkeit f; (Med) klarer Verstand.

rationalization [ˌræʃnəlaɪˈzeɪʃən] n Rationalisierung f; (of problem) vernünftige Betrachtung f.

rationalize ['ræʃnəlaɪz] **1** vt **(a)** event, conduct etc rationalisieren; problem vernünftig sehen or betrachten. **(b)** (organize efficiently) industry, production, work rationali-sieren. **(c)** (Math) in eine rationale Gleichung umändern. **2** vi rationalisieren.

rationally ['ræʃnəlɪ] adv act, behave, think vernünftig, rational; (Med) bei klarem Verstand. ~, **it should be possible to** do it rational gesehen sollte es möglich sein.

rationing ['ræʃənɪŋ] n see vt Rationierung f; Bewirtschaftung f.

ratline, ratlin ['rætlɪn] n (Naut) Webeleine f.

rat: ~ **poison** n Rattengift nt; **~-race** n ständiger Konkurrenz-kampf.

rats' tails npl (pej) Zotteln pl (pej); (inf: bunches) Rat-tenschwänze pl (inf). **her hair was or hung in ~** ihr Haar war zottelig or hing zottelig herunter; **sie hatte Rattenschwänze.**

rattan ['rætæn] n (plant) Rotang m; (cane) spanisches Rohr.

rattle ['rætl] **1** vi klappern; (chains) rasseln, klirren; (bottles) klirren; (gunfire) knattern; (drums) schlagen; (hailstones) prasseln; (rattlesnake) klappern. **to ~ at the door** an der Tür rütteln; **there's something rattling** da klappert etwas; **to ~** along/away (vehicle) entlang-/davonrattern; **they ~d through** the village sie ratterten durch das Dorf.

2 vt **(a)** box, dice, keys schütteln; bottles, cans zusam-menschlagen; chains rasseln mit; windows rütteln an (+dat).

(b) (inf: alarm) person durcheinanderbringen. **don't get ~d!**

reg dich nicht auf!; **she was ~d at or by the news, the news ~d** her die Nachricht hat ihr einen Schock versetzt.

3 n **(a)** (sound) see vi Klappern nt no pl; Rasseln, Klirren nt no pl; Klirren nt no pl; Knattern nt no pl; Schlagen nt no pl; Pras-seln nt no pl; Klappern nt no pl; (Med: also death ~) Röcheln nt.

(b) (child's) Rassel, Klapper f; (sports fan's) Schnarre f.

♦**rattle down** vi herunterprasseln, herunterhageln.

♦**rattle off** vt sep poem, speech, list herunterrasseln.

♦**rattle on** vi (inf) (unentwegt) quasseln (inf) (about über +acc).

♦**rattle through** vi +prep obj speech etc herunterrasseln; work, music rasen durch.

rattle: ~**brain** n (inf) Spatzenhirn nt (inf); ~**snake** n Klap-perschlange f; ~**trap** n (hum inf) Klapperkiste f (hum inf).

rattling ['rætlɪŋ] **1** n see vi Klappern nt; Rasseln, Klirren nt; Knattern nt; Schlagen nt; Prasseln nt; Klappern nt.

2 adj see vi klappernd; rasselnd, klirrend; knatternd; schlagend; prasselnd; klappernd. **a ~ noise ein Klappern** nt/Rasseln nt etc; **at a ~ pace** (inf) in rasendem Tempo (inf).

3 adv: ~ **good** (dated inf) verdammt gut (inf).

rattrap, rat trap ['rættræp] n Rattenfalle f.

ratty ['rætɪ] adj (+er) (inf) **(a)** (irritable) gereizt. **(b)** (US: run-down) verlottert (inf).

raucous ['rɔːkəs] adj rauh, heiser.

raucously ['rɔːkəslɪ] adv shout rauh, heiser; sing mit rauher or heiserer Stimme.

raucousness ['rɔːkəsnɪs] n Rauheit, Heiserkeit f.

raunchy ['rɔːntʃɪ] adj (+er) (US inf) geil; novel rasant.

ravage ['rævɪdʒ] **1** n (of war) verheerendes Wüten no pl; (of dis-ease) Wüten nt no pl, Zerstörung f (of durch). ~**s** (of war) Ver-heerung f (of durch); (of disease) Zerstörung f (of durch); **the** ~**s of time** die Spuren pl der Zeit; **a face marked by the ~s of** time ein von der Zeit schwer gezeichnetes Gesicht.

2 vt (ruin) verwüsten, verheeren; (plunder) plündern. ~**d by** disease von Krankheit schwer gezeichnet.

rave [reɪv] **1** vi (be delirious) phantasieren, delirieren (spec); (talk wildly) phantasieren, spinnen (inf); (speak furiously) toben; (inf: speak, write enthusiastically) schwärmen (about, over von); (liter) (storm) toben; (wind) brausen; (sea) toben. **to** ~ **against sb/sth** gegen jdn/etw wettern; **he ~d at the children** for breaking the window er donnerte die Kinder wegen der eingeworfenen Fensterscheibe an; **see rant.**

2 n **(a)** (Brit sl: also ~-up) Fete f (sl), tolle Party.

(b) (sl: praise) Schwärmerei f. **to have a ~ about sth von etw** schwärmen or ganz weg sein (sl); **the play got a ~ review** (inf) das Stück bekam eine glänzende or begeisterte Kritik.

(c) (Brit sl: fashion) **it's all the ~** das ist große Mode.

ravel ['rævəl] **1** vt **(a)** (disentangle) see **ravel out** 2. **(b)** (old: entangle) verwirren. **2** vi (become tangled) sich verwirren; (fray) ausfransen.

♦**ravel out 1** vi ausfransen; (rope) faserig werden. **2** vt sep material ausfransen; threads entwirren; knitting auftrennen, aufziehen; (fig) difficulty klären.

raven ['reɪvən] n Rabe m. ~**-black** rabenschwarz; ~**-haired** mit rabenschwarzem Haar.

ravening ['rævnɪŋ] adj beutehungrig, räuberisch.

ravenous ['rævənəs] adj animal ausgehungert; person also heißhungrig; appetite, hunger gewaltig. **I'm ~ ich habe einen** Bärenhunger (inf).

ravenously ['rævənəslɪ] adv **to be ~ hungry** (animal) ausgehungert sein; (person also) einen Heißhunger or Bärenhunger haben (inf).

raver ['reɪvəʳ] n (Brit sl) flotte Biene (sl). **she's a real little ~** sie führt ein flottes Leben.

rave-up ['reɪvʌp] n (Brit sl) see **rave** 2 **(a)**.

ravine [rəˈviːn] n Schlucht, Klamm f.

raving ['reɪvɪŋ] **1** adj **(a)** (frenzied) wahnsinnig, verrückt; (delirious) im Delirium, phantasierend attr. **his ~ fantasies** seine verrückten Phantastereien; **a ~ lunatic** (inf) ein kom-pletter Idiot (inf).

(b) (inf: remarkable) success toll (inf); beauty hinreißend.

2 adv ~ **mad** (inf) total verrückt (inf).

3 n ~**(s)** Phantasien pl, Delirien pl.

ravioli [ˌrævɪˈəʊlɪ] n Ravioli pl.

ravish ['rævɪʃ] vt **(a)** (delight) hinreißen. **(b)** (old, liter: rape) schänden (geh); (obs: abduct) rauben.

ravisher ['rævɪʃəʳ] n (old, liter) Schänder m (geh).

ravishing ['rævɪʃɪŋ] adj woman, sight atemberaubend; beauty also, meal hinreißend.

ravishingly ['rævɪʃɪŋlɪ] adv beautiful hinreißend, atem-beraubend; dressed, decorated atemberaubend schön.

ravishment ['rævɪʃmənt] n see vt **(a)** atemloses Staunen, Hingerissenheit f. **(b)** Schändung f (geh); Raub m.

raw [rɔː] **1** adj (+er) **(a)** (uncooked) meat, food roh; (unpro-cessed) ore, sugar, silk, brick also Roh-; spirit, alcohol rein, unvermischt; cloth ungewalkt; leather ungegerbt; (fig) statis-tics nackt. **it's a ~ deal** (inf) das ist eine Gemeinheit (inf); **to** give sb a ~ deal (inf) jdn benachteiligen, jdn unfair behandeln; **to get a ~ deal schlecht wegkommen** (inf); **the old get a ~ deal** from the state (inf) alte Leute werden vom Staat stiefmütter-lich behandelt; ~ **edge** (of cloth etc) ungesäumte Kante; ~ **material** Rohstoff m; ~ **spirits** reiner Alkohol.

(b) (inexperienced) troops, recruit neu, unerfahren. ~ **recruit** (fig) blutiger Anfänger (inf).

(c) (sore) wound offen; skin wund; nerves empfindlich.

(d) climate, wind, air rauh.

(e) (esp US: coarse) humour, story, person derb; colour grell.

2 n **(a)** **to touch or get sb on the ~** (Brit) bei jdm einen wunden Punkt berühren.

(b) **in the ~** (inf: naked) im Naturzustand; **life/nature in the ~** die rauhe Seite des Lebens/der Natur.

raw: ~**boned** adj mager, knochig; ~**hide** n (leather) ungegerbtes Leder; (whip) Lederpeitsche f.

Rawlplug ['rɔːlplʌg] ® n Dübel m.

rawness ['rɔːnɪs] n (a) (of meat, food) Roheit f. (b) (lack of experience) Unerfahrenheit f. (c) (soreness) Wundheit f. (d) (of weather) Rauheit f. (e) (esp US: coarseness) Derbheit f.

ray[1] [reɪ] n (a) Strahl m. a ~ of hope/solace ein Hoffnungsschimmer or -strahl m/ein kleiner Trost; ~ **gun** Strahlenpistole f. (b) (of fish) Flossenstrahl m; (of starfish) Arm m.

ray[2] n (fish) Rochen m.

rayon ['reɪɒn] 1 n Reyon m. 2 adj Reyon-, aus Reyon.

raze [reɪz] vt zerstören; (Mil) schleifen. to ~ to the ground dem Erdboden gleichmachen.

razor ['reɪzəʳ] n Rasierapparat m; (cutthroat) Rasiermesser nt. electric ~ Elektrorasierer m; ~'s edge (fig) see ~-**edge** (b).

razor-: ~**back** n (Zool) Finnwal m; ~**bill** n (Zool) Tordalk m; ~**blade** n Rasierklinge f; ~-**cut** n Messerschnitt m; 2 vt mit dem Messer schneiden; ~-**edge** n (a) (mountain ridge) Grat m; (b) (fig) our fate is poised/we stand poised on a ~-**edge** our fate steht auf Messers Schneide/wir stehen vor einem Abgrund; the decision rests on a ~-**edge** die Entscheidung steht auf Messers Schneide; the ~-**edge** that divides belief and unbelief der schmale Grat zwischen Glaube und Unglaube; on the ~-**edge** of virtue auf dem schmalen Grat der Tugend; ~-**sharp** adj knife scharf (wie ein Rasiermesser); (fig) person sehr scharfsinnig; mind, wit messerscharf.

razz [ræz] vt (US inf) aufziehen (inf), verhohnepiepeln (inf).

razzle ['ræzl] n (dated sl): to go on the ~ auf die Pauke hauen (inf).

razzle-dazzle ['ræzl'dæzl], **razzmatazz** ['ræzmə'tæz] n Rummel, Trubel m.

RC abbr of Roman Catholic rk, r.-k.

Rd abbr of Road Str.

RE abbr of Religious Education.

re[1] [reɪ] n (Mus) re nt.

re[2] [riː] prep (Admin, Comm etc: referring to) betreffs (+gen), bezüglich (+gen); (Jur: also in ~) in Sachen gegen. ~ your letter of 16th Betr(eff): Ihr Brief vom 16.

re- [riː-] pref wieder-.

reach [riːtʃ] 1 n (a) (act of reaching) to make a ~ for sth nach etw greifen; he managed to get it with a long ~ es gelang ihm, es mit langgestrecktem Arm zu erreichen.
(b) (denoting accessibility) within/out of sb's ~ in/außer jds Reichweite (dat), in/außer Reichweite für jdn; within arm's ~ in greifbarer Nähe; put it out of the children's ~ or out of the ~ of children stellen Sie es so, daß Kinder es nicht erreichen können; keep out of ~ of children von Kindern fernhalten; cars are within everyone's ~ nowadays Autos sind heute für jeden erschwinglich; mountains within easy ~ Berge, die leicht erreichbar sind; within easy ~ of the sea in unmittelbarer Nähe des Meers; this town is within easy ~ of London for a day trip man kann von dieser Stadt aus gut Tagesflüge nach London machen; I keep it within easy ~ ich habe es in greifbarer Nähe; she was beyond (the) ~ of human help für sie kam jede menschliche Hilfe zu spät; this subject is beyond his ~ dieses Thema geht über seinen Horizont (inf).
(c) (distance one can ~) Reichweite f; (Boxing) Aktionsradius m. a long ~ lange Arme pl; ein großer Aktionsradius.
(d) (sphere of action, influence) Einflußbereich m. beyond the ~ of the law außerhalb des Gesetzes.
(e) (stretch) (of beach, river) Strecke f; (of canal) Wasserhaltung f; (of woodland) Gebiet nt.
2 vt (a) (arrive at) erreichen; place, goal also, point ankommen an (+dat); town, country ankommen in (+dat); perfection also erlangen; agreement, understanding erzielen, kommen zu; conclusion kommen or gelangen zu. we ~ed London at 3pm wir kamen um 15 Uhr in London an; when we ~ed him he was dead als wir zu ihm kamen, war er tot; to ~ the terrace you have to cross the garden um auf die Terrasse zu kommen, muß man durch den Garten gehen; to ~ page 50 bis Seite 50 kommen; this advertisement is geared to ~ the under 25's diese Werbung soll Leute unter 25 ansprechen; you can ~ me at my hotel Sie erreichen mich in meinem Hotel.
(b) (stretch to get or touch) to be able to ~ sth an etw (acc) (heran)reichen können, bis zu etw langen können (inf); can you ~ it? kommen Sie dran?; can you ~ the ceiling? kannst du bis an die Decke reichen or langen? (inf).
(c) (come up to, go down to) reichen or gehen bis zu. he ~es her shoulder er reicht or geht ihr bis zur Schulter.
(d) (inf: get and give) langen (inf), reichen. ~ me (over) that book reiche or lang (inf) mir das Buch (herüber); ~ (over) the salt for Richard gib or lang (inf) Richard das Salz hinüber.
(e) (US Jur) witness bestechen.
3 vi (a) (to, as far as bis) (territory etc) sich erstrecken, gehen, reichen; (voice, sound) tragen.
(b) (stretch out hand or arm) greifen. to ~ for sth nach etw greifen or langen (inf); he ~ed to grasp the door handle er griff or langte (inf) nach dem Türgriff; to ~ for the sky! (US) Hände hoch!; to ~ for the moon (fig) nach den Sternen greifen.
(c) can you ~? kommen Sie dran?

♦**reach across** vi hinüber-/herübergreifen or -langen (inf).

♦**reach back** vi (in time) zurückreichen, zurückgehen (to bis).

♦**reach down 1** vi (clothes, curtains, hair etc) hinunter-/herunterreichen (to bis); (person) hinunter-/heruntergreifen or -langen (inf) (for nach). 2 vt sep hinunter-/herunterreichen.

♦**reach out 1** vt sep he ~ed ~ his hand to take the book er streckte die Hand aus, um das Buch zu nehmen; he ~ed ~ his hand for the cup er griff nach der Tasse.
2 vi die Hand/Hände ausstrecken. to ~ ~ for sth nach etw greifen or langen (inf); he ~ed ~ to grasp the door handle er griff or langte (inf) nach dem Türgriff; she ~ed ~ and slapped

---

him sie holte aus und haute ihm eine runter (inf).

♦**reach over** vi see reach across.

♦**reach up 1** vi (a) (water, level etc) (hinauf-/herauf)reichen or -gehen (to bis). (b) (person) hinauf-/heraufgreifen (for nach). 2 vt sep (inf) herauf-/hinaufreichen. can you ~ me ~ the box? kannst du mir die Schachtel heraufreichen or -geben?

reachable ['riːtʃəbl] adj erreichbar.

reach-me-down ['riːtʃmɪˌdaʊn] n (inf) see hand-me-down.

react [riː'ækt] vi (a) (respond, Chem, Phys) reagieren (to auf +acc). slow to ~ (Chem) reaktionsträge; she was slow to ~ to my offer sie reagierte nur langsam auf mein Angebot; to ~ against negativ reagieren auf (+acc).
(b) (have an effect) wirken (on, upon auf +acc). to ~ upon sb's mood sich auf jds Stimmung (acc) auswirken.

reaction [riː'ækʃən] n (a) (response, Chem, Phys) Reaktion f (to auf +acc, against gegen). what was his ~ to your suggestion? wie hat er auf Ihren Vorschlag reagiert?, wie war seine Reaktion auf Ihren Vorschlag?; a ~ against violence eine Absage an die Gewalt; action and ~ Wirkung und Gegenwirkung (+pl vb).
(b) (Pol) Reaktion f. forces of ~ reaktionäre Kräfte pl.
(c) (Mil) Gegenschlag m.
(d) (St Ex) Umschwung, Rückgang m.

reactionary [riː'ækʃənrɪ] adj reaktionär.

reactivate [riː'æktɪveɪt] vt reaktivieren.

reactive [riː'æktɪv] adj (Chem, Phys) reaktiv.

reactor [riː'æktəʳ] n (Phys) Reaktor m; (Chem also) Reaktionsapparat m; (Elec) Blindwiderstand m.

read[1] [riːd] (vb: pret, ptp read [red]) 1 vt (a) book, letter, bad handwriting, hieroglyphics lesen; (to sb) vorlesen (to dat). do you ~ music? können Sie Noten lesen?; I read him to sleep ich las ihm vor, bis er einschlief; to ~ sb a lesson (fig inf) jdm eine Strafpredigt halten; to take sth as read (fig) (as self-evident) etw als selbstverständlich voraussetzen; (as agreed) etw für abgemacht halten; they took the minutes as read (in meeting) sie setzten das Protokoll als bekannt voraus; for "meet" ~ "met" anstelle von „meet" soll „met" stehen; see paper.
(b) (interpret) thoughts, feelings lesen; dream deuten; words verstehen. to ~ sb's thoughts/mind jds Gedanken lesen; to ~ sb's hand jdm aus der Hand lesen; to ~ the tea leaves or the teacups ≈ aus dem Kaffeesatz lesen; these words can be read in several ways diese Wörter können unterschiedlich verstanden werden; to ~ something into a text etwas in einen Text (hinein)lesen.
(c) (Univ: study) studieren.
(d) thermometer, barometer etc sehen auf (+acc), ablesen. to ~ a meter einen Zähler(stand) ablesen.
(e) (meter) (an)zeigen, stehen auf (+dat); (flight etc instruments) anzeigen. the thermometer ~s 37° das Thermometer steht auf or zeigt 37°.
(f) (Telec) verstehen. do you ~ me? (Telec) können Sie mich verstehen?; (fig) haben Sie mich verstanden?
2 vi (a) lesen; (to sb) vorlesen (to dat). she ~s well sie liest gut; (learner, beginner) sie kann schon gut lesen; to ~ aloud or out loud laut lesen; to ~ to oneself für sich lesen; he likes being read to er läßt sich (dat) gern vorlesen; will you ~ to me, mummy? Mutti, liest du mir etwas vor?
(b) (convey impression when read) this book ~s well/badly das Buch liest sich gut/nicht gut; this ~s like an official report/a translation das klingt wie ein offizieller Bericht/eine Übersetzung; that's how it ~s to me so verstehe ich das.
(c) (have wording) lauten. the letter ~s as follows or thus der Brief geht so or lautet folgendermaßen or besagt folgendes.
(d) (Univ: study) to ~ for an examination sich auf eine Prüfung vorbereiten; see bar[1].
3 n she enjoys a good ~ sie liest gern; to have a quiet/little ~ ungestört or in Ruhe/ein wenig lesen; this book is quite a good ~ das Buch liest sich gut.

♦**read back** vt sep shorthand lesen; one's notes etc noch einmal lesen; (to sb) noch einmal vorlesen.

♦**read off** vt sep ablesen; (without pause) herunterlesen.

♦**read on** vi weiterlesen.

♦**read out** vt sep vorlesen; instrument readings ablesen.

♦**read over** or **through** vt sep durchlesen.

♦**read up 1** vt sep nachlesen über (+acc), sich informieren über (+acc). 2 vi nachlesen, sich informieren (on über +acc).

read[2] [red] 1 pret, ptp of read[1]. 2 adj he is well/badly ~ er ist sehr/wenig belesen.

readable ['riːdəbl] adj (legible) handwriting lesbar; (worth reading) book etc lesenswert. not very ~ schlecht lesbar/nicht besonders lesenswert.

readdress [ˌriːə'dres] vt letter, parcel umadressieren.

reader ['riːdəʳ] n (a) Leser(in f) m. publisher's ~ Lektor(in f) m.
(b) (Brit Univ) ≈ Dozent(in f) m.
(c) (schoolbook) Lesebuch nt; (to teach reading) Fibel f; (foreign language text) Text m, Lektüre f; (anthology) Sammelband m. a ~ in the Classics eine Klassikersammlung; "first French ~" „Französisches Lesebuch für Anfänger".

readership ['riːdəʃɪp] n (a) (of newspaper, magazine) Leserschaft f, Leser pl. a big or wide ~/a ~ of millions eine große Leserschaft/Millionen Leser. (b) (Brit Univ) ≈ Dozentur f.

readily ['redɪlɪ] adv bereitwillig; (easily) leicht. ~ to hand griffbereit.

readiness ['redɪnɪs] n (a) Bereitschaft f. ~ for war Kriegsbereitschaft f; to be (kept) in ~ (for sth) (für etw) bereitgehalten werden; his ~ to help seine Hilfsbereitschaft.
(b) (ease) Leichtigkeit f. his ~ of mind/speech seine geistige Gewandtheit/seine Redegewandtheit.

reading ['riːdɪŋ] n (a) (action) Lesen nt.
(b) (~ matter) Lektüre f. this book is or makes very interesting ~ dieses Buch ist sehr interessant zu lesen; have you any light ~? haben Sie eine leichte Lektüre?

(c) (*recital, excerpt*) Lesung *f*. **play** ~ **Lesen** *nt* mit verteilten Rollen.

(d) (*interpretation*) Interpretation *f*, Verständnis *nt*. **my** ~ **of this sentence** so wie ich den Satz verstehe, mein Verständnis des Satzes; **his** ~ **of the part** (*Film, Theat*) seine Interpretation *or* sein Verständnis der Rolle.

(e) (*variant*) Version *f*.

(f) (*from meter*) Thermometer-/Barometer-/Zählerstand *etc m*; (*from flight etc instruments*) Anzeige *f*. **to take a** ~ den Thermometerstand *etc* ablesen; die Anzeige ablesen; **the** ~ **is** ... das Thermometer *etc* steht auf ...; die Anzeige ist ...

(g) (*Parl: of bill*) Lesung *f*. **the Senate gave the bill its first/a second** ~ der Senat beriet das Gesetz in erster/zweiter Lesung.

(h) (*knowledge*) Belesenheit *f*. **a man of wide** ~ ein sehr belesener Mann.

reading: ~ **book** *n* Lesebuch *nt*; ~ **desk** *n* (Lese)tisch *m*; ~ **glass** *n* Lupe *f*; ~ **glasses** *npl* Lesebrille *f*; ~ **knowledge** *n* **to have a** ~ **knowledge of Spanish** Spanisch lesen können; ~ **lamp** *n* Leselampe *f*; ~ **matter** *n* Lesestoff *m*; ~ **room** *n* Lesesaal *m*.

readjust [ˌriːəˈdʒʌst] **1** *vt* *instrument, mechanism* neu einstellen; (*correct*) nachstellen; *prices, salary* anpassen, neu regeln; *opinion* korrigieren. **2** *vi* sich neu *or* wieder anpassen (*to* an +*acc*), sich neu *or* wieder einstellen (*to* auf +*acc*).

readjustment [ˌriːəˈdʒʌstmənt] *n see vb* Neueinstellung *f*; Nachstellung *f*; Anpassung, Neuregelung *f*; Korrektur *f*; Wiederanpassung *f*.

ready [ˈrɛdɪ] **1** *adj* (a) (*prepared*) *person, thing* bereit, fertig; (*finished, cooked etc*) fertig. ~ **to leave** abmarschbereit; (*for journey*) abfahrtbereit, reisefertig; ~ **to use** *or* **for use** gebrauchsfertig; ~ **to serve** tischfertig; ~ **for battle** kampfbereit; ~ **for anything** zu allem bereit; **dinner is** ~ das Essen ist fertig; **"dinner's** ~**"** „essen kommen", „zum Essen"; **are you** ~ **to go?** sind Sie soweit?, kann es losgehen? (*inf*); **are you** ~ **to push?** alles fertig zum Schieben?; **are you** ~ **to take the weight?** können Sie das Gewicht jetzt übernehmen?; **well, I think we're** ~ ich glaube, wir sind soweit; **I'm not quite** ~ **yet** ich bin noch nicht ganz fertig; **I'm** ~ **for him!** ich warte nur auf ihn, er soll nur kommen; **everything is** ~ **for his visit** alles ist für seinen Besuch bereit *or* fertig; **everything is** ~ **for the journey** alles ist für die Reise fertig *or* vorbereitet; **to be** ~ **with an excuse** eine Entschuldigung bereit haben *or* bereithalten; **to get** (**oneself**) ~ sich fertigmachen, sich fertigmachen, sich richten (*S Ger*); **to get** ~ **to do sth** sich bereitmachen, etw zu tun; **to get** ~ **to go out/play tennis** sich zum Ausgehen/Tennisspielen fertigmachen; **to get** ~ **for sth** sich auf etw (*acc*) vorbereiten; **get** ~ **for it!** (*before blow etc*) Achtung!, paß auf!; (*before momentous news*) mach dich auf was gefaßt (*inf*); **to get** *or* **make sth** ~ etw fertigmachen, etw bereitmachen; *room, bed, breakfast etc* etw vorbereiten; ~ **about!** (*Naut*) klar zum Wenden!; ~**, steady, go!** Achtung *or* auf die Plätze, fertig, los!

(b) ~ **to do sth** (*willing*) bereit, etw zu tun; (*quick*) schnell dabei, etw zu tun; **he's always** ~ **to find fault** er ist immer schnell dabei, wenn es gilt, Fehler zu finden; **don't be so** ~ **to criticize** kritisieren Sie doch nicht so schnell; **I'm** ~ **to believe it** ich möchte das fast glauben; **he was** ~ **to cry** er war den Tränen nahe; **he's always** ~ **with an answer** er ist mit einer Antwort immer schnell bei der Hand.

(c) (*prompt*) *reply* prompt; *wit* schlagfertig. **to have a** ~ **tongue/pen** schlagfertig sein/die Feder zu führen wissen.

(d) (*available*) ~ **money** jederzeit verfügbares Geld; ~ **cash** Bargeld *nt*; **to pay in** ~ **cash** auf die Hand bezahlen; ~ **to hand** zur Hand; **"now** ~**"** „jetzt zu haben".

(e) (*practical*) *solution* sauber; (*competent*) *speaker* gewandt. **to have a** ~ **sale** (*Comm*) guten Absatz finden.

2 *n* (a) (*Mil*) **to come to the** ~ das Gewehr in Anschlag nehmen; **at the** ~ (*Mil*) mit dem Gewehr im Anschlag; (*fig*) marsch-/fahrbereit *etc*; **with his pen at the** ~ mit gezücktem Federhalter.

(b) (*money*) **the** ~ (*inf*) das nötige Kleingeld (*inf*).

ready in *cpds* fertig-; ~**-cooked** *adj* vorgekocht; ~**-furnished** *adj* fertig eingerichtet; ~**-made** *adj* *curtains* fertig; *clothes* Konfektions-; *solution* Patent-; *answer, ideas* vorgefertigt; ~**-mix** *adj* attr (*Cook*) aus einer Packung; ~**-reckoner** *n* Rechentabelle *f*; ~**-to-serve** *adj* tischfertig; ~**-to-wear** *adj, pred* ~ **to wear** Konfektions-, von der Stange (*inf*).

reaffirm [ˌriːəˈfɜːm] *vt* (a) (*assert again*) wieder *or* erneut versichern, beteuern. (b) (*strengthen, reconfirm*) *suspicion, doubts* bestätigen; *principles, wish* bestärken.

reafforest [ˌriːəˈfɒrɪst] *vt* wieder aufforsten.

reafforestation [ˌriːəfɒrɪsˈteɪʃən] *n* Wiederaufforstung *f*.

reagent [riːˈeɪdʒənt] *n* (*Chem*) Reagens *nt*.

real [rɪəl] **1** *adj* (a) (*genuine*) *gold, flowers, silk etc, sympathy, joy, desire* echt; *need, improvement also* wirklich; (*as opposed to substitute*) richtig; *name* richtig; (*true, as opposed to apparent*) *owner, boss, reason, purpose, state of affairs* wirklich, tatsächlich, eigentlich; (*not imaginary*) *creature, object, life, world* wirklich, real (*esp Philos*); (*Phys, Math*) reell; (*Econ*) real. **you can touch it, it's** ~ das können Sie anfassen, es ist wirklich da; **was the unicorn ever a** ~ **creature?** gab es das Einhorn je wirklich *or* tatsächlich? (*inf*); ~ **coffee** Bohnenkaffee *m*; ~ **ale** Ale *nt*; **I prefer the** ~ **sun to the sunlamp** mir ist die richtige Sonne lieber als Höhensonne; **in** ~ **life** im wirklichen Leben; **in** ~ **terms** effektiv; **he has no** ~ **power** er hat keine wirkliche Macht; **his grief was very** ~ sein Schmerz war echt, er empfand seinen Schmerz zutiefst; **it's the** ~ **thing** *or* **McCoy, this whisky!** dieser Whisky ist der Echte; **it's not the** ~ **thing** das ist nicht das Wahre; (*not genuine*) das ist nicht echt; **climbing this hill isn't much when you've done the** ~ **thing** dieser Hügel ist gar nichts, wenn man schon einmal richtig geklettert hat; **R**~ **Presence** (*Rel*) Realpräsenz *f*.

(b) (*proper, complete, through and through*) richtig; *sportsman, gentleman, coward also* echt; *champion, friend, friendship* wahr, echt; *threat* echt, wirklich; *idiot, disaster* komplett. **it's a** ~ **miracle** das ist wirklich *or* echt (*inf*) ein Wunder, das ist ein wahres Wunder; **he doesn't know what** ~ **contentment/family life is** er weiß ja nicht, was Zufriedenheit/Familienleben wirklich ist; **that's what I call a** ~ **car** das nenne ich ein Auto; **that's a** ~ **racket** das ist wirklich ein Schwindel.

(c) ~ **estate** Immobilien *pl*, unbewegliches Vermögen; ~ **estate developer** (*US*) Immobilienhändler(in *f*) *m*; ~ **estate office** (*US*) Immobilienbüro *nt*; ~ **estate register** (*US*) Grundbuch *nt*; ~ **property** Grundbesitz *m*.

2 *adv* (*esp US inf*) echt (*inf*), wirklich. **we had a** ~ **good laugh** wir haben so gelacht.

3 *n* (a) **for** ~ wirklich, echt (*inf*); **is that invitation for** ~? ist die Einladung ernst gemeint?; **he's not for** ~ (*not sincere*) er meint es nicht wirklich; (*not genuine*) er ist nicht echt; **is this for** ~ **or is it another practice?** ist das echt (*inf*) *or* ernst oder schon wieder eine Übung?

(b) (*Philos*) **the** ~ das Reale, die Wirklichkeit.

realism [ˈrɪəlɪzəm] *n* Realismus *m*.

realist [ˈrɪəlɪst] *n* Realist *m*.

realistic [rɪəˈlɪstɪk] *adj* realistisch; *painting also* naturgetreu, wirklichkeitsgetreu.

realistically [rɪəˈlɪstɪkəlɪ] *adv see adj*.

reality [riːˈælɪtɪ] *n* (a) Wirklichkeit, Realität *f*. **to become** ~ sich verwirklichen; (**the**) ~ **is somewhat different** die Wirklichkeit *or* Realität sieht etwas anders aus; **in** ~ (*in fact*) in Wirklichkeit; (*actually*) eigentlich; **to bring sb back to** ~ jdn auf den Boden der Tatsachen zurückbringen; **the realities of the situation** der wirkliche Sachverhalt.

(b) (*trueness to life*) Naturtreue *f*.

realizable [ˈrɪəlaɪzəbl] *adj* *assets* realisierbar, zu verflüssigen *pred*; *hope, plan* realisierbar, zu verwirklichen *pred*.

realization [ˌrɪəlaɪˈzeɪʃən] *n* (a) (*of assets*) Realisation, Verflüssigung *f*; (*of hope, plan*) Realisierung, Verwirklichung *f*. (b) (*awareness*) Erkenntnis *f*.

realize [ˈrɪəlaɪz] **1** *vt* (a) (*become aware of*) erkennen, sich (*dat*) klarwerden (+*gen*), sich (*dat*) bewußt werden (+*gen*); (*be aware of*) sich (*dat*) klar sein über (+*acc*), sich (*dat*) bewußt sein (+*gen*); (*appreciate, understand*) begreifen, jdm wird klar; (*notice*) (be)merken; (*discover*) feststellen. **does he** ~ **the problems?** sind ihm die Probleme bewußt *or* klar?; **he had not fully** ~**d that she was dead** es war ihm nicht voll bewußt, daß sie tot war; **I** ~**d what he meant** es ist mir klargeworden *or* ich habe begriffen, was er meinte; **I** ~**d how he had done it** ich erkannte *or* mir wurde klar, wie er es gemacht hatte; **I hadn't** ~**d you were going away** mir war nicht klar, daß Sie weggehen; **I've just** ~**d I won't be here** mir ist eben aufgegangen *or* klargeworden, daß ich dann nicht hier sein werde; **when will you** ~ **you can't ...?** wann werden Sie endlich begreifen *or* wann wird Ihnen endlich klar, daß Sie ... nicht können?; **I hadn't** ~**d how late it was** ich habe gar nicht gemerkt, wie spät es war; **I'd** ~**d it was raining** ich hatte gemerkt, daß es regnete; **he didn't** ~ **she was cheating him** er hat nicht gemerkt, daß sie ihn betrog; **when the parents** ~**d their child was deaf** als die Eltern (be)merkten *or* feststellten, daß ihr Kind taub war; **I** ~**d I didn't have any money on me** ich stellte fest, daß ich kein Geld dabei hatte; **I made her** ~ **that I was right** ich machte ihr klar, daß ich recht hatte; **you couldn't be expected to** ~ **that** das konnten Sie nicht wissen; **yes, I** ~ **that** ja, das ist mir klar *or* bewußt; **yes, I** ~ **that I was wrong** ja, ich sehe ein, daß ich unrecht hatte.

(b) *hope, plan* verwirklichen, realisieren.

(c) (*Fin*) *assets* realisieren, verflüssigen; *price* bringen, erzielen; *interest* abwerfen, erbringen; (*goods*) einbringen. **how much did you** ~ **on your Rembrandt?** wieviel hat Ihr Rembrandt (ein)gebracht?

2 *vi* **didn't you** ~? war Ihnen das nicht klar?; (*notice*) haben Sie das nicht gemerkt?; **I've just** ~**d** das ist mir eben klargeworden; (*noticed*) das habe ich eben gemerkt; **I should have** ~**d** das hätte ich wissen müssen; **I thought you'd never** ~ ich dachte, Sie merken es nie; **he'll never** ~ (*notice*) das wird er nie merken; (*understand*) das wird ihm nie klarwerden.

really [ˈrɪəlɪ] **1** *adv* (a) (*in reality*) wirklich, tatsächlich. **I** ~ **don't know what to think** ich weiß wirklich *or* tatsächlich nicht, was ich davon halten soll; **I don't** ~ **know what I'm going to do** ich weiß eigentlich nicht, was ich machen werde; **I don't** ~ **think so** das glaube ich eigentlich nicht; **well yes, I** ~ **think we should** ich finde eigentlich schon, daß wir das tun sollten; **before he** ~ **knew/understood** bevor er richtig *or* wirklich wußte/verstand; ~ **and truly** wirklich.

(b) (*intensifier*) wirklich, echt (*inf*); *happy, glad, disappointed also* richtig. **he** ~ **is an idiot** er ist wirklich *or* echt (*inf*) ein Idiot; **you** ~ **must visit Paris** Sie müssen wirklich Paris besuchen; **I** ~ **must say ...** ich muß schon sagen ...

2 *interj* (*in doubt, disbelief, surprise*) wirklich, tatsächlich; (*in protest, indignation*) also wirklich! **not** ~! ach wirklich?

realm [rɛlm] *n* (*liter: kingdom*) Königreich *nt*; (*fig*) Reich *nt*. **within the** ~**s of possibility** im Bereich des Möglichen.

real: ~ **number** *n* reelle Zahl; ~ **tennis** *n* Ballhaustennis *nt*.

realtor [ˈrɪəltɔːʳ] *n* (*US*) Grundstücksmakler *m*.

realty [ˈrɪəltɪ] *n, no pl* (*Jur*) Immobilien *pl*.

ream [riːm] *n* (*of paper*) (altes) Ries. **he always writes** ~**s** (*inf*) er schreibt immer ganze Bände (*inf*).

reanimate [ˌriːˈænɪmeɪt] *vt* (*Med form*) *patient, person* wiederbeleben; (*fig*) *party, conversation also* neu beleben.

reap [riːp] **1** *vt* (a) *corn* (*cut*) schneiden, mähen; (*harvest*) ernten; *field* abernten. (b) (*fig*) *profit* ernten; *reward* bekommen. **to** ~ **the fruit of one's labours** die Früchte seiner Arbeit ernten; **to** ~ **what one has sown** ernten, was man gesät hat; *see* **sow**[1]. **2** *vi* schneiden, mähen; (*person*) ernten.

reaper ['riːpə^r] n (person) Schnitter(in f) m; (machine) Mähbinder m. **the R~** (fig: death) der Schnitter.

reaping ['riːpɪŋ] n see vt (a) Schneiden, Mähen nt; Ernten nt; Abernten nt.

reaping: ~ **hook** n Sichel f; ~ **machine** n Mähbinder m.

reappear [ˌriːə'pɪə^r] vi wiedererscheinen, wiederauftauchen; (person, sun also) sich wieder zeigen; (in public) wiedererscheinen; (character in novel) wiederauftauchen.

reappearance [ˌriːə'pɪərəns] n see vt Wiedererscheinen, Wiederauftauchen nt; Wiedererscheinen nt; Wiederauftauchen nt.

reappoint [ˌriːə'pɔɪnt] vt (to a job) wieder einstellen (to als); (to a post) wiederernennen or -bestellen (to zu).

reappointment [ˌriːə'pɔɪntmənt] n see vt Wiedereinstellung f; Wiederernennung or -bestellung f.

reapportion [ˌriːə'pɔːʃən] vt money, food, land neu aufteilen; duties neu zuteilen.

reappraisal [ˌriːə'preɪzəl] n see vt Neubeurteilung f; Neubewertung f.

reappraise [ˌriːə'preɪz] vt situation, problem von neuem beurteilen; author, film etc also neu bewerten.

rear[1] [rɪə^r] 1 n (a) (back part) hinterer Teil m; (inf: buttocks) Hintern m (inf). **in or at the** ~ hinten (of in +dat); **to be situated at/to(wards) the** ~ **of the plane** hinten im Flugzeug/am hinteren Ende des Flugzeugs sein; **at or to the** ~ **of the building** (outside) hinter dem Haus; (inside) nach hinten; **go to the** ~ **of the house** (behind the house) geh hinter das Haus; (inside the house) geh nach hinten; **from the** ~ von hinten.

(b) (Mil) Schwanz m (der Truppe). **to attack an army in the** ~ eine Armee im Rücken angreifen; **to bring up the** ~ (lit, fig) die Nachhut bilden.

2 adj Hinter-, hintere(r, s); (Aut) engine, window Heck-. ~ **door** (of car) hintere Tür; ~ **wheel/lights** (Aut) Hinterrad nt/Rücklichter pl.

rear[2] 1 vt (a) animals, family großziehen, aufziehen.

(b) **to** ~ **its head** (animal) den Kopf zurückwerfen; (snake) sich aufstellen; violence/racialism ~**ed its ugly head** (again) die Gewalt/der Rassismus kam (wieder) zum Durchbruch; sex ~**s its ugly head** der Trieb meldet sich.

2 vi (also ~ **up**) (horse) sich aufbäumen.

rear: ~ **admiral** n Konteradmiral m; ~**-engined** adj (Aut) mit Heckmotor, heckmotorig; ~**guard** n (Mil) Nachhut f; ~**guard action** n Nachhutgefecht nt; ~ **gunner** n (Mil) Heckschütze m.

rearm [ˌriː'ɑːm] 1 vt country wiederbewaffnen; forces, troops neu ausrüsten or ausstatten. **2 vi** wieder aufrüsten; neue Ausrüstung anschaffen, sich neu ausrüsten.

rearmament [ˌriː'ɑːməmənt] n see vb Wiederbewaffnung, Wiederaufrüstung f; Neuausrüstung, Neuausstattung f; see moral.

rearmost ['rɪəməʊst] adj hinterste(r, s). **we were** ~ **in the queue** wir waren die letzten in der Schlange.

rear: ~ **mounted engine** n (Aut) Heckmotor m; ~ **projection** n (Film, Theat) Rückprojektion f.

rearrange [ˌriːə'reɪndʒ] vt furniture, system umstellen; plans also, layout, formation, order, ideas ändern; appointment, meeting neu abmachen.

rearrangement [ˌriːə'reɪndʒmənt] n see vt Umstellung f; Änderung f; Neuabmachung f.

rear-view mirror [ˌrɪə'vjuː'mɪrə^r] n Rückspiegel m.

rearward ['rɪəwəd] 1 adj part hintere(r, s); position am Ende; movement nach hinten, rückwärtig. **2 adv** (also ~**s**) rückwärts.

rear-wheel drive ['rɪəˌwiːl'draɪv] n Heckantrieb m.

reason ['riːzn] 1 n (a) (cause, justification) Grund m (for für). **my** ~ **for going, the** ~ **for my going** (der Grund,) weshalb ich gehe/gegangen bin; **to give sb** ~ **for complaint** jdm Anlaß or Grund zu Klagen geben; **the police had no** ~ **to interfere** die Polizei hatte keinen Grund einzugreifen; (but did) die Polizei hat ohne Grund eingegriffen; **what's the** ~ **for this celebration?** aus welchem Anlaß wird hier gefeiert?; **I want to know the** ~ **why** ich möchte wissen, weshalb; **and that's the** ~ **why ...** und deshalb ...; **and that's the** ~ **why!** und das ist der Grund dafür!; **I have (good)/every** ~ **to believe that ...** ich habe (guten) Grund/allen Grund zu glauben, daß ...; **there is** ~ **to believe that ...** es gibt Gründe, zu glauben, daß ...; **there is every** ~ **to believe ...** es spricht alles dafür ..., man kann zurecht annehmen ...; **for that very** ~ **(that)** eben deswegen(, weil); **with (good)** ~ **mit gutem Grund, mit Recht; without any** ~ **ohne jeden Grund or Anlaß, grundlos; for no** ~ **at all grundlos, ohne ersichtlichen Grund; for no particular** ~ **ohne einen bestimmten Grund; why did you do that?** — **no particular** ~ warum haben Sie das gemacht? — einfach nur so; **for no other** ~ **than that ...** aus keinem anderen Grund, als daß ...; **for some** ~ **or (an)other** aus irgendeinem Grund; **for** ~**s best known to himself/myself** aus unerfindlichen/bestimmten Gründen; **all the more** ~ **for doing it** or **to do it** um so mehr Grund, das zu tun; **by** ~ **of** wegen (+gen); **for** ~**s of State this was never disclosed** die Staatsräson machte die Geheimhaltung erforderlich.

(b) no pl (mental faculty) Verstand m. **to lose one's** ~ den Verstand verlieren; **to reach the age of** ~ verständig werden; **the Age of R~** (Hist) das Zeitalter der Vernunft.

(c) no pl (common sense) Vernunft f. **to listen to** ~ auf die Stimme der Vernunft hören; **he won't listen to** ~ er läßt sich (dat) nichts sagen; **he's beyond** ~ ihm ist mit Vernunft nicht beizukommen; **that stands to** ~ das ist logisch; **we'll do anything within** ~ to ... wir tun alles, was in unserer Macht steht, um zu ...; **you can have anything within** ~ Sie können alles haben, solange es sich in Grenzen hält.

2 vi (a) (think logically) vernünftig or logisch denken. **the ability to** ~ logisches Denkvermögen.

(b) (argue) **to** ~ **(with sb)** vernünftig mit jdm reden; **there's no** ~**ing with him** mit ihm kann man nicht vernünftig reden.

---

3 vt (a) to ~ **sb out of/into sth** jdm etw ausreden/jdn zu etw überreden; **to** ~ **why/what ... sich (dat) klarmachen, warum/was ...; he could** ~**ed that we could get there by 6 o'clock** er rechnete vor, daß wir bis 6 Uhr dort sein könnten.

(b) (also ~ **out**) (deduce) schließen, folgern; (verbally) argumentieren; (work out) problem durchdenken.

reasonable ['riːznəbl] adj (a) vernünftig; price also, chance reell; claim berechtigt, billig; amount angemessen; (acceptable) excuse, offer akzeptabel, angemessen. **be** ~! sei vernünftig; **vegetables are** ~ **(in price) just now** Gemüse ist momentan preiswert; ~ **doubt** berechtigter Zweifel; **guilty beyond (all)** ~ **doubt** (Jur) hinreichend schuldig; **it would be** ~ **to assume that ...** man könnte durchaus annehmen, daß ...

(b) (quite good) ordentlich, ganz gut. **his work was only** ~ seine Arbeit war nur einigermaßen (gut); **with a** ~ **amount of luck** mit einigem Glück.

reasonableness ['riːznəblnɪs] n see adj Vernünftigkeit f; Berechtigung, Billigkeit f; Angemessenheit f; Angemessenheit f; Ordentlichkeit f.

reasonably ['riːznəblɪ] adv (a) behave, act, think vernünftig. **one could** ~ **think/argue that ...** man könnte durchaus annehmen/anführen, daß ...; ~ **priced** preiswert. (b) (quite, fairly) ziemlich, ganz.

reasoned ['riːznd] adj durchdacht. ~ **thought** Vernunftdenken nt.

reasoning ['riːznɪŋ] n logisches Denken; (arguing) Argumentation f. ~ **is not his strong point** logisches Denken ist nicht gerade seine starke Seite; **I don't follow your** ~ ich kann Ihrem Gedankengang or Ihrer Argumentation nicht folgen; **this (piece of)** ~ **is faulty** das Argument ist falsch; **his** ~ **is all wrong** er argumentiert ganz falsch, seine Argumente sind falsch.

reassemble [ˌriːə'sembl] 1 vt (a) people, troops wieder versammeln.

(b) tool wieder zusammenbauen; car, machine also wieder montieren.

2 vi sich wieder versammeln; (troops) sich wieder sammeln.

reassert [ˌriːə'sɜːt] vt mit Nachdruck behaupten. **to** ~ **oneself** seine Autorität wieder geltend machen.

reassess [ˌriːə'ses] vt neu überdenken; proposals, advantages neu abwägen; (for taxation) neu veranlagen; damages neu schätzen.

reassume [ˌriːə'sjuːm] vt work wiederaufnehmen; office also wieder übernehmen.

reassurance [ˌriːə'ʃʊərəns] n (a) (feeling of security) Beruhigung f. **safe in the** ~ **that he would soon be here** sicher in dem beruhigenden Wissen, daß er bald dasein würde; **to give sb** ~ jdn beruhigen; **a mother's presence gives a child the** ~ **it needs** die Gegenwart der Mutter gibt dem Kind das nötige Gefühl der Sicherheit.

(b) (renewed confirmation) Bestätigung f. **despite his** ~**(s)** trotz seiner Versicherungen; (of lover etc) trotz seiner Beteuerungen.

(c) see reinsurance.

reassure [ˌriːə'ʃʊə^r] vt (a) (relieve sb's mind) beruhigen; (give feeling of security to) das Gefühl der Sicherheit geben (+dat).

(b) (verbally) versichern (+dat); (lover) beteuern (+dat). **to** ~ **sb of sth** jdm etw versichern/beteuern; **she needs to be constantly** ~**d that her work is adequate** man muß ihr ständig versichern or bestätigen, daß ihre Arbeit gut genug ist.

(c) see reinsure.

reassuring adj, ~**ly** adv [ˌriːə'ʃʊərɪŋ, -lɪ] beruhigend.

reawaken [ˌriːə'weɪkən] 1 vt (a) person wiedererwecken; love, passion, interest also neu erwecken, wieder aufleben lassen. **2 vi** wieder aufwachen, wiedererwachen; (interest, love, passion) wieder aufleben, wiedererwachen.

reawakening [ˌriːə'weɪknɪŋ] n (of person) Wiedererwachen nt; (of ideas, interest also) erneutes Aufleben.

rebarbative [rɪ'bɑːbətɪv] adj (form) abstoßend.

rebate ['riːbeɪt] n (discount) Rabatt, (Preis)nachlaß m; (money back) Rückvergütung, Rückzahlung f.

rebel ['rebl] 1 n Rebell(in f), Aufrührer(in f) m; (by nature) Rebell m. **2 adj** attr rebellisch; forces, troops also aufständisch. **3** [rɪ'bel] vi rebellieren; (troops, forces also) sich erheben.

rebellion [rɪ'beljən] n Rebellion f, Aufstand m. **to rise (up) in** ~ einen Aufstand machen, sich erheben.

rebellious [rɪ'beljəs] adj soldiers, peasants etc rebellisch, aufrührerisch; child, nature rebellisch, widerspenstig.

rebelliousness [rɪ'beljəsnɪs] n (of troops, subordinates etc) Rebellion f; (nature, of child etc) Widerspenstigkeit f.

rebirth [ˌriː'bɜːθ] n Wiedergeburt f; (of desire) Wiederaufflackern nt.

rebore [ˌriː'bɔː^r] 1 vt wieder bohren; hole noch einmal bohren; (Aut) engine ausbohren. **2** ['riːˌbɔː^r] n (Aut) **this engine needs a** ~ der Motor muß ausgebohrt werden.

reborn [ˌriː'bɔːn] adj **to be** ~ wiedergeboren werden; **to be** ~ **in** (fig) weiterleben in (+dat); **to feel** ~ sich wie neugeboren fühlen.

rebound [rɪ'baʊnd] 1 vi (ball, bullet) zurückprallen, abprallen (against, off von). **your violent methods will** ~ **(on you)** Ihre rauhen Methoden werden auf Sie zurückfallen.

2 ['riːbaʊnd] n (of ball, bullet) Rückprall m. **to hit a ball on the** ~ den zurück- or abgeprallten Ball schlagen; **to be on the** ~ (fig) sich über eine Enttäuschung hinwegtrösten; **she married him on the** ~, **she was on the** ~ **when she married him** sie heiratete ihn, um sich über einen anderen hinwegzutrösten.

rebroadcast [ˌriː'brɔːdkɑːst] 1 n Wiederholung(ssendung) f. **2** vt wiederholen, noch einmal senden.

rebuff [rɪ'bʌf] 1 n Abfuhr f, kurze Zurückweisung. **to meet with a** ~ zurück- or abgewiesen werden, eine Abfuhr bekommen; (from opposite sex) einen Korb bekommen (inf). **2** vt zurückweisen or abweisen; einen Korb geben (+dat) (inf).

rebuild [,ri:'bɪld] *vt* (a) (*restore*) *house, wall* wieder aufbauen; (*fig*) *society, relationship* wiederherstellen; *country* wiederaufbauen. (b) (*convert*) *house* umbauen; *society* umorganisieren.

rebuilding [,ri:'bɪldɪŋ] *n* see *vt* Wiederaufbau *m*; Wiederherstellung *f*; Umbau *m*; Umorganisation *f*.

rebuke [rɪ'bju:k] 1 *n* Verweis, Tadel *m*. 2 *vt* zurechtweisen (*for* wegen), tadeln (*for* für). **to ~ sb for having spoken unkindly** jdn für seine unfreundlichen Worte tadeln, jdn dafür tadeln, daß er so unfreundlich gesprochen hat.

rebukingly [rɪ'bju:kɪŋlɪ] *adv* tadelnd.

rebus ['ri:bəs] *n* Bilderrätsel *nt*, Rebus *m or nt*.

rebut [rɪ'bʌt] *vt argument, contention* widerlegen.

rebuttal [rɪ'bʌtl] *n* Widerlegung *f*.

rec *abbr of* **recommended** empf.

recalcitrance [rɪ'kælsɪtrəns] *n* Aufsässigkeit *f*.

recalcitrant [rɪ'kælsɪtrənt] *adj* aufsässig.

recall [rɪ'kɔ:l] 1 *vt* (a) (*summon back*) zurückrufen; *ambassador also* abberufen; *library book* zurückfordern; (*Fin*) *capital* zurückfordern, einziehen. **this music ~s the past** diese Musik ruft die Vergangenheit zurück; **to ~ sb to life** jdn ins Leben zurückrufen; **her voice ~ed him to the present** ihre Stimme brachte ihn in die Wirklichkeit zurück.
(b) (*remember*) sich erinnern an (+*acc*), sich entsinnen (+*gen*). **I cannot ~ meeting him** ich kann mich nicht daran erinnern, daß ich ihn kennengelernt habe.
2 *n* (a) see *vt* (a) Rückruf *m*; Abberufung *f*; Rückforderung, Einmahnung *f*; Rückforderung *f*, Einzug *m*. **to sound the ~** (*Mil*) zum Rückzug blasen; **this book is on ~** das Buch wird zurückgefordert; **~ slip** Aufforderung *f* zur Rückgabe eines/des Buches; **beyond or past ~** für immer vorbei.
(b) (*remembrance*) **powers of ~** Erinnerungsvermögen *nt*.

recant [rɪ'kænt] 1 *vt religious belief* widerrufen; *statement also* zurücknehmen. **to ~ one's opinion** seiner Meinung abschwören. 2 *vi* widerrufen.

recantation [rɪːkæn'teɪʃən] *n* see *vt* Widerruf *m*; Zurücknahme *f*.

recap¹ ['ri:kæp] (*inf*) 1 *n* kurze Zusammenfassung. **can we have a quick ~?** können wir kurz rekapitulieren *or* zusammenfassen? 2 *vti* rekapitulieren, kurz zusammenfassen.

recap² [,ri:'kæp] (*US Aut*) 1 *n* laufflächenerneuerter Reifen. 2 *vt* die Laufflächen erneuern von.

recapitulate [,ri:kə'pɪtjuleɪt] 1 *vt* rekapitulieren, kurz zusammenfassen; (*Mus*) *theme* wiederaufnehmen. 2 *vi* rekapitulieren, kurz zusammenfassen; (*Mus*) eine Reprise bringen.

recapitulation ['ri:kə,pɪtju'leɪʃən] *n* Rekapitulation *f*, kurze Zusammenfassung; (*Mus*) Reprise *f*.

recapture [,ri:'kæptʃəʳ] 1 *vt animal* wieder einfangen; *prisoner* wiederergreifen; *town, territory* wiedererobern; (*fig*) *atmosphere, emotion, period* wieder wachwerden lassen. **they ~d the spark that had originally united them** sie entzündeten den Funken, der einst da war, noch einmal.
2 *n* see *vt* Wiedereinfangen *nt*; Wiederergreifung *f*; Wiedereroberung *f*; Heraufbeschwörung *f*.

recast [,ri:'kɑ:st] 1 *vt* (a) (*Metal*) neu gießen, umgießen. (b) *play, film* eine neue Besetzung wählen für; *parts, roles* umbesetzen, neu besetzen. (c) (*rewrite*) umformen. 2 *n* (*Metal*) Neuguß, Umguß *m*.

recce ['rekɪ] *n, vi* (*Brit Mil sl*) *abbr of* **reconnaissance, reconnoitre**.

recd *abbr of* **received** erh.

recede [rɪ'si:d] *vi* (a) (*tide*) zurückgehen; (*fig*) sich entfernen. **to ~ into the distance** in der Ferne verschwinden; **all hope is receding** jegliche Hoffnung schwindet.
(b) **his chin/forehead ~s a bit** er hat ein leicht fliehendes Kinn/eine leicht fliehende Stirn; **his hair is receding** er hat eine leichte Stirnglatze; see also **receding**.
(c) (*price*) zurückgehen.
(d) **to ~ from** *opinion, view etc* abgehen von, aufgeben.

receding [rɪ'si:dɪŋ] *adj chin, forehead* fliehend; *hairline* zurückweichend.

receipt [rɪ'si:t] 1 *n* (a) *no pl* Empfang *m*; (*Comm also*) Erhalt, Eingang *m*. **to acknowledge ~ of sth** den Empfang *etc* einer Sache (*gen*) bestätigen; **on ~ of your remittance/the goods, we shall be pleased to ...** nach Empfang *etc* Ihrer Zahlung/der Waren, werden wir gerne ...; **to pay on ~ (of the goods)** bei Empfang *etc* (der Waren) bezahlen; **I am in ~ of** (*on letter*) ich bin im Besitz (+*gen*); **~ stamp** Empfangsstempel *m*.
(b) (*paper*) Quittung *f*, Beleg *m*; (*for parcel, letter also*) Empfangsschein *m*; (**~ of posting**) Einlieferungsschein *m*. **~ book** Quittungsbuch *nt*.
(c) (*Comm, Fin: money taken*) **~s** Einnahmen, Einkünfte *pl*.
2 *vt* bill quittieren.

receivable [rɪ'si:vəbl] *adj* (*Jur*) zulässig. **accounts/bills ~** (*Comm*) Außenstände *pl*/Wechselforderungen *pl*.

receive [rɪ'si:v] 1 *vt* (a) (*get*) bekommen, erhalten; (*take possession or delivery of*) *letter, present, salary, orders etc also* empfangen; *punch* (ab)bekommen; *refusal, setback* erfahren; *impression* gewinnen, bekommen; *recognition* finden; (*Jur*) *stolen goods* hehlen; (*Tennis*) *ball, service* zurückschlagen; *sacrament* empfangen. **to ~ 2 years or 2 years' imprisonment** 2 Jahre (Gefängnis) bekommen; **to ~ nothing but abuse** nichts als Beleidigungen hören; **he ~d nothing worse than a few bruises** er bekam nur ein paar blaue Flecke ab; **"~d with thanks"** (*Comm*) „dankend erhalten".
(b) (*welcome*) *person* empfangen; (*into group, the Church*) aufnehmen; *offer, proposal, news* aufnehmen. **to ~ sb into one's family** jdn in seine Familie aufnehmen.
(c) (*Telec, Rad, TV*) empfangen. **are you receiving me?** hören Sie mich?

2 *vi* (a) (*form*) (*Besuch*) empfangen. **Mrs X ~s on Mondays** Mrs X empfängt an Montagen.
(b) (*Jur*) Hehlerei treiben.
(c) (*Tennis*) rückschlagen. **Borg to ~** Rückschläger Borg.
(d) (*Telec*) empfangen.

received [rɪ'si:vd]: **~ opinion** *n* die allgemeine Meinung; **~ pronunciation** *n* hochsprachliche Aussprache (*nach Daniel Jones*).

receiver [rɪ'si:vəʳ] *n* (a) (*of letter, goods*) Empfänger(in *f*) *m*; (*Jur: of stolen property*) Hehler(in *f*) *m*. (b) (*Fin, Jur*) official ~ Konkursverwalter *m*. (c) (*Telec*) Hörer *m*. **~ rest** Gabel *f*. (d) (*Rad*) Empfänger *m*. (e) (*Tennis*) Rückschläger *m*.

receiving [rɪ'si:vɪŋ] *n* (*Jur: of stolen goods*) Hehlerei *f*.

receiving: ~ end (*inf*): **to be on the ~ end (of it)/of sth** derjenige sein, der es/etw abkriegt (*inf*); **~ set** *n* Empfangsgerät *nt*.

recency ['ri:sənsɪ] *n* Neuheit *f*.

recension [rɪ'senʃən] *n* Rezension *f*.

recent ['ri:sənt] *adj* kürzlich (*usu adv*); *event, development, closure* jüngste(r, s), neueste(r, s); *news* neueste(r, s), letzte(r, s); *acquaintance, invention, edition, addition* neu; *publication* Neu-. **the ~ improvement** die vor kurzem eingetretene Verbesserung; **their ~ loss** ihr vor kurzem erlittener Verlust; **a ~ decision** eine Entscheidung, die erst vor kurzem gefallen ist; **most ~** neueste(r, s); **he is a ~ acquaintance of mine** ich kenne ihn erst seit kurzem; **his ~ arrival/holiday** seine Ankunft vor kurzem/sein erst kurz zurückliegender Urlaub; **he is a ~ arrival** er ist erst vor kurzem angekommen, er ist erst kurz hier; **in the ~ past** in jüngerer *or* jüngster Zeit (*geh*), erst vor kurzem; **in ~ years/times** in den letzten Jahren/in letzter *or* jüngster (*geh*) Zeit; **of ~ date** neueren Datums; **~ developments** jüngste Entwicklungen, Entwicklungen in jüngster Zeit.

recently ['ri:sntlɪ] *adv* (*a short while ago*) vor kurzem, kürzlich; (*the other day also*) neulich; (*during the last few days or weeks*) in letzter Zeit. **~ he has been doing it differently** seit kurzem macht er das anders; **as ~ as** erst; **quite ~** erst vor kurzem, erst kürzlich; **until (quite) ~** (noch) bis vor kurzem; **he lived there until as ~ as last year** er hat bis letztes Jahr noch dort gelebt.

receptacle [rɪ'septəkl] *n* Behälter *m*.

reception [rɪ'sepʃən] *n* (a) *no pl* (*receiving, welcome*) (*of person*) Empfang *m*; (*into group, of play, book etc*) Aufnahme *f*. **the play met with or had a very favourable ~** das Stück fand gute Aufnahme, das Stück wurde gut aufgenommen; **what sort of ~ did you get?** wie sind Sie empfangen *or* aufgenommen worden?; **to give sb a warm/chilly ~** jdm einen herzlichen/kühlen Empfang bereiten, jdn herzlich/kühl empfangen; **~ area/camp/centre** Empfangsbereich *m*/Aufnahmelager *nt*/Durchgangslager *nt*; **~ desk** Empfang *m*, Rezeption *f*; **~ room** Wohnzimmer *nt*; (*in hotel*) Aufenthaltsraum *m*.
(b) (*party, ceremony*) Empfang *m*.
(c) (*in hotel etc*) der Empfang. **at/to ~** am/zum Empfang.
(d) (*Rad, TV*) Empfang *m*.
(e) (*Brit Sch: also ~ class*) Anfängerklasse *f*.

receptionist [rɪ'sepʃənɪst] *n* (*in hotel*) Empfangschef *m*, Empfangsdame *f*; (*with firm*) Herr *m*/Dame *f* am Empfang, Portier *m*, Empfangssekretärin *f*; (*at airport*) Bodenhostess *f*; (*at doctor's, dentist's etc*) Sprechstundenhilfe *f*.

receptive [rɪ'septɪv] *adj person, mind* aufnahmefähig; *audience* empfänglich. **~ to** empfänglich für.

receptiveness [rɪ'septɪvnɪs] *n* see *adj* Aufnahmefähigkeit *f*; Empfänglichkeit *f*. **~ to** Empfänglichkeit *f* für.

receptor [rɪ'septəʳ] *n* (*nerve*) Rezeptor *m*.

recess [rɪ'ses] 1 *n* (a) (*cessation*) (*of Parliament*) (Sitzungs)pause *f*; (*of lawcourts*) Ferien *pl*; (*US Sch*) Pause *f*.
(b) (*alcove*) Nische *f*.
(c) (*secret place*) Winkel *m*. **in the (deepest) ~es of my heart** in den (tiefsten) Tiefen meines Herzens.
2 *vt* (*set back*) in eine/die Nische stellen; *cupboard, cooker* einbauen; *windows* vertiefen; *lighting* versenken; (*make a ~ in*) *wall etc* eine Nische machen in (+*acc*), vertiefen.

recession [rɪ'seʃən] *n* (a) *no pl* (*receding*) Zurückweichen *n*, Rückgang *m*; (*Eccl*) Auszug *m*.
(b) (*Econ*) Rezession *f*, (wirtschaftlicher) Rückgang.

recessional [rɪ'seʃənl] (*Eccl*) 1 *n* während des Auszugs gesungene Schlußhymne. 2 *adj hymn* Schluß-.

recessive [rɪ'sesɪv] *adj* zurückweichend; (*Econ, Biol*) rezessiv.

recharge [,ri:'tʃɑ:dʒ] *vt battery* aufladen; *gun* neu *or* wieder laden, nachladen.

recheck [,ri:'tʃek] *vt* nochmals prüfen *or* kontrollieren.

recherché [rə'ʃeəʃeɪ] *adj* gewählt; *book, subject* ausgefallen; *expression* gesucht.

rechristen [,ri:'krɪsən] *vt* umtaufen. **it was ~ed Leningrad** es wurde in Leningrad umbenannt *or* umgetauft.

recidivism [rɪ'sɪdɪvɪzəm] *n* Rückfälligkeit *f*.

recidivist [rɪ'sɪdɪvɪst] 1 *n* Rückfällige(r) *mf*. 2 *adj* rückfällig.

recipe ['resɪpɪ] *n* Rezept *nt*; (*fig also*) Geheimnis *nt*. **an easy ~ for ...** (*fig*) ein Patentrezept für ...

recipient [rɪ'sɪpɪənt] *n* Empfänger(in *f*) *m*. **Susan, as the ~ of his attentions** Susan, der die Aufmerksamkeiten galten.

reciprocal [rɪ'sɪprəkəl] 1 *adj* (*mutual*) gegenseitig; *favour* Gegen-; (*Gram, Math*) reziprok. **the ~ relationship between these two phenomena** die Wechselbeziehung zwischen diesen zwei Phänomenen; **~ trade** Handel untereinander. 2 *n* (*Math*) reziproker Wert.

reciprocally [rɪ'sɪprəkəlɪ] *adv* gegenseitig, help gegenseitig; *correspond* untereinander, miteinander; (*Gram*) reziprok.

reciprocate [rɪ'sɪprəkeɪt] 1 *vt* (a) *smiles, wishes* erwidern; *help, kindness also* sich revanchieren für.
(b) (*Tech*) hin- und herbewegen; *piston* auf- und abbewegen.
2 *vi* (a) sich revanchieren. **she ~d by throwing the saucepan at him** sie warf ihm den Topf nach.

(b) (*Tech*) hin- und hergehen; (*piston*) auf- und abgehen. **reciprocating engine** Kolbenmotor *m*.

reciprocation [rɪ͵sɪprə'keɪʃən] *n* **(a)** (*of help, kindness*) Erwiderung *f* (*of gen*), Revanche *f* (*of* für). **(b)** (*Tech*) Hin und Her *nt*; (*of pistons*) Auf und Ab *nt*.

reciprocity [͵resɪ'prɒsɪtɪ] *n* (*of feelings, kindness etc*) Gegenseitigkeit *f*; (*of favours*) Austausch *m*; (*Pol*) Gegenseitigkeit, Reziprozität (*form*) *f*.

recital [rɪ'saɪtl] *n* **(a)** (*of music, poetry*) Vortrag *m*; (*piano* ~ *etc*) Konzert *nt*. **song** ~ Matinee *f*, Liederabend *m*. **(b)** (*account*) Schilderung *f*; (*of details*) Aufführung, Aufzählung *f*.

recitation [͵resɪ'teɪʃən] *n* Vortrag *m*.

recitative [͵resɪtə'tiːv] *n* Rezitativ *nt*.

recite [rɪ'saɪt] **1** *vt* **(a)** *poetry* vortragen, rezitieren. **(b)** *facts* hersagen; *details* aufzählen. **2** *vi* vortragen, rezitieren.

reckless ['reklɪs] *adj* leichtsinnig; *driver, driving* rücksichtslos; *speed* gefährlich; *attempt* gewagt. ~ **of the danger** (*liter*) ungeachtet der Gefahr (*liter*).

recklessly ['reklɪslɪ] *adv see adj*.

recklessness ['reklɪsnɪs] *n see adj* Leichtsinn *m*; Rücksichtslosigkeit *f*; Gefährlichkeit *f*; Gewagtheit *f*.

reckon ['rekən] **1** *vt* **(a)** (*calculate*) *time, numbers, points, costs, area* ausrechnen, berechnen. he ~ed the cost to be £40.51 er berechnete die Kosten auf £ 40,51.
(b) (*judge*) rechnen, zählen (*among* zu). she is ~ed a beautiful woman sie gilt als schöne Frau.
(c) (*think, suppose*) glauben; (*estimate*) schätzen. what do you ~? was meinen Sie?; I ~ we can start ich glaube, wir können anfangen; I ~ he must be about forty ich schätze, er müßte so um die Vierzig sein; he ~s himself to be one of the great golf players er hält sich für einen der größten Golfspieler.
(d) (*sl*) (*like*) gutfinden (*inf*); (*think likely to succeed*) große Chancen geben (+*dat*).
2 *vi* (*calculate*) rechnen. it's difficult to ~ (*eg how far/long etc*) das ist schwer zu schätzen; ~ing from tomorrow ab morgen gerechnet.

♦**reckon in** *vt sep* mitrechnen, einrechnen.

♦**reckon on** *vi* +*prep obj* rechnen or zählen auf (+*acc*). you can ~ ~ 30 Sie können mit 30 rechnen; I was ~ing doing that tomorrow ich wollte das morgen machen; I wasn't ~ing ~ having to do that ich habe nicht damit gerechnet, daß ich das tun muß.

♦**reckon up 1** *vt sep* zusammenrechnen. **2** *vi* abrechnen (*with* mit).

♦**reckon with** *vi* +*prep obj* rechnen mit. if you insult him you'll have the whole family to ~ ~ wenn Sie ihn beleidigen, müssen Sie mit der ganzen Familie rechnen; he's a person to be ~ed ~ er ist nicht zu unterschätzen.

♦**reckon without** *vi* +*prep obj* nicht rechnen mit. he ~ed ~ the fact that ... er hatte nicht damit gerechnet, daß ...; you must ~ ~ my being there to help you du mußt damit rechnen, daß ich nicht da bin(, um dir zu helfen).

reckoner ['rekənə'] *n see* ready ~.

reckoning ['rekənɪŋ] *n* **(a)** (*calculation*) (Be)rechnung *f*; (*old: bill, account*) Rechnung *f*. to be out in one's ~ sich ziemlich verrechnet haben; the day of ~ der Tag der Abrechnung; to the best of my ~ nach meiner Schätzung; in your ~ Ihrer Meinung or Schätzung nach. **(b)** (*Naut*) see dead ~.

reclaim [rɪ'kleɪm] **1** *vt* **(a)** *land* gewinnen; (*with manure etc*) kultivieren. to ~ land from the sea dem Meer Land abringen, Land gewinnen.
(b) (*liter*) *person* abbringen (*from* von).
(c) (*from waste*) wiedergewinnen, regenerieren (*from* aus).
(d) (*demand or ask back*) *rights, privileges* zurückverlangen; *lost item, baggage* abholen.
2 *n* **(a)** *past or beyond* ~ rettungslos *or* für immer verloren. **(b)** *baggage or luggage* ~ Gepäckausgabe *f*.

reclaimable [rɪ'kleɪməbl] *adj* *land* nutzbar *m*; *by-products* regenerierbar.

reclamation [͵reklə'meɪʃən] *n see vt* **(a)** Gewinnung *f*; Kultivierung *f*. **(b)** Abbringung *f*. **(c)** Wiedergewinnung, Regeneration *f*. **(d)** (Rück)gewinnung *f*.

recline [rɪ'klaɪn] **1** *vt* *arm* zurücklegen (*on* auf +*acc*); *head also* zurücklehnen (*on* an +*acc*); *seat* zurückstellen.
2 *vi* (*person*) zurücklehnen; (*seat*) sich verstellen lassen. she was reclining on the sofa sie ruhte auf dem Sofa; reclining in his bath im Bade liegend; **reclining chair** Ruhesessel *m*; **reclining seat** verstellbarer Sitz; (*in car, on boat*) Liegesitz *m*; **reclining figure** (*Art*) Liegende(r) *mf*.

recliner [rɪ'klaɪnə'] *n* Ruhesessel *m*.

recluse [rɪ'kluːs] *n* Einsiedler(in *f*) *m*.

recognition [͵rekəg'nɪʃən] *n* **(a)** (*acknowledgement, Pol*) Anerkennung *f*. in ~ of in Anerkennung (+*gen*); his ~ of these facts daß er diese Tatsachen akzeptierte; by or on your own ~ wie Sie selbst zugeben; to gain/receive ~ Anerkennung finden.
(b) (*identification*) Erkennen *nt*. the baby's ~ of its mother/ mother's voice das Baby das seine Mutter/die Stimme seiner Mutter erkennt/erkannte; he has changed beyond or out of all ~ er ist nicht wiederzuerkennen; he has changed it beyond or out of all ~ er ist nicht wiederzuerkennen.

recognizable ['rekəgnaɪzəbl] *adj* erkennbar. you're scarcely ~ with that beard Sie sind mit dem Bart kaum zu erkennen; Poland is no longer ~ as the country I knew in 1940 Polen ist nicht mehr das Land, das ich 1940 kannte.

recognizance [rɪ'kɒgnɪzəns] *n* (*Jur*) Verpflichtung *f*; (*for debt*) Anerkenntnis *f*; (*sum of money*) Sicherheitsleistung *f*. to enter into ~ (*for sb*) für jdn Kaution stellen.

recognize ['rekəgnaɪz] *vt* **(a)** (*know again*) *person, town, face, voice etc* wiedererkennen; (*identify*) erkennen (*by* an +*dat*). you wouldn't ~ him/the house *etc* Sie würden ihn/das Haus *etc*

nicht wiedererkennen; do you ~ this tune? erkennen Sie die Melodie?; I wouldn't have ~d him in his disguise ich hätte ihn in der Verkleidung nicht erkannt.
(b) (*acknowledge, Pol*) anerkennen (*as, to be* als). she doesn't ~ me any more when she goes past sie kennt mich nicht mehr, wenn sie mich trifft; he doesn't even ~ my existence er nimmt mich nicht einmal zur Kenntnis.
(c) (*be aware*) erkennen; (*be prepared to admit*) zugeben, eingestehen. you must ~ what is necessary Sie müssen erkennen, was notwendig ist; I ~ that I am not particularly intelligent ich gebe zu, daß ich nicht besonders intelligent bin.
(d) (*US: let speak*) das Wort erteilen (+*dat*, an +*acc*).

recognized ['rekəgnaɪzd] *adj* anerkannt.

recoil [rɪ'kɒɪl] **1** *vi* **(a)** (*person*) (*from* vor +*dat*) zurückweichen; (*in fear*) zurückschrecken; (*in disgust*) zurückschaudern. he ~ed from (the idea of) doing it ihm graute davor, das zu tun.
(b) (*gun*) zurückstoßen; (*spring*) zurückschnellen. the gun will ~ das Gewehr hat einen Rückstoß.
(c) (*fig: actions*) to ~ on sb auf jdn zurückfallen, sich an jdm rächen.
2 ['riːkɒɪl] *n* (*of gun*) Rückstoß *m*; (*of spring*) Zurückschnellen *nt no pl*.

recollect [͵rekə'lekt] **1** *vt* sich erinnern an (+*acc*), sich entsinnen (+*gen*). **2** *vi* sich erinnern, sich entsinnen. as far as I can ~ soweit ich mich erinnern kann.

recollection [͵rekə'lekʃən] *n* (*memory*) Erinnerung *f* (*of an* +*acc*). to the best of my ~ soweit ich mich erinnern kann; his ~ of it is vague er erinnert sich nur vage daran; I have some/no ~ of it ich kann mich schwach/nicht daran erinnern.

recommence [͵riːkə'mens] *vti* wiederbeginnen.

recommend [͵rekə'mend] *vt* **(a)** empfehlen (*as* als). to ~ sb for a job jdn für eine Stelle empfehlen; what do you ~ for (curing) a cough? was empfehlen *or* raten Sie gegen Husten?; to ~ sb sth *or* sth to sb jdm etw empfehlen; it is not to be ~ed es ist nicht zu empfehlen; ~ed price empfohlener Richtpreis.
(b) (*make acceptable*) sprechen für. she has much/little to ~ her es spricht sehr viel/wenig für sie; his manners do little to ~ him seine Manieren sind nicht gerade eine Empfehlung für ihn; this book has little/a great deal to ~ it das Buch ist nicht gerade/sehr empfehlenswert.
(c) (*old, liter: entrust*) *child, one's soul* empfehlen (*to sb* jdm).

recommendable [͵rekə'mendəbl] *adj* empfehlenswert; *course of action, measures also* ratsam. it is not ~ reading das ist als Lesestoff nicht zu empfehlen.

recommendation [͵rekəmen'deɪʃən] *n* Empfehlung *f*. on the ~ of auf Empfehlung von; to make a ~ jemanden/etwas empfehlen; letter of ~ Empfehlung(sschreiben *nt*) *f*.

recommendatory [͵rekə'mendətərɪ] *adj* empfehlend. ~ letter Empfehlungsschreiben *nt*.

recompense ['rekəmpens] **1** *n* **(a)** (*reward*) Belohnung *f*. as a ~ als *or* zur Belohnung; in ~ for als Belohnung für.
(b) (*Jur, fig*) Entschädigung *f*; (*of loss*) Wiedergutmachung *f*.
2 *vt* **(a)** (*reward*) belohnen.
(b) (*Jur, fig: repay*) *person* entschädigen; *damage, loss* wiedergutmachen.

recompose [͵riːkəm'pəʊz] *vt* **(a)** (*rewrite*) umschreiben; (*Mus also*) umkomponieren. **(b)** (*calm*) to ~ oneself sich wieder beruhigen.

reconcilable ['rekənsaɪləbl] *adj* *people* versöhnbar; *ideas, opinions* miteinander vereinbar.

reconcile ['rekənsaɪl] *vt* **(a)** *people* versöhnen, aussöhnen; *differences* beilegen; *dispute* schlichten. they became *or* were ~d sie versöhnten sich, sie söhnten sich aus.
(b) (*make compatible*) *facts, ideas, theories, principles* miteinander in Einklang bringen, miteinander vereinbaren. to ~ sth with sth etw mit etw in Einklang bringen, etw mit etw vereinbaren; these ideas cannot be ~d diese Ideen sind unvereinbar; how do you ~ that with the fact that you said no last week? wie läßt sich das damit vereinbaren, daß Sie letzte Woche nein gesagt haben?
(c) (*make accept*) to ~ sb to sth jdn mit etw versöhnen; to ~ oneself to sth, to become ~d to sth sich mit etw abfinden; what ~d him to it was ... was ihn damit versöhnte, war ...

reconciliation [͵rekənsɪlɪ'eɪʃən] *n* (*of persons*) Versöhnung, Aussöhnung *f*; (*of opinions, principles*) Vereinbarung, Versöhnung (*esp Philos*) *f*; (*of differences*) Beilegung *f*.

recondite [rɪ'kɒndaɪt] *adj* abstrus.

recondition [͵riːkən'dɪʃən] *vt* generalüberholen. a ~ed engine ein Austauschmotor *m*.

reconnaissance [rɪ'kɒnɪsəns] *n* (*Aviat, Mil*) Aufklärung *f*. ~ plane Aufklärer *m*, Aufklärungszeug *nt*; ~ flight/patrol Aufklärungsflug *m*/Spähtrupp *m*; ~ mission Aufklärungseinsatz *m*; to be on ~ bei einem Aufklärungseinsatz sein.

reconnoitre, (*US*) **reconnoiter** [͵rekə'nɔɪtə'] **1** *vt* (*Aviat, Mil*) *region* auskundschaften, erkunden, aufklären. **2** *vi* das Gelände erkunden *or* aufklären.

reconquer [͵riː'kɒŋkə'] *vt* *town, territory* zurückerobern; *enemy* erneut *or* wieder besiegen.

reconquest [͵riː'kɒŋkwest] *n see vt* Zurückeroberung *f*; erneuter Sieg (*of* über +*acc*).

reconsider [͵riːkən'sɪdə'] **1** *vt* *decision, judgement* noch einmal überdenken; (*change*) revidieren; *facts* neu erwägen; (*Jur*) *case* wiederaufnehmen. won't you ~ your decision and come? wollen Sie es sich (*dat*) nicht überlegen und doch kommen?; I have ~ed my decision, I'd rather not accept ich habe es mir noch einmal überlegt, ich lehne lieber ab.
2 *vi* ask him to ~ sagen Sie ihm, er soll es sich (*dat*) noch einmal überlegen; there's still time to ~ es ist noch nicht zu spät, seine Meinung zu ändern *or* es sich anders zu überlegen; won't you ~ and come? wollen Sie es sich (*dat*) nicht (noch einmal) überlegen und doch kommen?

reconsideration ['ri:kən,sıdə'reıʃən] n see vt Überdenken nt; Revision f; erneute Erwägung; Wiederaufnahme f. **following his** ~ da er es sich (dat) anders überlegt hat/hatte.

reconstitute [,ri:'konstıtju:t] vt **(a)** assembly, committee neu einrichten, rekonstituieren (form); (reconstruct) wiederherstellen. **(b)** food aus einem Konzentrat zubereiten; solution in Wasser auflösen. **this medicine is** ~d **by the addition of 4 parts of water to 1 of granules** diese Medizin wird im Verhältnis 1:4 in Wasser aufgelöst.

reconstitution ['ri:,konstı'tju:ʃən] n see vt **(a)** Rekonstitution f (form); Wiederherstellung f. **(b)** Zubereitung f aus einem Konzentrat; Auflösen nt in Wasser.

reconstruct [,ri:kən'strʌkt] vt rekonstruieren; cities wiederaufbauen; building wieder aufbauen. **to** ~ **one's life** (im Leben) noch einmal von vorn anfangen.

reconstruction [,ri:kən'strʌkʃən] n see vt Rekonstruktion f; Wiederaufbau m.

record [rı'kɔ:d] **1** vt **(a)** facts, story, events (diarist, person) aufzeichnen; (documents, diary etc) dokumentieren; (in register) eintragen; (keep minutes of) protokollieren; one's thoughts, feelings etc festhalten, niederschreiben; protest, disapproval zum Ausdruck bringen. **these facts are not** ~ed **anywhere** diese Tatsachen sind nirgends festgehalten; **it's not** ~ed **anywhere** das ist nirgends dokumentiert or belegt; **to** ~ **sth photographically** etw im Bild festhalten; **to** ~ **one's vote** seine Stimme abgeben; **his speech as** ~ed **in the newspapers** seine Rede, wie sie in den Zeitungen wiedergegeben wurde; **history/the author** ~s **that ...** es ist geschichtlich dokumentiert/der Verfasser berichtet, daß ...

(b) (thermometer, meter etc) verzeichnen, registrieren; (needle) aufzeichnen, registrieren; (pen needle) aufzeichnen.

(c) (on tape, cassette etc) music, person aufnehmen; programme, speech also aufzeichnen. **a** ~ed **programme** eine Aufzeichnung; ~ing **apparatus** Aufnahmegerät nt.

2 vi (Tonband)aufnahmen machen. **he is** ~ing **at 5 o'clock** er hat um 5 Uhr eine Aufnahme; **his voice does not** ~ **well** seine Stimme läßt sich nicht gut aufnehmen; **the tape-recorder won't** ~ man kann mit dem Tonbandgerät nicht aufnehmen.

3 ['rekɔ:d] n **(a)** (account) Aufzeichnung f; (of attendance) Liste f; (of meeting) Protokoll nt; (official document) Unterlage, Akte f; (lit, fig: of the past, of civilization) Dokument nt. **(public)** ~s **im** Staatsarchiv gelagerte Urkunden; **a photographic** ~ eine Bilddokumentation; **it's nice to have a photographic** ~ **of one's holidays** es ist nett, den Urlaub im Bild festgehalten zu haben; **to keep a** ~ **of sth** über etw (acc) Buch führen; (official, registrar) etw registrieren; (historian, chronicler) etw aufzeichnen; **to keep a personal** ~ **of sth** sich (dat) etw notieren; **it is on** ~ **that ...** es gibt Belege dafür, daß ...; (in files) es ist aktenkundig, daß ...; **there is no similar example on** ~ es ist kein ähnliches Beispiel bekannt; **I'm prepared to go on** ~ **as saying that ...** ich stehe zu der Behauptung, daß ...; **he's on** ~ **as having said ...** es ist belegt, daß er gesagt hat, ...; **last night the PM went on** ~ **as saying ...** gestern abend hat sich der Premier dahingehend festgelegt, daß ...; **to put sth on** ~ etw schriftlich festhalten; **there is no** ~ **of his having said it** es ist nirgends belegt, daß er es gesagt hat; **to put or set the** ~ **straight** für klare Verhältnisse sorgen; **just to set the** ~ **straight** nur damit Klarheit herrscht; **for the** ~ der Ordnung halber; (for the minutes) zur Mitschrift; **this is strictly off the** ~ dies ist nur inoffiziell; (strictly) off the ~ **he did come** ganz im Vertrauen: er ist doch gekommen.

(b) (police ~) Vorstrafen pl. ~s (files) Strafregister nt; **he's got a** ~ er ist vorbestraft; **a** ~ **of previous convictions** Vorstrafen pl; **he's got a clean** ~, **he hasn't got a** ~ er ist nicht vorbestraft; **to keep one's** ~ **clean** sich (dat) nichts zuschulden kommen lassen.

(c) (history) Vorgeschichte f; (achievements) Leistungen pl. **to have an excellent** ~ ausgezeichnete Leistungen vorweisen können; **the applicant with the best** ~ der Bewerber mit den besten Voraussetzungen; **with a** ~ **like yours you should be able to handle this job** mit den Leistungen, die Sie vorzuweisen haben or mit Ihren Voraussetzungen müßten Sie sich in dieser Stelle leicht zurechtfinden; **he has a good** ~ **of service** er ist ein verdienter Mitarbeiter; **service** ~ (Mil) militärisches Führungszeugnis; **his attendance** ~ **is bad** er fehlt oft; **his past** ~ seine bisherigen Leistungen; **to have a good** ~ **at school** ein guter Schüler sein; **to have a good safety** ~ in bezug auf Sicherheit einen guten Ruf haben; **to have a dubious** ~ **as far as sth is concerned** in bezug auf etw (acc) einen zweifelhaften Ruf haben; **he's got quite a** ~ (has done bad things) er hat so einiges auf dem Kerbholz; **he left a splendid** ~ **of achievements behind him** er hat sich sehr verdient gemacht, er hat sehr viel geleistet; **to spoil one's** ~ es sich (dat) verderben, sich (dat) ein Minus einhandeln (inf); **I've been looking at your** ~, **Jones** ich habe mir Ihre Akte angesehen, Jones.

(d) (Mus) (Schall)platte f; (~ing) (of voice, music etc) Aufnahme f, (of programme, speech) Aufzeichnung, Aufnahme f. **to make or cut a** ~ eine Schallplatte machen.

(e) (Sport, fig) Rekord m. **to beat or break the** ~ den Rekord brechen; **to hold the** ~ den Rekord halten or innehaben; **long-jump** ~ Weitsprungrekord, Rekord im Weitsprung; **a** ~ **amount/time/result** ein Rekordbetrag m/eine Rekordzeit/ein Rekordergebnis nt.

(f) (on seismograph etc) Aufzeichnung, Registrierung f.

record ['rekɔ:d]: ~ **album** n Plattenalbum nt; ~ **breaker** n (Sport) Rekordbrecher(in f) m; ~-**breaking** adj (Sport, fig) rekordbrechend; ~ **cabinet** n Plattenschrank m; ~ **card** n Karteikarte f; ~ **changer** n Plattenwechsler m; ~ **dealer** n Schallplattenhändler(in f) m.

recorded [rı'kɔ:dıd] adj **(a)** music, programme aufgezeichnet. ~ **delivery** (Brit) eingeschriebene Sendung; **by** ~ **delivery** or

post (Brit) per Einschreiben. **(b)** fact, occurrence schriftlich belegt. **in all** ~ **history** seit unserer Geschichtsschreibung.

recorder [rı'kɔ:dər] n **(a)** (apparatus) Registriergerät nt. **cassette/tape** ~ Kassettenrekorder m/Tonbandgerät nt. **(b)** (Mus) Blockflöte f. **(c)** (of official facts) Berichterstatter m; (historian) Chronist m. **(d)** (Brit Jur) nebenher als Richter tätiger Rechtsanwalt.

record holder n (Sport) Rekordhalter(in f) or -inhaber(in f) m.

recording [rı'kɔ:dıŋ] n (of sound) Aufnahme f; (of programme) Aufzeichnung f.

recording: ~ **angel** n Engel, der die guten und bösen Taten aufschreibt; ~ **artist** n Musiker(in f) m, der/die Schallplattenaufnahmen macht; Plattensänger(in f) m; ~ **session** n Aufnahme f; ~ **studio** n Aufnahmestudio nt; ~ **tape** n Tonband nt; ~ **van** n (Rad, TV) Aufnahmewagen m.

record [rekɔ:d]: ~ **library** n Plattenverleih m; (collection) Plattensammlung f; ~-**player** n Plattenspieler m; ~ **token** n Plattengutschein m.

recount [rı'kaunt] vt (relate) erzählen, wiedergeben.

re-count [,ri:'kaunt] **1** vt nachzählen. **2** ['ri:,kaunt] n (of votes) Nachzählung f.

recoup [rı'ku:p] vt **(a)** (make good) money, amount wieder einbringen or hereinbekommen; losses wiedergutmachen, wettmachen. **(b)** (reimburse) entschädigen. **to** ~ **oneself** sich entschädigen. **to** ~ (Jur) einbehalten.

recourse [rı'kɔ:s] n Zuflucht f. **to have** ~ **to sb/sth** sich an jdn wenden/Zuflucht zu etw nehmen; **without** ~ **to his books** ohne seine Bücher zu konsultieren; **without** ~ (Fin) ohne Regreß.

recover[1], **re-cover** [,ri:'kʌvər] vt chairs, pillow, umbrella neu beziehen or überziehen; book neu einbinden.

recover[2] [rı'kʌvər] **1** vt sth lost wiederfinden; one's appetite, balance also wiedergewinnen; sth lent zurückbekommen; health wiedererlangen; goods, property, lost territory zurückgewinnen, zurückbekommen; space capsule, wreck bergen; (Ind etc) materials gewinnen; debt eintreiben, beitreiben; (Jur) damages Ersatz erhalten für; losses wiedergutmachen; expenses decken, wieder einholen. **to** ~ **one's breath/strength** wieder zu Atem/Kräften kommen; **to** ~ **consciousness** wieder zu Bewußtsein kommen or gelangen, das Bewußtsein wiedererlangen (geh); **to** ~ **one's sight** wieder sehen können, sein Augenlicht wiedererlangen (geh); **to** ~ **land from the sea** dem Meer Land abringen; **to** ~ **lost ground** (fig) aufholen; **to** ~ **oneself** or **one's composure** sich wieder fassen, seine Fassung wiedererlangen; **to be quite** ~ed sich ganz erholt haben.

2 vi **(a)** (after shock, accident etc, St Ex, Fin) sich erholen; (from illness also) genesen (geh); (from falling) sich fangen; (regain consciousness) wieder zu sich kommen.

(b) (Jur) (den Prozeß) gewinnen.

recoverable [rı'kʌvərəbl] adj (Fin) debt ein- or beitreibbar; losses, damages ersetzbar; deposit zurückzahlbar.

recovery [rı'kʌvərı] n **(a)** see vt Wiederfinden nt; Wiedergewinnung f; Zurückbekommen nt; Wiedererlangung f; Zurückgewinnung f; Bergung f; Gewinnung f; Ein- or Beitreibung f; Ersatz m (of für); Wiedergutmachung f; Deckung f. ~ **vehicle/service** Abschleppwagen m/-dienst m.

(b) see vi Erholung f; Genesung f (geh); Zusichkommen nt; Prozeßgewinn m; (Golf) Schlag m vom Rauh zum Fairway. **to be on the road or way to** ~ auf dem Weg der Besserung sein; **he is making a good** ~ er erholt sich gut; **past** ~ nicht mehr zu retten; **to make a** ~ (regain strength etc) sich erholen; (gymnast) sich fangen.

recreant ['rekrıənt] (liter) **1** n (coward) Memme f; (traitor) Verräter m. **2** adj see n memmenhaft; verräterisch.

recreate [,ri:krı'eıt] vt (reproduce) atmosphere wiederschaffen; scene nachschaffen; love, friendship etc wiederbeleben.

recreation [,rekrı'eıʃən] n **(a)** (leisure) Erholung, Entspannung f; (pastime) Hobby nt. **is gardening a** ~ **to you or hard work?** ist Gartenarbeit für Sie ein Hobby oder harte Arbeit?; **for** ~ **I go fishing** zur Erholung gehe ich Angeln; ~ **centre** Freizeitzentrum nt; ~ **facilities** Möglichkeiten pl zur Freizeitgestaltung; ~ **period** Freistunde f; ~ **room** Freizeitraum m; ~ **ground** Spielplatz m.

(b) (Sch) Pause f.

recreational [,rekrı'eıʃənəl] adj facilities, activity Freizeit-.

recreative ['rekrı,eıtıv] adj erholsam, entspannend.

recriminate [rı'krımıneıt] vi Gegenbeschuldigungen vorbringen.

recrimination [rı,krımı'neıʃən] n Gegenbeschuldigung f; (Jur) Gegenklage f. (mutual) ~s gegenseitige Beschuldigungen pl; **there's no point in all these** ~s es hat keinen Sinn, sich gegenseitig zu beschuldigen.

recrudesce [,ri:kru:'des] vi (form) (wound) wieder aufbrechen; (illness) wieder ausbrechen; (problems) wieder beginnen.

recruit [rı'kru:t] **1** n (Mil) Rekrut m (to gen); (to party, club) neues Mitglied (to in +dat); (to staff) Neue(r) m/(to in +dat).

2 vt soldier rekrutieren; member werben; staff einstellen, anstellen. **to be** ~ed **from** (member, staff) sich rekrutieren aus; **he** ~ed **me to help** er hat mich dazu herangezogen.

3 vi see vt Rekruten ausheben or anwerben; Mitglieder werben; neue Leute einstellen.

recruiting [rı'kru:tıŋ] n see vt Rekrutierung f; Werben nt; Einstellung f. ~ **office** (Mil) Rekrutierungsbüro nt; ~ **officer** Aushebungsoffizier, Werbeoffizier (Hist) m.

recruitment [rı'kru:tmənt] n (of soldiers) Rekrutierung, Aushebung f; (of members) Werbung f; (of staff) Einstellung f. **a large** ~ eine Menge Rekruten/neue Mitglieder pl/neue Leute pl; ~ **drive** Anwerbungskampagne f.

recta ['rektə] pl of rectum.

rectal ['rektəl] adj rektal (spec), des Mastdarms. ~ **passage** Mastdarm m.

rectangle ['rek͵tæŋgl] n Rechteck nt.

rectangular [rek'tæŋgjulə^r] adj rechteckig; *coordinates* rechtwinklig.

rectifiable ['rektɪfaɪəbl] adj (a) korrigierbar; *instrument* richtig einstellbar; *omission* nachholbar; *abuse* abstellbar. (b) (*Chem, Math*) rektifizierbar.

rectification [͵rektɪfɪ'keɪʃən] n see vt (a) Korrektur, Verbesserung f; Richtigstellung, Berichtigung f; Korrektur f; richtige Einstellung, Berichtigung f; Nachholen nt, Wiedergutmachung f; Abhilfe f (of für). (b) Gleichrichtung f. (c) Rektifikation f.

rectifier ['rektɪ͵faɪə^r] n (*Elec*) Gleichrichter m.

rectify ['rektɪfaɪ] vt (a) korrigieren, verbessern; *error, statement also* richtigstellen, berichtigen; *position, anomaly* korrigieren; *instrument* richtig einstellen, korrigieren; *omission* nachholen, wiedergutmachen; *abuse* abhelfen (+dat). (b) (*Elec*) gleichrichten. (c) (*Chem, Math*) rektifizieren.

rectilineal [͵rektɪ'lɪnɪəl], **rectilinear** [͵rektɪ'lɪnɪə^r] adj geradlinig. in a ~ direction geradlinig.

rectitude ['rektɪtjuːd] n Rechtschaffenheit f.

rector ['rektə^r] n (a) (*Rel*) Pfarrer m (*der Church of England*). (b) (*Scot*) (*Sch*) Direktor(in f) m; (*Univ*) Rektor(in f) m.

rectorship ['rektə͵ʃɪp] n see rector Zeit f als Pfarrer; Direktorat nt; Rektorat nt.

rectory ['rektərɪ] n (*house*) Pfarrhaus nt.

rectum ['rektəm] n, pl -s or **recta** Rektum nt (*spec*), Mastdarm m. a kick up the ~ (*inf*) ein Tritt in den Hintern (*inf*).

recumbent [rɪ'kʌmbənt] adj (*form*) ruhend attr, liegend attr. ~ figure (*Art*) liegende Figur, Liegende(r) mf; to be ~ liegen.

recuperate [rɪ'kuːpəreɪt] 1 vi sich erholen; (*from illness also*) genesen (geh). 2 vt *losses* wettmachen, wiedergutmachen.

recuperation [rɪ͵kuːpə'reɪʃən] n see vb Erholung f; Genesung f (geh); Wiedergutmachung f. after my ~ nachdem ich mich erholt hatte/habe.

recuperative [rɪ'kuːpərətɪv] adj erholsam; *treatment* Heil-. he has amazing ~ powers er erholt sich erstaunlich schnell.

recur [rɪ'kɜː^r] vi (a) (*happen again*) wiederkehren; (*error also, event*) sich wiederholen, wieder passieren; (*opportunity*) sich wieder bieten, sich noch einmal bieten; (*problem, symptoms also*) wieder auftreten; (*idea, theme also*) wieder auftauchen. (b) (*Math*) sich periodisch wiederholen; see recurring. (c) (*come to mind again*) wieder einfallen (*to sb* jdm); (*thought, idea*) wiederkommen (*to sb* jdm).

recurrence [rɪ'kʌrəns] n see vi Wiederkehr f; Wiederholung f; erneutes Auftreten; Wiederauftauchen nt. let there be no ~ of this das darf nie wieder vorkommen.

recurrent [rɪ'kʌrənt] adj (a) *idea, theme, illness, symptom(s)* (ständig) wiederkehrend attr; *error, problem also* häufig (vorkommend); *event(s)* sich wiederholend attr; *expenses* regelmäßig wiederkehrend. (b) (*Anat*) sich zurückziehend.

recurring [rɪ'kɜːrɪŋ] adj attr (a) see recurrent (a). (b) (*Math*) ~ decimal periodische Dezimalzahl; four point nine three ~ vier Komma neun Periode drei.

recusant ['rekjuzənt] adj (*Rel Hist*) der/die sich weigert, dem anglikanischen Gottesdienst beizuwohnen; (*fig liter*) renitent.

recycle [͵riː'saɪkl] vt *waste, paper etc* wiederaufbereiten.

recycling [͵riː'saɪklɪŋ] n Wiederaufbereitung f, Recycling nt.

red [red] 1 adj (+er) (*also Pol*) rot. ~ meat Rind-/Lammfleisch nt; ~ as a beetroot rot wie eine Tomate; was my face ~! da habe ich vielleicht einen roten Kopf bekommen; there'll be some ~ faces in the town hall das wird einigen Leuten im Rathaus sauer aufstoßen (*inf*); to see ~ (*fig*) rot sehen.
2 n (*colour*) Rot nt; (*Pol: person*) Rote(r) mf; (*Billiards*) Karambole f, roter Ball; (*Roulette*) Rot, Rouge nt. to underline mistakes in ~ Fehler rot unterstreichen; to go through the lights on ~, to go through on ~ bei Rot über die Ampel fahren; to be (£100) in the ~ (*inf*) (mit £ 100) in den roten Zahlen or in den Roten (*inf*) sein; to get out of the ~ (*inf*) aus den roten Zahlen or aus den Roten (*inf*) herauskommen.

red in cpds Rot-, rot; ~ admiral n Admiral m; R~ Army n Rote Armee; ~-blooded adj heißblütig; ~breast n Rotkehlchen nt; ~brick university n (*Brit*) neugebackene Universität (*inf*); ~cap n (*Brit Mil sl*) Militärpolizist, MP m; (*US*) Gepäckträger m; (*Orn*) Stieglitz m; ~ carpet n (*lit, fig*) roter Teppich; a ~ carpet reception ein Empfang m mit rotem Teppich; (*fig also*) ein großer Bahnhof; to roll out the ~ carpet for sb, to give sb the ~ carpet treatment (*inf*) jdn mit großem Bahnhof empfangen; ~ cedar n Bleistiftzeder f, Virginischer Wacholder; ~ cent n (*US inf*) roter Heller (*inf*); R~ China n Rotchina nt; ~coat n (*Brit Hist*) Rotrock m (*britischer Soldat im amerikanischen Unabhängigkeitskrieg*); R~ Crescent n Roter Halbmond; R~ Cross 1 n Rotes Kreuz; 2 attr Rotkreuz-, Rote-Kreuz-; ~currant n (rote) Johannisbeere; ~ deer n Rothirsch m; pl Rotwild nt.

redden ['redn] 1 vt röten; *sky, foliage* rot färben. 2 vi (*face*) sich röten; (*person*) rot werden; (*sky, foliage*) sich rot färben.

reddish ['redɪʃ] adj rötlich.

red duster n (*Naut inf*) see red ensign.

redecorate [͵riː'dekəreɪt] vti (*paper*) neu tapezieren; (*paint*) neu streichen. we'll have to ~ wir müssen das Haus/die Wohnung etc neu machen (*inf*).

redecoration [͵riːdekə'reɪʃən] n see vb (*action*) Neutapezieren nt; Neustreichen nt; (*result*) neue Tapeten pl; neuer Anstrich.

redeem [rɪ'diːm] vt *pawned object, trading stamps, coupons, bill etc* einlösen (*for* gegen); *promise also, obligation* einhalten, erfüllen; (*Fin*) *debt* abzahlen, tilgen; *mortgage* tilgen, abzahlen; *shares* verkaufen; (*US*) *banknote* wechseln (*for* in +acc); *one's honour, situation* retten; (*Rel*) *sinner* erlösen; (*compensate for*) *failing, fault* wettmachen, ausgleichen. to ~ oneself sich reinwaschen.

redeemable [rɪ'diːməbl] adj (a) *debt* tilgbar; *pawned object, trading stamps, coupons, bill* einlösbar. ~ for cash/goods gegen Bargeld/Waren einzulösen. (b) (*Rel*) erlösbar.

Redeemer [rɪ'diːmə^r] n (*Rel*) Erlöser, Retter, Heiland m.

redeeming [rɪ'diːmɪŋ] adj quality ausgleichend. ~ feature aussöhnendes Moment; the only ~ feature of this novel is ... das einzige, was einen mit diesem Roman aussöhnt, ist ...

redemption [rɪ'dempʃən] n see vt Einlösung f; Einhaltung, Erfüllung f; Abzahlung, Löschung f; Tilgung f; Verkauf m; Wechsel m; Rettung f; (*Rel*) Erlösung f; Ausgleich m. beyond or past ~ (*fig*) (*object*) nicht mehr zu retten; (*situation, person*) rettungslos, verloren; ~ centre (*Comm*) Einlösestelle f.

redemptive [rɪ'demptɪv] adj (*Rel*) erlösend, rettend.

red ensign n (*Naut*) britische Handelsflagge.

redeploy [͵riːdɪ'plɔɪ] vt *troops* umverlegen; *workers* anders einsetzen; *staff* umsetzen.

redeployment [͵riːdɪ'plɔɪmənt] n see vt Umverlegung f; Einsatz m an einem anderen Arbeitsplatz; Umsetzung f.

redevelop [͵riːdɪ'veləp] vt *building, area* sanieren.

redevelopment [͵riːdɪ'veləpmənt] n Sanierung f. ~ area Sanierungsgebiet nt.

red: ~-eye n (*US sl*) Fusel m (*inf*), schlechter Whisky; ~-eyed adj mit geröteten or roten Augen; ~-faced adj mit rotem Kopf; R~ Flag n Rote Fahne; ~-haired adj rothaarig; ~-handed adv: to catch sb ~-handed jdn auf frischer Tat ertappen; (*esp sexually*) jdn in flagranti erwischen (*inf*); ~head n Rothaarige(r) mf, Rotschopf m; ~-headed adj rothaarig; ~ heat n Rotglut f; to bring iron to ~ heat Eisen auf Rotglut erhitzen; ~ herring n (*lit*) Räucherhering m; (*fig*) Ablenkungsmanöver nt; (*in thrillers, historical research*) falsche Spur; that's a ~ herring (*irrelevant*) das führt vom Thema ab; ~-hot adj (a) (*lit*) rotglühend; (*very hot*) glühend heiß; (b) (*fig inf*) (*enthusiastic*) Feuer und Flamme pred (*inf*); (*very recent*) news brandaktuell; ~hot poker n (*Bot*) Fackellilie f; R~ Indian n Indianer(in f) m.

redirect [͵riːdaɪ'rekt] vt *letter, parcel* umadressieren; (*forward*) nachsenden; *traffic* umleiten.

rediscover [͵riːdɪs'kʌvə^r] vt wiederentdecken.

rediscovery [͵riːdɪs'kʌvərɪ] n Wiederentdeckung f.

redistribute [͵riːdɪs'trɪbjuːt] vt *wealth* umverteilen, neu verteilen; (*re-allocate*) *work* neu zuteilen.

redistribution [͵riːdɪstrɪ'bjuːʃən] n see vt Umverteilung, Neuverteilung f; Neuzuteilung f.

red: ~ lead n Bleirot nt, Bleimennige f; ~-letter day n besonderer Tag, Tag, den man im Kalender rot anstreichen muß; ~ light n (*lit*) (*warning light*) rotes Licht; (*traffic light*) Rotlicht nt; to go through the ~ light (*Mot*) bei Rot über die Ampel fahren, die Ampel überfahren (*inf*); to see the ~ light (*fig*) die Gefahr erkennen; a ~-light district die Strichgegend, der Strich (*inf*); (*with night-clubs*) das Amüsierviertel.

redness ['rednɪs] n Röte f.

redo [͵riː'duː] vt (a) noch einmal machen, neu machen; *hair* in Ordnung bringen. (b) see redecorate.

redolence ['redəʊləns] n (*liter*) Duft m.

redolent ['redəʊlənt] adj (*liter*) duftend. ~ of or with lavender nach Lavendel duftend; to be ~ of the 19th century/my youth stark an das 19. Jahrhundert/meine Jugend erinnern.

redouble [͵riː'dʌbl] 1 vt (a) *efforts, zeal etc* verdoppeln. (b) (*Bridge*) rekontrieren. 2 vi (*zeal, efforts*) sich verdoppeln. 3 n (*Bridge*) Rekontraansage f.

redoubt [rɪ'daʊt] n (*Mil*) Redoute f; (*inside a fort*) Kasematte f.

redoubtable [rɪ'daʊtəbl] adj (*formidable*) *task* horrend; (*to be feared*) *person, teacher* respektgebietend attr.

redound [rɪ'daʊnd] vi to ~ to sb's honour/advantage jdm zur Ehre/zum Vorteil gereichen (*geh*); to ~ to sb's credit jdm hoch angerechnet werden; to ~ upon wieder treffen.

red: ~ pepper n roter Paprika, rote Paprikaschote; ~ pine n Südkiefer f; (*wood*) Redpine nt.

redraft [͵riː'drɑːft] 1 n see vt Neuentwurf m; Neufassung f; Umschrift f. 2 vt nochmals or neu entwerfen; *speech also* nochmals or neu abfassen; *literary work* umschreiben.

red rag n rotes Tuch. it's like a ~ to a bull das ist ein rotes Tuch für ihn/sie etc.

redress [rɪ'dres] 1 vt *one's errors, wrongs* wiedergutmachen, sühnen; *situation* bereinigen; *grievance* beseitigen; *abuse* abhelfen (+dat); *balance* wiederherstellen.
2 n see vt Wiedergutmachung f; Bereinigung f; Beseitigung f; Abhilfe f. to seek ~ for Wiedergutmachung verlangen für; he set out to seek ~ for these grievances er wollte zu seinem Recht kommen; there is no ~ das steht unumstößlich fest; legal ~ Rechtshilfe f; to have no ~ in law keinen Rechtsanspruch haben; but what ~ does a manager have against an employee? aber welche Wege stehen dem Manager offen, gegen den Arbeitnehmer zu klagen?; to gain ~ zu seinem Recht kommen.

red: (Little) R~ Riding Hood n Rotkäppchen nt; ~ salmon n Pazifiklachs m; R~ Sea n Rotes Meer; ~ setter n (Roter) Setter; ~shank n (*Orn*) Rotschenkel m; ~ shift n Rotverschiebung f; ~skin n Rothaut f; ~ spider mite n Rote Spinne f; R~ Spot n (*Astron*) roter Punkt; ~ squirrel n Eichhörnchen nt; ~start n (*Orn*) Rotschwanz m; ~ tape n (*fig*) Papierkrieg m (*inf*); (*with authorities also*) Behördenkram m (*inf*).

reduce [rɪ'djuːs] 1 vt (a) *pressure, weight, swelling* verringern, reduzieren; *speed also* verlangsamen; *authority also* schwächen; (*lower also*) *standards, temperatures* herabsetzen; *prices* ermäßigen, herabsetzen; *taxes* senken; (*shorten*) *expenses, wages* kürzen; (*in size*) *width, staff, drawing, photo* verkleinern, reduzieren; *scale of operations* einschränken; *temperature* senken; (*Cook*) *sauce* einkochen lassen; *output* drosseln, reduzieren; (*Mil etc: in rank*) degradieren. to ~ one's weight abnehmen; to ~ the strength of a solution eine Lösung abschwächen; to ~ speed (*Mot*) langsamer fahren; "~ speed now" (*Mot*) ≈ langsam; the facts may all be ~d to four main headings die Tatsachen können alle auf vier Hauptpunkte reduziert werden.

(b) (*in price*) *goods, item* heruntersetzen, herabsetzen. **(c)** (*change the form of*) (*Chem*) reduzieren; (*Math*) zerlegen (*to in* +*acc*). **to ~ sth to a powder/to its parts** etw pulverisieren/in seine Einzelteile zerlegen; **to ~ sth to a common denominator** (*Math, fig*) etw auf einen gemeinsamen Nenner bringen; **to ~ an argument to its simplest form** ein Argument auf die einfachste Form bringen; **it has been ~d to a mere ...** es ist jetzt nur noch ein...; **it has been ~d to nothing** es ist zu nichts zusammengeschmolzen; **he's ~d to a skeleton** er ist zum Skelett abgemagert; **to ~ sb to silence/obedience/despair/tears** jdn zum Schweigen/Gehorsam/zur Verzweiflung/zum Weinen bringen; **to ~ sb to begging/to slavery** jdn zum Betteln/zur Sklaverei zwingen; **are we ~d to this!** so weit ist es also gekommen!; **to be ~d to submission** aufgeben müssen. **(d)** (*Med*) *joint* wieder einrenken.

2 *vi* (*esp US: slim*) abnehmen. **to be reducing** eine Schlankheitskur machen.

reduced [rɪ'djuːst] *adj price, fare* ermäßigt, *goods* herabgesetzt; *scale, version* kleiner; *circumstances* beschränkt.

reducer [rɪ'djuːsə'] *n* (*Phot*) Abschwächer *m*.

reducible [rɪ'djuːsəbl] *adj* (*to* auf +*acc*) (*Chem, fig*) reduzierbar; (*Math*) zerlegbar; *drawing, scale also* verkleinerbar; *time also* verkürzbar; *costs* herabsetzbar. **to be ~ to sth** sich auf etw (*acc*) reduzieren lassen.

reduction [rɪ'dʌkʃən] *n* **(a)** *no pl* (*in sth gen*) Reduzierung, Reduktion, Verringerung *f*; (*in speed also*) Verlangsamung *f*; (*in authority*) Schwächung *f*; (*in standards, temperatures also*) Herabsetzung *f*; (*in prices also*) Ermäßigung, Herabsetzung *f*; (*in taxes also*) Senkung *f*; (*in expenses, wages*) Kürzung *f*; (*in size*) Verkleinerung *f*; (*shortening*) Verkürzung *f*; (*in output also*) Drosselung *f*; (*in scale of operations*) Einschränkung *f*; (*of goods, items*) Herabsetzung *f*; (*of fever*) Senkung *f*; (*of joint*) Wiedereinrenken *nt*. **to make a ~ on an article** einen Artikel heruntersetzen; **~ for cash** Preisabschlag *m* bei Barzahlung; **~ of taxes** Steuersenkung *f*; **~ in rank** Degradierung *f*. **(b)** (*to another state*) (*Chem*) Reduktion *f*; (*Math also*) Zerlegung *f* (*to in* +*acc*). **~ of sth to powder/to a pulp** Zermahlung *f* einer Sache (*gen*) zu Pulver/zu Brei; **by the ~ of the argument to its simplest form** indem man die Argumentation auf die einfachste Form bringt. **(c)** (*amount reduced*) (*in sth gen*) (*in pressure, temperature, output*) Abnahme *f*, Rückgang *m*; (*of speed also*) Verlangsamung *f*; (*in size*) Verkleinerung *f*; (*in length*) Verkürzung *f*; (*in taxes*) Nachlaß *m*; (*in prices*) Ermäßigung *f*; (*Jur: of sentence*) Kürzung *f*; (*of swelling*) Rückgang *m*. **to sell (sth) at a ~** etw verbilligt or zu ermäßigtem Preis verkaufen; **what a ~!** wie billig!; **~ of strength** Nachlassen *nt* der Kräfte. **(d)** (*copy*) Verkleinerung *f*.

reductionism [rɪ'dʌkʃənɪzəm] *n* Reduktionismus *m*.

reductive [rɪ'dʌktɪv] *adj* verkürzt, zu kurz gegriffen; (*Philos*) reduktiv.

redundancy [rɪ'dʌndənsɪ] *n* Überflüssigkeit *f*; (*of style*) Weitschweifigkeit, Redundanz *f* (*geh*); (*Ind*) Arbeitslosigkeit *f*. **redundancies** Entlassungen *pl*; **the depression caused a lot of ~ or many redundancies** der Konjunkturrückgang brachte viel Arbeitslosigkeit mit sich; **he feared ~** er hatte Angst, seinen Arbeitsplatz zu verlieren; **~ payment** Abfindung *f*.

redundant [rɪ'dʌndənt] *adj* überflüssig; *style* zu wortreich, redundant (*geh*); (*Ind: out of work*) arbeitslos. **to become/to be made ~** (*Ind*) den Arbeitsplatz verlieren; **he found himself ~** er war plötzlich ohne Arbeitsplatz.

reduplicate [rɪ'djuːplɪkeɪt] **1** *vt* wiederholen; (*Ling*) reduplizieren. **2** *adj* (*Ling*) redupliziert.

reduplication [rɪ,djuːplɪ'keɪʃən] *n see vt* Wiederholung *f*; Reduplikation *f*.

reduplicative [rɪ'djuːplɪkətɪv] *adj* (*Ling*) reduplizierend.

red: **~wing** *n* Rotdrossel *f*; **~wood** *n* Redwood *nt*.

re-echo [,riː'ekəʊ] **1** *vi* widerhallen. **2** *vt* echoen. **he ~ed his wife's opinion** er war wie das Echo seiner Frau.

reed [riːd] *n* **(a)** (*Bot*) Schilf(rohr), Ried *nt*. **in the ~s** im Schilf or Ried; **a broken ~** (*fig*) ein schwankendes Rohr. **(b)** (*of wind instrument*) Rohrblatt *nt*; (*of harmonium*) Durchschlagzunge *f*; (*of organ*) Zungenpfeife *f*. **~s** Rohrblattinstrumente *pl*.

reed: **~ basket** *n* Korb *m* aus Schilfrohr; **~ bunting** *n* Rohrammer *f*; **~ instrument** *n* Rohrblattinstrument *nt*.

re-edit [,riː'edɪt] *vt* neu herausgeben; *book, text* noch einmal redigieren; *film, tape* neu schneiden.

reed: **~ organ** *n* Harmonium *nt*; **~ pipe** *n* Schalmei *f*; **~ stop** *n* Zungenregister *nt*.

re-educate [,riː'edjʊkeɪt] *vt* (um)erziehen. **to ~ one's palate** sich in seinem Geschmack umstellen.

re-education [,riː,edjʊ'keɪʃən] *n* (Um)erziehung *f*.

reed-warbler ['riːdwɔːblə'] *n* Rohrsänger *m*.

reedy ['riːdɪ] *adj* (+*er*) schilfig; *instrument* Rohrblatt-; *sound* näselnd; *voice* durchdringend.

reef[1] [riːf] *n* (*in sea*) Riff *nt*. **(b)** (*Min*) Ader *f*, Gang *m*.

reef[2] (*Naut*) **1** *n* Reff *nt*. **~ knot** Kreuz- or Weberknoten *m*. **2** *vt* *sail* reffen.

reefer ['riːfə'] *n* (*jacket*) Seemannsjacke *f*; (*sl*) Reefer *m* (*sl*).

reek [riːk] **1** *n* Gestank *m*. **2** *vi* stinken (*of* nach).

reel [riːl] **1** *n* (*a*) (*of thread, wire etc*) Rolle, Spule *f*; (*of film, magnetic tape*) Spule *f*; (*Fishing*) (Angel)rolle *f*. **(b)** (*dance*) Reel *m*. **2** *vt* (*Tech*) *thread* aufspulen. **3** *vi* (*person*) taumeln; (*drunk also*) torkeln, schwanken. **he went ~ing down the street** er torkelte or schwankte die Straße hinunter; **the blow made him ~ or sent him ~ing** er taumelte unter dem Schlag; **the street ~ed before his eyes** die Straße drehte sich ihr vor den Augen; **my head is ~ing** mir dreht sich der Kopf; **the news made him or his mind ~** bei der Nachricht drehte sich ihm alles; **I ~ed at the very thought of it** schon beim Gedanken daran wurde mir ganz schwindlig; **the whole country is still ~ing from the shock** das ganze Land ist noch tief erschüttert von diesem Schock.

◆**reel in** *vt sep* (*Fishing*) einrollen; *fish* einholen.

◆**reel off** *vt sep list* herunterrasseln (*inf*); (*monotonously*) herunterleiern (*inf*); *thread* abwickeln, abspulen.

◆**reel up** *vt sep* (*Fishing*) aufrollen, aufspulen.

re-elect [,riː'ɪlekt] *vt* wiederwählen.

re-election [,riː'ɪlekʃən] *n* Wiederwahl *f*.

reeling ['riːlɪŋ] **1** *n see vi* Taumeln *nt*; Torkeln, Schwanken *nt*. **2** *adj head* brummend (*inf*).

re-embark [,riːɪm'bɑːk] **1** *vt* wieder einschiffen. **2** *vi* sich wieder einschiffen. **to ~ on an enterprise** ein Unternehmen von neuem beginnen.

re-embarkation [,riːembɑː'keɪʃən] *n* Wiedereinschiffung *f*.

re-emerge [,riːɪ'mɜːdʒ] *vi* (*object, swimmer*) wieder auftauchen; (*facts*) (wieder) herauskommen, sich (wieder) herausstellen, an den Tag kommen.

re-enact [,riːɪ'nækt] *vt* **(a)** (*Jur*) wieder in Kraft setzen. **(b)** (*repeat*) *scene* nachspielen; *crime, meeting* nachvollziehen; (*for police purposes*) einen Lokaltermin abhalten wegen.

re-enactment [,riːɪ'næktmənt] *n* (*of law etc*) Wiederinkraftsetzung *f*; (*of scene*) Nachspiel *nt*; (*repetition*) Nachvollzug *m*; (*of crime for police purposes*) Lokaltermin *m*.

re-engage [,riːɪn'geɪdʒ] *vt employee* wieder einstellen; (*Tech*) *gear wheels* wieder ineinandergreifen lassen; *gear* wieder einlegen; *clutch* wieder kommen lassen.

re-enlist [,riːɪn'lɪst] **1** *vi* (*Mil*) sich wieder melden or verpflichten. **2** *vt* (*Mil*) neu verpflichten. **to ~ sb's help** jds Hilfe erneut in Anspruch nehmen.

re-enter [,riː'entə'] **1** *vi* **(a)** wieder hereinkommen/hineingehen; (*walk in*) wieder eintreten; (*drive in*) wieder einfahren; (*penetrate: bullet etc*) wieder eindringen; (*climb in*) wieder einsteigen; (*cross border*) wieder einreisen; (*ship*) wieder einlaufen. **(b)** (*Theat*) wieder auftreten. **(c)** (*for race, exam etc*) sich wieder melden (*for* zu). **2** *vt* **(a)** *room* wieder hereinkommen/hineingehen in (+*acc*), wieder betreten; (*Space*) *atmosphere* wieder eintreten in (+*acc*); *club etc* wieder beitreten (+*dat*). **(b)** *name* (*on list etc*) wieder eintragen.

re-entrant [,riː'entrənt] *n* Wiederholungskandidat(in *f*) *m*.

re-entry [,riː'entrɪ] *n* **(a)** (*also Space*) Wiedereintritt *m*; (*for exam*) Wiederantritt *m* (*for* zu). **~ is timed for 16.00** der Wiedereintritt in die Erdatmosphäre ist für 16⁰⁰ festgesetzt; **~ point, point of ~** (*Space*) Wiedereintrittsstelle *f*. **(b)** (*Jur*) Wiederinbesitznahme *f*.

re-erect [,riːɪ'rekt] *vt building, bridge* wieder aufbauen; *scaffolding also* wieder aufstellen.

re-establish [,riːɪ'stæblɪʃ] *vt order* wiederherstellen; *custom* wieder einführen. **to ~ sb as sth/in a position** jdn wieder als etw/in eine Stelle einsetzen.

re-establishment [,riːɪ'stæblɪʃmənt] *n see vt* Wiederherstellung *f*; Wiedereinführung *f*; (*in a position, office*) Wiedereinsetzung *f*.

reeve[1] [riːv] *n* **(a)** (*Hist*) Vogt *m*. **(b)** (*in Canada*) = Gemeindevorsteher *m*.

reeve[2] *vt* (*Naut*) (*thread*) einscheren; (*fasten*) festmachen.

re-examination ['riːɪg,zæmɪ'neɪʃən] *n* Überprüfung *f*, erneute or nochmalige Prüfung; (*Jur: of witness*) erneute or nochmalige Vernehmung.

re-examine [,riːɪg'zæmɪn] *vt* überprüfen, erneut or nochmals prüfen; (*Jur*) *witness* erneut or nochmals vernehmen.

ref[1] [ref] *n* (*Sport inf*) *abbr of* **referee** Schiri *m* (*sl*).

ref[2] *abbr of* **reference (number)**.

refectory [rɪ'fektərɪ] *n* (*in college*) Mensa *f*; (*in monastery*) Refektorium *nt*.

refer [rɪ'fɜː'] **1** *vt* **(a)** (*pass*) *matter, problem* weiterleiten (*to an* +*acc*); *decision* übergeben (*to sb* jdm). **the dispute was ~red to arbitration** der Streit wurde einem Schiedsgericht übergeben; **it was ~red to us for** (*a*) **decision** es wurde uns (*dat*) zur Entscheidung übergeben; **I ~red him to the manager** ich verwies ihn an den Geschäftsführer; **to ~ sb to the article on ...** jdn auf den Artikel über (+*acc*) ... verweisen; **the reader is ~red to page 10** der Leser wird auf Seite 10 verwiesen; **to ~ a cheque to drawer** (*Comm*) einen Scheck an den Aussteller zurücksenden. **(b)** (*Brit Univ*) *thesis* zur Änderung zurückgeben. **2** *vi* **(a)** **to ~ to** (*allude to*) sprechen von; (*mention also*) erwähnen; (*words*) sich beziehen auf (+*acc*); **I am not ~ring to you** ich meine nicht Sie; **we shall not ~ to it again** wir wollen es nicht mehr erwähnen, wir wollen nicht mehr davon sprechen; **what can he be ~ring to?** was meint er wohl?, wovon spricht er wohl?; **the letter ~s to you all** der Brief gilt euch allen; **~ring to your letter** (*Comm*) mit Bezug auf Ihren Brief. **(b)** (*apply to*) **to ~ to** (*orders, rules*) gelten für; (*criticism, remark*) sich beziehen auf (+*acc*). **(c)** (*consult*) **to ~ to** *notes, book* nachschauen in (+*dat*), konsultieren (*geh*); **to ~ person** sich wenden an (+*acc*); **you must ~ to the original** Sie müssen aufs Original zurückgreifen.

◆**refer back** **1** *vi* (*person, remark*) sich beziehen (*to* auf +*acc*). **(b)** (*check back, consult again*) zurückgehen (*to* zu). **2** *vt sep* (*pass back*) *decision etc* zurückgeben (*to an* +*acc*). **he ~red me ~ to you** er hat mich an Sie zurückverwiesen.

referee [,refə'riː] **1** *n* **(a)** (*Ftbl, Rugby, fig*) Schiedsrichter *m*; (*Boxing*) Ringrichter *m*; (*Judo, Wrestling*) Kampfrichter *m*. **(b)** (*Jur*) Schiedsrichter *m*. **(c)** (*Brit: person giving a reference*) Referenz *f*. **to be a ~ for sb** jdm als Referenz dienen. **2** *vt* (*Sport, fig*) Schiedsrichter sein bei; *match also* (als Schieds-/Ring-/Kampfrichter) leiten; (*Ftbl also*) pfeifen (*inf*). **3** *vi* (*Sport, fig*) Schiedsrichter sein, (den) Schiedsrichter machen or spielen (inf); (Ftbl also) pfeifen (inf).

reference ['refrəns] *n* (a) (act of mentioning) Erwähnung *f* (to sb/sth jds/einer Sache); (allusion) (direct) Bemerkung *f* (to über +acc); (indirect) Anspielung *f* (to auf +acc). to make (a) ~ to sth etw erwähnen; (a) ~ was made to his illness man erwähnte seine Krankheit; ~ to any such delicate issue should be avoided eine so delikate Sache sollte nicht erwähnt werden; this was not said with ~ to you diese Worte waren nicht auf dich gemünzt; in or with ~ to was ... anbetrifft; (Comm) bezüglich (+gen); ~ your letter ... (Comm) mit Bezug auf Ihren Brief (form); without ~ to age/to one's notes ungeachtet des Alters/ohne seine Aufzeichnungen zu Hilfe zu nehmen.
(b) no pl see vt (a) (to an +acc) Weiterleitung *f*; Übergabe *f*.
(c) (testimonial: also ~s) Referenz(en pl) *f*, Zeugnis nt. to give sb a good ~ or good ~s jdm gute Referenzen or ein gutes Zeugnis ausstellen; a banker's ~ eine Bankauskunft or -referenz; I've been asked to give a ~ for him man hat mich gebeten, ihm eine Referenz zu geben.
(d) (note redirecting reader) (in book, on map etc) Verweis *m*; (Comm) Zeichen nt; see cross-reference.
(e) (connection) to have ~ to in Beziehung stehen mit or zu; this has no/little ~ to das steht in keiner/kaum in Beziehung zu.
(f) (authority, scope: of committee, tribunal) Zuständigkeitsbereich *m*; see term.
(g) (esp US) see referee 1(c).

reference: ~ book *n* Nachschlagewerk nt; ~ library *n* Präsenzbibliothek *f*; ~ mark *n* Zeichen, das auf Fußnoten hinweist; ~ number *n* Aktenzeichen nt; (of subscriber etc) Nummer *f*.

referendum [,refə'rendəm] *n*, *pl* **referenda** [,refə'rendə] Volksentscheid *m*, Referendum nt. to hold a ~ einen Volksentscheid durchführen, ein Referendum abhalten.

refill [,ri:'fɪl] **1** *vt* nachfüllen, wieder füllen.
2 ['ri:fɪl] *n* (for fountain pen, lighter) Nachfüllpatrone *f*; (for ballpoint) Nachfüll- or Ersatzmine *f*; (lipstick) Nachfüllstift *m*; (for propelling pencil) Ersatzmine *f*; (for notebook) Nachfüllblätter *pl*. would you like a ~? (inf: drink) darf ich nachschenken?; he wants another ~ er will noch einmal nachgeschenkt haben.

refine [rɪ'faɪn] *vt* (a) metal, oil, sugar raffinieren. (b) language, manners verfeinern, kultivieren; taste(s) also bilden. (c) techniques, methods verfeinern, verbessern.
♦**refine upon** *vi* +prep obj point, detail näher ausführen; method verbessern, verfeinern.

refined [rɪ'faɪnd] *adj* (a) metal, oil raffiniert, rein. ~ sugar Raffinade *f*. (b) taste fein; person, style also vornehm.

refinement [rɪ'faɪnmənt] *n* (a) no pl (of metal, oil, sugar) Raffination, Raffinierung, Reinigung *f*.
(b) no pl (of person, language, style) Vornehmheit, Feinheit *f*. a person of no ~ ein ganz unkultivierter Mensch.
(c) (improvement: in technique, machine etc) Verfeinerung, Verbesserung *f* (in sth gen). a ~ of cruelty/torture subtile Grausamkeit/Folterung.

refinery [rɪ'faɪnərɪ] *n* (metal, oil, sugar ~) Raffinerie *f*.

refit [,ri:'fɪt] **1** *vt* ship neu ausrüsten; factory neu ausstatten. **2** *vi* (ship) neu ausgerüstet werden. **3** ['ri:fɪt] *n* (Naut) Neuausrüstung *f*.

refitting [,ri:'fɪtɪŋ], **refitment** [,ri:'fɪtmənt] *n see* **refit 3**.

reflate [,ri:'fleɪt] **1** *vt* (Econ) bewußt inflationieren, ankurbeln.
2 *vi* (economy) sich beleben, angekurbelt werden. they decided to ~ man beschloß, die Konjunktur anzukurbeln.

reflation [ri:'fleɪʃən] *n* (Econ) Reflation *f*, Ankurbelung *f* der Konjunktur.

reflationary [ri:'fleɪʃnərɪ] *adj* (Econ) bewußt or gewollt inflationär.

reflect [rɪ'flekt] **1** *vt* (a) (cast back) light, image, heat, sound zurückwerfen, reflektieren; (surface of water, mirror also) spiegeln; (fig) views, reality etc widerspiegeln. the moon was ~ed in the lake der Mond spiegelte sich im See; I saw him/myself ~ed in the mirror ich sah ihn/mich im Spiegel; ~ing prism Spiegelprisma nt; to bask in ~ed glory sich in jds Glanz (dat) sonnen; the many difficulties ~ed in his report/attitude die vielen Schwierigkeiten, die sich in seinem Bericht/seiner Haltung spiegeln; to ~ credit (up)on sb ein gutes Licht auf jdn werfen; his music ~s his love for her in seiner Musik spiegelt sich seine Liebe zu ihr wider.
(b) (think) I ~ed that thus was the way of the world ich dachte bei mir, daß das eben der Lauf der Welt sei; do you ever ~ that ...? denken Sie je darüber nach, daß ...?
2 *vi* (meditate) nachdenken, reflektieren (geh) (on, about über +acc).
♦**reflect (up)on** *vi* insep etwas aussagen über (+acc); person also ein gutes/schlechtes Licht werfen auf (+acc); motives, reasons also in gutem/schlechtem Licht erscheinen lassen; reputation, sb's honour sich auswirken auf (+acc); (unfavourably) schaden (+dat), schlechtes Licht werfen auf (+acc).

reflectingly [rɪ'flektɪŋlɪ] *adv see* **reflectively.**

reflecting telescope [rɪ'flektɪŋ'telɪskəup] *n* Spiegelteleskop nt.

reflection [rɪ'flekʃən] *n* (a) no pl (reflecting) Reflexion *f*; (by surface of lake, mirror) Spiegelung *f*; (fig) Widerspiegelung *f*.
(b) (image) Spiegelbild nt, Reflexion *f*; (fig) Widerspiegelung *f*. to see one's ~ in a mirror sich im Spiegel sehen; a pale ~ of ... ein matter Abglanz (+gen).
(c) no pl (consideration) Überlegung *f*; (contemplation) Reflexion, Betrachtung *f*. (up)on ~ wenn man sich (dat) das recht überlegt; on serious ~ bei ernsthafter Überlegung; he did it without sufficient ~ er tat es, ohne richtig darüber nachzudenken.
(d) (thoughts, comments) ~s. on language Reflexionen or Betrachtungen *pl* über die Sprache.

(e) (adverse criticism) a ~ on his honour ein Schatten auf seiner Ehre; this is a ~ on your motives das zeigt Ihre Motive in schlechtem Licht; this is no ~ on your motives damit soll gar nichts über Ihre Motive gesagt sein.
(f) (Anat) Zurückbiegung *f*.

reflective [rɪ'flektɪv] *adj* (a) (Phys etc) surface reflektierend, spiegelnd; light reflektiert. (b) faculty, powers Denk-, der Reflexion; person nachdenklich. (c) (Gram) see **reflexive.**

reflectively [rɪ'flektɪvlɪ] *adv* say, speak überlegt.

reflectiveness [rɪ'flektɪvnɪs] *n* (of person) Nachdenklichkeit *f*.

reflectivity [riflek'tɪvɪtɪ] *n* (Phys) Reflexionsvermögen nt.

reflector [rɪ'flektə^r] *n* (on car, cycle) Rückstrahler *m*; (telescope) Reflektor *m*.

reflex ['ri:fleks] **1** *adj* (Physiol, Psych, Phys, fig) Reflex-; (Math) angle überstumpf. ~ action Reflex *m*; ~ camera (Phot) Spiegelreflexkamera *f*. **2** *n* (Physiol, Psych, Phys, fig) Reflex *m*; (Phys: image) Reflexion *f*; see **condition.**

reflexion [rɪ'flekʃən] *n see* **reflection.**

reflexive [rɪ'fleksɪv] (Gram) **1** *adj* reflexiv. **2** *n* Reflexiv nt.

reflexively [rɪ'fleksɪvlɪ] *adv* see adj.

refloat [,ri:'fləut] *vt* ship, business wieder flottmachen.

reflux ['ri:flʌks] *n* Rückfluß *m*.

reforestation [,ri:fɒrɪ'steɪʃən] *n* (US) see **reafforestation.**

reform[1] [rɪ'fɔ:m] **1** *n* Reform *f* (in sth gen); (of person) Besserung *f*. ~ measures Reformmaßnahmen *pl*; ~ school Besserungsanstalt *f*; see **land** ~. **2** *vt* law, institutions, services, spelling system reformieren; society also verbessern; conduct, person bessern. **3** *vi* (person) sich bessern.

reform[2], **re-form** [,ri:'fɔ:m] **1** *vt* (a) (form again) wieder bilden; (Mil) ranks, troops neu formieren. the solution has ~ed crystals aus der Lösung haben sich erneut Kristalle gebildet.
(b) (give new form to) umformen, umgestalten (into zu).
2 *vi* sich wieder or erneut bilden; (Mil) sich neu formieren.

reformable [rɪ'fɔ:məbl] *adj* person, conduct besserungsfähig.

reformation [rɪ'fɔ:meɪʃən] *n* (of person) Reformierung, Besserung *f*. the R~ die Reformation.

reformative [rɪ'fɔ:mətɪv] *adj* effect reformierend; fervour Reform-.

reformatory [rɪ'fɔ:mətərɪ] *n* Besserungsanstalt *f*.

reformed [rɪ'fɔ:md] *adj* church, spelling reformiert; person also gewandelt; behaviour gebessert. he's a ~ character er hat sich gebessert.

reformer [rɪ'fɔ:mə^r] *n* (Pol) Reformer *m*; (Rel) Reformator *m*.

reformism [rɪ'fɔ:mɪzəm] *n* Reformismus *m*.

reformist [rɪ'fɔ:mɪst] **1** *n* Reformist *m*. **2** *adj* reformistisch.

refract [rɪ'frækt] *vt* brechen.

refracting telescope [rɪ'fræktɪŋ'telɪskəup] *n* Refraktor *m*.

refraction [rɪ'frækʃən] *n* Brechung, Refraktion (spec) *f*. angle of ~ Brechungswinkel *m*.

refractive [rɪ'fræktɪv] *adj* material, surface brechend. ~ index Brechzahl *f*, Brechungsindex *m*.

refractor [rɪ'fræktə^r] *n* (a) (Phys) brechendes Medium. (b) (telescope) Refraktor *m*.

refractoriness [rɪ'fræktərɪnɪs] *n* see adj Eigensinn *m*, störrische Art; Hartnäckigkeit *f*; Hitzebeständigkeit *f*.

refractory [rɪ'fræktərɪ] *adj* (a) person eigensinnig, störrisch. (b) (Med) hartnäckig. (c) (Chem, Miner) hitzebeständig.

refrain[1] [rɪ'freɪn] *vi* please ~! bitte unterlassen Sie das!; he ~ed from comment er enthielt sich eines Kommentars; they ~ed from such measures sie sahen von solchen Maßnahmen ab; I couldn't ~ from laughing ich konnte mir das Lachen nicht verkneifen; kindly ~ from saying that in front of the children würden Sie das bitte nicht vor den Kindern sagen; please ~ from smoking bitte unterlassen Sie das Rauchen!

refrain[2] *n* (Mus, Poet, fig) Refrain *m*.

refrangible [rɪ'frændʒəbl] *adj* brechbar.

refresh [rɪ'freʃ] *vt* (drink, bath, sleep, rest) erfrischen; (meal) stärken. to ~ oneself (with drink) eine Erfrischung zu sich (dat) nehmen; (with a bath) sich erfrischen; (with food) sich stärken; (with sleep, rest) sich ausruhen; to ~ oneself with a glass of beer zur Erfrischung ein Glas Bier trinken; to ~ one's memory sein Gedächtnis auffrischen; let me ~ your memory ich will Ihrem Gedächtnis nachhelfen.

refresher [rɪ'freʃə^r] *n* (a) (Brit Jur) zusätzliches Anwaltshonorar. (b) ~ course (Univ etc) Auffrischungskurs *m*. (c) (inf: drink) to have a ~ etwas trinken.

refreshing *adj*, ~ly *adv* [rɪ'freʃɪŋ, -lɪ] (lit, fig) erfrischend.

refreshment [rɪ'freʃmənt] *n* (a) (of mind, body) Erfrischung *f*; (through food) Stärkung *f*. (b) (food, drink) (light) ~s (kleine) Erfrischungen *pl*; ~ bar or stall Büffett nt.

refrigerant [rɪ'frɪdʒərənt] **1** *n* Kühlmittel nt; (Med) kühlendes Mittel; (fluid in fridge) Kältemittel nt. **2** *adj* kühlend.

refrigerate [rɪ'frɪdʒəreɪt] *vt* (chill) kühlen; (freeze) tiefkühlen. "~ after opening" „nach dem Öffnen kühl aufbewahren".

refrigeration [rɪ,frɪdʒə'reɪʃən] *n* see vt Kühlung *f*; Tiefkühlung *f*.

refrigerator [rɪ'frɪdʒəreɪtə^r] *n* Kühlschrank, Eisschrank *m*; (room) Kühlraum *m*.

refuel [,ri:'fjuəl] *vti* auftanken.

refuelling [,ri:'fjuəlɪŋ] *n* Auftanken nt. ~ stop Zwischenstopp *m* zum Auftanken.

refuge ['refju:dʒ] *n* (a) (lit, fig) Zuflucht *f* (from vor +dat). place of ~ Zufluchtsort *m*; to seek ~ Zuflucht suchen; to take ~ Zuflucht nehmen (in in +dat), sich flüchten (in in +acc); to take ~ in lying sich in Lügen flüchten, zu Lügen Zuflucht nehmen. (b) (for climbers, pedestrians) Unterstand *m*.

refugee [,refju'dʒi:] *n* Flüchtling *m*. ~ camp Flüchtlingslager nt.

refulgence [rɪ'fʌldʒəns] *n* (liter) Strahlen nt.

refund [rɪ'fʌnd] **1** *vt* money zurückzahlen, zurückerstatten; expenses erstatten; postage vergüten, zurückerstatten.

2 [ˈriːfʌnd] n see vt Rückzahlung, Rückerstattung f; Erstattung f; Vergütung f. **they wouldn't give me a ~** man wollte mir das Geld nicht zurückgeben; **I'd like a ~ on this blouse, please** ich hätte gern mein Geld für diese Bluse zurück; **we will send (you) a ~** wir senden Ihnen das Geld zurück.

refundable [rɪˈfʌndəbl] adj money, payment(s) zurückzahlbar, zurückerstattbar. **these expenses are/postage is ~** diese Ausgaben werden erstattet/das Porto wird vergütet.

refurbish [ˌriːˈfɜːbɪʃ] vt aufpolieren; hat, dress, furniture also verschönern; house renovieren.

refurnish [ˌriːˈfɜːnɪʃ] vt neu möblieren, ummöblieren.

refusal [rɪˈfjuːzəl] n **(a)** Ablehnung f; (of offer also) Zurückweisung f; (of food, permission, visa, permit) Verweigerung f; (to do sth) Weigerung f. **to meet with or get a ~** eine Absage erhalten; **to give (sb) a flat ~** jdm eine glatte Absage erteilen; **to give sb first ~ of sth** jdm etw als erstem or zuerst anbieten; **to have (the) first ~ of sth** etw als erster angeboten bekommen. **(b)** (Show-jumping) Verweigerung f.

refuse¹ [rɪˈfjuːz] **1** vt invitation, candidate, proposal ablehnen; (stronger) abweisen, zurückweisen; offer also ausschlagen; request also abschlagen, nicht gewähren; visa, permit, permission verweigern. **to ~ to do sth** sich weigern, etw zu tun; etw nicht tun wollen; **I ~ to believe it** ich weigere mich, das zu glauben, ich glaube das einfach nicht; **I ~/he ~d to be blackmailed** ich lasse mich nicht erpressen/er wollte sich nicht erpressen lassen; **he was ~d a visa** ihm wurde kein Visum erteilt, ihm wurde das Visum verweigert; **to be ~d sth** etw nicht bekommen; **they were ~d permission (to leave)** es wurde ihnen nicht gestattet (wegzugehen), sie bekamen nicht die Erlaubnis (wegzugehen); **he ~d food** or verweigerte die Nahrungsaufnahme; **he/his request was ~d** seine Bitte wurde abgelehnt; **she ~d him** sie wies ihn ab or zurück; **the horse ~d the fence** das Pferd hat am Hindernis verweigert.

2 vi ablehnen; (to do sth) sich weigern, es ablehnen; (horse) verweigern.

refuse² [ˈrefjuːs] n Müll m; (food waste) Abfall m. **household ~** Haus(halts)müll m; **garden ~** Gartenabfälle pl.

refuse [ˈrefjuːs] in cpds Müll-; **~ bin** n Mülleimer m; **~ chute** n Müllschlucker m; **~ collection** n Müllabfuhr f; **~ collector** n Müllmann m; **~ destructor** n Müllvernichtungsanlage f; **~ disposal** n Müllbeseitigung f; **~ disposal service** n Müllabfuhr f; **~ disposal unit** n Müllzerkleinerer m; **~ dump** n Müllablageplatz m; **~ lorry** n Müllwagen m.

refutable [rɪˈfjuːtəbl] adj widerlegbar.

refutation [ˌrefjuˈteɪʃən] n Widerlegung f.

refute [rɪˈfjuːt] vt widerlegen.

regain [rɪˈgeɪn] vt **(a)** wiedererlangen; lost time aufholen; control, one's sight also wiedergewinnen; territory zurückbekommen. **to ~ one's strength/health** wieder zu Kräften kommen/wieder gesund werden; **to ~ one's footing** wieder Stand finden; (fig) wieder auf die Beine kommen; **to ~ possession of sth** wieder in den Besitz einer Sache (gen) gelangen. **(b)** (reach again) main road/firm ground wieder gelangen an (+acc)/auf (+acc).

regal [ˈriːgəl] adj königlich; (fig) hoheitsvoll.

regale [rɪˈgeɪl] vt (with food, drink) verwöhnen; (with stories) ergötzen (geh).

regalia [rɪˈgeɪlɪə] npl Insignien pl. **she was in full ~** (hum) sie war in großer Gala or Aufmachung (hum).

regally [ˈriːgəlɪ] adv königlich; say hoheitsvoll.

regard [rɪˈgɑːd] **1** vt **(a)** (consider) betrachten. **to ~ sb/sth as sth** jdn/etw für etw halten, jdn/etw als etw betrachten; **to ~ sb/sth with favour** jdn/etw wohlwollend betrachten; **to ~ sth with horror** mit Schrecken an etw (acc) denken; **to be ~ed as ... als ...** angesehen werden; **he is ~ed as a great poet** er wird als großer Dichter angesehen, er gilt als großer Dichter; **it's not generally ~ed as worth doing** es wird im allgemeinen angenommen, daß sich das nicht lohnt; **we ~ it as worth doing** wir glauben, daß es sich lohnt(, das zu tun); **we don't ~ it as necessary/our responsibility** wir halten es nicht für notwendig/wir betrachten es nicht als unsere Verantwortung; **to ~ sb/sth highly or with great esteem** jdn/etw hochschätzen or sehr schätzen; **he is highly ~ed** er ist hoch angesehen; **his work is highly ~ed** seine Arbeit wird sehr geschätzt; **he is generally ~ed with great esteem** er wird allgemein sehr geschätzt. **(b)** (concern) **as ~s that/him/your application** was das/ihn/Ihren Antrag betrifft or anbelangt; see also **regarding**. **(c)** (liter: look at) betrachten. **(d)** (heed) berücksichtigen. **without ~ing his wishes** ohne Rücksicht auf seine Wünsche.

2 n **(a)** (attention, concern) Rücksicht f (for auf +acc). **to have some ~ for sb/sth** auf jdn/etw Rücksicht nehmen; **to show little/no ~ for sb/sth** wenig/keine Rücksichtnahme für jdn/etw zeigen; **with no ~ for his safety** ohne Rücksicht auf seine Sicherheit (zu nehmen); **without ~ to or for her advice/what people might think** ohne sich um ihren Rat zu kümmern/ohne sich darum zu kümmern, was die Leute denken mochten. **(b)** in this ~ diesbezüglich (form), in diesem Zusammenhang; **with or in ~ to** in bezug auf (+acc). **(c)** (respect) Achtung f. **to hold sb in high ~** jdn achten or sehr schätzen; **to have a great ~ for sb** jdn hochachten. **(d)** ~s pl (in message) Gruß m. **to send sb one's ~s** jdn grüßen lassen; **give him my ~s** grüßen Sie ihn von mir; **(kindest) ~s, with kind ~s** mit freundlichen Grüßen. **(e)** (liter: look) Blick m.

regardful [rɪˈgɑːdfʊl] adj (form) ~ of (one's) duty sich (dat) seiner Pflicht (gen) bewußt, pflichtbewußt; **to be ~ of sb's feelings/the interests of State** jds Gefühle achten or respektieren/die Staatsinteressen wahren.

regarding [rɪˈgɑːdɪŋ] prep in bezug auf (+acc), bezüglich (+gen).

regardless [rɪˈgɑːdlɪs] **1** adj ~ of ohne Rücksicht auf (+acc), ungeachtet (+gen); **to do sth ~ of the consequences** etw ohne Rücksicht auf die Folgen tun; ~ **of what it costs** egal, was es kostet; ~ **of the fact that ...** ungeachtet dessen, daß ... **2** adv trotzdem. **he did it ~** er hat es trotzdem getan.

regatta [rɪˈgætə] n Regatta f.

regd abbr of **registered** reg.

regency [ˈriːdʒənsɪ] n Regentschaft f. **the R~ (period)** (Brit Art etc) der Regency; **R~ furniture/style** Regencymöbel pl/-stil m.

regenerate [rɪˈdʒenəreɪt] **1** vt **(a)** (renew, re-create) erneuern; tissue also neu bilden, regenerieren. **to be ~d** sich erneuern; sich neu bilden, sich regenerieren; (fig: person) (by holiday etc) sich erholen; (esp Rel) erneuert werden. **(b)** (Elec) rückkoppeln. **2** vi (esp Sci) sich regenerieren; (tissue also) sich neu bilden. **3** [rɪˈdʒenərɪt] adj regeneriert.

regeneration [rɪˌdʒenəˈreɪʃən] n see vb Erneuerung f; Neubildung, Regeneration f; Erholung f; Erneuerung f; Rückkoppelung f.

regenerative [rɪˈdʒenərətɪv] adj **(a)** tissue sich regenerierend; (esp Rel) erneuernd. **(b)** (Elec) positiv rückgekoppelt.

regent [ˈriːdʒənt] n Regent m; (US Univ) Mitglied nt des Universitäts- or Schulverwaltungsrats; see **prince**.

reggae [ˈregeɪ] n Reggae m.

regicide [ˈredʒɪsaɪd] n (act) Königsmord m; (person) Königsmörder(in f) m.

regime [reɪˈʒiːm] n **(a)** (Pol) Regime nt; (fig: management, social system etc) System nt. **(b)** see **regimen**.

regimen [ˈredʒɪmen] n (Med) Kur f.

regiment [ˈredʒɪmənt] **1** n (Mil) Regiment nt; (fig) Kompanie f. **2** vt (fig) reglementieren.

regimental [ˌredʒɪˈmentl] **1** adj (Mil) Regiments-. **2** n ~s pl (Mil) Uniform f; (of particular regiment) Regimentsuniform f.

regimentation [ˌredʒɪmenˈteɪʃən] n (fig) Reglementierung f.

region [ˈriːdʒən] n (of country) Gebiet nt, Region f (also Admin, TV); (of body) Gegend, Region f; (of atmosphere, fig) Bereich m. **the lower ~s** die Unterwelt; **in the ~ of 5 kg** um die 5 kg.

regional [ˈriːdʒənl] adj regional. ~ **development** Gebietserschließung f; ~ **television** Regionalfernsehen nt.

regionalism [ˈriːdʒənəlɪzəm] n Regionalismus m; (division into regions) Einteilung f in Regionen; (loyalty) Lokalpatriotismus m; (word also) nur regional verwendeter Ausdruck.

regionalist [ˈriːdʒənəlɪst] **1** adj regionalistisch. **2** n Regionalist(in f) m.

register [ˈredʒɪstəʳ] **1** n **(a)** (book) Register nt; (at school) Namensliste f; (in hotel) Gästebuch nt; (of members etc) Mitgliedsbuch nt. **to take the ~** die Namen aufrufen; **electoral ~** Wählerverzeichnis nt; ~ **of births, deaths and marriages** Personenstandsbuch nt; ~ **of wills** (US: person) Testamentsbeamte(r) m. **(b)** (Tech) (recording device) Registriergerät nt; (for controlling airflow) Klappe f; see **cash ~**. **(c)** (Mus) Register nt; (organ stop) Registerzug m. **(d)** (Ling) (Sprach)ebene f, Register nt (geh). **(e)** (Typ) Register nt.

2 vt **(a)** (authorities: record formally) registrieren; (in book, files) eintragen; fact, figure also erfassen. **he is ~ed as disabled** er ist anerkannter Schwerbeschädigter; see **registered**. **(b)** (individual: have recorded) birth, marriage, death, (Comm) company, trademark anmelden, eintragen lassen; vehicle, child at school etc, candidate anmelden; student einschreiben. **to ~ a protest** Protest anmelden. **(c)** (indicate) (machines) speed, quantity, rainfall, temperature registrieren; (face, expression) happiness, disapproval zum Ausdruck bringen. **he ~ed surprise** or zeigte sich überrascht; **he ~ed no emotion** er zeigte keine Gefühlsbewegung. **(d)** (Typ) in Register bringen. **(e)** (Post) letter einschreiben; see **registered**. **(f)** (realize) registrieren. **I ~ed the fact that he had gone** ich registrierte, daß er gegangen war.

3 vi **(a)** (on electoral list etc) sich eintragen; (in hotel) sich anmelden; (student) sich einschreiben, sich immatrikulieren. **to ~ with a doctor/dentist** sich bei einem Arzt/Zahnarzt auf die Patientenliste setzen lassen; **to ~ with the police** sich polizeilich melden; **to ~ for military service** sich zum Militärdienst melden; **to ~ for a course/for maths** einen Kurs/Mathematik belegen. **(b)** (Tech) (part of machine) passen (with zu); (two parts) zueinander passen. **(c)** (Typ) Register halten. **(d)** (inf: be understood) **it hasn't ~ed (with him)** er hat es noch nicht registriert.

registered [ˈredʒɪstəd] adj **(a)** student eingeschrieben; voter, company, name eingetragen; vehicle amtlich zugelassen. ~ **nurse** (US) staatlich geprüfte Krankenschwester, staatlich geprüfter Pfleger; ~ **shareholder** Inhaber m von Namensaktien; ~ **trademark** gesetzlich geschütztes Warenzeichen, eingetragenes Warenzeichen. **(b)** (Post) letter eingeschrieben, Einschreib-. **by ~ post** per Einschreiben.

register ton n (Naut) Registertonne f.

registrar [ˌredʒɪˈstrɑːʳ] n (Admin) Standesbeamte(r) m; (Univ) höchster Verwaltungsbeamter, Kanzler m; (Med) Krankenhausarzt m/-ärztin f. ~'s **office** (Brit Admin) Standesamt nt; **to be married by the ~** sich standesamtlich trauen lassen.

registration [ˌredʒɪˈstreɪʃən] n see vt **(a)** Registrierung f; Eintragung f; Erfassung f. **(b)** Anmeldung f; Einschreibung f. ~ **fee** Anmeldegebühr f; (for evening class) Kursgebühr f; (Univ) Einschreib(e)gebühr f; ~ **number** (Aut) Kraftfahrzeugkennzeichen nt, polizeiliches Kennzeichen; ~ **document** (Aut) Kraftfahrzeugbrief m.

(c) Registrierung f; Ausdruck m.
(d) Aufgabe f als Einschreiben. ~ **fee** Einschreibegebühr f.
registry ['redʒɪstrɪ] n Sekretariat nt; (in church) Sakristei f; (Brit: also ~ **office**) Standesamt nt. **to get married in a ~ office** standesamtlich heiraten; **port of ~** Heimathafen m.
regius ['riːdʒəs] adj: (Brit Univ) ~ **professor** Inhaber m eines von einem Monarchen eingerichteten Lehrstuhls.
regorge [rɪ'gɔːdʒ] 1 vt (form) erbrechen. 2 vi sich ergießen.
regress [rɪ'gres] vi (lit form: move backwards) sich rückwärts bewegen; (fig) (society) sich rückläufig entwickeln; (Biol, Psych, Med) sich zurückentwickeln. **he is** ~ing **into childhood** er fällt wieder ins Kindesalter zurück.
regression [rɪ'greʃən] n (lit form) see vt Rückwärtsbewegung f; rückläufige Entwicklung; Zurückentwicklung f. **his ~ into his childhood** sein Rückfall in die Kindheit.
regressive [rɪ'gresɪv] adj regressiv; trend rückläufig.
regret [rɪ'gret] 1 vt bedauern; one's youth, lost opportunity nachtrauern (+dat). **I ~ that we will not be coming** ich bedauere, daß wir nicht kommen können; **I ~ to say that ...** ich muß Ihnen leider mitteilen, daß ...; **he is very ill, I ~ to say** er ist leider or bedauerlicherweise sehr krank; **we ~ to hear that ...** wir hören mit Bedauern, daß ...; **it is to be ~ted that ...** es ist bedauerlich, daß ...; **you won't ~ it!** Sie werden es nicht bereuen; **the President ~s he cannot see you today** der Präsident bedauert, Sie heute nicht empfangen zu können; **he is much ~ted** er wird sehr vermißt.
2 n Bedauern nt no pl. **to feel ~ for one's past** youth seiner vergangenen Jugend (dat) nachtrauern; **much to my ~** sehr zu meinem Bedauern; **I have no ~s** ich bereue nichts; **to do sth with ~** (sadly) etw mit Bedauern tun; (reluctantly) etw widerstrebend tun; **please give her my ~s that I cannot come** bitte, sagen Sie ihr, daß ich leider nicht kommen kann; **he sends his ~s** er läßt sich entschuldigen, er muß leider absagen.
regretful [rɪ'gretfʊl] adj look, attitude bedauernd attr. **he was extremely ~** es tat ihm sehr leid, er bedauerte es sehr.
regretfully [rɪ'gretfəlɪ] adv (sadly) mit Bedauern; (reluctantly) widerstrebend. **very ~ I must announce ...** sehr zu meinem Bedauern muß ich bekanntgeben, ...
regrettable [rɪ'gretəbl] adj bedauerlich.
regrettably [rɪ'gretəblɪ] adv bedauerlicherweise, leider. **a ~ poor turnout** eine bedauerlich schwache Beteiligung.
regroup [ˌriː'gruːp] 1 vt um- or neugruppieren. 2 vi sich umgruppieren, sich neu gruppieren.
regrouping [ˌriː'gruːpɪŋ] n see vt Um- or Neugruppierung f.
regt abbr of **regiment** Reg.
regular ['regjʊlə'] 1 adj **(a)** (symmetrical) regelmäßig; features also ebenmäßig; surface gleichmäßig; (Geometry) gleichseitig.
(b) (recurring at even intervals) service, bus, reminders regelmäßig; footsteps also gleichmäßig; employment fest, regulär; way of life, bowel movements geregelt. **is the bus ~?** fährt der Bus regelmäßig?; **to be ~ in one's habits** ein geregeltes Leben führen; **to eat ~ meals** regelmäßig essen; **to keep ~ hours** feste Zeiten haben; **she is as ~ as clockwork** bei ihr geht alles auf die Minute genau; **his visits are as ~ as ~ as** clockwork nach seinen Besuchen kann man die Uhr stellen.
(c) (habitual) size, price, time normal; staff, customer, pub, butcher Stamm-; listener, reader regelmäßig. **our ~ cleaning woman** unsere normale Reinemachefrau; **my ~ dentist** mein Hauszahnarzt m.
(d) (permissible, accepted) action, procedure richtig. ~ **procedure demands that ...** der Ordnung halber muß man ...; **it is quite ~ to apply in person** es ist ganz in Ordnung, sich persönlich zu bewerben.
(e) (Mil) soldier, army, officer Berufs-, regulär.
(f) (Gram) noun, declension regelmäßig.
(g) (Rel) ~ **clergy** Ordensgeistlichkeit f.
(h) (inf) echt (inf). **he's a ~ idiot** er ist ein regelrechter Idiot; ~ **guy** (US) ein klasse or echter Kerl (inf).
2 n (Mil) Berufssoldat m, regulärer Soldat; (habitual customer etc) Stammkunde m, Stammkundin f; (in pub, hotel) Stammgast m. **he's one of the ~s on that programme** er ist einer der Stammgäste dieser Sendung.
regularity [ˌregjʊ'lærɪtɪ] n **(a)** see adj **(a)** Regelmäßigkeit f; Ebenmäßigkeit f; Gleichmäßigkeit f; Gleichseitigkeit f. **(b)** see adj **(b)** Regelmäßigkeit f; Gleichmäßigkeit f; Festheit f; Geregeltheit f. **(c)** see adj **(d)** Richtigkeit f. **(d)** (Gram) Regelmäßigkeit f.
regularize ['regjʊləraɪz] vt breathing, service regulieren; situation, relationship normalisieren.
regularly ['regjʊləlɪ] adv regelmäßig; breathe, beat also gleichmäßig.
regulate ['regjʊleɪt] vt **(a)** (control) regulieren; flow, expenditure also, traffic, life-style regeln. **these things happen in even the best ~d families** so etwas kommt in den besten Familien vor. **(b)** machine, mechanism regulieren; clock richtig stellen.
regulation [ˌregjʊ'leɪʃən] 1 n **(a)** (regulating) see vt Regulierung f; Regelung f. **(b)** (rule) Vorschrift f. **the ~s of the society** die Satzung der Gesellschaft; **according to (the)** ~s laut Vorschrift/Satzung; **to be contrary to or against (the)** ~s gegen die Vorschrift(en)/Satzung verstoßen; **fire/safety ~s** Feuer-/Sicherheitsvorschriften pl.
2 attr boots, dress vorgeschrieben. **army ~ boots** vorgeschriebene Armeestiefel pl.
regulative ['regjʊlətɪv] adj regulativ, regulierend.
regulator ['regjʊleɪtə'] n (instrument) Regler m; (in clock, watch) Gangregler m; (for manual adjustment) Rücker m.
regurgitate [rɪ'gɜːdʒɪteɪt] vt wieder hochbringen, wieder von sich geben (fig); information wiederkäuen. **this animal's young feed on ~d insects** die Jungen dieses Tiers leben von vorverdauten Insekten.

regurgitation [rɪˌgɜːdʒɪ'teɪʃən] n see vt Wiederhochbringen nt; Wiederkäuen nt.
rehabilitate [ˌriːə'bɪlɪteɪt] vt **(a)** (to everyday life) refugee, demobilized troops (in die Gesellschaft) eingliedern; ex-criminal, the disabled also rehabilitieren. **(b)** (restore position to) rehabilitieren.
rehabilitation ['riːəˌbɪlɪ'teɪʃən] n see vt Eingliederung f in die Gesellschaft; Rehabilitation f. ~ **centre** (Admin) Rehabilitationszentrum nt.
rehash [riː'hæʃ] 1 vt literary material etc aufbereiten. 2 ['riːhæʃ] n (action) Aufbereitung f; (result) Aufguß m.
rehearsal [rɪ'hɜːsəl] n **(a)** (Theat, Mus) Probe f. **this play is in ~** das Stück wird geprobt. **(b)** (recital: of facts) Aufzählung f.
rehearse [rɪ'hɜːs] 1 vt **(a)** (Theat, Mus) play, concert proben; person proben lassen. **to ~ what one is going to say** einüben, was man sagen will. **(b)** (recite) facts, grievances aufzählen. 2 vi proben.
reheat [ˌriː'hiːt] vt aufwärmen.
rehouse [ˌriː'hauz] vt unterbringen.
reify ['reɪfaɪ] vt verdinglichen, reifizieren (Philos).
reign [reɪn] 1 n (lit, fig) Herrschaft f; (of monarch also) Regentschaft f. **Queen Victoria had a long ~** Königin Viktoria übte eine lange Herrschaft aus; **the R~ of Terror** die Schreckensherrschaft. 2 vi (lit, fig) herrschen (over über +acc). **silence ~s** es herrscht Ruhe; see **supreme**.
reigning ['reɪnɪŋ] adj attr regierend; champion herrschend, amtierend (hum). **the ~ beauty** die Schönheitskönigin.
reimburse [ˌriːɪm'bɜːs] vt person entschädigen; loss ersetzen; expenses, costs (zurück)erstatten, ersetzen. **to ~ sb for his expenses** jdm die Auslagen zurückerstatten.
reimbursement [ˌriːɪm'bɜːsmənt] n see vt Entschädigung f; Ersatz m; (Rück)erstattung f, Ersatz m.
reimport [ˌriːɪm'pɔːt] vt wiedereinführen, reimportieren.
reimpose [ˌriːɪm'pəuz] vt task, conditions neu aufzwingen or auferlegen (on sb jdm); sanctions, fine erneut verhängen (on gegen); one's will, authority erneut aufzwingen (on sb jdm). **to ~ a tax on sth** etw erneut besteuern.
rein [reɪn] n (lit, fig) Zügel m. ~s (for child) Laufgurt m; **to hold the ~s** (lit, fig) die Zügel or das Heft in der Hand haben; **he kept the horse on a long/short** ~ er ließ die Zügel lang/hielt die Zügel kurz; **to keep a tight ~ on sb/sth** (lit, fig) bei jdm/etw die Zügel kurz halten; **to give free ~ to sb/sth, to allow sb/sth free ~** (fig) jdm/einer Sache freien Lauf lassen (+dat).
♦**rein back** vti sep zügeln.
♦**rein in** 1 vt sep horse zügeln; (fig) passions also im Zaum halten. **to ~ the horse ~ to a trot/canter** das Pferd im Trab/leichten Galopp gehen lassen. 2 vi zügeln.
♦**rein up** vti sep zügeln.
reincarnate [ˌriːɪn'kɑːneɪt] 1 vt reinkarnieren (liter). **to be ~d** wiedergeboren werden; **the belief that man is ~d** (after death) der Glaube an die Reinkarnation des Menschen or an die Wiedergeburt. 2 [ˌriːɪn'kɑːnɪt] adj wiedergeboren.
reincarnation [ˌriːɪnkɑː'neɪʃən] n die Wiedergeburt, die Reinkarnation.
reindeer ['reɪndɪə'] n, pl - Ren(tier) nt. **Rudolph the red-nosed ~** Rudolf Rotnase m.
reinforce [ˌriːɪn'fɔːs] vt (lit, fig, Psych) verstärken; concrete also armieren (spec); sb's demands stärken, stützen; evidence, statement stützen, bestätigen; opinion bestätigen. **to ~ sb's decision/determination** jdn in seiner Entscheidung/Absicht bestärken; ~d concrete Stahlbeton m.
reinforcement [ˌriːɪn'fɔːsmənt] n **(a)** no pl (act) see vt Verstärkung f; Armierung f; Stärkung, Stützung f; Bestätigung f. ~ **troops** (Mil) Verstärkungstruppen pl. **(b)** (thing) Verstärkung f. ~s (Mil, fig) Verstärkung f.
reinsert [ˌriːɪn'sɜːt] vt wieder einfügen; thermometer wieder einführen; coin wieder einwerfen; filing card zurückstecken; needle wieder einstecken; zip wieder einsetzen. **to ~ an advert in a paper** erneut in einer Zeitung inserieren.
reinstate [ˌriːɪn'steɪt] vt person wieder einstellen (in in +acc); law and order wiederherstellen (in in +dat).
reinstatement [ˌriːɪn'steɪtmənt] n see vt Wiedereinstellung f; Wiederherstellung f.
reinsurance [ˌriːɪn'ʃuərəns] n Weiterversicherung f.
reinsure [ˌriːɪn'ʃuə'] vt weiterversichern.
reintegrate [ˌriː'ɪntɪgreɪt] vt wiedereingliedern, wieder or erneut integrieren (into in +acc).
reintegration ['riːˌɪntɪ'greɪʃən] n Wiedereingliederung, Reintegration f.
reissue [ˌriː'ɪʃuː] 1 vt book neu auflegen; stamps, recording, coins neu herausgeben. 2 n see vt Neuauflage f; Neuausgabe f.
reiterate [riː'ɪtəreɪt] vt wiederholen.
reiteration [riːˌɪtə'reɪʃən] n Wiederholung f.
reiterative [riː'ɪtərətɪv] adj comments sich wiederholend attr; style repetitiv.
reject [rɪ'dʒekt] 1 vt **(a)** damaged goods etc (customer) ablehnen, zurückweisen; (maker, producer) aussortieren, ausschießen.
(b) (turn down) application, request etc ablehnen; (stronger) abweisen, zurückweisen; candidate (through vote) durchfallen lassen; suitor, advances abweisen, zurückweisen; plea also abschlagen; possibility verwerfen.
(c) (Med) food nicht vertragen, ablehnen; transplant also abstoßen; (stomach) food verweigern.
2 ['riːdʒekt] n (Comm) Ausschuß m no pl. ~ **goods** Ausschußware f; **society's** ~s die Ausgestoßenen pl.
rejection [rɪ'dʒekʃən] n see vt **(a)** Ablehnung, Zurückweisung f; Aussortierung, Ausschießung f.
(b) Ablehnung f; Abweisung, Zurückweisung f; Abweisung, Zurückweisung f; Verwerfen nt. ~ **slip** Absage f.
(c) (Med) Ablehnung f; Abstoßung f; Verweigerung f.

rejoice [rɪ'dʒɔɪs] **1** vt (liter) person erfreuen. **2** vi sich freuen; (jubilate) jubeln; (Rel) jauchzen. ~ **in the Lord!** freut euch im Herrn!; **he ~s in the name of Marmaduke** (hum) er erfreut sich des Namens Marmaduke.

rejoicing [rɪ'dʒɔɪsɪŋ] n Jubel m. **~s** Jubel m.

rejoin[1] [ˌriː'dʒɔɪn] vt person, regiment sich wieder anschließen (+dat). **to ~ ship** (Naut) wieder aufs Schiff kommen; **then we ~ed the motorway** danach kamen wir wieder auf die Autobahn; **the road ~s the motorway** die Straße trifft wieder auf die Autobahn.

rejoin[2] [rɪ'dʒɔɪn] vt (reply) erwidern; (Jur) duplizieren.

rejoinder [rɪ'dʒɔɪndə'] n Erwiderung f; (Jur) Duplik f.

rejuvenate [rɪ'dʒuːvɪneɪt] vt verjüngen; (fig) erfrischen.

rekindle [ˌriː'kɪndl] **1** vt (lit) fire, flame wieder anzünden; (fig) passions, love wieder entzünden or entflammen; hope wiedererwecken. **2** vi (lit) wieder aufflackern; (fig) (passion, love also) wieder entflammen; (hope) wiedererwachen.

relapse [rɪ'læps] **1** n (Med) Rückfall, Rückschlag m; (fig) (in economy) Rückschlag m; (into vice, crime) Rückfall m (into in +acc). **to have a ~** einen Rückfall haben.
2 vi (Med) einen Rückfall haben; (economy) einen Rückschlag erleiden. **to ~ (into crime/vice)** rückfällig werden; **to ~ into unconsciousness** wieder bewußtlos werden.

relate [rɪ'leɪt] **1** vt **(a)** (recount) story erzählen; details aufzählen. **strange to ~** so unglaublich es klingt.
(b) (associate) in Verbindung or Beziehung or Zusammenhang bringen (to, with mit). **to try to ~ events** (to each other) versuchen, die Dinge im Zusammenhang zu sehen; **it is often difficult to ~ the cause to the effect** der Zusammenhang zwischen Ursache und Wirkung ist oft schwer zu erkennen.
2 vi **(a)** zusammenhängen (to mit).
(b) (form relationship) eine Beziehung finden (to zu).

related [rɪ'leɪtɪd] adj **(a)** (in family) verwandt (to mit). **(b)** (connected) zusammenhängend; elements, theories, languages etc verwandt. **to be ~ to sth** mit etw zusammenhängen/verwandt sein.

relating [rɪ'leɪtɪŋ] adj **~ to** in Zusammenhang mit.

relation [rɪ'leɪʃən] n **(a)** (relative) Verwandte(r) mf. **he's a/no ~ (of mine)** er ist/ist nicht mit mir verwandt; **what ~ is she to you?** wie ist sie mit Ihnen verwandt?; **is he any ~ to you?** ist er mit Ihnen verwandt?
(b) (relationship) Beziehung f. **to bear a ~ to** in Beziehung stehen zu; **to bear no ~ to** in keinerlei Beziehung stehen zu, keinerlei Beziehung haben zu; **in ~ to** (as regards) in bezug auf (+acc); (compared with) im Verhältnis zu.
(c) **~s** pl (dealings, ties, sexual **~s**) Beziehungen pl; **to have business ~s with sb** geschäftliche Beziehungen zu jdm haben; **~s are rather strained** die Beziehungen sind etwas gespannt.
(d) no pl (of story) Erzählung f; (of details) Aufzählung f.

relationship [rɪ'leɪʃənʃɪp] n **(a)** Verwandtschaft f (to mit). **what is your ~ (to him)?** wie sind Sie (mit ihm) verwandt?
(b) (connection: between events etc) Beziehung, Verbindung f; (relations) Verhältnis nt, Beziehungen pl; (in business) Verbindung f. **to have a (sexual) ~ with** ein Verhältnis haben mit; **what kind of a ~ do you have with him?** (is it good or bad) wie ist Ihr Verhältnis zu ihm?; (on what footing) in welchem Verhältnis stehen Sie zu ihm?; **to have a good ~ with sb** ein gutes Verhältnis or gute Beziehungen zu jdm haben; **they have a good ~** sie haben ein gutes Verhältnis (zueinander); **friendly ~** freundschaftliches Verhältnis; **we have a business ~** wir haben geschäftlich miteinander zu tun; **it is a strictly business ~** es ist eine rein geschäftliche Beziehung.

relative ['relətɪv] **1** adj **(a)** (comparative, not absolute, Sci) relativ; (respective) respektiv. **happiness is ~** Glück ist relativ; **~ to him, she is in a very happy position** verglichen mit ihm ist sie gut dran; **fuel consumption is ~ to speed** der Benzinverbrauch hängt von der Geschwindigkeit ab; **to live in ~ luxury** verhältnismäßig or relativ luxuriös leben; **the ~ merits of A and B** die respektiven Verdienste von A und B.
(b) (relevant) **~ to** sich beziehend auf (+acc); **the documents ~ to the problem** die mit dem Problem befaßten (geh) or sich auf das Problem beziehenden Dokumente.
(c) (Gram) pronoun, clause Relativ-.
(d) (Mus) minor, major parallel.
2 n **(a)** (person) see relation (a).
(b) (Gram) (clause) Relativsatz m; (pronoun) Relativpronomen nt.

relatively ['relətɪvlɪ] adv relativ, verhältnismäßig. **~ speaking** relativ.

relativism ['relətɪvɪzəm] n Relativismus m.

relativist ['relətɪvɪst] n Relativist(in f) m.

relativistic [ˌrelətɪ'vɪstɪk] adj relativistisch.

relativity [ˌrelə'tɪvɪtɪ] n (Phys, Philos) Relativität f. **~ theory, the theory of ~** die Relativitätstheorie.

relax [rɪ'læks] **1** vt lockern; muscles also, person, one's mind entspannen; attention, effort nachlassen in (+dat). **to ~ the bowels** (Med) den Stuhlgang fördern; **his face ~ed into a smile** sein Gesicht entspannte sich zu einem Lächeln.
2 vi (entspannen; (rest) (sich) ausruhen; (calm down) sich beruhigen. **let's just ~!** ganz ruhig!; **~! reg dich nicht auf!**, immer mit der Ruhe!

relaxant [rɪ'læksənt] n (Med) Relaxans nt.

relaxation [ˌriːlæk'seɪʃən] n **(a)** see vt Lockerung f; Entspannung f; Nachlassen nt.
(b) (rest) Entspannung f; (recreation also) Erholung f. **you need some ~ after work** Sie sollten sich nach der Arbeit entspannen; Sie brauchen ein wenig Erholung nach der Arbeit; **books are her ~** zur Entspannung or Erholung liest sie.

relaxed [rɪ'lækst] adj locker; person, smile, voice entspannt, ruhig; atmosphere zwanglos, gelockert; throat (Med) angegriffen. **to feel ~** (physically) entspannt sein; (mentally)

sich wohl fühlen; **to feel ~ about sth** etw ganz gelassen sehen.

relaxing [rɪ'læksɪŋ] adj entspannend; climate erholsam.

relay ['riːleɪ] **1** n **(a)** (of workers etc) Ablösung f; (of horses) frisches Gespann. **to work in ~s** sich ablösen. **(b)** (Sport: also ~ race) Staffel(lauf m) f. **(c)** (Rad, TV) Relais nt. **2** vt **(a)** (Rad, TV etc) programme, signal (weiter)übertragen. **(b)** message ausrichten (to sb jdm).

re-lay [ˌriː'leɪ] vt carpet, cable neu verlegen.

release [rɪ'liːs] **1** vt **(a)** animal, person freilassen; (from prison also) entlassen; employee, football player etc freigeben; (rescue) befreien; (from obligation, promise, vow) entbinden, befreien; (from pain) erlösen. **to ~ sb on bail** (Jur) jdn gegen Kaution freilassen; **to ~ sb from a debt** jdm eine Schuld erlassen; **can you ~ him for a few hours each week?** können Sie ihn für ein paar Stunden pro Woche freistellen?
(b) (let go of) loslassen; spring also zurückspringen lassen; handbrake losmachen; (Phot) shutter auslösen; bomb abwerfen; grip, clasp lösen; (police) confiscated articles freigeben. **to ~ the (foot)brake/clutch** den Fuß von der Bremse/Kupplung nehmen, die Kupplung kommen lassen; **to ~ one's hold** or **grip (on sth)** (etw) loslassen.
(c) (Comm: issue) film, goods herausbringen; record also veröffentlichen.
(d) (make known) news, statement veröffentlichen.
(e) (emit) gas, energy freisetzen; smell ausströmen; (let off, into atmosphere) pressure, steam ablassen.
(f) (Jur) property, title aufgeben, verzichten auf (+acc).
2 n see vt **(a)** Freilassung f; Entlassung f; Freigabe f; Befreiung f; Entbindung, Befreiung f; Erlösung f. **death was a happy ~ for him** der Tod war eine Erlösung für ihn.
(b) (act) Loslassen nt; Lösen nt; Auslösen nt; Abwurf m; Lösen nt; Freigabe f; (mechanism) Auslöser m; see shutter.
(c) (act) Herausbringen nt; Veröffentlichung f; (film) Film m; (record) Platte f. **this film is now on general ~** dieser Film ist nun überall zu sehen; **a new ~ from the Beatles/XYZ Films Inc.** eine Neuerscheinung der Beatles/ein neu herausgekommener Film der XYZ Filmgesellschaft.
(d) (act) Veröffentlichung f; (statement) Verlautbarung f.
(e) Freisetzung f. **~ valve** Entlastungsventil nt.
(f) Aufgabe f (of gen), Verzicht m (of auf +acc).

relegate ['relɪgeɪt] vt **(a)** (lit, fig: downgrade) degradieren; (Sport) team absteigen lassen (to in +acc); old toys, furniture verbannen (to in +acc). **to be ~d** (Sport) absteigen; **~d to second place** (fig) auf zweite Stelle abgeschoben or verbannt.
(b) (hand over) matter, question weiterleiten (to an +acc).

relegation [ˌrelɪ'geɪʃən] n see vt **(a)** Degradierung f; Abstieg m; Verbannung f. **(b)** Weiterleitung f.

relent [rɪ'lent] vi (person) nachgeben; (pace, pain) nachlassen; (weather) sich bessern.

relentless [rɪ'lentlɪs] adj erbarmungslos; person also unerbittlich; attitude, opposition also unnachgiebig; pain, cold nicht nachlassend.

relentlessly [rɪ'lentlɪslɪ] adv unerbittlich, erbarmungslos; oppose, maintain unnachgiebig; hurt, rain unaufhörlich.

relet [ˌriː'let] vt neu vermieten.

relevance ['reləvəns], **relevancy** ['relɪvənsɪ] n Relevanz f. **what is the ~ of your question to the problem?** inwiefern ist Ihre Frage für das Problem relevant?

relevant ['reləvənt] adj relevant (to für); information, document also entsprechend attr, sachdienlich (form); course, study also sachbezogen; authority, person zuständig. **a course ~ to one's studies** ein studienbezogener or für sein Studium relevanter Kurs; **that is not ~** das ist nicht relevant, das gehört nicht zur Sache; **the police are looking for any ~ information** die Polizei bittet um sachdienliche Hinweise.

reliability [rɪˌlaɪə'bɪlɪtɪ] n see adj Zuverlässigkeit f; Verläßlichkeit f; Seriosität, Vertrauenswürdigkeit f.

reliable [rɪ'laɪəbl] adj zuverlässig; person also verläßlich; firm, company serio, vertrauenswürdig.

reliably [rɪ'laɪəblɪ] adv zuverlässig. **I am ~ informed that ...** ich weiß aus zuverlässiger Quelle, daß ...

reliance [rɪ'laɪəns] n (trust, confidence) Vertrauen nt (on auf +acc). **to place ~ on sth** sich auf etw (acc) verlassen; **his ~ on his memory rather than his notes always gets him into difficulties** er verläßt sich auf sein Gedächtnis statt auf seine Notizen und kommt dadurch immer in Schwierigkeiten.

reliant [rɪ'laɪənt] adj (dependent) angewiesen (on, upon auf +acc); see self-reliant.

relic ['relɪk] n Überbleibsel, Relikt nt; (Rel) Reliquie f. **a ~ of** or **from a past age** ein Überbleibsel aus vergangener Zeit; **an old ~** (pej inf) (person) ein alter Knochen (inf); (car, wardrobe etc) ein vorsintflutlicher Karren/Schrank etc (pej inf).

relief [rɪ'liːf] **1** n **(a)** (from anxiety, pain) Erleichterung f. **to bring sb ~** (drug) jdm Erleichterung verschaffen; (news) jdn erleichtern; **that brought him some ~ from his headache** das hat seine Kopfschmerzen etwas gelindert; **that's a ~!** mir fällt ein Stein vom Herzen; **it was a ~ to find it** ich/er etc war erleichtert, als ich/er etc es fand.
(b) (from monotony, boredom) Abwechslung f. **to provide a little light/comic ~** eine kleine Abwechslung/komische Erleichterung schaffen.
(c) (assistance) Hilfe f. **to go/come to sb's ~** jdm zu Hilfe eilen/kommen; **~ was available in the form of blankets and cups of tea** für Decken und heißen Tee war gesorgt; **to send ~ in the form of food** to sb jdm mit Nahrungsmitteln zu Hilfe kommen; **~ of the poor** Armenfürsorge f; **to provide ~ for the poor** für die Armen sorgen; **to be on ~** (US) Fürsorge bekommen, von der Fürsorge leben.
(d) (esp Mil: act of relieving, replacement forces) Entsatz m; (substitute) Ablösung f; **~ watchman/driver etc** Ablösung f; **~ train/bus** Entlastungszug m/-bus m.

(e) (*Art, Geog*) Relief *nt*; (*Typ also*) Hochdruck *m*. **high/low ~** Hoch-/Flachrelief *nt*; **in ~ erhaben**; **to stand out in ~ against sth** (*lit*) sich (deutlich) von etw abheben; (*fig*) im Gegensatz zu etw stehen; **to bring** *or* **throw sth into ~** (*lit*) etw (deutlich) hervortreten lassen; (*fig*) etw hervorheben.

(f) (*Jur*) Rechtshilfe *f* (*of* bei).

2 *attr* **(a)** *fund, organization* Hilfs-. **~ supplies** Hilfsgüter *pl*.

(b) *watchman, driver* Ablöse-; *troops* Entsatz-; *bus, train, road* Entlastungs-. **~ valve** Ausgleichsventil *nt*.

(c) *map* Relief-; *printing also* Hoch-.

relieve [rɪ'liːv] *vt* **(a)** *person* erleichtern; (*of pain*) helfen (+*dat*). **to feel ~d** erleichtert sein; **he was ~d to learn that er** war erleichtert, als er das hörte; **to ~ sb's mind** jdn beruhigen.

(b) to ~ sb of sth *of burden, pain* jdn von etw befreien; *of duty, post, command* jdn einer Sache (*gen*) entheben (*geh*); *of coat, suitcase* jdm etw abnehmen; (*hum*) *of wallet, purse etc* jdn um etw erleichtern (*hum*).

(c) (*mitigate*) *anxiety* mildern, schwächen; *pain* lindern; (*completely*) stillen; *tension* abbauen; *monotony* (*interrupt*) unterbrechen; (*liven things up*) beleben; *poverty* erleichtern; (*Med*) *congestion* abhelfen (+*dat*); (*completely*) beheben. **to ~ one's feelings** seinen Gefühlen Luft machen; **the black of her dress was ~d by a white collar** das Schwarz ihres Kleides wurde durch einen weißen Kragen etwas aufgelockert; **the new road ~s peak-hour congestion** die neue Straße entlastet den Berufsverkehr; **to ~ oneself** (*euph*) sich erleichtern.

(d) (*help*) *stricken country, refugees etc* helfen (+*dat*).

(e) (*take over from, also Mil*) ablösen.

(f) (*Mil*) *town* entsetzen, befreien.

religion [rɪ'lɪdʒən] *n* Religion *f*; (*set of beliefs*) Glaube(n) *m*. **the Christian ~** der christliche Glaube; **wars of ~** Glaubenskriege *pl*; **her name in ~** ihr Klostername *m*; **to get ~** (*pej inf*) fromm werden; **that's against my ~** (*lit*) das verstößt gegen meine Religion; (*hum inf*) das hat mir der Arzt verboten; **to make a ~ of doing sth** (*fig*) sich (*dat*) ein Gewissen daraus machen, etw zu tun; **it's an absolute ~ with him, it's his ~** (*fig*) das ist ihm heilig.

religiosity [rɪˌlɪdʒɪ'ɒsɪtɪ] *n* Frömmlertum *nt*.

religious [rɪ'lɪdʒəs] **1** *adj* **(a)** religiös; *order* geistlich; *freedom also, wars* Glaubens-, Religions-. **~ instruction** (*Sch*) Religionsunterricht *m*.

(b) (*having ~ beliefs*) *person* gläubig; (*pious*) fromm.

(c) (*fig: conscientious*) gewissenhaft; *silence* ehrfürchtig.

2 *n* Ordensmann *m*, Ordensfrau *f*; **the ~** *pl* die Ordensleute *pl*.

religiously [rɪ'lɪdʒəslɪ] *adv* **live** fromm, gottesfürchtig; (*fig: conscientiously*) gewissenhaft, treu und brav.

religiousness [rɪ'lɪdʒəsnɪs] *n* (*piety*) Frömmigkeit *f*; (*fig: conscientiousness*) Gewissenhaftigkeit *f*.

reline [ˌriː'laɪn] *vt* *coat, jacket* neu füttern; *brakes* neu belegen.

relinquish [rɪ'lɪŋkwɪʃ] *vt* **(a)** (*give up*) *hope, habit, plan* aufgeben; *right, possessions, power, post also* verzichten auf (+*acc*). **to ~ sth to sb** jdm etw abtreten *or* überlassen.

(b) (*let go*) **to ~ one's hold on sb/sth** (*lit, fig*) jdn/etw loslassen; **he ~d his hold on life/reality** er gab seinen Willen zum Leben auf/er verlor jeden Bezug zur Realität; **to ~ one's hold over sb** (*fig*) jdn freigeben.

relinquishment [rɪ'lɪŋkwɪʃmənt] *n* (*form: of claim, possessions etc*) Verzicht *m* (*of* auf +*acc*).

reliquary [ˈrelɪkwərɪ] *n* Reliquiar *nt*, Reliquienschrein *m*.

relish ['relɪʃ] **1** *n* **(a)** (*enjoyment*) Geschmack, Gefallen *m* (*for* an +*dat*). **to do sth with (great) ~** etw mit (großem) Genuß tun; **he ate with (great) ~** er aß mit großem Genuß *or* Appetit; **he had no further ~ for such activities** er fand an solchen Dingen keinen Geschmack *or* Gefallen mehr.

(b) (*Cook*) Soße *f*; (*spiciness*) Würze *f*; (*fig: charm*) Reiz *m*. **tomato-/fruit ~** Tomaten-/Obstchutney *nt*; **hunger is the best ~** (*Prov*) Hunger ist der beste Koch (*Prov*); **it had lost all ~ (for me)** (*fig*) das hatte für mich jeglichen Reiz verloren.

2 *vt* genießen; *food, wine also* sich (*dat*) schmecken lassen. **I don't ~ doing that** (*enjoy*) das ist gar nicht nach meinem Geschmack; (*look forward to*) darauf freue ich mich überhaupt nicht; **I don't ~ the thought of getting up at 5 a.m.** der Gedanke, um 5 Uhr aufzustehen, behagt *or* schmeckt (*inf*) mir gar nicht.

relive [ˌriː'lɪv] *vt* *life* noch einmal leben; *experience, one's childhood* noch einmal erleben *or* durchleben.

reload [ˌriː'ləʊd] *vt* neu beladen; *gun* nachladen, neu laden.

relocate [ˌriːləʊ'keɪt] *vt* umsiedeln, verlegen.

relocation [ˌriːləʊ'keɪʃən] *n* Umzug *m*; (*of refugees etc*) Umsiedlung *f*. **~ allowance** Umzugsbeihilfe *f*.

reluctance [rɪ'lʌktəns] *n* **(a)** Widerwillen *m*, Abneigung *f*. **to do sth with ~** etw widerwillig *or* ungern tun; **to make a show of ~** sich widerwillig geben. **(b)** (*Phys*) magnetischer Widerstand.

reluctant [rɪ'lʌktənt] *adj* unwillig, widerwillig; *admission, consent, praise* widerwillig. **he is ~ to do it** es widerstrebt ihm, es zu tun; **I'm ~ to go, as he may not even be there** ich gehe nur ungern, denn er ist vielleicht nicht einmal da; **he seems ~ to admit it** er scheint es nicht zugeben zu wollen; **he is a ~ soldier/student** er ist nur widerwillig Soldat/Student.

reluctantly [rɪ'lʌktəntlɪ] *adv* widerwillig.

rely [rɪ'laɪ] *vi* **to ~ (up)on sb/sth** sich auf jdn/etw verlassen; (*be dependent on*) auf jdn/etw angewiesen sein; **she relied on the trains being on time** sie verließ sich darauf, daß die Züge pünktlich waren; **I ~ on him for my income** ich bin finanziell auf ihn angewiesen; **you can ~ (up)on my help** du kannst dich darauf verlassen, auf dir helfe; **you can ~ on me not to say anything about it** Sie können sich darauf verlassen, daß ich nichts davon sage; **she is not to be relied upon** man kann sich nicht auf sie verlassen.

REM *abbr of* **rapid eye movement**.

remain [rɪ'meɪn] *vi* **(a)** bleiben; (*be left over*) übrigbleiben. **what ~s if you take 2 from 4?** was bleibt übrig, wenn man 2 von 4

abzieht?; **much ~s to be done** es ist *or* bleibt noch viel zu tun; **nothing ~s to be said** es gibt *or* bleibt nichts mehr zu sagen; **nothing ~s but to accept** wir/sie *etc* brauchen nur noch anzunehmen; (*no alternative*) es bleibt uns nichts anderes übrig, als anzunehmen; **all that ~s is for me to wish you every success** ich möchte Ihnen nur noch viel Erfolg wünschen; **all that ~s (for me/us etc to do) is to lock up** ich brauche/wir brauchen jetzt nur noch abzuschließen; **that ~s to be seen** das wird sich zeigen, das bleibt abzuwarten; **the fact ~s that he is wrong** das ändert nichts an der Tatsache, daß er unrecht hat.

(b) (*stay*) bleiben. **~ seated!** bleiben Sie sitzen, behalten Sie Platz (*geh*); **to ~ silent** weiterhin schweigen; **to ~ behind/up** zurück-/aufbleiben; **let the matter ~ as it is** lassen Sie die Sache so, wie sie ist; **it ~s the same** das bleibt sich gleich; **"I ~ yours faithfully John Smith"** „mit besten Grüßen verbleibe ich Ihr John Smith".

remainder [rɪ'meɪndə^r] **1** *n* **(a)** Rest *m* (*also Math*). **the ~** (*remaining people*) der Rest, die übrigen (Leute); **for the ~ of the week** für den Rest der Woche, für die übrige Woche.

(b) ~s *pl* (*Comm*) Restbestände *pl*; (*books also*) Remittenden *pl* (*spec*).

(c) (*Jur*) Erbanwartschaft *f*.

2 *vt books* als Remittenden abgeben.

remaining [rɪ'meɪnɪŋ] *adj* übrig, restlich. **the ~ four, the four ~** die übrigen vier, die vier übrigen; **I have only one ~** ich habe nur noch einen/eine/eins (übrig).

remains [rɪ'meɪnz] *npl* (*of meal*) Reste *pl*; (*of fortune, army*) Rest *m*; (*of building*) Überreste *pl*; (*archaeological*) ~ Ruinen *pl*. *literary* **~** literarischer Nachlaß; **his (mortal) ~** seine sterblichen Überreste; **human ~** menschliche Überreste *pl*.

remake [ˌriː'meɪk] (*vb: pret, ptp* **remade** [ˌriː'meɪd]) **1** *vt* wieder *or* nochmals machen; (*in new form*) neu machen. **to ~ a film** ein Thema neu verfilmen. **2** ['riːmeɪk] *n* (*Film*) Neuverfilmung *f*, Remake *nt* (*spec*).

remand [rɪ'mɑːnd] **1** *vt* (*Jur*) *case* vertagen. **to ~ sb (in custody/on bail)** jdn weiterhin in Untersuchungshaft behalten/unter Kaution halten; **to ~ sb to a higher court** jdm an eine höhere Instanz verweisen; **he was ~ed in custody/on bail** er blieb in Untersuchungshaft/unter Kaution; **the man ~ed in custody** der Untersuchungsgefangene.

2 *n* (*of person*) Aufrechterhaltung *f* der Untersuchungshaft/der Erhebung von Kaution (*of* gegen); (*form: of case*) Vertagung *f*. **to be on ~** in Untersuchungshaft sein; (*on bail*) auf Kaution freigelassen sein; **~ home** *or* **centre** (*Brit*) Untersuchungsgefängnis *nt* für Jugendliche.

remark [rɪ'mɑːk] **1** *n* **(a)** (*comment*) Bemerkung *f*. **I have a few/no ~s to make on that subject** ich habe einiges zu diesem Thema zu bemerken/nichts zu diesem Thema zu sagen; **~s were passed about our absence** man redete über unsere Abwesenheit.

(b) *no pl* (*notice*) **worthy of ~** bemerkenswert; **without ~** unbemerkt.

2 *vt* **(a)** (*say*) bemerken.

(b) (*old, liter: notice*) bemerken, wahrnehmen.

3 *vi* **to ~ (up)on sth** über etw (*acc*) eine Bemerkung machen, sich zu etw äußern (+*acc*); **nobody/everybody ~ed on it** niemand hat etwas dazu gesagt/alle haben ihre Bemerkungen dazu gemacht; **he ~ed on it to me** er äußerte sich mir gegenüber dazu.

remarkable [rɪ'mɑːkəbl] *adj* (*notable*) bemerkenswert; *intelligence, talent, wit also* beachtlich; (*extraordinary*) außergewöhnlich. **to be ~ for sth** sich durch etw auszeichnen.

remarkably [rɪ'mɑːkəblɪ] *adv* außergewöhnlich.

remarriage [ˌriː'mærɪdʒ] *n* Wiederverheiratung *f* (*to* mit).

remarry [ˌriː'mærɪ] *vi* wieder heiraten.

remediable [rɪ'miːdɪəbl] *adj situation* rettbar; *fault, defect* behebbar.

remedial [rɪ'miːdɪəl] *adj attr action, measures* Hilfs-; (*Med*) Heil-. **~ exercises** Heilgymnastik *f*; **to teach ~ English/reading** einen/den Förderkurs in Englisch/im Lesen leiten; **~ teaching/work** Förder- *or* Hilfsunterricht *m*/Förderaufgaben *pl*; **~ class** Förderklasse *f* (für Lernschwache).

remedy ['remədɪ] **1** *n* (*Med, fig*) Mittel *nt* (*for* gegen); (*medication*) Heilmittel *nt* (*for* gegen); (*Jur*) Rechtsmittel *nt*. **the situation is past** *or* **beyond ~** die Lage ist hoffnungslos verloren *or* irreparabel; **unless we can find a ~** wenn wir keinen Ausweg *or* keine Lösung finden; **the ~ for boredom is work** das beste Mittel gegen Langeweile ist Arbeit.

2 *vt* (*Med*) heilen; (*fig*) *defect, fault* beheben; *situation* bessern; *abuse, evil* abhelfen (+*dat*). **his faults cannot be remedied** man kann ihn nicht von seinen Fehlern heilen; **the situation cannot be remedied** die Lage ist hoffnungslos.

remember [rɪ'membə^r] **1** *vt* **(a)** (*recall*) sich erinnern an (+*acc*); *person, occasion also* sich entsinnen (+*gen*) (*geh*), sich besinnen auf (+*acc*) (*geh*); (*bear in mind*) denken an (+*acc*); (*learn*) *formula, facts, vocabulary* sich (*dat*) merken. **I ~ that he was very tall** ich erinnere mich (daran), daß er sehr groß war; **I ~ her as a beautiful girl** ich habe sie als schönes Mädchen in Erinnerung; **I ~ her as a young girl** *or* **when she was young** ich erinnere mich noch, wie sie als kleines Mädchen war; **we must ~ that he's only a child** wir sollten bedenken *or* daran denken, daß er noch ein Kind ist; **to ~ to do sth** daran denken, etw zu tun; **I ~ doing it** ich erinnere mich daran, daß ich es getan habe, ich weiß noch, daß ich es getan habe; **I can't ~ the word at the moment** das Wort fällt mir im Moment nicht ein; **I've just ~ed his name** mir ist gerade sein Name wieder eingefallen; **don't you ~ me?** erinnern Sie sich nicht an mich?; **here's something to ~ me by** da habe ich dir etwas, das dich (immer) an mich erinnern wird; **do you ~ when ...?** (*reminiscing*) weißt du noch, als ...?; (*asking facts*) weißt du (noch), wann ...?; **I don't ~ a thing about it** ich kann mich überhaupt or absolut nicht daran erinnern; (*about lecture, book*) ich weiß nichts mehr davon; **I can never ~ phone numbers** ich kann mir Telefonnummern einfach nicht merken; **we can't always ~ everything** wir können nicht immer an alles denken; **~ where/who you are!** denken Sie daran or bedenken Sie, wo/wer Sie sind!; **to ~ sb in one's prayers/one's will** jdn in sein Gebet einschließen/jdn in seinem Testament bedenken.

(b) (*commemorate*) *the fallen, a battle* gedenken (+*gen*).

(c) (*give good wishes to*) **~ me to your mother** grüßen Sie Ihre Mutter von mir; **he asks to be ~ed to you** er läßt Sie grüßen.

2 *vi* sich erinnern. **I can't ~** ich weiß das nicht mehr, ich hab's vergessen; **not as far as I ~** soweit ich mich erinnere, nicht!; **if I ~ right(ly)** or **aright** wenn ich mich recht erinnere or entsinne.

remembrance [rɪˈmembrəns] *n* **(a)** Erinnerung *f* (*of an* +*acc*). **R~Day** (*Brit*) ≈ Volkstrauertag *m*; **~ service** Gedenkgottesdienst *m*; **in ~ of** zur Erinnerung an (+*acc*); **to the best of my ~** soweit ich mich erinnern kann; **I have no ~ of that** ich habe keinerlei Erinnerung daran.

(b) (*keepsake*) Andenken *nt* (*of an* +*acc*).

(c) **~s** *pl* (*old form: greetings*) Empfehlungen *pl*.

remind [rɪˈmaɪnd] *vt* erinnern (*of an* +*acc*). **you are ~ed that ...** wir weisen darauf hin, daß ...; **to ~ sb to do sth** jdn daran erinnern, etw zu tun; **that ~s me!** da(bei) fällt mir was ein.

reminder [rɪˈmaɪndəʳ] *n* (*note, knot etc*) Gedächtnisstütze *f*. **(letter of ~)** (~*Comm*) Mahnung *f*; **as a ~ that ...** um dich/ihn *etc* daran zu erinnern, daß ...; **to give sb a ~ to do sth** jdn daran erinnern, etw zu tun; **his presence was a ~** seine Gegenwart erinnerte mich/dich *etc* an (+*acc*) ...; **a gentle ~** ein zarter Wink; **give him a gentle ~** weis ihn sachte darauf hin.

reminisce [ˌremɪˈnɪs] *vi* sich in Erinnerungen ergehen (*about* über +*acc*).

reminiscence [ˌremɪˈnɪsəns] *n* (*action*) Zurückgehen *nt* (*of* zu); (*thought*) Reminiszenz, Erinnerung (*of an* +*acc*) *f*.

reminiscent [ˌremɪˈnɪsənt] *adj* **(a) to be ~ of sth** an etw (*acc*) erinnern; **a style ~ of Shakespeare** ein an Shakespeare erinnernder Stil. **(b)** (*reminiscing*) *style, chapter* nostalgisch. **to be feeling ~, to be in a ~ mood** in nostalgischer Stimmung sein.

reminiscently [ˌremɪˈnɪsəntlɪ] *adv* smile, sigh etc in der Erinnerung. **to think ~ of sth** nostalgisch an etw (*acc*) zurückdenken; **he talked ~ of the war** er erzählte von seinen Kriegserinnerungen.

remiss [rɪˈmɪs] *adj* nachlässig. **he has been ~ in not doing it** es war nachlässig von ihm, das zu unterlassen.

remission [rɪˈmɪʃən] *n* (*form*) *see* **remit¹ (a)** Erlassen *nt*; (*Jur*) (*Straf*)erlaß *m*; (*Rel*) Nachlaß *m*. **he got 3 years' ~ for good behaviour** ihm wurden wegen guter Führung 3 Jahre erlassen; **there can be no ~ of the fees** Gebührenerlaß ist nicht möglich.

(b) Überweisung *f*.

(c) Verschiebung, Vertagung *f*.

(d) Verweisung *f*.

(e) Nachlassen *nt*; (*Med*) Besserung, Remission (*spec*) *f*.

remissness [rɪˈmɪsnɪs] *n* Nachlässigkeit *f*.

remit¹ [rɪˈmɪt] (*form*) **1** *vt* **(a)** (*cancel, pardon*) *debt, sentence, sins* erlassen. **(b)** (*send*) *money* überweisen. **(c)** (*postpone*) verschieben, vertagen (*to auf* +*acc, till bis*). **(d)** (*Jur: transfer*) *case* verweisen (*to an* +*acc*). **2** *vi* (*become less*) nachlassen.

remit² [ˈriːmɪt] *n* (*form*) Aufgabe *f*, Auftrag *m*. **that is outside our ~** das liegt außerhalb unseres Aufgabenbereiches.

remittal [rɪˈmɪtl] *n see* **remission (b–d)**.

remittance [rɪˈmɪtəns] *n* Überweisung *f* (*to an* +*acc*).

remittee [rɪmɪˈtiː] *n* (*Comm*) Empfänger *m* einer/der Überweisung.

remittent [rɪˈmɪtənt] *adj* (*Med*) *symptoms, fever* remittierend (*spec*). **~ fever** Wechselfieber *nt*.

remitter [rɪˈmɪtəʳ] *n* (*sender*) Überweiser *m*.

remnant [ˈremnənt] *n* Rest *m*; (*fig: of splendour, custom*) Überrest *m*. **the ~ of his fortune/~s of his former glory** was von seinem Vermögen/Ruhm übriggeblieben war; **~ day** (*Comm*) Resteverkaufstag *m*; **~ sale** Resteausverkauf *m*.

remodel [ˌriːˈmɒdl] *vt* (*also Art, Tech*) umformen; *nose* richten; (*fig*) *society, constitution also* umgestalten.

remonstrance [rɪˈmɒnstrəns] *n* Protest *m* (*with bei, against* gegen).

remonstrant [rɪˈmɒnstrənt] *adj* protestierend.

remonstrate [ˈremənstreɪt] *vi* protestieren (*against* gegen). **to ~ with sb (about sth)** jdm Vorhaltungen (wegen etw) machen.

remorse [rɪˈmɔːs] *n* Reue *f* (*at, over* über +*acc*). **he is completely without ~** er zeigt überhaupt keine Reue; **without ~** (*merciless*) erbarmungslos.

remorseful [rɪˈmɔːsful] *adj* reumütig, reuig. **to feel ~** Reue spüren.

remorsefully [rɪˈmɔːsfəlɪ] *adv see adj*.

remorsefulness [rɪˈmɔːsfulnɪs] *n* Reue *f*; (*of person also*) Reumütigkeit *f*.

remorseless [rɪˈmɔːslɪs] *adj* reulos, ohne Reue; (*fig: merciless*) unbarmherzig.

remorselessly [rɪˈmɔːslɪslɪ] *adv see adj*.

remorselessness [rɪˈmɔːslɪsnɪs] *n see adj* Reuelosigkeit *f*; Unbarmherzigkeit *f*.

remote [rɪˈməut] *adj* (+*er*) **(a)** (*in place*) (*distant*) entfernt, fern (*geh*) *attr*; (*isolated*) entlegen, abgelegen. **in the ~st parts of Africa** in den abgelegensten Teilen Afrikas; **in a ~ spot** an einer entlegenen or abgelegenen Stelle; **a house ~ from the main road** ein von der Hauptstraße abgelegenes Haus.

(b) (*in time*) *past, future* fern. **~ antiquity** die früheste Antike; **a ~ ancestor** ein Urahn *m*/eine Urahne.

(c) *relative*, (*fig*) *connection, relevance etc* entfernt. **what he said was rather ~ from the subject in hand** was er sagte, war weit vom eigentlichen Thema entfernt.

(d) (*aloof*) unnahbar, unzugänglich.

(e) (*slight*) *possibility, resemblance* entfernt; *chance* gering, winzig. **I haven't the ~st idea** ich habe nicht die leiseste Idee.

remote: **~ control** *n* Fernsteuerung, Fernlenkung *f*; **~-controlled** *adj* ferngesteuert, ferngelenkt.

remotely [rɪˈməutlɪ] *adv* situated, related entfernt. **it's just ~ possible** es ist gerade eben noch möglich; **if it's ~ possible** wenn es auch nur irgend möglich ist; **they're not even ~ similar** sie sind sich nicht im entferntesten ähnlich.

remoteness [rɪˈməutnɪs] *n see adj* **(a)** Ferne *f*; Abgelegenheit *f*. **(b)** (*weite*) Ferne. **(c)** Entferntheit *f*. **his ~ from everyday life** seine Lebensfremdheit. **(d)** Unnahbarkeit, Unzugänglichkeit *f*. **(e)** Entferntheit *f*; Winzigkeit *f*.

remould [ˌriːˈməuld] **1** *vt* (*Tech*) *tyre* runderneuern. **2** [ˈriːməuld] *n* (*tyre*) runderneuerter Reifen.

remount [ˌriːˈmaunt] **1** *vt* **(a)** *horse, bicycle* wieder besteigen; *ladder* wieder hinaufsteigen or -klettern. **(b)** *picture, photo* wieder aufziehen. **2** *vi* wieder aufsitzen.

removable [rɪˈmuːvəbl] *adj* cover, lid, attachment abnehmbar; *button, trimming* abtrennbar; *lining* abknöpfbar; *stain* zu entfernen *pred* or entfernend *attr*; (*from container*) herausnehmbar. **the motor is easily ~** der Motor ist leicht auszubauen.

removal [rɪˈmuːvəl] *n see vt* **(a)** Entfernung *f*; Abnahme *f*; Beseitigung *f*; Abtrennung *f*; Abknöpfen *nt*. **his ~ to hospital** seine Einlieferung ins Krankenhaus.

(b) Herausnehmen *nt*; Entfernung *f*; Streichen *nt*; Ausbau *m*.

(c) Beseitigung *f*; Aufhebung *f*; Ausräumung *f*; Beseitigung *f*; Zerstreuung *f*; Beseitigung *f*.

(d) Entfernung *f*.

(e) (*move from house*) Umzug *m*. **our ~ to this house/to York** unser Umzug in dieses Haus/nach York; **"Brown & Son, ~s"** „Spedition Brown & Sohn", „Brown & Sohn, Umzüge".

removal: **~ allowance** *n* Umzugsbeihilfe *f*; **~ expenses** *npl* Umzugskosten *pl*; **~ firm** *n* Spedition *f*; **~ man** *n* Möbelpacker *m*; **~ van** *n* Möbelwagen *m*.

remove [rɪˈmuːv] **1** *vt* **(a)** (*take off, take away etc*) entfernen; *cover, lid, attachments also* abnehmen; *splint, bandage, tie* abnehmen; *stain also* beseitigen; *buttons, trimmings also* abtrennen; *lining* abknöpfen. **to ~ sth from sb** jdm etw wegnehmen; **to ~ one's clothes** die Kleider ablegen; **to ~ sb to hospital/the cells** jdn ins Krankenhaus einliefern/jdn in die Zelle bringen; **to ~ a child from school** ein Kind von or aus der Schule nehmen; **he ~d himself to another room** er begab sich in ein anderes Zimmer; **to ~ one's make-up** das Make-up entfernen.

(b) (*take out*) (*from container*) herausnehmen (*from* aus); (*Med*) *lung, kidney also* entfernen (*from* aus); *paragraph, word, item on list also* streichen; (*Tech*) ausbauen (*from* aus).

(c) (*eradicate*) *threat* beseitigen (*usu pass*), Schluß machen mit; *tax* aufheben; *objection, obstacle* aus dem Weg schaffen or räumen; *difficulty, problem* beseitigen, ein Ende machen or setzen (+*dat*); *doubt, suspicion, fear* zerstreuen; *abuse, evil* abstellen, beseitigen; (*euph: kill*) beseitigen. **to ~ all obstacles from one's path** (*fig*) alle Hindernisse aus dem Weg räumen.

(d) (*form: dismiss*) *official* entfernen.

(e) (*form: to another house*) transportieren.

(f) to be far ~d from ... weit entfernt sein von ...; **a cousin once/twice ~d** ein Cousin ersten/zweiten Grades; **but he's several times ~d** (*inf*) ich bin mit ihm verwandt, aber um ein paar Ecken herum (*inf*).

2 *vi* (*form: move house*) **to ~ to London/to larger premises** nach London/in größere Geschäftsräume (um)ziehen.

3 *n* **(a) to be only a few ~s from ...** nicht weit entfernt sein von ...; **this is but one ~ from disaster** das kommt einer Katastrophe nahe; **it's a far ~ from ...** es ist weit entfernt von ...

(b) (*Brit Sch*) Klasse *f* für lernschwache Schüler.

remover [rɪˈmuːvəʳ] *n* **(a)** (*for nail varnish, stains etc*) Entferner *m*. **(b)** (*removal man*) Möbelpacker *m*.

remunerate [rɪˈmjuːnəreɪt] *vt* (*pay*) bezahlen, vergüten; (*reward*) belohnen.

remuneration [rɪˌmjuːnəˈreɪʃən] *n* Bezahlung, Vergütung *f*; (*reward*) Belohnung *f*.

remunerative [rɪˈmjuːnərətɪv] *adj* lohnend, einträglich.

renaissance [rɪˈneɪsɑːns] *n* (*liter*) Wiedergeburt *f*; (*of nature*) Wiedererwachen *nt*. **the R~** (*Hist*) die Renaissance; **R~ man** der Renaissancemensch; (*fig*) der Humanist.

renal [ˈriːnl] *adj* Nieren-, renal (*spec*).

rename [ˌriːˈneɪm] *vt* umbenennen, umtaufen. **Petrograd was ~d Leningrad** Petrograd wurde in Leningrad umbenannt.

renascence [rɪˈnæsns] *n see* **renaissance**.

renascent [rɪˈnæsnt] *adj* (*liter*) wiedererwachend.

rend [rend] *pret, ptp* **rent** *vt* (*liter*) *cloth* zerreißen; *armour* aufreißen. **to ~ sth from sb/sth** jdm/einer Sache etw entreißen; **a country rent by civil war** ein vom Bürgerkrieg zerrissenes Land; **a cry rent the silence** ein Schrei zerriß die Stille; **to ~ sb's heart** jdm das Herz zerreißen.

render [ˈrendəʳ] *vt* **(a)** (*form: give*) *service, help* leisten; *judgement, explanation* abgeben; *homage* erweisen. **~ unto Caesar the things which are Caesar's** (*Bibl, prov*) gebet dem Kaiser, was des Kaisers ist (*Bibl*); **to ~ thanks to sb/God** jdm/Gott Dank sagen or abstatten; **to ~ assistance** Hilfe leisten; **to ~ an account of one's expenditure** Rechenschaft über seine Ausgaben ablegen.

(b) (*Comm*) **to ~ account** Rechnung legen or vorlegen; **(to) account ~ed £10** £ 10 laut früherer Rechnung.

(c) (*interpret, translate*) wiedergeben; (*in writing*) übertragen; *music, poem also* vortragen.

(d) (*form: make*) machen. **his accident ~ed him helpless** der Unfall hat ihn hilflos gemacht.

(e) (*also ~ down*) *fat* auslassen.

(f) (*Build*) verputzen.

♦**render up** *vt sep* fortress, prisoner übergeben.

rendering ['rendərɪŋ] n (a) Wiedergabe f; (in writing) Übertragung f; (of piece of music, poem also) Vortrag m. (b) (Build) Putz m.

rendez-vous ['rɒndɪvuː] 1 n (place) Treffpunkt m; (agreement to meet) Stelldichein (dated), Rendezvous nt. 2 vi sich treffen (with mit).

rendition [ren'dɪʃən] n (form) see **rendering** (a).

renegade ['renɪgeɪd] 1 n Renegat(in f) m, Abtrünnige(r) mf. 2 adj abtrünnig.

renege [rɪ'niːg] vi nicht Wort halten; (Cards) nicht bedienen. to ~ on a promise/an agreement ein Versprechen/eine Übereinkunft brechen.

renew [rɪ'njuː] vt erneuern; contract, passport etc (authority also) verlängern; (holder) erneuern or verlängern lassen; negotiations, discussions, attack, attempts wiederaufnehmen; one's strength wiederherstellen; supplies auffrischen. to ~ a library book ein Buch verlängern lassen; to ~ one's acquaintance with sb seine Bekanntschaft mit jdm erneuern or auffrischen; with ~ed enthusiasm mit neuem Schwung; ~ed efforts/strength/courage neue Anstrengungen/frische Kraft/frischer Mut; ~ed outbreaks of rioting erneute Krawalle pl; to feel spiritually ~ed sich wie ein neuer Mensch fühlen.

renewable [rɪ'njuːəbl] adj erneuerbar; contract also, passport, bill of exchange verlängerbar; (must be renewed) zu erneuern; zu verlängern. some library books are not ~ einige Bibliotheksbücher können nicht verlängert werden.

renewal [rɪ'njuːəl] n see vt Erneuerung f; Verlängerung f; Wiederaufnahme f; Wiederherstellung f; Auffrischung f. spiritual ~ geistige Erneuerung.

rennet ['renɪt] n (Cook) Lab nt.

renounce [rɪ'naʊns] 1 vt title, right, one's liberty verzichten auf (+acc), aufgeben; religion, devil abschwören (+dat); (Rel) world entsagen (+dat); opinions, cause, treaty leugnen, abschwören (+dat); friend verleugnen. 2 vi (Cards) renoncieren.

renouncement [rɪ'naʊnsmənt] n see **renunciation**.

renovate ['renəʊveɪt] vt building renovieren; painting, furniture restaurieren.

renovation [ˌrenəʊ'veɪʃən] n see vt Renovierung, Renovation f; Restaurierung f.

renown [rɪ'naʊn] n guter Ruf, Ansehen nt. of high ~ von hohem Ansehen, sehr berühmt.

renowned [rɪ'naʊnd] adj berühmt (for für).

rent¹ [rent] 1 n (for house, room) Miete f; (for farm, factory) Pacht f. for ~ (US) zu vermieten/verpachten/verleihen.
2 vt (a) (also vi) house, room mieten; farm, factory pachten; TV, car etc leihen. we don't own it, we only ~ it es gehört uns (dat) nicht; wir haben es nur gemietet etc.
(b) (also ~ out) vermieten; verpachten; verleihen.

rent² 1 pret, ptp of **rend**. 2 n (lit, fig) Riß m; (in rock) Spalte f.

rental ['rentl] n (amount paid) (for house) Miete f; (for TV, car, boat etc also) Leihgebühr f; (for land) Pacht f; (income from rents) Miet-/Pacht-/Leihgebühreinnahmen pl. ~ library (US) Leihbücherei f.

rent: ~ collector n Mietkassierer(in f) m; ~ control n Mietkontrolle f, Mieterschutz m; ~-controlled adj bewirtschaftet (form), mit gebundener Miete; ~-free adj mietfrei; ~-man n (inf) see ~ collector; ~ rebate n Mietrückzahlung f; ~ tribunal n Mieterschiedsgericht nt.

renumber [ˌriː'nʌmbəʳ] vt umnumerieren.

renunciation [rɪˌnʌnsɪ'eɪʃən] n see **renounce** Verzicht m (of auf +acc), Aufgabe f; Abschwören nt; Entsagung f; Leugnung f; Verleugnung f.

reoccupy [ˌriː'ɒkjʊpaɪ] vt post, position wieder innehaben or bekleiden; house, hotel room etc wieder belegen.

reopen [ˌriː'əʊpən] 1 vt wieder öffnen, wieder aufmachen; school, shop, theatre, fight, hostilities wiedereröffnen; debate, discussion, negotiations wiederaufnehmen; (Jur) case wieder aufrollen, wiederaufnehmen.
2 vi wieder aufgehen; (shop, theatre etc) wieder eröffnen or aufmachen; (school after holidays) wieder beginnen; (negotiations) wiederbeginnen; (case) wieder aufgerollt werden; (wound) wieder aufgehen.

reopening [ˌriː'əʊpnɪŋ] n (of shop etc) Wiedereröffnung f; (of school after holiday) Wiederbeginn m; (of negotiations, debate, case) Wiederaufnahme f.

reorder [ˌriː'ɔːdəʳ] vt (a) (also vi) goods, supplies nachbestellen; (because first order is lost etc) neu bestellen. (b) (reorganize) neu ordnen, umordnen; books, names on a list also umstellen; people in a row umstellen; appointments umlegen.

reorganization [ˌriːˌɔːgənaɪ'zeɪʃən] n see vt Neu- or Umorganisation f; Neu- or Umordnung f; Neueinteilung f; Neuaufbau m.

reorganize [ˌriː'ɔːgənaɪz] 1 vt neu organisieren, umorganisieren; furniture, books umordnen; work, time neu einteilen; essay neu aufbauen. 2 vi (Pol) sich neu organisieren.

rep¹ [rep] abbr of (a) (Theat) **repertory** Repertoire-Theater nt. (b) (Comm) **representative** Vertreter(in f) m.

rep² n (Tex) Rips m.

Rep abbr of (a) **Republic** Rep. (b) **Republican** Rep., rep.

repaid [ˌriː'peɪd] pret, ptp of **repay**.

repaint [ˌriː'peɪnt] vt neu streichen.

repair¹ [rɪ'peəʳ] 1 vt (lit, fig) reparieren; tyre also, clothes flicken; roof, wall also, road ausbessern; (fig) error, wrong, damage wiedergutmachen.
2 n (a) see vt Reparatur f; Flicken nt; Ausbesserung f; Wiedergutmachung f. to be under ~ (car, ship, machine) in Reparatur sein; to put sth in for ~ etw zur Reparatur bringen; the road is under ~ an der Straße wird gerade gearbeitet; beyond ~ nicht mehr zu reparieren/zu flicken/auszubessern/wiedergutzumachen; damaged beyond ~ irreparabel,

nicht mehr zu reparieren; closed for ~s wegen Reparaturarbeiten geschlossen; "road ~s" „Straßenbauarbeiten"; "~s while you wait" „Sofortdienst", „Sofortreparaturen".
(b) no pl (condition) to be in good/bad ~ in gutem Zustand or in Schuß (inf) sein/in schlechtem Zustand sein; to keep sth in good ~ etw in gutem Zustand or in Schuß (inf) halten.

repair² vi (liter: go) sich begeben (to nach).

repairable [rɪ'peərəbl] adj see vt zu reparieren, reparabel; zu flicken, auszubessern pred. is that ~? läßt sich das reparieren?

repairer [rɪ'peərəʳ] n (watch/boot) ~ Uhr-/Schuhmacher m.

repair: ~ kit n Flickzeug nt; ~-man n (in house) Handwerker m; she took her shoes to the ~-man sie brachte ihre Schuhe zum Schuster; ~ shop n Reparaturwerkstatt m.

repaper [ˌriː'peɪpəʳ] vt neu tapezieren.

reparable ['repərəbl] adj damage reparabel, wiedergutzumachen; loss ersetzbar.

reparation [ˌrepə'reɪʃən] n (for damage) Entschädigung f; (usu pl: after war) Reparation f; (for wrong, misdeed) Wiedergutmachung f. to make ~ for sth etw wiedergutmachen.

repartee [ˌrepɑː'tiː] n Schlagabtausch m; (retort) schlagfertige Antwort. to be good at ~ schlagfertig sein; renowned for his ~ bekannt für seine Schlagfertigkeit.

repast [rɪ'pɑːst] n (liter) Mahl nt (geh).

repatriate [ˌriː'pætrɪeɪt] 1 vt in das Heimatland zurücksenden, repatriieren. 2 n [ˌriː'pætrɪət] Repatriierte(r) mf.

repatriation [ˈriːˌpætrɪ'eɪʃən] n Repatriierung f.

repay [ˌriː'peɪ] pret, ptp **repaid** vt money zurückzahlen; expenses erstatten; debt abzahlen; kindness vergelten; visit erwidern. if you lend me £2 I'll ~ it or you on Saturday leih mir doch mal 2 Pfund, ich zahle sie dir am Samstag zurück; I shall ~ my obligation to you one day ich werde es dir eines Tages vergelten or lohnen; to ~ sb for his generosity sich für jds Großzügigkeit revanchieren; to be repaid for one's efforts für seine Mühen belohnt werden.

repayable [ˌriː'peɪəbl] adj rückzahlbar.

repayment [ˌriː'peɪmənt] n (of money) Rückzahlung f; (of effort, kindness) Lohn m. ~s can be spread over 3 years die Rückzahlung kann über 3 Jahre verteilt werden; in ~ als Rückzahlung/Lohn.

repeal [rɪ'piːl] 1 vt law aufheben. 2 n Aufhebung f.

repeat [rɪ'piːt] 1 vt wiederholen; (tell to sb else) weitersagen (to sb jdm). to ~ oneself sich wiederholen; he wasn't keen to ~ the experience er war nicht darauf aus, die Erfahrung noch einmal zu machen; he ~ed his lesson to the teacher er sagte seine Lektion vor dem Lehrer auf; to ~ an order (Comm) nachbestellen; this offer will never be ~ed! dies ist ein einmaliges Angebot!
2 vi (a) (say again) wiederholen. I ~, it is impossible ich wiederhole, es ist unmöglich; ~ after me sprecht mir nach.
(b) (Mus) wiederholen. ~! (conductor) noch einmal!
(c) radishes ~ on me Radieschen stoßen mir auf.
(d) (gun, clock etc) repetieren.
(e) (Math) periodisch sein.
3 n (a) (Rad, TV) Wiederholung f.
(b) (Mus) (section repeated) Wiederholung f; (~ sign) Wiederholungszeichen nt.

repeated adj, **~ly** adv [rɪ'piːtɪd, -lɪ] wiederholt.

repeater [rɪ'piːtəʳ] n (gun) Repetier- or Mehrladegewehr nt; (watch) Repetieruhr f.

repeating [rɪ'piːtɪŋ] adj (Math) see **recurring** (b).

repeat: ~ order n (Comm) Nachbestellung f; ~ performance n (Theat) Wiederholungsvorstellung f; he gave a ~ performance (fig) er machte es noch einmal, (pej) er machte noch einmal das gleiche Theater (inf); ~ sign n (Mus) Wiederholungszeichen nt.

repel [rɪ'pel] vt (a) enemy, attack zurückschlagen; sb's advance, insects, flies abwehren; water abstoßen. (b) (also vi) (disgust) abstoßen.

repellent [rɪ'pelənt] 1 adj (a) ~ to water wasserabstoßend. (b) (disgusting) abstoßend. 2 n (also ~) Mittel nt zur Abwehr von Insekten; (for body) Mückensalbe f.

repelling [rɪ'pelɪŋ] adj see **repellent** 1 (b).

repent [rɪ'pent] 1 vi Reue empfinden (of über +acc). 2 vt bereuen.

repentance [rɪ'pentəns] n Reue f.

repentant [rɪ'pentənt] adj look, expression reuig, reuevoll. he was very ~ es reute ihn sehr; to feel ~ Reue empfinden; a ~ sinner ein reuiger Sünder.

repercussion [ˌriːpə'kʌʃən] n (a) (consequence) Auswirkung f (on auf +acc). ~s pl (of misbehaviour etc) Nachspiel nt; it is bound to have ~s das wird Kreise ziehen; to have ~s on sth sich auf etw (acc) auswirken. (b) (of shock) Erschütterung f; (of sounds) Widerhall m.

repertoire ['repətwɑːʳ] n (Theat, Mus) Repertoire nt.

repertory ['repətərɪ] n (a) (also ~ theatre) Repertoire-Theater nt. ~ company Repertoire-Ensemble nt; to act in ~, to play ~ Repertoire-Stücke spielen; he was in ~ er spielte an einem Repertoire-Theater. (b) (songs, plays) see **repertoire**.

repetition [ˌrepɪ'tɪʃən] n Wiederholung f. there are six ~s of the pattern das Muster wiederholt sich sechsmal.

repetitious [ˌrepɪ'tɪʃəs] adj sich wiederholend.

repetitive [rɪ'petɪtɪv] adj sich dauernd wiederholend. to be ~ sich dauernd wiederholen; standing in a production line is such ~ work die Arbeit am Fließband ist äußerst eintönig.

repine [rɪ'paɪn] vi (liter) hadern (geh) (at, against mit).

replace [rɪ'pleɪs] vt (a) (put back) zurücksetzen; (on end, standing up) zurückstellen; (on its side, flat) zurücklegen. to ~ the receiver (Telec) (den Hörer) auflegen.
(b) (provide or be substitute for) person, thing, ingredient, goods ersetzen; employee (permanently also) die Stelle einnehmen (+gen), (temporarily) vertreten. the boss has ~d Smith with Jones der Chef hat Smith durch Jones ersetzt.

(c) *(renew) components, parts* austauschen, ersetzen.

replaceable [rɪ'pleɪsəbl] *adj person* ersetzbar, zu ersetzen; *(renewable) components, parts also* austauschbar.

replacement [rɪ'pleɪsmənt] *n* **(a)** *see vt (a)* Zurücksetzen *nt*; Zurückstellen *nt*; Zurücklegen *nt*; *(of receiver)* Auflegen *nt*.
   (b) *(substituting)* Ersatz *m*; *(by deputy)* Vertretung *f*.
   (c) *(person or thing replacing)* Ersatz *m*; *(deputy)* Vertretung *f*. ~ **engine/clutch** Austauschmotor *m*/-kupplung *f*; ~ **part** Ersatzteil *nt*.

replant [,ri:'plɑ:nt] *vt cabbages, trees etc* umpflanzen; *garden, field* neu bepflanzen.

replay ['ri:pleɪ] *(Sport)* **1** *n (recording)* Wiederholung *f*; *(match also)* Wiederholungsspiel *nt*; *see action* ~. **2** [,ri:'pleɪ] *vt match, game* wiederholen, nochmals austragen.

replenish [rɪ'plenɪʃ] *vt* ergänzen; *(when badly depleted)* wieder auffüllen; *glass* auffüllen.

replenishment [rɪ'plenɪʃmənt] *n see vt* Ergänzung *f*; Wiederauffüllen *nt*; Auffüllen *nt*.

replete [rɪ'pli:t] *adj (form)* reichlich versehen *or* ausgestattet *(with* mit); *(well-fed) person* gesättigt.

repletion [rɪ'pli:ʃən] *n (form)* Sättigung *f*. **to eat to** ~ essen, bis man gesättigt ist.

replica ['replɪkə] *n (of painting, statue)* Reproduktion, Kopie *f*; *(of document)* Kopie *f*; *(of ship, building etc)* Nachbildung *f*. **she is a** ~ **of her sister** sie ist das Ebenbild ihrer Schwester.

reply [rɪ'plaɪ] **1** *n (letter)* Antwort *f*; *(spoken also)* Erwiderung *f*. **in** ~ (als Antwort) darauf; **in** ~ **to your letter/remarks** in Beantwortung Ihres Briefes *(form)*, auf Ihren Brief/Ihre Bemerkungen; ~ **coupon** Antwortschein *m*; **to send a letter** ~ **paid** einen Brief gebührenfrei senden; ~**-paid envelope** freigemachter Briefumschlag, Freiumschlag *m*.
   2 *vt* **to** ~ **(to sb) that** ... (jdm) antworten, daß ...
   3 *vi (to sth* auf etw *+acc)* antworten; *(spoken also)* erwidern.

repoint [,ri:'pɔɪnt] *vt (Build)* neu verfugen.

repopulate [,ri:'pɒpjʊleɪt] *vt area* neu besiedeln.

report [rɪ'pɔ:t] **1** *n* **(a)** *(account, statement)* Bericht *m (on* über *+acc)*; *(Press, Rad, TV also)* Reportage *f (on* über *+acc)*. **to give a** ~ **on sth** Bericht über etw *(acc)* erstatten/eine Reportage über etw *(acc)* machen; **an official** ~ **on the motor industry** ein Gutachten *nt* über die Autoindustrie; **(school)** ~ Zeugnis *nt*; **chairman's** ~ Bericht *m* des Vorsitzenden; ~ **card** *(Sch)* Zeugnis(blatt) *nt*; **the bill has reached the** ~ **stage** *(Brit Parl)* der Gesetzentwurf kommt nach seiner Beratung im Ausschuß zur Berichterstattung wieder vors Parlament.
   (b) *(rumour)* **to know sth only by** ~ etw nur vom Hörensagen kennen; **there is a** ~ **that** ... es wird gesagt, daß ...
   (c) *(reputation)* Ruf *m*. **of good** ~ von gutem Ruf.
   (d) *(of gun)* Knall *m*. **with a loud** ~ mit lautem Knall.
   2 *vt* **(a)** *results, findings* berichten über *(+acc)*; *(announce officially also)* melden; *(tell to particular person also)* melden *(to sb* jdm*)*. **to** ~ **that** ... berichten, daß ...; **he** ~**ed to me that** ... er meldete mir, daß ...; **to** ~ **progress** einen Tätigkeitsbericht abgeben; **the papers** ~**ed the crime as solved** laut Presseberichten ist das Verbrechen aufgeklärt; **he is** ~**ed as having said** ... er soll gesagt haben ...; **it is** ~**ed that a prisoner has escaped**, a prisoner is ~**ed to have escaped** ein Gefangener wird als geflüchtet gemeldet *or* gilt als vermißt; **it is** ~**ed from the White House that** ... es wird vom Weißen Haus berichtet *or* gemeldet, daß ...
   (b) *(to sb* jdm*) (notify authorities of) accident, crime, suspect, criminal, culprit* melden; *(to police also)* anzeigen; *one's position* angeben. **to** ~ **sb for sth** jdn wegen etw melden; **to** ~ **sb sick** jdn krank melden; **to** ~ **sb missing** als vermißt gemeldet; **nothing to** ~ keine besonderen Vorkommnisse!
   3 *vi* **(a)** *(announce oneself)* sich melden. ~ **to the director on Monday** melden Sie sich am Montag beim Direktor; **to** ~ **for duty** sich zum Dienst melden; **to** ~ **to one's unit** *(Mil)* sich bei seiner Einheit melden; **to** ~ **sick** sich krank melden.
   (b) *(give a* ~*)* berichten, Bericht erstatten *(on* über *+acc)*; *(work as journalist)* Reporter(in *f*) *m* sein. **the committee is ready to** ~ der Ausschuß hat seinen Bericht fertig; **this is Michael Brown** ~**ing (from Rome)** *(Rad, TV)* Michael Brown (mit einem Bericht aus Rom).
   ♦**report back** *vi* **(a)** *(announce one's return)* sich zurückmelden. **you must** ~ ~ **at 6 o'clock** melden Sie sich um 6 Uhr zurück. **(b)** *(give report)* Bericht erstatten *(to sb* jdm*)*.

reportage [,repɔ:'tɑ:ʒ] *n* Reportage *f*; *(style)* Reporterstil *m*.

reported [rɪ'pɔ:tɪd] *adj* **(a)** gemeldet. **(b)** *(Gram)* ~ **speech** indirekte Rede.

reportedly [rɪ'pɔ:tɪdlɪ] *adv* wie verlautet.

reporter [rɪ'pɔ:təʳ] *n* **(a)** *(Press, Rad, TV)* Reporter(in *f*), Berichterstatter(in *f*) *m*; *(on the spot)* Korrespondent(in *f*) *m*. **special** ~ Sonderberichterstatter *m*; ~**s' gallery** *(Jur, Parl)* Pressetribüne *f*. **(b)** *(Jur, Parl: stenographer)* Stenograph(in *f*), Gerichtsschreiber(in *f*) *(old) m*.

repose [rɪ'pəʊz] **1** *n (liter) (rest, peace)* Ruhe *f*; *(composure)* Gelassenheit *f*. **in** ~ in Ruhe. **2** *vt (form, liter)* **(a)** *trust* setzen *(in* in *or* auf *+acc)*. **(b)** **to** ~ **oneself** *(rest)* sich ausruhen. **3** *vi (form, liter)* **(a)** *(rest, be buried)* ruhen. **(b)** *(be based)* beruhen *(upon* auf *+dat)*.

repository [rɪ'pɒzɪtərɪ] *n (warehouse)* Lager, Magazin *nt*; *(fig) (of facts etc)* Quelle *f (of* für*)*; *(book, library)* Fundgrube *f (of* für*)*; *(liter: of secret)* Hüter(in *f*) *m*.

repossess [,ri:pə'zes] *vt* wieder in Besitz nehmen.

repp *n see* **rep²**.

reprehend [,reprɪ'hend] *vt* tadeln, rügen.

reprehensible [,reprɪ'hensɪbl] *adj* verwerflich, tadelnswert.

reprehensibly [,reprɪ'hensɪblɪ] *adv* verwerflich.

reprehension [,reprɪ'henʃən] *n* **(a)** *no pl (act)* Tadeln, Rügen *nt*. **(b)** *(rebuke)* Tadel *m*, Rüge *f*.

represent [,reprɪ'zent] *vt* **(a)** darstellen; *(stand for also)* stehen

---

für; *(symbolize also)* symbolisieren. **he** ~**s all that is best in** ... er verkörpert das Beste *(+gen)* ...
   (b) *(act or speak for, Parl, Jur)* vertreten. **he** ~**s their firm in London** er vertritt *or* repräsentiert die Firma in London; **many countries were** ~**ed at the ceremony** viele Länder waren bei der Feier vertreten; **the foreign tourist should never forget that he** ~**s his country** ein Tourist sollte im Ausland nie vergessen, daß er sein Land repräsentiert.
   (c) *(declare to be)* *(as als) person, event, risk etc* darstellen; *(falsely)* hinstellen. **he** ~**ed me as a fool/a saint** er stellte mich als Narren/Engel hin; **I am not what you** ~ **me to be** ich bin nicht so, wie du mich hinstellst; **it is exactly as** ~**ed in the advertisement** es ist genau, wie in der Anzeige dargestellt.
   (d) *(set forth, explain)* vor Augen führen *(to sb* jdm*)*.
   (e) *(Theat) character, part* darstellen.

re-present [,ri:prɪ'zent] *vt* nochmals vorlegen.

representation [,reprɪzen'teɪʃən] *n* **(a)** *no pl (representing) see vt (a-c)* Darstellung *f*; Symbolisierung *f*; Vertretung *f*; Darstellung *f*; Hinstellung *f*.
   (b) *(drawing, description, Theat)* Darstellung *f*.
   (c) ~**s** *pl (esp Pol: remonstrations)* Vorstellungen, Vorhaltungen *pl*; **the ambassador made** ~**s to the government** der Botschafter wurde bei der Regierung vorstellig.

representational [,reprɪzen'teɪʃənl] *adj art, picture* gegenständlich. **in** ~ **form** symbolisch; **these matchsticks are a purely** ~ **device to show** ... diese Streichhölzer sind nur ein Mittel, um ... darzustellen; **a** ~ **party of** eine Vertretung *(+gen)*.

representative [,reprɪ'zentətɪv] **1** *adj* **(a)** *(of* für*)* *(typical) cross-section, sample* repräsentativ; *attitude also* typisch; *(symbolic)* symbolisch.
   (b) *(acting for)* repräsentativ; *delegation* Repräsentativ-. **a** ~ **body** eine Vertretung.
   (c) *(Parl) government* repräsentativ. ~ **assembly** Abgeordneten-Versammlung *f*.
   2 *n (Comm)* Vertreter(in *f*) *m*; *(Jur)* Bevollmächtigte(r), Beauftragte(r) *mf*; *(US Pol)* Abgeordnete(r) *mf*. **authorized** ~ Bevollmächtigte(r) *mf*; *see* **house**.

repress [rɪ'pres] *vt revolt, rebellion, population* unterdrücken; *emotions, desires also* zurückdrängen; *laugh, sneeze also* zurückhalten; *(Psych)* verdrängen.

repressed [rɪ'prest] *adj* unterdrückt; *(Psych)* verdrängt.

repression [rɪ'preʃən] *n* Unterdrückung *f*; *(Psych)* Verdrängung *f*.

repressive [rɪ'presɪv] *adj* repressiv.

reprieve [rɪ'pri:v] **1** *n (Jur)* Begnadigung *f*; *(postponement)* Strafaufschub *m*; *(fig)* Gnadenfrist *f*.
   2 *vt* **he was** ~**d** *(Jur)* er wurde begnadigt; *(sentence postponed)* seine Strafe wurde aufgeschoben; **the building/firm has been** ~**d for a while** das Gebäude/die Firma ist vorerst noch einmal verschont geblieben.

reprimand ['reprɪmɑ:nd] **1** *n* Tadel *m*; *(official also)* Verweis *m*. **2** *vt* tadeln; maßregeln *(geh)*.

reprint [,ri:'prɪnt] **1** *vt* neu auflegen, neu abdrucken, nachdrucken. **2** ['ri:prɪnt] *n* Neuauflage *f*, Nachdruck *m*.

reprisal [rɪ'praɪzəl] *n (for* gegen*)* Vergeltungsmaßnahme *f*; *(Mil, between companies, countries etc also)* Repressalie *f*. **to take** ~**s** zu Repressalien greifen; **as a** ~ **for** als Vergeltung für; **by way of** ~ als Vergeltungsmaßnahme.

repro ['reprəʊ] *n (inf) abbr of* **reproduction** Repro *f or nt*.

reproach [rɪ'prəʊtʃ] **1** *n* **(a)** *(rebuke)* Vorwurf *m*. **to heap** ~**es on sb** jdn mit Vorwürfen überhäufen; **a term/look of** ~ ein Vorwurf *m*/ein vorwurfsvoller Blick; **above or beyond** ~ über jeden Vorwurf erhaben.
   (b) *(discredit)* **to be a** ~ **to sb/sth** eine Schande für jdn/etw sein; **to bring** ~ **(up)on sb/sth** jdn/etw in schlechten Ruf bringen; **to bring** ~ **(up)on oneself** in schlechten Ruf kommen.
   2 *vt* Vorwürfe machen *(+dat)*. **to** ~ **sb for his mistake** jdn einen Fehler vorwerfen *or* zum Vorwurf machen; **to** ~ **sb for having done sth** jdm Vorwürfe dafür machen, daß er etw getan hat; **he has nothing to** ~ **himself for or with** er hat sich *(dat)* nichts vorzuwerfen.

reproachful *adj*, ~**ly** *adv* [rɪ'prəʊtʃfʊl, -fəlɪ] vorwurfsvoll.

reprobate ['reprəʊbeɪt] **1** *adj action* ruchlos, verwerflich; *person* verkommen; *(Eccl)* verdammt. **2** *n* verkommenes Subjekt, Gestrauchelte(r) *mf (geh)*; *(Eccl)* Verdammte(r) *mf*. **3** *vt (form)* verdammen.

reprobation [,reprəʊ'beɪʃən] *n* Verdammung *f*.

reprocess [,ri:'prəʊses] *vt* wiederverwerten; *sewage, atomic waste* wiederaufbereiten.

reproduce [,ri:prə'dju:s] **1** *vt* **(a)** wiedergeben; *(Art, mechanically, electronically also)* reproduzieren; *(Typ)* abdrucken.
   (b) *(Biol)* **to** ~ **its kind** sich *or* seine Art fortpflanzen.
   (c) *(Theat) play* neu inszenieren.
   2 *vi* **(a)** *(Biol)* sich fortpflanzen *or* vermehren. **(b)** *(Typ)* **this picture won't** ~ **well** dieses Bild läßt sich nicht gut reproduzieren.

reproducible [,ri:prə'dju:sɪbəl] *adj* reproduzierbar.

reproduction [,ri:prə'dʌkʃən] *n* **(a)** *(procreation)* Fortpflanzung *f*.
   (b) *(copying)* Reproduktion *f*; *(of documents also)* Vervielfältigung *f*. **sound** ~ Klang- *or* Tonwiedergabe *f*; **this radio has good** ~ das Radio gibt den Ton gut wieder.
   (c) *(copy)* Reproduktion *f*; *(photo)* Kopie *f*; *(sound* ~*)* Wiedergabe *f*. ~ **furniture** *(modern)* Stilmöbel *pl*.

reproductive [,ri:prə'dʌktɪv] *adj* Fortpflanzungs-.

reproof¹ [rɪ'pru:f] *vt garment* frisch *or* neu imprägnieren.

reproof² [rɪ'pru:f] *n* Tadel *m*, Rüge *f*.

reproval [rɪ'pru:vəl] *n* **(a)** *no pl (act)* Tadeln, Rügen *nt*. **(b)** *see* **reproof²**.

reprove [rɪ'pru:v] *vt person, action* tadeln, rügen.

reproving *adj*, ~**ly** *adv* [rɪ'pru:vɪŋ, -lɪ] tadelnd.

reptile ['reptaɪl] 1 n Reptil, Kriechtier nt; (fig pej) Kriecher m (pej). 2 adj Reptilien-, reptilartig.

reptilian [rep'tɪlɪən] 1 adj Reptilien-, reptilartig; (fig pej) kriecherisch (pej). 2 n Reptil, Kriechtier nt.

republic [rɪ'pʌblɪk] n Republik f.

republican [rɪ'pʌblɪkən] 1 adj republikanisch. 2 n Republikaner(in f) m.

republicanism [rɪ'pʌblɪkənɪzəm] n Republikanismus m.

republication ['riː,pʌblɪ'keɪʃən] n see **republish** Wieder- or Neuveröffentlichung f; erneutes Aushängen.

republish [,riː'pʌblɪʃ] vt book wieder or neu veröffentlichen or herausbringen; banns wieder aushängen.

repudiate [rɪ'pjuːdɪeɪt] vt person verstoßen; authorship, (government etc) debt, obligation nicht anerkennen; accusation zurückweisen.

repudiation [rɪ,pjuːdɪ'eɪʃən] n see vt Verstoßung f; Nichtanerkennung f; Zurückweisung f.

repugnance [rɪ'pʌgnəns] n Widerwille m, Abneigung f (towards, for gegen).

repugnant [rɪ'pʌgnənt] adj widerlich, abstoßend.

repulse [rɪ'pʌls] 1 vt (Mil) enemy, attack zurückschlagen, abwehren; (fig) person, help, offer abweisen, zurückweisen. 2 n (Mil) Abwehr f, Zurückschlagen nt; (fig) Abweisung, Zurückweisung f. to meet with or suffer a ~ abgewiesen or zurückgewiesen werden.

repulsion [rɪ'pʌlʃən] n (a) (distaste) Widerwille m (for gegen). (b) (Phys) Abstoßung f.

repulsive [rɪ'pʌlsɪv] adj (a) (loathsome) abstoßend, widerwärtig. (b) (Phys) forces abstoßend, Repulsiv-.

repulsively [rɪ'pʌlsɪvlɪ] adv abstoßend, widerwärtig. ~ ugly abstoßend häßlich.

repulsiveness [rɪ'pʌlsɪvnɪs] n see adj (a) Abstoßende(s) nt (of an +dat), Widerwärtigkeit f.

repurchase [,riː'pɜːtʃɪs] 1 n Rückkauf, Wiedererwerb m. 2 vt zurückkaufen, wieder erwerben.

reputable ['repjʊtəbl] adj ehrenhaft; occupation ordentlich, anständig; dealer, firm seriös.

reputation [,repjʊ'teɪʃən] n Ruf, Name m; (bad ~) schlechter Ruf. what sort of ~ does she have? wie ist ihr Ruf?; he has a ~ for being … er hat den Ruf, … zu sein; I know his ~ ich kenne seinen Ruf; to have a ~ for honesty als ehrlich gelten; you don't want to get (yourself) a ~, you know du willst dich doch sicherlich nicht in Verruf bringen.

repute [rɪ'pjuːt] 1 n Ruf m, Ansehen nt. to know sb by ~ von jdm schon viel gehört haben; to be of good ~ einen guten Ruf genießen; a restaurant of ~ ein angesehenes Restaurant; a house of ill ~ ein Haus von zweifelhaftem Ruf; to hold sb in high ~ eine hohe Meinung von jdm haben; to be held in high ~ in hohem Ruf or Ansehen stehen.

2 vt (pass only) he is ~d to be … man sagt, daß er … ist; to be ~d rich als reich gelten; he is ~d to be the best er gilt als der Beste, er steht in dem Ruf, der Beste zu sein.

reputed [rɪ'pjuːtɪd] adj angenommen. he is the ~ writer of two epic poems er soll zwei epische Gedichte geschrieben haben; the ~ father (Jur) der vermutliche Vater.

reputedly [rɪ'pjuːtɪdlɪ] adv wie man annimmt. he is ~ the best player in the world er gilt als der beste Spieler der Welt.

request [rɪ'kwest] 1 n Bitte f, Wunsch m, Ersuchen nt (geh). at sb's ~ auf jds Bitte etc; on/by ~ auf Wunsch; no parking by ~ bitte nicht parken; to make a ~ for sth um etw bitten; I have a ~ to make of or to you ich habe eine Bitte an Sie, ich muß eine Bitte an Sie richten; record ~s Plattenwünsche pl.

2 vt bitten, ersuchen (geh); (Rad) record sich (dat) wünschen. to ~ silence um Ruhe bitten or ersuchen (geh); to ~ sth of or from sb jdn um etw bitten or ersuchen (geh); "you are ~ed not to smoke" „bitte nicht rauchen"; see presence, pleasure.

request: ~ programme n (Rad) Wunschsendung f; ~ stop n (Brit) Bedarfshaltestelle f.

requiem ['rekwɪəm] n Requiem nt. ~ mass Totenmesse f.

require [rɪ'kwaɪəʳ] vt (a) (need) brauchen, benötigen; thing also nötig haben; work, action erfordern; (desire) wünschen, mögen. I have all I ~ ich habe alles, was ich brauche; the journey will ~ 3 hours man braucht or benötigt 3 Stunden für die Reise; it ~s great care das erfordert große Sorgfalt; this plant ~s frequent watering diese Pflanze braucht viel Wasser; what qualifications are ~d? welche Qualifikationen werden verlangt or sind erforderlich?; to be ~d to do sth etw müssen; that is not ~d das ist nicht nötig or erforderlich; if you ~ me wenn Sie mich benötigen; if ~d falls notwendig or erforderlich; when (it is) ~d auf Wunsch, wenn es gewünscht wird; as and when ~d nach Bedarf; dilute as ~d nach Bedarf verdünnen.

(b) (order) verlangen. to ~ sb to do sth von jdm verlangen, daß er etw tut; you are ~d to report to the boss immediately Sie sollen sich sofort beim Chef melden; to ~ sth of sb etw von jdm verlangen; as ~d by law den gesetzlichen Bestimmungen gemäß or entsprechend.

required [rɪ'kwaɪəd] adj erforderlich; date vorgeschrieben; (desired) gewünscht. the ~ amount die benötigte Menge; ~ reading (Sch, Univ) Pflichtlektüre f.

requirement [rɪ'kwaɪəmənt] n (a) (need) Bedürfnis nt, Bedarf m no pl; (desire) Wunsch, Anspruch m. to meet sb's ~s jds Bedürfnisse erfüllen; jds Wünschen entsprechen, jds Ansprüchen gerecht werden; there isn't enough bread to meet the ~s es ist nicht genügend Brot da, um den Bedarf zu decken. (b) (condition, thing required) Erfordernis nt. to fit the ~s den Erfordernissen entsprechen.

requisite ['rekwɪzɪt] 1 n Artikel m; (necessary thing) Erfordernis nt. bath/toilet/travel ~s Bade-/Toiletten-/Reiseartikel pl or -utensilien pl. 2 adj erforderlich, notwendig. the ~ time die dazu erforderliche Zeit.

requisition [,rekwɪ'zɪʃən] 1 n Anforderung f; (act: of objects) Requisition f. to make a ~ for sth etw anfordern. 2 vt sb's services anfordern; supplies, food requirieren.

requital [rɪ'kwaɪtl] n (repayment) Vergeltung f; (revenge also) Rache f.

requite [rɪ'kwaɪt] vt (a) (repay) person es vergelten (+dat); action vergelten. ~d love erwiderte Liebe. (b) (avenge) action vergelten; person rächen.

reran [,riː'ræn] pret of **rerun**.

reread [,riː'riːd] pret, ptp **reread** [,riː'red] vt wieder or nochmals lesen.

reredos ['rɪədɒs] n Retabel nt.

reroute [,riː'ruːt] vt train, bus umleiten.

rerun [,riː'rʌn] (vb: pret **reran**, ptp ~) 1 vt film wieder or nochmals aufführen; tape wieder or nochmals abspielen; race wiederholen. 2 ['riːrʌn] n see vt Wiederaufführung f; Wiederabspielen nt; Wiederholung f.

resale [,riː'seɪl] n Weiterverkauf m. "not for ~" „nicht zum Weiterverkauf bestimmt"; (on free sample) „unverkäufliches Muster"; ~ price maintenance Preisbindung f.

resat [,riː'sæt] pret, ptp of **resit**.

rescind [rɪ'sɪnd] vt decision rückgängig machen, widerrufen; judgement, contract also aufheben; law, act aufheben.

rescission [rɪ'sɪʒən] n see **rescind** Widerruf m; Annullierung f; Aufhebung f.

rescript ['riːskrɪpt] n (Hist, Rel) Erlaß m, Edikt nt.

rescue ['reskjuː] 1 n (saving) Rettung f; (freeing) Errettung, Befreiung f. ~ was difficult die Rettung war schwierig; to go/come to sb's ~ jdm zu Hilfe kommen; to the ~! zu Hilfe!; it was Bob to the ~ Bob war unsere/seine etc Rettung; ~ attempt/operation/party Rettungsversuch m/-aktion f/ -mannschaft f; see air-sea ~.

2 vt (save) retten; (free) erretten, befreien. you ~d me from a difficult situation du hast mich aus einer schwierigen Lage gerettet; the ~d were taken to hospital die Geretteten wurden ins Krankenhaus gebracht.

rescuer ['reskjuəʳ] n see vt Retter(in f) m; Befreier(in f) m.

research [rɪ'sɜːtʃ] 1 n Forschung f (into, on über +acc). a piece of ~ eine Forschungsarbeit; to do ~ forschen, Forschung betreiben; to carry out ~ into the effects of sth Forschungen über die Auswirkungen einer Sache (gen) anstellen.

2 vi forschen, Forschung betreiben. to ~ into or on sth etw erforschen, über etw (acc) forschen or Forschung betreiben.

3 vt erforschen, untersuchen.

research in cpds Forschungs-; ~ assistant n wissenschaftlicher Assistent, wissenschaftliche Assistentin.

researcher [rɪ'sɜːtʃəʳ] n Forscher(in f) m.

research: ~ establishment n Forschungsstätte f; ~ fellow n (Univ) Forschungsstipendiat(in f) m; ~ fellowship n Forschungsstipendium nt; ~ student n (Univ) Student, der Forschungen für einen höheren akademischen Grad betreibt, ≈ Doktorand(in f) m; ~ worker n Forscher m.

reseat [,riː'siːt] vt (a) person umsetzen. to ~ oneself sich wieder setzen; when everyone was ~ed als sich alle wieder gesetzt hatten. (b) chair einen neuen Sitz geben (+dat); trousers einen neuen Hosenboden anfertigen für. (c) (Tech) valve neu einschleifen.

resell [,riː'sel] vt weiterverkaufen, wieder verkaufen.

resemblance [rɪ'zembləns] n Ähnlichkeit f. to bear a strong/a faint/no ~ to sth/sb starke/leichte/wenig Ähnlichkeit mit jdm/etw haben; there's not the slightest ~ between them es besteht nicht die geringste Ähnlichkeit zwischen ihnen, sie sind sich (dat) nicht im geringsten ähnlich.

resemble [rɪ'zembl] vt ähneln, gleichen. they ~ each other sie ähneln or gleichen sich or einander.

resent [rɪ'zent] vt remarks, behaviour übelnehmen, sich ärgern über (+acc); person ein Ressentiment haben gegen. he ~ed her for the rest of his life er nahm ihr das sein Leben lang übel; he ~ed my having or me for having got the job er nahm es mir übel, daß ich die Stelle bekommen hatte; he ~ed the fact that … er ärgerte sich darüber, daß …; to ~ sb's success jdm seinen Erfolg mißgönnen; I ~ that das gefällt mir nicht; he may ~ my being here es könnte ihn ärgern, daß ich hier bin.

resentful [rɪ'zentfʊl] adj ärgerlich (of sb auf jdn); (of stepmother, younger brother etc) voller Ressentiment (of gegen). to be ~ of sb's success jdm seinen Erfolg nicht gönnen; ~ of the criticisms levelled at him die an ihm geübte Kritik übelnehmend; he felt ~ about her promotion er nahm es ihr übel, daß sie befördert worden war; feeling ~ he walked out of the room grollend verließ er das Zimmer.

resentfully [rɪ'zentfʊlɪ] adv ärgerlich.

resentment [rɪ'zentmənt] n Ärger, Groll (of über +acc) m no pl.

reservation [,rezə'veɪʃən] n (a) (qualification of opinion) Vorbehalt m; (Philos) Mentalreservation f (spec). without ~ ohne Vorbehalt, vorbehaltlos; with ~s unter Vorbehalt(en); to have ~s about sth/sb Bedenken in bezug auf jdn/etw haben.

(b) (booking) Reservierung f. to make a ~ at the hotel/on the boat ein Zimmer im Hotel/einen Platz auf dem Schiff reservieren lassen or bestellen; how many ~s did you make? für wieviele Personen haben Sie reservieren lassen?; to have a ~ (for a room) ein Zimmer reserviert haben.

(c) (area of land) Reservat nt, Reservation f. (central) ~ (Brit: on motorway) Mittelstreifen m.

reserve [rɪ'zɜːv] 1 vt (a) (keep) aufsparen, aufheben. to ~ one's strength seine Kräfte sparen; to ~ judgement/one's decision mit einem Urteil/seiner Entscheidung zurückhalten; to ~ the right to do sth sich (dat) (das Recht) vorbehalten, etw zu tun; to ~ a warm welcome for sb einen herzlichen Empfang für jdn bereithalten; to ~ oneself for sth sich für etw schonen; a great career is ~d for him ihm ist eine große Karriere sicher.

(b) (book in advance: client) reservieren lassen. the box

office lady ~d 4 seats for us die Dame an der Kasse hat uns 4 Plätze reserviert; **are you reserving these seats for anyone?** haben Sie diese Plätze für jdn reserviert?
2 n (a) (store) (of an +dat) Reserve f, Vorrat m; (Fin) Reserve f. **to have great ~s of energy** große Kraftreserven haben; **cash ~** Barreserve f; **~ fund** Rücklage f, Reservefonds m; **world ~s of copper** die Weltkupferreserven pl, die Weltreserven pl an Kupfer; **to have/keep in ~** in Reserve haben/halten.
(b) without ~ ohne Vorbehalt, vorbehaltlos; **with certain ~s** unter or mit gewissen Vorbehalten.
(c) see ~ **price.**
(d) (piece of land) Reservat nt, Reservation f; see **game** ~, **nature** ~.
(e) (coolness, reticence) Reserve, Zurückhaltung f. **he treated me with some ~** er behandelte mich etwas reserviert.
(f) (Mil) (force) Reserve f; (soldier) Soldat m der Reserve. **the ~s** die Reserveeinheiten.
(g) (Sport) Reservespieler(in f) m.

reserve in cpds Reserve-; **~ currency** n Leitwährung f.
reserved [rɪ'zɜːvd] adj (a) (reticent) zurückhaltend, reserviert (about in bezug auf +acc). **(b)** room, seat reserviert, belegt. **(c)** (Publishing) all rights ~ alle Rechte vorbehalten.
reservedly [rɪ'zɜːvɪdlɪ] adv zurückhaltend, reserviert.
reserve: ~ **list** n (Mil) Reserveliste f; ~ **player** n Reserve-spieler(in f) m; ~ **price** n Mindest- or Ausrufpreis m; ~ **tank** n Reservetank m; ~ **team** n Reserve(mannschaft) f.
reservist [rɪ'zɜːvɪst] n (Mil) Reservist m.
reservoir ['rezəvwɑː'] n (lit) (for water) Reservoir nt; (for gas) Speicher m; (fig: of knowledge, facts, talent etc) Fundgrube f.
reset [,riː'set] pret, ptp ~ vt precious stone neu (ein)fassen; watch neu stellen (to auf +acc); dial, gauge zurückstellen (to auf +acc); (Med) limb, bone wieder einrichten; dislocated shoulder wieder einrenken; (Typ) text neu setzen.
resettle [,riː'setl] vt refugees umsiedeln; land neu or wieder besiedeln.
resettlement [,riː'setlmənt] n see vt Umsiedlung f; Neubesied(e)lung f.
reshape [,riː'ʃeɪp] vt dough, clay etc umformen, neu formen; text umschreiben; policy umstellen.
reshuffle [,riː'ʃʌfl] **1** vt cards neu mischen; (fig) Cabinet umbilden; board of directors umbilden, umbesetzen. **2** n (of cards) erneutes Mischen; (fig: of board) Umbesetzung, Umbildung f. **Cabinet ~** (Pol) Kabinettsumbildung f.
reside [rɪ'zaɪd] vi (a) (form: live) seinen Wohnsitz haben; monarch, ambassador etc residieren. **(b)** (fig form) to ~ in sth in etw (dat) liegen; **the power ~s in the President** die Macht liegt or ruht beim Präsidenten.
residence ['rezɪdəns] n (a) (house) Wohnhaus nt; (hostel: for students, nurses) Wohnheim nt; (of monarch, ambassador etc) Residenz f. **the President's official ~** der Amtssitz des Präsidenten; see **hall.**
(b) no pl (stay, living) country/place of ~ Aufenthaltsland nt/Wohnort m; **after 5 years' ~ in Britain** nach 5 Jahren Aufent-halt in Großbritannien; **to take up ~ in the capital** sich in der Hauptstadt niederlassen; ~ **in the country** is restricted to nationals nur Staatsangehörige können im Land Wohnsitz nehmen (form); **to be in ~** (monarch, governor etc) anwesend sein; **poet etc in ~** (Univ) ansässiger Dichter etc; **the students are now in ~** das Semester hat angefangen; **there is always a doctor in ~** es ist immer ein Arzt am Ort; ~ **permit** Aufent-haltsgenehmigung f.
residency ['rezɪdənsɪ] n (a) (US) see **residence (b). (b)** (Brit) Residenz f. **(c)** (of doctor) Assistenzzeit f im Krankenhaus.
resident ['rezɪdənt] **1** n (a) Bewohner(in f) m; (in town also) Einwohner(in f) m; (of institution also) Insasse m, Insassin f; (in hotel) Gast m. **"access restricted to ~s only"** „Anlieger frei"; **parking for ~s only** Parkplatz nur für Mieter; (on road) Parken nur für Anlieger gestattet; (at hotel) Parkplatz nur für Gäste. **(b)** (doctor) Anstaltsarzt m/-ärztin f.
2 adj (a) (in country, town) wohnhaft; (attached to institu-tion) ansässig, Haus-; chaplain, tutor, physician Haus-. **they are ~ in Germany** sie haben ihren Wohnsitz in Deutschland; **the ~ population** die ansässige Bevölkerung; **are you ~ in the hotel?** sind Sie Hotelgast/Hotelgäste? **(b) to be ~ in sb/sth** see **reside (b).**
residential [,rezɪ'denʃəl] adj area Wohn-; job im Haus; college mit einem Wohnheim verbunden; course mit Wohnung im Heim. ~ **requirements for voting** Meldevoraussetzungen zur Ausübung des Wahlrechts.
residual [rɪ'zɪdjʊəl] **1** adj restlich, Rest-; (Chem) Rückstands-, rückständig. ~ **soil** (Geol) Alluvialboden m; (by erosion) Verwitterungsboden m. **2** n (Chem) Rückstand m; (Statistics, Math) Abweichung f.
residuary [rɪ'zɪdjʊərɪ] adj restlich, Rest-; (Chem) rückständig. ~ **legatee** (Jur) Empfänger m des nach Abzug sämtlicher Verbindlichkeiten verbleibenden Nachlasses.
residue ['rezɪdjuː] n Rest m; (Chem) Rückstand m; (Jur) Nachlaß m nach Abzug sämtlicher Verbindlichkeiten.
residuum [rɪ'zɪdjʊəm] n (Chem) Rückstand m, Residuum nt; (Jur) see **residue.**
resign [rɪ'zaɪn] **1** vt (a) (give up) office, post zurücktreten von, abgeben; claim, rights aufgeben, verzichten auf (+acc). **to ~ power** abtreten; **he ~ed the leadership to his colleague** or **übergab or überließ die Leitung seinem Kollegen; to ~ one's commission** (Mil) seinen Abschied nehmen.
(b) to ~ oneself to sth/to doing sth sich mit etw abfinden/sich damit abfinden, etw zu tun; see also **resigned.**
2 vi (from public appointment, committee) zurücktreten; (employee) kündigen; (civil servant, clergyman) sein Amt niederlegen; (teacher) aus dem Dienst ausscheiden. **to ~ from office** sein Amt niederlegen; **he ~ed from (his job with) "The**

Times" er hat (seine Stelle) bei der „Times" gekündigt; **the Prime Minister was forced to ~** der Premierminister wurde zum Rücktritt gezwungen.
resignation [,rezɪg'neɪʃən] n (a) see vi Rücktritt m; Kündigung f; Amtsniederlegung f; Ausscheiden nt aus dem Dienst. **to hand in** or **tender** (form) **one's ~** seinen Rücktritt/seine Kündigung einreichen/sein Amt niederlegen/aus dem Dienst ausscheiden.
(b) (mental state) Resignation (to gegenüber +dat), Ergebung (to in +acc) f.
(c) (form: of right, claim etc) Verzicht m (of auf +acc).
resigned [rɪ'zaɪnd] adj person resigniert. **to become ~ to sth** sich mit etw abfinden; **I was ~ to walking, when ... ich hatte mich schon damit abgefunden, zu Fuß gehen zu müssen, als ...; to be ~ to one's fate** sich in sein Schicksal ergeben haben.
resignedly [rɪ'zaɪnɪdlɪ] adv see adj.
resilience [rɪ'zɪlɪəns] n see adj Federn nt; Unverwüstlichkeit f.
resilient [rɪ'zɪlɪənt] adj (a) material federnd attr. **to be ~** federn. **(b)** (fig) person, nature unverwüstlich.
resin ['rezɪn] n Harz nt.
resinous ['rezɪnəs] adj harzig, Harz-.
resist [rɪ'zɪst] **1** vt (a) sich widersetzen (+dat); arrest, sb's advances, enemy, attack also Widerstand leisten gegen, sich wehren gegen; (fig) proposal, change also sich entgegenstellen (+dat), sich sträuben or wehren gegen.
(b) temptation, sb, sb's charms widerstehen (+dat). **I couldn't ~ (eating) another cake** ich konnte der Versuchung nicht widerstehen, noch ein Stück Kuchen zu essen.
(c) (wall, door) standhalten (+dat). **the lock ~ed my attempts at opening it** das Schloß widerstand meinen Versuchen, es zu öffnen; **to ~ corrosion** korrosionsbeständig sein.
2 vi see vt (a) sich widersetzen; Widerstand leisten, sich wehren; sich sträuben or wehren.
(b) widerstehen.
(c) standhalten.
resistance [rɪ'zɪstəns] n (to gegen) Widerstand m (also Elec, Phys, Mil); (Med) Widerstandsfähigkeit, Resistenz (geh) f. ~ **to water/heat** Wasser-/Hitzebeständigkeit f; **his ~ of this tempta-tion** daß er dieser Versuchung widerstanden hat; **to meet with ~** auf Widerstand stoßen; **to offer no ~ (to sb/sth)** (to attacker, advances etc) (jdm/gegen etw) keinen Widerstand leisten, (to proposals) sich (jdm/einer Sache) nicht entgegenstellen or widersetzen; ~ **fighter** Widerstandskämpfer m; **the (French) R~** (Hist) die Résistance; **the R~ movement** (Hist) die fran-zösische Widerstandsbewegung; see **line[1], passive.**
resistant [rɪ'zɪstənt] adj material, surface strapazierfähig; (Med) immun (to gegen). **water-~** wasserbeständig.
resistor [rɪ'zɪstə'] n (Elec) Widerstand m.
resit [,riː'sɪt] (vb: pret, ptp **resat**) **1** vt exam wiederholen. **2** vi die Prüfung wiederholen. **3** ['riːsɪt] n Wiederholung(sprüfung) f.
resole [,riː'səʊl] vt neu besohlen.
resolute ['rezəluːt] adj energisch, entschlossen; answer entschieden, bestimmt.
resolutely ['rezəluːtlɪ] adv see adj.
resoluteness ['rezəluːtnɪs] n see adj Entschlossenheit f; Entschiedenheit, Bestimmtheit f.
resolution [,rezə'luːʃən] n (a) (decision) Beschluß m; (Pol, Admin etc also) Resolution f; (governing one's behaviour) Vor-satz m. **good ~s** gute Vorsätze pl.
(b) no pl (resoluteness) Entschlossenheit, Bestimmtheit f.
(c) no pl (solving: of problem, puzzle) Lösung f.
(d) (Phys, Mus) Auflösung f (into in +acc).
(e) (Med: of swelling) Rückgang m.
resolvable [rɪ'zɒlvəbl] adj see vt (a, c) lösbar; zerstreubar; zer-legbar; auflösbar.
resolve [rɪ'zɒlv] **1** vt (a) problem lösen; doubt zerstreuen.
(b) (decide) **to ~ that ...** beschließen, daß ...; **to ~ to do sth** beschließen, etw zu tun; **that ~d me to ...** das hat mich zu dem Entschluß veranlaßt zu ...
(c) (break up: into elements) zerlegen (into in +acc); (con-vert) auflösen (also Phys) (into in +acc).
(d) (Mus) chord, harmony auflösen (into in +acc).
(e) (Med) zum Rückgang bringen.
2 vi (a) (decide) **to ~ (up)on sth** etw beschließen.
(b) (into in +acc) (break up) zerfallen; (be converted) sich auflösen. **the question ~s into 4 points** die Frage zerfällt in 4 Punkte.
3 vr (into in +acc) sich zerlegen lassen; (be converted) sich auflösen.
4 n (a) (decision) Beschluß m. **to make a ~ to do sth** den Be-schluß fassen, etw zu tun.
(b) no pl (resoluteness) Entschlossenheit f. **to do sth with ~** etw fest entschlossen tun.
resolved [rɪ'zɒlvd] adj (fest) entschlossen.
resonance ['rezənəns] n Resonanz f; (of voice) voller Klang.
resonant ['rezənənt] adj sound voll; voice klangvoll; room mit Resonanz. ~ **with the sound of singing/a thousand voices** von Gesang/vom Klang von tausend Stimmen erfüllt.
resonator ['rezəneɪtə'] n Resonator m.
resort [rɪ'zɔːt] **1** n (a) (recourse) Ausweg m; (thing, action resorted to also) Rettung f. **without ~ to violence** ohne Gewaltanwendung; **as a last ~** als letztes; **in the last ~** im schlimmsten Fall, wenn alle Stricke reißen (inf); **you were my last ~** du warst meine letzte Rettung.
(b) (place) Urlaubsort m. **coastal ~** Seebad nt; **seaside/summer ~** Seebad nt/Sommerurlaubsort m; **winter sports ~** Wintersportort m; see **health** ~, **holiday** ~.
2 vi (a) (have recourse) **to ~ to sth** zu etw greifen/sich an jdn wenden; **to ~ to violence** Gewalt anwenden, gewalttätig werden; **to ~ to beggary/stealing/swearing** sich aufs Betteln/Stehlen/Fluchen verlegen.

(b) (frequent) to ~ to a place häufig an einem Ort verkehren.

resound [rɪˈzaund] vi (wider)hallen (with von). my ears were still ~ing with the noise mir tönten noch die Ohren von dem Lärm; his name ~ed throughout the land (fig) sein Name war in aller Munde; his speech will ~ throughout the country (fig) seine Rede wird im ganzen Land widerhallen.

resounding [rɪˈzaundɪŋ] adj noise, shout widerhallend; laugh, voice schallend; (fig) triumph, victory, failure gewaltig; success durchschlagend; defeat haushoch. the response was a ~ "no" die Antwort war ein überwältigendes „Nein".

resoundingly [rɪˈzaundɪŋlɪ] adv the play was ~ successful das Stück war ein durchschlagender Erfolg.

resource [rɪˈsɔːs] n (a) ~s pl (wealth, supplies, money etc) Mittel, Ressourcen pl; financial/mineral/natural ~s Geldmittel pl/Bodenschätze pl/Naturschätze pl; ~s in or of men and materials Reserven pl an Menschen und Material; he has no inner ~s er weiß sich (dat) nie zu helfen; he has no ~s against boredom er weiß sich (dat) gegen Langeweile nicht zu helfen; left to his own ~s sich (dat) selbst überlassen; a man of ~s ein Mensch, der sich (dat) immer zu helfen weiß.
(b) (expedient) Ausweg m, Mittel nt. as a last ~ als letzter Ausweg; you are my last ~ du bist meine letzte Rettung.

resourceful [rɪˈsɔːsful] adv person einfallsreich, findig; scheme genial.

resourcefully [rɪˈsɔːfəlɪ] adv see adj.

resourcefulness [rɪˈsɔːsfulnɪs] n see adj Einfallsreichtum m, Findigkeit f; Genialität f.

respect [rɪˈspekt] 1 n (a) (esteem) Respekt m, Achtung f (for vor +dat). to have/show ~ for Respekt or Achtung haben/ zeigen vor (+dat); for the law achten; I have the highest ~ for his ability ich halte ihn für außerordentlich fähig; to behave with ~ sich respektvoll verhalten; to hold sb in (great) ~ jdn (sehr) achten; he commands ~ er ist eine Respektsperson or (public figure) respektgebietende Persönlichkeit; to command the ~ of the nation dem Volk Respekt or Achtung abnötigen; you should have a bit more ~ for his right hook du solltest etwas mehr auf seinen rechten Haken achten.
(b) (consideration) Rücksicht f (for auf +acc). to treat with ~ person rücksichtsvoll behandeln; dangerous person etc sich in acht nehmen vor (+dat); toys, clothes etc schonend behandeln; nitroglycerine should be treated with ~ Nitroglyzerin muß mit äußerster Vorsicht behandelt werden; she has or shows no ~ for other people's feelings sie nimmt keine Rücksicht auf die Gefühle anderer; out of ~ for aus Rücksicht auf (+acc); with (due) ~, I still think that ... bei allem Respekt or mit Verlaub (form), meine ich dennoch, daß ...; without ~ to the consequences ohne Rücksicht auf die Folgen.
(c) (reference) with ~ to ... was ... anbetrifft, in bezug auf ... (+acc); good in ~ of content inhaltlich gut.
(d) (aspect) Hinsicht, Beziehung f. in some/other ~s in gewisser/anderer Hinsicht or Beziehung; in many ~s in vieler Hinsicht; in this ~ in der or dieser Hinsicht or Beziehung; in what ...? in welcher Hinsicht or Beziehung?
(e) ~s pl (regards) Empfehlungen (geh), Grüße pl; to pay one's ~s to sb jdm seine Aufwartung machen; give my ~s to meine Empfehlung an (+acc) (geh); to pay one's last ~s to sb jdm die letzte Ehre erweisen.
2 vt (a) respektieren; person, customs, the law, sb's integrity, privacy also achten; ability anerkennen. a ~ed company eine angesehene Firma.
(b) as ~s was ... anbelangt or betrifft.

respectability [rɪˌspektəˈbɪlɪtɪ] n see adj (a) Ehrbarkeit f; Ehrenhaftigkeit f; Anständigkeit f; Angesehenheit, Geachtetheit f; Korrektheit, Anständigkeit f.

respectable [rɪˈspektəbl] adj (a) (estimable) person ehrbar; motives also ehrenhaft; (decent) life, district, club anständig, bieder (pej); (socially approved) person angesehen, geachtet, bieder (pej); clothes, behaviour korrekt, anständig. they are very ~ people sie sind sehr ehrbare Leute; he was outwardly ~ but ... er wirkte sehr ehrbar, aber ...; in ~ society in guter Gesellschaft; that's not ~ das schickt or gehört sich nicht.
(b) (large) size, income, sum ansehnlich, beachtlich.
(c) (fairly good) advantage beträchtlich; score, lead beachtlich. a ~ writer ein ganz ordentlicher Schriftsteller.

respectably [rɪˈspektəblɪ] adv dress, behave anständig.

respecter [rɪˈspektəʳ] n death/the law is no ~ of persons vor dem Tod/dem Gesetz sind alle gleich; death is no ~ of wealth der Tod nimmt keine Rücksicht auf Reichtum; he is no ~ of persons er läßt sich von niemandem beeindrucken.

respectful [rɪˈspektful] adj respektvoll (towards gegenüber).

respectfully [rɪˈspektfəlɪ] adv (a) see adj. (b) (in letters) I remain ~ yours or yours ~ ich verbleibe mit vorzüglicher Hochachtung Ihr ... (form).

respectfulness [rɪˈspektfulnɪs] n Respekt m. ~ of others Rücksicht f auf andere.

respecting [rɪˈspektɪŋ] prep bezüglich (+gen).

respective [rɪˈspektɪv] adj jeweilig. we took our ~ partners/glasses wir nahmen jeder unseren Partner/unser Glas, wir nahmen jeder unsere jeweiligen Partner/Gläser; they each have their ~ merits jeder von ihnen hat seine eigenen Vorteile.

respectively [rɪˈspektɪvlɪ] adv beziehungsweise. the girls' dresses are green and blue ~ die Mädchen haben grüne beziehungsweise blaue Kleider; and then allocate the funds ~ und die Mittel dann dementsprechend verteilen.

respiration [ˌrespɪˈreɪʃən] n (Bot, Med) Atmung f.

respirator [ˈrespɪreɪtəʳ] n (Med) Respirator m; (Mil) Atemschutzmaske f.

respiratory [rɪˈspaɪərətərɪ] adj Atem-, respiratorisch (spec); organs, problem Atmungs-; infection, disease der Atemwege. ~ system Atmungssystem nt; ~ tract Atemwege pl.

respire [rɪˈspaɪəʳ] vti (Med, form) atmen, respirieren (spec).

respite [ˈrespaɪt] n (a) (rest) Ruhepause f (from von); (easing off) Nachlassen nt. without (a) ~ ohne Unterbrechung or Pause. (b) (reprieve) Aufschub m.

resplendence [rɪˈsplendəns] n see adj Glanz m, Strahlen nt; Pracht f; Funkeln nt.

resplendent [rɪˈsplendənt] adj person, face glänzend, strahlend; clothes prächtig. the hills shone ~ in the evening sun die Berge erglänzten or erstrahlten im Schein der Abendsonne; there he was, ~ in his new uniform da war er, in seiner funkelnden neuen Uniform; the stage, ~ in blue and gold die Bühne in einer Pracht von Gold- und Blautönen.

respond [rɪˈspɒnd] vi (a) (reply) antworten. to ~ to a question eine Frage beantworten, auf eine Frage antworten or erwidern; to ~ to a toast einen Toast erwidern.
(b) (show reaction) (to auf +acc) reagieren; (brakes, meter also) ansprechen. to ~ to an appeal eine Appell beantworten; to ~ to an appeal for money einem Spendenaufruf folgen; they ~ed well to the appeal for money der Spendenaufruf fand ein großes Echo; to ~ to a call einem Ruf folgen; the patient did not ~ to the treatment/his mother's voice der Patient sprach auf die Behandlung nicht an/reagierte nicht auf die Stimme seiner Mutter; the illness ~ed to treatment die Behandlung schlug an.

respondent [rɪˈspɒndənt] n (Jur) Scheidungsbeklagte(r) mf.

response [rɪˈspɒns] n (a) (reply) Antwort, Erwiderung f; (Eccl) Antwort f. in ~ (to) als Antwort (auf +acc), in Erwiderung (+gen) (geh).
(b) (reaction) Reaktion f. £50,000 was raised in ~ to the radio appeal auf den Aufruf im Rundfunk hin gingen Spenden in Höhe von 50.000 Pfund ein; we had hoped for a bigger ~ from the public wir hatten uns ein stärkeres Echo aus or größere Resonanz in der Öffentlichkeit erhofft; my appeals met with no ~ meine Bitten fanden kein Echo or keine Resonanz.

responsibility [rɪˌspɒnsəˈbɪlɪtɪ] n (a) no pl Verantwortung f. to lay or put or place the ~ for sth on sb jdm die Verantwortung für etw übertragen; to take or assume (full) ~ (for sth) die (volle) Verantwortung (für etw) übernehmen; the management takes no ~ for objects left here die Firma haftet nicht für liegengelassene Gegenstände; that's his ~ dafür ist er verantwortlich; it's not my ~ to do that ich bin nicht dafür verantwortlich, das zu tun; on my own ~ auf eigene Verantwortung; he has no sense of ~ for his family er hat kein Verantwortungsgefühl für seine Familie.
(b) (duty, burden) Verpflichtung f (to für). the responsibilities of state/office die Pflichten eines Staatsmanns/die Dienstpflichten pl.

responsible [rɪˈspɒnsəbl] adj (a) (denoting cause of) verantwortlich; (to blame also) schuld (for an +dat). bad workmanship/he was ~ for the failure schlechte Arbeit/er war für das Versagen verantwortlich/an dem Versagen schuld; what's ~ for the hold-up? woran liegt die Verzögerung?
(b) (liable, answerable) verantwortlich. she is not ~ for her actions sie ist für ihre Handlungen nicht voll verantwortlich; to be ~ to sb for sth jdm gegenüber für etw verantwortlich sein; to be directly ~ to sb jdm unmittelbar unterstellt sein; to hold sb ~ for sth jdn für etw verantwortlich machen.
(c) (trustworthy) person, attitude verantwortungsbewußt; firm seriös, zuverlässig.
(d) (involving responsibility) job verantwortungsvoll.

responsibly [rɪˈspɒnsəblɪ] adv act, behave verantwortungsbewußt; carry out one's duties zuverlässig.

responsive [rɪˈspɒnsɪv] adj person, audience interessiert, mitgehend; class, pupil also mitmachend; steering, brakes, motor leicht reagierend or ansprechend. to be ~ to sth auf etw (acc) reagieren or ansprechen; to be ~ to sb's pleas jds Bitten (dat) nachkommen; he wasn't very ~ when I suggested it to him er war nicht sehr begeistert, als ich ihm das vorschlug; the pupils weren't very ~ die Schüler machten nicht richtig mit; he wasn't very ~ (to my complaint) er ging kaum darauf ein.

responsiveness [rɪˈspɒnsɪvnɪs] n because of the tremendous ~ of the audiences weil das Publikum so hervorragend mitging; a class not noted for its ~ eine Klasse, die dafür bekannt ist, daß sie kaum mitmacht; they have improved the ~ of the steering es ist ein leichteres Ansprechen der Steuerung erzielt worden; I was somewhat surprised at their ~ to my sugggestion ich war über ihre positive Reaktion auf meinen Vorschlag einigermaßen überrascht.

rest¹ [rest] 1 n (a) (relaxation) Ruhe f; (pause) Pause, Unterbrechung f; (in ~ cure, on holiday etc) Erholung f. a day of ~ ein Ruhetag m; to need ~ Ruhe brauchen; I need a ~ ich muß mich ausruhen; (vacation) ich brauche Urlaub; to go to the mountains for a ~ zur Erholung in die Berge fahren; to have or take a ~ (relax) (sich) ausruhen; (pause) (eine) Pause machen; she took or had an hour's ~ (relaxation) sie ruhte sich eine Stunde aus; (pause) sie machte eine Stunde Pause; take a ~! mach mal Pause!; to have a good night's ~ sich ordentlich ausschlafen; to give one's eyes a ~ seine Augen ausruhen; to give sb/the horses a ~ jdn/die Pferde ausruhen lassen; give it a ~! hör doch auf!
(b) to be at ~ (peaceful) ruhig sein; (immobile) sich in Ruhelage/-stellung befinden; (euph: dead) ruhen; to lay to ~ (euph) zur letzten Ruhe betten; to set at ~ fears, doubts beschwichtigen; to put or set sb's mind at ~ jdn beruhigen; you can set or put your mind at ~ Sie können sich beruhigen, Sie können beruhigt sein; to come to ~ (ball, car etc) zum Stillstand kommen; (bird, insect) sich niederlassen; (gaze, eyes) hängenbleiben (upon an +dat).
(c) (support) Auflage f; (of telephone) Gabel f; (Billiards) Steg m; see armrest, footrest.
(d) (Mus) Pause f; (Poet) Zäsur f.
2 vi (a) (lie down, take ~) ruhen (geh); (relax, be still) sich ausruhen; (pause) Pause machen, eine Pause einlegen; (on

walk, in physical work) rasten, Pause machen; (*euph: be buried*) ruhen. **you must ~ for an hour** Sie sollten eine Stunde ausruhen; **she never ~s** sie arbeitet ununterbrochen; **he will not ~ until** he discovers the truth er wird nicht (rasten und) ruhen, bis er die Wahrheit gefunden hat; **to ~ easy (in one's bed)** ruhig schlafen; **to be ~ing ruhen** (*geh*); (*euph: out of work*) ohne Engagement sein; **to let a field ~** einen Acker brachliegen lassen; **(the case for) the prosecution ~s** das Plädoyer der Anklage ist abgeschlossen; **to let a matter ~** eine Sache auf sich beruhen lassen; **let the matter ~!** laß es dabei!; **may he ~ in peace** er ruhe in Frieden; **to ~ in the Lord** im Herrn ruhen.

(b) (*remain*) (*decision, authority, blame, responsibility etc*) liegen (*with* bei). **the matter must not ~ there** man kann die Sache so nicht belassen; **and there the matter ~s for the moment** und damit ist die Sache momentan erledigt; **(you may) ~ assured that** ... Sie können versichert sein, daß ...

(c) (*lean*) (*person, head, ladder*) lehnen (*on* an +*dat*, *against* gegen); (*be supported: roof etc*) ruhen (*on* auf +*dat*); (*fig: eyes, gaze*) ruhen (*on* auf +*dat*); (*fig: be based*) (*argument, case*) sich stützen (*on* auf +*acc*); (*reputation*) beruhen (*on* auf +*dat*); (*responsibility*) liegen, ruhen (*on* auf +*dat*). **her elbows were/head was ~ing on the table** ihre Ellbogen waren auf dem Tisch gestützt/ihr Kopf lag auf dem Tisch.

3 *vt* **(a)** *one's eyes* ausruhen; *voice* schonen; *horses* ausruhen lassen. **to ~ oneself** sich ausruhen; **to be/feel ~ed** ausgeruht sein/sich ausgeruht fühlen; (*may*) **God ~ his soul** Gott hab ihn selig!; **to ~ one's case** (*Jur*) das Plädoyer abschließen.

(b) (*lean*) *ladder* lehnen (*against* gegen, *on* an +*acc*); *elbow*, (*fig*) *theory, suspicions* stützen (*on* auf +*acc*). **to ~ one's hand on sb's shoulder** jdm die Hand auf die Schulter legen; **to ~ one's head on the table** den Kopf auf den Tisch legen; **he ~ed his head against the wall** er lehnte den Kopf an die Wand.

♦**rest up** *vi* (*inf*) sich ausruhen.

rest² *n* (*remainder*) **the ~** der Rest, das übrige/die übrigen; **the ~ of the money/meal** der Rest des Geldes/Essens, das übrige Geld/Essen; **the ~ of the boys** der Rest der Jungen, die übrigen Jungen; **you go off and the ~ of us will wait here** ihr geht, und der Rest von uns wartet hier; **he was as drunk as the ~ of them** er war so betrunken wie der Rest *or* die übrigen; **she's no different from the ~** sie ist wie alle anderen; **all the ~ of the money** der ganze Rest des Geldes, das ganze übrige Geld; **all the ~ of the books** alle übrigen Bücher; **and all the ~ of it** (*inf*) und so weiter und so fort; **Mary, Jane and all the ~ of them** Mary, Jane und wie sie alle heißen; **for the ~** im übrigen.

restart [ˌriːˈstɑːt] **1** *vt job, activity* wiederaufnehmen; *negotiations, career also* wieder beginnen *or* anfangen; *engine* wieder anlassen; *machine* wieder anschalten. **to ~ work** wieder zu arbeiten anfangen. **2** *vi* wieder anfangen *or* beginnen; (*machine*) wieder starten; (*engine*) wieder anspringen.

restate [ˌriːˈsteɪt] *vt* **(a)** (*express again*) *reasons* wieder *or* erneut nennen; *problem, argument, theory* wieder *or* erneut vortragen; *case, one's position* wieder *or* erneut darstellen; (*Mus*) *theme* wiederaufnehmen. **(b)** (*express differently*) umformulieren; *case, one's position* neu darstellen.

restatement [ˌriːˈsteɪtmənt] *n see vt* **(a)** erneute Nennung; erneuter Vortrag; erneute Darstellung; Wiederaufnahme *f*. **(b)** Umformulierung *f*; Neudarstellung *f*.

restaurant [ˈrestərɔ̃ːŋ] *n* Restaurant *nt*, Gaststätte *f*. **~ food/prices** Gaststättenessen *nt*/-preise *pl*; **~ car** (*Brit Rail*) Speisewagen *m*.

restaurateur [ˌrestərəˈtɜː(r)] *n* Gastwirt, Gastronom *m*.

rest: **~ cure** *n* Erholung *f*; (*in bed*) Liegekur *f*; **~ day** *n* Ruhetag *m*.

restful [ˈrestfʊl] *adj occupation, pastime etc* erholsam; *colour* ruhig; *place* friedlich. **she is very ~ to be with** es ist sehr gemütlich, mit ihr zusammen zu sein.

rest-home [ˈresthəʊm] *n* Altersheim, Pflegeheim *nt*.

resting-place [ˈrestɪŋpleɪs] *n* Rastplatz *m*; (*euph: grave*) Ruhestätte *f*.

restitution [ˌrestɪˈtjuːʃən] *n* **(a)** (*giving back*) Rückgabe *f*; (*of objects, money also*) Rückerstattung *f*. **to make ~ of sth** (*form*) etw zurückgeben/zurückerstatten; **~ of conjugal rights** (*Jur*) Wiederherstellung *f* der ehelichen Gemeinschaft. **(b)** (*reparation*) Schadenersatz *m*, Entschädigung *f*.

restive [ˈrestɪv] *adj horse* (*stubborn*) störrisch; (*nervous*) unruhig; (*restless*) *person, manner* rastlos; *tribes* widerspenstig, aufsässig.

restiveness [ˈrestɪvnɪs] *n see adj* störrische Art; Unruhe *f*; Rastlosigkeit *f*; Widerspenstigkeit, Aufsässigkeit *f*.

restless [ˈrestlɪs] *adj person, manner, sea, night* unruhig; (*not wanting to stay in one place*) rastlos.

restlessly [ˈrestlɪslɪ] *adv see adj*.

restlessness [ˈrestlɪsnɪs] *n see adj* Unruhe *f*; Rastlosigkeit *f*.

restock [ˌriːˈstɒk] *vt shop* wieder auffüllen; *pond* wieder (mit Fischen) besetzen; *farm* den Viehbestand (+*gen*) erneuern.

restoration [ˌrestəˈreɪʃən] *n* **(a)** (*return*) Rückgabe *f* (*to* an +*acc*); (*of property also*) Rückerstattung *f* (*to* an +*acc*); (*of confidence, order etc*) Wiederherstellung *f*; (*to office*) Wiedereinsetzung *f* (*to* in +*acc*). **(b)** **the R~** (*Hist*) die Restauration. **(c)** (*of monument, work of art*) Restaurierung *f*.

restorative [rɪˈstɔːrətɪv] **1** *adj* stärkend; *remedy also* Stärkungs-. **2** *n* Stärkungsmittel *nt*.

restore [rɪˈstɔː(r)] *vt sth lost, borrowed, stolen* (*give back*) zurückgeben; (*bring back*) *confidence, order, calm* wiederherstellen. **to ~ sb's health, to ~ sb to health** jds Gesundheit *or* jdn wiederherstellen, jdn wieder gesund machen; **~d to health** wiederhergestellt; **to ~ sb to freedom** jdm die Freiheit wiedergeben; **to ~ sb to life** jdn ins Leben zurückrufen; **to ~ sth to its former condition** etw wiederherstellen; **the brandy ~d my strength** *or* **me** der Weinbrand hat mich wiederhergestellt; **he was ~d to them safe and sound** er

---

wurde ihnen gesund und munter wieder zurückgebracht.

(b) (*to former post*) wiedereinsetzen (*to* in +*acc*). **to ~ sb to the throne** jdn als König wiedereinsetzen; **to ~ to power** wieder an die Macht bringen.

(c) (*repair*) *building, painting, furniture, text* restaurieren.

restorer [rɪˈstɔːrə(r)] *n* (*Art*) Restaurator(in *f*) *m*; *see* **hair ~**.

restrain [rɪˈstreɪn] *vt person* zurückhalten; *prisoner* mit Gewalt festhalten; *animal, unruly children, madman* bändigen; *radicals* in Schranken halten; *sb's activities, power* einschränken; *emotions, laughter* unterdrücken. **to ~ sb from doing sth** jdn davon abhalten, etw zu tun; **to ~ oneself** sich beherrschen.

restrained [rɪˈstreɪnd] *adj emotions* unterdrückt; *manner, words* beherrscht; *tone, voice, colour* verhalten; *criticism* maßvoll, gezügelt. **he was very ~ when he heard the news** er war sehr beherrscht, als er die Nachricht hörte.

restraint [rɪˈstreɪnt] *n* **(a)** (*restriction*) Einschränkung, Beschränkung *f*. **without ~** unbeschränkt; *develop* ungehemmt; **~ of trade** Handelsbeschränkung *f*; **to place under ~** (*Jur*) in Haft nehmen.

(b) (*moderation*) Beherrschung *f*. **to show a lack of ~** wenig Beherrschung zeigen; **he said with great ~ that** ... er sagte sehr beherrscht, daß ...; **to express oneself without ~** sich zwangslos ausdrücken.

restrict [rɪˈstrɪkt] *vt* beschränken (*to* auf +*acc*); *freedom, authority also* einschränken; *time, number also* begrenzen (*to* auf +*acc*). **all speakers are ~ed to three hours** die Redezeit ist auf drei Stunden beschränkt; **~ing clothes** beengende Kleidungsstücke.

restricted [rɪˈstrɪktɪd] *adj view* beschränkt, begrenzt; (*Admin, Mil*) *document, information* geheim; *locality* nur bestimmten Gruppen zugänglich; *admission* begrenzt. **within a ~ area** auf begrenztem Gebiet; **~ area** (*Brit Mot*) Strecke *f* mit Geschwindigkeitsbeschränkung; (*US*) Sperrgebiet *nt*.

restriction [rɪˈstrɪkʃən] *n see vt* (*on* gen) Beschränkung *f*; Einschränkung *f*; Begrenzung *f*. **to place ~s on sth** etw beschränken *or* einschränken; **~s of space** räumliche Beschränktheit; **without ~s** uneingeschränkt; **speed ~** (*Mot*) Geschwindigkeitsbegrenzung *or* -beschränkung *f*; **price ~** Preisbeschränkung *f*.

restrictive [rɪˈstrɪktɪv] *adj* restriktiv, einschränkend *attr*. **~ practices** (*Jur, Ind*) wettbewerbsbeschränkende Geschäftspraktiken *pl*; **~ clause** (*Gram*) restriktiver *or* einschränkender Nebensatz.

restring [ˌriːˈstrɪŋ] *pret, ptp* **restrung** [ˌriːˈstrʌŋ] *vt instrument* neu besaiten; *bow, racket* neu bespannen; *pearls* neu aufziehen.

rest-room [ˈrestruːm] *n* (*US*) Toilette *f*.

result [rɪˈzʌlt] **1** *n* **(a)** Folge *f*. **as a ~ he failed** folglich fiel er durch; **as a ~ of this** und folglich; **as a ~ of which he ... was** zur Folge hatte, daß er ...; **to be the ~ of** resultieren aus.

(b) (*outcome: of election, exam, race, Math etc*) Ergebnis, Resultat *nt*; (*good ~*) Resultat *nt*. **~s** (*of test, experiment*) Werte *pl*; **I want to see ~s** ich möchte einen Erfolg *or* ein Resultat sehen; **to get ~s** (*person*) Erfolg *or* Resultate erzielen; **we had very good ~s with this** wir hatten damit großen Erfolg *or* sehr gute Resultate; **as a ~ of my inquiry** auf meine Anfrage (hin); **what was the ~?** (*Sport*) wie ist es ausgegangen?; **without ~** ergebnislos.

2 *vi* sich ergeben, resultieren (*from* aus). **from which it ~s that** ... woraus folgt, daß ...

♦**result in** *vi* +*prep obj* führen zu. **this ~ed ~ his being late** das führte dazu, daß er zu spät kam.

resultant [rɪˈzʌltənt] **1** *adj* resultierend, sich daraus ergebend. **2** *n* (*Phys*) Resultierende *f*.

resume [rɪˈzjuːm] **1** *vt* **(a)** (*restart*) *activity* wiederaufnehmen, weitermachen mit; *tale, account also* fortfahren in (*dat*); *journey* fortsetzen. **to ~ work** die Arbeit wiederaufnehmen; **well?, he ~d** nun?, fuhr er fort.

(b) *command, possession* wieder übernehmen; *name* wieder annehmen. **to ~ one's seat** seinen Platz wieder einnehmen; **to ~ possession of sth** etw wieder in Besitz nehmen.

(c) (*sum up*) zusammenfassen.

2 *vi* (*classes, work etc*) wieder beginnen.

résumé [ˈreɪzjʊmeɪ] *n* Resümee *nt*, Zusammenfassung *f*; (*US: curriculum vitae*) Lebenslauf *m*.

resumption [rɪˈzʌmpʃən] *n* (*of activity*) Wiederaufnahme *f*; (*of command, possession*) erneute Übernahme *f*; (*of journey*) Fortsetzung *f*; (*of classes*) Wiederbeginn *m*.

resurface [ˌriːˈsɜːfɪs] **1** *vt road* neu belegen. **2** *vi* (*diver, submarine, fig*) wieder auftauchen.

resurgence [rɪˈsɜːdʒəns] *n* Wiederaufleben, Wiedererstehen *nt*.

resurgent [rɪˈsɜːdʒənt] *adj* wieder auflebend.

resurrect [ˌrezəˈrekt] *vt* **(a)** (*lit*) *person* wiederbeleben; (*Rel*) auferstehen lassen. **to be ~ed** auferstehen. **(b)** (*fig*) *law* wieder zurückbringen *or* einführen; *ideology, institution* wieder ins Leben rufen, wiederbeleben; *custom, fashion, style* wiederbeleben; *ideas, memories* wieder aufleben lassen; (*inf*) *dress, chair* ausgraben (*inf*).

resurrection [ˌrezəˈrekʃən] *n see vt* **(a)** Wiederbelebung *f*; Auferstehung *f*. **the R~** (*Rel*) die Auferstehung. **(b)** Wiedereinführung *f*; Wiederbelebung *f*; Auflebenlassen *nt*; Ausgraben *nt* (*inf*).

resuscitate [rɪˈsʌsɪteɪt] *vt* (*Med*) wiederbeleben; (*fig*) beleben, neue Lebensgeister geben (+*dat*).

resuscitation [rɪˌsʌsɪˈteɪʃən] *n see vt* Wiederbelebung *f*; Belebung *f*.

retail [ˈriːteɪl] **1** *n* Einzelhandel, Kleinhandel, Detailhandel (*dated*) *m*. **~ and wholesale** Einzel- und Großhandel *m*.

2 *vt* im Einzel- *or* Kleinhandel *or* en detail (*dated*) verkaufen; (*fig*) *gossip* weitererzählen.

3 vi (goods) to ~ at ... im Einzelhandel ... kosten.
4 adv im Einzelhandel. to sell ~ im Einzelhandel or en detail (dated) verkaufen.
retail in cpds Einzelhandels-; ~ **business** n Einzel- or Kleinhandel m; ~ **shop** Einzelhandelsgeschäft nt; ~ **dealer** n Einzelhändler, Detailhändler (dated) m.
retailer ['riːteɪləʳ] n Einzelhändler, Kleinhändler m.
retailing ['riːteɪlɪŋ] n der Einzelhandel.
retail: ~ **outlet** n Einzelhandelsverkaufsstelle f; ~ **price** n Einzelhandelspreis m.
retain [rɪ'teɪn] vt (a) (keep) behalten; money, possession, person zurück(be)halten; custom beibehalten, bewahren; urine zurückhalten; colour behalten; flavour beibehalten; (battery) charge halten; (dam) water stauen. to ~ water (soil, body) Wasser speichern; (sponge) Wasser halten; to ~ control (of sth) etw weiterhin in der Gewalt haben; to ~ the use of a limb/ one's eyes ein Glied/seine Augen noch gebrauchen können.
(b) (remember) sich (dat) merken; (computer) information speichern. facts that should be ~ed Tatsachen, die man sich merken sollte.
(c) (engage) lawyer beauftragen.
retainer [rɪ'teɪnəʳ] n (a) (old: servant) Faktotum nt. (b) (fee) Vorschuß m.
retaining: ~ **fee** n Vorschuß m; ~ **nut** n Befestigungsschraube f; ~ **wall** n Stützmauer f.
retake [,riː'teɪk] (vb: pret retook, ptp retaken [,riː'teɪkən]) **1** vt (a) (Mil) town zurückerobern. he was ~n (prisoner) er wurde wieder gefangengenommen.
(b) (Film) nochmals aufnehmen.
(c) (Sport) penalty wiederholen.
2 ['riːteɪk] n (Film) Neuaufnahme f. we need a ~ of that scene wir müssen die Szene noch einmal filmen.
retaliate [rɪ'tælɪeɪt] vi Vergeltung üben; (for bad treatment, insults etc) sich revanchieren (against sb an jdm); (in battle) zurückschlagen; (Sport, in fight, with measures in argument) kontern. he ~d by pointing out that ... er konterte, indem er darauf hinwies, daß ...; he ~d by kicking him on the shins er hat sich mit einem Tritt gegen das Schienbein revanchiert; then she ~d by calling him a pig sie revanchierte sich damit or zahlte es ihm damit heim, daß sie ihn ein Schwein nannte; how will the unions ~? wie werden die Gewerkschaften kontern?
retaliation [rɪ,tælɪ'eɪʃən] n Vergeltung f; (in fight also) Vergeltungsschlag m; (in argument, diplomacy etc) Konterschlag m. his ~ was vicious er hat sich auf üble Weise revanchiert; in ~ zur Vergeltung; that's my ~ for what you did to me das ist meine Revanche für das, was Sie mir angetan haben; in ~ for your unkindness um mich für Ihre Unfreundlichkeit zu revanchieren; policy of ~ Vergeltungspolitik f.
retaliatory [rɪ'tælɪətərɪ] adj ~ insults Retourkutschen pl (inf); ~ measures Vergeltungsmaßnahmen pl; a ~ assassination ein Vergeltungsmord m.
retard [rɪ'taːd] vt development verlangsamen, verzögern; explosion, (Aut) ignition verzögern; (Biol, Phys) retardieren.
retarded [rɪ'taːdɪd] adj zurückgeblieben. ~ ignition (Aut) Spätzündung f; mentally ~ geistig zurückgeblieben.
retch [retʃ] **1** vi würgen. **2** n Würgen nt.
retching ['retʃɪŋ] n Würgerei f, Gewürge nt.
ret(d) abbr of retired a.D.
retell [,riː'tel] pret, ptp retold vt wiederholen; (novelist) old legend nacherzählen.
retention [rɪ'tenʃən] n (a) (Beibehaltung f; (of possession) Zurückhaltung f; (of water) Speicherung f; (of facts) Behalten nt; (of information by computer) Speicherung f; (of lawyer) Beauftragung f; (Med: also ~ of urine) Harnverhaltung f.
(b) (memory) Gedächtnis nt. his powers of ~ sein Gedächtnis nt, seine Merkfähigkeit.
retentive [rɪ'tentɪv] adj memory aufnahmefähig. he is very ~ er hat ein gutes Gedächtnis.
retentiveness [rɪ'tentɪvnɪs] n (of memory) Aufnahmefähigkeit f; (of person) Merkfähigkeit f.
rethink [,riː'θɪŋk] (vb: pret, ptp rethought [,riː'θɔːt]) **1** vt überdenken. **2** ['riːθɪŋk] n (inf) Überdenken nt. we'll have to have a ~ wir müssen das noch einmal überdenken.
reticence ['retɪsəns] n Zurückhaltung f.
reticent ['retɪsənt] adj zurückhaltend. to be ~ about sth in bezug auf etw (acc) nicht sehr gesprächig sein.
reticently ['retɪsəntlɪ] adv see adj.
reticle ['retɪkl] n (Opt) Meßkreuz nt.
reticulate [rɪ'tɪkjʊlɪt], **reticulated** [rɪ'tɪkjʊleɪtɪd] adj netzartig, retikular.
retina ['retɪnə] n, pl -e ['retɪniː] or -s Netzhaut, Retina (spec) f.
retinue ['retɪnjuː] n Gefolge nt.
retire [rɪ'taɪəʳ] **1** vi (a) (give up work) aufhören zu arbeiten; (civil servant, military officer) in Pension gehen, sich pensionieren lassen, in den Ruhestand treten; (self-employed) sich zur Ruhe setzen; (soldier) aus der Armee ausscheiden; (singer, player etc) (zu singen/spielen etc) aufhören. to ~ from business sich zur Ruhe setzen, sich aus dem Geschäftsleben zurückziehen.
(b) (withdraw, Mil) sich zurückziehen; (Sport) aufgeben; (Ftbl, Rugby etc) vom Feld gehen. to ~ into oneself sich in sich (acc) selbst zurückziehen; to ~ from the world/from public life sich von der Welt/aus dem öffentlichen Leben zurückziehen.
(c) (old, form: go to bed) sich zurückziehen.
2 vt aus Altersgründen entlassen; civil servant, military officer pensionieren, in den Ruhestand versetzen; soldier verabschieden; (Fin) bond aus dem Verkehr ziehen.
retired [rɪ'taɪəd] adj (a) (no longer working) worker, employee aus dem Arbeitsleben ausgeschieden (form); civil servant, military officer pensioniert, im Ruhestand; soldier aus der Armee ausgeschieden. he is ~ er arbeitet nicht mehr, er ist

Rentner/ist pensioniert or im Ruhestand/nicht mehr in der Armee; a ~ worker/teacher/soldier ein Rentner/pensionierter Lehrer/ehemaliger Soldat; "occupation — ~" „Beruf — Rentner/Pensionär/Veteran"; ~ **list** (Mil) Liste f der aus dem aktiven Dienst Geschiedenen; ~ **pay** Rente f; Pension f, Ruhegehalt nt.
(b) (secluded) life zurückgezogen.
retirement [rɪ'taɪəmənt] n (a) (stopping work) Ausscheiden nt aus dem Arbeitsleben (form); (of civil servant, military officer) Pensionierung f; (of soldier) Verabschiedung f. ~ at 60/65 Altersgrenze bei 60/65; to announce one's ~ aus dem Arbeitsleben ausscheiden wollen; sich pensionieren lassen wollen.
(b) (period) how will you spend your ~? was tun Sie, wenn Sie einmal nicht mehr arbeiten/wenn Sie pensioniert or im Ruhestand sind?; to come out of ~ wieder zurückkommen.
(c) (seclusion) Zurückgezogenheit f. to live in ~ zurückgezogen leben.
(d) (Mil) Rückzug m; (Sport) Aufgabe f; (Ftbl, Rugby etc) Abgang m vom Spielfeld.
retirement: ~ **age** n Altersgrenze f; (of civil servant also) Pensionsalter nt; ~ **benefit** n Altenhilfe f; ~ **pay** n Altersrente f; ~ **pension** n Altersruhegeld nt (form).
retiring [rɪ'taɪərɪŋ] adj (a) (shy) zurückhaltend. (b) ~ **age** see retirement age.
retold [,riː'təʊld] pret, ptp of retell.
retook [,riː'tʊk] pret of retake.
retort [rɪ'tɔːt] **1** n (a) (answer) scharfe Erwiderung or Antwort.
(b) (Chem) Retorte f. ~ **stand** Retortenhalter m or -stand m. **2** vt scharf erwidern, zurückgeben. **3** vi scharf erwidern.
retouch [,riː'tʌtʃ] vt (Art, Phot) retuschieren.
retrace [rɪ'treɪs] vt past, argumentation zurückverfolgen; development also nachgehen (+dat), nachvollziehen. to ~ one's path or steps denselben Weg zurückgehen.
retract [rɪ'trækt] **1** vt (a) (withdraw) offer zurückziehen; statement zurücknehmen. (b) (draw back) claws, (Aviat) undercarriage einziehen. **2** vi (a) (withdraw) einen Rückzieher machen.
(b) (claws, undercarriage) eingezogen werden.
retractable [rɪ'træktəbl] adj see vt (a) zurückziehbar; zurücknehmbar. (b) einziehbar.
retraction [rɪ'trækʃən] n see vt (a) (act) Rückzug m; Rücknahme f; (that retracted) Rückzieher m. (b) Einziehen nt.
retrain [,riː'treɪn] **1** vt umschulen. **2** vi umlernen, umgeschult werden, sich umschulen lassen.
retraining [,riː'treɪnɪŋ] n see vb Umschulung f; Umlernen nt.
retransmit [,riːtrænz'mɪt] vt weiterübertragen.
retread [,riː'tred] **1** vt tyre die Laufflächen erneuern von. **2** ['riːtred] n (tyre) laufflächenerneuerter Reifen.
retreat [rɪ'triːt] **1** n (a) (Mil) Rückzug m. to sound the ~ zum Rückzug blasen; the army is in ~ die Armee befindet sich or ist auf dem Rückzug; to make or beat a (hasty or swift) ~ (Mil) (schnell) den Rückzug antreten; (fig) (schleunigst) das Feld räumen; his ~ into silence seine Zuflucht zum Schweigen.
(b) (place) Zuflucht(sort m) f; (hiding place) Schlupfwinkel m. this is my ~ hierhin ziehe ich mich zurück; he has gone to his country ~ er hat sich aufs Land zurückgezogen.
2 vi (Mil) den Rückzug antreten; (in fear) zurückweichen; (flood, glacier) zurückgehen, zurückweichen. to ~ within oneself sich in sich (acc) selbst zurückziehen.
3 vti (Chess) zurückziehen.
retrench [rɪ'trentʃ] **1** vt expenditure einschränken, kürzen; personnel einsparen; book kürzen. **2** vi sich einschränken.
♦**retrench on** vi +prep obj see retrench 1.
retrenchment [rɪ'trentʃmənt] n see vt Einschränkung, Kürzung f; Einsparung f; Kürzung f.
retrial [rɪ'traɪəl] n (Jur) Wiederaufnahmeverfahren nt. to subject a case to (a) ~ einen Fall wiederaufnehmen; he requested a ~ er verlangte eine Wiederaufnahme des Verfahrens.
retribution [,retrɪ'bjuːʃən] n Vergeltung f. in ~ als Vergeltung.
retributive [rɪ'trɪbjʊtɪv] adj action Vergeltungs-, vergeltend; justice ausgleichend.
retrievable [rɪ'triːvəbl] adj (a) see vt (a) zurück-/hervor-/ heraus-/herunterholbar; rettbar; zu bergen; rückgewinnbar; abfragbar; wiedererlangbar; wiedergutmachbar. (b) error wiedergutmachbar; situation zu retten.
retrieval [rɪ'triːvəl] n see vt (a) Zurück-/Hervor-/Heraus-/ Herunterholen nt; Rettung f; Bergung f; Rückgewinnung f; Abfragen nt; Wiedererlangen nt; Wiedergutmachen nt. (b) Wiedergutmachung f; Rettung f. beyond or past ~ hoffnungslos. (c) Apportieren nt.
retrieve [rɪ'triːv] **1** vt (a) (recover) zurück-/hervor-/heraus-/ herunterholen; (rescue) retten; (from wreckage etc) bergen; material from waste zurückgewinnen; (Computers) information abfragen; fortune, honour, position, money, investment wiedererlangen; loss wiedergutmachen. to ~ a writer's work from oblivion das Werk eines Schriftstellers der Vergessenheit entreißen; we shall ~ nothing from this disaster wir werden bei dieser Katastrophe nichts retten können.
(b) (set to rights) error wiedergutmachen; situation retten.
(c) (dog) apportieren.
2 vi (dog) apportieren.
retriever [rɪ'triːvəʳ] n (race) Retriever m. he is a good ~ er ist ein guter Apportierhund.
retro ['retrəʊ] n pref rück-, Rück-. **2** n abbr of retrorocket.
retroactive [,retrəʊ'æktɪv] adj rückwirkend. a ~ effect eine Rückwirkung.
retrograde ['retrəʊgreɪd] **1** adj rückläufig; order umgekehrt; policy rückschrittlich; (Phys, Biol, Astron also) retrograd (spec). ~ **step** Rückschritt m. **2** vi (Biol) sich zurückentwickeln; (Astron) sich retrograd bewegen.
retrogress [,retrəʊ'gres] vi (go backwards) sich rückwärts bewegen; (deteriorate) sich zurückentwickeln.

retrogression [ˌretrəʊ'greʃən] *n see vi* rückläufige Bewegung; Rückentwicklung *f*.

retrogressive [ˌretrəʊ'gresɪv] *adj* (*moving backwards*) *motion etc* rückläufig, Rückwärts-; (*fig*) *plan, policy* rückschrittlich; (*Biol*) rückläufig. ~ **step** Rückschritt *m*.

retrorocket ['retrəʊ'rɒkɪt] *n* Bremsrakete *f*.

retrospect ['retrəʊspekt] *n* **in** ~, **what would you have done differently?** was hätten Sie rückblickend *or im* Rückblick anders gemacht?; **everything looks different in** ~ im nachhinein *or im* Rückblick sieht alles anders aus.

retrospection [ˌretrəʊ'spekʃən] *n* Zurückblicken *nt*.

retrospective [ˌretrəʊ'spektɪv] **1** *adj thought* rückblickend; *wisdom* im nachhinein; (*Admin, Jur*) *pay rise* rückwirkend. ~ **effect** Rückwirkung *f*; **a** ~ **look (at)** ein Blick zurück (auf +*acc*). **2** *n* Retrospektive *f*.

retrospectively [ˌretrəʊ'spektɪvlɪ] *adv act* rückwirkend. **to look** ~ **at sth** (*fig*) auf etw (*acc*) zurückblicken.

retry [riː'traɪ] *vt* (*Jur*) *case* wiederaufnehmen, neu verhandeln; *person* neu verhandeln gegen, wieder vor Gericht bringen.

retsina [ret'siːnə] *n* Retsina *m*.

return [rɪ'tɜːn] **1** *vi* (*come back: person, vehicle*) zurück- *or* wiederkommen, zurück- *or* wiederkehren (*geh*); (*go back*) (*person*) zurückgehen; (*vehicle*) zurückfahren; (*symptoms, doubts, fears*) wiederkommen, wieder auftreten; (*property: pass back to*) zurückfallen (*to an* +*acc*). **to** ~ **to London/the town/the group** nach London/in die Stadt/zur Gruppe zurückkehren; **to** ~ **to school** wieder in die Schule gehen; **to** ~ **to (one's) work** (*after short pause*) wieder an seine Arbeit gehen; (*after strike*) die Arbeit wiederaufnehmen; **to** ~ **to a subject** auf ein Thema zurückkommen; **to** ~ **to what we were talking about** um auf unser Gespräch zurückzukommen; **to** ~ **to one's old ways** in seine alten Gewohnheiten zurückfallen; **to** ~ **home** nach Hause kommen/gehen, heimkehren (*geh*); **have they** ~**ed?** sind Sie zurück(gekommen)?; (*gone back*) sind Sie zurückgegangen/-gefahren?; **his good spirits** ~**ed** seine gute Laune kehrte wieder; **to** ~ **to health** wieder gesund werden; **to** ~ **to dust** wieder zu Staub werden.

2 *vt* **(a)** (*give back*) *sth borrowed, stolen, lost* zurückgeben (*to sb* jdm); (*bring or take back*) zurückbringen (*to sb* jdm); (*put back*) zurücksetzen/-legen; (*send back*) (*to an* +*acc*) *letter etc* zurückschicken *or* -senden; (*refuse*) *cheque* zurückweisen; *ball* zurückschlagen/-werfen; *sound, light* zurückwerfen; *salute, visit, sb's love, compliment* erwidern. **to** ~ **a/sb's blow** zurückschlagen; **to** ~ **a book to the library** ein Buch in die Bücherei zurückbringen; **to** ~ **a book to the shelf/box** ein Buch auf das Regal zurückstellen/in die Kiste zurücklegen; **he** ~**ed it to his pocket** er steckte es wieder in die Tasche; **to** ~ **goods to the shop** Waren in das Geschäft zurückbringen; **to** ~ **thanks** (*form*) danksagen; **to** ~ **thanks to sb** jdm Dank sagen; **I hope to** ~ **your kindness/favour** ich hoffe, daß ich mich einmal bei Ihnen revanchieren kann; **to** ~ **good for evil** Böses mit Gutem vergelten; **to** ~ **like for like** Gleiches mit Gleichem vergelten; **to** ~ **fire** (*Mil*) das Feuer erwidern; **to** ~ **hearts** (*Bridge*) Herz nachspielen.

(b) (*reply*) erwidern, zurückgeben.

(c) (*declare*) *details of income* angeben. **to** ~ **a verdict of guilty (on sb)** (*Jur*) sich an jdm (*jdn*) schuldig sprechen, einen Schuldspruch (gegen jdn) fällen; **to** ~ **a verdict of murder** (*Jur*) jdn des Mordes für schuldig erklären; **he was** ~**ed guilty** (*Jur*) er wurde schuldig gesprochen.

(d) (*Fin*) *income* einbringen; *profit, interest* abwerfen.

(e) (*Brit Parl*) *candidate* wählen.

3 *n* **(a)** (*coming/going back*) (*of person, vehicle, seasons*) Rückkehr, Wiederkehr *f* (*geh*); (*of illness*) Wiederauftreten *nt*. **on my** ~ bei meiner Rückkehr; ~ **to home** Heimkehr *f*; ~ **to school** Schulbeginn *m*; **by** ~ (*of post*) postwendend; ~ **to work** (*after strike*) Wiederaufnahme *f* der Arbeit; ~ **to health** Genesung *f*; **a** ~ **to one's old habits** ein Rückfall *m* in seine alten Gewohnheiten; **many happy** ~**s (of the day)!** herzlichen Glückwunsch zum Geburtstag!; *see* **point**.

(b) (*giving/bringing/taking/sending back*) *see vt* **(a)** Rückgabe *f*; Zurückbringen *nt*; Zurücksetzen/-stellen/-legen *nt*; Zurückschicken *or* -senden *nt*; Zurückweisen *nt*; Zurückschlagen *nt*/-werfen *nt*; Zurückwerfen *nt*; Erwiderung *f*.

(c) (*Brit: also* ~ **ticket**) Rückfahrkarte *f*; (*Aviat*) Flugschein *m* für Hin- und Rückreise.

(d) (*profit: from investments, shares*) (*on* aus) Einkommen *nt*; (*on capital also*) Ertrag, Gewinn *m*; (*product: from land, mine etc*) Ertrag *m*. ~**s** (*profits*) Gewinn *m*; (*receipts*) Einkünfte *pl*; ~ **on capital** (*Fin*) Kapitalertrag *m*; *see* **diminish**.

(e) (*fig: recompense*) **in** ~ dafür; **in** ~ **for für**; **to do sb a kindness in** ~ sich für einen Gefallen revanchieren.

(f) (*act of declaring*) (*of verdict, election results*) Verkündung *f*; (*report*) Bericht *m*. **the population** ~**s show that ...** die Bevölkerungszahlen zeigen, daß ...; **the** ~ **of the jury** = das Urteil der Schöffen; **the (election)** ~**s** das Wahlergebnis; **tax** ~ Steuererklärung *f*.

(g) (*Brit Parl: of candidate*) Wahl *f* (*to* in +*acc*).

(h) (*Sport*) (*game, match*) Rückspiel *nt*; (*stroke*) Rückschlag *m*; (*throw*) Rückwurf *m*; (~ *pass*) Rückpaß *m*. **to make a good** ~ den Ball gut zurückschlagen/-werfen.

(i) (*Comm:* ~**ed item**) zurückgebrachte Ware.

returnable [rɪ'tɜːnəbl] *adj bottle* zurückzugeben *attr*; (*with deposit*) mit Flaschenpfand.

return: ~ **fare** *n* Preis *m* für eine Rückfahrkarte *or* (*Aviat*) einen Flugschein; ~ **flight** *n* Rückflug *m*; (*both ways*) Hin- und Rückflug *m*; ~ **half** *n* (*of ticket*) Abschnitt *m* für die Rückreise.

returning officer [rɪ'tɜːnɪŋ'ɒfɪsəʳ] *n* (*Brit Parl*) Wahlleiter *m*.

return: ~ **journey** *n* Rückreise *f*; (*both ways*) Hin- und Rückreise *f*; ~ **match** *n* Rückspiel *nt*; ~ **pass** *n* (*Sport*) Rückpaß *m*; ~

ticket *n* (*Brit*) Rückfahrkarte *f*; (*Aviat*) Rückflugschein *m*.

reunification [riːˌjuːnɪfɪ'keɪʃən] *n* Wiedervereinigung *f*.

reunify [riː'juːnɪfaɪ] *vt* wiedervereinigen.

reunion [riː'juːnjən] *n* **(a)** (*coming together*) Wiedervereinigung *f*. **(b)** (*gathering*) Treffen *nt*, Zusammenkunft *f*. **a family/an office** ~ ein Familien-/Belegschaftstreffen *nt*.

reunite [ˌriːjuː'naɪt] **1** *vt* wiedervereinigen. **they were** ~**d at last** sie waren endlich wieder vereint. **2** *vi* (*countries, parties*) sich wiedervereinigen; (*people*) wieder zusammenkommen.

Rev [rev] *abbr of* **Reverend**.

rev [rev] **1** *n abbr of* **revolution** (*Aut*) Umdrehung *f*. **the number of** ~**s per minute** die Dreh- *or* Tourenzahl pro Minute; **4,000** ~**s per minute** 4.000 Umdrehungen *or* Touren (*inf*) pro Minute; ~**counter** Drehzahlmesser, Tourenzähler *m*.

2 *vti* **to** ~ **(up)** (*driver*) den Motor auf Touren bringen; (*noisily*) den Motor aufheulen lassen; (*engine*) aufheulen.

revaluation [riːˌvæljʊ'eɪʃən] *n* (*Fin*) Aufwertung *f*.

revalue [ˌriː'væljuː] *vt* (*Fin*) aufwerten.

revamp [ˌriː'væmp] *vt* (*inf*) *book, play* aufpolieren (*inf*); *company* auf Vordermann bringen (*inf*); *house, room* aufmöbeln (*inf*).

revanchist [rɪ'væntʃɪst] *adj* revanchistisch.

reveal [rɪ'viːl] *vt* **(a)** (*make visible*) zum Vorschein bringen; (*show*) zeigen. **stripping off the plaster** ~**ed an old frieze** das Abschlagen des Putzes hatte einen alten Fries zum Vorschein gebracht; **a nightdress that** ~**ed her slender form** ein Nachthemd, das ihre schlanke Gestalt abzeichnete; **a neckline that** ~**ed her bosom** ein Ausschnitt, der ihren Busen freigab.

(b) (*make known*) *truth, facts* enthüllen, aufdecken; *one's identity* zu erkennen geben, enthüllen; *ignorance, knowledge* erkennen lassen. **I cannot** ~ **to you what he said** ich kann Ihnen nicht verraten, was er gesagt hat; **he** ~**ed himself as being ...** er verriet sich als ...; (*deliberately*) er gab sich als ... zu erkennen; **he could never** ~ **his feelings for her** er konnte seine Gefühle für sie nie zeigen; **what does this** ~ **about the motives of the hero?** was sagt das über die Motive des Helden aus?; **Nixon** ~**s all** Nixon packt aus (*inf*); **the doctor did not** ~ **to him how hopeless his situation was** der Arzt hat ihn nicht darüber aufgeklärt, wie hoffnungslos sein Zustand war.

(c) (*Rel*) offenbaren (*to sb* jdm). ~**ed religion** Offenbarungsreligion *f*.

revealing [rɪ'viːlɪŋ] *adj* **(a)** aufschlußreich. **(b)** *material, slit skirt etc* viel zeigend; *dress, neckline also* offenherzig (*hum*).

reveille [rɪ'vælɪ] *n* (*Mil*) Reveille *f*, Wecksignal *nt*. **(the)** ~ **is at 6** um 6 Uhr ist Wecken.

revel ['revl] **1** *vi* **(a)** (*make merry*) feiern.

(b) (*delight*) **to** ~ **in gossip/one's freedom** seine wahre Freude an Klatschgeschichten haben/seine Freiheit aus ganzem Herzen genießen; **to** ~ **in doing sth** seine wahre Freude daran haben, etw zu tun; **like it? I** ~ **in it** gefallen? es macht mir Riesenspaß.

2 *n* ~**s** *pl* Feiern *nt*.

revelation [ˌrevə'leɪʃən] *n* Enthüllung *f*; (*Rel*) Offenbarung *f*. **(the book of) R**~**s** die Offenbarung (des Johannes); **it was a** ~ **to me** das hat mir die Augen geöffnet; **what a** ~! unglaublich!

reveller ['revləʳ] *n* Feiernde(r) *mf*.

revelry ['revlrɪ] *n usu pl* Festlichkeit *f*.

revenge [rɪ'vendʒ] **1** *n* Rache *f*; (*Sport*) Revanche *f*. **to take** ~ **on sb (for sth)** sich an jdm (für etw) rächen; **to get one's** ~ sich rächen, seine Rache bekommen; (*Sport*) sich revanchieren, seine Revanche bekommen; **out of** ~ aus Rache; **he killed him in** ~ er tötete ihn aus Rache; **in** ~ **for als Rache für**; ~ **is sweet** Rache ist süß *or* Blutwurst (*hum inf*).

2 *vt insult, murder, sb* rächen. **to** ~ **oneself or to be** ~**d (for sth)** sich (für etw) rächen; **to** ~ **oneself on sb (for sth)** sich (für etw) an jdm rächen.

revengeful [rɪ'vendʒfʊl] *adj* rachsüchtig. ~ **act** Racheakt *m*.

revengefully [rɪ'vendʒfəlɪ] *adv* rachsüchtig; *act* aus Rache.

revenger [rɪ'vendʒəʳ] *n* Rächer(in *f*) *m*.

revenue ['revənjuː] *n* (*of state*) Staatseinkünfte, öffentliche Einnahmen *pl*; (*tax* ~) Steueraufkommen *nt*; (*of individual*) Einnahmen, Einkünfte *pl*; (*department*) Finanzbehörde *f*, Fiskus *m*. ~ **man** *or* **officer** Finanzbeamter *m*; ~ **stamp** (*US*) Steuermarke *or* -banderole *f*; *see* **inland, internal**.

reverberate [rɪ'vɜːbəreɪt] **1** *vi* (*sound*) widerhallen, nachhallen; (*light, heat*) zurückstrahlen, reflektieren. **2** *vt sound, light, heat* zurückwerfen, reflektieren.

reverberation [rɪˌvɜːbə'reɪʃən] *n* (*of sound*) Widerhall, Nachhall *m*; (*of light, heat*) Zurückstrahlen *nt*, Reflexion *f*.

revere [rɪ'vɪəʳ] *vt* verehren.

reverence ['revərəns] **1** *n* **(a)** Ehrfurcht, Reverenz (*geh*) *f*; (*veneration*) Verehrung *f* (*for* für). **to have** ~ **for sb, to hold sb in** ~ jdn verehren; **to treat sth with** ~ etw ehrfürchtig behandeln; **to show** *or* **pay** ~ **to** Ehrfurcht bezeigen (+*dat*). **(b)** **your R**~ (Euer) Hochwürden. **(c)** (*obs: bow*) Reverenz *f*. **2** *vt* verehren.

reverend ['revərənd] **1** *adj* **the R**~ **Robert Martin** = Pfarrer Robert Martin; **the Most R**~ **John Smith** Erzbischof John Smith; **the Very R**~ **John Smith** Dekan John Smith; **the Right R**~ **John Smith** Bischof John Smith; **the R**~ **Mother** die Mutter Oberin. **2** *n* (*inf*) = Pfarrer *m*.

reverent ['revərənt] *adj* ehrfürchtig, ehrfurchtsvoll.

reverential [ˌrevə'renʃəl] *adj awe, respect* ehrerbietig; *bow, gesture etc* ehrerbietig.

reverently ['revərəntlɪ] *adv see adj*.

reverie ['revərɪ] *n* (*liter*) Träumereien *pl*. **he fell into a** ~ er kam ins Träumen.

revers [rɪ'vɪəʳ] *n, pl* - Revers *nt or* **m**.

reversal [rɪ'vɜːsəl] *n see vt* **(a)** Umkehren *nt*; Umstellen *nt*; Vertauschung *f*; Wenden *nt*; Umdrehen *nt*; Umkehren *nt*. **(b)** Rückwärtslaufenlassen *nt*; Zurückstellen *nt*. **(c)** Umstoßung *f*;

Aufhebung f; Umkehrung f; völlige Umstellung. **(d) to suffer a** ~ einen Rückschlag erleiden.

reverse [rɪ'vɜːs] **1** adj **(a)** (opposite) umgekehrt; direction entgegengesetzt; (Opt) image seitenverkehrt. **in ~ order in** umgekehrter Reihenfolge.

(b) ~ **gear** (Aut) Rückwärtsgang m; ~ **motion** or **action** (Tech) (backwards) Rückwärtsbewegung f; (opposite direction) entgegengesetzte Bewegung.

2 n **(a)** (opposite) Gegenteil nt. **quite the ~!** ganz im Gegenteil; **he is the ~ of polite** er ist alles andere als höflich; **he did everything one expected, but in ~** er hat alles immer genau andersherum gemacht, als man (von ihm) erwartete.

(b) (back) Rückseite f; (of cloth also) Abseite f, linke Seite; (of coin, medal also) Kehrseite f.

(c) (setback, loss) Rückschlag m; (defeat) Niederlage f. **the ~s of fortune** die Mißgeschicke pl.

(d) (on typewriter) Rücktelltaste f; (on tape-recorder) Rücklauftaste f; (Aut) Rückwärtsgang m. **in ~** (Aut) im Rückwärtsgang; **to go into ~** (Aut) in den Rückwärtsgang schalten.

3 vt **(a)** (turn the other way round) order, situation, procedure umkehren; objects, sentences, words also umstellen, vertauschen; garment wenden; result also umdrehen; (Phot) negative umkehren. **to ~ the order of sth** etw herumdrehen; **to ~ the position of words in a sentence** die Wörter in einem Satz umstellen or vertauschen; **to ~ the charges** (Brit Telec) ein R-Gespräch führen; **~d charge call** R-Gespräch nt.

(b) (cause to move backwards) moving belt rückwärts laufen lassen; typewriter ribbon zurückleiten. **to ~ one's car into the garage/down the hill/into a tree** rückwärts in die Garage fahren or setzen/rückwärts den Berg hinunter fahren/rückwärts gegen einen Baum fahren.

(c) verdict, judgement, decision umstoßen; decree aufheben; trend umkehren; policy völlig umstellen.

4 vi (move backwards) (car) rückwärts fahren; (dancer) rückwärts tanzen; (machine) rückwärts laufen. **to ~ into the garage** rückwärts in die Garage fahren; **reversing lights** Rückfahrscheinwerfer pl.

reversibility [rɪˌvɜːsɪ'bɪlɪtɪ] n see adj Umstoßbarkeit f; Umkehrbarkeit f.

reversible [rɪ'vɜːsəbl] adj decision umstoßbar; (Phys, Chem) umkehrbar; garment Wende-. ~ **cloth** Doubleface m or nt.

reversion [rɪ'vɜːʃən] n **(a)** (return to former state: of person) Umkehr f (to zu); (to bad state) Rückfall m (to in + acc). **the ~ of this country to a republic** die Rückverwandlung dieses Landes in eine Republik; ~ **to type** (Biol) (Arten)rückschlag m; **his ~ to type** das erneute Durchbrechen seiner alten Natur.

(b) (Jur: of property) Zurückfallen nt (to an + acc).

reversionary [rɪ'vɜːʃnərɪ] adj **(a)** (Jur) Anwartschafts-. **(b)** (Biol) atavistisch (spec).

revert [rɪ'vɜːt] vi (return) (to former state) zurückkehren (to zu); (to bad state) zurückfallen (to in + acc); (to topic) zurückkommen (to auf + acc); (Jur: property) zurückfallen (to an + acc). **he has ~ed to being a child** er ist wieder ins Kindheitsalter zurückgefallen; **but to ~ to the question** aber um auf die Frage zurückzukommen; **to ~ to type** (Biol) in der Art zurückschlagen; **he has ~ed to type** (fig) seine alte Natur ist wieder durchgebrochen; **fields ~ing to moorland/woodland** Felder, die wieder versumpfen/zu Wäldern werden.

review [rɪ'vjuː] **1** n **(a)** (look back) Rückblick m (of auf + acc); (report) Überblick m (of über + acc). **he gave a ~ of recent developments** er gab einen Überblick über die jüngsten Entwicklungen; **I shall keep your case under ~** ich werde Ihren Fall genau verfolgen or im Auge behalten; **to pass one's life in ~** das Leben noch einmal an sich (dat) vorüberziehen lassen.

(b) (re-examination) nochmalige Prüfung. **the agreement comes up for ~ or comes under ~** next year das Abkommen wird nächstes Jahr nochmals geprüft; **salary due for ~ in** January Gehaltsaufbesserung f im Januar geplant; **there will be a ~ of the situation in 3 months' time** in 3 Monaten wird die Lage noch einmal überprüft.

(c) (Mil: inspection) Inspektion f. **to hold a ~** eine Inspektion vornehmen.

(d) (of book, film, play etc) Kritik, Besprechung, Rezension f. ~ **copy** (of book) Rezensionsexemplar nt.

(e) (magazine) Zeitschrift f.

2 vt **(a)** (look back at) one's life, the past etc zurückblicken auf (+ acc), überdenken.

(b) (re-examine) situation, case erneut (über)prüfen.

(c) (Mil) troops inspizieren, mustern.

(d) book, play, film besprechen, rezensieren.

reviewer [rɪ'vjuːə^r] n Kritiker(in f), Rezensent(in f) m.

revile [rɪ'vaɪl] **1** vt schmähen, verunglimpfen. **2** vi **to ~ against** sb/sth gegen jdn/etw schmähen.

revise [rɪ'vaɪz] **1** vt **(a)** (change) opinion, estimate überholen, revidieren.

(b) (correct) proof, text revidieren, überarbeiten. **~d edition** überarbeitete Ausgabe; **the R~d Version** (Brit), **the R~d Standard Version** (US) die revidierte Übersetzung der Bibel.

(c) (Brit: learn up) wiederholen.

2 vi (Brit) (den Stoff) wiederholen.

reviser [rɪ'vaɪzə^r] n Bearbeiter m; (of translations etc) Korrektor m.

revision [rɪ'vɪʒən] n **(a)** (of opinion, estimate) Überholen, Revidieren nt. **(b)** (of proofs) Revision, Überarbeitung f. **(c)** (Brit: for exam) Wiederholung f (des Stoffs). **(d)** (revised version) überarbeitete Ausgabe.

revisionism [rɪ'vɪʒənɪzəm] n Revisionismus m.

revisionist [rɪ'vɪʒənɪst] **1** adj revisionistisch. **2** n Revisionist(in f) m.

revisit [ˌriː'vɪzɪt] vt place, person wieder or nochmals besuchen.

revitalize [ˌriː'vaɪtəlaɪz] vt neu beleben.

revival [rɪ'vaɪvəl] n **(a)** (bringing back) (of custom, usage) Wiedererwecken, Wiederauflebenlassen nt; (of old ideas, affair) Wiederaufnahme, Wiederaufgreifen nt; (from faint, fatigue) Wiederbeleben nt, Wiederbelebung f; (of play) Wiederaufnahme f; (of law) Wiederinkrafttreten nt.

(b) (coming back, return: of old ideas etc) Wiederaufleben nt; (of custom, usage also) Wiederaufblühen nt, Renaissance f (geh); (from faint, fatigue) Wiederbelebung f. **there has been a ~ of interest in** ... das Interesse an ... ist wieder wach geworden or erwacht; **the dollar experienced a slight ~** der Dollar verzeichnete wieder einen leichten Aufschwung; **an economic ~** ein wirtschaftlicher Aufschwung.

(c) (Rel) Erweckung f. ~ **meeting** Erweckungsversammlung f.

revivalism [rɪ'vaɪvəlɪzəm] n (Rel) Erweckungsbewegung f.

revivalist [rɪ'vaɪvəlɪst] (Rel) **1** adj erneuernd. **2** n Anhänger(in f) m der Erweckungsbewegung.

revive [rɪ'vaɪv] **1** vt person (from fainting, from fatigue) (wieder or neu) beleben; munter machen (inf); (from near death) wiederbeleben; fashion, custom, usage, conversation, hatred wiederbeleben; friendship, hobby, old usage, word wiederaufgreifen; wiederaufnehmen; old play wiederaufnehmen. **a glass of brandy will ~ you** ein Glas Weinbrand wird Sie wieder beleben or wieder auf die Beine bringen.

2 vi (person) (from fainting) wieder zu sich kommen; (from fatigue) wieder aufleben, wieder munter werden; (hope, feelings) wiederaufleben; (business, trade) wiederaufblühen.

revivify [riː'vɪvɪfaɪ] vt person wieder beleben or munter machen; (restore to life) wiederbeleben.

revocation [ˌrevə'keɪʃən] n see revoke Aufhebung f; Zurückziehen nt; Widerruf m; Entzug m.

revoke [rɪ'vəuk] **1** vt law aufheben; order, promise zurückziehen; decision widerrufen, rückgängig machen; licence entziehen. **2** vi (Cards) nicht Farbe bekennen. **3** n (Cards) Nichtfarbebekennen nt.

revolt [rɪ'vəult] **1** n Empörung, Revolte f, Aufstand m. **to rise (up) in ~, to break out in ~** einen Aufstand or eine Revolte machen, sich erheben; **to be in ~ (against)** rebellieren (gegen).

2 vi **(a)** (rebel) (against gegen) revoltieren, rebellieren.

(b) (be disgusted) (at, against bei, gegen) (one's nature, sensibilities) sich empören; (stomach) rebellieren.

3 vt abstoßen, anekeln (inf). **I was ~ed by it** es hat mich angeekelt or abgestoßen.

revolting [rɪ'vəultɪŋ] adj (repulsive, disgusting) abstoßend; meal, story ekelhaft; (inf: unpleasant) weather, colour, dress scheußlich, abscheulich; person widerlich.

revolution [ˌrevə'luːʃən] n **(a)** (Pol, fig) Revolution f; (radical change also) Umwälzung f (in + gen). **(b)** (turn) (around own axis) Umdrehung f; (of planet around sun) Umlauf m. **4,000 ~s** per minute eine Drehzahl von 4.000 pro Minute.

revolutionary [ˌrevə'luːʃnərɪ] **1** adj (lit, fig) revolutionär. **2** n Revolutionär, Revoluzzer (pej) m.

revolutionize [ˌrevə'luːʃənaɪz] vt revolutionieren.

revolve [rɪ'vɒlv] **1** vt drehen. **2** vi sich drehen. **to ~ on an axis/around the sun** sich um eine Achse/um die Sonne drehen; **he thinks everything ~s around him** (fig) er glaubt, alles drehe sich nur um ihn.

revolver [rɪ'vɒlvə^r] n Revolver m.

revolving [rɪ'vɒlvɪŋ] in cpds Dreh-; ~ **chair** n Drehstuhl m; ~ **door** n Drehtür f; ~ **light** n Drehleuchtfeuer nt; ~ **stage** n Drehbühne f.

revue [rɪ'vjuː] n (Theat) Revue f; (satirical) Kabarett nt. ~ **artist** Revuestar m; Kabarettist(in f) m.

revulsion [rɪ'vʌlʃən] n **(a)** (disgust) Abscheu, Ekel m (at vor + dat). **(b)** (sudden change) Umschwung m; (reaction) Empörung f.

reward [rɪ'wɔːd] **1** n Belohnung f; (money) Entgelt nt (form). **as a ~ for your honesty** als Belohnung or Lohn für Ihre Ehrlichkeit; **as a ~ for helping me** als Belohnung für Ihre Hilfe; **DM 1,000 ~** 1.000 DM Belohnung; ~ **offered for the return of** ... Finderlohn für ...; **the ~s of this job** die Vorzüge dieser Arbeit.

2 vt belohnen. **"finder will be ~ed"** „Finderlohn (ist) ausgesetzt".

rewarding [rɪ'wɔːdɪŋ] adj (financially) lohnend, einträglich; (mentally, morally) experience lohnend; task, work dankbar. **this is a very ~ book** es lohnt sich wirklich, dieses Buch zu lesen/diesen Film zu sehen; **bringing up a child is ~** ein Kind großzuziehen ist eine dankbare or lohnende Aufgabe.

rewind [ˌriː'waɪnd] pret, ptp **rewound** vt thread wieder aufwickeln; watch wieder aufziehen; film, tape zurückspulen. ~ **button** Rückspultaste f.

rewire [ˌriː'waɪə^r] vt neu verkabeln.

reword [ˌriː'wɜːd] vt explanation, question umformulieren, anders ausdrücken; paragraph, sentence also neu abfassen.

rework [ˌriː'wɜːk] vt (use again) theme wieder verarbeiten; (revise) neu fassen.

rewound [ˌriː'waʊnd] pret, ptp of **rewind**.

rewrite [ˌriː'raɪt] vb: pret **rewrote** [ˌriː'rəut], ptp **rewritten** [ˌriː'rɪtn] **1** vt (write out again) nochmals or neu schreiben; (recast) umschreiben. **2** ['riːraɪt] n this is just a ~ of his first novel dies ist nur ein Neuaufguß m seines ersten Romans; **it needs a complete ~** es muß vollständig neu geschrieben werden.

Rhaeto-Romanic ['riːtəurəu'mænɪk] n Rätoromanisch nt.

rhapsodic [ræp'sɒdɪk] adj (Mus) rhapsodisch; (fig) ekstatisch.

rhapsodize ['ræpsədaɪz] vi überschwenglich schwärmen (over, about von).

rhapsody ['ræpsədɪ] n (Mus) Rhapsodie f; (fig) Schwärmerei f.

rhd abbr of **right hand drive**.

rhea ['riːə] n Nandu, Pampasstrauß m.

Rhenish ['renɪʃ] adj wine Rhein-; region also rheinisch.

rheostat ['ri:əʊstæt] n Regelwiderstand, Rheostat (spec) m.

rhesus ['ri:səs] n Rhesus m. ~ **baby** Rhesus-geschädigtes Baby; ~ **monkey** Rhesusaffe m; ~ **factor** Rhesusfaktor m; ~-**negative/-positive** Rhesus negativ/positiv; ~-**negative baby** Baby nt mit Rhesus negativ.

rhetoric ['retərɪk] n Rhetorik f; (pej) Phrasendrescherei f (pej).

rhetorical [rɪ'tɒrɪkəl] adj rhetorisch; (pej) phrasenhaft, schwülstig (pej). ~ **question** rhetorische Frage.

rhetorically [rɪ'tɒrɪkəlɪ] adv (pej) schwülstig; ask rhetorisch.

rhetorician [ˌretə'rɪʃən] n Rhetoriker m; (pej) Phrasendrescher m (pej).

rheumatic [ruː'mætɪk] **1** n (a) (person) Rheumatiker(in f) m. **(b)** ~**s** sing Rheumatismus m. **2** adj pains rheumatisch; joint rheumakrank. ~ **fever** rheumatisches Fieber, akuter Rheumatismus.

rheumatism ['ruːmətɪzəm] n Rheuma(tismus m) nt.

rheumatoid ['ruːmətɔɪd] adj ~ **arthritis** chronischer Rheumatismus, Gelenkrheumatismus m.

rheumy ['ruːmɪ] adj eyes wäßrig.

Rhine [raɪn] n Rhein m. ~ **wine** Rheinwein m.

Rhine: ~**land** n Rheinland nt; r~**stone** n Rheinkiesel m.

rhino ['raɪnəʊ] n abbr of **rhinoceros**.

rhinoceros [raɪ'nɒsərəs] n Nashorn, Rhinozeros nt.

rhizome ['raɪzəʊm] n Rhizom nt, Wurzelstock m.

Rhodes [rəʊdz] n Rhodos nt. in ~ auf Rhodos.

Rhodesia [rəʊ'diːʒə] n Rhodesien nt.

Rhodesian [rəʊ'diːʒən] **1** adj rhodesisch. **2** n Rhodesier(in f) m.

rhododendron [ˌrəʊdə'dendrən] n Rhododendron m or nt.

rhomb [rɒm] n Rhombus m.

rhombic ['rɒmbɪk] adj rhombisch.

rhomboid ['rɒmbɔɪd] **1** n Rhomboid nt. **2** adj rhomboid.

rhombus ['rɒmbəs] n Rhombus m.

Rhone [rəʊn] n Rhone f.

rhubarb ['ruːbɑːb] n Rhabarber m. "~, ~, ~" (Theat hum) „Rhabarbarhabarbarhabarba".

rhyme [raɪm] **1** n (a) (word) Reim m. for (the sake of) the ~ damit es sich reimt, des Reimes willen; ~ **scheme** Reimschema nt; without ~ or reason ohne Sinn und Verstand; there seems to be neither ~ nor reason to it, that has neither ~ nor reason das hat weder Sinn noch Verstand.

(b) (poem) Gedicht nt. in ~ in Reimen or Versen; to put into ~ in Reime or Verse bringen or setzen.

2 vt reimen.

3 vi (a) sich reimen.

(b) (pej: write verse) reimen, Verse schmieden.

rhymester ['raɪmstər], **rhymer** ['raɪmər] n (pej) Verseschmied (pej), Dichterling (pej) m.

rhyming ['raɪmɪŋ] adj ~ **couplets** Reimpaare pl; ~ **dictionary** Reimwörterbuch nt; ~ **slang** Slang, bei dem ein Wort durch ein sich darauf reimendes Wort ersetzt wird.

rhythm ['rɪðm] n Rhythmus m. the ~ **method** (of contraception) die Knaus-Ogino-Methode; ~ **section** (of band) Rhythmusgruppe f; ~ **and blues** Rhythm-and-Blues m.

rhythmic(al) ['rɪðmɪk(əl)] adj rhythmisch; breathing, pulse gleichmäßig.

rhythmically ['rɪðmɪkəlɪ] adv rhythmisch; gleichmäßig.

RI abbr of **Religious Instruction**.

rib [rɪb] **1** n (a) (Anat, Cook) Rippe f. to dig or poke sb in the ~s jdn in die Rippen stoßen. **(b)** (of leaf, ceiling, ship, shell) Rippe f; (of umbrella) Speiche f. **(c)** (Knitting) Rippen pl. in ~ in Rippen. **2** vt (tease) necken, foppen.

RIBA ['riːbə] abbr of **Royal Institute of British Architects**.

ribald ['rɪbəld, 'raɪbəld] adj deftig, zotig (pej); behaviour derb; company liederlich. ~ **talk** Ferkeleien pl.

ribaldry ['rɪbəldrɪ] n Ferkeleien, Schweinereien pl.

riband ['rɪbənd] n (obs) see **ribbon**.

ribbed [rɪbd] adj knitting gerippt; shell, ceiling Rippen-, mit Rippen.

ribbon ['rɪbən] n (a) (for hair, dress) Band nt; (for typewriter) Farbband nt; (on medal) Ordensband nt; (fig: narrow strip) Streifen m. ~ **development** (Brit) Zeilenbauweise f.

(b) ~**s** pl (tatters) Fetzen pl; to tear sth to ~**s** etw zerfetzen or zerreißen; (fig) play etc etw in der Luft zerreißen.

riboflavin ['raɪbəʊfleɪvɪn] n Riboflavin nt.

ribonucleic acid ['raɪbəʊnjuː'kliːɪkæsɪd] n Ribonukleinsäure f.

ribwort ['rɪbwɜːt] n Spitzwegerich m.

rice [raɪs] n Reis m.

rice in cpds Reis-; ~**field** n Reisfeld nt; ~ **growing** n Reis(an)bau m; ~-**growing** adj reisanbauend; ~ **paper** n Reispapier nt; ~ **pudding** n Milchreis m; ~ **wine** n Reiswein m.

rich [rɪtʃ] **1** adj (+er) (a) (wealthy) reich.

(b) (splendid) furniture, decoration, style, clothes prächtig; gift teuer; banquet großartig.

(c) food schwer. ~ **tea biscuit** ≈ Butterkeks m; a ~ **diet** reichhaltige Kost.

(d) (fertile) soil fett; land fruchtbar, reich.

(e) (full) colour satt; sound also, voice voll; wine schwer.

(f) (inf: amusing) köstlich. that's ~! (iro) das ist ja großartig!

(g) (Aut) mixture fett.

(h) ~ **in vitamins** vitaminreich; ~ **in corn/minerals** reich an Getreide/Bodenschätzen; ~ **in detail/illustrations/examples** sehr detailliert/mit vielen Abbildungen/Beispielen; to be ~ **in spirit** ein gutes Herz haben.

2 n (a) **the** ~ pl die Reichen pl. **(b)** ~**es** Reichtümer pl.

Richard ['rɪtʃəd] n Richard m. ~ (**the**) **Lionheart** Richard Löwenherz.

richly ['rɪtʃlɪ] adv dress, decorate prächtig. he ~ **deserves it** er hat es mehr als verdient; he was ~ **rewarded** (lit) er wurde reich belohnt; (fig) er wurde reichlich belohnt.

richness ['rɪtʃnɪs] n see adj (a-e, g, h) **(a)** Reichtum m. **(b)** Pracht f; Großartigkeit f. **(c)** Schwere f. the ~ of the diet die reichhaltige Kost. **(d)** Fruchtbarkeit f. **(e)** Sattheit f; Schwere f. the ~ of his voice seine volle Stimme. **(f)** Fettheit f. **(g)** Reichtum m (in an +dat).

Richter scale ['rɪktə'skeɪl] n Richterskala f.

rick[1] [rɪk] n Schober m.

rick[2] n, vt see **wrick**.

rickets ['rɪkɪts] n sing Rachitis f, die englische Krankheit.

rickety ['rɪkɪtɪ] adj (a) furniture etc wackelig. (b) (Med) rachitisch.

rickshaw ['rɪkʃɔː] n Rikscha f.

ricochet ['rɪkəʃeɪ] **1** n see vi Abprall m; Rikoschettieren nt (spec). **2** vi (off von) abprallen; (bullet also) rikoschettieren (spec). the stone ~ed off the water der Stein hüpfte auf dem Wasser.

rictus ['rɪktəs] n (Anat, Zool) Sperrweite f.

rid [rɪd] pret, ptp ~ or ~ded vt to ~ of (of pests, disease) befreien von; (of bandits etc) säubern von; to ~ oneself of sb/sth jdn/etw loswerden; (of pests also) sich von etw befreien; (of ideas, prejudice etc) sich von etw lösen; to get ~ of sb/sth jdn/etw loswerden; to be ~ of sb/sth etw los sein; get ~ of it sieh zu, daß du das loswirst; (throw it away) schmeiß es weg (inf); you are well ~ of him ein Glück, daß du den los bist.

riddance ['rɪdəns] n good ~ (to bad rubbish)! (inf) ein Glück, daß wir das/den etc los sind.

ridden ['rɪdn] **1** ptp of **ride**. **2** adj ~ **by fears, fear-**~ angsterfüllt; **strike-**~ streikgeschüttelt; **disease-**~ von Krankheiten befallen; **doubt-**~ von Zweifeln zernagt; **strife-**~ zerstritten; ~ **by prejudice** von Vorurteilen beherrscht.

riddle[1] ['rɪdl] **1** n (sieve) (Schüttel)sieb nt.

2 vt (a) soil etc sieben; coal also schütteln.

(b) to ~ sb/sth with bullets jdn/etw mit Kugeln durchlöchern; ~**d with holes** völlig durchlöchert; ~**d with woodworm** wurmzerfressen; ~**d with corruption** von der Korruption zerfressen; ~**d with troublemakers** von Störenfrieden durchsetzt; ~**d with mistakes** voller Fehler.

riddle[2] n Rätsel nt. I'll ask you a ~ ich werde Ihnen ein Rätsel aufgeben; to speak in ~**s** in Rätseln sprechen.

ride [raɪd] (vb: pret rode, ptp ridden) **1** n (a) (in vehicle, on bicycle) Fahrt f; (on horse) Ritt m; (for pleasure) Ausritt m. to go for a ~ eine Fahrt machen/reiten gehen; after a hard ~ across country nach einer langen Überlandfahrt/einem langen Ritt querfeldein; he gave the child a ~ on his back er ließ das Kind auf den Schultern reiten; cycle/car/coach ~ Rad-/Auto-/Busfahrt f; to go for a ~ in the car mit dem Auto wegfahren, eine Fahrt (mit dem Auto) machen; to take sb for a ~ (in car etc) mit jdm eine Fahrt machen; (inf) jdn anschmieren (inf); he gave me a ~ into town in his car er nahm mich im Auto in die Stadt mit; it's my first ~ in a Rolls/in a train ich fahre zum ersten Mal in einem Rolls Royce/Zug; can I have a ~ on your bike? kann ich mal mit deinem Rad fahren?; 3 ~**s** on the merry-go-round 3 Karussellfahrten; to have a ~ in a helicopter in einem Hubschrauber fliegen; we had a ~ in a taxi/train wir sind in einem Taxi/Zug gefahren; it's a 20p ~ from the station ab Bahnhof kostet die Fahrt 20 Pence; the R~ of the Valkyries der Ritt der Walküren; to steal a ~ schwarzfahren.

(b) (quality of ~) this car gives a smooth/bumpy ~ mit diesem Auto fährt es sich sanft/unsanft.

(c) (path for horses) Reitweg m.

2 vi (a) (on a horse etc, Sport) reiten (on auf +dat). to go riding reiten gehen; the jockey was riding just under 65 kilos der Jockey brachte knapp 65 kg auf die Waage; Harold Wilson ~**s** again! (fig hum) Harold Wilson ist wieder da!

(b) (go in vehicle, by cycle etc) fahren. he was riding on a bicycle er fuhr mit einem Fahrrad; to ~ on a bus/in a car/in a train/in a cart in einem Bus/Wagen/Zug/Schubkarren fahren; to ~ away or off/down weg- or davon-/hinunterfahren.

(c) (fig: float) the seagull ~**s** on the wind die Möwe läßt sich vom Wind tragen; the moon was riding high in the sky der Mond zog hoch am Himmel dahin; he's riding high (fig) er schwimmt ganz oben; to ~ at anchor (ship) vor Anker liegen; we'll just have to let the matter or to let things ~ for a while wir müssen einfach für eine Weile den Dingen ihren Lauf lassen; but I'll let it ~ ich lasse es vorerst einmal.

(d) (horse) to ~ well gut laufen.

3 vt (a) horse, donkey etc reiten mit or auf (+dat), reiten; bicycle, motorbike fahren mit, fahren. I have never ridden a bicycle/a motorbike ich bin noch nie Rad/Motorrad gefahren; may I ~ your bike? darf ich mit deinem Fahrrad fahren?; he rode his horse away/back etc er ritt mit seinem Pferd weg/zurück etc; he rode him hard er ritt es scharf; he rode the horse into the stable er ritt das Pferd in den Stall; Jason will be ridden by H. Martin Jason wird unter H. Martin laufen; to ~ a race bei einem Rennen reiten; to ~ a good race (bei einem Rennen) gut reiten; they had ridden 10 km sie waren 10 km geritten/gefahren; they had ridden all the way sie waren den ganzen Weg geritten/gefahren; he rode the country-looking for ... er durchritt/durchfuhr das ganze Land auf der Suche nach ...; the birds riding the wind die Vögel, die sich vom Wind tragen lassen; the ship rode the waves das Schiff trieb auf den Wellen; witches ~ broomsticks Hexen reiten auf einem Besen; to ~ a horse to death ein Pferd zu Tode reiten; to ~ an argument to death ein Argument totreiten; see also **ridden**.

(b) (US inf: torment) piesacken (inf), schikanieren, zusetzen (+dat). don't ~ him too hard treibt's nicht so toll mit ihm.

♦**ride about** or **around** vi (on horse etc) herumreiten; (in vehicle, on motorcycle) herumfahren; (on bicycle) herumradeln (inf), herumfahren.

♦**ride behind** vi (on same horse, bicycle) hinten sitzen; (on different horse/bicycle) hinterherreiten; hinterherfahren.

♦**ride down** *vt sep* (a) (*trample*) umreiten. (b) (*catch up with*) einholen.

♦**ride out 1** *vt sep* überstehen. **to ~ ~ the storm** (*lit, fig*) den Sturm überstehen. **2** *vi* (*on horse*) ausreiten, einen Ausritt machen.

♦**ride up** *vi* (a) (*horseman*) heranreiten; (*motorcyclist etc*) heranfahren. (b) (*skirt etc*) hochrutschen.

rider ['raɪdə^r] *n* (a) (*person*) (*on horse*) Reiter(in *f*) *m*; (*on bicycle, motorcycle*) Fahrer(in *f*) *m*. (b) (*addition*) Zusatz *m*; (*to document, will etc*) Zusatzklausel *f*; (*to bill*)Allonge *f*; (*to jury's verdict*) zusätzliche Empfehlung. **I'd just like to add one ~ to that** zusätzlich (dazu) möchte ich noch sagen.

ridge [rɪdʒ] **1** *n* (a) (*raised strip*) (*on fabric, cardboard etc*) Rippe *f*; (*on corrugated iron*) Welle *f*; (*on sand*) Rippelmarke *f*; (*on ploughed land*) Grat *m*; (*in sea: reef*) Riff *nt*. **a ~ of hills/mountains** eine Hügelkette/in Höhenzug *m*; **a ~ of high pressure** (*Met*) ein Hochdruckkeil *m*.

(b) (*of hills, mountains*) Rücken, Kamm *m*; (*pointed, steep*) Grat *m*; (*of roof*) First *m*; (*of nose*) Rücken *m*.

2 *vt rocks, land, sand* zerfurchen.

ridge: **~ pole** *n* (*of tent*) Firststange *f*; **~ tent** *n* Firstzelt *nt*; **~ tile** *n* Firstziegel *m*; **~way** *n* Gratweg *m*.

ridicule ['rɪdɪkjuːl] **1** *n* Spott *m*. **to hold sb/sth up to ~** sich über jdn/etw lustig machen; **she's an object of ~** alles macht sich über sie lustig; **to become an object of ~** der Lächerlichkeit preisgegeben werden. **2** *vt* verspotten, verlachen.

ridiculous [rɪ'dɪkjʊləs] *adj* lächerlich. **don't be ~** red keinen Unsinn; **to make oneself (look) ~** sich lächerlich machen.

ridiculously [rɪ'dɪkjʊləslɪ] *adv see adj.*

ridiculousness [rɪ'dɪkjʊləsnɪs] *n* Lächerlichkeit *f*.

riding ['raɪdɪŋ] *n* Reiten *nt*. **I enjoy ~** ich reite gern.

riding in *cpds* Reit-; **~ breeches** *npl* Reithosen, Breeches *pl*; **a pair of ~ breeches** eine Reithose; **~ crop** *n* Reitgerte *f*; **~ habit** *n* Reitkostüm, Reitkleid *nt*; **~-light** *n* (*Naut*) Ankerlicht *nt*; **~ master** *n* Reitlehrer *m*.

rife [raɪf] *adj* (a) (*widespread*) *disease, corruption* weit verbreitet. **to be ~** grassieren; (*rumour*) umgehen. (b) (*full of*) **~ with** voll von, voller +*gen*; **the garden was ~ with weeds** der Garten strotzte vor Unkraut.

riffle ['rɪfl] *vt* (*also ~ through*) *pages* blättern durch; *cards* mischen.

riffraff ['rɪfræf] *n* Pöbel *m*, Gesindel *nt*.

rifle[1] ['raɪfl] *vt town* plündern; (*also ~ through*) *sb's pockets, drawer, till, house* durchwühlen.

rifle[2] *n* (*gun*) Gewehr *nt*; *mit gezogenem Lauf*; (*for hunting*) Büchse *f*. **the R~s** (*Mil*) = die Schützen *pl*.

rifle: **~ butt** *n* Gewehrkolben *m*; **~man** *n* (Gewehr)schütze *m*; **~ range** *n* Schießstand *m*; **~ shot** *n* Gewehrschuß *m*; **within ~ range** *or shot* in Schußweite (eines Gewehrs).

rift [rɪft] *n* (a) *Spalt m*. **~ valley** Grabenbruch *m*. (b) (*fig: in friendship*) Riß *m*; (*Pol also*) Spalt *m*.

rig [rɪg] **1** *n* (a) (*Naut*) Takelage, Takelung *f*.
(b) (*oil ~*) (Öl)förderturm *m*; (*offshore*) Ölbohrinsel *f*.
(c) (*inf: outfit: also ~-out*) Ausrüstung *f*. **in full ~** in großer Aufmachung, in voller Montur (*inf*).
(d) (*US inf: articulated lorry*) Sattelschlepper *m*.

2 *vt* (a) (*Naut*) auftakeln.
(b) (*fig*) *election, market etc* manipulieren. **it was ~ged!** das war Manipulation.

♦**rig out** *vt sep* (*inf*) (*equip*) ausstaffieren (*inf*); (*dress*) auftakeln (*inf*).

♦**rig up** *vt sep ship* auftakeln; *equipment* aufbauen; (*fig*) (*make*) improvisieren; (*arrange*) arrangieren.

rigger ['rɪgə^r] *n* (*Naut*) Takler *m*.

rigging ['rɪgɪŋ] *n* (a) (*Naut*) (*action*) Auftakeln *nt*; (*ropes*) Tauwerk *nt*. (b) (*inf: dishonest interference*) Manipulation, Schiebung (*inf*) *f*.

right [raɪt] **1** *adj* (a) (*just, fair, morally good*) richtig, recht (*S Ger*). **it isn't ~ to lie** es ist nicht richtig *or* recht zu lügen; **he thought it ~ to warn me** er hielt es für richtig, mich zu warnen; **it seemed only ~ to give him the money** es schien richtig, ihm das Geld zu geben; **it's only ~ (and proper)** es ist nur recht und billig; **it is only ~ to point out that ...** es ist nur recht und billig, wenn man darauf hinweist, daß ...; **to do the ~ thing by sb** sich jdm gegenüber anständig benehmen.

(b) (*true, correct*) *answer, solution, time, train* richtig. **to be ~** (*person*) recht haben; (*answer, solution*) richtig sein, stimmen; (*clock*) richtig gehen; **you're quite ~** Sie haben ganz recht; **how ~ you are!** (*inf*) da haben Sie ganz recht! **is the clock ~?**; geht die Uhr richtig?; **you were ~ to refuse** *or* in refusing Sie hatten recht, als Sie ablehnten; **the ~ road** (*lit*) der richtige Weg; **on the ~ road** *or* track (*fig*) auf dem rechten Weg; **my guess was ~** ich habe richtig geraten; **let's get it ~ this time!** mach es dieses Mal richtig; (*in reporting facts etc*) sag es dieses Mal richtig; **to put** *or* **set ~** *error* korrigieren; *clock* richtig stellen; *situation* wieder in Ordnung bringen; **I tried to put things ~ after their quarrel** ich versuchte, nach ihrem Streit wieder einzulenken; **to put** *or* **set sb ~** jdn berichtigen; **put me ~ if I'm wrong** korrigieren *or* verbessern Sie mich, wenn ich unrecht habe; *see also category* (d).

(c) (*proper*) *clothes, document* richtig. **what's the ~ thing to do in this case?** was tut man da am besten?; **to come at the ~ time** zur rechten Zeit kommen; **to do sth the ~ way** etw richtig machen; **that is the ~ way of looking at it** das ist die richtige Einstellung; **the ~ word** das rechte *or* richtige Wort; **the ~ man for the job** der richtige *or* richtige Mann für die Stelle; **Mr/Miss R~** (*inf*) der/die Richtige (*inf*); **we will do what is ~ for the country** wir werden tun, was für das Land gut ist; **to know the ~ people** die richtigen Leute kennen; **more than is ~** mehr als recht ist.

(d) (*well*) **the medicine soon put** *or* **set him ~** die Medizin hat

ihn schnell wiederhergestellt *or* wieder auf die Beine gebracht; **I don't feel quite ~ today** ich fühle mich heute nicht ganz wohl; **to be as ~ as rain** (*Brit*) kerngesund sein; (*after accident*) keine Schramme abbekommen haben (*inf*); **to put the engine ~** den Motor reparieren; **the plumber put things ~** der Klempner brachte alles wieder in Ordnung; **to be in one's ~ mind** klar bei Verstand sein; **he's not ~ in the head** (*inf*) bei ihm stimmt's nicht im Oberstübchen (*inf*); *see* all right.

(e) (*phrases*) **~!, ~-oh!** (*Brit inf*), **~ you are!** (*Brit inf*) gut, schön, okay (*inf*); **~ on!** (*esp US sl*) super! (*sl*); **that's ~!** (*correct, true*) das stimmt!; **that's ~, dear, put it on the table** schön, stell es bitte auf den Tisch; **so they came in the end — is that ~?** und so kamen sie schließlich — wirklich?; **~ enough!** (*das*) stimmt!; **it's a ~ mess in there** (*inf*) das ist vielleicht ein Durcheinander hier (*inf*); **he's a ~ fool!** (*inf*) er ist wirklich doof (*inf*); **you're a ~ one** (*inf*) du bist mir der Richtige (*inf*).

(f) (*opposite of left*) rechte(r, s). **~ hand** rechte Hand; **I'd give my ~ hand to know** the answer ich würde was drum geben, wenn ich die Antwort wüßte (*inf*); **on your ~ hand** you see the **bridge** rechter Hand *or* rechts sehen Sie die Brücke.

2 *adv* (a) (*straight, directly*) direkt; (*exactly also*) genau. **~ in front/ahead of you** direkt *or* genau vor Ihnen; **go ~ on gehen/fahren Sie geradeaus weiter; **~ away, ~ off** (*immediately*) sofort, schnurstracks (*inf*); **~ off** (*at the first attempt*) auf Anhieb (*inf*); **~ now** (*at this very moment*) in diesem Augenblick; (*immediately*) sofort; **~ here** genau hier; **~ in the middle** genau *or* direkt in die/der Mitte; **~ at the beginning** gleich am Anfang; **I'll be ~ with you** ich bin gleich da; **it hit me ~ on the face** der Schlag traf mich genau *or* voll ins Gesicht.

(b) (*completely, all the way*) ganz. **~ round the house** ganz um das Haus herum; (*inside*) durch das ganze Haus; **rotten ~ through** durch und durch verfault *or* (*fig*) verdorben; **pierced ~ through** mitten durchgestochen.

(c) (*correctly*) richtig. **to guess/answer ~** richtig raten/antworten; **if I remember ~** wenn ich mich recht *or* richtig erinnere; **you did ~ to refuse** es war richtig (von Ihnen), abzulehnen; **if everything goes ~** wenn alles klappt (*inf*); **nothing goes ~ for them** nichts klappt bei ihnen (*inf*), bei ihnen läuft alles schief (*inf*); **if I get you ~** (*inf*) wenn ich Sie (da) richtig verstehe; **I'll see you ~** (*inf*) ich werde aufpassen, daß Sie nicht zu kurz kommen (*inf*); *see* serve.

(d) (*old, dial: very*) sehr. **the R~ Honourable John Smith MP** (*not old, dial*) der Abgeordnete John Smith.

(e) (*opposite of left*) rechts. **it is ~ of the bridge** es ist rechts von der Brücke; **turn ~** biegen Sie rechts ab; **~ of centre** (*Pol*) rechts von der Mitte; **~, left and centre** (*everywhere*) überall; **to be cheated ~, left and centre** (*inf*) *or* **~ and left** (*inf*) von vorne bis hinten betrogen werden (*inf*); **to owe money ~, left and centre** (*inf*) bei Gott und der Welt Schulden haben (*inf*).

3 *n* (a) *no pl* (*moral, legal*) Recht *nt*. **he doesn't know ~ from wrong** er kann Recht und Unrecht nicht auseinanderhalten; **I want to know the ~s and wrongs of it first** ich möchte erst beide Seiten kennenlernen; **to be in the ~** im Recht sein.

(b) (*entitlement*) Recht *nt*; (*to sth also*) Anrecht *nt*, Anspruch *m*. **to (have) a ~ to sth** ein (An)recht *or* einen Anspruch auf etw (*acc*) (haben); **to have a** *or* **the ~ to do sth** ein *or* das Recht haben, etw zu tun; **what ~ have you to say that?** mit welchem Recht sagen Sie das?, was berechtigt Sie, das zu sagen?; **by what ~?** mit welchem Recht?; **he is within his ~s** das ist sein gutes Recht; **by ~s** rechtmäßig, von Rechts wegen; **in one's own ~** selber, selbst; **to have the (sole) ~s of sth** (*Comm*) die (alleinigen) Rechte für etw haben; **the divine ~ (of kings)** das Gottesgnadentum; **the queen has the divine ~ to ...** die Königin hat das von Gott gegebene Recht, zu ...; *see* civil ~s.

(c) **to put** *or* **set sth to ~s** etw (wieder) in Ordnung bringen; **to put things** *or* **the world to ~s** die Welt verbessern.

(d) (*not left*) rechte Seite. **to drive on the ~** rechts fahren; **to keep to the ~** sich rechts halten, rechts bleiben; **on my ~** rechts (von mir); **on** *or* **to the ~ of the church** rechts von der Kirche; **the R~** (*Pol*) die Rechte; **those to the ~ of him** (*Pol*) diejenigen, die weiter rechts stehen/standen als er.

4 *vt* (a) (*return to upright position*) aufrichten.
(b) (*make amends for*) *wrong* wiedergutmachen.
(c) **the problem should ~ itself** (*fig*) das Problem müßte sich von selbst lösen.

right: **~ angle** *n* rechter Winkel; **at ~ angles (to)** rechtwinklig (zu); **~-angled** ['raɪtæŋgld] *adj* rechtwinklig.

righteous ['raɪtʃəs] *adj* (a) rechtschaffen; (*pej*) selbstgerecht (*pej*). (b) *indignation* gerecht; *anger also* heilig.

righteously ['raɪtʃəslɪ] *adv* rechtschaffen.

righteousness ['raɪtʃəsnɪs] *n* Rechtschaffenheit *f*.

rightful ['raɪtfʊl] *adj* (a) *heir, owner* rechtmäßig. (b) *punishment* gerecht.

rightfully ['raɪtfʊlɪ] *adv* rechtmäßig; gerechterweise.

right: **~-hand drive** *adj* rechtsgesteuert; **~-handed** *adj person* rechtshändig; *punch, throw also* mit der rechten Hand; **~-hander** *n* (*punch*) Rechte *f*; (*person*) Rechtshänder(in *f*) *m*; **~-hand man** *n* rechte Hand; **~-hand side** *n* rechte Seite.

rightist ['raɪtɪst] **1** *n* (*Pol*) Rechte(r) *mf*. **2** *adj* rechtsorientiert.

rightly ['raɪtlɪ] *adv* (a) (*correctly*) he said, **~, that ...** er sagte sehr richtig, daß ...; **I don't ~ know** ich weiß nicht genau. (b) (*justifiably*) mit *or* zu Recht. **~ or wrongly** ob das nun richtig ist/war oder nicht; **and ~ so** und zwar mit Recht.

right: **~-minded** *adj* vernünftig; **~ of way** *n* (*across property*) Durchgangsrecht *nt*; (*Mot: priority*) Vorfahrt(srecht *nt*) *f*; **it's his ~ of way, he has the ~ of way** (*Mot*) er hat Vorfahrt; **~-thinking** *adj* vernünftig; **~ wing** *n* (*Sport, Pol*) rechter Flügel; **he's the ~ wing** (*Sport*) er ist (der) Rechtsaußen; **~-wing** *adj* (*Pol*) rechtsorientiert; **~-winger** *n* (*Sport*) Rechtsaußen *m*; (*Pol*) Rechte(r) *mf*.

rigid ['rɪdʒɪd] *adj* (*lit*) *board, material, frame* starr, steif; (*fig*) *person, character* strikt, streng, stur *(pej); discipline, principles* streng, strikt; *(inflexible)* unbeugsam; *interpretation* genau, stur *(pej); specifications* genau festgelegt, strikt; *system* starr, unbeugsam. ~ **with fear** starr *or* steif vor Angst.

rigidity [rɪ'dʒɪdɪtɪ] *n see adj* Starrheit, Steifheit *f;* Striktheit, Strenge, Sturheit *(pej) f;* Strenge, Striktheit *f;* Unbeugsamkeit *f;* Genauigkeit, Sturheit *(pej) f;* Starrheit, Unbeugsamkeit *f.*

rigidly ['rɪdʒɪdlɪ] *adv stand etc* starr, steif; *(fig) behave, treat* streng, strikt; *oppose* star, strikt; *(inflexibly)* unbeugsam.

rigmarole ['rɪgmərəʊl] *n* Gelaber *nt; (process)* Gedöns *nt (inf).*
   to go through the whole *or* **same** ~ **again** nochmal mit demselben Gelaber/Gedöns anfangen.

rigor *n (US) see* **rigour.**

rigor mortis ['rɪgə'mɔːtɪs] *n* die Toten- *or* Leichenstarre.

rigorous ['rɪgərəs] *adj (strict) person, character, discipline, rule, structure, method* streng, strikt; *measures* rigoros; *(accurate) book-keeping, work* peinlich genau; *analysis, tests* gründlich; *(harsh) climate* streng. **with** ~ **precision/accuracy** mit äußerster Präzision/peinlicher Genauigkeit.

rigour, (US) rigor ['rɪgə'] *n (a) no pl (strictness)* Strenge, Striktheit *f.* **to punish with** ~ hart *or* streng bestrafen; **the full** ~ **of the law** die ganze Strenge des Gesetzes. **(b)** ~**s** *pl (of climate, famine etc)* Unbilden *pl.*

rig-out ['rɪgaʊt] *n (inf) see* **rig 1 (c).**

rile [raɪl] *vt (inf)* ärgern, reizen.

rill [rɪl] *n (poet)* Bächlein *nt.*

rim [rɪm] *n (of cup, bowl)* Rand *m; (of hat also)* Krempe *f; (of spectacles also)* Fassung *f; (of wheel)* Felge *f,* Radkranz *m.*

rime¹ [raɪm] *n see* **rhyme.**

rime² *n (liter)* (Rauh)reif *m.*

rimless ['rɪmlɪs] *adj spectacles* randlos.

rimmed [rɪmd] *adj* mit Rand; *wheel* Felgen-. **gold-**~ **spectacles** Brille *f* mit Goldfassung *or* -rand.

rind [raɪnd] *n (of cheese)* Rinde *f; (of bacon)* Schwarte *f; (of fruit)* Schale *f.*

ring¹ [rɪŋ] **1** *n (a)* Ring *m; (for swimmer)* Schwimmring *or* -reifen *m.*
   (b) *(circle)* Ring *m; (in tree trunk)* Jahresring *m.* **the** ~**s of Saturn** die Saturnringe *pl;* **to have** ~**s round one's eyes** (dunkle) Ringe unter den Augen haben; **to stand in a** ~ im Kreis stehen; **to run** ~**s round sb** *(inf)* jdn in die Tasche stecken *(inf).*
   (c) *(group) (Pol)* Gruppe *f; (of dealers, spies)* Ring *m.*
   (d) *(enclosure) (at circus)* Manege *f; (at exhibition)* Ring *m; (Horseracing)* Buchmacherring *m; (boxing* ~) (Box)ring *m.*

   2 *vt (surround)* umringen; *(in game: with hoop)* einen/den Ring werfen über (+*acc*); *(put* ~ *on or round) item on list etc* einkreisen, einen Kreis machen um; *bird* beringen; *bear, bull* einen/den Nasenring verpassen (+*dat*); *tree* ringeln.

ring² [vb: pret **rang**, ptp **rung**] **1** *n (a) (sound)* Klang *m;* (~*ing: of bell, alarm bell)* Läuten *nt; (of electric bell, also alarm clock, phone)* Klingeln *nt; (metallic sound: of swords etc)* Klirren *nt; (of crystal)* Klang *m.* **there was a** ~ **at the door** es hat geklingelt *or* geläutet; **to hear a** ~ **at the door** die Türklingel hören; **give two** ~**s for the maid** für das Zimmermädchen zweimal läuten; **the** ~ **of the hammers** der Schall der Hämmer.
   (b) *(esp Brit Telec)* Anruf *m.* **to give sb a** ~ jdn anrufen.
   (c) *(fig)* Klang *m.* **his voice had an angry** ~ **(in** *or* **to it)** seine Stimme klang etwas böse; **that has the** *or* **a** ~ **of truth (to** *or* **about it)** das klingt sehr wahrscheinlich.
   (d) *(set)* ~ **of bells** Glockenspiel *nt.*

   2 *vi (a) see n (a)* klingen; läuten; klingeln; klirren; klingen; *(hammers)* schallen. **the (door)bell rang** es hat geläutet *or* geklingelt; **the bell rang for dinner** es hat zum Essen geläutet; **when the bell** ~**s** wenn es klingelt *or* läutet; *(churchbell)* wenn die Glocke läutet; **to** ~ **for sb** (nach) jdm läuten; **to** ~ **for sth** für etw läuten; **you rang, sir?** (gnädiger Herr,) Sie haben geläutet?; **please** ~ **for attention** bitte läuten; **to** ~ **at the door** (an der Tür) klingeln *or* läuten.
   (b) *(esp Brit Telec)* anrufen.
   (c) *(sound, resound) (words, voice)* tönen, schallen; *(music, singing)* erklingen *(geh),* tönen. **to** ~ **false/true** falsch/wahr klingen; **my ears are** ~**ing** mir klingen die Ohren; **the valley rang with their shouts** das Tal hallte von ihren Rufen wider *(geh);* **the town rang with his praises** *(liter)* die ganze Stadt sang sein Lob; **his voice rang with emotion** seine Rührung klang (bei seinen Worten) deutlich durch; **his words still** ~ **in my ears** seine Worte klingen mir noch im Ohr.

   3 *vt (a) bell* läuten. **to** ~ **the doorbell** (an der Tür) läuten *or* klingeln; **that/his name** ~**s a bell** *(fig inf)* das/sein Name kommt mir bekannt vor; **to** ~ **the hours** die Stunden schlagen; **to** ~ **the changes (on sth)** *(lit: on bells)* (etw) im Wechsel läuten; *(fig)* etw in allen Variationen durchspielen.
   (b) *(also* ~ **up)** anrufen.

♦**ring back** *vti sep (esp Brit)* zurückrufen.

♦**ring down** *vt sep* **to** ~ **the curtain** ~ *(Theat)* den Vorhang niedergehen lassen; **to** ~ ~ **the curtain on sth** *(fig) on project* einen Schlußstrich unter etw *(acc)* ziehen; *on era* den Vorhang über etw *(acc)* fallen lassen.

♦**ring in 1** *vi (a) (esp Brit Telec)* sich telefonisch melden *(to* in +*dat).* **(b)** *(US: clock in)* (zu Beginn der Arbeit) stempeln *or* stechen. **2** *vt sep* **to** ~ **the New Year** das neue Jahr einläuten.

♦**ring off** *vi (esp Brit Telec)* aufhängen, (den Hörer) auflegen.

♦**ring out 1** *vi (a)* ertönen; *(bell also)* laut erklingen; *(shot also)* krachen; *(sound above others)* herausklingen. **2** *vt sep* **to** ~ ~ **the Old Year** das alte Jahr ausläuten.

♦**ring up** *vt sep (a) (esp Brit Telec)* anrufen. **(b)** **to** ~ ~ **the curtain** *(Theat)* den Vorhang hochgehen lassen; **to** ~ ~ **the curtain on sth** *(fig)* den Vorhang zu etw hochgehen lassen. **(c)** *(cashier)* eintippen.

ring: ~**-a-**~**-o'-roses** *n* Ringelreihen *m;* ~ **binder** *n* Ringbuch *nt;*

~**bolt** *n* Ringbolzen *m;* ~ **circuit** *n* Ringverzweigung *f;* ~**dove** *n* Ringeltaube *f.*

ringer ['rɪŋə'] *n (a) (bell* ~) Glöckner *m.* **(b) to be a dead** ~ **for sb** *(sl)* jdm aufs Haar gleichen.

ring-finger ['rɪŋ'fɪŋgə'] *n* Ringfinger *m.*

ringing ['rɪŋɪŋ] **1** *adj bell* läutend; *voice, tone* schallend. ~ **tone** *(Brit Telec)* Rufzeichen *nt.* **2** *n (of bell)* Läuten *nt; (of electric bell also, of phone)* Klingeln *nt; (in ears)* Klingen *nt.*

ringleader ['rɪŋ‚liːdə'] *n* Anführer(in *f) m.*

ringlet ['rɪŋlɪt] *n* Ringellocke, Korkenzieherlocke *f.*

ring: ~**master** *n* Zirkusdirektor *m;* ~ **road** *n* Umgehung(s- straße) *f;* ~**side** *n* **at the** ~**side** am Ring; ~**side seat** *n (Boxing)* Ringplatz *m;* ~**side seat** *n;* **to have a** ~**side seat** *(fig)* einen Logenplatz haben; ~ **spanner** *n* Ringschlüssel *m;* ~**tailed** *adj* mit Ringelschwanz; ~**worm** *n* Scherpilzflechte *f.*

rink [rɪŋk] *n* Eisbahn *f; (roller-skating* ~) Rollschuhbahn *f.*

rinse [rɪns] **1** *n (a) (act)* Spülung *f.* **to give sth a** ~ *see vt (a);* **have a** ~ *(dentist)* bitte spülen.
   (b) *(for hair)* Spülung *f; (colorant)* Tönung *f.*

   2 *vt (a) clothes, hair* spülen; *plates* abspülen; *cup, mouth, basin* ausspülen. **to** ~ **one's hands** sich *(dat)* die Hände abspülen; **to** ~ **the soap off one's hands** sich *(dat)* die Seife von den Händen abspülen.
   (b) *(colour with a* ~) hair tönen. **she** ~**d her hair black** sie hat sich *(dat)* das Haar schwarz getönt.

♦**rinse down** *vt sep car, wall* abspülen. **to** ~ **sth** ~ **the plughole** etw den Abfluß hinunterspülen.

♦**rinse out** *vt sep (a) hair, tint, colour, soap, cup* ausspülen, auswaschen. **to** ~ ~ **one's mouth** sich *(dat)* den Mund ausspülen. **(b)** *(wash quickly) clothes* auswaschen.

Rio (de Janeiro) ['rɪəʊ(dədʒə'nɪərəʊ)] *n* Rio (de Janeiro) *nt.*

riot ['raɪət] **1** *n (a) (Pol)* Aufstand, Aufruhr *m no pl; (by mob, football fans etc)* Krawall *m; (fig: wild occasion)* Orgie *f.* **there'll be a** ~ **if you announce that** wenn Sie das verkünden, gibt es einen Aufstand; **to run** ~ *(people)* randalieren; *(vegetation)* wuchern; **his imagination runs** ~ seine Phantasie geht mit ihm durch; **ivy had run** ~ **all over the house** Efeu hatte das ganze Haus überwuchert; **the R** ~ **Act** *(Hist)* die Aufruhrakte; **to read sb the** ~ **act** *(fig)* jdm die Leviten lesen; **the** ~ **police/ squad** die Bereitschaftspolizei/das Überfallkommando; ~ **shield** Schutzschild *m.*
   (b) a ~ **of colour(s)** eine Farbenexplosion, eine Farbenorgie; **a** ~ **of reds and blues** eine Explosion von Rot- und Blautönen; **a** ~ **of flowers** ein wildes Blumenmeer.
   (c) **to be a** ~ *(inf)* zum Schießen *or* Schreien sein *(inf).*

   2 *vi* randalieren, Krawall machen; *(revolt)* einen Aufruhr machen.

rioter ['raɪətə'] *n* Randalierer *m; (rebel)* Aufrührer *m.*

rioting ['raɪətɪŋ] *n* Krawalle *pl; (Pol also)* Aufstände *pl.* ~ **in the streets** Straßenkrawalle *or* -schlachten *pl.*

riotous ['raɪətəs] *adj (a) person, crowd* randalierend; *living, behaviour, child* wild. **(b)** *(inf)* wild *(inf); (hilarious)* urkomisch *(inf).* **we had a** ~ **time** es ging hoch her *(inf);* **a** ~ **success** ein Riesen- *or* Bombenerfolg *(inf) m.*

riotously ['raɪətəslɪ] *adv behave, live* wild. **it was** ~ **funny** *(inf)* es war zum Schreien *(inf).*

RIP *abbr of* **rest in peace** R.I.P.

rip [rɪp] **1** *n* Riß *m; (made by knife etc)* Schlitz *m.*
   2 *vt material, clothes* einen Riß machen in (+*acc); (stronger)* zerreißen; *(vandalize) pictures etc* zerschlitzen. **you've** ~**ped your jacket** du hast einen Riß in der Jacke; du hast dir die Jacke zerrissen; **to** ~ **sth down the middle** etw mitten durchreißen; **to** ~ **open** aufreißen; *(with knife)* aufschlitzen.
   3 *vi (a) (cloth, garment)* reißen.
   (b) *(inf)* **the car** ~**s along** der Wagen rast dahin; **let her** ~! volle Pulle! *(inf);* **to let** ~ loslegen *(inf);* **he let** ~ **a stream of complaints** er hat einen Schwall Beschwerden vom Stapel gelassen *(inf);* **he let** ~ **at me** er ist auf mich losgegangen *(inf).*

♦**rip down** *vt sep* herunterreißen; *old buildings* abreißen.

♦**rip off** *vt sep (a) (lit)* abreißen *(prep obj* von); *clothing* herunterreißen. **he** ~**ped** ~ **her dress** er riß ihr das Kleid vom Leib. **(b)** *(sl) object, goods* mitgehen lassen *(inf); bank, shop, house* ausrauben; *person* schröpfen *(inf),* ausnehmen *(sl).*

♦**rip out** *vt sep* herausreißen *(of* aus).

♦**rip up** *vt sep* zerreißen; *road* aufreißen.

riparian [raɪ'pɛərɪən] *adj (form)* Ufer-. ~ **right** Uferanlieger recht *nt.*

rip-cord ['rɪp‚kɔːd] *n* Reißleine *f.*

ripe [raɪp] *adj (+er) (a) fruit, cheese* reif; *(fig) lips* voll. **(b)** *(mature)* reif. **to live to a** ~ **old age** ein hohes Alter erreichen; **to be** ~ **for sth** *(fig)* für etw reif sein; **when the time is** ~ wenn die Zeit dafür reif ist.

ripen ['raɪpən] **1** *vt (lit, fig)* reifen lassen. **2** *vi* reifen.

ripeness ['raɪpnɪs] *n* Reife *f*

rip-off ['rɪpɒf] *n (inf)* Wucher, Nepp *(inf) m; (cheat)* Schwindel *m.* **it's a** ~ das ist Wucher *or* Nepp *(inf)/*Schwindel; **he'd been the victim of a** ~ er war ausgenommen worden *(inf).*

riposte [rɪ'pɒst] **1** *n (retort)* scharfe Antwort, Gegenschlag *m; (Fencing)* Riposte *f.* **2** *vi (retort)* scharf erwidern, parieren; *(Fencing)* parieren und eine Riposte bringen.

ripper ['rɪpə'] *n (murderer)* Frauenmörder *m.*

ripping ['rɪpɪŋ] *adj (dated Brit inf)* herrlich, wunderbar.

ripple ['rɪpl] **1** *n (a) (in water)* kleine Welle; *(of crops)* sanftes Wogen *no pl.* **little** ~**s spread out in the water** das Wasser kräuselte sich; **the wind blew across the grass in** ~**s** das Gras wogte im Wind.
   (b) *(noise)* Plätschern *nt; (of waves)* Klatschen *nt.* **a** ~ **of laughter** ein kurzes Lachen; *(girls')* ein perlendes Lachen.

   2 *vi (a) (undulate) (water)* sich kräuseln; *(crops)* wogen.
   (b) *(murmur: water)* plätschern; *(waves)* klatschen.

   3 *vt water* kräuseln; *corn* wogen lassen.

rip: ~-**roaring** adj (inf) sagenhaft (inf); ~**tide** n Kabbelung f.
rise [raɪz] (vb: pret **rose**, ptp **risen**) 1 n (a) (increase) (in gen) (in temperature, pressure, of tide, river, barometer) Anstieg m, Steigen nt no pl; (in number) Zunahme f; (in prices, wages, bank rate also) Steigerung f; (St Ex) Aufschwung m. a (pay) ~ (Brit) eine Gehaltserhöhung; prices are on the ~ die Preise steigen; there has been a ~ in the number of participants die Zahl der Teilnehmer ist gestiegen; a ~ in the population ein Bevölkerungszuwachs m, eine Bevölkerungszunahme.
   (b) (upward movement) (of theatre curtain) Hochgehen, Heben nt; (of sun) Aufgehen nt; (Mus: in pitch) Erhöhung f (in gen); (fig: to fame, power etc) Aufstieg m (to zu). the ~ of the working classes der soziale Aufstieg der Arbeiterklasse; the ~ and fall of an empire der Aufstieg und Niedergang eines Weltreichs; to get a ~ out of sb (inf) jdn zur Reaktion bringen.
   (c) (small hill) Erhebung f; (slope) Steigung f.
   (d) (origin) (of river) Ursprung m. the river has its ~ in der Fluß entspringt in (+dat); to give ~ to sth etw verursachen; to questions etw aufwerfen; to complaints Anlaß zu etw geben.
   2 vi (a) (get up) (from sitting, lying) aufstehen, sich erheben (geh), um zu gehen; to ~ (up) on tiptoe sich auf die Zehenspitzen stellen; to ~ from the table vom Tisch aufstehen, sich (geh), um zu gehen; to ~ (up) on tiptoe sich auf die Zehenspitzen stellen; to ~ from the table vom Tisch aufstehen, sich vom Tisch erheben (geh); to ~ in the saddle sich im Sattel heben; he rose from his sickbed to go and see her er verließ sein Krankenlager, um sie zu sehen; ~ and shine! (inf) raus aus den Federn! (inf); the horse rose on its hind legs das Pferd stellte sich auf die Hinterbeine; (rear up) das Pferd bäumte sich auf; to ~ from the dead (liter, Bibl) von den Toten auferstehen.
   (b) (go up) steigen; (smoke, mist etc also) aufsteigen, emporsteigen; (prices, temperature, pressure etc also) ansteigen (to auf +acc); (balloon, aircraft, bird) (auf)steigen, sich heben (geh); (lift) hochfahren, nach oben fahren; (theatre curtain) hochgehen, sich heben; (sun, moon, bread, dough) aufgehen; (wind, storm) aufkommen, sich erheben; (voice) (in volume) sich erheben; (in pitch) höher werden; (swimmer, fish) hochkommen; (new buildings) entstehen; (fig: hopes) steigen; (anger) wachsen, zunehmen; (stomach) sich heben. to ~ to the surface an die Oberfläche kommen; the fish are rising well die Fische beißen gut; he won't ~ to any of your taunts er läßt sich von dir nicht reizen; the idea/image rose in his mind kam der Gedanke/das Bild tauchte vor ihm auf; I can't ~ to £10 ich kann nicht bis £ 10 gehen; to ~ in price (goods) im Preis steigen; to ~ above a certain temperature über eine gewisse Temperatur steigen; his spirits rose ihre Stimmung hob sich; his voice rose to screaming pitch seine Stimme wurde kreischend or shrill; to ~ to a crescendo zu einem Crescendo anschwellen; the colour rose to her cheeks die Röte stieg ihr ins Gesicht; things rose to a climax die Dinge kamen zu einem Höhepunkt.
   (c) (ground) ansteigen; (mountains, hills, castle) sich erheben. the mountain ~s to 3,000 metres der Berg erhebt sich auf 3.000 m; the mountains rising (up) before him die Berge, die sich vor ihm erhoben; where the hills ~ against the sky wo sich die Berge gegen den Himmel abheben.
   (d) (fig: in society, rank) to ~ in the world/in society es zu etwas bringen; to ~ from nothing sich aus dem Nichts emporor hocharbeiten; he rose to be President/a captain er stieg zum Präsidenten/Kapitän auf; see rank¹.
   (e) (adjourn) (assembly) auseinandergehen; (meeting) beendet sein. the House rose at 2 a.m. (Parl) das Haus beendete die Sitzung um 2 Uhr morgens; Parliament will ~ on Thursday next das Parlament geht kommenden Donnerstag in Ferien.
   (f) (originate: river) entspringen.
   (g) (also ~ up) (revolt: people) sich empören, sich erheben; (rebel: one's soul etc) sich empören. to ~ (up) in protest/anger (at sth) (people) sich protestierend (gegen etw) erheben/sich (gegen etw) empören; (one's soul, inner being etc) sich (gegen etw) auflehnen/zornig empören; to ~ (up) in revolt (against sb/sth) (gegen jdn/etw) rebellieren, sich gegen jdn erheben.
♦ **rise above** vi +prep obj insults etc erhaben sein über (+acc), stehen über (+dat).
♦ **rise up** vi (person) aufstehen, sich erheben (geh); (mountain etc) sich erheben; see also rise 2 (g).
risen [ˈrɪzn] 1 ptp of rise. 2 adj (Rel) the ~ Lord der Auferstandene; Jesus Christ is ~! Christ ist erstanden!
riser [ˈraɪzə⁾] n (a) (person) to be an early ~ Frühaufsteher(in f) m sein, früh aufstehen; to be a late ~ spät aufstehen, ein Langschläfer or eine Langschläferin sein (inf). (b) (of stair) Setzstufe f. (c) (for gas, water etc) Steigrohr nt, Steigleitung f.
risibility [ˌrɪzɪˈbɪlɪtɪ] n (liter: disposition) Lachlust f.
risible [ˈrɪzɪbl] adj (liter: laughable) lächerlich, lachhaft.
rising [ˈraɪzɪŋ] 1 n (a) (rebellion) Erhebung f, Aufstand m.
   (b) (of sun, star) Aufgehen nt, Aufgang m; (of barometer, prices, river) (An)steigen nt; (from dead) Auferstehung f; (of theatre curtain) Hochgehen nt; (of ground) Steigung f, Anstieg m. the ~ and falling of ... das Auf und Ab (+gen).
   (c) (adjournment: of Parliament etc) Auseinandergehen nt.
   2 adj (a) sun aufgehend; tide, barometer, prices, hopes steigend; wind aufkommend; anger, fury wachsend. ~ damp Bodenfeuchtigkeit f; the ~ sap der aufsteigende Saft.
   (b) (fig) a ~ young doctor ein aufstrebender junger Arzt; a ~ politician ein kommender Politiker; the ~ generation die kommende Generation.
   3 adv (inf) she's ~ sixteen sie ist fast sechzehn.
risk [rɪsk] 1 n (a) Risiko nt; (in cpds) -gefahr f. to take or run ~s/a ~ Risiken/ein Risiko eingehen; to take or run the ~ of doing sth das Risiko eingehen, etw zu tun; you'll run the ~ of losing a lot of money Sie laufen dabei Gefahr, eine Menge Geld zu verlieren; there is no ~ of his coming or that he will

come es besteht keine Gefahr, daß er kommt; at one's own ~ auf eigene Gefahr, auf eigenes Risiko; goods sent at sender's ~ Warenversand auf Risiko des Senders; at the ~ of seeming stupid auf die Gefahr hin, dumm zu erscheinen; at the ~ of his life unter Einsatz seines Lebens; children at ~ gefährdete Kinder; some jobs are at ~ einige Stellen sind gefährdet; to put sb/sth at ~ jdn gefährden/etw riskieren.
   (b) (Insur) Risiko nt. fire ~ Feuerrisiko; he's a bad accident ~ bei ihm besteht ein hohes Unfallrisiko; see security ~.
   2 vt (a) career, future, reputation, savings riskieren, aufs Spiel setzen; life also wagen; see neck.
   (b) defeat, quarrel, accident riskieren; (venture) criticism, remark also wagen. you'll ~ losing your job/falling Sie riskieren dabei, Ihre Stelle zu verlieren/hinzufallen; she won't ~ coming today sie wird es heute nicht riskieren, zu kommen; I'll ~ it das riskiere ich, ich lasse es darauf ankommen.
riskiness [ˈrɪskɪnɪs] n Riskantheit f.
risky [ˈrɪskɪ] adj (+er) (a) enterprise, deed riskant. it's ~, it's a ~ business das ist riskant. (b) joke, story pikant, gewagt.
risotto [rɪˈzɒtəu] n Risotto m.
risqué [ˈriːskeɪ] adj pikant, gewagt.
rissole [ˈrɪsəul] n = Frikadelle f.
rite [raɪt] n Ritus m. burial ~s Bestattungsriten pl.
ritual [ˈrɪtjuəl] 1 adj rituell; laws, objects Ritual-.
   2 n Ritual nt; (pej also) Zeremoniell nt no pl. he went through the same old ~ (fig) er durchlief dasselbe alte Ritual or Zeremoniell; he went through the ~ of checking all the locks er überprüfte nach dem üblichen Zeremoniell or Ritual, ob alles abgeschlossen war.
ritualism [ˈrɪtjuəlɪzəm] n Ritualismus m.
ritualist [ˈrɪtjuəlɪst] n Ritualist(in f) m; (expert) Ritualienforscher(in f) m.
ritualistic [ˌrɪtjuəˈlɪstɪk] adj rituell.
ritzy [ˈrɪtsɪ] adj (+er) (sl) nobel (inf), protzig (pej inf).
rival [ˈraɪvəl] 1 n Rivale m, Rivalin f (for um, to für); (in love also) Nebenbuhler(in f) m (old); (Comm) Konkurrent(in f) m.
   2 adj (to für) claims, attraction konkurrierend; firm, enterprise also Konkurrenz-.
   3 vt (in love, for affections) rivalisieren mit; (Comm) konkurrieren mit. he can't ~ her in intelligence er kann sich mit ihr in bezug auf Intelligenz nicht messen; his achievements ~ even yours seine Leistungen können sich sogar mit deinen messen; I can't ~ that da kann ich nicht mithalten.
rivalry [ˈraɪvəlrɪ] n Rivalität f; (Comm) Konkurrenzkampf m.
rive [raɪv] pret ~d, ptp riven [ˈrɪvn] vt (old, liter) spalten. riven by grief (fig) von Schmerz zerrissen.
river [ˈrɪvə⁾] n Fluß m; (major) Strom m. down ~ fluß-/stromabwärts; up ~ fluß-/stromaufwärts; the ~ Rhine (Brit), the Rhine ~ (US) der Rhein; ~s of blood/lava Blut-/Lavaströme pl; see sell.
river in cpds Fluß-; ~ basin n Flußbecken nt; ~bed n Flußbett nt; ~ fish n Flußfisch m; ~-head n Flußquelle f.
riverine [ˈrɪvəraɪn] adj (form) (of river) Fluß-; (like river) flußartig; people am.Fluß wohnend.
river: ~ mouth n Flußmündung f; ~ police n Wasserschutzpolizei f; ~side 1 n Flußufer nt; the ~side is cool and shady am Fluß ist es kühl und schattig; on/by the ~side am Fluß; 2 adj am Fluß(ufer); ~ traffic n Flußschiffahrt f.
rivet [ˈrɪvɪt] 1 n Niete f.
   2 vt (lit) nieten; two things vernieten; (fig) audience, attention fesseln. his eyes were ~ed to the screen sein Blick war auf die Leinwand geheftet; it ~ed our attention das fesselte uns or unsere Aufmerksamkeit; ~ed (to the spot) with fear vor Angst wie festgenagelt; ~ joint Nietnaht, Nietung f.
riveter [ˈrɪvɪtə⁾] n Nieter(in f) m; (tool) Nietmaschine f.
rivet(t)ing [ˈrɪvɪtɪŋ] 1 n Nieten nt. 2 adj (fig) fesselnd.
Riviera [ˌrɪvɪˈɛərə] n the (French)/Italian ~ die französische/italienische Riviera.
rivulet [ˈrɪvjulɪt] n Flüßchen nt, Bach m.
rm abbr of room Zim.
RM abbr of Royal Marines.
RN abbr of Royal Navy.
RNA abbr of ribonucleic acid.
RNR abbr of Royal Navy Reserve.
RNVR abbr of Royal Navy Volunteer Reserve.
roach [rəutʃ] n Plötze f; (inf: cock~) Schabe f.
road [rəud] n (a) Straße f."~ up" „Straßenbauarbeiten"; "~ narrows" „Straßenverengung"; by ~ (send sth) per Spedition; (travel) mit dem Bus/Auto etc; she lives across the ~ (from us) sie wohnt über der Straße, sie wohnt gegenüber (von uns); just across the ~ is a bakery gerade gegenüber ist eine Bäckerei; my car is off the ~ just now ich kann mein Auto momentan nicht benutzen; my car has never been/is never off the ~ mein Auto war noch nie/ist nie in der Werkstatt; I hope to put the car back on the ~ soon ich hoffe, das Auto bald wieder fahren zu können; this vehicle shouldn't be on the ~ das Fahrzeug ist nicht verkehrstüchtig; he is a danger on the ~ er ist eine Gefahr für den Straßenverkehr; to take to the ~ sich auf den Weg machen, losfahren; (as tramp) Vagabund werden; to be on the ~ (travelling) unterwegs sein; (theatre company) auf Tournee sein; (car) fahren; is this the ~ to London? geht es hier nach London?; the London ~ die Straße nach London; "Westlands/London ~" „Westlandsstraße/Londoner Straße"; to have one for the ~ (inf) zum Abschluß noch einen trinken; gentleman of the ~ Vagabund m.
   (b) (fig) Weg m. you're on the right ~ (lit, fig) Sie sind auf dem richtigen Weg; on the ~ to ruin/success auf dem Weg ins Verderben/zum Erfolg; somewhere along the ~ he changed his mind irgendwann hat er seine Meinung geändert; you're in my ~ (dial inf) du bist mir im Weg; (get) out of the ~! (dial inf) geh weg!; any ~ (dial inf) see anyhow.

(c) ~s pl (Naut) Reede f.
(d) (US) abbr of railroad.
road in cpds Straßen-; ~ **accident** n Verkehrsunfall m; ~**block** n Straßensperre f; ~-**book** n Straßenatlas m; ~ **construction** n Straßenbau m; ~ **fund licence** n (Brit) = Verkehrssteuer f; ~ **haulage** n Spedition f; ~ **haulier** n Spediteur m; ~**hog** n (inf) Verkehrsrowdy m (inf); ~**holding** (ability) n Straßenlage f; (of tyres) Griffigkeit f; ~**house** n Rasthaus nt; ~**making** n Straßenbau m; ~**man** n (inf) Straßenbauarbeiter m; ~**mender** n Straßenbauarbeiter m; ~ **metal** n Straßenschotter m; ~**roller** n Straßenwalze f; ~ **safety** n Verkehrssicherheit f, Sicherheit f im Straßenverkehr; ~ **sense** n Verkehrssinn m; ~ **show** n (Theat) Tournee f; ~**side** 1 n Straßenrand m; **along** or **by the** ~**side** am Straßenrand; 2 adj **stall, toilet** an der Straße; **inn, pub** also Straßen-; ~**side repairs** (professional) Sofortdienst m; (done alone) Reparatur f am Straßenrand; ~**sign** n (Straßen)verkehrszeichen nt; ~**stead** n (Naut) Reede f.
roadster ['rəʊdstə'] n (old) (car) Vehikel nt (inf); (bicycle) Drahtesel m (inf).
road: ~**sweeper** n (person) Straßenkehrer(in f) m; (vehicle) Straßenkehrmaschine f; ~-**test** 1 n Straßentest m; 2 vt probefahren; ~ **transport** n Straßengüterverkehr m; ~-**trials** npl (~-**test**) Straßentest m; (rally) Straßenwettbewerb m; ~-**user** n Verkehrsteilnehmer m; ~**way** n Fahrbahn f; ~**work** n (Sport) Straßentraining nt; ~**works** npl Straßenbauarbeiten pl; ~**worthy** adj verkehrstüchtig.
roam [rəʊm] 1 vt streets, countryside wandern or ziehen durch. to ~ **the** (seven) **seas** die sieben Meere durchkreuzen; to ~ **the streets** (child, dog) (in den Straßen) herumstreunen.
2 vi (herum)wandern; (hum: hands) wandern, sich verirren. to ~ **about the house/streets** durch das Haus/die Straßen wandern; to ~ **about the world** in der Welt herumziehen.
♦**roam about** or **around** vi herumwandern; (dogs, looters) herumstreunen.
roamer ['rəʊmə'] n Vagabund m; (dog) Herumstreuner m; (child) Stromer m (inf).
roaming ['rəʊmɪŋ] 1 adj (fig) thoughts wandernd. 2 n Herumwandern nt. **this life of** ~ dieses Vagabundenleben.
roan [rəʊn] 1 adj horse rötlich-grau. 2 n Rotschimmel m.
roar [rɔː'] 1 vi (person, crowd, lion, bull) brüllen (with vor +dat); (fire in hearth) prasseln; (wind, engine, plane) heulen; (sea, waterfall) tosen; (thunder, forest fire) toben; (gun) donnern. to ~ **at sb** jdn anbrüllen; **the trucks** ~**ed past** die Lastwagen donnerten vorbei; **the car** ~**ed up the street** der Wagen donnerte die Straße hinauf; **to make the engine** ~ den Motor aufheulen lassen; **he had them** ~**ing** (with laughter) sie brüllten vor Lachen.
2 vt (also ~ **out**) order, song etc brüllen. **to** ~ **oneself hoarse** sich heiser brüllen.
(b) engine aufheulen lassen.
3 n (a) no pl see vi Gebrüll nt; Prasseln nt; Heulen nt; Tosen nt; Toben nt; Donnern nt.
(b) ~**s of laughter** brüllendes Gelächter; **the** ~**s of the crowd/lion** das Brüllen der Menge/des Löwen.
roaring ['rɔːrɪŋ] 1 adj see vi brüllend; prasselnd; heulend; tosend; tobend; donnernd. **the R~ Forties, the** ~ **forties** (Geog) stürmischer Teil des Ozeans (zwischen dem 39. und 50. Breitengrad); ~ **drunk** (inf) sternhagelvoll (inf); **the** ~ **Twenties** die wilden zwanziger Jahre; **a** ~ **success** ein voller Erfolg, ein Bombenerfolg m (inf); **to do a** ~ **trade** (in sth) ein Riesengeschäft nt (mit etw) machen.
2 n see roar 3.
roast [rəʊst] 1 n Braten m. **pork** ~ Schweinebraten m.
2 adj pork, veal gebraten; chicken Brat-, gebraten; potatoes in Fett im Backofen gebraten. ~ **beef** Roastbeef nt; **we had** ~ **pork** es gab Schweinebraten.
3 vt (a) meat braten; chestnuts, coffee beans, ore rösten. **the sun was** ~**ing the city** die Sonne brannte auf der Stadt herab; **to** ~ **oneself by the fire/in the sun** sich am Feuer/in der Sonne braten lassen; **to be** ~**ed alive** (fig) sich totschwitzen (inf); (by sun) gebraten werden (inf); see also roasting.
(b) (inf: criticize) ins Gericht gehen mit (inf).
4 vi (meat) braten; (inf: person) irrsinnig schwitzen (inf); (in sun) in der Sonne braten; see also roasting.
roaster ['rəʊstə'] n (oven) Bratofen m, Bratröhre f; (dish) Bräter m; (coffee ~) Röstapparat m; (for ore) Röstofen m; (chicken) Brathähnchen nt; (pig) Spanferkel nt. **it's a real** ~ **today!** (inf) das ist heute eine richtige Affenhitze (inf).
roasting ['rəʊstɪŋ] 1 n (a) (lit) Braten nt. ~ **spit** Bratspieß m.
(b) (inf) (criticism) Verriß m; (telling-off) Standpauke f. **to give sb/sth a** ~ jdn/etw verreißen; jdm eine Standpauke halten.
2 adj (a) (inf: hot) days, weather knallheiß (inf).
(b) (Cook) zum Braten; chicken Brat-; meat Braten-.
rob [rɒb] vt person bestehlen; (more seriously) berauben; shop bank ausrauben; orchard plündern. **to** ~ **sb of sth** (lit, fig) jdn einer Sache (gen) berauben (geh), jdm etw rauben; (lit also) jdm etw stehlen; **I've been** ~**bed!** ich bin bestohlen worden!; (had to pay too much) ich bin genepppt worden (inf); **to** ~ **the till** die Ladenkasse ausräumen or plündern; **he was** ~**bed of the pleasure of seeing her** es war ihm nicht vergönnt, sie zu sehen; **the shock** ~**bed him of speech** er hat vor Schreck die Stimme verloren; (briefly also) der Schreck hat ihm die Sprache verschlagen; **our team was** ~**bed** (sl) das ist nicht fair(, wir hätten gewinnen müssen).
robber ['rɒbə'] n Räuber m.
robbery ['rɒbərɪ] n Raub m no pl; (burglary) Einbruch m (of in +acc). ~ **with violence** (Jur) Raubüberfall m; **at that price it's sheer** ~! (inf) das ist der reinste Nepp (inf), das ist reiner Wucher (inf); **the bank** ~ der Überfall auf die Bank.
robe [rəʊb] 1 n (a) (garment) (of office) Robe f, Talar m; (for priest also) Rock m; (for baby) langes Kleidchen nt; (esp US: for house wear) Morgenrock, Haus- or Bademantel m; (obs: gown) Kleid nt. **he was wearing his** ~ **of office** er war im Ornat; **ceremonial** ~**s** Festgewänder pl; **christening** ~ Taufkleid nt.
(b) (US: wrap) Decke f.
2 vt (lit) ankleiden, die Amtsrobe or den Ornat anlegen (+dat). **to** ~ **sb/sth in sth** (lit, fig) jdn/etw kleiden in (+acc).
3 vi (judge etc) die Amtsrobe or den Ornat anlegen.
robin ['rɒbɪn] n Rotkehlchen nt; see round ~.
robot ['rəʊbɒt] n Roboter m; (fig also) Automat m. ~ **guidance,** ~ **pilot** Selbststeuerung f.
robust [rəʊ'bʌst] adj person, material, toy, machine robust, widerstandsfähig; build kräftig, robust; exercise hart; defence stark; appetite, humour gesund, unverwüstlich; structure massiv, stabil; style markig; wine kernig.
robustness [rəʊ'bʌstnɪs] n see adj Robustheit f, Widerstandsfähigkeit f; Kräftigkeit f, Robustheit f; Härte f; Stärke f; Gesundheit, Unverwüstlichkeit f; Massivität, Stabilität f; Markigkeit f; Kernigkeit f.
rock¹ [rɒk] 1 vt (a) (swing) schaukeln; (gently: lull) wiegen. **to** ~ **a child to sleep** ein Kind in den Schlaf wiegen; ~**ed by the waves** von den Wellen hin und her geschaukelt.
(b) (shake) town erschüttern, zum Beben bringen; building also ins Wanken bringen; ship hin und her werfen; (fig inf) person erschüttern. **to** ~ **the boat** (fig) für Unruhe sorgen.
2 vi (a) (gently) schaukeln. **he was** ~**ing back and forth (in his chair)** er schaukelte (auf seinem Stuhl) vor und zurück.
(b) (violently) (building, tree, post) schwanken; (ship) hin und her geworfen werden; (ground) beben. **they** ~**ed with laughter** sie schüttelten sich or bebten vor Lachen.
(c) (~ and roll) rocken.
3 n (pop music) Rock m; (dance) Rock 'n' Roll m. ~-**and-roll** Rock and Roll, Rock 'n' Roll m; **to do the** ~-**and-roll** Rock 'n' Roll tanzen, rocken.
rock² n (a) (substance) Stein m; (~ face) Fels(en) m; (Geol) Gestein nt. **caves hewn out of the** ~ aus dem Fels(en) gehauene Höhlen; **hewn out of solid** ~ aus massivem Stein/Fels gehauen; **built on** ~ (lit, fig) auf Fels gebaut; porous/volcanic ~ poröses/vulkanisches Gestein; **the study of** ~**s** Gesteinskunde f.
(b) (large mass) Fels(en) m; (boulder also) Felsbrocken m; (smaller) (großer) Stein. **the R~** (of Gibraltar) der Felsen von Gibraltar; **on the R~** (inf) in Gibraltar; **as solid as a** ~ structure massiv wie ein Fels; firm, marriage unerschütterlich wie ein Fels; **the ship went on the** ~**s** das Schiff lief (auf der Felsen) auf; **on the** ~**s** (inf) (with ice) mit Eis; (ruined: marriage etc) kaputt (inf); (broke) bankrott; **danger, falling** ~**s** Vorsicht Steinschlag.
(c) (sl: diamond) Diamant m. ~**s** (jewels) Klunker pl (inf).
(d) no pl (Brit: sweet) Zuckerstange f.
rock: ~-**bottom** 1 n der Tiefpunkt; **to touch/reach** ~-**bottom** auf dem Nullpunkt or Tiefpunkt sein/den Nullpunkt or Tiefpunkt erreichen; **his spirits reached** ~-**bottom** ihre Stimmung sank auf den Nullpunkt or Tiefpunkt; **this is** ~-**bottom** (inf) schlimmer kann es nicht werden; 2 adj ~-**bottom prices** niedrigste(r, s), Niedrigst-; ~ **bun,** ~ **cake** n = Rosinenhäufchen m; ~ **carving** n Felszeichnung f; (writing) Felsschrift f; (action) Ritzen nt in Fels; ~-**climber** n (Felsen)kletterer(in f) m; ~ **climbing** n Klettern nt (im Fels); ~ **crystal** n Bergkristall m.
rocker ['rɒkə'] n (a) (of cradle etc) Kufe f. **to be/go off one's** ~ (sl) übergeschnappt sein (inf)/überschnappen (inf). (b) (sl: person) Rocker m. (c) (Aut: also ~ **arm**) Kipphebel, Unterbrecherhebel m.
rockery ['rɒkərɪ] n Steingarten m.
rocket ['rɒkɪt] 1 n (a) Rakete f.
(b) (Brit inf: reprimand) (from boss) Zigarre f (inf); (from parent) Anschiß m (sl). **to get a** ~ eine Zigarre (inf)/einen Anschiß (sl) bekommen; **to give sb a** ~ jdm eine Zigarre verpassen (inf)/jdm einen Anschiß geben (sl).
2 vi (prices) hochschießen, hochschnellen. **to** ~ **to fame** über Nacht berühmt werden; (person also) kometenhaft aufsteigen; **he went** ~**ing past my door** (inf) er zischte or schoß (wie ein geölter Blitz) an meiner Tür vorbei (inf).
rocket in cpds Raketen-; ~ **launcher** n Raketenabschußgerät nt; (on plane) Raketenwerfer m; (multiple) Stalinorgel f; ~ **plane** n Raketenflugzeug nt; ~-**propelled** adj mit Raketenantrieb; ~ **propulsion** n Raketenantrieb m; ~ **range** n Raketenversuchsgelände nt; **within** ~-**range** mit Raketen zu erreichen; ~ **research** n Raketenforschung f.
rocketry ['rɒkɪtrɪ] n Raketentechnik f; (rockets) Raketen pl.
rocket ship n Raketenträger m; (rocket propelled) Raketenschiff nt.
rock: ~ **face** n Felswand f; ~ **fall** n Steinschlag m; ~ **garden** n Steingarten m.
rocking ['rɒkɪŋ]: ~ **chair** n Schaukelstuhl m; ~ **horse** n Schaukelpferd nt.
rock: ~ **plant** n Steinpflanze f; ~ **rose** n Sonnenröschen nt; ~ **salmon** n (Brit) Dorsch m; ~ **salt** n Steinsalz nt.
rocky¹ ['rɒkɪ] adj (unsteady) wackelig (also fig inf).
rocky² adj (+er) mountain, hill felsig; road, path steinig. **the R~ Mountains, the Rockies** die Rocky Mountains pl.
rococo [rəʊ'kəʊkəʊ] 1 n Rokoko nt. 2 adj Rokoko-, Rokoko pred. ~ **period** Rokoko nt, Rokokozeit f.
rod [rɒd] n (a) Stab m, Stange f; (switch) Rute, Gerte f; (in machinery) Stange f; (for punishment, fishing) Rute f; (symbol of authority) Stab m. ~ **bacterium** Stäbchenbakterie f.
(b) (measure) = Rute f (5, 5 yards).
(c) (US sl: gun) Schießeisen nt (sl).
rode [rəʊd] pret of ride.
rodent ['rəʊdənt] n Nagetier nt.
rodeo ['rəʊdɪəʊ] n Rodeo nt.
rodomontade [ˌrɒdəmɒn'teɪd] n (liter) Prahlerei f, Bramarbasieren nt (geh).

roe[1] [rəʊ] *n, pl* **-(s)** (*species: also* ~ **deer**) Reh *nt.* ~ **buck** Rehbock *m;* ~ **deer** (*female*) Reh *nt,* Ricke *f* (*spec*).

roe[2] *n, pl* - (*of fish*) Rogen *m.* **hard** ~ Rogen *m;* **soft** ~ Milch *f;* **herring** ~ Heringsrogen *m.*

roentgen ['rɒntjən] 1 *n* Röntgen *nt.* 2 *adj* Röntgen-.

rogation [rəʊˈɡeɪʃən] *n* (*Eccl*) (*litany*) Litanei *f;* (*period: also* R~ *or* R~-**tide**) Bittwoche *f.* **R~ Days** Bittage, Rogationstage *pl;* **R~ Sunday** (*Sonntag m*) Rogate *no art.*

Roger ['rɒdʒə[r]] *n* Rüdiger *m.* "**r~**" „verstanden"; *see* **Jolly ~.**

rogue [rəʊɡ] *n* (**a**) (*scoundrel*) Gauner, Schurke *m;* (*scamp*) Schlingel, Spitzbube *m.* ~**s' gallery** (*Police inf*) Verbrecheralbum *nt;* **they look like a real ~s' gallery** sie sehen wie Gauner aus. (**b**) (*Zool*) Einzelgänger(in *f*) *m.* ~ **elephant** Einzelgänger(-Elefant) *m.*

roguery ['rəʊɡərɪ] *n no pl* (*wickedness*) Gaunerei, Schurkerei *f;* (*mischief*) Spitzbüberei *f.*

roguish ['rəʊɡɪʃ] *adj* spitzbübisch; (*old: wicked*) schurkisch.

roguishly ['rəʊɡɪʃlɪ] *adv see adj.*

roister ['rɔɪstə[r]] *vi* (*revel*) herumtollen; (*brag*) prahlen, aufschneiden.

roisterer ['rɔɪstərə[r]] *n* Krawallmacher *m;* (*braggart*) Prahlhans (*dated*), Aufschneider *m,* Großmaul *nt* (*inf*).

role [rəʊl] *n* (*Theat, fig*) Rolle *f.* ~-**playing** Rollenspiel *nt;* ~ **reversal** (*Psych*) Rollentausch *m;* **in the ~ of Ophelia** in der Rolle der Ophelia.

roll [rəʊl] 1 *n* (**a**) (*of paper, netting, tobacco, wire, hair etc*) Rolle *f;* (*of fabric*) Ballen *m;* (*of banknotes*) Bündel *nt;* (*of butter*) Röllchen *nt;* (*of flesh, fat*) Wulst *m,* Röllchen *nt.* **a ~ of paper/banknotes** eine Rolle Papier/ein Bündel *nt* Banknoten; **a ~ of film** (*Phot*) eine Rolle Film.
(**b**) (*Cook: also* **bread ~**) Brötchen *nt.* **ham/cheese ~** Schinken-/Käsebrötchen *nt;* **see sausage ~** etc.
(**c**) (*movement, of sea, waves*) Rollen *nt;* (*of ship also*) Schlingern *nt;* (*somersault, Aviat*) Rolle *f;* (*of person's gait*) Schaukeln, Wiegen *nt.* **to walk with a ~** einen schaukelnden Gang haben; **to do a ~** eine Rolle machen; **the ship gave a sudden ~** das Schiff schlingerte plötzlich; **the dog was having a ~ on the grass** der Hund wälzte sich im Gras; **to have a ~ in the hay with sb** (*inf*) mit jdm ins Heu gehen (*inf*); **the farmer caught them having a ~ in the hay** (*inf*) der Bauer hat sie miteinander im Heu erwischt (*inf*).
(**d**) (*sound*) (*of thunder*) Rollen *nt;* (*of drums*) Wirbel *m;* (*of organ*) Brausen *nt.*
(**e**) (*list, register*) Liste *f,* Register *nt;* (*of solicitors*) Anwaltsliste *f.* **we have 60 pupils on our ~(s)** bei uns sind 60 Schüler angemeldet; **to call the ~** die Namensliste verlesen, die Namen aufrufen; ~ **of honour** Ehrenliste *f;* (*plaque*) Ehrentafel *f;* **to strike sb** *or* **sb's name off the ~s** jdn *or* jds Name von der Liste streichen; *see* **electoral ~.**
2 *vi* (**a**) rollen; (*from side to side: ship*) schlingern; (*presses*) laufen; (*Aviat*) eine Rolle machen. **to ~ over and over** rollen und rollen, kullern und kullern (*inf*); **the children/stones ~ed down the hill** die Kinder/Steine rollten *or* kugelten (*inf*) den Berg hinunter; **tears were ~ing down her cheeks** Tränen rollten *or* kullerten (*inf*) ihr über die Wangen; **the waves were ~ing onto the beach** die Wellen rollten über den Strand; **the newspapers were ~ing off the presses** die Zeitungen rollten von den Druckerpressen; **heads will ~!** (*fig*) da werden die Köpfe rollen!; **to keep the show ~ing** (*Theat inf*) die Show in Gang halten; **can you keep the ball** *or* **things ~ing while I'm away?** (*inf*) können Sie den Laden in Schwung halten, solange ich weg bin? (*inf*); **the dog ~ed in the mud** der Hund wälzte sich im Schlamm; **he's ~ing in money** *or* **in it** (*inf*) er schwimmt im Geld (*inf*); **the words just ~ed off his tongue** die Worte flossen ihm nur so von der Zunge; **he ~s from side to side as he walks** er hat einen schaukelnden Gang.
(**b**) (*sound*) (*thunder*) rollen, grollen; (*drum*) wirbeln; (*organ*) brausen; (*echo*) rollen.
3 *vt* barrel, hoop, ball, car rollen; umbrella aufrollen; cigarette drehen; pastry, dough ausrollen; metal, lawn, road walzen. **to ~ one's eyes** die Augen rollen *or* verdrehen; **to ~ one's r's** das R rollen; **to ~ sth between one's fingers** etw zwischen den Fingern drehen; **to ~ one's own** (*cigarettes*) sich (*dat*) seine eigenen drehen; **to ~ wool into a ball** Wolle zu einem Knäuel aufwickeln; **the hedgehog ~ed itself into a ball** der Igel rollte sich zu einer Kugel zusammen; **he ~ed himself in a blanket** er wickelte sich in eine Decke; *see also* **rolled.**

♦**roll about** *vi* (*balls*) herumrollen *or* -kugeln (*inf*); (*ship*) schlingern; (*person, dog*) sich herumwälzen, sich wälzen; (*inf: with laughter*) sich kugeln (vor Lachen) (*inf*).

♦**roll along 1** *vi* (*ball*) entlang- *or* dahinrollen. **we were ~ing ~ at 100 mph/enjoying the countryside** wir fuhren mit 160 Stundenkilometern/wir rollten dahin und genossen die Landschaft. (**b**) (*inf: arrive*) aufkreuzen (*inf*), eintrudeln (*inf*). 2 *vt sep* rollen.

♦**roll away 1** *vi* (*ball, vehicle*) wegrollen; (*clouds, mist*) abziehen. 2 *vt sep* trolley, table wegrollen.

♦**roll back 1** *vi* zurückrollen; (*eyes*) nach innen rollen. 2 *vt sep* object, carpet zurückrollen; sheet zurückschlagen. **if only we could ~ ~ the years** wenn wir nur die Uhr zurückdrehen könnten.

♦**roll by** *vi* (*vehicle, procession*) vorbeirollen; (*clouds*) vorbeiziehen; (*time, years*) dahinziehen.

♦**roll down 1** *vi* (*ball, person, tears*) hinunter-/herunterrollen *or* -kugeln (*inf*). 2 *vt sep* cart hinunter-/herunterrollen.

♦**roll in 1** *vi* herein-/hineinrollen; (*letters, money, contributions, suggestions*) hereinströmen; (*inf: person*) eintrudeln (*inf*). 2 *vt sep* barrel, trolley hinein-/hereinrollen.

♦**roll off** *vi* (**a**) (*vehicle, procession*) weg- *or* davonrollen. (**b**) (*fall off*) (*object, person*) herunter-/hinunterrollen.

♦**roll on** *vi* weiterrollen; (*time*) verfliegen; ~ **~ the holidays!**

wenn doch nur schon Ferien wären! **2** *vt sep* stockings (die Beine) hochrollen.

♦**roll out 1** *vt sep* (**a**) barrel hinaus-/herausrollen. (**b**) pastry, dough ausrollen; metal auswalzen. (**c**) (*inf*) sentence, verse produzieren (*inf*). 2 *vi* hinaus-/herausrollen.

♦**roll over 1** *vi* herumrollen; (*vehicle*) umkippen; (*person*) sich umdrehen. **the dog ~ed ~ onto his back** der Hund rollte auf den Rücken. 2 *vt sep person, animal, object* umdrehen; patient auf die andere Seite legen.

♦**roll past** *vi see* **roll by.**

♦**roll up 1** *vi* (*animal*) sich zusammenrollen (*into* zu).
(**b**) (*inf: arrive*) antanzen (*inf*).
(**c**) (*at fairground etc*) ~ ~! treten Sie näher!
2 *vt sep* cloth, paper, map, umbrella auf- *or* zusammenrollen; sleeves, trouser legs hochkrempeln.

roll: ~-**bar** *n* Überrollbügel *m;* ~**call** *n* (*Sch*) Namensaufruf *m;* (*Mil*) (Anwesenheits)appell *m;* ~ **collar** *n* Rollkragen *m.*

rolled [rəʊld] *adj* blanket, paper etc zusammengerollt; tobacco gerollt, gedreht. ~ **gold** Dubleegold *nt;* ~ **oats** Haferflocken *pl.*

roller ['rəʊlə[r]] *n* (**a**) (*for pressing, smoothing*) Rolle *f;* (*pastry* ~) Nudelholz *nt;* (*for lawn, road, Ind*) Walze *f;* (*paint* ~) Rolle *f.*
(**b**) (*for winding sth round*) Rolle *f;* (*hair* ~) (Locken)wickler *m.* **to put one's hair in ~s** sich (*dat*) die Haare aufdrehen *or* eindrehen; **with her ~s in** mit Lockenwicklern (im Haar).
(**c**) (*for moving things*) Rolle *f;* (*log-shaped*) Rollklotz *m.*
(**d**) (*wave*) Brecher *m.*

roller: ~ **bandage** *n* Rollbinde *f;* ~ **bearing** *n* Rollenlager *nt;* ~ **blind** *n* Rollo, Rouleau *nt;* ~ **coaster** *n* Achterbahn, Berg-und-Talbahn *f;* ~ **skate** *n* Rollschuh *m;* ~-**skate** *vi* Rollschuh laufen; **he ~-skated down the street** er lief *or* fuhr mit seinen Rollschuhen die Straße entlang; ~-**skating** *n* Rollschuhlaufen *nt;* ~ **towel** *n* Rollhandtuch *nt.*

rollick ['rɒlɪk] *vi* (*also* ~ **about**) herumtollen.

rollicking ['rɒlɪkɪŋ] *adj* person ausgelassen; play, farce Klamauk-; occasion, life wild. ~ (**good**) **fun** Mordsspaß *m* (*inf*); **to have a ~ time** richtig auf die Pauke hauen (*inf*).

rolling ['rəʊlɪŋ] *adj* ship schlingernd; sea rollend, wogend; waves rollend; countryside wellig. **to have a ~ gait** einen schaukelnden Gang haben; **a ~ stone gathers no moss** (*Prov*) wer rastet, der rostet (*Prov*); **he's a ~ stone** er ist ein unsteter Bursche.

rolling: ~ **mill** *n* (*factory*) Walzwerk *nt;* (*machine*) Walze *f;* ~ **pin** *n* Nudelholz *nt,* Teigrolle *f;* ~ **stock** *n* (*Rail*) rollendes Material, Fahrzeuge *pl;* ~ **train** *n* Walzstraße *f.*

roll: ~**mop** (**herring**) *n* Rollmops *m;* ~-**neck** *n* Rollkragen *m;* ~-**neck(ed)** *adj* Rollkragen-; ~-**on** *n* (**a**) Elastikschlüpfer *m;* (**b**) (*deodorant*) Roller *m;* ~-**on**--**off,** ~-**on**/~-**off** *adj* Roll-on-roll-off-; ~-**top** *n* Rolladen *m;* ~-**top desk** *n* Rollschreibtisch *m;* ~-**up** *n* Selbstgedrehte *f;* **to have a ~-up** sich (*dat*) eine drehen.

roly-poly ['rəʊlɪ'pəʊlɪ] 1 *adj* (*inf*) kugelrund, mopsig (*inf*). 2 *n* (**a**) (*Brit: also* ~ **pudding**) mit Nierentalg hergestellter Strudel, der gebacken oder im Wasserbad gekocht wird. (**b**) (*inf: plump child*) Rollmops (*inf*), Pummel (*inf*) *m.* (**c**) (*inf: somersault*) Purzelbaum *m* (*inf*).

Roman ['rəʊmən] 1 *n* (**a**) (*Hist*) Römer(in *f*) *m.* (**b**) (*Typ: also* ~ type) Magerdruck *m.* 2 *adj* römisch; (~ *Catholic*) römisch-katholisch. **r~** (*Typ*) mager; **r~ letters** (*Typ*) Magerdruck *m.*

roman à clef ['rəʊmɑ̃ːˈkleɪ] *n* Schlüsselroman *m.*

Roman: ~ **candle** *n* Goldrausch *m;* ~ **Catholic 1** *adj* (römisch-)katholisch; **the ~ Catholic Church** die (römisch-)katholische Kirche; **2** *n* Katholik(in *f*) *m,* (Römisch-)Katholische(r) *mf.*

romance [rəʊˈmæns] 1 *n* (**a**) (*book*) Phantasieerzählung *f,* Roman *m;* (*love-story*) Liebesgeschichte *f or* -roman *m;* (*adventure story*) Abenteuerroman *m;* (*tale of chivalry*) Ritterroman(ze *f*) *m;* (*no pl: romantic fiction*) Liebesromane *pl;* (*fig: lies*) Märchen *nt.* **it's pure ~** es ist das reinste Märchen.
(**b**) (*love affair*) Romanze *f.* **it's quite a ~** das ist eine richtige Liebesgeschichte.
(**c**) *no pl* (*romanticism*) Romantik *f.* **an air of ~ pervaded the village** ein romantischer Zauber umgab das Dorf; **the ~ of foreign lands** der Zauber ferner Länder.
(**d**) (*Mus*) Romanze *f.*
(**e**) **R~** (**R~ languages**) die romanischen Sprachen *pl.*
2 *adj* **R~ language** etc romanisch.
3 *vi* phantasieren, fabulieren.

romancer [rəʊˈmænsə[r]] *n* (*fig*) Phantast *m.*

Romanesque [ˌrəʊməˈnesk] *adj* romanisch.

Roman holiday *n* Spaß *m* auf Kosten anderer.

Romania [rəʊˈmeɪnɪə] *n* Rumänien *nt.*

Romanian [rəʊˈmeɪnɪən] 1 *adj* rumänisch. 2 *n* (**a**) Rumäne *m,* Rumänin *f.* (**b**) (*language*) Rumänisch *nt.*

Romanic [rəʊˈmænɪk] *adj* language romanisch.

romanize ['rəʊmənaɪz] *vt* (*Hist*) romanisieren; (*Rel*) nach dem Katholizismus ausrichten; (*Typ*) in Magerdruck umsetzen.

Roman: ~ **law** *n* Römisches Recht; ~ **nose** *n* Römernase *f;* ~ **numeral** *n* römische Ziffer.

Romansh [rəʊˈmænʃ] 1 *adj* romantsch. 2 *n* Romantsch *nt.*

romantic [rəʊˈmæntɪk] 1 *adj* (*Art, Liter, Mus: also* R~) romantisch; person also romantisch veranlagt. ~ **novel** Liebes-/Abenteuerroman *m;* **he played the ~ lead in several plays** er spielte in mehreren Stücken den romantischen Liebhaber.
2 *n* (*Art, Liter, Mus: also* R~) Romantiker(in *f*) *m.*

romantically [rəʊˈmæntɪkəlɪ] *adv* romantisch.

romanticism [rəʊˈmæntɪsɪzəm] *n* (*Art, Liter, Mus: also* R~) Romantik *f.* **his ~** sein romantisches Wesen.

Romanticist [rəʊˈmæntɪsɪst] *n* (*Art, Liter, Mus: also* R~) Romantiker(in *f*) *m.*

romanticize [rəʊˈmæntɪsaɪz] 1 *vt* romantisieren, zu romantisch sehen. 2 *vi* phantasieren.

Romany ['rɒmənɪ] 1 *n* (**a**) Zigeuner(in *f*) *m.* (**b**) (*language*) die Zigeunersprache, Romani *nt.* 2 *adj* Zigeuner-.

Rome [rəʊm] n Rom nt. **when in ~ (do as the Romans do)** (prov) = andere Länder, andere Sitten (Prov); **~ wasn't built in a day** (Prov) Rom ist auch nicht an einem Tag erbaut worden (Prov); **all roads lead to ~** (Prov) viele Wege führen nach Rom (prov); **the Church of ~** die römische Kirche.

Romeo ['rəʊmɪəʊ] n Romeo m; (fig) Herzensbrecher m. **a Latin ~** ein Pappagallo m (inf).

Romish ['rəʊmɪʃ] adj (pej) Katholen- (pej), papistisch (pej).

romp [rɒmp] **1** n Tollerei f. **the play was just a ~** das Stück war reiner Klamauk; **to have a ~** herumtollen or -toben.

2 vi **(a)** (children, puppies) herumtollen or -toben. **to ~ away** weghopsen; **he came ~ing up to me** er kam auf mich zugetollt.
(b) (to ~ **home** (win) spielend gewinnen.
(c) **to ~ through sth** mit etw spielend fertig werden, etw mit der linken Hand erledigen.

rompers ['rɒmpəz] npl (also **pair of ~**) einteiliger Spielanzug.

rondeau ['rɒndəʊ], **rondel** ['rɒndəl] n (Mus) Rondeau nt; (Liter also) Rondel nt.

rondo ['rɒndəʊ] n (Mus) Rondo nt.

Roneo ® ['rəʊnɪəʊ] **1** vt (mit Matrize) kopieren. **2** n Kopie f.

rood [ruːd] n **(a)** (Archit) Kruzifix nt. **~ screen** Lettner m (spec).
(b) (Brit: measure) Rute f, = Viertelmorgen m.

roof [ruːf] **1** n **(a)** Dach nt; (of car also) Verdeck nt; (of cave, tunnel) Gewölbe nt. **the vast ~ of the sky** (liter) das gewaltige Himmelsgewölbe (geh); **the ~ of the mouth** der Gaumen; **the ~ of the world** das Dach der Welt; **a ~ of branches** ein Blätterdach nt; **without a ~ over one's head** ohne Dach über dem Kopf; **a room in the ~** ein Zimmer unter dem Dach; **to live under the same ~ as sb** mit jdm unter demselben Dach wohnen; **as long as you live under my ~** solange du deine Beine unter meinen Tisch streckst; **to go through the ~** (inf) (person) an die Decke gehen (inf); (prices etc) untragbar werden; see **hit, raise**.

2 vt house mit einem Dach decken. **red-~ed** mit rotem Dach.

♦**roof in** or **over** vt sep überdachen.

roof in cpds Dach-; **~-garden** n Dachgarten m.

roofing ['ruːfɪŋ] n Material nt zum Dachdecken; (action) Dachdecken nt. **~ felt** Dachpappe f.

roof: **~-rack** n Dachträger m; **~-top** n Dach nt; **to shout** or **scream sth from the ~-tops** (fig) etw überall herumposaunen (inf), etw an die große Glocke hängen (inf).

rook [rʊk] **1** n **(a)** (bird) Saatkrähe f. **(b)** (swindler) Betrüger, Gauner m. **(c)** (Chess) Turm m. **2** vt (swindle) übers Ohr hauen (inf), betrügen. **to ~ sb of £5** jdm £5 abgaunern. **3** vi (Chess) mit dem Turm ziehen.

rookery ['rʊkərɪ] n Kolonie f.

rookie ['rʊkɪ] n (esp Mil sl) Grünschnabel m (inf).

room [ruːm] **1** n **(a)** (in house, building) Zimmer nt, Raum m (geh); (public hall, ball~ etc) Saal m; (hotel bed~) Zimmer nt; (office) Büro nt. **the whole ~ laughed** alle im Zimmer lachten; **der ganze Saal lachte; "~s to let"** „Zimmer zu vermieten"; **~ and board** Unterkunft mit Verpflegung; (in lodgings also) Zimmer mit Pension; **they used to live in ~s** sie haben früher in möbliierten Zimmern gewohnt; **I'll come to your ~s** ich komme in deine Wohnung or auf deine Bude (esp Univ inf).

(b) no pl (space) Platz m; (fig) Spielraum m. **is there (enough) ~?** ist da genügend Platz?; **there is ~ for two (people)** es ist genügend Platz für zwei (Leute); **there is no ~ (for you/that box)** es ist nicht genug Platz (für dich/die Kiste); **to make ~ for sb/sth** für jdn/etw Platz machen or schaffen; **there is still ~ for hope** es besteht immer noch Hoffnung; **there is little ~ for hope** es besteht wenig Hoffnung; **there is no ~ for doubt** es kann keinen Zweifel geben; **there is ~ for improvement in your work** Ihre Arbeit könnte um einiges besser sein.

2 vi zur Untermiete wohnen. **~ing house** (esp US) Mietshaus nt (mit möblierten Wohnungen).

room: **~ clerk** n (US) Empfangschef m, Empfangsdame f; **~ divider** n Raumteiler m.

-roomed [-ruːmd] adj suf **a 6-~ house** ein Haus mit 6 Zimmern; **a two-~ flat** eine Zweizimmerwohnung.

roomer ['ruːmə'] n (US) Untermieter(in f) m.

roomful ['ruːmfʊl] n **there was quite a ~** das Zimmer war ganz schön voll; **a ~ of people** ein Zimmer voll(er) Leute.

roominess ['ruːmɪnɪs] n Geräumigkeit f; (of garment) Weite f.

room: **~-mate** n Zimmergenosse m, Zimmergenossin f; **~ service** n Zimmerservice, Etagendienst m; **to ring for ~ service** nach dem Zimmerkellner/-mädchen klingeln; **~ temperature** n Zimmertemperatur f; **wine at ~ temperature** Wein mit or auf Zimmertemperatur.

roomy ['ruːmɪ] adj (+er) geräumig; garment weit.

roost [ruːst] **1** n (pole) Stange f; (henhouse) Hühnerhaus nt or -stall m. **at ~** auf der Stange; **to come home to ~** (fig) auf den Urheber zurückfallen; see **cock, rule**. **2** vi (settle) sich auf die Stange setzen; (sleep) auf der Stange schlafen.

rooster ['ruːstə'] n Hahn m.

root [ruːt] **1** n **(a)** (of plant, hair, tooth) Wurzel f. **~s** (fig: of person) Wurzeln; **by the ~s** mit der Wurzel; **to take ~** (lit, fig) Wurzeln schlagen; **her ~s are in Scotland** sie ist in Schottland verwurzelt; **she has no ~s** sie ist nirgends zu Hause; **to put down ~s in a country** in einem Land Fuß fassen; **~ and branch** (fig) mit Stumpf und Stiel; see **grass-roots, pull up**.
(b) (fig) (source: of evil, of trouble etc) Wurzel f. **the ~ of the matter** der Kern der Sache; **to get to the ~(s) of the problem** dem Problem auf den Grund gehen; **that is** or **lies at the ~ of his behaviour** das ist der eigentliche Grund für sein Benehmen.
(c) (Math, Ling) Wurzel f; (of equation) Lösung f; (Ling: base form also) Stamm m; see **cube, square ~**.

2 vt plant Wurzeln schlagen lassen bei. **deeply ~ed** (fig) tief verwurzelt; **~ed objections** grundsätzliche Einwände pl; **to be** or **stand ~ed to the spot** (fig) wie angewurzelt dastehen.

3 vi (plants etc) Wurzeln schlagen or fassen.

♦**root about** or **around** vi herumwühlen (for nach).

♦**root for** vi +prep obj team anfeuern. **to ~ ~ sb** jdm die Daumen drücken; (esp Sport: cheer on) jdn anfeuern.

♦**root out** vt sep **(a)** (lit) see **root up**. **(b)** (fig) (remove) evil mit der Wurzel ausreißen; (find) aufspüren, ausgraben (inf).

♦**root up** vt sep plant herausreißen; (dig up) ausgraben.

root in cpds Wurzel-; **~ beer** n (US) Art f Limonade; **~ cause** n eigentlicher Grund m; **~ crop** n Wurzelgemüse nt no pl; **~less** adj plant wurzellos; (fig) person ohne Wurzeln; **~ sign** n (Math) Wurzelzeichen nt; **~ stock** n (Bot) Wurzelstock m; **~ vegetable** n Wurzelgemüse nt; **~ word** n (Ling) Wortwurzel f; (base form also) Wortstamm m.

rope [rəʊp] **1** n **(a)** Seil nt; (Naut) Tau nt; (of bell) Glockenstrang m; (hangman's ~) Strang, Strick m. **a ~ of pearls** eine Perlenschnur; **a ~ of onions** eine Schnur Zwiebeln; **to give sb more/plenty of ~** (fig) jdm mehr/viel Freiheit lassen; **give him enough ~ and he'll hang himself** (fig) der dreht sich (dat) schon selbst seinen Strick.
(b) (Mountaineering) Seil nt. **a ~ of climbers** eine Seilschaft; **to put on the ~s** anseilen; **to be on the ~** angeseilt sein; **there were three of them on the ~** sie waren zu dritt am Seil.
(c) the ~s (Boxing etc) die Seile pl; **to be on the ~s** (boxer) in den Seilen hängen; (inf) in der Klemme sein; **to know the ~s** (inf) sich auskennen; **to show sb the ~s** (inf) jdn in alles einweihen; **to learn the ~s** (inf) sich einarbeiten.

2 vt **(a)** box, case verschnüren. **to ~ sb to a tree** jdn an einen Baum binden; **to ~ sb's feet together** jdm die Füße zusammenbinden; **to ~ climbers (together)** Bergsteiger anseilen.
(b) (lasso) mit dem Lasso fangen.

♦**rope in** vt sep **(a)** area (mit einem Seil) abgrenzen; cattle mit einem Seil einfrieden. **(b)** (fig) rankriegen (inf). **how did you get ~ed ~to that?** wie bist du denn da reingeraten? (inf); **I don't want to get ~ed ~to helping** ich will nicht, daß die mich zum Helfen rankriegen (inf).

♦**rope off** vt sep area mit einem Seil abgrenzen.

♦**rope together** vt sep objects zusammenbinden; climbers an(einander)seilen.

♦**rope up 1** vi (climbers) sich anseilen. **2** vt sep anseilen.

rope in cpds Seil-; **~ ladder** n Strickleiter f; **~ maker** n Seiler m; **~ sole** n (aus Seil) geflochtene Sohle; **~-soled** adj mit (aus Seil) geflochtener Sohle; **~ walker** n Seiltänzer(in f) m.

rop(e)y ['rəʊpɪ] adj (+er) (inf) (bad) miserabel (inf); (worn) mitgenommen. **the battery is a bit ~** die Batterie pfeift auf dem letzten Loch (inf).

rosary ['rəʊzərɪ] n (Rel) Rosenkranz m. **to say the ~** den Rosenkranz beten.

rose¹ [rəʊz] pret of **rise**.

rose² **1** n **(a)** Rose f. **wild ~** Wildrose f; **~-bush/-tree** Rosenbusch m/-bäumchen nt; **my life isn't all ~s** (inf) ich bin auch nicht auf Rosen gebettet; **life/marriage isn't all ~s** (inf) das Leben/die Ehe hat auch seine/ihre Schattenseiten; **no ~ without a thorn** (prov) keine Rose ohne Dornen (prov); **an English ~** (fig) eine englische Schöne; **that will put the ~s back in your cheeks** davon bekommst du wieder etwas Farbe im Gesicht; **under the ~** (fig liter) unter dem Siegel der Verschwiegenheit; **the Wars of the R~s** die Rosenkriege pl.
(b) (nozzle) Brause f; (rosette, Archit) Rosette f.
(c) (colour) Rosarot, Rosenrot nt.

2 adj rosarot, rosenrot.

rosé ['rəʊzeɪ] **1** adj rosé. **2** n Rosé m.

roseate ['rəʊzɪɪt] adj (liter) rosenfarben.

rose in cpds Rosen-; **~bay** n Oleander m; **~bowl** n Rosenpokal m; **~-bud** n Rosenknospe f; **~-bud mouth** Rosenmund m; **~-coloured** adj rosarot, rosenrot; **to see everything/life through ~-coloured spectacles** alles/das Leben durch die rosarote Brille sehen; **~-cut** adj mit Rosetteschliff; **~ garden** n Rosengarten m; **~-grower** n Rosenzüchter m. ... **~hip n Hagebutte f.**

rosemary ['rəʊzmərɪ] n Rosmarin m.

rose: **~ petal** n Rosen(blüten)blatt nt; **~-pink 1** adj rosarot; **2** n Rosarot nt; **~ quartz** n Rosenquarz m; **~-red** adj rosenrot; **~ tree** n Rosenstrauch m.

Rosetta stone [rəʊ'zetə'stəʊn] n Stein m von Rosette.

rosette [rəʊ'zet] n Rosette f.

rose: **~-water** n Rosenwasser nt; **~ window** n (Fenster)rosette f; **~-wood** n Rosenholz nt.

rosin ['rɒzɪn] **1** n Harz, Kolophonium (esp Mus) nt. **2** vt mit Harz/Kolophonium behandeln.

roster ['rɒstə'] n Dienstplan m; see **duty ~**.

rostrum ['rɒstrəm] n, pl **rostra** ['rɒstrə] Tribüne f, Rednerpult nt; (for conductor) Dirigentenpult nt; (Roman Hist) Rostra f.

rosy ['rəʊzɪ] adj (+er) (pink) rosarot; complexion, cheeks rosig; (rose-covered) fabric mit Rosenmuster; design Rosen-; (fig: promising) future, situation rosig. **to paint a ~ picture of sth** etw in den rosigsten Farben ausmalen.

rot [rɒt] **1** n **(a)** (in teeth, plants) Fäulnis f no pl; (in wood also) Moder m no pl. **to stop the ~** (lit, fig) den Fäulnisprozeß aufhalten; **then the ~ set in** (fig) dann setzte der Fäulnisprozeß or Verfall ein; see **dry ~**.
(b) (inf: rubbish) Quatsch (inf), Blödsinn (inf) m. **that's utter ~, that's a lot of ~** das ist doch kompletter Blödsinn (inf).

2 vi (wood, material, rope) verrotten, faulen; (teeth, plant) verfaulen; (fig) verrotten. **to ~ in jail** im Gefängnis verrotten; **let him ~!** (inf) soll er doch vor die Hunde gehen! (inf).

3 vt verfaulen lassen; wood modrig machen.

♦**rot away** vi verfaulen, vermodern; (teeth) verfaulen; (plants) verwesen.

rota ['rəʊtə] n **(a)** Dienstplan m. **(b)** (Eccl) R~ Rota f.

Rotarian [rəʊ'teərɪən] **1** adj Rotarier-; **2** n Rotarier m.

rotary ['rəʊtərɪ] adj **(a)** motion rotierend, Dreh-; wheel Rotations-. **~ iron** Heißmangel f; **~ (printing) press** Rotationsmaschine f; **~ printer** Rotationsdrucker m; **~ pump** Kreiselpumpe f. **(b)** R~ **Club** Rotary Club m.

rotate [rəʊˈteɪt] **1** vt **(a)** (around axis) drehen, rotieren lassen; (Math) rotieren lassen. **(b)** crops im Wechsel anbauen; work, jobs turnusmäßig erledigen. **2** vi **(a)** sich drehen, rotieren; (Math) rotieren. **(b)** (crops) im Wechsel angebaut werden; (people: take turns) sich (turnusmäßig) abwechseln.

rotating [rəʊˈteɪtɪŋ] adj (revolving) rotierend, sich drehend; crops im Wechsel angebaut.

rotation [rəʊˈteɪʃən] n **(a)** no pl Drehung, Rotation (also Math) f; (of crops) Wechsel m, Rotation f; (taking turns) turnusmäßiger Wechsel. **in** or **by** ~ abwechselnd im Turnus; ~ **of** crops, crop ~ Fruchtwechsel m. **(b)** (turn) (Um)drehung, Rotation f.

rotatory [rəʊˈteɪtərɪ] adj **(a)** movement Dreh-, rotierend. **(b)** schedule turnusmäßig; cultivation abwechselnd.

rote [rəʊt] n: **by** ~ learn auswendig; recite mechanisch.

rotgut [ˈrɒtgʌt] n (pej inf) Fusel m (inf).

rotogravure [ˌrəʊtəʊgrəˈvjʊəʳ] n Kupferdruck m.

rotor [ˈrəʊtəʳ] n (Aviat, Elec, Aut) Rotor m. ~ **arm** Verteilerfinger m; ~ **blade** Flügelblatt nt.

rot-proof [ˈrɒtpruːf] adj fäulnissicher.

rotten [ˈrɒtn] adj **(a)** vegetation, egg, tooth faul; wood also morsch; fruit also verdorben; (fig: corrupt) korrupt, verdorben. ~ **to the core** (fig) durch und durch verdorben. **(b)** (inf) (bad) scheußlich (inf); weather, book, film, piece of work also mies (inf); (mean) gemein, eklig; (unwell) mies, mies (inf). **what** ~ **luck!** so ein Pech!; **it's a** ~ **business** das ist eine üble Sache; **a** ~ **thing to have to do** eine scheußliche Aufgabe; **that was a** ~ **trick/a** ~ **thing to do** das war ein übler Trick/eine Gemeinheit.

rottenness [ˈrɒtnɪs] n see adj **(a)** Faulheit f; Morschheit f; Verdorbenheit f; Korruptheit f, Verdorbenheit f.

rotter [ˈrɒtəʳ] n (dated Brit inf) Lump m.

rotting [ˈrɒtɪŋ] adj meat verfaulend; wood also modrig; carcass, bones also verwesend.

rotund [rəʊˈtʌnd] adj person rund(lich); object rund; speech, literary style bombastisch, hochtrabend; voice voll.

rotunda [rəʊˈtʌndə] n Rotunde f, Rundbau m.

rotundity [rəʊˈtʌndɪtɪ] n see adj Rund(lich)keit f; Bombast m; Vollheit f.

rouble, (US) **ruble** [ˈruːbl] n Rubel m.

roué [ˈruːeɪ] n (dated) Lebemann m.

rouge [ruːʒ] **1** n Rouge nt. **2** vt **to** ~ **one's cheeks** Rouge auflegen.

rough [rʌf] **1** adj (+er) **(a)** (uneven) ground uneben; path, road also holprig; surface, skin, hands, cloth rauh. **(b)** (harsh) sound hart; voice, tone rauh; taste, wine sauer; words grob, hart. **to have** ~ **luck** schweres Pech haben; **to have a** ~ **tongue** (fig) eine scharfe Zunge haben; **he got the** ~ **side of her tongue** er bekam (von ihr) den Marsch geblasen. **(c)** (coarse, unrefined) person ungehobelt; manners also, speech grob, roh. **(d)** (violent) person, child grob, roh; treatment, handling grob, hart; life wüst; children's game wild; match, sport, work hart; neighbourhood, manners, pub rauh; sea, weather, wind rauh, stürmisch; sea crossing stürmisch. **to be** ~ **with sb** grob mit jdm umgehen, unsanft mit jdm umspringen (inf); ~ **play** (Sport) Holzerei f (inf); **the children love a bit of** ~ **play with their father** die Kinder balgen gern mit ihrem Vater; ~ **stuff** Schlägereien pl/eine Schlägerei f; **he had a** ~ **time (of it)** (fig inf) es ging ihm ziemlich dreckig (inf); **to be in for a** ~ **time (of it)** (inf) harten Zeiten entgegensehen; **the examiners gave him a** ~ **time** (inf) die Prüfer haben ihn ganz schön rangenommen (inf); **to make things** ~ **for sb** (inf) jdm Schwierigkeiten machen; **to be** ~ **on sb** (Brit inf) grob mit jdm umspringen; **it's** ~ **on him** (Brit inf) das ist hart für ihn. **(e)** (approximate, rudimentary) plan, calculation, estimate, translation grob, ungefähr; draft also Roh-; workmanship schludrig; guess grob. ~ **copy** Konzept nt; ~ **sketch** Faustskizze f; ~ **paper** Konzeptpapier nt; **in its** ~ **state** im Rohzustand; **do your** ~ **work on the paper provided** macht euer Konzept auf dem dafür bereitgestellten Papier. **(f)** (inf: unwell) **to feel** ~ sich mies fühlen; **the engine sounds pretty** ~ der Motor hört sich nicht gerade gut an. **2** adv live wüst; play wild. **to sleep** ~ im Freien übernachten. **3** n **(a)** unwegsames Gelände; (Golf) Rauh nt. ~ **or smooth?** (Sport) untere oder obere Seite? (des Schlägers, die durch einen roten Faden gekennzeichnet ist; zum Bestimmen, wer anfängt) **(b)** (unpleasant aspect) **to take the** ~ **with the smooth** das Leben nehmen, wie es kommt. **(c)** (draft, sketch) Rohentwurf m. **in the** ~ im Rohzustand. **(d)** (person) Rowdy, Schläger m. **4** vt **to** ~ **it** (inf) primitiv leben.

◆**rough out** vt sep plan, drawing grob entwerfen.

◆**rough up** vt sep hair zersausen, verstrubbeln (inf); (sl) person zusammenschlagen.

roughage [ˈrʌfɪdʒ] n Ballaststoffe pl.

rough: ~**-and-ready** adj method, installation, equipment provisorisch; work zusammengehauen (inf), zusammengepfuscht (inf); person rauh(beinig); ~**-and-tumble** n (play) Balgerei f; (fighting) Keilerei f; **after the** ~**-and-tumble of life in the navy** nach seinem wilden Leben in der Marine; ~ **book** n (Sch) Schmierheft nt; ~**cast** (inf: pret, ptp ~**cast**) **1** n Rauhputz m; **2** vt rauh verputzen; ~ **diamond** n (lit) Rohdiamant m; **he's a** ~ **diamond** er ist rauh, aber herzlich; ~**-dry** vt einfach trocknen.

roughen [ˈrʌfn] **1** vt ground uneben machen; skin, cloth rauh machen, rauh werden lassen; surface aufrauhen. **living in that district has** ~**ed his manners/speech** seit er in diesem Bezirk wohnt, sind seine Sitten/ist seine Sprechweise ganz verroht. **2** vi **(a)** (skin) rauh werden. **(b)** (sound) hart werden; (voice) rauh werden.

(c) (treatment) hart werden; (neighbourhood) verrohen; (sea, wind, weather) rauh or stürmisch werden.

rough: ~**-hew** vt timber grob behauen; ~**-house** (inf) **1** n Schlägerei f; **2** vt herumstoßen.

roughly [ˈrʌflɪ] adv **(a)** (not gently) grob, roh; play rauh; answer, order grob, hart. **(b)** (not finely) make, sew, sketch grob. **(c)** (approximately) ungefähr. ~ **(speaking)** grob gesagt.

roughneck [ˈrʌfˌnek] n (inf) Grobian m; (thug) Schläger m.

roughness [ˈrʌfnɪs] n see adj **(a)** Unebenheit f; Holprigkeit f; Rauheit f. **(b)** Härte f; Rauheit f; saurer Geschmack; Grobheit, Härte f. **(c)** Ungehobeltheit f; Grobheit, Roheit f. **(d)** Grobheit, Roheit f; Grobheit, Härte f; Wüstheit f; Wildheit f; Härte f; Rauheit f. **(e)** Grobheit f.

rough: ~ **note book** n (Sch) Schmierheft nt; ~**rider** n Zureiter m; ~**shod** adv: **to ride** ~**shod over sb/sth** rücksichtslos über jdn/etw hinweggehen; ~**-spoken** adj **to be** ~**-spoken** (sich) ungehobelt (ausdrücken).

roulette [ruːˈlet] n Roulett(e) nt; see Russian.

Roumania [ruːˈmeɪnɪə] etc see **Romania** etc.

round [raʊnd] **1** adj (+er) **(a)** rund; (Ling) vowel gerundet. **in rich** ~ **tones** mit vollem, rundem Klang; ~ **arch** (Archit) Rundbogen m; **a** ~ **dozen** ein rundes Dutzend; ~ **figure**, ~ **number** runde Zahl; **in** ~ **figures, that will cost 20 million** es kostet rund (gerechnet) or runde 20 Millionen. **(b)** (dated) (unequivocal) oath kräftig; (considerable) sum rund; pace flott. **in** ~ **terms** klar und deutlich. **2** adv **there was a wall right** ~ **or all** ~ **rings-** or rundherum war eine Mauer; **he went** ~ **by the bridge** er nahm den (Um)weg über die Brücke; **you can't get through here, you'll have to go** ~ Sie können hier nicht durch, Sie müssen außen herum gehen; **the long way** ~ der Umweg, der längere Weg; **that's a long way** ~ (detour) das ist ein großer Umweg; (round field, town) das ist eine ganz schöne Strecke; **for 5 km** ~ **in Umkreis von 5 km**; ~ **and** ~ (in circles, round field etc) rundherum; (all over the place) überall herum; **I asked him** ~ **for a drink** ich lud ihn auf ein Glas Wein/Bier etc bei mir ein; **I'll be** ~ **at 8 o'clock** ich werde um 8 Uhr da sein; **spring will soon be** ~ **again** der Frühling steht bald wieder vor der Tür; **for the second time** ~ zum zweitenmal; **all (the) year** ~ das ganze Jahr über or hindurch; **all** ~ (lit) ringsherum; (fig: for everyone) für alle; **drinks all** ~! eine Runde!; **taking things all** ~, **taken all** ~ insgesamt gesehen, wenn man alles zusammennimmt; **a pillar 2 m** ~ eine Säule mit 2 m Umfang; see also vbs.

3 prep **(a)** (of place etc) um (... herum). ~ **the table/fire** um den Tisch/das Feuer (herum); **the ribbon** ~ **her hat** das Band um ihren Hut; **all** ~ **the house** (inside) im ganzen Haus; (outside) um das ganze Haus herum; ~ **and** ~ **the field** rings um das Feld herum; **the villages** ~ **Wigan** die Dörfer um Wigan (herum) or rund um Wigan; **to go** ~ **a corner/bend** um eine Ecke/Kurve gehen/fahren etc; **if you're** ~ **this way** wenn Sie in der Gegend sind; **to look or see** ~ **a house** sich (dat) ein Haus ansehen; **they went** ~ **the castle** sie sahen sich (dat) die Burg an; **to show sb** ~ **a town** jdm eine Stadt zeigen, jdn in einer Stadt herumführen; **they went** ~ **the cafés looking for him** sie gingen in alle Cafés, um nach ihm zu suchen; **to talk** ~ **a subject** um ein Thema herumreden; **she's 75 cm** ~ **the waist** um die Taille mißt or ist sie 75 cm. **(b)** (approximately) ungefähr. ~ **(about)** 7 o'clock ungefähr um 7 Uhr; ~ **(about) £800** um die £ 800.

4 n **(a)** (circle etc) Kreis, Ring m; (slice: of bread, meat) Scheibe f. **a** ~ **of toast** eine Scheibe Toast; **a** ~ **of beef** sandwiches ein belegtes Brot mit Braten, eine Bratenschnitte. **(b)** (delivery ~) Runde f. ~**(s)** (of policeman, watchman, doctor) Runde f; **to do or make one's** ~**(s)** seine Runde machen; (doctor also) Hausbesuche machen; **to be (out) on one's** ~**(s)** auf seiner Runde sein; (doctor also) Hausbesuche machen; **to go or make or do the** ~**s** (visiting relatives etc) die Runde machen; **to do the** ~**s of the clubs** etc (inf) durch die Klubs etc ziehen, die Klubs abklappern (inf); **he does a paper** ~ er trägt Zeitungen aus; **the daily** ~ (fig) die tägliche Arbeit, der tägliche Trott (pej); **her life was one long** ~ **of parties** ihr Leben war eine einzige Folge von Partys. **(c)** **to go the** ~**s** (story etc) reihum gehen; **the story went the** ~**s of the club** die Geschichte ging im ganzen Verein reihum; **this coat has gone the** ~**s of the family** dieser Mantel ist durch die ganze Familie gegangen. **(d)** (Sport, of election, talks) Runde f; (Showjumping) Durchgang m. **a** ~ **(of drinks)** eine Runde; **a new** ~ **of negotiations** eine neue Verhandlungsrunde; ~ **of ammunition** Ladung f; **10** ~**s of bullets** 10 Schuß; **a** ~ **of 5 shots** eine Folge von 5 Schüssen; **a** ~ **of applause** Applaus m. **(e)** (Mus) Kanon m. **(f)** **in the** ~ (as a whole) insgesamt; theatre/sculpture **in the** ~ Arenatheater nt/Rund- or Vollplastik f.

5 vt **(a)** (make ~) runden. **(b)** (go ~) corner, bend gehen/fahren um; cape umfahren, herumfahren um; obstacle herumgehen/-fahren etc um.

◆**round down** vt sep price, number abrunden.

◆**round off** vt sep **(a)** edges etc abrunden. **(b)** (complete, perfect) list, series voll machen; speech, sentence, meal abrunden; debate, meeting, one's career beschließen, abschließen. **and now, to** ~ ~, **I would like to say** ... und zum Abschluß möchte ich nun sagen ...

◆**round on** vi +prep obj (verbally) anfahren; (in actions) herumfahren zu.

◆**round out** **1** vt sep story etc runden. **2** vi sich runden.

◆**round up** vt sep **(a)** (bring together) people zusammentrommeln (inf); cattle zusammentreiben; criminals hochnehmen (inf); facts zusammentragen. **(b)** price, number aufrunden.

◆**round upon** vi +prep obj see **round on**.

roundabout [ˈraʊndəbaʊt] **1** adj ~ **route** Umweg m; **we came a**

~ way or by a ~ route wir sind auf Umwegen gekommen, wir haben einen Umweg gemacht; he has a ~ way of going about things er geht sehr umständlich an die Dinge heran; what a ~ way of doing things! wie kann man nur so umständlich sein!; I found out in a ~ way ich habe es auf Umwegen herausgefunden; by ~ means auf Umwegen, hintenherum; a very ~ way of putting it eine sehr umständliche Art, es auszudrücken; ~ phrase (umständliche) Umschreibung.

2 n (Brit) (merry-go-round) Karussell nt; (Mot) Kreisverkehr m; see swing.

round: ~-cheeked ['raund'tʃi:kt] adj mit runden Backen; ~-dance n Reigen m; (ballroom dance) Rundtanz m.

rounded ['raundɪd] adj rundlich; edges abgerundet; vowel gerundet. (well-)~ sentences, style (wohl) abgerundet; bosom, figure wohlgerundet.

roundelay ['raundɪleɪ] n (Mus) Lied mit Refrain.

rounder ['raundə'] n (Brit Sport) to score a ~ einen Lauf machen.

rounders ['raundəz] n sing (Brit Sport) ≈ Schlagball m.

round: ~-eyed adj großäugig; ~-faced adj rundgesichtig, mit rundem Gesicht; R~head n (Brit Hist) Rundkopf m; ~house n (esp US Rail) Lokomotivschuppen m.

roundly ['raundlɪ] adv (fig) (bluntly) ohne Umschweife; (dated: conscientiously) gründlich, gewissenhaft.

round-necked ['raund'nekt] adj mit rundem Ausschnitt.

roundness ['raundnɪs] n Rundheit f; (of sound also) Vollheit f; (of vowel) Gerundetheit f.

round: ~ robin n (a) (petition) gemeinsamer Antrag(, bei dem die Unterschriften (oft) im Kreis angeordnet sind); (b) (esp US Sport) Wettkampf m, in dem jeder gegen jeden spielt; ~-shouldered ['raund'ʃəʊldəd] adj mit runden Schultern; to be ~-shouldered runde Schultern haben.

roundsman ['raundzmən] n, pl -men [-mən] (Brit) Austräger m. milk ~ Milchmann(, der an die Tür kommt).

round: R~ Table n (Hist) (König Artus') Tafelrunde f; ~-discussion/conference Diskussion f/Konferenz f am runden Tisch; ~-the-clock adj rund um die Uhr not attr; ~ trip n Rundreise f; ~-trip ticket n (US) Rückfahrkarte f; (Aviat) Hin- und Rückflug-Ticket nt; ~-up n (a) (act) (of cattle) Zusammentreiben nt; (of people) Zusammentrommeln nt (inf); (of criminals) Hochnehmen nt (inf); (of facts) Sammlung f, Zusammentragen nt; a ~-up of today's news eine Zusammenfassung der Nachrichten vom Tage; (b) (group) zusammengetriebene Herde; Versammlung f; ausgehobene Bande; Sammlung f.

rouse [rauz] 1 vt (a) (from sleep, daydream etc) wecken. (b) (stimulate) person bewegen; feeling, admiration, interest wecken, wachrufen; hatred, indignation erregen; suspicions erwecken, erregen. to ~ sb (to anger) jdn reizen; to ~ sb to enthusiasm/hatred jds Begeisterung entfachen/jds Haß anstacheln; to ~ sb to action jdn zum Handeln bewegen; to ~ sb out of his/her apathy jdn aus seiner Apathie aufrütteln; to ~ the masses die Massen aufrütteln; ~ yourself! raff dich auf! 2 vi (waken) wach werden; (become active) lebendig werden.

rousing ['rauzɪŋ] adj speech, sermon zündend, mitreißend; cheers, applause stürmisch; music schwungvoll.

roustabout ['raustəbaut] n (a) (US Naut) (deckhand) Deckhelfer m; (in dock) Werft- or Hafenarbeiter m. (b) (US: unskilled labourer) Hilfsarbeiter m. (c) (Austral) Helfer m beim Scheren.

rout[1] [raut] 1 n (a) (defeat) Schlappe f. to put to ~ in die Flucht schlagen. (b) (Jur: mob) Bande, Rotte f. 2 vt (defeat) in die Flucht schlagen.

rout[2] vi (pig: also ~ about) herumwühlen.

♦**rout out** vt sep (find) aufstöbern; (force out) (heraus)jagen (of aus).

route [ruːt], (US) [raut] 1 n (a) Strecke, Route f; (bus service) Linie f. shipping/air ~s Schiffahrtsstraßen or -wege/Flugwege; what ~ does the 39 bus take? welche Strecke or Route fährt der 39er-Bus?; we live on a bus ~ wir wohnen an einer Buslinie; the ~ to the coast goes through Easthampton der Weg zur Küste führt durch Easthampton; "all ~s" (Mot) „alle Richtungen"; ~ map Straßenkarte f. (b) (Mil) Marschbefehl m. ~ march Geländemarsch m. (c) (US: delivery round) Runde f. he has a paper ~ er trägt Zeitungen aus. (d) (Med: of drug) Weg m.

2 vt train, coach, bus legen. my luggage was ~d through Amsterdam mein Gepäck wurde über Amsterdam geschickt; the train is ~d (to go) through Birmingham der Zug wird durch Birmingham geführt or über Birmingham gelegt; complaints should be ~d through the service department Beschwerden sollten über die Kundendienstabteilung gehen.

routine [ruːˈtiːn] 1 n (a) Routine f. business or office ~ Büroroutine f; as a matter of ~ routinemäßig. (b) (Dancing, Skating) Figur f; (Gymnastics) Übung f. he gave me the old ~ about his wife not understanding him er kam mit der alten Geschichte, daß seine Frau ihn nicht versteht. 2 adj Routine-, routinemäßig. ~ duties tägliche Pflichten pl; to be ~ procedure Routine(sache) sein; it was quite ~ es war eine reine Formsache.

roux [ruː] n Mehlschwitze, Einbrenne f.

rove [rəʊv] 1 vi (person) umherwandern or -ziehen; (eyes) umherwandern or -schweifen. to ~ over sth (eyes) über etw (acc) schweifen or wandern. 2 vt countryside, streets wandern or ziehen durch, durchwandern or -ziehen. his eyes ~d the room seine Augen wanderten durch das Zimmer.

rover ['rəʊvə'] n (a) (wanderer) Vagabund m. (b) (also R~ Scout) Rover m.

roving ['rəʊvɪŋ] 1 adj he has a ~ eye er riskiert gern ein Auge; ~ life Vagabundenleben nt; ~ ambassador Botschafter m für mehrere Vertretungen; ~ reporter Reporter, der ständig unterwegs ist; rasender Reporter (hum); ~ commission weitläufiges Mandat; (travelling) Reisemandat nt.

2 n Vagabundieren nt no pl.

row[1] [rəʊ] n Reihe f. 4 failures in a ~ 4 Mißerfolge hinter- or nacheinander; arrange them in ~s stell sie in Reihen or reihenweise auf.

row[2] 1 vti (in boat) rudern. to ~ sb across jdn hinüber-/herüberrudern; to ~ away/back weg-/zurückrudern; to ~ stroke Schlagmann sein. 2 n I enjoy a ~ ich rudere gern; to go for a ~ rudern gehen; it will be a hard ~ upstream flußaufwärts wird es hart zu rudern sein.

row[3] [rau] 1 n (a) (noise) Lärm, Krach (inf) m. to make a or kick up (inf) a ~ Krach schlagen (inf). (b) (quarrel) Streit, Krach (inf) m. to have a ~ with sb mit jdm Streit or Krach (inf) haben; to start a ~ Streit anfangen. (c) (scolding) to get into a ~ Krach bekommen (inf). 2 vi (quarrel) (sich) streiten.

rowan ['rauən] n (tree) Eberesche f, Vogelbeere f. ~ berry Vogelbeere f.

rowboat ['rəʊ,bəʊt] n (US) Ruderboot nt.

rowdiness ['raudɪnɪs] n see adj Krawall m; Rüpel- or Flegelhaftigkeit f; Randalieren, Rowdytum nt.

rowdy ['raudɪ] 1 adj (+er) (noisy) laut; football fans randalierend. the party got a bit ~ die Party artete in Krawall aus. 2 n Krawallmacher m. football rowdies Fußballrowdys pl.

rowdyism ['raudɪɪzəm] n Rowdytum nt.

rower ['rəʊə'] n Ruderer m.

row house ['rəʊ,haus] n (US) Reihenhaus nt.

rowing[1] ['rəʊɪŋ] n Rudern nt.

rowing[2] ['rauɪŋ] n (quarrelling) Streiterei f, Streitereien pl.

rowing ['rəʊɪŋ] ~ boat n (Brit) Ruderboot nt; ~ club n Ruderklub or -verein m.

rowlock ['rəʊ,lɒk] n (esp Brit) Dolle f.

royal ['rɔɪəl] 1 adj königlich; family, palace also Königs-; (fig also) fürstlich. the ~ road to freedom/success etc (fig) der sichere Weg or der Königsweg (geh) zur Freiheit/zum Erfolg etc. 2 n (a) (inf) Angehörige(r) mf der königlichen Familie. (b) (stag) kapitaler Bock.

royal: R~ Academy n (Brit) Königliche Akademie; R~ Air Force n (Brit) Königliche Luftwaffe; ~ assent n (Brit) königliche Zustimmung; ~ blue 1 adj königsblau; 2 n Königsblau nt; R~ Canadian Mounted Police n kanadische berittene Polizei; R~ Commission n (Brit) königliche Untersuchungskommission; R~ Engineers n (Brit Mil) Königliches Pionierkorps; ~ flush n (Cards) Royal Flush m; R~ Highness n Your/His R~ Highness Eure/Seine Königliche Hoheit; ~ household n königlicher Haushalt.

royalism ['rɔɪəlɪzəm] n Royalismus m, Königstreue f.

royalist ['rɔɪəlɪst] 1 adj royalistisch, königstreu. 2 n Royalist(in f) m, Königstreue(r) mf.

royally ['rɔɪəlɪ] adv königlich; (fig also) fürstlich.

Royal Navy (Brit) 1 n Königliche Marine. 2 attr der Königlichen Marine.

royalty ['rɔɪəltɪ] n (a) (dignity, rank) das Königtum; (collectively: royal persons) das Königshaus, die königliche Familie. symbols of ~ Wahrzeichen pl der Königswürde; he's ~ er gehört zur königlichen Familie.

(b) royalties pl (sing + acc) (from book, records) Tantiemen pl; (from patent) Patent- or Lizenzgebühren pl; (from oil well) Förderabgaben pl.

rozzer ['rɒzə'] n (Brit sl) Bulle, Polyp (sl) m.

RPM (Brit) abbr of resale price maintenance vertikale Preisbindung.

rpm abbr of revolutions per minute Umdr. p. min.

RR (US) abbr of Railroad.

RSPCA abbr of Royal Society for the Prevention of Cruelty to Animals ≈ Tierschutzverein m.

RSVP abbr of répondez s'il vous plaît u.A.w.g.

Rt Hon abbr of Right Honourable.

rub [rʌb] 1 n (a) Reiben nt; (with duster etc) Polieren nt. with a ~ on the magic lantern he ... indem er an der Zauberlampe rieb ...; to give sth a ~ etw reiben; furniture, shoes, silver etw polieren; ~-a-dub(-dub)! (inf) rubbel-rubbel! (inf). (b) (fig) there's the ~! da liegt der Hase im Pfeffer.

2 vt reiben; (with towel also) frottieren; (polish) polieren; (Art) brass, inscription durchzeichnen, durchschummern. to ~ sth/oneself with a lotion etw/sich mit einer Lotion einreiben; to ~ sth with sandpaper etw (mit Sandpapier) abschmirgeln; to ~ one's hands (together) sich (dat) die Hände reiben; to ~ sth dry etw trockenreiben or -rubbeln (inf); to ~ a hole in sth ein Loch in etw (acc) reiben or rubbeln (inf); to ~ noses (as greeting) Nasen reiben; to ~ sb's nose in sth (fig) jdm etw dauernd unter die Nase reiben or halten; to ~ shoulders with all sorts of people (fig) mit allen möglichen Leuten in Berührung kommen.

3 vi (thing) (against an + dat) reiben; (shoes, collar) scheuern. you must have ~bed against some wet paint da mußt du an feuchte Farbe gekommen sein; the cat ~bed against my legs/the tree die Katze strich mir um die Beine/scheuerte sich am Baum.

♦**rub along** vi (inf) (manage) sich durchschlagen (inf). to ~ ~ (together) recht und schlecht miteinander auskommen.

♦**rub away** vt sep wegreiben.

♦**rub down** vt sep horse (dry) abreiben; (clean) striegeln; person abrubbeln (inf), abfrottieren; wall, paintwork (clean) abwaschen; (sandpaper) abschmirgeln.

♦**rub in** vt sep (a) oil, lotion einreiben (prep obj, -to in + acc). (b) (fig) sb's stupidity herumreiten auf (+dat). he's always ~bing ~ how rich he is (inf) er reibt es uns/ihnen etc immer unter die Nase, wie reich er ist (inf).

♦**rub off** 1 vt sep dirt wegreiben; writing ausradieren; tape löschen; (from blackboard) aus- or wegwischen; paint, gold-plating abreiben; (through wear) abwetzen.

2 vi (lit, fig) abgehen; (through wear also) sich abwetzen. to ~ ~ on(to) sb (fig) auf jdn abfärben.

♦**rub out 1** vt sep stain etc herausreiben; (with eraser) ausradieren; (sl: kill) auslöschen. **2** vi herausgehen; (with eraser) sich ausradieren lassen.

♦**rub up 1** vt sep (a) vase, table blank reiben, (auf)polieren.
(b) to ~ sb ~ **the wrong way** bei jdm anecken; **you should learn to** ~ **him** ~ **the right way** Sie sollten lernen, ihn richtig zu behandeln.
2 vi **the cat** ~**bed** ~ **against my leg** die Katze strich mir um die Beine; to ~ ~ **against all sorts of people** (fig) mit allen möglichen Leuten in Berührung kommen.

rubber[1] ['rʌbər] n (a) (material) Gummi m; (unprocessed, synthetic also) Kautschuk m (spec); (Brit: eraser) (Radier)gummi m; (sl: contraceptive) Gummi m (inf). ~s (shoes) Turnschuhe pl; (overshoes) (Gummi)überschuhe pl; (clothing) Ölzeug nt. **2** adj Gummi-; Kautschuk- (spec). **is that cheque** ~? (sl) platzt der Scheck?; ~ **goods** Gummiwaren.

rubber[2] n (Cards) Robber m.

rubber: ~ **band** n Gummiband nt; ~-**covered** adj mit Gummiüberzug.

rubberize ['rʌbəraɪz] vt (cover) mit Gummi überziehen; (impregnate) gummieren.

rubber: ~**neck** (US inf) **1** n Gaffer m (inf); **2** vi gaffen (inf); ~ **plant** n Gummibaum m; ~ **plantation** n Kautschukplantage f; ~ **stamp** n Stempel m; ~-**stamp** vt (lit) stempeln; (fig inf) genehmigen; ~ **tree** n Kautschukbaum m; ~-**tyred** ['rʌbə'taɪəd] adj mit Gummireifen.

rubbery ['rʌbəri] adj material gummiartig; meat zäh, wie Gummi pred; (hum) lips wulstig.

rubbing ['rʌbɪŋ] n (a) (action) Reiben nt; (of shoes, collar also) Scheuern nt; (with towel) Frottieren nt; (polishing) Polieren nt; (with sandpaper) Schmirgeln nt. **(b)** (Art) see **brass** ~.

rubbish ['rʌbɪʃ] **1** n (waste material) Abfall m, Abfälle pl; (household ~, in factory also) Müll m; (on building site) Schutt m; (fig) (trashy goods, record etc) Mist m; (nonsense) Quatsch (inf), Blödsinn m. **household** ~ Hausmüll m; **garden** ~ Gartenabfälle pl; **most modern furniture is** ~ die meisten modernen Möbel sind nichts wert; **don't talk** ~! red keinen Quatsch! (inf); **he talked a lot** or **a load of** ~ er hat eine Menge Blödsinn verzapft (inf); **(what a lot of)** ~! (so ein) Quatsch! (inf); **this book is** ~ das Buch ist Quatsch (inf).
2 attr (inf) see **rubbishy**.

rubbish in cpds (esp Brit) Müll-; ~ **bin** n Mülleimer m; ~ **cart** n Müllwagen m; ~ **chute** n Müllschlucker m; ~ **collection** n Müllabfuhr f; ~ **dump** n Müllabladeplatz m; (in garden: also ~ **heap**) Abfallhaufen m; ~ **tip** n Müllabladeplatz m.

rubbishy ['rʌbɪʃɪ] adj (inf) (worthless) goods wertlos; (nonsensical) ideas blödsinnig. ~ **shoes** Schuhe, die nichts taugen; **this is** ~ **stuff** (article) das taugt nichts or ist Mist; (book, theory) das ist Quatsch (inf).

rubble ['rʌbl] n Trümmer pl; (smaller pieces) Schutt m; (Geol) Geröll m.

rub-down ['rʌb'daʊn] n **to give sb/sth a** ~ see **rub down**; **after a** ~ (horse) nachdem es abgerieben/gestriegelt war; (child) nachdem er/sie abfrottiert war.

rube [ru:b] n (US sl) (Bauern)tölpel m (inf).

rubella [ru:'belə] n Röteln pl.

Rubicon ['ru:bɪkən] n: **to cross the** ~ den Rubikon überschreiten.

rubicund ['ru:bɪkənd] adj rot.

ruble (US) see **rouble**.

rubric ['ru:brɪk] n (heading) Überschrift, Rubrik f; (Eccl) (liturgische) Anweisungen pl; (on exam paper) Prüfungsanweisungen pl. **under the** ~ ... in der Rubrik ...

ruby ['ru:bɪ] **1** n (stone) Rubin m; (colour: also ~ **red**) Rubinrot nt. **2** adj (~-coloured) wine, lips rubinrot; (made of rubies) necklace, ring Rubin-. ~ **red** rubinrot; ~ **wedding** (anniversary) vierzigster Hochzeitstag.

ruche [ru:ʃ] n Rüsche f.

ruched [ru:ʃt] adj Rüschen-, gerüscht.

ruching ['ru:ʃɪŋ] n Rüschen pl.

ruck[1] [rʌk] n (Racing) Pulk m. **the (common)** ~ (fig) die (breite) Masse; **to get out of the** ~ (fig) sich von der breiten Masse absetzen.

ruck[2] n (wrinkle) Falte f.

♦**ruck up 1** vt sep seam zusammenziehen; rug verschieben. **his shirt is all** ~**ed** ~ sein Hemd hat sich hochgeschoben. **2** vi (seam) sich zusammenziehen; (shirt etc) sich hochschieben; (rug) Falten schlagen.

rucksack ['rʌksæk] n (esp Brit) Rucksack m.

ruckus ['rʌkəs] n (inf) Krawall m.

ruction ['rʌkʃən] n (inf: usu pl) (dispute, scolding) Krach m no pl; (uproar also) Krawall m no pl. **there'll be** ~s **if you do that** es gibt Krach, wenn du das tust; **that'll cause** ~s das gibt Krach.

rudder ['rʌdə'] n (Naut, Aviat) Ruder nt.

rudderless ['rʌdəlɪs] adj ohne Ruder; (fig) führungslos.

ruddiness ['rʌdɪnɪs] n Röte f. **the** ~ **of his complexion** seine gesunde Gesichtsfarbe.

ruddy ['rʌdɪ] adj (+er) (a) complexion gesund, rot; sky, glow rötlich. **(b)** (Brit sl) verdammt (inf).

rude [ru:d] adj (+er) (a) (bad-mannered) unhöflich; (stronger) unverschämt; (rough, uncouth) grob. **it's** ~ **to stare** es gehört sich nicht, Leute anzustarren, man starrt andere Leute nicht an; **don't be so** ~! so was sagt man/tut man nicht!; **talk about** ~! der/die hat vielleicht einen Ton am Leib! (inf).
(b) (obscene) unanständig, unflätig (geh). **to make a** ~ **noise/smell** (euph) pup(s)en (inf).
(c) (harsh) shock bös, hart; blast, weather wüst, rauh; reminder unsanft; see **awakening**.
(d) (liter: primitive) primitiv; fare einfach, schlicht.

(e) (liter: vigorous) strength gewaltig. **he is in** ~ **health/strength** er strotzt (nur so) vor Gesundheit/Kraft.

rudely ['ru:dlɪ] adv see adj (a–d).

rudeness ['ru:dnɪs] n see adj (a) Unhöflichkeit f; Unverschämtheit f; Grobheit f. **(b)** Unanständigkeit, Unflätigkeit (geh) f. **(c)** Härte f; Wüstheit, Rauheit f. **(d)** Primitivität f; Einfachheit, Schlichtheit f. **(e)** gewaltige Größe.

rudiment ['ru:dɪmənt] n (a) ~s pl Anfangsgründe, Grundlagen pl. **(b)** (Biol) Rudiment nt.

rudimentary [,ru:dɪ'mentəri] adj (basic) knowledge, principles elementar; language, system rudimentär; (Biol) rudimentär. **a** ~ **sort of building** ein primitives Gebäude.

rue[1] [ru:] vt (liter) bereuen. **to** ~ **the day that** ... den Tag verwünschen, an dem ...

rue[2] n (Bot) Raute f.

rueful ['ru:fʊl] adj look reuig, reuevoll; situation beklagenswert.

ruefully ['ru:fəlɪ] adv reuevoll.

ruff[1] [rʌf] n (a) (on dress etc, of bird, animal) Halskrause f. **(b)** (bird) Kampfläufer m.

ruff[2] (Cards) **1** n Trumpfen nt. **2** vti (mit einem Trumpf) stechen.

ruffian ['rʌfɪən] n Rüpel, Grobian m; (violent) Schläger m. **you little** ~! du kleiner Halbstarker!

ruffianly ['rʌfɪənlɪ] adj (liter, old) grob, roh.

ruffle [rʌfl] **1** n (on dress) Rüsche f; (on water) Kräuseln nt no pl.
2 vt (a) (disturb) hair, feathers zerzausen; surface, water kräuseln; bedspread, clothes verkrumpeln (inf). **the bird** ~**d (up) its feathers** der Vogel plusterte sich auf.
(b) (fig) (upset, disturb) aus der Ruhe bringen; (annoy also) verärgern, aufbringen. **to** ~ **sb's calm/temper** jdn aus der Ruhe bringen/jdn wütend machen; **to get** ~**d** aus der Ruhe kommen.

rug [rʌg] n (a) Teppich m; (rectangular also) Läufer m; (valuable also) Brücke f; (bedside) (Bett)vorleger m. **fireside** ~ Kaminvorleger m. **(b)** (blanket) (Woll)decke f.

rugby ['rʌgbɪ] n (also ~ **football**) Rugby nt. ~ **league** Rugbyliga f; ~ **footballer, ~ player** Rugbyspieler m.

rugged ['rʌgɪd] adj rauh; country, landscape also wild; cliff, rocks, mountains zerklüftet; ground felsig; statue grob; face, features markig; determination wild; resistance verbissen. **a** ~ **test** eine harte Prüfung.

ruggedness ['rʌgɪdnɪs] n see adj Rauheit f; Wildheit f; Zerklüftetheit f; Felsigkeit f; Grobheit f; Markigkeit f; Wildheit f; Verbissenheit f.

rugger ['rʌgə'] n (Brit inf) see **rugby**.

ruin ['ru:ɪn] **1** n (a) no pl (of thing, person) Untergang m; (of event) Ende nt; (financial, social) Ruin m. **the palace was going to** ~ or **falling into** ~ der Palast verfiel (zur Ruine); ~ **stared him in the face** er stand vor dem (finanziellen/gesellschaftlichen) Ruin.
(b) (cause of ~) Ende nt; (of person also) Ruin m. **the** ~ **of my hopes** das Ende meiner Hoffnungen; **it will be the** ~ **of him** das wird ihn ruinieren; **you will be the** ~ **of me** du bist mein Ruin.
(c) (ruined building) Ruine f; (fig: person) Wrack nt. ~s (of building) Ruinen pl; (of reputation, beauty) Reste pl; (of hopes, career) Trümmer pl; **to be** or **lie in** ~s (lit) eine Ruine sein; (fig) zerstört sein; (life: financially, socially) ruiniert sein.
2 vt (destroy) building, hopes zerstören; reputation, health, sb's life also ruinieren; (financially, socially) person ruinieren; (spoil) clothes, event, enjoyment, child, horse verderben. **they** ~**ed my birthday party** sie haben (mir) die Geburtstagsfeier verdorben.

ruination [,ru:ɪ'neɪʃən] n see vt Zerstörung f; Ruinierung f; Verderben nt. **to be the** ~ **of sb** jds Ruin sein.

ruined ['ru:ɪnd] adj building in Ruinen pred, zerfallen; person ruiniert.

ruinous ['ru:ɪnəs] adj (financially) ruinös; price extrem.

ruinously ['ru:ɪnəslɪ] adv ~ **expensive** wahnsinnig teuer (inf).

rule [ru:l] **1** n (a) Regel f; (Sport, Cards also) Spielregel f; (Admin also) Vorschrift, Bestimmung f. **the** ~s **of the game** (lit, fig) die Spielregeln; **to play by the** ~s (lit, fig) die Spielregeln einhalten; **running is against the** ~s, **it's against the** ~s **to run** Rennen ist nicht erlaubt; ~s **and regulations** Regeln und Bestimmungen; **it's a** ~ **that** ... es ist Vorschrift, daß ...; **that's the** ~ **of the road** (Mot) das ist im Straßenverkehr üblich; **the Franciscan** ~ die Regel des Franziskanerordens; **to do sth by** ~ etw vorschriftsmäßig tun; ~ **of three** (Math) der Dreisatz; **by** ~ **of thumb** über den Daumen gepeilt; ~ **book** Regelheft nt; Vorschriftenbuch nt; **to throw the** ~ **book at sb** (fig) jdn wegen jeder Kleinigkeit drankriegen (inf).
(b) (custom) Regel f. **I make it a** ~ **to get up early** ich habe es mir zur Regel gemacht, früh aufzustehen; **to make tidiness a** or **one's** ~ sich (dat) Ordentlichkeit zur Regel machen; **as a (general)** ~ in der Regel; **ties are the** ~ **at the office** Krawatten sind im Büro die Regel; **violence is the** ~ **rather than the exception** Gewalt ist eher (die) Regel als (die) Ausnahme.
(c) (authority, reign) Herrschaft f; (period also) Regierungszeit f. **the** ~ **of law** die Rechtsstaatlichkeit.
(d) (for measuring) Metermaß nt, Maßstab m. **a foot** ~ (1 foot long) ein (30 cm langes) Lineal; (showing feet) ein Maßstab m mit Fußeinteilung; **folding** ~ Zollstock m; see **slide** ~.
2 vt (a) beherrschen, regieren; (individual also) herrschen über; (fig) passions, emotion beherrschen, zügeln; person beherrschen. **to** ~ **the roost** (fig) Herr im Haus sein (inf); **to be** ~**d by** jealousy/destiny von Eifersucht/vom Schicksal beherrscht werden; **if you would only be** ~**d by what I say** wenn du nur auf mich hören würdest; **I won't be** ~**d by what he wants** ich richte mich nicht nach seinen Wünschen.
(b) (Jur, Sport, Admin: give decision) entscheiden. **his question was** ~**d out of order** seine Frage wurde als unzulässig

abgewiesen; **the judge ~d the defence out of order** (*Jur*) der Richter rügte die Verteidigung.

(c) (*draw lines on*) paper linieren; (*draw*) *line, margin* ziehen. **~d paper** liniertes Papier.

3 *vi* (a) (*lit, fig: reign*) herrschen (*over* über +*acc*), regieren (*over acc*).

(b) (*Fin: prices*) notieren. **the prices ruling in London** die in London notierten Preise.

(c) (*Jur*) entscheiden (*against* gegen, *in favour of* für, *on* in +*dat*).

♦**rule off** *vt sep* einen Schlußstrich ziehen unter (+*acc*).

♦**rule out** *vt sep word, sentence* einen Strich ziehen durch; (*fig: exclude, dismiss*) ausschließen.

ruler ['ruːlə^r] *n* (a) (*for measuring*) Lineal *nt*. (b) (*sovereign*) Herrscher *m*.

ruling ['ruːlɪŋ] **1** *adj principle* leitend, Leit-; *factor* ausschlaggebend; *passion* vorherrschend; (*prevalent*) (vor)herrschend; (*Fin, St Ex*) *prices* notiert. **the ~ class** die herrschende Klasse; **the ~ party** (*Pol*) die Regierungspartei.

2 *n* (*Admin, Jur*) Entscheid *m*. **to receive/give a ~** einen Bescheid erhalten/einen Entscheid fällen.

rum¹ [rʌm] *n* Rum *m*. **~ toddy** Grog *m*.

rum² *adj* (*dated Brit inf*) komisch (*inf*); *person also* kauzig.

Rumania [ruːˈmeɪnɪə] *etc see* **Romania** *etc*.

rumba ['rʌmbə] *n* Rumba *m or f*.

rumble ['rʌmbl] **1** *n* (a) *see vi* Grollen *nt*; Donnern *nt*; Knacken *nt*; Rumpeln, Knurren *nt*; Rumpeln *nt* (*all no pl*). **his stomach gave a ~** sein Magen rumpelte *or* knurrte.

(b) (*sl: fight*) Schlägerei *f*.

2 *vi* (*thunder*) grollen; (*cannon*) donnern; (*pipes*) knacken; (*stomach*) rumpeln, knurren; (*train, truck*) rumpeln. **to ~ past/along/off** vorbei-/entlang-/davonrumpeln.

3 *vt* (*inf: see through*) swindle, trick, *person* durchschauen. **I soon ~d him** *or* **his game** *or* **what he was up to** ich bin ihm bald auf die Schliche gekommen (*inf*).

rumbling ['rʌmblɪŋ] *n see vi* Grollen *nt*; Donnern *nt*; Knacken *nt*; Rumpeln, Knurren *nt*; Rumpeln *nt* (*all no pl*).

rumbustious [rʌmˈbʌstʃəs] *adj* derb.

ruminant ['ruːmɪnənt] **1** *n* Wiederkäuer *m*. **2** *adj* (*lit*) wiederkäuend, Wiederkäuer-; (*fig*) grübelnd.

ruminate ['ruːmɪneɪt] **1** *vi* (*lit*) wiederkäuen; (*fig*) grübeln (*over, about, on* über +*acc*). **2** *vt* wiederkäuen.

rumination [ˌruːmɪˈneɪʃən] *n* (*lit*) Wiederkäuen *nt no pl*; (*fig*) Grübeln *nt no pl*.

ruminative *adj*, **~ly** *adv* ['ruːmɪnətɪv, -lɪ] (*fig*) grübelnd.

rummage ['rʌmɪdʒ] **1** *n* (a) **to have a good ~ in sth/around** etw gründlich durchstöbern *or* durchwühlen/gründlich herumstöbern *or* herumwühlen. (b) (*jumble*) Ramsch *m*. **~ sale** (*US*) Ramschverkauf *m*. **2** *vi* (*also ~ around*) herumstöbern, herumwühlen (*among, in* in +*dat, for* nach).

rummy ['rʌmɪ] *n* (*Cards*) Rommé *nt*.

rumour, (*US*) **rumor** ['ruːmə^r] **1** *n* Gerücht *nt*. **~ has it that** ... es geht das Gerücht um, daß ...; **as ~ has it** wie es Gerüchten zufolge heißt; **there is a ~ of war** es gehen Kriegsgerüchte um.

2 *vt* **it is ~ed that** ... es geht das Gerücht, daß ...; (*through gossip*) man munkelt, daß ...; **he is ~ed to be in London** Gerüchten zufolge ist er in London; **he is ~ed to be rich** er soll angeblich reich sein; **his ~ed resignation/death** das Gerücht von seiner Abdankung/seinem Tod.

rump [rʌmp] *n* (*of animal*) Hinterbacken *pl*; (*of fowl*) Bürzel *m*; (*inf: of person*) Hinterteil *nt*, Allerwerteste(r) *m* (*hum*). **~ (steak)** Rumpsteak *nt*; **The R~** (*Brit Hist*) das Rumpfparlament (*im 17. Jahrhundert in England*).

Rumpelstiltskin ['rʌmpəlˈstɪltskɪn] *n* Rumpelstilzchen *nt*.

rumple ['rʌmpl] *vt* (*also ~ up*) *clothes, paper* zerknittern; *hair* verwuscheln, zerzausen.

rumpus ['rʌmpəs] *n* (*inf*) (*noise*) Spektakel (*inf*), Krach *m*; (*quarrel*) Krach *m* (*inf*). **to kick up a ~, to make a ~** (*noise*) einen Spektakel *or* Heidenlärm machen (*inf*); (*complain*) Krach schlagen (*inf*); **to have a ~ with sb** (*inf*) sich mit jdm in die Haare geraten; **~ room** (*US*) Spielzimmer *nt*.

run [rʌn] (*vb: pret* **ran**, *ptp* **~**) **1** *n* (a) (*act of running, Cricket, Baseball*) Lauf *m*. **to go for a 2-km ~** einen 2 km-Lauf machen; **his ~ is slower than my walk** ich kann schneller gehen, als er laufen kann; **let the dog have a ~** laß den Hund laufen; **he came in at a ~** er kam hereingelaufen; **he took the fence at a ~** nahm die Hürde im Lauf; **to break into a ~** zu laufen *or* rennen anfangen; **to take a ~ at a hurdle** auf eine Hürde loslaufen; **to make a ~ for it** weglaufen, wegrennen; **he made a ~ for the door** er lief *or* rannte zur Tür; **on the ~** (*from the police etc*) auf der Flucht; **we have the enemy on the ~** der Feind ist auf der Flucht; **to keep the enemy on the ~** den Feind weiter zur Flucht zwingen; **the house and family keep you on the ~** Haus und Familie halten einen ganz schön auf Trab; **she has so much to do she's always on the ~** (*fig*) sie hat so viel zu tun, daß sie immer auf Trab ist; **we've given him a good ~ for his money, he has had a good ~ for his money** (*inf*) er hat was für sein Geld bekommen; (*competition*) er hat einen ordentlichen Kampf bekommen; (*pleasure*) er kann sich nicht beklagen; **my old car has given me a good ~ for my money** (*inf*) mein altes Auto hat mir gute Dienste geleistet; **the theory had a good ~ for its money** (*inf*) die Theorie hat sich lange gehalten.

(b) (*journey: in vehicle*) Fahrt *f*; (*outing also*) Ausflug *m*. **to go for a ~ in the car** eine Fahrt/einen Ausflug im Auto machen; **to take a ~ up to London** eine Fahrt nach London machen; **I'll give you a ~ up to town** ich fahre Sie in die Stadt.

(c) (*distance travelled*) (*in bus, tram, boat, car*) Fahrt *f*; (*in plane*) Flug *m*; (*route*) Strecke *f*. **it's a 30-minute ~** es ist eine Fahrt von 30 Minuten; **the boat no longer does that ~** das Schiff fährt die Strecke nicht mehr; **on the outward/inward ~** auf der Hinfahrt/Rückfahrt; **the ferries on**

the Dover-Calais ~ die Fähren der Linie Dover-Calais; **the ships on the China ~** die Schiffe der China-Linie.

(d) (*Aviat*) Flug *m*. **approach ~** Anflug *m*; **bombing ~** Bombenzielanflug *m*; **the plane made a low ~ over the village** das Flugzeug flog im Tiefflug über das Dorf.

(e) **to have the ~ of a place** einen Ort zur freien Verfügung haben; **to give sb the ~ of one's house** jdm sein Haus überlassen.

(f) **in the short/long ~** fürs nächste/auf die Dauer; *plan etc* **auf kurze/lange Sicht**.

(g) (*series*) Folge, Reihe, Serie *f*; (*Cards*) Sequenz *f*; (*Theat*) Spielzeit *f*; (*of film*) Laufzeit *f*. **a ~ on the red** (*Roulette*) eine Serie von roten Zahlen; **the ~ of the cards** die Verteilung der Karten; **this fashion is having a long ~** diese Mode hat sich lange gehalten; **when the London ~ was over** (*Theat*) als das Stück in London abgelaufen war; **the play had a long ~** das Stück lief sehr lange; **a two-year ~** in office eine zweijährige Amtszeit; **a ~ of luck/of bad luck** eine Glücks-/Pechsträhne; **a ~ of misfortunes** eine Serie von Mißgeschicken.

(h) (*rush, great demand*) **on** Ansturm *m auf* (+*acc*); (*St Ex, Fin also*) Run *m auf* (+*acc*); **there has been a ~ on sugar** (*Comm*) es gab einen Ansturm auf Zucker.

(i) (*average type*) **the common ~ of mankind** der Durchschnittsmensch; **the usual ~ of students** die gewöhnliche Sorte Studenten.

(j) (*trend: of market, opinion*) Tendenz *f*; (*course: of events*) Lauf *m*. **the ordinary ~ of things** der normale Gang der Dinge.

(k) **the ~ of the grain** die Maserung; (*of paper*) die Faserrichtung.

(l) (*track for sledging, skiing etc*) Bahn *f*. **ski ~** Abfahrt(strecke) *f*.

(m) (*animal enclosure*) Gehege *nt*; (*chicken*) Hühnerhof *m*.

(n) (*in stocking*) Laufmasche *f*.

(o) (*Mus*) Lauf *m*.

(p) **the ~s** (*inf: diarrhoea*) der flotte Otto (*inf*), die Renneritis (*hum inf*).

(q) (*Typ: printing ~*) Auflage *f*.

2 *vi* (a) laufen, rennen; (*in race*) laufen. **to ~ past/off** vorbei-/davonlaufen *or* -rennen; **she came ~ning out** sie kam herausgelaufen *or* -gerannt; **to ~ down a slope** einen Abhang hinunterlaufen *or* -rennen; **he is always ~ning about the streets** er treibt sich immer auf der Straße herum; **~! lauf!**; **walk don't ~** du sollst gehen, nicht rennen!; **to ~ for the bus** zum Bus laufen *or* rennen; **she ran to meet him** sie lief *or* rannte ihm entgegen; **she ran to help him** sie kam ihm schnell zu Hilfe; **he used to ~ for his school** er lief früher für seine Schule; **to ~ in the 100 metres** die 100 Meter laufen; **eleven ran** (*Horseracing*) elf (Pferde) waren am Start; **X, Y, Z also ran** (*Horseracing*) X, Y, Z waren ebenfalls am Start; **this horse will ~ in the National** das Pferd startet im National; *see* **also-ran**.

(b) (*flee*) davonlaufen, weglaufen, wegrennen. **to ~ for one's life** um sein Leben laufen *or* rennen; **~ for it!** lauft *or* rennt, was ihr könnt!; **to ~ to earth** (*fox, criminal*) sich verkriechen; **go on then, ~ to mummy!** na, lauf doch schon zu deiner Mutti!

(c) (*fig*) (*news, rumour etc*) umgehen. **the news ran like wildfire through the crowd** die Nachricht ging wie ein Lauffeuer durch die Menge; **a rumour ran through the school** ein Gerücht ging in der Schule um; **the order ran down the column** der Befehl wurde von Mund zu Mund weitergegeben; **he ran down the list** er ging die Liste durch; **laughter ran round the room** einer nach dem anderen fing an zu lachen; **a shiver ran down her spine** ein Schauer lief ihr über den Rücken; **a ripple of fear ran through the town** ein Schaudern durchlief die Stadt; **his eyes/fingers ran over the sculpture** seine Augen/Finger glitten über die Plastik; **the idea ran through my head that** ... der Gedanke *or* es ging mir durch den Kopf, daß ...

(d) (*story, words*) gehen, lauten; (*tune*) gehen. **how does the last sentence ~?** wie lautet der letzte Satz?; **so the story ~s** die Geschichte geht so; **the wording ran as follows** es hieß *or* lautete folgendermaßen; **the conversation ran on that very subject** das Gespräch drehte sich um eben das Thema; **my thoughts ran on my sister** ich dachte an meine Schwester.

(e) (*stand as candidate*) kandidieren, sich aufstellen lassen. **to ~ for President** *or* **for the Presidency** für die Präsidentschaft kandidieren, sich als Präsidentschaftskandidat aufstellen lassen; **to ~ against sb** jds Gegenkandidat sein.

(f) (*become*) **to ~ dry** (*river*) austrocknen; (*pen*) leer werden; (*resources*) ausgehen; **he ran dry of ideas** ihm gingen die Ideen aus; **supplies are ~ning short** *or* **low** die Vorräte werden knapp; *see* **seed, short, wild**.

(g) (*roll, slide: things*) (*drawer, curtains, rope*) laufen, gleiten; (*vehicle*) rollen. **to ~ on a rod/on rollers/in a groove** auf einer Stange/auf Rädern/in einer Rille laufen; **it ~s on wheels** es läuft *or* fährt auf Rädern; **money just ~s through his fingers** das Geld zerrinnt ihm einfach zwischen den Fingern.

(h) (*flow*) (*water, tears, tap, nose, butter, cheese*) laufen; (*river, electric current*) fließen; (*eyes*) tränen; (*sore, abscess*) eitern; (*paint, colour*) zerfließen, ineinanderfließen; (*colour, dye: in washing*) färben; (*ink*) fließen. **my shirt has ~** mein Hemd hat gefärbt; **my ice cream is ~ning** mein Eis schmilzt; **this pen doesn't ~ very well** dieser Kuli schreibt nicht sehr gut; **where the river ~s into the sea** wo der Fluß ins Meer mündet; **the street ~s into the square** die Straße mündet auf den Platz; **interest rates are ~ning at record levels/15%** die Zinssätze sind auf Rekordhöhe/stehen auf 15%; **inflation is ~ning at 20%** die Inflationsrate beträgt 20%; **a heavy sea was ~ning** die See ging hoch; **where the tide is ~ning strongly** wo die Gezeiten sehr stark sind; **let the tap/water ~ hot** laß das Wasser laufen, bis es heiß kommt; **your bath is ~ning** Ihr Badewasser läuft ein; **the floor was ~ning with water** der Fußboden schwamm vor Wasser; **the walls were ~ning with moisture** die Wände tropften vor Feuchtigkeit; ~ning with sweat schweißüberströmt; his blood ran cold das Blut gefror ihm in den Adern.

(i) (*extend in time*) (*play, film, contract, Jur: sentence*) laufen; (*Fin: interest rate*) gelten. **the contract has 10 months to ~** der Vertrag läuft noch 10 Monate; **the expenditure ~s into thousands of pounds** die Ausgaben gehen in die Tausende (von Pfund); **the book has ~ into three editions** das Buch hat schon drei Auflagen erreicht; **the poem ~s (in)to several hundred lines** das Gedicht geht über mehrere hundert Zeilen.

(j) to ~ to (*afford*) **I can't ~ to a new car** ich kann mir kein neues Auto leisten; **the funds won't ~ to a party** die Finanzen reichen nicht für eine Party.

(k) (*Naut*) **to ~ before the wind** vor dem Wind segeln; **to ~ onto the rocks** (auf die Felsen) auflaufen; **to ~ into port** in den Hafen einlaufen.

(l) (*drive*) fahren.

(m) (*provide service: bus, train etc*) fahren, verkehren. **this train ~s between London and Manchester** dieser Zug verkehrt zwischen London und Manchester; **the buses ~ once an hour** die Busse fahren *or* verkehren stündlich; **the train doesn't ~ on Sundays** der Zug fährt sonntags nicht; **no trains ~ there any more** dorthin gibt es keine Zugverbindung mehr.

(n) (*function*) (*machine, wheel*) laufen; (*factory*) arbeiten; (*fig: ceremony*) laufen. **when the central heating is ~ning** wenn die Zentralheizung angeschaltet ist; **the car is ~ning smoothly** der Wagen läuft ohne Schwierigkeiten; **my sewing machine doesn't ~ very well** meine Nähmaschine funktioniert nicht besonders gut; **you mustn't leave the engine ~ning** Sie dürfen den Motor nicht laufen lassen; **this model ~s on diesel** dieses Auto fährt mit Diesel; **the radio ~s off the mains/off batteries** das Radio läuft auf Netz/Batterie; **things are ~ning smoothly/badly for them** bei ihnen läuft zur Zeit alles wunschgemäß/alles schief; **the principle on which democracy ~s** das Prinzip, auf dem die Demokratie basiert; **all planes/trains are ~ning late** die Flugzeuge/Züge haben Verspätung; **the project is ~ning late** *or* **to schedule** das Projekt hat sich verzögert/geht ganz nach Plan voran.

(o) (*extend in space*) (*road*) gehen, führen; (*mountains*) sich ziehen, sich erstrecken; (*river*) fließen. **the main road ~s north and south** die Hauptstraße geht *or* führt nach Norden und Süden; **he has a scar ~ning across his chest** eine Narbe zieht sich quer über seine Brust; **a wall ~s round the garden** um den Garten zieht sich *or* läuft eine Mauer; **the river ~s for 300 km** der Fluß ist 300 km lang; **this theme ~s right through his work** dieses Thema zieht sich durch sein ganzes Werk.

(p) to ~ in the family in der Familie liegen.

(q) (*stocking*) eine Laufmasche bekommen; (*stitch*) laufen.

3 *vt* **(a)** *distance* laufen, rennen; *race* laufen. **he ~s 3 km every day** er läuft jeden Tag 3 km; **the first race will be ~ at 2 o'clock** das erste Rennen findet um 2 Uhr statt; **to ~ errands/messages** Botengänge machen; **to ~ the streets** (*child, dog*) sich auf der Straße herumtreiben; **to ~ a blockade** eine Blockade brechen; **they ran the rapids** sie meisterten die Stromschnellen; **to ~ sb a close second** (*Sport*) nur knapp von jdm auf den zweiten Platz verwiesen werden; **to ~ sb close** (*Sport, fig*) nur knapp von jdm geschlagen werden.

(b) (*fig*) **to ~ its/their course** (*events, disease*) seinen/ihren Lauf nehmen; **to ~ a temperature** *or* **a fever** Fieber haben; **he was ~ning a high temperature** er hatte Fieber; **see gauntlet.**

(c) (*chase, hunt*) *fox, deer* treiben; (*make run*) *person, animal* jagen. **to ~ sb off the house** sie jagten ihn aus dem Haus; **to ~ sb off his feet** (*inf*) jdn ständig in Trab halten (*inf*); **she is absolutely ~ off her feet** (*inf*) sie ist ständig in Trab (*inf*); **to ~ oneself out of breath** außer Atem kommen; **that will ~ him into trouble** das wird ihn in Schwierigkeiten bringen; **that will ~ you into a lot of expense** das wird Sie eine ganze Menge *or* schöne Stange (*inf*) kosten; **to ~ sb into debt** jdn in Schulden stürzen; **see earth, ground¹.**

(d) *candidate* aufstellen; (*Sport*) *horse* laufen lassen.

(e) (*cause to flow*) **to ~ water into a bath** Wasser in die Badewanne einlaufen lassen; **I'll ~ you a bath** ich lasse Ihnen ein Bad einlaufen; **he ~s his words together** bei ihm fließen alle Wörter ineinander über, er schnuddelt (*dial*).

(f) (*transport*) *person, thing* fahren, bringen; (*drive*) *vehicle* fahren. **he ran her home** er brachte *or* fuhr sie nach Hause; **I'll ~ your luggage to the station** ich fahre Ihr Gepäck zum Bahnhof; **he ran the car into the garage/a tree** er fuhr das Auto in die Garage/gegen einen Baum.

(g) *buses, trains* unterhalten; *extra buses, trains* einsetzen. **this company ~s a bus service** diese Firma unterhält einen Busdienst; **they ~ trains to London every hour** es besteht stündlicher Zugverkehr nach London; **how many machines does this factory ~?** wie viele Maschinen laufen in dieser Fabrik?

(h) (*operate, cause to function*) *machine, engine* betreiben (*on* mit); (*person*) bedienen. **to ~ a radio off the mains** ein Radio auf Netz laufen lassen.

(i) I can't afford to ~ a car ich kann es mir nicht leisten, ein Auto zu unterhalten; **he ~s a Rolls** er fährt einen Rolls Royce; **this car is cheap to ~** dieses Auto ist billig im Unterhalt.

(j) (*conduct*) *experiment, test* durchführen; (*manage*) *business, hotel* führen, leiten; *shop* führen; *mine* betreiben; *school, organization, newspaper* leiten; (*organize*) *course of study, competition* veranstalten, durchführen; (*be in charge of*) *course, competition, department, project* leiten. **a well-~ hotel** ein gutgeführtes Hotel; **he ~s a small hotel/shop in the village** er hat ein kleines Hotel/Geschäft im Dorf; **to ~ a house** einen Haushalt führen; **a house which is easy to ~** ein Haus, das leicht in Schuß gehalten werden kann; **who will ~ your house now?** wer führt Ihnen nun den Haushalt?; **I want to ~ my own life** ich möchte mein eigenes Leben leben; **she's**

the one who really ~s everything sie ist diejenige, die den Laden schmeißt (*inf*); **I'm ~ning this show!** (*inf*) ich bestimme, was gemacht wird.

(k) (*smuggle*) *guns etc* schmuggeln.

(l) (*move, put*) **to ~ one's fingers over the piano keys** die Finger über die (Klavier)tasten gleiten lassen; **to ~ one's finger down a list** mit dem Finger eine Liste durchgehen; **to ~ one's fingers/a comb through one's hair** sich (*dat*) mit den Fingern/einem Kamm durch die Haare fahren; **to ~ one's eye over a page** eine Seite überfliegen; **he ran the vacuum cleaner over the carpet** er ging mit dem Staubsauger über den Teppich; **she ran her pencil through the word** sie strich das Wort durch.

(m) (*take, lead etc*) *rope, road* führen; *piece of elastic, line, ditch* ziehen; *pipe, wires* (ver)legen; (*above ground*) führen. **to ~ a rope round a tree** ein Seil um einen Baum legen.

(n) (*thrust*) **he ran a sword into his side** er stieß ihm das Schwert in die Seite, er durchbohrte ihn mit dem Schwert.

(o) (*issue*) (*Press*) *article, series* bringen; (*Film also*) zeigen, spielen; (*Comm*) verkaufen.

♦ **run about** *or* **around** *vi* (*lit, fig*) herumlaufen *or* -rennen. **to ~ ~ with sb** sich mit jdm herumtreiben; **the children were ~ning ~ all over the house** die Kinder liefen *or* rannten im ganzen Haus herum; **I'm not going to ~ ~ after you cleaning up** ich putze doch nicht dauernd hinter dir her.

♦ **run across 1** *vi* **(a)** (*lit*) hinüber-/herüberlaufen *or* -rennen. **(b)** (*go to see*) kurz rüberlaufen *or* -gehen (*to* zu). **2** *vi* +*prep obj* (*meet*) *person* zufällig treffen; (*find*) *object, reference* stoßen auf (+*acc*).

♦ **run after 1** *vi* **to come ~ning ~** hinterherlaufen *or* -rennen. **2** *vi* +*prep obj* nachlaufen *or* -rennen (+*dat*). **I'm not going to spend my days ~ning ~ you!** (*fig*) ich denke gar nicht daran, nur immer für dich dazusein!

♦ **run along** *vi* laufen, rennen; (*go away*) gehen. **~ ~!** nun geht mal schön!

♦ **run around** *vi* **see run about.**

♦ **run at** *vi* +*prep obj* zu- *or* loslaufen auf (+*acc*); (*attack*) losstürzen auf (+*acc*).

♦ **run away 1** *vi* **(a)** (*child, animal*) weglaufen, wegrennen; (*person*) weglaufen; (*horse*) durchgehen. **to ~ ~ from home** von zu Hause weglaufen; **don't ~ ~, I need your advice** (*inf*) gehen Sie nicht weg, ich möchte Sie um Rat fragen; **~ ~ and play!** geht (mal schön) spielen! **(b)** (*water*) auslaufen. **2** *vt sep* *water* auslaufen lassen.

♦ **run away with** *vi* +*prep obj* (*use up*) *funds, money, resources* verschlucken (*inf*), verbrauchen; (*steal*) *money, object* durchgehen *or* durchbrennen mit (*inf*); (*Sport etc: win easily*) *race, prize* spielend gewinnen. **don't ~ ~ ~ the idea that ...** (*fig*) kommen Sie nur nicht auf den Gedanken, daß ...; **he lets his imagination/enthusiasm ~ ~ ~ him** seine Phantasie/seine Begeisterung geht leicht mit ihm durch.

♦ **run back 1** *vi* (*lit*) zurücklaufen, zurückrennen. **let's just ~ ~ over what we've agreed** gehen wir noch einmal durch, was wir vereinbart haben; **she'll come ~ning ~** sie wird reumütig zurückkommen. **2** *vt sep* **(a)** *person* zurückfahren *or* -bringen. **(b)** (*rewind*) *tape, film* zurückspulen.

♦ **run down 1** *vi* **(a)** (*lit: person*) hinunter-/herunterlaufen *or* -rennen. **(b)** (*watch, clock*) ablaufen; (*battery*) leer werden. **to let stocks ~ ~** das Lager leer werden lassen; (*deliberately*) das Lager abbauen. **2** *vt sep* **(a)** (*knock down*) umfahren; (*run over*) überfahren. **(b)** (*Naut*) *ship* rammen; (*in battle*) versenken. **(c)** (*limit, reduce*) *factory, shop* (allmählich) auflösen; *department, stocks, staff* abbauen; *battery* zu stark belasten. **(d)** (*disparage*) schlechtmachen, runtermachen (*inf*). **(e)** (*pursue and capture*) *stag* zur Strecke bringen; *criminal also* zu fassen kriegen; *person* ausfindig machen.

♦ **run in 1** *vi* hinein-/hereinlaufen *or* -rennen. **2** *vt sep* **(a)** *car* einfahren. **"~ning ~, please pass"** (*Brit Mot*) „bitte überholen, Wagen wird eingefahren". **(b)** (*inf: arrest*) sich (*dat*) schnappen.

♦ **run into** *vi* +*prep obj* (*meet*) zufällig treffen; (*collide with*) rennen/fahren gegen. **to ~ ~ difficulties/trouble/problems** Schwierigkeiten/Ärger bekommen/auf Probleme stoßen; **to ~ ~ danger/debt** in Gefahr/Schulden geraten; **see also run 2 (h).**

♦ **run off 1** *vi* **see run away 1 (a).** **2** *vt sep* **(a)** *water* ablassen. **(b)** *poem, letter, article* herunterschreiben, hinhauen (*inf*). **(c)** (*reproduce*) *copy* abziehen. **(d)** (*Sport*) **to ~ ~ the heats** die Ausscheidungskämpfe durchführen. **(e)** (*excess weight*) sich (*dat*) ablaufen *or* abrennen. **(f)** (*on machine*) *a few dresses, a sample* schnell machen.

♦ **run on 1** *vi* **(a)** (*lit*) weiterlaufen, weiterrennen. **you ~ ~, I'll catch up** geh schon mal voraus, ich komme nach. **(b)** (*fig: in speaking*) **he does ~ ~ so!** er redet wie ein Buch!; **it ran ~ for four hours** das zog sich über vier Stunden hin. **(c)** (*handwriting, letters*) verbunden sein; (*words*) fortlaufend geschrieben sein; (*line of type*) ohne Absatz gedruckt sein. **~ ~** (*instruction*) ohne Absatz! **(d)** (*time*) weitergehen. **2** *vt sep letters* verbinden; *words* fortlaufend schreiben; *line of type* ohne Absatz drucken.

♦ **run out 1** *vi* **(a)** (*person*) hinaus-/herauslaufen *or* -rennen; (*rope, chain*) ablaufen; (*liquid*) herauslaufen; (*through leak*) auslaufen. **the pier ~s ~ into the sea** der Landungssteg geht ins Meer hinaus. **(b)** (*come to an end*) (*lease, contract, period of time*) ablaufen; (*money, supplies*) ausgehen, zu Ende gehen. **my patience is ~ning ~** mir geht langsam die Geduld aus.

2 vt sep (a) rope, chain abwickeln.
(b) (Cricket) ausschlagen (während der Schlagmann seinen Lauf macht).

♦**run out of** vi + prep obj he ran ~ ~ supplies/money/patience/time ihm gingen die Vorräte/ging das Geld/die Geduld aus/er hatte keine Zeit mehr; we're ~ning ~ ~ time wir haben nicht mehr viel Zeit.

♦**run over 1** vi (a) (to neighbour etc) kurz hinüberlaufen or hinübergehen or rübergehen (inf).
(b) (overflow) liquid, container) überlaufen.
(c) (Rad, TV etc) the play ran ~ by 10 minutes das Stück hatte 10 Minuten Überlänge; we're ~ning ~ ~ wir überziehen.
2 vi + prep obj story, part in play, details durchgehen; text, notes durchsehen. I'll ~ ~ your part with you ich gehe Ihre Rolle kurz mit Ihnen durch.
3 vt sep (in vehicle) überfahren.

♦**run round** vi kurz vorbeigehen. to ~ ~ and see sb kurz bei jdm vorbeigehen; see also run about.

♦**run through 1** vi (lit) durchlaufen. **2** vi + prep obj (a) (use up) money, fortune durchbringen. (b) (rehearse) piece of music, play durchspielen; ceremony also, part durchgehen. (c) see run over 2. **3** vt sep to ~ sb ~ (with a sword) jdn (mit einem Schwert) durchbohren.

♦**run up 1** vi (lit) (up mountain, upstairs) hinauf-/herauflaufen (towards sb/sth); hin-/herlaufen or -rennen (to zu). to ~ ~ against difficulties auf Schwierigkeiten stoßen.
2 vt sep (a) flag hissen, hochziehen. they ran the flag ~ (the mast) sie hißten die Fahne.
(b) (incur) machen. to ~ ~ one's account sein Kreditkonto belasten; to ~ ~ a debt Schulden machen.
(c) (sew quickly) schnell zusammennähen.

run: ~about n (car) kleiner Flitzer (inf); (boat) kleines Motorboot; ~around n (inf): to give sb the ~around jdn an der Nase herumführen (inf); to get the ~around (from sb) (von jdm) an der Nase herumgeführt werden (inf); ~away 1 n Ausreißer(in f) m; **2** adj slave entlaufen; person, couple, horse durchgebrannt (inf), ausgerissen; car, railway truck der/die/das sich selbständig gemacht hat; inflation unkontrollierbar; the ~away child der kleine Ausreißer; they planned a ~away wedding sie beschlossen, wegzulaufen und zu heiraten; he had a ~away victory er hatte einen sehr leichten Sieg; ~down 1 n (a) (of factory, shop) (allmähliche) Auflösung; (of department, stock, personnel) Abbau m; (b) (inf: summary) Zusammenfassung f, Bericht m; to give sb a ~down on sth jdn über etw (acc) informieren, jdm einen Bericht über etw (acc) geben; **2** adj (dilapidated) heruntergekommen; (tired) abgespannt; battery leer; to be (feeling) ~down abgespannt sein.

rune [ruːn] n Rune f.
rung¹ [rʌŋ] ptp of ring².
rung² n (of ladder) Sprosse f; (of chair) Querstab m.
runic [ˈruːnɪk] adj runisch, Runen-.
runner [ˈrʌnəʳ] n (a) (athlete) Läufer(in f) m; (horse) Rennpferd nt; (messenger) Bote, Laufbursche m; (smuggler) Schmuggler m. (Bow Street) R~s (Brit Hist) = Büttel pl; it's a good ~, this car (inf) das Auto läuft wirklich einwandfrei.
(b) (on sledge, skate) Kufe f; (for curtain) Vorhangröllchen nt; (for drawer, machine part) Laufschiene f.
(c) (carpet, for table) Läufer m.
(d) (Bot) Ausläufer m. ~ bean (Brit) Stangenbohne f.
runner-up [ˈrʌnərˈʌp] n Zweite(r), Zweitplazierte(r) mf. the runners-up die weiteren Plätze; (in competition) die weiteren Gewinner.
running [ˈrʌnɪŋ] 1 n (a) Laufen, Rennen nt. ~ style, style of ~ Laufstil m; to make the ~ (lit, fig) das Rennen machen; to be in the ~ (for sth) im Rennen (für etw) liegen; to be out of the ~ aus dem Rennen sein; to take up the ~ (lit, fig) sich an die Spitze setzen.
(b) (functioning: of machine, vehicle) Laufen nt.
(c) (management) see run 3 (j) Führung, Leitung f; Führung f; Betrieb m; Leitung f; Veranstaltung, Durchführung f; Leitung f.
(d) (smuggling) Schmuggel m.
2 adj (a) ~ jump Sprung m mit Anlauf; to take a ~ jump at sth mit Anlauf über etw springen; go and take a ~ jump (inf) du kannst mich gern haben (inf); ~ kick Schuß m aus vollem Lauf; ~ commentary (Rad, TV) fortlaufender Kommentar; we don't need a ~ commentary (inf) wir brauchen keinen Kommentar; ~ account (Fin) laufendes Konto; see also cpds.
(b) (after n) 4 days ~ 4 Tage hintereinander or nacheinander.
(c) (flowing) water, stream, handwriting fließend; tap, nose laufend; eyes tränend; ~ water (in every room) fließend(es) Wasser in allen Zimmern; ~ sore (Med) eiternde Wunde; (fig) Eiterbeule f; ~ cold schwerer Schnupfen.
(d) (current) prices momentan; costs laufend.
running: ~ battle n (Mil) Gefecht nt, bei dem eine Seite immer weiter zurückgedrängt wird; (fig) Kleinkrieg m; to fight a ~ battle (fig) einen Kleinkrieg führen; ~board n Trittbrett nt; ~ costs npl Betriebskosten pl; (of car) Unterhaltskosten pl; ~head n (Typ) Kolumnentitel m; ~knot n Schlaufenknoten m; ~mate n (US Pol) Kandidat m für die Vizepräsidentschaft; ~ order n: in ~ order betriebsbereit; ~ stitch n (Sew) Vorstich, Reihstich m; ~ title n see ~ head; ~ track n Aschenbahn f.
runny [ˈrʌnɪ] adj (+er) flüssig; nose laufend; eyes wässerig, tränend. I've got a ~ nose mir läuft die Nase, meine Nase läuft.
run: ~-off n (Sport) Entscheidungslauf m, Stechen nt; ~-of-the-mill adj durchschnittlich, gewöhnlich; theme, novel Feld-Wald-Wiesen- (inf); ~-on n fortlaufender Eintrag; ~-on line/entry fortlaufende Zeile/fortlaufender Eintrag; ~-proof adj tights etc laufmaschenfest, laufmaschensicher.
runt [rʌnt] n kleinstes Ferkel (eines/des Wurfes); (pej) Wicht m; (despicable) Fiesling m (inf).

run: ~-through n Durchgehen nt; let's have a final ~-through gehen wir das noch einmal durch; to give sth a ~-through etw durchgehen; ~-up n (Sport) Anlauf m; (fig) Vorbereitungszeit f; ~way n (Aviat) Start- und Landebahn f, Runway m.
rupee [ruːˈpiː] n Rupie f.
rupture [ˈrʌptʃəʳ] 1 n (lit, fig) Bruch m; (Pol: of relations) Abbruch m. **2** vt brechen. to ~ oneself (inf) sich (dat) einen Bruch heben (inf). **3** vi brechen.
rural [ˈrʊərəl] adj ländlich; population, life also Land-. ~ dean (Brit Rel) Dekan, der mehrere Landgemeinden betreut; ~ district (Brit Admin) Landkreis m; ~ depopulation Abwanderung f der Landbevölkerung, Landflucht f; ~ deprivation Strukturschwäche f in ländlichen Gebieten.
ruse [ruːz] n List f.
rush¹ [rʌʃ] 1 n (a) (rapid movement) (of crowd) Andrang m, Gedränge nt; (of air) Stoß m; (Mil: attack) Sturm m. he was caught in the ~ for the door die zur Tür drängende Menge riß ihn mit; it got lost in the ~ das ging im Gedränge verloren; they made a ~ for the door sie drängten zur Tür; to make a ~ at losstürzen auf (+acc); there was a ~ for the empty seats alles stürzte sich auf die leeren Sitze; there's been a ~ on these goods diese Waren sind rasend weggegangen; we have a ~ on in the office just now bei uns im Büro herrscht zur Zeit Hochbetrieb; the Christmas ~ der Weihnachtsbetrieb; we've had a ~ of orders wir hatten eine Flut von Aufträgen; there was a ~ of water Wasser strömte or schoß herein/heraus etc; water streamed out in a ~ das Wasser schoß in einem Schwall heraus; a ~ of blood to the head Blutandrang m im Kopf; see gold ~.
(b) (hurry) Eile f; (stronger) Hetze, Hast f. the ~ of city life die Hetze des Stadtlebens; to be in a ~ in Eile sein; I had a ~ to get here on time ich mußte ganz schön hetzen, um rechtzeitig hier zu sein; I did it in a ~ ich habe es sehr schnell or hastig gemacht; what's (all) the ~? wozu die Eile/Hetzerei?; is there any ~ for this? eilt das?; it all happened in such a ~ das ging alles so plötzlich.
(c) ~es pl (Film) erste Kopie.
2 vi (hurry) eilen; (stronger) hetzen, hasten; (run) stürzen; (wind) brausen; (water) schießen, stürzen; (make ~ing noise) rauschen. they ~ed to help her sie eilten ihr zu Hilfe; I ~ed to her side ich eilte an ihre Seite; I'm ~ing to finish it ich beeile mich, es fertigzumachen; don't ~, take your time überstürzen Sie nichts, lassen Sie sich Zeit; the train went ~ing into the tunnel der Zug brauste in den Tunnel; you shouldn't just go ~ing into things Sie sollten die Dinge nicht so überstürzen; to ~ through book hastig lesen; meal hastig essen; museum, town hetzen durch; work hastig erledigen; to ~ past (person) vorbeistürzen; (vehicle) vorbeischießen; to ~ in/out/back etc hinein-/hinaus-/zurückstürzen or -stürmen; the ambulance ~ed to the scene der Krankenwagen raste zur Unfallstelle; to ~ to the attack auf ihn/sie etc losgehen; to ~ into print vorzeitig veröffentlichen; the blood ~ed to his face das Blut schoß ihm ins Gesicht; memories ~ed into his mind Erinnerungen schossen ihm durch den Kopf.
3 vt (a) to ~ sb to hospital jdn schnellstens ins Krankenhaus bringen; they ~ed more troops to the front sie schickten eilends mehr Truppen an die Front; they ~ed him out (of the room) sie brachten ihn eilends aus dem Zimmer; they ~ed the bill through Parliament sie peitschten die Gesetzesvorlage durch das Parlament; to ~ a book into print ein Buch eilends in Druck geben.
(b) (force to hurry) hetzen, drängen. don't ~ me! hetz mich nicht; he won't be ~ed er läßt sich nicht drängen or treiben; to be ~ed off one's feet dauernd auf Trab sein; to ~ sb off his feet jdn dauernd auf Trab halten; to ~ sb into a decision jdn zu einer hastigen Entscheidung treiben; to ~ sb into doing sth jdn dazu treiben, etw überstürzt zu tun.
(c) (charge at) stürmen; fence zustürmen auf (+acc). the mob ~ed the line of policemen der Mob stürmte auf den Polizeikordon zu; to ~ one's fences (fig) die Sache überstürzen.
(d) (do hurriedly) job, task hastig machen, schnell machen; (do badly) schludern bei (pej). you can't ~ this sort of work für solche Arbeit muß man sich (dat) Zeit lassen.
(e) (sl: charge exorbitantly) schröpfen (inf). what were you ~ed for it? wieviel haben sie dir dafür abgeknöpft? (inf).
♦**rush about** or **around** vi herumhasten or -hetzen.
♦**rush at** vi + prep obj (a) losstürzen auf (+acc), sich stürzen auf (+acc). (b) don't ~ ~ the job, take it slowly überstürzen Sie die Arbeit nicht, machen Sie langsam; he tends to ~ ~ things er neigt dazu, die Dinge überstürzt zu machen.
♦**rush down** vi hinunter-/heruntereilen; (very fast) hinunter-/herunterstürzen; (stream) hinunter-/herunterstürzen.
♦**rush out 1** vi hinaus-/herauseilen; (very fast) hinaus-/herausstürzen. he ~ed ~ and bought one er kaufte sofort eines. **2** vt sep order eilends wegschicken; troops, supplies eilends hintransportieren.
♦**rush through** vt sep order durchjagen; goods, supplies eilends durchschleusen. they ~ed medical supplies ~ to him sie schickten eilends Medikamente zu ihm.
♦**rush up 1** vi (lit) hinauf-/heraufeilen; (very fast) hinauf-/heraufstürzen. **2** vt sep help, reinforcements eilends schicken.
rush² n (Bot) Binse f. in the ~es im Schilf.
rush: ~-hour(s pl) n Hauptverkehrszeit(en pl), Stoßzeit(en pl), Rush-hour f; ~-hour traffic Stoßverkehr m; ~ job n eiliger Auftrag; (pej: bad work) Schluderarbeit f (inf); can you do a ~ job for me? können Sie das ganz schnell für mich machen?; ~light n aus Binsen und Talg hergestellte Kerze; ~ mat, ~ matting n Binsenmatte f; ~ order n (Comm) Eilauftrag m.
rusk [rʌsk] n Zwieback m.
russet [ˈrʌsɪt] 1 n (a) (colour) gelbliches Rotbraun. (b) (apple) Boskop m. **2** adj gelblich rotbraun.
Russia [ˈrʌʃə] n Rußland nt.

Russian ['rʌʃən] **1** *adj* russisch. ~ **leather** Juchten *nt*; ~ **roulette** russisches Roulette; ~ **salad** russischer Salat. **2** *n* **(a)** Russe *m*, Russin *f*. **(b)** (*language*) Russisch *nt*.
Russky ['rʌskɪ] *n* (*pej*) Iwan *m*. **the Russkies** der Iwan.
rust [rʌst] **1** *n* Rost *m*; (*Bot*) Brand *m*. ~**-proof/-resistant** rostfrei/nicht rostend; **covered in** ~ völlig verrostet. **2** *adj* (*also* ~**-coloured**) rostfarben. **3** *vt* (*lit*) rosten lassen. **4** *vi* rosten; (*talent*) verkümmern; (*brain, language*) (ein)rosten.
♦**rust in** *vi* (*screw*) einrosten.
♦**rust over** *vi* verrosten. **to be** ~**ed** ~ verrostet sein.
♦**rust through 1** *vi* durchrosten. **2** *vt sep* durchrosten lassen.
♦**rust up** *vi* festrosten.
rustic ['rʌstɪk] **1** *n* Bauer *m*. **2** *adj* bäuerlich; *furniture, style* rustikal; *manners* bäurisch (*pej*).
rusticate ['rʌstɪkeɪt] **1** *vi* (*form, liter*) (*go to country*) aufs Land ziehen; (*stay in country*) auf dem Land leben; (*become rustic*) bäurisch werden. **2** *vt* **(a)** (*form, liter*) (*send to country*) aufs Land schicken; (*make rustic*) bäurisch machen. **(b)** (*Brit Univ*) vorübergehend von der Universität verweisen.
rustiness ['rʌstɪnɪs] *n* Rostigkeit *f*; (*fig*) eingerostete Kenntnisse (*of* in +*dat*).
rustle ['rʌsl] **1** *n* Rascheln *nt*; (*of foliage*) Rauschen *nt*.
2 *vi* (*leaves, silk, papers*) rascheln; (*foliage, skirts*) rauschen. **the wind** ~**d through the leaves** der Wind rauschte in den Blättern; (*on the ground*) der Wind raschelte mit den Blättern.
3 *vt* **(a)** *paper, skirt, leaves on ground etc* rascheln mit; *leaves on tree* rauschen in (+*dat*).

(b) (*US: steal*) *cattle* klauen (*inf*).
♦**rustle up** *vt sep* (*inf*) *meal* improvisieren (*inf*). **can you ~ ~ a cup of coffee?** können Sie eine Tasse Kaffee auftreiben?
rustler ['rʌslər] *n* (*US*) (*cattle-thief*) Viehdieb *m*; (*inf: energetic person*) Geschäftlhuber *m* (*dial inf*).
rusty ['rʌstɪ] *adj* (+*er*) (*lit*) rostig; (*fig*) *mind, maths* eingerostet; *talent* verkümmert. **I'm a bit** ~ ich bin etwas aus der Übung.
rut[1] [rʌt] (*Zool*) **1** *n* Brunft, Brunst *f*. **2** *vi* brunften, brunsten. ~**ting call** Brunftschrei *m*; ~**ting season** Brunftzeit *f*.
rut[2] **1** *n* (*in track, path*) Spur, Furche *f*; (*fig: routine*) Trott *m* (*inf*). **to be in a** ~ (*fig*) im Trott sein (*inf*); **to get into/out of a** ~ (*fig*) (*person*) in einen Trott geraten (*inf*)/aus dem Trott herauskommen (*inf*); (*mind*) sich in einem eingefahrenen Gleis bewegen/aus dem eingefahrenen Gleis herauskommen.
2 *vt* furchen.
rutabaga [ˌruːtəˈbeɪgə] *n* (*US*) Steckrübe *f*.
ruthless ['ruːθlɪs] *adj* *person* rücksichtslos; *cuts, treatment, self-analysis* schonungslos; *irony, sarcasm* unbarmherzig, schonungslos. **you'll have to be** ~ man muß hart sein.
ruthlessly ['ruːθlɪslɪ] *adv see adj.*
ruthlessness ['ruːθlɪsnɪs] *n see adj* Rücksichtslosigkeit *f*; Schonungslosigkeit *f*; Unbarmherzigkeit, Schonungslosigkeit *f*; Härte *f*.
RV *abbr of* **Revised Version.**
rye [raɪ] *n* (*grain*) Roggen *m*; (*US inf*) Roggenwhiskey, Rye-(whiskey) *m*; (*bread*) Roggenbrot *nt*.
rye: ~ **bread** *n* Roggenbrot *nt*; ~ **whisk(e)y** *n* Roggen- *or* Ryewhiskey *m*.

S

S, s [es] *n* S, s *nt*.
S *abbr of* **(a)** south S. **(b)** Saint St. **(c)** small.
s (*Brit old*) *abbr of* shilling.
's (a) he's *etc* = he is/has; what's = what is/has/does? **(b)** (*genitive*) John's book Johns Buch; my brother's car das Auto meines Bruders; at the Browns'/butcher's bei den Browns/beim Fleischer. **(c)** let's = let us.
SA *abbr of* **(a)** South Africa. **(b)** South America. **(c)** South Australia. **(d)** Salvation Army.
Sabbatarian [ˌsæbəˈtɛərɪən] *n* strenger Befürworter des Sonntagsgebots *or* (*Jewish*) Sabbatgebots.
Sabbath ['sæbəθ] *n* Sabbat *m*; *see* witch.
sabbatical [səˈbætɪkəl] **1** *adj* **(a)** (*Rel*) Sabbat-. **(b)** (*Univ*) *year, term* Forschungs-. **he is on** ~ **leave** er hat akademischen Urlaub *or* Forschungsurlaub. **2** *n* (*Univ*) akademischer Urlaub, Forschungsurlaub *m*. **to have a/be on** ~ Forschungsurlaub *or* akademischen Urlaub haben.
saber *n* (*US*) *see* **sabre.**
Sabine ['sæbaɪn] **1** *adj* sabinisch. **2** *n* Sabiner(in *f*) *m*.
sable ['seɪbl] **1** *n* Zobel *m*; (*fur*) Zobelfell *nt or* -pelz *m*; (*liter: colour*) Schwarz *nt*. **2** *adj* Zobel-; (*liter: black*) schwarz.
sabot ['sæbəʊ] *n* Holzschuh *m*.
sabotage ['sæbətɑːʒ] **1** *n* Sabotage *f*. **2** *vt* (*lit, fig*) sabotieren.
saboteur [ˌsæbəˈtɜːr] *n* Saboteur *m*.
sabre, (*US*) **saber** ['seɪbər] *n* Säbel *m*.
sabre: ~**-rattler** *n* Säbelraßler *m*; ~**-rattling** *n* Säbelrasseln *nt*; ~**-tooth**, ~**-toothed tiger** *n* Säbelzahntiger *m*.
sac [sæk] *n* (*Anat*) Sack *m*; (*pollen* ~) Staubbeutel *m*.
saccharin(e) ['sækərɪn] *n* Saccharin *nt*.
saccharine ['sækəriːn] *adj* Saccharin-; (*fig liter*) zuckersüß.
sacerdotal [ˌsæsəˈdəʊtl] *adj* Priester-; *robes, dignity also* priesterlich.
sachet ['sæʃeɪ] *n* Beutel *m*; (*of powder*) Päckchen *nt*; (*of shampoo, cream*) Briefchen *nt*; (*lavender*) Kissen *nt*.
sack[1] [sæk] **1** *n* **(a)** Sack *m*. **2** ~**s of coal** 2 Säcke *or* Sack Kohlen; **to buy sth by the** ~ etw sackweise *or* in Säcken kaufen.
(b) (*inf: dismissal*) Entlassung *f*, Rausschmiß *m* (*inf*). **to get the** ~ rausgeschmissen werden (*inf*), rausfliegen (*inf*); **to give sb the** ~ jdn rausschmeißen (*inf*); **it's the** ~ **for him** er wird rausgeschmissen (*inf*), er fliegt raus (*inf*).
(c) (*sl: bed*) **to hit the** ~ sich in die Falle *or* Klappe hauen (*sl*).
2 *vt* **(a)** (*put in* ~s) einsacken.
(b) (*inf: dismiss*) rausschmeißen (*inf*), entlassen.
sack[2] **1** *n* (*pillage*) Plünderung *f*. **2** *vt* plündern.
sack[3] *n* (*old*) Sherry *m*.
sackbut ['sækbʌt] *n* (*Hist*) Posaune *f*.
sackcloth ['sækklɒθ] *n* Sackleinen *nt*. **in** ~ **and ashes** in Sack und Asche.
sackful ['sækfʊl] *n* Sack *m*. **two** ~**s of potatoes** zwei Sack Kartoffeln.
sacking ['sækɪŋ] *n* **(a)** (*material*) Sackleinen *nt*. **(b)** (*inf: dismissal*) Entlassung *f*.
sack-race ['sækreɪs] *n* Sackhüpfen *nt*.

sacral ['seɪkrəl] *adj* **(a)** (*Rel*) sakral. **(b)** (*Anat*) Kreuzbein-.
sacrament ['sækrəmənt] *n* Sakrament *nt*. **the** (Blessed *or* Holy) **S~** das heilige Sakrament; **to receive the the Holy S~** die heilige Kommunion *or* (*Protestant*) das heilige Abendmahl empfangen; **the last** ~**s** die Sterbesakramente *pl*.
sacramental [ˌsækrəˈmentl] *adj* *vows, rites, significance* sakramental; *wine, bread, rites* Opfer-.
sacred ['seɪkrɪd] *adj* heilig; *music, poetry* geistlich; *building* sakral. ~ **to the memory of** ... zum Gedenken *or* Andenken an (+*acc*) ...; **a statue** ~ **to Venus** eine der Venus geweihte Statue; **these memories are** ~ **to me** diese Erinnerungen sind mir heilig; **is nothing** ~? (*inf*) ist denn nichts mehr heilig?; ~ **cow** (*lit, fig*) heilige Kuh.
sacrifice ['sækrɪfaɪs] **1** *n* (*lit, fig*) Opfer *nt*; (*thing sacrificed also*) Opfergabe *f*. **to make a** ~ **of sb/sth** jdn/etw opfern *or* zum Opfer bringen; **to make** ~**s** (*lit, fig*) Opfer bringen; **what a** ~ (**to make**)! welch ein Opfer!; **the** ~ **of quality to speed** wenn Qualität der Geschwindigkeit geopfert wird *or* zum Opfer fällt; **to sell sth at a** ~ (*inf*) etw mit Verlust verkaufen.
2 *vt* opfern (*sth to sb* jdm etw).
sacrificial [ˌsækrɪˈfɪʃəl] *adj* Opfer-.
sacrilege ['sækrɪlɪdʒ] *n* Sakrileg *nt*; (*fig also*) Frevel *m*. **that would be** ~ das wäre ein Sakrileg *nt or* Frevel *m*.
sacrilegious [ˌsækrɪˈlɪdʒəs] *adj* (*lit*) gotteslästerlich, sakrilegisch (*geh*); (*fig*) frevelhaft, frevlerisch.
sacristan ['sækrɪstən] *n* Sakristan *m*.
sacristy ['sækrɪstɪ] *n* Sakristei *f*.
sacrosanct ['sækrəʊˌsæŋkt] *adj* (*lit, fig*) sakrosankt.
sacrum ['sækrəm] *n* Kreuzbein *nt*.
sad [sæd] *adj* (+*er*) traurig; *loss* schmerzlich; *colour* trist; *disappointment* schlimm; *result also, mistake, luck* bedauerlich. **to feel** ~ traurig sein; **to be** ~ **at heart** (*liter*) zutiefst betrübt sein (*geh*); **he left a** ~**der and wiser man** er ging betrübt und geläutert weg; **the** ~ **death of our father** der schmerzliche Verlust unseres Vaters; **how** ~ **for you!** wie schrecklich für Sie!, wie traurig!; **it's pretty** ~ **stuff for a writer of his ability** für einen Schriftsteller seines Formats ist das traurig.
sadden ['sædn] *vt* betrüben.
saddle ['sædl] **1** *n* (*also of hill*) Sattel *m*; (*of meat*) Rücken *m*. **to be in the** ~ (*lit*) im Sattel sein; (*fig*) im Sattel sitzen. **2** *vt* **(a)** *horse* satteln. **(b)** (*inf*) **to** ~ **sb/oneself with sth** jdm/sich jdn/etw aufhalsen (*inf*); **to be/have been** ~**d with sb/sth** jdn/etw auf dem *or* am Hals haben (*inf*).
♦**saddle up** *vti sep* aufsatteln.
saddle: ~**-backed** *adj hill* sattelförmig; *pig, gull* mit sattelförmiger Markierung am Rücken; ~**bag** *n* Satteltasche *f*; ~**cloth** *n* Satteldecke *f*; ~**-horse** *n* Reitpferd *nt*.
saddler ['sædlər] *n* Sattler *m*.
saddle roof *n* Satteldach *nt*.
saddlery ['sædlərɪ] *n* Sattlerei *f*; (*articles*) Sattelzeug *nt*.
saddle: ~ **shoes** *npl* (*US*) Sportschuhe *pl* aus hellem Leder mit andersfarbigem Einsatz; ~ **soap** *n* Seife *f* für die Behandlung von Sätteln; ~ **sore** *n* wundgescheuerte Stelle; ~**-sore** *adj*

person wundgeritten; *horse* wundgescheuert; to get ~-sore sich wund reiten/scheuern.

Sadducee ['sædʒusiː] *n* Sadduzäer *m*.

sadism ['seɪdɪzəm] *n* Sadismus *m*.

sadist ['seɪdɪst] *n* Sadist(in *f*) *m*.

sadistic *adj*, ~ally *adv* [sə'dɪstɪk, -əlɪ] sadistisch.

sadly ['sædlɪ] *adv* (a) traurig; (*unfortunately*) traurigerweise. (b) (*regrettably*) bedauerlich. ~ enough he has ... bedauerlicherweise hat er ...; he is ~ lacking in any sense of humour ihm fehlt jeglicher Humor; the house had been ~ neglected es war traurig, wie vernachlässigt das Haus war.

sadness ['sædnɪs] *n* Traurigkeit *f*. our ~ at his death unsere Trauer über seinen Tod.

sadomasochism [ˌseɪdəʊˌmæsəʊ'kɪzəm] *n* Sadomasochismus *m*.

sae *abbr of* **stamped addressed envelope.**

safari [sə'fɑːrɪ] *n* Safari *f*. to be/go on ~ eine Safari machen, auf Safari sein/gehen; to go on ~ to Kenya nach Kenia auf Safari fahren; ~ **jacket** Safarijacke *f*; ~ **park** Safaripark *m*.

safe[1] [seɪf] *n* (*for valuables*) Safe *m or nt*, Panzerschrank, Tresor *m*; (*for meat*) Fliegenschrank *m*.

safe[2] 1 *adj* (+er) (a) (*not in danger*) sicher; (*out of danger*) in Sicherheit; (*not injured*) unverletzt. to be ~ from sb/sth vor jdm/etw sicher sein; no girl is ~ with him bei ihm ist kein Mädchen sicher; to keep sth ~ etw sicher aufbewahren; all the passengers/climbers are ~ alle Passagiere/Bergsteiger sind in Sicherheit *or* (*not injured*) wohlbehalten *or* unverletzt; you're not ~ without a seat-belt es ist gefährlich *or* nicht sicher, ohne Gurt zu fahren; ~ journey! gute Fahrt/Reise!; journey home! komm gut nach Hause!; we've found him — is he ~?! wir haben ihn gefunden! — ist ihm etwas passiert?; thank God you're ~ Gott sei Dank ist dir nichts passiert; he was ~ at home all the time *or* saß die ganze Zeit wohlbehalten zu Hause; ~ and sound gesund und wohlbehalten; the patient is ~ now der Patient ist jetzt außer Gefahr; my life's not ~ here ich bin hier meines Lebens nicht sicher; your reputation is ~ Ihr Ruf ist nicht in Gefahr; the secret is ~ with me bei mir ist das Geheimnis sicher; the thieves are now ~ in prison die Diebe sind jetzt in sicherem Gewahrsam.

(b) (*not likely to cause harm, not dangerous, not presenting risks*) ungefährlich; (*stable, secure*) *building, roof etc* sicher. not ~ gefährlich; this car is not ~ to drive das Auto ist nicht verkehrssicher; she is not ~ on the roads sie ist eine Gefahr im Straßenverkehr; the roof doesn't look ~ to me das Dach sieht mir nicht sehr sicher aus *or* sieht ziemlich gefährlich aus; is 120 km/h ~ on this road? kann man auf dieser Straße gefahrlos 120 km/h fahren?; is this beach ~ for bathing? kann man an diesem Strand gefahrlos *or* ohne Gefahr baden?; it is ~ to leave it open/tell him man kann es unbesorgt *or* ohne weiteres auflassen/es ihm unbesorgt *or* ohne weiteres erzählen; is it ~ to touch that/drive so fast/light a fire? ist es auch nicht gefährlich, das anzufassen/so schnell zu fahren/ein Feuer anzumachen?; the dog is ~ with children der Hund tut Kindern nichts.

(c) (*reliable*) *job, contraceptive, driver* sicher; *mountain guide, method also, player* zuverlässig, verläßlich. ~ period sichere *or* ungefährliche Zeit.

(d) (*not likely to be/go wrong*) *investment, theory* sicher; *policy* vorsichtig, risikolos; *estimate* realistisch. it's a ~ assumption that ... man kann mit ziemlicher Sicherheit annehmen, daß ...; it's a ~ guess es ist so gut wie sicher; they appointed a ~ man as headmaster sie bestimmten einen gemäßigten Mann als Rektor; he plays a ~ game (of tennis) er spielt (Tennis) auf Sicherheit; I think it's ~ to say ... ich glaube, man kann wohl *or* ruhig sagen ...; is it ~ to generalize/draw that conclusion? kann man das ohne weiteres verallgemeinern/kann man diesen Schluß aus ihm ohne weiteres ziehen?; do you feel ~ just taking on three extra staff? haben Sie keine Bedenken, wenn Sie nur drei extra Leute einstellen?; just to be ~ *or* on the ~ side um ganz sicher zu sein, um sicherzugehen.

(e) (*certain*) a ~ seat (*Pol*) ein sicherer Sitz; he is ~ to win/get the job er wird sicher gewinnen/die Stelle sicher bekommen.

2 *adv* to play (it) ~ (*inf*) auf Nummer Sicher gehen (*inf*).

safe: ~-**blower**, ~-**breaker** *n* Schränker (*sl*), Safeknacker (*inf*) *m*; ~-**conduct** *n* freies *or* sicheres Geleit; (*document*) Geleitbrief *m*; ~-**cracker** *n* (*inf*) Schränker (*sl*), Safeknacker (*inf*) *m*; ~-**deposit** *n* Tresorraum *m*; ~-**deposit box** *n* Banksafe *m or nt*; ~-**guard** 1 *n* Schutz *m*; as a ~**guard against** zum Schutz gegen; double-check these figures as a ~**guard** überprüfen Sie diese Zahlen zur Sicherheit noch einmal; 2 *vt* schützen (*against* vor +*dat*); *interests* wahrnehmen; 3 *vi* to ~**guard against** sth sich gegen etw absichern; ~-**keeping** *n* sichere Verwahrung; to give sb sth for ~-**keeping** jdm etw zur (sicheren) Aufbewahrung geben; ~-**light** *n* (*Phot*) Dunkelkammerlicht *nt*.

safely ['seɪflɪ] *adv* (*unharmed*) *arrive, get home* wohlbehalten, heil; (*without problems also*) sicher, gut; (*without running risks*) unbesorgt, gefahrlos; *drive* vorsichtig; (*solidly, firmly*) sicher, fest; (*not dangerously*) ungefährlich. we can ~ estimate that ... wir können mit einiger Sicherheit annehmen, daß ...; I think I can ~ say/claim/assume ... ich glaube, ich kann wohl *or* ruhig sagen/behaupten/annehmen ...; I got ~ through the first interview ich bin gut *or* heil durch das erste Interview gekommen; money ~ deposited in the bank sicher auf der Bank deponiertes Geld; ~ invested sicher angelegt; to put sth away ~ etw an einem sicheren Ort verwahren; he put it ~ away in a drawer er verwahrte es sicher in einer Schublade; put it ~ out of the reach of the children bringen Sie es vor den Kindern in Sicherheit; he's ~ locked away in prison er sitzt hinter Schloß und Riegel; once the children are ~ tucked up in bed wenn die Kinder erst mal im Bett sind; he was ~ tucked up in bed er lag wohlvermummt im Bett.

safeness ['seɪfnɪs] *n* Sicherheit *f*.

safety ['seɪftɪ] *n* Sicherheit *f*. in a place of ~ an einem sicheren Ort; for ~'s sake aus Sicherheitsgründen; with complete ~ vollkommen sicher; I think I can say with complete ~ that ... ich glaube, ich kann mit Sicherheit behaupten, daß ...; to play for ~ (*Sport*) auf Sicherheit spielen; (*fig*) sichergehen; (there's) ~ in numbers zu mehreren ist man sicherer; to reach ~ in Sicherheit gelangen; when we reached the ~ of the opposite bank als wir sicher das andere Ufer erreicht hatten; to leap to ~ sich in Sicherheit bringen; to seek ~ in flight sein Heil in der Flucht suchen.

safety: ~ **belt** *n* Sicherheitsgurt *m*; ~ **bicycle** *n* (*old*) Sicherheitsrad (*old*), Niederrad (*old*) *nt*; ~ **catch** *n* (*on gun*) (Abzugs)sicherung *f*, Sicherungsbügel *m*; was the ~ **catch on/off?** war das Gewehr gesichert/entsichert?; ~ **chain** *n* Sicherheitskette *f*; ~ **curtain** *n* (*Theat*) eiserner Vorhang; ~ **first** *n* to believe in ~ **first** der Sicherheit den Vorrang geben; ~ **first** campaign Unfallverhütungskampagne *f*; "~ **first**" (*as slogan*) „Sicherheit geht vor"; ~ **glass** *n* Sicherheitsglas *nt*; ~ **harness** *n* Sicherheitsgurt *m*; ~ **lamp** *n* Grubenlampe *f*; ~ **match** *n* Sicherheitsholz *nt or* -zünder *m*; ~ **measure** *n* Sicherheitsmaßnahme *f*; ~ **net** *n* Sprung- *or* Sicherheitsnetz *nt*; ~ **pin** *n* Sicherheitsnadel *f*; ~ **precaution** *n* Sicherheitsvorkehrung *f*; ~ **razor** *n* Rasierapparat, Naßrasierer (*inf*) *m*; ~ **valve** *n* Sicherheitsventil *nt*; (*fig*) Ventil *nt*.

saffron ['sæfrən] 1 *n* Safran *m*; (*colour*) Safrangelb *nt*. 2 *adj* Safran-; (*in colour*) safrangelb.

sag [sæg] 1 *n* there's a bit of a ~ in the bed/ceiling das Bett/die Decke hängt etwas durch; if the ~ in the roof gets any worse ... wenn das Dach noch weiter durchhängt ...; the ~ of her shoulders ihre herabhängenden Schultern; as a result of the recent ~ in prices als Folge des jüngsten Preisabfalls.

2 *vi* absacken; (*in the middle*) durchhängen; (*shoulders*) herabhängen; (*breasts*) schlaff herunterhängen; (*production, rate*) zurückgehen; (*price, spirit*) sinken; (*conversation*) abflauen. don't ~, stand up straight steh nicht so schlaff da (*inf*), stell dich gerade hin; a drink will revive his ~ging spirits ein Drink wird seine Stimmung wieder heben.

saga ['sɑːgə] *n* Saga *f*; (*novel also*) Generationsroman *m*; (*fig*) Geschichte, Story (*sl*) *f*.

sagacious *adj*, ~ly *adv* [sə'geɪʃəs, -lɪ] weise, klug.

sagacity [sə'gæsɪtɪ] *n* Weisheit, Klugheit *f*.

sage[1] [seɪdʒ] 1 *n* Weise(r) *m*. 2 *adj* (+er) weise.

sage[2] *n* (*Bot*) Salbei *m*.

sage-green ['seɪdʒ'griːn] 1 *n* Graugrün *nt*. 2 *adj* graugrün.

sagely ['seɪdʒlɪ] *adv* weise.

sageness ['seɪdʒnɪs] *n* Weisheit *f*.

Sagittarian [ˌsædʒɪ'tɛərɪən] 1 *n* Schütze *m*. 2 *adj* des Schützen.

Sagittarius [ˌsædʒɪ'tɛərɪəs] *n* Schütze *m*.

sago ['seɪgəʊ] *n* Sago *m*.

Sahara [sə'hɑːrə] *n* Sahara *f*. the ~ **Desert** die (Wüste) Sahara.

sahib ['sɑːhɪb] *n* Sahib *m*.

said [sed] 1 *pret, ptp of* **say.** 2 *adj* (*form*) besagt.

sail [seɪl] 1 *n* (a) Segel *nt*; (*of windmill*) Flügel *m*. under ~ mit aufgezogenen Segeln; in *or* under full ~ mit vollen Segeln; with all ~s set mit gesetzten Segeln; to make ~ (*hoist*) Segel setzen; to set *or* make ~ (*for ...*) los- *or* abfahren (*nach ...*); (*with* sailing boat) absegeln (*nach ...*).

(b) (*trip*) Fahrt *f*. it's (a) 3 days' ~ from here von hier aus fährt *or* (*in yacht*) segelt man 3 Tage; to go for a ~ segeln gehen; to take sb for a ~ mit jdm segeln gehen; have you ever had a ~ in his yacht? sind Sie schon einmal auf seiner Jacht gefahren *or* gesegelt?

(c) (*boat*) (Segel)schiff *nt*; (*small*) (Segel)boot *nt*. 20 ~ 20 Schiffe/Boote; there was not a ~ in sight kein einziges Schiff war zu sehen.

2 *vt ship* segeln mit; *liner etc* steuern. they ~ed the ship to Cadiz sie segelten nach Cadiz; he ~s his own yacht er hat eine eigene Jacht; to ~ the seas die Meere befahren.

3 *vi* (a) (*Naut*) fahren; (*with yacht*) segeln. are you flying? — no, ~ing fliegen Sie? — nein, ich fahre mit dem Schiff; I went ~ing for a week ich ging eine Woche segeln; to ~ round the world um die Welt segeln, die Erde umsegeln; to ~ round a headland eine Landzunge umfahren/umsegeln.

(b) (*leave*) (*for* nach) abfahren; (*yacht, in yacht*) absegeln. passengers ~ing for New York Passagiere nach New York.

(c) (*fig: glider, swan etc*) gleiten; (*moon, clouds*) ziehen; (*ball, object*) fliegen. she ~ed past/out of the room/into the room sie rauschte vorbei/aus dem Zimmer/sie kam ins Zimmer gerauscht (*all inf*); she ~ed through all her exams sie schaffte alle Prüfungen spielend *or* mit Leichtigkeit; all the heat just ~s out of the window (*inf*) die ganze Wärme verpufft (durchs Fenster) (*inf*); the holidays just ~ed by (*inf*) die Ferien vergingen wie im Flug.

♦ **sail in** *vi* (*inf: enter argument*) sich einschalten.

♦ **sail into** *vi* +*prep obj* (*inf*) *person* anfahren; *discussion* sich einschalten in (+*acc*).

sail: ~ **boat** *n* (*US*) Segelboot *nt*; ~**cloth** *n* Segeltuch *nt*; ~ **fish** *n* Fächerfisch *m*.

sailing ['seɪlɪŋ] *n* (a) Segeln *nt*; (*as sport also*) Segelsport *m*. (b) (*departure*) when is the next ~ for Arran? wann fährt das nächste Schiff nach Arran?; *see* **plain.**

sailing: ~ **boat** *n* (*Brit*) Segelboot *nt*; ~ **date** *n* Abfahrtstermin *m*; ~ **school** *n* Segelschule *f*; ~ **ship** *n* Segelschiff *nt*; ~ **time** *n* Abfahrtszeit *f*; ~ **vessel** *n* Segelschiff *nt*.

sail maker *n* Segelmacher *m*.

sailor ['seɪlə'] *n* (a) Seemann *m*; (*in navy*) Matrose *m*; (*sportsman*) Segler(in *f*) *m*. ~ **suit** Matrosenanzug *m*; hello ~ (*hum*) hallo Süßer. (b) to be a bad/good ~ (*get seasick*) nicht seefest/seefest sein.

sailplane ['seɪlpleɪn] *n* Segelflugzeug *nt*.

saint [seɪnt] *n* (a) Heilige(r) *mf*.

(b) (*before name abbr to* St [snt]) **St John** der heilige Johannes, Sankt Johannes, St. Johannes; **St Francis** der heilige Franziskus; **St Mark's (Church)** die Markuskirche.

(c) (*fig*) Heilige(r) *mf.* **she is a ~ to put up with that** sie muß ja eine Engelsgeduld haben, daß sie sich das gefallen läßt.

sainted ['seɪntɪd] *adj* heiliggesprochen. **my ~ aunt!** (*inf*) heiliger Strohsack! (*inf*), heiliger Bimbam! (*inf*).

sainthood ['seɪnthʊd] *n* Heiligkeit *f.* **martyrs who were elevated to ~** Märtyrer, die in die Gemeinschaft der Heiligen aufgenommen wurden.

saintliness ['seɪntlɪnɪs] *n* Heiligmäßigkeit *f*; (*fig pej: of person*) frömmlerisches Wesen. **the ~ of his smile** sein lammfrommes Lächeln.

saintly ['seɪntlɪ] *adj* (*+er*) heiligmäßig; (*fig pej*) *person* frömmlerisch; *smile* lammfromm. **he stood there with a ~ look on his face** (*lit*) er hatte ein verklärten Gesichtsausdruck; (*iro*) er sah aus, als ob er kein Wässerchen trüben könnte.

saint's day *n* Heiligenfest *nt*, Tag *m* des/der heiligen ... **when is your ~?** wann ist Ihr Namenstag?

saith [seθ] (*old*) = **says**.

sake¹ [seɪk] *n* **for the ~ of ...** um (*+gen*) ... willen; **for my ~** meinetwegen; (*to please me*) mir zuliebe; **for your own ~** dir selbst zuliebe; **for your family's ~** um Ihrer Familie willen, Ihrer Familie wegen; **for heaven's or Christ's ~!** (*inf*) um Gottes willen!; **for heaven's or Christ's ~** shut up (*inf*) nun halt doch endlich die Klappe (*inf*); **for old times' ~** in Erinnerung an alte Zeiten; **for the ~ of those who ...** für diejenigen, die ...; **for whose ~ is the writer writing, his own or the public's?** für wen schreibt der Schriftsteller, (für) sich selbst oder den Leser?; **I'd do anything for your ~** für dich tue ich alles; (*to keep you happy*) dir zuliebe tue ich alles; **I did it just for the ~ of having a new experience** ich habe es nur getan, um eine neue Erfahrung zu machen; **and all for the ~ of a few pounds** und alles wegen ein paar Pfund; **to talk for talking's ~** reden, nur damit etwas gesagt wird; **I do the job for its own ~** ich mache die Arbeit um ihrer selbst willen *or* ihrer selbst wegen.

sake², saki ['sɑːkɪ] *n* (*drink*) Sake *m.*

sal *abbr of* **salary** Geh.

salaam [sə'lɑːm] **1** *n, interj* Salem *m.* **2** *vi* mit Salem begrüßen.

salable *adj* (*US*) **see saleable.**

salacious [sə'leɪʃəs] *adj* schlüpfrig; *picture* aufreizend; *chuckle* anzüglich.

salaciousness [sə'leɪʃəsnɪs] *n see adj* Schlüpfrigkeit *f*; aufreizende Darstellung; Anzüglichkeit *f.*

salad ['sæləd] *n* Salat *m.*

salad: **~ bowl** *n* Salatschüssel *f*; **~ cream** *n* ≈ Mayonnaise *f*; **~ days** *npl* unschuldige Jugendtage *pl*; **in the ~ days of his youth** als er noch jung und unschuldig war; **~ dressing** *n* Salatsoße *f*; **lettuce with ~ dressing** angemachter Salat; **~ oil** *n* Salatöl *m.*

salamander ['sælə,mændə^r] *n* Salamander *m*; (*Myth*) Feuergeist *m.*

salami [sə'lɑːmɪ] *n* Salami *f.*

sal ammoniac [,sælə'məʊnɪæk] *n* Ammoniumsalz *nt*, Salmiak *m.*

salaried ['sælərɪd] *adj* **~ post** Angestelltenposten *m*; **~ employee** Gehaltsempfänger *m*; **~ staff** Gehaltsempfänger *pl.*

salary ['sælərɪ] *n* Gehalt *nt.* **~ earner** Gehaltsempfänger *m*; **~ increase** Gehaltserhöhung *f*; **he earns a good ~** er hat ein gutes Gehalt; **what is his ~?** wie hoch ist sein Gehalt?

sale [seɪl] *n* **(a)** (*selling*) Verkauf *m.* **for ~** zu verkaufen; **to put sth up for ~** etw zum Verkauf anbieten; **is it up for ~?** steht es zum Verkauf?; **not for ~** nicht verkäuflich; **going cheap for a quick ~** umständehalber billig abzugeben; **to be on ~** verkauft werden; **on ~ at all bookshops** in allen Buchhandlungen erhältlich; **there is a very slow ~ in these goods** diese Waren verkaufen sich schlecht; **on ~ or return, on a ~ or return basis** auf Kommission(sbasis).

(b) (*instance*) Geschäft *nt*; (*of insurance, bulk order*) Abschluß *m.* **~s pl** (*turnover*) der Absatz; **how many ~s have you made?** wieviel (Stück) haben Sie verkauft/wie viele Abschlüsse haben Sie gemacht?; **we've made no ~ to China** mit China haben wir keine Geschäfte abgeschlossen; **"no ~"** (*on till*) ≈ Nullbon.

(c) **~s department** (*department*) Verkaufsabteilung *f.*

(d) (*at reduced prices*) Ausverkauf *m*; (*at end of season also*) Schlußverkauf *m*; (*clearance*) ≈ Räumungsverkauf *m.* **to go to the ~s** zum Ausverkauf gehen; **they've got a ~ on** da ist Ausverkauf; **to buy in or at the ~s** im Ausverkauf kaufen.

(e) (*auction, selling off*) Auktion *f.* **~ of work** Basar *m.*

saleable, (*US*) **salable** ['seɪləbl] *adj* (*marketable*) absatzfähig; (*in ~ condition*) verkäuflich. **not in a ~ condition** nicht zum Verkauf geeignet.

sale: **~ price** *n* Ausverkaufspreis *m*; **~room** *n* Auktionsraum *m.*

sales: **~ clerk** *n* (*US*) Verkäufer(in *f*) *m*; **~ department** *n* Verkaufsabteilung *f*; **~ director** *n* Verkaufsdirektor *m*; **~ figures** *npl* Verkaufs- *or* Absatzziffern *pl*; **~ force** *n* Verkäufer- *or* Absatzstab *m*; **~girl, ~lady** *n* Verkäuferin *f*; **~man** *n* Verkäufer *m*; (*representative*) Vertreter, Repräsentant *m*; **~ manager** *n* Verkaufsleiter, Salesmanager *m.*

salesmanship ['seɪlzmənʃɪp] *n* Verkaufstechnik *f.*

sales: **~ pitch** *n* Verkaufstechnik *or* -masche (*inf*) *f*; **he gave me a long ~ pitch** (*inf*) er hat mir einen langen Sermon (*inf*) *or* eine lange Story (*sl*) erzählt; **~ representative** *n* Vertreter(in *f*) *m*; **~ resistance** *n* Kaufunlust *f*; **to meet with ~ resistance** auf Absatzschwierigkeiten stoßen; **~room** *n see* **saleroom**; **~ talk** *n* Verkaufsgespräch *nt*; **his ~ talk won me over** der Art, wie er die Ware angepriesen hat, hat mich überzeugt; **that's just ~ talk** er/sie macht nur Reklame; **~ tax** *n* (*US*) Verkaufssteuer *f*; **~woman** *n* Verkäuferin *f.*

salient ['seɪlɪənt] *adj* (*lit*) hervorstehend; (*fig*) hervorstechend. **the ~ points of his argument** die Hauptpunkte *pl* seiner

Argumentation; **the very ~ print on this page** der stark hervortretende Druck auf dieser Seite.

saline ['seɪlaɪn] *adj* salzig. **~ solution** Salzlösung *f.*

salinity [sə'lɪnɪtɪ] *n* Salzigkeit *f*; (*content*) Salzgehalt *m.*

saliva [sə'laɪvə] *n* Speichel *m.*

salivary ['sælɪvərɪ] *adj* Speichel-. **~ gland** Speicheldrüse *f.*

salivate ['sælɪveɪt] *vi* Speichel produzieren; (*animal*) geifern; (*old people, baby*) sabbern; (*with lust*) lüstern geifern.

salivation [,sælɪ'veɪʃən] *n* Speichelfluß *m.*

sallow ['sæləʊ] *adj* bleich, teigig; *colour* fahl.

sallowness ['sæləʊnɪs] *n* Blässe *f*; Fahlheit *f.*

sally ['sælɪ] **1** *n* Ausbruch *m*; (*of troops*) Ausfall *m.* **to make a ~** (*troops*) einen Ausfall machen; (*fig: verbally*) eine Tirade loslassen; **I made a ~ into town** ich habe einen Trip in die Stadt gemacht; **another ~ of violent prose** ein weiterer Erguß gewalttätiger Prosa.

2 *vi* (*old, hum*) **to ~ forth** (*Mil*) einen Ausfall machen; (*rush out*) hinaus-/herausstürmen; (*set out*) sich aufmachen.

Sally Army ['sælɪ'ɑːmɪ] *n* (*Brit inf*) *see* **Salvation Army.**

salmon ['sæmən] **1** *n, pl* **-** Lachs, Salm *m*; (*colour*) Lachs(rosa) *nt.* **2** *adj* (*in colour*) lachs(farben).

salmon: **~ leap** *n* Lachssprung *m*; (*man-made*) Lachsleiter *or* -treppe *f*; **~ pink** **1** *n* Lachsrosa *nt*; **2** *adj* lachsrosa; **~ river** *n* Fluß *m*, in dem Lachse vorkommen; **~ trout** *n* Lachsforelle *f.*

salon ['sælɒn] *n* (*all senses*) Salon *m.*

saloon [sə'luːn] *n* **(a)** Saal *m*; (*Naut*) Salon *m.* **(b)** (*Brit Aut*) Limousine *f*; (*in motor racing*) Tourenwagen *m.* **(c)** (*US: bar*) Wirtschaft *f*; (*in Westerns*) Saloon *m.*

saloon: **~ bar** *n* (*Brit*) vornehmerer Teil eines Lokals; **~ car** *n* (*Brit*) Limousine *f.*

Salop ['sæləp] *abbr of* **Shropshire.**

salsify ['sælsɪfɪ] *n* Schwarzwurzel *f.*

salt [sɔːlt] **1** *n* **(a)** (*Cook, Chem*) Salz *nt.* **~ of the earth** (*fig*) Salz der Erde; **to be worth one's ~** (*fig*) etwas taugen; **to take sth with a pinch or grain of ~** (*fig*) etw nicht ganz für bare Münze *or* so wörtlich nehmen; **see old ~.**

(b) **~s pl** (*smelling ~s*) Riechsalz *nt*; (*for bowels*) salinisches Abführmittel; **that drink went through me like a dose of ~s** (*inf*) das Getränk hat mich richtig durchgeputzt (*inf*); **the new director went through the board like a dose of ~s** (*inf*) der neue Direktor hat im Vorstand mit eisernem Besen ausgekehrt.

(c) (*fig: zest, flavour*) Würze *f.*

2 *adj meat, water etc* Salz-; *butter* gesalzen; *taste* Salz-, salzig. **it's very ~** es ist sehr salzig.

3 *vt* (*cure*) einsalzen; (*flavour*) salzen. **~ed herrings** Salzheringe *pl.*

♦ **salt away** *vt sep* (*inf*) *money* auf die hohe Kante legen (*inf*).

SALT [sɔːlt] *abbr of* **Strategic Arms Limitation Treaty.**

salt: **~ cellar** *n* Salzfäßchen *nt*; (*shaker*) Salzstreuer *m*; **~ flats** *npl* Salztonebene *f.*

saltiness ['sɔːltɪnɪs] *n* Salzigkeit *f.*

salt: **~ lake** *n* Salzsee *m*; **~-lick** *n* Salzlecke *f*; **~-marsh** *n* Salzsumpf *m*; **~-mine** *n* Salzbergwerk *nt.*

saltness ['sɔːltnɪs] *n* Salzigkeit *f.*

salt: **~-pan** *n* Salzpfanne *f*; **~petre,** (*US*) **~peter** [,sɔːlt'piːtə^r] *n* Salpeter *m*; **~ shaker** *n* Salzstreuer *m*; **~ water** *n* Salzwasser *nt*; **~-water** *adj fish etc* Meeres-; *lake* Salz-; **~ works** *n sing or pl* Saline *f.*

salty ['sɔːltɪ] *adj* (*+er*) salzig.

salubrious [sə'luːbrɪəs] *adj* **(a)** (*form*) *air, climate* gesund. **(b)** (*inf*) *district, friends* ersprießlich. **not a very ~ pub** eine recht zweifelhafte Kneipe.

salutary ['sæljʊtərɪ] *adj* **(a)** (*healthy*) gesund. **(b)** (*beneficial*) *advice* nützlich; *experience* heilsam, lehrreich; *effect* günstig.

salutation [,sæljʊ'teɪʃən] *n* Begrüßung *f*; (*in letters*) Anrede *f.* **he raised his hand in ~** er hob die Hand zum Gruß.

salutatorian [səlˌuːtə'tɔːrɪən] *n* (*US*) *Student, der die Begrüßungsrede hält.*

salutatory [sə'luːtətərɪ] *adj oration, gesture* Begrüßungs-.

salute [sə'luːt] **1** *n* Gruß *m*; (*of guns*) Salut *m.* **flags were raised in ~** zur Begrüßung wurden die Fahnen gehißt; **to stand at the ~** salutieren; **a 21-gun ~** 21 Salutschüsse; **to take the ~** die Parade abnehmen; **he gave a smart ~** er salutierte zackig.

2 *vt* (*Mil*) *flag etc* grüßen; *person also* salutieren vor (*+dat*); (*fig liter: welcome*) begrüßen; *courage* bewundern, den Hut ziehen vor (*+dat*). **to ~ the arrival of sb/sth** jdn/etw begrüßen; **we ~ the glorious dead** wir gedenken der gefallenen Helden.

3 *vi* (*Mil*) salutieren, grüßen.

salutories [sə'luːtərɪz] *npl* (*US*) Begrüßungsrede *f* (*bei Semesterabschluß und Zeugnisüberreichung*).

salvage ['sælvɪdʒ] **1** *n* (*act*) Bergung *f*; (*objects*) Bergungsgut *nt*; (*payment*) Bergelohn *m*; (*proceeds from ~d goods*) Wert *m* der geretteten Waren. **to collect newspapers for ~** Zeitungen zur Wiederverwertung sammeln.

2 *vt* (*from wreck, building*) bergen (*from aus*); (*fig*) retten (*from von*). **to ~ sth from the fire** etw aus den Flammen retten; **~ what you can** (*lit, fig*) rettet, was ihr retten könnt; **a few happy memories can be ~d from the marriage** ein paar glückliche Erinnerungen können aus den Trümmern der Ehe geborgen werden; **there is not much in this theory/bill/manuscript that's worth salvaging** an der Theorie/dem Gesetzentwurf/Manuskript ist nicht viel zu retten.

salvage: **~ operation** *n* Bergungsaktion *f*; (*fig*) Rettungsaktion *f*; **~ tug** *n* Bergungsschlepper *m*; **~ vessel** *n* Bergungsschiff *nt.*

salvation [sæl'veɪʃən] *n* (*act of saving*) Rettung *f*; (*state of being saved also, esp Rel*) Heil *nt.* **he found ~ in the Church** er fand sein Heil in der Kirche; **he found a kind of emotional ~ in this poetry** er fand Erlösung in dieser Dichtung; **the path to ~** der Weg des Heils; **you were/that was my ~** du warst/das war meine Rettung; **everyone has to work out his own ~** jeder muß für sein eigenes Heil sorgen; **these days every company has to**

figure out its own means of ~ heutzutage muß jede Firma eigene Wege finden, um zu überleben.
Salvation Army 1 n Heilsarmee f. **2** attr hostel, band, meeting der Heilsarmee.
salvationist [sæl'veɪʃənɪst] n Heilsprediger(in f) m; (usu S~: of Salvation Army) Angehörige(r) mf der Heilsarmee.
salve[1] [sælv] vt (liter) see **salvage**.
salve[2] **1** n Salbe f; (fig liter) Balsam m. **as a** ~ **for his conscience** um sein Gewissen zu beruhigen. **2** vt (rare lit) (ein)salben; (fig) conscience beruhigen.
salver ['sælvə'] n Tablett nt.
salvo ['sælvəʊ] n (of guns, fig) Salve f. **a** ~ **of applause** ein Beifallssturm m.
sal volatile [ˌsælvə'lætəlɪ] n Riechsalz nt.
Samaritan [sə'mærɪtən] n Samariter m. **good** ~ (lit, fig) barmherziger Samariter.
samba ['sæmbə] **1** n Samba f or m. **2** vi Samba tanzen.
sambo ['sæmbəʊ] n (pej) Kaffer m.
same [seɪm] **1** adj **the** ~ der/die/das gleiche; (one and the ~, numerically identical also) derselbe/dieselbe/dasselbe; **they were both wearing the** ~ **dress** sie hatten beide das gleiche Kleid an; **they both live in the** ~ **house** sie wohnen beide in demselben or im selben Haus; **they are all the** ~ sie sind alle gleich; **that's the** ~ **tie as I've got** so eine Krawatte habe ich auch, ich habe die gleiche Krawatte; **she just wasn't the** ~ **person** sie war ein anderer Mensch; **it's the** ~ **thing** das ist das gleiche; **see you tomorrow,** ~ **time** zur gleichen Zeit bis morgen, gleicher Ort, gleiche Zeit or Ort und Zeit wie gehabt; **we sat at the** ~ **table as usual** wir saßen an unserem üblichen Tisch; **how are you?** — ~ **as usual** wie geht's? — wie immer; **I've made the** ~ **mistake myself** den Fehler habe ich auch gemacht, ich habe den gleichen Fehler gemacht; **this** ~ **person** eben dieser Mensch; (Jur) besagte Person; **she was killed with this** ~ **knife** sie wurde mit eben or genau diesem Messer erstochen; **he is the** ~ **age as his wife** er ist (genau) so alt wie seine Frau; **it happened the** ~ **day** es ist am gleichen or selben Tag passiert; **if you can do the two jobs in the** ~ **day** wenn sie die beiden Arbeiten an einem Tag erledigen können; **in the** ~ **way** (genau) gleich; (by the ~ token) ebenso; see **time**.
2 pron **(a)** **the** ~ der/die/das gleiche; derselbe/dieselbe/dasselbe; **and I would do the** ~ **again** und ich würde es wieder tun; **he left and I did the** ~ er ist gegangen, und ich auch or ebenfalls; **they are one and the** ~ das ist doch dasselbe; (people) das ist doch ein und derselbe/dieselbe; **another drink?** — **thanks, (the)** ~ **again** noch etwas zu trinken? — ja bitte, das gleiche noch mal; ~ **again, Joe** und noch einen, Joe; **she's much the** ~ sie hat sich kaum geändert; (in health) es geht ihr ziemlich gleich; **you're not the** ~ **any more** du bist nicht mehr derselbe/dieselbe; **I'm not the** ~ **as my brother** ich bin nicht so wie mein Bruder; **it's always the** ~ es ist immer das gleiche.
(b) no art (Comm) for repairing chair: **£10, for recovering** ~: **£15** Stuhlreparatur: £ 10, Beziehen: £ 15.
(c) (in adverbial uses) **the** ~ gleich; **to pay/treat everybody the** ~ alle gleich bezahlen/behandeln; **things go on just the** ~ (as always) es ändert sich nichts; **it's not the** ~ **as before** es ist nicht wie früher; **I don't feel the** ~ **about it** ich sehe das nicht so; **I used to love you but I don't feel the** ~ **any more** ich habe dich mal geliebt, aber das ist nicht anders; **I still feel the** ~ **about you** an meinen Gefühlen dir gegenüber hat sich nichts geändert; **if it's all the** ~ **to you** wenn es Ihnen egal ist or nichts ausmacht; **it's all the** ~ **to me** (what you do) es ist mir egal(, was du tust); **it comes or amounts to the** ~ das kommt or läuft aufs gleiche hinaus.
(d) (phrases) **all or just the** ~ (nevertheless) trotzdem; ~ **here** ich/wir auch; ~ **to you** (danke) gleichfalls; **I'd have hit him,** ~ (inf) or **the** ~ **as you did** ich hätte ihn (an Ihrer Stelle) auch geschlagen; **we left our country the** ~ **as you did** wir haben unsere Heimat verlassen, wie Sie auch.
sameness ['seɪmnɪs] n Eintönigkeit f.
samey ['seɪmɪ] adj (inf) eintönig, dasselbe in Grün (inf).
Samoa [sə'məʊə] n Samoa nt.
Samoan [sə'məʊən] **1** adj samoanisch. **2** n **(a)** Samoaner(in f) m. **(b)** (language) Samoanisch nt.
samovar [ˌsæməʊ'vɑː'] n Samowar m.
sampan ['sæmpæn] n Sampan m.
sample ['sɑːmpl] **1** n (example) Beispiel nt (of für); (for tasting, fig: of talent, behaviour) Kostprobe f; (Comm) (of cloth etc) Muster nt; (of commodities, urine, blood etc) Probe f; (Statistics) (Zufalls)stichprobe f, Sample nt. **that's a typical** ~ **of her cooking/the local dialect/Japanese tourists** so kocht sie immer/das ist ein typisches Beispiel für den örtlichen Dialekt/das ist ein typischer japanischer Tourist; **give us a** ~ **of your playing/singing** spielen/singen Sie uns etwas vor; **up to** ~ (Comm) dem Muster entsprechend; **a representative** ~ **of the population** eine repräsentative Auswahl aus der Bevölkerung; **to take** ~s **of public opinion/of goods produced** Stichproben aus öffentlicher Meinung/bei der gefertigten Ware machen.
2 adj attr pieces, books Muster-; pages, copy Probe-; bottle, sachet etc Probier-. ~ **survey** Stichprobenerhebung f; **a** ~ **section of the population** eine Auswahl aus der Bevölkerung.
3 vt wine, food probieren, kosten; pleasures kosten. **to** ~ **wines** eine Weinprobe machen.
sampler ['sɑːmplə'] n **(a)** (person) Probierer(in f) m. **(b)** (Sew) Stickmustertuch nt. **(c)** (record) Auswahlplatte f.
sampling ['sɑːmplɪŋ] **1** n (of food) Kostprobe f; (of wine) Weinprobe f; (Statistics) Stichprobenverfahren nt. **2** attr methods, techniques Stichproben-.
Samson ['sæmsn] n (lit) Samson m; (fig) Herkules m.
Samurai ['sæmjuraɪ] **1** n Samurai m. **2** attr Samurai-.
sanatorium [ˌsænə'tɔːrɪəm] n, pl **sanatoria** [ˌsænə'tɔːrɪə] Sanatorium nt; (in cpds) -heilanstalt f.

sanctification [ˌsæŋktɪfɪ'keɪʃən] n see vt Heiligung f; Weihe f; Annahme f.
sanctify ['sæŋktɪfaɪ] vt (make holy) heiligen; (give quasi-moral sanction to also) sanktionieren; (consecrate) weihen; (make binding) vows annehmen. **a custom sanctified by tradition** ein durch die Tradition geheiligter Brauch.
sanctimonious [ˌsæŋktɪ'məʊnɪəs] adj frömmlerisch. **don't be so** ~ **about it** tu doch nicht so fromm.
sanctimoniously [ˌsæŋktɪ'məʊnɪəslɪ] adv see adj.
sanctimoniousness [ˌsæŋktɪ'məʊnɪəsnɪs] n frömmlerisches Wesen.
sanction ['sæŋkʃən] **1** n **(a)** (permission, approval) Zustimmung f. **to give one's** ~ **to sth** etw sanktionieren, seine Zustimmung zu etw geben; **rituals which have received the** ~ **of tradition** Rituale, die durch die Tradition sanktioniert sind. **(b)** (enforcing measure) Sanktion f. **2** vt sanktionieren.
sanctity ['sæŋktɪtɪ] n Heiligkeit f; (of rights) Unantastbarkeit f. **a man of great** ~ ein sehr heiliger Mann; **through time these customs have acquired an unquestionable** ~ im Laufe der Jahre sind diese Sitten zur geheiligten Tradition geworden.
sanctuary ['sæŋktjʊərɪ] n **(a)** (holy place) Heiligtum nt; (altar ~) Altarraum m. **(b)** (refuge) Zuflucht f. **to seek** ~ **with** Zuflucht suchen bei. **(c)** (for animals) Schutzgebiet nt.
sanctum ['sæŋktəm] n **(a)** (holy place) heiliger Ort. **(b)** (fig: private place) Allerheiligste(s) nt.
sand [sænd] **1** n Sand m no pl. ~s (of desert) Sand m; (beach) Sandstrand m; **the** ~s **are running out** (fig) die Zeit or Uhr läuft ab; **the** ~s **of time** (fig) die Zeit. **2** vt (smooth) schmirgeln; (sprinkle with ~) streuen.
♦ **sand down** vt sep (ab)schmirgeln.
sandal ['sændl] n Sandale f.
sandalled ['sændəld] adj in her ~ feet in or mit Sandalen.
sandalwood ['sændlwʊd] **1** n Sandelholz nt. **2** attr Sandelholz-.
sand: ~**bag** n Sandsack m; **2** vt mit Sandsäcken schützen; ~**bank** n Sandbank f; ~**bar** n Sandbank f; ~**blast** vt sandstrahlen; ~**blaster** n Sandstrahler m; ~**blasting** n Sandstrahlen nt; ~**box** n (Rail) Sandstreuer m; (Metal) Sandform f; (for playing) Sandkasten m; ~**boy** n: **as happy as a** ~boy quietschvergnügt (inf); ~**castle** n Sandburg f; ~ **dune** n Sanddüne f; ~**flea** n Strandfloh m; (harmful) Sandfloh m; ~**fly** n Sandfliege f; ~**glass** n Sanduhr f; ~**hopper** n Sandhüpfer m.
sandiness ['sændɪnɪs] n Sandigkeit f. **noted for the** ~ **of its beaches** berühmt für seine Sandstrände.
sand: ~**lot** adj (US) ~lot baseball auf einem nicht als Spielfeld markierten Gelände und zum Spaß gespielter Baseball; ~**man** n Sandmann m; ~**martin** n Uferschwalbe f; ~**paper** **1** n Sand- or Schmirgelpapier nt; **2** vt schmirgeln; ~**paper down** vt sep abschmirgeln; ~**piper** n Strandläufer m; ~**pit** n Sandkasten m or -kiste f; ~**shoe** n Stoffschuh m; (for beach) Strandschuh m; ~**stone** **1** n Sandstein m; **2** adj Sandstein-, aus Sandstein; ~**storm** n Sandsturm m; ~**table** n (Mil) Sandkasten m.
sandwich ['sænwɪdʒ] **1** n Doppelschnitte or -stulle (N Ger) f, Sandwich nt. **open** ~ belegtes Brot; **he has** ~es **for lunch** er ißt Brote or Schnitten or Stullen (N Ger) zum Mittagessen.
2 vt (also ~ **in**) hineinzwängen; car einkeilen. **to be** ~ed **between two things/people** (car, house) zwischen zwei Dingen/Menschen eingekeilt sein; (person also, small object) zwischen zwei Dingen/Menschen eingezwängt sein; ~ed **between two slices of bread** zwischen zwei Brotscheiben.
sandwich: ~**board** n Reklametafel f, Sandwich nt (dated); ~ **course** n Ausbildungsgang m, bei dem sich Theorie und Praxis abwechseln; ~**man** n Plakatträger, Sandwichmann (hum) m.
sandy ['sændɪ] adj (+er) **(a)** (sandy) beach, soil Sand-, sandig pred. **(b)** (in colour) rötlich; hair rotblond.
sand-yacht ['sændjɒt] n Segelwagen m.
sane [seɪn] adj (+er) person normal; (Med, Psych etc) geistig gesund; (Jur) zurechnungsfähig; world, society etc gesund; (sensible) advice, policy, person vernünftig. **it's simply not** ~ **to ...** es ist doch verrückt, zu ...
sang [sæŋ] pret of **sing**.
sangfroid ['sɑːŋ'frwɑː] n Gelassenheit f, Seelenruhe f.
sangria [sæŋ'griːə] n Sangria f.
sanguinary ['sæŋgwɪnərɪ] adj (liter) battle blutig; person blutrünstig; expression etc derb. ~ **language** (hum) ≈ Fäkalsprache f.
sanguine ['sæŋgwɪn] adj **(a)** (optimistic) optimistisch. **to have a** ~ **nature or disposition** von Natur aus ein Optimist sein; **I remain** ~ **about his chances** was seine Chancen betrifft, bin ich noch immer zuversichtlich; ~ **that we shall succeed** zuversichtlich, daß wir Erfolg haben werden.
(b) ~ **complexion** rote or gesunde (euph) Gesichtsfarbe.
sanguinely ['sæŋgwɪnlɪ] adv optimistisch; say zuversichtlich.
sanguinity [sæŋ'gwɪnɪtɪ] n Optimismus m. **the** ~ **of his outlook** seine optimistische Einstellung.
sanies ['seɪnɪːz] n (Med) Jauche f.
sanitariness ['sænɪtərɪnɪs] n Hygiene f. **the** ~ **of conditions** die hygienischen Zustände; **the** ~ **of the toilets is not up to standard** bei den Toiletten läßt die Hygiene zu wünschen übrig.
sanitarium [ˌsænɪ'teərɪəm] n (US) see **sanatorium**.
sanitary ['sænɪtərɪ] adj hygienisch; arrangements, installations sanitär attr; regulations, expert, commission Gesundheits-; recommendations in bezug auf die Hygiene; questions, principles der Hygiene.
sanitary: ~ **belt** n Bindengürtel m; ~ **inspector** n Gesundheitsaufseher m; ~ **towel**, (US) ~ **napkin** n Damenbinde f.
sanitation [ˌsænɪ'teɪʃən] n Hygiene f; (toilets etc) sanitäre Anlagen pl; (sewage disposal) Kanalisation f. **the** ~ **department** das Amt für Stadtreinigung or Stadthygiene; ~ **man** (US) Stadtreiniger m.
sanitize ['sænɪtaɪz] vt (esp US) keimfrei machen.

sanity ['sænɪtɪ] n (a) (mental balance) geistige Gesundheit; (of individual also) gesunder Verstand; (Jur) Zurechnungsfähigkeit f. to lose one's ~ den Verstand verlieren; to doubt sb's ~ an jds Verstand (dat) zweifeln; the line between ~ and insanity die Grenze zwischen gesundem und krankem Verstand.
(b) (sensibleness) Vernünftigkeit f. ~ of judgement ein gesundes Urteilsvermögen; the obvious financial ~ of the plan der aus finanzieller Sicht eindeutig vernünftige Plan; ~ demands that it be done soon die Vernunft gebietet, es bald zu tun; to return to ~ zur Vernunft annehmen.

sank [sæŋk] pret of **sink**[1].

San Marino [ˌsænməˈriːnəʊ] n San Marino nt.

sanserif [ˌsænseˈriːf] n serifenlose Schrift; (character) serifenloser Buchstabe.

Sanskrit ['sænskrɪt] 1 adj sanskritisch. 2 n Sanskrit nt.

Santa (Claus) ['sæntə('klɔːz)] n der Weihnachtsmann.

sap[1] [sæp] n (Bot) Saft m; (fig) Lebenskraft f. heavy taxation which sucks all the ~ out of industry die hohe Besteuerung, die der Industrie das Mark aus den Knochen saugt; the ~ is rising (lit) der Saft steigt, (fig) die Triebe erwachen.

sap[2] 1 n (Mil) Sappe f. 2 vt (a) (Mil) unterminieren, untergraben; fortification also Sappen graben unter (+dat). (b) (fig) untergraben; confidence also schwächen. to ~ sb's strength jdn entkräften, jds Kräfte angreifen; to ~ sb's energy/enthusiasm jdm die Energie/Begeisterung nehmen.

sap[3] n (sl) Trottel m (inf).

sapling ['sæplɪŋ] n junger Baum.

sapper ['sæpə[r]] n (Mil) Pionier m.

Sapphic ['sæfɪk] adj sapphisch.

sapphire ['sæfaɪə[r]] 1 n Saphir m; (colour) Saphirblau nt. 2 adj ring Saphir-; (liter) sky strahlend blau.

saraband ['særəbænd] n Sarabande f.

Saracen ['særəsn] 1 adj Sarazenen-. 2 n Sarazene m, Sarazenin f.

sarcasm ['sɑːkæzəm] n Sarkasmus m. ~s sarkastische Bemerkungen pl.

sarcastic [sɑːˈkæstɪk] adj sarkastisch. he has a ~ tongue er hat eine sarkastische Art; are you being ~? sind Sie jetzt sarkastisch?, das soll wohl ein Witz sein (inf).

sarcastically [sɑːˈkæstɪkəlɪ] adv sarkastisch.

sarcophagus [sɑːˈkɒfəgəs] n, pl **sarcophagi** [sɑːˈkɒfəgaɪ] Sarkophag m.

sardine [sɑːˈdiːn] n Sardine f. packed in like ~s wie die Sardinen.

Sardinia [sɑːˈdɪnɪə] n Sardinien nt.

Sardinian [sɑːˈdɪnɪən] 1 adj sardisch, sardinisch. 2 n Sarde m, Sardin f, Sardinier(in f) m.

sardonic adj, **~ally** adv [sɑːˈdɒnɪk, -əlɪ] süffisant; grin, laugh also sardonisch (liter).

sari ['sɑːrɪ] n Sari m.

sarky ['sɑːkɪ] adj (+er) (Brit inf) sarkastisch.

sarong [səˈrɒŋ] n Sarong m.

sarsaparilla [ˌsɑːsəpəˈrɪlə] n (plant) Sarsaparille f; (drink) dunkelbraunes Limonadengetränk aus Sarsaparillenwurzeln.

sartorial [sɑːˈtɔːrɪəl] adj his ~ elegance sein elegantes Aussehen, seine elegante Art, sich zu kleiden; the very last word in ~ elegance der letzte Schrei in der Herrenmode; his unusual ~ preferences seine Vorliebe für ungewöhnliche Kleidung; ~ styles Herrenmoden pl.

sartorially [sɑːˈtɔːrɪəlɪ] adv dressed elegant, stilvoll.

sash[1] [sæʃ] n Schärpe f.

sash[2] n (window ~) Schiebefenster nt.

sashay ['sæʃeɪ] vi (esp US inf) stolzieren. I'll just ~ down to the bar ich latsche mal eben zur Bar (inf).

sash: ~-cord n Gewichtsschnur f; ~-window n Schiebefenster nt.

sass [sæs] (US inf) 1 n Frechheit f. 2 vt frech antworten (+dat).

sassafras ['sæsəfræs] n Sassafras m.

Sassenach ['sæsənæx] n, adj (Scot pej, hum) Bezeichnung der Schotten für die Engländer/Englisches.

sassy ['sæsɪ] adj (+er) (US inf) frech.

sat [sæt] pret, ptp of **sit**.

Sat abbr of **Saturday** Sa.

Satan ['seɪtn] n Satan m.

satanic [səˈtænɪk] adj satanisch.

Satanism ['seɪtənɪzəm] n Satanismus, Satanskult m.

satchel ['sætʃəl] n Schultasche f, Schulranzen m.

sate [seɪt] vt (liter) appetite, desires stillen (geh), befriedigen. now that he was ~d nun, da seine Lüste gestillt waren (geh); a nation ~d with every luxury ein Volk, von jedem erdenklichen Luxus übersättigt; to ~ oneself (with food) sich sättigen (on an +dat) (liter); (sexually) seine Lust befriedigen.

sateen [sæ'tiːn] n Baumwollsatin m.

satellite ['sætəlaɪt] n Satellit m; (natural also, fig) Trabant m.

satellite: ~ country, ~ state n Satellitenstaat m; ~ town n Satelliten- or Trabantenstadt f.

satiate ['seɪʃɪeɪt] vt appetite, desires, lust etc stillen (geh); person, animal sättigen; (to excess) übersättigen. we were ~d with food and drink wir hatten unseren Hunger und Durst zur Genüge gestillt; I'm quite ~d (liter, hum) mein Bedarf ist gedeckt (hum inf), ich bin gesättigt (hum, geh).

satiation [ˌseɪʃɪˈeɪʃən] n (act) Befriedigung f. a state of ~ ein Zustand der Sättigung or (excessive) Übersättigung.

satiety [səˈtaɪətɪ] n (liter) Sättigung f. they fed to ~ sie aßen sich satt; to do sth to (the point of) ~ etw bis zum Überdruß tun; I've achieved a point of ~ ich habe meinen Sättigungsgrad erreicht.

satin ['sætɪn] 1 n Satin m. 2 adj Satin-; skin samtig.

satin: ~ stitch n Plattstich m; ~wood n Satinholz nt.

satiny ['sætɪnɪ] adj seidig; skin samtig.

satire ['sætaɪə[r]] n Satire f (on auf +acc). the (tone of) ~ in his voice die Ironie in seiner Stimme.

satirical [səˈtɪrɪkəl] adj literature, film etc satirisch; (mocking, joking) ironisch.

satirically [səˈtɪrɪkəlɪ] adv see adj.

satirist ['sætərɪst] n Satiriker(in f) m.

satirize ['sætəraɪz] vt satirisch darstellen or (written also) beschreiben. his novel ~s or in his novel he ~s contemporary American life sein Roman ist eine Satire auf die zeitgenössische amerikanische Lebensart.

satisfaction [ˌsætɪsˈfækʃən] n (a) (act: of person, needs, creditors, curiosity etc) Befriedigung f; (of debt) Begleichung, Tilgung f; (of employer) Zufriedenstellung f; (of ambition) Verwirklichung f; (of conditions, contract) Erfüllung f.
(b) (state) Zufriedenheit f (at mit). the ~ of having solved a difficult problem die Genugtuung or das befriedigende Gefühl, ein schwieriges Problem gelöst zu haben; to feel a sense of ~ at sth Genugtuung über etw (acc) empfinden; at least you have the ~ of seeing him pay Sie haben wenigstens die Genugtuung, daß er zahlen muß; he did it just for the ~ of seeing him suffer er tat es nur, um sie leiden zu sehen; we hope the meal was to your complete ~ wir hoffen, Sie waren mit dem Essen zufrieden or das Essen ist zu Ihrer vollen Zufriedenheit ausgefallen (form); has it been done to your ~? sind Sie damit zufrieden?, ist es zu Ihrer Zufriedenheit erledigt worden? (form); if anything in the hotel is not to your ~ sollte irgend etwas im Hotel nicht zu Ihrer Zufriedenheit sein; our aim, your ~ bei uns ist der Kunde König, it gives every or full ~ es fällt zur vollständigen Zufriedenheit aus; the machine is guaranteed to give complete ~ wir garantieren mit diesem Gerät vollste Zufriedenheit; we aim to give full ~ (to our customers) wir wollen, daß Sie/unsere Kunden zufrieden sind; it gives me much ~ to introduce ... es ist mir eine besondere Freude, ... vorstellen zu können; to get ~ out of sth Befriedigung in etw (dat) finden; (find pleasure) Freude an etw (dat) haben; I can't get any ~ ich bin unbefriedigt; he gets ~ out of his job seine Arbeit befriedigt ihn; I get a lot of ~ out of listening to music Musik gibt mir viel; what ~ do you get out of climbing mountains? was gibt Ihnen das Bergsteigen?; what particular ~ did you get from the course? was hat Ihnen der Kurs gegeben?; he proved to my ~ that ... er hat überzeugend bewiesen, daß ...; he has shown to the examiners'/court's ~ that ... der Prüfungsausschuß hat befunden, daß er .../er hat dem Gericht überzeugend dargelegt, daß ...
(c) (satisfying thing) your son's success must be a great ~ to you der Erfolg Ihres Sohnes muß für Sie sehr befriedigend or eine große Freude sein; it is no ~ to me to know that ... es ist kein Trost (für mich) zu wissen, daß ...; what ~ is that supposed to be! das ist ein schwacher Trost.
(d) (redress) Genugtuung, Satisfaktion (old) f. to demand/obtain ~ from sb Genugtuung or Satisfaktion (old) von jdm verlangen/erhalten; to give sb ~ jdm Genugtuung or Satisfaktion (old) geben.

satisfactorily [ˌsætɪsˈfæktərɪlɪ] adv zufriedenstellend. does that answer your question ~? ist damit Ihre Frage hinreichend or hinlänglich beantwortet?; was it done ~? waren Sie damit zufrieden?; he is progressing ~ er macht zufriedenstellende Fortschritte pl.

satisfactory [ˌsætɪsˈfæktərɪ] adj befriedigend, zufriedenstellend; account, completion of contract zufriedenstellend; (only just good enough) ausreichend, hinlänglich attr; reason triftig, einleuchtend; excuse angemessen, annehmbar; (in exams) ausreichend; befriedigend. work is proceeding at a ~ pace die Arbeit geht zufriedenstellend voran; how ~ do you find the new conditions? wie sind Sie mit den neuen Verhältnissen zufrieden?; his work is only just ~ seine Arbeit ist gerade noch annehmbar or gerade or (Sch) ist gerade noch befriedigend; this is just not ~! das geht so nicht!; (not enough) das reicht einfach nicht (aus)!; it's hardly ~ being given only one hour's notice das geht doch nicht, wenn einem nur eine Stunde vorher Bescheid gesagt wird; an offer of 8% is simply not ~ ein Angebot von 8% reicht einfach nicht; your attitude ist not ~ Ihre Einstellung läßt zu wünschen übrig.

satisfy ['sætɪsfaɪ] 1 vt (a) (make contented) befriedigen; employer, customers etc zufriedenstellen; (meal) person sättigen. to be satisfied with sth (mit etw) zufrieden sein; you'll have to be satisfied with that Sie werden sich damit zufriedengeben or begnügen or bescheiden (geh) müssen; that won't ~ the boss damit wird der Chef nicht zufrieden sein; not satisfied with that he ... damit noch immer nicht zufrieden, ... er ...; nothing satisfies him ihn kann nichts befriedigen; (always wants more) er ist mit nichts zufrieden; with a satisfied look on his face mit einem zufriedenen Gesichtsausdruck; more pudding? — no thank you, I'm quite satisfied noch etwas Nachtisch? — nein danke, ich bin satt or gesättigt (geh); this little drink didn't ~ him/his thirst das bißchen hat ihn nicht gereicht/hat seinen Durst nicht gelöscht; you've really upset her now, I hope you're satisfied sie ist ganz außer sich, bist du jetzt zufrieden?
(b) needs, wishes, lust, demand, also (sexually) befriedigen; wants, curiosity also, hunger stillen; contract, conditions erfüllen; requirements genügen (+dat); ambitions verwirklichen. to do sth to ~ one's pride etw nur aus reinem Stolz tun.
(c) (convince) überzeugen. they were not satisfied with the answers sie waren mit den Antworten nicht zufrieden; if you can ~ him that ... wenn Sie ihn davon überzeugen können, daß ...; X has satisfied the examiners that ... der Prüfungsausschuß hat befunden, daß X ...; X has satisfied the examiners in the following subjects X hat in den folgenden Fächern die Prüfung abgelegt.
(d) (Comm) debt begleichen, tilgen; claims nachkommen (+dat); creditors befriedigen.
(e) (Math) equation erfüllen.
2 vr to ~ oneself about sth sich von etw überzeugen; to ~

oneself that ... sich davon überzeugen, daß ...; **have you satisfied yourself as to the validity of the claim?** haben Sie sich von der Rechtmäßigkeit der Forderungen überzeugt?

3 *vi* (*meal*) sättigen. **we aim to** ~ wir bemühen uns, allen Wünschen zu entsprechen; **pleasures which no longer** ~ Genüsse, die einen nicht mehr befriedigen; **riches do not always** ~ Reichtum macht nicht immer zufrieden.

satisfying ['sætɪsfaɪɪŋ] *adj* befriedigend; *food, meal* sättigend. **a** ~ **experience** ein befriedigendes Erlebnis; **they had the** ~ **experience of seeing him fail** es tat ihnen gut, seinen Mißerfolg zu erleben; **sounds which are very** ~ **to the ear** angenehme Klänge *pl*; **a cool** ~ **lager** ein kühles, durststillendes Bier.

satsuma [ˌsæt'su:mə] *n* Satsuma *f*.

saturate ['sætʃəreɪt] *vt* (**a**) (*with liquid*) (durch)tränken; (*rain*) durchnässen. **I'm** ~**d** (*inf*) ich bin klatschnaß (*inf*).

(**b**) (*Chem*) sättigen. **a** ~**d solution/colour** eine gesättigte Lösung/Farbe.

(**c**) (*fig*) *market* sättigen. **this area is** ~**d with a sense of history** dies ist eine geschichtsträchtige Gegend; **he** ~**d himself in French literature until the exam was over** er hat sich mit französischer Literatur vollgepfropft, bis die Prüfung vorbei war; **the government** ~**d the area with troops** die Regierung entsandte massenhaft *or* pumpte (*inf*) Truppen in das Gebiet; **the area is** ~**d with troops** die Gegend wimmelt von Soldaten.

saturation [ˌsætʃə'reɪʃən] *n* Sättigung *f*. **after** ~ **in a red dye** nach Tränkung mit einem roten Farbstoff.

saturation: ~ **bombing** *n* völliges Zerbomben; ~ **point** *n* Sättigungspunkt *m*; (*fig*) Sättigungsgrad *m*; **to have reached** ~ **point** seinen Sättigungsgrad erreicht haben; **I couldn't drink any more coffee, I've reached** ~ **point** (*inf*) ich kann keinen Kaffee mehr trinken, ich habe schon mehr als genug gehabt.

Saturday ['sætədɪ] *n* Sonnabend, Samstag *m*; *see also* **Tuesday**.

Saturn ['sætən] *n* (*Astron, Myth*) Saturn *m*.

saturnalia [ˌsætə'neɪlɪə] *npl* **a** S~ Saturnalien *pl*. (**b**) (*liter: wild revelry*) wilde Feste *pl*, Freudenfeste *pl*.

saturnine ['sætənaɪn] *adj* (*liter*) finster, düster.

satyr ['sætəʳ] *n* Satyr *m*.

sauce [sɔ:s] *n* (**a**) (*Cook*) Soße, Sauce *f*. **white** ~ Mehlsoße *f*; **what's** ~ **for the goose is** ~ **for the gander** (*Prov*) was dem einen recht ist, ist dem anderen billig (*prov*). (**b**) *no pl* (*inf: cheek*) Frechheit *f*. **none of your** ~! werd bloß nicht frech! (*inf*).

sauce: ~**-boat** *n* Sauciere *f*; ~**box** *n* (*inf*) Frechdachs *m*.

saucepan ['sɔ:spən] *n* Kochtopf *m*.

saucer ['sɔ:səʳ] *n* Untertasse *f*.

saucily ['sɔ:sɪlɪ] *adv see* **adj**.

sauciness ['sɔ:sɪnɪs] *n, no pl* Frechheit *f*.

saucy ['sɔ:sɪ] *adj* (+*er*) frech. **don't be** ~! sei nicht so frech!; **with her hat at a** ~ **angle** mit frech *or* keck aufgesetztem Hut.

Saudi Arabia ['saʊdɪə'reɪbɪə] *n* Saudi-Arabien *nt*.

Saudi (Arabian) ['saʊdɪ(ə'reɪbɪən)] **1** *n* Saudi(araber) *m*, Saudiaraberin *f*. **2** *adj* saudisch, saudiarabisch.

Saul [sɔ:l] *n* Saul(us) *m*.

sauna ['sɔ:nə] *n* Sauna *f*. **to have a** ~ in die Sauna gehen.

saunter ['sɔ:ntəʳ] **1** *n* Bummel *m*. **to have a** ~ **in the park** einen Parkbummel machen, durch den Park schlendern.

2 *vi* schlendern. **he** ~**ed through the bazaar** er schlenderte *or* bummelte durch den Basar; **he** ~**ed up to me** er schlenderte auf mich zu; **she came** ~**ing in four hours late** sie tanzte vier Stunden zu spät an (*inf*).

saurian ['sɔ:rɪən] *n* Echse *f*; (*dinosaur etc*) Saurier *m*.

sausage ['sɒsɪdʒ] *n* (**a**) Wurst *f*. **you can't judge a** ~ **by its skin** (*prov*) man kann nicht nach dem Äußeren urteilen; **not a** ~ (*inf*) †ein gar nichts (*inf*). (**b**) (*Brit inf: silly person*) Dummerchen (*inf*), Schäfchen (*inf*) *nt*.

sausage: ~ **dog** *n* (*Brit hum*) Dackel *m*; ~ **machine** *n* Wurstfüllmaschine *f*; (*fig hum: school*) Bildungsfabrik *f*; ~**meat** *n* Wurstbrät *nt*; ~ **roll** *n* = Bratwurst *f* im Schlafrock.

sauté ['saʊteɪ] **1** *adj* ~ **potatoes** Brat- *or* Röstkartoffeln *pl*. **2** *vt potatoes* rösten; (*sear*) (kurz) anbraten.

sauterne [saʊ'tɜ:n] *n* Sauternes *m*.

savable ['seɪvəbl] *adj* zu retten *pred*; *goal* haltbar, zu halten *pred*.

savage ['sævɪdʒ] **1** *adj* wild; *sport, fighter, guard, punch, revenge* brutal; *custom* grausam; *animal* gefährlich; *competition* scharf, brutal (*inf*); (*drastic, severe*) *cuts, measures* rigoros, drastisch, brutal (*inf*); *changes* drastisch; *criticism* schonungslos, brutal (*inf*). **the** ~ **people of New Guinea** die Wilden Neuguineas; **to put up a** ~ **fight** sich wütend *or* grimmig (*geh*) *or* wild (*inf*) verteidigen, sich verbissen wehren; **with a** ~ **snap of its jaws the crocodile ...** wütend biß das Krokodil ...; **the dog became a** ~ **beast** der Hund wurde zur reißenden Bestie; **the guard dogs are** ~ die Wachhunde sind scharf *or* gefährlich; **to make a** ~ **attack on sb** brutal über jdn herfallen; (*fig*) jdn scharf angreifen; **the** ~ **wildness of Scotland** die rauhe Wildheit Schottlands; **he has a** ~ **temper** er ist ein äußerst jähzorniger Mensch; **he is in a** ~ **temper** er ist fuchsteufelswild (*inf*); **the critics were really** ~ **with her new play** die Kritiker haben ihr neues Stück wirklich schonungslos verrissen; **there was no need to be so** ~ es wäre nicht notwendig gewesen, so scharf zu reagieren.

2 *n* Wilde(r) *mf*.

3 *vt* (*animal*) anfallen; (*fatally*) zerfleischen.

savagely ['sævɪdʒlɪ] *adv attack, fight, punch* brutal; *bite* gefährlich; *reduce services* drastisch, rigoros; *criticize* schonungslos, brutal (*inf*). **he glared at her** ~ er warf ihr einen wilden Blick zu.

savageness ['sævɪdʒnɪs] *n see* **adj** Wildheit *f*; Brutalität *f*; Grausamkeit *f*; Gefährlichkeit *f*; Schärfe, Brutalität (*inf*) *f*; drastische *or* brutale (*inf*) Härte; Schonungslosigkeit, Brutalität (*inf*) *f*. **the** ~ **of these changes** diese drastischen Veränderungen.

savagery ['sævɪdʒərɪ] *n* (**a**) (*of tribe, people*) Wildheit *f*. (**b**) (*cruelty*) Grausamkeit *f*; (*of attack*) Brutalität *f*; (*of treatment, prison life*) brutale Härte. **the savageries committed** ~ die Grausamkeiten *or* Greueltaten *pl* ...; **they were accused of** ~ **in their economic cuts** ihnen wurde bei den wirtschaftlichen Kürzungen brutale Härte vorgeworfen.

savanna(h) [sə'vænə] *n* Savanne *f*.

save[1] [seɪv] **1** *n* (*Ftbl etc*) Ballabwehr *f*. **what a** ~! hervorragend gehalten!; **he made a fantastic** ~ er hat den Ball prima abgewehrt *or* gehalten.

2 *vt* (**a**) (*rescue, Rel*) retten. **to** ~ **sb from sth** jdn vor etw (*dat*) retten; **to** ~ **sb from disaster/ruin** jdn vor einer Katastrophe/dem Ruin bewahren *or* retten; **he** ~**d me from falling/making that mistake** er hat mich davor bewahrt, hinzufallen/den Fehler zu machen; **to** ~ **sth from sth** etw aus etw retten; **his goal** ~**d the match** sein Tor hat das Spiel gerettet *or* herausgerissen (*inf*); **to** ~ **the day (for sb)** jds Rettung sein; **God** ~ **the Queen** Gott schütze die Königin; **to** ~ **a building for posterity** ein Gebäude der Nachwelt erhalten.

(**b**) (*put by*) aufheben, aufbewahren, aufsparen; *money* sparen; (*collect*) *stamps etc* sammeln. ~ **some of the cake for me** laß mir etwas Kuchen übrig; ~ **me a seat** halte mir einen Platz frei; ~ **it for later, I'm busy now** (*inf*) spar dir's für später auf, ich habe jetzt zu tun (*inf*); ~ **it!** (*inf*) spar dir das! (*inf*).

(**c**) (*avoid using up*) *fuel, time, space, money* sparen; (*spare*) *strength, eyes, battery* schonen; (~ *up*) *strength, fuel etc* aufsparen. **that will** ~ **you £2 a week** dadurch sparen Sie £ 2 die Woche; **you don't** ~ **much by taking this short cut** Sie gewinnen nicht viel, wenn Sie diese Abkürzung nehmen; **he's saving himself for the big match** er schont sich für das große Spiel; **she's saving herself for the right man** sie spart sich für den Richtigen auf.

(**d**) (*prevent*) *bother, trouble* ersparen. **at least it** ~**d the rain coming in** es hat wenigstens den Regen abgehalten; **it'll** ~ **a lot of hard work if we ...** es erspart uns (*dat*) sehr viel Mühe, wenn wir ...; **it** ~**d us having to do it again** da brauchten wir es (wenigstens) nicht noch einmal zu machen, das hat es uns (*dat*) erspart, es noch einmal machen zu müssen; **I've been** ~**d a lot of expense** mir blieben *or* wurden sehr viel Ausgaben erspart.

(**e**) *goal* verhindern; *shot, penalty* halten. **well** ~**d!** gut gehalten!

3 *vi* (**a**) (*with money*) sparen. **to** ~ **for sth** für *or* auf etw (*acc*) sparen; ~ **as you earn** (*Brit: savings scheme*) Sparprogramm *nt*, bei dem der monatliche Beitrag unversteuert bleibt.

(**b**) (*inf: keep*) (*food*) sich halten; (*news*) warten können.

♦**save up 1** *vi* sparen (*for* für, *auf* +*acc*). **2** *vt sep* (*not spend*) sparen; (*not use*) aufheben, aufbewahren. **he's saving himself** ~ **for the big match** er schont sich für das große Spiel.

save[2] **1** *prep* außer + *dat*. **2** *conj* (**a**) (*old, liter*) es sei denn (*geh*). (**b**) ~ **that** nur daß.

saveable *adj see* **savable**.

saveloy ['sævələɪ] *n* Zervelatwurst *f*.

saver ['seɪvəʳ] *n* (**a**) Retter(in *f*) *m*. **a** ~ **of souls** ein Seelenretter *m*. (**b**) (*with money*) Sparer(in *f*) *m*.

-saver *n suf* **it is a time-/money-**~ es spart Zeit/Geld.

saving ['seɪvɪŋ] **1** *adj* (**a**) (*redeeming*) **the book has the** ~ **quality of brevity** was aber für das Buch spricht, ist seine Kürze; **the one** ~ **feature of the scheme** das einzig Gute an dem Plan, das einzige, was für den Plan spricht; **his/the book's** ~ **sense of humour** sein Humor/der Humor in dem Buch, der manches wettmacht; **a self-confident man with a** ~ **air of modesty** ein selbstbewußter Mensch, dessen bescheidenes Auftreten aber für ihn spricht; **the** ~ **beauty of a pair of lovely eyes in an otherwise unattractive face** die Schönheit der Augen, durch die das sonst unscheinbare Gesicht gewinnt; **his** ~ **grace** was einen mit ihm versöhnt.

(**b**) *sparsam*. **she's not the** ~ **sort** sie ist nicht gerade sparsam.

(**c**) ~ **clause** Sicherheitsklausel *f*, einschränkende Klausel.

2 *n* (**a**) *no pl* (*act: rescue, Rel*) Rettung *f*.

(**b**) *no pl* (*of money*) Sparen *nt*. **to encourage** ~ zum Sparen ermutigen.

(**c**) (*of cost etc*) (*act*) Einsparung *f*; (*amount saved*) Ersparnis *f*. **how much of a** ~ **is there?** wieviel wird eingespart?; **we must make** ~**s** wir müssen sparen.

(**d**) ~**s** *pl* Ersparnisse *pl*; (*in account*) Spareinlagen *pl*; **post-office** ~**s** Postsparguthaben *nt*.

3 *prep, conj see* **save**[2].

-saving *adj suf* -sparend.

savings *in cpds* Spar-; ~ **account** *n* Sparkonto *nt*; ~ **bank** *n* Sparkasse *f*; ~ **book** *n* Sparbuch *nt*; ~ **stamp** *n* (*Brit*) Sparmarke *f*.

saviour, (*US also*) **savior** ['seɪvjəʳ] *n* Retter(in *f*) *m*; (*Rel also*) Erlöser, Heiland *m*. **Our** S~ unser Erlöser.

savoir-faire ['sævwɑ:'feəʳ] *n* Gewandtheit *f*; (*in social matters*) gute Umgangsformen *pl*. **it's a question of** ~ es ist nur eine Frage, wie man es anfaßt.

savor *etc* (*US*) *see* **savour** *etc*.

savory ['seɪvərɪ] *n* (*Bot*) Bohnenkraut *nt*.

savour, (*US*) **savor** ['seɪvəʳ] **1** *n* (**a**) Geschmack *m*. **a** ~ **of garlic** ein Knoblauchgeschmack *m*.

(**b**) (*slight trace*) Spur *f*. **there is a** ~ **of pride in everything he says** in allem, was er sagt, schwingt ein gewisser Stolz mit.

(**c**) (*enjoyable quality*) Reiz *m*.

2 *vt* (**a**) (*form*) kosten (*geh*), verkosten (*form*); *aroma* (*of food*) riechen.

(**b**) (*fig liter*) genießen, auskosten.

3 *vi* **to** ~ **of sth** (*fig liter*) etw ahnen lassen.

savouriness, (*US*) **savoriness** ['seɪvərɪnɪs] *n* (**a**) (*tastiness*) Schmackhaftigkeit *f*. **the** ~ **of the smells/taste** die leckeren Gerüche/der leckere Geschmack. (**b**) (*spiciness*) Würzigkeit, Pikantheit *f*. **the excessive** ~ **of all the food** das zu stark gewürzte Essen.

savourless, (US) **savorless** ['seɪvəlɪs] adj geschmacklos.
savoury, (US) **savory** ['seɪvərɪ] **1** adj **(a)** (appetizing) lecker; meal also schmackhaft.
(b) (not sweet) pikant. ~ omelette gefülltes Omelett; ~ biscuits Salzgebäck nt.
(c) (fig) angenehm, ersprießlich; sight also einladend; joke fein. **that was not the most ~ adjective to have chosen** das war ja nicht gerade das feinste Adjektiv.
2 n Häppchen nt. **would you like a sweet or a ~?** hätten Sie gern etwas Süßes oder etwas Pikantes or Salziges?
savoy (cabbage) [sə'vɔɪ(ˈkæbɪdʒ)] n Wirsing(kohl) m.
savvy ['sævɪ] (sl) **1** n (common sense) Grips m (inf), Köpfchen nt (inf); (know-how) Können, Know-how nt. **he hasn't got much ~** er hat keine Ahnung (inf) or keinen Dunst (inf); **show a bit of ~, use your ~!** streng mal dein Köpfchen or deinen Grips an (inf).
2 vt kapieren (inf). ~? **kapiert?** (inf), kapisko? (inf); **no ~** keine Ahnung (inf); (don't understand) kapier' ich nicht (inf).
saw[1] [sɔ:] pret of **see**[1].
saw[2] n Spruch m, Weisheit f.
saw[3] (vb: pret: ~ed, ptp ~ed or sawn) **1** n Säge f. musical or singing ~ singende Säge.
2 vt **(a)** sägen. **to ~ sth through** etw durchsägen; **to ~ sth in two** etw entzweisägen; ~ **the wood into smaller logs** zersägen Sie das Holz in kleinere Scheite; ~n **timber** Schnittholz nt.
(b) (the bird/the bird's wings ~ed the air der Vogel schlug wild mit den Flügeln; **he/his arms ~ed the air** er schlug wild um sich, er fuchtelte mit den Armen (durch die Luft).
3 vi **(a)** (person, saw) sägen; (wood) sich sägen lassen.
(b) to ~ (away) at the violin auf der Geige herumsägen; **to ~ (away) at the meat** am Fleisch herumsäbeln (inf).
♦**saw down** vt sep um- or absägen.
♦**saw off** vt sep absägen. **a ~n-~ shotgun** ein Gewehr mit abgesägtem Lauf.
♦**saw up** vt sep zersägen (into in +acc).
saw: ~**bones** n (dated sl) Medizinmann m (inf); ~**buck** n (US) Sägebock m; (sl) Zehndollarschein m; ~**dust** n Sägemehl nt; ~**fish** n Sägefisch m; ~**horse** n Sägebock m; ~**mill** n Sägewerk nt.
sawn [sɔ:n] ptp of **saw**[3].
saw-toothed [sɔ:'tu:θt] adj gezähnt.
sawyer ['sɔ:jə*] n Sägewerker m.
sax [sæks] n (inf: saxophone) Saxophon nt.
saxifrage ['sæksɪfrɪdʒ] n Steinbrech m.
Saxon ['sæksn] **1** n **(a)** Sachse m, Sächsin f; (Hist) (Angel)sachse m/-sächsin f. **(b)** (Ling) Sächsisch nt. **2** adj sächsisch; (Hist) (angel)sächsisch. ~ **genitive** sächsischer Genitiv.
Saxony ['sæksənɪ] n Sachsen nt.
saxophone ['sæksəfəʊn] n Saxophon nt.
saxophonist [ˌsæk'sɒfənɪst] n Saxophonist(in f) m.
say [seɪ] (vb: pret, ptp said) **1** vt **(a)** (what a person has to ~) let him have his ~ laß ihn mal reden or seine Meinung äußern; **everyone should be allowed to have his ~** jeder sollte seine Meinung äußern dürfen, jeder sollte zu Wort kommen; **you've had your ~, now let the others speak** Sie haben Ihre Meinung äußern können, nun lassen Sie einmal die anderen reden.
(b) (right to decide etc) Mitspracherecht nt (in bei). **to have no/a ~ in sth** bei etw nichts/etwas zu sagen haben, bei etw kein/ein Mitspracherecht haben; **I want more ~ in determining ...** ich möchte mehr Mitspracherecht bei der Entscheidung ... haben; **to have the last or final ~ (in sth)** (etw) letztlich entscheiden; (person also) das letzte Wort (bei etw) haben.
2 vti **(a)** sagen; poem aufsagen; prayer, text sprechen; (pronounce) aussprechen. ~ **after me ...** sprechen Sie mir nach ...; **he didn't have much to ~ for himself** er sagte or redete nicht viel; (in defence) er konnte nicht viel (zu seiner Verteidigung) sagen; **what have you got to ~ for yourself?** was haben Sie zu Ihrer Verteidigung zu sagen?; **who shall I ~?** wen darf ich melden?; **you can ~ what you like ...** Sie können sagen, was Sie wollen, ...; **that's not for him to ~** es steht ihm nicht zu, sich darüber zu äußern; (to decide) das kann ich/er nicht entscheiden; **I never thought I'd hear him ~ that** daß word ich hätte nie gedacht, daß er das sagen or dieses Wort aussprechen würde; **if you see her, ~ I haven't changed my mind** wenn du sie siehst, sag ihr or richte ihr aus, daß ich es mir nicht anders überlegt habe; **he said to wait here** er hat gesagt, ich soll/wir sollen etc.hier warten; **I'm not ~ing it's the best, but ...** ich sage or behaupte ja nicht, daß es das beste ist, aber ...; **never let it be said that I didn't try** es soll keiner sagen können or mir soll keiner nachsagen, ich hätte es nicht versucht; **well, all I can ~ is ...** na ja, da kann ich nur sagen ...; **do it this way — if you ~ so** machen Sie es so — wenn Sie meinen, ganz wie Sie meinen; **if you don't like it, ~ so** wenn Sie es nicht mögen, dann sagen Sie es doch; **why don't you ~ so?** warum sagen Sie es dann nicht?; **you'd better do it — who ~s?** tun Sie das lieber — wer sagt das?; **well, what do you want me to ~?** na ja, was soll ich da schon sagen?; **well, what can I ~?** na ja, was kann man da sagen?; **what does it mean? — I wouldn't like to ~** was bedeutet das? — das kann ich auch nicht sagen; **having said that, I must point out ...** ich muß allerdings darauf hinweisen ...; **so ~ing, he sat down** und mit den Worten setzte er sich.
(b) (weather forecast, newspaper, dictionary, clock, horoscope) sagen (inf); (thermometer also) anzeigen; (law, church, Bible, computer) sagen. **it ~s in the papers that ... in** den Zeitungen steht, daß ...; **what does the paper/this book/your horoscope etc ~?** was steht in der Zeitung/diesem Buch/deinem Horoskop etc?; **the rules ~ that ...** in den Regeln heißt es, daß ...; **what does the weather forecast ~?** wie ist or lautet (form) der Wetterbericht?; **the weather forecast said that ... es** hieß im Wetterbericht, daß ..., laut Wetterbericht ...; **what does your watch ~?** wie spät ist es auf Ihrer Uhr?, was sagt Ihre Uhr? (hum); **did the news ~ anything about**

the strike? kam in den Nachrichten etwas über den Streik?; **they weren't allowed to ~ anything about it in the papers** sie durften in den Zeitungen nichts darüber schreiben.
(c) (tell) sagen. **it's hard to ~ what's wrong** es ist schwer zu sagen, was nicht stimmt; **what does that ~ about his intentions/the main character?** was sagt das über seine Absichten/die Hauptperson aus?; **that ~s a lot about his character/state of mind** das läßt tief auf seinen Charakter/Gemütszustand schließen; **these figures ~ a lot about recent trends** diese Zahlen sind in bezug auf neuere Tendenzen sehr aufschlußreich or sagen viel über neuere Tendenzen aus; and **that's ~ing a lot** und das will schon etwas heißen; that's not ~ing much das will nicht viel heißen; **that doesn't ~ much for him** das spricht nicht für ihn; that ~s a lot for him das spricht für ihn; **there's no ~ing** das weiß keiner; **she blushed? that ~s a lot** sie ist rot geworden? das läßt tief blicken.
(d) what would you ~ **to a whisky/holiday/game of tennis?** wie wär's mit einem Whisky/mit Urlaub/, wenn wir Tennis spielen würden?; **I wouldn't ~ no to a cup of tea** ich hätte nichts gegen eine Tasse Tee; **he never ~s no to a drink** er schlägt einen Drink nie aus, er sagt nie nein zu einem Drink; **what did he ~ to your plan?** was hat er zu Ihrem Plan gesagt?; **I'll offer £500, what do you ~ to that?** ich biete £ 500, was meinen Sie dazu?; **what do you ~ we go now?** (inf) was hieltest du davon or wie wär's, wenn wir jetzt gingen?, was meinst du, sollen wir jetzt gehen?; **shall we ~ Tuesday/£50?** sagen wir Dienstag/£ 50?; **let's try again, what d'you ~?** (inf) was meinste (inf), versuchen wir's noch mal?; **what do you ~?** was meinen Sie?
(e) (exclamatory) well, I must ~! na, ich muß schon sagen!; I ~! (dated) na so was!; (to attract attention) hallo!; **I ~, are you serious?** (dated) das ist doch wohl nicht Ihr Ernst?; **I ~, thanks awfully, old stick!** (dated) na dann vielen Dank, altes Haus! (dated); **I ~, are you crazy?** (dated) sag mal, bist du denn wahnsinnig?; ~, **what a great idea!** (esp US) Mensch, tolle Idee! (inf); ~, **buddy!** (esp US) he, Mann! (inf); **I should ~ (so)!** das möchte ich doch meinen!; **you don't ~!** (also iro) nein wirklich?, was du nicht sagst!; **well said!** (ganz) richtig!; **you('ve) said it!** Sie sagen es!; **you can ~ that again!** das kann man wohl sagen!; ~ **no more!** ich weiß Bescheid!; ~s **you!** (inf) das meinst auch nur du! (inf); ~s **who?** (inf) wer sagt das?; **and so ~ all of us** und wir stimmen alle zu; **though I ~ it myself, though I ~s it as shouldn't** (inf) wenn ich das mal selbst sagen darf.
(f) (it's) easier said than done das ist leichter gesagt als getan; **no sooner said than done** gesagt, getan; **when all is said and done** letzten Endes; **he is said to be very rich** er soll sehr reich sein, es heißt, er sei sehr reich; **a building said to have been built by ...** ein Gebäude, das angeblich von ... gebaut wurde or das von ... gebaut worden sein soll; **it goes without ~ing that ...** es versteht sich von selbst or ist selbstverständlich, daß ...; **that goes without ~ing** das ist selbstverständlich; **that is to ~** das heißt; (correcting also) beziehungsweise; **to ~ nothing of the noise/costs** etc von dem Lärm/den Kosten etc ganz zu schweigen or mal ganz abgesehen; **to ~ nothing of being ...** davon, daß ich/er etc ..., ganz zu schweigen or mal ganz abgesehen; **that's not to ~ that ...** das soll nicht heißen, daß ...; **they ~ ..., it is said ...** es heißt ...; **enough said!** (na ja) genug!
(g) (suppose) ~ **it takes three men to ...** angenommen, man braucht drei Leute, um zu ...; ~ **you need more time** angenommen, Sie brauchen mehr Zeit; **if it happens on, ~, Wednesday** wenn es am, sagen wir mal Mittwoch, passiert?
sayest ['seɪəst] (obs) 2nd pers sing of **say**.
saying ['seɪɪŋ] n Redensart f; (proverb) Sprichwort nt. **as the ~ goes** wie man so sagt, wie es so schön heißt.
say-so ['seɪsəʊ] n (inf) (assertion) Wort nt; (authority) Plazet nt. **on whose ~?** wer sagt das? (inf); **mit welchem Recht?**
scab [skæb] **1** n **(a)** (on cut) Schorf, Grind m. **(b)** (scabies) Krätze f. **(c)** (inf: strikebreaker) Streikbrecher(in f) m. ~ **labour** Streikbrecher pl. **2** vi **(a)** (inf) den Streik brechen. **(b)** (wound) **to ~ over** Schorf bilden.
scabbard ['skæbəd] n Scheide f.
scabby ['skæbɪ] adj (+er) **(a)** skin, hands schorfig, grindig. **(b)** (having scabies) räudig.
scabies ['skeɪbi:z] n Krätze, Skabies (spec) f; (of animal also) Räude, Schäbe f.
scabious ['skeɪbɪəs] adj (having scabies) räudig.
scabrous ['skeɪbrəs] adj (indecent) geschmacklos.
scaffold ['skæfəld] n (on building) Gerüst nt; (for execution) Schafott nt.
scaffolding ['skæfəldɪŋ] n Gerüst nt. **to put up ~** ein Gerüst aufbauen.
scalawag ['skæləwæg] n (US) see **scallywag**.
scald [skɔ:ld] **1** n Verbrühung f. **2** vt **(a)** oneself, skin etc verbrühen. **he was ~ed to death** er erlitt tödliche Verbrennungen pl. **(b)** instruments, vegetables abbrühen; milk abkochen.
scalding ['skɔ:ldɪŋ] adj siedend; (inf: also ~ hot) siedend heiß.
scale[1] [skeɪl] **1** n (of fish, snake, skin) Schuppe f; (of rust) Flocke f; (of paint) Plättchen nt; (kettle ~) Kesselstein m no pl. **to take the ~s from sb's eyes** jdm die Augen öffnen; **the ~s fell from his eyes** es fiel ihm wie Schuppen von den Augen.
2 vt fish (ab)schuppen.
3 vi (also ~ off) sich schuppen; (paint, rust) abblättern.
scale[2] **1** n (pair of) ~s pl, ~ (form) Waage f; **the S~s** (Astron) die Waage; ~-**pan** Waagschale f; **he turns or tips the ~s at 80 kilos** er bringt 80 Kilo auf die Waage; **the extra votes have tipped or turned the ~s in favour of Labour** die zusätzlichen Stimmen gaben den Ausschlag für die Labour Party. **2** vi wiegen.
scale[3] n **(a)** Skala f; (on thermometer etc also) Gradeinteilung f; (on ruler) (Maß)einteilung f; (fig) Leiter f; (social ~) Stufenleiter f; (list, table) Tabelle f. ~ **of charges** Gebührenordnung f, Tarife pl; **he ranks at the top of the ~ of contemporary violinists** er steht an der Spitze der zeitgenössischen Geiger.

(b) (*instrument*) Meßgerät *nt*.
(c) (*Mus*) Tonleiter *f*. the ~ of G die G(-Dur)-Tonleiter.
(d) (*of map etc*) Maßstab *m*. on a ~ of 5 km to the cm in einem Maßstab von 5 km zu 1 cm; what is the ~? welchen Maßstab hat es?, in welchem Maßstab ist es?; to draw sth to ~ etw im Maßstab *or* maßstabgerecht zeichnen.
(e) (*fig: size, extent*) Umfang *m*, Ausmaß *nt*. to entertain on a large/small/different ~ Feste im größeren/im kleineren/in einem anderen Rahmen geben; large stores buy on a different ~ from small shops große Kaufhäuser kaufen in ganz anderen Mengen als kleine Geschäfte; inflation on an unprecedented ~ Inflation von bisher nie gekanntem Ausmaß; they differ enormously in ~ sie haben völlig verschiedene Größenordnungen; a house designed on a magnificent ~ ein in großem Stil *or* großzügig angelegtes Haus; it's similar but on a smaller ~ es ist ähnlich, nur kleiner; on a national ~ auf nationaler Ebene.
◆**scale down** *vt sep* (*lit*) verkleinern; (*fig*) verringern. a sort of ~d-~ Parthenon eine Art Parthenon im Kleinformat.
◆**scale up** *vt sep* (*lit*) vergrößern; (*fig*) erhöhen.
scale⁴ *vt mountain, wall* erklettern.
scale: ~ drawing *n* maßstabgerechte *or* maßstabgetreue Zeichnung; ~ model *n* maßstäbliches *or* maßstabgetreues Modell.
scalene ['skeɪliːn] *adj triangle* ungleichseitig; *cone* schief.
scaliness ['skeɪlɪnɪs] *n* Schuppigkeit *f*.
scaling ladder ['skeɪlɪŋˌlædə'] *n* Sturmleiter *f*.
scallop ['skɒləp] **1** *n* **(a)** (*Zool*) Kammuschel, Jakobsmuschel (*esp Cook*) *f*. ~ shell (*for cooking*) Muschelschale *f*.
(b) ['skæləp] (*loop*) Bogen *m*, bogenförmige Verzierung; (*on linenware*) Feston *m*.
2 ['skæləp] *vt* (*decorate with loops*) mit Bögen *or* einem Bogenrand versehen; *pastry also* bogenförmig eindrücken; *linenware* festonieren.
scalloped ['skæləpt] *adj* **(a)** mit einem Bogenrand; *linenware* festoniert. ~ edge Bogen-/Festonrand *m*. **(b)** ['skɒləpt] (*Cook*) überbacken.
scallywag ['skælɪwæg] *n* (*inf*) Schlingel (*inf*), Strolch (*inf*) *m*.
scalp [skælp] **1** *n* Kopfhaut *f*; (*as Indian trophy*) Skalp *m*. to want *or* be after *or* be out for sb's ~ (*fig*) jdn fertigmachen wollen (*inf*). **2** *vt* skalpieren; (*hum: by barber*) kahlscheren (*inf*). you've really been ~ed (*hum*) du bist wohl die Treppe runtergefallen (*inf*).
scalpel ['skælpəl] *n* Skalpell *nt*.
scaly ['skeɪlɪ] *adj* (+*er*) schuppig; *walls* abblätternd.
scamp¹ [skæmp] *n* Frechdachs, Lausebengel (*inf*) *m*.
scamp² *vt work* pfuschen *or* schludern (*inf*) bei.
scamper ['skæmpə'] **1** *n* they can go for a ~ in the garden sie können im Garten herumtollen; take the dog/children out for a ~ dem Hund/den Kindern Auslauf verschaffen.
2 *vi* (*person, child, puppy*) trippeln, trappeln; (*squirrel, rabbit*) hoppeln; (*mice*) huschen. the rabbit ~ed down its hole das Kaninchen verschwand blitzschnell in seinem Loch.
scampi ['skæmpɪ] *npl* Scampi *pl*.
scan [skæn] **1** *vt* **(a)** (*search with sweeping movement*) schwenken über (+*acc*); (*person*) seine Augen wandern lassen über (+*acc*); *newspaper, book* überfliegen; (*examine closely*) *horizon* absuchen; (*by radar*) absuchen, abtasten. he ~ned her face for a sign of emotion er suchte in ihrem Gesicht nach Anzeichen einer Gefühlsregung.
(b) (*TV*) abtasten, rastern.
(c) *verse* in Versfüße zerlegen.
2 *vi* (*verse*) das richtige Versmaß haben, sich reimen (*inf*). he couldn't make it ~ er konnte es nicht ins richtige Versmaß bringen; stressed differently so that the line ~s anders betont, um das richtige Metrum in der Zeile zu bekommen.
3 *n* (*Med*) Scan *m*; (*in pregnancy*) Ultraschall-Untersuchung *f*; (*picture*) Ultraschallaufnahme *f*.
scandal ['skændl] *n* **(a)** Skandal *m*. the ~ of our overcrowded hospitals unsere skandalös überfüllten Krankenhäuser; to cause/create a ~ einen Skandal verursachen; (*amongst neighbours etc*) allgemeinen Aufsehen erregen; it's a ~! (das ist) ein Skandal!; it is a ~ that ... es ist skandalös, daß ...
(b) *no pl* (*gossip*) Skandalgeschichten *pl*; (*piece of gossip*) Skandalgeschichte *f*, Skandälchen *nt*. the latest ~ der neueste Klatsch *or* Tratsch (*inf*).
scandalize ['skændəlaɪz] *vt* schockieren. she was ~d sie war entrüstet *or* empört (*by* über +*acc*).
scandal: ~monger *n* Klatschmaul *nt* (*inf*), Lästerzunge *f*; ~mongering *n* Klatschsucht *f*; (*by press*) Skandalsucht *f*.
scandalous ['skændələs] *adj* skandalös. ~ talk böswilliger Klatsch; a ~ report/tale eine Skandalgeschichte.
scandalously ['skændələslɪ] *adv* skandalös. to talk ~ about sb über jdn böswillig klatschen, böse *or* üble Gerüchte über jdn verbreiten; she's ~ neglectful of her children es ist skandalös *or* ein Skandal, wie sie ihre Kinder vernachlässigt.
scandal sheet *n* Skandalblatt, Revolverblatt (*inf*) *nt*.
Scandinavia [ˌskændɪˈneɪvɪə] *n* Skandinavien *nt*.
Scandinavian [ˌskændɪˈneɪvɪən] **1** *adj* skandinavisch. **2** *n* Skandinavier(in *f*) *m*.
scanner ['skænə'] *n* (*Rad*) Richtantenne *f*; (*TV*) Abtaststrahl *m*.
scansion ['skænʃən] *n* (*Poet*) metrische Gliederung; (*Sch*) Zerlegung *f* in Versfüße.
scant [skænt] *adj* (+*er*) wenig *inv; satisfaction, attention, respect also, chance* gering; *success* gering, mager; *supply, grazing, amount* dürftig, spärlich. to do ~ justice to sth einer Sache (*dat*) wenig *or* kaum gerecht werden; a ~ 3 hours knappe *or* kaum 3 Stunden.
scantily ['skæntɪlɪ] *adv* spärlich. ~ provided with ... mit einem knappen *or* spärlichen *or* dürftigen Vorrat an (+*dat*) ...
scantiness ['skæntɪnɪs] *n see* **scanty** Spärlichkeit, Dürftigkeit *f*; Kärglichkeit *f*; Schütterkeit *f*; Knappheit *f*.
scanty ['skæntɪ] *adj* (+*er*) *amount, supply* spärlich, dürftig;

---

vegetation, meal also kärglich; *harvest also* mager; *hair* schütter; *piece of clothing, supply* knapp.
scapegoat ['skeɪpgəʊt] *n* Sündenbock *m*. to be a ~ for sth für etw der Sündenbock sein; to use sb/sth as a ~, to make sb/sth one's ~ jdn/einer Sache die Schuld zuschieben.
scapegrace ['skeɪpgreɪs] *n* (*obs*) Tunichtgut *m* (*old*).
scapula ['skæpjʊlə] *n* (*Anat*) Schulterblatt *nt*.
scar [skɑ:'] **1** *n* (*on skin, tree*) Narbe *f*; (*scratch*) Kratzer *m*; (*burn*) Brandfleck *m*, Brandloch *nt*; (*fig*) (*emotional*) Wunde *f*; (*on good name*) Makel *m*. ~ tissue vernarbtes Fleisch.
2 *vt skin, tree* Narben/eine Narbe hinterlassen auf (+*dat*); *furniture* zerkratzen; Brandflecken hinterlassen auf (+*dat*); (*fig*) *person* zeichnen. he was ~red for life (*lit*) er behielt bleibende Narben zurück; (*fig*) er war fürs Leben gezeichnet; her ~red face ihr narbiges Gesicht; the table was ~red with cigarette burns der Tisch war mit Brandlöchern *or* Brandflecken von Zigaretten übersät; his mind was ~red forever by this tragic occurrence dieses tragische Ereignis hatte bei ihm tiefe Wunden hinterlassen.
3 *vi* Narben/eine Narbe hinterlassen.
scarab ['skærəb] *n* Skarabäus *m*.
scarce [skeəs] **1** *adj* (+*er*) (*in short supply*) knapp; (*rare*) selten. to make oneself ~ (*inf*) sich rar machen (*inf*). **2** *adv* (*old*) *see* **scarcely**.
scarcely ['skeəslɪ] *adv* **(a)** kaum. ~ anybody kaum einer *or* jemand; ~ anything fast *or* beinahe nichts; ~ ever kaum jemals, fast *or* beinahe nie; I ~ know what to say ich weiß nicht recht, was ich sagen soll.
(b) (*not really*) wohl kaum. you can ~ expect him to believe that Sie erwarten doch wohl nicht *or* kaum, daß er das glaubt; he's ~ the most polite of men er ist nicht gerade *or* er ist wohl kaum der Höflichste.
scarceness ['skeəsnɪs], **scarcity** ['skeəsɪtɪ] *n* (*shortage*) Knappheit *f*; (*rarity*) Seltenheit *f*. because of the ~ of talent among the singers/pupils weil so wenige Sänger/Schüler wirklich begabt sind; his pictures are expensive because of their ~ seine Bilder sind teuer, weil es so wenige davon gibt; a ~ of qualified people ein Mangel *m* an qualifizierten Kräften; in years of ~ in schlechten Jahren; there are many scarcities in wartime in Kriegszeiten ist vieles knapp; scarcity value Seltenheitswert *m*.
scare [skeə'] **1** *n* (*fright, shock*) Schreck(en) *m*; (*general alarm*) Panikstimmung, Hysterie *f* (*about* in bezug auf +*acc*, wegen). to give sb a ~ jdm einen Schrecken einjagen; (*make sb jump also*) jdn erschrecken; the devaluation ~ die Abwertungshysterie; to create *or* cause a ~ eine Panik auslösen, allgemeine Hysterie auslösen.
2 *vt* einen Schrecken einjagen (+*dat*); (*worry also*) Angst machen (+*dat*); (*frighten physically*) *person, animal* erschrecken; *birds* aufschrecken. to be ~d Angst haben (*of* vor +*dat*); to be easily ~d sehr schreckhaft sein; (*easily worried*) sich (*dat*) leicht Angst machen lassen; (*timid: deer etc*) sehr scheu sein; to be ~d stiff *or* to death *or* out of one's wits (*all inf*) Todesängste ausstehen, fürchterliche Angst haben; she was too ~d to speak sie konnte vor Angst nicht sprechen; she was always too ~d to speak in public sie getraute sich nie, in der Öffentlichkeit zu sprechen; he's ~d of telling her the truth er getraut sich nicht, ihr die Wahrheit zu sagen; I'm ~d at the thought ich habe Angst davor.
3 *vi* I don't ~ easily ich bekomme nicht so schnell Angst.
◆**scare away** *vt sep* verscheuchen; *people* verjagen.
◆**scare off** *vt sep* **(a)** *see* **scare away**. **(b)** (*put off*) abschrecken (*prep obj* von).
scare: ~crow *n* (*lit, fig*) Vogelscheuche *f*; ~head *n* (*US*) Sensationsschlagzeile *f*; ~monger *n* Panikmacher *m*; ~mongering *n* Panikmache(rei) *f* (*inf*); ~ story *n* Schauergeschichte *f*; ~ tactics *npl* Panikmache(rei) (*inf*), Verängstigungstaktik *f*.
scarf [skɑ:f] *n, pl* **scarves** Schal *m*; (*neck* ~) Halstuch *nt*; (*head*~) Kopftuch *nt*; (*round the shoulders*) Schultertuch *nt*. ~ pin Brosche, Busen- *or* Vorstecknadel *f*.
scarifying ['skeərɪfaɪɪŋ] *adj* (*inf*) beängstigend; *film* grus(e)lig (*inf*). that was really ~ da konnte man Angst kriegen (*inf*).
scarlatina [ˌskɑ:ləˈtiːnə] *n* Scharlach *m*.
scarlet ['skɑ:lɪt] **1** *n* Scharlach(rot) *nt*. ~ fever Scharlach *m*, Scharlachfieber *nt*. **2** *adj* (scharlach)rot, hochrot. to turn ~ hochrot werden, rot anlaufen (*inf*); he was ~ with rage er war rot *or* knallrot (*inf*) vor Wut; a ~ woman (*old, hum*) eine verrufene *or* liederliche Frau.
scarp [skɑ:p] *n* Abhang *m*.
scarper ['skɑ:pə'] *vi* (*Brit sl*) abhauen (*inf*), verduften (*sl*).
scarves [skɑ:vz] *pl of* **scarf**.
scary ['skeərɪ] *adj* (+*er*) (*inf*) **(a)** unheimlich; *house also, film* grus(e)lig (*inf*). it was pretty ~ da konnte man schon Angst kriegen (*inf*). **(b)** (*nervous*) *horse, person* schreckhaft; (*easily worried*) ängstlich.
scat [skæt] *interj* (*inf*) verschwinde; verschwindet!
scathing ['skeɪðɪŋ] *adj* bissig; *remark also* schneidend; *attack* scharf, schonungslos; *look* vernichtend; *criticism* beißend, vernichtend. to be ~ bissige *or* schneidende Bemerkungen *pl* machen (*about* über +*acc*).
scathingly ['skeɪðɪŋlɪ] *adv* answer mit schneidendem Hohn; *look* vernichtend; *criticize, attack* scharf, schonungslos. a ~ critical review eine Rezension, die vernichtende Kritik übt.
scatology [skəˈtɒlədʒɪ] *n* (*Med*) Koprologie *f* (*spec*); (*fig*) Fäkalsprache, Skatologie (*geh*) *f*.
scatter ['skætə'] **1** *n see* **scattering**.
2 *vt* **(a)** (*distribute at random*) verstreuen; *seeds, gravel*, (*Phys*) *light* streuen (*on, onto* auf +*acc*); *money* verschleudern; (*not group together*) (unregelmäßig) verteilen; *votes* verteilen (*between* auf +*acc*). to ~ sth around *or* about etw überall

umherstreuen or verstreuen; to ~ sth with sth etw mit etw bestreuen; **the books were ~ed (about)** all over the room die Bücher lagen im ganzen Zimmer herum or verstreut; **white material ~ed with blue stars** weißer Stoff mit blauen Sternen besät; **she knocked the table over, ~ing glasses all over the room** sie stieß den Tisch um, und die Gläser flogen durch das ganze Zimmer; **don't ~ your investments here and there** investieren Sie nicht so kleckerweise.

(b) (disperse) auseinandertreiben; army etc also zersprengen; (demonstrators, crowd also) zerstreuen. **his friends were ~ed all over the country** seine Freunde waren über das ganze Land verstreut or zerstreut; **the division was ~ed all over the countryside** die Division war über das ganze Gebiet versprengt; see also **scattered.**

3 vi sich zerstreuen (to in +acc); (in a hurry, in fear) auseinanderlaufen.

scatter: ~**brain** n (inf) Schussel m (inf); ~**brained** ['skætə,breɪnd] adj (inf) schußlig (inf), schusselig (inf), zerfahren, flatterhaft; ~ **cushion** n (Sofa)kissen nt.

scattered ['skætəd] adj population gestreut; villages verstreut; clouds, showers vereinzelt.

scattering ['skætərɪŋ] n (of people) vereinzeltes Häufchen; (Phys: of light, waves) Streuung f. **a ~ of books/houses/dots** vereinzelte Bücher pl/Häuser pl/Punkte pl; **a thin ~ of snow on the hillside** dünner Schneefall auf dem Hügel.

scatty ['skætɪ] adj (+ er) (inf) **(a)** (scatterbrained) schußlig (inf), schusselig (inf). **(b)** (mad) verrückt, närrisch (inf).

scavenge ['skævɪndʒ] **1** vt (lit, fig) ergattern. **the scraps are ~d by hungry gulls** hungrige Möwen ergattern or holen sich (dat) die Essensreste; **the tramp ~d food from the bins** der Landstreicher plünderte die Abfalleimer; **the car had been completely ~d** das Auto war völlig ausgeschlachtet worden.

2 vi (lit) Nahrung suchen. **jackals live by scavenging** Schakale leben von Aas; **to ~ in the bins** die Abfalleimer plündern; **he's always scavenging around in the scrapyards** er durchstöbert dauernd die Schrottplätze.

scavenger ['skævɪndʒəʳ] n (animal) Aasfresser m; (fig: person) Aasgeier m.

scenario [sɪ'nɑːrɪəʊ] n Szenar(ium) nt; (fig) Szenario nt.

scene [siːn] n **(a)** (place, setting) Schauplatz m; (of play, novel) Ort m der Handlung. **the ~ of the crime** der Tatort, der Schauplatz des Verbrechens; **the ~ of the battle was a small hill** die Schlacht fand auf einem kleinen Hügel statt; **to set the ~** (lit, fig) den richtigen Rahmen geben; **the ~ is set in Padua** Ort der Handlung ist Padua, das Stück/der Roman etc spielt in Padua; **a change of ~** does you good ein Tapetenwechsel m tut dir gut; **to come or appear on the ~** auftauchen, auf der Bildfläche erscheinen; **after the accident the police were first on the ~** nach dem Unfall war die Polizei als erste zur Stelle.

(b) (description, incident) Szene f.

(c) (Theat) Szene f. **Act II, ~ i** Akt II, 1. Auftritt or Szene.

(d) (Theat: scenery) Bühnenbild nt, Kulisse f. **the stagehands move the ~s** die Bühnenarbeiter wechseln die Kulissen; **behind the ~s** (lit, fig) hinter den Kulissen.

(e) (sight) Anblick m; (landscape) Landschaft f; (tableau) Szene f. **colourful ~s of Parisian life** bunte Szenen aus dem Pariser Leben; **favourite Glasgow ~s** die beliebtesten Ansichten von Glasgow; **they left behind a ~ of destruction** sie hinterließen eine Stätte der Verwüstung.

(f) (fuss, argument) Szene f.

(g) (inf) **the London drug/pop etc ~** die Londoner Drogen-/ Popszene etc (sl); **on the fashion ~** in der Modewelt; **that's not my ~** da steh' ich nicht drauf (sl); **to know the ~ or what the ~ is** wissen, was läuft (sl); **it's a whole different ~ here** hier sieht alles ganz anders aus, hier läuft alles ganz anders (inf); **to make the ~** groß herauskommen (inf); **he knew he'd made the ~ when ...** er wußte, daß er es geschafft hatte, als ... (inf).

scene: ~ **change** n Szenenwechsel m; ~ **painter** n Bühnen- or Kulissenmaler(in f) m.

scenery ['siːnərɪ] n **(a)** (landscape) Landschaft f. **there was no ~ at all to look at** die Landschaft bot überhaupt nichts Sehenswertes; **do you like the ~?** gefällt Ihnen die Gegend?; **the new typist has improved the ~ in the office** (hum) seit wir die neue Schreibkraft haben, bietet unser Büro einen erfreulicheren Anblick; **I'm tired of all the city ~** ich bin stadtmüde.

(b) (Theat) Bühnendekoration f, Kulissen pl.

scene shifter n Kulissenschieber m.

scenic ['siːnɪk] adj **(a)** (of landscape) landschaftlich. ~ **shots** (Phot) Landschaftsaufnahmen pl.

(b) (picturesque) malerisch. ~ **railway** Touristenbahnlinie f durch landschaftlich schönes Gebiet, ≈ Berg- und Talbahn f.

(c) (theatrical) bühnentechnisch; filmtechnisch. ~ **effects** (Theat) Bühneneffekte pl; (Film) landschaftliche Effekte pl.

scent [sent] **1** n **(a)** (smell) Duft, Geruch m. **there was the ~ of danger in the air** es roch nach Gefahr.

(b) (perfume) Parfüm nt.

(c) (of animal) Fährte f. **to be on the ~** (lit, fig) auf der Fährte or Spur sein (of sb/sth jdm/einer Sache); **to lose the ~** (lit, fig) die Spur or Fährte verlieren; **to put or throw sb off the ~** (lit, fig) jdn von der Spur or Fährte abbringen or ablenken.

(d) (sense of smell) Geruchssinn m; (fig) (Spür)nase f.

2 vt **(a)** (smell, suspect) wittern.

(b) (perfume) parfümieren. **roses ~ed the air** der Duft von Rosen erfüllte die Luft; **beautifully/lightly ~ed** hair, skin duftend/leicht parfümiert.

♦ **scent out** vt sep (lit, fig) aufspüren; story ausfindig machen.

scent: ~ **bottle** n Parfümfläschchen nt; ~ **gland** n (pleasant smell) Duftdrüse f; (unpleasant smell) Stinkdrüse f; ~**less** adj flower duftlos, geruchlos; ~ **spray** n Parfümzerstäuber m.

scepter n (US) see **sceptre.**

sceptic, (US) **skeptic** ['skeptɪk] n Skeptiker(in f) m.

sceptical, (US) **skeptical** ['skeptɪkəl] adj skeptisch. **he was ~ about it** er stand der Sache skeptisch gegenüber, er war skeptisch; **I'm ~ about the necessity of this** ich bin skeptisch or ich bezweifle, ob das nötig ist.

sceptically, (US) **skeptically** ['skeptɪkəlɪ] adv skeptisch.

scepticism, (US) **skepticism** ['skeptɪsɪzəm] n Skepsis f (about gegenüber).

sceptre, (US) **scepter** ['septəʳ] n Szepter nt.

sch abbr of **school** Sch.

schedule ['ʃedjuːl, (esp Brit),'skedʒʊəl] **1** n **(a)** (of events) Programm nt; (of work) Zeitplan m; (of lessons) Stundenplan m; (esp US: timetable) Fahr-/Flugplan m; (US: list) Verzeichnis nt. **what's on the ~ for today?** was steht für heute auf dem Programm?; **according to ~** planmäßig; (work also) nach Plan; **the train is behind ~** der Zug hat Verspätung; **the bus was on ~** der Bus war pünktlich or kam fahrplanmäßig an; **the building will be opened on ~** das Gebäude wird wie geplant eröffnet werden; **the work is up to ~** die Arbeit verläuft nach Zeitplan; **the work is ahead of ~** wir/sie sind (mit der Arbeit) dem Zeitplan voraus/in Verzug or im Rückstand; **we are working to a very tight ~** wir arbeiten nach einem knapp bemessenen or sehr knappen Zeitplan.

(b) (insurance, mortgage ~) Urkunde f; (US Jur: appendix) Anhang m.

2 vt planen; (put on programme, timetable) ansetzen; (US: list) aufführen. **the work is ~d for completion in 3 months** die Arbeit soll (nach dem or laut Zeitplan) in 3 Monaten fertig(gestellt) sein; **this is not ~d for this year** das steht für dieses Jahr nicht auf dem Programm; **this building is ~d for demolition** es ist geplant, dieses Gebäude abzureißen; **you are ~d to speak for 20 minutes/tomorrow** für Sie sind 20 Minuten Sprechzeit vorgesehen/Ihre Rede ist für morgen geplant or angesetzt; **trains/buses to New York will be ~d differently** die Abfahrtszeiten der Züge/Busse nach New York werden geändert; **the plane is ~d for 2 o'clock** planmäßige Ankunft/planmäßiger Abflug ist 2 Uhr; **the journey is ~d to last 7 hours** die Fahrt soll 7 Stunden dauern; **this stop was not ~d** dieser Aufenthalt war nicht eingeplant.

scheduled ['ʃedjuːld (esp Brit), 'skedʒʊəld] adj vorgesehen, geplant; departure etc planmäßig. ~ **flight** (not charter) Linienflug m; (on timetable) planmäßiger Flug.

schema ['skiːmə] n, pl **-ta** ['skiːmətə] Darstellung f; (Philos) Schema nt.

schematic adj, ~**ally** adv [skɪ'mætɪk, -əlɪ] schematisch.

scheme [skiːm] **1** n **(a)** (plan) Plan m, Programm nt; (project) Projekt nt; (insurance ~, savings ~) Programm nt; (pension ~) Pensionsprogramm nt or -plan m; (idea) Idee f. **was that your ~?** hatten Sie das beabsichtigt or geplant?; **the ~ for the new ring road** das neue Umgehungsstraßenprojekt; **a ~ of work** ein Arbeitsprogramm nt or -plan m.

(b) (plot) (raffinierter) Plan; (political also) Komplott nt; (at court, in firm etc) Intrige f. **a ~ to overthrow the government** ein Komplott gegen die Regierung, Pläne pl, die Regierung zu stürzen; **the CIA's ~s to discredit Castro** die Machenschaften pl des CIA, um Castro zu diskreditieren.

(c) (arrangement, layout) (of town centre etc) Anlage f; (of room etc) Einrichtung f. **rhyme ~** Reimschema nt.

(d) (housing ~) Siedlung f.

2 vi Pläne schmieden or aushecken (inf); (at court, in firm etc) intrigieren. **to ~ for sth auf etw** (acc) hinarbeiten.

schemer ['skiːməʳ] n raffinierter Schlauner; (at court, in firm etc) Intrigant(in f), Ränkeschmied (liter) m. **my mother's a real ~** meine Mutter schmiedet immer ganz raffinierte Pläne.

scheming ['skiːmɪŋ] **1** n raffiniertes Vorgehen, Tricks pl (inf); (of politicians, businessmen etc) Machenschaften, Schliche pl; (at court, in firm etc) Intrigen, Ränke (liter) pl.

2 adj girl, methods, businessman raffiniert, durchtrieben; colleague, courtier, politician intrigant. **what's in your ~ little mind?** was führst du im Schild?; **her ~ mother-in-law** ihre hinterhältige Schwiegermutter.

scherzo ['skɜːtsəʊ] n Scherzo nt.

schism ['sɪzəm] n (Eccl) Schisma nt; (general also) Spaltung f.

schismatic [sɪz'mætɪk] **1** adj schismatisch. **2** n Schismatiker(in f) m.

schist [ʃɪst] n Schiefer m.

schizo ['skɪtsəʊ] (inf) **1** n (schizophrenic) Schizophrene(r) mf; (crazy) Verrückte(r) mf (inf). **2** adj (schizophrenic) schizophren; (crazy) verrückt (inf).

schizoid ['skɪtsɔɪd] **1** adj schizoid. **2** n Schizoide(r) mf.

schizophrenia [,skɪtsəʊ'friːnɪə] n Schizophrenie f, Spaltungsirresein nt.

schizophrenic [,skɪtsəʊ'frenɪk] **1** adj person, reaction schizophren. **his symptoms are ~** er zeigt die Symptome eines Schizophrenen; **a ~ illness** eine Art Schizophrenie. **2** n Schizophrene(r) mf.

schizophrenically [,skɪtsəʊ'frenɪkəlɪ] adv schizophren. **a ~ disturbed person** ein Mensch mit Bewußtseinsspaltung.

schmal(t)z [ʃmɔːlts] n (inf) Schmalz m (inf).

schnap(p)s [ʃnæps] n Schnaps m.

schnitzel ['ʃnɪtsəl] n (Wiener) Schnitzel nt.

schnorkel ['ʃnɔːkl] n see **snorkel.**

schnozzle ['ʃnɒzəl] n (esp US sl) Zinken m (sl).

scholar ['skɒləʳ] n **(a)** (learned person) Gelehrte(r) mf. **the foremost ~s of our time** die führenden Wissenschaftler unserer Zeit; **a famous Shakespeare ~** ein bekannter Shakespearekenner; **I'm no ~** ich bin ja kein Gelehrter.

(b) (student) Student(in f) m; Schüler(in f) m.

(c) (scholarship holder) Stipendiat(in f) m.

scholarliness ['skɒləlɪnɪs] n (of person, work) Gelehrtheit, Gelehrsamkeit f. **the air of ~ in the library** die Atmosphäre der Gelehrsamkeit in der Bibliothek; **the ~ of his interests** sein

Interesse an hochgeistigen Dingen; **the ~ of his appearance** sein gelehrtes Aussehen.

scholarly ['skɒləlɪ] *adj* wissenschaftlich; *(learned)* gelehrt; *interests* hochgeistig. **he's not at all ~** er hat keinen Hang zum Hochgeistigen; *(in his approach)* er geht überhaupt nicht wissenschaftlich vor; **his way of life was very ~** er führte ein sehr beschauliches Leben.

scholarship ['skɒləʃɪp] *n* **(a)** *(learning)* Gelehrsamkeit *f*. ~ **flourished during the Renaissance** die Gelehrsamkeit entfaltete sich in der Renaissance zur vollen Blüte.
 (b) *(money award)* Stipendium *nt*, Begabtenförderung *f*. **to win a ~ to Cambridge** ein Stipendium *nt* für Cambridge bekommen; **on a ~** mit einem Stipendium; ~ **holder** Stipendiat(in *f*) *m*.

scholastic [skə'læstɪk] *adj* **(a)** *(relative to school)* schulisch, Schul-; *(Univ)* Studien-. **the ~ profession** der Lehrberuf. **(b)** *(relative to scholasticism)* scholastisch.

scholasticism [skə'læstɪsɪzəm] *n* Scholastik *f*.

school[1] [skuːl] **1** *n* **(a)** Schule *f*; *(US: college, university)* College *nt*; Universität *f*. **at ~** in der Schule/im College/an der Universität; **to go to ~** in die Schule/ins College/zur Universität gehen; **there's no ~ tomorrow morgen** ist schulfrei *or* keine Schule; ~ **of art/dancing** Kunst-/Tanzschule *f*; **to learn in a tough ~** *(fig)* durch eine harte Schule gehen.
 (b) *(Univ: department)* Fachbereich *m*; *(of medicine, law)* Fakultät *f*. **S~ of Arabic Studies** Institut *nt* für Arabistik.
 (c) *(group of artists, philosophers etc)* Schule *f*. **Plato and his ~** Platon und seine Schüler(schaft); **I'm not one of that ~** ich gehöre nicht zu den Leuten, die das meinen; **he belongs to a different ~ of thought** er vertritt eine andere Lehrmeinung.
 2 *vt* lehren; *animal* dressieren; *one's temper* zügeln. **to ~ sb in a technique** jdn eine Technik lehren, jdn in einer Technik unterrichten *or* unterweisen; **he had been ~ed by poverty to ...** Armut hatte ihn gelehrt, ...; **he ~ed himself to control his temper** er hatte sich dazu erzogen, sich zu beherrschen.

school[2] *n* *(of fish)* Schule *f*; *(of herrings)* Schwarm *m*.

school *in cpds* Schul-; ~ **age** *n* schulpflichtiges Alter, Schulalter *nt*; **is he of ~ age yet?** ist er schon schulpflichtig *or* im schulpflichtigen Alter?; ~ **bag** *n* Schultasche *f*; ~ **board** *n* *(US)*, Schulbehörde *f*; *(Brit old)* Schulaufsichtsrat *m* *(der sich aus geachteten Bürgern zusammensetzt)*; ~**boy** **1** *n* Schuljunge, Schüler *m*; **2** *adj attr* Pennäler-, Schulbuben-; ~**children** *npl* Schulkinder, Schüler *pl*; ~**days** *npl* Schulzeit *f*; ~ **fees** *npl* Schulgeld *nt*; ~**girl** *n* Schulmädchen *nt*, Schülerin *f*; ~**house** *n* *(teacher's house)* Lehrerhaus *nt*; *(school)* Schulhaus *nt*.

schooling ['skuːlɪŋ] *n* *(education)* Ausbildung *f*. **compulsory ~ was introduced in 1870** 1870 wurde die Schulpflicht eingeführt; **compulsory ~ lasts 11 years** die (gesetzlich) vorgeschriebene Schulzeit dauert 11 Jahre.

school: ~**-leaving age** *n* Schulabgangsalter, Schulentlassungsalter *nt*; ~**ma'am**, ~**marm** *n* *(pej)* Schulmeisterin *f* *(pej)*; ~**master** *n* Lehrer, Schulmeister *(dated)* *m*; **village ~master** Dorfschulleiter, Dorfschulmeister *(dated)* *m*; ~**mate** *n* Schulkamerad(in *f*), Schulfreund(in *f*) *m*; ~**mistress** *n* Lehrerin, Schulmeisterin *(dated)* *f*; ~**room** *n* *(in school)* Klassenzimmer *nt*; *(in private house)* Schulzimmer *nt*; **his youngest daughter is still in the ~room** *(old)* seine jüngste Tochter ist noch nicht in die Gesellschaft eingeführt; ~**teacher** *n* Lehrer(in *f*) *m*; ~ **yard** *n* Schulhof *m*; ~ **year** *n* Schuljahr *nt*.

schooner ['skuːnə'] *n* **(a)** *(boat)* Schoner *m*. **(b)** *(sherry glass)* großes Sherryglas; *(US, Austral: beer* ~*)* hohes Pint-Glas.

schuss [ʃus] *(Ski)* **1** *n* Schuß *m*. **2** *vi* (im) Schuß fahren.

schwa [ʃwaː] *n* *(Phon)* Schwa *nt*.

sciatic [saɪ'ætɪk] *adj* Ischias-, ischiadisch *(spec)*.

sciatica [saɪ'ætɪkə] *n* Ischias *m or nt*.

science ['saɪəns] *n* **(a)** Wissenschaft *f*; *(natural ~)* Naturwissenschaft *f*. **to study ~** Naturwissenschaften studieren; **a man of ~** ein Wissenschaftler *m*; **things that ~ cannot explain** Dinge, die man nicht naturwissenschaftlich erklären kann; **on the ~ side of the school** im naturwissenschaftlichen Zweig der Schule; **the ~ of cooking** die Kochkunst; **the ~ of life/astrology** die Lehre vom Leben/von den Gestirnen.
 (b) *(systematic knowledge or skill)* Technik *f*. **it wasn't luck that helped me to do it, it was ~!** das war kein Zufall, daß mir das gelungen ist, das war Können; **there's a lot of ~ involved in that** dazu gehört großes Können.

science fiction *n* Science-fiction *f*. ~ **novel** Zukunftsroman, Science-fiction-Roman *m*.

scientific [ˌsaɪən'tɪfɪk] *adj* **(a)** *(of natural sciences)* naturwissenschaftlich; *apparatus, equipment* wissenschaftlich. **(b)** *(systematic, exact)* classification, methods etc wissenschaftlich. **a keen but not ~ football player** ein begeisterter, doch technisch schwacher Fußballspieler; **his ~ boxing technique** seine gekonnte Boxtechnik.

scientifically [ˌsaɪən'tɪfɪkəlɪ] *adv* wissenschaftlich; *(relating to natural sciences)* naturwissenschaftlich; *box, fence etc* technisch gekonnt. **he approaches sport very ~** der Sport wird bei ihm zur Wissenschaft; ~, **his work is ...** vom naturwissenschaftlichen Standpunkt aus ist seine Arbeit ...

scientist ['saɪəntɪst] *n* (Natur)wissenschaftler(in *f*) *m*.

scientology [ˌsaɪən'tɒlɪdʒɪ] *n* Scientology *f*.

sci-fi ['saɪfaɪ] *n* *(inf)* *see* **science fiction**.

Scillies ['sɪlɪz], **Scilly Isles** ['sɪlɪˌaɪlz] *npl* Scilly-Inseln *pl*.

scimitar ['sɪmɪtə'] *n* Krummschwert *nt*.

scintilla [sɪn'tɪlə] *n* *(liter)* Quentchen *nt*.

scintillate ['sɪntɪleɪt] *vi* *(diamonds, stars)* funkeln; *(fig: person, conversation)* vor Geist sprühen.

scintillating ['sɪntɪleɪtɪŋ] *adj* funkelnd *attr*; *(fig)* *(witty, lively)* wit, humour sprühend *attr*; *person, speech* vor Geist sprühend *attr*; *(fascinating)* information faszinierend. **to be ~** funkeln; sprühen; vor Geist sprühen; faszinierend sein.

scintillatingly ['sɪntɪleɪtɪŋlɪ] *adv* ~ **witty** vor Geist sprühend.

scion ['saɪən] *n* **(a)** *(Bot)* Schößling *m*; *(for grafting)* (Pfropf)reis *nt*. **(b)** *(form)* Nachkomme, Nachfahr *m*.

scissors ['sɪzəz] *n* **(a)** *pl* Schere *f*. **a pair of ~** eine Schere. **(b)** *sing (Sport)* *(also ~ jump)* Schersprung *m*; *(also ~ hold)* Schere *f*. ~ **kick** *(Swimming, Ftbl)* Scherenschlag *m*.

sclerosis [sklɪ'rəusɪs] *n* Sklerose *f*; *see* **multiple** ~.

scoff[1] [skɒf] **1** *n* verächtliche *or* abschätzige Bemerkung. **2** *vi* spotten. **to ~ at sb/sth** jdn/etw verachten; *(verbally)* sich verächtlich *or* abschätzig über jdn/etw äußern.

scoff[2] *(inf)* **1** *n* *(food)* Fressalien *pl* *(inf)*; *(eating)* Fresserei *f* *(inf)*. **2** *vt* futtern *(inf)*, in sich *(acc)* hineinstopfen *(inf)*. **she ~ed (up) the lot** sie hat alles verputzt *(inf)* *or* verdrückt *(inf)*.

scoffer ['skɒfə'] *n* Spötter(in *f*) *m*.

scoffing ['skɒfɪŋ] **1** *n* Spötterei *f*, verächtliche Bemerkungen *pl*. **2** *adj* spöttisch, verächtlich.

scoffingly ['skɒfɪŋlɪ] *adv* *see adj*.

scold [skəuld] **1** *vt* (aus)schelten, ausschimpfen *(for wegen)*. **she ~ed him for coming home late** sie schimpfte ihn aus, weil er so spät heimgekommen war. **2** *vi* schimpfen. **3** *n* *(person)* Beißzange *f* *(inf)*; *(woman also)* Xanthippe *f*. **don't be such a ~, mother!** schimpf doch nicht dauernd, Mutter!

scolding ['skəuldɪŋ] *n* Schelte *f no pl*; *(act)* Schimpferei *f*. **to give sb a ~** jdn ausschimpfen, jdn (aus)schelten.

scollop *n* *see* **scallop 1 (a)**.

sconce [skɒns] *n* Wandleuchter *m*.

scone [skɒn] *n* brötchenartiges Buttergebäck.

scoop [skuːp] **1** *n* **(a)** *(instrument)* Schaufel *f*; *(for ice cream, potatoes etc)* Portionierer *m*; *(ball of ice-cream, potato)* Kugel *f*. **at one ~** *(lit, fig)* auf einmal.
 (b) *(inf: lucky gain)* Fang *m* *(inf)*.
 (c) *(Press)* Knüller *m* *(inf)*.
 2 *vt* **(a)** schaufeln; *liquid* schöpfen.
 (b) **The Times ~ed the other papers** die Times ist den anderen Zeitungen zuvorgekommen; **they ~ed the market** *(inf)* sie haben den Markt abgeschöpft.
 ♦**scoop out** *vt sep* **(a)** *(take out)* herausschaufeln; *liquid* herausschöpfen. **the cat ~ed ~ the goldfish with its paw** die Katze hat den Goldfisch mit ihrer Pfote herausgefischt. **(b)** *(hollow out)* melon, marrow etc aushöhlen; *hole* graben.
 ♦**scoop up** *vt sep* aufschaufeln; *liquid* aufschöpfen. **she ~ed the child/cards/money ~** sie raffte das Kind/die Karten/das Geld an sich *(acc)*.

scoop: ~ **neck** *n* U-Ausschnitt *m*; ~**-necked** ['skuːp'nekt] *adj* mit U-Ausschnitt.

scoot [skuːt] *vi* *(inf)* *(scram)* abzischen *(sl)*; *(walk quickly)* rennen. ~ **across and get it!** spritz mal rüber und hol's! *(inf)*.

scooter ['skuːtə'] *n* (Tret)roller *m*; *(motor ~)* (Motor)roller *m*.

scope [skəup] *n* **(a)** *(of topic, idea, investigation)* Umfang *m*; *(of law, measures)* Reichweite *f*; *(of sb's duties, department, tribunal)* Kompetenzbereich *m*. **sth is within the ~ of sth** etw hält sich *or* bleibt im Rahmen einer Sache *(gen)*; **sth is within the ~ of sb's duties/a department** etw fällt in jds Aufgabenbereich *(acc)*/in den Kompetenzbereich einer Abteilung etc; **sth is beyond** *or* **outside the ~ of sth** etw geht über etw *(acc)* hinaus; **that's beyond the ~ of his duties/this department** das geht über seinen Aufgabenbereich/den Kompetenzbereich dieser Abteilung hinaus; **it's not within the ~ of my power to authorize that** das überschreitet meine Kompetenzen.
 (b) *(extent of one's perception, grasp)* Fassungsvermögen *nt*; *(of talents, knowledge)* Umfang *m*. **that job would be beyond my ~** diese Arbeit würde meine Fähigkeiten übersteigen; **that is beyond my ~** *or* **the ~ of my understanding** das übersteigt mein Fassungsvermögen; **that job is within his ~** diese Arbeit liegt im Bereich seiner Fähigkeiten.
 (c) *(opportunity)* Möglichkeit(en *pl*) *f*; *(to develop one's talents)* Entfaltungsmöglichkeit *f*; *(to use one's talents)* Spielraum *m*. **there is ~ for improvement** es könnte noch verbessert werden; **there is ~ for further projects** es ist Spielraum für weitere Vorhaben; **to give sb ~ to do sth** jdm den nötigen Spielraum geben, etw zu tun; **that job gave his ability/imaginative powers full ~** in diesem Beruf konnten sich seine Fähigkeiten/konnte sich seine Phantasie frei entfalten; **he was given full ~ to start new projects** man gab ihm freie Hand, neue Vorhaben durchzuführen.
 (d) *(inf)* *see* **microscope, periscope** etc.

scorbutic [skɔː'bjuːtɪk] *adj* skorbutisch.

scorch [skɔːtʃ] **1** *n* *(also ~ mark)* verbrannte *or* versengte Stelle, Brandfleck *m*.
 2 *vt* versengen. **the sun ~ed our faces** die Sonne brannte auf unsere Gesichter; ~**ed earth policy** *(Mil)* Politik der verbrannten Erde.
 3 *vi* **(a)** **the sun ~ed down** die Sonne brannte herunter.
 (b) *(become ~ed)* **that dress will ~ easily** das Kleid kann man leicht versengen.
 (c) *(inf: go fast)* rasen *(inf)*. **to ~ along** entlangrasen *(inf)*.

scorcher ['skɔːtʃə'] *n* *(inf)* **yesterday/last summer was a real ~** gestern war eine Knallhitze *(inf)*/im letzten Sommer war es wirklich heiß; **his speech was quite a ~** das war eine gepfefferte Rede *(inf)*.

scorching ['skɔːtʃɪŋ] *adj* *(very hot)* sun, iron glühend heiß; *day, weather* brütend heiß, knallheiß *(inf)*; *(fig: very fast)* speed rasend; *driver* rasant; *(fig: scathing)* gepfeffert *(inf)*.

score [skɔː'] **1** *n* **(a)** *(number of points)* (Punkte)stand *m*; *(of game, Sport also)* Spielstand *m*; *(final ~)* Spielergebnis *nt*. **what was your ~ in the test?** wie viele Punkte hast du bei dem Test erreicht *or* gemacht? *(inf)*; **England didn't get a very good ~** England hat nicht sehr gut abgeschnitten; *(in game, test also)* England hat nicht sehr viele Punkte erzielt; *(Ftbl etc also)* England hat nicht sehr viele Tore erzielt *or* geschossen; **the ~ was Celtic 2, Rangers 1** es stand 2:1 für Celtic (gegen Rangers);

(final ~) Celtic schlug Rangers (mit) 2:1; **there was no ~ at half-time** zur Halbzeit stand es 0:0; **to keep (the) ~** (mit)zählen; (officially) Punkte zählen; (on scoreboard) Punkte anschreiben; **what's the ~?** wie steht es?; (fig also) wie sieht es aus? (on mit) (inf); **he doesn't know the ~** (lit) er weiß nicht, wie es steht; (fig) er weiß nicht, was gespielt wird (inf); **to make a ~ with sb** (fig) jdn stark beeindrucken; **to make a ~ off sb** (fig) jdm eins auswischen (inf).

(b) (reckoning, grudge) Rechnung f. **what's the ~?** was bin ich schuldig?, wieviel macht das?; **to pay off old ~s** alte Schulden begleichen; **to have a ~ to settle with sb** mit jdm eine alte Rechnung zu begleichen haben.

(c) (Mus) (printed music) Noten pl; (of classical music also) Partitur f; (of film, musical) Musik f.

(d) (line, cut) Rille, Kerbe f; (on body) Kratzer m; (weal) Striemen m.

(e) (20) zwanzig. **~s of ...** (many) Hunderte von ..., jede Menge ... (inf); **a ~ of people** zwanzig Leute; **3 ~ years and 10** (old) 70 Jahre; **~s and ~s** Hunderte, jede Menge (inf); **~s of times** hundertmal, zigmal (inf); **by the ~** massenweise (inf).

(f) (reason, ground) Grund m. **on the ~ of illness** wegen Krankheit; **on that ~** aus diesem Grund, deshalb.

2 vt **(a)** erzielen; marks, points also bekommen; goals also schießen; runs also schaffen. **he ~d an advantage over his opponent** er war gegenüber seinem Gegner im Vorteil; **our last contestant ~d one hundred points** unser letzter Kandidat hat hundert Punkte; **each correct answer ~s five points** jede richtige Antwort zählt fünf Punkte; **to ~ a point off sb** (fig) auf jds Kosten (acc) glänzen, jdn ausstechen; **to ~ a hit with sb** jdn stark beeindrucken; **he ~d a hit with his book** er hatte einen durchschlagenden Erfolg mit seinem Buch; **that remark ~d a hit** diese Bemerkung hat ins Schwarze getroffen.

(b) (groove) einkerben, Rillen/eine Rille machen in (+acc); (mark) Kratzer/einen Kratzer machen in (+acc); (Cook) fat, meat etc einschneiden. **the wall is heavily ~d with lines** die Wand weist tiefe Rillen auf; **the mountainside had been ~d by glaciers** Gletscher hatten ihre Spuren am Berg hinterlassen.

(c) (Mus) schreiben.

3 vi **(a)** einen Punkt erzielen or machen (inf); (Sport also) punkten; (Ftbl etc) ins Tor schießen. **to ~ well/badly** gut/schlecht abschneiden; (in game, test etc also) eine gute/keine gute Punktzahl erreichen; (Ftbl etc also) viele/wenig Tore schießen; **the batsman didn't ~ off the fast balls** der Schlagmann konnte die schnellen Bälle nicht verwandeln; **that's where he ~s** (fig) das ist sein großes Plus.

(b) (keep ~) (mit)zählen.

(c) (sl: sexually) **did you ~ with her?** hast du sie aufs Kreuz gelegt? (sl).

(d) (sl: obtain drugs) sich (dat) Stoff beschaffen.

♦**score off 1** vt sep (delete) ausstreichen. **2** vi +prep obj **to ~ ~ sb** jdn als dumm hinstellen.

♦**score out** or **through** vt sep aus- or durchstreichen.

♦**score up** vt sep anschreiben (to sb für jdn). **~ it ~ to me** (fig) eins zu null für mich (inf).

score: ~board n Anzeigetafel f; (on TV) Tabelle f der Spielergebnisse; **~card** n Spielprotokoll nt; (Golf) Zählkarte f; **~keeper** n (official) (Sport) Anschreiber m; (in quiz etc) Punktezähler m; **who's the ~keeper?** wer zählt (mit)?

scorer ['skɔ:rəʳ] n **(a)** (Ftbl etc: player) Torschütze m. **Chelsea were the highest ~s** Chelsea schoß die meisten Tore; **the leading ~ in the quiz** der, der die meisten Punkte im Quiz erzielt. **(b)** see scorekeeper.

score sheet n Spielbericht(sbogen) m, Protokoll nt.

scoring ['skɔ:rɪŋ] **1** n Erzielen nt eines Punktes; (Sport also) Punkten nt; (Fußball etc) Tor(schuß m) nt; (scorekeeping) Zählen nt. **rules for ~** Regeln über die Zählweise; **X did most of the ~** X erzielte or machte (inf) die meisten Punkte; (Ftbl etc) X schoß die meisten Tore.

2 adj suf **a low-/high-~ match** ein Spiel, in dem wenig/viele Punkte/Tore erzielt wurden; **a fast-/high-~ batsman** ein Schlagmann, der schnell/viele Punkte erzielt.

scorn ['skɔ:n] **1** n (disdain) Verachtung f; (verbal also) Hohn m. **to laugh sb/sth to ~** jdn höhnisch verlachen/etw mit Hohnlachen quittieren; **to pour ~ on sth** etw verächtlich abtun; **to be the ~ of sb** von jdm verachtet werden.

2 vt (treat scornfully) verachten; (condescendingly) verächtlich behandeln; (turn down) gift, advice verschmähen; idea mit Verachtung von sich weisen. **to ~ to do sth** es für seiner (gen) unwürdig halten, etw zu tun; **to ~ sb as sth** jdn verächtlich als etw abtun.

scornful ['skɔ:nfʊl] adj verächtlich; laughter also, person spöttisch, höhnisch. **to be ~ of sb/sth** jdn/etw verachten; (verbally) jdn/etw verhöhnen; **to be ~ about sb/sth** sich über jdn/etw verächtlich äußern.

scornfully ['skɔ:nfəlɪ] adv see adj.

scornfulness ['skɔ:nfʊlnɪs] n Verachtung f (of für). **her ~ at the mere mention of his name** ihre verächtliche or höhnische Reaktion bei der bloßen Erwähnung seines Namens.

Scorpio ['skɔ:pɪəʊ] n (Astrol) Skorpion m.

scorpion ['skɔ:pɪən] n Skorpion m.

Scot [skɒt] n Schotte m, Schottin f.

Scotch [skɒtʃ] **1** adj schottisch. **~ broth** Gemüsesuppe f mit Gerstengraupen und Hammelfleischbrühe; **~ egg** hartgekochtes Ei in Wurstbrät, paniert und ausgebacken; **~ fir** Föhre f, (gemeine) Kiefer; **~ tape** ® Tesafilm ® m; **~ terrier** Scotchterrier m, schottischer Terrier.

2 n **(a)** (~ whisky) Scotch m. **(b) the ~** pl die Schotten pl.

scotch [skɒtʃ] vt rumour aus der Welt schaffen; idea, plan unterbinden, einen Riegel vorschieben (+dat). **the rain has ~ed that** der Regen hat uns (dat) einen Strich durch die Rechnung gemacht (inf).

Scotchman ['skɒtʃmən], **Scotchwoman** ['skɒtʃwʊmən] n see **Scotsman, Scotswoman**.

scot-free ['skɒt'fri:] adv ungeschoren. **to get off ~** ungeschoren davonkommen.

Scotland ['skɒtlənd] n Schottland nt.

Scots [skɒts] **1** adj schottisch. **2** n (dialect) Schottisch nt. **the ~** (people) die Schotten pl.

Scots: ~man n Schotte m; **~ pine** n Föhre f, (gemeine) Kiefer; **~woman** n Schottin f.

Scotticism ['skɒtɪsɪzm] n schottischer Ausdruck.

scotticize ['skɒtɪsaɪz] vt schottifizieren, verschotten (hum).

Scottie ['skɒtɪ] n **(a)** (also ~ dog) Scotchterrier m, schottischer Terrier. **(b)** (inf: Scotsman) Schotte m.

Scottish ['skɒtɪʃ] **1** adj schottisch. **2** n **(a)** (dialect) Schottisch nt. **(b) the ~** pl die Schotten pl.

scoundrel ['skaʊndrəl] n (dated) Schurke m; (inf) Bengel m.

scoundrelly ['skaʊndrəlɪ] adj schurkisch.

scour[1] ['skaʊəʳ] **1** vt scheuern. **2** n Scheuern nt. **give the pan a good ~** scheuern Sie den Topf gründlich.

♦**scour away** or **off** vt sep abscheuern; rust abreiben.

♦**scour out** vt sep pan ausscheuern.

scour[2] vt area, town, shops absuchen, abkämmen (for nach).

♦**scour about** or **around** vi herumsuchen (for nach).

scourer ['skaʊərəʳ] n Topfkratzer m.

scourge [skɜ:dʒ] **1** n (lit, fig) Geißel f. **2** vt **(a)** geißeln. **(b)** (fig) (punish) (be)strafen; (devastate) heimsuchen; (verbally) geißeln (geh).

scouse [skaʊs] n Liverpooler Dialekt.

scout[1] [skaʊt] **1** n **(a)** (Mil) (person) Kundschafter, Späher m; (ship, plane) Aufklärer m.

(b) (reconnaissance) Erkundung f; (Mil) Aufklärung f; (search) Suche f. **on the ~** auf Erkundung/auf der Suche; **a week's ~ in the desert** eine einwöchige Erkundungsexpedition in der Wüste; **to have** or **take a ~ about** or **(a)round for sth** sich nach etw umsehen.

(c) Pfadfinder m; (US: girl ~) Pfadfinderin f.

(d) (football ~ etc) Kundschafter, Spion m; (talent ~) Talentsucher m.

(e) (employed by motoring organization) Pannenhelfer m.

(f) (Brit Univ) Diener m für die College-Studenten.

2 vi erkunden, auskundschaften. **they were ~ing inside enemy territory** sie waren auf Erkundung in feindlichem Gebiet; **to ~ for sth** nach etw etw Ausschau or Umschau halten; **he was ~ing for new talent** er war auf Talentsuche.

♦**scout about** or **around** vi sich umsehen (for nach).

♦**scout out** vt sep (Mil) auskundschaften; (inf) aufstöbern.

scout[2] vt proposal verwerfen; rumour etc aus der Welt schaffen.

scout car n Aufklärungsfahrzeug nt; (heavier) Aufklärungs- or Spähpanzer m.

scouting ['skaʊtɪŋ] **1** n **(a)** Erkunden, Auskundschaften nt; (Mil) Aufklärung f; (looking) Suche f (for nach); (for talent) Talentsuche f. **(b)** (scout movement) Pfadfinderei f (inf), Pfadfindertum nt. **2** adj attr Pfadfinder-.

scout: ~ master n Gruppenführer m; **~ movement** n Pfadfinderbewegung f; **~ troop** n Pfadfindergruppe f.

scow [skaʊ] n Prahm m.

scowl [skaʊl] **1** n unmutiger Ausdruck, finsterer Blick, böses Gesicht. **to give sb a ~** jdn böse ansehen. **2** vi ein böses or finsteres Gesicht machen. **to ~ at sb** jdn böse ansehen; **what are you ~ing about** or **at?** warum machst du so ein böses Gesicht?

scowling ['skaʊlɪŋ] adj mißmutig.

scrabble ['skræbl] vi (also ~ about) (herum)tasten; (among movable objects) (herum)wühlen. **the hens ~d (about) in the earth** die Hühner wühlten im Boden herum.

scrag [skræg] **1** n (also ~ end) Hals m. **2** vt (sl) person abmurksen (inf).

scragginess ['skrægɪnɪs] n Magerkeit f; (of meat) minderwertige Qualität, Sehnigkeit f.

scraggy ['skrægɪ] adj (+er) dürr; meat minderwertig, sehnig.

scram [skræm] vi (inf) abhauen (sl). **~!** ab!, verschwinde/verschwindet!

scramble ['skræmbl] **1** n **(a)** (climb) Kletterei f. **we went for a ~ in the hills** wir sind in den Bergen herumgeklettert.

(b) (mad dash) Gerangel, Gedrängel nt. **a ~ for the better-paid jobs** die Jagd nach den besser bezahlten Stellen.

(c) (Motor sport) Querfeldeinrennen nt.

2 vt **(a)** pieces, letters untereinander- or ver)mischen. **(b)** eggs verquirlen, verrühren. **~d eggs** Rührei(er pl) nt. **(c)** (Telec) message chiffrieren, verschlüsseln; line an das Verschlüsselungsgerät anschließen.

3 vi **(a)** (climb) klettern; (over mountains, rocks also) kraxeln (inf). **to ~ out heraus-/hinausklettern; he ~d to his feet** er rappelte sich auf (inf); **to ~ through the hedge** durch die Hecke kriechen or krabbeln (inf); **to ~ up sth** auf etw (acc) hinaufklettern or hinaufkraxeln (inf).

(b) (struggle) **to ~ for sth/to get sth** sich um etw balgen or raufen/um etw balgen or raufen, um etw zu bekommen; for ball etc um etw kämpfen/darum kämpfen, etw zu bekommen; for bargains, job, good site sich um etw drängeln/sich drängen, um etw zu bekommen; **they ~d for the escalator** sie drängelten sich zur Rolltreppe vor.

(c) (Aviat) einen Soforteinsatz fliegen. **~!** höchste Alarmstufe.

scrambler ['skræmbləʳ] n (Telec) Verschlüsselungs- or Chiffriergerät nt.

scrap[1] [skræp] **1** n **(a)** (small piece) Stückchen nt; (fig) bißchen no pl; (of papers etc also) Fetzen m; (of conversation, news) Fetzen m; (of truth) Fünkchen nt, Spur f; (of poetry) Fragment nt. **there isn't a ~ of food in the house** es ist überhaupt nichts or kein Bissen zu essen im Haus; **his few ~s of German** seine paar Brocken Deutsch; **his few ~s of knowledge** das bißchen Wissen, das er hat; **a few ~s of information** ein paar magere Auskünfte; **it's a ~ of comfort** es ist wenigstens ein kleiner Trost; **not a ~!** nicht die Spur!; **not a ~ of evidence** nicht der geringste Beweis; **he was not a ~ of help** er war überhaupt keine Hilfe, er war nicht die geringste Hilfe; **that won't help a ~** das hilft kein bißchen.

(b) (*usu pl: leftover*) Rest *m*.

(c) (*waste material*) Altmaterial *nt*, Altwaren *pl*; (*metal*) Schrott *m*; (*paper*) Altpapier *nt*. **these bits are ~** diese Sachen werden nicht mehr gebraucht; **are these notes ~?** können die Notizen weggeworfen werden?; **to sell a ship for ~** ein Schiff als Schrott *or* zum Verschrotten verkaufen; **what is your car worth as ~?** wie hoch ist der Schrottwert Ihres Autos?

2 *vt* car, ship etc verschrotten; *furniture, clothes* ausrangieren; *idea, plan etc* fallenlassen; *piece of work* wegwerfen. **~ that** (*inf: forget it*) vergiß es!

scrap² (*inf*) **1** *n* Balgerei *f*; (*verbal*) Streiterei *f*. **to get into** *or* **have a ~ with sb** mit jdm in die Wolle geraten (*inf*). **2** *vi* sich balgen; (*verbal*) sich streiten.

scrap: **~book** *n* Sammelalbum *nt*; **~ dealer** *n* Altwarenhändler *m*; (*in metal*) Schrott- *or* Altmetallhändler *m*.

scrape [skreɪp] **1** *n* (a) (*act*) **to give sth a ~** *see vt (a, b)*.

(b) (*mark, graze*) Schramme *f*.

(c) (*sound*) Kratzen *nt*. **the ~ of his feet on the gravel** das Knirschen seiner Füße auf dem Kies; **a nasty ~ as she caught the lamppost** ein ekelhaftes Ratschen, als sie den Laternenpfahl streifte.

(d) (*difficulty*) Schwulitäten *pl* (*inf*). **he goes from one ~ to another** er handelt sich (*dat*) dauernd Ärger ein (*inf*); **to get sb out of a ~** jdm aus der Patsche *or* Klemme helfen (*inf*).

2 *vt* (a) (*make clean or smooth*) *potatoes, carrots etc* schaben; *plate, wall, shoes* abkratzen; *dish, saucepan* auskratzen. **that's really scraping the (bottom of the) barrel** (*fig*) das ist wirklich das Letzte vom Letzten.

(b) *car* schrammen; *wall, gatepost* streifen; *arm, knee* auf- *or* abschürfen. **the paint was ~d in the crash** der Lack bekam bei dem Unfall Kratzer.

(c) (*grate against*) kratzen an (+*dat*). **he ~d his bow across the violin** er kratzte mit dem Bogen auf der Geige; **he ~d his nail along the glass** er kratzte mit dem Nagel über das Glas.

(d) (*make by scraping*) *hole* scharren. **to ~ a living** gerade so sein Auskommen haben; **he ~d a living as a freelance reporter** er hielt sich als freier Reporter gerade so über Wasser (*inf*); **he was trying to ~ (up) an acquaintance with him** er versuchte mit allen Mitteln, seine Bekanntschaft zu machen.

3 *vi* (a) (*make clean*) kratzen. **he ~d at the paint for hours** er kratzte stundenlang an der Farbe herum.

(b) (*rub*) streifen (*against acc*); (*grate*) kratzen (*against an* +*dat*). **the bird's broken wing ~d along the ground** der gebrochene Flügel des Vogels schleifte am Boden; **as he ~d past me** als er an mir vorbeizwängte; **the car ~d past the gatepost** der Wagen fuhr um Haaresbreite am Torpfosten vorbei; *see* bow².

(c) (*be economical*) knapsen (*inf*), knausern. **they ~d for years to pay the debt** sie mußten jahrelang daran knapsen, die Schulden zu bezahlen (*inf*).

♦**scrape along** *vi* sich schlecht und recht durchschlagen (*inf*) (**on** mit).

♦**scrape away 1** *vi* herumkratzen (**at** an +*dat*). **2** *vt sep* abkratzen.

♦**scrape by** *vi* (*lit*) sich vorbeizwängen; (*fig*) sich durchwursteln (*inf*) (**on** mit).

♦**scrape in** *vi* **he just managed to ~ ~** er ist gerade noch hineingerutscht (*inf*).

♦**scrape off 1** *vi* sich abkratzen lassen. **2** *vt sep* abkratzen (*prep obj* von).

♦**scrape out** *vt sep* auskratzen, ausschaben; *eyes of potato, bad parts* ausschneiden.

♦**scrape through 1** *vi* (*lit*) (*object*) gerade so durchgehen; (*person*) sich durchzwängen; (*in exam*) durchrutschen (*inf*). **2** *vi* +*prep obj* *narrow gap* sich durchzwängen durch; *exam* durchrutschen durch (*inf*).

♦**scrape together** *vt sep leaves* zusammenharken, zusammenrechen; *money* zusammenkratzen; *people* zusammenbringen, organisieren; *support* organisieren.

♦**scrape up** *vt sep* (*lit*) aufkratzen, zusammenkratzen; *money* auftreiben (*inf*); *support* organisieren.

scraper ['skreɪpə'] *n* (*tool*) Spachtel *m*; (*at door*) Kratzeisen *nt*.

scrap heap *n* **to be thrown on the ~** (*thing*) zum Schrott geworfen werden; (*person*) zum alten Eisen geworfen werden; (*idea*) über Bord geworfen werden.

scrapings ['skreɪpɪŋz] *npl* (*of food*) Reste *pl*; (*potato ~*) Schalen *pl*; (*carrot ~*) Schababfälle, Schabsel *pl*; (*metal ~*) Späne *pl*. **~ of old paint/of rust** abgekratzte alte Farbe/abgekratzter Rost.

scrap: **~ iron** *n* Alteisen *nt*; **~ merchant** *n* Schrotthändler(in *f*) *m*; **~ metal** *n* Schrott *m*, Altmetall *nt*.

scrappiness ['skræpɪnɪs] *n* (*of knowledge*) Lückenhaftigkeit *f*. **she apologized for the ~ of the meal** sie entschuldigte sich für das zusammengestoppelte Essen; **his essay/book was criticized for its ~** sein Aufsatz/Buch wurde als zusammengestückelt *or* zusammengestoppelt kritisiert.

scrappy ['skræpɪ] *adj* (+*er*) zusammengestückelt, zusammengestoppelt (*inf*); *knowledge* lückenhaft.

scrap yard *n* Schrottplatz *m*.

scratch [skrætʃ] **1** *n* (a) (*mark*) Kratzer *m*.

(b) (*act*) **to give sb a ~** jdn kratzen; **to have a ~** sich kratzen; **the dog enjoys a ~** der Hund kratzt sich gern; **a ~ of the pen** ein Federstrich *m*.

(c) (*sound*) Kratzen *nt no pl*.

(d) **to start from ~** (*lit*) (ganz) von vorn(e) anfangen; (*Sport*) ohne Vorgabe anfangen; **to start sth from ~** etw ganz von vorne anfangen; *business* etw aus dem Nichts aufbauen; **to learn a**

language/a new trade from ~ eine Sprache ganz von Anfang an *or* von Grund auf erlernen/einen neuen Beruf von der Pike auf *or* von Grund auf erlernen; **to be** *or* **come up to ~** (*inf*) die Erwartungen erfüllen, den Anforderungen entsprechen; **he/it is not quite up to ~** yet (*inf*) er/es läßt noch zu wünschen übrig; **to bring sb up to ~** jdn auf Vordermann bringen (*inf*).

2 *adj attr* (a) *meal* improvisiert; *crew, team* zusammengewürfelt. (b) (*with no handicap*) ohne Vorgabe.

3 *vt* (a) kratzen; *hole* scharren; (*leave ~es on*) zerkratzen. **the spots will get worse if you ~ them** die Pickel werden nur schlimmer, wenn du (daran) kratzt; **she ~ed the dog's ear** sie kratzte den Hund am Ohr; **to ~ sth away** etw abkratzen; **we ~ed our names in the wood** wir ritzten unsere Namen ins Holz; **to ~ a living** sich (*dat*) einen kümmerlichen Lebensunterhalt verdienen; **he ~ed a living out of** *or* **from the soil** er konnte sich nur mühsam von den Erträgen des Bodens ernähren; **to ~ one's head** (*lit, fig*) sich am Kopf kratzen; **if you ~ my back, I'll ~ yours** (*fig*) eine Hand wäscht die andere; **to ~ the surface of sth** (*fig*) etw oberflächlich berühren.

(b) **to ~ sth through** etw durchstreichen; **to ~ sb/sb's name off a list** jdn/jds Namen von *or* aus einer Liste streichen.

(c) (*Sport etc*) (*withdraw*) streichen; *horse* zurückziehen.

4 *vi* (a) (*make ~ing movement/noise*) kratzen; (*in soil etc*) scharren; (*~ oneself*) sich kratzen.

(b) (*become ~ed*) **the new paint will ~ easily/won't ~** die neue Farbe bekommt leicht Kratzer/bekommt keine Kratzer.

(c) (*Sport*) zurücktreten. **to ~ from** nicht antreten zu.

♦**scratch about** *or* **around** *vi* (*lit*) herumscharren; (*fig inf*) sich umtun (*inf*) *or* umsehen (*for* nach).

♦**scratch out** *vt sep* auskratzen; (*cross out*) ausstreichen.

♦**scratch together** *see* scratch up (b).

♦**scratch up** *vt sep* (a) (*lit*) ausscharren. (b) (*fig*) *money* zusammenkratzen; *team* zusammenbringen, auftreiben (*inf*).

scratchily ['skrætʃɪlɪ] *adv* kratzend.

scratchiness ['skrætʃɪnɪs] *n* Kratzen *nt*.

scratch: **~ line** *n* (*US*) (*in races*) Startlinie *f*; (*jumping*) Absprunglinie *f*; (*throwing*) Abwurflinie *f*; **~ method** *n* (*Med*) (*test*) Skarifikation *f* (*spec*); (*inoculation*) Ritzmethode *f*; **~ pad** *n* (*US*) Notizblock *m*; **~ paper** *n* (*US*) Notizpapier *nt*; **~ test** *n* (*Med*) Kutanreaktionstest, Einreibungstest *m*.

scratchy ['skrætʃɪ] *adj* (+*er*) *sound, pen* kratzend *attr*; *record* zerkratzt; *feel, sweater* kratzig. **does his beard feel ~?** kratzt sein Bart?; **my old record-player has a rather ~ tone** mein alter Plattenspieler kracht ziemlich.

scrawl [skrɔːl] **1** *n* Krakelei *f*, Gekrakel *nt* (*inf*); (*handwriting*) Klaue *f* (*inf*); (*inf: message*) gekritzelte Nachricht. **the word finished in a ~** das Wort hörte mit einem Krakel auf (*inf*).

2 *vt* hinschmieren (*inf*), hinkritzeln. **it's been ~ed all over** es war ganz vollgeschmiert.

3 *vi* krakeln (*inf*), schmieren.

scrawny ['skrɔːnɪ] *adj* (+*er*) dürr.

scream [skriːm] **1** *n* (a) Schrei *m*; (*of saw, tyres*) Kreischen *nt*; (*of engines, siren*) Heulen *nt*. **there were ~s of laughter from the audience** das Publikum kreischte vor Lachen; **to give a ~** einen Schrei ausstoßen; **a ~ of pain/fear** ein Schmerzensschrei/ein Aufschrei *m*; **the car stopped with a ~ of tyres** das Auto hielt mit quietschenden *or* kreischenden Reifen an.

(b) (*fig inf*) **to be a ~** zum Schreien sein (*inf*).

2 *vt* schreien; *command* brüllen; (*fig: headlines*) ausschreien. **to ~ sth at sb** jdm etw zuschreien; **you idiot, she ~ed at me** du Idiot, schrie sie mich an; **she ~ed insults at him** sie schrie ihm Beleidigungen ins Gesicht; **to ~ one's head off** (*inf*) sich (*dat*) die Lunge aus dem Leib *or* Hals schreien; **to ~ oneself hoarse** sich heiser schreien *or* brüllen.

3 *vi* schreien; (*saw, tyres*) kreischen; (*wind, engine, siren*) heulen. **to ~ at sb** jdn anschreien; **to ~ for sth** nach etw schreien; **to ~ with pain** vor Schmerzen schreien; **to ~ with laughter** vor Lachen kreischen; **an ambulance ~ed past** ein Krankenwagen heulte vorbei; **the newspaper headlines ~ed at him** (*fig*) die Schlagzeilen schrien ihm entgegen.

♦**scream out 1** *vi* aufschreien. **to ~ ~ for sth** (*lit, fig*) nach etw schreien. **2** *vt sep* ausschreien; (*person*) hinausschreien; *name* schreien, rufen; *warning* ausstoßen.

screaming ['skriːmɪŋ] *adj* (*lit, fig*) schreiend; *saw, tyres* kreischend; *wind, engine, siren* heulend.

screamingly ['skriːmɪŋlɪ] *adv*: **~ funny** (*inf*) zum Schreien komisch (*inf*).

scree [skriː] *n* Geröll *nt*. **~ slope** Geröllhalde *f*, Geröllfeld *nt*.

screech [skriːtʃ] **1** *n* Kreischen *nt no pl*; (*of women, tyres also, of brakes*) Quietschen *nt no pl*; (*of owl*) Schrei *m*; (*of whistle*) Schrillen *nt no pl*. **the car stopped with a ~ of brakes** das Auto hielt mit quietschenden Bremsen; **to give a ~ of laughter/anger** vor Lachen/zornig kreischen; **~ owl** Schleiereule *f*.

2 *vt* schreien; *high notes* quietschen; (*fig: headlines*) ausschreien.

3 *vi* kreischen; (*women, brakes, tyres also*) quietschen. **to ~ with pain** vor Schmerzen schreien; **to ~ with laughter/anger** vor Lachen/zornig kreischen; **to ~ with delight** vor Vergnügen quietschen; **jet planes ~ing over the housetops** Düsenflugzeuge, die heulend über die Hausdächer fliegen.

screed [skriːd] *n* Roman *m* (*inf*). **to write ~s (and ~s)** (*inf*) ganze Romane schreiben (*inf*).

screen [skriːn] **1** *n* (a) (*protective*) Schirm *m*; (*for privacy etc*) Wandschirm *m*; (*as partition*) Trennwand *f*; (*against insects*) Fliegenfenster *nt*; (*against light*) Verdunklungsschutz *m*; (*fig*) (*for protection*) Schutz *m*; (*of trees*) Wand *f*; (*of mist, secrecy*) Schleier *m*; (*of indifference*) Mauer *f*. **behind a ~ of cavalry** im Schutz der Kavallerie, von der Kavallerie abgeschirmt; **~ of smoke** Rauchschleier *m*, Nebelwand *f*; **protected by a ~ of destroyers** durch eine Zerstörerflotte geschützt.

(b) (*Film*) Leinwand *f*; (*TV, radar ~*) (Bild)schirm *m*. **stars of**

the ~ Filmstars pl; **to write for the** ~ für den Film/das Fernsehen schreiben; **the small** ~ die Mattscheibe. **(c)** (sieve) (Gitter)sieb nt. **(d)** (in church) Lettner m. **(e)** (Cricket) see **sight** ~.
2 vt **(a)** (hide) verdecken; (protect) abschirmen; (fig) schützen (from vor +dat), abschirmen (from gegen). **to** ~ **the windows/doors** (with screen) einen Schirm vor die Fenster/Türen stellen; (with fabric) die Fenster/Türen verhängen; (against light) die Fenster/Türen verdunkeln; (against insects) Fliegenfenster an den Fenstern/Türen anbringen; **to** ~ **sth from the enemy** etw vor dem Feind tarnen or verbergen; he ~ed his eyes from the sun er schützte die Augen vor der Sonne. **(b)** TV programme senden; film vorführen. **they gave permission for the conference to be** ~ed sie genehmigten die Vorführung der Filmaufzeichnungen von der Konferenz. **(c)** (sift) sieben. **(d)** (investigate) applicants, security risks überprüfen.
♦ **screen off** vt sep (durch einen Schirm/Vorhang/eine Wand etc) abtrennen.
screening ['skri:nɪŋ] n **(a)** (of applicants, security risks) Überprüfung f. **(b)** (of film) Vorführung f; (TV) Sendung f.
screen: ~play n Drehbuch nt; ~ **-print** 1 n Siebdruck m; 2 vt im Siebdruckverfahren drucken; ~**-printing** n Siebdruck(verfahren nt) m; ~ **test** n Probeaufnahmen pl.
screw [skru:] 1 n **(a)** (Mech) Schraube f. **he's got a** ~ **loose** (inf) bei dem ist eine Schraube locker (inf); **to put the** ~**s on sb** (inf) jdm die Daumenschrauben anlegen (inf). **(b)** (Naut, Aviat) Schraube f, Propeller m. **(c)** (action) Drehung f. **to give sth a** ~ **an** etw (dat) drehen. **(d)** (Brit dated: of salt etc) Salz-/Tabaksbeutelchen or -tütchen nt (mit zusammengezwirbelten Ende). **(e)** (sl: sexual intercourse) Nummer f (sl). **he/she is a good** ~ er/sie bumst gut (inf); **to have a** ~ **vögeln** (sl), bumsen (sl). **(f)** (Brit sl: wage) **he earns a good** ~ er verdient einen schönen Zaster (sl) or ganz schön viel Kies (sl); **that's not a bad** ~ **bei dem Job stimmen die Piepen** (sl). **(g)** (Brit sl: prison officer) Schließer (inf), Kapo (dial) m.
2 vt **(a)** schrauben (to an +acc, onto auf +acc). **he** ~ed her **head round** er drehte seinen Kopf herum; **she** ~ed her **handkerchief into a ball** sie knüllte ihr Taschentuch zu einem Knäuel zusammen; **he** ~ed his face into a smile er verzog das Gesicht zu einem Lächeln. **(b)** (inf: put pressure on) in die Mangel nehmen (inf). **to** ~ **sb for sth** etw aus jdm herausquetschen (inf). **(c)** (sl: have intercourse with) bumsen (inf), vögeln (sl).
3 vi **(a)** (can be ~ed) sich schrauben lassen; (fasten with screw) angeschraubt werden. **(b)** (sl: have intercourse) bumsen (inf), vögeln (sl).
♦ **screw down** vt sep an- or festschrauben.
♦ **screw in** 1 vt sep (hin)einschrauben (prep obj, -to in +acc). 2 vi (hin)eingeschraubt werden (prep obj, -to in +acc).
♦ **screw off** 1 vt sep abschrauben (prep obj von). 2 vi abgeschraubt werden (prep obj von).
♦ **screw on** 1 vt sep anschrauben. **to** ~ **sth** ~**(to) sth** etw an etw (acc) schrauben; lid, top etw auf etw (acc) schrauben; **it was** ~ed ~ **tightly** es war festgeschraubt; (lid, top) es war fest zugeschraubt; **to have one's head** ~ed ~ **(the right way)** (inf) ein vernünftiger Mensch sein. 2 vi aufgeschraubt werden; (be fastened with screws) angeschraubt werden.
♦ **screw out** 1 vt sep herausschrauben (of aus). **to** ~ **sth** ~ **of sb** (inf) money etw aus jdm herausquetschen (inf); concessions etw aus jdm herauspressen. 2 vi herausgeschraubt werden.
♦ **screw together** 1 vt sep zusammenschrauben. 2 vi zusammengeschraubt werden.
♦ **screw up** vt sep **(a)** screw, nut anziehen. **(b)** (crush) paper, material zusammenknüllen, zerknüllen. **(c)** eyes zusammenkneifen; face verziehen. **to** ~ ~ **one's courage** seinen ganzen Mut zusammennehmen; **to** ~ **oneself** ~ **to do sth** sich aufraffen, etw zu tun. **(d)** (sl: spoil) vermasseln (inf). **(e)** (sl: make uptight) sb neurotisch machen. **he's so** ~ed ~ er ist total verkorkst (inf), der hat einen Knacks weg (sl); **to be** ~ed ~ **about sth** in bezug auf etw (acc) total neurotisch sein; **to get** ~ed ~ **about sth** sich in etw (acc) hineinsteigern.
screw: ~**ball** (esp US sl) 1 n Spinner(in f) m (inf); 2 adj hirnverbrannt (inf); ~**driver** n Schraubenzieher m.
screwed [skru:d] adj (Brit sl: drunk) voll (sl), fett (sl).
screw: ~ **top** n Schraubverschluß m; ~**-topped** ['skru:ˌtɒpt] adj mit Schraubverschluß.
screwy ['skru:ɪ] adj (+er) (inf) verrückt, bekloppt (sl); person, humour komisch, schrullig. **you must be** ~! du bist wohl bekloppt (sl) or verrückt!; **what a** ~ **thing to do!** so was Verrücktes (inf) or Beklopptes (sl)!
scribal ['skraɪbl] adj Schreib-; (copying) Abschreib-.
scribble ['skrɪbl] 1 n Gekritzel nt no pl; (note) schnell hingekritzelte Nachricht. **covered in** ~(s) vollgekritzelt.
2 vt hinkritzeln. **to** ~ **sth on sth** etw auf etw (acc) kritzeln; **paper** ~d (over) **with notes** mit Notizen vollgekritzeltes Papier; **to** ~ **sth down** etw hinkritzeln.
3 vi **(a)** kritzeln. **the children** ~d all over the **wallpaper** die Kinder haben die ganze Tapete vollgekritzelt. **(b)** (inf: write novel etc) schreiben. **he** ~**s away all day at his novel** er schreibt den ganzen Tag an seinem Roman herum.
scribbler ['skrɪblər] n (inf) Schreiberling m.
scribbling block ['skrɪblɪŋˌblɒk], **scribbling pad** ['skrɪblɪŋˌpæd] n (Brit) Schreibblock, Notizblock m.
scribe [skraɪb] n Schreiber m; (Bibl) Schriftgelehrte(r) m.
scrimmage ['skrɪmɪdʒ] 1 n (US Ftbl) Gedränge nt; (inf: struggle also) Rangelei f (inf); (Rugby) offenes Gedränge. ~s

with the police Handgemenge nt mit der Polizei. 2 vi sich drängen.
scrimp [skrɪmp] vi sparen, knausern. **to** ~ **on sth** an etw (dat) sparen; **to** ~ **and save** geizen und sparen.
script [skrɪpt] 1 n **(a)** (style of writing) Schrift f; (joined writing) Schreibschrift f; (handwriting) Handschrift f; (Typ: cursive) Kursivdruck m. **(b)** (Sch, Univ) (schriftliche) Arbeit. **(c)** (of play, documentary) Text m; (screenplay) Drehbuch nt; (of talk etc) (Manu)skript nt.
2 vt den Text schreiben zu/das Drehbuch/(Manu)skript schreiben für. **a** ~ed discussion eine vorbereitete Diskussion.
script girl n (Film) Scriptgirl n.
scriptorium [skrɪp'tɔ:rɪəm] n, pl **scriptoria** [skrɪp'tɔ:rɪə] Schreibstube f (eines Klosters).
scriptural ['skrɪptʃərəl] adj Bibel-; characters biblisch. **that isn't strictly** ~ das entspricht nicht genau der Bibel.
scripture ['skrɪptʃər] n **(a)** S~, **the** S~**s** die (Heilige) Schrift; **the Hindu** ~**s** die heiligen Schriften or Bücher der Hindus. **(b)** (Sch) Religion f.
scriptwriter ['skrɪptˌraɪtər] n Textautor(in f) m/Drehbuchautor(in f) m/Verfasser(in f) m des (Manu)skripts.
scrivener ['skrɪvnər] n (Hist) Schreiber m.
scrofula ['skrɒfjʊlə] n (dated Med) Skrofulose, Skrofel f.
scroll [skrəʊl] n Schriftrolle f; (decorative) Schnörkel m; (volute, of violin) Schnecke f.
Scrooge [skru:dʒ] n Geizhals m.
scrotum ['skrəʊtəm] n (Anat) Hodensack m, Skrotum nt (spec).
scrounge [skraʊndʒ] (inf) 1 vi **(a)** (sponge) schnorren (inf) (off, from bei). **he** ~d off his parents for years er lag seinen Eltern jahrelang auf der Tasche (inf). **(b)** (hunt) **to** ~ **around for sth** nach etw herumsuchen.
2 vt schnorren (inf), abstauben (inf) (from, off bei).
3 n (inf) **to be on the** ~ am Schnorren or Abstauben sein (inf); **he's always on the** ~ **for cigarettes** er schnorrt dauernd Zigaretten (inf); **to have a** ~ **round for sth** sich nach etw umgucken (inf).
scrounger ['skraʊndʒər] n (inf) Schnorrer m (inf).
scrounging ['skraʊndʒɪŋ] n (inf) Schnorrerei f (inf).
scrub¹ [skrʌb] n Gebüsch, Gestrüpp nt; (also ~land) Gestrüpp nt; (tropical) Busch(land nt) m.
scrub² 1 n Schrubben nt no pl. **to give sth a** ~/a good ~ etw schrubben/gründlich abschrubben; ~**woman** (US) Scheuer- or Putzfrau f. 2 vt schrubben; vegetables putzen; (inf: cancel) abblasen (inf); idea abschreiben (inf). **to** ~ **oneself down** abschrubben; **to** ~ **off a dirty mark** einen Schmutzfleck wegschrubben.
♦ **scrub up** vi sich (dat) die Hände waschen or schrubben (inf).
scrubber ['skrʌbər] n (Brit sl) (billiges) Flittchen.
scrubbing brush ['skrʌbɪŋˌbrʌʃ] n Schrubbürste, Wurzelbürste f.
scrubby ['skrʌbɪ] adj (+er) bushes, beard struppig; countryside Busch-, mit Buschwerk bewachsen; chin stoppelig.
scruff¹ [skrʌf] n by the ~ **of the neck** am Genick.
scruff² n (inf: scruffy person) schlampig or vergammelt (inf) aussehende Person; (woman also) Schlampe f (inf); (man also) abgerissener Typ (inf).
scruffily ['skrʌfɪlɪ] adv (inf) vergammelt (inf).
scruffiness ['skrʌfɪnɪs] n (inf) vergammelter Zustand (inf), vergammeltes Aussehen (inf).
scruffy ['skrʌfɪ] adj (+er) (inf) vergammelt (inf); house, park also verlottert (inf), verwahrlost.
scrum [skrʌm] n (Rugby) Gedränge nt. **loose** ~ offenes Gedränge; **set** ~ Gedränge nt; ~ **half** Gedrängehalbspieler m.
scrummage ['skrʌmɪdʒ] n offenes Gedränge.
scrump [skrʌmp] 1 vt apples stehlen. 2 vi Äpfel stehlen.
scrumptious ['skrʌmpʃəs] adj (inf) meal etc lecker; girl zum Anbeißen (inf).
scrumpy ['skrʌmpɪ] n = Most m (S Ger, Aus, Sw) (starker Cider in Südwestengland).
scrunch [skrʌntʃ] 1 n Knirschen nt. **the car came up the snowy road with a** ~ **of tyres** die Reifen des Wagens knirschten auf der schneebedeckten Straße.
2 vt his feet ~ed the gravel/snow der Kies/Schnee knirschte unter seinen Füßen.
3 vi (gravel, snow) knirschen. **he came** ~ing up the garden **path** er ging mit knirschenden Schritten den Gartenweg hinauf; **they** ~ed through the fallen leaves das Laub raschelte unter ihren Schritten.
scruple ['skru:pl] 1 n Skrupel m. ~**s** (doubts) (moralische) Bedenken pl; **I have certain** ~**s about that** ich habe da meine Bedenken; **to be without** ~, **to have no** ~**s** keine Skrupel haben. 2 vi not to ~ **to do sth** keine Skrupel haben, etw zu tun.
scrupulous ['skru:pjʊləs] adj (person) gewissenhaft; honesty, fairness unbedingt, kompromißlos; cleanliness peinlich; account (peinlich) genau. **he can't afford to be too** ~ er kann sich keine allzu großen Skrupel leisten; **he is not too** ~ **in his business dealings/in matters of cleanliness** er hat keine allzu großen Skrupel bei seinen Geschäften/er nimmt es mit der Sauberkeit nicht so genau.
scrupulously ['skru:pjʊləslɪ] adv (honestly, conscientiously) gewissenhaft; (meticulously) exact, clean peinlich; fair, careful äußerst. **he's** ~ **careful about telling the truth** er nimmt es mit der Wahrheit äußerst or peinlich genau.
scrupulousness ['skru:pjʊləsnɪs] n (honesty, fairness) Gewissenhaftigkeit f; (meticulousness) (peinliche) Genauigkeit f.
scrutineer [ˌskru:tɪ'nɪər] n (Brit Pol) Wahlprüfer(in f) m.
scrutinize ['skru:tɪnaɪz] vt (examine) (genau) untersuchen; (check) genau prüfen; votes prüfen; (stare at) prüfend ansehen, mustern. **to** ~ **sth for sth** etw auf etw (acc) untersuchen or prüfen.

scrutiny ['skru:tɪnɪ] n (a) (examination) Untersuchung f; (checking) (Über)prüfung f; (of person) Musterung f; (stare) prüfender or musternder Blick. everyone was subject to police ~ jeder wurde einer Überprüfung durch die Polizei unterzogen; it does not stand up to ~ es hält keiner genauen Untersuchung or Prüfung stand. (b) (Pol) Wahlprüfung f.

scuba ['sku:bə] n (Schwimm)tauchgerät nt. ~ **diver** (Sport-) taucher(in f) m.

scud [skʌd] vi flitzen; (clouds) jagen.

scuff [skʌf] 1 vt abwetzen. don't ~ your feet like that! schlurf nicht so! 2 vi schlurfen. the children ~ed through the pile of leaves die Kinder raschelten or wateten durch den Laubhaufen. 3 n (a) (~ mark) abgewetzte Stelle. (b) (US: slipper) Pantolette f.

scuffle ['skʌfl] 1 n (skirmish) Rauferei f (inf), Handgemenge nt. 2 vi (have skirmish) sich raufen; (make noise) poltern; (mice etc) trippeln. to ~ with the police ein Handgemenge nt mit der Polizei haben.

scull [skʌl] 1 n (oar) Skull nt; (boat) Skullboot nt. 2 vt rudern. 3 vi rudern, skullen (spec).

scullery ['skʌlərɪ] n Spülküche f. ~-**maid** Küchenmagd f.

sculpt [skʌlpt] 1 vt see sculpture. 2 vi bildhauern (inf). he ~s for a living er verdient sich (dat) seinen Lebensunterhalt als Bildhauer, er lebt vom Bildhauern (inf).

sculptor ['skʌlptə^r] n Bildhauer(in f) m.

sculptress ['skʌlptrɪs] n Bildhauerin f.

sculptural ['skʌlptʃərəl] adj plastisch; (of statues) bildhauerisch. the ~ **work** on the cathedral die Skulpturenarbeit der Kathedrale; ~ **details** plastisch gearbeitete Details pl; the ~ **triumphs** of Ancient Greece die Meisterwerke der altgriechischen Bildhauerkunst.

sculpture ['skʌlptʃə^r] 1 n (art) Bildhauerkunst, Skulptur f; (work) Bildhauerei f; (object) Skulptur, Plastik f. 2 vt formen, arbeiten; (in stone) hauen, meißeln; (in clay etc) modellieren. decorated with ~d flowers mit plastisch gearbeiteten Blumen verziert; he ~d the tombstone out of marble er haute den Grabstein in Marmor.

scum [skʌm] n (a) (on liquid) Schaum m; (residue) Rand m. a pond covered in green ~ ein mit einer grünen Schleimschicht bedeckter Teich; a greasy ~ floated on the soup auf der Suppe schwamm eine Fettschicht. (b) (pej inf) (collective) Abschaum m; (one individual) Dreck(s)kerl m (inf). the ~ of the earth der Abschaum der Menschheit.

scupper ['skʌpə^r] 1 n Speigatt nt. 2 vt (a) (Naut) versenken. (b) (Brit inf) (ruin) zerschlagen. if he finds out, we'll be ~ed wenn er das erfährt, sind wir erledigt (inf).

scurf [skɜ:f] n Schuppen pl.

scurrility [skʌˈrɪlɪtɪ] n (abusiveness) Ehrenrührigkeit f; (of person) verleumderische Art; (abusive remark) Verleumdung, Verunglimpfung f; (indecency) Zotigkeit, Unflätigkeit f; (indecent remark) zotige or unflätige Bemerkung.

scurrilous ['skʌrɪləs] adj (abusive) verleumderisch; remark, attack, story also ehrenrührig; (indecent) unflätig, zotig.

scurrilously ['skʌrɪləslɪ] adv see adj.

scurry ['skʌrɪ] 1 n (hurry) Hasten nt; (sound) Trippeln nt. we had quite a ~ to get there in time wir mußten uns ziemlich beeilen, um rechtzeitig dort zu sein; there was a ~ to leave the room alle hatten es eilig, das Zimmer zu verlassen. 2 vi (person) hasten; (with small steps) eilig trippeln; (animals) huschen. to ~ along entlanghasten/entlangtrippeln/entlanghuschen; they scurried out of the classroom sie hatten es alle eilig, aus dem Klassenzimmer zu kommen; to ~ for shelter sich (dat) eilig einen Unterschlupf suchen; she scurried through her work hastig erledigte sie ihre Arbeit.

scurvy ['skɜ:vɪ] 1 n Skorbut m. 2 adj (obs) knave schändlich.

scut [skʌt] n Stummelschwanz m; (of rabbit also) Blume f (Hunt); (of deer also) Wedel m (Hunt).

scutcheon ['skʌtʃən] n see escutcheon.

scuttle¹ ['skʌtl] n Kohleneimer m.

scuttle² n (person) trippeln; (animals) hoppeln; (spiders, crabs etc) krabbeln. she/it ~d off in a hurry sie/es flitzte davon.

scuttle³ (Naut) 1 n Luke f. 2 vt versenken.

scythe [saɪð] 1 n Sense f. 2 vt (mit der Sense) mähen.

Scythia ['sɪθɪə] n Skythien nt.

SE abbr of south-east SO.

sea [si:] n (a) Meer nt, See f. beyond/from beyond the ~s (dated) überm großen Meer (old), in Übersee/übers große Meer (old), von or aus Übersee; by ~ auf dem Seeweg; to travel by ~ mit dem Schiff fahren; a town by or on the ~ eine Stadt am Meer or an der See; (out) at ~ auf See; as I looked out to ~ als ich aufs Meer hinausblickte; to be all at ~ (fig) nicht durchblicken (with bei) (inf); I'm all at ~ about how to answer this question ich habe keine Ahnung, wie ich die Frage beantworten soll; that left him all at ~ er hatte überhaupt keinen Durchblick (inf); to go to ~ zur See gehen; to put to ~ in See stechen. (b) (state of the ~) See f no pl, Seegang m. heavy/strong ~s schwere/rauhe See. (c) (fig) Meer nt. a ~ of faces ein Meer von Gesichtern; a ~ of flame ein Flammenmeer.

sea: ~ **air** n Seeluft f; ~ **anemone** n Seeanemone f; ~ **animal** n Meerestier nt; ~ **bathing** n Baden nt im Meer; ~ **battle** n Seeschlacht f; ~**bed** n Meeresboden, Meeresgrund (geh) m; ~ **bird** n Seevogel m; ~**board** n (US) Küste f; ~**borne** adj trade See-; fruit, articles etc auf dem Seeweg befördert; ~**borne goods** Seefrachtgüter pl; ~ **breeze** n Seewind m; ~ **calf** n Meerkalb nt, Seehund m; ~ **coast** n Meeresküste f; ~ **cow** n Seekuh f; ~ **cucumber** n Seegurke, Seewalze f; ~ **dog** n (inf: sailor) Seebär m; (seal) Seehund m; ~ **elephant** n Elefantenrobbe f, See-Elefant m; ~**farer** n Seefahrer m; ~**faring** 1 adj nation, people

seafaring; boat hochseetüchtig; ~**faring man** Seefahrer m; 2 n Seefahrt f; ~ **fight** n Seegefecht nt; ~**fish** n See- or Meeresfisch m; ~**fog** n Küstennebel, Seenebel m; ~**food** n Meeresfrüchte pl; ~**food cocktail** Cocktail m aus Meeresfrüchten; ~**food restaurant** Fischrestaurant nt; ~**front** n (beach) Strand m; (promenade) Strandpromenade f; ~ **god** n Meer(es)gott m; ~**going** adj boat etc hochseetüchtig; nation, family Seefahrer-; ~-**green** adj meergrün; ~**gull** n Möwe f; ~**horse** n Seepferdchen nt; ~**kale** n See- or Strandkohl m.

seal¹ [si:l] n (Zool) Seehund m, (~skin) Seal m. 2 vi Seehunde jagen. to go ~ing auf Seehundfang or -jagd gehen; to go on a ~ing expedition an einer Seehundjagd teilnehmen.

seal² 1 n (a) (impression in wax etc) Siegel nt; (against unauthorized opening) Versiegelung f; (of metal) Plombe f; (die) Stempel m; (ring) Siegelring m; (decorative label) Aufkleber m. the police put ~s on the door die Polizei versiegelte die Tür; under the ~ of secrecy unter dem Siegel der Verschwiegenheit; the ~ of the confessional das Beichtgeheimnis; ~ of quality Gütesiegel nt; to put one's or the ~ of approval on sth einer Sache (dat) seine offizielle Zustimmung geben; to set one's ~ to sth (lit, fig) unter etw (acc) sein Siegel setzen; this set the ~ on their friendship das besiegelte ihre Freundschaft; as a ~ of friendship zum Zeichen der Freundschaft.
(b) (airtight closure) Verschluß m; (washer) Dichtung f. 2 vt versiegeln; envelope, parcel also zukleben; (with wax) siegeln; (make air- or watertight) joint, container abdichten; porous surface versiegeln; (fig: settle, finalize) besiegeln. ~ed envelope verschlossener Briefumschlag; ~ed orders versiegelte Order; ~ the meat before adding the stock Poren (durch rasches Anbraten) schließen und dann Fleischbrühe hinzufügen; my lips are ~ed meine Lippen sind versiegelt; this ~ed his fate dadurch war sein Schicksal besiegelt.
♦**seal in** vt sep einschließen. this process ~s all the flavour ~ dieses Verfahren erhält das volle Aroma.
♦**seal off** vt sep absperren, abriegeln.
♦**seal up** vt sep versiegeln; parcel, letter zukleben; crack, windows abdichten.

sea legs npl: to get or find one's ~ (inf) standfest werden.

sealer¹ ['si:lə^r] n (boat) Robbenfänger m; (person also) Robbenjäger m.

sealer² n (varnish) (Ver)siegeler m.

sea level n Meeresspiegel m. above/below ~ über/unter dem Meeresspiegel.

sealing wax ['si:lɪŋˌwæks] n Siegelwachs nt.

sea lion n Seelöwe m.

seal: ~ **ring** n Siegelring m; ~**skin** n Seehundfell nt, Seal m.

Sealyham ['si:lɪəm] n Sealyham-Terrier m.

seam [si:m] 1 n (a) Naht f; (furrow in skin) Falte, Furche f; (scar) Narbe f; (Naut) Fuge f. are my ~s straight? sitzen meine Nähte gerade?; to come apart at the ~s aus den Nähten gehen; to be bursting at the ~s (lit, fig) aus allen Nähten platzen (inf).
(b) (Geol) Flöz nt.
2 vt (sew, join) nähen; (fig: mark with lines) durchziehen. a face ~ed by suffering ein von Kummer zerfurchtes Gesicht.

seaman ['si:mən] n, pl -men [-mən] Seemann m.

seaman-: ~**like** adj seemännisch; ~**ship** n Seemannschaft f.

sea mile n Seemeile f.

seamless ['si:mlɪs] adj stockings nahtlos; cardigan ohne Nähte.

seamstress ['semstrɪs] n Näherin f.

seam-welding ['si:mˌweldɪŋ] n Nahtverschweißung f.

seamy ['si:mɪ] adj (+er) düster. the ~ side of life die Schattenseite des Lebens.

séance ['seɪɑ̃:ns] n spiritistische Sitzung, Séance f.

sea: ~ **pink** n (gemeine) Grasnelke; ~ **plane** n Wasserflugzeug nt; ~ **port** n Seehafen m; ~ **power** n Seemacht f.

sear [sɪə^r] vt (a) (burn: hot metal, water etc) verbrennen; (pain) durchzucken; (Med: cauterize) ausbrennen; (Cook: brown quickly) rasch anbraten; (fig) zutiefst treffen. his mind was ~ed by his childhood experiences er war von seinen Kindheitserlebnissen zutiefst gezeichnet.
(b) (scorch, wither: sun, wind) ausdörren, austrocknen.

search [sɜ:tʃ] 1 n (hunt: for lost object, missing person etc) Suche f (for nach); (examination: of cupboard, luggage, suspect etc) Durchsuchung f (of gen); (esp Jur: of documents) Nachforschungen pl (of über + acc). right of ~ Durchsuchungsrecht nt; to go in ~ of sb/sth auf die Suche nach jdm/etw gehen; to make a ~ in or of a house eine Haus(durch)suchung machen; a ~ through the drawers revealed nothing er etc durchsuchte die Schubladen ohne Erfolg; I found an interesting book in my ~ bei meiner Suche or beim Suchen habe ich ein interessantes Buch gefunden; to make a ~ for sb/sth nach jdm/etw suchen; they arranged a ~ for the missing child sie veranlaßten eine Suchaktion nach dem vermißten Kind.
2 vt (for nach) durchsuchen; archives, records suchen in (+ dat), durchforschen; conscience erforschen; memory, sb's face durchforschen. to ~ a place for sb/sth einen Ort nach jdm absuchen/nach etw durch- or absuchen; ~ me! (inf) was weiß ich? (inf); if you ~ your heart ... wenn Sie Ihr Herz fragen, ...
3 vi suchen (for nach).
♦**search about** or **around** vi herumstöbern.
♦**search out** vt sep heraussuchen; person ausfindig machen, aufspüren; cause herausfinden.
♦**search through** vi +prep obj durchsuchen; papers, books durchsehen.

searcher ['sɜ:tʃə^r] n (customs, police etc) Durchsuchungsbeamte(r) m, Durchsuchungsbeamtin f. the ~s (search party) die Suchmannschaft f.

searching adj, ~**ly** adv ['sɜ:tʃɪŋ, -lɪ] look prüfend, forschend; question durchdringend, sondierend.

search: ~**light** n Suchscheinwerfer m; ~ **party** n Suchmannschaft f; ~ **warrant** n Durchsuchungsbefehl m.

searing ['sɪərɪŋ] *adj heat* glühend; *pain also* scharf; *wind* glühend heiß; *(fig) grief, sense of loss* quälend.

sea: ~**scape** *n* Seestück *nt*; ~ **serpent** *n* Seeschlange *f*; ~ **shanty** *n* Seemannslied *nt*; ~ **shell** *n* Muschel(schale) *f*; ~**shore** *n* Strand *m*; **on the** ~**shore** am Strand; **the life of the** ~**shore** die Strandflora und -fauna; ~**sick** *adj* seekrank; ~**sickness** *n* Seekrankheit *f*; ~**side 1** *n* **at the** ~**side** am Meer; **to go to the** ~**side** ans Meer fahren; **2** *attr resort, town* See-; *concert* Strand-; ~**side holidays/activities** Ferien/Vergnügungsmöglichkeiten am Meer; ~ **snake** *n* (*Zool*) Seeschlange *f*.

season ['siːzn] **1** *n* **(a)** *(of the year)* Jahreszeit *f*. **rainy/monsoon** ~ Regen-/Monsunzeit *f*.
(b) *(social* ~, *sporting* ~ *etc)* Saison *f*. **holiday** ~ Urlaubszeit *f*; **nesting/hunting** ~ Brut-/Jagdzeit *f*; **the football** ~ die Fußballsaison; **the strawberry** ~ die Erdbeerzeit; **strawberries are in** ~/**out of** ~ **now** für Erdbeeren ist jetzt die richtige/nicht die richtige Zeit; **their bitch is in** ~ ihre Hündin ist läufig; **in and out of** ~ andauernd, jahrein (und) jahraus; **at the height of the** ~/**London** ~ in der *or* zur Hochsaison/auf dem Höhepunkt der Londoner Saison; **the** ~ **of good will** *(Christmas)* die Zeit der Nächstenliebe; "**S**~**'s greetings**" „fröhliche Weihnachten und ein glückliches neues Jahr".
(c) *(Theat)* Spielzeit *f*. **they did a** ~ **at La Scala** sie spielten eine Saison lang an der Scala; **for a** ~ eine Spielzeit lang.
(d) *(fig liter)* **in due** ~ zu gegebener Zeit; **in good** ~ rechtzeitig; **if I might offer a word in** ~ wenn ich dazu meinen Rat anbieten darf.
2 *vt* **(a)** *food* würzen; *(fig: temper)* durchsetzen.
(b) *wood* ablagern; *(fig: inure)* **troops** stählen.

seasonable ['siːzənəbl] *adj* **(a)** *dress, weather etc* der Jahreszeit entsprechend *attr.* **to be** ~ der Jahreszeit entsprechen. **(b)** *(form: timely)* **advice, rebuke** zur rechten Zeit.

seasonal ['siːzənl] *adj* **employment, workers, rates etc** Saison-; **disease** jahreszeitlich bedingt.

seasoned ['siːznd] *adj* **(a)** *food* gewürzt. **(b)** *timber* abgelagert.
(c) *(fig: experienced)* erfahren; **troops** *also* kampfgestählt.

seasoning ['siːznɪŋ] *n* **(a)** *(Cook)* Gewürz *nt*; *(fig)* Würze *f*. **a serious lecture with a** ~ **of jokes** eine ernstzunehmende Vorlesung, die mit einigen Witzen durchsetzt ist/war.

season ticket *n* *(Rail)* Zeitkarte *f*; *(Theat)* Abonnement *nt*. ~ **holder** Inhaber(in *f*) *m* einer Zeitkarte; Abonnent(in *f*) *m*.

seat [siːt] **1** *n* **(a)** *(place to sit)* (Sitz)platz *m*; *(actual piece of furniture)* Sitz *m*; *(usu pl:* ~**ing)** Sitzgelegenheit *f*. **to have a front** ~ **at the opera** in der Oper in den vorderen Reihen sitzen; **we had to use boxes as** ~**s** wir mußten Kisten als Sitze *or* Sitzgelegenheiten verwenden; **driver's** *or* **driving** ~ Fahrersitz *m*; **an aircraft with 250** ~**s** ein Flugzeug mit 250 Plätzen *or* Sitzen; **we'll have to borrow some** ~**s** wir werden uns wohl ein paar Stühle borgen müssen; **we haven't enough** ~**s** wir haben nicht genügend Sitzgelegenheiten; **to lose one's** ~ seinen Platz verlieren *or* loswerden *(inf)*; **will you keep my** ~ **for me?** würden Sie mir meinen Platz freihalten?; **I've booked two** ~**s** ich habe zwei Plätze reservieren lassen; *see* **take**.
(b) *(of chair etc)* Sitz *m*, Sitzfläche *f*; *(of trousers)* Hosenboden *m*; *(buttocks)* Hinterteil *nt*. **he picked him up by the** ~ **of his pants** er packte ihn beim Hosenboden; **to fly by the** ~ **of one's pants** *(Aviat sl)* mit dem Hintern fliegen *(inf)*.
(c) *(on committee)* Sitz *m*. **a** ~ **in Parliament** ein Sitz im Parlament, ein Mandat *nt*; **to win a** ~ ein Mandat gewinnen; **his** ~ **is in Devon** sein Wahlkreis *m* ist in Devon.
(d) *(centre)* *(of government, commerce etc)* Sitz *m*; *(of fire, trouble)* Herd *m*. ~ **of emotions** Sitz der Gefühle; ~ **of learning** Stätte *f* der Gelehrsamkeit.
(e) *(country* ~, *bishop's* ~ *etc)* Sitz *m*.
(f) *(of rider)* Sitz *m*. **to keep/lose one's** ~ im Sattel bleiben/aus dem Sattel fallen.
2 *vt* **(a)** *person etc* setzen. **to** ~ **oneself** sich setzen; **to be** ~**ed** sitzen; **please be** ~**ed** bitte, setzen Sie sich; **to remain** ~**ed** sitzen bleiben.
(b) *(have sitting room for)* **the car/table/sofa** ~**s 4** im Auto/am Tisch/auf dem Sofa ist Platz für 4 Personen; **the theatre** ~**s 900** das Theater hat 900 Sitzplätze.
(c) *(Tech: fix in place)* einpassen.
(d) *(base)* **the development board was** ~**ed in Edinburgh** die Entwicklungsbehörde hatte ihren Sitz in Edinburgh.
3 *vi* *(skirt etc: go baggy)* ausbeulen, sich durchsitzen.

seat belt *n* Sicherheits- *or* Sitzgurt *m*. **to fasten one's** ~, **to put one's** ~ **on** sich anschnallen, einen Sicherheitsgurt anlegen; "**fasten** ~**s**" „bitte anschnallen".

-seater [-siːtə²] *suf* **1** *n* -sitzer *m*. **2** *attr* **car, plane** -sitzig.

seating ['siːtɪŋ] *n* Sitzgelegenheiten, Sitzplätze *pl*. ~ **arrangements** Sitzordnung *f*; ~ **plan** *(Theat etc)* Sitzplan, Bestuhlungsplan *m*; ~ **room** Platz *m* zum Sitzen.

SEATO ['siːtəʊ] *abbr of* **South-East Asia Treaty Organization** SEATO *f*.

sea: ~ **transport** *n* Seetransport *m*; ~ **trip** *n* Seereise *f*; ~ **trout** *n* Meerforelle *f*; ~ **urchin** *n* Seeigel *m*; ~ **wall** *n* Deich *m*; ~**ward** **1** *adj* direction, course aufs Meer hinaus; ~**ward wind** Seewind *m*; **2** *adv* *(also* ~**wards)** see- *or* meerwärts; ~ **water** *n* Meer- *or* Seewasser *nt*; ~**way** *n* *(route)* Seestraße *f*; *(waterway)* Wasserweg *m* *or* -straße *f*; ~**weed** *n* (Meeres)alge *f*, (See)tang *m*, Seegras *nt*; ~**worthy** *adj* seetüchtig.

sebaceous [sɪ'beɪʃəs] *adj* Talg-. ~ **glands** Talgdrüsen *pl*.

seborrhoea, *(US)* **seborrhea** [sebə'rɪə] *n* Seborrhö(e) *f*.

sebum ['siːbəm] *n* Talg *m*.

sec [sek] *abbr of* **second(s)** Sek. **wait a** ~ *(inf)* Augenblick *or* Moment mal.

secant ['siːkənt] *n* **(a)** Sekans *m*. **(b)** *(line)* Sekante *f*.

secateurs [sekə'tɜːz] *npl* Gartenschere *f*.

secede [sɪ'siːd] *vi* sich abspalten.

secession [sɪ'seʃən] *n* Abspaltung *f*; *(US Hist)* Sezession *f*.

secessionist [sɪ'seʃənɪst] **1** *adj* Sezessions-, sezessionistisch. **2** *n* Sezessionist(in *f*) *m*.

seclude [sɪ'kluːd] *vt* absondern.

secluded [sɪ'kluːdɪd] *adj* **spot, house** abgelegen; **life** zurückgezogen, abgeschieden.

seclusion [sɪ'kluːʒən] *n (act of secluding)* Absondern *nt*, Absonderung *f*; *(being secluded)* Abgeschlossenheit, Zurückgezogenheit, Abgeschiedenheit *f*; *(of house, spot)* Abgelegenheit *f*. **in** ~ **from the world** in Weltabgeschiedenheit *or* Weltabgeschlossenheit.

second[1] ['sekənd] **1** *adj* zweite(r, s). **the** ~ **floor** *(Brit)* der zweite Stock; *(US)* der erste Stock; **a** ~ **Goethe** ein zweiter Goethe; **every** ~ **house** jedes zweite Haus; **to be** ~ Zweite(r, s) sein; **to be** ~ **to none** übertroffen *or* unerreicht sein; **in** ~ **place** *(Sport etc)* an zweiter Stelle; **in the** ~ **place** *(secondly)* zweitens; **to be** ~ **in command** *(Mil)* stellvertretender Kommandeur sein; *(fig)* der zweite Mann sein; ~ **violin/tenor** zweite Geige/zweiter Tenor; **will you have a** ~ **cup?** möchten Sie noch eine Tasse?; **I won't tell you a** ~ **time** ich sage dir das kein zweites Mal; **you won't get a** ~ **chance** die Möglichkeit kriegst du so schnell nicht wieder *(inf)*; **the** ~ **thing he did was (to) get himself a drink** als zweites holte er sich etwas zu trinken; *see* **fiddle, string, wind**[1].
2 *adv* *(+adj)* zweit-; *(+vb)* an zweiter Stelle. **the speaker against a motion always speaks** ~ der Gegenredner spricht immer als zweiter; **to come/lie** ~ *(in race, competition)* Zweite(r) werden/an zweiter Stelle liegen, Zweite(r) sein; **to go** *or* **travel** ~ *(by rail, bus etc)* zweiter Klasse fahren *or* reisen.
3 *vt* **motion, proposal** unterstützen. **I'll** ~ **that!** *(at meeting)* ich unterstütze das; *(in general)* (genau) meine Meinung.

second[2] *n* **(a)** *(of time, Math, Sci)* Sekunde *f*; *(inf: short time)* Augenblick *m*. **just a** ~**!** (einen) Augenblick!; **it won't take a** ~ es dauert nicht lange, es geht ganz schnell; **I'll only be a** ~ **(or two)** ich komme gleich; *(back soon)* ich bin gleich wieder da; **at that very** ~ genau in dem Augenblick.
(b) **the** ~ *(in order)* der/die/das zweite; *(in race, class etc)* der/die/das Zweite; **you're the** ~ **to say that ...** Sie sind (schon) der/die zweite, der/die sagt ...; **to come a poor/good** ~ einen schlechten/guten zweiten Platz belegen; **Elizabeth the S**~ Elizabeth die Zweite.
(c) *(Aut)* der zweite Gang. **to drive in** ~ im zweiten Gang *or* im Zweiten fahren.
(d) *(Mus: interval)* Sekunde *f*.
(e) *(Brit Univ: degree)* **mittlere Noten bei Abschlußprüfungen. he got an upper/a lower** ~ ≃ er hat mit Eins bis Zwei/Zwei bis Drei abgeschnitten.
(f) *(Sport, in duel)* Sekundant *m*. ~**s out!** Ring frei!
(g) ~**s** *pl* *(inf:* ~ **helping)** Nachschlag *m* *(inf)*; **there aren't any** ~**s** es ist nichts mehr da; **can I have a** ~? kann ich noch etwas nachbekommen?; **you can't have any** ~**s** du kannst nicht mehr nachbekommen.
(h) *(Comm)* **this is a** ~ das ist zweite Wahl; ~**s are much cheaper** Waren zweiter Wahl sind viel billiger.

second[3] [sɪ'kɒnd] *vt* abordnen, abstellen.

secondarily ['sekəndərɪlɪ] *adv* in zweiter Linie.

secondary ['sekəndərɪ] *adj* **(a)** sekundär, Sekundär- *(also Sci)*; **road, route, effect, stress** Neben-; **industry** verarbeitend; **reason** weniger bedeutend. **of** ~ **importance** von untergeordneter *or* sekundärer Bedeutung; **that was only** ~ **to our need to save money** das kam erst an zweiter Stelle, nach der Notwendigkeit, Geld zu sparen; ~ **picketing** Aufstellung von Streikposten vor nur indirekt beteiligten Firmen; ~ **feather** Armschwinge *f*.
(b) *(higher)* **education, school** höher. ~ **modern (school)** *(Brit)* ≃ Realschule *f*.

second: ~-**best 1** *n* Zweitbeste(r, s); **(the)** ~-**best isn't good enough for him das Beste ist gerade gut genug für ihn; 2** *adj* zweitbeste(r, s); **she always felt she was** ~-**best** sie hatte immer das Gefühl, zweite Wahl zu sein; **he was always** ~-**best to his older brother** er stand immer im Schatten seines älteren Bruders; **that job was** ~-**best for him** diese Stelle war eine Ausweichlösung für ihn; **3** *adv* **to come off** ~-**best** es nicht so gut haben; *(come off badly)* den kürzeren ziehen; ~ **chamber** *n* zweite Kammer; ~ **childhood** *n* zweite Kindheit; ~ **class** *n* *(Rail etc, mail)* zweite Klasse; ~-**class 1** *adj* **(a)** **travel, mail, citizen** zweiter Klasse *(after noun)*; **~-class degree** *(Brit Univ) see* **second**[2] **(e)**; **(b)** *see* ~-**rate; 2** *adv* zweiter Klasse; **S**~ **Coming** *n* Wiederkunft *f*; ~ **cousin** *n* Cousin *m*/Cousine *f* zweiten Grades; ~-**degree burn** *n* Verbrennung *f* zweiten Grades.

seconder ['sekəndə²] *n* Befürworter(in *f*) *m*.

second: ~ **hand** *n* *(of watch)* Sekundenzeiger *m*; ~-**hand 1** *adj* gebraucht; **car** Gebraucht-; **dealer** Gebrauchtwaren-; *(for cars)* Gebrauchtwagen-; **bookshop** Antiquariats-; **clothes** getragen, second hand *(esp Comm)*; *(fig)* **information** indirekt, aus zweiter Hand; **knowledge** aus zweiter Hand; **2** *adv* gebraucht, aus zweiter Hand; **I only heard it** ~-**hand, but I am sure it's true** ich habe es nur aus zweiter Hand, aber ich bin sicher, daß es stimmt; ~ **lieutenant** *n* Leutnant *m*.

secondly ['sekəndlɪ] *adv* zweitens; *(secondarily)* an zweiter Stelle, in zweiter Linie.

secondment [sɪ'kɒndmənt] *n* Abordnung *f*. **to be on** ~ abgeordnet sein.

second: ~ **nature** *n* zweite Natur; **to become** ~ **nature (to sb)** (jdm) in Fleisch und Blut übergehen; ~ **person** *n* *(Gram)* zweite Person; ~-**rate** *adj (pej)* zweitklassig, zweitrangig; ~ **sight** *n* das Zweite Gesicht; **you must have** ~ **sight** du mußt hellsehen können; ~ **thoughts** *npl* **to have** ~ **thoughts about sth** sich *(dat)* etw anders überlegen; **on** ~ **thoughts I decided not to** dann habe ich mich doch dagegen entschieden; **on** ~ **thoughts maybe I'd better do it myself** vielleicht mache ich es, genau besehen, doch lieber selbst.

secrecy ['si:krəsɪ] n (of person) (ability to keep secrets) Verschwiegenheit f; (secretiveness) Geheimnistuerei, Heimlichtuerei f; (of event, talks) Heimlichkeit f. in ~ im geheimen; in strict ~ ganz im geheimen; see swear.

secret ['si:krɪt] **1** adj geheim; negotiations, treaty, code also Geheim-; door, drawer also Geheim-, verborgen; pocket versteckt. the ~ ingredient die geheimnisvolle Zutat; (fig: of success etc) die Zauberformel; **to keep sth ~ (from sb)** etw (vor jdm) geheimhalten; **it's all highly ~** es ist alles streng geheim.
2 n Geheimnis nt. to keep sb/sth a ~ from sb jdn/etw vor jdm geheimhalten; ~ im geheimen; I told you that in ~ or as a ~ ich habe Ihnen das im Vertrauen erzählt; they always met in ~ sie trafen sich immer heimlich; (society etc) sie hatten immer geheime Versammlungen; she pretended to hate London, but in ~ she loved the place sie gab vor, London zu hassen, aber insgeheim liebte sie die Stadt; to be in on the ~ (in das Geheimnis) eingeweiht sein; there's no ~ about it das ist kein Geheimnis; to keep a ~ ein Geheimnis bewahren; can you keep a ~? kannst du schweigen?; to make no ~ of sth kein Geheimnis or keinen Hehl aus etw machen; the ~ of being a good teacher das Geheimnis eines guten Lehrers; I have no ~s from you ich habe keine Geheimnisse vor dir.
secret agent n Geheimagent(in f) m.
secretaire [,sekrə'teəʳ] n Sekretär m.
secretarial [,sekrə'teərɪəl] adj Sekretärinnen-; job, qualifications als Sekretärin/Sekretär; work, job Sekretariats-. ~ staff Sekretärinnen und Schreibkräfte pl; (of politician) Stab m; she joined his ~ staff sie wurde Sekretärin bei ihm; basic ~ skills grundlegende Fertigkeiten pl einer Sekretärin.
secretariat [,sekrə'teərɪət] n Sekretariat nt.
secretary ['sekrətrɪ] n (a) Sekretär(in f) m; (of society) Schriftführer(in f) m; (esp US Pol: minister) Minister(in f) m. ~ to the board Schriftführer(in f) m. (b) (desk) see secretaire.
secretary: ~ bird n Sekretär m; S~-General n, pl Secretaries-General, S~-Generals Generalsekretär m; S~ of State n (Brit) Minister(in f) m; (US) Außenminister(in f) m; ~ship n (office) Amt nt des Schriftführers; (period) Zeit f als Schriftführer.
secrete [sɪ'kri:t] **1** vt (a) (hide) verbergen. (b) (Med) absondern. **2** vi (Med) absondern.
secretion [sɪ'kri:ʃən] n (a) (hiding) Verbergen nt. (b) (Med) (act) Absonderung, Sekretion f; (substance) Sekret nt.
secretive[1] [sɪ'kri:tɪv] adj (Med) sekretorisch.
secretive[2] ['si:krətɪv] adj person (by nature) verschlossen; (in action) geheimnistuerisch; smile, behaviour geheimnisvoll. to be ~ about sth mit etw geheimnisvoll tun.
secretively ['si:krətɪvlɪ] adv geheimnisvoll. to behave ~ geheimnistuerisch sein.
secretiveness ['si:krətɪvnɪs] n (character trait) Verschlossenheit f; (secretive behaviour) Geheimnistuerei f. the ~ of his smile/behaviour sein geheimnisvolles Lächeln/Benehmen.
secretly ['si:krətlɪ] adv (in secrecy) im geheimen; meet heimlich; (privately) insgeheim, im stillen. he was ~ concerned insgeheim war er beunruhigt.
secretory [sɪ'kri:tərɪ] adj gland etc sekretorisch.
secret: ~ police n Geheimpolizei f; ~ service n Geheimdienst m; ~ society n Geheimgesellschaft f.
sect [sekt] n Sekte f.
sectarian [sek'teərɪən] **1** adj policy, politics, views konfessionsgebunden; school, education also konfessionell; war, troubles, differences Konfessions-, zwischen den Konfessionen. it was a ~ killing/bombing der Mord/der Bombenanschlag hing mit den Konfessionsstreitigkeiten zusammen; ~ loyalties konfessionelles Zugehörigkeitsgefühl.
2 n Konfessionalist(in f) m.
sectarianism [sek'teərɪənɪzəm] n Konfessionalismus m.
section ['sekʃən] **1** n (a) (part) Teil m; (wing of building also) Trakt m; (of book) Abschnitt m; (of document, law) Absatz m; (of motorway etc) Abschnitt m; (under construction) Trakt m; (of railway) Streckenabschnitt m; (of orange) Stück nt. ~ mark (Typ) Paragraphenzeichen nt; the brass/string ~ of the orchestra die Blechbläser pl/Streicher pl des Orchesters; the sports ~ (Press) der Sportteil; all ~s of the public alle Teile der Öffentlichkeit; the Indian ~ of the community die Gruppe der Inder in der Gesellschaft.
(b) (department, Mil) Abteilung f; (esp of academy etc) Sektion f. passports ~ Paßabteilung f.
(c) (diagram) Schnitt m. in ~ im Schnitt; vertical/longitudinal ~ Quer-/Längsschnitt m.
(d) (cutting: of rock, tissue) Schnitt m; (Med: operation) Sektion f. he took a horizontal ~ of the tissue er machte einen Horizontalschnitt von dem Gewebe.
2 vt (a) (cut to show a ~) einen Schnitt machen durch.
(b) (divide into ~s) teilen.
♦**section off** vt sep abteilen; (cordon off) absperren.
sectional ['sekʃənl] adj (a) (in sections) road-building abschnittsweise; furniture, pipe, fishing rod zerlegbar, zusammensetzbar. ~ drawing Darstellung f im Schnitt. (b) differences, rivalries zwischen den Gruppen; interests partikularistisch.
sectionalism ['sekʃənəlɪzəm] n Partikularismus m.
sector ['sektəʳ] n Sektor m.
secular ['sekjʊləʳ] adj weltlich, säkular; music, art profan; court, education weltlich. ~ priest Weltgeistliche(r) m.
secularism ['sekjʊlərɪzəm] n Säkularismus m; (of attitude) Weltlichkeit f.
secularization [,sekjʊləraɪ'zeɪʃən] n Säkularisation f; (of education, court, Sunday also) Säkularisierung f.
secularize ['sekjʊləraɪz] vt säkularisieren.
secure [sɪ'kjʊəʳ] **1** adj (+er) sicher; (emotionally) geborgen; (firm, well-fastened) grip, knot, tile fest. ~ in the knowledge that ... ruhig in dem Bewußtsein,

daß ...; in the ~ trust that he would return fest darauf vertrauend, daß er wiederkommen würde; to be ~ against or from sth vor etw (dat) sicher sein; to feel ~ sich sicher fühlen; (emotionally) sich geborgen fühlen; to feel ~ about one's future der Zukunft sicher or beruhigt entgegensehen; is the window/lid ~? ist das Fenster fest zu/ist der Deckel fest drauf?; to make a door/window/rope ~ eine Tür/ein Fenster/ein Seil sichern; to make a tile ~ einen Ziegel befestigen.
2 vt (a) (fasten, make firm) festmachen; (tie up also) befestigen; window, door fest zumachen; (with chain, bolt etc) sichern; tile befestigen; (make safe) sichern (from, against gegen), schützen (from, against vor +dat). they ~d the prisoner in his cell sie haben den Gefangenen sicher in der Zelle untergebracht.
(b) (obtain) sich (dat) sichern; majority of votes, order erhalten; profits, higher prices erzielen; share, interest in business erwerben; (buy) erstehen; cook, employee verpflichten. to ~ sb's services jdn verpflichten.
(c) (guarantee) sichern, garantieren; loan (ab)sichern.
securely [sɪ'kjʊəlɪ] adv (firmly) fest; (safely) sicher. the prisoner was kept ~ in his cell der Gefangene wurde streng gesichert in seiner Zelle gehalten.
secureness [sɪ'kjʊənɪs] n see adj Sicherheit f; (emotional) Geborgenheit f.
security [sɪ'kjʊərɪtɪ] n (a) Sicherheit f; (emotional) Geborgenheit f. (~ measures) Sicherheitsvorkehrungen or -maßnahmen pl. for ~ zur Sicherheit; ~ of tenure Kündigungsschutz m; airports have tightened their ~ die Flughäfen haben ihre Sicherheitsvorkehrungen verschärft; in the ~ of one's own home sicher im eigenen Heim; (from emotional point of view) in der Geborgenheit des eigenen Heims; the child never experienced emotional ~ das Kind hat nie Geborgenheit erfahren.
(b) (~ department) Sicherheitsdienst m.
(c) (Fin) (guarantee) Sicherheit f; (guarantor) Bürge m. up to £100 without ~ bis zu £100 ohne Sicherheit; to lend money on ~ Geld gegen Sicherheit leihen; to stand ~ for sb für jdn Bürge sein or Bürgschaft leisten.
(d) (Fin) securities pl Effekten, (Wert)papiere pl.
security in cpds Sicherheits-; (Fin) Effekten-, Wertpapier-; ~ check n Sicherheitskontrolle f; S~ Council n Sicherheitsrat m; S~ Force n Friedenstruppe f; S~ Forces npl Friedensstreitmacht f; ~ guard, ~ man n Wache f, Wächter m; (for ~ checks) Sicherheitsbeamte(r) m; one of the ~ men einer der Sicherheitsleute; ~ risk n Sicherheitsrisiko nt.
sec(y) abbr of secretary.
sedan [sɪ'dæn] n (a) (also ~ chair) Sänfte f. (b) (US Aut) Limousine f.
sedate [sɪ'deɪt] **1** adj (+er) gesetzt; little girl, colour ruhig; furnishings, décor gediegen; life geruhsam; speed gemächlich; answer ruhig, gelassen; prose bedächtig. **2** vt Beruhigungsmittel geben (+dat), sedieren (spec). he was heavily ~d er stand stark unter dem Einfluß von Beruhigungsmitteln.
sedately [sɪ'deɪtlɪ] adv see adj.
sedateness [sɪ'deɪtnɪs] n see adj Gesetztheit f; ruhige Art; (of colour) ruhiger Ton; Gediegenheit f; Geruhsamkeit f; Gemächlichkeit f; Ruhe, Gelassenheit f; Bedächtigkeit f.
sedation [sɪ'deɪʃən] n Beruhigungsmittel pl. to put sb under ~ jdm Beruhigungsmittel geben; drugs used for ~ Drogen zur Beruhigung.
sedative ['sedətɪv] **1** n Beruhigungsmittel, Sedativum (spec) nt. **2** adj beruhigend, sedativ (spec).
sedentariness ['sedntərɪnɪs] n (a) as a result of the ~ of the job durch das dauernde Sitzen bei der Arbeit; the excessive ~ of his daily life das übermäßige tägliche Sitzen. (b) (of tribe) Seßhaftigkeit f; (of bird) Verbleiben nt am Nistort.
sedentary ['sedntərɪ] adj (a) job, occupation sitzend attr; worker Sitz-. to lead a ~ life sehr viel sitzen; any job of a ~ nature jede im Sitzen ausgeübte Tätigkeit. (b) tribe seßhaft; bird Stand-.
sedge [sedʒ] n Riedgras nt, Segge f. ~-warbler Seggenrohrsänger m.
sediment ['sedɪmənt] n (Boden)satz m; (in river) Ablagerung f; (in chemical solution) Niederschlag m, Sediment nt.
sedimentary [,sedɪ'mentərɪ] adj sedimentär. ~ rocks Sedimentgestein nt.
sedimentation [,sedɪmen'teɪʃən] n Ablagerung, Sedimentation f.
sedition [sə'dɪʃən] n Aufwiegelung, Verhetzung f.
seditious [sə'dɪʃəs] adj aufrührerisch, aufwieglerisch.
seduce [sɪ'dju:s] vt verführen. to ~ sb into doing sth jdn zu etw verleiten, jdn dazu verleiten, etw zu tun; to ~ sb (away) from his duty/a party/his wife/a place jdn seine Pflichten vergessen lassen/jdn einer Partei/seiner Frau abspenstig machen/jdn von einem Ort weglocken.
seducer [sɪ'dju:səʳ] n Verführer m.
seducible [sɪ'dju:sɪbl] adj verführbar.
seduction [sɪ'dʌkʃən] n Verführung f.
seductive [sɪ'dʌktɪv] adj verführerisch; salary, offer, suggestion verlockend.
seductively [sɪ'dʌktɪvlɪ] adv see adj.
seductiveness [sɪ'dʌktɪvnɪs] n verführerische Art. the ~ of the offer etc das verlockende Angebot etc.
seductress [sɪ'dʌktrɪs] n Verführerin f.
sedulous adj, ~ly adv ['sedjʊləs, -lɪ] unermüdlich, unentwegt.
see[1] [si:] pret saw, ptp seen **1** vt (a) sehen; (in newspaper etc also) lesen; (check also) nachsehen, gucken (inf); (go and ~) film, show, sights sich (dat) ansehen. worth ~ing sehenswert; to ~ sb do sth sehen, wie jd etw macht; I've never ~n him swim(ming) ich habe ihn noch nie schwimmen sehen;

he was ~n to enter the building man hat ihn gesehen *or* er wurde gesehen, wie er das Gebäude betrat; **I saw it happen** ich habe gesehen, wie es passiert ist; **I've ~n it done three times** das habe ich schon dreimal gesehen; **I wouldn't ~ you starve** ich würde doch nicht zusehen, wie du verhungerst; **I don't like to ~ people mistreated** ich kann es nicht sehen, wenn Menschen schlecht behandelt werden; **I wouldn't like to ~ you unhappy** ich möchte doch nicht, daß du unglücklich bist; **I'll go and ~ who it is** ich gehe mal nachsehen *or* ich gucke mal, wer das ist); → **page 8** siehe Seite 8; **there was nothing to be ~n** es war nichts zu sehen; **I don't know what she ~s in him** ich weiß nicht, was sie an ihm findet; **we don't ~ much of them nowadays** wir sehen sie zur Zeit nur selten; **I shall be ~ing them for dinner** ich treffe sie beim Abendessen; **~ you (soon)!** bis bald!; **be ~ing you!, ~ you later!** bis später!, bis nachher!; **~ you on Sunday!** bis Sonntag!; **she doesn't want to ~ me any more** sie will mich nicht mehr sehen; **I want to ~ (a bit of) the world** ich möchte etwas von der Welt sehen *or* kennenlernen; **I'll ~ him damned *or* in hell first** (*inf*) ich denke nicht (im Schlaf) daran; **she won't ~ 40 again** sie ist gut und gern 40; **I/you must be ~ing things** ich sehe/du siehst wohl Gespenster!; **I must be ~ing things, if it isn't Peter!** ich glaub', ich seh' nicht richtig, das ist doch der Peter!; **am I ~ing things or is ...?** seh' ich richtig, das ist das nicht ...?; **can you ~ your way without a torch?** findest du den Weg ohne Taschenlampe?; **I can't ~ my way (clear) to doing that** ich sehe mich nicht in der Lage, das zu tun; **I saw myself obliged to/faced with the need to ...** ich sah mich gezwungen, zu ...; **I suddenly saw myself being cheated** ich sah *or* erkannte plötzlich, daß man mich betrog/betrügen wollte.

(b) (*visit*) besuchen; (*on business*) aufsuchen. **to call *or* go and ~ sb** jdn besuchen (gehen); **to ~ the doctor** zum Arzt gehen, einen Arzt aufsuchen; **he is the man you ought to ~ about this** Sie sollten sich damit an ihn wenden.

(c) (*meet with*) sehen; (*have a word with, talk to*) sprechen; (*receive visit of*) empfangen. **the boss can't ~ you now, you can't ~ the boss now** Sie können den Chef jetzt nicht sprechen, Sie können jetzt nicht zum Chef (*inf*); **the boss/doctor will ~ you now** der Chef/Herr Doktor ist jetzt frei; **what did he want to ~ you about?** weswegen wollte er Sie sprechen?; **I'll have to ~ my wife about that** das muß ich mit meiner Frau besprechen; **have you ~n Personnel yet?** waren Sie schon bei der Personalabteilung?; **the minister saw the Queen yesterday** der Minister war gestern bei der Königin; **the Queen will ~ the minister tomorrow** die Königin wird den Minister morgen empfangen; **she refused to ~ us** sie wollte uns nicht empfangen *or* sehen; **there was only one applicant worth ~ing** es war nur ein Bewerber dabei, den es sich anzusehen lohnte.

(d) (*accompany*) begleiten, bringen. **to ~ sb to the door** jdn zur Tür bringen; *see also phrasal vbs.*

(e) **we'll/he'll ~ if we can help** mal sehen/er wird mal sehen, ob wir helfen können; **we'll soon ~ who is right** wir werden ja bald sehen, wer recht hat; **that remains to be ~ das wird sich zeigen; **let's just ~ what happens** wollen wir mal sehen *or* abwarten, was passiert; **I don't ~ any way I can help** ich sehe nicht, wie ich da helfen kann; **now let me ~ how we can solve this** lassen Sie mich mal überlegen, wie wir das lösen können; **give me a week, let me ~** if I can fix up something mal eine Woche, und ich werde mal sehen, ob sich etwas arrangieren läßt; **let me ~** if I can't find a better way mal sehen, ob ich nicht etwas Besseres finden kann.

(f) (*visualize*) sich (*dat*) vorstellen. **I can't *or* don't ~ that working/him winning/myself living there** ich kann mir kaum vorstellen, daß das klappt/daß er gewinnt/daß ich da leben möchte; **I can't ~ myself in that job** ich glaube nicht, daß das eine Stelle für mich wäre; **he saw himself as the saviour** er sah sich als Retter; **I can ~ it happening** ich sehe es kommen; **I don't ~ that happening** das kann ich mir kaum vorstellen *or* denken; **I can't ~ any chance of that happening** das halte ich für unwahrscheinlich *or* kaum möglich.

(g) (*experience*) erleben. **he lived to ~ the beginning of a new age** er hat den Anfang eines neuen Zeitalters miterlebt; **now I've ~n everything!** ist das denn zu fassen *or* die Möglichkeit?!; **what a cheek, I've never ~n anything like it!** so eine Frechheit, so etwas habe ich ja noch nie gesehen *or* erlebt!; **it's ~n a lot of hard wear** das ist schon sehr strapaziert worden.

(h) (*hear, notice*) sehen. **I ~ you still haven't done that/he's got married again** wie ich sehe, hast du das immer noch nicht gemacht/hat er wieder geheiratet.

(i) (*understand*) verstehen; (*understand the reason for*) einsehen; (*realize*) erkennen. **I don't ~ the importance of doing it/the need for the change** ich sehe nicht ein, warum das unbedingt gemacht werden muß/warum das geändert werden muß; **I can ~ that it might be a good thing** ich sehe ja ein, daß das eine gute Idee wäre; **I can ~ I'm going to be busy** ich sehe schon, ich werde viel zu tun haben; **I fail to *or* don't ~ how anyone could ...** ich begreife einfach nicht, wie jemand nur ... kann; **I don't ~ how it works** es ist mir nicht klar, wie das funktioniert; **I don't ~ where the problem is** ich sehe das Problem nicht; **I ~ from this report that ...** ich ersehe aus diesem Bericht, daß ...; (*do you*) **~ what I mean?** verstehst du(, was ich meine)?; (*didn't I tell you!*) siehst du's jetzt!; **I ~ what you mean ich verstehe** *or* verstehe, was du meinst; (*you're quite right*) ja, du hast recht; **to make sb ~ sth** jdm etw klarmachen; **I saw only too clearly that ...** ich sah *or* erkannte nur zu deutlich, daß ...

(j) (*look at*) problem sehen. **as I ~ it** so, wie ich das sehe; **this is how I ~ it** ich sehe das so; **that's how I ~ it** so sehe ich das jedenfalls; **try to ~ it my way** versuchen Sie doch einmal, es aus meiner Sicht zu sehen; **I don't ~ it that way** ich sehe das anders.

(k) (*ensure*) **~ that it is done by tomorrow** sieh zu, daß es bis morgen fertig ist; (*done by sb else also*) sorge dafür, daß es bis

morgen fertig ist; **~ that it doesn't happen again** sieh zu *or* paß auf, daß das nicht noch mal passiert.

(l) (*Cards*) **I'll ~ you** ich halte.

2 *vi* **(a)** (*have sight*) sehen.

(b) (*look*) sehen. **let me ~, let's ~** lassen Sie mich mal sehen; **can you ~ if I sit here?** können Sie (etwas) sehen, wenn ich hier sitze?; **it was so dark I couldn't ~** es war so dunkel, ich konnte nichts sehen; **who was it? — I couldn't/didn't ~** wer war das? — ich konnte es nicht sehen; **can you ~ to read?** ist es Ihnen hell genug zum Lesen?; **as far as the eye can ~** so weit das Auge reicht; **~ for yourself!** sieh doch selbst!; **now ~ here!** nun hören Sie mal her!

(c) (*check, find out*) nachsehen, gucken (*inf*). **is he there? — I'll ~ ist er da?** — ich sehe mal nach *or* ich guck mal (*inf*); **I'll go and ~ ich gehe mal nachsehen; **~ for yourself!** sieh doch selbst (nach)!; **let me ~** lassen Sie mich mal nachsehen.

(d) (*discover*) sehen. **will he come? — we'll soon ~** kommt er? — das werden wir bald sehen *or* rausfinden (*inf*); **what kind of person is she? — you'll soon ~ for yourself** was für ein Mensch ist sie? — das werden Sie bald selbst sehen *or* feststellen.

(e) (*understand*) verstehen. **as I can ~** ... so wie ich das sehe ...; **it's all over, ~?** es ist vorbei, verstehst du?; **it's logical, do you ~?** es ist logisch, nicht wahr?; **he's dead, don't you ~?** er ist tot, begreifst du das denn nicht?; **as I ~ from your report** wie ich in Ihrem Bericht ersehe; **it's too late,** (*you*) ~ (*explaining*) weißt du, es ist zu spät; (*I told you so*) siehst du, es ist zu spät!; (*you*) ~, **it's like this** es ist nämlich so; (*you*) ~, **we can't do that** weißt du, das können wir nicht machen; **that's the way he is,** (*you*) ~ das ist eben seine Art(, weißt du); **but this still has to be improved, you ~** das muß natürlich nicht verbessert werden; **and we went out,** ~, **and saw this film,** ~, **and ...** (*dial*) und wir sind weggegangen, weißte (*inf*) *or* nich (*inf*), und haben uns den Film angesehen, weißte *etc*, und ...; **I ~!** aha!; (*after explanation*) ach so!; (*to keep conversation going, I'm with you*) ja; **yes, I ~** ja, aha.

(f) (*consider*) **we'll ~** (wir werden *or* wollen) mal sehen; **I don't know, I'll have to ~** ich weiß nicht, ich muß mal sehen; **will you be there? — I'll ~** bist du da? — mal sehen; **he said he'll ~** er sagt, er will mal sehen; **let me ~, let's ~** warten Sie mal, lassen Sie mich mal überlegen.

♦**see about** *vi* +*prep obj* **(a)** (*attend to*) sich kümmern um. **I'll have to ~ getting the roof mended** ich muß mich darum kümmern, daß das Dach repariert wird; **he came to ~ the TV** er kam, um sich (*dat*) den Fernseher anzusehen; **I've still a few things to ~** ich muß noch ein paar Dinge erledigen; **he came to ~ the rent** er ist wegen der Miete gekommen; **we'd better ~ going now** wir sehen besser zu, daß wir jetzt gehen.

(b) (*consider*) **I'll ~** ~ it ich will mal sehen *or* schauen (*esp S Ger*); **we'll ~ ~ that!** (*iro*) das wollen wir mal sehen.

♦**see across** *vt always separate* hinüberbegleiten *or* -bringen (*prep obj* über +*acc*).

♦**see in 1** *vi* (*look in*) herein-/hineinsehen. **2** *vt sep* (*show in*) herein-/hineinbringen. **to ~ the New Year** das Neue Jahr begrüßen.

♦**see into** *vi* +*prep obj* **(a)** house, room hineinsehen in (+*acc*). **(b)** (*investigate*) untersuchen, prüfen, nachgehen (+*dat*). **this needs ~ing** das muß geprüft *or* untersucht werden.

♦**see off** *vt sep* **(a)** (*bid farewell to*) verabschieden. **are you coming to ~ me ~?** kommt ihr mit mir (zum Flughafen *etc*)? **(b)** (*chase off*) Beine machen (+*dat*) (*inf*). ~ **him, boy!** verjag ihn! **(c)** (*sl: be better than*) in die Tasche stecken (*inf*).

♦**see out 1** *vi* (*look out*) heraus-/hinaussehen. **I can't ~ ~ of the window** ich kann nicht zum Fenster hinaussehen.

2 *vt sep* (*show out*) hinausbringen *or* -begleiten (*of* aus). **I'll ~ myself ~** ich finde (schon) alleine hinaus.

(b) (*last to the end of*) coat, car) winter *etc* überdauern; (*old man, invalid*) wife, year *etc* überleben. **to ~ the old year ~** das alte Jahr verabschieden.

♦**see over** *or* **round** *vi* +*prep obj* house *etc* sich (*dat*) ansehen.

♦**see through 1** *vi* **(a)** (*lit*) (hin)durchsehen (*prep obj* durch). **(b)** +*prep obj* (*fig: not be deceived by*) durchschauen. **I can ~ right ~ you** ich habe dich durchschaut *or* erkannt.

2 *vt always separate* **(a)** (*help through difficult time*) beistehen (+*dat*). **to ~ sb ~ a bad time** jdm über eine schwierige Zeit hinweghelfen; **he had £10 to ~ him ~ the term** er hatte £ 10 für das ganze Semester; **I hope £10 will ~ you ~** die £ 10 reichen dir hoffentlich.

(b) job zu Ende bringen; (*Parl*) bill durchbringen.

♦**see to** *vi* +*prep obj* sich kümmern um. **these shoes need/that cough needs ~ing** ~ mit den Schuhen muß etwas gemacht werden/um den Husten muß man sich kümmern; ~ ~ **it that you don't/he doesn't forget** sieh zu, daß du das nicht vergißt/sieh zu *or* sorge dafür, daß er das nicht vergißt; **there's no chance now, the rain has ~n ~ that** es ist aussichtslos, dafür hat der Regen schon gesorgt.

♦**see up 1** *vi* (*look up*) herauf-/hinaufsehen (*prep obj* acc). **I could ~ ~ her skirt** ich konnte ihr unter den Rock sehen. **2** *vt sep* (*show up*) herauf-/hinaufbringen.

see² *n* Bistum *nt*; (*Catholic also*) Diözese *f*; (*Protestant in Germany*) Landeskirche *f*. **Holy S~, S~ of Rome** Heiliger Stuhl.

seed [siːd] **1** *n* **(a)** (*Bot*) (*one single*) Same(n) *m*; (*of grain, poppy, sesame etc*) Korn *nt*; (*within fruit*) Same(n) *pl*; (*for birds*) Körner *pl*; (*grain*) Saat *f*, Saatgut *nt*; (*liter: sperm*) Samen *pl*; (*liter: offspring*) Nachkommen *pl*; (*fig: of unrest, idea etc*) Keim *m* (*of* zu). **to go or run to ~** (*vegetables*) schießen; (*flowers*) einen Samenstand bilden; (*fig: person*) herunterkommen; **to sow the ~s of doubt (in sb's mind)** (bei jdm) Zweifel säen *or* den Keim des Zweifels legen; **he sowed the ~ from which ... developed** er hat den Keim gelegt, aus dem sich ... entwickelte; **I don't want to make a direct proposal, just to sow the ~s** ich möchte keinen direkten

seedbed

Vorschlag machen, ich möchte nur den Boden dafür bereiten. **(b)** (Sport) to be the third ~ als dritter plaziert or gesetzt sein; **the number one** ~ der/die Erstplazierte.

2 vt **(a)** (sow with ~) besäen.

(b) (extract ~s from) entkernen.

(c) (Sport) setzen, plazieren. **~ed number one** als Nummer eins gesetzt; **~ed players** gesetzte or plazierte Spieler.

3 vi (vegetables) schießen; (flowers) Samen entwickeln.

4 vr to ~ itself (plant) sich aussäen.

seed: ~**bed** n Saatbeet, Saatbett nt; ~**cake** n Kümmelkuchen m; ~**case** n Samenkapsel f; ~ **corn** n Samenkorn nt; ~**drill** n Sämaschine f; ~ **leaf** n Keimblatt nt; ~**less** adj kernlos.

seedling ['si:dlɪŋ] n Sämling m.

seed: ~ **pearl** n Staubperle f; ~ **plant** n Samenpflanze f; ~ **potato** n Saatkartoffel f.

seedsman ['si:dzmən] n, pl **-men** [-mən] Samenhändler m.

seedtime ['si:dtaɪm] n Saatzeit f.

seedy ['si:dɪ] adj (+er) **(a)** (disreputable) person, character zweifelhaft, zwielichtig; area, place übel; clothes schäbig, abgerissen. **(b)** (inf: unwell) **I feel** ~ mir ist flau (inf) or nicht gut; **to look** ~ abgeschlagen (inf) or nicht gut aussehen.

seeing ['si:ɪŋ] **1** n Sehen nt. **I'd never have thought it possible but** ~ **is believing** (prov) ich hätte es nie für möglich gehalten, aber ich habe es mit eigenen Augen gesehen; **look,** ~ **is believing, you can't deny it now** da haben Sie den Beweis vor Augen, jetzt können Sie es nicht mehr abstreiten.

2 conj ~ **(that)** da.

seek [si:k] pret, ptp **sought** vt **(a)** suchen; fame, wealth erlangen wollen, streben nach. **to** ~ **sb's advice** jdn um Rat fragen; **the reason is not far to** ~ der Grund liegt auf der Hand; **the quarrel is not of my** ~ing ich habe den Streit nicht gesucht.

(b) (liter: attempt) suchen (geh). **they sought to kill him** sie suchten ihn zu töten (liter), sie trachteten ihm nach dem Leben; **those who sought his downfall** die(jenigen), die ihn zu Fall bringen wollten.

♦ **seek after** vi +prep obj **(a)** suchen. **(b)** see **sought-after**.

♦ **seek for** vi +prep obj suchen nach; reforms, changes anstreben. **long-sought-**~ **reforms/changes** langerstrebte Reformen pl/Veränderungen pl.

♦ **seek out** vt sep ausfindig machen; opinion herausfinden. ~ **him** ~, **discover what he thinks** (liter) erforschen Sie ihn, finden Sie heraus, was er denkt (geh).

seeker ['si:kəʳ] n Suchende(r) mf; (pursuer) Verfolger m. ~ **of justice** nach Gerechtigkeit Suchende(r) mf; ~ **of or after truth** Wahrheitssucher(in f) m.

seem [si:m] vi **(a)** scheinen. **he** ~s **(to be) honest/a nice young man** er scheint ehrlich/ein netter junger Mann zu sein; **he may** ~ **poor but** ... er mag arm scheinen or wirken, aber ...; **he** ~s **younger than he is** er wirkt jünger, als er ist; **that makes it** ~ **longer** dadurch wirkt es länger or kommt es einem länger vor; **he doesn't** ~ **(to be) able to concentrate** er scheint sich nicht konzentrieren zu können; **he is not what he** ~s **to be** er ist nicht (das), was er zu sein scheint; **things aren't always what they** ~ vieles ist anders, als es aussieht; **I** ~ **to have heard that before** das habe ich doch schon mal gehört; **what** ~s **to be the trouble?** worum geht es denn?; (doctor) was kann ich für Sie tun?; **there** ~s **to be no need/solution** das scheint nicht nötig zu sein/da scheint es keine Lösung zu geben; **it** ~s **to me that I'll have to do that again** mir scheint, ich muß das noch einmal machen; **he has left, it** ~s **or so it seems** anscheinend weggegangen, es scheint, er ist weggegangen; **we are not welcome, it** ~s **or so it seems** wir sind anscheinend or scheinbar (inf) nicht willkommen; **so it** ~s **as** (ganz) so aus; **he is, so it** ~s, ... er scheint ... zu sein; **it** ~s **or would** ~ **that he is coming after all** es sieht so aus, als ob er doch noch kommt, es scheint, er kommt doch noch; **it doesn't** ~ **that he'll be coming** es sieht nicht so aus, als ob er kommt; **it** ~s **that he's forgotten, he** ~s **to have forgotten** er hat es anscheinend or scheinbar (inf) vergessen, es sieht so aus, als ob er es vergessen hat; **if it** ~s **right to you** wenn Sie es für richtig halten; **it** ~s **or would** ~ **(to be) advisable** das scheint ratsam (zu sein); **how does it** ~ **to you?** was meinen Sie?; **it** ~s **a shame to leave it unfinished** es ist doch irgendwie or eigentlich schade, das nicht fertig zu machen; **it just doesn't** ~ **right somehow** das ist doch irgendwie nicht richtig; **it would** ~ **that** ... es scheint fast so, als ob ...; **I can't** ~ **to do it** ich kann das anscheinend or scheinbar (inf) or irgendwie nicht.

(b) it only ~s like **it das kommt einem nur so vor; I** ~ **to be floating in space** es kommt mir so vor, als ob ich schwebe würde; **it all** ~s **so unreal to him/me** es kommt ihm/mir alles so unwirklich vor; **I** ~ **to remember that you had that problem before** es kommt mir so vor, als hätten Sie das Problem schon einmal gehabt; **I** ~ **to have heard his name before** es kommt mir so vor, als hätte ich seinen Namen schon einmal gehört.

seeming ['si:mɪŋ] adj attr scheinbar.

seemingly ['si:mɪŋlɪ] adv scheinbar (inf), anscheinend.

seemliness ['si:mlɪnɪs] n Schicklichkeit f.

seemly ['si:mlɪ] adj (+er) schicklich. **it isn't** ~ **(for sb to do sth)** es schickt sich nicht (für jdn, etw zu tun).

seen [si:n] ptp of **see**[1].

seep [si:p] vi sickern. **to** ~ **through/into sth** durch etw durch-sickern/in etw (acc) hineinsickern.

seepage ['si:pɪdʒ] n (out of sth) Aussickern nt; (through sth) Durchsickern nt; (into sth) Hineinsickern nt. **there is an excessive amount of** ~ es läuft zuviel aus/es dringt zuviel ein; (Comm) die Leckage ist zu groß.

seer [sɪəʳ] n Seher m.

seeress ['sɪərɛs] n Seherin f.

seersucker ['sɪəˌsʌkəʳ] n Krepp, Seersucker m.

seesaw ['si:sɔ:] **1** n Wippe f; (fig) (back and forth) Hin und Her nt; (up and down) Auf und Ab nt. **2** adj schaukelnd. ~ **changes** ständiges Hin und Her; **the boat rolled with a** ~

motion das Schiff schlingerte or schaukelte. **3** vi wippen; (fig) (emotional states) auf und ab gehen; (prices, public opinion) schwanken.

seethe [si:ð] vi (boil) sieden; (surge) schäumen; (fig) (be crowded) wimmeln (with von); (be angry) kochen (inf). **to** ~ **with anger** vor Wut schäumen or kochen; **the crowd** ~**d forward** die Menge drängte sich vor.

see-through ['si:θru:] adj durchsichtig.

segment ['segmənt] **1** n Teil m; (of worm) Glied, Segment nt; (of orange) Stück nt, Rippe f, Schnitz m (dial); (of circle) Abschnitt m, Segment nt. **2** [seg'ment] vt zerlegen, segmentieren. **3** [seg'ment] vi sich teilen.

segmental [ˌseg'mentl] adj (Ling) Segment-.

segmentation [ˌsegmən'teɪʃən] n Zerlegung, Segmentierung f; (Biol) Zellteilung f.

segregate ['segrɪgeɪt] vt individuals absondern; group of population nach Rassen/Geschlechtern/Konfessionen trennen. **to be** ~**d** from sb/sth von jdm/etw abgesondert sein; ~**d** (racially) school, church nur für Weiße/Schwarze; schools, society mit Rassentrennung.

segregation [ˌsegrɪ'geɪʃən] n Trennung f. **racial/sexual** ~ Rassentrennung f/Geschlechtertrennung f.

segregationist [ˌsegrɪ'geɪʃənɪst] n Befürworter(in f) m der Rassentrennung.

seine [seɪn] n Wade f.

seismic ['saɪzmɪk] adj seismisch. ~ **focus** Erdbebenherd m.

seismograph ['saɪzməgrɑ:f] n Seismograph m.

seismography [saɪz'mɒgrəfɪ] n Seismologie f.

seismologist [saɪz'mɒlədʒɪst] n Seismologe m, Seismologin f.

seismology [saɪz'mɒlədʒɪ] n Seismologie, Seismik, Erdbeben-kunde f.

seize [si:z] **1** vt **(a)** (grasp) packen, ergreifen; (as hostage) nehmen; (confiscate) beschlagnahmen; passport einziehen; ship (authorities) beschlagnahmen; (pirates) kapern; (capture) town einnehmen; train, building besetzen; criminal fassen. **to** ~ **sb's arm, to** ~ **sb by the arm** jdn am Arm packen.

(b) (fig) (lay hold of: panic, fear, desire) packen, ergreifen; power, leadership an sich (acc) reißen; (leap upon) idea, suggestion aufgreifen; opportunity ergreifen.

2 vi see **seize up**.

♦ **seize on** or **upon** vi +prep obj **(a)** (clutch at) idea, offer sich stürzen auf (+acc); excuse beim Schopf packen. **(b)** (pick out for criticism) herausgreifen.

♦ **seize up** vi **(a)** (engine, brakes) sich festfressen. **(b)** (inf) my back ~**d** ~ es ist mir in den Rücken gefahren (inf); **she talks so much it's a miracle her jaw doesn't** ~ ~ sie redet so viel, es ist ein Wunder, daß ihr Mundwerk nicht ausleiert (inf).

seizure ['si:ʒəʳ] n **(a)** (confiscation) Beschlagnahmung f; (of passport) Einzug m; (of ship) Beschlagnahme f; (by pirates) Kapern nt; (capture) Einnahme f; (of train, building) Besetzung f. **(b)** (Med) Anfall m; (apoplexy) Schlaganfall m.

seldom ['seldəm] adv selten. **I** ~ **go there** ich gehe (nur) selten dorthin; ~ **have I** ... ich habe selten ...; ~, **if ever, does he do that** er tut das nur äußerst selten.

select [sɪ'lekt] **1** vti (aus)wählen; (in buying also) aussuchen; (Sport) auswählen; (for football match etc) aufstellen. ~**ed poems** ausgewählte Gedichte pl. **2** adj (exclusive) exklusiv; (carefully chosen) auserwählt, auserlesen; tobacco aus-erlesen; fruit ausgesucht. ~ **committee** Sonderausschuß m.

selection [sɪ'lekʃən] n **(a)** (choosing) (Aus)wahl f; (Biol) Auslese, Selektion f.

(b) (person, thing selected) Wahl f; (likely winner) Tip m. **to make one's** ~ seine Wahl treffen; **he took his** ~ **to the assistant** er ging mit den gewählten Artikeln zum Verkäufer; ~**s from Rossini/Goethe** ausgewählte Stücke pl von Rossini/eine Auswahl aus Goethe; ~ **committee** Auswahlkomitee nt.

(c) (range, assortment) Auswahl f (of an +dat).

selective [sɪ'lektɪv] adj **(a)** wählerisch; reader kritisch, anspruchsvoll; examination, processes Auslese-; school Elite-. **we can't treat everything, we have to be** ~ wir können nicht alles abhandeln, wir müssen eine Auswahl treffen or selektiv vorgehen (geh) or (choose carefully) wählerisch sein; **the bigger the range the more** ~ **one must be** je größer das Angebot, desto kritischer muß man auswählen; **a more** ~ **approach to the available material** ... wenn Sie aus dem vor-handenen Material etwas kritischer auswählen würden ...; **a very** ~ **admission procedure** ein stark aussiebendes Aufnahmeverfahren; **the computer program has to be made more** ~ man sollte mehr Wahlmöglichkeiten in das Computerprogramm einbauen; ~ **service** (US) Wehrdienst m.

(b) radio trennscharf, selektiv.

selectively [sɪ'lektɪvlɪ] adv wählerisch; read also, operate selektiv. **to read/buy** ~ beim Lesen/Einkaufen wählerisch sein; **if he had proceeded more** ~ wenn er eine bessere Auswahl ge-troffen hätte; **if you approach the material more** ~ wenn Sie das Material besser auswählen or selektier behandeln (geh); **he built up his collection very** ~ er wählte bei der Zusammenstellung seiner Sammlung sorgfältig aus.

selectivity [ˌsilek'tɪvɪtɪ] n **(a)** Selektivität f; (of reader, buyer) kritisches Auswählen. **his collection shows great** ~ seine Sammlung ist mit viel Sorgfalt ausgewählt; **to develop** ~ kritisches Bewußtsein entwickeln; **to show** ~ anspruchsvoll or wählerisch sein; **to show** ~ **in one's taste** einen anspruchsvollen Geschmack haben; **it diminishes the level of** ~ es verringert die (Aus)wahlmöglichkeiten pl; **the less sophisticated** ~ **of this computer** die weniger verfeinerten Sortiereinrichtungen dieses Computers.

(b) (of radio) Trennschärfe, Selektivität f.

selectman [sɪ'lektmən] n, pl **-men** [-mən] (US) Stadtrat m.

selector [sɪ'lektəʳ] n **(a)** (Tech) Wählschalter m; (lever) Schaltgriff m; (knob) Schaltknopf m; (TV) Programmtaste f;

(*Rad*) Stationstaste *f*; (*on record-player*) Geschwindigkeits-regler *m*; (*Aut*) Schalthebel *m*; (*of computer*) Selektor *m*.
(**b**) (*Sport*) *jd, der die Mannschaftsaufstellung vornimmt.*

selenium [sɪ'liːnɪəm] *n* Selen *nt*.

self [self] **1** *n, pl* **selves** Ich, Selbst (*esp Psych*) *no pl nt*; (*side of character*) Seite *f*. **he showed his worst** ~ er zeigte sich von der schlechtesten Seite; **one's other/better** ~ sein anderes/besseres Ich; **my whole** ~ **revolted at the idea** alles in mir lehnte sich gegen diese Idee auf; **he's quite his old** ~ **again, he's back to his usual** ~ er ist wieder ganz der alte (*inf*); **back to her usual cheerful** ~ wieder fröhlich wie immer; **to be all** ~ (*inf*), **to think of nothing but** ~ nur an sich (*acc*) selbst denken; **with no thought of** ~ ohne an sich (*acc*) selbst denken; **my humble** ~ meine Wenigkeit; **how is your good** ~? wie geht es Ihnen?
2 *pron* (*Comm*) **pay** ~ zahlbar an selbst; **a room for wife and** ~ ein Zimmer für meine Frau und mich.
3 *adj attr* lining aus gleichem Material. **in a** ~ **colour** in uni.

self: ~**-abasement** *n* Selbsterniedrigung *f*; ~**-absorbed** *adj* mit sich selbst beschäftigt; ~**-abuse** *n* (*euph*) Selbstbefleckung *f* (*euph*); ~**-accusation** *n* Selbstanklage, Selbstbeschuldigung *f*; ~**-accusing** *adj* selbstanklagend; ~**-acting** *adj* automatisch, selbsttätig; ~**-activating** *adj* **bomb** selbstzündend; ~**-addressed** *adj* envelope adressiert; ~**-adhesive** *adj* selbstklebend; ~**-adjusting** *adj* selbstregulierend *attr*; **brakes** selbst-nachstellend *attr*; **to be** ~**-adjusting** sich selbst regulieren/nachstellen; ~**-admiration** *n* Selbstbewunderung *f*; ~**-advertisement** *n* Eigenreklame *f*; ~**-aggrandizement** *n* Selbstverherrlichung *f*; ~**-appointed** *adj* selbsternannt; **he is the** ~**-appointed spokesman of the group** er hat sich selbst zum Sprecher der Gruppe gemacht; ~**-approval** *n* Selbstgefälligkeit *f*; ~**-assertion** *n* Durchsetzungsvermögen *nt*; (*pej*) Überheblichkeit *f*, Eigenommenheit *f* von sich selbst; ~**-assertive** *adj* selbstbewußt; (*pej*) von sich selbst eingenommen; ~**-assurance** *n* Selbstsicherheit *f*; ~**-assured** *adj* selbstsicher; **to be** ~ sich (*dat*) seiner selbst bewußt, selbstbewußt sein; ~**-awareness** *n* Selbsterkenntnis *f*, Selbstbewußtsein *nt*.

self: ~**-cancelling** *adj* indicator sich automatisch abschaltend *attr*; ~**-catering** *adj* für Selbstversorger; ~**-centred**, (*US*) ~**-centered** *adj* egozentrisch, ichbezogen; ~**-centredness**, (*US*) ~**-centeredness** *n* Egozentrik, Ichbezogenheit *f*; ~**-cleaning** *adj* selbstreinigend; ~**-closing** *adj* automatisch or von selbst schließend *attr*; ~**-coloured**, (*US*) ~**-colored** *adj* einfarbig, uni; ~**-complacent** *adj* selbstgefällig; ~**-composed** *adj* ruhig, gelassen; ~**-conceit** *n* Eingebildetheit *f*; ~**-confessed** *adj* selbsterklärt *attr*; ~**-confidence** *n* Selbstvertrauen, Selbstbewußtsein *nt*; ~**-confident** *adj* selbstbewußt; ~**-conscious** *adj* befangen, gehemmt; *piece of writing, style etc* bewußt; (*Philos*: ~**-aware**) selbstbewußt; ~**-consciousness** *n* see *adj* Befangenheit, Gehemmtheit *f*; Bewußtheit *f*; Selbstbewußtsein *nt*; ~**-contained** *adj* person distanziert; (~**-sufficient**) selbstgenügsam; *flat* separat; *community* unabhängig; ~**-contradictory** *adj* sich (*dat*) selbst widersprechend *attr*; *alibi* widersprüchlich; **his argument is** ~**-contradictory** seine Argumente widersprechen sich (*dat*); ~**-control** *n* Selbstbeherrschung *f*; ~**-controlled** *adj* selbstbeherrscht; ~**-correcting** *adj* selbstregulierend *attr*; *computer* sich selbst korrigierend *attr*; **to be** ~**-correcting** sich selbst regulieren/korrigieren; ~**-critical** *adj* selbstkritisch; ~**-criticism** *n* Selbstkritik *f*.

self: ~**-deception** *n* Selbsttäuschung *f*, Selbstbetrug *m*; ~**-defeating** *adj* sinnlos, unsinnig; *argument* sich selbst widerlegend *attr*; **the government's plan was** ~**-defeating** dieser Plan der Regierung hat die Gegenteil erzielt; **a** ~**-defeating move** ein Eigentor *nt*; ~**-defence**, (*US*) ~**-defense** *n* Selbstverteidigung *f*; (*Jur*) Notwehr *f*; **to act in** ~**-defence** in Notwehr handeln; **the noble art of** ~**-defence** Boxen *nt*; ~**-denial** *n* Selbstzucht *f*; (*Rel*) Selbstverleugnung *f*; ~**-denying** *adj* sich selbst einschränkend *attr*; (*Rel*) sich selbst verleugnend *attr*; **to be** ~**-denying** sich einschränken/verleugnen; ~**-deprecating** *adj* bescheiden; ~**-destruct** *vi* sich selbst zerstören; ~**-destruction** *n* Selbstzerstörung *f*; (*of person, race*) Selbstmord *m*; ~**-determination** *n* Selbstbestimmung *f* (*also Pol*); ~**-discipline** *n* Selbstdisziplin *f*; ~**-doubt** *n* Zweifel *m* an sich (*dat*) selbst; ~**-dramatization** *n* his tendency towards ~**-dramatization** seine Neigung, sich in Szene zu setzen; ~**-drive** *adj* car für Selbstfahrer.

self: ~**-educated** *adj* autodidaktisch; ~**-educated person** Autodidakt(in *f*) *m*; **he is** ~**-educated** er ist Autodidakt; ~**-effacement** *n* Zurückhaltung *f*; ~**-effacing** *adj* zurückhaltend; ~**-employed** *adj* selbständig; *artist* freischaffend; *journalist* freiberuflich; ~**-esteem** *n* (~**-respect**) Selbstachtung *f* (*conceit*) Selbstüberschätzung *f*; ~**-evident** *adj* offensichtlich, (*not needing proof*) selbstverständlich; **we'll need more money** — **that's** ~**-evident** wir brauchen mehr Geld — das versteht sich von selbst; ~**-explanatory** *adj* unmittelbar verständlich; **this word is** ~**-explanatory** das Wort erklärt sich selbst; ~**-expression** *n* Selbstdarstellung *f*.

self: ~**-fertilization** *n* Selbstbefruchtung *f*; ~**-flagellation** *n* Selbstgeißelung *f*; ~**-fulfilling** *adj* **a** ~**-fulfilling prophecy** eine sich selbst bewahrheitende Voraussage, eine self-fulfilling prophecy (*Sociol*); **the** ~**-fulfilling prophecy of war** der herbeigeredete Krieg; **to be** ~**-fulfilling** sich selbst bewahrheiten; ~**-fulfilment** *n* Erfüllung *f*.

self: ~**-governed**, ~**-governing** *adj* selbstverwaltet, sich selbst verwaltend *attr*; **to become** ~**-governing** eine eigene Regierung bekommen; ~**-government** *n* Selbstverwaltung *f*.

self-help [,self'help] *n* Selbsthilfe *f*. **she never was one for** ~ sie konnte sich noch nie selbst behelfen; **why not practise a little** ~? warum (be)helfen Sie sich (*dat*) nicht selbst?.

self: ~**-importance** *n* Eigendünkel *m*; ~**-important** *adj* dün-

kelhaft; *person also* aufgeblasen (*inf*); ~**-imposed** *adj* selbstauferlegt *attr*; **his exile is** ~**-imposed** er hat sich (*dat*) sein Exil selbst auferlegt; ~**-improvement** *n* Weiterbildung *f*; ~**-induced** *adj* selbstverursacht *attr*; **her miscarriage was** ~**-induced** sie hat die Fehlgeburt selbst verursacht; ~**-induction** *n* (*Elec*) Selbstinduktion *f*; ~**-indulgence** *n* see *adj* Nachgiebigkeit *f* gegen sich selbst; Hemmungslosigkeit *f*; Maßlosigkeit *f*; **go on, take one, a little** ~**-indulgence never hurt anyone** nehmen Sie doch einen, jeder darf sich doch einmal verwöhnen or gehenlassen; **the distinction between humorous style and pure** ~**-indulgence** der Unterschied zwischen humorvollem Stil und reiner Selbstbefriedigung; ~**-indulgent** *adj* nachgiebig gegen sich selbst; (*sexually*) hemmungslos; (*in eating, drinking also*) maßlos; **his columns grew ever more** ~**-indulgent** er schrieb seine Spalten immer mehr zum eigenen Vergnügen; **be** ~**-indulgent, have another slice** verwöhnen Sie sich, nehmen Sie noch ein Stück; ~**-inflicted** *adj* wounds sich (*dat*) selbst zugefügt or beigebracht *attr*; *task, punishment* sich (*dat*) freiwillig auferlegt; **his wounds are** ~**-inflicted** er hat sich (*dat*) die Wunden selbst beigebracht; ~**-interest** *n* (*selfishness*) Eigennutz *m*; (*personal advantage*) eigenes Interesse; **in our own** ~**-interest** in unserem eigenen Interesse; ~**-invited** *adj* selbsteingeladen *attr*; **he is a** ~**-invited guest** er hat sich selbst eingeladen.

selfish *adj*, ~**ly** *adv* ['selfɪʃ, -lɪ] egoistisch, selbstsüchtig.
selfishness ['selfɪʃnɪs] *n* Egoismus *m*, Selbstsüchtigkeit *f*.
self: ~**-justification** *n* Rechtfertigung *f*; **he felt no need for** ~**-justification** er sah keinen Grund, sich zu rechtfertigen; ...; **he said in** ~**-justification** ..., sagte er zu seiner eigenen Rechtfertigung; ~**-justifying** *adj* sachlich gerechtfertigt; ...; **he added in a** ~**-justifying way** ..., fügte er zur eigenen Rechtfertigung an; ~**-knowledge** *n* Selbsterkenntnis *f*.
selfless ['selfl̩s] *adj* selbstlos.
selflessly ['selflɪslɪ] *adv* selbstlos, in selbstloser Weise.
selflessness ['selflɪsnɪs] *n* Selbstlosigkeit *f*.
self: ~**-loading** *adj* ~**-loading gun** Selbstlader *m*; ~**-locking** *adj* von selbst schließend *attr*; *attachment* von selbst einrastend *attr*; ~**-locking door** Tür mit Schnappschloß; ~**-love** *n* Eigenliebe, Selbstliebe (*also Philos*) *f*.
self: ~**-made** *adj* ~**-made man** Selfmademan *m*; ~**-mutilation** *n* Selbstverstümmelung *f*.
self-neglect [,selfnɪ'glekt] *n* Vernachlässigung *f* seiner (*gen*) selbst. **as a result of** ~ weil er sich selbst vernachlässigt hat.
self: ~**-opinionated** *adj* rechthaberisch; *nonsense, drivel* selbstherrlich; **he's too** ~**-opinionated to change his mind** er ist viel zu sehr von sich selbst überzeugt, um seine Meinung zu ändern; ~**-opinionatedness** *n* rechthaberisches und selbstherrliches Wesen; **this stream of** ~**-opinionatedness** dieses selbstherrliche Gerede.
self: ~**-perpetuating** *adj* selbst erneuernd or erhaltend *attr*; ~**-perpetuating poverty/dictatorship** sich ständig fortsetzende Armut/Diktatur; **the system is** ~**-perpetuating** das System erhält sich selbst or entwickelt sich aus sich selbst weiter; ~**-perpetuation** *n* Selbstperpetuierung *f*; ~**-pity** *n* Selbstmitleid *nt*; ~**-pitying** *adj* selbstbemitleidend; ~**-pollination** *n* Selbstbestäubung *f*; ~**-portrait** *n* Selbstporträt or -bildnis *nt*; ~**-possessed** *adj* selbstbeherrscht; ~**-possession** *n* Selbstbeherrschung *f*; ~**-praise** *n* Eigenlob *nt*; ~**-preservation** *n* Selbsterhaltung *f*; **the instinct for** ~**-preservation** der Selbsterhaltungstrieb; ~**-propagating** *adj* flower sich selbst aussäend *attr*; *poverty, bad state of affairs* aus sich selbst weiterentwickelnd *attr*; ~**-propelled** *adj* selbstangetrieben *attr*, mit Selbstantrieb.
self: ~**-raising**, (*US*) ~**-rising** *adj* flour selbsttreibend, mit bereits beigemischtem Backpulver; ~**-realization** *n* Selbstverwirklichung *f*; ~**-regulating** *adj* selbstregulierend *attr*; **this mechanism is** ~**-regulating** dieser Mechanismus reguliert sich selbst; ~**-reliance** *n* Selbständigkeit *f*; ~**-reliant** *adj* selbständig; ~**-reproach** *n* Selbstvorwurf *m*; **all this** ~**-reproach** diese Selbstvorwürfe *pl*; ~**-respect** *n* Selbstachtung *f*; **have you no** ~**-respect?** schämen Sie sich gar nicht?; ~**-respecting** *adj* anständig; **no** ~**-respecting person would** ... niemand, der etwas auf sich hält, würde ...; ~**-restraint** *n* Selbstbeherrschung *f*; ~**-righteous** *adj* selbstgerecht; ~**-righteousness** *n* Selbstgerechtigkeit *f*; ~**-righting** *adj* boat sich (von) selbst aufrichtend *attr*; ~**-rising** *adj* (*US*) see ~**-raising**.
self: ~**-sacrifice** *n* Selbstaufopferung *f*; **it should not be too much of a** ~**-sacrifice** das sollte kein zu großes Opfer sein; ~**-sacrificing** *adj* aufopfernd; ~**-same** *adj* genau der/die/das gleiche, der-/die-/dasselbe; **on the** ~**-same day** noch am selben Tag; ~**-satisfaction** *n* Selbstzufriedenheit *f*; (*smugness*) Selbstgefälligkeit *f*; ~**-satisfied** *adj* (*smug*) selbstgefällig, selbstzufrieden; ~**-sealing** *adj* envelope selbstklebend; *tyre* selbstdichtend; ~**-seeking** **1** *adj* selbstsüchtig; **2** *n* Selbstsucht *f*; ~**-serve** (*esp US*), ~**-service** **1** *adj* Selbstbedienungs-; **the petrol station has gone** ~**-service** die Tankstelle hat jetzt auf Selbstbedienung umgestellt; **2** *n* Selbstbedienung *f*; ~**-starter** *n* Selbstanlasser *m*; ~**-styled** *adj* selbsternannt; ~**-sufficiency** *n* (*of person*) Selbständigkeit *f*; (*emotional*) Selbstgenügsamkeit *f*; (*of country*) Autarkie *f*; (*of community*) Selbstversorgung *f*; ~**-sufficient** *adj* person selbständig, (*emotionally*) selbstgenügsam; *country* autark; **they are** ~**-sufficient in oil** sie können ihren Ölbedarf selbst decken; **a** ~**-sufficient community** eine Gemeinde, die sich selbst versorgen kann; ~**-supporting** *adj* person finanziell unabhängig; *structure* freitragend; *chimney* freistehend; **the newspaper/club is** ~**-supporting** die Zeitung/der Club trägt sich selbst; **our commune is** ~**-supporting** wir sind in unserer Kommune Selbstversorger.
self: ~**-tapping screw** *n* selbstschneidende Schraube, Treibschraube *f*; ~**-taught** *adj* skills selbsterlernt; **he is**

~-taught er hat sich (dat) das selbst beigebracht; (intellectu-ally) er hat das autodidaktisch erlernt; he's a ~-taught guitarist er hat sich das Gitarrespielen selbst beigebracht.

self: ~-will n Eigenwilligkeit f, Eigensinn m (pej); ~-willed adj eigenwillig, eigensinnig (pej); ~-winding adj watch Automatik-.

sell [sel] (vb: pret, ptp sold) 1 vt (a) verkaufen (sb sth, sth to sb jdm etw, etw an jdn); insurance policy abschließen (to mit); (business) goods absetzen. I was sold this in Valencia man hat mir das in Valencia verkauft; the book sold 3,000 copies von dem Buch wurden 3.000 Exemplare verkauft; to ~ a fridge to an Eskimo er könnte einem Eskimo einen Eisschrank andrehen (inf) or aufschwatzen (inf); to ~ insurance (for a living) Versicherungsvertreter sein; to ~ one's life dearly sein Leben teuer verkaufen; he sold himself to the enemy er hat sich an den Feind verkauft; to ~ one's soul to sb/sth jdm/einer Sache seine Seele verschreiben; modern man has sold his soul der moderne Mensch hat seine Seele verloren; how much do you want to ~ it for? wieviel verlangen Sie dafür?, wieviel wollen Sie dafür haben?; I can't remember what I sold it for ich weiß nicht mehr, für wieviel ich es verkauft habe.

(b) (stock) führen, haben (inf); (deal in) vertreiben.

(c) (promote the sale of) zugkräftig machen, einen guten Absatz verschaffen (+dat). you need advertising to ~ your product Sie müssen werben, um Ihr Produkt zu verkaufen or abzusetzen; nothing will ~ this product, it's so bad das Produkt ist so schlecht, daß es sich nicht verkaufen or an den Mann bringen (inf) läßt; she finished up ~ing toothpaste on television sie warb schließlich im Fernsehen für Zahnpasta.

(d) (inf: gain acceptance for) schmackhaft machen (to sb jdm), gewinnen für (to sb jdn); religion aufschwatzen (inf), ver-kaufen (inf) (to sb jdm). you'll never ~ them that idea dafür sind sie nicht zu haben; I know I'll never be able to ~ it to him ich weiß, daß ich ihn dafür nicht erwärmen kann or daß er dafür nicht zu haben ist; to ~ oneself (put oneself across) sich pro-filieren (to bei), sich verkaufen (to an +acc).

(e) (inf: convince of the worth of) to ~ sb on sth jdn von etw überzeugen; to be sold on sb/sth von jdm/etw begeistert sein; how sold is he on the idea? wie sehr hat es ihm diese Idee angetan? (inf).

(f) (fig: betray) verraten. to ~ sb down the river (inf) jdn ganz schön verschaukeln (inf).

2 vi (person) verkaufen (to sb an jdn); (article) sich ver-kaufen (lassen). his book is ~ing well/won't ~ sein Buch ver-kauft sich gut/läßt sich nicht verkaufen; the house sold for £15,000 das Haus wurde für £ 15.000 verkauft; what are they ~ing at or for? wieviel kosten sie?; the idea didn't ~ (fig) die Idee kam nicht an or fand keinen Anklang.

3 n (a) (Comm inf: sales appeal) Zugkraft, Attraktivität f. (b) (selling technique) Verkaufstaktik or -methode f; see hard ~, soft ~.

(c) (dated inf: disappointment) Reinfall m, Pleite f (inf).

♦ **sell off** vt sep verkaufen; (get rid of quickly, cheaply) ab-stoßen; (at auction) versteigern.

♦ **sell out** 1 vt sep (a) (sell entire stock of) ausverkaufen. sorry, sold ~ wir sind leider ausverkauft; we're sold ~ of ice-cream/size 10 wir haben kein Eis/keine Größe 10 mehr, das Eis/Größe 10 ist ausverkauft.

(b) share, interest verkaufen, abgeben.

(c) (inf: betray) verraten (to an +acc).

2 vi (a) (sell entire stock) alles verkaufen or absetzen. this book/we sold ~ in two days das Buch war/wir waren in zwei Tagen ausverkauft.

(b) (in business) sein Geschäft/seine Firma/seinen Anteil etc verkaufen or abstoßen.

(c) (inf: betray) the union leader sold ~ to the bosses der Gewerkschaftsführer verkaufte die Arbeiter an die Bosse (inf); he sold ~ to the right wing/the enemy er hat sich an den rechten Flügel/den Feind verkauft.

♦ **sell up** 1 vt sep zu Geld machen (inf); (Brit Fin) zwangsver-kaufen. he was sold ~ by his creditors die Gläubiger ließen seinen Besitz zwangsverkaufen. 2 vi sein Haus/seinen Besitz/seine Firma etc verkaufen or zu Geld machen (inf).

seller ['selə'] n (a) Verkäufer(in f) m. you should take faulty goods back to the ~ du solltest fehlerhafte Ware (zum Händler) zurückbringen; it's a ~s' market in housing just now zur Zeit bestimmen die Verkäufer die Hauspreise.

(b) (thing sold) big ~ Verkaufsschlager m; bad ~ schlecht gehender or verkäuflicher Artikel; (in shop also) Ladenhüter m; this book is a good/slow ~ das Buch verkauft sich gut/schlecht; it's the best/worst ~ we've had das ist der best-gehende/am schlechtesten gehende Artikel, den wir je hatten.

selling ['selɪŋ] 1 n Verkauf m, Verkaufen nt. they get a special training in ~ sie werden besonders im Verkaufen ausgebildet.
2 adj Verkaufs-. ~ price Verkaufspreis m; ~ point Verkaufsanreiz m.

sellotape ® ['seləʊteɪp] (Brit) 1 n Tesafilm ® m. 2 vt mit Tesafilm ® festkleben.

sell-out ['selaʊt] n (a) (inf: betrayal) fauler Kompromiß or Handel (to mit); (of one's ideals etc) Ausverkauf m (to an +acc). (b) (Theat, Sport) ausverkauftes Haus. to be a ~ ausverkauft sein. (c) (Comm) Verkaufsschlager m.

seltzer (water) ['seltsə('wɔːtə')] n Selterswasser nt.

selvage, selvedge ['selvɪdʒ] n Web(e)kante f.

selves [selvz] pl of self.

semantic adj, ~ally adv [sɪ'mæntɪk, -əlɪ] semantisch.

semanticist [sɪ'mæntɪsɪst] n Semantiker(in f) m.

semantics [sɪ'mæntɪks] n sing Semantik f. the discussion got bogged down in ~ die Diskussion blieb in Wortklaubereien stecken; it's just a question of ~ es ist nur eine Frage der For-mulierung or (interpretation) Auslegung.

---

semaphore ['seməfɔːr] 1 n (a) (Rail) Semaphor nt, Signalmast m. (b) (system) Signalsprache f, Winken nt. transmitted by ~ durch optische Signale übermittelt; to learn ~ das Winker-alphabet lernen. 2 vti durch Winkzeichen signalisieren.

semblance ['sembləns] n (with def art) Anschein m (of von); (with indef art) Anflug m (of von). without a ~ of regret/fear/a smile ohne den leisesten Anflug von Bedauern/Angst/eines Lächelns; I saw in him the ~ of his father (liter) ich konnte in ihm die Ähnlichkeit mit seinem Vater erkennen; it possessed more the ~ of a dream than reality (liter) es war von eher traumhaftem als wirklichem Charakter (liter); to put on a ~ of gaiety (liter) eine fröhliche Miene zur Schau tragen (geh).

semen ['siːmən] n Samenflüssigkeit f, Sperma nt.

semester [sɪ'mestə'] n Semester nt.

semi¹ ['semɪ] n (Brit inf) see semidetached.

semi² n (US inf) see semitrailer.

semi- pref halb-, Halb-.

semi: ~breve n (esp Brit) ganze Note f; ~circle n Halbkreis m; ~circular adj halbkreisförmig; ~circular canal (Anat) Bogen-gang m; ~colon n Strichpunkt m, Semikolon nt; ~conductor n Halbleiter m; ~conscious adj halb bewußtlos; he's ~conscious now, you can talk to him er ist zwar noch nicht ganz bei Bewußt-sein, Sie können aber jetzt mit ihm reden; ~darkness n Halb-dunkel nt; ~detached 1 adj ~detached house halbes Dop-pelhaus; 2 n halbes Doppelhaus nt; ~final n Halb- or Semifinalspiel nt; ~finals Halb- or Semifinale nt; ~finalist n Teilnehmer(in f) m am Halbfinale.

seminal ['seminəl] adj (a) ~ fluid Samenflüssigkeit f. (b) (embryonic) keimhaft (geh). to be present in a ~ state im Keim vorhanden sein. (c) (generative) ideas ertragreich.

seminar ['seminɑː'] n Seminar nt.

seminarian [ˌsemɪ'nɛərɪən], **seminarist** ['semɪnərɪst] n Seminarist m.

seminary ['semɪnərɪ] n Priesterseminar nt.

semiofficial ['semɪə'fɪʃl] adj halbamtlich, offiziös; rule halboffiziell.

semiotic [semɪ'ɒtɪk] adj semiotisch.

semiotics [semɪ'ɒtɪks] n sing Semiotik f.

semi: ~precious adj ~precious stone Halbedelstein m; ~quaver n (esp Brit) Sechzehntel(note f) nt; ~skilled adj worker angelernt; job Anlern-; ~skilled labour (workforce) Angelernte pl; (work) Arbeit f für Angelernte; ~solid 1 adj halbfest; 2 n halbfeste Substanz.

Semite ['siːmaɪt] n Semit m, Semitin f.

Semitic [sɪ'mɪtɪk] adj semitisch.

semi: ~tone n Halbton m; ~trailer n (US) Sattelschlepper m; (part) Sattelauflieger m; ~vowel n Halbvokal m.

semolina [ˌseməˈliːnə] n Grieß m.

sempiternal [ˌsempɪ'tɜːnl] adj (liter) immerwährend (liter).

sempstress ['sempstrɪs] n Näherin f.

Sen (US) abbr of Senator.

SEN (Brit) abbr of State Enrolled Nurse.

senate ['senɪt] n Senat m.

senator ['senɪtə'] n Senator m; (as address) Herr Senator.

senatorial [ˌsenə'tɔːrɪəl] adj des/eines Senators. a family with a long ~ tradition eine Familie, aus der schon viele Senatoren hervorgegangen sind.

send [send] pret, ptp sent 1 vt (a) schicken; letter, messenger also senden (geh); (~ off) letter abschicken; (Rad) radio wave ausstrahlen; signal, SOS senden; (through wires) übermitteln. the gods sent it as a punishment die Götter schickten or sandten (geh) das als Strafe; the satellite ~s signals (to us) der Satellit sendet Signale aus/sendet uns Signale; to ~ sb to pris-on/to his death jdn ins Gefängnis/in den Tod schicken; to ~ sb on a course/tour jdn auf einen or zu einem Kurs/auf eine Tour schicken; to ~ sb to university jdn studieren lassen; to ~ sb for sth jdn nach etw schicken.

(b) she ~s her love/congratulations/apologies etc sie läßt grüßen/Ihnen ihre Glückwünsche ausrichten/sich entschul-digen etc; ~ him my love/best wishes grüßen Sie ihn von mir.

(c) (propel, make sb) arrow, ball schießen; (hurl) schleudern; (conveyor belt) leiten, befördern. he/the explosion sent every-thing crashing to the ground er/die Explosion ließ alles krachend zu Boden fallen; the blow sent him sprawling der Schlag schleuderte ihn zu Boden; the fire sent everyone run-ning out of the building das Feuer ließ alle das Gebäude flucht-artig verlassen; the blue ball sent the red across the table die blaue Kugel ließ die rote über den Tisch rollen; the particle is sent off at an angle das Teilchen fliegt schräg zur Seite weg; this ~s a spark into the engine das leitet einen Funken zum Motor; his speech sent a wave of excitement through the audi-ence seine Rede ließ eine Woge der Aufregung durch die Zu-schauer gehen; the explosion had sent the spaceship off course die Explosion hatte das Raumschiff vom Kurs abgebracht.

(d) (cause to become, cause to go) it's enough to ~ you round the bend da kann man ja wirklich verrückt werden; this sent him into such a temper das machte ihn fürchterlich wütend; this sent him off into one of his diatribes/into fits of laughter das ließ ihn in eine seiner Schimpfkanonaden vom Stapel las-sen/in einen Lachkrampf ausbrechen.

(e) (sl) hinreißen. that tune/he ~s me ich bin ganz weg von der Melodie/von ihm (inf); see also sent.

(f) (old) geben. ~ her victorious möge sie siegreich sein (liter).

2 vi we have to say that ... sie ließ sagen or ausrichten or be-stellen, daß ...; the mail-order firm suddenly stopped ~ing die Versandfirma lieferte plötzlich nicht mehr.

♦ **send across** vt sep herüber-/hinüberschicken; (+prep obj) schicken über (+acc).

♦ **send after** 1 vt sep to ~ sb ~ sb jdn jdm nachschicken. 2 vi +prep obj they sent ~ him sie schickten ihm jemanden nach.

◆**send along** *vt sep* her-/hinschicken.

◆**send away 1** *vt sep* **(a)** wegschicken, fortschicken; *letter etc also* abschicken. **his parents sent him ~ to Europe/to school** seine Eltern schickten ihn nach Europa/ins Internat.
(b) **I had to ~ him ~ without an explanation** ich mußte ihn ohne Erklärung weggehen lassen *or* wegschicken.
2 *vi* schreiben. **the number of people who sent ~ when they saw the TV advert** die Anzahl von Leuten, die auf die Fernsehreklame hin schrieben; **to ~ ~ for sth** etw anfordern.

◆**send back 1** *vt sep* zurückschicken; *food in restaurant* zurückgehen lassen. **2** *vi* **to ~ ~ for reinforcements** nach Verstärkung schicken, Verstärkung holen lassen.

◆**send down** *vt sep* **(a)** *temperature, prices* fallen lassen; *(gradually)* senken. **(b)** *(Brit Univ: expel)* relegieren. **(c)** *prisoner* verurteilen *(for zu)*.

◆**send for** *vi +prep obj* **(a)** *person* kommen lassen; *doctor, police, priest also* rufen; *help* herbeirufen; *reinforcements* herbeiordern; *food* bringen lassen; *(person in authority)* *pupil, secretary, minister* zu sich bestellen. **I'll ~ ~ you/these books when I want you/them** ich lasse Sie rufen/ich schicke nach den Büchern, wenn ich Sie/sie brauche; **to ~ ~ sb to do sth** jdn herbeiholen *or* zu jdm schicken, um etw zu tun; **has the doctor been sent ~ yet?** ist der Arzt schon gerufen worden?
(b) *copy, catalogue* anfordern, sich *(dat)* kommen lassen.

◆**send forth** *vt sep (liter)* aussenden *(geh)*; *blossom* hervorbringen; *smell* verströmen *(geh)*; *heat, light* ausstrahlen.

◆**send in 1** *vt sep* einschicken, einsenden; *person* herein-/hineinschicken; *troops* einsetzen. **2** *vi* see **send away 2**.

◆**send off 1** *vt sep* **(a)** *letter, parcel* abschicken.
(b) *children to school* wegschicken. **he sent his son ~ to Paris** er schickte seinen Sohn nach Paris.
(c) see **send away 1** **(b)**.
(d) *(Sport)* vom Platz verweisen *(for wegen)*; *(Ice hockey)* auf die Strafbank schicken. **he was sent ~ the pitch** er wurde vom Platz verwiesen; **~ him, ~, ref!** Platzverweis!
(e) *(see off)* verabschieden.
2 *vi* see **send away 2**.

◆**send on** *vt sep* **(a)** *(forward)* *letter* nachschicken; *(pass on)* *memo* weiterleiten. **(b)** *(in advance)* *troops, luggage etc* vorausschicken. **(c)** *substitute* aufs Feld schicken, einsetzen; *actor* auf die Bühne schicken.

◆**send out** *vt sep* **(a)** *(out of house, room)* hinaus-/herausschicken *(of aus)*. **he sent me ~ to the shop/to buy a paper** er hat mich zum Geschäft geschickt/losgeschickt, um eine Zeitung zu kaufen; **the company started ~ing work** ~ die Firma hat angefangen, Arbeit außer Haus zu geben.
(b) *(emit)* *rays, radio signals* aussenden; *light, heat, radiation* ausstrahlen, abgeben; *smoke* ausstoßen, abgeben.
(c) *leaflets, invitations, application forms* verschicken.

◆**send out for 1** *vi +prep obj* holen lassen. **2** *vt sep* **to ~ sb ~ ~ sth** jdn nach etw schicken.

◆**send up** *vt sep* **(a)** *rocket* hochschießen lassen; *balloon* steigen lassen; *flare* in die Luft schießen.
(b) *prices, temperature* hochtreiben, in die Höhe treiben; *pressure* steigen lassen.
(c) *(destroy)* in die Luft gehen lassen. **to ~ sth ~ in flames** etw in Flammen aufgehen lassen.
(d) *(Brit inf: satirize)* verulken *(inf)*.
(e) *(US inf: send to prison)* hinter Gitter bringen *(inf)*.

sender ['sendə^r] *n* Absender(in *f*) *m*. **return to ~** zurück an Absender.

send: **~-off** *n* Abschied *m*, Verabschiedung *f*; **to give sb a good ~-off** jdn ganz groß verabschieden *(inf)*; **~-up** *n* *(Brit inf)* Verulkung *f (inf)*; **to do a ~-up of sb/sth** jdn/etw verulken *(inf)*.

Senegal [,senɪ'gɔːl] *n* Senegal *nt*.
Senegalese [,senɪgə'liːz] **1** *adj* senegalesisch. **2** *n* Senegalese *m*, Senegalesin *f*.
senescence [sɪ'nesəns] *n (form)* Alterungsprozeß *m*, Seneszenz *f (spec)*.
senescent [sɪ'nesənt] *adj (form)* alternd.
senile ['siːnaɪl] *adj person* senil; *(physically)* altersschwach. **~ decay** Altersabbau *m*; **he must be getting** ~ er wird langsam senil *or (physically)* ein richtiger Tattergreis *(inf)*.
senility [sɪ'nɪlɪtɪ] *n* Senilität *f*; *(physical)* Altersschwäche *f*.
senior ['siːnɪə^r] **1** *adj* *(in age)* älter; *(in rank)* vorgesetzt, übergeordnet; *(with longer service)* dienstälter; *rank, civil servant* höher; *officer* ranghöher; *position* höher, leitend; *designer, editor, executive, accountant etc* leitend; *doctor, nurse etc* Ober-. **he is ~ to me** *(in age)* er ist älter als ich; *(in rank)* er ist mir übergeordnet; *(in length of service)* er ist *or* arbeitet schon länger hier als ich; **~ section** ältere *or* höhere Altersgruppe; **the ~ management** die Geschäftsleitung; **~ partner** Seniorpartner *m*; **~ consultant** Chefarzt *m*/-ärztin *f*; **~ citizen** älterer Bürger, Altbürger *m*; **~ service** *(Brit)* Kriegsmarine *f*; **~ school, ~ high school** *(US)* Oberstufe *f*; **~ pupil** Oberstufenschüler(in *f*) *m*; **my ~ officer** mein Vorgesetzter; **a very ~ officer** ein sehr hoher Offizier; **he's very/not very ~** er hat eine ziemlich hohe/keine sehr hohe Stellung; **can I speak to somebody more ~?** könnte ich bitte jemanden sprechen, der verantwortlich ist?; **J. B. Schwartz, S~** J. B. Schwartz senior.
2 *n (Sch)* Oberstufenschüler(in *f*) *m*; *(US Univ)* Student(in *f*) *m* im 4./letzten Studienjahr; *(in club etc)* Senior *m*. **he is my ~** *(in age)* er ist älter als ich; *(in rank)* er ist mir übergeordnet; *(in length of service)* er ist *or* arbeitet schon länger hier als ich; **he is two years my ~**, **he is my ~ by two years** er ist zwei Jahre älter als ich.
seniority [,siːnɪ'ɒrɪtɪ] *n* *(in age)* (höheres) Alter; *(in rank)* (höhere) Position; *(Mil)* (höherer) Rang; *(in civil service etc)* (höherer) Dienstgrad; *(in service)* (längere) Betriebszugehörigkeit; *(in civil service etc)* (höheres) Dienstalter. **promotion on the basis of ~** Beförderung *f* nach Länge der

Dienstjahre/Betriebszugehörigkeit.

senna ['senə] *n (drug)* Sennesblätter *pl*; *(plant)* Sennespflanze *f*.
sennight ['senɪt] *n (obs)* Woche *f*.
sen(r) *abbr of* **senior** sen.
sensation [sen'seɪʃən] *n* **(a)** *(feeling)* Gefühl *nt*; *(of heat, cold etc)* Empfindung *f*; *(of the external world)* Sinneseindruck *m*. **a/the ~ of falling** das Gefühl zu fallen; **a ~ of fear/hunger** ein Gefühl *nt* der Angst, ein Angst-/Hungergefühl *nt*; **how can one describe the ~ of touching silk?** wie kann man beschreiben, was man beim Berühren von Seide empfindet?
(b) *(great success)* Sensation *f*. **to cause** *or* **create a ~** (großes) Aufsehen erregen.
sensational [sen'seɪʃənl] *adj* **(a)** sensationell, aufsehenerregend; *newspaper, film, book* reißerisch aufgemacht, auf Sensation bedacht; *news item* Sensations-; *style, writing* reißerisch; *journalist* sensationsgierig *or* -lüstern *(inf)*. **(b)** *(inf: very good etc)* sagenhaft *(inf)*.
sensationalism [sen'seɪʃnəlɪzəm] *n (of paper, reporter etc)* Sensationsmache *f (inf)*; *(of reader)* Sensationsgier *f*. **the cheap ~ of his style** die billige Effekthascherei in seinem Stil; **to edit out the ~** die zu reißerisch aufgemachten Stellen herausstreichen.
sensationally [sen'seɪʃnəlɪ] *adv* **(a)** *write, report* in einem reißerischen Stil. **(b)** *(inf: amazingly)* sagenhaft *(inf)*.
sense [sens] **1** *n* **(a)** *(bodily)* Sinn *m*. **~ of hearing** Gehör(sinn *m*) *nt*; **~ of sight** Sehvermögen *nt*; **~ of smell** Geruchssinn *m*; **~ of taste** Geschmack(sinn) *m*; **~ of touch** Tastsinn *m*.
(b) **~s** *pl (right mind)* Verstand *m*; **no man in his ~s** ... kein einigermaßen vernünftiger Mensch ...; **to be out of one's ~s** nicht ganz bei Trost sein, von Sinnen sein *(geh)*; **to frighten sb out of his ~s** jdn zu Tode erschrecken; **his ~s were deranged by** ... er war durch ... völlig verstört; **to bring sb to his ~s** jdn zur Vernunft *or* Besinnung bringen; **to come to one's ~s** zur Vernunft *or* Besinnung kommen, Vernunft annehmen.
(c) *(feeling)* Gefühl *nt*. **~ of duty** Pflichtbewußtsein *or* -gefühl *nt*; **a ~ of pleasure** ein Gefühl der Freude; **he has an exaggerated ~ of his own importance** er nimmt sich selbst übertrieben wichtig; **imbued with a ~ of history** von Geschichte durchtränkt *(liter)*; **there's a ~ of impermanence in these buildings** diese Gebäude haben etwas Unbeständiges an sich; **these buildings create a ~ of space** diese Gebäude vermitteln den Eindruck von Weite.
(d) *(instinct, appreciation)* Sinn *m*. **his ~ for what is appropriate** sein Gefühl *nt or* Gespür *nt* dafür, was angebracht ist; **~ of colour/justice** Farben-/Gerechtigkeitssinn.
(e) *(good ~)* *(common)* ~ gesunder Menschenverstand; **haven't you ~ enough** *or* **enough ~ to stop when you're tired?** bist du eigentlich zu dumm dazu aufzuhören, wenn du müde bist?; **he had the (good) ~ to** ... er war so vernünftig *or* klug *or* gescheit und ...; **she didn't even have the ~ to take a key** sie war should have had more ~ than to ... du hättest vernünftiger sein sollen und nicht ...; **there is no ~/a lot of ~ in that** das hat keinen Sinn, es ist zwecklos/das hat Hand und Fuß, das ist ganz vernünftig; **what's the ~ of or in doing this?** welchen Sinn hat es denn, das zu tun?; **there is no ~ in doing that** es ist zwecklos *or* sinnlos, das zu tun; **there is no ~ in what he says/in doing that** was er heulen; **there's some ~ in what he says/in doing that** was er sagt, ist ganz vernünftig/es wäre ganz vernünftig, das zu tun; **a man of good ~** ein (ganz) vernünftiger Mann; **to talk ~** vernünftig sein; **you're just not talking ~** du bist doch völlig unvernünftig; **now you're talking ~** das läßt sich schon eher hören; **he hasn't the ~ he was born with** er hat nicht für fünf Pfennig Verstand *(inf)*; **to make sb see ~** jdn zur Vernunft bringen.
(f) **to make ~** *(sentence etc)* (einen) Sinn ergeben; *(be sensible, rational etc)* sinnvoll *or* vernünftig sein, Sinn machen *(inf)*; **it doesn't make ~ doing it that way/to spend all that money** es ist doch Unsinn *or* unvernünftig, es so zu machen/soviel Geld auszugeben; **why did he decide that?** **— I don't know, it doesn't make ~** warum hat er das beschlossen? — ich weiß es nicht, das ist mir unverständlich *or* ich verstehe das nicht; **the whole scheme fails to make ~ to me** die ganze Sache leuchtet mir nicht ein; **it makes good or sound ~** das scheint sehr vernünftig; **it makes good financial/political ~ to ...** aus finanzieller/politischer Sicht gesehen ist es sehr vernünftig, zu ...; **sometimes it just doesn't make ~** manchmal ergibt das Leben einfach keinen Sinn; **her behaviour doesn't make ~ (to me)** man wird/ich werde aus ihrem Verhalten nicht schlau *(inf)*; **he/his theory doesn't make ~/er/seine Theorie ist völlig unverständlich; **it all makes ~ now** jetzt wird einem alles klar; **it doesn't make ~, the jewels were there a minute ago** das ist ganz unverständlich, die Juwelen waren doch eben noch da; **to make ~ of sth** etw verstehen, aus etw schlau werden *(inf)*; **you're not making ~** *(in explaining sth, in plans, intentions etc)* das ist doch Unsinn; *(in behaviour, attitude)* ich werde aus Ihnen nicht schlau *(inf)*; **now you're making ~** *(in explaining sth)* jetzt verstehe ich, was Sie meinen; *(in plans, intentions etc)* das ist endlich eine vernünftige Idee.
(g) *(meaning)* Sinn *m no pl*. **in the full ~ of the word** im wahrsten Sinn des Wortes; **in the ~ which Keats is using the term** in dem Sinn, in dem Keats den Ausdruck benutzt; **it has three distinct ~s** es hat drei verschiedene Bedeutungen; **in what ~ are you using the word?** in welchem Sinn *or* welcher Bedeutung gebrauchen Sie das Wort?; **he is an amateur in the best ~** er ist Amateur im eigentlichen Sinn des Wortes; **in every ~ of the word** in der vollen Bedeutung des Wortes.
(h) *(way, respect)* **in a ~** in gewisser Hinsicht, gewissermaßen; **in every ~** in jeder Hinsicht; **in what ~?** inwiefern?; **there are ~s in which that may be true** in mancher Hinsicht mag das wahr sein; **there is a ~ in which what he claims is true

in einer Hinsicht hat er mit seiner Behauptung recht.
 2 *vt* fühlen, spüren. **I could ~ someone there in the dark** ich fühlte *or* spürte, daß da jemand in der Dunkelheit war.
sense datum *n* Sinnesdatum *nt*.
senseless ['senslɪs] *adj* **(a)** *(unconscious)* besinnungslos, bewußtlos. **to knock sb ~** jdn bewußtlos schlagen. **(b)** *(stupid)* unvernünftig, unsinnig; *(futile)* waste, discussion sinnlos. **what a ~ thing to do/say** *etc* welch ein Unsinn.
senselessly ['senslɪslɪ] *adv see adj* (b).
senselessness ['senslɪsnɪs] *n see adj* (b) Unvernunft, Unsinnigkeit *f*; Sinnlosigkeit *f*.
sense organ *n* Sinnesorgan *nt*.
sensibility [ˌsensɪ'bɪlɪtɪ] *n* (*to beauty etc*) Empfindsamkeit *f*; (*artistic ~ also*) Sensibilität *f*; (*emotional ~, susceptibility to insult*) Empfindlichkeit, Sensibilität *f*. **sensibilities** Zartgefühl *nt*; **his ~ of the problems involved/of her feelings** sein (Fein)gefühl für die damit verbundenen Probleme/sein Verständnis für ihre Gefühle; **the body's ~ to touch/cold** die Empfindlichkeit des Körpers für Berührungen/gegen/(über) Kälte.
sensible ['sensəbl] *adj* **(a)** vernünftig. **be ~ about it** seien Sie vernünftig; **that's the ~ thing to do** das ist vernünftig.
 (b) (*liter: aware*) **to be ~ of sth** sich (*dat*) einer Sache (*gen*) bewußt sein; **he seems not to be ~ of the cold** er scheint gegen Kälte unempfindlich zu sein.
 (c) (*rare: appreciable*) spürbar, merklich.
sensibleness ['sensəblnɪs] *n* Vernünftigkeit *f*.
sensibly ['sensəblɪ] *adv* vernünftig. **he very ~ ignored the question** er hat die Frage vernünftigerweise ignoriert.
sensitive ['sensɪtɪv] *adj* **(a)** (*emotionally*) person sensibel, empfindsam; (*easily hurt*) empfindlich; (*understanding*) einfühlsam; *novel, film, remark* einfühlend. **to be ~ about sth** in bezug auf etw (*acc*) empfindlich sein; **she is very ~ to criticism/the mention of that** sie reagiert sehr empfindlich auf Kritik/darauf, wenn das erwähnt wird.
 (b) (*physically*) *instruments, part of body, leaves, plants* empfindlich; (*Phot*) *emulsion, film* lichtempfindlich; (*delicate*) *balance, adjustment* fein; (*fig*) *topic, issue* heikel, prekär. **~ to heat/light** wärme-/lichtempfindlich.
sensitiveness ['sensɪtɪvnɪs], **sensitivity** [ˌsensɪ'tɪvɪtɪ] *n see adj* **(a)** Sensibilität, Empfindsamkeit *f*; Empfindlichkeit *f*; Einfühlsamkeit *f*; Einfühlungsvermögen *nt*. **(b)** Empfindlichkeit *f*; Lichtempfindlichkeit *f*; Feinheit *f*; heikle Natur. **~ to heat/light** Wärme-/Lichtempfindlichkeit *f*.
sensitize ['sensɪtaɪz] *vt* (*Phot*) sensibilisieren.
sensor ['sensə‍ʳ] *n* Sensor, Fühler *m*.
sensorimotor ['sensərɪ'məʊtə‍ʳ] *adj* sensomotorisch.
sensory ['sensərɪ] *adj* sensorisch; *data, organs* Sinnes-.
sensual ['sensjʊəl] *adj* sinnlich, wollüstig (*pej*); *person, life also* sinnesfreudig, lustbetont. **~ moments** Augenblicke *pl* der Lust.
sensualism ['sensjʊəlɪzəm] *n* Sinnlichkeit, Wollüstigkeit (*pej*) *f*; (*Philos*) Sensualismus *m*.
sensualist ['sensjʊəlɪst] *n* Genußmensch, sinnlicher Mensch, Lüstling (*pej*) *m*; (*Philos*) Sensualist *m*.
sensuality [ˌsensjʊ'ælɪtɪ] *n* Sinnlichkeit, Wollüstigkeit (*pej*) *f*; (*of person also*) Sinnesfreudigkeit *f*.
sensually ['sensjʊəlɪ] *adv* sinnlich, wollüstig (*pej*).
sensuous *adj*, **~ly** *adv* ['sensjʊəs, -lɪ] sinnlich, sinnenhaft.
sensuousness ['sensjʊəsnɪs] *n* Sinnlichkeit, Sinnenhaftigkeit *f*.
sent [sent] **1** *pret, ptp of* **send**. **2** *adj* (*inf*) *look* hingerissen (*inf*). **he's ~** er ist ganz weg (*inf*).
sentence ['sentəns] **1** *n* **(a)** (*Gram*) Satz *m*. **~ structure** Satzbau *m*; (*of particular ~*) Satzaufbau *m*, Satzstruktur *f*.
 (b) (*Jur*) Strafe *f*. **to be under ~ of death** zum Tode verurteilt sein; **the judge gave him a 6-month ~** der Richter verurteilte ihn zu 6 Monaten Haft *or* Freiheitsentzug; **to pass ~ (on sb)** (über) jdn das Urteil verkünden; (*fig*) jdn verurteilen.
 2 *vt* (*Jur*) verurteilen. **he was ~d to life imprisonment** er wurde zu lebenslänglichem Freiheitsentzug verurteilt.
sententious *adj*, **~ly** *adv* ['sen'tenʃəs, -lɪ] salbungsvoll.
sententiousness [sen'tenʃəsnɪs] *n* **the ~ of the lecture/speaker** der salbungsvolle Vortrag/Redner; **..., he said with great ~ ...**, sagte er salbungsvoll.
sentience ['sentɪəns] *n* Empfindungsvermögen *nt*. **the ~ of approaching death** das Vorgefühl des nahenden Todes.
sentient ['sentɪənt] *adj* empfindungsfähig.
sentiment ['sentɪmənt] *n* **(a)** (*feeling, emotion*) Gefühl *nt*. **(b)** (*sentimentality*) Sentimentalität, Rührseligkeit *f*. **(c)** (*opinion*) Ansicht, Meinung *f*. **my ~s exactly!** genau meine Ansicht *or* Meinung! **(d)** (*thought behind words or deeds*) Gedanke *m*.
sentimental [ˌsentɪ'mentl] *adj* sentimental; *person, mood* gefühlvoll; *novel, song, music also* gefühlsselig, kitschig (*pej*), schmalzig (*pej*); *value* Gefühls-. **for ~ reasons** aus Sentimentalität; **to make a ~ visit to a place** einem Ort aus Sentimentalität einen Besuch abstatten; **a certain ~ attachment** eine gewisse gefühlsmäßige Bindung.
sentimentalism [ˌsentɪ'mentəlɪzəm] *n* Sentimentalität *f*.
sentimentalist [ˌsentɪ'mentəlɪst] *n* Gefühlsmensch *m*, sentimentaler Mensch.
sentimentality [ˌsentɪmen'tælɪtɪ] *n* Sentimentalität *f*.
sentimentalize [ˌsentɪ'mentəlaɪz] **1** *vt* sentimental *or* gefühlvoll darstellen. **2** *vi* sentimental sein.
sentimentally [ˌsentɪ'mentəlɪ] *adv* important, attached *etc* gefühlsmäßig; *say, reminisce* sentimental; *sing, play music* gefühlvoll; (*pej*) sentimental, kitschig, schmalzig.
sentinel ['sentɪnl] *n* Wache *f*. **to stand ~ over sth** (*liter*) über etw (*acc*) wachen *or* Wacht halten.
sentry ['sentrɪ] *n* Wache *f*, Wachtposten *m*. **to be on ~ duty** auf Wache sein; **~ box** Wachhäuschen *nt*.
sep *abbr of* **separate**.
sepal ['sepəl] *n* Kelchblatt *nt*.

separability [ˌseprə'bɪlɪtɪ] *n* Trennbarkeit *f*.
separable ['seprəbl] *adj* trennbar.
separate ['seprət] **1** *adj* **(a)** getrennt, gesondert (*from* von); *section, piece also* extra *attr inv*; *organization, unit also* eigen *attr*; *two organizations, issues, parts* gesondert *attr*, voneinander getrennt, verschieden *attr*; *provisions, regulations* besonder(r, s) *attr*, separat, gesondert; *beds, rooms, accounts* getrennt; *account, bill, agreement, department* gesondert, extra *attr inv*; *entrance, toilet, flat* separat; *treaty, peace* Separat-, Sonder-; *existence* eigen. **that is a ~ question/issue** das ist eine andere Frage, das ist eine Frage für sich; **on two ~ occasions** bei zwei verschiedenen Gelegenheiten; **on a ~ occasion** bei einer anderen Gelegenheit; **there will be ~ discussions on this question** diese Frage wird extra *or* separat *or* gesondert diskutiert; **they live ~ lives** sie gehen getrennte Wege; **a ~ sheet of paper** ein anderes Blatt Papier; (*additional*) ein gesondertes *or* extra Blatt Papier; **this is quite ~ from his job** das hat mit seinem Beruf nichts zu tun; **to keep two things ~** zwei Dinge nicht zusammentun; *questions, issues* zwei Dinge auseinanderhalten; **always keep your cheque book ~ from your banker's card** bewahren Sie Scheckbuch und Scheckkarte immer getrennt auf; **keep this book/problem ~ from the others** halten Sie dieses Buch von den anderen getrennt/betrachten Sie dieses Problem getrennt.
 (b) (*individual*) einzeln. **all the ~ sections/pieces/units/questions** alle einzelnen Abschnitte/Teile/Einheiten/Fragen; **everybody has a ~ cup/task** jeder hat eine Tasse/Aufgabe für sich *or* seine eigene Tasse/Aufgabe.
 2 ~s *pl* Röcke, Blusen, Hosen *etc*.
 3 ['sepəreɪt] *vt* trennen; (*Chem also*) scheiden; (*milk*) zentrifugieren; (*divide up*) aufteilen (*into* in + *acc*). **to ~ the good from the bad** die Guten von den Schlechten trennen *or* scheiden; **he can't ~ his private life from his work** er kann das Privatleben und Arbeit nicht (voneinander) trennen, er kann das Privatleben nicht von der Arbeit trennen; **he is ~d from his wife** er lebt von seiner Frau getrennt.
 4 ['sepəreɪt] *vi* sich trennen; (*Chem also*) sich scheiden. **it ~s into four parts** es läßt sich in vier Teile auseinandernehmen; (*fig: problem etc*) es zerfällt in vier Teile.
 ♦ **separate out 1** *vt sep* trennen (*from* von), absondern (*from* von), aussondern. **2** *vi* getrennt werden.
separated ['sepəreɪtɪd] *adj* getrennt; *couple* getrennt lebend *attr*. **the couple are ~** das Paar lebt getrennt.
separately ['seprətlɪ] *adv* getrennt, gesondert, separat; *live* getrennt; (*singly*) einzeln.
separateness ['seprətnɪs] *n* Getrenntheit, Gesondertheit *f*.
separation [ˌsepə'reɪʃən] *n* Trennung *f*; (*Chem also*) Scheidung *f*; (*of rocket etc*) Abtrennung *f* (*from* von).
separation allowance *n* Trennungsentschädigung *f*.
separatism ['sepərətɪzəm] *n* Separatismus *m*.
separatist ['sepərətɪst] **1** *adj* separatistisch. **2** *n* Separatist(in *f*) *m*.
separator ['sepəreɪtə‍ʳ] *n* Separator *m*.
sepia ['siːpjə] **1** *n* Sepia *f*. **2** *adj* paint, pigment, drawing Sepia-; (*also ~-coloured*) sepia(farben).
sepoy ['siːpɔɪ] *n* Sepoy *m*.
sepsis ['sepsɪs] *n* Vereiterung, Sepsis (*spec*) *f*.
Sept *abbr of* **September** Sept.
September [sep'tembə‍ʳ] **1** *n* September *m*. **the first/tenth of ~** der erste/zehnte September; **on ~ 1st/19th** (*written*), **on 1st/19th ~** (*written*), **on the 1st/19th of ~** (*spoken*) am 1./19. September; **~ 3rd, 1979, 3rd ~ 1979** (*on letter*) 3. September 1979; **in ~** im September; **during ~** im September; **every** *or* **each ~** jeden September; **at the beginning/end of ~** Anfang/Ende September; **~ is a pleasant month** der September ist ein angenehmer Monat; **there are 30 days in ~** der September hat 30 Tage.
 2 *adj attr* September-; *weather, mists etc also* septemberlich.
septennial [sep'tenɪəl] *adj* siebenjährig; (*every seven years*) alle sieben Jahre stattfindend, siebenjährlich.
septet [sep'tet] *n* Septett *nt*.
septic ['septɪk] *adj* vereitert, septisch. **the wound turned ~** die Wunde eiterte; **~ tank** Faulbehälter, Klärbehälter *m*.
septicaemia, (US) septicemia [ˌseptɪ'siːmɪə] *n* Vergiftung *f* des Blutes, Septikämie *f* (*spec*).
septuagenarian [ˌseptjʊədʒɪ'neərɪən] **1** *adj* siebzigjährig. **2** *n* Siebzigjährige(r) *mf*. **to be a ~** ein(e) Siebziger(in) sein.
Septuagesima [ˌseptjʊə'dʒesɪmə] *n* Sonntag *m* Septuagesima.
septuplet [sep'tjuːplɪt] *n* (*baby*) Siebenling *m*; (*Mus*) Septimole *f*.
sepulcher *n* (*US*) *see* **sepulchre**.
sepulchral [sɪ'pʌlkrəl] *adj* (*liter*) sepulkral (*liter*); (*fig*) düster; *voice* Grabes-; *atmosphere* Friedhofs-.
sepulchre, (US) sepulcher ['sepəlkə‍ʳ] *n* Grabstätte *f*. **the Holy S~** das Heilige Grab; *see* **whited ~**.
sequel ['siːkwəl] *n* Folge *f* (*to* von). **it had a tragic ~** es hatte ein tragisches Nachspiel.
sequence ['siːkwəns] *n* **(a)** (*order*) Folge, Reihenfolge *f*. **~ of tenses/words** Zeiten-/Wortfolge *f*; **in ~** der Reihe nach; **to do sth in logical ~** etw in der logisch richtigen Reihenfolge tun.
 (b) (*things following*) Reihe, Folge *f*; (*Mus, Cards, Eccl*) Sequenz *f*; (*Math*) Reihe *f*. **(c)** (*Film, dance ~*) Sequenz *f*.
sequential [sɪ'kwenʃəl] *adj* (*form*) der Reihe nach, in regelmäßiger Folge; (*following*) folgend. **to be ~ to** *or* **upon sth** auf etw (*acc*) folgen; **a ~ alphabetical arrangement** eine Anordnung in alphabetischer Reihenfolge.
sequester [sɪ'kwestə‍ʳ] *vt* **(a)** (*liter: isolate*) abkapseln. **(b)** (*Jur*) *see* **sequestrate**.
sequestered [sɪ'kwestəd] *adj* (*liter*) *village* abgeschieden; *spot* abgelegen; *life* zurückgezogen.
sequestrate [sɪ'kwestreɪt] *vt* (*Jur*) sequestrieren.

sequestration [ˌsiːkwe'streɪʃən] n (Jur) Sequestration f; (in bankruptcy case also) Zwangsverwaltung f.
sequin ['siːkwɪn] n Paillette f.
sequined ['siːkwɪnd] adj mit Pailletten besetzt.
sequoia [sɪ'kwɔɪə] n Mammutbaum m, Sequoie f.
seraglio [se'rɑːlɪəʊ] n Serail nt.
seraph ['serəf] n, pl -s or -im Seraph m.
seraphic [sə'ræfɪk] adj verklärt, verzückt.
seraphim ['serəfɪm] pl of seraph.
Serb [sɜːb] n Serbe m, Serbin f.
Serbia ['sɜːbɪə] n Serbien nt.
Serbian ['sɜːbɪən] 1 adj serbisch. 2 n (a) Serbe m, Serbin f. (b) (language) Serbisch nt.
Serbo-Croat ['sɜːbəʊ'krəʊæt] n (language) Serbokroatisch nt. the ~s pl (people) die Serben und Kroaten.
Serbo-Croatian ['sɜːbəʊkrəʊ'eɪʃən] 1 adj serbokroatisch. 2 n the ~s pl die Serben und Kroaten.
serenade [ˌserə'neɪd] 1 n Serenade f. 2 vt ein Ständchen nt bringen (+dat).
serendipity [ˌserən'dɪpɪtɪ] n Spürsinn m (fig), mehr Glück als Verstand.
serene [sə'riːn] adj gelassen; sea ruhig; sky heiter, klar. His S~ Highness seine Durchlaucht, Serenissimus.
serenely [sə'riːnlɪ] adv gelassen. ~ indifferent to the noise gleichmütig dem Lärm gegenüber.
serenity [sɪ'renɪtɪ] n Gelassenheit f; (as title: also S~) Durchlaucht f.
serf [sɜːf] n Leibeigene(r) mf.
serfdom ['sɜːfdəm] n Leibeigenschaft f; (fig) Knechtschaft f.
serge [sɜːdʒ] n Serge, Sersche f.
sergeant ['sɑːdʒənt] n (Mil) Feldwebel m; (police) Polizeimeister m. ~ at arms (Hist) Waffenmeister m; (Brit Parl) Exekutivbeamte(r) m des Parlaments; ~ first class (US) Oberfeldwebel m; ~ major Oberfeldwebel m.
serg(t) abbr of sergeant.
serial ['sɪərɪəl] 1 adj Serien-; novel Fortsetzungs-; story, radio etc programme etc in Fortsetzungen; writer von Fortsetzungsromanen; music seriell; computer mit Stapelbetrieb. **published in** ~ **form** in Fortsetzungen veröffentlicht; ~ **number** fortlaufende Nummer; (on manufactured goods) Fabrikationsnummer f; ~ **rights** Rechte pl für die Veröffentlichung in Fortsetzungen; ~ **processing** (Computers) Stapelbetrieb m.
2 n (novel) Fortsetzungsroman m; (Rad) Sendereihe f (in Fortsetzungen); (TV) Sendefolge f; (spec: magazine) (periodisch erscheinende) Zeitschrift. **it was published/broadcast as a** ~ es wurde in Fortsetzungen veröffentlicht/gesendet.
serialization [ˌsɪərɪəlaɪ'zeɪʃən] n (Rad, TV) Sendung f (in Fortsetzungen; (in magazines etc) Fortsetzung(sreihe) f; (serializing) Umarbeitung f in Fortsetzungen.
serialize ['sɪərɪəlaɪz] vt in Fortsetzungen veröffentlichen; (Rad, TV) in Fortsetzungen senden; (put into serial form) in Fortsetzungen umarbeiten.
serially ['sɪərɪəlɪ] adv publish, broadcast in Fortsetzungen; (in order) number fortlaufend; (Mus) seriell.
seriatim [ˌsɪərɪ'eɪtɪm] adv (form) der Reihe nach.
sericulture ['serɪˌkʌltʃəʳ] n Seidenraupenzucht f.
series ['sɪərɪz] n, pl - Serie f; (Rad) Sendereihe f; (TV) Sendefolge f; (of books, lectures etc also, of films, talks, Math, Mus, Elec) Reihe f; (of events also, succession of things) Reihe, Folge f. a ~ **of articles** eine Artikelserie or -reihe; a ~ **of visitors** eine Besucherserie; **in** ~ der Reihe nach; (Elec) in Reihe; (Comm) serienmäßig; **publish** als Serie.
series-wound ['sɪəriːˌwaʊnd] adj (Elec) in Serie or Reihe geschaltet.
serif ['serɪf] 1 n Serife f. 2 adj Serifen-.
serio-comic(al) ['sɪərɪəʊ'kɒmɪk(l)] adj halb ernst, halb heiter.
serious ['sɪərɪəs] adj (a) ernst; person, manner (not frivolous) ernsthaft; (subdued) ernst; consideration, discussion, conversation also ernsthaft; newspaper, publication, interest ernsthaft, seriös; offer, suggestion ernstgemeint attr, ernst gemeint pred, seriös; doubts also ernstlich, ernsthaft. **to be** ~ **about doing sth** etw im Ernst tun wollen; **I'm** ~ (**about it**) ich meine das ernst, das ist mein Ernst; **he is** ~ **about her** er meint es ernst mit ihr; **be** ~ **about your studies** du mußt dein Studium ernst nehmen; **you can't be** ~! das meinst du doch nicht ernst!, das kann nicht dein Ernst sein!; **to give** ~ **thought to sth** sich (dat) etw ernsthaft or ernstlich überlegen; **the** ~ **student of** jazz will ... wer sich ernsthaft mit Jazz beschäftigt, wird ...
(b) (critical) accident, flooding, deficiencies, loss schwer; mistake, injury, damage also schlimm; problem also ernst, ernstzunehmend attr; illness also, situation ernst, schlimm; patient's condition ernst, bedenklich; threat, shortage, lack ernst, ernstlich; situation, deterioration bedenklich. **it's** ~ **das ist schlimm; it's getting** ~ es wird ernst; **inflation is getting** ~ die Inflation nimmt ernste Ausmaße an.
seriously ['sɪərɪəslɪ] adv (a) ernst; talk, interested, work ernsthaft; (not jokingly) im Ernst. **to take sb/sth** ~ jdn/etw ernst nehmen; **do you** ~ **want to do that?** wollen Sie das wirklich or im Ernst tun?; ~ **now/though** ... jetzt/aber mal ganz im Ernst ...; do **you mean that** ~? meinen Sie das ernst?, ist das Ihr Ernst?; **he offered it quite** ~ er hat das ernstlich angeboten.
(b) wounded, flooded schwer; ill also, worried ernstlich; damaged, injured also schlimm; deteriorate bedenklich. **he/the take-off went** ~ **wrong** er hat einen schweren Fehler gemacht/beim Start ist etwas schlimm daneben gegangen; **we are** ~ **short of water** bei uns herrscht schwerer or schlimmer Wassermangel.
seriousness ['sɪərɪəsnɪs] n see adj (a) Ernst m; Ernsthaftigkeit f; Seriosität f; Ernstlichkeit f. **in all** ~ ganz im Ernst. (b) Schwere f; Ernst m; Bedenklichkeit f.

serjeant ['sɑːdʒənt] n see **sergeant**.
sermon ['sɜːmən] n (Eccl) Predigt f; (homily) Moralpredigt f; (scolding) Strafpredigt f. **the S~ on the Mount** die Bergpredigt.
sermonize ['sɜːmənaɪz] vi Vorträge halten; (reproving) Moralpredigten halten.
serous ['sɪərəs] adj serös; fluid Serum-.
serpent ['sɜːpənt] n (a) (liter) Schlange f (also fig). (b) (Mus) Serpent nt.
serpentine ['sɜːpəntaɪn] adj lane, river gewunden, mit vielen Windungen; road also kurvenreich.
serrated [se'reɪtɪd] adj gezackt; leaves also gesägt. ~ **knife** Sägemesser nt.
serration [se'reɪʃən] n Zacke f; (edge) gezackter Rand; (on knife) Sägerand m; (of leaves) gesägter Rand.
serried ['serɪd] adj: ~ **ranks** enggeschlossene Reihen pl.
serum ['sɪərəm] n Serum nt.
servant ['sɜːvənt] n (lit, fig) Diener(in f) m; (also ~ **girl**) Dienstmädchen nt; (domestic) Bedienstete(r) mf, Dienstbote m. **to keep or have** ~s Bedienstete or Diener haben; ~s' **quarters** Gesinderäume (Hist), Dienstbotenräume pl; **your devoted or humble or obedient** ~ (old) Ihr ergebenster or untertänigster Diener (old); see **public** ~, **civil** ~.
serve [sɜːv] v **1** vt (a) dienen (+dat); (be of use) dienlich sein (+dat), nützen (+dat). **he** ~**d his country/the firm well** er hat sich um sein Land/die Firma verdient gemacht; **he has** ~**d our cause faithfully** er hat sich um unsere Sache verdient gemacht, er hat unserer Sache treue Dienste geleistet; **if my memory** ~s **me right** wenn ich mich recht erinnere; **to** ~ **its/sb's purpose** seinen Zweck erfüllen, jds Zwecken (dat) dienen; **it** ~s **a variety of purposes** es hat viele verschiedene Verwendungsmöglichkeiten; **it** ~s **no useful purpose** es hat keinen praktischen Wert; **my needs das ist genau (das), was ich brauche; **to** ~ **sb as sth** jdm als etw dienen; **this box has** ~**d us as a table** diese Kiste hat uns (dat) als Tisch gedient; **can I** ~ **you in any way?** kann ich Ihnen irgendwie behilflich sein?; **it has** ~**d us well** es hat uns gute Dienste geleistet; **his knowledge of history** ~**d him well** seine Geschichtskenntnisse kamen ihm sehr zugute.
(b) (work out) abdienen, ableisten; term of office durchlaufen; apprenticeship durchmachen; sentence verbüßen, absitzen (inf). **when he** ~**d his term as Prime Minister** während seiner Amtszeit als Premierminister.
(c) (supply: transport, gas etc) versorgen.
(d) (in shop) bedienen. **to** ~ **sb with 5 kilos of potatoes** jdm 5 kg Kartoffeln bringen or geben; **I'm being** ~**d, thank you** danke, ich werde schon bedient or ich bekomme schon (inf).
(e) (esp in restaurant) food, drink servieren; (bring to table also) auftragen; (put on plate) aufgeben; guests bedienen; (waiter) bedienen, servieren (+dat); (pour drink for) einschenken (+dat); wine etc einschenken; rations verteilen (to an +acc). **dinner is** ~**d** (butler) das Essen or es ist aufgetragen; (hostess) darf ich zu Tisch bitten?; "~s **three**" (on packet etc) „(ergibt) drei Portionen".
(f) Mass, Communion ministrieren bei.
(g) (Tennis etc) ball aufschlagen. **he** ~**d a double fault** er hat einen Doppelfehler gemacht.
(h) (Jur) zustellen (on sb jdm). **to** ~ **a summons on sb**, **to** ~ **sb with a summons** jdn vor Gericht laden; **the landlord** ~**d notice (to quit) on his tenants** der Vermieter kündigte den Mietern.
(i) (old: treat) behandeln. **to** ~ **sb ill** jdm einen schlechten Dienst erweisen, jdm übel mitspielen; (it) ~s **you right!** (inf) das geschieht dir (ganz) recht!; **it** ~s **him right for being so greedy** (inf) das geschieht ihm ganz recht, was muß er auch so gierig sein!; **it would have** ~**d you right if** ... (inf) es wäre dir ganz recht geschehen, wenn ...
(j) (stallion etc) decken.
2 vi (a) dienen. **to** ~ **on the jury** Geschworene(r) mf sein; **to** ~ **on a committee/the council/in Parliament** einem Ausschuß angehören/im Stadt- or Gemeinderat/Parlament sein; **to** ~ **in an office** ein Amt bekleiden (form) or innehaben; **to** ~ **as chairman** das Amt des Vorsitzenden innehaben or bekleiden (form); **he** ~s **here as a gardener** er ist hier Gärtner.
(b) (Mil) dienen.
(c) (at table) aufgeben; (waiter, butler etc) servieren (at table bei Tisch). **is there anyone serving at this table?** bedient hier jemand?
(d) **to** ~ **as**, **to** ~ **for** dienen als; **it will** ~ **das tut's; it** ~s **to show/explain** ... das zeigt/erklärt ...; **these facts merely** ~ **to prove my point** diese Fakten dienen lediglich dazu, mein Argument zu beweisen; **when the occasion** ~s wenn es gerade paßt.
(e) (Eccl) ministrieren.
(f) (Tennis etc) aufschlagen.
3 n (Tennis etc) Aufschlag m. **whose** ~ **is it?** wer hat Aufschlag?
♦ **serve out** vt sep (a) food ausgeben; rations etc vergeben, verteilen. (b) (work out) time in army ableisten; apprenticeship beenden, abschließen; sentence absitzen.
♦ **serve up** vt sep (a) food servieren; rations verteilen. **you can't** ~ **this muck** ~ (inf) so etwas kann man doch niemandem vorsetzen! (b) (inf: present) servieren (inf); excuse auftischen.
server ['sɜːvəʳ] n (a) (tray) Servierbrett nt. (b) (spoon, fork) Servierlöffel, Vorlegelöffel m/-gabel f; (pie ~) Tortenheber m; (fish ~) Fischvorlegelöffel m. **a pair of** ~s **in** Vorlegebesteck nt; salad ~s Salatbesteck nt. (c) (Tennis) Aufschläger(in f) m. **he's a strong** ~ er hat einen guten Aufschlag. (d) (Eccl) Ministrant, Meßdiener m.
service ['sɜːvɪs] **1** n (a) (liter, fig) Dienst m. **his faithful** ~ seine treuen Dienste; ~s **to God** Dienst an Gott; ~s **to one's country/the Queen** (soldier etc) Dienst an seinem Vaterland/für die Königin; **his** ~s **to industry/the country** (politician, industrialist) seine Verdienste in der Industrie/um das Land; **he died**

in the ~ of his country er starb in Pflichterfüllung für sein Vaterland; **he has ten years' ~ behind him** er hat zehn Jahre Dienstzeit hinter sich (*dat*); **to do sb a ~** jdm einen Dienst erweisen; **to do *or* see good ~** gute Dienste leisten; **this box did ~ as a table** diese Kiste hat schon als Tisch gedient; **to be of ~** nützlich sein; **to be of ~ to sb** jdm nützen; **it's of no ~ in an emergency** im Notfall nützt es nichts; **to be at sb's ~** jdm zur Verfügung stehen; (*person also*) jdm zu Diensten stehen; **can I be of ~ to you?** kann ich Ihnen behilflich sein?; **out of ~** außer Betrieb; **to need the ~s of a doctor/lawyer** einen Arzt/Anwalt brauchen, einen Arzt/Anwalt zuziehen müssen; **on Her/His Majesty's S~** (*abbr* OHMS) *Aufdruck auf Dienstsachen, Umschlägen von Behörden etc*; ≈ Dienstsache *f*.

(b) (*operation*) Betrieb *m*. **to be out of ~** außer Betrieb sein; **to bring sth into ~** etw in Betrieb nehmen; **to come into ~** in Betrieb genommen werden.

(c) (*Mil*) Militärdienst *m*. **to see ~ as a soldier/sailor** beim Militär/in der Marine dienen; **when I was in the ~s** als ich beim Militär war; **the three ~s** die drei Waffengattungen.

(d) (*with adj attr: branch, department etc*) -dienst *m*. **telephone ~** Telefondienst *m*; **postal ~** Postwesen *nt*, Postdienst *m*; **medical ~(s)** ärztliche Versorgung.

(e) (*to customers*) Service *m*; (*in shop, restaurant etc*) Bedienung *f*.

(f) (*bus, train, plane etc*) Bus-/Zug-/Flugverbindung *f*. **to increase ~s in rural areas** den Verkehr *or* die Verkehrslage in ländlichen Gebieten verbessern; **there's no ~ to Oban on Sundays** sonntags besteht kein Zug-/Busverkehr nach Oban; **the number 12 (bus) ~** die Linie 12.

(g) (*domestic ~*) Dienst *m*, Stellung *f*. **to be in ~ (with sb)** (bei jdm) in Stellung sein, in jds Dienst (*dat*) stehen; **to go into ~ (with sb)** (bei jdm) in Stellung gehen, in jds Dienst (*acc*) treten; **to take sb into ~** jdn in Stellung *or* in seine Dienste nehmen.

(h) (*Eccl*) Gottesdienst *m*.

(i) (*of machines*) Wartung *f*; (*Aut: major ~*) Inspektion *f*. **my car is in for/has had a ~** mein Auto wird/wurde gewartet; **mein Auto ist/war zur *or* bei der Inspektion.**

(j) (*tea or coffee set*) Service *nt*.

(k) (*Tennis*) Aufschlag *m*. **to lose one's ~** seinen Aufschlag *or* sein Aufschlagspiel abgeben; **whose ~ is it?** wer hat Aufschlag?, wer schlägt auf?

(l) (*Jur*) Zustellung *f*.

(m) **~s pl** (~ industries) Dienstleistungen *pl*; (*gas, electricity, water*) Versorgungsnetz *nt*; **all the ~s have been cut off** Gas, Wasser und Strom sind abgestellt worden; **the house is close to all ~s** das Haus ist in günstiger Lage.

(n) (*Mot*) **~s pl** Tankstelle und Raststätte (+*pl vb*).

2 vt (a) *car, machine* warten. **to send a car to be ~d** ein Auto warten lassen; (*major ~*) ein Auto zur Inspektion geben.

(b) *area* bedienen; *committee etc* zuarbeiten (+*dat*).

(c) *cow, mare* decken.

serviceability [ˌsɜːvɪsəˈbɪlɪtɪ] *n see adj* Strapazierfähigkeit *f*; Zweckmäßigkeit *f*; Brauchbarkeit *f*.

serviceable [ˈsɜːvɪsəbl] *adj* (*durable, sturdily made*) strapazierfähig; (*practical*) praktisch, zweckmäßig; (*usable*) brauchbar.

service: **~ area** *n* Tankstelle und Raststätte (+*pl vb*); **~ bus** *n* Linienbus *m*; **~ charge** *n* Bedienung(sgeld *nt*) *f*; (*of bank*) Bearbeitungsgebühr *f*; **~ court** *n* (*Tennis etc*) Aufschlagfeld *nt*; **~ department** *n* Kundendienst(abteilung *f*) *m*; **~ dress** *n* Dienstkleidung *f*; **~ elevator** *n* (*esp US*) Lasten- *or* Warenaufzug *m*; **~ engineer** *n* Servicemechaniker *m*; **~ entrance** *n* Dienstboteneingang *m*; **~ family** *n* Familie *f* von Militärpersonal; **~ flat** *n* (*Brit*) Appartement *nt* mit vollem Service (*Portier, Hausmeister etc*); **~ game** *n* Aufschlagspiel *nt*; **~ hatch** *n* Durchreiche *f*; **~ industry** *n* Dienstleistungsbranche *f*; **~ lift** *n* (*Brit*) Lasten- *or* Warenaufzug *m*; **~ line** *n* (*Tennis etc*) Aufschlaglinie *f*; **~man** *n* Militärangehörige(r) *m*; **~ module** *n* (*Space*) Versorgungsteil *nt*; **~ road** *n* (*for access*) Zufahrtsstraße *f*; (*for works traffic*) Versorgungsstraße *f*; (*for delivery*) Andienungsstraße *f*; **~ station** *n* Tankstelle *f* (mit Reparaturwerkstatt); **~woman** *n* Militärangehörige *f*.

serviette [ˌsɜːvɪˈet] *n* Serviette *f*. **~ ring** Serviettenring *m*.

servile [ˈsɜːvaɪl] *adj* unterwürfig; *obedience* sklavisch.

servility [sɜːˈvɪlɪtɪ] *n* Unterwürfigkeit *f*.

serving [ˈsɜːvɪŋ] *n* (*helping of food*) Portion *f*. **~ hatch** Durchreiche *f*; **~ spoon** Vorlegelöffel *m*.

servitude [ˈsɜːvɪtjuːd] *n* Knechtschaft *f*.

servo [ˈsɜːvəʊ] **1** *n* (*inf*) Servomechanismus *m*. **2** *adj attr* Servo-. **~-assisted brakes** Servobremsen *pl*; **~mechanism** Servomechanismus *m*.

sesame [ˈsesəmɪ] *n* (a) (*Bot*) Sesam *m*. **~ seed roll** Sesambrötchen *nt*. **(b) open ~!** Sesam, öffne dich!; **an open ~** (*fig*) ein Sesam-öffne-dich *nt*.

sessile [ˈsesaɪl] *adj* (*Bot*) festgewachsen, sessil (*spec*).

session [ˈseʃən] *n* (a) (*meeting*) Sitzung *f*; (*Jur, Parl: period*) Sitzungsperiode *f*; (*Parl: term of office*) Legislaturperiode *f*. **to be in ~** eine Sitzung abhalten; (*Jur, Pol*) tagen; **to go into secret ~** eine Geheimsitzung abhalten; **a ~ of talks, negotiations** Gespräche *pl*/Verhandlungen *pl*; *see* **quarter ~s, court**.

(b) (*with psychiatrist etc, period devoted to activity*) Sitzung *f*; (*at doctor's, dentist's*) Behandlung *f*; (*discussion, meeting*) Besprechung *f*. **recording ~** Aufnahme *f*; **we're in for a long ~** das wird lange dauern; **we're going to have a card/manicure etc ~ tonight** (*inf*) heute abend treffen wir uns zum Kartenspielen/zur Maniküre *etc*; **I'll have a cleaning ~ tomorrow** (*inf*) morgen werde ich mal ausgiebig putzen (*inf*); **to have a ~ with one's girlfriend** (*inf*) mit seiner Freundin zusammensein.

(c) (*academic year*) (*Univ*) Studienjahr *nt*; (*Sch*) Schuljahr *nt*; (*term*) Semester/Trimester *nt*; (*esp Sch*) Halbjahr *nt*; (*division of course*) Stunde, Sitzung (*esp Univ*) *f*. **the afternoon**

~s begin ... der Nachmittagsunterricht fängt ... an.

sestet [sesˈtet] *n* (*Mus*) Sextett *nt*; (*Poet*) Sestine *f*.

set [set] (*vb:* pret, ptp **~**) **1 n (a)** (*of two*) Paar *nt*; (*of underwear, cutlery, furniture, hairbrushes etc*) Garnitur *f*; (*tea-~ etc*) Service *nt*; (*of tablemats etc*) Set *nt*; (*chess or draughts ~ etc, of knitting needles*) Spiel *nt*; (*chemistry ~ etc*) Bastelkasten *m*; (*painting ~*) Malkasten *m*; (*meccano, construction ~*) Baukasten *m*; (*of books*) (*on one subject*) Reihe, Serie *f*; (*by one author*) gesammelte Ausgabe; (*gift or presentation ~*) Kassette *f*; (*of rooms*) Zimmerflucht *f*. **a ~ of tools** Werkzeug *nt*; **a ~ of teeth** ein Gebiß *nt*; **a complete ~ of Dickens' novels/the "Times" for 1972** eine Gesamtausgabe von Dickens/eine vollständige Sammlung der „Times" von 1972.

(b) (*batch, large number*) Reihe *f*; (*of contradictions also*) Kette *f*. **he had a whole ~ of questions to ask** er hatte eine ganze Menge *or* Reihe Fragen; **a strange ~ of morals/ideas** eigenartige Moralanschauungen/Ideen.

(c) (*group of people*) Kreis *m*; (*pej*) Bande *f*; (*Brit Sch: stream*) Kurs *m*. **the literary ~** die Literaten *pl*; **the golfing ~** die Golffreunde *pl*; **that ~ of people** dieser Personenkreis; **a nice ~ of people** nette Leute *pl*; **that ~ of idiots** dieser Haufen von Idioten; **they're a ~ of thieves** das sind Gauner.

(d) (*Tennis*) Satz *m*; (*Table-tennis*) Spiel *nt*. **~ point** Set- *or* Satzpunkt *m*.

(e) (*Math*) Reihe *f*; (*in set theory*) Menge *f*.

(f) (*performance of songs, poems*) Programmnummer *f*.

(g) (*Telec, Rad, TV*) Gerät *nt*, Apparat *m*; (*head~*) Paar *nt*. **~ of headphones** Kopfhörer *m*.

(h) (*Dancing*) Gruppe *f*. **to make up a ~** eine Gruppe bilden; **they then move up the ~** sie rücken (in der Gruppe) auf.

(i) (*Hunt*) Vorstehen *nt*. **to make a dead ~ at sb** (*dated: try to attract*) sich an jdn ranmachen (*inf*); **to make a dead ~ for sb** (*head for*) sich auf jdn stürzen, auf jdn losstürzen.

(j) (*fit of garment*) Sitz *m*; (*position of head, shoulders etc*) Haltung *f*; (*of wind*) Richtung *f*. **the ~ of sb's mouth** Mundstellung *f*.

(k) (*hair~*) Frisur, Form *f*. **to have a (shampoo and) ~** sich (*dat*) die Haare (waschen und) legen lassen.

(l) (*Theat*) Bühnenbild *nt*; (*Film*) Szenenaufbau *m*. **to be on the ~** bei den Dreharbeiten sein.

(m) (*US*) *see* **sett**.

2 adj (a) *pred* (*ready*) fertig, bereit. **all ~?** alles klar?; **are we all ~?** sind wir alle startklar?; **to be all ~ for sth** für etw gerüstet *or* auf etw (*acc*) vorbereitet sein; (*mentally prepared*) auf etw (*acc*) eingestellt sein; **to be all ~ to do sth** (*have made all the arrangements*) sich darauf eingerichtet haben, etw zu tun; (*mentally prepared*) fest entschlossen *or* drauf und dran sein, etw zu tun; **we're all ~ to go** wir sind soweit *or* startklar; **with their cameras all ~** mit schußbereiter Kamera.

(b) (*rigid*) starr; *face, expression* also unbeweglich; *forms* also fest; *habit, custom* fest; (*prescribed*) festgesetzt, fest; *task* bestimmt; *essay topic* vorgegeben, bestimmt; (*pre-arranged*) *time, place* festgesetzt, bestimmt, ausgemacht (*inf*). **~ book(s)** Pflichtlektüre *f*; **~ menu** Tageskarte *f*; **~ lunch/meal** Tagesgericht *nt*; **~ speech** Standardrede *f*; **~ phrase** starrer Ausdruck; (*idiom*) feststehender Ausdruck; **~ piece** Standardstück *nt*; (*Sch: for exam etc*) Pflichtstück *nt*; (*fireworks*) Feuerwerksstück *nt*; (*attached to frame*) (Feuerwerks)bild *nt*; **one of my ~ tasks is ...** eine der mir übertragenen Aufgaben ist es, ...; **~ hours for studying** feste Zeiten zum Lernen; **his ~ purpose was to annoy me** er war fest entschlossen, mich zu ärgern; **to be ~ in one's ways *or* habits** in seinen Gewohnheiten festgefahren sein.

(c) (*resolved*) entschlossen. **to be (dead) ~ on sth/doing sth** etw auf Biegen oder Brechen haben/tun wollen; **to be (dead) ~ against sth/doing sth/sb doing sth** (absolut) gegen etw sein/etw (absolut) nicht tun wollen/(absolut) dagegen sein, daß jd etw tut; **she is far too ~ on getting her own way** sie will immer nur ihren eigenen Kopf durchsetzen.

3 vt (a) (*put, place*) stellen; (*on its side, flat*) legen; (*deliberately, carefully*) setzen. **to ~ the chairs by the window** die Stühle ans Fenster setzen *or* stellen; **he ~ the stones carefully on top of each other** er setzte *or* legte die Steine vorsichtig aufeinander; **to ~ the child in his chair/on his feet** das Kind in sein Stühlchen setzen/auf die Beine stellen; **to ~ a plan before a committee** einem Ausschuß einen Plan vorlegen; **I ~ him on his way** (*lit*) ich schickte ihn los; (*fig*) ich habe ihm zu einem guten Anfang verholfen; **I ~ him/his books above all others** ich schätze ihn/seine Bücher höher ein als alle anderen.

(b) (*regulate, adjust*) einstellen (*at auf* +*acc*); *clock* stellen (*by nach, to auf* +*acc*); (*fix*) *trap, snare* aufstellen; (*fig*) stellen (*for sb jdm*). **to ~ fair** (*barometer*) auf „schön" stehen; (*weather*) beständig *or* freundlich sein; **everything is ~ fair for sth** für etw steht einer Sache (*dat*) im Wege; **to ~ the alarm for a certain time** den Wecker auf eine bestimmte Zeit stellen.

(c) (*prescribe, impose*) *target, limit etc* festsetzen, festlegen; *task, question* stellen (*sb jdm*); *homework* aufgeben; *exam, exam questions* zusammenstellen; *book for exam* vorschreiben; (*arrange*) *time, date* festsetzen, ausmachen (*inf*), anberaumen (*form*); *place* bestimmen, ausmachen (*inf*); (*establish*) *record* aufstellen; *fashion* bestimmen. **he was supposed to ~ an example (to the others)** er sollte den anderen ein Beispiel geben *or* Vorbild sein; **Hamlet is not ~ this year** Hamlet steht dieses Jahr nicht auf dem Lehrplan; **he was ~ a target** ihm wurde ein Soll vorgeschrieben; **England was ~ then 75 to win** (*Sport*) England brauchte 75 (Punkte), um zu gewinnen; **to ~ the date (of the wedding)** die Hochzeit festsetzen; **to ~ a value/price on sth** einen Wert/Preis für etw festsetzen; **to ~ a high value on sth** einer Sache (*dat*) großen Wert beimessen, etw hoch bewerten; **to ~ sb a problem** (*lit*) jdm ein Problem aufgeben; (*fig*) jdn vor ein Problem stellen;

the attack was ~ for midnight der Angriff war für Mitternacht geplant.

(d) (*mount*) *gem* fassen (*in* +*dat*); *piece of jewellery* besetzen (*with* mit); *windowpane* einsetzen (*in in* +*acc*); (*embed firmly*) einlegen (*in in* +*dat*); (*in ground*) einlassen (*in* in +*acc*). **to ~ stones in concrete** Steine einzementieren.

(e) *usu pass* **to be ~ in the valley** im Tal liegen; **a house ~ on a hillside** ein am Berghang gelegenes Haus.

(f) (*Liter*) **the book etc is ~ in Rome** das Buch *etc* spielt in Rom; **he ~ the book in 19th century France/in Rome** er wählte das Frankreich des 19. Jahrhunderts/Rom als Schauplatz für sein Buch; **she ~ the action in the 16th century/in Vienna** sie verlegte die Handlung in 16. Jahrhundert/nach Wien.

(g) (*Med*) *bone* einrichten; *dislocated joint* einrenken.

(h) (*lay with cutlery*) *table* decken. **to ~ places for 14 für 14** decken, 14 Gedecke auflegen.

(i) (*station*) *guard* aufstellen. **to ~ a guard on sth** etw bewachen lassen.

(j) (*Typ*) setzen, absetzen (*spec*).

(k) *hair* legen, eindrehen.

(l) *jam* fest werden *or* gelieren lassen; *dye* fixieren.

(m) **to ~ a dog/the police after sb** einen Hund/die Polizei auf jdn ansetzen *or* hetzen.

(n) (*Mus*) **to ~ sth to music** etw vertonen.

(o) **to ~ sth going/in motion** in Gang/Bewegung bringen; **to ~ sb doing sth** jdn dazu veranlassen, etw zu tun; **to ~ sb laughing** jdn zum Lachen bringen; **that ~ me thinking das gab mir zu denken**; **that ~ me thinking that ...** das ließ mich denken, daß ...; **to ~ people talking** Anlaß zu Gerede geben; **what ~ the dog barking?** warum bellt der Hund?; **to ~ sb/oneself to doing** *or* **do sth** jdn etw tun lassen/sich daranmachen, etw zu tun.

(p) (*phrases*) *see also other elements* **to ~ a match to sth** ein (brennendes) Streichholz an etw (*acc*) halten, etw anzünden; **to ~ sb free** jdn freilassen; **to ~ sb ashore** jdn an Land setzen; **to ~ things in order** (die) Dinge in Ordnung bringen; **to ~ sth/things right** etw/die Dinge in Ordnung bringen; **to ~ sb right (about sth)** jdn (in bezug auf etw *acc*) berichtigen.

4 *vi* **(a)** (*sun etc*) untergehen. **his star is ~ting** (*fig*) sein Stern ist im Sinken.

(b) (*jelly, cement*) hart *or* fest werden; (*jam also*) gelieren. (*dye*) farbbeständig werden; (*bone*) zusammenwachsen.

(c) (*Dancing*) **to ~ to one's partner** sich dem Partner zuwenden.

(d) (*Hunt*) vorstehen.

♦**set about** *vi* +*prep obj* **(a)** (*begin*) sich machen an (+*acc*), anfangen; (*tackle*) anfassen, anpacken (*inf*), anstellen (*inf*). **to ~ doing sth** (*begin*) sich daranmachen, etw zu tun; **how do I ~ ~ getting a loan?** wie fasse *or* packe (*inf*) ich es an, um ein Darlehen zu bekommen? **(b)** (*attack*) herfallen über (+*acc*).

♦**set against** *vt sep* +*prep obj* **(a)** (*influence against*) einnehmen gegen; (*cause trouble between*) Zwietracht säen zwischen (+*dat*). **to ~ oneself ~ sth** sich einer Sache entgegenstellen; **the civil war ~ friend ~ friend/father ~ son** der Bürgerkrieg ließ Freunde/Väter und Söhne zu Feinden werden; *see also* **set 2 (c)**.

(b) (*balance against*) gegenüberstellen (+*dat*). **his story must be ~ ~ the evidence of the police** man muß seine Darstellung den Aussagen der Polizei gegenüberhalten.

♦**set apart** *vt sep* **(a)** (*distinguish*) abheben, unterscheiden. **he felt ~ ~ from the other boys** er fühlte, daß er nicht so war wie die anderen Jungen. **(b)** (*save*) *money* beiseite legen, auf die Seite legen; *time* einplanen.

♦**set aside** *vt sep* **(a)** *work, money* beiseite legen; *time* einplanen; *plans* aufschieben; *differences, quarrels, hostilities* beiseite schieben, begraben; *dislike* vergessen; *mistrust, bitterness* sich freimachen von; *formality* verzichten auf (+*acc*); *rules, protest* übergehen, außer acht lassen.

(b) (*Jur*) aufheben; *will* für nichtig *or* ungültig erklären.

♦**set back** *vt sep* **(a)** (*place at a distance*) zurücksetzen. **the house is ~ ~ from the road** das Haus liegt etwas von der Straße ab *or* liegt nicht direkt an der Straße.

(b) (*retard*) verzögern, behindern; (*by a certain length of time*) zurückwerfen. **the programme has been ~ ~ (by) 2 years** das Programm ist um 2 Jahre zurückgeworfen.

(c) (*inf: cost*) kosten. **the dinner ~ me ~ £15** das Essen hat mich 15 Pfund gekostet *or* ärmer gemacht (*inf*).

♦**set down** *vt sep* **(a)** (*put down*) *suitcase* absetzen; *passenger also* aussteigen lassen. **(b)** (*in writing*) (schriftlich) niederlegen. **(c)** (*attribute*) zuschreiben (*to dat*). **(d)** (*classify as*) **to ~ sb/sth ~ as sth** jdn/etw für etw halten.

♦**set forth** **1** *vt sep* (*expound*) *theory, plan* darlegen. **2** *vi* (*liter*) ausziehen (*old*).

♦**set in** **1** *vi* (*start*) einsetzen; (*panic*) ausbrechen; (*night*) anbrechen; (*Med: gangrene, complications*) sich einstellen. **2** *vt sep* **(a)** (*Typ: indent*) einrücken. **(b)** (*Sew*) *sleeve* einsetzen; *pocket* einarbeiten (*into* in +*acc*).

♦**set off** **1** *vt sep* **(a)** (*ignite*) *bomb, firework* losgehen lassen. **(b)** (*start*) führen zu; *speculation, quarrel* auslösen. **that ~ us all ~ laughing** das brachte uns (*acc*) alle zum Lachen; **to ~ sb ~ on a new line of thought** jdn auf einen neuen Gedanken bringen; **her remark ~ him ~ on a story** ihre Bemerkung ließ ihn erzählte er eine Geschichte; **don't ~ him ~!** laß ihn nur nicht damit anfangen!; **that really ~ him ~** daraufhin legte er richtig los *or* war er nicht mehr zu halten *or* bremsen (*inf*).

(c) (*offset*) **to ~ sth ~ against sth** etw einer Sache (*dat*) gegenüberstellen.

(d) (*enhance*) hervorheben. **to ~ sth ~ from sth** etw von etw abheben.

2 *vi* (*depart*) sich auf den Weg machen, aufbrechen; (*car, in car etc*) losfahren. **to ~ ~ on a journey** eine Reise antreten; **to ~ ~ for Spain** nach Spanien abfahren; **the police ~ ~ in pur-**

suit die Polizei nahm die Verfolgung auf.

♦**set on** **1** *vt sep* +*prep obj dogs* hetzen *or* ansetzen auf (+*acc*); *see* **eye**. **2** *vi* +*prep obj see* **set upon**.

♦**set out** **1** *vt sep* **(a)** (*display*) ausbreiten; (*arrange*) *chess pieces* aufstellen; *printed matter, essay* anordnen, anlegen; (*state*) darlegen, darstellen. **2** *vi* **(a)** (*depart*) *see* **set off 2**. **(b)** (*intend*) beabsichtigen, sich (*dat*) vorgenommen haben; (*start*) sich daranmachen.

♦**set to** **1** *vi* (*start working, fighting*) loslegen (*inf*); (*start eating also*) reinhauen (*inf*). **they ~ ~ and repaired it** sie machten sich an die Arbeit *or* daran (*inf*) und reparierten es. **2** *vi* +*prep obj* **to ~ ~ work** sich an die Arbeit machen.

♦**set up** **1** *vi* (*establish oneself*) **to ~ ~ as a doctor** sich als Arzt niederlassen; **to ~ ~ in business** sein eigenes Geschäft aufmachen; **to ~ ~ for oneself** sich selbständig machen.

2 *vt sep* **(a)** (*place in position*) *statue, post* aufstellen; (*assemble, get ready to work*) *tent, stall, apparatus* aufbauen; (*Typ*) einrichten; (*fig: arrange*) *meeting* arrangieren, vereinbaren; *robbery* planen, vorbereiten. **to ~ sth ~ for sb** etw für jdn vorbereiten; **one comic ~s ~ the joke, the other ...** ein Komiker liefert das Stichwort (für den Witz), der andere ...

(b) (*establish*) gründen; *school, office, control system* einrichten; *inquiry* veranlassen, anordnen; *record* aufstellen. **to ~ sb ~ in business/a flat** jdm zu einem Geschäft verhelfen/jdm eine Wohnung einrichten; **to ~ sb ~ as sth** (*es*) jdm ermöglichen, etw zu werden; **to ~ oneself ~ as sth** *or* **to be sth** sich als jd/etw aufspielen; **to be ~ ~ for life** für sein ganzes Leben ausgesorgt haben; **to be well ~ ~** sich gut stehen; *see* **house, shop**.

(c) (*restore to health*) guttun (+*dat*). **a holiday will ~ you ~ again** ein Urlaub wird dich schon wieder auf die Beine bringen.

(d) (*raise*) *cry, protest, cheer* anstimmen. **to ~ ~ a commotion** allgemeinen Aufruhr auslösen *or* hervorrufen; (*make noise*) Krach machen.

(e) (*cause*) *infection, reaction* auslösen, verursachen.

(f) (*inf: frame*) **to ~ sb ~** jdm etw anhängen; **I've been ~ ~** das will mir einer anhängen (*inf*) *or* in die Schuhe schieben.

(g) (*inf: rig*) **the fight had been ~ ~** der Kampf war von vornherein eine abgekartete Sache.

♦**set upon** *vt* +*prep obj* überfallen; (*animal*) anfallen.

set: **~-back** *n* Rückschlag *m*; **~-down** *n* (*dated*) Rüffel *m*; **to give sb a ~-down** jdm den Kopf zurechtsetzen *or* einen Rüffel erteilen; **~-in** *adj* *sleeve* eingesetzt; *pocket* eingearbeitet; **~ square** *n* Zeichendreieck *nt*.

sett, (*US*) **set** [set] *n* (*badger's den*) Bau *m*.

settee [se'ti:] *n* Couch *f*, Sofa *nt*.

setter ['setə'] *n* **(a)** (*type-~*) Setzer(in *f*) *m*. **(b)** (*dog*) Setter *m*.

set theory *n* Mengenlehre *f*.

setting ['setɪŋ] *n* **(a)** (*of sun, moon*) Untergang *m*.
(b) (*background, atmosphere*) Rahmen *m*; (*environment, surroundings*) Umgebung *f*; (*of novel etc*) Schauplatz *m*. **a film with a medieval ~** ein Film, der im Mittelalter spielt.
(c) (*of jewel*) Fassung *f*.
(d) (*place ~*) Gedeck *nt*.
(e) (*position on dial etc*) Einstellung *f*.
(f) (*musical arrangement*) Vertonung *f*.
(g) (*hair*) Legen *nt*. **~ lotion** (Haar)festiger *m*.

settle¹ ['setl] *n* (Wand)bank *f*.

settle² **1** *vt* **(a)** (*decide*) entscheiden; (*sort out*) regeln, erledigen; *problem, question, points* klären; *dispute, differences, quarrel* beilegen, schlichten; *doubts* ausräumen, beseitigen; *date, place* vereinbaren, festlegen, ausmachen (*inf*); *venue* festlegen *or* -setzen; *deal* abschließen; *price* sich einigen auf (+*acc*), aushandeln; *terms* aushandeln, vereinbaren. **that should ~ the winner** damit müßte es sich entscheiden, wer gewinnt; **the result of the game was ~d in the first half** das Ergebnis des Spiels stand schon in der ersten Halbzeit fest; **when my future is ~d** wenn sich meine Zukunft entschieden hat; **to ~ one's affairs** seine Angelegenheiten in Ordnung bringen; **to ~ an estate** (*Jur*) die Verteilung des Nachlasses regeln; **to ~ a case out of court** einen Fall außergerichtlich klären; **that's ~d then** das ist also klar *or* geregelt; **that ~s it** damit wäre der Fall (ja wohl) erledigt; (*angry*) jetzt reicht's.

(b) (*pay*) *bill* begleichen, bezahlen; *account* ausgleichen.

(c) *sediment* sich setzen lassen; *liquid* sich klären *or* absetzen lassen; (*fig: calm*) *nerves, stomach* beruhigen. **we need rain to ~ the dust/soil** wir brauchen Regen, damit sich der Staub setzt/die Erde liegen bleibt.

(d) (*place carefully*) legen; (*in upright position*) stellen; (*make comfortable for sleep etc*) *child, invalid* versorgen; *pillow* zurechtlegen. **to ~ oneself comfortably in an armchair** es sich (*dat*) in einem Sessel bequem machen; **to ~ oneself to doing sth** sich daranmachen, etw zu tun.

(e) (*establish*) (*in house*) unterbringen; (*in business also*) etablieren. **to get one's daughter ~d with a husband** seine Tochter verheiraten *or* unter die Haube bringen (*inf*).

(f) **to ~ sb into a house/job** jdm helfen, sich häuslich einzurichten/sich in eine Stellung einzugewöhnen; **we'd just ~d the children into a new school** wir hatten die Kinder gerade in einer neuen Schule gut untergebracht; *see* **~ in 2**.

(g) (*colonize*) *land* besiedeln; (*set up*) *people* ansiedeln.

(h) (*form*) **to ~ money/property on sb** jdm Geld/Besitz überschreiben *or* übertragen; (*in will*) jdm Geld/Besitz vermachen; **to ~ an annuity on sb** für jdn eine Rente aussetzen.

(i) (*inf: put an end to*) **I'll soon ~ his nonsense** ich werde ihm schon die Flausen austreiben; **I'll soon ~ him** dem werd' ich's geben (*inf*); (*verbally also*) dem werd' ich was erzählen (*inf*); **that ~d him!** da hatte er sein Fett weg (*inf*).

2 *vi* **(a)** (*put down roots*) seßhaft werden; (*in country, town, profession*) sich niederlassen; (*as settler*) sich ansiedeln; (*in* *house*) sich häuslich niederlassen, sich einrichten; (*feel at home in house, town, country*) sich einleben (*into in* +*dat*); (*in job, surroundings*) sich eingewöhnen (*into in* +*dat*). **to ~ into a way of life** sich an einen Lebensstil gewöhnen; **to ~ into a habit** sich (*dat*) etw angewöhnen; **as he ~d into middle age** als er älter und reifer wurde.

  (b) (*become less variable: weather*) beständig werden. **the wind ~d in the east** der Wind kam schließlich aus dem Osten.

  (c) (*become calm*) (*child, matters, stomach*) sich beruhigen; (*panic, excitement*) sich legen; (*become less excitable or restless*) zur Ruhe kommen, ruhiger werden. **he couldn't ~ to anything** er konnte sich auf nichts konzentrieren.

  (d) (*come to rest, sit down*) (*person, bird, insect*) sich niederlassen *or* setzen; (*dust*) sich setzen *or* legen; (*sink slowly, subside*) (*building, walls*) sich senken; (*ground, liquid, sediment, coffee grounds*) sich setzen; (*wine*) sich beruhigen. **to ~ comfortably in an armchair** es sich (*dat*) in einem Sessel gemütlich *or* bequem machen; **the boat ~d in the water** das Boot hörte auf zu schaukeln; **fog/silence ~d over the city** Nebel/Stille legte sich über die Stadt *or* breitete sich über der Stadt aus; **gloom ~d over the meeting** eine bedrückte Stimmung breitete sich in der Versammlung aus; **the cold ~d on his chest** die Erkältung setzte sich auf der Brust fest.

  (e) (*Jur*) **to ~ (out of court)** sich vergleichen.

  (f) (*pay*) bezahlen; *see also* **~ with.**

♦ **settle back** *vi* sich (gemütlich) zurücklehnen.

♦ **settle down 1** *vi* **(a)** *see* **settle 2** (a). **it's time he ~d ~** es ist Zeit, daß er ein geregeltes Leben anfängt *or* zur Ruhe kommt; **to marry and ~ ~** heiraten und seßhaft *or* häuslich werden; **to ~ ~ at school/in a new house/job** sich an einer Schule/in einem Haus einleben/sich in einer Stellung eingewöhnen; **he ought to ~ ~ in a steady job** er sollte sich (*dat*) endlich eine feste Stellung suchen; **~ ~, children!** ruhig, Kinder!

  (b) *see* **settle 2** (c).

  (c) **to ~ ~ to work** sich an die Arbeit machen *or* setzen; **to ~ ~ for a chat/for the night** sich zu einem Schwatz (gemütlich) zusammensetzen/sich schlafen legen; **to ~ ~ to watch TV** es sich (*dat*) vor dem Fernseher gemütlich machen.

  2 *vt sep* **(a)** (*calm down*) *baby* hinlegen; *patient* versorgen. **to ~ oneself ~ to work/to finish the job** sich an die Arbeit machen *or* setzen/sich daranmachen, die Arbeit fertigzumachen; **the cat ~d itself ~ for the night** die Katze kuschelte sich zum Schlafen zurecht; **the campers ~d themselves ~ for the night** die Zeltenden richteten alles für die Nacht her.

♦ **settle for** *vi* +*prep obj* sich zufriedengeben mit. **I'd ~ ~ a diamond necklace** ich wäre schon mit einem Diamanthalsband zufrieden; **I think I'll ~ ~ this one** ich glaube, ich nehme doch das da; **she won't ~ ~ anything less** mit weniger gibt sie sich nicht zufrieden; **he was glad to ~ ~ a bronze medal** er war schon mit einer Bronzemedaille zufrieden.

♦ **settle in 1** *vi* (*in house, town*) sich einleben; (*in job, school*) sich eingewöhnen. **how are you settling ~?** haben Sie sich schon eingelebt/eingewöhnt? **2** *vt sep* **to ~ sb ~** jdm helfen, sich einzuleben/sich einzugewöhnen.

♦ **settle on** *or* **upon** *vi* +*prep obj* sich entscheiden für *or* entschließen zu; (*agree on*) sich einigen auf (+*acc*).

♦ **settle up 1** *vi* (be)zahlen. **to ~ ~ with sb** (*lit, fig*) mit jdm abrechnen. **2** *vt sep* bill bezahlen.

♦ **settle with 1** *vi* +*prep obj* (*lit, fig*) abrechnen mit. **2** *vt sep* +*prep obj* **(a)** *debt etc* abrechnen mit. **to ~ one's account ~ sb** (*lit, fig*) mit jdm abrechnen. **(b)** (*come to agreement with*) **to ~ sth ~ sb** sich mit jdm auf etw (*acc*) einigen.

settled ['setld] *adj weather* beständig; *way of life* geregelt; *opinions* fest; *procedure* feststehend, festgelegt. **to be ~ in geregelten** Verhältnissen leben, etabliert sein; (*in place*) seßhaft sein; (*have permanent job etc*) festen Fuß gefaßt haben; (*in a house*) sich häuslich niedergelassen haben; (*be less restless*) ruhiger *or* gesetzter sein; **to feel ~** sich wohl fühlen; **I don't feel very ~ at the moment** ich hänge zur Zeit in der Luft (*inf*), ich fühle mich zur Zeit verunsichert.

settlement ['setlmənt] *n* **(a)** (*act*) (*deciding*) Entscheidung *f*; (*sorting out*) Regelung, Erledigung *f*; (*of problem, question etc*) Klärung *f*; (*of dispute, differences etc*) Beilegung, Schlichtung *f*; (*of estate*) Regelung *f*; (*of bill, claim*) Bezahlung *f*; (*of account*) Ausgleich *m*; (*contract, agreement etc*) Übereinkunft *f*, Übereinkommen *nt*. **a ~ out of court** (*Jur*) ein außergerichtlicher Vergleich; **to reach a ~** sich einigen, einen Vergleich treffen; **the terms of the** (*Jur*) **~ die Bedingungen des Übereinkommens; this payment is made in ~ of all claims** mit dieser Zahlung werden alle Forderungen beglichen.

  (b) (*settling of money*) Übertragung, Überschreibung *f* (*on* auf +*acc*); (*in will also*) Vermächtnis *nt*; (*of annuity, income*) Aussetzung *f*; (*document, agreement*) Schenkungsvertrag *m*. **he receives £10,000 by the ~** auf ihn wurden £ 10.000 übertragen *or* überschrieben; ihm wurden £ 10.000 vermacht.

  (c) (*of building*) Senkung *f*; (*of sediment*) Absetzen *nt*. **the discoloration is caused by ~ of the powder** die Verfärbung entsteht dadurch, daß sich das Pulver setzt.

  (d) (*colony, village*) Siedlung, Niederlassung *f*; (*act of settling persons*) Ansiedlung *f*; (*colonization*) Besiedlung *f*.

  (e) (*US: also* **~ house**) (*institution*) Wohlfahrtseinrichtung *f*; (*building*) Gemeindezentrum *nt*.

settler ['setlə'] *n* Siedler(in *f*) *m*.

set: **~-to** *n* (*inf*) Krach *m*, Streiterei *f* (*inf*); **to have a ~-to with sb** sich mit jdm in die Wolle kriegen (*inf*); **~-up** *n* **(a)** (*inf*) (*situation*) Zustände, Umstände *pl*; (*way of organizing things*) Organisation *f*, Arrangement, Drum und Dran (*inf*) *nt*; **it's a funny ~-up** das sind (vielleicht) komische Zustände!; **what's the ~-up here?** wie verhält sich *or* läuft (*inf*) das hier (alles)?; **she didn't quite understand the ~-up** sie verstand die Sachlage

nicht ganz; **(b)** (*equipment*) Geräte, Instrumente *pl*; **(c)** (*US: for drinks*) Zubehör *nt* für Cocktails *etc*; **(d)** (*inf: rigged contest*) abgekartete Sache.

seven ['sevn] **1** *adj* sieben. **to sail the ~ seas** die sieben Meere befahren; **he's got the ~-year itch** (*inf*) er ist im verflixten siebenten Jahr; **~-league boots** Siebenmeilenstiefel *pl.* **2** *n* Sieben *f*; *see also* **six.**

sevenfold ['sevnfəʊld] **1** *adj* siebenfach. **2** *adv* um das Siebenfache.

seventeen ['sevn'ti:n] **1** *adj* siebzehn. **2** *n* Siebzehn *f*; *see also* **sixteen.**

seventeenth ['sevn'ti:nθ] **1** *adj* siebzehnte(r, s). **a ~ part** ein Siebzehntel *nt*. **2** *n* (*fraction*) Siebzehntel *nt*; (*of series*) Siebzehnte(r, s).

seventh ['sevnθ] **1** *adj* siebte(r, s). **a ~ part** ein Siebtel *nt*; **S~-day Adventist** Adventist(in *f*) *m* vom Siebenten Tag. **2** *n* (*fraction*) Siebtel *nt*; (*in series*) Siebte(r, s); (*Mus*) (*interval*) Septime *f*; (*chord*) Septimenakkord *m*; *see also* **sixth.**

seventhly ['sevnθlı] *adv* siebtens.

seventieth ['sevntııθ] **1** *adj* siebzigste(r, s). **2** *n* (*fraction*) Siebzigstel *nt*; (*in series*) Siebzigste(r, s).

seventy ['sevntı] **1** *adj* siebzig. **2** *n* Siebzig *f*. **~-eight** Achtundsiebzig *f*; (*record*) Achtundsiebziger(platte *f*), 78er-Platte *f*.

sever ['sevə'] **1** *vt* (*cut through*) durchtrennen; (*violently*) durchschlagen; (*cut off*) abtrennen; (*violently*) abschlagen; (*fig*) (*break off*) ties, bonds of friendship lösen; *relations, links, connections, friendship* abbrechen; *communications, telephone links* unterbrechen; (*divide*) nation, area teilen. **the wires were ~ed in the storm** beim Sturm sind die Leitungen (durch)gerissen; **to ~ sb from sb/sth** jdn von jdm/etw trennen; **to ~ sth from etw** von etw abtrennen.

  2 *vi* (durch)reißen.

several ['sevrəl] **1** *adj* **(a)** (*some*) einige, mehrere; (*different, diverse, various*) verschiedene. **I went with ~ others** ich ging mit einigen *or* ein paar anderen zusammen; **I've seen him ~ times/~ times already** ich habe ihn einige Male gesehen/schon mehrmals *or* mehrere Male gesehen; **there are ~ ways of doing it** das kann man auf mehrere *or* verschiedene Arten machen; **I'll need ~ more** ich brauche noch mehr.

  (b) (*dated: respective*) jeweilig. **they went their ~ ways** jeder ging seinen Weg, sie gingen ihrer Wege (*old*).

  2 *pron* einige. **~ of the houses** einige (der) Häuser; **~ of us** einige von uns.

severally ['sevrəlı] *adv* einzeln.

severance ['sevərəns] *n see vt* **(a)** Durchtrennen *nt*; Durchschlagen *nt*; Abtrennen *nt*; Abschlagen *nt*; Lösen *nt*; Abbruch *m*; Unterbrechung *f*; Teilung *f*; Abschneiden *nt*, Absonderung *f*. **~ pay** eine Abfindung.

severe [sı'vıə'] *adj* (+*er*) (*strict*) person, appearance, style streng; (*harsh*) critic, law, winter also, punishment, competition, test hart; criticism scharf; reprimand ernst, scharf; test hart, schwer; (*serious*) expression, crime, warning ernst; illness, injury, blow, frost, drought, storm, loss schwer, schlimm; pain, storm stark, heftig; weather rauh. **to be ~ with sb** streng mit jdm sein; **to be ~ on sb** hart über jdn urteilen.

severely [sı'vıəlı] *adv see adj.* **to be ~ critical of sth** sich äußerst kritisch über etw (*acc*) äußern; **to leave sb/sth ~ alone** sich sehr *or* schwer vor jdm/etw hüten.

severeness [sı'vıənıs], **severity** [sı'verıtı] *n see adj* Strenge *f*; Härte *f*, Schärfe *f*; Ernst *m*, Schärfe *f*; Härte *f*, Ernst *m*; Schwere *f*; Stärke, Heftigkeit *f*; Rauheit *f*. **the ~ of the cold/drought/frost/loss** die große *or* schwere Kälte/Dürre/der starke *or* schwere Frost/der schwere *or* große *or* schlimme Verlust; **severities** Härte *f*.

Seville [sə'vıl] *n* Sevilla *nt*. **~ orange** Bitterorange, Pomeranze *f*.

sew [səʊ] *pret* **~ed,** *ptp* **~n** *vti* nähen. **to ~ sth on/down/together** etw an-/auf-/zusammennähen; **she's been ~ing that seam all evening** an dem Saum hat sie den ganzen Abend genäht.

♦ **sew up** *vt sep* **(a)** nähen (*also Med*); *opening* zunähen. **to ~ sth ~ in sth** etw in etw (*acc*) einnähen.

  (b) (*fig*) unter Dach und Fach bringen. **it's all ~n ~** es ist unter Dach und Fach; **we've got the game all ~n ~** das Spiel ist gelaufen (*inf*).

sewage ['sju:ıdʒ] *n* Abwasser *nt*. **~ disposal** Abwasserbeseitigung *f*; **~ farm/works** Rieselfeld *nt*/Kläranlage *f*.

sewer[1] ['səʊə'] *n* Näher(in *f*) *m*.

sewer[2] ['sjʊə'] *n* (*pipe*) Abwasserleitung *f or* -rohr *nt*; (*main ~*) Abwasserkanal *m*; (*fig*) (*smelly place*) Kloake *f*; (*evil place*) Sündenpfuhl *m*, Kloake *f* (*liter*). **~ gas** Faulschlammgas *nt*; **~ rat** Wanderratte *f*; **he has a mind like a ~** (*inf*) er hat eine schmutzige *or* dreckige (*inf*) Phantasie.

sewerage ['sjʊərıdʒ] *n* Kanalisation *f*; (*service*) Abwasserbeseitigung *f*; (*sewage*) Abwässer *pl*.

sewing ['səʊıŋ] *n* (*activity*) Nähen *nt*; (*piece of work*) Näharbeit *f*. **~ basket** Nähkorb *m*; **~ machine** Nähmaschine *f*.

sewn [səʊn] *ptp of* **sew.**

sex [seks] **1** *n* **(a)** (*Biol*) Geschlecht *nt*. **what ~ is the baby?** welches Geschlecht hat das Baby? **(b)** (*sexuality*) Sexualität *f*, Sex *m*; (*sexual intercourse*) Sex (*inf*), Geschlechtsverkehr (*form*) *m*. **to teach pupils (about) ~** Schüler aufklären; **to have ~** (Geschlechts)verkehr haben.

  2 *adj attr* Geschlechts-; *hormone, organs, drive also, hygiene* Sexual-; *crime* Trieb-, Sexual-; *aids, film, scandal* Sex-.

  3 *vt* das Geschlecht (+*gen*) bestimmen.

sexagenarian [,seksədʒı'neərıən] **1** *adj* sechzigjährig. **~ member of the club** Clubmitglied, die in den Sechzigern sind. **2** *n* Sechzigjährige(r) *mf*. **to be a ~** in den Sechzigern sein.

Sexagesima [,seksə'dʒesımə] *n* Sonntag *m* Sexagesima.

sex: **~ appeal** *n* Sex-Appeal *m*; **~ discrimination** *n* Diskriminierung *f* auf Grund des Geschlechts.

sexed [sekst] *adj* to be highly ~ einen starken Geschlechtstrieb haben; *see* oversexed, undersexed.

sex education *n* Sexualerziehung *f*; *(Sch also)* Aufklärungsunterricht *m*.

sexily ['seksɪlɪ] *adv* aufreizend, sexy *(inf)*.

sexist ['seksɪst] **1** *n* Sexist(in *f*) *m*. **2** *adj* sexistisch.

sex: ~ **kitten** *n* *(inf)* Sexkätzchen *nt* *(inf)*, Sexmieze *f* *(inf)*; ~**less** *adj* geschlechtslos; ~ **life** *n* Geschlechtsleben *nt*; *(of people also)* Liebesleben *nt*; ~**linked** *adj* geschlechtsgebunden; ~ **maniac** *n* *(criminal)* Triebverbrecher *or* -täter *m*; he/she is a ~ **maniac** *(inf)* er/sie ist ganz verrückt nach *or* wild auf Sex *(inf)*; you're a ~ **maniac** *(inf)* du denkst aber auch nur an Sex.

sexpert ['sekspɜːt] *n* *(hum)* Experte *m* in Sachen Sex *(inf)*, Sex-perte *m* *(hum)*.

sexploit ['seksplɔɪt] *n* *(hum)* Liebesabenteuer *nt*.

sex: ~**pot** *n* *(inf)* *(woman)* Sexbombe *f* *(inf)*; to be a real little ~**pot** unheimlich sexy sein *(inf)*; ~ **symbol** *n* Sexsymbol *nt*.

sextant ['sekstənt] *n* Sextant *m*.

sextet(te) [seks'tet] *n* Sextett *nt*.

sexton ['sekstən] *n* Küster *m*.

sextuplet [seks'tjuːplɪt] *n* Sechsling *m*.

sexual ['seksjʊəl] *adj* geschlechtlich; *behaviour, attraction, excitement* sexuell; *intercourse, maturity* Geschlechts-; *crime* Sexual-, Trieb-. his ~ **exploits** seine Liebesabenteuer *pl*; ~ **characteristics** Geschlechtsmerkmale *pl*.

sexuality [ˌseksjʊˈælɪtɪ] *n* Sexualität *f*.

sexually ['seksjʊəlɪ] *adv* sexuell. ~ **mature** geschlechtsreif; ~ **transmitted diseases** durch Geschlechtsverkehr übertragene Krankheiten.

sexy ['seksɪ] *adj* (+*er*) *(inf)* sexy *pred*; *smile, pose also* aufreizend; *joke, film* erotisch. **the sexiest girl in the class** das Mädchen in der Klasse, das am meisten Sex-Appeal hat.

SF *abbr of* science fiction.

s.g. *abbr of* specific gravity.

sgraffito [sgræˈfiːtəʊ] *n* Sgraffito *nt*.

sgt *abbr of* sergeant.

sh [ʃ] *interj* sch(t).

shabbily ['ʃæbɪlɪ] *adv* *(lit, fig)* schäbig.

shabbiness ['ʃæbɪnɪs] *n* *(lit, fig)* Schäbigkeit *f*.

shabby ['ʃæbɪ] *adj* (+*er*) *(lit, fig)* schäbig. they were ~-**genteel** sie gehörten zur verarmten Oberschicht.

shack [ʃæk] **1** *n* Hütte *f*, Schuppen *m*. **2** *vi* *(inf)* to ~ **up with sb** mit jdm zusammenziehen; to ~ **up together** zusammenziehen.

shackle ['ʃækl] **1** *n* (a) *usu pl* Kette, Fessel *(also fig)* *f*.
(b) *(Tech)* Schäkel *m*.
2 *vt* in Ketten legen. they were ~d **together/to the wall** sie waren aneinandergekettet/an die Wand (an)gekettet; to ~ one-self with sth sich mit etw belasten; to be ~d by sth *(fig)* an etw *(acc)* gebunden sein; to be ~d with sth die Belastung einer Sache *(gen)* haben.

shad [ʃæd] *n* Alse *f*.

shade [ʃeɪd] **1** *n* (a) Schatten *m*. 30° **in the** ~ 30 Grad im Schatten; to give ~ Schatten spenden; **the** ~**s of night were falling fast** *(liter)* der Schatten der Nacht senkte sich hernieder *(liter)*; to put *or* cast sb/sth in the ~ *(fig)* jdn/etw in den Schatten stellen.
(b) *(lamp~)* (Lampen)schirm *m*; *(eye ~)* Schild *nt*, Schirm *m*; *(esp US: blind)* Jalousie *f*; *(roller blind)* Springrollo *nt*; *(outside house)* Markise *f*. ~**s** *pl* *(esp US: sunglasses)* Sonnenbrille *f*.
(c) *(of colour)* (Farb)ton *m*; *(fig) (of opinion)* Schattierung *f*; *(of meaning)* Nuance *f*. **turquoise is a** ~ **of blue** Türkis ist ein blauer Farbton; **a brighter** ~ **of red** ein leuchtenderer Rotton; **a new** ~ **of lipstick** eine neuer Farbton für Lippenstifte; ~-**card** Farb(en)probe *f*; **of all** ~**s and hues** *(lit)* in den verschiedensten Farben, in allen Schattierungen; *(fig)* aller Schattierungen.
(d) *(small quantity)* Spur *f*. **it's a** ~ **long/too long** es ist etwas lang/etwas *or* eine Spur zu lang.
(e) *(liter: ghost)* Schatten *m*. **the** ~**s** *(Myth)* die Bewohner *pl* des Schattenreiches; *(Hades)* das Reich der Schatten, das Schattenreich; ~**s of Professor Jones!** *(inf)* wie mich das an Professor Jones erinnert!
2 *vt* (a) *(cast shadow on)* Schatten werfen auf (+*acc*), be-schatten *(geh)*; *(protect from light, sun)* abschirmen; *lamp, window* abdunkeln. **that part is** ~d by a tree der Teil liegt im Schatten eines Baumes; to be ~d **from the sun** im Schatten liegen *or* sein; *(protected against sun)* vor der Sonne geschützt sein; he ~d **his eyes with his hand** er hielt die Hand vor die Augen(, um nicht geblendet zu werden).
(b) *(darken with lines)* schraffieren; *(for artistic effect)* schattieren. to ~ **sth in** etw ausschraffieren; *(colour in)* etw ausmalen; to ~ **one colour into another** eine Farbe langsam in die andere übergehen lassen.
3 *vi* *(lit, fig)* übergehen. to ~ **off** allmählich blasser werden; **blue that** ~**s (off) into black** Blau, das in Schwarz übergeht.

shadeless ['ʃeɪdlɪs] *adj* schattenlos.

shadiness ['ʃeɪdɪnɪs] *n* Schattigkeit *f*; *(fig)* Zwielichtigkeit *f*. they **retreated to the** ~ **of the house** sie zogen sich in den Schatten des Hauses zurück.

shading ['ʃeɪdɪŋ] *n* *(shaded area)* Schraffierung, Schraffur *f*; *(Art)* Schattierung *f*.

shadow ['ʃædəʊ] **1** *n* (a) *(lit, fig)* Schatten *m* *(also Med, Art)*; *(growth of beard)* Anflug *m* von Bartstoppeln; *(fig: threat)* (Be)drohung *f*. **in the** ~ im Schatten, im Dunkel; **the valley of the** ~ **of death** das finstere Tal des Todes; **sb lives under the** ~ **of sth** etw liegt *or* lastet wie ein Schatten auf jdm; **he's been living under the** ~ **of death for 2 years** seit 2 Jahren liegt der Schatten des Todes auf ihm; to be in sb's ~ *(fig)* in jds *(dat)* Schatten stehen; to be **afraid of one's own** ~ sich vor seinem eigenen Schatten fürchten; to wear oneself to a ~ sich aufreiben, sich zugrunde richten; to be just a ~ of one's former self nur noch ein Schatten seiner selbst sein; a ~ of his

former power ein Abglanz *m* seiner früheren Macht; to catch at *or* chase ~**s** *(fig)* einem Phantom *or* Schatten nachjagen.
(b) *(trace)* Spur *f*. a ~ **of hope** ein Hoffnungsschimmer *m*; without a ~ **of a doubt** ohne den geringsten Zweifel.
(c) *(person)* Schatten *m*. he's **his older brother's** ~ er folgt seinem älteren Bruder wie ein Schatten; to put a ~ **on sb** jdn beschatten lassen *(inf)*.
2 *attr* *(Brit Pol)* Schatten-. **the** ~ **Foreign Secretary** der Außenminister des Schattenkabinetts.
3 *vt* (a) *(darken)* Schatten werfen auf (+*acc*); *(fig)* überschatten. **the room is** ~ed **by a high wall** das Zimmer bekommt den Schatten *or* liegt im Schatten einer hohen Mauer.
(b) *(follow)* beschatten *(inf)*.

shadow: ~-**boxing** *n* *(lit, fig)* Schattenboxen *nt*; ~ **cabinet** *n* *(Brit)* Schattenkabinett *nt*.

shadowy ['ʃædəʊɪ] *adj* schattig; *(blurred)* outline, form schat-tenhaft, verschwommen; *(vague)* thought, fear unbestimmt, vage. **the** ~ **world beyond the grave** die dunkle Welt nach dem Tode; a ~ **existence** ein Schattendasein *nt*.

shady ['ʃeɪdɪ] *adj* (+*er*) (a) *place* schattig; *tree, hat* schatten-spendend. (b) *(inf: of dubious honesty)* zwielichtig, zweifelhaft. to be on the ~ **side of the law** dunkle Geschäfte treiben; on the ~ **side of forty** *(US inf)* vierzig vorbei *(inf)*; there's **something** ~ **about it** da ist etwas faul dran *(inf)*.

shaft [ʃɑːft] *n* (a) Schaft *m*; *(of tool, golf club etc)* Stiel *m*; *(of cart, carriage)* Deichsel *f*; *(of light)* Strahl *m*; *(Mech)* Welle *f*; *(liter: arrow)* Pfeil *m*; *(liter: spear)* Speer *m*; *(fig: remark)* Spitze *f*. ~**s of wit/malice** geistreiche/boshafte Spitzen *pl*; the ~**s of Cupid** Amors Pfeile *pl*. (b) *(of lift, mine etc)* Schacht *m*.

shag¹ [ʃæg] *n* (a) *(tobacco)* Shag *m*. (b) *(of carpet etc)* Flor *m*. ~-**pile carpet** langfloriger Teppich.

shag² *n* *(Orn)* Krähenscharbe *f*.

shag³ *(sl)* **1** *n* *(intercourse, partner)* Nummer *f* *(sl)*. to have a ~ eine Nummer machen *(sl)*. **2** *vti* (a) *(have sex)* bumsen *(inf)*.
(b) to be ~**ged out** ausgebufft sein *(sl)*.

shaggy ['ʃægɪ] *adj* (+*er*) *(long-haired)* zottig; *(unkempt)* zottelig. ~ **carpet** zotteliger Teppich; ~ **dog story** breitgewalzte Geschichte mit schwacher Pointe.

shagreen [ʃæˈgriːn] *n* Chagrin(leder) *nt*.

Shah [ʃɑː] *n* Schah *m*.

shake [ʃeɪk] *(vb: pret* **shook**, *ptp* **shaken)** **1** *n* (a) *(act of shaking)* Schütteln *nt*. to give a rug a ~ einen Läufer ausschüt-teln; give the paint a ~ die Farbe (gut) durchschütteln; to give sb/oneself a good ~ jdn/sich kräftig schütteln; with a ~ **of her head** mit einem Kopfschütteln; **in his voice** mit zit-ternder Stimme; to be **all of a** ~ *(inf)* am ganzen Körper zittern.
(b) *(milk~)* Shake *m*, Mixgetränk *nt*.
(c) *(inf: moment)* Minütchen *nt* *(inf)*. **in two** ~**s (of a lamb's tail)** in zwei Sekunden; **in half a** ~ sofort.
(d) to be **no great** ~**s** *(inf)* nicht umwerfend sein *(at* in +*dat)*.
(e) **the** ~**s** *(inf)* der Tatterich *(inf)*; *(esp with fear)* das Zittern; he's **got the** ~**s** er hat einen Tatterich *(inf)*; *(due to alcoholism also)* ihm zittern die Hände, er hat einen Flattermann *(sl)*; *(esp with fear)* er hat das große Zittern *(inf)*; *(esp with cold, emo-tion)* er zittert am ganzen Körper.
2 *vt* (a) schütteln; *building* erschüttern; *cocktail* durchschüt-teln. "~ **well before using"** „vor Gebrauch gut schütteln"; to be ~n **to pieces** total durchgeschüttelt werden; **she shook the door-handle which seemed to have stuck** sie rüttelte an der Türklinke, die zu klemmen schien; to ~ **pepper on a steak** Pfeffer auf ein Steak streuen; to ~ **one's fist at sb** jdm mit der Faust drohen; to ~ **oneself/itself free** sich losmachen; to ~ **hands** sich *(dat)* die Hand geben; *(for longer time, in congratulations etc)* sich *(dat)* die Hand schütteln; to ~ **hands with sb** jdm die Hand geben/schütteln; **I'd like to** ~ **him by the hand** ihm würde ich gern die Hand schütteln *or* drücken; **English people don't often** ~ **hands** Engländer begrüßen sich selten mit Handschlag, Engländer geben sich *(dat)* selten die Hand; ~ **hands** *(to dog)* gib) Pfötchen; *(to child)* gib mal die Hand; to ~ **a leg** *(inf)* *(hurry)* Dampf machen *(inf)*; *(dated: dance)* das Tanzbein schwingen *(dated)*.
(b) *(weaken)* faith, foundation of society erschüttern; *evi-dence, reputation, courage, resolve* ins Wanken bringen. so-ciety was ~n **to its very core** die Gesellschaft wurde bis in ihre Grundfesten erschüttert.
(c) *(shock, amaze)* erschüttern. **that shook him!** da war er platt *(inf)*; **it shook me rigid** *(inf)* da war ich schwer geschockt *(inf)*; **it was a nasty accident, he's still rather badly** ~n ein schlimmer Unfall, der Schreck sitzt ihm noch in den Knochen; **she was badly** ~n **by the news** die Nachricht hatte sie sehr mitgenommen *or* erschüttert; **her nerves are badly** ~n sie ist mit den Nerven am Ende.
(d) *(inf)* see ~ **off.**
3 *vi* wackeln; *(hand, voice)* zittern; *(earth, voice)* beben. **the whole boat shook as the waves hit** das ganze Boot wurde vom Aufprall der Wellen erschüttert; **the trees shook in the wind** die Bäume schwankten im Wind; to ~ **like a leaf** zittern wie Espen-laub; to ~ **with fear/cold** vor Angst/Kälte zittern; he was **shaking all over** er zitterte am ganzen Körper; to ~ **with laughter** vor Lachen schütteln; to ~ **in one's shoes** *(inf)* das große Zittern kriegen *(inf)*; ~!, ~ **on it!** *(inf)* Hand drauf; ~! *(me too)* da können wir uns ja die Hand reichen!; **they shook on the deal** sie bekräftigten das Geschäft mit Handschlag.

♦**shake down** **1** *vt sep* (a) *fruit* herunterschütteln.
(b) *(US sl: extort money from)* ausnehmen *(inf)*. to ~ **sb** ~ **for** $500 jdn um 500 Dollar erleichtern *(inf)*.
(c) *(US sl: search)* absuchen, durchsuchen *(for* nach).
2 *vi sep* (a) *(sleep)* kampieren, sein Lager aufschlagen.
(b) *(settle)* *(people)* sich eingewöhnen; *(machinery)* sich ein-laufen; *(situation)* sich einspielen.

♦**shake off** *vt sep* dust, snow, pursuer abschütteln; *visitor, cold* loswerden. to ~ the dust (of a place) ~ one's feet (fig) den Staub (eines Ortes) von seinen Schuhen schütteln.

♦**shake out 1** vt sep **(a)** tablecloth, rug ausschütteln; crumbs, creases herausschütteln; (out of container) herausschütteln. she took off her hat and shook ~ her long hair sie nahm den Hut ab und schüttelte sich (dat) die langen Haare zurecht.
(b) (fig: out of complacency etc) aufrütteln (of aus).
2 vi (Mil: spread out) ausschwärmen.

♦**shake up** vt sep **(a)** bottle, liquid schütteln; pillow aufschütteln. they were really ~n ~ by the rough crossing sie wurden bei der stürmischen Überfahrt durchgeschüttelt.
(b) (upset) erschüttern. he was badly ~n ~ by the accident der Unfall hat ihm einen schweren Schock versetzt; she's still a bit ~n ~ sie ist immer noch ziemlich mitgenommen.
(c) management, recruits auf Zack bringen (inf); ideas revidieren. your ideas could do with a bit of shaking ~ deine Aussichten müßten auch mal wieder revidiert werden.

shakedown ['ʃeɪkdaʊn] **1** n (bed) Lager, Notbett nt; (US sl: extortion) Gaunerei f; (US sl: search) Razzia (inf), Durchsuchung f. he slept on a ~ in the living room er hatte sein Lager im Wohnzimmer aufgeschlagen, er kampierte im Wohnzimmer; to give a room a ~ ein Zimmer auf den Kopf stellen. **2** adj trial, cruise Probe-.

shaken ['ʃeɪkən] ptp of **shake**.

shake-out ['ʃeɪkaʊt] n (inf) Gesundschrumpfung f (inf).

shaker ['ʃeɪkər] n (cocktail ~) Mix- or Schüttelbecher, Shaker m; (flour/salt ~) Mehl-/Salzstreuer m.

Shakespearean, Shakespearian [ʃeɪk'spɪərɪən] **1** adj Shakespearesch, Shakespearisch; style shakespearesch, shakespearisch; actor Shakespeare-. **2** n Shakespeareforscher(in f) m.

shake-up ['ʃeɪkʌp] n (inf) (reorganization) Umbesetzung f. to give a department etc a good ~ (revitalization) eine Abteilung etc auf Zack bringen (inf); (reorganization) eine Abteilung etc umbesetzen or umorganisieren.

shakily ['ʃeɪkɪlɪ] adv wackelig; talk, say mit zitteriger Stimme; walk mit wackeligen Schritten; pour etc zitterig.

shakiness ['ʃeɪkɪnɪs] n see adj Wackeligkeit f; Fragwürdigkeit, Unsicherheit f; Zittern, Beben nt; Zitterigkeit f; Unsicherheit f; Holprigkeit f. the ~ of their position ihre wackelige Position.

shaking ['ʃeɪkɪŋ] n Zittern nt. to give sb/sth a good ~ jdn/etw kräftig schütteln; (fig) jdn kräftig treten; a nasty experience, it gave me a bit of a ~ ein unangenehmes Erlebnis, das sitzt mir immer noch in den Knochen.

shako ['ʃækoʊ] n Tschako m.

shaky ['ʃeɪkɪ] adj (+er) chair, position wackelig; evidence fragwürdig, unsicher; voice, hands, writing zitterig; knowledge unsicher, wackelig. in rather ~ French in ziemlich holprigem Französisch; his Spanish is rather ~ sein Spanisch ist ziemlich wackelig or holprig; to be ~ on one's legs wackelig auf den Beinen sein; to feel ~ (physically) sich ganz schwach fühlen; I still feel a bit ~ about this theory diese Theorie sitzt bei mir noch nicht.

shale [ʃeɪl] n Schiefer m. ~ oil Schieferöl nt.

shall [ʃæl] pret should modal aux vb **(a)** (future) I/we ~ or I'll/we'll go to France this year ich werde/wir werden dieses Jahr nach Frankreich fahren, ich fahre/wir fahren dieses Jahr nach Frankreich; ~ do (inf) wird gemacht (inf); no, I ~ not or I shan't/yes, I ~ nein, das werde ich nicht tun or das tue ich nicht/jawohl, das werde ich tun or das tue ich!
(b) (determination, obligation) you ~ pay for this! dafür sollst or wirst du büßen!; but I say you shall do it! aber ich sage dir, du wirst das machen!; the directors ~ not be disturbed (form) die Direktoren dürfen nicht gestört werden; the court ~ rise das Gericht muß sich erheben; (command) erheben Sie sich!; thou shalt not kill (Bibl) du sollst nicht töten; I want to go too — and so you ~ ich will auch mitkommen — aber gewiß doch or (in fairy stories) es sei!
(c) (in questions, suggestions) what ~ we do? was sollen wir machen?, was machen wir?; let's go in, ~ we? komm, gehen wir hinein!; ~ I go now? soll ich jetzt gehen?; I'll buy 3, ~ I? soll ich 3 kaufen?, ich kaufe 3, oder?

shallot [ʃə'lɒt] n Schalotte f.

shallow ['ʃæloʊ] **1** adj (+er) water also seicht; (fig) oberflächlich; talk, person, novel seicht, oberflächlich. in the ~ end of the pool am flachen or niedrigen Ende des Beckens. **2** n ~s pl seichte or flache Stelle (im Wasser), Untiefe f.

shallowness ['ʃæləʊnɪs] n see adj Flachheit f; Seichtheit f; Oberflächlichkeit f.

shalt [ʃælt] (obs) 2nd pers sing of **shall**.

sham [ʃæm] **1** n (a) (pretence) Heuchelei f. he's not really sorry, it's all a big ~ es tut ihm nicht wirklich leid, er heuchelt nur or das ist geheuchelt; this so-called emotion is all ~ dieses sogenannte Gefühl ist reine Heuchelei; their marriage had become a ~ ihre Ehe war zur Farce geworden or bestand nur noch zum Schein; these discussions are a complete ~ diese Diskussionen sind eine reine Farce; his life seemed a ~ sein Leben erschien ihm als Lug und Trug; this lighthouse is just a ~, built to deceive enemy bombers dieser Leuchtturm ist nur eine Attrappe, die die feindlichen Bomber täuschen soll.
(b) (person) Scharlatan, Blender (inf) m. you don't really feel anything, you big ~! du empfindest überhaupt nichts, du Heuchler!
2 adj diamonds, leather, oak etc unecht, imitiert; sympathy, piety, politeness etc vorgetäuscht, geheuchelt, gespielt. ~ battle Scheingefecht nt.
3 vt vortäuschen, vorgeben; illness also simulieren; emotions, sympathy heucheln.
4 vi so tun; (esp with illness) simulieren; (with feelings) heucheln. he's just ~ming er tut nur so.

shamble ['ʃæmbl] vi trotten; (people also) latschen (inf). every

morning he ~s in half an hour late er kommt jeden Morgen eine halbe Stunde zu spät angelatscht (inf).

shambles ['ʃæmblz] n sing heilloses Durcheinander; (esp of room etc) Tohuwabohu nt. the room was a ~ im Zimmer herrschte das reinste Tohuwabohu or ein heilloses Durcheinander; the economy/country is a ~ die Wirtschaft/das Land befindet sich in einem Chaos; they left the house in a ~ sie hinterließen das Haus wie ein Schlachtfeld; the game was a ~ das Spiel war das reinste Kuddelmuddel (inf); he made a ~ of that job da hat er vielleicht einen Mist gebaut! (inf).

shame [ʃeɪm] **1** n (a) (feeling of ~) Scham f; (cause of ~) Schande f. to feel ~ at sth sich für etw schämen; he hung his head in ~ er senkte beschämt den Kopf; (fig) er schämte sich; to bring ~ upon sb/oneself jdm/sich Schande machen; he is without ~, he is lost to all sense of ~ er hat keinerlei Schamgefühl, ihm fehlt jegliches Schamgefühl; she is past all (sense of) ~ sie hat jegliches Schamgefühl verloren; she has no ~, dancing around like that sie hat nicht mehr schämt, so herumzutanzen; to put sb/sth to ~ (lit) jdm/etw Schande machen; (fig) jdn/etw in den Schatten stellen; by working so hard he puts us to ~ er arbeitet so schwer, daß er uns alle beschämt; to my (eternal) ~ zu meiner (ewigen) Schande; I'll never forget the ~ of that defeat ich werde die Schande or Schmach dieser Niederlage nie vergessen; I'll never forget the ~ of it ich werde nie vergessen, wie ich mich schämte; to cry ~ on sb sich über jdn entrüsten; the ~ of it all die Schande or Schmach; the ~ of it! was für eine Schande!, diese Schande!; the street is the ~ of the town die Straße ist der Schandfleck or die Schande dieser Stadt; have you no ~? schämst du dich (gar) nicht?; for ~! schäm dich!/schämt euch!; the didn't! for ~! nein! sie sollte sich schämen!; ~ on you! du solltest dich schämen!/ihr solltet euch schämen!
(b) (pity) it's a ~ you couldn't come schade, daß du nicht kommen konntest; it's a (great) ~ we have to leave so early es ist (so) schade or ein Jammer, daß wir schon so früh gehen müssen; what a ~! (das ist aber) schade!, wie schade!; what a ~ he ... schade, daß er ...; see crying.
2 vt Schande machen (+dat); (fig: by excelling) in den Schatten stellen. he ~d us by working so hard er hat uns alle durch sein hartes Arbeiten beschämt; by giving so much he ~d me into making a bigger contribution dadurch, daß er soviel gab, fühlte ich mich moralisch gezwungen, mehr zu spenden; see if you can ~ him into changing his mind appelliere an sein besseres Ich, dann überlegt er es sich vielleicht anders.

shamefaced ['ʃeɪm'feɪst] adj, ~ly ['ʃeɪm'feɪsɪdlɪ] adv betreten.

shamefacedness ['ʃeɪm'feɪstnɪs] n Betretenheit f.

shameful ['ʃeɪmfʊl] adj schändlich. another ~ day for the pound noch ein schmachvoller Tag für das Pfund Sterling; how ~! was für eine Schande!; what ~ prices/behaviour! diese Preise sind/dieses Benehmen ist eine Schande.

shamefully ['ʃeɪmfəlɪ] adv schändlich. he is ~ ignorant es ist eine Schande, wie wenig er weiß.

shamefulness ['ʃeɪmfʊlnɪs] n Ungeheuerlichkeit f.

shameless ['ʃeɪmlɪs] adj schamlos. are you completely ~? hast du gar kein Schamgefühl?; he was quite ~ about it er schämte sich überhaupt nicht; he was quite ~ about lying to his parents er belog seine Eltern schamlos.

shamelessly ['ʃeɪmlɪslɪ] adv see adj.

shamelessness ['ʃeɪmlɪsnɪs] n Schamlosigkeit f.

shaming ['ʃeɪmɪŋ] adj beschämend.

shammy (leather) ['ʃæmɪ('leðər)] n Fenster-/Autoleder nt.

shampoo [ʃæm'puː] **1** n (liquid) Shampoo(n), Schampun nt; (for hair also) Haarwaschmittel nt; (act of washing) Reinigung f; (of hair) Waschen nt. to give the carpet a ~ den Teppich reinigen or shampoonieren or schampunieren; ~ and set Waschen und Legen nt; to have a ~ and set sich (dat) die Haare waschen und legen lassen.
2 vt person die Haare waschen (+dat); hair waschen; carpet, upholstery reinigen, shampoonieren, schampunieren. to have one's hair ~ed sich (dat) die Haare waschen lassen.

shamrock ['ʃæmrɒk] n Klee m; (leaf) Kleeblatt nt.

shandy ['ʃændɪ] n Bier nt mit Limonade. lemonade ~ Alsterwasser nt (N Ger), Radlermaß nt (S Ger).

shanghai [ʃæŋ'haɪ] vt (Naut) schanghaien. to ~ sb into doing sth (fig inf) jdn zwingen, etw zu tun.

shank [ʃæŋk] n (a) (part of leg) (of person) Unterschenkel m; (of horse) Unterarm m; (of beef) Hachse f. ~s (inf: legs) Hachsen pl (inf); (to go) on S~s' pony auf Schusters Rappen (reiten). **(b)** (of anchor, key etc) Schaft m; (of spoon) Stiel m.

shan't [ʃɑːnt] contr of **shall not**. ~! (inf) will nicht! (inf).

shantung [ʃæn'tʌŋ] n Schantungseide f.

shanty¹ ['ʃæntɪ] n (hut) Baracke, Hütte f. ~ town Slum(vor)stadt, Bidonville f.

shanty² n (Mus) Seemannslied, Shanty nt.

SHAPE [ʃeɪp] abbr of **Supreme Headquarters Allied Powers in Europe**.

shape [ʃeɪp] **1** n (a) (geometrical form, outline) Form f. what ~ is it? welche Form hat es?; it's rectangular etc in ~ es ist rechteckig etc; that dress hasn't much/has lost its ~ das Kleid hat keine richtige Form/hat seine Form verloren; she has the right ~ for a model sie hat die richtige Figur für ein Mannequin; to hammer metal into ~ Metall zurechthämmern or -schlagen; to knock sth out of ~ etw zerbeulen; to take ~ (lit) Form bekommen; (fig) Gestalt annehmen; a flowerbed in the ~ of a circle ein Blumenbeet in der Form eines Kreises; government action took the ~ of a ban on die Regierung griff mit einem Verbot ein; help in the ~ of a cheque Hilfe in Form eines Schecks; of all ~s and sizes, of every ~ and size aller Art, jeder Art, in allen Variationen; I don't accept gifts in any ~ or form ich nehme überhaupt keine Geschenke an; we do not know the ~ of things to come wir wissen nicht, wie sich die Zukunft gestalten wird; **this may be the** ~ **of things to come** so könnte das vielleicht in Zukunft sein.

(b) (*unidentified figure*) Gestalt *f*; (*object*) Form *f*.

(c) (*guise*) Gestalt *f*. **in human** ~ in Menschengestalt, in menschlicher Gestalt.

(d) (*fig: order, condition*) **in good/bad** ~ (*sportsman*) in Form/ nicht in Form; (*mentally, healthwise*) in guter/schlechter Verfassung; (*things*) in gutem/schlechtem Zustand; (*business*) gut/schlecht in Schuß (*inf*), in gutem/schlechtem Zustand; **what sort of** ~ **is your boxer in?** in welchem Zustand ist Ihr Boxer?; **what sort of** ~ **was the business in?** in welchem Zustand war das Unter- nehmen?; **to get sb/a business into** ~ jdn/ein Geschäft *or* Unter- nehmen auf Vordermann bringen (*inf*); **to get a house into** ~ ein Haus in Ordnung bringen; **to get one's affairs into** ~ seine Angelegenheiten ordnen.

(e) (*mould*) (*for hats*) Hutform *f*; (*for dressmaking*) Schneiderpuppe *f*; (*for cutting*) Form *f*; (*for cutting*) Ausstecher *m*.

2 *vt* (*lit*) *stone, wood etc* bearbeiten; *clay etc* formen (*into*:*zu*); (*fig*) *character, ideas* formen, prägen; *one's life* gestalten. **he** ~**d the wood/stone into the desired form** er verlieh dem Holz/ Stein die gewünschte Form; **the factors which** ~ **one's life** die Faktoren, die das Leben prägen *or* bestimmen; **those who** ~ **the course of history** die(jenigen), die den Lauf der Geschichte bestimmen; **those who have helped** ~ **our society** die(jenigen), die unsere Gesellschaft mitgeformt haben; **we must** ~ **our strategy according to our funds** wir müssen unsere Strategie nach den zur Verfügung stehenden Mitteln ausrichten.

3 *vi* (*also* ~ **up**) sich entwickeln. **to** ~ **up well** sich gut ent- wickeln, vielversprechend sein; **he is shaping (up) nicely as a goalkeeper** er ist ein vielversprechender Torwart; **things are shaping up well** es sieht sehr gut aus.

shaped [ʃeɪpt] *adj* geformt. **an oddly** ~ **hat** ein Hut mit einer komischen Form; ~ **like a ...** in der Form einer/eines ...

-shaped [-ʃeɪpt] *adj suf* -förmig.

shapeless [ˈʃeɪplɪs] *adj* formlos; (*ugly*) unförmig.

shapelessly [ˈʃeɪplɪslɪ] *adv* unförmig.

shapeliness [ˈʃeɪplɪnɪs] *n* (*of figure*) Wohlproportiertheit *f*; (*of legs, bust*) Wohlgeformtheit *f*.

shapely [ˈʃeɪplɪ] *adj* (+*er*) *figure, woman* wohlproportioniert; *legs, bust* wohlgeformt.

shard [ʃɑːd] *n* (Ton)scherbe *f*.

share¹ [ʃɛəʳ] **1** *n* **(a)** (*portion*) Anteil *m* (*in or of* an +*dat*). **we want fair** ~**s for all** wir wollen, daß gerecht geteilt wird; **I want my fair** ~ ich will meinen (An)teil, ich will, was mir zusteht; **he didn't get his fair** ~ er ist zu kurz gekommen; **I've had more than my fair** ~ **of bad luck** ich habe mehr (als mein Teil an) Pech gehabt; **I'll give you a** ~ **in the profit** ich beteilige Sie am Gewinn; **in equal** ~**s** zu gleichen Teilen; **your** ~ **is £5** du bekommst £ 5; **du mußt £ 5 bezahlen; how much is my** ~? wie groß ist mein Anteil?, wieviel fällt für mich ab?; **to come in for one's full** ~ seinen vollen Anteil bekommen; **he came in for his full** ~ **of criticism** er hat sein Teil an Kritik abbekommen; **to fall to sb's** ~ (*liter*) jdm zufallen (*liter*); **to go** ~**s** (*inf*) teilen; **to bear one's** ~ **of the cost** seinen Anteil an den Kosten tragen; **to take one's** ~ **of the proceeds/blame** sich (*dat*) seinen Anteil am Gewinn nehmen/sich mitschuldig erklären; **to pay one's** ~ seinen (An)teil bezahlen; **to do one's** ~ sein(en) Teil *or* das Seine tun *or* beitragen; **to have a** ~ **in sth** an etw (*dat*) beteiligt sein; **I had no** ~ **in that** damit hatte ich nichts zu tun.

(b) (*Fin*) (*general*) (Geschäfts)anteil *m*; (*in a public limited company*) Aktie *f*. **to hold** ~**s in a company** (Geschäfts)anteile *pl* an einem Unternehmen besitzen/Aktien eines Unter- nehmens besitzen.

2 *vt* (*divide*) teilen; (*have in common also*) gemeinsam haben; *responsibility* gemeinsam tragen. **we** ~ **the same name/birthday** wir haben den gleichen Namen/am gleichen Tag Geburtstag; **they** ~ **a room** sie teilen ein Zimmer, sie haben gemeinsam ein Zimmer *or* ein gemeinsames Zimmer; **I do not** ~ **that view** diese Ansicht teile ich nicht.

3 *vi* **(a)** teilen. **there were no rooms free so I had to** ~ es gab keine freien Zimmer mehr, also mußte ich (ein Zimmer) mit jemandem teilen; **children have to learn to** ~ Kinder müssen lernen, mit anderen zu teilen; **to** ~ **and** ~ **alike** (brüderlich) mit (den) anderen teilen; **now children,** ~ **and** ~ **alike** Kinder, teilt brüderlich!

(b) to ~ **in sth** sich an etw (*dat*) beteiligen; (*in profit*) an etw (*dat*) beteiligt werden; (*in enthusiasm*) etw teilen; (*in success, sorrow*) an etw (*dat*) Anteil nehmen.

♦**share out** *vt sep* verteilen.

share² *n* (Agr) (Pflug)schar *f*.

share: ~ **certificate** *n* Aktienzertifikat *nt*; ~**cropper** *n* (*US etc Agr*) (Farm)pächter *m* (*der Pacht in Form eines Ernteanteils zahlt*); ~**holder** *n* Aktionär(in *f*) *m*; ~ **index** *n* Aktienindex *m*; ~**-out** *n* Verteilung *f*; (*St Ex*) (Dividenden)ausschüttung *f*.

shark [ʃɑːk] *n* **(a)** Hai(fisch) *m*. **(b)** (*inf: swindler*) Schlitzohr *nt* (*inf*). **loan/property** ~ Kredit-/Grundstückshai *m* (*inf*).

sharp [ʃɑːp] **1** *adj* (+*er*) **(a)** *knife, blade etc* scharf; *needle, point etc* spitz.

(b) (*clear-cut, not blurred*) *outline, photo, contrast* scharf.

(c) (*observant, keen*) *eyes, wits, glance, mind* scharf; *nose* gut, empfindlich; *observation, remark* scharfsinnig, schlau; (*intelligent*) *person* schlau, gewieft, auf Draht (*inf*); *child* schlau, aufgeweckt. **that was pretty** ~ **of you** das war ganz schön schlau *or* clever (*inf*); **to keep a** ~ **watch for mistakes** gut *or* scharf auf Fehler aufpassen; **keep a** ~ **watch for him/the train** paß gut auf, ob du ihn/den Zug siehst.

(d) (*sudden, intense*) *whistle, cry* durchdringend, schrill; *drop in prices* steil; *frost* scharf; *shower, desire, pain* heftig; *hunger* nagend (*geh*), groß. **after a short,** ~ **struggle** nach kurzem, heftigem Kampf; **be** ~ **about it!** (*inf*) (ein bißchen) dalli! (*inf*), zack, zack! (*inf*).

(e) (*acute*) *angle* spitz; *bend, turn by car* scharf.

(f) (*pej: cunning*) *person* gerissen, raffiniert, clever (*inf*); *trick etc* raffiniert. ~ **practice** unsaubere Geschäfte *pl*; **there's some** ~ **practice going on there** da sind Gaunereien im Gange; **that was a pretty** ~ **move** das war ein raffinierter Schachzug.

(g) (*harsh, fierce*) *tongue, retort* scharf; *person* schroff; *temper* hitzig. **he has a** ~ **temper** er ist jähzornig.

(h) (*acidic, pungent*) *taste* scharf; *apple* sauer; *wine* herb, sauer (*pej*); (*fig: biting*) *air* schneidend kalt; *wind also* beißend.

(i) (*Mus*) *note* (*too high*) zu hoch; (*raised a semitone*) (um einen Halbton) erhöht. **her voice goes** ~ **on the higher notes** sie singt die höheren Töne zu hoch.

(j) (*inf: stylish*) *person, clothes* toll (*inf*), todschick (*inf*); *piece of driving* clever (*inf*).

2 *adv* (+*er*) **(a)** (*Mus*) zu hoch.

(b) (*punctually*) pünktlich, genau. **at 5 o'clock** ~ Punkt 5 Uhr.

(c) look ~! dalli! (*inf*), zack, zack! (*inf*); **if you don't look** ~ ... wenn du nicht schnell machst ...; **to pull up** ~ plötzlich anhalten; **to turn** ~ **left** scharf nach links abbiegen.

3 *n* (*Mus*) Kreuz *nt*. **you played F natural instead of a** ~ du hast f statt fis gespielt.

sharp-edged [ˌʃɑːpˈedʒd] *adj knife, outline etc* scharf; *piece of furniture etc* scharfkantig.

sharpen [ˈʃɑːpən] **1** *vt* **(a)** *knife* schleifen, schärfen, wetzen; *razor* wetzen; *pencil* spitzen; (*fig*) *appetite* anregen; *wits* schärfen; *sensation* erhöhen. **(b)** (*Mus*) (*by a semitone*) (um einen Halbton) erhöhen; (*raise pitch*) höher singen/spielen/ stimmen. **2** *vi* **her voice** ~**s** sie singt zu hoch.

sharpener [ˈʃɑːpnəʳ] *n* Schleifgerät *nt*; (*in rod shape*) Wetz- stahl *m*; (*pencil* ~) (Bleistift)spitzer *m*.

sharper [ˈʃɑːpəʳ] *n* Gauner *m*; (*card* ~) Falschspieler *m*.

sharp: ~**-eyed** *adj* scharfsichtig; **to be** ~**-eyed** scharfe *or* gute Augen haben; **it was** ~**-eyed of you to see that** du hast ja Augen wie ein Luchs; ~**-faced** *adj* spitzschnäuzig; (*alert*) pfiffig aussehend; ~**-featured** *adj* mit scharfen (Gesichts)zügen.

sharpness [ˈʃɑːpnɪs] *n see adj* **(a)** Schärfe *f*; Spitzheit *f*. **(b)** Schärfe *f*. **(c)** Schärfe *f*; Empfindlichkeit *f*; Scharfsinnigkeit *f*; Schläue, Gewieftheit (*inf*) *f*; Aufgewecktheit *f*. **(d)** Schrillheit *f*; Schärfe *f*; Heftigkeit *f*; Größe *f*. **because of the unexpected** ~ **of the drop in prices** wegen des unerwartet steilen Preissturzes. **(e)** Spitzheit *f*; Schärfe *f*. **(f)** Gerissenheit *f*, Raffiniertheit, Cleverneß (*inf*) *f*. **(g)** Schärfe *f*; Schroffheit *f*; Hitzigkeit *f*. **(h)** Schärfe *f*; Säure *f*; Herbheit, Säure *f*; schneidende Kälte; Schärfe *f*. **there is a** ~ **in the air** es ist sehr frisch.

sharp: ~**shooter** *n* Scharfschütze *m*; ~**-sighted** *adj see* ~**-eyed**; ~**-tongued** *adj* scharfzüngig; ~**-witted** *adj* scharfsinnig.

shat [ʃæt] *pret, ptp of* shit¹.

shatter [ˈʃætəʳ] **1** *vt* **(a)** (*lit*) zertrümmern, zerschmettern; *hopes, dreams* zunichte machen; *nerves* zerrütten. **he hurled a brick at the window,** ~**ing** it into a thousand pieces er schleuderte einen Ziegel gegen das Fenster, das in tausend Stücke zersplitterte *or* zersprang; **the blast** ~**ed all the win- dows** durch die Explosion zersplitterten alle Fensterscheiben; **to** ~ **sth against a wall** etw gegen eine Wand schmettern, etw an einer Wand zerschmettern; **his hopes were** ~**ed** seine Hoff- nungen hatten sich zerschlagen.

(b) (*fig inf: exhaust*) erledigen, fertigmachen (*inf*); (*run down mentally*) mitnehmen. **she was absolutely** ~**ed by the divorce** proceedings das Scheidungsverfahren hatte sie schwer mitgenommen.

(c) (*inf: flabbergast*) erschüttern. **I've won the pools? I'm** ~**ed!** ich habe im Toto gewonnen? ich bin platt! (*inf*).

2 *vi* zerbrechen, zerspringen; (*windscreen*) (zer)splittern.

shattering [ˈʃætərɪŋ] *adj* **(a)** *blow* wuchtig, gewaltig; *explosion* gewaltig; *defeat* vernichtend. **it had a** ~ **effect on the state of the pound** es wirkte sich verheerend auf das Pfund aus.

(b) (*fig inf: exhausting*) erschöpfend, anstrengend; (*psychologically*) niederschmetternd. **a** ~ **blow to his ego** ein schwerer Schlag für sein Ich; **I had a** ~ **day at the office** der Tag im Büro hat mich wahnsinnig geschlaucht (*inf*), ich bin total erledigt vom Büro (*inf*); **the divorce was a** ~ **experience for her** die Scheidung hat sie unheimlich mitgenommen (*inf*).

(c) (*inf: flabbergasting*) *news, realization, ignorance, frank- ness* erschütternd; *effect* umwerfend (*inf*). **this new film is a** ~ **experience** dieser neue Film ist ein umwerfendes Erlebnis (*inf*); **a few** ~ **changes in the cabinet** ein paar aufsehener- regende Veränderungen im Kabinett; **it must have been absolutely** ~ **for you to have found out that** ... das war bestimmt entsetzlich für Sie, als Sie erfuhren, daß ...

shatterproof [ˈʃætəpruːf] *adj* splitterfest *or* -frei.

shave [ʃeɪv] (*vb: pret* ~**d**, *ptp* ~**d** *or* **shaven**) **1** *n* Rasur *f*. **to have a** ~ sich rasieren; (*at a barber's*) sich rasieren lassen; **this new razor gives you a good** ~ dieser neue Rasierapparat rasiert gut; **a close** ~ (*lit*) eine glatte Rasur; **to have a close** *or* **narrow** ~ (*fig*) gerade noch *or* mit knapper Not davonkommen, gerade noch Glück haben; **he got a place at university, but it was a close** ~ er bekam einen Studienplatz, aber nur mit knapper Not; **that was a close** ~ das war knapp.

2 *vt face, legs* rasieren; *leather* (ab)falzen; *wood* hobeln; (*graze*) streifen.

3 *vi* (*person*) sich rasieren; (*razor*) rasieren, schneiden.

♦**shave off** *vt sep her beard* sich (*dat*) abrasieren; *sb's beard* abrasieren; *wood* abhobeln.

shaven [ˈʃeɪvn] *adj head etc* rasiert. ~**-headed** kahlgeschoren.

shaver [ˈʃeɪvəʳ] *n* **(a)** (*razor*) Rasierapparat *m*. **(b)** (*inf*) *young* ~ junger Bengel (*inf*); (*as address*) junger Freund.

Shavian [ˈʃeɪvɪən] *adj* Shawsch.

shaving [ˈʃeɪvɪŋ] *n* **(a)** Rasieren *nt*. **(b)** ~**s** *pl* Späne *pl*.

shaving in cpds Rasier-; ~ **brush** n Rasierpinsel m; ~ **cream** n Rasiercreme f; ~ **mug** n Rasierschale f; ~ **point** n Steckdose f für Rasierapparate; ~ **soap** or **stick** n Rasierseife f.

shawl [ʃɔːl] n (round shoulders) (Umhänge)tuch nt; (tailored) Umhang m; (covering head) (Kopf)tuch nt.

she [ʃiː] **1** pron sie; (of boats, cars etc) er/sie/es. ~ **who** ... (liter) diejenige, die ...; **it is** ~ (form) sie ist es. **2** n Sie f.

she- pref weiblich. ~-**bear** weiblicher Bär, Bärin f.

sheaf [ʃiːf] n, pl **sheaves** (of wheat, corn) Garbe f; (of arrows etc, papers, notes) Bündel nt.

shear [ʃɪəʳ] pret ~**ed**, ptp **shorn 1** vt sheep scheren; wool (ab)scheren; see **shorn. 2** vi the knife ~s through the metal das Messer zerschneidet das Metall; the bird ~ed through the air der Vogel segelte durch die Luft; the motorboat ~ed through the water das Motorboot durchpflügte das Wasser.

♦**shear off 1** vt sep sheep's wool abscheren. the ship had its bows shorn ~ in the collision beim Zusammenstoß wurde dem Schiff der Bug abrasiert. **2** vi (break off) abbrechen.

shearer [ʃɪərəʳ] n (Schaf)scherer m.

shearing [ʃɪərɪŋ] n (Schaf)schur f. ~s Schur- or Scherwolle f.

shearing: ~ **machine** n Schermaschine f; ~ **time** n Schurzeit f, Zeit f der Schafschur.

shears [ʃɪəz] npl (große) Schere f; (for hedges) Heckenschere f; (for metal) Metallschere f.

shearwater [ʃɪəwɔːtəʳ] n Sturmtaucher m.

sheath [ʃiːθ] n (for sword etc) Scheide f; (Bot) (Blatt)scheide f; (on cable) Mantel m, Armierung f; (contraceptive) Gummischutz m, Kondom m or nt; (dress) Futteralkeid nt. the cat withdrew its claws into their ~s die Katze zog die Krallen ein; the wing-~ of an insect die Flügeldecke eines Insekts.

sheathe [ʃiːð] vt sword in die Scheide stecken; claws einziehen; cables armieren. **to** ~ **sth in metal** etw mit Metall verkleiden.

sheathing [ʃiːðɪŋ] n (on roof, house) Verkleidung f; (on ship also) Beschlag m; (with wood) Verschalung f; (on cables) Armierung, Bewehrung f.

sheath knife n Fahrtenmesser nt.

sheaves [ʃiːvz] pl of **sheaf.**

shebang [ʃəˈbæŋ] n (sl) the whole ~ die ganze Chose (inf), der ganze Kram (inf) or Laden (inf).

shebeen [ʃɪˈbiːn] n (Ir) Kaschemme, Spelunke f.

shed¹ [ʃed] pret, ptp ~ **1** vt (a) leaves, hair etc verlieren; horns abwerfen; clothes ausziehen, ablegen. the dancer slowly ~ another layer die Tänzerin schälte sich langsam aus einer weiteren Hülle; **to** ~ **its skin** sich häuten; **you should** ~ **a few pounds** Sie sollten ein paar Pfund abnehmen.
(b) tears, blood vergießen. **he** ~ **his blood** sein Blut floß; (die also) sein Blut wurde vergossen; **why should I** ~ **my blood?** warum sollte ich Leib und Leben einsetzen?; **I won't** ~ **any tears over him** ich weine ihm keine Träne nach.
(c) burden, leader loswerden; cares ablegen; friend fallenlassen. **he has now** ~ **his childish notions** er hat jetzt seine kindischen Vorstellungen abgelegt; **an actress who** ~s **husbands like a snake** ~s **skins** eine Schauspielerin, die die Ehemänner wechselt wie andere das Hemd.
(d) light, perfume verbreiten. **to** ~ **light on sth** (fig) etw erhellen, Licht auf etw (acc) werfen.
2 vi (dog, cat etc) sich haaren.

shed² n Schuppen m; (industrial also) Halle f; (cattle ~) Stall m; (night shelter also) Unterstand m; see **watershed.**

she'd [ʃiːd] contr of **she would; she had.**

sheen [ʃiːn] n Glanz m.

sheep [ʃiːp] n, pl - (lit, fig) Schaf nt. the vicar and his ~ der Pfarrer und seine Schäfchen; **to count** ~ Schäfchen zählen; **to separate the** ~ **from the goats** (fig) die Schafe von den Böcken trennen; **to make** ~'s **eyes at sb** jdn anhimmeln; **you might as well be hanged for a** ~ **as a lamb** (prov) das macht den Kohl auch nicht fett (inf).

sheep: ~-**dip** n Desinfektionsbad nt für Schafe; (for mange) Räudebad nt; ~**dog** n Hütehund m; ~**dog trials** npl Gehorsamkeits- und Geschicklichkeitsprüfungen pl für Hütehunde; ~ **farm** n Schaffarm f; ~**fold** n Schafhürde f.

sheepish [ʃiːpɪʃ] adv verlegen. **I felt a bit** ~ **about it** das war mir ein bißchen peinlich.

sheepishly [ʃiːpɪʃlɪ] adv verlegen.

sheep: ~-**run** n Schafweide f; ~**shearing** n Schafschur f; ~**skin** n (a) Schaffell nt; ~**skin (jacket)** Schaffelljacke f; (b) (US inf: diploma) Pergament nt.

sheer [ʃɪəʳ] **1** adj (+er) (a) (absolute) rein; nonsense also bar, glatt; madness also glatt. **by the** ~ **force of his own muscles** durch bloße Muskelkraft; **by** ~ **chance** rein zufällig; **by** ~ **hard work** durch nichts als harte Arbeit; **the** ~ **impossibility of doing that** die schiere Unmöglichkeit, das zu tun; **that's** ~ **robbery!** das ist der reinste Nepp! (inf).
(b) (steep) cliff, drop steil, jäh (geh). **there is a** ~ **drop of 200 metres** es fällt 200 Meter steil or senkrecht ab.
(c) (of cloth etc) (hauch)dünn, (hauch)zart. ~ **nylon stockings** hauchdünne Nylonstrümpfe pl.
2 adv steil, jäh (geh); (vertically) senkrecht.
3 vi (Naut) ausscheren.

♦**sheer away** vi (a) (ship, plane) ausweichen. (b) (avoid) **to** ~ **from sb/sth** jdm/einer Sache ausweichen.

♦**sheer off** vi (a) (ship) ausscheren. (b) (person: make off) sich davonmachen.

sheerness [ʃɪənɪs] n (of cliffs) Steilheit f.

sheet¹ [ʃiːt] n (a) (for bed) (Bett)laken, Lein- or Bettuch nt; (waterproof ~) Gummidecke f; (for covering furniture) Tuch nt. **between the** ~s (inf) im Bett (inf); **the furniture was covered with (dust)** ~s die Möbel waren verhängt.
(b) (of paper, inf: a newspaper) Blatt nt; (big, as of wrapping paper, stamps etc, Typ) Bogen m. ~ **of music** Notenblatt nt.
(c) (of plywood) Platte f; (of glass also) Scheibe f; (of metal

---

also) Blech nt; (baking ~) (Back)blech nt; (Geol) Schicht f; (of water, ice etc) Fläche f; (of flame) Flammenmeer nt. **a** ~ **of ice covered the lake** eine Eisschicht bedeckte den See; **the** ~ **of water covering the lawn** das Wasser, das auf dem Rasen stand; **the lake, a glasslike** ~ **of water** der See, eine spiegelblanke Wasserfläche; **a huge** ~ **of flame engulfed the building** das Gebäude ging in einem Flammenmeer unter; ~s **of flame leapt from the burning tanker** riesige Flammen schlugen aus dem brennenden Tanker; **the rain was coming down in** ~s es regnete in Strömen.

sheet² n (Naut: rope) Schot, (Segel)leine f. ~s (space) Vorder-/ Achterteil nt.

sheet: ~ **anchor** n Notanker m; (fig) Rettungsanker m; ~ **anchor man** n Eckpfeiler m; ~**bend** n Schotstek m; ~ **glass** n Flach- or Scheibenglas nt.

sheeting [ʃiːtɪŋ] n (cloth) Leinen nt; (metal etc) Verkleidung f; (wood) Verschalung f. **plastic** ~ Plastiküberzug m/-überzüge pl.

sheet: ~ **lightning** n Wetterleuchten nt; ~ **metal** n Walzblech nt; ~ **music** n Notenblätter pl.

sheik(h) [ʃeɪk] n Scheich m.

sheik(h)dom [ʃeɪkdəm] n Scheichtum nt.

sheila [ʃiːlə] n (Austral inf) Biene (inf), Puppe (inf) f.

shekel [ʃekl] n Sekel, Schekel m. ~s (sl) Moneten pl (sl).

sheldrake [ʃeldreɪk] n Brandente f.

shelf [ʃelf] n, pl **shelves** (a) Brett, Bord nt; (for books) Bücherbrett or -bord nt. **shelves** (unit of furniture) Regal nt; **book**~ or -**shelves** Bücherregal or -bord; **to be on the** ~ (girl) eine alte Jungfer sein, sitzengeblieben sein; (worker) zum alten Eisen gehören; **she was left on the** ~ sie ist eine alte Jungfer geworden, sie ist sitzengeblieben.
(b) (ledge of rock etc) (on rock face) Gesims nt, (Fels-) vorsprung m; (under water) (Felsen)riff nt, Felsbank f; (sandbank) Sandbank f, Untiefe f.

shelf: ~ **mark** n Standortzeichen nt; ~ **room** n Platz m in den Regalen.

shell [ʃel] **1** n (a) (of egg, nut, mollusc) Schale f; (on beach) Muschel f; (of pea etc) Hülse f; (of snail) (Schnecken)haus nt; (of tortoise, turtle, insect) Panzer m; (pastry ~) Form f. **to come out of one's** ~ (fig) aus seinem Schneckenhaus kommen, aus sich (dat) herausgehen; **to retire into one's** ~ (fig) sich in sein Schneckenhaus verkriechen; **I'm just an empty** ~ (fig) ich bin nur noch eine leere Hülse.
(b) (frame) (of building) Mauerwerk nt, Mauern pl; (gutted also) (leere) Schale; (unfinished) Rohbau m; (ruin) Gemäuer nt, Ruine f; (of car) (unfinished) Karosserie f; (gutted) Wrack nt; (of ship) Gerippe nt, Rumpf m; (gutted) Wrack nt.
(c) (Mil) Granate f; (esp US: cartridge) Patrone f.
(d) (boat) Rennruderboot nt.
2 vt (a) peas etc enthülsen; eggs, nuts schälen; egg abschälen.
(b) (Mil) (mit Granaten) beschießen. **the town is still being** ~ed die Stadt steht immer noch unter Beschuß.

♦**shell out** (inf) **1** vt sep blechen (inf). **2** vi **to** ~ ~ **for sth** für etw blechen (inf).

she'll [ʃiːl] contr of **she will; she shall.**

shellac [ʃəˈlæk] **1** n Schellack m. **2** vt (a) (varnish) mit Schellack behandeln. (b) (US sl: defeat utterly) in die Pfanne hauen (sl); (beat) vermöbeln (inf), verwichsen (inf). **to get a** ~**king** eins auf die Schnauze kriegen (sl)/eine Tracht Prügel kriegen.

shell: ~**fire** n Granatfeuer nt; ~**fish** n Schaltier(e pl) nt; (Cook) Meeresfrüchte pl; ~**hole** n Granattrichter m.

shelling [ʃelɪŋ] n Granatfeuer nt (of auf + acc), Granatbeschuß m.

shell: ~**proof** adj bombensicher; ~ **shock** n Kriegsneurose f; ~-**shocked** adj **to be** ~-**shocked** (lit) unter einer Kriegsneurose leiden; (fig) verstört sein.

shelter [ʃeltəʳ] **1** n (protection) Schutz m; (place) Unterstand m; (air-raid ~) (Luftschutz)keller or -bunker m; (bus ~) Wartehäuschen nt; (mountain ~) (Berg- or Schutz)hütte f; (for the night) Obdach nt (liter), Unterkunft f. **a night** ~ **for homeless people** ein Obdachlosenheim or -asyl nt; **in the** ~ **of one's home** in der Geborgenheit des Hauses; **under the** ~ **of the rock** im Schutze des Felsens; **under** ~ **of night** im Schutze der Nacht; **when the ship reached** ~ als das Schiff den sicheren or schützenden Hafen erreichte; **to get under** ~, **to take** ~ sich in Sicherheit bringen; (from rain, hail etc) sich unterstellen; **to seek** ~/**to run for** ~ Schutz or Zuflucht suchen; **to give sb** ~ jdn beherbergen; **to provide** ~ **for sb** jdm Schutz bieten; (accommodation) jdn beherbergen; **the peasants offered the guerrillas** ~ die Bauern boten den Partisanen Zuflucht.
2 vt schützen (from vor + dat); criminal verstecken. **to** ~ **sb from blame** jdn gegen Vorwürfe in Schutz nehmen; **to** ~ **sb from harm** jdn vor Schaden bewahren; **the police think he's trying to** ~ **someone** die Polizei glaubt, daß er jemanden deckt; **parents** ~**ing their children from harsh reality** Eltern, die ihre Kinder vor der rauhen Wirklichkeit behüten.
3 vi **there was nowhere to** ~ man konnte nirgends Schutz finden; (from rain etc) man konnte sich nirgends unterstellen; **a good place to** ~ eine Stelle, wo man gut geschützt ist; **we** ~**ed in a shop doorway** wir stellten uns in einem Ladeneingang unter; **we** ~**ed behind the rocks** wir stellten uns zum Schutz hinter die Felsen; **to** ~ **behind a friend/one's reputation** (fig) sich hinter einem Freund/seinem Ansehen verstecken.

sheltered [ʃeltəd] adj place geschützt; life behütet. ~ **from the wind** windgeschützt; ~ **housing** Wohnungen pl für Behinderte/Senioren; ~ **workshop** Behindertenwerkstatt f.

shelve [ʃelv] **1** vi (slope) abfallen. **2** vt (a) room mit Regalen versehen, Regale einbauen in (+acc). (b) problem aufschieben; plan, project ad acta legen.

shelves [ʃelvz] pl of **shelf.**

shelving [ʃelvɪŋ] n Regale pl; (material also) Bretter pl.

shenanigans [ʃəˈnænɪgən(z)] n pl (inf) (tomfoolery) Faxen pl (inf), Mumpitz m (inf); (goings-on) Dinger (inf), Sachen (inf) pl; (trickery) üble Tricks (inf) or Dinger (inf) pl.

shepherd [ˈʃepəd] 1 n (a) Schäfer, (Schaf)hirt m. ~ boy Hütejunge m; the Good S~ der Gute Hirte; ~'s pie Auflauf m aus Hackfleisch und Kartoffelbrei; ~'s plaid schwarz-weiß karierter Wollstoff; ~'s purse Hirtentäschel(kraut) nt. (b) (US) see German ~. 2 vt führen.

shepherdess [ˈʃepədɪs] n Schäferin f.

sherbet [ˈʃɜːbət] n (powder) Brausepulver nt; (drink) Brause f, Sorbet(t) m or nt; (US: water ~ ice) Fruchteis nt.

sherd [ʃɜːd] n see shard.

sheriff [ˈʃerɪf] n Sheriff m; (Scot) Friedensrichter m.

Sherpa [ˈʃɜːpə] n Sherpa m.

sherry [ˈʃerɪ] n Sherry m.

she's [ʃiːz] contr of she is; she has.

Shetland Islands [ˈʃetlənd ˈaɪləndz] npl Shetlandinseln pl.

Shetland pony [ˈʃetlənd ˈpəʊnɪ] n Shetlandpony nt.

Shetlands [ˈʃetləndz] npl Shetlandinseln pl.

shew [ʃəʊ] vti (old) ptp **shewn** [ʃəʊn] see show.

shibboleth [ˈʃɪbəleθ] n (custom) Gepflogenheit, Konvention f; (catchword) Losung, Parole f, Schibboleth nt (rare, liter).

shield [ʃiːld] 1 n (Mil, Her) Schild m; (Zool also) Panzer m; (sporting trophy also) Trophäe f; (on machine) Schutzschirm or -schild m; (eye~, radiation ~) Schirm m; (fig) Schutz m. riot ~ Schutzschild m; God is our ~ Gott ist unser Schild; see dress ~. 2 vt schützen (sb from sth jdn vor etw dat); industry absichern, abschirmen. she tried to ~ him from the truth sie versuchte, ihm die Wahrheit zu ersparen.

shift [ʃɪft] 1 n (a) (change) Änderung f; (in policy, opinion also) Wandel m; (Ling) Verschiebung f; (Mus) Lagenwechsel m; (from one place to another) Verlegung f. a ~ of scene ein Szenenwechsel m; a ~ in direction eine Richtungsänderung; a ~ in public opinion ein Meinungsumschwung m in der Bevölkerung; a ~ of emphasis eine Gewichtsverlagerung; a population ~ eine Bevölkerungsverschiebung; this shows a ~ away from the government dies läßt eine für die Regierung ungünstige Tendenz erkennen; a new ~ towards liberalism ein neuer Trend zum Liberalismus.
(b) (Aut: gear~) Schaltung f; (on typewriter: also ~ key) Umschalttaste f. ~ lock Umschaltfeststeller m.
(c) (period at work, group of workers) Schicht f. to work in ~s in Schichten arbeiten; to do ~ work Schicht arbeiten.
(d) (stratagem) List f, Kniff m; (expedient) Ausweg m. to make ~ with/without sth sich mit/ohne etw behelfen.
(e) (dress) Hemdkleid nt; (old: undergarment) Hemd nt.
2 vt (a) (move) (von der Stelle) bewegen; screw, nail loskriegen, rauskriegen; lid abkriegen; cork rauskriegen; furniture also verrücken; head, arm wegnehmen; (from one place to another) verlagern, verschieben; offices etc verlegen; rubble, boulder also wegräumen. to ~ scenery Kulissen schieben; to ~ one's ground seinen Standpunkt ändern; to ~ sb from an opinion jdn von einer Meinung abbringen; he stood ~ing his weight from foot to foot er trat von einem Fuß auf den anderen; to ~ the blame onto sb else die Verantwortung auf jd anderen schieben; to ~ sth to another room etw in ein anderes Zimmer schaffen; ~ the table over to the wall rück den Tisch an die Wand (rüber)!; can you ~ your car back a bit? können Sie ein Stück zurücksetzen?; they ~ed him to Munich sie haben ihn nach München versetzt; we'll ~ all this junk up to the attic/out of the cupboard wir schaffen das ganze Gerümpel auf den Boden/räumen das ganze Gerümpel aus dem Schrank.
(b) (inf: get rid of) loswerden.
(c) (US Aut) to ~ gears schalten.
(d) (inf) food verputzen (inf); drink schlucken (sl).
3 vi (a) (move) sich bewegen; (ballast, cargo, scene) sich verlagern; (scene) wechseln; (wind) umspringen; (from one's opinion) abgehen. he ~ed out of the way er ging aus dem Weg; he was ~ing about in his chair er rutschte auf seinem Stuhl hin und her; ~ over, you're taking up too much room rück mal rüber, du nimmst zuviel Platz weg; he ~ed onto his back er drehte sich auf den Rücken; he ~s around all over the country er reist im ganzen Land herum; he refused to ~ (fig) er war nicht umzustimmen; ~ing sands (Geol) Flugsand m.
(b) (Aut) schalten.
(c) (inf: move quickly) (cars, runners) flitzen (inf), rasen. that's really ~ing! das nenne ich Tempo!
(d) (manage) to ~ for oneself sich (dat) (selbst) behelfen.

shiftily [ˈʃɪftɪlɪ] adv see adj zwielichtig, nicht ganz sauber (inf); verstohlen; ausweichend; behave verdächtig.

shiftiness [ˈʃɪftɪnɪs] n see adj Zwielichtigkeit f; Fragwürdigkeit f; Verstohlenheit f; Ausweichen nt. there was a certain ~ in his manner sein Verhalten hatte etwas Verdächtiges.

shiftless [ˈʃɪftlɪs] adj träge, energielos.

shiftlessness [ˈʃɪftlɪsnɪs] n Trägheit, Energielosigkeit f.

shifty [ˈʃɪftɪ] adj (+er) zwielichtig, nicht ganz sauber (inf); person, character also fragwürdig; glance verstohlen; reply ausweichend. there was something ~ about ... mit ... war etwas faul (inf); he has a ~ look in his eyes er hat so einen unsicheren Blick; a ~ expression came over his face sein Gesicht nahm einen gerissenen Ausdruck an; a ~ little man ein verdächtiger kleiner Kerl.

shillelagh [ʃəˈleɪlə] n (Ir) (Schlehdorn- or Eichen)knüppel m.

shilling [ˈʃɪlɪŋ] n (Brit old, Africa etc) Shilling m.

shilly-shally [ˈʃɪlɪˌʃælɪ] vi (inf) unschlüssig sein. stop ~ing laß das Fackeln; you've shilly-shallied long enough du hast lange genug gezögert.

shimmer [ˈʃɪmər] 1 n Schimmer m. 2 vi schimmern.

shin [ʃɪn] 1 n Schienbein nt; (of meat) Hachse f. to kick sb on the ~ jdm or jdn vors Schienbein treten. 2 vi to ~ up/down (geschickt) hinauf-/hinunterklettern.

shinbone [ˈʃɪnbəʊn] n Schienbein nt.

shindig [ˈʃɪndɪg] n (inf) Remmidemmi nt (inf).

shindy [ˈʃɪndɪ] n (inf) Radau m (inf); (noise also, dispute) Krach m (inf).

shine [ʃaɪn] (vb: pret, ptp **shone**) 1 n Glanz m. to give one's shoes a ~ seine Schuhe polieren or blank putzen; ~, sir? Schuhe putzen, der Herr?; to have a ~ glänzen; to put a ~ on sth etw blank polieren; to take the ~ off sth (lit, fig) einer Sache (dat) den Glanz nehmen; she's taken a real ~ to Oxford/my brother (inf) Oxford/mein Bruder hat es ihr wirklich angetan; see rain.
2 vt (a) pret, ptp usu ~d (polish: also ~ up) blank putzen; shoes also polieren.
(b) (direct a light) to ~ a light on sth etw beleuchten; ~ the torch this way! leuchte einmal hierher!; don't ~ it in my eyes! blende mich nicht!
3 vi (a) leuchten; (stars, eyes, face also, metal, nose, paint) glänzen; (moon, sun, lamp) scheinen; (glass) blitzblank sein. to ~ like a beacon (fig) wie ein Licht in der Dunkelheit sein or leuchten; (hum: face, nose) wie ein Lampion leuchten.
(b) (fig: excel) glänzen. to ~ at/in sth (lit etc) glänzen; he doesn't exactly ~ at sports/his work er ist keine or nicht gerade eine Leuchte im Sport/bei der Arbeit.
♦**shine down** vi herabscheinen (on auf +acc).
♦**shine out** vi (a) (light) the light shining ~ from the windows across the lawn das durch die Fenster auf den Rasen fallende Licht; a light (suddenly) shone ~ from the darkness in der Dunkelheit blitzte (plötzlich) ein Licht auf; the sun shone ~ from behind a cloud die Sonne schien hinter einer Wolke hervor.
(b) (fig: qualities) his courage ~s ~ sein Mut ragt heraus.

shiner [ˈʃaɪnər] n (sl: black eye) Veilchen nt (sl).

shingle[1] [ˈʃɪŋgl] 1 n (a) (tile) Schindel f; (US inf: signboard) Schild nt. to put up one's ~ (US) ein Geschäft eröffnen; (doctor, lawyer) sich niederlassen.
(b) (hairstyle) Herrenschnitt, Bubikopf m.
2 vt (a) roof etc mit Schindeln decken.
(b) hair einen Herrenschnitt or Bubikopf machen (+dat).

shingle[2] n, no pl (pebbles) Kiesel m, Kieselsteine pl; (~ beach) Kiesel(strand) m.

shingles [ˈʃɪŋglz] n sing (Med) Gürtelrose f.

shingly [ˈʃɪŋglɪ] adj beach steinig, voller Kieselsteine.

shin-guard [ˈʃɪngɑːd] n Schienbeinschützer m.

shining [ˈʃaɪnɪŋ] adj (lit, fig) leuchtend; light strahlend; eyes also, nose, metal, paint glänzend; car blitzend, blitzblank. a ~ light (fig) eine Leuchte; ~ white leuchtend or strahlend weiß.

shinty [ˈʃɪntɪ] n dem Hockey ähnliches Spiel.

shiny [ˈʃaɪnɪ] adj (+er) glänzend; elbows, trousers also blank.

ship [ʃɪp] 1 n (a) Schiff nt. the good ~ Venus die gute Venus; on board ~ an Bord; to take ~ (for) (liter) sich einschiffen (nach); when my ~ comes home or in (fig) wenn ich das große Los ziehe; ~ of the line Kriegsschiff nt; ~ of the desert Wüstenschiff nt; the great ~ of state das Staatsschiff.
(b) ~'s articles Heuervertrag m, Schiffsartikel pl; ~'s biscuit, (US) ~ biscuit Schiffszwieback m; ~'s company (Schiffs)besatzung f; ~'s doctor Schiffsarzt m; ~'s papers Schiffspapiere pl.
(c) (US inf: plane) Maschine f; (space~) (Raum)schiff nt.
2 vt (a) (take on board) goods an Bord nehmen or bringen, laden; crew, passengers an Bord nehmen; mast setzen. to ~ oars die Riemen einlegen; to ~ water leck sein; we're ~ping water unser Boot leckt or ist leck.
(b) (transport) versenden; coal, grain etc verfrachten; (by sea also) verschiffen.
3 vi (take employment) anheuern.
♦**ship off** vt sep versenden; coal, grain etc verfrachten; (by ship also) verschiffen. they ~ped their sons ~ to boarding school sie steckten ihre Söhne ins Internat (inf).
♦**ship out** vt sep versenden; coal, grain etc verfrachten. to ~ supplies ~ to sb jdn (per Schiff) mit Vorräten versorgen.

ship-: ~board n: on ~board an Bord; a ~board romance eine Romanze auf See; ~breaker n Schiffsverschrotter m; ~builder n Schiffbauer m; a firm of ~builders eine Schiffbaufirma; ~building n Schiffbau m; ~ canal n (See)kanal m; ~load n Schiffsladung f; the tourists were arriving by the ~load or in ~loads (inf) ganze Schiffsladungen von Touristen kamen an; ~mate n Schiffskamerad m.

shipment [ˈʃɪpmənt] n Sendung f; (of coal, grain, tractors) Transport m; (transporting by sea) Verschiffung f; (taking on board) Verladen nt.

shipowner [ˈʃɪpəʊnər] n Schiffseigner m; (of many ships) Reeder m.

shipper [ˈʃɪpər] n (company) Speditionsfirma f, Spediteure pl; (sender) Absender m.

shipping [ˈʃɪpɪŋ] 1 n, no pl (a) (ships) Schiffahrt f; (ships) Schiffe pl. the Suez Canal has been reopened to ~ der Suezkanal ist wieder für die Schiffahrt or den Schiffsverkehr geöffnet.
(b) (transportation) Verschiffung f; (by rail etc) Versand m.
2 adj attr ~ agent Reedereivertreter m; ~ business Reederei- or Schiffahrtsgeschäft nt; ~ clerk Expedient(in f) m, Angestellte(r) mf in der Versandabteilung; ~ costs Frachtkosten pl; ~ company, ~ line Schiffahrtsgesellschaft or -linie, Reederei f; ~ lane Schiffahrtsstraße f; ~ losses Verluste pl von or an Schiffen; ~ office (agent's office) Büro nt einer Reedereivertretung; (place where seamen get jobs) Heuerbüro nt; ~ route Schiffahrtslinie f.

ship-: ~shape adj, adv tipptopp (inf); to get everything ~shape alles tipptopp machen (inf); we'll soon have you ~shape again, said the doctor Sie werden bald wieder auf dem Damm (inf) sein, sagte der Arzt; ~shape and Bristol fashion in bester Ordnung; ~way n (support for a ship under construction) Stapel m; (ship canal) (See)kanal, Schiffahrtsweg m; ~wreck 1 n (lit, fig) Schiffbruch m; (fig also) Scheitern nt;

in the ~**wreck** bei dem Schiffbruch; **to suffer** ~**wreck** Schiffbruch erleiden; **2** vt (lit) schiffbrüchig werden lassen; (fig) zum Scheitern bringen, scheitern lassen; **to be** ~**wrecked** (lit) schiffbrüchig sein; (fig) Schiffbruch erleiden, scheitern; ~**wright** n Schiffbauer m; ~**yard** n (Schiffs)werft f.

shire ['ʃaɪə'] n (Brit old) Grafschaft f. ~ **horse** Zugpferd nt.

shirk [ʃɜːk] **1** vt sich drücken vor (+dat), ausweichen (+dat). **2** vi sich drücken. you're ~**ing**! du willst dich drücken!

shirker ['ʃɜːkə'] n Drückeberger(in f) m.

shirking ['ʃɜːkɪŋ] n Drückebergerei f.

shirr [ʃɜː'] vt kräuseln.

shirring ['ʃɜːrɪŋ] n Kräuselarbeit f. ~ **elastic** Gummizug m.

shirt [ʃɜːt] n (men's) (Ober)hemd nt; (Ftbl) Hemd, Trikot nt; (women's: also US ~**waist**) Hemdbluse f. **keep your** ~ **on** (inf) reg dich nicht auf!; **to put one's** ~ **on a horse** (inf) den letzten Pfennig auf ein Pferd setzen; **I'm putting my** ~ **on him to get the job** (inf) ich gehe jede Wette ein, daß er die Stelle bekommt; **to lose the** ~ **off one's back** (inf) alles bis aufs Hemd verlieren (inf); **he'd give you the** ~ **off his back** (inf) er würde einem sein letztes Hemd geben; **he'll have the** ~ **off your back!** (inf) er zieht dich aus bis aufs letzte Hemd! (inf).

shirt: ~ **collar** n Hemdkragen m; ~**front** n Hemdbrust f.

shirting ['ʃɜːtɪŋ] n Hemdenstoff m.

shirt-sleeve ['ʃɜːtsliːv] **1** adj hemdsärmelig. **it's real** ~ **weather now** jetzt kann man wirklich in Hemdsärmeln gehen. **2** n ~**s** pl Hemdsärmel pl; **in his/their** ~**s** in Hemdsärmeln.

shirttail ['ʃɜːtteɪl] n Hemd(en)schoß m.

shirtwaister ['ʃɜːtweɪstə'], (US) **shirtwaist** ['ʃɜːtweɪst] n Hemdblusenkleid nt.

shirty ['ʃɜːtɪ] adj (+er) (esp Brit inf) sauer (inf), verärgert; (as characteristic) griesgrämig (inf). **he got pretty** ~ **about it** er wurde ganz schön sauer (inf); **now don't get** ~ **with me!** nun werd nicht gleich sauer! (inf).

shit¹ [ʃɪt] (vb: pret, ptp ~ or (hum) shat) (vulg) **1** n **(a)** (excrement) Scheiße f (sl). **to have a** ~ scheißen (sl).
(b) (person) Arschloch nt (vulg).
(c) (nonsense) Scheiße f (sl), Scheiß m (sl). **don't give me that** ~! erzähl mir nicht solche Scheiße (sl) or solchen Scheiß (sl)!
(d) ~**s** pl (state of fear) Schiß m (sl), Muffensausen nt (sl); **to have/get the** ~**s** Schiß or Muffensausen haben/kriegen (sl); **it gives me the** ~**s** da krieg' ich Schiß (sl).
(e) to be up ~ **creek (without a paddle)** bis zum Hals in der Scheiße sitzen (vulg); **to be in the** ~ in der Scheiße sitzen (vulg).
2 vi scheißen (sl). **to** ~ **on sb** (inform) jdn verpfeifen (inf); **all offenders will be shat on from a great height** (vulg hum) wer nicht spurt, wird unheimlich zur Sau gemacht (sl) or zusammengeschissen (sl).
3 vr **to** ~ **oneself** sich vollscheißen (vulg); (with fear) sich (dat) vor Angst in die Hose scheißen (sl).
4 interj Scheiße (sl).

shit² [ʃɪt] n (sl: drugs) Shit m (sl).

shite [ʃaɪt] n vir, interj (vulg) see **shit¹**.

shitless ['ʃɪtlɪs] adj: **to be scared** ~ (vulg) sich (dat) vor Angst in die Hosen scheißen (sl).

shitty ['ʃɪtɪ] adj (+er) (sl) beschissen (sl), Scheiß- (sl).

shiver¹ ['ʃɪvə'] **1** n **(a)** (of cold) Schauer m; (of horror also) Schauder m. **a** ~ **of cold** ein kalter Schauer; **a** ~ **ran down my spine** es lief mir kalt den Rücken hinunter; **a little** ~ **of fear ran down my spine** ein Angstschauer überlief mich; **the sight sent** ~**s down my back** bei dem Anblick überlief es mich kalt or lief es mir kalt den Rücken hinunter; **his touch sent** ~**s down her spine** es durchzuckte sie bei seiner Berührung.
(b) (fig) **to get/have the** ~**s** eine Gänsehaut kriegen/haben; **it gives me the** ~**s** ich kriege eine Gänsehaut.
2 vi zittern (with vor +dat); (with fear also) schaudern.

shiver² **1** n Splitter m, Scherbe f. **2** vti zersplittern, zerbrechen.

shivery ['ʃɪvərɪ] adj **to feel** ~ frösteln; **the 'flu made him a bit** ~ wegen seiner Grippe fröstelte er leicht; **she's a** ~ **person** sie friert leicht.

shoal¹ [ʃəʊl] n (shallow place) Untiefe f; (sandbank) Sandbank f.

shoal² n (of fish) Schwarm m. **in** ~**s** (letters, applications etc) massenweise, in Massen; (people) in hellen Scharen; ~**s of applications** Unmengen pl von Bewerbungen.

shock¹ [ʃɒk] n **(a)** (of explosion, impact) Wucht f; (of earthquake) (Erd)stoß m.
(b) (Elec) Schlag m; (Med) (Elektro)schock m. **to get a** ~ einen Schlag bekommen.
(c) (emotional disturbance) Schock, Schlag m; (state) Schock(zustand) m. **to suffer from** ~ einen Schock (erlitten) haben; **to be in (a state of)** ~ unter Schock stehen, sich in einem Schockzustand befinden; **the** ~ **killed him** den Schock hat er nicht überlebt; **rabbits can die of** ~ für ein or bei einem Kaninchen kann ein Schock tödlich sein; **a feeling of** ~ **spread through the town** Entsetzen verbreitete sich in der Stadt; **our feeling is one of** ~ wir sind zutiefst bestürzt; **a** ~ **to one's system** ein Kreislaufschock; **it comes as a** ~ **to hear that ...** ich dachte, mich trifft der Schlag (inf), als ich hörte ...; **he is in for a** ~! (inf) der wird sich wundern (inf); ~ **horror story** (Press, hum) Horrorgeschichte f.
2 vt (affect emotionally) erschüttern, bestürzen; (make indignant) schockieren, empören. **to be** ~**ed by sth** über etw (acc) erschüttert or bestürzt sein; (morally) über etw (acc) schockiert or empört sein; **she is easily** ~**ed** sie ist leicht or schnell schockiert; **I was** ~**ed to hear the news** or **at the news** ich war bestürzt über die Nachricht, die Nachricht bestürzte mich; **he was** ~**ed when they took his passport away** es hat ihn

geschockt, daß man ihm den Paß abgenommen hat (inf); **to** ~ **sb into doing sth** jdm eine solche Angst einjagen, daß er etw tut/unternimmt etc; **to** ~ **sb into acting/out of his lethargy** jdn zum Handeln/aus seiner Lethargie aufrütteln.
3 vi (film, writer etc) schockieren, schocken (inf).

shock² n (Agr) Garbenbündel nt, Hocke f.

shock³ n (also ~ of hair) (Haar)schopf m.

shock absorber ['ʃɒkæb,zɔːbə'] n Stoßdämpfer m.

shocked [ʃɒkt] adj erschüttert, bestürzt; (indignant, outraged) schockiert, empört; (amazed) geschockt (inf). **to be** ~ (Med) unter Schock stehen, in einem Schockzustand sein; **the patient is badly** ~ der Patient hat einen schweren Schock (erlitten).

shocker ['ʃɒkə'] n (inf) Reißer (inf), Schocker (inf) m. **he told me a** ~ **about conditions in jail** er erzählte mir eine Schauergeschichte über die Zustände im Gefängnis; **it's a** ~ das haut einen um (inf); **I have a** ~ **of a cold** ich habe eine grausige (inf) or entsetzliche Erkältung; **he's a** ~ er ist ein ganz Schlimmer (hum); **he's a** ~ **for drink/women** er ist vielleicht ein Schluckspecht (inf)/Weiberheld (inf).

shockheaded ['ʃɒk,hedɪd] adj: **to be** ~ strubbeliges or zotteliges Haar haben, ein Struwwelpeter sein (inf).

shocking ['ʃɒkɪŋ] adj **(a)** news, report erschütternd, schockierend. ~ **pink** knallrosa (inf), pink (Fashion).
(b) (very bad) entsetzlich, furchtbar. **what a** ~ **thing to say/way to behave!** wie kann man bloß so etwas Schreckliches sagen/wie kann man sich bloß so schrecklich benehmen!; **isn't it** ~! es ist doch furchtbar!

shockingly ['ʃɒkɪŋlɪ] adv **(a)** (badly) schrecklich, furchtbar. **to behave** ~ **(towards sb)** sich (jdm gegenüber) haarsträubend or miserabel benehmen. **(b)** (extremely) entsetzlich, schrecklich.

shock: ~**proof** adj stoßfest or -sicher; ~ **tactics** npl (Mil) Stoß- or Durchbruchstaktik f; (fig) Schocktherapie f; ~ **therapy** or **treatment** n Schocktherapie or -behandlung f; ~ **troops** npl Stoßtruppen pl; ~ **wave** n (lit) Druckwelle f; (fig) Erschütterung f, Schock m.

shod [ʃɒd] pret, ptp of **shoe**.

shoddily ['ʃɒdɪlɪ] adv schäbig.

shoddiness ['ʃɒdɪnɪs] n Schäbigkeit f; (of work) Schludrigkeit f; (of goods also) Minderwertigkeit f.

shoddy ['ʃɒdɪ] **1** adj (+er) schäbig; work schludrig; goods also minderwertig. **2** n (cloth) Shoddy nt or m.

shoe [ʃuː] (vb: pret, ptp shod) **1** n **(a)** Schuh m. **I wouldn't like to be in his** ~**s** ich möchte nicht in seiner Haut stecken; **to put oneself in sb's** ~**s** sich in jds Lage (acc) versetzen; **to step into** or **fill sb's** ~**s** an jds Stelle (acc) treten or rücken; **where the** ~ **pinches** (fig) wo mich/uns der Schuh drückt.
(b) (horse~) (Huf)eisen nt.
(c) (brake ~) Bremsschuh m.
(d) (for electric power cable) (Gleit)schuh m; (for mast) Schuh m; (on sledge) Beschlag m.
2 vt horse beschlagen. **to be well-shod** (of person) gut beschuht sein (hum, geh).

shoe: ~**black** n Schuhputzer m; ~**brush** n Schuhbürste f; ~**horn** n Schuhanzieher or -löffel m; ~**lace** n Schnürsenkel m; ~ **leather** n Schuhleder nt; **to wear out one's** ~ **leather** seine Schuhe auftragen; **save** ~ **leather by taking the bus** fahr mit dem Bus und schone deine Schuhsohlen; ~**less** adj ohne Schuhe; ~**maker** n Schuhmacher, Schuster m; ~**mender** n (Flick)schuster m; ~ **polish** n Schuhcreme f; ~**shine** n (US) Schuh(e)putzen nt; **to have a** ~**shine** sich (dat) die Schuhe putzen lassen; ~**shine boy** n Schuhputzer m; ~**shop** n Schuhgeschäft nt; ~**string** n (a) (US: ~lace) Schnürsenkel m, Schnürband nt; (b) (fig) **to live on a** ~**string** von der Hand in den Mund leben; **to do sth on a** ~**string** etw mit ein paar Pfennigen or Mark tun; **the project is run on a** ~**string** das Projekt wird mit ganz wenig Geld finanziert; ~**string budget** n Minibudget nt (inf); ~**tree** n (Schuh)spanner m.

shone [ʃɒn] pret, ptp of **shine**.

shoo [ʃuː] **1** interj sch; (to dog etc) pfui; (to child) husch. **2** vt **to** ~ **sb away** jdn ver- or wegscheuchen; **I** ~**ed the children into the garden** ich scheuchte die Kinder in den Garten.

shook¹ [ʃʊk] pret of **shake**.

shook² n (of corn) Garbenbündel nt, Hocke f.

shoot [ʃuːt] (vb: pret, ptp shot) **1** n **(a)** (Bot) Trieb m; (sprouting from seed, potato etc also) Keim m; (out of ground: of bushes, trees) Schößling, Schoß m; (young branch) Reis nt.
(b) (hunting expedition) Jagd f; (~ing party) Jagdgesellschaft f; (competition) (Wett)schießen nt; (land) (Jagd)revier nt, Jagd f.
2 vt **(a)** (Mil etc) schießen; bullet, gun abfeuern.
(b) person, animal (hit) anschießen; (wound seriously) niederschießen; (kill) erschießen. **to** ~ **sb dead** jdn erschießen; **he shot himself** er hat sich erschossen; **he accidentally shot himself in the foot** er schoß sich (dat) versehentlich in den Fuß; **he was shot in the leg** er wurde ins Bein getroffen; **the bird had been shot through the wing** dem Vogel war ein Flügel durchschossen worden; **he was fatally shot in the neck** ihn traf ein tödlicher Genickschuß; **you'll get me shot** (fig inf) du bringst mich um Kopf und Kragen (inf); **you'll get shot for doing that!** (fig inf) das kann dich Kopf und Kragen kosten! (inf); **people have been shot for less!** (hum inf) es sind schon Leute für weniger an den Galgen gekommen! (inf).
(c) (throw, propel) schleudern. **to** ~ **a question at sb** eine Frage auf jdn abfeuern; **to** ~ **a glance at sb**, **to** ~ **sb a glance** jdm einen (schnellen) Blick zuwerfen; **to** ~ **a line** (inf) aufschneiden, sich wichtig tun (of bei jdm).
(d) to ~ **the bolt** den Riegel vorlegen; **to** ~ **one's bolt** (fig) sein Pulver verschießen; **to** ~ **the rapids** über die Stromschnellen jagen; **to** ~ **the lights** eine Ampel (bei Rot) überfahren.
(e) (Sport) schießen; ball also (with foot) schlagen; (US sl: play) craps, pool spielen. **to** ~ **dice** würfeln, Würfel spielen.

(f) (Phot) film, scene drehen; snapshot schießen; subject aufnehmen.

(g) (sl: inject) drug schießen (sl), drücken (sl).

3 vi **(a)** schießen; (as hunter) jagen. **to ~ to kill** gezielt schießen; (police) einen gezielten Todesschuß/gezielte Todesschüsse abgeben; **don't ~!** nicht schießen!; **stop or I'll ~!** stehenbleiben oder ich schieße!; **to ~ at sb/sth** auf jdn/etw schießen; **to ~ straight/wide** genau/daneben schießen; **to ~ from the hip** aus der Hüfte schießen; **~!** (fig inf) schieß los!

(b) (move rapidly) schießen (inf). **to ~ ahead/into the lead** an die Spitze vorpreschen; **he shot ahead of the other boys in maths** er ließ die anderen Jungen in Mathe weit hinter sich (dat); **the car shot along the track** der Wagen schoß or jagte die Piste entlang; **he shot down the stairs** er schoß or jagte die Treppe hinunter; **to ~ by or past** vorbeischießen or -jagen; **to ~ in** (he)reingeschossen kommen.

(c) (Sport) schießen. **to ~ at goal** aufs Tor schießen.

(d) (pain) **the pain shot up his leg** der Schmerz durchzuckte sein Bein; **~ing pains** stechende Schmerzen pl.

(e) (Bot) treiben.

(f) (Film) drehen.

♦**shoot away 1** vi **(a)** (move rapidly) davonschießen, losjagen. **(b)** (shoot continuously) schießen. **we shot ~ at them for two hours** wir beschossen sie zwei Stunden lang; **~ ~!** (fig inf) schieß los! **2** vt sep wegschießen.

♦**shoot down** vt sep plane abschießen; (fig inf) person fertigmachen (inf); suggestion abschmettern (inf); argument in der Luft zerreißen. **the plane was shot ~ in flames** die Maschine wurde in Brand geschossen und stürzte ab.

♦**shoot off 1** vi **(a)** davonschießen, losjagen (inf).
(b) (sl: ejaculate) abspritzen (vulg).
2 vt sep weapons; gun etc also abfeuern. **to ~ one's mouth ~** (sl) (indiscreetly) tratschen (inf); (boastfully) das Maul aufreißen (sl); **he'll start ~ing his mouth ~ to the police** er wird bei der Polizei anfangen zu quatschen (inf).

♦**shoot out 1** vi (emerge swiftly) herausschießen (of aus).
2 vt sep **(a)** (put out swiftly) hand etc blitzschnell ausstrecken; tongue etc hervor- or herausschnellen (lassen); (inf: eject) an die Luft setzen (inf), raussetzen (inf). **they were shot ~ of the car** sie wurden aus dem Auto geschleudert.
(b) **to ~ it ~** sich (dat) ein (Feuer)gefecht liefern; **the cowboys shot it ~** die Cowboys machten die Sache mit ihren Colts aus (inf); **nobody dared to ~ it ~ with Bad Jake** keiner wagte es, sich mit Bad Jake zu schießen (inf).

♦**shoot up 1** vi (hand, prices, temperature) in die Höhe schnellen; (grow rapidly) (children, plant) in die Höhe schießen; (new towns, buildings etc) aus dem Boden schießen.
2 vt sep **(a) to ~ ~ a town** (inf) in einer Stadt herumballern (inf) or -knallen (inf); **the aerodrome was shot ~** das Flugfeld wurde heftig beschossen; **he was badly shot ~ in the war** er ist im Krieg übel zusammengeschossen worden.
(b) drug schießen (sl).

shooter ['ʃuːtəʳ] n (sl: gun) Ballermann m (sl).

shooting ['ʃuːtɪŋ] n **(a)** (shots) Schießen nt; (by artillery) Feuer nt. **was there any ~?** gab es Schießereien?
(b) (murder, execution) Erschießung f. **there was a ~ last night** gestern nacht ist jemand erschossen worden; **"new outbreak of ~s in Belfast"** „Schießereien in Belfast wieder aufgeflammt"; **the police are investigating the ~** die Polizei untersucht den Mord.
(c) (Sport: Ftbl etc, with guns) Schießen nt; (Hunt) Jagen nt, Jagd f; (~ rights) Jagdrecht(e pl) nt; (land) Jagd f, Jagdrevier nt. **there is good ~ in Scotland** in Schottland kann man gut jagen; **to go ~** auf die Jagd gehen; **good ~!** Weidmannsheil!
(d) (Film) Drehen nt. **~ script** Drehplan m; **~ was interrupted** die Dreharbeiten wurden unterbrochen.

shooting: **~ box** n Jagdhütte f; **~ brake** n (Aut) Kombiwagen m; **~ club** n Schießklub m; **~ gallery** n Schießstand m, Schießbude f; **~ iron** n (US sl) Schießeisen nt (sl), Schießprügel m (sl); **~ jacket** n Jagdrock m; **~ lodge** n see **~ box**; **~ match** n Wett- or Preisschießen nt; **the whole ~ match** (inf) der ganze Laden (inf); **~ party** n Jagdgesellschaft f; **~ range** n Schießplatz m; **~ rights** npl Jagdrecht(e pl) nt; **~ star** n Sternschnuppe f; **~ stick** n Jagdstuhl m; **~ war** n offener or heißer Krieg.

shootout ['ʃuːtaʊt] n Schießerei f.

shop [ʃɒp] **1** n **(a)** Geschäft nt, Laden m; (esp Brit: large store) Kaufhaus nt. **I have to go to the ~s** ich muß einkaufen gehen; **~!** Bedienung!; **to set up ~** ein Geschäft or einen Laden eröffnen; **you've come to the wrong ~** (fig inf) da sind Sie an der falschen Adresse; **all over the ~** (inf) in der ganzen Gegend herum (inf); **to talk ~** über die or von der Arbeit reden; (of professional people also) fachsimpeln; **no ~, please!** wir wollen nicht von der Arbeit reden/keine Fachsimpelei, bitte!
(b) (work~) Werkstatt f; (workers) Arbeiter pl, Arbeiterschaft f.
2 vi einkaufen, Einkäufe machen. **to go ~ping** einkaufen gehen; **we usually spend Saturday mornings ~ping** Samstagvormittag gehen wir immer einkaufen; **to ~ at Macfarlane's!** kaufen Sie bei Macfarlane!; **to ~ for fish** Fisch kaufen gehen.
3 vt (Brit sl) **to ~ sb (to sb)** jdn (bei jdm) verpfeifen (inf).

♦**shop around** vi (lit, fig) sich umsehen (for nach).

shop: **~ assistant** n (Brit) Verkäufer(in f) m; **~ breaker** n Einbrecher m; **~breaking** n Ladeneinbruch m; **~ fitter** n Geschäftsausstatter m; **~fittings** npl Ladeneinrichtungen pl; **~ floor** n **(a)** (place) Produktionsstätte f; (for heavier work) Werkstatt f; **the manager's son started off working on the ~ floor** der Sohn des Direktors hat (ganz unten) in der Fabrik or Produktion angefangen; **on the ~ floor** in der Fabrik etc; **bei** or unter den Arbeitern; **(b)** (workers) Arbeiter pl, Leute pl in der Produktion; **~-floor opinion** die Meinung der

Arbeiter; **~ front** n Ladenfassade f; **~girl** n (Brit) Ladenmädchen nt; **~ hours** npl Öffnungszeiten pl; **~keeper** n Geschäfts- or Ladeninhaber m; **a nation of ~keepers** ein Krämervolk nt; **~lifter** n Ladendieb(in f) m; **~lifting** n Ladendiebstahl m.

shopper ['ʃɒpəʳ] n Käufer(in f) m. **she's a good ~** sie kann gut einkaufen; **the streets were thronged with ~s** in den Straßen drängten sich die Kauflustigen.

shopping ['ʃɒpɪŋ] n **(a)** Einkaufen nt; (goods bought) Sachen pl. **she had her ~ in a plastic bag** sie hatte ihre Einkäufe in einer Plastiktüte; **to do one's ~** einkaufen, Einkäufe machen.

shopping: **~ bag** n Einkaufstasche f; **~ basket** n Einkaufskorb m; **~ cart** n Einkaufswagen m; **~ centre**, (US) **~ center** n Einkaufszentrum nt; **~ list** n Einkaufszettel m; **~ spree** n Einkaufsbummel m; **~ street** n Einkaufsstraße f.

shop: **~-soiled** adj clothes, furniture, wallpaper angestaubt, angeschmutzt; goods, material leicht angestoßen or beschädigt; **~ steward** n (gewerkschaftlicher) Vertrauensmann m (im Betrieb); **~ talk** n Reden nt über die Arbeit; (of professional people also) Fachsimpelei f; **~walker** n (Brit) Aufsichtsperson (form), Aufsicht f; **~ window** n (lit, fig) Schaufenster nt; (glass also) Schaufensterscheibe f; **~-worn** adj goods, furniture etc leicht beschädigt.

shore¹ [ʃɔːʳ] n **(a)** (sea, lake ~) Ufer, Gestade (liter) nt; (beach) Strand m. **these ~s** (fig) dieses Land, diese Gestade pl (liter); **he returned to his native ~s** er kehrte zurück zu heimatlichen Gefilden; **a house on the ~s of the lake** ein Haus am Seeufer; **no invader has since set foot on these ~s** seitdem hat kein Eroberer mehr diesen Boden betreten.
(b) (land) Land nt. **on ~** an Land.

shore² n (Min, Naut) Stützbalken m, Strebe(balken m) f. **2** vt (also ~ up) (ab)stützen; (fig) stützen.

shore: **~ dinner** n (US) Meeresfrüchte pl; **~ leave** n (Naut) Landurlaub m; **~line** n Wasserlinie, Uferlinie f; **~ pass** n (Naut) Landurlaubsschein m; **~ patrol** n (US) Küstenstreife, Küstenpatrouille f (der US-Marine); **~ward(s)** **1** adj wind See-; **in a ~ward(s) direction** in Richtung Küste or Land, landwärts; **2** adv landwärts, zum Land (hin).

shorn [ʃɔːn] **1** ptp of **shear. 2** adj **(a) to be ~ of sth** einer Sache (gen) entkleidet sein. **(b)** sheep geschoren; head also kahlgeschoren. **her ~ locks** ihr kurzgeschorenes Haar.

short [ʃɔːt] **1** adj (+er) **(a)** kurz; steps also, person klein; waist (of dress) hoch. **a ~ way off** nicht weit entfernt; **to be ~ in the leg** (person) kurze Beine haben; (trousers) zu kurz sein; **to be in ~ trousers** in kurzen Hosen herumlaufen; (fig) ein kleiner Junge sein; **to have/get sb by the ~ and curlies** (inf) jdn am Wickel haben/kriegen (inf); **a ~ time ago** vor kurzer Zeit, vor kurzem; **in a ~ time or while** in Kürze, in kurzer Zeit; **time is getting/is ~** die Zeit wird/ist knapp; **it took us only one ~ hour** wir brauchten nur eine knappe Stunde dazu; **to take the ~ view** die Sache auf kurze Sicht betrachten; **in ~ order** (US inf) sofort; **~ drink** Kurze(r) (inf), Schnaps m.
(b) (Ling) vowel, syllable kurz; (unstressed) unbetont.
(c) (brief) kurz. **~ and sweet** schön kurz, kurz und ergreifend (iro); **the ~ answer is that** he refused kurz gesagt, er lehnte ab; **in ~** kurz gesagt; **she's called Pat for ~** sie wird kurz or einfach Pat genannt; **Pat is ~ for Patricia** Pat steht für or ist die Kurzform von Patricia.
(d) (curt) reply knapp; (rude) barsch, schroff; manner, person schroff, kurz angebunden (inf). **to have a ~ temper** unbeherrscht sein; **his ~ temper** seine Unbeherrschtheit; **to be ~ with sb** jdn schroff behandeln, kurz angebunden sein (inf).
(e) (insufficient) zuwenig inv; rations knapp. **to be ~** supply knapp sein; (Comm) beschränkt lieferbar sein; **to be ~ (in ~ supply)** knapp sein; (shot, throw) zu kurz sein, nicht weit genug sein; **we are (five/£3) ~, we are ~ (of five/£3)** wir haben (fünf/£ 3) zuwenig, uns (dat) fehlen fünf/£ 3; **it's five/£3 ~** es fehlen fünf/£ 3; **we are ~ of books/staff** wir haben zuwenig Bücher/Personal; **we are not ~ of volunteers** wir haben genug Freiwillige, uns fehlt es nicht an Freiwilligen; **to be ~ of time** wenig Zeit haben; **I'm a bit ~ (of cash)** (inf) ich bin etwas knapp bei Kasse (inf); **we are £2,000 ~ of our target** wir liegen £ 2.000 unter unserem Ziel; **we are not far ~ of our destination** now wir sind nicht mehr weit von unserem Ziel entfernt; **not far/much ~ of £100** nicht viel weniger als £ 100, beinahe £ 100, knapp unter £ 100; **to be ~ on experience/examples** wenig Erfahrung/Beispiele haben; **to give sb ~ change** jdm zuwenig herausgeben or zuwenig Wechselgeld geben; see **measure**.
(f) (Fin) sale ohne Deckung, ungedeckt, Blanko-. **~ stock** auf Baisse gekaufte Aktien.
(g) pastry mürbe.

2 adv **(a)** (below the expected amount) **to fall ~** (arrow etc) zu kurz landen; (shot) zu kurz sein; (supplies etc) nicht ausreichen; **that's where the book falls ~** daran fehlt es dem Buch; **to fall ~ of sth** etw nicht erreichen; **of expectations** nicht erfüllen; **it fell 10 metres ~ of the target** es fehlten 10 Meter zum Ziel, es war 10 Meter zu kurz; **it falls far ~ of what we require** das bleibt weit hinter unseren Bedürfnissen zurück; (in quantity) das bleibt weit unter unseren Bedürfnissen; **production has fallen ~ by 100 tons** die Produktion ist um 100 Tonnen zu niedrig; **to go ~ (of money/food etc)** zuwenig (Geld/zu essen etc) haben; **the parents went ~ of food so that the children could eat** die Eltern haben an sich (dat) selbst gespart, damit die Kinder zu essen hatten; **they never let the children go ~** sie ließen es den Kindern an nichts fehlen; **we are running ~ (of petrol/supplies/time)** wir haben nicht mehr viel (Benzin/Vorräte/Zeit); **I'm running ~ of ideas** mir gehen die Ideen aus; **my patience is running ~** meine Geduld ist bald zu Ende; **sugar/petrol is running ~** Zucker/Benzin ist knapp; **to sell sb ~ (in shop)** jdm zuwenig geben; (betray, cheat) jdn betrügen; **to sell ~** (Fin) ungedeckt or ohne Deckung verkaufen; see **cut, bring up**.

(b) (*abruptly, suddenly*) plötzlich, abrupt. **to pull up** *or* **stop ~** (*while driving*) plötzlich *or* abrupt anhalten; (*while walking also*) plötzlich *or* abrupt stehenbleiben; **to stop ~** (*while talking*) sich plötzlich *or* unvermittelt unterbrechen; **to stop a conversation ~** eine Unterhaltung plötzlich *or* unvermittelt abbrechen; **to stop sb ~** jdn unterbrechen; **I'd stop ~ of** *or* **at murder** vor Mord würde ich haltmachen; **he stopped ~ of** actually calling me a liar er ging nicht soweit, mich tatsächlich einen Lügner zu nennen; **to be caught ~** (*inf*) (*unprepared*) überrascht werden; (*without money, supplies*) zu knapp (dran) sein; (*need the toilet*) dringend mal müssen (*inf*); **to catch sb ~** (*inf*) jdn in einer Verlegenheit antreffen; **to be caught ~ by sth** auf etw (*acc*) nicht vorbereitet sein.

(c) **~ of** (*except*) außer (+*dat*); **it is nothing ~ of robbery** das ist glatter Diebstahl; **nothing ~ of a revolution can ... nur eine Revolution kann ...; it's little ~ of madness** das grenzt an Wahnsinn; **it's little ~ of suicide** das kommt ja Selbstmord gleich; **I don't see what you can do ~ of asking him yourself** ich sehe keine andere Möglichkeit, außer daß *or* als daß Sie ihn selbst fragen; **~ of telling him a lie ...** außer ihn zu belügen ...

3 *n* (~ *circuit*) Kurzschluß, Kurze(r) (*inf*) *m*; (*inf: ~ drink*) Kurze(r) *m* (*inf*); (*inf: ~ film*) Kurzfilm *m*; see **long**².

4 *vt* (*Elec*) kurzschließen.

5 *vi* (*Elec*) einen Kurzschluß haben.

shortage [ˈʃɔːtɪdʒ] *n* (*of goods, objects*) Knappheit *f no pl* (*of an* +*dat*); (*of people*) Mangel *m no pl* (*of an* +*dat*). **the housing ~** die Wohnungsknappheit; **a ~ of staff** ein Mangel *m* an Arbeitskräften, Personalmangel *m*; **in times of ~** in Zeiten der Knappheit; **there are always ~s** irgend etwas ist immer knapp; **there is no ~ of advice/water/money** es fehlt nicht an guten Ratschlägen/Wasser/Geld.

short: **~ arse** *n* (*sl*) (kleiner) Pimpf (*inf*), Knirps (*inf*), Murkel (*dial inf*) *m*; **~bread** *n* Shortbread *nt*, ≈ Butterkeks *m*; **~cake** *n* (*Brit: ~bread*) Butterkeks *m*; (*US: sponge*) Biskuittörtchen *nt*; **strawberry ~cake** Erdbeertörtchen *nt*; **~-change** *vt* **to ~-change sb** (*lit*) jdm zuwenig Wechselgeld geben, jdm zuwenig herausgeben; (*fig inf*) jdn übers Ohr hauen (*inf*); **~-circuit 1** *n* Kurzschluß *m*; **2** *vt* kurzschließen; (*fig: bypass*) umgehen; **3** *vi* einen Kurzschluß haben; **~coming** *n* (*esp pl*) Mangel *m*; (*of person*) Fehler *m*; **~crust** *n* (*also ~crust pastry*) Mürbeteig *m*; **~ cut** *n* Abkürzung *f*; (*fig*) Schnellverfahren *nt*; (*easy solution*) Patentlösung *f*; **there's no ~ cut to success** der Erfolg fällt einem nicht in den Schoß; **~-dated** *adj* (*Fin*) stock kurzfristig.

shorten [ˈʃɔːtn] **1** *vt* (a) verkürzen; *dress, rope* kürzer machen, kürzen; *book, programme, letter, syllabus etc* kürzen; *odds* verringern; *sail* reffen. (b) *pastry* Fett beigeben (+*dat*). **2** *vi* (*evenings, days*) kürzer werden; (*odds*) sich verringern.

shortening [ˈʃɔːtnɪŋ] *n* (*Cook*) (Back)fett *nt*.

short: **~fall** *n* Defizit *nt*; **~-haired** *adj* kurzhaarig; **~hand** *n* Kurzschrift, Stenographie *f*; **in ~hand** in Kurzschrift; **to write ~hand** stenographieren; **to take sth down in ~hand** etw stenographieren; **~-handed** *adj* **to be ~-handed** zuwenig Personal haben; **~hand notebook** *n* Stenoblock *m*; **~hand notes** *npl* stenographische Notizen *pl*; **~hand typist** *n* Stenotypist(in *f*) *m*; **~hand writer** *n* Stenograph(in *f*) *m*; **~ haul** *n* Nahtransport *m*; **~-haul jet** *n* Kurzstreckenflugzeug *nt*; **~horn** *n* Kurzhornrind, Shorthorn *nt*; **~horn cattle** Kurzhornrinder *pl*.

shortie [ˈʃɔːtɪ] *n* (a) (*inf: also ~ nightie*) Shorty *nt*, kurzes Nachthemd. (b) *see* **shorty**.

shortish [ˈʃɔːtɪʃ] *adj* ziemlich kurz; (*scarce*) ziemlich knapp.

short: **~ list** *n* (*esp Brit*) Auswahlliste *f*; **to be on the ~ list** in der engeren Wahl sein; **~-list** *vt* (*esp Brit*) **to ~-list sb** jdn in die engere Wahl nehmen *or* ziehen; **he has not been ~-listed** er ist nicht in die engere Wahl gekommen; **~-lived** *adj* (*lit, fig*) kurzlebig; *protests, attempts* nicht lange andauernd; **to be ~-lived** (*success, happiness*) von kurzer Dauer sein.

shortly [ˈʃɔːtlɪ] *adv* (a) (*soon*) bald, in Kürze; *after, before, afterwards* kurz. (b) (*briefly*) kurz. (c) (*curtly*) barsch.

shortness [ˈʃɔːtnɪs] *n* (a) Kürze *f*; (*of person*) Kleinheit *f*. **~ of sight/breath** Kurzsichtigkeit/Kurzatmigkeit *f*. (b) (*curtness*) Schroffheit, Barschheit *f*. (c) (*of supplies, money*) Knappheit *f*.

short: **~-order** *adj* (*US*) dishes Schnell-; *cook* im Schnellimbiß; **~ pastry** *n* Mürbeteig *m*; **~-range** *adj* gun Nahkampf-; *missile, aircraft* Kurzstrecken-; (*fig*) plans kurzfristig; **~-range weather forecast** Wetterbericht *m* für die nächsten Tage.

shorts [ʃɔːts] *npl* (a) (*short trousers*) Shorts *pl*, kurze Hose(n *pl*). (b) (*esp US: underpants*) Unterhose *f*.

short: **~-sighted** *adj*, **~-sightedly** *adv* (*lit, fig*) kurzsichtig; **~-sightedness** *n* (*lit, fig*) Kurzsichtigkeit *f*; **~-sleeved** *adj* kurzärmelig; **~-staffed** *adj* **to be ~-staffed** zuwenig Personal haben; **~ story** *n* Kurzgeschichte, Short story, Erzählung *f*; **a ~-story writer** ein Kurzgeschichtenautor *m*; **~-tempered** *adj* (*in general*) unbeherrscht; (*in a bad temper*) gereizt; **to be ~-tempered with sb** mit jdm ungeduldig sein; **~-temperedly** *adv* unbeherrscht; *reply* unwirsch, ungeduldig; **~ term** *n* for the **~ term** auf kurze Frist gesehen, vorläufig; **plans for the ~ term** kurzfristige Pläne; **in the ~ term** auf kurze Sicht; **~-term** *adj* kurzfristig; **~ time** *n* Kurzarbeit *f*; **to be on ~ time, to work ~ time** kurzarbeiten, Kurzarbeit haben; **~ ton** *n* Tonne von 2000 Pounds = 907,18 *kg*; **~-waisted** *adj* person mit kurzer Taille; *coat* hochtailliert; **to be ~-waisted** eine kurze/hohe Taille haben; **~-wave 1** *n* (*also ~wave radio*) Kurzwelle *f*; **2** *adj* transmission auf Kurzwelle; **a ~wave radio** ein Kurzwellenempfänger *m*; **~-winded** *adj* (*breathless*) kurzatmig.

shorty [ˈʃɔːtɪ] *n* (*inf*) Kleine(r) *mf*, Knirps *m* (*inf*).

shot¹ [ʃɒt] **1** pret, ptp of **shoot**.

2 *n* (a) (*from gun, bow etc*) Schuß *m*. **to fire** *or* **take a ~ at sb/sth** einen Schuß auf jdn/etw abfeuern *or* abgeben; **a ~ across the bows** (*lit, fig*) ein Schuß vor den Bug; **to exchange ~s** sich (*dat*) einen Schußwechsel liefern; **the first ~s in the election campaign** (*fig*) die ersten scharfen Schüsse im Wahlkampf; **to**

call the ~s (*fig sl*) das Sagen haben (*inf*); *see* **long ~, parting**.

(b) (*projectile*) Kugel *f*; (*no pl: lead ~*) Schrot(kugeln *pl*) *m*.

(c) (*person*) Schütze *m*; *see* **big ~**.

(d) (*attempt*) Versuch *m*. **at the first ~** beim ersten Versuch, auf Anhieb; **to make** *or* **take a ~ at (it)** (*try*) es (mal) versuchen; (*guess*) (auf gut Glück) raten; **I had a ~ at waterskiing** ich habe auch mal versucht, Wasserski zu laufen; **it's your ~** du bist dran; *see* **dark**.

(e) (*space-~*) (Raum)flug *m*; (*launch*) Start *m*.

(f) (*inf: quickly*) **like a ~** run away, be off wie der Blitz (*inf*); **do sth** sofort; **agree** sofort, ohne zu überlegen.

(g) (*injection*) Spritze *f*; (*immunization*) Impfung *f*; (*of alcohol*) Schuß *m*. **he gave him a ~ of morphine** er gab ihm eine Morphiumspritze; **a ~ of rum** ein Schuß *m* Rum; **to give sb/sth a ~ in the arm** (*fig*) jdm/einer Sache eine Vitaminspritze geben.

(h) (*Phot*) Aufnahme *f*. **out of ~** nicht im Bild.

(i) (*Sport*) (*Ftbl, Hockey etc*) Schuß *m*; (*throw*) Wurf *m*; (*Tennis, Golf*) Schlag *m*. **to take a ~ at goal** aufs Tor schießen.

(j) (*~-putting*) **the ~** (*discipline*) Kugelstoßen *nt*; (*weight*) die Kugel; **to put the ~** kugelstoßen.

shot² *adj* (a) (*variegated*) durchzogen, durchschossen (*with* mit); *silk* eingeschossen, changierend. (b) (*inf: rid*) **to be/get ~ of sb/sth** jdn/etw los sein/loswerden.

shot: **~gun** *n* Schrotflinte *f*; **~gun wedding** *n* Mußheirat *f*; **~-put** *n* (*event*) Kugelstoßen *nt*; (*throw*) Wurf, Stoß *m*; **~-putter** *n* Kugelstoßer(in *f*) *m*; **~ tower** *n* Schrotturm *m*.

should [ʃʊd] pret of **shall**, modal aux vb (a) (*expressing duty, advisability, command*) I/you/he/we/you/they **~ do that** ich sollte/du solltest/er sollte/wir sollten/ihr solltet/sie sollten das tun; **you ~n't do that** Sie sollten das nicht tun; **I ~ have done it** ich hätte es tun sollen *or* müssen; **I ~n't have done it** ich hätte es nicht tun sollen *or* dürfen; **all is as it ~ be** alles ist so, wie es sein sollte *or* muß; **which is as it ~ be** und so soll(te) es auch sein; **he ~ know that it's wrong to lie** er sollte *or* müßte wissen, daß man nicht lügen darf; **you really ~ see that film** den Film sollten *or* müssen Sie wirklich sehen; **~ I go too?** yes you **~** sollte ich auch gehen? — ja, das sollten Sie schon; **was it a good film? — I ~ think it was** war der Film gut? — und ob; **he's coming to apologize — I ~ think so** er will sich entschuldigen — das möchte ich auch meinen *or* hoffen; **... and I ~ know ...** und ich müßte es ja wissen; **how ~ I know?** woher soll ich das wissen?

(b) (*expressing probability*) **he ~ be there by now** er müßte eigentlich schon da sein; **they ~ arrive tomorrow** sie müßten morgen ankommen; **this ~ be enough** das müßte eigentlich reichen; **why ~ he suspect me?** warum sollte er mich verdächtigen?; **this book ~ help you** dieses Buch wird Ihnen bestimmt helfen; **this ~ be good!** (*inf*) das wird bestimmt gut!

(c) (*in tentative statements*) **I ~n't like to say** das möchte ich nicht gern sagen; **I ~ hardly have called him an idiot** ich hätte ihn wohl kaum einen Idioten genannt; **I ~ think there were about 40** ich würde etwa 40 schätzen; **~ I open the window?** soll ich das Fenster aufmachen?; **I ~ like to disagree** da möchte ich widersprechen; **I ~ like to know** ich wüßte gern, ich möchte gern wissen; **I ~ like to apply for the job** ich würde mich gern um die Stelle bewerben; **thanks, I ~ like to** danke, gern.

(d) (*expressing surprise*) **who ~ I see/~ it be but Anne!** und wen sehe ich/und wer war's? Anne!; **what ~ he do next but propose to me** und was tut er? er macht mir einen Heiratsantrag!; **why ~ he want to know/do that?** warum will er das wohl wissen/machen?; **why ~ he have done it, if ...?** warum hat er es dann gemacht, wenn ...?

(e) (*subjunc, cond*) I/you/he/we/you/they **~ go if ...** ich würde/du würdest/er würde/wir würden/ihr würdet/sie würden gehen, wenn ...; **we ~ have come if ...** wir wären gekommen, wenn ...; **I ~ not have come if ...** ich wäre nicht gekommen, wenn ...; **it seems unbelievable that he ~ have failed/be so young** es scheint unglaublich, daß er versagt hat/so jung ist; **I don't know why he ~ behave so strangely** ich weiß nicht, warum er sich so eigenartig benimmt; **I don't see why he ~n't have paid by now** ich verstehe nicht, warum er bis jetzt noch nicht bezahlt hat; **if they ~ send for me** wenn *or* falls sie nach mir schicken sollten; **if he ~ come, ~ he come** falls er kommen sollte, sollte er kommen; **~ it not be true** sollte das nicht wahr sein; **I ~n't be surprised if he comes** *or* **came** *or* **were to come** ich wäre nicht *or* keineswegs überrascht, wenn er kommen würde *or* käme; **I ~n't (do it)** if I were you ich würde das an Ihrer Stelle nicht tun; **I ~n't worry about it** ich würde mir darüber keine Gedanken machen; **it is necessary that he ~ be told** es ist nötig, daß man es ihm sagt; **unless he ~ change his mind** falls er es sich (*dat*) nicht anders überlegt.

shoulder [ˈʃəʊldəʳ] **1** *n* (a) (*of person, animal*) Schulter *f*; (*of bird*) Schultergürtel *m*; (*of meat*) Bug *m*; (*of pork*) Schulter *f*, Schulterstück *nt*; (*of garment*) Schulter(partie) *f*. **to shrug one's ~s** mit den Schultern *or* Achseln zucken; **to have broad ~s** (*lit*) breite Schultern haben; (*fig also*) einen breiten Rücken *or* Buckel (*inf*) haben; **to put one's ~ to the wheel** (*fig*) sich ins Zeug legen; **to cry** *or* **weep on sb's ~** sich an jds Brust (*dat*) ausweinen; **a ~ to cry on** jemand, bei dem man sich ausweinen kann; **~ to ~** Schulter an Schulter; *see* **cold, rub, straight**.

(b) (*of mountain*) Schulter *f*; (*of road*) Seitenstreifen *m*, Bankett *nt*; (*of vase, bottle*) Ausbuchtung *f*.

2 *vt* (a) schultern, auf die Schulter nehmen; (*fig*) responsibilities, blame, task auf sich (*acc*) nehmen; *expense* tragen. **~ arms!** (*Mil*) das Gewehr über!; **the fans ~ed him off the pitch** die Fans trugen ihn auf den Schultern vom Platz.

(b) (*push*) (mit der Schulter) stoßen. **to ~ sb aside** (*lit*) jdn zur Seite stoßen; (*fig*) jdn beiseite drängen; **to ~ one's way through (the crowd)** sich durch die Menge drängen *or* boxen.

shoulder: **~ bag** *n* Umhängetasche *f*; **~ blade** *n* Schulterblatt *nt*; **~ flash** *n* (*Mil*) Dienstgradabzeichen, Schulterstück *nt*; **~-high** *adv* **to carry sb ~-high** jdn auf den Schultern tragen;

to stand ~-high to sb jdm bis an die Schultern reichen; **~-length** adj hair schulterlang; **~ loop** n Dienstgradabzeichen nt; **~ pad** n Schulterpolster nt; **~ strap** n (Mil) Schulterklappe f; (of dress) Träger m; (of satchel, bag etc) (Schulter)riemen m.

shouldn't ['ʃʊdnt] contr of **should not**.

shout [ʃaʊt] **1** n Ruf, Schrei m. **a ~ of protest/joy/pain** ein Protestruf m/Freuden-/Schmerzensschrei m; **a ~ of excitement** ein aufgeregter Schrei; **~s of applause/laughter** Beifallsrufe pl/Lachsalven pl, brüllendes Gelächter; **to give a ~** einen Schrei ausstoßen; **to give sb a ~, give me a ~ when you're ready** (inf) sag Bescheid, wenn du fertig bist; **his voice rose to a ~** seine Stimme steigerte sich bis zum Brüllen; **it's my ~** (inf: turn) ich bin dran.

2 vt schreien; (call) rufen; order brüllen; protest, disapproval etc laut(stark) kundtun. **to ~ abuse at sb** jdn (laut) beschimpfen; **to ~ a warning to sb** jdm eine Warnung zurufen.

3 vi (call out) rufen; (very loudly) schreien; (angrily, commanding) brüllen. **to ~ for sb/sth** nach jdm/etw rufen or schreien; **she ~ed for Jane to come** sie rief, Jane solle kommen; **to ~ at sb** (mit jdm) schreien; (abusively) jdn anschreien or anbrüllen; **don't ~!** schrei nicht (so)!; **to ~ to sb** jdm zurufen; **he ~ed to me to open the door** er rief mir zu, ich sollte die Tür öffnen; **to ~ for help** um Hilfe rufen; **to ~ for joy** einen Freudenschrei/Freudenschreie ausstoßen; **to ~ with laughter** vor Lachen brüllen; **it was nothing to ~ about** (inf) es war nichts umwerfend.

4 vr **to ~ oneself hoarse/silly** sich heiser/krumm und dusselig (inf) schreien.

♦**shout down** vt sep person niederbrüllen; play ausbuhen.

♦**shout out 1** vi einen Schrei ausstoßen; (in pain, rage, protest) aufschreien. **to ~ ~ in delight** Freudenrufe/einen Freudenruf ausstoßen; **~ ~ when you're ready** ruf, wenn du fertig bist. **2** vt sep ausrufen; order brüllen.

shouting ['ʃaʊtɪŋ] n (act) Schreien nt; (sound) Geschrei nt. **it's all over bar the ~** (inf) es ist so gut wie gelaufen (inf).

shove [ʃʌv] **1** n Schubs(er) (inf), Stoß m. **to give sb a ~** jdn schubsen (inf) or stoßen; **to give sth a ~** etw rücken; door gegen etw stoßen; ball etw anstoßen; car etw anschieben; **one more ~** noch einmal schieben, noch einen Ruck.

2 vt **(a)** (push) schieben; (with one short push) stoßen, schubsen (inf); (jostle) drängen. **stop shoving me** hör auf zu drängeln or mich zu schubsen (inf); **to ~ sb against a wall** jdn gegen die Wand drücken; **to ~ sb off the pavement** jdn vom Bürgersteig herunterschubsen (inf); jdn vom Bürgersteig herunterdrängen; **to ~ a door open** eine Tür aufstoßen.

(b) (inf: put) **to ~ sth on(to) sth** etw auf etw (acc) werfen (inf); **to ~ sth in(to) sth/between sth** etw in etw (acc)/zwischen etw (acc) stecken; **he ~d his head through the window** er steckte den Kopf durchs Fenster; **he ~d a book into my hand** er drückte mir ein Buch in die Hand.

3 vi stoßen; (to move sth) schieben; (jostle) drängeln.

♦**shove about** or **around** vt sep (inf) herumstoßen.

♦**shove away** vt sep (inf) wegstoßen, wegschubsen (inf).

♦**shove back** vt sep (inf) chair etc zurückschieben; sb, plate zurückstoßen, zurückschubsen (inf); (replace) zurücktun; (into pocket etc) wieder hineinstecken.

♦**shove down** vt sep (inf) (put) hinlegen, hinwerfen (inf); (write) hinschmieren (inf), aufschreiben.

♦**shove off 1** vt sep (Naut) vom Ufer abstoßen. **2** vi **(a)** (in boat) ablegen. **(b)** (inf: leave) abschieben (inf).

♦**shove on** vt sep (inf) coat anziehen; hat aufsetzen; record auflegen.

♦**shove out** vt sep boat abstoßen; person rausschmeißen (inf).

♦**shove over** (inf) **1** vt sep rüberwerfen (inf), rüberschmeißen (inf). **2** vi (also shove up) rutschen.

shove-halfpenny [,ʃʌv'heɪpnɪ] n Spiel, bei dem Münzen in auf einer Platte gezeichnete Felder gestoßen werden.

shovel ['ʃʌvl] **1** n Schaufel f; (with long handle also) Schippe f; (on power-~) Löffel m; (power-~) Löffelbagger m. **a ~ of coal** eine Schaufel Kohle.

2 vt schaufeln; coal, snow also schippen; path schaufeln. **to ~ food into one's mouth** (inf) Essen in sich (acc) hineinschaufeln; **to ~ a path clear of snow** einen Pfad vom Schnee freischaufeln.

shovelful ['ʃʌvlfʊl] n Schaufel f. **a ~ of coal** eine Schaufel Kohle; **they dug up ~s** of potatoes sie gruben schaufelweise or haufenweise Kartoffeln aus.

show [ʃəʊ] (vb: pret ~ed, ptp shown) **1** n **(a)** (display) Schau f. **a ~ of roses** eine Rosenpracht; **the dahlias make a fine ~ this year** die Dahlien sind dieses Jahr eine Pracht; **~ of force** or **power** Machtdemonstration f; **~ of hands** Handzeichen, Hand(er)heben nt.

(b) (outward appearance) Schau f; (trace) Spur f; (of hatred, affection) Kundgebung f. **it's just for ~** das ist nur zur Schau da; (pretence) das ist nur Schau (inf); **to do sth for ~** etw tun, um Eindruck zu schinden (inf) or zu machen; **it's all done for ~** das ist alles nur dazu da, um Eindruck zu machen; **to make a great ~ of being impressed/overworked/pleased** sich (dat) ganz den Anschein geben, beeindruckt/überarbeitet/erfreut zu sein; **to make a great ~ of resistance/sympathy** ganz Ablehnung/Mitleid sein; **they made a great ~ of their wealth** sie protzten mit ihrem Reichtum (inf); **without any ~ of emotion** ohne irgendwelche Gefühle zu zeigen; **it was all ~** es war alles nur Schau (inf); **to be fond of ~** gerne prunken.

(c) (exhibition) Ausstellung f. **flower/dog/fashion ~** Blumen-/Hunde-/Modenschau f; **to be on ~** ausgestellt or zu sehen sein.

(d) (Theat) Aufführung f; (TV, variety or pop ~) Show f; (Rad) Sendung f; (Film) Vorstellung f. **to go to a ~** ins Theater gehen; **the ~ must go on** es muß trotz allem weitergehen; **on with the ~!** anfangen!; (continue) weitermachen!; **to stop the ~**

(lit) die Aufführung unterbrechen; (fig) alle plötzlich innehalten lassen; see steal.

(e) (esp Brit inf) (jolly) **good ~!** ausgezeichnet!, bravo!; **bad ~!** schwaches Bild (inf); (what a pity) so ein Pech!; **to put up a good/poor ~** eine gute/schwache Leistung zeigen; **to make a poor ~** eine traurige Gestalt abgeben; **it's a pretty poor ~ when** ... das ist vielleicht traurig or ein schwaches Bild (inf), wenn ...

(f) (inf: undertaking, organization) Laden m (inf). **he runs the ~** er schmeißt hier den Laden (inf); **to give the (whole) ~ away** alles verraten.

2 vt **(a)** zeigen; (at exhibition also) ausstellen; (demonstrate) dog also vorführen; slides, film also vorführen; passport, ticket vorzeigen. **to ~ sth, to ~ sth to sb** jdm etw zeigen; **~ me how to do it** zeigen Sie mir, wie man das macht; **it's been ~n on television** das kam im Fernsehen; **the film was first ~n in 1978** der Film wurde 1978 uraufgeführt; **to ~ one's face** sich zeigen; **he had nothing to ~ for it** er hatte am Ende nichts vorzuweisen; **there was nothing to ~ for it** man/er etc hatte immer noch nichts vorzuweisen; **he has nothing to ~ for all his effort** seine ganze Mühe hat nichts gebracht; **I'll ~ him!** (inf) dem werd' ich's zeigen!; **that ~ed him!** (inf) dem habe ich's aber gezeigt! (inf); see hand, heel¹.

(b) (register) (an)zeigen; loss, profit haben, verzeichnen; rise in numbers aufzeigen; (thermometer, speedometer) stehen auf (+dat); (calendar) zeigen. **it ~s that** ... es zeigt, daß ...; **as ~n in the illustration/diagram** wie in der Illustration/Skizze dargestellt; **the roads are ~n in red** die Straßen sind rot (eingezeichnet); **to ~ a speed of 80 miles per hour** eine Geschwindigkeit von 80 Meilen pro Stunde anzeigen; **what time does your watch ~?** wie spät ist es nach Ihrer Uhr?; **the dial will ~ red if** ... der Zeiger zeigt auf Rot, wenn ...

(c) (indicate) zeigen; (prove) beweisen; kindness, favour erweisen; courage also, loyalty, taste, tact, intelligence beweisen; respect bezeigen; proof erbringen. **to ~ one's gratitude** sich dankbar zeigen; **this ~s him to be a thief** das zeigt/beweist, daß er ein Dieb ist; **I hope I have ~n how silly it is** ich habe hoffentlich (auf)gezeigt, wie dumm das ist; **it all** or **just goes to ~ that** ... das zeigt doch nur, daß ...

(d) (reveal) zeigen. **that dress ~s her bra** bei dem Kleid sieht man ihren BH; **it was ~ing signs of rain** es sah nach Regen aus; **it ~ed signs of having been used** man sah, daß es gebraucht worden war; **to ~ signs of wear/tiredness** Abnutzungserscheinungen pl/Ermüdungserscheinungen pl zeigen; **~ a leg!** (inf) raus aus den Federn! (inf); **she's beginning to ~ her age** man sieht ihr allmählich das Alter an; **the carpet ~s the dirt** auf dem Teppich sieht man den Schmutz.

(e) (direct) zeigen. **to ~ sb the way** jdm den Weg zeigen; **to ~ sb in/out** jdn hereinbringen/hinausbringen or -begleiten; **to ~ sb out of/into a room** jdn hinausbegleiten, jdn aus dem Zimmer begleiten/jdn hereinbringen, jdn ins Zimmer bringen; **to ~ sb to his seat/to the door** jdn an seinen Platz/an die or zur Tür bringen; **to ~ sb over** or **round the house** jdm das (ganze) Haus zeigen; **they were ~n over** or **round the factory** ihnen wurde die Fabrik gezeigt, sie wurden in der Fabrik herumgeführt.

3 vi **(a)** (be visible) zu sehen sein, sichtbar sein; (petticoat etc) vorsehen, rausgucken (inf); (film) gezeigt werden, laufen; (exhibit: artist) ausstellen. **the dirt doesn't ~** man sieht den Schmutz nicht; **his anger ~ed in his eyes** man sah ihm den Ärger an den Augen an; **don't let your anger ~** lassen Sie sich (dat) den Ärger nicht anmerken!; **the tulips are beginning to ~** die Tulpen kommen langsam heraus; **his bad leg ~s when he walks** beim Gehen merkt man, daß er ein schlimmes Bein hat; **it only ~s when** ... (be visible) man sieht es nur, wenn ...; (be noticed) man merkt es nur, wenn ...; **to ~ through** durchkommen; **the house ~s through the gap** durch den Spalt kann man das Haus sehen; **he didn't ~** (inf) er hat sich nicht blicken lassen (inf).

(b) (prove) **it just goes to ~!** da sieht man's mal wieder!

(c) (Horse-racing) sich plazieren.

4 vr **to ~ oneself** sich blicken lassen (inf); **to ~ oneself (to be) incompetent** sich (als) unfähig erweisen; **he ~ed himself to be a coward** es zeigte sich, daß er ein Feigling war; **it ~s itself in his speech** das merkt man an seiner Sprache.

♦**show off 1** vi angeben (to, in front of vor +dat).

2 vt sep **(a)** (flaunt) knowledge, medal angeben mit; new car, son vorführen (to sb jdm); wealth protzen mit (inf).

(b) (enhance) beauty, picture etc hervorheben; figure also betonen. **to ~ sth ~ to advantage** etw vorteilhaft wirken lassen; **the dress ~s her ~ to advantage** das Kleid ist sehr vorteilhaft für sie.

♦**show up 1** vi (be seen) zu sehen or zu erkennen sein; (stand out) hervorstechen. **the stain ~s** ~ man sieht den Fleck; **the tower ~ed ~ clearly against the sky** der Turm zeichnete sich deutlich gegen den Himmel ab; **to ~ ~ well/badly** (fig) eine gute/schlechte Figur machen.

(b) (inf: turn up) auftauchen, sich blicken lassen (inf).

2 vt sep **(a)** (highlight) (deutlich) erkennen lassen. **the bright light ~ed ~ the faded wallpaper** in dem hellen Licht konnte man sehen, wie verblichen die Tapete war.

(b) (reveal) flaws, bad condition, errors zum Vorschein bringen; sb's character, intentions deutlich zeigen; impostor entlarven; fraud aufdecken; person bloßstellen; (shame) blamieren. **my question ~ed him ~ to be a liar** meine Frage entlarvte ihn als Lügner; **his bad manners ~ his parents ~** mit seinen schlechten Manieren blamiert er seine Eltern.

(c) (direct) heraufbringen.

show: ~ biz n (inf) see **~ business**; **~ boat** n (esp US) Dampfer m, auf dem eine Schauspieltruppe etc Vorstellungen gibt; **~ business** n Showbusineß, Showgeschäft, Schaugeschäft nt; **to be in ~ business** im Showgeschäft (tätig) sein; **~ business personalities** Persönlichkeiten pl aus dem Showgeschäft; **~case** n

Schaukasten *m*, Vitrine *f*; *(fig)* Schaufenster *nt*; ~**down** *n (inf)* Kraftprobe, Machtprobe *f*, Showdown *(sl) m*; **there was a ~down between the two rivals** zwischen den Rivalen kam es zur Machtprobe *or* Kraftprobe; **to have a ~down with sb** sich mit jdm auseinandersetzen.

shower ['ʃaʊə'] **1** *n* **(a)** *(of rain etc)* Schauer *m*; *(of arrows, stones, blows, bullets etc)* Hagel *m*; *(of curses, questions)* Schwall *m*. **a ~ of sparks** ein Funkenregen *m*; **~ of water** Dusche *f*, Wasserstrahl *m*.

(b) *(~ bath)* Dusche *f*; *(device also)* Brause *f*. **to take** *or* **have a ~** duschen.

(c) *(Brit fig inf)* Blödmänner *pl (inf)*. **what a ~!** so ein lausiges Volk! *(inf)*.

(d) *(US inf: party)* Party, *auf der jeder ein Geschenk für den Ehrengast mitbringt;* *(for bride-to-be)* ≈ Polterabend *m*.

2 *vt* **to ~ sb with sth, to ~ sth on sb** *curses* etw auf jdn niederregnen lassen; *blows* etw auf jdn niederprasseln *or* niederhageln lassen; *honours, presents* jdn mit etw überschütten *or* überhäufen; **the broken pipe ~ed** water on the passers-by das Wasser aus dem kaputten Rohr bespritzte die Passanten; **to ~ abuse on sb, to ~ sb with abuse** einen Schwall von Beschimpfungen gegen jdn loslassen.

3 *vi* **(a)** *(wash)* duschen, brausen *(dated)*.

(b) *(descend: also ~ down)* niedergehen auf (+*acc*).

shower: ~**bath** *n* Dusche *f*; ~**cabinet** *n* Duschkabine *f*; ~**cap** *n* Duschhaube *f*; ~**curtain** *n* Duschvorhang *m*; ~**proof** *adj* regenfest.

showery ['ʃaʊərɪ] *adj* regnerisch.

show: ~**girl** *n* Revuegirl *nt*; ~**ground** *n* Ausstellungsgelände *nt*; *(for circus)* Zirkusgelände(nt; ~ **house** *n* Musterhaus *nt*.

showily ['ʃaʊɪlɪ] *adv* protzig; *furnished also*, *produced* bombastisch; *behave* theatralisch. ~ **dressed** aufgeputzt.

showiness ['ʃaʊɪnɪs] *n see adj* Protzigkeit *f (inf)*; auffallende Art; Aufgeputztheit *f*; theatralische Art; bombastische Art; Auffälligkeit *f*; Effekthascherei *f*.

showing ['ʃaʊɪŋ] *n* **(a)** *(exhibition)* Ausstellung *f*.

(b) *(performance)* Aufführung *f*; *(of film)* Vorstellung *f*; *(of programme)* Ausstrahlung *f*.

(c) *(standard of performance)* Leistung *f*. **to make a good/poor ~** eine gute/schwache Leistung zeigen; **on his present ~** mit seinen jetzigen Leistungen; **on the present ~** so, wie die Dinge zur Zeit stehen.

(d) **on his own ~** nach eigenen Angaben.

showing-off ['ʃaʊɪŋ'ɒf] *n* Angeberei *f*.

show: ~**jumper** *n* Springreiter(in *f*) *m*; ~**-jumping** *n* Springen, Springreiten *nt*.

showman ['ʃaʊmən] *n*, *pl* **-men** [-mən] Showman *m*; *(fig)* Schausteller *m*.

showmanship ['ʃaʊmənʃɪp] *n* *(skill)* *(of person)* Talent *nt* für effektvolle Darbietung; *(of act)* effektvolle Darbietung; *(fig)* Talent *nt*, sich in Szene zu setzen; **he knows nothing about ~** er hat keine Ahnung, wie man etwas effektvoll darbietet *or* in Szene setzt; **it's nothing but ~** das ist reine Schau *or* Effekthascherei.

shown [ʃaʊn] *ptp of* **show**.

show: ~**-off** *n (inf)* Angeber(in *f*) *m*; ~**piece** *n* Schaustück *nt*; *(fine example)* Paradestück *nt*; ~**place** *n (tourist attraction)* Sehenswürdigkeit *f*; ~**room** *n* Ausstellungsraum *m*; **in ~room condition** in makellosem Zustand; ~**-stopper** *n (inf)* Publikumshit *m (inf)*; *(fig)* Clou *m* des Abends/der Party *etc*; ~**trial** *n* Schauprozeß *m*.

showy ['ʃaʊɪ] *adj* (+*er*) protzig; *person* auffallend; *(as regards clothes)* protzig angezogen; *manner* theatralisch; *ceremony also*, *decor* bombastisch; *colour* grell, auffällig; *production* bombastisch, auf Schau *(inf)* *or* Effekte gemacht.

shrank [ʃræŋk] *pret of* **shrink**.

shrapnel ['ʃræpnl] *n* Schrapnell *nt*.

shred [ʃred] **1** *n (scrap)* Fetzen *m*; *(of paper also)* Schnipsel, Schnippel *(inf) m*; *(of vegetable, meat)* Stückchen *nt*; *(fig)* Spur *f*; *(of truth)* Fünkchen *nt*. ~ **of cloth** Stoffetzen *m*; **not a ~ of evidence** keinerlei Beweis; **without a ~ of clothing on** splitter(faser)nackt; **to be** *or* **hang in ~s** zerfetzt sein; **her dress hung in ~s** ihr Kleid hing ihr in Fetzen vom Leib; **his reputation was in ~s** sein (guter) Ruf war ruiniert; **to tear sth to ~s** etw total zerreißen, etw in Stücke reißen; *(fig)* etw verreißen; *argument* etw total zerpflücken; **to tear sb to ~s** keinen guten Faden an jdm lassen.

2 *vt* **(a)** *food* zerkleinern, schnitzeln; *(grate)* *carrots* raspeln; *cabbage* hobeln; *paper* zerstückeln, schnitzeln; *(in shredder)* in den Papierwolf geben.

(b) *(tear)* in kleine Stücke reißen; *(with claws)* zerfetzen.

shredder ['ʃredə'] *n* Zerkleinerungsmaschine *f*; *(grater)* Reibe *f*; *(in electric mixer)* Gemüseschneider *m*; *(for waste paper)* Papierwolf, Reißwolf *m*.

shredding machine ['ʃredɪŋmə'ʃiːn] *n* Zerkleinerungsmaschine *f*; *(for wastepaper)* Papierwolf, Reißwolf *m*.

shrew [ʃruː] *n* Spitzmaus *f*; *(fig)* Xanthippe *f*.

shrewd [ʃruːd] *adj* (+*er*) *person* gewitzt, klug, clever *(inf)*; *businessman also*, *plan*, *move* clever *(inf)*, raffiniert, geschickt; *investment*, *argument* taktisch geschickt, klug; *assessment*, *observer* scharf, genau; *smile* verschmitzt, wissend; *eyes* schlau; *mind* scharf; *glance* durchdringend, prüfend. **I can make a ~ guess** ich kann ja mal raten; **that was a ~ guess** das war gut geraten; **I have a ~ idea that ...** ich habe so das bestimmte Gefühl, daß ...; **I have a ~ idea of what he'll say** ich kann mir gut denken, was er sagen wird; **to have a ~ understanding of sth** in bezug auf etw (*acc*) Durchblick haben.

shrewdly ['ʃruːdlɪ] *adv* geschickt, clever *(inf)*. **he ~ guessed that/what ...** er hat gut geraten, daß/was ...; **~, he decided ...** gewitzt *or* clever *(inf)* wie er ist, hat er beschlossen ...; **... he said ~ ...** sagte er schlau *or* clever *(inf)*.

shrewdness ['ʃruːdnɪs] *n see adj* Gewitztheit, Klugheit *f*; Cleverneß *(inf)*; Raffiniertheit, Geschicktheit *f*; Klugheit *f*; Schärfe, Genauigkeit *f*; Verschmitztheit *f*; Schläue *f*; Schärfe *f*; durchdringende Art; *(of guess)* Treffsicherheit *f*.

shrewish ['ʃruːɪʃ] *adj* zänkisch, boshaft, giftig.

shrewishly ['ʃruːɪʃlɪ] *adv* giftig.

shrewishness ['ʃruːɪʃnɪs] *n* Boshaftigkeit, Giftigkeit *f*.

shriek [ʃriːk] **1** *n* *(schriller)* Schrei *m*; *(of whistle)* schriller Ton *m*; *(of brakes, hinges)* Quietschen *nt no pl*. **a ~ of pain/horror** ein Schmerzens-/Schreckensschrei *m*; **~s of laughter** kreischendes Lachen; **to give a ~** einen schrillen Schrei ausstoßen.

2 *vt* kreischen, schreien. **to ~ abuse at sb** jdn ankeifen.

3 *vi* aufschreien. **to ~ at sb** jdn ankreischen; **to ~ with pain** vor Schmerz aufschreien; **to ~ with laughter** vor Lachen quietschen; **to ~ out** aufschreien, einen Schrei ausstoßen; **this colour really ~s** die Farbe tut einem richtig weh.

shrift [ʃrɪft] *n* **to give sb/sth short ~** jdn/etw kurz abfertigen.

shrike [ʃraɪk] *n* Würger *m*.

shrill [ʃrɪl] **1** *adj* (+*er*) schrill; *criticism*, *speech* scharf. **2** *vi* schrillen. **3** *vt* kreischen, schrill schreien.

shrillness ['ʃrɪlnɪs] *n* Schrillheit *f*.

shrilly ['ʃrɪlɪ] *adv* schrill.

shrimp [ʃrɪmp] **1** *n* Garnele, Krevette *f*. **that ~ of a child** der kleine Steppke *(inf)*. **2** *vi* **to go ~ing** auf Krevetten- *or* Garnelenfang gehen; **~ing net** Reuse *f (für den Garnelenfang)*.

shrine [ʃraɪn] *n* Schrein *m*; *(sacred place also)* heilige Stätte, Heiligtum *nt*; *(tomb)* Grab *nt*, Grabstätte *f*; *(chapel)* Grabkapelle *f*; *(altar)* Grabaltar *m*. **to worship at sb's ~** *(fig inf)* jdm zu Füßen liegen.

shrink [ʃrɪŋk] *(vb: pret* **shrank**, *ptp* **shrunk**) **1** *vt* eingehen *or* einlaufen lassen. **the fabric is shrunk before it is used** der Stoff wird vor Gebrauch gewaschen, damit er danach nicht mehr einläuft; **to ~ a part on** *(Tech)* ein Teil aufschrumpfen.

2 *vi* **(a)** *(get smaller)* kleiner werden, schrumpfen; *(clothes etc)* eingehen, einlaufen; *(metal etc)* sich zusammenziehen, schrumpfen; *(wood)* schwinden; *(fig)* *(popularity)* abnehmen, schwinden; *(trade)* zurückgehen. **to ~ away to nothing** auf ein Nichts zusammenschrumpfen; **a ~ing violet** *(fig)* ein schüchternes Pflänzchen; **~-proof/-resistant** nicht einlaufend.

(b) *(fig: recoil)* zurückschrecken. **to ~ from doing/saying sth** davor zurückschrecken, etw zu tun/sich davor scheuen, etw zu sagen; **to ~ from the truth** vor der Wahrheit die Augen verschließen; **to ~ back** zurückweichen; **to ~ away from sb** vor jdm zurückweichen.

3 *n (sl)* Klapsdoktor *(inf)*, Pyschater *(inf) m*.

shrinkage ['ʃrɪŋkɪdʒ] *n* *(of material, clothes)* Einlaufen, Eingehen *nt*; *(of wood)* Schwund *m*; *(of metal)* Schrumpfung *f*; *(fig: of tourism, economic growth etc)* Schrumpfung *f*, Rückgang *m*; *(Comm)* Schwund *m*, Rechnungsverlust ... Einbuße *pl*. **there will be ~ with this material** dieser Stoff geht *or* läuft noch ein; **you'd better buy extra material to allow for ~** kaufen Sie lieber mehr von dem Stoff, falls er noch eingeht.

shrink-wrap ['ʃrɪŋkræp] *vt* einschweißen.

shrive [ʃraɪv] *pret* **shrove**, *ptp* **shriven** *vt* die Beichte abnehmen (+*dat*).

shrivel ['ʃrɪvl] **1** *vt* *plants (frost, dryness)* welk werden lassen; *(heat)* austrocknen; *skin, fruit* runzlig werden lassen; *nylon* zusammenschrumpfen lassen.

2 *vi* kleiner werden, schrumpfen; *(balloon)* zusammenschrumpfen; *(plants)* welk werden; *(through heat)* austrocknen; *(fruit, skin)* runzlig werden; *(nylon)* zusammenschrumpfen; *(worries, problems)* sich verflüchtigen. **~(l)ed old lady** eine kleine, vertrocknete Dame.

♦**shrivel away** *vi* zusammenschrumpfen; *(leaves)* verwelken, vertrocknen; *(nylon)* zusammenschmelzen; *(worries, problems)* sich in Luft auflösen.

♦**shrivel up 1** *vt sep see* **shrivel 1**.

2 *vi* **(a)** *see* **shrivel 2**.

(b) *(fig: become timid)* **I just want to ~ ~ when he looks at me like that** wenn er mich so ansieht, möchte ich am liebsten in den Boden versinken; **he just ~led ~ when the boss questioned him** bei den Fragen des Chefs wurde er ganz klein.

shriven ['ʃrɪvn] *ptp of* **shrive**.

shroud [ʃraʊd] **1** *n* **(a)** Leichentuch, Totenhemd *nt*.

(b) *(fig)* Schleier *m*. **a ~ of mist** ein Nebelschleier *m*; **a ~ of mystery** der Schleier eines Geheimnisses.

(c) **~s** *pl (Naut)* Wanten *pl*.

2 *vt* **(a)** *(lit)* in ein Leichentuch hüllen.

(b) *(fig)* hüllen. **the whole thing is ~ed in mystery** die ganze Angelegenheit ist von einem Geheimnis umgeben.

shrove [ʃraʊv] *pret of* **shrive**.

Shrovetide ['ʃraʊvtaɪd] *n* Fastnacht *f (die drei Tage vor Aschermittwoch)*.

Shrove Tuesday *n* Faschingsdienstag *(S Ger)*, Fastnachtsdienstag *m*.

shrub [ʃrʌb] *n* Busch, Strauch *m*.

shrubbery ['ʃrʌbərɪ] *n (shrub bed)* Strauchrabatte *f*; *(shrubs)* Büsche, Sträucher *pl*, Buschwerk *nt*. **the ball got lost in the ~** der Ball ging im Gebüsch verloren.

shrug [ʃrʌg] **1** *n* Achselzucken *nt no pl*. **to give a ~** die *or* mit den Schultern *or* Achseln zucken; **a ~ of despair** ein verzweifeltes Achselzucken. **2** *vt* *shoulders* zucken (mit). **she ~ged herself out of the coat** sie schüttelte den Mantel ab.

♦**shrug off** *vt sep* mit einem Achselzucken abtun; *coat* abschütteln. **he simply ~ged the whole affair ~** er hat die ganze Sache einfach von sich abgeschüttelt.

shrunk [ʃrʌŋk] *ptp of* **shrink**.

shrunken ['ʃrʌŋkən] *adj* (ein)geschrumpft; *old person* geschrumpft; *profits, savings* zusammengeschrumpft. **~ head** Schrumpfkopf *m*.

shuck [ʃʌk] *(US)* **1** *n* Schale *f*; *(of corn, peas)* Hülse *f*. **2** *vt* **(a)**

schälen; *peas* enthülsen. **(b)** (*inf*) he ~ed his jacket er warf seine Jacke ab.

shucks [ʃʌks] *interj* (*US*) verflixt, Mist (*inf*); (*rubbish*) Unsinn, Quatsch (*inf*). ~, **I'm sorry** Mist!, tut mir leid (*inf*); ~ **to you** (*inf*) bätsch! (*inf*).

shudder [ˈʃʌdər] **1** *n* Schauer, Schauder *m*. **to give a** ~ (*person*) sich schütteln, erschaudern (*geh*); (*ground*) beben; **she gave a** ~ **of revulsion** sie schüttelte sich vor Ekel; **the dying man gave a last great** ~ ein letztes Zucken lief durch den Körper des Sterbenden; **a** ~ **ran through her/her body** ein Schauer überlief sie; **she realized with a** ~ **that ...** schaudernd erkannte sie, daß ...; **a** ~ **of fear/cold** ein Angst-/Kälteschauer; **with a** ~ **of anticipation/pleasure** zitternd *or* bebend vor Erwartung/Freude; **a** ~ **went through the building as the heavy lorry passed by** das Gebäude bebte, als der schwere Lastwagen vorbeifuhr; **with a** ~ **the old car moved into second gear** der alte Wagen vibrierte, als der zweite Gang eingelegt wurde; **that gives me the** ~s (*inf*) da läuft's mir kalt den Buckel runter (*inf*); **he gives me the** ~s (*inf*) er ist mir unheimlich.

2 *vi* (*person*) schaudern, schauern; (*house, ground*) beben, zittern; (*car, train*) rütteln, geschüttelt werden. **her whole body was** ~ing sie zitterte am ganzen Körper; **the train** ~ed **to a halt** der Zug kam rüttelnd zum Stehen; **I** ~ **to think** mir graut, wenn ich nur daran denke.

shudderingly [ˈʃʌdərɪŋlɪ] *adv* (*with fear etc*) schaudernd; (*with cold*) zitternd. **the rocket climbed** ~ **into the sky** die Rakete stieg zitternd zum Himmel auf.

shuffle [ˈʃʌfl] **1** *n* **(a)** Schlurfen *nt no pl*. **to walk with a** ~ schlurfen.

(b) (*dance*) Shuffle *m*.

(c) (*Cards*) **to give the cards a** ~ die Karten mischen.

(d) (*change round*) Umstellung *f*; (*of jobs*) Umbesetzung *f*. **the latest** ~ **in the cabinet** die letzte Kabinettsumbildung; **the recent management** ~ die jüngsten personellen Verschiebungen im Management.

2 *vt* **(a)** he ~d **his feet as he walked** er schlurfte beim Gehen; **he sat there shuffling his feet** er saß da und scharrte mit den Füßen.

(b) *cards* mischen. **he** ~d **the papers on his desk** er durchwühlte die Papiere auf seinem Schreibtisch.

(c) (*fig: change round*) *cabinet* umbilden; *jobs* umbesetzen. **top men are** ~d **around quite often** die Männer an der Spitze werden oft von einem Ressort ins andere versetzt.

3 *vi* **(a)** (*walk*) schlurfen. **the dancers** ~d **round on the floor** die Tänzer schoben sich über die Tanzfläche; **he** ~d **into his slippers** er schlüpfte umständlich in seine Pantoffeln; **to** ~ **out of one's responsibilities** seine Verantwortung von sich (*ab*)wälzen; **he just** ~s **through life** er läßt sich einfach treiben.

(b) (*Cards*) mischen.

♦**shuffle off** *vt sep* *skin, dress* abstreifen; *worries, fear* ablegen; *responsibility* abwälzen, abschieben (*onto* auf +*acc*).

shuffling [ˈʃʌflɪŋ] *adj* *walk, steps* schlurfend. **the** ~ **movement of a badger** das Watscheln eines Dachses.

shun [ʃʌn] *vt* meiden; *publicity, light* scheuen. **to feel** ~ned **by the world** sich ausgestoßen fühlen.

'shun [ʃʌn] *interj* (*Mil*) Achtung.

shunt [ʃʌnt] **1** *n* Stoß *m*; (*sl: car crash*) Bums *m* (*inf*). **they gave the waggon a** ~ **into the siding** sie schoben *or* rangierten den Waggon auf das Abstellgleis; **the lorry gave the car a** ~ **into the back of another car** der Lastwagen schob das Auto auf ein anderes drauf; **to give sth a** ~ etw anstoßen, einer Sache (*dat*) einen Stoß geben.

2 *vt* **(a)** (*Rail*) rangieren, verschieben. **they** ~ed **the train off the main line** sie schoben den Zug auf ein Nebengleis.

(b) (*inf*) *person* schieben; (*out of the way*) abschieben. **to** ~ **sb to and fro** jdn herumschubsen (*inf*); **our department then has to** ~ **the papers back for signing** unsere Abteilung muß die Papiere dann zur Unterschrift zurückverfrachten (*inf*).

(c) (*sl: crash*) *car* einen Unfall bauen mit (*sl*).

3 *vi* (*Rail*) (*train*) rangiert *or* verschoben werden; (*person*) rangieren. **a line of trucks** ~ed **past** eine Reihe Güterwagen schob sich vorbei.

shunter [ˈʃʌntər] *n* (*Rail*) Rangierer *m*.

shunting [ˈʃʌntɪŋ] *n* (*Rail*) Rangieren *nt*. ~ **engine** Rangierlokomotive *f*; ~ **yard** Rangier- *or* Verschiebebahnhof *m*.

shush [ʃʊʃ] **1** *interj* pst, sch. **2** *vt* beruhigen, zum Schweigen bringen. **the teacher** ~ed **the excited children** der Lehrer brachte die aufgeregten Kinder mit einem "Pst!" zum Schweigen. **3** *vi* still sein. **oh** ~, **will you!** sei doch still!, pst!

shut [ʃʌt] (*vb: pret, ptp* ~) **1** *vt* **(a)** zumachen; *box, door, book, shop, office* also, *sportsground* also schließen; *penknife, book, wallet* also zuklappen. **they** ~ **the office at 6.00** das Büro wird um 18⁰⁰ geschlossen; **the strike** ~ **the factory for a week** der Streik legte die Fabrik für eine Woche still; **they** ~ **the tennis courts to the public during the tournament** während des Turniers sind die Tennisplätze für die Öffentlichkeit geschlossen; ~ **your eyes** mach die Augen zu; **to** ~ **one's ears to sth** vor etw (*dat*) die Ohren verschließen; **to** ~ **one's mind to sth** sich einer Sache (*dat*) verschließen; **he** ~ **his mind to thoughts of the past** Gedanken an die Vergangenheit schob er weit von sich; ~ **your mouth** (*sl*) *or* **face** (*sl*) halt's Maul! (*sl*).

(b) **to** ~ **sb/sth in(to) sth** jdn/etw in etw (*dat*) einschließen; **she was** ~ **in the cellar as a punishment** sie wurde zur Strafe im Keller eingesperrt; **to** ~ **one's fingers in the door** sich (*dat*) die Finger in der Tür einklemmen.

2 *vi* (*door, window, box*) schließen, zugehen; (*shop, factory*) schließen, geschlossen werden, zumachen (*inf*); (*sportsground*) geschlossen werden. **the suitcase just won't** ~ der Koffer will einfach nicht zugehen; **it** ~s **very easily** es läßt sich ganz leicht schließen *or* zumachen; **it** ~s **with a zip** es hat einen Reißverschluß; **when do the shops** ~? wann schließen die

Geschäfte?, wann machen die Geschäfte zu? (*inf*); **the door** ~ **in the wind** der Wind schlug die Tür zu.

3 *adj* geschlossen, zu (*inf*). **sorry sir, we're** ~ wir haben leider geschlossen; **the door swung** ~ die Tür schlug zu; **to find the door** ~ vor verschlossener Tür stehen; ~ **in his dungeon** in seinem Kerker eingeschlossen; ~ **in his own little world** abgekapselt in seiner eigenen kleinen Welt; **the** ~ **mind of a reactionary** der Verbohrtheit eines Reaktionärs; **his mind is** ~ **to anything new** er verschließt sich allem Neuen.

♦**shut away** *vt sep* (*put away*) wegschließen; (*in sth*) einschließen (*in* in +*dat*); (*keep locked away*) *books, papers etc* aufbewahren; (*safely*) verwahren; *persons* verborgen halten. **to keep sb** ~ **from sth** jdn von etw fernhalten; **he was** ~ **in a mental hospital** er wurde in eine Nervenklinik gesteckt.

♦**shut down 1** *vt sep* *shop, factory* zumachen (*inf*), schließen. **Heathrow is completely** ~ ~ Heathrow ist zu.

2 *vi* (*shop, factory etc*) zumachen (*inf*), schließen. **we** ~ ~ **with a poem by X** wir schließen (unser Programm) mit einem Gedicht von X; **the television service** ~s ~ **at midnight** um Mitternacht ist Sendeschluß im Fernsehen.

♦**shut in** *vt sep* einschließen (*also fig*), einsperren (*inf*) (*prep obj, -to* in +*dat*). **close the door and** ~ **the heat** ~ schließe die Tür, damit die Wärme drinnen bleibt.

♦**shut off 1** *vt sep* **(a)** *gas, water, electricity* abstellen; *light, engine* ab- *or* ausschalten; *street* (ab)sperren. **the kettle** ~s **itself** ~ der Wasserkessel schaltet von selbst ab.

(b) (*isolate*) (ab)trennen. **I feel very** ~ ~ **on this island** ich fühle mich auf dieser Insel sehr abgeschlossen; **I feel** ~ ~ **from my friends/civilization** ich komme mir von meinen Freunden/der Zivilisation abgeschnitten vor; **they tried to** ~ **their daughter** ~ **from the evil things in life** sie versuchten, ihre Tochter von allem Bösen fernzuhalten.

2 *vi* abschalten. **the heater** ~s ~ **automatically** das Heizgerät schaltet (sich) automatisch ab.

♦**shut out** *vt sep* **(a)** *person, oneself* aussperren (*of* aus); *view* versperren; *light* nicht hereinlassen (*of* in +*acc*). **the child was** ~ ~ **of the house** das Kind war ausgesperrt; **don't** ~ **the sun** ~ laß doch die Sonne herein; **draw the curtains to** ~ ~ **the light** zieh die Vorhänge zu, damit das Licht nicht hereinfällt; **she closed the door to** ~ ~ **the noise/draught** sie schloß die Tür, damit kein Lärm hereinkam/damit es nicht zog.

(b) (*fig*) *foreign competition* ausschalten; *memory* loswerden, unterdrücken. **I can't** ~ **her** ~ **of my life** ich kann sie nicht von meinem Leben ausschließen; **the censors' attempts to** ~ ~ **all news from abroad** die Versuche der Zensoren, sämtliche Nachrichten aus dem Ausland zu unterdrücken.

(c) (*US Sport*) *opponent* nicht zum Zuge kommen lassen. **they** ~ **the opponents** ~ **with two hits** sie schalteten ihre Gegner mit zwei Treffern aus; **they** ~ **them** ~ **1–0** sie warfen sie mit 1:0 aus dem Rennen.

♦**shut to** *vt sep* ganz *or* richtig zumachen; (*not quite closed*) anlehnen. **the door wasn't** ~ ~ die Tür war nicht ganz zu.

♦**shut up 1** *vt sep* **(a)** *house* verschließen. **to** ~ ~ **shop** (*lit*) das Geschäft schließen; (*fig*) Feierabend machen (*inf*).

(b) (*imprison*) einsperren. **you can't spend your whole life** ~ ~ **in libraries** Sie können sich doch nicht Ihr ganzes Leben in Bibliotheken vergraben.

(c) (*inf: silence*) zum Schweigen bringen. **that'll soon** ~ **him** ~ das wird ihm schon den Mund stopfen (*inf*); **every time I try to say something she always tries to** ~ **me** ~ jedes Mal, wenn ich etwas sagen will, fährt sie mir über den Mund.

2 *vi* (*inf*) den Mund (*inf*) *or* die Klappe (*sl*) halten.

shut: ~**down** *n* Stillegung *f*; (*TV, Rad*) Sendeschluß *m*; ~-**eye** *n* (*inf*) Schlaf *m*; **I need some** ~-**eye** ich brauche etwas *or* ein paar Stunden Schlaf; ~-**in** **1** *adj* **(a)** (*US*) ans Haus/ans Bett gefesselt; **(b) a** ~-**in feeling** des Eingeschlossenseins; **these small rooms give me a** ~-**in feeling** in diesen kleinen Räumen fühle ich mich beengt *or* wie in einem Gefängnis; **2** *n* (*US*) **he is a** ~-**in** er ist ans Haus/ans Bett gefesselt; ~-**off** **1** *n* (*of gas, water*) Abstellen *nt*; **we regret the temporary water** ~-**off** **yesterday** wir bedauern, daß wir gestern vorübergehend das Wasser abstellen mußten; **2** *adj* **(a) a** ~-**off feeling** ein Gefühl des Abgeschlossenseins *or* Abgeschnittenseins; **(b)** ~-**off switch** (*of electricity, engine*) Hauptschalter *m*.

shutter [ˈʃʌtər] **1** *n* (*Fenster*)laden *m*; (*Phot*) Verschluß *m*. **to put up the** ~s (*lit*) die (Fenster)läden anmachen; (*fig*) den Laden dichtmachen (*inf*); ~ **release** (*Phot*) Auslöser *m*. **2** *vt* **the** ~ed **windows of the old mansion** die geschlossenen (Fenster)läden der alten Villa; **the** ~ **windows** mach die (Fenster)läden zu; **a** ~ed **look** ein verschlossener Blick.

shuttle [ˈʃʌtl] **1** *n* **(a)** (*of loom, sewing machine*) Schiffchen *nt*.

(b) Pendelverkehr *m*; (*plane, train etc*) Pendelflugzeug *nt*/-zug *m etc*; (*space* ~) Raumtransporter *m*.

2 *vt* *passengers, goods* hin- und hertransportieren. **to** ~ **sb about** jdn herumschieben; **the form was** ~d **about between different departments** das Formular wurde in den verschiedenen Abteilungen herumgereicht.

3 *vi* (*people*) pendeln; (*goods*) hin- und hertransportiert werden; (*forms*) herumgereicht werden.

shuttle: ~**cock** *n* Federball *m*; ~ **service** *n* Pendelverkehr *m*.

shy¹ [ʃaɪ] **1** *adj* (+*er*) **(a)** schüchtern; *smile* also, *animal* scheu. **don't be** ~ nur keine Hemmungen! (*inf*); **to be** ~ **of/with sb** Hemmungen vor/gegenüber jdm haben; **to be** ~ **of doing sth** Hemmungen haben, etw zu tun; **to feel** ~ schüchtern sein; **don't be** ~ **of telling me if there's anything you need** sagen Sie mir ruhig, wenn Sie etwas brauchen; **to make sb** ~ jdn verschüchtern; *see* **fight.**

(b) (*esp US inf: short*) **we're $3** ~ wir haben 3 Dollar zuwenig.

2 *vi* (*horse*) scheuen (*at* vor +*dat*).

♦**shy away** *vi* (*horse*) zurückscheuen; (*person*) zurückweichen. **to** ~ ~ **from sb/sth** vor jdm zurückweichen/vor etw (*dat*) zurückschrecken; **he shies ~ from accepting respon-sibilities** er scheut sich, Verantwortung zu übernehmen.

shy² **1** *n* (*throw*) Wurf *m*. **to have** *or* **take a ~ at sth** nach etw werfen; **to have a ~ at sth** (*fig*) sich an etw (*dat*) versuchen; **I'll have a ~ at it** ich kann's ja mal versuchen; **to have a ~ at doing sth** etw zu tun versuchen. **2** *vt* werfen.

Shylock ['ʃaɪlɒk] *n* (*fig*) (*mean person*) Geizhals *m*; (*dated: moneylender*) Wucherer *m*.

shyly ['ʃaɪlɪ] *adv see adj*.

shyness ['ʃaɪnɪs] *n* Schüchternheit *f*; (*esp of animals*) Scheu *f*. **his ~ of meeting people/of strangers** seine Scheu, andere Leute kennenzulernen/vor Fremden.

shyster ['ʃaɪstə'] *n* (*US sl*) Gauner *m*; (*lawyer*) Rechtsverdreher *m* (*inf*).

Siam [saɪ'æm] *n* Siam *nt*.

Siamese [,saɪə'miːz] **1** *adj* siamesisch. **~ cat** Siamkatze *f*, siamesische Katze; **~ twins** siamesische Zwillinge *pl*. **2** *n* **(a)** Siamese *m*, Siamesin *f*. **(b)** (*language*) Siamesisch *nt*. **(c)** (*cat*) Siamkatze *f*, siamesische Katze.

Siberia [saɪ'bɪərɪə] *n* Sibirien *nt*.

Siberian [saɪ'bɪərɪən] **1** *adj* sibirisch. **2** *n* Sibirier(in *f*) *m*.

sibilant ['sɪbɪlənt] **1** *adj* zischend; *hiss* scharf; (*Phon*) Zisch-, gezischt. **2** *n* (*Phon*) Zischlaut *m*.

sibling ['sɪblɪŋ] *n* Geschwister *nt* (*form*).

sibyl ['sɪbɪl] *n* (*lit*) Sibylle *f*; (*fig*) Prophetin *f*, Weissagerin *f*.

sibylline ['sɪbɪlaɪn] *adj* (*lit*) sibyllinisch; (*fig*) prophetisch.

sic [sɪk] *adv* sic.

Sicilian [sɪ'sɪljən] **1** *adj* sizilianisch. **2** *n* **(a)** Sizilianer(in *f*) *m*. **(b)** (*dialect*) Sizilianisch *nt*.

Sicily ['sɪsɪlɪ] *n* Sizilien *nt*.

sick [sɪk] **1** *n* (*vomit*) Erbrochene(s) *nt*.
2 *adj* (+er) **(a)** (*ill*) krank (*also fig*). **the ~ die** Kranken *pl*; **to be (off) ~** (*wegen Krankheit*) fehlen; **to fall** *or* **take** *or* **be taken ~** krank werden; **to go ~** krank werden; **he was ~ at heart** (*liter*) er war von Kummer verzehrt (*liter*).
(b) (*vomiting or about to vomit*) **to be ~** brechen, sich übergeben, kotzen (*sl*); (*esp cat, baby, patient*) spucken; **he was ~ all over the carpet** er hat den ganzen Teppich vollgespuckt *or* vollgekotzt (*sl*); **I think I'm going to be ~** ich glaube, ich muß brechen *or* mich übergeben (*form*) *or* kotzen (*sl*); **I felt ~** mir war schlecht *or* übel; **I get ~ in aeroplanes** im Flugzeug wird mir immer schlecht *or* übel; **that smell/that food makes me ~** bei dem Geruch/von dem Essen wird mir übel *or* schlecht; **to make sb ~** (*fig inf*) jdn (ganz) krank machen (*inf*); **it makes you ~ the way** he's always right es ist zum Weinen *or* zum Kotzen (*sl*), daß er immer recht hat; **to be ~ at sth** (*fig*) (*disgusted*) voll etw angewidert sein; (*upset*) wegen etw geknickt sein; **~ with envy** grün vor Neid.
(c) (*inf: fed up*) **to be ~ of doing sth** es satt haben, etw zu tun; **I'm ~ and tired of it** ich habe davon die Nase (gestrichen) voll (*inf*), ich habe es gründlich satt; **I get ~ of listening to her complaining** ich habe es langsam satt, immer ihr Gejammer hören zu müssen.
(d) (*inf*) geschmacklos; *joke also* übel, makaber; *person* abartig, pervers. **~ humour** schwarzer Humor; **he has a ~ mind** er ist abartig; **a comedy about life in Dachau, how ~ can you get!** eine Komödie über das Leben in Dachau, das ist ja schon pervers!

sick: **~-bag** *n* Spucktüte *f*; **~ bay** *n* Krankenrevier *nt*; **~-bed** *n* Krankenlager *nt*.

sicken ['sɪkn] **1** *vt* (*turn sb's stomach*) anekeln, anwidern; (*upset greatly*) erschüttern, krank machen (*inf*); (*disgust*) anwidern. **the sight of blood ~s me** wenn ich Blut sehe, wird mir übel; **what they saw in the camp ~ed them** sie waren entsetzt über das, was sie im Lager sahen; **it ~s me the way he treats her** es macht mich krank, wie er sie behandelt (*inf*); **doesn't it ~ you?** das ist doch unerträglich *or* zum Kotzen (*sl*).
2 *vi* **(a)** (*feel ill*) **to ~ at sth** sich vor etw (*dat*) ekeln; **I ~ at the sight of blood** mir wird übel, wenn ich Blut sehe.
(b) (*become ill*) krank werden. **he's definitely ~ing for something** er wird bestimmt krank; **you must be ~ing for something** (*lit, iro*) ist mit dir was nicht in Ordnung?; **he's ~ing for measles** bei ihm sind die Masern im Anzug; **to ~ for want of love** (*liter*) nach Liebe verzehren (*liter*).
(c) **to ~ of sth** einer Sache (*gen*) müde (*geh*) werden *or* sein, etw satt haben; **to ~ of doing sth** es müde werden, etw zu tun.

sickening ['sɪknɪŋ] *adj* (*lit*) ekelerregend; *smell, sight also* widerlich, ekelhaft; (*upsetting*) entsetzlich, erschütternd; (*disgusting, annoying*) ekelhaft, zum Kotzen (*sl*); *treatment* abscheulich; *delays, price increase* unerträglich. **his ~ habit of always being right** seine unerträgliche Angewohnheit, immer recht zu haben.

sickeningly ['sɪknɪŋlɪ] *adv* (*lit*) ekelerregend; (*fig*) unerträglich. **his English is ~ good** es ist schon unerträglich, wie gut sein Englisch ist; **we had all that ~ good weather during the exams** es war richtig gemein, daß wir ausgerechnet während des Examens so schönes Wetter hatten; **now it's all ~ obvious** das schreit ja schon zum Himmel (*inf*).

sick headache *n* ~ Migräne(anfall *m*) *f*.

sickle ['sɪkl] *n* Sichel *f*. **~-cell anaemia** Sichelzellenanämie *f*.

sick-leave ['sɪkliːv] *n* **to be on ~** krank geschrieben sein; **employees are allowed six weeks' ~ per year** Angestellte dürfen insgesamt sechs Wochen pro Jahr wegen Krankheit fehlen; **he has three months' ~ because of his accident** aufgrund seines Unfalls hat er drei Monate Genesungsurlaub; **he only gets two weeks' paid ~** im Krankheitsfall wird sein Gehalt nur zwei Wochen weitergezahlt.

sickliness ['sɪklɪnɪs] *n see adj* Kränklichkeit *f*; Blässe *f*; Widerlichkeit, Ekelhaftigkeit *f*; Mattheit *f*; Schwachheit *f*.

sick-list ['sɪklɪst] *n* (*because of illness*) Krankenliste *f*; (*because of injury*) Verletztenliste *f*. **to be on/off the ~** (*Mil, Sport*) auf der/nicht mehr auf der Kranken-/Verletztenliste stehen; (*inf*) (wegen Krankheit) fehlen/wieder im Einsatz sein (*inf*).

sickly ['sɪklɪ] *adj* (+er) *person, appearance* kränklich; *complexion, light* blaß; *smell, taste, food, sentimentality, colour* widerlich, ekelhaft; *smile* matt; *grin* schwach; *climate* ungesund. **~ sweet smell** unangenehm süßer Geruch; **~ sweet smile** übersüßes *or* zuckersüßes Lächeln.

sick-making ['sɪkmeɪkɪŋ] *adj* (*inf*) gräßlich (*inf*).

sickness ['sɪknɪs] *n* (*Med*) Krankheit *f* (*also fig*); (*nausea*) Übelkeit *f*; (*vomiting*) Erbrechen *nt*; (*of joke, book, film*) Geschmacklosigkeit *f*. **there is ~ on board** an Bord geht eine Krankheit um; **the ~ of his mind** seine Abartigkeit; **~ benefit** Krankengeld *nt*.

sick: **~-pay** *n* Bezahlung *f* im Krankheitsfall; **~-room** *n* Krankenzimmer *nt*.

side [saɪd] **1** *n* **(a)** (*wall, vertical surface*) (*of car, box, hole, ditch*) Seite *f*; (*of cave, artillery trench, mining shaft, boat, caravan*) Wand *f*; (*of cliff, mountain*) Hang *m*. **the ~s of the hill** die Berghänge *pl*.
(b) (*flat surface, line*) (*of triangle, cube, coin, paper, material, record*) Seite *f*. **this ~ up!** (*on parcel etc*) oben!; **right/wrong ~** (*of cloth*) rechte/linke Seite; **this sock is right/wrong ~ out** dieser Strumpf ist rechts/links (herum).
(c) (*edge*) Rand *m*. **at the ~ of the road** am Straßenrand; **the body was found in the ~ of the wood** nearest to the road die Leiche wurde am Waldrand neben der Straße gefunden; **at** *or* **on the ~ of his plate** auf dem Tellerrand.
(d) (*not back or front, area to one ~*) Seite *f*. **by/at the ~ of sth** seitlich von etw; **the destroyer rammed the ~ of the boat** der Zerstörer rammte das Boot seitlich; **to drive on the left ~ of the road** auf der linken Straßenseite fahren; **the path goes down the ~ of the house** der Weg führt seitlich am Haus entlang; **it's this/the other ~ of London** (*out of town*) es ist auf dieser/auf der anderen Seite Londons; (*in town*) es ist in diesem Teil/am anderen Ende von London; **the south/respectable ~ of Glasgow** der Süden/der vornehme Teil Glasgows; **the debit/credit ~ of an account** die Soll-/Habenseite eines Kontos; **the enemy attacked them on** *or* **from all ~s** der Feind griff sie von allen Seiten an; **this statement was attacked on** *or* **from all ~s** diese Behauptung wurde von allen angegriffen; **he stood** *or* **moved to one ~** er trat zur Seite; **the car moved to one ~ of the road and stopped** der Wagen fuhr seitlich heran und hielt; **he stood to one ~ and did nothing** (*lit*) er stand daneben und tat nichts; (*fig*) er hielt sich raus; **to put sth on one ~** etw beiseite *or* auf die Seite legen; (*shopkeeper*) etw zurücklegen; **I'll put that question on one ~** ich werde diese Frage vorerst zurückstellen; **to take sb to** *or* **on one ~** jdn beiseite nehmen; **just this ~ of the boundary** (*lit*) (noch) diesseits der Grenze; (*fig*) gerade an der Grenze; **just this ~ of respectability** gerade noch annehmbar; **just this ~ of the line between sanity and madness** gerade an der Grenze zum Wahnsinn; **on the other ~ of death/the boundary** nach dem Tod/jenseits der Grenze; **with one's head on one ~** mit zur Seite geneigtem Kopf.
(e) **to be on the safe ~** sichergehen; **we'll take an extra £50 just to be on the safe ~** wir werden vorsichtshalber *or* für alle Fälle 50 Pfund mehr mitnehmen; **to get/stay on the right ~ of sb** jdn für sich einnehmen/es (sich *dat*) mit jdm nicht verderben; **to get on the wrong ~ of sb** es (sich *dat*) mit jdm verderben; **to be on the right/wrong ~ of 40** noch nicht/über 40 sein; **on the right ~ of the law** auf dem Boden des Gesetzes; **only just on the right ~ of the law** an der Grenze der Legalität; **to make a bit (of money) on the ~** (*inf*) sich (*dat*) etwas nebenher *or* nebenbei verdienen (*inf*); **to have a bit on the ~** (*inf*) einen Seitensprung machen; (*for longer*) noch nebenher etwas laufen haben (*inf*).
(f) (*of person, Anat*) Seite *f*. **~ of bacon** Speckseite *f*; **by sb's ~** neben jdm; **~ by ~** nebeneinander, Seite an Seite; **to stand/sit ~ by ~ with sb** direkt neben jdm stehen/sitzen; **to fight ~ by ~ with sb** Seite an Seite mit jdm kämpfen; **I'll be by your ~** (*fig*) ich werde Ihnen zur Seite stehen; *see* **split**.
(g) (*branch*) (*of family*) Seite *f*; (*of business, school*) Zweig *m*. **the Catholic/intellectual ~ of the family** der katholische Teil/die Intelligenz der Familie; **on one's father's/mother's ~** väterlicherseits/mütterlicherseits; **there's French blood on the paternal/maternal ~** von väterlicher/mütterlicher Seite *f* französisches Blut da.
(h) (*aspect*) Seite *f*. **a problem with many ~s** to it ein vielschichtiges Problem; **there are always two ~s to every story** alles hat seine zwei Seiten; **let's hear your ~ of the story** erzählen Sie mal Ihre Version (der Geschichte); **the management's ~ of the story was quite different** die Geschichte hörte sich von seiten des Managements ganz anders an; **to hear both ~s of the question** bei einer Frage beide Seiten (an)hören; **the bright/seamy ~ of life** die Sonnen-/Schattenseite des Lebens; **to look on the bright ~** (*be optimistic*) zuversichtlich sein; (*look on the positive ~*) etw von der positiven Seite betrachten; **you don't know his cruel ~** Sie kennen ihn nicht von seiner grausamen Seite.
(i) **(a bit) on the large/high/formal** *etc* **~** etwas groß/hoch/förmlich *etc*; (*for somebody*) etwas zu groß/hoch/förmlich *etc*; **he errs on the ~ of over-generosity** er ist eher etwas zu großzügig.
(j) (*opposing team*) (*Sport, in quiz*) Mannschaft *f*; (*fig*) Seite *f*. **there are two ~s in the dispute** in dem Streit stehen sich zwei Parteien gegenüber; **the management ~ refused to give in die** Managementseite weigerte sich nachzugeben; **with a few concessions on the government ~** mit einigen Zugeständnissen von seiten der Regierung; **to change ~s** sich auf die andere Seite schlagen; (*Sport*) **die Seiten ~s wechseln**; **to take ~s** Partei ergreifen; **he's on our ~** er steht auf unserer Seite; **whose ~ are you on?** (*supporting team*) für wen sind Sie?; (*playing for team*) bei wem

spielen Sie mit?; (in argument) zu wem halten Sie eigentlich?
 (k) (dated inf: superiority) there's no ~ about or to him er sitzt nicht auf dem hohen Roß; to put on ~ sich aufplustern.
 2 adj attr (on one ~) window, door, entrance, road, street Seiten-; (not main) entrance, room, door, road, street, job Neben-; (to one ~) punch seitlich, Seiten-.
 3 vi to ~ with/against sb jds Partei (acc)/Partei gegen jdn ergreifen.
side: ~ **arm** n an der Seite getragene Waffe; (sword etc) Seitenwaffe f; ~**board** n Anrichte f, Sideboard nt; ~**boards**, ~**burns** npl Koteletten pl; (longer) Backenbart m; ~**car** n Beiwagen m; (esp Sport) Seitenwagen m.
-sided [-saɪdɪd] adj suf -seitig.
side: ~**dish** n Beilage f; ~ **drum** n kleine Trommel; ~ **effect** n Nebenwirkung f; ~ **elevation** n Seitenansicht f, Seitenriß m; ~ **issue** n Randproblem nt; that's just a ~ issue das ist Nebensache; ~**kick** n (esp US inf) Kumpan (inf), Kumpel (inf) m; (assistant) Handlanger m (pej); the rancher and his ~kicks der Farmer und seine Leute; ~**light** n (Aut) Parklicht nt, Parkleuchte f; (incorporated in headlight) Standlicht nt; that was an interesting ~light on his character das warf ein neues Licht auf seinen Charakter; ~**line** n (extra business) Nebenerwerb m; it's just a ~line das läuft so nebenher (inf); to do sth as a ~line etw nebenher or nebenbei tun; ~**lines** npl Seitenlinien pl; the trainer sat at the ~lines der Trainer saß am Spielfeldrand; to keep to the ~lines (fig) im Hintergrund bleiben; to be or stand or sit on the ~lines (fig) unbeteiligter Außenstehender or Zuschauer sein; ~**long** adj, adv glance Seiten-; (surreptitious) verstohlen, versteckt; to give sb a ~long glance, to glance ~long at sb jdn kurz aus den Augenwinkeln anblicken.
sidereal [saɪˈdɪərɪəl] adj (spec) siderisch.
side: ~**saddle** 1 n Damensattel m; 2 adv to ride ~saddle im Damensattel or Damensitz reiten; ~ **salad** n Salat m (als Beilage); ~ **show** n Nebenvorstellung f; (exhibition) Sonderausstellung f; ~ **slip** n (Aviat) Slippen nt, Seitenrutsch m.
sidesman [ˈsaɪdzmən] n, pl -men [-mən] ≃ (ehrenamtlicher) Kirchendiener.
side: ~**splitting** adj urkomisch, zum Totlachen (inf); ~**step 1** n Schritt m zur Seite; (dancing) Seitenschritt m; (Sport) Ausfallschritt m; (fig: dodge) Ausweichmanöver nt; a master of the dribble and ~step ein Meister im Dribbeln und Ausweichen; 2 vt tackle, punch (seitwärts) ausweichen (+dat); person ausweichen (+dat); (fig) ausweichen (+dat), umgehen; 3 vi (seitwärts or zur Seite) ausweichen; (fig) ausweichen, ausweichende Antworten geben; ~ **street** n Seitenstraße f; ~**stroke** n Seitenschwimmen nt; to do the ~stroke seitenschwimmen; ~**swipe** n Puff m (inf); (fig) Seitenhieb m (at gegen); to take a ~swipe at sb (lit) jdm einen Puff geben; (verbally) jdm einen Seitenhieb versetzen; ~ **table** n Beistelltisch m; ~**track 1** n (esp US) see siding; 2 vt ablenken; I got ~tracked onto something else ich wurde durch irgend etwas abgelenkt; (from topic) ich wurde irgendwie vom Thema abgebracht or auf ein anderes Thema gebracht; to ~track sb onto sth jdn auf etw (acc) bringen; she's easily ~tracked sie läßt sich leicht ablenken; ~ **view** n Seitenansicht f; to have a ~ **view** of sth etw von der Seite sehen; I just caught a ~ view of the queen's head ich konnte die Königin nur kurz im Profil sehen; ~**walk** n (US) Bürgersteig, Gehsteig m, Trottoir (S Ger) nt; ~ **wall** n Seitenwand f; ~**ward** adj see ~wards 1; ~**wards**, ~**ways** 1 adj movement zur Seite; glance von der Seite; to give sb/sth a ~**wards** or ~**ways** glance jdn/etw von der Seite ansehen; 2 adv move zur Seite, seitwärts; look at sb von der Seite; it goes in ~**ways** or ~**wards** es geht seitwärts hinein; ~**ways** on seitlich (to sth zu etw); ~ **whiskers** npl Backenbart m; ~ **wind** n Seitenwind m; ~**winder** n (US: blow) Schlag m.
siding [ˈsaɪdɪŋ] n Rangiergleis nt; (dead end) Abstellgleis nt.
sidle [ˈsaɪdl] vi (sich) schleichen. to ~ away (sich) wegschleichen; he must have ~d off er muß sich verdrückt haben (inf); to ~ up to sb sich an jdn heranschleichen.
siege [siːdʒ] n (of town) Belagerung f; (by police) Umstellung f. to lay ~ to a town/a house eine Stadt/ein Haus belagern/umstellen; he attempted to lay ~ to her emotions er versuchte, ihr Herz zu erobern.
sienna [sɪˈenə] 1 n (earth) Sienaerde f; (colour) Ockergelb nt. raw ~ Ockergelb nt; burnt ~ gebrannte Siena. 2 adj ockergelb. raw ~ ockergelb; burnt ~ siena(braun), rotbraun.
sierra [sɪˈerə] n Sierra f.
Sierra Leone [sɪˈerəlɪˈəʊn] n Sierra Leone f.
siesta [sɪˈestə] n Siesta f. to have or take a ~ Siesta halten or machen.
sieve [sɪv] 1 n Sieb nt. to have a memory like a ~ (inf) ein Gedächtnis wie ein Sieb haben (inf). 2 vt see **sift** 1 (a).
sift [sɪft] 1 vt (a) sieben; coal schütteln. ~ the sugar onto the cake den Kuchen mit Zucker besieben.
 (b) (fig: search) sichten, durchgehen; (separate) trennen.
 2 vi (fig) sieben. to ~ through the evidence das Beweismaterial durchgehen; a ~ing process ein Siebverfahren n.
♦ **sift out** vt sep (a) stones, seed, wheat aussieben. (b) (fig) herausfinden, herauskristallisieren; (eliminate) absondern; applicants aussieben.
sifter [ˈsɪftə^r] n Mehl-/Zuckerstreuer m.
sigh [saɪ] 1 n (of person) Seufzer m; (of wind) (murmur) Säuseln nt no pl; (moan) Seufzen nt no pl (liter). a ~ of relief ein Seufzer der Erleichterung; to ~ breathe.
 2 vti seufzen; (wind) (murmur) säuseln; (moan) seufzen (liter). to ~ with relief erleichtert aufatmen; to ~ with contentment zufrieden seufzen; to ~ for sb/sth sich nach jdm/etw sehnen.
sighing [ˈsaɪɪŋ] n see vti Seufzen nt; Säuseln nt; Seufzen nt (liter).

sight [saɪt] 1 n (a) (faculty) Sehvermögen nt. the gift of ~ die Gabe des Sehens; long/short ~ Weit-/Kurzsichtigkeit f; to have long/short ~ weit-/kurzsichtig sein; to lose/regain one's ~ sein Augenlicht verlieren/wiedergewinnen; he has very good ~ er sieht sehr gut; ~ is the most valuable sense das Auge ist das wertvollste Sinnesorgan.
 (b) (glimpse, seeing) it was my first ~ of Paris das war das erste, was ich von Paris gesehen habe; to hate sb at first ~ or on ~ jdn vom ersten Augenblick an nicht leiden können; at first ~ I hated him, but then ... als ich ihn zum erstenmal sah, or zuerst konnte ich ihn gar nicht leiden, aber dann ...; at first ~ it seemed easy auf den ersten Blick erschien es einfach; to shoot at or on ~ sofort schießen; to translate at or on ~ vom Blatt übersetzen; he played the music by or at ~ er hat vom Blatt gespielt; love at first ~ Liebe auf den ersten Blick; at the ~ of the police they ran away als sie die Polizei sahen, rannten sie weg; to know sb by ~ jdn vom Sehen kennen; to catch ~ of sb/sth jdn/etw entdecken or erblicken; if I catch ~ of you round here again ... wenn du mir hier noch einmal unter die Augen kommst, ...; don't let me catch ~ of you with her again ich möchte dich nicht noch einmal mit ihr erwischen; to get or have a ~ of sb/sth jdn/etw zu sehen or zu Gesicht bekommen; we had a glorious ~ of the mountains wir hatten einen herrlichen Blick auf die Berge; to lose ~ of sb/sth (lit, fig) jdn/etw aus den Augen verlieren; don't lose ~ of the fact that ... Sie dürfen nicht außer acht lassen, daß ...; payable at ~ (Comm) zahlbar bei Sicht; 30 days' ~ (Comm) 30 Tage nach Sicht; ~ unseen (Comm) unbesehen, ohne Besicht (form); see second ~.
 (c) (sth seen) Anblick m. the ~ of blood/her makes me sick wenn ich Blut/sie sehe, wird mir übel; that is the most beautiful ~ I've ever seen das ist das Schönste, was ich je gesehen habe; I hate or can't bear the ~ of him/his greasy hair ich kann ihn (einfach) nicht ausstehen/ich finde seine fettigen Haare widerlich; to be a ~ to see or behold ein herrlicher Anblick sein; (funny) ein Bild or Anblick für die Götter sein (inf); what a horrible ~! das sieht ja furchtbar aus!; it was a ~ for sore eyes war eine wahre Augenweide; you're a ~ for sore eyes es ist schön, dich zu sehen.
 (d) (inf) to be or look a ~ (funny) zum Schreien aussehen (inf); (horrible) fürchterlich aussehen; he looks a ~ der sieht vielleicht aus (inf); what a ~ you are! wie siehst du denn aus!
 (e) (range of vision) Sicht f. to be in or within ~ in Sicht or in Sichtweite sein; land in ~! Land in Sicht!; our goal is in ~ unser Ziel ist in greifbare Nähe gerückt; we are in ~ of victory unser Sieg liegt in greifbarer Nähe; we came in ~ of the coast die Küste kam in Sicht; at last we were in ~ of land endlich war Land in Sicht; to keep sb in ~ jdn im Auge behalten; to keep out of ~ sich verborgen halten; to keep sb/sth out of ~ jdn/etw nicht sehen lassen; keep out of my ~! laß dich bloß bei mir nicht mehr sehen or blicken; to be out of or lost to ~ nicht mehr zu sehen sein, außer Sicht sein; the minute I was out of ~ of the school/the headmaster sobald ich von der Schule aus nicht mehr zu sehen war/sobald mich der Rektor nicht mehr sehen konnte; when he's out of our ~ wenn wir ihn nicht sehen; somewhere out of ~ a cat was mewing irgendwo miaute eine (unsichtbare) Katze; don't let the children out of your ~ laß die Kinder nicht aus den Augen; the first time I let him out of my ~ he was almost run over als ich einmal nicht auf ihn aufpaßte, wurde er fast überfahren; darling, I'll never let you out of my ~ again Schatz, ich lasse dich nie mehr fort; to drop out of (sb's) ~ langsam verschwinden, (jds Blick dat) entschwinden (geh); to be lost to ~ nicht mehr zu sehen sein; out of ~, out of mind (Prov) aus den Augen, aus dem Sinn (Prov).
 (f) (fig: opinion) in sb's ~ in jds Augen (dat); in the ~ of God vor Gott.
 (g) usu pl (of city etc) Sehenswürdigkeit f. to see the ~s of a town etc eine Stadt etc besichtigen.
 (h) (on gun, telescope etc) Visiereinrichtung f; (on gun also) Visier nt. to set one's ~s too high (fig) seine Ziele zu hoch stecken; to lower one's ~s (fig) seine Ansprüche herabsetzen or herunterschrauben; to set one's ~s on sth (fig) ein Auge auf etw (acc) werfen; to have sb/sth in one's ~s (fig) jdn/etw im Fadenkreuz haben.
 (i) (aim, observation) to take a ~ with a gun etc at sth etw mit einem Gewehr etc anvisieren.
 (j) (inf) not by a long ~ bei weitem nicht; we're not finished yet, not by a long ~ wir sind noch lange nicht fertig; a ~ better/cheaper einiges besser/billiger; he's a damn ~ cleverer than you think er ist ein ganzes Ende gescheiter als du meinst (inf).
 (k) (sl) out of ~ sagenhaft (sl), 'ne Wucht (sl).
 2 vt (a) (see) sichten (also Mil); person ausmachen.
 (b) gun (provide with ~s) mit Visier versehen; (adjust ~s) richten.
sight bill n Sichtwechsel m.
sighted [ˈsaɪtɪd] adj sehend.
-sighted adj suf -sichtig.
sighting [ˈsaɪtɪŋ] n Sichten nt. at the first ~ of land als zum ersten Mal Land gesichtet wurde; another ~ of the monster was reported das Ungeheuer soll erneut gesehen or gesichtet worden sein.
sightless [ˈsaɪtlɪs] adj blind. worms are completely ~ Würmer haben kein Sehvermögen (form), Würmer können überhaupt nicht sehen; with ~ eyes mit blicklosen (geh) or toten Augen.
sightlessness [ˈsaɪtlɪsnɪs] n Blindheit f.
sightly [ˈsaɪtlɪ] adj ansehnlich.
sight: ~**read** vti vom Blatt spielen/lesen/singen; ~ **screen** n (Cricket) Sichtblende f hinter dem Tor; ~**seeing** 1 n Besichtigungen pl; I hate ~seeing ich hasse Sightseeing; ~seeing in Ruritania eine Rundreise durch Ruritania; (list of sights) Sehenswürdigkeiten pl von Ruritanien; to go ~seeing auf Besichtigungstour gehen; 2 adj ~seeing tour Rundreise f; (in

town) (Stadt)rundfahrt *f;* **~seeing tourists** Touristen *pl (auf Besichtigungstour);* **~seer** *n* Tourist(in *f) m.*

sign [saɪn] **1** *n* **(a)** *(with hand etc)* Zeichen *nt.* **he nodded as a ~ of recognition** er nickte zum Zeichen, daß er mich/ihn *etc* erkannt hatte; **to give sb a ~** jdm ein Zeichen geben; **to make a ~ to sb** jdm ein Zeichen machen *or* geben; **he gave** *or* **made me a ~** to stay er gab mir durch ein Zeichen zu verstehen, ich solle bleiben; **he made a rude ~** er machte eine unverschämte Geste.

(b) *(indication, Med)* Anzeichen *nt (of* für, *gen); (evidence)* Zeichen *nt (of* von, *gen); (trace)* Spur *f.* **a sure/good/bad ~** ein sicheres/gutes/schlechtes Zeichen; **it's a ~ of the times** es ist ein Zeichen unserer Zeit; **it's a ~ of the true expert** daran erkennt man den wahren Experten; **at the slightest/first ~ of disagreement** beim geringsten/ersten Anzeichen von Uneinigkeit; **there is no ~ of their agreeing** nichts deutet darauf hin, daß sie zustimmen werden; **to show ~s of** sth Anzeichen von etw erkennen lassen; **he shows ~s of doing it** es sieht so aus, als ob er es tun würde; **our guest showed no ~s of leaving** unser Gast machte keine Anstalten zu gehen; **the rain showed no ~s of stopping** nichts deutete darauf hin, daß der Regen aufhören würde; **there was no ~ of life in the village** es gab keine Spur *or* kein Anzeichen von Leben im Dorf; **there was no ~ of him/the book anywhere** von ihm/von dem Buch war keine Spur zu sehen; **is there any ~ of him yet?** ist er schon im Zeichen gekommen?

(c) *(road~, inn ~, shop ~)* Schild *nt.*

(d) *(written symbol)* Zeichen *nt; (Astron)* (Stern- *or* Tierkreis)zeichen *nt.*

2 *vt* **(a)** **to ~ one's name** unterschreiben; **~ your name, don't type it** schreiben Sie Ihren Namen von Hand, nicht mit der Maschine; **to ~ one's name in a book** sich in ein Buch eintragen; **he ~s himself J.G. Jones** er unterschreibt mit J.G. Jones.

(b) *letter, contract, cheque* unterschreiben, unterzeichnen *(form); picture, book* signieren. **to ~ the guest book** sich ins Gästebuch eintragen; **to ~ the register** sich eintragen; **~ed and sealed** (unterschrieben und) besiegelt; **~ed, sealed and delivered** unter Dach und Fach, fix und fertig *(inf);* **~ed copy** handsigniertes Exemplar.

3 *vi* **(a)** *(signal)* **to ~ to sb to do sth** jdm einen Zeichen geben, etw zu tun, jdm bedeuten, etw zu tun *(geh).*

(b) *(with signature)* unterschreiben.

♦ **sign away** *vt sep* verzichten auf (+*acc).* **she felt she was ~ing ~ her life** sie hatte den Eindruck, ihr Leben abzuschreiben; **I'm not going to ~ my life ~ with a mortgage** ich werde mich nicht ein Leben lang mit einer Hypothek belasten.

♦ **sign for** *vi* +*prep obj* den Empfang (+*gen)* bestätigen.

♦ **sign in 1** *vt sep person* eintragen. **to ~ sb ~ at a club** jdn als Gast in einen Klub mitnehmen. **2** *vi* sich eintragen.

♦ **sign off** *vi (Rad, TV)* sich verabschieden; *(in letter)* Schluß machen.

♦ **sign on 1** *vt sep see* **sign up 1. 2** *vi* **(a)** *see* **sign up 2. (b)** *(for unemployment benefit etc) (apply)* beantragen *(for* acc); *(register regularly)* sich melden. **(c)** *(disc jockey etc)* sich melden.

♦ **sign out 1** *vi* sich austragen. **to ~ ~ of a hotel** (aus einem Hotel) abreisen. **2** *vt sep* austragen.

♦ **sign over** *vt sep* überschreiben *(to sb* jdm).

♦ **sign up 1** *vt sep (employ, enlist)* verpflichten; *workers, employees* anstellen; *mercenaries* anwerben; *sailors* anheuern. **2** *vi* sich verpflichten; *(mercenaries)* sich melden *(with* zu); *(employees, players also)* sich verschreiben; *(sailors)* anheuern; *(for evening class etc)* sich einschreiben.

signal¹ [ˈsɪɡnl] **1** *n* **(a)** *(sign)* Zeichen *nt; (as part of code)* Signal *nt; (message)* Nachricht *f.* **engaged** *or* **busy** *(US)* **~** *(Telec)* Besetztzeichen *nt;* **to give the ~ for sth** das Zeichen/Signal zu etw geben; **to make a ~ to sb** jdm ein Zeichen geben.

(b) *(apparatus, Rail)* Signal *nt.* **the ~ is at red** das Signal steht auf Rot.

(c) *(Telec)* Signal *nt.*

(d) *(Brit Mil)* **S~s** = Fernmelder *pl,* Angehörige *pl* der britischen Fernmeldetruppe *Royal Corps of Signals.*

2 *vt* **(a)** *(indicate)* anzeigen; *arrival, (fig) future event, spring etc* ankündigen. **to ~ sb to do sth** jdm ein Zeichen geben, etw zu tun; **the policeman ~led the cars on** der Polizist gab den Autos das Zeichen weiterzufahren; **to ~ a turn to the right/left** nach rechts/links anzeigen; **he ~led that he was going to turn left** er zeigte an, daß er (nach) links abbiegen wollte; **the train was ~led onto another line** der Zug wurde durch Signale auf ein anderes Gleis gewiesen *or* geleitet; **the green light ~led the train on** das grüne Licht gab dem Zug freie Fahrt.

(b) *message* signalisieren.

3 *vi* Zeichen/ein Zeichen geben. **he ~led to the waiter** er winkte dem Ober; **he ~led for his bill** er winkte zum Zeichen, daß er zahlen wollte; **the driver didn't ~** der Fahrer hat kein Zeichen gegeben *or* hat nicht angezeigt; **the general ~led for reinforcements** der General forderte Verstärkung an.

signal² *adj attr (liter) victory, courage* beachtlich, bemerkenswert; *failure, stupidity* eklatant *(geh).*

signal: ~ box *n* Stellwerk *nt;* **~ flag** *n* Signalflagge *f.*

signalize [ˈsɪɡnəlaɪz] *vt* kennzeichnen.

signal lamp *n* Signallampe *f.*

signaller [ˈsɪɡnələ^r] *n (Mil)* Fernmelder, Funker *m.*

signalling [ˈsɪɡnəlɪŋ] *n (Mil)* Nachrichtenübermittlung *f.*

signally [ˈsɪɡnəlɪ] *adv (liter) see adj* bemerkenswert; eklatant.

signal: ~man *n (Rail)* Stellwerkswärter *m; (Mil)* Fernmelder, Funker *m;* **~ red** *n* signalrot.

signatory [ˈsɪɡnətərɪ] **1** *adj* Signatar-. **the ~ powers to an agreement** die Signatarmächte eines Abkommens. **2** *n* Unterzeichnete(r) *mf (form),* Signatar *m (form).* **the signatories** *or* **to the EEC treaty** die Signatarstaaten des EWG-Abkommens.

signature [ˈsɪɡnətʃə^r] *n* **(a)** Unterschrift *f; (of artist)* Signatur *f.*

(b) *(Mus)* Vorzeichnung *f.* **~ tune** *(Brit)* Erkennungsmelodie *f.*

(c) *(Typ)* Signatur *f.*

signboard [ˈsaɪnbɔːd] *n* Schild *nt; (hoarding)* Anschlagtafel *f.*

signer [ˈsaɪnə^r] *n* Unterzeichner *m.*

signet ring [ˈsɪɡnɪtˌrɪŋ] *n* Siegelring *m.*

significance [sɪɡˈnɪfɪkəns] *n* Bedeutung *f; (of action also)* Tragweite *f; (of one special event also)* Wichtigkeit *f.* **what is the ~ of this?** was bedeutet das?, welche Bedeutung hat das?; **all films should have some ~ for our times** alle Filme sollten für unsere Zeit bedeutsam sein; **of no ~** belanglos, bedeutungslos; **to attach great ~ to sth** einer Sache *(dat)* große Bedeutung beimessen; **he attaches great ~ to us arriving on time** er legt großen Wert darauf, daß wir pünktlich sind.

significant [sɪɡˈnɪfɪkənt] *adj (considerable, having consequence)* bedeutend; *(important)* wichtig; *(meaningful)* bedeutungsvoll; *look* vielsagend, bedeutsam. **is it of any ~ interest?** ist das von wesentlichem Interesse?; **it is ~ that …** es ist bezeichnend, daß …; **to be ~ to** *or* **for sth** eine bedeutende *or* wichtige Rolle in etw *(dat)* spielen; **he doubted whether the marks on the wall were ~** er bezweifelte, daß die Zeichen an der Wand irgendeine Bedeutung hatten; **he wondered whether her glance was ~** er fragte sich, ob ihr Blick etwas zu bedeuten habe; **to be ~ of sth** *(liter)* ein (An)zeichen für etw sein.

significantly [sɪɡˈnɪfɪkəntlɪ] *adv (considerably)* bedeutend; *(meaningfully)* bedeutungsvoll; *look* vielsagend, bedeutsam. **it is not ~ different** das ist kaum anders, da besteht kein wesentlicher Unterschied; **~ enough, they both had the same name** bezeichnenderweise trugen sie beide denselben Namen.

signification [ˌsɪɡnɪfɪˈkeɪʃən] *n* **(a)** *(meaning)* Sinn *m,* Bedeutung *f.* **(b)** *(indication)* Bezeichnung *f.* **he gave us no ~ of what he was going to do** er machte uns gegenüber keine Andeutung, was er tun würde; **a ~ of one's intentions** eine Absichtsbekundung *or* -erklärung.

signify [ˈsɪɡnɪfaɪ] **1** *vt* **(a)** *(mean)* bedeuten. **(b)** *(indicate)* andeuten, erkennen lassen; *(person also)* zu erkennen geben. **2** *vi (dated)* **it/he doesn't ~** das/er spielt keine Rolle.

sign: ~ language *n* Zeichensprache *f;* **~ painter** *n* Plakat- *or* Schildermaler *m;* **~post 1** *n* Wegweiser *m;* **2** *vt way* beschildern; *diversion, special route* ausschildern; **~posting** *n* Beschilderung *f; (of special route, diversion)* Ausschilderung *f;* **~writer** *n* Schriften- *or* Schildermaler *m.*

Sikh [siːk] *n* Sikh *mf.*

silage [ˈsaɪlɪdʒ] *n* Silage *f,* Silofutter *nt.*

silence [ˈsaɪləns] **1** *n* Stille *f; (quietness also)* Ruhe *f; (absence of talk also, of letters etc)* Schweigen *nt; (on a particular subject)* (Still)schweigen *nt.* **~!** Ruhe!; **in ~** still; *(not talking also)* schweigend; **there was ~** alles war still; **there was a short ~** es herrschte für kurze Zeit Stille; **the conversation was full of awkward ~s** die Unterhaltung kam immer wieder ins Stocken; **radio ~** *(Mil)* Funkstille *f;* **to break the/one's ~** die Stille durchbrechen/sein Schweigen brechen; **the ~ of the night** die Stille der Nacht, die nächtliche Stille.

2 *vt (lit, fig)* zum Schweigen bringen. **to ~ sb's tongue** jdn zum Schweigen bringen.

silencer [ˈsaɪlənsə^r] *n (on gun, Brit: on car)* Schalldämpfer *m; (whole fitting on car)* Auspufftopf *m.*

silent [ˈsaɪlənt] *adj* still; *(not talking also)* schweigsam; *engine, machine etc (running quietly)* ruhig; *agreement, disapproval* (still)schweigend *attr.* **~ movie/letter** Stummfilm *m*/stummer Buchstabe; **~ partner** *(US)* stiller Teilhaber *or* Gesellschafter; **the ~ majority** die schweigende Mehrheit; **to be ~ (about sth)** (über etw acc) schweigen; **to keep** *or* **remain ~** still sein *or* bleiben, sich still verhalten; *(about sth)* nichts sagen, sich nicht äußern; **he kept completely ~ when questioned** er sagte kein einziges Wort *or* überhaupt nichts, als man ihn verhörte; **everyone kept ~** keiner sagte etwas; **be ~!** sei/seid still!; **to become ~** still werden; *(people also, guns)* verstummen.

silently [ˈsaɪləntlɪ] *adv* lautlos; *(without talking)* schweigend; *(with little noise)* leise.

silhouette [ˌsɪluːˈet] **1** *n* Silhouette *f; (picture)* Schattenriß, Scherenschnitt *m.* **2** *vt* **to be ~d against sth** sich (als Silhouette) gegen *or* von etw abzeichnen.

silica [ˈsɪlɪkə] *n* Kieselerde *f.* **~ gel** Kieselgel *nt.*

silicate [ˈsɪlɪkɪt] *n* Silikat, Silicat *nt.*

siliceous [sɪˈlɪʃəs] *adj* kiesig, Kies-.

silicon [ˈsɪlɪkən] *n* Silicium *nt.* **~ chip** Siliciumchip *nt.*

silicone [ˈsɪlɪkəʊn] *n* Silikon *nt.* **~ treatment** Silikonbehandlung *f.*

silicosis [ˌsɪlɪˈkəʊsɪs] *n (Med)* Staublunge, Silikose *(spec) f.*

silk [sɪlk] **1** *n* **(a)** Seide *f; (~ dress)* Seidene(s), Seidenkleid *nt.* **dressed in beautiful ~s** in herrliche Seidengewänder gekleidet; **dressed in ~s and satins** in Samt und Seide (gekleidet).

(b) *(Brit Jur) (barrister)* Kronanwalt *m; (gown)* Seidengewand *nt.* **to take ~** Kronanwalt werden.

(c) **~s** *pl (racing colours)* (Renn)farben *pl.*

2 *adj* Seiden-, seiden. **the dress is ~** das Kleid ist aus Seide.

silken [ˈsɪlkən] *adj (old: of silk)* seiden; *(like silk also)* seidig; *manner* glatt; *voice* (bedrohlich) sanft.

silk hat *n* Zylinder *m.*

silkiness [ˈsɪlkɪnɪs] *n (appearance)* seidiger Glanz; *(feeling)* seidige Weichheit; *(of voice)* Sanftheit *f; (of manner)* Glätte *f.*

silk: ~ moth *n* Seidenspinner *m;* **~ screen** *n* Seidensieb *nt; (also* **~-screen printing)** Seidensiebdruck *m;* **~ stocking** *n* Seidenstrumpf *m;* **~-stocking** *adj (US)* vornehm; **~worm** *n* Seidenraupe *f.*

silky [ˈsɪlkɪ] *adj (+er) (also)* seidig; *voice* samtig; *manner* glatt.

sill [sɪl] *n* Sims *m or nt; (window~)* (Fenster)sims *m or nt; (esp of wood)* Fensterbrett *nt; (door~)* Schwelle *f; (on car)* Türleiste *f.*

sillabub *n see* **syllabub.**

silliness [ˈsɪlɪnɪs] *n* Albernheit *f.* **no ~ while we're out, children!** macht keine Dummheiten, wenn wir nicht da sind!

silly ['sɪlɪ] **1** adj (+er) albern, dumm, doof (inf). ~ **season** närrische Zeit; (Press) Sauregurkenzeit f; **you ~ child!** du Kindskopf!; **don't be ~** (do ~ things) mach keinen Quatsch (inf); (say ~ things) red keinen Unsinn; (ask ~ questions) frag nicht so dumm; **that was ~ of you, that was a ~ thing to do** das war dumm (von dir); **I've done a ~ thing and come without the key** ich war so dumm, ohne Schlüssel zu kommen, ich Dussel bin ohne Schlüssel gekommen (inf); **I've done a ~ thing and told you a pointless lie** ich habe dich ohne Grund angelogen, das war dumm von mir; **I feel ~ in this hat** mit diesem Hut komme ich mir albern or lächerlich vor; **to make sb look ~** jdn lächerlich machen; **that remark of yours made him look/left him looking a bit ~** nach dieser Bemerkung von dir stand er ziemlich dumm da; **to knock sb ~** jdn windelweich schlagen (inf).
2 n (Brit: also ~-billy) Dussel m (inf). **you big ~** du Dummerchen (inf); **don't be such a ~** sei nicht albern.
silo ['saɪləʊ] n Silo nt; (for missile) unterirdische Startrampe.
silt [sɪlt] **1** n Schwemmsand m; (river mud) Schlick m. **2** vt (also ~ up) mit Schlick/Schwemmsand füllen. **3** vi (also ~ up) verschlammen.
Silurian [saɪ'ljuːrɪən] adj (Geol) silurisch, Silur-.
silver ['sɪlvəʳ] **1** n (a) (metal) Silber nt.
(b) (coins) Silber(geld) nt, Silbermünzen pl. **£10 in ~** £ 10 in Silber; **a ~ collection** eine Sammlung.
(c) (tableware, articles) Silber nt.
2 adj Silber-, silbern. **to be born with a ~ spoon in one's mouth** (prov) mit einem silbernen Löffel im Mund geboren sein (prov).
3 vt metal, mirror versilbern. **old age had ~ed his hair** das Alter hatte sein Haar silbergrau werden lassen.
silver: ~ **birch** n Weißbirke f; ~ **fir** n Weiß- or Silbertanne f; ~**fish** n Silberfischchen nt; ~ **foil** n (kitchen foil) Alu(minium)folie f; (~ paper) Silberpapier nt; ~ **fox** n Silberfuchs m; ~**grey** adj silbergrau; **hair** silberweiß; ~**-haired** adj silberhaarig; **he is ~-haired** er hat silberweißes Haar.
silveriness ['sɪlvərɪnɪs] n silbriger Schimmer; (of sound, voice) silberheller Klang.
silver: ~ **jubilee** n 25jähriges Jubiläum; ~ **nitrate** n Silbernitrat nt; ~ **paper** n Silberpapier nt; ~ **plate** n (plating) Silberauflage, Versilberung f; (articles) versilberte Sachen pl; **is that ~ plate?** ist das versilbert?; ~**-plate** vt versilbern; ~**plating** n Versilberung f; (layer also) Silberauflage f; ~ **screen** n Leinwand f; ~**side** n (Cook) quergeschnittenes Stück aus der Rindskeule; ~**smith** n Silberschmied m; ~**smith's (shop)** n Silberschmiede f; ~ **standard** n Silberstandard m; ~**-tongued** adj (liter) wort- or redegewandt; ~**ware** n Silber(zeug inf) nt; (in shop also) Silberwaren pl; ~ **wedding** n Silberhochzeit f.
silvery ['sɪlvərɪ] adj silbern, silbrig; sound, voice silberhell.
simian ['sɪmɪən] **1** adj (form) der Affen; appearance affenartig.
2 n Affe m.
similar ['sɪmɪləʳ] adj ähnlich (also Math); amount, size fast or ungefähr gleich. **this is ~ to what happened before** etwas Ähnliches ist schon einmal geschehen; **she and her sister are very ~, she is very ~ to her sister** ihre Schwester und sie sind sich sehr ähnlich, sie ähnelt ihrer Schwester sehr; **the two sisters are very ~ in appearance/character** die beiden Schwestern ähneln sich äußerlich/charakterlich sehr; ~ **in size** ungefähr or fast gleich groß; **in a ~ way** ähnlich; (likewise) genauso, ebenso.
similarity [ˌsɪmɪ'lærɪtɪ] n Ähnlichkeit f (to mit).
similarly ['sɪmɪləlɪ] adv ähnlich; (equally) genauso, ebenso. **a ~ abstruse expression** ein genauso wirrer Ausdruck; **~, you could maintain ...** genausogut or ebensogut könnten Sie behaupten ...
simile ['sɪmɪlɪ] n Gleichnis nt. **his use of ~** sein Gebrauch von Gleichnissen.
similitude [sɪ'mɪlɪtjuːd] n (liter) Ähnlichkeit f.
simmer ['sɪməʳ] **1** n to be on the ~ (Cook) simmern, sieden; (fig) (with rage) kochen (inf); (with excitement) fiebern; **he was on the ~** es kochte in ihm; **to keep sb/sth on the ~** (lit) etw (weiter)simmern or -sieden lassen; (fig) jdn/etw nicht zur Ruhe kommen lassen; **his outrageous behaviour kept her anger on the ~** sie konnte sich über sein unerhörtes Benehmen einfach nicht beruhigen.
2 vt simmern or sieden lassen.
3 vi simmern, sieden; (fig) (with rage) kochen (inf); (with excitement) fiebern.
♦**simmer down** vi sich beruhigen, sich abregen (inf).
simnel cake ['sɪmnlkeɪk] n (Brit) marzipanüberzogener Früchtekuchen.
simonize ® ['saɪmənaɪz] vt polieren.
simony ['saɪmənɪ] n (old, Eccl) Simonie f.
simper ['sɪmpəʳ] **1** n her ~s and poses ihr Gehabe und Getue; ... **she said with a ~** sagte sie affektiert. **2** vi (smile) geziert or albern lächeln; (talk) säuseln. **3** vt säuseln.
simpering ['sɪmpərɪŋ] adj geziert, albern.
simperingly ['sɪmpərɪŋlɪ] adv geziert, albern; talk säuselnd.
simple ['sɪmpl] adj (+er) **(a)** (easy, not complicated, Math, Med, Gram) einfach; (Fin) interest also gewöhnlich. ~ **time** (Mus) gerader Takt; **it's as ~ as ABC** das ist kinderleicht, das ist ein Kinderspiel; **"chemistry made ~"** „Chemie leichtgemacht".
(b) (plain, not elaborate) einfach; decor, dress also schlicht. **the ~ fact or truth is ...** es ist einfach so, daß ...
(c) (unsophisticated, unworldly) einfach, schlicht. **I'm a ~ soul** ich bin (nur) ein einfacher Mensch.
(d) (foolish, mentally deficient) einfältig.
simple: ~**-minded** adj einfältig; ~**-mindedness** n Einfältigkeit, Einfalt f.
simpleton ['sɪmpltən] n Einfaltspinsel m.
simplex ['sɪmpleks] n (Ling) Simplex nt.
simplicity [sɪm'plɪsɪtɪ] n (a) Einfachheit f; (unworldliness, lack of sophistication, of decor, dress also) Schlichtheit f. **it's ~**

itself das ist das Einfachste, das ist die einfachste Sache der Welt.
(b) (foolishness) Einfalt, Einfältigkeit f.
simplifiable ['sɪmplɪfaɪəbl] adj zu vereinfachend attr, zu vereinfachen pred, simplifizierbar.
simplification [ˌsɪmplɪfɪ'keɪʃən] n Vereinfachung, Simplifizierung f.
simplify ['sɪmplɪfaɪ] vt vereinfachen, simplifizieren.
simplistic [sɪm'plɪstɪk] adj simpel, simplistisch (geh).
simply ['sɪmplɪ] adv einfach; (merely) nur, bloß. **but you ~ must!** aber du mußt einfach!
simulate ['sɪmjʊleɪt] vt (a) (feign) amazement, emotions vortäuschen; enthusiasm also spielen; illness simulieren. **to ~ (the appearance of) sth** (material) etw imitieren; (animal, person) sich als etw tarnen; ~**d leather/sheepskin** Lederimitation f/falsches Schafsfell.
(b) (reproduce) conditions, environment simulieren.
simulation [ˌsɪmjʊ'leɪʃən] n (a) Vortäuschung f; (simulated appearance) Imitation f; (of animals) Tarnung f. **his ~ of epilepsy** seine simulierte Epilepsie. **(b)** (reproduction) Simulation f.
simulator ['sɪmjʊleɪtəʳ] n Simulator m.
simultaneity [ˌsɪmltə'nɪɪtɪ] n Gleichzeitigkeit, Simultan(e)ität (geh) f.
simultaneous [ˌsɪml'teɪnɪəs] adj gleichzeitig, simultan (geh). ~ **equations** (Math) Simultangleichungen pl; ~ **translation** Simultanübersetzung f.
simultaneously [ˌsɪml'teɪnɪəslɪ] adv gleichzeitig, zur gleicher Zeit, simultan (geh).
sin [sɪn] **1** n (Rel, fig) Sünde f. **to live in ~** (inf) in wilder Ehe leben; (Rel) in Sünde leben; **I've been chosen to organize the office party, for my ~s** (hum) man hat mich drangekriegt (inf), ich darf die Büroparty organisieren; **is that your work/family?** — **yes for my ~s** (hum) haben Sie das gemacht/ist das Ihre Familie? — ja, leider; **to cover a multitude of ~s** (hum) viele Schandtaten verdecken; **this hat is covering a multitude of ~s,** she said (hum) aber fragen Sie bloß nicht, wie es unter dem Hut aussieht!, sagte sie; **isn't it a ~!** ist das nicht unerhört or eine (Sünde und) Schande!
2 vi sündigen (against gegen, an +dat), sich versündigen (against an +dat); (against principles, standards etc) verstoßen (gegen). **he was more ~ned against than ~ning** er hat mehr Unrecht erlitten als begangen.
Sinai ['saɪneɪɪ] n Sinai m. ~ **Peninsula** Sinaihalbinsel f; **Mount ~** der Berg Sinai.
since [sɪns] **1** adv (in the meantime) inzwischen; (up to now) seitdem. **ever ~** seither; **a long time ~,** long ~ schon lange; **he died long ~** er ist schon lange tot; **not long ~** erst vor kurzem.
2 prep seit. **ever ~ 1900** (schon) seit 1900; **he had been living there ~ 1900** er lebte da schon seit 1900; **I've been coming here ~ 1972** ich komme schon seit 1972 hierher; **it's a long time ~ ...** then das ist schon lange her; **how long is it ~ the accident?** wie lange ist der Unfall schon her?
3 conj (a) (time) seit(dem). **ever ~ I've known him** seit(dem) ich ihn kenne.
(b) (because) da.
sincere [sɪn'sɪəʳ] adj aufrichtig, lauter (liter); person also offen; intention also ernst, ehrlich. **a ~ friend** ein wahrer Freund; **it is our ~ hope that ...** wir hoffen aufrichtig, daß ...
sincerely [sɪn'sɪəlɪ] adv see adj aufrichtig; offen; ernsthaft. **yours ~** mit freundlichen Grüßen, hochachtungsvoll (form).
sincerity [sɪn'serɪtɪ] n see adj Aufrichtigkeit, Lauterkeit (liter) f; Offenheit f; Ernsthaftigkeit f. **in all ~** in aller Offenheit; **I was acting in all ~ when ...** ich habe es ganz aufrichtig or ehrlich gemeint, als ...
sine [saɪn] n (Math) Sinus m.
sinecure ['saɪnɪkjʊəʳ] n Pfründe, Sinekure (geh) f. **this job is no ~!** diese Arbeit ist kein Ruheposten.
sine die [ˌsaɪnɪ'daɪiː, 'sɪneɪ'diːeɪ] adv **to adjourn ~** auf unbestimmte Zeit vertagen.
sine qua non [ˌsɪnɪkwɑː'nəʊn] n unerläßliche Voraussetzung, Conditio sine qua non f (to, for für).
sinew ['sɪnjuː] n Sehne f. ~**s** pl (fig) Kräfte pl, Stärke f.
sinewy ['sɪnjʊɪ] adj sehnig; (fig) plant, tree knorrig; prose style kraftvoll, kernig.
sinfonia [sɪn'fəʊnɪə] n (symphony) Sinfonie, Symphonie f; (overture) Opernsinfonia f; (orchestra) Sinfonie- or Symphonieorchester nt, Sinfoniker, Symphoniker pl.
sinfonietta [ˌsɪnfəʊnɪ'etə] n (music) Sinfonietta f; (orchestra) kleines Sinfonie- or Symphonieorchester.
sinful ['sɪnfʊl] adj sündig; person, act, thought also sündhaft (geh). **it is ~ to ...** es ist eine Sünde, zu ...
sinfully ['sɪnfəlɪ] adv sündig, sündhaft (geh).
sinfulness ['sɪnfʊlnɪs] n Sündigkeit, Sündhaftigkeit (geh) f.
sing [sɪŋ] (vb: pret **sang**, ptp **sung**) **1** n to have a (good) ~ (tüchtig) singen; **I used to go there for a ~** ich ging immer zum Singen hin.
2 vt singen. **to ~ a child to sleep** ein Kind in den Schlaf singen; **to ~ the praises of sb/sth** ein Loblied auf jdn/etw singen.
3 vi singen; (ears) dröhnen; (kettle) summen.
♦**sing along** vi mitsingen.
♦**sing away 1** vi (person, bird) (ununterbrochen) singen; (kettle) summen; (to oneself) vor sich (acc) hin trällern. **2** vt sep troubles fortsingen.
♦**sing of** vi +prep obj singen von (poet), besingen.
♦**sing out 1** vi (a) (sing loudly) (person, bird) laut or aus voller Kehle singen; (voice) rufen, tönen; (angrily) schimpfen. **come on, ~ ~,** let's hear you na los, singt mal tüchtig, wir wollen was hören (inf); **their voices sang ~ through the church** ihr Singen tönte durch die Kirche.
(b) (inf: shout) schreien (inf).

2 *vt sep words, tune* singen, hervorbringen; *(shout out)* (mit singender Stimme) ausrufen.
♦**sing up** *vi* lauter singen.
singable ['sɪŋəbl] *adj* sangbar *(geh)*. **that tune is (not/very)** ~ diese Melodie läßt sich (nicht/sehr) gut singen.
Singapore [,sɪŋgə'pɔː^r] *n* Singapur *nt*.
singe [sɪndʒ] **1** *vt* sengen; *clothes also* versengen; *(slightly)* ansengen; *hair-ends, poultry also* absengen. **2** *vi* versengt/ angesengt werden, sengen. **3** *n* (on clothes etc) versengte/angesengte Stelle. **there's a slight** ~ **on the sleeve** der Ärmel ist leicht angesengt.
singer ['sɪŋə^r] *n* Sänger(in *f*) *m*.
Singhalese [,sɪŋgə'liːz] **1** *adj* singhalesisch. **2** *n* **(a)** Singhalese *m*, Singhalesin *f*. **(b)** *(language)* Singhalesisch *nt*.
singing ['sɪŋɪŋ] *n* Singen *nt*; *(of person, bird also)* Gesang *m*; *(in the ears)* Dröhnen *nt*; *(of kettle)* Summen *nt*. **he teaches** ~ er gibt Sing- or Gesangstunden, er gibt Singen *(inf)*; **do you like my** ~? gefällt dir, wie ich singe?, gefällt dir mein Gesang?
singing: ~ **lesson** *n* Sing- or Gesangstunde *f*; ~ **voice** *n* Singstimme *f*.
single ['sɪŋgl] **1** *adj* **(a)** *(one only)* einzige(r, s). **not a** ~ **one spoke up** nicht ein einziger äußerte sich dazu; **every** ~ **day was precious** jeder (einzelne) Tag war kostbar; **I've missed the bus every** ~ **day this week** diese Woche habe ich jeden Tag den Bus verpaßt; **every** ~ **book I looked at** (aber auch) jedes Buch, das ich mir ansah; **with a** ~ **voice they cried out for reform** wie mit einer Stimme riefen sie nach Reformen; **not a** ~ **thing** überhaupt nichts.
  (b) *(not double etc)* einzeln; *bed, room* Einzel-; *(Typ)*, carburettor, *(Brit)* ticket einfach. **a** ~-**tank aqualung** ein Preßluftatmer *m* mit nur einer Sauerstofflasche.
  (c) *(not married)* unverheiratet, ledig. **he was tired of the** ~ **life** er hatte das Junggesellendasein satt; ~ **people** Ledige, Unverheiratete *pl*; **I'm a** ~ **man/girl** ich bin ledig.
  2 *n* **(a)** *(Cricket)* Schlag *m* für einen Lauf; *(Baseball)* Lauf *m* zum ersten Mal; *(Golf)* Zweier *m*.
  (b) *(ticket)* Einzelfahrschein *m*; *(Rail also)* Einzelfahrkarte *f*; *(room)* Einzelzimmer *nt*; *(record)* Single *f*; *(bank note)* Einpfund-/-dollarschein *m*. **a** ~/**two** ~**s to Xanadu** einmal/ zweimal einfach nach Xanadu.
  (c) *(unmarried person)* Single *m*. ~**s holiday/apartment** Urlaub *m*/Wohnung *f* für Singles; ~**s bar** Singles-Bar *f*.
♦**single out** *vt sep (choose)* auswählen; *victim, prey* sich *(dat)* herausgreifen; *(distinguish, set apart)* herausheben *(from* über *+acc)*. **to** ~ **sb** ~ **for special attention** jdm besondere Aufmerksamkeit zuteil werden lassen; **he always gets** ~**d** ~ **for all the worst jobs** er wird immer zu den schlimmsten Arbeiten herangezogen; **you couldn't** ~ **any one pupil** ~ **as the best** es wäre unmöglich, einen einzelnen Schüler als den besten hinzustellen.
single: ~-**action** *adj rifle* Einzelfeuer-; ~-**barrelled** [,sɪŋgl-'bærld] *adj gun* mit einem Lauf; ~-**breasted** *adj jacket* einreihig; ~-**breasted suit** Einreiher *m*; ~-**cell(ed)** *adj (Biol)* einzellig; ~-**chamber** *adj (Pol)* Einkammer-; ~ **combat** *n* Nah- or Einzelkampf *m*; *(esp of knights etc)* Kampf *m* Mann gegen Mann, Zweikampf *m*; ~ **cream** *n* Sahne *f (mit geringem Fettgehalt)*; ~-**decker** *n* einstöckiger Omnibus/einstöckige Straßenbahn, Eindecker *m*; ~-**engined** *adj plane* einmotorig; ~-**entry book-keeping** *n* einfache Buchführung; ~ **file** *n* **in** ~ **file im** Gänsemarsch; ~-**handed 1** *adj (ganz)* allein *(after noun)* *achievement* allein or ohne (fremde) Hilfe vollbracht; *arrest* allein or ohne (fremde) Hilfe durchgeführt; *struggle* einsam; **his** ~-**handed attempts to write a dictionary** seine Versuche, ganz allein or im Alleingang ein Wörterbuch zu schreiben; **2** *adj (also* ~-**handedly)** ohne Hilfe, im Alleingang; **to sail** ~-**handed round the world** ganz allein or als Einhandsegler um die Welt fahren; ~-**lens-reflex (camera)** *n* (einäugige) Spiegelreflexkamera; ~-**line** *adj* eingleisig; *railway also, traffic* einspurig; **there was** ~-**line traffic only on the main road** die Hauptstraße konnte nur einspurig befahren werden; ~-**masted** *adj ship* einmastig; ~-**masted ship** Einmaster *m*; ~-**minded** *adj* zielbewußt, zielstrebig, beharrlich; *devotion* unbeirrbar; **his** ~-**minded pursuit of money** sein ausschließlich auf Geld gerichtetes Streben; ~-**mindedness** *n* Zielstrebigkeit, Beharrlichkeit *f*; *see adj* Unbeirrbarkeit *f*.
singleness ['sɪŋglnɪs] *n* ~ **of purpose** Zielstrebigkeit *f*; **his** ~ **of purpose caused him to neglect his family** er ging so vollkommen in der Sache auf, daß er seine Familie vernachlässigte.
single: ~-**party** *adj* Einparteien-; ~-**phase** *adj* einphasig, Einphasen-.
singles ['sɪŋglz] *n sing or pl (Sport)* Einzel *nt*. **the** ~ **finals** das Finale im Einzel; ~ **is more tiring** Einzel sind anstrengender.
single-seater ['sɪŋgl'siːtə^r] *n* Einsitzer *m*.
singlet ['sɪŋglɪt] *n (Brit) (Sport)* ärmelloses Trikot; *(underclothing)* (ärmelloses) Unterhemd, Trikothemd *nt*.
singleton ['sɪŋgltən] *n (Cards)* Single *nt (einzige Karte einer Farbe)*.
single: ~-**tongue** *vti* mit einfachem Zungenschlag spielen; ~-**tonguing** *n* der einzelne Zungenschlag; ~-**track** *adj (Rail)* einspurig; *(Rail also)* eingleisig.
singly ['sɪŋgli] *adv* einzeln; *(solely)* einzig, nur.
singsong ['sɪŋsɒŋ] **1** *adj* **the** ~ **Welsh accent** die walisische Singsang; **in his** ~ **voice** mit or in seinem Singsang. **2** *n* Liedersingen *nt no indef art, no pl*. **we often have a** ~ **down the pub in der Wirtschaft** singen wir oft zusammen.
singular ['sɪŋgjolə^r] **1** *adj* **(a)** *(Gram)* im Singular, singularisch *(form)*. **a** ~ **noun** ein Substantiv im Singular, ein im Singular stehendes Substantiv.
  (b) *(odd)* sonderbar, eigenartig. **how very** ~! das ist aber sehr sonderbar or eigenartig!

(c) *(outstanding)* einzigartig, einmalig.
  2 *n* Singular *m*. **in the** ~ im Singular.
singularity [,sɪŋgjʊ'lærɪtɪ] *n (oddity)* Sonderbarkeit, Eigenartigkeit *f*.
singularly ['sɪŋgjolɑlɪ] *adv* **(a)** außerordentlich. **(b)** *(dated: strangely)* sonderbar, eigenartig.
Sinhalese [sɪnhə'liːz] *see* **Singhalese.**
sinister ['sɪnɪstə^r] *adj* **(a)** unheimlich; *person, night, scheme also* finster; *music, look also* düster; *atmosphere, meaning also* unheilverkündend; *fate* böse. **(b)** *(Her)* linke(r, s).
sink¹ [sɪŋk] *pret* **sank,** *ptp* **sunk 1** *vt* **(a)** *ship* versenken.
  (b) *(fig: ruin)* theory zerstören; *hopes also* zunichte machen. **now we're sunk!** *(inf)* jetzt sind wir geliefert *(inf)*.
  (c) *shaft* senken, teufen *(spec)*; *hole* ausheben. **to** ~ **a post in the ground** einen Pfosten in den Boden einlassen; **they sank a pipe under the riverbed** sie versenkten ein Rohr unter dem Flußbett; *see* **well¹.**
  (d) *(inf) drink* hinunterschütten *(inf)*, hinunterspülen *(inf)*.
  (e) *teeth, claws* schlagen. **I'd like to** ~ **my teeth into a juicy steak** ich möchte in ein saftiges Steak reinbeißen *(inf)*.
  (f) *differences* begraben. **to** ~ **one's identity in that of a group** vollkommen in der Anonymität einer Gruppe aufgehen.
  (g) **to** ~ **money in sth** Geld in etw *(acc)* stecken.
  (h) *golf ball* einlochen; *billiard ball* in das Loch treiben.
  (i) *(lower) eyes, voice, value of currency* senken. **he sank his hands deep in his pockets** er vergrub die Hände in der Tasche; **he sank his head in his hands** er stützte den Kopf auf die Hände.
  (j) **to be sunk in thought** in Gedanken versunken sein; **to be sunk in a book** in ein Buch vertieft sein; **sunk in depression** völlig deprimiert; **to be sunk in debt** tief in Schulden stecken.
  2 *vi* **(a)** *untergehen; (ship also)* sinken. **to** ~ **to the bottom auf den Grund sinken; he was left to** ~ **or swim** *(fig)* er war ganz auf sich allein angewiesen; **if I go down I'll make sure you all** ~ **with me** wenn es mich erwischt, werde ich euch alle mitreißen.
  (b) *(go down, subside)* sinken; *(sun also)* versinken; *(voice)* sich senken; *(building, land etc)* sich senken, absinken. **the building is gradually** ~**ing into the mud** das Gebäude versinkt allmählich im Schlamm; **he sank up to his knees in the mud** er sank bis zu den Knien im Schlamm ein; **to** ~ **(down) into a chair/ back into the cushions** in einen Sessel (nieder)sinken/in die Kissen versinken; **the flames sank lower and lower** das Feuer fiel immer mehr in sich zusammen; **the sun sank beneath the horizon** die Sonne versank am Horizont; **the record has sunk to the bottom of the charts** die Platte ist ans Ende der Liste gerutscht; **to** ~ **to one's knees** auf die Knie sinken; **to** ~ **out of sight** *(fig)* jds Augen *(dat)* entschwinden; **to** ~ **into a deep sleep/a depression** in tiefen Schlaf/in Schwermut versinken; **my spirits or my heart sank at the sight of the work** beim Anblick der Arbeit verließ mich der Mut; **with** ~**ing heart** mutlos; **the sick man is** ~**ing fast** der Kranke verfällt zusehends.
  (c) *(deteriorate, lessen: output, shares, standards)* sinken. **to** ~ **into insignificance** zur Bedeutungslosigkeit herabsinken; **to** ~ **deeper into degradation** immer tiefer sinken.
♦**sink away** *vi (seabed, ground)* abfallen.
♦**sink in 1** *vi* **(a)** *(into mud etc)* einsinken *(prep obj, -to* in *+acc)*.
  (b) *(inf: be understood)* kapiert werden *(inf)*. **it's only just sunk** ~ **that it really did happen** ich kapiere er kapiert etc erst jetzt, daß das tatsächlich passiert ist *(inf)*; **can't you get this to** ~ ~**(to your thick head)!** kannst du das denn nicht in deinen dicken Schädel bekommen? *(inf)*; **repeat each line so that the words** ~ ~ wiederhole jede Zeile, damit du's dir merkst *(inf)*.
  2 *vt sep stakes, pylons etc* einlassen *(prep obj, -to* in *+acc)*.
sink² *n* Ausguß *m*; *(in kitchen also)* Spülbecken *nt*. ~ **unit** Spültisch *m*, Spüle *f*; ~ **of iniquity** Sündenpfuhl *m*, Stätte *f* des Lasters; *see* **kitchen** ~.
sinker ['sɪŋkə^r] *n (Fishing)* Senker *m*, Senkgewicht *nt*.
sinking ['sɪŋkɪŋ] **1** *n (of ship)* Untergang *m*; *(deliberately)* Versenkung *f*; *(of shaft)* Senken, Abteufen *(spec)*; *(of well)* Bohren *nt*. **2** *adj* ~ **feeling** flaues Gefühl (im Magen) *(inf)*; **I got that horrible** ~ **feeling when I realized ...** mir wurde ganz anders, als ich erkannte ...; ~ **fund** Tilgungsfonds *m*.
sinless ['sɪnlɪs] *adj person* ohne Sünde, frei von Sünde; *life also* sündenlos, sündenfrei.
sinner ['sɪnə^r] *n* Sünder(in *f*) *m*.
Sino- ['saɪnəʊ-] *pref* chinesisch-, Sino- *(form)*.
sinologist [,saɪ'nɒlədʒɪst] *n* Sinologe *m*, Sinologin *f*.
sinology [saɪ'nɒlədʒɪ] *n* Sinologie *f*.
sinuosity [,sɪnjʊ'ɒsɪtɪ] *n (liter)* Schlangenbewegungen *pl*; *(of river)* Windungen *pl*; *(fig)* Gewundenheit *f*.
sinuous ['sɪnjʊəs] *adj (lit, fig)* gewunden; *motion of snake* schlängelnd *attr*; *dancing etc* geschmeidig, schlangenartig. **the lane follows a** ~ **course between ...** der Pfad schlängelt sich zwischen *(+dat)* ... durch.
sinuously ['sɪnjʊəslɪ] *adv see adj.*
sinus ['saɪnəs] *n (Anat)* Sinus *m (spec)*; *(in head)* (Nasen)nebenhöhle, Stirnhöhle *f*.
sinusitis [,saɪnə'saɪtɪs] *n* Stirnhöhlenkatarrh *m*, Sinusitis *f*.
Sioux [suː] **1** *n* Sioux *mf*. **2** *adj* Sioux-, der Sioux.
sip [sɪp] **1** *n* Schluck *m*; *(very small)* Schlückchen *nt*. **2** *vt* kleinen Schlucken trinken; *(suspiciously, daintily)* nippen an *(+dat)*; *(savour)* schlürfen. **3** *vi* **to** ~ **at sth** an etw *(dat)* nippen.
siphon ['saɪfən] **1** *n* Heber *m*; *(soda* ~*)* Siphon *m*. **2** *vt* absaugen; *(into tank)* (mit einem Heber) umfüllen.
♦**siphon off** *vt sep* **(a)** *(lit)* abziehen, absaugen; *petrol* abzapfen; *(into container)* (mit einem Heber) umfüllen or abfüllen. **(b)** *(fig) staff, money* abziehen; *profits* abschöpfen.
♦**siphon out** *vt sep liquid* mit einem Heber herausleiten.
sir [sɜː^r] *n* **(a)** *(in direct address)* mein Herr *(form)*, Herr X. **no,** ~ **nein(, Herr X)**; *(Mil)* nein, Herr Leutnant/General etc; **you will apologize,** ~! *(dated)* dafür werden Sie sich entschuldigen

(müssen); S~ (to editor of paper) wird nicht übersetzt; Dear S~ (or Madam), ... sehr geehrte (Damen und) Herren!; my dear or good ~! (dated) mein (lieber) Herr! (dated).
(b) (knight etc) S~ Sir m.
(c) (Sch sl: teacher) er (Sch sl). I'll tell ~ ich sag's ihm.
sire [saɪəʳ] **1** n **(a)** (Zool) Vater(tier nt) m; (stallion also) Deck- or Zuchthengst, Beschäler (form) m.
(b) (old: to monarch etc) S~ Majestät f, Sire m.
(c) (old, poet: father, forebear) Erzeuger, Ahn m. ~ of a great nation Vater m einer großen Nation.
2 vt zeugen. the horse A, ~d by B Pferd A, Vater B; he ~d 49 children (hum) er hat 49 Kinder in die Welt gesetzt.
siren [saɪərən] n (all senses) Sirene f.
sirloin [ˈsɜːlɔɪn] n Filet nt.
sirocco [sɪˈrɒkəʊ] n Schirokko m.
sirrah [ˈsɪrə] n (obs) Bube m (obs).
sirup n (US) see syrup.
sis [sɪs] n (inf) Schwesterherz nt (inf).
sisal [ˈsaɪsəl] n Sisal m.
sissified [ˈsɪsɪfaɪd] adj weibisch, wie ein Weib.
sissy [ˈsɪsɪ] **1** n Waschlappen m (inf), Memme f. **2** adj weibisch.
sister [ˈsɪstəʳ] n **(a)** Schwester f; (in trade union) Kollegin f; (ship) Schwesterschiff nt. to be ~ to (form) or the ~ of sb jds Schwester sein. **(b)** (nun) (Ordens)schwester f; (before name) Schwester f. **(c)** (Brit: senior nurse) Oberschwester f.
sisterhood [ˈsɪstəhʊd] n **(a)** Schwesterschaft f. she emphasized the ~ of women all over the world sie betonte, daß alle Frauen der ganzen Welt Schwestern seien. **(b)** (Eccl) Schwesternorden m. **(c)** (association of women) Frauenvereinigung f.
sister in cpds Schwester-; ~-in-law, pl ~s-in-law Schwägerin f.
sisterly [ˈsɪstəlɪ] adj schwesterlich.
Sistine [ˈsɪstiːn] adj Sixtinisch.
Sisyphus [ˈsɪsɪfəs] n Sisyphus m.
sit [sɪt] (vb: pret, ptp sat) **1** vi **(a)** (be ~ting) sitzen (in/on in/auf +dat); (~ down) sich setzen (in/on in/auf +acc). ~! (to dog) sitz!; a place to ~ ein Sitzplatz m; ~ by/with me setz dich zu mir/neben mich; to ~ for a painter für einen Maler Modell sitzen; to ~ for an exam eine Prüfung ablegen (form) or machen; to be ~ting pretty (fig inf) gut dastehen (inf); he's ~ting pretty for the directorship der Direktorsposten ist ihm so gut wie sicher; don't just ~ there, do something! sitz nicht nur tatenlos da (herum), tu (endlich) was!; see still[1].
(b) (assembly) tagen; (have a seat) einen Sitz haben. he ~s for Liverpool (Brit Parl) er ist der Abgeordnete für Liverpool; to ~ in parliament/on a committee einen Sitz im Parlament haben/in einem Ausschuß sitzen.
(c) (object: be placed, rest) stehen. the car sat in the garage das Auto stand in der Garage; the parcel is ~ting in the hall das Päckchen liegt im Flur; this food ~s heavy on the stomach dieses Essen liegt schwer im Magen; the cares ~ heavy on his brow (liter) die Sorgen lasten schwer auf ihm.
(d) (bird: hatch) sitzen, brüten. the hen is ~ting on two eggs das Huhn brütet zwei Eier aus, das Huhn sitzt auf zwei Eiern.
(e) (fig: clothes) sitzen (on sb bei jdm).
(f) how ~s the wind? (liter) wie steht der Wind?
(g) (inf) see babysit.
2 vt **(a)** setzen (in in +acc, on auf +acc); (place) object also stellen. to ~ a child on one's knees sich (dat) ein Kind auf die Knie setzen; the table/car ~s 5 people an dem Tisch/in dem Auto haben 5 Leute Platz.
(b) horse sitzen auf (+dat). to ~ a horse well gut zu Pferde sitzen.
(c) examination ablegen (form), machen.
3 vr to ~ oneself down sich gemütlich niederlassen or hinsetzen; ~ you down (dial) setz dich hin.
4 n to have a ~ sitzen.
♦ **sit about** or **around** vi herumsitzen.
♦ **sit back** vi (lit, fig) sich zurücklehnen; (fig: do nothing, not take action) die Hände in den Schoß legen.
♦ **sit down** vi **(a)** sich (hin)setzen. to ~ ~ in a chair sich auf einen Stuhl setzen. **(b)** (fig) to take sth/an insult ~ting ~ etw einfach hinnehmen/eine Beleidigung einfach schlucken.
♦ **sit in** vi **(a)** (demonstrators) ein Sit-in machen or veranstalten. **(b)** (take place of) to ~ ~ (for sb) jdn vertreten. **(c)** (attend as visitor) dabeisein, dabeisitzen (on sth bei etw). **(d)** (stay in) zu Hause or im Haus sitzen.
♦ **sit on** vi **(a)** (continue sitting) sitzen bleiben.
2 vi +prep obj **(a)** (committee, panel, jury) sitzen in (+dat). I was asked to ~ ~ the committee man bat mich, Mitglied des Ausschusses zu werden.
(b) (not deal with) sitzen auf (+dat).
(c) (inf: suppress) idea, invention, product unterdrücken, nicht hochkommen lassen; person einen Dämpfer aufsetzen (+dat) (inf). to get sat ~ eins draufkriegen (inf).
♦ **sit out** vi draußen sitzen. **2** vt sep **(a)** (stay to end) play, film, meeting bis zum Schluß or Ende (sitzen)bleiben bei, bis zum Schluß or Ende durch- or aushalten (pej); storm auf das Ende (+gen) warten. we'd better ~ it ~ wir bleiben besser bis zum Ende (hier). **(b)** dance auslassen.
♦ **sit through** vi +prep obj durchhalten, aushalten (pej).
♦ **sit up** vi **(a)** (be sitting upright) aufrecht sitzen; (action) sich aufrichten, sich aufsetzen. to ~ ~ (and beg) (dog etc) Männchen machen (inf).
(b) (sit straight) aufrecht or gerade sitzen. ~ ~! setz dich gerade hin!, sitz gerade!; to make sb ~ ~ (and take notice) (fig inf) jdn aufhorchen lassen.
(c) (not go to bed) aufbleiben, aufwachen (dated). she sat ~ with the sick child sie wachte bei dem kranken Kind; to ~ ~ for sb aufbleiben und auf jdn warten.
(d) to ~ ~ to table sich an den Tisch setzen.
2 vt sep aufrichten, aufsetzen; doll also, baby hinsetzen.

♦ **sit upon** vi +prep obj see sit on 2.
sitar [sɪˈtɑːʳ] n Sitar m.
sitcom [ˈsɪtkɒm] n (inf) Situationskomödie f.
sit-down [ˈsɪtdaʊn] **1** n (inf: rest) Verschnaufpause f (inf). **2** attr to have a ~ strike einen Sitzstreik machen.
site [saɪt] **1** n **(a)** Stelle f, Platz m; (Med: of infection) Stelle f.
(b) (Archeol) Stätte f.
(c) (building) (Bau)gelände nt, Baustelle f. missile ~ Raketenbasis f; ~ foreman Polier m; ~ office Büro nt der Bauleitung f.
(d) (camping ~) Campingplatz m.
2 vt legen, anlegen. to be ~d liegen, (gelegen) sein; a badly ~d building ungünstig gelegenes Gebäude.
sit-in [ˈsɪtɪn] n Sit-in nt. to hold or stage a ~ ein Sit-in veranstalten.
siting [ˈsaɪtɪŋ] n Legen nt. the ~ of new industries away from London is being encouraged man fördert die Errichtung neuer Betriebe außerhalb Londons; the ~ of the town here was a mistake es war ein Fehler, die Stadt hierher zu legen.
sitter [ˈsɪtəʳ] n **(a)** (Art) Modell nt; (baby-~) Babysitter m; (bird) brütender Vogel; (Sport sl) todsicherer Ball (inf).
sitting [ˈsɪtɪŋ] **1** adj sitzend; bird brütend; conference tagend, in Sitzung. ~ and standing room Sitz- und Stehplätze pl.
2 n (of committee, parliament, for portrait) Sitzung f. they have two ~s for lunch sie servieren das Mittagessen in zwei Schüben; the first ~ for lunch is at 12 o'clock die erste Mittagessenzeit ist um 12 Uhr; at one ~ (fig) auf einmal.
sitting: ~ duck n (fig) leichte Beute; ~ member n (Brit Parl) (derzeitiger) Abgeordneter, (derzeitige) Abgeordnete; ~ room n (lounge) Wohnzimmer nt; (in guest house etc) Aufenthaltsraum m; ~ tenant n (derzeitiger) Mieter.
situate [ˈsɪtjʊeɪt] vt legen.
situated [ˈsɪtjʊeɪtɪd] adj gelegen; person (financially) gestellt, situiert (geh). it is ~ in the High Street es liegt an der Hauptstraße; a pleasantly ~ house ein schön gelegenes Haus, ein Haus in angenehmer Lage; how are you ~ (for money)? wie sind Sie finanziell gestellt?, wie ist Ihre finanzielle Lage?; he is well ~ to appreciate the risks er ist sehr wohl (dazu) in der Lage, die Risiken abzuschätzen.
situation [ˌsɪtjʊˈeɪʃən] n **(a)** (state of affairs) Lage, Situation f; (financial, marital etc) Lage f, Verhältnisse pl; (in play, novel) Situation f. to save the ~ die Lage or Situation retten; a 2-0 ~ eine 2:0-Situation; ~ comedy Situationskomödie f.
(b) (of house etc) Lage f.
(c) (job) Stelle f. "~s vacant/wanted" „Stellenangebote/Stellengesuche".
sit-up [ˈsɪtʌp] n (Sport) to do a ~ sich aus der Rückenlage aufsetzen.
sitz bath [ˈzɪtsbɑːθ] n Sitzbadewanne f.
six [sɪks] **1** adj sechs. she is ~ (years old) sie ist sechs (Jahre alt); at (the age of) ~ im Alter von sechs Jahren, mit sechs Jahren; it's ~ (o'clock) es ist sechs (Uhr); there are ~ of us wir sind sechs; it cost ~ pounds es kostete sechs Pfund; ~ and a half/ quarter sechseinhalb/sechseinviertel; in ~-eight time (Mus) im Sechsachteltakt; to be ~ foot under (hum) sich (dat) die Radieschen von unten besehen (hum); it's ~ of one and half a dozen of the other (inf) das ist Jacke wie Hose (inf), das ist gehupft wie gesprungen (inf).
2 n **(a)** (Math, figure, mark, tram) Sechs f; (bus) Sechser m. ~ and a half/quarter Sechseinhalb/-einviertel f.
(b) (Cards, on dice, Golf) Sechs f; (Cricket also) Sechserschlag m; (team of ~ also) Sechsermannschaft f. to divide sth into ~ etw in sechs Teile teilen; we divided up into ~es wir teilten uns in Sechsergruppen auf; they are sold in ~es wie werden in Sechserpackungen verkauft; to be at ~es and sevens (things) wie Kraut und Rüben durcheinanderliegen (inf); (person) völlig durcheinander sein; to knock sb for ~ (inf) jdn umhauen.
six: ~fold **1** adj sechsfach; **2** adv um das Sechsfache; ~-footer n to be a ~-footer über 1,80 (gesprochen: einsachtzig) sein; ~ hundred **1** adj sechshundert; **2** n Sechshundert f.
sixish [ˈsɪksɪʃ] adj um sechs herum.
six: ~ million adj, n sechs Millionen; ~pack n Sechserpackung f; ~pence n (old: coin) Sixpencestück nt; ~penny **1** adj für Sixpence; **2** n (fare) Fahrkarte für Sixpence; (stamp) Sixpence-Marke f; ~-shooter n (inf) sechsschüssiger Revolver.
sixteen [ˈsɪksˈtiːn] **1** adj sechzehn. **2** n Sechzehn f.
sixteenth [ˈsɪksˈtiːnθ] **1** adj sechzehnte(r, s). a ~ part ein Sechzehntel nt; a ~ note (esp US Mus) eine Sechzehntelnote, ein Sechzehntel nt. **2** n **(a)** (fraction) Sechzehntel nt; (in series) Sechzehnte(r, s). **(b)** (date) der Sechzehnte.
sixth [sɪksθ] **1** adj sechste(r, s). a ~ part ein Sechstel nt; he was or came ~ er wurde Sechster; he/it was ~ from the end/left er/es war der/das Sechste von hinten/von links.
2 n **(a)** (fraction) Sechstel nt; (in series) Sechste(r, s).
(b) (date) the ~ der Sechste; on the ~ am Sechsten; the ~ of September der sechste September.
(c) (Mus: interval) Sexte f; (chord) Sextakkord m.
(d) (Brit) see ~ form.
3 adv he did it ~ (the ~ person to do it) er hat es als Sechster gemacht; (the ~ thing he did) er hat es als sechstes or an sechster Stelle gemacht.
sixth: ~ form n (Brit) Abschlußklasse, ≈ Prima f; ~-former n (Brit) Schüler(in f) m der Abschlußklasse, ≈ Primaner(in f) m.
sixthly [ˈsɪksθlɪ] adv sechstens, als sechstes.
six thousand 1 adj sechstausend. **2** n Sechstausend f.
sixth sense n sechster Sinn.
sixtieth [ˈsɪkstɪθ] **1** adj sechzigste(r, s). a ~ part ein Sechzigstel nt. **2** n (fraction) Sechzigstel nt; (in series) Sechzigste(r, s).
sixty [ˈsɪkstɪ] **1** adj sechzig. **2** n Sechzig f. the sixties die sechziger Jahre; to be in one's sixties zwischen sechzig und

siebzig sein; **to be in one's late/early sixties** Ende/Anfang sech-zig sein; *see also* **six.**

sixty: ~-**fourth note** *n* (*esp US Mus*) Vierundsechzigstel(note *f*) *nt*; ~-**four thousand dollar question** *n* (*hum*) Zehntausend-markfrage *f* (*hum*).

sixtyish ['sɪkstɪɪʃ] *adj* um die Sechzig (*inf*), ungefähr sechzig.

sixty-one ['sɪkstɪ'wʌn] **1** *adj* einundsechzig. **2** *n* Einundsechzig *f*.

six-year-old ['sɪksjɪɐ,əʊld] **1** *adj* sechsjährig *attr*, sechs Jahre alt *pred*; *war* schon sechs Jahre dauernd. **2** *n* Sechsjährige(r) *mf*.

sizable *adj see* **sizeable.**

size[1] [saɪz] **1** *n* (*all senses*) Größe *f*; (*of problem, operation also*) Ausmaß *nt*. **collar/hip/waist** ~ Kragen-/Hüft-/Taillenweite *f*; **it's the** ~ **of a brick** es ist so groß wie ein Ziegelstein; **he's about your** ~ er ist ungefähr so groß wie du; **what** ~ **is it?** wie groß ist es?; (*clothes, shoes, gloves etc*) welche Größe ist es?; **it's quite a** ~ es ist ziemlich groß; **it's two** ~**s too big** es ist zwei Nummern zu groß; **to cut sth to** ~ etw auf die richtige Größe zurechtschneiden; **that's about the** ~ **of it** (*inf*) ja, so ungefähr kann man es sagen.
   2 *vt* größenmäßig ordnen.

♦**size up** *vt sep* abschätzen. **I can't quite** ~ **him** ~ ich werde aus ihm nicht schlau.

size[2] **1** *n* (Grundier)leim *m*. **2** *vt* grundieren.

sizeable ['saɪzəbl] *adj* ziemlich groß, größer; *car, estate, jewel also* ansehnlich; *sum, problem, difference also* beträchtlich.

sizeably ['saɪzəblɪ] *adv* beträchtlich.

-**size(d)** [-saɪz(d)] *adj suf* -groß. **medium-**~ mittelgroß, von mitt-lerer Größe.

sizzle ['sɪzl] **1** *vi* brutzeln. **2** *n* Brutzeln *nt*, Brutzelei *f*.

sizzling ['sɪzlɪŋ] **1** *adj* *fat, bacon* brutzelnd. **2** *adv*: ~ **hot** ko-chend heiß; **it was a** ~ **hot day** (*inf*) es war knallheiß (*inf*).

skate[1] [skeɪt] *n* (*fish*) Rochen *m*.

skate[2] **1** *n* (*shoe*) Schlittschuh *m*; (*blade*) Kufe *f*. **put or get your** ~**s on** (*fig inf*) mach/macht mal ein bißchen dalli! (*inf*); *see* **ice-skate, roller** ~.
   2 *vi* eislaufen, Schlittschuh laufen; (*figure-*~) eislaufen, Eiskunstlauf machen; (*roller-*~) Rollschuh laufen. **he** ~**d across the pond** er lief (auf Schlittschuhen) über den Teich; **she** ~**d up to him** sie lief auf ihn zu; **the next couple to** ~ das nächste Paar auf dem Eis; **it went skating across the room** (*fig*) es rutschte durch das Zimmer.

♦**skate over** *or* **round** *vi* + *prep obj* links liegenlassen; *difficulty, problem* einfach übergehen.

skateboard ['skeɪtbɔːd] *n* Skateboard, Rollbrett *nt*. ~ **park** Skateboard-Anlage *f*.

skateboarding ['skeɪtbɔːdɪŋ] *n* Skateboardfahren *nt*.

skater ['skeɪtəʳ] *n* (*ice-*~) Eisläufer(in *f*), Schlittschuhläufer(in *f*) *m*; (*figure-*~) Eiskunstläufer(in *f*) *m*; (*roller-*~) Rollschuh-läufer(in *f*) *m*.

skating ['skeɪtɪŋ] *n* (*ice-*~) Eislauf, Schlittschuhlauf *m*; (*figure-*~) Eiskunstlauf *m*; (*roller-*~) Rollschuhlauf *m*.

skating *in cpds* Eislauf-; Rollschuh-; ~ **rink** *n* Eisbahn/ Rollschuhbahn *f*.

skedaddle [skɪ'dædl] *vi* (*Brit inf*) Reißaus nehmen (*inf*), türmen (*inf*). ~! weg mit dir/euch!, verzieh dich/verzieht euch!

skein [skeɪn] *n* (*of wool etc*) Strang *m*; (*of geese*) Schwarm *m*; (*of evidence, lies etc*) Geflecht *nt*.

skeletal ['skelɪtl] *adj* Skelett-; *person* bis aufs Skelett abgemagert; *appearance* wie ein Skelett; *shapes of trees etc* skelettartig.

skeleton ['skelɪtn] **1** *n* (*lit, fig*) Skelett *nt*; (*esp of ship*) Gerippe *nt*. **a** ~ **in one's cupboard** ein dunkler Punkt (in der Familiengeschichte); (*of public figure*) eine Leiche im Keller.
   2 *adj* *plan, outline etc* provisorisch; *staff, service etc* Not-. ~ **key** Dietrich, Nachschlüssel *m*.

skep [skep] *n* (*old*) (*basket*) Korb *m*; (*bee* ~) Bienenkorb *m*.

skeptic *etc* (*US*) *see* **sceptic** *etc*.

sketch [sketʃ] **1** *n* (*Art, Liter*) Skizze *f*; (*Mus*) Impression *f*; (*Theat*) Sketch *m*; (*draft, design also*) Entwurf *m*. **2** *vt* (*lit, fig*) skizzieren. **2** *vi* Skizzen machen.

♦**sketch in** *vt sep* (*draw*) (grob) einzeichnen; (*verbally*) umreißen.

♦**sketch out** *vt sep* (*draw*) grob skizzieren; (*outline also*) umreißen.

sketch-book ['sketʃbʊk] *n* Skizzenbuch *nt*.

sketchily ['sketʃɪlɪ] *adv* flüchtig, oberflächlich.

sketchiness ['sketʃɪnɪs] *n* Flüchtigkeit, Oberflächlichkeit *f*; (*insufficiency*) Unzulänglichkeit *f*.

sketching ['sketʃɪŋ] *n* (*Art*) Skizzenzeichnen *nt*.

sketch: ~-**map** *n* Kartenskizze *f*; ~-**pad** *n* Skizzenblock *m*.

sketchy ['sketʃɪ] *adj* (+ *er*) (*inadequate*) *knowledge, plan, work, account* flüchtig, oberflächlich; (*incomplete*) *account, record* bruchstückhaft. **we had a** ~ **lunch** wir aßen nur eine Kleinig-keit zu Mittag.

skew [skjuː] **1** *n* **on the** ~ schief; (*on the diagonal*) schräg.
   2 *adj* (*lit, fig*) schief; (*diagonal*) schräg. ~-**whiff** (*lit, fig*) (wind)schief.
   3 *vt* (*turn round*) umdrehen; (*make crooked*) krümmen; (*fig: distort*) verzerren.
   4 *vi* **the car** ~**ed off the road** der Wagen kam von der Straße ab; **the road** ~**s to the right** die Straße biegt nach rechts ab; **he** ~**ed round** er drehte sich um.

skewbald ['skjuːbɔːld] **1** *n* Schecke *mf*. **2** *adj* gescheckt, scheckig.

skewer ['skjuːəʳ] **1** *n* Spieß *m*. **2** *vt* aufspießen.

ski [skiː] **1** *n* Ski, Schi *m*; (*Aviat*) Kufe *f*. **2** *vi* Ski laufen *or* fahren. **they** ~**ed down the slope/over the hill** sie fuhren (auf ihren Skiern) den Hang hinunter/sie liefen (mit ihren Skiern) über den Hügel.

ski *in cpds* Ski-, Schi-; ~-**bob** *n* Skibob *m*; ~ **boot** *n* Skistiefel *or* -schuh *m*.

skid [skɪd] **1** *n* (a) (*sliding movement*) (*Aut etc*) Schleudern *nt*. **to steer into/against a** ~ mitsteuern/gegensteuern; **to go into a** ~ ins Schleudern geraten *or* kommen; **to correct** *or* **get out of a** ~ das Fahrzeug abfangen *or* wieder in sein Gewalt bekommen; **to stop with a** ~ schleudernd zum Stehen kommen.
   (b) (*on wheel*) Rolle *f*.
   (c) (*runner*) Gleiter *m*; (*of plane, sledge etc*) Gleitkufe *f*.
   (d) ~**s** *pl* (*fig*) **he was on** *or* **hit the** ~**s** (*US inf*) es ging abwärts mit ihm; **to put the** ~**s under sb/sb's plans** (*inf*) jdn/jds Pläne zu Fall bringen, jdm die Suppe versalzen (*inf*).
   2 *vi* (*car, objects*) schleudern; (*person*) ausrutschen. **to** ~ **across the floor** über den Boden rutschen *or* schlittern; **the car** ~**ded into a tree** der Wagen schleuderte gegen einen Baum.

skid: ~ **lid** *n* (*sl*) Sturzhelm *m*; ~-**mark** *n* Reifenspur *f*; (*from braking*) Bremsspur *f*; ~-**pan** *n* Schleuderstrecke *f*; ~ **row** *n* (*esp US inf*) (Kaschemmen- und) Pennergegend *f* (*inf*); **to be on** *or* **in** ~ **row** heruntergekommen *or* verpennert (*sl*) sein; **he ended up in** ~ **row** er ist als Penner geendet (*inf*).

skier ['skiːəʳ] *n* Skiläufer(in *f*), Skifahrer(in *f*) *m*.

skiff [skɪf] *n* Skiff *nt*; (*Sport*) Einer *m*.

skiffle ['skɪfl] *n* Skiffle *m*. ~ **group** Skiffle Group *f*.

skiing ['skiːɪŋ] *n* Skilaufen, Skifahren *nt*.

ski: ~-**jump** *n* (*action*) Skisprung *m*; (*place*) Sprungschanze *f*; ~-**jumping** *n* Skispringen *nt*.

skilful, (*US*) **skillful** ['skɪlfʊl] *adj* geschickt; *piano-playing etc* also gewandt; *sculpture, painting etc* kunstvoll.

skilfully, (*US*) **skillfully** ['skɪlfəlɪ] *adv see* **adj.**

skilfulness, (*US*) **skillfulness** ['skɪlfʊlnɪs] *n see* **skill (a).**

ski-lift ['skiːlɪft] *n* Skilift *m*.

skill [skɪl] *n* (a) *no pl* (*skilfulness*) Geschick *nt*, Geschicklichkeit *f*; (*of sculptor etc*) Kunst(fertigkeit) *f*. **his** ~ **at billiards/in per-suading people** sein Geschick beim Billard/sein Geschick *or* seine Fähigkeit, andere zu überreden; **he shows no small** ~ er ist recht geschickt.
   (b) (*acquired technique*) Fertigkeit *f*; (*ability*) Fähigkeit *f*. **to learn new** ~**s** etwas Neues lernen; **it's a** ~ **that has to be acquired** so etwas muß gelernt sein.

skilled [skɪld] *adj* (*skilful*) geschickt, gewandt (*at in* + *dat*); (*trained*) ausgebildet, Fach-; (*requiring skill*) Fach-, fachmän-nisch. **he's** ~ **in persuading people** er versteht es, andere zu überreden; **a man** ~ **in diplomacy** ein geschickter Diplomat.

skillet ['skɪlɪt] *n* Bratpfanne *f*.

skillful *etc* (*US*) *see* **skilful** *etc*.

skim [skɪm] **1** *vt* (a) (*remove floating matter*) abschöpfen; *milk* entrahmen. ~**med** *or* (*US*) ~ **milk** Magermilch *f*.
   (b) (*pass low over*) streifen *or* streichen über (+ *acc*); (*fig: touch on*) berühren. **he** ~**med stones across the surface of the water** er ließ Steine übers Wasser hüpfen *or* springen; **he** ~**med his hat across the room** er schleuderte seinen Hut quer durchs Zimmer; **the book merely** ~**s the surface of the problem** das Buch berührt das Problem nur an der Oberfläche.
   (c) (*read quickly*) überfliegen.
   2 *vi* (*across, over* über + *acc*) (*move quickly*) fliegen; (*aircraft also*) rasch gleiten; (*stones*) springen, hüpfen.

♦**skim off** **1** *vt sep* abschöpfen; (*fig*) absahnen. **to** ~ **the cream** ~ **the milk** die Milch entrahmen. **2** *vi* (*birds*) davonfliegen; (*person*) lossausen.

♦**skim through** *vi* + *prep obj* *book etc* überfliegen.

skimmer ['skɪməʳ] *n* (a) Schaumlöffel *m*. (b) (*Orn*) Scherenschnabel *m*.

skimp [skɪmp] **1** *vt* *food, material* sparen an (+ *dat*), knausern mit; *work* hudeln bei (+ *dat*), nachlässig erledigen; *details* zu kurz kommen lassen. **2** *vi* sparen (*on an* + *dat*), knausern (*on* mit).

skimpily ['skɪmpɪlɪ] *adv* dürftig; *live, eat also* kärglich; *dressed* spärlich.

skimpy ['skɪmpɪ] *adj* (+ *er*) dürftig; *meal, existence also* kärg-lich; *clothes* knapp. **to be** ~ **with sth** mit etw sparsam *or* geizig sein.

skin [skɪn] **1** *n* (a) Haut *f*. **to be soaked to the** ~ bis auf die Haut naß sein; **he's nothing but** ~ **and bone(s)** nowadays er ist nur noch Haut und Knochen; **that's no** ~ **off his nose** (*inf*) das braucht ihn nicht zu stören; **that's no** ~ **off my nose** (*inf*) das juckt mich nicht (*inf*); **to get inside the** ~ **of a part** (*Theat*) in einer Rolle aufgehen; **all men/women are brothers/sisters under the** ~ im Grunde sind alle Menschen gleich; **to save one's own** ~ die eigene Haut retten; **to jump** *or* **leap out of one's** ~ (*inf*) erschrecke hochfahren; **to get under sb's** ~ (*inf*) (*irritate*) jdm auf die Nerven gehen (*inf*); (*fascinate*) (*music, voice*) jdm unter die Haut gehen; (*person*) jdn faszinieren; **I've got you under my** ~ du hast mir's angetan; **to have a thick/thin** ~ (*fig*) ein dickes Fell (*inf*)/eine dünne Haut haben; **by the** ~ **of one's teeth** (*inf*) mit knapper Not, mit Ach und Krach (*inf*).
   (b) (*hide*) Haut *f*; (*fur*) Fell *nt*; (*of small animals also*) Balg *m*.
   (c) (*oilskins*) Ölhaut *f*, Ölzeug *nt*.
   (d) (*for wine etc*) Schlauch *m*.
   (e) (*of fruit etc*) Schale *f*; (*of grape, tomato also*) Haut *f*.
   (f) (*on sausage etc*) Haut *f*, Darm *m*.
   (g) (*on milk etc*) Haut *f*.
   (h) (*for duplicating*) Matrize *f*.
   2 *vt* *animal* abziehen; *fruit* schälen; *grapes, tomatoes* enthäuten. **to** ~ **sb alive** (*inf*) jdm den Kopf abreißen (*hum inf*); *see* **eye.**

skin: ~-**deep** *adj see* **beauty;** ~ **disease** *n* Hautkrankheit *f*; ~-**diver** *n* Sporttaucher(in *f*) *m*; ~-**diving** *n* Sporttauchen *nt*; ~-**flick** *n* (*inf*) Pornofilm *m*; ~-**flint** *n* (*inf*) Geizkragen *m* (*inf*); ~ **food** *n* Nahrung *f* für die Haut.

skinful ['skɪnfʊl] *n* (*inf*) **to have had a** ~ einen über den Durst getrunken haben, einen sitzen haben (*inf*).

skin: ~ **game** *n* (*US inf*) Schwindel *m*; ~ **graft** *n*

Hauttransplantation *or* -verpflanzung *f*; ~**head** *n* (*Brit inf*) (kurzgeschorener) Rowdy; ~**less** *adj sausage* ohne Haut *or* Darm.

-skinned [-skɪnd] *adj suf* -häutig.

skinner ['skɪnə^r] *n* (*removing skins*) Abdecker *m*; (*preparing skins*) Gerber *m*.

skinny ['skɪnɪ] *adj* (+*er*) (*inf*) *person, legs, arms* dünn; *sweater* eng anliegend *attr*, hauteng.

skinny: ~-**dip** *vi* (*inf*) im Adams-/Evaskostüm baden (*hum*); ~-**rib** *adj sweater* Rippen-.

skint [skɪnt] *adj* (*Brit inf*) to be ~ pleite *or* blank sein (*inf*).

skin: ~ **test** *n* Hauttest *m*; ~-**tight** *adj* hauteng.

skip¹ [skɪp] **1** *n* (*kleiner*) Sprung, Hüpfer *m*; (*in dancing*) Hüpfschritt *m*. **she gave a little** ~ **of pleasure** sie machte einen Freudensprung.

2 *vi* **(a)** hüpfen; (*jump, gambol*) springen; (*with rope*) seilhüpfen, seilspringen. **she came** ~**ping up to us** sie kam auf uns zugesprungen; **she was** ~**ping** (*with rope*) sie sprang Seil.

(b) (*move from subject to subject*) springen.

(c) (*inf: abscond, flee*) abhauen (*inf*), türmen (*inf*).

3 *vt* **(a)** (*omit, miss*) *school, church etc* schwänzen (*inf*); *passage, chapter etc* überspringen, auslassen. **my heart** ~**ped a beat** mein Herzschlag setzte für eine Sekunde aus; **to** ~ **lunch** das Mittagessen ausfallen lassen; ~ **it!** ist ja auch egal!

(b) (*US*) **to** ~ **rope** seilhüpfen, seilspringen.

(c) (*US inf*) **to** ~ **town** aus der Stadt verschwinden (*inf*).

♦**skip about** *vi* (*lit*) herumhüpfen; (*fig: author, speaker*) springen.

♦**skip across** *vi* (*inf*) rüberspritzen (*inf*), rüberspringen (*inf*). ~ ~ **to the other office** spritz *or* spring doch mal rüber ins andere Büro!; **we** ~**ped** ~ **to Paris** wir machten eine Spritztour nach Paris (*inf*).

♦**skip off** *vi* (*inf*) abhauen (*inf*).

♦**skip over 1** *vi* (*inf*) *see* **skip across. 2** *vi* +*prep obj* (*pass over*) überspringen.

♦**skip through** *vi* +*prep obj book* durchblättern.

skip² *n* **(a)** (*Build*) Container *m*, Bauschuttmulde *f* (*form*); (*Min*) Förderkorb *m*. **(b)** *see* **skep.**

skip³ *n* (*Sport*) Kapitän *m*.

ski: ~ **pants** *npl* Skihose(n *pl*) *f*; ~**plane** *n* Flugzeug *nt* mit Schneekufen; ~ **pole** *n see* ~ **stick.**

skipper ['skɪpə^r] **1** *n* Kapitän *m*. a. *aye, aye* ~! jawohl, Käpt'n! **2** *vt* anführen. **the team was** ~**ed by X** Kapitän der Mannschaft war X.

skipping ['skɪpɪŋ] *n* Seilhüpfen, Seilspringen *nt*. ~ **rope** Hüpf- *or* Sprungseil *nt*.

skirl [skɜːl] *n* **the** ~ **of the bagpipes** das Pfeifen der Dudelsäcke.

skirmish ['skɜːmɪʃ] **1** *n* (*Mil*) Gefecht *nt*, Plänkelei *f*; (*scrap, fig*) Zusammenstoß *m*. **2** *vi* (*Mil*) kämpfen; (*scrap, fig*) zusammenstoßen.

skirmisher ['skɜːmɪʃə^r] *n* Kämpfende(r) *m*.

skirt [skɜːt] **1** *n* **(a)** Rock *m*; (*of jacket, coat*) Schoß *m*. **(b)** (*sl: woman*) Weibse *f* (*sl*). **a bit** *or* **piece of** ~ ein Weibsstück *nt* (*sl*). **2** *vt* (*also* ~ **a)round**) umgehen; (*encircle*) umgeben.

skirting (board) ['skɜːtɪŋ(ˌbɔːd)] *n* (*Brit*) Fuß- *or* Scheuerleiste, Lambrie (*dial*) *f*.

ski: ~-**run** *n* Skipiste *f*; ~ **school** *n* Skischule *f*; ~ **stick** *n* Skistock *m*.

skit [skɪt] *n* (*satirischer*) Sketch (*on* über +*acc*), Parodie *f* (*on gen*).

ski tow *n* Schlepplift *m*.

skitter ['skɪtə^r] *vi* rutschen.

skittish ['skɪtɪʃ] *adj* (*playful*) übermütig, schelmisch; (*flirtatious*) *woman* neckisch, kokett; (*nervous*) *horse* unruhig.

skittishly ['skɪtɪʃlɪ] *adv see adj.*

skittishness ['skɪtɪʃnɪs] *n see adj* Übermütigkeit *f*, Übermut *m*; Neckereien *pl*; Unruhe, Nervosität *f*.

skittle ['skɪtl] *n* (*Brit*) Kegel *m*. **to play** ~**s** kegeln; ~ **alley** Kegelbahn *f*.

skive [skaɪv] (*Brit sl*) **1** *n* **to be on the** ~ blaumachen (*inf*); (*from school etc*) schwänzen (*inf*); **to have a good** ~ sich (*dat*) einen schönen Tag machen (*inf*), sich vor der Arbeit drücken (*inf*). **2** *vi* blaumachen (*inf*); (*from school etc*) schwänzen (*inf*).

♦**skive off** *vi* (*Brit sl*) sich abseilen (*sl*), sich drücken (*inf*).

skiver ['skaɪvə^r] *n* (*Brit sl*) fauler Bruder (*inf*), faule Schwester (*inf*).

skivvy ['skɪvɪ] *n* (*Brit inf*) Dienstmagd *f*.

skua ['skjuːə] *n* Skua *f*, Große Raubmöwe.

skulduggery [skʌl'dʌgərɪ] *n* (*inf*) üble Tricks *pl* (*inf*). **a piece of** ~ ein übler Trick (*inf*); **what** ~ **are you planning?** (*hum*) na, was für Schandtaten hast du denn vor? (*inf*).

skulk [skʌlk] *vi* (*move*) schleichen, sich stehlen; (*lurk*) sich herumdrücken.

♦**skulk off** *vi* sich davonschleichen, sich davonstehlen.

skull [skʌl] *n* Schädel *m*. **I couldn't get it into his thick** ~ (*inf*) das wollte einfach nicht in seinen Schädel (*inf*); ~ **and crossbones** Totenkopf *m*; ~**cap** Scheitelkäppchen *nt*.

-skulled [-skʌld] *adj suf* -schädelig.

skunk [skʌŋk] *n* Skunk *m*, Stinktier *nt*; (*inf: person*) Schweinehund *m*.

sky [skaɪ] *n* Himmel *m*. **under the open** ~ unter freiem Himmel; **in the** ~ am Himmel; **the** ~'s **the limit!** nach oben sind keine Grenzen gesetzt; **out of a clear (blue)** ~ aus heiterem Himmel; **to praise** *or* **extol sb to the skies** jdn in den Himmel heben, jdn über den grünen Klee loben (*inf*).

sky: ~ **blue** *n* strahlendes Blau; ~-**blue** *adj* strahlend blau; ~-**diving** *n* Fallschirmspringen *nt*.

Skye terrier ['skaɪˌterɪə^r] *n* Skye-Terrier *m*.

sky: ~-**high 1** *adj prices* schwindelnd hoch; **2** *adv* zum Himmel; **to blow a bridge** ~-**high** (*inf*) eine Brücke in die Luft sprengen (*inf*); **to blow a theory** ~-**high** (*inf*) eine Theorie zum Einsturz

bringen; ~**jack 1** *vt* entführen; **2** *n* Flugzeugentführung *f*; ~**jacker** *n* Luftpirat(in *f*), Flugzeugentführer(in *f*) *m*; ~**lark 1** *n* Feldlerche *f*; **2** *vi* (*inf*) (*frolic*) tollen; (*fool around*) blödeln (*inf*); ~**larking** *n* (*inf*) Tollen *nt*; (*fooling around*) Blödelei *f* (*inf*); ~**light** *n* Oberlicht *nt*; (*in roof also*) Dachfenster *nt*; ~**line** *n* (*horizon*) Horizont *m*; (*of building, hills etc*) Silhouette *f*; (*of city*) Skyline, Silhouette *f*; ~ **pilot** *n* (*sl*) Schwarzrock *m* (*inf*); ~**rocket 1** *n* (*Feuerwerks*)rakete *f*; **2** *vi* (*prices, expenses*) in die Höhe schießen; **he** ~**rocketed to fame** er wurde mit einem Schlag berühmt; **3** *vt* in die Höhe schießen lassen; **the novel** ~**rocketed its author to fame der Roman machte den Autor mit einem Schlag berühmt; ~**scraper** *n* Wolkenkratzer *m*.

skyward(s) ['skaɪwəd(z)] **1** *adj* zum *or* gen (*geh*) Himmel gerichtet. **in a** ~ **direction** zum *or* gen (*geh*) Himmel. **2** *adv* zum *or* gen (*geh*) Himmel.

sky-writing ['skaɪˌraɪtɪŋ] *n* Himmelsschrift *f*.

slab [slæb] *n* (*of wood etc*) Tafel *f*; (*of stone, concrete etc*) Platte *f*; (*in mortuary*) Tisch *m*; (*slice*) dicke Scheibe; (*of cake, bread*) großes Stück; (*of chocolate*) Tafel *f*.

slack [slæk] **1** *adj* (+*er*) **(a)** (*not tight*) locker. **to keep a** ~ **rein on the horse/one's children/the economy** beim Pferd/bei seinen Kindern/in der Wirtschaft die Zügel locker *or* schleifen lassen.

(b) (*lazy*) bequem, träge; *student* verbummelt; (*negligent*) nachlässig, schlampig (*inf*). **they are very** ~ **about renewing contracts** die Erneuern der Verträge wird sehr nachlässig gehandhabt; **to be** ~ **about one's work** in bezug auf seine Arbeit nachlässig sein.

(c) (*not busy*) (*Comm*) *market* flau; *period, season also* ruhig. **business is** ~ das Geschäft geht schlecht.

(d) (*slow*) *water* träge; *wind* flau.

2 *n* **(a)** (*of rope etc*) durchhängendes Teil (des Seils/Segels etc), Lose(s) *nt* (*spec*). **to take up the** ~ (*on a rope/sail*) ein Seil/Segel straffen *or* spannen; **there is too much** ~ das Seil/Segel hängt zu sehr durch; **to take up the** ~ **in the economy** die brachliegenden Kräfte (der Wirtschaft) nutzen.

(b) (*coal*) Grus *m*.

3 *vi* bummeln.

♦**slack off** *vi see* **slacken off (b).**

slacken ['slækn] **1** *vt* **(a)** (*loosen*) lockern.

(b) (*reduce*) vermindern, verringern. **to** ~ **speed** langsamer werden, die Geschwindigkeit verlangsamen.

2 *vi* **(a)** (*become loose*) sich lockern.

(b) (*speed*) sich verringern; (*rate of development*) sich verlangsamen; (*wind, demand, market*) abflauen, nachlassen.

♦**slacken off** *vi* **(a)** (*diminish*) nachlassen; (*wind, trade also*) abflauen; (*work, trade*) abnehmen. **(b)** (*person: relax*) nachlassen; (*for health reasons*) sich schonen.

♦**slacken up** *vi see* **slacken off (b).**

slackening ['slækniŋ] *n* (*loosening*) Lockern *nt*; (*reduction*) Abnahme *f*; (*of rate of development, speed*) Verlangsamung *f*; (*of wind, efforts, market*) Abflauen *nt*. **there is no** ~ **off in the demand** die Nachfrage ist nicht zurückgegangen.

slacker ['slækə^r] *n* Bummelant *m*.

slackly ['slæklɪ] *adv hold* locker; *hang* lose.

slackness ['slæknɪs] *n* (*of rope, reins*) Schlaffheit *f*, Durchhängen *nt*; (*of business, market etc*) Flaute *f*; (*laziness*) Bummelei *f*; (*negligence*) Nachlässigkeit, Schlampigkeit (*inf*) *f*.

slacks [slæks] *npl* Hose *f*.

slag [slæg] *n* **(a)** Schlacke *f*. ~ **heap** Schlackenhalde *f*. **(b)** (*sl: woman*) Schlampe *f* (*inf*).

slain [sleɪn] *ptp of* **slay.**

slake [sleɪk] *vt* **(a)** (*liter: quench*) stillen. **(b)** *lime* löschen. ~**d lime** gelöschter Kalk, Löschkalk *m*.

slalom ['slɑːləm] *n* Slalom *m*.

slam [slæm] **1** *n* **(a)** (*of door etc*) Zuschlagen, Zuknallen *nt no pl*; (*of fist etc*) Aufschlagen *nt no pl*. **with a** ~ mit voller Wucht.

(b) (*Cards*) Schlemm *m*. **little** *or* **small** ~ Klein-Schlemm *m*; *see* **grand.**

2 *vt* **(a)** (*close violently*) zuschlagen, zuknallen. **to** ~ **the door** (*lit, fig*) die Tür zuschlagen; **to** ~ **sth shut** etw zuknallen; **to** ~ **the door in sb's face** jdm die Tür vor der Nase zumachen; **to** ~ **home a bolt** einen Riegel vorwerfen.

(b) (*inf: put, throw etc with force*) knallen (*inf*). **he** ~**med his fist into my face/on the table** er knallte mir die Faust ins Gesicht (*inf*)/er knallte mit der Faust auf den Tisch (*inf*); **to** ~ **the brakes on** (*inf*) auf die Bremse latschen (*inf*).

(c) (*inf: defeat*) vernichtend schlagen, am Boden zerstören.

(d) (*inf: criticize harshly*) verreißen; *person* herunterputzen (*inf*), miesmachen (*inf*).

3 *vi* (*door, window*) zuschlagen, zuknallen.

♦**slam down** *vt sep* (*put down violently*) hinknallen (*inf*); *phone* aufknallen (*inf*); *window* zuknallen. **to** ~ **sth** ~ **on the table** etw auf den Tisch knallen.

slander ['slɑːndə^r] **1** *n* Verleumdung *f*. **2** *vt* verleumden.

slanderer ['slɑːndərə^r] *n* Verleumder(in *f*) *m*.

slanderous ['slɑːndərəs] *adj* verleumderisch.

slang [slæŋ] **1** *n* Slang *m*; (*army* ~, *schoolboy* ~ *etc*) Jargon *m*. **thieves'** ~ Rotwelsch *nt*; **gipsy** ~ Zigeunersprache *f*. **2** *adj* Slang-. **3** *vt* (*inf: esp Brit*) jdn beschimpfen/über etw (*acc*) schimpfen; ~**ing match** Wettschimpfen *nt*.

slangy *adj* (+*er*), **slangily** *adv* ['slæŋɪ, -lɪ] salopp.

slant [slɑːnt] **1** *n* **(a)** Neigung *f*, Schräge *f*. **to be on the** ~ sich neigen, schräg sein; **pockets on the** ~ schräg aufgesetzte Taschen; **his handwriting has a definite** ~ **to the right/left** er schreibt stark nach rechts/links.

(b) (*fig*) (*bias, leaning*) Tendenz, Neigung *f*; (*point of view*) Anstrich *m*. **these newspapers have a right-wing** ~ diese Zeitungen sind rechts gerichtet; **to get a** ~ **on sth** sich (*dat*) einen Eindruck von etw verschaffen; ~-**eyed** mit schräggestellten Augen; **she is** ~-**eyed** sie hat schräggestellte Augen.

2 vt verschieben; report färben. the book is ~ed towards women das Buch ist auf Frauen ausgerichtet.
3 vi (road) sich neigen. the light ~ed in at the window das Licht fiel durch das Fenster herein; her eyes ~ up at the corners ihre Augen sind schräggestellt.
slanted ['slɑːntɪd] adj (fig) gefärbt.
slanting ['slɑːntɪŋ] adj schräg.
slap [slæp] **1** n Schlag, Klaps m. to give sb a ~ jdm einen Klaps geben; **a ~ in the face** (lit, fig) ein Schlag ins Gesicht; (lit also) eine Ohrfeige; **to give sb a ~ on the back** jdm (anerkennend) auf den Rücken klopfen; (fig) jdn loben; **~ and tickle** (hum inf) Balgerei (inf), Kalberei (inf) f.
2 adv (inf) direkt.
3 vt (a) schlagen. to ~ sb's face, to ~ sb on or round the face jdn ohrfeigen, jdm ins Gesicht schlagen, jdm eine runter hauen (inf); **to ~ sb on the back** jdm auf den Rücken klopfen; **to ~ one's knee(s)** sich (dat) auf die Schenkel schlagen.
(b) (put noisily) knallen (on(to) auf +acc).
(c) (inf: put carelessly) a piece of cheese ~ped between two slices of bread ein Stück Käse zwischen zwei Scheiben Brot geklatscht (inf).
♦**slap down** vt sep (inf) **(a)** (put down) hinknallen. **(b)** (fig) to ~ sb ~ jdm eins aufs Dach or auf den Deckel geben (inf); to be ~ped ~ eins aufs Dach or auf den Deckel bekommen (inf).
♦**slap on** vt sep (inf) **(a)** (apply carelessly) paint, make-up draufklatschen (inf). **(b)** (put on top) draufklatschen (inf); (fig) tax, money draufhauen (inf).
slap: ~**-bang** adv (inf) mit Karacho (inf); **it was ~-bang in the middle** es war genau in der Mitte; ~**dash** adj flüchtig, schludrig (pej); ~**-happy** adj unbekümmert; ~**jack** n (US) ≈ Pfannkuchen m; ~**stick** n Klamauk m (inf); ~**stick comedy** Slapstick m; ~**-up** adj (inf) super pred, Super- (inf); **meal** mit allem Drum und Dran (inf).
slash [slæʃ] **1** n **(a)** (action) Streich m; (wound) Schnitt m; (made with sword etc also) Schmiß m.
(b) (Sew) Schlitz m. **a velvet dress with ~es of silk** ein Samtkleid mit seidenunterlegten Schlitzen.
(c) (sl) to go for/have a ~ schiffen gehen (sl)/schiffen (sl).
2 vt **(a)** (cut) zerfetzen; face also aufschlitzen; undergrowth abhauen, wegschlagen; (with sword) hauen auf (+acc), schlagen. **to ~ sth to ribbons** etw zerfetzen; **he ~ed the air with his sword** er ließ das Schwert durch die Luft sausen; see wrist.
(b) (strike) schlagen, einschlagen auf (+acc).
(c) (inf: reduce drastically) price radikal herabsetzen; estimate, budget zusammenstreichen (inf).
(d) (Sew) mit Schlitzen versehen. ~**ed sleeves** Schlitzärmel pl; ~**ed doublet** Schlitzwams nt.
3 vi to ~ at sb/sth nach jdm/etw schlagen.
♦**slash off** vt sep abschlagen. to ~ £100 ~ the budget £ 100 aus dem Etat streichen.
slashing ['slæʃɪŋ] adj blow zerschmetternd; attack also scharf; criticism vernichtend.
slat [slæt] n Leiste f; (wooden also) Latte f; (in grid etc) Stab m.
slate [sleɪt] **1** n **(a)** (rock) Schiefer m; (roof ~) Schieferplatte f; (writing ~) (Schiefer)tafel f. **~ quarry** Schieferbruch m; **he has a ~ loose** (inf) bei ihm ist eine Schraube locker (inf); **put it on the ~** (inf) schreiben Sie es mir an; **to have a clean ~** (fig) eine reine Weste haben, nichts auf dem Kerbholz haben (inf); **to wipe the ~ clean** (fig) reinen Tisch machen.
(b) (US Pol) (Kandidaten)liste f.
2 adj Schiefer-, schief(e)rig. **the roof is ~** das Dach ist aus Schiefer.
3 vt **(a)** roof (mit Schiefer) decken.
(b) (US) (propose) vorschlagen; (schedule) ansetzen. **it is ~d to start at nine** es ist für neun Uhr angesetzt.
(c) (inf: criticize harshly) play, performance verreißen; person zusammensaucken (inf).
slate: ~**-blue** adj blaugrau; ~**-coloured** adj schiefergrau, schieferfarben; ~**-grey** adj schiefergrau; ~ **pencil** n Griffel m.
slater ['sleɪtə'] n Dachdecker, Schieferdecker (rare) m.
slating ['sleɪtɪŋ] n (inf) Verriß m. **to give sb a ~** jdn zusammenstauchen (inf); **to get a ~** zusammengestaucht werden (inf); (play, performance etc) verrissen werden.
slatted ['slætɪd] adj see slat aus Leisten/Latten/Stäben bestehend. **a ~ fence** ein Lattenzaun m.
slattern ['slætən] n Schlampe f.
slatternly ['slætənlɪ] adj liederlich, schlampig.
slaty ['sleɪtɪ] adj material schief(e)rig; (in colour) schieferfarben. ~ **blue** eyes graublaue Augen pl.
slaughter ['slɔːtə'] **1** n (of animals) Schlachten nt no pl; (of persons) Gemetzel, Abschlachten (liter) nt no pl. **the S~ of the Innocents** (Bibl) der Mord der Unschuldigen Kinder; **the ~ on the roads** das Massensterben auf den Straßen.
2 vt schlachten; persons (lit) abschlachten; (fig) fertigmachen (inf).
slaughterer ['slɔːtərə'] n (lit) Schlachter m; (fig) Schlächter m.
slaughterhouse ['slɔːtəhaʊs] n Schlachthof m or -haus nt.
Slav [slɑːv] **1** adj slawisch. **2** n Slawe m, Slawin f.
slave [sleɪv] **1** n Sklave m, Sklavin f. **to be a ~ to sb/sth** jds Sklave sein/Sklave von etw sein. **2** vi sich abplagen, schuften (inf). **to ~ (away)** at sth sich mit etw herumschlagen; **to ~ over a hot stove** den ganzen Tag am Herd stehen.
slave: ~ **driver** n (lit, fig) Sklaventreiber m; ~ **labour** n **(a)** (work) Sklavenarbeit f. **(b)** (work force) Sklaven pl.
slaver[1] ['sleɪvə'] n (ship) Sklavenschiff nt; (person) Sklavenhändler m.
slaver[2] ['slævə'] **1** vi speicheln (geh), geifern. **the dog ~ed at the mouth** der Hund hatte Schaum vor dem Maul; **he began to ~ at the thought of food** bei dem Gedanken ans Essen lief ihm das Wasser im Munde zusammen. **2** n Speichel, Geifer m.
lavery ['sleɪvərɪ] n Sklaverei f; (condition) Sklavenleben nt;

(fig: addiction) sklavische Abhängigkeit (to von). **she was tired of domestic ~** sie hatte es satt, sich immer im Haushalt abrackern zu müssen.
slave: ~**-ship** n Sklavenschiff nt; ~**-trade** n Sklavenhandel m; ~**-trader** n see slaver[1].
slavey ['sleɪvɪ] n (dated Brit inf) (Dienst)mädchen nt.
Slavic ['slɑːvɪk] **1** adj slawisch. **2** n das Slawische.
slavish adj, ~**ly** adv ['sleɪvɪʃ, -lɪ] sklavisch.
slavishness ['sleɪvɪʃnɪs] n sklavische Abhängigkeit; (submissiveness) Unterwürfigkeit f. **the ~ with which she imitated him** die sklavische Art, in der sie ihn nachahmte.
Slavonic [slə'vɒnɪk] **1** adj slawisch. **2** n das Slawische.
slaw [slɔː] n (US) Krautsalat m.
slay [sleɪ] pret **slew**, ptp **slain** vt erschlagen; (with gun etc) ermorden. **this will ~ you** (inf) da lachst du dich tot! (inf); **he really ~s me** (inf) ich könnte mich über ihn totlachen (inf).
slayer ['sleɪə'] n (liter) Mörder, Töter (old liter) m.
sleazy ['sliːzɪ] adj (+er) (inf) schäbig.
sled [sled], **sledge** [sledʒ] **1** n Schlitten m. **2** vi Schlitten fahren.
sledge(hammer) ['sledʒ(,hæmə')] n Vorschlaghammer m.
sleek [sliːk] adj (+er) hair, fur, animal geschmeidig, glatt; (of general appearance) gepflegt; car also schnittig, elegant; behaviour aalglatt (pej), glatt. **2** vt glätten; (cat) lecken. **to ~ one's hair down/back** sich (dat) die Haare glätten or zurechtstreichen/zurückstreichen.
sleekness ['sliːknɪs] n see adj Geschmeidigkeit f; Gepflegtheit f; Schnittigkeit, Eleganz f; aaglatte Art (pej), Glätte f.
sleep [sliːp] (vb: pret, ptp **slept**) **1** n Schlaf m. **to go to ~** (person, limb), **to drop off to ~** (person) einschlafen; **I couldn't get to ~ last night** ich konnte letzte Nacht nicht einschlafen; **try and get some ~** versuche, etwas zu schlafen; **to have a ~** (etwas) schlafen; **to have a good night's ~** sich richtig ausschlafen, richtig schlafen; **to put sb to ~** (person, cocoa etc) jdn zum Schlafen bringen; (drug) jdn einschläfern; **to put an animal to ~** (euph) ein Tier einschläfern; **that film sent me to ~** bei dem Film bin ich eingeschlafen; **to walk/talk in one's ~** schlafwandeln/im Schlaf sprechen.
2 vt **(a)** to ~ the hours away vor sich hin dösen (inf); (all day) den ganzen Tag verschlafen; **to ~ the clock round** rund um die Uhr schlafen; **to ~ the sleep of the just/the sleep of the dead** or **the last sleep** den Schlaf des Gerechten/den ewigen (liter) or letzten Schlaf (liter) schlafen.
(b) unterbringen. **the house ~s 10** in dem Haus können 10 Leute schlafen or übernachten.
3 vi schlafen. **to ~ like a log** or **top** or **baby** wie ein Klotz or wie ein Murmeltier or unschuldig wie ein Kind schlafen; **to ~ late** lange schlafen; **the village slept** (liter) das Dorf schlief (geh); **you must have been ~ing** (fig) da mußt du geschlafen haben.
♦**sleep around** vi (inf) mit jedem schlafen (inf).
♦**sleep in** vi **(a)** ausschlafen; (inf: oversleep) verschlafen. **(b)** (live in) im Hause wohnen.
♦**sleep off** vt sep (inf) hangover etc ausschlafen. **to ~ it ~** seinen Rausch ausschlafen; cold etc sich gesund schlafen; **to ~ one's lunch** ein Verdauungsschläfchen nt halten.
♦**sleep on** vi (continue sleeping) weiterschlafen. **2** vi +prep obj problem etc überschlafen. **let's ~ ~ it** schlafen wir erst einmal darüber, überschlafen wir die Sache erst einmal.
♦**sleep out** vi **(a)** (in open air) draußen or im Freien schlafen. **(b)** (hotel staff: live out) außer Haus wohnen.
♦**sleep through** vi **1** vi durchschlafen. **2** vi +prep obj weiterschlafen bei. **to ~ ~ the alarm** (clock) den Wecker verschlafen.
♦**sleep together** vi zusammen schlafen.
♦**sleep with** vi +prep obj schlafen mit.
sleeper ['sliːpə'] n **(a)** (person) Schlafende(r) mf, Schläfer(in f) m. **to be a heavy/light ~** einen festen/leichten Schlaf haben.
(b) (Brit Rail: on track) Schwelle f.
(c) (Rail) (train) Schlafwagenzug m; (coach) Schlafwagen m; (berth) Platz m im Schlafwagen. **I've booked a ~** ich habe Schlafwagen gebucht.
(d) (earring) einfacher Ohrring, der das Zuwachsen des Loches im Ohrläppchen verhindern soll.
sleepily ['sliːpɪlɪ] adv see adj (a) schläfrig, müde; verschlafen.
sleepiness ['sliːpɪnɪs] n see adj **(a)** Müdigkeit, Schläfrigkeit f; Verschlafenheit f. **(b)** Lahmheit (inf), Müdigkeit f; Verschlafenheit f; Einschläfernde(s) nt; Schläfrigkeit f.
sleeping ['sliːpɪŋ] **1** adj schlafend. ~ **Beauty** Dornröschen nt; **let ~ dogs lie** (Prov) schlafende Hunde soll man nicht wecken (Prov). **2** n Schlafen nt. **between ~ and waking** zwischen Schlaf und Wachen.
sleeping: ~ **accommodation** n Schlafgelegenheit f; ~ **bag** n Schlafsack m; ~ **car** n Schlafwagen m; ~ **draught** n Schlaftrunk m; ~ **partner** n (Brit) stiller Teilhaber or Gesellschafter; ~ **pill** n Schlaftablette f; ~ **quarters** npl Schlafräume pl; Schlafsaal m; ~ **sickness** n Schlafkrankheit f.
sleepless ['sliːplɪs] adj schlaflos.
sleeplessness ['sliːplɪsnɪs] n Schlaflosigkeit f.
sleep: ~**walk** vi schlafwandeln; **he was ~walking** er hat or ist geschlafwandelt; ~**walker** n Schlafwandler(in f) m; ~**walking** **1** n Schlafwandeln nt; **2** attr schlafwandlerisch.
sleepy ['sliːpɪ] adj (+er) **(a)** (drowsy) person, voice etc müde, schläfrig; (not yet awake) verschlafen. **to be/look ~** müde sein/aussehen; **I feel very ~ at midnight** um 12 Uhr werde ich immer sehr müde.
(b) (inactive) person lahm (inf), müde; place, atmosphere verschlafen; climate schläfrig machend; afternoons schläfrig.
sleepyhead ['sliːpɪhed] n (inf) Schlafmütze f.
sleet [sliːt] **1** n Schneeregen m. **2** vi **it was ~ing** es gab Schneeregen.
sleeve [sliːv] n **(a)** (on garment) Ärmel m. **to roll up one's ~s** (lit) sich (dat) die Ärmel hochkrempeln; (fig) die Ärmel aufkrem-

peln (*inf*); **to have sth/a card up one's ~** (*fig inf*) etw/etwas in petto haben *or* auf Lager haben; *see* **laugh.**
  (b) (*for record, on book*) Hülle *f*.
  (c) (*Tech*) Muffe, Manschette *f*.
-sleeved [-sliːvd] *adj suf* -ärmelig.
sleeveless [ˈsliːvlɪs] *adj* ärmellos.
sleigh [sleɪ] *n* (Pferde)schlitten *m*. **~-bell** Schlittenglocke *or* -schelle *f*; **~ ride** Schlittenfahrt *f*.
sleighing [ˈsleɪɪŋ] *n* Schlittenfahren *nt*.
sleight [slaɪt] *n*: **~ of hand** Fingerfertigkeit *f*; **by ~ of hand** durch Taschenspielertricks.
slender [ˈslendəʳ] *adj* schlank; *hand, waist also* schmal; *resources, income* knapp, mager; *chance, hope* schwach, gering; *excuse* dürftig, schwach.
slenderize [ˈslendəraɪz] *vt* (*US*) schlank machen.
slenderly [ˈslendəlɪ] *adv*: **~ built** *or* **made** schlank.
slenderness [ˈslendənɪs] *n see adj* Schlankheit *f*; Schmalheit *f*; Schwäche *f*; Dürftigkeit *f*. **the ~ of his income/of the margin** sein geringes Einkommen/der knappe Abstand.
slept [slept] *pret, ptp of* **sleep.**
sleuth [sluːθ] (*inf*) **1** *n* Spürhund *m* (*inf*). **2** *vi* Detektiv spielen.
slew¹, (*US*) **slue** [sluː] (*also* **~ round**) **1** *vt crane, lorry* (herum)schwenken; *head* drehen. **to ~ sth to the left** etw nach links schwenken. **2** *vi* (herum)schwenken.
slew² (*US inf: also* **slue**) *n* Haufen *m* (*inf*).
slew³ *pret of* **slay.**
slewed [sluːd] *adj pred* (*sl*) voll (*inf*), besoffen (*sl*). **to get ~** sich vollaufen lassen (*sl*).
slice [slaɪs] **1** *n* (**a**) Scheibe *f*; (*of bread also*) Schnitte *f*.
  (b) (*fig: portion*) (*of population, profits*) Teil *m*; (*of land*) Stück *nt*. **a ~ of life in contemporary Paris** ein Ausschnitt aus dem Leben im heutigen Paris; **a ~ of luck** eine Portion Glück; **that was a ~ of luck!** das war ein glücklicher Zufall.
  (c) (*esp Brit: food server*) Wender *m*. **cake ~** Tortenheber *m*.
  (d) (*Sport*) angeschnittener Ball. **to put a bit of ~ on the ball** den Ball etwas anschneiden.
  2 *vt* (**a**) durchschneiden; *bread, meat etc* (in Scheiben) schneiden. **to ~ sth in two** etw in zwei Teile schneiden.
  (b) *ball* (an)schneiden.
  3 *vi* (**a**) schneiden. **to ~ through sth** etw durchschneiden.
  (b) (*Sport*) schneiden.
♦**slice off** *vt sep* abschneiden. **he ~d ~ the top of his egg** er köpfte sein Ei (*inf*).
♦**slice up** *vt sep* (ganz) in Scheiben schneiden; *bread, meat, sausage also* aufschneiden; (*divide*) aufteilen.
sliced [slaɪst] *adj* (in Scheiben) geschnitten; *loaf, bread, sausage* (auf)geschnitten.
slicer [ˈslaɪsəʳ] *n* (*cheese-*, *cucumber-~ etc*) Hobel *m*; (*machine*) (*bread-~*) Brot(schneide)maschine *f*, Brotschneider *m*; (*bacon-~*) ≈ Wurstschneidemaschine *f*.
slick [slɪk] **1** *adj* (*+er*) (*inf*) (**a**) (*usu pej: clever, smart*) gewieft (*inf*), clever (*inf*); *answer, solution* glatt; *show, performance, translation, style* glatt, professionell. **a ~ novel** ein glatt *or* professionell geschriebener Roman; **a ~ customer** ein ganz gewiefter Kerl (*inf*); **he's a ~ operator** er geht raffiniert vor; **these ~ young people who know all the answers** diese neunmalklugen jungen Leute, die auf alles eine Antwort haben.
  (b) *hair* geschniegelt.
  (c) (*US: slippery*) glatt, schlüpfrig.
  2 *n* (**a**) (*oil~*) (Öl)teppich *m*, Schlick *m*.
  (b) (*US inf: glossy magazine*) Hochglanzmagazin *nt*.
  (c) (*racing tyre*) Slick *m* (*inf*).
♦**slick back** *vt sep* **to ~ one's hair ~** sich (*dat*) die Haare anklatschen (*inf*); **the ~ed-~ hairstyles of the 50s** die geschniegelten Frisuren der 50er Jahre.
slicker [ˈslɪkəʳ] *n* (*US*) (**a**) (*coat*) Regenjacke *f*. **(b)** (*inf: swindler*) Gauner (*inf*), Ganove (*inf*) *m*. **(c)** *see* **city ~.**
slickly [ˈslɪklɪ] *adv* (*see adj*) (**a**) (**a**).
slickness [ˈslɪknɪs] *n* (*inf*) *see adj* (**a**) Gewieftheit (*inf*), Cleverneß (*inf*) *f*. **we were impressed by the ~ with which he answered** wir waren davon beeindruckt, wie glatt er antwortete. **(b)** (*appearance*) geschniegeltes Aussehen.
slide [slaɪd] (*vb: pret, ptp* **slid** [slɪd]) **1** *n* (**a**) (*slide for sliding, chute*) Rutschbahn *f*; (*in playground, for logs etc*) Rutsche *f*.
  (b) (*fig: fall, drop*) Abfall *m*. **the ~ in share prices** der Preisrutsch bei den Aktien; **the ~ in the temperature** der Temperaturabfall; **his slow ~ into dishonesty** sein langsamer Abstieg in die Unehrlichkeit.
  (c) (*land~*) Rutsch *m*, Rutschung *f* (*spec*).
  (d) (*of trombone*) Zug *m*; (*sequence of notes*) Schleifer *m*.
  (e) (*Tech: part*) gleitendes Teil, Schlitten *m*.
  (f) (*esp Brit: for hair*) Spange *f*.
  (g) (*Phot*) Dia, Diapositiv (*form*) *nt*; (*microscope ~*) Objektträger *m*. **a lecture with ~s** ein Diavortrag, ein Lichtbildervortrag *m*.
  2 *vt* (*push*) schieben; (*slip*) gleiten lassen. **he slid the gun into the holster** er ließ den Revolver ins Halfter gleiten; **to ~ the top (back) onto a box** den Deckel auf eine Kiste zurückschieben; **to ~ the drawer (back) into place** die Schublade (wieder) zurück- *or* zuschieben.
  3 *vi* (**a**) rutschen; (*deliberately also*) schlittern. **to ~ down the banisters** das Treppengeländer hinunterrutschen; **suddenly it all slid into place** plötzlich paßte alles zusammen.
  (b) (*move smoothly: machine part etc*) sich schieben lassen. **it slid into its place** es glitt *or* rutschte an die richtige Stelle.
  (c) (*person*) schleichen. **he slid into the room** er kam ins Zimmer geschlichen; **he slid off into the dark** er verschwand in der Dunkelheit.
  (d) (*fig*) **the days slid by** *or* **past** die Tage schwanden dahin (*geh*); **to ~ into bad habits** (allmählich) in schlechte Gewohn-

heiten verfallen; **to let sth ~** etw schleifen lassen, etw vernachlässigen; **to let things/everything ~** die Dinge laufen *or* schleifen lassen/sich um nichts mehr kümmern.
slide: **~ control** *n* Schieberegler *m*; **~ fastener** *n* (*US*) Reißverschluß *m*; **~ film** *n* Diafilm *m*; **~ projector** *n* Diaprojektor *m*; **~ rule** *n* Rechenschieber, Rechenstab (*form*) *m*.
sliding [ˈslaɪdɪŋ] *adj part* gleitend; *door, roof, seat* Schiebe-; *seat* (*in rowing boat*) Roll-. **~ scale** gleitende Skala.
slight [slaɪt] **1** *adj* (*+er*) (**a**) *person, build* zierlich.
  (b) (*small, trivial*) leicht; *improvement also, change, possibility* geringfügig; *importance, intelligence* gering; *error also* klein; *pain also* schwach; *acquaintance* flüchtig. **the wound is only ~** es ist nur eine leichte Verwundung; **to a ~ extent** in geringem Maße; **he showed some ~ optimism** er zeigte gewisse Ansätze von Optimismus; **just the ~est bit short** ein ganz kleines bißchen zu kurz; **the ~est optimism/criticism/possibility** das gering(fügig)ste Zeichen von Optimismus/die geringste Kritik/die allergeringste Möglichkeit; **he takes offence at the ~est thing** er ist wegen jeder kleinsten Kleinigkeit gleich beleidigt; **I haven't the ~est idea** ich habe nicht die geringste *or* leiseste (*) Ahnung; **not in the ~est** nicht im geringsten *or* mindesten (*geh*); **without the ~est difficulty** ohne die kleinste *or* mindeste Schwierigkeit.
  2 *n* (*affront*) Affront *m* (*on* gegen). **a ~ on one's/sb's character** eine persönliche Kränkung *or* Beleidigung.
  3 *vt* (*offend*) kränken, beleidigen; (*ignore*) ignorieren. **to feel ~ed** gekränkt *or* beleidigt sein.
slighting [ˈslaɪtɪŋ] *adj* (*offensive*) kränkend; (*disparaging*) *behaviour* geringschätzig; *remark* abschätzig, abfällig.
slightingly [ˈslaɪtɪŋlɪ] *adv speak* abschätzig, abfällig; *treat* geringschätzig.
slightly [ˈslaɪtlɪ] *adv* (**a**) **~ built** *or* **made** *person* zierlich. **(b)** (*to a slight extent*) etwas, ein klein(es) bißchen; *know* flüchtig; *smell* leicht, etwas.
slightness [ˈslaɪtnɪs] *n* (**a**) (*of person, build*) Zierlichkeit *f*. **(b)** (*triviality*) Geringfügigkeit *f*; (*of acquaintance*) Flüchtigkeit *f*.
slim [slɪm] **1** *adj* (*+er*) (**a**) schlank; *ankle, waist etc* schmal; *volume* schmal, dünn. **(b)** *resources, profits* mager; *excuse, hope also* schwach; *chances* gering. **2** *vi* eine Schlankheitskur machen. **3** *vt* (*also* **~ down**) schlank(er) machen; (*fig*) *demands etc* schrumpfen.
slime [slaɪm] *n* Schleim *m*. **trail of ~** Schleimspur *f*.
sliminess [ˈslaɪmɪnɪs] *n see adj* Schleimigkeit *f*; Glitschigkeit *f*; Schmierigkeit *f*; Schleimigkeit *f*; Öligkeit *f*.
slimmer [ˈslɪməʳ] *n* Kalorienzähler(in *f*) *m* (*hum*). **special meals for ~s** spezielle Gerichte für Leute, die abnehmen wollen.
slimming [ˈslɪmɪŋ] **1** *adj* schlankmachend *attr.* **crispbread is ~** Knäckebrot macht schlank; **to be on a ~ diet** eine Schlankheitskur machen; **~ club** Diätklub, Schlankheitsklub *m*; **~ foods** kalorienarme Nahrungsmittel *pl*. **2** *n* Abnehmen *nt*. **is ~ really worth it?** lohnt es sich wirklich abzunehmen?
slimness [ˈslɪmnɪs] *n see adj* (**a**) Schlankheit *f*; Schmalheit *f*, Dünne *f*. **(b)** Magerkeit *f*. **the thought of the ~ of their chances/hopes** der Gedanke daran, wie gering ihre Chancen/schwach ihre Hoffnungen waren.
slimy [ˈslaɪmɪ] *adj* (*+er*) *liquid, secretion, deposit* schleimig; *stone, wall* glitschig; *hands* schmierig; (*fig*) schleimig; *smile, person also* ölig.
sling [slɪŋ] (*vb: pret, ptp* **slung**) **1** *n* (**a**) (*Med*) Schlinge *f*. **to have one's arm in a ~** den Arm in der Schlinge tragen.
  (b) (*for hoisting*) Schlinge, Schlaufe *f*; (*for rifle*) (Trag)riemen *m*; (*for baby*) (Baby)tragetuch *nt*, (Baby)trageschlinge *f*. **to carry a rifle/baby in a ~** ein Gewehr am Riemen/ein Baby in einer *or* der Schlinge tragen.
  (c) (*weapon*) Schleuder *f*.
  2 *vt* (**a**) (*throw*) schleudern; (*inf*) schmeißen (*inf*). **to ~ sth away** etw wegschleudern/wegschmeißen (*inf*); **with sth over to sb** (*inf*) jdm etw zuschmeißen (*inf*); **he slung his coat over his arm/the box onto his back** er warf sich (*dat*) den Mantel über den Arm/die Kiste auf den Rücken; **to ~ one's hook** (*fig inf*) Leine ziehen (*inf*).
  (b) (*hoist with a ~*) in einer Schlinge hochziehen.
  (c) (*hang*) aufhängen.
♦**sling out** *vt sep* (*inf*) rausschmeißen (*inf*).
sling: **~back 1** *adj* **~back shoes** Slingpumps *pl*; (*sandals*) Sandaletten *pl*; **2** *n* **~backs** Slings, Slingpumps *pl*; **~ bag** *n* (*US*) Schultertasche *f*; **~shot** *n* (*US*) (Stein)schleuder *f*.
slink [slɪŋk] *pret, ptp* **slunk** *vi* schleichen. **to ~ away** *or* **off** sich davonschleichen; **to ~ along the wall** sich an der Wand entlangdrücken; **to ~ off with one's tail between one's legs** (*fig inf*) mit eingezogenem Schwanz abziehen (*inf*).
slinky *adj* (*+er*), **slinkily** *adv* [ˈslɪŋkɪ, -lɪ] (*inf*) aufreizend; *walk etc also* katzenhaft.
slip [slɪp] **1** *n* (**a**) (*slide*) she broke her leg after a **~ on the icy road** sie rutschte auf der eisigen Straße aus und brach sich das Bein; **she had a nasty ~** sie ist ausgerutscht und bös gefallen.
  (b) (*mistake*) Ausrutscher, Patzer *m*. **to make a (bad) ~** sich (übel) vertun (*inf*), einen (ganz schönen) Bock schießen (*inf*); **a ~ of the pen/tongue** ein Schreibfehler *m*/Versprecher *m*; **it was just a ~ of the pen** da habe ich mich nur verschrieben; **there's many a ~** ('twixt cup and lip) (*Prov*) man soll den Tag nicht vor dem Abend loben (*Prov*), zwischen Lipp' und Kelchesrand (schwebt der finster'n Mächte Hand) (*liter*).
  (c) **to give sb the ~** jdm entwischen.
  (d) (*pillow~*) Kissenbezug *m*.
  (e) (*undergarment*) Unterrock *m*. **waist ~** Halbunterrock *m*; **full-length ~** Unterkleid *nt*.
  (f) (*of paper*) Zettel *m*. **~s of paper** Zettel *pl*; **withdrawal ~** Auszahlungsschein *m*; **sales ~** Kassenzettel *m*.
  (g) (*person*) **a (mere) ~ of a girl** (*slightly built*) ein zierliches Persönchen; (*young*) eine halbe Portion (*inf*).

(h) *(Hort) (for planting)* Steckling *m*; *(for grafting)* Reis *nt*.

(i) *(Cricket) (position/area)* Position *f*/Gebiet *nt* neben dem Torwächter; *(fielder)* Eckmann *m*.

(j) ~s *pl (Theat)* Bühnenloge *f*.

(k) *(Pottery)* geschlämmter Ton.

(l) *(Aviat: side-~)* Schlipp *m*.

2 *vt* **(a)** schieben; *(slide)* gleiten *or* rutschen lassen. to ~ sth across to sb jdm etw zuschieben; *(unobtrusively)* jdm etw zuschmuggeln; she ~ped the dress over her head sie streifte sich *(dat)* das Kleid über den Kopf; to ~ one's arm round sb's waist jdm den Arm um die Taille legen; to ~ one over on sb *(inf)* jdn reinlegen *(inf)*; to ~ sb a fiver jdm einen Fünfer zustecken.

(b) *(escape from)* sich losreißen. the dog ~ped its chain der Hund hat sich (von der Kette) losgerissen; the boat had ~ped its moorings das Boot hatte sich losgerissen; to ~ anchor *(Naut)* den Anker kappen *(form)*; it/his birthday ~ped my mind or memory ich habe es/seinen Geburtstag vergessen *or* verschwitzt *(inf)*; it ~ped my notice es ist mir entgangen.

(c) *(loose)* losmachen. he ~ped the dog from its chain er machte den Hund (von der Kette) los.

(d) *(Med)* to ~ a disc sich *(dat)* einen Bandscheibenschaden zuziehen; a ~ped disc ein Bandscheibenschaden, ein Bandscheibenvorfall *or* -prolaps *(spec) m*.

(e) *(Aut) clutch* schleifen lassen.

(f) to ~ a stitch eine Masche (ungestrickt) abheben.

3 *vi* **(a)** *(person)* (aus)rutschen; *(feet, tyres)* (weg)rutschen; *(become loose: knot, nut)* sich lösen; *(Aut: clutch)* schleifen. the car ~ped into the ditch das Auto rutschte in den Graben; the knife ~ped das Messer rutschte ab; it ~ped from her hand es rutschte ihr aus der Hand; the secret ~ped out before he realized ene er sich's versah, war ihm das Geheimnis herausgerutscht; a few errors have ~ped into the text in den Text haben sich ein paar Fehler eingeschlichen; the beads ~ped through my fingers die Perlen glitten durch meine Finger; money ~s through her fingers das Geld zerrinnt ihr in den Händen; suddenly everything ~ped into place plötzlich paßte alles zusammen.

(b) *(move quickly)* schlüpfen; *(time smoothly)* rutschen. I'll ~ round to the shop ich spring' schnell zum Laden; the motor-cycle ~s through the traffic das Motorrad schlängelt sich durch den Verkehr.

(c) to let (it) ~ that ... fallenlassen, daß ...; he let ~ an oath ihm entfuhr ein Fluch; to let a secret/chance ~ ein Geheimnis ausplaudern/eine Gelegenheit vorübergehen lassen; the police let the thief ~ through their fingers die Polizei ließ sich *(dat)* den Dieb in letzter Minute durch die Finger schlüpfen.

(d) *(decline: standards, morals etc)* fallen. you're ~ping! *(inf)* du läßt nach *(inf)*.

♦**slip away** *vi* sich wegschleichen, sich wegstehlen; *(time)* verstreichen, vergehen; *(chances)* (allmählich) schwinden; *(opportunity)* dahinschwinden. her life was ~ping ~ from her ihr Leben schwand dahin.

♦**slip back** *vi* **(a)** *(return unobtrusively)* unbemerkt zurückgehen; *(quickly)* schnell zurückgehen. **(b)** *(deteriorate)* *(production)* zurückgehen; *(patient)* einen Rückfall haben.

♦**slip by** *vi* *(pass unobtrusively)* *(person)* sich vorbeischleichen *or* vorbeischmuggeln *(prep obj* an *+dat)*; *(mistake)* durchgehen; *(years)* verfliegen, nur so dahinschwinden.

♦**slip down** *vi* *(fall)* ausrutschen, ausgleiten; *(go down)* hinunterlaufen. this wine ~s ~ easily dieser Wein rutscht *or* kullert so schön (die Kehle hinunter) *(inf)*.

♦**slip in 1** *vi (enter unobtrusively)* (sich) hineinschleichen; *(burglar also, mistake)* sich einschleichen.

2 *vt sep (mention casually)* einfließen lassen. to ~ the clutch ~ die Kupplung schleifen lassen; to ~ sth ~to sb's pocket jdm etw in die Tasche gleiten lassen; to ~ a coin ~to a slot eine Münze einwerfen; she ~ped the car ~to first gear sie legte den ersten Gang ein.

♦**slip off 1** *vi* sich wegschleichen, sich wegstehlen. **2** *vt sep clothes* ausziehen, abstreifen, schlüpfen aus.

♦**slip on** *vt sep* schlüpfen in *(+acc)*; *dress, gloves also* überstreifen, überziehen; *ring* aufziehen; *lid* drauftun *(prep obj auf +acc)*. he ~ped the ring ~ to her finger er steckte ihr den Ring an den Finger.

♦**slip out** *vi* **(a)** *(leave unobtrusively)* kurz weggehen *or* rausgehen. **(b)** *(be revealed)* herauskommen. the secret ~ped ~ das Geheimnis ist durchgesickert.

♦**slip past** *vi see* slip by.

♦**slip up** *vi (inf: err)* sich vertun *(inf)*, (einen) Schnitzer machen *(over,* in bei*)*. you really ~ped ~ there! da hast du aber wirklich Murks gemacht *(inf)*; he usually ~s ~ on spelling meistens stolpert er über die Rechtschreibung *(inf)*.

slip: ~ case *n* Schuber *m*; ~cover *n (esp US)* Schonbezug *m*; ~knot *n* Schlippstek *m (spec)*; ~ons *npl (also* ~-on shoes*)* Slipper *pl; (for women also)* Trotteurs *pl*; ~over *n* Pullunder *m*.

slippage ['slɪpɪdʒ] *n* **(a)** *(Mech)* Schlupf *m*, Spiel *nt*. **(b)** *(fig)* Rückstand *m*. to prevent ~ um Rückstände zu vermeiden.

slipper ['slɪpə^r] *n (bedroom ~)* Pantoffel, Hausschuh *m*; *(dancing ~)* Pumps, Slipper *m*.

slipperiness ['slɪpərɪnɪs] *n see adj* **(a)** Schlüpfrigkeit *f*; Glätte *f*; Glitschigkeit *f*. **(b)** Glätte *f*, aalglatte Art.

slippery ['slɪpərɪ] *adj* **(a)** schlüpfrig; *rope, road, ground* glatt, rutschig; *fish also* glitschig. to be on ~ ground *(fig)* sich auf unsicherem Boden bewegen.

(b) *(pej inf) person* glatt, windig *(inf)*. a ~ customer ein aalglatter Kerl *(inf)*; he's as ~ as they come or as an eel er ist aalglatt; he's on the ~ slope er ist auf der schiefen Bahn; it's a ~ slope das ist ein gefährlicher Weg.

slippy ['slɪpɪ] *adj (inf)* **(a)** *(slippery)* glatt. **(b)** *(esp Brit)* to be *or* look ~ einen Zahn zulegen *(inf) (about sth* bei etw*)*; ... and look ~ (about it)! ... und zwar flott *or* ein bißchen dalli! *(inf)*.

slip-road ['slɪprəud] *n (Brit)* Zufahrtsstraße *f*; *(for entering motorway)* (Autobahn)auffahrt *f*; *(for leaving motorway)* (Autobahn)ausfahrt *f*.

slipshod ['slɪpʃɒd] *adj* schludrig.

slip: ~stream *n (Aviat)* Sog *m*; *(Aut)* Windschatten *m*; ~-up *n* Schnitzer *m*; *(more serious)* Patzer *m*; there's been a ~-up somewhere da muß irgend etwas schiefgelaufen sein; ~way *n (Aut)* Ablaufbahn, Gleitbahn *f*.

slit [slɪt] *(vb: pret, ptp ~)* **1** *n* Schlitz *m; (in castle wall also)* Schießscharte *f*. **2** *vt* (auf)schlitzen. to ~ a sack open einen Sack aufschlitzen; to ~ sb's throat jdm die Kehle aufschlitzen.

slit-eyed ['slɪtaɪd] *adj (pej)* schlitzäugig.

slither ['slɪðə^r] *vi* rutschen. to ~ about on the ice auf dem Eis herumschlittern *or* -rutschen.

slit trench *n* Splittergraben *m*.

sliver ['slɪvə^r] *n (of wood, glass etc)* Splitter *m; (thin slice)* Scheibchen *nt*.

slob [slɒb] *n (inf) (man)* Dreckschwein *nt (sl); (woman)* Schlampe *f (inf)*.

slobber ['slɒbə^r] **1** *n* Sabber *m (inf)*. **2** *vi* sabbern, sabbeln *(also fig); (dog)* geifern. to ~ over sb jdn schwärmen; *(kiss)* jdn abküssen; to ~ over sth *(fig inf)* etw anschmachten; *(dirty old man etc)* sich an etw *(dat)* aufgeilen *(sl)*.

slobbery ['slɒbərɪ] *adj (inf)* naß. the newspaper is all ~ die Zeitung ist ganz vollgesabbert *(inf)*.

sloe [sləu] *n (fruit)* Schlehe *f; (tree)* Schlehdorn *m*. ~-gin Schlehdornschnaps *m*; ~-eyed *person* dunkeläugig.

slog [slɒg] *(inf)* **1** *n* **(a)** *(effort)* Schinderei, Plackerei *f (inf)*.

(b) *(stroke)* wuchtiger Schlag. to give sb/sth a ~ jdm/etw einen (ordentlichen) Schlag versetzen; to take a ~ at sb/sth auf jdn/etw (ein)dreschen.

2 *vt ball* dreschen *(inf); opponent* hart schlagen *or* treffen.

3 *vi* **(a)** to ~ at sth *(hit)* auf etw *(acc)* (ein)dreschen *(inf); (work)* an etw *(dat)* schuften *(inf)*; to ~ away (at sth) sich (mit etw) abrackern.

(b) *(walk)* to ~ on/along sich weiter-/dahinschleppen.

slogan ['sləugən] *n* Slogan *m; (motto)* Motto *nt*, Wahlspruch *m; (political also)* Schlagwort *nt*, Parole *f*. advertising ~ Werbeslogan, Werbespruch *m*.

slogger ['slɒgə^r] *n (inf)* Arbeitstier *nt*.

sloop [slu:p] *n* Slup, Schlup *f*.

slop [slɒp] **1** *vi* **(a)** *(spill)* (über)schwappen. to ~ over (into sth) überschwappen (in *+acc*).

(b) *(splash)* to ~ about herumschwappen *(inf)*.

(c) to ~ about *(fig inf: in slippers etc)* herumschlurfen *(inf)*.

2 *vt (spill)* verschütten; *(pour out)* schütten.

3 *n* **(a)** *(inf: sentimental)* rührseliges Zeug, Schmalz *m*.

(b) *(tasteless food: also* ~s*)* Schlabber *m (inf)*.

(c) *usu pl (waste)* Schmutzwasser, Abwasser *nt; (swill)* Schweinetrank *m.* ~ pail Eimer *m* für Schmutzwasser.

slop basin, slop bowl *n* Abgußschale *f (Teil des Teeservice, in das Teereste gegossen werden)*.

slope [sləup] **1** *n* **(a)** *(angle)* Neigung *f; (downwards also)* Gefälle *nt; (of roof also)* Schräge *f*.

(b) *(sloping ground)* (Ab)hang *m.* on a ~ am Hang; halfway up the ~ auf halber Höhe; there is a ~ down to the town es fällt zur Stadt hin ab; he broke his leg on the (ski) ~s er hat sich das Bein auf der Piste gebrochen.

(c) *(Mil)* with his rifle at the ~ mit geschultertem Gewehr.

2 *vt* neigen, schräg (an)legen. ~ arms! *(Mil)* schultert Gewehr!

3 *vi* **(a)** geneigt sein; *(road, garden, floor)* sich neigen. the picture is sloping to the left/right das Bild hängt schief; his handwriting ~s to the left/backwards seine Handschrift ist nach links/nach hinten geneigt.

(b) *(inf: move casually)* schlendern *(inf)*.

♦**slope away** *vi* **(a)** sich abfallen. **(b)** *(slip away)* abziehen *(inf)*.

♦**slope down** *vi* sich neigen, abfallen.

♦**slope off** *vi* abziehen *(inf)*.

♦**slope up** *vi* **(a)** *(road etc)* ansteigen. **(b)** *(person)* herschlendern. to ~ ~ to sb auf jdn zuschlendern.

sloping ['sləupɪŋ] *adj hill, road (upwards)* ansteigend; *(downwards)* abfallend; *roof, floor* schräg, geneigt; *shoulders* abfallend; *garden, field etc* am Hang; *(not aligned)* schief.

sloppily ['slɒpɪlɪ] *adv see adj* to write/talk English ~ nachlässig *or* schlampig *(inf)* Englisch schreiben/sprechen.

sloppiness ['slɒpɪnɪs] *n see adj* **(a)** Schlampigkeit *f (inf)*; Nachlässigkeit, Schlud(e)rigkeit *(inf) f*. **(b)** Rührseligkeit *f*. **(c)** Schlabberigkeit *f (inf)*.

sloppy ['slɒpɪ] *adj (+er)* **(a)** *(inf: careless)* schlampig *(inf); work also* nachlässig, schlud(e)rig *(inf)*. ~ joe *(pullover)* Schlabberpullover *m (inf)*.

(b) *(inf: sentimental)* rührselig; *film, novel also* schmalzig.

(c) *(inf: slopping around)* liquid schlabberig *(inf)*.

slosh [slɒʃ] *(inf)* **1** *vt* **(a)** *(Brit: hit)* person eine schmieren *(+dat) (inf); ball* dreschen *(inf)*. **(b)** *(splash)* klatschen. don't ~ the milk about schwapp nicht so mit der Milch herum. **2** *vi* to ~ about *(children)* (herum)planschen; *(water)* (herum)schwappen.

sloshed [slɒʃt] *adj pred (esp Brit sl)* blau *(inf)*, voll *(sl)*. to get ~ sich besaufen *(inf)*.

slot [slɒt] *n (opening)* Schlitz *m; (groove)* Rille *f; (inf: place)* Plätzchen *nt; (TV inf)* (gewohnte) Sendezeit. ~ machine Münzautomat *m; (for gambling)* Spielautomat *m*; ~ meter Münzzähler *m*; do we have a ~ for this in our range? können wir das in unser Programm einbauen?

♦**slot in 1** *vt sep* hineinstecken. to ~ sth ~to sth etw in etw *(acc)* stecken; to ~ sb ~to the firm/a stereotype jdn in der Firma unterbringen/in einen bestimmten Typ einordnen; to ~ ~ commercials/graduates *(inf)* Werbespots einbauen/Studienabsolventen unterbringen *(inf)*; to ~ people/jobs ~to a scale Leute/Arbeiten in eine Skala einordnen.

2 *vi* sich einfügen lassen. **suddenly everything ~ted ~to place** plötzlich paßte alles zusammen.

♦**slot together** 1 *vi (parts, object)* sich zusammenfügen lassen; *(fig: pieces of mystery etc)* sich zusammenfügen, zusammenpassen. 2 *vt sep parts, object* zusammenfügen.

sloth [sləʊθ] *n* (a) *(laziness)* Trägheit, Faulheit *f*. (b) *(Zool)* Faultier *nt*.

slothful ['sləʊθfʊl] *adj* faul; *person, life also* träge.

slothfully ['sləʊθfəlɪ] *adv see adj*.

slothfulness ['sləʊθfʊlnɪs] *n* Trägheit, Faulheit *f*.

slouch [slaʊtʃ] 1 *n* (a) *(posture)* krumme Haltung; *(of shoulders)* Hängen *nt*; *(gait)* latschiger Gang *(inf)*. **to walk with a ~** latschen, latschig gehen *(inf)*; **~ hat** Schlapphut *m*. (b) *(inf: incompetent or lazy person)* Niete *f (inf)*. **to be no ~ at** sth etw ganz schön gut können *(inf)*.

2 *vi (stand, sit)* herumhängen, sich lümmeln *(inf)*; *(move)* latschen. **to ~ off** davonzockeln *(inf)*; **he was ~ed over his desk** er hing über seinem Schreibtisch, er war über den Schreibtisch gebeugt; **he sat ~ed on a chair** er hing auf einem Stuhl.

slough¹ [slaʊ] *n (liter)* Morast *m*; *(swamp also)* Sumpf *m (also fig liter)*. **the news cast him into the S~ of Despond** die Nachricht stürzte ihn in tiefe Verzweiflung *(liter)*.

slough² [slʌf] 1 *n (Zool)* abgestreifte Haut; *(Med)* Schorf *m*. 2 *vt (snake) skin* abstreifen. **it ~s (off)** its skin sie häutet sich.

♦**slough off** *vt sep habits, cares* abwerfen, abschütteln; *(hum) husband* den Laufpaß geben (+*dat*).

Slovak ['sləʊvæk] 1 *adj* slowakisch. 2 *n* (a) Slowake *m*, Slowakin *f*. (b) *(language)* Slowakisch *nt*.

Slovakia [sləʊ'vækɪə] *n* die Slowakei.

sloven ['slʌvn] *n* Schlampe *f (pej inf)*; *(man)* Schlamper *m (inf)*.

Slovene ['sləʊviːn], **Slovenian** [sləʊ'viːnɪən] 1 *adj* slowenisch. 2 *n* (a) Slowene *m*, Slowenin *f*, Slowenier(in *f*) *m*. (b) *(language)* Slowenisch *nt*.

slovenliness ['slʌvnlɪnɪs] *n* Schlampigkeit *f*; *(of person, work also)* Schlud(e)rigkeit *f (inf)*.

slovenly ['slʌvnlɪ] *adj* schlud(e)rig *(inf)*, schlampig *(inf)*; *appearance, person* verlottert *(inf)*.

slow [sləʊ] 1 *adj* (+*er*) (a) langsam. **it's ~ work** das braucht seine Zeit; **he is a ~ worker/learner/reader** er arbeitet/ lernt/liest langsam; **it was ~ going** es ging nur langsam voran; **to get off to a ~ start** *(race)* schlecht vom Start kommen; *(project)* nur langsam in Gang kommen; **to be ~/not to be ~ to do sth** sich *(dat)* mit etw Zeit lassen/etw prompt erledigen; **he is ~ to make up his mind/~ to anger** er braucht lange, um sich zu entscheiden/er wird nicht so leicht wütend; **they were ~ to act** sie ließen sich *(dat)* Zeit; **to be (20 minutes) ~** *(clock)* (20 Minuten) nachgehen.

(b) *(stupid) person* langsam, begriffsstutzig; *see* uptake. (c) *(dull) person, place, event* langweilig; *(Comm)* flau. (d) *(~ing down movement) surface, track, pitch* langsam; *(because of rain etc)* schwer; *(~-burning) fire* langsam brennend. **bake in a ~ oven** bei schwacher Hitze backen.

2 *adv* (+*er*) langsam. **to go ~** *(driver)* langsam fahren; *(workers)* einen Bummelstreik machen; **~-spoken** langsam sprechend; **~ (on sign)** langsam fahren.

3 *vi* **to ~ (to a stop/standstill)** langsam zum Halten/zum Stillstand kommen.

4 *vt* verlangsamen. **he ~ed his horse to a walk** er ließ sein Pferd langsamer gehen.

♦**slow down** *or* **up** 1 *vi* sich verlangsamen; *(drive/walk)* langsamer fahren/gehen; *(worker)* langsamer arbeiten; *(inflation)* abnehmen. **if you don't ~ you'll make yourself ill** Sie müssen zurückstecken, sonst werden Sie krank; **my mind has ~ed ~** ich werde immer langsamer im Denken.

2 *vt sep (lit)* verlangsamen; *engine* drosseln; *machine* herunterschalten; *(fig) programme, project* verzögern, verlangsamen. **to ~ ~ the car** langsamer fahren; **you just ~ me ~** du hältst mich nur auf.

slow: **~-burning** *adj candle* langsam herunterbrennend; *fire also* langsam brennend; *stove* Dauerbrand-; **~coach** *n (Brit inf)* Langweiler *m*; *(mentally)* Transuse *f (inf)*; **~down** *n* (a) *(slowing)* Verlangsamung *f*, *(of gen)*; (b) *(US: go-slow)* Bummelstreik *m*; **~ film** *n* unempfindlicher Film; **~ fuse** *n* Zündschnur *f*; **~ handclap** *n* rhythmisches Klatschen *(zum Zeichen des Protests)*. **to give sb the ~ handclap** durch Klatschen gegen ihn protestieren.

slowly ['sləʊlɪ] *adv* langsam.

slow: **~ march** *n* Trauermarsch *m*; **~ motion** *n* Zeitlupe *f*; **in ~ motion** in Zeitlupe; **a ~-motion shot** eine Einstellung in Zeitlupe; **~-moving** *adj* sich (nur) langsam bewegend; *traffic* kriechend; *plot* langatmig.

slowness ['sləʊnɪs] *n see adj* (a) Langsamkeit *f*. **their ~ to act** ihr Zaudern. (b) Begriffsstutzigkeit *f*. **~ of mind** Begriffsstutzigkeit *f*. (c) Lahmheit, Langweiligkeit *f*; Flaute *f*. (d) Langsamkeit *f*; Schwere *f*.

slow: **~ poison** *n* schleichendes Gift; **~poke** *n (US inf) see* **~coach**; **~ train** *n (Brit)* Personenzug, Bummelzug *m (inf)*; **~-witted** *adj* begriffsstutzig, schwer von Begriff; **~worm** *n* Blindschleiche *f*.

sludge [slʌdʒ] *n* Schlamm, Matsch *(inf)* *m*; *(sediment)* schmieriger Satz.

slue *n*, *vti (US) see* **slew¹**, **slew²**.

slug¹ [slʌg] *n* Nacktschnecke *f*. **~s and snails** Schnecken *pl* (mit und ohne Gehäuse).

slug² *n* (a) *(bullet)* Kugel *f*. (b) *(Typ) (piece of metal)* Reglette *f*; *(line)* (Setzmaschinen)zeile *f*. (c) *(inf)* **a ~ of whisky** ein Schluck *m* Whisky.

slug³ *(inf: hit)* 1 *vt (eine)* knallen (+*dat*) *(inf)*. 2 *n gehöriger or* tüchtiger Schlag *(inf)*. **to give sb a ~** jdm eine knallen *(inf)*.

sluggard ['slʌgəd] *n* Faulpelz *m*.

sluggardly ['slʌgədlɪ] *adj* faul, träge.

slugger ['slʌgəʳ] *n (inf)* Schläger *m (inf)*.

sluggish ['slʌgɪʃ] *adj (indolent, Med)* träge; *engine, car* lahm, langsam; *temperament* phlegmatisch; *steps also* schwerfällig; *business* flau; *market, stock exchange* flau, lustlos.

sluggishly ['slʌgɪʃlɪ] *adv move, flow* träge; *walk also* schwerfällig; *(Comm)* flau, lustlos.

sluggishness ['slʌgɪʃnɪs] *n see adj* Trägheit *f*; Lahmheit *f*; Phlegma *nt*; Schwerfälligkeit *f*. **the ~ of the market/business** die Flaute am Markt/die geschäftliche Flaute.

sluice [sluːs] 1 *n* Schleuse *f*; *(Min)* (Wasch)rinne *f*. **to give the car/wall a ~ down** Auto oder Wand schütten; *(with hose)* das Auto/die Wand abspritzen. 2 *vt ore* waschen. **to ~ sth (down)** etw abspritzen. 3 *vi* **to ~ out** herausschießen.

sluice: **~ gate** *n* Schleusentor *nt*; **~way** *n* (Schleusen)kanal *m*.

slum [slʌm] 1 *n (usu pl: area)* Slum *m*, Elendsviertel *nt*; *(house)* Elendsquartier *nt*. **to live in the ~s** im Slum *or* in den Slums leben; **~ schools/streets/children** Schulen *pl*/Straßen *pl* in den Slums/Slumkinder *pl*; **~ clearance** ≈ (Stadt)sanierung *f*, Beseitigung *f* der Slums; **~ dweller** Slumbewohner(in *f*) *m*.

2 *vi (also go ~ming)* sich unters gemeine Volk mischen.

3 *vti (inf: also ~ it)* primitiv leben. **we don't often see you round here — I'm ~ming it** du läßt dich doch sonst kaum hier sehen! — ich will mich eben mal unters gemeine Volk mischen.

slumber ['slʌmbəʳ] *(liter)* 1 *n* Schlummer *m (geh)*, Schlaf *m*. **~s** Schlummer *m*, Träume *pl*; *(fig: intellectual etc)* Dornröschenschlaf *m*; **to disturb sb's ~s** jds Schlummer stören. 2 *vi* schlummern *(geh)*; *(fig also)* im Dornröschenschlaf liegen.

slumb(e)rous ['slʌmb(ə)rəs] *adj (liter) (sleepy)* schläfrig; *(inducing sleep)* einschläfernd, einlullend.

slummy ['slʌmɪ] *adj* (+*er*) *(inf)* verwahrlost; *district also* Slum-.

slump [slʌmp] 1 *n (in gen) (in numbers, popularity, morale etc)* *(plötzlich)* Abnahme; *(in production, sales)* Rückgang *m*; *(state)* Tiefstand *m*; *(Fin)* Sturz *m*, Baisse *f (spec)*; *(of prices)* plötzliches Absinken. **~ in prices** Preissturz *m (of bei)*; **the 1929 S~** die Weltwirtschaftskrise von 1929.

2 *vi* (a) *(Fin, Comm) (prices)* stürzen, fallen; *(sales, production)* plötzlich zurückgehen; *(fig: morale etc)* sinken, fallen. (b) *(sink)* fallen, sinken. **to ~ into a chair** sich in einen Sessel fallen *or* plumpsen *(inf)* lassen; **he was ~ed over the wheel/on the floor** er war über dem Steuer zusammengesackt/er lag in sich *(dat)* zusammengesunken auf dem Fußboden.

slung [slʌŋ] *pret, ptp of* **sling**.

slunk [slʌŋk] *pret, ptp of* **slink**.

slur [slɜːʳ] 1 *n* (a) *(Makel,* Schandfleck *m*; *(insult)* Beleidigung *f*. **to cast a ~ on sb/sth** jdn/etw in schlechtem Licht erscheinen lassen; *(person)* jdn/etw verunglimpfen; **it is no ~ on him to say that ...** es geht nicht gegen ihn, wenn man sagt, daß ... (b) *(Mus) (mark)* Bindebogen *m*; *(notes)* Bindung *f*. (c) **to speak with a ~** unartikuliert sprechen.

2 *vt* (a) *(pronounce indistinctly)* undeutlich artikulieren; *words, syllable* (halb) verschlucken, verschleifen. (b) *(Mus)* binden, gebunden spielen/singen.

♦**slur over** *vi* +*prep obj* hinweggehen über (+*acc*).

slurp [slɜːp] 1 *vti (inf)* schlürfen. 2 *n* Schlürfen *nt*. **to drink sth with a ~** etw schlürfen.

slurred [slɜːd] *adj* undeutlich; *(Mus) note* gebunden.

slush [slʌʃ] *n (watery snow)* (Schnee)matsch *m*; *(mud)* Matsch, Morast *m*; *(inf: sentimental nonsense)* Kitsch *m*. **~ fund** Schmiergelder *pl*, Schmiergeldfonds *m*.

slushy ['slʌʃɪ] *adj* (+*er*) *snow, mud, path* matschig; *mud, path also* morastig; *(inf: sentimental)* kitschig.

slut [slʌt] *n (liederliche)* Schlampe.

sluttish ['slʌtɪʃ] *adj* liederlich.

sly [slaɪ] 1 *adj* (+*er*) schlau, gerissen; *person, look also* verschlagen; *(artful) look, wink* verschmitzt; *humour* versteckt. **to be (very) ~ about sth** etw schlau anstellen.

2 *n* **on the ~** heimlich, still und leise *(hum)*, ganz heimlich.

slyly ['slaɪlɪ] *adv see adj*.

slyness ['slaɪnɪs] *n see adj* Schlauheit, Gerissenheit *f*; Verschlagenheit *f*; Verschmitztheit *f*; Verstecktheit *f*.

smack¹ [smæk] 1 *n (taste)* (leichter) Geschmack *(of nach)*, Spur *f (of von)*; *(smell)* (leichter) Geruch *(of nach)*, Hauch *m (of von)*; *(fig)* Spur *f (of von)*. 2 *vi* **to ~ of** *(taste)* leicht schmecken nach; *(smell)* leicht riechen nach; *(fig)* riechen nach.

smack² 1 *n (klatschender)* Schlag; *(slap also)* fester Klaps; *(sound)* Klatschen *nt*. **to give a child/the ball a (hard) ~** einem Kind eine knallen *(inf)*/(fest) auf den Ball dreschen *(inf)*; **you'll get a ~** du fängst gleich eine *(inf)*; **a ~ in the eye** *(fig)* ein Schlag ins Gesicht; **to have a ~ at sth** *(esp Brit fig inf)* an etw *(acc)* rangehen *(inf)*, etw mal probieren *(inf)*; **to have a ~ at the title/record** einen Anlauf auf den Titel/Rekord machen.

2 *vt (slap)* knallen *(inf)*. **to ~ a child/one's thigh** einem Kind eine runterhauen *(inf)*/sich *(dat)* auf den Schenkel klatschen; **I'll ~ your bottom, you'll get a ~ed bottom** ich versohl' dir gleich den Hintern! *(inf)*; *see* lip.

3 *adv (inf)* direkt. **he kissed her ~ on the lips** er gab ihr einen Schmatzer *(inf)*, er küßte sie mit Schmackes *(dial)*.

smack³ *n (Naut)* Schmack(e) *f*.

smacker ['smækəʳ] *n (inf)* (a) *(kiss)* Schmatzer *m (inf)*. (b) *(blow)* Klaps *m*. (c) *(money)* Pfund *nt*; Dollar *m*.

smacking ['smækɪŋ] *n* Tracht *f* Prügel. **to give sb a good ~** jdn tüchtig verdreschen *(inf)*.

small [smɔːl] 1 *adj* (+*er*) (a) klein; *supply, stock also* gering; *waist* schmal; *(not much) reason, desire* wenig, gering; *letter* Klein-; *(humble) voice* kleinlaut. **the ~est possible number of books** so wenig Bücher wie möglich; **to have a ~ appetite/be a ~ eater** wenig Appetit *or* keinen großen Appetit haben/kein großer Esser sein; **~ capitals** Kapitälchen *pl*; **no ~ success** ein beachtlicher Erfolg; **to feel/look ~** *(fig)* sich (ganz) klein (und häßlich) vorkommen/schlecht aussehen *or* dastehen; **he/it**

made me feel/look pretty ~ da kam ich mir ziemlich klein vor/da sah ich ziemlich schlecht aus.
  (b) (*unimportant, minor*) klein; *present, sum also* bescheiden; *importance, consequence* gering. **a few ~ matters/problems** ein paar Kleinigkeiten; **to help/contribute in a ~ way** bescheidene Hilfe/einen bescheidenen Beitrag leisten; **to start in a ~ way** bescheiden or klein anfangen.
  (c) (*fig: mean, petty*) *person* kleinlich.
  2 *n* **(a)** **the ~ of the back** das Kreuz.
  (b) **~s** *pl* (*Brit inf*) Unterwäsche *f*.
  3 *adv* **to chop sth up ~** etw kleinhacken.
small: **~ ad** *n* (*Brit*) Kleinanzeige *f*; **~ arms** *npl* Handfeuerwaffen *pl*; **~ beer** *n* (*old*) Dünnbier *nt*; **he's very ~ beer** (*inf*) er ist ein kleiner Fisch (*inf*); **~ change** *n* Kleingeld *nt*; **~ fry** *npl* *see* fry¹; **~holder** *n* Kleinbauer *m*; **~holding** *n* kleiner Landbesitz; **~ hours** *npl* früher Morgen; **in the ~ hours** in den frühen Morgenstunden; **~ intestine** *n* Dünndarm *m*.
smallish ['smɔːlɪʃ] *adj* (*eher*) kleiner. **he is ~** er ist eher klein.
small: **~-minded** *adj person, attitude* engstirnig; **~-mindedness** *n* Engstirnigkeit *f*.
smallness ['smɔːlnɪs] *n* Kleinheit *f*; (*of waist*) Schmalheit *f*; (*of sum, present*) Bescheidenheit *f*; (*pettiness*) Kleinlichkeit *f*. **surprised at the ~ of his** stock/appetite/success/voice erstaunt, wie klein sein Lager/schlecht sein Appetit/gering sein Erfolg/kleinlaut seine Stimme war.
small: **~pox** *n* Pocken, Blattern (*old*) *pl*; **~pox vaccination** *n* Pockenimpfung *f*; **the ~ print** *n* das Kleingedruckte; **~-scale** *adj map, model* in verkleinertem Maßstab; *project* kleinangelegt; *war* begrenzt; **~ screen** *n* (*TV*) **on the ~ screen** auf dem Bildschirm; **~talk** *n* oberflächliche Konversation, Smalltalk *m*; **she has no ~talk** oberflächliche or höfliche Konversation liegt ihr nicht; **to engage in ~talk with sb** höflich mit jdm Konversation machen; **~-time** *adj* (*inf*) mickerig (*inf*), armselig; *crook* klein; *politician* Schmalspur-; **~-town** *adj* Kleinstadt-, kleinstädtisch; *mentality also, morality* kleinbürgerlich.
smarm [smɑːm] (*Brit inf*) **1** *vt* **to ~ one's hair down** sich (*dat*) das Haar anklatschen (*inf*) or an den Kopf kleben. **2** *vi* **to ~ all over sb** sich an jdn heranschmeißen (*inf*); **to ~ one's way into sb's confidence** sich in jds Vertrauen (*acc*) einschleichen.
smarmy ['smɑːmɪ] *adj* (+er) (*Brit inf*) kriecherisch (*pej*); *voice* einschmeichelnd.
smart [smɑːt] **1** *adj* (+er) **(a)** *schick*; *person, clothes, car also* flott; *society* fein; (*not shabby also*) *appearance* gepflegt. **a ~-looking girl/garden** ein flott aussehendes Mädchen/ein gepflegter Garten; **the ~ set** die Schickeria (*inf*).
  (b) (*bright, clever*) clever (*inf*), schlau, gewitzt; *thief, trick also* raffiniert; *young people also* hell (*inf*); (*pej*) *person, answer* superklug, neunmalklug (*pej inf*). **to get ~** (*US inf*) sich am Riemen reißen (*inf*); (*get cheeky*) frech kommen (*with dat*); **don't be so ~** (*to child*) sei nicht so vorlaut or vorwitzig; **he thinks it's ~ to run down his parents** er kommt sich toll vor, wenn er seine Eltern schlechtmacht.
  (c) (*quick*) (blitz)schnell; *pace, work* rasch, flott (*inf*); *work also* flink, fix (*inf*). **and look ~** (**about it**)! und zwar ein bißchen fix or plötzlich! (*inf*).
  2 *n* Schmerz *m* (*also fig*); (*of ointment, from wound also*) Brennen *nt*.
  3 *vi* brennen. **it will make your mouth/cut ~** es wird (dir) im Mund/in der Wunde brennen; **to ~ under sth** (*fig*) unter etw (*dat*) leiden; **his injured vanity still ~ed** er spürte immer noch den Schmerz gekränkter Eitelkeit; **to ~ from sth** (*from blow etc*) von etw brennen; (*fig*) unter etw (*dat*) leiden.
smart: **~-aleck** (*inf*) **1** *n* Schlauberger (*inf*), Besserwisser *m*; **2** *adj remarks* besserwisserisch, superschlau (*inf*); **~ ass 1** *n* (*sl*) Klugscheißer *m* (*sl*); **2** *adj* klugscheißerisch (*sl*).
smarten ['smɑːtn] (*also ~ up*) **1** *vt house, room* herausputzen; *appearance* (her)richten, aufmöbeln (*inf*). **to ~ oneself up** (*dress up*) sich in Schale werfen (*inf*); (*generally improve appearance*) mehr Wert auf sein Äußeres legen; **you'd better ~ up your ideas** (*inf*) du solltest dich am Riemen reißen (*inf*).
  2 *vi* (*dress up*) sich in Schale werfen (*inf*); (*improve appearance*) sich herausmachen, (*pace*) schneller or flotter (*inf*) werden. **he's ~ed up in his ideas/appearance** seine Ansichten haben/sein Aussehen hat sich gemacht.
smartly ['smɑːtlɪ] *adv see adj* **(a)** schick; *dress also* flott. **(b)** clever, schlau, gewitzt; (*pej*) superschlau (*inf*), neunmalklug (*inf*). **... the child replied ~** ... antwortete das Kind vorlaut or vorwitzig. **(c)** (blitz)schnell, fix (*inf*); *walk* rasch.
smartness ['smɑːtnɪs] *n* **(a)** *see adj* **(a)** Schick *m*; Feinheit *f*; Gepflegtheit *f*.
  (b) (*brightness, cleverness*) Cleverneß (*inf*), Schlauheit *f*, Gewitztheit *f*; (*of thief, trick*) Raffiniertheit *f*; (*pej*) (*of person*) Besserwisserei *f* (*pej*); (*of answer*) Vorwitzigkeit *f*.
  (c) *see adj* **(c)** Schnelligkeit, Fixheit (*inf*) *f*; Raschheit *f*; Flinkheit, Fixheit (*inf*) *f*.
smarty ['smɑːtɪ] *n* (*inf*) Schlaumeier, Schlauberger (*inf*) *m*.
smash [smæʃ] **1** *vt* **(a)** (*break into pieces*) zerschlagen; *window also* einschlagen. **I ~ed my glasses** ich habe mir die Brille zerschlagen or kaputtgeschlagen.
  (b) (*defeat or destroy*) zerschlagen; *rebellion, revolution also* niederschlagen; *fascism, the enemy also, opponent* zerschmettern; *record* haushoch schlagen; *business* ruinieren.
  (c) (*strike, also Tennis*) schmettern. **he ~ed his fist into his face** er schlug ihm mit der Faust ins Gesicht; **he ~ed him on the nose** er schlug ihm auf die Nase; **he ~ed his way through the mob** er mußte sich (*dat*) gewaltsam einen Weg durch den Mob bahnen; **to ~ one's way into a building** gewaltsam in ein Gebäude eindringen.
  2 *vi* **(a)** (*break*) zerschlagen, zerbrechen. **it ~ed into a thousand pieces** es (zer)sprang in tausend Stücke.

  (b) (*crash*) prallen. **the car ~ed into the wall** das Auto krachte gegen die Mauer; **the terrified animal ~ed through the fence** das verängstigte Tier durchbrach das Gatter; **the plane ~ed into the houses** das Flugzeug raste in eine Häusergruppe; **the ship ~ed onto the rocks** das Schiff prallte gegen die Felsen; **the sound of the waves ~ing against the rocks** das Geräusch der gegen die Felsen klatschenden Wellen.
  (c) (*Fin inf*) bankrott gehen, kaputtgehen (*inf*).
  3 *n* (*noise*) Scheppern *nt*; (*of waves*) Klatschen *nt*. **there was a ~** es hat gekracht or (*of broken glass*) gescheppert.
  (b) (*collision*) Unfall *m*; (*with another vehicle also*) Zusammenstoß *m*. **rail ~** Zugunglück *nt*.
  (c) (*blow*) Schlag *m*; (*Tennis*) Smash, Schmetterball *m*. **to give sb a ~ on the nose** jdm auf die Nase schlagen; **he hit his head an awful ~ against the wall** er ist mit dem Kopf ganz fürchterlich gegen die Wand geschlagen.
  (d) (*Fin inf*) (finanzieller) Zusammenbruch, Pleite *f* (*inf*).
  4 *adv* (*inf*) mit Karacho (*inf*). **to go or run ~ into sth** mit Karacho gegen etw (*acc*) fahren/stoßen *etc* (*inf*).
♦**smash in** *vt sep* einschlagen. **the firemen had to ~ their way ~** die Feuerwehrleute mußten gewaltsam eindringen; **to ~ sb's face ~** (*sl*) jdm die Schnauze einschlagen (*sl*).
♦**smash up 1** *vt sep* zertrümmern; *face* übel zurichten; *car* kaputtfahren. **2** *vi* kaputtgehen. **the capsule completely ~ed ~ on landing** die Kapsel zerschellte bei der Landung.
smash-and-grab (raid) [ˌsmæʃən'græb(reɪd)] *n* Schaufenstereinbruch *m*.
smashed [smæʃt] *adj pred* (*sl: drunk*) stockvoll (*sl*).
smasher ['smæʃə'] *n* (*esp Brit inf*) toller Typ (*inf*); (*woman also*) Klasseweib *nt* (*inf*). **to be a ~** eine Wucht (*inf*) or (ganz große) Klasse sein (*inf*).
smash hit *n* (*inf*) Superhit *m* (*inf*). **her new boyfriend was a ~ with her family** ihr neuer Freund kam bei ihrer Familie unwahrscheinlich gut an (*inf*).
smashing ['smæʃɪŋ] *adj* (*esp Brit inf*) klasse *inv*, Klasse *pred*, dufte (*all inf*). **isn't it ~!** unheimlich dufte!
smash-up ['smæʃʌp] *n* (*Aut, Rail*) übler Unfall; (*with another vehicle also*) Karambolage *f*; (*Fin inf*) Pleite *f*.
smattering ['smætərɪŋ] *n* **a ~ of French** ein paar Brocken Französisch.
smear [smɪə'] **1** *n* verschmierter Fleck; (*fig*) Beschmutzung, Verleumdung *f*; (*Med*) Abstrich *m*. **he had ~s of blood/grease on his hands** er hatte blut-/fettbeschmierte Hände; **this left a ~ on his name** das hinterließ einen Fleck auf seinem Namen; **he angrily repudiated their ~s** empört wies er ihre Verleumdungen zurück; **~ campaign** Verleumdungskampagne *f*; **~word** Schimpfwort *nt*; **~-test** (*Med*) Abstrich *m*.
  2 *vt* **(a)** *grease, cream, ointment* schmieren; (*spread*) verschmieren; (*mark, make dirty*) beschmieren; *face, body* einschmieren. **to ~ grease over sth** Fett auf etw (*acc*) schmieren; **don't ~ the paint** verschmiere die Farbe nicht!
  (b) (*fig*) *person* verunglimpfen; *sb's reputation* beschmutzen, besudeln.
  3 *vi* (*glass*) verschmieren; (*print*) verschmiert, verwischt werden; (*biro*) schmieren; (*paint, ink*) verlaufen.
smeary ['smɪərɪ] *adj* (+er) *glass* verschmiert; *clothes* schmierig; (*likely to smear*) *paint, ink* schmierend.
smell [smel] (*vb: pret, ptp ~ed or smelt*) **1** *n* (*sense of ~, odour*) Geruch *m*; (*unpleasant also*) Gestank *m*; (*fragrant also*) Duft *m*. **it has a nice ~** es riecht gut or angenehm; **there's a funny ~ in here** hier riecht es komisch; **to have or take a ~ at sth** an etw (*acc*) riechen or (*dog etc*) schnuppern.
  2 *vt* **(a)** riechen. **can or do you ~ burning?** riechst du, daß etwas brennt or (*Cook*) anbrennt?; **just ~ this meat** riech mal an diesem Fleisch!; **first he ~s the wine** zunächst einmal riecht er an dem Wein.
  (b) (*fig*) *danger, treason* wittern. **to ~ trouble** Ärger or Stunk (*inf*) kommen sehen; **to ~ a rat** (*inf*) Lunte or den Braten riechen, etw spitzkriegen; **aha, I can ~ a rat** (*inf*) da scheint mir doch etwas faul zu sein!
  3 *vi* riechen; (*unpleasantly also*) stinken; (*fragrantly also*) duften. **that ~s!** (*lit, fig*) das stinkt!; **to ~ of sth** (*lit, fig*) nach etw riechen; **to ~ at sth** an etw (*dat*) riechen or (*dog etc*) schnuppern; **his breath ~s** er riecht aus dem Mund, er hat Mundgeruch; **can fish ~?** können die Fische riechen?
♦**smell out** *vt sep* **(a)** *rabbit, traitor etc* aufspüren; *plot* aufdecken. **(b)** **these onions are ~ing the house ~!** die Zwiebeln verpesten das ganze Haus!
smelling bottle ['smelɪŋbɒtl] *n* Riechfläschchen *nt*.
smelling salts ['smelɪŋsɔːlts] *npl* Riechsalz *nt*.
smelly ['smelɪ] *adj* (+er) übelriechend, stinkend. **it's ~ in here** hier drin stinkt es; **you've got ~ feet** deine Füße stinken.
smelt¹ [smelt] *pret, ptp of* smell.
smelt² *vt ore* schmelzen; (*refine*) verhütten.
smelt³ *n, pl* -(s) (*fish*) Stint *m*.
smelter ['smeltə'] *n* (*furnace*) Schmelzhütte, Schmelzerei *f*; (*person*) Schmelzer *m*.
smile [smaɪl] **1** *n* Lächeln *nt*. **there was a sarcastic ~ on his face** ein sarkastisches Lächeln ging über sein Gesicht; **to be all ~s** übers ganze Gesicht strahlen; **to give sb a ~** jdm zulächeln; **come on, give me a ~** lach doch mal!; **take that ~ off your face!** hör auf, so zu grinsen!
  2 *vi* lächeln. **we tried to make the baby ~** wir versuchten, das Baby zum Lachen zu bringen; **come on, ~** lach mal!; **~ for the camera!** bitte recht freundlich!; **he's always smiling** er lacht immer; **keep smiling!** keep smiling!; **he kept smiling through all his troubles** trotz aller Schwierigkeiten ließ er den Kopf nicht hängen; **to ~ at sb** jdn anlächeln; (*cheerful person*) jdn anlachen; **to ~ at sth** über etw (*acc*) lächeln; **to ~ at danger** der Gefahr (*dat*) ins Gesicht lachen; **to ~ with joy/happiness** *etc* vor Freude/Glück *etc* strahlen; **fortune ~d on him**

(liter) ihm lachte das Glück; **all nature ~d** *(liter)* die Natur hatte ihr schönstes Kleid angelegt.

3 *vt* **she ~d her thanks** sie lächelte dankbar; **he ~d a bitter smile** er lächelte bitter.

smiling *adj*, **~ly** *adv* ['smaɪlɪŋ, -lɪ] lächelnd.

smirch [smɜːtʃ] *(liter)* **1** *n* Schmutz- *or* Schandfleck, Makel *(geh)* m. **2** *vt* beflecken *(liter)*, besudeln *(geh)*.

smirk [smɜːk] **1** *n* Grinsen *nt*. **2** *vi* grinsen, süffisant lächeln.

smite [smaɪt] *pret* **smote**, *ptp* **smitten** *vt (old, liter)* schlagen. **he smote off his head** er schlug *or* hieb *(old, liter)* ihm den Kopf ab; **whosoever shall ~ thee on thy right cheek, ...** *(Bibl)* wenn dir jemand einen Streich gibt auf deine rechte Backe, ...; **the sound of gun-fire smote our ears** der Lärm von Schüssen schlug an unsere Ohren; **the light smote our eyes as we emerged from the dark** das Licht schlug uns *(dat)* in die Augen, als wir aus der Dunkelheit traten; **and the Lord shall ~ them down** und der Herr wird sie zerschmettern.

smith [smɪθ] *n* Schmied *m*.

smithereens [ˌsmɪðəˈriːnz] *npl* **to smash sth to ~** etw in tausend Stücke schlagen; **in ~** in tausend Stücken.

smithy ['smɪðɪ] *n* Schmiede *f*.

smitten ['smɪtn] **1** *ptp of* **smite**.

2 *adj* **to be ~ with the plague/remorse/fear** von der Pest heimgesucht/von Reue/Angst geplagt werden; **he's really ~ with her** *(inf)* er ist wirklich vernarrt in sie; **he's really ~ this time** *(inf)* diesmal hat's ihn erwischt *(inf)*; **I've never seen him so ~** *(inf)* ich habe ihn noch nie so vernarrt gesehen.

smock [smɒk] **1** *n* Kittel *m*; *(as top)* Hänger *m*. **2** *vt* smoken.

smocking ['smɒkɪŋ] *n* Smokarbeit *f*.

smog [smɒg] *n* Smog *m*.

smoke [sməʊk] **1** *n* **(a)** Rauch *m*. **there's no ~ without fire** *(prov)* kein Rauch ohne Flamme *(prov)*; **to go up in ~** in Rauch (und Flammen) aufgehen; *(fig)* sich in Wohlgefallen auflösen; *(inf: get angry)* in die Luft gehen *(inf)*.

(b) *(cigarette etc)* was zu rauchen *(inf)*. **have you got a ~?** hast du was zu rauchen? *(inf)*; **it's a nice ~, this tobacco** dieser Tabak raucht sich gut; **~s** *(inf)* Glimmstengel *pl (dated inf)*.

(c) *(act)* **to have a ~** eine rauchen; **I'm dying for a ~** ich muß unbedingt eine rauchen; **the condemned were allowed a final ~** die Verurteilten durften eine letzte Zigarette rauchen.

2 *vt* **(a)** *tobacco* rauchen.

(b) *bacon, fish etc* räuchern.

3 *vi* rauchen; *(oil-lamp etc)* qualmen. **to ~ like a chimney** wie ein Schlot rauchen.

♦ **smoke out** *vt sep* ausräuchern; *(fill with smoke)* einräuchern, einnebeln *(inf)*.

smoke-bomb ['sməʊkbɒm] *n* Rauchbombe *f*.

smoked [sməʊkt] *adj* *bacon, fish* geräuchert, Räucher-. **~ glass** Rauchglas *nt*; **~ glasses** Gläser *pl* aus Rauchglas.

smoke-dried ['sməʊkdraɪd] *adj* geräuchert.

smokeless ['sməʊklɪs] *adj* *zone* rauchfrei; *fuel* rauchlos.

smoker ['sməʊkə(r)] *n* **(a)** *(person)* Raucher(in *f*) *m*. **to be a heavy ~** stark rauchen, starker Raucher sein; **~'s cough** Raucherhusten *m*. **(b)** *(Rail)* Raucher(abteil *nt*) *m*. **(c)** *(entertainment)* Herrenabend *m*.

smoke: **~-ring** *n* (Rauch)ring *m*; **~-room** *n* Rauchsalon *m*, Rauchzimmer *nt*; **~-screen** *n* Nebelwand *f*, Rauchvorhang *m*; *(fig)* Deckmantel, Vorwand *m*; **a ~-screen of words** ein Schwall von Worten; **his answer was just a ~-screen** seine Antwort war nur ein Ablenkungsmanöver; **~ signal** *n* Rauchzeichen *nt*; **~-stack** *n* Schornstein *m*; *(on factory also)* Schlot *m*.

smoking ['sməʊkɪŋ] **1** *adj* rauchend. **2** *n* Rauchen *nt*. **"no ~"** „Rauchen verboten".

smoking: **~ compartment**, *(US)* **~ car** *n* Raucherabteil *nt*; **~ jacket** *n* Rauchjacke, Hausjacke *f*; **~ room** *n* Rauchzimmer *nt*.

smoky ['sməʊkɪ] *adj* (+*er*) *chimney, fire* rauchend; *room, atmosphere* verraucht; *(stained by smoke)* verräuchert; *(like smoke) flavour* rauchig; *colour* rauchfarben. **~ blue** rauchblau.

smolder *vi (US) see* **smoulder**.

smooch [smuːtʃ] *(inf)* **1** *vi* knutschen *(inf)*. **2** *n* **to have a ~** rumknutschen *(inf)*.

smoochy ['smuːtʃɪ] *adj* (+*er*) *(inf)* *music, record* Knutsch- *(inf)*, zum Knutschen *(inf)*; romantisch.

smooth [smuːð] **1** *adj* (+*er*) **(a)** *(in texture, surface etc)* glatt; *sea also* ruhig; *road, surface also* eben; *outline* sanft; *skin also, hair* weich. **as ~ as silk** weich wie Seide, seidenweich; **as ~ as glass** spiegelglatt; *worn ~ steps* glattgetreten; *knife* abgeschliffen; *type* abgefahren; **this razor gives you a really ~ shave** dieser Apparat rasiert wirklich sanft.

(b) *(in consistency)* *paste* sämig; *sauce* glatt. **whisk sauce until ~** Soße glattrühren.

(c) *motion, flight, crossing* ruhig; *gear-change* weich, leicht; *take-off, landing* glatt; *breathing* gleichmäßig. **the car came to a ~ stop** der Wagen kam glatt *or* ruhig zum Stehen; **he is a very ~ driver** er ist ein sehr angenehmer, ruhiger Fahrer; **to ensure a ~ fit** damit es genau paßt.

(d) *(trouble-free) transition, functioning* reibungslos, glatt. **the bill had a ~ passage through Parliament** der Gesetzentwurf kam glatt durchs Parlament; **we want the move to the new offices to be as ~ as possible** wir wollen, daß der Umzug in die neuen Büroräume so reibungslos wie möglich verläuft.

(e) *(not harsh in taste) whisky, Guinness* weich.

(f) *style of writing* glatt, flüssig; *tones* sanft; *diction* flüssig, geschliffen. **the ~, relaxing voice of the hypnotist** die sanft beruhigende Stimme des Hypnotiseurs.

(g) *(polite, often pej) manners, diplomat, salesman* glatt; *person also* aalglatt *(pej)*; *manners also* geschliffen; *(unruffled)* kühl, cool *(inf)*. **to be a ~ talker** schönreden können; **he's too ~ to be sincere** er ist bestimmt nicht ehrlich, er redet zu schön; **a ~ operator** ein Schlawiner *(inf)* *m*.

(h) *(inf) restaurant, furniture, car, person* gepflegt.

(i) *(Tennis)* glatt.

2 *n* **to give sth a ~** etw glattstreichen; *see* **rough 3**.

3 *vt* *surface* glätten, glatt machen; *dress, hair* glätten, glattstreichen; *wood* glatthobeln; *(fig) feelings* besänftigen, beruhigen. **to ~ the way for sb** jdm den Weg ebnen.

♦ **smooth away** *vt sep* glätten; *(fig) fears* besänftigen.

♦ **smooth back** *vt sep* *hair* zurückstreichen.

♦ **smooth down** **1** *vt sep* *hair* glatt machen; *feathers, hair, dress* glattstreichen; *(fig) person, feelings* besänftigen, beschwichtigen. **to ~ things ~** die Wogen glätten. **2** *vi (fig)* sich beruhigen.

♦ **smooth out** *vt sep (make smooth) crease, surface* glätten; *(fig) difficulty* ausräumen, aus dem Weg räumen.

♦ **smooth over** *vt sep (fig) quarrel* in Ordnung bringen, geradebiegen *(inf)*. **to ~ things ~** die Sache geradebiegen *(inf)*.

smooth: **~-bore 1** *adj* **2** *n* Gewehr *nt* mit glattem Lauf; **~-faced** *adj* zarthäutig; *(fig)* scheinheilig.

smoothly ['smuːðlɪ] *adv* **(a)** *shave* sanft.

(b) *land* weich; *change gear* weich, leicht; *drive* ruhig; *fit* genau.

(c) *(without problems)* **to go ~** glatt über die Bühne gehen; **~ running organization** reibungslos laufende Organisation.

(d) *(flowing prose)* flüssige Prosa; **the music passes ~ from one mood to another** die Musik fließt unmerklich von einer Stimmung in die andere über.

(e) *talk* schön; *behave* aalglatt *(pej)*. **he handled the situation very ~** er hat die Lage sehr kühl gemeistert.

smoothness ['smuːðnɪs] *n see adj* **(a)** Glätte *f*; Ruhe *f*; Ebenheit *f*; Sanftheit *f*; Weichheit *f*. **it has the ~ of silk** es ist seidenweich.

(b) Sämigkeit *f*; Glätte *f*.

(c) Ruhe *f*; Weichheit *f*; Glätte *f*; Gleichmäßigkeit *f*; *(of fit)* Genauigkeit *f*.

(d) Reibungslosigkeit *f*.

(e) Weichheit *f*.

(f) Flüssigkeit *f*; Sanftheit *f*.

(g) Glätte *f*; *(aal)*glatte Art *(pej)*.

smooth: **~-running** *adj engine, car* ruhig laufend; **~-spoken**, **~-tongued** *adj (pej)* schönredend *(pej)*, schönrednerisch *(pej)*.

smoothy ['smuːðɪ] *n (inf)* Lackaffe *m (pej inf)*.

smote [sməʊt] *pret of* **smite**.

smother ['smʌðə(r)] **1** *vt* **(a)** *(stifle) person, fire, criticism* ersticken; *(fig) criticism also, yawn, sob, laughter* unterdrücken. **to ~ sb with affection** jdn mit seiner Liebe erdrücken.

(b) *(cover)* bedecken, überschütten. **fruit ~ed in cream** Obst, das in Sahne schwimmt; **~ed in dirt** schmutzstarrend; **~ed in dust** völlig eingestaubt; **she ~ed his face in kisses** sie bedeckte *or* übersäte sein Gesicht mit Küssen.

2 *vi* ersticken.

smother-love ['smʌðəˌlʌv] *n (inf)* übertriebene Mutterliebe.

smoulder, *(US)* **smolder** ['sməʊldə(r)] *vi (lit, fig)* glimmen, schwelen. **his eyes were ~ing with anger/passion** seine Augen glühten vor Zorn/Leidenschaft; **a ~ing look** ein glühender Blick; **~ing hatred** glimmender *or* schwelender Haß.

smudge [smʌdʒ] **1** *n* **(a)** Fleck *m*; *(of ink)* Klecks *m*.

(b) *(US: fire)* qualmendes Feuer *(gegen Insekten)*.

2 *vt* *ink, lipstick, paint* verwischen. **he had chocolate ~d all over his face** er hatte sich *(dat)* das ganze Gesicht mit Schokolade vollgeschmiert.

3 *vi* verlaufen, verschmieren.

smudgy ['smʌdʒɪ] *adj* (+*er*) verschmiert; *outline* verwischt, verschwommen.

smug [smʌg] *adj* (+*er*) selbstgefällig; *grin, remark also* süffisant. **~ self-confidence** eitle Selbstzufriedenheit.

smuggle ['smʌgl] *vti (lit, fig)* schmuggeln. **to ~ sb/sth in** jdn/etw einschmuggeln, jdn einschleusen; **to ~ sb/sth out** jdn/etw herausschmuggeln, jdn herausschleusen.

smuggler ['smʌglə(r)] *n* Schmuggler(in *f*) *m*.

smuggling ['smʌglɪŋ] *n* Schmuggel *m*.

smugly ['smʌglɪ] *adv* selbstgefällig; *grin, say also* süffisant.

smugness ['smʌgnɪs] *n* Selbstgefälligkeit *f*.

smut [smʌt] *n* **(a)** *(piece of dirt)* Rußflocke *f*. **there's a ~ on your nose/in your eye** du hast da was an der Nase/im Auge; **~s from the stove** Ruß *m* aus dem Ofen. **(b)** *(fig)* Schmutz *m*. **to talk ~** Schweinereien erzählen. **(c)** *(Bot)* Brand *m*.

smuttiness ['smʌtɪnɪs] *n (fig)* Schmutz *m*; *(of joke, language)* Anstößigkeit, Unflätigkeit *f*.

smutty ['smʌtɪ] *adj* (+*er*) *(lit, fig)* schmutzig.

snack [snæk] *n* Kleinigkeit *f* (zu essen), Imbiß *m*. **to have a ~** eine Kleinigkeit essen; **~ einen Imbiß zu sich *(dat)* nehmen; **~ bar** Imbißstube *f*; **for us lunch is just a ~** mittags essen wir nicht viel *or* groß *(inf)*; **too many ~s between meals ...** wenn man zwischen den Mahlzeiten zuviel ißt ...

snaffle¹ ['snæfl] *n (also* **~-bit**) Trense *f*.

snaffle² *vt (Brit inf)* sich *(dat)* unter den Nagel reißen *(inf)*.

♦ **snaffle up** *vt sep (Brit inf) bargain* wegschnappen *(inf)*.

snafu [snæˈfuː] *(US sl)* **1** *n* Schlamassel *m (inf)*. **2** *vt* total durcheinanderbringen.

snag [snæg] **1** *n* **(a)** *(hidden difficulty)* Haken *m*, Schwierigkeit *f*. **there's a ~** die Sache hat einen Haken; **what's the ~?** woran liegt es?, was ist das Problem?; **to run into *or* hit a ~** in Schwierigkeiten *(acc)* kommen.

(b) *(flaw in clothes etc)* gezogener Faden.

(c) *(in water)* Baumstumpf *m* (im Wasser).

2 *vt* sich *(dat)* einen Faden ziehen. **I ~ged my tights** ich habe mir an den Strumpfhosen einen Faden gezogen.

3 *vi* Fäden ziehen.

snail [sneɪl] *n* Schnecke *f*. **edible ~** Weinbergschnecke *f*; **at a ~'s pace** im Schneckentempo.

snake [sneɪk] **1** *n* Schlange *f*. **a ~ in the grass** *(fig) (woman)* eine listige Schlange; *(man)* ein heimtückischer Kerl. **2** *vi* sich schlängeln.

snake: ~**bite** n Schlangenbiß m; ~ **charmer** n Schlangenbe-
schwörer m; ~**skin** 1 n Schlangenhaut f; (leather) Schlangenleder nt; 2 adj Schlangenleder-, aus Schlangenleder.
snaky ['sneɪkɪ] adj windings schläng(e)lig; movements
schlangenartig.
snap [snæp] 1 n (a) (sound) Schnappen nt; (with fingers)
Schnippen, Schnalzen nt; (of sth breaking) Knacken nt; (click)
Klicken nt; (of whip) Knall m. the dog made a ~ at the biscuit
der Hund schnappte nach dem Keks.
  (b) (fastener) Druckknopf m.
  (c) (Phot) Schnappschuß m.
  (d) (Cards) = Schnipp-Schnapp nt.
  (e) (inf: vigour) Schwung m. put a bit of ~ into it mach ein
bißchen zackig! (inf).
  (f) (biscuit) Plätzchen nt.
  (g) cold ~ Kälteeinbruch m.
  2 adj attr plötzlich, spontan, Blitz-. ~ **vote** Blitzabstimmung
f; ~ **decision** plötzlicher Entschluß.
  3 adv to go ~ schnapp/knack(s)/klick machen.
  4 interj I bought a green one — ~! (inf) ich hab' mir ein grünes
gekauft — (ätsch,) ich auch!
  5 vt (a) fingers schnipsen or schnalzen mit; whip knallen mit.
to ~ a book shut ein Buch zuklappen; he ~**ped** the lid down er
ließ den Deckel runterklappen; to ~ sth into place etw
einschnappen lassen; to ~ one's fingers at sb/sth (fig) auf
jdn/etw pfeifen (inf).
  (b) (break) zerbrechen, entzweibrechen; bone brechen.
  (c) (also ~ out) to ~ an order befehlend etwas ausbellen; she
~**ped** a few words at the children sie pfiff die Kinder an.
  (d) (Phot) knipsen.
  6 vi (a) (click) (zu)schnappen, einschnappen; (crack, break)
entzweibrechen, zerbrechen; (of whip) knallen. to ~ **shut** zuschnappen; my patience finally ~**ped** dann ist mir aber der
Geduldsfaden gerissen.
  (b) (speak sharply) bellen (inf), schnappen (inf). to ~ at sb
jdn anpfeifen or anschnauzen (inf); there's no need to ~ du
brauchst nicht gleich so zu schnauzen!
  (c) (of dog, fish etc, fig) schnappen (at nach). to ~ at the
opportunity die Gelegenheit beim Schopf packen.
  (d) to ~ to attention Haltung annehmen; ~ to it! mach 'n
bißchen zackig! (inf).
  (e) (inf: crack up) durchdrehen (inf). something ~**ped** (in
him) da hat (bei ihm) etwas ausgehakt (inf).
♦**snap off** 1 vt sep (break off) abbrechen; (bite off) abbeißen. to
~ sb's head ~ (fig inf) jdm ins Gesicht springen (inf). 2 vi
(break off) abbrechen.
♦**snap out** 1 vt sep order brüllen, bellen. 2 vi to ~ ~ **of** sth sich
aus etw (dat) herausreißen, mit etw Schluß machen; it's time he
~**ped** ~ **of** this depression es wird höchste Zeit, daß er aus
dieser Depression rauskommt; ~ ~ **of** it! reiß dich zusammen
or am Riemen! (inf); (cheer up) Kopf hoch!
♦**snap up** vt sep (lit, fig) wegschnappen.
snap: ~**dragon** n Löwenmaul nt; ~**fastener** n Druckknopf m.
snappish ['snæpɪʃ] adj (lit, fig) bissig.
snappishness ['snæpɪʃnɪs] n (lit, fig) Bissigkeit f.
snappy ['snæpɪ] adj (+er) (a) (inf: quick) flott (inf), zackig (inf).
and be ~ about it!, and make it ~! und zwar ein bißchen flott or
zackig! (inf). (b) (lit, fig) dog, person bissig. (c) (inf) translation kurz und treffend; phrase zündend.
snap: ~**shot** n Schnappschuß m.
snare[1] [sneəʳ] 1 n (lit, fig: trap) Falle f; (fig also) Fallstrick m. 2
vt (lit, fig) (ein)fangen.
snare[2] n (a) (of drum) Schnarrsaite f. (b) (also ~ **drum**) kleine
Trommel.
snarl[1] [snɑːl] 1 n Knurren nt no pl. ..., he said with a ~ ..., sagte er
knurrend. 2 vi knurren. to ~ at sb jdn anknurren.
snarl[2] 1 n (in wool) Knoten m, verhedderte Stelle. 2 vt wool
verheddern.
♦**snarl up** (inf) 1 vt sep traffic, system durcheinanderbringen;
plan also vermasseln (sl). the new one-way system merely ~**s**
the traffic ~ das neue Einbahnstraßensystem führt bloß zu
einem Verkehrschaos; traffic always gets ~**ed** ~ at the bridge
an der Brücke ist der Verkehr immer chaotisch; I got ~**ed** ~ in
a traffic jam ich bin im Verkehr steckengeblieben.
  2 vi (traffic) chaotische Formen annehmen.
snarl-up ['snɑːlʌp] n (inf) (in traffic) (Verkehrs)chaos nt; (in
system, on switchboard etc) Kuddelmuddel nt (inf). ~**s** ein
großes Kuddelmuddel (inf); the ~**s** at rush-hour periods das
Chaos in den Stoßverkehrszeiten.
snatch [snætʃ] 1 n (a) (act) Griff m. to make a ~ at sth nach etw
greifen; (animal) zuschnappen.
  (b) (Brit inf) (robbery) Raub m; (kidnapping) Entführung f.
  (c) (snippet) Stück nt, Brocken m; (of conversation also)
Fetzen m; (of music) ein paar Takte. to do sth in ~**es** etw in
Etappen tun.
  (d) (Weightlifting) Reißen nt.
  (e) (US sl: female genitals) Möse (vulg), Pflaume (vulg) f.
  2 vt (a) (grab) greifen. to ~ sth from sb jdm etw entreißen; to
~ hold of sth nach etw greifen, etw packen; to ~ sth out of sb's
hand jdm etw aus der Hand reißen.
  (b) some sleep etc ergattern. to ~ a quick meal schnell etwas
essen; the Ferrari ~**ed** the lead on the last lap der Ferrari riß in
der letzten Runde die Führung an sich; to ~ an opportunity
eine Gelegenheit ergreifen or beim Schopf packen; they ~**ed** a
quick kiss sie gaben sich (dat) schnell einen Kuß; he ~**ed** a kiss
while she wasn't looking als sie gerade wegsah, stahl er ihr
schnell einen Kuß.
  (c) (Brit inf) (steal) money klauen (inf); handbag aus der
Hand reißen; (kidnap) entführen.
  3 vi greifen (at nach). don't ~! nicht grapschen! (inf); to ~ at
an opportunity eine Gelegenheit ergreifen.

♦**snatch away** vt sep wegreißen (sth from sb jdm etw). death
~**ed** him ~ from us der Tod hat ihn uns (dat) entrissen.
♦**snatch up** vt sep schnappen. he ~**ed** ~ his camera er
schnappte sich (dat) seine Kamera; the mother ~**ed** her child
~ die Mutter riß ihr Kind an sich (acc).
snazzy adj (+er), **snazzily** adv ['snæzɪ, -lɪ] (sl) flott, schnieke
(inf).
sneak [sniːk] 1 n Schleicher m; (Sch sl) Petze(r) mf (Sch sl). ~
preview (of film etc) Vorschau f; (of new car etc) Vorbesichtigung f; ~ **thief** Langfinger (inf), Einschleichdieb m.
  2 vt he ~**ed** a cake off the counter er klaute or klemmte einen
Kuchen vom Tresen (inf); to ~ sth into a room etw in ein
Zimmer schmuggeln; to ~ a look at sb/sth verstohlen auf
jdn/etw schielen.
  3 vi (a) to ~ about herumschleichen; to ~ away or off sich
wegschleichen or -stehlen; to ~ in sich einschleichen; to ~ past
sb (sich) an jdm vorbeischleichen.
  (b) (Sch sl: tell tales) petzen (inf). to ~ on sb jdn verpetzen
(inf).
sneakers ['sniːkəz] npl (esp US) Freizeitschuhe, Leisetreter
(hum), Schleicher (inf) pl.
sneaking ['sniːkɪŋ] adj attr geheim attr; suspicion also leise.
sneaky ['sniːkɪ] adj (+er) (inf) raffiniert, schlau.
sneer [snɪəʳ] 1 n (expression) spöttisches or höhnisches
Lächeln; (remark) spöttische or höhnische Bemerkung.
  2 vi spotten; (look sneering) spöttisch or höhnisch grinsen.
adolescents often ~ at what they cannot understand Jugendliche spotten oft über das, was sie nicht verstehen können; to ~
at sb jdn verhöhnen; (facially also) jdn auslachen.
sneerer ['snɪərəʳ] n Spötter m.
sneering adj, ~**ly** adv ['snɪərɪŋ, -lɪ] höhnisch, spöttisch.
sneeze [sniːz] 1 n Nieser m. ~**s** Niesen nt. 2 vi niesen. not to be
~**d** at nicht zu verachten.
snick [snɪk] 1 n (small cut) Kerbe f. 2 vt (with razor) schneiden;
(with knife) schnitzen; (with tweezers) zupfen; (Cricket) ball
auf Kante schlagen.
snicker ['snɪkəʳ] n, vi see **snigger**.
snide [snaɪd] adj (inf) abfällig.
sniff [snɪf] 1 n Schniefen nt no pl (inf); (disdainful) Naserümp-
fen nt no pl; (of dog) Schnüffeln nt no pl. to go out for a ~ of air
frische Luft schnappen gehen; we never got a ~ of the vodka
wir durften noch nicht einmal an dem Wodka riechen; one ~ of
the cyanide and ... einmal an dem Zyankali gerochen, und ...;
have a ~ at this riech mal hieran; he had a good ~ to try to clear
his nose er zog kräftig hoch, um die Nase frei zu kriegen.
  2 vt (test by smelling) riechen, schnuppern an (+dat) (inf);
smelling salts einziehen; glue einatmen, schnüffeln (inf); snuff
schnupfen; (fig: detect) wittern, riechen. the dogs ~**ed** each
other die Hunde beschnupperten sich; ~ these flowers riech
mal an den Blumen.
  3 vi (person) schniefen (inf); (dog) schnüffeln, schnuppern.
to ~ at sth (lit) an etw (dat) schnuppern; (fig) die Nase über etw
(acc) rümpfen; not to be ~**ed** at nicht zu verachten.
♦**sniff out** vt sep (lit, fig) aufspüren; crime, plot aufdecken.
sniffle ['snɪfl] n, vi see **snuffle**.
sniffy ['snɪfɪ] adj (+er) (inf) (disdainful) naserümpfend; (put
out) verschnupft, eingeschnappt (inf). she was rather ~ about
the plan sie hat über den Plan nur die Nase gerümpft.
snifter ['snɪftəʳ] n (dated inf) Kurze(r) m (inf). to have a ~ einen
Kurzen trinken or nehmen (inf).
snigger ['snɪgəʳ] 1 n Kichern, Gekicher nt. to give a ~ los-
kichern. 2 vi kichern (at, about wegen).
snip [snɪp] 1 n (a) (cut, cutting action) Schnitt m; (sound)
Schnipsen, Klappern nt no pl.
  (b) (of cloth) Stück nt; (of paper) Schnipsel, Schnippel (inf) m
or nt; (from newspaper) Ausschnitt m.
  (c) (esp Brit inf: bargain) Schnäppchen nt, günstiger Kauf. at only
£2 it's a real ~ für nur £ 2 ist es unheimlich günstig.
  (d) (US inf: insignificant person) Nichts nt (pej inf).
  2 vt schnippeln (inf). to ~ sth off etw abschnippeln (inf).
  3 vi to ~ at schnippeln an (+dat) (inf).
snipe [snaɪp] 1 n, pl - (Orn) Schnepfe f. 2 vi to ~ at sb (lit, fig) aus
dem Hinterhalt auf jdn schießen.
sniper ['snaɪpəʳ] n Heckenschütze m. ~**-fire** Heckenschützen-
feuer nt.
snippet ['snɪpɪt] n Stückchen nt; (of paper also) Schnipsel m or
nt; (of information) (Bruch)stück m. ~**s** of a conversation Gesprächsfetzen pl.
snitch [snɪtʃ] (sl) 1 vt klauen (inf), klemmen (inf). 2 vi to ~ on sb
über jdn plaudern (inf) or klatschen.
snivel ['snɪvl] vi heulen, flennen (inf).
snivelling ['snɪvlɪŋ] 1 adj heulend, flennend (inf). 2 n
Geheul(e), Geflenne (inf) nt.
snob [snɒb] n Snob m. ~ **appeal** or **value** Snobappeal m.
snobbery ['snɒbərɪ] n Snobismus m.
snobbish adj, ~**ly** adv ['snɒbɪʃ, -lɪ] snobistisch, versnobt (inf).
snobbishness ['snɒbɪʃnɪs] n Snobismus m, Versnobtheit f (inf).
snog [snɒg] (Brit sl) 1 n Knutscherei f (inf). to have a ~ with sb
mit jdm rumknutschen (inf). 2 vi rumknutschen (inf).
snood [snuːd] n Haarnetz nt.
snook [snuːk] n see **cock** 2 (h).
snooker ['snuːkəʳ] 1 n Snooker nt. 2 vt to ~ sb jdn sperren; to be
~**ed** (fig inf) festsitzen (inf).
snoop [snuːp] 1 n (a) see **snooper**. (b) (act) I'll have a ~ around
ich gucke mich mal (ein bißchen) um. 2 vi schnüffeln. to ~
about or around herumschnüffeln.
snooper ['snuːpəʳ] n Schnüffler(in f) m.
snootily ['snuːtɪlɪ] adv (inf) hochnäsig, von oben herab.
snooty ['snuːtɪ] adj (+er) (inf) hochnäsig.
snooze [snuːz] 1 n Schläfchen, Nickerchen nt. to have a ~ ein
Schläfchen machen. 2 vi dösen, ein Nickerchen machen.

snore [snɔː^r] **1** *n* Schnarchen *nt no pl.* **2** *vi* schnarchen.
snorer ['snɔːrə^r] *n* Schnarcher(in *f*) *m*.
snoring ['snɔːrɪŋ] *n* Schnarchen *nt*.
snorkel ['snɔːkl] **1** *n* Schnorchel *m*. **2** *vi* schnorcheln. **to go ~ling** schnorcheln gehen.
snort [snɔːt] **1** *n* Schnauben *nt no pl*; (*of boar*) Grunzen *nt no pl*; (*of person also*) Prusten *nt no pl.* **with a ~ of rage** wutschnaubend; **he gave a ~ of** contempt/rage/laughter er schnaubte verächtlich/vor Wut/er prustete los.
   2 *vti* schnauben; (*boar*) grunzen; (*person also*) prusten.
snorter ['snɔːtə^r] *n* (a) (*Brit sl*) schwierige Kiste (*sl*), hartes Ding (*sl*). (b) (*dated inf: drink*) Kurze(r) *m* (*inf*).
snot [snɒt] *n* (*inf*) Rotz *m* (*inf*).
snotty ['snɒtɪ] *adj* (+*er*) (*inf*) (a) *handkerchief, nose* Rotz- (*inf*); *child* rotznäsig (*inf*). **~-nose** Rotznase *f* (*inf*); **~-nosed** rotznäsig (*inf*). (b) (*fig: snooty*) rotzig (*sl*), pampig (*inf*).
snout [snaut] *n* (a) (*of animal*) Schnauze *f*; (*of pig also, of insect*) Rüssel *m*; (*inf: of person*) Rüssel (*inf*), Zinken (*inf*) *m*. (b) (*sl: informer*) Spitzel *m*. (c) (*Brit sl: tobacco*) Knaster *m* (*inf*).
snow [snəʊ] **1** *n* (a) (*also sl: cocaine or heroin*) Schnee *m*; (~*fall*) Schneefall *m*. **the ~s that lie on the plains** der Schnee in der Ebene; **the heavy ~s last winter** die heftigen Schneefälle im letzten Winter; **a ~ of confetti** ein Konfettiregen *m*; **as white as ~** schneeweiß, blütenweiß; **as pure as the driven ~** engelrein. (b) (*TV*) Geflimmer *nt*, Schnee *m*.
   2 *vi* schneien.
♦**snow in** *vt sep* (*usu pass*) **to be** *or* **get ~ed ~** einschneien; **we are ~ed ~** wir sind eingeschneit.
♦**snow off** *vt sep* (*usu pass*) **to be ~ed ~** wegen Schnee abgesagt werden *or* ausfallen.
♦**snow under** *vt sep* (*inf: usu pass*) **to be ~ed ~** (*with work*) reichlich eingedeckt sein; (*with requests*) überhäuft werden.
♦**snow up** *vt sep* (*usu pass*) *see* **snow in**.
snow: **~ball 1** *n* Schneeball *m*; (*drink*) Snowball *m*; **he doesn't stand a ~ball's chance in hell** (*sl*) er hat nicht die geringste Chance *or* gleich Null; **2** *vt* Schneebälle werfen auf (+*acc*); **3** *vi* eskalieren; **we must take action now otherwise things will ~ball and get out of control** wir müssen jetzt etwas unternehmen, sonst wachsen uns die Dinge über den Kopf; **opposition to the referendum just ~balled** die Opposition gegen die Volksabstimmung wuchs lawinenartig an; **~ball effect** *n* Schneeballeffekt *m*; **~-blind** *adj* schneeblind; **~ blindness** *n* Schneeblindheit *f*; **~bound** *adj* eingeschneit; **~-capped** *adj* schneebedeckt; **~ chains** *npl* Schneeketten *pl*; **~-clad** (*poet*), **~-covered** *adj* verschneit; **~drift** *n* Schneewehe *f*; **~drop** *n* Schneeglöckchen *nt*; **~fall** *n* Schneefall *m*; **~field** *n* Schneefeld *nt*; **~flake** *n* Schneeflocke *f*; **~-in-summer** *n* (*Bot*) Hornkraut *nt*; **~ leopard** *n* Schneeleopard *m*; **~ line** *n* Schneegrenze *f*; **~man** *n* Schneemann *m*; *see* **abominable**; **~mobile** *n* (*US*) Schneemobil *nt*; **~plough**, (*US*) **~plow** *n* (*also Ski*) Schneepflug *m*; **~shed** *n* (*US*) Schneedach *nt*; **~shoe** *n* Schneeschuh *m*; **~slide** *n* (*US*) Schneerutsch *m*; **~storm** *n* Schneesturm *m*; **~suit** *n* (*US*) gefütterter Overall; **S~ White** *n* Schneewittchen *nt*; **~-white** *adj* schneeweiß; *hair also* schlohweiß.
snowy ['snəʊɪ] *adj* (+*er*) (a) *weather, region* schneereich; *hills* verschneit. **it was very ~ yesterday** gestern hat es viel geschneit. (b) (*white as snow*) schneeweiß.
SNP *abbr of* **Scottish National Party**
snub [snʌb] **1** *n* Brüskierung *f*. **to give sb a ~** jdn brüskieren, jdn vor den Kopf stoßen; *subordinate, pupil etc* (*verbally*) jdm über den Mund fahren; **to get a ~ from sb** von jdm brüskiert *or* vor den Kopf gestoßen werden.
   2 *vt* (a) *person* brüskieren, vor den Kopf stoßen; *subordinate, pupil* (*verbally*) über den Mund fahren (+*dat*); *suggestion, proposal* kurz abtun.
   (b) (*ignore, not greet*) schneiden.
snub: **~ nose** *n* Stupsnase *f*; **~-nosed** *adj* stumpfnasig; *person also* stupsnasig.
snuff [snʌf] **1** *n* Schnupftabak *m*. **to take ~** schnupfen. **2** *vt* *candle* (*extinguish: also* ~ **out**) auslöschen; (*trim wick*) putzen, schneuzen (*old*); (*fig*) *revolt* ersticken; *hopes* zunichte machen, zerschlagen. **to ~ it** (*Brit sl: die*) abkratzen (*sl*).
snuff box *n* Schnupftabakdose, Tabatiere (*geh*) *f*.
snuffer ['snʌfə^r] *n* Kerzenlöscher *m*. **~s, a pair of ~s** Lichtputzschere *f*.
snuffle ['snʌfl] **1** *n* Schniefen *nt no pl.* **to have a touch of the ~s** (*inf*) einen leichten Schnupfen haben. **2** *vi* (*person, animal*) schnüffeln; (*with cold, from crying also*) schniefen (*inf*).
snug [snʌg] **1** *adj* (+*er*) (*cosy, comfortable*) behaglich, gemütlich; (*cosy and warm*) *bed, garment, room etc* mollig warm, behaglich warm; (*sheltered*) *spot, harbour* geschützt; (*close-fitting*) gut sitzend *attr*; (*tight*) eng; *income* ganz annehmbar *or* passabel, hübsch (*inf*). **to be ~ in bed/in one's sleeping bag** es im Bett/Schlafsack mollig *or* behaglich warm haben; **I was as ~ as a bug in a rug** (*inf*) es war urgemütlich; **it is a good ~ fit** es paßt gut; **it was a ~ fit with 6 of us in the car** wir paßten zu sechst noch gerade in den Wagen.
   2 *n* (*Brit: in pub*) kleines Nebenzimmer.
snuggle ['snʌgl] **1** *vi* sich schmiegen, sich kuscheln. **to ~ down in bed** sich ins Bett kuscheln; **to ~ up (to sb)** sich (an jdn) anschmiegen *or* ankuscheln; **I like to ~ up with a book** ich mache es mir gern mit einem Buch gemütlich; **to ~ into sth** sich in etw (*acc*) einkuscheln; **the cottages ~d in the valley** die Häuschen schmiegten sich ins Tal.
   2 *vt* an sich (*acc*) schmiegen.
snugly ['snʌglɪ] *adv* (*cosily*) gemütlich, behaglich. **~ tucked in**, **~ tucked up (in bed)** mollig warm eingepackt (im Bett); **it fits ~** es paßt wie angegossen.
snugness ['snʌgnɪs] *n see adj* Behaglichkeit, Gemütlichkeit *f*; mollige *or* behagliche Wärme *f*; Geschütztheit *f*; guter Sitz.
So *abbr of* **south** S.

so [səʊ] **1** *adv* (a) so. **~ much tea/~ many flies** so viel Tee/so viele Fliegen; **he was ~ stupid (that)** er war so *or* dermaßen *or* derart dumm(, daß); **he's ~ quick I can't keep up with him** er ist so schnell, daß ich nicht mithalten kann; **not ~ ... as nich so ...** wie; **he is not ~ fast a runner as you** er ist kein so schneller Läufer wie Sie, er kann nicht so schnell laufen wie Sie; **I am not ~ stupid as to believe that** so dumm bin ich nicht, daß ich das glaube(n würde); **he was ~ stupid as to tell her** er war so dumm und hat es ihr gesagt; **would you be ~ kind as to open the door?** wären Sie bitte so freundlich und würden die Tür öffnen?; **~ great a writer as Shakespeare** ein so großer Dichter wie Shakespeare; **he's not been ~ well recently** in letzter Zeit geht es ihm nicht so sonderlich; **how are things?** — **not ~ bad!** wie geht's? — nicht schlecht!; **not ~ as you'd notice** aber das fällt kaum auf.
   (b) (*emphatic*) *glad, sorry, sure, rich, hurt* so; *pleased, relieved, hope, wish* sehr; *love* so sehr; *hate* so sehr, derart. **that's ~ true** das ist ja so wahr, das ist wirklich wahr; **I'm ~ very tired** ich bin ja so müde; **it's not ~ very difficult** es ist gar nicht so schwer; **it would be ~ much better/nicer etc** es wäre soviel besser/netter etc; **~ much the better/worse (for sb)** um so besser/schlechter (für jdn); **that's ~ kind of you** das ist wirklich sehr nett von Ihnen; **I ~ hope you're right!** ich hoffe (wirklich) sehr, daß Sie recht haben!
   (c) (*replacing longer sentence*) das, es. **I hope ~** hoffentlich; (*emphatic*) das hoffe ich doch sehr; **I think ~** ich glaube schon; **I never said ~** das habe ich nie gesagt; **I told you ~** ich habe es dir doch *or* ja gesagt; **I told you ~ yesterday** das habe ich dir gestern gesagt; **why should I do it?** — **because I say ~** warum muß ich das tun? — weil ich es sage, darum; **I didn't say ~** das habe ich nicht gesagt; **can I go/will you do it?** — **I suppose ~** darf ich gehen/machen Sie es? — na ja, meinetwegen; **is that right/can I do it like that?** — **I suppose ~** stimmt das/kann ich es so machen? — ich glaube schon; **~ I believe ja**, ich glaube schon; **~ I see** das, ja, das sehe ich; **please, do ~** bitte(, tun Sie es ruhig); **perhaps ~** vielleicht; **it may be ~** es kann schon sein; **~ be it** nun gut; **if ~** wenn ja; **he said he would finish it this week, and ~ he did** er hat gesagt, er würde es diese Woche fertigmachen, und das hat er auch (gemacht); **how or why ~?** wieso *or* warum das?; **or ~ they say** oder so heißt es jedenfalls; **he's a millionaire, or ~ he says** er ist Millionär, zumindest *or* jedenfalls behauptet er das; **it is ~!** (*contradiction*) doch!; **I can ~!** (*contradiction*) und ob (ich das kann)!, doch!; **I didn't say that** — **you did ~** das habe ich nicht gesagt — doch, das hast du (sehr wohl gesagt)!; **you've got the papers?** — **yes, that's ~** haben Sie die Papiere? — jawohl; **that is ~** das stimmt; **if that's ~** wenn das stimmt; **he's coming by plane** — **is that ~?** er kommt mit dem Flugzeug - ach so, ja?, tatsächlich?; **you're a fool** — **is that ~?** du bist ein Idiot — ach, wirklich?; **... — it is/I have/he did etc** — (ja) tatsächlich; **it was terrible** — **~ it was** ja, wirklich; **he's a nice chap** — **~ he is** er ist ein netter Kerl — ja, wirklich *or* ja, das ist er auch.
   (d) (*thus, in this way*) so. **perhaps it was better ~** vielleicht war es auch besser so; **~ it was that ... so kam es, daß ...**; **and ~ it was und so war es auch**; **by ~ doing he has ...** dadurch hat er ...; **bother them! he exclaimed, and ~ saying walked out** zum Kuckuck! rief er, und damit ging er hinaus; **... and ~ to bed ...** und dann ins Bett.
   (e) (*unspecified amount*) **how high is it?** — **oh, about ~ high** (*accompanied by gesture*) wie hoch ist das? — oh, ungefähr so; **~ much per head** soviel pro Kopf; **they looked like ~ many gypsies** sie sahen wie so viele andere Zigeuner auch aus; **how long will it take?** — **a week or ~** wie lange dauert das? — ungefähr eine Woche, so eine Woche; **50 or ~** etwa 50.
   (f) (*likewise*) auch. **~ am/would/do/could etc I** ich auch; **he's wrong and ~ are you** ihr irrt euch beide; **as A is to B, ~ D is to E** A verhält sich zu B wie D zu E.
   (g) **he walked past and didn't ~ much as look at me** er ging vorbei, ohne mich auch nur anzusehen; **without saying ~ much as hello** ohne auch nur „guten Tag" zu sagen; **he didn't say ~ much as thank you** er hat nicht einmal danke gesagt; **I haven't ~ much as a penny** ich habe keinen Pfennig; **~ much for that!** (*inf*) das wär's ja wohl gewesen! (*inf*); **~ much for him/his help** (*inf*) das war ja wohl nichts mit ihm! (*inf*)/schöne Hilfe! (*inf*); **~ much for his ambition to be a doctor/for our holidays** aus der Traum vom Arztwerden/von den Ferien; **~ much for his promises/fine words** und er hat solche Versprechungen gemacht/so große Töne gespuckt (*inf*); *see* **ever**, **far 1** (d), **just**[1], **long**[2] 2 (a, c), **more** 1 (b), **quite** (a).
   2 *conj* (a) (*expressing purpose*) damit. **~ (that)** you don't have to do it again damit Sie es nicht noch einmal machen müssen; **we hurried ~ as not to be late** wir haben uns beeilt, um nicht zu spät zu kommen.
   (b) (*expressing result, therefore*) also. **it rained (and) ~ we couldn't go out** es regnete, also konnten wir nicht weggehen *or* und deshalb konnten wir nicht weggehen; **he refused to move ~ that (finally) the police had to carry him away** er weigerte sich wegzugehen, so daß ihn die Polizei schließlich wegtragen mußte; **he was standing in the doorway ~ (that) no-one could get past** er stand in der Tür, so daß niemand vorbeikonnte; **I told him to leave and ~ he did** ich habe ihm gesagt, er solle gehen, und das hat er auch getan; **~ I told him he could get lost** da habe ich ihm gesagt, er kann *or* könnte mir den Buckel runterrutschen; **the roads are busy ~ be careful** es ist viel Verkehr, also fahre vorsichtig; **~, far from helping us, he ... nicht** nur, daß er uns nicht geholfen hat, sondern ...; **~ you see ...** wie du siehst, ...
   (c) (*in questions, exclamations*) also. **~ you're Spanish/leaving?** Sie sind also Spanier(in)/Sie gehen also?; **~ that's his wife/the reason!** das ist also seine Frau/der Grund!; **~ you lost it, did you?** du hast es also verloren, wie?; **~ you *did* do it!** du

hast es also doch gemacht!; ~ **there you are!** hier steckst du also!; ~ **what did you do?** und was haben Sie (da) gemacht?; ~ **what do we do now?** und was machen wir jetzt?; ~ **(what)?** (*inf*) (na) und?; ~ **what if you don't do it?** (*inf*) (na) und wenn du's nicht machst?; **I'm not going,** ~ **there!** (*inf*) ich geh' nicht, fertig, aus!

soak [səʊk] **1** *vt* (**a**) (*wet*) durchnässen. **to be/get** ~**ed** patschnaß *or* völlig durchnäßt sein/werden; **to be** ~**ed to the skin, to be** ~**ed through** bis auf die Haut *or* völlig durchnäßt sein.

(**b**) (*steep*) einweichen (**in** in +*dat*). **a town** ~**ed in history** eine geschichtsträchtige Stadt; **to** ~ **oneself in sunshine** sich von der Sonne bescheinen lassen; **to** ~ **oneself in sth** (*fig*) sich in etw (*acc*) vertiefen.

(**c**) (*inf*) **the rich** *etc* schröpfen. **to** ~ **sb for sth** jdn um etw angehen.

2 *vi* (**a**) (*steep*) leave it **to** ~ weichen Sie es ein; (*in dye*) lassen Sie die Farbe einziehen; **to** ~ **in a bath** sich einweichen (*inf*).

(**b**) (*penetrate*) **rain has** ~**ed through the ceiling** der Regen ist durch die Decke gesickert; **the coffee was** ~**ing into the carpet** der Kaffee saugte sich in den Teppich; **blood was** ~**ing out of the wound** aus der Wunde sickerte Blut.

3 *n* (**a**) (*act of soaking*) **give the washing a good** ~ lassen Sie die Wäsche gut einweichen; **the sheets are in** ~ die Laken sind eingeweicht; **the garden needs a** ~ der Garten muß gründlich bewässert werden.

(**b**) (*inf: drunkard*) Schluckbruder (*inf*), Säufer(in *f*) *m*.

♦ **soak in** *vi* (*stain, dye etc*) einziehen. **to leave sth to** ~ ~ etw einziehen lassen; **I just hope that it has** ~**ed** ~ (*fig*) ich hoffe nur, daß er/sie *etc* das kapiert hat (*inf*).

♦ **soak off 1** *vt sep* ablösen. **2** *vi* sich (ab)lösen (*prep obj* von).

♦ **soak out 1** *vt sep* **mark, stain** durch Einweichen entfernen. **2** *vi* beim Einweichen herausgehen.

♦ **soak up** *vt sep* **liquid** aufsaugen; **sunshine** genießen; *alcohol* in sich (*acc*) hineinkippen; **sound** schlucken; (*fig*) in sich (*acc*) hineinsaugen; *information* aufsaugen.

soaking ['səʊkɪŋ] **1** *adj* **person** klitschnaß, patschnaß; *object also* triefend.

2 *adv* ~ **wet** triefend naß, klitschnaß; **a** ~ **wet day** ein völlig verregneter Tag.

3 *n* (*steeping*) Einweichen *nt no indef art*. **to get a** ~ patschnaß werden; **to give sth a** ~ etw einweichen.

so-and-so ['səʊənsəʊ] *n* (*inf*) (**a**) (*unspecified person*) Soundso *no art*. ~ **up at the shop** Herr/Frau Soundso im Laden. (**b**) (*pej*) **he's a real/an old** ~ das ist ein gemeiner Kerl; **you old** ~ du bist vielleicht eine/einer.

soap [səʊp] **1** *n* (*substance*) Seife *f*. **2** *vt* einseifen, abseifen.

soap: ~**box** *n* (*lit: packing case*) Seifenkiste *f*; (*fig: platform*) Apfelsinenkiste *f*; (*as cart*) Seifenkiste *f*; **to get up on one's** ~**box** (*fig*) Volksreden halten; ~**box derby** *n* Seifenkistenrennen *nt*; ~**box evangelist** *n* Wanderprediger *m*; ~**box orator** *n* Volksredner *m*; ~-**bubble** *n* Seifenblase *f*; ~**dish** *n* Seifenschale *f*; ~**flakes** *npl* Seifenflocken *pl*; ~ **opera** *n* (*TV, Rad inf*) rührseliges (Familien)drama; ~ **powder** *n* Seifenpulver *nt*; ~**stone** *n* Speckstein *m*; ~**suds** *npl* Seifenschaum *m*.

soapy ['səʊpɪ] *adj* (+*er*) seifig.

soar [sɔːʳ] *vi* (**a**) (*rise: also* ~ **up**) aufsteigen; (*bird also*) sich in die Lüfte schwingen. **to** ~ **(up) into the sky** zum Himmel steigen.

(**b**) (*fig*) (*building, tower*) hochragen; (*price, cost, profit*) hochschnellen; (*ambition, popularity, reputation, hopes*) einen Aufschwung nehmen; (*morale, spirits*) einen Aufschwung bekommen. **the tower/hill** ~**ed above the town** der Turm/Hügel ragte über die Stadt hinaus.

soaring ['sɔːrɪŋ] *adj* **bird, plane** aufsteigend, in die Luft steigend; **tower** hoch aufragend; *imagination, ideas, ambition* hochfliegend; *popularity, reputation* schnell zunehmend; *prices* in die Höhe schnellend; *inflation* unaufhaltsam; *pride, hopes* wachsend. **I watched the lark's** ~ **flight** ich sah, wie sich die Lerche in die Lüfte schwang.

sob [sɒb] **1** *n* Schluchzer *m*, Schluchzen *nt no pl*. **to give a** ~ (auf)schluchzen; ..., **he said with a** ~ ..., sagte er schluchzend. **2** *vi* schluchzen (**with** *vor* +*dat*). ~, ~ (*inf*) schluchz-schluchz. **3** *vt* schluchzen. **to** ~ **oneself to sleep** sich in den Schlaf weinen.

♦ **sob out** *vt sep* **information** schluchzend hervorstoßen; *story* schluchzend erzählen. **to** ~ **one's heart** ~ sich (*dat*) die Seele aus dem Leib weinen.

sobbing ['sɒbɪŋ] **1** *n* Schluchzen *nt*. **2** *adj* schluchzend.

sober ['səʊbəʳ] *adj* (**a**) (*not drunk*) nüchtern. **to be as** ~ **as a judge** stocknüchtern sein (*inf*).

(**b**) (*sedate, serious*) **life, expression, mood, occasion** ernst; *person also* solide; (*sensible, moderate*) **opinion, judgement** vernünftig; *assessment, statement, advice, facts* nüchtern. **in** ~ **earnest** sehr ernst, tiefernst.

(**c**) (*not bright or showy*) schlicht, dezent; *colour* gedeckt.

♦ **sober down** *vi* ruhiger werden.

♦ **sober up 1** *vt sep* (*lit*) nüchtern machen; (*fig*) zur Vernunft bringen. **2** *vi* (*lit*) nüchtern werden; (*fig*) ruhiger werden; (*after laughing, joking etc*) sich beruhigen.

soberly ['səʊbəlɪ] *adv* nüchtern; *behave* vernünftig; *dress, furnish* schlicht, dezent.

sober-minded ['səʊbə'maɪndɪd] *adj* nüchtern, vernünftig.

soberness ['səʊbənɪs] *n see* **sobriety**.

sobersides ['səʊbəsaɪdz] *n* (*dated inf*) Fadian *m* (*inf*).

sobriety [sə'braɪətɪ] *n* (**a**) (*not being drunk*) Nüchternheit *f*. (**b**) (*seriousness, sedateness*) Solidität *f*; (*of dress etc*) Schlichtheit, Dezentheit *f*; (*of colour*) Gedecktheit *f*.

sobriquet ['səʊbrɪkeɪ], **soubriquet** *n* Spitzname *m*.

sob: ~-**sister** *n* (*esp US inf*) Briefkastentante *f* (*inf*); ~**story** *n* (*inf*) rührselige Geschichte (*inf*); ~-**stuff** *n* (*inf*) Schmalz *m* (*inf*); (*book, film*) Tränendrüsendrücker *m* (*inf*); (*heart-rending tale*) todtraurige Geschichte (*inf*).

soc *abbr of* **society** Ges.

Soc *abbr of* **Socialist** Soz.

so-called ['səʊ'kɔːld] *adj* sogenannt; (*supposed*) angeblich.

soccer ['sɒkəʳ] *n* Fußball *m*. ~ **player** Fußballer, Fußballspieler(in *f*) *m*.

sociability [ˌsəʊʃə'bɪlɪtɪ] *n* Geselligkeit *f*.

sociable ['səʊʃəbl] *adj* (*gregarious*) gesellig; (*friendly*) freundlich. ... **just to be** ~ ..., man möchte sich ja nicht ausschließen; **I'm not feeling very** ~ **today** mir ist heute nicht nach Geselligkeit (zumute).

sociably ['səʊʃəblɪ] *adv* **invite, say** freundlich. **he didn't behave very** ~ er war nicht gerade umgänglich; **to be** ~ **inclined** ein geselliger Mensch sein.

social ['səʊʃəl] **1** *adj* (**a**) (*relating to community*, *Admin, Pol*) sozial; *history, reform, legislation, policy* Sozial-; *evils of the* Gesellschaft; *order, system, realism* Gesellschafts-, Sozial-; *structure, development, conditions also* gesellschaftlich. **the** ~ **services** die Sozialeinrichtungen *pl*; **the** ~ **contract** (*Hist*) der Gesellschaftsvertrag; (*Brit Pol*) das Tarifabkommen; **to suffer from** ~ **deprivation** sozial benachteiligt sein.

(**b**) *engagements, pleasures, ambitions, life, equal, superior* gesellschaftlich; *behaviour* in Gesellschaft; *distinctions, advancement, rank, status also* sozial. ~ **class** gesellschaftliche Klasse, Gesellschaftsklasse *f*; ~ **climber** Emporkömmling *m* (*pej*), sozialer Aufsteiger; ~ **snobbery** Standesdünkel *m*; **to be sb's** ~ **inferior/superior** gesellschaftlich unter/über jdm stehen; **a room for** ~ **functions** ein Gesellschaftsraum *m*; (*larger*) ein Saal *m* für Gesellschaften; **there isn't much** ~ **life around here** hier in der Gegend wird gesellschaftlich nicht viel geboten; **how's your** ~ **life these days?** (*inf*) und was treibst du so privat? (*inf*); **a job which leaves no time for one's/a** ~ **life** ein Beruf, bei dem man keine Zeit für Geselligkeiten hat.

(**c**) (*gregarious*) **evening, person** gesellig; (*living in groups*) **animals, bees, ants** *etc* gesellig lebend, sozial. **man is a** ~ **animal** der Mensch ist ein Gesellschaftswesen.

2 *n* Gesellschaftsabend *m*.

social: ~ **anthropology** *n* Sozialanthropologie *f*; ~ **club** *n* Verein *m*, Klub *m* für gesellige Beisammensein; ~ **column** *n* Gesellschaftsspalte *f*; ~ **democrat** *n* Sozialdemokrat(in *f*) *m*; ~ **democratic** *adj* sozialdemokratisch; ~ **disease** *n* (**a**) (*euph: VD*) Geschlechtskrankheit *f*; (**b**) (*caused by* ~ *conditions*) Volksseuche *f*; ~ **insurance** *n* Sozialversicherung *f*.

socialism ['səʊʃəlɪzəm] *n* Sozialismus *m*.

socialist ['səʊʃəlɪst] **1** *adj* sozialistisch. **2** *n* Sozialist(in *f*) *m*.

socialistic [ˌsəʊʃə'lɪstɪk] *adj* (*esp pej*) sozialistisch angehaucht.

socialite ['səʊʃəlaɪt] *n* (*inf*) Angehörige(r) *mf* der Schickeria *or* der feinen Gesellschaft; (*man also*) Salonlöwe *m* (*inf*). **a famous London** ~ eine bekannte Figur der Londoner Schikkeria.

socialization [ˌsəʊʃəlaɪ'zeɪʃən] *n* (*Pol*) Vergesellschaftung, Sozialisierung *f*; (*Sociol, Psych*) Sozialisation *f*.

socialize ['səʊʃəlaɪz] **1** *vt* sozialisieren; *means of production* vergesellschaften.

2 *vi* **to** ~ **with sb** (*meet socially*) mit jdm gesellschaftlich verkehren; (*chat to*) sich mit jdm unterhalten; **I don't** ~ **much these days** ich komme zur Zeit nicht viel unter die Leute; **she** ~**s a lot** sie hat ein reges gesellschaftliches Leben.

socially ['səʊʃəlɪ] *adv see adj* (**a**) gesellschaftlich, aus sozialer Sicht; *deprived, structured etc* sozial. (**b**) gesellschaftlich; *meet* privat.

social: ~ **science** *n* Sozialwissenschaft *f*; ~ **scientist** *n* Sozialwissenschaftler(in *f*) *m*; ~ **secretary** *n* persönlicher Sekretär, persönliche Sekretärin; (*of club*) Veranstaltungsklubwart *m*; ~ **security** *n* Sozialunterstützung *f*; (~ *security office*) Sozialamt *nt*; **to be on** ~ **security** Sozialhilfeempfänger sein; ~ **welfare** *n* soziales Wohl; ~ **work** *n* Sozialarbeit *f*; ~ **worker** *n* Sozialarbeiter(in *f*) *m*.

societal [sə'saɪətl] *adj* gesellschaftlich.

society [sə'saɪətɪ] *n* (**a**) (*social community*) die Gesellschaft. **modern industrial** ~ die moderne Industriegesellschaft.

(**b**) (*company*) Gesellschaft *f*. **I enjoy her** ~ ich bin gerne in ihrer Gesellschaft; **everyone needs human** ~ jeder braucht die Gesellschaft anderer Menschen.

(**c**) (*high* ~) die Gesellschaft. **London** ~ die Londoner Gesellschaft, die gesellschaftlichen Kreise Londons; **to go into** ~ in die Gesellschaft eingeführt werden; **to try to get into** ~ in die Gesellschaft *or* in gesellschaftliche Kreise vordringen wollen; **the years she spent in** ~ die Jahre, die sie in gesellschaftlichen *or* feinen Kreisen verbracht hat.

(**d**) (*club, organization*) Verein *m*; (*learned, Comm*) Gesellschaft *f*; (*debating, history, dramatic etc*) (*Sch*) Arbeitsgemeinschaft *f*; (*Univ*) Klub *m*. **S~ for the Prevention of Cruelty to Animals/Children** Tierschutzverein *m*/Kinderschutzbund *m*; **charitable** ~ Wohltätigkeitsverein *m*; **cooperative** ~ Genossenschaft *f*; **S~ of Jesus** Gesellschaft Jesu; *see* **friendly, friend, provident, building** ~.

society *in cpds* Gesellschafts-; ~ **column** *n* Gesellschaftsspalte *f*; ~ **gossip** *n* Gesellschaftsklatsch *m*; ~ **man** *n* Mann *m* der Gesellschaft; ~ **wedding** *n* Hochzeit *f* in den besseren Kreisen.

socio- [ˌsəʊsɪəʊ-] *pref* sozio-. ~**economic** *adj* sozioökonomisch; ~**linguistics** Soziolinguistik *f*.

sociological *adj*, ~**ly** *adv* [ˌsəʊsɪə'lɒdʒɪkəl, -ɪ] soziologisch.

sociologist [ˌsəʊsɪ'ɒlədʒɪst] *n* Soziologe *m*, Soziologin *f*.

sociology [ˌsəʊsɪ'ɒlədʒɪ] *n* Soziologie *f*.

sociopolitical [ˌsəʊsɪəʊpə'lɪtɪkəl] *adj* sozialpolitisch.

sock[1] [sɒk] *n* Socke *f*, Socken *m* (*inf*); (*knee-length*) Kniestrumpf *m*; (*insole*) Einlegesohle *f*; (*wind* ~) Wind- *or* Luftsack *m*. **to pull one's** ~ **up** (*inf*) sich am Riemen reißen (*inf*); **put a** ~ **in it!** (*Brit inf*) hör auf!

sock[2] **1** *n* (*inf*) Schlag *m* (mit der Faust). **to give sb a** ~ **on the jaw/in the eye** jdm eine aufs Kinn/aufs Auge verpassen (*inf*).

2 vt **(a)** (inf: hit) hauen (inf). ~ **him one!** knall ihm eine! (inf), hau ihm eine rein! (sl); he ~ed her right it. the eye er verpaßte ihr eine aufs Auge (inf).
(b) (sl) ~ **it to me** dreh/dreht auf (sl).

socket ['sɒkɪt] n **(a)** (of eye) Augenhöhle f; (of joint) Gelenkpfanne f; (of tooth) Zahnhöhle f. **to pull sb's arm out of its** ~ jdm den Arm auskugeln. **(b)** (Elec) Steckdose f; (for lightbulb) Fassung f; (Mech) Sockel m, Fassung f.

Socrates ['sɒkrətiːz] n Sokrates m.

Socratic [sɒ'krætɪk] adj sokratisch.

sod¹ [sɒd] n (turf) Grassode f. **beneath the** ~ (liter) unter dem grünen Rasen (liter).

sod² (Brit sl) **1** n (mean, nasty) Sau f (sl). **the poor** ~s die armen Schweine (inf); **you stupid** ~ blöde Sau! (sl). **2** vt ~ **it!** verdammte Scheiße! (sl); ~ **him/you** der kann/du kannst mich mal (am Arsch lecken vulg)! (sl).

♦ **sod off** vi (Brit sl) Leine ziehen (sl). ~ ~! zieh Leine, du Arsch! (sl).

soda ['səʊdə] n **(a)** (Chem) Soda nt; (sodium oxide) Natriumoxyd nt; (caustic ~) Ätznatron nt. **(b)** (drink) Soda(wasser) nt.

soda: ~ **biscuit**, (US) ~ **cracker** n Cracker m; ~ **bread** n mit Backpulver gebackenes Brot; ~ **crystals** npl (Wasch)soda nt; ~-**fountain** n (US: café) Erfrischungshalle f; ~ **siphon** n Siphon m; ~-**water** n Sodawasser nt.

sodden ['sɒdn] adj durchnäßt, triefnaß; ground durchnäßt, durchweicht. **to be** ~ **with drink** sinnlos betrunken sein.

sodding ['sɒdɪŋ] adj (Brit sl) verflucht (inf), Scheiß- (sl). **what a** ~ **nuisance** verdammte Scheiße (sl).

sodium ['səʊdɪəm] n Natrium nt. ~ **bicarbonate** n Natron nt, doppeltkohlensaures Natrium; ~ **carbonate** n Natriumkarbonat, Soda nt; ~ **chloride** n Natriumchlorid, Kochsalz nt; ~ **hydroxide** n Natriumhydroxid, Ätznatron nt; ~ **nitrate** n Natriumnitrat nt.

Sodom ['sɒdəm] n Sodom nt. ~ **and Gomorrha** Sodom und Gomorr(h)a.

sodomite ['sɒdəmaɪt] n jd, der Analverkehr betreibt, Päderast m.

sodomy ['sɒdəmɪ] n Analverkehr m.

sofa ['səʊfə] n Sofa nt, Couch f. ~ **bed** Schlafcouch f.

soft [sɒft] adj (+er) **(a)** weich; meat zart; (pej: flabby) muscle schlaff. **a photo taken in** ~ **focus** ein Foto mit weichen Kontrasten; ~-**focus lens** Weichzeichner m; **a book in** ~ **covers** ein kartoniertes Buch; ~ **cheese** Weichkäse m.
(b) (smooth) skin zart; surface glatt; material, velvet weich; hair seidig. **as** ~ **as silk** seidenweich.
(c) (gentle, not harsh) sanft; (subdued) light, sound also, music gedämpft; (not loud) leise; rain, breeze, tap, pressure also leicht; steps leicht, leise; heart weich.
(d) (Ling) consonant weich.
(e) (weak) character, government schwach; treatment nachsichtig; (lenient) teacher, parent nachsichtig, gutmütig; judge, punishment mild(e). **to be** ~ **with** or **on sb** jdm gegenüber nachgiebig sein; **with children also** jdm alles durchgehen lassen.
(f) (not tough) verweichlicht. **a** ~ **and effeminate youth** ein verweichlichter Jugendlicher; **he thinks it's** ~ **for a boy to play the violin** er hält es für unmännlich, wenn ein Junge Geige spielt; **to make sb** ~ jdn verweichlichen.
(g) (easy) job, life bequem. **he has a** ~ **time of it** er hat's leicht or bequem; **that's a** ~ **option** das ist der Weg des geringsten Widerstandes.
(h) currency weich.
(i) drink alkoholfrei; drug, pornography weich.
(j) (inf: foolish) doof (inf), nicht ganz richtig im Kopf (inf). **he's** ~ **(in the head)** er ist nicht ganz richtig im Kopf (inf); **you must be** ~! du spinnst wohl! (inf); **I must be going** ~ ich fange wohl an zu spinnen (inf).
(k) (inf: feeling affection) **to be** ~ **on sb** für jdn schwärmen; **to have a** ~ **spot for sb** eine Schwäche für jdn haben.

soft: ~-**ball** n (US) Softball m; ~-**boiled** adj egg weich(gekocht); ~-**centred** adj mit Cremefüllung.

soften ['sɒfn] **1** vt weich machen; water also enthärten; light, sound, colour dämpfen; effect, sb's anger, reaction, impression mildern; outline weicher machen; resistance schwächen; person verweichlichen. **to** ~ **the blow** (fig) den Schock mildern.
2 vi (material, person, heart) weich werden; (voice, look) sanft werden; (anger, resistance) nachlassen; (outlines) weicher werden.

♦ **soften up 1** vt sep **(a)** weich machen.
(b) (fig) person, opposition milde stimmen; (by flattery etc) schmeicheln (+dat); customer kaufwillig stimmen; (by bullying) einschüchtern, weichmachen; enemy, resistance zermürben; enemy position schwächen; prisoner weichmachen.
2 vi (material) weich werden; (person, attitude) nachgiebiger werden. **to** ~ ~ **on sb** jdm gegenüber nachgiebig or schwach werden.

softener ['sɒfnəʳ] n Weichmacher m; (for water also) Enthärtungsmittel nt; (fabric ~) Weichspüler m, Weichspülmittel nt.

softening ['sɒfnɪŋ] n **(a)** see vt Weichmachen nt; Enthärten nt; Dämpfen nt; Mildern nt; Weicherwachen nt; Schwächung f; Verweichlichung f.
(b) see vi Erweichen nt; Nachlassen nt; Weicherwerden nt. ~ **of the brain** (Med) Gehirnerweichung f; **there has been a** ~ **of his attitude** er ist nachgiebiger geworden.

soft: ~-**footed** adj tiger, person auf leisen Sohlen schleichend attr; tread leise, lautlos; **to be** ~-**footed** leise gehen; ~ **fruit** n Beerenobst nt; ~ **furnishings** npl (Brit) Vorhänge, Teppiche, Kissen etc; ~-**headed** adj (inf) doof (inf); ~-**hearted** adj weichherzig; ~-**heartedness** n Weichherzigkeit f.

softie ['sɒftɪ] n (inf) (too tender-hearted) gutmütiger Trottel (inf); (sentimental) sentimentaler Typ (inf); (effeminate, cowardly) Schlappschwanz (inf), Weichling (inf) m.

softly ['sɒftlɪ] adv **(a)** (gently, tenderly) sanft; (not loud) leise; rain, blow leicht, sacht. **her hair falls** ~ **round her shoulders** ihr Haar fällt weich auf die Schultern; **a** ~ **blowing breeze** ein sanfter or schwacher Wind. **(b)** (leniently) nachsichtig.

softness ['sɒftnɪs] n see adj **(a)** Weichheit f; Zartheit f; Schlaffheit f.
(b) Zartheit f; Glätte f; Weichheit f; Seidigkeit f.
(c) Sanftheit f; Gedämpftheit f; leiser Klang; Leichtheit f; Weichheit f.
(d) Weichheit f.
(e) Schwäche f; Nachsichtigkeit f; Nachsichtigkeit f, Gutmütigkeit f; Milde f.
(f) Verweichlichung f.
(g) Bequemlichkeit f.
(h) Weichheit f.

soft: ~ **palate** n weicher Gaumen; ~-**pedal 1** vt (Mus) note, passage mit Dämpfer spielen; (fig inf) demands etc herunterschrauben; **2** vi zurückstecken; ~ **sell** n Softsell m, weiche Verkaufstaktik; **he's a master of the** ~ **sell** er kann die Leute auf sanfte Art or auf die sanfte Tour (inf) überreden; ~-**shelled** adj weichschalig; ~-**soap** (fig) **1** n Schmeichelei f; **2** vt einseifen (inf), um den Bart gehen (+dat); **they** ~-**soaped him into doing it** sie sind ihm so lange um den Bart gegangen, bis er es getan hat (inf); ~-**spoken** adj person leise sprechend attr; **to be** ~-**spoken** leise sprechen; ~ **toy** n Stofftier nt; ~ **verges** npl nicht befahrbare Bankette; (on sign) Seitenstreifen nicht befahrbar; ~**ware** n Software f; ~ **wood** n Weichholz nt.

softy n (inf) see **softie**.

SOGAT ['səʊgæt] abbr of **Society of Graphical and Allied Trades.**

sogginess ['sɒgɪnɪs] n see adj triefende Nässe; Aufgeweichtheit f; Matschigkeit f (inf); Klitschigkeit f.

soggy ['sɒgɪ] adj (+er) durchnäßt, triefnaß; soil durchweicht; food matschig (inf); cake, bread klitschig, matschig (inf).

soi-disant [ˌswaːˈdiːzɑ̃] adj sogenannt, angeblich.

soigné [ˈswaːnjeɪ] adj gepflegt, soigniert (geh).

soil¹ [sɔɪl] n (earth, ground) Erde f, Erdreich nt, Boden m. **cover it with** ~ bedecken Sie es mit Erde; native/foreign/British ~ heimatlicher/fremder/britischer Boden, heimatliche/fremde britische Erde; **the** ~ (fig: farmland) die Scholle; **a man of the** ~ ein mit der Scholle verwachsener Mensch.

soil² **1** vt (lit) beschmutzen, schmutzig machen; (fig) reputation beschmutzen, beflecken; honour beflecken; oneself besudeln; minds verderben. **the baby has** ~ed **its nappy** der Säugling hat eine schmutzige Windel or hat in die Windel gemacht.
2 vi schmutzig werden, verschmutzen.

soiled [sɔɪld] adj schmutzig, verschmutzt; sanitary towel gebraucht. ~ **linen** Schmutzwäsche f.

soil-pipe ['sɔɪlpaɪp] n Abflußrohr nt.

soirée [ˈswaːreɪ] n (form) Soirée f (geh).

soixante-neuf [ˈswæsɑ̃ːntˈnɜːf] n Neunundsechzig, Soixanteneuf no art.

sojourn ['sɒdʒɜːn] **1** n (liter) Aufenthalt m; (place) Aufenthaltsort m. **2** vi (ver)weilen (liter) (in in +dat).

solace ['sɒlɪs] **1** n Trost m. **2** vt trösten.

solar ['səʊləʳ] adj Sonnen-, Solar-. ~ **battery** Sonnen- or Solarbatterie f; ~ **cell** Solarzelle f; ~ **constant** Solarkonstante f; ~ **eclipse** Sonnenfinsternis f; ~ **energy** Sonnenenergie f; ~ **heat** Sonnenwärme f; ~ **panel** Sonnenkollektor m; ~ **plexus** Solarplexus m (spec), Magengrube f; ~ **system** Sonnensystem nt.

solarium [səʊˈlɛərɪəm] n, pl **solaria** [səʊˈlɛərɪə] Solarium nt.

sold [səʊld] pret, ptp of **sell**.

solder ['səʊldəʳ] **1** n Lötmittel, Lötzinn nt. **2** vt löten; (~ together) verlöten. ~ed **joint** Lötstelle f.

soldering-iron ['səʊldərɪŋˌaɪən] n Lötkolben m.

soldier ['səʊldʒəʳ] **1** n **(a)** Soldat m. ~ **of fortune** Söldner m; **to play (at)** ~s Soldaten or Krieg spielen; old ~ altgedienter Soldat; (fig) alter Kämpe; old ~s never die(,they only fade away) (prov) manche Leute sind nicht totzukriegen (inf).
(b) (Zool) Soldat m.
2 vi Soldat sein, (in der Armee) dienen. **after 6 years'** ~ing nach 6 Jahren Dienst in der Armee; **tired of** ~ing des Soldatenlebens müde.

♦ **soldier on** vi unermüdlich weitermachen. **two of them** ~ed ~ **to the top** zwei kämpften sich bis zum Gipfel vor.

soldierly ['səʊldʒəlɪ] adj soldatisch.

soldiery ['səʊldʒərɪ] n Soldaten pl, Soldateska f (pej geh).

sole¹ [səʊl] **1** n Sohle f. **2** vt besohlen.

sole² n (fish) Seezunge f.

sole³ adj einzig; heir also, agency Allein-; rights alleinig.

solecism ['sɒlɪsɪzəm] n (linguistic) Solözismus (geh), Fehler m; (in behaviour etc) Fauxpas m.

-soled [-səʊld] adj suf mit ... Sohlen.

solely ['səʊllɪ] adv (einzig und) allein, nur. **he is** ~ **responsible** er allein trägt die Verantwortung, er ist alleinverantwortlich; ~ **because of this** ... nur or allein deswegen ...

solemn ['sɒləm] adj feierlich; face, mood, music also, person, plea, warning ernst; prose also, architecture ehrwürdig, erhaben; promise, duty, oath heilig; (drab) colour trist. **I give you my** ~ **assurance** ich verspreche es hoch und heilig.

solemnity [səˈlemnɪtɪ] n see adj Feierlichkeit f; Ernst m; Ehrwürdigkeit f, Erhabenheit f; heiliger Ernst; Tristheit f. **with all** ~ feierlich (und würdig).

solemnization [ˌsɒləmnaɪˈzeɪʃən] n feierlicher Vollzug.

solemnize ['sɒləmnaɪz] vt feierlich begehen; marriage (feierlich) vollziehen.

solemnly ['sɒləmlɪ] adv feierlich; walk gemessenen Schrittes, würdevoll; look, warn, plead ernst; promise hoch und heilig; swear bei allem, was einem heilig ist.

solenoid ['səʊlənɔɪd] n Magnetspule f. ~ **switch** Magnetschalter m.

solfa ['sɒl'fɑ:] n Solmisation f.

solicit [sə'lɪsɪt] **1** vt support etc erbitten, bitten um; person anflehen, inständig bitten; votes werben; (prostitute) ansprechen. **to ~ sb for sth, to ~ sth of sb** jdn um etw bitten, etw von jdm erbitten; **to ~ custom/trade** um Kunden werben.
2 vi (prostitute) Kunden anwerben, zur Unzucht auffordern (form). **~ing** Aufforderung f zur Unzucht.

solicitation [sə,lɪsɪ'teɪʃən] n (form) Flehen nt no pl (geh).

solicitor [sə'lɪsɪtər] n (Jur) (Brit) Rechtsanwalt m/-anwältin f (der/die nicht vor Gericht plädiert); (US) Justizbeamte(r) m/-beamtin f. **S~ General** (Brit) zweiter Kronanwalt; (US) ≈ Generalstaatsanwalt m.

solicitous [sə'lɪsɪtəs] adj (form) (concerned) besorgt (about um); (eager) dienstbeflissen. **to be ~ to do sth** eifrig darauf bedacht sein, etw zu tun.

solicitude [sə'lɪsɪtjuːd] n see adj (form) Besorgtheit f; Dienstbeflissenheit f.

solid ['sɒlɪd] **1** adj (a) (firm, not liquid) fuel, food, substance fest. **~ body** Festkörper m; **to be frozen ~** hartgefroren sein; **to be stuck ~** festsitzen; **when the glue is ~** wenn der Klebstoff fest (geworden) ist; **the soup/pudding is rather ~** die Suppe ist ziemlich dick/der Nachtisch ist ziemlich schwer; **~ figure** (Geometry) Körper m; **~ geometry** Raumlehre f.
(b) (pure, not hollow, not broken) block, gold, oak, rock massiv; matter fest; crowd etc dicht; stretch, row, line ununterbrochen; queue, line of people etc geschlossen; week ganz. **~ ball/tyre** Vollgummiball m/-reifen m; **the square was packed ~ with cars** die Autos standen dicht an dicht auf dem Platz; **the garden was a ~ mass of colour** der Garten war ein einziges Farbenmeer; **it will take a ~ week's work** dazu braucht man eine volle or ganze Arbeitswoche; **they worked for two ~ days** or **for two days ~** sie haben zwei Tage ununterbrochen gearbeitet, sie haben zwei volle Tage gearbeitet; **he was 6 ft of ~ muscle** er war 2 Meter groß und bestand nur aus Muskeln; **a man of ~ build** ein kräftig or massiv gebauter Mann.
(c) (stable, secure) bridge, house, car stabil; furniture also, piece of work, character solide; foundations also, (lit, fig) ground fest; business, firm gesund, solide, reell. **he's a good ~ worker** er ist ein solider or guter Arbeiter; **he's a good ~ bloke** er ist ein verläßlicher Kerl.
(d) reason, argument handfest, stichhaltig; grounds gut, fundiert. **it makes ~ good sense** das leuchtet durchaus ein; **~ common sense** gesunder Menschenverstand.
(e) (unanimous) vote einstimmig; support voll, geschlossen. **to be ~ on sth** (accept/reject) etw einstimmig or geschlossen annehmen/ablehnen; **we are ~ behind you/that proposal** wir stehen voll und ganz hinter Ihnen/diesem Vorschlag; **we are ~ for peace** wir sind hundertprozentig für den Frieden; **Newtown/he is ~ for Labour** Newtown wählt fast ausschließlich Labour/er ist überzeugter Labour-Anhänger.
(f) (valuable, substantial) education, knowledge, grounding solide; relationship stabil; meal kräftig, nahrhaft.
2 n **(a)** fester Stoff. **~s and liquids** feste und flüssige Stoffe pl; (Sci) Festkörper und Flüssigkeiten pl.
(b) (Geometry) Körper m.
(c) (usu pl: food) feste Nahrung no pl.

solidarity [,sɒlɪ'dærɪtɪ] n Solidarität f.

solid fuel n fester Brennstoff; (for rockets) Feststoff m.

solidification [sə,lɪdɪfɪ'keɪʃən] n see vi Festwerden nt, Verfestigung f; Erstarrung f; Erhärtung f; Gerinnung f; Festigung f.

solidify [sə'lɪdɪfaɪ] **1** vi fest werden; (planet, lava etc) erstarren; (metal also) hart werden; (blood) gerinnen; (fig: support) sich festigen. **2** vt see vi fest werden lassen; erstarren lassen; hart werden lassen; gerinnen lassen; festigen.

solidity [sə'lɪdɪtɪ] n see adj **(a)** Festigkeit f.
(b) Massivität f; Festigkeit f; Dichtheit f.
(c) Stabilität f; solide Art; Festigkeit f; Solidheit f.
(d) Handfestigkeit, Stichhaltigkeit f; Fundiertheit f.
(e) Einstimmigkeit f; Geschlossenheit f.
(f) Solidheit f; Stabilität f; Kräftigkeit f.

solidly ['sɒlɪdlɪ] adv **(a)** (firmly) stuck, secured fest. **~ built** house fest or solide gebaut; person kräftig or massiv gebaut.
(b) reasoned, argued stichhaltig.
(c) (uninterruptedly) work ununterbrochen.
(d) (unanimous) vote einstimmig; support geschlossen. **to be ~ behind sb** geschlossen hinter jdm stehen.

solid-state ['sɒlɪd'steɪt] adj Festkörper-; (Elec) Halbleiter-.

soliloquize [sə'lɪləkwaɪz] **1** vi monologisieren; (talk to oneself) Selbstgespräche führen. **2** vt zu sich selbst sagen.

soliloquy [sə'lɪləkwɪ] n Monolog m (also Theat), Zwiegespräch nt mit sich selbst.

solipsism ['sɒlɪpsɪzəm] n Solipsismus m.

solipsist ['sɒlɪpsɪst] n Solipsist(in f) m.

solipsistic [,sɒlɪp'sɪstɪk] adj solipsistisch.

solitaire [,sɒlɪ'teər] n (game) Solitär nt; (gem) Solitär m.

solitary ['sɒlɪtərɪ] **1** adj **(a)** (alone, secluded) life, person einsam; place also abgelegen, abgeschieden. **a few ~ houses** ein paar einzelne or vereinzelte Häuser; **to take a ~ walk** allein einen Spaziergang machen; **do you enjoy this ~ life?** gefällt Ihnen das Leben so allein?; **a ~ person** ein Einzelgänger m; **in ~ confinement** in Einzelhaft.
(b) (sole) case, example einzig. **not a ~ one** kein einziger.
2 n (~ confinement) Einzelhaft f.

solitude ['sɒlɪtjuːd] n Einsamkeit f; (of place also) Abgelegenheit, Abgeschiedenheit f.

solo ['səʊləʊ] **1** n Solo nt. **2** adj flight Allein-; violinist, violin Solo-. **3** adv solo. **to fly ~** einen Alleinflug machen.

soloist ['səʊləʊɪst] n Solist(in f) m.

Solomon ['sɒləmən] n Salomo(n) m. **the ~ Islands** die Salomonen pl.

solstice ['sɒlstɪs] n Sonnenwende f, Solstitium nt (spec).

solubility [,sɒljʊ'bɪlɪtɪ] n see adj **(a)** Löslichkeit f. **(b)** Lösbarkeit f.

soluble ['sɒljʊbl] adj **(a)** löslich, auflösbar. **~ in water** wasserlöslich. **(b)** problem lösbar.

solution [sə'luːʃən] n **(a)** Lösung f (to gen); (of crime) Aufklärung f. **a problem incapable of ~** ein unlösbares Problem. **(b)** (Chem) (liquid) Lösung f; (act) Auflösen nt.

solvable ['sɒlvəbl] adj see soluble.

solve [sɒlv] vt problem, equation lösen; mystery enträtseln; crime, murder aufklären. **that question remains to be ~d** diese Frage muß noch geklärt werden.

solvency ['sɒlvənsɪ] n (Fin) Zahlungsfähigkeit, Solvenz f.

solvent ['sɒlvənt] **1** adj **(a)** (Chem) lösend; agent Lösungs-. **(b)** (Fin) zahlungsfähig, solvent. **2** n (Chem) Lösungsmittel nt.

Somali [səʊ'mɑːlɪ] **1** adj somali. **2** n Somali mf, Somalier(in f) m.

Somalia [səʊ'mɑːlɪə] n Somalia nt.

Somaliland [səʊ'mɑːlɪlænd] n Somaliland nt.

somatic [səʊ'mætɪk] adj somatisch.

sombre, (US) **somber** ['sɒmbər] adj **(a)** (dark) dunkel; (gloomy) düster. **(b)** mood, prospect trüb, düster; face düster; person düster, finster; music trist, trauervoll.

sombrely, (US) **somberly** ['sɒmbəlɪ] adv see adj.

sombreness, (US) **somberness** ['sɒmbənɪs] n see adj **(a)** Dunkelheit f; Düsterkeit f. **(b)** Trübheit, Düsterkeit f; Düsterkeit f; finsteres or düsteres Wesen; trauervoller or trister Klang.

sombrero [sɒm'breərəʊ] n Sombrero m.

some [sʌm] **1** adj **(a)** (with plural nouns) einige; (a few, emphatic) ein paar; (any: in "if" clauses, questions) meist nicht übersetzt. **if you have ~ questions** wenn Sie Fragen haben; **did you bring ~ records?** hast du Schallplatten mitgebracht?; **~ records of mine** einige meiner Platten; **would you like ~ more biscuits?** möchten Sie noch (ein paar) Kekse?; **take ~ nuts** nehmen Sie sich (dat) doch (ein paar) Nüsse; **~ few people** einige wenige Leute; **~ suggestions, please!** Vorschläge bitte!
(b) (with singular nouns) etwas, meist nicht übersetzt; (a little, emph) etwas, ein bißchen. **there's ~ ink on your shirt** Sie haben Tinte auf dem Hemd; **would you like ~ cheese?** möchten Sie (etwas) Käse?; **~ more (tea)?** noch etwas (Tee)?; **leave ~ cake for me** laß mir ein bißchen or etwas Kuchen übrig; **did they give you ~ money/sugar?** hat sie Ihnen Geld/Zucker gegeben?; **have you got ~ money?** haben Sie Geld?; **well yes, it was ~ help** es war eine gewisse Hilfe; **we played ~ golf** wir haben ein bißchen Golf gespielt.
(c) (certain, in contrast) manche(r, s). **~ people say ...** manche Leute sagen ...; **~ people just don't care** es gibt Leute, denen ist das einfach egal; **there are ~ things you just don't say** es gibt (gewisse or manche) Dinge, die man einfach nicht sagt; **~ questions were really difficult** manche (der) Fragen waren wirklich schwierig; **~ work can be rewarding** manche Arbeit ist sehr lohnend; **~ butter is salty** manche Buttersorten sind salzig; **in ~ ways** in gewisser Weise; **to ~ extent** in gewissem Maße.
(d) (vague, indeterminate) irgendein. **~ book/man or other** irgendein Buch/Mann; **~ woman rang up** da hat eine Frau angerufen; **~ woman, whose name I forget ...** eine Frau, ich habe ihren Namen vergessen, ...; **~ idiot of a driver** irgend so ein Idiot von (einem) Autofahrer; **at ~ place in Africa** irgendwo in Afrika; **in ~ way or another** irgendwie; or **~ such** oder so etwas ähnliches; or **~ such name** oder so ein ähnlicher Name; **(at) ~ time before midnight/last week** irgendwann vor Mitternacht/letzte Woche; **~ time or other** irgendwann einmal; **~ other time** ein andermal; **~ day** eines Tages; **~ day next week** irgendwann nächste Woche.
(e) (intensifier) ziemlich; (in exclamations) vielleicht ein (inf). **it took ~ courage** dazu brauchte man schon (einigen) or ziemlichen Mut; **(that was) ~ argument/party!** das war vielleicht ein Streit/eine Party! (inf); **that's ~ whisky** das ist vielleicht ein Whisky! (inf); **it's ~ size!** das ist vielleicht ein Ding!; **this might take ~ time** das könnte einige Zeit dauern; **quite ~ time** ganz schön lange (inf), ziemlich lange; **to speak at ~ length** ziemlich lange sprechen; **it's ~ distance from the house** es ist ziemlich weit vom Haus entfernt.
(f) (iro) vielleicht ein (inf). **~ experts!** das sind vielleicht Experten! (inf); **~ help** you are/this is du bist/das ist mir vielleicht eine Hilfe (inf); **~ people!** Leute gibt's!
2 pron **(a)** (~ people) einige; (certain people) manche; (in "if" clauses, questions) welche. **~ ..., others ...** manche ..., andere ...; **~ of my friends** einige or manche meiner Freunde; **there are still ~ who will never understand** es gibt immer noch Leute or welche, die das nicht begreifen werden; **~ of them were late** einige kamen zu spät.
(b) (referring to plural nouns) (a few) einige; (certain ones) manche; (in "if" clauses, questions) welche. **~ of these books** einige dieser Bücher; **~ of them have been sold** einige sind verkauft worden; **I've only seen ~ of the mountains** ich habe nur ein paar Berge gesehen; **they're lovely, try ~** die schmecken gut, probieren Sie mal; **I've still got ~** ich habe noch welche; **he took ~** er hat welche genommen; **tell me if you see ~** sagen Sie mir Bescheid, wenn Sie welche sehen; **would you like ~?** möchten Sie welche?
(c) (referring to singular nouns) (a little) etwas; (a certain amount, in contrast) manches; (in "if" clauses, questions) welche(r, s). **here is the milk, if you feel thirsty drink ~** hier ist die Milch, wenn du Durst hast, trinke etwas; **I drank ~ of the milk** ich habe (etwas) von der Milch getrunken; **I drank ~ of the milk but not all** ich habe etwas von der Milch getrunken, aber nicht alles; **have ~!** nehmen Sie sich (dat), bedienen Sie sich; **it's good cake, would you like ~?** das ist ein guter Kuchen, möchten Sie welchen?; **try ~ of this cake** probieren Sie doch mal diesen Kuchen; **would you like ~ money/tea?** — no, I've got

~ möchten Sie Geld/Tee? — nein, ich habe Geld/ich habe noch; **have you got money?** — no, but he has ~ haben Sie Geld? — nein, aber er hat welches; ~ of it had been eaten einiges (davon) war gegessen worden; he only **believed/read** ~ of it er hat es nur teilweise geglaubt/gelesen; ~ of his speech was excellent manches or einiges in seiner Rede war ausgezeichnet; ~ of his work is good manches, was er macht, ist gut.

(d) this is ~ of the oldest rock in the world dies gehört zum ältesten Gestein der Welt; ~ of the finest poetry in the English **language** einige der schönsten Gedichte in der englischen Sprache; this is ~ of the finest scenery in Scotland dies ist eine der schönsten Landschaft Schottlands.

3 adv **(a)** ungefähr, etwa, zirka. ~ **20 people** ungefähr 20 Leute; ~ **few difficulties** einige Schwierigkeiten.

(b) (US inf) (a little) etwas, ein bißchen; (a lot) viel. it sure **bothered us** das hat uns ziemlich zu schaffen gemacht; he's **travelling** ~ er fährt schnell; I really **drank** ~ last night ich habe gestern abend ganz schön was getrunken (inf); that's **going** ~ das ist ganz schön schnell (inf).

somebody ['sʌmbədɪ] **1** pron jemand; (dir obj) jemand(en); (indir obj) jemandem. ~ **else** jemand anders; ~ **or other** irgend jemand; ~ **knocked at the door** es klopfte jemand an die Tür; **we need** ~ **German** wir brauchen einen Deutschen; **everybody needs** ~ **to talk to** jeder braucht einen, mit dem er sprechen kann; ~ **or other irgend jemand; you must have seen** somebody Sie müssen doch irgend jemand(en) gesehen haben.

2 n to be ~ etwas vorstellen, wer (inf) or jemand sein; he **thinks he's** ~ now er bildet sich (dat) ein, er wäre jetzt jemand or wer (inf).

somehow ['sʌmhaʊ] adv irgendwie. it must be done ~ or other es muß irgendwie gemacht werden; ~ (or other) I never liked **him** irgendwie habe ich ihn nie gemocht or leiden können.

someone ['sʌmwʌn] pron see **somebody 1**.

someplace ['sʌmpleɪs] adv (US inf) be irgendwo; go irgendwohin.

somersault ['sʌməsɔ:lt] **1** n Purzelbaum m; (Sport, fig) Salto m; (fig also) Salto mortale m. **to do** or **turn a** ~ einen Purzelbaum schlagen/einen Salto/Salto mortale machen; (car) sich überschlagen, einen Salto machen (inf).

2 vi (person) einen Purzelbaum schlagen; (Sport) einen Salto machen; (car) sich überschlagen, einen Salto machen (inf). the **car** ~ed into a lamppost das Auto hat sich überschlagen und ist gegen einen Laternenpfahl geprallt.

something ['sʌmθɪŋ] **1** pron a etwas. ~ **nice/unpleasant/ serious** etc etwas Nettes/Unangenehmes/Ernstes; ~ **or other** irgend etwas, irgendwas; **did you say** ~? hast du (et)was **gesagt?**; ~ **of the kind** so etwas (Ähnliches); that's ~ I don't **know** das weiß ich nicht; there's ~ I don't like about him irgend etwas or irgendwas gefällt mir an ihm nicht; **let's see** ~ of you **soon** laß dich (doch) bald einmal sehen; **do you want to make** ~ **of it?** willst du dich mit mir anlegen? (inf); **there's** ~ **in what you say** an dem, was du sagst, ist (schon) was dran; **well, that's** ~ (das ist) immerhin etwas; **he's** ~ **to do with the Foreign Office** er ist irgendwie beim Außenministerium; **she's called Rachel** ~ sie heißt Rachel Soundso or Sowieso; **there were thirty** ~ es waren etwas über dreißig; **three hundred and** ~ dreihundert und ein paar (Zerquetschte inf); **we left at five** ~ wir sind etwas nach fünf gegangen.

(b) (inf: ~ special or unusual) it was ~ else (US) or quite ~ das war schon toll (inf); **it's** ~ **to be Prime Minister at 35** es will schon was heißen, mit 35 Premierminister zu sein; **what a beautiful dress! that's really** ~ so ein schönes Kleid! ganz große Klasse! (inf).

(c) or ~ (inf) oder so (was); **are you drunk** or ~? (inf) bist du betrunken oder was? (inf).

2 n **a little** ~ eine Kleinigkeit (als Geschenk); **a/the certain** ~ ein gewisses/das gewisse Etwas; **that certain** ~ **that makes all the difference** das gewisse Etwas, auf das es ankommt.

3 adv **(a)** ~ **over 200** etwas über 200, etwas mehr als 200; ~ **like 200** ungefähr 200, um die 200 herum; **you look** ~ **like him** du siehst ihm irgendwie ähnlich; **this is** ~ **like the one I wanted** so (et)was Ähnliches wollte ich haben; **now that's** ~ **like a rose!** das nenne ich eine Rose!; **another £500, now that's** ~ **like it** noch £ 500, und wir kommen der Sache schon näher.

(b) it's ~ of a problem das ist schon ein Problem; I feel ~ of a **stranger here** ich fühle mich hier irgendwie fremd; **he's** ~ of a **musician** er ist ein recht guter Musiker; ~ of a surprise/ **drunkard** eine ziemliche Überraschung/ein ziemlicher Säufer.

(c) (dial) it's ~ chronic das ist schon krankhaft (inf); the **weather was** ~ shocking das Wetter war einfach schrecklich.

sometime ['sʌmtaɪm] **1** adv irgendwann. ~ or other it will have **to be done** irgendwann muß es gemacht werden; **write to me** ~ **soon** schreib mir (doch) bald (ein)mal; ~ **before tomorrow** bis morgen, heute noch; ~ **next year** irgendwann nächstes or im nächsten Jahr. **2** adj attr (form) ehemalig, früher, einstig.

sometimes ['sʌmtaɪmz] adv manchmal.

someway ['sʌmweɪ] adv (US) irgendwie.

somewhat ['sʌmwɒt] adv ein wenig. more than ~! mehr als das!, und ob! (inf); **we were more than** ~ disappointed wir waren mehr als enttäuscht; ~ of a surprise/ **disappointment/drunkard** eine ziemliche or arge Überraschung/eine arge Enttäuschung/ein arger Trinker.

somewhere ['sʌmweəʳ] adv ~ be irgendwo; go irgendwohin. ~ **else** irgendwo anders, anderswo; irgendwo andershin, anderswohin; **from** ~/~ **else** von irgendwo, irgendwoher/von irgendwo anders, anderswoher; **I left it** ~ or other ich habe es irgendwo liegen-/stehenlassen; **I left it in the garden** or ~ ich habe es im Garten oder irgendwo (anders) gelassen; **I know** ~ **where** ... ich weiß, wo ...

(b) (fig) the temperature was ~ about 40°C die Temperatur betrug ungefähr 40°C or war um die 40° (inf); ~ about £50 or

in the region of £50 um (die) £ 50 herum; **she is** ~ **in her fifties** sie muß in den Fünfzigern sein; ~ **between midnight and one o'clock** irgendwann zwischen Mitternacht und ein Uhr.

somnambulism [sɒm'næmbjʊlɪzəm] n Nacht- or Schlafwandeln nt, Mondsüchtigkeit f, Somnambulismus m (spec).

somnambulist [sɒm'næmbjʊlɪst] n Nacht- or Schlafwandler(in f) m, Mondsüchtige(r), Somnambule (spec) mf.

somnolence ['sɒmnələns] n Schläfrigkeit f. the heavy ~ of this **summer's day** die bleierne Schwere dieses Sommertages.

somnolent ['sɒmnələnt] adj **(a)** (sleepy) schläfrig. **(b)** (causing sleep) einschläfernd.

son [sʌn] n (lit, fig) Sohn m; (as address) mein Junge. **S~ of God/Man** Gottes-/Menschensohn m; **the ~s of men** (liter) die Menschen; **a** ~ **of the soil** ein mit der Erde verwachsener Mensch, ein Sohn der Scholle (liter); **he's ~ his father's** ~ er ist ganz der Vater; ~ **of a bitch** (esp US sl) Scheißkerl m (sl); (thing) Scheißding nt (sl); ~ **of a gun** (esp US sl) Schlawiner m (inf).

sonar ['səʊnɑːʳ] n Sonar(gerät), Echolot nt.

sonata [sə'nɑːtə] n Sonate f. **in ~ form** in Sonatenform.

son et lumière ['sɒneɪ'lu:mjeəʳ] n Son et Lumière nt.

song [sɒŋ] n **(a)** Lied nt; (modern ballad also) Chanson nt; (folk-also, blues-~) Song m. **give us a** ~! sing uns etwas vor!; one of **Brecht's** ~s ein Brechtsong m; **to burst into** ~ ein Lied anstimmen; ~-and-dance act Gesangs- und Tanznummer f; **S~ of S~s, S~ of Solomon** Lied der Lieder, Hohelied Salomos nt. **(b)** (singing, bird~) Gesang m. **(c)** (fig inf) **to make a** ~ **and dance about sth** eine Haupt- und Staatsaktion aus etw machen (inf); **to sell/buy sth for a** ~ etw für einen Apfel und ein Ei or ein Butterbrot verkaufen/kaufen.

song: ~**bird** n Singvogel m; ~**book** n Liederbuch nt; ~ **cycle** n Liederzyklus m; ~**less** adj bird nicht singend attr.

songster ['sɒŋstəʳ] n Sänger m.

songstress ['sɒŋstrɪs] n Sängerin f.

song: ~ **thrush** n Singdrossel f; ~**writer** n Texter(in f) und Komponist(in f) m; (of modern ballads) Liedermacher(in f) m.

sonic ['sɒnɪk] adj Schall-. ~ **barrier** Schallmauer f; ~ **boom** Schallknall, Düsenknall m, Knallschleppe f (Aviat sl); **was that a** ~ **boom?** hat da jemand die Schallmauer durchbrochen?; ~ **depth finder** Echolot nt.

son-in-law ['sʌnɪnlɔː] n, pl **sons-in-law** Schwiegersohn m.

sonnet ['sɒnɪt] n Sonett nt. ~ **form** Sonettform f.

sonny ['sʌnɪ] n (inf) kleiner Mann. ~ **Jim** (inf) mein Junge m.

sonority [sə'nɒrɪtɪ] n Klangfülle f.

sonorous ['sɒnərəs] adj volltönend, sonor (geh); language, **poem** klangvoll.

sonorously ['sɒnərəslɪ] adv volltönend, sonor (geh). the French **horns echoing** ~ in the background das volle Echo der Hörner im Hintergrund.

sonorousness ['sɒnərəsnɪs] n Klangfülle f.

sons-in-law pl of **son-in-law**.

soon [suːn] adv **(a)** (in a short time from now) bald; (early) früh; (quickly) schnell. it will ~ be Christmas bald ist Weihnachten; ~ **after his death** kurz nach seinem Tode; ~ **afterwards** kurz or bald danach; **how** ~ **can you be ready?** wann kannst du fertig sein?; **how** ~ **would you like it back?** wann or bis wann möchtest du es wiederhaben?; **how** ~ **is the next performance?** wann fängt die nächste Vorstellung an?; **we got there too** ~ wir' kamen zu früh an; **Friday is too** ~ Freitag ist zu früh; **all too** ~ viel zu schnell; **we were none too** ~ wir kamen gerade rechtzeitig; **as** ~ **as sobald; as** ~ **as possible** so schnell wie möglich; **when can I have it?** — **as** ~ **as you like** wann kann ich's kriegen? — wann du willst!

(b) I would as ~ not go (prefer not to) ich würde lieber nicht **gehen**; (don't mind) es ist mir egal, wenn ich nicht gehe; I would **as** ~ **you didn't tell him** es wäre mir lieber, wenn du es ihm nicht erzählen würdest.

sooner ['suːnəʳ] adv **(a)** (time) früher, eher. ~ **or later** früher oder später; **the** ~ **the better** je eher or früher, desto besser; **no** ~ **had we arrived than** ... wir waren gerade or kaum angekommen, da ...; **in 5 years** or **at his death, whichever is the** ~ in 5 Jahren bzw. bei seinem Tode, je nachdem, was früher eintrifft; **no** ~ **said than done** gesagt, getan.

(b) (preference) lieber. I would ~ not do it ich würde es lieber nicht tun; **which would you** ~? was möchtest du lieber?

soot [sʊt] n Ruß m. **black as** ~ rußschwarz.

sooth [suːθ] n: in ~ (obs, liter) wahrlich (obs).

soothe [suːð] **1** vt beruhigen; pain lindern, mildern. **2** vi beruhigen; (relieve pain) lindern. an ointment which ~s eine schmerzlindernde Salbe.

soothing ['suːðɪŋ] adj beruhigend, besänftigend; (pain-relieving) schmerzlindernd; massage wohltuend; bath entspannend.

soothingly ['suːðɪŋlɪ] adv see adj beruhigend, besänftigend; schmerzlindernd; wohltuend. she rubbed his bruised arm ~ sie rieb ihm am Arm, um den Schmerz zu lindern.

soothsayer ['suːθseɪəʳ] n (old) Wahrsager(in f) m.

soothsaying ['suːθseɪɪŋ] n (old) Wahrsagerei f.

sooty ['sʊtɪ] adj (+er) rußig, Ruß-. buildings covered with a ~ **deposit** mit einer Rußschicht bedeckte Gebäude; a dull ~ black ein trübes, rußfarbenes Schwarz.

sop [sɒp] n **(a)** (food) eingetunktes Brotstück. **(b)** (to pacify) Beschwichtigungsmittel nt. they're just **offering you that as a** ~ **to keep you quiet** die bieten euch das nur an, damit ihr ruhig bleibt: mit Speck fängt man Mäuse!; as **a** ~ **to his pride** als Trost (, um seinen Stolz nicht zu verletzen).

♦**sop up** vt sep gravy etc aufnehmen.

sophism ['sɒfɪzəm] n Sophismus m.

sophist ['sɒfɪst] n Sophist(in f) m.

sophistic(al) [sə'fɪstɪk(əl)] adj sophistisch.

sophisticate [sə'fɪstɪkɪt] n the ~s who haunt the fashionable restaurants die Schickeria, die sich in den richtigen Restaurants zeigt.

sophisticated [sə'fɪstɪkeɪtɪd] adj (a) (worldly, cultivated) kultiviert; manners, taste also verfeinert; cabaret act, audience also anspruchsvoll, niveauvoll; person, restaurant also, hairdo gepflegt, elegant; dress raffiniert, schick. she's a very ~ young lady considering she's only twelve für eine Zwölfjährige ist sie schon sehr weit; she thinks she looks more ~ with a cigarette-holder sie glaubt, mit einer Zigarettenspitze mehr darzustellen.
  (b) (complex, advanced) hochentwickelt; electronics, techniques also raffiniert; method also durchdacht; device also ausgeklügelt.
  (c) (subtle, refined) subtil; mind also differenziert; prose, style also anspruchsvoll; discussion von or auf hohem Niveau, anspruchsvoll; plan, plot ausgeklügelt, raffiniert; system, approach differenziert, komplex. the conversation was a bit too ~ for me mir war die Unterhaltung etwas zu hochgestochen.

sophistication [sə,fɪstɪ'keɪʃən] n see adj (a) Kultiviertheit f; Verfeinerung f; hohes Niveau; Gepflegtheit, Eleganz f; Raffiniertheit f, Schick m.
  (b) hoher Entwicklungsstand or -grad; Raffiniertheit f; Durchdachtheit f; Ausgeklügeltheit f.
  (c) Subtilität f; Differenziertheit f; hohe Ansprüche; hohes Niveau; Ausgeklügeltheit, Raffiniertheit f; Differenziertheit, Komplexheit f.

sophistry ['sɒfɪstrɪ] n Sophisterei f.
Sophocles ['sɒfəkliːz] n Sophokles m.
sophomore ['sɒfəmɔːʳ] n (US) Student(in f) m im 2. Jahr.
soporific [,sɒpə'rɪfɪk] 1 adj einschläfernd. 2 n (drug) Schlafmittel nt.
sopping ['sɒpɪŋ] adj (also ~ wet) durchnäßt, triefend; person klitschnaß.
soppy ['sɒpɪ] adj (inf) (sentimental) book, song schmalzig (inf); person sentimental; look schmachtend; (effeminate) weibisch. she dresses her little boy in really ~ clothes sie zieht ihren kleinen Jungen immer so püppchenhaft an.
soprano [sə'prɑːnəʊ] 1 n Sopran m; (person also) Sopranist(in f) m; (voice also) Sopranstimme f; (part) Sopran(partie f) m. 2 adj Sopran-. ~ saxophone Sopransaxophon nt. 3 adv im Sopran.
Sorb [sɔːb] n Sorbe m, Sorbin f.
sorbet ['sɔːbeɪ] n Fruchteis nt.
sorcerer ['sɔːsərəʳ] n Hexenmeister, Hexer m.
sorceress ['sɔːsərɛs] n Hexe f.
sorcery ['sɔːsərɪ] n Hexerei f.
sordid ['sɔːdɪd] adj eklig; place, room also verkommen, heruntergekommen; motive schmutzig, niedrig, gemein; conditions, life, story elend, erbärmlich; crime gemein. he considers it ~ to discuss money er hält es für unfein, über Geld zu sprechen.
sordidness ['sɔːdɪdnɪs] n see adj Ekligkeit f; Verkommenheit f; Schmutzigkeit, Niedrigkeit, Gemeinheit f; Elend nt, Erbärmlichkeit f; Gemeinheit f.
sore [sɔːʳ] 1 adj (+er) (a) (hurting) weh, schlimm (inf); (inflamed) wund, entzündet. to have a ~ throat Halsschmerzen haben; my eyes are ~ mir tun die Augen weh; my wrist feels ~ mein Handgelenk schmerzt (geh) or tut weh; I'm ~ all over mir tut alles weh; where are you ~? wo tut es (dir/Ihnen) weh?, was tut (dir/Ihnen) weh?; to be ~ at heart (liter) betrübt sein (geh); her heart was ~ (liter) ihr war weh ums Herz (liter).
  (b) (fig) a ~ point ein wunder Punkt; a ~ subject ein heikles Thema.
  (c) (inf: angry, upset) verärgert, sauer (inf) (about sth über etw acc), at sb über jdn). now don't get ~ at me werd doch nicht gleich sauer! (inf).
  (d) (great) to be in ~ need of sth etw unbedingt or dringend brauchen; in ~ distress (liter) in arger Not (liter).
  2 adv (obs: greatly) arg (old), gar sehr (obs). and when they saw the angel they were ~ afraid (Bibl) und als sie den Engel sahen, fürchteten sie sich sehr.
  3 n (Med) wunde Stelle; (caused by friction) wund(ge-scheuert)e Stelle. to open old ~s (fig) alte Wunden aufreißen.
sorehead ['sɔːhɛd] n (US sl) Brummbär m (inf).
sorely ['sɔːlɪ] adv tempted sehr, arg (S Ger, Aus, Sw); needed dringend; missed schmerzlich; (liter) afflicted, troubled, offended zutiefst; wounded schwer. he has been ~ tried seine Geduld wurde auf eine sehr harte Probe gestellt.
soreness ['sɔːnɪs] n (a) (ache) Schmerz m; (rawness) Wundsein nt. (b) (inf: anger) Verärgerung f (at über +acc).
sorghum ['sɔːgəm] n Sorghum m.
sororicide [sə'rɒrɪsaɪd] n Schwestermord m; (person) Schwestermörder(in f) m.
sorority [sə'rɒrɪtɪ] n (US Univ) Studentinnenvereinigung f.
sorrel ['sɒrəl] 1 n (a) (Bot) großer Sauerampfer; (wood-~) Sauerklee m. (b) (horse) Fuchs m. 2 adj horse rotbraun.
sorrow ['sɒrəʊ] 1 n (no pl: sadness) Traurigkeit f; (no pl: grief) Trauer f, Kummer m; (trouble, care) Sorge, Kümmernis f; (affliction, suffering) Leiden nt. more in ~ than in anger eher aus Betrübnis als aus Zorn; to my (great) ~ zu meinem größten Kummer; this was a great ~ to me das hat mir großen Kummer bereitet; a feeling of ~ ein Gefühl von Traurigkeit, ein wehes Gefühl (liter); the deep sense of ~ which pervades his writing die tiefe Trauer, die sein Werk durchzieht; teenage ~s Sorgen und Nöte pl der Teenager; to drown one's ~s seine Sorgen ertränken; the ~s of the war years/their race das Leid der Kriegsjahre/die Leiden ihres Volkes.
  2 vi sich grämen (geh) (at, for, over über +acc).
sorrowful adj, **~ly** adv ['sɒrəʊfʊl, -fəlɪ] traurig.
sorry ['sɒrɪ] adj (+er) (a) pred (sad) traurig. I was ~ to hear that es tat mir leid, das zu hören or hören zu müssen; we were ~ to hear about your mother's death es tat uns leid, daß deine

Mutter gestorben ist; he wasn't in the least bit ~ to hear the news das machte ihm überhaupt nichts aus, das kümmerte ihn überhaupt nicht; I can't say I'm ~ he lost es tut mir wirklich nicht leid, daß er verloren hat; I'm not ~ I did it es tut mir nicht leid, es getan zu haben; this work is no good, I'm ~ to say diese Arbeit taugt nichts, das muß ich leider sagen; to be or feel ~ for sb/oneself jdn/sich selbst bemitleiden; I feel ~ for the child das Kind tut mir leid; I feel ~ for him having to ... es tut mir leid, daß er ... muß; I'm only ~ I didn't do it sooner es tut mir nur leid, daß ich es nicht eher getan habe; don't feel ~ for me, I don't need your pity! du brauchst mich nicht zu bedauern, kein Mitleid, bitte!; you'll be ~ for this! das wird dir noch leid tun!
  (b) (in apologizing, repentant) ~! Entschuldigung!, Verzeihung!; I'm/he's ~ es tut mir/ihm leid; I'm so ~! entschuldige(n Sie) bitte!; (iro) tut mir leid!; can you lend me £5? — ~ kannst du mir £ 5 leihen? — bedaure, leider nicht; ~? (pardon) wie bitte?; to say ~ (to sb for sth) sich (bei jdm für etw) entschuldigen; I'm ~ to hurt you es tut mir leid, daß ich dir weh tun muß; I'm ~ but ... (es) tut mir leid, aber ...; I'm ~ about that vase/your dog es tut mir leid um die Vase/um Ihren Hund; I'm ~ about Thursday, but I can't make it es tut mir leid mit Donnerstag, aber ich kann nicht; I'm ~ about (what happened on) Thursday es tut mir leid wegen Donnerstag.
  (c) (pitiful) condition, plight traurig; sight, figure also jämmerlich; excuse faul. it was a ~ tale of defeat es war eine traurige Niederlage.
sort [sɔːt] 1 n (a) (kind) Art f; (species, type, model also) Sorte f. a ~ of eine Art (+nom), so ein/so eine, so 'n/so 'ne (inf); this ~ of house diese Art Haus, so ein Haus; an odd ~ of novel ein komischer Roman; I felt a ~ of shame ich schämte mich irgendwie; the Mambo is a ~ of dance der Mambo ist eine Art Tanz; a ~ of silly smile so ein or so 'n (inf) albernes Grinsen; I have a ~ of idea that ... ich habe das or so ein Gefühl, daß ...; what ~ of was für ein; what ~ of man is he? was für ein Mensch ist er?; he's not the ~ of man to do that er ist nicht der Mensch, der das täte; this ~ of thing so etwas; all ~s of things alles mögliche; people of all ~s alle möglichen Leute; he's a painter of a ~ or of ~s das ist ein Maler, sozusagen; it's coffee of a ~ or of ~s das ist Kaffee oder so etwas ähnliches; perfect of its ~ vollkommen in seiner Art; something of the ~ (irgend) so (et)was; he's some ~ of administrator er hat irgendwie in der Verwaltung zu tun; he's got some ~ of job with ... er hat irgendeinen Job bei ...; nothing of the ~! von wegen!; you'll do nothing of the ~! von wegen!, das wirst du schön bleiben lassen!; that's the ~ of person I am ich bin nun mal so!; I'm not that ~ of girl ich bin nicht so eine.
  (b) (person) he's a good ~ er ist ein prima Kerl; she sounds a good ~ sie scheint in Ordnung zu sein; he's not my ~ er ist nicht mein Typ; I don't trust his ~ solchen Leuten traue ich nicht; I know your ~ euch Brüder kenn' ich! (inf); your ~ never did any good du und deinesgleichen, ihr habt noch nie etwas zustande gebracht; it takes all ~s (to make a world) es gibt so 'ne und solche.
  (c) to be out of ~s nicht ganz auf der Höhe or dem Posten (inf) or dem Damm (inf) sein.
  2 adv ~ of (inf) irgendwie; it's ~ of heavy es ist irgendwie schwer (inf); is it tiring? — ~ of ist das anstrengend? — irgendwie schon; it's ~ of finished es ist so ziemlich or eigentlich schon fertig; aren't you pleased? — ~ of freust du dich nicht? — doch, eigentlich schon; is this how he did it? — well, ~ of hat er das so gemacht? — ja, so ungefähr.
  3 vt sortieren. to ~ the ripe tomatoes from the unripe ones die reifen und die unreifen Tomaten aussortieren.
  4 vi (a) to ~ through sth etw durchsehen.
  (b) to ~ well/ill with passen zu/nicht passen zu.
♦**sort out** vt sep (a) (arrange) sortieren, ordnen; (select) aussortieren, aussuchen. to ~ sth ~ from sth etw von etw trennen; to ~ red apples ~ from green ones rote und grüne Äpfel aussortieren.
  (b) (straighten out) muddle in Ordnung bringen; problem lösen; situation klären. the problem will ~ itself ~ das Problem wird sich von selbst lösen or erledigen; to ~ oneself ~ zur Ruhe kommen, sich (dat) über sich (acc) selbst klar werden; you must come and visit us in the new house once we've ~ed ourselves ~ or once we're ~ed ~ wenn wir uns in dem neuen Haus erst mal richtig eingerichtet haben, mußt du uns unbedingt besuchen.
  (c) (inf) to ~ sb ~ sich (dat) jdn vorknöpfen (inf) or kaufen (sl).
sorta ['sɔːtə] adv (sl) = sort of; see sort 2.
sorter ['sɔːtəʳ] n (person) Sortierer(in f) m; (machine) Sortiermaschine f; (Post: person) Briefverteiler(in f) m.
sortie ['sɔːtɪ] n (Mil) Ausfall m; (Aviat) (Einzel)einsatz, Feindflug m. a ~ into town/literary criticism ein Ausflug or Abstecher m in die Stadt/Literaturkritik.
sorting office ['sɔːtɪŋ'ɒfɪs] n Sortierstelle f.
SOS n SOS nt.
so-so ['səʊ'səʊ] adj pred, adv (inf) soso, so la la.
sot [sɒt] n (pej) Säufer, Trunkenbold (dated) m.
sottish ['sɒtɪʃ] adj dem Trunk ergeben; grin benebelt.
sotto voce ['sɒtəʊ'vəʊtʃɪ] adv leise; (conspiratorial) mit unterdrückter Stimme; (Mus) sotto voce.
sou [suː] n (inf) I haven't a ~ ich habe keinen Pfennig.
sou' [saʊ] (Naut) abbr of south.
soubrette [suː'brɛt] n (dated) Soubrette f (dated).
soubriquet ['suːbrɪkeɪ] n see sobriquet.
Soudanese adj, n see Sudanese.
soufflé ['suːfleɪ] n Soufflé nt.
sough [saʊ] (liter) 1 n Rauschen nt. 2 vi (wind) rauschen.
sought [sɔːt] pret, ptp of seek.
sought-after ['sɔːtɑːftəʳ] adj begehrt. much ~ vielbegehrt; rare object gesucht.

soul [səʊl] n (a) Seele f. upon my ~! (dated), (God) bless my ~! meiner Treu (dated), na so was!; All S~s' Day Allerheiligen nt; God rest his ~! Gott hab ihn selig!; see body (a).

(b) (inner being) Innerste(s), Wesen nt. he may not be a brilliant intellect, but he has a great ~ er ist vielleicht kein großer Geist, aber er hat innere Werte; he loved her with all his ~ er liebte sie von ganzem Herzen or heiß und innig; he loved her with all his heart and with all his ~ er liebte sie mit jeder Faser seines Herzens; the priest urged them to search their ~s der Priester drängte sie, ihr Gewissen zu erforschen; a little humility is good for the ~ ein bißchen Bescheidenheit tut der Seele gut; she felt a stirring in her ~ sie war im Innersten or bis ins Innerste aufgewühlt; the ~ of the city has been destroyed by modernization durch die Modernisierung ist die Stadt in ihrem innersten Wesen zerstört worden; at least the old slum had ~ der alte Slum hatte wenigstens (noch) Herz; to have a ~ above sth über etw (acc) hoch erhaben sein; the music lacks ~ der Musik fehlt echter Ausdruck; freedom is the ~ of democracy Freiheit ist das Wesen der Demokratie.

(c) (finer feelings) Herz, Gefühl nt. complete lack of ~ vollkommene Gefühllosigkeit; a musician of considerable technical skill, but lacking ~ ein Musiker von beachtlichem technischem Können, aber ohne echtes Gefühl; you've got to have ~ (US sl) du mußt Feeling haben (sl); ~ brother/sister Bruder/Schwester; he's a ~ brother er ist einer von uns.

(d) (person) Seele f. 3,000 ~s 3.000 Seelen (geh); poor ~! (inf) Ärmste(r)!; how is she, the wee ~? wie geht's denn unsrer Kleinen?; he's a good ~ er ist ein guter Mensch; she's a simple ~ sie hat ein schlichtes Gemüt; not a ~ keine Menschenseele; every living ~ was indoors keine Menschenseele war auf der Straße; the ship was lost with all ~s das Schiff ging mit (der ganzen Besatzung und) allen Passagieren unter.

(e) he's the ~ of generosity/discretion er ist die Großzügigkeit/Diskretion in Person.

(f) (music) Soul m.

soul-destroying ['səʊldɪˌstrɔɪɪŋ] adj geisttötend; factory work etc nervtötend.

soulful ['səʊlfʊl] adj look seelenvoll; person gefühlvoll; song also inbrünstig.

soulfully ['səʊlfəlɪ] adv see adj.

soulless ['səʊllɪs] adj person seelenlos; work also eintönig.

soul: ~ mate n Seelenfreund m; ~ music n Soul m; ~-searching n Gewissensprüfung f; ~-stirring adj speech bewegend; music also aufwühlend.

sound[1] [saʊnd] 1 adj (+er) (a) (in good condition) person, animal, tree gesund; constitution, lungs also kräftig; condition also, building, chassis, appliance einwandfrei. to be as ~ as a bell kerngesund sein; to be ~ in wind and limb gesund und munter sein; to be of ~ mind (esp Jur) bei klarem Verstand sein, im Vollbesitz seiner geistigen Kräfte sein (Jur); the windows were broken, but the frames were ~ die Fensterscheiben waren zerbrochen, aber die Rahmen waren heil.

(b) (valid, good, dependable) solide; business also gesund; argument, analysis also vernünftig, fundiert; scholarship also gründlich; economy, currency also stabil; person, goal-keeper verläßlich; idea gesund, vernünftig; move vernünftig; advice wertvoll, vernünftig. he's ~ on financial policy er hat gründliche Kenntnisse in der Finanzpolitik; a ~ scholar ein ernstzunehmender Gelehrter; that's ~ sense das ist vernünftig.

(c) (thorough) gründlich, solide; beating gehörig; defeat vernichtend.

(d) (Jur) decision rechtmäßig; claim also berechtigt.

(e) (deep) sleep tief, fest. I'm a very ~ sleeper ich schlafe sehr tief or fest, ich habe einen gesunden Schlaf.

2 adv (+er) to be ~ asleep fest schlafen; I shall sleep the ~er for it ich werde nur um so besser schlafen.

sound[2] 1 n (a) (noise) Geräusch nt; (Ling) Laut m; (Phys) Schall m; (Mus, of instruments) Klang m; (verbal, TV, Rad, Film) Ton m. don't make a ~ still!; the speed of ~ die Schallgeschwindigkeit; within ~ of in Hörweite (+gen); to the ~(s) of the national anthem zu den Klängen der Nationalhymne; French has a soft ~ die französische Sprache hat einen weichen Klang; would you still recognize the ~ of Karin's voice? würdest du Karins Stimme immer noch erkennen?; not a ~ was to be heard man hörte keinen Ton; ~s/the ~ of laughter Gelächter nt; we heard the ~ of voices on the terrace wir hörten Stimmen auf der Terrasse; vowel ~ Vokallaut m; ~ and fury leerer Schall.

(b) (impression) I don't like the ~ of it das klingt gar nicht gut; from the ~ of it he had a hard time es hört sich so an or klingt, als sei es ihm schlecht gegangen; his remarks had a familiar ~ seine Bemerkungen klangen vertraut.

2 vt (a) (produce ~ from) ~ your horn hupen!; the trumpeter ~ed a high note der Trompeter spielte einen hohen Ton; to ~ the alarm Alarm schlagen; (mechanism) die Alarmanlage auslösen; to ~ the retreat zum Rückzug blasen; to ~ the "r" in "cover" das „r" in „cover" aussprechen; his speech ~ed a note of warning in seiner Rede klang eine Warnung an; I think we need to ~ a note of warning ich finde, wir sollten eine vorsichtige Warnung aussprechen.

(b) (test by tapping, Med) abklopfen.

3 vi (emit ~) erklingen, ertönen. feet ~ed in the corridor im Flur waren Schritte zu hören; a gun ~ed a long way off in der Ferne hörte man einen Schuß.

(b) (give aural impression) klingen, sich anhören. it ~s hollow es klingt hohl; the children ~ happy es hört sich so an, als ob die Kinder ganz lustig sind; he ~s angry es hört sich so an, als wäre er wütend; he ~ed depressed on the phone am Telefon klang er deprimiert; he ~s French (to me) er hört sich (für mich) wie ein Franzose an; it ~s like Spanish to me ich finde, das klingt wie Spanisch or hört sich wie Spanisch an.

(c) (seem) sich anhören. that ~s very odd das hört sich sehr seltsam an; he ~s like a nice man er scheint ein netter Mensch zu sein; it ~s like a sensible idea das klingt ganz vernünftig; how does it ~ to you? wie findest du das?

♦ **sound off** vi (inf) sich verbreiten or auslassen (about über +acc). don't listen to him, he's just ~ing ~ hör nicht auf ihn, er spielt sich nur auf!

sound[3] vt (Naut) loten, ausloten; (Met) messen. ~ing line Lot, Senkblei nt; ~ing balloon Versuchs- or Registrierballon m; to ~ sb (out) about or on sth jdn vorsichtig ausfragen, bei jdm auf den Busch klopfen (inf).

♦ **sound out** vt sep person aushorchen, ausfragen; intentions, opinions herausfinden, herausbekommen.

sound[4] n (Geog) Meerenge f, Sund m.

sound: ~ archives npl Tonarchiv nt; ~ barrier n Schallmauer f; ~-board n see sounding board (a); ~-box n (Mus) Schallkörper, Schallkasten m; ~ effects npl Toneffekte pl; ~ engineer n Toningenieur(in f) m; ~-hole n Schalloch nt.

sounding ['saʊndɪŋ] n (Naut) Loten nt, Peilung f. to take ~s (lit) Lotungen vornehmen; (fig) sondieren.

sounding-board ['saʊndɪŋbɔːd] n (a) (on instrument) Resonanzboden m; (over platform etc) Schalldeckel m. (b) (fig) Resonanzboden m. he used the committee as a ~ for his ideas er benutzte den Ausschuß, um die Wirkung seiner Vorschläge zu sondieren.

soundless ['saʊndlɪs] adj lautlos. her mouth opened in a ~ scream ihr Mund öffnete sich zu einem stummen Schrei.

soundlessly ['saʊndlɪslɪ] adv lautlos.

soundly ['saʊndlɪ] adv built, made solide; argue, reason, invest also vernünftig; thrash tüchtig, gehörig; train gründlich. our team was ~ beaten unsere Mannschaft wurde eindeutig or klar geschlagen; to sleep ~ tief und fest schlafen.

soundness ['saʊndnɪs] n (a) (good condition) gesunder Zustand; (of building, chassis, appliance) guter Zustand.

(b) (validity, dependability) Solidität f; (of argument, analysis also) Vernünftigkeit, Fundiertheit f; (of scholarship) Gründlichkeit f; (of economy, currency also) Stabilität f; (of idea, advice, move, policy) Vernünftigkeit f; (of person, goal-keeper) Verläßlichkeit f.

(c) (thoroughness) Gründlichkeit, Solidität f.

(d) (Jur: of decision, claim) Rechtmäßigkeit f.

(e) (of sleep) Tiefe f.

sound: ~-proof 1 adj schalldicht; 2 vt schalldicht machen, gegen Schall isolieren; ~-proofing n Schallisolierung f; ~ radio n Rundfunk, Hörfunk m; ~ recording n Tonaufnahme, Tonaufzeichnung f; ~ shift n Lautverschiebung f; ~-track n Tonspur f; (sound, recording) Ton m; Filmmusik f; ~-wave n Schallwelle f.

soup [suːp] n Suppe f. to be in the ~ (inf) in der Tinte or Patsche sitzen (inf).

♦ **soup up** vt sep (inf) car, engine (hoch)frisieren (inf).

soupçon ['suːpsɔ̃] n (of spice etc) Spur f; (of irony etc) Anflug m; (of melancholy also) Hauch m. sauce? — just a ~ Soße? — (ja bitte, nur) eine Idee!

soup: ~-kitchen n Volksküche f; (for disaster area etc) Feldküche f; ~-plate n Suppenteller m, tiefer Teller; ~ spoon n Suppenlöffel m; ~ tureen n Suppenterrine f.

sour ['saʊəʳ] 1 adj (+er) (a) fruit, soil sauer; wine, vinegar säuerlich. whisky ~ (esp US) Whisky mit Zitrone.

(b) (bad) milk sauer; smell also streng, säuerlich. to go or turn ~ (lit) sauer werden; to go or turn ~ (on sb) (fig) (relationship, marriage) jdn anöden; (plan, investment) sich als Fehlschlag erweisen.

(c) (fig) person verdrießlich, griesgrämig; expression also sauer; remark bissig. he's feeling ~ about being demoted er ist über seine Absetzung verbittert; it's just ~ grapes die Trauben sind sauer or hängen zu hoch; it sounds like ~ grapes to me das kennt man: der Fuchs und die sauren Trauben.

2 vt milk sauer or dick werden lassen; person verdrießlich or griesgrämig machen; soil sauer or kalkarm machen.

3 vi (milk) sauer or dick werden; (person) verbittern, griesgrämig werden; (soil) sauer or kalkarm werden. his character had ~ed er war verbittert.

source [sɔːs] n (of river, light information) Quelle f; (of troubles, problems etc) Ursache f, Ursprung m. a ~ of vitamin C ein Vitamin-C-Spender m; they tried to trace the ~ of the gas leak sie versuchten, das Leck in der Gasleitung ausfindig zu machen; he is a ~ of embarrassment to us er bringt uns ständig in Verlegenheit; ~ of supply Bezugsquelle f; to have its ~ in sth seine Ursache or seinen Ursprung in etw (dat) haben; I have it from a good ~ that ... ich habe es aus sicherer Quelle, daß ...; at ~ (Tax) unmittelbar, direkt; these rumours must be stopped at ~ diese Gerüchte darf man gar nicht erst aufkommen lassen; ~s (in book etc) Quellen, Literaturangaben pl; from reliable ~s aus zuverlässiger Quelle.

source: ~-book n Quellenwerk nt, Quellensammlung f; ~ language n Ausgangssprache f; ~ material n Quellenmaterial nt.

sourdough ['saʊədəʊ] n (esp US) Sauerteig m.

sour(ed) cream ['saʊə(d)'kriːm] n saure Sahne, Sauerrahm m.

sour-faced ['saʊəfeɪst] adj (inf) vergrätzt (inf).

sourly ['saʊəlɪ] adv (fig) verdrießlich, griesgrämig.

sourness ['saʊənɪs] n (of lemon, milk) saurer Geschmack; (of wine, vinegar also, of smell) Säuerlichkeit f; (of soil) saure Beschaffenheit; (fig) (of person, expression) Verdrießlichkeit, Griesgrämigkeit f; (of remark) Bissigkeit f.

sourpuss ['saʊəpʊs] n (inf) Miesepeter (inf), Sauertopf (old) m; (woman) miesepetrige Frau/miesepetriges Mädchen nt.

sousaphone ['suːzəfəʊn] n Sousaphon nt.

souse [saʊs] vt (a) (cover with water) naß machen; fire löschen. he ~d himself with water er übergoß sich mit Wasser.

(b) (pickle) fish einlegen, marinieren.

(c) to be/get ~d (sl) sternhagelvoll sein (inf)/sich vollaufen lassen (sl).

soutane [suːˈtæn] n (Eccl) Soutane f.

south [sauθ] 1 n Süden, Süd (liter, Met) m. **in the ~ of** im Süden +gen; **to the ~ of** im Süden or südlich von; **from the ~** aus dem Süden; (wind) aus Süden; **to veer to the ~** in südliche Richtung or nach Süden drehen; **the wind is in the ~** es ist Südwind; **the S~ of France** Südfrankreich nt.

  2 adj südlich, Süd-; (liter) Süd-.

  3 adv im Süden; (towards the ~) nach Süden, gen Süden (liter), südwärts (Liter, Naut); (Met) in südliche Richtung. **to be further ~** weiter im Süden or weiter südlich sein; **~ of** südlich von, im Süden von.

south in cpds Süd-; S~ Africa n Südafrika nt; S~ African 1 adj südafrikanisch; 2 n Südafrikaner(in f) m; S~ America n Südamerika nt; S~ American 1 adj südamerikanisch; 2 n Südamerikaner(in f) m; ~bound adj (in) Richtung Süden; ~-east 1 n Südosten, Südost (esp Naut) m; 2 adj südöstlich; (in names) Südost-; ~-east wind Südost(wind) m, Wind m aus Südost or südöstlicher Richtung; 3 adv nach Südosten; ~-east of südöstlich von; ~-easter, sou'-easter n (esp Naut) Südostwind, Südost m; ~-easterly 1 adj direction südöstlich; wind also aus (wind) Südostwind m; ~-eastern adj südöstlich, im Südosten; the ~-eastern States die Südoststaaten pl; ~-eastward(s) adv nach Südosten; (Met, Naut also) südostwärts.

southerly [ˈsʌðəlɪ] 1 adj südlich; course also nach Süden; wind aus Süden or südlicher Richtung. 2 adv nach Süden, südwärts (esp Naut). 3 n Südwind m.

southern [ˈsʌðən] adj südlich; (in names) Süd-; (Mediterranean) südländisch. **~ people** Südländer pl; **a ~ belle** eine Schönheit aus dem Süden; **S~ Cross** Kreuz des Südens nt; **~ lights** Südlicht nt; S~ Africa das südliche Afrika; S~ Europe Südeuropa nt; S~ Ireland (Süd)irland nt; S~ States (US) Südstaaten pl.

southerner [ˈsʌðənər] n Bewohner(in f) m des Südens; Südengländer(in f) m/-deutsche(r) mf etc; (from the Mediterranean) Südländer(in f) m; (US) Südstaatler(in f) m.

southernmost [ˈsʌðənməʊst] adj südlichste(r, s).

south: S~ Korea n Südkorea nt; S~ Korean 1 adj südkoreanisch; 2 n Südkoreaner(in f) m; ~paw n (Boxing) Linkshänder, Rechtsausleger m; S~ Pole n Südpol m; S~ Sea Islands npl Südseeinseln pl; ~-south-east 1 n Südsüdosten, Südsüdost (esp Naut) m; 2 adj Südsüdost-, südsüdöstlich; 3 adv nach Südsüdost(en); ~-south-west 1 n Südsüdwesten, Südsüdwest (esp Naut) m; 2 adj Südsüdwest-, südsüdwestlich; 3 adv nach Südsüdwest(en); ~-south-west of südsüdwestlich von; S~ Vietnam n Südvietnam nt; ~ward(s) 1 adj südlich; 2 adv nach Süden, südwärts; ~-west 1 n Südwesten, Südwest (esp Naut) m; 2 adj Südwest-, südwestlich; wind aus südwestlicher Richtung, Südwest-; 3 adv nach Südwest(en); ~-west of südwestlich von; ~-wester n (esp Naut) Südwest(wind) m; ~-westerly adj südwestlich, Südwest-; wind aus südwestlicher Richtung, Südwest-; ~-western adj südwestlich, Südwest-; ~-westward(s) adv nach Südwesten.

souvenir [ˌsuːvəˈnɪər] n Andenken, Souvenir nt (of an +acc).

sou'wester [sauˈwestər] n (a) (hat) Südwester m. (b) (Naut: wind) Südwest(wind) m.

sovereign [ˈsɒvrɪn] 1 n (monarch) Souverän m, Herrscher(in f) m; (Brit old: coin) 20-Shilling-Münze f.

  2 adj (a) (supreme) höchste(r, s), oberste(r, s); state, power souverän; contempt tiefste(r, s), äußerste(r, s). **the ~ power of the Pope** die Oberhoheit or Suprematie des Papstes; **our ~ Lord the King** (old) unser gnädiger Herr, der König.

  (b) ~ cure (lit, fig) Allheilmittel nt.

sovereignty [ˈsɒvrəntɪ] n Oberhoheit, Oberherrschaft f; (right of self-determination) Souveränität f. **the ~ of papal decrees** die unumschränkte Gültigkeit der päpstlichen Erlasse.

soviet [ˈsəʊvɪət] 1 n Sowjet m. **the S~s** (people) die Sowjets. 2 adj attr sowjetisch, Sowjet-. **~ power** Sowjetmacht f; **~ citizen** Sowjetbürger(in f) m.

sovietize [ˈsəʊvɪətaɪz] vt sowjetisieren.

sovietologist [ˌsəʊvɪəˈtɒlədʒɪst] n Sowjetologe m, Sowjetologin f.

Soviet: ~ Russia n Sowjetrußland nt; ~ Union n Sowjetunion f.

sow¹ [səʊ] pret ~ed, ptp ~n or ~ed vt (a) corn, plants säen; seed aussäen; (Mil) mine legen. **to ~ the garden with grass im Garten Gras (aus)säen**; **to ~ a field with seed** auf einem Feld säen; **this field has been ~n with barley** auf diesem Feld ist Gerste gesät; **to ~ mines in a strait** eine Meerenge verminen.

  (b) (fig) **to ~ (the seeds of) hatred/discord/rebellion** Haß/Zwietracht säen/Aufruhr stiften, die Saat des Hasses/Aufruhrs/der Zwietracht säen (liter); **to ~ the wind and reap the whirlwind** (Prov) wer Wind sät, wird Sturm ernten (Prov); **as you ~ so shall you reap** (Prov) was der Mensch säet, das wird er ernten (Prov); see seed.

sow² [saʊ] n (a) (pig) Sau f; (of wild boar) (Wild)sau f; (of badger) Dächsin f. (b) (Tech) (block of iron) Massel f; (channel) Masselgraben m.

sower [ˈsəʊər] n (person) Säer(in f), Sämann m; (machine) Sämaschine f. **a ~ of discord/rebellion** ein Mensch, der Zwietracht sät/Aufruhr stiftet.

sowing [ˈsəʊɪŋ] n (action) (Aus)säen nt, Aussaat f; (quantity sown) Saat f. **the ~ of a field** die Aussaat auf einem Feld.

sown [səʊn] ptp of sow¹.

sox [sɒks] npl (US Comm sl) = socks.

soya [ˈsɔɪə], (US) **soy** [sɔɪ] n Soja f. ~ bean Sojabohne f; ~ flour Sojamehl nt; ~ sauce Sojasoße f.

sozzled [ˈsɒzld] adj (Brit inf) **to be ~** angetütert sein (N Ger inf), einen sitzen haben (inf); **to get ~** beschwipst werden, sich (dat) einen antürken (N Ger inf).

spa [spɑː] n (town) (Heil- or Mineral)bad nt, (Bade)kurort m; (spring) (Heil- or Mineral)quelle f.

space [speɪs] 1 n (a) Raum m (also Phys); (outer ~ also) der Weltraum, das Weltall. **time and ~** Zeit und Raum; **to stare or gaze into ~** ins Leere starren; **to vanish into ~** sich in Luft or in nichts auflösen; see outer.

  (b) no pl (room) Platz, Raum m; (Typ) (between letters) Spatien pl; (between lines) Durchschuß m. **to take up a lot of ~** viel Platz wegnehmen or einnehmen; **to clear/leave some ~ for sb/sth** für jdn/etw Platz schaffen/lassen; **to buy/sell ~** (Press) Platz für Anzeigen kaufen/verkaufen; (TV) Sendezeit kaufen/verkaufen; **parking ~** Platz m zum Parken.

  (c) (gap, empty area) Platz m no art; (between objects, words, lines) Zwischenraum m; (Mus: on stave) Zwischenraum m; (parking ~) Lücke f. **to leave a ~ for sb/sth** für jdn Platz lassen/für etw Platz (frei)lassen; **leave a ~ for the name** laß Platz für den Namen; **there was a (blank) ~ at the end of the document** am Ende des Dokuments war Platz gelassen; **please answer in the ~ provided** bitte an der dafür vorgesehenen Stelle beantworten; **to leave an empty ~ in a room/sb's heart** eine Lücke in einem Zimmer/jds Herz hinterlassen; **indent the first line a few ~s** rücken Sie die erste Zeile ein paar Stellen ein; **the wide open ~s** das weite, offene Land.

  (d) (Typ: piece of metal) (between words) Spatienkeil m; (between lines) Reglette f.

  (e) (of time) Zeitraum m. **in a short ~ of time** in kurzer Zeit; **in the ~ of one hour/three generations** innerhalb einer Stunde/in drei Generationen; **there's a 5-year ~ between the two children** die Kinder sind 5 Jahre auseinander; **for a ~** eine Weile or Zeitlang.

  2 vt (also ~ out) in Abständen verteilen; chairs also in Abständen aufstellen; seedlings also in Abständen setzen; visits verteilen; words Zwischenraum or Abstand lassen zwischen (+dat); (Typ) spatiieren (spec). **~ them out more, ~ them further out or further apart** lassen Sie etwas mehr Zwischenraum or Abstand (dazwischen); **houses ~d (out) along the road** Häuser, die sich entlang der Straße verteilen; **well ~d-out houses** genügend weit auseinander gebaute Häuser; **to ~ payments nach und nach zahlen; **to ~ the family/children (out)** in vernünftigen (Zeit)abständen Kinder bekommen; **their children are well ~d out** ihr Kinder sind genügend weit auseinander; see spaced-out.

space in cpds (Welt)raum-; ~ age n (Welt)raumzeitalter nt; ~-age adj attr des Raumzeitalters; ~-bar n (Typ) Leertaste f; ~ capsule n (Welt)raumkapsel f; ~craft n Raumfahrzeug nt; (unmanned) Raumkörper m.

spaced-out [ˈspeɪstˈaʊt] adj (sl) high (sl); (on drugs also) auf Trip (sl).

space: ~ fiction n Zukunftsromane pl über den Weltraum; ~ flight n Weltraumflug m; ~ heater n (esp US) Heizgerät nt; ~ helmet n Astronautenhelm m; ~ lab(oratory) n Weltraumlabor nt; ~man n (Welt)raumfahrer m; ~ platform n Raumstation f; ~port n Raumflugzentrum nt; ~ probe n Raumsonde f; ~ programme n Raumfahrtprogramm nt.

spacer [ˈspeɪsər] n see space-bar.

space: ~ rocket n Weltraumrakete f; ~-saving adj equipment, gadget platzsparend; furniture also raumsparend; a ~-saving kitchen eine Küche, in der Platz voll ausgenutzt wird; ~-seller n (Press) Anzeigenakquisiteur(in f) m; (TV) Werbungspromoter(in f) m; ~-ship n Raumschiff nt; ~ shot n (launching) Abschuß m eines Raumfahrzeugs/-körpers; (flight) Raumflug m; ~ shuttle n Raumfähre f, Raumtransporter m; ~ sickness n Weltraumkrankheit f; ~ station n (Welt)raumstation f; ~ suit n Raumanzug m; ~-time (continuum) n Raum-Zeit-Kontinuum nt; ~ travel n die Raumfahrt; ~ vehicle n Raumfahrzeug nt; ~ walk 1 n Weltraumspaziergang m; 2 vi im Weltraum spazierengehen; ~woman n (Welt)raumfahrerin f; ~ writer n (Press) Korrespondent(in), der/die nach der Länge seiner/ihrer Artikel bezahlt wird.

spacing [ˈspeɪsɪŋ] n Abstände pl; (between two objects) Abstand m; (also ~ out) Verteilung f; (of payments) Verteilung f über längere Zeit. **single/double ~** (Typ) einzeiliger/zweizeiliger Abstand.

spacious [ˈspeɪʃəs] adj geräumig; garden, park weitläufig.

spaciousness [ˈspeɪʃəsnɪs] n see adj Geräumigkeit f; Weitläufigkeit f.

spade [speɪd] n (a) (tool) Spaten m; (children's ~) Schaufel f. **to call a ~ a ~** (prov) das Kind beim Namen nennen (prov). (b) (Cards) Pik nt. **the Queen/two of ~s** die Pik-Dame/Pik-Zwei; **to play in ~s** Pik spielen; **~s are trumps** Pik ist Trumpf. (c) (pej sl) Nigger m (pej sl).

spadeful [ˈspeɪdfʊl] n **a ~ of earth** ein Spaten m or eine Schaufel (voll) Erde; **by the ~** spaten- or schaufelweise.

spadework [ˈspeɪdwɜːk] n Vorarbeit f.

spaghetti [spəˈgetɪ] n Spaghetti pl. **~ western** (inf) Italowestern m.

Spain [speɪn] n Spanien nt.

spake [speɪk] (obs) pret of speak.

spam ® [spæm] n Frühstücksfleisch nt.

span¹ [spæn] 1 n (a) (of hand) Spanne f; (wing~, of bridge etc) Spannweite f; (arch of bridge) (Brücken)bogen m. **a single-~ bridge** eine eingespannte Bogenbrücke.

  (b) (time) ~ Zeitspanne f, Zeitraum m; (of memory) Gedächtnisspanne f; (of attention) Konzentrationsspanne f; (range) Umfang m. **within his ~** zu seinen Lebzeiten; **for a brief ~** eine kurze Zeit lang; **the whole ~ of world affairs** die Weltpolitik in ihrer ganzen Spannweite.

  (c) (of oxen) Gespann nt.

  (d) (old: measurement) Spanne f.

  2 vt (rope, rainbow) sich spannen über (+acc); (bridge also) überspannen; (plank) führen über (+acc); (Mus) octave etc

greifen; (*encircle*) umfassen; (*in time*) sich erstrecken über (+*acc*), umfassen. **to ~ a river/valley with a bridge** eine Brücke über einen Fluß/ein Tal führen *or* bauen.

span² (*old*) *pret of* spin.

spangle ['spæŋgl] **1** *n* Paillette *f*. **2** *vt* mit Pailletten besetzen. **~d with stars/flowers** mit Sternen/Blumen übersät.

Spaniard ['spænjəd] *n* Spanier(in *f*) *m*.

spaniel ['spænjəl] *n* Spaniel *m*.

Spanish ['spænɪʃ] **1** *adj* spanisch. **the ~** die Spanier *pl*. **2** *n* (*language*) Spanisch *nt*.

Spanish: **~ America** *n* die spanischsprachigen Länder Mittel- *und Südamerikas*; **~-American 1** *n* spanischsprachiger Lateinamerikaner, spanischsprachige Lateinamerikanerin; (*in US*) spanischstämmiger Amerikaner, spanischstämmige Amerikanerin; **2** *adj* spanisch-amerikanisch; **~ chestnut** *n* Edelkastanie *f*; **~ Main** *n* Karibik *f*; **~ moss** *n* (*US*) Spanisches Moos, Greisenbart *m*; **~ omelette** *n* Omelett *nt* mit Piment, Paprika und Tomaten; **~ onion** *n* Gemüsezwiebel *f*.

spank [spæŋk] **1** *n* Klaps *m*. **to give sb a ~** jdm einen Klaps geben; (*spanking*) jdm den Hintern versohlen. **2** *vt* versohlen. **to ~ sb's bottom** jdm den Hintern versohlen. **3** *vi* **to ~ along** dahinjagen, dahinrasen.

spanker ['spæŋkəʳ] *n* (**a**) (*Naut: sail*) Besan *m*. (**b**) (*dated inf*) (*horse*) Renner *m*. **a real ~** (*blow*) ein Schlag, der nicht von Pappe war (*inf*).

spanking ['spæŋkɪŋ] **1** *n* Tracht *f* Prügel. **to give sb a ~** jdm eine Tracht Prügel verpassen, jdm den Hintern versohlen. **2** *adj pace* scharf, schnell. **3** *adv* (*dated inf: exceedingly*) **~ new** funkelnagelneu; **~ clean** blitzsauber; **we had a ~ good time** wir haben uns blendend amüsiert.

spanner ['spænəʳ] *n* (*Brit*) Schraubenschlüssel *m*. **to put or throw a ~ in the works** (*fig*) jdm Knüppel *or* einen Knüppel zwischen die Beine werfen; **that's a real ~ in the works** das ist wirklich ein Hemmschuh.

span roof *n* Satteldach *nt*.

spar¹ ['spaːʳl] *n* (*Naut*) Spiere *f*.

spar² *vi* (*Boxing*) ein Sparring *nt* machen; (*fig*) sich kabbeln (*inf*) (*about* um).

spar³ *n* (*Miner*) Spat *m*.

spare [spɛəʳ] **1** *adj* (**a**) den/die/das man nicht braucht, übrig *pred*; (*surplus*) überzählig, übrig *pred*; *bed, room* Gäste-; (*replacement*) *part etc* Ersatz-. **have you any ~ string?, have you any string ~?** kannst du mir (einen) Bindfaden geben?, hast du (einen) Bindfaden für mich?; **I can give you a racket/ pencil, I have a ~** one ich kann dir einen Schläger/Bleistift geben, ich habe noch einen *or* ich habe einen übrig; **take a ~ pen** in case that one doesn't work nehmen Sie noch einen Füller mit, falls dieser nicht funktioniert; **take some ~ clothes** nehmen Sie Kleider zum Wechseln mit; **it's all the ~ cash I have** mehr Bargeld habe ich nicht übrig; **if you have any ~ cash** wenn Sie Geld übrig haben; **should you have any ~ time or a ~ minute** sollten Sie Zeit (übrig) haben; **when you have a few ~ minutes or a few minutes ~** wenn Sie mal ein paar freie Minuten haben *or* ein paar Minuten übrig haben; **we have two ~ seats** wir haben zwei Plätze übrig; **I still have one ~ place in the car** ich habe noch einen Platz im Auto (frei); **there are two seats (going)** ~ es sind noch zwei Plätze frei; *see also cpds*.
(**b**) (*thin*) hager; (*meagre*) dürftig.
(**c**) **to drive sb ~** (*inf*) jdn wahnsinnig machen (*inf*); **to go ~** durchdrehen (*inf*), wild werden (*inf*).
2 *n* Ersatzteil *nt*.
3 *vt* (**a**) *usu neg* (*grudge, use sparingly*) sparen mit; *expense, pains, effort* scheuen. **don't ~ the horses** schone die Pferde nicht; **we must ~ no effort in trying to finish this job** wir dürfen keine Mühe scheuen, um diese Arbeit zu erledigen; **there was no expense ~d in building this hotel** beim Bau dieses Hotels ist an nichts gespart worden *or* hat man keine Kosten gescheut; **no expense ~d** es wurden keine Kosten gescheut; **she doesn't ~ herself** sie schont sich nicht; **he never ~d himself in the service of his country** er setzte sich selbstlos für sein Land ein; **~ the rod and spoil the child** (*Prov*) wer mit der Rute spart, verzieht das Kind (*Prov*).
(**b**) (*give*) *money etc* übrig haben; *space, room also* frei haben; *time* (übrig) haben. **to ~ sb sth** jdm etw überlassen *or* geben; *money* jdm etw geben; **can you ~ the time to do it?** haben Sie Zeit, das zu machen?; **I can ~ you five minutes** ich habe fünf Minuten Zeit für Sie (übrig); **can you ~ a penny for a poor old man?** haben Sie einen Groschen für einen armen alten Mann?; **there is none to ~** es ist keine(r, s) übrig; **to have sth to ~** etw übrig haben; **there are three to ~** es sind drei übrig *or* überzählig; **there's enough and to ~** es ist mehr als genug da; **to have a few minutes/hours to ~** ein paar Minuten/Stunden Zeit haben; **I got to the theatre/airport with two minutes to ~** ich war zwei Minuten vor Beginn der Vorstellung im Theater/vor Abflug am Flughafen.
(**c**) (*do without*) *person, object* entbehren, verzichten auf (+*acc*). **I can't ~ him/it** ich kann ihn/es nicht entbehren, ich kann auf ihn/es nicht verzichten, ich brauche ihn/es unbedingt; **can you ~ this for a moment?** brauchst du das gerade?, kannst du das im Moment entbehren?; **if you can ~ it** wenn Sie es nicht brauchen; **to ~ a thought for sb/sth** an jdn/etw denken.
(**d**) (*show mercy to*) verschonen; (*refrain from upsetting*) *sb, sb's feelings* schonen. **the fire ~d nothing** nichts blieb vom Feuer verschont; **the plague/soldiers ~d** no-one die Pest verschonte/die Soldaten verschonten keinen; **if we're ~d** wenn wir (dann) noch leben.
(**e**) (*save*) **to ~ sb/oneself sth** jdm/sich etw ersparen; **~ me the details** verschone mich mit den Einzelheiten; **to ~ him embarrassment** um ihn nicht in Verlegenheit zu bringen.

sparely ['spɛəlɪ] *adv* **~ built** schlank gebaut.

spare: ~ part *n* Ersatzteil *nt*; **~-part surgery** *n* (*inf*) Ersatzteil-

chirurgie *f* (*inf*); **~rib** *n* Rippchen *nt*, Spare Rib *no art*; **~ room** *n* Gästezimmer *nt*; **~ time 1** *n* (*leisure time*) Freizeit *f*; **2** *adj attr* Freizeit-; **~ tyre** *n* Ersatzreifen *m*; (*fig inf*) Pölsterchen *pl*, Rettungsring *m*; **~ wheel** *n* Ersatzrad *nt*.

sparing ['spɛərɪŋ] *adj* sparsam. **to be ~ of (one's) praise/one's time** mit Lob/seiner Zeit geizen, mit seiner Zeit knausern; **to be ~ of words** nicht viel sagen, wortkarg sein.

sparingly ['spɛərɪŋlɪ] *adv* sparsam; *spend, drink, eat* in Maßen. **to use sth ~** mit etw sparsam umgehen.

spark [spaːk] **1** *n* (**a**) (*from fire, Elec*) Funke *m*; (*fig: glimmer*) Fünkchen *nt*, Funke(n) *m*. **not a ~ of life** kein Fünkchen Leben, kein Lebensfunke; **a ~ of interest** ein Fünkchen *or* Funke(n) Interesse; **there were a few ~s of wit** towards the end of the speech es gab ein paar geistreiche Bemerkungen am Ende der Rede; **when the ~s start to fly** (*fig*) wenn die Funken anfangen zu fliegen.
(**b**) (*dated inf: person*) Stutzer *m* (*dated*). **a bright ~** (*iro*) ein Intelligenzbolzen *m* (*iro*); (*clumsy*) ein Tolpatsch *m*.
2 *vt* (*also* **~ off**) entzünden; *explosion* verursachen; (*fig*) auslösen; *quarrel also* entfachen, auslösen; *interest, enthusiasm* wecken, anfachen.
3 *vi* Funken sprühen; (*Elec*) zünden.

spark: **~ coil** *n* Zündspule *f*; **~ gap** *n* Funkenstrecke *f*.

spark(ing) plug ['spaːk(ɪŋ)plʌg] *n* Zündkerze *f*.

sparkle ['spaːkl] **1** *n* Funkeln, Glitzern *nt*; (*of eyes*) Funkeln *nt*. **the speech had a few ~s of wit** seine Rede war stellenweise recht geistreich; **he has no or lacks ~** ihm fehlt der (rechte) Schwung.
2 *vi* funkeln, glitzern; (*eyes*) blitzen, funkeln (*with* vor +*dat*); (*fig: person*) vor Leben(sfreude) sprühen; (*with intelligence, wit etc*) brillieren. **her eyes ~d with intelligence** ihre Augen blitzten vor Gescheitheit; **she was so happy she really ~d** sie sprühte geradezu vor Glück; **his conversation ~d (with wit)** seine Unterhaltung sprühte vor Geist.

sparkler ['spaːkləʳ] *n* (**a**) (*firework*) Wunderkerze *f*. (**b**) (*inf: diamond*) Klunker *m* (*inf*).

sparkling ['spaːklɪŋ] *adj lights* glänzend, funkelnd; *eyes* funkelnd; *wit* sprühend; (*lively*) *person* vor Leben sprühend; (*witty*) *person, speech, conversation* vor Geist sprühend; (*bubbling*) *lemonade etc* perlend; *wine* perlend, moussierend. **~ wine** (*as type*) Schaumwein *m*; (*slightly ~*) Perlwein *m*; **the car was ~ (clean)** das Auto blitzte vor Sauberkeit.

spark plug *n see* **spark(ing) plug**.

sparring ['spaːrɪŋ]: **~ match** *n* (*lit*) Sparringkampf *m*; (*fig*) (*Wort*)geplänkel, Wortgefecht *nt*; **~ partner** *n* (*lit*) Sparringpartner *m*; (*fig also*) Kontrahent(in *f*) *m*.

sparrow ['spærəʊ] *n* Sperling, Spatz *m*. **house ~** Haussperling.

sparrowhawk ['spærəʊhɔːk] *n* (*European*) Sperber *m*; (*N American*) amerikanischer Falke.

sparse [spaːs] *adj* (+*er*) spärlich; *covering, vegetation also, population* dünn; *furnishings also* dürftig; (*infrequent*) *references also* rar.

sparsely ['spaːslɪ] *adv* spärlich; *wooded also, populated* dünn; *furnished also* dürftig. **a hillside ~ covered with trees** ein Hang mit spärlichem Baumwuchs.

sparseness ['spaːsnɪs] *n* Spärlichkeit *f*; (*of furnishings also*) Dürftigkeit *f*; (*of population*) geringe Dichte.

Sparta ['spaːtə] *n* Sparta *nt*.

Spartan ['spaːtən] **1** *adj* (*fig*: s~) spartanisch. **2** *n* Spartaner(in *f*) *m*.

spasm ['spæzəm] *n* (*Med*) Krampf, Spasmus (*spec*) *m*; (*of asthma, coughing, fig*) Anfall *m*. **~s of coughing** krampfartige Hustenanfälle *pl*; **a ~ of fear** ein Anfall *m* von Angst; **there was a (sudden) ~ of activity** es entwickelte sich (plötzlich) fieberhafte Aktivität; **~s of interest** sporadisch auftretendes Interesse; **to work in ~s** sporadisch arbeiten.

spasmodic [spæz'mɒdɪk] *adj* (*Med*) krampfartig, spasmisch, spasmodisch (*spec*); (*fig: occasional*) sporadisch; *growth* schubweise. **his generosity was ~** er hatte Phasen *or* Anfälle von Großzügigkeit.

spasmodically [spæz'mɒdɪkəlɪ] *adv* (*Med*) krampfartig; (*fig*) sporadisch, hin und wieder; *grow* in Schüben, schubweise.

spastic ['spæstɪk] **1** *adj* spastisch; (*fig sl*) schwach (*inf*). **2** *n* Spastiker(in *f*) *m*.

spasticity [spæ'stɪsɪtɪ] *n* spastische Lähmung.

spat¹ [spæt] **1** *n* (*of oyster etc*) Muschellaich *m*. **2** *vi* (*oyster etc*) laichen.

spat² *n* Halbgamasche *f*.

spat³ (*US inf*) **1** *n* (*quarrel*) Knatsch (*inf*), Krach (*inf*) *m*. **2** *vi* (*quarrel*) zanken, streiten.

spat⁴ *pret, ptp of* **spit¹**.

spate [speɪt] *n* (*of river*) Hochwasser *nt*; (*fig*) (*of letters, orders etc*) Flut *f*; (*of burglaries, accidents*) Serie *f*; (*of words, abuse*) Schwall *m*. **the river is in (full) ~** der Fluß führt Hochwasser; **a ~ of words** ein Wortschwall *m*; **a ~ of excited talk** aufgeregtes Stimmengewirr; **a ~ of work** ein Arbeitsandrang *m*.

spatial ['speɪʃəl] *adj* räumlich. **~ sense** räumliches Vorstellungsvermögen.

spatially ['speɪʃəlɪ] *adv* räumlich.

spatio-temporal ['speɪʃɪəʊ'tempərəl] *adj* räumlich-zeitlich, Raum-Zeit-.

spatter ['spætəʳ] **1** *vt* bespritzen. **to ~ water over sb, to ~ sb with water** jdn naß spritzen; **a wall ~ed with blood** eine blutbespritzte Wand.
2 *vi* **to ~ over sth** etw vollspritzen; **it ~ed all over the room** es verspritzte im ganzen Zimmer; **the rain ~ed (down) on the roof** der Regen klatschte aufs Dach.
3 *n* (*mark*) Spritzer *pl*; (*sound: of rain*) Klatschen *nt*. **a ~ of rain** ein paar Tropfen Regen; **a ~ of applause** kurzer Beifall.

spatula ['spætjʊlə] *n* Spachtel *m*; (*Med*) Spatel *m*.

spavin ['spævɪn] *n* Spat *m*.

spavined [spə'viːnd] *adj horse* spatkrank.
spawn [spɔːn] **1** *n* **(a)** (*of fish, shellfish, frogs*) Laich *m*. **(b)** (*of mushrooms*) Fadengeflecht, Myzelium (*spec*) *nt*. **2** *vi* laichen.
3 *vt* (*fig*) hervorbringen, erzeugen. **bad living conditions ~ crime** schlechte Wohnverhältnisse sind Brutstätten des Verbrechens.
spay [speɪ] *vt cat* sterilisieren.
SPCA *abbr of* **Society for the Prevention of Cruelty to Animals** ≃ Tierschutzverein *m*.
speak [spiːk] *pret* **spoke** *or* (*obs*) **spake**, *ptp* **spoken** *or* (*obs*) **spoke 1** *vt* **(a)** (*utter*) sagen; *one's thoughts* aussprechen, äußern; *one's lines* aufsagen. **to ~ one's mind** seine Meinung sagen; **nobody spoke a word** niemand sagte ein Wort, keiner sagte etwas; **his eyes spoke his love** sein Blick verriet seine Liebe; *see* volume.
(b) *language* sprechen. **English spoken here** wird Englisch gesprochen.
2 *vi* **(a)** (*talk, be on ~ing terms*) sprechen, reden (*about* über + *acc*, von); (*converse*) reden, sich unterhalten (*with* mit); (*fig: guns, drums*) sprechen, ertönen. **to ~ to** *or* (*esp US*) **with sb** mit jdm sprechen *or* reden; **did you ~?** haben Sie etwas gesagt?; **to ~ in a whisper** flüstern; **~, don't shout** nun schreien Sie doch nicht (so)!; **we don't ~** (**to one another**) wir reden *or* sprechen nicht miteinander; **I'm not ~ing to you** mit dir rede *or* spreche ich nicht mehr; **she never spoke to me again** seitdem hat sie nie wieder mit mir geredet *or* gesprochen; **to ~ to oneself** Selbstgespräche führen; **I'll ~ to him about it** (*euph: admonish*) ich werde ein Wörtchen mit ihm reden; **I'll have to ~ to my lawyer about it** das muß ich mit meinem Anwalt besprechen; **~ when you're spoken to** antworte, wenn man mit dir redet *or* spricht; **servants should only ~ when spoken to** Diener sollten nur dann etwas sagen, wenn man sie anspricht; **I don't know him to ~ to** ich kenne ihn nicht näher *or* nur vom Sehen; **music ~s directly to the soul** Musik spricht die Seele an; **this novel ~s to the rebel in all of us** dieser Roman spricht den Rebellen in uns an; **~ing of dictionaries ...** da *or* wo wir gerade von Wörterbüchern sprechen ..., apropos Wörterbücher ...; **not to ~ of ...** ganz zu schweigen von ...; **it's nothing to ~ of** es ist nicht weiter erwähnenswert, es ist nichts weiter; **no money/trees** *etc* **to ~ of** so gut wie kein Geld/keine Bäume *etc*; **to ~ well of sb/sth** jdn/etw loben, (nur) Gutes über jdn/etw sagen; **he is well spoken of** er genießt große Achtung; **so to ~** sozusagen, eigentlich; **roughly ~ing** grob gesagt; **strictly ~ing** genau genommen; **legally/biologically ~ing** rechtlich/biologisch gesehen; **generally ~ing** im allgemeinen; **~ing personally ...** wenn Sie mich fragen ..., was mich betrifft ...; **~ing as a member of the club I have ...** als Mitglied des Vereins habe ich ...; **to ~ down to sb** jdn von oben herab behandeln.
(b) (*make a speech*) reden (*on* zu), sprechen (*on* zu); (*give one's opinion*) sich äußern (*on, to* zu). **to ~ in public** in der Öffentlichkeit reden; **~ to the subject!** bleiben Sie beim Thema!; **to ~ in the debate** in der Debatte das Wort ergreifen; **to ask sb to ~** jdm das Wort erteilen; **Mr X will ~ next** als nächster wird Herr X sprechen *or* hat Herr X das Wort; **then Geoffrey rose to ~** dann stand Geoffrey auf, um das Wort zu ergreifen.
(c) (*Telec*) **~ing!** am Apparat!; **Jones ~ing!** (hier) Jones!; **who is that ~ing?** wer ist da, bitte?; (*on extension phone, in office*) **wer ist am Apparat?**
(d) (*fig: suggest*) zeugen (*of* von). **their appearance ~s of poverty** ihre Erscheinung verrät Armut *or* zeugt von Armut.
♦**speak against** *vi* + *prep obj* (*in debate*) sprechen gegen, sich aussprechen gegen; (*criticize*) etwas sagen gegen, kritisieren.
♦**speak for** *vi* + *prep obj* **(a)** (*in debate*) unterstützen.
(b) **to ~ sb** (*on behalf of*) in jds Namen (*dat*) sprechen; (*in favour of*) sich für jdn verwenden, ein gutes Wort für jdn einlegen; **he ~s for the miners/delegation** er ist der Sprecher der Bergleute/Abordnung; **I know I ~ for all of us** ich bin sicher, daß ich im Namen aller spreche; **~ing ~ myself** ... was mich angeht ...; **let her ~ herself** laß sie selbst reden; **~ ~ yourself!** (*I don't agree*) das meinst auch nur du!; (*don't include me*) du vielleicht!; **I can ~ ~ his honesty** ich kann mich für seine Ehrlichkeit verbürgen; **that ~s well ~ him** das spricht für ihn; **to ~ well/badly ~ sth** ein Beweis *m*/nicht gerade ein Beweis *m* für etw sein.
(c) **to ~ ~ itself** (*be obvious*) für sich sprechen, alles sagen.
(d) to be spoken ~ (*dated: girl*) versprochen sein (*old*), vergeben sein (*hum*); **the chair had already been spoken ~** (*hum*) der Stuhl war schon reserviert (*hum*); **that's already spoken ~** (*hum*) das ist schon vergeben.
♦**speak out** *vi* (*audibly*) deutlich sprechen; (*give one's opinion*) seine Meinung deutlich vertreten. **to ~ ~ in favour of sth** für etw eintreten; **to ~ ~ against sth** sich gegen etw aussprechen.
♦**speak up** *vi* **(a)** (*raise one's voice*) lauter sprechen *or* reden; (*talk loudly*) laut (und verständlich) sprechen *or* reden. **~ ~!** sprich lauter!; **if you want anything ~ ~** mach den Mund auf *or* sag, wenn du etwas willst.
(b) (*fig*) seine Meinung sagen *or* äußern. **don't be afraid to ~ ~** sagen Sie ruhig Ihre Meinung, äußern Sie sich ruhig; **to ~ ~ for sb/sth** für jdn/etw eintreten; **what's wrong? ~ ~!** was ist los? heraus mit der Sprache!
speakeasy ['spiːkiːzɪ] *n* (*US*) Mondscheinkneipe *f* (*inf*) (*Lokal, in dem während der Prohibition Alkohol ausgeschenkt wurde*).
speaker ['spiːkə^r] *n* **(a)** (*of language*) Sprecher *m*. **all ~s of German** alle, die Deutsch sprechen, alle Deutschsprechenden; (*native ~s also*) alle Deutschsprachigen; **are you an English-~?** ist Englisch Ihre Muttersprache?
(b) (*in discussion also, in lecture, public ~*) Redner(in *f*) *m*. **the last** *or* **previous ~** der Vorredner; **our ~ today is ...** der heutige Referent ist ...; **he's a good/poor ~** er ist ein guter/schlechter Redner.

(c) (*loud~, in record-player*) Lautsprecher *m*; (*on hi-fi etc*) Box *f*.
(d) (*Parl*) **S~** Sprecher *m*; **Mr S~** Herr Vorsitzender.
speaking ['spiːkɪŋ] **1** *n* (*act of ~*) Sprechen *nt*; (*speeches*) Reden *pl*. **the art of ~** die Redekunst. **2** *adj attr* **doll** sprechend, **Mama-** (*inf*); (*fig*) *likeness* verblüffend. **~ voice** Sprechstimme *f*; **to be within ~ distance** nahe genug sein, daß man sich verständigen kann.
-speaking *adj suf* -sprechend; (*with native language also*) -sprachig.
speaking: ~ clock *n* (*Brit*) telefonische Zeitansage; **~ terms** *npl* **to be on ~ terms with sb** mit jdm sprechen *or* reden; **~ trumpet** *n* (*old*) Hörrohr *nt*; **~ tube** *n* Sprachrohr *nt*.
spear [spɪə^r] **1** *n* Speer *m*; (*leaf*) Lanzettenblatt *nt*; (*of grass*) Halm *m*; (*of grain*) Keim *m*. **~s of broccoli/asparagus** Brokkoliköpfe *pl*/Stangen *pl* Spargel.
2 *vt* aufspießen; (*wound, kill*) durchbohren; (*catch with ~*) mit Speeren fangen. **he ~ed him through the arm** er durchbohrte ihm den Arm; **he ~ed the meat with** *or* **onto his fork** er spießte das Fleisch auf die Gabel.
spear: ~head 1 *n* (*of spear*) Speerspitze *f*; (*Mil*) Angriffsspitze *f*; (*fig: person, thing*) Bahnbrecher *m* (*of* für); **2** *vt* (*lit, fig*) anführen; **~man** *n* Speerträger *m*; **~mint** *n* (*plant, flavour*) Grüne Minze; **~mint chewing gum** Spearmint-Kaugummi *m*.
spec [spek] *n* (*inf*) **on ~** auf Verdacht, auf gut Glück.
special ['speʃəl] *n* **1** *adj* **(a)** besondere(r, s); (*specific*) *purpose, use, person, date also* bestimmt, speziell; (*exceptional*) *friend, favour, occasion also* speziell. **I have no ~ person in mind** ich habe eigentlich an niemanden Bestimmtes gedacht; **in this one ~ instance** in diesem einen Fall; **take ~ care of it** passen Sie besonders gut darauf auf; **nothing ~** nichts Besonderes; **he expects ~ treatment** er will besonders behandelt werden, er will eine Extrawurst gebraten haben (*inf*); **this is rather a ~ day for me** heute ist ein ganz besonderer Tag für mich; **he uses the word in a ~ sense** er gebraucht das Wort in einer speziellen Bedeutung; **he's a very ~ person to her** er bedeutet ihr sehr viel; **you're extra ~!** (*inf*) du bist was ganz Besonderes! (*inf*); **what's so ~ about her/the house?** was ist denn an ihr/an dem Haus so besonders?; **what's so ~ about that?** na und? (*inf*), **das ist doch nichts Besonderes!**; **I do that my own ~ way** ich mache das ganz auf meine (eigene) Weise; **he has his own ~ way with children/the garden** er kann gut mit Kindern umgehen/er hat ein Händchen fürs Gärtnern; **it's my ~ chair** das ist *mein* Stuhl; **everyone has his ~ place** jeder hat seinen eigenen Platz; **to feel ~** sich als etwas ganz Besonderes vorkommen; **make him feel ~** seien Sie besonders nett zu ihm.
(b) (*out of the ordinary*) *permission, fund, supplement, edition,* (*Pol*) *powers, legislation* Sonder-; *arrangement, wish, order also* besondere(r, s). **~ feature** (*Press*) Sonderartikel *m*.
(c) (*specialized*) *subject, dictionary, tool* Spezial-.
(d) (*inf: separate*) *place, book etc* gesondert.
2 *n* (*constable*) Hilfspolizist(in *f*) *m*; (*TV, Rad*) Sonderprogramm *nt*; (*train*) Sonderzug *m*; (*Cook*) Tagesgericht *nt*; (*edition*) Sonder- *or* Extraausgabe *f*. **chef's ~** Spezialität *f* des Küchenchefs.
special: ~ agent *n* (*spy*) Agent(in *f*) *m*; **S~ Branch** *n* (*Brit*) Sicherheitspolizei *f*, Sicherheitsdienst *m*; **~ case** *n* (*also Jur*) Sonderfall *m*; **~ constable** *n* Hilfspolizist *m*; **~ correspondent** *n* (*Press*) Sonderberichterstatter(in *f*) *m*; **~ delivery** *n* Eilzustellung *f*; **a ~-delivery letter** ein Eilbrief *m*; **by ~ delivery** durch Eilzustellung, durch Eilboten (*inf*); **~ drawing rights** *npl* Sonderziehungsrechte *pl*; **~ edition** *n* Sonderausgabe *f*; **~ effects** *npl* Tricks *pl*; **~ investigator** *n* Sonderbeauftragte(r) *mf*, Untersuchungsbeamte(r) *m*.
specialism ['speʃəlɪzəm] *n* (*specializing*) Spezialisierung *f*; (*special subject*) Spezialgebiet *nt*.
specialist ['speʃəlɪst] *n* **1** Fachmann *m* (*in* für); (*Med*) Spezialist(in *f*) *m*, Facharzt *m*/-ärztin *f*. **a ~ in tropical diseases** ein Facharzt *or* Spezialist für Tropenkrankheiten.
2 *adj attr* *knowledge, dictionary* Fach-. **it's ~ work** dazu braucht man einen Fachmann.
speciality [,speʃɪ'ælɪtɪ], (*US*) **specialty** ['speʃəltɪ] *n* Spezialität *f*; (*subject also*) Spezialgebiet *nt*. **to make a ~ of sth** sich auf etw (*acc*) spezialisieren; **a ~ of the house** eine Spezialität des Hauses.
specialization [,speʃəlaɪ'zeɪʃən] *n* Spezialisierung *f* (*in auf* + *acc*); (*special subject*) Spezialgebiet *nt*.
specialize ['speʃəlaɪz] **1** *vi* sich spezialisieren (*in auf* + *acc*). **2** *vt* **the species/tail has been ~d** die Art/der Schwanz hat sich gesondert entwickelt.
specialized ['speʃəlaɪzd] *adj* spezialisiert. **a ~ knowledge of biology** Fachkenntnisse *pl* in Biologie.
special licence *n* (*Brit*) (Ehe)dispens *f* (*des Bischofs von Canterbury*).
specially ['speʃəlɪ] *adv* besonders; (*specifically*) extra; (*for a particular purpose*) speziell, extra. **a ~ difficult task** eine besonders schwierige Aufgabe; **I had it ~ made** ich habe es extra machen lassen; **we asked for it ~** wir haben extra darum gebeten; **a book ~ written for the competition** ein Buch, das speziell für den Wettbewerb geschrieben wurde; **he brought it ~ for me** er hat es eigens für mich gebracht; **don't go to the post office ~/~ for me** gehen Sie deswegen/meinetwegen nicht extra zur Post.
special: ~ messenger *n* Expreßbote *m*; (*Mil*) Kurier *m*; **~ offer** *n* Sonderangebot *nt*; **~ pleading** *n* (*Jur*) Beibringung *f* neuen Beweismaterials; (*fig*) Berufung *f* auf einen Sonderfall; **you might try some ~ pleading** (*fig*) du kannst dich ja darauf berufen, daß das ein Sonderfall ist; **~ pleading is no use** (*fig*) es hilft nichts, zu sagen, daß das ja ein Ausnahmefall ist; **~ prosecutor** *n* (*US*) Sonderstaatsanwalt *m*; **~ school** *n* Sonderschule *f*; (*for physically handicapped*) Behindertenschule *f*.

specialty ['speʃəltɪ] n (US) see **speciality**.

specie ['spiːʃiː] n, no pl Hartgeld, Münzgeld nt. **payment in ~** Zahlung in Hartgeld.

species ['spiːʃiːz] n, pl - Art f; (Biol also) Spezies f. **the human ~** der Mensch.

specific [spə'sɪfɪk] **1** adj (a) (definite) bestimmt, speziell; (precise) statement, instructions genau; example ganz bestimmt. **9.3, to be ~** 9,3, um genau zu sein; **can you be a bit more ~?** können Sie sich etwas genauer äußern?
(b) (Biol, Chem, Phys, Med) spezifisch. **~ gravity** spezifisches Gewicht, Wichte f.
2 n (a) (old Med) Spezifikum nt.
(b) **~s** pl nähere or genauere Einzelheiten pl.

specifically [spə'sɪfɪkəlɪ] adv warn, order, state, mention ausdrücklich; (specially) designed, request speziell; (precisely) genau. **~, we need three** wir brauchen genau drei.

specification [ˌspesɪfɪ'keɪʃən] n (a) (specifying) Angabe f. **his ideas need more ~** seine Ideen müssen noch genauer ausgeführt werden.
(b) (detailed statement) (of requirements) genaue Angabe, Aufstellung f; (for patent) (genaue) Beschreibung; (design) (for car, machine) (detaillierter) Entwurf; (for building) Bauplan m. **~s** pl genaue Angaben pl; (of car, machine) technische Daten or Angaben pl; (of new building) Raum- und Materialangaben pl, Baubeschreibung f, Baubeschrieb m; **the new ~ includes ...** (model) die neue Ausführung hat auch ...
(c) (stipulation) Bedingung f; (for building) Bestimmung, Vorschrift f.

specify ['spesɪfaɪ] **1** vt angeben; (list individually or in detail) spezifizieren, (einzeln) aufführen; (stipulate) vorschreiben; (blueprint, contract etc) vorsehen. **in the order specified** in der angegebenen or vorgeschriebenen Reihenfolge; **to ~ how to do it** genauer or näher ausführen, wie es gemacht werden soll.
2 vi genaue Angaben machen. **unless otherwise specified** wenn nicht anders angegeben.

specimen ['spesɪmən] **1** n Exemplar nt; (of urine, blood etc) Probe f; (sample) Muster nt. **a beautiful or fine ~** ein Prachtexemplar nt; **if that's a ~ of your work/intelligence** wenn das eine Probe deines Könnens/deiner Intelligenz ist; **he's an odd ~** (inf) er ist ein komischer Kauz (inf); **you're a pretty poor ~** (inf) du hast ja nicht viel zu bieten (inf).
2 adj attr page Probe-. **a ~ copy** ein Beleg- or Probeexemplar nt; **a ~ signature** eine Unterschriftenprobe.

specious ['spiːʃəs] adj argument, proposal vordergründig bestechend; excuse vordergründig, fadenscheinig; claim unfundiert, fadenscheinig; charm, phrases leer.

speciousness ['spiːʃəsnɪs] n see adj Vordergründigkeit f; Fadenscheinigkeit f; Unfundiertheit f; Hohlheit f.

speck [spek] **1** n Fleck m; (of blood, paint, mud also) Spritzer m; (of dust) Körnchen nt; (of soot) Flocke f, Flöckchen nt; (of gold, colour etc) Sprenkel m; (small portion) (of drink etc) Tropfen m, Tröpfchen nt; (of sugar, butter) kleines bißchen; (fig: of truth, confidence) Fünkchen, Quentchen nt. **his reputation is without a ~** sein Ruf ist ohne Makel; **a ~ on the horizon** ein Punkt m or Pünktchen nt am Horizont.
2 vt **to be ~ed with black** schwarze Fleckchen haben; (bird, eyes etc) schwarz gesprenkelt sein; **his face was ~ed with** dust/dirt er hatte Staub-/Schmutzflecken im Gesicht; **to be ~ed with blood** blutbespritzt sein.

speckle ['spekl] **1** n Sprenkel, Tupfer, Tupfen m. **2** vt sprenkeln. **to be ~d with sth** mit etw gesprenkelt sein; **to be ~d with brown** braun gesprenkelt sein.

specs [speks] npl (inf) Brille f.

spectacle ['spektəkl] n (a) (show) Schauspiel nt. **a sad/ridiculous ~** ein trauriger/lächerlicher Anblick; **to make a ~ of oneself** unangenehm auffallen. (b) **~s** pl (also pair of **~s**) Brille f.

spectacle case n Brillenetui or -futteral nt.

spectacled ['spektəkld] adj bebrillt; (Zool) Brillen-, brillenähnlich gezeichnet.

spectacular [spek'tækjʊləʳ] **1** adj sensationell; improvement, success also spektakulär; race, finish, jump, fall also atemberaubend. **2** n (Theat) Show f.

spectacularly [spek'tækjʊləlɪ] adv sensationell; improve, fail also spektakulär. **he was ~ wrong** er hat einen Riesenfehler gemacht.

spectate [spek'teɪt] vi (inf: esp Sport) zuschauen (at bei).

spectator [spek'teɪtəʳ] n Zuschauer(in f) m. **~ sport** Publikumssport m.

specter n (US) see **spectre**.

spectra ['spektrə] pl of **spectrum**.

spectral ['spektrəl] adj (a) (of ghosts) geisterhaft, gespenstisch. (b) (of the spectrum) spektral, Spektral-.

spectre, (US) **specter** ['spektəʳ] n Gespenst nt; (fig) (Schreck)gespenst nt. **the ~ of a woman in white** die Erscheinung einer Frau in Weiß.

spectroscope ['spektrəskəʊp] n Spektroskop nt.

spectroscopic [ˌspektrəʊ'skɒpɪk] adj spektroskopisch; analysis Spektral-.

spectrum ['spektrəm] n, pl **spectra** Spektrum nt; (fig: range also) Palette, Skala f. **~ analysis** Spektralanalyse f.

specula ['spekjʊlə] pl of **speculum**.

speculate ['spekjʊleɪt] vi (a) (meditate, ponder) (nach)grübeln, nachdenken (on über +acc); (conjecture) Vermutungen anstellen, spekulieren (about, on über +acc). **I ~ that ...** ich vermute, daß ... (b) (Fin) spekulieren (in mit, on an +dat).

speculation [ˌspekjʊ'leɪʃən] n (all senses) Spekulation f (on über +acc); (guesswork also) Vermutung f. **it is the subject of much ~** darüber sind viele Spekulationen or Vermutungen angestellt worden; **it's pure ~** das ist reine Vermutung; **to buy sth as a ~** etw als Spekulationsobjekt kaufen.

speculative ['spekjʊlətɪv] adj (a) spekulativ (esp Philos); approach, suggestions, ideas rein theoretisch; mind also, expression, look grüblerisch. (b) (Fin) Spekulations-. **~ builder** Bauspekulant m; **~ building** Bauspekulation f; **a ~ building** ein Beispiel von Bauspekulation.

speculatively ['spekjʊlətɪvlɪ] adv spekulativ, theoretisch; look, say grüblerisch. **to invest ~ in sth** mit etw spekulieren.

speculator ['spekjʊleɪtəʳ] n Spekulant(in f) m.

speculum ['spekjʊləm] n, pl **specula** (Med) Spekulum nt; (in telescope) Metallspiegel m.

sped [sped] pret, ptp of **speed**.

speech [spiːtʃ] n (a) no pl (faculty of ~) Sprache f; (act of speaking) Sprechen nt; (manner of speaking) Sprechweise f. **to be slow of ~** langsam sprechen; **his ~ was very indistinct** er sprach sehr undeutlich; **he expresses himself better in ~ than in writing** er drückt sich mündlich besser aus als schriftlich; **to burst into ~** in einen Redeschwall ausbrechen; **to lose/recover the power of ~** die Sprache or Sprechfähigkeit verlieren/zurückgewinnen; **~ is silver, silence is golden** (Prov) Reden ist Silber, Schweigen ist Gold (Prov); **freedom of ~** Redefreiheit f.
(b) (language) Sprache f. **in dockers' ~** in der Sprache der Werftarbeiter.
(c) (oration, Theat) Rede f (on, about über +acc); (address also) Ansprache f; (in court) Plädoyer nt. **to give or make a ~** eine Rede etc halten; **the actor had three ~es** der Schauspieler hat dreimal gesprochen; **the chairman invited ~es from the floor** der Vorsitzende forderte das Publikum zu Meinungsäußerungen auf; **the ~ from the throne** die Thronrede.
(d) (Brit Gram) direct/indirect or reported ~ direkte/indirekte Rede; see **figure, part**.
(e) (US Sch, Univ: study of ~) Sprechkunde f.

speech: ~ act n Sprechakt m; **~ community** n Sprachgemeinschaft f; **~ day** n (Brit) Schulfeier f; **~ defect** n Sprachfehler m.

speechify ['spiːtʃɪfaɪ] vi salbadern, Volksreden halten.

speechifying ['spiːtʃɪfaɪɪŋ] n Volksreden pl, Schwätzerei f.

speechless ['spiːtʃlɪs] adj (a) (at a loss for words) sprachlos (with vor); anger stumm. **everybody was ~** at this darüber waren alle völlig sprachlos; **his remark left me ~** seine Bemerkung machte mich sprachlos or verschlug mir die Sprache.
(b) (lit: dumb) stumm. **to be ~** nicht sprechen können.

speechlessly ['spiːtʃlɪslɪ] adv wortlos; (from surprise, shock etc) sprachlos.

speechlessness ['spiːtʃlɪsnɪs] n (a) Sprachlosigkeit f. (b) (lit) Stummheit f; (loss of speech) Sprachverlust m.

speech: ~making n (making speeches) Redenhalten nt; (pej: speechifying) Schwätzerei f, Gelabere nt (inf); **~ organ** n Sprechwerkzeug nt; **~ sound** n Sprachlaut m; **~ therapist** n Sprachtherapeut(in f) m, Logopäde m, Logopädin f; **~ therapy** n Sprachtherapie f; (treatment) logopädische Behandlung, Logopädie f; **~ writer** n Verfasser(in f) m von Reden.

speed [spiːd] (vb: pret, ptp **sped** or **~ed**) **1** n (a) Geschwindigkeit f; (fast ~ also) Schnelligkeit f; (of moving object or person also) Tempo nt. **at ~** äußerst schnell; **at a high/low ~** mit hoher/niedriger Geschwindigkeit; **at full or top ~** mit Höchstgeschwindigkeit; **at a ~ of 50 mph** mit einer Geschwindigkeit or einem Tempo von 50 Meilen pro Stunde; **the ~ of light/sound** die Lichtgeschwindigkeit/Schallgeschwindigkeit; **at the ~ of light** mit Lichtgeschwindigkeit; **walking/reading ~** Schritttempo nt/Lesegeschwindigkeit f; **to pick up or gather ~** beschleunigen, schneller werden; (fig: development) sich beschleunigen; (person) schneller werden; **to lose ~** (an) Geschwindigkeit verlieren; **what ~ were you doing?** wie schnell sind Sie gefahren?; **her typing/shorthand ~ is good** sie kann schnell maschineschreiben/stenographieren; **what is her typing/shorthand ~?** wieviele Anschläge/Silben (pro Minute) schreibt sie?; **a secretary with good ~s** eine Sekretärin, die schnell schreiben kann; **with all possible ~** so schnell wie möglich; **with such ~** so schnell; **full ~ ahead!** (Naut) volle Kraft voraus!
(b) (Aut, Tech: gear) Gang m. **three-~ bicycle** Fahrrad mit Dreigangschaltung; **a three-~ gear** ein Dreiganggetriebe nt.
(c) (Phot) (film ~) Lichtempfindlichkeit f; (shutter ~) Belichtungszeit f.
(d) (sl: drug) Speed nt (sl), Schnellmacher m (sl).
2 vt **to ~ sb on his way** (person) jdn verabschieden; (iro) jdn hinauskomplimentieren; (good wishes etc) jdn auf seinem Weg begleiten; **if you fetch the vistors' coats it may ~ them on their** way wenn du die Mäntel der Gäste holst, machen sie sich vielleicht auf den Weg; **to ~ an arrow** (old) einen Pfeil abschießen; **God ~ you!** (old) Gott (sei) mit dir! (old).
3 vi (a) pret, ptp **sped** (move quickly) jagen, flitzen; (arrow) sausen, flitzen. **the years sped by** die Jahre verflogen or vergingen wie im Fluge; **God ~** (old) Gott mit dir (old).
(b) pret, ptp **~ed** (Aut: exceed ~ limit) zu schnell fahren, die Geschwindigkeitsbegrenzung überschreiten.

♦**speed along** pret, ptp **~ed** or **sped ~ 1** vi sep work etc beschleunigen. **2** vi entlangjagen or -flitzen (+prep obj acc); (work) vorangehen.

♦**speed off** pret, ptp **~ed** or **sped ~** vi davonjagen; (car also) davonbrausen; (person also) davonflitzen.

♦**speed up** pret, ptp **~ed ~ 1** vi (car, driver etc) beschleunigen; (person) Tempo zulegen, schneller machen; (work, production etc) schneller werden. **their pace ~ ~** ihr Tempo wurde schneller; **with practice you'll ~ ~** wenn du erst mehr Übung hast, wirst du schneller.
2 vt sep beschleunigen; person antreiben, auf Trab bringen (inf); research also vorantreiben. **that ~ed me ~** das hat mir Antrieb gegeben; **tell her to ~ ~ that coffee** (inf) sag ihr, sie soll sich mit dem Kaffee beeilen.

speed: ~boat n Renn- or Schnellboot nt; ~ cop n (inf) weiße Maus (inf), Verkehrsbulle m (inf).

speeder ['spiːdəʳ] n Temposünder(in f) m (inf), Raser m (inf).

speedily ['spiːdɪlɪ] adv schnell; reply, return prompt.

speediness ['spiːdɪnɪs] n Schnelligkeit f.

speeding ['spiːdɪŋ] n Geschwindigkeitsüberschreitung f.

speed: ~ limit n Geschwindigkeitsbegrenzung f; a 30 mph ~ limit eine Geschwindigkeitsbegrenzung von 50 km/h; (inf: area) eine Strecke mit einer Geschwindigkeitsbegrenzung von 50 km/h; ~ merchant n (inf) Raser (inf), Todesfahrer(in f) (inf) m; Nicholas is a real ~ merchant Nicholas fährt wie der Henker (inf).

speedo ['spiːdəʊ] n (Brit inf) Tacho m (inf).

speedometer [spɪˈdɒmɪtəʳ] n Geschwindigkeitsmesser, Tachometer m.

speed: ~-read vti nach der Schnellesemethode lesen; a class in ~-reading ein Kurs zum Erlernen der Schnellesemethode.

speedster ['spiːdstəʳ] n (inf) (car) Flitzer m; (person) rasanter Fahrer, rasante Fahrerin, Raser m (inf).

speed: ~ trap n Radarfalle f (inf); ~-up n (inf) schnelleres Tempo (inf) (in bei), Beschleunigung f (in gen); (in research) Vorantreiben nt (in gen); (in rate of inflation) Steigerung f (in gen); ~way n (a) (Sport) Speedwayrennen nt; (track) Speedway- or Aschenrennbahn f; (b) (US) (race-track) Rennstrecke f; (expressway) Schnellstraße f; ~well n (Bot) Ehrenpreis m or nt, Veronika f; ~-writing n Schnellschreiben nt.

speedy ['spiːdɪ] adj (+er) schnell; answer, service also prompt; remedy schnell wirkend.

speleologist [ˌspiːlɪˈɒlədʒɪst] n Höhlenkundler(in f) m.

speleology [ˌspiːlɪˈɒlədʒɪ] n Höhlenkunde, Speläologie (spec) f.

spell[1] [spel] n (lit, fig) Zauber m; (incantation) Zauberspruch m. to be under a ~ (lit) unter einem Zauber stehen, verzaubert or verhext sein; (fig) wie verzaubert sein; to put a ~ on sb, to cast a ~ over sb, to put sb under a ~ (lit) jdn verzaubern or verhexen; (fig) jdn in seinen Bann ziehen, jdn verzaubern; to be under sb's ~ (fig) in jds Bann (dat) stehen; to break the ~ (lit, fig) den Bann brechen, den Zauber lösen.

spell[2] n (period) Weile f, Weilchen nt. for a ~ eine Weile, eine Zeitlang; cold/hot ~ Kälte-/Hitzewelle f; dizzy ~ Schwächeanfall m; a short ~ of sunny weather eine kurze Schönwetterperiode; we had or spent a ~ in Chile wir hielten uns eine Zeitlang in Chile auf; to do a ~ on the assembly line/as a waitress sich kurzzeitig am Fließband/als Serviererin betätigen; he did or had a ~ in prison er hat eine Zeitlang (im Gefängnis) gesessen; to take a ~ at the wheel eine Zeitlang or ein Weilchen das Steuer übernehmen; they're going through a bad ~ sie machen eine schwierige Zeit durch.

   2 vt to ~ sb (at sth) jdn (bei etw) ablösen.

spell[3] pret, ptp ~ed or spelt 1 vi (in writing) (orthographisch) richtig schreiben; (aloud) buchstabieren. she can't ~ sie kann keine Rechtschreibung; children should learn to ~ Kinder sollten richtig schreiben lernen.

   2 vt (a) schreiben; (aloud) buchstabieren. how do you ~ "onyx"? wie schreibt man „Onyx"?; how do you ~ your name? wie schreibt sich Ihr Name?, wie schreiben Sie sich?; what do these letters ~? welches Wort ergeben diese Buchstaben?

   (b) (denote) bedeuten. it ~s disaster (for us) das bedeutet Unglück (für uns).

♦ **spell out** vt sep (spell aloud) buchstabieren; (read slowly) entziffern; (explain) verdeutlichen, klarmachen. to ~ sth ~ for sb jdm etw klarmachen; he needs everything ~ed ~ to him man muß ihm alles überdeutlich machen; do I have to ~ it ~ for you? (inf) muß ich noch deutlicher werden?

spellbinder ['spelbaɪndəʳ] n fesselnder Redner/Schauspieler/Sänger; (film) fesselnder Film, Knüller m (inf). to be a ~ das Publikum fesseln.

spellbound ['spelbaʊnd] adj, adv (fig) wie verzaubert, gebannt; (lit) princess, castle verzaubert. to hold sb ~ jdn fesseln; (person also) jdn in seinen Bann schlagen.

speller ['speləʳ] n to be a good/bad ~ in Rechtschreibung gut/schlecht sein.

spelling ['spelɪŋ] n Rechtschreibung, Orthographie f; (of a word) Schreibweise f; (activity) Rechtschreiben nt; (Sch: lesson) Rechtschreibunterricht m. the correct ~ is ... die richtige Schreibweise ist ...

spelling: ~ bee n (Sch) Buchstabierwettbewerb m; ~ book n Fibel f; ~ mistake n (Recht)schreibfehler m, orthographischer Fehler; ~ pronunciation n buchstabengetreue Aussprache.

spelt[1] [spelt] n (Bot) Spelz(weizen), Dinkel m.

spelt[2] pret, ptp of spell[3].

spelunker [spɪˈlʌŋkəʳ] n Hobby-Höhlenforscher(in f) m.

spend [spend] pret, ptp spent 1 vt (a) (use) money ausgeben (on für); energy, strength verbrauchen; time brauchen. I've spent all my energy/strength ich habe meine ganze Energie/Kraft aufgebraucht; we spent a lot of time in useless discussion wir haben sehr viel Zeit mit nutzlosen Diskussionen vertan; I've spent three hours on this job/journey ich habe drei Stunden für diese Arbeit/Reise gebraucht; time well spent sinnvoll verwendete Zeit; see penny.

   (b) (pass) time, holiday, evening etc verbringen. he ~s all his spare time on his car/with his friends er verbringt jede freie Minute an seinem Auto/mit seinen Freunden; I ~ my weekends sleeping ich verschlafe meine Wochenenden; he ~s his time reading er verbringt seine Zeit mit Lesen.

   (c) to ~ money/time/effort on sth (devote to) Geld/Zeit/Mühe für etw aufbringen or in etw (acc) investieren; I spent a lot of effort on that das hat mich viel Mühe gekostet.

   (d) (exhaust) to have spent itself (anger, fury) sich erschöpft or gelegt haben; the storm had spent itself or its fury der Sturm hatte sich ausgetobt or gelegt; see also spent.

   2 vi Geld ausgeben. he was ~ing somewhat too freely er gab

das Geld mit vollen Händen aus.

spender ['spendəʳ] n he is a big/free ~ bei ihm sitzt das Geld locker; the Arabs are the big ~s nowadays heutzutage haben die Araber das große Geld; the last of the big ~s (iro) ein echter Großkapitalist (hum).

spending ['spendɪŋ] n, no pl Ausgaben pl. government ~ cuts Kürzungen im Etat.

spending: ~ money n Taschengeld nt; ~ power n Kaufkraft f; ~ spree n Großeinkauf m; to go on a ~ spree groß einkaufen, viel Geld ausgeben.

spendthrift ['spendθrɪft] 1 adj verschwenderisch. 2 n Verschwender(in f) m.

spent [spent] 1 pret, ptp of spend.

   2 adj ammunition, cartridge, match verbraucht; bullets also verschossen; person erschöpft. to be/look ~ erschöpft sein/aussehen; (prematurely aged) müde und verbraucht sein/aussehen; as a poet he was ~ at 25 mit 25 war seine dichterische Schaffenskraft verbraucht; to be a ~ force nichts mehr zu sagen haben; (movement) sich totgelaufen haben; (ideology) keine Zugkraft mehr haben.

sperm [spɜːm] n Samenfaden m, Spermatozoon, Spermium nt; (fluid) Samenflüssigkeit f, Sperma nt.

spermaceti [ˌspɜːməˈsetɪ] n Spermazet, Walrat nt.

spermatic [spɜːˈmætɪk] adj Samen-.

spermatozoon [ˌspɜːmætəʊˈzʊɒn] n, pl **spermatozoa** [ˌspɜːmætəˈzəʊə] Spermatozoon, Spermium nt.

spermicide [ˈspɜːmɪsaɪd] n Spermizid nt.

sperm: ~ oil n Walratöl nt; ~ whale n Pottwal m.

spew [spjuː] 1 vi (a) (sl: vomit) brechen, spucken. it makes me ~ (fig) es kotzt mich an (sl).

   (b) (flow: also ~ forth (form) or out) sich ergießen (geh); (liquid also) hervorsprudeln. flames/water ~ed out of or from the cave Flammen schlugen or züngelten aus der Höhle hervor/Wasser sprudelte aus der Höhle hervor, Wasser ergoß sich aus der Höhle (geh).

   2 vt (a) (also ~ up) (sl: vomit) erbrechen, ausspucken; blood spucken, speien.

   (b) (fig: also ~ out) flames spucken, speien; lava also auswerfen; waste water etc ablassen. the popular press ~s out lies die Boulevardpresse überschüttet ihre Leser mit Lügen.

sphagnum ['sfægnəm] n Torf- or Bleichmoos nt.

sphere [sfɪəʳ] n (a) Kugel f; (heavenly ~) Gestirn nt (geh); (old Astron) Sphäre f (old). the celestial ~ (poet) das Himmelszelt (poet); to be a ~ kugelförmig sein; see music.

   (b) (fig) Sphäre, Welt f; (of person, personal experience) Bereich m; (of knowledge etc) Gebiet, Feld nt; (social etc circle) Kreis m. in the ~ of politics/poetry in der Sphäre or Welt der Politik/Welt der Dichtung; his ~ of interest/influence sein Interessen-/Einflußbereich; ~ of activity (job, specialism) Wirkungskreis m; that's outside my ~ das geht über meinen Horizont; (not my responsibility) das ist nicht mein Gebiet.

spherical ['sferɪkəl] adj (in shape) kugelförmig, (kugel)rund; (Math, Astron) sphärisch.

spheroid ['sfɪərɔɪd] n (Geometry) Rotationsellipsoid nt.

sphincter ['sfɪŋktəʳ] n (Anat) Schließmuskel, Sphinkter (spec) m.

sphinx [sfɪŋks] n Sphinx f.

sphinx-like ['sfɪŋkslaɪk] adj sphinxhaft.

spice [spaɪs] 1 n (a) Gewürz nt. ~ rack Gewürzbord or -regal nt; ~ trade Gewürzhandel m; mixed ~ Gewürzmischung f.

   (b) (fig) Würze f; (trace: of irony, humour) Anflug, Hauch m. the ~ of life die Würze des Lebens; stories with some ~ pikante Geschichten pl.

   2 vt (lit, fig) würzen. a highly ~d account (fig) ein reichlich ausgeschmückter Bericht.

spiciness ['spaɪsɪnɪs] n (quality) Würzigkeit, Würze f; (taste) Würze f; (fig) Pikanterie f. because of its ~ weil das so stark gewürzt ist.

spick-and-span ['spɪkən'spæn] adj house etc blitzsauber, tipptopp in Ordnung pred. to look ~ (person) wie aus dem Ei gepellt aussehen; (house) blitzsauber sein.

spicy ['spaɪsɪ] adj (+er) würzig; sauce, food also stark gewürzt; (fig) story etc pikant.

spider ['spaɪdəʳ] n Spinne f. ~'s web Spinnwebe f, Spinnengewebe, Spinnennetz nt.

spider: ~ crab n Spinnenkrabbe f or -krebs m; ~man n (inf) (a) (building worker) Gerüstbauer m; (b) (steeplejack) Schornsteinarbeiter m; ~ monkey n Klammeraffe m; ~web n (US) Spinnwebe f, Spinnengewebe, Spinnennetz nt.

spidery ['spaɪdərɪ] adj writing krakelig; outline, drawing, pattern fein, spinnwebartig; limbs etc spinnenhaft.

spiel [ʃpiːl] n (inf) Sermon m (inf), Blabla m (inf); (tall story, excuse) Geschichte f (inf).

spiffing ['spɪfɪŋ] adj (dated inf) famos (dated inf).

spigot ['spɪgət] n (on cask) Spund, Zapfen m; (in tap) Abschlußkörper m; (US: faucet) Hahn m.

spike [spaɪk] 1 n (a) (on wall, railing etc) Spitze f; (nail) Nagel m; (on plant) Stachel m; (on helmet, shield) Spitze f; (on shoe, tyre etc) Spike m; (for letters, wastepaper etc) Dorn m. ~ heel Pfennigabsatz m; see also spikes.

   (b) (Bot) Ähre f.

   2 vt (a) aufspießen; (with weapon also) durchbohren. the editor ~d the story (Press) der Redakteur ließ die Story in der Schublade verschwinden.

   (b) (fig: frustrate) rumours den Boden entziehen (+dat). to ~ sb's guns (inf) jdm den Wind aus den Segeln nehmen.

   (c) (US: lace) drink einen Schuß zusetzen (+dat). ~d with rum mit einem Schuß Rum.

spiked [spaɪkt] adj shoe mit Spikes; drink mit Schuß.

spikes [spaɪks] npl (inf: running shoes) Spikes pl.

spiky ['spaɪkɪ] adj (+er) (a) (having spikes) railings, top of wall

mit Metallspitzen; *bush, animal* stach(e)lig; *branch* dornig.
 (b) (*like spikes*) *grass* spitz, stach(e)lig; *flower* mit spitzen Blütenblättern; *plant* spitzblättrig; *leaf* spitz; *writing* steil.
 (c) (*fig*) *person* empfindlich, leicht eingeschnappt (*inf*).

spill¹ [spɪl] (*vb: pret, ptp* ~**ed** *or* **spilt**) **1** *n* (*fall*) Sturz *m*. **to have a** ~ stürzen.
 2 *vt* **(a)** verschütten; *liquid also, blood* vergießen. **to** ~ **the beans (to sb)** (*inf*) (jdm gegenüber) nicht dichthalten (*inf*); **to** ~ **the beans about sth** etw ausplaudern.
 (b) (*horse*) abwerfen. **the lorry** ~**ed its load onto the road** die Ladung fiel vom Lastwagen herunter auf die Straße.
 3 *vi* verschüttet werden; (*large quantity*) sich ergießen; (*tears*) strömen, laufen; (*fig: people*) strömen. **the milk** ~**ed all over the carpet** die Milch war auf dem ganzen Teppich verschüttet; **the blood** ~**ed onto the floor** das Blut floß auf den Boden.
 ◆**spill out 1** *vi* (*out of aus*) (*liquid*) herausschwappen; (*grain*) herausrieseln; (*money, jewels*) herausfallen; (*fig: people*) (heraus)strömen. **clothes were** ~**ing** ~ **of the drawer** Kleidungsstücke quollen aus der Schublade hervor.
 2 *vt sep* ausschütten; (*by accident also*) verschütten; *liquid also* vergießen.
 ◆**spill over** *vi* (*liquid*) überlaufen; (*grain etc, assembly*) überquellen; (*fig*) (*population*) sich ausbreiten (*into auf* +*acc*); (*meeting*) sich hinziehen (*into bis in* +*acc*).

spill² *n* (*of wood*) (Kien)span *m*; (*of paper*) Fidibus *m*.

spillage [ˈspɪlɪdʒ] *n* (*act*) Verschütten *nt*; (*of liquid also*) Vergießen *nt*; (*quantity*) verschüttete Menge, Spillage *f* (*Comm*). **the** ~ **amounted to ...** es waren ... verschüttet worden.

spillikin [ˈspɪlɪkɪn] *n* **(a)** (*old: spill*) Kienspan *m*. **(b)** ~**s** *pl* (*game*) Mikado *nt*.

spill-over [ˈspɪləʊvəʳ] *n* Überschuß *m*. ~ **population** überquellende Bevölkerung.

spillway [ˈspɪlweɪ] *n* Überlaufrinne *f*.

spilt [spɪlt] *pret, ptp of* **spill¹**.

spin [spɪn] (*vb: pret* **spun** *or* (*old*) **span**, *ptp* **spun**) **1** *n* **(a)** (*revolution*) Drehung *f*; (*washing machine programme*) Schleudern *nt no pl*. **to give sth a** ~ etw (schnell) drehen; *spinning top* etw treiben lassen; (*in washing machine etc*) etw schleudern; **to give sth a long/short** ~ (*in washing machine*) etw lange/kurz schleudern; **to be in a** (*flat*) ~ (*fig inf*) am Rotieren *or* Durchdrehen sein (*inf*) (*about wegen*); **to send sb into a** (*flat*) ~ (*fig inf*) jdn zum Rotieren bringen (*inf*).
 (b) (*on ball*) Drall *m*, Drall *m*; (*Billiards*) Effet *m*. **to put a** ~ **on the ball** dem Ball einen Drall/Effet geben; (*with racquet*) den Ball anschneiden.
 (c) (*Aviat*) Trudeln *nt no pl*. **to go into a** ~ zu trudeln anfangen.
 (d) (*dated: trip*) Spritztour *f*. **to go for a** ~ eine Spritztour machen.
 2 *vt* **(a)** spinnen; *see* **yarn**.
 (b) (*turn*) *wheel* drehen; (*fast*) herumwirbeln; *top* tanzen lassen, treiben; (*in washing machine*) schleudern; (*toss*) *ball, coin* (hoch)werfen; (*Sport*) *ball* einen Drall/Effet geben (+*dat*); (*with racquet*) (an)schneiden.
 3 *vi* **(a)** spinnen.
 (b) (*revolve*) sich drehen; (*fast*) (herum)wirbeln; (*plane etc*) trudeln; (*in washing machine*) schleudern. **to** ~ **round and round** sich im Kreis drehen; (*dancer*) im Kreis herumwirbeln; **the ball spun into the air/past him** der Ball flog wirbelnd in die Luft/an ihm vorbei; **the car spun out of control** der Wagen begann, sich unkontrollierbar zu drehen; **to send sb/sth** ~**ing** jdn/etw umwerfen; **my head is** ~**ing** mir dreht sich alles; **the wine/noise makes my head** ~ von dem Wein dreht sich mir alles/mir schwirrt der Kopf von dem Lärm.
 ◆**spin along** *vi* (*move quickly*) (dahin)rasen, (dahin)sausen.
 ◆**spin out** *vt sep* (*inf*) *money, food* strecken (*inf*); *holiday, meeting* in die Länge ziehen; *story* ausspinnen.
 ◆**spin round 1** *vi* (*revolve*) sich drehen; (*very fast*) (herum)wirbeln; (*in surprise*) herumwirbeln, herumfahren. **2** *vt sep* (schnell) drehen; (*very fast*) herumwirbeln.

spina bifida [ˈspaɪnəˈbɪfɪdə] **1** *n* offene Wirbelsäule, Spina bifida *f* (*spec*). **2** *adj attr baby* mit einer offenen Wirbelsäule.

spinach [ˈspɪnɪdʒ] *n* Spinat *m*.

spinal [ˈspaɪnl] *adj vertebrae* Rücken-; *injury, muscle* Rückgrat-, spinal (*spec*); *nerves, anaesthesia* Rückenmark(s)-. ~ **column** Wirbelsäule *f*; ~ **cord** Rückenmark *nt*.

spin bowler *n* (*Cricket*) Werfer, der dem Ball einen Drall gibt.

spindle [ˈspɪndl] *n* (*for spinning, Mech*) Spindel *f*.

spindleshanks [ˈspɪndlʃæŋks] *n* (*inf*) **(a)** *pl* (*legs*) Streichholzbeine (*inf*), Stelzen (*inf*) *pl*. **(b)** *sing* (*person*) Langbein *nt* (*inf*).

spindly [ˈspɪndlɪ] *adj* (+*er*) *legs, arms, plant* spindeldürr (*inf*); *chairs* zierlich.

spin: ~**-drier**, ~**-dryer** *n* (*Brit*) (Wäsche)schleuder *f*; ~**drift** *n* Gischt *f*; ~**-dry** *vti* schleudern; ~**-dryer** *n see* ~**-drier**.

spine [spaɪn] *n* **(a)** (*Anat*) Rückgrat *nt*; (*of book*) (Buch)rücken *m*; (*of mountain range*) (Gebirgs)grat *m*. **(b)** (*spike*) Stachel *m*; (*of plant also*) Dorn *m*.

spine: ~**-chiller** *n* (*inf*) Gruselgeschichte *f*; Gruselfilm *m*; ~**chilling** *adj* (*inf*) schaurig, gruselig; *noise also* unheimlich.

spineless [ˈspaɪnlɪs] *adj* **(a)** (*Anat*) wirbellos; (*fig*) *person* ohne Rückgrat; *compromise, refusal* feige. **don't be so** ~ beweisen Sie mal, daß Sie Rückgrat haben! **(b)** (*Zool*) ohne Stacheln; *stachellos*; (*Bot also*) ohne Dornen, dornenlos.

spinelessly [ˈspaɪnlɪslɪ] *adv* (*fig*) feige.

spinet [spɪˈnet] *n* **(a)** (*Hist*) Spinett *nt*. **(b)** (*US*) Kleinklavier *nt*.

spinnaker [ˈspɪnəkəʳ] *n* (*Naut*) Spinnaker *m*.

spinner [ˈspɪnəʳ] *n* **(a)** (*of cloth*) Spinner(in *f*) *m*. **(b)** (*inf*) *see* **spin-drier**. **(c)** (*Fishing*) Spinnköder *m*. **(d)** (*Cricket*) Werfer, der den Bällen einen Drall gibt.

spinney [ˈspɪnɪ] *n* (*esp Brit*) Dickicht *nt*.

spinning [ˈspɪnɪŋ] *n* Spinnen *nt*.

spinning *in cpds* Spinn-; ~ **jenny** *n* Jenny-Maschine *f*; ~ **top** *n* Kreisel *m*; ~ **wheel** *n* Spinnrad *nt*; ~ **works** *n sing or pl* Spinnerei, Spinnstoffabrik *f*.

spin-off [ˈspɪnɒf] *n* (*side-product*) Nebenprodukt *nt*.

spinster [ˈspɪnstəʳ] *n* Unverheiratete, Ledige *f*; (*pej*) alte Jungfer (*pej*). **Mary Jones,** ~ die ledige Mary Jones; **to be a** ~ unverheiratet *or* ledig *or* eine alte Jungfer (*pej*) sein.

spinsterhood [ˈspɪnstəhʊd] *n* Ehelosigkeit *f*, Jungfernstand *m* (*old*). **she preferred** ~ sie wollte lieber unverheiratet bleiben.

spinsterish [ˈspɪnstərɪʃ] *adj* (*pej*) altjüngferlich (*pej*).

spiny [ˈspaɪnɪ] *adj* (+*er*) stach(e)lig, Stachel-; *plant also* dornig. ~ **lobster** (*Zool*) Languste *f*, Stachelhummer *m*.

spiracle [ˈspaɪrəkl] *n* (*of shark, ray etc*) Atemloch *nt*; (*of insect also*) Stigma *nt* (*spec*); (*of whale, dolphin*) Spritzloch *nt*.

spiral [ˈspaɪərəl] **1** *adj* spiralförmig, spiralig; *shell also* gewunden; *nebula, spring* Spiral-; *movement, descent* in Spiralen. **a** ~ **curve** eine Spirale; ~ **staircase** Wendeltreppe *f*.
 2 *n* (*lit, fig*) Spirale *f*. **price/inflationary** ~ Preis-/Inflationsspirale *f*.
 3 *vi* (*also* ~ **up**) sich (hoch)winden; (*smoke also, missile etc*) spiralförmig *or* in einer Spirale aufsteigen; (*plane, bird also*) sich in die Höhe schrauben; (*prices*) (nach oben) klettern.
 ◆**spiral down** *vi* spiralförmig *or* in einer Spirale herunterkommen; (*staircase also*) sich abwärts winden; (*plane also*) sich herunterschrauben, sich nach unten schrauben.

spirally [ˈspaɪərəlɪ] *adv* in einer Spirale, spiralförmig.

spire [spaɪəʳ] *n* (*of church*) Turmspitze *f*, Turm *m*.

spirit [ˈspɪrɪt] **1** *n* **(a)** (*soul*) Geist *m*. **the life of the** ~ das Seelenleben; **he was troubled in** ~ (*liter*) etwas lastete auf seiner Seele (*geh*); **I'll be with you in** ~ im Geiste werde ich bei euch sein; **the** ~ **is willing (but the flesh is weak)** der Geist ist willig, aber das Fleisch ist schwach.
 (b) (*supernatural being, ghost*) Geist *m*.
 (c) (*leading person*) (*of age, movement etc*) Geist *m*; (*of party, enterprise*) Kopf *m*.
 (d) *no pl* (*courage*) Mut, Schneid *m*; (*vitality, enthusiasm*) Elan, Schwung *m*. **the** ~ **of a lion** das Herz eines Löwen; **a man of** ~ (*courageous*) ein mutiger Mensch; **a horse with plenty of** ~ ein feuriges Pferd; **to break sb's** ~ jdn *or* jds Mut brechen; **to sing/reply with** ~ mit Inbrunst singen/mutig antworten; **to put** ~ **into sb** jdm Mut machen.
 (e) (*mental attitude: of country, group of people, doctrine, reform etc*) Geist *m*; (*mood*) Stimmung *f*. **pioneering/team/community** ~ Pionier-/Mannschaftsgeist *m*/Gemeinschaftssinn *m*; **Christmas** ~ (*Rel*) weihnachtlicher Geist; (*mood*) weihnachtliche Stimmung; **party** ~ Partystimmung *f*; **fighting** ~ Kampfgeist; **a** ~ **of optimism/despair/rebellion** eine optimistische/verzweifelte/rebellische Stimmung; **to do sth in a** ~ **of optimism/humility** etw voll Optimismus/voller Demut tun; **in a** ~ **of forgiveness/revenge** aus einer vergebenden/rachsüchtigen Stimmung heraus; **Christian** ~ Christlichkeit; **the** ~ **of the age** der Zeitgeist; **he has the right** ~ er hat die richtige Einstellung; **to enter into the** ~ **of sth** bei etw mitmachen *or* dabeisein; **when the** ~ **moves him** wenn es ihn überkommt; **that's the** ~! (*inf*) so ist's recht! (*inf*).
 (f) *no pl* (*intention*) Geist *m*. **the** ~ **of the law** der Geist *or* Sinn des Gesetzes; **to take sth in the right/wrong** ~ etw richtig/falsch auffassen; **to take sth in the** ~ **in which it was meant/given** etw so nehmen, wie es gemeint war; **the** ~ **in which it is done** wie es getan wird.
 (g) ~**s** *pl* (*state of mind*) Stimmung, Laune *f*; (*courage*) Mut *m*; **to be in good/bad/out of** ~**s** guter/schlechter Laune/niedergeschlagen sein; **to keep one's** ~**s den Mut nicht verlieren; **my** ~**s rose/fell** ich bekam (neuen) Mut/mir sank der Mut; **to raise sb's** ~**s** jdn aufmuntern; **to revive sb's** ~**s** jds Lebensgeister wiedererwecken.
 (h) ~**s** *pl* (*alcohol*) Branntwein *m*, Spirituosen, geistige Getränke *pl*; *raw* ~ reiner Alkohol.
 (i) (*Chem*) Spiritus *m*. ~**s of ammonia** Salmiakgeist *m*; ~**(s) of turpentine** Terpentinöl *nt*.
 2 *vt* **to** ~ **sb/sth away** *or* **off** jdn/etw verschwinden lassen *or* wegzaubern; **to** ~ **sb out of a room** *etc* jdn aus einem Zimmer *etc* wegzaubern.

spirited [ˈspɪrɪtɪd] *adj* temperamentvoll; *horse also* feurig; *book, performance* lebendig; (*courageous*) *person, reply, attack, attempt etc* beherzt, mutig.

spiritedly [ˈspɪrɪtɪdlɪ] *adv* *see adj*.

spiritedness [ˈspɪrɪtɪdnɪs] *n see adj* Temperament *nt*; Feurigkeit *f*; Lebendigkeit *f*; Beherztheit *f*, Mut *m*.

spirit: ~ **gum** *n* Mastix(gummi) *m*; ~ **lamp** *n* Petroleumlampe *f*; ~**less** *adj person, performance, book* saft- und kraftlos; *agreement, acceptance, reply* lustlos; *animal* brav, lahm (*inf*); ~ **level** *n* Wasserwaage *f*; ~ **stove** *n* Spirituskocher *m*.

spiritual [ˈspɪrɪtjʊəl] **1** *adj* geistig; *expression* vergeistigt; (*Eccl*) geistlich. ~ **life** Seelenleben *nt*; **my** ~ **home** meine geistige Heimat; **Lords** ~ geistliche Lords (im Oberhaus). **2** *n* (*Mus*) Spiritual *nt*.

spiritualism [ˈspɪrɪtjʊəlɪzəm] *n* Spiritismus *m*.

spiritualist [ˈspɪrɪtjʊəlɪst] *n* Spiritist(in *f*) *m*.

spirituality [ˌspɪrɪtjʊˈælɪtɪ] *n see adj* Geistigkeit *f*; Vergeistigung *f*.

spiritually [ˈspɪrɪtjʊəlɪ] *adv* geistig. ~, **he is ...** in geistiger Hinsicht ist er ...

spirituous [ˈspɪrɪtjʊəs] *adj* (*form*) alkoholisch, spirituos (*rare*).

spit¹ [spɪt] (*vb: pret, ptp* **spat**) **1** *n* **(a)** (*action*) (Aus)spucken *nt*; (*saliva*) Spucke *f*. **to have a** ~ ausspucken; **there was just a** ~ **of rain** es tröpfelte nur; ~ **and polish** (*inf*) Wienern *nt* (*inf*); **to give sth a bit of** ~ **and polish** (*inf*) etw wienern (*inf*); **it needs a bit of** ~ **and polish** (*inf*) es müßte einmal tüchtig gewienert werden (*inf*).

(b) (inf: image) see **spitting image**.

2 vt spucken, speien (geh); curses ausstoßen (at gegen).

3 vi spucken, speien (geh); (fat) spritzen; (fire) zischen; (person: verbally, cat) fauchen, zischen. **to ~ at sb** jdn anspucken, jdn anspeien (geh); jdn anfauchen, jdn anzischen; **to ~ with rage** vor Wut schäumen; **to ~ in sb's face/eye** jdm ins Gesicht spucken; (fig) auf jdn pfeifen (inf); **it is ~ting (with rain)** es tröpfelt.

♦ **spit out** vt sep ausspucken, ausspeien (geh); words ausstoßen. **~ it ~!** (fig inf) spuck's aus! (inf), heraus mit der Sprache!

spit² **1** n **(a)** (Cook) (Brat)spieß m. **on the ~** am Spieß. **(b)** (of land) Landzunge f. **2** vt meat (auf)spießen.

spite [spaɪt] **1** n **(a)** (ill will) Boshaftigkeit, Gehässigkeit f. **to do sth out of or from ~** etw aus reiner Boshaftigkeit tun.
(b) **in ~ of** (despite) trotz (+gen); **it was a success/we went in ~ of him** es war dennoch ein Erfolg/wir gingen dennoch; **he did it in ~ of himself** er konnte nicht anders; **in ~ of the fact that he ... obwohl** er ...; **in ~ of that** I'll still go ich gehe trotzdem.
2 vt ärgern. **she just does it to ~ me** sie tut es nur mir zum Trotz, sie tut es nur, um mich zu ärgern.

spiteful [ˈspaɪtfʊl] adj boshaft, gemein; (gloating also) schadenfroh, gehässig.

spitefully [ˈspaɪtfəlɪ] adv see adj. **~, she told him** voll Bosheit/voll Schadenfreude erzählte sie es ihm.

spitefulness [ˈspaɪtfʊlnɪs] n Boshaftigkeit, Gemeinheit f; (gloating) Schadenfreude, Gehässigkeit f.

spitfire [ˈspɪtfaɪə²] n feuerspeiender Drache; (woman also) Giftnudel f (inf).

spitting image [ˈspɪtɪŋˈɪmɪdʒ] n (inf) Ebenbild nt. **to be the ~ of sb** jdm wie aus dem Gesicht geschnitten sein, jdm zum Verwechseln ähnlich sehen.

spittle [ˈspɪtl] n Speichel m, Spucke f.

spittoon [spɪˈtuːn] n Spucknapf m.

spiv [spɪv] n (Brit sl) schmieriger Typ (sl).

splash [splæʃ] **1** n **(a)** (spray) Spritzen nt no pl; (noise) Platschen nt no pl, Platscher m (inf). **he dived in with a ~** es spritzte/platschte, als er hineinsprang; **it made a great ~ as it hit the water** das Wasser spritzte nach allen Seiten, als es hineinfiel; (noise) es fiel laut platschend ins Wasser; **to make a ~** (fig) Furore machen; (news) wie eine Bombe einschlagen; (book) einschlagen; **to make a ~ with sth** mit etw Furore machen; **a great ~ of publicity** großes Tamtam (inf).
(b) (sth ~ed) Spritzer m; (in drink etc also) Schuß m; (of colour, light) Tupfen m; (patch) Fleck m. **~es of paint** Farbspritzer pl.
2 vt **(a)** water etc spritzen; (pour) gießen; person, object bespritzen. **to ~ sb with water, to ~ water over sb** jdn mit Wasser bespritzen; **to ~ paint on sth** etw mit Farbe bespritzen; (with brush) Farbe auf etw (acc) klatschen (inf); **to ~ one's way through a stream** platschend einen Bach durchqueren.
(b) (Press inf) story groß rausbringen (inf). **the story was ~ed all over the papers** die Geschichte wurde in allen Zeitungen groß rausgebracht (inf).
3 vi (liquid) spritzen; (rain, waves) klatschen; (tears) tropfen; (when diving, walking etc) platschen; (when playing) planschen.

♦ **splash about 1** vi herumspritzen; (in water) herumplanschen; (while walking) herumplatschen. **2** vt sep water herumspritzen mit; (fig inf) money um sich werfen mit (inf); story groß aufziehen or rausbringen (inf).

♦ **splash down** vi **(a)** (Space) wassern. **(b)** (rain) herunterrinnen (prep obj an +dat).

♦ **splash out** vi (inf) tüchtig in die Tasche greifen (inf); (on reception, giving presents etc) sich nicht lumpen lassen (inf). **to ~ ~ on sth** sich (dat) etw spendieren (inf).

splash: **~back**, **~board** n Spritzschutz m; **~down** n (Space) Wasserung f; **~ guard** n (US Aut) Schmutzfänger m.

splat [splæt] **1** n Platschen nt. **2** adv **to go ~ into sth** gegen etw platschen.

splatter [ˈsplætə²] **1** n Spritzen nt no pl; (of rain) Prasseln nt no pl; (sth ~ed) Fleck m; (of ink, paint etc) Klecks m; (Art: ~ technique) Spritztechnik f.
2 vi spritzen; (rain also) prasseln; (ink, paint also) klecksen.
3 vt bespritzen; (with ink, paint etc) beklecksen. **to ~ mud over sb** jdn mit Schlamm bespritzen.

splay [spleɪ] **1** vt **(a)** (spread out) legs, fingers, toes spreizen; feet nach außen stellen. **the wheels are ~ed** die Räder stehen nach außen, die Räder haben negativen Sturz.
(b) (Tech) pipe weiten; window frame ausschrägen.
2 vi nach außen gehen; (table, pillars also) sich nach außen biegen; (window frame) ausgeschrägt sein. **he lay ~ed out on the ground** er lag auf der Erde und hatte alle viere von sich gestreckt.
3 n (Archit) Ausschrägung f.

splay: **~foot** n nach außen gestellter Fuß; **~ footed** adj mit nach außen gestellten Füßen; **to be ~footed** nach außen gehen.

spleen [spliːn] n (Anat) Milz f; (fig) Zorn m, Rage f. **a fit of ~** ein Zornesausbruch m; **to vent one's ~** seinem Ärger Luft machen; **to vent one's ~ on sb** seine Wut an jdm auslassen.

splendid [ˈsplendɪd] adj **(a)** (magnificent) clothes, sunset, music herrlich; occasion, scale, villain großartig. **(b)** (excellent) hervorragend; rider etc, chance, idea, amusement glänzend, ausgezeichnet; joke also herrlich. **that's (simply) ~!** (das ist ja) ausgezeichnet!

splendidly [ˈsplendɪdlɪ] adv **(a)** (magnificently) herrlich. **(b)** (excellently) hervorragend, glänzend, ausgezeichnet.

splendiferous [splenˈdɪfərəs] adj (dated inf) fabelhaft.

splendour, (US) **splendor** [ˈsplendə²] n Pracht f no pl; (of music, achievement) Großartigkeit f. **the ~ of his victory** sein ruhmreicher Sieg; **the ~s of the Roman Empire** der Glanz or die Pracht des Römischen Reiches.

---

splenetic [splɪˈnetɪk] adj **(a)** (Anat) Milz-. **(b)** (liter: peevish) unwirsch. **his ~ anger** seine Galligkeit.

splice [splaɪs] n Verbindung f; (of ropes also) Spleiß m (spec); (of tapes, film also) Klebung f; (of wood also) Fuge f. **2** vt ropes spleißen (spec); tapes, film (zusammen)kleben; pieces of wood etc verfugen. **to get ~d** (inf) sich verehelichen (hum).

splint [splɪnt] **1** n Schiene f. **to put a ~ on sb/sth** jdn/etw schienen; **to be in ~s** geschient sein. **2** vt schienen.

splinter [ˈsplɪntə²] **1** n Splitter m; (wooden ~ in finger etc also) Spließ, Spreißel (S Ger) m. **2** vt (zer)splittern; (with axe) wood zerhacken; (fig) party spalten. **3** vi (zer)splittern; (party) sich spalten. **to ~ off** absplittern; (fig) sich abspalten.

splinter: **~ group** n Splittergruppe f; **~proof** adj splitterfrei.

splintery [ˈsplɪntərɪ] adj splitt(e)rig.

split [splɪt] (vb: pret, ptp ~) **1** n **(a)** Riß m (in in +dat); (in wall, rock, wood also) Spalt m (in in +dat).
(b) (fig: division) Bruch m (in in +dat), Entzweiung f (+gen); (Pol, Eccl) Spaltung f (in gen). **there is a ~ in the party over ...** die Partei ist in der Frage (+gen) ... gespalten; **there is a three-way ~ in the party over ...** die Partei zerfällt in der Frage (+gen) ... in drei Lager, die Partei ist in der Frage (+gen) ... dreigeteilt; **a three-way ~ of the profits** eine Drittelung des Gewinns; **I want my ~** ich will meinen Schnitt (inf).
(c) (distinction: in meaning) Aufteilung f.
(d) pl **the ~s** Spagat m; **to do the ~s** (einen) Spagat machen.
(e) (inf: sweet) (also banana ~) (Bananen-)Split m. **jam/cream ~** mit Marmelade/Sahne gefülltes Gebäckstück.
(f) (esp US: bottle) kleine Flasche.
2 adj gespalten (on, over in +dat).
3 vt **(a)** (cleave) (zer)teilen; wood also, atom spalten; stone zerbrechen; fabric, garment zerreißen, zerschlitzen; seam aufplatzen lassen. **the sea had ~ the ship in two** in dem Sturm zerbrach das Schiff in zwei Teile; **I ~ the seam** die Naht ist (auf)geplatzt; **to ~ hairs** (inf) Haarspalterei treiben (inf); **to ~ one's sides (laughing)** (inf) vor Lachen fast platzen (inf); **to ~ sth open** etw aufbrechen; **his lip had been ~ open** seine Lippe war aufgeplatzt; **his head was ~ open when he fell** er hatte sich (dat) beim Fallen den Kopf aufgeschlagen.
(b) (divide) spalten; (share) work, costs etc (sich dat) teilen. **to ~ sth into three parts** etw in drei Teile aufteilen; **to ~ the vote** die Abstimmung zum Scheitern bringen; **a party ~ three ways** eine in drei Lager gespaltene Partei; **to ~ one's vote** or (US) **ticket** panaschieren; **they ~ the profit three ways** sie haben den Gewinn gedrittelt or in drei Teile geteilt; **to ~ the difference** (fig: in argument etc) sich auf halbem Wege einigen; (lit: with money etc) sich (dat) die Differenz teilen.
4 vi **(a)** (wood, stone) (entzwei)brechen; (hair) sich spalten; (trousers, seam etc) platzen; (fabric) zerreißen; (ship) auseinanderbrechen. **to ~ open** aufplatzen, aufbrechen; **to ~ at the seams** (lit) an den Nähten aufplatzen; (fig) aus allen or den Nähten platzen; **my head is ~ting** (fig) mir platzt der Kopf.
(b) (divide) sich teilen; (people) sich aufteilen; (Pol, church) sich spalten (on, over wegen).
(c) (sl: leave) abhauen (inf).
(d) (inf: tell tales) **to ~ on sb** jdn verpfeifen (inf).

♦ **split off 1** vt sep abtrennen (prep obj von); (with axe also) abspalten (prep obj von); (break) abbrechen (prep obj von). **2** vi abbrechen; (rock also) sich lösen; (fig) sich trennen (from von).

♦ **split up 1** vt sep money, work (auf)teilen; meanings aufteilen; party, organization spalten; meeting ein Ende machen (+dat); two people trennen; crowd zerstreuen. **2** vi zerbrechen; (divide) sich teilen; (meeting, crowd) sich spalten; (partners) sich voneinander trennen.

split: **~ decision** n (Boxing) nicht einstimmige Entscheidung; **~ ends** npl gespaltene Haarspitzen pl, Spliß m; **~ infinitive** n (Gram) getrennter Infinitiv; **~-level** adj (Archit) mit Zwischenstock; **~-level cooker** Herdkombination, bei der Koch- und Backteil getrennt in Sichthöhe sind; **~ peas** npl getrocknete (halbe) Erbsen pl; **~-pea soup** n Erbsensuppe f; **~ personality** n (Psych) gespaltene Persönlichkeit; **~ pin** n (cotter pin) Splint m; (on envelope) Musterklammer f; **~ second 1** n Bruchteil m einer Sekunde; **in a ~ second** in Sekundenschnelle; **2** adj **~-second timing** Abstimmung f auf die Sekunde; (of actor) Gefühl nt für den richtigen Moment.

splitting [ˈsplɪtɪŋ] **1** n Zerteilung f; (of wood) Spalten nt. **the ~ of the atom** die Kernspaltung. **2** adj headache rasend, heftig. **there was a ~ sound** (of wood) es klang, als ob etwas zerbräche; (of cloth) es klang, als ob etwas zerrisse.

split-up [ˈsplɪtʌp] n (of friends) Bruch m (of zwischen +dat); (of partners) Trennung f (of gen); (of party) Spaltung f (of gen).

splodge [splɒdʒ], **splotch** [splɒtʃ] **1** n Fleck, Klecks m; (of cream etc) Klacks m. **2** vt clothes bespritzen; (with paint, ink also) beklecksen; mud spritzen; paint klecksen.

splurge [splɜːdʒ] n (inf) (shopping spree) Kauforgie f (pej inf). **I felt like a ~** ich wollte mir was leisten; **to go on a ~** groß einkaufen gehen; **a big publicity ~** eine groß aufgemachte Werbekampagne; **we had a big ~ on the reception** unser Empfang war ein Riesentamtam.

♦ **splurge out on** vi +prep obj (inf) sich in Unkosten stürzen mit.

splutter [ˈsplʌtə²] **1** n (of engine) Stottern nt; (of fire) Zischen nt; (of sausages) Zischen nt; (while talking) Prusten nt no pl.
2 vi (person) (spit) prusten, spucken; (stutter) stottern; (engine) stottern; (fire, lamp, fat) zischen; (sausages) brutzeln, zischen. **to ~ with indignation** vor Entrüstung prusten.
3 vt (hervor)stoßen. **that's not true, he ~ed** das ist nicht wahr, platzte er los.

spoil [spɔɪl] (vb: pret, ptp ~ed or spoilt) **1** n usu pl **~s** Beute f no pl; (fig: profits also) Gewinn m. **the ~s of war/office** Kriegsbeute f/Amtsausbeute f; **~s system** (US Pol) Ämterpatronage, Filzokratie (inf) f.

2 vt (a) (ruin, detract from) verderben; view also, town, looks etc verschandeln; peace of mind zerstören; life ruinieren; ballot papers ungültig machen. to ~ sb's fun jdm den Spaß verderben; it ~ed our evening das hat uns (dat) den Abend verdorben; if you eat now you'll ~ your lunch wenn du jetzt etwas ißt, verdirbst du dir den Appetit fürs Mittagessen; ~ed ballot papers ungültige Stimmzettel.
(b) person verwöhnen; children also verziehen. to ~ sb for sth (inf) jdn für etw verderben; to be ~t for choice eine übergroße Auswahl haben, die Qual der Wahl haben.
3 vi (food) verderben. to be ~ing for trouble/a fight Ärger/Streit suchen.
spoiler ['spɔɪlə'] n (Aut) Spoiler m.
spoilsport ['spɔɪlspɔːt] n (inf) Spielverderber m (inf).
spoilt [spɔɪlt] **1** pret, ptp of spoil. **2** adj child verwöhnt, verzogen; meal verdorben.
spoke¹ [spəuk] n Speiche f. to put a ~ in sb's wheel (inf) jdm Knüppel zwischen die Beine werfen (inf).
spoke² pret of speak.
spoken ['spəukən] **1** ptp of speak. **2** adj language gesprochen. his ~ English is better than ... er spricht Englisch besser als ...
spokeshave ['spəukʃeɪv] n Schabhobel, Speichenhobel m.
spokesman ['spəuksmən] n, pl -men [-mən] Sprecher m. to act as (a) ~ for a group als Sprecher einer Gruppe auftreten.
spokesperson ['spəukspɜːsən] n Sprecher(in f) m.
spokeswoman ['spəukswumən] n, pl -women [-wimin] Sprecherin f.
spoliation [ˌspəulɪ'eɪʃən] n (liter) Plünderung f.
spondee ['spɒndiː] n Spondeus m.
sponge [spʌndʒ] **1** n (a) Schwamm m; see throw in.
(b) (sponging) to give sth a ~ floor etw aufwischen; car etw waschen; walls etw abwaschen; table etw abwischen; to give sb a ~ jdn kurz (ab)waschen.
(c) (Cook) (also ~ cake) Rührkuchen m; (fatless) Biskuit(kuchen) m; (~ mixture) Rührteig m; Biskuitmasse f. jam ~ Biskuit(kuchen) mit Marmeladenfüllung.
2 vt (a) (clean) abwischen; wound abtupfen.
(b) (inf: scrounge) schnorren (inf) (from bei).
♦**sponge down** vt sep person (schnell) waschen; walls also abwaschen; horse abreiben.
♦**sponge off** vt sep stain, liquid abwischen.
♦**sponge off** or **on** vi +prep obj (inf) to ~ ~ sb jdm auf der Tasche liegen (inf).
♦**sponge out** vt sep (remove) stain herausreiben, herausmachen; (clean out) drawer auswaschen; wound austupfen.
♦**sponge up** vt sep aufwischen.
sponge: ~ bag n (Brit) Waschbeutel, Kulturbeutel m; ~ bath n (esp US) to give sb a ~ bath jdn (gründlich) waschen; ~ cake n Rührkuchen m; (fatless) Biskuit(kuchen) m; ~ down n kurze Wäsche; to give sb/sth a ~ down jdn/etw kurz abwaschen; ~ pudding n Mehlpudding m.
sponger ['spʌndʒə'] n (inf) Schmarotzer, Schnorrer (inf) m.
sponginess ['spʌndʒɪnɪs] n see adj Nachgiebigkeit, Weichheit f; Lockerheit f; Schwammigkeit f.
spongy ['spʌndʒɪ] adj (+er) nachgiebig, weich; (light) pudding locker; skin etc schwammig.
sponsor ['spɒnsə'] **1** n (a) Förderer m, Förderin f; (for membership) Bürge m, Bürgin f; (for event) Schirmherr(in f) m; (Rad, TV, Sport etc) Geldgeber(in f), Sponsor(in f) m; (for fundraising) Spender(in f) m; (Parl: of bill) Befürworter(in f) m. to stand ~ for sb jdn für jdn bürgen.
(b) (godparent) Pate m, Patin f. to stand ~ for a child Pate/Patin eines Kindes sein.
2 vt (a) unterstützen; (financially also) fördern; event also die Schirmherrschaft (+gen) übernehmen; future member bürgen für; membership, bill befürworten, empfehlen; (Rad, TV, Sport etc) programme finanzieren. he ~ed him at 5p a mile er verpflichtete sich, ihm 5 Pence pro Meile zu geben.
(b) (as godparent) die Patenschaft (+gen) übernehmen.
sponsored ['spɒnsəd] adj (for charity etc) walk, silence etc: zur Geldbeschaffung abgehalten, wobei die Leistung pro Einheit vom Spender mit einem abgemachten Einsatz honoriert wird.
sponsorship ['spɒnsəʃɪp] n see vt (a) Unterstützung f; Förderung f; Schirmherrschaft f; Bürgschaft f; Befürwortung, Empfehlung f; Finanzierung f. he got into the club under my ~ durch or auf meine Empfehlung kam er in den Klub. (b) Patenschaft f.
spontaneity [ˌspɒntə'neɪətɪ] n see adj Spontaneität f; Ungezwungenheit f.
spontaneous [spɒn'teɪnɪəs] adj spontan; style ungezwungen. ~ combustion Selbstentzündung f.
spontaneously [spɒn'teɪnɪəslɪ] adv spontan; (voluntarily also) von sich aus, von selbst.
spoof [spuːf] (inf) **1** n (a) (parody) Parodie f (of auf +acc). (b) (hoax) Ulk (inf), (April)scherz (inf) m. **2** adj attr poem, programme etc parodiert; version verballhornt. **3** vt (parody) novel parodieren; poem also verballhornen.
spook [spuːk] n (inf) Gespenst nt.
spooky ['spuːkɪ] adj (+er) (inf) (a) gespenstisch, gruselig (inf). (b) (esp US: strange) sonderbar. it was really ~ das war wirklich ein sonderbares or eigenartiges Gefühl.
spool [spuːl] n (Phot, on sewing machine) Spule f; (on fishing line) Rolle f; (for thread) (Garn)rolle f; (of thread) Rolle f.
spoon [spuːn] **1** n Löffel m; see silver. **2** vt löffeln. **3** vi (dated inf) schmusen, poussieren (dated inf).
♦**spoon out** vt sep (löffelweise) ausschöpfen.
♦**spoon up** vt sep löffeln; (eat up) auslöffeln; spillage auflöffeln.
spoonbill ['spuːnbɪl] n Löffler, Löffelreiher m.
spoonerism ['spuːnərɪzəm] n lustiger Versprecher, Dreckfuhler m (hum inf).

spoon-feed ['spuːnfiːd] pret, ptp **spoon-fed** ['spuːnfed] vt baby, invalid füttern; (fig) (do thinking for) gängeln; (supply with) füttern (inf).
spoonful ['spuːnful] n Löffel. m. a ~ of soup ein Löffel Suppe.
sporadic [spə'rædɪk] adj sporadisch; (occasional also) gelegentlich. we heard ~ gun-fire wir hörten gelegentlich Schüsse.
sporadically [spə'rædɪkəlɪ] adv sporadisch; (occasionally also) gelegentlich. snow fell ~ es fiel vereinzelt Schnee.
spore [spɔː'] n Spore f.
sporran ['spɒrən] n (über dem Schottenrock getragene) Felltasche.
sport [spɔːt] **1** n (a) (games collectively) Sport m no pl; (type of ~) Sportart f. to be good at ~(s) gut im Sport sein, sportlich sein; tennis is my ~ Tennis ist mein Lieblingssport; the ~ of kings der königliche Sport, der Pferderennsport; to offer good ~ gute Jagd-/Angelmöglichkeiten pl bieten.
(b) ~s pl (also ~s meeting) Sportveranstaltung f.
(c) (amusement) Spaß m. to do sth for/in ~ etw zum Spaß tun; it was great ~ es hat großen Spaß gemacht; to say sth in ~ etw aus or im or zum Spaß sagen; to make ~ of sb/sth (old) sich über jdn/etw lustig machen; the ~ of Fortune (liter) der Spielball des Schicksals (liter).
(d) (inf: person) feiner or anständiger Kerl (inf); (Austral) Junge m. to be a (good) ~ alles mitmachen; they are such good ~s mit ihnen kann man Pferde stehlen (inf); he's a good ~, he doesn't mind losing er ist kein Spielverderber, er macht sich nichts daraus, wenn er verliert; be a ~! sei kein Spielverderber!, sei nicht so! (inf).
(e) (Biol, Zool) Spielart, Abart f.
2 vt tie, dress anhaben; (show off) ring etc protzen mit; black eye herumlaufen mit (inf).
3 vi (frolic) (herum)tollen; (kitten) (herum)spielen.
4 adj attr (US) see sports.
sporting ['spɔːtɪŋ] adj (a) person, interests sportlich; equipment also Sports-; dog, gun Jagd-. ~ events Wettkämpfe pl; a great ~ man ein großer Sportsmann.
(b) (sportsmanlike) sportlich; spirit also Sports-; (fig) offer, solution fair; (decent) anständig. it's ~ of you to ... es ist anständig von dir, zu ...; to give sb a ~ chance jdm eine faire Chance geben; there is a ~ chance that ... die Chancen stehen nicht schlecht, daß ...
sporting editor n (US) Sportredakteur(in f) m.
sportingly ['spɔːtɪŋlɪ] adv fair; (decently) anständig. he ~ gave his opponent a start er gab seinem Gegner fairerweise einen Vorsprung.
sportive adj, ~**ly** adv ['spɔːtɪv, -lɪ] (liter) fidel, launig (liter).
sports, (US also) **sport** in cpds Sport-; ~ car n Sportwagen m; ~cast n Sportübertragung or -sendung f; ~caster, ~ commentator n Sportreporter(in f), (Sport)kommentator(in f) m; ~coat n see ~ jacket; ~ day n (Brit) (Schul)sportfest nt; ~ department n Sportabteilung f; ~ editor n Sportredakteur(in f) m; ~field, ~ ground n Sportplatz m; ~ jacket n Sportjackett nt, Sakko m or nt; ~man [-mən] n (player) Sportler m; (good ~man) anständiger or feiner Kerl (inf); (hunter) Jäger m; ~man of the year Sportler m des Jahres; ~manlike [-mənlaik] adj sportlich; (fig) behaviour, act etc fair; ~manship [-mənʃɪp] n (skill) Sportlichkeit f; (fairness also) sportliches Verhalten, Fairneß f; ~ page n Sportseite f; ~ programme n Sportprogramm nt; ~wear n (for sport) Sportkleidung f; (leisure wear) Freizeitkleidung f; ~woman n Sportlerin f; ~ writer n Sportjournalist(in f) m.
sporty ['spɔːtɪ] adj (+er) (inf) (a) person sportbegeistert, sportlich; clothes sportlich. (b) (jaunty) flott.
spot [spɒt] **1** n (a) (dot) Tupfen, Punkt m; (on dice) Punkt m; (Zool, Bot also, stain, on fruit) Fleck m; (fig: on reputation, good name) Makel m (on an +dat). a dress with ~s ein getupftes or gepunktetes Kleid; ~s of blood/grease Blutflecken pl/ Fettflecken pl; ~s of ink Tintenklecks or -flecke pl; to knock ~s off sb/sth (fig inf) jdn/etw in den Schatten stellen, jdn in die Tasche stecken (inf); to have ~s before one's eyes Sternchen sehen; without a ~ or stain (fig liter) makellos.
(b) (Med etc) Fleck m; (pimple) Pickel m; (place) Stelle f. to break or come out in ~s Flecken/Pickel bekommen.
(c) (place) Stelle f; (point) Punkt m. this is the ~ where Rizzio was murdered an dieser Stelle or hier ist Rizzio ermordet worden; a pleasant ~ ein schönes Fleckchen (inf); good in ~s stellenweise ganz gut; on the ~ (at the scene) an Ort und Stelle; (at once) auf der Stelle, sofort; our man on the ~ unser Mann am Ort (des Geschehens) or vor Ort; on-the-~ inquiry/investigation (at the scene) Untersuchung f an Ort und Stelle; (immediate) sofortige Untersuchung; an on-the-~ report/broadcast ein Bericht vom Ort des Geschehens; our on-the-~ reporter will now ... vom Ort des Geschehens berichtet nun ...
(d) (Brit inf: small quantity) a/the ~ of ein/das bißchen; we had a ~ of rain/a few ~s of rain wir hatten ein paar Tropfen Regen; there was a ~ of trouble/bother es gab etwas Ärger; we're in a ~ of bother wir haben Schwierigkeiten; why don't you do a ~ of work? warum arbeiten Sie nicht mal ein bißchen?; after a ~ of difficulty nach einigen Schwierigkeiten; would you like to do a ~ of driving? möchten Sie ein bißchen fahren?
(e) (fig: characteristic) Punkt m, Stelle f. weak ~ schwache Stelle.
(f) (difficulty) Klemme f. to be in a (tight) ~ in der Klemme sitzen (inf), in Schwulitäten sein (inf); to put sb in a ~ or on the ~ jdn in Verlegenheit or Schwulitäten (inf) bringen.
(g) (in show) Nummer f; (Rad, TV) (ein paar Minuten) Sendezeit f; (for advertisement) Werbespot m; (announcement) Kurzmeldung f. he's got a ~ in that show er tritt in dieser Show auf; a three-minute TV ~ drei Minuten Sendezeit im

Fernsehen; ein dreiminütiger Werbespot im Fernsehen.

(h) ~s *pl* (*Comm*) Lokowaren (*spec*), sofort lieferbare Waren *pl*.

(i) (*Billiards*) (*on table*) Marke *f*; (*also* ~ ball) Spielball *m*.

(j) (*esp Theat, inf: spotlight*) Scheinwerfer *m*.

2 *vt* (**a**) (*notice, see*) entdecken, sehen; (*pick out*) erkennen; (*find*) mistake, bargain finden; (*Mil: pinpoint*) ausmachen. to ~ a winner (*lit, fig*) richtig tippen (*inf*); train/plane ~ting Hobby, das darin besteht, möglichst viele verschiedene Zug-/Flugzeugtypen zu sehen und zu notieren.

(b) (*stain*) besprühen. blue material ~ted with white blauer Stoff mit weißen Tupfen.

(c) (*Billiards*) ball auf die Marke(n) setzen.

3 *vi* (**a**) it's ~ting (with rain) es tröpfelt.

(b) (*stain*) Flecken bekommen, schmutzen.

spot: ~ cash *n* sofortige Bezahlung; for ~ cash gegen sofortige Bezahlung; ~ check *n* Stichprobe *f*; ~-check *vt* stichprobenweise untersuchen (*for auf* +*acc*); motorists Stichproben machen bei (*for in bezug auf* +*acc*); ~ goods *npl* sofort lieferbare Waren, Lokowaren (*spec*) *pl*; ~ height *n* Höhenangabe *f*.

spotless [ˈspɒtlɪs] *adj* person, house, clothes tadellos or makellos sauber, pikobello (*inf*); (*fig*) reputation makellos, untadelig. ~ white strahlend weiß.

spotlessly [ˈspɒtlɪslɪ] *adv*: ~ clean blitzsauber.

spotlessness [ˈspɒtlɪsnɪs] *n* (*of person, house etc*) tadellose or makellose Sauberkeit; (*fig: of reputation*) Makellosigkeit, Untadeligkeit *f*.

spot: ~light (*vb: pret, ptp ~lighted*) **1** *n* (*lamp*) Scheinwerfer *m*; (*light*) Scheinwerferlicht, Rampenlicht (*also fig*) *nt*; (*on car etc*) Suchscheinwerfer *m*; to be in the ~light (*lit*) im Scheinwerferlicht or Rampenlicht stehen; (*fig*) im Rampenlicht der Öffentlichkeit stehen; to turn the ~light on sb/sth (*lit*) die Scheinwerfer auf jdn/etw richten; (*fig*) die Aufmerksamkeit auf jdn/etw lenken; **2** *vt* anstrahlen; (*fig*) aufmerksam machen auf (+*acc*); ~ market *n* Kassamarkt *m*; ~-on *adj* (*Brit inf*) answer, analysis exakt, haarscharf richtig (*inf*); ~-on! richtig!, genau!; his guess was ~-on er hat es haarscharf getroffen; ~ remover *n* Fleck(en)entferner *m*; ~ survey *n* Stichprobenuntersuchung *f*.

spotted [ˈspɒtɪd] *adj* gefleckt; (*with dots*) getüpfelt; material getüpfelt, getupft; (*marked, stained*) fleckig.

spotted: ~ dick *n* (*Brit*) = Kochpudding *m* mit Rosinen; ~ hyena *n* Tüpfelhyäne *f*.

spotter [ˈspɒtə*r*] *n* (**a**) (*Aviat: also* ~ plane) Aufklärer *m*; see trainspotter. **(b)** (*US inf: detective*) Detektiv *m*.

spottiness [ˈspɒtɪnɪs] *n* (*Med*) Fleckigkeit *f*, Flecken *pl*, fleckige Haut; (*pimples*) Pickeligkeit *f* (*inf*), Pickel *pl*, pickelige Haut.

spotty [ˈspɒtɪ] *adj* (+*er*) (*stained*) fleckig; (*Med*) fleckig, voller Flecken; (*pimply*) pick(e)lig, voller Pickel.

spot-weld [ˈspɒtweld] *vti* punktschweißen.

spouse [spaʊs] *n* (*form*) Gemahl(in *f*) *m* (*geh*), Gatte *m*, Gattin *f* (*all form*).

spout [spaʊt] **1** *n* (**a**) Ausguß *m*, Tülle *f*; (*on teapot, cup also*) Schnabel *m*; (*of jug, kettle also*) Schnauze *f*; (*on gargoyle, guttering*) Speirohr *nt*; (*on pump, tap*) Ausflußrohr *nt*; (*on pipe*) Ausfluß *m*; (*on watering can*) Rohr *nt*. up the ~ (*sl*) (*plans, building, schedule etc*) im Eimer (*sl*); she is up the ~ (*sl: pregnant*) sie hat's erwischt (*inf*).

(b) (*of whale: also* ~-hole) Spritzloch, Atemloch *nt*.

(c) (*jet of water etc*) Fontäne *f*; (*Met: water*~) Wasserhose *f*.

2 *vt* (**a**) (*gush*) (*fountain etc*) (heraus)spritzen; (*whale also*) ausstoßen; (*lava, gargoyle*) speien.

(b) (*inf: declaim*) poetry, speeches vom Stapel lassen (*inf*), loslassen (*at sb auf* jdn) (*inf*); words hervorsprudeln; figures herunterrasseln (*inf*); nonsense von sich geben.

3 *vi* (**a**) (*water, fountain etc, whale*) spritzen (*from aus*); (*gargoyle*) speien. to ~ out (of sth) (aus etw) hervorspritzen; (*lava*) (aus etw) ausgespieen werden; to ~ up (from sth) (aus etw) hochspritzen or herausschießen.

(b) (*fig inf: declaim*) palavern (*inf*), salbadern (*pej*). to ~ about sth über etw (*acc*) salbadern.

sprain [spreɪn] **1** *n* Verstauchung *f*. **2** *vt* verstauchen. to ~ one's wrist/ankle sich (*dat*) das Handgelenk/den Fuß verstauchen.

sprang [spræŋ] pret of spring.

sprat [spræt] *n* Sprotte *f*. to set or use a ~ to catch a mackerel or whale (*prov*) mit der Wurst nach der Speckseite werfen (*prov*).

sprawl [sprɔːl] **1** *n* (*posture*) Lümmeln (*inf*), Flegeln (*inf*) *nt no pl*; (*mass: of buildings, town etc*) Ausbreitung *f*. urban ~ wildwuchernde Ausbreitung des Stadtgebietes; in the urban ~ in der riesigen Stadtlandschaft.

2 *vi* (*person*) (*fall*) der Länge nach hinfallen; (*lounge*) (herum)lümmeln (*inf*), sich hinflegeln (*inf*); (*plant, town*) (wild) wuchern. he was ~ing (out) on the floor/in a chair er lag ausgestreckt auf dem Fußboden/er hatte sich in einem Sessel breitgemacht, er hatte sich in einen Sessel geflegelt; to send sb ~ing jdn zu Boden werfen, jdn der Länge nach umwerfen.

3 *vt* to be ~ed over sth/on sth (*body*) ausgestreckt auf etw (*dat*) liegen; his legs were ~ed over the arm of the chair seine Beine hingen zwanglos über der Sessellehne.

sprawling [ˈsprɔːlɪŋ] *adj* city, suburbs wildwuchernd; figure hingeflegelt; body ausgestreckt; handwriting riesig.

spray[1] [spreɪ] *n* (*bouquet*) Strauß *m*; (*buttonhole*) Ansteckblume *f*; (*shoot, twig*) Zweig *m*; (*brooch*) Brosche *f* (in Form eines Sträußchens).

spray[2] **1** *n* (**a**) Sprühnebel, Sprühregen *m*; (*of sea*) Gischt *m*. the ~ from the lorries makes it difficult to see die Lastwagen spritzen so, daß man kaum etwas sehen kann.

(b) (*implement*) Sprühdose, Sprühflasche *f*; (*insecticide* ~, *for irrigation*) Spritze *f*, Sprühgerät *nt*; (*scent* ~) Zerstäuber *m*; (*on shower*) Brause(kopf *m*) *f*.

(c) (*preparation, Med, hair*~ *etc*) Spray *m or nt*.

(d) (*act of* ~*ing*) (Be)sprühen *nt*. to give sth a ~ etw besprühen; (*with paint, insecticide*) etw spritzen; (*with hair*~ *etc*) etw sprayen.

2 *vt* plants, insects etc besprühen; garden, crops (*with paint, insecticide*) spritzen; hair sprayen; room aussprühen; water, paint, foam sprühen, spritzen; perfume zerstäuben, (ver)sprühen. to ~ insecticide on plants Pflanzen (mit Insektenmittel) spritzen; to ~ sth with water/bullets etw mit Wasser besprühen/mit Kugeln übersäen.

3 *vi* sprühen; (*water, mud*) spritzen. to ~ out herausprühen/-spritzen.

sprayer [ˈspreɪə*r*] *n* see spray[2] **1** (c).

spray-gun [ˈspreɪgʌn] *n* Spritzpistole *f*.

spread [spred] (*vb: pret, ptp* ~) **1** *n* (**a**) (*of wings*) Spannweite, Flügelspanne *f*; (*range*) (*of marks*) Verteilung, Streuung *f*; (*of prices*) Spanne *f*; (*of ideas, interests*) Spektrum *nt*; (*distribution of wealth*) Verteilung *f*; (*scope: of theory, ideas*) Umfang *m*. middle-age ~ Fülligkeit *f*, Altersspeck *m* (*inf*); Gerry's beginning to get a middle-age ~ Gerry setzt Speck an (*inf*).

(b) (*growth*) Ausbreitung, Verbreitung *f*; (*spatial*) Ausdehnung *f*. the ~ of nuclear weapons die zunehmende Verbreitung von Atomwaffen.

(c) (*inf: of food etc*) Festessen *nt*, Festschmaus *m*. that was an excellent ~ das war prima, was du etc da aufgetischt hast.

(d) (*cover*) Decke *f*.

(e) (*for bread*) (Brot)aufstrich *m*. anchovy ~ Sardellenpaste *f*; cheese ~ Streichkäse *m*.

(f) (*Press, Typ: two pages*) Doppelseite *f*. a full-page/double ~ ein ganz-/zweiseitiger Bericht; (*advertisement*) eine ganz-/zweiseitige Anzeige; a picture ~ ein ganzseitiger Bildbericht; the centre ~ of a paper die Mittelseite einer Zeitung.

2 *vt* (**a**) (*open or lay out: also* ~ out) rug, nets, hay, wings ausbreiten; fan öffnen; arms also ausstrecken; goods also auslegen; hands, legs spreizen. the peacock ~ its tail der Pfau schlug ein Rad; he was lying with his arms and legs ~ out er lag mit ausgestreckten Armen und Beinen da; the fields were ~ (out) below us die Felder breiteten sich unter uns aus; the view which was ~ before us die Sicht, die sich uns bot; the yacht ~ its sails die Segel des Bootes blähten sich.

(b) bread, canvas, surface bestreichen; butter, paint etc (ver-or auf)streichen; table decken. ~ the paint evenly verteilen Sie die Farbe gleichmäßig; he ~ the plaster over the wall er verstrich den Gips auf der Wand; to ~ a cloth/blanket on sth, to ~ sth with a cloth/blanket ein Tuch/eine Decke über etw (*acc*) breiten or etw (*dat*) ausbreiten; the table was ~ with food der Tisch war reichlich or üppig gedeckt.

(c) (*distribute: also* ~ out) forces, writing, objects, payments verteilen; sand, fertilizer also, muck streuen; (*in time*) verteilen (*over über* +*acc*). our resources are ~ very thin unsere Mittel sind maximal beansprucht.

(d) (*disseminate*) news, knowledge, panic, disease, smell verbreiten; rumour also ausstreuen. I'll ~ the news to everyone in the office ich werde es allen im Büro mitteilen.

3 *vi* (**a**) (*extend*) (*spatially*) sich erstrecken, sich ausdehnen (*over, across über* +*acc*); (*with movement*) (*weeds, liquid, fire, smile, industry*) sich ausbreiten (*over, across über* +*acc*); (*towns, settlements*) sich ausdehnen; (*knowledge, fear etc, smell*) sich verbreiten; (*disease, trouble, fire*) sich verbreiten, um sich greifen. the course ~s over four months der Kurs erstreckt sich über vier Monate; to ~ to sth etw erreichen; (*disease etc*) auf etw (*acc*) übergreifen; to ~ into sth sich in etw (*acc*) erstrecken; (*in time*) sich bis in etw (*acc*) erstrecken; under the ~ing trees unter den ausladenden Bäumen; he's worried about his ~ing waistline (*inf*) er macht sich Sorgen, weil er in die Breite geht (*inf*); see wildfire.

(b) (*butter etc*) sich streichen or schmieren (*inf*) lassen.

4 *vr* to ~ oneself (*physically*) sich ausstrecken; ~ one's things sich ausbreiten; (*in speech, writing*) sich verbreiten.

♦**spread about** or **around** *vt sep* news, rumours, disease verbreiten, unters Volk bringen (*inf*); toys, seeds etc verstreuen.

♦**spread out 1** *vt sep* see spread **2** (a, c).

2 *vi* (**a**) (*countryside etc*) sich ausdehnen.

(b) (*troops, runners*) sich verteilen.

spread-eagle [ˈspred ˌiːgl] *vt* he ~d his opponent against the wall er drückte seinen Gegner, Arme und Beine gespreizt, an die Wand; to be or lie ~d mit ausgestreckten Armen und Beinen daliegen, alle viere von sich (*dat*) strecken (*inf*); the policeman outlined the ~d body der Polizist zeichnete die Umrisse des ausgestreckt daliegenden Toten.

spreader [ˈspredə*r*] *n* Spachtel *m*; (*for butter etc*) Messer *nt*.

spree [spriː] *n* spending or shopping or buying ~ Großeinkauf *m*; drinking/gambling ~ Zech-/Spieltour *f* (*inf*); to be/go (out) on a ~ (*drinking*) eine Zechtour machen; (*gambling*) auf Spieltour sein/gehen; (*spending*) groß einkaufen/groß einkaufen gehen.

sprig [sprɪg] *n* Zweig *m*. embroidered with ~s of flowers mit Blütenzweigen bestickt.

sprightliness [ˈspraɪtlɪnɪs] *n* see adj Munterkeit, Lebhaftigkeit *f*, Schwung *m*; Rüstigkeit *f*; Leichtigkeit *f*; Lebhaftigkeit *f*.

sprightly [ˈspraɪtlɪ] *adj* (+*er*) person, tune munter, lebhaft; old person rüstig; walk leicht, schwungvoll; dance lebhaft, schwungvoll.

spring [sprɪŋ] (*vb: pret sprang or (US) sprung, ptp sprung*) **1** *n* (**a**) (*lit, fig liter: source*) Quelle *f*. ~s (*fig liter: origins*) Ursprung *m*; the inner ~s of his being sein Innerstes.

(b) (*season*) Frühling *m*, Frühjahr *nt*, Lenz *m* (*poet*). in (the) ~ im Frühling, im Frühjahr; ~ is in the air der Frühling liegt in der Luft, der Lenz hält seinen Einzug (*poet*); in the ~ of his life im Frühling seines Lebens, im Lenz des Lebens (*poet*).

(c) (*leap*) Sprung, Satz *m*. in one ~ mit einem Sprung or Satz; to make a ~ at sb/sth sich auf jdn/etw stürzen.

(d) (*Mech*) Feder *f*; (*in mattress, seat etc also*) Sprungfeder *f*. ~s (*Aut*) Federung *f*.

(e) *no pl* (*bounciness*) (*of chair*) Federung *f*; (*of wood, grass etc*) Nachgiebigkeit, Elastizität *f*. **the floor has no/a good ~** der Boden federt nicht/federt gut; **to walk with a ~ in one's step** mit federnden Schritten gehen; **the news put a new ~ into his step** die Nachricht beflügelte seine Schritte.

2 *adj attr* **(a)** (*seasonal*) Frühlings-.

(b) (*with springs*) gefedert; **mattress** Federkern-.

3 *vt* **(a)** (*leap over*) überspringen, springen über (+*acc*).

(b) (*put springs in*) federn.

(c) (*cause to operate*) auslösen; **mine** *also* explodieren lassen; **lock, mousetrap etc** zuschnappen lassen. **to ~ a leak** (*pipe*) (plötzlich) undicht werden; (*ship*) (plötzlich) ein Leck bekommen; **to ~ sth on sb** (*fig*) **idea, decision** jdn mit etw konfrontieren; **to ~ a piece of news on sb** jdn mit einer Neuigkeit überraschen; **to ~ a surprise on sb** jdn völlig überraschen.

(d) (*sl: free*) rausholen (*inf*).

4 *vi* **(a)** (*leap*) springen; (*be activated*) ausgelöst werden; (*mousetrap*) zuschnappen. **to ~ at sb** jdn anspringen; **to ~ out at sb** auf jdn lospringen; **to ~ open** aufspringen; **to be poised to ~** (*lit, fig*) sprungbereit sein; **to ~ into the saddle** in den Sattel schwingen; **to ~ to one's feet** aufspringen; **to ~ out of bed** aus dem Bett hüpfen; **a blush sprang to her cheeks** das Blut schoß ihr in die Wangen; **tears sprang to her eyes** ihr schossen die Tränen in die Augen; **his hand sprang to his gun** er griff (schnell) zur Waffe; **an oath sprang to his lips** ein Fluch drängte sich auf seine Lippen (*geh*); **to ~ into action** aktiv werden; (*police, fire brigade etc*) in Aktion treten; **to ~ to attention** (*Mil*) Haltung annehmen; **to ~ to arms** zu den Waffen eilen; **to ~ into view** plötzlich in Sicht kommen; **to ~ to mind** einem einfallen; **to ~ to sb's aid/defence** jdm zu Hilfe eilen; **to ~ to fame** er wurde plötzlich berühmt; **to ~ (in)to life** (plötzlich) lebendig werden; **the old man/the debate sprang (in)to life** es kam plötzlich Leben in den alten Mann/in die Debatte; **they sprang into the public eye** die Augen der Öffentlichkeit waren plötzlich auf sie gerichtet.

(b) (*issue: also ~ forth*) (*liter*) (*water, blood*) (hervor)quellen (*from aus*); (*fire, sparks*) sprühen (*from aus*); (*shoot*) (hervor)sprießen (*from aus*); (*from family etc*) abstammen (*from von*); (*fig*) (*idea*) entstehen (*from aus*); (*interest, irritability etc*) herrühren (*from von*). **a man sprang from the people** ein Mann aus dem Volk; **where did you ~ from?** (*inf*) wo kommst du denn her?; **to ~ into existence** (plötzlich *or* rasch) entstehen.

♦**spring back** *vi* (*person*) zurückspringen; (*in fear*) zurückschrecken; (*object*) zurückschnellen.

♦**spring up** *vi* (*plant*) hervorsprießen; (*weeds*) aus dem Boden schießen; (*person*) hoch- *or* aufspringen; (*wind*) aufkommen; (*building, settlement*) aus dem Boden schießen; (*fig*) (*suspicion, friendship*) erwachen, (plötzlich) entstehen; (*firm, magazine*) (plötzlich) entstehen; (*problem, rumour*) auftauchen. **doubts sprang ~ in his mind** ihm kamen (plötzlich) Zweifel.

spring: ~**-back file** *n* (*Brit*) Klemmhefter *m*; ~ **balance** *n* Federwaage *f*; ~ **binder** *n* Klemmhefter *m*; ~**board** *n* (*lit, fig*) Sprungbrett *nt*.

springbok ['sprɪŋbɒk] *n* Springbock *m*.

spring: ~ **chicken** *n* Stubenküken *nt*; **he's no ~ chicken** (*fig inf*) er ist nicht mehr feucht hinter den Ohren (*inf*); ~**-clean 1** *vt* gründlich putzen; **to ~-clean a house** (in einem Haus) Frühjahrsputz machen; **2** *vi* Frühjahrsputz machen; ~**cleaning** *n* Frühjahrsputz *m*.

springer (spaniel) ['sprɪŋə^r-] *n* Springerspaniel *m*.

spring fever *n* **(a)** (*energetic feeling*) Frühlingsgefühle *pl*. **it must be ~!** das muß der Frühling sein!, es muß am Frühling liegen! **(b)** (*lassitude*) Frühjahrsmüdigkeit *f*.

springiness ['sprɪŋɪnɪs] *n* Elastizität *f*; (*of turf, wood, grass, track also*) Nachgiebigkeit *f*; (*of springboard also*) Sprungkraft *f*; (*of bed*) Federung *f*. **the ~ of his step** sein federnder Gang.

spring: ~**less** *adj* ungefedert; ~**-like** *adj* frühlingshaft; ~**-loaded** *adj* mit einer Sprungfeder. **to be ~-loaded** eine Sprungfeder haben; ~ **onion** *n* Frühlingszwiebel *f*; ~ **tide** *n* **(a)** Springflut *f*; **(b)** (*poet:* ~*time*) Lenz *m* (*poet*); ~**time** *n* Frühling(szeit *f*) *m*, Frühjahr *nt*; (*fig*) Frühling, Lenz (*poet*) *m*; ~ **water** *n* Quellwasser *nt*; ~ **wheat** *n* Sommerweizen *m*.

springy ['sprɪŋɪ] *adj* (+*er*) **step** federnd; **plank, turf, grass** *also* nachgiebig, elastisch; **rubber, wood, plastic etc, hair** elastisch; **bed** weich gefedert.

sprinkle ['sprɪŋkl] **1** *vt* **water** sprenkeln, sprengen; **lawn, plant**, (*with holy water*) besprengen; **salt, dust, sugar etc** streuen; **dish, cake** bestreuen. **a rose ~d with dew** eine taubenetzte Rose; **a lawn ~d with daisies** ein mit Gänseblümchen durchzogener Rasen; **his hair was ~d with grey** sein Haar war grau meliert; **churches/pubs are ~d about over the town** man findet Kirchen/Gasthäuser über die ganze Stadt verstreut; ~**d with quotations** mit Zitaten durchsetzt.

2 *n* (*of liquid, vinegar*) ein paar Spritzer; (*of salt etc*) Prise *f*. **a ~ of rain** ein paar Regentropfen; **he gave the roses a ~ with the hose** er bespritzte *or* besprengte die Rosen mit dem Schlauch.

sprinkler ['sprɪŋklə^r] *n* **(a)** (*Hort, Agr*) Berieselungsapparat, Sprinkler *m*; (*in garden also*) (Rasen)sprenger *m*; (*for fire-fighting*) Sprinkler *m*; (*on watering can etc*) Sprenger, Gießkannenkopf *m*; (*on shower*) Brause *f*; (*sugar* ~) Streudose *f*, Streuer *m*. **(b)** (*Eccl*) Weihwasserwedel *m*.

sprinkler: ~ **head** *n* Sprinkler *m*; (*on watering can*) Sprenger, Gießkannenkopf *m*; (*on shower*) Brause *f*; ~ **system** *n* Berieselungsanlage *f*; (*for fire-fighting also*) Sprinkleranlage *f*.

sprinkling ['sprɪŋklɪŋ] *n* (*of rain, dew etc*) ein paar Tropfen; (*of sugar etc*) Prise *f*; (*fig*) (*of humour, comedy etc*) Anflug *m*; (*of common sense*) Spur *f*. **there was a ~ of grey in his hair** ein paar graue Fäden durchzogen sein Haar; **there was a ~ of young**

people es waren ein paar vereinzelte junge Leute da; **a ~ of freckles** ein paar Sommersprossen; **to give sth a ~** (*with water*) etw besprengen *or* besprenkeln.

sprint [sprɪnt] **1** *n* **(a)** (*race*) Sprint *m*; (*burst of speed*) Spurt, Sprint *m*. **the 100-m ~** der 100-m-Lauf; **to put on a ~** einen Sprint *or* Spurt vorlegen, sprinten, spurten; **he made a ~ for safety/for the bus** er rannte in Sicherheit/er sprintete *or* spurtete zum Bus; **to ~ finish** ein Endspurt *m*; **he has a good ~ finish** er legt einen guten Endspurt vor.

2 *vi* (*in race*) sprinten; (*dash*) rennen; (*for train etc also*) spurten.

sprinter ['sprɪntə^r] *n* Kurzstreckenläufer(in *f*), Sprinter(in *f*) *m*.

sprit [sprɪt] *n* Spriet *nt*.

sprite [spraɪt] *n* Kobold *m*. **water/wood ~** Wasser-/Waldgeist *m*.

spritsail ['sprɪtsəl] *n* Sprietsegel *nt*.

sprocket ['sprɒkɪt] *n* **(a)** (*tooth*) Zahn *m*. **(b)** (~ *wheel*) Kettenrad *nt*; (*on bicycle*) Kettenzahnrad *nt*, Zahnkranz *m*; (*Film*) Greifer *m*.

sprout [spraʊt] **1** *n* **(a)** (*shoot*) (*of plant*) Trieb *m*; (*of tree also*) Schoß, Schößling, Sproß *m*; (*from seed*) Keim *m*.

(b) (*Brussels* ~) (Rosenkohl)röschen *nt*. ~**s** *pl* Rosenkohl *m*.

2 *vt* **leaves, buds, shoots etc** treiben; **horns etc** entwickeln; **seeds, wheat etc** keimen lassen; (*inf*) **beard sich** (*dat*) wachsen lassen. **the town is ~ing new buildings** in der Stadt sprießen neue Gebäude hervor; **he suddenly started ~ing hairs on his chest** er bekam plötzlich Haare auf der Brust.

3 *vi* **(a)** (*grow*) wachsen, sprießen; (*seed, wheat etc*) keimen; (*potatoes, trees etc*) Triebe bekommen.

(b) (*lit, fig: also ~ up*) (*plants, weeds*) emporschießen, sprießen; (*new sects, new buildings*) wie die Pilze aus dem Boden schießen.

spruce[1] [spru:s] *n* (*also ~ fir*) Fichte *f*.

spruce[2] *adj* (+*er*) **person, appearance** proper, gepflegt; **men's clothes** flott, schmuck (*dated*); **women, children, women's clothes, appearance** adrett; **building sidewalk; lawn, flower beds** gepflegt. **he was looking very ~** er sah geschniegelt und gebügelt *or* geschniegelt und gestriegelt aus.

♦**spruce up** *vt sep* **child** herausputzen, schniegeln (*inf*); **house, garden** auf Vordermann bringen (*inf*). **to ~ oneself ~** (*in general*) sein Äußeres pflegen; (*get dressed up*) sich in Schale werfen; (*woman*) sich schön- *or* zurechtmachen; **he looks much better now that he has ~d himself ~** so gepflegt sieht er wesentlich besser aus; **all ~d** children, **men** geschniegelt und gestriegelt; **women** schön zurechtgemacht; **house** auf Hochglanz.

sprucely ['spru:slɪ] *adv* **dressed** (*man*) flott, schmuck (*dated*); (*woman, child*) adrett; **painted, decorated etc** schmuck; **laid out** sauber und ordentlich. ~ **kept gardens** gepflegte Gärten.

spruceness ['spru:snɪs] *n see adj* Gepflegtheit *f*; Schmuckheit (*dated*), Flottheit *f*; Adrettheit *f*; Schmuckheit *f*; Gepflegtheit *f*.

sprung [sprʌŋ] **1** *ptp of* **spring**. **2** *adj* gefedert.

spry [spraɪ] *adj* rüstig.

spud [spʌd] *n* (*inf: potato*) Kartoffel *f*. ~**-bashing** (*Brit Mil sl*) Küchendienst *m*.

spume [spju:m] *n* (*liter*) Gischt *m*.

spun [spʌn] **1** *pret, ptp of* **spin**. **2** *adj* **gold, silver, silk** gesponnen. ~ **sugar** (*candy floss*) Zuckerwatte *f*.

spunk [spʌŋk] *n* **(a)** (*inf*) Mumm *m* (*inf*), Courage *f*. **(b)** (*Brit sl: semen*) Soße *f* (*sl*).

spunky ['spʌŋkɪ] *adj* (+*er*) (*inf*) couragiert.

spur [spɜ:^r] **1** *n* **(a)** (*Sport*) Sporn *m*; (*fig*) Ansporn, Antrieb *m* (*to für*). **he urged the horse on with his ~s** er gab dem Pferd die Sporen; **to win** *or* **gain one's ~s** (*fig*) sich (*dat*) die Sporen verdienen; **the ~ of hunger** bohrender Hunger; **this might act as a ~ to his memory** das könnte seinem Gedächtnis einen Stoß geben; **this was a new ~ to his ambition** das gab seinem Ehrgeiz neuen Antrieb *or* Ansporn.

(b) **on the ~ of the moment** ganz spontan; **a ~-of-the-moment decision** ein spontaner Entschluß.

(c) (*Geol*) Vorsprung *m*.

(d) (*Zool*) Sporn *m*.

(e) (*Rail*) Nebengleis, Rangiergleis *nt*.

2 *vt* **(a)** die Sporen geben (+*dat*).

(b) (*urge on: also ~ on*) (vorwärts) treiben, vorantreiben; (*fig*) anspornen. ~**red (on) by greed/ambition** von Habgier/vom Ehrgeiz getrieben.

3 *vi* (*also ~ on*) galoppieren, sprengen (*dated*).

spurge [spɜ:dʒ] *n* (*Bot*) Wolfsmilch *f*. ~ **laurel** Lorbeer-Seidelbast *m*.

spurious ['spjʊərɪəs] *adj* **claim, claimant** unberechtigt; **document, account** falsch; **anger, interest, affection** nicht echt.

spuriousness ['spjʊərɪəsnɪs] *n see adj* mangelnde Berechtigung; mangelnde Echtheit.

spurn [spɜ:n] *vt* verschmähen.

spurred [spɜ:d] *adj* gespornt.

spurt [spɜ:t] **1** *n* **(a)** (*flow*) Strahl *m*. ~**s of flame** Stichflammen. **(b)** (*burst of speed*) Spurt *m*. **a final ~** (*lit, fig*) ein Endspurt *m*; **to put a ~ on** (*lit, fig*) einen Spurt vorlegen; **there was a ~ of activity** es brach plötzliche Aktivität aus; **in a sudden ~ of energy** in einer plötzlichen Energieanwandlung.

2 *vi* **(a)** (*gush: also ~ out*) (heraus)spritzen (*from aus*).

(b) (*run*) spurten.

3 *vt* **the wound ~ed blood** aus der Wunde spritzte Blut; **the pipe ~ed water** aus dem Rohr spritzte das Wasser.

spur wheel *n* Stirnrad *nt*.

sputnik ['spʊtnɪk] *n* Sputnik *m*.

sputter ['spʌtə^r] *vi* zischen; (*in frying pan*) brutzeln; (*fat*) spritzen; (*engine*) stottern; (*in speech*) sich ereifern (*about über* +*acc*). **he was ~ing with rage** er geiferte (vor Zorn); **the candle ~ed out** die Kerze ging flackernd aus.

sputum ['spju:təm] *n* (*Med*) Auswurf *m*, Sputum *nt* (*spec*).

spy [spaɪ] **1** n Spion(in f) m; (police ~) Spitzel m. ~ **in the cab** (inf: tachograph) Fahrtenschreiber m.

2 vt sehen, erspähen (geh). **finally I spied him coming** endlich sah ich ihn kommen; **I ~ with my little eye something ...** ≃ ich sehe was, was du nicht siehst, und ...

3 vi spionieren, Spionage treiben. **to ~ into sth** in etw (dat) herumspionieren; **to ~ on sb** jdn bespitzeln; **on neighbours** jdm nachspionieren; **I S ~** (game) ich sehe was, was du nicht siehst.

♦ **spy out** vt sep ausfindig machen. **to ~ ~ the land** (Mil) die Gegend auskundschaften; (fig) die Lage peilen.

spy: ~ **glass** n Fernglas nt; ~ **hole** n Guckloch nt, Spion m; ~ **plane** n Spionageflugzeug nt; ~ **story** n Spionagegeschichte f.

Sq abbr of **Square**.

sq abbr of **square** ~ m qm, m².

squab [skwɒb] n **(a)** (Orn) Jungtaube f. **(b)** (Aut) Bank f.

squabble ['skwɒbl] **1** n Zank, Streit m. ~**s** Zankereien, Streitigkeiten pl. **2** vi (sich) zanken, (sich) streiten (about, over um).

squabbling ['skwɒblɪŋ] n Zankerei, Streiterei f.

squad [skwɒd] n (Mil) Korporalschaft f; (special unit of police etc) Kommando nt; (police department) Dezernat nt; (of workmen) Trupp m; (Sport, fig) Mannschaft f.

squad car n Streifenwagen m.

squadron ['skwɒdrən] n (of cavalry) Schwadron f; (Aviat) Staffel f; (Naut) Geschwader nt.

squadron leader n (Brit Aviat) Luftwaffenmajor m.

squalid ['skwɒlɪd] adj room, house schmutzig und verwahrlost; existence, conditions elend, erbärmlich; motive, manoeuvres, deed, idea etc gemein, niederträchtig; dispute, gossip entwürdigend; affair schmutzig.

squalidly ['skwɒlɪdlɪ] adv live in elenden or erbärmlichen Verhältnissen; behave, treat sb gemein, niederträchtig.

squall [skwɔːl] **1** n **(a)** (storm) Bö(e) f; (fig) Gewitter nt, Sturm m. **there are ~s ahead** (fig) wir gehen stürmischen Zeiten entgegen. **(b)** (cry) Schrei m. **2** vi schreien.

squally ['skwɔːlɪ] adj (+er) stürmisch; wind also böig.

squalor ['skwɒlə'] n Schmutz m; (moral ~) Verkommenheit f. **the ~ of the conditions** die elenden or erbärmlichen Verhältnisse; **to live in ~** in unbeschreiblichen Zuständen leben.

squander ['skwɒndə'] vt verschwenden, vergeuden (on an +acc); inheritance, fortune also durchbringen (on mit); opportunity vertun.

square [skweə'] **1** n **(a)** (shape, Geometry, on graph paper) Quadrat nt. **a 6 metre ~** 6 Meter im Quadrat.

(b) (piece of material, paper etc) Quadrat, Viereck nt; (on chessboard etc) Feld nt; (on paper) Kästchen, Karo nt; (in crossword) Kästchen nt; (check on material etc) Karo nt; (head~) Kopftuch nt. **form yourselves into a ~** stellen Sie sich im Viereck auf; **cut it in ~s** schneiden Sie es quadratisch or in Quadrate zu; **cut a 6 cm ~** schneiden Sie ein Quadrat or Viereck 6 cm × 6 cm aus; **to go back to ~ one** (fig) noch einmal von vorne anfangen; **we're back ~ one** jetzt sind wir wieder da, wo wir angefangen haben.

(c) (in town) Platz m; (US: of houses) Block m; (Mil: barrack ~) (Kasernen)platz m.

(d) (Math) Quadrat(zahl f) nt. **the ~ of 3 is 9** 3 hoch 2 or 3 (im) Quadrat ist 9.

(e) (Tech) Winkel(maß nt) m; (set ~) Zeichendreieck nt; (T-~) Reißschiene f. **to be out of ~** schief or nicht rechtwinklig sein; **to cut sth on the ~** etw rechtwinklig schneiden; **to be on the ~** (fig inf: above board) in Ordnung sein.

(f) (Mil: battle formation) Karree nt.

(g) (inf: old-fashioned person) Spießer m (inf). **to be a ~ von** (vor)gestern sein.

2 adj (+er) **(a)** (in shape) quadratisch; picture, lawn etc also, nib viereckig; file Vierkant-; block of wood etc vierkantig. **to be a ~ peg in a round hole** am falschen Platz sein.

(b) (forming right angle) angle rechtwinklig; corner rechtwinklig; bracket, shoulder eckig; chin, jaw kantig, eckig; build vierschrötig.

(c) (Math) Quadrat-. **3 ~ kilometres** 3 Quadratkilometer; **3 metres ~** 3 Meter im Quadrat; **there wasn't a ~ inch of space left** es war kein Zentimeter Platz mehr.

(d) attr (complete) meal anständig, ordentlich.

(e) (fair) deal gerecht, fair; dealings, game, person ehrlich. **to give sb a ~ deal** jdn gerecht or fair behandeln; **I'll be ~ with you** ich will ehrlich or offen mit dir sein.

(f) (fig: even) **to be ~** (accounts etc) in Ordnung sein; **to get ~ with sb** mit jdm abrechnen; **we are (all) ~** (Sport) wir stehen beide/alle gleich; (fig) jetzt sind wir quitt; **he wanted to be ~ with his creditors** er wollte mit seinen Gläubigern im reinen sein; **we can start again all ~** wir sind wieder quitt.

(g) (inf: old-fashioned) überholt, verstaubt; person, ideas spießig (inf); fashion also passé. **he's ~** er ist von (vor)gestern.

3 adv (+er) **(a)** (at right angles) rechtwinklig. ~ **with sth** im rechten Winkel or senkrecht zu etw.

(b) (directly) direkt, genau.

(c) (honestly) ehrlich, fair; see **fair¹**.

4 vt **(a)** (make ~) quadratisch machen; (make a right angle) rechtwinklig machen. **to ~ one's shoulders** die Schultern straffen; **to ~ a block of wood/stone** (cut ~) einen Holzklotz vierkantig zuschneiden/einen Steinblock vierkantig behauen; **to try to ~ the circle** die Quadratur des Kreises versuchen.

(b) (Math) number quadrieren. **3 ~d is 9** 3 hoch 2 or 3 (im) Quadrat ist 9.

(c) (adjust) debts begleichen; creditors abrechnen mit; (reconcile) in Einklang bringen. **to ~ one's accounts abrechnen** (with mit); **to ~ one's accounts with God/the world** mit Gott/der Welt ins reine kommen; **to ~ sth with one's conscience** etw mit seinem Gewissen vereinbaren or in Einklang bringen; **I'll ~ it with the porter** (inf) ich mache das mit dem Portier ab (inf).

(d) (inf: bribe) schmieren (inf).

5 vi übereinstimmen.

♦ **square off 1** vt sep **(a)** (make square) corner rechtwinklig machen. **(b)** (draw squares on) in Quadrate einteilen. **2** vi (esp US) in Kampfstellung gehen, Kampfstellung annehmen.

♦ **square up** vi in Kampfstellung gehen, Kampfstellung annehmen. **to ~ ~ to sb** sich vor jdm aufpflanzen (inf); (boxer) vor jdm in Kampfstellung gehen; (fig) jdm die Stirn bieten. **to ~ ~ to sth** sich einer Sache (dat) stellen.

(b) (lit, fig: settle) abrechnen.

square: ~**-bashing** n (Brit Mil sl) Drill m; ~**-built** adj stämmig or breit gebaut; man vierschrötig; house quadratisch gebaut.

squared [skweəd] adj paper kariert.

square: ~ **dance** n Square-Dance m; ~ **knot** n (US) Kreuzknoten m.

squarely ['skweəlɪ] adv **(a)** (directly) direkt, genau; (fig: firmly) fest. **we must face this ~** wir müssen dieser Sache (dat) (fest) ins Auge sehen. **(b)** (honestly) ehrlich; (fairly) gerecht, fair. **to deal ~ with sb** jdn gerecht or fair behandeln. **(c)** ~ **built** stämmig or breit gebaut.

square: ~ **measure** n Flächenmaß nt; **the children are studying ~ measure** die Kinder lernen Flächenmaße; ~ **number** n Quadratzahl f; ~**-rigged** adj vollgetakelt; ~ **root** n Quadratwurzel f, zweite Wurzel; **to work out the ~ root of** sth die zweite Wurzel or Quadratwurzel aus etw ziehen; ~ **sail** n Rahsegel nt; ~ **shooter** n (US inf) ehrlicher Kerl (inf); ~**-shouldered** adj mit eckigen Schultern; ~**-toed** adj shoes mit breiter Kappe.

squash¹ [skwɒʃ] **1** n **(a)** (Brit) (fruit concentrate) Fruchtsaftkonzentrat, Squash nt; (drink) Fruchtsaft m. **a glass of orange ~** ein Glas (verdünnter) Orangensaft. **(b)** (crowd) (Menschen)menge f; (crush) Gedränge nt. **it's a bit of a ~** es ist ziemlich eng.

2 vt (also ~ **up**) zerdrücken, zerquetschen; box etc zusammendrücken. **to be ~ed to a pulp** zu Brei gequetscht or zerquetscht werden; **my hat was ~ed flat** or in mein Hut war völlig zerdrückt.

(b) (fig inf) (silence) person über den Mund fahren (+dat); (squash) protest, argument vom Tisch fegen (inf). ~**ed again!** schon wieder kein Erfolg; **I felt completely ~ed** ich kam mir ganz klein und häßlich vor (inf).

(c) (squeeze) quetschen. **to ~ sb/sth in** jdn einquetschen/etw hineinquetschen; **to be ~ed up against sb** gegen jdn gequetscht or gepreßt werden; **to be ~ed together** eng zusammengepreßt or -gequetscht sein.

3 vi (get ~ed) zerdrückt or zerquetscht werden.

(b) (squeeze) sich quetschen. **to ~ in** sich hinein-/hereinquetschen; **could you ~ up?** könnt ihr etwas zusammenrücken?; (one person) kannst du dich etwas kleiner machen?

squash² n or (Sport: also ~ **racquets** or (US) **rackets**) Squash, Squash-Racket nt.

squash³ n, no pl (US) (Pâtisson-)Kürbis m.

squashy ['skwɒʃɪ] adj (+er) matschig; cushion weich.

squat [skwɒt] **1** adj (+er) gedrungen, kompakt; chair niedrig; figure, person gedrungen.

2 vi (a) (person) hocken, kauern; (animal) hocken. **(b)** (also ~ **down**) sich (hin)hocken or (hin)kauern. **(c)** (on land) sich (illegal) ansiedeln. **to ~ in a house** sich in einem Haus eingenistet haben, ein Haus besetzt haben; **(inf); they are not tenants, they're just ~ting** das sind keine Mieter, das sind Squatter or Hausbesetzer.

3 n (inf: place) Unterschlupf m (für Hausbesetzer). **after their ~ in that house ...** nachdem sie sich in dem Haus eingenistet hatten ... (inf), nachdem sie das Haus als Unterschlupf benutzt hatten ...

squatter ['skwɒtə'] n (on land) Squatter m, illegaler Siedler; (in house) Squatter, Hausbesetzer m.

squaw [skwɔː] n Squaw f.

squawk [skwɔːk] **1** n heiserer Schrei; (fig inf: complaint) Protest m. **he let out a ~** er kreischte auf; **the ~s of the hens** das aufgeregte Gackern der Hühner. **2** vi (bird, person) schreien, kreischen; (fig inf: complain) protestieren.

squeak [skwiːk] **1** n (of hinge, wheel etc, shoe, pen) Quietschen nt no pl; (of person) Quiekser m; (of small animal) Quieken nt no pl; (of mouse, bird) Piepsen nt no pl; (fig inf: sound) Pieps (inf), Mucks (inf) m. **she gave a ~ of surprise/delight** sie quiekste überrascht/entzückt; **the door opened with a ~** die Tür ging quietschend auf; see **narrow**.

2 vi (door, hinge, shoes etc) quietschen; (person) quieksen; (small animal) quieken, quieksen; (mouse, bird) piepsen.

3 vt quieksen.

squeaky ['skwiːkɪ] adj (+er) quietschend; voice piepsig.

squeal [skwiːl] **1** n Schrei m; (of person, tyre, brakes) Kreischen nt no pl; (of protest) (Auf)schrei m; (of pig) Quieken nt no pl. **with a ~ of brakes/tyres** mit kreischenden Bremsen/Reifen; **a ~ of pain** ein Schmerzensschrei m; ~**s of protest** Protestgeschrei nt; ~**s/a ~ of laughter** schrilles Gelächter.

2 vi **(a)** schreien, kreischen; (brakes, tyres) kreischen, quietschen; (pig, puppy) quieken; (fig inf) jammern. **to ~ with pain/pleasure/laughter** vor Schmerz aufheulen or kreischen/vor Vergnügen quietschen/laut auflachen; **to ~ for help** um Hilfe schreien.

(b) (inf: confess, inform) (criminal) singen (sl) (to bei); (schoolboy etc) petzen (inf) (to bei).

3 vt schreien, kreischen.

squeamish ['skwiːmɪʃ] adj person (easily nauseated) empfindlich, heikel (dial); (easily shocked) zartbesaitet, empfindlich. **I felt a bit ~** (sick) mir war leicht übel; **it gave me a ~ feeling in my stomach** mein Magen revoltierte; **I felt a bit ~ about telling him the bad news** mir war gar nicht wohl dabei, daß ich ihm die schlechte Nachricht mitteilen mußte; **I'm not ~** (not easily nauseated) mir wird nicht so schnell schlecht or übel; (not easily shocked) ich bin nicht so zartbesaitet (or

squeamishness ['skwi:mɪʃnɪs] n (nausea) Übelkeit f; (disgust) Ekel m; (prudishness) Zimperlichkeit f. **a feeling of** ~ (nausea) leichte Übelkeit; **his** ~ **when he sees blood** die Übelkeit, die ihn beim Anblick von Blut überkommt; **you have to overcome your** ~ (prudishness, reluctance) Sie dürfen nicht so zimperlich sein; (disgust) Sie müssen Ihren Ekel überwinden; **I feel a certain** ~ **when I see blood/porn films** wenn ich Blut sehe, wird mir schlecht or übel/Pornofilmen gegenüber bin ich empfindlich.

squeegee [ˌskwiˈdʒiː] n (Gummi)wischer m; (Phot) Rollen-quetscher m.

squeeze [skwiːz] **1** n **(a)** (act of squeezing) Drücken nt no pl; (hug) Umarmung f; (of hand) Händedruck m; (in bus etc) Gedränge nt. **to give sth a** ~ etw drücken, etw pressen; (lemon, sponge etw ausdrücken; **to give sb/sb's hand a** ~ jdn an sich (acc) drücken/die Hand drücken; **it was a terrible** or **tight** ~ es war fürchterlich eng; **getting into that dress was a bit of a** ~ es war nicht so leicht, mich in das Kleid zu zwängen; **we are in a tight** ~ (inf: in difficulty) wir sind in der Klemme (inf). **(b)** (amount) Spritzer m. **put a** ~ **of toothpaste on the brush** drücken Sie etwas Zahnpaste auf die Bürste. **(c)** (credit ~) Kreditbeschränkung f. **(d)** **to put the** ~ **on sb** (inf) jdm die Daumenschrauben ansetzen (inf).
2 vt drücken; sponge, tube ausdrücken; orange auspressen, ausquetschen; (squash) person, hand einquetschen. **to** ~ **clothes into a case** Kleider in einen Koffer zwängen; **to** ~ **liquid out of** or **from sth** Flüssigkeit aus etw (heraus)pressen; **to** ~ **out water/juice** Wasser/Saft herauspressen (from aus); **he** ~**d the trigger** er drückte ab; **to** ~ **out a tear** eine Träne zerdrücken; **to** ~ **sth dry** (lit) etw auswringen; (fig) das Letzte aus etw herausholen; **to** ~ **sb dry** (fig) jdn ausbluten; **to** ~ **money/information** etc **out of sb** Geld/Informationen etc aus jdm herausquetschen; **to** ~ **the rich** die Reichen schröpfen; **to be** ~**d to death** erdrückt werden; **I'll see if we can** ~ **you in** vielleicht können wir Sie noch unterbringen.
3 vi **you'll get through if you** ~ wenn du dich klein machst, kommst du durch; **to** ~ **in/out** sich hinein-/hinausdrängen; **to** ~ **past sb** sich an jdm vorbeidrücken; **to** ~ **into the bus** sich in den Bus hineinzwängen; **to** ~ **through a crowd/hole/underneath a fence** sich durch eine Menge/ein Loch zwängen/sich unter einem Zaun durchzwängen; **to** ~ **over into another lane** (car) sich in eine andere Spur drängen; **you'll have to** ~ **up a bit** Sie müssen ein bißchen zusammenrücken.

squeeze-box ['skwiːzbɒks] n (inf) Quetschkommode f (inf).
squeezer ['skwiːzəʳ] n Presse f.
squeezy ['skwiːzɪ] adj (+er) (inf) nachgiebig.
squelch [skweltʃ] **1** n glucksendes or quatschendes (inf) Geräusch. **I heard the** ~ **of his footsteps in the mud** ich hörte, wie er quatschend (inf) or platschend durch den Schlamm lief; **the tomato hit the floor with a** ~ die Tomate schlug mit einem satten Platsch auf den Boden auf.
2 vt **to** ~ **one's way through sth** durch etw p(l)atschen.
3 vi patschen, platschen; (shoes, mud) quatschen. **water** ~**ed in his boots** das Wasser gluckste or quatschte in seinen Stiefeln.
squib [skwɪb] n (firework) Knallfrosch m; see **damp**.
squid [skwɪd] n Tintenfisch m.
squiffy ['skwɪfɪ] adj (+er) (Brit inf) angesäuselt (inf).
squiggle ['skwɪgl] **1** n Schnörkel m. **2** vt **to** ~ **a line under sth** eine Wellenlinie unter etw (acc) machen.
squiggly ['skwɪglɪ] adj (+er) schnörkelig. ~ **tail** Ringelschwanz m.
squint [skwɪnt] **1** n **(a)** (Med) Schielen nt no pl, Silberblick m (inf). **to have a** ~ leicht schielen, einen Silberblick haben (inf); **he has a terrible** ~ **in his left eye** er schielt furchtbar auf dem linken Auge. **(b)** (look) Blick m; (sidelong glance) Seitenblick m. **to have** or **take a** ~ **at sb/sth** einen Blick auf jdn/etw werfen; (obliquely) jdn/etw von der Seite ansehen, nach jdm/etw schielen.
2 vi schielen; (in strong light etc) blinzeln; (inf: look also) linsen (inf). **to** ~ **at sb/sth** nach jdm/etw schielen; (quickly) einen kurzen Blick auf jdn/etw werfen.
3 adj (crooked) schief.
squint-eyed ['skwɪntˈaɪd] adj person schielend attr; look schräg, schief. **to be** ~ schielen.
squire ['skwaɪəʳ] **1** n **(a)** (esp Brit: landowner) Gutsherr, ≈ Junker (Hist) m. **right,** ~ (Brit sl) jawohl, der Herr (dated), in Ordnung, Chef (inf); **the** ~ **of the manor** der Herr of Gutes. **(b)** (Hist: knight's attendant) Knappe m. **(c)** (dated: escort) Kavalier m (dated).
2 vt (dated) begleiten, eskortieren (dated).
squirearchy ['skwaɪərɑːkɪ] n Gutsbesitzer pl, ≈ Landjunkertum nt (Hist).
squirm [skwɜːm] **1** n Winden nt. **to give a** ~ sich winden.
2 vi sich winden; (in distaste) schaudern; (with embarrassment) sich (drehen und) winden; (from discomfort) hin und her rutschen. **blood/her poetry makes me** ~ wenn ich Blut sehe,/bei ihren Gedichten dreht sich in mir alles herum; **spiders make me** ~ vor Spinnen graust es mir.
squirrel ['skwɪrəl] **1** n Eichhörnchen nt. **2** adj attr coat, fur Eichhörnchen-.
squirt [skwɜːt] **1** n **(a)** Spritzer m. **(b)** (implement) Spritze f. **(c)** (pej inf: person) Fatzke m (inf); (small) Pimpf m (inf). **2** vt liquid spritzen; object, person bespritzen. **to** ~ **water at sb, to** ~ **sb with water** jdn mit Wasser bespritzen. **3** vi spritzen.
squish [skwɪʃ] vt (inf) zermatschen (inf).
squishy ['skwɪʃɪ] adj (+er) (inf) matschig (inf); fruit also zermatscht (inf).

Sr abbr of **senior** sen., Sr.
Sri Lanka [ˌsriːˈlæŋkə] n Sri Lanka nt.
Sri Lankan [ˌsriːˈlæŋkən] **1** adj srilankisch. **2** n Srilanker(in f) m.
SRN (Brit) abbr of **State Registered Nurse**.
SS abbr of **steamship**.
SSE abbr of **south-south-east** SSO.
SSW abbr of **south-south-west** SSW.
St. abbr of **(a) Street** Str. **(b) Saint** hl., St. **(c) Strait**.
st abbr of **stone(s)**.

stab [stæb] **1** n **(a)** (with knife etc, wound, of pain) Stich m. ~ **wound** Stichwunde f; **a** ~ **of rheumatism** ein rheumatischer Schmerz; **to feel a** ~ **of pain** einen stechenden Schmerz empfinden; **to feel a** ~ **of conscience/guilt/remorse** ein schlechtes Gewissen haben, Gewissensbisse haben; **he felt a** ~ **of grief/pity** der Kummer/das Mitleid schnitt ihm in die Seele; **a** ~ **in the back** (fig) ein Dolchstoß m. **(b)** (inf: try) Versuch m. **to have a** ~ **at sth** etw probieren.
2 vt person einen Stich versetzen (+dat); (several times) einstechen auf (+acc); (wound seriously) niederstechen; food durchstechen. **to** ~ **sb (to death)** jdn erstechen; (with dagger also) jdn erdolchen; **to** ~ **sb with a knife, to** ~ **a knife into sb** jdn mit einem Messerstich/mit Messerstichen verletzen; **he** ~**bed his penknife into the desk** er stach sein Taschenmesser in den Tisch; **the knife** ~**bed her arm** das Messer drang ihr in den Arm; **he was** ~**bed through the arm/heart** er hatte eine Stichwunde am Arm/der Stich traf ihn ins Herz; **to** ~ **a knife/fork into sth** ein Messer in etw (acc) hineinstoßen/mit einer Gabel in etw (acc) hineinstechen; **to** ~ **sb in the back** (lit) jdm in den Rücken stechen; (fig) jdm in den Rücken fallen; **he** ~**bed the air with his fork** er fuchtelte mit der Gabel in der Luft herum (inf).
3 vi **to** ~ **at sb/sth** (with knife etc) nach jdm/etw stechen; (with finger) auf jdn/etw zeigen.
stabbing ['stæbɪŋ] **1** n Messerstecherei f. **2** adj pain stechend.
stability [stəˈbɪlɪtɪ] n Stabilität f; (of relationship also, of job) Beständigkeit, Dauerhaftigkeit f. **(mental)** ~ (seelische) Ausgeglichenheit, innere Festigkeit.
stabilization [ˌsteɪbəlaɪˈzeɪʃən] n Stabilisierung f.
stabilize ['steɪbəlaɪz] **1** vt (Fin, Naut, Aviat) stabilisieren. **2** vi sich stabilisieren.
stabilizer ['steɪbəlaɪzəʳ] n (Naut, Chem) Stabilisator m; (Aviat) Stabilisierungsfläche f; (US Aviat) Höhenflosse f; (on bicycle) Stützrad nt.
stable[1] ['steɪbl] adj (+er) stabil; ladder, structure also sicher; relationship also, job beständig, dauerhaft; character gefestigt. **mentally** ~ ausgeglichen, innerlich gefestigt.
stable[2] **1** n (building) Stall m; (group of racehorses) (Renn)stall m. **riding** ~s Reitstall m; **to be out of the same** ~ (fig) aus dem gleichen Stall stammen; **it's no good locking the** ~ **door after the horse has bolted** (prov) jetzt ist die Katze schon den Bach hinab (inf).
2 vt (put in ~) in den Stall bringen; (keep in ~) im Stall halten. **he** ~**s his horses with the trainer** seine Pferde stehen im Stall des Trainers.
stable: ~**boy,** ~**-lad,** ~**man** n Stallbursche, Stallknecht m; (young man also) Stalljunge m.
stabling ['steɪblɪŋ] n Stallungen, Ställe pl.
staccato [stəˈkɑːtəʊ] adj, adv (Mus) staccato, stakkato; (fig) abgehackt.
stack [stæk] **1** n **(a)** (pile) Haufen m; (neatly piled) Stoß, Stapel m; (of hay also) Schober m; (of rifles) Pyramide f. **to be in the** ~ (Aviat) kreisen, Warteschleifen ziehen (over über +dat). **(b)** (inf: lots) Haufen m (inf). ~**s** jede Menge (inf); **we have** ~**s of time/helpers/money** etc wir haben jede Menge (inf) Zeit/Hilfskräfte/Geld etc. **(c)** (in library: also ~s) Magazin nt. **(d)** see **chimneystack, smokestack**. **(e)** (Geol) Felssäule f.
2 vt **(a)** stapeln. **to** ~ **up** aufstapeln. **(b)** (Aviat) incoming planes had to be ~**ed** ankommende Maschinen mußten kreisen or Warteschleifen ziehen. **(c)** (US Cards) packen, beim Mischen betrügen. **the cards** or **odds are** ~**ed against us** (fig) wir haben keine großen Chancen.
3 vi sich stapeln lassen. ~**ing chairs** Stühle, die sich (gut) stapeln lassen.
stacked [stækt] adj (sl) **to be (well)** ~ einen großen or üppigen Vorbau haben (inf), Holz vor der Hütte haben (inf).
stadium ['steɪdɪəm] n, pl stadia ['steɪdɪə] or -s Stadion nt.
staff [stɑːf] **1** n **(a)** (personnel) Personal nt; (Sch, Univ) Lehrpersonal nt, Lehrkörper m (form); (of one department, on one project) Mitarbeiterstab m. **the** ~ **wear red uniforms** das Personal trägt rote Uniformen; **all the** ~ **are behind this idea** die ganze Belegschaft or (Sch, Univ) das ganze Kollegium steht hinter diesem Vorschlag; **a large** ~ viel Personal/ein großes Kollegium/ein großer Mitarbeiterstab; **we don't have enough** ~ **to complete the project** wir haben nicht genügend Mitarbeiter, um das Projekt zu beenden; **editorial** ~ Redaktion f, Redaktionsstab m; **administrative** ~ Verwaltungsstab m, Verwaltungspersonal nt; **a member of** ~ ein Mitarbeiter m; (Sch) ein Kollege m; **my fellow members of** ~ meine Kollegen; **we have 30 typists on the** ~ bei uns sind 30 Schreibkräfte angestellt; **to be on the** ~ zum Personal/Kollegium/Mitarbeiterstab gehören; **are you** ~? (inf) arbeiten Sie hier?; **he joined the** or **our** ~ **in 1976** er arbeitet seit 1976 bei uns; **he has left our** ~ er arbeitet nicht mehr hier.
(b) pl -s or (old) staves (stick, symbol of authority) Stab m; (flag~) Stock m; (fig liter: support) Stütze f. ~ **of office** Amtsstab m; **the** ~ **of life** das wichtigste Nahrungsmittel.
(c) (Mil: general ~) Stab m.
(d) pl staves (Mus) Notenlinien pl, Notensystem nt.

2 vt department Mitarbeiter finden für; hospital, shop, hotel mit Personal besetzen, Personal finden für; school mit Lehrpersonal besetzen. **to be well ~ed** gut besetzt sein, ausreichend Personal haben; **the kitchens are ~ed by foreigners** das Küchenpersonal besteht aus Ausländern.

staff college n Generalstabsakademie f.

staffer [ˈstɑːfɚ] n (Press inf) ständiger Mitarbeiter, ständige Mitarbeiterin.

staffing [ˈstɑːfɪŋ] n Stellenbesetzung f.

staffing: ~ **costs** npl Personalkosten pl; ~ **problem** n Problem nt mit der Stellenbesetzung.

staff: ~ **notation** n Notenschrift f; ~ **nurse** n (Brit) (voll)ausgebildete Krankenschwester, Vollschwester f (inf); ~ **officer** n Stabsoffizier m; ~ **problem** n Personalproblem nt; **~room** n Lehrerzimmer nt.

stag [stæg] **1** n (a) (Zool) (deer) Hirsch m; (male animal) Bock, Bulle m. (b) (Brit Fin) Spekulant m (der junge Aktien aufkauft). (c) (inf) Mann, der solo ist (inf). **2** adj Herren-, nur für Männer. **3** adv **to go** ~ solo ausgehen (inf).

stag beetle n Hirschkäfer m.

stage [steɪdʒ] **1** n (a) (Theat, fig) Bühne f. **the** ~ (profession) das Theater, die Bühne; **to be/go on/leave the** ~ (as career) beim Theater sein/zum Theater gehen/das Theater verlassen; **to go on** ~ (actor) die Bühne betreten; (play) anfangen; **to come off** ~, **to leave the** ~ von der Bühne abtreten; **to put a play on the** ~ ein Stück aufführen or auf die Bühne bringen; **his play never reached the** ~ sein Stück wurde nie aufgeführt; **to write for the** ~ Theater- or Bühnenstücke schreiben; **to adapt a novel for the** ~ einen Roman fürs Theater bearbeiten; **to hold** or **dominate the** ~ (lit, fig) die Szene beherrschen; **the** ~ **was set** (lit) das Bühnenbild war aufgebaut; (fig) alles war vorbereitet; **the** ~ **was set for a confrontation** die Situation war reif für eine Auseinandersetzung.

(b) (platform in hall) Podium nt.

(c) (period) Stadium nt; (of disease, process also, of operation, development) Phase f. **at this** ~ **such a thing is/was impossible** zum gegenwärtigen Zeitpunkt ist das/zum damaligen Zeitpunkt war das unmöglich; **at this** ~ **in the negotiations** an diesem Punkt der Verhandlungen; **at this** ~ **in the game** (fig) zu diesem Zeitpunkt; **in the early/final** ~(s) im Anfangs-/ Endstadium; **at an early** ~ **in its history** ganz zu Anfang seiner Geschichte; **what** ~ **is your thesis at?** wie weit sind Sie mit Ihrer Dissertation?; **we have reached a** ~ **where ...** wir sind an einem Punkt angelangt, wo ...; **the child has reached the talking** ~ das Kind ist jetzt im Alter, wo es zu reden anfängt; **to go through a difficult** ~ eine schwierige Phase durchmachen; **to be at the experimental** ~ im Versuchsstadium sein.

(d) (part of journey, race etc) Abschnitt m, Etappe f; (fare~) Teilstrecke, Fahrzone f; (actual bus stop) Zahlgrenze f. **in** or **by** (easy) ~s (lit) etappenweise; (fig also) Schritt für Schritt.

(e) (section of rocket) Stufe f. **a three-~ rocket** eine dreistufige Rakete.

(f) (old inf: ~coach) Postkutsche f.

2 vt play aufführen, auf die Bühne bringen; (fig) accident, scene etc inszenieren; welcome arrangieren; demonstration, strike etc inszenieren, veranstalten. **to** ~ **a recovery/comeback** sich erholen/sein Comeback machen; **the play is** ~d **in the 19th century** das Stück spielt im 19. Jahrhundert.

stage: ~ **box** n Bühnen- or Proszeniumsloge f; **~coach** n Postkutsche f; ~ **craft** n dramaturgisches Können; (of actor) schauspielerisches Können; ~ **direction** n Bühnen- or Regieanweisung f; ~ **door** n Bühneneingang m; ~ **effect** n Bühneneffekt m; ~ **fright** n Lampenfieber nt; **to have an attack of** ~ **fright** Lampenfieber haben; ~ **hand** n Bühnenarbeiter(in f) m; **~-manage** vt (lit) Inspizient sein bei; (fig) demonstration, argument inszenieren; ~ **manager** n Inspizient m; ~ **name** n Künstlername m.

stager [ˈsteɪdʒɚ] n: **old** ~ alter Hase (inf).

stage: **~-struck** adj theaterbesessen; **to be ~-struck** unbedingt zum Theater wollen; ~ **whisper** n Bühnenflüstern nt; **to say sth in a** ~ **whisper** etw hörbar flüstern.

stagey adj see **stagy**.

stagger [ˈstægɚ] **1** vi schwanken, taumeln; (because of illness, weakness) wanken; (drunkenly) torkeln. **he was ~ing along the street** er taumelte die Straße entlang.

2 vt (a) (fig: amaze) (news, events etc) den Atem verschlagen (+dat), umhauen (inf). **he was ~ed to hear of his promotion** die Nachricht von seiner Beförderung verschlug ihm die Sprache or haute ihn um (inf); **you ~ me!** da hat es ihm aber die Sprache verschlagen; **you ~ me!** da bin ich aber platt! (inf).

(b) hours, holidays staffeln, stufen; seats, spokes versetzt anordnen, versetzen.

3 n Taumeln nt. **to give a** ~ taumeln, schwanken; **with a** ~ taumelnd, schwankend; **~s** (Vet: of horses) (Dumm)koller m.

staggered [ˈstægɚd] adj (a) (amazed) verblüfft, platt (inf). (b) working hours etc gestaffelt, gestuft. **they work** ~ **hours** ihre Arbeitszeit ist gestaffelt; **a** ~ **junction** eine Kreuzung mit versetzten or versetzt angeordneten Straßen.

staggering [ˈstægɚɪŋ] adj (a) **to give sb a** ~ **blow** (lit) jdm einen Schlag versetzen, der ihn taumeln läßt; (fig) jdm einen harten or schweren Schlag versetzen.

(b) (amazing) atemberaubend, umwerfend (inf); news, beauty also umwerfend.

staggeringly [ˈstægɚɪŋlɪ] adv (amazingly) umwerfend (inf), erstaunlich.

stag: **~hound** n (für die Hirschjagd bestimmter) Jagdhund; ~ **hunt,** ~ **hunting** n Hirschjagd f.

stagily [ˈsteɪdʒɪlɪ] adv dressed, made up auffallend.

staginess [ˈsteɪdʒɪnɪs] n auffällige Art.

staging [ˈsteɪdʒɪŋ] n (a) (production) Inszenieren nt; (scenery etc) Inszenierung f. (b) (stage) Bühne f.

stagnancy [ˈstægnənsɪ] n Stagnieren nt; (of trade also) Stagnation f, Stocken nt.

stagnant [ˈstægnənt] adj (still, not moving) air, water (still-) stehend attr, gestaut; (foul, stale) water abgestanden; air verbraucht; trade stagnierend, stockend; mind träge.

stagnate [stægˈneɪt] vi (not circulate) stagnieren; (become foul) (water) abstehen; (air) verbraucht werden; (trade) stagnieren, stocken; (person) verdummen; (mind) einrosten.

stagnation [stægˈneɪʃən] n (of water) Stagnieren nt; (of air) Stau m; (of trade also) Stagnation f, Stocken nt; (of person) Verdummung f; (of mind) Verlangsamung f.

stag: ~ **night** n Saufabend m des Bräutigams mit seinen Kumpeln; ~ **party** n (a) Herrenabend m; (b) see ~ **night**.

stagy [ˈsteɪdʒɪ] adj (+er) theatralisch; appearance auffallend.

staid [steɪd] adj (+er) seriös, gesetzt; answer bedächtig; colour gedeckt.

staidly [ˈsteɪdlɪ] adv gesetzt; answer in seiner etc gesetzten Art; dressed gedeckt.

staidness [ˈsteɪdnɪs] n Gesetztheit f.

stain [steɪn] **1** n (a) Fleck m; (fig also) Makel m. **a blood/grease/mud** ~ ein Blutfleck m/Fettfleck m/Schlammspritzer m; ~ **remover** Fleckenentferner m; **without a** ~ **on his character** ohne (einen) Makel.

(b) (colorant) (Ein)färbemittel nt; (wood~) Beize f.

2 vt beflecken; (colour) einfärben; (with wood~) beizen.

3 vi (a) (leave a ~) Flecken hinterlassen or geben (inf).

(b) (become ~ed) fleckig werden, Flecken bekommen.

stained [steɪnd] adj dress, floor fleckig, befleckt (geh); glass bunt, bemalt; reputation befleckt. **~-glass window** Buntglasfenster nt, farbiges Glasfenster; ~ **with blood** blutbefleckt.

stainless [ˈsteɪnlɪs] adj (a) (character) tadellos.

(b) (rust-resistant) rostfrei. ~ **steel** rostfreier (Edel)stahl, Nirosta ® no art (dated); (esp for dishes, cutlery also) Cromargan ® nt; **"~ steel"** „rostfrei"; ~ **steel cutlery** rostfreies Besteck, Cromarganbesteck ® nt.

stair [steɚ] n (a) (step) Stufe f. (b) usu pl (~way) Treppe f. **at the top of the ~s** oben an der Treppe; **below ~s** (Brit dated) beim (Haus)personal; see **flight**[1].

stair: ~ **carpet** n Treppenläufer m; **~case** n Treppe f; (~way) Treppenhaus nt; ~ **rod** n Teppichstab m; **~way** n Treppenhaus nt; **~well** n Treppenauge nt.

stake [steɪk] **1** n (a) (post) Pfosten, Pfahl m; (for vampires) Pfahl m; (for plant) Stange f; (for animal) Pflock m; see **pull up**.

(b) (place of execution) Scheiterhaufen m. **to go to** or **to die at the** ~ auf dem Scheiterhaufen sterben, verbrannt werden; **he was ready to be burnt at the** ~ **for his principles** er war bereit, sich für seine Prinzipien ans Kreuz nageln zu lassen.

(c) (bet) Einsatz m; (financial interest) Anteil m. **to be at** ~ auf dem Spiel stehen; **he has a lot at** ~ er hat viel zu verlieren; **to have a** ~ **in sth** in business einen Anteil an etw (dat) haben; **in the future** von etw betroffen werden; **he has a big** ~ **in the success of the plan** für ihn hängt viel vom Erfolg des Planes ab; **I don't understand the issue at** ~ ich verstehe nicht, worum es geht; **that's precisely the issue at** ~ genau darum geht es; **the issue at** ~ **is not** ... es steht nicht zur Debatte, ob ...

(d) ~s pl (prize) Gewinn m; **the Newmarket ~s** der Große Preis von Newmarket.

2 vt (a) animal anpflocken.

(b) (also ~ up) plant hochbinden; fence abstützen.

(c) (bet, risk) setzen (on auf +acc); (esp US: back financially) finanziell unterstützen. **to** ~ **one's life/reputation on sth** seine Hand für etw ins Feuer legen/sein Wort für etw verpfänden; **to** ~ **a/one's claim to sth** sich (dat) ein Anrecht auf etw (acc) sichern.

♦ **stake off** or **out** vt sep land abstecken.

♦ **stake out** vt sep (US sl) place umstellen; person überwachen.

stakeout [ˈsteɪkaʊt] n (US sl) Überwachung f.

stalactite [ˈstæləktaɪt] n Stalaktit m.

stalagmite [ˈstæləgmaɪt] n Stalagmit m.

stale [steɪl] adj (+er) (a) (old, musty) alt; cake also trocken; bread, biscuit also altbacken; (in taste, smell also) muffig; water, beer, wine abgestanden, schal; air verbraucht.

(b) (fig) news veraltet; joke abgedroschen; athlete, pianist etc ausgepumpt, verbraucht. **to be** ~ (person) alles nur noch routinemäßig machen; **I'm getting** ~ ich mache langsam alles nur noch routinemäßig; **don't let yourself get** ~ paß auf, daß du nicht in Routine verfällst.

stalemate [ˈsteɪlmeɪt] **1** n (Chess) Patt nt; (fig) Patt(situation f) nt, Sackgasse f. **to reach** (a) ~ (lit) ein Patt erreichen; (fig) in eine Sackgasse geraten; **to end in** (a) ~ (lit) mit (einem) Patt enden, patt enden; (fig) in einer Sackgasse enden.

2 vt (Chess) patt setzen; (fig) matt setzen; negotiations zum Stillstand bringen.

staleness [ˈsteɪlnɪs] n (a) (lit) (of beer, water etc) Schalheit, Abgestandenheit f; (of bread, biscuit) Altbackenheit f; (of taste, smell) Muffigkeit f. **the** ~ **of the air made them sleepy** die verbrauchte Luft machte sie schläfrig.

(b) (fig) (of joke) Abgedroschenheit f. **the** ~ **of the news** die veraltete Nachricht; **he practised to the point of** ~ er übte, bis er langsam alles nur noch routinemäßig machte.

stalk[1] [stɔːk] **1** vt game sich anpirschen an (+acc); person sich anschleichen an (+acc); (animal) beschleichen, sich heranschleichen an (+acc). **evil ~ed the streets** (liter) das Böse ging in den Straßen um. **2** vi (a) (walk haughtily) stolzieren. (b) (Hunt) pirschen. **to go** ~ing auf die Pirsch gehen.

stalk[2] n (of plant, leaf) Stiel m; (cabbage~) Strunk m. **his eyes came out on ~s** (inf) er bekam Stielaugen (inf).

stalker [ˈstɔːkɚ] n Pirschjäger(in f) m.

stalking-horse [ˈstɔːkɪŋhɔːs] n (fig) (person) Strohmann m; (pretext) Vorwand m.

stall [stɔːl] **1** n (a) (in stable) Box, Bucht f; (old: stable) Stall m.

(b) (*at market etc*) Stand *m*.
(c) ~s *pl* (*Brit Theat, Film*) Parkett *nt*; **in the** ~**s** im Parkett.
(d) (*Eccl*) Kirchenstuhl *m*. ~**s** Chorgestühl *nt*.
(e) (*Aviat*) überzogener Flug. **to do a** ~ **turn** (*Aviat*) ein Flugzeug auffangen und neu starten.
2 *vt* **(a)** *horse, cow* einstellen.
(b) (*Aut*) abwürgen; (*Aviat*) überziehen.
(c) (*also* ~ **off**) *person* hinhalten; *decision* hinauszögern.
3 *vi* **(a)** (*engine*) absterben; (*Aviat*) überziehen.
(b) (*delay*) Zeit schinden (*inf*). **stop** ~**ing!** hören Sie auf auszuweichen *or* drum rumzureden (*inf*)!; **to** ~ **on a decision** eine Entscheidung hinauszögern; **to** ~ **for time** versuchen, Zeit zu gewinnen *or* zu schinden (*inf*).
stallion ['stæljən] *n* Hengst *m*; (*for breeding*) Zuchthengst *m*.
stalwart ['stɔːlwət] **1** *adj* **(a)** (*in spirit*) treu, unentwegt; *supporter also* getreu; *belief* unerschütterlich. **(b)** (*in build*) kräftig, robust. **2** *n* (*supporter*) (getreuer) Anhänger. **the party leader and his** ~**s** der Parteichef und seine Getreuen.
stalwartly ['stɔːlwətlɪ] *adv fight, oppose* tapfer, unentwegt; *support* treu; *believe* unerschütterlich; *built* kräftig.
stamen ['steɪmen] *n* Staubgefäß *nt*, Staubfaden *m*.
stamina ['stæmɪnə] *n* Stehvermögen, Durchhaltevermögen *nt*.
stammer ['stæməʳ] **1** *n* Stottern *nt*. **to speak with a** ~ stottern; **he has a bad** ~ er stottert stark. **2** *vt* (*also* ~ **out**) stammeln. **3** *vi* stottern. **to start** ~**ing** ins Stottern geraten.
stammerer ['stæmərəʳ] *n* Stotterer *m*, Stotterin *f*.
stammering ['stæmərɪŋ] **1** *adj excuse, apology* gestammelt; *person* stammelnd. **2** *n* (*act*) Stottern, Stammeln *nt*; (*stammered speech*) Gestotter(e), Gestammel(e) *nt*.
stammeringly ['stæmərɪŋlɪ] *adv* stammelnd, stotternd.
stamp [stæmp] **1** *n* **(a)** (*postage* ~) (*Brief*)marke *f*, (*Post*)wertzeichen *nt* (*form*); (*insurance* ~, *revenue* ~ *etc*) Marke *f*; (*trading* ~) (*Rabatt*)marke *f*; (*charity* ~, *airmail* ~, *sticker*) Aufkleber *m*. **to collect** (*postage*) ~**s** Briefmarken sammeln; **to save** (*trading*) ~**s** Rabattmarken sammeln.
(b) (*rubber* ~, *die, impression*) Stempel *m*.
(c) (*fig*) **a man of his** ~ ein Mann seines Schlags; **to bear the** ~ **of the expert/of authenticity** den Stempel des Experten/die Züge der Echtheit tragen.
2 *vt* **(a)** **to** ~ **one's foot** (mit dem Fuß) (auf)stampfen; **to** ~ **the ground** (mit dem Fuß/den Füßen) auf den Boden stampfen; **he** ~**ed the turf back into place** er stampfte die Sode wieder an ihrem Platz fest.
(b) (*put postage* ~ *on*) frankieren. **a** ~**ed addressed envelope** ein frankierter Rückumschlag.
(c) *paper, document etc* (*with rubber* ~) stempeln; (*with embossing machine*) prägen; *name, pattern* aufstempeln; aufprägen (*on* auf +*acc*); (*fig*) ausweisen (*as* als). **the new leader has** ~**ed his personality on the party** der neue Vorsitzende hat der Partei seine Persönlichkeit aufgeprägt.
3 *vi* (*walk*) sta(m)pfen, trampeln; (*disapprovingly, in dancing*) (mit dem Fuß) (auf)stampfen; (*horse*) aufstampfen. **must you** ~ **about like that?** mußt du so (rum)trampeln?; **he was** ~**ing about the house** er trampelte im Haus herum; **to** ~ **in/out** hinein-/hinausstapfen.
♦**stamp on 1** *vt sep pattern, design* aufprägen. **to** ~ **a pattern** ~ **sth** auf etw (*acc*) ein Muster (auf)prägen; **to be** ~**ed** ~ **sb's memory** sich jdm eingeprägt haben. **2** *vi* +*prep obj* (*put one's foot on*) treten auf (+*acc*).
♦**stamp out 1** *vt sep* **(a)** *fire* austreten; (*fig: eradicate*) *epidemic, crime* ausrotten; *opposition* unterdrücken, zunichte machen; *trouble* niederschlagen; *rebels* unschädlich machen. **(b)** (*punch or cut out*) *pattern, shape* ausstanzen. **(c)** *rhythm* (mit)stampfen. **2** *vi* herausstampfen, herausta(m)pfen.
stamp: ~ **album** *n* Briefmarkenalbum *nt*; ~ **collecting** *n* Briefmarkensammeln *nt*; ~ **collection** *n* Briefmarkensammlung *f*; ~ **collector** *n* Briefmarkensammler(in *f*) *m*; ~ **dealer** *n* Briefmarkenhändler(in *f*) *m*; ~ **duty** *n* (Stempel)gebühr *f*.
stampede [stæm'piːd] **1** *n* (*of horses, cattle*) wilde Flucht; (*of people*) Massendrang, Massenansturm *m* (*on* auf +*acc*); (*to escape*) wilde *or* panikartige Flucht. **the exodus turned into a** ~ der Exodus geriet zur Panik.
2 *vt cattle, horses, crowd* in (wilde *or* helle) Panik versetzen. **to** ~ **sb into doing sth** (*fig*) jdn dazu drängen, etw zu tun; **let's not be** ~**d** (*fig*) wir wollen uns nicht kopfscheu machen lassen.
3 *vi durchgehen*; (*crowd*) losstürmen (*for* auf +*acc*).
stamping ground ['stæmpɪŋ‚graʊnd] *n* his old ~s seine alten Jagdgründe; **it's the** ~ **of a lot of students** es ist der Treff(punkt) vieler Studenten.
stamp machine *n* Briefmarkenautomat *m*.
stance [stæns] *n* (*posture, Sport*) Haltung *f*; (*mental attitude also*) Einstellung *f*; (*Cricket, Golf etc also*) Stand *m*. **to take up a** ~ (*lit*) in Stellung gehen; (*fig*) eine Haltung einnehmen.
stand [stænd] (*vb: pret, ptp stood*) **1** *n* **(a)** (*position*) Platz, Standort *m*; (*fig*) Standpunkt *m*, Einstellung *f* (*on* zu). **my** ~ **is that ...** ich stehe auf dem Standpunkt, daß ...; **ich vertrete die Einstellung, daß ...**; **to take a** ~ (*on a matter*) (zu einer Angelegenheit) eine Einstellung vertreten; **to take a firm** ~ einen festen Standpunkt vertreten (*on* zu).
(b) (*Mil*) (*resistance*) Widerstand *m*; (*battle*) Gefecht *nt*. **to make a** ~ (*lit, fig*) sich widersetzen, Widerstand leisten.
(c) (*taxi* ~) Stand *m*.
(d) (*Theat*) Gastspiel *nt*; (*of pop group etc*) Konzert *nt*.
(e) (*furniture, lamp* ~, *music* ~) Ständer *m*.
(f) (*market stall etc*) Stand *m*.
(g) (*band*~) Podium *m*.
(h) (*Sport*) Tribüne *f*; (*US Jur*) Zeugenstand *m*. **(we sat) in the** ~ (wir saßen) auf der Tribüne; **to take the** ~ (*Jur*) in den Zeugenstand treten.
2 *vt* **(a)** (*place*) stellen; *see* **stead, head**.
(b) (*withstand*) *pressure, close examination etc* (*object*)

(b) (*person*) gewachsen sein (+*dat*); *test* bestehen; *climate* vertragen; *heat, noise* ertragen, aushalten; *loss, cost* verkraften. **the wall could** ~ **another coat of paint** (*inf*) die Wand könnte noch einen Anstrich vertragen.
(c) (*inf: put up with*) *person, noise, interruptions etc* aushalten. **I can't** ~ **him/it** (*don't like*) ich kann ihn nicht leiden *or* ausstehen/ich kann das nicht ausstehen *or* vertragen; **I can't** ~ **being kept waiting** ich kann es nicht leiden *or* ausstehen, wenn man mich warten läßt; **I can't** ~ **it any longer** ich halte das nicht mehr (länger) aus.
(d) (*inf: treat*) **to** ~ **sb a drink/a meal** jdm einen Drink/ein Essen spendieren.
3 *vi* **(a)** (*be upright*) stehen; (*get up*) aufstehen. **all** ~**!** alles aufstehen!; **don't just** ~ **there!** stehen Sie nicht nur (dumm) rum! (*inf*); **to** ~ **still** stillstehen; **we stood talking** wir standen da und unterhielten uns; ~ **and deliver!** (*old, hum*) anhalten, her mit dem Zeug! (*inf*); *see* **attention, ease**.
(b) (*measure*) (*person*) groß sein; (*tree etc*) hoch sein.
(c) (*be situated*) stehen. **it has stood there for 600 years** es steht da schon seit 600 Jahren.
(d) (*remain unchanged*) stehen; (*fig*) bestehen (bleiben).
(e) **to** ~ **as a candidate** kandidieren; *see also* ~ **for** (a).
(f) (*continue to be valid*) (*offer, promise*) gelten; (*argument, objection, contract also*) gültig bleiben; (*decision, record, account*) stehen. **the theory** ~**s or falls by this** damit steht und fällt die Theorie.
(g) (*be at a level of*) (*thermometer, record*) stehen (*at* auf +*dat*); (*sales*) liegen (*at* bei).
(h) (*fig: be in a position*) **we** ~ **to lose/gain a lot** wir laufen Gefahr, eine Menge zu verlieren/wir können sehr viel gewinnen; **he** ~**s to earn a lot of money** er wird wohl eine Menge Geld (dabei) verdienen; **what do we** ~ **gain by it?** was springt für uns dabei heraus? (*inf*), was bringt uns (*dat*) das ein?
(i) (*fig: be placed*) **how do we** ~? wie stehen wir?; **I'd like to know where I** ~ (*with him*) ich möchte wissen, woran ich (bei ihm) bin; **where do you** ~ **with him?** wie stehen Sie sich mit ihm?; **as things** ~ nach Lage der Dinge; **as it** ~**s** so wie die Sache aussieht; **to** ~ **alone** (*be best*) unerreicht sein.
(j) (*fig: be, continue to be*) **to** ~ **firm or fast** festbleiben; **to** ~ **ready** sich bereithalten; **to** ~ **in need of help** Hilfe brauchen; **to** ~ **together** zusammenhalten; **to** ~ **(as) security for sb** für jdn bürgen *or* Bürge sein; **nothing now** ~**s between us** es steht nichts mehr zwischen uns; *see also other elements*.
♦**stand about** *or* **around** *vi* herumstehen.
♦**stand apart** *vi* (*lit*) abseits stehen; (*fig*) sich fernhalten. **to** ~ ~ **from the others** abseits stehen.
♦**stand aside** *vi* (*lit*) zur Seite treten; (*fig*) (*withdraw*) zurücktreten; (*play no part*) (tatenlos) danebenstehen.
♦**stand back** *vi* (*move back*) zurücktreten; (*be situated at a distance*) zurückstehen, abliegen, zurückliegen; (*fig*) (*distance oneself*) Abstand nehmen; (*play no part*) (tatenlos) danebenstehen. **to** ~ ~ **and do nothing** tatenlos zusehen.
♦**stand by 1** *vi* **(a)** (*remain uninvolved*) (unbeteiligt) danebenstehen. **to** ~ ~ **and do nothing** tatenlos zusehen. **(b)** (*be on alert*) sich bereithalten. **to** ~ ~ **for further news** auf weitere Nachrichten warten. **2** *vi* +*prep obj* **to** ~ ~ **a promise/sb** ein Versprechen/zu jdm halten.
♦**stand down** *vi* **(a)** (*retire, withdraw*) verzichten. **(b)** (*Jur*) den Zeugenstand verlassen. **(c)** (*Mil*) aufgelöst werden.
♦**stand for** *vi* +*prep obj* **(a)** (*be candidate for*) kandidieren für, sich zur Wahl stellen für. **to** ~ ~ **Labour** für Labour *or* für die Labour-Partei kandidieren; **to** ~ ~ **(the post of) chairman** für den Posten des Vorsitzenden kandidieren, sich zur Wahl stellen; **to** ~ ~ **election** (in einer Wahl) kandidieren, sich zur Wahl stellen; **to** ~ ~ **re-election** sich zur Wiederwahl stellen; **to** ~ ~ **election to sth** für etw kandidieren; **she is** ~**ing** ~ **election to Parliament** sie kandidiert in den Parlamentswahlen.
(b) (*be abbreviation for, represent*) stehen für, bedeuten.
(c) (*put up with*) hinnehmen, sich (*dat*) gefallen lassen.
♦**stand in** *vi* einspringen.
♦**stand off** *vi* (*Naut*) seewärts anliegen.
♦**stand out** *vi* **(a)** (*project*) hervorstehen; (*land, balcony*) herausragen.
(b) (*contrast, be noticeable*) hervorstechen, auffallen. **to** ~ ~ **against sth** sich gegen etw *or* von etw abheben; **to** ~ ~ **from the others** hervorstechen, auffallen.
(c) (*hold out*) **to** ~ ~ **against sth** weiterhin gegen etw Widerstand leisten; **to** ~ ~ **for sth** auf etw (*acc*) bestehen.
♦**stand over 1** *vi* (*work, project*) liegenbleiben. **to let sth** ~ ~ etw liegenlassen. **2** *vi* +*prep obj* (*supervise*) auf die Finger sehen (+*dat*). **I can't work with you** ~**ing** ~ **me** ich kann nicht arbeiten, wenn du mir (dauernd) über die Schulter siehst.
♦**stand to** *vi* (*Mil*) in Bereitschaft *or* in Waffen stehen.
♦**stand up 1** *vi* **(a)** (*get up*) aufstehen; (*be standing*) stehen. ~ ~ **straight!** stell dich gerade hin; **to** ~ ~ **and be counted** sich zu seiner Meinung *or* seinen Überzeugungen bekennen.
(b) (*be valid*) (*argument*) überzeugen; (*Jur*) bestehen.
(c) **to** ~ ~ **for sb/sth** für jdn/etw eintreten; **to** ~ ~ **to sth** *to test, pressure* (*object*) einer Sache (*dat*) standhalten; (*person*) einer Sache (*dat*) gewachsen sein; **to** ~ **to hard wear** etw vertragen *or* aushalten; **to** ~ ~ **to sb** sich jdm gegenüber behaupten.
2 *vt sep* **(a)** (*put upright*) hinstellen.
(b) (*inf*) *boyfriend etc* versetzen.
standard ['stændəd] **1** *n* **(a)** (*average, established norm*) Norm *f*; (*criterion*) Maßstab *m*. **to set a good** ~ Maßstäbe setzen; **to be above/below** ~ über/unter der Norm sein *or* liegen; **to be up to** ~ den Anforderungen genügen.
(b) *usu pl* (*moral* ~s) (*sittliche*) Maßstäbe *pl*. **his (moral)** ~**s are abysmally low** er hat eine erschreckend niedere Moral; **to conform to society's** ~**s** den Wertvorstellungen der

Gesellschaft entsprechen; **he sets himself very high ~s** er stellt hohe Anforderungen an sich (acc) selbst.

(c) (degree, level) Niveau nt. **~ of living** Lebensstandard m; **~ of culture** kulturelles Niveau; **first-year university ~** Wissensstand m des ersten Studienjahrs; **of high/low ~** von hohem/niedrigem Niveau.

(d) (Measurement) (Maß)einheit f, Standard m; (monetary ~) (Währungs)standard m. **these coins don't contain enough silver to conform to the monetary ~** diese Münzen enthalten weniger Silber, als dem Münzfuß entspräche.

(e) (flag) Flagge, Fahne f; (on car) Stander m; (royal ~) (königliche) Standarte.

(f) (pole) Mast m.

(g) (Hort) (Hoch)stamm m. **~ rose** Stammrose f.

2 adj (a) (usual, customary) üblich; (Comm also) handelsüblich; model, price, practice, reply Standard-; size, measure Normal-; (average) performance, work Durchschnitts-, durchschnittlich; (widely referred to) author, reference book Standard-; (generally established as a measure) weight, size Norm-; conditions, pressure, temperature, time Normal-; gauge Regel-, Normal-. **such requirements are not ~** solche Forderungen sind nicht die Norm or Regel.

(b) (Ling) (allgemein) gebräuchlich. **~ English** korrektes Englisch; **~ German** Hochdeutsch nt; **that word is hardly ~** dieses Wort ist ziemlich ungebräuchlich.

standard-bearer ['stændəd,bɛərə^r] n Fahnenträger(in f), Bannerträger (old, fig) m.

standardization [,stændədaɪ'zeɪʃən] n see vt Vereinheitlichung f; Normung, Standardisierung f.

standardize ['stændədaɪz] vt education, style, approach vereinheitlichen; format, sizes etc normen, standardisieren.

standard-lamp ['stændəd'læmp] n Stehlampe f.

stand-by ['stændbaɪ] **1 n (a)** (person) Ersatz, Ersatzmann m; (Sport also) Ersatz- or Auswechselspieler(in f) m; (thing) Reserve f; (Aviat) (plane) Entlastungsflugzeug nt; (ticket) Standby-Ticket nt; (passenger) Passagier, der mit einem Standby-Ticket reist.

(b) (state of readiness) **on ~** in Bereitschaft; (ready for action) in Einsatzbereitschaft; **to be on 24-hour ~** 24 Stunden Bereitschaftsdienst haben.

2 adj attr troops, player, generator Reserve-, Ersatz-; (Aviat) plane Entlastungs-; passenger, ticket Standby-.

standee [stæn'diː] n (esp US) jd, der steht or einen Stehplatz hat.

stand-in ['stændɪn] n (Film, Theat) Ersatz m.

standing ['stændɪŋ] **1 n (a)** (social) Rang m, (gesellschaftliche) Stellung; (professional) Position f; (financial) (finanzielle) Verhältnisse pl; (repute) Ruf m, Ansehen nt. **of high ~** von hohem Rang; (repute) von hohem Ansehen; **a man of some ~** ein angesehener Mann; **what is his ~ locally?** was hält man in der Gegend von ihm?; **to be in good ~ with sb** gute Beziehungen zu jdm haben.

(b) (duration) Dauer f. **a treaty/her husband of only six months' ~** ein Vertrag, der erst seit sechs Monaten besteht/ihr Mann, mit dem sie erst seit sechs Monaten verheiratet ist; **of long ~** alt, langjährig; relationship, agreement etc also von langer Dauer.

2 adj attr (a) (established, permanent) ständig; rule, custom bestehend; army also stehend. **it's a ~ joke** es ist schon ein Witz geworden; **to pay sth by ~ order** etw per Dauerauftrag bezahlen; **~ committee** ständiger Ausschuß; **the ~ orders of an association** die Geschäftsordnung einer Gesellschaft.

(b) (from a standstill) aus dem Stand; (not sitting) ticket Stehplatz-; (erect) corn auf dem Halm (stehend); stone (aufrecht) stehend. **~ room only** nur Stehplätze; **to give sb a ~ ovation** jdm im Stehen Beifall klatschen or eine Ovation darbringen; **to receive a ~ ovation** stürmischen Beifall ernten.

stand-: **~-offish** [,stænd'ɒfɪʃ] adj, **~-offishly** [-lɪ] adv (inf) hochnäsig; **~-offishness** [-nɪs] n (inf) Hochnäsigkeit f; **~ pipe** n Steigrohr nt; **~point** n Standpunkt m; **from the ~point of the teacher** vom Standpunkt des Lehrers (aus) gesehen; **~still** n Stillstand m; **to be at a ~still** (plane, train) stehen; (machines, traffic) stillstehen; (trade, factory, production) ruhen; **to bring production to a ~still** die Produktion lahmlegen or zum Erliegen bringen; **to come to a ~still** (person) stehenbleiben, anhalten; (vehicle) zum Stehen kommen, anhalten; (traffic, machines) zum Stillstand kommen; (industry etc) zum Erliegen kommen; **~-up** adj attr buffet, collar Steh-; meal im Stehen; **~-up fight** Schlägerei f.

stank [stæŋk] pret of **stink**.

stannic ['stænɪk] adj Zinn-.

stanza ['stænzə] n Strophe f.

staple[1] ['steɪpl] **1 n** Klammer f; (for paper) Heftklammer f; (for wires, cables etc) Krampe f. **2 vt** heften; wire mit Krampen befestigen. **to ~ sth together** etw zusammenheften.

staple[2] **1 adj** diet, food Grund-, Haupt-; product, topic Haupt-. **2 n (a)** (main product) Hauptartikel m; (main element) Ausgangsmaterial nt; (main food) Hauptnahrungsmittel nt.

(b) (of cotton) Rohbaumwolle f; (of wool) Rohwolle f.

stapler ['steɪplə^r] n Heftmaschine f.

star [stɑː^r] **1 n (a)** Stern m; (asterisk also, Sch) Sternchen nt. **the S~s and Stripes** das Sternenbanner; **to be born under a lucky/an unlucky ~** unter einem glücklichen/unglücklichen Stern geboren sein; **you can thank your lucky ~s that ...** Sie können von Glück sagen, daß ...; **it's all in the ~s** es steht (alles) in den Sternen; **to see ~s** Sterne sehen; **a three-~ general** (US Mil) ein Drei-Sterne-General m.

(b) (person) Star m.

2 adj attr attraction Haupt-; performer, pupil, player Star-.

3 vt (a) (mark with ~s) mit einem Stern/mit Sternen versehen; (fig: scatter) besäen or übersäen.

(b) (Film etc) **to ~ sb** (film) jdn in der Hauptrolle zeigen; a

film **~ring** Greta Garbo ein Film mit Greta Garbo (in der Hauptrolle); **~ring ...** in der Hauptrolle/den Hauptrollen ...

4 vi (Film etc) die Hauptrolle spielen or haben.

star: **~ billing** n **to get ~ billing** auf Plakaten groß herausgestellt werden; **~board 1 n** Steuerbord nt; **to ~board** (direction) (nach) Steuerbord; (place) (in) Steuerbord; **2 adj** Steuerbord-; **3 adv** (nach) Steuerbord.

starch [stɑːtʃ] **1 n** Stärke f. **~-reduced** stärkearm. **2 vt** stärken.

starchily ['stɑːtʃɪlɪ] adv (fig) steif.

starchy ['stɑːtʃɪ] adj (+er) stärkehaltig; (fig) steif.

star-crossed ['stɑːkrɒst] adj **they were ~ lovers** ihre Liebe stand unter einem Unstern.

stardom ['stɑːdəm] n Berühmtheit f, Ruhm m. **where he hoped to find ~** wo er hoffte, ein Star zu werden.

stare [stɛə^r] **1 n** (starrer) Blick. **the village idiot looked at me with a vacant ~** der Dorftrottel sah mich mit stierem Blick an; **to give sb a ~** jdn anstarren.

2 vt **the answer/his guilt was staring us in the face** die Antwort/seine Schuld lag klar auf der Hand.

3 vi (vacantly etc) (vor sich hin) starren; (cow, madman) stieren, glotzen (inf); (in surprise) große Augen machen; (eyes) weit aufgerissen sein. **he ~d in disbelief** er starrte ungläubig; **it's rude to ~** es ist unhöflich, andere Leute anzustarren; **to ~ at sb/sth** jdn/etw anstarren; (cow, madman also) jdn/etw anstieren or anglotzen (inf); **don't ~ (at me)!** starr (mich) nicht so (an)!; **to ~ at sb in horror/amusement/disbelief** etc jdn entsetzt/verblüfft/ungläubig etc anstarren; **to ~ after sb** jdm nachstarren or hinterherstarren.

♦ **stare out** or **down** vt sep **they were trying to ~ each other ~** sie versuchten, sich so lange gegenseitig anzustarren, bis einer aufgab; **I bet I can ~ you ~** wetten, daß du zuerst wegguckst (inf); **this idiot standing there trying to ~ me ~** der Blödmann da glotzt mich so herausfordernd an (inf); **the teacher just sat there and ~d him ~** der Lehrer saß da und fixierte ihn.

star: **~fish** n Seestern m; **~gazer** n (hum inf) Sterngucker m (hum inf).

staring ['stɛərɪŋ] adj starrend attr. **~ eyes** starrer Blick.

stark [stɑːk] **1 adj** (+er) realism, contrast, ignorance, poverty kraß; reality, poverty also, white, truth, terror nackt; clothing, simplicity schlicht; madness schier, rein, hell; landscape, cliffs, branches nackt, kahl; light, bulb grell; colour eintönig; (glaring) grell; black trist; silhouette hart.

2 adv **~ raving** or **staring mad** (inf) total verrückt (inf); **~ naked** splitternackt.

starkers ['stɑːkəz] adj pred (inf) im Adamskostüm/Evaskostüm (hum); children nackig (inf).

starkly ['stɑːklɪ] adv lit grell; described kraß, schonungslos. **~ dressed in black** in tristes Schwarz gekleidet; **trees ~ silhouetted against the winter sky** Bäume, die sich hart gegen den Winterhimmel abhoben.

starkness ['stɑːknɪs] n (of clothing) Schlichtheit f; (of colour) Eintönigkeit f; (glaring) Grellheit f; (of truth, contrast) Härte, Kraßheit f; (of landscape) Nacktheit, Kahlheit f.

starless ['stɑːlɪs] adj sternenlos.

starlet ['stɑːlɪt] n (Film)sternchen, Starlet nt.

starlight ['stɑːlaɪt] n Sternenlicht nt.

starling ['stɑːlɪŋ] n Star m.

star: **~lit** adj sky, night stern(en)klar; woods, hills von Sternen beschienen; **~ part** n Hauptrolle f.

starred [stɑːd] adj mit (einem) Sternchen bezeichnet.

starriness ['stɑːrɪnɪs] n (of night, sky) Stern(en)klarheit f; (of eyes) Leuchten, Strahlen nt. **the ~ of the sky** der stern(en)klare Himmel.

star role n see **star part**.

starry ['stɑːrɪ] adj (+er) night stern(en)klar; sky Sternen-; eyes strahlend, leuchtend.

starry-eyed ['stɑːrɪ'aɪd] adj idealist romantisch, blauäugig; (naively trusting) arglos, blauäugig. **to go all ~** glänzende Augen kriegen.

star: **~ shell** n Leuchtkugel f, Leuchtgeschoß nt; **~-spangled** adj **(a)** (liter) sky stern(en)übersät (liter); **(b)** The **S~-spangled Banner** das Sternenbanner; **~-studded** adj **(a)** (liter) night stern(en)klar, voller Sterne; sky also stern(en)übersät (liter); **(b)** (fig) **~-studded cast** Starbesetzung f.

start[1] [stɑːt] **1 n** (fright etc) Zusammenfahren nt; Auffahren, Aufschrecken nt; (of horse) Scheuen nt. **to give a ~** zusammenfahren; auffahren, aufschrecken; (horse) scheuen; **to give sb a ~** jdn erschrecken, jdm einen Schreck(en) einjagen; **to wake with a ~** aus dem Schlaf hochschrecken; **he looked up with a ~** er blickte erschreckt hoch; see **fit**[2].

2 vi (a) aufschrecken, hochschrecken; zusammenfahren. **to ~ from one's chair/out of one's sleep** aus dem Stuhl hochfahren/aus dem Schlaf hochschrecken.

(b) **tears ~ed to his eyes** Tränen traten ihm in die Augen; **his eyes were ~ing out of his head** die Augen traten ihm fast aus dem Kopf.

3 vt pheasant etc aufscheuchen (from aus).

start[2] **1 n (a)** (beginning) Beginn, Anfang m; (departure) Aufbruch m; (of race) Start m; (of rumour, trouble, journey) Ausgangspunkt m. **at the ~** am Anfang, zu Beginn; (Sport) am Start; **we are at the ~ of something big** wir stehen am Anfang or Beginn einer großen Entwicklung; **for a ~** (to begin with) fürs erste; (firstly) zunächst einmal; **from the ~** von Anfang an; **from ~ to finish** von Anfang bis Ende, von vorn bis hinten (inf); **to get off to a good** or **flying ~** gut vom Start wegkommen; (fig) (person) die richtige Starthilfe bekommen; (project, business) sich gut anlassen; **to get sb/sth off to a good ~** jdm einen guten Start verschaffen/etw gut anlaufen lassen; **to give sb a (good) ~ in life** jdm eine (gute) Starthilfe geben; **the review gave the book a good ~** die Rezension war eine gute Starthilfe für das Buch; **to make a ~ (on sth)** (mit etw) anfangen; **to make**

an early ~/a ~ for home frühzeitig aufbrechen/sich auf den Heimweg machen; **to make a fresh** or **new ~ (in life)** (noch einmal) von vorn anfangen.

(b) (advantage, Sport) Vorsprung m (over vor +dat).

2 vt **(a)** (begin) anfangen mit; argument, career, new life, negotiations beginnen, anfangen; new job, journey antreten. **to ~ work** anfangen zu arbeiten; **he ~ed life as a miner** er hat/hatte als Bergmann angefangen; **don't ~ that again!** fang nicht schon wieder (damit) an!; **to ~ smoking** das or mit dem Rauchen anfangen; **he ~ed coming late** er fing an, zu spät zu kommen.

(b) (runners) starten zu; (cause to begin) runners, race starten; train abfahren lassen; rumour im Umlauf setzen; conversation anfangen, anknüpfen; fight anfangen; blaze, collapse, chain reaction auslösen; coal fire etc anzünden; (arsonist) legen; (found) enterprise, newspaper gründen, starten (inf). **to ~ sb thinking/on a subject** jdn nachdenklich machen/jdn auf ein Thema bringen; **to ~ sb in business/on a career** jdn zu einem Start im Geschäftsleben/zu einer Karriere verhelfen; **the discovery ~ed a new line of research** mit der Entdeckung kam eine neue Forschungsrichtung in Gang; **I don't want to ~ anything but ...** ich will keinen Streit anfangen, aber ...; **just to ~ you getting used to it** nur damit Sie sich erst mal daran gewöhnen; **as soon as she ~ed the baby** (inf) sobald sich das Baby angekündigt hatte; **when she wore the first miniskirt she didn't realize what she was ~ing** als sie den ersten Minirock trug, war ihr nicht bewußt, was sie damit auslösen würde; **look what you've ~ed now!** da hast du was Schönes angefangen (inf).

(c) car starten; engine also anlassen; clock in Gang setzen; machine, motor also anwerfen.

(d) **to ~ a horse in a race** eine Nennung für ein Pferd abgeben.

3 vi **(begin)** anfangen, beginnen; (car, engine) starten; (plane) starten; (move off) anfahren; (bus, train) abfahren; (boat) ablegen; (rumour) in Umlauf kommen; (violins, cellos etc) einsetzen. **~ing from Tuesday** ab Dienstag; **to ~ for home** (nach Hause) aufbrechen, sich auf den Heimweg machen; **to ~ for work** zur Arbeit gehen/fahren; **to ~ for London** nach London losfahren; **to ~ (off) with** (adv) (firstly) erstens, erst einmal; (at the beginning) zunächst; **what shall we have to ~ (off) with?** was nehmen wir als Vorspeise?; **I'd like soup to ~ (off) with** ich möchte erst mal eine Suppe; **to ~ after sb** jdn verfolgen; **to get ~ed** anfangen; (on journey) aufbrechen; **he finds it difficult to get ~ed in the morning** er kommt morgens nur schwer in Schwung or Gang; **to ~ on a task/journey/the food** sich an eine Aufgabe/auf eine Reise/ans Essen machen; **to ~ talking** or **to talk** zu sprechen beginnen or anfangen; **he ~ed by saying ...** er sagte zunächst ...; **don't you ~!** fang du nicht auch noch an!

♦**start back** vi sich auf den Rückweg machen. **we ~ed ~ for home** wir machten uns auf den Heimweg; **the rocket ~ed ~ to earth** die Rakete trat die Rückreise zur Erde an.

♦**start in** vi (inf) **(a)** (begin to scold) loslegen (inf), vom Leder ziehen (inf) (on sb gegen jdn). **(b)** **to ~ on sth** sich an etw (acc) machen.

♦**start off** **1** vi (begin) anfangen; (begin moving: person) losgehen, (on journey) aufbrechen; (run) loslaufen; (drive) losfahren; (esp Sport) starten; (begin talking etc) anfangen, loslegen (inf) (on mit). **to ~ ~ with** (adv) see start² 3.

2 vt sep sth anfangen. **to ~ sb ~ (talking)** jdm das Stichwort geben; **to ~ the baby ~ (crying)** das Baby zum Schreien bringen; **whatever you do, don't ~ her ~** sieh bloß zu, daß sie nicht damit anfängt; **that ~ed the dog ~** da fing der Hund an zu bellen; **to ~ sb ~ on sth/doing sth** jdn auf etw (acc) bringen/jdn dazu bringen, etw zu tun; **a few stamps to ~ you ~** ein paar Briefmarken für den Anfang; **I'll play a few bars to ~ you ~** ich spiele ein paar Takte, um Sie einzustimmen.

♦**start out** vi (begin) (zunächst) beginnen or anfangen; (begin a journey) aufbrechen (for nach). **we ~ed ~ on a long journey/new enterprise** wir machten uns auf eine lange Reise/an ein neues Unternehmen; **we ~ed ~ with great hopes for the future** wir hatten mit großen Zukunftshoffnungen begonnen.

♦**start over** vi (US) noch (ein)mal von vorn anfangen.

♦**start up** vi **1** vi **(a)** (move suddenly) **a rabbit ~ed ~ out of the undergrowth** ein Kaninchen schoß aus dem Unterholz hervor; **he ~ed ~ in bed at the noise** bei dem Geräusch schreckte or fuhr er im Bett hoch.

(b) (begin: music etc) anfangen; (machine) angehen (inf), in Gang kommen; (motor) anspringen; (siren) losheulen. **when I ~ed ~ in business** als ich als Geschäftsmann anfing; **he ~ed ~ by himself when he was 21** er machte sich mit 21 selbständig.

2 vt sep **(a)** (cause to function) anmachen (inf), in Gang bringen; engine also anlassen, starten; machine also anwerfen.

(b) (begin) eröffnen; business also anfangen; conversation anfangen, anknüpfen; (amongst other people) in Gang bringen.

starter ['staːtə^r] n **(a)** (Sport) Starter(in f) m (also horse); (competitor) Teilnehmer(in f) m; (runner also) Läufer(in f) m am Start. **to be under ~'s orders** auf das Startkommando warten.

(b) (Aut etc: self-~) Starter, Anlasser m.

(c) (inf: person) **to be a late ~ in the presidential race/with girls** sich erst spät an den Präsidentschaftswahlen beteiligen/ein Spätzünder sein, was Mädchen betrifft (inf); **she is a slow ~ in the morning** sie kommt morgens nur langsam in Schwung.

(d) (inf: first course) Vorspeise f.

(e) for ~s (sl) für den Anfang (inf).

starting ['staːtɪŋ] n in cpds (Sport) line, post Start-; **~ block** n Startblock m; **~ gate** n Startmaschine f; **~ grid** n Start(platz) m; **~ gun** n Startpistole f; **~ handle** n Anlasserkurbel f; **~ point** n (lit, fig) Ausgangspunkt m; **~ post** n Startpflock m; **~ price** n (Horseracing) letzter Kurs vor dem Start.

startle ['staːtl] **1** vt erschrecken; animal also aufschrecken. **I was ~d to see how old he looked** ich stellte entsetzt fest, wie alt er aussah. **2** vi **she ~s easily** sie ist sehr schreckhaft.

startling ['staːtlɪŋ] adj news überraschend; (bad) alarmierend, bestürzend; coincidence, resemblance erstaunlich, überraschend; colour, originality aufregend, erregend; dress aufregend; discovery aufregend, sensationell.

startlingly ['staːtlɪŋlɪ] adv simple überraschend; loud erschreckend; alike erstaunlich, überraschend; dressed aufregend. **nothing ~ new/original** nichts besonders or allzu Neues/Originelles.

star turn n Sensation, Hauptattraktion f.

starvation [staːˈveɪʃən] n (act) Hungern nt; (of besieged people) Aushungern nt; (condition) Hunger m. **to die of ~** verhungern, Hungers or den Hungertod sterben (geh); **to live on a ~ diet** Hunger leiden; **the prisoners were kept on a ~ diet** for months man ließ die Gefangenen monatelang fast verhungern; **the ~ diet we get at this school** die erbärmlichen Portionen, die es in dieser Schule gibt; **to go on a ~ diet** (hum) eine Hungerkur machen; **~ wages** Hungerlohn m, Hungerlöhne pl.

starve [staːv] **1** vt **(a)** (deprive of food) hungern lassen; (also ~ out) aushungern; (kill: also ~ to death) verhungern lassen, Hungers sterben lassen (geh). **to ~ oneself** hungern; **to ~ a town into surrender** eine Stadt durch Aushungern zur Kapitulation zwingen; **he ~d his way through college** er hat sich (dat) das Studium am Mund abgespart.

(b) (fig) **to ~ sb of sth** jdm etw vorenthalten or verweigern; **to be ~d of capital/graduates** an akutem Kapital-/Akademikermangel leiden; **to be ~d of affection** zuwenig Zuneigung erfahren, an Liebesentzug leiden.

2 vi hungern; (die: also ~ to death) verhungern. **I'm simply starving!** (inf) ich sterbe vor Hunger! (inf); **you must be starving!** du mußt doch halb verhungert sein! (inf); **to ~ for sth** (fig) nach etw hungern.

♦**starve out** vt sep garrison etc aushungern.

starveling ['staːvlɪŋ] n (dated) Hungerleider m.

starving ['staːvɪŋ] adj (lit) hungernd attr; (fig) hungrig.

stash [stæʃ] vt (also ~ away) (sl) loot verschwinden lassen (inf), bunkern (sl); money beiseite schaffen.

stasis ['steɪsɪs] n Stauung, Stase (spec) f; (Liter) Stillstand m.

state [steɪt] **1** n **(a)** (condition) Zustand m. **~ of health/mind/war/siege** Gesundheits-/Geistes-/Kriegs-/Belagerungszustand m; widowed/married/single **~** Witwer- or Witwen-/Ehe-/Ledigenstand m; **to be in a ~ of grace/weightlessness** im Stand der Gnade sein/sich im Zustand der Schwerelosigkeit befinden; **the ~ of the nation** die Lage der Nation; **the present ~ of the economy** die gegenwärtige Wirtschaftslage; **in a liquid/solid ~** im flüssigen/festen Zustand, in flüssigem/festem Zustand; **where animals live in their natural ~** wo Tiere im Naturzustand leben; **in a good/bad ~** in gutem/schlechtem Zustand; **he's in no (fit) ~/~ of mind to do that** er ist nicht in dem (richtigen) Zustand dafür or dazu; **what a ~ of affairs!** was sind das für Zustände!; **look at the ~ of your hands!** guck dir bloß mal deine Hände an!; **my business papers are in such a ~!** meine Geschäftspapiere sind in einem furchtbaren Durcheinander!; **the room was in a terrible ~** im Zimmer herrschte ein fürchterliches Durcheinander.

(b) (inf: anxiety) **to get into a ~ (about sth)** (inf) wegen etw durchdrehen (inf); **to be in a great ~ (inf)** in heller Aufregung or ganz durchgedreht (inf) sein.

(c) (rank) Stand, Rang m. **~ of bishop** Bischofswürde f; **men in all ~s of life** Menschen or Angehörige aller Stände.

(d) (pomp) Aufwand, Pomp m. **to be received in great ~** mit großem Staat empfangen werden; **to travel in ~** aufwendig or pompös reisen; **to lie in ~** (feierlich) aufgebahrt sein.

(e) (Pol) Staat m; (federal ~) (Bundes)staat m; (in BRD, Austria) (Bundes)land nt. **the S~s** die (Vereinigten) Staaten; **the S~ of Florida** der Staat Florida; **a ~ within a ~** ein Staat im Staate; **affairs of ~** Staatsangelegenheiten pl.

2 vt darlegen, vortragen; name, price, amount nennen, angeben; purpose angeben. **to ~ that ...** feststellen or erklären, daß ...; **to ~ one's case** seine Sache vortragen; **it must be clearly ~d in the records ...** es muß aus den Akten einwandfrei hervorgehen, ...; **to ~ the case for the prosecution** (Jur) die Anklage vortragen; **the theme is ~d in the first few bars** das Thema wird in den ersten paar Takten vorgestellt; **unless otherwise ~d** wenn nicht ausdrücklich anders festgestellt; **as ~d in my letter I ...** wie in meinem Brief erwähnt, ... ich ...

state in cpds Staats-; control also, industry staatlich; (US etc) des Bundes- or Einzelstaates, bundesstaatlich; (ceremonial) Staats-; **~-aided** adj school, project staatlich gefördert; **~ apartment** n Prunksaal m; **~ bank** n Staatsbank f; **~ craft** n die Staatskunst.

stated ['steɪtɪd] adj **(a)** (declared) sum, date angegeben, genannt; limits bestimmt. **(b)** (fixed, regular) times, amount fest(gesetzt). **at the ~ intervals** in den festgelegten Abständen; **on the ~ date** or **the date ~** zum festgesetzten Termin.

state: S~ **Department** n (US) Außenministerium nt; **~ education** n staatliche Erziehung; (system) staatliches Erziehungswesen.

statehood ['steɪthʊd] n Eigenstaatlichkeit f. **to achieve ~** ein eigener or selbständiger Staat werden; **when was Alaska granted ~?** wann wurde Alaska zum Bundesstaat erklärt?

state: **~house** n (US) Parlamentsgebäude, Kapitol nt; **~less** adj staatenlos; **~less person** Staatenlose(r) mf.

stateliness ['steɪtlɪnɪs] n see adj Würde f; Gemessenheit f; Pracht f.

stately ['steɪtlɪ] adj (+er) person, bearing würdevoll; pace, walk gemessen; palace, tree prächtig. **~ home** herrschaftliches Anwesen, Schloß nt.

statement ['steɪtmənt] n **(a)** (putting forward: of thesis etc)

Darstellung *f*; (*of problem also*) Darlegung *f*. **a masterpiece of careful** ~ eine meisterhaft formulierte Darstellung; **a clear** ~ **of the facts** eine klare Feststellung der Tatsachen.

(b) (*that said*) Feststellung *f*; (*claim*) Behauptung *f*; (*Mus: of theme*) Vorstellen *nt*; (*official, Government* ~) Erklärung, Stellungnahme *f*; (*in court, to police*) Aussage *f*; (*written*) Protokoll *nt*, Aussage *f*. **to make a** ~ **to the press** eine Presseerklärung abgeben.

(c) (*Philos*) Behauptung, These *f*; (*Logic*) Satz *m*; (*Gram*) Feststellung *f*.

(d) (*Fin*) (*tradesman's*) Rechnung *f*; (*also bank* ~) Auszug *m*.

state: ~ **occasion** *n* Staatsanlaß *m*, Staatsfeierlichkeit *f*; ~**-owned** *adj* staatseigen; ~ **registered nurse** *n* staatlich anerkannte Krankenschwester; ~**room** *n* (*Naut*) Kabine *f*; (*US Rail*) Privat(schlafwagen)abteil *nt*; ~ **school** *n* öffentliche Schule; ~ **secret** *n* Staatsgeheimnis *nt*; **S**~'**s evidence** *n* (*US*) Aussage *f* eines Kronzeugen; **to turn S**~'**s evidence** als Kronzeuge auftreten; ~**side** (*US inf*) **1** *adj* in den Staaten (*inf*); *newspaper* aus den Staaten (*inf*); **2** *adv* heim, nach Hause; **when I'm back** ~**side** ... wenn ich wieder zu Hause in den Staaten bin, ...

statesman ['steɪtsmən] *n*, *pl* **-men** [-mən] Staatsmann *m*.

statesmanlike ['steɪtsmənlaɪk] *adj* staatsmännisch.

statesmanship ['steɪtsmənʃɪp] *n* Staatskunst *f*. **skills of** ~ staatsmännische Fähigkeiten *pl*.

state: ~ **trooper** *n* (*US*) Soldat *m* der amerikanischen Nationalgarde; ~ **visit** *n* Staatsbesuch *m*; ~**wide** *adj* (*US*) im ganzen Bundesstaat, landesweit.

static ['stætɪk] **1** *adj* **(a)** (*Phys*) statisch.

(b) (*not moving or changing*) konstant; (*stationary*) feststehend *attr*; *condition, society* statisch. **if the development of a civilization remains** ~ ... wenn eine Kultur sich nicht mehr weiterentwickelt, ...; **after a lively beginning the novel becomes rather** ~ nach dem lebendigen Anfang tritt der Roman fast nur noch an der Stelle; **their relationship became** ~ ihre Beziehung stagnierte *or* trat auf der Stelle.

2 *n* (*Phys*) Reibungselektrizität *f*; (*Rad also*) atmosphärische Störungen *pl*.

statics ['stætɪks] *n sing* Statik *f*.

station ['steɪʃən] **1** *n* **(a)** Station *f*; (*police* ~, *fire* ~) Wache *f*; (*space* ~) (Raum)station *f*; (*US: gas* ~) Tankstelle *f*. **work** ~ (*in office*) Position *f*, Platz *m*; (*in factory*) Station *f*.

(b) (*railway* ~, *bus* ~) Bahnhof *m*; (*stop*) Station *f*.

(c) (*Mil: post*) Stellung *f*, Posten *m*. **frontier/naval** ~ Grenzstellung *f*/Flottenstützpunkt *m*.

(d) (*esp Austral: ranch*) Farm *f*. **sheep/cattle** ~ Schafs-/Rinderzuchtfarm *f*; ~**-hand** Farmgehilfe *m*.

(e) (*Rad, TV*) Sender *m*, Sendestation *f*; (*channel*) Sender *m*.

(f) (*position*) Platz *m*. **to take up one's** ~ sich (*dat*)stellen, seinen Platz einnehmen; **the S**~**s of the Cross** die Stationen *pl* des Kreuzwegs.

(g) (*rank*) Stand, Rang *m*. ~ **in life** Stellung *f* (im Leben), Rang *m*; **to marry below/above one's** ~ nicht standesgemäß/über seinem Stand heiraten; **he has got ideas above his** ~ er hat Ideen, die jemandem aus seinem Stand gar nicht zukommen.

2 *vt* (auf)stellen, postieren; (*Mil*) stationieren.

station agent *n* (*US*) *see* **station-master**.

stationary ['steɪʃənərɪ] *adj* (*not moving*) *car* parkend *attr*; haltend *attr*; (*not movable*) fest(stehend *attr*). **to be** ~ (*vehicles*) stehen; (*traffic, fig*) stillstehen; **to remain** ~ sich nicht bewegen; (*traffic*) stillstehen; **the bird didn't remain** ~ **long enough for me to get a good aim** der Vogel saß nicht lange genug still, um mir ein gutes Ziel zu bieten; **he never remains** ~ **for long** er bleibt nirgendwo lange.

stationer ['steɪʃənər] *n* Schreibwarenhändler *m*. ~'**s (shop)** Schreibwarenhandlung *f*.

stationery ['steɪʃənərɪ] *n* (*notepaper*) Briefpapier *nt*; (*writing materials*) Schreibwaren *pl*. **office** ~ Büromaterial *nt*.

station: ~ **house** *n* (*US: police*) (Polizei)wache *f*, (Polizei)revier *nt*; ~**-master** *n* Bahnhofsvorsteher, Stationsvorsteher (*dated*) *m*; ~ **police** *n* Bahnpolizei *f*; ~ **selector** *n* (*Rad*) Sendereinstellung *f*; ~ **wagon** *n* Kombi(wagen) *m*.

statistic [stə'tɪstɪk] *n* Statistik *f*.

statistical *adj*, ~**ly** *adv* [stə'tɪstɪkəl, -l] statistisch.

statistician [ˌstætɪ'stɪʃən] *n* Statistiker(in *f*) *m*.

statistics [stə'tɪstɪks] *n* **(a)** *sing* Statistik *f*. **(b)** *pl* (*data*) Statistiken *pl*; *see* **vital**.

stator ['steɪtər] *n* (*Elec*) Stator *m*.

statuary ['stætjʊərɪ] (*form*) **1** *adj* statuarisch (*geh*). ~ **art** Plastik *f*. **2** *n* (*Art*) Plastik, Bildhauerei *f*; (*statues*) Plastiken, Statuen *pl*.

statue ['stætju:] *n* Statue *f*, Standbild *nt*. **S**~ **of Liberty** Freiheitsstatue *f*.

statuesque [ˌstætjʊ'esk] *adj* standbildhaft, statuesk (*liter*). **a woman of** ~ **proportions/beauty** eine Frau mit klassischen Maßen/von klassischer Schönheit.

statuette [ˌstætjʊ'et] *n* Statuette *f*.

stature ['stætʃər] *n* **(a)** Wuchs *m*; (*esp of man*) Statur *f*. **of short** ~ von kleinem Wuchs. **(b)** (*fig*) Format *nt*.

status ['steɪtəs] *n* Stellung *f*; (*legal* ~, *social* ~ *also*) Status *m*. **equal** ~ Gleichstellung *f*; **marital** ~ Familienstand *m*; **many people who merely desire** ~ viele Menschen, die bloß nach Prestige streben; **unsupported statements have no** ~ **in law** unbewiesene Behauptungen sind rechtlich irrelevant; **he hasn't got enough** ~ **for this position** für diese Position stellt er nicht genug dar *or* hat er nicht den richtigen Zuschnitt.

status-conscious ['steɪtəsˌkɒnʃəs] *adj* statusbewußt.

status quo ['steɪtəs'kwəʊ] *n* Status quo *m*.

status symbol *n* Statussymbol *nt*.

statute ['stætju:t] *n* Gesetz *nt*; (*of organization*) Satzung *f*, Statut *nt*. **by** ~ gesetzlich; statutarisch, satzungsgemäß.

statute: ~ **book** *n* Gesetzbuch *nt*; **to put sth in the** ~ **book** etw zum Gesetz machen *or* erheben; ~ **law** *n* Gesetzesrecht, Statute Law *nt*; ~ **mile** *n* britische Meile.

statutory ['stætjʊtərɪ] *adj* gesetzlich; *holiday also, quarantine* gesetzlich vorgeschrieben; (*in organization*) satzungsgemäß, statutarisch; *right also* verbrieft; *punishment* (vom Gesetz) vorgesehen. ~ **rape** Notzucht *f*; **this is** ~ das ist Gesetz.

staunch[1] [stɔ:ntʃ] *adj* (+*er*) *Catholic, loyalist* überzeugt; *Republican also* loyal; *member, supporter* ergeben, getreu; *support* standhaft, zuverlässig. **to be** ~ **in one's belief** fest *or* unerschütterlich im Glauben sein; **those who were the** ~**est supporters of the king** die getreuesten Anhänger des Königs.

staunch[2] *vt flow* stauen; *bleeding* stillen. **to** ~ **a wound** die Blutung einer Wunde stillen.

staunchly ['stɔ:ntʃlɪ] *adv* treu, standhaft. **a** ~ **devout Catholic** ein treu ergebener Katholik.

staunchness ['stɔ:ntʃnɪs] *n see adj* Überzeugung *f*; Loyalität *f*; Treue *f*; Standhaftigkeit *f*.

stave [steɪv] *n* **(a)** (*of barrel*) (Faß)daube *f*; (*rung*) (Leiter)sprosse *f*; (*stick*) Knüppel, Knüttel (*old*) *m*. **(b)** (*Mus: staff*) Notenlinien *pl*. *(Liter: stanza)* Strophe *f*, Vers *m*.

♦**stave in** *pret, ptp* ~**d** *or* **stove in 1** *vt sep* eindrücken; *head* einschlagen. **2** *vi* eingedrückt werden.

♦**stave off** *vt sep* **(a)** *attack* zurückschlagen; *crisis, cold* abwehren; *hunger* lindern. **(b)** (*delay*) *person* hinhalten; *crisis* hinausschieben.

staves [steɪvz] *pl of* **staff 1 (b, d)**.

stay[1] [steɪ] **1** *n* **(a)** Aufenthalt *m*. **come for a longer** ~ **next year** komm nächstes Jahr für länger; **a short** ~ **in hospital** ein kurzer Krankenhausaufenthalt.

(b) (*Jur*) Aussetzung *f*. ~ **of execution** Aussetzung *f*, Vollstreckungsaufschub *m*; (*fig*) Galgenfrist *f*; (*of death penalty*) Hinrichtungsaufschub *m*.

2 *vt* **(a)** (*old, liter: stop*) Einhalt gebieten (+*dat*) (*geh*); *hunger* stillen. **to** ~ **one's/sb's hand** sich/jdn zurückhalten.

(b) (*Jur*) *order, sentence* aussetzen.

(c) to ~ **the course** (*lit, fig*) durchhalten.

3 *vi* **(a)** (*remain*) bleiben. **to** ~ **for or to supper** zum Abendessen bleiben; **to have come to** ~ (*fashion etc*) sich halten; **has unemployment come to** ~? ist die Arbeitslosigkeit nun ein Dauerzustand?; **if it** ~**s fine** wenn es schön bleibt; **if he can** ~ **with the others** wenn er mit den anderen mithalten kann; ~ **with it!** nicht aufgeben!; *see* **put**[2].

(b) (*reside*) wohnen; (*at youth-hostel etc*) übernachten. **to** ~ **at a hotel** im Hotel wohnen *or* übernachten; **I** ~**ed in Italy for a few weeks** ich habe mich ein paar Wochen in Italien aufgehalten; **when I/Goethe was** ~**ing in Italy** als ich/Goethe in Italien war *or* weilte (*liter*); **where are you** ~**ing?** wo wohnen Sie?; **he is** ~**ing at Chequers for the weekend** er verbringt das Wochenende in Chequers; **he went to** ~ **in the country for a while** er ist für einige Zeit aufs Land gefahren; **we would** ~ **at a different resort each year** wir waren jedes Jahr an einem anderen Urlaubsort; **it was a nice place to** ~ **in the summer** dort konnte man gut den Sommer verbringen; **my brother came to** ~ **for a week** mein Bruder ist für eine Woche gekommen; **my brother came to** ~ mein Bruder ist zu Besuch gekommen.

(c) (*old: wait*) ~! stehenbleiben!; ~, **wanderer!** halt inne, Wanderer! (*old, liter*).

♦**stay away** *vi* (*from* von) wegbleiben; (*from person*) sich fernhalten. **to** ~ **from a girl** von einem Mädchen die Finger lassen; **he can't** ~ ~ **from the pub** ihn zieht es immer wieder in die Wirtschaft.

♦**stay behind** *vi* zurückbleiben; (*Sch: as punishment*) nachsitzen. **I** ~**ed** ~ **after the party** ich blieb nach der Party noch da.

♦**stay down** *vi* (*keep down*) unten bleiben; (*Sch*) wiederholen.

♦**stay in** *vi* (*at home*) zu Hause bleiben; (*in position, in book etc*) drinbleiben; (*Sch*) nachsitzen. **he had to** ~ ~ **as a punishment** (*at home*) er kriegte zur Strafe Stubenarrest *or* Hausarrest.

♦**stay off 1** *vi* **(a)** (*rain*) ausbleiben. **(b)** (*from work etc*) zu Hause bleiben. **2** *vi* + *prep obj* **(a)** (*not go on*) nicht betreten. ~ **my patch!** komm mir nicht ins Gehege! **(b) to** ~ ~ **work/school** nicht zur Arbeit/Schule gehen; **to** ~ ~ **the bottle** (*inf*) die Flasche nicht anrühren (*inf*).

♦**stay on** *vi* (*lid etc*) draufbleiben; (*light*) anbleiben; (*people*) (noch) bleiben. **he** ~**ed** ~ **for another year** er blieb noch ein Jahr; **to** ~ ~ **at school/as manager** (in der Schule) weitermachen/(weiterhin) Geschäftsführer bleiben.

♦**stay out** *vi* draußen bleiben; (*on strike*) weiterstreiken; (*not come home*) wegbleiben. **to** ~ ~ **of sth** sich aus etw heraushalten; **he never managed to** ~ ~ **of trouble** er war dauernd in Schwierigkeiten; **you** ~ ~ **of this!** halt du dich da raus!

♦**stay up** *vi* **(a)** (*person*) aufbleiben. **don't** ~ ~ **for me!** bleib nicht meinetwegen auf!

(b) (*tent, fence, pole*) stehen bleiben; (*picture, decorations*) hängen bleiben; (*swimmer*) oben bleiben; (*roof*) draufbleiben. **his trousers won't** ~ ~ seine Hosen rutschen immer.

(c) (*at university*) (an der Uni) bleiben.

(d) **he's still** ~**ing** ~ **with the front runners** er liegt immer noch auf gleicher Höhe mit den Läufern an der Spitze.

stay[2] *n* (*guy-rope*) Stütztau, Halteseil *nt*; (*Naut*) Stag *nt*. **the** ~ **of one's old age** (*fig*) die Stütze seines Alters; ~**s** *pl* (*old: corsets*) Korsett *nt*.

stay-at-home ['steɪətˌhəʊm] **1** *n* Stubenhocker *m*. **2** *adj attr* stubenhockerisch.

stayer ['steɪər] *n* (*horse*) Steher *m*; (*person*) beständiger *or* ausdauernder Mensch. **it's the** ~**s rather than the geniuses** ... es sind die Ausdauernden, nicht die Genies ...

staying power ['steɪŋˌpaʊər] *n* Stehvermögen, Durchhaltevermögen *nt*, Ausdauer *f*.

St Bernard [sənt'bɜ:nəd] *n* Bernhardiner *m*.

STD (*Brit Telec*) *abbr of* **subscriber trunk dialling** der Selbstwählfernverkehr, der Selbstwählferndienst. **~ number/ code** Vorwahl(nummer) *f*.

stead [sted] *n* **in his ~** an seiner Stelle *or* Statt (*liter, form*); **to stand ~ in good ~** jdm zugute *or* zustatten kommen.

steadfast ['stedfəst] *adj* fest; *look also* unverwandt; *person, refusal also* standhaft; *person also*, *belief* unerschütterlich. **to remain ~ in adversity/in one's faith** allen Unbilden zum Trotz (*liter*) in seinem Glauben nicht schwanken.

steadfastly ['stedfəstli] *adv* fest; *look* unverwandt; *adhere, refuse* standhaft, unerschütterlich.

steadfastness ['stedfəstnıs] *n see adj* Festigkeit *f*; Unverwandtheit *f*; Standhaftigkeit *f*; Unerschütterlichkeit *f*.

steadily ['stedɪlɪ] *adv* **(a)** (*firmly*) ruhig; *balanced* fest; *gaze* fest, unverwandt. **(b)** (*constantly*) ständig; *rain* ununterbrochen. **(c)** (*reliably*) zuverlässig, solide.

steadiness ['stedɪnɪs] *n* (*stability*) Festigkeit *f*; (*of hand, eye*) Ruhe *f*; (*regularity*) Stetigkeit *f*; (*of gaze also*) Unverwandtheit *f*; (*of character*) Zuverlässigkeit, Solidität *f*.

steady ['stedɪ] **1** *adj* (+*er*) **(a)** (*firm, not wobbling*) *hand, nerves, eye* ruhig; *gaze* fest, unverwandt. **with a ~ hand** mit ruhiger Hand; **~ on one's legs/feet** fest *or* sicher auf den Beinen; **to hold sth ~** etw ruhig halten; *ladder* etw festhalten; **the chair is not very ~** der Stuhl ist wacklig.

(b) (*constant*) *wind, progress, demand etc* ständig, stet (*geh*); *drizzle* ununterbrochen; *temperature* beständig. **at a ~ pace/70** in gleichmäßigem Tempo/ständig mit 70.

(c) (*reliable, regular*) *worker* zuverlässig, solide. **he plays a ~ game** er ist ein zuverlässiger Spieler.

(d) *job, boyfriend* fest.

2 *adv* **~!** (*carefully, gently*) vorsichtig!; **~ (on)!**, **~ the buffs!** immer mit der Ruhe (*inf*), sachte! (*inf*); **to go ~ (with sb)** (*inf*) mit jdm (fest) gehen (*inf*); **they're going ~** (*inf*) sie gehen fest miteinander, sind seit fest zusammen.

3 *n* (*inf*) fester Freund (*inf*), feste Freundin (*inf*).

4 *vt plane, boat* wieder ins Gleichgewicht bringen; (*stabilize*) *nerves, person* beruhigen; (*in character*) ausgleichen. **to ~ oneself** festen Halt finden; **she had a ~ing influence on him** durch ihren Einfluß wurde er ausgeglichener.

5 *vi* sich beruhigen; (*person: also* **~ up**) ruhig(er) werden.

steady state theory *n* Theorie *f* des stationären Kosmos.

steak [steɪk] *n* Steak *nt*; (*of fish*) Filet *nt*. **a ham/bacon ~** eine Scheibe gebackener Schinken/Speck; **~ and kidney pie** Fleischpastete *f* mit Nieren; **~ dinner** Steak-Menü *nt*; **~house** Steakhouse *nt*; **~ knife** Steakmesser *nt*; **~ tartare** Tatarbeefsteak *nt*.

steal [stiːl] (*vb: pret* **stole**, *ptp* **stolen**) **1** *vt object, idea, kiss, heart* stehlen. **to ~ sth from sb** jdm etw stehlen; **he's had his car stolen again** sein Auto ist wieder gestohlen worden; **to ~ sb's girlfriend** jdm die Freundin ausspannen (*inf*); **to ~ the show/sb's thunder/a march on sb** die Schau stehlen/jdm den Wind aus den Segeln nehmen/jdm zuvorkommen; **the baby stole all the attention** das Kind zog die ganze Aufmerksamkeit auf sich; **to ~ a glance at sb** verstohlen zu jdm hinschauen.

2 *vi* **(a)** stehlen.

(b) (*move quietly etc*) sich stehlen; schleichen. **to ~ away** *or* **off/into a room** sich weg- *or* davonstehlen/sich in ein Zimmer stehlen; **to ~ about/up on sb** herumschleichen/sich an jdn heranschleichen; **old age was ~ing up on her** das Alter machte sich allmählich bei ihr bemerkbar; **the mood/feeling which was ~ing over the country** die Stimmung, die sich allmählich im Land verbreitete; **he could feel the depression ~ing over him** er fühlte, wie ihn ein Gefühl der Niedergeschlagenheit beschlich; **to ~ home** (*Baseball*) ungehindert zur Ausgangsbase vorrücken.

3 *n* (*US inf: bargain*) Geschenk *nt* (*inf*). **it's a ~!** das ist (ja) geschenkt! (*inf*).

stealth [stelθ] *n* List *f*; (*of fox also*) Schläue *f*. **by ~** durch List.

stealthily ['stelθɪlɪ] *adv* verstohlen.

stealthiness ['stelθɪnɪs] *n* Verstohlenheit *f*.

stealthy ['stelθɪ] *adj* (+*er*) verstohlen; *footsteps* verhalten.

steam [stiːm] **1** *n* Dampf *m*; (*from swamp also*) Dunst *m*. **the windows were covered with ~** die Fensterscheiben waren beschlagen; **driven by ~** dampfgetrieben; **full ~ ahead!** (*Naut*) volle Kraft voraus!; **to get up ~** (*lit*) feuern, Dampf aufmachen (*dated*); (*fig*) in Schwung kommen; **to let off ~** (*lit, fig*) Dampf ablassen; (*fig also*) sich (*dat*) Luft machen; **to run out of ~** (*lit*) Dampf verlieren; (*fig*) Schwung verlieren; **he has run out of ~** ihm ist die Puste ausgegangen (*inf*); **the project has run out of ~** aus der Sache ist der Dampf raus (*inf*); **the ship went on under its own ~** das Schiff fuhr mit eigener Kraft weiter; **under one's own ~** (*fig*) allein, ohne Hilfe.

2 *vt* dämpfen; *food also* dünsten. **to ~ open an envelope** einen Briefumschlag über Dampf öffnen; **~ed pudding** Kochpudding *m*.

3 *vi* **(a)** (*give off ~*) dampfen.

(b) (*move*) dampfen. **we were ~ing along at 12 knots** wir fuhren mit 12 Knoten; **the ship ~ed into the harbour** das Schiff kam in den Hafen gefahren; **the train ~ed out** der Zug dampfte ab; **the runner came ~ing round the last bend** (*inf*) der Läufer kam mit Volldampf um die letzte Kurve (*inf*).

♦ **steam ahead** *vi* (*inf: project, work*) gut vorankommen.

♦ **steam off 1** *vt sep stamp* über Dampf ablösen; *dirt* über Dampf entfernen; *excess flab* (*inf*) sich (*dat*) abschwitzen. **2** *vi* abfahren; (*train also*) losdampfen.

♦ **steam over** *vi* (*window*) beschlagen.

♦ **steam up 1** *vt sep window* beschlagen lassen. **to be/get (all) ~ed** (*ganz*) beschlagen sein/(*ganz*) beschlagen; (*fig inf*) sich aufregen, hochgehen (*inf*); **look at you, all ~ed ~ about nothing** deine ganze Aufregung war umsonst. **2** *vi* beschlagen.

steam: **~boat** *n* Dampfschiff *nt*, Dampfer *m*; **~-driven** *adj* mit

---

Dampfantrieb, dampfgetrieben; **~ engine** *n* Dampflok *f*; (*stationary*) Dampfmaschine *f*.

steamer ['stiːmə^r] *n* (*ship*) Dampfer *m*; (*Cook*) Dampf(koch)topf *m*.

steam: **~hammer** *n* Dampfhammer *m*; **~ iron** *n* Dampfbügeleisen *nt*; **~ radio** *n* (*hum*) Dampfradio *nt* (*hum*); **~roller** 1 *n* Dampfwalze *f*; 2 *vt road* glattwalzen; **to ~roller a bill through parliament** (*fig*) ein Gesetz im Parlament durchpeitschen; 3 *adj* **~roller tactics** Holzhammermethode *f* (*inf*); **~ room** *n* Saunaraum *m*; (*in Turkish bath*) Dampfraum *m*; **~ship** *n* Dampfschiff *nt*, Dampfer *m*; **~ship company** *n* Dampfschiffahrtsgesellschaft *f*; **~ship line** *n* Schiffahrtslinie, Dampferlinie *f*; **~ shovel** *n* Löffelbagger *m*; **~ turbine** *n* Dampfturbine *f*.

steamy ['stiːmɪ] *adj* (+*er*) dampfig, dunstig; *jungle, swamp* dunstig; *room, atmosphere* dampfig, voll Dampf; *window, mirror* beschlagen. **it is so ~ in here** hier ist vielleicht ein Dampf!

steed [stiːd] *n* (*liter*) Roß *nt*.

steel [stiːl] **1** *n* Stahl *m*; (*for sharpener*) Wetzstahl *m*; (*for striking spark*) Feuerstahl *m*. **to fight with cold ~** mit dem blanken Messer kämpfen; **he felt cold ~ between his ribs** er spürte den kalten Stahl zwischen den Rippen; **a man of ~** ein stahlharter Mann; **as hard as ~** stahlhart, so hart wie Stahl; *see* **nerve**.

2 *adj attr* Stahl-.

3 *vt* **to ~ oneself** sich wappnen (*for* gegen); (*physically*) sich stählen (*for* für); **to ~ oneself to do sth** allen Mut zusammennehmen, um etw zu tun; **he had ~ed himself/his heart against her/their suffering** er hatte sich gegen sie/ihre Not innerlich hart gemacht; **he ~ed his troops for the battle** er machte seiner Truppe Mut für den Kampf; (*physically*) er stählte seine Truppe für den Kampf.

steel in *cpds* Stahl-, stahl-; **~ band** *n* Band aus der Karibik, die Schlaginstrumente aus Metall benutzt; **~-clad** *adj* stahlgepanzert; **~ grey** 1 *n* Stahlgrau *nt*; 2 *adj* stahlgrau; **~ guitar** *n* Hawaii-Gitarre *f*; **~ mill** *n* Stahlwalzwerk *nt*; **~-plated** *adj* mit Stahlüberzug; (*for protection*) stahlgepanzert; **~ wool** *n* Stahlwolle *f*; **~ worker** *n* (Eisen- und) Stahlarbeiter *m*; **~works** *n sing or pl* Stahlwerk *nt*.

steely ['stiːlɪ] *adj* (+*er*) *grip* stahlhart; *smile, expression* hart; *gaze* hart, stählern; *determination* eisern, ehern; *blue* Stahl-. **~-eyed** *adj* mit hartem *or* stählernem Blick.

steel yard *n* Handwaage *f*.

steep[1] [stiːp] *adj* (+*er*) **(a)** steil. **it's a ~ climb** es geht steil hinauf; **there's been a ~ drop in the value of the pound** das Pfund ist stark gefallen.

(b) (*fig inf*) *demand* unverschämt; *price also, bill* gepfeffert (*inf*), gesalzen (*inf*). **that's pretty ~!** das ist allerhand; **it seems a bit ~ that ...** es ist ein starkes Stück, daß ...

steep[2] **1** *vt* **(a)** (*in liquid*) eintauchen; (*in marinade, dye*) ziehen lassen; *dried food, washing* einweichen.

(b) (*fig*) **to be ~ed in sth** von etw durchdrungen sein; **~ed in history** geschichtsträchtig; **~ed in ignorance/vice/prejudice** durch und durch unwissend/verdorben/voreingenommen; **he is so ~ed in his own methods** er ist so auf seine eigenen Methoden geeicht; **a scholar ~ed in the classics** ein Gelehrter, der sich in die Klassiker versenkt hat.

2 *vi* **to leave sth to ~** etw einweichen; (*in marinade, dye*) etw ziehen lassen.

steepen ['stiːpən] **1** *vt* steiler machen. **2** *vi* steiler werden.

steeple ['stiːpl] *n* Kirchturm *m*.

steeple: **~chase** *n* (*for horses*) Jagdrennen, Hindernisrennen *nt*; (*for runners*) Hindernislauf *m*; **~chaser** *n* (*horse*) Steepler *m*; (*jockey*) Reiter(in *f*) *m* in einem Jagdrennen; (*runner*) Hindernisläufer(in *f*) *m*; **~jack** *n* Turmarbeiter, Klettermaxe (*inf*) *m*.

steeply ['stiːplɪ] *adv* steil.

steepness ['stiːpnɪs] *n* **(a)** Steile, Steilheit *f*. **(b)** (*fig inf*) Unverschämtheit *f*.

steer[1] [stɪə^r] **1** *vt* (*lit, fig*) lenken; *car also, ship* steuern; *person also* lotsen. **to ~ an erratic course** (*lit, fig*) einen Zickzackkurs steuern; **to ~ a course for sth** (*Naut*) auf etw (*acc*) Kurs halten; (*fig*) auf etw (*acc*) zusteuern; **this car is easy to ~** der Wagen läßt sich leicht lenken.

2 *vi* (*in car*) lenken; (*in ship*) steuern. **to ~ due north** Kurs nach Norden halten; **~ left a bit lenken** *or* (*in ship*) steuern Sie etwas nach links; **to ~ for sth** auf etw (*acc*) zuhalten; (*Naut*) etw ansteuern; *auf etw* (*acc*) Kurs halten; (*fig*) auf etw (*acc*) zusteuern; *see* **clear**.

steer[2] *n* junger Ochse.

steerage ['stɪərɪdʒ] *n* Zwischendeck *nt*.

steerageway ['stɪərɪdʒweɪ] *n* Steuerkraft *f*.

steering ['stɪərɪŋ] *n* (*in car etc*) Lenkung *f*; (*Naut*) Steuerung *f*.

steering: **~ column** *n* Lenksäule *f*; **~ committee** *n* vorbereitender Ausschuß; **~ gear** *n* (*of plane*) Leitwerk *nt*; (*of boat*) Ruderanlage *f*; (*of car*) Lenkung *f*; **~ lock** *n* (*Aut*) radschloß *nt*; **~ wheel** *n* Steuer(rad) *nt*; (*of car also*) Lenkrad *nt*.

steersman ['stɪəzmən] *n, pl* **-men** [-mən] Steuermann *m*.

stein [ʃtaɪn] *n* Maßkrug *m*.

stele ['stiːlɪ] *n* (*Archeol*) Stele *f*.

stellar ['stelə^r] *adj* stellar.

stem [stem] **1** *n* **(a)** (*of plant*) Stiel *m*; (*of woody plant, shrub*) Stamm *m*; (*of grain*) Halm *m*; (*fig: of family tree*) Hauptlinie *f*, Hauptzweig *m*.

(b) (*of glass*) Stiel *m*; (*of pipe*) Hals *m*; (*Mus: of note*) (Noten)hals *m*; (*in watch*) Welle *f*; (*of thermometer*) Röhre *f*.

(c) (*of word*) Stamm *m*.

(d) (*Naut*) Vordersteven *m*. **from ~ to stern** von vorne bis achtern.

2 *vt* (*check, stop*) aufhalten; *flood, tide* eindämmen; *bleeding* zum Stillstand bringen; *flow of words* Einhalt gebieten (+*dat*).

3 *vi* **to ~ from sth** (*result from*) von etw kommen, von etw herrühren; *(have as origin)* aus etw (her)stammen, auf etw *(acc)* zurückgehen; **what does this increase in inflation ~ from?** welche Ursachen hat diese Zunahme der Inflation?

stemmed [stemd] *adj* Stiel-.

stem-turn ['stemtɜ:n] *n* Stemmbogen *m*.

stench [stentʃ] *n* Gestank *m*. **~ trap** Geruchsverschluß *m*.

stencil ['stensl] **1** *n* Schablone *f*; *(Printing: for duplicating)* Matrize *f*. **2** *vt* mit Schablonen zeichnen; auf Matrize schreiben.

sten gun ['stenʌn] *n (Mil)* leichtes Maschinengewehr.

stenographer [stə'nɒgrəfər] *n (form)* Stenograph(in *f*) *m*.

stenography [stə'nɒgrəfi] *n (form)* Stenographie *f*.

stentorian [sten'tɔ:rɪən] *adj* schallend; *voice* Stentor- *(geh)*.

step [step] **1** *n* **(a)** *(pace, in dancing)* Schritt *m*; *(sound of ~ also)* Tritt *m*. **to take a ~** einen Schritt machen; **~ by ~** *(lit, fig)* Schritt für Schritt; **we followed his ~s in the snow** wir folgten seinen Fußstapfen im Schnee; **to follow in sb's ~s** in jds Fußstapfen *(acc)* treten; **I recognized you from your ~** ich habe Sie am Schritt erkannt; **he watched my every ~** *(fig)* er beobachtete mich auf Schritt und Tritt; **to watch one's ~** achtgeben; *(fig also)* sich vorsehen.

(b) to be in ~ *(lit)* im Gleichschritt *or* Tritt sein *(with* mit); *(in dancing)* im Takt sein *(with* mit); *(fig)* im Gleichklang sein *(with* mit); **to be out of ~** *(lit)* nicht im Tritt *or* im gleichen Schritt sein *(with* mit); *(in dancing)* nicht im gleichen Takt sein *(with* wie); *(fig)* nicht im Gleichklang sein *(with* mit); **to get out of ~** *(lit)* aus dem Schritt *or* Tritt kommen; *(in dancing)* aus dem Takt kommen; *(fig)* von der gemeinsamen Linie abkommen; **to keep in/break ~** *(lit)* Tritt halten/aus dem Tritt kommen; *(fig)* Schritt halten/aus dem Schritt kommen; **to fall into ~** *(lit)* in Gleichschritt fallen *(with* mit); *(fig)* in den gleichen Takt kommen *(with* wie).

(c) *(distance)* **it's (quite) a good ~ (to the village)** es ist ein ziemlich weiter Weg (bis zum Dorf), es ist ziemlich weit (bis zum Dorf); **it's only a few ~s** es sind nur ein paar Schritte.

(d) *(move)* Schritt *m*; *(measure also)* Maßnahme *f*. **the first ~ is to form a committee** als erstes muß ein Ausschuß gebildet werden; **it's a great ~ forward** es ist ein großer Schritt nach vorn; **that would be a ~ back/in the right direction for him** das wäre für ihn ein Rückschritt/ein Schritt in die richtige Richtung; **one can't take a single ~ without having to consult somebody** man kann (rein) gar nichts unternehmen, ohne fragen zu müssen; **to take ~s to do sth** Maßnahmen ergreifen, (um) etw zu tun; **to take legal ~s** gerichtlich vorgehen.

(e) *(in process, experiment)* Abschnitt *m*, Stufe *f*; *(in learning, course also)* Lernschritt *m*.

(f) *(stair, fig: in scale, hierarchy)* Stufe *f*. **~s** *(outdoors)* Treppe *f*. **mind the ~** Vorsicht Stufe.

(g) ~s *pl* (*~-ladder: also* **pair of ~s**) Tritt- *or* Stufenleiter *f*.

2 *vt* **(a)** *(old)* dance tanzen.

(b) *(arrange in ~s)* terrassenförmig anlegen, abstufen.

(c) ~ two paces to the left treten Sie zwei Schritte nach links.

3 *vi* **when. to ~ into/out of sth** *house, room, puddle* in etw *(acc)*/aus etw treten; *train, dress* in etw *(acc)*/aus etw steigen; **to ~ on(to) sth** *plane, train* in etw *(acc)* steigen; *platform, ladder* auf etw *(acc)* steigen; **to ~ on sth** *object, toy* auf etw *(acc)* treten; **he ~ped on my foot** er ist mir auf den Fuß getreten; **to ~ over sb/sth** über jdn/etw steigen; **please mind where you ~** geben Sie acht, wo Sie hintreten; **~ this way, please** hier entlang, bitte!; **he ~ped into the road** er trat auf die Straße; **he ~ped into his father's job/shoes** er übernahm die Stelle seines Vaters; **to ~ on board** an Bord gehen; **to ~ inside** herein-/hineintreten; **to ~ outside** heraus-/hinaustreten; *(for fight)* *(mal eben)* vor die Tür gehen; **just ~ outside a moment** kommen/gehen Sie einen Moment hinaus; **~ on it!** mach mal ein bißchen (schneller)! *(inf)*; *(in car)* gib Gas!

♦ **step aside** *vi* **(a)** *(lit)* zur Seite treten. **(b)** *(fig)* Platz machen. **to ~ ~ to make way for sb** jdm Platz machen.

♦ **step back** *vi* **(a)** *(lit)* zurücktreten. **(b)** *(fig)* **to ~ ~ from sth** von etw Abstand gewinnen; **let us ~ ~ into the 18th century** versetzen wir uns einmal ins 18. Jahrhundert zurück.

♦ **step down** *vi* **(a)** *(lit)* herab-/hinabsteigen. **(b)** *(fig)* **to ~ ~ in favour of sb** *or* **for sb** jdm Platz machen, zu jds Gunsten zurücktreten; **he decided to ~ ~ and not stand again/not stand for the presidency** er beschloß, seine Kandidatur für die Wiederwahl/für das Amt des Präsidenten zurückzuziehen. **(c)** *(resign)* zurücktreten.

♦ **step forward** *vi* vortreten, nach vorne treten; *(fig)* sich melden.

♦ **step in** *vi* **(a)** *(lit)* eintreten (*-to*, *+ prep obj* in *+ acc*). **she suddenly ~ped ~to a totally new world** sie fand sich plötzlich in einer ganz neuen Welt wieder. **(b)** *(fig)* eingreifen, einschreiten; *(interferingly)* dazwischenkommen.

♦ **step off** **1** *vi* *+ prep obj* *(off bus, plane, boat)* aussteigen *(prep obj* aus). **to ~ ~ the pavement** vom Bürgersteig treten. **2** *vi* *(begin to march)* losmarschieren.

♦ **step out** **1** *vt sep* *(measure)* abschreiten. **2** *vi* **(a)** *(go out)* hinausgehen. **(b)** *(walk briskly)* zügig *or* schnell gehen, forsch ausschreiten *(liter)*; *(speed up)* schneller gehen. **(c)** **to be ~ping ~ with sb** *(dated)* mit jdm gehen.

♦ **step up** **1** *vt sep* steigern; *efforts also, security arrangements, campaign* verstärken; *volume, number* erhöhen.
  2 *vi* **(a)** *(come forward)* vortreten. **to ~ ~ to sb** auf jdn zugehen/zukommen; **ladies and gentlemen** treten Sie näher, meine Damen und Herren; **he ~ped ~ onto the stage** er trat auf die Bühne; **he ~ped ~ another rung** er stieg eine Sprosse höher.
  (b) *(increase)* zunehmen; *(rate, pressure)* ansteigen.

step- *pref* brother, mother *etc* Stief-.

step-down ['step'daʊn] *adj* *(Elec)* heruntertransformierend.

Stephen ['sti:vn] *n* Stephan *m*.

step-ladder ['step,lædər] *n* Stufenleiter, Trittleiter *f*.

---

steppe [step] *n* Steppe *f*.

stepping stone ['stepɪŋ,stəʊn] *n* (Tritt)stein *m*; *(fig)* Sprungbrett *nt*.

step-up ['step'ʌp] **1** *n* *(inf: increase)* Anstieg *m*, Zunahme *f* *(in* gen). **2** *adj* *(Elec)* herauftransformierend.

stereo ['sterɪəʊ] **1** *n* Stereo *nt*; *(record-player)* Stereoanlage *f*. **in/on ~** in Stereo/auf einem Stereogerät. **2** *adj* Stereo-.

stereophonic [,sterɪəʊ'fɒnɪk] *adj* stereophon.

stereophony [sterɪ'ɒfənɪ] *n* Stereophonie *f*, Raumklang *m*.

stereoscope ['sterɪəʊˌskəʊp] *n* Stereoskop *nt*.

stereoscopic [,sterɪəʊ'skɒpɪk] *adj* stereoskop(isch); *film, screen also* 3-D-.

stereotype ['sterɪəˌtaɪp] **1** *n* **(a)** *(fig)* Klischee(vorstellung *f*), Stereotyp *nt*; *(~ character)* stereotype Figur. **the ~ of the Englishman** der typische Engländer.
  (b) *(Typ)* *(plate)* Stereotypplatte *f*; *(process)* Plattendruck *m*.
  2 *attr* stereotyp; *ideas, thinking also* klischeehaft.
  3 *vt* **(a)** *(fig: character)* klischeehaft *or* als Typ zeichnen *or* darstellen. **the plot of the Western has become ~d** die Handlung des Westerns ist zu einem Klischee geworden; **I don't like being ~d** ich laß mich nicht gern in ein Klischee zwängen.
  (b) *(Typ)* stereotypieren.

stereotyped ['sterɪəˌtaɪpt] *adj see* **stereotype 2**.

sterile ['steraɪl] *adj* **(a)** *animal, soil* unfruchtbar; *person also* steril; *(fig: fruitless also)* ergebnislos, nutzlos. **(b)** *(germ-free)* steril, keimfrei; *(fig)* steril.

sterility [ste'rɪlɪtɪ] *n see adj* **(a)** Unfruchtbarkeit *f*; Sterilität *f*; Ergebnislosigkeit, Nutzlosigkeit *f*. **(b)** Sterilität *f*.

sterilization [,sterɪlaɪ'zeɪʃən] *n* Sterilisierung, Sterilisation *f*.

sterilize ['sterɪlaɪz] *vt* person, instruments sterilisieren.

sterilizer ['sterɪlaɪzər] *n* *(for instruments)* Sterilisator *m*.

sterling ['stɜ:lɪŋ] **1** *adj* **(a)** *(Fin)* Sterling-. **in pounds ~** in Pfund Sterling; **~ area** Sterlingländer *pl*.
  (b) *(fig)* gediegen; *character* lauter.
  (c) ~ silver Sterlingsilber *nt*; **~ cutlery** Silberbesteck *nt*.
  2 *n* **(a)** *no art* *(money)* das Pfund Sterling, das englische Pfund. **in ~** in Pfund Sterling.
  (b) *(silver)* (Sterling)silber *nt*.
  3 *adj attr* aus (Sterling)silber.

stern[1] [stɜ:n] *n (Naut)* Heck *nt*; *(fig hum: of person)* Hinterteil *nt*, Achtersteven *(N Ger hum)* *m*. **the ~ of the ship** das Achterschiff.

stern[2] *adj* *(+ er)* *(strict)* streng; *words also, character, warning* ernst. **with a ~ face** mit strenger Miene; **made of ~er stuff** aus härterem Holz geschnitzt.

sternly ['stɜ:nlɪ] *adv see adj*.

sternmost ['stɜ:nməʊst] *adj* achterste(r, s).

sternness ['stɜ:nnɪs] *n see adj* Strenge *f*; Ernst *m*.

sternum ['stɜ:nəm] *n* Brustbein, Sternum *(spec)* *nt*.

steroid ['stɪərɔɪd] *n* Steroid *nt*.

stertorous ['stɜ:tərəs] *adj* *(liter)* breathing röchelnd, rasselnd.

stet [stet] *(Typ)* **1** *interj* stehenlassen *(drei Punkte unter falscher Korrektur)*. **2** *vt* die Korrektur *(+ gen)* rückgängig machen.

stethoscope ['steθəskəʊp] *n* Stethoskop *nt*.

stetson ['stetsən] *n* Stetson, Texashut *m*.

stevedore ['sti:vɪdɔ:r] *n* Stauer, Schauermann *m*.

Steven ['sti:vn] *n* Stefan *m*.

stew [stju:] **1** *n* **(a)** Eintopf(gericht *nt*) *m*; *see* **Irish**.
  (b) *(inf)* **to be in a ~** *(about sth)* (über etw *(acc)* *or* wegen etw) (ganz) aufgeregt sein.
  (c) *(obs: brothel)* Bordell *nt*.
  2 *vt* **(a)** *meat* schmoren; *fruit* dünsten. **~ed apples** Apfelkompott *nt*; **the tea was ~ed** der Tee war bitter geworden.
  (b) **to be/get ~ed** *(sl: drunk)* voll sein *(inf)*/sich vollaufen lassen *(inf)*.
  3 *vi* *(meat)* schmoren; *(fruit)* dünsten; *(inf: tea)* bitter werden. **to let sb ~** *(in his/her own juice)* jdn (im eigenen Saft) schmoren lassen.

steward ['stju:əd] *n* Steward *m*; *(on estate etc)* Verwalter *m*; *(at dance, meeting)* Ordner *m*; *(shop ~)* (gewerkschaftlicher) Vertrauensmann (im Betrieb).

stewardess [,stju:ə'des] *n* Stewardeß *f*.

stewardship ['stju:ədʃɪp] *n* Verwaltung *f*; *(rank, duties)* Verwalteramt *nt*.

stewing ['stju:ɪŋ] :- **pan** *n* Kasserolle *f*, Bratentopf *m*; **~ steak** *n* Rindfleisch *nt* für Eintopf.

stick[1] [stɪk] **1** *n* **(a)** Stock *m*; *(twig)* Zweig *m*; *(conductor's baton)* Taktstock *m*; *(hockey)* Schläger *m*; *(drum~)* Schlegel *m*. **to give sb the ~, to take the ~ to sb** jdm eine Tracht Prügel geben; **to give sb/sth (a lot of) ~** *(inf: criticize)* jdn/etw heruntermachen *(inf)* *or* -putzen *(inf)*; **to take (a lot of) ~** *(inf)* viel einstecken (müssen); **just a few ~s of furniture** nur ein paar Möbelstücke; **they adopted the policy of the big ~** sie holten den großen Knüppel raus *(inf)*; **to get hold of the wrong end of the ~** *(fig inf)* etw falsch verstehen.
  (b) *(of sealing wax, celery, rhubarb, dynamite)* Stange *f*; *(of chalk, shaving soap)* Stück *nt*; *(Aviat: joy~)* Steuerknüppel *m*; *(of bombs)* Bombenladung *f* für Reihenabwurf; *(Typ)* Winkelhaken *m*. **a ~ deodorant** ein Deodorant-Stift *m*; **a ~ of rock** eine Zuckerstange.
  (c) *(inf: person)* Kerl *m* *(inf)*. **he's/she's a funny old ~** er/sie ist ein komischer Kauz; **he's/she's such a dry old ~** er/sie ist ein solcher Stockfisch.
  (d) **the ~s** *(Horseracing inf)* die Hürden *pl*.
  (e) **in the ~s** *(esp US: backwoods)* in der hintersten *or* finstersten Provinz.
  2 *vt* plants stützen.

stick[2] *pret, ptp* **stuck** **1** *vt* **(a)** *(with glue etc)* kleben. **to ~ a stamp on sth** eine Briefmarke auf etw *(acc)* kleben; **please ~ the posters to the walls with pins not sellotape** bitte die Poster mit Stecknadeln und nicht mit Tesafilm an den

Wänden befestigen; **is this glue strong enough to ~ it?** wird dieser Klebstoff das halten?; **to ~ the blame on sb** jdm die Schuld zuschieben.

  (b) *(pin)* stecken. **he stuck a badge on his lapel** er steckte sich *(dat)* ein Abzeichen ans Revers; **he stuck a badge on her** er steckte ihr ein Abzeichen an.

  (c) *(jab)* knife, sword etc stoßen. **he stuck a knife through her arm** er stieß ihr ein Messer in den Arm; *see also* **~ in.**

  (d) *pig* (ab)stechen. **he stuck him with his bayonet** er spießte ihn mit dem Bajonett auf.

  (e) *(inf: place, put)* tun *(inf)*; *(in sth also)* stecken *(inf)*. **~ it on the shelf** tu's ins *or* aufs Regal; **he stuck his head round the corner** er steckte seinen Kopf um die Ecke; **to ~ one's hat on** sich *(dat)* den Hut aufsetzen; **he stuck a drink in my hand and a record on the turntable** er drückte mir ein Glas in die Hand und legte eine Platte auf; **you know where you can ~ that** *(sl)* du kannst mich am Arsch lecken! *(vulg)*; **I'll tell him where he can ~ his complaint in a minute!** *(sl)* die Beschwerde kann er sich *(dat)* wohin stecken *(inf)*; **if he doesn't want it he can ~ it** *(sl)* wenn er nicht will, dann hat er halt Pech gehabt *(inf)*.

  (f) *(decorate: with pearls)* besetzen.

  (g) *(esp Brit inf: tolerate)* aushalten; *pace, pressure of work* durchhalten. **I can't ~ him/that** ich kann ihn/das nicht ausstehen *(inf)*; **I can't ~ it any longer!** ich halte das nicht mehr *(länger)* aus!

  (h) to ~ sb with sth *(inf: lumber)* jdm etw aufladen *or* aufhalsen *(inf)*; *(with bill)* jdm etw andrehen.

  2 *vi* **(a)** *(glue, burr etc)* kleben *(to* an + *dat)*. **to make a charge ~** genügend Beweismaterial haben; **you'll never make it ~!** damit kommen Sie nie durch!; **how do they hope to make the charge ~?** wie wollen sie das (je) beweisen?; **the name seems to have stuck** der Name scheint ihm/ihr geblieben zu sein.

  (b) *(become caught, wedged etc)* steckenbleiben; *(drawer, window)* klemmen; *see* **stuck.**

  (c) *(sth pointed)* stecken *(in* in + *dat)*. **it stuck in my foot** das ist mir im Fuß steckengeblieben.

  (d) *(Cards)* halten.

  (e) *(project)* **his toes are ~ing through his socks** seine Zehen kommen durch die Socken; **we could see Manfred's head ~ing over the wall** wir sahen Manfreds Kopf über die Mauer gucken *(inf)*.

  (f) *(stay)* bleiben; *(slander)* haftenbleiben. **to ~ in sb's mind** jdm im Gedächtnis bleiben; **to make sth ~ in one's mind** sich *(dat)* etw einprägen; **I just can't make the dates ~** ich kann mir einfach die Daten nicht einprägen *or* merken; **a teacher must be able to make things ~** der Lehrer muß den Stoff so bringen, daß er haftenbleibt.

◆**stick around** *vi (inf)* hier/da bleiben. **~ ~!** wart's ab!; **he decided to ~ ~ Bonn** er beschloß, noch in Bonn zu bleiben.

◆**stick at** *vi + prep obj* **(a)** *(persist)* bleiben an (+ *dat*) *(inf)*. **to ~ it** dranbleiben *(inf)*. **(b)** *(stop at)* zurückschrecken vor (+ *dat*). **he will ~ ~ nothing** er macht vor nichts halt.

◆**stick by** *vi + prep obj* sb halten zu; *promise* stehen zu.

◆**stick down** *vt sep* **(a)** *(glue)* ankleben; *envelope* zukleben. **(b)** *(inf: put down)* abstellen; *(write down)* aufschreiben.

◆**stick in 1** *vt sep* **(a)** *stamps etc* einkleben. **to ~ stamps ~(to) an album** Briefmarken in ein Album kleben.

  (b) hineinstecken; *knife etc* einstechen. **to ~ sth ~(to) sth** etw in etw *(acc)* stecken; *(prick)* knife, pin etc mit etw in etw *(acc)* stechen; **he stuck his knife ~(to) the table** er stieß das Messer in den Tisch; **she stuck a knife ~(to) him** sie stieß ihm ein Messer in den Leib.

  2 *vi (knife, arrow)* stecken(bleiben).

◆**stick on 1** *vt sep* **(a)** *label, cover* aufkleben *(prep obj* auf + *acc)*. **(b)** *(add)* money draufschlagen; *(+ prep obj)* aufschlagen auf (+ *acc*). **2** *vi* **(a)** *(label etc)* kleben, haften *(prep obj* an + *dat)*. **(b)** *(inf: on horse)* oben bleiben. **to ~ ~ the horse** auf dem Pferd bleiben.

◆**stick out 1** *vi* vorstehen *(of* aus); *(ears, hair)* abstehen; *(fig: be noticeable)* auffallen. **his head was ~ing ~ of the turret** sein Kopf sah aus dem Turm vor. **2** *vt sep* hinaus-/herausstrecken.

◆**stick out for** *vi + prep obj* sich stark machen für.

◆**stick to** *vi + prep obj* **(a)** bleiben bei; *(remain faithful to)* principles etc treubleiben (+ *dat*).

  (b) the photographers stuck ~ her wherever she went die Fotografen hefteten sich ihr überall an die Fersen.

  (c) *(persist with)* task bleiben an (+ *dat*).

◆**stick together** *vi* zusammenkleben; *(fig: partners etc)* zusammenhalten.

◆**stick up 1** *vt sep* **(a)** *(with tape etc)* zukleben.

  (b) *(inf: raise)* **~ 'em ~!** Hände hoch!; **~ your hand if you want to go** Hand hoch, wer gehen will; **three pupils stuck ~ their hands** drei Schüler meldeten sich.

  (c) *(inf: rob)* bank überfallen.

  (d) *(inf)* **she just stuck ~ her nose and marched off** sie stolzierte erhobenen Hauptes weg; **don't ~ your nose ~ at my cooking** rümpf bloß nicht die Nase über meine Kochkünste.

  2 *vi (nail etc)* vorstehen; *(hair)* abstehen; *(collar)* hochstehen.

◆**stick up for** *vi + prep obj sb, one's principles* eintreten für. **to ~ ~ ~ oneself** sich behaupten.

◆**stick with** *vi + prep obj* bleiben bei; *(remain loyal to)* halten zu; *the leaders* mithalten mit.

sticker ['stɪkə^r] *n* **(a)** *(label)* Aufkleber *m*; *(price ~)* Klebeschildchen *nt*. **(b)** *(inf: determined person)* **he's a ~** er ist zäh.

stickiness ['stɪkɪnɪs] *n (lit)* Klebrigkeit *f*; *(of atmosphere, weather)* Schwüle *f*; *(of air)* Stickigkeit *f*. **the ~ of the situation** die heikle Situation.

sticking ['stɪkɪŋ]: **~ plaster** *n (Brit)* Heftpflaster *nt*; **~ point** *n* **you can push her so far, then she reaches her ~ point** man kann sie bis zu einem gewissen Punkt überreden, dann macht sie einfach nicht mehr mit.

stick insect *n* Gespenstheuschrecke *f*.

stick-in-the-mud ['stɪkɪnðə‚mʌd] *(inf)* **1** *n* Muffel *m (inf)*. **2** *adj* rückständig; *parents etc also* muffelig *(inf)*.

stickleback ['stɪklbæk] *n* Stichling *m*.

stickler ['stɪklə^r] *n* **to be a ~ for sth** es mit etw peinlich genau nehmen.

stick: ~-on *adj* label (Auf)klebe-; **~ pin** *n (US)* Krawattennadel *f*; **~-up** *n (inf)* Überfall *m*.

sticky ['stɪkɪ] *adj (+ er)* **(a)** klebrig; *label* Klebe-; *paint* feucht; *atmosphere, weather* schwül; *air* stickig; *(sweaty)* hands feucht, verschwitzt. **I'm all hot and ~** ich bin total verschwitzt; **~ tape** Klebeband *nt*.

  (b) *(fig inf)* problem, person schwierig; *situation, moment* heikel. **he was a bit ~ about it** er hat dabei Schwierigkeiten gemacht; **we had a ~ time in the discussion** wir hatten in der Diskussion ein paar heikle Augenblicke; **to come to a ~ end** ein böses Ende nehmen; **to be on a ~ wicket** in der Klemme sein; **he's got ~ fingers** *(fig)* er hat lange Finger *(inf)*.

stiff [stɪf] **1** *adj (+ er)* **(a)** steif; *corpse also* starr; *brush* hart; *dough, paste* fest.

  (b) *resistance, drink, dose* stark; *fight* zäh, hart; *competition* hart; *breeze* steif; *climb, test* schwierig; *examination, task* schwer, schwierig; *penalty, punishment* schwer; *price, demand* hoch. **that's a bit ~** das ist ganz schön happig *(inf)*.

  2 *adv* steif.

  3 *n (sl)* Leiche *f*.

stiffen ['stɪfn] *(also ~ up)* **1** *vt* steif machen; *shirt etc* stärken, steifen; *(disease)* limb steif werden lassen; *resistance etc* verstärken. **2** *vi* steif werden; *(fig: resistance)* sich verhärten; *(breeze)* auffrischen. **when I said this she ~ed (up)** als ich das sagte, wurde sie ganz starr.

stiffener ['stɪfnə^r] *n (for collar)* Kragenstäbchen *nt*; *(starch etc)* Stärke *f*.

stiffening ['stɪfnɪŋ] *n* Einlage *f*.

stiffly ['stɪflɪ] *adv* steif.

stiff-necked ['stɪf‚nekt] *adj (fig)* halsstarrig.

stiffness ['stɪfnɪs] *n see adj* **(a)** Steifheit *f*; Starre *f*; Härte *f*; Festigkeit *f*. **(b)** Stärke *f*; Zähigkeit *f*; Härte *f*; Steifheit *f*; Schwierigkeit *f*; Schwierigkeit *f*; Schwere *f*; Höhe *f*.

stifle ['staɪfl] **1** *vt (suffocate)* ersticken; *(fig)* laugh, cough also, rage, opposition unterdrücken. **the heat nearly ~d them** sie sind fast umgekommen vor Hitze. **2** *vi* ersticken.

stifling ['staɪflɪŋ] *adj* **(a)** fumes, smoke erstickend; *heat* drückend. **it's ~ in here** es ist ja zum Ersticken hier drin *(inf)*.

  (b) *(fig)* beengend.

stigma ['stɪgmə] *n* **(a)** *pl* **-s** *(mark of shame)* Brandmal, Stigma *nt*. **(b)** *pl* **-ta** *[stɪg'mɑːtə]* Wundmal *nt*; *(Rel)* Stigmatisierung *f*. **(c)** *pl* **-s** *(Bot)* Narbe *f*, Stigma *nt*.

stigmatize ['stɪgmətaɪz] *vt* **(a)** *(Rel)* stigmatisieren. **(b) to ~ sb as sth** jdn als etw brandmarken.

stile [staɪl] *n* (Zaun)übertritt *m*.

stiletto [stɪ'letəu] *n* **(a)** *(knife)* Stilett *nt*. **(b)** *(also ~ heel)* Bleistift- *or* Pfennigabsatz, Stiletto-Absatz *m*. **(c)** *(also ~-heeled shoe)* Schuh *m* mit Bleistift- *or* Pfennigabsatz.

still[1] [stɪl] **1** *adj, adv (+ er)* **(a)** *(motionless)* bewegungslos; *person also* reglos; *sea, waters* ruhig. **to keep ~** stillhalten, sich nicht bewegen; **to hold sth ~** etw ruhig *or* still halten; **to be ~** *(vehicle, measuring needle etc)* stillstehen; **to lie ~** still *or* reglos daliegen; **to stand/sit ~** still stehen/sitzen; **my heart stood ~** mir stockte das Herz; **~ waters run deep** *(Prov)* stille Wasser sind tief *(Prov)*.

  (b) *(quiet, calm)* still. **be ~!** *(US)* sei still!; **a ~ small voice** ein leises Stimmchen.

  2 *adj* wine nicht moussierend; *drink* ohne Kohlensäure. **a ~ photograph** ein Standfoto *nt*.

  3 *n* **(a)** Stille *f*. **in the ~ of the night** in der nächtlichen Stille, in der Stille der Nacht.

  (b) *(Film)* Standfoto *nt*.

  4 *vt (liter)* calm beruhigen; *anger* besänftigen; *sounds* zum Verstummen bringen; *passion, pain* abklingen lassen, stillen. **in order to ~ the waves/wind** damit sich die Wogen glätten/der Wind abflaut *or* sich legt; **to ~ sb's fear** jdm die Furcht nehmen.

still[2] **1** *adv* **(a)** *(temporal)* noch; *(for emphasis, in exasperation, used on its own)* immer noch; *(in negative sentences)* noch immer, immer noch; *(now as in the past)* nach wie vor. **is he ~ coming?** kommt er noch?; **she is ~ in the office** sie ist noch im Büro; *(with emphasis)* sie ist immer noch im Büro; **do you mean you ~ don't believe me?** willst du damit sagen, daß du mir immer noch nicht *or* noch immer nicht glaubst?; **it ~ hasn't come** es ist immer noch nicht gekommen; **I will ~ be here** ich werde noch da sein; **will you ~ be here at 6?** bist du um 6 noch da?; **there will ~ be objections, no matter ...** es wird nach wie vor *or* auch weiterhin Einwände geben, egal ...

  (b) *(nevertheless, all the same)* trotzdem. **~, it was worth it** es hat sich trotzdem gelohnt; **~, he's not a bad person** na ja, er ist eigentlich kein schlechter Mensch; **~, he is my brother** er ist trotz allem mein Bruder; **rich but ~ not happy** reich und doch nicht glücklich; **~, at least we didn't lose anything** na ja, wir haben wenigstens nichts dabei verloren; **~, what can you expect?** was kann man auch anderes erwarten?

  (c) *(with comp)* noch. **~ better** noch besser; **better ~, do it this way** oder noch besser, mach es so; **~ more (so) because ...** und um so mehr, als ..., und um so mehr, weil ...

  2 *conj* (aber) dennoch.

still[3] *n* Destillierapparat *m*; *(small distillery)* Brennerei *f*.

still: ~birth *n* Totgeburt *f*; **~born** *adj (lit, fig)* totgeboren *attr*; **the child was ~born** das Kind war eine Totgeburt, das Kind kam tot zur Welt; **~ life** *n*, *pl* **~ lifes** Stilleben *nt*; **~-life** *adj attr* **a ~-life picture/composition** ein Stilleben *nt*.

stillness ['stɪlnɪs] *n* **(a)** *(motionlessness)* Unbewegtheit *f*; *(of person)* Reglosigkeit *f*. **(b)** *(quietness)* Stille, Ruhe *f*.

stillroom ['stɪlruːm] n (pantry) Vorratskammer f.

stilt [stɪlt] n Stelze f; (Archit) Pfahl m. **a house built on** ∼**s** ein Pfahlbau m.

stilted adj, ∼**ly** adv ['stɪltɪd, -lɪ] gestelzt, gespreizt, geschraubt.

stiltedness ['stɪltɪdnɪs] n Gestelztheit, Gespreiztheit, Geschraubtheit f.

stimulant ['stɪmjʊlənt] 1 n Stimulans, Anregungsmittel nt; (fig) Ansporn m. 2 adj anregend, belebend.

stimulate ['stɪmjʊleɪt] vt (a) (excite) body, circulation, mind anregen; (cold shower, coffee etc) sb beleben; (Med also) stimulieren; nerve reizen; (sexually) erregen, stimulieren; (fig) person animieren, anspornen; (mentally, intellectually) stimulieren; sb's interest erregen. **to** ∼ **sb to do sth** jdn anspornen or dazu animieren, etw zu tun; **to** ∼ **sb into activity** jdn aktiv werden lassen.
(b) (increase) economy, sales etc ankurbeln; (incite) response hervorrufen; criticism anregen zu.

stimulating ['stɪmjʊleɪtɪŋ] adj anregend; drug also stimulierend; bath, shower, walk, music belebend; prospect ermunternd, animierend, beflügelnd; experience (physically) erfrischend, ermunternd; (mentally) stimulierend.

stimulation [,stɪmjʊ'leɪʃən] n (a) (act) (physical, mental) Anregung f; (from shower, walk etc) belebende Wirkung; (Med also) Stimulation f; (sexual) Stimulieren, Erregen nt; (state) Angeregtheit, Erregung f; (sexual) Erregung f; (fig: incentive) Anreiz, Ansporn m; (intellectual) Stimulation f.
(b) (of economy, sales etc) Ankurbelung f (to gen); (of criticism) Anregung f (to zu); (of response) Hervorrufen nt.

stimulative ['stɪmjʊlətɪv] adj anregend, belebend; (esp Physiol) stimulierend.

stimulus ['stɪmjʊləs], pl **stimuli** ['stɪmjʊlaɪ] Anreiz, Ansporn m; (inspiration) Anregung f, Stimulus m; (Physiol) Reiz m; (Psych) Stimulus m. **under the** ∼ **of their encouragement** angespornt von ihrer Ermunterung; **it gave the trade new** ∼ das hat dem Handel neuen Aufschwung gegeben.

stimy vt see **stymie**.

sting [stɪŋ] (vb: pret, ptp **stung**) 1 n (a) (Zool, Bot: organ) (of insect) Stachel m; (of jellyfish) Brennfaden m; (of nettle) Brennhaar nt.
(b) (of insect) (act, wound) Stich m; (of nettle, jellyfish) (act) Brennen nt; (wound) Quaddel f.
(c) (pain) (from needle etc) Stechen nt, stechender Schmerz; (of antiseptic, ointment, from nettle etc) Brennen nt; (of whip) brennender Schmerz. **there might be a bit of a** ∼ das brennt jetzt vielleicht ein bißchen; **we felt the** ∼ **of the hail on our faces** wir spürten den Hagel wie Nadeln im Gesicht.
(d) (fig) (of remark, irony) Stachel m; (of attack, criticism etc) Schärfe f. **a** ∼ **of remorse** Gewissensbisse pl; **a** ∼ **of regret** schmerzliches Bedauern; **to take the** ∼ **out of sth** etw entschärfen; (out of remark, criticism also) einer Sache (dat) den Stachel nehmen; **to have a** ∼ **in its tail** (story, film) ein unerwartet fatales Ende nehmen; (remark) gesalzen sein; **death, where now thy** ∼? Tod, wo ist dein Stachel?
2 vt (a) (insect) stechen; (jellyfish) verbrennen. **she was stung by the nettles** sie hat sich an den Nesseln verbrannt.
(b) **the hail stung our faces** der Hagel stach uns wie mit Nadeln im Gesicht.
(c) (comments, sarcasm etc) treffen, schmerzen; (remorse, conscience) quälen. **he was stung by their insults** ihre Beleidigungen haben ihn sehr getroffen or geschmerzt; **to** ∼ **sb into doing sth** jdn antreiben, etw zu tun; **he was stung into replying** er ließ sich dazu hinreißen zu antworten; **to** ∼ **sb into action** jdn aktiv werden lassen.
(d) (inf) **to** ∼ **sb for sth** jdn bei etw ausnehmen (inf) or schröpfen (inf); **could I** ∼ **you for a fiver?** kann ich dir einen Fünfer abknöpfen? (inf).
3 vi (a) (insect) stechen; (nettle, jellyfish etc) brennen; (burn: eyes, cut, ointment etc) brennen. **smoke makes your eyes** ∼ Rauch brennt in den Augen.
(b) (hail etc) wie mit Nadeln stechen.
(c) (comments, sarcasm etc) schmerzen.

stingaree ['stɪŋəriː] n (US, Austral) Stachelrochen m.

stingily ['stɪndʒɪlɪ] adv (inf) knauserig (inf), knickerig (inf). **he** ∼ **donated a mere 20p** knauserig or knickerig, wie er ist, hat er nur 20 Pence gespendet.

stinginess ['stɪndʒɪnɪs] n (inf) see adj Geiz m, Knauserigkeit (inf), Knickerigkeit (inf) f; Schäbigkeit, Popeligkeit (inf) f.

stinging ['stɪŋɪŋ] adj pain stechend; cut, ointment brennend.

stinging nettle n Brennessel f.

stingray ['stɪŋreɪ] n Stachelrochen m.

stingy ['stɪndʒɪ] adj (+er) (inf) person geizig, knauserig (inf), knickerig (inf); sum, portion, donation schäbig, popelig (inf). **to be** ∼ **with sth** mit etw knausern.

stink [stɪŋk] (vb: pret **stank**, ptp **stunk**) 1 n (a) Gestank m (of nach); (fig: of corruption etc) (Ge)ruch m.
(b) (inf: fuss, scandal) Knatsch (inf), Stunk (inf) m. **to kick up or make or create a** ∼ Stunk machen (inf).
(c) ∼**s** sing (Brit Sch inf) Chemie f; S∼**s** (teacher) der Chemielehrer.
2 vi (a) stinken. **it** ∼**s in here** hier (drin) stinkt's; **it** ∼**s to high heaven** das stinkt zum Himmel.
(b) (fig inf: be bad) sauschlecht or miserabel sein (inf). **the idea** ∼**s** das ist eine sauschlechte or miserable Idee (inf); **the whole business** ∼**s** die ganze Sache stinkt (inf).

♦**stink out** vt sep (a) (inf) room verstänkern (inf). (b) fox etc ausräuchern.

♦**stink up** vt sep (inf) room verstänkern (inf).

stink bomb n Stinkbombe f.

stinker ['stɪŋkəʳ] n (inf) (person) Ekel nt, Fiesling m (sl); (problem, question) harter Brocken, harte Nuß; (letter) gesalzener or geharnischter Brief. **that problem/meeting was a** ∼

das war ein ganz verzwicktes (inf) Problem/eine äußerst schwierige Besprechung.

stinking ['stɪŋkɪŋ] 1 adj (a) (lit) stinkend. (b) (inf) beschissen (sl). **you can keep your** ∼ **money!** du kannst dein Scheißgeld behalten! (sl); **what a** ∼ **thing to do** so was Fieses (sl). 2 adv (inf) ∼ **rich** stinkreich (inf); ∼ **awful** sauschlecht (inf).

stint [stɪnt] 1 n (a) (allotted amount of work) Arbeit, Aufgabe f; (share) Anteil m, Teil nt or m (of an +dat). **to do one's** ∼ (daily work) seine Arbeit leisten or tun; (one's share) sein(en) Teil beitragen or tun; **my** ∼ **was from 3 to 6/lasted two hours** ich war von 3 bis 6/zwei Stunden lang dran; **he has done his** ∼ **of washing up/at the wheel** er hat seinen (An)teil am Abwaschen geleistet/er ist lange genug gefahren; **would you like to do a** ∼ **with the lawn-mower/at the wheel?** wie wär's, wenn du dich auch mal mit dem Rasenmäher betätigen würdest/auch mal fahren würdest or das Steuer übernehmen würdest?; **that was a long** ∼ das hat vielleicht lange gedauert!; **I've finished my** ∼ **for today** für heute habe ich genug getan; **he does a** ∼ **in the gym/at the typewriter every day** er betätigt sich jeden Tag eine Weile in der Turnhalle/an der Schreibmaschine.
(b) without ∼ ohne Einschränkung.
2 vt sparen mit, knausern mit. **to** ∼ **sb of sth** jdm gegenüber mit etw knausern; of praise, reward jdm etw vorenthalten; **to** ∼ **oneself (of sth)** sich (mit etw) einschränken, an sich (dat) sparen; **it's silly to** ∼ **yourself of the little extra luxuries** es ist dumm, sich (dat) das bißchen Extraluxus nicht zu gönnen.
3 vi **to** ∼ **on sth** mit etw sparen or knausern.

stipend ['staɪpend] n (for official, clergyman) Gehalt nt; (liter: for scholar) Stipendium nt.

stipendiary [staɪ'pendɪərɪ] adj official, magistrate, duty nicht ehrenamtlich. ∼ **allowance** Gehalt nt, Bezüge pl.

stipple ['stɪpl] 1 vt picture in der Tupfentechnik malen; paint tupfen, in Tupfen auftragen. 2 vi die Tupfentechnik anwenden. 3 n Tupfen pl; (technique) Tupfentechnik f.

stipulate ['stɪpjʊleɪt] vt (a) (make a condition) zur Auflage machen, verlangen. (b) delivery date, amount, price festsetzen, sich (dat) ausbedingen; size, quantity vorschreiben, festsetzen; conditions stellen, fordern, stipulieren (geh).

stipulation [,stɪpjʊ'leɪʃən] n (a) (condition) Auflage f. **with or on the** ∼ **that ...** unter der Bedingung or mit der Auflage, daß ...
(b) see vt (b) Festsetzung, Ausbedingung f; Festsetzung f; Stellen, Fordern nt, Stipulation f (geh).

stir [stɜːʳ] 1 n (a) Rühren nt. **to give sth a** ∼ etw rühren; tea etc etw umrühren.
(b) (fig: excitement) Aufruhr m. **to cause or create or make a** ∼ Aufsehen erregen.
2 vt (a) tea, paint, soup umrühren; cake mixture rühren. **to** ∼ **sugar into the mixture** den Zucker darunterrühren; **he sat there thoughtfully** ∼**ring his tea** er saß da und rührte gedankenverloren in seinem Tee.
(b) (move) bewegen; limbs rühren; water, waves kräuseln. **come on,** ∼ **yourself or your stumps, we're late** (inf) komm, beweg dich, wir sind ohnehin schon spät dran; **if you want to pass the exam you'd better** ∼ **yourself** wenn du die Prüfung bestehen willst, solltest du dich besser dranhalten (inf).
(c) (fig) emotions aufwühlen; passion wachrufen; imagination anregen; curiosity anstacheln, erregen; blood in Wallung versetzen; (incite) person anstacheln; (move) person, heart rühren, bewegen. **to** ∼ **sb to do sth** jdn bewegen, etw zu tun; (incite) jdn dazu anstacheln, etw zu tun; **that'll** ∼ **things** ∼ das kann heiter werden!; **he's always trying to** ∼ **things** ∼ **among the workers** er versucht immer, die Arbeiter aufzuhetzen.
3 vi sich regen; (person also) sich rühren; (leaves, curtains, animal etc) sich bewegen; (emotion, anger etc) wachwerden; (pity, love) sich rühren, wachwerden.

♦**stir up** vt sep (a) liquid, mixture umrühren; cream rühren, schlagen; mud aufwühlen.
(b) (fig) curiosity, attention, anger erregen; imagination anregen; memories, the past wachrufen; opposition, discord entfachen, erzeugen; hatred schüren; revolution, revolt anzetteln; mob aufstacheln; lazy person aufrütteln. **to** ∼ **sb** ∼ **to sth/to do sth** jdn zu etw anstacheln/jdn dazu anstacheln, etw zu tun; **that'll** ∼ **things** ∼ das kann heiter werden!; **he's always trying to** ∼ **things** ∼ **among the workers** er versucht immer, die Arbeiter aufzuhetzen.

stirrer ['stɜːrəʳ] n (inf: trouble-maker) Scharfmacher(in f) (inf), Agitator(in f) m.

stirring ['stɜːrɪŋ] adj speech, music, scene, poetry bewegend; (stronger) aufwühlend; days, times bewegt.

stirrup ['stɪrəp] n Steigbügel m (also Anat).

stirrup: ∼ **cup** n Abschiedstrunk m; ∼ **pump** n Handspritze f.

stitch [stɪtʃ] 1 n (a) Stich m; (in knitting etc) Masche f; (kind of ∼) (in knitting etc) Muster nt; (in embroidery) Stichart f. **to put a few** ∼**es in sth** etw mit ein paar Stichen nähen; **to put** ∼**es in a wound** eine Wunde nähen; **he had to have** ∼**es** er mußte genäht werden; **he needed** ∼**es in his arm** sein Arm mußte genäht werden; **to have the** ∼**es taken out** die Fäden gezogen bekommen; **a** ∼ **in time saves nine** (Prov) was du heute kannst besorgen, das verschiebe nie auf morgen (Prov).
(b) (inf: piece of clothing) **she hadn't a** ∼ **on** sie war splitter(faser)nackt (inf); **I haven't a** ∼ **to wear** ich habe überhaupt nichts anzuziehen.
(c) (pain) Seitenstiche pl.
(d) **to be in** ∼**es** (inf: from laughing) sich schieflachen (inf); **the story had us all in** ∼**es** wir haben uns alle darüber schiefgelacht (inf); **he had us all in** ∼**es** er brachte uns alle zum Lachen (inf).
2 vt (Sew, Med) nähen; book (zusammen)heften, broschieren; (mend) hole, tear zunähen, stopfen; (embroider) sticken.

3 *vi* nähen (*at* an +*dat*); (*embroider*) sticken (*at* an +*dat*).
♦**stitch down** *vt sep* festnähen.
♦**stitch on** *vt sep* aufnähen; *button* annähen.
♦**stitch up** *vt sep seam, wound, patient* nähen; (*mend*) *hole etc* zunähen, stopfen; (*sew up*) *hem* hochnähen.
stitching ['stɪtʃɪŋ] *n* (*seam*) Naht *f*; (*ornamental*) Zierstiche *pl*, Ziernaht *f*; (*embroidery*) Stickerei *f*; (*of book*) Broschur *f*.
stoat [stəʊt] *n* Wiesel *nt*.
stock [stɒk] **1** *n* **(a)** (*supply*) Vorrat *m* (*of* an +*dat*); (*Comm*) Bestand *m* (*of* an +*dat*). ~ **of knowledge/information** Wissensschatz *m*/Informationsmaterial *nt*; **to get** *or* **lay in a** ~ **of** *wood/candles etc* sich (*dat*) einen Holzvorrat/Kerzenvorrat *etc* anlegen; **to have sth in** ~ etw vorrätig haben; **to be in** ~/**out of** ~ vorrätig/nicht vorrätig sein; **to keep sth in** ~ etw auf Vorrat haben; **to get sth from** ~ etw vom Lager holen; **to take** ~ (*Comm*) Inventur machen; **to take** ~ **of sb** jdn abschätzen; **to take** ~ **of sth** of situation, prospects sich (*dat*) klarwerden über etw (*acc*), sich (*dat*) von etw ein Bild machen; *of one's life* Bilanz aus etw (*dat*) ziehen; **surplus** ~ Überschuß *m*; **the** ~ **was auctioned** die Bestände wurden versteigert.
(b) (*live*~) Viehbestand *m*. **some good** ~ schönes Vieh.
(c) (*Cook*) Brühe *f*.
(d) (*Fin*) (*capital raised by company*) Anleihekapital, Aktienkapital *nt*; (*shares held by investor*) Anteil *m*; (*government* ~) Staatsanleihe *f*. **to have** *or* **hold** ~ **in oil companies** Ölaktien haben; ~**s and shares** (Aktien und) Wertpapiere *pl*, Effekten *pl*; **his** ~ **is going up/is falling** (*fig*) sein Kurswert steigt/fällt; **she puts great** ~ **in what you say** (*fig*) sie mißt allem, was Sie sagen, große Bedeutung bei.
(e) (*Hort*) (*of tree, plant*) Stamm *m*; (*of vine, rose*) Stock *m*; (*for grafting onto*) Wildling *m*, Unterlage *f*; (*for supplying grafts*) das Edelreis liefernde Pflanze.
(f) (*Bot*) Levkoje *f*.
(g) (*tribe, race etc*) Stamm *m*; (*descent*) Abstammung, Herkunft *f*; (*Ling*) (Sprach)familie, (Sprach)gruppe *f*. **to be** *or* **come of good** ~ guter Herkunft sein; **to be from good farming** ~ aus einer alten Bauernfamilie stammen.
(h) (*handle*) Griff *m*; (*of rifle*) Schaft *m*.
(i) to be on the ~**s** (*ship*) im Bau sein; (*book etc*) in Arbeit sein.
(j) ~**s** *pl* (*Hist: for punishment*) Stock *m*.
(k) (*neckcloth*) Halsbinde *f*.
(l) (*Rail*) rollendes Material.
(m) (*esp US Theat*) **to play in summer** ~ bei den Sommeraufführungen mitwirken; **this play is in their** ~ dieses Stück gehört zu ihrem Repertoire.
2 *adj attr* (*Comm*) *size etc* Standard-; *model* Serien-; (*fig*) *phrase, remark, response etc* Standard-, stereotyp.
3 *vt* **(a)** (*shop etc*) goods führen.
(b) (*provide with* ~) *cupboard* füllen; *shop also, library* ausstatten; *pond, river* (mit Fischen) besetzen; *farm* mit einem Viehbestand versehen. **the freezer is** ~**ed with vegetables** die Kühltruhe ist mit Gemüse gefüllt.
♦**stock up 1** *vi* sich eindecken (*on* mit); (*squirrel etc*) einen Vorrat anlegen. **I must** ~ ~ **on rice, I've almost run out** mein Reis ist fast alle, ich muß meinen Vorrat auffüllen.
2 *vt sep shop, larder etc* auffüllen; *library* anreichern; *farm* den Viehbestand (+*gen*) vergrößern; *lake, river* den Fischbestand vergrößern in (+*dat*).
stockade [stɒ'keɪd] *n* (*fence*) Palisade(nzaun *m*) *f*; (*area*) Einfriedung, Umzäunung *f*.
stock: ~**breeder** *n* Viehzüchter *m*; ~**breeding** *n* Viehzucht *f*; ~**broker** *n* Börsenmakler *m*; **the** ~**broker belt** = die reichen Villenvororte *pl*; ~**broking** *n* Effektenhandel, Wertpapierhandel *m*; ~ **car** *n* (*a*) (*for racing*) Stock Car *nt* (*frisierter, verstärkter Serienwagen*); **(b)** (*US Rail: cattle truck*) Viehwaggon, Viehwagen *m*; ~**car racing** *n* Stock-Car-Rennen *nt*; ~ **character** *n* (*Theat*) Typ *m* (im Rollenfach); ~ **company** *n* (a) (*Fin*) Aktiengesellschaft *f*; **(b)** (*US Theat*) Repertoiretheater *nt*; ~ **cube** *n* Brüh- *or* Suppenwürfel *m*; ~ **exchange** *n* Börse *f*; ~ **farmer** *n* Viehhalter *m*; ~ **fish** *n* Stockfisch *m*; ~**holder** *n* Aktionär(in *f*) *m*.
stockily ['stɒkɪlɪ] *adv* ~ **built** stämmig.
stockiness ['stɒkɪnɪs] *n* Stämmigkeit *f*.
stockinet(te) [‚stɒkɪ'net] *n* (Baumwoll)trikot *m*.
stocking ['stɒkɪŋ] *n* Strumpf *m*; (*knee-length*) Kniestrumpf *m*; (*of horse*) Fessel *f*. **in one's** ~(**ed**) **feet** in Strümpfen.
stocking: ~ **filler** *n* kleines Geschenk (*für den Weihnachtsstrumpf*); ~ **mask** *n* Strumpfmaske *f*; ~ **stitch** *n* glatt rechts gestricktes Muster; **in** ~ **stitch** glatt rechts gestrickt.
stock-in-trade [‚stɒkɪn'treɪd] *n* (*tools, materials, fig*) Handwerkszeug *nt*. **that joke is part of his** ~ den Witz hat er ständig auf Lager.
stockist ['stɒkɪst] *n* (*Brit*) (Fach)händler *m*.
stock: ~**jobber** *n* (*Brit*) Börsenhändler *m*; (*US pej*) Börsenjobber, Börsenspekulant *m*; ~ **list** *n* (a) (*Comm*) Warenliste *f*; **(b)** (*Fin*) Börsenzettel *m*; ~**man** *n* (a) (*US, Austral*) Viehzüchter *m*; (*farmhand*) Farmarbeiter *m*; **(b)** (*US: in shop etc*) Lagerist, Lagerverwalter *m*; ~ **market** *n* Börse *f*(nmarkt *m*) *f*; ~**pile 1** *n* Vorrat *m* (*of an* +*dat*); (*of weapons*) Lager *nt*; **the nuclear** ~**pile** das Atomwaffenlager, das Kernwaffenarsenal; **2** *vt* Vorräte an (+*dat*) ... anlegen; (*pej*) horten; **to** ~**pile weapons** Waffenlager *or* Waffenarsenale anlegen; ~ **play** *n* (*Theat*) gängiges Repertoirestück; ~ **prices** *npl* (*St Ex*) Börsenkurse, Effektenkurse *pl*; ~ **room** *n* Lager(raum *m*) *nt*; ~**-still** *adj, adv* **to be/stand** ~**-still** stockstill sein/stehen; ~**taking** *n* Inventur *f*; (*fig*) Bestandsaufnahme *f*; ~**taking sale** *n* Ausverkauf *m* wegen Inventur, = Jahresschlußverkauf *m*.
stocky ['stɒkɪ] *adj* (+*er*) stämmig.
stockyard ['stɒkjɑːd] *n* Viehhof, Schlachthof *m*.
stodge [stɒdʒ] *n* (*inf*) Pampe *f* (*inf*).

stodgy ['stɒdʒɪ] *adj* (+*er*) *food* pampig (*inf*), schwer; *style* schwerfällig; *subject* trocken; *book* schwer verdaulich; *person* langweilig, fad.
stoic ['stəʊɪk] (*Philos:* S~) **1** *n* Stoiker *m*. **2** *adj* stoisch.
stoical *adj*, ~**ly** *adv* ['stəʊɪkəl, -lɪ] stoisch.
stoicism ['stəʊɪsɪzəm] *n* (*Philos:* S~) Stoizismus *m*; (*fig*) stoische Ruhe, Gelassenheit *f*, Gleichmut *m*.
stoke [stəʊk] *vt furnace* (be)heizen, beschicken (*spec*); *fire*, (*fig*) schüren.
♦**stoke up 1** *vt sep furnace* (be)heizen, beschicken (*spec*); *fire* schüren. **2** *vi* (*eat*) sich satt essen; (*drink*) tanken (*inf*).
stoke: ~**hold** *n* (*Naut*) Heizraum *m*; ~**hole** *n* (a) (*Naut*) Heizraum *m*; **(b)** (*in furnace*) Schürloch *nt*.
stoker ['stəʊkə'] *n* Heizer *m*; (*device*) Beschickungsanlage *f*.
stole¹ [stəʊl] *n* Stola *f*.
stole² *pret of* **steal**.
stolen ['stəʊlən] **1** *ptp of* **steal**. **2** *adj* gestohlen; *pleasures* heimlich. ~ **goods** Diebesgut *nt*; **to receive** ~ **goods** Hehler sein; **receiving** ~ **goods** Hehlerei *f*.
stolid ['stɒlɪd] *adj person* phlegmatisch, stur (*pej*); *indifference* stumpf; *determination, silence* beharrlich, stur (*pej*).
stolidly ['stɒlɪdlɪ] *adv* phlegmatisch, stur (*pej*); *remain silent, work* beharrlich, stur (*pej*).
stolidness ['stɒlɪdnɪs] *n see adj* Phlegma *nt*, Sturheit *f* (*pej*); Stumpfheit *f*; Beharrlichkeit, Sturheit (*pej*) *f*. **the** ~ **of his manner** sein Phlegma *nt*, seine sture Art (*pej*).
stoma ['stəʊmə] *n, pl* **-ta** (*Bot*) Stoma *nt* (*spec*).
stomach ['stʌmək] **1** *n* (*abdomen*) Magen *m*; (*belly, paunch*) Bauch *m*; (*fig: appetite*) Lust *f* (*for auf* +*acc*), Interesse *nt* (*for* an +*dat*). **to lie on one's** ~ auf dem Bauch liegen; **hold your** ~ **in** zieh den Bauch ein!; **to have a pain in one's** ~ Magen-/Bauchschmerzen haben; **to hit sb in the** ~ jdn in die Magengrube/Bauchgegend schlagen *or* (*bullet etc*) treffen; **on an empty** ~ *drink, take medicine etc* auf leeren *or* nüchternen Magen; **on an empty/full** ~ *swim, drive etc* mit leerem *or* nüchternem/vollem Magen; **an army marches on its** ~ (*prov*) mit leerem Magen kann man nichts Ordentliches zustande bringen; **I have no** ~ **for that** das ist mir zuwider; *for party, journey etc* mir ist nicht danach (zumute), ich habe keine Lust dazu; **he doesn't have the** ~ **for it** (*guts*) dazu hat er nicht den Mumm (*inf*).
2 *vt* (*inf*) *behaviour, rudeness, cruelty* vertragen; *person, film, music etc* ausstehen.
stomach *in cpds* Magen-; ~**-ache** *n* Magenschmerzen *pl*; ~**pump** *n* Magenpumpe *f*; ~ **trouble** *n* Magenbeschwerden *pl*; ~ **upset** *n* Magenverstimmung *f*.
stomata [stəʊ'mɑːtə] *pl of* **stoma**.
stomp [stɒmp] *vi* stapfen.
stone [stəʊn] **1** *n* **(a)** Stein *m*. **a heart of** ~ ein Herz aus Stein; **a** ~**'s throw from the station** nur einen Steinwurf *or* Katzensprung vom Bahnhof entfernt; **within a** ~**'s throw of success** kurz vor dem Erfolg, den Erfolg in greifbarer Nähe; **to leave no** ~ **unturned** nichts unversucht lassen; **to have a** ~ **in one's kidney/gall-bladder** einen Nieren-/Gallenstein haben.
(b) (*Brit: weight*) britische Gewichtseinheit = 6.35 kg.
2 *adj* Stein-, aus Stein.
3 *vt* **(a)** (*throw* ~**s** *at*) mit Steinen bewerfen; (*kill*) steinigen. ~ **the crows!** (*Brit sl*) jetzt brat mir einer einen Storch! (*inf*).
(b) *fruit* entsteinen.
(c) (*sl*) **to be** ~**d** (*out of one's mind*) (*on drugs*) (total) weg (*inf*) *or* stoned (*sl*) sein; (*drunk*) mächtig unter Strom stehen (*sl*).
stone: S~ **Age** *n* Steinzeit *f*; ~**-blind** *adj* stockblind (*inf*); ~**-broke** *adj* (*US inf*) *see* **stony-broke**; ~**-cold** *adj* eiskalt; **2** *adv* ~**-cold sober** stocknüchtern (*inf*); ~**-dead** *adj* mausetot (*inf*); **to kill sb/sth** ~**-dead** jdm/einer Sache den Garaus machen (*inf*); ~**-deaf** *adj* stocktaub (*inf*); ~**mason** *n* Steinmetz *m*; ~ **pit**, ~ **quarry** *n* Steinbruch *m*; ~**wall** *vi* (*fig: esp Parl*) obstruieren; (*in answering questions*) ausweichen; (*Sport*) mauern (*sl*); ~**ware** **1** *n* Steingut *nt*; **2** *adj attr* Steingut-; ~**work** *n* Mauerwerk *nt*.
stonily ['stəʊnɪlɪ] *adv* (*fig*) *suit* mit steinerner Miene, starr.
stoniness ['stəʊnɪnɪs] *n* (*of ground etc*) Steinigkeit *f*; (*fig: of look etc*) Versteinertheit *f*.
stony ['stəʊnɪ] *adj* (+*er*) *ground, path, beach* steinig; *substance, texture* steinartig; (*fig*) *glance, silence, heart* steinern; *person, welcome* kalt.
stony: ~**-broke** *adj* (*Brit inf*) völlig abgebrannt (*inf*), total blank *or* pleite (*inf*); ~**-faced** ['stəʊnɪ'feɪst] *adj* (*solemn*) ernst; (*impassive*) mit steinerner Miene; ~**-hearted** *adj* kaltherzig.
stood [stʊd] *pret, ptp of* **stand**.
stooge [stuːdʒ] *n* (*inf*) Handlanger *m*; (*comedian's* ~) Stichwortgeber *m*.
stook [stuːk] *n* Hocke *f*.
stool [stuːl] *n* **(a)** (*seat*) Hocker *m*; (*foot-, kitchen* ~, *milking* ~ *also*) Schemel *m*; (*folding*) Stuhl *m*. **to fall between two** ~**s** sich zwischen zwei Stühle setzen; (*be neither one thing nor the other*) weder dem einen noch dem anderen gerecht werden.
(b) (*esp Med: faeces*) Stuhl *m*.
stool pigeon *n* **(a)** (*lit, fig: decoy*) Lockvogel *m*. **(b)** (*inf: informer*) Spitzel *m* (*inf*).
stoop¹ [stuːp] **1** *n* Gebeugtheit *f*; (*deformity*) krummer Rücken, Buckel *m*. **to walk with a** ~ gebeugt gehen; **to have a** ~ einen Buckel *or* einen krummen Rücken haben.
2 *vi* beugen; *head* (*to avoid sth*) einziehen.
3 *vi* sich beugen *or* neigen (*over über* +*acc*); (*also* ~ **down**) sich bücken; (*have a* ~, *walk with a* ~) gebeugt gehen. ~**ing shoulders** krumme Schultern *pl*; **to** ~ **to sth/to doing sth** (*fig*) sich zu etw herablassen *or* hergeben/sich dazu herablassen *or* hergeben, etw zu tun.
stoop² *n* (*US*) Treppe *f*.
stop [stɒp] **1** *n* **(a)** (*act of* ~*ping*) Halt *m*, Stoppen *nt*. **the signal is at** ~ das Signal steht auf Halt *or* Stop; **to be at a** ~ stillstehen; **to**

bring sth to a ~ (*lit*) etw anhalten *or* stoppen, etw zum Stehen bringen; *traffic* etw zum Erliegen bringen; (*fig*) *project, meeting, development* einer Sache (*dat*) ein Ende machen; *conversation* etw verstummen lassen; **to come to a ~** (*car, machine*) anhalten, stoppen; (*traffic*) stocken; (*fig*) (*meeting, rain*) aufhören; (*research, project*) eingestellt werden; (*conversation*) verstummen; **to come to a dead/sudden ~** (*vehicle*) abrupt anhalten *or* stoppen; (*traffic*) völlig/plötzlich zum Erliegen kommen; (*rain*) ganz plötzlich aufhören; (*research, project, meeting*) ein Ende *nt*/ein abruptes Ende finden; (*conversation*) völlig/abrupt verstummen; **the aircraft has come to a complete ~** wenn die Maschine völlig zum Stillstand gekommen ist; **to make a ~** (*bus, train, tram*) (an)halten; (*plane, ship*) (Zwischen)station machen; **to put a ~ to sth** einer Sache (*dat*) einen Riegel vorschieben.

(b) (*stay*) Aufenthalt *m*; (*break*) Pause *f*; (*Aviat: for refuelling etc*) Zwischenlandung *f*. **to have a ~ for coffee** eine Kaffeepause machen; **to have a ~** haltmachen; **we had *or* made three ~s** wir haben dreimal haltgemacht; **to work for eight hours without a ~** acht Stunden ohne Unterbrechung arbeiten.

(c) (~ping place) Station *f*; (*for bus, tram, train*) Haltestelle *f*; (*for ship*) Anlegestelle *f*; (*for plane*) Landeplatz *m*.

(d) (*esp Brit: punctuation mark*) Punkt *m*.

(e) (*Mus*) (*of wind instruments*) (Griff)loch *nt*; (*on organ: also ~knob*) Registerzug *m*; (*organ pipe*) Register *nt*. **to pull out all the ~s** (*fig*) alle Register ziehen.

(f) (*stopper*) (*for door, window*) Sperre *f*; (*on typewriter*) Feststelltaste *f*.

(g) (*Phot: f number*) Blende *f*.

(h) (*Phon*) Verschlußlaut *m*; (*glottal ~*) Knacklaut *m*.

2 vt (a) (~ *when moving*) *person* anhalten; *vehicle, clock also, ball* stoppen; *engine, machine etc* abstellen; *blow* abblocken, auffangen; (~ *from going away, from moving on*) *runaway, thief etc* aufhalten; *attack, enemy, progress* aufhalten, hemmen; *traffic* (*hold up*) aufhalten; (*bring to complete standstill*) zum Stehen *or* Erliegen bringen; (*policeman*) anhalten; (*keep out*) *noise, light* abfangen, auffangen. **~ thief!** haltet den Dieb!; **to ~ a bullet** (*be shot*) eine Kugel verpaßt kriegen (*inf*); **to ~ sb dead *or* in his tracks** jdn urplötzlich anhalten lassen; (*in conversation*) jdn plötzlich verstummen lassen; *see* **rot, show**.

(b) (~ *from continuing*) *activity, rumour, threat, crime* ein Ende machen *or* setzen (+*dat*); *nonsense, noise* unterbinden; *match, conversation, work* beenden; *development* aufhalten; (*temporarily*) unterbrechen; *flow of blood* stillen, unterbinden; *progress, inflation* aufhalten, hemmen; *speaker, speech* unterbrechen; *production* zum Stillstand bringen; (*temporarily*) unterbrechen. **he was talking and talking, we just couldn't ~ him** er redete und redete, und wir konnten ihn nicht dazu bringen, endlich aufzuhören; **the referee ~ped play** der Schiedsrichter hat das Spiel abgebrochen; (*temporarily*) der Schiedsrichter hat das Spiel unterbrechen lassen; **this will ~ the pain** das hilft gegen die Schmerzen.

(c) (*cease*) aufhören mit; *noise, nonsense also* unterlassen. **to ~ doing sth** aufhören, etw zu tun; etw nicht mehr tun; **she never ~s talking** sie redet ununterbrochen *or* in einer Tour (*inf*); **to ~ smoking** mit dem Rauchen aufhören; (*temporarily*) das Rauchen einstellen; **I'm trying to ~ smoking** ich versuche, das Rauchen aufzugeben *or* nicht mehr zu rauchen; ~ **saying that** nun sag das doch nicht immer; ~ **it!** laß das!, hör auf!; **I just can't ~ it** ich kann es nicht lassen.

(d) (*suspend*) stoppen; *payments, delivery of goods also, production, activity, fighting* einstellen; *leave, cheque, electricity, water supply, wages* sperren; *privileges* unterbinden; *subsidy, allowances, grant etc* jdm streichen; *battle, negotiations, proceedings* abbrechen; (*cancel*) *subscription* kündigen; (*temporarily*) *delivery, newspaper* abbestellen. **the money was ~ped out of his wages** das Geld wurde von seinem Lohn einbehalten *or* zurückbehalten.

(e) (*prevent from happening*) *sth* verhindern; *trouble also* unterbinden; (*prevent from doing*) *sb* abhalten. **to ~ oneself** sich beherrschen, sich zurückhalten, sich bremsen (*inf*); **can't you ~ him?** können Sie ihn nicht davon abhalten *or* daran hindern?; **there's no ~ping him** (*inf*) er ist nicht zu bremsen (*inf*); **there's nothing ~ping you *or* to ~ you** es hindert Sie nichts, es hält Sie nichts zurück.

(f) (*in participial construction*) **to ~ sb (from) doing sth** jdn davon abhalten *or* (*physically*) daran hindern, etw zu tun; (*put a ~ to*) dafür sorgen, daß jd etw nicht mehr tut *or* daß jd aufhört, etw zu tun; **to ~ sth (from) happening** (*prevent, put a ~ to*) (es) verhindern, daß etw geschieht; **that will ~ it (from) hurting** (*prevent*) dann wird es nicht weh tun; (*put a ~ to*) dann wird es nicht mehr weh tun; **how can we ~ the baby (from) crying?** (*prevent*) was können wir tun, damit das Baby nicht schreit?; **that'll ~ the gas (from) escaping/the pipe (from) leaking** das wird verhindern, daß Gas entweicht/das Rohr leckt; **to ~ the thief (from) escaping** den Dieb an der Flucht hindern; **it will ~ you from worrying/getting wet** dann brauchen Sie sich (*dat*) keine Sorgen zu machen/dann werden Sie nicht naß; **to ~ oneself from doing sth** sich zurückhalten und etw nicht tun.

(g) (*block*) verstopfen; (*with cork, bung, cement etc also*) zustopfen (*with mit*); (*fill*) *tooth* plombieren, füllen; (*fig*) *gap* füllen, stopfen; *leak of information* stopfen; (*Mus*) *string* greifen; *finger hole* zuhalten. **to ~ sb's mouth** (*inf*) jdm den Mund stopfen (*inf*); **to ~ one's ears with one's fingers/cotton wool** sich (*dat*) die Finger in die Ohren stecken/sich (*dat*) die Ohren mit Watte zustopfen.

3 vi (a) (*halt*) anhalten; (*train, car also*) halten, stoppen; (*traveller, driver, hiker*) haltmachen; (*pedestrian, clock, watch*) stehenbleiben; (*engine, machine*) nicht mehr laufen. ~! halt!, stopp!; ~ **right there!** halt!, stopp!; **we ~ped for a drink at the pub** wir sind in der Wirtschaft eingekehrt, um etwas zu

trinken; **to ~ at nothing (to do sth)** (*fig*) vor nichts haltmachen(, um etw zu tun); **to ~ dead *or* in one's tracks** plötzlich *or* abrupt *or* auf der Stelle stehenbleiben; *see* **short**.

(b) (*finish, cease*) aufhören; (*pain, headache also*) weggehen; (*heart*) aufhören zu schlagen, stehenbleiben; (*production, payments, delivery*) eingestellt werden; (*programme, show, match, film*) zu Ende sein; (*music, speaker also*) verstummen. **to ~ doing sth** aufhören, etw zu tun, mit etw aufhören; **when the film has ~ped** wenn der Film zu Ende ist; **ask him to ~** sag ihm, er soll aufhören; **he ~ped in mid sentence** er brach mitten im Satz ab; **I will not ~ until I find him/convince you** ich gebe keine Ruhe, bis ich ihn gefunden habe/dich überzeugt habe; **he would ~ at nothing** er macht vor nichts halt; **if you had ~ped to think** wenn du nur einen Augenblick nachgedacht hättest; ~ **to think** before you speak erst denken, dann reden; **he never knows when *or* where to ~** er weiß nicht, wann er aufhören muß *or* Schluß machen muß; **my enjoyment/ worry has ~ped** ich genieße das/sorge mich nicht mehr.

(c) (*inf: stay*) bleiben (*at* in +*dat*, *with* bei). **to ~ for *or* to supper** zum Abendessen bleiben.

♦ **stop away** *vi* (*inf*) wegbleiben. **to ~ ~ from school/the lecture** die Schule/Vorlesung schwänzen (*inf*).

♦ **stop behind** *vi* (*inf*) (noch) dableiben, länger bleiben; (*Sch: as punishment*) nachsitzen.

♦ **stop by** *vi* kurz vorbeikommen *or* vorbeischauen. **to ~ ~ (at) sb's house** bei jdm hereinschauen (*inf*).

♦ **stop down** *vi* (*Phot*) abblenden, eine niedrigere Blende einstellen.

♦ **stop in** *vi* (*inf*) drinbleiben (*inf*); (*Sch: as punishment*) nachsitzen, dableiben.

♦ **stop off** *vi* (kurz) haltmachen (*at sb's place* bei jdm); (*on travels also*) Zwischenstation machen (*at* in +*dat*).

♦ **stop on** *vi* (*inf*) (noch) dableiben, länger bleiben. **to ~ ~ at school** in der Schule weitermachen.

♦ **stop out** *vi* (*inf*) wegbleiben, streiken.

♦ **stop over** *vi* kurz haltmachen; (*on travels*) Zwischenstation machen (*in* in +*dat*); (*Aviat*) zwischenlanden.

♦ **stop up 1** *vt sep* verstopfen; *crack, hole also* zustopfen. **2 vi (a)** (*inf: stay up*) aufbleiben. **(b)** (*Phot*) eine größere Blende einstellen.

stop: ~ **button** *n* Halteknopf *m*; ~**cock** *n* Absperrhahn *m*; ~**gap** *n* (*thing*) Notbehelf *m*; (*scheme*) Notlösung *f*; (*person*) Lückenbüßer *m*; ~**gap measure** *n* Überbrückungsmaßnahme *f*; ~**-go** *adj attr* ~**-go policies** Politik *f* des ewigen Hin und Her; ~**light** *n* (*brakelight*) Bremslicht, Stopplicht *nt*; (*esp US: traffic light*) rotes Licht; ~**over** *n* Zwischenstation *f*; (*Aviat*) Zwischenlandung *f*; **to have a ~over** Zwischenstation/Zwischenlandung machen; ~**over ticket** *n* (*Aviat*) Rundreiseticket *nt*.

stoppage ['stɒpɪdʒ] *n* (a) (*in work, game*) Unterbrechung *f*; (*in traffic*) Stockung *f*; (*in production etc*) (*temporary, because of mechanical problems*) Unterbrechung *f*; (*for longer time, because of strike etc*) Stopp *m*; (*strike*) Streik *m*.

(b) (*of pay, leave, cheque*) Sperrung *f*; (*of delivery, supplies etc*) Stopp *m*; (*deduction*) Abzug *m*.

(c) (*blockage*) Verstopfung *f*, Stau *m*.

stopper ['stɒpə'] **1** *n* (*plug*) Stöpsel *m*; (*cork also*) Pfropfen *m*. **2** *vt* verstöpseln.

stopping ['stɒpɪŋ] *n* (a) ~ **and starting** (*in driving*) stückchenweises Vorwärtskommen, Stop- und Go-Verkehr *m*; (*in work*) ständige Unterbrechungen *pl*. (b) (*in tooth*) Füllung, Plombe *f*.

stopping: ~ **place** *n* (*of bus, train etc*) Haltestelle *f*; **this is an ideal ~ place** das ist ein idealer Platz zum Haltmachen; ~ **train** *n* Personenzug *m*.

stop: ~**-press** *n* (*esp Brit*) (*space*) Spalte *f* für letzte Meldungen; (*news*) letzte Meldungen *pl*; ~ **sign** *n* Stoppschild *nt*; ~**watch** *n* Stoppuhr *f*.

storage ['stɔːrɪdʒ] *n* (*of goods, food*) Lagerung *f*; (*of books, documents, in household*) Aufbewahrung *f*; (*of water, electricity, data*) Speicherung *f*, Speichern *nt*; (*cost*) Lagergeld *nt*. **to put sth into ~** etw unterstellen, etw (ein)lagern; *see* **cold ~**.

storage: ~ **battery** *n* Akkumulator *m*; ~ **capacity** *n* (*of computer*) Speicherkapazität *f*; ~ **charge** *n* Lagergeld *nt*; ~ **heater** *n* (Nachtstrom)speicherofen *m*; ~ **problems** *npl* Lagerungsprobleme *pl*; (*in house*) Probleme *pl* mit der Aufbewahrung, Platzmangel *m*; ~ **space** *n* Lagerraum *m*; (*in house*) Schränke und Abstellräume *pl*; ~ **tank** *n* Vorratstank *m*.

store [stɔː'] **1** *n* (a) (*stock*) Vorrat *m* (*of an* +*dat*); (*fig*) Fülle *f*, Schatz, Reichtum *m* (*of an* +*dat*). ~**s** *pl* (*supplies*) Vorräte, Bestände *pl*; **to lay *or* get in a ~ of food/coal** einen Lebensmittel-/Kohlenvorrat anlegen; **to have *or* keep sth in ~** etw lagern, einen Vorrat von etw haben; **to be in ~ for sb** jdm bevorstehen, auf jdn warten; **to have a surprise in ~ for sb** für jdn eine Überraschung auf Lager haben; **that's a treat in ~ (for you)** da habt ihr noch was Schönes vor euch, das ist etwas, worauf ihr euch freuen könnt; **what has the future in ~ for us?** was wird uns (*dat*) die Zukunft bringen?; **to set great/little ~ by sth** viel/wenig von etw halten, einer Sache (*dat*) viel/wenig Bedeutung beimessen; **a fine ~ of knowledge** ein großer Wissensschatz, eine große Fülle *or* ein großer Reichtum an Wissen.

(b) (*place*) Lager *nt*; (~**room also**) Lagerraum *nt*, Lagerhalle *f*; (~**room also**) Lagerraum *m*. **he is *or* works in the ~s** er ist im Lager tätig; **to put one's furniture in ~** seine Möbel unterstellen *or* (ein)lagern.

(c) (*esp Brit Computers*) (Daten)speicher *m*.

(d) (*large shop, book* ~) Geschäft *nt*; (*department* ~) Kaufhaus, Warenhaus *nt*; (*esp US: shop*) Laden *m*.

2 adj attr (*US*) *clothes* von der Stange; *bread* aus der Fabrik.

3 vt lagern; *documents* aufbewahren; *furniture* unterstellen; (*in depository*) einlagern; *information, electricity, heat* speichern; (*in one's memory*) sich (*dat*) merken;

(*keep in reserve, collect: also* ~ **up**) Vorräte an (+*dat*) ...
anschaffen; (*equip, supply*) *larder etc* auffüllen. **the cellar can**
~ **enough coal for the winter** der Keller hat genügend Platz für
die Winterkohle; **to** ~ **sth away** etw verwahren; **squirrels** ~
away nuts for the winter Eichhörnchen legen einen Vorrat von
Nüssen für den Winter an; **to** ~ **sth up** einen Vorrat von etw
anlegen; (*fig*) etw anstauen; **surprise** etw auf Lager haben;
hatred ~**d up over years** jahrelang angestauter Haß.
   4 *vi* (*fruit, vegetables*) sich lagern or aufbewahren lassen.
store: ~**house** *n* Lager(haus) *nt*; (*fig*) Fundgrube, Schatzkammer *f*; ~ **keeper** *n* (*in* ~**house**) Lagerverwalter or (*esp US:*
shopkeeper) Ladenbesitzer(in *f*), Geschäftsinhaber(in *f*) *m*; ~
man *n* Lagerverwalter *m*; (*esp US: shopkeeper*) Ladenbesitzer
m; ~**room** *n* Lagerraum *m*; (*for food*) Vorratskammer *f*.
storey, (*esp US*) **story** ['stɔːrɪ] *n*, *pl* -**s** or (*US*) **stories** Stock-
(werk *nt*) *m*, Etage *f*. **a nine-**~ **building** ein neunstöckiges
Gebäude, ein Gebäude mit neun Stockwerken or Etagen; **on the**
second ~ im zweiten Stock(werk), auf der zweiten Etage; (*US*)
im ersten Stock(werk), auf der ersten Etage; **he fell from the**
third-~ **window** er fiel aus dem Fenster des dritten or (*US*)
zweiten Stock(werk)s or der dritten or (*US*) zweiten Etage.
-storeyed, (*esp US*) **-storied** [-'stɔːrɪd] *adj suf* -stöckig. **an**
eight-~ **building** ein achtstöckiges Gebäude.
stork [stɔːk] *n* Storch *m*.
storm [stɔːm] **1** *n* **(a)** (*thunder*~) Unwetter *nt*; (*thunder*~) Gewitter *nt*;
(*strong wind*) Sturm *m*. **there is a** ~ **blowing** es stürmt; **come in**
out of the ~ kommen Sie herein ins Trockene; **to brave the** ~
dem Unwetter/Gewitter/Sturm trotzen; (*fig*) das Gewitter über
sich (*acc*) ergehen lassen; **a** ~ **in a teacup** (*fig*) ein Sturm im
Wasserglas.
   (b) (*fig*) (*of abuse, insults*) Flut *f* (*of* von); (*of applause,*
indignation, criticism) Sturm *m* (*of* gen); (*of blows, arrows,*
missiles) Hagel *m* (*of* von); (*outcry*) Aufruhr *m*. ~ **of protest**
Proteststurm *m*; **a** ~ **of cheering** stürmischer Jubel; ~ **and**
stress Sturm und Drang *m*.
   (c) to take sth/sb by ~ (*Mil, fig*) etw/jdn im Sturm erobern.
   2 *vt* stürmen.
   3 *vi* **(a)** (*talk angrily*) toben, wüten (*at* gegen). **he** ~**ed on for**
an hour about the government er schimpfte eine Stunde lang
wütend über die Regierung.
   (b) (*move violently*) stürmen. **to** ~ **out of/into a room** aus
einem/in ein Zimmer stürmen.
   (c) (*esp US: Met*) stürmen.
storm: ~**bound** *adj* vom Sturm aufgehalten; ~ **centre** or (*US*)
center *n* Sturmzentrum *nt*; (*fig*) (Unruhe)herd *m*; ~ **cloud** *n* (*lit,*
fig) Gewitterwolke *f*; ~ **cone** *n* Sturmkegel *m*; ~ **door** *n* äußere
Windfangtür; ~ **force** *n* Windstärke *f*.
stormily ['stɔːmɪlɪ] *adv* (*lit, fig*) stürmisch; *weep* heftig; *protest,*
reply, answer, react heftig, heftig.
storminess ['stɔːmɪnɪs] *n* (*of reaction, temper, feelings*) Heftigkeit *f*. **the** ~ **of the weather/wind/sea** das stürmische Wet-
ter/der stürmische Wind/die stürmische See; **the** ~ **of his**
reception sein stürmischer Empfang.
storm: ~ **lantern** *n* Sturmlaterne *f*; ~ **petrel** *n* Sturmschwalbe *f*;
~**proof** *adj* sturmsicher; ~ **signal** *n* Sturmsignal *nt*; ~**-tossed**
adj (*liter*) sturmgepeitscht (*liter*); ~ **trooper** *n* (*NS*) SA-Mann
m; ~**troopers** *npl* (*fig*) (Sonder)einsatzkommando *nt*; ~ **troops**
npl Sturmtruppe *f*; ~ **warning** *n* Sturmwarnung *nt*; ~ **window** *n*
äußeres Doppelfenster.
stormy ['stɔːmɪ] *adj* (+*er*) (*lit, fig*) stürmisch; *discussion also,*
temper hitzig; *protests* heftig. **he has a** ~ **temper** er ist
jähzornig.
stormy petrel *n* Sturmschwalbe *f*; (*fig*) Unglücksbote *m*.
story[1] ['stɔːrɪ] *n* **(a)** (*tale, account*) Geschichte *f*; (*Liter also*)
Erzählung *f*; (*joke*) Witz(geschichte *f*) *m*. **it's a long** ~ das ist
eine lange Geschichte; **the** ~ **of her life** ihre Lebensgeschichte;
that's another ~ das ist eine andere Geschichte; **the** ~ **goes**
that ... man erzählt sich, daß ...; **his** ~ **is that** ... er behauptet, daß
...; **according to your** ~ dir zufolge; **I've heard his** ~ ich habe
seine Version gehört; **the full** ~ **still has to be told** die ganze
Wahrheit muß noch ans Licht kommen; **that's not the whole** ~
das ist nicht die ganze Wahrheit; **the marks tell their own** ~ die
Flecke sprechen für sich; **to cut** or **make a long** ~ **short** um es
kurz zu machen, kurz und gut; **it's the (same) old** ~ es ist das
alte Lied; **but it's another** ~ **now** aber jetzt sieht die Sache
anders aus; **that's the** ~ **of my life** (*inf*) wem sagen Sie das!
(*inf*).
   (b) (*Press*) (*event*) Geschichte *f*; (*newspaper* ~) Artikel *m*.
it'll make a good ~ das gibt einen guten Artikel.
   (c) (*plot*) Handlung *f*.
   (d) (*inf: lie*) Märchen *nt*. **to tell stories** Märchen erzählen.
story[2] *n* (*US*) *see* **storey**.
story: ~**book** *n* Geschichtenbuch *nt*; **2** *adj attr castles, sights*
etc märchenhaft; *romance* Märchen-; ~**book ending** Ende *nt*
wie im Märchen, Happy-End *nt*; **their romance had a** ~**book**
ending ihre Romanze endete wie im Märchen; ~**line** *n* Handlung *f*; ~**teller** *n* (*a*) (*narrator*) Geschichtenerzähler(in *f*) *m*; **(b)**
(*inf: liar*) Lügenheld *m*.
stoup [stuːp] *n* (*Eccl*) Weihwasserbecken *nt*.
stout [staʊt] **1** *adj* (+*er*) **(a)** (*corpulent*) korpulent; *woman also*
füllig; *man also* untersetzt.
   (b) (*strong*) *stick, horse etc* kräftig; *door, rope also, wall, gate*
stark; *shoes* fest; *coat* dick.
   (c) (*brave*) *heart* tapfer; *fellow, resistance also* beherzt,
unerschrocken, mannhaft (*liter*); *refusal, denial* entschieden;
belief fest. ~ **fellow!** (*dated inf*) tapferer Kerl! (*dated inf*); **it**
takes a ~ **man to** ... man muß tapfer or beherzt sein, um ...; **with**
~ **heart** tapferen Herzens.
   2 *n* Starkbier *nt*; (*sweet* ~) Malzbier *nt*.
stout-hearted *adj*, ~**ly** *adv* ['staʊt'hɑːtɪd, -lɪ] tapfer,
unerschrocken, mannhaft (*liter*).

stoutly ['staʊtlɪ] *adv* (*strongly*) *made* solide; (*resolutely*) *resist,*
defend, fight tapfer, beherzt, mannhaft; (*liter*) *believe, main-*
tain fest, steif und fest (*pej*); *resist, refuse, deny* entschieden;
built *person* stämmig, kräftig (gebaut); *wall, door* stark,
kräftig; *house* solide gebaut.
stoutness ['staʊtnɪs] *n see adj* **(a)** Korpulenz *f*; Fülligkeit *f*;
Untersetztheit *f*. **(b)** Kräftigkeit *f*; Stärke *f*; Festigkeit *f*; Dicke
f. **(c)** Tapferkeit *f*; Beherztheit, Mannhaftigkeit (*liter*) *f*;
Entschiedenheit *f*; Festigkeit *f*. **the** ~ **of his resistance** sein tapferer or beherzter Widerstand.
stove [stəʊv] *n* Ofen *m*; (*for cooking*) Herd *m*. **electric/gas** ~
Elektro-/Gasherd *m*.
stove: ~**pipe** *n* Ofenrohr *nt*; ~**pipe hat** *n* (*esp US inf*) Angströhre
f (*inf*), Zylinder *m*.
stow [stəʊ] *vt* **(a)** (*Naut*) *cargo* verladen, (ver)stauen; *ship*
(be)laden. **(b)** (*put away: also* ~ **away**) verstauen (*in* in +*dat*).
he ~**ed the money (away) behind the clock** er versteckte das
Geld hinter der Uhr. **(c)** (*sl: desist*) ~ **it!** hör auf!
♦ **stow away** *vi* als blinder Passagier fahren.
stowage ['stəʊɪdʒ] *n* (*stowing*) (Be)laden, Stauen *nt*; (*space*)
Stauraum *m*; (*charge*) Staugeld *nt*, Staugebühr *f*.
stowaway ['stəʊəweɪ] *n* blinder Passagier.
strabismus [strəˈbɪzməs] *n* (*Med*) Schielen *nt*.
straddle ['strædl] **1** *vt* (*standing*) breitbeinig or mit gespreizten
Beinen stehen über (+*dat*); (*sitting*) rittlings sitzen auf (+*dat*);
(*jumping*) grätschen über (+*acc*); (*fig*) *differences* überbrücken; **two continents** überspannen. **he/his legs** ~**d the**
fence/horse *etc* er saß rittlings auf dem Zaun/Pferd *etc*; **to** ~
the border/river sich über beide Seiten der Grenze/beide Ufer
des Flusses erstrecken; **to** ~ **an issue** (*US inf*) in einer Frage
zwischen zwei Lagern schwanken.
   2 *n* (*Sport*) Grätsche *f*, Grätschsprung *m*; (*in high jump*)
Scherprung *m*.
strafe [strɑːf] *vt* unter Beschuß nehmen; (*with machine guns*
also) mit Geschützfeuer bestreichen (*spec*); (*with shells also*)
mit Granaten bewerfen; (*with bombs*) bombardieren.
straggle ['strægl] *vi* **(a)** (*spread untidily*) (*houses, trees*) verstreut liegen; (*hair*) (*unordentlich*) hängen; (*plant*) in die
Länge) wuchern, in die Höhe schießen. **the town** ~**s on for miles**
die Stadt zieht sich über Meilen hin.
   (b) to ~ **behind** zurückbleiben, hinterherzockeln (*inf*); **to** ~
behind the leader in weitem Abstand hinter dem Führer
zurückbleiben or hinterherzockeln (*inf*); **to** ~ **along the road**
die Straße entlangbummeln or -zockeln (*inf*); **to** ~ **in/out**
vereinzelt kommen/gehen; **to** ~ **away from the main group** sich
nach und nach von der Hauptgruppe entfernen; **stop**
straggling bleibt beieinander.
straggler ['stræglə^r] *n* Nachzügler *m*.
straggling ['stræglɪŋ] *adj* **(a)** *children, cattle etc* weit verteilt;
(~ *behind*) zurückgeblieben, hinterherzottelnd (*inf*); *village*
sich lang hinziehend; *houses* zerstreut liegend; *group, row of*
houses auseinandergezogen. **(b)** (*inf: also* **straggly**) *hair*
unordentlich, zottig; *plant* hochgeschossen.
straight [streɪt] **1** *adj* (+*er*) **(a)** *line* gerade; *shot, pass* direkt;
stance, posture also aufrecht; *hair* glatt; *skirt, trousers* gerade
geschnitten. **your tie isn't** ~ deine Krawatte sitzt schief; **the**
picture isn't ~ das Bild hängt schief; **your hem isn't** ~ dein
Saum zipfelt or ist nicht gerade; **to pull sth** ~ etw
geradeziehen; **is my hat on** ~? sitzt mein Hut gerade?; **please**
put the picture ~ bitte hängen Sie das Bild gerade hin; **hold**
yourself ~ gerade!; **as** ~ **as a die** kerzengerade; *road*
schnurgerade; (*honest*) grundehrlich; **to keep a** ~ **face, to keep**
one's face ~ ernst bleiben, das Gesicht nicht verziehen; ~
left/right (*Boxing*) gerade Linke/Rechte.
   (b) (*clear*) *thinking* klar.
   (c) (*frank*) *answer, talking, question* offen, direkt; *piece of*
advice offen, ehrlich; *denial, refusal* offen, ohne Umschweife;
(*honest*) *person, dealings* ehrlich. **to be** ~ **with sb** offen und
ehrlich zu jdm sein; **to keep sb** ~ dafür sorgen, daß jd ehrlich
bleibt or nicht auf die schiefe Bahn gerät (*inf*).
   (d) (*plain,* ~*forward*) *drink* pur; (*Pol*) *fight* direkt; **yes or no,**
choice, exam pass einfach. ~ **A's** glatte Einsen; **to vote the** ~
ticket (*US Pol*) seine Stimme einer einzigen Partei (*dat*) geben;
he's a ~ **Democrat** er ist ein hundertprozentiger Demokrat; **to**
have a ~ **choice between** ... nur die Wahl zwischen ... haben.
   (e) (*continuous*) ununterbrochen. ~ **run** (*Cards*) Sequenz *f*;
for the third ~ **day** (*US*) drei Tage ohne Unterbrechung; **the** ~
line of succession to the throne die Thronfolge in der direkten
Linie; **our team had ten** ~ **wins** unsere Mannschaft gewann
zehnmal hintereinander or in ununterbrochener Folge.
   (f) (*Theat*) *production* konventionell; *actor* ernsthaft. **a** ~
play ein reines Drama.
   (g) *pred* (*in order*) **to be (all)** ~ in Ordnung sein; (*fig: clarified*
also) (*völlig*) geklärt sein; **now we're** ~ jetzt haben wir die
Sache geklärt; (*tidy*) jetzt ist alles in Ordnung; **to put things** ~
(*tidy*) alles in Ordnung bringen; (*clarify*) alles klären; **let's get**
this ~ das wollen wir mal klarstellen; **and get this** ~ und damit
wir uns richtig verstehen; **to put** or **set sb** ~ **about sth** jdm etw
klarmachen.
   (h) (*sl*) (*heterosexual*) normal, hetero (*inf*); (*conventional*)
etabliert, spießig (*pej*).
   2 *adv* **(a)** *hold, walk, fly, shoot, grow* gerade; *sit up, stand up*
also aufrecht; *hit* genau; *leap at, aim for* direkt; *above* genau,
direkt; *across* direkt. ~ **through sth** gerade durch etw; **he came** ~
at me er kam direkt or geradewegs auf mich zu; **it went** ~ **up in**
the air es flog senkrecht in die Luft; **to look** ~ **ahead** geradeaus
sehen; **the town lay** ~ **ahead of us** die Stadt lag direkt or genau
vor uns; **the airport is** ~ **ahead** der Flughafen ist geradeaus; **go**
~ **ahead with your plan** führen Sie Ihren Plan wie vorgesehen
durch; **to drive** ~ **on** geradeaus weiterfahren; **he drove** ~ **into a**
tree er fuhr direkt or voll (*inf*) gegen einen Baum; **the arrow**

went ~ to the target der Pfeil traf genau ins Ziel; to go ~ (criminal) keine krummen Sachen (mehr) machen (inf).

(b) (directly) direkt. I went ~ home ich ging direkt or sofort nach Hause; to look sb ~ in the eye jdm direkt or genau in die Augen sehen.

(c) (immediately) sofort. ~ after this sofort or unmittelbar danach; ~ away or off sofort, gleich, auf der Stelle; he said ~ off that ... er sagte ohne Umschweife or sofort, daß ...; to come ~ to the point sofort or gleich zur Sache kommen.

(d) (clearly) think, see klar.

(e) (frankly) offen, rundheraus, ohne Umschweife. I'll give it to you ~, you're fired ich sage es Ihnen rundheraus or ohne Umschweife, Sie sind entlassen; ~ out (inf) unverblümt (inf), rundheraus; to give or tell sb sth/it ~ from the shoulder jdm etw/es jdm unverblümt or ohne Umschweife sagen.

(f) (Theat) play, produce konventionell.

(g) drink pur.

3 *n* **(a)** (~ part, on race track) Gerade f; (road, rail) gerade Strecke. the final ~ die Zielgerade; the ~ and narrow der Pfad der Tugend; to keep sb on the ~ and narrow dafür sorgen, daß jd ehrlich bleibt or nicht auf die schiefe Bahn kommt.

(b) (~ line) Gerade f. to cut sth on the ~ etw gerade (ab)schneiden; (cloth) am Faden(lauf) entlang schneiden.

straight: ~ angle *n* gestreckter Winkel, Winkel von 180°; ~away (US) **1** *n* Gerade f; (road, rail) gerade Strecke; **2** *adv see* **straight 2 (c)**; ~ edge *n* Lineal nt.

straighten ['streɪtn] **1** *vt* **(a)** (make straight) gerademachen; picture gerade hinhängen; road, river begradigen; hat gerade aufsetzen; tablecloth, sheet, rope, clothes, tie geradeziehen; wire geradebiegen; one's shoulders straffen; hair glätten.

(b) (tidy) in Ordnung bringen.

2 *vi* (road, plant etc) gerade werden; (hair) glatt werden; (person) sich aufrichten.

3 *vr* ~ oneself sich aufrichten.

♦**straighten out 1** *vt sep* **(a)** (make straight) gerade machen; road begradigen; wire geradebiegen; rope geradeziehen; hair glätten.

(b) (put right) problem, situation klären; one's ideas ordnen; one's affairs in Ordnung bringen; misunderstanding (auf)klären; person (by discipline) auf die richtige Bahn bringen. to ~ oneself ~ ins richtige Gleis kommen; the problem will soon ~ itself ~ das Problem wird sich bald von selbst erledigen; to ~ things ~ die Sache in Ordnung bringen or geradebiegen; (clarify) Klarheit in die Sache bringen.

2 *vi* (road etc) gerade werden; (hair) glatt werden.

♦**straighten up 1** *vi* sich aufrichten. **2** *vt sep* **(a)** (make straight) gerade machen; papers ordentlich hinlegen; picture gerade hinhängen; hat gerade aufsetzen; lines also begradigen. **(b)** (tidy) in Ordnung bringen, aufräumen.

straight: ~faced [streɪt'feɪst] **1** *adj* ohne eine Miene zu verziehen; **2** *adj* to be ~faced keine Miene verziehen; ~forward *adj* (honest) person aufrichtig; explanation, look also offen, freimütig; (simple) question, problem einfach; I'm a ~ forward soldier ich bin ein einfacher Soldat; ~forwardly *adv see adj*; ~forwardness *n see adj* Aufrichtigkeit f, Offenheit f, Freimütigkeit f; Einfachheit, Klarheit f; ~ man *n* (Theat) Stichwortgeber *m* für einen Komiker; ~out **1** *adj* (esp US inf) resentment, threat unverblümt (inf), offen; opposition also kompromißlos; refusal glatt (inf); he's a ~out Democrat er ist durch und durch Demokrat; **2** *adv see* **straight 2 (e)**; ~way *adv* (liter) sogleich (liter).

strain¹ [streɪn] **1** *n* **(a)** (Mech) Beanspruchung f; (on rope, arch also) Spannung f; (on beams, floor also) Druck m. the ~ on a rope die Seilspannung; can you take some of the ~? können Sie mal mit festhalten/mit ziehen?; to put a (great) ~ on sth etw (stark) belasten; the wind put a ~ on the ship's rigging der Wind zerrte am Takelwerk (des Schiffes); to show signs of ~ Zeichen von Überlastung or Überbeanspruchung zeigen; to take the ~ off sth etw entlasten.

(b) (fig: mental, economic etc) Belastung f (on für); (effort) Anstrengung f; (pressure) (of job etc also) Beanspruchung f (of durch); (of responsibility) Last f. to be under a lot of ~ stark beansprucht sein; to suffer from (nervous) ~ (nervlich) überlastet sein, im Streß sein; I find her/that a bit of a ~ ich finde sie/das ziemlich anstrengend; to put a (great) ~ on sb/sth jdn/etw stark belasten; to put too great a ~ on sb/sth jdn/etw überlasten; to show signs of ~ Zeichen von Überlastung or Überanstrengung zeigen; to take the ~ off sb/sth jdn/etw entlasten; to be under ~ großen Belastungen ausgesetzt sein; the ~s of modern life die Belastungen or der Streß des heutigen Lebens; the ~ of six hours at the wheel die Anstrengung, sechs Stunden am Steuer zu sitzen.

(c) (muscle-~) (Muskel)zerrung f; (on eyes, heart etc) Überanstrengung f (on sen). back-/eye-/~ überanstrengter Rücken/überanstrengte Augen; new glasses will relieve the ~ eine neue Brille wird die Augen entlasten.

(d) ~s *pl* (of instrument, tune) Klänge *pl*; to the ~s of zu den Klängen (+gen).

2 *vt* **(a)** (stretch) spannen.

(b) (put ~ on) rope, beams, relationship, faith, budget belasten; nerves, patience also strapazieren; (put too much ~ on) überlasten; meaning, word dehnen. it ~s my nerves das zerrt an meinen Nerven; to ~ one's ears/eyes to ... angestrengt lauschen/gucken, um zu ...; to ~ every nerve jeden Nerv anspannen; to ~ oneself sich anstrengen; (excessively) sich überanstrengen; don't ~ yourself! (iro inf) überanstrenge dich bloß nicht!, reiß dir bloß kein Bein aus! (inf).

(c) (Med) muscle zerren; ankle, arm verrenken; back, eyes, voice anstrengen, strapazieren; (excessively) überanstrengen; heart belasten; (excessively) überlasten.

(d) (filter) (durch)sieben, (durch)seihen; (pour water off)

vegetables abgießen. to ~ off water Wasser abgießen; to ~ out solids feste Stoffe aussieben.

3 *vi* (exert effort) sich anstrengen, sich abmühen; (pull) zerren, ziehen; (fig: strive) sich bemühen, streben. to ~ to do sth sich anstrengen or abmühen, etw zu tun; to ~ at sth sich mit etw abmühen; (pull) an etw (dat) zerren or ziehen; to ~ at the leash (dog) an der Leine zerren; (fig) aufmucken, aufmüpfig werden (inf); to ~ after sth nach etw streben, sich um etw bemühen; to ~ after effects auf Effekte aus or erpicht sein; to ~ against sb sich an jdn drücken; to ~ against sth sich gegen etw stemmen; to ~ at a gnat and swallow a camel (prov) Mücken seihen und Kamele verschlucken.

strain² *n* **(a)** (streak) Hang, Zug m; (hereditary) Veranlagung f. a ~ of madness eine Veranlagung zum Wahnsinn; a ~ of weakness ein Hang m zur Schwäche.

(b) (style) Anflug m. there is a humorous ~ in his writing seine Schriften haben einen humorvollen Anflug or Zug.

(c) (breed) (animals) Rasse f; (of plants) Sorte f; (of virus etc) Art f; (old: race) Geschlecht nt (old).

strained [streɪnd] *adj* **(a)** liquids durchgesiebt, durchgeseiht; solids ausgesiebt; vegetables abgegossen.

(b) muscle gezerrt; back, eyes überanstrengt, strapaziert. to have a ~ ankle sich (dat) den Knöchel verrenkt haben.

(c) (unnatural) expression, performance, style unnatürlich, gekünstelt; laugh, smile, conversation gezwungen; meeting steif; voice, relations, atmosphere, nerves (an)gespannt. he looked rather ~ er sah ziemlich abgespannt aus.

strainer ['streɪnəʳ] *n* **(a)** (Cook) Sieb nt. **(b)** (Tech) Filter m.

strait [streɪt] *n* **(a)** (Geog) Meerenge, Straße f. the ~s of Dover/Gibraltar die Straße von Dover/Gibraltar.

(b) ~s *pl* (fig) Nöte, Schwierigkeiten *pl*; to be in dire or desperate ~s in großen Nöten sein, in einer ernsten Notlage sein.

straitened ['streɪtnd] *adj* means beschränkt; circumstances also bescheiden, dürftig.

strait: ~jacket *n* (lit, fig) Zwangsjacke f; ~-laced [streɪt'leɪst] *adj* prüde, puritanisch, spießig (inf).

strand¹ [strænd] **1** *n* (liter: beach) Gestade nt (liter).

2 *vt* ship, fish stranden lassen; person (in place) verschlagen, geraten lassen; (without money, help etc) seinem Schicksal überlassen. to be ~ed (ship, fish, shipwrecked person) gestrandet sein; to be (left) ~ed (person) festsitzen; (without money also) auf dem trockenen sitzen (inf); to leave sb ~ed jdn seinem Schicksal überlassen.

strand² *n* Strang m; (of hair) Strähne f; (of thread, wool) Faden m; (of wire) Litze f; (of vine etc) Ranke f; (of beads) Schnur f; (fig) (in melody etc) Melodienfolge f; (in story) Handlungsfaden m. a three-~ necklace eine dreireihige Halskette.

strange [streɪndʒ] *adj* (+er) **(a)** seltsam, sonderbar, merkwürdig. he told me the ~st story er erzählte mir eine sehr seltsame etc Geschichte; by a ~ chance eigenartigerweise, komischerweise; ~ to say so seltsam or komisch (inf) es klingen mag.

(b) (unfamiliar) country, surroundings, bed fremd; (unusual, unaccustomed) work, activity nicht vertraut, ungewohnt. I felt rather ~ at first zuerst fühlte ich mich ziemlich fremd; I feel ~ in a skirt ich komme mir in einem Rock komisch vor (inf); I am ~ to the work die Arbeit ist mir fremd or ist ungewohnt für mich; the boys are ~ to the school die Schule ist den Jungen noch nicht vertraut or noch fremd.

strangely ['streɪndʒlɪ] *adv* (oddly) seltsam, sonderbar, merkwürdig; act, behave also komisch (inf). ~ enough seltsamerweise, sonderbarerweise, merkwürdigerweise.

strangeness ['streɪndʒnɪs] *n* **(a)** (oddness) Seltsamkeit, Merkwürdigkeit f. **(b)** (unfamiliarity) Fremdheit f (of surroundings also, of work, activity) Unvertrautheit (of mit), Ungewohntheit f.

stranger ['streɪndʒəʳ] *n* Fremde(r) *mf*. he's a perfect ~ to me ich kenne ihn überhaupt nicht; I'm a ~ here myself ich bin selbst fremd hier; he is no ~ to London or kennt sich in London aus; he is no ~ to vice kein Laster ist ihm fremd; he is no ~ to misfortune Leid ist ihm nicht fremd; to be a ~ to this kind of work mit dieser Art von Arbeit nicht vertraut sein; hullo, ~! (inf) hallo, lange nicht gesehen; you're quite a ~ here (inf) man kennt dich ja gar nicht mehr; the little ~ (hum) der kleine Neuankömmling; S~s' Gallery (Brit Parl) Besuchergalerie f.

strangle ['stræŋgl] *vt* (murder) erwürgen, erdrosseln, strangulieren (form); (fig) cry, freedom, originality ersticken; impulse, protests abwürgen, ersticken. a ~d cry ein erstickter Schrei; this collar is strangling me (inf) dieser Kragen schnürt mir den Hals zu or ein.

stranglehold ['stræŋglhəʊld] *n* (lit) Würgegriff m, Manschette f; (fig) absolute Machtposition (on gegenüber). they have a ~ on us sie haben uns in der Zange.

strangler ['stræŋgləʳ] *n* Würger(in f) m.

strangling ['stræŋglɪŋ] *n* **(a)** (murder) Würgmord m. **(b)** (act of ~) Erwürgen, Erdrosseln, Strangulieren (form) nt; (fig) Ersticken nt.

strangulate ['stræŋgjʊleɪt] *vt* (Med) abschnüren, abbinden.

strangulation [ˌstræŋgjʊ'leɪʃən] *n* **(a)** (being strangled) Ersticken nt; (act of strangling) Erwürgen, Erdrosseln, Strangulieren (form) nt. death was due to ~ der Tod trat durch Ersticken ein. **(b)** (Med) Abschnürung, Abbindung f.

strap [stræp] **1** *n* Riemen m; (for safety also) Gurt m; (in bus etc also) Schlaufe, Lasche f; (shoe ~ also) Riemchen nt; (on ski-pants etc) Steg m; (watch ~) Band nt; (shoulder ~) Träger m. to give sb the ~ jdn verprügeln, jdn züchtigen.

2 *vt* **(a)** (fasten with ~) festschnallen (to an +dat). to ~ sth onto sth etw auf etw (acc) schnallen; he ~ped on his rucksack er schnallte sich (dat) den Rucksack auf; to ~ sb/sth down jdn/etw festschnallen; to ~ on one's watch/belt sich (dat) die Uhr umbinden/sich (dat) den Gürtel umschnallen; to ~ sb/on-

self in (in car, plane) jdn/sich anschnallen; to ~ up a suitcase einen Koffer zuschnallen.
  (b) (Med: also ~ up) bandagieren; dressing festkleben.
  (c) (punish) person verprügeln, züchtigen.
  (d) (US inf) to be ~ped (broke) pleite or blank sein (inf).

strap: ~-hang vi (inf) I had to ~-hang ich mußte stehen; ~-hanger n (inf) Pendler(in f) m; ~-hanging n (inf) Pendeln nt; ~less adj trägerlos, schulterfrei.

strapping ['stræpɪŋ] adj (inf) stramm; woman also drall.

Strasbourg ['stræzbɔːg] n Straßburg nt.

strata ['strɑːtə] pl of **stratum**.

stratagem ['strætɪdʒəm] n (Mil) Kriegslist f; (artifice) List f.

strategic [strə'tiːdʒɪk] adj strategisch; (strategically important) strategisch wichtig; (fig also) taktisch.

strategically [strə'tiːdʒɪkəlɪ] adv strategisch; (fig also) taktisch. to be ~ placed eine strategisch günstige Stellung haben; ~, his move was a mistake strategisch gesehen war das falsch.

strategist ['strætɪdʒɪst] n Stratege m; (fig also) Taktiker m.

strategy ['strætɪdʒɪ] n (a) (Mil) Strategie f; (Sport, fig also) Taktik f. (b) (art of ~) (Mil) Feldherrnkunst, Kriegskunst f; (fig) Taktieren nt.

stratification [ˌstrætɪfɪˈkeɪʃən] n (lit, fig) Schichtung f; (stratifying also) Schichtenbildung f; (Geol) Stratifikation f.

stratify ['strætɪfaɪ] 1 vt schichten; (Geol also) stratifizieren. a highly stratified society eine vielschichtige Gesellschaft. 2 vi (Geol) Schichten bilden, sich aufschichten; (fig) Schichten herausbilden, in Schichten zerfallen.

stratosphere ['strætəʊsfɪəʳ] n Stratosphäre f.

stratospheric [ˌstrætəʊsˈferɪk] adj stratosphärisch.

stratum ['strɑːtəm] n, pl **strata** (Geol, fig) Schicht f.

stratus ['strɑːtəs] n (Met) Stratus(wolke f) m, Schichtwolke f.

straw [strɔː] 1 n (a) (stalk) Strohhalm m; (collectively) Stroh nt no pl. it's the last ~ that breaks the camel's back (prov) das ist der Tropfen, der das Faß zum Überlaufen bringt (Prov); it's the last or final ~! (inf) das ist der Gipfel! (inf); it's a ~ in the wind das ist ein Vorzeichen; to clutch or grasp at ~s sich an einen Strohhalm klammern; man of ~ Strohmann m; (in politics) Marionette f; (set-up opponent) Scheingegner m; not worth a ~ (inf) keinen Pfifferling wert; see **drowning**.
  (b) (drinking ~) Trink- or Strohhalm m.
  2 adj attr Stroh-; basket aus Stroh.

strawberry ['strɔːbərɪ] n (plant, fruit) Erdbeere f.

strawberry in cpds Erdbeer-; ~ blonde 1 n Rotblonde(r) mf; she's a ~ blonde sie hat rotblondes Haar; 2 adj rotblond; ~ mark n (rotes) Muttermal.

straw: ~ boss n (US inf) Pro-forma-Vorgesetzte(r) m; ~-coloured adj strohfarben, strohfarbig; hair strohblond; ~ hat n Strohhut m; ~ man n Strohmann m; (in politics) Marionette f; (set-up opponent) Scheingegner m; ~ mattress n Strohsack m; ~ poll, ~ vote n Probeabstimmung f; (in election) Wählerbefragung f.

stray [streɪ] 1 vi (also ~ away) sich verirren, abirren; (also ~ about) (umher)streunen; (fig: thoughts, speaker) abschweifen. to ~ (away) from sth (lit, fig) von etw abkommen; to ~ from or off a path von einem Weg abkommen; to ~ from the path of virtue vom rechten Weg or vom Pfad der Tugend abkommen; the cattle ~ed into the road die Rinder haben sich auf die Straße verirrt; they ~ed into the enemy camp sie verirrten sich ins feindliche Lager; his thoughts ~ed to happier times seine Gedanken wanderten or schweiften zurück zu glücklicheren Zeiten.
  2 adj child, bullet, cattle verirrt; cat, dog etc streunend attr; (ownerless) herrenlos; (isolated) remarks, houses, customers, cases vereinzelt; (single) remark, success einzeln; (occasional) gelegentlich; thoughts flüchtig. a ~ car or two ein paar vereinzelte Autos.
  3 n (a) (dog, cat) streunendes Tier; (ownerless) herrenloses Tier. that cat's a ~ das ist eine herrenlose Katze; see **waif**.
  (b) ~s pl (Rad) (atmosphärische) Störungen pl.

streak [striːk] 1 n Streifen m; (of light) Strahl m; (in hair) Strähne f; (of fat also) Schicht f; (fig: trace) Spur f; (of jealousy, meanness etc) Zug m; (of madness, humour) Anflug m. ~ of lightning Blitz(strahl) m; there was a ~ of blood on his arm eine Blutspur zog sich über seinen Arm; there's a ~ of Spanish blood in her sie hat spanisches Blut in den Adern; his ~ of luck, his lucky ~ seine Glückssträhne; a winning/losing ~ eine Glücks-/Pechsträhne; he went past like a ~ (of lightning) er sauste vorbei wie der Blitz.
  2 vt streifen. to be ~ed gestreift sein; the sky was ~ed with red der Himmel hatte rote Streifen; hair ~ed with blonde/grey Haar mit blonden/grauen Strähnen, graumeliertes Haar; ~ed with dirt/paint schmutzverschmiert/mit Farbe beschmiert; ~ed with tears tränenverschmiert; meat ~ed with fat von Fett durchsetztes Fleisch; rock ~ed with quartz von Quarzadern durchzogener Stein.
  3 vi (a) (lightning) zucken; (inf: move quickly) flitzen (inf). to ~ along/past entlang-/vorbeiflitzen (inf).
  (b) (run naked) blitzen, flitzen.

streaker ['striːkəʳ] n Blitzer(in f), Flitzer(in f) m.

streaky ['striːkɪ] adj (+er) bacon durchwachsen; face verschmiert; window, mirror streifig, verschmiert.

stream [striːm] 1 n (a) (small river) Bach m, Flüßchen nt; (current) Strömung f. to go with/against the ~ (lit, fig) mit dem/gegen den Strom schwimmen.
  (b) (flow) (of liquid, air, people, cars) Strom m; (of light, tears) Flut f; (of words, excuses, abuse) Schwall m, Flut f. people were coming out in ~s Menschen strömten heraus; ~ of consciousness (Liter) Bewußtseinsstrom m.
  (c) (Brit Sch) Leistungsgruppe f.
  (d) (Tech) to be/come on ~ (oil well) in Betrieb sein/genommen werden; (oil) fließen/zu fließen anfangen.

2 vt (a) (liter) the walls ~ed water von den Wänden rann das Wasser; his face ~ed blood Blut rann or strömte ihm übers Gesicht.
  (b) (Brit Sch) in (Leistungs)gruppen einteilen.
  3 vi (a) (flow) (liquid) strömen, fließen, rinnen; (eyes: because of cold, gas etc) tränen; (air, sunlight) strömen, fluten; (people, cars etc) strömen. the wound was ~ing with blood Blut strömte or rann aus der Wunde; the walls were ~ing with water die Wände trieften vor Nässe; her eyes/cheeks were ~ing with tears Tränen strömten ihr aus den Augen/ihre Wangen waren tränenüberströmt.
  (b) (wave: flag, hair) wehen.

♦**stream down** vi (liquid) in Strömen fließen; herunterströmen; (cars) in Strömen herunterfahren; (hair) wallend herunterfallen (prep obj über +acc). the rain was ~ing ~ es regnete in Strömen; tears ~ed ~ her face Tränen rannen or strömten or liefen über ihr Gesicht.

♦**stream in** vi herein-/hineinströmen.

♦**stream out** vi heraus-/hinausströmen (of aus); (liquid also) herausfließen (of aus). her hair ~ed ~ behind her ihre Haare wehten nach hinten.

♦**stream past** vi vorbeiströmen (prep obj an +dat); (cars) in Strömen vorbeifahren (prep obj an +dat). the cars kept ~ing ~ der Strom der Autos brach nicht ab.

streamer ['striːməʳ] n (flag) Banner nt; (made of paper) Papier- or Luftschlange f; (made of cloth, as decoration) Band nt. ~ headline (US) Balkenüberschrift f.

streaming ['striːmɪŋ] 1 n (Brit Sch) Einteilung f in Leistungsgruppen.
  2 adj nose, windows triefend; eyes also tränend. I have a ~ cold ich habe einen fürchterlichen Schnupfen.

streamlet ['striːmlət] n (poet) Bächlein, Rinnsal (liter) nt.

streamline ['striːmlaɪn] vt racing car, aeroplane windschlüpfig machen, Stromlinienform geben (+dat); (fig) rationalisieren.

streamlined ['striːmlaɪnd] adj wing windschlüpfig; car, plane also stromlinienförmig; (fig) rationalisiert.

street [striːt] 1 n (a) Straße f. in or on the ~ auf der Straße, to live in or on a ~ in einer Straße wohnen; it's right up my ~ (fig inf) das ist genau mein Fall (inf); to be ~s ahead of or better than sb (fig inf) jdm haushoch überlegen sein (inf); ~s apart (fig) grundverschieden; he's not in the same ~ as her (fig inf) zwischen ihm und ihr ist ein himmelweiter Unterschied (inf); to take to the ~s (demonstrators) auf die Straße gehen; to be/go on the ~s (inf) auf den Strich gehen (inf); a woman of the ~s ein Mädchen von der Straße, ein Straßenmädchen nt; see **man**.
  (b) (inf: residents) Straße f.
  2 adj attr Straßen-.

street: ~ arab n (dated) herumstreunendes Gassenkind; ~ car n (US) Straßenbahn f; ~ cleaner n (esp US) Straßenkehrer(in f) or -feger(in f) m; ~ cry n Anpreisung f or Ausruf m (eines Straßenhändlers); ~ door n Tür f zur Straße hin; ~ fighting n Straßenkämpfe pl; ~ lamp n Straßenlaterne f; ~ level n at ~ level zu ebener Erde; ~ life n (inf) Leben nt auf der Straße; ~ light n Straßenlaterne f; ~ lighting n Straßenbeleuchtung f; ~ map n Stadtplan, Straßenplan m; ~ market n Straßenmarkt m; ~ musician n Straßenmusikant(in f) m; ~ plan n Straßen- or Stadtplan m; ~ sweeper n (person) Straßenkehrer(in f) or -feger(in f) m; (machine) Kehrmaschine f; ~ theatre or (US) theater n Straßentheater nt; ~ urchin n Straßen- or Gassenjunge m; ~walker n Prostituierte f, Straßenmädchen nt.

strength [streŋθ] n (a) (lit, fig) Stärke f; (of person, feelings) Kraft f; (of table, bolt, nail, wall) Stabilität f; (of material, character also, of conviction, shoes) Festigkeit f; (of views) Überzeugtheit f; (of imagination) Lebhaftigkeit f; (of reason, argument, evidence) Überzeugungskraft f; (of plea, protest) Eindringlichkeit f; (of letter) geharnischte or starke Ausdrucksweise; (of measure) Drastik f. ~ of character/will or mind Charakter-/Willensstärke f; to increase in or gain ~ stärker werden; he was swept away by the ~ of the current die Strömung war so stark, daß er abgetrieben wurde; on the ~ of sth auf Grund einer Sache (gen); he decided to be a writer on the ~ of selling one short story er beschloß, Schriftsteller zu werden, nachdem er eine einzige Kurzgeschichte verkauft hatte; his ~ failed him seine Kräfte versagten, ihn verließen die Kräfte; to be beyond sb's ~ über jds Kräfte (acc) gehen; to save one's ~ mit seinen Kräften haushalten; you don't know your own ~! du weißt gar nicht, wie stark du bist!; to argue from a position of ~ von einer starken Position aus argumentieren; to go from ~ to ~ einen Erfolg nach dem anderen erzielen or haben; he was a great ~ to me er war mir eine große Stütze.
  (b) (health) (of constitution) Robustheit, Kräftigkeit f; (of eyes, heart) Stärke f. the patient is recovering his or gaining ~ der Patient kommt wieder zu Kräften; when she has her ~ back wenn sie wieder bei Kräften ist.
  (c) (of colour) Kräftigkeit, Intensität f; (of acid, bleach) Stärke f; (of diluted solution) Konzentration f.
  (d) (numbers) (An)zahl f; (Mil) Stärke f. to be at full/bring up to ~ vollzählig sein/machen; to be up to/below ~ (die) volle Stärke/nicht die volle Stärke haben; to come in ~ in großer Zahl kommen, zahlreich erscheinen; the police were there in ~ ein starkes Polizeiaufgebot war da.
  (e) (of currency) Stärke f; (of market prices) Stabilität f; (of economy) Gesundheit f.

strengthen ['streŋθən] 1 vt stärken; material, shoes, building, protest verbessern; eyesight verbessern; muscles, patient also kräftigen; person (lit) Kraft geben (+dat); (fig) bestärken; currency, market festigen; affection also, effect vergrößern. to ~ sb's hand (fig) jdn bestärken or ermutigen; this only ~ed her determination das bestärkte sie nur in ihrem Entschluß.
  2 vi stärker werden; (wind, desire also) sich verstärken.

strenuous ['strenjʊəs] adj (a) (exhausting) anstrengend; march, game also ermüdend. (b) (energetic) attempt, supporter, support unermüdlich, energisch; attack, effort, denial hartnäckig; opposition, conflict, protest heftig.

strenuously ['strenjʊəslɪ] adv see adj (b).

strep throat ['strep'θrəʊt] n (esp US inf) Halsentzündung f.

streptococcus [,streptəʊ'kɒkəs] n, pl **streptococci** [,streptəʊ'kɒksaɪ] Streptokokkus m.

stress [stres] 1 n (a) (strain) Belastung f, Streß m; (Med) Überlastung f, Streß m. the **~es and strains of modern life** die Belastungen or der Streß des heutigen Lebens; **times of ~** Krisenzeiten pl, Zeiten pl großer Belastung; **to be under ~** großen Belastungen ausgesetzt sein; (as regards work) unter Streß stehen, im Streß sein; **to put sb under great ~** jdn großen Belastungen aussetzen; **to break down under ~/the ~** unter Streß or bei Belastung/unter dem Streß or unter der Belastung zusammenbrechen.

(b) (accent) Betonung f, Ton m; (fig: emphasis) Akzent m, (Haupt)gewicht nt. **to put or lay (great) ~ on sth** großen Wert auf etw (acc) legen, einer Sache (dat) großes Gewicht beimessen; fact, detail etw (besonders) betonen.

(c) (Mech) Belastung f, Beanspruchung f; (pressure) Belastung f, Druck m; (tension also) Spannung f. the **~ acting on the metal** die Belastung or Beanspruchung, der das Metall ausgesetzt ist.

2 vt (a) (lit, fig: emphasize) betonen; innocence also beteuern; good manners, subject großen Wert legen auf (+acc); fact, detail also hervorheben.

(b) (Mech) belasten, beanspruchen.

stress disease n Streßkrankheit, Managerkrankheit (inf) f.

stressed [strest] adj (a) syllable, word betont. (b) (under stress) person gestreßt, über(be)lastet.

stress fracture n Spannungsriß m.

stressful ['stresfʊl] adj anstrengend, stark beanspruchend attr. **a ~ situation** eine angespannte Lage.

stress mark n Akzent m, Betonungszeichen nt.

stretch [stretʃ] 1 n (a) (act of ~ing) Strecken, Dehnen nt. **to have a ~**, **to give oneself a ~** sich strecken or dehnen; (person also) sich recken; **to give sth a ~** (make wider) etw dehnen; (make longer also) etw strecken; **to be at full ~** (lit: material) bis zum äußersten gedehnt sein; (fig) (person) mit aller Kraft arbeiten; (factory etc) auf Hochtouren arbeiten (inf); (engine, production, work) auf Hochtouren laufen; **by no ~ of the imagination** beim besten Willen nicht; **only by some ~ of the imagination** nur mit viel Phantasie; **not by a long ~** bei weitem nicht.

(b) (elasticity) Elastizität, Dehnbarkeit f. **a fabric with plenty of ~** ein stark dehnbares or sehr elastisches Material; **there's not much ~ left in this elastic** das Gummi ist ziemlich ausgeleiert.

(c) (expanse) (of road etc) Strecke f, Stück nt; (on racecourse) Gerade f; (of wood, river, countryside etc) Stück nt; (of journey) Abschnitt, Teil m. **a straight ~ of road** eine gerade Strecke; **that ~ of water is called ...** dieser Gewässerlauf heißt ...; **in that ~ of the river** in dem Teil des Flusses; **for a long ~** über eine weite Strecke.

(d) (~ of time) Zeit(raum m or -spanne f) f. **for a long ~ of time** für (eine) lange Zeit, lange Zeit; **for hours at a ~** stundenlang; **three days at a ~** drei Tage an einem Stück or ohne Unterbrechung; **to do a ~** (sl: in prison) im Knast sein (sl).

2 adj attr dehnbar, Stretch-; socks, trousers, track suit etc Stretch-, ≈ Helanca-®; esp ski pants Lastex-.

3 vt (a) (extend, lengthen) strecken; (widen) jumper, gloves also, elastic, shoes dehnen; (spread) wings, blanket etc ausbreiten; (tighten) rope, canvas spannen. **to become ~ed** ausleiern; **a curtain was ~ed across the room** ein Vorhang war quer durchs Zimmer gezogen; **she ~ed the bedspread over the bed** sie breitete die Tagesdecke übers Bett; **to ~ sth tight** etw straffen, etw straffziehen; cover etw strammziehen; **to ~ one's legs** (go for a walk) sich (dat) die Beine vertreten (inf); **to ~ one's neck** den Hals recken.

(b) (make go further) meal, money strecken; (use fully) resources voll (aus)nutzen; credit voll beanspruchen; athlete, student etc fordern; one's abilities bis zum äußersten fordern. **to be fully ~ed** (person) voll ausgelastet sein.

(c) (strain) meaning, word äußerst weit fassen; truth, law, rules so sehr or so genau nehmen mit, großzügig auslegen. **this clause/law could be ~ed to allow ...** diese Klausel/dieses Gesetz könnte so weit gedehnt werden, daß sie/es ... zuläßt; **to ~ a point** ein Auge zudrücken, großzügig sein; **that's ~ing it too far/a bit** (far) das geht zu weit/fast zu weit.

4 vi (after sleep etc) sich strecken, sich dehnen; (person also) sich recken; (be elastic) sich dehnen, dehnbar sein; (extend) (time, area, authority, influence) sich erstrecken (to bis, over über +acc); (be enough: food, money, material) reichen (to für); (become looser) weiter werden; (become longer) länger werden. **the rope won't ~ to that** post das Seil reicht nicht bis zu dem Pfosten (hinüber); **to ~ to reach sth** sich recken, um etw zu erreichen; **she ~ed up to pick the apple** sie reckte sich, um den Apfel zu pflücken; **he ~ed down and touched his toes** er beugte sich nieder und berührte seine Zehen; **he ~ed across and touched her cheek** er reichte herüber und berührte ihre Wange; **to ~ back to** zurückreichen bis; **the fields ~ed away into the distance** die Felder dehnten sich bis in die Ferne aus; **the years ~ed (out) ahead of him** die Jahre dehnten sich vor ihm aus; **a life of misery ~ed (out) before her** vor ihr breitete sich ein Leben voll Kummer und Leid aus; **I can't/my purse won't ~ to that** so viel kann ich mir nicht erlauben/das läßt mein Geldbeutel nicht zu.

5 vr (a) (after sleep etc) sich strecken or dehnen; (person also) sich recken.

(b) (strain oneself) sich verausgaben. **if only he'd ~ himself** a little wenn er sich nur etwas anstrengen würde.

♦**stretch out** 1 vt sep arms, wings, blanket ausbreiten; leg, hand ausstrecken; foot vorstrecken; rope spannen; meeting, discussion, essay, story ausdehnen. **to ~ oneself ~** (on the ground) sich auf den Boden legen.

2 vi sich strecken; (inf: lie down) sich hinlegen; (countryside) sich ausbreiten; (in time) sich erstrecken, sich hinziehen (over über +acc). **her arm ~ed ~** sie streckte den Arm aus; **he ~ed ~/lay ~ed ~ on the bed** er legte sich (ausgestreckt) aufs Bett/er lag ausgestreckt auf dem Bett.

stretcher ['stretʃər] n (Med) (Trag)bahre f; (for shoes, gloves) Spanner m; (Art: for canvas) Rahmen m.

stretcher: **~-bearer** n Krankenträger m; **~ case** n Kranke(r) mf/Verletzte(r) mf, der/die nicht gehen kann; (Mil) Schwerverwundete(r) mf; **by the time I've finished this work I'll be a ~ case** (hum) bis ich diese Arbeit fertig habe, bin ich krankenhausreif (inf); **~ party** n Team nt von Krankenträgern.

stretch: **~ mark** n Dehnungsstreifen m; (through pregnancy) Schwangerschaftsstreifen m or -narbe f; **~ nylon** n Stretchnylon, Helanca ® nt; (esp for ski pants) Lastex nt.

stretchy ['stretʃɪ] adj (+er) elastisch, dehnbar.

strew [struː] pret, ptp **strewn** or **~ed** vt (scatter) verstreuen; flowers, gravel, sand streuen; (cover with) floor etc bestreuen. **to ~ one's clothes around (the room)** seine Kleider im Zimmer verstreuen; **dresses were ~n about the room** Kleider lagen im ganzen Zimmer verstreut herum; **the floor was ~n with ...** ... lagen überall auf dem Boden verstreut.

strewth interj (sl) see struth.

striated [straɪ'eɪtɪd] adj (form) (striped) gestreift; (furrowed) gefurcht; (Geol) mit Schliffen or Schrammen.

striation [straɪ'eɪʃən] n (form) (stripes) Streifen pl; (furrows) Furchen pl, Furchung f; (Geol) Schliffe, Schrammen pl.

stricken ['strɪkən] 1 (old) ptp of strike.

2 adj (liter: wounded) verwundet; (afflicted) leidgeprüft, schwergeprüft attr, schwer geprüft pred; (with grief) schmerzerfüllt, gramgebeugt (liter); (ill) leidend (geh); ship, plane in Not. **~ with guilt/fear** etc von Schuld/Angst etc erfüllt, von Angst ergriffen; **he gave me a ~ look** er sah mich schmerzerfüllt or (with guilt) schuldbewußt an; **~ in years** hochbetagt (geh); **to be ~ with illness** leidend sein (geh); **to be ~ with blindness** mit Blindheit geschlagen sein (geh).

-stricken adj suf (with emotion) -erfüllt; (by catastrophe) von ... heimgesucht. **panic-~** von Panik ergriffen.

strict [strɪkt] adj (+er) (a) (stern, severe) law, parent, principles, judge etc streng; order, ban, discipline also strikt; (obedience absolut, strikt; Catholic strenggläubig. **they're very ~ about time-keeping** es wird streng auf Pünktlichkeit geachtet.

(b) (precise) streng; accuracy, neutrality, secrecy also absolut; translation, meaning genau. **in the ~ sense of the word** genau genommen; **in ~ confidence** streng vertraulich; **there is a ~ time limit** on that das ist zeitlich genau begrenzt.

strictly ['strɪktlɪ] adv (a) streng. **smoking is ~ forbidden** Rauchen ist streng or strengstens verboten.

(b) (precisely) genau; (absolutely) absolut, streng. **to be ~ accurate** um ganz genau zu sein; **~ in confidence** ganz im Vertrauen; **~ personal/confidential** privat/streng vertraulich; **~ speaking** genau genommen; **not ~ true** nicht ganz richtig; **~ between ourselves** ganz unter uns.

strictness ['strɪktnɪs] n (a) Strenge f; (of order, discipline also) Striktheit f. (b) (preciseness) Genauigkeit f. the **~ of their neutrality/secrecy** ihre strenge or absolute Neutralität/Geheimhaltung.

stricture ['strɪktʃər] n (a) usu pl (criticism) (scharfe) Kritik no pl. **to make or pass ~s upon sb** jdn (scharf) kritisieren. (b) (Med) Verengung, Striktur (spec) f.

stride [straɪd] (vb: pret strode, ptp stridden ['strɪdn]) 1 n (step) Schritt m; (gait also) Gang m; (fig) Fortschritt m. **to get into one's/its ~** (fig) in Schwung or in Fahrt kommen; **to take sth in one's ~** mit etw spielend fertigwerden; exam, interview etw spielend schaffen; **to put sb off his ~** jdn aus dem Konzept bringen; **he took the disasters in his ~** die Katastrophen schienen spurlos an ihm vorübergegangen zu sein.

2 vi schreiten (geh), mit großen Schritten gehen. **to ~ along** ausschreiten (geh); **to ~ away or off** sich mit schnellen Schritten entfernen, davonschreiten (geh); **to ~ up to sb** (mit großen Schritten) auf jdn zugehen, auf jdn zuschreiten (geh); **to ~ up and down** auf- und abgehen or -schreiten (geh).

stridency ['straɪdənsɪ] n see adj Schrillheit, Durchdringlichkeit f; Grellheit f; Streitbarkeit f; Schärfe f; Stärke f.

strident ['straɪdənt] adj sound, voice schrill, durchdringend; colour grell; person streitbar; protest, criticism, tone scharf; demand, protest lautstark.

stridently ['straɪdəntlɪ] adv talk etc schrill, durchdringend; object, protest scharf, lautstark; demand, behave lautstark.

strife [straɪf] n Unmut (geh), Unfriede m; (in family, between friends) Zwietracht f (geh). **armed ~** bewaffneter Konflikt; **party ~** Zwietracht f (geh) or Zwistigkeiten pl in der Partei; **internal ~** innere Kämpfe pl; **civil/industrial ~** Auseinandersetzungen pl in der Bevölkerung/Industrie; **to cease from ~** (liter) allen Zwist begraben (geh).

strike [straɪk] (vb: pret struck, ptp struck or (old) **stricken**) 1 n (a) Streik, Ausstand m. **official/unofficial ~** offizieller/ wilder Streik; **to be on ~** streiken, im Ausstand sein; **to be on official/unofficial ~** offiziell/wild streiken; **to come out or go on ~** in den Streik or Ausstand treten; **to bring sb out on ~** jdn zum Streik veranlassen; see hunger.

(b) (discovery of oil, gold etc) Fund m. **a big oil ~** ein großer Ölfund; **to make a ~** fündig werden; **a lucky ~** ein Treffer, ein Glücksfall m; **to make a lucky ~** Glück haben, einen Treffer landen (inf).

(c) (*Baseball*) verfehlter Schlag; (*Ten-pin bowling*) alle zehne. **to get a ~** alle zehne werfen, abräumen (*inf*); **to have the ~** (*Cricket*) schlagen.

(d) (*Fishing*) **he got three ~s** drei haben angebissen.

(e) (*Mil: attack*) Angriff *m*.

(f) (*act of striking*) Schlag *m*.

2 *vt* **(a)** (*hit*) schlagen; *door* schlagen an *or* gegen (+*acc*); *nail, table* schlagen auf (+*acc*); *metal, hot iron etc* hämmern; (*stone, blow, bullet etc*) treffen; (*snake*) beißen; (*pain*) durchzucken, durchfahren; (*misfortune, disaster*) treffen; (*disease*) befallen. **to ~ one's fist on the table, to ~ the table with one's fist** mit der Faust auf den Tisch schlagen; **to ~ sb/sth a blow** jdm/einer Sache einen Schlag versetzen; **who struck the first blow?** wer hat zuerst (zu)geschlagen?; **to ~ a blow for sth** (*fig*) eine Lanze für etw brechen; **to ~ a blow (at sth)** (*fig*) einen Schlag (gegen etw) führen; **to ~ one's hands together** in die Hände klatschen; **to be struck by lightning** vom Blitz getroffen werden; **he struck his forehead in surprise** er schlug sich (*dat*) überrascht an die Stirn; **to ~ 38 (per minute)** 38 Ruderschläge (pro Minute) machen.

(b) (*collide with, meet*) (*person*) stoßen gegen; (*spade*) stoßen auf (+*acc*); (*car*) fahren gegen; *ground* aufschlagen *or* auftreffen auf (+*acc*); (*ship*) auflaufen auf (+*acc*); (*sound, light*) *ears, eyes* treffen; (*lightning*) *person* treffen; *tree* einschlagen in (+*acc*), treffen. **to ~ one's head against sth** mit dem Kopf gegen etw *or* sich (*dat*) den Kopf an etw (*acc*) stoßen; **to ~ difficulties/obstacles** (*fig*) in Schwierigkeiten geraten/auf Hindernisse stoßen; **a terrible sight struck my eyes** plötzlich sah ich etwas Schreckliches.

(c) (*sound*) *instrument* zu spielen anfangen; *string, chord, note* anschlagen; (*clock*) schlagen. **to ~ the piano/guitar** in die Tasten/Saiten greifen; **to ~ the hour** die volle Stunde schlagen; **that struck a familiar note** das kam mir/ihm *etc* bekannt vor; *see* **note**.

(d) (*Hort*) *cutting* schneiden; (*plant*) *roots* schlagen.

(e) (*occur to*) in den Sinn kommen (+*dat*). **to ~ sb as cold/unlikely** *etc* jdm kalt/unwahrscheinlich *etc* vorkommen; **that ~s me as a good idea** das kommt mir sehr vernünftig vor; **has it ever struck you that ...?** (*occurred to you*) haben Sie je daran gedacht, daß ...?; (*have you noticed*) ist Ihnen je aufgefallen, daß ...?; **it ~s me that ...** (*I have the impression*) ich habe den Eindruck, daß ...; (*I am noticing*) mir fällt auf, daß ...; **it struck me how ...** (*occurred to me*) mir ging plötzlich auf, wie ...; (*I noticed*) mir fiel auf, wie ...; **the funny side of it struck me later** erst später ging mir auf, wie lustig das war; **a thought struck me** mir kam plötzlich ein Gedanke.

(f) (*impress*) beeindrucken. **to be struck by sth** von etw beeindruckt sein; **how does it ~ you?** wie finden Sie das?, was halten Sie davon?; **how did the film ~ you?** wie fanden Sie den Film?; **how does she ~ you?** welchen Eindruck haben Sie von ihr?; **she struck me as being very competent** sie machte auf mich einen sehr fähigen Eindruck; *see also* **struck**.

(g) (*produce, make*) *coin, medal* prägen; (*fig*) *agreement, truce* sich einigen auf (+*acc*), aushandeln. **to ~ a light/match** Feuer machen/ein Streichholz anzünden; **to ~ sparks from sth** Funken aus etw schlagen; **to be struck blind/deaf/dumb** blind/taub/stumm werden, mit Blindheit/Taubheit/Stummheit geschlagen werden (*geh*); **to ~ fear** *or* **terror into sb's heart** jdn mit Angst *or* Schrecken erfüllen; **~ a light!** (*sl*) ach du grüne Neune! (*inf*), hast du da noch Töne! (*inf*).

(h) (*find*) *gold, oil, correct path* finden, stoßen auf (+*acc*). **to ~ it rich** das große Geld machen; *see* **oil**.

(i) (*make*) *path* hauen.

(j) (*take down*) *camp, tent* abbrechen; (*Naut*) *flag, sail* einholen, streichen; *mast* kappen, umlegen; (*Theat*) *set* abbauen.

(k) (*remove*) streichen. **to be struck** *or* (*US*) **stricken from a list/the record** von einer Liste/aus dem Protokoll gestrichen werden.

3 *vi* **(a)** (*hit*) treffen; (*lightning*) einschlagen; (*snake*) zubeißen; (*tiger*) die Beute schlagen; (*attack, Mil etc*) zuschlagen, angreifen; (*disease*) zuschlagen; (*panic*) ausbrechen. **to ~ against sth** gegen etw stoßen; **to ~ at sb/sth** (*hit*) nach jdm/etw schlagen; (*fig: at democracy, existence*) an etw (*dat*) rütteln; **they struck at his weakest point** sie trafen ihn an seinem wundesten Punkt; **to ~ at the roots of sth** etw an der Wurzel treffen; **they were within striking distance of the enemy camp/success** das feindliche Lager/der Erfolg war in greifbarer Nähe; **the chill struck through to his very bones** die Kälte ging ihm bis aufs Mark; **the snake struck at me** die Schlange fuhr auf mich los; **we're waiting for the blow to ~** wir warten darauf, daß es uns trifft; *see* **home, iron**.

(b) (*clock*) schlagen. **when midnight ~s** wenn es Mitternacht schlägt.

(c) (*workers*) streiken.

(d) \(*match*) zünden, angehen.

(e) (*Naut: run aground*) auflaufen (*on* auf +*acc*).

(f) (*Fishing*) anbeißen.

(g) inspiration struck er/sie *etc* hatte eine Eingebung; **to ~ on a new idea** eine neue Idee haben, auf eine neue Idee kommen.

(h) (*take root*) Wurzeln schlagen.

(i) (*go in a certain direction*) **to ~ across country** querfeldein gehen; **to ~ into the woods** sich in die Wälder schlagen; **to ~ right/left** sich nach rechts/links wenden; (*road*) nach rechts/links abbiegen; **the sun struck through the mist** die Sonne brach durch den Dunst.

♦**strike back 1** *vi* zurückschlagen; (*fig also*) sich wehren, sich zur Wehr setzen. **to ~ ~ at sb** jds Angriff (*acc*) erwidern; (*fig*) sich gegen jdn wehren *or* zur Wehr setzen. **2** *vt sep* zurückschlagen.

♦**strike down** *vt sep* niederschlagen; (*God*) *enemies* ver-

nichten; (*fig*) zu Fall bringen. **to be struck ~** niedergeschlagen werden; (*by illness*) getroffen werden; (*by blow*) zu Boden gestreckt werden; **he was struck ~ in his prime** er wurde in seiner Blüte dahingerafft.

♦**strike in** *vi* (*inf: interrupt*) sich einmischen, dazwischenplatzen (*inf*).

♦**strike off 1** *vt sep* **(a)** (*cut off*) abschlagen.

(b) (*remove*) (*from list*) (aus)streichen; *solicitor* die Lizenz entziehen (+*dat*); *doctor* die Zulassung entziehen (+*dat*); (*from price*) abziehen (*prep obj* von). **to be struck ~** (*Med*) die Zulassung verlieren; (*Jur*) die Lizenz verlieren.

(c) (*print*) drucken. **to ~ ~ a proof** einen Bürstenabzug machen.

2 *vi* (*set off*) gehen; (*road etc also*) abbiegen.

♦**strike out 1** *vi* **(a)** (*hit out*) schlagen. **to ~ ~ wildly** wild um sich schlagen; **to ~ ~ at sb** (*lit, fig*) jdn angreifen *or* attackieren.

(b) (*change direction*) zuhalten (*for, towards* auf +*acc*); (*set out*) sich aufmachen, losziehen (*inf*) (*for* zu). **to ~ ~ for home** sich auf den Heimweg machen; **to ~ ~ on one's own** (*lit*) allein losziehen; (*fig*) eigene Wege gehen; **to ~ ~ in a new direction** (*fig*) neue Wege gehen.

(c) (*Baseball*) „aus" sein.

2 *vt sep* (*aus*)streichen. **to ~ sth ~ of the record** etw aus dem Protokoll streichen.

♦**strike through** *vt sep* durchstreichen.

♦**strike up 1** *vi* (*band etc*) einsetzen, anfangen (zu spielen). **2** *vt insep* **(a)** (*band*) *tune* anstimmen. **~ ~ the band!** Musik! **(b)** *friendship* schließen, anknüpfen; *conversation* anfangen.

strike: **~ action** *n* Streikmaßnahmen *pl*; **~ ballot** *n* Urabstimmung *f*; **~-bound** *adj* bestreikt, vom Streik betroffen; **~breaker** *n* Streikbrecher *m*; **~breaking** *n* Streikbruch *m*; **~ call** *n* Aufruf *m* zum Streik; **~ force** *n* (*Mil*) Kampftruppe *f*; **~ fund** *n* Streikkasse *f*; **~-leader** *n* Streikführer *m*; **~ pay** *n* Streikgeld(er *pl*) *nt*.

striker ['straikə[r]] *n* **(a)** (*worker*) Streikende(r), Ausständige(r) *mf*. **(b)** (*Ftbl*) Stürmer *m*.

striking ['straikiŋ] *adj* **(a)** (*arresting*) *contrast, colour, resemblance etc* auffallend, bemerkenswert; *difference* verblüffend, erstaunlich; *appearance, beauty* eindrucksvoll. **a ~ example of sth** ein hervorragendes Beispiel für etw.

(b) *attr worker* streikend.

(c) *attr clock* mit Schlagwerk. **the ~ clock keeps me awake** das Schlagen der Uhr läßt mich nicht schlafen; **~ mechanism** Schlagwerk *nt*.

strikingly ['straikiŋli] *adv see adj* (a).

strine [strain] *n* (*hum inf*) Australisches Englisch.

string [striŋ] (*vb: pret, ptp* **strung**) **1** *n* **(a)** (*pl rare: cord*) Schnur, Kordel *f*, Bindfaden *m*; (*on apron etc*) Band *nt*; (*on anorak, belt*) Kordel *f*; (*of puppet*) Faden *m*, Schnur *f*, Draht *m*. **to have sb on a ~** (*fig inf*) jdn am Gängelband halten (*inf*); **to pull ~s** (*fig inf*) Fäden ziehen, Beziehungen spielen lassen; **without ~s, with no ~s attached** ohne Bedingungen; **a relationship with no ~s attached** eine völlig lockere Beziehung; **he wants a girlfriend but no ~s attached** er möchte eine Freundin, will sich aber in keiner Weise gebunden fühlen; **the offer is without ~s** an das Angebot sind keinerlei Bedingungen geknüpft.

(b) (*row*) (*of beads, onions etc*) Schnur *f*; (*of racehorses etc*) Reihe *f*; (*of people*) Schlange *f*; (*of vehicles*) Kette, Schlange *f*; (*fig: series*) Reihe *f*; (*of lies, curses*) Haufen *m*, Reihe *f*.

(c) (*of musical instrument, tennis racquet etc*) Saite *f*; (*of bow*) Sehne *f*. **the ~s** *pl* (*instruments*) die Streichinstrumente *pl*; (*players*) die Streicher *pl*; **he plays in the ~s** ist Streicher, er gehört zu den Streichern; **a twelve-~ guitar** eine zwölfsaitige Gitarre; **to have two ~s** *or* **a second ~** *or* **more than one ~ to one's bow** zwei Eisen im Feuer haben; **history/translating is my second ~** ich kann jederzeit auf Geschichte/Übersetzungen als zweite Möglichkeit zurückgreifen.

(d) (*Bot*) Faden *m*.

2 *vt* **(a)** (*put on ~*) aufreihen, auffädeln, aufziehen. **to ~ objects/sentences etc together** Gegenstände zusammenbinden *or* -schnüren/Sätze *etc* aneinanderreihen; **she can't even ~ two sentences together** sie bringt keinen vernünftigen Satz zusammen; **she can't ~ her thoughts together coherently** sie ist unfähig, zusammenhängend zu denken.

(b) *violin etc, tennis racquet* (mit Saiten) bespannen, besaiten; *bow* spannen; *see* **highly-strung**.

(c) *beans* abfasern, (die) Fäden (+*gen*) abziehen.

(d) (*space out*) aufreihen. **they strung lights in the trees** sie haben Lampen in die Bäume gehängt.

♦**string along** (*inf*) **1** *vt sep* **to ~ sb ~** jdn hinhalten. **2** *vi* (*go along, play along with*) sich anschließen (*with dat*).

♦**string out 1** *vi* sich verteilen. **the children strung ~ behind the teacher** die Kinder gingen in weiten Abständen hinter dem Lehrer her. **2** *vt sep lanterns, washing* aufhängen; *guards, posts* verteilen.

♦**string up** *vt sep* **(a)** (*suspend with string*) aufhängen; (*inf: hang*) aufknüpfen (*inf*). **(b)** (*excite*) **to be strung ~** aufgeregt sein; **to ~ oneself ~ to do sth** sich seelisch und moralisch darauf vorbereiten, etw zu tun.

string: **~ bag** *n* (*esp Brit*) Einkaufsnetz *nt*; **~ band** *n* Streichorchester *nt*; **~ bass** *n* Kontrabaß *m*; **~ bean** *n* (*esp US*) (*bean*) grüne Bohne; (*fig: person*) Bohnenstange *f* (*hum inf*).

stringed [striŋd] *adj instrument* Saiten-; (*played with bow also*) Streich-.

stringency ['strindʒənsi] *n see adj* Strenge *f*; Härte *f*; Schärfe *f*. **economic ~** strenge Sparmaßnahmen *pl*.

stringent ['strindʒənt] *adj standards, laws, discipline* streng; *rules, testing, training etc also* hart; *measures also* schärfste(r, s), energisch; *market* gedrückt. **~ economies**

schärfste Sparmaßnahmen *pl*; **they have to practise ~ economy** sie müssen eisern sparen.

stringently ['strindʒəntlɪ] *adv control* streng; *enforce, train also* hart; *deal with* schärfstens, energisch; *economize* eisern.

stringer ['strɪŋəʳ] *n (Press sl)* Lokalreporter(in *f*) *m*.

string: **~ instrument** *n* Saiteninstrument *nt*; *(played with bow also)* Streichinstrument *nt*; **~ player** *n* Streicher(in *f*) *m*; **~-puller** *n* Drahtzieher *m*; **~-pulling** *n* Spielenlassen *nt* von Beziehungen; **~ quartet** *n* Streichquartett *nt*; **~ vest** *n* Netzhemd *nt*.

stringy ['strɪŋɪ] *adj (+er) meat* sehnig, zäh, faserig; *vegetable* faserig, voller Fäden; *person* sehnig; *plant, seaweed, root* lang und dünn. **the cheese goes ~ when it melts** der Käse zieht beim Schmelzen Fäden.

strip [strɪp] **1** *n* **(a)** *(narrow piece)* Streifen *m*; *(of land also)* (schmales) Stück; *(of metal)* Band *nt*; *see* comic, tear off.
(b) *(Brit Sport)* Trikot *nt*, Dreß *m*.
(c) *(inf: air~)* Start- und Landebahn, Piste *(inf) f*.
(d) *(inf: ~tease)* **to do a ~** strippen *(inf)*.
2 *vt* **(a)** *(remove clothes etc from) person* ausziehen; *bed* abziehen; *wall (remove paint from)* abkratzen; *(remove paper from)* die Tapeten abziehen von; *wallpaper* abziehen; *(remove contents from)* ausräumen. **to ~ sb of his clothes** jdm die Kleider ausziehen; **to ~ sb naked** *or* **to the skin** jdn bis auf die Haut *or* nackt ausziehen; **to ~ a house of its contents** ein Haus ausräumen; **to ~ a room of all its pictures** alle Bilder aus einem Zimmer entfernen; **to ~ sth from** *or* **off sth** etw von etw entfernen; **to ~ a tree of fruit, to ~ the fruit off** *or* **from a tree** einen Baum abernten; **the wind ~ped the leaves from** *or* **off the trees** der Wind wehte die Blätter von den Bäumen; **to ~ the bark from the trees** Bäume schälen *or* entrinden; **to ~ sth away** *(lit, fig)* etw wegnehmen, etw entfernen; **~ped of sth** ohne etw; **~ped of official language, this means ...** in einfachen Worten heißt das ...
(b) *(fig: deprive of)* berauben *(of gen)*; *honours, title also* entkleiden *(geh) (of gen)*. **he was ~ped of his titles** seine Titel wurden ihm aberkannt.
(c) *(Tech) (damage) gear* kaputtmachen *(inf)*, beschädigen; *screw* überdrehen; *(dismantle) engine, car, gun* auseinandernehmen, zerlegen. **to ~ the thread (off a screw)** eine Schraube überdrehen.
3 *vi (remove clothes)* sich ausziehen; *(at doctor's)* sich freimachen; *(perform ~tease)* strippen *(inf)*. **to ~ naked** sich bis auf die Haut *or* ganz ausziehen; **to ~ to the waist** den Oberkörper freimachen; **~ped to the waist** mit nacktem Oberkörper.

♦**strip down** *vt sep engine* auseinandernehmen, zerlegen.

♦**strip off 1** *vt sep clothes* ausziehen; *berries, leaves* abmachen *(prep obj* von*)*; *(wind)* herunterwehen *(prep obj* von*)*; *paper* abziehen *(prep obj* von*)*; *buttons, ornaments* entfernen, abmachen *(prep obj* von*)*; *fruit skin, bark* abschälen, ablösen *(prep obj* von*)*. **to ~ ~ the branches** die Blätter vom Zweig entfernen; die Äste entfernen.
2 *vi* **(a)** *(take one's clothes off)* sich ausziehen; *(at doctor's)* sich freimachen; *(in striptease)* strippen *(inf)*.
(b) *(bark)* sich abschälen lassen; *(paper)* sich abziehen lassen.

strip: **~ cartoon** *n* Comic(strip) *m*; **~ club** *n* Striptease-Club *m*; **~ cropping** *n* Streifenpflanzung *f*.

stripe [straɪp] *n* **(a)** Streifen *m*.
(b) *(Mil)* (Ärmel)streifen, Winkel *m*. **to gain** *or* **get/lose one's ~s** befördert/degradiert werden.
(c) *(old: stroke)* Schlag, Hieb *m*.
(d) *(US: kind) (of politics)* Färbung, Richtung *f*; *(of character, opinion)* Art *f*, Schlag *m*.
(e) **~s** *pl (US inf: prison uniform)* Sträflingsanzug *m (inf)*.

striped [straɪpt] *adj* gestreift, Streifen-. **~ with ... mit ...** Streifen; **to be ~ with grey** graue Streifen haben, grau gestreift sein.

strip: **~ light** *n (esp Brit)* Neonröhre *f*; **~ lighting** *n (esp Brit)* Neonlicht *nt or* -beleuchtung *f*.

stripling ['strɪplɪŋ] *n (liter)* Bürschchen *nt*; *(pej also)* Grünschnabel *m*.

strip: **~ mill** *n* Walzwerk *nt*; **~ mining** *n (esp US)* Abbau *m* über Tage.

stripper ['strɪpəʳ] *n* **(a)** *(performer)* Stripper(in *f*), Stripteasetänzer(in *f*) *m*. **(b)** *(paint-~)* Farbentferner *m*; *(wallpaper ~)* Tapetenlöser *m*.

strip: **~ poker** *n* Strip-Poker *nt*; **~ show** *n* Striptease(schau *or* -show *f*) *m or nt*; **~tease 1** *n* Striptease *m or nt*; **to do a ~tease** strippen *(inf)*, einen Striptease machen; **2** *adj attr* Striptease-.

stripy ['straɪpɪ] *adj (+er) (inf)* gestreift.

strive [straɪv] *pret* **strove**, *ptp* **striven** ['strɪvn] *vi (exert oneself)* sich bemühen; *(fight)* kämpfen. **to ~ to do sth** bestrebt *or* bemüht sein, etw zu tun; **to ~ for** *or* **(old) after sth** etw anstreben, nach etw streben; **to ~ against sth** gegen etw (an)kämpfen; **to ~ with sb/sth** mit jdm/etw ringen *or* kämpfen.

strobe [strəub] **1** *adj* stroboskopisch. **2** *n* stroboskopische Beleuchtung.

stroboscope ['strəubəskəup] *n* Stroboskop *nt*.

stroboscopic [‚strəubəu'skɒpɪk] *adj* stroboskopisch.

strode [strəud] *pret of* **stride**.

stroke [strəuk] **1** *n* **(a)** *(blow)* Schlag, Hieb *m*; *(of sword also)* Streich *m (old)*. **a ~ of lightning** ein Blitz(schlag) *m*.
(b) *(Cricket, Golf, Rowing, Tennis)* Schlag *m*; *(Billiards)* Stoß *m*; *(Swimming) (movement)* Zug *m*; *(type of ~)* Stil *m*. **they are rowing (at) a fast ~** sie rudern mit hoher Schlagzahl; **to put sb off his ~** *(fig)* jdn aus dem Takt *or* Konzept bringen.
(c) *(Rowing: person)* Schlagmann *m*.
(d) *(of pen, brush etc)* Strich *m*; *(fig) (of work)* Schlag *m*; *(in diplomacy, business)* Schachzug *m*. **he doesn't do a ~ (of work)**

er tut keinen Schlag *(inf)*, **er rührt keinen Finger** *(inf)*; **a ~ of genius** ein genialer Einfall; **a ~ of luck** ein Glücksfall *m*; **we had a ~ of luck** wir hatten Glück; **with one ~ of the pen** *(lit, fig)* mit einem Federstrich; **at a** *or* **one ~** mit einem Schlag.
(e) *(of clock)* Schlag *m*. **on the ~ of twelve** Punkt zwölf (Uhr).
(f) *(of piston)* Hub *m*. **two-~ engine** Zweitaktmotor *m*.
(g) *(Med)* Schlag *m*. **to have a ~** einen Schlag(anfall) bekommen.
(h) *(caress)* Streicheln *nt no pl*. **to give sb/sth a ~** jdn/etw streicheln; **with gentle ~s** mit sanftem Streicheln.
2 *vt* **(a)** streicheln. **he ~d his chin** er strich sich *(dat)* übers Kinn; **to ~ one's hair down** sich *(dat)* das Haar glattstreichen.
(b) **to ~ a boat (to victory)** als Schlagmann (ein Boot zum Sieg) rudern.

stroke play *n (Golf)* Zählspiel *nt*.

stroll [strəul] **1** *n* Spaziergang, Bummel *m*. **to go for** *or* **have** *or* **take a ~** einen Spaziergang *or* Bummel machen.
2 *vi* spazieren, bummeln. **to ~ along/around** herumspazieren *or* -bummeln *or* -schlendern; **to ~ along the road** die Straße entlangspazieren *or* -bummeln *or* -schlendern; **to ~ around the house/town** um das Haus herumspazieren/durch die Stadt bummeln; **to ~ up to sb** auf jdn zuschlendern; **to ~ in/(to the room)** (ins Zimmer) herein-/hineinspazieren *or* -schlendern; **to ~ out (of the room)** (aus dem Zimmer) hinaus-/herausspazieren *or* -schlendern; **to ~ up and down (the road)** die Straße auf und ab spazieren *or* bummeln *or* schlendern.

stroller ['strəuləʳ] *n* **(a)** *(walker)* Spaziergänger(in *f*) *m*. **(b)** *(esp US: push-chair)* Sportwagen *m*.

strolling ['strəulɪŋ] *adj attr actor, minstrel* fahrend.

strong [strɒŋ] **1** *adj (+er)* **(a)** stark; *(physically) person, material, kick, hands, grip also, voice* kräftig; *table, bolt, nail, wall* stabil, solide; *shoes* fest; *(strongly marked) features* ausgeprägt. **you need a ~ stomach to be a nurse** als Krankenschwester muß man allerhand verkraften können.
(b) *(healthy)* kräftig; *person, constitution also* robust; *teeth also, eyes, eyesight, heart, nerves* gut. **when you're ~ again** wenn Sie wieder bei Kräften sind; **he's getting ~er every day** er wird mit jedem Tag wieder kräftiger.
(c) *(powerful, effective)* stark; *character, conviction, views* fest; *country* mächtig; *candidate, case* aussichtsreich; *influence, temptation* groß, stark; *reason, argument, evidence* überzeugend; *protest, plea* energisch; *measure* drastisch; *letter* geharnischt, in starken Worten abgefaßt; *(Liter) plot, sequence, passage* gut, stark *(sl)*. **to have ~ feelings/views about sth** in bezug auf etw stark engagiert sein; **I didn't know you had such ~ feelings about it** ich habe nicht gewußt, daß Ihnen so viel daran liegt *or* daß Ihnen das so viel bedeutet; *(against it)* ich habe nicht gewußt, daß Sie so dagegen sind; **she has very ~ feelings about him** sie hat sehr viel für ihn übrig; *(as candidate etc)* sie hält sehr viel von ihm; *(against him)* sie ist vollkommen gegen ihn; **to have ~ feelings for** *or* **about sth** eine starke Bindung an etw *(acc)* haben; **he rules (his country) with a ~ hand** er regiert (sein Land) mit starker Hand; **his ~ point** seine Stärke; **to protest in ~ terms** energisch protestieren; **I had a ~ sense of déjà-vu** ich hatte ganz den Eindruck, das schon einmal gesehen zu haben.
(d) *(in numbers)* stark. **a group 20 ~** eine 20 Mann starke Gruppe.
(e) *(capable)* gut, stark *(inf)*. **he is ~ in/on sth** etw ist seine Stärke *or* starke Seite.
(f) *(enthusiastic, committed)* begeistert; *supporter, Catholic, socialist* überzeugt; *belief, faith* unerschütterlich, stark. **he's very ~ for Smith** *(inf)* er ist (ein) Smith-Fan *(inf)*.
(g) *food, smell, perfume etc* stark; *(pungent, unpleasant) smell, taste* streng; *(of butter)* ranzig; *colour, light* kräftig; *acid, bleach* stark; *solution* konzentriert. **~ breath** *(euph)* schlechter Atem, Mundgeruch *m*; **a ~ drink/whisky** ein steifer Drink/ein starker Whisky; **~ meat** *(fig)* starker Tobak *(inf)*.
(h) *accent, verb, rhyme* stark; *syllable etc* betont.
(i) *(Fin) market, economy* gesund; *price* stabil; *currency also* stark.
2 *adv (+er)* **(a)** *(inf)* **to be going ~** *(old person, thing)* gut in Schuß sein *(inf)*; *(runner)* gut in Form sein *(inf)*; *(party, rehearsals)* in Schwung sein *(inf)*; **that's coming** *or* **going it a bit ~!** das ist ein starkes Stück!; **he pitched it pretty ~** *(inf)* er drückte sich ziemlich drastisch aus.
(b) *(Fin)* in einer starken Position.

strong: **~-arm** *(inf) tactics etc* brutal, Gewalt-; **~-arm man** Schläger *m*; **2** *vt (esp US) (beat up)* zusammenschlagen; *(intimidate)* unter Druck setzen; **they were ~-armed into paying** sie wurden so unter Druck gesetzt, daß sie zahlten; **~-box** *n* (Geld)kassette *f*; **~ breeze** *n (Met)* starke Winde *pl*, Windstärke 6; **~ gale** *n (Met)* Windstärke 9; **~hold** *n (castle, fortress)* Festung *f*; *(town etc)* Stützpunkt *m*; *(fig)* Hochburg *f*.

strongly ['strɒŋlɪ] *adv* **(a)** *(physically)* stark; *kick, grip, shine* kräftig; *fight, attack* heftig, energisch; *built, made* solide, stabil; *built (person)* kräftig; *marked* stark.
(b) *(mentally) influence, suspect, tempt* stark; *desire also* heftig; *interest also* brennend; *believe* fest. **to feel very ~ about sth** in bezug auf etw *(acc)* stark engagiert sein; **I didn't know that you felt so ~ about it** ich habe nicht gewußt, daß Ihnen das so viel bedeutet *or* so sehr am Herzen liegt; *(against it)* ich habe nicht gewußt, daß Sie so dagegen sind; **she feels very ~ about him** sie hat sehr viel für ihn übrig; *(as candidate etc)* sie hält sehr viel von ihm; *(against him)* sie ist vollkommen gegen ihn.
(c) *(powerfully)* stark; *protest, defend* heftig, energisch; *plead* inständig; *support* kräftig; *sense* zutiefst; *answer, worded* in starken Worten. **he spoke ~ against it** er sprach sich entschieden dagegen aus; **I ~ advise you ...** ich möchte Ihnen dringend(st) raten ...

strongman ['strɒŋmæn] n, pl -men [-men] (lit, fig) starker Mann.

strong-minded adj, ~ly adv ['strɒŋ'maɪndɪd, -lɪ] willensstark.

strong-mindedness ['strɒŋ'maɪndɪdnɪs] n Willensstärke f.

strong: ~ point n Stärke f; ~room n Tresorraum m, Stahlkammer f; ~-willed ['strɒŋ'wɪld] adj willensstark, entschlossen; (pej) eigensinnig, trotzig.

strontium ['strɒntɪəm] n Strontium nt.

strop [strɒp] 1 n Streichriemen m. 2 vt abziehen.

strophe ['strəʊfɪ] n Strophe f.

stroppy ['strɒpɪ] adj (+er) (Brit inf) fuchtig (inf); answer, children pampig (inf). to be ~ about doing sth fuchtig/pampig sein, weil man etw tun soll (inf).

strove [strəʊv] pret of strive.

struck [strʌk] 1 pret, ptp of strike.
2 adj (a) pred to be ~ with sb/sth (impressed) von jdm/etw begeistert or angetan sein; I wasn't very ~ with him er hat keinen großen Eindruck auf mich gemacht; to be ~ on sb/sth (keen) auf jdn/etw stehen (inf), auf jdn/etw versessen sein.
(b) (US attr) (striking) workers streikend; factory, employers vom Streik betroffen, bestreikt.

structural ['strʌktʃərəl] adj (a) (relating to structure) strukturell; (of building) alterations, damage, requirements baulich; fault, defect Konstruktions-; material, element, part Bau-; weight Konstruktions-; (fig) Struktur-. the bridge suffered ~ damage die Struktur der Brücke wurde beschädigt.
(b) (weight-bearing) wall, beam tragend; (fig: essential) essentiell, notwendig.

structural: ~ engineering n Bautechnik f; ~ formula n (Chem) Strukturformel f.

structuralism ['strʌktʃərəlɪzəm] n der Strukturalismus.

structuralist ['strʌktʃərəlɪst] 1 n Strukturalist(in f) m. 2 adj attr strukturalistisch.

structurally ['strʌktʃərəlɪ] adv strukturell. ~ the novel is excellent vom Aufbau her ist der Roman ausgezeichnet; ~ sound sicher; ~ the building is in good condition was das rein Bauliche betrifft, ist das Haus in gutem Zustand.

structure ['strʌktʃəʳ] 1 n (a) (organization) Struktur f; (Sociol also) Aufbau m; (Ling also) Bau m; (Liter) Aufbau m; (Tech: of bridge, car etc) Konstruktion f. bone ~ Knochenbau m.
(b) (thing constructed) Konstruktion f; (building also) Gebäude nt.
2 vt strukturieren; essay, argument aufbauen, gliedern; layout, life gestalten. highly ~d society stark gegliedert; novel etc sorgfältig (auf)gebaut or gegliedert.

strudel ['ʃtruːdl] n (esp US) Strudel m.

struggle ['strʌgl] 1 n (lit, fig) Kampf m (for um); (fig: effort) Anstrengung f. without a ~ kampflos; you won't succeed without a ~ ohne Anstrengung wird Ihnen das nicht gelingen; to put up a ~ sich wehren; the ~ for survival/existence/to feed her seven children der Überlebenskampf/der Daseinskampf/der Kampf, ihre sieben Kinder zu ernähren; the ~ to find somewhere to live der Kampf or die Schwierigkeiten, bis man eine Wohnung gefunden hat; it is/was a ~ es ist/war mühsam; she finds life a ~ sie findet das Leben mühsam; I had a ~ to persuade him es war gar nicht einfach, ihn zu überreden; life feels like one long ~ das Leben scheint ein einziger Kampf zu sein.
2 vi (a) (contend) kämpfen; (in self-defence) sich wehren; (writhe) sich winden; (financially) in Schwierigkeiten sein, krebsen (inf); (fig: strive) sich sehr bemühen or anstrengen, sich abmühen. the police were struggling with the burglar zwischen der Polizei und dem Einbrecher gab es ein Handgemenge; to ~ to do sth sich sehr anstrengen, etw zu tun; to ~ for sth um etw kämpfen, sich um etw bemühen; to ~ against sb/sth gegen jdn/etw kämpfen; to ~ with sb mit jdm kämpfen; to ~ with sth with problem, difficulty sich mit etw herumschlagen; with language, subject, homework sich mit etw abmühen; with doubts, one's conscience mit etw ringen; can you manage? — I'm struggling schaffst du's? — mit Müh und Not; he was struggling to make ends meet er hatte seine liebe Not durchzukommen.
(b) (move with difficulty) sich quälen. to ~ to one's feet mühsam aufstehen or auf die Beine kommen, sich aufrappeln (inf); to ~ to get up sich hochquälen; he ~d through the tiny window er zwängte sich durch das kleine Fenster; to ~ on (lit) sich weiterkämpfen; (fig) weiterkämpfen; to ~ along/through (lit, fig) sich durchschlagen or -kämpfen.

struggling ['strʌglɪŋ] adj artist etc am Hungertuch nagend.

strum [strʌm] 1 vt tune klimpern; guitar klimpern auf (+dat). to ~ out a song ein Liedchen klimpern. 2 vi klimpern (on auf +dat).

strumpet ['strʌmpɪt] n (old) Hure, Dirne f.

strung [strʌŋ] pret, ptp of string.

strut[1] [strʌt] 1 vi stolzieren. to ~ about (the yard) (auf dem Hof) herumstolzieren; to ~ past vorbeistolzieren. 2 n angeberischer Gang, Stolzieren nt. to walk with a ~ stolzieren.

strut[2] n (horizontal) Strebe f; (sloping also) Stütze f; (vertical) Pfeiler m.

struth [struːθ] interj (sl) heiliger Strohsack (inf).

stub [stʌb] 1 n (of candle, pencil, tail) Stummel m; (of cigarette also) Kippe f; (of cheque, ticket) Abschnitt m; (of tree) Stumpf m. ~-axle Achsschenkel m.
2 vt to ~ one's toe (on or against sth) sich (dat) den Zeh (an etw dat) stoßen, mit dem Zeh an or gegen etw (acc) stoßen; to ~ out a cigarette eine Zigarette ausdrücken.

stubble ['stʌbl] n, no pl Stoppeln pl. a field of ~ ein Stoppelfeld nt.

stubbly ['stʌblɪ] adj (+er) field Stoppel-; chin, beard also stoppelig.

stubborn ['stʌbən] adj (a) (obstinate) person, insistence stur; animal also, child störrisch. to be ~ about sth stur auf etw (dat) beharren. (b) refusal, resistance, campaign etc hartnäckig. (c) lock, material widerspenstig; weeds, cough hartnäckig.

stubbornly ['stʌbənlɪ] adv see adj.

stubbornness ['stʌbənnɪs] n see adj (a) Sturheit f; störrische Art. (b) Hartnäckigkeit f. (c) Widerspenstigkeit f; Hartnäckigkeit f.

stubby ['stʌbɪ] adj (+er) revolver etc kurz; tail stummelig; pencil, vase kurz und dick; person gedrungen, stämmig, untersetzt; legs kurz und stämmig. ~ fingers Wurstfinger pl.

stucco ['stʌkəʊ] 1 n, pl -(e)s Stuck m; (also ~ work) Stuckarbeit, Stukkatur f. 2 adj attr Stuck-. 3 vt mit Stuck verzieren.

stuck [stʌk] 1 pret, ptp of stick[2].
2 adj (a) (baffled) (on, over mit) to be ~ nicht klarkommen, nicht zurechtkommen; to get ~ nicht weiterkommen, nicht zurechtkommen.
(b) (inf) he/she is ~ for sth es fehlt ihm/ihr an etw (dat), ihm/ihr fehlt etw; I'm a bit ~ for cash ich bin ein bißchen knapp bei Kasse; he wasn't exactly ~ for something to say man kann nicht gerade sagen, daß ihm der Gesprächsstoff fehlte.
(c) (inf) to get ~ into sb/sth jdn richtig in die Mangel nehmen (inf)/sich in etw (acc) richtig reinknien (inf); Stephen got ~ into his steak Stephen nahm sein Steak in Angriff; get ~ in! schlag zu! (inf).
(d) (inf: infatuated) to be ~ on sb in jdn verknallt sein (inf).
(e) (inf) to be ~ with sb/sth mit jdm/etw dasitzen, jdn/etw am Hals haben.

stuck-up ['stʌk'ʌp] adj (inf) person, attitude, voice hochnäsig. to be ~ about sth sich (dat) viel auf etw (acc) einbilden.

stud[1] [stʌd] 1 n (a) (nail) Beschlagnagel m; (decorative) Ziernagel m; (on boots) Stollen m. ~ reflector ~ Katzenauge nt.
(b) (collar ~) Kragenknopf m.
(c) (earring) Ohrstecker m.
2 vt (usu pass) besäen; (with jewels) (dicht) besetzen. their family tree is ~ded with generals in ihrem Stammbaum wimmelt es von Generälen.

stud[2] n (group of horses) (for breeding) Gestüt nt, Zucht f; (for racing etc) Stall m; (stallion) (Zucht)hengst m; (sl: man) Sexprotz m (inf). the stallion is at ~ der Hengst wird zur Zucht benutzt; to put to ~ zu Zuchtzwecken verwenden.

stud-book ['stʌdbʊk] n Gestüt- or Zuchtbuch nt.

student ['stjuːdənt] 1 n (Univ) Student(in f) m, Studierende(r) mf; (esp US: at school, night school) Schüler(in f) m. he is a ~ of French life/human nature er studiert die französischen Lebensart/die menschliche Natur; he is a ~ of French or a French ~ (Univ) er studiert Französisch; (Sch) er lernt Französisch; medical/law ~s Medizin-/Jurastudenten pl.
2 adj attr Studenten-; activities also, protest movement studentisch. ~ driver (US) Fahrschüler(in f) m.

student: ~ship n (Brit: grant) Stipendium nt; ~ teacher n Referendar(in f) m; ~ union n (a) (organization) Studentenvereinigung f; (political also) Studentenbund m; (b) (building) Gebäude nt der Studentenvereinigung/des Studentenbundes.

stud: ~ farm n Gestüt nt; ~ horse n Zuchthengst m.

studied ['stʌdɪd] 1 pret, ptp of study. 2 adj (carefully considered) reply durchdacht, wohlüberlegt; simplicity bewußt, ausgesucht; prose, style kunstvoll; (deliberate) berechnet; calm, politeness gewollt; insult beabsichtigt, bewußt; avoidance sorgfältig; pose einstudiert.

studio ['stjuːdɪəʊ] n (all senses) Studio nt; (of painter, photographer also) Atelier nt; (broadcasting ~ also) Senderaum m.

studio: ~ audience n Publikum nt im Studio; ~ couch n Schlafcouch f.

studious ['stjuːdɪəs] adj person fleißig, eifrig; life, habits gelehrsam; pupil also, turn of mind lernbegierig; attention, piece of work, research gewissenhaft, sorgfältig; avoidance gezielt, sorgsam; politeness bewußt; effort eifrig, beflissen (geh). a ~ atmosphere eine eifrige Lernatmosphäre.

studiously ['stjuːdɪəslɪ] adv fleißig, eifrig; (painstakingly) sorgsam, sorgfältig; polite bewußt; avoid gezielt, sorgsam; (deliberate) absichtlich, bewußt. he is not ~ inclined er hat keinen Hang zum Studieren.

studiousness ['stjuːdɪəsnɪs] n see adj Lerneifer, Fleiß m; Gelehrsamkeit f; Lernbegierde f; Gewissenhaftigkeit, Sorgfältigkeit f; Bewußtheit f; Bewußtheit f; Eifer m.

study ['stʌdɪ] 1 n (a) (studying, branch of ~) (esp Univ) Studium nt; (at school) Lernen nt; (of situation, evidence, case) Untersuchung f; (of nature) Beobachtung f. the ~ of cancer die Krebsforschung; the ~ of Chinese das Chinesischstudium; African studies (Univ) afrikanische Sprache und Kultur; to make a ~ of sth etw untersuchen; (academic) etw studieren; to spend one's time in ~ seine Zeit mit Studieren/Lernen verbringen; fond of ~ lernbegierig; during my studies während meines Studiums; his face was a ~ (inf) sein Gesicht war sehenswert; see brown ~.
(b) (piece of work) Studie f (of über +acc); (Art, Phot) Studie f (of gen); (Liter, Sociol also) Untersuchung f (of über +acc); (Mus) Etüde f.
(c) (room) Arbeits- or Studierzimmer nt.
2 vt studieren; (Sch) lernen; nature also, stars beobachten; author, particular tune, text etc sich befassen mit; (research into) erforschen; (examine also) untersuchen; clue, evidence prüfen, untersuchen.
3 vi studieren; (esp Sch) lernen. to ~ to be a teacher/doctor ein Lehrerstudium/Medizinstudium machen; to ~ for an exam sich auf eine Prüfung vorbereiten, für eine Prüfung lernen; he has to ~ a lot er muß viel lernen; to ~ for the medical profession Medizin studieren; to ~ under sb bei jdm studieren.

study: ~ group n Arbeitsgruppe or -gemeinschaft f; ~ visit n Studienreise f.

stuff [stʌf] **1** n (a) Zeug nt. green/sweet etc ~ Grünzeug nt/süßes etc Zeug; **the ~ that heroes/dreams are made of** der Stoff, aus dem Helden gemacht sind/die Träume sind; **the ~ of tragedy** echte Tragik; **show him what kind of ~ you're made of** zeig ihm, aus welchem Holz du geschnitzt bist; **there was a lot of rough ~** es ging ziemlich rauh zu; **there is some good ~ in that book** in dem Buch stecken ein paar gute Sachen; **it's poor/good ~** das ist schlecht/gut; **this tea/book is strong ~** der Tee ist ziemlich stark/das Buch ist starker Tobak; **I can't read his ~** ich kann sein Zeug nicht lesen; **his later ~ is less original** seine späteren Sachen sind weniger originell; **he brought me some ~ to read/to pass the time with** er hat mir etwas zum Lesen/zur Unterhaltung mitgebracht; **books and ~** Bücher und so (inf); **and ~ like that und so was** (inf); **all that ~ about how he wants to help us** all das Gerede, daß er uns helfen will; **~ and nonsense** Quatsch (inf), Blödsinn m; **all this ~ about Father Christmas** (inf) all der Quatsch vom Weihnachtsmann (inf).

(b) (inf) **she's a nice bit of ~** die ist nicht ohne (inf); **a drop of the hard ~** ein Schluck von dem scharfen Zeug; **that's the ~ (to give the troops)** so ist's richtig!, weiter so!; **to do one's ~** seine Nummer abziehen (inf); **go on, do your ~!** nun mach mal or doch! (inf); **he did his ~ well** er hat seine Sache gut gemacht; **to know one's ~** wissen, wovon man redet, sich auskennen; *see* **hot ~**.

(c) (possessions) Zeug nt, Sachen pl.

(d) (inf: drugs) Stoff m (sl).

(e) (old: cloth) Material nt, Stoff m.

2 vt (a) (fill) container, room, person vollstopfen; hole zustopfen, verstopfen; contents, object, books (hinein)stopfen (into in +acc); (into envelope) stecken (into in +acc). **to ~ a person with food** jdn mit Essen vollstopfen, jdn mästen (inf); **to ~ sth away** etw wegstecken; **he ~ed it away in his pocket** er stopfte es in seine Tasche; **he ~ed some money into my hand** er drückte mir Geld in die Hand; **to ~ one's fingers into one's ears** sich (dat) die Finger in die Ohren stecken; **to ~ sb's/one's head with nonsense** jdm/sich den Kopf mit Unsinn vollstopfen; **to be ~ed up (with a cold)** verschnupft sein, eine verstopfte Nase haben; **my nose is ~ed up** ich habe eine verstopfte Nase.

(b) (Cook) füllen.

(c) cushion etc füllen; toy also (aus)stopfen; (in taxidermy) ausstopfen. **a ~ed toy** ein Stofftier nt.

(d) (sl) **~ it** (be quiet) halt's Maul!, Schnauze! (sl); **get ~ed!** du kannst mich mal (sl)!; **I told him to ~ it** or **to get ~ed** ich habe ihm gesagt, er kann mich mal (sl); **you can ~ that (idea)** die Idee kannst du dir an den Hut stecken (inf); **you can ~ your money/advice** etc du kannst dein blödes Geld etc behalten (inf)/du kannst dir deinen Rat schenken or an den Hut stecken (inf); **~ him!** der kann mich mal! (sl).

3 vi (inf: eat) sich vollstopfen (inf).

4 vr **to ~ oneself (with food/on cakes)** sich (mit Essen/Kuchen) vollstopfen (inf).

stuffed shirt [stʌft'ʃɜːt] n (inf) Stockfisch m (inf).

stuffily ['stʌfɪlɪ] adv (narrow-mindedly) spießig; (prudishly) prüde; (stiffly) steif, gezwungen; (dully) langweilig.

stuffiness ['stʌfɪnɪs] n see adj (a) Stickigkeit, Dumpfheit f. (b) Spießigkeit f; Prüderie, Zimperlichkeit f. (c) Steifheit f; Gezwungenheit f; Langweiligkeit, Fadheit f.

stuffing ['stʌfɪŋ] n (of pillow, quilt, Cook) Füllung f; (of furniture) Polstermaterial nt; (in taxidermy, toys) Füllmaterial, Stopfmaterial nt. **he's got no ~** (fig) er hat keinen Mumm in den Knochen (inf); **to knock** or **take the ~ out of sb** (inf) jdn fertigmachen (inf), jdn schaffen (inf).

stuffy ['stʌfɪ] adj (+er) (a) room, atmosphere stickig, dumpf. (b) (narrow-minded) spießig; (prudish) prüde, zimperlich. (c) (stiff) steif; atmosphere also gezwungen; (dull) langweilig, öde, fad.

stultify ['stʌltɪfaɪ] **1** vt lähmen; mind, person verkümmern or verdummen lassen. **to become stultified** verkümmern, verdummen. **2** vi verkümmern, verdummen.

stultifying ['stʌltɪfaɪɪŋ] adj lähmend; boredom, inactivity also abstumpfend. **to have a ~ effect on sb/sb's mind** jdn verkümmern lassen.

stumble ['stʌmbl] **1** n Stolpern nt no pl, no indef art; (in speech etc) Stocken nt no pl, no indef art.

2 vi (lit, fig) stolpern; (in speech) stocken. **to ~ against sth** gegen etw stoßen; **to ~ on sth** (lit) über etw (acc) stolpern; (fig) auf etw (acc) stoßen; **he ~d through a waltz/his speech** stokkend or holperig spielte er einen Walzer/hielt er seine Rede.

stumbling-block ['stʌmblɪŋˌblɒk] n (fig) Hürde f, Hindernis, Problem nt. **to be a ~ to sth** einer Sache (dat) im Weg stehen.

stump [stʌmp] **1** n (a) (of tree, limb) Stumpf m; (of tooth, candle also, of pencil, tail, cigar) Stummel m; (Cricket) Stab m. **to stir one's ~s** (inf) sich rühren, sich regen.

(b) (US Pol: platform) Rednertribüne f. **~ speaker** Wahlredner(in f) m.

2 vt (a) (Cricket) (durch Umwerfen der Stäbe) ausschalten. (b) (fig inf) **you've got me ~ed** da bin ich überfragt; **I'm ~ed, that problem's got me ~ed** ich bin mit meiner Weisheit or meinem Latein am Ende (inf); **to be ~ed for an answer** um eine Antwort verlegen sein.

(c) (US Pol) **to ~ the country** Wahl(kampf)reisen durch das Land machen.

3 vi (inf) stapfen. **to ~ along/about** entlang-/herumstapfen; **to ~ up to sb** auf jdn zustapfen.

♦**stump up** (Brit inf) **1** vt insep springen lassen (inf), locker machen (inf). **2** vi blechen (inf).

stumpy ['stʌmpɪ] adj (+er) pencil, candle stummelig (inf), kurz; person stämmig, untersetzt; tree klein und gedrungen; legs kurz. **a ~ tail** ein Stummelschwanz m.

stun [stʌn] vt (make unconscious) betäuben; (noise also, daze) benommen machen; (fig) (shock) fassungslos machen;

(amaze) erstaunen, verblüffen. **he was ~ned by the news** (bad news) er war über die Nachricht fassungslos or wie gelähmt; (good news) die Nachricht hat ihn überwältigt; **he was ~ned by his good fortune** er war sprachlos über sein Glück.

stung [stʌŋ] pret, ptp of **sting**.

stunk [stʌŋk] ptp of **stink**.

stunned [stʌnd] adj (unconscious) betäubt; (dazed) benommen; (fig) (shocked) fassungslos; (amazed) sprachlos.

stunner ['stʌnəʳ] n (inf) (thing) Wucht f (inf); (woman) tolle Frau, tolles Weib (inf); (man) toller Mann or Kerl (inf).

stunning ['stʌnɪŋ] adj (lit) blow wuchtig, betäubend; (fig) news, dress, girl etc phantastisch, toll (inf), atemberaubend; shock überwältigend.

stunningly ['stʌnɪŋlɪ] adv atemberaubend, phantastisch.

stunt[1] [stʌnt] n Kunststück nt, Nummer f; (publicity ~, trick) Gag m; (Aviat) Kunststück nt. **to do ~s** (be ~man) ein Stuntman sein, doubeln; **he does most of his own ~s** gefährliche Szenen spielt er meist selbst.

stunt[2] vt (lit, fig) growth, development hemmen; trees, mind etc verkümmern lassen.

stunted ['stʌntɪd] adj plant, mind verkümmert; child unterentwickelt. **the ~ growth of these trees** die verkümmerten Bäume; **his ~ growth** seine Verwachsungen.

stunt: **~ flying** n Kunstflug m; **~man** n Stuntman m, Double nt.

stupefaction [ˌstjuːpɪˈfækʃən] n Verblüffung f. **he looked at me in ~** er sah mich verblüfft or voller Verblüffung an.

stupefy ['stjuːpɪfaɪ] vt benommen machen; (fig: amaze, surprise) verblüffen. **to be stupefied by drink** vom Alkohol benommen sein.

stupefying ['stjuːpɪfaɪɪŋ] adj betäubend; (fig: amazing) verblüffend.

stupendous [stjuːˈpendəs] adj phantastisch; effort enorm.

stupendously [stjuːˈpendəslɪ] adv phantastisch; hard enorm.

stupid ['stjuːpɪd] **1** adj (a) dumm; (foolish also, boring) blöd(e) (inf). **don't be ~** sei nicht so blöd (inf); **I've done a ~ thing** ich habe etwas ganz Dummes or Blödes (inf) gemacht; **you ~ idiot!** du blöder Idiot!; **take that ~ look off your face** guck nicht so dumm or blöd (inf)!; **that was ~ of you, that was a ~ thing to do** das war dumm (von dir).

(b) (stupefied) benommen, benebelt. **to drink oneself ~** sich sinnlos betrinken; **the blow knocked him ~** der Schlag hat ihn völlig benebelt.

2 adv (inf) **to talk ~** Quatsch reden (inf); **to act ~** sich dumm stellen.

3 n (inf: person) Blödmann (inf), Dummkopf (inf) m.

stupidity [stjuːˈpɪdɪtɪ] n Dummheit f; (silliness also) Blödheit f (inf). **of all the ~!** so was Dummes!

stupidly ['stjuːpɪdlɪ] adv (unintelligently) dumm; (foolishly also) blöd (inf). **~ I'd forgotten my keys** dummerweise hatte ich meine Schlüssel vergessen; **he ~ refused** er war so dumm or blöd (inf) abzulehnen.

stupor ['stjuːpəʳ] n Benommenheit f. **he lay/sat there in a ~** er lag/saß benommen or apathisch or teilnahmslos da; **to be in a drunken ~** sinnlos betrunken or im Vollrausch sein.

sturdily ['stɜːdɪlɪ] adv (a) stabil. **~ built** person kräftig or stämmig gebaut; chair, ship etc stabil gebaut. (b) (fig). unerschütterlich, standhaft.

sturdiness ['stɜːdɪnɪs] n see adj (a) Kräftigkeit, Stämmigkeit f; Kräftigkeit, Robustheit f; Stabilität f. (b) Unerschütterlichkeit, Standhaftigkeit f.

sturdy ['stɜːdɪ] adj (+er) (a) person, body, plant kräftig, stämmig; material kräftig, robust; building, ship, car stabil. (b) (fig) opposition unerschütterlich, standhaft.

sturgeon ['stɜːdʒən] n Stör m.

stutter ['stʌtəʳ] **1** n (of person, engine) Stottern nt no pl; (of guns) Trommeln nt. **he has a bad ~** er stottert sehr; **to say sth with a ~** etw stotternd sagen, etw stottern.

2 vti stottern. **he was ~ing with rage** er stotterte vor Wut; **she ~ed (out) an apology** sie entschuldigte sich stotternd.

stutterer ['stʌtərəʳ] n Stotterer m, Stotterin f.

stuttering ['stʌtərɪŋ] n Stottern nt.

sty [staɪ] n (lit, fig) Schweinestall m.

sty(e) [staɪ] n (Med) Gerstenkorn nt.

stygian ['stɪdʒɪən] adj (liter) gloom, darkness stygisch (liter).

style [staɪl] **1** n (a) (Art, Mus, Liter, personal etc) Stil m. **~ of painting** Malstil m; **the ~ of his writing** sein Stil m; **~ of life** Lebensstil m; **a poem in the Romantic ~** ein Gedicht im Stil der Romantik; **he won in fine ~** er gewann souverän or überlegen; **in his own inimitable ~** (iro) in seiner unnachahmlichen Art or Manier, auf die ihm typische Art; **that house is not my ~** so ein Haus ist nicht mein Stil; **hillwalking/flattering people is not his ~** Bergwanderungen liegen ihm nicht/es ist nicht seine Art zu schmeicheln; **that's the ~** (inf) so ist's richtig.

(b) (elegance) Stil m. **the man has (real) ~** der Mann hat Klasse or Format; **in ~** stilvoll; **to do things in ~** alles im großen Stil tun; **to celebrate in ~** groß feiern; **to get married in ~** eine Hochzeit großen Stils or im großen Stil feiern.

(c) (sort, type) Art f. **a new ~ of house/car** etc ein neuer Haus-/Autotyp etc; **just the ~ of book/car I like** ein Buch/Auto in der Art, die mir gefällt.

(d) (Fashion) Stil m no pl (liter) gloom, darkness (cut) Schnitt m; (hair~) Frisur f. **these coats are available in two ~s** diese Mäntel gibt es in zwei verschiedenen Schnitten or Macharten; **I want something in that ~** ich hätte gern etwas in der Art or in dem Stil; **all the latest ~s** die neue(ste) Mode, Mode im neue(ste)n Stil; **the latest ~s in shoes** die neue(ste)n Schuhmoden.

(e) (~ of address) Anrede f; (title) Titel m.

(f) (Bot) Griffel m.

2 vt (a) (designate) nennen.

(b) (design) entwerfen; clothes, interior etc also gestalten; hair schneiden und frisieren. **a smartly ~d dress** ein elegant geschnittenes Kleid; **it is ~d for comfort not elegance** es ist auf Bequemlichkeit und nicht Eleganz zugeschnitten.

-style adj suf nach ... Art, auf (+acc) ... Art. **American-~ fried chicken** Brathühnchen nach amerikanischer Art; **cowboy-~** auf Cowboyart, nach Art der Cowboys; **Swedish-~ furniture/design** Möbel/Design im schwedischen Stil; **the old-~ cricketer** der Cricketspieler der alten Schule.

stylebook ['staɪlbʊk] n (Typ) Stilvorschriften pl; (Fashion) Modeheft nt; (for hairstyles) Frisurenheft nt.

styli ['staɪlaɪ] pl of stylus.

styling ['staɪlɪŋ] n (of car etc) Design nt; (of dress) Machart f, Schnitt m; (of hair) Schnitt m.

stylish ['staɪlɪʃ] adj person elegant; car, hotel, district also vornehm; furnishings stilvoll; (fashionable) modisch; wedding großen Stils; way of life großartig, im großen Stil.

stylishly ['staɪlɪʃlɪ] adv elegant; furnished stilvoll; (fashionably) modisch; live im großen Stil; travel mit allem Komfort.

stylishness ['staɪlɪʃnɪs] n see adj Eleganz f; Vornehmheit f; stilvolle Art; modische Finesse; großangelegter Stil. **the ~ of his way of life** sein großartiger Lebensstil.

stylist ['staɪlɪst] n (a) (Fashion) Modeschöpfer(in f) m, Modestylist(in f) m; (hair~) Friseur m, Friseuse f, Coiffeur m (geh), Coiffeuse f (geh). (b) (Liter, Sport) Stilist(in f) m.

stylistic [staɪ'lɪstɪk] adj stilistisch. ~ **device** Stilmittel nt.

stylistically [staɪ'lɪstɪkəlɪ] adv see adj. ~ **it lacks polish** stilistisch gesehen or vom Stil her fehlt es am letzten Schliff.

stylistics [staɪ'lɪstɪks] n sing Stilistik f.

stylite ['staɪlaɪt] n Säulenheilige(r), Stylit (spec) m.

stylize ['staɪlaɪz] vt stilisieren.

stylus ['staɪləs] n, pl **styli** (a) (on record-player) Nadel f. (b) (writing instrument) Griffel, Stilus (Hist) m.

stymie ['staɪmɪ] vt (fig inf) matt setzen (inf). **to be ~d** aufgeschmissen sein (inf).

styptic ['stɪptɪk] 1 n blutstillendes Mittel. 2 adj pencil Blutstill-.

suave adj, **~ly** adv ['swɑːv, -lɪ] liebenswürdig, weltmännisch, aalglatt (pej).

suaveness ['swɑːvnɪs], **suavity** ['swɑːvɪtɪ] n Liebenswürdigkeit, Gewandtheit f, aalglatte Art (pej).

sub [sʌb] abbr of (a) **sub-edit, sub-editor**. (b) **submarine**. (c) **subscription**. (d) **substitute**.

sub- pref (under, subordinate, inferior) Unter-, unter-; (esp with foreign words) Sub-, sub-. **~alpine** subalpin.

subaltern ['sʌbltən] n (Brit Mil) Subalternoffizier m.

sub: **~aqua** adj attr Unterwasser-; equipment, club Taucher-; **~arctic** adj subarktisch; **~atomic** adj particle subatomar; **~basement** n Kellergeschoß nt; **~class** n Unterabteilung f; **~classify** vti unterteilen; **~committee** n Unterausschuß m; **~conscious** 1 adj unterbewußt; 2 n the **~conscious** das Unterbewußtsein; **in his ~conscious** im Unterbewußtsein; **~consciously** adv im Unterbewußtsein; **~continent** n Subkontinent m; **~contract** 1 vt (vertraglich) weitervergeben (to an +acc); 2 n Nebenvertrag, Untervertrag m; **~contractor** n Unterkontrahent m; **~culture** n Subkultur f; **~cutaneous** adj subkutan; **~divide** 1 vt unterteilen; 2 vi sich aufteilen; **~division** n (act) Unterteilung f; (~group) Unterabteilung f; **~dominant** 1 n Subdominante f; 2 attr chord Subdominant-.

subdue [səb'djuː] vt rebels, country unterwerfen; rioters überwältigen; wilderness besiegen; (make submissive) gehorsam or fügsam or gefügig machen; (fig) anger, desire unterdrücken, zähmen; noise, light, high spirits dämpfen; animals, children bändigen; pain lindern.

subdued [səb'djuːd] adj (quiet) colour, lighting, voice gedämpft; manner, person ruhig, still; mood, atmosphere gedrückt; (submissive) voice, manner, person fügsam, gehorsam, gefügig; (repressed) feelings, excitement unterdrückt.

sub: **~edit** vti (esp Brit) redigieren; **~editor** n (esp Brit) Redakteur(in f) m; **~family** n Unterfamilie f; **~group** n Unterabteilung f; **~head** (inf), **~heading** n Untertitel m; **~human** adj treatment etc unmenschlich; **they were treated as if they were ~human** sie wurden behandelt, als seien sie Untermenschen.

subject ['sʌbdʒɪkt] 1 n (a) (Pol) Staatsbürger(in f) m; (of king etc) Untertan m, Untertanin f.
(b) (Gram) Subjekt nt, Satzgegenstand m.
(c) (topic, Mus) Thema nt. **the ~ of the picture is** ... das Thema or Sujet (geh) des Bildes ist ...; **he paints urban ~s** er malt städtische Motive; **the author takes for his ~ the civil war** der Autor macht den Bürgerkrieg zu seinem Thema; **to change the ~** das Thema wechseln; **on the ~ of** ... zum Thema (+gen) ...; **while we're on the ~** da wir gerade beim Thema sind; **while we're on the ~ of mushrooms** wo wir gerade von Pilzen reden, apropos Pilze; **that's off the ~** das gehört nicht zum Thema.
(d) (discipline) (Sch, Univ) Fach nt; (specialist ~) (Spezial)gebiet nt.
(e) (reason) Grund, Anlaß m (for zu).
(f) (object) Gegenstand m (of gen); (in experiment) (person) Versuchsperson f, Versuchsobjekt nt; (animal) Versuchstier, Versuchsobjekt nt; (esp Med: for treatment) Typ m. **he is the ~ of much criticism** er wird stark kritisiert, er ist Gegenstand häufiger Kritik; **he's a good ~ for treatment by hypnosis** er läßt sich gut hypnotisch behandeln; **he's a good ~ for research into hypnosis** an ihm läßt sich Hypnose gut studieren; **the survey team asked 100 ~s** die Meinungsforscher befragten 100 Personen.
(g) (Philos: ego) Subjekt, Ich nt.
2 adj (a) (conquered) unterworfen.
(b) ~ **(unter the control of)** unterworfen (+dat); **provinces ~ to foreign rule** Provinzen unter Fremdherrschaft; **to be ~ to sth** to law, constant change, sb's will einer Sache (dat) unterworfen sein; **to illness** für etw anfällig sein; **to consent, approval** von etw abhängig sein; **northbound trains are ~ to**

delays bei Zügen in Richtung Norden muß mit Verspätung gerechnet werden; **prices/opening times are ~ to change** or **alteration without notice** Preisänderungen sind vorbehalten/bezüglich Öffnungszeiten sind Änderungen vorbehalten; **all these plans are ~ to last minute changes** all diese Pläne können in letzter Minute noch geändert werden; **these roads are ~ to fog** auf diesen Straßen muß mit Nebel gerechnet werden; **~ to flooding** überschwemmungsgefährdet; **to be ~ to taxation** besteuert werden; **~ to correction** vorbehaltlich Änderungen; **~ to confirmation in writing** vorausgesetzt, es wird schriftlich bestätigt.

3 [səb'dʒekt] vt (a) (subjugate) unterwerfen; terrorists, guerrillas zerschlagen.
(b) **to ~ sb to sth** to questioning, analysis, treatment jdn einer Sache (dat) unterziehen; to test also jdn einer Sache (dat) unterwerfen; to torture, suffering, heat, ridicule, criticism jdn einer Sache (dat) aussetzen; **to ~ sb to insults** jdn beschimpfen; **to ~ sb/a book to criticism** jdn/ein Buch unter Kritik nehmen, jdn/ein Buch kritisieren.
4 [səb'dʒekt] vr **to ~ oneself to sth** to insults, suffering etw hinnehmen; to criticism, ridicule sich einer Sache (dat) aussetzen; to examination, test, questioning sich einer Sache (dat) unterziehen.

subject: ~ **catalogue** n Schlagwortkatalog m; ~ **heading** n Überschrift f; (in index) Rubrik f; ~ **index** n Sachregister nt.

subjection [səb'dʒekʃən] n (a) (state) Abhängigkeit f. **to bring a people into ~** ein Volk unterwerfen; **to hold** or **keep a people in ~** ein Volk unterdrücken. (b) (act) Unterwerfung f; (of terrorists, guerrillas etc) Zerschlagung f. (c) **the ~ of sb to sth** see **subject** 3 (b).

subjective [səb'dʒektɪv] adj (a) subjektiv. (b) (Gram) ~ **case** Nominativ m.

subjectively [səb'dʒektɪvlɪ] adv subjektiv.

subjectivism [səb'dʒektɪvɪzəm] n Subjektivismus m.

subjectivity [ˌsʌbdʒek'tɪvɪtɪ] n Subjektivität f.

subject-matter ['sʌbdʒɪkt'mætəʳ] n (theme) Stoff m; (content) Inhalt m.

sub judice [ˌsʌb'djuːdɪsɪ] adj **to be ~** verhandelt werden.

subjugate ['sʌbdʒʊgeɪt] vt unterwerfen, unterjochen.

subjugation [ˌsʌbdʒʊ'geɪʃən] n Unterwerfung, Unterjochung f.

subjunctive [səb'dʒʌŋktɪv] 1 adj konjunktivisch. **a/the ~ verb/the ~ mood** der Konjunktiv; ~ **form** Konjunktiv(form f) m. 2 n (mood, verb) Konjunktiv m.

sub: **~lease** 1 n (contract) (on farm etc) Unterpachtvertrag m (on für); (on house etc) Untermietvertrag m (on für); **they have a ~lease on that house/farm** das Haus ist an sie untervermietet worden/sie haben den Hof als Unterpächter; 2 vt land unter- or weiterverpachten (to an +acc); house unter- or weitervermieten (to an +acc); **she has ~leased the flat from the tenants** sie hat die Wohnung in Untermiete; **~let** pret, ptp **~let** 1 vt house, room unter- or weitervermieten (to an +acc); 2 vi untervermieten; **~letting** n Untervermietung f; **~-lieutenant** n (esp Brit) Leutnant m zur See.

sublimate ['sʌblɪmeɪt] 1 n (Chem) Sublimat nt. 2 vt (Chem, Psych) sublimieren.

sublimation [ˌsʌblɪ'meɪʃən] n Sublimierung f.

sublime [sə'blaɪm] adj (a) poetry, beauty, scenery erhaben; thoughts, feelings also sublim; achievement, courage, genius also überragend. **this was the ~ moment of his life** das war der erhabenste Augenblick or die Krönung seines Lebens; **that's going from the ~ to the ridiculous** (inf) or the gorblimey (hum sl) das nenne ich tief sinken (inf).
(b) (iro: extreme) chaos, ignorance vollendet; impertinence, confidence also unglaublich, hanebüchen; indifference also, contempt souverän.

sublimely [sə'blaɪmlɪ] adv erhaben; unaware, ignorant ergreifend (iro), vollkommen; foolish, drunk unglaublich. ~ **beautiful** von erhabener Schönheit; **a ~ contented expression on his face** ein überglücklicher Gesichtsausdruck; ~ **contemptuous/indifferent** he ... mit souveräner Verachtung/Gleichgültigkeit ... er ...

subliminal [ˌsʌb'lɪmɪnl] adj (Psych) unterschwellig.

sublimity [sə'blɪmɪtɪ] n (liter) Erhabenheit f.

submachine gun [ˌsʌbmə'ʃiːn'gʌn] n Maschinenpistole f.

submarine ['sʌbmə,riːn] 1 n Unterseeboot, U-Boot nt. 2 adj life, equipment, cable unterseeisch, submarin.

submerge [səb'mɜːdʒ] 1 vt untertauchen; (flood) überschwemmen. **to ~ sth in water** etw in Wasser (ein)-tauchen; **the house was completely ~d** das Haus stand völlig unter Wasser. 2 vi (diver, submarine) tauchen.

submerged [səb'mɜːdʒd] adj rocks unter Wasser; wreck gesunken; city versunken. **she is ~ in work** sie erstickt in Arbeit.

submersible [səb'mɜːsəbl] 1 adj versenkbar; submarine tauchfähig. 2 n Tauchboot nt.

submersion [səb'mɜːʃən] n Untertauchen nt; (of submarine) Tauchen nt; (by flood) Überschwemmung f. ~ **in liquid** Eintauchen nt in Flüssigkeit; **prolonged ~ in water** langes Liegen im Wasser.

submission [səb'mɪʃən] n (a) (yielding) Unterwerfung f (to unter +acc); (submissiveness) Gehorsam m; (Sport) Aufgabe f. **to force sb into ~** jdn zwingen, sich zu ergeben; **to starve sb into ~** jdn aushungern.
(b) (presentation) Eingabe f; (documents submitted) Vorlage f. **to make a ~ to sb** jdm eine Vorlage machen or unterbreiten; **his ~ to the appeals tribunal** seine Berufung.
(c) (contention) Einwurf m (to gegenüber). **it is our ~ that** ... wir behaupten, daß ...

submissive [səb'mɪsɪv] adj demütig, gehorsam, unterwürfig (pej) (to gegenüber). ~ **to authority** autoritätsgläubig.

submissively [səbˈmɪsɪvlɪ] *adv see adj.*

submissiveness [səbˈmɪsɪvnɪs] *n* Demut *f*, Gehorsam *m*, Unterwürfigkeit *f (pej)* (*to* gegenüber).

submit [səbˈmɪt] **1** *vt* **(a)** *(put forward)* vorlegen (*to dat*); *application, claim etc* einreichen (*to* bei). **to ~ that ...** *(esp Jur)* behaupten, daß ...; **to ~ an entry to a competition** *(participate)* an einem Wettbewerb teilnehmen.
(b) *(refer to)* verweisen an (+*acc*). **to ~ sth to scrutiny/investigation/tests** *etc* etw einer Prüfung/einer Untersuchung/Tests *(dat) etc* unterziehen; **to ~ sth to heat/ cold** etw der Hitze/Kälte *(dat)* etc aussetzen.
2 *vi (yield)* sich beugen, nachgeben; *(Mil)* sich ergeben (*to* dat); *(Sport)* aufgeben. **to ~ to sb's orders, judgement, God's will** sich einer Sache *(dat)* beugen *or* unterwerfen; **to humiliations, indignity** sich *(dat)* etw gefallen lassen, etw erdulden; **to demands, threats, pressure** einer Sache *(dat)* nachgeben; **to separation** etw auf sich *(acc)* nehmen; **to ~ to blackmail/questioning** sich erpressen/verhören lassen.
3 *vr* **to ~ oneself to sth** *to examination, operation, questioning etc* sich einer Sache *(dat)* unterziehen.

subnormal [sʌbˈnɔːməl] *adj intelligence, temperature* unterdurchschnittlich; *person* minderbegabt; *(inf)* schwachsinnig.

subordinate [səˈbɔːdɪnɪt] **1** *adj officer* rangniedriger; *rank, position, (secondary) importance* untergeordnet. **~ clause** *(Gram)* Nebensatz *m*; **to be ~ to sb/sth** jdm/einer Sache untergeordnet sein; **to be ~ in importance** to weniger wichtig sein als; **~ in rank** rangniedriger (*to* als).
2 *n* Untergebene(r) *mf*.
3 [səˈbɔːdɪneɪt] *vt* unterordnen (*to dat*). **subordinating conjunction** unterordnende Konjunktion *f*.

subordination [sə,bɔːdɪˈneɪʃən] *n (subjection)* Unterordnung *f* (*to* unter +*acc*).

suborn [sʌˈbɔːn] *vt (Jur) witness* beeinflussen.

sub-plot [ˈsʌb,plɒt] *n* Nebenhandlung *f*.

subpoena [səbˈpiːnə] *(Jur)* **1** *n* Vorladung *f*. **to serve a ~ on sb** jdn vorladen. **2** *vt witness* vorladen. **he was ~ed to give evidence** er wurde als Zeuge vorgeladen.

sub: **~polar** *adj* subpolar; **~-postmaster/-postmistress** *n (Brit)* Vorstand *m* einer Zweigstelle der Post; **~-post office** *n (Brit)* Zweigstelle *f* der Post; **~ rosa** [,sʌbˈrəʊzə] *(form)* **1** *adj* geheim, sub rosa *(geh)*; **2** *adv* im geheimen, sub rosa *(geh)*.

subscribe [səbˈskraɪb] **1** *vt (to appeal) money* zeichnen *(form)*; spenden (*to* für). **to ~ one's signature** *or* **name to a document** *(form)* ein Dokument (unter)zeichnen; **to ~ oneself M. Rogers** *(form)* mit M. Rogers zeichnen *(form)*.
2 *vi* **(a)** *(contribute, promise to contribute)* spenden, geben (*to dat*). **to ~ to an appeal** sich an einer Spendenaktion beteiligen; **to ~ to** *or (form)* **for a gift** sich an einem Geschenk beteiligen, etwas zu einem Geschenk beisteuern; **to ~ for a book** ein Buch vorbestellen; **to ~ for shares in a company** Aktien einer Gesellschaft zeichnen.
(b) **to ~ to a magazine** *etc* eine Zeitschrift *etc* abonnieren.
(c) *(support)* **to ~ to sth** *to proposal* etw gutheißen, etw billigen; *to opinion, theory* sich einer Sache *(dat)* anschließen.

subscriber [səbˈskraɪbəʳ] *n (to paper)* Abonnent(in *f*) *m*; *(to fund)* Spender(in *f*), Zeichner(in *f*) *(form)*; *(Telec)* Teilnehmer(in *f*) *m*; *(to opinion)* Befürworter(in *f*) *m*; *(of shares)* Zeichner *m*. **~ trunk dialling** *(Brit)* der Selbstwählferndienst.

subscription [səbˈskrɪpʃən] *n* Subskription *(form)*, Zeichnung *(form) f*; *(money subscribed)* Beitrag *m*; *(to newspaper, concert etc)* Abonnement *nt* (*to* gen). **to take out a ~** *to* sth abonnieren; **to pay one's ~** (*to a club)* seinen (Vereins)beitrag bezahlen; **by public ~** mit Hilfe von *or* durch Spenden; **by ~** durch Subskription(en *pl*) *f*.

subscription rate *n* Abonnements- *or* Bezugspreis *m*. **to buy sth at a ~** etw zum Bezugspreis bekommen.

subsection [ˈsʌbˌsekʃən] *n* Unterabteilung *f*; *(Jur)* Paragraph *m*.

subsequent [ˈsʌbsɪkwənt] *adj* (nach)folgend, anschließend; *(in time)* später, anschließend. **~ to** *(form)* im Anschluß an (+*acc*).

subsequently [ˈsʌbsɪkwəntlɪ] *adv (afterwards)* später, anschließend; *(from that time on)* von da an.

subserve [səbˈsɜːv] *vt (form)* dienen (+*dat*), dienlich *or* förderlich sein (+*dat*) *(form)*.

subservience [səbˈsɜːvɪəns] *n (pej)* Unterwürfigkeit *f* (*to* gegenüber); *(form)* Unterworfenheit *f* (*to* unter +*acc*).

subservient [səbˈsɜːvɪənt] *adj (pej)* unterwürfig (*to* gegenüber); *(form)* unterworfen (*to* dat).

subserviently [səbˈsɜːvɪəntlɪ] *adv* unterwürfig.

subset [ˈsʌbˌset] *n (Math)* Teilmenge *f*.

subside [səbˈsaɪd] *vi* **(a)** *(flood, river)* sinken; *(land, building, road)* sich senken, absacken *(inf)*. **the lorry ~d into the mud** der Lastwagen sank im Schlamm ein; **to ~ into a chair** auf einen Stuhl sinken.
(b) *(storm, wind)* abflauen, nachlassen, sich legen; *(anger, excitement, laughter, noise also)* abklingen; *(fever)* sinken.

subsidence [səbˈsaɪdəns] *n* Senkung *f*, Absacken *nt (inf)*. **there's a lot of ~ in the area** in der Gegend senkt sich die Erdreich; **"danger: ~"** „Achtung: Bodensenkung"; **we can't get a mortgage because of the ~** wir bekommen keine Hypothek, weil sich das Gelände senkt.

subsidiary [səbˈsɪdɪərɪ] **1** *adj role, interest, subject* Neben-; *company* Tochter-. **to be ~ to sth** einer Sache *(dat)* untergeordnet sein; **my role is ~** ich spiele eine Nebenrolle *or* eine untergeordnete Rolle. **2** *n* Tochtergesellschaft *f*.

subsidize [ˈsʌbsɪdaɪz] *vt company etc*, *(inf) sb's habits* subventionieren; *(inf) person* unterstützen.

subsidy [ˈsʌbsɪdɪ] *n* Subvention *f*. **there is a ~ on butter** Butter wird subventioniert; **rent ~** Wohnungsbeihilfe *f*; **housing subsidies** *(for building, renovation etc)* Wohnungsbaubeihilfen *pl*.

subsist [səbˈsɪst] *vi (form)* sich ernähren, leben (*on* von).

subsistence [səbˈsɪstəns] *n (living)* Leben *nt (on* von); *(means of ~)* Existenz *f*, (Lebens)unterhalt *m*. **enough for ~** genug zum (Über)leben; **~ on £11 is impossible** es ist unmöglich, von £ 11 zu leben; **rice is their chief means of ~** sie ernähren sich hauptsächlich von Reis.

subsistence: **~ allowance** *n* Unterhaltszuschuß *m*; **~ farmer** *n* Bauer, der nur für den Eigenbedarf anbaut; **~ farming** *n* Ackerbau *m* für den Eigenbedarf; **~ level** *n* Existenzminimum *nt*; **at ~ level** auf dem Existenzminimum; **~ wage** *n* Minimallohn *m*.

sub: **~soil** *n* Untergrund *m*; **~sonic** *adj* Unterschall-; **~species** *n* Unterart, Subspezies *f*.

substance [ˈsʌbstəns] *n* **(a)** Substanz, Materie *f*, Stoff *m*. **what is this ~?** was ist das für eine Substanz?; **a yellow ~ on the wound** er rieb eine gelbe Masse auf die Wunde; **the meal lacked ~** das Essen war nicht sehr gehaltvoll.
(b) *no pl (subject matter)* Substanz *f*, Gehalt *m*; *(essence)* Kern *m*. **in ~** im wesentlichen, im großen und ganzen; **I agree with the ~ of his proposals** im wesentlichen stimme ich seinen Vorschlägen zu.
(c) *no pl (weight, importance)* Gewicht *nt*. **the book/argument lacks ~** das Buch hat keine Substanz/das Argument hat keine Durchschlagskraft; **there is some ~ in his claim** seine Behauptung ist nicht unfundiert.
(d) *no pl* **a man of ~** ein vermögender Mann.

substandard [,sʌbˈstændəd] *adj work, goods* minderwertig; *quality also, housing, achievement* unzulänglich; *(Ling)* nicht korrekt.

substantial [səbˈstænʃəl] *adj* **(a)** *meal, person, cloth* kräftig; *furniture also, building, firm* solide; *rope also* stark; *book* umfangreich.
(b) *(considerable) income, loss, gain, amount* beträchtlich; *erheblich; sum also* namhaft; *part, majority, contribution, improvement* also wesentlich, bedeutend; *(rich) landowner, businessman* vermögend, kapitalkräftig.
(c) *(weighty, important)* bedeutend; *proof, argument* überzeugend, stichhaltig; *difference* wesentlich, bedeutend. **~ agreement** im wesentlichen übereinstimmen.
(d) *(real, material)* körperlich, wesenhaft.

substantially [səbˈstænʃəlɪ] *adv* **(a)** *(solidly)* solide; *(considerably)* erheblich, beträchtlich, wesentlich. **~ built** *house* solide gebaut; *person* kräftig gebaut. **(b)** *(essentially, basically)* im wesentlichen.

substantiate [səbˈstænʃɪeɪt] *vt* erhärten, untermauern.

substantiation [səb,stænʃɪˈeɪʃən] *n* Erhärtung, Untermauerung *f*. **as yet this theory lacks ~** diese Theorie ist bisher noch nicht erhärtet; **in ~ of** zur Erhärtung (+*gen*).

substantival [,sʌbstənˈtaɪvəl] *adj (Gram)* substantivisch, Substantiv-.

substantive [ˈsʌbstəntɪv] **1** *adj* **(a)** *evidence, argument, reason* überzeugend, stichhaltig. **(b)** *(considerable) contribution, improvement, progress* beträchtlich, wesentlich, bedeutend. **(c)** **~ motion** endgültige Formulierung des Antrags. **(d)** *(Gram) see* **substantival**. **2** *n (Gram)* Substantiv, Hauptwort *nt*.

substantivize [ˈsʌbstəntɪ,vaɪz] *vt* substantivieren.

substation [ˈsʌb,steɪʃən] *n (Elec)* Umspann(ungs)werk *nt*.

substitute [ˈsʌbstɪtjuːt] **1** *n* Ersatz *m no pl*; *(representative also)* Vertretung *f*; *(male person also)* Ersatzmann *m*; *(Sport)* Ersatzspieler(in *f*), Auswechselspieler(in *f*) *m*. **to find a ~ for sb** für jdn Ersatz finden; **to use sth as a ~** etw als Ersatz benutzen; **coffee ~** Kaffee-Ersatz *m*; **various coffee ~s** verschiedene Sorten Kaffee-Ersatz.
2 *adj attr* Ersatz-.
3 *vt* **to ~ A for B** B durch A ersetzen; *(Sport also)* B gegen A austauschen *or* auswechseln; **~ 3 for X** setze für X 3 ein, substituiere 3 für X.
4 *vi* **to ~ for sb/sth** jdn vertreten, für jdn einspringen/etw ersetzen.

substitution [,sʌbstɪˈtjuːʃən] *n* Ersetzen *nt (of X for Y* von Y durch X); *(Sport)* Austausch *m (of X for Y* von Y gegen X); *(Math)* Substitution *f*, Einsetzen *nt (of X for Y* von X für Y). **the ~ of margarine for butter** der Gebrauch von Margarine statt Butter.

substratum [ˈsʌbˌstrɑːtəm], *n, pl* **substrata** [ˈsʌbˌstrɑːtə] Substrat *nt*; *(Geol)* Untergrund *m*; *(Sociol)* Substratum *nt*.

substructure [ˈsʌbˌstrʌktʃəʳ] *n* Unterbau *m*; *(fig also)* Grundlage *f*; *(Build)* Fundament *nt*; *(of bridge)* Widerlager *nt*.

subsume [səbˈsjuːm] *vt* **to ~ sth under sth** etw unter etw *(dat)* zusammenfassen *or* subsumieren *(geh)*.

subsystem [ˈsʌbˌsɪstəm] *n* Untersystem *nt*.

sub-teen [ˈsʌbˈtiːn] *n (esp US)* Schulkind *nt*.

sub-teenage [ˈsʌbˈtiːneɪdʒ] *adj attr (esp US)* Schulkinder-. **~ drinking** der Alkoholkonsum von (Schul)kindern.

subtenancy [,sʌbˈtenənsɪ] *n during his ~ of the flat/farm** während er Untermieter in der Wohnung/Unterpächter des Bauernhofes war.

subtenant [,sʌbˈtenənt] *n (of flat etc)* Untermieter(in *f*) *m*; *(of land)* Unterpächter(in *f*) *m*.

subtend [səbˈtend] *vt* gegenüberliegen (+*dat*).

subterfuge [ˈsʌbtəfjuːdʒ] *n (trickery)* Täuschung, List *f*; *(trick)* Trick *m*, List *f*. **to resort to ~** zu einer List greifen; **to be incapable of ~** *(zu)* keiner Falschheit *or* List fähig sein.

subterranean [,sʌbtəˈreɪnɪən] *adj* unterirdisch.

subtitle [ˈsʌbˌtaɪtl] **1** *n* Untertitel *m (also Film)*. **2** *vt film* mit Untertiteln versehen; *book etc* einen Untertitel geben (+*dat*). **the film is ~d in English** der Film hat englische Untertitel; **the book is ~d ...** das Buch hat den Untertitel ...

subtle [ˈsʌtl] *adj* **(a)** *(delicate, gentle)* fein; *irony, distinction also* subtil *(geh)*; *perfume, flavour also* zart; *hint, allusion* zart, leise; *charm* leise, unaufdringlich.

(b) (*ingenious, not obvious*) *remark, argument, point* scharfsinnig, spitzfindig; *design, construction, proof* raffiniert, fein ausgedacht *or* ausgetüftelt (*inf*). **he has a very ~ mind** er ist ein sehr subtiler Denker (*geh*); **be ~ about it** gehen Sie mit Zartgefühl vor.

(c) (*quick at seeing fine distinctions*) fein; *observer also* aufmerksam; *critic also* subtil (*geh*).

subtlety ['sʌtltɪ] *n see adj* **(a)** Feinheit *f*; Subtilität *f* (*geh*); Zartheit *f*; Unaufdringlichkeit *f*.

(b) Scharfsinn(igkeit *f*) *m*, Spitzfindigkeit *f*; Raffiniertheit *f*. **his methods lack ~** seinen Methoden fehlt (die) Finesse *or* Subtilität (*geh*); **the subtleties of the novel** die Feinheiten *pl* des Romans; **~ is wasted on him** feine Andeutungen nützen bei ihm nichts.

(c) Feinheit *f*; Aufmerksamkeit *f*; Subtilität *f* (*geh*).

subtly ['sʌtlɪ] *adv* fein; *flavoured also* delikat; *argue, reply* scharfsinnig, subtil (*geh*); *analyse, think* scharfsinnig; *achieve one's ends* auf raffinierte Weise. **~ different** auf subtile Weise verschieden *or* unterschiedlich; **he ~ suggested or schlug geschickt vor; his mind works very ~** er ist ein sehr subtiler Denker (*geh*); **it's just very ~ wrong** es ist schwer zu fassen, was falsch daran ist.

subtotal ['sʌb,təʊtl] *n* Zwischen- *or* Teilsumme *f*, Zwischen- *or* Teilergebnis *nt*.

subtract [səb'trækt] *vti* abziehen, subtrahieren (*from* von).

subtraction [səb'trækʃən] *n* Subtraktion *f*; (*act also*) Abziehen *nt*.

subtrahend ['sʌbtrə,hend] *n* (*Math form*) Subtrahend *m*.

subtropical [,sʌb'trɒpɪkəl] *adj* subtropisch.

subtype ['sʌb,taɪp] *n* Unterart *f*.

suburb ['sʌbɜːb] *n* Vorort *m*. **in the ~s** am Stadtrand.

suburban [sə'bɜːbən] *adj* Vorort-; *area also* vorstädtisch; (*pej*) spießig, kleinbürgerlich. **the area is becoming increasingly ~** die Gegend nimmt immer mehr vorstädtischen Charakter an; **~ line** (*Rail*) Vorortbahn *f*.

suburbia [sə'bɜːbɪə] *n* (*usu pej*) die Vororte *pl*. **to live in ~** am Stadtrand wohnen; **that's typical of ~!** typisch Spießbürger!

subvention [səb'venʃən] *n* Subvention *f*.

subversion [səb'vɜːʃən] *n, no pl* Subversion *f*; (*of rights, freedom etc*) Untergrabung, Unterminierung *f*. **the US was accused of ~** in Chile die USA wurden subversiver *or* umstürzlerischer Tätigkeiten in Chile beschuldigt; **~ is rife in the army** die Armee ist voll(er) subversiver Elemente.

subversive [səb'vɜːsɪv] **1** *adj* subversiv, umstürzlerisch. **~ elements** subversive Elemente *or* Kräfte *pl*. **2** *n* Umstürzler(in *f*) *m*, Subversive(r) *mf*.

subvert [səb'vɜːt] *vt government* zu stürzen versuchen; *faith, morals etc* untergraben, unterminieren; *person* zum Umsturz anstacheln.

subway ['sʌbweɪ] *n* Unterführung *f*; (*for cars also*) Tunnel *m*; (*US Rail*) U-Bahn *f*.

subzero ['sʌb'zɪərəʊ] *adj temperature* unter Null, unter dem Nullpunkt.

succeed [sək'siːd] **1** *vi* **a** (*be successful*) (*person*) erfolgreich sein, Erfolg haben; (*plan etc also*) gelingen. **to ~ in business/in a plan** geschäftlich/mit einem Plan erfolgreich sein; **I ~ed in doing it** es gelang mir, es zu tun; **you'll only ~ in making things worse** damit erreichst du nur, daß alles noch schlimmer wird; **nothing ~s like success** (*prov*) nichts ist so erfolgreich wie der Erfolg; **if at first you don't ~**(*, try, try, try again*) (*Prov*) wirf die Flinte nicht gleich ins Korn (*prov*).

(b) (*come next*) **to ~ to an office** in einem Amt nachfolgen; **he ~ed to his father's position** er wurde (der) Nachfolger seines Vaters, er trat die Nachfolge seines Vaters an (*geh*); **to ~ to the throne** die Thronfolge antreten; **to ~ to an estate** einen Besitz erben; **there ~ed a period of peace** (*form*) es folgte eine Zeit des Friedens.

2 *vt* (*come after, take the place of*) folgen (+*dat*), folgen auf (+*acc*); (*person also*) Nachfolger(in *f*) *m* werden (+*gen*). **to ~ sb in a post/in office** jds Nachfolger werden, jds Stelle (*acc*) übernehmen/jdm im Amt nachfolgen; **who ~ed James I?** wer kam nach *or* folgte auf Jakob I.?

succeeding [sək'siːdɪŋ] *adj* folgend. **~ generations** spätere *or* nachfolgende Generationen *pl*.

success [sək'ses] *n* Erfolg *m*. **without ~** ohne Erfolg, erfolglos; **wishing you every ~ in your exams/new career** mit besten Wünschen für eine erfolgreiche Prüfung/viel Erfolg im neuen Beruf; **to make a ~ of sth** mit *or* bei etw Erfolg haben, mit *or* bei etw erfolgreich sein; **they made a ~ of their marriage** ihre Ehe war ein Erfolg; **to be a ~ with sb** bei jdm ankommen; **the new car is not a ~** das neue Auto ist nicht gerade ein (durchschlagender) Erfolg; **the plan was a ~** der Plan war erfolgreich *or* ein voller Erfolg; **to meet with ~** Erfolg haben, erfolgreich sein; **I was ~ in doing it** es gelang mir, es zu tun; **~ story** Erfolgsstory *f*; (*person*) Erfolg *m*.

successful [sək'sesfʊl] *adj* erfolgreich. **to be ~** erfolgreich sein, Erfolg haben (*in* mit, bei); **to be entirely ~** ein voller Erfolg sein; **I was ~ in doing it** es gelang mir, es zu tun.

successfully [sək'sesfəlɪ] *adv* erfolgreich, mit Erfolg.

succession [sək'seʃən] *n* **(a)** Folge, Serie *f*; (*with no intervening period*) (Aufeinander)folge, Kette *f*. **a ~ of visitors** eine Kette *or* Serie von Besuchern; **life is a ~ of joys and sorrows das Leben ist in steter Wechsel von Kummer und Freude; **in ~** nacheinander, hintereinander; **in quick *or* rapid ~** in rascher Folge, schnell hintereinander.

(b) (*to post*) Nachfolge *f*; (*to throne*) Thronfolge *f*; (*to title, estate*) Erbfolge *f*. **his ~ to the office/title/throne** seine Amtsübernahme/seine Übernahme des Titels/seine Thronbesteigung; **in ~ to sb** als jds Nachfolger(in *f*) *m*, in jds Nachfolge (*dat*) (*geh*); **fourth in ~ to the throne** an vierter Stelle in der Thronfolge; *see* **apostolic**.

succession state *n* Nachfolgestaat *m*.

successive [sək'sesɪv] *adj* aufeinanderfolgend *attr*. **4 ~ days** 4 Tage nacheinander *or* hintereinander, 4 aufeinanderfolgende Tage; **he was sacked from 3 ~ jobs** er wurde nacheinander *or* hintereinander aus 3 verschiedenen Stellen hinausgeworfen.

successively [sək'sesɪvlɪ] *adv* nacheinander, hintereinander.

successor [sək'sesəʳ] *n* Nachfolger(in *f*) *m* (*to gen*); (*to throne*) Thronfolger(in *f*) *m*.

succinct [sək'sɪŋkt] *adj* knapp, kurz und bündig *pred*.

succinctly [sək'sɪŋktlɪ] *adv* kurz und bündig, in kurzen *or* knappen Worten *or* Zügen; (*write*) in knappem *or* gedrängtem Stil. **as he very ~ put it** wie er so treffend bemerkte.

succinctness [sək'sɪŋktnɪs] *n* Knappheit, Kürze *f*. **with great ~** kurz und bündig, in kurzen Worten; (*write*) in knappem Stil.

succour, (*US*) **succor** ['sʌkəʳ] (*liter*) **1** *n* Beistand *m*. **she was his ~** sie war ihm ein Beistand. **2** *vt* beistehen (+*dat*).

succubus ['sʌkjʊbəs] *n, pl* **succubi** ['sʌkjʊbaɪ] Sukkubus *m*.

succulence ['sʌkjʊləns] *n* Saftigkeit *f*.

succulent ['sʌkjʊlənt] **1** *adj peach, steak* saftig; (*Bot*) *plant, stem* fleischig, sukkulent (*spec*). **2** *n* (*Bot*) Fettpflanze, Sukkulente (*spec*) *f*.

succumb [sə'kʌm] *vi* erliegen (*to dat*); (*to threats*) sich beugen (*to dat*).

such [sʌtʃ] **1** *adj* **(a)** (*of that kind*) solche(r, s). **~ a person** so *or* solch ein Mensch; **~ a book** so ein Buch, ein solches Buch; **~ people/books** solche Leute/Bücher; **many/few/all ~ people/books** viele/wenige/all solche Leute/Bücher; **all ~ books are very expensive** solche Bücher sind sehr teuer; **do you have ~ a book?** haben Sie so ein Buch?; **~ a thing** so etwas, so was (*inf*); **there's ~ a thing as divorce** es gibt so etwas wie eine Scheidung; **I said no ~ thing** das habe ich nie gesagt; **no ~ thing** nichts dergleichen; **(I'll) do no ~ thing** ich werde mich/du wirst dich hüten; **there's no ~ thing as a unicorn** so etwas wie ein Einhorn gibt es nicht; **... or some ~ idea** ... oder so etwas, ... oder so was in der Richtung (*inf*), ... oder so ähnlich; **... or some ~ name/place** ... oder so (ähnlich); **he was ~ a one/just ~ another** er war einer von ihnen/auch (so) einer; **in ~ a case** in einem solchen Fall; **men/books ~ as these, ~ men/books as these** Männer/Bücher wie diese, solche Männer/Bücher; **writers ~ as Agatha Christie, ~ writers as Agatha Christie** (*solche*) Schriftsteller wie Agatha Christie; **he's not ~ a fool as you think** er ist nicht so dumm, wie Sie denken; **I'm not ~ a fool as to believe that *or* that I'd believe that** ich bin nicht so dumm *or* kein solcher Dummkopf, daß ich das glaube; **only ~ a fool as John would do that** nur (solch) ein Dummkopf wie John würde das tun; **~ people as attended** die(jenigen), die anwesend waren; **I'll give you ~ books/money as I have** was ich an Büchern/Geld habe, gebe ich Ihnen.

(b) (*so much, so great etc*) (*with uncountable nouns*) solche(r, s); (*with countable nouns*) so, solch, derartige(r, s). **he's ~ a liar** er ist so *or* solch ein Lügner, er ist ein derartiger *or* solcher Lügner; **he did it in ~ a way that ...** er machte es so, daß ...; **~ wealth/beauty!** welch (ein) Reichtum/welche Schönheit!; **he's always in ~ a hurry** er hat es immer so eilig.

(c) *pred* **his surprise was ~ that ..., ~ was his surprise that ...** seine Überraschung war so groß, daß ..., er war so überrascht, daß ...; **his manner was ~ that ...** er benahm sich so, daß ...; **her speech was ~ that ...** ihre Rede war so gehalten, daß ...

(d) *see* **such-and-such**.

2 *adv* so, solch (*geh*). **nobody else makes ~ a good cup of tea as you** niemand kocht so guten Tee wie du; **it's ~ a long time ago** es ist so lange her.

3 *pron* **rabbits and hares and ~** Kaninchen, Hasen und dergleichen; **~ being the case ...** in diesem Fall ...; **~ was not my intention** dies war nicht meine Absicht; **~ is not the case** dies ist nicht der Fall; **~ is life!** so ist das Leben!; **those and ~ as those** (*hum inf*) die oberen Zehntausend (*hum*); **may all ~ perish!** mögen sie alle verderben!; **as ~** an sich; **~ as?** (*wie*) zum Beispiel?; **~ as it is** so, wie es nun mal ist; **the food, ~ as there was of it** ... das Essen, soweit vorhanden ..., was an Essen da war, ...; **I'll give you ~ as I have** ich gebe Ihnen, was ich habe.

such-and-such ['sʌtʃənsʌtʃ] (*inf*) **1** *adj* **~ a time/town** die und die Zeit/Stadt. **2** *n* das und das *nt*.

suchlike ['sʌtʃlaɪk] (*inf*) **1** *adj* solche. **2** *pron* dergleichen.

suck [sʌk] **1** *n* **to have *or* take a ~** (*at straw*) saugen, ziehen (*at an* +*dat*); (*at lemonade etc*) nuckeln (*inf*), ziehen (*at an* +*dat*); (*at lollipop*) lutschen (*at an* +*dat*); **to give ~** (*to a baby*) (*old*) (ein Baby) stillen.

2 *vt* saugen; *breast, straw* saugen an (+*dat*); *sweet, pastille* lutschen; *lollipop* lutschen an (+*dat*); *thumb* lutschen *or* nukkeln (*inf*) an (+*dat*). **to ~ one's teeth** an den Zähnen saugen; **to ~ the juice out of *or* from sth** den Saft aus etw heraussaugen; **to ~ sb dry** (*fig*) jdn bis aufs Blut aussaugen; **don't teach your grandmother to ~ eggs** (*prov*) da will das Ei wieder klüger sein als die Henne (*prov*).

3 *vi* (*at an* +*dat*) saugen; (*at bottle also, at dummy*) nuckeln (*inf*); (*at lollipop*) lutschen; (*at thumb*) lutschen, nuckeln (*inf*); (*at pipe, at straw, through straw*) ziehen. **he always makes a ~ing noise when he eats his soup** er schlürft seine Suppe immer.

♦**suck down** *vt sep* hinunterziehen.

♦**suck in** *vt sep liquid, dust* aufsaugen; *air* (*ventilator*) ansaugen; (*person*) in tiefen Zügen einatmen; *cheeks* einziehen; (*fig*) *knowledge, facts* (in sich *acc*) aufsaugen.

♦**suck off** *vt sep* (*vulg*) **to ~ sb ~** jdm einen (ab)lutschen (*sl*).

♦**suck under** *vt sep* hinunterziehen; (*completely*) verschlingen.

♦**suck up** **1** *vt sep liquid, dust* aufsaugen. **the child ~ed ~ his milk** das Kind trank seine Milch (mit einem Strohhalm) aus. **2** *vi* (*inf*) **to ~ ~ to sb** jdm schöntun (*inf*).

sucker ['sʌkəʳ] *n* **(a)** (*rubber ~, Zool*) Saugnapf *m*; (*Bot*) unterirdischer Ausläufer; (*on creeper*) Häkchen *nt*.

(b) (*US inf: lollipop*) Lutscher *m*. **all-day ~** Dauerlutscher *m*.

(c) (*sl: fool*) Simpel (*S Ger*), Trottel (*inf*) *m*. **to be a ~ for sth** (immer) auf etw (*acc*) hereinfallen; **to be had for a ~** zum Narren gehalten werden, für dumm verkauft werden; **he's looking for some ~** who'll lend him £20 er sucht einen Dummen, der ihm £ 20 leiht.

sucking-pig ['sʌkɪŋpɪg] *n* Spanferkel *nt*.

suckle ['sʌkl] **1** *vt child* stillen; *animal* säugen. **2** *vi* saugen, trinken.

suckling ['sʌklɪŋ] *n* (*old*) Säugling *m*; (*animal*) Jungtier *nt*. **out of the mouths of babes and ~s** (*Bibl*) aus dem Mund von Kindern und Säuglingen; (*fig*) Kindermund tut Wahrheit kund (*Prov*).

sucrose ['suːkrəʊz] *n* Saccharose *f*, pflanzlicher Zucker.

suction ['sʌkʃən] *n* Saugwirkung *f*; (*caused by air or water currents*) Sog *m*. **~-pump** Saugpumpe *f*.

Sudan [suˈdɑːn] *n* (the) **~** der Sudan.

Sudanese [ˌsuːdəˈniːz] **1** *adj* sudanesisch, sudanisch. **2** *n* Sudanese *m*, Sudanesin *f*, Sudaner(in *f*) *m*.

sudden ['sʌdn] **1** *adj* plötzlich; *movement also* jäh, abrupt; *drop, silence also* jäh; (*unexpected*) *bend, change of direction* unerwartet. **there was a ~ bend** da war plötzlich eine Kurve, da war eine unerwartete Kurve; **~ death** (*play-off*) Stich- or Entscheidungskampf *m*; (*Ftbl*) Elfmeterschießen *nt*.

2 *n* **all of a ~** (ganz) plötzlich, urplötzlich (*inf*).

suddenly ['sʌdnlɪ] *adv* plötzlich; *move also* jäh, abrupt.

suddenness ['sʌdnɪs] *n* Plötzlichkeit *f*; (*of movement also*) Jäheit, Abruptheit *f*.

Sudetenland [suːˈdeɪtənˌlænd] *n* Sudetenland *nt*.

suds [sʌdz] *npl* Seifenwasser *nt* or -lauge *f*; (*lather*) (Seifen)schaum *m*; (*US sl: beer*) Bier *nt*.

sue [suː] **1** *vt* (a) (*Jur*) verklagen, (gerichtlich) belangen. **to ~ sb for sth** jdn auf etw (*acc*) or wegen etw verklagen; **to ~ sb for divorce** gegen jdn die Scheidung einreichen; **to ~ sb for damages** jdn auf Schadenersatz verklagen; **I'll ~ you for every penny you've got** ich werde (vor Gericht) den letzten Pfennig aus dir herausholen.

(b) (*liter: ask*) bitten, anflehen (*for* um).

2 *vi* (a) (*Jur*) klagen, einen Prozeß anstrengen, Klage erheben. **to ~ for divorce** die Scheidung einreichen.

(b) (*liter*) **to ~ for peace/mercy** um Frieden/Gnade bitten.

suede [sweɪd] **1** *n* Wildleder *nt*; (*soft, fine also*) Veloursleder *nt*. **2** *adj shoes, boots* Wildleder-, aus Wildleder; (*of finer quality*) *gloves, coat etc also* Veloursleder-, aus Veloursleder.

suet ['sʊɪt] *n* Nierenfett *nt*, Nierentalg *m*. **~ pudding** (*sweet*) im Wasserbad gekochte Süßspeise, zu der Nierenfett verwendet wird; (*savoury*) Pastetenteig mit Nierenfett.

Suetonius [swiːˈtəʊnɪəs] *n* Sueton(ius) *m*.

suety ['sʊɪtɪ] *adj* talgig.

Suez ['suːɪz] *n* Sues, Suez *nt*. **~ Canal** Sueskanal, Suezkanal *m*.

suffer ['sʌfə^r] **1** *vt* (a) (*undergo, be subjected to*) *pain, loss, setback* erleiden; *hardship also, hunger* leiden; *headache, stress, effects etc* leiden unter or an (+*dat*); *shock* haben. **to ~ defeat/death** eine Niederlage/den Tod (*geh*) erleiden; **the pound ~ed further losses** das Pfund mußte weitere Einbußen hinnehmen; **her popularity ~ed** a decline ihre Beliebtheit hat gelitten.

(b) (*tolerate*) dulden, ertragen. **he doesn't ~ fools gladly** Dummheit ist ihm ein Greuel.

(c) (*liter: allow*) zulassen, dulden. **to ~ sth to be done** zulassen or dulden, daß etw geschieht; **~ the little children to come unto me** (*Bibl*) lasset die Kindlein zu mir kommen (*Bibl*).

2 *vi* (*physically, mentally, fig*) leiden (*from* unter +*dat*, *from illness* an +*dat*); (*as punishment, in hell etc*) büßen. **he's still ~ing from the effects** er leidet immer noch an or unter den Folgen; **he was ~ing from shock** er hatte einen Schock (erlitten); **your health/work will ~** deine Gesundheit/Arbeit wird darunter leiden; **the runners are clearly ~ing in this heat** die Hitze macht den Läufern sichtlich zu schaffen; **the regiment ~ed badly** das Regiment erlitt schwere Verluste; **the town ~ed badly in the raids** die Stadt wurde bei den Luftangriffen schwer in Mitleidenschaft gezogen; **how I ~ed!** was ich alles durchgemacht habe!; **to ~ for one's sins** für seine Sünden büßen; **you'll ~ for this!** das wirst du büßen!; **we will see that you don't ~ by the changes** wir werden zusehen, daß Ihnen aus den Umstellungen keine Nachteile entstehen.

sufferance ['sʌfərəns] *n* Duldung *f*. **on ~** (nur or stillschweigend) geduldet; **he's allowed to sleep here on ~ only** es wird nur geduldet, daß er hier schläft.

sufferer ['sʌfərə^r] *n* (*Med*) Leidende(r) *mf* (*from* an +*dat*). **diabetes ~s, ~s from diabetes** Diabeteskranke, an Diabetes Leidende *pl*; **he's been a ~ from arthritis for several years** er leidet seit mehreren Jahren an Arthritis; **the ~s from the earthquake** die Erdbebenopfer *pl*; **my fellow ~s at the concert** meine Leidensgenossen bei dem Konzert.

suffering ['sʌfərɪŋ] *n* Leiden *nt*; (*hardship, deprivation*) Leid *nt* no *pl*.

suffice [səˈfaɪs] (*form*) **1** *vi* genügen, (aus)reichen. **2** *vt* genügen (+*dat*) (*geh*); *sb also* zufriedenstellen. **~ it to say ...** es reicht wohl, wenn ich sage, ...

sufficiency [səˈfɪʃənsɪ] *n* (*adequacy*) Hinlänglichkeit *f*. **to have a ~** genügend haben; **to have (an) ample ~** mehr als genug haben.

sufficient [səˈfɪʃənt] *adj* genügend, ausreichend, genug *inv*; *maturity, temperature* genügend *attr*, ausreichend; *reason, condition, explanation, translation* hinreichend. **is that ~ reason for his dismissal?** ist das Grund genug or ein ausreichender Grund, ihn zu entlassen?; **to be ~** genügen, ausreichen, genug sein; **thank you, that's ~** danke, das genügt or reicht; **I think you have drunk quite ~** ich glaube, Sie haben genug getrunken; **we haven't got ~ to live on** wir haben nicht genug zum Leben.

sufficiently [səˈfɪʃəntlɪ] *adv* genug. **~ good/warm** *etc* gut/warm *etc* genug *pred*, genügend or ausreichend gut/warm *etc*; **a ~ large number** eine ausreichend große Anzahl; **it's not ~ cooked** es ist nicht gar.

suffix ['sʌfɪks] **1** *n* (*Ling*) Suffix *nt*, Nachsilbe *f*; (*in code etc*) Zusatz *m*. **2** *vt* anfügen, anhängen (*to* an +*acc*).

suffocate ['sʌfəkeɪt] *vti* (*lit, fig*) ersticken. **this existence/he is suffocating me** dieses Leben/er erdrückt mich; **he felt ~d in that environment** er hatte das Gefühl, in dieser Umgebung zu ersticken; **he was ~d by the smoke** er erstickte am Rauch.

suffocating ['sʌfəkeɪtɪŋ] *adj* (*lit*) erstickend *attr*; (*fig also*) erdrückend *attr*; *heat* drückend *attr*, brütend *attr*. **intellectually ~** geisttötend.

suffocation [ˌsʌfəˈkeɪʃən] *n* (*lit, fig*) Ersticken *nt*.

suffragan ['sʌfrəgən] **1** *adj* Suffragan-. **2** *n* Suffragan(bischof) *m*.

suffrage ['sʌfrɪdʒ] *n* Wahl- or Stimmrecht *nt*; (*form: vote*) Stimme *f*. **universal ~** das allgemeine Wahlrecht; **female ~** das Frauenstimmrecht.

suffragette [ˌsʌfrəˈdʒet] *n* Suffragette, Stimmrechtlerin *f*.

suffuse [səˈfjuːz] *vt* erfüllen; (*light*) durchfluten. **~d with light** in Licht getaucht, lichtdurchflutet (*geh*); **eyes ~d with tears** Augen voller Tränen, tränenerfüllte Augen; **a blush ~d her face** Schamröte or (eine) Röte überzog ihr Gesicht.

sugar ['ʃʊgə^r] **1** *n* (a) Zucker *m*. (b) (*inf: term of affection*) (meine) Süße, (mein) Süßer *m*, Schätzchen *nt* (*all inf*). **2** *vt* zuckern, süßen; (*fig*) *criticism etc* versüßen, mildern. **to ~ the pill** die bittere Pille versüßen.

sugar in *cpds* Zucker-; **~ basin** *n* Zuckerdose *f*; **~ beet** *n* Zuckerrübe *f*; **~ bowl** *n* Zuckerdose *f*; **~ candy** *n* Kandis(zucker) *m*; (*US: sweet*) Bonbon *nt* or *m*; **~ cane** *n* Zuckerrohr *nt*; **~-coated** *adj* mit Zucker überzogen; **~-daddy** *n* (*inf*) she's looking for a **~-daddy** sie sucht einen alten Knacker, den sie aushält (*inf*); **~ diabetes** *n* Zuckerkrankheit, Diabetes (*spec*) *f*, Zucker *m* (*inf*).

sugared ['ʃʊgəd] *adj* gezuckert; *almonds* Zucker-; *words* (honig)süß.

sugar: ~ loaf *n* Zuckerhut *m*; **S~ Loaf Mountain** der Zuckerhut; **~ maple** *n* Zuckerahorn *m*; **~plum** *n* Bonbon *nt* or *m*, Süßigkeit *f*; **~plum fairy** Zuckerfee *f*; **~ tongs** *npl* Zuckerzange *f*.

sugary ['ʃʊgərɪ] *adj taste* süß; (*full of sugar*) zuckerig; (*fig*) *style, music etc* süßlich.

suggest [səˈdʒest] **1** *vt* (a) (*propose*) *candidate, place etc* vorschlagen; *plan, idea also* anregen. **I ~ that we go, I ~ going** ich schlage vor, zu gehen or (daß) wir gehen; **what do you ~ we do?** was schlagen Sie vor?; **are you ~ing I should tell a deliberate lie?** soll das heißen, daß ich bewußt lügen soll?; **I am ~ing nothing of the kind** das habe ich nicht gesagt.

(b) (*put forward for consideration*) *explanation, theory* nahelegen, vorbringen. **I ~ (to you) that ...** (*esp Jur*) ich möchte (Ihnen) nahelegen, daß ...

(c) (*insinuate, hint at*) andeuten; (*unpleasantly*) unterstellen. **what are you trying to ~?** worauf wollen Sie hinaus?, was wollen Sie damit sagen?; **I'm not trying to ~ that** he's lying ich will damit nicht unterstellen or sagen, daß er lügt.

(d) (*indicate: facts, data, sb's action*) andeuten, hindeuten auf (+*acc*); (*evoke*) (*music, poem*) denken lassen an (+*acc*); (*symbolism, colours*) andeuten. **these incredible coincidences do certainly ~ complicity** diese unwahrscheinlichen Zufälle deuten zweifellos auf Mittäterschaft hin; **the symptoms would ~ an operation** die Symptome lassen eine Operation angeraten erscheinen.

(e) (*Psych*) **to ~ sth to sb** jdm etw suggerieren.

2 *vr* (*idea, thought, plan*) sich aufdrängen, sich anbieten, naheliegen.

suggestibility [səˌdʒestɪˈbɪlɪtɪ] *n* Beeinflußbarkeit *f*.

suggestible [səˈdʒestɪbl] *adj person* beeinflußbar.

suggestion [səˈdʒestʃən] *n* (a) (*proposal, recommendation*) Vorschlag *m*, Anregung *f*. **my ~ is that ...** mein Vorschlag lautet ..., ich schlage vor, daß ...; **following your ~** auf Ihren Vorschlag or Ihre Anregung hin; **Rome was your ~** Rom war deine Idee; **his ~ of John as a candidate** daß er John als Kandidaten vorgeschlagen hat; **John was his ~ as candidate** er schlug John als Kandidaten vor; **I'm open to ~s** Vorschläge sind or jeder Vorschlag ist willkommen.

(b) (*theory, explanation*) Vermutung *f*. **he made the ~ that ...** er äußerte die Vermutung, daß ...; **that theory was Professor Higgins' ~** die Theorie stammt von Professor Higgins.

(c) (*insinuation, hint*) Andeutung, Anspielung *f*; (*unpleasant*) Unterstellung *f*. **I resent that ~** ich weise diese Unterstellung zurück; **I intended no ~ that ...** ich wollte damit nicht andeuten or unterstellen, daß ...; **there is no ~ that he was involved** (*nobody is suggesting it*) niemand deutet an or unterstellt, daß er beteiligt war; (*no indication*) es gibt keinen Hinweis darauf or Anhaltspunkt dafür, daß er beteiligt war.

(d) (*trace*) Spur *f*. **with a ~ of irony in his voice** mit einer Spur or einem Anflug von Ironie in der Stimme.

(e) (*impression*) Eindruck *m*, Vorstellung *f*. **to create a ~ of depth** um den Eindruck von Tiefe zu erwecken.

(f) (*also indecent ~*) unsittlicher Antrag.

(g) (*Psych*) Suggestion *f*.

suggestions-box [səˈdʒestʃənzˌbɒks] *n* Kasten *m* für Verbesserungsvorschläge, Kummerkasten (*inf*) *m*.

suggestive [səˈdʒestɪv] *adj* (a) **to be ~ of sth** an etw (*acc*) denken lassen; (*create impression of*) den Eindruck von etw erwecken or vermitteln; (*be indicative of*) auf etw (*acc*) hindeuten.

(b) (*Psych*) suggestiv, Suggestiv-.

(c) (*indecent*) *joke, remark etc* zweideutig, anzüglich; *movements, gesture* aufreizend.

suggestively [səˈdʒestɪvlɪ] *adv* vielsagend, anzüglich; *move, dance* aufreizend.

suggestiveness [səˈdʒestɪvnɪs] n Zweideutigkeit, Anzüglichkeit f. the ~ of her dancing ihr aufreizendes Tanzen.

suicidal [ˌsuɪˈsaɪdl] adj selbstmörderisch. that would be ~ das wäre glatter Selbstmord; to have ~ tendencies zum Selbstmord neigen; I feel ~ this morning ich möchte heute morgen am liebsten sterben.

suicide [ˈsuɪsaɪd] n Selbstmord, Freitod (euph), Suizid (spec) m; (person) Selbstmörder(in f), Suizidär(in f) (spec) m. to commit ~ Selbstmord begehen; to contemplate ~ sich mit Selbstmordgedanken tragen; ~ attempt or bid Selbstmord- or Suizidversuch m; ~ pact Selbstmordabkommen nt; ~ squad Selbstmorddezernat nt.

sui generis [ˌsuːaɪˈdʒenərɪs] adj sui generis (geh), einzig(artig).

suit [suːt] 1 n (a) Anzug m; (woman's) Kostüm nt. ~ of clothes Garnitur f (Kleider); they bought him a new ~ of clothes sie kleideten ihn von Kopf bis Fuß neu ein; ~ of armour Rüstung f.
(b) (Jur) Prozeß m, Verfahren nt. to bring a ~ (against sb for sth) (wegen etw gegen jdn) Klage erheben or einen Prozeß anstrengen; he lost his ~ er hat seinen Prozeß verloren.
(c) (Cards) Farbe f. short ~kurze Farbe; long/strong ~ lange/starke Farbe; (fig) starke Seite, Stärke f; to follow ~ (lit) Farbe bedienen; (fig) jds Beispiel (dat) folgen.
(d) (old, liter: in marriage) Werbung f. to press one's ~ seiner Werbung (dat) Nachdruck verleihen; he failed in his ~ seine Werbung wurde zurückgewiesen.
(e) (form: request) Anliegen nt (form), Bitte f. to press one's ~ seinem Anliegen or seiner Bitte Nachdruck verleihen.
2 vt (a) (be convenient, pleasing to) (arrangement, date, price) passen (+dat); (climate, food) bekommen (+dat); (occupation, job) gefallen (+dat). ~s me! (inf) ist mir recht (inf), mir soll's recht sein (inf); that ~s me fine! (inf) das ist mir recht; that would ~ me nicely (time, arrangement) das würde mir gut (in den Kram inf) passen; (house, job etc) das wäre genau das richtige für mich; when would it ~ you to come? wann würde es Ihnen passen?, wann wäre es Ihnen recht?; I know what ~s me best ich weiß, was für mich das beste ist.
(b) (be suitable, right for) geeignet sein für. the hall wasn't ~ed to such a meeting die Halle war für eine solche Versammlung nicht geeignet; he is very well ~ed to the job er eignet sich sehr gut für die Stelle; he is not ~ed to be or for a doctor er eignet sich nicht zum Arzt; they are well ~ed (to each other) sie passen gut zusammen.
(c) (clothes, hairstyle) (gut) stehen (+dat), passen zu. you ~ a beard/fringe ein Bart/Pony steht dir gut; such behaviour hardly ~s you so ein Benehmen steht dir nicht an.
(d) (adapt) anpassen (to dat). to ~ one's style to the audience sich dem Publikumsgeschmack anpassen, sich nach dem Publikum richten; he makes the music ~ the mood of the poem er stimmt die Musik auf die Stimmung des Gedichts ab; ~ing the action to the word he ... er setzte seine Worte in die Tat um und...
(e) (please) gefallen (+dat), zufriedenstellen. you can't ~ everybody man kann es nicht jedem recht machen; we try to ~ every taste wir versuchen, für jeden Geschmack zu finden or jedem Geschmack gerecht zu werden.
3 vr he ~s himself er tut, was er will or was ihm paßt; you can ~ yourself whether you come or not du kannst kommen oder nicht, ganz wie du willst; ~ yourself! wie du willst!, mach, was du willst!; I like to be able to ~ myself ich möchte gern tun und lassen können, was ich will.
4 vi (be suitable) passen.

suitability [ˌsuːtəˈbɪlɪtɪ] n Angemessenheit f; (of person for job) Eignung f. they discussed his ~ as a husband for their daughter sie diskutierten darüber, ob er sich als Ehemann für ihre Tochter eignete; the ~ of a film for children ob ein Film für Kinder geeignet ist.

suitable [ˈsuːtəbl] adj (convenient, practical, right for the purpose) geeignet, passend; (socially, culturally appropriate to the occasion) angemessen. to be ~ for sb (date, place) jdm passen; (film, job) für jdn geeignet sein; (hairstyle, clothes) das richtige für jdn sein; to be ~ for sth für etw geeignet sein, sich für etw eignen; (socially appropriate) einer Sache (dat) angemessen sein; the most ~ man for the job der am besten geeignete Mann für den Posten; would 8 o'clock be a ~ time? würde Ihnen etc 8 Uhr passen?, wäre Ihnen etc 8 Uhr recht?; Tuesday is the most ~ day Dienstag ist der günstigste or beste Tag, Dienstag paßt am besten; she's not ~ for him sie paßt nicht zu ihm; she's not a ~ person to have care of children sie eignet sich nicht zur Betreuung von Kindern.

suitably [ˈsuːtəblɪ] adv angemessen; behave also, apologize geziemend (geh), wie es sich gehört. he was ~ impressed er war geziemend beeindruckt; I'm ~ impressed ich bin ja auch beeindruckt; a ~ elegant room ein Raum von angemessener Eleganz; we camped ~ close to the hills wir zelteten in günstiger Nähe der Berge.

suitcase [ˈsuːtˌkeɪs] n Koffer m. to live out of a ~ aus dem Koffer leben.

suite [swiːt] n (of retainers) Gefolge nt; (of furniture) Garnitur f; (chairs and sofa) Sitzgarnitur f; (of rooms) Suite, Zimmerflucht f; (Mus) Suite f. bedroom ~ Schlafzimmergarnitur or -einrichtung f.

suiting [ˈsuːtɪŋ] n (fabric) Anzugstoff m.

suitor [ˈsuːtər] n (a) (old: of woman) Freier m (old). (b) (Jur) Kläger(in f) m.

sulfa etc (US) see **sulpha** etc.

sulk [sʌlk] 1 vi schmollen, eingeschnappt sein, beleidigt sein. 2 n Schmollen nt. to have a ~/the ~s schmollen, den Eingeschnappten/die Eingeschnappte spielen; to go into a ~ sich in den Schmollwinkel zurückziehen, einschnappen.

sulkily [ˈsʌlkɪlɪ] adv see adj.

sulkiness [ˈsʌlkɪnɪs] n Schmollen nt. the ~ of his expression sein eingeschnappter or schmollender Gesichtsausdruck.

sulky[1] [ˈsʌlkɪ] adj (+er) answer eingeschnappt, beleidigt; person, expression also schmollend.

sulky[2] n (Sport) Sulky nt.

sullen [ˈsʌlən] adj (a) (morose) mürrisch, mißmutig, verdrießlich. (b) (fig) landscape, sky etc düster, finster.

sullenly [ˈsʌlənlɪ] adv see adj (a).

sullenness [ˈsʌlənnɪs] n see adj (a) Mißmutigkeit, Verdrießlichkeit f. (b) (liter) Düsterkeit f.

sully [ˈsʌlɪ] vt reputation besudeln.

sulpha, (US) **sulfa** [ˈsʌlfə] adj ~ drug Sulfonamid nt.

sulphate, (US) **sulfate** [ˈsʌlfeɪt] n Sulfat nt, schwefelsaures Salz. copper ~ Kupfersulfat or -vitriol nt.

sulphide, (US) **sulfide** [ˈsʌlfaɪd] n Sulfid nt.

sulphite, (US) **sulfite** [ˈsʌlfaɪt] n Sulfit nt.

sulphonamide, (US) **sulfonamide** [sʌlˈfɒnəmaɪd] n Sulfonamid nt.

sulphur, (US) **sulfur** [ˈsʌlfər] n Schwefel m. ~ dioxide Schwefeldioxid nt.

sulphureous, (US) **sulfureous** [sʌlˈfjʊərɪəs] adj see **sulphurous.**

sulphuretted, (US) **sulfuretted** [ˈsʌlfjʊˌretɪd] adj geschwefelt. ~ hydrogen Schwefelwasserstoff m.

sulphuric, (US) **sulfuric** [sʌlˈfjʊərɪk] adj Schwefel-. ~ acid Schwefelsäure f.

sulphurize, (US) **sulfurize** [ˈsʌlfjʊˌraɪz] vt schwefeln.

sulphurous, (US) **sulfurous** [ˈsʌlfərəs] adj schwefelig, Schwefel-, schwefelhaltig. ~ acid schwefelige Säure.

sultan [ˈsʌltən] n Sultan m.

sultana [sʌlˈtɑːnə] n (a) (person) Sultanin f. (b) (fruit) Sultanine f.

sultanate [ˈsʌltənɪt] n Sultanat nt.

sultriness [ˈsʌltrɪnɪs] n (lit) Schwüle f; (fig) Heißblütigkeit f; (of look) Glut f.

sultry [ˈsʌltrɪ] adj weather, atmosphere schwül; woman heißblütig, temperamentvoll; beauty, look glutvoll, schwül (liter).

sum [sʌm] n (a) (total) Summe f. that was the ~ (total) of his achievements das war alles, was er geschafft hatte; the ~ total of my ambitions das Ziel meiner Wünsche.
(b) (of money) Betrag m, Summe f.
(c) (esp Brit: calculation) Rechenaufgabe f. to do ~s (in one's head) (im Kopf) rechnen; I was bad at ~s ich war schlecht im Rechnen.
(d) (essence) in ~ mit einem Wort, zusammengefaßt.

♦**sum up** 1 vt sep (a) (review, summarize) zusammenfassen.
(b) (evaluate rapidly) ab- or einschätzen, taxieren. she ~med me ~ at a glance sie taxierte mich mit einem Blick.
2 vi (also Jur) zusammenfassen, resümieren. to ~ ~ , we can say that ... zusammenfassend or als Resümee können wir feststellen, daß ...; the judge hasn't ~med ~ yet der Richter hat sein Resümee noch nicht gegeben.

sumac(h) [ˈsuːmæk] n (plant) Sumach, Gerberstrauch m; (preparation) Schmack m.

Sumatra [suːˈmɑːtrə] n Sumatra nt.

Sumatran [suːˈmɑːtrən] 1 adj von/aus Sumatra. 2 n Bewohner(in f) m von Sumatra.

Sumerian [suːˈmɪərɪən] 1 adj sumerisch. 2 n Sumerer(in f) m; (language) Sumerisch nt.

summa cum laude [ˈsʊmɑːkʊmˈlaʊdeɪ] adv (US) summa cum laude.

summarily [ˈsʌmərɪlɪ] adv (briefly) knapp, kurzgefaßt; (fast, without ceremony) kurz und bündig, ohne viel Federlesen(s); (Jur) punish, try summarisch; read flüchtig, kursorisch (geh).

summarize [ˈsʌməraɪz] vt zusammenfassen.

summary [ˈsʌmərɪ] 1 n Zusammenfassung f; (Sci also) Abriß m. here is a ~ of the main points of the news hier eine Zusammenfassung der or ein Überblick m über die wichtigsten Meldungen; he gave us a short ~ of the film er gab uns eine kurze Inhaltsangabe des Films; ~ of contents Inhaltsangabe f.
2 adj (a) (brief) account knapp, gedrängt, kurzgefaßt.
(b) (fast, without ceremony) treatment kurz, knapp; perusal flüchtig; (Jur) trial, punishment summarisch; dismissal fristlos. the court dealt out ~ justice das Gericht sprach Recht im Schnellverfahren; ~ offence (Jur) ≈ Übertretung f.

summation [sʌˈmeɪʃən] n (act) Addition f; (total) Summe f; (summary) Zusammenfassung f; (US Jur) Plädoyers pl. in ~ zusammenfassend.

summer [ˈsʌmər] 1 n Sommer m. in (the) ~ im Sommer; two ~s ago im Sommer vor zwei Jahren; a girl of seventeen ~s (liter) ein Mädchen von siebzehn Lenzen (liter); a ~'s day ein Sommertag m.
2 adj attr Sommer-. ~ resort Ferien- or Urlaubsort m (für die Sommersaison).
3 vi den Sommer verbringen; (birds also) übersommern.

summer: ~house n Gartenhaus nt, (Garten)laube f; ~ lightning n Wetterleuchten nt.

summersault n, vi see **somersault.**

summer: ~time n Sommer(szeit f) m; (daylight-saving time) Sommerzeit f; ~weight adj suit sommerlich, Sommer-.

summery [ˈsʌmərɪ] adj sommerlich.

summing-up [ˈsʌmɪŋˈʌp] n (Jur) Resümee nt.

summit [ˈsʌmɪt] 1 n (lit) Gipfel m; (fig also) Höhepunkt m; (~ conference) Gipfel(konferenz f) m. 2 adj attr Gipfel-.

summon [ˈsʌmən] vt adv (a) (servant etc) (herbei)rufen, kommen lassen, herbeizitieren; police, fire brigade etc (herbei)rufen, help holen; meeting, Parliament einberufen. to ~ sb to do sth (order) jdn auffordern, etw zu tun; the King ~ed his ministers der König rief seine Minister zusammen; he was ~ed back or wurde zurückgerufen; to be ~ed into sb's presence zu jdm befohlen or zitiert (iro) werden; a bell ~ed them to their work eine Glocke rief sie zur Arbeit.

(b) *(Jur)* vorladen. ~ **the next witness!** rufen Sie den nächsten Zeugen (auf)!

♦ **summon up** *vt sep courage* zusammennehmen, zusammenraffen; *strength* aufbieten; *enthusiasm, energy* aufbieten, aufbringen. ~**ing** ~ **all his strength** he lifted it up unter Aufbietung aller Kräfte hob er es hoch.

summons ['sʌmənz] **1** n **(a)** *(Jur)* Vorladung *f.* **to take out a ~ against sb** jdn vorladen lassen, jdn vor Gericht laden.
(b) *(order to appear etc)* Aufruf m, Aufforderung *f.* **he received a ~ from the boss** er wurde zum Chef gerufen, er wurde aufgefordert, zum Chef zu kommen.
2 *vt (Jur)* vorladen.

sump [sʌmp] n *(Brit Aut)* Ölwanne *f; (Min)* Sumpf *m.*

sumptuary ['sʌmptjʊərɪ] *adj law* Aufwands-, Luxus-.

sumptuous ['sʌmptjʊəs] *adj (splendid)* luxuriös; *(costly)* aufwendig, kostspielig; *food etc* üppig, verschwenderisch.

sumptuously ['sʌmptjʊəslɪ] *adv see adj.*

sumptuousness ['sʌmptjʊəsnɪs] *n see adj* Luxus m; Aufwand m, Kostspieligkeit *f;* Üppigkeit *f.*

Sun *abbr of* **Sunday** So.

sun [sʌn] **1** n Sonne *f.* **I've got the ~ in my eyes** die Sonne scheint mir in die Augen *or* blendet mich; **he was up with the ~** er stand in aller Frühe auf; **to have a touch of the ~** einen Sonnenstich haben *(also fig);* **you've caught the ~** dich hat die Sonne erwischt; **there is no reason under the ~ why** ... es gibt keinen Grund auf Erden, warum ...; **he's tried everything under the ~** er hat alles Menschenmögliche versucht; **nothing under the ~ would help him** nichts auf Erden konnte ihm helfen; **nobody under the ~ would agree to that** kein Mensch würde dem zustimmen; **a place in the ~** *(fig)* ein Platz an der Sonne; **there's nothing new under the ~** *(Prov)* es ist alles schon einmal dagewesen *(prov).*
2 *vt* der Sonne aussetzen.
3 *vr* sich sonnen.

sun: ~**-baked** *adj* ausgedörrt; ~ **bath** n Sonnenbad *f;* ~**bathe** *vi* in der Sonne liegen, sonnenbaden; ~**bather** n Sonnenanbeter(in f) m *(hum);* **all the** ~**bathers in the park** all die Leute, die sich im Park sonnen *or* die im Park in der Sonne liegen; ~**bathing** n Sonnenbaden nt; ~**beam** n Sonnenstrahl m; ~ **blind** n *(awning)* Markise *f; (venetian blind)* Jalousie *f;* ~ **bonnet** n Sonnenhut m; ~**burn** n Bräune *f; (painful)* Sonnenbrand m; ~**burnt** *adj* sonnengebräunt, sonnenverbrannt; *(painfully)* von der Sonne verbrannt; **to get** ~**burnt** braun werden; (einen) Sonnenbrand bekommen; ~**burst** n **(a)** *(US)* plötzlicher Sonnenschein; **(b)** *(pattern)* Sonnenrad nt.

sundae ['sʌndeɪ] n Eisbecher m.

sun dance n Sonnenanbetungstanz m.

Sunday ['sʌndɪ] **1** n Sonntag m. **a month of** ~**s** *(inf)* ewig (lange), eine Ewigkeit; **never in a month of** ~**s** *(inf)* nie im Leben; *see also* **Tuesday**.
2 *adj attr* Sonntags-. ~ **best** Sonntagskleider *pl,* Sonntagsstaat m *(old, hum);* ~ **school** Sonntagsschule *f;* ~ **driver** Sonntagsfahrer(in f) m; ~ **painter** Sonntagsmaler(in f) m.

sun deck n Sonnendeck nt.

sunder ['sʌndər] *(liter)* **1** *vt* brechen; *chains* sprengen; *(fig) connection* abbrechen. **2** *vi* brechen; *(fig)* sich trennen.

sun: ~**dew** n *(Bot)* Sonnentau m; ~**dial** n Sonnenuhr *f;* ~**down** n Sonnenuntergang m; **at/before** ~**down** bei/vor Sonnenuntergang; ~**downer** n **(a)** *(Austral inf: tramp)* Penner *(inf),* Vagabund m; **(b)** *(drink)* Abendtrunk m; ~**drenched** *adj beaches* sonnenüberflutet, in Sonne getaucht; ~**dress** n leichtes Sonnenkleid; ~**dried** *adj fruit* an *or* in der Sonne getrocknet.

sundry ['sʌndrɪ] **1** *adj* verschiedene. **2** *pron* **all and** ~ jedermann. **3** n **sundries** *pl* Verschiedenes (+*sing vb*).

sun: ~**fast** *adj (esp US)* lichtecht; ~**flower** n Sonnenblume *f.*

sung [sʌŋ] *ptp of* **sing.**

sun: ~**glasses** *npl* Sonnenbrille *f;* ~**god** n Sonnengott m; ~ **hat** n Sonnenhut m; ~ **helmet** n Tropenhelm m.

sunk [sʌŋk] *ptp of* **sink¹.**

sunken ['sʌŋkən] *adj wreck, ship* gesunken, versunken; *treasure* versunken; *garden* tiefliegend *attr; bath* eingelassen; *cheeks* eingefallen, hohl; *eyes* eingesunken.

sun: **S**~ **King** n Sonnenkönig m; ~ **lamp** n Höhensonne *f;* ~**less** *adj garden* ohne Sonne; *room* also dunkel; *day* also trübe; ~**light** n Sonnenlicht nt; **in the** ~**light** in der Sonne, im Sonnenlicht; ~**lit** *adj room* sonnig; *fields etc* also sonnenbeschienen; ~ **lounge** n Wintergarten m, Glasveranda *f.*

sunnily ['sʌnɪlɪ] *adv* heiter; *smile* also sonnig.

sunny ['sʌnɪ] *adj* (+*er*) *place, room, day etc* sonnig; *(fig) smile, disposition* also, *answer, face* heiter. ~ **intervals** *(Met)* Aufheiterungen *pl;* **on the** ~ **side of the house** auf der Sonnenseite (des Hauses); ~**side up** nur auf einer Seite gebraten; **the outlook is** ~ *(Met)* die Wetteraussichten sind gut; *(fig)* die Aussichten sind rosig; **to look on the** ~ **side (of things)** die Dinge von der angenehmen Seite nehmen; **to be on the** ~ **side of forty** noch nicht vierzig sein, unter vierzig sein.

sun: ~ **parlor** n *(US)* Wintergarten m, Glasveranda *f;* ~ **porch** n Veranda *f;* ~**ray 1** n Sonnenstrahl m; **2** *adj attr* ~**ray lamp** Höhensonne *f;* ~**ray treatment** Ultraviolett-/Infrarot-(strahlen)behandlung *f;* ~**rise** n Sonnenaufgang m; **at** ~**rise** bei Sonnenaufgang; ~**roof** n *(of car)* Schiebedach nt; *(of hotel etc)* Sonnenterrasse *f;* ~**set** n Sonnenuntergang m; **at** ~**set** bei Sonnenuntergang; ~**shade** n *(lady's, over table)* Sonnenschirm m; *(awning)* Markise, Sonnenblende *f;* ~**shine** n **(a)** Sonnenschein m; **hours of** ~**shine** Sonnenstunden *pl;* **a daily average of 5 hours'** ~**shine** durchschnittlich 5 Stunden Sonne täglich; **(b)** *(inf: person)* mein Lieber, meine Liebe; ~**shine roof** n Schiebedach nt; ~**spot** n **(a)** Sonnenfleck m; **(b)** *(inf: for holiday)* Ferienparadies nt; ~**stroke** n Sonnenstich m; **to get** ~**stroke** einen Sonnenstich bekommen; ~**suit** n Spiel- *or* Sonnenanzug m; ~**tan** n Sonnenbräune *f;* **to get a** ~**tan** braun

werden; ~**tan lotion/oil** n Sonnenöl nt; ~**tanned** *adj* braungebrannt; ~**trap** n sonniges Eckchen; ~**-up** n Sonnenaufgang m; **at** ~**-up** bei Sonnenaufgang; ~**worship** n Sonnenanbetung *f;* ~**worshipper** n Sonnenanbeter(in f) m.

sup [sʌp] **1** *vt (esp N Engl, Scot)* trinken. **2** *vi (old: dine)* zu Abend essen. **to** ~ **off or on sth** etw zu Abend essen; **he that** ~**s with the devil must have a long spoon** *(Prov)* wer den Teufel zum Freund hat, kommt leicht in die Hölle *(Prov).* **3** n *(drink)* Schluck m.

♦ **sup up** *vti sep (esp N Engl, Scot)* austrinken.

super¹ ['suːpər] *adj (inf)* phantastisch, sagenhaft, klasse *inv (inf).* ~! Klasse! *(inf);* **we had a** ~ **time** es war große Klasse *(inf) or* phantastisch *or* sagenhaft.

super² n **(a)** *(inf: abbr of* **superintendent**) Aufseher(in f) m; *(of police)* = Kommissar(in f) m. **(b)** *(Theat, Film: abbr of* **supernumerary**) Statist(in f) m.

super- *pref* super-, Super-.

superable ['suːpərəbl] *adj* überwindbar, überwindlich.

superabundance [ˌsuːpərə'bʌndəns] n *(of* an +*dat)* großer Reichtum; *(excessive amount)* Überfluß, Überschuß m; *(of enthusiasm)* Überschuß m.

superabundant [ˌsuːpərə'bʌndənt] *adj* überreichlich; *enthusiasm* überströmend.

superannuate [ˌsuːpə'rænjʊeɪt] *vt* pensionieren, in den Ruhestand versetzen.

superannuated [ˌsuːpə'rænjʊeɪtɪd] *adj* pensioniert, im Ruhestand; *(fig inf)* veraltet, überholt.

superannuation [ˌsuːpəˌrænjʊ'eɪʃən] n *(act)* Pensionierung *f,* Versetzung *f* in den Ruhestand; *(state)* Pension *f,* Ruhestand m; *(pension)* Rente *f; (for civil servants, teachers)* Ruhegehalt nt *(form).* ~ **contribution** Beitrag m zur Altersversicherung.

superb [suː'pɜːb] *adj* großartig; *engineering, design, painting* also meisterhaft; *quality, food* also vorzüglich, superb *(dated, geh).*

superbly [suː'pɜːblɪ] *adv see adj.* ~ **fit/self-confident** ungemein fit/selbstbewußt.

superbness [suː'pɜːbnɪs] *n see adj* Großartigkeit *f;* Vorzüglichkeit *f.*

supercargo ['suːpəkɑːgəʊ] n, *pl* -es Frachtaufseher m.

supercharged ['suːpətʃɑːdʒd] *adj gas* vorverdichtet; *engine* aufgeladen; *(fig) atmosphere* gereizt.

supercharger ['suːpətʃɑːdʒər] n Lader m.

supercilious *adj,* ~**ly** *adv* ['suːpə'sɪliəs, -lɪ] hochnäsig.

superciliousness [ˌsuːpə'sɪliəsnɪs] n Hochnäsigkeit *f.*

supercool [ˌsuːpə'kuːl] *vt* unterkühlen.

super-duper ['suːpə'duːpə'] *adj (hum inf)* ganz toll *(inf).*

superego [ˌsuːpər'iːgəʊ] n Über-Ich nt.

supererogation [ˌsuːpərˌerə'geɪʃən] n *(form)* Mehrleistung, Supererogation *(form) f; (Eccl)* freiwillige Gebete *pl;* gute Werke *pl.* **an act of** ~ eine Mehrleistung *or* Supererogation *(form).*

superficial [ˌsuːpə'fɪʃəl] *adj person, behaviour, injury, treatment* oberflächlich; *characteristics, resemblance* äußerlich; *measurements* Oberflächen-.

superficiality ['suːpəˌfɪʃɪ'ælɪtɪ] *n see adj* Oberflächlichkeit *f;* Äußerlichkeit *f.*

superficially [ˌsuːpə'fɪʃəlɪ] *adv see adj* oberflächlich; äußerlich. ~ **this may be true** oberflächlich gesehen mag das stimmen.

superfine ['suːpəfaɪn] *adj (esp Comm) quality, goods* hochfein, superfein *(inf); (pej) distinction* übertrieben fein.

superfluity [ˌsuːpə'fluːɪtɪ] n Überfluß m. **his** ~ **of style, the** ~ **of his style** sein verschwenderischer Stil.

superfluous [suː'pɜːfluəs] *adj* überflüssig; *style* verschwenderisch. **it is** ~ **to say** ... es erübrigt sich *or* es ist überflüssig, zu sagen ...

superfluously [suː'pɜːfluəslɪ] *adv see adj.* **he added** ~ er fügte überflüssigerweise hinzu.

super: ~**heat** *vt* überhitzen; ~**hero** n Superheld m; ~**highway** n *(US)* = Autobahn *f;* ~**human** *adj* übermenschlich.

superimpose [ˌsuːpərɪm'pəʊz] *vt* **to** ~ **sth on sth** etw auf etw *(acc)* legen; *(Phot)* etw über etw *(acc)* photographieren; *(Film)* etw über etw *(acc)* filmen; *(Geol)* etw über etw *(acc)* lagern; *(fig)* etw mit etw überlagern; **by superimposing one image on another** indem man zwei Bilder aufeinanderlegt; **the images became** ~**d** die Bilder hatten sich überlagert.

superintend [ˌsuːpərɪn'tend] *vt* beaufsichtigen, überwachen.

superintendence [ˌsuːpərɪn'tendəns] n (Ober)aufsicht *f.*

superintendent [ˌsuːpərɪn'tendənt] n Aufsicht *f; (in swimming-pool)* Bademeister m; *(in park also)* Parkwärter m; *(of hostel, Sunday school etc)* Leiter(in f) m; *(of police)* *(Brit)* = Kommissar(in f) m; *(US)* = Polizeipräsident m.

superior [suː'pɪərɪər] **1** *adj* **(a)** *(better) quality, equipment* besser *(to* als); *intellect, ability, skill, technique* überlegen *(to sb/sth* jdm/einer Sache). **he thinks he's so** ~ er hält sich für so überlegen *or* für soviel besser.
(b) *(excellent) work(manship), technique* großartig, hervorragend; *craftsman* ausgezeichnet; *intellect* überragend. **goods of** ~ **quality,** ~ **quality goods** Waren *pl* bester Qualität.
(c) *(higher in rank etc)* höher. ~ **officer** Vorgesetzte(r) mf; ~ **court** höheres Gericht; **to be** ~ **to sb/sth** jdm/etw übergeordnet sein, höher stehen als jd/etw.
(d) *(greater)* überlegen *(to sb/sth* jdm/etw); *forces* also stärker *(to* als); *strength* also größer *(to* als). **they were** ~ **to us in number(s)** sie waren uns zahlenmäßig überlegen.
(e) *(snobbish) person, manner* überheblich; *tone, smile* also überlegen; *(smart) restaurant, clientèle* fein, vornehm.
(f) *(Typ) figure, letter* hochgestellt. ~ **number** Hochzahl *f.*
2 n **(a)** *(in rank)* Vorgesetzte(r) mf.
(b) *(in ability)* Überlegene(r) mf. **to be sb's** ~ jdm überlegen sein; **he has few** ~**s when it comes to that** was das anbelangt, sind ihm wenige überlegen.

(c) (*Eccl*) **Father/Mother** S~ Vater Superior/Mutter Superiorin *or* Oberin.

(d) (*Typ*) (*figure*) hochgestellte Zahl, Hochzahl *f*; (*letter*) hochgestellter Buchstabe.

superiority [suˌpɪərɪˈɒrɪtɪ] *n* **(a)** (*of cloth etc*) bessere Qualität; (*of technique, ability etc*) Überlegenheit *f*. **its ~ as a holiday resort** seine bessere Klasse als Ferienort.

(b) (*excellence*) Großartigkeit *f*; (*of intellect*) überragende Eigenschaft.

(c) (*in rank*) höhere Stellung, höherer Rang.

(d) (*in numbers etc*) Überlegenheit *f*.

(e) (*conceitedness*) Überheblichkeit *f*; (*of tone, smile also*) Überlegenheit *f*. **~ complex** Superioritätskomplex *m*.

superlative [suˈpɜːlətɪv] **1** *adj* (*excellent*) überragend, unübertrefflich; *happiness* größte(r, s), höchste(r, s); *indifference* höchste(r, s); (*Gram*) superlativisch, im Superlativ; (*exaggerated*) *style* überschwenglich. **2** *n* Superlativ *m*. **to talk in ~s** in Superlativen sprechen.

superlatively [suˈpɜːlətɪvlɪ] *adv* (*excellently*) überragend, unübertrefflich; *happy, fit* höchst.

superman [ˈsuːpəmæn] *n, pl* **-men** [-men] Übermensch *m*. **S~** (*in comics*) Supermann *m*.

supermarket [ˈsuːpəˌmɑːkɪt] *n* Supermarkt *m*.

supernatural [ˌsuːpəˈnætʃərəl] *adj* übernatürlich. **the ~** das Übernatürliche.

supernormal [ˌsuːpəˈnɔːməl] *adj* übermenschlich.

supernova [ˌsuːpəˈnəʊvə] *n, pl* **-e** [-ˈnəʊviː] *or* **-s** Supernova *f*.

supernumerary [ˌsuːpəˈnjuːmərərɪ] **1** *adj* zusätzlich; (*superfluous*) überzählig. **2** *n* Zusatzperson *f*, Supernumerar *m* (*form*); (*Theat, Film*) Statist(in *f*) *m*.

superpower [ˈsuːpəˌpaʊəʳ] *n* (*Pol*) Supermacht *f*.

supersede [ˌsuːpəˈsiːd] *vt* ablösen; *person, belief also* an die Stelle treten von. **old, ~d ideas** alte, überholte Ideen.

supersensitive [ˌsuːpəˈsensɪtɪv] *adj* hochempfindlich; *person* überempfindlich.

supersonic [ˌsuːpəˈsɒnɪk] *adj* Überschall-. **~ travel** Reisen *nt* mit Überschallgeschwindigkeit.

superstar [ˈsuːpəˌstɑːʳ] *n* (Super)star *m*.

superstition [ˌsuːpəˈstɪʃən] *n* Aberglaube *m no pl*. **this is a ~** das ist Aberglaube.

superstitious *adj*, **~ly** *adv* [ˌsuːpəˈstɪʃəs, -lɪ] abergläubisch.

superstitiousness [ˌsuːpəˈstɪʃəsnɪs] *n* Aberglaube *m*, Abergläubigkeit *f*.

superstratum [ˌsuːpəˈstrɑːtəm] *n, pl* **-strata** [-ˈstrɑːtə] (*Geol*) obere Schicht; (*Ling*) Superstrat *nt*.

superstructure [ˈsuːpəˌstrʌktʃəʳ] *n* Überbau *m* (*also Sociol*); (*of ship*) Aufbauten *pl*.

supertanker [ˈsuːpəˌtæŋkəʳ] *n* Super- *or* Riesentanker *m*.

supertax [ˈsuːpəˌtæks] *n* Höchststeuer *f*.

supervene [ˌsuːpəˈviːn] *vi* dazwischenkommen, hinzukommen.

supervise [ˈsuːpəvaɪz] **1** *vt* beaufsichtigen; *work also* überwachen. **2** *vi* Aufsicht führen, die Aufsicht haben.

supervision [ˌsuːpəˈvɪʒən] *n* Aufsicht *f*; (*action*) Beaufsichtigung *f*; (*of work*) Überwachung, Beaufsichtigung *f*. **under the ~ of** unter der Aufsicht von.

supervisor [ˈsuːpəvaɪzəʳ] *n* (*of work*) Aufseher(in *f*) *m*, Aufsicht *f*; (*of research*) Leiter(in *f*) *m*; (*Brit Univ*) ≈ Tutor(in *f*) *m*; (*for PhD*) Doktorvater *m*.

supervisory [ˈsuːpəvaɪzərɪ] *adj* role beaufsichtigend, überwachend. **in a ~ post** in einer Aufsichtsposition; **in his ~ capacity** in seiner Eigenschaft als Aufsichtsperson.

supine [ˈsuːpaɪn] **1** *adj* zurückliegend; (*fig liter*) lethargy träge, gleichgültig. **in a ~ position** auf dem Rücken liegend; **to be/lie ~** auf dem Rücken liegen. **2** *n* (*Gram*) Supinum *nt*.

supper [ˈsʌpəʳ] *n* (*evening meal*) Abendessen, Abendbrot, Abendmahl (*liter*) *nt*; (*late evening snack*) (später) Imbiß. **they were at ~** sie waren beim Abendessen; **to have ~** zu Abend essen, Abendbrot essen.

supper: **~ club** *n* (*US*) Luxusnachtklub *m*; **~time** *n* Abendessenszeit, Abendbrotzeit *f*; **at ~time** zur Abendbrotzeit; **when is ~time?** wann wird zu Abend gegessen?

supplant [səˈplɑːnt] *vt* ablösen, ersetzen; (*forcibly*) verdrängen; (*by ruse*) *rival* ausstechen.

supple [ˈsʌpl] *adj* (+*er*) *body, material etc* geschmeidig, elastisch; *shoes* weich; *mind, intellect* beweglich, flexibel.

supplement [ˈsʌplɪmənt] **1** *n* **(a)** Ergänzung *f* (*to gen*); (*of book*) Ergänzungsband *m* (*to zu*); (*food ~*) Zusatz *m*; (*at end of book*) Anhang, Nachtrag *m*. **a ~ to his income** eine Aufbesserung seines Einkommens; **family income ~s** Kindergeld *nt*.

(b) (*colour ~ etc*) Beilage *f*, Magazin *nt*.

2 *vt* ergänzen; *income also* aufbessern.

supplementary [ˌsʌplɪˈmentərɪ] *adj* zusätzlich, ergänzend; *volume, report also* Zusatz-, Ergänzungs-. **~ question** (*Parl*) Zusatzfrage *f*; **~ angle** Supplement- *or* Ergänzungswinkel *m*; **~ benefit** (*Brit*) Fürsorgeunterstützung, Sozialhilfe *f*.

suppleness [ˈsʌplnɪs] *n see adj* Geschmeidigkeit, Elastizität *f*; Weichheit *f*; Beweglichkeit, Flexibilität *f*.

suppliant [ˈsʌplɪənt], **supplicant** [ˈsʌplɪkənt] **1** *adj* flehend *attr*. **2** *n* Flehende(r) *mf*, Bittsteller(in *f*) *m*.

supplicate [ˈsʌplɪkeɪt] *vt* (*form*) flehen.

supplication [ˌsʌplɪˈkeɪʃən] *n* Flehen *nt no pl*.

supplier [səˈplaɪəʳ] *n* (*Comm*) Lieferant(in *f*) *m*.

supply [səˈplaɪ] **1** *n* **(a)** (*supplying*) Versorgung *f*; (*Comm: delivery*) Lieferung *f* (*to an* +*acc*); (*Econ*) Angebot *nt*. **electricity ~** Stromversorgung *f*; **the ~ of blood to the brain** die Versorgung des Gehirns mit Blut; **~ and demand** Angebot und Nachfrage (+*pl vb*).

(b) (*what is supplied*) Lieferung *f*. **to cut off the ~** (*of gas, water etc*) das Gas/Wasser abstellen; **our wholesaler has cut off our ~** (*of goods, paper etc*) unser Großhändler hat die Lieferungen eingestellt; **where does the badger get its food ~?** woher bekommt der Dachs seine Nahrung?

(c) (*stock*) Vorrat *m*. **supplies** *pl* (*food*) Vorräte *pl*; (*for expedition also, for journey*) Proviant *m*; **a good ~ of coal** ein guter Kohlenvorrat; **to get** *or* **lay in supplies** *or* **a ~ of** sich (*dat*) einen Vorrat an (+*dat*) anlegen *or* zulegen; **a month's ~** ein Monatsbedarf *m*; **to be in short ~** knapp sein; **our ~ is running out** unser Vorrat geht *or* unsere Vorräte gehen zu Ende; **fresh supplies** (*Mil*) Nachschub *m*; **office supplies** Bürobedarf *m*, Büromaterial *nt*; **medical supplies** Arzneimittel *pl*; (*including bandages*) Ärztebedarf *m*; **electrical supplies** Elektrowaren *or* -artikel *pl*.

(d) (**~ teacher**) Aushilfslehrer(in *f*) *m*. **to be on ~** aushilfsweise *or* vertretungsweise unterrichten.

(e) (*Parl*) (Militär- und Verwaltungs)etat *m*.

2 *vt* **(a)** *material, food, tools etc* sorgen für; (*deliver*) *goods* liefern; *clue, evidence, gas, electricity* liefern; (*put at sb's disposal*) stellen. **pens and paper are supplied by the firm** Schreibmaterial wird von der Firma gestellt.

(b) (*with* mit) *person, army, city* versorgen; (*Comm*) beliefern. **she supplies the humour in the office** sie sorgt für (den) Humor im Büro; **this supplied me with the chance ...** das gab mir die Chance ...; **we were not supplied with a radio** wir hatten/bekamen kein Radio.

(c) (*satisfy, make good*) *need* befriedigen; *want, deficiency* abhelfen (+*dat*); (*Comm*) *demand* decken.

supply: **~ base** *n* Vorratslager *nt*; **~ day** *n* (*Parl*) Tag *m*, an dem der Haushaltsplan vorgelegt wird; **~ depot** *n* Versorgungslager *nt*; **~ industry** *n* Zulieferungsindustrie *f*; **~ lines, ~ routes** *npl* (*Mil, fig*) Versorgungslinien *pl*; **~ ship** *n* Versorgungsschiff *nt*; **~ teacher** *n* Aushilfslehrer(in *f*) *m*; **~ train** *n* Versorgungszug *m*.

support [səˈpɔːt] **1** *n* **(a)** (*lit*) Stütze *f*. **to give ~ to sb/sth** jdn/etw stützen; **the ceiling will need some kind of ~** die Decke muß irgendwie abgestützt werden; **the bridge ~s** die Stützpfeiler *pl* der Brücke; **~ corset** Stützkorsett *nt*; **to lean on sb for ~** sich auf jdn stützen.

(b) (*fig*) (*no pl: moral, financial backing*) Unterstützung *f*; (*person*) Stütze *f*. **in ~ of** zur Unterstützung (+*gen*); **in ~ of an allegation** zur Untermauerung *or* Stützung einer Behauptung; **to speak in ~ of a candidate** einen Kandidaten unterstützen; **to depend on sb for financial ~** von jdm finanziell abhängig sein, auf jds finanzielle Unterstützung angewiesen sein; **our ~ comes from the workers** wir stützen uns auf die Arbeiterschaft.

2 *attr* (*Mil*) *troops, vessel etc* Hilfs-.

3 *vt* **(a)** (*lit*) stützen; (*Tech also*) abstützen; (*bear the weight of*) tragen. **it is ~ed on 4 columns** es wird von 4 Säulen getragen *or* gestützt.

(b) (*fig*) unterstützen; *plan, motion, sb's application also* befürworten; *cause also* eintreten für; (*give moral ~ to also*) beistehen (+*dat*), Rückhalt geben (+*dat*); (*corroborate*) *claim, theory* erhärten, untermauern; (*financially*) *family* unterhalten; *party, orchestra* finanziell unterstützen. **he ~s Arsenal** er ist Arsenal-Anhänger *m*; **which team do you ~?** für welche Mannschaft bist du?; **without his family to ~ him** ohne die Unterstützung seiner Familie; **Burton and Taylor, ~ed by X and Y** Burton und Taylor, mit X und Y in den Nebenrollen; **his parents ~ed him through university** seine Eltern haben ihn während seines Studiums finanziell unterstützt.

(c) (*endure*) *bad behaviour, tantrums* dulden, ertragen.

4 *vr* (*physically*) sich stützen (*on* auf +*acc*); (*financially*) seinen Unterhalt (selbst) bestreiten.

supportable [səˈpɔːtəbl] *adj* erträglich.

supporter [səˈpɔːtəʳ] *n* Anhänger(in *f*) *m*; (*of theory, cause, opinion also*) Befürworter(in *f*) *m*; (*Sport also*) Fan *m*. **~s' club** Fanclub *m*.

supporting [səˈpɔːtɪŋ] *adj film* Vor-; *part, role* Neben-. **with full ~ cast/programme** mit vielen anderen (bedeutenden) Darstellern/mit vollem Nebenprogramm.

supportive [səˈpɔːtɪv] *adj* stützend *attr*. **if his parents had been more ~** wenn seine Eltern ihn mehr gestützt hätten.

suppose [səˈpəʊz] *vt* **(a)** (*imagine*) sich (*dat*) vorstellen; (*assume, postulate also*) annehmen. **let us ~ we are living in the 8th century** stellen wir uns einmal vor, wir lebten im 8. Jahrhundert; **let us ~ that X equals 3** angenommen, X sei gleich 3; **even supposing it were** *or* **was true** (sogar) angenommen, daß es wahr ist, angenommen, es sei wahr; **always supposing he comes** immer vorausgesetzt, (daß) er kommt.

(b) (*believe, think*) annehmen, denken. **I ~ he'll come** ich nehme an, (daß) er kommt, er wird wohl *or* vermutlich kommen; **I don't ~ he'll come** ich glaube kaum, daß er kommt; **I ~ he won't come** ich denke, er wird nicht kommen, er wird wohl nicht kommen; **I ~ that's the best thing, that's the best thing, I ~** das ist *or* wäre vermutlich das Beste; **he's rich, I ~** er muß wohl reich sein; **you're coming, I ~?** ich nehme an, du kommst?; **I don't ~ you could lend me a pound?** Sie könnten mir nicht zufällig ein Pfund leihen?; **will he be coming? — I ~ so** kommt er? — ich denke *or* glaube schon; **you ought to be leaving — I ~ so** du solltest jetzt gehen — stimmt wohl; **don't you agree with me? — I ~ so** bist du da nicht meiner Meinung? — na ja, schon; **I don't ~ so** ich glaube kaum; **isn't he coming? — I ~ not** kommt er nicht? — ich glaube kaum, wohl kaum; **so you see, it can't be true — I ~ not** da siehst du selbst, es kann nicht stimmen — du wirst wohl recht haben; **he can't very well refuse, can he? — I ~ not** er kann wohl kaum ablehnen, oder? — eigentlich nicht *or* kaum; **I never ~d him (to be) a hero** ich habe ihn nie für einen Helden gehalten; **it is not to be ~d that ...** man sollte nicht annehmen, daß ...; **he is generally ~d to be rich** er gilt als reich; **he's ~d to be coming** er soll (angeblich) kommen; **and he's ~d to be an expert!** und der soll (angeblich) (ein) Experte sein!

(c) *(modal use in pass: ought)* to be ~d to do sth etw tun sollen; he's the one who's ~d to do it er müßte es eigentlich tun; you're ~d to be in bed du solltest eigentlich im Bett sein, du gehörst eigentlich ins Bett; he isn't ~d to find out er darf es nicht erfahren; you're not ~d to (do that) das darfst du nicht tun; I am ~d to start work here today ich soll hier heute anfangen; you're ~d to report to the police Sie müssen sich bei der Polizei melden.

(d) *(in imper: I suggest)* ~ we have a go? warum versuchen wir es nicht einmal?; ~ we buy it? wie wäre es, wenn wir es kauften?; ~ you have a wash? wie wär's, wenn du dich mal wäschst?; ~ they could see us now! wenn sie uns jetzt sehen könnten!

(e) *(presuppose)* voraussetzen. that ~s unlimited resources das setzt unbegrenzte Vorräte voraus.

supposed [sə'pəʊzd] *adj* vermutet; *date of birth, site of temple, author also* mutmaßlich.

supposedly [sə'pəʊzɪdlɪ] *adv* angeblich. the ~ brave James Bond der angeblich so mutige James Bond; the atom was ~ indivisible das Atom galt als unteilbar.

supposing [sə'pəʊzɪŋ] *conj* angenommen. but ~ ... aber wenn ...; ~ he can't do it? und wenn er es nicht schafft?; even ~ that ... sogar wenn ...; always ~ ... immer unter der Annahme, daß ...

supposition [,sʌpə'zɪʃən] *n (no pl: hypothesizing)* Mutmaßung, Spekulation *f*; *(thing supposed)* Annahme *f*. based on (a) pure ~ auf reiner Spekulation; acting on the ~ that you are right vorausgesetzt, daß Sie recht haben; to maintain the ~ of innocence until guilt is proved so lange davon ausgehen, daß jemand unschuldig ist, bis seine Schuld bewiesen ist.

suppository [sə'pɒzɪtərɪ] *n* Zäpfchen, Suppositorium *(spec) nt.*

suppress [sə'pres] *vt* **(a)** unterdrücken. **(b)** *(Elec)* entstören.

suppression [sə'preʃən] *n* **(a)** Unterdrückung *f*. **(b)** *(Elec)* Entstörung *f*.

suppressive [sə'presɪv] *adj* Unterdrückungs-, repressiv.

suppressor [sə'presə'] *n (Elec)* Entstörungselement *nt.*

suppurate ['sʌpjʊəreɪt] *vi* eitern.

suppuration [,sʌpjʊə'reɪʃən] *n* Eiterung *f.*

supra- ['su:prə-] *pref* über-; *(esp with foreign words)* supra-. ~national überstaatlich, supra- or übernational.

supremacy [sʊ'preməsɪ] *n* Vormachtstellung *f*; *(Pol, Eccl, fig)* Supremat *nt or m*. air/naval ~ Luft-/Seeherrschaft *f.*

supreme [sʊ'pri:m] **1** *adj* **(a)** *(highest in authority)* höchste(r, s); *court, Soviet* oberste(r, s). S~ Being Höchstes Wesen; S~ Commander Oberbefehlshaber *m.*

(b) *(ultimate)* to make the ~ sacrifice das höchste Opfer bringen; the ~ moment of the opera der Höhepunkt der Oper.

(c) *(very great)* courage, indifference etc äußerste(r, s), größte(r, s). with ~ indifference äußerst or völlig unbeteiligt.

2 *adv* to rule or reign ~ *(monarch)* absolut herrschen; *(champion, justice)* unangefochten herrschen; *(silence)* überall herrschen.

supremely [sʊ'pri:mlɪ] *adv* confident, self-satisfied, indifferent zutiefst.

supremo [sʊ'pri:məʊ] *n (Brit inf)* Oberboß *m (inf).*

Supt *abbr of* **Superintendent.**

surcharge ['sɜ:tʃɑ:dʒ] **1** *n* Zuschlag *m*; *(postal)* Nachporto, Strafporto *(inf) nt.* **for a small** ~ gegen einen geringen Aufschlag. **2** *vt* Zuschlag erheben auf (+acc). parcels sent airmail are ~d Luftpostpakete kosten Zuschlag.

surd [sɜ:d] *n (Math)* irrationaler Ausdruck.

sure [ʃʊə'] **1** *adj* (+er) **(a)** *(reliable, steady, safe)* hand, touch, marksman, footing sicher; *criterion, proof, facts also* eindeutig; *method also, remedy, friend* zuverlässig, verläßlich. his aim was ~ er traf sicher ins Ziel.

(b) *(definite)* sicher. it is ~ that he will come es ist sicher, daß er kommt, er kommt ganz bestimmt; it's ~ to rain es regnet ganz bestimmt; be ~ to tell me/to turn the gas off sag mir auf jeden Fall Bescheid/dreh ganz bestimmt das Gas ab; be ~ to go and see her du mußt sie unbedingt besuchen; you're ~ of a good meal/of success ein gutes Essen/der Erfolg ist Ihnen sicher; I want to be ~ of seeing him ich möchte ihn auf jeden Fall sehen; to make ~ *(check)* nachsehen, kontrollieren; make ~ you get the leads the right way round achten Sie darauf, daß die Kabel richtig herum sind; make ~ you take your keys denk daran, deine Schlüssel mitzunehmen; it's best to make ~ sicher ist sicher; to make ~ of one's facts sich der Fakten (gen) versichern; to make ~ of a seat sich (dat) einen Platz sichern; I've made ~ of having enough coffee for everyone ich habe dafür gesorgt, daß genug Kaffee für alle da ist; ~ thing! *(esp US inf)* klare Sache! *(inf)*; he's a ~ thing for president *(esp US inf)* ist ein todsicherer Tip für die Präsidentschaft; he'll quit for ~ er kündigt ganz bestimmt; I'll find out for ~ ich werde das genau herausfinden; do you know for ~? wissen Sie das ganz sicher?; to be ~! Mensch!, tatsächlich!; and there he was, to be ~ *(esp Ir)* und da war er doch tatsächlich!

(c) *(positive, convinced)* sicher. I'm perfectly ~ ich bin (mir da) ganz sicher; to be ~ about sth sich (dat) einer Sache (gen) sicher sein; I'm not so ~ about that da bin ich so nicht sicher; to be ~ of one's facts seiner or der Fakten sicher sein; to be ~ of oneself sich (dat) seiner Sache sicher sein; *(generally self-confident)* selbstsicher sein; I'm ~ I don't know, I don't know, I'm ~ ich habe keine Ahnung; I'm not ~ how/why ... ich bin (mir) nicht sicher or ich weiß nicht genau, wie/warum ...

2 *adv* **(a)** will you do it? — ~! machst du das? — klar! *(inf)*; that meat was ~ tough or ~ was tough das Fleisch war vielleicht zäh!; that's ~ pretty *(US)* das ist doch schön, nicht?

(b) and ~ enough he did come und er ist tatsächlich gekommen; he'll come ~ enough er kommt ganz bestimmt, er kommt schon; it's petrol ~ enough es ist tatsächlich Benzin.

(c) as ~ as sure can be *(inf)*, as ~ as I'm standing here *(inf)* garantiert, todsicher.

sure: ~-**fire** *adj (inf)* todsicher *(inf)*, bombensicher *(inf)*; ~-**footed** *adj* (tritt)sicher.

surely ['ʃʊəlɪ] *adv* **(a)** bestimmt, sicher. ~ you don't mean it? das meinen Sie doch bestimmt or sicher nicht (so)?; ~ he's come(, hasn't he?) er ist doch bestimmt gekommen(, oder?); ~ he hasn't come(, has he?) er ist doch bestimmt or sicher nicht gekommen(, oder?); ~ they'll let you go out sie werden dich doch bestimmt ausgehen lassen(, oder?); ~ not! das kann doch nicht stimmen!; ~ someone must know the answer irgend jemand muß doch die Antwort wissen; there must ~ be something we can do irgend etwas müssen wir doch (sicher) tun können; I can't ~ — oh, ~ you can ich kann (es) nicht — aber sicher kannst du das!; ~ I've met you before ich habe Sie bestimmt schon einmal gesehen; but ~ you can't expect us to believe that Sie können doch wohl nicht erwarten, daß wir das glauben!; ~ if a = b, then c must ... also, wenn a = b ist, dann muß c doch sicherlich ...

(b) *(esp US: gladly)* gern, mit Vergnügen.

(c) *(inevitably, with certainty)* zweifellos.

sureness ['ʃʊənɪs] *n* **(a)** *(positiveness, conviction)* Überzeugung, Sicherheit *f*. **(b)** *(reliability, steadiness, sure-footedness)* Sicherheit *f*; *(of method, cure)* Verläßlichkeit, Zuverlässigkeit *f*; *(of sb's judgement also)* Untrüglichkeit *f.*

surety ['ʃʊərətɪ] *n* **(a)** *(sum)* Bürgschaft, Sicherheit *f*; *(person)* Bürge *m*. to go or stand ~ for sb für jdn bürgen; he was granted bail in his own ~ of £50 er hinterlegte eine Kaution von £50. **(b)** *(obs: certainty)* Sicherheit, Gewißheit *f*. of a ~ gewiß, sicherlich.

surf [sɜ:f] **1** *n* Brandung *f*. **2** *vi* surfen.

surface ['sɜ:fɪs] **1** *n* **(a)** *(lit, fig)* Oberfläche *f*; *(of road)* Decke *f*, Belag *m*. on the ~ it seems that ... oberflächlich sieht es so aus, als ...; on the ~ he is friendly enough nach außen hin ist er sehr freundlich; we never got beneath the ~ of the subject wir haben immer nur die Oberfläche des Themas berührt.

(b) *(Math: of cube etc)* Fläche *f*; *(area also)* Flächeninhalt *m.*

(c) *(Min)* at/on/up to the ~ über Tage.

(d) *(Aviat)* Tragfläche *f.*

2 *adj attr* **(a)** oberflächlich; *measurements, hardening* Oberflächen-.

(b) *(not by air)* travel auf dem Land-/Seeweg.

(c) *(Min)* worker, job über Tage.

3 *vt* **(a)** road mit einem Belag versehen; *wall* verblenden.

(b) *submarine* auftauchen lassen.

4 *vi (lit, fig)* auftauchen.

surface: ~ **area** *n* Fläche *f*; *(Math)* Flächeninhalt *m*; ~ **dressing** *n (on roads) (method)* Straßenreparatur *f* mit Rollsplitt; *(material)* Rollsplitt *m*; ~ **mail** *n* Post *f* auf dem Land-/Seeweg; by ~ **mail** auf dem Land-/Seeweg; ~ **noise** *n* Rauschen *nt*; ~ **structure** *n (Ling)* Oberflächenstruktur *f*; ~ **tension** *n* Oberflächenspannung *f*; ~-**to-air** *adj attr missile* Boden-Luft-; ~-**to-surface** *adj attr missile* Boden-Boden-; ~ **vessel** *n* Schiff *nt (im Gegensatz zu Unterseeboot).*

surfacing ['sɜ:fɪsɪŋ] *n* what did they use as ~ for the roads/walls? was für ein Material wurde für den Straßenbelag/als Wandbelag verwendet?

surfboard ['sɜ:fbɔ:d] *n* Surfboard *nt.*

surfeit ['sɜ:fɪt] **1** *n* Übermaß, Zuviel *nt (of an +dat).* **2** *vt sb, oneself* übersättigen, überfüttern *(on, with* mit).

surfer ['sɜ:fə'] *n* Wellenreiter(in *f*) *m.*

surfing ['sɜ:fɪŋ], **surfriding** ['sɜ:fraɪdɪŋ] *n* Wellenreiten, Surfen *nt*. a good ~ beach ein guter Strand zum Wellenreiten.

surge [sɜ:dʒ] **1** *n (of sea)* Wogen *nt*; *(of floodwater)* Schwall *m*. a ~ of people eine wogende Menschenmenge; there was a ~ of sympathy for him es gab eine Sympathiewelle für ihn; he felt a sudden ~ of rage er fühlte, wie die Wut in ihm aufstieg.

2 *vi (sea)* branden; *(floods, river)* anschwellen. blood ~d into her face ihr schoß das Blut ins Gesicht; they ~d towards/(a)round him sie drängten auf ihn zu, sie umdrängten ihn/sie wogten um ihn *(liter)*; people ~d in/out eine Menschenmenge flutete herein/heraus; to ~ ahead vorpreschen.

surgeon ['sɜ:dʒən] *n* Chirurg(in *f*) *m*; *(Mil)* Stabsarzt *m*/-ärztin *f*; *(Naut)* Marinearzt *m*/-ärztin *f*; *see* **dental, veterinary.**

surgery ['sɜ:dʒərɪ] *n* **(a)** Chirurgie *f*. to have ~ operiert werden; to need (heart) ~ (am Herzen) operiert werden müssen; to undergo major heart ~ sich einer größeren Herzoperation unterziehen; he's had ~ on his stomach er ist am Magen operiert worden; ~ is the only solution nur ein operativer Eingriff kann helfen, Operieren ist die einzige Lösung; a fine piece of ~ eine großartige chirurgische Leistung.

(b) *(Brit) (room)* Sprechzimmer *nt* ; *(consultation)* Sprechstunde *f*. ~ **hours** Sprechstunden *pl*; when is his ~? wann hat er Sprechstunde?

surgical ['sɜ:dʒɪkəl] *adj* treatment operativ; *procedures, technique, instrument* chirurgisch; *training, skill* Chirurgen-, eines Chirurgen. ~ **appliance** Stützapparat *m*; *(false limb)* Prothese *f*; ~ **boot** orthopädischer Schuh; ~ **goods shop** orthopädisches Fachgeschäft; ~ **spirit** Wundbenzin *nt*; ~ **ward** chirurgische Station, Chirurgie *f (inf).*

surgically ['sɜ:dʒɪkəlɪ] *adv* treat, remove operativ. ~, we have advanced a long way wir haben in der Chirurgie große Fortschritte gemacht.

surging ['sɜ:dʒɪŋ] *adj* water, corn, crowd wogend. a ~ flood of emotion eine Woge des Gefühls.

surliness ['sɜ:lɪnɪs] *n* Verdrießlichkeit, Mürrischkeit, Mißmutigkeit *f.*

surly ['sɜ:lɪ] *adj* (+er) verdrießlich, mürrisch, mißmutig.

surmise ['sɜ:maɪz] **1** *n* Vermutung, Mutmaßung *f*. **2** [sɜ:'maɪz] *vt* vermuten, mutmaßen. I ~d as much das hatte ich (schon) vermutet; as one could ~ from his book wie man nach seinem Buch vermuten or mutmaßen konnte.

surmount [sɜː'maʊnt] vt (a) difficulty, obstacle überwinden. (b) (esp Archit, Her etc) ~ed by sth von or mit etw gekrönt.
surmountable [sɜː'maʊntəbl] adj überwindlich, zu überwinden.
surname ['sɜːneɪm] n Nachname, Familienname m. what is his ~? wie heißt er mit Nachnamen?
surpass [sɜː'pɑːs] 1 vt (a) (be better than) übertreffen. (b) (exceed) comprehension hinausgehen über (+acc). 2 vr sich selbst übertreffen.
surpassing [sɜː'pɑːsɪŋ] adj (liter) beauty unvergleichlich.
surplice ['sɜːpləs] n Chorrock m, Chorhemd nt.
surplus ['sɜːpləs] 1 n Überschuß m (of an +dat). a balance of trade ~ ein Überschuß m in der Handelsbilanz.
  2 adj überschüssig; (of countable objects) überzählig. ~ value Mehrwert m; to use up one's ~ energy seine überschüssige Energie verbrauchen; Army ~ goods Stegwaren pl; Army ~ anoraks Anoraks pl aus Armeerestbeständen; sale of ~ stock Verkauf m von Lagerbeständen; have you any ~ sheets I could borrow? hast du Laken übrig, die ich mir borgen könnte?; it is ~ to my requirements das benötige ich nicht; ~ store Geschäft, das billig Lagerbestände verkauft.
surprise [sə'praɪz] 1 n Überraschung f. in ~ voller Überraschung, überrascht; much to my ~, to my great ~ zu meiner großen Überraschung; with a look of ~ mit überraschtem Gesicht; it was a ~ (for or to me) to find that ... ich war überrascht, als ich entdeckte, daß ...; it came as a ~ to us wir waren überrascht, es hat uns überrascht; what a ~! was für eine Überraschung!; to give sb a ~ jdn überraschen; to take sb by ~ jdn überraschen; ~, ~, it's me! rate mal, wer hier ist?; ~, ~! (iro) was du nicht sagst!
  2 attr attack, defeat, visit, decision Überraschungs-; parcel, gift, phone call überraschend.
  3 vt überraschen; (catch unawares also) army, sentry überrascht, das zu hören; I wouldn't be ~d if ... es würde mich nicht wundern, wenn ...; don't be ~d if he refuses wundere dich nicht, wenn er ablehnt; it's nothing to be ~d at das ist nicht weiter verwunderlich; I'm ~d at or by his ignorance ich bin überrascht über seine Unkenntnis; I'm ~d you didn't think of that es wundert mich, daß du nicht daran gedacht hast; go on, ~ me! ich lass' mich überraschen!; he ~d me into agreeing er hat mich so verblüfft, daß ich zugestimmt habe.
surprising [sə'praɪzɪŋ] adj überraschend, erstaunlich. there's nothing ~ about that das ist nicht weiter verwunderlich; it's hardly ~ he said no es ist kaum verwunderlich, daß er nein gesagt hat.
surprisingly [sə'praɪzɪŋlɪ] adv see adj. ~ (enough), he was right er hatte erstaunlicherweise recht; and then ~ he left und dann ist er zu unserer/ihrer etc Überraschung gegangen.
surreal [sə'rɪəl] adj unwirklich.
surrealism [sə'rɪəlɪzəm] n Surrealismus m.
surrealist [sə'rɪəlɪst] 1 adj surrealistisch. 2 n Surrealist(in f) m.
surrealistic [sə,rɪə'lɪstɪk] adj surrealistisch.
surrender [sə'rendər] 1 vi sich ergeben (to dat); (to police) sich stellen (to dat). I ~! ich ergebe mich!
  2 vt (Mil) übergeben; goods, firearms also ausliefern, herausgeben; insurance policy einlösen; lease kündigen; claim, right, hope aufgeben.
  3 vr to ~ oneself to sth sich einer Sache (dat) hingeben; to fate sich in etw (acc) ergeben.
  4 n (a) Kapitulation f (to vor +dat). because of the gunman's quick ~ weil der Schütze sich so schnell ergab.
  (b) see vt Übergabe f (to an +acc); Auslieferung, Aushändigung f (to an +acc); Einlösen nt; Kündigung f; Aufgabe, Preisgabe f. ~ value (Insur) Rückgabe- or Rückkaufswert m.
surreptitious [,sʌrəp'tɪʃəs] adj heimlich; whisper, glance, kiss also verstohlen. he made a few ~ changes er machte heimlich ein paar Änderungen.
surreptitiously [,sʌrəp'tɪʃəslɪ] adv see adj.
surrey ['sʌrɪ] n (US) zweisitzige Kutsche.
surrogate ['sʌrəgɪt] 1 n (substitute) Ersatz m, Surrogat nt (geh); (Brit Eccl) ~ Weihbischof m. 2 attr Ersatz-; (Eccl) bishop ~ Weih-.
surround [sə'raʊnd] 1 n Umrandung f; (floor round carpet) Ränder pl. 2 vt umgeben; (Mil) umstellen, umzingeln. she was ~ed by children/suitors sie war von Kindern umgeben/von Verehrern umgeben or umschwärmt.
surrounding [sə'raʊndɪŋ] adj umliegend. in the ~ countryside in der Umgebung or Umgegend; in the ~ darkness in der Dunkelheit, die mich/ihn etc umgab.
surroundings [sə'raʊndɪŋz] npl Umgebung f.
surtax ['sɜːtæks] n Steuerzuschlag m.
surveillance [sɜː'veɪləns] n Überwachung, Observation (form) f. to be under ~ überwacht or observiert (form) werden; to keep sb under ~ jdn überwachen or observieren (form).
survey ['sɜːveɪ] 1 n (a) (Surv) (of land, coast) Vermessung f; (report) (Vermessungs)gutachten nt; (of house) Begutachtung f; (report) Gutachten nt. they are doing a ~ for a new motorway sie machen die Vermessungsarbeiten für eine neue Autobahn; to have a ~ done on a house ein Gutachten über ein Haus erstellen lassen.
  (b) (comprehensive look, review) (of surroundings, countryside) Musterung f (of gen), Überblick m (of über +acc); (of subject, recent development) Überblick m.
  (c) (inquiry) Untersuchung f (of, on über +acc); (by opinion poll, market research etc) Umfrage f (of, on über +acc).
  2 [sɜː'veɪ] vt (a) (look at) countryside, view, scene, person, crowd, prospects, plans betrachten, sich (dat) ansehen; (appraisingly also) begutachten; person, goods, crowd

mustern. he is monarch of all he ~s er beherrscht das Land, soweit er blicken kann.
  (b) (study) prospects, plans, developments untersuchen; institutions einer Prüfung (gen) unterziehen; (take general view of) events, trends einen Überblick geben über (+acc).
  (c) (Surv) site, land vermessen; building inspizieren.
surveying [sɜː'veɪɪŋ] n (a) see vt (c) Vermessung f; Inspektion f. (b) (profession) Landvermessung f; (of buildings) Inspektion f von Gebäuden.
surveyor [sɜː'veɪər] n (land ~) Landvermesser(in f) m; (building ~) Bauinspektor(in f), Baugutachter(in f) m.
survival [sə'vaɪvəl] n (a) Überleben nt; (of species also) Fortbestand m; (of customs, usages) Weiterleben nt. the ~ of the whale is in jeopardy der Wal ist in Gefahr, ausgerottet zu werden; the ~ of the fittest das Überleben der Stärkeren; his ~ as prime minister seems unlikely es ist unwahrscheinlich, daß er sich als Premierminister halten kann; ~ kit Überlebensausrüstung f.
  (b) (relic) Überbleibsel nt (of, from aus).
survive [sə'vaɪv] 1 vi (person, animal etc) überleben, am Leben bleiben; (in job) sich halten (können); (house, treasures, book, play) erhalten bleiben; (custom, religion) weiterleben, fortbestehen. only five copies ~ or have ~d nur fünf Exemplare sind erhalten; will this play ~ despite the critics? wird sich das Stück trotz der Kritiken halten?; you'll ~ (iro) das wirst du schon überleben!; he ~d to tell the tale er hat als Zeuge überlebt; (hum) er hat es überlebt (hum).
  2 vt überleben; experience, disease, accident, operation also (lebend) überstehen; (house, objects) fire, flood etc überstehen; (inf) heat, boredom etc aushalten. to ~ the ages die Jahrhunderte überdauern; he was ~d by his wife seine Frau überlebte ihn.
survivor [sə'vaɪvər] n Überlebende(r) mf; (Jur) Hinterbliebene(r) mf.
Susan ['suːzn] n Susanne f.
susceptibility [sə,septə'bɪlɪtɪ] n (a) no pl see adj (a) Beeindruckbarkeit f. ~ to sth Empfänglichkeit f für etw; Ausgesetztsein nt gegenüber etw; Anfälligkeit f für etw; their ~ to trickery ihre Gutgläubigkeit; ~ to pain/treatment Schmerzempfindlichkeit f/Behandelbarkeit f; ~ to unkind remarks Empfindlichkeit f in bezug auf unfreundliche Bemerkungen; his ~ to her tears/pleas daß er sich durch ihre Tränen/Bitten erweichen läßt/ließ.
  (b) susceptibilities pl (sensibilities) Feingefühl nt.
susceptible [sə'septəbl] adj (a) (impressionable) beeindruckbar, leicht zu beeindrucken pred. ~ to sth to charms, flattery etc für etw empfänglich; to kindness, suggestion, influence etc einer Sache (dat) zugänglich; to attack einer Sache (dat) ausgesetzt; to rheumatism, colds für etw anfällig; to be ~ to trickery sich leicht täuschen lassen, gutgläubig sein; ~ to pain/treatment schmerzempfindlich/behandelbar; he's very ~ to remarks about his big nose er reagiert sehr empfindlich auf Anspielungen auf seine große Nase; he was ~ to her tears/pleas er ließ sich von ihren Tränen/Bitten erweichen.
  (b) (form) to be ~ of proof/corroboration/change etc beweisbar/untermauerbar/änderbar etc sein.
suspect ['sʌspekt] 1 adj verdächtig, suspekt.
  2 n Verdächtige(r) mf.
  3 [sə'spekt] vt (a) person verdächtigen (of sth einer Sache gen), in Verdacht haben; plot, swindle vermuten, ahnen, argwöhnen (geh). he is ~ed of having stolen it/written it ich habe sie im Verdacht or ich verdächtige sie, es gestohlen/geschrieben zu haben; he is ~ed of being a member of this sect, he is a ~ed member of this sect er steht im Verdacht or man verdächtigt ihn, Mitglied dieser Sekte zu sein; he ~s nothing er ahnt nichts; does he ~ anything? hat er Verdacht geschöpft?
  (b) (doubt) truth bezweifeln, anzweifeln; motive argwöhnisch sein gegenüber.
  (c) (think likely) vermuten. I ~ed as much das habe ich doch vermutet or geahnt, das habe ich mir doch gedacht; a ~ed case of measles, a case of ~ed measles ein Fall, bei dem Verdacht auf Masern besteht.
  4 vi einen Verdacht haben.
suspend [sə'spend] vt (a) (hang) (auf)hängen (from an +dat); (Chem) suspendieren. to be ~ed in sth in etw (dat) hängen; in etw (dat) suspendiert sein; to hang ~ed from sth/in sth von/in etw (dat) hängen.
  (b) (stop, defer) publication, payment (zeitweilig) einstellen; judgement aufschieben, aussetzen; sentence zur Bewährung aussetzen. he was given a ~ed sentence seine Strafe wurde zur Bewährung ausgesetzt; to be in a state of ~ed animation im Zustand vorübergehender Leblosigkeit sein.
  (c) person suspendieren; member, pupil, student zeitweilig ausschließen; (Sport) sperren; licence zeitweilig einziehen; law, privileges aussetzen. to ~ from duty suspendieren.
suspender [sə'spendər] n usu pl (a) (Brit) (for stockings) Strumpfhalter, Straps m; (for socks) Sockenhalter m. ~ belt Strumpf(halter)gürtel m. (b) (US) ~s pl Hosenträger pl.
suspense [sə'spens] n (a) (in book, film etc) Spannung f. the ~ is killing me ich bin gespannt wie ein Regenschirm (hum inf); to keep sb in ~ jdn in Spannung halten, jdn auf die Folter spannen (inf); to wait in ~ gespannt or voller Spannung warten.
  (b) (form) to be in ~ (question, matter) unentschieden or in der Schwebe sein.
suspension [sə'spenʃən] n (a) see suspend (b) zeitweilige Einstellung; Aufschub m, Aussetzung f; Aussetzung f (zur Bewährung).
  (b) see suspend (c) Suspendierung f; zeitweiliger Ausschluß; Sperrung f; zeitweiliger Einzug; Aussetzen nt.
  (c) (Aut) Federung f; (of wheels) Aufhängung f.
  (d) (Chem) Suspension f.

(e) (*Mus*) to be in ~ suspendiert sein, gehalten werden.
suspension: ~ **bridge** *n* Hängebrücke *f*; ~ **point** *n* (*Typ*) Auslassungspunkt *m*.

suspensory [səˈspensərɪ] *adj ligament, muscle* Aufhänge-; *bandage* Schlingen-.

suspicion [səˈspɪʃən] *n* **(a)** Verdacht, Argwohn (*geh*) *m no pl*. to arouse sb's ~s jds Verdacht *or* Argwohn (*geh*) erregen; **I had no** ~ that ... der Verdacht, daß ..., wäre mir nie gekommen; **I have a** ~ **that** ... ich habe den Verdacht *or* das Gefühl, daß ...; **to have one's** ~s **about sth** seine Zweifel bezüglich einer Sache (*gen*) haben; **I was right in my** ~s mein Verdacht hat sich bestätigt; **to be above (all)/under** ~ über jeden Verdacht erhaben sein/ unter Verdacht stehen; **to arrest sb on** ~/on ~ **of murder** jdn wegen Tatverdachts/Mordverdachts festnehmen; **to lay one-self open to** ~ sich verdächtig machen; ~ **fell on him** der Verdacht fiel auf ihn; **to view sb/sth with** ~ jdn/etw argwöhnisch *or* mißtrauisch betrachten.
(b) (*trace, touch*) Hauch *m*, Spur *f*.

suspicious [səˈspɪʃəs] *adj* **(a)** (*feeling suspicion*) argwöhnisch, mißtrauisch (*of* gegenüber) (*causing suspicion*) Sie sind aber mißtrauisch; **to be** ~ **about sth** etw mit Mißtrauen *or* Argwohn (*geh*) betrachten. **(b)** (*causing suspicion*) verdächtig; *actions also* verdächterregend *attr*.

suspiciously [səˈspɪʃəslɪ] *adv see adj* **(a)** argwöhnisch, mißtrauisch. **(b)** verdächtig. it looks ~ like measles to me das sieht mir verdächtig nach Masern aus.

suspiciousness [səˈspɪʃəsnɪs] *n see adj* **(a)** Verdacht, Argwohn (*geh*) *m*. **(b)** Verdächtigkeit *f*.

suss [sʌs] *vt* (*Brit inf*) **(a)** (*suspect*) *plan* kommen hinter (+*acc*) (*inf*). **to** ~ **it** dahinterkommen (*inf*); as soon as he ~ed what was going on sobald er dahinterkam, was da gespielt wurde (*inf*).
(b) **to** ~ **sb out** jdm auf den Zahn fühlen (*inf*); **I can't** ~ **him out** bei ihm blicke ich nicht durch (*inf*); **I've got him** ~ed **(out)** ich habe ihn durchschaut; **to** ~ **sth out** etw herausbekommen; **to** ~ **things out** die Lage peilen (*inf*).

sustain [səˈsteɪn] *vt* **(a)** (*support*) *load, weight* aushalten, tragen; *life* erhalten; *family* unterhalten; *charity* unterstützen; (*nourish*) *body* bei Kräften halten. not enough to ~ life nicht genug zum Leben; that isn't enough food to ~ you das wird Ihnen nicht reichen; his support ~ed her in her hour of need seine Hilfe gab ihr Kraft in der Stunde der Not (*liter*).
(b) (*keep going, maintain*) *pretence, argument, theory* aufrechterhalten; *effort also* nicht nachlassen in (+*dat*); (*Mus*) *note* (aus)halten; (*Theat*) *accent, characterization* durchhalten; (*Jur*) *objection* stattgeben (+*dat*). objection ~ed Einspruch stattgegeben; *see also* sustained.
(c) (*receive*) *injury, damage, loss* erleiden. **to** ~ **an attack** angegriffen werden.

sustained [səˈsteɪnd] *adj effort* ausdauernd; *applause also* anhaltend; (*Mus*) *note* (aus)gehalten.

sustaining [səˈsteɪnɪŋ] *adj food* nahrhaft, kräftig. ~ **pedal** (*Mus*) Fortepedal *nt*; ~ **program** (*US Rad, TV*) nichtkommerzielle Sendung.

sustenance [ˈsʌstɪnəns] *n* (*food and drink*) Nahrung *f*; (*nutritive quality*) Nährwert *m*. to get one's ~ from sth sich von etw ernähren; you don't get much ~ from strawberries Erdbeeren haben keinen großen Nährwert.

susurration [ˌsjuːsəˈreɪʃən] *n* (*liter*) Säuseln *nt* (*liter*).
suture [ˈsuːtʃər] (*Med*) **1** *n* Naht *f*. **2** *vt* (ver)nähen.
suzerainty [ˈsuːzəreɪntɪ] *n* Suzeränität *f*.
svelte [svelt] *adj* (*slender*) grazil; (*sophisticated*) vornehm, elegant.
SW *abbr of* **(a)** **South-West** SW. **(b)** **short wave** KW.
swab [swɒb] **1** *n* **(a)** (*Med*) Tupfer *m*; (*specimen*) Abstrich *m*. to take a ~ einen Abstrich machen. **(b)** (*Naut*) Mop *m*. **2** *vt* **(a)** (*Med*) *wound etc* (ab)tupfen. **(b)** (*Naut: also* ~ **down**) wischen.
Swabia [ˈsweɪbɪə] *n* Schwaben *nt*.
swaddle [ˈswɒdl] *vt baby* wickeln (*in* in +*acc*). **swaddling clothes** (*esp Bibl*) Windeln *pl*.
swag [swæg] *n* (*inf*) Beute *f*.
swagger [ˈswægər] **1** *n* (*gait*) Stolzieren *nt*; (*behaviour*) Angeberei, Großtuerei *f*. **to walk with a** ~ stolzieren. **2** *vi* (*a*) stolzieren. **he** ~ed **down the street/over to our table** er stolzierte die Straße hinunter/zu unserem Tisch herüber. **(b)** (*boast, act boastfully*) angeben.
swaggering [ˈswægərɪŋ] **1** *adj gait, manner* forsch. **(b)** (*boastful*) großtuerisch, angeberisch. **2** *n* Großtuerei, Angeberei *f*. his ~ **about** seine angeberische Art.
swagger-stick [ˈswægəstɪk] *n* Offiziersstöckchen *nt*.
swain [sweɪn] *n* (*old*) (*suitor*) Freier *m*; (*lad*) Bursch(e) *m*.
swallow¹ [ˈswɒləʊ] **1** *n* Schluck *m*. after several ~s nachdem er etc ein paarmal geschluckt hatte.
2 *vt food, drink* (hinunter)schlucken; (*fig*) *story, evidence, insult* schlucken. **to** ~ **one's pride** seinen Stolz schlucken; **to** ~ **sth whole** (*lit*) etw ganz schlucken; (*fig*) etw ohne weiteres schlucken; **that's a bit hard to** ~ das glaubt ja kein Mensch (*inf*); **to** ~ **one's words** (*speak indistinctly*) seine Worte verschlucken; (*remain silent*) hinunterschlucken, was er/sie etc sagen wollte; (*retract*) seine Worte zurücknehmen; *see* bait.
3 *vi* schlucken. **to** ~ **hard** (*fig*) kräftig schlucken.
♦**swallow down** *vt sep* hinunterschlucken.
♦**swallow up** *vt sep* (*fig*) verschlingen. **the mist/darkness seemed to** ~ **them** ~ der Nebel/die Dunkelheit schien sie zu verschlucken; **I wished the ground would open and** ~ **me** ich könnte vor Scham in den Boden versinken.
swallow² *n* (*bird*) Schwalbe *f*. **one** ~ **doesn't make a summer** (*Prov*) eine Schwalbe macht noch keinen Sommer (*Prov*).
swallow: ~-**dive** *n* Schwalbensprung *m*; ~-**tail** *n* (*butterfly*) Schwalbenschwanz *m*; ~-**tailed coat** *n* Schwalbenschwanz *m*.
swam [swæm] *pret of* **swim.**
swamp [swɒmp] **1** *n* Sumpf *m*. **2** *vt* unter Wasser setzen,

überschwemmen; (*fig: overwhelm*) überschwemmen. to be ~ed with sth mit etw überschwemmt werden.
swamp: ~ **buggy** *n* Sumpffahrzeug *nt*; ~ **fever** *n* Sumpffieber *nt*; ~**land** *n* Sumpf(land *nt*) *m*.
swampy [ˈswɒmpɪ] *adj* (+*er*) sumpfig. to become ~ versumpfen.
swan [swɒn] **1** *n* Schwan *m*. ~ -**dive** (*US*) Schwalbensprung *m*. **2** *vi* (*inf*) **to** ~ **off** abziehen (*inf*); **to** ~ **around New York in New York** herumziehen (*inf*); **to** ~ **around (the house)** zu Hause herumschweben (*inf*); **a** ~**ning job** ein gemütlicher Posten.
swank [swæŋk] (*inf*) **1** *n* **(a)** (*boastfulness*) Angabe, Protzerei (*inf*) *f*; (*ostentation also*) Schau *f* (*inf*). **it's just a lot of** ~ das ist doch nur Angabe/Schau. **(b)** (*person*) Angeber(in *f*) *m*. **2** *vi* angeben (*about* mit).
swanky [ˈswæŋkɪ] *adj* (+*er*) (*inf*) *manner, words* großspurig; *car etc* protzig (*inf*), Angeber-.
swannery [ˈswɒnərɪ] *n* Schwanenteich *m*.
swansdown [ˈswɒnzˌdaʊn] *n* (*feathers*) Schwanendaunen *pl*; (*fabric*) wolliges Material.
swan: ~**song** *n* (*fig*) Schwanengesang *m*; ~**-upping** [ˌswɒnˈʌpɪŋ] *n* feierliche Zeichnung der jungen Schwäne.
swap [swɒp] **1** *n* Tausch, Tauschhandel *m*. ~**s** (*stamps*) Tauschmarken *pl*; **it's a fair** ~ das ist ein fairer Tausch; **to do a** ~ **(with sb)** (mit jdm) tauschen.
2 *vt stamps, cars, houses etc* tauschen; *stories, reminiscences* austauschen. **to** ~ **sth for sth** etw für etw eintauschen; **to** ~ **places with sb** mit jdm tauschen; **I'll** ~ **you!** (*inf*) ich tausch' mit dir (*inf*).
3 *vi* tauschen. **I wouldn't** ~ **with anyone** ich würde *or* möchte mit niemandem tauschen.
sward [swɔːd] *n* (*obs, poet*) Rasen *m*.
swarm [swɔːm] **1** *n* (*of insects, birds*) Schwarm *m*; (*of people also*) Schar *f*. **they came in (their)** ~s sie kamen scharenweise *or* in Scharen.
2 *vi* (*bees, flies, people*) schwärmen. **the place was** ~ing **with insects/people** es wimmelte von Insekten/Leuten; **the main street was** ~ing (*inf*) auf der Hauptstraße herrschte Hochbetrieb (*inf*); **tourists were** ~ing **everywhere** es wimmelte überall von Touristen; **children** ~ed **all round the car** Kinder schwärmten um das Auto herum.
♦**swarm up** *vi* +*prep obj* hinauf- *or* hochklettern.
swarthiness [ˈswɔːðɪnɪs] *n* (*of skin*) Dunkelheit *f*; (*of person also*) Dunkelhäutigkeit *f*, dunkle Farbe.
swarthy [ˈswɔːðɪ] *adj* (+*er*) *skin* dunkel; *person also* dunkelhäutig.
swash [swɒʃ] *vti* schwappen.
swashbuckler [ˈswɒʃˌbʌklər] *n* verwegener Kerl.
swashbuckling [ˈswɒʃˌbʌklɪŋ] *adj person, manner* verwegen.
swastika [ˈswɒstɪkə] *n* Hakenkreuz *nt*; (*religious symbol also*) Swastika *f*.
swat [swɒt] **1** *vt fly* totschlagen; *table* schlagen auf (+*acc*). **2** *vi* **to** ~ **at a fly** nach einer Fliege schlagen. **3** *n* **(a)** (*blow*) Schlag *m*. **(b)** (*fly* ~) Fliegenklatsche *f*.
swatch [swɒtʃ] *n* (*Textil*)muster *nt*; (*collection of samples*) Musterbuch *nt*.
swath [swɔːθ], **swathe** [sweɪð] *n* Schwade *f*. **to cut a** ~ **through sth** eine Bahn durch etw schneiden.
swathe [sweɪð] *vt* wickeln (*in* in +*acc*); (*in bandages also*) umwickeln (*in* mit). **to** ~ **oneself in sth** sich in etw (*acc*) einwikkeln *or* einhüllen, etw um sich wickeln.
swatter [ˈswɒtər] *n* (*fly* ~) Fliegenklatsche *f*.
sway [sweɪ] **1** *n* **(a)** (*movement*) *see vi* Sich-Wiegen *nt*; Schwingen *nt*; Schwanken *nt*; Schaukeln *nt*; Wackeln *nt*; Schwenken *nt*. **the graceful** ~ **of the dancer's body** das anmutige Wiegen der Tänzerin; **the bridge has quite a** ~ die Brücke schwankt beträchtlich.
(b) (*influence, rule*) Macht *f* (*over* über +*acc*). **to bring sb/a people under one's** ~ jdn seinem Willen/ein Volk seiner Macht unterwerfen; **to hold** ~ *over* sb/a nation jdn/ein Volk beherrschen *or* in seiner Macht haben.
2 *vi* (*trees*) sich wiegen; (*hanging object*) schwingen; (*building, mast, bridge etc, unsteady person*) schwanken; (*train, boat*) schaukeln; (*hips*) wackeln; (*fig*) schwenken. **the ladder** ~ed **away from the wall** die Leiter bewegte sich von der Mauer weg; **she** ~s **as she walks** sie wiegt beim Gehen die Hüften; **the drunk** ~ed **up the road** der Betrunkene schwankte die Straße entlang; **public opinion** ~ed **over to the conservatives** die öffentliche Meinung schwenkte zu den Konservativen über; **to** ~ **between two alternatives** zwischen zwei Alternativen schwanken.
3 *vt* **(a)** schwenken; (*wind*) hin und her bewegen.
(b) (*influence*) beeinflussen; (*change sb's mind*) umstimmen.
swear [sweər] (*vb: pret* swore, *ptp* sworn) **1** *vt* **(a)** *allegiance, love, revenge* schwören; *oath also* leisten, ablegen. **I** ~ **it!** ich kann das beschwören!
(b) (*Jur*) *witness, jury* vereidigen. **to** ~ **sb to secrecy** jdn schwören lassen, daß er nichts verrät; **I've been sworn to secrecy** ich habe schwören müssen, daß ich nichts sage.
2 *vi* **(a)** (*use solemn oath*) schwören. **to** ~ **on the Bible** auf die Bibel schwören; **to** ~ **by all one holds dear** schwören bei allem, was einem lieb ist; **to** ~ **to sth** etw beschwören, einen Eid auf etw (*acc*) ablegen; **to** ~ **blind that** ... (*inf*) Stein und Bein schwören, daß ... (*inf*).
(b) (*use swearwords*) fluchen (*about* über +*acc*). **to** ~ **at sb/sth** jdn/etw beschimpfen.
3 *n* **to have a (good)** ~ (tüchtig) fluchen.
♦**swear by** *vi* +*prep obj* (*inf*) schwören auf (+*acc*).
♦**swear in** *vt sep witness, jury, president* vereidigen.
♦**swear off** *vi* +*prep obj* (*inf*) abschwören (+*dat*).
swearing [ˈsweərɪŋ] *n* Fluchen *nt*.
swearing-in [ˌsweərɪŋˈɪn] *n* Vereidigung *f*.

swearword ['swɛə,wɜːd] n Fluch, Kraftausdruck m.
sweat [swet] **1** n (a) Schweiß m no pl; (on walls) (Kondens)-wasser nt. **drops/beads of** ~ Schweißtropfen pl/-perlen pl; **his face was running with** ~ der Schweiß rann ihm von der Stirn; **all of a** ~ schweißgebadet; **by the** ~ **of one's brow** (fig) im Schweiße seines Angesichts (liter); **to be in a** ~ (lit, fig inf) schwitzen; **to get into a** ~ **about sth** (fig) wegen etw ins Schwitzen geraten or kommen; **no** ~ (inf) kein Problem; **the walls are running with** ~ die Wände schwitzen; see **cold.**
(b) (inf: work) **what a** ~ **that was!** das war eine Heidenarbeit! (inf); **we had a real** ~ **to do it** wir haben dabei wirklich geschuftet (inf); **that's too much** ~ **for me** das ist mir zu anstrengend.
2 vi (person, animal, wall) schwitzen (with vor +dat); (fig inf) (work hard) sich abrackern (inf) (over mit); (worry) zittern, schwitzen (inf) (with vor +dat). **to** ~ **like a pig** (inf) wie ein Affe schwitzen (inf).
3 vt horse, athlete schwitzen lassen; (pej) worker für einen Hungerlohn arbeiten lassen; recruit schleifen (inf). **to** ~ **blood** (with worry) Blut und Wasser schwitzen; (with effort, work) sich abrackern (inf); **to** ~ **blood trying to do sth** sich abrackern, um etw zu tun (inf).
◆**sweat out** vt sep (a) illness, fever herausschwitzen. (b) **to** ~ **it** ~ (fig inf) durchhalten; (sit and wait) abwarten.
sweatband ['swet,bænd] n Schweißband nt.
sweated ['swetɪd] adj worker völlig unterbezahlt, ausgebeutet; goods für einen Hungerlohn hergestellt. ~ **labour** billige Arbeitskräfte pl; **it was** ~ **labour!** (inf) das war Ausbeutung.
sweater ['swetəʳ] n Pullover m.
sweat: ~ **gland** n Schweißdrüse f; ~**shirt** n Sweatshirt nt; (Sport) Trainingspullover m; ~**shop** n (pej, hum inf) Ausbeuterbetrieb m (pej).
sweaty ['swetɪ] adj (+er) hands schweißig; feet, smell also Schweiß-; brow schweißbedeckt; body, person, socks verschwitzt; weather, day, work zum Schwitzen. **digging is** ~ **work** beim Graben kommt man leicht ins Schwitzen; **to have a** ~ **smell** nach Schweiß riechen.
swede [swiːd] n (Brit) Kohlrübe, Steckrübe f.
Swede [swiːd] n Schwede m, Schwedin f.
Sweden ['swiːdn] n Schweden nt.
Swedish ['swiːdɪʃ] **1** adj schwedisch. **2** n Schwedisch nt.
sweep [swiːp] (vb: pret, ptp **swept**) **1** n (a) **to give the floor a** ~ den Boden kehren or fegen; **the chimney needs a** ~ der Schornstein muß gekehrt or gefegt werden.
(b) (chimney ~) Schornsteinfeger, Kaminkehrer m.
(c) (of arm, pendulum) Schwung m; (of sword also) Streich m; (of dress) Rauschen nt no pl; (of oars) Durchziehen nt no pl; (of light, radar) Strahl m. **at or in one** ~ (fig) auf einen Schwung; **with a** ~ **of her skirts** mit rauschenden Gewändern; **to make a** ~ **for mines** nach Minen suchen; **the police made a** ~ **of the district** die Polizei hat die Gegend abgesucht; **to make a clean** ~ (fig) gründlich aufräumen or Ordnung schaffen; **the Russians made a clean** ~ **of the athletic events** die Russen haben beim Leichtathletikkampf tüchtig abgeräumt (inf) or alle Preise eingesteckt.
(d) (range) Bereich m; (of gun also) Schußbereich m.
(e) (curve, line) (of road, river) Bogen m; (of facade, contour, hair) Schwung m. **the** ~ **of the plains** die Weite der Ebene; **a wide** ~ **of country** eine sich weit ausdehnende Landschaft; **a beautiful** ~ **of hills** herrliche Berge pl.
(f) see **sweepstake.**
2 vt (a) floor, street, chimney kehren, fegen; room also auskehren, ausfegen; dust, snow wegfegen. **to** ~ **a passage through the snow** einen Weg durch den Schnee bahnen; **to** ~ **sth under the carpet** (fig) etw unter den Teppich kehren.
(b) (scan, move searchingly over) absuchen (for nach); (lights also, bullets) streichen über (+acc); minefield durchkämmen; mines räumen. **to** ~ **a channel clear of mines** einen Kanal von Minen säubern; **the fleet swept the seas in search of ...** die Flotte durchkämmte die Meere auf der Suche nach ...; **to** ~ **a road with bullets** eine Straße beschießen or bestreichen (spec).
(c) (move quickly over) (wind, skirt) fegen über (+acc); (waves) deck, sand etc überrollen, überschwemmen; (glance) gleiten über (+acc); (fig) (wave of protest, violence, fashion) überrollen; (disease) um sich greifen in (+dat).
(d) (remove with ~ing movement) (wave) spülen, schwemmen; (current) reißen; (wind) fegen; person reißen. **to** ~ **sth off the table/onto the floor/into a bag** etw vom Tisch/zu Boden fegen/etw in eine Tasche raffen; **the crowd swept him into the square** er wurde von der Menge zum Platz hin mitgerissen; **he swept the obstacles from his path** er stieß die Hindernisse aus dem Weg; **the army swept the enemy before them** die Armee jagte die feindlichen Truppen vor sich her.
(e) (triumph) große Triumphe feiern in (+dat). **to** ~ **the polls** (Pol) die Wahlen haushoch gewinnen; **to** ~ **all before one** (fig) alle in die Tasche stecken (inf); **to** ~ **the board** (fig) alle Preise/Medaillen gewinnen, abräumen (inf).
3 vi (a) (with broom) kehren, fegen; see **broom.**
(b) (move) (person) rauschen; (vehicle, plane) (quickly) schießen; (majestically) gleiten; (skier) fegen; (road, river) in weitem Bogen führen. **panic/the disease swept through Europe** Panik/die Krankheit griff in Europa um sich or breitete sich in Europa aus; **the tornado swept across the fields** der Wirbelwind fegte über die Felder.
◆**sweep along 1** vi dahin- or entlangrauschen; (majestically) dahin- or entlanggleiten. **2** vt sep (lit, fig) mitreißen.
◆**sweep aside** vt sep (lit, fig) beiseite fegen.
◆**sweep away 1** vi see **sweep off. 2** vt sep dust, leaves etc wegfegen; (storm also, avalanche) wegreißen; (flood etc) wegspülen, wegschwemmen; (fig) old laws aufräumen mit; work, accomplishments zunichte machen.

◆**sweep down 1** vi hinunter-/herunterrauschen; (car, plane) hinunter-/herunterschießen; (majestically) hinunter-/heruntergleiten; (road, hill) in sanftem Bogen abfallen. **to** ~ ~ **on sb** sich auf jdn stürzen, über jdn herfallen.
2 vt sep abkehren, abfegen.
◆**sweep off 1** vi davonrauschen; (car, plane) davonschießen; (majestically) davongleiten; (skier) davonfegen.
2 vt sep vase, clock hinunter-/herunterfegen. **to** ~ ~ **sb** ~ **somewhere** jdn irgendwohin entführen; **the children were swept** ~ **to bed** die Kinder wurden schleunigst ins Bett gesteckt (inf) or geschickt; **to** ~ **sb** ~ **his/her feet** (lit) jdn umreißen; (fig) audience jdn begeistern; **he swept her** ~ **her feet** sie hat sich Hals über Kopf in ihn verliebt (inf).
◆**sweep out 1** vi hinaus-/herausrauschen; (car) hinaus-/herausschießen; (majestically) hinaus-/herausgleiten. **to** ~ ~ **of a room** aus einem Zimmer rauschen. **2** vt sep room auskehren, ausfegen; dust hinaus-/herauskehren or -fegen.
◆**sweep up 1** vi (a) (with broom) zusammenkehren or -fegen. **to** ~ ~ **after sb** hinter jdm herfegen.
(b) (move) **he swept** ~ **to me** er rauschte auf mich zu; **the car swept** ~ **to the house** der Wagen rollte aufs Haus zu; **she swept** ~ **in a Rolls Royce** sie rollte in einem Rolls Royce vor; **a broad driveway** ~**s** ~ **to the manor** ein breiter Zufahrtsweg schwingt sich zum Herrenhaus hinauf.
2 vt sep zusammenkehren or -fegen; (collect up) objects zusammenraffen; person hochreißen; hair hochbinden.
sweepback ['swiːp,bæk] n (Aviat) Pfeilform f.
sweeper ['swiːpəʳ] n (a) (road ~) Straßenkehrer(in f) or -feger(in f) m; (machine) Kehrmaschine f; (carpet ~) Teppichkehrer m. (b) (Ftbl) Ausputzer m.
sweep hand n Sekundenzeiger m.
sweeping ['swiːpɪŋ] adj (a) gesture weitausholend; stroke also mächtig; bow, curtsey, lines schwungvoll; glance streifend. **the steady** ~ **movement of his oars** das gleichmäßige Durchziehen der Ruder.
(b) (fig) change, reduction radikal, drastisch; statement pauschal; victory überragend, glänzend. **to make a** ~ **condemnation of sth** etw in Bausch und Bogen verdammen.
sweepingly ['swiːpɪŋlɪ] adv gesture schwungvoll; speak verallgemeinernd; condemn in Bausch und Bogen.
sweepings ['swiːpɪŋz] npl Kehricht, Dreck m; (fig: of society etc) Abschaum m.
sweepstake ['swiːp,steɪk] n (race) Rennen nt, in dem die Pferdebesitzer alle Einsätze machen; (prize) aus allen Einsätzen gebildeter Preis; (lottery) Wette, bei der die Preise aus den Einsätzen gebildet werden.
sweet [swiːt] **1** adj (+er) (a) süß. **to like** ~ **things** gern Süßes essen; **to have a** ~ **tooth** gern Süßes essen, naschhaft sein.
(b) (fresh) food, water frisch; air, breath also rein; soil nicht sauer; (fragrant) smell süß. **the air was** ~ **with the scent of roses** die Luft war erfüllt vom Duft der Rosen.
(c) (fig) süß; (kind also) lieb. **that's very** ~ **of you** das ist sehr lieb von dir; **that car/horse is a** ~ **little runner** das Auto/Pferd läuft prächtig; **to be** ~ **on sb** (dated inf) in jdn vernarrt sein; **to keep sb** ~ (inf) jdn bei Laune halten; **the water tasted** ~ **to him** (liter) das Wasser schmeckte (ihm) so gut; **success was doubly** ~ **to him** er genoß den Erfolg doppelt; **once he caught the** ~ **smell of success** als erst der Erfolg lockte; **the words were** ~ **to his ear** die Worte klangen lieblich in seinen Ohren; **at his own** ~ **will** (iro) wie es ihm gerade paßt or einfällt; **in his own** ~ **way** (iro) auf seine unübertroffene Art; ~ **Fanny Adams or FA** (sl) nix (inf), nicht die Bohne (sl); see **dream, nothing.**
2 n (a) (Brit: candy) Bonbon nt.
(b) (Brit: dessert) Nachtisch m, Dessert nt. **for** ~ zum or als Nachtisch or Dessert.
(c) yes, (my) ~ (inf) ja, (mein) Schätzchen or Liebling.
(d) ~**s** pl (fig: pleasures) **the** ~**s of country life/youth/solitude** etc die Freuden pl des Landlebens/der Jugend/Einsamkeit etc; **once he had tasted the** ~**s of success** nachdem er einmal erfahren hatte, wie süß der Erfolg sein kann.
sweet: ~**-and-sour** adj süßsauer; ~**bread** n Bries nt; ~**-brier** n Weinrose f; ~ **chestnut** n Edelkastanie f; ~ **corn** n Mais m.
sweeten ['swiːtn] **1** vt coffee, sauce süßen; air, breath reinigen; (fig) temper bessern; task versüßen. **to** ~ **sb** (inf) jdn gnädig stimmen; (sl: bribe) jdn schmieren (inf). **2** vi (temper) sich bessern; (person) gute Laune bekommen.
sweetener ['swiːtnəʳ] n (Cook) Süßungsmittel nt; (artificial) Süßstoff m; (sl: bribe) Schmiergeld nt (inf).
sweetening ['swiːtnɪŋ] n (Cook) Süßungsmittel nt; (artificial) Süßstoff m.
sweetheart ['swiːt,hɑːt] n Schatz m, Liebste(r) mf. **soon they were** ~**s** (dated) bald waren sie ein Pärchen; **Vera Lynn, the Forces'** ~ Vera Lynn, der Liebling der Armee.
sweetie ['swiːtɪ] n (a) (inf: also ~-**pie**) yes, ~ ja, Schatzi (inf) or Süße(r); **she's/he's a** ~ sie/er ist ein Engel or ist süß (inf). (b) (baby-talk, Scot: candy) Bonbon m.
sweetish ['swiːtɪʃ] adj taste, smell süßlich.
sweetly ['swiːtlɪ] adv sing, play süß; smile also, answer lieb. **the engine was running** ~ der Motor ist prächtig gelaufen; **rather** ~, **he offered to drive me** there er bot an, mich hinzufahren, was wirklich süß or lieb von ihm war.
sweet: ~**meat** n (old) Leckerei f; ~**-natured** adj lieb.
sweetness ['swiːtnɪs] n (lit) Süßigkeit, Süße f; (fig) Süße f; (of smile, nature) Liebenswürdigkeit f; (of person) liebe Art; (freshness) (of food, water) Frische f; (of air, breath) Reinheit, Frische f. **she has real** ~ **of character** sie hat eine wirklich liebe Art; **now all is** ~ **and light** (usu iro) nun herrscht eitel Freude und Sonnenschein; **to go around spreading** ~ **and light** Freundlichkeit ausstrahlen.
sweet: ~ **pea** n Gartenwicke f; ~ **potato** n Süßkartoffel, Batate f; ~**-scented** adj süß-duftend; ~**-shop** n (Brit) Süßwarenladen m

or -geschäft *nt*; ~-**smelling** *adj* süß riechend *attr*; ~-**talk** (*inf*) 1 *n* süße Worte *pl*; 2 *vt* to ~-**talk** sb **into doing sth** jdn mit süßen Worten dazu bringen, etw zu tun; ~-**tempered** *adj* verträglich; ~ **william** *n* Bartnelke *f*.

swell [swel] (*vb: pret* ~ **ed**, *ptp* **swollen** *or* ~ **ed**) 1 *n* (a) (*of sea*) Wogen *nt no pl*; (*wave*) Woge *f*. **there was a heavy** ~ es herrschte hoher Seegang *or* schwere See; *see* **groundswell**.

(b) (*dated inf*) (*stylish person*) feine Dame, feiner Herr; (*important person*) hohes Tier; (*of high society*) Größe *f*. **the** ~**s** *pl* die feinen Leute.

(c) (*Mus*) (*sound*) Crescendo *nt* mit gleich anschließendem Decrescendo; (*control, knob*) Schweller *m*; (*mechanism*) Schwellwerk *nt*.

2 *adj* (*inf*) (a) (*dated: stylish*) fein, vornehm; *house, restaurant also* nobel (*inf*).

(b) (*esp US: excellent*) klasse (*inf*), prima (*inf*).

3 *vt* ankle, river, sound *etc* anschwellen lassen; *stomach* (auf)blähen; *wood* (auf)quellen; *sail* blähen; *numbers, population* anwachsen lassen; *sales* steigern. **to be swollen with pride/rage** stolzgeschwellt sein/vor Wut (beinahe) platzen; **he was too swollen with rage/pride to listen** er war zu wütend/zu sehr von sich selbst eingenommen, um zuzuhören; **your praise will only** ~ **her head** dein Lob wird ihr nur zu Kopf steigen.

4 *vi* (a) (*ankle, arm, eye etc: also* ~ **up**) (an)schwellen; (*balloon, air bed, tyre*) sich füllen. **to** ~ (**up**) **with rage/pride/vor** Wut rot anlaufen/vor Stolz anschwellen; **the childrens' bellies had swollen with hunger** die Bäuche der Kinder waren vom Hunger (auf)gebläht.

(b) (*river, lake, sound etc*) anschwellen; (*cheers also*) anwachsen; (*sails: also* ~ **out**) sich blähen; (*wood*) quellen; (*in size, number: population, debt etc*) anwachsen. **to** ~ **into a crowd** sich zu einer Menschenmenge auswachsen; **the cheers** ~**ed to a roar** der Jubel schwoll zu einem Begeisterungssturm an; **the debt had swollen to a massive sum** die Schuld war zu einer riesigen Summe angewachsen; *see also* **swollen**.

swell-box ['swel,bɒks] *n* (*Mus*) Schwellwerk *nt*.
swellhead ['swel,hed] *n* (*esp US inf*) aufgeblasener Typ (*inf*).
swell-headed ['swel,hedɪd] *adj* (*inf*) aufgeblasen (*inf*).
swelling ['swelɪŋ] 1 *n* (a) Verdickung *f*; (*Med*) Schwellung *f*.

(b) (*act*) *see vi* Anschwellen *nt*; Anwachsen *nt*; Blähen *nt*; Quellen *nt*; Anwachsen *nt*.

2 *adj attr* ankle etc (an)schwellend; *sails* gebläht; *sound* anschwellend; *numbers* steigend, anwachsend, zunehmend; *line, curve* geschwungen. **the** ~ **curve of her bosom** die Wölbung ihrer Brüste.

swelter ['sweltə^r] *vi* (vor Hitze) vergehen, verschmachten (*inf*).
sweltering ['sweltərɪŋ] *adj* day, weather glühend heiß; heat glühend. **it's** ~ **in here** (*inf*) hier verschmachtet man ja! (*inf*).
swept [swept] *pret, ptp of* **sweep**.
swept: ~-**back** *adj wing* Delta-, Dreieck-; ~**wing** *adj aircraft* mit Delta- *or* Dreieckflügeln.
swerve [swɜːv] 1 *n* Bogen *m*; (*of road, coastline also*) Schwenkung *f*; (*of car etc also*) Schlenker *m* (*inf*); (*spin on ball*) Effet *m*. **with a** ~ **he avoided his opponent** er wich seinem Gegner mit einer geschickten Bewegung aus; **to put a** ~ **on the ball** einen Ball anschneiden; **to make a** ~ (*lit*) *see vi*.

2 *vi* einen Bogen machen; (*car, driver*) ausschwenken; (*boxer*) ausweichen; (*horse*) ausbrechen; (*ball also*) im Bogen fliegen; (*fig*) (*from truth*) abweichen; (*from chosen path*) abschwenken. **to** ~ **round sth** einen Bogen um etw machen; **the road** ~**s** (**round**) **to the right** die Straße schwenkt nach rechts; **he** ~**d in front of me** er schwenkte plötzlich vor mir ein; **the car** ~**d in and out of the traffic** der Wagen schoß im Slalom durch den Verkehrsstrom.

3 *vt car etc* herumreißen; *ball* anschneiden.
swift [swɪft] 1 *adj* (+*er*) schnell; *movement, steps also* flink; *reaction, reply also, revenge* prompt; *runner also* flink, flott; *pace* flott, rasch. ~ **of foot** (*liter*) schnellfüßig; **to be** ~ **to anger** jähzornig sein; **to be** ~ **to do sth** etw schnell tun. 2 *n* (*bird*) Mauersegler *m*.
swift: ~-**flowing** *adj* schnellfließend *attr*; ~-**footed** *adj* (*liter*) schnellfüßig.
swiftly ['swɪftlɪ] *adv see adj*. **time passes** ~ die Zeit vergeht wie im Flug.
swiftness ['swɪftnɪs] *n see adj* Schnelligkeit *f*; Flinkheit *f*; Promptheit *f*; Flinkheit *f*, Flottheit *f*; Flottheit, Raschheit *f*. **the** ~ **of the current** die reißende Strömung.
swig [swɪg] (*inf*) 1 *n* Schluck *m*. **to have** *or* **take a** ~ **of beer/at** *or* **from a bottle** einen Schluck Bier/aus einer Flasche nehmen; **have a** ~ **of this** trinken Sie mal einen Schluck (davon) (*inf*); **to down a drink in one** ~ das Glas in einem Zug leeren.

2 *vt* (*also* ~ **down**) herunterkippen (*inf*). **to sit** ~**ging beer all evening** den ganzen Abend ein Bier nach dem anderen runterkippen (*inf*).
swill [swɪl] 1 *n* (a) (*animal food*) (Schweine)futter *nt*; (*garbage, slops*) (*solid*) Abfälle *pl*; (*liquid*) Spülicht, Schmutzwasser *nt*; (*fig pej*) (Schweine)fraß *m* (*inf*); (*liquid*) Abwaschwasser *nt* (*inf*), Brühe *f* (*inf*).

(b) (*cleaning*) *see vt* (a) Auswaschen *nt*; Ausschwenken *nt*; Abspülen *nt*; Waschen *nt*. **the barn needs a good** ~ (**out**) die Scheune muß mal gründlich ausgewaschen werden; **to give sth a** ~ (**out/down**) *see vt* (a).

2 *vt* (a) (*also* ~ **out**) auswaschen; *cup, dish* ausschwenken. **to** ~ **sth down** etw abspülen; *floor* etw waschen.

(b) (*inf*) *beer etc* kippen (*inf*). **he** ~**ed it down with beer** er hat es mit Bier runtergespült (*inf*).
swim [swɪm] (*vb: pret* **swam**, *ptp* **swum**) 1 *n* (a) **after a 2 km** ~ nach 2 km Schwimmen, nachdem ich *etc* 2 km geschwommen bin/war; **it's a long** ~ es ist weit (zu schwimmen); **that was a nice** ~ das (Schwimmen) hat Spaß gemacht!; **I like** *or* **enjoy a** ~ ich gehe gern (mal) schwimmen, ich schwimme

gern (mal); **to have a** ~ schwimmen.

(b) (*inf*) **to be in the/out of the** ~ up to date/nicht mehr up to date sein; (*socially active*) mitmischen (*inf*)/den Anschluß verloren haben; **to keep sb in the** ~ jdn auf dem laufenden halten.

2 *vt* schwimmen; *river, Channel* durchschwimmen.

3 *vi* (*all senses*) schwimmen. **to** ~ **back** zurückschwimmen; **we shall have to** ~ **for it** wir werden schwimmen müssen; **the room swam before my eyes** das Zimmer verschwamm vor meinen Augen; **my head is** ~**ming** mir dreht sich alles, mir ist ganz schwummrig (*inf*).
swim-bladder ['swɪm,blædə^r] *n* Schwimmblase *f*.
swimmer ['swɪmə^r] *n* Schwimmer(in *f*) *m*.
swimming ['swɪmɪŋ] 1 *n* Schwimmen *nt*. **do you like** ~? schwimmen Sie gern? 2 *adj* (*for* ~) Schwimm-; (*dizzy*) *feeling* schwummrig (*inf*).
swimming: ~ **bath** *n usu pl see* ~ **pool**; ~ **cap** *n* Badekappe, Bademütze *f*; ~ **costume** *n* Badeanzug *m*; ~ **gala** *n* Schwimmfest *nt*.
swimmingly ['swɪmɪŋlɪ] *adv* (*inf*) glänzend. **how are your plans?** — **they're going** ~ wie entwickeln sich Ihre Pläne? — glänzend!
swimming: ~ **pool** *n* Schwimmbad *nt*, Badeanstalt *f* (*form*); (*indoor also*) Hallenbad *nt*; ~ **ring** *n* Schwimmring *m*; ~ **trunks** *npl* Badehose *f*.
swimsuit ['swɪmsuːt] *n* Badeanzug *m*.
swindle ['swɪndl] 1 *n* Schwindel, Betrug *m*. **it's a** ~! das ist (reiner) Schwindel!

2 *vt* person beschwindeln, betrügen. **to** ~ **sb out of sth** (*take from*) jdm etw abschwindeln *or* abgaunern (*inf*); (*withhold from*) jdn um etw beschwindeln *or* betrügen; **to** ~ **sth out of sb** jdm etw abschwindeln *or* abgaunern (*inf*).
swindler ['swɪndlə^r] *n* Schwindler(in *f*), Gauner(in *f*) (*inf*) *m*.
swine [swaɪn] *n* (a) *pl* - (*old, form*) Schwein *nt*. (b) *pl* -**s** (*pej inf*) (*man*) (gemeiner) Hund (*inf*); (*woman*) gemeine Sau (*sl*). **this translation is a** ~ diese Übersetzung ist wirklich gemein (*inf*).
swine: ~ **fever** *n* Schweinepest *f*; ~**herd** *n* (*old*) Schweinehirt *m*.
swing [swɪŋ] (*vb: pret, ptp* **swung**) 1 *n* (a) (*movement*) Schwung *m*; (*to and fro*) Schwingen *nt*; (*of needle*) Ausschlag *m*; (*distance*) Ausschlag, Schwung(weite *f*); (*Boxing etc: blow*) Schwinger *m*; (*Golf, Skiing etc*) Schwung *m*; (*fig, Pol*) (Meinungs)umschwung *m*. **to take a** ~ **at sb** nach jdm schlagen; **the golfer took a big** ~ **at the ball** der Golfer holte weit aus und schlug den Ball; **my** ~ **is too short** ich hole nicht weit genug aus; **a** ~ **in opinion** ein Meinungsumschwung.

(b) (*rhythm*) Schwung *m*; (*kind of music, dance*) Swing *m*. **a tune with a** ~ eine Melodie mit Schwung; **they swayed to the** ~ **of the music** sie bewegten sich im Rhythmus *or* im Takt der Musik; **to walk with a** ~ schwungvoll gehen; **to go with a** ~ (*fig*) ein voller Erfolg sein (*inf*); **to be in full** ~ voll im Gang sein; **to get into the** ~ **of things** (*inf*) reinkommen (*inf*).

(c) (*seat for* ~**ing**) Schaukel *f*. **to give sb a** ~ jdn anstoßen *or* anschubsen (*inf*); **to have a** ~ schaukeln; **what you gain on the** ~**s** (**you lose on the roundabouts**) (*prov*) was man auf der einen Seite gewinnt, verliert man auf der anderen; **it's a** ~**s and roundabouts situation** (*inf*) es ist gehupft wie gesprungen.

(d) (*esp US: scope, freedom*) **he gave his imagination full** ~ er ließ seiner Phantasie (*dat*) freien Lauf; **he was given full** ~ **to make decisions** man hat ihm bei allen Entscheidungen freie Hand gelassen.

2 *vt* (a) schwingen; (*to and fro*) hin und her schwingen; (*on swing, hammock*) schaukeln; *arms, legs* (*vigorously*) schwingen (mit); (*dangle*) baumeln mit; *propeller* einen Schwung geben (+*dat*). **to** ~ **a child** ein Kind schaukeln; **to** ~ **one's hips** sich in den Hüften wiegen; **to** ~ **the lead** (*Brit inf*) sich drücken (*inf*); *see* **cat**.

(b) (*move*) **he swung his axe at the tree/at me** er schwang die Axt gegen den Baum/gegen mich; **he swung his racket at the ball** er holte mit dem Schläger aus; **to** ~ **a door open/shut** eine Tür aufstoßen/zustoßen; **he swung the case (up) onto his shoulder** er schwang sich (*dat*) die Kiste auf die Schulter; **he swung himself over the stream/wall/up into the saddle** er schwang sich über den Bach/über die Mauer/in den Sattel.

(c) (*influence*) election, decision, voters beeinflussen; opinion umschlagen lassen; person umstimmen, herumkriegen (*inf*). **his speech swung the decision in our favour** seine Rede ließ die Entscheidung zu unseren Gunsten ausfallen; **what swung it for me was the fact that** ... (*inf*) was dann letzten Endes den Ausschlag gegeben hat, war, daß ...; **to** ~ **it** (**so that** ...) (*inf*) es so drehen *or* deichseln (*inf*) (, daß ...); **he managed to** ~ **it in our favour** es gelang ihm, es zu unseren Gunsten zu drehen; **he managed to** ~ **the deal** (*inf*) er hat das Geschäft gemacht (*inf*).

(d) (*Mus*) tune (*arrange*) Schwung geben (+*dat*); (*play*) schwungvoll spielen.

(e) (*turn: also* ~ **round**) plane, car herumschwenken.

3 *vi* (a) schwingen; (*to and fro*) (hin und her) schwingen; (*hanging object also*) pendeln; (*pivot*) sich drehen; (*on swing*) schaukeln; (*arms, legs: dangle*) baumeln. **he was left** ~**ing by his hands** er hing *or* (*dangerously*) baumelte nur noch an den Händen; **the boat was** ~**ing at anchor** das Boot lag schaukelnd vor Anker; **he swung at me with his axe** er schwang die Axt gegen mich; **the golfer swung at the ball** der Golfer holte aus.

(b) (*move*: into saddle, along rope etc) sich schwingen. **to** ~ **from tree to tree** sich von Baum zu Baum schwingen; **to** ~ **open/shut** aufschwingen/zuschlagen; **to** ~ **into action** in Aktion treten; **the car swung into the square** der Wagen schwenkte auf den Platz ein; **opinion/the party has swung to the right** die Meinung/die Partei hat einen Rechtsschwenk gemacht.

(c) (*music, tune*) Schwung haben. **the town/club began to** ~ in der Stadt/im Klub kam Stimmung auf (*inf*); **London really swung in the sixties** in den sechziger Jahren war in London schwer was los (*inf*).

(d) (*inf: be hanged*) he'll ~ for it dafür wird er baumeln (*inf*); I'll ~ for him (yet) ich bring ihn noch um (*inf*); he's not worth ~ing for es lohnt sich nicht, sich an ihm die Hände schmutzig zu machen (*inf*).

♦**swing across** *vi* hinüber-/herüberschwingen; (*hand-over-hand*) sich hinüber-/herüberhangeln; (*+prep obj*) schwingen über (*+acc*); (*person, animal*) sich schwingen über (*+acc*); (*hand-over-hand*) sich hangeln über (*+acc*).

♦**swing back 1** *vi* zurückschwingen; (*opinion*) zurückschlagen. **2** *vt sep* zurückschwingen; *opinion* zurückschlagen lassen.

♦**swing round 1** *vi* (*person*) sich umdrehen, herumfahren (*inf*); (*car, ship, plane, crane*) herumschwenken; (*needle*) ausschlagen; (*fig: voters, opinion*) umschwenken. he has swung ~ in favour of the idea er hat sich doch noch für diese Idee entschieden.

2 *vt sep* herumschwenken; *voters* umstimmen; *opinion* umschlagen lassen.

♦**swing to** *vi* (*door*) zuschlagen.

swing: ~ band *n* (*Mus*) Swingband *f*; ~-boat *n* Schiffschaukel *f*; ~ bridge *n* Drehbrücke *f*; ~-door *n* (*Brit*) Pendeltür *f*.

swingeing ['swɪndʒɪŋ] *adj* (*Brit*) *blow* hart; *attack* scharf; *defeat* vernichtend; *taxation, price increases* extrem hoch; *cuts* extrem.

swinger ['swɪŋəʳ] *n* (*inf*) lockerer Typ (*sl*).

swinging ['swɪŋɪŋ] *adj step* schwungvoll; *movement* schaukelnd; *music* schwungvoll, swingend; (*fig inf*) *person* locker (*sl*). ~ door (*US*) Pendeltür *f*; **London was a ~ place then** in London war damals wirklich was los (*inf*); **the ~ sixties** die flotten sechziger Jahre, die „swinging sixties" (*sl*).

swing-wing ['swɪŋˈwɪŋ] *adj aircraft* mit ausfahrbaren Tragflächenteilen.

swinish ['swaɪnɪʃ] *adj* (*fig*) gemein.

swipe [swaɪp] **1** *n* (*blow*) Schlag *m*. **to take or make a ~ at sb/sth** nach jdm/etw schlagen. **2** *vt* (**a**) *person, ball etc* schlagen. he ~d the wasp with the towel er schlug mit dem Handtuch auf die Wespe. (**b**) (*inf: to steal*) mopsen (*inf*), klauen (*inf*). **3** *vi* **to ~ at sb/sth** nach jdm/etw schlagen.

swirl [swɜːl] **1** *n* Wirbel *m*; (*whorl in pattern also*) Spirale *f*. **the ~ of the dancers' skirts** die wirbelnden Röcke der Tänzerinnen; **she put a ~ of cream on the cake** sie spritzte ein Sahnehäufchen auf den Kuchen.

2 *vt water, dust etc* wirbeln. **to ~ sth along/away etc** (*river*) etw wirbelnd mitreißen/etw wegwirbeln; **he ~ed his partner round the room** er wirbelte seine Partnerin durchs Zimmer. **3** *vi* wirbeln. **to ~ around** herumwirbeln.

swish [swɪʃ] **1** *n see* vi Zischen, Sausen *nt*; Rascheln *nt*; Rauschen *nt*; Zischen, Pfeifen *nt*; Wischen *nt*.

2 *adj* (+er) (*esp Brit inf: smart*) (tod)schick.

3 *vt cane* zischen *or* sausen lassen; *tail* schlagen mit; *skirt* rauschen mit; *water* schwenken. **she ~ed water round the bowl** sie schwenkte die Schüssel mit Wasser aus.

4 *vi* (*whip, cane*) zischen, sausen; (*grass*) rauschen; (*skirts*) rauschen, rascheln; (*water*) rauschen; (*tyres*) zischen, pfeifen; (*windscreen wipers*) wischen.

Swiss [swɪs] **1** *adj* Schweizer, schweizerisch. **the ~-German part of Switzerland** die deutschsprachige Schweiz; **~ cheese** Schweizer Käse; ~ roll Biskuitrolle *f*; **the/a ~ Guard** die Schweizergarde/ein Schweizer *m*.

2 *n* Schweizer(in *f*) *m*. **the ~ pl** die Schweizer *pl*; **~ French/German** (*person*) Französisch-/Deutschschweizer(in *f*) *m*; (*language*) Schweizer Französisch *nt*/Schweizerdeutsch, Schwyzerdütsch *nt*.

switch [swɪtʃ] **1** *n* (**a**) (*Elec etc*) Schalter *m*.

(**b**) (*US Rail*) Weiche *f*.

(**c**) (*change*) Wechsel *m*; (*in plans, policies*) Änderung, Umstellung *f* (*in gen*); (*in opinion*) Änderung *f* (*in gen*); (*exchange*) Tausch *m*. **a rapid ~ of plan** eine schnelle Änderung der Pläne; **to do *or* make a ~** tauschen.

(**d**) (*stick, cane*) Rute, Gerte *f*; (*riding-whip*) Gerte *f*.

(**e**) (*of hair*) falscher Zopf.

2 *vt* (**a**) (*change, alter*) wechseln; *direction, plans* ändern; *allegiance* übertragen (*to* auf *+acc*); *attention, conversation* lenken (*to* auf *+acc*). **to ~ schools** die Schule wechseln.

(**b**) (*move*) *production* verlegen; *object* umstellen.

(**c**) (*exchange*) tauschen; (*transpose: also* ~ **over**, ~ **round**) *objects, letters in word, figures in column* vertauschen. **I ~ed hats with him** ich tauschte meinen Hut mit ihm; **we ~ed hats** wir tauschten die Hüte; **to ~ A for B** A für *or* gegen B (ein)tauschen; **to ~ A and B (over)** A und B vertauschen.

(**d**) (*Elec*) (um)schalten. **to ~ the radio to another programme** schalten Sie auf ein anderes Radioprogramm um.

(**e**) *tail, cane* schlagen mit. **he ~ed the rope out of my hands** er wand mir das Seil aus der Hand.

(**f**) (*esp US Rail*) rangieren.

3 *vi* (**a**) (*change: also* ~ **over**) (über)wechseln (*to* zu); (*Elec, TV, Rad*) umschalten (*to* auf *+acc*); (*exchange: also* ~ **round**, ~ **over**) tauschen. **to ~ (over) from Y to Z** von Y auf Z (*acc*) (über)wechseln; **we've ~ed (over) to gas** wir haben auf Gas umgestellt; **the wind ~ed to the east** der Wind hat (sich) nach Osten gedreht; **he ~ed to another line of attack** er wechselte seine Angriffstaktik; **she ~ed to being in favour of it** sie änderte ihre Meinung und war auf einmal dafür.

(**b**) (*Rail*) rangieren.

♦**switch back 1** *vi* (*to original plan, product, allegiance etc*) zum Alten zurückkehren; (*for the Alte zurückgreifen*); (*Elec, Rad, TV*) zurückschalten (*to* zu). **to ~ to one's original plans** auf die ursprünglichen Pläne zurückgreifen.

2 *vt sep heater, cooker* zurückschalten (*to* auf *+acc*). **to ~ the light ~ on** das Licht wieder anschalten.

♦**switch off 1** *vt sep* (**a**) *light* ausschalten; *radio, TV, machine*

also, *engine* abschalten; *gas, water supply* abstellen. **the oven ~es itself ~** der Backofen schaltet sich selbsttätig ab *or* aus.

(**b**) (*inf*) ~ **him ~ for goodness' sake!** (*inf*) kann man niemand abstellen, um Himmels willen; **that/he ~es me right ~** dabei/bei ihm schalte ich gleich ab (*inf*).

2 *vi* (**a**) *see vt* (a) ausschalten; abschalten; abstellen. **the TV won't ~ ~** der Fernseher läßt sich nicht aus- *or* abschalten.

(**b**) (*inf: person*) abschalten.

♦**switch on 1** *vt sep* (**a**) *gas, water* anstellen; *machine, radio, TV also, light* einschalten, anschalten; *engine also* anlassen. **please leave the TV ~ed ~** laß den Fernseher bitte an.

(**b**) (*sl*) *person* (*interest*) munter machen, begeistern; (*emotionally, by drugs*) anturnen (*sl*), high machen (*sl*); (*sexually*) auf Touren bringen (*inf*). ~**ed ~** begeistert; (*emotionally, on drugs*) high (*sl*); (*sexually*) auf Touren (*inf*); (*up-to-date*) in (*sl*); **to be ~ed ~ to jazz** auf Jazz stehen (*inf*).

2 *vi see vt* (a) einschalten, anschalten; anlassen. **the cooker will ~ ~ at 10** der Herd schaltet sich um 10 Uhr ein *or* an; **the record-player won't ~ ~** der Plattenspieler läßt sich nicht einschalten *or* anstellen.

♦**switch over 1** *vi see* **switch 3** (a). **2** *vt sep* (**a**) *see* **switch 2** (b). (**b**) (*TV, Rad*) **to ~ the programme ~** auf ein anderes Programm umschalten.

♦**switch round 1** *vt sep* (*swap round*) vertauschen; (*rearrange*) umstellen. **2** *vi see* **switch 3** (a).

♦**switch through** *vt sep* (*Telec*) durchstellen (*to* zu), verbinden (*to* mit).

switch: ~back *n* Berg- und Talbahn *f*; (*Brit: roller-coaster also*) Achterbahn *f*; ~**blade** *n* (*US*) Schnappmesser *nt*; ~**board** *n* (*Telec*) (*exchange*) Vermittlung *f*; (*in office etc*) Zentrale *f*; (*actual panel, Elec*) Schalttafel *f*; ~**board operator** *n* (*in office*) Telephonist(in *f*) *m*; ~**man** *n* (*US Rail*) Weichensteller *m*; ~**over** *n* Wechsel *m* (*to* auf *+acc*, zu); (*exchange*) Tausch *m*; (*of letters, figures etc*) Vertauschung *f*; ~**round** *n* Tausch *m*; (*of letters, figures etc*) Vertauschung *f*; (*rearrangement*) Umstellen *f*; ~**yard** *n* (*US Rail*) Rangierbahnhof, Verschiebebahnhof *m*.

Switzerland ['swɪtsələnd] *n* die Schweiz. **to ~** in die Schweiz; **French-/German-/Italian-speaking ~** die französische Schweiz/die deutsch-/italienischsprachige Schweiz.

swivel ['swɪvl] **1** *n* Drehgelenk *nt*. **2** *attr* Dreh-. **3** *vt* (*also* ~ **round**) (herum)drehen. **4** *vi* (*also* ~ **round**) sich drehen; (*person*) sich herumdrehen.

swizz [swɪz], **swizzle** ['swɪzl] *n* (*Brit inf*) (*swindle*) Bauernfängerei *f* (*inf*); (*disappointment*) Gemeinheit *f* (*inf*).

swizzle-stick ['swɪzlˈstɪk] *n* Sektquirl *m*.

swollen ['swəʊlən] **1** *ptp of* **swell**.

2 *adj ankle, face, glands etc* (an)geschwollen; *stomach* aufgedunsen, aufgebläht; *wood* verquollen, gequollen; *sails* gebläht; *river* angeschwollen, angestiegen; *numbers* (an)gestiegen, angewachsen. **her eyes were ~ with tears** ihre Augen waren verweint; **he has a ~ head** (*fig*) er ist so aufgeblasen.

swollen-headed ['swəʊlənˈhedɪd] *adj* aufgeblasen.

swollen-headedness ['swəʊlənˈhedɪdnɪs] *n* Aufgeblasenheit *f*.

swoon [swuːn] **1** *n* (*old*) Ohnmacht *f*. **to fall in(to)/be in a ~** in Ohnmacht fallen *or* sinken (*geh*)/ohnmächtig sein.

2 *vi* (*old: faint*) in Ohnmacht fallen, ohnmächtig werden; (*fig: over pop star etc*) beinahe ohnmächtig werden (*over sb/sth* wegen jdm/einer Sache).

swoop [swuːp] **1** *n* (*lit: also* ~ **down**) (*bird*) herabstoßen, niederstoßen (*on* auf *+acc*); (*plane*) einen Sturzflug machen; (*fig: police*) einen Überraschungsangriff machen (*on* auf *+acc*) *or* landen (*inf*) (*on* bei); (*person*) sich stürzen (*on* auf *+acc*). **the plane ~ed (down) low over the village** das Flugzeug flog im Sturzflug auf das Dorf zu; **the police ~ed on 8 suspects** die Polizei schlug überraschend bei 8 Verdächtigen zu; **they're just waiting to ~** die lauern nur darauf zuzuschlagen.

2 *n* (*bird, plane*) Sturzflug *m*; (*by police*) Razzia *f* (*on* in *+dat*, *on sb* bei jdm). **to make a ~** (*bird*) herabstoßen (*on* auf *+acc*); **at one (fell) ~** auf einen Schlag.

swoosh [swuːʃ] **1** *vi* rauschen; (*air*) brausen; (*tyres in rain etc*) pfeifen, sirren; (*skirts, curtains*) rauschen. **2** *n see* vi Rauschen *nt*; Brausen *nt*; Pfeifen, Sirren *nt*; Rauschen *nt*. **his sword cut the air with a ~** sein Schwert pfiff durch die Luft.

swop *n, vti see* **swap.**

sword [sɔːd] *n* Schwert *nt*. **to cross ~s with sb** (*lit, fig*) mit jdm die Klinge(n) kreuzen; **by fire and (the) ~** mit Feuer und Schwert; **to put people to the ~** (*old*) Menschen mit dem Schwert töten; **those that live by the ~ die by the ~** (*prov*) wer das Schwert ergreift, der soll durchs Schwert umkommen.

sword *in cpds* Schwert-; ~**bearer** *n* Schwertträger *m*; ~**cane** *n* Stockdegen *m*; ~**-dance** *n* Schwert(er)tanz *m*; ~**fish** *n* Schwertfisch *m*; ~**play** *n* (Schwert)fechten *nt*; ~**-point** *n* **at ~-point** mit vorgehaltener Klinge.

swordsman ['sɔːdzmən] *n, pl* **-men** [-mən] Schwertkämpfer *m*; (*fencer*) Fechter *m*.

swordsmanship ['sɔːdzmənʃɪp] *n* Fechtkunst *f*.

sword: ~**stick** *n* Stockdegen *m*; ~**-swallower** *n* Schwertschlucker *m*.

swore [swɔːʳ] *pret of* **swear.**

sworn [swɔːn] **1** *ptp of* **swear**. **2** *adj enemy* eingeschworen; *friend also* verschworen; (*Jur*) *evidence, statement* beschworen, eidlich, unter Eid.

swot [swɒt] (*Brit inf*) **1** *vti* büffeln (*inf*), pauken (*inf*). **to ~ up (on) one's maths** Mathe pauken (*inf*); **to ~ for an exam** für eine Prüfung büffeln (*inf*) *or* pauken (*inf*); **to ~ at sth** etw pauken (*inf*) *or* büffeln (*inf*). **2** *n* (*pej*) *person* Streber(in *f*) *m*.

swotting ['swɒtɪŋ] *n* (*Brit inf*) Büffeln (*inf*), Pauken (*inf*) *nt*. **to do some ~** büffeln (*inf*), pauken (*inf*).

swum [swʌm] *ptp of* **swim.**

swung [swʌŋ] 1 pret, ptp of **swing**. 2 adj (Typ) ~ **dash** Tilde f.

sybarite ['sɪbəraɪt] n (form) Genußmensch m.

sybaritic [ˌsɪbə'rɪtɪk] adj (form) person genußsüchtig; way of life schwelgerisch.

sycamore ['sɪkəmɔːʳ] n Bergahorn m; (US: plane tree) nordamerikanische Platane; (wood) Ahorn m.

sycophancy ['sɪkəfənsɪ] n Kriecherei, Speichelleckerei f.

sycophant ['sɪkəfənt] n Kriecher, Speichellecker m.

sycophantic [ˌsɪkə'fæntɪk] adj kriecherisch, unterwürfig.

syllabary ['sɪləbərɪ] n Syllabar nt, Silbentabelle f.

syllabic [sɪ'læbɪk] adj silbisch, Silben-.

syllable ['sɪləbl] n Silbe f. a two-~(d) word ein zweisilbiges Wort; did he tell you anything about it? — not a ~ hat er dir etwas darüber gesagt? — nein, kein Wort; don't breathe a ~ of it sag keinen Ton darüber; in words of one ~ (hum) in einfachen Worten.

syllabub ['sɪləbʌb] n (dessert) Obstspeise f mit Sahne.

syllabus ['sɪləbəs] n, pl -es or **syllabi** ['sɪləbaɪ] (Sch, Univ) Lehrplan m; (of club etc) Programm nt. the S~ (of Errors) (Eccl) der Syllabus (von Zeitirrtümern).

syllogism ['sɪlədʒɪzəm] n Syllogismus m.

syllogistic [ˌsɪlə'dʒɪstɪk] adj syllogistisch.

syllogize ['sɪlədʒaɪz] vi syllogistisch folgern.

sylph [sɪlf] n (Myth) Sylphe mf; (fig: girl) Sylphide, Nymphe f.

sylphid ['sɪlfɪd] n Sylphide f.

sylphlike ['sɪlf,laɪk] adj figure etc grazil, sylphidenhaft.

sylvan, silvan ['sɪlvən] adj (liter) Wald-; shade, goddess also des Waldes; surroundings waldig.

symbiosis [ˌsɪmbɪ'əʊsɪs] n Symbiose f.

symbiotic [ˌsɪmbɪ'ɒtɪk] adj symbiotisch.

symbol ['sɪmbəl] n Symbol, Zeichen nt (of für).

symbolic(al) [sɪm'bɒlɪk(əl)] adj symbolisch (of für). to be ~ of sth etw symbolisieren, ein Symbol für etw sein; ~ logic mathematische Logik.

symbolically [sɪm'bɒlɪkəlɪ] adv see adj.

symbolism ['sɪmbəlɪzəm] n Symbolik f; (Art, Liter: movement) Symbolismus m.

symbolist ['sɪmbəlɪst] 1 n Symbolist(in f) m. 2 adj symbolistisch.

symbolization [ˌsɪmbəlaɪ'zeɪʃən] n Symbolisierung f.

symbolize ['sɪmbəlaɪz] vt symbolisieren.

symmetrical adj, **~ly** adv [sɪ'metrɪkəl, -ɪ] symmetrisch.

symmetry ['sɪmɪtrɪ] n Symmetrie f.

sympathetic [ˌsɪmpə'θetɪk] adj (a) (showing pity) mitfühlend, teilnahmsvoll; (understanding) verständnisvoll; (well-disposed) wohlwollend, wohlgesonnen (geh); look, smile verbindlich, freundlich. to be or feel ~ to(wards) sb mit jdm mitfühlen; jdm Verständnis entgegenbringen, für jdn Verständnis haben; mit jdm sympathisieren; he was most ~ when I told him all my troubles er zeigte sehr viel Mitgefühl für all meine Sorgen; a ~ ear ein offenes Ohr; ~ strike Sympathie- or Solidaritätsstreik m.

(b) (likeable) sympathisch.

(c) (Physiol, Phys) sympathisch. ~ vibration Mitschwingung f; ~ string mitschwingende Saite, Bordunsaite f; ~ magic Sympathiezauber m.

sympathetically [ˌsɪmpə'θetɪkəlɪ] adv (showing pity) mitfühlend; (with understanding) verständnisvoll; (well-disposed) wohlwollend. to be ~ inclined towards sb/sth jdm/einer Sache wohlwollend gegenüberstehen; to respond/vibrate ~ (Phys etc) mitreagieren/mitschwingen.

sympathize ['sɪmpəθaɪz] vi (feel compassion) mitfühlen, Mitleid haben (with mit); (understand) Verständnis haben (with für); (agree) sympathisieren (with mit; esp Pol); (express sympathy) sein Mitgefühl aussprechen; (on bereavement) sein Beileid aussprechen. to ~ with sb over sth (feel sorry) mit jdm in einer Sache mitfühlen können; to ~ with sb's views jds Ansichten teilen; to ~ with sb's troubles mit jdm mitfühlen; I really do ~ (have pity) das tut mir wirklich leid; (understand your feelings) ich habe wirklich vollstes Verständnis; I ~ with you or with what you say/feel, but ... ich teile Ihre Ansichten/Gefühle, aber ..., ich kann Ihnen das nachfühlen, aber ...; to ~ with sb in his bereavement/grief jds Verlust/Schmerz teilen; (express sympathy) jdm sein Beileid/Mitgefühl aussprechen.

sympathizer ['sɪmpəθaɪzəʳ] n Mitfühlende(r) mf; (at death also) Kondolierende(r) mf; (with cause) Sympathisant(in f) m.

sympathy ['sɪmpəθɪ] n (a) (pity, compassion) Mitgefühl, Mitleid nt (for mit); (at death) Beileid nt. to feel or have ~ for sb Mitgefühl or Mitleid mit jdm haben; a letter of ~ ein mitfühlender Brief, ein Beileidsbrief m; you have our deepest or heartfelt ~ or sympathies wir fühlen mit Ihnen, (unser) aufrichtiges or herzliches Beileid; you have my ~! (hum) herzliches Beileid (hum); my sympathies are with her family mir tut ihre Familie leid; to express one's ~ sein Mitgefühl aussprechen; sein Beileid aussprechen; you won't get any ~ from me erwarte kein Mitleid von mir.

(b) (understanding) Verständnis nt; (fellow-feeling, agreement) Sympathie f. to be in/out of ~ with sb/sth mit jdm/etw einhergehen/nicht einhergehen; the sympathies of the crowd were with him (in match, discussion) die Zuschauer waren auf seiner Seite; he has Democratic sympathies er sympathisiert mit or seine Sympathien gehören den Demokraten; politically there wasn't much ~ between them sie verstanden sich politisch nicht gut; to come out or strike in ~ (Ind) in Sympathiestreik treten; the dollar fell and the pound fell in ~ der Dollar fiel und das Pfund fiel mit; to resonate/vibrate in ~ mitklingen/mitschwingen; to strike Sympathiestreik m.

symphonic [sɪm'fɒnɪk] adj symphonisch, sinfonisch. ~ poem symphonische Dichtung.

symphony ['sɪmfənɪ] n Symphonie, Sinfonie f. ~ orchestra Symphonie- or Sinfonieorchester nt; the London S~ (inf) or S~

Orchestra die Londoner Symphoniker pl; a ~ of colours (liter) eine Sinfonie von Farben, eine Farbensinfonie.

symposium [sɪm'pəʊzɪəm] n, pl -s or **symposia** [sɪm'pəʊzɪə] Symposium, Symposion nt.

symptom ['sɪmptəm] n (lit, fig) Symptom nt.

symptomatic [ˌsɪmptə'mætɪk] adj symptomatisch (of für).

synagogue ['sɪnəgɒg] n Synagoge f.

sync [sɪŋk] n (Film, TV, Computers inf) abbr of **synchronization. in/out of** ~ synchron/nicht synchron.

synchromesh ['sɪŋkrəʊˌmeʃ] n Synchrongetriebe nt.

synchronic [sɪŋ'krɒnɪk] adj (Ling) synchronisch.

synchronization [ˌsɪŋkrənaɪ'zeɪʃən] n (a) see vt Abstimmung f; Synchronisation f; Gleichstellung f. (b) see vi Synchronisation f; Gleichgehen nt; Zusammenfall m, gleichzeitiger Ablauf; Übereinstimmung f.

synchronize ['sɪŋkrənaɪz] 1 vt abstimmen (with auf +acc); two actions, movements aufeinander abstimmen; (Film) synchronisieren (with mit); clocks gleichstellen (with mit). ~ your watches! Uhrenvergleich!

2 vi (Film) synchron sein (with mit); (clocks) gleichgehen; (actions) zusammenfallen, gleichzeitig ablaufen (with mit); (movements) in Übereinstimmung sein (with mit).

synchronous ['sɪŋkrənəs] adj gleichzeitig; events also zeitlich parallel.

syncopate ['sɪŋkəpeɪt] vt (Mus) synkopieren; (Ling also) zusammenziehen.

syncopation [ˌsɪŋkə'peɪʃən] n Synkope f; (act) Synkopierung f.

syncope ['sɪŋkəpɪ] n (Ling, Med) Synkope f.

syncretism ['sɪŋkrɪtɪzəm] n (Ling) Synkretismus m.

syndicalism ['sɪndɪkəlɪzəm] n Syndikalismus m.

syndicate ['sɪndɪkɪt] 1 n Interessengemeinschaft f; (for gambling) Wettgemeinschaft f; (Comm) Syndikat nt, Verband m; (Press) (Presse)zentrale f; (crime ~) Ring m.

2 ['sɪndɪkeɪt] vt (Press) an mehrere Zeitungen verkaufen. there are several ~d articles in this newspaper mehrere Artikel dieser Zeitung stammen aus einer Pressezentrale.

syndrome ['sɪndrəʊm] n (Med) Syndrom nt; (fig, Sociol) Phänomen nt.

synecdoche [sɪ'nekdəkɪ] n Synekdoche f.

synod ['sɪnəd] n Synode f.

synonym ['sɪnənɪm] n Synonym nt.

synonymous [sɪ'nɒnɪməs] adj synonym, synonymisch. her name was ~ with sex ihr Name war gleichbedeutend mit Sex.

synonymy [sɪ'nɒnəmɪ] n Synonymik f.

synopsis [sɪ'nɒpsɪs] n, pl **synopses** [sɪ'nɒpsiːz] Abriß m der Handlung; (of article, book) Zusammenfassung f.

synoptic [sɪ'nɒptɪk] adj zusammenfassend. ~ view Überblick m, Übersicht f; S~ Gospels die Evangelien des Markus, Matthäus und Lukas; ~ chart (Met) synoptische Karte.

syntactic(al) [sɪn'tæktɪk(əl)] adj syntaktisch.

syntax ['sɪntæks] n Syntax f; (of sentence also) Satzbau m.

synthesis ['sɪnθəsɪs] n, pl **syntheses** ['sɪnθəsiːz] Synthese f; (artificial production also) Synthetisieren nt.

synthesize ['sɪnθəsaɪz] vt synthetisieren; speech synthetisch bilden; theories etc zusammenfassen.

synthesizer ['sɪnθəsaɪzəʳ] n (Mus) Synthesizer m.

synthetic [sɪn'θetɪk] 1 adj (a) synthetisch; fibre, silk Kunst-. ~ smile künstliches or gekünsteltes Lächeln. (b) (Ling, Philos) synthetisch. 2 n Kunststoff m, synthetischer Stoff.

synthetically [sɪn'θetɪkəlɪ] adv synthetisch, künstlich; (fig) smile gekünstelt.

syphilis ['sɪfɪlɪs] n Syphilis f.

syphilitic [ˌsɪfɪ'lɪtɪk] adj syphilitisch. 2 n Syphilitiker(in f) m.

syphon n see **siphon**.

Syria ['sɪrɪə] n Syrien nt.

Syrian ['sɪrɪən] 1 adj syrisch. 2 n Syr(i)er(in f) m.

syringa [sɪ'rɪŋgə] n (Bot) Falscher Jasmin, Pfeifenstrauch m; (lilac) Flieder m, Syringe f.

syringe [sɪ'rɪndʒ] 1 n (Med) Spritze f; (garden ~ also) Spritzgerät nt. 2 vt (Med) (aus)spülen.

syrup, (US also) **sirup** ['sɪrəp] n Sirup m; (preservative also) Saft m. ~ of figs Feigensaft m; fruit ~ Fruchtsirup m; cough ~ (Med) Hustensaft or -sirup m.

syrupy, (US also) **sirupy** ['sɪrəpɪ] adj siruppartig, sirupähnlich; (pej) smile, voice zucker- or honigsüß; (sentimental) voice, song schmalzig.

system ['sɪstəm] n (a) System nt. new teaching ~s neue Lehrmethoden pl; the democratic ~ of government das demokratische (Regierungs)system; the Pitman ~ of shorthand die Kurzschriftmethode nach Pitman; there's no ~ in his work er hat kein System bei seiner Arbeit.

(b) (working whole) System nt. digestive ~ Verdauungsapparat m; respiratory ~ Atmungsapparat m; it's bad for the ~ das ist ungesund; to pass through the ~ den Körper auf natürlichem Wege verlassen; to be absorbed into the ~ aufgenommen werden; it was a shock to his ~ er hatte schwer damit zu schaffen; to get sth out of one's ~ (fig inf) sich (dat) etw von der Seele schaffen, etw loswerden (inf); it's all ~s go! (inf) jetzt heißt es: volle Kraft voraus!

(c) (established authority) the ~ das System; you can't beat or buck the ~ gegen das System kommst du or kommt man einfach nicht an.

systematic [ˌsɪstə'mætɪk] adj systematisch; liar, cruelty ständig. he works in a ~ way er arbeitet mit System.

systematically [ˌsɪstə'mætɪkəlɪ] adv see adj.

systematization [ˌsɪstəmətaɪ'zeɪʃən] n Systematisierung f.

systematize ['sɪstəmətaɪz] vt systematisieren.

systemic adj [sɪ'stiːmɪk] systemisch.

systems: ~ **analysis** n Systemanalyse f; ~ **analyst** n Systemanalytiker(in f) m.

systole ['sɪstəlɪ] n (Physiol) Systole f.

T

T, t [tiː] *n* T, t *nt*. **it suits him to a T** es ist genau das richtige für ihn; **that's him/it to a T** das ist er, wie er leibt und lebt/genau so ist es; **he got him to a T** er hat ihn haargenau getroffen.

TA (*Brit*) *abbr of* **Territorial Army**.

ta [taː] *interj* (*Brit inf*) danke.

tab¹ [tæb] *n* (**a**) (*loop on coat etc*) Aufhänger *m*; (*on back of boot, book*) Schlaufe *f*; (*fastener on coat etc*) Riegel *m*; (*name* ~) (*of owner*) Namensschild *nt*; (*of maker*) Etikett *nt*; (*on collar*) Verschluß(riegel) *m*; (*Mil*) Spiegel *m*; (*on shoulder, pocket*) Klappe, Patte *f*; (*on filing cards*) Reiter *m*. **to keep** ~**s on sb/sth** (*inf*) jdn/etw genau im Auge behalten.
(**b**) (*Aviat*) Klappe *f*.
(**c**) (*US inf: bill*) Rechnung *f*.

tab² (*inf*) *abbr of* **tabulator**.

tabard [ˈtæbəd] *n* (*of knight, herald*) Heroldsrock, Wappenrock, Tappert *m*; (*Fashion*) ärmelloser, an den Seiten offener Kasak.

tabasco [təˈbæskəʊ] *n* Tabasco(soße *f*) *m*.

tabby [ˈtæbɪ] *n* (**a**) (*also* ~ **cat**) getigerte Katze; (*female cat*) (weibliche) Katze. (**b**) (*inf: old maid*) Tantchen *nt* (*inf*).

tabernacle [ˈtæbənækl] *n* (*church*) Gotteshaus *nt*; (*receptacle*) Tabernakel *m or nt*. **the T**~ (*Bibl*) die Stiftshütte.

table [ˈteɪbl] **1** *n* (**a**) Tisch *m*; (*banquet* ~) Tafel *f*. **at the** ~ am Tisch; **at** ~ (*form*) bei Tisch; **to sit down to or at** ~ sich zu Tisch setzen; **he was sitting at the Mayor's** ~ er saß am Bürgermeisterstisch; **who was on your** ~? wer saß an Ihrem Tisch *or* bei Ihnen am Tisch?; **to eat at sb's** ~ seine Beine *or* Füße unter jds Tisch strecken (*inf*); **to be under the** ~ (*drunk*) unter dem Tisch liegen; **to drink sb under the** ~ jdn unter den Tisch trinken; **the motion is on the** ~ (*Brit Parl*) der Antrag liegt vor *or* ist eingebracht; **on the** ~ (*US: postponed*) zurückgestellt, aufgeschoben; **to turn the** ~**s (on sb)** (*gegenüber jdm*) den Spieß umdrehen *or* umkehren.
(**b**) (*people at a* ~) Tisch *m*, Tischrunde *f*. **the whole** ~ **laughed** der ganze Tisch *or* die ganze Runde lachte.
(**c**) (*of figures, prices etc, Sport*) Tabelle *f*; (*log* ~) Logarithmentafel *f*. (**multiplication**) ~**s** Einmaleins *nt*; (*up to 10*) kleines Einmaleins; (*from 11 to 20*) großes Einmaleins; **to say one's three/five times** ~ das Einmal-Drei/Einmal-Fünf aufsagen; ~ **of contents** Inhaltsverzeichnis *nt*; ~ **of fares** Preistabelle *f*.
(**d**) (*Bibl: tablet*) Tafel *f*.
(**e**) (*Geog*) **water** ~ Grundwasserspiegel *m*.
(**f**) (~**land**) Tafelland, Plateau *nt*, Hochebene *f*.
2 *vt* (**a**) *motion* einbringen.
(**b**) (*US: postpone*) *bill* zurückstellen.
(**c**) (*put in tabular form*) tabellarisieren (*form*), in einer Tabelle zusammenstellen.

tableau [ˈtæbləʊ] *n, pl* **-s** *or* **-x** [ˈtæbləʊ(z)] (*Art, Theat*) Tableau *nt*; (*fig*) Bild *nt*, Szene *f*.

table: ~**cloth** *n* Tischdecke *f or* -tuch *nt*; ~ **d'hôte** [ˈtɑːblˈdəʊt] *n* Tagesmenü *or* -gedeck *nt*; **to eat** ~ **d'hôte** das Tagesgedeck *or* -menü nehmen, Menü essen; ~ **d'hôte menu** *n* Tagesmenü *or* -gedeck *nt*; ~ **lamp** *n* Tischlampe *f*; ~**land** *n* Tafelland, Plateau *nt*, Hochebene *f*; ~ **licence** *n* Schankerlaubnis *f* bei Abgabe von Speisen; ~**lifting** *n* Anheben *nt* von Tischen, Levitation *f* (*form*); ~ **linen** *n, no pl* Tischwäsche *f*; ~ **manners** *npl* Tischmanieren *pl*; ~ **mat** *n* Untersetzer *m*; (*of cloth*) Set *nt*; **T**~ **Mountain** *n* Tafelberg *m*; ~ **napkin** *n* Serviette *f*; ~**-rapping** *n* Tischrücken *nt*; ~ **salt** *n* Tafelsalz *nt*; ~**spoon** *n* Eßlöffel *m*; ~**spoonful** *n* Eßlöffel(voll) *m*.

tablet [ˈtæblɪt] *n* (**a**) (*Pharm*) Tablette *f*. (**b**) (*of paper*) Block *m*; (*of wax, clay*) Täfelchen *nt*; (*of soap*) Stückchen *nt*. (**c**) (*on wall etc*) Tafel, Platte *f*.

table: ~ **talk** *n, no pl* Tischgespräch *nt*; ~ **tennis** *n* Tischtennis *nt*; ~ **top** *n* Tischplatte *f*; ~**-turning** *n* Drehen *nt* von Tischen, Levitation *f* (*form*); ~**ware** *n, no pl* Tisch- *or* Tafelgeschirr *nt* und -besteck *nt*; ~ **water** *n* Tafelwasser *nt*; ~ **wine** *n* Tisch- *or* Tafelwein *m*.

tabloid [ˈtæblɔɪd] *n* (*also* ~ **newspaper**) bebilderte, kleinformatige Zeitung; (*pej*) Boulevardzeitung *f*, Revolverblatt *nt* (*inf*). ~ **journalism** Sensations- *or* Boulevardpresse *f*; **news presented in** ~ **form** Nachrichten, die im Stil der Boulevardpresse aufgemacht sind.

taboo, tabu [təˈbuː] **1** *n* Tabu *nt*. **to be under a** ~ tabu sein, unter einem Tabu stehen. **2** *adj* tabu. ~ **words** Tabuwörter *pl*. **3** *vt* für tabu erklären, tabui(sier)en.

tabo(u)ret [ˈtæbʊreɪ] *n* (*Sew*) Stickrahmen *m*.

tabu *n, adj, vt see* **taboo**.

tabular [ˈtæbjʊləʳ] *adj* tabellenförmig, Tabellen-, tabellarisch. **in** ~ **form** in Tabellenform, tabellarisch.

tabulate [ˈtæbjʊleɪt] *vt* tabellarisch aufzeichnen *or* darstellen, tabellarisieren.

tabulation [ˌtæbjʊˈleɪʃən] *n* tabellarische Aufstellung, Tabellarisierung *f*.

tabulator [ˈtæbjʊleɪtəʳ] *n* (*on typewriter*) Tabulator *m*.

tachograph [ˈtækəɡrɑːf] *n* Fahrtenschreiber, Tachograph *m*.

tachometer [tæˈkɒmɪtəʳ] *n* Drehzahlmesser *m*.

tacit *adj*, ~**ly** *adv* [ˈtæsɪt, -lɪ] stillschweigend.

taciturn [ˈtæsɪtɜːn] *adj* schweigsam, wortkarg.

taciturnity [ˌtæsɪˈtɜːnɪtɪ] *n* Schweigsamkeit, Wortkargheit *f*.

tack¹ [tæk] **1** *n* (**a**) (*nail*) kleiner Nagel; (*with small head also*) Stift *m*; (*for shoes*) Täcks *m*; (*esp US: drawing pin*) Reiß- *or* Heftzwecke *f*, Reißnagel *m*.
(**b**) (*Brit Sew*) Heftstich *m*.
(**c**) (*Naut: course*) Schlag *m*; (*fig*) Richtung *f*, Weg *m*. **to be on the port/starboard** ~ auf Backbord-/Steuerbordbug segeln; **they are on a new/different** ~ (*fig*) sie haben eine neue/andere Richtung eingeschlagen; **to be on the right/wrong** ~ (*fig*) auf der richtigen/falschen Spur sein, richtig/falsch liegen (*inf*); **to try another** ~ (*fig*) es anders versuchen.
(**d**) (*Naut: zigzag*) Aufkreuzen *nt*. **to make a** ~ **towards land** landwärts kreuzen.
(**e**) (*for horse*) Sattel- und Zaumzeug *nt*.
2 *vt* (**a**) (*with nail*) annageln (*to an* +*dat or acc*); (*with clip, pin*) feststecken (*to an* +*dat*). (**b**) (*Brit Sew*) heften.
3 *vi* (**a**) (*Naut*) aufkreuzen. **to** ~ **to port** mit Backbordbug kreuzen. (**b**) (*Brit Sew*) heften.

♦**tack about** *vi* (*Naut*) wenden.

♦**tack down** *vt sep* festnageln; (*Brit Sew*) festheften.

♦**tack on** *vt sep* annageln (*-to an* +*acc or dat*); (*with drawing pin*) anstecken (*-to an* +*acc or dat*); (*with clips*) anheften, anstecken (*-to an* +*acc or dat*); (*Sew*) anheften; (*fig*) anhängen (*-to dat*).

♦**tack together** *vt sep* (*with nails*) zusammennageln; (*with clips*) zusammenstecken *or* -heften; (*Sew*) zusammenheften.

♦**tack up** *vt sep* (*Brit*) hem heften.

tack² *n* (*Naut: biscuits*) Schiffszwieback *m*.

tacking [ˈtækɪŋ] *n* (**a**) (*Brit Sew*) Heften *nt*. ~ **stitches** Heftstiche *pl*; ~ **thread** Heftfaden *m*. (**b**) (*Naut*) Aufkreuzen *nt*.

tackle [ˈtækl] **1** *n* (**a**) (*lifting gear*) Flaschenzug *m*; (*Naut*) Talje *f*, Takel *nt*, Zugwinde *f*.
(**b**) (*Naut: rigging*) Tauwerk *nt*.
(**c**) (*equipment*) Ausrüstung *f*, Zeug *nt* (*inf*). **fishing** ~ Angelausrüstung *f or* -zeug *nt* (*inf*); **shaving** ~ Rasierzeug *nt*.
(**d**) (*Sport*) Angriff *m*, Tackling *nt*.
2 *vt* (**a**) (*physically, Sport*) angreifen, angehen (*geh*); (*Rugby*) fassen; *thief also* sich stürzen auf (+*acc*); (*verbally*) zur Rede stellen (*about wegen*).
(**b**) (*undertake*) *job* in Angriff nehmen; *new challenge* sich versuchen an (+*dat*); *problem* angehen, anpacken (*inf*); (*manage to cope with*) bewältigen, fertig werden mit. **could you** ~ **another ice cream?** (*inf*) schaffst du noch ein Eis? (*inf*); **I don't know how to** ~ **it** ich weiß nicht, wie ich es anfangen soll.
3 *vi* angreifen.

tacky¹ [ˈtækɪ] *adj* (+*er*) klebrig. **the paint is still** ~ die Farbe klebt noch.

tacky² *adj* (+*er*) (*US inf*) verlottert (*inf*); (*cheap*) billig.

tact [tækt] *n, no pl* Takt *m*.

tactful *adj*, ~**ly** *adv* [ˈtæktfʊl, -fəlɪ] taktvoll.

tactfulness [ˈtæktfʊlnɪs] *n* Takt *m*; (*of person*) Feingefühl *nt*.

tactic [ˈtæktɪk] *n* Taktik *f*.

tactical *adj*, ~**ly** *adv* [ˈtæktɪkəl, -ɪ] (*Mil, fig*) taktisch.

tactician [tækˈtɪʃən] *n* Taktiker(in *f*) *m*.

tactics [ˈtæktɪks] *n sing* (*art, science*) (*Mil*) Taktik *f*; (*fig also*) Taktiken *pl*.

tactile [ˈtæktaɪl] *adj* Tast-, taktil (*spec*); (*tangible*) greifbar, fühlbar.

tactless *adj*, ~**ly** *adv* [ˈtæktlɪs, -lɪ] taktlos.

tactlessness [ˈtæktlɪsnɪs] *n* Taktlosigkeit *f*.

tactual [ˈtæktjʊəl] *adj* taktil (*spec*). ~ **pleasure** Berührungslust *f*.

tactually [ˈtæktjʊəlɪ] *adv* (*by touch*) durch Berühren *or* Fühlen. **to be** ~ **pleasing** sich angenehm anfühlen; ~ **oriented** berührungsorientiert.

tadpole [ˈtædpəʊl] *n* Kaulquappe *f*.

taffeta [ˈtæfɪtə] *n* Taft *m*.

taffrail [ˈtæfreɪl] *n* (*Naut*) Heckreling *f*.

Taffy [ˈtæfɪ] *n* (*inf*) Waliser *m*.

taffy [ˈtæfɪ] *n* (*US*) Toffee *nt*.

tag [tæɡ] **1** *n* (**a**) (*label*) Schild(chen) *nt*; (*on clothes*) (*maker's name*) Etikett *nt*; (*owner's name*) Namensschild(chen) *nt*; (*loop*) Aufhänger *m*. **the cattle had metal** ~**s in their ears** die Rinder hatten Blechmarken in den Ohren.
(**b**) (*hackneyed phrase*) stehende Redensart.
(**c**) (*Gram: question* ~) Bestätigungsfrage *f*.
(**d**) (*game*) Fangen *nt*.
(**e**) *see* ~ **wrestling**.
2 *vt* (**a**) *specimen* mit Schildchen versehen; *cattle* (mit Blechmarke) zeichnen; *garment, goods* etikettieren; (*with price*) auszeichnen; (*with owner's name*) (mit Namensschild-chen) zeichnen; *suitcase* mit einem Anhänger versehen.
(**b**) (*US Mot inf*) einen Strafzettel verpassen (+*dat*).
3 *vi* **to** ~ **behind** *or* **after sb** hinter jdm hertrotten *or* -zockeln (*inf*); **with her husband** ~**ging after her** mit ihrem Mann im Schlepptau (*inf*).

♦**tag along** *vi* (*unwillingly, unwanted*) mittrotten (*inf*) *or* -zockeln (*inf*). **to** ~ ~ **behind sb** hinter jdm herzockeln (*inf*) *or*

-trotten (*inf*); **why don't you ~ ~?** (*inf*) warum kommst *or* gehst du nicht mit?

♦ **tag around with** *vi* + *prep obj* (*inf*) immer zusammensein mit; (*unwanted, unwillingly*) mittrotten *or* -zockeln mit (*inf*).

♦ **tag on** 1 *vi* sich anhängen (*to* an + *acc*). 2 *vt sep* (*attach*) anhängen (*to* an + *acc*), befestigen (*to* an + *dat*); (*add as after-thought*) anhängen (*to* an + *acc*).

♦ **tag together** *vt sep* (*fasten*) zusammenheften.

tag: ~ **end** *n see* fag end; ~ **question** *n* Bestätigungsfrage *f*; ~**rope** *n* (*Sport*) Seil *nt* (*beim Tagwrestling*); ~ **wrestler** *n* Ringer *m* (*beim Tagwrestling*); ~ **wrestling** *n* Ringkampf *m* zwischen 2 Ringerpaaren, wobei immer 2 auf der Matte sind, während die 2 Auswechselkämpfer an den Seilen warten.

Tahiti [taːˈhiːtɪ] *n* Tahiti *nt*.

Tahitian [taːˈhiːʃən] 1 *adj* tahitisch. 2 *n* (a) Tahitianer(in *f*) *m*. (b) (*language*) Tahitisch *nt*.

tail [teɪl] 1 *n* (a) (*of animal*) Schwanz *m*; (*of horse also*) Schweif *m* (*liter*); (*hum inf: of person*) Hinterteil *nt* (*inf*), Allerwerteste(r) *m* (*hum inf*). **with his ~ between his legs** (*fig*) wie ein geprügelter Hund, mit eingezogenem Schwanz (*inf*); **to turn ~** ausreißen, die Flucht ergreifen; **keep your ~ up!** (*fig inf*) halt die Ohren steif, laß dich nicht unterkriegen! (*inf*); **he was right on my ~** er saß mir direkt im Nacken.

(b) (*of aeroplane, kite, procession, list*) Schwanz *m*; (*of comet*) Schweif *m*; (*of shirt*) Zipfel *m*; (*of jacket, coat*) Schoß *m*; (*of letter*) Schleife *f*; (*Mus: of note*) Notenhals *m*.

(c) (*inf: person following sb*) Schatten (*inf*), Beschatter(in *f*) *m* (*inf*). **to put a ~ on sb** jdn beschatten lassen.

(d) (*sl*) **they were out looking for ~** sie hielten nach Weibern Ausschau (*sl*); **a nice piece of ~** ein dufter Arsch (*sl*).

(e) ~**s** (*on coin*) Rück- *or* Zahlseite *f*; ~**s I win!** bei Zahl gewinne ich; **it came down ~s** die Zahl kam nach oben.

(f) ~**s** *pl* (*jacket*) Frack, Schwalbenschwanz (*inf*) *m*; "~**s** (**will be worn**)" „Frackzwang" *m*.

2 *vt* (a) (*person, suspect*) beschatten (*inf*); (*on one journey*) folgen (+ *dat*). (b) *see* top[1].

♦ **tail after** *vi* + *prep obj* hinterherzockeln (+ *dat*) (*inf*).

♦ **tail away** *vi see* tail off (a).

♦ **tail back** *vi* (*traffic*) sich gestaut haben.

♦ **tail off** *vi* (a) (*diminish*) abnehmen, schrumpfen; (*interest*) abflauen, abnehmen, schwinden; (*sounds*) sich verlieren, schwächer werden; (*sentence*) mittendrin abbrechen. **his voice ~ed ~ into silence** seine Stimme wurde immer schwächer, bis sie schließlich verstummte.

(b) (*deteriorate*) sich verschlechtern, nachlassen. **the article ~ed ~ into a jumble of figures** der Artikel war zum Schluß nur noch ein Gewirr von Zahlen.

tail: ~**back** *n* Rückstau *m*; ~**board** *n* Ladeklappe *f*; ~ **coat** *n* Frack *m*.

-**tailed** [-teɪld] *adj suf* -schwänzig.

tail: ~ **end** *n* Ende *nt*; (*of procession also*) Schwanz *m* (*inf*); **to come in at the ~ end** (*of discussion etc*) erst am Ende dazukommen; (*of race*) den Schwanz bilden; ~**fin** *n* (*Aut*) Heckflosse *f*; ~**gate** 1 *n* (*of car*) Hecktür *f*; (*of lorry*) Ladeklappe *f*; 2 *vi* (*inf*) zu dicht auffahren, schieben (*inf*); ~ **gun** *n* Heckkanone *f*; ~ **gunner** *n* Heckschütze *m*; ~**less** *adj* schwanzlos; ~**-light** *n* (*Aut*) Rücklicht *nt*.

tailor [ˈteɪləʳ] 1 *n* Schneider *m*. ~**'s chalk** Schneiderkreide *f*; ~**'s dummy** (*lit*) Schneiderpuppe *f*; (*fig inf*) Ölgötze *m* (*inf*); ~**('s) tack** Schlinge *f* beim Durchschlagen eines Musters.

2 *vt* (a) *dress etc* schneidern. **the dress was ~ed to reveal her figure** das Kleid war so geschnitten, daß es ihre Figur betonte.

(b) (*fig*) *plans, insurance, holiday* zuschneiden (*to* auf + *acc*); *products, salary structure* abstimmen (*to* auf + *acc*). ~**ed to meet his needs** auf seine Bedürfnisse abgestimmt.

tailored [ˈteɪləd] *adj* (*classically styled*) klassisch; (*made by tailor*) vom Schneider gemacht. **a well-~ suit** ein gut gearbeiteter Anzug; **his personally ~ clothes** seine für ihn persönlich gefertigten Kleider.

tailoring [ˈteɪlərɪŋ] *n* Verarbeitung *f*; (*profession*) Schneiderei *f*. **this is a nice bit of ~** das ist sehr gut gearbeitet.

tailor-made [ˈteɪləˈmeɪd] *adj* (a) maßgeschneidert, nach Maß gearbeitet. ~ **suit/costume** Maßanzug *m*/Schneiderkostüm *nt*.

(b) (*fig*) *role* zugeschnitten (*for* auf + *acc*). **the job was ~ for him** die Stelle war ihm wie auf den Leib geschnitten; **she seemed ~ for the part** sie schien für die Rolle wie geschaffen.

tail: ~ **piece** *n* (a) Anhang *m*, Anhängsel *nt* (*inf*); (b) (*Aviat*) Heck *nt*; (c) (*on violin*) Saitenhalter *m*; (d) (*Typ*) Schlußvignette *f*; ~**pipe** *n* (*US*) Auspuffrohr *nt*; ~**plane** *n* (*Aviat*) Höhenleitwerk *nt*; ~ **side** *n* (*of coin*) Zahlseite *f*; ~ **skid** *n* (a) (*Aviat*) Schwanzsporn *m*; (b) (*Aut*) Schleudern *nt no pl* der Hinterräder; **to go into a ~ skid** mit den Hinterrädern herumrutschen *or* schleudern; ~**spin** *n* (*Aviat*) Trudeln *nt*; ~ **wheel** *n* (*Aviat*) Spornrad *nt*; ~**wind** *n* Rückenwind *m*.

taint [teɪnt] 1 *n* (a) (*lit: of food etc*) Stich *m*. **meat free from ~** einwandfreies Fleisch.

(b) (*fig*) (*blemish*) Makel *m*; (*trace*) Spur *f*. **a ~ of madness** eine Anlage zum Irrsinn; **the hereditary ~** die krankhafte Erbanlage; **the ~ of sin** der Makel der Sünde; **a nasty ~ of fascism** ein übler faschistischer Beigeschmack.

2 *vt* (a) *food* verderben. **to become ~ed** schlecht werden, verderben.

(b) *air, atmosphere* verderben, verpesten.

(c) (*fig*) *reputation* beflecken, beschmutzen. **not ~ed by prejudice** von Vorurteilen unbelastet; **to be ~ed with sth** mit etw belastet *or* behaftet sein.

take [teɪk] (*vb: pret* **took**, *ptp* **taken**) 1 *vt* (a) (*remove, steal*) nehmen; (~ *away with one*) mitnehmen; (*remove from its place*) wegnehmen. **to ~ sth from a drawer** etw aus einer Schublade nehmen; **to ~ sth from sb** jdm etw wegnehmen; **I took it by mistake** ich habe es aus Versehen mitgenommen;

the thieves took everything die Einbrecher haben alles mitgenommen; **that man has ~n my wallet** der Mann hat mir meine Brieftasche weggenommen *or* gestohlen; **how much did he ~ off you for that?** wieviel hat er dir dafür abverlangt *or* abgenommen?

(b) (*carry, transport, accompany*) bringen; (~ *along with one*) *person, things* mitnehmen. **I'll ~ you to the station** ich bringe Sie zum Bahnhof; **I'll ~ you** (**with me**) **to the party** ich nehme dich zur Party mit; **let me ~ your case** komm, ich nehme *or* trage deinen Koffer; **you can't ~ it with you when you're dead** wenn du tot bist, nützt es dir auch nichts mehr; **he took me a new way to the coast** er ist mit mir eine neue Strecke zur Küste gefahren; **to ~ sb/the dog for a walk** mit jdm spazierengehen *or* einen Spaziergang machen/den Hund ausführen; **to ~ sb to the cinema** (*treat*) jdn ins Kino einladen; (~ *along with one*) mit jdm ins Kino gehen; **I'll ~ you for a meal** ich lade Sie zum Essen ein; **to ~ sb on holiday** mit jdm Urlaub machen; **this bus will ~ you to the town hall** der Bus fährt zum Rathaus; **this road will ~ you to Paris** diese Straße führt *or* geht nach Paris; **if it won't ~ you out of your way** wenn es kein Umweg für Sie ist; **what ~s you to London this time?** was führt Sie diesmal nach London?; **his ability took him to the top of his profession** seine Begabung brachte ihn in seinem Beruf bis an die Spitze.

(c) (*get hold of, seize*) nehmen. **to ~ sb's arm/hand** jds Arm/Hand nehmen; **to ~ sb by the throat** jdn am Kragen (*inf*) *or* an der Kehle packen; **to ~ a knife by the handle** ein Messer am Griff (an)fassen *or* beim Griff nehmen; ~ **three eggs** (*Cook*) man nehme drei Eier; **how does that ~ you?** (*inf*) wie finden Sie das?; *see* **bait**.

(d) (*capture*) *person* fassen, fangen, festnehmen; *animal* fangen; *town, country etc* einnehmen, erobern; *ship* kapern; (*Chess etc*) schlagen, nehmen; (*Cards*) stechen. **to ~ sb prisoner** jdn gefangennehmen; **they took 200 prisoners** sie machten 200 Gefangene; **to be ~n alive** lebend gefaßt werden.

(e) (*accept, receive*) nehmen; *job, dye, perm* annehmen; *command, lead, second position, role* übernehmen. **to ~ that!** da!; (*hold that*) halt mal; **I won't ~ less than £200** ich verkaufe es nicht unter £ 200; **I'd ~ £150 for it** ich würde es für £ 150 verkaufen; **would you ~ an offer?** kann ich Ihnen ein Angebot machen?; **she took paying guests** sie vermietete Zimmer an Gäste; **to ~ things as they come** die Dinge nehmen, wie sie kommen; **to ~ a bet** eine Wette annehmen; **I wouldn't ~ a bet on it** darauf würde ich keine Wette eingehen; **~ it from me!** das können Sie mir glauben; ~ **it from me, he'll never ...** eines können Sie mir glauben, er wird nie ...; (*you can*) ~ **it or leave it** ja oder nein, ganz wie Sie wollen); **I can ~ it or leave it** ich mache mir nicht besonders viel daraus; **he took the blow on his left arm** der Schlag traf ihn am linken Arm; (*in defence*) **er wehrte den Schlag mit dem linken Arm ab**; **to ~ sb into partnership/the business** jdn zu seinem Partner machen/jdn ins Geschäft aufnehmen; **will it ~ a British plug?** paßt da ein englischer Stecker (rein)?; **do you ~ me/my meaning?** verstehen Sie mich/, was ich meine?; **the school only ~s boys/private pupils** die Schule nimmt nur Jungen/Privatschüler (auf); **he ~s** (*private*) **pupils** er gibt (Privat)stunden; *see* **advice, lawful**.

(f) (*get for oneself*) sich (*dat*) nehmen; (*purchase, rent*) nehmen. ~ **a seat/chair!** nehmen Sie Platz!, setzen Sie sich doch!; ~ **your seats!** nehmen Sie Ihre Plätze ein!; **this seat is ~n** dieser Platz ist besetzt; **I'll ~ a pound of apples** ich nehme ein Pfund Äpfel; **I think I'll ~ the steak** ich glaube, ich nehme das Steak; **to ~ a wife** (*old*) sich (*dat*) eine Frau nehmen (*old*); **he took her** (*sexually*) er nahm sie; ~ **your partners for a waltz** führen Sie Ihre Partnerinnen zum Walzer.

(g) (*buy regularly*) *newspaper etc* immer nehmen *or* kaufen, bekommen; (*on subscription*) beziehen, bekommen.

(h) (*gain, obtain*) *prize, honours etc* bekommen; *game, match* gewinnen; (*Comm*) £500 einnehmen.

(i) *exam* machen, ablegen; *driving test* machen. **to ~ a PhD** promovieren, den Doktor machen (*inf*); **he took his degree in 1965** er hat 1965 Examen gemacht *or* sein Examen abgelegt.

(j) (*teach*) *lesson* halten, geben; *subject* unterrichten, geben; *class* unterrichten, nehmen. **he ~s 25 classes a week** er hat *or* gibt 25 Wochenstunden; **who ~s you for Latin?** bei wem habt ihr Latein?, wer unterrichtet *or* gibt bei euch Latein?

(k) (*study, learn*) *course, French* machen;· (*as optional subject*) wählen; *lessons, private tuition* nehmen.

(l) (*conduct, run*) *census, poll* durchführen; *church service* (ab)halten. **to ~ (the chair at) a meeting** den Vorsitz bei einer Versammlung führen; **he ~s a scout troop in the evenings** abends hat er eine Pfadfindergruppe.

(m) (*go on*) *walk, stroll* machen; *trip also* unternehmen.

(n) (*consume*) *drink, food* zu sich (*dat*) nehmen; *drugs, pill, medicine* nehmen; (*on directions for use*) einnehmen. **to ~ sugar in one's tea** den Tee mit Zucker trinken; **to ~ a sip or nip/a drink** ein Schlückchen/einen Schluck trinken; **do you ~ sugar?** nehmen Sie Zucker?; **to ~ a meal** (*old*) (etwas) essen, speisen (*geh*); **I took tea with her** (*dated form*) ich war bei ihr zum Tee; **the three friends took tea together once a week** (*old*) die drei Freundinnen trafen sich einmal wöchentlich zum Tee; **they took coffee on the veranda** sie tranken den Kaffee auf der Veranda; **will you ~ coffee or tea?** möchten Sie Kaffee oder Tee?; **I always ~ coffee in the morning** morgens trinke ich immer Kaffee; **not to be ~n** (**internally**) (*Med*) nur zur äußeren Anwendung.

(o) (*Film*) *scene* drehen; (*Phot*) *photo* machen. **he took the whole group** er nahm die ganze Gruppe auf; *see* **photograph**.

(p) (*write down, record*) *letter, dictation* aufnehmen; *address, details, particulars* (sich *dat*) aufschreiben, (sich *dat*) notieren. **to ~ notes** sich (*dat*) Notizen machen; *see* **minute**[1].

(q) (*measure*) *temperature, pulse* messen. **to ~ sb's**

measurements bei jdm Maß nehmen; **to ~ the measurements of a room** ein Zimmer ausmessen; **to ~ sb's temperature/pulse** jds Temperatur *or* bei jdm Fieber/den Puls messen.

(r) (*put up with*) sich (*dat*) gefallen lassen; (*endure, stand up to*) (*person*) alcohol, climate vertragen; (*long journey*) aushalten; *emotional experience, shock* fertig werden mit, verkraften; (*thing*) aushalten. **I can ~ it** ich kann's verkraften, ich werde damit fertig; **I just can't ~ any more/it** any more ich bin am Ende/das halte ich nicht mehr aus; **I won't ~ any nonsense!** ich dulde keinen Unsinn!

(s) (*respond to, regard*) *news, blow* aufnehmen, reagieren auf (+*acc*); *person* nehmen. **she knows how to ~ him** sie versteht es, ihn von der richtigen Seite zu nehmen; **she took his death very badly** sein Tod hat sie sehr mitgenommen.

(t) (*understand, interpret*) auffassen, verstehen. **I would ~ that to mean** ... ich würde das so auffassen *or* verstehen ; **how am I meant to ~ that?** wie soll ich das auffassen *or* verstehen?; **she took what he said as a compliment** sie hat das, was er sagte, als Kompliment aufgefaßt.

(u) (*assume*) annehmen. **to ~ sb/sth for** *or* **to be** ... jdn/etw für ... halten; **how old do you ~ him to be?** für wie alt halten Sie ihn?, wie alt schätzen Sie ihn?; **what do you ~ me for?** wofür hältst du mich eigentlich?; **may I ~ it that** ...? darf ich annehmen, daß ...?; **I ~ it you don't want to come** ich nehme an, du willst nicht mitkommen, du willst wohl keinen mitkommen.

(v) (*consider*) *case, example* nehmen. **~ (the case of) England in the 17th century** nehmen Sie zum Beispiel England im 17. Jahrhundert; **taking all things together, it's been a very successful day** alles in allem (genommen,) war es ein sehr erfolgreicher Tag; **taking one year with another** wenn man die Jahre zusammen betrachtet.

(w) (*extract*) entnehmen (*from dat*). **he ~s his examples from real life** seine Beispiele sind aus dem Leben gegriffen; **to ~ a quotation from a text** eine Stelle aus einem Text zitieren.

(x) (*require*) brauchen; *clothes size* haben. **it ~s five hours/men** ... man braucht *or* benötigt fünf Stunden/Leute ...; **it ~s me five hours** ... ich brauche fünf Stunden ...; **it took ten men to complete the job** zehn Leute waren nötig *or* es wurden zehn Leute benötigt, um diese Arbeit zu erledigen; **it took him** *or* **he took two hours to write a page,** it took two hours for him to write a page er brauchte zwei Stunden, um eine Seite zu schreiben; **the journey ~s 3 hours** die Fahrt dauert 3 Stunden; **the wound took five weeks to heal** es dauerte fünf Wochen, bis die Wunde verheilt war; **it took a lot of courage/intelligence** dazu gehörte viel Mut/Intelligenz; **it ~s two to quarrel** (*prov*) zu einem Streit gehören immer zwei; **it ~s more than that to make me angry** deswegen werde ich noch lange nicht wütend; **it ~s time** es braucht (seine) Zeit, es dauert (eine Weile); **it took a long time** es hat lange gedauert; **it took me a long time** ich habe lange gebraucht; **I took a long time over it** ich habe lange dazu gebraucht; **it won't ~ long** das dauert nicht lange; **it won't ~ long to convince him** er ist schnell *or* leicht überzeugt; **that'll ~ some explaining** das wird schwer zu erklären sein; **it ~s some believing** (*inf*) das kann man kaum glauben; **she's got what it ~s** (*inf*) sie ist nicht ohne (*inf*), die bringt's (*sl*); (*is capable also*) sie kann was (*inf*); **it's a difficult job but he's got what it ~s** (*inf*) es ist eine schwierige Arbeit, aber er hat der Zeug dazu.

(y) (*support*) *weight* aushalten; (*have capacity or room for*) *50 people, 200 books* Platz haben für; *5 gallons* fassen. **the road can ~ 3,500 cars an hour** die Straße bewältigt eine Verkehrsdichte von 3.500 Autos pro Stunde; **the bridge can only ~ five tons** die Brücke hat eine Höchstbelastung von fünf Tonnen.

(z) *taxi, train* nehmen, fahren mit; *motorway, country roads* nehmen, fahren auf (+*dat*); *plane* nehmen. **to ~ the plane/next plane** fliegen/das nächste Flugzeug nehmen; **we took a wrong turning** wir sind falsch abgebogen.

(aa) (*negotiate*) *obstacle* nehmen; *hurdle, fence also* überspringen; *bend, corner* (*person*) nehmen; (*car*) fahren um; (*Ski also*) fahren; *hill* hinauffahren.

(bb) (*sing, dance, play etc*) **let's ~ it from the beginning of Act 2** fangen wir mit dem Anfang vom zweiten Akt an; **let's ~ that scene again** die Szene machen wir noch einmal; **the orchestra took that passage too quickly** das Orchester hat die Stelle zu schnell gespielt; **the director took her through her lines** der Regisseur ging die Rolle mit ihr durch.

(cc) (*Math: subtract*) abziehen (*from von*).

(dd) (*Gram*) stehen mit; (*preposition*) *case* gebraucht werden mit, haben (*inf*). **verbs that ~ "haben"** Verben, die mit „haben" konjugiert werden; **this word ~s the accent on the first syllable** dieses Wort wird auf der ersten Silbe betont.

(ee) (*old, dial*) *illness* bekommen. **to ~ a cold** sich erkälten.

(ff) **to be ~n sick** *or* **ill** krank werden; **she has been ~n ill with pneumonia** sie hat eine Lungenentzündung bekommen.

(gg) **to be ~n with sb/sth** (*attracted by*) von jdm/etw angetan sein.

(hh) *in phrases see other element* **to ~ sb by surprise** jdn überraschen; **to ~ one's time** sich (*dat*) Zeit lassen (*over* mit); **to ~ a bath** baden, ein Bad nehmen (*form*); **to ~ a holiday** Urlaub machen; **to ~ one's holidays** seinen Urlaub nehmen; **to ~ a pitch** (*Baseball*) einen Ball durchlassen.

2 *vi* **(a)** (*fire*) angehen; (*dye, perm, graft*) angenommen werden; (*vaccination*) anschlagen; (*plant*) anwachsen; (*seeds*) kommen; (*fish: bite*) anbeißen. **the ink won't ~ on this paper** dieses Papier nimmt die Druckfarbe nicht an.

(b) (*fig*) (*gimmick*) ankommen (*inf*); (*novel, idea also*) Anklang finden.

(c) she took ill (*inf*) sie wurde krank.

(d) (*detract*) **that doesn't ~ from his merit** das tut seinen Verdiensten keinen Abbruch, das schmälert seine Verdienste

nicht; **that ~s from its usefulness/attraction** das vermindert den Gebrauchswert/die Anziehungskraft.

3 *n* **(a)** (*Film*) Aufnahme *f*. **after several ~s they** ... nachdem sie die Szene mehrmals gedreht hatten, ... sie ....

(b) (*Hunt*) Beute *f*; (*Fishing*) Fang *m*.

(c) (*US inf: takings*) Einnahmen *pl*.

♦**take aback** *vt sep* überraschen. **I was completely ~n ~** mir hatte es völlig den Atem verschlagen, ich war völlig perplex.

♦**take after** *vi* +*prep obj* nachschlagen (+*dat*); (*in looks*) ähneln (+*dat*), ähnlich sein (+*dat*).

♦**take along** *vt sep* mitnehmen.

♦**take apart** *vt sep* auseinandernehmen; (*dismantle also*) zerlegen; (*fig inf*) *person, team etc* auseinandernehmen (*sl*).

♦**take around** *vt sep* mitnehmen; (*show around*) herumführen.

♦**take aside** *vt sep* beiseite nehmen.

♦**take away** **1** *vi* **to ~ ~ from sth** etw schmälern; *merit, reputation also* Abbruch tun (+*dat*); *worth* mindern, verringern; *pleasure, fun etc also* beeinträchtigen.

2 *vt sep* **(a)** (*subtract*) abziehen. **6 ~ ~ 2** 6 weniger 2.

(b) (*remove*) *child, thing, privilege* wegnehmen (*from sb* jdm); (*from school etc*) nehmen (*from* aus); (*lead, transport, carry away*) weg- *or* fortbringen (*from* von); *prisoner* abführen (*to in* +*acc*). **to ~ sb/sth ~ (with one)** jdn/etw mitnehmen; **to ~ ~ sb's pain/pleasure/freedom etc** jdm die Schmerzen/Freude/Freiheit *etc* nehmen; **they've come to ~ him ~** sie sind da, um ihn abzuholen; **to ~ a child ~ from a school** ein Kind von einer Schule nehmen; **"not to be ~n ~"** (*on library book*) „nicht für die Ausleihe"; **what ~s you ~ so early?** warum müssen Sie denn schon so früh gehen?

(c) *food* mitnehmen. **pizza to ~ ~** Pizza zum Mitnehmen.

(d) from the 15th bar, ~ it ~! noch mal von Takt 15, los!

♦**take back** *vt sep* **(a)** (*reclaim, get back*) sich (*dat*) zurückgeben lassen; *toy etc* wieder wegnehmen; (*fig: retract*) *threat, statement* zurücknehmen.

(b) (*return*) zurückbringen. **he took us ~ (home)** er brachte uns (nach Hause) zurück, er brachte uns wieder heim.

(c) (*agree to receive again*) *thing* zurücknehmen; *employee* wieder einstellen; *husband* wieder aufnehmen; *boyfriend* wieder gehen mit; *tenant* wieder vermieten an (+*acc*).

(d) (*remind*) **to ~ sb ~ to his childhood** jdn in seine Kindheit zurückversetzen, jdn an seine Kindheit erinnern; **this photograph/that ~s me ~** dieses Foto/das ruft Erinnerungen wach; **that ~s me ~ fifteen years** das erinnert mich an die Zeit vor fünfzehn Jahren.

♦**take down** *vt sep* **(a)** (*lit*) (*off high shelf etc*) herunternehmen; *curtains* abhängen, abnehmen; *decorations* abnehmen; *Christmas cards* wegräumen; *picture* abhängen; *flag* einholen. **to ~ one's/sb's trousers ~** seine/jdm die Hose herunterlassen.

(b) (*dismantle*) *scaffolding etc* abbauen; *tent also* abbrechen; *railing, gate* entfernen.

(c) (*write down*) (sich *dat*) notieren *or* aufschreiben; *notes* (sich *dat*) machen; *letter* aufnehmen; *speech, lecture* mitschreiben. **anything you say will be ~n ~ and** ... alles, was Sie sagen, wird festgehalten und ...; **~ this ~ please** notieren Sie bitte, bitte schreiben Sie.

(d) (*humble*) einen Dämpfer geben (+*dat*); *see* peg.

♦**take home** *vt insep* **£100 per week** netto verdienen *or* bekommen.

♦**take in** *vt sep* **(a)** (*bring in*) *thing, person* hinein-/hereinbringen *or* -nehmen; *harvest* einbringen, bergen (*esp DDR*). **I'll ~ the car ~ (to work) on Monday** ich fahre am Montag mit dem Auto (zur Arbeit); **when are you taking the car ~ (to the garage)?** wann bringen Sie das Auto in die Werkstatt?; **to ~ a lady ~ to dinner** eine Dame zu Tisch führen.

(b) (*receive in one's home*) *refugee* (bei sich) aufnehmen, beherbergen; *child, stray dog* zu sich nehmen, ins Haus nehmen; (*for payment*) *student* (Zimmer) vermieten an (+*acc*). **she ~s ~ lodgers** sie vermietet (Zimmer).

(c) (*receive*) *money* einnehmen. **to ~ ~ laundry/sewing** Wasch-/Näharbeiten übernehmen.

(d) (*make narrower*) *dress* enger machen. **to ~ ~ sail** die Segel reffen.

(e) (*usu insep: include, cover*) einschließen. **the lecture took ~ all the more recent developments** der Vortrag berücksichtigte auch alle neueren Entwicklungen.

(f) (*note visually*) *surroundings, contents, occupants* wahrnehmen, registrieren (*inf*); *area, room* überblicken; (*grasp, understand*) *meaning, lecture, difficult subject* begreifen; *impressions, sights etc* aufnehmen; *situation* erfassen. **the children were taking it all ~** die Kinder haben alles mitbekommen *or* mitgekriegt (*inf*); **his death was so sudden that she couldn't ~ it ~** sein Tod kam so plötzlich, daß sie es gar nicht fassen konnte.

(g) (*deceive*) hereinlegen. **to be ~n ~** hereinfallen, hereingelegt werden; **to be ~n ~ by sb/sth** auf jdn/etw hereinfallen; **to be ~n ~ by appearances** sich vom äußeren Schein täuschen lassen; **you won't ~ him ~ with that** damit kannst du ihn nicht hereinlegen, darauf fällt er nicht herein.

(h) (*go to*) *film, party, town* mitnehmen (*inf*).

♦**take off** **1** *vi* **(a)** (*plane, passengers*) starten, abfliegen; (*plane: leave the ground*) abheben; (*Sport*) abspringen; (*fig*) (*project, sales*) anlaufen; (*film, product*) ankommen.

(b) (*inf: leave*) sich absetzen, sich davonmachen (*inf*).

2 *vt sep* **(a)** (*remove, cut off: person*) abmachen (*prep obj* von); *beard, hat, lid* abnehmen (*prep obj* von); *tablecloth, bedspread* herunternehmen, entfernen (*prep obj* von); *pillowcases etc* abziehen (*prep obj* von); *coat, gloves etc* (sich *dat*) ausziehen; *leg, limb* abnehmen, amputieren; *play* absetzen; *food from menu, train, bus* streichen (*prep obj* von); *service, tax* abschaffen; (*remove from duty, job*) *detective,* *journalist etc* abziehen (*prep obj* von); *waitress, driver* ablösen. **to ~ sth ~ sb** jdm etw abnehmen; **the sun will ~ the paint ~ the wood** von der Sonne geht *or* blättert die Farbe ab; **double deckers have been ~n ~ this route** Doppeldecker werden auf dieser Strecke nicht mehr eingesetzt; **to ~ the receiver ~ (the hook)** den Hörer abnehmen, den Hörer von der Gabel nehmen; **he/she took her dress ~** er zog ihr das Kleid aus/sie zog ihr Kleid *or* (*sich dat*) das Kleid aus; **he took his/her clothes off** er zog sich/sie aus; **would you like to ~ your coat ~**? möchten Sie ablegen?, legen Sie doch bitte ab; **he had two inches ~ ~** (his hair) er hat sich (*dat*) die Haare 5 cm kürzer schneiden lassen; **please ~ a little ~ the top** bitte oben etwas kürzer; **the barber took too much ~** der Friseur hat zu viel abgeschnitten; **the 5 o'clock train has been ~n ~ today/for the summer** der 5-Uhr-Zug ist heute ausgefallen/wurde den Sommer über (vom Fahrplan) gestrichen.

(b) (*deduct*) abziehen (*prep obj* von); (*from price*) *5%, 50p* nachlassen. **he took 50p ~ (the price)** er hat 50 Pence nachgelassen, er hat es 50 Pence billiger gemacht.

(c) (*lead away, go away with*) mitnehmen; (*under arrest etc*) abführen. **he was ~n ~ to hospital** er wurde ins Krankenhaus gebracht; **to ~ oneself ~** (*inf*) sich auf den Weg machen.

(d) (*from ship, wreck*) von Bord holen; (+*prep obj*) holen von; (*from island, mountain*) herunterholen (*prep obj* von).

(e) (*have free*) *week, Monday* frei nehmen. **to ~ time/a day ~ work** sich (*dat*) frei nehmen/einen Tag freimachen.

(f) (*imitate*) nachmachen, nachahmen.

(g) +*prep obj* (*in phrases*) **to ~ sb's mind** *or* **thoughts ~ sth** jdn von etw ablenken; **to ~ the weight ~ one's feet** seine Beine ausruhen; **to ~ sb/sth ~ sb's hands** jdm jdn/etw abnehmen; **to ~ years/ten years ~ sb** jdn um Jahre/zehn Jahre verjüngen.

♦**take on 1** *vi* **(a)** (*inf: become upset*) sich aufregen.

(b) (*become popular: song, fashion etc*) sich durchsetzen.

2 *vt sep* **(a)** (*undertake*) *job, work* an- *or* übernehmen; *responsibility* auf sich (*acc*) nehmen *or* laden, übernehmen; *sick person, backward child* sich annehmen (+*gen*); *bet* annehmen. **when he married her he took ~ more than he bargained for** als er sie heiratete, hat er sich (*dat*) mehr aufgeladen *or* aufgebürdet, als er gedacht hatte; **he took ~ the fund-raising** er hat es übernommen, das Geld aufzutreiben.

(b) (*Sport etc: accept as opponent*) antreten gegen; *union, shop steward* sich anlegen mit. **I could ~ ~ someone twice your size** ich könnte es mit einem aufnehmen, der zweimal so groß ist wie Sie; **I'll ~ you ~ at tennis** ich werde gegen Sie im Tennis antreten; **I bet you £50 — OK, I'll ~ you ~** ich wette mit Ihnen um 50 Pfund — gut, die Wette gilt.

(c) (*employ*) einstellen, anstellen; *apprentice* annehmen.

(d) (*take aboard*) (*coach, train etc*) *passengers* einsteigen lassen, aufnehmen; (*plane, ship*) an Bord nehmen, übernehmen; *cargo, stores* (über)nehmen, laden; *fuel* tanken.

(e) (*assume*) *colour, aspect, expression* bekommen, annehmen. **her face/eyes took ~ a doleful expression** ihr Gesicht nahm/ihre Augen nahmen einen traurigen Ausdruck an; **his face took ~ a greenish tinge** sein Gesicht verfärbte sich grün *or* bekam einen grünen Schimmer; **he took ~ an air of importance** er gab sich (*dat*) eine gewichtige Miene.

♦**take out** *vt sep* **(a)** (*bring or carry out*) (hinaus)bringen (*of* aus); (*out of house etc also*) nach draußen bringen; (*out of garage etc*) car hinaus-/herausfahren (*of* aus); (*for drive etc*) *car, boat* wegfahren mit. **the children were ~n ~ of the city** die Kinder wurden aus der Stadt gebracht; **the current took the boat ~ to sea** die Strömung trieb das Boot aufs Meer hinaus.

(b) (*to theatre etc*) ausgehen mit, ausführen. **to ~ the children/dog ~ (for a walk)** mit den Kindern/dem Hund spazierengehen *or* einen Spaziergang machen, den Hund ausführen; **to ~ sb ~ for a drive** mit jdm eine Autofahrt machen; **to ~ sb ~ to** *or* **for dinner/to the cinema** jdn zum Essen/ins Kino einladen *or* ausführen; **he has been taking her ~ for several months** er geht schon seit einigen Monaten mit ihr.

(c) (*pull out, extract*) herausnehmen; (*out of pocket, bag, cupboard etc also*) herausholen; *tooth also* ziehen; *appendix etc* herausnehmen, entfernen; *nail, screw* herausziehen (*of* aus). **to ~ sth ~ of** *or* **from sth** etw aus etw (heraus)nehmen/-holen; **~ your hands ~ of your pockets** nimm die Hände aus der Tasche.

(d) (*cause to disappear*) *stain* entfernen (*from* aus). **cold water will ~ the stain ~ of the tablecloth** mit kaltem Wasser geht der Fleck aus dem Tischtuch heraus.

(e) (*withdraw from bank etc*) abheben.

(f) (*deduct*) **~ it ~ of the housekeeping** nimm es vom Haushaltsgeld.

(g) (*procure*) *insurance* abschließen. **to ~ ~ a subscription for sth** etw abonnieren; **to ~ ~ a patent on sth** etw patentieren lassen; **to ~ ~ a summons against sb** jdn gerichtlich vorladen lassen; **to ~ ~ a licence for sth** eine Lizenz für etw erwerben, sich (*dat*) eine Lizenz für etw geben lassen.

(h) **to ~ sb ~ of himself** jdn auf andere Gedanken bringen.

(i) (*inf*) **to ~ sth ~ on sb** etw an jdm auslassen (*inf*) *or* abreagieren (*inf*); **to ~ it ~ on sb** sich an jdm abreagieren.

(j) (*tire*) **to ~ it/a lot ~ of sb** jdn ziemlich/sehr schlauchen (*inf*).

(k) (*Mil, fig: Sport*) außer Gefecht setzen; *village* angreifen.

(l) (*US*) **see take away 2 (c)**.

♦**take over 1** *vi* (*assume government*) an die Macht kommen; (*military junta etc*) die Macht ergreifen; (*party*) an die Regierung kommen; (*new boss etc*) die Leitung übernehmen; (*in a place: tourists, guests etc*) sich breitmachen (*inf*). **to ~ ~ (from sb)** jdn ablösen; **can you ~ ~?** können Sie mich/ihn *etc* ablösen?; **he's ill so I have to ~ ~** da er krank ist, muß ich (für ihn) einspringen; **his wife has ~n ~ completely** seine Frau führt das Regiment; **the next shift ~s ~ at 6 o'clock** die nächste Schicht übernimmt um 6 Uhr; **the Martians have ~n ~** die

Marsmenschen haben die Erde/Stadt *etc* besetzt.

2 *vt sep* **(a)** (*take control or possession of*) übernehmen. **tourists ~ Edinburgh ~ in the summer** im Sommer machen sich die Touristen in Edinburgh breit (*inf*); **she took ~ the whole show** (*inf*) sie riß das Regiment an sich.

(b) (*escort or carry across*) *person* hinüberbringen; (+*prep obj*) bringen über (+*acc*); (*in boat also*) übersetzen; (*to visit town, people etc*) mitnehmen (*to* nach, *to sb* zu jdm).

(c) **to ~ sb ~ sth** (*show round*) jdn durch etw führen, jdm etw zeigen; (*tell about*) *facts* etw mit jdm durchgehen.

♦**take to** *vi* +*prep obj* **(a)** (*form liking for*) *person* mögen, sympathisch finden. **sb ~s ~ a game/subject/place** ein Spiel/Fach/Ort sagt jdm zu; **the children soon took ~ their new surroundings** den Kindern gefiel es bald in der neuen Umgebung; **I'll never ~ ~ it** dafür werde ich mich nie erwärmen *or* begeistern können; **I don't know how she'll ~ ~ him/it** ich weiß nicht, wie sie auf ihn/darauf reagieren wird; **I don't ~ kindly ~ that/you doing that** ich kann das nicht leiden/es nicht leiden, wenn Sie das tun.

(b) (*form habit of*) **to ~ ~ doing sth** anfangen, etw zu tun; **to ~ ~ drink** zu trinken anfangen, sich (*dat*) das Trinken angewöhnen; **to ~ ~ drugs** anfangen, Drogen zu nehmen; **she took ~ telling everyone that ...** sie erzählte allen Leuten, daß ...

(c) (*escape to*) *woods, hills* sich flüchten *or* zurückziehen in (+*acc*), Zuflucht suchen in (+*dat*). **to ~ ~ the boats** sich in die Boote retten; **to ~ ~ one's bed** sich ins Bett legen; *see* **heel[1]**.

♦**take up 1** *vi* (*continue*) (*person*) weitermachen. **chapter 3 ~s ~ where chapter 1 left off** das dritte Kapitel schließt thematisch an erste an.

2 *vt sep* **(a)** (*raise, lift*) aufnehmen; *carpet, floor-boards* hochnehmen; *road* aufreißen; *dress* kürzer machen, kürzen; *pen* zur Hand nehmen, greifen zu. **~ ~ your bed and walk** (*Bibl*) nimm dein Bett und wandle.

(b) (*lead or carry upstairs etc*) *invalid, child* hinauf-/heraufbringen; *visitor* (mit) hinauf-/heraufnehmen; *thing also* hinauf-/herauftragen.

(c) (*vehicles*) *passengers* mitnehmen, einsteigen lassen.

(d) (*occupy*) *time, attention* in Anspruch nehmen, beanspruchen; *space* einnehmen.

(e) (*absorb*) (*in sich acc*) aufnehmen; *liquids also* aufsaugen.

(f) *matter, point* (*raise*) besprechen, zur Sprache bringen; (*go into*) eingehen auf (+*acc*). **I'll ~ that ~ with the headmaster** das werde ich beim Rektor zur Sprache bringen *or* mit dem Rektor besprechen; **I'd like to ~ ~ the point you made earlier** on ich möchte auf das eingehen, was Sie vorhin sagten.

(g) (*start doing as hobby*) *photography, archaeology* zu seinem Hobby machen; *a hobby* sich (*dat*) zulegen; *a language* (anfangen zu) lernen. **to ~ ~ painting/pottery/the guitar** anfangen zu malen/zu töpfern/Gitarre zu spielen.

(h) (*adopt*) *cause* sich einsetzen für, verfechten; *idea* aufgreifen; *case* sich annehmen (+*gen*). **to ~ ~ an attitude** eine Haltung einnehmen; **the speaker took ~ a conciliatory attitude** der Sprecher schlug einen versöhnlichen Ton an; **to ~ ~ a person** (*as protégé*) sich eines Menschen annehmen, einen Menschen unter seine Fittiche nehmen; **to ~ ~ a position** (*lit*) eine Stellung einnehmen; (*fig*) eine Haltung einnehmen.

(i) (*accept*) *challenge, invitation* annehmen; *suggestion also* aufgreifen.

(j) (*start*) *job, employment* annehmen; *new job, post* antreten; *one's duties* übernehmen; *career* einschlagen. **he left to ~ ~ a job as a headmaster** er ist gegangen, um eine Stelle als Schulleiter zu übernehmen; **to ~ ~ residence** sich niederlassen (*at, in* in +*dat*); (*in house*) einziehen (*in* in +*acc*); (*sovereign etc*) Residenz beziehen (*in* in +*dat*).

(k) (*continue*) *story* aufnehmen; *conversation* fortfahren mit, weiterführen; (*join in*) *chorus, chant* einstimmen in (+*acc*). **the crowd took ~ the cry** die Menge nahm den Schrei auf.

(l) **to ~ sb ~ on an invitation/offer** von jds Einladung/Angebot Gebrauch machen; **to ~ sb ~ on a promise/boast** jdn beim Wort nehmen; **I'll ~ you ~ on that** ich werde davon Gebrauch machen; (*on promise etc*) ich nehme Sie beim Wort.

(m) (*question, argue with*) **I would like to ~ you ~ there** *or* **on that** ich möchte gern etwas dazu sagen; **he took me ~ on that point** dagegen hatte er etwas einzuwenden; **I would like to ~ you ~ on what you said about strikes** zu Ihrer Bemerkung über Streiks hätte ich noch etwas zu sagen; **he took his critics ~ on their narrow-mindedness** er warf seinen Kritikern ihre Engstirnigkeit vor; **to ~ sb ~ short** jdm das Wort abschneiden.

(n) (*Fin*) **to ~ ~ an option** Bezugsrecht ausüben; **to ~ ~ a bill** einen Wechsel einlösen; **to ~ ~ shares** Aktien beziehen.

(o) *collection* durchführen.

(p) **to be ~n ~ with sb/sth** (*involved with*) mit jdm/etw sehr beschäftigt sein; (*busy with also*) von jdm/etw sehr beansprucht werden.

♦**take upon** *vt* +*prep obj* **he took that job ~ himself** er hat das völlig unnötig getan; **he took it ~ himself to answer for me** er meinte, er müsse für mich antworten.

♦**take up with** *vi* +*prep obj person* sich anfreunden mit. **to ~ ~ ~ bad company** in schlechte Gesellschaft geraten.

take: **~-away** (*esp Brit*) **1** *n* **(a)** (*meal*) Speisen *pl* zum Mitnehmen; **let's get a ~-away** wir können uns ja etwas (zu essen) holen *or* mitnehmen; **(b)** (*restaurant*) Imbißstube *f*/Restaurant *nt* für Außer-Haus-Verkauf; **2** *adj attr* Außer-Haus-; **the ~-away menu is quite different** für Gerichte zum Mitnehmen gibt es eine ganz andere Speisekarte; **~-home pay** *n* Nettolohn *m*; **~-in** *n* (*inf*) Schwindel *m*.

taken ['teɪkən] *ptp of* **take**.

take: **~-off** *n* **(a)** (*Aviat*) Start, Abflug *m*; (*moment of leaving ground also*) Abheben *nt*; (*Sport*) Absprung *m*; (*place*)

Absprungstelle f or -brett nt; **the plane was ready for ~-off** das Flugzeug war startbereit or flugklar; at **~-off** beim Start or Abheben; **at the moment of ~-off** beim Abheben; **to be cleared for ~-off** Starterlaubnis haben/bekommen; **(b)** (imitation) Parodie, Nachahmung f; **to do a ~-off of sb** jdn nachahmen or nachmachen (inf); **~-over** n (Fin, Comm) Übernahme f; **~-over bid** n Übernahmeangebot nt.

taker ['teɪkəʳ] n (Betting) Wettende(r) mf; (at auction: fig) Interessent(in f) m. **any ~s?** wer wettet?; (at auction) wer bietet?; (fig) wer ist daran interessiert?; **there were no ~s** (Betting) niemand wettete or schloß eine Wette ab; (at auction) es wurden keine Angebote gemacht, niemand bot; (fig) niemand war daran interessiert.

take-up ['teɪkʌp] n **(a)** Inanspruchnahme f. **there is a very low ~ of rent allowances** nur wenige nehmen Mietzuschüsse in Anspruch. **(b)** (Tech: of tape etc) Aufwickeln, Aufspulen nt. **the rate of ~** die Aufwickel- or Aufspulgeschwindigkeit; **~ spool** Aufwickelspule f.

taking ['teɪkɪŋ] **1** n **(a)** it's yours for the ~ das können Sie (umsonst) haben.
   (b) ~s pl (Comm) Einnahmen pl.
   (c) (old: of town) Einnahme f, Eroberung f.
   (d) (old: distress) Aufregung, Erregung f. **to be in a ~** aufgeregt or erregt sein.
   2 adj manners, ways einnehmend, gewinnend; person sympathisch, anziehend.

talc [tælk] **1** n (also talcum ['tælkəm]) **(a)** Talk m. **(b)** (also **talcum powder**) Talkumpuder m; (perfumed also) (Körper)puder m. **2** vt pudern.

tale [teɪl] n **(a)** Geschichte f; (Liter) Erzählung f. **fairy ~** Märchen nt; **T~s of King Arthur** Artussagen pl; **he had quite a ~ to tell** er hatte einiges zu erzählen, der hatte vielleicht was zu erzählen (inf); **I bet he/that bed could tell a ~ or two** (inf) der/das Bett könnte bestimmt so einiges erzählen; **it tells its own ~** das spricht für sich; **thereby hangs a ~** das ist eine lange/hübsche/pikante etc Geschichte; **I've heard a fine ~ about you** (iro) von dir hört man ja schöne Geschichten!
   (b) to tell ~s petzen (inf) (to dat); (dated: fib) flunkern; **to tell ~s out of school** (inf) aus der Schule plaudern; **to tell ~s about sb** jdn verpetzen (inf) (to bei).

tale-bearing ['teɪlbɛərɪŋ] n see **taletelling**.

talent ['tælənt] n **(a)** Begabung f, Talent nt. **to have a ~ for drawing/mathematics** Begabung zum Zeichnen/für Mathematik haben; **a painter of great ~** ein hochbegabter or sehr talentierter Maler.
   (b) (talented people) Talente pl.
   (c) (inf) (girls) Miezen (inf), Bräute (sl) pl; (boys) Typen (sl), Jungs (inf) pl. **they went to inspect the local ~** sie zogen los, um zu sehen, wie die Miezen etc dort waren.
   (d) (Hist) Talent nt.

talented ['tæləntɪd] adj person begabt, talentiert. **a ~ book/painting** ein Buch/Gemälde, das von großer Begabung zeugt.

talent scout, talent spotter n Talentsucher m. **they send ~s round** sie schicken (ihre) Leute auf Talent- or Nachwuchssuche.

tale: **~teller** n (Sch) Petzer(in f) m (inf); **~telling** n (Sch) Petzerei f (inf).

talisman ['tælɪzmən] n, pl -s Talisman m.

talk [tɔːk] **1** n **(a)** Gespräch nt (also Pol); (conversation also) Unterhaltung f; (private also) Unterredung f; (heart-to-heart also) Aussprache f. **to have a ~** ein Gespräch führen/sich unterhalten/eine Unterredung haben/sich aussprechen (with sb about sth mit jdm über etw acc); **could I have a ~ with you?** könnte ich Sie mal sprechen?; **to hold or have ~s** Gespräche führen; **to have a friendly ~ with sb** sich mit jdm nett unterhalten, mit jdm plaudern; (giving advice, warning) mit jdm (mal) in aller Freundschaft reden; **I have enjoyed our ~** ich habe mich gern mit Ihnen unterhalten; **to meet for ~s** sich zu Gesprächen treffen.
   (b) no pl (~ing) Reden nt, Rederei f; (rumour) Gerede nt. **he's all ~** er ist ein fürchterlicher Schwätzer; (and no action) der führt bloß große Reden; **there is some ~ of his returning** es heißt, er kommt zurück; **there is too much ~ of going on strike in this factory** in dieser Fabrik wird zu viel vom Streiken geredet; **it's the ~ of the town** es ist Stadtgespräch; **she's the ~ of the town** sie ist zum Stadtgespräch geworden.
   (c) (lecture) Vortrag m. **to give a ~** einen Vortrag halten (on über +acc); **a series of ~s** eine Vortragsreihe; **her ~ on the dangers ...** ihre (kurze) Rede über die Gefahren ...
   2 vi **(a)** sprechen, reden (of von, about über +acc); (have conversation also) sich unterhalten (of, about über +acc); (bird, doll, child) sprechen. **to ~ to or with** (esp US) **sb** mit jdm sprechen or reden (about über +acc); (converse also) sich mit jdm unterhalten (about über +acc); (reprimand also) mit jdm ein ernstes Wort reden; **could I ~ to Mr Smith please?** kann ich bitte Herrn Smith sprechen?; **don't ~ silly!** (inf) red keinen Stuß! (inf), red nicht so blöd (daher) (inf); **it's easy or all right for you to ~** (inf) du hast gut reden (inf); **don't (you) ~ to me like that!** wie redest du denn mit mir?; **who do you think you're ~ing to?** was meinst du denn, wen du vor dir hast?; **that's no way to ~ to your parents** so redet man doch nicht mit seinen Eltern!; **hey, that's no way to ~** hör mal, sag doch so was nicht!; **he sat there without ~ing** er saß da und sagte kein Wort; **~ to me!** erzähl mir was!; **to get/be ~ing to sb** mit jdm ins Gespräch kommen/im Gespräch sein; **I'm not ~ing to you** (we're on bad terms) mit dir spreche or rede ich nicht mehr; (I mean somebody else) ich spreche nicht mit dir; **he ~s very highly of you** er spricht sehr lobend von Ihnen; **he knows/doesn't know what he's ~ing about** er weiß (schon)/weiß (doch) nicht, wovon er spricht, er hat (davon) ziemlich Ahnung (inf)/(doch) überhaupt keine Ahnung; **you can or should ~!** (inf) du kannst

gerade reden!; **to keep sb ~ing** jdn (mit einem Gespräch) hinhalten; **to ~ to oneself** Selbstgespräche führen; **today I'm going to ~ about impressionism** heute möchte ich über den Impressionismus sprechen or reden; **now you're ~ing!** das läßt sich schon eher hören!
   (b) (mention) sprechen, reden. **he's been ~ing of going abroad** er hat davon gesprochen or geredet, daß er ins Ausland fahren will; **~ing of salaries/films ...** da or wo (inf) wir gerade von Gehältern/Filmen sprechen ...; **~ about impertinence/rude/hot!** so was von Frechheit/unverschämt/heiß! (inf).
   (c) (chatter) reden, schwatzen. **stop ~ing!** sei/seid ruhig!
   (d) (gossip) reden, klatschen. **everyone was ~ing about them** sie waren in aller Munde; (because of scandal also) alle haben über sie geredet or geklatscht; **to get oneself ~ed about** von sich reden machen; (because of scandal) ins Gerede kommen.
   (e) (reveal secret) reden. **the spy refused to ~** der Spion schwieg beharrlich or weigerte sich zu reden; **to make sb ~** jdn zum Reden bringen; **OK, Kowalski, ~!** OK!, Kowalski, raus mit der Sprache! (inf).
   3 vt **(a)** (speak) a language, slang sprechen; nonsense reden. **~ sense!** red keinen solchen Unsinn!; **he simply wasn't ~ing sense** er hat bloß Unsinn geredet or verzapft (inf).
   (b) (discuss) politics, cricket, business reden über (+acc) or von, sich unterhalten über (+acc). **we ~ to ~ business for a while** wir müssen mal kurz etwas Geschäftliches besprechen; **then they got down to ~ing business** dann sind sie zum geschäftlichen Teil übergegangen; **let's ~ business** kommen wir zur Sache; **now you're ~ing business** das läßt sich schon eher hören; see **shop**.
   (c) (persuade) **to ~ sb/oneself into doing sth** jdn überreden or jdn/sich dazu bringen, etw zu tun; (against better judgement) jdm/sich einreden, daß man etw tut; **he ~ed himself into believing she was unfaithful** er hat sich eingeredet, sie sei ihm nicht treu; **to ~ sb out of sth/doing sth** jdn von etw abbringen/davon abbringen, etw zu tun, jdm etw ausreden/jdm ausreden, etw zu tun.
   (d) (achieve by ~ing) **he ~ed himself out of that job** durch sein Reden hat er sich (dat) diese Stelle verscherzt; **you won't be able to ~ your way out of this** jetzt können Sie sich nicht mehr herausreden; **he ~ed himself out of trouble** er redete sich (geschickt) heraus; **he ~ed himself into this situation** er hat sich da hineingeredet; **to ~ sb into a better humour/out of his bad temper** jdn in eine bessere Laune bringen/jdm die schlechte Laune vertreiben.
   (e) to ~ oneself hoarse sich heiser reden; see **head**.

♦**talk at** vi +prep obj person einreden auf (+acc).
♦**talk away 1** vi ununterbrochen reden, schwatzen. **we ~ed ~ for hours** wir haben stundenlang geschwatzt or uns stundenlang unterhalten; **may I talk to you for a minute?** — certainly, **~ ~!** kann ich Sie einen Augenblick sprechen? — natürlich, schießen Sie los! (inf).
   2 vt sep **(a)** (spend talking) im Gespräch verbringen. **we ~ed the evening ~** wir haben den ganzen Abend lang geredet, wir haben die Abend im Gespräch verbracht.
   (b) debts, problems etc wegdiskutieren.
♦**talk back** vi (be cheeky) frech antworten (to sb jdm).
♦**talk down 1** vi **to ~ ~ to sb** mit jdm herablassend or von oben herab reden or sprechen.
   2 vt sep **(a)** (reduce to silence) über den Haufen reden (inf); niederreden.
   (b) (Aviat) pilot, plane zur Landung einweisen.
♦**talk on** vi weiterreden. **they ~ed ~ and on** sie redeten und redeten.
♦**talk out** vt sep **(a)** (discuss) problems, differences ausdiskutieren. **(b)** (Parl) **to ~ ~ a bill** die rechtzeitige Verabschiedung eines Gesetzes verschleppen.
♦**talk over** vt sep **(a)** question, problem bereden (inf), besprechen. **let's ~ it ~** quietly wir wollen jetzt einmal in aller Ruhe darüber reden. **(b)** (persuade) see **talk round 1**.
♦**talk round 1** vt always separate umstimmen. **I ~ed her ~ to my way of thinking** ich habe sie zu meiner Anschauung bekehrt. **2** vi +prep obj problem, subject herumreden um.

talkative ['tɔːkətɪv] adj gesprächig, redselig.
talkativeness ['tɔːkətɪvnɪs] n Gesprächigkeit, Redseligkeit f.
talkback ['tɔːkbæk] n (device) Gegensprechanlage f; (talking) Anweisungen pl im Hintergrund.
talked-of ['tɔːktɒv] adj: **much ~** berühmt; plans also vielbesprochen; **his much ~ brilliance was apparent** seine vielgerühmte Brillanz wurde offensichtlich.
talker ['tɔːkəʳ] n Redner m. **the parrot was a good ~** der Papagei konnte gut sprechen; **he's just a ~** er ist ein Schwätzer m.
talkie ['tɔːkɪ] n (dated inf) Tonfilm m.
talking ['tɔːkɪŋ] n Reden, Sprechen nt. **no ~ please!** bitte Ruhe!, Sprechen verboten!; **I'll let you do the ~** ich überlasse das Reden Ihnen; **he did all the ~** er übernahm das Reden; **his constant ~ will drive me mad** sein dauerndes Gerede or Geschwätz macht mich noch verrückt; **that's enough ~!** Ruhe jetzt!, Schluß mit dem Reden!
talking: **~ bird** n sprechender Vogel; **~ doll** n sprechende Puppe, Sprechpuppe f; **~ picture** n (old) Tonfilm m; **~ point** n Gesprächsthema nt; **~-to** n (inf) Standpauke f (inf); **to give sb a good ~-to** jdm eine Standpauke halten (inf).
talk show n Talkshow f.
tall [tɔːl] adj (+er) **(a)** person groß, lang (inf). **how ~ are you?** wie groß bist Du?; **he is 1 m 80 ~** er ist 1,80 m groß; **how ~ he is growing!** wie groß er wird!; **to feel ten foot or feet ~** (inf) riesig stolz sein (inf); (after compliment also) um einen halben Meter wachsen (inf).
   (b) building, tree, grass hoch; mast also lang. **~ ship** Klipper m.
   (c) (inf) **that's a ~ order** das ist ganz schön viel verlangt;

(*indignant also*) das ist eine Zumutung; **a ~ story** ein Märchen *nt* (*inf*).

tallboy ['tɔːlbɔɪ] *n* (*Brit*) hohe Schlafzimmerkommode.

tallish ['tɔːlɪʃ] *adj person* ziemlich groß; *building* ziemlich hoch.

tallness ['tɔːlnɪs] *n see adj* (**a**) Größe, Länge (*inf*) *f*. (**b**) Höhe *f*; Länge *f*.

tallow ['tæləu] *n* Talg, Unschlitt (*old*) *m*. **~ candle** Talglicht *nt*.

tallowy ['tæləuɪ] *adj* talgig.

tally ['tælɪ] **1** *n* (**a**) (*Hist: stick*) Kerbholz *nt*. (**b**) (*count, account*) **to keep a ~ of** Buch führen über (+ *acc*). (**c**) (*result of counting, number*) (An)zahl *f*. **what's the ~?** wieviel ist/sind es? **2** *vi* übereinstimmen; (*reports etc also*) sich decken. **they don't ~** sie stimmen nicht (miteinander) überein. **3** *vt* (*also ~ up*) zusammenrechnen *or* -zählen.

tally clerk *n* Kontrolleur *m*.

tally-ho ['tælɪ'həu] **1** *interj* halali. **2** *n* Halali *nt*.

Talmud ['tælmuːd] *n* Talmud *m*.

talon ['tælən] *n* Kralle, Klaue *f*; (*fig: of person*) Kralle *f*.

tamable *adj see* **tameable**.

tamarind ['tæmərɪnd] *n* Tamarinde *f*; (*tree also*) Tamarindenbaum *m*.

tamarisk ['tæmərɪsk] *n* Tamariske *f*.

tambour ['tæm,buə^r] *n* (**a**) (*old Mus*) Trommel *f*. (**b**) (*on desk etc*) Rouleau, Rollo *nt*.

tambourine [,tæmbə'riːn] *n* Tamburin *nt*.

tame [teɪm] **1** *adj* (+ *er*) (**a**) *animal, person* zahm. **the village has its own ~ novelist** (*hum*) der Ort hat seinen dorfeigenen Schriftsteller (*inf*); **I'll get my ~ lawyer to do that** (*hum*) ich beauftrage meinen treuer Rechtsanwalt damit.
(**b**) (*dull*) *person, life, adventure etc* lahm (*inf*); *story, film, answer, criticism, joke, shot, tennis service etc also* zahm. **2** *vt animal, person* zähmen, bändigen; *passion* (be)zähmen, zügeln; *garden* unter Kontrolle bringen.

tameable ['teɪməbl] *adj* zähmbar.

tamely ['teɪmlɪ] *adv see adj* (**a**) zahm. (**b**) lahm (*inf*); zahm.

tameness ['teɪmnɪs] *n see adj* (**a**) Zahmheit *f*. (**b**) Lahmheit *f* (*inf*); Zahmheit *f*.

tamer ['teɪmə^r] *n* (*of animals*) Bändiger, Dompteur *m*.

taming ['teɪmɪŋ] *n* Zähmung, Bändigung *f*. **"The T~ of the Shrew"** „Der Widerspenstigen Zähmung".

tam o'shanter [,tæmə'ʃæntə^r], **tammy** ['tæmɪ] *n* (schottische) Baskenmütze.

tamp [tæmp] *vt* (**a**) (*block up*) *drill hole etc* (ver)stopfen. (**b**) (*ram down*) *earth* (fest)stampfen. **to ~ (down) tobacco in a pipe** die Pfeife (fest) stopfen.

tamper ['tæmpə^r] *n* (*for soil etc*) Stampfer *m*; (*for tobacco*) Stopfer *m*.

♦ **tamper with** *vi* + *prep obj* herumhantieren an (+ *dat*); (*with evil intent*) sich (*dat*) zu schaffen machen an (+ *dat*); (*plan, schedule*) herumpfuschen an (+ *dat*) (*inf*); *document* verfälschen; (*Jur*) *witness* beeinflussen; (*bribe*) bestechen. **the car had been ~ed** jemand hatte sich am Auto zu schaffen gemacht.

tampon ['tæmpən] *n* Tampon *m*.

tan [tæn] **1** *n* (**a**) (*suntan*) Bräune *f*. **to get a ~** braun werden; **she's got a lovely ~** sie ist so schön braun; **what a ~!** du bist/er ist *etc* aber schön braun! (**b**) (*colour*) Hellbraun *nt*.
2 *adj* hellbraun.
3 *vt* (**a**) *skins* gerben. **to ~ sb's hide** (*fig inf*) jdm das Fell gerben. (**b**) (*sun*) *face, body etc* bräunen, braun werden lassen. **4** *vi* braun werden. **she ~s easily** sie wird schnell braun.

tandem ['tændəm] **1** *n* (*cycle*) Tandem *nt*. **the horses were in ~** die Pferde liefen hintereinander im Gespann; **in ~** (*fig*) zusammen. **2** *adv* hintereinander im Gespann.

tang [tæŋ] *n* (*smell*) scharfer Geruch; (*taste*) starker Geschmack. **the fish has a salty ~** der Fisch schmeckt salzig.

tangent ['tændʒənt] *n* (*Math*) Tangente *f*. **to go or fly off at a ~** (*fig*) (plötzlich) vom Thema abkommen *or* abschweifen; **he went off at a ~ about flowers** er schweifte plötzlich ab und fing an, über Blumen zu reden.

tangential [tæn'dʒɛnʃəl] *adj* (*Math*) tangential. **this is merely ~ to the problem** dies berührt das Problem nur am Rande.

tangerine [,tændʒə'riːn] **1** *n* (*also ~ orange*) Mandarine *f*. **2** *adj* (*in colour*) stark orange, rötlich orange.

tangibility [,tændʒɪ'bɪlɪtɪ] *n* Greifbarkeit *f*.

tangible ['tændʒəbl] *adj* (**a**) (*lit*) greifbar, berührbar. (**b**) (*fig*) *result* greifbar; *proof also* handfest, handgreiflich; *assets* handfest, real.

tangibly ['tændʒəblɪ] *adv* greifbar. **he would prefer to be rewarded more ~** ihm wäre etwas Handfesteres als Belohnung lieber.

Tangier(s) [tæn'dʒɪə(z)] *n* Tanger *nt*.

tangle ['tæŋgl] **1** *n* (**a**) (*lit*) Gewirr *nt*. **the string was in a ~** die Schnur hatte sich verheddert; **the ~s in her hair** ihr verheddertes Haar; **to get into a ~** sich verheddern.
(**b**) (*fig: muddle*) Wirrwarr *m*, Durcheinander *nt*. **to get into a ~** sich verheddern; **I'm in such a ~ with my tax forms** ich komme bei meinen Steuerformularen überhaupt nicht klar; **an emotional ~** eine Verstrickung der Gefühle; **she has got herself into an emotional ~** sie hat sich gefühlsmäßig verstrickt.
(**c**) (*fig: trouble*) Ärger *m*, Schwierigkeiten *pl*. **she's in a real ~ this time** diesmal hat sie sich aber böse hineingeritten; **he got into a ~ with the police** er ist mit der Polizei aneinandergeraten, er hat Schwierigkeiten mit der Polizei gehabt.
2 *vt* (*lit, fig*) verwirren, durcheinanderbringen; *wool, string also* verheddern; *hair* durcheinanderbringen. **to get ~d** (*lit, fig*) sich verheddern; (*ropes*) sich verknoten; **the hedges were ~d with wild roses** die Hecken waren von wilden Rosen durchflochten; **a ~d web** ein Gespinst *nt*.

♦ **tangle up** *vt sep* (*lit, fig*) verwirren, durcheinanderbringen; *wool, string also* verheddern. **to get ~d ~** durcheinan-

dergeraten; (*wool etc also*) sich verheddern; (*ropes*) sich verknoten; (*person*) (*in talking, explaining etc*) sich verstricken *or* verheddern; (*become involved*) verwickelt *or* verstrickt werden; **the paper got all ~d ~ in the machine** das Papier hat sich in der Maschine verheddert; **she got ~d ~ with a married man** sie hat sich mit einem verheirateten Mann eingelassen.

♦ **tangle with** *vi* + *prep obj* (*inf*) aneinandergeraten mit. **I'm not tangling ~ him** mit ihm laß ich mich (doch) nicht ein.

tango ['tæŋgəu] **1** *n* Tango *m*. **2** *vi* Tango tanzen. **they ~ed across the room** sie tanzten im Tangoschritt durch das Zimmer.

tangy ['tæŋɪ] *adj* (+ *er*) *taste* scharf, streng; *smell also* durchdringend.

tank [tæŋk] *n* (**a**) (*container*) Tank *m*; (*for water also*) Wasserspeicher *m*; (*of boiler also*) Kessel *m*; (*Naut: for water supply*) Kessel *m*; (*in submarines*) Tauchtank *m*; (*Rail: in engine*) Kessel *m*; (*for diver: oxygen* ~) Flasche *f*; (*Phot*) Wanne *f*. **fill up the ~, please** (*Aut*) volltanken, bitte.
(**b**) (*Mil*) Panzer, Tank *m*.
(**c**) (*US sl*) Kittchen *nt* (*inf*), Knast *m* (*sl*).

♦ **tank up** **1** *vi* (**a**) (*ship, plane*) auftanken; (*car, driver also*) volltanken. (**b**) (*Brit sl: get drunk*) sich vollaufen lassen (*sl*). **2** *vt sep* (**a**) *ship, plane* auftanken; *car also* volltanken. (**b**) (*Brit sl*) **to get/be ~ed ~** sich vollaufen lassen (*on* mit)/voll sein.

tankard ['tæŋkəd] *n* Humpen *m*; (*for beer also*) Seidel *m*.

tank car *n* (*Rail*) Kesselwagen *m*.

tanker ['tæŋkə^r] *n* (**a**) (*boat*) Tanker *m*, Tankschiff *nt*. (**b**) (*vehicle*) Tankwagen *m*.

tank farm *n* (*US*) Tanklager *nt*.

tankful ['tæŋkful] *n* (**a**) Tank(voll) *m*. (**b**) (*Brit sl: drink*) he's had a ~ der ist total voll (*inf*).

tank: ~**top** *n* Pullunder *m*; ~ **town** *n* (*US*) Wasser(auffüll)station *f*; (*fig*) Kuhnest *nt* (*inf*); ~ **trap** *n* Panzersperre *f*; ~ **wagon** *n* (*Rail*) Kesselwagen *m*.

tanned [tænd] *adj* (**a**) *person* braun(gebrannt). (**b**) *skins* gegerbt.

tanner[1] ['tænə^r] *n* Gerber *m*.

tanner[2] *n* (*old Brit inf*) Sixpence *m*.

tannery ['tænərɪ] *n* Gerberei *f*.

tannic ['tænɪk] *adj* Gerb-.

tannin ['tænɪn] *n* Tannin *f*.

tanning ['tænɪŋ] *n* (**a**) (*of hides*) Gerben *nt*; (*craft*) Gerberei *f*. (**b**) (*punishment*) Tracht *f* Prügel. **to give sb a ~** jdm das Fell gerben.

Tannoy ® ['tænɔɪ] *n* Lautsprecheranlage *f*. **over or on the ~** über den Lautsprecher.

tansy ['tænzɪ] *n* Rainfarn *m*.

tantalize ['tæntəlaɪz] *vt* reizen; (*torment also*) quälen. **to be ~d** Tantalusqualen ausstehen.

tantalizing ['tæntəlaɪzɪŋ] *adj* *smell, promise, blouse* verlockend, verführerisch; *behaviour also* aufreizend. **he spoke with ~ slowness** er sprach aufreizend langsam; **it is ~ to think that ... es** ist zum Verrücktwerden, zu denken, daß ... (*inf*).

tantalizingly ['tæntəlaɪzɪŋlɪ] *adv* verlockend, verführerisch. **success was ~ near** der Erfolg schien zum Greifen nahe.

tantamount ['tæntəmaunt] *adj:* **to be ~ to sth** einer Sache (*dat*) gleichkommen, auf etw (*acc*) hinauslaufen.

tantrum ['tæntrəm] *n* Koller, Wutanfall *m*. **to be in/have or throw a ~** einen Koller *or* Wutanfall haben/bekommen.

Tanzania [,tænzə'nɪə] *n* Tansania *nt*.

Tanzanian [,tænzə'nɪən] **1** *adj* tansanisch. **2** *n* Tansanier(in *f*) *m*.

tap[1] [tæp] **1** *n* (*esp Brit*) Hahn *m*. **don't leave the ~s running** laß das Wasser nicht laufen!, dreh die Hähne zu!; **on ~** (*lit: beer etc*) vom Faß; (*fig*) zur Hand; **he has plenty of ideas on ~** er hat immer Ideen auf Lager (*inf*).
2 *vt* (**a**) *cask, barrel* anzapfen, anstechen; *tree* anzapfen. **to ~ a pine for resin** einer Kiefer (*dat*) Harz abzapfen.
(**b**) (*fig*) *resources* erschließen. **to ~ an electric current** eine Stromleitung anzapfen; **to ~ telephone wires** Telephonleitungen anzapfen; **the wires are ~ped here** die Leitung hier wird abgehört; **to ~ sb for money/a loan** (*inf*) jdn anzapfen (*inf*), jdn anpumpen (*inf*); **he tried to ~ me for information** er wollte mich aushorchen.

tap[2] **1** *n* (**a**) (*light knock*) Klopfen *nt*.
(**b**) (*light touch*) Klaps *m*, leichter Schlag. **to give sb a ~ on the shoulder** jdn *or* jdm auf die Schulter klopfen.
(**c**) ~**s** *sing or pl* (*Mil*) Zapfenstreich *m*.
2 *vt* klopfen. **he ~ped me on the shoulder** er klopfte mir auf die Schulter; **to ~ in/out a nail** einen Nagel ein-/ausschlagen; **he ~ped his foot impatiently** er klopfte ungeduldig mit dem Fuß auf den Boden.
3 *vi* klopfen. **to ~ on or at the door** sachte an die Tür klopfen *or* pochen (*geh*), leise anklopfen; **she sat ~ping away at the typewriter** sie klapperte auf der Schreibmaschine herum; **he ~ped with his fingers on the table** er trommelte mit den Fingern auf den Tisch.

♦ **tap out** *vt sep* (**a**) *pipe* ausklopfen. (**b**) *rhythm* klopfen. **to ~ a message** (*in Morse*) eine Nachricht morsen.

tap: ~**-dance 1** *n* Steptanz *m*; **2** *vi* steppen; ~**-dancer** *n* Steptänzer(in *f*), Stepper(in *f*) *m*; ~**-dancing** *n* Steppen *nt*.

tape [teɪp] **1** *n* (**a**) (*of cloth*) Band *nt*; (*sticky paper*) Klebeband *nt*; (*Sellotape etc*) Kleb(e)streifen, Tesafilm ® *m*; (*ticker-~, computer ~ etc*) Lochstreifen *m*; (*Sport*) Zielband *nt*. **the message was coming through on the ~** die Nachricht kam über den Fernschreiber; **to break or breast the ~** (*Sport*) durchs Ziel gehen.
(**b**) (*magnetic*) (Ton)band, Magnetband *nt*. **on ~** auf Band; **to put or get sth on ~** etw auf Band aufnehmen.
2 *vt* (**a**) *parcel* (mit Kleb(e)streifen/-band) verkleben *or* zukleben. **to ~ together two documents** zwei Dokumente mit Kleb(e)streifen/-band zusammenkleben.

(b) (~-*record*) *song, message* (auf Band) aufnehmen.
(c) (*inf*) **I've got the situation** ~d ich habe die Sache im Griff (*inf*); **I've got him** ~d ich kenne mich mit ihm aus.
◆**tape back** *vt sep* (mit Kleb(e)streifen/-band) zurückkleben.
◆**tape down** *vt sep* (mit Kleb(e)streifen/-band) festkleben.
◆**tape on** *vt sep* (mit Kleb(e)streifen/-band) ankleben *or* -heften. **to** ~ **sth** ~(**to**) **sth** etw auf etw (*acc*) kleben.
◆**tape up** *vt sep sth broken* mit Kleb(e)streifen/-band zusammenkleben; *parcel* mit Kleb(e)streifen/-band verkleben; *gap, windows, mouth* zukleben.
tape: ~ **cassette** *n* Tonbandkassette *f*; ~ **deck** *n* Tapedeck *nt*; ~ **measure** *n* Maßband, Bandmaß *nt*.
taper ['teɪpə'] **1** *n* (*candle*) (dünne) Kerze.
2 *vt end of plank, stick etc* zuspitzen; *edge* abschrägen; *hair* spitz zuschneiden; *pair of trousers* (nach unten) verengen.
3 *vi* sich zuspitzen; (*tower, vase also*) sich verjüngen; (*trousers*) nach unten enger werden; (*hair*) (im Nacken) spitz zulaufen. **to** ~ **to a point** spitz zulaufen.
◆**taper off 1** *vi* (**a**) spitz zulaufen, sich zuspitzen; (*tower also, vase*) sich verjüngen; (*road, trousers*) sich verengen.
(b) (*fig: decrease gradually*) langsam aufhören; (*numbers*) langsam zurückgehen; (*production*) langsam auslaufen.
2 *vt sep edge* abschrägen; *end of plank, stick etc* zuspitzen; (*fig*) *production* zurückschrauben; (*bring to an end*) langsam auslaufen lassen.
tape: ~ **reader** *n* (*Computers*) Lochstreifenleser *m*; ~**-record** *vt* auf Band aufnehmen; ~**-recorder** *n* Tonbandgerät *nt*; ~**-recording** *n* Bandaufnahme *f*.
tapered ['teɪpəd] *adj* spitz zulaufend. ~ **trousers** Hosen, die unten enger werden.
tapering ['teɪpərɪŋ] *adj* spitz zulaufend.
tapestry ['tæpɪstrɪ] *n* Wand- *or* Bildteppich *m*; (*fabric*) Gobelin *m*. **the chairs were upholstered in** ~ die Stühle hatten Gobelinbezüge; ~**-making,** ~**-weaving** Tapisserie *f*.
tapeworm ['teɪpwɜːm] *n* Bandwurm *m*.
tapioca [,tæpɪ'əʊkə] *n* Tapioka *f*.
tapir ['teɪpə'] *n* Tapir *m*.
tappet ['tæpɪt] *n* (*Aut*) Stößel *m*.
tap: ~**room** *n* Schankstube, Schenke (*old*) *f*; ~**root** *n* (*Bot*) Pfahlwurzel *f*.
tapster ['tæpstə'] *n* (*old*) Schankkellner(in *f*), Zapfer(in *f*) *m*.
tap water *n* Leitungswasser *nt*.
tar[1] ['tɑː'] **1** *n* Teer *m*. **2** *vt road, fence* teeren. **they are all** ~**red with the same brush** (*fig*) sie sind alle vom gleichen Schlag; **to** ~ **and feather sb** jdn teeren und federn.
tar[2] *n* (*old Naut sl*) Teerjacke *f* (*hum*), Seemann *m*.
tarantella [,tærən'telə] *n* Tarantella *f*.
tarantula [tə'ræntjʊlə] *n* Tarantel *f*.
tarbrush ['tɑːbrʌʃ] *n*: **a touch of the** ~ (*hum inf*) schwarzes Blut.
tardily ['tɑːdɪlɪ] *adv see adj* (**a**) (reichlich) spät. (**b**) zu spät.
tardiness ['tɑːdɪnɪs] *n. adj* (*of person*) Säumigkeit *f* (*geh*). **the** ~ **of his reply/offer** *etc* seine reichlich späte Antwort/sein reichlich spätes Angebot *etc*. (**b**) (*US: lateness*) Zuspätkommen *nt*; (*of train etc*) Verspätung *f*.
tardy ['tɑːdɪ] *adj* (+*er*) (**a**) (*belated*) *reply, arrival, offer to help* (reichlich) spät; *person* säumig (*geh*). **to be** ~ **in doing sth** etw erst reichlich spät tun.
(b) (*US: late*) **to be** ~ (*person*) zu spät kommen; (*train etc*) Verspätung haben; **the train was** ~ (**in arriving at New York**) der Zug kam mit Verspätung (in New York) an.
tare[1] [teə'] *n* (*Bot*) Wicke *f*.
tare[2] *n* (*Comm*) Tara *f*; (*of vehicle*) Leergewicht *nt*.
target ['tɑːgɪt] *n* (**a**) (*person, object, Mil*) Ziel *nt*; (*Sport: board*) Ziel- *or* Schießscheibe *f*; (*fig: of joke, criticism etc*) Zielscheibe *f*. **he was a** ~ **for their mockery** er war Zielscheibe ihres Spotts; **his shot was off/on** ~ (*Mil*) sein Schuß ist daneben gegangen/hat getroffen; (*Ftbl etc*) sein Schuß war ungenau/sehr genau; **the bombs landed on/off** ~ die Bomben haben getroffen/sind daneben niedergegangen; **Apollo III is on** ~ **for the moon** Apollo III ist auf direktem Kurs zum Mond.
(b) (*objective, goal*) Ziel *nt*; (*in production*) (Plan)soll *nt*. **industrial production** ~ Produktionssoll *nt no pl*; **production is above/on/below** ~ das Produktionssoll ist überschritten/erfüllt/nicht erfüllt; **we set ourselves the** ~ **of £10,000** wir haben uns £ 10.000 zum Ziel gesetzt.
target: ~ **area** *n* Zielbereich *m*, Zielgebiet *nt*; ~ **date** *n* angestrebter Termin; ~ **language** *n* Zielsprache *f*; ~ **practice** *n* (*Mil*) Zielschießen *nt*.
tariff ['tærɪf] **1** *n* (**a**) (Gebühren)tarif *m*; (*in hotels*) Preisverzeichnis *nt*, Preisliste *f*. (**b**) (*Econ: tax*) Zoll *m*; (*table*) Zolltarif *m*. **2** *attr* (*Econ*) ~ **reform** Zolltarifreform *f*; (*Hist*) Einführung *f* von Schutzzöllen; ~ **walls** Zollschranken *pl*.
tarmac ['tɑːmæk] **1** *n* (**a**) Makadam *m*; (*generally*) Asphalt, Makadam (*spec*) *m*. (**b**) (*esp Brit Aviat*) Rollfeld *nt*. **2** *vt road* (*generally*) asphaltieren, makadamisieren (*spec*).
tarmacadam [,tɑːmə'kædəm] *n* Makadam *m*.
tarn [tɑːn] *n* kleiner Berg- *or* Gebirgssee.
tarnish ['tɑːnɪʃ] **1** *vt* (**a**) *metal* stumpf werden lassen. **the silver was** ~**ed by exposure to air** das Silber war an der Luft angelaufen. (**b**) (*fig*) *reputation, glory* beflecken; *ideals* trüben, den Glanz nehmen (+*dat*). **2** *vi* (*metal*) anlaufen. **3** *n* Beschlag *m*. **to prevent** ~ das Anlaufen verhindern.
taro ['tɑːrəʊ] *n* Taro *m*.
tarot card ['tɑːrəʊkɑːd] *n* Tarockkarte *f*.
tarp [tɑːp] *n* (*US inf*) *see* **tarpaulin**.
tar paper *n* (*US*) Dachpappe, Teerpappe *f*.
tarpaulin [tɑː'pɔːlɪn] *n* (**a**) (*waterproof sheet*) Plane *f*; (*Naut*) Persenning *f*. (**b**) ~**s** *pl* (*clothes*) Ölzeug *nt*.
tarpon ['tɑːpɒn] *n* Atlantischer Tarpon, Silberkönig *m*.
tarragon ['tærəgən] *n* Estragon *m*.

tarry[1] ['tɑːrɪ] *adj* teerig.
tarry[2] ['tærɪ] *vi* (*old, liter*) (**a**) (*remain*) verweilen (*old, liter*). (**b**) (*delay*) säumen (*old, liter*), zögern.
tarsus ['tɑːsəs] *n* Tarsus *m*.
tart[1] [tɑːt] *adj* (+*er*) (**a**) *flavour, wine* herb, sauer (*pej*); *fruit* sauer. (**b**) (*fig*) *remark, manner* scharf; *humour* beißend; *person* schroff.
tart[2] *n* (*Cook*) Obstkuchen *m*, Obsttorte *f*; (*individual*) Obsttörtchen *nt*. **apple/jam** ~ Apfelkuchen *m*/Marmeladenkuchen *m*; Apfeltörtchen *nt*/Marmeladentörtchen *nt*.
tart[3] *n* (*inf*) (*prostitute*) Nutte *f* (*sl*); (*loose woman*) Flittchen *nt* (*pej*); (*pej: woman*) Schachtel *f* (*inf*).
◆**tart up** *vt sep* (*esp Brit inf*) aufmachen (*inf*); *oneself* auftakeln (*inf*), aufdonnern (*inf*). **there she was, all** ~**ed** ~ da stand sie, aufgetakelt wie eine Fregatte (*inf*).
tartan ['tɑːtən] **1** *n* (*pattern*) Schottenkaro *nt*; (*material*) Schottenstoff *m*. **what** ~ **are you?** welches Clan-Muster tragen Sie? **2** *adj skirt* im Schottenkaro *or* -muster.
tartar[1] ['tɑːtə'] *n* (*of wine*) Weinstein *m*; (*in kettle*) Kesselstein *m*; (*on teeth*) Zahnstein *m*.
Tartar ['tɑːtə'] *n* Tatar *m*. **t**~ (*fig*) Tyrann *m*; **to catch a** ~ (*fig*) sich (*dat*) etwas Übles einhandeln.
tartare [tɑː'tɑː'] *adj see* **steak.**
tartaric [tɑː'tærɪk] *adj* ~ **acid** Weinsäure *f*.
tartar sauce *n* = Remouladensoße *f*.
Tartary ['tɑːtərɪ] *n* Tatarei *f*.
tartly ['tɑːtlɪ] *adv speak* scharf.
tartness ['tɑːtnɪs] *n see adj* (**a**) Herbheit, Säure (*pej*) *f*; Säure *f*. (**b**) Schärfe *f*; Beißende(s) *nt*; Schroffheit *f*.
task [tɑːsk] *n* Aufgabe *f*. **to set** *or* **give sb a** ~ jdm eine Aufgabe stellen *or* geben; **it is the** ~ **of the politician to …** es ist Aufgabe des Politikers zu …; **to take sb to** ~ jdn ins Gebet nehmen, sich (*dat*) jdn vornehmen (*inf*) (*for, about* wegen). **2** *vt see* **tax 2** (**b**).
task: ~ **force** *n* Sondereinheit, Spezialeinheit *f*; ~**master** *n* (*stronger*) Arbeitgeber; **he's a hard** ~**master** er ist ein strenger Meister.
Tasmania [tæz'meɪnɪə] *n* Tasmanien *nt*.
Tasmanian [tæz'meɪnɪən] **1** *adj* tasmanisch. **2** *n* Tasmanier(in *f*) *m*.
Tasman Sea ['tæzmən'siː] *n* Tasmansee *f*.
tassel ['tæsəl] *n* Quaste, Troddel *f*.
taste [teɪst] **1** *n* (**a**) (*sense*) Geschmack(sinn) *m*. **the organ of** ~ das Geschmacksorgan; **to be sweet to the** ~ süß schmecken, einen süßen Geschmack haben.
(b) (*flavour*) Geschmack *m*. **I don't like the** ~ **of it** das schmeckt mir nicht; **her cooking has no** ~ ihr Essen schmeckt nach nichts; **a** ~ **of onions** ein Zwiebelgeschmack *m*; **to leave a bad** ~ **in the mouth** (*lit, fig*) einen üblen Nachgeschmack hinterlassen.
(c) (*small amount*) Kostprobe *f*, Versucherchen *nt* (*inf*); (*fig: as an example*) Kostprobe *f*; (*of sth in the future*) Vorgeschmack *m*. **would you like some?** — **just a** ~ möchten Sie etwas? — nur eine Idee; **to have a** ~ (*of sth*) (*lit*) (etw) probieren *or* kosten; (*fig*) eine Kostprobe (von etw) bekommen; (*of sth to come*) einen Vorgeschmack (von etw) haben; **two years in the army will give him a** ~ **of discipline** zwei Jahre bei der Armee werden ihm zeigen *or* ihn spüren lassen, was Disziplin ist; **to give sb a** ~ **of the whip** jdn die Peitsche *or* Knute spüren lassen; **he gave them a** ~ **of his bad temper** er gab ihnen eine (Kost)probe seiner schlechten Laune; **a** ~ **of what was to come** ein Vorgeschmack dessen, was noch kommen sollte.
(d) (*liking*) Geschmack *m no pl*. **to have a** ~ **for sth** eine Vorliebe für etw haben; **to acquire** *or* **develop a** ~ **for sth** Geschmack an etw (*dat*) finden; **it's an acquired** ~ das ist etwas für Kenner; **she has expensive** ~**s in hats** was Hüte anbelangt, hat sie einen teuren Geschmack; **my** ~ **in music has changed over the years** mein musikalischer Geschmack hat sich mit der Zeit geändert; **to be to sb's** ~ nach jds Geschmack sein; **it is a matter of** ~ das ist Geschmack(s)sache; **there is no accounting for** ~**s** über Geschmack läßt sich (nicht) streiten; ~**s differ** die Geschmäcker sind verschieden; **sweeten to** ~ (*Cook*) nach Geschmack *or* Bedarf süßen.
(e) (*discernment*) Geschmack *m*. **she has very good** ~ **in furniture** was Möbel anbelangt, hat sie einen sehr guten Geschmack; **she has no** ~ **at all when it comes to choosing friends** sie ist nicht sehr wählerisch in der Auswahl ihrer Freunde; **a man of** ~ ein Mann mit Geschmack; **in good/bad** ~ geschmackvoll/geschmacklos; **to be in doubtful** ~ von zweifelhaftem Geschmack zeugen; **that joke shows very poor** ~ dieser Witz ist geschmacklos.
2 *vt* (**a**) (*perceive flavour of*) schmecken; *blood* lecken. **I can't** ~ **anything** ich schmecke überhaupt nichts; **I can't** ~ **anything wrong** ich kann nichts Besonderes schmecken; **once you've** ~**d real champagne** wenn Sie einmal echten Sekt getrunken haben; **I've never** ~**d caviar** ich habe noch nie Kaviar gekostet (*geh*) *or* gegessen; **wait till you** ~ **this** warten Sie mal, bis Sie das probiert haben; **he hadn't** ~**d food for a week** er hatte seit einer Woche nichts zu sich genommen.
(b) (*take a little*) versuchen, probieren, kosten.
(c) (*test*) *wine* verkosten; *food products* probieren; (*official*) prüfen. ~ **the sauce before adding salt** schmecken Sie die Soße ab, bevor Sie Salz zugeben.
(d) (*fig*) *power, freedom* erfahren, erleben. **once the canary had** ~**d freedom …** als der Kanarienvogel erst einmal Geschmack an der Freiheit gefunden hatte …
3 *vi* (**a**) schmecken. **to** ~ **good** *or* **nice** (gut) schmecken; **it** ~**s all right to me** ich schmecke nichts; **I like it** ich finde, das schmeckt nicht schlecht; **to** ~ **of sth** nach etw schmecken.
(b) **to** ~ **of** (*liter*) erfahren; **those who have** ~**d of the knowledge of Zen** diejenigen, denen die Weisheit des Zen zuteil geworden ist (*geh*).

taste bud n Geschmacksknospe f.
tasteful adj, ~ly adv ['teistfʊl, -fəli] geschmackvoll.
tastefulness ['teistfʊlnis] n guter Geschmack.
tasteless ['teistlis] adj geschmacklos; food also fade; joke also abgeschmackt.
tastelessly ['teistlisli] adv see adj.
tastelessness ['teistlisnis] n see adj Geschmacklosigkeit f; Fadheit f; Abgeschmacktheit f.
taster ['teistə'] n (of wine) Prüfer, Probierer m; (of tea) Schmecker m; (of tobacco) Prüfer m; (as bodyguard) Vorkoster m.
tastily ['teistili] adv see adj.
tastiness ['teistinis] n Schmackhaftigkeit f.
tasty ['teisti] adj (+er) dish schmackhaft. a ~ morsel (lit) ein Leckerbissen m; his new girlfriend is a ~ morsel (inf) seine neue Freundin ist zum Anbeißen (inf).
tat¹ [tæt] **1** vi Okkispitze or Schiffchenspitze machen. **2** vt in Okkispitze or Schiffchenspitze arbeiten. **she ~ted a strip of lace** sie stellte eine Spitze in Okkiarbeit her.
tat² n see **tit²**.
ta-ta ['tæ'taː] interj (Brit inf) tschüs (inf), ada-ada (baby-talk).
tattered ['tætəd] adj clothes, person zerlumpt; book, sheet zerfleddert, zerfetzt; (fig) pride, reputation angeschlagen.
tatters ['tætəz] npl Lumpen, Fetzen pl. **to be in** ~ in Fetzen sein or hängen; **his jacket hung in** ~ sein Jackett war zerrissen or hing ihm in Fetzen vom Leib; **his reputation/pride was in** ~ sein Ruf/Stolz war sehr angeschlagen or hatte sehr gelitten.
tattily ['tætili] adv (inf) see adj.
tattiness ['tætinis] n (inf) see adj Schmuddeligkeit f; Schäbigkeit f.
tatting ['tætiŋ] n Okki- or Schiffchenspitze, Frivolitätenarbeit f.
tattle ['tætl] **1** vi tratschen (inf), klatschen. **2** n Geschwätz, Gerede nt. **office** ~ Büroklatsch or -tratsch (inf) m.
tattler ['tætlə'] n Klatschmaul nt (pej sl), Klatschbase f (inf).
tattoo¹ ['tæ'tuː] **1** vt tätowieren. **2** n Tätowierung f.
tattoo² n **(a)** (military pageant) Musikparade f. **(b)** (Mil: on drum or bugle) Zapfenstreich m. **to beat or sound the** ~ den Zapfenstreich blasen; **to beat a** ~ **on the table** (with one's fingers) auf den Tisch trommeln.
tatty ['tæti] adj (+er) (inf) schmuddelig; clothes schäbig.
taught [tɔːt] pret, ptp of **teach**.
taunt [tɔːnt] **1** n Spöttelei f, höhnische Bemerkung. **he paid no attention to their** ~s **of "traitor"** er kümmerte sich nicht darum, daß sie ihn als Verräter verhöhnten. **2** vt person verspotten, aufziehen (inf) (about wegen). **to** ~ **sb with cowardice** jdm höhnisch or spöttisch Feigheit vorwerfen.
taunting ['tɔːntiŋ] adj höhnisch, spöttisch.
tauntingly ['tɔːntiŋli] adv see adj. **a** ~ **insolent remark** eine Bemerkung von herausfordernder Unverschämtheit.
Taurean [tɔː'riən] **1** adj Stier-. **2** n Stier m.
Taurus ['tɔːrəs] n (Astron, Astrol) Stier m.
taut [tɔːt] adj (+er) **(a)** rope straff (gespannt); muscles stramm, gestrafft. ~ **round thighs** pralle Oberschenkel pl; **to haul** ~ (Naut) straff spannen.
    (b) (fig: tense) nerves, situation (an)gespannt.
    (c) (fig: precise, economical) style, prose knapp.
tauten ['tɔːtn] **1** vt rope spannen, straff anziehen, straffen; sail straffen. **2** vi sich spannen or straffen, straff werden.
tautly ['tɔːtli] adv see adj.
tautness ['tɔːtnis] n (of skin, rope) Straffheit f; (of muscles) Strammheit f; (fig) (of atmosphere) Gespanntheit f; (of nerves) Anspannung f; (of style) Knappheit f.
tautological [ˌtɔːtə'lɒdʒikəl], **tautologous** [tɔː'tɒləgəs] adj tautologisch, doppelt gemoppelt (inf).
tautology [tɔː'tɒlədʒi] n Tautologie f, weißer Schimmel (inf).
tavern ['tævən] n (old) Taverne, Schenke (old) f.
tawdrily ['tɔːdrili] adv billig und geschmacklos. ~ **dressed** aufgedonnert.
tawdriness ['tɔːdrinis] n (of jewellery, decorations etc) ordinäre Protzigkeit. **the** ~ **of her appearance** ihre billige und geschmacklose Aufmachung.
tawdry ['tɔːdri] adj (+er) clothes billig und geschmacklos; hat, jewellery, splendour, decorations ordinär; person, appearance aufgedonnert. **a** ~ **little dress** ein knalliges Fähnchen (inf), ein knalliger Fummel (inf); **all this cheap and** ~ **jewellery** all dieser billige Flitterkram.
tawny ['tɔːni] adj (+er) gelbbraun, goldbraun. ~ **port** bräunlicher Portwein, Tawny-Portwein m; ~ **owl** Waldkauz m; (in Brownies) Helferin f der Wichtelmutter.
tax [tæks] **1** n **(a)** (Fin, Econ) Steuer f; (on a company's profit) Abgabe f; (import ~) Gebühr f. **before/after** ~ brutto-/Nettoverdienst m; **that's done for** ~ **purposes** das wird aus steuerlichen Gründen getan; **free of** ~ steuer-/abgaben-/gebührenfrei; **to put a** ~ **on sb/sth** jdn/etw besteuern, mit einer Steuer belegen; **the heavy** ~ **on the rich** die hohe Besteuerung der Reichen; **the** ~ **on alcohol/cars** etc die Getränke-/Kraftfahrzeugsteuer etc.
    (b) (fig) Belastung f (on sth gen, on sb für jdn).
    2 vt **(a)** (Fin, Econ) besteuern; goods also mit einer Steuer belegen; country mit Steuern belegen. **this government is going to** ~ **us all out of existence** diese Regierung zieht uns den letzten Pfennig aus der Tasche (inf).
    (b) (fig) brain, imagination strapazieren; one's patience, nerves also auf eine harte Probe stellen; strength stark beanspruchen; savings, resources angreifen, schmälern.
    (c) (accuse) **to** ~ **sb with sth** jdn einer Sache (gen) beschuldigen or bezichtigen or zeihen (liter); **to** ~ **sb with having lied** jdn einer Lüge zeihen (liter).
taxable ['tæksəbl] adj person steuerpflichtig; income also (be)steuerbar (form); goods besteuert, abgabenpflichtig.

tax in cpds Steuer-; ~ **allowance** n Steuervergünstigung f; (tax-free income) Steuerfreibetrag m.
taxation [tæk'seiʃən] n Besteuerung f; (taxes also) Steuern pl. **money acquired from** ~ Steuereinnahmen or -einkünfte pl; **exempt from** ~ nicht besteuert; goods, income also steuerfrei; **subject to** ~ steuerpflichtig.
tax: ~ **avoidance** n Steuerumgehung f; ~ **bracket** n Steuergruppe or -klasse f; ~ **collecting** n Steuereinziehung f; ~ **collector** n Finanz- or Steuerbeamte(r) m; (Bibl, Hist) Zöllner m; ~**-deductible** adj (von der Steuer) absetzbar; mortgage steuerbegünstigt; ~ **dodge** n Trick m, um Steuern zu umgehen; ~**-dodger** n Steuerhinterzieher m; (who goes abroad) Steuerflüchtling m; ~ **evasion** n Steuerhinterziehung f; (by going abroad) Steuerflucht f; ~**-exempt** adj (US) person steuerbefreit; business abgabenfrei; income steuerfrei; ~ **exile** n Steuerexil nt; ~ **form** n Steuerformular nt; ~**-free** adj, adv steuer-/abgabenfrei; ~ **haven** n Steuerparadies nt.
taxi ['tæksi] **1** n Taxi nt, Taxe f. **to go by** ~ mit dem Taxi or der Taxe fahren. **2** vi (Aviat) rollen. **the plane** ~**ed to a halt** das Flugzeug rollte aus.
taxi: ~**cab** n Taxi nt, (Auto)taxe, Kraftdroschke (form) f; ~ **dancer** n (US) Tanzdame f, Taxigirl nt.
taxidermist ['tæksidɜːmist] n Präparator, Tierausstopfer m.
taxidermy ['tæksidɜːmi] n Taxidermie f.
taxi: ~**-driver** n Taxifahrer(in f), Taxichauffeur m; ~ **meter** n Fahrpreisanzeiger, Taxameter (form) m; ~ **plane** n (US) Lufttaxi nt; ~ **rank**, ~ **stand** n Taxistand m.
taxman ['tæksmæn] n Steuer- or Finanzbeamte(r) m. **the** ~ **gets 35%** das Finanzamt bekommt 35%.
taxonomy [tæk'sɒnəmi] n Taxonomie f.
tax: ~**payer** n Steuerzahler m; ~ **rebate** n Steuervergütung or -rückzahlung f; ~ **relief** n Steuervergünstigung f; ~ **relief of 5% ein Steuernachlaß von 5%**; **it qualifies for** ~ **relief** das ist steuerbegünstigt; ~ **return** n Steuererklärung f; ~ **structure** n Steuersystem nt; ~ **system** n Steuerwesen, Steuer- or Besteuerungssystem nt.
TB abbr of tuberculosis Tb, Tbc f.
T-bar ['tiːbaː'] n Bügel m; (lift) Schlepplift m.
T-bone steak ['tiːbəʊn'steik] n T-bone-Steak nt.
tbs(p) abbr of tablespoonful(s), tablespoon(s) Eßl.
TD abbr of touchdown.
T.D. (US) abbr of Treasury Department Fin-Min.
tea [tiː] n **(a)** (substance, drink) Tee m. **to make (the)** ~ (den) Tee machen; **a cup of** ~ eine Tasse Tee; **not for all the** ~ **in China** nicht um alles Gold der Welt.
    (b) (also ~ **plant**) Tee(strauch) m.
    (c) ≈ Kaffee und Kuchen; (meal) Abendbrot nt. **we have** ~ **at five** wir essen um 5 Uhr Abendbrot or zu Abend.
    (d) (infusion of herbs etc) Tee m.
tea: ~ **bag** n Tee- or Aufgußbeutel m; ~ **ball** n (esp US) Tee-Ei nt; ~ **biscuit** n Butterkeks m; ~ **biscuits** npl Teegebäck nt; ~**boy** n Stift m; ~ **break** n Pause f; ~ **caddy** n Teebüchse or -dose f; (dispenser) Teespender m; ~**cake** n Rosinenbrötchen nt; ~ **cart** n (US) Tee- or Serviergwagen m.
teach [tiːtʃ] (vb: pret, ptp **taught**) **1** vt subject, person unterrichten, lehren (geh); animal abrichten. **to** ~ **sth to sb** jdm etw beibringen; (teacher) jdn in etw (dat) unterrichten, jdm Unterricht in etw (dat) geben; **to** ~ **sb to do sth** jdm beibringen, etw zu tun; **this accident taught me to be careful** durch diesen Unfall habe ich gelernt, vorsichtiger zu sein; **you can't** ~ **somebody how to be happy** man kann niemanden lehren, glücklich zu sein; **to** ~ **sb how to do sth** jdm zeigen, wie man etw macht, jdm etw beibringen; **he** ~**es French** er unterrichtet or gibt (inf) or lehrt (geh) Französisch; **who taught you to drive?** bei wem haben Sie Fahren gelernt?; **to** ~ **school** (US) Lehrer(in) sein/werden; **to** ~ **oneself sth** sich (dat) etw beibringen; **let that** ~ **you not to** ... laß dir das eine Lehre sein und ...nicht; **that'll** ~ **him a thing or two!** da werden ihm die Augen aufgehen, da wird er erst mal sehen (inf); **it taught me a thing or two** es war sehr lehrreich, da habe ich einiges gelernt; **that'll** ~ **him!** das hat er nun davon!; **make her pay, that'll** ~ **her** laß sie bezahlen, das wird ihr eine Lehre sein; **that'll** ~ **you to break the speed limit** das hast du (nun) davon, daß du die Geschwindigkeitsbegrenzung überschritten hast; **that'll** ~ **you not to pay your insurance** das hast du nun davon, daß du die Versicherung nicht bezahlt hast, das kommt davon, wenn man die Versicherung nicht bezahlt; **I'll** ~ **you to speak to me like that** ich werde dir schon austreiben (inf) or werde dich lehren, so mit mir zu sprechen!; **you can't** ~ **him anything about that** darüber können Sie ihm nichts Neues mehr erzählen.
    2 vi unterrichten, Unterricht geben. **he wants to** ~ er möchte Lehrer werden; **he can't** ~ (not allowed) er darf nicht unterrichten; (no ability) er hat keine guten Unterricht.
    3 n (sl: teacher: as address) Herr/Frau X.
teachability [ˌtiːtʃə'biliti] n (of pupil) Lernfähigkeit f; (of subject) Lehrbarkeit f.
teachable ['tiːtʃəbl] adj animal, child lernfähig. **music is a very** ~ **subject** Musik ist ein Fach, das sich gut unterrichten or lehren (geh) läßt; **things in life which are not** ~ Dinge, die man niemandem beibringen kann.
teacher ['tiːtʃə'] n Lehrer(in f) m. **university** ~s Hochschullehrer pl, Lehrkräfte pl an (den) Universitäten (form); ~s **of English, English** ~s Englischlehrer pl; **she is a German** ~ sie ist Deutschlehrerin.
teacher-training ['tiːtʃə'treiniŋ] n Lehrer(aus)bildung f; (for primary teachers) Studium nt or Ausbildung f an einer/der pädagogischen Hochschule; (for secondary teachers) Referendarausbildung f. ~ **certificate or qualification** (document) Zeugnis nt über die Prüfung für das Lehramt; **to do a** ~ **certificate or qualification** die Lehrerausbildung machen; **to get a** ~ **certificate** die Lehrbefähigung erhalten; ~ **college** (for

primary teachers) pädagogische Hochschule; (*for secondary teachers*) Studienseminar *nt*.

tea-chest ['ti:tʃest] *n* Kiste *f*.

teach-in ['ti:tʃɪn] *n* Teach-in *nt*.

teaching ['ti:tʃɪŋ] *n* (a) das Unterrichten *or* Lehren (*geh*); (*as profession*) der Lehrberuf. **to take up** ~ den Lehrberuf ergreifen (*form*), Lehrer werden; **she enjoys** ~ sie unterrichtet gern; **he is no good at** ~ er ist kein guter Lehrer.
(b) (*doctrine: also* ~s) Lehre *f*. **his** ~ **on this subject was somewhat vague** seine Ausführungen zu diesem Thema waren ziemlich vage.

teaching: ~ **aid** *n* Lehr- *or* Unterrichtsmittel *nt*; ~ **hospital** *n* Ausbildungskrankenhaus *nt*; ~ **machine** *n* Lernmaschine *f*, Lehrmittel *nt* für den programmierten Unterricht; ~ **profession** *n* Lehrberuf *m*; (*all teachers*) Lehrer *pl*; ~ **staff** *n* Lehrerkollegium *nt*, Lehrkörper *m* (*form*).

tea: ~ **cloth** *n* Geschirrtuch *nt*; ~ **cosy** *n* Teewärmer *m*; ~**cup** *n* (a) Teetasse *f*; *see* storm 1(a); (b) (*also* ~**cupful**) Tasse *f* (voll); ~ **dance** *n* Tanztee *m*; ~ **garden** *n* Gartencafé *nt*; ~**house** *n* Teehaus *nt*.

teak [ti:k] *n* (*wood*) Teak(holz) *nt*; (*tree*) Teakbaum *m*.

tea-kettle ['ti:ketl] *n* Wasserkessel *m*.

teal [ti:l] *n, pl* - Krickente *f*.

tea: ~ **lady** *n* Frau, die in Büros etc für die Angestellten Tee zubereitet; ~**leaf** *n* (a) Teeblatt *nt*; *see* read¹ 1 (b); (b) (*Brit sl: thief*) Langfinger *m* (*inf*).

team [ti:m] 1 *n* (a) Team *nt*; (*Sport also*) Mannschaft *f*. **football** ~ Fußballmannschaft *or* -elf *f*; **they work as a** ~ sie arbeiten im *or* als Team; **they make a good** ~ sie sind ein gutes Team *or* (*two also*) Gespann, sie arbeiten gut zusammen; **research** ~ Forschungsgruppe *or* -gemeinschaft *f or* -team *nt*; **a** ~ **of scientists** eine Gruppe *or* ein Team *nt* von Wissenschaftlern.
(b) (*of horses, oxen etc*) Gespann *nt*.
2 *vt horses, oxen* zusammenspannen; (*fig*) zusammentun.

♦ **team up** *vi* (*people*) sich zusammentun (*with* mit); (*join group*) sich anschließen (*with sb* jdm, an jdn). **I see that John and Mary have** ~**ed** ~ John und Mary gehen jetzt (anscheinend) miteinander (*inf*).

team: ~ **effort** *n* Teamarbeit *f*; ~ **game** *n* Mannschaftsspiel *nt*; ~**-mate** *n* Mannschaftskamerad *m*; ~ **spirit** *n* Gemeinschaftsgeist *m*; (*Sport*) Mannschaftsgeist *m*.

teamster ['ti:mstə*r*] *n* (a) (*US: truck driver*) Lastwagenfahrer, LKW- Fahrer *m*. (b) (*old Agr*) Fuhrmann *m*.

teamwork ['ti:mwɜ:k] *n* Gemeinschaftsarbeit, Teamarbeit *f*, Teamwork *nt*.

tea: ~ **party** *n* Teegesellschaft *f*; ~**pot** *n* Teekanne *f*.

tear¹ [teə*r*] (*vb: pret* **tore**, *ptp* **torn**) 1 *vt* (a) *material, paper, dress* zerreißen; *flesh* verletzen, aufreißen; *hole* reißen. **I've torn a muscle** ich habe mir einen Muskel gezerrt; **the nail tore a gash in his arm** er hat sich (*dat*) an dem Nagel eine tiefe Wunde am Arm beigebracht; **to** ~ **sth in two** etw (in zwei Stücke *or* Hälften) zerreißen, etw in der Mitte durchreißen; **to** ~ **sth to pieces** etw in Stücke reißen; **the critics tore the play to pieces** die Kritiker haben das Stück total verrissen; **his reputation was torn to shreds by his critics** die Kritiker ließen keinen guten Faden an ihm; **clothes torn to rags** völlig zerrissene Kleidung; **to** ~ **sth open** etw aufreißen; **that's torn it!** (*fig inf*) das hat alles verdorben!
(b) (*pull away*) **the wind tore the tent from the pole** der Wind riß das Zelt von der Stange; **her child was torn from her/her arms** das Kind wurde ihr entrissen/ihr aus den Armen gerissen; **he tore it out of my hand** er riß es mir aus der Hand; **he was torn from his seat** er wurde vom Stuhl gerissen *or* geschleudert; **to** ~ **one's hair (out)** sich (*dat*) die Haare raufen.
(c) (*fig: usu pass*) **country torn by war** ein vom Krieg zerrissenes Land; **a heart torn with remorse** ein von Reue gequältes Herz; **to be torn between two things/people** zwischen zwei Dingen/Menschen hin- und hergerissen sein; **she was completely torn** sie war innerlich zerrissen.
2 *vi* (a) (*material etc*) (zer)reißen. **her coat tore on a nail** sie zerriß sich (*dat*) den Mantel an einem Nagel; ~ **along the dotted line** an der gestrichelten Linie abtrennen.
(b) (*move quickly*) rasen. **to** ~ **past** vorbeirasen.
3 *n* (*in material etc*) Riß *m*.

♦ **tear along** *vi* entlangrasen. **he tore** ~ **the street** er raste die Straße entlang *or* hinunter.

♦ **tear apart** *vt sep place, house* völlig durcheinanderbringen; *meat, flesh, zebra, country* zerreißen.

♦ **tear at** *vi +prep obj* zerren an (+*dat*). **he tore** ~ **the walls of his cell** er verkrallte sich in die Wände seiner Zelle; **the thorns tore** ~ **her hands** die Dornen zerkratzten ihr die Hände; **the waves tore** ~ **the cliffs** die Wellen peitschten gegen die Klippen.

♦ **tear away** 1 *vi* davonrasen.
2 *vt sep wrapping* abreißen, wegreißen (*from* von). **to** ~ ~ **sb's mask** jdm die Maske vom Gesicht reißen; **to** ~ **sth** ~ **from sb** jdm etw wegreißen *or* entreißen (*geh*); **if you can** ~ **yourself** ~ **from the paper** wenn du dich von der Zeitung losreißen kannst; **if you can** ~ **him** ~ **from the party** wenn du ihn von der Party wegkriegen *or* loseisen kannst (*inf*).

♦ **tear down** 1 *vi* hinunter-/herunterrasen (*prep obj* acc). 2 *vt sep poster* herunterreißen; *house* abreißen, abbrechen.

♦ **tear into** *vi +prep obj* (a) (*shell, rocket*) ein Loch reißen in (+*acc*); (*animals*) *deer etc* zerfleischen; *meat* sich hermachen über (+*acc*); (*person*) *food* sich hermachen über (+*acc*); (*saw*) *wood* sich fressen durch.
(b) (*attack physically*) herfallen über (+*acc*).
(c) (*attack verbally*) abkanzeln, zur Schnecke machen (*inf*); (*critic*) keinen guten Faden lassen an (+*dat*).

♦ **tear off** 1 *vi* (a) wegrasen. **he tore** ~ **down the street** er raste die Straße hinunter.
(b) **the carbon** ~**s** ~ die Durchschrift läßt sich abtrennen.

2 *vt sep label, wrapping, calendar leaf* abreißen; *cover* wegreißen; *clothes* herunterreißen. **please** ~ ~ **this part and complete** bitte hier abtrennen und ausfüllen; **he tore a strip** ~ **me** (*inf*), **he tore me** ~ **a strip** (*inf*) er hat mich zur Minna *or* Schnecke gemacht (*inf*).

♦ **tear out** 1 *vi* heraus-/hinausrasen, wegrasen. **he tore** ~ **through the front door** er raste *or* rannte zur Vordertür hinaus.
2 *vt sep* (her)ausreißen (*of* aus). **the tree was torn** ~ **by the roots** der Baum wurde entwurzelt.

♦ **tear up** 1 *vi* angerast kommen. **he tore** ~ **the hill/road** er raste den Berg hinauf/die Straße entlang.
2 *vt sep* (a) *paper etc* zerreißen.
(b) (*fig: cancel*) *contract, agreement* zerreißen.
(c) (*pull from ground*) *post, stake, plant* (her)ausreißen.
(d) (*break surface of ground*) aufwühlen; *road* aufreißen.

tear² [tɪə*r*] *n* Träne *f*. **in** ~**s** in Tränen aufgelöst; **wet with** ~**s** tränenfeucht; **there were** ~**s in her eyes** ihr standen Tränen in den Augen; **the news brought** ~**s to her eyes** als sie das hörte, stiegen ihr die Tränen in die Augen; **you are bringing** ~**s to my eyes** (*iro*) mir kommen die Tränen (*iro*); **the** ~**s were running down her cheeks** ihr Gesicht war tränenüberströmt; **smiling bravely through her** ~**s** unter Tränen tapfer lächelnd; **to laugh till the** ~**s come** Tränen lachen; **to weep** ~**s of joy** Freudentränen weinen *or* vergießen; *see* shed¹, burst.

tearaway ['teərəweɪ] *n* (*inf*) Rabauke *m* (*inf*). **I used to be a bit of a** ~ ich war ein ziemlicher Rabauke.

tear drop *n* Träne *f*.

tearful ['tɪəful] *adj look* tränenfeucht; *face* tränenüberströmt. **there were a few** ~ **moments** es gab ein paar tränenvolle Augenblicke; ..., **she said in a** ~ **voice** ..., sagte sie unter Tränen.

tearfully ['tɪəfəlɪ] *adv look* mit Tränen in den Augen; *say* unter Tränen.

teargas ['tɪəgæs] *n* Tränengas *nt*.

tearing ['teərɪŋ] *adj* (*inf*): **to be in a** ~ **hurry** es fürchterlich *or* schrecklich eilig haben.

tear: ~**-jerker** *n* (*inf*) Tränendrüsendrücker *m* (*inf*); **to be a** ~**-jerker** auf die Tränendrüsen drücken (*inf*); ~**-jerking** *adj* (*inf*) der/die/das auf die Tränendrüsen drückt (*inf*).

tearoff ['teərɒf] *adj sheet, form* zum Abtrennen *or* Abreißen. ~ **calendar** Abreißkalender *m*.

tea: ~**room** *n* Teestube *f*, Café *nt*; ~**-rose** *n* Teerose *f*.

tear-stained ['tɪəsteɪnd] *adj face* verweint, verheult (*pej inf*), tränenverschmiert; *pillow, handkerchief* naßgeweint.

tease [ti:z] 1 *vt* (a) *person* necken; *animal* reizen, quälen; (*make fun of, because of stutter etc*) aufziehen, hänseln (*about* wegen); (*pull leg, have on*) auf den Arm nehmen (*inf*), veralbern (*inf*). **a problem to** ~ **your brain** ein Problem, an dem Sie sich die Zähne ausbeißen können.
(b) *see* tease out (a).
(c) (*raise nap on*) *cloth* kämmen.
(d) (*backcomb*) *hair* toupieren.
(e) (*ease gently*) **he** ~**d the red into the pocket/the rope through the crack** er manipulierte die rote Kugel ins Loch/schob das Seil geschickt durch den Spalt.
2 *vi* (a) **give it back to her, don't** ~ gib es ihr zurück und neck sie nicht; **I'm only teasing** ich mache nur Spaß.
(b) (*joke*) Spaß machen.
3 *n* (*inf: person*) Schäker(in *f*) *m* (*inf*). **don't be a** ~, **give it back to her** neck sie nicht, gib's ihr zurück; **he's a real** ~ ihm sitzt der Schalk im Nacken (*hum*), er ist ein kleiner Schäker (*inf*); **she's just a** ~ sie foppt einen nur.

♦ **tease out** *vt sep* (a) *fibres* kardieren, karden; *wool* krempeln, kämmen; *flax* hecheln; *tangles* auskämmen.
(b) (*fig*) *significant factors etc* herausdestillieren. **to** ~ **sth** ~ **of sth** etw aus etw herauspusseln (*inf*); **he managed to** ~ **the information** ~ **of her** er hat ihr die Auskunft abgelockt.

teasel ['ti:zl] *n* (a) (*Bot*) Karde *f*. (b) (*Tech*) Karde, Krempel *f*.

teaser ['ti:zə*r*] *n* (a) (*difficult question*) harte Nuß (*inf*); (*riddle*) Denksportaufgabe, Knacknuß (*inf*) *f*. (b) (*person*) Schelm, Schäker(in *f*) *m* (*inf*). **don't be such a** ~, **tell me** neck mich nicht so, sag's schon; **he's a real** ~ ihm sitzt der Schalk im Nacken; **she's just a** ~ sie foppt einen nur.

tea: ~ **service**, ~ **set** *n* Teeservice *nt*; ~ **shop** *n* Teestube *f*.

teasing ['ti:zɪŋ] 1 *adj voice, manner* neckend; (*making fun*) hänselnd. 2 *n see vt* (a) Neckerei *f*; Reizen *nt*, Quälerei *f*; Hänselei *f*; Veralbern *nt*.

teasingly ['ti:zɪŋlɪ] *adv see adj*.

tea: ~**spoon** *n* (a) Teelöffel *m*; (b) (*also* ~**spoonful**) Teelöffel *m* (voll); ~ **strainer** *n* Teesieb *nt*.

teat [ti:t] *n* (*of animal*) Zitze *f*; (*of woman*) Brustwarze *f*; (*Brit: on baby's bottle*) (Gummi)sauger *m*.

tea: ~ **table** *n* **to lay the** ~ **table** dem Tisch zum Tee/fürs Abendessen decken; **at the** ~ **table** beim Tee/Abendessen; ~**time** *n* **when is** ~**time in your family?** wann trinkt Ihr Tee/eßt Ihr zu Abend?; **we'll talk about it at** ~**time** wir werden uns beim Tee/Abendessen darüber unterhalten; **I'll meet you at** ~**time** ich treffe Sie am späten Nachmittag; ~ **towel** *n* Geschirrtuch *nt*; ~ **tray** *n* Tablett, Teebrett *nt*; ~ **trolley** *n* Tee- *or* Servierwagen *m*; ~ **urn** *n* Teemaschine *f*; ~**-wagon** *n* (*US*) Tee- *or* Servierwagen *m*.

teazel *n see* teasel.

tech [tek] (*Brit*) *abbr of* **technical college**.

technical ['teknɪkəl] *adj* (a) (*concerning technology and technique*) technisch. ~ **hitch** technische Schwierigkeit, technisches Problem; ~ **school** Gewerbeschule, Fachshule *f*.
(b) (*of particular branch*) fachlich, Fach-; *adviser, journal, dictionary* Fach-; *problems, vocabulary* fachspezifisch; *details* formal. ~ **term** Fachausdruck, Terminus technicus *m* (*geh*); ~ **terminology** Fachsprache *f*; ~ **question** (*Jur*) Verfahrensfrage *f*; **for** ~ **reasons** (*Jur*) aus verfahrenstechnischen Gründen; **the book is a bit too** ~ **for me** in dem Buch sind mir zu

viele Fachausdrücke; **he uses very ~ language** er benutzt sehr viele Fachausdrücke; **am I getting too ~ for you?** benutze ich zu viele Fachausdrücke?; **a 2L 54, if you want to be ~** ein 2L 54, um den Fachausdruck zu gebrauchen; **that's true, if you want to be ~** das stimmt schon, wenn man's genau nimmt.

technical: ~ **college** n (Brit) Technische Fachschule; ~ **defeat** n (Mil) rein formale Niederlage.

technicality [ˌteknɪˈkælɪtɪ] n **(a)** no pl **the** ~ **of the** language/terms die Fülle von Fachausdrücken; **avoid** ~ vermeiden Sie Fachjargon; **the** ~ **of his style** (complex style) die formale Komplexität seines Stils; (technical terms) sein Fachjargon m (pej), seine Fachterminologie. **(b)** (technical detail, difficulty) technische Einzelheit; (fig, Jur) Formsache f. **because of a** ~ auf Grund einer Formsache; **that's just a** ~ das ist bloß ein Detail.

technical knockout n (Boxing) technischer K.o.

technically [ˈteknɪkəlɪ] adv **(a)** technisch. **(b)** (concerned with specialist field) vom Fachlichen her gesehen. **he spoke very** ~ er benutzte sehr viele Fachausdrücke. **(c)** (strictly speaking) ~ **you're right** genau genommen haben Sie recht.

technical: ~ **offence** n Verstoß m; ~ **sergeant** n (US) Oberfeldwebel m.

technician [tekˈnɪʃən] n Techniker(in f) m; (skilled worker) Facharbeiter(in f) m.

Technicolor ® [ˈteknɪˌkʌlər] n Technicolor nt.

technique [tekˈniːk] n Technik f; (method) Methode f.

technocracy [tekˈnɒkrəsɪ] n Technokratie f.

technocrat [ˈteknəʊkræt] n Technokrat(in f) m.

technocratic [ˌteknəʊˈkrætɪk] adj technokratisch.

technological [ˌteknəˈlɒdʒɪkəl] adj technologisch; details, information technisch.

technologist [tekˈnɒlədʒɪst] n Technologe m, Technologin f.

technology [tekˈnɒlədʒɪ] n Technologie f. **the** ~ **of printing** die Technik des Druckens, die Drucktechnik; **University/College of T~** Technische Universität/Fachschule; **the age of** ~ das technische Zeitalter, das Zeitalter der Technik.

techy adj see **tetchy.**

tectonics [tekˈtɒnɪks] n sing (Geol) Tektonik f.

Ted [ted] n dim of **Edward.**

ted [ted] n (dated Brit sl) Halbstarke(r) m.

tedder [ˈtedər] n Heuwender m.

Teddy [ˈtedɪ] n dim of **Edward.**

teddy (bear) [ˈtedɪ(ˌbeər)] n Teddy(bär) m.

teddy boy n Halbstarke(r) m; (referring to style of dress) Teddy-Boy m.

tedious [ˈtiːdɪəs] adj langweilig, öde.

tediously [ˈtiːdɪəslɪ] adv langweilig. **a** ~ **long journey** eine lange und langweilige Reise; **he talked** ~ **on and on** er erging sich in langweiligen Reden.

tediousness [ˈtiːdɪəsnɪs] n Lang(e)weile f. **his** ~ seine Langweiligkeit.

tedium [ˈtiːdɪəm] n Lang(e)weile f.

tee[1] [tiː] (Golf) **1** n Tee nt. **2** vt **ball** auf das Tee legen.

♦**tee off** vi einen Ball vom (ersten) Abschlag spielen.

♦**tee up** vi den Ball auf das Tee legen, aufteen (spec). **2** vt sep auf das Tee legen.

tee[2] n see **T.**

tee-hee [ˈtiːˈhiː] interj (giggle) hihi; (snigger) ätsch.

teem [tiːm] vi **(a)** (with people, insects etc) wimmeln (with von); (with mistakes, information etc) strotzen (with vor). **he/his mind was** ~**ing with ideas** er strotzte nur so von Ideen/in seinem Kopf wimmelte es nur so von Ideen. **(b)** (of rain: pour) **it's** ~**ing (with rain)** es regnet or gießt (inf) in Strömen; **the rain** ~**ed down** es regnete in Strömen; **he watched the rain** ~**ing down** er sah zu, wie der Regen vom Himmel strömte.

teeming [ˈtiːmɪŋ] adj **(a)** streets von Menschen wimmelnd; crowd wuselnd. **the world's** ~ **millions** die Millionen und Abermillionen von Menschen (auf der Erde). **(b)** (pouring) rain strömend.

teenage [ˈtiːnˌeɪdʒ] adj Jugend-, Teenager-; child, son halbwüchsig.

teenager [ˈtiːnˌeɪdʒər] n Junge m/Mädchen nt im Teenageralter; (esp girl) Teenager m. ~**s** Teenager pl; **now that you're a** ~ **... jetzt,** wo du 13 (Jahre alt) bist ...

teens [tiːnz] npl (age) Teenageralter nt. **to be in/reach one's** ~ im Teenageralter sein/ins Teenageralter kommen; **he is barely out of/still in his** ~ er ist knapp über/noch keine zwanzig (Jahre alt). **(b)** (inf: teenagers) Teenager pl.

teeny-bopper [ˈtiːnɪˌbɒpər] n Teenager m; (girl also) Pipimädchen nt (pej inf).

teeny(weeny) [ˈtiːnɪ(ˈwiːnɪ)] adj (inf) winzig (klein), klitzeklein (inf). **just a** ~ **drop** nur ein ganz klein wenig.

tee-shirt n see **T-shirt.**

teeter [ˈtiːtər] vi **(a)** taumeln, schwanken. **to** ~ **on the brink or edge of sth** (lit) am Rand von etw taumeln; (fig) am Rand von etw sein. **(b)** (US: seesaw) wippen, schaukeln.

teeterboard [ˈtiːtəˌbɔːd] n, **teeter-totter** [ˈtiːtəˌtɒtər] n (US) Wippe f.

teeth [tiːθ] pl of **tooth.**

teethe [tiːð] vi zahnen.

teething [ˈtiːðɪŋ] n Zahnen nt.

teething: ~ **ring** n Beißring m; ~ **troubles** npl (fig) Kinderkrankheiten pl.

teetotal [ˈtiːˈtəʊtl] adj person abstinent; party etc ohne Alkohol. **to be** ~ (grundsätzlich) keinen Alkohol trinken, abstinent sein.

teetotaler n (US) see **teetotaller.**

teetotalism [ˈtiːˈtəʊtəlɪzəm] n Abstinenz f.

teetotaller, (US) **teetotaler** [ˈtiːˈtəʊtlər] n Abstinenzler(in f), Nichttrinker(in f) m.

Teflon ® [ˈteflɒn] n Teflon ® nt.

tel abbr of **telephone (number)** Tel.

telecast [ˈtelɪkɑːst] **1** n Fernsehsendung f. **2** vt im Fernsehen übertragen or senden.

telecaster [ˈtelɪkɑːstər] n Fernsehjournalist(in f) m.

telecommunications [ˌtelɪkəˌmjuːnɪˈkeɪʃənz] n **(a)** pl Fernmeldewesen nt. **(b)** sing (science) Fernmeldetechnik f.

telegram [ˈtelɪɡræm] n Telegramm nt. **2** vti telegraphieren.

telegrammatic [ˌtelɪɡrəˈmætɪk] adj im Telegrammstil.

telegraph [ˈtelɪɡrɑːf] **1** n **(a)** (apparatus) Telegraph m. **(b)** (message) Telegramm nt. **2** vt telegraphisch übermitteln; message also telegraphieren; person telegraphieren (+dat). **3** vi telegraphieren.

telegraph boy n Telegrammbote m.

telegraphese [ˌtelɪɡrɑːˈfiːz] n Telegrammstil m.

telegraphic [ˌtelɪˈɡræfɪk] adj telegraphisch; address, style Telegramm-.

telegraphist [tɪˈleɡrəfɪst] n Telegraphist(in f) m.

telegraph: ~ **pole** n Telegraphenmast m or -stange f; ~ **wire** n Telegraphendraht m or -leitung f; (under ground) Telegraphenkabel nt.

telegraphy [tɪˈleɡrəfɪ] n Telegraphie f.

telekinesis [ˌtelɪkɪˈniːsɪs] n Telekinese f.

telemeter [ˈtelɪmiːtər] n Entfernungsmesser m, Telemeter nt.

telemetry [teˈlemɪtrɪ] n Telemetrie, Fernmessung f.

teleological [ˌtelɪəˈlɒdʒɪkl] adj teleologisch.

teleology [ˌtelɪˈɒlədʒɪ] n Teleologie f.

telepathic [ˌtelɪˈpæθɪk] adj telepathisch. **you must be** ~**!** du mußt ja ein Hellseher sein!

telepathically [ˌtelɪˈpæθɪkəlɪ] adv see adj.

telepathist [tɪˈlepəθɪst] n Telepath(in f) m; (believer in telepathy) Telepathiegläubige(r) mf.

telepathy [tɪˈlepəθɪ] n Telepathie f.

telephone [ˈtelɪfəʊn] **1** n Telefon nt, Fernsprecher (form) m; (apparatus also) Telefonapparat, Fernsprechapparat (form) m. **there's somebody on the** ~ **for you, you're wanted on the** ~ Sie werden am Telefon verlangt; **are you on the** ~?, **have you got a** ~? haben Sie Telefon?; (can you be reached by ~) sind Sie telefonisch zu erreichen?; **he's on the** ~ (is using the ~) er telefoniert gerade; (wants to speak to you) er ist am Telefon; **by** ~ telefonisch; **I've just been/I'll get on the** ~ **to him** ich habe eben mit ihm telefoniert/ich werde ihn anrufen; **we arranged it by** ~ or over the ~ wir haben es telefonisch vereinbart; **I heard a strange noise down the** ~ ich hörte ein merkwürdiges Geräusch im Telefon.

2 vt anrufen; message, reply telefonisch mitteilen or übermitteln. **he** ~**d the news (through) to his news-paper** er rief seine Mutter an, um ihr die Nachricht mitzuteilen/er gab die Nachricht telefonisch an die Zeitung durch; **would you** ~ **the office to say ...** würden Sie im Büro or das Büro anrufen und sagen ...

3 vi anrufen, telefonieren; (make ~ call) telefonieren. **he** ~**d with the good news** er hat angerufen or telefoniert und die gute Nachricht mitgeteilt; **to** ~ **for an ambulance/a taxi** einen Krankenwagen/ein Taxi rufen.

♦**telephone back** vti (vt: always separate) see **phone back.**

♦**telephone in** vti see **phone in.**

telephone in cpds Telefon-, Fernsprech- (form); ~**book** n see ~ **directory;** ~ **booth** or **box** n Telefonzelle, Fernsprechzelle f; ~ **call** n Telefongespräch nt, Telefonanruf m; ~ **directory** n Telefonbuch, Fernsprechbuch nt; ~ **exchange** n Fernsprechamt nt, Vermittlungsstelle f (form); ~ **kiosk** n Telefonzelle, Sprechzelle (form) f; ~ **line** n Fernsprechleitung, (Telefon)leitung f; ~ **message** n telefonische Nachricht; ~ **number** n Telefonnummer, Rufnummer (form), Fernsprechnummer (form) f; ~ **operator** n (esp US) Telefonist(in f) m.

telephonic [ˌtelɪˈfɒnɪk] adj telefonisch, Telefon-.

telephonically [ˌtelɪˈfɒnɪkəlɪ] adv fernsprechtechnisch; (by telephone) telefonisch.

telephonist [tɪˈlefənɪst] n Telefonist(in f) m.

telephony [tɪˈlefənɪ] n Fernsprechwesen nt.

telephotograph [ˌtelɪˈfəʊtəɡrɑːf] n (Telec) durch Bildtelegraphie übertragenes Photo.

telephoto (lens) [ˈtelɪˌfəʊtəʊ(ˈlenz)] n Teleobjektiv nt.

teleprinter [ˈtelɪˌprɪntər] n Fernschreiber m.

teleprompter ® [ˈtelɪˌprɒmptər] n Teleprompter m.

telerecord [ˌtelɪrɪˈkɔːd] vt fürs Fernsehen aufzeichnen.

telerecording [ˌtelɪrɪˈkɔːdɪŋ] n Fernsehaufzeichnung f.

telescope [ˈtelɪskəʊp] **1** n Teleskop, Fernrohr nt. **2** vi (also ~ **together**) (train carriages) sich ineinanderschieben; (aerial, umbrella) sich ineinanderschieben lassen. **3** vt (also ~ **together**) ineinanderschieben; umbrella, aerial zusammenschieben; (fig) komprimieren.

telescopic [ˌtelɪˈskɒpɪk] adj aerial etc ausziehbar, zusammenschiebbar; view teleskopisch. ~ **lens** Fernrohrlinse f; ~ **sight** Zielfernrohr nt; ~ **umbrella** Taschenschirm, Knirps ® m.

teletype ® [ˈtelɪtaɪp] n (US) (apparatus) Fernschreiber m; (message) Fernschreiben, Telex nt.

teletypewriter [ˌtelɪˈtaɪpraɪtər] n (US) Fernschreiber m.

televise [ˈtelɪvaɪz] vt (im Fernsehen) senden or übertragen.

television [ˈtelɪˌvɪʒən] n Fernsehen nt; (set) Fernseher, Fernsehapparat m. **to watch** ~ fernsehen; **to be on** ~ im Fernsehen sein; **what's on** ~ **tonight?** was gibt es heute abend im Fernsehen?; **jobs in** ~ Stellen pl beim Fernsehen.

television in cpds Fernseh-; ~ **camera** n Fernsehkamera f; ~ **personality** n bekannte Fernsehpersönlichkeit; ~ **screen** n Bildschirm m, Mattscheibe f (inf); ~ **set** n Fernsehapparat m, Fernsehgerät nt, Fernseher m; ~ **studio** n Fernsehstudio nt; ~ **viewer** n Fernsehzuschauer(in f) m.

telex [ˈteleks] **1** n (message) Fernschreiben, Telex nt; (machine) Fernschreiber m. **2** vt message über Fernschreiber *or* fernschriftlich mitteilen; *person* ein Fernschreiben *or* Telex schicken (+*dat*).

tell [tel] *pret, ptp* **told 1** *vt* **(a)** (*relate*) *story, experiences, adventures* erzählen (*sb sth, sth to sb* jdm etw *acc*); (*inform, say, announce*) sagen (*sb sth* jdm etw *acc*). **to ~ lies/tales/fortunes** lügen/petzen (*inf*)/wahrsagen; **to ~ sb's fortune** jdm wahrsagen *or* die Zukunft deuten; **to ~ the future** wahrsagen, die Zukunft deuten; **to ~ sb a secret** jdm ein Geheimnis anvertrauen *or* (*give away*) verraten; **to ~ sb about** *or* **of sth** jdm von etw erzählen; **I told my friend/boss about what had happened** ich erzählte meinem Freund/berichtete meinem Chef, was geschehen war; **... or so I've been told** ... so hat man es mir jedenfalls gesagt *or* erzählt; **I can't ~ you how pleased I am** ich kann Ihnen gar nicht sagen, wie sehr ich mich freue; **who told you that?** wer hat Ihnen denn das erzählt *or* gesagt?; **you can't ~ her anything** (*she can't keep a secret*) man kann ihr (aber auch) nichts sagen *or* anvertrauen; (*she's a know-all*) sie läßt sich (*dat*) nichts sagen; **to ~ sb the way** jdm den Weg sagen; **could you ~ me the way to the station, please?** könn(t)en Sie mir bitte sagen, wie ich zum Bahnhof komme?; **don't let me have to ~ you that again** ich will dir das nicht noch einmal sagen müssen; (**I'll**) **~ you what, let's go to the cinema** weißt du was, gehen wir doch ins Kino!; **don't~ me you can't come!** sagen Sie bloß nicht, daß Sie nicht kommen können!; **I won't do it, I ~ you!** und ich sage dir, das mache ich nicht!; **let me ~ you that ...** ich kann Ihnen sagen, daß ..., lassen Sie sich von mir sagen, daß ...; **it makes me ~ you** ich kann Ihnen dir sagen, das war vielleicht kalt!; **I told you so** ich habe es (dir) ja gesagt; **~ me another!** nicht möglich!, wer's glaubt! (*inf*); **that ~s me all I need to know** das sagt mir alles; **that ~s me a lot** das sagt mir allerlei; **no words could ~ how sad she was** es läßt sich nicht mit Worten sagen, wie traurig sie war.

(b) (*distinguish, discern*) erkennen. **to ~ the time** die Uhr kennen; **to ~ the time by the sun/stars** die Zeit an der Sonne/den Sternen ablesen; **to ~ the difference** den Unterschied sehen/fühlen/schmecken *etc*; **you can ~ that he's clever/a foreigner/getting worried** man sieht *or* merkt, daß er intelligent ist/Ausländer ist/sich Sorgen macht; **we couldn't ~ much from his letter** wir konnten aus seinem Brief nicht viel entnehmen; **you can't ~ whether it's moving** man kann nicht sagen *or* sehen, ob es sich bewegt; **to ~ sb/sth by sth** jdn/etw an etw (*dat*) erkennen; **I can't ~ butter from margarine** ich kann Butter nicht von Margarine unterscheiden; **to ~ right from wrong** wissen, was Recht und Unrecht ist, Recht von Unrecht unterscheiden; *see* **apart**.

(c) (*know, be sure*) wissen. **how can/could I ~ that?** wie soll ich das wissen?/wie hätte ich das wissen können?; **how can I ~ that/whether he will do it?** wie kann ich sicher sein, daß er es tut?/wie kann ich sagen *or* wissen, ob er es tut?

(d) (*order*) sagen (*sb* jdm). **we were told to bring sandwiches with us** es wurde uns gesagt, daß wir belegte Brote mitbringen sollten; **~ him to stop singing** sagen Sie ihm, er soll aufhören zu singen; **don't you ~ me what to do!** Sie haben mir nicht zu sagen, was ich tun soll!; **I told you not to do that** ich habe dir doch gesagt, du sollst das nicht tun!; **do as** *or* **what you are told!** tu, was man dir sagt!

(e) (*old: count*) **to ~ one's beads** den Rosenkranz beten.

2 *vi* +*indir obj* es sagen (+*dat*). **I won't ~ you again** ich sage es dir nicht noch einmal; **you know what?** — **don't ~, let me guess** weißt du was? — sag's mir nicht, laß mich raten; **she wouldn't be told** sie hat sich (ja) nichts sagen lassen; **you're ~ing me!** das kann man wohl sagen!, wem sagen Sie das!

3 *vi* **(a)** (*discern, be sure*) wissen. **who can ~?** wer weiß?; **how can I ~?** (*how should I know*) woher soll ich das wissen?; **how will I be able to ~?** wie kann ich das erkennen *or* wissen?; **no-one can/could ~** niemand kann/konnte das sagen, das weiß/wußte keiner; **you never can ~, you can never ~** man kann nie wissen.

(b) (*talk, ~ tales of*) sprechen. **his face told of his sorrow** aus seinem Gesicht sprach Kummer; **that would be ~ing!** das kann ich nicht verraten; **promise you won't ~** du mußt versprechen, daß du nichts sagst; **his cruelty hurt me more than words can ~** seine Grausamkeit hat mich mehr verletzt, als ich mit Worten ausdrücken kann.

(c) (*have effect*) sich bemerkbar machen. **his age told against him** (*in applying for job*) sein Alter war ein Nachteil für ihn; (*in competition*) sein Alter machte sich bemerkbar; **character always ~s in the end** zum Schluß schlägt doch die Veranlagung durch; **a boxer who makes every punch ~** ein Boxer, bei dem jeder Schlag sitzt; **you could see from the look in his eyes that the criticism had told** man konnte an seinem Blick sehen, daß ihn die Kritik getroffen hatte.

♦**tell off** *vt sep* **(a)** (*inf: scold*) schimpfen, schelten (*for* wegen). **he told me ~ for being late** er schimpfte (mich aus), weil ich zu spät kam. **(b)** (*Mil etc*) abkommandieren (*for* zu).

♦**tell on** *vi* +*prep obj* **(a)** (*inf: inform on*) verpetzen (*inf*). **(b)** (*have a bad effect on*) sich bemerkbar machen bei.

teller ['telə^r] *n* **(a)** (*in bank*) Kassierer(in *f*) *m*. **(b)** (*vote counter*) Stimmenauszähler(in *f*) *m*. **(c)** (*of story*) Erzähler(in *f*) *m*.

telling ['telɪŋ] **1** *adj* (*effective*) wirkungsvoll; *argument also* schlagend; *blow* (*lit, fig*) empfindlich; (*revealing*) aufschlußreich; *blush* verräterisch.

2 *n* **(a)** (*narration*) Erzählen *nt*. **it loses in the ~** das kann man gar nicht so schön erzählen.

(b) **there is no ~ what he may do** man kann nicht sagen *or* wissen, was er tut; **there's no ~** das läßt sich nicht sagen; **there's never any ~ with him** bei ihm läßt sich nie sagen.

telling-off ['telɪŋ'ɒf] *n* (*inf*) Standpauke *f* (*inf*). **to give sb a good ~** jdn kräftig ausschimpfen, jdm eine (kräftige) Standpauke halten (*inf*); **to get a good ~** kräftig ausgeschimpft werden, eine Standpauke bekommen (*inf*).

telltale ['telteɪl] **1** *n* **(a)** Petzer *m*, Petze *f*. **(b)** (*Tech*) Kontrollicht *nt*, Kontrollampe *f*. **2** *adj attr* verräterisch.

telly ['telɪ] *n* (*Brit inf*) Fernseher *m*, Röhre *f* (*inf*). **on ~** im Fernsehen; **to watch ~** fernsehen; *see also* **television**.

temerity [tɪ'merɪtɪ] *n* Kühnheit, Unerhörtheit (*pej*) *f*.

temp[1] *abbr of* **(a)** **temporary**. **(b)** **temperature** Temp.

temp[2] [temp] (*Brit*) **1** *n* Aushilfssekretärin *f*. **2** *vi* als Aushilfssekretärin arbeiten.

temper ['tempə^r] **1** *n* **(a)** (*disposition*) Wesen, Naturell *nt*; (*angry mood*) Wut *f*. **~ tantrum** Wutanfall *m*; **to be in a ~/good/bad ~** wütend sein/guter/schlechter Laune sein; **she's got a quick/terrible/foul/vicious ~** sie kann sehr jähzornig sein/unangenehm/ausfallend/tückisch werden; **what a ~ that child has!** was dieses Kind für Wutanfälle hat!; **to be in a ~/bad ~** with sb auf jdn wütend sein; **to lose one's ~** die Beherrschung verlieren (*with sb* bei jdm); **to keep one's ~** sich beherrschen (*with sb* bei jdm); **~, ~!** aber, aber, wer wird denn gleich so zornig werden!; **to fly into a ~** einen Wutanfall bekommen, in die Luft gehen (*inf*); **a fit of ~** ein Wutanfall *m*; **to put sb into a ~,** **to get sb's ~ up** jdn zur Weißglut bringen, jdn wütend machen; **he has quite a ~** er kann ziemlich aufbrausen; **to be out of ~** (*old*) verstimmt *or* übel gelaunt sein.

(b) (*of metal*) Härte(grad *m*) *f*.

2 *vt* **(a)** *metal* tempern.

(b) (*old: Mus*) *instrument* temperieren (*old*).

(c) (*fig*) *action, passion* mäßigen; *criticism* mildern. **to ~ justice with mercy** bei aller Gerechtigkeit Milde walten lassen.

tempera ['tempərə] *n* Temperafarbe *f*. **to paint in ~** in Tempera malen.

temperament ['tempərəmənt] *n* **(a)** (*disposition*) Veranlagung *f*; (*of race*) Temperament *nt*. **his ~ isn't suited to that job** er ist von seiner Veranlagung her nicht für diese Stelle geeignet; **he has an artistic ~** er ist eine Künstlernatur; **their ~s are quite different** sie sind völlig unterschiedlich veranlagt; **he has a happy ~** er hat ein fröhliches Wesen *or* Naturell. **(b)** (*no art: temper, excitability*) Temperament *nt*.

temperamental [,tempərə'mentl] *adj* **(a)** temperamentvoll, launenhaft (*pej*). **(b)** *machine, car* launisch (*hum*). **to be ~** Mucken haben (*inf*), launisch sein (*hum*). **(c)** (*caused by temperament*) *inability, unsuitability* veranlagungsmäßig; *laziness etc* angeboren.

temperamentally [,temprə'mentəlɪ] *adv* **(a)** *behave etc* temperamentvoll, launenhaft (*pej*). **(b)** (*of machine, car*) launisch (*hum*). **(c)** (*as regards disposition*) charakterlich, veranlagungsmäßig.

temperance ['tempərəns] *n* **(a)** (*moderation*) Mäßigung *f*; (*in speech etc also*) Zurückhaltung *f*; (*in eating, drinking also*) Maßhalten *nt*. **(b)** (*teetotalism*) Enthaltsamkeit, Abstinenz *f*.

temperance: ~ hotel *n* alkoholfreies Hotel; **~ movement** *n* Temperenzler- *or* Temperenzbewegung *f*; **~ society** *n* Temperenzverein *m or* -gesellschaft *f*.

temperate ['tempərɪt] *adj* **(a)** *person, language* gemäßigt; (*in eating, demands*) maßvoll. **(b)** *climate, zone* gemäßigt.

temperature ['temprɪtʃə^r] *n* Temperatur *f*; (*Med: above normal ~ also*) Fieber *nt*. **water boils at a ~ of 100°C** Wasser kocht bei einer Temperatur von 100°C; **to take sb's ~** jds Temperatur messen, bei jdm Fieber messen; **he has a ~/a slight/high ~** er hat Fieber/erhöhte Temperatur/hohes Fieber; **his ~ is high, he's running a high ~** er hat hohes Fieber; **he has a ~ of 39°C** er hat 39° Fieber; **his ~ is 37°/39°** seine Temperatur ist 37°/39°, er hat 39° Fieber.

temperature chart *n* (*Med*) Fiebertabelle *f*; (*curve of graph*) Fieberkurve *f*.

tempered ['tempəd] *adj steel* gehärtet, Temper- (*spec*).

-tempered *adj suf* -gelaunt; (*Mus*) temperiert.

tempest ['tempɪst] *n* (*liter*) Sturm *m* (*also fig*), Unwetter *nt*.

tempestuous [,tem'pestjʊəs] *adj* **(a)** (*lit liter*) *winds* stürmisch; *sea also* tobend, aufgewühlt. **(b)** (*fig*) stürmisch; *argument, rage* heftig; *speech* leidenschaftlich.

tempestuously [,tem'pestjʊəslɪ] *adv* (*lit liter, fig*) heftig.

tempestuousness [,tem'pestjʊəsnɪs] *n* (*lit liter, fig*) Heftigkeit *f*; (*of sea*) Aufgewühltheit *f*.

Templar ['templə^r] *n* (*also* **Knight ~**) Tempelherr, Templer *m*.

template, templet ['templɪt] *n* Schablone *f*.

temple[1] ['templ] *n* (*Rel*) Tempel *m*.

temple[2] *n* (*Anat*) Schläfe *f*.

templet *n see* **template**.

tempo ['tempəʊ] *n* (*Mus, fig*) Tempo *nt*.

temporal ['tempərəl] *adj* **(a)** zeitlich; (*Gram*) Zeit-, temporal. **(b)** (*Rel*) weltlich. **(c)** (*Anat*) Schläfen-.

temporarily ['tempərərɪlɪ] *adv* vorübergehend, für einige Zeit.

temporariness ['tempərərɪnɪs] *n* vorübergehender Charakter. **because of the ~ of her home** ... weil es nur vorübergehend ihr Zuhause war ...

temporary ['tempərərɪ] **1** *adj* vorübergehend; *job also* für kurze Zeit, befristet; *arrangement also, method, building, road surface* provisorisch; *powers also* zeitweilig, befristet. **our new secretary is only ~** unsere neue Sekretärin ist nur vorübergehend *or* für einige Zeit hier; **I'm only here for a ~ stay** ich bin nur für kurze Zeit hier. **2** *n* Aushilfe, Aushilfskraft *f*.

temporize ['tempəraɪz] *vi* (*delay*) ausweichen (um Zeit zu gewinnen), Verzögerungstaktiken anwenden. **to ~ with sb** jdn hinhalten; **a temporizing politician** ein Politiker, der Verzögerungstaktiken anwendet.

temporizer ['tempəraɪzə^r] *n* Verzögerungstaktiker *m*.

tempt [tempt] *vt* **(a)** in Versuchung führen; (*successfully*) verführen, verleiten. **to ~ sb to do** *or* **into doing sth** jdn dazu verleiten *or* verführen *or* dazu bringen, etw zu tun; **don't ~ me** bring *or* führ mich nicht in Versuchung!; **one is ~ed to believe that ...** man möchte fast glauben, daß ..., man ist versucht zu glauben, daß ...; **I am very ~ed to accept** ich bin sehr versucht anzunehmen; **try and ~ her to eat a little** versuchen Sie, ob Sie sie nicht dazu bringen können, etwas zu essen; **may I ~ you to a little more wine?** kann ich Sie noch zu etwas Wein überreden?; **are you sure you won't come? — go on, ~ me/no, I won't be ~ed!** willst du bestimmt nicht mitkommen? — wenn du so weitermachst, kriegst du mich vielleicht doch noch herum (inf)/nein, ich bleibe hart; **to ~ fate or providence** (fig) sein Schicksal herausfordern; (in words) den Teufel an die Wand malen.

(b) (Rel) versuchen, in Versuchung führen. **the devil ~s us to evil** der Teufel führt uns in Versuchung.

temptation [temp'teɪʃən] n Versuchung f (also Rel), Verlockung f. **to put ~ in sb's way** jdn in Versuchung führen; **lead us not into ~** (Bibl) führe uns nicht in Versuchung (Bibl); **to yield or give way to ~** der Versuchung erliegen.

tempter ['temptə'] n Versucher, Verführer m. **the T~** (Rel) der Versucher.

tempting adj, **~ly** adv ['temptɪŋ, -lɪ] verlockend, verführerisch.

temptress ['temptrɪs] n Verführerin f.

ten [ten] **1** adj zehn. **the T~ Commandments** die Zehn Gebote; **~ to one he won't come** (inf) zehn gegen or zu eins, daß er nicht kommt; **nine out of ~ people would agree with you** neun von zehn Leuten würden Ihnen zustimmen; **a packet of ~ (cigarettes)** eine Zehnerpackung (Zigaretten).

2 n Zehn f. **~s** (Math) Zehner pl; **to count in ~s** in Zehnern zählen; **you can only buy them in ~s** man kann sie nur in Zehnerpackungen kaufen; see also **six**.

tenability [,tenə'bɪlɪtɪ] n see adj (a) Haltbarkeit f; Vertretbarkeit f.

tenable ['tenəbl] adj **(a)** (Mil) position haltbar; (fig) opinion, theory also vertretbar. **(b)** pred **a post ~ for two years/for life** eine auf zwei Jahre befristete Stelle/eine Lebensstellung, eine Stelle auf Lebenszeit.

tenacious [tɪ'neɪʃəs] adj zäh, hartnäckig; character, person also beharrlich; memory unschlagbar. **he was ~ in the defence of his principles** er verteidigte hartnäckig or zäh or eisern seine Prinzipien; **inflation/the disease had a ~ hold on ...** die Inflation/Seuche hielt ... in eisernem Griff; **to be ~ of sth** (form) zäh an etw (dat) festhalten.

tenaciously [tɪ'neɪʃəslɪ] adv zäh, hartnäckig. **she held ~ to her principles** sie hielt zäh an ihren Prinzipien fest; **the dog held on ~ to the bone** der Hund hielt den Knochen zäh fest; **he clung ~ to life** er hielt zäh am Leben fest, er klammerte sich hartnäckig ans Leben.

tenacity [tɪ'næsɪtɪ] n Zähigkeit f, Hartnäckigkeit f; Beharrlichkeit f. **the ~ of his grip** sein eiserner Griff; **his ~ of life** sein zäher Lebenswille.

tenancy ['tenənsɪ] n right/conditions/problems **of ~** Mietrecht nt/-bedingungen pl/-probleme pl; (of farm) Pachtrecht nt/-bedingungen pl/-probleme pl. **a ~ can be established** (form) wenn ein Miet-/Pachtverhältnis nt nachgewiesen werden kann; **during his ~** während er (dort) Mieter/Pächter ist/war; **period of ~** Dauer f des Miet-/Pachtverhältnisses.

tenant ['tenənt] **1** n Mieter(in f) m; (of farm) Pächter(in f) m. **~ farmer** Pächter m. **2** vt (form) house zur Miete wohnen in (+dat); premises gemietet haben; farm in Pacht haben. **the house was ~ed by students** in dem Haus wohnten Studenten zur Miete.

tenantry ['tenəntrɪ] n, no pl (of estate) Pächter pl; (of building, premises) Mieter pl. **the law of ~** das Mietrecht; (of farm) das Pachtrecht.

tend¹ [tend] vt sick kümmern um; sheep hüten; sick person pflegen; land bestellen; machine bedienen.

tend² vi **(a)** **to ~ to be/do sth** (have a habit of being/doing sth) gewöhnlich or gern etw sein/tun, die Tendenz haben, etw zu sein/tun; (person also) dazu neigen or tendieren, etw zu sein/tun; **the lever ~s to stick** der Hebel bleibt oft hängen; **I ~ to believe** ich neige or tendiere dazu, ihm zu glauben; **that would ~ to suggest that ...** das würde gewissermaßen darauf hindeuten, daß ...

(b) **to ~ towards** (be directed, lead) (line) führen or streben (geh) nach; (measures, actions etc) führen zu, anstreben; (incline) (person, views, designs etc) neigen or tendieren or eine Tendenz haben zu; (prices, colours) tendieren or eine Tendenz haben zu; **prices are ~ing upwards** die Preise tendieren nach oben or haben eine steigende Tendenz; **his opinion is ~ing in our direction** seine Meinung tendiert in unsere Richtung.

tendency ['tendənsɪ] n Tendenz f (geh); (physical predisposition) Neigung f. **artistic tendencies** künstlerische Neigungen pl; **to have a ~ to be/do sth** gern or gewöhnlich etw sein/tun; (person, style of writing also) dazu neigen or tendieren, etw zu sein/zu tun; **he had an annoying ~ to forget things** er hatte die ärgerliche Angewohnheit, alles zu vergessen; **there is a ~ for business to improve in autumn** gewöhnlich nehmen die Geschäfte im Herbst einen Aufschwung; **a strong upward ~** (St Ex) eine stark steigende Tendenz.

tendentious adj, **~ly** adv [ten'denʃəs, -lɪ] tendenziös.

tendentiousness [ten'denʃəsnɪs] n tendenziöse Färbung.

tender¹ ['tendə'] n **(a)** Hüter(in f) m; (of sick person) Pfleger(in f) m. **machine ~** Maschinenwart m. **(b)** (Naut, Rail)Tender m.

tender² **1** vt money, services (an)bieten, geben; thanks aussprechen; resignation einreichen. **"please ~ exact fare"** „bitte Fahrgeld abgezählt bereithalten".

2 vi (Comm) sich bewerben (for um).

3 n **(a)** (Comm) Angebot nt. **to invite ~s for a job** Angebote pl für eine Arbeit einholen; **to put work out to ~** Arbeiten ausschreiben; **to make** or **put in** or **send in a ~ for sth** ein Angebot or eine Submissionsofferte (form) für etw machen or einreichen.

(b) (Fin) **legal ~** gesetzliches Zahlungsmittel.

tender³ adj **(a)** (sore, easily hurt) spot, bruise empfindlich; skin, plant also zart; (fig) subject heikel. **a child of ~ years/age** ein Kind im zarten Alter; **my arm still feels ~ (to the touch)** mein Arm ist noch sehr empfindlich; **she is a ~ plant** (fig) sie ist ein zartes Pflänzchen.

(b) meat zart.

(c) (affectionate) person, voice, look zärtlich, liebevoll; memories lieb, zärtlich; heart gut. **to bid sb a ~ farewell** liebevoll(en) or zärtlich(en) Abschied von jdm nehmen; **in sb's ~ care** in jds Obhut; **to leave sb to sb's ~ mercies** (iro) jdn jds liebevollen Händen anvertrauen.

tender: **~foot** n Neuling m; **~-hearted** adj gutherzig; **~-heartedness** n Gutherzigkeit f.

tenderize ['tendəraɪz] vt meat zart or weich machen; (by beating) klopfen.

tenderizer ['tendəraɪzə'] n Mürbesalz nt.

tenderloin ['tendə,lɔɪn] n Lendenstück nt.

tenderly ['tendəlɪ] adv zärtlich, liebevoll.

tenderness ['tendənɪs] n see adj **(a)** Empfindlichkeit f; Zartheit f. **(b)** Zartheit f. **(c)** Zärtlichkeit f; Güte f.

tendon ['tendən] n Sehne f.

tendril ['tendrɪl] n Ranke f; (of hair) Ringellocke f.

tenement ['tenɪmənt] n **(a)** (also ~ house) Mietshaus nt, Mietskaserne f (pej). **(b)** (Jur) Mietbesitz m; (farm) Pachtbesitz m.

Tenerife [,tenə'riːf] n Teneriffa nt.

tenet ['tenət] n Lehrsatz m; (Rel) Glaubenssatz m.

tenfold ['tenfəʊld] **1** adj zehnfach. **2** adv zehnfach, um das Zehnfache. **increase ~** sich verzehnfachen.

ten-gallon hat ['tengæln'hæt] n Cowboyhut m.

tenner ['tenə'] n (inf) Zehner m (inf).

tennis ['tenɪs] n Tennis nt.

tennis in cpds Tennis-; **~ club** n Tennisclub or -verein m; **~ court** n Tennisplatz m; **~ elbow** n (Med) Tennisarm m.

tennish ['tenɪʃ] adj (so) um zehn herum (inf).

tennis racket, tennis racquet n Tennisschläger m.

tenon ['tenən] n Zapfen m. **~ joint** Zapfenverbindung f; **~ saw** Zapfenschneidsäge f.

tenor ['tenə'] **1** n **(a)** (voice) Tenor(stimme f) m; (person) Tenor m. **(b)** (purport) Tenor m; (of theory) Tendenz f; (general nature) (of life) Stil m; (of events) (Ver)lauf m. **2** adj (Mus) part, voice Tenor-.

ten: **~pence** n zehn Pence; **~ pence, a ~penny piece** n ein Zehnpencestück nt; **~pin bowling,** (US) **~pins** n Bowling nt.

tense¹ [tens] n (Gram) Zeit f, Tempus nt. **present/past/future ~** Gegenwart f/Vergangenheit f/Zukunft f.

tense² **1** adj (+er) rope gespannt, straff; muscles (an)gespannt; person, expression, bearing (through stress, worry etc) angespannt; (through nervousness, fear etc) verkrampft; voice nervös; silence, atmosphere gespannt; (thrilling) scene spannungsgeladen. **~ headache** Spannungskopfschmerz m; **I've been feeling rather ~** ich bin schon den ganzen Tag so nervös; **in a voice ~ with emotion** mit vor Erregung erregter Stimme; **things are getting rather ~** die Lage wird gespannter.

2 vt anspannen.

3 vi sich (an)spannen, sich straffen.

tensely ['tenslɪ] adv (lit) stretch straff; (fig) listen angespannt; speak, wait (nervously) nervös; (excitedly) gespannt. **the diver stood ~ poised** der Taucher stand in angespannter Haltung da.

tenseness ['tensnɪs] n see adj Gespanntheit f, Straffheit f; (An)gespanntheit f; Angespanntheit f; Verkrampftheit f; Nervosität f; Gespanntheit f; Spannung f(geladenheit) f.

tensile ['tensaɪl] adj dehnbar, spannbar. **~ strength** or **stress** Zugfestigkeit f.

tension ['tenʃən] n **(a)** (lit) Spannung f; (of muscle) Anspannung f; (Knitting) Festigkeit f; (Sew) Spannung f. **to check the ~** die Spannung prüfen; (Knitting) eine Maschenprobe machen. **(b)** (nervous strain) nervliche Belastung, Anspannung f. **(c)** (strain: in relationship) Spannungen pl.

tensor (muscle) ['tensɔ:'-] n Tensor m.

tenspot ['tenspɒt] n (US sl) Zehner m (inf).

tent [tent] n Zelt nt. **~ peg** Zeltpflock, Hering m; **~ pole** Zeltstange f.

tentacle ['tentəkl] n (Zool) Tentakel m or nt (spec); (of octopus etc also) Fangarm m; (of snail also) Fühler m; (fig) Klaue f.

tentative ['tentətɪv] adj (not definite, provisional) vorläufig; offer unverbindlich; (hesitant) player, movement vorsichtig; conclusion, suggestion vorsichtig, zögernd. **this proposal or suggestion is only ~** das ist ja nur ein Vorschlag; **we've a ~ arrangement to play tennis tonight** wir haben halb abgemacht, heute abend Tennis zu spielen.

tentatively ['tentətɪvlɪ] adv see adj. **he ~ suggested a weekend in Brighton** er machte den Vorschlag, eventuell ein Wochenende in Brighton zu verbringen.

tenterhooks ['tentəhʊks] npl: **to be on ~** wie auf glühenden Kohlen sitzen (inf); **to keep sb on ~** jdn zappeln lassen.

tenth [tenθ] **1** adj (in series) zehnte(r, s). **a ~ part** n Zehntel nt. **2** n (fraction) Zehntel nt; (in series) Zehnte(r, s); (Mus) Dezime f; see also **sixth**.

tenthly ['tenθlɪ] adv zehntens.

tenuity [te'njuɪtɪ] n (lit) see **tenuousness**.

tenuous ['tenjʊəs] adj **(a)** (lit) thread etc dünn, fein; cobweb zart, fein; air dünn; gas flüchtig. **(b)** (fig) connection, distinction schwach; argument, evidence also wenig stichhaltig. **he kept a ~ grip on life** er hatte nur noch einen schwachen Lebenswillen.

tenuousness ['tenjʊəsnɪs] n see adj **(a)** Dünne, Feinheit f; Zartheit, Feinheit f; Dünne f; Flüchtigkeit f. **(b)** Schwäche f; mangelnde Stichhaltigkeit.

tenure ['tenjʊə'] n **(a)** (holding of office) Anstellung f; (period of office) Amtszeit f. **(b)** (of property) **during his ~ of the house/**

farm während er das Haus/die Farm innehat(te) *(geh)*; laws governing land ~ Landpachtgesetze *pl*.

tepee ['ti:pi:] *n* Tipi *nt*.

tepid ['tepid] *adj (lit, fig)* lau(warm).

tepidity [te'piditi], **tepidness** ['tepidnis] *n (lit, fig)* Lauheit *f*.

tercentenary [,tɜ:sen'ti:nəri] **1** *n (anniversary)* dreihundertster Jahrestag; *(celebration)* Dreihundertjahrfeier *f*, dreihundertjähriges Jubiläum. **2** *attr* für den dreihundertsten Jahrestag; *celebrations also* Dreihundertjahr-.

tercet ['tɜ:sit] *n (Poet)* Terzine *f*; *(Mus)* Triole *f*.

tergiversate ['tɜ:dʒɪvəseɪt] *vi (form, hum)* dauernd seine Gesinnung ändern.

tergiversation [,tɜ:dʒɪvə'seɪʃən] *n usu pl (form, hum)* (ständiger) Gesinnungswandel *no pl*.

term [tɜ:m] **1** *n* **(a)** *(period of time)* Dauer *f*, Zeitraum *m*; *(of contract)* Laufzeit *f*; *(limit)* Frist *f*. ~ of government/office Regierungszeit *f*/Amtsdauer *or* -zeit *f*; ~ of imprisonment Gefängnisstrafe *f*; ~ of service *(Mil)* Militärdienst(zeit *f*) *m*; to put *or* set a ~ *(of three years)* to sth etw (auf drei Jahre) befristen; elected for a three-year ~ auf *or* für drei Jahre gewählt; the contract is nearing its ~ der Vertrag läuft bald ab; in the long/short ~ auf lange/kurze Sicht; at ~ *(Fin)* bei Fälligkeit; *(Med)* zur rechten Zeit.

(b) *(Sch) (three in one year)* Trimester *nt*; *(four in one year)* Vierteljahr, Quartal *nt*; *(two in one year)* Halbjahr *nt*; *(Univ)* Semester *nt*. end-of-~ exam Examen *nt* am Ende eines Trimesters *etc*; during *or* in ~(-time) während der Schulzeit; *(Univ)* während des Semesters; out of ~(-time) in den Ferien.

(c) *(expression)* Ausdruck *m*. in plain *or* simple ~s in einfachen Worten; technical ~s Fachausdrücke *pl*; a legal ~ ein juristischer (Fach)ausdruck *or* Terminus *(geh)*; he spoke of her in the most flattering ~s er äußerte sich sehr schmeichelhaft über sie; a contradiction in ~s ein Widerspruch in sich.

(d) *(Math, Logic)* Term *m*. ~ in parentheses Klammerausdruck *m*; to express one thing in ~s of another eine Sache mit einer anderen erklären; in ~s of production we are doing well was die Produktion betrifft, stehen wir gut da; in ~s of money/time geldlich *or* finanziell/zeitlich; in ~s of energy/planning energiemäßig/planerisch.

(e) ~s *pl (conditions)* Bedingungen *pl*; ~s of surrender/service/sale/payment Kapitulations-/Arbeits-/Verkaufs-/Zahlungsbedingungen *pl*; ~s of reference *(of committee etc)* Aufgabenbereich *m*; *(of thesis etc)* Themenbereich *m*; to buy sth on credit/easy ~s etw auf Kredit/auf Raten kaufen; the hotel offered reduced ~s in winter das Hotel bot ermäßigte Winterpreise an; on what ~s? zu welchen Bedingungen?; not on any ~s unter gar keinen Umständen; to accept sb on his own ~s jdn nehmen, wie er ist; to come to ~s (with sb) sich (mit jdm) einigen; to come to ~s with sth sich mit etw abfinden.

(f) ~s *pl (relations)* to be on good/bad/friendly/neighbourly ~s with sb gut/nicht (gut) mit jdm auskommen/auf freundschaftlichem/gutnachbarlichem Fuß mit jdm stehen; they are not on speaking ~s sie reden nicht miteinander; what sort of ~s are they on? wie ist ihre Beziehung?

2 *vt* nennen, bezeichnen.

termagant ['tɜ:məgənt] *n* Furie *f*.

terminal ['tɜ:mɪnl] **1** *adj rhyme, syllable, station* End-; *accounts, report, exams* (Ab)schluß-; *(Elec) voltage* Klemmen-; *(Med: fatal) cancer, patient* unheilbar. ~ ward Sterbestation *f*; he's a ~ case er ist unheilbar krank.

2 *n* **(a)** *(Rail)* Endbahnhof *m*; *(of tramway, buses)* Endstation *f*; *(airport* ~*, container* ~*)* Terminal *m*.

(b) *(Elec)* Pol *m*.

terminate ['tɜ:mɪneɪt] **1** *vt* beenden, beschließen; *contract, lease etc* lösen; *pregnancy* unterbrechen; *friendship* beenden. **2** *vi* enden; *(contract, lease)* ablaufen. most plural nouns ~ in "s" die meisten Substantive enden im Plural auf „s".

termination [,tɜ:mɪ'neɪʃən] *n* **(a)** Ende *nt*; *(bringing to an end)* Beendigung *f*; *(of contract, lease etc) (expiry)* Ablauf *m*, Erlöschen *nt*; *(cancellation)* Lösung *f*. ~ of pregnancy Schwangerschaftsabbruch *m*. **(b)** *(Gram)* Endung *f*.

terminological [,tɜ:mɪnə'lodʒɪkəl] *adj* terminologisch.

terminology [,tɜ:mɪ'nolədʒɪ] *n* Terminologie *f*. all the technical ~ in the article all die Fachausdrücke in dem Artikel.

terminus ['tɜ:mɪnəs] *n (Rail, Bus)* Endstation *f*.

termite ['tɜ:maɪt] *n* Termite *f*.

tern [tɜ:n] *n (Zool)* Seeschwalbe *f*.

ternary ['tɜ:nərɪ] *adj* ternär.

terpsichorean [,tɜ:psɪkə'rɪən] *adj (form, hum)* Tanz-.

terrace ['terəs] **1** *n* **(a)** *(patio)* Terrasse *f*. **(b)** *(on hillside)* Terrasse *f*. ~ cultivation Terrassenfeldbau *m*. **(c)** ~s *pl (Sport)* Ränge *pl*. **(d)** *(row of houses)* Häuserreihe *f*; *(as street name)* = Weg *m*. **2** *vt garden, hill* in Terrassen *or* stufenförmig anlegen.

terraced ['terəst] *adj* **(a)** *hillside etc* terrassenförmig *or* stufenförmig angelegt. **(b)** ~ house *(Brit)* Reihenhaus *nt*.

terracotta ['terə'kɒtə] **1** *n* Terrakotta *f*. **2** *attr* Terrakotta-, aus Terrakotta.

terra firma ['terə'fɜ:mə] *n* fester Boden. to be on ~ again wieder festen Boden unter den Füßen haben.

terrain [te'reɪn] *n* Terrain *nt (esp Mil)*, Gelände *nt*; *(fig)* Boden *m*.

terrapin ['terəpɪn] *n* Sumpfschildkröte *f*.

terrazzo [te'rætsəu] *n* Terrazzo *m*.

terrestrial [tɪ'restrɪəl] **1** *adj* **(a)** *(of land)* plants, animals Land-, auf dem Land lebend. **(b)** *(of the planet Earth)* terrestrisch, irdisch. ~ globe Erdball, Globus *m*. **(c)** *(wordly)* problems irdisch, weltlich. **2** *n* Erdbewohner(in *f*) *m*.

terrible ['terəbl] *adj* schrecklich, furchtbar. he is ~ at golf er spielt schrecklich *or* furchtbar schlecht Golf *(inf)*.

terribleness ['terəblnɪs] *n* Schrecklichkeit, Fürchterlichkeit *f*.

terribly ['terəblɪ] *adv see adj*.

terrier ['terɪəʳ] *n* Terrier *m*.

terrific [tə'rɪfɪk] *adj shame, nuisance, shock* unheimlich *(inf)*; *person, success, idea, party also* sagenhaft *(sl)*, klasse *inv (inf)*; *speed, heat, strength, generosity* unwahrscheinlich *(inf)*.

terrifically [tə'rɪfɪkəlɪ] *adv (inf) (very)* unheimlich *(inf)*; *(very well)* unheimlich (gut) *(inf)*. the party went ~ die Party war klasse *(inf)*.

terrify ['terɪfaɪ] *vt (person)* fürchterliche *or* schreckliche Angst machen *or* einjagen (+*dat*), in Angst *or* Schrecken versetzen. flying/my driving terrifies him er hat schreckliche Angst vor dem Fliegen/, wenn ich fahre; to be terrified of sth vor etw schreckliche Angst haben; he was terrified when/in case ... er hatte fürchterliche Angst, als .../davor, daß ...; he was terrified by the ghost story die Geistergeschichte hat ihm schreckliche Angst eingejagt *(inf)*; a terrified look ein angstvoller Blick; you look terrified du hast Angst, das sieht man!

terrifying ['terɪfaɪɪŋ] *adj film, story* grauenerregend; *thought, sight* entsetzlich; *speed* angsterregend, furchterregend.

terrifyingly ['terɪfaɪɪŋlɪ] *adv* entsetzlich. he came ~ close to disaster er kam dem Unheil schrecklich nahe.

territorial [,terɪ'tɔ:rɪəl] **1** *adj* territorial, Gebiets-; *(Zool)* Revier-; *instincts* territorial. ~ sovereignty Gebietshoheit *f*; ~ possessions Territorialbesitz *m*; ~ rights Hoheitsrechte *pl*; ~ waters Territorialgewässer *pl*; T~ Army Territorialheer *nt*; a strongly ~ bird ein Vogel mit ausgeprägtem Territorialverhalten.

2 *n* T~ Soldat *m* der Heimatschutztruppe; the T~s die Heimatschutztruppe.

territory ['terɪtərɪ] *n* (Staats)gebiet, Territorium *nt*; *(in US, Austral)* Territorium *nt*; *(of animals)* Revier, Territorium *nt*; *(Comm: of agent etc)* Bezirk *m*; *(fig)* Revier, Gebiet *nt*.

terror ['terəʳ] *n* **(a)** *no pl (great fear)* panische Angst *(of vor* +*dat)*. in ~ in panischer Angst; to go in ~ of one's life um sein Leben bangen; it held no ~ for him er schreckte nicht davor zurück; reign of ~ *(Hist, fig)* Terror- *or* Schreckensherrschaft *f*; the IRA ~ der IRA-Terror.

(b) *(cause of ~, terrible event)* Schrecken *m*. he was the ~ of the other boys er terrorisierte die anderen Jungen; the headmaster was a ~ to boys who misbehaved der Rektor war der Schrecken aller Jungen, die sich schlecht benahmen.

(c) *(inf) (person)* Teufel *m*; *(child)* Ungeheuer, Scheusal *nt*. he's a ~ for punctuality/for wanting everything just so er ist fürchterlich pedantisch in bezug auf Pünktlichkeit/Ordnung; a ~ with the ladies ein Weiberheld *m (inf)*.

terrorism ['terərɪzəm] *n* Terrorismus *m*; *(acts of* ~*)* Terror *m*. an act of ~ ein Terrorakt *m*.

terrorist ['terərɪst] **1** *n* Terrorist(in *f*) *m*. **2** *attr* Terror-.

terrorize ['terəraɪz] *vt* terrorisieren.

terror-stricken, terror-struck *adj* starr vor Schreck(en).

terry cloth ['terɪ'klɒθ] *or* **towelling** [-'təuəlɪŋ] *n* Frottee *nt or m*.

terry towel *n* Frotteetuch, Frottier(hand)tuch *nt*.

terse [tɜ:s] *adj (+er)* knapp. he was very ~ er war sehr kurz angebunden.

tersely ['tɜ:slɪ] *adv* knapp, kurz; *say, answer* kurz (angebunden). to dismiss sth ~ etw kurzerhand verwerfen.

terseness ['tɜ:snɪs] *n* Knappheit *f*; *(of reply also, person)* Kürze, Bündigkeit *f*.

tertiary ['tɜ:ʃərɪ] *adj* tertiär; *colour* Misch-. T~ period *(Geol)* Tertiär *nt*; ~ burns Verbrennungen *pl* dritten Grades.

Terylene ® ['terɪli:n] *n* Terylen(e) *nt*, ≈ Trevira ®, Diolen ® *nt*.

tessellated ['tesɪleɪtɪd] *adj* Mosaik-.

test [test] **1** *n* **(a)** *(Sch)* Klassenarbeit *f*; *(Univ)* Klausur *f*; *(short)* Kurzarbeit *f*, Test *m*; *(intelligence* ~*, psychological* ~ *etc)* Test *m*; *(driving* ~*)* (Fahr)prüfung *f*. he gave them a vocabulary ~ er ließ eine Vokabel- *or* Wörterarbeit schreiben; *(orally)* er hat sie Vokabeln abgefragt; if we apply the ~ of public acceptability wenn wir die Probe machen, wie die Öffentlichkeit das aufnimmt; to pass the ~ of public acceptability von der Öffentlichkeit gutgeheißen werden; to put sb/sth to the ~ jdn/etw auf die Probe stellen; to stand the ~ die Probe bestehen; their marriage didn't stand up to the ~ of separation ihre Ehe hat die Trennung nicht verkraftet; to stand the ~ of time die Zeit überdauern; that was a real ~ of character/his endurance das war eine wirkliche Charakterprüfung/Belastungsprobe für ihn.

(b) *(on vehicle, product, weapon etc)* Test *m*; *(check)* Kontrolle *f*; *(on road also)* Testfahrt *f*; *(in air also)* Testflug *m*.

(c) *(chemical* ~*)* Test *m*, Untersuchung *f*. a skin ~ ein Hauttest *m*; to do a ~ for sugar/starch einen Zuckertest/Stärketest machen, eine Untersuchung auf Zucker/Stärke machen; the samples were sent for ~s die Proben wurden zur Untersuchung geschickt.

(d) *(Brit) see* ~ match.

2 *vt* **(a)** *(examine, check)* testen, prüfen; *(Sch) pupil* prüfen; *(orally)* abfragen; *person (with psychological* ~*s)*, *intelligence* testen; *(fig)* auf die Probe stellen. the teacher ~ed them on that chapter der Lehrer fragte sie das Kapitel ab; to ~ sb for a job jds Eignung für eine Stelle prüfen *or* testen; to ~ sb/sth for accuracy jdn/etw auf Genauigkeit prüfen; I just wanted to ~ your reaction ich wollte nur mal sehen, wie du reagierst.

(b) *(chemically)* gold prüfen; *water, contents of stomach etc* untersuchen. to ~ sth for sugar etw auf seinen Zuckergehalt untersuchen; the blood samples were sent for ~ing *or* to be ~ed die Blutproben wurden zur Untersuchung geschickt.

3 *vi* Tests/einen Test machen; *(chemically also)* untersuchen *(for auf* +*acc)*. ~ing, ~ing one, two! eins, zwei; we are ~ing for a gas leak/loose connection wir überprüfen die Leitung auf eine undichte Stelle, wir überprüfen, ob irgendwo Gas austritt/ein Anschluß locker ist.

♦**test out** *vt sep* ausprobieren *(on bei or an* +*dat)*.

testament ['testəmənt] *n* **(a)** *(old)* Testament *nt*, letzter Wille.

(b) (*Bibl*) **Old/New T~** Altes/Neues Testament.
testamentary [,testə'mentərɪ] *adj* testamentarisch.
testator [te'steɪtəʳ] *n* Erblasser *m* (*form*).
testatrix [te'steɪtrɪks] *n* Erblasserin *f* (*form*).
test: **~ ban** *n* Versuchsverbot *nt*; **~ ban treaty** *n* Teststoppabkommen *nt*; **~ bed** *n* Prüfstand *m*; **~ card** *n* (*TV*) Testbild *nt*; **~ case** *n* Musterfall *m*; **~ drive** *n* Probefahrt *f*; **~-drive** *vt* car probefahren.
tester ['testəʳ] *n* (*of product etc*) Prüfer(in *f*) *m*; (*machine*) Prüfgerät *nt*.
testes ['testi:z] *npl* Testikel, Hoden *pl*.
test flight *n* Test- *or* Probeflug *m*.
testicle ['testɪkl] *n* Testikel, Hoden *m*.
testify ['testɪfaɪ] **1** *vt* **to ~ that ...** (*Jur*) bezeugen, daß ...
2 *vi* (*Jur*) eine Zeugenaussage machen, aussagen. **to ~ against/in favour of sb** gegen/für jdn aussagen; **to ~ to sth** (*speak for*) etw bezeugen (*also Jur*); (*be sign of*) sincerity, efforts etc von etw zeugen, ein Zeichen für etw sein.
testily ['testɪlɪ] *adv see adj.*
testimonial [,testɪ'məʊnɪəl] *n* **(a)** (*character recommendation*) Referenz *f*. **(b)** (*gift*) Geschenk *nt* als Zeichen der Anerkennung *or* Wertschätzung (*geh*).
testimony ['testɪmənɪ] *n* Aussage *f*. **he gave his ~** er machte seine Aussage; **to bear ~ to sth** etw bezeugen; **accept this gift as ~ of my friendship** nehmen Sie dieses Geschenk als Zeichen *or* Beweis meiner Freundschaft; **according to the ~ of the medical profession** nach Aussagen der Ärzteschaft.
testiness ['testɪnɪs] *n* Gereiztheit *f*.
testing ['testɪŋ] *adj* hart. **I had a ~ time** es war hart (für mich).
testing ground *n* Test- *or* Versuchsgebiet *nt*; (*fig*) Versuchsfeld *nt*.
test match *n* (*Brit*) Testmatch *nt or m*.
testosterone [te'stɒstərəʊn] *n* Testosteron *nt*.
test: **~ paper** *n* (*Sch*) Klassenarbeit *f*; (*Chem*) Reagenzpapier *nt*; **~ pattern** *n* (*US*) see **~ card**; **~ piece** *n* (*of handwork*) Prüfungsstück *nt*; (*Mus*) Stück *nt* zum Vorspielen; **~ pilot** *n* Testpilot *m*; **~ tube** *n* Reagenzglas *nt*; **~-tube baby** *n* Kind *nt* aus der Retorte, Retortenbaby *nt*.
testy ['testɪ] *adj* (+*er*) unwirsch, gereizt.
tetanus ['tetənəs] *n* Wundstarrkrampf, Tetanus *m*. **anti-~ vaccine/vaccination** Tetanusimpfstoff *m*/Tetanusimpfung *f*.
tetchily ['tetʃɪlɪ] *adv see adj.*
tetchiness ['tetʃɪnɪs] *n see adj* Gereiztheit *f*; Reizbarkeit *f*.
tetchy, techy ['tetʃɪ] *adj* (+*er*) (*on particular occasion*) gereizt; (*as general characteristic*) reizbar.
tête-à-tête ['teɪtɑ:'teɪt] **1** *adj, adv* unter vier Augen. **2** *n* Tête-à-tête *nt*.
tether ['teðəʳ] **1** *n* (*lit*) Strick *m*; (*chain*) Kette *f*. **to be at the end of one's ~** (*fig inf*) am Ende sein (*inf*). **2** *vt* (*also ~ up*) animal an- *or* festbinden.
tetrahedron [,tetrə'hi:drən] *n* Tetraeder *nt*.
tetrameter [te'træmɪtəʳ] *n* (*Liter*) Tetrameter *m*.
tetrapod ['tetrəpɒd] *n* Tetrapode (*spec*), Vierfüßer *m*.
Teuton ['tju:tɒn] *n* Teutone *m*, Teutonin *f*.
Teutonic [tju'tɒnɪk] *adj* (*Hist, hum*) teutonisch.
Texan ['teksən] **1** *n* Texaner(in *f*) *m*. **2** *adj* texanisch.
Texas ['teksəs] *n* Texas *nt*.
text [tekst] *n* **(a)** Text *m*; (*of document also*) Wortlaut, Inhalt *m*. **to restore a ~** den Originaltext wiederherstellen. **(b)** (*of sermon*) Text *m*.
textbook ['tekstbʊk] *n* Lehrbuch *nt*. **~ case** Paradefall *m*.
textile ['tekstaɪl] **1** *adj* Textil-, textil. **2** *n* Stoff *m*. **~s** Textilien, Textilwaren *pl*.
textual ['tekstjʊəl] *adj* Text-.
texture ['tekstʃəʳ] *n* (*stoffliche*) Beschaffenheit, Textur *f*; (*of dough also*) Konsistenz *f*; (*of food*) Substanz, Textur *f*; (*of material, paper*) Griff *m* und Struktur, Textur *f*; (*of minerals also, fig: of music, poetry etc*) Gestalt *f*. **the ~ of velvet** wie sich Samt anfühlt; **the smooth ~ of silk makes it pleasant to wear** es ist angenehm, Seide zu tragen, weil sie so anschmiegsam ist; **this spongy/light ~ of the cake** dieser feuchte und lockere/leichte Kuchen; **a sculptor interested in ~** ein Bildhauer, der an der Materialgestalt *or* -beschaffenheit interessiert ist; **the ~ of one's life** seine Lebensqualität.
textured ['tekstʃəd] *adj* strukturiert, texturiert (*form*); paint Struktur-.
TGWU *abbr of* **Transport and General Workers' Union**.
Thai [taɪ] **1** *adj* thailändisch; (*Ling*) T(h)ai-. **2** *n* **(a)** Thailänder(in *f*) *m*, Thai *mf*. **(b)** (*language*) Thai *nt*; (*language family*) Tai *nt*.
Thailand ['taɪlænd] *n* Thailand *nt*.
thalidomide [θə'lɪdəʊmaɪd] *n* Contergan ®, Thalidomid *nt*. **~ baby** Contergankind *nt*.
Thames [temz] *n* Themse *f*. **he'll never set the ~ on fire** er hat das Pulver auch nicht erfunden.
than [ðæn, *weak form* ðən] *conj* als. **I'd rather do anything ~ that** das wäre das letzte, was ich tun wollte; **no sooner had I sat down ~ he** began to talk kaum hatte ich mich hingesetzt, als er auch schon anfing zu reden; **who better to help us ~ he?** wer könnte uns besser helfen als er?; **the whole story was nothing more ~ a lie** die ganze Geschichte war nichts als eine (einzige) Lüge; *see* **more, other 1** (c), **rather**.
thank [θæŋk] *vt* **(a)** danken (+*dat*), sich bedanken bei. **I'll never be able to ~ him (enough) for what he has done** ich kann ihm nie genug dafür danken, was er für mich getan hat; **I don't know how to ~ you** ich weiß nicht, wie ich Ihnen danken soll.
(b) (*phrases*) **he won't ~ you for it** er wird es Ihnen nicht danken; **I'll ~ you to mind your own business** ich wäre Ihnen dankbar, wenn Sie sich nicht einmischen würden; **he has his brother/he only has himself to ~ for this** das hat er seinem Bruder/sich selbst zu verdanken.

(c) **~ you danke** (schön); **~ you very much** vielen Dank; **no ~ you/yes, ~ you nein,** danke/ja, bitte *or* danke; **~ you for coming — not at all, ~ you!** vielen Dank, daß Sie gekommen sind — ich danke *Ihnen*, ich bin *froh*; **~ you for the present** vielen Dank für Ihr Geschenk; **~ you for nothing** (*iro*) ich danke (bestens)!; **to say ~ you** danke sagen (*to sb* jdm), sich bedanken (*to* bei).
(d) **~ goodness or heavens or God** (*inf*) Gott sei Dank! (*inf*).
thankee ['θæŋki:] *interj* (*dial*) = **thank you;** *see* **thank (c).**
thankful ['θæŋkfʊl] *adj* dankbar (*to sb* jdm). **I'm only ~ that it didn't happen** ich bin bloß froh, daß es nicht passiert ist.
thankfully ['θæŋkfəlɪ] *adv* dankbar, voller Dankbarkeit. **~, no real harm has been done** zum Glück ist kein wirklicher Schaden entstanden.
thankfulness ['θæŋkfʊlnɪs] *n* Dankbarkeit *f*.
thankless ['θæŋklɪs] *adj* undankbar. **a ~ task** eine undankbare Aufgabe.
thank-offering ['θæŋk,ɒfərɪŋ] *n* (*lit*) Dankopfer *nt*; (*fig*) Dankesgabe *f*.
thanks [θæŋks] **1** *npl* **(a)** Dank *m*. **to accept sth with ~** etw dankend *or* mit Dank annehmen; **and that's all the ~ I get** und das ist jetzt der Dank dafür; **to give ~ to God** Gott danksagen *or* Dank sagen; **~ be to God** (*Eccl*) Dank sei Gott.
(b) **~ to wegen** (+*gen*); (*with positive cause also*) dank (+*gen*); **~ to his coming early everything was finished on time** weil er so früh kam, wurde alles rechtzeitig fertig; **it's all ~ to you that we're so late** bloß deinetwegen kommen wir so spät; **it was no ~ to him that ...** ich hatte/wir hatten *etc* es nicht ihm zu verdanken, daß ...; **you managed it then — no ~ to you** du hast es also doch geschafft — ja, und das habe ich nicht dir zu verdanken.
2 *interj* (*inf*) danke (*for* für). **many ~** vielen *or* herzlichen Dank (*for* für); **~ a lot or a million** vielen *or* tausend Dank; (*iro*) (na,) vielen Dank (*inf*); **will you have some more? — no ~/yes, ~** etwas mehr? — nein/ja, danke.
thanksgiving ['θæŋks,gɪvɪŋ] *n* **(a)** Dankbarkeit *f*. **(b)** (*US*) **T~ (Day)** Thanksgiving Day *m*.
thank-you ['θæŋkju:] **1** *n* Dankeschön *nt*. **he grabbed the book without even a ~** er riß das Buch ohne ein Dankeschön *nt or* ohne ein Wort *nt* des Dankes an sich. **2** *attr letter* Dank-.
that¹ [ðæt, *weak form* ðət] **1** *dem pron, pl* **those (a)** das. **what is ~?** was ist das?; **they all say ~** das sagen alle; **~ is Joe** (over there) das (dort) ist Joe; **who is ~?** wer ist das?; **who is ~ speaking?** wer spricht (denn) da?; (*on phone*) **wer ist am Apparat?;** **~'s what I say or think too** das finde ich auch; **... ~'s what I say or think** das ist jedenfalls meine Meinung; **~'s what they've been told** das hat man ihnen gesagt; **if she's as unhappy/stupid etc as (all) ~** wenn sie so derart unglücklich/dumm *etc* ist; **she's not as stupid as all ~** so dumm ist sie nun auch (wieder) nicht; **I didn't think she'd get/be as angry as ~** ich hätte nicht gedacht, daß sie sich so ärgern würde; **... and all ~** ... so und (*inf*); **like ~** so; **with luck/weather/talent like ~** mit solchem *or* so einem (*inf*) Glück/Wetter/Talent ...; **~'s got ~/him out of the way** so, das wäre geschafft/so, den wären wir los; **~ is** (to say) das heißt; **oh well, ~'s ~** nun ja, damit ist der Fall erledigt; **there, ~'s ~** so, das wär's; **you can't go and ~'s ~** du darfst nicht gehen, und damit hat sich's *or* und damit basta (*inf*); **well, ~'s ~ then** das wär's dann also; **so ~ was ~** damit hatte sich's; **~'s it!** das ist es!; (*the right way*) gut so!, richtig!; (*finished*) so, das wär's!; (*the last straw*) jetzt reicht's!; **will he come? — ~ he will** (*dial*) kommt er? — (der?) bestimmt.
(b) (*after prep*) after/before/below/over **~** danach/davor/darunter/darüber; **and ... at ~** und dabei ...; (*on top of that*) und außerdem ...; **you can get it in any supermarket and quite cheaply at ~** man kann es in jedem Supermarkt, und zwar ganz billig, bekommen; **my watch is broken already and it was a good one at ~** meine Uhr ist schon kaputt und dabei war es eine gute; **what do you mean by ~?** (*not understanding*) was wollen Sie damit sagen?; (*amazed, annoyed*) was soll (denn) das heißen?; **as for ~** was das betrifft *or* angeht; **if things have or it has come to ~** wenn es (schon) so weit gekommen ist; **with ~ she got up and left/burst into tears** damit stand sie auf und ging/brach sie in Tränen aus; *see* **leave**.
(c) (*opposed to "this" and "these"*) das (da), jenes (*old, geh*). **I prefer this to ~** dies ist mir lieber als das (da); **~'s the one I like, not this one** das (dort) mag ich, nicht dies (hier).
(d) (*followed by rel pron*) **this theory is different from ~ which ...** diese Theorie unterscheidet sich von derjenigen, die ...; **~ which we call ...** das, was wir ... nennen.
2 *dem adj, pl* **those (a)** der/die/das, jene(r, s). **what was ~ noise?** was war das für ein Geräusch?; **~ child/dog!** dieses Kind/dieser Hund!; **~ poor girl!** das arme Mädchen!; **I only saw him on ~ one occasion** ich habe ihn nur bei dieser einen Gelegenheit gesehen; **everyone agreed on ~ point** alle waren sich in dem Punkt einig; **I like ~ one** ich mag das da.
(b) (*in opposition to this*) der/die/das. **I'd like ~ one, not this one** ich möchte das da, nicht dies hier; **she was rushing this way and ~** sie rannte hierhin und dorthin.
(c) (*with poss*) **~ dog of yours!** Ihr Hund, dieser Hund von Ihnen (*inf*); **what about ~ plan of yours now?** wie steht es denn jetzt mit Ihrem Plan?, was ist denn nun mit Ihrem Plan?
3 *dem adv* (*inf*) so. **he was at least ~ much taller than me** er war mindestens (um) soviel größer als ich; **it's not ~ good/cold etc** so gut/kalt *etc* ist es auch wieder nicht; **you're not ~ stupid** so dumm bist du auch wieder nicht; **it's not ~ good a film** so ein guter Film ist es nun auch wieder nicht; **he was ~ angry** er hat sich *derart* (ig) geärgert.
that² *rel pron* **(a)** der/die/das; die. **all/nothing/everything etc ~ ...** alles/nichts/alles *etc*, was ...; **the best/cheapest etc ~ ...** das Beste/Billigste *etc*, das *or* was ...; **fool ~ I am** Idiot; **the girl ~ I told you about** das Mädchen, von dem ich Ihnen erzählt

habe; no-one has come ~ I know of meines Wissens or soviel ich weiß, ist niemand gekommen.
(b) *(with expressions of time)* the minute ~ he came the phone rang genau in dem Augenblick, als er kam, klingelte das Telefon; the day ~ we spent on the beach was one of the hottest der Tag, den wir am Strand verbrachten, war einer der heißesten; the day ~ ... an dem Tag, als ...
that³ *conj* **(a)** daß. ~ he should behave like this is quite incredible daß er sich so benehmen kann, ist kaum zu glauben; she promised ~ she would come sie versprach zu kommen; he said ~ it was wrong er sagte, es sei *or* wäre *(inf)* falsch, er sagte, daß es falsch sei *or* wäre *(inf)*; not ~ I want to do it ich will es nicht (etwa), daß ich das tun wollte; *see* **so**.
(b) *(in exclamations)* ~ things *or* it should come to this! daß es soweit kommen konnte!; oh ~ I could only see you again *(liter)* oh, daß ich dich doch wiedersehen könnte! *(liter)*.
(c) *(obs, liter: in order ~)* auf daß *(old)*.
thatch [θætʃ] **1** *n* **(a)** *(material)* *(straw)* Stroh *nt*; *(reed)* Reet *nt*; *(roof)* Strohdach *nt*; Reetdach *nt*. **(b)** *(inf: hair)* Mähne *f*. **2** *vt* roof mit Stroh/Reet decken.
thatched [θætʃt] *adj* roof *(with straw)* Stroh-; *(with reed)* Reet-; cottage mit Stroh-/Reetdach, mit Stroh-/Reet gedeckt. to be ~ ein Stroh-/Reetdach haben, mit Stroh-/Reet gedeckt sein.
thatcher [ˈθætʃəʳ] *n* Dachdecker *m*.
thatching [ˈθætʃɪŋ] *n (act, skill)* Stroh-/Reetdachdecken *nt*; *(roofing)* Stroh-/Reetdach *nt*.
thaw [θɔː] **1** *vt* auftauen (lassen); ice, snow also tauen lassen; *(make warm)* person, hands aufwärmen; *(fig: make friendly)* person auftauen *or* warm werden lassen; *relations* entspannen.
2 *vi (lit, fig)* auftauen; *(ice, snow)* tauen; *(person: become warmer also)* sich aufwärmen. it is ~ing es taut.
3 *n (lit, fig)* Tauwetter *nt*. before the ~/a ~ sets in bevor das Tauwetter einsetzt.
♦**thaw out 1** *vi (lit, fig)* auftauen. **2** *vt sep (lit)* frozen food etc auftauen (lassen); *person, hands* aufwärmen; *(fig) person* aus der Reserve locken. it took several whiskies to ~ him ~ *(inf)* er brauchte mehrere Whiskys, bis er auftaute *or* warm wurde.
the [ðə, *before vowels* ði:] **1** *def art* **(a)** der/die/das. in ~ room im *or* in dem Zimmer; on ~ edge am *or* an dem Rand; he went up on ~ stage er ging aufs *or* auf das Podium; to play ~ piano/guitar, Klavier/Gitarre spielen; all ~ windows all die *or* alle Fenster; have you invited ~ Browns? haben Sie die Browns *or* (with children) die Familie Brown eingeladen?; in ~ 20s in den zwanziger Jahren; Henry ~ Eighth Heinrich der Achte; how's ~ leg/wife? *(inf)* wie geht's dem Bein/Ihrer Frau? *(inf)*.
(b) *(with adj used as n)* das; die; *(with comp or superl)* der/die/das. ~ **Good** das Gute; ~ **poor/rich** die Armen *pl*/Reichen *pl*; translated from ~ **German** aus dem Deutschen übersetzt; she was ~ prettier/prettiest sie war die hübschere/hübscheste.
(c) *(denoting whole class)* der/die/das. ~ **elephant** is in danger of extinction der Elefant ist vom Aussterben bedroht.
(d) *(distributive use)* twenty pence ~ pound zwanzig Pence das *or* pro Pfund; by ~ hour pro Stunde; the car does thirty miles to ~ gallon das Auto braucht eine Gallone auf dreißig Meilen.
(e) [ði:] *(stressed)* der/die/das. it's *the* restaurant in this part of town das ist *das* Restaurant in diesem Stadtteil.
2 *adv (with comp adj or adv)* all ~ more/better/harder um so mehr/besser/schwieriger; ~ more he has ~ more he wants je mehr er hat, desto mehr will er; (all) ~ more so because ... um so mehr, als ...; *see* **better², worse**.
theatre, *(US)* **theater** [ˈθɪətəʳ] *n* **(a)** Theater *nt*; *(esp in names, ~ company also)* Bühne *f*. to go to the ~ ins Theater gehen; what's on at the ~? was wird im Theater gegeben?
(b) *no pl (theatrical business, drama)* Theater *nt*. he's always been keen on (the) ~ er war schon immer theaterbegeistert; he has been in (the) ~ all his life er war sein Leben lang beim Theater; not all Shaw's plays are good ~ nicht alle Stücke von Shaw eignen sich für die Bühne.
(c) *(Brit: operating ~)* Operationssaal *m*.
(d) *(scene of events)* Schauplatz *m*. ~ of war Kriegsschauplatz *m*; ~ of operations Schauplatz *m* der Handlungen.
theatre: ~ **company** *n* Theaterensemble *nt*; *(touring)* Schauspiel- *or* Theatertruppe *f*; ~ **critic** *n* Theaterkritiker(in *f*) *m*; ~**goer** *n* Theaterbesucher(in *f*) *m*; ~**land** *n* Theatergegend *f*; **in ~land** in der Theatergegend; ~ **nurse** *n (Brit Med)* Operationsschwester *f*.
theatrical [θɪˈætrɪkəl] **1** *adj* **(a)** Theater-; *company also* Schauspiel-; *experience also* schauspielerisch.
(b) *(pej)* behaviour etc theatralisch.
2 *n* ~s *pl* Theaterspielen *nt*; most people have taken part in ~s die meisten Menschen haben schon mal Theater gespielt.
theatricality [θɪˈætrɪkælɪtɪ] *n* theatralische Art.
theatrically [θɪˈætrɪkəlɪ] *adv* **(a)** schauspielerisch. ~ it was a disaster vom Theaterstandpunkt war das eine Katastrophe.
(b) *(pej)* behave, speak theatralisch.
thee [ðiː] *pron (old, dial: objective case of thou)* *(dir obj, with prep +acc)* Euch *(obs)*, Dich *(also Eccl)*; *(indir obj, with prep +dat)* Euch *(obs)*, Dir *(also Eccl)*. God be with ~ Gott sei mit Dir; for ~ and thine für Dich und die Deinen.
theft [θeft] *n* Diebstahl *m*.
their [ðɛəʳ] *poss adj* **(a)** ihr. **(b)** *(inf: belonging to him or her)* seine(r, s). everyone knows ~ rights nowadays jeder kennt heutzutage seine Rechte; *see also* **my 1**.
theirs [ðɛəz] *poss pron* **(a)** ihre(r, s). **(b)** *(inf: belonging to him or her)* seine(r, s). ~ **is not to reason why** es ist nicht an ihnen, zu fragen; ~ **is a wretched life** sie führen ein elendes Leben; ~ **is the Kingdom of Heaven** ihrer ist das Himmelreich; *see also* **mine¹ 1**.
theism [ˈθiːɪzəm] *n* Theismus *m*.

theist [ˈθiːɪst] *n* Theist(in *f*) *m*.
theistic [θiːˈɪstɪk] *adj* theistisch.
them [ðem, *weak form* ðəm] **1** *pers pron pl* **(a)** *(dir obj, with prep +acc)* sie; *(indir obj, with prep +dat)* ihnen. both/neither of ~ saw me beide haben/keiner von beiden hat mich gesehen; give me a few of ~ geben Sie mir ein paar davon; none of ~ keiner/keinen (von ihnen); he's one of ~ das ist einer von ihnen; *(homosexual)* er ist andersrum *(inf)*.
(b) *(emph)* sie. ~ **and us** *(inf)* sie *or* die *(inf)* und wir; it's ~ sie sind's; it's ~ **who did it** *sie or die* haben es gemacht.
(c) *(dial: incorrect)* ~ **as wants to** die, die wollen.
2 *adj (incorrect)* diese.
thematic *adj*, ~**ally** *adv* [θɪˈmætɪk, -əlɪ] thematisch.
theme [θiːm] *n* **(a)** *(subject)* Thema *nt*. **(b)** *(US Sch: essay)* Aufsatz *m*. **(c)** *(Mus)* Thema *nt*; Leitmotiv *nt*; *(Film, TV)* Melodie *f (from aus)*.
theme: ~ **music** *n (Film)* Titelmusik *f*; *(TV)* Erkennungsmelodie *f*; ~ **song** *n (Film)* Titlesong *m*; *(TV)* Erkennungssong *m*; *(of opera)* Leitmotiv *nt*; ~ **tune** *n* *see* ~ **music**.
themselves [ðəmˈselvz] *pers pron pl* **(a)** *(reflexive)* sich. **(b)** *(emph)* selbst. the figures ~ die Zahlen selbst *or* an sich; *see also* **myself**.
then [ðen] **1** *adv* **(a)** *(next, afterwards)* dann. and ~ what happened? und was geschah dann?
(b) *(at this particular time)* da; *(in those days also)* damals. it was ~ 8 o'clock da war es 8 Uhr; I was/will be on holiday ~ ich war da (gerade) in Urlaub/werde da in Urlaub sein; he did it ~ and there *or* there and ~ er hat es auf der Stelle getan; *see* **now**.
(c) *(after prep)* from ~ on(wards) von da an; before ~ vorher, zuvor; but they had gone by ~ aber da waren sie schon weg; we'll be ready by ~ bis dahin sind wir fertig; since ~ seitdem, seit der Zeit; between now and ~ bis dahin; (up) until ~ I had never tried it bis dahin hatte ich es nie versucht.
(d) *(in that case)* dann. I don't want that — ~ what do you want? ich will das nicht — was willst du denn?; what are you going to do, ~? was wollen Sie dann tun?; but ~ that means that ... das bedeutet ja aber dann, daß ...; all right, ~ also *or* dann meinetwegen; so it's true ~ dann ist es (also) wahr, es ist also wahr; (so) I was right ~ ich hatte also recht; you don't want it ~? Sie wollen es also nicht?, dann wollen Sie es (also) nicht?; where is it ~? wo ist es denn?
(e) *(furthermore, and also)* dann, außerdem. (and) ~ there's my aunt und dann ist da noch meine Tante; but ~ ... aber ... auch; but ~ he's my son aber er ist (eben) auch mein Sohn; but ~ again he is my friend aber er ist doch mein Freund.
(f) *(phrases)* now ~, what's the matter? na, was ist denn los?; come on ~ nun komm doch.
2 *adj attr* damalig. the ~ Prime Minister der damalige Premierminister.
thence [ðens] *adv* **(a)** *(old: from that place)* von dannen *(old)*, von dort *or* da *(weg)*.
(b) *(old: from that time)* which dated from ~ was aus der *(damaligen)* Zeit stammt; they met again a week ~ sie trafen eine Woche darauf wieder zusammen.
(c) *(form: for that reason)* infolgedessen.
thenceforth [ˌðensˈfɔːθ], **thenceforward** [ˌðensˈfɔːwəd] *adv* von da an, von der Zeit an.
theocracy [θɪˈɒkrəsɪ] *n* Theokratie *f*.
theocratic [θɪəˈkrætɪk] *adj* theokratisch.
theodolite [θɪˈɒdəlaɪt] *n* Theodolit *m*.
theologian [θɪəˈləʊdʒɪən] *n* Theologe *m*, Theologin *f*.
theological [θɪəˈlɒdʒɪkəl] *adj* theologisch. ~ college Priesterseminar *nt*; ~ student Theologiestudent(in *f*) *m*.
theology [θɪˈɒlədʒɪ] *n* Theologie *f*.
theorem [ˈθɪərəm] *n* Satz *m (also Math)*, Theorem *nt (geh, spec)*.
theoretic(al) [θɪəˈretɪk(əl)] *adj* theoretisch.
theoretically [θɪəˈretɪkəlɪ] *adv* theoretisch.
theoretician [θɪərəˈtɪʃən], **theorist** [ˈθɪərɪst] *n* Theoretiker(in *f*) *m*.
theorize [ˈθɪəraɪz] *vi* theoretisieren.
theorizer [ˈθɪəraɪzəʳ] *n* Theoretiker(in *f*) *m*.
theory [ˈθɪərɪ] *n* Theorie *f*. in ~ theoretisch, in der Theorie; ~ of colour/evolution Farben-/Evolutionslehre *or* -theorie *f*; he has a ~ that ... er hat die Theorie, daß ...; well, it's a ~ das ist eine Möglichkeit; he always goes on the ~ that ... er geht immer davon aus, daß ....
theosophical [θɪəˈsɒfɪkəl] *adj* theosophisch.
theosophist [θɪˈɒsəfɪst] *n* Theosoph(in *f*) *m*.
theosophy [θɪˈɒsəfɪ] *n* Theosophie *f*.
therapeutic(al) [ˌθerəˈpjuːtɪk(əl)] *adj* therapeutisch. to be ~ therapeutisch wirken.
therapeutics [ˌθerəˈpjuːtɪks] *n sing* Therapeutik *f*.
therapist [ˈθerəpɪst] *n* Therapeut(in *f*) *m*.
therapy [ˈθerəpɪ] *n* Therapie *f*.
there [ðɛəʳ] **1** *adv* **(a)** dort, da; *(with movement)* dorthin, dahin. look, ~'s Joe/~'s Joe coming guck mal, da ist/kommt Joe; it's under/over/in ~ es liegt dort *or* da drunter/drüben/drin; put it under/over/in/on ~ stellen Sie es dort *or* da drunter/rüber *or* hinüber/rein *or* hinein/drauf *or* hinauf; let's stop ~ hören wir doch da auf; *(travelling)* halten wir doch da *or* dort an; ~ and back hin und zurück; so ~ we were da waren wir nun also.
(b) *(fig: on this point)* da. ~ you are wrong da irren Sie sich; you've got me ~ da bin ich überfragt; I've got you ~ da *or* jetzt habe ich Sie.
(c) *(in phrases)* ~ is/are es *or* da ist/sind; *(~ exists/exist also)* es gibt; ~ were three of us wir waren zu dritt; ~ is a mouse in the room da ist eine Maus im Zimmer; ~ was once a castle here hier war *or* stand einmal eine Burg; ~ is a chair in the corner in der Ecke steht ein Stuhl; ~ is dancing afterwards danach ist Tanz *or* wird getanzt; ~'s a book I want to read da ist ein Buch, das ich lesen möchte; is ~ any wine left? — well, ~ was ist noch

Wein da? — gerade war noch welcher da; ~ isn't any food/time/point, is ~? — yes ~ is es gibt wohl nichts zu essen/dazu haben wir wohl keine Zeit/das hat wohl keinen Sinn, oder? — doch!; ~ seems to be no-one at home es scheint keiner zu Hause zu sein; ~ appears to be a flaw in your argument da scheint ein Fehler in Ihrer Beweisführung zu sein; how many mistakes were ~? wie viele Fehler waren es?; is ~ any beer? ist Bier da?; afterwards ~ was coffee anschließend gab es Kaffee; ~ is a page missing es or da fehlt eine Seite; ~ comes a time when ... es kommt eine Zeit, wo ...; ~ being no alternative solution da es keine andere Lösung gibt/gab; ~'ll be a picnic at the end of term am Ende des Semesters wird ein Picknick stattfinden; ~ will be an opportunity for shopping es wird Gelegenheit zum Einkaufen geben; God said: let ~ be light, and ~ was light und Gott sprach: es werde Licht! und es ward Licht; ~ you go again (inf) jetzt geht's schon wieder los; now ~'s a real woman das ist eine richtige Frau; ~'s gratitude for you! (iro) da haben Sie Ihren Dank!; now ~'s a good idea! (das ist) eine gute Idee!; ~ you are (giving sb sth) hier(, bitte)!; (on finding sb) da sind Sie ja!; ~ you or we are, you see, I knew he'd say that na, sehen Sie, ich habe es ja gewußt, daß er das sagen würde; wait, I'll help you ... ~ you are! warten Sie, ich helfe Ihnen, ... so(, das wär's)!; you press the switch and ~ you are! Sie brauchen nur den Schalter zu drücken, das ist alles.

2 interj ~! ~! na, na!; stop crying now, ~'s a good boy hör auf zu weinen, na komm; drop it, ~'s a good dog laß das fallen, komm, sei brav; now ~'s a good boy, don't tease your sister komm, sei ein braver Junge und ärgere deine Schwester nicht; hey, you ~! (inf) he, Sie da!; hurry up ~ (inf) Beeilung!, Tempo, Tempo! (inf); make way ~ Platz da!, machen Sie mal Platz!; ~ take this to your mother da, bring das deiner Mutter; but ~, what's the good of talking about it? was soll's, es hat doch keinen Zweck, darüber zu reden; ~! I knew it would break! da! ich hab's ja gewußt, daß es kaputt gehen würde!

thereabouts [ˌðɛərə'bauts] adv (a) (place) dort in der Nähe, dort irgendwo. (b) (quantity, degree) five pounds/fifteen or ~ so um die fünf Pfund/fünfzehn (herum).

thereafter [ðɛər'ɑːftə^r] adv (form) danach, darauf (geh).

thereby [ˌðɛə'baɪ] adv dadurch, damit. and ~ hangs a tale und da gibt es eine Geschichte dazu.

therefore ['ðɛəfɔː^r] adv deshalb, daher; (as logical consequence) also. so ~ I was wrong ich hatte also unrecht; we can deduce, ~, that ... wir können also or daher folgern, daß ....

therein [ðɛər'ɪn] adv (form) (a) (in that particular) darin, in dieser Hinsicht. (b) (in that place) darin, dort.

thereof [ˌðɛər'ɒv] adv (form) davon. this town and the citizens ~ diese Stadt und deren Bürger.

thereon [ˌðɛər'ɒn] adv (form) (on that) darauf; (on that subject) darüber.

there's [ðɛəz] contr of **there is**; **there has**.

thereupon [ˌðɛərə'pɒn] adv (a) (then, at that point) daraufhin). (b) (form: on that subject) darüber; (on that) darauf.

therewith [ˌðɛə'wɪθ] adv (form) (a) (with that) damit. (b) (thereupon) darauf.

therm [θɜːm] n (Brit) 100.000 Wärmeeinheiten (≈ 10⁸ Joules).

thermal ['θɜːməl] **1** adj a (Phys) capacity, unit Wärme-; neutron, reactor, equilibrium thermisch. (b) thermal. ~ springs Thermalquellen pl; ~ baths Thermalbäder pl. **2** n (Aviat, Met) Thermik f no pl.

thermic ['θɜːmɪk] adj thermisch.

thermionic [ˌθɜːmɪ'ɒnɪk] adj thermionisch, glühelektrisch. ~ valve (Brit) or tube (US) Glühelektronenröhre f.

thermo [ˌθɜːməu-]: ~dynamic adj thermodynamisch; ~dynamics npl Thermodynamik f; ~electric adj thermoelektrisch; ~electricity n Thermoelektrizität f.

thermometer [θə'mɒmɪtə^r] n Thermometer nt.

thermo: ~nuclear adj thermonuklear, Fusions-; ~pile n Thermosäule f; ~plastic 1 adj thermoplastisch; 2 n Thermoplast m.

thermos ® ['θɜːməs] n (also ~ flask or bottle US) Thermosflasche f.

thermostat ['θɜːməstæt] n Thermostat m.

thermostatic [ˌθɜːmə'stætɪk] adj thermostatisch. ~ regulator Temperaturregler m; ~ switch Temperaturschalter m.

thermostatically [ˌθɜːmə'stætɪkəli] adv thermostatisch.

thesaurus [θɪ'sɔːrəs] n Thesaurus m.

these [ðiːz] adj, pron diese; see this.

thesis ['θiːsɪs] n, pl **theses** ['θiːsiːz] (a) (argument) These f. (b) (Univ) (for PhD) Dissertation, Doktorarbeit (inf) f; (for diploma) Diplomarbeit f.

thespian ['θɛspɪən] (liter, hum) **1** adj dramatisch. ~ art Schauspielkunst f. **2** n Mime m, Mimin f.

they [ðeɪ] pers pron pl (a) sie. ~ are very good people es sind sehr gute Leute; it is ~ (form) sie sind es; ~ who diejenigen, die or welche, wer (+sing vb).

(b) (people in general) ~ say that ... man sagt, daß ...; ~ are going to build a new road man will or sie wollen eine neue Straße bauen; ~ are thinking of changing the law es ist beabsichtigt, das Gesetz zu ändern.

(c) (inf) if anyone looks at this closely, ~ will notice ... wenn sich das jemand näher ansieht, wird er bemerken ...

they'd [ðeɪd] contr of **they had**; **they would**.

they'd've ['ðeɪdəv] contr of **they would have**.

they'll [ðeɪl] contr of **they will**.

they're [ðɛə^r] contr of **they are**.

they've [ðeɪv] contr of **they have**.

thiamine ['θaɪəmiːn] n Thiamin nt.

thick [θɪk] **1** adj (+er) (a) dick; wall, thread, legs, arms also stark. a wall three feet ~ eine drei Fuß dicke or starke Wand; to give sb a ~ ear (inf) jdm ein paar hinter die Ohren hauen (inf); you'll get a ~ ear in a minute du kriegst gleich ein

---

paar hinter die Ohren! (inf); the shelves were ~ with dust auf den Regalen lag dick der Staub; to have a ~ head einen Brummschädel haben (inf), einen dicken Kopf haben (inf).

(b) hair, fog, smoke dick, dicht; forest, hedge, beard dicht; liquid, sauce, syrup etc dick(flüssig); mud dick; darkness tief; crowd dicht(gedrängt); air schlecht, dick (inf); accent stark, breit. they are ~/not exactly ~ on the ground (inf) die gibt es wie Sand am Meer (inf)/die sind dünn gesät; the hedgerows were ~ with wild flowers die Hecken strotzten von wilden Blumen; his voice was ~ with a cold/emotion/fear/drink er sprach mit belegter/bewegter/angstvoller Stimme/schwerer Zunge; the air was ~ with cries for help die Luft war von Hilfeschreien erfüllt; the air is pretty ~ in here hier ist eine Luft zum Schneiden or sehr schlechte Luft.

(c) (inf: stupid) person dumm, doof (inf).

(d) (inf: intimate) they are very ~ sie sind dicke Freunde (inf); to be very ~ with sb mit jdm eine dicke Freundschaft haben (inf).

(e) (inf: much) that's a bit ~! das ist ein starkes Stück (inf).

2 n (a) in the ~ of the crowd/the fight/it mitten in der Menge/im Kampf/mittendrin; he likes to be in the ~ of things er ist gern bei allem voll dabei; to stay with sb/stick together through ~ and thin mit jdm/zusammen durch dick und dünn gehen.

(b) (of finger, leg) dickste Stelle. the ~ of the calf die Wade.

3 adv (+er) spread, lie, cut dick; grow dicht. the snow lay ~ lag eine dichte Schneedecke; his blows fell ~ and fast seine Schläge prasselten nieder; offers of help poured in ~ and fast es kam eine Flut von Hilfsangeboten; they are falling ~ and fast sie fallen um wie die Fliegen (inf); to lay it on ~ (inf) (zu) dick auftragen (inf); that's laying it on a bit ~ (inf) das ist ja wohl etwas übertrieben.

thicken ['θɪkən] **1** vt sauce etc eindicken. **2** vi (a) dicker werden; (fog, hair also, crowd, forest) dichter werden; (smoke, fog also, darkness) sich verdichten; (sauce) dick werden. (b) (fig: plot, mystery) immer verwickelter or undurchsichtiger werden. aha, the plot ~s! aha, jetzt wird's interessant!

thickener ['θɪkənə^r], **thickening** ['θɪkənɪŋ] n (for sauces) Bindemittel nt.

thicket ['θɪkɪt] n Dickicht nt.

thick: ~-head n (inf) Dummkopf m; ~-headed adj (inf) dumm, doof (inf); ~-headedness n (inf) Dummheit, Doofheit (inf) f; ~-lipped adj mit dicken or wulstigen Lippen, mit Wulstlippen.

thickly ['θɪkli] adv (a) spread, paint, cut dick; populated, crowded, wooded dicht. (b) snow was falling ~ dichter Schnee fiel; the ~ falling snow der dicht fallende Schnee. (c) speak (with a cold) mit belegter Stimme; (with drink) mit schwerer Zunge; (with emotion) bewegt; (with fear) angstvoll.

thickness ['θɪknɪs] n sec adj (a) Dicke f; Stärke f. (b) Dicke, Dichte f; Dichte f; Dickflüssigkeit f; Dichte f; Stärke f. the ~ of his lips seine dicken or wulstigen Lippen; the ~ of his voice (through cold) seine belegte Stimme; (through drink) seine schwere Zunge; (through emotion) seine bewegte Stimme; (through fear) seine bebende Stimme; the ~ of the air die schlechte or verbrauchte Luft; it is sold in three different ~es es wird in drei verschiedenen Dicken or Stärken verkauft.

(c) Dummheit, Doofheit (inf) f.

(d) (layer) Lage, Schicht f.

thick: ~-set adj gedrungen; hedge dicht; ~-skinned adj (lit) dickhäutig; (fig) dickfellig.

thicky ['θɪki] n (inf) Dummkopf m, Doofkopf (inf) m.

thief [θiːf] n, pl **thieves** [θiːvz] Dieb(in f) m. to set a ~ to catch a ~ (prov) einen vom Fach benützen; to be as thick as thieves dicke Freunde sein (inf).

thieve [θiːv] vti stehlen.

thieving ['θiːvɪŋ] **1** adj jackdaw diebisch. a ~ disposition ein Hang m zum Stehlen; keep your ~ hands off my cigarettes laß die Finger weg von meinen Zigaretten (inf); this ~ lot (inf) diese Räuberbande (inf). **2** n (thefts) Stehlen nt, Diebstähle pl.

thievish ['θiːvɪʃ] adj diebisch attr.

thievishness ['θiːvɪʃnɪs] n diebische Art.

thigh [θaɪ] n (Ober)schenkel m.

thigh: ~ bone n Oberschenkelknochen m; ~-length adj boots übers Knie reichend.

thimble ['θɪmbl] n Fingerhut m.

thimbleful ['θɪmblful] n (fig) Fingerhut(voll) m.

thin [θɪn] **1** adj (+er) (a) (not thick) paper, slice, string, wall, blood dünn; dress, material also leicht; liquid dünn(flüssig); (narrow) line also, column schmal.

(b) (not fat) dünn.

(c) (sparse) hair, grass dünn, schütter; vegetation gering, spärlich, kümmerlich (pej); population, crowd klein, kümmerlich (pej). his hair is getting quite ~ sein Haar lichtet sich or wird schütter; he's a bit ~ on top bei ihm lichtet es sich oben schon ein wenig; to be ~ on the ground (fig) dünn gesät sein.

(d) (not dense) fog leicht; air dünn. to vanish into ~ air (fig) sich in Luft auflösen; the agent simply vanished into ~ air der Agent schien sich einfach in Luft aufgelöst zu haben.

(e) (fig: weak, poor) voice, smile schwach, dünn; excuse schwach, fadenscheinig; disguise, story-line, plot schwach. she had a ~ time of it (dated inf) es war nicht gerade schön für sie; to give sb a ~ time of it (inf) jdm das Leben schwermachen.

2 adv (+er) spread, cut dünn; lie dünn, spärlich.

3 vt paint, sauce verdünnen; trees lichten; hair ausdünnen; population verringern; blood dünner werden lassen.

4 vi (fog, crowd) sich lichten; (hair also) schütter werden.

♦**thin down 1** vi dünner werden; (person also) abnehmen, schlanker werden. **2** vt sep paint, sauce verdünnen.

♦**thin out 1** vi (fog) sich lichten, schwächer werden; (crowd) kleiner werden; (audience) sich lichten; (hair) sich lichten, schütter werden. the houses started ~ning ~ die Häuser wurden immer spärlicher. **2** *vt sep* hair ausdünnen; *seedlings also* verziehen; *forest* lichten; *population* verkleinern.

thine [ðaɪn] (*old, dial*) **1** *poss pron* der/die/das deine. **for thee and ~** für Dich und die Deinen; *see* **mine**¹. **2** *poss adj* (*only before vowel*) Euer/Eure/Euer (*obs*), Dein/Deine/Dein (*also Eccl*).

thing [θɪŋ] *n* **(a)** (*any material object*) Ding *nt*. **a ~ of beauty/ great value** etwas Schönes/etwas sehr Wertvolles; **she likes sweet ~s** sie mag Süßes *or* süße Sachen; **if you regard a number as some sort of ~** wenn man eine Zahl als eine Art Ding *or* Gegenstand betrachtet; **what's that ~?** was ist das?; **I don't have a ~ to wear** ich habe nichts zum Anziehen.

(b) (*clothes, equipment, belongings*) **~s** *pl* Sachen *pl*; **have you got your swimming ~s?** hast du dein Badezeug *or* deine Badesachen dabei?; **they washed up the breakfast ~s** sie spülten das Frühstücksgeschirr.

(c) (*non material: affair, subject*) Sache *f*. **you know, it's a funny ~** wissen Sie, es ist schon seltsam; **the odd/best ~ about it is** ... das Seltsame/Beste daran ist, ...; **it's a good ~ I came** nur gut, daß ich gekommen bin; **it's a bad/strange ~ but** ... es ist schlecht/seltsam, aber ...; **he's on to** *or* **onto a good ~** (*inf*) er hat da was Gutes aufgetan (*inf*); **he's got a good ~ going there** (*inf*) der hat da was Gutes laufen (*inf*); **what a (silly) ~ to do** wie kann man nur so was (Dummes) tun!; **you take the ~ too seriously** Sie nehmen die Sache *or* das zu ernst; **there is one/another ~ I want to ask you** eines/und noch etwas möchte ich Sie fragen; **and there's another ~, why didn't you** ...? und noch etwas, warum haben Sie nicht ...?; **the ~s you do/say!** was du so machst/sagst!; **I must be hearing/seeing ~s!** ich glaube, ich höre/sehe nicht richtig, ich glaube, ich spinne! (*inf*); **all the ~s I meant to say/do** alles, was ich sagen/tun wollte; **which ~s in life do you value most?** was *or* welche Dinge im Leben bewerten Sie am höchsten?; **to expect great ~s of sb/sth** Großes *or* große Dinge von jdm/etw erwarten; **I must think ~s over** ich muß mir die Sache *or* das überlegen; **~s are going from bad to worse** es wird immer schlimmer; **as ~s stand at the moment, as ~s are** ... so wie die Dinge im Moment liegen; **how are ~s with you?** wie geht's (bei) Ihnen?; **since that's how ~s are** ... wenn das so ist ..., in dem Fall ...; **it's bad enough as ~s are** es ist schon schlimm genug; **~s aren't what they used to be** es ist alles nicht mehr so wie früher; **to talk of one ~ and another** von diesem und jenem reden; **taking one ~ with another** im großen und ganzen, alles in allem; **it's been one ~ after the other** going wrong es kam eins zum anderen; **if it's not one ~ it's the other** es ist immer irgend etwas; **(what) with one ~ and another I haven't had time to do it yet** ich bin einfach noch nicht dazu gekommen; **it's neither one ~ nor the other** es ist weder das eine noch das andere; **for one ~ it doesn't make sense** erst einmal ergibt das überhaupt keinen Sinn; **to see/under-stand/know not a ~** (*absolut*) nichts sehen/verstehen/wissen, keine Ahnung haben; **to tell sb a ~ or two** jdm einiges erzählen; **he knows a ~ or two** er hat etwas auf dem Kasten (*inf*); **he knows a ~ or two about cars** er kennt sich mit Autos aus; **it's just one of those ~s** so was kommt eben vor (*inf*); **she was all ~s to all men** sie war der Wunschtraum aller Männer; *see* **teach**.

(d) (*person, animal*) Ding *nt*. **poor little ~** das arme (kleine) Ding!; **you poor ~!** du Arme(r)!; **she's a funny old ~** sie ist ein komisches altes Haus (*inf*); **I say, old ~** (*dated inf*) na, du altes Haus (*inf*); **lucky ~!** die *or* der Glückliche/du Glückliche(r).

(e) (*what is suitable, best*) **that's just the ~ for me** das ist genau das richtige für mich; **that's not the ~ to do so** was macht *or* tut man nicht; **his behaviour isn't quite the ~** (*dated*) sein Benehmen ist nicht gerade berückend (*inf*); **the latest ~ in ties** der letzte Schrei in der Krawattenmode; **the ~ to do now would be** ... wie wir jetzt machen sollten, wäre ...; **that would be the polite/honourable ~ to do** es wäre nur höflich/anständig, das zu tun; **it's the usual ~ to apologize** normalerweise entschuldigt man sich.

(f) (*in phrases*) **I'm not at my best first ~ in the morning** so früh am Morgen bin ich nicht gerade in Hochform; **I'll do that first ~ in the morning** ich werde das gleich *or* als erstes morgen früh tun; **I'll do it first ~** ich werde das zuerst *or* als erstes tun; **last ~ at night** vor dem Schlafengehen; **painting is his ~** das Malen liegt ihm (*inf*); **the ~ is to know when** ... man muß wissen, wann ...; **yes, but the ~ is** ... ja, aber ...; **the ~ is we haven't got enough money** die Sache ist die, wir haben nicht genug Geld; **the ~ is, you see, he loves her** das Problem ist, daß er sie liebt; **yes but the ~ is it won't work** ja, aber das Dumme ist, es funktioniert nicht; **to do one's own ~** (*sl*) tun, was man will; **when Jimi Hendrix starts doing his ~** (*sl*) wenn Jimi Hendrix seine Schau abzieht (*sl*); **she's got this ~ about Sartre/dogs** (*inf*) (*can't stand*) sie kann Sartre/Hunde einfach nicht ausstehen; (*is fascinated by*) sie hat einen richtigen Sartre-/Hundefimmel (*inf*); **she's got a ~ about spiders** (*inf*) bei Spinnen dreht sie durch (*inf*); **he's got this ~ about her** (*inf*) (*can't stand*) er kann sie nicht ausstehen; (*is infatuated*) er ist verrückt nach ihr.

(g) (*all*) **~s** German/mystical/mechanical alles Deut-sche/Geheimnisvolle/Mechanische.

(h) (*inf: for forgotten name of person*) Dings(bums) *mf* (*inf*).

thingummybob ['θɪŋəmɪˌbɒb], **thingamajig** ['θɪŋəmɪˌdʒɪg], **thingummy** ['θɪŋəmɪ] *n* Dings, Dingens, Dingsbums, Dingsda *nt or* (*for people*) *mf* (*all inf*).

think [θɪŋk] (*vb: pret, ptp thought*) **1** *vi* denken. **to ~ to oneself** sich (*dat*) denken; **I was just sitting there ~ing to myself** ich saß so in Gedanken da; **~ before you speak/act** denk nach *or* überleg, bevor du sprichst/handelst; **do animals ~?** können Tiere denken?; **to act without ~ing** unüberlegt handeln; (*stupidly also*) unbedacht handeln; **~ again!** denk noch mal nach; **so you ~ I'll give you the money?** well, you'd better **~ again!** du denkst also, ich gebe dir das Geld? das hast du dir (wohl) gedacht!; **to ~ in French** französisch *or* in Fran-

zösisch denken; **it makes you ~** es macht *or* stimmt einen nachdenklich; **I need time to ~** ich brauche Zeit zum Nach-denken; **wait a minute, give me time to ~** Augenblick, laß mir Zeit zum Nachdenken; **it's so noisy you can't hear yourself ~** bei so einem Lärm kann doch kein Mensch denken; **now let me ~** laß (mich) mal überlegen *or* nachdenken; **stop and ~ before you make a big decision** denke in aller Ruhe nach, bevor du eine schwerwiegende Entscheidung triffst; **it's a good idea, don't you ~?** es ist eine gute Idee, findest *or* meinst du nicht auch?; **just ~** stellen Sie sich (*dat*) bloß mal vor; **just ~, you too could be rich** stell dir vor *or* denk dir nur, auch du könntest reich sein; **~! denk mal nach!; where was it? ~, man, ~!** wo war es?, denk doch mal nach!; **listen, I've been ~ing,** ... hör mal, ich habe mir überlegt ...; **sorry, I just wasn't ~ing** Entschuldigung, da habe ich geschlafen (*inf*); **you just didn't ~, did you?** da hast du dir nichts gedacht, oder?; **you just don't ~, do you?** (*about other people*) du denkst auch immer nur an dich; (*about conse-quences*) was denkst du dir eigentlich?; *see* **big**.

2 *vt* **(a)** denken; (*be of opinion also*) glauben, meinen. **I ~ you'll find I'm right** ich glaube *or* denke, Sie werden zu der Überzeugung gelangen, daß ich recht habe; **I ~ it's too late** ich glaube, es ist zu spät; **I ~ I can do it** ich glaube *or* denke, daß ich es schaffen kann; **I ~ I'm old enough to make my own mind up!** ich denke, ich bin alt genug, um selbst zu entscheiden!; **well, I think it was there!** nun, ich glaube zumindest, daß es da war!; **and what do you ~?** asked the interviewer und was meinen Sie *or* und was ist Ihre Meinung? fragte der Interviewer; **you never know what he's ~ing** ich weiß nie, was er (sich) denkt; **I ~ you'd better go/accept/be careful** ich denke, Sie gehen jetzt besser/Sie stimmen lieber zu/Sie wären besser vorsichtig; **I ~ he'll understand** ich denke, er wird das verstehen; **well, I think he'll understand** na ja, ich nehme zumindest an, daß er ver-stehen wird; **I ~ so** ich denke *or* glaube (schon); **I ~ so too** das meine *or* denke ich auch; **I don't ~ so/I shouldn't ~ so/I ~ not** ich denke *or* glaube nicht; **I'll take this one then — I ~ not, Mr Green** dann nehme ich dieses — das glaube ich kaum, Herr Green; **I should ~ so/not!** das will ich (aber) auch gemeint haben/das will ich auch nicht hoffen; **I hardly ~/~ it** likely that ... ich glaube kaum/ich halte es nicht für wahrscheinlich, daß ...; **I wasn't even ~ing** it daran habe ich nicht einmal gedacht; **one would have thought there was an easier answer** man sollte eigentlich meinen, daß es da eine einfachere Lösung gäbe; **one would have thought you could have been more punctual** man könnte eigentlich erwarten, daß Sie etwas pünktlicher kommen; **I wouldn't have thought you would do such a thing** ich hätte nie gedacht *or* geglaubt, daß Sie so etwas tun würden; **one would have thought they'd have grasped it by now** man sollte eigentlich erwarten, daß sie das inzwischen begriffen haben; **what do you ~ I should do?** was, glauben Sie, soll ich tun?, was soll ich Ihrer Meinung nach tun?; **well, what do you ~, shall we leave now?** nun, was meinst du, sollen wir jetzt gehen?; **I ~ I'll go for a walk** ich glaube, ich mache einen Spaziergang; **do you ~ you can manage?** glauben Sie, daß Sie es schaffen?

(b) (*consider*) **you must ~ me very rude** Sie müssen mich für sehr unhöflich halten; **he ~s he's intelligent, he ~s himself intelligent** er hält sich für intelligent, er meint, er ist *or* sei intelligent; **they are thought to be rich** man hält sie für reich; **I wouldn't have thought it possible** das hätte ich nicht für mög-lich gehalten.

(c) (*imagine*) sich (*dat*) denken, sich (*dat*) vorstellen. **I don't know what to ~** ich weiß nicht, was ich davon halten soll; **that's what you ~!** denkste! (*inf*); **that's what he ~s** hat der eine Ahnung! (*inf*); **who do you ~ you are!** für wen hältst du dich eigentlich?, wofür hältst du dich eigentlich?; **you can't ~ how pleased I am to see you** Sie können sich (*dat*) (gar) nicht denken *or* vorstellen, wie froh ich bin, Sie zu sehen; **I can't ~ what he means!** ich kann mir (gar) nicht denken, was er meint; (*iro also*) was er damit bloß meinen kann *or* meint?; **anyone would ~ he was dying** man könnte beinahe glauben, er läge im Sterben; **one or you would ~ they'd already met** man könnte (geradezu) glauben *or* denken, sie seien alte Bekannte; **who would have thought it?** wer hätte das gedacht?; **to ~ that she's only ten!** wenn man bedenkt *or* sich (*dat*) vorstellt, daß sie erst zehn ist.

(d) (*reflect*) **to ~ how to do sth** sich (*dat*) überlegen, wie man etw macht; **I was ~ing to (myself) how ill he looked** ich dachte mir (im Stillen), daß er sehr krank aussah; **I never thought to ask you** ich habe gar nicht daran gedacht, Sie zu fragen.

(e) (*expect, intend: often neg or interrog*) **I didn't ~ to see you here** ich hätte nicht gedacht *or* erwartet, Sie hier zu treffen *or* daß ich Sie hier treffen würde; **I thought as much/I thought so** das habe ich mir schon gedacht.

(f) **to ~ one's way out of a difficulty** sich (*dat*) einen Ausweg aus einer Schwierigkeit überlegen; **you'll ~ yourself into a rage again** du steigerst dich (nur) wieder in eine Wut hinein.

3 *n* **have a ~ about it and let me know** denken Sie mal darüber nach *or* überlegen Sie es sich (*dat*) einmal, und geben Sie mir dann Bescheid; **to have a good/quiet ~** gründlich/in aller Ruhe nachdenken; **you've got another ~ coming** (*inf*) da irrst du dich aber gewaltig (*inf*), da bist du aber auf dem Holzweg (*inf*).

♦**think about** *vi + prep obj* **(a)** (*reflect on*) idea, suggestion nachdenken über (+*acc*). **OK, I'll ~ it** okay, ich überlege es mir; **what are you ~ing ~?** woran denken Sie gerade?; **it's worth ~ing ~** das ist überlegenswert, das wäre zu überlegen; **to ~ twice ~ sth** sich (*dat*) etw zweimal überlegen; **that'll give him something to ~ ~** das wird ihm zu denken geben.

(b) (*in progressive tenses: half intend to*) daran denken, vor-haben. **I was ~ing ~ coming to see you** ich habe vorgehabt *or* daran gedacht, Sie zu besuchen; **he was ~ing ~ suicide** er hat daran gedacht, Selbstmord zu begehen; **we're ~ing ~ a holiday in Spain** wir denken daran, in Spanien Urlaub zu machen.

(c) *see* **think of (a, b, f).**

♦**think ahead** vi vorausdenken; (*anticipate: driver etc*) Voraussicht walten lassen.

♦**think back** vi sich zurückversetzen (*to* in +acc).

♦**think of** vi +prep obj (a) (*consider, give attention to*) denken an (+acc). I've too many things to ~ ~ just now ich habe gerade zu viel um die Ohren (*inf*); I've enough things to ~ ~ as it is ich habe sowieso schon den Kopf voll *or* genug um die Ohren (*inf*); he has his family to ~ ~ er muß an seine Familie denken; to ~ ~ sb's feelings an jds Gefühle (*acc*) denken, auf jds Gefühle (*acc*) Rücksicht nehmen; he ~s nobody but himself er denkt bloß an sich; what am I ~ing ~! (*inf*) was habe ich mir da(bei) bloß gedacht?, was hab' ich bloß im Kopf? (*inf*).

(b) (*remember*) denken an (+acc). will you ~ ~ me sometimes? wirst du manchmal an mich denken?; I can't ~ ~ her name ich kann mich nicht an ihren Namen erinnern, ich komme nicht auf ihren Namen.

(c) (*imagine*) sich (*dat*) vorstellen, bedenken, sich (*dat*) denken. and to ~ ~ her going there alone! und wenn man bedenkt *or* sich (*dat*) vorstellt, daß sie ganz allein dorthin gehen will/geht(ging; ~ ~ the cost of all that! stell dir bloß vor *or* denk dir bloß, was das alles kostet; just ~ ~ him in a kilt! stellen Sie sich (*dat*) ihn mal in einem Schottenrock vor!

(d) (*entertain possibility of*) she'd never ~ ~ getting married sie denkt gar nicht daran zu heiraten; he'd never ~ ~ such a thing so etwas würde ihm nicht im Traum einfallen; would you ~ ~ lowering the price a little? würden Sie unter Umständen den Preis etwas ermäßigen?

(e) (*devise, suggest*) solution, idea, scheme sich (*dat*) ausdenken. who thought ~ that idea/plan? wer ist auf diese Idee gekommen *or* verfallen/wer hat sich diesen Plan ausgedacht?; the best thing I can ~ ~ is to go home ich halte es für das beste, nach Hause zu gehen; shoes for dogs! what will they ~ ~ next! Schuhe für Hunde! was sie sich wohl (nächstens) noch alles einfallen lassen!

(f) (*have opinion of*) halten von. what do you ~ ~ it/him? was halten Sie davon/von ihm?; to ~ well *or* highly ~ sb/sth eine gute *or* hohe Meinung von jdm/etw haben, viel von jdm/etw halten; to ~ little *or* not to ~ much ~ sb/sth wenig *or* nicht viel von jdm/etw halten; I told him what I thought ~ him ich habe ihm gründlich die *or* meine Meinung gesagt; he is very well thought ~ in his own town in seiner Heimatstadt hält man große Stücke auf ihn.

♦**think on** vi +prep obj (*old, dial*) see **think about (a)**.

♦**think out** vt sep plan durchdenken; (*come up with*) solution sich (*dat*) ausdenken. a person who likes to ~ things ~ for himself ein Mensch, der sich (*dat*) seine eigene Meinung bildet.

♦**think over** vt sep offer, suggestion nachdenken über (+acc), sich (*dat*) überlegen. can I ~ it ~? darf ich darüber nachdenken?, kann ich es mir nochmal überlegen?

♦**think through** vt sep (*gründlich*) durchdenken.

♦**think up** vt sep sich (*dat*) ausdenken. who thought ~ that idea? wer ist auf die Idee gekommen?

thinkable ['θɪŋkəbl] adj denkbar.

thinker ['θɪŋkə'] n Denker(in f) m.

thinking ['θɪŋkɪŋ] 1 adj denkend. he's not really a ~ man, he prefers action er ist kein Denker, sondern ein Macher; all ~ men will agree with me alle vernünftigen Menschen werden mit mir übereinstimmen; to put one's ~ cap on scharf überlegen *or* nachdenken.

2 n to do some hard ~ about a question sich (*dat*) etwas gründlich überlegen, etwas genau durchdenken; to my way of ~ meiner Meinung nach; that might be his way of ~ das mag seine Meinung sein; this calls for some quick ~ hier muß eine schnelle Lösung gefunden werden.

thin-lipped ['θɪnlɪpt] adj dünnlippig; smile dünn.

thinly ['θɪnlɪ] adv (a) (*in thin slices or layers*) dünn. (b) (*sparsely*) dünn; wooded spärlich. (c) (*lightly*) clad leicht, dünn. (d) (*fig*) veiled, disguised kaum, dürftig; smile schwach.

thinner ['θɪnə'] n Verdünner m, Verdünnungsmittel nt.

thinness ['θɪnnɪs] n (a) Dünnheit, Dünnigkeit f; (*of dress, material*) Leichtheit f; (*of liquid*) Dünnflüssigkeit f; (*of paper, line, thread*) Feinheit f; (*of column of print*) geringe Breite.

(b) (*of person*) Magerkeit f.

(c) (*sparseness*) the ~ of his hair/the grass/wood/population etc sein schütterer *or* spärlicher Haarwuchs/das spärlich wachsende Gras/die lichte Bewaldung/die geringe Bevölkerungsdichte etc; the ~ of the crowd die geringe Anzahl von Zuschauern.

(d) (*lack of density: of air*) Dünnheit f.

(e) (*fig*) (*of voice, smile*) Schwachheit f; (*of excuse, disguise, plot*) Dürftigkeit f.

thin-skinned ['θɪnskɪnd] adj (*fig*) empfindlich, dünnhäutig.

third [θɜːd] 1 adj (a) (*in series*) dritte(r, s). she was *or* came ~ in her class/in the race sie war die Drittbeste in der Klasse/sie machte *or* belegte den dritten Platz beim Rennen; ~ time lucky beim dritten Anlauf gelingt's!

(b) (*of fraction*) a ~ part ein Drittel nt.

2 n (a) (*of series*) Dritte(r, s); (*fraction*) Drittel nt.

(b) (*Mus*) Terz f.

(c) (*Aut*: ~ gear) dritter Gang; see also **sixth**.

third: ~-class 1 adv dritter Klasse; 2 adj (*lit*) dritter Klasse; (*fig*) drittklassig; ~ degree n to give sb the ~ degree (*lit*) (beim Verhör) Stufe drei einschalten; (*fig*) jdn in die Zange nehmen; ~-degree burns npl (*Med*) Verbrennungen pl dritten Grades.

thirdly ['θɜːdlɪ] adv drittens.

third: ~ party n Dritte(r) m, dritte Person; ~-party 1 adj attr Haftpflicht-; 2 adv to be insured ~-party in einer Haftpflichtversicherung sein, haftpflichtversichert sein; ~-person adj in der dritten Person; ~-rate adj drittklassig, drittrangig; T~ World 1 n Dritte Welt; 2 attr der Dritten Welt.

thirst [θɜːst] 1 n Durst m. ~ for knowledge/revenge/adventure/love Wissensdurst m/Rachsucht f/Abenteuerlust f/Liebeshunger m; he's got a real ~ on him (*inf*) er hat einen noblen Durst (am Leibe) (*inf*); to die of ~ verdursten.

2 vi (a) (*old*) I ~ er dürstet *or* durstet mich.

(b) (*fig*) to ~ for revenge/knowledge etc nach Rache/Wissen etc dürsten; the plants were ~ing for rain die Pflanzen dürsteten nach Regen.

thirstily ['θɜːstɪlɪ] adv (*lit*) durstig; (*fig*) begierig.

thirsty ['θɜːstɪ] adj (+er) (a) durstig. to be/feel ~ Durst haben; it made me ~ das machte mich durstig *or* mir Durst; ~ for praise/love/affection/revenge/knowledge/blood begierig auf Lob/nach Liebe/Zuneigung/Rache/Wissen/Blut dürstend *or* lechzend (*old, hum*); the land is ~ for rain das Land dürstet nach Regen.

(b) (*causing thirst*) it's ~ work diese Arbeit macht durstig.

thirteen [θɜː'tiːn] 1 adj dreizehn. 2 n Dreizehn f.

thirteenth [θɜː'tiːnθ] 1 adj (*in series*) dreizehnte(r, s). a ~ part ein Dreizehntel nt. 2 n (*in series*) Dreizehnte(r, s); (*fraction*) Dreizehntel nt; see also **sixth**.

thirtieth ['θɜːtɪθ] 1 adj (*in series*) dreißigste(r, s). a ~ part ein Dreißigstel nt. 2 n (*in series*) Dreißigste(r, s); (*fraction*) Dreißigstel nt; see also **sixth**.

thirty ['θɜːtɪ] 1 adj dreißig. ~-one/-two ein-/zweiunddreißig; a ~-second note (US Mus) ein Zweiunddreißigstel nt. 2 n Dreißig f. the thirties (*time*) die dreißiger Jahre; one's thirties (*age*) die Dreißiger; see also **sixty**.

thirtyish ['θɜːtɪʃ] adj um die dreißig.

this [ðɪs] 1 dem pron, pl these dies, das. what is ~? was ist das (hier)?; who is ~? wer ist das?; ~ is John das *or* dies ist John; these are my children das *or* dies sind meine Kinder; ~ is where I live hier wohne ich; ~ is what he showed me dies *or* das (hier) hat er mir gezeigt; do you like ~? gefällt dir das?; I prefer ~ ich mag das hier *or* dies(es) lieber; ~ is to certify that ... hiermit wird bestätigt, daß ...; under/in front of/against etc ~ darunter/davor/dagegen etc; it ought to have been done before ~ es hätte schon vorher getan werden sollen; with ~ he left us damit *or* mit diesen Worten verließ er uns; what's all ~? was soll das?; what's all ~ I hear about your new job? was höre ich da so (alles) über deine neue Stelle?; ~ and that mancherlei; we were talking of ~ and that wir haben von diesem und jenem *or* über dies und das geredet; ~, that and the other alles mögliche; will you take ~ or that? nehmen Sie dieses hier oder das da?; it was like ~ es war so; ~ is Friday the 13th heute ist Freitag der 13., heute haben wir Freitag den 13.; but ~ is May aber wir haben *or* es ist doch Mai!; and now ~! und jetzt (auch noch) dies *or* das!; ~ is Mary (speaking) hier (ist) Mary; ~ is what I mean! das meine ich (ja)!; ~ is it! (now) jetzt!; (showing sth) das da!, das ist er/sie/es!; (exactly) genau!

2 dem adj, pl these diese(r, s). ~ week/month/year diese Woche/diesen Monat/dieses Jahr; ~ evening heute abend; ~ day week/fortnight (heute) in einer Woche/in vierzehn Tagen; ~ time last week letzte Woche um diese Zeit; ~ coming week jetzt die (kommende) Woche; ~ time diesmal, dieses Mal; these days heutzutage; all ~ talk dieses ganze Gerede, all das *or* dies Gerede; to run ~ way and that hin und her rennen; I have been waiting for you ~ past half-hour ich habe bereits die letzte halbe Stunde auf dich gewartet; ~ boy of yours! also, Ihr Junge!; I met ~ guy who ... (*inf*) ich habe (so) einen getroffen, der ...; ~ friend of hers said ... dieser Freund von ihr (*inf*) *or* ihr Freund sagte ...

3 dem adv so. it was ~ long es war so lang; ~ far (*time*) bis jetzt; (*place*) so weit, bis hierher; ~ much is certain soviel ist sicher, eins steht fest.

thistle ['θɪsl] n Distel f.

thistledown ['θɪsldaʊn] n Distelwolle f. as light as ~ federleicht.

thither ['ðɪðə'] adv (*old*) dorthin, dahin; see **hither**.

tho' [ðəʊ] abbr of **though**.

thole [θəʊl] n (*Naut*) Dolle, Riemenauflage f.

Thomist ['təʊmɪst] 1 n Thomist m. 2 adj thomistisch.

thong [θɒŋ] n (*of whip*) Peitschenschnur f, Peitschenriemen m; (*fastening*) Lederriemen m.

thoracic [θɔː'ræsɪk] adj Brust-, thorakal (*spec*).

thorax ['θɔːræks] n Brustkorb, Brustkasten, Thorax (*spec*) m.

thorn [θɔːn] n Dorn m; (*shrub*) Dornbusch, Dornenstrauch m. to be a ~ in sb's flesh *or* side (*fig*) jdm ein Dorn im Auge sein.

thornless ['θɔːnlɪs] adj ohne Dornen.

thorny ['θɔːnɪ] adj (+er) (*lit*) dornig, dornenreich; (*fig*) haarig.

thorough ['θʌrə] adj (a) gründlich; knowledge also umfassend, solide; contempt also bodenlos; success voll, durchschlagend; fool, rascal ausgemacht. she's/it's a ~ nuisance sie ist wirklich eine Plage/das ist wirklich lästig.

thorough: ~bred 1 n reinrassiges Tier; (*horse*) Vollblut(pferd) nt, Vollblüter m; 2 adj reinrassig; horse Vollblut-, vollblütig; dog Rasse-; ~fare n Durchfahrts- *or* Durchgangsstraße f; it's the most famous ~fare of this town es ist die berühmteste Straße dieser Stadt; this isn't a public ~fare das ist keine öffentliche Verkehrsstraße; "no ~fare" (*cul-de-sac*) „Sackgasse"; (*not open to public*) „Durchfahrt verboten"; ~going adj changes gründlich; revision grundlegend, tiefgreifend; measure, reform durchgreifend; he is a ~going rascal er ist ein Spitzbube durch und durch.

thoroughly ['θʌrəlɪ] adv (a) gründlich, von Grund auf.

(b) (*extremely*) durch und durch, von Grund auf. a ~ nasty person ein Scheusal durch und durch; ~ modern durch und durch modern; ~ boring ausgesprochen langweilig; I'm ~ ashamed ich schäme mich zutiefst, ich bin zutiefst beschämt.

thoroughness ['θʌrənɪs] n Gründlichkeit, Sorgfältigkeit, Sorgfalt f; (*of knowledge also*) Umfang m, Solidität f.

Thos abbr of **Thomas**.

those [ðəʊz] *pl of* **that 1** *dem pron* das (da) *sing.* **what are ~?** was ist das (denn) da?, was sind das für Dinger? (*inf*); **whose are ~?** wem gehören diese da?; **~ are the girls/my suggestions** das (da) *or* dies(es) sind die Mädchen/das *or* dies sind meine Vorschläge; **on top of/above/after ~** darauf (*inf*) darüber hinaus/darüber/danach; (*place*) dahinter; **~ are the ones I like** das da *or* diese dort mag ich; **~ who want to go, may** wer möchte, kann gehen, diejenigen, die gehen möchten, können das tun (*form*); **one of ~ who ...** einer/eine von denen *or* denjenigen, die ...; **there are ~ who say ...** einige sagen ...
2 *dem adj* diese *or* die (da), jene (*old, liter*). **what are ~ men doing?** was machen diese Männer da?; **on ~ two occasions** bei diesen beiden Gelegenheiten; **it was just one of ~ days/things** das war wieder so ein Tag/so eine Sache; **he is one of ~ people who ...** er ist einer von den Leuten *or* von denjenigen, die ...; **~ dogs/sons of yours!** also, diese Hunde/deine Söhne!

thou [ðaʊ] *pers pron* (*old*) (*to friend, servant etc*) Er/Sie (*obs*); (*to stranger*) Ihr (*obs*); (*Rel*) Du; (*Brit: dial*) du.

though [ðəʊ] **1** *conj* **(a)** (*in spite of the fact that*) obwohl, obgleich, obschon. **even ~** obwohl *etc*; **~ poor** obwohl *etc* sie arm ist, ist sie großzügig; **strange ~ it may seem** ... so seltsam es auch scheinen mag ..., mag es auch noch so seltsam scheinen (*geh*) ...; **important ~ it may be/is** ... so wichtig es auch sein mag/ist, auch wenn es noch so wichtig ist ...
(b) (*liter: even if*) **I will go (even) ~ it should cost me my life** ich werde gehen, und sollte es mich (auch) das Leben kosten *or* und koste es das Leben (*liter*); **~ it take forever** (*liter*) und dauerte es auch ewig (*liter*).
(c) *see* **as.**
2 *adv* **(a)** (*nevertheless*) doch. **he didn't/did do it ~** er hat es aber (doch) nicht/aber doch gemacht; **I'm sure he didn't do it ~** ich bin aber sicher, daß er es nicht gemacht hat; **nice day — rather windy ~** schönes Wetter! — aber ziemlich windig!
(b) (*really*) **but will he ~?** tatsächlich?, wirklich?
(c) (*inf*) **hot, isn't it? — isn't it ~!** warm, was? — allerdings!

thought [θɔːt] **1** *pret, ptp of* **think.**
2 *n* **(a)** *no pl* (*act or process of thinking*) Denken *nt*. **to spend hours in ~** stundenlang in Gedanken (vertieft) sein; **to be lost in ~** in Gedanken *or* gedankenverloren (*geh*) sein; **to take ~** (*old*) denken; **logical ~** logisches Denken; **in ~** in Gedanken; **~ experiment** Gedankenexperiment *nt*.
(b) (*idea, opinion*) Gedanke *m*; (*sudden*) Einfall *m*. **she hasn't a ~ in her head** sie hat nichts im Hirn *or* Kopf; **the ~s of Chairman Mao** die Gedanken *pl* des Vorsitzenden Mao; **he didn't express any ~s on the matter** er hat keine Ansichten zu diesem Thema geäußert; **that's a ~!** (*amazing*) man stelle sich das mal vor!; (*problem to be considered*) das ist wahr!; (*good idea*) das ist eine (gute) Idee *or* ein guter Gedanke *or* Einfall; **what a ~!** was für ein Gedanke *or* eine Vorstellung!; **a ~ has just occurred to me, I've just had a ~** (*inf*) mir ist gerade ein Gedanke gekommen, mir ist gerade etwas eingefallen; **don't give it another ~** machen Sie sich (*dat*) keine Gedanken darüber; (*forget it*) denken Sie nicht mehr daran; **on second ~s** wenn man das noch mal überlegt; **his one ~ was ...** sein einziger Gedanke war ...; **to have no ~ of doing sth** gar nicht vorhaben *or* gar nicht daran denken, etw zu tun; **it's a shame it doesn't fit, but it's the ~ that counts** es ist zwar ein Jammer, daß es nicht paßt, aber es war gut gemeint; **it's the ~ that counts, not how much you spend** es kommt nur auf die Idee an, nicht auf den Preis; **to collect one's ~s** sich sammeln, seine Gedanken zusammennehmen; **her ~s were elsewhere** sie war in Gedanken woanders; **the mere or very ~ of it** der bloße Gedanke (daran), die bloße Vorstellung.
(c) *no pl* (*body of ideas*) Denken *nt.* **modern ~** das moderne Denken, das Denken der Moderne.
(d) *no pl* (*care, consideration*) Nachdenken *nt*, Überlegung *f*. **to give some ~ to sth** sich (*dat*) Gedanken über etw (*acc*) machen, etw bedenken *or* überlegen; **after much ~** nach langer Überlegung *or* langem Überlegen; **to act without ~** gedankenlos *or* ohne Überlegung handeln; **without ~ for sb/oneself/sth** ohne an jdn/sich selbst/etw zu denken; **to be full of ~ for sb** auf jdn große Rücksicht nehmen; **he was full of ~ for our comfort** er bemühte sich sehr um unser Wohlergehen; **he has no ~ for his parents' feelings** er nimmt keine Rücksicht auf die Gefühle seiner Eltern; **I never gave it a moment's ~** ich habe mir nie darüber Gedanken gemacht.
(e) **a ~** (*a little*) eine Idee, ein Ideechen *nt* (*inf*); **with a ~ more tact** mit einer Idee *or* einer Spur mehr Takt.

thoughtful [ˈθɔːtfʊl] *adj* **(a)** (*full of thought*) expression, person nachdenklich, gedankenvoll, grüblerisch; remark, analysis, book gut durchdacht, wohlüberlegt; present gut ausgedacht.
(b) (*considerate*) rücksichtsvoll; (*attentive, helpful*) aufmerksam. **to be ~ of sb's comfort/needs** an jds Wohlbefinden/Bedürfnisse denken; **to be ~ of/towards sb** jdm gegenüber aufmerksam/rücksichtsvoll sein; **it was very ~ of you to ...** es war sehr aufmerksam von Ihnen, zu ...

thoughtfully [ˈθɔːtfəlɪ] *adv* **(a)** say, look nachdenklich.
(b) (*with much thought*) mit viel Überlegung. **a ~ written book** ein wohldurchdachtes Buch.
(c) (*considerately*) rücksichtsvoll; (*attentively, helpfully*) aufmerksam. **she ~ provided rugs** sie war so aufmerksam, Decken bereitzustellen, aufmerksamerweise hatte sie Decken bereitgestellt.

thoughtfulness [ˈθɔːtfʊlnɪs] *n* **(a)** (*of expression, person*) Nachdenklichkeit *f*; (*of remark, analysis*) Tiefgang *m*. **the ~ of her present** der Gedanke, der hinter ihrem Geschenk steckt/steckte.
(b) (*consideration*) Rücksicht(nahme) *f*; (*attentiveness, helpfulness*) Aufmerksamkeit *f*. **his ~ of or for/towards his parents** seine Aufmerksamkeit/Rücksichtnahme seinen Eltern gegenüber.

thoughtless [ˈθɔːtlɪs] *adj* **(a)** (*without reflection*) gedankenlos, unüberlegt, unbesonnen. **~ of the danger, he leapt** ungeachtet der Gefahr, sprang er.
(b) (*inconsiderate*) person gedankenlos, rücksichtslos; (*inattentive, unhelpful*) gedankenlos, unachtsam. **he's very ~ of or about/to(wards) other people** er ist sehr gedankenlos/rücksichtslos anderen gegenüber.

thoughtlessly [ˈθɔːtlɪslɪ] *adv* **(a)** (*without reflection*) gedankenlos, unüberlegt. **he had ~ taken the key with him** er hatte aus Gedankenlosigkeit den Schlüssel mitgenommen. **(b)** *see adj (b).*

thoughtlessness [ˈθɔːtlɪsnɪs] *n* **(a)** (*lack of reflection*) Gedankenlosigkeit, Unüberlegtheit *f*. **(b)** *see adj (b)* Gedankenlosigkeit, Rücksichtslosigkeit *f*; Gedankenlosigkeit, Unaufmerksamkeit *f*.

thought: **~reader** *n* Gedankenleser(in *f*) *m*; **~reading** *n* Gedankenlesen *nt*; **~ transference** *n* Gedankenübertragung *f*.

thousand [ˈθaʊzənd] **1** *adj* tausend. **a ~/two ~** (ein)tausend/zweitausend; **a ~ times** tausendmal; **a ~ and one/two** tausend(und)eins/tausend(und)zwei; **I died a ~ deaths** (*inf*) (*embarrassed*) ich wäre fast in den Boden versunken; (*afraid*) ich habe tausend Ängste ausgestanden; **I have a ~ and one (different) things to do** (*inf*) ich habe tausenderlei *or* tausend Dinge zu tun.
2 *n* Tausend *nt*. **the ~s** (*Math*) die Tausender *pl*; **there were ~s of people present** es waren Tausende (von Menschen) anwesend; **the year three ~** das Jahr dreitausend; **people arrived in their ~s** die Menschen kamen zu Tausenden.

thousandfold [ˈθaʊzəndfəʊld] (*liter*) **1** *adj* tausendfach. **2** *adv* tausendfach, tausendfältig.

thousandth [ˈθaʊzəntθ] **1** *adj* (*in series*) tausendste(r, s). **a or one ~ part** ein Tausendstel *nt*. **2** *n* (*in series*) Tausendste(r, s); (*fraction*) Tausendstel *nt*; *see also* **sixth.**

thraldom, (*US*) **thralldom** [ˈθrɔːldəm] *n* (*liter*) Knechtschaft *f*. **he was held in ~ to her beauty** (*fig*) ihre Schönheit hatte ihn in ihren Bann geschlagen.

thrall [θrɔːl] *n* (*liter*) **(a)** (*slave*) Leibeigene(r), Sklave (*also fig*), Knecht *m*. **(b)** (*condition*) *see* **thraldom.**

thrash [θræʃ] **1** *vt* **(a)** (*beat*) verprügeln, verdreschen; donkey *etc* einschlagen auf (+*acc*). **to ~ the life out of sb** jdn grün und blau schlagen.
(b) (*Sport inf*) opponent (vernichtend) schlagen.
(c) (*move wildly*) arms schlagen mit, fuchteln mit; legs strampeln mit. **he ~ed his arms (about) angrily** er schlug wütend (mit den Armen) um sich.
(d) (*Agr*) *see* **thresh.**
2 *vi* **to ~ about or around** um sich schlagen; (*in bed*) sich herumwerfen; (*fish*) zappeln; **the branches ~ed against the panes** die Zweige schlugen gegen die Fensterscheiben.

◆ **thrash out** *vt sep* problem ausdiskutieren.

thrashing [ˈθræʃɪŋ] *n* **(a)** (*beating*) Prügel, Schläge *pl*, Dresche *f* (*inf*). **to give sb a good ~** jdm eine ordentliche Tracht Prügel verpassen. **(b)** (*Sport inf*) komplette Niederlage. **to give sb a ~** jdn vernichtend schlagen.

thread [θred] **1** *n* **(a)** (*of cotton, wool etc*) Faden *m*; (*Sew also*) Garn *nt*; (*strong ~*) Zwirn *m*. **to hang by a ~** (*fig*) an einem (seidenen *or* dünnen) Faden hängen.
(b) (*fig: of story*) (roter) Faden. **to follow the ~ of an argument/a story** dem Gedankengang einer Argumentation/dem roten Faden (in) einer Geschichte folgen; **he lost the ~ of what he was saying** er hat den Faden verloren; **to pick up the ~s of one's story/a conversation** den (roten) Faden/den Gesprächsfaden wiederaufnehmen; **to gather up or pick up the ~s of one's life** alte Fäden wieder anknüpfen.
(c) (*Tech: of screw*) Gewinde *nt*.
(d) (*fig: thin line: of light*) Strahl, Streifen *m*.
2 *vt* **(a)** needle einfädeln; beads aufreihen, auffädeln (*on* auf +*acc*); necklace aufziehen. **~ed with silver** von Silber(fäden) durchzogen, mit Silber(fäden) durchsetzt.
(b) **to ~ one's way through the crowd/trees** *etc* sich durch die Menge/zwischen den Bäumen *etc* hindurchschlängeln.
(c) (*Tech*) screw mit einem Gewinde versehen.
3 *vi* **he ~ed through the crowd** er schlängelte sich durch die Menge (hindurch).

threadbare [ˈθredbɛəʳ] *adj* abgewetzt, fadenscheinig; clothes also abgetragen; carpet also abgelaufen; argument fadenscheinig.

threaded [ˈθredɪd] *adj* (*Tech*) Gewinde-.

thread mark *n* Silberfaden *m* (*in Banknoten*).

threat [θret] *n* **(a)** Drohung *f*. **is that a ~?** soll das eine Drohung sein?; **is that a ~ or a promise?** soll das eine Strafe oder eine Belohnung sein?; **to make a ~** drohen, eine Androhung machen (*against sb* jdm); **under ~ of sth** unter Androhung von etw; **he is under ~ of expulsion** ihm wurde der Ausschluß angedroht.
(b) (*danger*) Bedrohung (*to gen*), Gefahr (*to für*) *f*. **this war is a ~ to civilization** dieser Krieg stellt eine Gefahr für die *or* eine Bedrohung der Zivilisation dar.

threaten [ˈθretn] **1** *vt* **(a)** person bedrohen, drohen (+*dat*); revenge, violence androhen, drohen mit. **don't you ~ me!** von Ihnen lasse ich mir nicht drohen!; **to ~ to do sth** (an)drohen, etw zu tun; **to ~ sb with sth** jdm etw androhen, jdm mit etw drohen; **to ~ sb with a weapon** jdn mit der Waffe bedrohen.
(b) (*put in danger*) bedrohen, gefährden. **the rain ~ed to spoil the harvest** der Regen drohte, die Ernte zu zerstören.
(c) (*Met: give warning of*) **the sky ~s rain** der Himmel sieht (bedrohlich) nach Regen aus; **it's ~ing to rain** es sieht (bedrohlich) nach Regen aus.
2 *vi* (*danger, storm etc*) drohen, im Anzug sein.

threatening [ˈθretnɪŋ] *adj* tone, gesture, voice drohend; weather, clouds also bedrohlich. **a ~ letter** ein Drohbrief *m*; **~ behaviour** Drohungen *pl.*

threateningly ['θretnɪŋlɪ] adv drohend. **the sky darkened ~** der Himmel verfinsterte sich bedrohlich.

three [θriː] **1** adj drei. **2** n (figure, tram, Cards) Drei f. **~'s a crowd** drei Leute sind schon zuviel, bei dreien ist einer zuviel; see also **six**.

three: **~-act play** n Dreiakter m; **~-colour(ed)** adj (Phot) Dreifarben-; **~-cornered** adj dreieckig; **~-cornered contest** or **fight** Kampf m mit drei Beteiligten or Parteien, Dreieckskampf m; **~-cornered hat** Dreispitz m; **~-D 1** n to be in **~-D** dreidimensional sein; **2** adj (also **~-dimensional**) dreidimensional; **~-fold** adj, adv dreifach; **~-legged** adj dreibeinig; **~-legged race** (Sport) Wettlauf, bei dem zwei an einem Bein zusammengebunden werden; **~-master** n Dreimaster m; **~penny** ['θrepənɪ] attr zu or für drei Pence; stamp also Dreipence-; **~penny bit** or **piece** n (Brit old) Dreipennystück nt; **~penny opera** n Dreigroschenoper f; **~-phase** adj (Elec) Dreiphasen-; **~-piece suit** n (man's) Anzug m mit Weste; (lady's) dreiteiliges Ensemble; **~-piece suite** n dreiteilige Polster- or Sitzgarnitur; **~-ply 1** n (wool) Dreifachwolle f; (wood) dreischichtiges Spanholz; **2** attr wool dreifach, Dreifach-; wood dreischichtig; **~-point landing** n (Aviat) Dreipunktlandung f; **~-point turn** n (Aut) volle Kehrtwende (bei der man zurücksetzen muß); **~-quarter 1** n (Sport) Dreiviertelspieler m; **2** attr dreiviertel; **~-quarter length** dreiviertellang; **~-quarter portrait** Halbbild nt; **~ quarters 1** n Dreiviertel nt; **2** adv dreiviertel, zu drei Vierteln; **~-ring circus** n (inf) Affenzirkus m; **~-score** adj sechzig; **~some** n Trio nt, Dreiergruppe f; (Golf) Dreier m; **in a ~some** zu dritt; **~-speed** adj attr **~-speed gears/gearbox** Dreigangschaltung f/ Dreiganggetriebe nt; **~-wheeler** n (Aut) dreirädriges Auto; (tricycle) Dreirad nt.

threnody ['θrenədɪ] n (Liter) Threnodie f.

thresh [θreʃ] vti dreschen.

thresher ['θreʃə'] n (a) (Agr: machine) Dreschmaschine f; (person) Drescher(in f) m. (b) (~ shark) Drescherhai m.

threshing ['θreʃɪŋ] n Dreschen nt. **~ floor** Dreschboden m, Tenne f; **~ machine** Dreschmaschine f.

threshold ['θreʃhəʊld] n (lit, fig, Psych) Schwelle f; (of door also) (Tür)schwelle f. **on the ~** an der Schwelle; **we are on the ~ of a great discovery** wir stehen unmittelbar vor or an der Schwelle zu einer großen Entdeckung; **the ~ of consciousness** die Bewußtseinsschwelle; **to have a high/low pain ~** eine hohe/niedrige Schmerzschwelle haben.

threw [θruː] pret of **throw**.

thrice [θraɪs] adv (old) dreimal. **he is ~ blessed** er ist dreifach or dreifältig gesegnet.

thrift [θrɪft] n Sparsamkeit f.

thriftily ['θrɪftɪlɪ] adv (a) sparsam, wirtschaftlich, haushälterisch. (b) (US) **his business is doing ~** sein Geschäft floriert.

thriftiness ['θrɪftɪnɪs] n (a) Sparsamkeit, Wirtschaftlichkeit f. (b) (US: prosperity) Gedeihen nt.

thriftless ['θrɪftlɪs] adj verschwenderisch.

thriftlessness ['θrɪftlɪsnɪs] n Verschwendung(ssucht) f.

thrifty ['θrɪftɪ] adj (+er) (a) (careful, economical) sparsam, wirtschaftlich, haushälterisch. (b) (US: thriving) blühend.

thrill [θrɪl] **1** n Erregung f. **all the ~s and spills of the circus** all die Sensationen und der Nervenkitzel des Zirkus; **the ~ of her touch** der erregende Reiz ihrer Berührung; **a ~ of joy/horror** eine freudige Erregung/ein Entsetzensschauder m; **she heard his voice with a ~ of excitement** sie hörte seine Stimme, und Erregung durchfuhr sie; **it gave me quite a~**, **it was quite a ~ for me** es war ein richtiges Erlebnis; **what a ~!** wie aufregend!; **he gets a ~ out of hunting** Jagen hat für ihn einen ganz besonderen Reiz; **the real ~ comes at the end of the book** die eigentliche Sensation kommt erst am Ende des Buches; **that's how he gets his ~s** das erregt ihn; **this will give you the ~ of a lifetime** das wird das Erlebnis deines Lebens (sein); **go on, give us a ~!** (inf) nun laß uns mal was sehen (inf).

2 vt person (story, crimes) mitreißen, fesseln, packen; (experience) eine Sensation sein für; (sb's touch, voice etc) freudig erzittern lassen; (sexually) erregen. **I was quite ~ed by the sight of the Alps** ich war ganz hingerissen beim Anblick der Alpen; **the thought of going to America ~ed her** der Gedanke an eine Amerikareise versetzte sie in freudige Erregung; **to be ~ed to bits** (inf) sich freuen wie ein Kind; (child esp) ganz aus dem Häuschen sein vor Freude.

3 vi **she ~ed at the sound of his voice/to his touch** ein freudiger Schauer durchlief sie, als sie seine Stimme hörte/bei seiner Berührung.

thriller ['θrɪlə'] n Reißer m (inf); (whodunnit) Krimi m.

thrilling ['θrɪlɪŋ] adj aufregend; book, film spannend, fesselnd; sensation überwältigend, hinreißend; music hinreißend, mitreißend; experience überwältigend, unwerfend (inf); (sexually) erregend. **we had a ~ time** es war richtig aufregend.

thrillingly ['θrɪlɪŋlɪ] adv spannungsgeladen. **~ new** aufregend neu; **the music rose ~ to a climax** die Musik steigerte sich einem erregenden Höhepunkt entgegen.

thrive [θraɪv] pret **throve** (old) or **~d**, ptp **thriven** ['θrɪvən] (old) or **~d** vi (be in good health: animal, plant) (gut) gedeihen; (child also) sich gut or prächtig entwickeln; (do well) (business) blühen, florieren; (businessman) erfolgreich sein.

♦**thrive on** vi +prep obj **the baby ~s ~ milk** mit Milch gedeiht das Baby prächtig; **this plant ~s ~ sun and light** bei Sonne und Licht gedeiht or entwickelt sich diese Pflanze prächtig; **he ~s ~ criticism/praise** Kritik/Lob bringt ihn erst zur vollen Entfaltung; **like it? I ~ ~ it** ob mir das gefällt? ich brauche das.

thriving ['θraɪvɪŋ] adj (a) plant prächtig gedeihend, kräftig; person blühend; child gut gedeihend. **he's ~!** ihm geht's prächtig; (child) er blüht und gedeiht! (b) business florierend, blühend, gutgehend; businessman erfolgreich, mit blühendem Geschäft.

thro' [θruː] abbr of **through**.

throat [θrəʊt] n (external) Kehle f; (internal also) Rachen m. **to grab sb by the ~** jdn bei or an der Kehle or Gurgel packen; **to cut sb's/one's ~** jdm/sich die Kehle or Gurgel durchschneiden; **to cut one's own ~** (fig) selbst das Wasser abgraben; **my ~ is really dry** ich habe einen völlig trockenen Hals or eine ganz trockene Kehle; **I've a fishbone stuck in my ~** mir ist eine Gräte im Hals steckengeblieben; **the doctor looked down her ~** der Arzt sah ihr in den Hals; **cancer of the ~** Kehlkopfkrebs m; **to clear one's ~** sich räuspern; **they've been pouring drink down my ~ all evening** (inf) sie haben den ganzen Abend lang Alkohol in mich hineingeschüttet (inf); **to thrust or ram or force one's ideas down sb's ~** (inf) jdm seine eigenen Ideen aufzwingen; **the words stuck in my ~** die Worte blieben mir im Halse stecken; **it sticks in my ~** (fig) das geht mir gegen den Strich (inf); **~ microphone** Kehlkopfmikrophon nt.

throaty adj (+er), **throatily** adv ['θrəʊtɪ, -ɪlɪ] kehlig, rauh.

throb [θrɒb] **1** vi (engine) klopfen, hämmern; (drums, gunfire) dröhnen; (heart, pulse) pochen, klopfen; (painfully: cut, wound) pochen, pulsieren, klopfen; (very strongly) hämmern; (fig: with life, activity) pulsieren (with vor +dat, mit). **his heart ~bed with joy** sein Herz klopfte vor Freude; **my head was still ~bing (with pain)** ich hatte immer noch dieses Pochen im Kopf; **my head is ~bing** ich habe rasende Kopfschmerzen; **a street ~bing with people** eine Straße, die von Menschen wimmelt.

2 n (engine) Klopfen, Hämmern nt; (drums, gunfire) Dröhnen nt; (heart, pulse, wound) Klopfen, Pochen nt; Hämmern nt. **the ~ of life** der Pulsschlag des Lebens.

throbbing ['θrɒbɪŋ] n see vi Klopfen, Hämmern nt; Dröhnen nt; Pochen, Klopfen nt; Pochen, Klopfen nt; Hämmern nt.

throes [θrəʊz] npl (a) **the ~ of childbirth** die (Geburts)wehen pl; **in the ~ of death** im Todeskampf, in Todesqualen pl; **to be in its final ~** (fig) in den letzten Zügen liegen.
(b) (fig) Wirren pl. **we are in the ~ of moving** wir stecken mitten im Umzug; **I was in the ~ of composition** ich war völlig vertieft in meine Kompositionen; **in the ~ of inspiration** in künstlerischer Versunkenheit.

thrombosis [θrɒm'bəʊsɪs] n Thrombose f.

thrombus ['θrɒmbəs] n Thrombus (form), Blutpfropf m.

throne [θrəʊn] **1** n Thron m; (Eccl) Stuhl m. **to come to the ~** den Thron besteigen; **to swear allegiance to the ~** der Krone den Treueid leisten; **the powers of the ~** die Macht der Krone. **2** vt (he is) **~d in glory** (Eccl) er sitzet or thronet in Herrlichkeit.

throneroom ['θrəʊnruːm] n Thronsaal m; (hum) Klo nt (inf).

throng [θrɒŋ] **1** n (of people) Scharen pl von Menschen, Menschenmenge f; (of angels) Heerschar f.
2 vi sich drängen. **to ~ round sb/sth** sich um jdn/etw drängen or scharen; **hundreds of people ~ed round** Hunderte von Leuten strömten herbei; **to ~ towards sb/sth** sich zu jdm/etw drängen, zu jdm/etw strömen.
3 vt belagern. **people ~ed the streets** die Menschen drängten sich in den Straßen; **to be ~ed with** wimmeln von or mit.

throttle ['θrɒtl] **1** vt (a) erdrosseln, erwürgen.
(b) (fig) feelings ersticken, unterdrücken; opposition ersticken, unterbinden. **to ~ the press** die Presse knebeln.
(c) (Tech) see **back**.
2 n (a) (on engine) Drossel f; (Aut etc) (lever) Gashebel m; (valve) Drosselklappe f. **at full ~** mit Vollgas; **to open/close the ~** die Drossel öffnen/schließen; (Aut etc) Gas geben/zurücknehmen.
(b) (hum: throat) Kehle f.
♦**throttle back** or **down 1** vt sep drosseln. **2** vi Gas zurücknehmen, den Motor drosseln.

through, (US) **thru** [θruː] **1** prep (a) (place) durch. **he got/couldn't get ~ the hedge** er schlüpfte durch die Hecke (hindurch)/er konnte nicht durch die Hecke durchkommen or (hin)durchschlüpfen; **to listen ~ the door** durch die (geschlossene) Tür mithören, lauschen; **he was shot ~ the head** er bekam einen Kopfschuß; **he went right ~ the red lights** er ist bei Rot einfach durchgefahren; **he has come ~ many hardships** er hat viel Schweres durchgemacht; **we're ~ that stage now** wir sind jetzt durch dieses Stadium hindurch; **to be halfway ~ a book** ein Buch halb or zur Hälfte durchhaben (inf); **that happens halfway/three-quarters of the way ~ the book** das passiert in der Mitte/im letzten Viertel des Buches; see vbs.
(b) (time) all **~ his life** sein ganzes Leben lang; **he won't live ~ the night** er wird die Nacht nicht überleben; **he worked ~ the night** er hat die Nacht durchgearbeitet; **he lives there ~ the week** er wohnt da während or unter (dial) der Woche or die Woche über; **he slept ~ the film** er hat den ganzen Film über or hindurch or lang geschlafen; all **~ the autumn** den ganzen Herbst über or hindurch.
(c) (US: up to and including) bis (einschließlich). **Monday ~ Friday** von Montag bis (einschließlich) Freitag.
(d) (means, agency) durch. **~ the post** mit der or per Post; **it happened ~ no fault of mine** es geschah nicht durch meine Schuld; **absent ~ illness** abwesend wegen Krankheit; **~ neglect** durch Nachlässigkeit; **to act ~ fear** aus Angst handeln.
2 adv (time, place) durch. **he's a gentleman/liar ~ and ~** er ist durch und durch ein Gentleman/verlogen; **to sleep all night ~** die ganze Nacht durchschlafen; **did you stay right ~?** sind Sie bis zum Schluß geblieben?; **they stayed ~ until Thursday** sie blieben bis Donnerstag (da); **he knew all ~ what I was getting at** er wußte die ganze Zeit (über), worauf ich hinauswollte; **to let sb ~** jdn durchlassen; **to be wet ~** durch und durch or bis auf die Haut naß sein; **to read sth ~** etw durchlesen; **he's ~ in the other office** er ist (drüben) im anderen Büro; **the train goes ~ to Berlin** der Zug fährt bis nach Berlin durch; see vbs.
3 adj pred (a) (finished) **to be ~ with sb/sth** mit jdm/etw fertig sein (inf); **we're ~** (have finished relationship) es ist (alles) aus zwischen uns; (have finished job) wir sind fertig; **I'm**

~ **with him** der ist für mich gestorben *or* erledigt, ich bin fertig mit ihm (*all inf*); I'm ~ **with that kind of work** ich habe genug von dieser Arbeit; you're ~, **Kowalski, fired** wir sind mit Ihnen fertig, Kowalski, Sie fliegen!; **are you** ~? sind Sie fertig?

   (**b**) (*Brit Telec*) **to be** ~ (**to sb/London**) mit jdm/London verbunden sein; **to get** ~ (**to sb/London**) zu jdm/nach London durchkommen; **you're** ~, **caller** Ihre Verbindung!, Ihr Gespräch!

through: ~ **coach** *n* (*Rail*) Kurswagen *m* (*for* nach); (*bus*) direkte Busverbindung; ~ **flight** *n* Direktflug *m*.

throughout [θru'aυt] **1** *prep* (**a**) (*place*) überall in (+*dat*). ~ **the country/world** im ganzen Land/in der ganzen Welt.

   (**b**) (*time*) den ganzen/die/das ganze ... hindurch *or* über. ~ **the war** den ganzen Krieg hindurch *or* über; ~ **his life** sein ganzes Leben lang.

   2 *adv* (**a**) (*in every part*) **the house is carpeted** ~ das Haus ist ganz *or* überall mit Teppichboden ausgelegt; **a house with electric light** ~ ein Haus, das in jedem Raum elektrisches Licht hat/hatte; **a block of flats with water and gas** ~ ein Wohnblock mit Wasser und Gas in allen Wohnungen; **the coat is lined** ~ der Mantel ist ganz gefüttert.

   (**b**) (*time*) die ganze Zeit hindurch *or* über.

through: ~**put** *n* (*Ind*) Durchsatz *m*; (*of computer*) Leistung *f*; ~ **ticket** *n* **can I get a** ~ **ticket to London?** kann ich bis London durchlösen?; ~ **traffic** *n* Durchgangsverkehr *m*; ~ **train** *n* durchgehender Zug; ~**way** *n* (*US*) Schnellstraße *f*.

throve [θrəuv] (*old*) *pret of* **thrive**.

throw [θrəu] (*vb: pret* **threw**, *ptp* **thrown**) **1** *n* (*of ball, javelin, dice*) Wurf *m*. **it's your** ~ du bist dran; **have another** ~ werfen Sie noch einmal; **to lose a** ~ (*dice*) den Wurf verlieren; **a 30-metre** ~ ein Dreißigmeterwurf *m*; **the first** ~ **went to the German** (*Wrestling*) der Deutsche brachte seinen Gegner als erster zu Boden.

   2 *vt* (**a**) *ball, stone* werfen; *water* schütten. **to** ~ **the dice/a six** würfeln/eine Sechs würfeln; **to** ~ **sth to sb** jdm etw zuwerfen; ~ **me those keys** werfen Sie mir die Schlüssel herüber; **to** ~ **sth at sb** etw nach jdm werfen; *mud, paint* etc mit etw bewerfen; **to** ~ **a ball 20 metres** einen Ball 20 Meter weit werfen; **to** ~ **sth across the room** etw (quer) durchs Zimmer werfen; **to** ~ **sb across the ring** jdn durch den Ring schleudern; **he threw himself to the floor** er warf sich auf den Boden *or* zu Boden; **to** ~ **oneself at sb** (*physically*) sich auf jdn werfen *or* stürzen; (*fig*) sich jdm an den Hals werfen *or* schmeißen (*inf*); **to** ~ **oneself into** sich in die Arbeit stürzen *or* hineinknien (*inf*); **to** ~ **one's voice** seine Stimme zum Tragen bringen.

   (**b**) (*send to ground*) *rider* abwerfen; *opponent* zu Boden werfen *or* bringen. **to be** ~**n from the saddle** aus dem Sattel geworfen werden.

   (**c**) (*put hastily*) werfen. **to** ~ **a coat over sb** jdm einen Mantel überwerfen; **to** ~ **a bridge across a river** eine Brücke über einen Fluß schlagen.

   (**d**) (*fig: cast*) werfen. **to** ~ **a glance at sb/sth** einen Blick auf jdn/etw werfen; **to** ~ **an angry look at sb/sth** jdm/einer Sache einen wütenden Blick zuwerfen; **she threw him an icy look** sie warf ihm einen eisigen Blick zu; **to** ~ **light** Licht geben; **to** ~ **sb/the dogs off the scent** *or* **trail** jdn abschütteln *or* abhängen/die Hunde von der Spur abbringen; **to** ~ **sb into prison** jdn ins Gefängnis werfen; **to** ~ **the blame on sb** jdm die Schuld zuschieben *or* in die Schuhe schieben; **he threw his troops into action** er warf seine Truppen ins Gefecht.

   (**e**) *switch, lever* betätigen.

   (**f**) (*inf: disconcert*) aus dem Konzept bringen.

   (**g**) *party* geben, schmeißen (*inf*).

   (**h**) *fit* bekommen, kriegen (*inf*).

   (**i**) *vase* töpfern, drehen; *silk* zwirnen.

   (**j**) (*snake*) **to** ~ **its skin** sich häuten.

   (**k**) (*animal: give birth to*) werfen.

   3 *vi* werfen; (~ *dice*) würfeln.

♦**throw about** *or* **around** *vt always separate* (**a**) (*scatter*) verstreuen; (*fig*) *money* um sich werfen mit.

   (**b**) (*toss*) herumwerfen; *one's arms* fuchteln mit; *one's legs* strampeln mit. **to** ~ **oneself** ~ (*in bed, on floor*) sich hin und her werfen, sich herumwerfen; (*wrestler etc*) sich nach allen Richtungen fallen lassen; **to** ~ **a ball** ~ ein bißchen Ball spielen; **he was** ~**n** ~ **in the car/accident** er wurde im Auto hin und her geschleudert/bei dem Unfall herumgeschleudert.

♦**throw away** *vt sep* (**a**) (*discard*) *rubbish* wegwerfen.

   (**b**) (*waste*) verschenken; *money* verschwenden (*on sb* auf *or* für etw, *on sb* an jdn), vergeuden (*on sth* für etw, *on sb* an jdn). **you are** ~**ing yourself** ~ **on him** Sie sind zu schade für ihn, Sie verschwenden sich an ihn (*geh*).

   (**c**) (*say casually*) *remark* nebenbei machen, beiläufig sagen.

♦**throw back 1** *vi* (*Biol*) **a type which** ~**s** ~ **to an earlier species** ein Typ, der Merkmale einer früheren Art aufweist.

   2 *vt sep* (**a**) (*send back*) *ball* zurückwerfen; *enemy* zurückwerfen, zurückdrängen.

   (**b**) (*backwards*) *head, bedclothes* zurückwerfen; *curtains* aufreißen. **to** ~ **oneself** ~ zurückweichen, zurückspringen.

   (**c**) (*fig*) **to be** ~**n** ~ **upon sth** auf etw (*acc*) wieder angewiesen sein, auf etw (*acc*) zurückgreifen müssen; **the crisis threw them** ~ **on their own resources** durch die Krise waren sie wieder auf sich selbst angewiesen.

   (**d**) **I don't want you** ~**ing that** ~ **at me** ich möchte nicht, daß du mir meine eigenen Worte/Taten wieder vorhältst.

♦**throw down** *vt sep* (*from a roof, the stairs etc*) herunterwerfen. ~ **your guns!** werfen Sie die Waffen weg!; **to** ~ **oneself** ~ sich zu Boden werfen, sich niederwerfen; **it's** ~**ing it** ~ (*inf: raining*) es gießt (in Strömen).

♦**throw in** *vt sep* (**a**) *extra* (gratis) dazugeben. **with a tour of London** ~**n** ~ mit einer Gratistour durch London dabei.

   (**b**) (*Sport*) *ball* einwerfen.

   (**c**) (*fig*) **to** ~ ~ **one's hand** aufgeben, sich geschlagen geben; **to** ~ ~ **the sponge** *or* **towel** das Handtuch werfen (*inf*).

   (**d**) (*say casually*) *remark* einwerfen (*to* in +*acc*).

♦**throw off** *vt sep* (**a**) (*get rid of*) *clothes* abwerfen; *disguise, habits* ablegen; *pursuer* abschütteln; *cold* loswerden; *the yoke of tyranny* abwerfen, abschütteln. (**b**) (*emit*) *sparks, smell* abgeben, von sich geben.

♦**throw on** *vt sep* *clothes* sich (*dat*) überwerfen.

♦**throw open** *vt sep* (**a**) *door, window* aufreißen. (**b**) *stately home etc* (öffentlich) zugänglich machen (*to* für). **membership was** ~**n** ~ **to the public** die Mitgliedschaft wurde für jedermann freigegeben.

♦**throw out** *vt sep* (**a**) (*discard*) *rubbish etc* wegwerfen.

   (**b**) (*reject*) *suggestion, bill* (*Parl*) verwerfen.

   (**c**) *person* hinauswerfen, rauswerfen (*inf*) (*of* aus). **to be** ~**n** ~ **of work** entlassen werden; **automation has** ~**n a lot of people** ~ **of work** die Automation hat viele Menschen arbeitslos gemacht *or* vielen Menschen ihren Arbeitsplatz genommen.

   (**d**) (*utter*) *hint* machen; *idea* äußern. **to** ~ ~ **a challenge** (**to sb**) jdn herausfordern.

   (**e**) (*plant*) *suckers, shoots* treiben; (*fire etc*) *heat* abgeben.

   (**f**) *one's chest* herausdrücken.

   (**g**) (*make wrong*) *calculations etc* über den Haufen werfen (*inf*), durcheinanderbringen. **to** ~ **sb** ~ **in his calculations** jdn bei seinen Berechnungen durcheinanderbringen.

♦**throw over** *vt sep* *plan* über den Haufen werfen (*inf*); *girlfriend* sitzenlassen (*for* wegen).

♦**throw together** *vt sep* (**a**) (*put hastily together*) *ingredients* zusammenwerfen; *clothes* zusammenpacken; (*make quickly*) *essay* hinhauen (*inf*), runterschreiben (*inf*).

   (**b**) (*bring together*) *people* (*fate etc*) zusammenführen; (*friends etc*) zusammenbringen.

♦**throw up 1** *vi* sich übergeben, brechen. **it makes you want to** ~ ~ da kann einem schlecht werden, da kommt einem das Kotzen (*sl*).

   2 *vt sep* (**a**) *ball, hands* hochwerfen.

   (**b**) (*abandon*) *job* aufgeben; *opportunity etc* verschenken. **I feel like** ~**ing everything** ~ ich würde am liebsten alles hinwerfen (*inf*).

   (**c**) (*vomit up*) von sich (*dat*) geben, ausbrechen.

   (**d**) (*produce*) hervorbringen. **the meeting threw** ~ **several good ideas** bei der Versammlung kamen ein paar gute Ideen zutage; **the new politicians** ~**n** ~ **by the war** die neuen Politiker, die der Krieg hervorgebracht hat.

throw: ~**away** *adj* (**a**) (*casual*) *remark* nebenbei gemacht; *style* unaufdringlich, leger; (**b**) *wrapping, packet* Wegwerf-, zum Wegwerfen; *bottle also* Einweg-; (**c**) (*cheap*) ~**away prices** Schleuderpreise *pl*; ~**back** *n* (**a**) **his height/selfishness is a** ~**back to an earlier generation** in ihm schlägt die Größe/Selbstsucht seiner Vorfahren wieder durch; **he's a** ~**back to his Irish ancestors** bei ihm kommen seine irischen Vorfahren wieder durch; (**b**) (*fig*) Rückkehr (*to* zu), (*fig*) Neubelebung (*to gen*) *f*, Rückgriff *m* (*to* auf +*acc*).

thrower [θrəuə] *n* Werfer(in *f*) *m*. **he's not a very good** ~ er kann nicht sehr gut werfen.

throw-in [θrəuɪn] *n* (*Sport*) Einwurf *m*.

thrown [θrəun] *ptp of* **throw**.

thru *prep, adv, adj* (*US*) = **through**.

thrum [θrʌm] **1** *vt* *guitar* klimpern auf (+*dat*), schlagen; *tune* (*auf der Gitarre etc*) klimpern. **he** ~**med the desk with his fingers** *or* ~**med his fingers on the desk** er trommelte mit seinen Fingern auf der Schreibtischplatte. **2** *vi* (*on guitar*) klimpern.

thrush[1] [θrʌʃ] *n* (*Orn*) Drossel *f*.

thrush[2] *n* (*Med*) Soor *m* (*spec*), Schwämmchen *nt*; (*of vagina*) Pilzkrankheit *f*; (*Vet: in horses*) Strahlfäule *f*.

thrust [θrʌst] (*vb: pret, ptp* ~) **1** *n* (**a**) *Stoß m*; (*of knife also*) Stich *m*; (*fig: of intellect*) Stoßkraft *f*.

   (**b**) (*Tech*) Druckkraft *f*; (*in rocket, turbine*) Schub(kraft *f*) *m*, Triebkraft *f*. ~ **bearing** Drucklager *nt*.

   (**c**) (*Mil: also* ~ **forward**) Vorstoß *m*.

   2 *vt* (**a**) (*push, drive*) stoßen. **the tree** ~ **its branches upward** der Baum streckte seine Äste in den Himmel; **to** ~ **sb into a room** jdn in ein Zimmer stoßen; **to** ~ **one's hands into one's pockets** die Hände in die Tasche stecken *or* stopfen (*inf*); **she** ~ **her books into the box** sie stopfte ihre Bücher in die Kiste; **she** ~ **the money into his hands/pocket** sie drückte ihm das Geld in die Hand/sie stopfte ihm das Geld in die Tasche.

   (**b**) (*fig*) **to** ~ **oneself** (**up**) **on sb** sich jdm aufdrängen; **I had the job** ~ **upon me** die Arbeit wurde mir aufgedrängt *or* aufgezwungen; **to** ~ **one's way through a crowd** sich durch die Menge drängen *or* schieben; **to** ~ **one's way to the front** sich nach vorne vordrängeln, sich nach vorne kämpfen.

   3 *vi* stoßen (*at* nach); (*with knife*) stechen (*at* nach); (*Fencing*) einen Ausfall machen, ausfallen (*at* gegen).

♦**thrust aside** *vt sep* wegstoßen, beiseite schieben; *person also* beiseite *or* zur Seite drängen; (*fig*) *objection* zurückweisen, beiseite schieben.

♦**thrust forward** *vt sep* **to** ~ **sb/oneself** ~ (*lit*) sich vorschieben, sich nach vorne durchdrängeln; (*fig*) sich einsetzen, Einsatz zeigen; (*pej*) sich in den Vordergrund drängen.

♦**thrust out** *vt sep* *leg* ausstrecken; *hand also* hinstrecken; *head, breasts* vorstrecken; *chest* herausdrücken, wölben. **she** ~ **her head** ~ (**of the window**) sie streckte ihren Kopf (zum Fenster) hinaus; **the goalie** ~ ~ **his legs** der Torwart streckte die Beine vor.

♦**thrust past** *vi* sich vorbeidrängen (*prep obj* an +*dat*).

thrustful [θrʌstfʊl], **thrusting** *adj person, behaviour* energisch, zielstrebig, resolut; (*pej*) (etwas) zu zielstrebig.

thrustfulness [θrʌstfʊlnɪs] *n* energische Art, Zielstrebigkeit, Resoluheit *f*; (*pej*) (etwas) zu große Zielstrebigkeit.

thrusting [θrʌstɪŋ] *adj see* **thrustful**.

thruway ['θru:weɪ] n (US) Schnellstraße f.

thud [θʌd] **1** n dumpfes Geräusch. **the ~ of his footsteps** seine dumpfen Schritte; **he fell to the ground with a ~** er fiel mit einem Plumps (inf) or dumpfen Aufschlag zu Boden; **the ~ of the sea against the hull** das dumpfe Schlagen des Wassers gegen den Schiffsrumpf.
2 vi dumpf aufschlagen; (move heavily) stampfen. **the blow ~ded against his chin** dumpf klatschte der Schlag gegen sein Kinn; **a ~ding noise** ein dumpfes Geräusch; **with ~ding heart** mit pochendem Herzen; **the heavy door ~ded into place** mit einem dumpfen Knall fiel die Tür zu.

thug [θʌg] n Schläger(typ) m.

thumb [θʌm] **1** n Daumen m. **to be under sb's ~** unter jds Pantoffel (dat) or Fuchtel (dat) stehen; **she has him under her ~** sie hat ihn unter ihrer Fuchtel; **to be all ~s** zwei linke Hände haben; **he gave me the ~s up/down** er gab mir durch ein Zeichen mit dem Daumen zu verstehen, daß alles in Ordnung war/ daß etwas nicht stimmte; **the idea was given the ~s up/ down** für den Vorschlag wurde grünes/rotes Licht gegeben; **it sticks out like a sore ~** das springt einem direkt ins Auge; **he sticks out like a sore ~** (doesn't fit) er ist auffallend anders.
2 vt **(a)** (inf) **to ~ a ride** or **lift** per Anhalter fahren; **let's ~ a lift with this lorry** wir wollen versuchen, diesen Lastwagen anzuhalten.
(b) to ~ one's nose at sb/sth jdm/einer Sache eine lange Nase machen; (fig) auf jdn/etw pfeifen.
(c) a well ~ed book ein Buch mit abgegriffenen Seiten.
◆**thumb through** vi +prep obj book durchblättern; card index durchgehen, durchsehen.

thumb: **~ index** n Daumenregister nt, Daumenindex m; **~nail** n Daumennagel m; **~nail sketch** (drawing) kleine Skizze; (description) kurze Skizze; **~ print** n Daumenabdruck m; **~screw** n (Tech) Flügelschraube f; (torture) Daumenschraube f; **~stall** n Daumenkappe f, Daumenschützer, Fingerling m; **~tack** n (US) Reißnagel m, Reiß- or Heftzwecke f.

thump [θʌmp] **1** n (blow) Schlag m; (noise) (dumpfes) Krachen, Bums m (inf). **the bus gave the car such a ~ ...** der Bus gab dem Auto einen solchen Stoß ...
2 vt table klopfen or schlagen auf (+acc); door klopfen or schlagen an (+acc); (repeatedly) trommeln auf/an (+acc); (accidentally) one's head sich (dat) anschlagen or anhauen (inf). **he ~ed the box down on my desk** er knallte die Schachtel auf meinen Tisch; **the prisoners started ~ing their stools on the floor** die Gefangenen schlugen mit ihren Hockern auf den Boden; **I ~ed him (one) on the nose** (inf) ich habe ihm eins auf die Nase verpaßt (inf); **I'll ~ you (one) if you don't shut up** (inf) wenn du nicht gleich den Mund hältst, knallt's (inf).
3 vi (person) schlagen (on the door/table gegen or an die Tür/auf den Tisch); (heart) heftig schlagen or pochen; (move heavily) stapfen; (object: fall loudly) plumpsen (inf). **ask the people upstairs to stop ~ing around** sag den Leuten über uns, sie sollen aufhören herumzutrampeln.
◆**thump out** vt sep tune hämmern.

thumping ['θʌmpɪŋ] adj (also ~ great) (inf) kolossal, enorm.

thunder ['θʌndəʳ] **1** n **(a)** Donner m. **a long roll of ~** ein langer rollender Donner, ein langes Donnergrollen; **there is ~ in the air** es liegt ein Gewitter nt in der Luft.
(b) (fig) (of applause) Sturm m; (of cannons) Donnern, Dröhnen nt; (of waves) Tosen nt. **he was greeted with a ~ of applause** er wurde mit donnerndem Applaus or einem Beifallssturm begrüßt; see **steal.**
2 vi (lit, fig) donnern; (guns, hooves also) dröhnen; (waves, sea) tosen, brausen; (applause also) brausen. **the horses came ~ing up to the gate** die Pferde kamen aufs Tor zugerescht; **the senator ~ed against them** der Senator wetterte gegen sie.
3 vi (shout) brüllen, donnern, mit Donnerstimme brüllen.
◆**thunder out 1** vt sep order mit donnernder Stimme geben. **2** vi (guns) losdonnern. **his voice ~ed ~** er donnerte los.
◆**thunder past** vi (train, traffic) vorbeidonnern.

thunder: **~bolt** n (lit) Blitz m, Blitz und Donner; **the news came as something of a ~bolt** (fig) die Nachricht schlug wie der Blitz ein or kam wie ein Donnerschlag; **~clap** n Donnerschlag m; **~cloud** n Gewitterwolke f.

thunderer ['θʌndərəʳ] n: **the T~** (Myth) der Blitzeschleuderer.

thundering ['θʌndərɪŋ] adj (inf) verteufelt (inf), verflixt (inf). **to be in a ~ rage** vor Wut kochen or schäumen.

thunderous ['θʌndərəs] adj stürmisch; applause also, voice donnernd.

thunder: **~storm** n Gewitter nt; **~struck** adj (fig) wie vom Donner gerührt.

thundery ['θʌndərɪ] adj weather gewitterig.

thurible ['θjʊərɪbl] n (Eccl) (Weih)rauchfaß, Räucherfaß nt.

Thurs abbr of **Thursday** Do.

Thursday ['θɜːzdɪ] n Donnerstag m; see also **Tuesday.**

thus [ðʌs] adv **(a)** (in this way) so, auf diese Art. **you must hold it ~** Sie müssen das so halten; **~ it was that ...** so kam es, daß ...
(b) (consequently) folglich, somit.
(c) (+ptp or adj) reassured, encouraged etc solchermaßen (geh), derart (geh). **~ far** so weit.

thwack [θwæk] **1** n (blow) Schlag m; (noise) Klatschen nt, Bums m (inf). **she gave her head a nasty ~ on the table** sie hat sich den Kopf ziemlich übel am Tisch angeschlagen (inf).
2 vt schlagen; (waves) klatschen gegen. **he ~ed his cane on the table** er ließ seinen Stock auf den Tisch heruntersausen.
3 vi schlagen (against gegen); (waves, cane) klatschen.

thwart¹ [θwɔːt] vt vereiteln; plan also durchkreuzen; robbery, attack also verhindern; person einen Strich durch die Rechnung machen (+dat). **he was ~ed** imm wurde ein Strich durch die Rechnung gemacht; **to ~ sb in sth** jdm etw vereiteln; **to be ~ed at every turn** überall auf Hindernisse stoßen; **~ed! wieder nichts!**

thwart² n (Naut) Ruderbank, Ducht f.

thy [ðaɪ] poss adj (old, dial) (before vowel **thine**) Euer/Eure/Euer (obs); (dial, to God) Dein/Deine/Dein.

thyme [taɪm] n Thymian m.

thyroid ['θaɪrɔɪd] **1** n (also ~ **gland**) Schilddrüse f. **2** adj Schilddrüsen-.

thyself [ðaɪ'self] pers pron (old, dial) **(a)** (reflexive, dir obj, with prep +acc) Euch (obs); (dial, to God) Dich; (indir obj, with prep +dat) Euch (obs); (dial, to God) Dir.
(b) (emph) Ihr selbst (obs); Du selbst (obs); (acc) Euch selbst (obs); Dich selbst; (dat) Ihnen selbst (obs); Dir selbst.

tiara [tɪ'ɑːrə] n Diadem nt; (of pope) Tiara f.

Tiber ['taɪbəʳ] n Tiber m.

Tibet [tɪ'bet] n Tibet nt.

Tibetan [tɪ'betən] **1** adj tibetanisch, tibetisch. **2** n **(a)** Tibeter(in f), Tibetaner(in f) m. **(b)** (language) Tibetisch nt.

tibia ['tɪbɪə] n, pl **-s** or **-e** ['tɪbiːiː] Schienbein nt, Tibia f (spec).

tic [tɪk] n (Med) Tick m, nervöses Zucken.

tich, titch [tɪtʃ] n (inf) Knirps m. **hey, ~!** he, Kleine(r)!

tichy, titchy ['tɪtʃɪ] adj (+er) (inf: also ~ **little**) person winzig, knirpsig (inf); things klitzeklein (inf), winzig.

tick¹ [tɪk] **1** n **(a)** (of clock etc) Ticken nt.
(b) (inf: moment) Augenblick m, Sekunde f, Minütchen nt (inf). **half a ~** eine Sekunde; **are you ready yet? — half a ~** or **two ~s!** sofort or noch eine Sekunde; **I'll be ready in a ~** or **two ~s** bin sofort fertig (inf); **he did it in two ~s** er hat es in Sekundenschnelle or im Handumdrehen getan.
(c) (mark) Häkchen nt, Haken m. **to put a ~ against a name/an answer** einen Namen/eine Antwort abhaken.
2 vi **(a)** (clock) ticken. **the minutes ~ed by** or **past/away** die Minuten vergingen or verstrichen.
(b) (inf) **what makes him ~?** was geht in ihm vor?
3 vt name, answer abhaken.
◆**tick off** vt sep **(a)** name etc abhaken. **(b)** (inf: scold) ausschimpfen (inf), anpfeifen (inf). **he got ~ed ~ for doing it** er wurde angepfiffen (inf) or er bekam einen Rüffel or Anpfiff (inf), weil er das getan hat.
◆**tick over** vi **(a)** (idle: engine) im Leerlauf sein. **the engine is ~ing ~ nicely** der Motor läuft ganz gut or ruhig. **(b)** (fig: business etc) ganz ordentlich laufen; (pej) auf Sparflamme sein (inf). **to keep things ~ing ~** die Sache in Gang halten.

tick² n (Zool) Zecke f.

tick³ n (Brit sl): **on ~** auf Pump (inf).

tick⁴ n (Tex: cover) (for mattress) Matratzenbezug m; (for pillow etc) Inlett nt.

ticker ['tɪkəʳ] n **(a)** (inf: heart) Pumpe f (sl). **(b)** (sl: watch) Zwiebel f (sl).

ticker tape n Lochstreifen m. **~ welcome/parade** Konfettibegrüßung f/Konfettiparade f.

ticket ['tɪkɪt] n **(a)** (rail) Fahrkarte f; (bus) Fahrschein m; (plane ~) Ticket nt, Flugkarte f, Flugschein m; (Theat, for football match etc) (Eintritts)karte f; (cloakroom) Garderobenmarke f; (library) = Buchzettel m; (for dry cleaners, cobbler etc) Abschnitt, Zettel m; (luggage office) (Gepäck)schein m; (raffle ~) Los nt; (price ~) Preisschild nt; (for car park) Parkschein, Parkzettel (inf) m. **admission by ~ only** Einlaß nur gegen Eintrittskarten.
(b) (US Pol) Wahlliste f. **he's running on the Democratic ~** er kandidiert für die Demokratische Partei; see **split, straight.**
(c) (Jur) Strafzettel m. **to give sb a ~** jdm einen Strafzettel geben or verpassen (inf).
(d) (dated Brit inf) **that's the ~!** das ist famos! (dated inf).

ticket: **~ agency** n (Theat) Vorverkaufsstelle f; (Rail etc) Verkaufsstelle f; **~ collector** n (Rail) (on train) Schaffner(in f) m; (in station) Bahnsteigschaffner(in f), Fahrkartenkontrolleur m; **~ holder** n (Theat etc) jd, der eine Eintrittskarte hat; **~holders only through this door** (Theat etc) Eingang nur für Besucher mit Eintrittskarten; **~ inspector** n (Fahrkarten)kontrolleur m; **~ office** n (Rail) Fahrkartenschalter m, Fahrkartenausgabe f; (Theat) Kasse f; **~ window** n (Rail) (Fahrkarten)schalter m; (Theat) Kasse f.

ticking ['tɪkɪŋ] n **(a)** (for mattress) Matratzendrell m; (for pillows etc) Inlett nt. **(b)** (of clock) Ticken nt.

ticking-off ['tɪkɪŋ'ɒf] n (inf) Rüffel, Anpfiff (inf) m. **he needs a good ~** dem muß man mal den Marsch blasen (inf).

tickle ['tɪkl] **1** vt **(a)** kitzeln. **to ~ sb in the ribs** jdn in der Seite kitzeln; **to ~ sb's toes** jdn an den Zehen kitzeln; **this wool ~s my skin** diese Wolle kratzt or juckt (auf der Haut).
(b) (fig inf) person (please) schmeicheln (+dat) und freuen; (amuse) belustigen, amüsieren. **to feel/be ~d** sich gebauchpinselt fühlen (inf); **here's a little story that might ~ your imagination** eine kleine Geschichte, die Sie wohl recht amüsant finden werden; **that story really ~d me** diese Geschichte fand ich wirklich köstlich; **to be ~d pink** or **to death** sich wie ein Schneekönig freuen (inf); see **fancy.**
2 vi kitzeln; (wool) kratzen, jucken. **stop it, you're tickling** aufhören, das kitzelt; **my ear is tickling** mein Ohr juckt.
3 n Kitzeln nt. **he gave the baby a little ~** er kitzelte das Baby ein bißchen; **to have a ~ in one's throat** einen Hustenreiz haben; **I didn't get a ~ all day** (Fishing) es hat den ganzen Tag keiner (an)gebissen.

tickler ['tɪkləʳ] n (inf) kitz(e)lige Angelegenheit, kitz(e)liges Problem. **this problem is a bit of a ~** dieses Problem ist ziemlich kitz(e)lig.

ticklish ['tɪklɪʃ] adj (lit) person kitz(e)lig; (fig) situation kitz(e)lig, heikel.

tick: **~-tack** n Zeichensprache f der Buchmacher; **~-tack man** n Buchmachergehilfe m; **~-tack-toe** n (US) Kreuzchen-und-Kringelspiel nt; **~-tock** n (sound) tick-tack; (baby-talk: clock) Ticktack f.

tidal ['taɪdl] adj river, harbour Tide-. **this river is not ~** in diesem

Fluß gibt es keine Gezeiten, das ist kein Tidefluß; ~ **wave** (*lit*) Flutwelle *f*; a great ~ **wave of enthusiasm** swept over the country eine Welle der Begeisterung ging durch das Land.

tidbit ['tɪdbɪt] *n* (*US*) see **titbit**.

tiddler ['tɪdlə^r] *n* (*Brit*) **(a)** (*fish*) winziger Fisch. **(b)** (*inf: child*) Knirps *m*. she teaches ~s sie unterrichtet die ganz Kleinen.

tiddly ['tɪdlɪ] *adj* (+*er*) (*inf*) **(a)** (*tiny*) winzig, klitzeklein (*inf*). a ~ **little scratch** ein klitzekleiner (*inf*) *or* winzig kleiner Kratzer. **(b)** (*tipsy*) angesäuselt (*inf*), beschwipst. **she gets** ~ **on half a glass of sherry** sie bekommt von einem halben Glas Sherry schon einen Schwips.

tiddlywinks ['tɪdlɪwɪŋks] *n* Floh(hüpf)spiel *nt*. to play ~ Flohhüpfen spielen.

tide [taɪd] *n* **(a)** (*lit*) Gezeiten *pl*, Tide (*N Ger*) *f*. (at) **high/low** ~ (bei) Hochwasser *nt or* Flut *f*/Niedrigwasser *nt or* Ebbe *f*; to utilize the rise and fall of the ~ Ebbe und Flut *or* den Tidenhub (*spec*) ausnutzen; **we'll sail on the next** ~ wir fahren mit der nächsten Flut; **the** ~ **is in/out** es ist Flut/Ebbe *or* Hochwasser (*form*)/Niedrigwasser (*form*); **the** ~ **comes in very far/fast** die Flut kommt sehr weit herein/schnell; **the** ~**s are influenced by the moon** Ebbe und Flut *or* die Gezeiten werden vom Mond beeinflußt; **stranded by the** ~ in der Ebbe gestrandet. **(b)** (*fig: trend*) **the** ~ **of history** der Lauf der Geschichte; **the** ~ **of public opinion** der Trend der öffentlichen Meinung; **carried away by the** ~ **of events** vom Strom der Ereignisse mitgerissen; **to go** *or* **swim against/with the** ~ gegen den/mit dem Strom schwimmen; **the** ~ **of the battle turned** das Glück (der Schlacht) wendete sich; *see* **turn, time.**
   (c) (*old: time*) Zeit *f*.
◆ **tide over** *vt always separate* **that will** ~ **me** ~ **until tomorrow** damit werde ich bis morgen auskommen; **is that enough to** ~ **you** ~? reicht Ihnen das vorläufig?

tide: ~ **gate** *n* Seeschleuse *f*; ~**land** *n* (*US*) Watt *nt*; ~**mark** *n* Flutmarke *f*; (*man-made*) Pegelstand *m*; (*hum: on neck, in bath*) schwarzer Rand; ~ **race** *n* Gezeitenstrom *m*; ~**water** *n* Flut *f*; (*US: lowlands*) Watt *nt*; ~**way** *n* Priel *m*.

tidily ['taɪdɪlɪ] *adv* ordentlich.

tidiness ['taɪdɪnɪs] *n see adj* Ordentlichkeit *f*; Sauberkeit *f*; Gepflegtheit *f*.

tidings ['taɪdɪŋz] *npl* (*old, liter*) Kunde (*old, liter*), Botschaft (*liter*), Nachricht *f*.

tidy ['taɪdɪ] **1** *adj* (+*er*) **(a)** (*orderly*) ordentlich; (*with* ~ **habits** *also*) sauber; *appearance also* gepflegt; *room also* aufgeräumt. she has very ~ **habits** sie ist ein sehr ordentlicher *or* ordnungsliebender Mensch; **to teach sb** ~ **habits** jdn zur Ordnung erziehen; **to keep/put sth** ~ etw in Ordnung halten/bringen; **to get a room** ~ ein Zimmer aufräumen; **she's very** ~ **in her dress** sie ist immer sehr ordentlich gekleidet; **to make oneself** ~ sich zurechtmachen; **to have a** ~ **mind** klar *or* logisch denken. **(b)** (*inf: considerable*) ordentlich (*inf*), ganz schön (*inf*). a ~ **sum** eine ordentliche Stange Geld (*inf*).
   2 *vt hair* in Ordnung bringen; *room also* aufräumen.
   3 *n* Behälter *m*.
◆ **tidy away** *vt sep* wegräumen, aufräumen.
◆ **tidy out** *vt sep* aufräumen, ausmisten (*inf*).
◆ **tidy up 1** *vi* **(a)** (*clear away*) aufräumen, Ordnung machen. **(b)** (*clean oneself*) sich zurechtmachen. **2** *vt sep books, room* aufräumen, in Ordnung bringen; *piece of work* in Ordnung bringen. **to** ~ **oneself** ~ sich zurechtmachen.

tie [taɪ] **1** *n* **(a)** (*also esp US:* neck~) Krawatte *f*, Schlips *m*, Binder *m* (*dated form*).
   (b) (*Archit, Build*) (*also* ~ **beam**) Binderbalken, Bundbalken *m*; (~ **piece**) Stichbalken *m*; (*Mus*) Haltebogen *m*; (*US Rail*) Schwelle *f*; (*cord*) Schnur *f*.
   (c) (*fig: bond*) Band *nt* (*liter*), Beziehung, (Ver)bindung *f*. ~**s of friendship** freundschaftliche Beziehungen *or* Bande (*liter*) *pl*; **the blood** ~ Blutsbande *pl*; **business** ~**s** Geschäftsverbindungen *pl*; **he's investigating the** ~**s between Pasternak and Rilke** er untersucht die Beziehung zwischen Pasternak und Rilke; **family** ~**s** familiäre Bindungen *pl*.
   (d) (*hindrance*) Belastung *f*. **family** ~**s** familiäre Bindungen *or* Fesseln *pl*; **I don't want any** ~**s** ich will keine Bindung, ich will mich nicht gebunden fühlen; **her children are a** ~ **on her** ihre Kinder sind für sie eine Belastung *or* ein Klotz *m* am Bein.
   (e) (*Sport etc: result of match*) Unentschieden *nt*; (*match, competition ending in draw*) unentschiedenes Spiel. **the match ended in a** ~ das Spiel endete mit einem Unentschieden; **the result of the election/competition was a** ~ bei der Wahl ergab sich eine Stimmengleichheit/der Wettkampf ging unentschieden aus; **there was a** ~ **for second place** es gab zwei zweite Plätze.
   (f) (*esp Ftbl: match*) Spiel *nt*.
   2 *vt* **(a)** (*fasten*) binden (*to* an +*acc*), befestigen (*to* an +*dat*). ~ **the string round the tree** binde die Schnur um den Baum; **my hands are** ~**d** (*fig*) mir sind die Hände gebunden.
   (b) (*knot*) *shoelace, tie, ribbon* binden. **to** ~ **a knot in sth** einen Knoten in etw (*acc*) machen; **to** ~ **a bow in a ribbon** *or* **a ribbon in a bow** ein Band zu einer Schleife binden.
   (c) (*fig: unite, link*) verbinden.
   (d) (*restrict*) *person* binden (*to* an +*acc*). **we're very** ~**d in the evenings** wir sind abends sehr gebunden; **are we** ~**d to this plan?** sind wir an diesen Plan gebunden?
   (e) (*Sport*) **the match was** ~**d** das Spiel ging unentschieden aus.
   3 *vi* **(a)** (*ribbon etc*) **it won't** ~ **properly** es läßt sich nicht richtig binden; **it** ~**s at the back** es wird hinten (zu)gebunden.
   (b) (*Sport*) unentschieden spielen; (*in competition, vote*) gleich stehen. **they're still tying** es steht immer noch unentschieden; **they** ~**d for first place** (*Sport, competition*) sie teilten sich den ersten Platz; (*Sch*) sie waren (mit den gleichen Noten) die Klassenbesten.

◆ **tie back** *vt sep hair, roses, door* zurückbinden.
◆ **tie down** *vt sep* **(a)** (*lit*) festbinden (*to* an +*dat*); *huts, tents* verankern (*to* in +*dat*); *horse* fesseln.
   (b) (*fig: restrict*) binden (*to* an +*acc*); *meaning* genau bestimmen. ~**d** ~ **to one's duties** durch seine Pflichten gebunden; **to** ~ **sb/oneself** ~ **to certain conditions** jdn/sich auf bestimmte Bedingungen festlegen; **to** ~ **oneself** ~ **to doing sth** sich verpflichten, etw zu tun; **marriage/owning property** ~**s you** ~ durch die Ehe/Eigentum ist man gebunden; **she's very** ~**d** ~ **because of the children, the children** ~ **her** ~ **a lot** durch die Kinder ist sie sehr gebunden.
◆ **tie in 1** *vi* dazu passen. **to** ~ ~ **with sth** zu etw passen, dazu passen; **it all** ~**s** ~ das paßt alles zusammen; **the new evidence didn't** ~ ~ das neue Beweismaterial paßte nicht ins Bild. **2** *vt sep plans* verbinden, in Einklang bringen.
◆ **tie on** *vt sep* anbinden, festbinden. **to** ~ **sth** ~(**to**) **sth** etw an etw (*dat*) anbinden.
◆ **tie up 1** *vi* **(a)** now **it all** ~**s** ~ jetzt paßt alles zusammen; **it all** ~**s** ~ **with his marital problems** das hängt alles mit seinen Eheproblemen zusammen.
   (b) (*Naut*) festmachen.
   2 *vt sep* **(a)** *parcel* verschnüren; *shoelaces* binden.
   (b) *boat* festmachen; *animal* festbinden, anbinden (*to* an +*dat*); *prisoner, hands etc* fesseln.
   (c) (*settle*) *deal, arrangements etc* unter Dach und Fach bringen. **to** ~ ~ **a few loose ends (of sth)** (bei einer Sache) ein paar Lücken schließen.
   (d) (*Fin*) *capital* (fest) anlegen, festlegen.
   (e) (*link*) **to be** ~**d** ~ **with sth** mit etw zusammenhängen; **are you still** ~**d** ~ **with that firm?** haben Sie noch Verbindungen zu der Firma?
   (f) (*keep busy*) beschäftigen; *machines* auslasten. **he's** ~**d** ~ **all tomorrow** er ist morgen den ganzen Tag belegt *or* beschäftigt; **he's** ~**d** ~ **with the manager at the moment** er hat momentan beim Betriebsleiter zu tun.
   (g) (*obstruct, hinder*) *production etc* stillegen.

tie: ~ **breaker** *n* (*Tennis*) Tiebreaker *m*; ~ **clip** *n* Krawattennadel *f*.
tied [taɪd]: ~ **cottage** *n* (*Brit*) Gesindehaus *nt*; ~ **house** *n* (*Brit*) Brauereigaststätte *f*, brauereieigene Gaststätte.
tie: ~-**in 1** *n* **(a)** (*connection, relationship*) Verbindung, Beziehung *f*, Zusammenhang *m*; **(b)** (*US: sale*) Kopplungsgeschäft *nt*; **2** *attr* ~-**in sale** (*US*) Kopplungsgeschäft *nt*; ~ **line** *n* (*Telec*) Direktverbindung *f*; ~-**on** *adj attr* Anhänge-, zum Anbinden *or* Anhängen; ~ **pin** *n* Krawatten- *or* Schlipsnadel *f*.
tier [tɪə^r] *n* (*of cake*) Etage, Stufe *f*; (*of amphitheatre*) Reihe *f*; (*Theat, of stadium*) Rang *m*; (*fig: in hierarchy, system etc*) Stufe *f*, Rang *m*. **first-**~ **box** Loge *f* im ersten Rang; **a cake with three** ~**s** ein dreistöckiger Kuchen; **a three-**~ **hierarchy** eine dreigestufte Hierarchie; **to arrange sth in** ~**s** etw stufenförmig aufbauen; **to rise in** ~**s** stufenförmig nach oben führen.
tiered [tɪəd] *adj* gestuft. **a three-**~ **cake** ein dreistöckiger Kuchen.
tie: ~ **rod** *n* (*Aut*) Lenkspurstange *f*; ~-**up** *n* **(a)** (*connection*) Verbindung *f*; **(b)** (*US: stoppage*) Stillstand *m*; **there is a** ~-**up in transportation** der Verkehr steht still *or* ist lahmgelegt.
tiff [tɪf] *n* (*inf*) Krach *m* (*inf*). **he's had a** ~ **with his girlfriend** er hat mit seiner Freundin Krach gehabt (*inf*).
tiger ['taɪgə^r] *n* Tiger *m*.
tiger: ~ **lily** *n* Tigerlilie *f*; ~ **moth** *n* Bärenspinner *m*; ~ **shark** *n* Tigerhai *m*.
tight [taɪt] **1** *adj* (+*er*) **(a)** (*close-fitting*) *clothes* eng; *join* dicht. **these jeans/shoes are too** ~ diese Jeans/Schuhe sind zu eng, diese Jeans spannen/Schuhe drücken.
   (b) (*stiff, difficult to move*) *screw, bolt* festsitzend, unbeweglich. **the top/cork/screw/bolt is (too)** ~ der Hahn ist zu fest zu/der Korken/die Schraube/der Bolzen sitzt fest; **the drawer/window is a bit** ~ die Schublade/das Fenster klemmt ein bißchen *or* geht schwer auf.
   (c) (*firm*) *screw* fest angezogen; *tap, window* dicht; *lid, embrace* fest; *control, discipline* streng; *organization* straff. **to keep a** ~ **hold on sth** (*lit*) etw gut festhalten; **to keep a** ~ **hold on the reins** (*fig*) die Zügel fest in der Hand halten; **to run a** ~ **ship** (*lit, fig*) ein strenges Regiment führen.
   (d) (*taut*) *rope, skin* straff; *knot* fest (angezogen). **she wears her hair in a** ~ **bun** sie trägt ihr Haar in einem festen Knoten; **a** ~ **feeling in the chest** ein beengtes Gefühl in der Brust.
   (e) (*leaving little space*) eng; *weave also* dicht. **things are getting rather** ~ **in this office** es wird ziemlich eng im Büro; **it's a** ~ **space for lorries** es ist eng hier für Lastwagen.
   (f) (*leaving little time*) *timing etc* knapp; *schedule* knapp bemessen. **4 o'clock is making it a bit** ~ **for me** 4 Uhr ist ein bißchen knapp für mich.
   (g) (*difficult*) *situation* schwierig. **in a** ~ **corner** *or* **spot** (*fig*) in der Klemme (*inf*); **things are getting a bit** ~ **for him** round here es wird langsam brenzlig für ihn (*inf*).
   (h) (*close*) *race, match* knapp.
   (i) (*Fin*) *money* knapp.
   (j) (*inf: miserly*) knick(e)rig (*inf*), geizig.
   (k) (*inf: drunk*) voll (*sl*), blau (*inf*). **to get** ~ voll *or* blau werden (*inf*).
   2 *adv* (+*er*) *hold, shut, screw, fasten* fest; *stretch* straff. **the suitcase/train was packed** ~ **with ...** der Koffer/Zug war vollgestopft mit ... *or* prallvoll/gerammelt voll von ... (*inf*); **he kept his mouth shut** ~ er schwieg eisern; (*at dentist etc*) er hielt den Mund fest geschlossen; **to hold sb/sth** ~ jdn/etw fest halten; **to do sth up** ~ etw festmachen *or* gut befestigen; **sleep** ~! schlaf(t) gut!; **hold** ~! festhalten!; **to sit** ~ sich nicht rühren.
   3 *adj suf* dicht. **water-**~/**air-**~ wasser-/luftdicht.
tight-assed ['taɪtɑːst] *adj* (*esp US sl*) verbohrt (*inf*), stur (*inf*).
tighten ['taɪtn] (*also* ~ **up**) **1** *vt* **(a)** *knot* fester machen, anziehen; *screw* anziehen; (*re-tighten*) nachziehen;

rope straffen, anziehen; (*stretch tighter*) straffer spannen. **to ~ the steering in a car** die Lenkung an einem Auto nachziehen. **(b)** *restrictions* verschärfen; *see* **belt**. **2** *vi* (*rope*) sich spannen, sich straffen; (*knot*) sich zusammenziehen. **whenever he's angry his mouth ~s** immer wenn er wütend ist, wird sein Mund schmal und verkniffen.

♦ **tighten up 1** *vi* **(a)** *see* **tighten 2. (b)** (*in discipline*) strenger werden, härter durchgreifen. **they've ~ed ~ on security** sie haben die Sicherheitsvorkehrungen verschärft. **2** *vt sep* **(a)** *see* **tighten 1 (a). (b)** *organization, procedure* straffen; *discipline, controls* verschärfen.

tight: **~-fisted** ['taɪt'fɪstɪd] *adj* knauserig, knickerig (*inf*); **to be ~-fisted** die Hand auf der Tasche halten; **~-fitting** *adj* eng anliegend; **~-knit** *adj community* eng miteinander verbunden *or* verwachsen; **~-lipped** *adj* (*lit*) schmallippig; (*silent*) verschwiegen, verschlossen; **he kept a ~-lipped silence** er wahrte absolutes *or* eisernes Schweigen.

tightness ['taɪtnɪs] *n see adj* **(a)** enges Anliegen; Dichtheit *f*. **(b)** Festsitzen *nt*, Unbeweglichkeit *f*. **the ~ of the drawer/window** das Klemmen der Schublade/des Fensters. **(c)** fester Sitz; Dichtheit *f*; Strenge *f*; Straffheit *f*. **the ~ of his embrace** seine feste Umarmung. **(d)** Straffheit *f*; Festigkeit *f*. **(e)** Enge *f*; Dichte *f*. **(f)** Knappheit *f*. **(g)** Schwierigkeit *f*. **(h)** Knappheit *f*. **(i)** Knappheit *f*. **(j)** Knick(e)rigkeit *f* (*inf*), Geiz *m*. **(k)** Besoffenheit *f* (*sl*).

tightrope ['taɪtrəʊp] *n* Seil *nt*. **to walk a ~** (*fig*) einen Balanceakt vollführen; **~ act** (*lit, fig*) Balanceakt *m*; **~ walker** Seiltänzer(in *f*) *m*.

tights [taɪts] *npl* (*esp Brit*) Strumpfhose *f*. **a pair of ~** ein Paar *nt* Strumpfhosen, eine Strumpfhose.

tightwad ['taɪtwɒd] *n* (*US*) Geizhals, Geizkragen (*inf*) *m*.

tigress ['taɪgrɪs] *n* Tigerin *f*.

tilde ['tɪldɪ] *n* Tilde *f*.

tile [taɪl] **1** *n* (*on roof*) (Dach)ziegel *m*; (*ceramic ~*) Fliese *f*; (*on wall also*) Kachel *f*; (*lino ~, cork ~, polystyrene ~ etc*) Platte, Fliese *f*; (*carpet ~*) (Teppich)fliese *f*. **to have a night on the ~s** (*inf*) einen draufmachen (*inf*). **2** *vt roof* (mit Ziegeln) decken; *floor* mit Fliesen/Platten auslegen; *wall* kacheln; mit Platten bedecken; *bathroom* kacheln, Fliesen anbringen in (+*dat*). **~d roof** Ziegel-.

tiling ['taɪlɪŋ] *n* **(a)** (*action*) (*of roof*) (Dach)decken *nt*; (*of floor*) Fliesenlegen *nt*; (*of wall*) Kacheln *nt*; Belegen *nt* mit Platten. **~ the floor** ... das Fliesenlegen *or* Legen der Bodenfliesen ... **(b)** (*tiled surface*) (*on roof*) Ziegel *pl*; (*on floor*) Fliesen *pl*; Platten *pl*; (*on wall*) Kacheln, Fliesen *pl*; Platten *pl*.

till¹ [tɪl] *prep, conj see* **until**.

till² *n* (*cash-register*) Kasse *f*; (*drawer*) (*in bank*) Geldkasse *f*, Geldkasten *m*; (*in shop*) Ladenkasse *f*. **pay at the ~** an der Kasse bezahlen; **to be caught with one's hand in the ~** (*fig*) beim Griff in die Kasse ertappt werden.

till³ *vt* (*Agr*) bestellen.

tillage ['tɪlɪdʒ] *n* (*act*) Bestellen *nt*; (*land*) bestelltes Land.

tiller¹ ['tɪlər] *n* (*Naut*) Ruderpinne *f*. **at the ~** am Ruder; **to take the ~** das Ruder übernehmen.

tiller² *n* (*Agr*) Landmann *m* (*old*). **~ of the soil** (*liter*) Ackersmann (*old*), Bebauer *m* der Scholle (*liter*).

tilt [tɪlt] **1** *n* **(a)** (*slope*) Neigung *f*. **the sideways ~ of his head** seine schräge Kopfhaltung; **if you increase the (angle of) ~ of the conveyor belt** ... wenn Sie das Fließband schräger stellen ...; (*sideways also*) wenn Sie das Fließband weiter kippen ...; **to have a ~** sich neigen; **the wall has developed rather a dangerous ~** die Wand neigt sich ziemlich gefährlich; **the bird's/plane's wings have a slight downwards ~** die Flügel des Vogels/Flugzeugs neigen sich leicht nach unten. **(b)** (*Hist: tournament*) Turnier *nt*; (*thrust*) Stoß *m*. **to have a ~ at sb/sth** (*fig*) jdn/etw aufs Korn nehmen; *see* **full. 2** *vt* kippen, schräg stellen; *head* (seitwärts) neigen. **3** *vi* **(a)** (*slant*) sich neigen. **this part of the machine ~s** dieser Teil der Maschine läßt sich kippen; **sit properly on your chair, don't ~** sitz anständig auf dem Stuhl und schaukle *or* kipp(le) nicht dauernd! **(b)** (*fig*) **to ~ at sb/sth** jdn/etw attackieren; *see* **windmill**.

♦ **tilt back 1** *vi* sich nach hinten neigen. **he ~ed ~ in his chair** er kippte mit seinem Stuhl nach hinten. **2** *vt sep* nach hinten neigen; *chair also, machine part* nach hinten kippen.

♦ **tilt forward 1** *vi* sich nach vorne neigen; *machine part* nach vorn kippen. **he ~ed ~ in his chair** er kippte mit seinem Stuhl nach vorne, er lehnte sich mit seinem Stuhl vor. **2** *vt sep* nach vorne neigen; *chair also, machine part* nach vorne kippen.

♦ **tilt over 1** *vi* (*lean*) sich neigen; (*fall*) (um)kippen. **2** *vt sep* (*slant*) neigen, schräg stellen; *barrel, chair* kippen.

♦ **tilt up 1** *vi* nach oben kippen. **the back of the lorry ~s ~** die Ladefläche des Lastwagens kippt. **2** *vt sep bottle* kippen; *kaleidoscope* schräg nach oben halten.

tilth [tɪlθ] *n* **(a)** (*topsoil*) (Acker)krume *f*. **(b)** (*cultivated land*) Ackerland *nt*.

Tim [tɪm] *n abbr of* **Timothy**; (*Brit Telec*) der Zeitservice.

timber ['tɪmbər] **1** *n* **(a)** Holz *nt*; (*for building also*) Bauholz *nt*; (*land planted with trees*) (Nutz)wald *m*. **to put land under ~** Land mit Bäumen bepflanzen; **standing ~** Nutzwald *m*; **~!** Baum fällt! **(b)** (*beam*) Balken *m*; (*Naut also*) Spant *nt*. **(c)** (*Hunt*) (Holz)zäune und -gatter *pl*. **(d)** (*esp US: character*) **a man of that/presidential ~** ein Mann dieses Kalibers/ein Mann, der das Zeug zum Präsidenten hat.

2 *vt house* mit Fachwerk versehen; *gallery* (*in mine*) abstützen, verzimmern.

timbered ['tɪmbəd] *adj house* Fachwerk-; *land* Wald-.

timber framing *n* Fachwerk *nt*.

timbering ['tɪmbərɪŋ] *n* (*inside house*) Gebälk, Balkenwerk *nt*; (*outside house*) Fachwerk *nt*; (*Naut*) Spanten *pl*; (*Min*) Stützbalken *pl*; (*material*) (Bau)holz *nt*.

timber: **~land** *n* (*US*) Waldland *nt*; **~ line** *n* Baumgrenze *f*; **~ mill** *n* Sägemühle *f*, Sägewerk *nt*; **~ wolf** *n* Timberwolf *m*; **~work** *n* (*beams*) Gebälk, Balkenwerk *nt*; (*~ framing*) Fachwerk *nt*; **~ yard** *n* Holzlager *nt*.

timbre ['tɪmbər] *n* Timbre *nt*; (*Phon*) Tonqualität *f*.

time [taɪm] **1** *n* **(a)** Zeit *f*. **how ~ flies!** wie die Zeit vergeht!; **only ~ will tell whether** ... es muß sich erst herausstellen, ob ...; **it takes ~ to do that** das erfordert *or* braucht (seine) Zeit; **to take (one's) ~ (over sth)** sich (*dat*) (bei etw) Zeit lassen; **it took me all my ~ to finish** ich bin gerade noch fertig geworden; **in (the course of) ~** mit der Zeit; **in (next to *or* less than) no ~** im Nu, im Handumdrehen; **at this (present) point *or* moment in ~** zu diesem *or* zum gegenwärtigen Zeitpunkt; **to have a lot of/no ~ for sb/sth** viel/keine Zeit für jdn/etw haben; (*fig: be for/against*) viel/nichts für jdn/etw übrig haben; **to find/make ~ (for sb/sth)** Zeit finden/sich (*dat*) Zeit (für jdn/etw) nehmen; **to have ~ on one's hands** viel freie Zeit haben; **too many people who have ~ on their hands** zu viele Leute, die zuviel freie Zeit haben; **having ~ on my hands I went into a café** da ich (noch) Zeit hatte, ging ich ins Café; **~ is on our side** die Zeit arbeitet für uns; **he lost no ~ in telling her** er verlor keine Zeit und sagte es ihr sofort; **my ~ is my own** ich kann frei über meine Zeit verfügen; **in one's own/the company's ~** in *or* während der Freizeit/Arbeitszeit; **to be in good ~** rechtzeitig dran sein; **don't rush, do it in your own ~** nur keine Hast, tun Sie es, wie Sie es können; **let me know in good ~** sagen Sie mir rechtzeitig Bescheid; **he'll let you know in his own good ~** er wird Ihnen Bescheid sagen, wenn er soweit ist; **he does everything in his own good ~** er läßt sich bei nichts hetzen; **all in good ~** alles zu seiner Zeit; **~ is money** (*prov*) Zeit ist Geld (*prov*); **~ and tide wait for no man** (*Prov*) das Rad der Zeit hält niemand auf (*Prov*); (**for) a long/short ~** lange/kurz; **I'm going away for a long ~** ich fahre für *or* auf längere Zeit weg; **it's a long ~ (since)** es ist schon lange her(, seit); **what a (long) ~ you have been!** du hast (aber) lange gebraucht!; **a short ~ later/ago** kurz darauf/vor kurzem; **in a short ~ they were all gone** nach kurzer Zeit waren alle gegangen; **for some ~ past** seit einiger Zeit; **all the ~** die ganze Zeit; **in two weeks' ~** in zwei Wochen; **for a ~** eine Zeitlang; **for the ~ being** (*provisionally*) vorläufig; (*temporarily*) vorübergehend; **to do ~** (*inf: in prison*) sitzen (*inf*).

(b) (*of clock, moment, season*) **what ~ is it?, what's the ~?** wie spät ist es?, wieviel Uhr ist es?; **what ~ do you make it?** wie spät haben Sie's?; **my watch keeps good ~** meine Uhr geht genau; **to tell the ~** (*person*) die Uhr kennen; (*instrument*) die Uhrzeit anzeigen; **can you tell the ~?** kennst du die Uhr?; **the ~ is 2.30** es ist 2^{30}, die Zeit: 2^{30}; **what was his ~?** (*in race*) welche Zeit hatte er?; **the winning ~ was** ... die Zeit des Siegers war ...; **it's ~ (for me/us *etc*) to go, it's ~ I was/we were *etc* going, it's ~ I/we went** es wird Zeit, daß ich gehe/wir gehen *etc*; **on ~/ahead of ~/behind ~** pünktlich/zu früh/zu spät; **we are ahead of ~/behind ~** wir sind früh/spät dran; **we're/the project is ahead of ~/behind ~** wir sind/das Projekt ist dem Zeitplan voraus/zeitlich im Rückstand; **to make good ~** gut *or* schnell vorankommen; **if we get to Birmingham by 3 we'll be making good ~** wenn wir um 3 Uhr in Birmingham sind, sind wir ziemlich schnell; **the trains are on ~ or running** die Züge fahren pünktlich; **to be in ~ for sth** rechtzeitig zu etw kommen; **it's about ~ he was here** (*he has arrived*) es wird (aber) auch Zeit, daß er kommt; (*he has not arrived*) es wird langsam Zeit, daß er kommt; **it's ~ for tea** es ist Teezeit; (**and) about ~ too!** das wird aber auch Zeit!; **at all ~s** jederzeit, immer; **at any ~ during the day** zu jeder Tageszeit; **not at this ~ of night!** nicht zu dieser nachtschlafenen Stunde!; **to pass the ~ of day (with sb)** (mit jdm) über Belanglosigkeiten reden; **I wouldn't even give him the ~ of day** ich würde ihm nicht einmal guten Tag sagen; **~ gentlemen please!** Feierabend! (*inf*), bitte, trinken Sie aus, wir schließen gleich; **there's a ~ and a place for everything** alles zu seiner Zeit; **this is hardly the ~ or the place to** ... dies ist wohl kaum die rechte Zeit oder der rechte Ort, um ...; **this is no ~ for quarrelling *or* to quarrel** jetzt ist nicht die Zeit, sich zu streiten; **well, this is a fine ~ to tell me that** (*iro*) Sie haben sich (*dat*) wahrhaftig eine gute Zeit ausgesucht, um mir das zu sagen; **there are ~s when** ... es gibt Augenblicke, wo *or* da (*geh*) ...; **at the *or* that ~** damals, zu der Zeit, seinerzeit; **at this (particular) ~, at the present ~** zur Zeit; **at one ~** früher, einmal; **at any/no ~** jederzeit/niemals; **come (at) any ~** du kannst jederzeit kommen; **at the same ~** (*lit*) gleichzeitig; **they arrived at the same ~ as us** sie kamen zur gleichen Zeit an wie wir; **sometimes** ... **(at) other ~s** ... (manch)mal ..., (manch)mal ...; **but at the same ~, you must admit that** ... aber andererseits müssen Sie zugeben, daß ...; **it was hard, but at the same ~ you could have tried** es war schwierig, aber Sie hätten es trotzdem versuchen können; **at ~s** manchmal; **at various ~s in the past** schon verschiedene Male *or* verschiedentlich; **by the ~ it had finished** als es zu Ende war; **by the ~ we arrive, there's not going to be anything left** bis wir ankommen, ist nichts mehr übrig; **by that ~ we knew/we'll know** da *or* inzwischen wußten wir es/dann *or* bis dahin wissen wir es; **by this ~** inzwischen; **by this ~ next year/tomorrow** nächstes Jahr/morgen um diese Zeit; **between ~s** (*inf*) zwischendurch; **from ~ to ~** dann und wann, von Zeit zu Zeit; **from that ~ on** von der Zeit an, von da an; **since that ~** seit der Zeit; **until such ~ as** ... so lange bis ...; **until such ~ as you apologize** solange du dich nicht entschuldigst, bis du dich entschuldigst; **this ~ of the**

day/year diese Tages-/Jahreszeit; **at this ~ of the week/month** zu diesem Zeitpunkt der Woche/des Monats; **this ~ last year/week** letztes Jahr/letzte Woche um diese Zeit; **to choose** or **pick one's ~** sich (dat) einen günstigen Zeitpunkt aussuchen; **now's the ~ to do it** jetzt ist der richtige Zeitpunkt or die richtige Zeit, es zu tun; **now's my/your** etc **~ to do it** jetzt habe ich/hast du etc Gelegenheit, es zu tun; **to die before one's ~** zu früh sterben; **when the ~ comes** wenn es soweit ist; **I never thought the ~ would come** when she says sorry ich hätte nie gedacht, daß sie sich wirklich einmal entschuldigen würde; **the ~ has come (to do sth)** es ist an der Zeit(, etw zu tun); **the ~ has come for us to leave** es ist Zeit für uns zu gehen; **when her ~ comes** (of pregnant woman) wenn ihre Zeit kommt; **when your ~ comes to be the leader** wenn Sie an der Reihe sind, die Führung zu übernehmen; **my ~ is (almost) up** meine or die Zeit ist (gleich) um; (fig: life) meine Zeit ist gekommen.

(c) (occasion) **this ~** diesmal, dieses Mal; **(the) next ~** nächstes Mal, das nächste Mal; **(the) next ~ I see you** wenn ich dich nächstes Mal or das nächste Mal sehe; **(the) last ~** letztes Mal, das letzte Mal; **(the) last ~ he was here** letztes Mal or das letzte Mal, als er hier war; **every** or **each ~ ...** jedesmal, wenn ...; **many a ~, many ~s** viele Male; **many's the ~ I have heard him say ...** ich habe ihn schon oft sagen hören ...; **for the last ~** zum letzten Mal; **it's not the first ~ and it won't be the last** es war nicht das erste, und es wird nicht das letzte Mal sein; **and he's not very bright at the best of ~s** und er ist ohnehin or sowieso nicht sehr intelligent; **the ~ before** das letzte or vorige Mal; **the ~ before last** das vorletzte Mal; **~ and (~) again**, **~ after ~** immer wieder, wieder und wieder (geh); **they came in one/three** etc **at a ~** sie kamen einzeln/immer zu dritt etc herein; **four at a ~** vier auf einmal; **for weeks at a ~** wochenlang; **he pays me £10 a ~** er zahlt mir jedesmal £ 10; **rides on the round-about cost 10p a ~** eine Fahrt auf dem Karussell kostet 10 Pence; **apples cost 3p a ~** Äpfel kosten 3 Pence pro Stück; **I've told you a dozen ~s** ich habe dir schon x-mal gesagt.

(d) (multiplication) **2 ~s 3 is 6** 2 mal 3 ist 6; **it was ten ~s as big as** or **ten ~s the size of ...** es war zehnmal so groß wie ...

(e) (rate) **Sunday is (paid) double ~/~ and a half** Sonntage werden doppelt bezahlt, sonntags gibt es 100% Zuschlag or 200%/sonntags gibt es 50% Zuschlag or 150%; **you're paid ~ and a half for overtime** Sie bekommen 50% Zuschlag or 150 Prozent für Überstunden.

(f) (era) **in Victorian ~s** im Viktorianischen Zeitalter; **in olden ~s** in alten Zeiten; **in my ~** zu meiner Zeit; **~s was when ...** es gab Zeiten, da ...; **he is ahead of** or **before his ~** er ist seiner Zeit (voit) voraus; **to be behind the ~s** rückständig sein, hinter dem Mond leben (inf); (outdated knowledge) nicht auf dem laufenden sein; **to keep up with the ~s** mit der Zeit gehen; (keep in touch) auf dem laufenden bleiben; **~s are hard** die Zeiten sind hart or schwer; **when ~s are hard** in harten or schweren Zeiten; **~s change** die Zeiten ändern sich; **~s are changing** es kommen andere Zeiten; **~s are changing for the better/worse** es kommen bessere/schlechtere Zeiten; **~s have changed for the better/worse** die Zeiten haben sich gebessert/verschlechtert.

(g) (experience) **we had a good ~** es war (sehr) schön, es hat uns (dat) gut gefallen; **he doesn't look as though he's having a good ~** es scheint ihm nicht besonders gut zu gefallen; **have a good ~!** viel Vergnügen or Spaß!; **to have the ~ of one's life** eine herrliche Zeit verbringen, sich glänzend amüsieren; **what a ~ we had** or **that was!** das war eine Zeit!; **what ~s we had!, what ~s they were!** das waren (noch) Zeiten!; **to have an easy/a hard ~** es leicht/schwer haben; **we had an easy/a hard ~ getting to the finals** es war leicht für uns/wir hatten Schwierigkeiten, in die Endrunde zu kommen; **was it difficult? — no, we had an easy ~ (of it)** war es schwierig? — nein, (es war) ganz leicht; **he didn't have an easy ~ of it** in the operating theatre er war im Operationssaal schlimm dran; **to have a bad/rough ~** viel mitmachen; **we had such a bad ~ with our holidays/travel agency** wir hatten solches Pech mit unserem Urlaub/Reisebüro; **I've been having a bad ~ with my ulcer** mein Magengeschwür hat mir schwer zu schaffen gemacht; **the goalkeeper had a rough ~** der Torwart hatte schwer zu kämpfen; **we've been having a rough ~ with the printers recently** wir hatten in letzter Zeit viel Ärger mit den Druckern; **to show sb a good ~** jdn ausführen; **she'll give you a good ~ for £30** bei ihr kannst du dich für £ 30 amüsieren; **to give sb a bad/rough ~** (of it) jdm das Leben schwermachen; **a good ~ girl** ein lebenslustiges Mädchen, ein vergnügungssüchtiges Mädchen (pej).

(h) (rhythm) Takt m. **(to be) in ~ (with)** im Takt (sein) (mit); **(to be/get) out of ~** aus dem Takt (sein/kommen); **you're singing out of ~ (with the others)** du singst nicht im Takt (mit den anderen); **3/4 ~** Dreivierteltakt m; **to keep ~ (beat ~)** den Takt angeben or schlagen; **(keep in ~)** (den) Takt halten.

2 vt (a) (choose ~ of) **to ~ sth perfectly** genau den richtigen Zeitpunkt für etw wählen; **you must learn to ~ your requests a little more tactfully** du mußt lernen, deine Forderungen zu einem geeigneteren Zeitpunkt vorzubringen; **he ~d his arrival to coincide with ...** er legte seine Ankunft so, daß sie mit ... zusammenfiel; **you ~d that well** du hast dir den richtigen Zeitpunkt (dafür) ausgesucht; **the bomb is ~d to explode at ...** die Bombe ist so eingestellt, daß sie um ... explodiert.

(b) (with stop-watch etc) stoppen; speed also messen. **to ~ sb (over 1000 metres)** jdn (auf 1000 Meter) stoppen, jds Zeit (auf or über 1000 Meter) nehmen; **~ how long it takes you, ~ yourself** sieh auf die Uhr, wie lange du brauchst; (with stop-watch) stopp, wie lange du brauchst; **to ~ an egg** auf die Uhr sehen, wenn man ein Ei kocht; **a computer that ~s its operator** ein Computer, der die Zeit mißt, die sein Operator braucht.

time: **~-and-motion expert** n Fachmann m für Zeitstudien, =

REFA-Fachmann m; **~-and-motion study** n Zeitstudie, Bewegungsstudie f; **~ bomb** n (lit, fig) Zeitbombe f; **~ capsule** n Kassette f mit Zeitdokumentationen; **~card** n (for workers) Stechkarte f; (US: **~table**) Fahrplan m; **~ check** n (general) Zeitkontrolle f; (Rad, TV) Zeitvergleich m; **~ clock** n Stechuhr f; **~-consuming** adj zeitraubend; **~ exposure** n Langzeitbelichtung f; (photograph) Langzeitaufnahme f; **~ fuse** or (US) **fuze** n Zeitzünder m; **~-honoured** or (US) **-honored** adj althergebracht, altehrwürdig; **~keeper** n (Sport) Zeitnehmer m; **this watch/employee is a good/bad ~keeper** diese Uhr geht richtig or genau/nicht richtig/dieser Angestellte erfüllt immer/nie das Zeitsoll; **~-keeping** n (in sports) Zeitmessung f; (in factories etc) Zeitkontrolle f; (of worker) Erfüllung f des Zeitsolls; **bad ~-keeping** ständiges Zuspätkommen; **~-lag** n Zeitdifferenz f; (delay) Zeitverschiebung f; **cultural/technical ~-lag** Unterschied m in der kulturellen/technischen Entwicklung; **~-lapse** adj Zeitraffer-.

timeless ['taɪmlɪs] adj zeitlos; (everlasting) immerwährend.

timelessly ['taɪmlɪslɪ] adv zeitlos; (eternally) immerfort.

timelessness ['taɪmlɪsnɪs] n Zeitlosigkeit f; (eternal nature) Unvergänglichkeit f.

time limit n zeitliche Begrenzung; (for the completion of a job) Frist f. **to put a ~ on sth** etw befristen.

timeliness ['taɪmlɪnɪs] n Rechtzeitigkeit f. **the ~ of his warning soon became apparent** man merkte bald, daß seine Warnung genau zum richtigen Zeitpunkt erfolgt war.

time lock n Zeitschloß nt.

timely ['taɪmlɪ] adj rechtzeitig. **a ~ piece of advice** ein Rat zur rechten Zeit; **that was very ~** das war genau zur rechten Zeit.

time: **~ machine** n Zeitmaschine f; **~-out** n (US) (a) (Ftbl, Basketball) Auszeit f; (b) (break) **to take ~-out** Pause machen; **~piece** n Uhr f, Chronometer nt (geh).

timer ['taɪmə^r] n Zeitmesser m; (switch) Schaltuhr f; (person) Zeitnehmer m.

time: **~saving** adj zeitsparend; **~ scale** n (in novel, drama etc) zeitlicher Rahmen; (perception of time) Zeitmaßstab m; **to think on a different ~ scale** einen anderen Zeitbegriff haben; **~-served** adj apprentice ausgelernt; **~server** n Opportunist, Gesinnungslump (inf) m (pej); **~serving 1** n Opportunismus m, Gesinnungslumperei (inf) f (pej); **2** adj opportunistisch; **~ sharing** n Teilnehmer-Rechensystem, Time-sharing nt; **~ sheet** n Stundenzettel m, Arbeitszeit-Kontrolliste f (form); **~ signal** n Zeitzeichen nt; **~ signature** n Taktvorzeichnung f; **~ span** n Zeitspanne f; **~ switch** n Schaltuhr f, Zeitschalter m; **~table** n (transport) Fahrplan m; (Brit Sch) Stundenplan m; **to have a busy ~table** ein volles Programm haben; **what's on the ~table?** was steht auf dem Programm?; **~ travel** n Zeitreise f, Reise f durch die Zeit; **~ traveller** n Zeitreisende(r) mf; **~worn** adj stones verwittert; (through use) abgetreten; cliché, joke abgedroschen; **~ zone** n Zeitzone f.

timid ['tɪmɪd] adj scheu, ängstlich; person, behaviour, words also schüchtern, zaghaft.

timidity [tɪ'mɪdɪtɪ], **timidness** ['tɪmɪdnɪs] n see adj Scheu, Ängstlichkeit f; Schüchternheit, Zaghaftigkeit f.

timidly ['tɪmɪdlɪ] adv see adj.

timing ['taɪmɪŋ] n (a) (choice of time) Wahl f des richtigen Zeitpunkts (of für), Timing nt; (Tennis, Ftbl also) (Ball)berechnung f. **it's all a question of ~** es ist eine Frage (der Wahl) des richtigen Zeitpunkts or des Timings; **perfect ~, I'd just opened a bottle** ihr kommt gerade richtig, ich habe eben eine Flasche aufgemacht; **the ~ of the statement was wrong/excellent** die Erklärung kam zum falschen/genau zum richtigen Zeitpunkt; **what's the ~ for this job?** wie sieht der Zeitplan für diese Arbeit aus?; **the actors' ~ was terrible** die Schauspieler zeigten erbärmliche Synchronisierung; **to improve one's ~** sein Timing verbessern; **the dancer showed a good sense of ~** der Tänzer bewies ein gutes Gefühl fürs Timing.

(b) (Aut) (mechanism) Steuerung f; (adjustment) Einstellung f. **~ mechanism** Steuermechanismus m.

(c) (measuring of time) Zeitnahme, Zeitmessung f (of bei); (of race, runners etc) Stoppen nt. **regular ~ of the factory workers** regelmäßige Zeitkontrollen bei den Fabrikarbeitern.

timorous ['tɪmərəs] adj furchtsam, ängstlich, scheu.

Timothy ['tɪməθɪ] n (Bibl) Timotheus m.

timpani ['tɪmpənɪ] npl (Mus) Timpani, Kesselpauken pl.

timpanist ['tɪmpənɪst] n Timpanist, Paukist m.

tin [tɪn] **1** n (a) Blech nt; (Chem: metal) Zinn nt.

(b) (esp Brit: can) Dose, Büchse f. **a ~ of beans/biscuits** eine Dose or Büchse Bohnen/eine Dose Kekse.

2 vt (a) (coat with ~) verzinnen.

(b) (esp Brit: can) in Dosen konservieren. **this factory ~s all sorts of fruit and vegetables** in dieser Fabrik werden Obst- und Gemüsekonserven aller Art hergestellt.

tin can n (a) (Brit) (Blech)dose, (Blech)büchse f. (b) (US Naut sl: destroyer) Zerstörer m.

tincture ['tɪŋktʃə^r] **1** n (a) (Pharm, Her) Tinktur f. **~ of iodine** Jodtinktur f. (b) (fig: tinge) Spur, Andeutung f. **2** vt views, opinions einen Anstrich or Beigeschmack geben (with von). **to be ~d with sth** einen Anstrich or Beigeschmack von etw haben.

tinder ['tɪndə^r] n Zunder m. **~box** n Zunderbüchse f; **to be (like) a ~box** wie Zunder brennen; (country etc) ein Pulverfaß sein.

tine [taɪn] n (of fork) Zinke f; (of antlers) Ende nt, Sprosse f.

tinfoil ['tɪnfɔɪl] n Stanniol(papier) nt; (aluminium foil) Aluminiumfolie f.

ting [tɪŋ] **1** vt bell läuten. **to ~ the bell** klingeln; **he ~ed his knife against the glass**, **he ~ed the glass with his knife** er schlug mit dem Messer an das Glas, daß es klirrte. **2** vi (bell) klingen. **3** n Klingen nt. **to give the bell a (quick) ~** (kurz) klingeln.

ting-a-ling ['tɪŋə'lɪŋ] **1** n Kling(e)ling nt. **2** interj kling(e)ling.

tinge [tɪndʒ] **1** n (a) (of colour) Hauch m, Spur f. **a ~ of red** ein (leichter) Rotstich, ein Hauch m von Rot.

(b) (fig: hint, trace) Spur f; (of sadness also) Anflug m.
2 vt **(a)** (colour) (leicht) tönen. **lavender water** ~d **with pink** Lavendelwasser, das leicht rosa getönt ist.
(b) (fig) **to** ~ **sth with sth** einer Sache (dat) eine Spur von etw geben; ~d **with** ... mit einer Spur von ...; **our happiness was** ~d **with sorrow** unser Glück war getrübt.

tingle ['tɪŋgl] **1** vi prickeln, kribbeln (inf) (with vor +dat); (with blows) leicht brennen (with von). ... **makes your mouth** ~ **with freshness** ... gibt Ihrem Mund prickelnde Frische; **to** ~ **with excitement** vor Aufregung beben, ganz kribbelig sein (inf).
2 n see vi Prickeln, Kribbeln (inf) nt; leichtes Brennen. **she felt a** ~ **of excitement** sie war ganz kribbelig, **a** ~ **of excitement** ran up her spine ihr lief (vor Aufregung) ein Schauer über den Rücken.

tingling ['tɪŋglɪŋ] **1** n see vi Prickeln, Kribbeln (inf) nt; leichtes Brennen. **2** adj (with cold, freshness, excitement) prickelnd; (with blows) brennend.

tingly ['tɪŋglɪ] adj prickelnd. **my arm feels (all)** ~ ich habe ein prickelndes Gefühl im Arm, mein Arm kribbelt (inf); **I feel** ~ **all over** es kribbelt mich überall; (with excitement) es prickelt mir unter der Haut, ich bin ganz kribbelig (inf).

tin: ~ **god** n (fig) Bonze m; (idol) Abgott, Götze m; ~ **hat** n (inf) Stahlhelm m, steifer Hut (inf); ~**horn** n (US sl) Angeber m (inf).

tinker ['tɪŋkə'] **1** n Kesselflicker m. **you little** ~! (inf) du kleiner Stromer or Zigeuner! (inf); **not to give a** ~'s **curse** or **cuss** or **damn about sb/sth** (inf) sich einen feuchten Kehricht um jdn/etw scheren (inf); **not to be worth a** ~'s **curse** or **cuss** or **damn** (inf) keinen Pfifferling wert sein (inf); (person) keinen Schuß Pulver wert sein (inf).
2 vi **(a)** (also ~ **about**) herumbasteln (with, on an +dat).
(b) (unskilfully) **to** ~ **with sth** an etw (dat) herumpfuschen.

tinkle ['tɪŋkl] **1** vt zum Klingen bringen. **he** ~d **the bell** er klingelte (mit der Glocke).
2 vi (bells etc) klingen, bimmeln (inf); (on piano) klimpern; (breaking glass) klirren.
3 n Klingen, Bimmeln (inf) nt no pl; (of breaking glass) Klirren nt no pl. **to give sb a** ~ (Brit inf: on telephone) jdn anbimmeln (inf).

tinkling ['tɪŋklɪŋ] **1** n (of bells etc) Klingen, Bimmeln (inf) nt; (of piano) Klimpern nt; (of broken glass) Klirren nt. **2** adj see n klingend, bimmelnd (inf); klimpernd; klirrend.

tin: ~ **lizzie** n (inf: car) Klapperkiste f; ~ **mine** n Zinnmine f, Zinnbergwerk nt.

tinned [tɪnd] adj (esp Brit) Dosen-, Büchsen-.

tinny ['tɪnɪ] adj (+er) sound blechern; instrument blechern klingend; taste nach Blech; (pej) typewriter etc schäbig. **these cars are so** ~ diese Autos bestehen fast nur aus Blech.

tin: ~**opener** n (esp Brit) Dosen- or Büchsenöffner m; ~ **pan alley** n die Schlagerindustrie; (district) das Zentrum der Schlagerindustrie; ~ **plate** n Zinnblech nt; ~**plate** vt verzinnen; ~**pot** adj (Brit inf) mickrig (inf).

tinsel ['tɪnsəl] n **(a)** (foil) Girlanden pl aus Rauschgold etc; (on dress) Lamé nt. **(b)** (pej) Talmi nt (pej), Tand m (geh).

tin: ~**smith** n Blechschmied m; ~ **soldier** n Zinnsoldat m.

tint [tɪnt] **1** n Ton m; (product for hair) Tönung(smittel nt) f. ~**s of autumn/purple** Herbst-/Violettöne pl. **2** vt tönen.

tintack ['tɪntæk] n Tapeziernagel m.

tintinnabulation ['tɪntɪ,næbjʊ'leɪʃən] n (liter, form) Klingeln nt or Geläut nt (von Glocken).

tin whistle n Blechflöte f.

tiny ['taɪnɪ] adj (+er) winzig, sehr klein; baby, child sehr or ganz klein. ~ **little** winzig klein; **a** ~ **mind** (pej) ein winziger Verstand, ein Zwergenverstand m.

tip¹ [tɪp] **1** n Spitze f; (of cigarette) Filter m; (inf: cigarette) Filter(zigarette) f. **from** ~ **to toe** von Kopf bis Fuß, vom Scheitel bis zur Sohle; **to stand on the** ~ **of one's toes** auf Zehenspitzen stehen; **it's on the** ~ **of my tongue** es liegt mir auf der Zunge; **it's just the** ~ **of the iceberg** (fig) das ist nur die Spitze des Eisbergs; see fingertip, wingtip.
2 vt (put ~ on) **to** ~ **sth with sth** etw mit einer Kupfer-/Stahlspitze versehen; **copper/steel** ~**ped** mit Kupfer-/Stahlspitze; ~**ped** (cigarette) mit Filter, Filter-.

tip² **1** n **(a)** (gratuity) Trinkgeld nt. **what do your** ~**s amount to?** wieviel Trinkgeld bekommen Sie (insgesamt)?; **£100 a week, plus** ~**s** £ 100 pro Woche, plus Trinkgeld(er); **10p is sufficient as a** ~ 10 Pence Trinkgeld reichen.
(b) (warning) Wink, Tip m; (advice) Tip, Hinweis, Ratschlag m; (Racing) Tip m. **if you take my** ~ wenn Sie meinen Tip or Wink beachten.
(c) (tap) **to give the ball a** ~ den Ball nur antippen; **to give a glass a** ~ **with one's finger** ein Glas mit dem Finger antippen, mit dem Finger an ein Glas tippen.
2 vt **(a)** (give gratuity to) Trinkgeld geben (+dat). **to** ~ **sb £1** jdm £ 1 Trinkgeld geben.
(b) (Racing) tippen auf (+acc), setzen auf (+acc). **he** ~**ped Red Rum for the 3.30** er setzte or tippte im 3³⁰-Rennen auf Red Rum; **they are** ~**ped to win the competition/election** (fig) sie sind die Favoriten in dem or für den Wettbewerb/in der or für die Wahl; **you** ~**ped a winner** (lit, fig) da hast du auf das richtige Pferd gesetzt; **Paul is** ~**ped for the job** Paul ist der Favorit or gilt als Favorit für diese Stelle.
(c) (tap) (with fingers) tippen or schnipsen an (+acc); (with bat, racket) antippen. **to** ~ **one's hat (to sb)** an den Hut tippen.
3 vi **Americans** ~ **better** Amerikaner geben mehr Trinkgeld.
♦ **tip off** vt sep einen Tip or Wink geben (+dat) (about über +acc). **he** ~**ped** ~ **the police as to her whereabouts** er verklickerte (inf) or verriet der Polizei, wo sie war; **they've been** ~**ped** ~ man hat ihnen einen Tip or Wink gegeben.

tip³ [tɪp] **1** vt (tilt, incline) kippen; (overturn) umkippen; (pour) liquid kippen, schütten; (empty) load, sand, rubbish schütten; books, clothes etc kippen. **to** ~ **sth backwards/forwards** etw nach

hinten/vorne kippen or neigen; **to** ~ **a load into a ship** eine Ladung in ein Schiff leeren or kippen; **he** ~**s the scales at 70kg** er bringt 70 kg auf die Waage; **it** ~**ped the scales in his favour** (fig) das hat für ihn den Ausschlag gegeben; **the car** ~**ped over and they were** ~**ped into the ditch** der Wagen kippte um, und sie landeten in einem Graben or im Graben; ~ **the case upside down** dreh die Kiste um, stell die Kiste auf den Kopf; **to** ~ **sb off his chair** jdn vom Stuhl kippen; **to** ~ **one's hat over one's eyes** sich (dat) den Hut über die Augen ziehen/schieben.
2 vi (incline) kippen; (dump rubbish) Schutt abladen. **the boat** ~**ped to and fro** das Boot schaukelte auf und ab; "no ~**ping**", "~**ping prohibited**" „Schutt abladen verboten".
3 n **(a)** (Brit) (for rubbish) Schuttabladeplatz, Müllplatz m; (for coal) Halde f; (inf: untidy place) Saustall m (inf).
(b) to give sb a ~ etw (um)kippen.
♦ **tip back 1** vi (chair, person, mirror) nach hinten (weg)kippen.
2 vt sep nach hinten kippen; person nach hinten legen.
♦ **tip out 1** vt sep auskippen; liquid, sand also ausschütten; load, objects, rubbish abladen, ausleeren. **they** ~**ped him** ~ **of bed** sie kippten ihn aus dem Bett. **2** vi herauskippen; (liquid) herauslaufen; (sand) herausrutschen; (load, objects, rubbish also) herausfallen.
♦ **tip over** vti sep (overturn) umkippen.
♦ **tip up** vti sep (tilt) kippen; (overturn) umkippen; (folding seat) hochklappen.

tip-off ['tɪpɒf] n (inf) Tip, Wink m.

tipper ['tɪpə'] n **(a)** (also ~ **lorry** (Brit), ~ **truck**) Kipplaster, Kipper m. **(b)** (person) **he's a generous** ~ er gibt großzügig Trinkgeld or großzügige Trinkgelder.

tippet ['tɪpɪt] n (old) (woman's) Schultertuch nt; (Eccl) Stola f.

tipple ['tɪpl] (inf) **1** n **he enjoys a** ~ er trinkt ganz gerne mal einen; **gin is his** ~ er trinkt am liebsten Gin. **2** vi (ganz schön) süffeln (inf), picheln (inf).

tippler ['tɪplə'] n (inf) Schluckspecht m (inf).

tippy-toe ['tɪpɪtəʊ] vi, n (US inf) see **tiptoe**.

tipsily ['tɪpsɪlɪ] adv beschwipst, angesäuselt (inf).

tipsiness ['tɪpsɪnɪs] n Beschwipstheit f.

tipstaff ['tɪpstɑːf] n (Brit Jur) ~ Ordnungsbeamte(r) m.

tipster ['tɪpstə'] n jd, der bei Pferderennen Wettips verkauft.

tipsy ['tɪpsɪ] adj (+er) beschwipst, angesäuselt (inf). ~ **cake** mit Alkohol getränkter Kuchen; **to be** ~ beschwipst or angesäuselt (inf) sein, einen Schwips haben.

tip: ~**toe 1** vi auf Zehenspitzen gehen; **2** n on ~**toe** auf Zehenspitzen; **they stood on/raised themselves on** ~**toe** sie standen auf Zehenspitzen/sie stellten sich auf die Zehenspitzen; ~**top** adj (inf: first-rate) tipp-topp (inf) pred, erstklassig, Spitzen-, Top-; ~**up lorry** (Brit), ~**up truck** n Kipplaster, Kipper m; ~**up seat** n Klappsitz m.

tirade [taɪ'reɪd] n Tirade, Schimpfkanonade f.

tire¹ [taɪə'] **1** vt ermüden, müde machen.
2 vi **(a)** (become fatigued) ermüden, müde werden.
(b) (become bored) **to** ~ **of sb/sth** jdn/etw satt haben, jds/einer Sache (gen) müde (geh) or überdrüssig (geh) werden; **she never** ~**s of talking about her son** sie wird es nie müde, über ihren Sohn zu sprechen (geh).
♦ **tire out** vt sep (völlig) erschöpfen.

tire² n (US) see **tyre**.

tired ['taɪəd] adj **(a)** (fatigued) müde; cliché abgegriffen. ~ **out** völlig erschöpft.
(b) to be ~ **of sb/sth** jds/einer Sache (gen) müde or überdrüssig sein (geh), jdn/etw leid sein or satt haben; **to get** ~ **of sb/sth** jdn/etw satt bekommen; **I'm** ~ **of telling you** ich habe es satt, dir das zu sagen; **you make me** ~! du regst mich auf!

tiredly ['taɪədlɪ] adv müde; say also mit müder Stimme; walk also mit müden Schritten.

tiredness ['taɪədnɪs] n Müdigkeit f. ~ **had got the better of him** (die) Müdigkeit hatte ihn übermannt; **the accident was a result of** (his) ~ (seine) Übermüdung war die Unfallursache.

tireless ['taɪəlɪs] adj unermüdlich; patience also unerschöpflich.

tirelessly ['taɪəlɪslɪ] adv see adj unermüdlich; unerschöpflich.

tirelessness ['taɪəlɪsnɪs] n Unermüdlichkeit f.

tiresome ['taɪəsəm] adj (irritating) lästig, leidig; (boring) fade, langweilig.

tiresomeness ['taɪəsəmnɪs] n see adj Lästigkeit, Leidigkeit f; Fadheit f.

tiring ['taɪərɪŋ] adj anstrengend, ermüdend. **looking after 6 children under 5 is** ~ es ist sehr anstrengend or es macht (einen) sehr müde, auf 6 Kinder unter 5 Jahren aufzupassen; **this is** ~ **work/a** ~ **job** diese Arbeit ist anstrengend.

tiro n see **tyro**.

Tirol n see **Tyrol**.

'tis [tɪz] (Poet, dial) contr of it is es ist.

tissue ['tɪʃuː] n **(a)** (Anat, Bot, fig) Gewebe nt. ~ **culture** Gewebekultur f; ~ **cell** Gewebe- or Gewebszelle f; **a** ~ **of lies** ein Lügengewebe, ein Lügengespinst nt. **(b)** (handkerchief) Papier(taschen)tuch nt. **(c)** (also ~ **paper**) Seidenpapier nt.

tit¹ [tɪt] n (bird) Meise f.

tit² n: ~ **for tat** wie du mir, so ich dir, Auge um Auge(, Zahn um Zahn); **it was** ~ **for tat** es ging Auge um Auge(, Zahn um Zahn); **he was repaid** ~ **for tat** er bekam es mit gleicher Münze heimgezahlt.

tit³ n (sl) (breast) Titte f (sl); (person) (blöde) Sau (sl). ~ **and bum press** (hum) Arsch-und-Titten-Presse f (hum).

Titan ['taɪtən] n (Myth) Titan m. **t~** (fig) Titan, Gigant m.

titanic [taɪ'tænɪk] adj (huge) gigantisch; (Chem) Titan-.

titanium [tɪ'teɪnɪəm] n Titan nt.

titbit ['tɪtbɪt] n (esp Brit) Leckerbissen m.

titfer ['tɪtfə'] n (Brit sl: hat) Deckel m (inf).

tithe [taɪð] n usu pl Zehnte m. **to pay** ~**s** or **the** ~ den Zehnten bezahlen or abgeben.

titillate ['tɪtɪleɪt] vt person, senses anregen, angenehm erregen; interest erregen. it ~s the palate es kitzelt den Gaumen.

titillation [ˌtɪtɪ'leɪʃən] n see vt Anregung f, angenehme Erregung; Erregen nt. such ~ is not for the serious-minded solcher Kitzel ist nichts für ernsthaft gesinnte Menschen.

titivate ['tɪtɪveɪt] (old, hum) 1 vi sich feinmachen. 2 vt oneself, hair etc, restaurant herausputzen, verschönern.

titivation [ˌtɪtɪ'veɪʃən] n (old, hum) Verschönerung f.

title ['taɪtl] n (a) Titel m (also Sport); (of chapter) Überschrift f; (Film) Untertitel m; (form of address) Anrede f. what ~ do you give a bishop? wie redet or spricht man einen Bischof an? (b) (Jur) (right) (Rechts)anspruch (to auf +acc), Titel (spec) m; (document) Eigentumsurkunde f.

titled ['taɪtld] adj person, classes mit (Adels)titel. is he ~? hat er einen Titel?

title: ~ **deed** n Eigentumsurkunde f; ~ **holder** n (Sport) Titelträger(in f) m; ~ **page** n (Typ) Titelseite f; ~ **role** n (Theat, Film) Titelrolle f.

titmouse ['tɪtmaʊs] n Meise f.

titrate ['taɪtreɪt] vt (Chem) titrieren.

titter ['tɪtə^r] 1 vti kichern. 2 n Kichern, Gekicher nt.

tittle ['tɪtl] n see jot.

tittle-tattle ['tɪtlˌtætl] 1 n Geschwätz nt; (gossip also) Klatsch, Tratsch (inf) m. 2 vi see n quatschen, schwatzen; klatschen, tratschen (inf).

titular ['tɪtjʊlə^r] adj (a) possessions zum Titel gehörend. (b) (without real authority) nominell, Titular-.

tizzy ['tɪzɪ], **tizwoz** ['tɪzwɒz] n (inf) to be in/get into a ~ höchst aufgeregt sein/sich schrecklich aufregen.

T-junction ['tiːˌdʒʌŋkʃən] n T-Kreuzung f.

TNT abbr of **trinitrotoluene** TNT nt.

to [tuː] 1 prep (a) (in direction of, towards) zu. to go ~ the station zum Bahnhof gehen/fahren; to go ~ the doctor('s)/greengrocer's etc zum Arzt/Gemüsehändler etc gehen; to go ~ the theatre/cinema etc ins Theater/Kino etc gehen; to go ~ France/London nach Frankreich/London gehen/fahren; to go ~ Switzerland in die Schweiz gehen/fahren; to go ~ school zur or in die Schule gehen; to go ~ bed ins or zu Bett gehen; ~ the left nach links; ~ the west nach Westen; he came ~ where I was standing er kam dahin or zu der Stelle, wo ich stand; to fall ~ the ground auf den or zu Boden fallen; to turn a picture/one's face ~ the wall ein Bild/sich mit dem Gesicht zur Wand drehen; hold it ~ the light halte es gegen das Licht.

(b) (as far as, until) bis. to count (up) ~ 20 bis 20 zählen; there were (from) 40 ~ 60 people es waren 40 bis 60 Leute da; it's 90 kms ~ Paris nach Paris sind es 90 km; it's correct ~ a millimetre es stimmt bis auf den Millimeter; 8 years ago ~ the day auf den Tag genau vor 8 Jahren; ~ this day bis auf den heutigen Tag; they perished ~ a man sie kamen alle bis auf den letzten Mann ums Leben.

(c) (with indir obj) to give sth ~ sb jdm etw geben; a present from me ~ you ein Geschenk für dich von mir or von mir an dich; who did you give it ~? ~, who(m) did you give it? wem haben Sie es gegeben?; I said ~ myself ich habe mir gesagt; he was muttering/singing ~ himself er murmelte/sang vor sich hin; what is it ~ you? was geht dich das an?; he is kind ~ everyone er ist zu allen freundlich; it's a great help ~ me das ist eine große Hilfe für mich; he has been a good friend ~ us er war uns (dat) ein guter Freund; to address sth ~ sb etw an jdn adressieren; "To ..." (on envelope etc) „An (+acc) ..."; welcome ~ you all seid alle willkommen; to pray ~ God zu Gott beten.

(d) (in toasts) auf (+acc). to drink ~ sb jdm zutrinken; to drink ~ sb's health auf jds Wohl (acc) trinken.

(e) (next ~, with position) bumper ~ bumper Stoßstange an Stoßstange; close ~ sb/sth nahe bei jdm/etw; at right angles/parallel ~ the wall im rechten Winkel/parallel zur Wand; ~ the west (of)/the left (of) westlich/links (von).

(f) (with expressions of time) vor. 20 (minutes) ~ 2 20 (Minuten) vor 2; at (a) quarter ~ 2 um Viertel vor 2; it was five ~ when we arrived es war fünf vor, als wir ankamen.

(g) (in relation ~) A is ~ B as C is ~ D A verhält sich zu B wie C zu D; 3 ~ the 4th (Math) 3 hoch 4; by a majority of 10 ~ 7 mit einer Mehrheit von 10 zu 7; they won by 4 goals ~ 2 sie haben mit 4:2 (spoken: vier zu zwei) Toren gewonnen.

(h) (per) pro; (in recipes, when mixing) auf (+acc). one person ~ a room eine Person pro Zimmer; 200 people ~ the square km 200 Einwohner pro Quadratkilometer.

(i) (in comparison ~) inferior/superior ~ schlechter/besser als, unter-/überlegen (+dat); that's nothing ~ what is to come das ist gar nichts verglichen mit dem, was noch kommt.

(j) (concerning) what do you say ~ the idea? was hältst du von der Idee?; what would you say ~ a beer? was hältst du von einem Bier?; there's nothing ~ it (it's very easy) es ist nichts dabei; that's all there is ~ it das ist alles; ~ repairing cooker £10 (Comm) (für) Reparatur eines Herdes £ 10.

(k) (according ~) ~ the best of my knowledge nach bestem Wissen; ~ all appearances allem Anschein nach; it's not ~ my taste das ist nicht nach meinem Geschmack.

(l) (accompanied by) to sing ~ the guitar zur Gitarre singen; to sing sth ~ the tune of ... etw nach der Melodie von ... singen; ~ the strains of Rule Britannia unter den Klängen von „Rule Britannia"; to dance ~ a tune/an orchestra zu einer Melodie/den Klängen or der Musik eines Orchesters tanzen.

(m) (of) ambassador ~ America/the King of France Botschafter in Amerika/am Hofe des Königs von Frankreich; secretary ~ the director Sekretärin des Direktors.

(n) (producing) ~ my delight zu meiner Freude; ~ everyone's surprise zu jedermanns Überraschung.

(o) (secure ~) he nailed it ~ the wall/floor etc er nagelte es an die Wand/auf den Boden etc; they tied him ~ the tree sie

banden ihn an den Baum or am Baum fest; they held him ~ the ground sie hielten ihn am Boden.

(p) (in) I have never been ~ Brussels/India ich war noch nie in Brüssel/Indien.

2 (in infin) (a) ~ begin ~ do sth anfangen, etw zu tun; he decided ~ come er beschloß zu kommen; I want ~ do it ich will es tun; I want him ~ do it ich will, daß er es tut.

(b) (in order ~) to eat ~ live essen, um zu leben; I did it ~ help you ich tat es, um dir zu helfen.

(c) (until) he lived ~ be 100 er wurde 100 Jahre alt; the firm grew ~ be the biggest in the world die Firma wurde zur größten der Welt.

(d) (infin as prp) ~ see him now, one would never think ... wenn man ihn jetzt sähe, würde man nicht glauben, ...; ~ be honest, ... ehrlich gesagt, ...; ~ tell the truth, ... um ehrlich zu sein, ...; ~ get to the point, ... um zur Sache zu kommen, ...; well, not ~ exaggerate ... ohne zu übertreiben, ...; not ~ be too detailed ... ohne zu sehr ins Detail zu gehen, ...

(e) (qualifying noun or pronoun) he is not the sort ~ do that er ist nicht der Typ, der das täte or der Typ dazu; I have done nothing ~ deserve this ich habe nichts getan, womit ich das verdient hätte; who is he ~ order you around? wer ist er denn, daß er dich so herumkommandiert?; he was the first ~ arrive er kam als erster an, er war der erste, der ankam; who was the last ~ see her? wer hat sie zuletzt gesehen?; there's no-one ~ help us er ist niemand da, der uns helfen könnte; there is much ~ be done es gibt viel zu tun; what is there ~ do here? was gibt es hier zu tun?; now is the time ~ do it jetzt ist die (beste) Zeit, es zu tun or dazu; the book is still ~ be written das Buch muß noch geschrieben werden; he's a big boy ~ be still in short trousers er ist so ein großer Junge und trägt noch kurze Hosen; I arrived ~ find she had gone als ich ankam, war sie weg; it disappeared, never ~ be found again es verschwand und wurde nie wieder gefunden.

(f) (adj + to + infin) to be ready ~ do sth (willing) bereit sein, etw zu tun; are you ready ~ go at last? bist du endlich fertig?; it's hard ~ understand/accept es ist schwer zu verstehen/es ist schwer, sich damit abzufinden; it's impossible ~ believe das kann man einfach nicht glauben; you are foolish ~ try it du bist dumm, das überhaupt zu versuchen or daß du das versuchst; is it good ~ eat? schmeckt es gut?; it's too heavy ~ lift es ist zu schwer zum Heben; too young ~ marry zu jung zum Heiraten.

(g) (omitting verb) I don't want ~ ich will nicht; I'll try ~ ich werde es versuchen; you have ~ du mußt; I should love ~ sehr gerne; I should love ~ but ... ich würde gerne, aber ...; we didn't want ~ but we were forced ~ wir wollten nicht, aber wir waren dazu gezwungen; I intended ~ do it, but I forgot ~, I intended ~, but I forgot ich wollte es tun, aber ich habe es vergessen; buy it, it would be silly not ~ kaufe es, es wäre dumm, es nicht zu tun; he often does things one doesn't expect him ~ er macht oft Dinge, die man nicht von ihm erwartet.

3 adj (slightly ajar) door angelehnt; (shut) zu.

4 adv ~ and fro hin und her; walk auf und ab.

toad [təʊd] n Kröte f; (fig: repulsive person) Ekel nt.

toad-in-the-hole ['təʊdɪnðə'həʊl] n in Pfannkuchenteig gebakkene Würste.

toadstool ['təʊdstuːl] n (nicht eßbarer) Pilz. poisonous ~ Giftpilz m.

toady ['təʊdɪ] 1 n (pej) Kriecher, Speichellecker m. 2 vi radfahren (pej inf). to ~ to sb vor jdm kriechen.

to-and-fro ['tuːən'frəʊ] n Hin und Her nt.

toast[1] [təʊst] 1 n Toast m. a piece of ~ ein Toast m, eine Scheibe Toast; on ~ auf Toast; as warm as ~ (fig) mollig warm; ~ rack Toastständer m.

2 vt bread toasten; (on open fire) rösten. ~ed teacakes getoastete Rosinenbrötchen; ~ed cheese überbackener Käsetoast; to ~ one's feet by the fire sich (dat) die Füße am Feuer wärmen.

3 vi (bread etc) sich toasten/rösten lassen; (inf: person) braten (inf), rösten (inf).

toast[2] 1 n (a) Toast, Trinkspruch m. to drink a ~ to sb auf jdn trinken; to propose a ~ einen Toast or Trinkspruch ausbringen (to auf +acc); they raised their glasses in a ~ sie hoben ihre Gläser (to um auf (+ acc) zu trinken). (b) she was the ~ of the town sie war der gefeierte Star der Stadt.

2 vt to ~ sb/sth auf jds Wohl or jdn/etw trinken; we ~ed the victory in champagne wir haben unseren Sieg mit Champagner gefeiert or begossen (inf); as a girl, she was much ~ed for her beauty als Mädchen war sie eine gefeierte Schönheit.

toaster ['təʊstə^r] n Toaster m.

toasting fork ['təʊstɪŋˌfɔːk] n Gabel f zum Brotrösten.

toastmaster ['təʊstˌmɑːstə^r] n jd, der bei Diners Toasts ankündigt oder ausbringt und Tischreden ansagt.

tobacco [tə'bækəʊ] n Tabak m.

tobacco: ~ **jar** n Tabaksdose f; ~ **leaf** n Tabakblatt nt.

tobacconist [tə'bækənɪst] n Tabak(waren)händler m; (shop) Tabak(waren)laden m. at the ~'s (shop) im Tabak(waren)laden.

tobacco: ~ **plantation** n Tabakplantage f; ~ **pouch** n Tabaksbeutel m.

to-be [tə'biː] adj zukünftig. the mother-/bride-/husband-~ die werdende Mutter/zukünftige Braut/der zukünftige Mann.

toboggan [tə'bɒgən] 1 n Schlitten, Rodel(schlitten) m. ~ run Schlitten- or Rodelbahn f. 2 vi Schlitten fahren, rodeln. to ~ down a slope mit dem Schlitten einen Hang hinunterfahren; to go ~ing Schlitten fahren, rodeln.

toby jug ['təʊbɪˌdʒʌg] n Figurkrug m.

toccata [tə'kɑːtə] n Tokkata f.

tocsin ['tɒksɪn] n (old) Alarm(glocke f) m.

tod [tɒd] n (Brit sl): on one's ~ ganz allein.

today [tə'deɪ] adv, n (a) heute. a week/fortnight ~ heute in einer

Woche/zwei Wochen; **he's been here a week** ~ heute ist er eine Woche da; **a year ago** ~ heute vor einem Jahr; ~ **is Monday** heute ist Montag; **from** ~ von heute an, vom heutigen Tag an, ab heute; **~'s paper/news** die heutige Zeitung/ heutigen Nachrichten, die Zeitung/Nachrichten von heute; **~'s rate** (Fin) der Tageskurs; **here** ~ **and gone tomorrow** (fig) heute hier und morgen da.

(b) (these days) heutzutage. **the cinema** ~ das Kino (von) heute; **the world/youth/writers of** ~ die Welt/Jugend/Schrift-steller von heute; **~'s world/youth** die heutige Welt/Jugend, die Welt/Jugend von heute; **live for** ~ **and let tomorrow take care of itself** lebe dem Heute und laß das Morgen morgen sein.

toddle ['tɒdl] **1** vi **(a)** wackeln. **the little boy** ~**d into the room** der kleine Junge kam ins Zimmer gewackelt.

(b) (inf) (walk) gehen; (leave: also ~ **off**) abzwitschern (inf). **well, I'd better be toddling (off)** ich zwitschere wohl besser mal ab (inf); **could you just** ~ **down to the shops and** ... könntest du mal zu den Geschäften runtergehen und ...

2 n (inf) **to go for a** ~ an die Luft gehen.

toddler ['tɒdlə^r] n Kleinkind nt.

toddy ['tɒdɪ] n Grog m.

to-do [tə'duː] n (inf) Theater (inf), Gedöns (inf) nt. **to make a** ~ ein Theater or Gedöns machen (inf); **she made quite a** ~ **about it** sie machte viel Wind or vielleicht ein Theater or Gedöns darum (inf); **what a** ~! so ein Theater! (inf); **what's all the** ~? was soll denn das ganze Theater or Getue or Gedöns? (inf).

toe [təʊ] **1** n **(a)** (on foot) Zehe f, Zeh m. **to tread** or **step on sb's** ~**s** (lit) jdm auf die Zehen treten; (fig) jdm ins Handwerk pfuschen (inf); **with so many of us we'll be treading on each other's** ~**s** wir sind so viele, daß wir uns gegenseitig ins Gehege kommen; **to be on one's** ~**s** (fig) auf Zack sein (inf); **to keep sb on his** ~**s** (fig) jdn auf Zack halten (inf).

(b) (of sock, shoe) Spitze f.

2 vt (fig) **to** ~ **the line** sich einfügen, spuren (inf); **to** ~ **the party line** (Pol) sich nach der Parteilinie richten.

toe: ~**cap** n (Schuh)kappe f; ~**clip** n (on bicycle)Rennbügel m.

-toed [-təʊd] adj suf -zehig. **two-**~ zweizehig, mit zwei Zehen.

toe: ~**-dance** vi (US) auf den Spitzen tanzen; ~**hold** n Halt m für die Fußspitzen; (fig) Einstieg m; ~**-in** n Vorlauf m; ~**nail** n Zehennagel m; ~**-out** n Nachlauf m; ~ **shoe** n (US) Spitzenschuh m.

toff [tɒf] n (Brit inf) feiner Pinkel (inf).

toffee ['tɒfɪ] n (substance) (Sahne)karamel m; (sweet) Toffee nt, (weiches) Karamelbonbon. **he can't sing for** ~ (inf) er kann überhaupt nicht or nicht die Bohne (inf) singen.

toffee: ~ **apple** n kandierter Apfel; ~**-nosed** adj (Brit inf) ein-gebildet, hochnäsig.

toga ['təʊgə] n Toga f.

together [tə'geðə^r] adv **(a)** zusammen. **to do sth** ~ etw zusammen tun; (with one another) discuss, play, dance etc also etw miteinander tun; (jointly) try, achieve sth, do research etc also etw gemeinsam tun; **to sit/stand** etc ~ zusammen or beieinander sitzen/stehen etc; **to be** ~/**all** ~ (people) (alle) zusammen or beieinander or beisammen sein; **to tie/fit/glue etc two things** ~ zwei Dinge zusammenbinden/-setzen/-kleben etc; **we're in this** ~ wir hängen da beide/alle zusammen or miteinander drin (inf); **they were both in it** ~ sie waren beide zusammen or miteinander daran beteiligt; **just you and me** ~ nur wir beide zusammen; **that makes £15 all** ~ das macht insgesamt or (alles) zusammen £ 15.

(b) (at the same time) zusammen. **all** ~ **now** jetzt alle zusammen; **you're now** ~ (Mus) ihr seid im Takt auseinander.

(c) (continuously) **for hours** ~ stundenlang; **can't you sit still for two minutes** ~! kannst du nicht mal zwei Minuten (lang) still sitzen?

togetherness [tə'geðənɪs] n (physical) Beisammensein nt; (mental, emotional) Zusammengehörigkeit f. **a feeling** or **sense of** ~ ein Gefühl der Zusammengehörigkeit, ein Zusammengehörigkeitsgefühl nt.

toggle ['tɒgl] n Knebel m; (on clothes) Knebelknopf m; (on tent) Seilzug m. ~ **switch** Kipp(hebel)schalter m.

Togo ['təʊgəʊ] n Togo nt.

Togoland ['təʊgəʊlænd] n Togo nt.

togs [tɒgz] npl (inf) Sachen, Klamotten pl (inf), Zeug nt. **his swimming** ~ sein Badezeug, seine Badesachen (inf).

♦**tog up** vt sep (inf) **to** ~ **oneself** ~, **to get** ~**ged** ~ sich in Schale werfen (inf); (for climbing, tennis etc) seine Kluft anlegen; **she was all** ~**ged** ~ sie hatte sich in Schale geworfen (inf); (for climbing, tennis etc) sie hatte ihre Kluft an; **to be** ~**ged** ~ **in one's best clothes** seine besten Sachen anhaben (inf).

toil [tɔɪl] **1** vi **(a)** (liter: work) sich plagen, sich abmühen (at, over mit). **(b)** (move with effort) sich schleppen. **to** ~ **up a hill** sich einen Berg hinaufschleppen. **2** n (liter: work) Mühe, Plage (geh) f. **after months of** ~ nach monatelanger Mühe or Plage.

toilet ['tɔɪlɪt] n **(a)** (lavatory) Toilette f, Klosett nt (dated). **to go to the** ~ auf die Toilette gehen; **she's in the** ~/~**s** sie ist auf or in der Toilette; **to put sth down the** ~ etw in die Toilette werfen.

(b) (old) Toilette f (geh).

toilet in cpds Toiletten-; ~ **bag** or **case** n Kulturbeutel m, Toilettentasche f; ~ **paper** n Toilettenpapier nt; ~ **requisites** npl Toilettenartikel pl.

toiletries ['tɔɪlɪtrɪz] npl Toilettenartikel pl.

toilet: ~ **roll** n Rolle f Toilettenpapier; ~ **seat** n Toilettensitz m, Brille f (inf); ~ **set** n (brush and comb) Toilettengarnitur f; (bathroom set) Badezimmergarnitur f; ~ **soap** n Toilettenseife f; ~ **training** n Erziehung f zur Sauberkeit; **has he started his** ~ **training yet?** geht er schon auf den Topf?; ~ **water** n Toilette(n)wasser, Eau de Toilette nt.

toils [tɔɪlz] npl (old liter) Netze pl; (fig) Maschen, Schlingen pl.

toilsome ['tɔɪlsəm] adj (liter) mühselig, mühsam.

to-ing and fro-ing ['tuːɪŋən'frəʊɪŋ] n Hin und Her nt.

Tokay [tə'kaɪ] n (wine) Tokaier m.

token ['təʊkən] **1** n **(a)** (sign) Zeichen nt. **as a** ~ **of/in** ~ **of** als or zum Zeichen (+gen); **by the same** ~ ebenso; (with neg) aber auch; ... **then by the same** ~ **you can't object to** ... dann können Sie aber auch nichts gegen ... einwenden.

(b) (counter: for gambling, jukebox etc) Marke f.

(c) (voucher, gift ~) Gutschein m.

2 attr Schein-, pro forma. **it was just a** ~ **offer** das hat er/sie etc nur pro forma or nur so zum Schein angeboten; ~ **payment** symbolische Bezahlung; ~ **resistance** Scheinwiderstand m; ~ **strike** Warnstreik m; ~ **rent/fine** nominelle or symbolische Miete/symbolische Strafe.

Tokyo ['təʊkɪəʊ] n Tokio nt.

told [təʊld] pret, ptp of **tell**. **there were 50 people there all** ~ es waren insgesamt or alles in allem 50 Leute da.

tolerable ['tɒlərəbl] adj (lit) pain, noise level etc erträglich; (fig: not too bad also) annehmbar, leidlich, passabel (inf). **how are you?** — ~ **wie geht's dir?** — ganz leidlich or passabel (inf).

tolerably ['tɒlərəblɪ] adv ziemlich. ~ **well** ganz leidlich or annehmbar, ziemlich gut; **they are** ~ **well-educated** sie sind leidlich gebildet or (rather well) ziemlich gebildet.

tolerance ['tɒlərəns] n **(a)** Toleranz, Duldsamkeit f (of, for, towards gegenüber); (towards children, one's juniors) Nach-sicht f (of mit). **racial** ~ Toleranz in Rassenfragen; **I have no** ~ **for such behaviour** für solch ein Benehmen habe ich kein Ver-ständnis.

(b) (Med, Tech) Toleranz f. **to work to fine** ~**s** mit kleinen or engen Toleranzen arbeiten.

tolerant ['tɒlərənt] adj (of, towards, with gegenüber) tolerant (also Tech), duldsam; (towards children, one's juniors) nach-sichtig. **the Lord is** ~ **of our mistakes** der Herr sieht uns unsere Schwächen nach.

tolerantly ['tɒlərəntlɪ] adv see adj.

tolerate ['tɒləreɪt] vt **(a)** pain, noise, weather etc ertragen.

(b) person dulden, tolerieren; behaviour, injustice etc also sich (dat) gefallen lassen, hinnehmen. **he can** ~ **anything except intolerance** er kann alles tolerieren, nur keine Intoleranz; **are we to** ~ **this?** müssen wir uns (dat) das gefallen lassen?; **it is not to be** ~**d** so etwas kann man nicht dulden or hinnehmen; **I won't** ~ **this disobedience!** ich dulde diesen Ungehorsam nicht!

toleration [,tɒlə'reɪʃən] n Dulden, Tolerieren nt.

toll[1] [təʊl] **1** vti läuten. **for whom the bell** ~**s** wem die Stunde schlägt. **2** n Läuten nt; (single stroke) Glockenschlag m.

toll[2] n **(a)** (tax) Maut f (esp Aus); (bridge ~, road ~ also) Zoll m, Benutzungsgebühr f; (US Telec) (Fernsprech)gebühr f.

(b) (deaths, loss etc) **the** ~ **on the roads** die Zahl der Verkehrsopfer; **the** ~ **of the floods continues to rise** (in terms of people) die Zahl der Opfer der Flutkatastrophe steigt ständig weiter; (in terms of property) das Ausmaß der Flutschäden wird immer größer; **the earthquake took a heavy** ~ **of human life** das Erdbeben forderte or kostete viele Menschenleben; **the** ~ **of the war** der Blutzoll des Krieges.

toll: ~**bar** n Mautschranke f (esp Aus); ~ **bridge** n gebührenpflichtige Brücke, Mautbrücke f (esp Aus); ~ **call** n (US) Ferngespräch nt; ~**-free call** n (US) gebührenfreier Anruf; ~**gate** n Schlagbaum m, Mautschranke f (esp Aus); ~**house** n Mauthaus nt (esp Aus).

tolling ['təʊlɪŋ] n, no pl Läuten nt.

toll: ~**keeper** n Mautner m (esp Aus); ~ **road** n Mautstraße f (esp Aus), gebührenpflichtige Straße.

Tom [tɒm] n dim of **Thomas**. **any** ~, **Dick** or **Harry** (inf) jeder x-beliebige; **you don't have to invite every** ~, **Dick and Harry** (inf) du brauchst ja nicht gerade Hinz und Kunz or Krethi und Plethi einzuladen (inf); **it's not every** ~, **Dick and Harry who can afford this** nicht jeder kann sich (dat) so was leisten; ~ **Thumb** der Däumling.

tom [tɒm] n (cat) Kater m.

tomahawk ['tɒməhɔːk] n Tomahawk m.

tomato [tə'mɑːtəʊ, (US) tə'meɪtəʊ] n, pl ~**es** Tomate f.

tomato in cpds Tomaten-; ~ **juice** n Tomatensaft m; ~ **ketchup** n (Tomaten)ketchup m or nt; ~ **sauce** n Tomatensoße f; (ketchup) (Tomaten)ketchup m or nt.

tomb [tuːm] n (grave) Grab nt; (building) Grabmal nt.

tombola [tɒm'bəʊlə] n Tombola f.

tomboy ['tɒmbɔɪ] n Wildfang m. **she is a real** ~ sie ist ein rich-tiger Junge or Wildfang.

tombstone ['tuːmstəʊn] n Grabstein m.

tomcat ['tɒmkæt] n Kater m.

tome [təʊm] n dickes Buch, Wälzer m (inf).

tomfool ['tɒm'fuːl] **1** n Blödian m. **2** adj attr blöd(sinnig).

tomfoolery [tɒm'fuːlərɪ] n Blödsinn, Unsinn m.

Tommy ['tɒmɪ] n dim of **Thomas**; (Mil sl) Tommy m (sl).

tommy: **T~ gun** n Maschinenpistole f; ~**rot** n (dated inf) dummes Zeug, Mumpitz m (dated).

tomorrow [tə'mɒrəʊ] adv, n morgen. ~ **week**, (esp Brit)/**fortnight** ~ morgen in einer Woche/zwei Wochen; **he'll have been here a week** ~ morgen ist er eine Woche da; **a year ago** ~ morgen vor einem Jahr; **the day after** ~ übermorgen; ~ **morning** morgen früh; ~ **is Monday, it's Monday** ~ morgen ist Montag; **(as) from** ~ ab morgen, von morgen an, vom morgigen Tag an; **see you** ~! bis morgen!; **~'s paper** die morgige Zeitung, die Zeitung von morgen; **the article will be in** ~**'s paper** der Artikel wird morgen in der Zeitung sein; **will** ~ **do?** (early enough) reicht es noch bis morgen?, hat es noch bis morgen Zeit?; (convenient) ist es morgen recht?; ~ **is another day** (prov) morgen ist auch noch ein Tag (prov); ~ **may never come** wer weiß, was morgen ist; ~ **never comes** (prov) es heißt immer „morgen, morgen, nur nicht heute"; **who knows what** ~ **will bring?** wer weiß, was das Morgen bringt?; **the science of** ~ die Wissenschaft von morgen; **~'s problems** die Probleme von morgen.

tom: ~**tit** n (Blau)meise f; ~**-tom** n Tamtam nt.
ton [tʌn] n (a) Tonne f. she/it weighs a ~ (fig inf) sie/das wiegt ja eine Tonne; see appendix.
  (b) ~s pl (inf: lots) jede Menge (inf); to have ~s of time/friends/money etc jede Menge (inf) or massenhaft (inf) Zeit/Freunde/Geld etc haben.
  (c) (sl: of speed) to do a or the ~ mit hundertsechzig Sachen fahren (inf).
tonal ['təʊnl] adj klanglich, Klang-; (Mus) (regarding form) tonal; (Art) farblich, Farb-. ~ **variation** Klangvariation f; (in colours) Farbabstufung f; ~ **effects in the music/painting** Klangeffekte in der Musik/Farbeffekte in dem Gemälde.
tonality [təʊ'nælɪtɪ] n (Mus) Tonalität f; (of voice) Klang m; (of poem) Tonart f; (of painting) Farbkomposition f.
tone [təʊn] 1 n (a) (of sound) (~ of voice, Phon) Ton m; (quality of sound also) Klang m. the soft ~s of a flute/her voice die sanften Töne einer Flöte/der sanfte Klang ihrer Stimme; she spoke in soft ~s sie sprach in sanftem Ton; ... he said in a friendly ~ ... sagte er in freundlichem Ton; I don't like your ~ (of voice) mir gefällt dein Ton nicht; don't speak to me in that ~ (of voice) in diesem Ton kannst du mit mir nicht reden; a dog can tell what you mean by your ~ (of voice) ein Hund erkennt am Ton (der Stimme), was man meint.
  (b) (of colour) (Farb)ton m.
  (c) (fig: mood, character) Ton m. what was the ~ of his letter? wie war denn der Ton seines Briefes?; the new people have lowered/raised the ~ of the neighbourhood die neuen Leute haben dem Ansehen or dem Ruf des Viertels geschadet/das Ansehen or den Ruf des Viertels verbessert; of course, Trevor had to lower the ~ (of the conversation) Trevor mußte natürlich ausfallend werden.
  (d) (Mus) Ton m; (US: note) Note f.
  (e) (Physiol) Tonus m (spec). to keep one's ~ sich fit halten.
2 vt (Phot: tint) einfärben, tonen (spec).
3 vi (colours) (im Farbton) harmonieren.
♦**tone down** vt sep (lit, fig) abmildern; colour also abschwächen; criticism also, language, demands mäßigen.
♦**tone in** vi (im Farbton) harmonieren.
♦**tone up** vt sep muscles kräftigen; person in Form bringen. cycling keeps you ~d ~ Radfahren hält einen in Form.
tone: ~ **arm** n (US) Tonarm m; ~ **control** n Klangfarbeneinstellung, Tonblende f; ~**-deaf** adj nicht in der Lage, Tonhöhen zu unterscheiden; he's ~**-deaf** er kann Töne verschiedener Höhen nicht unterscheiden, er hat kein Gehör für Tonhöhen; ~ **language** n Tonsprache, Tonhöhensprache f.
toneless ['təʊnlɪs] adj voice, answer tonlos; music eintönig; colour stumpf.
tonelessly ['təʊnlɪslɪ] adv reply tonlos; sing eintönig.
tone poem n Tongedicht nt.
tongs [tɒŋz] npl Zange f; (curling ~) (Hist) Brennschere f; (electric) Lockenstab m. a pair of ~ eine Zange.
tongue [tʌŋ] 1 n (a) Zunge f. to put or stick one's ~ out at sb jdm die Zunge herausstrecken; to lose/find one's ~ (fig) die Sprache verlieren/wiederfinden; to hold one's ~ den Mund halten; ~ in cheek witzelnd; is that ~ in cheek or are you serious? ist das nur Spaß or machst du nur Spaß/ist das ironisch gemeint oder ist das dein Ernst?; to have a ready/sharp ~ schlagfertig sein, nicht auf den Mund gefallen sein/eine scharfe Zunge haben; keep a civil ~ in your head! werden Sie nicht ausfallend!; I can't get my ~ round it dabei breche ich mir fast die Zunge ab; see slip, tip[1].
  (b) (liter: language) Sprache f; (old, Bibl) Zunge f. the gift of ~s (Bibl) die Gabe, in fremden Zungen zu reden.
  (c) (of shoe) Zunge, Lasche f; (of bell) Klöppel m; (of land) (Land)zunge f; (of wood) Spund, Zapfen m. a ~ of fire licked the building eine Flamme züngelte an dem Gebäude empor.
2 vt (Mus) note (mit der Zunge) stoßen.
tongue: ~**-and-groove joint** n Anschlitzzunge, Spundung f; ~-**in-cheek** adj attr remark witzelnd; ~**-tied** adj to be ~**-tied** keinen Ton herausbringen; she sat there ~**-tied** sie saß da und brachte keinen Ton heraus; ~ **twister** n Zungenbrecher m.
tonguing ['tʌŋɪŋ] n (Mus) Zungenschlag m; see double-~.
tonic ['tɒnɪk] 1 n (a) (Med) Tonikum nt; (hair ~) Haarwasser nt; (skin ~) Lotion f. it was a real ~ to see him again (fig) es hat richtig gutgetan, ihn wiederzusehen.
  (b) ~ (water) Tonic(water)nt; gin and ~ Gin (mit) Tonic.
  (c) (Mus) Tonika f, Grundton m. ~ **solfa** Solmisation f.
2 adj (a) (Med) stärkend, kräftigend, tonisch (spec). ~ **wine** Stärkungswein m.
  (b) (Phon) syllable Ton-; stress tontragend.
tonicity [tɒ'nɪsɪtɪ] n (of muscles) Tonus m (spec), Spannungszustand m.
tonight [tə'naɪt] 1 adv (this evening) heute abend; (during the coming night) heute nacht. see you ~! bis heute abend!
2 n (this evening) der heutige Abend; (the coming night) die heutige Nacht. ~'s party die Party heute abend; I'm looking forward to ~ ich freue mich auf heute abend or auf den heutigen Abend; ~ is the night we've been looking forward to heute ist der Abend, auf den wir uns gefreut haben; ~ is a night I'll remember all my life an den heutigen Abend werde ich mich mein ganzes Leben lang erinnern; ~'s weather: ~ will be clear but cold das Wetter heute nacht: heute nacht wird es klar, aber kalt sein; ~'s paper die heutige Abendzeitung, die Abendzeitung von heute.
tonnage ['tʌnɪdʒ] n Tonnage f.
tonne [tʌn] n Tonne f.
-tonner [-'tʌnər] n suf (inf) -tonner m.
tonsil ['tɒnsl] n Mandel, Tonsille (spec) f. to have one's ~s out sich (dat) die Mandeln herausnehmen lassen.
tonsillectomy [,tɒnsɪ'lektəmɪ] n Mandeloperation, Tonsillektomie (spec) f.

tonsillitis [,tɒnsɪ'laɪtɪs] n Mandelentzündung, Tonsillitis (spec) f.
tonsorial [tɒn'sɔːrɪəl] adj (hum, rare form) Barbier- (hum). ~ **artist** Barbier m.
tonsure ['tɒnʃər] 1 n Tonsur f. 2 vt scheren, die Tonsur erteilen (+dat) (spec).
ton-up ['tʌnʌp] adj (sl) ~ **kids** Motorradrocker pl (inf).
too [tuː] adv (a) (+adj or adv) zu. that's ~/not ~ **difficult a question to answer** diese Frage ist zu/nicht zu schwer zu beantworten; ~ **much/many** zuviel inv/zu viele; too much/many zu viel/zu viele; he's had ~ **much to drink** er hat zuviel getrunken; you can have ~ **much of a good thing** allzuviel ist ungesund (prov); it's ~ **much for her** es ist zuviel für sie; don't worry ~ **much** mach dir nicht zuviel Sorgen; ~ **much!** (sl) dufte!, Klasse! (sl); ~ **right!** (inf) das kannste laut sagen (inf).
  (b) (very) zu. all ~ ... allzu ...; only ~ ... nur zu ...; none ~ ... gar nicht ..., keineswegs ...; not ~/not any ~ ... nicht zu/allzu ...; I'm not/none ~ **sure** ich bin nicht ganz/gar nicht or keineswegs sicher; (that's) ~ **kind of you** (iro) (das ist) wirklich zu nett von Ihnen; none/all ~ **soon** keineswegs zu/allzu früh.
  (c) (also) auch. he can swim, ~ he ~ can swim er kann auch schwimmen, auch er kann schwimmen; he can swim ~ er kann auch schwimmen, schwimmen kann er auch.
  (d) (moreover, into the bargain) auch noch. it was really cheap, and it works ~! es war wirklich billig, und es funktioniert sogar or auch noch!; they asked for a price-reduction ~! sie wollten auch noch einen Preisnachlaß!
toodle-pip ['tuːdlpɪp] interj (dated Brit inf) tschau (inf).
took [tʊk] pret of take.
tool [tuːl] 1 n (a) Werkzeug nt; (gardening ~) (Garten)gerät nt. ~s Werkzeuge pl; (set) Werkzeug nt; that's one of the ~s of the trade das gehört zum Handwerkszeug; to have the ~s for the job das richtige or nötige Werkzeug haben; see down[1].
  (b) (fig: person) Werkzeug nt.
  (c) (sl: penis) Ding nt (sl), Apparat m (sl).
2 vt book, leather punzen.
♦**tool up** vt sep factory (mit Maschinen) ausrüsten.
tool: ~**bag** n Werkzeugtasche f; ~**box**, ~ **chest** n Werkzeugkasten m.
tooling ['tuːlɪŋ] n Punzarbeit f.
tool: ~ **kit** n Werkzeug(ausrüstung f) nt; ~**shed** n Geräteschuppen m.
toot [tuːt] 1 vt to ~ **a horn** auf dem Horn blasen or (child's trumpet) tuten; (in car, on bicycle) auf die Hupe drücken, hupen; to ~ **a whistle** pfeifen, auf der Pfeife blasen.
2 vi (in car, on bicycle) hupen; (train) pfeifen; (ship) tuten.
3 n (in car, on bicycle) Hupen nt; (of train) Pfiff m, Pfeifsignal nt. give a quick ~ (on car horn) drück mal kurz auf die Hupe.
tooth [tuːθ] n, pl teeth (a) (of person, animal) Zahn m. to have a ~ out/filled sich (dat) einen Zahn ziehen/plombieren lassen; to get one's teeth into sth (lit) etw zwischen die Zähne bekommen; (fig) sich in etw (dat) festbeißen; to be armed to the teeth bis an die Zähne bewaffnet sein; to show one's teeth die Zähne zeigen (also fig) or fletschen; to fight ~ and nail bis aufs Blut kämpfen; in the teeth of the wind/all opposition gegen den Wind/ungeachtet allen Widerstands; to lie in one's teeth das Blaue vom Himmel herunterlügen; I'm fed up to the (back) teeth with that (inf) or sick to the (back) teeth of that (inf) ich habe die Nase gestrichen voll davon (inf), es hängt mir zum Hals heraus (inf); to give a law/an organization some teeth (fig) einem Gesetz/einer Organisation Wirksamkeit verleihen; I'd give my back or eye teeth for that ich würde viel darum geben; to kick sb or give sb a kick in the teeth (fig) jdn vor den Kopf stoßen.
  (b) (of zip, wheel etc) Zahn m; (small also) Zähnchen nt; (of comb, rake also) Zinke f.
tooth in cpds Zahn-. ~**ache** n Zahnweh nt, Zahnschmerzen pl; ~**brush** n Zahnbürste f; ~**brush moustache** (Zahn)bürste f.
toothed [tuːθt] adj gezahnt, mit Zähnen.
tooth: ~**less** adj zahnlos; ~**paste** n Zahnpasta or -creme f; ~**pick** n Zahnstocher m; ~ **powder** n Zahnpulver nt; ~**some** adj schmackhaft, wohlschmeckend.
toothy ['tuːθɪ] adj (+er) she's a bit ~ sie hat ein ziemliches Pferdegebiß (pej inf); he gave me a ~ **smile** er lächelte mich an und zeigte dabei seine Zähne/Zahnlücken.
toothypeg ['tuːθɪpeg] n (baby-talk) Beißerchen nt (baby-talk).
tootle ['tuːtl] 1 vi (a) (on whistle etc also: ~ away) vor sich hin dudeln (inf).
  (b) (drive) juckeln (inf); (go) trotten, zotteln. I'll just ~ (down) to the shops ich geh' bloß mal eben (runter) einkaufen; it's time I was tootling off es wird Zeit, daß ich abzottele (inf).
2 vt whistle etc (he)rumdudeln auf (+dat) (inf). he ~d the car horn er hupte mehrmals.
3 n to give a ~ on the car horn/a whistle hupen/auf einer Flöte herumdudeln (inf).
♦**tootle along** vi (dated inf) dahinzuckeln (inf). I'd better ~ ~ now ich zottele jetzt mal lieber ab (inf); I thought I'd ~ ~ to the garden party (inf) ich dachte, ich zottel' mal mit zu der Gartenparty (inf).
too-too ['tuː'tuː] 1 adj pred (dated inf: marvellous) pfundig (inf); (iro: affected) affig (inf). 2 adv (excessively) zu.
toots [tuːts] n (inf) Schätzchen nt.
tootsy ['tʊtsɪ] n (baby-talk) Füßchen nt.
top[1] [tɒp] 1 n (a) (highest part) oberer Teil; (of spire, pyramid, cone etc, fig: of league, company etc) Spitze f; (of mountain) Gipfel m; (of tree) Krone, Spitze f; (of pine tree) Wipfel m, Spitze f; (of branch) oberes Ende; (of wave) Kamm m; (of carrots, radishes) Ende nt; (leafy part) Kraut nt; (detachable part of cupboard etc) Aufsatz m; (head end) (of table, bed, sheet) Kopfende nt, oberes Ende; (of road, beach) oberes Ende. which

is the ~? wo ist oben?; **the ~ of the tree/page/list/wall** etc is ... der Baum/die Seite/Liste/Wand etc ist oben ...; **the ~ of the milk** die Rahmschicht (auf der Milch); **at the ~** oben; **at the ~ of the page/list/league/pile/stairs/wall/hill/tree** etc oben auf der Seite/Liste/in der Tabelle/im Stapel/an der Treppe/Wand/am Berg/Baum etc; **at the ~ of the table/road** am oberen Ende des Tisches/der Straße; **to be (at the) ~ of the class** Klassenbeste(r) or -erste(r) sein, der/die Beste in der Klasse sein; **to come out at the ~ of the list** Erste(r) sein; **near the ~** (ziemlich) weit oben; **he's near the ~ in English** in Englisch gehört er zu den Besten; **the liquid was cloudy near the ~** die Flüssigkeit war oben wolkig; **she bashed the ~ of her head on the luggage rack** sie schlug sich (dat) den Kopf an der Gepäckablage an; **he looked over the ~ of his spectacles** er sah über den Brillenrand (hinweg); **he curled his fingers over the ~ of the window** er klammerte sich mit den Fingern an den oberen Fensterrand; **she fell from the ~ of the stairs to the bottom** sie fiel die ganze Treppe von oben bis unten hinunter; **five lines from the ~** in der fünften Zeile von oben; **from ~ to toe** von Kopf bis Fuß; **from ~ to bottom** von oben bis unten; **the system is rotten from ~ to bottom** das System ist von vorn bis hinten schlecht (inf); **to scream at the ~ of one's voice** aus vollem Hals or aus Leibeskräften brüllen; **they were talking at the ~(s) of their voices** sie haben sich in voller Lautstärke unterhalten; **to be at the ~ of the ladder** or **the tree** (fig) auf dem Gipfel (des Erfolgs) sein; **go to the ~ of the class** (inf) du bist gar nicht so dumm!; **to go over the ~** (in trenches) aus dem Schützengraben klettern; (exaggerate) zu viel des Guten tun; **he's over the ~** er ist auf dem absteigenden Ast; **he's over the ~ with happiness** er ist ganz außer sich (dat) vor Glück; **~ of the pops** (record) Spitzenreiter m (in der Hitparade); **the ~ of the morning to you!** (Ir) grüß Gott! (S Ger, Aus), (schönen) guten Morgen! see bill[3].

(b) (upper surface) Oberfläche f. **to be on** ~ oben sein or liegen; (fig) obenauf sein; **it was on** ~ **of/on the** ~ **of the cupboard/pile** etc es war auf/oben auf dem Schrank/Stapel etc; **put it on** ~ **of/the** ~ **of the cupboard** etc leg es oben auf den Schrank etc; **to go up on** ~ (on boat) an Deck gehen; **seats on** ~! (in bus) oben sind noch Sitzplätze!; **to see London from the** ~ **of a bus** London vom Oberdeck eines Busses aus sehen; **on** ~ **of** (in addition to) zusätzlich zu; **things are getting on** ~ **of me** die Dinge wachsen mir über den Kopf; **then, on** ~ **of all that ...** und dann, um das Maß vollzumachen ...; **and, on** ~ **of that ...** und zusätzlich, und außerdem; **it's just one thing on** ~ **of another** es kommt eines zum anderen; **he didn't see it until he was right on** ~ **of it** er sah es erst, als er ganz nah dran war; **he felt he was on** ~ **of the situation** er hatte das Gefühl, die Situation im Griff or unter Kontrolle zu haben; **to come out on** ~ sich durchsetzen; (over rival) die Oberhand gewinnen; **to be on the** ~ **of one's form** in Höchstform sein; **to talk off the** ~ **of one's head** (inf) nur so daherreden.

(c) (inf: of body) Oberkörper m. **to blow one's** ~ in die Luft or an die Decke gehen (inf), aus der Haut fahren (inf); **she's rather big round the** ~ sie ist oben herum ganz schön füllig (inf).

(d) (working surface) Arbeitsfläche f.

(e) (bikini ~) Oberteil nt; (blouse also) Top nt.

(f) (lid) (of jar, suitcase) Deckel m; (of beer bottle also) Kronkorken m; (of pen) Hülle f; (of car) Dach nt. **hard/soft** ~ Hardtop nt/Weichverdeck nt.

(g) (Aut: ~ gear) höchster Gang. **in** ~ im vierten/fünften, im höchsten Gang.

(h) (inf: big ~) Großzelt, Zirkuszelt nt.

(i) (inf) **to be (the)** ~**s** Klasse or Spitze sein (inf).

(j) (Naut) Mars m.

2 adj (upper) obere(r, s); (highest) oberste(r, s); branches, note, honours, price höchste(r, s); (best) driver, athlete, competitor, job Spitzen-; pupil, school, marks beste(r, s); entertainer, management Top-. ~ **prices** Höchstpreise pl; **on the** ~ **floor** im obersten Stockwerk; **a** ~-**floor corner** eine Wohnung im obersten Stockwerk; **the** ~ **right-hand corner** die obere rechte Ecke; **he's out of the** ~ **drawer** (fig) er gehört zu den oberen Zehntausend; **the car has a** ~ **speed of 120** das Auto hat eine Höchstgeschwindigkeit von 120; **at** ~ **speed** mit Höchstgeschwindigkeit; **~ in form** in Höchstform; **to be** ~ (Sch) Beste(r) or Erste(r) sein; **the** ~ **men in the party/government/firm** die Parteispitze/Führungsspitze in der Regierung/des Unternehmens; **the newspaper for** ~ **people** die Zeitung für Führungskräfte; **the** ~ **people** (in a company) die Leute an der Spitze; (in society) die oberen Zehntausend.

3 adv **to come** ~ (Sch) Beste(r) sein.

4 vt **(a)** (cover, cap) bedecken. **~ped by a dome** gekrönt von einer Kuppel; **fruit ~ped with cream** Obst mit Sahne darauf.

(b) (reach ~ of) just as the car/he **~ped the hill** gerade, als das Auto/er oben auf dem Berg angekommen war or den Gipfel des Berges erreicht hatte.

(c) (be at ~ of) his name **~ped the list** sein Name stand ganz oben auf der Liste or an der Spitze der Liste; see bill[3].

(d) (be higher than, fig: surpass) übersteigen. **that ~s the lot** (inf) das übertrifft alles; **and to ~ it all ...** (inf) und um das Maß vollzumachen ...

(e) **to ~ a tree/radish/carrot** die Spitze eines Baumes/das Ende eines Rettichs/einer Mohrrübe abschneiden; **to ~ and tail gooseberries** Stachelbeeren putzen.

(f) **to ~ oneself** (inf) sich umbringen.

♦ **top off** vt sep abrunden.

♦ **top out** vt sep **to ~ a building** den letzten Stein legen; **~ping ~ ceremony** = Richtfest nt.

♦ **top up** vt sep glass, battery, tank auffüllen. **to ~ ~ the oil** Öl nachfüllen; **can I ~ you ~ ?** (inf) darf ich dir nachschenken?

top[2] n Kreisel m. **to sleep like a** ~ wie ein Murmeltier schlafen.

topaz ['təʊpæz] n Topas m.

top-: **~coat** n **(a)** (overcoat) Mantel m; (for men also) Überzieher

m; **(b)** (coat of paint) Deckanstrich m, letzter Anstrich; ~ **copy** n Original nt; ~ **dog** n (fig) he always has to be ~ dog er muß immer das Sagen haben; ~-**dress** vt (Agr) mit Kopfdünger düngen; ~ **dressing** n (Agr) Kopfdünger m.

topee, topi ['təʊpiː] n Tropenhelm m.

top-: ~-**fermented** adj obergärig; ~-**flight** adj Spitzen-, erstklassig; ~ **gear** n höchster Gang; **to be in** ~ gear (lit) im höchsten Gang or im vierten/fünften (Gang) sein; (fig) auf Hochtouren sein; ~ **hat** n Zylinder m; ~-**hatted** ['tɒp'hætɪd] adj mit Zylinder; ~-**heavy** adj (lit, fig) kopflastig; **she's a bit** ~-**heavy** (hum inf) sie hat einen ziemlichen Vorbau (inf); ~-**hole** adj, interj (dated inf) (dated), erstklassig (dated).

topiary ['təʊpɪərɪ] n (Hort) Formschnitt m.

topic ['tɒpɪk] n Thema nt. ~ **of conversation** Gesprächsthema nt.

topical ['tɒpɪkəl] adj **(a)** problem, speech, event aktuell. he **made a few** ~ **remarks/allusions** er ging kurz auf aktuelle Geschehnisse ein/spielte kurz auf aktuelle Geschehnisse an. **(b)** (according to subject) index Sach-.

topicality [,tɒpɪ'kælɪtɪ] n (of problem, event) Aktualität f.

topically ['tɒpɪkəlɪ] adv **(a)** aktuell. **(b)** (according to subject) nach Sachgebieten.

top-: ~**knot** n Dutt m; ~**less** adj (mit) oben ohne, Oben-ohne-; waitress also topless pred; ~**less waitress** Oben-ohne-Bedienung f; ~-**level** adj Spitzen-; ~**mast** n (Naut) Toppmast m, Marsstenge f; ~**most** adj oberste(r, s); **the** ~**most room in the house** das Zimmer unter dem Dach; ~-**notch** adj (inf) eins a (oben) (dated inf), prächtig.

topographer [tə'pɒgrəfə'] n Topograph(in f), Vermessungsingenieur(in f) m.

topographic(al) [,tɒpə'græfɪk(əl)] adj topographisch.

topography [tə'pɒgrəfɪ] n Topographie f.

toponym ['tɒpənɪm] n Ortsname m.

topper ['tɒpə'] n (inf) Angströhre f (inf).

topping ['tɒpɪŋ] **1** adj (dated Brit inf) famos (dated).

2 n (Cook) with a ~ of cream/nuts etc mit Sahne/Nüssen etc (oben) darauf; recipes for various different ~s for ice cream verschiedene Rezepte, wie man Eis überziehen kann; artificial cream ~ Schlagschaum m.

topple ['tɒpl] **1** vi wackeln; (fall) fallen; (fig: from power) gestürzt werden. **2** vt umwerfen; (from a height) hinunterkippen or -werfen; (fig) government etc stürzen. **to ~ sb from power** jdn stürzen or entmachten.

♦ **topple down** vi umfallen; (thing also) umkippen; (group of objects) runterpurzeln; (from chair, top of stairs etc) herunterfallen; (+prep obj) hinunterfallen. **they all came toppling** ~ sie kamen alle runtergepurzelt.

♦ **topple over** vi schwanken und fallen (prep obj über +acc).

top-: ~-**ranking** adj von hohem Rang; civil servant, officer also hohe(r); personality hochgestellt; author, singer Spitzen-; ~**sail** n (Naut) Marssegel nt; ~-**secret** adj streng geheim; ~**side** n (of beef) Oberschale f; ~**soil** n (Agr) Ackerkrume f; ~**spin** n Topspin m.

topsy-turvy ['tɒpsɪ'tɜːvɪ] (inf) **1** adj (lit) (upside down) umgedreht; (in disorder) kunterbunt durcheinander pred; (fig) auf den Kopf gestellt. **it's a** ~ **world** es ist eine verkehrte Welt.

2 adv **to turn sth** ~ (lit, fig) etw auf den Kopf stellen; room, house also etw völlig durcheinanderbringen; plans etw über den Haufen werfen.

top-up ['tɒpʌp] n (inf) **the battery/oil needs a** ~ die Batterie muß aufgefüllt/es muß Öl nachgefüllt werden; **would you like a** ~? darf man dir noch nachschenken?

toque [təʊk] n Toque f.

tor [tɔː'] n (esp in names) Berg m.

torch [tɔːtʃ] n (lit, fig) Fackel f; (Brit: flashlamp) Taschenlampe f; (blowlamp) Schweißbrenner m. **the** ~ **of learning** die Fackel der Wissenschaft; **to carry a** ~ **for sb** nach jdm schmachten.

torch-: ~ **battery** n (Brit) Taschenlampenbatterie f; ~**bearer** n (lit) Fackelträger m; (fig also) Herold m; ~**light** n Licht nt der Fackel/Taschenlampe; ~**light procession** n Fackelzug m.

tore [tɔː'] pret of tear[1].

toreador ['tɒrɪədɔː'] n Torero m.

torment ['tɔːment] **1** n Qual f; (inf: person) Qualgeist m. **to be in** ~, **to suffer** ~(**s**) Qualen leiden. **2** [tɔː'ment] vt quälen; (annoy, tease) plagen. ~**ed by remorse** von Reue gequält or geplagt.

tormentor [tɔː'mentə'] n Peiniger(in f) m.

torn [tɔːn] ptp of tear[1].

tornado [tɔː'neɪdəʊ] n, pl **-es** Tornado m.

torpedo [tɔː'piːdəʊ] **1** n, pl **-es** Torpedo m. ~ **boat** Torpedoboot nt; ~ **tube** Torpedoausstoßrohr nt. **2** vt torpedieren.

torpid ['tɔːpɪd] adj (lethargic) träge; (apathetic) abgestumpft; (Zool) torpid.

torpidity [tɔː'pɪdɪtɪ], **torpor** ['tɔːpə'] n see adj Trägheit f; Abgestumpftheit f; Torpidität f.

torque [tɔːk] n (Mech) Drehmoment nt.

torrent ['tɒrənt] n (river) reißender Strom; (fig) (of lava) Strom m; (of words, insults) Sturzbach, Schwall m, Flut f. **the rain came down in ~s** der Regen kam in wahren Sturzbächen herunter; **a** ~ **of abuse** ein Schwall m von Beschimpfungen.

torrential [tɒ'renʃəl] adj rain sintflutartig.

torrid ['tɒrɪd] adj (lit, fig) heiß; heat, air, sun sengend.

torsion ['tɔːʃən] n Drehung, Torsion (spec) f. **degree of** ~ Drehbeanspruchung, Torsionsschwingung (spec) f.

torso ['tɔːsəʊ] n Körper m; (Art) Torso m.

tort [tɔːt] n (Jur) Delikt nt.

tortoise ['tɔːtəs] n Schildkröte f.

tortoiseshell ['tɔːtəsʃel] n (a) Schildpatt m; (esp for spectacle frames) Horn nt. (b) (~ cat) Schildpattkatze f.

tortuous ['tɔːtjʊəs] adj (lit) path gewunden; (fig) verwickelt; methods also, person umständlich. **he has a** ~ **mind** er hat komplizierte Gedankengänge.

torture ['tɔːtʃə'] **1** n Folter f; (fig) Qual f. ~ **chamber** Folter-

kammer *f*; **instrument of ~** Folterwerkzeug *nt*; **it was sheer ~!** (*inf*) es war eine wahre Qual *or* Folter.
2 *vt* (a) (*lit*) foltern.
(b) (*fig: torment*) quälen, peinigen (*geh*).
(c) (*fig: distort*) verzerren; *language* vergewaltigen. **~d language/sentences** verkrampfte Sprache/Sätze *pl*; **~d steel** grotesk verbogener Stahl; **her hair had been ~d into elaborate curls** ihr Haar war mühsam in kunstvolle Locken gedreht.
torturer ['tɔːtʃərəʳ] *n* (*lit*) Folterknecht *m*; (*fig: tormentor*) Peiniger(in *f*) *m*.
Tory ['tɔːrɪ] (*Brit Pol*) **1** *n* Tory *m*. **2** *adj* konservativ, Tory-.
Toryism ['tɔːrɪɪzəm] *n* (*Brit Pol*) Konservativismus *m*.
tosh [tɒʃ] *n* (*dated Brit inf*) dummes Zeug.
toss [tɒs] **1** *n* (a) (*throw*) Wurf *m*. **to take a ~** (*from horse*) abgeworfen werden; **with a proud ~ of her head** mit einer stolzen Kopfbewegung.
(b) (*of coin*) Münzwurf *m*. **to win/lose the ~** (*esp Sport*) die Seitenwahl gewinnen/verlieren; **there is no point in arguing the ~ (with me)** es hat keinen Sinn, (mit mir) darüber zu streiten *or* mit mir herumzustreiten; **there'll always be somebody who'll want to argue the ~** es gibt immer einen, der Einwände hat.
2 *vt* (a) (*throw*) *ball* werfen; *salad* anmachen; *pancake* wenden (*durch Hochwerfen*); *rider* abwerfen. **to ~ sth to sb** jdm etw zuwerfen; **~ it over!** wirf es herüber, schmeiß mal her (*inf*); **to ~ sth aside/(up)** into the air etw zur Seite werfen/hochwerfen *or* in die Luft werfen; **to ~ sb aside** jdn fallenlassen; **~ing the caber** Baumstammwerfen *nt*; **to be ~ed by a bull/horse** auf die Hörner genommen werden/vom Pferd (ab)geworfen werden.
(b) (*move: wind*) schütteln, zerren an (+*dat*). **the boat, ~ed (about) by the waves ...** das Boot, von den Wellen hin und her geworfen, ...; **to ~ (back) one's head** den Kopf zurückwerfen *or* hochwerfen.
(c) **to ~ a coin** eine Münze (zum Losen) hochwerfen; **we settled it by ~ing a coin** wir haben eine Münze hochgeworfen und es ausgeknobelt; **to ~ sb for sth** mit jdm (durch Münzenwerfen) um etw knobeln; **I'll ~ you for it** laß uns darum knobeln.
3 *vi* (a) (*ship*) rollen; (*corn also*) wogen; (*plumes*) flattern. **to ~ in one's sleep** sich im Schlaf wälzen *or* herumwerfen; **to ~ and turn (in bed)** sich (im Bett) hin und her wälzen *or* hin und her werfen; *see* **pitch²**.
(b) (*with coin*) (durch Münzenwerfen) knobeln. **to ~ for sth** um etw knobeln.
♦ **toss about 1** *vi* sich heftig hin und her bewegen; (*person*) sich hin und her werfen. **2** *vt sep* (*move*) hin und her schütteln, durchschütteln; *boat* schaukeln; (*throw*) *ball* herumwerfen; (*fig*) *ideas* zur Debatte stellen.
♦ **toss away** *vt sep* wegwerfen.
♦ **toss back** *vt sep head* zurückwerfen, hochwerfen; *drink* hinunterstürzen, (runter)kippen (*inf*).
♦ **toss off 1** *vt sep* (a) *drink* hinunterstürzen, (runter)kippen (*inf*). (b) (*inf: produce quickly*) *essay* hinhauen (*inf*); *remark* hinwerfen. (c) (*sl: masturbate*) einen runterholen (+*dat*) (*sl*). **2** *vi* (*sl*) sich (*dat*) einen runterholen (*sl*).
♦ **toss out** *vt sep rubbish* wegschmeißen (*inf*) *or* -werfen; *person* hinauswerfen, rausschmeißen (*inf*).
♦ **toss up 1** *vi* knobeln (*for* um). **2** *vt sep* werfen. **to ~ sth ~ (into the air)** etw hochwerfen, etw in die Luft werfen.
toss-up ['tɒsʌp] *n* (*lit*) Knobeln *nt durch Münzenwerfen*. **it was a ~ whether ...** (*inf*) es war völlig offen, ob ...
tot [tɒt] *n* (a) (*child: also tiny ~*) Steppke (*inf*), Knirps (*inf*) *m*.
(b) (*esp Brit: of alcohol*) Schlückchen *nt*.
♦ **tot up** *vt sep* (*esp Brit inf*) zusammenzählen *or* -rechnen.
total ['təʊtl] **1** *adj* (*complete*) völlig, absolut; (*comprising the whole*) *sum, loss, number* Gesamt-; *war, eclipse* total; *disaster* absolut, total. **what is the ~ number of rooms you have?** wie viele Zimmer haben Sie (insgesamt)?; **the ~ effect of all this worry was ...** im Endeffekt haben seine Sorgen bewirkt, daß ...; **to be in ~ ignorance (of sth)** (von etw) überhaupt nichts wissen; **it's a ~ waste of time** das ist absolute *or* totale Zeitverschwendung; **the silence was ~** es herrschte völlige *or* vollkommene *or* totale Stille; **my bewilderment was ~** meine Verwirrung war vollkommen *or* komplett.
2 *n* Gesamtmenge *f*; (*money, figures*) Endsumme *f*. **a ~ of 50 people** insgesamt 50 Leute; *see* **grand, sum**.
3 *vt* (a) (*amount to*) sich belaufen auf (+*acc*). **the visitors ~ed 5,000** insgesamt kamen 5 000 Besucher.
(b) (*add: also ~ up*) zusammenzählen *or* -rechnen.
totalitarian [,təʊtælɪˈtɛərɪən] *adj* totalitär.
totalitarianism [,təʊtælɪˈtɛərɪənɪzəm] *n* Totalitarismus *m*.
totality [təʊˈtælɪtɪ] *n* Gesamtheit, Totalität (*esp Philos*) *f*; (*Astron*) totale Finsternis.
totalizator ['təʊtəlaɪˌzeɪtəʳ], **totalizer** ['təʊtəlaɪzəʳ] *n* (*Horseracing*) Totalisator *m*.
totally ['təʊtəlɪ] *adv* völlig, total.
tote¹ [təʊt] *n* (*inf*) **the ~** der Totalisator.
tote² *vt* (*inf: carry*) *sth heavy* schleppen; *gun* bei sich haben. **to ~ sth around** etw herumschleppen.
tote bag *n* (*US*) (Einkaufs)tasche *f*.
tote board *n* Totalisator *m*.
totem ['təʊtəm] *n* Totem *nt*.
totemism ['təʊtəmɪzəm] *n* Totemismus *m*.
totem pole *n* Totempfahl *m*.
totter ['tɒtəʳ] *vi* (a) (*wobble before falling*) wanken, schwanken; (*stagger*) taumeln; (*unsicher gehen*); (*old man, baby*) tapsen; (*invalid*) schwanken, taumeln. **to ~ about** *or* **around** herumwanken-/taumeln/-tapsen.
(b) (*fig*) schwanken; (*economy*) kränkeln. **the country was ~ing on the brink of war** das Land befand sich am Rande eines Krieges.

tottering ['tɒtərɪŋ] *adj* schwankend, wankend; *person also* taumelnd; *regime* bröckelig; *economy* wack(e)lig, kränklich. **a ~ monarch** ein Monarch auf einem wackeligen Thron.
tottery ['tɒtərɪ] *adj* wack(e)lig; *person* tatterig. **a ~ old man** ein Tattergreis *m* (*inf*).
toucan ['tuːkən] *n* Tukan, Pfefferfresser *m*.
touch [tʌtʃ] **1** *n* (a) (*sense of ~*) (Tast)gefühl *nt*. **to be cold/soft to the ~,** to have a cold/soft ~ sich kalt/weich anfühlen.
(b) (*act of ~ing*) Berühren *nt*, Berührung *f*; (*of pianist, typist, typewriter*) Anschlag *m*. **I felt a ~ on my arm** ich spürte, daß jd/etw meinen Arm berührte; **she thrilled to his ~** es durchzuckte sie, als er sie berührte; **it opens at a ~** es öffnet sich auf Fingerdruck *or* auf leichten Druck; **the wheel responds to the slightest ~** das Lenkrad reagiert sofort *or* auf jede Bewegung; **braille is read by ~** Blindenschrift wird durch Abtasten gelesen.
(c) (*skill*) Hand *f*; (*style also*) Stil *m*. **the ~ of a master** die Hand eines Meisters; **it has the ~ of genius/the professional ~** es hat etwas Geniales/Professionelles *or* einen genialen/professionellen Anstrich; **he's losing his ~** er wird langsam alt; **to have the right ~ with sb/sth** mit jdm/etw umgehen können; **a personal ~** eine persönliche Note.
(d) (*stroke*) (*Art*) Strich *m*; (*fig*) Einfall *m*. **a book with humorous ~es** ein stellenweise humorvolles Buch; **a nice ~** eine hübsche Note; (*gesture*) eine nette Geste; **it was a nice ~ inviting them** es war nett, sie einzuladen; **to put the final *or* finishing ~es to sth** letzte Hand an etw (*acc*) legen, einer Sache (*dat*) den letzten Schliff geben; **the house lacks a woman's ~** es fehlt eine Frau im Haus.
(e) (*small quantity*) Spur *f*; (*of irony, sadness etc also*) Anflug *m*. **a ~ of flu/fever** eine leichte Grippe/leichtes Fieber; **a ~ of spring** ein Hauch *m* (von) Frühling; **he gave the horse a ~ of the whip** er ließ das Pferd die Peitsche fühlen *or* spüren; *see* **sun**.
(f) (*communication*) **to be in (constant) ~ with sb** mit jdm in (ständiger) Verbindung stehen; **they were in ~ with us** yesterday sie haben sich gestern mit uns in Verbindung gesetzt; **to be/keep in ~ with (political) developments** (politisch) auf dem laufenden sein/bleiben; **I'll be in ~!** ich lasse von mir hören!, ich melde mich!; **keep in ~!** laß/laßt wieder einmal von dir/euch hören!; **to be out of ~ with sb** keine Verbindung mehr zu jdm haben; **to be completely out of ~ (with sth)** (in bezug auf etw *acc*) überhaupt nicht auf dem laufenden sein; **you can get in ~ with me at this number** Sie können mich unter dieser Nummer erreichen; **you ought to get in ~ with the police** Sie sollten sich mit der Polizei in Verbindung setzen; **to lose ~ (with sb/sth)** den Kontakt (zu jdm) verlieren (in bezug auf etw *acc*) nicht mehr auf dem laufenden sein; **a husband and wife who have lost ~ with each other** ein Ehepaar, das sich fremd geworden ist *or* sich entfremdet hat; **I'll put you in ~ with Mr Brown** ich werde Sie mit Herrn Brown in Verbindung bringen.
(g) (*Ftbl*) Aus *nt*; (*Rugby also*) Mark *f*. **in ~** im Aus; **in der** Mark; **to kick for ~** (*Rugby*) in die Mark schlagen.
(h) (*sl*) **to make a ~** Geld schnorren (*inf*); **he's usually good for a ~** ihn kann man normalerweise gut anpumpen (*inf*) *or* anzapfen (*inf*); **to be an easy *or* soft ~** leicht anzupumpen (*inf*) *or* anzuzapfen (*inf*) sein.
2 *vt* (a) (*be in *or* make contact with*) berühren; (*get hold of also*) anfassen; (*press lightly also*) *piano keys* anschlagen, leicht drücken; (*strike lightly*) *harp strings* streichen über (+*acc*); (*brush against*) streifen. **to ~ glasses** anstoßen; **don't ~ that!** faß das nicht an!; **he ~ed his hat to me** er tippte (zum Gruß) an den Hut; **the speedometer needle ~ed 100** die Tachonadel ging auf 100; **I was ~ing 100 most of the way** ich fuhr fast immer 100; **once I ~ed 100** einmal habe ich 100 geschafft.
(b) (*lay hands on*) anrühren, anfassen. **the police/tax authorities can't ~ me** die Polizei/das Finanzamt kann mir nichts anhaben; **the paintings weren't ~ed by the fire** die Gemälde blieben vom Feuer verschont.
(c) *food, drink* anrühren; *capital also* herankommen an (*+acc*) (*inf*); (*use*) antasten. **I haven't ~ed the piano/accordion for months** ich habe seit Monaten nicht mehr Klavier gespielt/das Akkordeon nicht mehr in der Hand gehabt.
(d) (*equal*) herankommen an (+*acc*), erreichen. **there's nothing to ~ hot lemon for a cold** bei einer Erkältung geht nichts über heiße Zitrone.
(e) (*deal with*) *problem etc* anrühren. **everything he ~es turns to gold** ihm gelingt einfach alles; **I wouldn't ~ those shares** ich würde meine Finger von den Aktien lassen; **an ordinary detergent won't ~ dirt like that** mit normales Reinigungsmittel wird mit diesem Schmutz nicht fertig; **I couldn't ~ the third question** mit der dritten Frage konnte ich nichts anfangen; **I asked them not to ~ my desk** ich bat sie, nicht an meinen Schreibtisch zu gehen; **they hadn't even ~ed my desk** sie hatten überhaupt nichts an meinem Schreibtisch gemacht.
(f) (*concern*) berühren, betreffen.
(g) (*move emotionally*) rühren, bewegen; (*affect*) berühren; (*wound*) *pride* treffen. **deeply ~ed** tief gerührt *or* bewegt.
(h) **to ~ sb for a loan/£10** (*sl*) jdn um einen Kredit angehen/jdn um £ 10 anpumpen (*inf*).
3 *vi* (*come into contact*) sich berühren; (*estates etc: be adjacent also*) aneinanderstoßen, aneinandergrenzen. **don't ~!** Finger weg!; **"please do not ~"** „bitte nicht berühren".
♦ **touch at** *vi +prep obj* (*Naut*) anlaufen.
♦ **touch down 1** *vi* (a) (*Aviat, Space*) aufsetzen. (b) (*Rugby, US Ftbl*) einen Versuch erzielen. **2** *vt sep ball* niederlegen.
♦ **touch in** *vt sep details, shading etc* einfügen.
♦ **touch off** *vt sep explosion, argument etc* auslösen.
♦ **touch up** *vt sep* (a) *colour* auffrischen; *make-up also* frisch machen; *picture, paintwork also* ausbessern; *photo* retuschieren; *essay, article* ausbessern. (b) (*inf*) *woman, man*

betatschen (*inf*), befummeln (*sl*).

♦ **touch (up)on** *vi* + *prep obj* *subject* kurz berühren, antippen. **but he barely ~ed ~ the question** aber er hat die Frage kaum berührt.

touch-and-go ['tʌtʃən'gəʊ] *adj* **to be ~** riskant *or* prekär sein; **it's ~ whether ...** es steht auf des Messers Schneide, ob ...; **he won eventually but it was ~ for a while** er gewann schließlich, aber es stand eine Zeitlang auf des Messers Schneide; **it's ~ if we'll make it** es ist noch vollkommen offen, ob wir es schaffen; **it was ~ with the project** das Projekt stand auf des Messers Schneide; **after his operation it was ~** nach der Operation hing sein Leben an einem Faden.

touchdown ['tʌtʃdaʊn] *n* **(a)** (*Aviat, Space*) Aufsetzen *nt*. **(b)** (*Rugby, US Ftbl*) Versuch *m* (*Niederlegen des Balles im Malfeld des Gegners*).

touché [tu:'ʃeɪ] *interj* (*Fencing*) Treffer; (*fig inf*) eins zu null für dich (*inf*).

touched [tʌtʃt] *adj pred* **(a)** (*moved*) gerührt, bewegt. **(b) to be a bit ~** (*inf: mad*) einen leichten Stich haben (*inf*).

touch football *n* (*US*) sanftere Art des Football, bei der der Gegner berührt wird, anstatt zu Fall gebracht zu werden.

touchiness ['tʌtʃɪnɪs] *n* Empfindlichkeit *f* (*on* in bezug auf +*acc*); (*irritability also*) leichte Reizbarkeit. **because of the ~ of this subject** weil dieses Thema so heikel ist/war.

touching ['tʌtʃɪŋ] **1** *adj* rührend, bewegend. **2** *prep* (*form*) bezüglich (*form*).

touchingly ['tʌtʃɪŋlɪ] *adv* rührend, bewegend.

touch: **~ judge** *n* (*Rugby*) Seitenrichter *m*; **~line** *n* (*Sport*) Seitenlinie, Auslinie *f*; **~paper** *n* Zündpapier *nt*; **~stone** *n* (*fig*) Prüfstein *m*; **~-type** *vti* blindschreiben; **~-typing** *n* Blindschreiben *nt*; **~-up paint** *n* Tupflack *m*.

touchy ['tʌtʃɪ] *adj* empfindlich (*about* in bezug auf +*acc*); (*irritable also*) leicht reizbar; *subject* heikel, kitzlig (*inf*).

tough [tʌf] **1** *adj* (+*er*) **(a)** zäh; *resistant* widerstandsfähig; *cloth* strapazierfähig; (*towards others*) hart, knallhart (*inf*); *bargaining, negotiator, opponent, fight, struggle, lesson* hart; *district, city* hart, rauh. **as ~ as leather** zäh wie Leder (*inf*); **they want their son to be ~** sie wollen ihren Sohn abhärten *or* zur Härte erziehen; **he'll get over it, he's pretty ~** er wird schon dar-. über hinwegkommen, er ist hart im Nehmen (*inf*); **you need to be ~ to work here** man muß schon etwas aushalten können *or* hart im Nehmen sein (*inf*), wenn man hier arbeitet; **to get ~ (with sb)** (*physically*) grob werden (mit jdm *or* gegen jdn), handgreiflich werden (gegen jdn); (*fig*) hart durchgreifen (gegen jdn); **~ guy** (*inf*) (knall)harter Kerl *or* Bursche (*inf*). **(b)** (*difficult*) *task, problem* hart; *journey* strapaziös, anstrengend. **it was ~ going** (*lit, fig*) es war eine Strapaze *or* ein Schlauch *m* (*inf*); **to have a ~ time of it** nichts zu lachen haben. **(c)** (*strict*) *policy, controls* hart. **(d)** (*inf*) **that's pretty ~!** das ist ganz schön hart!; **it was ~ on the others** das war hart für die andern; **~ (luck)!** Pech! **2** *n* (*inf*) Schlägertyp *m* (*pej inf*), (knall)harter Bursche (*inf*). **3** *adv* (+*er*) (*inf*) **to treat sb ~** jdn hart rannehmen.

toughen ['tʌfn] **1** *vt* **(a)** *glass, metal* härten. **(b)** (*fig*) *person* zäh *or* hart machen; (*physically also*) abhärten; *laws* verschärfen. **2** *vi* (*glass, metal*) aushärten, hart werden; (*meat*) zäh werden; (*attitude*) sich verhärten.

♦ **toughen up 1** *vt sep* *person* hart *or* zäh machen, stählen (*geh*); *muscles* trainieren; *sportsman* also fit machen; *regulations* verschärfen. **2** *vi* hart *or* zäh werden; (*attitude*) sich verhärten. **to ~ ~ on sb/sth** härter gegen jdn/etw vorgehen.

toughie ['tʌfɪ] *n* (*inf*) (*person*) (*ruffian*) Rauhbein *nt*; (*child*) Rabauke *m*; (*problem, question*) harte Nuß. **she thinks she's a ~ and can take it** sie hält sich für hart genug, das auszuhalten.

toughly ['tʌflɪ] *adv* *made* robust; *built also* stabil; *say* fest. **~ worded** geharnischt; **to bring sb up ~** jdn zur Härte erziehen; **to behave ~** (*like a tough guy*) den harten Mann spielen *or* markieren (*inf*); (*decisively*) hart auftreten.

toughness ['tʌfnɪs] *n see adj* **(a)** (*of meat etc*) Zähheit *f*; (*of person*) Zähigkeit *f*; Widerstandsfähigkeit *f*; Strapazierfähigkeit *f*; Härte *f*; Rauheit *f*. **(b)** (*difficulty*) Schwierigkeit *f*; (*of journey*) Strapazen *pl*. **(c)** Härte *f*.

toupee ['tu:peɪ] *n* Toupet *nt*.

tour [tʊəʳ] **1** *n* **(a)** (*journey, walking ~ etc*) Tour *f*; (*by bus, car etc also*) Fahrt, Reise *f*; (*of town, building, exhibition etc*) Rundgang *m* (*of* durch); (*also guided ~*) Führung *f* (*of* durch); (*by bus*) Rundfahrt *f* (*of* durch). **to go on/make a ~ of Scotland** eine Schottlandreise gehen/eine Schottlandreise machen/an einer Schloßführung teilnehmen/einen Rundgang durch das Schloß machen; **he took us on a ~ of the Highlands** er machte mit uns eine Reise durch die Highlands. **(b)** (*also ~ of inspection*) Runde *f* (*of* durch); (*on foot also*) Rundgang *m* (*of* durch). **he had a 3-year ~ (of duty) in East Africa** er wurde für drei Jahre nach Ostafrika versetzt; **two months leave between ~s (of duty)** zwei Monate Urlaub zwischen zwei Versetzungen; **to make a ~ of the site/border posts** einen Rundgang durch das Gelände/eine Runde bei den Grenzposten machen. **(c)** (*Theat*) Gastspielreise, Tournee *f* (*of* durch); (*Sport*) Tournee *f*. **to go/be on ~** auf Gastspielreise *or* Tournee gehen/sein; **to take a company/play on ~** mit einer Truppe/einem Stück auf Gastspielreise *or* Tournee gehen. **2** *vt* **(a)** *country, district etc* fahren durch; (*on foot*) ziehen durch (*inf*); (*travel around also*) bereisen, eine Reise *or* Tour machen durch. **(b)** (*visit*) *town, building, exhibition* einen Rundgang machen durch, besichtigen; (*by bus etc*) eine Rundfahrt machen durch. **(c)** (*Theat*) eine Gastspielreise *or* Tournee machen durch; (*Sport*) eine Tournee machen durch. **3** *vi* **(a)** (*on holiday*) eine Reise *or* Tour *or* Fahrt machen; (*on foot also*) ziehen. **we're ~ing (around)** wir reisen herum;

to go ~ing Touren/eine Tour machen. **(b)** (*Theat*) eine Gastspielreise *or* Tournee machen. **to go/be ~ing** (*Theat*) auf Gastspielreise *or* Tournee gehen/sein; (*Sport*) auf Tournee gehen/sein.

tour de force ['tʊədə'fɔːs] *n* Glanzleistung *f*.

touring ['tʊərɪŋ] *n* (Herum)reisen, (Herum)fahren *nt*.

touring: **~ club** *n* Touring-Club *m*; **~ company** *n* (*Theat*) Tourneetheater *nt*; **~ holiday** *n* Reiseurlaub *m*; **~ party** *n* Reisegruppe *f*; **~ team** *n* Gastmannschaft *f*.

tourism ['tʊərɪzəm] *n* Fremdenverkehr, Tourismus *m*.

tourist ['tʊərɪst] **1** *n* (*person*) Tourist(in *f*) *m*, Fremde(r) *mf*; (*Sport*) Gast *m*; (*~ class*) Touristenklasse *f*. **to travel ~** in der Touristenklasse reisen. **2** *attr* *class, hotel, shop* Touristen-; *guide* Fremden-; *bureau, office, industry* Fremdenverkehrs-. **~ season** Reisesaison *or* -zeit *f*; **~ trade** Fremdenverkehrsgewerbe *nt*; **~ traffic** Reiseverkehr *m*.

touristy ['tʊərɪstɪ] *adj* (*pej*) auf Tourismus getrimmt; *resorts, shops, souvenirs* für Touristen.

tournament ['tʊənəmənt] *n* (*Sport etc, also Hist*) Turnier *nt*.

tournedos [tʊə'neɪdəʊ] *n* (*Cook*) Tournedos *nt*.

tourney ['tʊənɪ] *n* (*Hist, US Sport*) Turnier *nt*.

tourniquet ['tʊənɪkeɪ] *n* Aderpresse *f*, Tourniquet *nt* (*spec*).

tour operator *n* Reiseveranstalter *m*.

tousle ['taʊzl] *vt* *hair* zerzausen; (*affectionately also*) zausen.

tousled ['taʊzld] *adj* *hair* zerzaust, wuschelig (*inf*). **~ head** Wuschelkopf *m* (*inf*).

tout [taʊt] (*inf*) **1** *n* (*tipster*) Wettberater *m*; (*esp Brit: spy*) Schnüffler (*inf*), Spion (*inf*) *m*; (*ticket ~*) (Karten)schwarzhändler *m*; (*for business*) Kundenfänger, Schlepper (*sl*) *m*. **2** *vt* (*Racing*) *horse* als Favorit angeben, als heißen Tip nennen; (*spy*) *stables* ausspionieren (*inf*); *horse* herumschnüffeln bei (*inf*); (*sell: also ~ around*) *information* anbieten; *tickets* anbieten, schwarz verkaufen (*inf*); *goods* (den Leuten) aufschwatzen (*inf*); *ideas* propagieren. **to ~ business for sb/sth** für etw (aufdringlich) Reklame machen. **3** *vi* (*Racing*) (*offer tips*) Wettips geben; (*spy*) herumspionieren, herumschnüffeln (*inf*). **to ~ for business/customers** (aufdringlich) Reklame machen/auf Kundenfang sein (*inf*), Kunden schleppen (*sl*).

tow¹ [taʊ] *n* Werg *nt*, Hede *f*.

tow² [taʊ] **1** *n* **to take a car/yacht in ~** ein Auto abschleppen/eine Jacht schleppen *or* ins Schlepptau nehmen; **to give sb/a car a ~** (*in car*) jdn/ein Auto abschleppen; (*to start*) jdn/ein Auto anschleppen; **to give sb/a yacht a ~** jdn/eine Jacht schleppen *or* ins Schlepptau nehmen; **do you want a ~?** soll ich Sie abschleppen/anschleppen?; **"on ~"** = „Fahrzeug wird abgeschleppt"; **in ~** (*fig*) im Schlepptau. **2** *vt* *boat, glider* schleppen; *car* also abschleppen; (*to start*) anschleppen; *trailer* ziehen. **he was ~ing a huge dog behind him** er zog *or* schleifte einen riesigen Hund hinter sich her.

♦ **tow away** *vt sep* *car* (*of meat etc*) (to start) abschleppen.

towage ['taʊdʒ] *n* **(a)** (*of ships*) Bugsieren, Schleppen *nt*; (*of cars*) Abschleppen *nt*. **(b)** (*fee*) (*for ships*) Schlepp- *or* Bugsiergebühr *f*; (*for cars*) Abschleppgebühr *f*. **~ charges** (*for ships*) Schlepp- *or* Bugsiergebühren *pl*; (*for cars*) Abschleppgebühren, Abschleppkosten *pl*.

toward [tə'wɔːd] *adj* (*form: favourable*) angemessen.

toward(s) [tə'wɔːd(z)] *prep* **(a)** (*in direction of*) (*with verbs of motion*) auf (+*acc*) ... zu. **they walked ~ the town** sie gingen auf die Stadt zu; **we sailed ~ China** wir segelten in Richtung China; **it's further north, ~ Dortmund** es liegt weiter im Norden, Richtung Dortmund; **~ the south** nach *or* gen (*liter*) Süden; **he turned ~ her** er wandte sich ihr zu; **with his back ~ the wall** mit dem Rücken zur Wand; **you should read with your back ~ the light** Sie sollten mit dem Rücken zum Licht lesen; **on the side (facing) ~ the sea** zum Meer hin; **a hotel facing ~ the sea** ein Hotel mit Blick aufs Meer; **they are working ~ a solution** sie arbeiten auf eine Lösung hin; **if it helps ~ a solution** wenn es zur Lösung beiträgt; **the latest move went a long way ~ solving the problem** die letzte Maßnahme trug beträchtlich zur Lösung des Problems bei; **~ a better understanding of ...** zum besseren Verständnis von ...; **~ a new theory of knowledge** (Ansätze *pl*) zu einer neuen Erkenntnistheorie. **(b)** (*in relation to*) ... (*dat*) gegenüber. **what are your feelings ~ him?** was empfinden Sie ihm gegenüber *or* für ihn? **(c)** **~ ten o'clock** gegen zehn Uhr; **~ the end of the 60's/the year** gegen Ende der sechziger Jahre/des Jahres.

tow: **~-bar** *n* Anhängerkupplung *f*; **~boat** *n* Schleppschiff *nt*, Schlepper *m*; **~-car** *n* (*US*) Abschleppwagen *m*.

towel ['taʊəl] **1** *n* Handtuch *nt*. **~ rail** Handtuchhalter *m*; *see* **throw in. 2** *vt* (mit einem Handtuch) (ab)trocknen.

♦ **towel down** *vt sep* (ab)trocknen, trockenreiben.

towelling ['taʊəlɪŋ] *n* Frottee(stoff) *m*.

tower ['taʊəʳ] **1** *n* **(a)** Turm *m*. **(b)** (*fig: person*) **a ~ of strength** eine Stütze, ein starker (Rück)halt. **2** *vi* ragen. **the buildings ~ into the sky** die Gebäude ragen in den Himmel.

♦ **tower above** *or* **over** *vi* + *prep obj* **(a)** (*buildings etc*) emporragen über (+*acc*). **(b)** (*lit, fig: people*) überragen.

♦ **tower up** *vi* hinaufragen, emporragen.

tower block *n* Hochhaus *nt*.

towering ['taʊərɪŋ] *adj* **(a)** *building* hochragend, alles überragend; *mountain* (steil) aufragend; *tree* hochgewachsen. **the boy stood before the ~ figure of the headmaster** der Schüler stand vor der hoch aufragenden Gestalt des Rektors. **(b)** (*fig*) **a ~ rage** eine rasende *or* unbändige Wut; **one of the ~ giants of literature** eine der einsamen Größen der Literatur, ein Titan der Literatur.

tow-headed ['taʊ'hedɪd] *adj* flachsblond.

towline ['taʊlaɪn] *n* (*Aut*) Abschleppseil *nt*; (*Naut, for glider*) Schleppseil *nt*.

town [taʊn] n **(a)** Stadt f. the ~ of Brighton (die Stadt) Brighton; to go into or down ~ in die Stadt gehen; to live in ~ in der Stadt wohnen; guess who's in ~? raten Sie mal, wer zur Zeit hier (in der Stadt) ist?; he's out of ~ er ist nicht in der Stadt, er ist außerhalb; ~ and gown (Univ) (die) Bevölkerung und (die) Studenten; to have a night on the ~ (inf) die Nacht durchmachen (inf), einen draufmachen (sl); you didn't know, but it's all over ~ du hattest keine Ahnung, das ist doch stadtbekannt; it's all over ~ now that he has ... es hat sich herumgesprochen, daß er ...; to go to ~ on sth (fig inf) (go to great trouble with) sich bei etw einen abbrechen (inf); (to please) sich bei etw ins Zeug legen; (exaggerate) etw übertreiben; you've really gone to ~ on this essay bei diesem Aufsatz sind Sie wirklich ins Detail gegangen; John's really gone to ~ on his new house John hat bei seinem neuen Haus wirklich keine Kosten gescheut.
(b) (Brit: London) London nt. to go up to ~ nach London gehen or fahren; he is out of ~ er ist nicht in London.

town: ~ centre n Stadtmitte f, (Stadt)zentrum, Stadtinnere(s) nt; ~ clerk n Stadtdirektor, Stadtschreiber (old, Sw) m; (of bigger town) Oberstadtdirektor m; ~ council n Stadtrat m; ~ councillor n Stadtrat m, Stadträtin f; ~ crier n Ausrufer m; ~ dweller n Städter, Stadtbewohner m.
townee, townie ['taʊni:] n Städter, Stadtmensch m; (Univ) Bewohner einer Universitätsstadt, der nicht der Universität angehört.
town: ~ gas n Stadtgas nt; ~ hall n Rathaus nt; ~ house n Stadthaus nt, Haus nt in der Stadt; (type of house) Wohnhaus nt; ~ life n Stadtleben nt, Leben nt in der Stadt; ~ planner n Stadt- or Städteplaner m; ~ planning n Stadtplanung, Städteplanung f; ~scape n Stadtbild nt or -landschaft f; (Art) Stadtansicht f.
townsfolk ['taʊnzfəʊk] npl Städter, Stadtmenschen pl, Stadtbevölkerung f; (citizens) Bürger pl.
township ['taʊnʃɪp] n (Stadt)gemeinde f; (US) Verwaltungsbezirk m; (US Surv) 6 Meilen großes Gebiet.
towns: ~man n Städter, Stadtmensch m; (citizen) Bürger m; my fellow ~men meine (lieben) Mitbürger; ~people npl Städter, Stadtmenschen pl; (citizens) Bürger pl; ~woman n Bürgerin f; the ~women of Paisley die Bewohnerinnen or Bürgerinnen pl von Paisley; ~women's guild (US) Frauenvereinigung f mit gesellschaftlichen Aufgaben.
tow: ~path n Treidelpfad m; ~plane n Schleppflugzeug nt; ~rope n see ~line; ~ start n (Aut) Anschleppen nt; to give sb a ~ start jdn anschleppen; ~truck n (US) Abschleppwagen m.
toxaemia, (US) **toxemia** [tɒk'si:mɪə] n Blutvergiftung, Sepsis (spec) f.
toxic ['tɒksɪk] adj giftig, Gift-, toxisch.
toxicity [tɒk'sɪsɪtɪ] n Giftigkeit f, Giftgehalt m.
toxicological [,tɒksɪkə'lɒdʒɪkəl] adj toxikologisch.
toxicology [,tɒksɪ'kɒlədʒɪ] n Toxikologie f.
toxin ['tɒksɪn] n Gift(stoff m), Toxin nt.
toy [tɔɪ] **1** n Spielzeug nt. ~s Spielsachen pl, Spielzeug nt; (in shops also) Spielwaren pl; it's not a ~! das ist kein (Kinder)spielzeug!
2 vi to ~ with an object/idea mit einer Sache/Idee etc spielen; to ~ with one's food mit dem Essen (herum)spielen.
toy in cpds gun, car, soldier Spielzeug-; ~ dog n Zwerghund m; (of material) Stoffhund m; ~shop n Spielwarenladen m.
trace[1] [treɪs] **1** n **(a)** (sign) Spur f. I can't find any ~ of your file Ihre Akte ist spurlos verschwunden; there's no ~ of it keine Spur davon; to vanish without ~ spurlos verschwinden; to lose ~ of sb/sth jdn/etw aus den Augen verlieren.
(b) (small amount: of poison) Spur f; (of spice also) Idee f; (of irony etc also) Hauch m.
2 vt **(a)** (draw) zeichnen; (copy) nachzeichnen, nachzeichnen; (with tracing paper) durchpausen, durchzeichnen. he ~d his name in the sand er malte seinen Namen in den Sand.
(b) (follow trail of) trail, progress, developments verfolgen; steps folgen (+dat). she was ~d to a house in Soho ihre Spur führte zu einem Haus in Soho.
(c) (find) ausfindig machen, auffinden. I can't ~ your file ich kann Ihre Akte nicht finden.
♦**trace back 1** vi zurückgehen (to auf +acc).
2 vt sep descent zurückverfolgen; rumour auf seinen Ursprung zurückverfolgen; neurosis etc zurückführen (to auf +acc). he can ~ his family ~ to Henry VIII seine Familie läßt sich bis zu Heinrich VIII. zurückverfolgen; we ~d the rumour ~ to one of the secretaries wir fanden heraus, daß das Gerücht von einer der Sekretärinnen in die Welt gesetzt worden war.
♦**trace out** vt sep (copy) nachzeichnen; (with tracing paper) durchpausen (onto auf +acc); (draw) zeichnen. we ~d ~ the route on the map wir zeichneten die Route auf der Karte ein.
trace[2] n (of harness) Zuggurt, Zugriemen m; see kick over.
traceable ['treɪsəbl] adj **(a)** (can be found) auffindbar. **(b)** a characteristic ~ through the centuries eine Eigenschaft, die sich durch viele Jahrhunderte hindurch zurückverfolgen läßt; to be ~ to sth sich auf etw (acc) zurückführen lassen.
trace element n Spurenelement nt.
tracer ['treɪsə'] n **(a)** (Mil: also ~ bullet) Leuchtgeschoß nt. **(b)** (Med) Isotopenindikator m. **(c)** (enquiry form) Suchzettel, Laufzettel m.
tracery ['treɪsərɪ] n (Archit) Maßwerk nt; (pattern: of threads, branches etc) Filigranmuster nt.
trachea [trə'kɪə] n Luftröhre f; (of insects) Trachea f.
tracheotomy [,trækɪ'ɒtəmɪ] n Luftröhrenschnitt m.
trachoma [trə'kəʊmə] n Körnerkrankheit f, (hartnäckige) Bindehautentzündung.
tracing ['treɪsɪŋ] n (drawing) Durchpausen, Durchzeichnen nt; (result) Pause f. ~ paper Pauspapier nt.
track [træk] **1** n **(a)** (trail) Fährte, Spur f; (of tyres) (Fahr)spur f. to be on sb's ~ jdm auf der Spur sein; you can't expect to keep ~ of your friends if you never write to them du kannst nicht

erwarten, Kontakt zu deinen Freunden zu behalten, wenn du nie schreibst; to keep ~ of sb/sth (watch, follow) jdn/etw im Auge behalten; situation also etw verfolgen; (keep up to date with) über jdn/etw auf dem laufenden bleiben; I can't keep ~ of his movements or him ich weiß nie, wo er sich gerade aufhält; how do you keep ~ of the time without a watch? wie können Sie wissen, wie spät es ist, wenn Sie keine Uhr haben?; I can't keep ~ of your arguments/girlfriends du hast so viele Argumente/Freundinnen, da komme ich nicht mit (inf); no-one can keep ~ of the situation niemand hat mehr einen Überblick über die Lage; the Americans kept ~ of the Russian moonrocket die Amerikaner verfolgten die Bahn der sowjetischen Mondrakete; to lose ~ of sb/sth (lose contact with, lose sight of) jdn/etw aus den Augen verlieren; (lose count of, be confused about) über Leute/etw den Überblick verlieren; (not be up to date with) über jdn/etw nicht mehr auf dem laufenden sein; he/I lost ~ of what he was saying er hat den Faden verloren/ich habe nicht (mehr) mitbekommen, was er gesagt hat.
(b) (fig) we must be making ~s (inf) wir müssen uns auf die Socken (inf) or auf den Weg machen; to make ~s for home sich auf den Nachhauseweg machen; he made ~s for London er ging/fuhr nach London; he stopped dead in his ~s er blieb abrupt stehen; to cover (up) one's ~s seine Spuren verwischen.
(c) (path) Weg, Pfad m. off the ~ (fig) abwegig; to be on the right/wrong ~ (fig) auf der richtigen/falschen Spur sein, auf dem richtigen Weg/Holzweg (inf) or falschen Weg sein.
(d) (course) (of hurricane) Weg m; (of comet) (Lauf)bahn f; (of rocket) Bahn f, Kurs m.
(e) (Rail) Gleise pl; (US: platform) Bahnsteig m. a new section of ~ eine neue (Gleis)strecke; the ~ to Paisley die (Bahn)strecke nach Paisley; "keep off the ~" Betreten der Gleise verboten; two miles of new ~ zwei Meilen neuer Gleise or Schienen; to leave the ~(s) entgleisen; double/single ~ line zwei-/eingleisige Strecke; to be born on the wrong side of the ~s (US fig) aus niedrigem Milieu stammen.
(f) (Sport) Rennbahn f; (Athletics) Bahn f; (Motorsport) Piste, Bahn f; (circuit) Rennstrecke f; (Cycling) Radrennbahn f.
(g) (on tape) Spur f; (on record: song etc) Stück nt. four-~ tape-recorder Vierspurgerät nt.
(h) (also caterpillar ~) Raupenkette f.
(i) (Aut: between wheels) Spur(weite) f.
2 vt **(a)** (follow) person, animal verfolgen; (Space) rocket die Flugbahn (+gen) verfolgen.
(b) (US) the children ~ed dirt all over the carpet die Kinder hinterließen überall auf dem Teppich Schmutzspuren.
3 vi **(a)** (follow trail) Fährten lesen.
(b) (Aut) spurgenau laufen.
(c) (Film, TV) fahren.
(d) (move: hurricane etc) ziehen; (stylus) sich bewegen.
♦**track down** vt sep aufspüren (to in +dat); thing aufstöbern, auftreiben (inf), finden; reference, source of infection ausfindig machen.
♦**track in** vi (Film, TV) heranfahren (on an +acc).
track: ~-and-field adj Leichtathletik-; ~ athletics n sing Laufdisziplinen pl.
tracked [trækt] adj vehicle Ketten-, Raupen-.
tracker ['trækə'] n (Indian etc) Fährtenleser m; (Hunt) Tracker m. ~ dog Spürhund m.
track event n Laufwettbewerb m.
tracking ['trækɪŋ] n Verfolgen m. ~ station Bodenstation f.
track: ~-laying vehicle n Kettenfahrzeug nt; ~less adj **(a)** vehicle ohne Ketten; **(b)** forest weglos; snow ohne Spuren, unbetreten; ~ maintenance n (Rail) Streckenwartung f; ~ meeting or meet (US) Leichtathletikwettbewerb or -wettkampf m; ~ race n Rennen nt; (Motorsport, Athletics also) Lauf m; ~ racing n Laufwettbewerb m; (Motorsport) Rennen nt; (Cycling) Radrennen nt; ~ record n (fig) what's his ~ record? was hat er vorzuweisen?; ~ rod n Spurstange f; ~ shoe n Rennschuh m; ~suit n Trainingsanzug m; ~walker n (US) Streckenläufer m.
tract[1] [trækt] n **(a)** (of land) Gebiet nt. narrow ~ Streifen m. **(b)** (respiratory) Wege pl; (digestive) Trakt m.
tract[2] n Traktat nt, Schrift f.
tractability [træktə'bɪlɪtɪ] n see adj Formbarkeit, Bearbeitbarkeit f; Fügsamkeit, Lenkbarkeit f.
tractable ['træktəbl] adj (lit) metal etc leicht zu bearbeiten, formbar; (fig) child, animal, disposition fügsam, lenkbar.
traction ['trækʃən] n Zugkraft, Ziehkraft, Zugleistung f; (of wheels) Bodenhaftung f; (Med) Streckverband m. in ~ im Streckverband; ~ engine Zugmaschine f, Dampftraktor m.
tractor ['træktə'] n **(a)** Traktor, Trecker m, Zugmaschine f. ~ driver Traktorfahrer(in f), Traktorist(in f) m. **(b)** (of truck) Sattelschlepper m.
trad [træd] (inf), **trad jazz** n Traditional, Old-time m.
trade [treɪd] **1** n **(a)** (commerce) Handel m, Gewerbe nt; (hotel ~, catering ~) Gewerbe nt; (turnover: of shop, hotel etc) die Geschäfte pl. he used to be in ~ er war Geschäftsmann; how's ~? wie gehen die Geschäfte?; to do ~ with sb mit jdm Handel treiben; to do a good ~ gute Geschäfte machen; ~ was good last summer im letzten Sommer waren die Geschäfte gut; to do a brisk ~ in sth einen reißenden Absatz an etw (dat) haben.
(b) (line of business) Branche f, Geschäftszweig m. he's in the wool ~ er ist in der Wollbranche, er ist im Wollhandel tätig; what ~ are you in? in welcher Branche sind Sie (tätig)?; he's in the ~ er ist in der Branche, er ist vom Fach; as we call it in the ~ wie es in unserer Branche heißt.
(c) (job) Handwerk nt. he's a bricklayer by ~ er ist Maurer von Beruf; a lawyer by ~ (hum) ein gelernter Rechtsanwalt (hum); every man to his ~ (prov) Schuster, bleib bei deinen Leisten (prov); what's your ~? was machen Sie beruflich?; to put sb to a ~ (old) jdn ein Handwerk erlernen lassen.

(d) (*people*) Geschäftsleute *pl*, Branche *f*. special terms for the ~ Vergünstigungen *pl* für Leute aus der Branche; **to sell to the ~** an Gewerbetreibende verkaufen.

(e) (*exchange*) Tausch(geschäft *nt or* -handel *m*) *m*.

(f) the T~s *pl* (*Geog*) der Passat.

2 *vt* tauschen. **to ~ sth for** sth else etw gegen etw anderes (ein)tauschen; **to ~ secrets** Geheimnisse austauschen.

3 *vi* **(a)** (*Comm*) Handel treiben, handeln. **to ~ in sth** mit etw handeln; **to ~ with sb** mit jdm Geschäfte machen *or* Handel treiben.

(b) (*US inf*) einkaufen (at bei).

♦**trade in** *vt sep* in Zahlung geben (*for* für).

♦**trade (up)on** *vi* +*prep obj* ausnützen.

trade: ~ **directory** *n* Branchenverzeichnis, Firmenverzeichnis *nt*; ~ **discount** *n* Händlerrabatt *m*; ~ **fair** *n* Handelsmesse *f*; ~ **figures** *npl* Handelsziffern *pl*; ~ **gap** *n* Außenhandelsdefizit *nt*; ~**-in** *n* Altgerät *nt*; (*car*) in Zahlung gegebenes Auto; **we offer £10 for a ~-in** if you buy a new cooker beim Kauf eines neuen Herds nehmen wir Ihren alten für £ 10 in Zahlung; **we will take your old car as a ~-in** wir nehmen Ihren alten Wagen in Zahlung; **2** *attr* ~**-in value** Gebrauchtwert *m*; **they don't give very good ~-in** terms sie bezahlen nicht sehr viel für Altgeräte/Gebrauchtwagen; ~**mark** *n* (*lit*) Warenzeichen *nt*; **honesty was his ~mark** er war für seine Ehrlichkeit bekannt; **although it was anonymous it had the director's ~mark on it** obwohl es anonym war, trug es die Handschrift des Direktors; ~ **name** *n* Handelsname *m*; ~ **paper** *n* Fachzeitschrift *f*, Fachblatt *nt*; ~ **price** *n* Großhandelspreis *m*.

trader ['treɪdə'] *n* **(a)** (*person*) Händler *m*. **(b)** (*ship*) Handelsschiff *nt*.

trade route *n* Handelsweg *m*, Handelsstraße *f*.

tradescantia [,trædə'skæntɪə] *n* Tradeskantie *f*.

trade: ~ **school** *n* Gewerbe- *or* Berufsschule *f*; ~ **secret** *n* (*lit, fig*) Betriebsgeheimnis *nt*.

trades: ~**man** *n* (*delivery man*) Lieferant *m*; (*shopkeeper*) Händler, Ladenbesitzer *m*; (*plumber, electrician etc*) Handwerker *m*; ~**man's entrance** Lieferanteneingang *m*; ~**people** *npl* Geschäftsleute, Händler *pl*; ~ **union** *n see* trade union; T~ **Union Congress** (*britischer*) Gewerkschaftsbund.

trade: ~ **union** *n* Gewerkschaft *f*; ~ **unionism** *n* Gewerkschaftsbewegung *f*; ~ **unionist** *n* Gewerkschaft(l)er(in *f*) *m*; ~ **wind** *n* Passat *m*.

trading ['treɪdɪŋ] *n* Handel *m*, Handeln *nt* (*in* mit).

trading in *cpds* Handels-; ~ **estate** *n* Industriegelände *nt*; ~ **licence** *n* Gewerbeerlaubnis *f*, Gewerbeschein *m*; ~ **post** *n* Laden *m*; ~ **profits** *npl* Geschäfts- *or* Handelsgewinn *m*; ~ **stamp** *n* Rabattmarke *f*.

tradition [trə'dɪʃən] *n* Tradition *f*. **village** ~**s** Dorfbräuche *or* -traditionen *pl or* -brauchtum *nt*; **it has become a ~ for** the chairman to propose the first toast es ist jetzt so üblich *or* ist zum festen Brauch geworden, daß der Vorsitzende den ersten Toast ausbringt; **according to ~** he ..., ~ **has it that he** ... es ist überliefert, daß er ...; **there is a ~** in the village that Queen Mary slept here im Dorf erzählt man sich, daß Königin Maria dort übernachtet hat; **in the French ~** in der französischen Tradition; **in the best ~** nach bester Tradition.

traditional [trə'dɪʃənl] *adj* traditionell; *story, custom also* alt; *virtues also* überkommen; *jazz* Old-time-, traditional. **it's ~ for us to spend New Year's Day at my mother's** es ist bei uns so üblich *or* Brauch, daß wir den Neujahrstag bei meiner Mutter verbringen.

traditionalism [trə'dɪʃnəlɪzəm] *n* Festhalten *nt* am Alten, Traditionalismus *m*.

traditionalist [trə'dɪʃnəlɪst] **1** *n* Traditionalist(in *f*) *m*. **2** *adj* traditionsgebunden, an Traditionen hängend *or* festhaltend.

traditionally [trə'dɪʃnəlɪ] *adv* traditionell; (*customarily*) üblicherweise, normalerweise. **middle-class people have ~** voted Conservative der Mittelstand hat schon immer konservativ gewählt; ~ **New Year's day is a holiday** der Neujahrstag ist schon immer ein Feiertag gewesen; **turkey is ~ eaten at Christmas** es ist Tradition *or* ein Brauch, Weihnachten Truthahn zu essen.

trad jazz *n see* trad.

traduce [trə'dju:s] *vt* (*liter*) verleumden.

traducer [trə'dju:sə'] *n* (*liter*) Ehrabschneider *m* (*geh*).

traffic ['træfɪk] **1** *n* **(a)** Verkehr *m*; (*Aviat*) Flug- *or* Luftverkehr *m*. **a policeman was directing ~** ein Polizist regelte den Verkehr; ~ **coming into London is advised to avoid Putney Bridge** Fahrern in Richtung Innenstadt London wird empfohlen, Putney Bridge zu meiden.

(b) (*business: of port, airport*) Umschlag *m*. ~ **in steel** Stahlumschlag *m*; **freight** ~ Frachtumschlag *m*.

(c) (*usu pej: trading*) Handel *m* (*in* mit); (*in drugs also*) Dealen *nt* (*in* mit); (*in pornography*) Vertrieb *m* (*in* von); (*in illegal alcohol*) Schieberei *f* (*in* von).

2 *vi* (*usu pej*) handeln (*in* mit); (*in drugs also*) dealen (*in* mit); (*in pornography*) vertreiben (*in* acc); (*in illegal alcohol*) verschieben (*in* acc).

trafficator ['træfɪkeɪtə'] *n* (Fahrt)richtungsanzeiger *m* (*form*).

traffic in *cpds* Verkehrs-; ~ **circle** *n* (*US*) Kreisverkehr *m*; ~ **control tower** *n* (*Aviat*) Kontrollturm, Tower *m*; ~ **cop** *n* (*US inf*) Verkehrspolizist *m*; ~ **diversion** *n* Umleitung *f*; ~ **hold-up** *n see* ~ jam; ~ **indicator** *n* (Fahrt)richtungsanzeiger *m* (*form*); (*flashing*) Blinker *m*; ~ **island** *n* Verkehrsinsel *f*; ~ **jam** *n* Verkehrsstockung *or* -stauung *f*.

trafficker ['træfɪkə'] *n* (*usu pej*) Händler, Schieber (*pej*) *m*; (*in drugs also*) Dealer *m*.

trafficking ['træfɪkɪŋ] *n* Handel *m* (*in* mit); (*in drugs also*) Dealen *nt* (*in* mit); (*in illegal alcohol*) Schieberei *f* (*in* von); (*in pornography*) Vertrieb *m* (*in* von).

traffic: ~ **lights** *npl* Verkehrsampel *f*; ~ **police** *npl* Ver-

kehrspolizei *f*; ~ **policeman** *n* Verkehrspolizist *m*; ~ **signals** *npl see* ~ lights; ~ **warden** *n* ≈ Verkehrspolizist *m* ohne polizeiliche Befugnisse; (*woman*) ≈ Politesse *f*.

tragedian [trə'dʒi:dɪən] *n* (*writer*) Tragödiendichter *m*; (*actor*) Tragöde *m* (*geh*), Darsteller *m* tragischer Rollen.

tragedienne [trə,dʒi:dɪ'en] *n* (*actress*) Tragödin (*geh*), Darstellerin *f* tragischer Rollen.

tragedy ['trædʒɪdɪ] *n* (*tragic incident*) Tragödie *f*; (*Theat also*) Trauerspiel *nt*; (*no pl: tragicalness*) Tragische(s) *nt*. **he often acts in ~** er tritt oft in Tragödien auf; **a life/voice/look full of ~** ein tragisches Leben/eine tragische Stimme/ein tragischer Blick, ein Leben/eine Stimme/ein Blick voller Tragik; **six killed in holiday crash ~** tragischer Urlaubsunfall forderte sechs Todesopfer; **the ~ of it is that ...** das Tragische daran ist, daß ...; **it is a ~ that ...** es ist (wirklich) tragisch *or* ein Unglück, daß ...

tragic ['trædʒɪk] *adj* tragisch. **the ~ and the comic** (*Theat*) das Tragische und das Komische.

tragically ['trædʒɪkəlɪ] *adv* ~, **he was killed before he ...** tragischerweise kam er ums Leben, bevor er ...; **she was ~ unaware of what had happened** tragischerweise wußte sie nicht, was geschehen war; **don't take it too ~!** nehmen Sie es nicht zu tragisch!

tragicomedy ['trædʒɪ'kɒmɪdɪ] *n* Tragikomödie *f*.

tragicomic ['trædʒɪ'kɒmɪk] *adj* tragikomisch.

trail [treɪl] **1** *n* **(a)** Spur *f*; (*of meteor*) Schwanz, Schweif *m*. ~ **of blood** Blutspur *f*; ~ **of smoke/dust** Rauchfahne *f*/Staubwolke *f*; **the hurricane left a ~ of destruction** der Hurrikan hinterließ eine Spur der Verwüstung.

(b) (*track*) Fährte, Spur *f*. **hot on the ~** dicht auf den Fersen; **to be on the ~ of an animal** die Spur eines Tieres verfolgen; **the police are on his ~** die Polizei ist ihm auf der Spur.

(c) (*path*) Weg, Pfad *m*; (*nature ~ etc*) (Wander)weg *m*.

2 *vt* **(a)** (*follow*) person folgen (+*dat*), verfolgen. **to ~ an animal** ein Tier *or* die Spur eines Tieres verfolgen; **they ~ed him to his hideout** sie folgten ihm bis zu seinem Versteck.

(b) (*drag*) schleppen, schleifen. **the bird ~ed its broken wing** der Vogel zog seinen gebrochenen Flügel nach.

(c) (*US: tow*) ziehen, schleppen.

3 *vi* **(a)** (*on floor*) schleifen.

(b) (*plant*) sich ranken. **with ivy ~ing round the windows** von Efeu umrankte Fenster.

(c) (*walk*) zuckeln, trotten.

(d) (*be behind: in competition etc*) weit zurückliegen, hinterherhinken; (*Sport*) weit zurückgefallen sein. **our team is ~ing at the bottom of the league** unsere Mannschaft rangiert in der Tabelle unter „ferner liefen" *or* auf den letzten Plätzen.

♦**trail along 1** *vi* entlangzuckeln. **the child ~ed ~ behind his mother** das Kind trottete *or* zuckelte hinter der Mutter her.

2 *vt* entlangschleppen *or* -schleifen. **the child ~ed his coat ~ behind him** das Kind schleifte *or* schleppte seinen Mantel hinter sich (*dat*) her.

♦**trail away** *or* **off** *vi* (*voice*) sich verlieren (*into* in +*dat*), verhallen. **his voice ~ed off** its voice *or* in silence er verstummte.

♦**trail behind 1** *vi* hinterhertrotten *or* -zuckeln (+*prep obj* hinter +*dat*); (*in competition etc*) zurückgefallen sein (+*prep obj* hinter +*acc*). **2** *vt sep* hinter sich (*dat*) herziehen.

trailblazer ['treɪl'bleɪzə'] *n* (*fig*) Wegbereiter, Bahnbrecher *m*.

trailer ['treɪlə'] *n* **(a)** (*Aut*) Anhänger *m*; (*esp US: of lorry*) Sattelauflieger *m*. **(b)** (*US*) Wohnwagen, Caravan *m*. ~ **camp** Platz *m* für Wohnwagen *or* Caravans. **(c)** (*Bot*) Hängepflanze *f*. **(d)** (*Film, TV*) Vorschau *f*.

trailing ['treɪlɪŋ] *adj* **(a)** *plant* Hänge-. **(b)** (*Aviat*) ~ **edge** Hinterkante, Achterkante *f*.

train[1] [treɪn] *n* **(a)** (*Rail*) Zug *m*. **to go/travel by ~** mit dem Zug *or* der (Eisen)bahn fahren/reisen; **a ~ journey** eine Bahn- *or* Zugfahrt; **to take** *or* **catch** *or* **get the 11 o'clock ~** den Elfuhrzug nehmen; **to change ~s** umsteigen; **on the ~** im Zug.

(b) (*line*) Kolonne *f*; (*of people*) Schlange *f*; (*of camels*) Karawane *f*; (*retinue*) Gefolge *nt*. **in his ~** in seinem Gefolge; **the war brought famine in its ~** der Krieg brachte eine Hungersnot mit sich; **to put sth in ~** (*form*) etw einleiten *or* in Gang setzen; **to be in ~** (*form*) im Gang(e) sein.

(c) (*of events*) Folge, Kette *f*. **he interrupted my ~ of thought** er unterbrach meinen Gedankengang.

(d) (*of dress*) Schleppe *f*.

(e) ~ **of gunpowder** Pulverspur *f*.

train[2] **1** *vt* **(a)** ausbilden; *child* erziehen; *apprentice, new employee also* unterrichten, unterweisen; *animal* abrichten, dressieren; *mind* schulen; (*Sport*) trainieren. **to ~ sb as sth** jdn als *or* zu etw ausbilden; **to ~ oneself to do sth** sich dazu erziehen, etw zu tun; **to ~ a child to be polite** ein Kind zur Höflichkeit erziehen; **to ~ an animal to do sth** ein Tier dazu abrichten, etw zu tun; **this dog has been ~ed to kill** dieser Hund ist aufs Töten abgerichtet; **a lion ~ed to do tricks** ein dressierter Löwe, der Kunststücke macht; **she has her dog/husband** (*hum*) **well ~ed** sie hat ihren Hund/Mann (*hum*) gut erzogen; **he was ~ed for the ministry** er wurde zum Geistlichen ausgebildet.

(b) (*aim*) *gun, telescope* richten (*on* auf +*acc*).

(c) *plant* wachsen lassen (*over* über +*acc*). **she ~ed her roses along/up the trellis** sie ließ ihre Rosen am Gitter entlang-/hochwachsen.

2 *vi* **(a)** (*esp Sport*) trainieren (*for* für).

(b) (*study*) ausgebildet werden. **he ~ed as a teacher** er hat eine Lehrerausbildung gemacht, er ist ausgebildeter Lehrer; **where did you ~?** wo haben Sie Ihre Ausbildung erhalten?, sind Sie ausgebildet worden?

♦**train up** *vt sep* heranbilden (*to* zu); *team* trainieren.

train: ~**bearer** *n* Schleppenträger(in *f*) *m*; ~ **driver** *n* Zug- *or* Lokführer(in *f*) *m*.

trained [treɪnd] *adj* *worker* gelernt, Fach-; *nurse, teacher* ausgebildet; *animal* dressiert; *dog* abgerichtet, dressiert;

mind, ear geschult; *eye* geübt, geschult; *voice* ausgebildet. **a well-~ child** ein guterzogenes Kind.

trainee [treɪ'ni:] *n* Auszubildende(r) *mf*; (*in office, shop etc*) Anlernling *m*; (*academic, technical*) Praktikant(in *f*) *m*; (*nurse*) Krankenpflegeschüler(in *f*) *m*, Schwesternschülerin *f*; (*management*) Trainee *mf*. **I am a ~** ich bin *or* befinde mich in der Ausbildung.

trainee-: **~ manager** *n* Management-Trainee *mf*; **~ mechanic** *n* Schlosserlehrling *m*; **~ nurse** *n* Krankenpflegeschüler(in *f*) *m*, Schwesternschülerin *f*; **~ teacher** *n* (*in primary school*) ≈ Praktikant(in *f*) *m*; (*in secondary school*) ≈ Referendar(in *f*) *m*.

trainer ['treɪnə'] *n* (*Sport, of racehorse*) Trainer *m*; (*of animals*) Dresseur *m*, (*in circus*) Dompteur *m*, Dompteuse *f*. **~ plane** (*Aviat*) Schulflugzeug *nt*.

train ferry *n* Eisenbahnfähre *f*.

training ['treɪnɪŋ] *n* **(a)** Ausbildung *f* (*also Mil*); (*of staff*) Schulung *f*; (*of animal*) Dressur *f*, Abrichten *nt*. **it's good ~ for the mind** es ist eine gute Denkschulung.
　(b) (*Sport*) Training *nt*. **to be in ~** im Training stehen *or* sein, trainieren; (*be fit*) gut in Form *or* fit *or* durchtrainiert sein; **to be out of ~** nicht in Form sein, aus dem Training sein; **to go into ~** das Training beginnen, anfangen zu trainieren.

training-: **~ camp** *n* Trainingslager *or* -camp *nt*; **~ centre** *n* Lehr- *or* Ausbildungszentrum *nt*; **~ college** *n* (*for teachers*) Pädagogische Hochschule; **~ course** *n* Ausbildungskurs *m*; **~ manual** *n* Lehrbuch *nt*; **~ period** *n* Ausbildungsdauer *f*; **~ plane** *n* Schulflugzeug *nt*; **~ scheme** *n* Ausbildungsweg *m or* -programm *nt*; **~ ship** *n* Schulschiff *nt*; **~ shoes** *npl* Trainingsschuhe *pl*.

train-: **~load** *n* (*of goods*) Zugladung *f*; **~loads** *of holidaymakers* ganze Züge voller Urlauber; **soldiers were sent there by the ~load** ganze Zugladungen Soldaten wurden hingeschickt; **~man** *n* (*US*) Eisenbahner *m*; (*brakeman*) Bremser *m*; **~ oil** *n* Tran *m*; **~ service** *n* Zugverkehr *m*; (*between two places*) (Eisen)bahnverbindung *f*; **~ set** *n* (Spielzeug)eisenbahn *f*; **~sick** *adj* **he gets ~sick** ihm wird beim Zugfahren schlecht *or* übel; **~sickness n I've never suffered from ~sickness** mir ist beim Zugfahren noch nie schlecht *or* übel geworden; **~spotter** *n* Eisenbahnfan *m*; **~spotting** *n Hobby nt, bei dem Züge beguatachtet und deren Nummern notiert werden*.

traipse [treɪps] (*inf*) **1** *vi* latschen (*inf*). **to ~ round the shops** in den Geschäften rumlatschen (*inf*); **to ~ round the shops for sth** die Geschäfte nach etw abklappern (*inf*). **2** *n* **it's a long ~** da muß man lange latschen (*inf*).

trait [treɪt, treɪ] *n* Eigenschaft *f*; (*of particular person also*) Charakter- *or* Wesenszug *m*.

traitor ['treɪtə'] *n* Verräter *m*. **to be a ~ to one's country** sein Vaterland verraten, Verrat an seinem Vaterland üben; **to turn ~** zum Verräter werden; **to be a ~ to the cause** die Sache verraten.

traitorous ['treɪtərəs] *adj behaviour, action* verräterisch; *coward also* treulos.

traitorously ['treɪtərəslɪ] *adv* verräterisch, in verräterischer Weise.

traitress ['treɪtrɪs] *n* Verräterin *f*.

trajectory [trə'dʒektərɪ] *n* Flugbahn *f*.

tram [træm] *n* **(a)** (*Brit*) Straßenbahn, Tram(bahn) (*S Ger, Sw, Aus*) *f*. **Blackpool still has ~s** in Blackpool gibt es noch Straßenbahnen *or* eine Straßenbahn; **to go by/take the ~** mit der Straßenbahn fahren/die Straßenbahn nehmen; **I saw her on a ~** ich habe sie in einer Straßenbahn gesehen.
　(b) (*Min*) Grubenbahn *f*.

tram-: **~car** *n* Straßenbahn *f*; (*single car*) Straßenbahnwagen *m*; **~ driver** *n* Straßenbahnfahrer(in *f*) *m*; **~ line** *n* (*track*) Straßenbahnschiene *f*; (*route*) Straßenbahnlinie *f*; **~lines** *npl* (*Tennis*) Linien *pl* des Doppelspielfelds.

trammel ['træməl] **1** *vt* einengen. **to feel ~led by sth** sich durch etw behindert *or* eingeengt fühlen. **2** *n* **~s** *pl* Fesseln *pl*.

tramp [træmp] **1** *vi* **(a)** (*walk heavily, trudge*) stapfen, mit schweren Schritten gehen, stampfen; **the soldiers ~ed along for hours** die Soldaten marschierten stundenlang (mit schweren Schritten); **I've been ~ing round town all day** ich bin den ganzen Tag in der Stadt herumgestiefelt (*inf*); **to ~ up and down the platform** auf dem Bahnsteig auf und ab marschieren; **they ~ed about in the garden** sie trampelten *or* stapften im Garten herum; **feet ~ing up and down** Füße, die herumtrampeln *or* -stapfen.
　(b) (*hike*) marschieren, wandern; (*as vagabond*) umherziehen. **to ~ across the hills** über die Berge marschieren; **he ~ed all over Europe** er wanderte in ganz Europa umher.
　2 *vt* **(a)** (*spread by walking*) herumtreten. **don't ~ that mud into the carpet** tritt den Dreck nicht in den Teppich.
　(b) (*walk*) *streets* latschen durch (*inf*).
　3 *n* **(a)** (*vagabond*) Landstreicher(in *f*), Tramp *m*; (*in town*) Stadtstreicher(in *f*) *m*.
　(b) (*sound*) Stapfen *nt*, schwere Schritte *pl*.
　(c) (*walk*) Wanderung *f*. **it's a long ~** es ist ein weiter Weg.
　(d) (*Naut*) Trampdampfer *m*.
　(e) (*inf: loose woman*) Flittchen *nt* (*pej*).

♦**tramp down** *vt sep* feststampfen, festtreten; *corn, flowers etc* platttreten, niedertrampeln.

♦**tramp in** *vt sep* festtreten, in den Boden treten.

trample ['træmpl] **1** *vt* niedertrampeln, niedertreten, zertrampeln. **to ~ sth underfoot** auf etw (*dat*) herumtrampeln; **she ~s her husband underfoot** (*fig*) sie macht ihren Mann zur Schnecke (*inf*); **he was ~d to death by a bull** er wurde von einem Bullen zu Tode getrampelt; **to ~ sth into the ground** etw in den Boden treten *or* trampeln.
　2 *vi* stapfen, trampeln. **he lets his wife ~ all over him** (*fig*) er läßt sich (*dat*) von seiner Frau auf dem Kopf herumtanzen.
　3 *n* Getrampel, Trampeln *nt*.

♦**trample about** *vi* herumtrampeln.

♦**trample down** *vt sep* heruntertreten, niedertreten.

♦**trample on** *vi* +*prep obj* herumtreten auf (+*dat*). **several children were ~d ~ by people escaping from the fire** mehrere Kinder wurden getreten, als sich die Leute vor dem Feuer retteten; **to ~ ~ everybody/sb** (*fig*) über Leichen gehen/jdn herumschikanieren; **to ~ ~ sb's feelings** (*fig*) jds Gefühle mit Füßen treten.

trampoline ['træmpəlɪn] *n* Trampolin *nt*.

tramp steamer *n* Trampdampfer *m*.

tram-: **~ride** *n* Straßenbahnfahrt *f*; **~way** *n* Straßenbahn *f*; (*route*) Straßenbahnstrecke *f*.

trance [trɑːns] *n* Trance *f*; (*Med*) tiefe Bewußtlosigkeit. **to go into a ~** in Trance verfallen; **to put sb into a ~** jdn in Trance versetzen; **she's been going about in a ~ for the past few days** die letzten paar Tage ist sie wie in Trance *or* im Tran (*inf*) durch die Gegend gelaufen.

tranny ['trænɪ] *n* (*Brit sl*) Transistor *m* (*inf*), Kofferradio *nt*.

tranquil ['træŋkwɪl] *adj* ruhig, friedlich, still; *life* friedlich, ohne Aufregung; *mind* ruhig, gelassen; *music* ruhig, sanft; *person* ruhig, gelassen, ausgeglichen.

tranquillity, (*US*) **tranquility** [træŋ'kwɪlɪtɪ] *n see adj* Ruhe, Friedlichkeit, Stille *f*; Friede *m*; Ruhe, Gelassenheit *f*; Sanftheit *f*; Ruhe, Gelassenheit, Ausgeglichenheit *f*. **the ~ of the home** die friedliche Atmosphäre des Hauses; **he was soothed by the ~ of the music** die sanfte Musik beruhigte ihn.

tranquillize, (*US*) **tranquilize** ['træŋkwɪlaɪz] *vt* beruhigen. **tranquillizing** dart Betäubungspfeil *m*.

tranquillizer, (*US*) **tranquilizer** ['træŋkwɪlaɪzə'] *n* Beruhigungstablette *f*; Beruhigungsmittel *nt*.

tranquilly ['træŋkwɪlɪ] *adv see adj*.

trans- [trænz-] *pref* trans-, Trans-.

transact [træn'zækt] *vt* abwickeln; *business also* abschließen, durchführen; *deal* abschließen. **to ~ business with sb** Geschäfte mit jdm abschließen.

transaction [træn'zækʃən] *n* **(a)** (*act*) *see vt* Abwicklung *f*; Abschluß *m*, Durchführung *f*; Abschluß *m*. **~ of business** Geschäftsbetrieb *m*; **the bank will be closed for the ~ of business at 3 p.m.** die Bank hat *or* ist ab 15⁰⁰ Uhr geschlossen.
　(b) (*piece of business*) Geschäft *nt*; (*Fin, St Ex*) Transaktion *f*.
　(c) **~s** *pl* (*of society*) Sitzungsbericht *m*.

transalpine [trænz'ælpaɪn] *adj* transalpin.

transatlantic ['trænzət'læntɪk] *adj journey, phone call* transatlantisch, Transatlantik-; *customs* auf der anderen Seite (des Atlantiks); *cousins, accent* amerikanisch; (*for Americans*) britisch.

transceiver [træn'si:və'] *n* Sender-Empfänger *m*, Sende-Empfangsgerät *nt*.

transcend [træn'send] *vt* übersteigen, überschreiten, hinausgehen über (+*acc*); (*Philos*) transzendieren.

transcendence [træn'sendəns], **transcendency** [træn'sendənsɪ] *n* Erhabenheit *f*; (*Philos*) Transzendenz *f*.

transcendent [træn'sendənt] *adj* (*Philos*) transzendent; (*supreme*) hervorragend, alles übersteigend, überragend.

transcendental [,trænsen'dentl] *adj* überirdisch; (*Philos*) transzendental; *vision* transzendierend. **an almost ~ experience** eine fast transzendentale Erfahrung; **~ meditation** transzendentale Meditation; **~ number** (*Math*) transzendente Zahl, Transzendente *f*.

transcendentalism [,trænsen'dentəlɪzəm] *n* transzendentale Philosophie, Transzendentalismus *m*.

transcontinental ['trænz,kɒntɪnentl] *adj* transkontinental.

transcribe [træn'skraɪb] *vt manuscripts* abschreiben, transkribieren; (*from shorthand*) (in Langschrift) übertragen; *speech, proceedings etc* niederschreiben, mitschreiben; (*Mus*) transkribieren. **to ~ sth phonetically** etw in phonetische (Um)schrift übertragen; **to ~ a record** onto tape eine Schallplatte auf Band aufnehmen *or* überspielen.

transcript ['trænskrɪpt] *n* **(a)** (*of court proceedings*) Protokoll *nt*; (*of tapes*) Niederschrift *f*; (*copy*) Kopie, Abschrift *f*. **(b)** (*US: academic record*) Zeugnis *nt* bzw *f* (*Studienunterlagen*).

transcription [træn'skrɪpʃən] *n* (*Mus, Phon*) Transkription *f*; (*copy, of shorthand notes*) Abschrift *f*; (*act*) Abschrift *f*, Abschreiben *nt*; (*of speech, proceedings*) Niederschrift *f*, Protokoll *nt*; (*Rad, TV: recording*) Aufnahme *f*. **phonetic ~** Lautschrift *f*, phonetische (Um)schrift.

transducer [,trænz'dju:sə'] *n* Umformer, Umwandler *m*.

transept ['trænsept] *n* Querschiff, Transept (*spec*) *nt*.

trans-European ['trænz,jʊərə'pi:ən] *adj railway* Trans-Europ(a)-; *journey* quer durch Europa.

transfer [træns'fɜː'] **1** *vt* übertragen (*to auf* +*acc*); *prisoner* überführen (*to in* +*acc*), verlegen (*to nach*); *premises, soldiers* verlegen (*to in* +*acc, to town* nach); (*soldier, employee*) versetzen (*to in* +*acc, to town, country* nach); (*Sport*) *player* transferieren (*to zu*), abgeben (*to an* +*acc*); (*Fin*) *funds, money* überweisen (*to auf* +*acc*), transferieren (*to nach*); *account* verlegen; *stocks* transferieren; (*Jur*) *property* übertragen, überschreiben (*to auf* +*acc*); *right* übertragen (*to auf* +*acc*), abtreten (*to an* +*acc*). **he ~red the bigger engine into his old car** er baute den größeren Motor in sein altes Auto ein; **it's difficult to ~ one's concentration from one task to another so quickly** es ist schwierig, seine Konzentration so schnell von einer Aufgabe auf eine andere umzustellen; **he ~red his capital into gold shares** er investierte sein Kapital in Goldaktien, er legte sein Kapital in Goldaktien an; **he ~red the money from the box to his pocket** er nahm das Geld aus der Schachtel und steckte es in die Tasche; **the magician had somehow ~red the rabbit from the hat to the box** der Zauberer hatte das Kaninchen irgendwie aus dem Hut in die Kiste praktiziert; **he ~red his weight from one foot to the other** er verlagerte sein Gewicht von einem Fuß auf den anderen; **she ~red**

her affections to another man sie schenkte ihre Zuneigung einem anderen.

2 *vi* **(a)** überwechseln (*to* zu); (*to new system, working conditions*) umstellen (*to* auf +*acc*). **he can easily ~ from one language to another** er kann leicht von einer Sprache auf eine andere überwechseln *or* umschalten.

(b) (*Fin*) umsteigen (*into* auf +*acc*). **just before the crash he ~red into government bonds** gerade rechtzeitig vor dem Zusammenbruch stieg er auf Regierungsanleihen um.

(c) (*in travelling*) umsteigen (*to* in +*acc*); (*Univ*) das Studienfach wechseln, umsatteln (*inf*) (*from ... to* von ... auf +*acc*).

3 ['trænsfɜ:ʳ] *n* **(a)** *see vt* Übertragung *f*; Überführung, Verlegung *f*; Verlegung *f*; Versetzung *f*; Transfer, Wechsel *m*; Überweisung *f*; Verlegung *f*; Transfer *m*; Übertragung, Überschreibung *f*; Übertragung, Abtretung *f*. **he asked for a ~** (*soldier, employee*) er bat um Versetzung; (*footballer*) er bat, auf die Transferliste gesetzt zu werden.

(b) (*person ~red*) **he's a ~ from another regiment/Chelsea** er ist von einem anderen Regiment hierher versetzt *or* verlegt worden/er ist von Chelsea gekommen *or* hierher gewechselt; **Chelsea's latest ~** Chelseas jüngste Neuerwerbung.

(c) (*picture*) Abziehbild *nt*.

(d) (*in travelling*) Umsteigen *nt*. **during the ~ to the train** beim Umsteigen auf die Bahn.

(e) (*~ ticket*) Umsteige(fahr)karte *f*.

transferable [træns'fɜːrəbl] *adj* übertragbar; *money, stocks* transferierbar.

transference ['trænsfərəns] *n* **(a)** (*Psych*) Übertragung *f*. **(b)** (*Fin*) (*of holdings, real estate*) Übertragung, Überschreibung *f* (*to sb* auf jdn); (*of money*) Transfer *m*.

transfer: **~ fee** *n* (*Ftbl*) Transfersumme *f*; **~ list** *n* (*Ftbl*) Transferliste *f*; **~ ticket** *n* Umsteige(fahr)karte *f*.

transfiguration [ˌtrænsfɪɡəˈreɪʃən] *n* **(a)** (*transformation*) Wandel *m*, Wandlung *f*. **(b)** (*Rel*) Verklärung Jesu, Transfiguration *f*.

transfigure [træns'fɪɡəʳ] *vt* verklären; (*transform*) verwandeln.

transfix [træns'fɪks] *vt* **(a)** (*fix*) annageln, feststecken (*to an* +*acc*); *butterflies* aufspießen. **(b)** (*fig*) **to be** *or* **stand ~ed with horror** starr vor Entsetzen sein; **he stood as though ~ed (to the ground)** er stand da wie angewurzelt.

transform [træns'fɔːm] *vt* umwandeln, umformen, umgestalten (*into* zu); *ideas, views* (von Grund auf) verändern; *person* verwandeln; *caterpillar* verwandeln; (*Phys*) umwandeln, verwandeln (*into* in +*acc*); (*Elec*) (um)wandeln, umformen (*into* in +*acc*), transformieren (*into* in +*acc*). **the old house was ~ed into three luxury flats** das alte Haus wurde in drei Luxuswohnungen umgebaut; *authority* **~ed him from a kind man into a tyrant** die Autorität machte aus ihm, dem freundlichen Menschen, einen Tyrannen; **when she came out of the beauty parlour she was ~ed** als sie aus dem Schönheitssalon kam, sah sie wie umgewandelt aus; **a coat of paint ~ed the dull old room** ein Anstrich ließ den langweiligen alten Raum in neuem Glanz erstrahlen.

transformation [ˌtrænsfəˈmeɪʃən] *n* Umwandlung, Umgestaltung, Umformung *f*; (*of ideas, views etc*) (grundlegende) Veränderung; (*of person also*) (grundlegende) Verwandlung; (*of person, caterpillar etc*) Verwandlung *f*; (*Phys*) Umwandlung *f*; (*Elec*) Umwandlung, Umformung, Transformation *f*; (*Ling*) Umformung, Transformation *f*. **~ scene** (*Theat*) Verwandlungsszene *f*.

transformational [ˌtrænsfəˈmeɪʃənl] *adj* (*Ling*) *grammar, rules* Transformations-.

transformer [træns'fɔːməʳ] *n* (*Elec*) Transformator *m*.

transfuse [træns'fjuːz] *vt* (*Med*) *blood* übertragen; (*fig*) erfüllen, durchdringen.

transfusion [træns'fjuːʒən] *n* (*also* **blood ~**) Blutübertragung, Transfusion *f*. **to give sb a ~** jdm eine Blutübertragung *or* Transfusion geben; (*blood*) **~ service** Blutspendedienst *m*; **a ~ of public money into ...** eine Finanzspritze aus öffentlichen Geldern für ...; **it was like a ~ of new life into their friendship** es war, als ob ihre Freundschaft von neuem Leben durchdrungen *or* erfüllt würde.

transgress [træns'ɡres] **1** *vt* *standards* verstoßen gegen, verletzen; *law also* überschreiten. **2** *vi* sündigen. **to ~ against the Lord** gegen Gottes Gebote sündigen *or* verstoßen.

transgression [træns'ɡreʃən] *n* **(a)** (*of law*) Verletzung, Überschreitung *f*. **(b)** (*sin*) Sünde *f*, Verstoß *m*.

transgressor [træns'ɡresəʳ] *n* Übeltäter(in *f*), Missetäter(in *f*) *m*; (*sinner*) Sünder(in *f*) *m*. **a ~ against the laws of God** einer, der gegen die Gesetze Gottes verstößt *or* sündigt.

tranship [træn'ʃɪp] *vt* umladen, umschlagen.

transhipment [træn'ʃɪpmənt] *n* Umladung *f*.

transience ['trænzɪəns], **transiency** ['trænzɪənsɪ] *n* (*of life*) Kürze, Vergänglichkeit *f*; (*of grief, joy*) Kurzlebigkeit *f*; (*of interest*) Kurzlebigkeit, Flüchtigkeit *f*.

transient ['trænzɪənt] **1** *adj* **(a)** *life* kurz; *grief, joy* kurzlebig, vergänglich, vorübergehend; *interest* kurzlebig, flüchtig, vorübergehend. **(b)** (*US*) **~** *population* nichtansässiger Teil der Bevölkerung eines Ortes. **2** *n* (*US*) Durchreisende(r) *mf*.

transistor [træn'zɪstəʳ] *n* **(a)** (*Elec*) Transistor *m*. **(b)** (*also* **~ radio**) Transistorradio, Kofferradio *nt*, Transistor *m* (*inf*).

transistorize [træn'zɪstəraɪz] *vt* transistorisieren, transistorieren.

transistorized [træn'zɪstəraɪzd] *adj* *circuit* transistorisiert.

transit ['trænzɪt] *n* Durchfahr *f*, Transit *m* (*esp DDR*); (*of goods*) Transport *m*. **the books were damaged in ~** die Bücher wurden auf dem Transport beschädigt; **passengers in ~ for New York** Transitreisende nach New York; **goods in ~ for New York** Güter für den Weitertransport nach New York; **they are stationed here in ~** sie sind hier zwischendurch stationiert.

transit: **~ camp** *n* Durchgangslager *nt*; **~ desk** *n* Transitschalter *m*.

transition [træn'zɪʃən] *n* Übergang *m* (*from ... to* von ... zu); (*of weather*) Wechsel, Umschwung *m*; (*Mus*) (*act*) Übergang *m*; (*passage*) Überleitung *f*. **period of ~** Übergangsperiode *or* -zeit *f*; **~ stage** Übergangsstadium *nt*; **~ element** (*Chem*) Übergangselement *nt*.

transitional [træn'zɪʃənl] *adj* Übergangs-.

transitive ['trænzɪtɪv] *adj* transitiv. **~ verb** transitives Verb, Handlungsverb, Transitiv(um) *nt*.

transitively ['trænzɪtɪvlɪ] *adv* transitiv.

transitivity [ˌtrænzɪˈtɪvɪtɪ] *n* transitive Eigenschaft *or* Funktion.

transit lounge *n* Warteraum, Transitraum *m*.

transitory ['trænzɪtərɪ] *adj* *life* kurz; *grief, joy* kurzlebig, vergänglich, vorübergehend; *interest* kurzlebig, flüchtig.

transit: **~ passenger** *n* Durchgangsreisende(r), Transitreisende(r) *mf*; **~ visa** *n* Durchreisevisum, Transitvisum *nt*.

translatable [trænz'leɪtəbl] *adj* übersetzbar.

translate [trænz'leɪt] **1** *vt* **(a)** übersetzen; *work of literature also* übertragen. **to ~ a text from German (in)to English** einen Text aus dem Deutschen ins Englische übersetzen; **it is ~d as ...** es wird mit ... übersetzt.

(b) **to ~ words into action** Worte in die Tat umsetzen.

(c) (*Eccl*) *bishop* in eine andere Diözese berufen; (*Rel: to heaven*) aufnehmen.

(d) (*rare: transfer*) übertragen; *person* versetzen.

2 *vi* übersetzen. **his novels ~ well (into English)** seine Romane lassen sich gut (ins Englische) übersetzen *or* übertragen.

translation [trænz'leɪʃən] *n* **(a)** (*act, translated work*) Übersetzung *f* (*from* aus); (*of work of literature also*) Übertragung *f*. **to do a ~ of sth** von etw eine Übersetzung machen *or* anfertigen; **errors in ~** Übersetzungsfehler *pl*; **it loses in ~** es verliert bei der Übersetzung; **a ~ problem** ein Übersetzungsproblem *nt*; **he is not good at ~** er kann nicht gut übersetzen.

(b) (*Eccl*) Berufung *f* in eine andere Diözese; (*to heaven*) Himmelfahrt *f*.

translational [trænz'leɪʃənl] *adj* Übersetzungs-.

translator [trænz'leɪtəʳ] *n* Übersetzer(in *f*) *m*.

transliterate [trænz'lɪtəreɪt] *vt* transliterieren.

transliteration [ˌtrænzlɪtəˈreɪʃən] *n* Transliteration *f*.

translucence [trænz'luːsns], **translucency** [trænz'luːsnsɪ] *n* Lichtdurchlässigkeit, Durchsichtigkeit *f*.

translucent [trænz'luːsnt], **translucid** [trænz'luːsɪd] *adj* *glass etc* lichtdurchlässig; *skin* durchsichtig. **~ glass** Milchglas *nt*; **~ prose of ~ clarity** eine Prosa von brillanter Klarheit.

transmigrate [ˌtrænzmaɪˈɡreɪt] *vi* (*Rel*) wiedergeboren werden.

transmigration [ˌtrænzmaɪˈɡreɪʃən] *n* (*Rel*) (Seelen)wanderung, Transmigration (*spec*) *f*. **the ~ of souls** die Seelenwanderung; **the ~ of a human soul into an animal body** die Wiedergeburt einer menschlichen Seele in einem Tierleib.

transmissible [trænz'mɪsəbl] *adj* übertragbar.

transmission [trænz'mɪʃən] *n* **(a)** (*transmitting*) Übertragung *f*; (*through heredity*) Vererbung *f*; (*of news*) Übermittlung *f*; (*of heat*) Leitung *f*; (*programme also*) Sendung *f*. **(b)** (*Aut*) Getriebe *nt*. **~ shaft** Kardanwelle *f*.

transmit [trænz'mɪt] **1** *vt* (*convey*) *message* übermitteln; *sound waves* übertragen; *information, knowledge* weiter- *or* übermitteln; *illness* übertragen; (*by heredity*) vererben; *heat etc* leiten; *radio/TV programme* übertragen, senden. **2** *vi* senden, Programme ausstrahlen.

transmitter [trænz'mɪtəʳ] *n* (*Tech*) Sender *m*; (*in telephone*) Mikrophon *nt*.

transmitting [trænz'mɪtɪŋ]: **~ set** *n* Sender *m*; **~ station** *n* (*of broadcasting company*) Sendestation *f*; (*general also*) Sendestelle *f*.

transmogrification [ˌtrænzmɒɡrɪfɪˈkeɪʃən] *n* (*hum*) wunderbare Wandlung (*hum*).

transmogrify [trænz'mɒɡrɪfaɪ] *vt* (*hum*) auf wunderbare Weise verwandeln *or* umwandeln (*hum*).

transmutable [trænz'mjuːtəbl] *adj* verwandelbar.

transmutation [ˌtrænzmjuːˈteɪʃən] *n* Verwandlung, Umwandlung *f*; (*Biol*) Umbildung, Transmutation *f*.

transmute [trænz'mjuːt] *vt* umwandeln, verwandeln (*into* in +*acc*); *metal* umwandeln (*into* in +*acc*).

transoceanic [ˌtrænzəʊfiːˈænɪk] *adj* Übersee-; *countries* transozeanisch; *migration* über den Ozean.

transom ['trænsəm] *n* (*~ window*) Oberlicht *nt*; (*cross-piece*) Querbalken *m*.

transpacific [ˌtrænzpəˈsɪfɪk] *adj* über den Pazifik; *countries* jenseits des Pazifik.

transparency [træns'pærənsɪ] *n* **(a)** Transparenz, Durchsichtigkeit *f*. **(b)** (*of lies, excuses etc*) Durchschaubarkeit *f*. **(c)** (*Phot*) Dia(positiv) *nt*. **colour ~** Farbdia *nt*.

transparent [træns'pærənt] *adj* **(a)** durchsichtig, lichtdurchlässig, transparent; *blouse* durchsichtig.

(b) (*fig: obvious*) *lie, intentions* durchschaubar, durchsichtig; *personality* durchschaubar; *guilt, meaning* klar, eindeutig, offensichtlich. **it became ~ that ...** es wurde offensichtlich, daß ...; **you're so ~** du bist so leicht zu durchschauen.

transparently [træns'pærəntlɪ] *adv* *lie* durchschaubar, offensichtlich, offenkundig. **it was ~ obvious that ...** es war so offensichtlich *or* klar zu erkennen, daß ...

transpiration [ˌtrænspɪˈreɪʃən] *n* (*Anat*) Schweißabsonderung, Transpiration *f*; (*Bot*) Transpiration, Ausdunstung *f*.

transpire [træn'spaɪəʳ] **1** *vi* **(a)** (*become known*) bekannt werden; (*slowly*) durchsickern, ruchbar werden (*geh*).

(b) (*happen*) passieren (*inf*). **new developments had ~d** es hatten sich neue Entwicklungen ergeben *or* angebahnt.

(c) (*Anat*) schwitzen, transpirieren (*geh*); (*Bot*) Feuchtigkeit abgeben *or* verdunsten, transpirieren (*spec*).

2 *vt* (*Bot*) moisture verdunsten, abgeben.

transplant [træns'plɑːnt] 1 *vt* (a) (*Hort*) umpflanzen, umsetzen, verpflanzen.

(b) (*Med*) verpflanzen, transplantieren (*spec*).

(c) (*fig*) people verpflanzen. his wealth ~ed him into a new world sein Reichtum versetzte ihn in eine neue Welt.

2 ['trɑːnsplɑːnt] *n* (*operation*) Verpflanzung, Transplantation *f*; (*organ*) Transplantat *nt*, transplantiertes *or* verpflanztes Organ. to have a ~ sich einer Organverpflanzung unterziehen.

transplantation [ˌtrænsplɑːn'teɪʃən] *n* (*Hort*) Umpflanzung, Verpflanzung *f*; (*Med*) Transplantation, Verpflanzung *f*.

transpolar [træns'pəʊləʳ] *adj* über den (Nord-/Süd)pol *or* das Polargebiet, Transpolar-. the ~ route die Polroute.

transport ['trænspɔːt] 1 *n* (a) (*of goods*) Transport *m*, Beförderung *f*; (*of troops*) Transport *m*. road ~ Straßentransport *m*; rail ~ Beförderung *or* Transport per Bahn, (Eisen)bahntransport *m*; Ministry of T~ Verkehrsministerium *nt*.

(b) (*vehicle*) have you got your own ~? hast du einen fahrbaren Untersatz? (*inf*), bist du motorisiert?; public ~ öffentliche Verkehrsmittel *pl*; what are we going to do about ~? wie lösen wir die Transportfrage?; I am without (means of) ~ ich bin nicht motorisiert, ich habe keinen fahrbaren Untersatz (*inf*); ~ will be provided für An- und Abfahrt wird gesorgt.

(c) (*Mil*) (*ship*) (Truppen)transporter *m*; (*plane*) Transportflugzeug *nt*.

(d) (*US: shipment*) (Schiffs)fracht, Ladung *f*.

(e) (*liter*) ~ of delight/joy freudige Entzückung *or* (*Rel*) Entrückung (*liter*); it sent her into ~s of delight es erfüllte sie mit freudigem Entzücken (*liter*).

2 [træn'spɔːt] *vt* (a) goods befördern, transportieren; people befördern.

(b) (*Hist*) convict deportieren.

(c) (*liter*) to be ~ed with joy freudig entzückt sein (*liter*).

transportable [træn'spɔːtəbl] *adj* transportabel, transportierbar.

transportation [ˌtrænspɔː'teɪʃən] *n* (a) Beförderung *f*, Transport *m*; (*means*) Beförderungsmittel *nt*; (*public*) Verkehrsmittel *nt*; (*cost*) Transport- *or* Beförderungskosten *pl*. Department of T~ (*US*) Verkehrsministerium *nt*. (b) (*Hist: of criminal*) Deportation *f*.

transport café *n* (*Brit*) Fernfahrerlokal *nt*.

transporter [træn'spɔːtəʳ] *n* (*car* ~) Transporter *m*; (~ *crane*) Verladebrücke *f*; (*in factory*) Transportband *nt*.

transport: ~ line *n* (*in factory*) Transportband *nt*; ~ plane *n* Transportflugzeug *nt*; ~ ship *n* (Truppen)transporter *m*; ~ system *n* Verkehrswesen *nt*.

transpose [træns'pəʊz] *vt* vertauschen, umstellen; (*Mus*) transponieren.

transposition [ˌtrænspə'zɪʃən] *n* Umstellung, Vertauschung *f*; (*Mus*) Transponierung *f*.

transsexual [træns'seksjʊəl] *n* Transsexuelle(r) *mf*.

transship [træns'ʃɪp] *vt see* tranship.

transshipment [træns'ʃɪpmənt] *n see* transhipment.

transubstantiate [ˌtrænsəb'stænʃɪeɪt] *vt* (*Rel*) verwandeln.

transubstantiation ['trænsəbˌstænʃɪ'eɪʃən] *n* (*Rel*) Wandlung, Transsubstantiation (*spec*) *f*.

transverse ['trænzvɜːs] *adj* beam, bar, section Quer-; muscles transversal; position horizontal; engine querstehend.

transversely [trænz'vɜːslɪ] *adv* quer; divided diagonal.

transvestism [trænz'vestɪzəm] *n* Transve(s)tismus *m*.

transvestite [trænz'vestaɪt] *n* Transvestit *m*.

trap [træp] 1 *n* (a) (*for animal, fig*) Falle *f*. to set *or* lay a ~ for an animal eine Falle für ein Tier (auf)stellen; to set a ~ for sb (*fig*) jdm eine Falle stellen; be careful of this question, there is a ~ in it paß bei dieser Frage auf, da ist ein Haken dabei; to be caught in a ~ in der Falle sitzen; the lawyer had caught him in a ~ er war dem Rechtsanwalt in die Falle gegangen; to fall into a ~ in die Falle gehen; the soldiers fell straight into the ~ die Soldaten liefen geradewegs in die Falle.

(b) (*in greyhound racing*) Box *f*; (*shooting*) Wurftaubenanlage, Wurfmaschine *f*.

(c) (*in drainpipe*) Siphon, Geruchsverschluß *m*.

(d) (*vehicle*) zweirädriger Pferdewagen.

(e) (*also* ~door) Falltür *f*; (*Theat*) Versenkung *f*.

(f) (*sl: mouth*) Klappe (*inf*), Fresse (*sl*), Schnauze (*sl*) *f*. shut your ~! (halt die) Klappe! (*inf*), halt die Fresse (*sl*) *or* Schnauze (*sl*)!; keep your ~ shut about this darüber hältst du aber die Klappe (*inf*), halt ja die Schnauze! (*sl*).

2 *vt* (a) *animal* (mit einer Falle) fangen.

(b) (*fig*) person in die Falle locken. he realized he was ~ped er merkte, daß er in der Falle saß; to ~ sb into saying sth jdn dazu bringen, etw zu sagen; I was ~ped into saying I would organize the party ich hatte mich darauf eingelassen, die Party zu organisieren; she ~ped him into marriage sie hat ihn geködert (*inf*), sie hat ihn ins Netz gelockt.

(c) (*block off, leave no way of escape*) in die Enge treiben. the miners are ~ped die Bergleute sind eingeschlossen; the ship was ~ped in the harbour by the storm das Schiff saß wegen des Sturms im Hafen fest; to be ~ped in the snow im Schnee festsitzen; he feels ~ped in suburbia/his marriage er empfindet die Vorstadt/seine Ehe als Gefängnis; the soldiers found themselves ~ped at the end of the gully am Ende des Hohlweges stellten die Soldaten fest, daß sie in der Falle saßen; I get this ~ped feeling ich fühle mich wie gefangen *or* im Gefängnis *or* eingeschlossen; my arm was ~ped behind my back mein Arm war hinter meinem Rücken eingeklemmt.

(d) (*catch*) (*Sport*) *ball* stoppen. to ~ one's finger/one's foot in the door sich (*dat*) den Finger/Fuß in der Tür einklemmen.

(e) gas, liquid stauen. pools of water lay ~ped among the rocks as the tide receded als die Flut zurückging, blieben Wasserpfützen zwischen den Felsen zurück.

3 *vi* (*trapper*) Trapper sein.

trapdoor ['træp'dɔːʳ] *n* Falltür *f*; (*Theat*) Versenkung *f*.

trapeze [trə'piːz] *n* (*in circus*) Trapez *nt*. ~ artist Trapezkünstler(in *f*) *m*.

trapezium [trə'piːzɪəm] *n* (*Brit*) Trapez *nt*; (*US*) Trapezoid *nt*.

trapezoid ['træpɪzɔɪd] *n* (*Brit*) Trapezoid *nt*; (*US*) Trapez *nt*.

trapper ['træpəʳ] *n* Fallensteller, Trapper *m*.

trappings ['træpɪŋz] *npl* (a) (*of admiral, chieftain etc*) Rangabzeichen *pl*; (*of horse*) Schmuck *m*.

(b) (*fig*) äußere Aufmachung, äußeres Drum und Dran (*inf*). ~ of office Amtsinsignien *pl*; shorn of all its ~ aller Ausschmückungen entkleidet; he surrounded himself with all the ~ of power er umgab sich mit allen Insignien der Macht.

Trappist ['træpɪst] *n* (*also* ~ monk) Trappist *m*.

trapse *vi see* traipse.

trap-shooting ['træpˌʃuːtɪŋ] *n* Wurftaubenschießen *nt*.

trash [træʃ] *n* (a) (*US: refuse*) Abfall *m*.

(b) (*goods*) Schund, Ramsch *m*, billiges Zeug; (*book, play etc*) Schund *m*; (*pop group etc*) Mist *m* (*inf*). don't talk ~ red kein Blech (*sl*) *or* nicht so einen Quatsch (*inf*).

(c) (*pej inf: people*) Gesindel, Pack *nt*. ~ like her Gesindel wie sie; she/he is ~ sie/er taugt nichts; *see* white ~.

trash-can ['træʃkæn] *n* (*US*) Abfalleimer *m*.

trashy ['træʃɪ] *adj* (+er) goods minderwertig, wertlos; novel, play Schund-, minderwertig. clothes for teenagers are often ~ Teenagerkleidung ist oft Schund *or* billiges Zeug.

trauma ['trɔːmə] *n* (*Psych*) Trauma *nt*, seelischer Schock.

traumatic [trɔː'mætɪk] *adj* traumatisch.

travail ['træveɪl] 1 *n* (a) usu *pl* (toils) Mühen *pl*. after all the ~s of Watergate nach den schweren Belastungen durch die Watergate-Affäre.

(b) (*old, liter: exhausting labour*) Plackerei, Mühsal *f*.

(c) (*old: childbirth*) (Geburts)wehen *pl*. a woman in ~ eine Frau, die in den Wehen liegt.

2 *vi* (a) (*old, liter: toil*) sich plagen (*old*). he ~ed in the depths of despair er litt in tiefer Verzweiflung.

(b) (*old: in childbirth*) in den Wehen liegen, Wehen haben.

travel ['trævl] 1 *vi* (a) (*make a journey*) reisen. they have ~led a lot sie sind viel gereist, sie haben viele Reisen gemacht; he ~s to work by car er fährt mit dem Auto zur Arbeit; she is ~ling to London tomorrow sie fährt morgen nach London; the President is ~ling to Paris tomorrow der Präsident reist morgen nach Paris; they have ~led a long way sie haben eine weite Reise *or* lange Fahrt hinter sich; (*fig*) sie haben es weit gebracht (im Leben); they ~led for 300 kms sie fuhren 300 km; to ~ round the world eine Reise um die Welt machen; to ~ around a country ein Land durchreisen *or* bereisen.

(b) (*go, move*) sich bewegen; (*sound, light*) sich fortpflanzen. light ~s at ... die Lichtgeschwindigkeit beträgt ...; we were ~ling at 80 kph wir fuhren 80 km/h; the parts ~ along the conveyor belt die Teile werden vom Förderband weiterbefördert; the electricity ~s along the wire der Strom fließt durch den Draht; you were ~ling too fast Sie sind zu schnell gefahren; he was certainly ~ling! (*inf*) er hatte vielleicht einen Zahn drauf! (*sl*); wow! that's ~ling! (*inf*) Mann, das ist aber schnell!

(c) (*Comm*) Vertreter sein. he ~s for a Berlin insurance firm er reist für eine *or* ist Vertreter einer Berliner Versicherungsgesellschaft; he ~s in ladies' underwear er reist in Damenunterwäsche.

(d) (*wine etc*) some wines do not ~ well manche Weine vertragen den Transport nicht.

(e) (*pass*) his eye ~led over the scene seine Augen wanderten über die Szene.

(f) (*Tech*) sich hin- und herbewegen. as the piston ~s from A to B während sich der Kolben von A nach B bewegt; it doesn't ~ freely es bewegt sich schwer; the sliding doors don't ~ freely diese Schiebetüren gleiten nicht gut; the current ~s along this wire der Strom läuft durch diesen Draht.

(g) (*Basketball*) einen Schrittfehler machen.

2 *vt* area bereisen; distance zurücklegen, fahren; route fahren.

3 *n* (a) no *pl* Reisen *nt*. to be fond of ~ gerne reisen; ~ was difficult in the 18th century im 18. Jahrhundert war das Reisen beschwerlich.

(b) ~s *pl* (*in country*) Reisen *pl*; (*hum: in town, building*) Ausflüge, Gänge *pl*; if you meet him on your ~s wenn Sie ihm auf einer Ihrer Reisen begegnen; he's off on his ~s again tomorrow er verreist morgen wieder.

(c) (*Tech*) Weg *m*; (*of instrument's needle etc*) Ausschlag *m*; (*of piston*) Hub *m*.

travel: ~ agency *n* Reisebüro *nt*; ~ agent *n* Reisebürokaufmann *m*; (*of package tours*) Reiseveranstalter *m*; ~ agent's *n* Reisebüro *nt*; ~ brochure *n* Reiseprospekt *m*; ~ bureau *n* Reisebüro *nt*.

travelled, (*US*) **traveled** ['trævld] *adj* well-~ person weitgereist attr, weit gereist pred; route vielbefahren attr, viel befahren pred; widely ~ weitgereist attr, weit gereist pred; a much-~ road eine stark befahrene *or* vielbefahrene Straße.

traveller, (*US*) **traveler** ['trævləʳ] *n* (a) Reisende(r) *mf*. I am a very poor *or* bad ~ ich vertrage das Reisen nicht. (b) (*also* commercial ~) Vertreter, (Handels)reisende(r) *m*. a ~ in toys ein (Handels)vertreter für Spielsachen, ein Reisender in Spielsachen.

traveller's cheque, (*US*) **traveler's check** *n* Reisescheck, Travellerscheck *m*.

travelling, (*US*) **traveling** ['trævlɪŋ] *n* Reisen *nt*. I hate ~ ich reise sehr ungern, ich hasse das Reisen.

travelling: ~ bag *n* Reisetasche *f*; ~ circus *n* Wanderzirkus *m*; ~ clock *n* Reisewecker *m*; ~ crane *n* Lauf- *or* Rollkran *m*;

~ **exhibition** n Wanderausstellung f; ~ **expenses** npl Reisekosten pl; (on business) Reisespesen pl; ~ **rug** n Reisedecke f; ~ **salesman** n Vertreter, Handelsreisende(r) m; ~ **scholarship** n Auslandsstipendium nt; ~ **theatre** n Wandertheater, Tourneetheater nt.

travel: ~ **literature** n Reisebeschreibung f; ~ **novel** n Reisebeschreibung f.

travelogue, (US) **travelog** ['trævəlɒg] n (film) filmischer Reisebericht; (slides) Lichtbildervortrag m (über eine Reise); (lecture) Reisebericht m.

travel: ~**-sick** adj reisekrank; ~**-sickness** n Reisekrankheit f; ~**-sickness pill** n Pille f gegen Reisekrankheit; ~**-weary,** ~**-worn** adj von der Reise ermüdet or erschöpft.

traverse ['trævɜːs] 1 vt (a) (cross) land durchqueren; (river also) durchfließen; (bridge, person) water überqueren. **the searchlight** ~d **the sky** from east to west der Suchscheinwerfer leuchtete den Himmel von Osten nach Westen ab.

(b) (cross and recross) **the searchlight** ~d **the sky** der Suchscheinwerfer leuchtete den Himmel ab.

(c) (extend over) period überdauern.

(d) (Mountaineering) ice, slope queren, traversieren.

2 vi (Mountaineering, Ski) sich quer zum Hang bewegen, (den Hang/die Wand etc) traversieren.

3 n (on mountain) (movement) Queren, Traversieren nt; (place) Quergang m; (Archit) Querbalken m, Traverse f.

travesty ['trævɪstɪ] 1 n (Liter) Travestie f. a ~ of justice ein Hohn m auf die Gerechtigkeit; **the elections were a** ~ die Wahlen waren ein Hohn m or eine Farce; **the ageing actress was only a** ~ **of her former self** die alternde Schauspielerin war nur noch eine Karikatur or ein Zerrbild nt ihrer selbst.

2 vt ins Lächerliche ziehen, travestieren (Liter).

trawl [trɔːl] 1 n (also ~ net) Schleppnetz, Trawl nt; (US: ~ line) Grundleine f.

2 vi mit dem Schleppnetz fischen; (US) mit einer Grundleine fischen.

3 vt fish mit dem Schleppnetz fangen. **they** ~ed **the sea-bottom** sie fischten mit Schleppnetzen auf dem Meeresboden; **they** ~ed **the net along the sea-bottom** sie schleppten das Netz über den Meeresboden.

trawler ['trɔːləʳ] n (boat) Fischdampfer, Trawler m.

trawlerman ['trɔːləmən] n, pl **-men** [-mən] Trawlerfischer m.

trawling ['trɔːlɪŋ] n Dampfer- or Trawlfischerei f.

tray [treɪ] n Tablett nt; (tea-~) Teebrett, Servierbrett nt; (of cakes) (small) Platte f; (big) Brett nt; (for display) Auslagekästchen nt; (baking ~) (Back)blech nt; (for pencils etc) (Feder)schale f; (for papers, mail) Ablage(korb m) f; (of street vendor etc) Bauchladen m; (drawer) (Schub)fach nt; (in suitcase, trunk) Einsatz m; (Phot, ice ~) Schale f; (for ash) Kasten m. ~ **cloth** Deckchen nt für ein Tablett.

treacherous ['tretʃərəs] adj (a) person, action verräterisch.

(b) (unreliable) trügerisch, irreführend; memory trügerisch. **my memory is rather** ~ **now** mein Gedächtnis läßt mich neuerdings ziemlich im Stich. (c) (dangerous) tückisch; corner also gefährlich; ice trügerisch.

treacherously ['tretʃərəslɪ] adv see adj (a) verräterisch, in verräterischer Weise.

(b) trügerisch, irreführend. **at times he can be** ~ **convincing** er wirkt manchmal gefährlich überzeugend.

(c) sharp corner, icy or wet road tückisch. **rocks hidden** ~ **beneath the surface** Felsen, die gefährlich dicht unter der Wasseroberfläche liegen; **in** ~ **bad conditions** unter gefährlich schlechten Bedingungen.

treacherousness ['tretʃərəsnɪs] n see adj (a) **the** ~ **of these generals** diese verräterischen Generäle. (b) (of memory etc) Unzuverlässigkeit f. (c) Tücke, Gefährlichkeit f. **because of the** ~ **of the snow** wegen der trügerischen Schneeverhältnisse.

treachery ['tretʃərɪ] n Verrat m; (of weather) Tücke f. **an act of** ~ Verrat, eine verräterische Tat.

treacle ['triːkl] n (Brit) Sirup m. **a voice like** ~ eine zucker- or honigsüße Stimme; ~ **pudding** im Dampfbad gekochter, mit Sirup angereicherter Teig.

treacly ['triːklɪ] adj (+er) (lit) sirupartig; (fig) voice, smile honig- or zuckersüß; song, sentiment schmalzig.

tread [tred] (vb: pret **trod,** ptp **trodden**) 1 n (a) (act) over the years the ~ of feet has worn the steps away über die Jahre sind die Stufen völlig ausgetreten worden.

(b) (gait, noise) Schritt, Tritt m. **to walk with a heavy/springy** ~ mit schweren/hüpfenden Schritten gehen, einen schweren/hüpfenden Gang haben; **I could hear his** ~ **on the stairs** ich konnte seine Schritte auf der Treppe hören.

(c) (of stair) Stufe f.

(d) (of shoe, tyre) Profil nt, Lauffläche f.

2 vi (a) (walk) gehen.

(b) (bring foot down) treten (on auf +acc). **mind you don't** ~ **on it!** passen Sie auf, daß Sie nicht darauftreten!; **will you** ~ **on that cigarette-end?** könnten Sie den Zigarettenstummel austreten?; **he trod on my foot** er trat mir auf den Fuß; **to** ~ **on sb's heels** (lit) jdm auf die Fersen treten; (fig) an jds Fersen hängen; **to** ~ **softly or lightly** (lit) leise or leicht auftreten; **to** ~ **carefully** (lit) vorsichtig gehen; (fig) vorsichtig vorgehen; **to** ~ **in sb's footsteps** (fig) in jds Fuß(s)tapfen treten; see air.

3 vt path (make) treten; (follow) gehen. **he's** ~**ing the same path as his father** (fig) er hat den gleichen Weg wie sein Vater eingeschlagen; **he's** ~**ing a risky path there** (fig) da hat er aber einen gefährlichen Weg eingeschlagen; **it got trodden underfoot** es wurde zertreten; **to** ~ **grapes** Trauben stampfen; **he trod his cigarette into the sand** er trat seine Zigarette im Sand aus; **to** ~ **water** Wasser treten; **don't** ~ **that earth into the carpet** treten Sie die Erde nicht in den Teppich.

♦**tread down** vt sep festtreten.

♦**tread in** vt sep festtreten.

♦**tread out** vt sep fire, cigarette austreten.

treadle ['tredl] 1 n (of sewing machine) Tretkurbel f, Pedal nt; (of lathe also) Fußhebel m. 2 vi treten.

treadmill ['tredmɪl] n (lit) Tretwerk nt; (fig) Tretmühle f.

treas abbr of **treasurer.**

treason ['triːzn] n Verrat m (to an +dat). **an act of** ~ Verrat m.

treasonable ['triːzənəbl], **treasonous** ['triːzənəs] adj verräterisch.

treasure ['treʒəʳ] 1 n (lit) Schatz m; (fig also) Kostbarkeit f; (dear person) Schatz m. **many** ~s **of modern art** viele moderne Kunstschätze; **she's a real** ~ sie ist eine Perle or ein Juwel nt.

2 vt (hoch)schätzen, zu schätzen wissen. **he really** ~s **his books** diese Bücher bedeuten ihm sehr viel; **I shall always** ~ **this memory** ich werde das immer in lieber Erinnerung behalten.

♦**treasure up** vt sep horten, ansammeln, anhäufen; (in memory) aufbewahren. **he** ~d ~ **the money for future use** er legte das Geld für die Zukunft zurück.

treasure: ~ **house** n (lit) Schatzkammer f; **a** ~ **house of knowledge** eine Fundgrube des Wissens; ~ **hunt** n Schatzsuche f.

treasurer ['treʒərəʳ] n (of club) Kassenwart, Kassenverwalter(in f) m; (city ~) Stadtkämmerer m; (of business) Leiter m der Finanzabteilung; (of king) Schatzmeister m.

treasure trove n Schatzfund m; (place where treasures are found) Schatzgrube, Fundgrube f.

treasury ['treʒərɪ] n (a) (Pol) T~, (US also) T~ **Department** Finanzministerium nt; **First Lord of the T**~ (Brit) der Premierminister. (b) (of society) Kasse f. (c) (anthology) Schatzkästlein nt, Schatzgrube f.

Treasury: ~ **bench** n (Brit) Regierungsbank f (im Parlament); ~ **bill** n kurzfristiger Schatzwechsel m; ~ **note** n (US) Schatzschein m or -anweisung f or -wechsel m.

treat [triːt] 1 vt (a) (behave towards) person, animal behandeln; (handle) books behandeln, umgehen mit.

(b) (consider) betrachten (as als). **you should** ~ **your work more seriously** Sie sollten Ihre Arbeit ernster nehmen.

(c) (Med) behandeln. **which doctor is** ~**ing you?** bei welchem Arzt sind Sie in Behandlung?, welcher Arzt behandelt Sie?; **the doctor is** ~**ing him for nervous exhaustion** er ist wegen Nervenüberlastung in Behandlung.

(d) (process) behandeln (with mit); leather bearbeiten, behandeln (with mit); sewage klären; wastepaper verarbeiten.

(e) subject behandeln; (scientifically, philosophically also) abhandeln.

(f) (pay for, give) einladen. **to** ~ **sb to sth** jdn zu etw einladen, jdm etw spendieren; **to drink, ice-cream also** jdm etw ausgeben; **I'm** ~**ing you** ich lade Sie ein; **to** ~ **oneself to sth** sich (dat) etw gönnen; **he** ~**ed his wife to a weekend in Paris** er spendierte seiner Frau ein Wochenende in Paris; **he** ~**ed us to a preview of the exhibition** er machte uns (dat) eine Freude und zeigte uns die Ausstellung vorher; **for once she** ~**ed us to the sight of her knees** endlich einmal gönnte sie uns den Anblick ihrer Knie; **he** ~**ed us to a display of his temper** (iro) er gab uns eine Kostprobe seiner Launenhaftigkeit.

2 vi (deal) **to** ~ **with sb** for sth mit jdm über etw (acc) Verhandlungen führen, mit jdm um or über etw (acc) verhandeln; **the general decided to** ~ **for peace** der General entschloß sich, Friedensverhandlungen zu führen.

3 n (a) besondere Freude. **well, folks, tomorrow we're going on our Christmas** ~ also Leute, morgen machen wir unsere Weihnachtsfeier (inf); **children's** ~ Kinderfest nt, Kindernachmittag m; **I thought I'd give myself a** ~ ich dachte, ich gönne mir mal etwas; **I'm taking them to the circus as or for a** ~ ich mache ihnen eine Freude und lade sie in den Zirkus ein or nehme sie in den Zirkus mit; **it's my** ~ das geht auf meine Kosten or Rechnung, ich lade Sie ein; **I want to give them a** ~ ich möchte ihnen eine besondere Freude machen, ich möchte ihnen etwas Gutes tun; **our uncle's** ~ **was to give us tickets for the cinema** unser Onkel hat uns Kinokarten spendiert; **that trip was a great** ~ **for her** dieser Ausflug war etwas ganz Besonderes für sie or hat ihr riesige Freude gemacht; **that was a** ~! das war ein Genuß!; **what a** ~ **to have a quiet afternoon** das ist ein Genuß or tut gut, mal einen ruhigen Nachmittag zu verbringen; **it's a** ~ **in store** das ist etwas, worauf wir uns noch freuen können; **this time you can carry the bags as a** ~! (iro) dieses Mal darfst du ausnahmsweise die Taschen tragen; **it's a (real)** ~ **to see you again** was für eine Freude, Sie mal wiederzusehen!

(b) (inf) **it's coming on a** ~ es macht sich prima (inf).

♦**treat of** vi +prep obj (form) handeln von, behandeln.

treatise ['triːtɪz] n Abhandlung f (on über +acc).

treatment ['triːtmənt] n (a) (of person, animal) Behandlung f; (of books etc also) Umgang m (of mit). **their** ~ **of foreigners** ihre Art, Ausländer zu behandeln; **to give sb the** ~ (inf: violently, sexually) es jdm ordentlich besorgen (inf); **he went for a two-day interview, they really gave him the** ~ (inf) bei seinem zweitägigen Einstellungsgespräch wurde er ganz schön in die Mangel genommen (inf); **she went to the beauty parlour and they really gave her the** ~ (inf) sie ging in den Schönheitssalon und wurde dort nach allen Regeln der Kunst bearbeitet (inf); **when the foreign delegates visited the factory, they were given the full** ~ (inf) als die ausländischen Delegierten die Firma besichtigten, wurde ein enormes Tamtam gemacht (inf) or eine große Schau abgezogen (sl); **John was really giving her the** ~ **at that party!** (inf) John hat sich bei der Party ganz schön an sie rangemacht (inf); (giving her a bad time) John hat sie bei der Party ganz schön mies behandelt (inf).

(b) (Med) Behandlung f. **there are many** ~s **for rheumatism** es gibt viele Behandlungsarten or Heilverfahren für Rheumatismus; **to be having** ~ **for sth** wegen etw in Behandlung sein.

(c) (processing) Behandlung f; (of leather also) Bearbeitung f; (of sewage) Klärung f; (of wastepaper) Verarbeitung f.
(d) (of subject) Behandlung, Bearbeitung f.

treaty ['tri:tɪ] n Vertrag m. ~ **port** Vertragshafen m.

treble[1] ['trebl] **1** adj dreifach. **his mortgage repayments are in** ~ **figures** seine Hypothekenraten erreichen dreistellige Summen; ~ **chance (pools)** eine Variante des Fußballtotos mit dreifacher Gewinnchance.
2 adv **they had** ~ **our numbers** sie waren dreimal so viele wie wir; **clothes are** ~ **the price** Kleider kosten dreimal soviel.
3 vt verdreifachen.
4 vi sich verdreifachen.
5 n (on dartboard etc) Dreifache(s) nt.

treble[2] **1** n (Mus) (boy's voice) Knabensopran m or -stimme f; (highest part) Oberstimme f; (of piano) Diskant m; (child's speaking voice) Diskantstimme f.
2 adj **voice** Knabensopran-; **part** Oberstimmen-; (of piano, children speaking) Diskant-. ~ **clef** Violinschlüssel m; ~ **recorder** Altflöte f; ~ **instrument** Instrument nt für die oberen Stimmlagen.

trebly ['treblɪ] adv dreifach. **the child was** ~ **dear to him** er liebte das Kind dreimal mehr.

tree [tri:] **1** n **(a)** Baum m. **an oak/a cherry** ~ eine Eiche/ein Kirschbaum m; **rose** ~ Rosenstämmchen nt; ~ **of knowledge** ~ **of life** Baum des Lebens; **money doesn't/good teachers don't grow on** ~s das Geld fällt/gute Lehrer fallen nicht vom Himmel; **to be up a** ~ (inf) in der Patsche or Tinte or Klemme sitzen (inf); **he's at the top of the** ~ (fig inf) er ist ganz oben (an der Spitze).
(b) (family ~) Stammbaum m.
(c) (shoe-~) Spanner, Leisten m.
(d) (Rel: cross) Kreuz nt.
2 vt auf einen Baum jagen or treiben.

tree in cpds Baum-; ~-**covered** adj baumbestanden; ~ **fern** n Baumfarn m; ~ **frog** n Laub- or Baumfrosch m; ~ **house** n Baumhaus nt; ~-**less** adj baumlos; ~-**lined** adj baumbestanden, von Bäumen gesäumt (geh); ~ **surgeon** n Baumchirurg m; ~**top** n Baumkrone f, Wipfel m; ~ **trunk** n Baumstamm m.

trefoil ['trefɔɪl] n (Bot) Klee m; (symbol of Girl Guide movement) Kleeblatt nt; (Archit) Dreipaß m.

trek [trek] **1** vi trecken; (inf) latschen (inf). **they** ~**ked across the desert** sie zogen durch die Wüste; **I had to** ~ **up to the top floor** ich mußte bis ins oberste Stockwerk latschen (inf). **2** n Treck, Zug m; (inf) anstrengender Weg or Marsch.

trellis ['trelɪs] **1** n Gitter nt; (for plants also) Spalier nt. ~-**work** Gitterwerk nt. **2** vt (furnish with ~) mit einem Gitter or Spalier versehen; **vines etc** an Spalier ziehen.

tremble ['trembl] **1** vi (person, hand etc) zittern (with vor); (voice also) beben (with vor); (ground, building) beben, zittern. **I** ~ **to think what** or **at the thought of what might have happened** mir wird angst or ich zittere, wenn ich daran denke, was hätte geschehen können; **to** ~ **for sb's safety/the future** um jds Sicherheit/die Zukunft zittern or bangen.
2 n Zittern, Beben nt. **to be all of a** ~ (inf) am ganzen Körper zittern, das große Zittern haben (inf).

trembling ['tremblɪŋ] **1** adj hands zitternd; voice also bebend.
2 n see vi Zittern nt; Beben nt; see fear 1 (a).

tremendous [trɪ'mendəs] adj **(a)** gewaltig, enorm; difference also riesengroß; size, number, crowd also riesig; storm, explosion also ungeheuer stark; success Riesen-, enorm, unglaublich. **he's a** ~ **eater** er ißt unglaublich viel.
(b) (very good) klasse, prima, toll (all inf). **we had a** ~ **time** wir haben uns prima or ganz toll amüsiert; **he's a** ~ **person** er ist ein toller Mensch, er ist klasse or prima.

tremendously [trɪ'mendəslɪ] adv sehr; fat, tall, long etc also enorm; relieved, upset, grateful, dangerous also ungeheuer, äußerst; pretty also äußerst; intelligent, difficult also enorm, äußerst. **it was** ~ **good** es war einfach prima or umwerfend gut or sagenhaft (all inf); **they enjoyed themselves** ~ sie haben sich prächtig or prima or ausgezeichnet amüsiert (all inf).

tremolo ['tremələʊ] n (Mus) Tremolo nt.

tremor ['tremə[r]] n Zittern, Beben nt; (Med) Tremor m; (of emotion) Zittern, Zucken nt; (earth ~) Beben nt, Erschütterung f. **a** ~ **of fear** ein Schaudern nt; **without a** ~ völlig ruhig, unbewegt.

tremulous ['tremjʊləs] adj (trembling) voice zitternd, bebend; hand zitternd; (timid) smile, person zaghaft, schüchtern.

tremulously ['tremjʊləslɪ] adv zaghaft, ängstlich.

trench [trentʃ] **1** n Graben m; (Mil) Schützengraben m. **in the** ~**es** (Mil) im Schützengraben; ~ **warfare** Stellungskrieg, Grabenkrieg m. **2** vt Gräben ziehen in (+dat); (Mil) Schützengräben ausheben in (+dat).

trenchancy ['trentʃənsɪ] n see adj Treffsicherheit f; Prägnanz f; Bissigkeit f; Pointiertheit f; Schärfe f.

trenchant ['trentʃənt] adj language treffsicher; style prägnant; satire beißend; speech pointiert; wit, criticism scharf.

trenchantly ['trentʃəntlɪ] adv see adj. **he made his point** ~ er argumentierte sicher; **a** ~ **witty remark** eine scharfe, geistreiche Bemerkung.

trench coat n Trenchcoat, Regenmantel m.

trencher ['trentʃə[r]] n (old: platter) Tranchierbrett nt.

trencherman ['trentʃəmən] n, pl -men [-mən] good/poor ~ guter/schlechter Esser.

trend [trend] **1** n **(a)** (tendency) Tendenz, Richtung f, Trend m. **the** ~ **towards violence** der Trend or die Tendenz zur Gewalttätigkeit; **upward** ~ steigende Tendenz, Aufwärtstrend m; **the downward** ~ **in the birth rate** die Rückläufigkeit or der Abwärtstrend der Geburtenrate; **the** ~ **away from materialism** die zunehmende Abkehr vom Materialismus; **to set a** ~ eine neue Richtung setzen, richtungweisend sein.
(b) (fashion) Mode f, Trend m. **that is the** ~/**the latest** ~ **among young people** das ist bei jungen Leuten jetzt Mode/der

letzte Schrei (inf); **to follow a** ~ einem Trend folgen; (fashion) eine Mode mitmachen.
(c) (Geog) Verlauf m.
2 vi verlaufen (towards nach). **the direction in which events are** ~**ing** die Richtung, die die Dinge nehmen; **prices are** ~**ing upwards** die Preise haben eine steigende Tendenz; **his views are** ~**ing towards the anarchistic** seine Auffassungen neigen or tendieren zum Anarchismus.

trendily ['trendɪlɪ] adv modern. **to dress** ~ sich nach der neuesten Mode kleiden.

trendy ['trendɪ] **1** adj (+er) modern, in pred (inf). **to be** ~ als schick gelten, große Mode sein; **a pub where all the** ~ **people go** eine Kneipe, in der sich die Schickeria trifft; **this is a** ~ **pub** diese Kneipe ist zur Zeit in (inf).
2 n (inf) **the trendies** die Schickeria sing; **he looks a real** ~ der macht vielleicht auf modern!

trepan [trɪ'pæn] **1** vt (Med) trepanieren. **2** n Trepan m.

trepidation [ˌtrepɪ'deɪʃən] n Bangigkeit, Beklommenheit, Ängstlichkeit f. **full of** ~ **he knocked on the door** voll ängstlicher Erwartung klopfte er an die Tür; **a look of** ~ ein banger or beunruhigter or ängstlicher Blick; **a feeling of** ~ ein beklommenes Gefühl, ein Gefühl der Bangigkeit or Verzagtheit; **I am writing, not without some** ~, **to tell you** ... nicht ohne ein Gefühl der Beklommenheit teile ich Ihnen mit ...

trespass ['trespəs] **1** vi **(a)** (on property) unbefugt betreten (on sth etw acc). **"no** ~**ing"** „Betreten verboten"; **you're** ~**ing** Sie dürfen sich hier nicht aufhalten.
(b) ~ **to** ~ **(up)on sb's rights/area of responsibility** in jds Rechte/Verantwortungsbereich (acc) eingreifen; **to** ~ **(up)on sb's privacy** jds Privatsphäre verletzen; **to** ~ **(up)on sb's kindness/time** jds Freundlichkeit/Zeit überbeanspruchen.
(c) (Eccl) **as we forgive them that** ~ **against us** wie wir vergeben unseren Schuldigern.
2 n **(a)** (Jur) unbefugtes Betreten.
(b) (Eccl) **forgive us our** ~**es** und vergib uns unsere Schuld.

trespasser ['trespəsə[r]] n Unbefugte(r) mf. **"**~**s will be prosecuted"** „widerrechtliches Betreten wird strafrechtlich verfolgt"; **the farmer found a** ~ **on his land** der Bauer fand einen Eindringling auf seinem Land.

tress [tres] n (liter) Locke f (liter).

trestle ['tresl] n (Auflage)bock m.

trestle: ~ **bridge** n Bockbrücke f; ~ **table** n auf Böcken stehender Tisch; (decorator's) Tapeziertisch m.

trews [tru:z] npl (Scot) enganliegende Hose im Schottenkaro; (inf: trousers) Hose f. **a pair of** ~ eine Hose.

triad ['traɪəd] n Triade, Trias f; (Mus) Dreiklang m; (Chem) dreiwertiges Element.

trial ['traɪəl] n **(a)** (Jur) (Gerichts)verfahren nt, Prozeß m; (actual hearing) (Gerichts)verhandlung f. **to be on** ~ angeklagt sein, unter Anklage stehen; **he goes on** ~ **tomorrow** seine Verhandlung ist morgen; **to be on** ~ **for theft** des Diebstahls angeklagt sein, wegen Diebstahls unter Anklage stehen; **to be on** ~ **for one's life** wegen eines mit Todesstrafe bedrohten Verbrechens angeklagt sein or unter Anklage stehen; **at the** ~ bei or während der Verhandlung; **to bring sb to** ~ jdn vor Gericht stellen, jdm den Prozeß machen; **the case comes up for** ~ **next month** der Fall wird nächsten Monat verhandelt; **please don't feel you are on** ~, **we're just asking a few questions** betrachten Sie sich bitte nicht als Angeklagten, wir wollen Ihnen nur ein paar Fragen stellen.
(b) (test) Versuch m, Probe, Erprobung f. ~**s** (of machine, aeroplane) Test(s pl) m, (Über)prüfung f; (Sport) Qualifikationsspiel nt; **horse** ~**s** Querfeldeinrennen nt; **to give sth a** ~ ausprobieren; **the manager has promised to give me a** ~ **as a clerk** der Betriebsleiter hat versprochen, mir eine Chance als Büroangestellter zu geben; **to take sth on** ~ etw zur Probe or Prüfung or etw probeweise nehmen; **to put sb/sth to the** ~ jdn/etw testen or auf die Probe stellen; **the new clerk is on** ~ der neue Büroangestellte ist auf Probe eingestellt; ~ **of strength** Kraftprobe f; **by** ~ **and error** durch Ausprobieren; **a system of** ~ **and error** ein System der empirischen Lösung.
(c) (hardship) Widrigkeit, Unannehmlichkeit f; (nuisance) Plage f, Problem nt (to für). **he's a** ~ **to his mother** er macht seiner Mutter sehr viel Kummer, er ist ein Problem für seine Mutter; ~**s and tribulations** Aufregungen, Schwierigkeiten, Drangsale (liter) pl.

trial: ~ **flight** n Testflug m; ~ **marriage** n Ehe f auf Probe; ~ **offer** n Einführungsangebot nt; ~ **period** n (for people) Probezeit f; (for goods) Zeit, die man etw zur Probe or Prüfung hat; ~ **run** n Generalprobe f; (with car etc) Versuchsfahrt, Probefahrt f; (of machine) Probelauf m; **give the new method a** ~ **run** probieren Sie diese neue Methode einmal aus or durch.

triangle ['traɪæŋgl] n Dreieck nt; (set square) (Zeichen)dreieck nt; (Mus) Triangel m; (fig: relationship) Dreiecksbeziehung f.

triangular [traɪ'æŋgjʊlə[r]] adj (Math) dreieckig. ~ **relationship** Dreiecksverhältnis nt; ~ **contest** Dreipersonenwettkampf m; (between nations) Dreinationenwettkampf m.

triangulate [traɪ'æŋgjʊleɪt] **1** adj (Math) triangulär (form). **2** [traɪ'æŋgjʊleɪt] vt in Dreiecke einteilen; (Surv) triangulieren.

triangulation [traɪˌæŋgjʊ'leɪʃən] n (Surv) Triangulation, Triangulierung f. ~ **point** Vermessungspunkt m.

tribal ['traɪbəl] adj customs, dance, life Stammes-. **Celtic society was basically** ~ die Gesellschaftsordnung der Kelten war stammesgebunden; ~ **loyalties** Stammestreue f.

tribalism ['traɪbəlɪzm] n Stammesstruktur f.

tribe [traɪb] n **(a)** Stamm m; (Bot, Zool) Gattung f. **(b)** (fig inf) Korona f.

tribesman ['traɪbzmən] n, pl -men [-mən] Stammesangehörige(r) m.

tribulation [ˌtrɪbjʊ'leɪʃən] n Kummer m no pl. ~**s** Sorgen pl; (less serious) Kümmernisse pl; **to bear one's** ~**s bravely** sein

Leid tapfer tragen; **that is the least of our ~s** das ist unsere geringste Sorge; **to have such unwelcome visitors must have been quite a ~ for you** so unliebsame Gäste zu haben, muß eine ziemliche Last *or* Plage für Sie gewesen sein; *see* **trial**.

tribunal [traɪˈbjuːnl] *n* Gericht(shof *m*) *nt*; (*inquiry*) Untersuchungsausschuß *m*; (*held by revolutionaries etc*) Tribunal *nt*. **before the ~ of public opinion** (*fig*) vor dem Tribunal der öffentlichen Meinung.

tribune[1] [ˈtrɪbjuːn] *n* (*Hist*) (Volks)tribun *m*.

tribune[2] *n* (*platform*) Tribüne *f*.

tributary [ˈtrɪbjutərɪ] **1** *adj state* tributpflichtig; *river* Neben-. **2** *n* (*state*) tributpflichtiger Staat; (*river*) Nebenfluß *m*.

tribute [ˈtrɪbjuːt] *n* (a) (*Hist: payment*) Tribut *m*. (b) (*admiration*) Tribut *m*. **to pay ~ to sb/sth** jdm/einer Sache (den schuldigen) Tribut zollen; **they stood in silent ~ to him** sie zollten ihm (stehend) ihren stillen Tribut; **after her performance/his victory ~s came flooding in** nach ihrer Vorstellung wurde sie mit Ehrungen *or* Zeichen der Hochachtung überschüttet/nach seinem Sieg wurde er mit Ehrungen *or* Zeichen der Anerkennung überschüttet; **~s have been coming in from all over the world for the new champion** aus aller der ganzen Welt kamen Zeichen der Anerkennung für den neuen Champion; **a floral ~** Blumen als Zeichen der Hochachtung/Anerkennung/des Dankes; **to be a ~ to one's parents/school** seinen Eltern/seiner Schule (alle) Ehre machen.

trice[1] [traɪs] *n*: **in a ~** im Handumdrehen, im Nu.

trice[2] *vt* (*Naut: also ~ up*) *sail* aufholen.

Tricel ® [ˈtraɪsel] *n* Tricel *nt*.

triceps [ˈtraɪseps] *n*, *pl* **(-es)** Trizeps *m*.

trichina [trɪˈkaɪnə] *n*, *pl* **-e** [-iː] Trichine *f*.

trichinosis [trɪkɪˈnəʊsɪs] *n* Trichinenkrankheit, Trichinose *f*.

trick [trɪk] **1** *n* (a) (*ruse*) Trick *m*. **to get sth by a ~** etw durch einen Trick *or* eine List bekommen; **be careful, it's a ~** paß auf, das ist eine Falle!; **be careful with this question, there's a ~ in it** sei vorsichtig bei dieser Frage, sie enthält eine Falle!; **he knows a ~ or two** (*inf*) der kennt sich aus, der weiß, wie der Hase läuft; **I know a ~ worth two of that** (*inf*) ich kenne da noch einen viel besseren Trick; **he never misses a ~** er läßt sich (*dat*) nichts entgehen; **he knows all the ~s of the trade** er ist ein alter Hase; (*is crafty*) er ist mit allen Wassern gewaschen; **he is full of ~s** (*child, footballer etc*) er steckt voller Tricks; (*salesman, politician etc*) er hat es faustdick hinter den Ohren; **it's a ~ of the light** da täuscht das Licht.

(b) (*mischief*) Streich *m*. **to play a ~ on sb** jdm einen Streich spielen; **the car started playing ~s again** der Wagen fängt wieder an zu mucken (*inf*); **unless my eyes are playing ~s on** *or* **with me** wenn meine Augen mich nicht täuschen; **a dirty ~** ein ganz gemeiner Trick; **he's up to his (old) ~s again** jetzt macht er wieder seine (alten) Mätzchen (*inf*); **how's ~s?** (*inf*) wie geht's?

(c) (*skilful act*) Kunststück *nt*. **to teach a dog to do ~s** einem Hund Kunststücke beibringen; **once you get the ~ of adjusting it** wenn du einmal den Dreh *or* Trick heraushast, wie man das einstellt; **there's a special ~ to it** da ist ein Trick dabei; **that should do the ~** (*inf*) das müßte eigentlich inhauen (*inf*).

(d) (*habit*) Eigenart *f*. **to have a ~ of doing sth** die Eigenart haben, etw zu tun; **he has a ~ of always arriving as I'm pouring out the tea** er hat eine merkwürdige Art, immer gerade dann zu erscheinen, wenn ich den Tee einschenke; **history has a ~ of repeating itself** die Geschichte hat die merkwürdige Eigenschaft, sich immer zu wiederholen.

(e) (*Cards*) Stich *m*. **to take a ~** einen Stich machen.

(f) (*sl: of prostitute*) Nummer *f* (*sl*).

2 *attr cigar* Scherz-; *spider, glass* als Scherzartikel.

3 *vt* einen Trick betrügen, hereinlegen (*inf*). **I've been ~ed!** ich bin hereingelegt *or* übers Ohr gehauen (*inf*) worden!; **to ~ sb into doing sth** jdn (mit einem Trick *or* mit List) dazu bringen, etw zu tun; **he ~ed the old lady into giving him her life savings** er hat die alte Dame mit einem Trick um all ihre Ersparnisse betrogen; **to ~ sb out of sth** jdn um etw prellen, jdm etw abtricksen (*inf*).

♦**trick out** *vt sep* herausputzen. **~ed ~ in her Sunday best/all her finery** in ihrem Sonntagsstaat/in vollem Staat.

trick cyclist *n* Kunstradfahrer(in *f*) *m*; (*fig inf*) Püschater *m* (*hum*).

trickery [ˈtrɪkərɪ] *n* Tricks *pl* (*inf*). **a piece of ~** ein Trick *m*; **another piece of his ~** wieder einer seiner Tricks; **legal ~** Rechtsverdrehung *f*; **beware of verbal ~ in the contract** passen Sie auf, daß der Vertragstext nicht irgendwelche Fallen enthält!; **that's just verbal ~** das ist bloß ein raffinierter Trick mit Worten.

trickiness [ˈtrɪkɪnɪs] *n* (a) (*difficulty*) Schwierigkeit *f*; (*fiddliness also*) Knifflligkeit *f*. (b) (*of situation*) Schwierigkeit, Kitzligkeit *f*. **the ~ of the present industrial situation** ... die heikle *or* kitzlige (*inf*) augenblickliche Lage in der Industrie ... (c) (*slyness*) Durchtriebenheit, Gerissenheit *f*.

trickle [ˈtrɪkl] **1** *vi* (a) (*liquid*) tröpfeln, tropfen. **tears ~d down her cheeks** Tränen kullerten ihr über die Wangen; **the rain ~d down his neck** der Regen tropfte ihm in den Kragen; **if you don't fix the leak the water will all ~ away/out** wenn Sie die undichte Stelle nicht abdichten, tropft das ganze Wasser heraus; **the sand ~d through his fingers** der Sand rieselte ihm durch die Finger; **the waves broke and ~d back over the pebbles** die Wellen brachen sich und rieselten über die Kiesel zurück.

(b) (*fig*) **people/escapees began to ~ in/out/back** die Leute/ Flüchtlinge begannen, vereinzelt herein-/hinaus-/zurückzukommen; **the ball ~d into the net** der Ball trudelte (langsam) ins Netz; **reports/donations are beginning to ~ in** so langsam trudeln die Berichte/Spenden ein (*inf*).

2 *vt liquid* tröpfeln, träufeln, tropfenweise gießen.

3 *n* (a) (*of liquid*) Tröpfeln *nt*; (*stream*) Rinnsal *nt*.

(b) (*fig*) **a constant ~ of people** gradually filled the lecture hall der Hörsaal füllte sich langsam aber stetig mit Leuten; **news reports from the occupied country have dwindled to a mere ~** Meldungen aus dem besetzten Land kommen *or* (*secretively*) sickern nur noch ganz selten durch; **profits have been reduced/arms deliveries have shrunk to a ~** die Gewinne/Waffenlieferungen sind spärlich geworden; **we cut their supplies to a ~** wir haben ihren Nachschub drastisch reduziert.

trickle charger *n* (*Elec*) Kleinlader *m*.

trick: **~ photography** *n* Trickphotographie *f*; **~ question** *n* Falle *f*; **to ask sb a ~ question** jdm eine Falle stellen.

trickster [ˈtrɪkstəʳ] *n* Schwindler, Betrüger *m*.

tricksy [ˈtrɪksɪ] *adj* (+*er*) (*inf*) *see* **tricky** (c).

tricky [ˈtrɪkɪ] *adj* (+*er*) (a) (*difficult*) schwierig; (*fiddly also*) knifflig. **he is a very ~ person to get on with** es ist äußerst schwierig, mit ihm auszukommen. (b) (*requiring tact*) *situation, problem* heikel, kitzlig. (c) (*sly, crafty*) *person, plan* durchtrieben, gerissen; *question* Fang-, gemein (*inf*).

tricolour, (*US*) **tricolor** [ˈtrɪkʌləʳ] *n* Trikolore *f*.

tricorn [ˈtraɪkɔːn] *n* Dreispitz *m*.

tricot [ˈtriːkəʊ] *n* (*Tex*) Trikot *m*.

tricuspid [traɪˈkʌspɪd] *adj* trikuspidal (*spec*).

tricycle [ˈtraɪsɪkl] *n* Dreirad *nt*.

trident [ˈtraɪdənt] *n* Dreizack *m*.

Tridentine [traɪˈdentaɪn] *adj* Tridentinisch.

tried [traɪd] *adj* erprobt, bewährt.

triennial [traɪˈenɪəl] *adj* (*lasting 3 years*) dreijährig; (*every 3 years*) dreijährlich, alle drei Jahre stattfindend.

triennially [traɪˈenɪəlɪ] *adv* alle drei Jahre, dreijährlich.

triennium [traɪˈenɪəm] *n* Zeitraum *m* von drei Jahren.

trier [ˈtraɪəʳ] *n*: **to be a ~** sich (*dat*) (ernsthaft) Mühe geben.

trifle [ˈtraɪfl] *n* (a) Kleinigkeit *f*; (*trivial matter also*) Lappalie (*inf*), Nichtigkeit *f*. **the merest ~ upsets** her die geringste *or* kleinste Kleinigkeit regt sie auf; **I'm so sorry — a ~, don't let it worry you** es tut mir außerordentlich leid — das ist doch nicht der Rede wert, machen Sie sich deswegen keine Sorgen!

(b) (*small amount*) Kleinigkeit *f*. **have some more cake — just a ~, thank you** noch etwas Kuchen? — bloß ein ganz kleines Stückchen, bitte; **a ~ hot/small etc** ein bißchen heiß/klein etc; **a ~ too ...** ein wenig *or* eine Spur zu ...

(c) (*Cook*) Trifle *m*.

♦**trifle away** *vt sep* vergeuden.

♦**trifle with** *vi* +*prep obj* (a) *person* zu leicht nehmen; *affections* spielen mit. **he is not a person to be ~d ~** mit ihm ist nicht zu spaßen. (b) *one's food* spielen mit, herumstochern in (+*dat*).

trifling [ˈtraɪflɪŋ] *adj* unbedeutend, geringfügig.

trifoliate [traɪˈfəʊlɪət] *adj* dreiblättrig.

trigger [ˈtrɪgəʳ] **1** *n* (*of gun*) Abzug(shahn), Drücker (*inf*) *m*; (*of cine-camera, machine*) Auslöser *m*; (*Elec*) Trigger *m*. **to pull the ~** abdrücken; **to be quick on the ~** schnell abdrücken.

2 *vt* (*also ~ off*) auslösen.

trigger: **~ finger** *n* Zeigefinger *m*; **my ~ finger's itching** es juckt mich abzudrücken; **~ grip** *n* Pistolengriff *m*; **~ guard** *n* Abzugsbügel *m*; **~-happy** *adj* (*inf*) schießfreudig (*inf*), schießwütig (*pej*); (*hum*) *photographer* knipswütig (*inf*).

trigonometric(al) [ˌtrɪgənəˈmetrɪk(əl)] *adj* trigonometrisch.

trigonometry [ˌtrɪgəˈnɒmɪtrɪ] *n* Trigonometrie *f*.

trihedron [ˌtraɪˈhiːdrən] *n* Dreiflächner *m*, Trieder *nt*.

trike [traɪk] *n* (*inf*) *abbr of* **tricycle**.

trilateral [ˌtraɪˈlætərəl] *adj* dreiseitig; *conference, agreement also* Dreier-.

trilby [ˈtrɪlbɪ] *n* (*also ~ hat*) weicher Filzhut.

trilingual [ˌtraɪˈlɪŋgwəl] *adj* dreisprachig.

trill [trɪl] **1** *n* (a) (*of bird*) Trillern *nt*; (*of voice*) Tremolo *nt*. (b) (*Mus*) Triller *m*. (c) (*Phon*) Rollen *nt*, rollende Aussprache. **2** *vt* (a) (*birds*) trillern, tirilieren (*geh*); (*person*) trällern. (b) (*Mus*) *note* trillern. (c) (*Phon*) *consonant* rollen, rollend aussprechen. **3** *vi* (a) (*bird*) trillern, tirilieren (*geh*); (*person*) trällern. (b) (*Mus*) trillern.

trillion [ˈtrɪljən] *n* (*Brit*) Trillion *f*; (*US*) Billion *f*. **there were ~s of them there** (*fig*) es waren Millionen und Abermillionen da.

trilogy [ˈtrɪlədʒɪ] *n* Trilogie *f*.

trim [trɪm] **1** *adj* (+*er*) sauber; *appearance also* adrett; *hair, haircut* gepflegt. **he keeps his lawn/garden/house very ~** sein Rasen/Garten/Haus ist immer sehr gepflegt; **she has a ~ little figure** sie hat ein niedliches Figürchen.

2 *n* (a) (*condition*) Zustand *m*, Verfassung *f*; (*fitness*) Form *f*. **in good ~** (*house, car etc*) in gutem Zustand; (*person*) gut in Form; **financially in good ~** finanziell in guter Verfassung; **to get things into ~** Ordnung machen *or* schaffen; **to get into ~** sich trimmen *or* in Form bringen; **in fighting ~** kampfbereit.

(b) (*inf*) **to give sth a ~** etw schneiden; (*tree, hedge, beard also*) etw stutzen; **your hair needs a ~** du mußt dir die Haare etwas nachschneiden lassen; **just a light ~, please** nur etwas kürzen *or* nachschneiden, bitte.

(c) (*Aut*) (*outside*) Zierleisten *pl*; (*inside*) Innenausstattung *f*. (d) (*Naut*) Trimm *m*, Gleichgewichtslage *f*. **in/out of ~** (*ship*) in/nicht in Trimm *or* Gleichgewichtslage.

(e) (*Aviat*) Trimm(lage *f*) *m*, Fluglage *f*.

3 *vt* (a) (*cut*) *hair* nachschneiden; *beard, hedge, branch* stutzen; *dog* trimmen; *wick, roses* beschneiden; *piece of wood* zurechtschneiden/-sägen/-hobeln.

(b) (*fig: cut down*) *budget* kürzen; *essay also* zurechtstutzen.

(c) (*decorate*) *dress* besetzen; *Christmas tree* schmücken.

(d) *boat, plane* trimmen; *sails* richtig stellen.

(e) (*US inf*) (*defeat*) schlagen; (*cheat*) übers Ohr hauen (*inf*)

♦ **trim away** vt sep weg- or abschneiden; details etc entfernen.
♦ **trim back** vt sep hedge, roses zurückschneiden.
♦ **trim down** vt sep wick, budget kürzen (to auf +acc); essay also, hedge (zurecht)stutzen; roses zurückschneiden. **to ~ ~ one's/sb's figure** etwas für seine/jds Figur tun.
♦ **trim off** vt sep bits of beard, ends of branch abschneiden; rough edges abschneiden/-sägen/-hobeln/-feilen.
♦ **trim up** vt sep beard stutzen.
trimaran ['traɪməræn] n Dreirumpfboot nt, Trimaran m.
trimester [trɪ'mestə‍ʳ] n Trimester nt.
trimming ['trɪmɪŋ] n (a) on clothes Besatz m. ~s Verzierung(en pl) f.
  (b) ~s pl (cuttings) Abfälle pl; (of paper also) (Papier)schnitzel, Schnipsel (inf) pl.
  (c) ~s pl (accessories) Zubehör nt; the car costs £10,000 with all the ~s das Auto kostet £ 10.000 mit allen Extras or mit allem Zubehör; **roast beef with all the ~s** Roastbeef mit allem Drum und Dran (inf) or allen Beilagen.
trimness ['trɪmnɪs] n (of hair, lawn etc) Gepflegtheit f, gepflegtes Aussehen; (of figure) Schlankheit f.
Trinidad ['trɪnɪdæd] n Trinidad nt.
trinitrotoluene [traɪ,naɪtrəʊ'tɒljuːiːn] n Trinitrotoluol nt.
Trinity ['trɪnɪtɪ] n (a) Trinität, Dreieinigkeit, Dreifaltigkeit f. ~ **Sunday** Trinitatis(fest), Dreieinigkeitsfest, Dreifaltigkeitsfest nt. **(b)** (~ term) Sommertrimester nt.
trinket ['trɪŋkɪt] n Schmuckstück nt; (ornament) Schmuckgegenstand m. ~ **box** Schmuckkästchen nt; **the little ~s** hanging from her bracelet die kleinen Anhänger an ihrem Armband.
trinomial [traɪ'nəʊmɪəl] **1** adj trinomisch, dreigliedrig. **2** n Trinom nt.
trio ['triːəʊ] n Trio nt.
trip [trɪp] **1** n (a) (journey) Reise f; (excursion) Ausflug m, Tour f; (shorter also) Trip m. let's go for a ~ **to the seaside** machen wir doch einen Ausflug ans Meer!, fahren wir doch ans Meer!; when was your last ~ **to the dentist's?** wann waren Sie zuletzt beim Zahnarzt?; **that's his fifth ~ to the bathroom already!** er geht jetzt schon zum fünften Mal auf die Toilette! (inf); **he is away on a ~/a ~ to Canada** er ist verreist or auf Reisen/macht zur Zeit eine Reise nach Kanada; **to take a ~** eine Reise machen, verreisen.
  (b) (sl: on drugs) Trip m (sl). **to go on a ~** auf einen Trip or die Reise gehen (sl).
  (c) (stumble) Stolpern nt. that was a nasty ~ da sind Sie aber übel gestolpert.
  (d) (esp Sport) Beinstellen nt. he didn't fall, it was a ~ er ist nicht (von selbst) hingefallen, man hat ihm ein Bein gestellt.
  (e) (mistake) Fehler, Ausrutscher (inf) m.
  (f) (Mech) Auslösung f.
  2 vi (a) (stumble) stolpern (on, over über +acc).
  (b) (fig) see trip up 1 (b).
  (c) (skip) trippeln. **to ~ in/out** hinein-/hinaustrippeln; a phrase which ~s off the tongue ein Ausdruck, der einem leicht von der Zunge geht; **the notes should come ~ping off the tongue** die Töne müssen richtig perlend kommen.
  3 vt (a) (make fall) stolpern lassen; (deliberately also) ein Bein stellen (+dat). **I was ~ped** jemand hat mir ein Bein gestellt; (fig) see trip up 2 (b).
  (b) (Mech) lever betätigen; mechanism auslösen.
  (c) (old: dance) tanzen. **to ~ the light fantastic** (hum) das Tanzbein schwingen (inf).
♦ **trip over** vi stolpern (+prep obj über +acc).
♦ **trip up 1** vi (a) stolpern.
  (b) (fig) sich vertun.
  2 vt sep (a) (make fall) stolpern lassen; (deliberately also) zu Fall bringen.
  (b) (fig: cause to make a mistake etc) eine Falle stellen (+dat), aufs Glatteis führen. he was trying to ~ **me ~ with his ad-libbing** er versuchte, mich mit seinem Improvisieren aus dem Konzept zu bringen; **question six was a very tricky one and it managed to ~ most of the candidates** ~ die sechste Frage war sehr verzwickt, und die meisten Prüflinge sind auch tatsächlich über sie gestolpert.
tripartite [,traɪ'pɑːtaɪt] adj agreement, talks dreiseitig; division Drei-.
tripe [traɪp] n (a) (Cook) Kaldaunen, Kutteln (S Ger, Aus, Sw) pl. **(b)** (fig inf) Quatsch, Stuß (inf) m.
triphammer ['trɪp,hæmə‍ʳ] n Aufwerfhammer m.
triplane ['traɪpleɪn] n Dreidecker m.
triple ['trɪpl] **1** adj dreifach. ~ **jump** Dreisprung m.
  2 adv dreimal soviel. it's ~ **the distance** es ist dreimal so weit; **at ~ the speed** mit dreifacher Geschwindigkeit; **it costs ~ what it used to** es kostet dreimal soviel wie früher, es kostet das Dreifache von früher.
  3 n Dreifache(s) nt.
  4 vt verdreifachen.
  5 vi sich verdreifachen.
triplet ['trɪplɪt] n (a) (baby) Drilling m. **(b)** (Mus) Triole f; (Poet) Dreireim m.
triple time n (Mus) Dreiertakt m.
triplex ® ['trɪpleks] n Verbundglas nt.
triplicate ['trɪplɪkɪt] **1** n: in ~ in dreifacher Ausfertigung. **2** adj in dreifacher Ausfertigung. **3** ['trɪplɪkeɪt] vt document dreifach or in drei Exemplaren ausfertigen.
triply ['trɪplɪ] adv dreimal. ~ **expensive** dreimal so teuer.
tripod ['traɪpɒd] n (Phot) Stativ nt; (Hist) Dreifuß m.
tripos ['traɪpɒs] n Abschlußexamen nt an der Universität Cambridge.
tripper ['trɪpə‍ʳ] n Ausflügler(in f) m; see day ~.
tripping ['trɪpɪŋ] adj (a) walk trippelnd; notes perlend; metre fließend. **(b)** (Mech) ~ **device** Auslösemechanismus m.

trippingly ['trɪpɪŋlɪ] adv see adj (a).
trip recorder n (Aut) Tageszähler m.
triptych ['trɪptɪk] n Triptychon nt.
tripwire ['trɪpwaɪə‍ʳ] n Stolperdraht m.
trireme ['traɪriːm] n Triere, Trireme f.
trisect [traɪ'sekt] vt in drei Teile teilen, dreiteilen; angle in drei gleiche Teile teilen.
trisection [traɪ'sekʃən] n Dreiteilung f; (of angle) Einteilung f in drei gleiche Teile.
trisyllabic ['traɪsɪ'læbɪk] adj dreisilbig.
trisyllable [,traɪ'sɪləbl] n dreisilbiges Wort.
trite [traɪt] adj (+er) (trivial, banal) banal, nichtssagend; (hackneyed) abgedroschen.
tritely ['traɪtlɪ] adv see adj. **to talk ~** banales/abgedroschenes Zeug reden, Phrasen dreschen; **a ~ obvious remark** eine Binsenweisheit; **nobody is perfect, he said ~** er machte die banale Bemerkung: niemand ist vollkommen.
triteness ['traɪtnɪs] n see adj Banalität f; Abgedroschenheit f. his conversation was notable for its ~ seine Unterhaltung war bemerkenswert banal or nichtssagend or abgedroschen.
tritium ['trɪtɪəm] n Tritium nt.
triumph ['traɪʌmf] **1** n (a) Triumph m. **in ~** triumphierend, im Triumph; **shouts of ~** Triumphgeschrei pl; **to win or score a ~ over sb/sth** einen Triumph über jdn/etw erzielen.
  (b) (Hist: procession) Triumphzug m.
  2 vi den Sieg davontragen (over über +acc). **to ~ over sb/sth** über jdn/etw triumphieren; **they ~ed over incredible odds** sie setzten sich gegen unglaubliche Widerstände durch; **we've made it! he ~ed** wir haben's geschafft! triumphierte er.
triumphal [traɪ'ʌmfəl] adj triumphal. ~ **arch** Triumphbogen m.
triumphant [traɪ'ʌmfənt] adj (victorious) siegreich; (rejoicing) triumphierend; moment triumphal. **to be ~ (over sth)** triumphieren (over über +acc); **he was ~ in his success** er jubelte triumphierend or triumphierte über seinen Erfolg; **his book was a ~ success** sein Buch war ein triumphaler Erfolg or ein Triumph; **in our ~ hour** in unserer Stunde des Triumphs.
triumphantly [traɪ'ʌmfəntlɪ] adv triumphierend. **it was a ~ successful expedition** die Expedition war ein triumphaler Erfolg.
triumvir ['traɪəmvɪ:r] n (Hist) Triumvir m.
triumvirate [traɪ'ʌmvɪrɪt] n (Hist) Triumvirat nt.
triune ['traɪjuːn] adj (Rel) dreieinig.
trivalent [,traɪ'veɪlənt] adj (Chem) dreiwertig.
trivia ['trɪvɪə] npl triviales Zeug. **the ~ of daily life** die Trivialitäten des täglichen Lebens.
trivial ['trɪvɪəl] adj (a) trivial; objection, loss, details, matters also geringfügig, belanglos. **look, your health is not something ~** hör mal, mit der Gesundheit ist nicht zu spaßen!; **the ~ round** das triviale Einerlei. **(b)** person oberflächlich.
triviality [,trɪvɪ'ælɪtɪ] n see adj (a) Trivialität f; Geringfügigkeit, Belanglosigkeit f.
trivialize ['trɪvɪəlaɪz] vt trivialisieren.
trochaic [trɒ'keɪɪk] adj trochäisch.
trochee ['trəʊkiː] n Trochäus m.
trod [trɒd] pret of tread.
trodden ['trɒdn] ptp of tread.
troglodyte ['trɒglədaɪt] n Höhlenbewohner, Troglodyt (liter) m; (fig: recluse) Einsiedler m.
troika ['trɔɪkə] n Troika f.
Trojan ['trəʊdʒən] **1** n (Hist) Trojaner(in f), Troer(in f) m. **to work like a ~** (fig) wie ein Pferd arbeiten; **he's a real ~** (fig) er ist wirklich eine treue Seele. **2** adj trojanisch; (fig) übermenschlich. ~ **Horse** (lit, fig) Trojanisches Pferd; ~ **War** Trojanischer Krieg.
troll[1] [trəʊl] n (Myth) Troll m.
troll[2] vi (inf: walk) laufen.
trolley ['trɒlɪ] n (a) (cart) (four wheels) Handwagen m; (in supermarket) Einkaufswagen m; (in station) Gepäckwagen, Ladekasten m; (for passengers) Kofferkuli m; (two wheels) (for golf clubs) Caddy m; (in station, factory etc) Sackkarre f.
  (b) (tea-~) Teewagen m.
  (c) (Rail) Lore f, Förderkarren m; (hand-driven) Draisine f.
  (d) (Elec) (~ pole) Kontaktarm m, Stromabnehmerstange f; (~-wheel) Kontaktrolle f, Rollenstromabnehmer m.
  (e) (~bus or -car (US)) see trolleybus, trolley-car.
trolley: ~**bus** n Obus, Oberleitungsomnibus (form), Trolleybus (dated) m; ~-**car** n (US) Straßenbahn f; ~ **pole** n Kontaktarm m, Stromabnehmerstange f.
trollop ['trɒləp] n (dated: prostitute) leichtes Mädchen, Straßenmädchen nt; (pej) Schlampe f.
trombone [trɒm'bəʊn] n (Mus) Posaune f.
trombonist [trɒm'bəʊnɪst] n Posaunist m.
troop [truːp] **1** n (a) (Mil: of cavalry) Trupp m; (unit) Schwadron f.
  (b) (Mil) ~s pl Truppen pl; **a dozen of our best ~s** zwölf unserer besten Soldaten; **200 ~s** 200 Soldaten.
  (c) (of scouts) Stamm m.
  (d) (of people) Horde (pej), Schar f.
  2 vi **to ~ out/in** hinaus-/hineinströmen; **to ~ upstairs** nach oben strömen; **to ~ past sth** an etw (dat) vorbeiziehen; **to ~ away or off** abziehen (inf); **to ~ up** herbeiströmen.
  3 vt (Mil) **to ~ the colours** die Fahnenparade abhalten; **the colours being ~ed today** die Fahnen bei der heutigen Parade; **the ~ing of the colours** die Fahnenparade.
troop-carrier ['truːp,kærɪə‍ʳ] n (vehicle) Truppentransport m.
trooper ['truːpə‍ʳ] n (Mil) berittener Soldat, Kavallerist m; (US: state ~) Polizist m. **to swear like a ~** wie ein Kutscher fluchen.
troop: ~-**ship** n (Truppen)transportschiff nt; ~ **train** n Truppentransportzug m.
trope [trəʊp] n (Liter) Trope f.
trophy ['trəʊfɪ] n (Hunt, Mil, Sport) Trophäe f.

tropic ['trɒpɪk] n (a) Wendekreis m. T~ of Cancer/Capricorn Wendekreis des Krebses/Steinbocks. (b) ~s pl Tropen pl.

tropical ['trɒpɪkəl] adj tropisch, Tropen-. ~ medicine/diseases Tropenmedizin f/Tropenkrankheiten pl.

tropism ['trəʊpɪzəm] n (Biol) Tropismus m.

trot [trɒt] 1 n (a) (pace) Trab m. to go at a ~ traben; to go for a ~ einen Ausritt machen; to keep sb on the ~ (fig inf) jdn in Trab halten; I've been on the ~ all day (fig inf) ich bin schon den ganzen Tag auf Trab.
(b) (inf) for five days on the ~ fünf Tage lang in einer Tour.
(c) (inf: diarrhoea) the ~s die Renneritis (hum inf).
2 vi (horse, person) traben; (pony) zockeln; (small child) trippeln. he ~ted obediently round the shops after her er zottelte folgsam hinter ihr her durch die Geschäfte.
3 vt horse traben lassen.
♦ **trot along** vi see trot 2 traben; zockeln; trippeln; (go away) abmarschieren. to ~ ~ behind sb hinter jdm hertraben etc.
♦ **trot away** or **off** vi see trot 2 davon- or wegtraben; davon- or wegzockeln; davon- or wegtrippeln.
♦ **trot out** 1 vi see trot 2 hinaus-/heraustraben; hinaus-/herauszockeln; hinaus-/heraustrippeln. 2 vt sep excuses, theories, names, list aufwarten mit.
♦ **trot over** or **round** vi (go quickly) hinüberlaufen. to ~ ~ to the grocer's zum Kaufmann laufen.

troth [trəʊθ] n (old) see plight¹.

trotter¹ ['trɒtə'] n (horse) Traber m.

trotter² n (of animal) Fuß m. pigs' ~s (Cook) Schweinsfüße pl.

troubadour ['tru:bədɔ:'] n Troubadour m.

trouble ['trʌbl] 1 n (a) Schwierigkeiten pl; (bothersome also) Ärger m. did you have any ~ (in) getting it? hatten Sie Schwierigkeiten, es zu bekommen?; to be in ~ in Schwierigkeiten sein; you'll be in ~ for this da bekommen Sie Ärger or Schwierigkeiten; to be in ~ with sb mit jdm Schwierigkeiten or Ärger haben; to get into ~ in Schwierigkeiten geraten; (with authority) Schwierigkeiten or Ärger bekommen (with mit); to get sb into ~ jdn in Schwierigkeiten bringen (with mit); to get a girl into ~ (euph) ein Mädchen ins Unglück bringen; to get out of/sb out of ~ aus den Schwierigkeiten herauskommen/jdm aus seinen Schwierigkeiten heraushelfen; to keep or stay out of ~ nicht in Schwierigkeiten kommen, sauber bleiben (inf); now we're out of ~ jetzt sind wir aus den Schwierigkeiten heraus; the children are never out of ~ die Kinder stellen dauernd etwas an; to make ~ (cause a row etc) Krach schlagen (inf), Ärger machen; to make ~ (for sb/oneself) (with authority) jdn/sich selbst in Schwierigkeiten bringen; that's/you're asking for ~ das kann ja nicht gutgehen; are you looking for ~? Sie wollen wohl Ärger?; to look for ~, to go around looking for ~ sich (dat) Ärger einhandeln; there'll be ~ if he finds out wenn er das erfährt, gibt's Ärger or Trouble (inf); here comes ~ (inf) jetzt geht es los! (inf), jetzt gibt es Ärger or Trouble! (inf); what's the ~? was ist los?; (to sick person) wo fehlt's?; the ~ is that ... das Problem ist, daß ...; that's the ~ das ist das Problem; family/money ~s Familien-/Geldsorgen pl; his ~s are not yet over seine Sorgen or Probleme sind noch nicht vorbei.
(b) (bother, effort) Mühe f. it's no ~ (at all)! das mache ich doch gern; thank you — (it was) no ~ vielen Dank — (das ist) gern geschehen; it's no ~ to do it properly man kann es genausogut ordentlich machen; it's not worth the ~ das ist nicht der Mühe wert; nothing is too much ~ for her nichts ist ihr zuviel; to go to the ~ (of doing sth), to take the ~ (to do sth) sich (dat) die Mühe machen(, etw zu tun); to go to/to take a lot of ~ (over or with sth) sich (dat) (mit etw) viel Mühe geben; you have gone to a lot of ~ over the food Sie haben sich (dat) solche Umstände mit dem Essen gemacht; he went to enormous ~ to get it for me er hat alles nur Erdenkliche getan, um mir das zu besorgen; to put sb to the ~ of doing sth jdn bemühen, etw zu tun; to put sb to the ~ of making unnecessary preparations jdm unnötig Umstände machen; to put sb to a lot of ~ jdm viel Mühe machen.
(c) (nuisance) to be a ~ (to sb) (jdm) Mühe machen; (dependent person also) (jdm) zur Last fallen; the child is a ~ to his parents das Kind macht seinen Eltern nur Sorgen.
(d) (Med: illness) Leiden nt; (fig) Schaden m. heart/back ~ Herz-/Rückenleiden nt; my back is giving me ~ mein Rücken macht mir zu schaffen; engine ~ (ein) Motorschaden m.
(e) (unrest, upheaval) Unruhe f. labour ~s Arbeiterunruhen pl; there's ~ at the factory/in Iran in der Fabrik/im Iran herrscht Unruhe; he caused/made ~ between them er hat Unruhe zwischen ihnen gestiftet; see stir up.
2 vt (a) (worry) beunruhigen; (disturb, grieve) bekümmern. to be ~d by sth wegen etw besorgt or beunruhigt/bekümmert sein; his eyes ~ him seine Augen machen ihm zu schaffen; he's ~d with a bad back er leidet an Rückenschmerzen.
(b) (bother) bemühen, belästigen. I'm sorry to ~ you, but could you tell me if ... entschuldigen Sie die Störung, aber könnten Sie mir sagen, ob ...; may I ~ you for a light? darf ich Sie um Feuer bemühen?; will it ~ you if I smoke? stört es Sie, wenn ich rauche?; I shan't ~ you with the details ich werde Ihnen die Einzelheiten ersparen; we are ~d with mice just now wir werden zur Zeit von Mäusen geplagt; I'll ~ you to remember who you're speaking to! (iro) würden Sie bitte daran denken, mit wem Sie sprechen.
(c) (take the trouble) to ~ to do sth sich bemühen, etw zu tun; please don't ~ yourself bitte bemühen Sie sich nicht; don't ~ to write until you've settled down schreib erst, wenn du dich eingelebt hast; if you had ~d to ask, you might have found out the truth wenn du dir die Mühe gemacht und gefragt hättest, hättest du wahrscheinlich die Wahrheit erfahren; oh, don't ~ to apologize! (iro) bemüh dich nicht, dich zu entschuldigen!
3 vi sich bemühen.

troubled ['trʌbld] adj person, look unruhig, beunruhigt; (grieved) bekümmert; times unruhig; water aufgewühlt. the ~ waters of industrial relations die gestörte Beziehung zwischen Arbeitgebern und Arbeitnehmern; see oil.

trouble: ~-free adj period, process, car problemlos; relationship also reibungslos; area ruhig; machine störungsfrei; ~maker n Tunichtgut m; (deliberate) Unruhestifter(in f) m; ~shooter n Störungssucher(in f) m; (Pol, Ind: mediator) Vermittler(in f) m; ~some adj (bothersome) lästig; person, problem schwierig; John is the most ~some boy in the school John ist der schwierigste Junge in der Schule; (troublemaker) John ist der größte Störenfried in der Schule; don't be ~some! sei nicht so schwierig!; ~ spot n Unruhherd m; (in system) Störung f.

troublous ['trʌbləs] adj (liter) unruhig.

trough [trɒf] n (a) (container) Trog m. drinking ~ Wassertrog m. (b) (depression) Furche, Rille f; (between waves, on graph) Tal nt; (Met) Trog m. ~ of depression Tiefdrucktrog m.

trounce [traʊns] vt verprügeln; (Sport) vernichtend schlagen.

trouncing ['traʊnsɪŋ] n Prügel pl (also Sport). to give sb a ~ jdm Prügel verpassen.

troupe [tru:p] n (Theat) Truppe f.

trouper ['tru:pə'] n (Theat) Mime m, Mimin f (dated). an old ~ (fig) ein alter Hase; a good ~ (fig) ein treuer Mitarbeiter.

trouser ['traʊzə] ~ clip n Hosenklammer f; ~ leg n Hosenbein nt; ~ press n Hosenpresse f.

trousers ['traʊzɪz] npl (esp Brit: also pair of ~) Hose f. she was wearing ~ sie hatte Hosen or eine Hose an; to wear the ~ (fig inf) die Hosen anhaben (inf).

trouser-suit ['traʊzəˌsu:t] n (Brit) Hosenanzug m.

trousseau ['tru:səʊ] n Aussteuer f.

trout [traʊt] n Forelle f. ~ fishing Forellenfang m, Forellenangeln nt; silly old ~! (inf) blöde alte (Zimt)ziege (inf).

trove [trəʊv] n see treasure ~.

trowel ['traʊəl] n Kelle f. to lay sth on with a ~ (inf) bei etw dick auftragen.

Troy [trɔɪ] n (Hist) Troja nt; see Helen.

troy [trɔɪ] n (also ~ weight) Troygewicht nt.

truancy ['truənsɪ] n (Schule)schwänzen nt, unentschuldigtes Fehlen (in der Schule) (form), (Schul)schwänzerei f (inf). ~ officer Sozialarbeiter, der sich um Schulschwänzer kümmert.

truant ['truənt] n (Schul)schwänzer(in f) m. to play ~ (from sth) (bei etw) unentschuldigt fehlen, (etw) schwänzen (inf).

truce [tru:s] n (Mil, fig) Waffenstillstand m; (Mil: interrupting fighting) Waffenruhe f. ~! Friede!

truck¹ [trʌk] 1 n (a) (Rail) Güterwagen m. (b) (barrow) Karren, Wagen m; (for luggage) Gepäckkarren m; (motorized) Elektrokarren m. (c) (lorry) Last(kraft)wagen m; (van, pick-up) Lieferwagen m. 2 vt (US) transportieren, spedieren. 3 vi (US) Lastwagen fahren.

truck² n (a) (fig: dealings) to have no ~ with sb/sth mit jdm/etw nichts zu tun haben. (b) (Hist: payment) ~ (system) Trucksystem nt (spec); they were paid in ~ sie wurden in Waren bezahlt. (c) (US) (garden produce) (für den Verkauf angebautes) Gemüse.

truckage ['trʌkɪdʒ] n (US: transport) Transport m, Spedition f; (charge) Transportkosten pl. ~ company Spedition(sfirma) f, Transportunternehmen nt.

truck driver n Lastwagenfahrer(in f) m.

trucker ['trʌkə'] n (US) (a) (truck-driver) Lastwagenfahrer(in f) m; (haulage contractor) Spediteur m. (b) (farmer) Gemüsegärtner(in f) m.

truck (US): ~ farm n Gemüseanbaubetrieb m, Gemüsefarm f; ~ farmer n Gemüsegärtner(in f), Gemüseanbauer(in f) m; ~ garden n Gemüsegärtnerei f.

trucking ['trʌkɪŋ] n (US) Spedition f, Transport m.

truckle ['trʌkl] vi klein beigeben (to sb jdm gegenüber).

truckle bed n niedriges Rollbett.

truck: ~load n Wagenladung f; they came by the ~load sie kamen in ganzen Wagenladungen; ~man n Lastwagenfahrer m.

truculence ['trʌkjʊləns] n Trotzigkeit, Aufsässigkeit f.

truculent ['trʌkjʊlənt] adj trotzig, aufsässig.

trudge [trʌdʒ] 1 vi to ~ in/out/along etc hinein-/hinaus-/entlangtrotten etc; to ~ through the mud durch den Matsch stapfen; we ~d round the shops wir sind durch die Geschäfte getrottet or gelatscht (inf). 2 vt streets, town trotten durch; (looking for sth) abklappern. 3 n mühseliger Marsch.

true [tru:] 1 adj (a) (not false) story, rumour, statement wahr. to come ~ (dream, wishes) Wirklichkeit werden, wahr werden; (prophecy) sich verwirklichen; (fears) sich bewahrheiten; it is ~ that ... es stimmt, daß ..., es ist wahr or richtig, daß ...; that's ~ das stimmt, das ist wahr; if it is ~ that ... wenn es stimmt or wahr ist, daß ...; can it be ~ (that he didn't know)? kann es stimmen or sein(, daß er das nicht wußte)?; the same is or holds ~ for ... dasselbe gilt auch für ..., dasselbe trifft auch auf ... (acc) zu; ~! richtig!; too ~! (das ist nur) zu wahr!; wie wahr!; we mustn't generalize, (it's) ~, but ... wir sollten natürlich nicht verallgemeinern, aber ...; that's wrong! — ~, but ... das ist falsch! — stimmt or richtig, aber ...
(b) (accurate) description, report, account wahrheitsgetreu; likeness (lebens)getreu; copy getreu.
(c) (real, genuine) feeling, friendship, friend, Christian, heir, opinion wahr, echt; reason wirklich; leather, antique echt. the frog is not a ~ reptile der Frosch ist kein echtes Reptil; in a ~ spirit of friendship/love im wahren Geist der Freundschaft/ Liebe; ~ love die wahre Liebe; (person) Schatz m, Herzallerliebste(r) mf (old); the path of ~ love ne'er did run smooth (prov) die Pfade der Liebe sind gewunden; what is the ~ situation? wie verhält es sich wirklich?; in ~ life im wirklichen Leben; the one ~ God der einzige wahre Gott.
(d) (faithful) friend, follower treu. to be ~ to sb jdm treu

sein/bleiben; **to be ~ to one's word** (treu) zu seinem Wort stehen, seinem Wort treu bleiben; **~ to life** lebensnah; (*Art*) lebensecht; **the horse ran ~ to form** das Pferd lief erwartungsgemäß; **~ to type** erwartungsgemäß; (*Bot*) artgetreu.
  (e) *wall, surface* gerade; *join* genau; *circle* rund; (*Mus*) *note* rein.
  (f) (*Phys*) tatsächlich. **~ North** der eigentliche *or* tatsächliche *or* geographische Norden.
  2 *n* **out of ~** *upright, beam, wheels* schief; *join* verschoben.
  3 *adv* *aim* genau; *sing* richtig. **to ~** sich reinrassig fortpflanzen; **he speaks ~** (*old*) er spricht die Wahrheit; *see* ring².
♦**true up** *vt sep machinery* genau einstellen; *beam* genau ausrichten; *wheel* einrichten. **to ~ ~ the edges of the planks** die Bretterkanten plan machen.
true: **~ blue 1** *adj* waschecht (*inf*), echt; **2** *n* (*Brit: Tory*) echter Tory; **~-born** *adj* echt, gebürtig; (*legitimate*) rechtmäßig; **~-bred** *adj* wahr, echt; *cattle* reinrassig; **~-hearted** *adj* ehrlich, aufrichtig; **~-life** *adj attr* aus dem Leben gegriffen; **~ rib** *n* wahre Rippe.
truffle ['trʌfl] *n* Trüffel *f or m*.
trug [trʌg] *n* Korb *m*.
truism ['truːɪzəm] *n* (*obvious truth*) Binsenwahrheit *f*; (*platitude*) Platitüde *f*, Gemeinplatz *m*.
truly ['truːlɪ] *adv* (**a**) (*truthfully, genuinely*) wirklich, wahrhaftig. **(really and) ~?** wirklich und wahrhaftig?; **he did it, ~ he did!** er hat es wirklich und wahrhaftig getan!; **a ~ great writer** ein wirklich *or* wahrhaft großer Schriftsteller; *see* well².
  (**b**) (*faithfully*) *serve* treu; *love also* getreu(lich) (*geh*); *reflect* wahrheitsgetreu.
trump¹ [trʌmp] **1** *n* (*Cards, fig*) Trumpf *m*; (*dated inf: person*) prima Kerl (*dated inf*). **spades are ~s** Pik ist Trumpf; **what's ~s?** was ist Trumpf?; **to hold all the ~s** (*fig*) alle Trümpfe in der Hand halten; **~ card** (*Cards*) Trumpf(karte *f*) *m*; (*fig*) Trumpf *m*; **to play one's ~ card** (*lit, fig*) seinen Trumpf ausspielen; **he's absolutely ~s** (*dated inf*) er ist große Klasse (*inf*); **to turn up ~s** (*inf*) alles rausreißen (*inf*).
  2 *vt* (*Cards, fig*) übertrumpfen.
♦**trump up** *vt sep* erfinden.
trump² *n* (*liter*) Trompete *f*. **at the Last T~** wenn die Posaunen des Jüngsten Gerichts erklingen.
trumpery ['trʌmpərɪ] **1** *n* Plunder *m no pl*; (*ornaments*) Kitsch *m*; (*jewellery*) Flitterkram *m*; (*nonsense*) Unsinn *m*. **2** *adj* billig; *ornaments also* kitschig.
trumpet ['trʌmpɪt] **1** *n* (**a**) (*Mus*) Trompete *f*. **~ major** Stabstrompeter *m*; *see* blow².
  (**b**) (*noise of elephant*) Trompeten *nt no pl*.
  (**c**) (*of flower*) Trompete *f*; (*hearing ~*) Hörrohr *m*; (*speaking ~*) Sprachrohr, Megaphon *nt*; *see* ear-trumpet.
  2 *vt* (*rare: also ~ forth*) hinaustrompeten.
  3 *vi* (*elephant*) trompeten.
trumpeter ['trʌmpɪtəʳ] *n* Trompeter(in *f*) *m*.
trumpeting ['trʌmpɪtɪŋ] *n* (*of elephant*) Trompeten *nt*
truncate [trʌŋ'keɪt] **1** *vt* kürzen, beschneiden; *tree* stutzen. **2** ['trʌŋkeɪt] *adj cone* stumpf; *leaf* abgestumpft.
truncated [trʌŋ'keɪtɪd] *adj tree* gestutzt; *article, speech* gekürzt; *cone* stumpf; *leaf* abgestumpft.
truncation [trʌŋ'keɪʃən] *n see vt* Kürzung, Beschneidung *f*; Stutzung *f*.
truncheon ['trʌntʃən] *n* (Gummi)knüppel *m*; (*esp of riot police*) Schlagstock *m*.
trundle ['trʌndl] **1** *vt* (*push*) rollen; (*pull*) ziehen. **2** *vi* **to ~ in/along/down** hinein-/entlang-/hinunterzockeln; (*clatter*) hinein-/entlang-/hinunterrumpeln.
trundle bed *n* (*US*) Rollbett *nt*.
trunk [trʌŋk] *n* (**a**) (*of tree*) Stamm *m*; (*of body*) Rumpf *m*.
  (**b**) (*of elephant*) Rüssel *m*.
  (**c**) (*case*) Überseekoffer, Schrankkoffer *m*; (*US Aut*) Kofferraum *m*.
  (**d**) **~s** *pl* (*for swimming*) Badehose *f*; (*for sport*) Shorts *pl*; (*dated Brit: underwear*) Unterhose *f*; **a pair of ~s** eine Badehose/(ein Paar) Shorts/eine Unterhose.
trunk: **~ call** *n* (*Brit: Tele*) Ferngespräch *nt*; **~ line** *n* (*Rail*) Hauptstrecke *f*; (*Telec*) Fernleitung *f*; **~ road** *n* (*Brit*) Fernstraße *f*.
truss [trʌs] **1** *n* (**a**) (*Brit: bundle*) Bündel *nt*, Garbe *f*.
  (**b**) (*Build*) (*of bridge*) Fachwerk *nt*; (*of roof*) Gesparre *nt*; (*single beam*) Dachsparren *m*; (*vertical*) Dachbalken *m*.
  (**c**) (*Med*) Bruchband *nt*.
  2 *vt* (**a**) (*tie*) hay bündeln.
  (**b**) (*Cook*) *chicken etc* dressieren.
  (**c**) (*Build*) (ab)stützen.
♦**truss up** *vt sep* (*Cook*) *chicken etc* dressieren; (*inf*) *person* fesseln.
trust [trʌst] **1** *n* (**a**) (*confidence, reliance*) Vertrauen *nt* (*in* zu) I **have every ~ in him** ich habe volles Vertrauen zu ihm; **to put** *or* **place one's ~ in sb** Vertrauen in jdn setzen; **to take sth on ~** etw einfach glauben; **to give sb sth on ~** (*without payment*) jdm etw auf sein ehrliches Gesicht hin (*inf*) *or* im guten Glauben geben; **position of ~** Vertrauensstellung *f*.
  (**b**) (*charge*) Verantwortung *f*. **to commit sth to** *or* **place sth in sb's ~** jdm etw anvertrauen.
  (**c**) (*Jur, Fin*) Treuhand(schaft) *f*; (*property*) Treuhandeigentum *nt*; (*charitable fund*) Fonds *m*, Stiftung *f*. **to hold sth in ~** for sb etw für jdn treuhänderisch verwalten; **all his money was tied up in a ~** sein ganzes Geld wurde treuhänderisch verwaltet; **~ fund** Treuhandvermögen *nt*; Stiftungsgelder *pl*; **~ territory** (*Pol*) Treuhandgebiet *nt*.
  (**d**) (*Comm: also ~ company*) Trust *m*.
  2 *vt* (**a**) (*have confidence in*) trauen (+*dat*); *person also* vertrauen (+*dat*); *words* glauben. **to ~ sb to do sth** (*believe him*

honest etc) jdm vertrauen, daß er etw tut; (*believe him capable*) jdm zutrauen, daß er etw tut; **don't you ~ me?** vertraust du mir nicht?; **to ~ sb with sth**, **to ~ sth to sb** jdm etw anvertrauen; **I don't ~ her** with her boyfriend ich traue ihr und ihrem Freund nicht; **can he be ~ed not to lose it?** kann man sich darauf verlassen, daß er es nicht verliert?; **can we ~ him to go shopping alone?** können wir ihn allein einkaufen gehen lassen?; **he's not a man to be ~ed** man kann ihm nicht trauen; **you can't ~ a word he says** man kann ihm kein Wort glauben; **she won't ~ us out of her sight** sie läßt uns nicht aus den Augen; **I wouldn't ~ him (any) farther than I can throw him** (*inf*) ich traue ihm nicht über den Weg (*inf*).
  (**b**) (*iro inf*) **~ you/him!** typisch!; **~ him to break it!** er muß es natürlich kaputtmachen.
  (**c**) (*hope*) hoffen. **I ~ not** hoffentlich nicht, ich hoffe nicht; **you're going to help, I ~** du wirst doch hoffentlich mithelfen.
  3 *vi* (**a**) (*have confidence*) vertrauen. **to ~ in sb** auf jdn vertrauen.
  (**b**) (*rely on*) **to ~ to sth** sich auf etw (*acc*) verlassen, auf etw (*acc*) vertrauen; **to ~ to luck** *or* **chance** sich auf sein Glück verlassen; **I'll have to ~ to luck to find it** ich kann nur hoffen, daß ich es finde.
trusted ['trʌstɪd] *adj method* bewährt; *friend, servant* getreu.
trustee [trʌs'tiː] *n* (**a**) (*of estate*) Treuhänder(in *f*), Vermögensverwalter(in *f*) *m*.
  (**b**) (*of institution*) Kurator, Verwalter *m*. **~s** Vorstand *m*; **T~ Savings Bank** ≈ Sparkasse *f*.
trusteeship [trʌs'tiːʃɪp] *n* (**a**) Treuhandschaft *f*. (**b**) (*of a territory*) Treuhandschaft *f*, Mandat *nt*. (**c**) (*also ~ territory*) Treuhandgebiet, Mandat(sgebiet) *nt*.
trustful ['trʌstfʊl] *adj look, expression* vertrauensvoll; *person also* gutgläubig, arglos.
trustfully ['trʌstfəlɪ] *adv* vertrauensvoll.
trusting ['trʌstɪŋ] *adj see* trustful.
trustworthiness ['trʌst̩wɜːðɪnɪs] *n see adj* Vertrauenswürdigkeit *f*; Glaubhaftigkeit, Glaubwürdigkeit *f*.
trustworthy ['trʌst̩wɜːðɪ] *adj person* vertrauenswürdig; *statement, account* glaubhaft, glaubwürdig.
trusty ['trʌstɪ] *adj* (+*er*) (*liter, hum*) getreu (*liter*).
truth [truːθ] *n*, *pl* **-s** [truːðz] (**a**) *no pl* Wahrheit *f*. **you must always tell the ~** du mußt immer die Wahrheit sagen; **to tell the ~ ...**, **to tell ...** um ehrlich zu sein ..., um die Wahrheit zu sagen ...; **the ~ of it** *or* **the matter is that ...** die Wahrheit ist, daß ..., in Wahrheit ...; **there's no ~** *or* **not a word of ~ in what he says** es ist kein Wort wahr von dem, was er sagt; **there's some ~ in that** es ist etwas Wahres daran, da ist etwas Wahres dran (*inf*); **the ~, the whole ~ and nothing but the ~** (*Jur*) die Wahrheit, die reine Wahrheit und nichts als die Wahrheit; **in ~** in Wahrheit, in Wirklichkeit; **~ will out** (*prov*) die Wahrheit wird ans Licht kommen, die Sonne wird es an den Tag bringen (*prov*); **~ drug** *or* **serum** Wahrheitsdroge *f*; **~ value** (*Logic*) Wahrheitswert *m*.
  (**b**) (*belief, fact*) Wahrheit *f*. **I told him a few ~s about his behaviour** ich habe ihm mal gesagt, was ich von seinem Benehmen halte; *see* home **~**.
truthful ['truːθfʊl] *adj person* ehrlich; *statement* ehrlich, wahrheitsgetreu. **to be ~** *about* sth ehrlich sein.
truthfully ['truːθfəlɪ] *adv* ehrlich; *answer, say also, explain* wahrheitsgemäß, der Wahrheit entsprechend.
truthfulness ['truːθfʊlnɪs] *n* Ehrlichkeit, Aufrichtigkeit *f*; (*of statement*) Wahrheit *f*.
try [traɪ] **1** *n* (**a**) (*attempt*) Versuch *m*. **to have a ~** es versuchen; **let me have a ~** laß mich mal versuchen!, laß mich mal! (*inf*); **to have a ~ at doing sth** (*sich daran*) versuchen, etw zu tun, (es) probieren, etw zu tun; **have another ~ (at it)** versuch's noch mal; **to have a ~ for sth** sich um etw bemühen; **I'll give it a ~** (*will attempt it*) ich werde es mal versuchen; (*will test it out*) ich werde es ausprobieren; **I'll give him a ~** ich werde ihm eine Chance geben; **it was a good ~** das war schon ganz gut; **it's worth a ~** es ist einen Versuch wert; **at the first ~** beim ersten Versuch, auf Anhieb; **can I have a ~ at your bicycle?** kann ich mal dein Rad ausprobieren?
  (**b**) (*Rugby*) Versuch *m*. **to score a ~** einen Versuch erzielen.
  2 *vt* (**a**) (*attempt*) versuchen. **you have only tried two questions** du hast dich nur an zwei Fragen versucht (*inf*), du hast nur zwei Fragen zu beantworten versucht; **to ~ one's hardest** *or* **one's best** sein Bestes tun *or* versuchen; **do ~ to understand** bitte versuche doch zu verstehen!; **I've given up ~ing to help** him ich habe es aufgegeben, ihm helfen zu wollen; **it's ~ing to rain** (*inf*) es sieht aus, als würde es regnen; **the sun's ~ing to come out** es sieht so aus, als wollte die Sonne rauskommen; **to ~ one's hand at sth** etw probieren; **I'll ~ anything once** ich probiere alles einmal; **just you ~ it!** (*dare*) versuch's bloß!
  (**b**) (**~ out**) *new detergent, bicycle etc* ausprobieren; *job applicant* eine Chance geben (+*dat*), es versuchen mit (*inf*); (**~ it with**) *glue, aspirin* es versuchen mit; (**~ to buy** *or* **get sth at**) *newsagent, next door* es versuchen (bei); (**~ to open**) *door, window* ausprobieren. **I can't shut this case — ~** sitting on it ich kriege diesen Koffer nicht zu — setz dich doch mal drauf! (*inf*); **you could ~ seeing whether John would help** Sie könnten doch John mal um Hilfe angehen; **I've tried everything** ich habe alles versucht *or* probiert; **~ whether ...** probieren Sie, ob ...; **~ this for size** probieren Sie mal, ob dieser/diese etc paßt; (*fig inf*) wie wär's denn damit? (*inf*); **to ~ one's hand at sth** etw *or* sich an etw (*dat*) versuchen; **to ~ one's strength** seine Kraft erproben; **to ~ one's strength against sb** seine Kräfte mit jdm messen.
  (**c**) (*sample, taste*) *beer, olives* probieren.
  (**d**) (*test*) *courage, patience* auf die Probe stellen; (*strain*) *eyes* anstrengen. **he was tried and found wanting** (*liter*) er wurde gewogen und zu leicht befunden (*liter*); (*just*) **~ me!** (*inf*) willst du's wetten?, wetten, daß?; **tried and tested** (*Comm*)

erprobt, bewährt; **this product was tried and tested in our laboratories** dieses Produkt ist in unseren Labors getestet und geprüft worden; **theirs was a tried and tested friendship** ihre Freundschaft hatte sich bewährt; **they have been sorely tried** sie sind schwer geprüft (worden); **these things are sent to ~ us** ja, ja, das Leben ist so einfach.

(e) (*Jur*) *person* vor Gericht *or* unter Anklage stellen; *case* verhandeln. **he will be/is being tried for theft** er wird wegen Diebstahls vor Gericht gestellt/er steht wegen Diebstahls vor Gericht.

3 *vi* versuchen. **~ and arrive on time** versuch mal, pünktlich zu sein; **~ as he might**, he didn't succeed sosehr er es auch versuchte *or* sosehr er sich auch bemühte, er schaffte es einfach nicht; **he wasn't even ~ing** er hat sich (*dat*) überhaupt keine Mühe gegeben; *(didn't attempt it)* er hat es überhaupt nicht versucht; **you can't say I didn't ~** du kannst nicht sagen, ich hätte es nicht versucht; *see* **succeed**.

♦**try for** *vi* +*prep obj* sich bemühen um.

♦**try on** *vt sep* (a) *clothes* anprobieren; *hat* aufprobieren.
(b) *(fig inf)* **to ~ it ~ with sb** probieren, wie weit man bei jdm gehen kann, jdn provozieren; **the policeman warned the thief not to ~ anything ~** der Polizist warnte den Dieb, keine Mätzchen (*inf*) *or* Dummheiten zu machen; **he's ~ing it ~** er probiert, wie weit er gehen *or* es treiben kann; **don't you ~ it ~ with me**, I'm not taking any excuses versuch nicht, mir etwas vorzumachen, ich dulde keine Ausreden.

♦**try out** *vt sep* ausprobieren (*on* bei, an +*dat*); *person* eine Chance geben (+*dat*), einen Versuch machen mit.

♦**try out for** *vi* +*prep obj* **two of their players are ~ing ~ ~** Arsenal zwei ihrer Spieler versuchen sich bei Arsenal.

♦**try over** *vt sep* (*Mus*) *piece* proben.

trying ['traɪɪŋ] *adj* schwierig, anstrengend; *work, day, time* anstrengend, aufreibend; *experience* schwer. **they've had a ~ time of it recently** sie haben es in letzter Zeit sehr schwer gehabt; **how ~!** wie ärgerlich!

try: ~-on *n* (*inf*) **do you think he'll do what he threatened?** — **no, it was just a ~-on** glaubst du, er wird seine Drohung wahr machen? — nein, er wollte uns nur auf den Arm nehmen (*inf*); **~out** *n* (*of car*) Probefahrt *f*; (*of actor*) Probevortrag *m*; **to give sb/sth a ~out** jdm eine Chance geben/etw ausprobieren.

tryst [trɪst] *n* (*old*) Stelldichein *nt* (*dated*).

trysting place ['trɪstɪŋpleɪs] *n* (*old*) Stelldichein *nt* (*dated*).

tsar [zɑːʳ] *n* Zar *m*.

tsarina [zɑːˈriːnə] *n* Zarin *f*.

tsarist ['zɑːrɪst] **1** *n* Zarist *m*. **2** *adj* zaristisch.

tsetse (fly) ['tsetsɪ'flaɪ] *n* Tsetsefliege *f*.

T-shirt ['tiːʃɜːt] *n* T-Shirt *nt*.

tsp(s) *abbr of* **teaspoonful(s), teaspoon(s)** Teel.

T-square ['tiːskweəʳ] *n* Reißschiene *f*.

TT *abbr of* (a) **teetotal**. (b) **teetotaller**. (c) (*Mot*) **Tourist Trophy**. (d) (*Agr*) **tuberculin-tested**.

TU (*Brit*) *abbr of* **Trade Union** Gew.

tub [tʌb] *n* (a) Kübel *m*; (*for rainwater*) Tonne, Traufe *f*; (*for washing*) Zuber, Bottich, Trog *m*; (*of ice-cream, margarine*) Becher *m*. (b) (*inf: bath ~*) Wanne *f*. (c) (*inf: boat*) Kahn *m*.

tuba ['tjuːbə] *n* Tuba *f*.

tubby ['tʌbɪ] *adj* (+*er*) (*inf*) dick; *woman* mollig, rundlich; *child* pummelig, kugelrund; *man* rundlich. **he is getting quite ~** er geht immer mehr in die Breite, er wird immer runder.

tube [tjuːb] *n* (a) (*pipe*) Rohr *nt*; (*of rubber, plastic*) Schlauch *m*; (*speaking ~*) Sprachrohr *nt*; (*torpedo ~*) (Torpedo)rohr *nt*.
(b) (*container*) (*of toothpaste, paint, glue*) Tube *f*; (*of sweets*) Röhrchen *nt*, Rolle *f*.
(c) (*London underground*) U-Bahn *f*. **to travel by ~** mit der U-Bahn fahren; **~ station** U-Bahnstation *f*; **~ train** U-Bahnzug *m*.
(d) (*Elec, TV, US Rad*) Röhre *f*. **the ~** (*US inf*) die Röhre (*inf*).
(e) (*Anat*) Röhre *f*; (*Fallopian*) Eileiter *m*. **the bronchial ~s** die Bronchien *pl*.

tubeless ['tjuːblɪs] *adj tyre* schlauchlos.

tuber ['tjuːbəʳ] *n* (*Bot*) Knolle *f*.

tubercle ['tjuːbɜːkl] *n* (*Bot*) Knoten *m*, Knötchen *nt*; (*Med also*) Tuberkel *m*.

tubercular [tjuˈbɜːkjʊləʳ] *adj* tuberkulös.

tuberculin [tjuˈbɜːkjʊlɪn] *n* Tuberkulin *nt*. **~-tested** tuberkulingetestet.

tuberculosis [tjuˌbɜːkjʊˈləʊsɪs] *n* Tuberkulose *f*.

tuberculous [tjuˈbɜːkjʊləs] *adj* tuberkulös.

tubing ['tjuːbɪŋ] *n* Schlauch *m*.

tub: ~-thumper *n* (*pej*) Demagoge, Volksredner *m*; **~-thumping 1** *n* Demagogie *f*. **2** *adj* demagogisch.

tubular ['tjuːbjʊləʳ] *adj* röhrenförmig, Röhren-. **~ bells** Glockenspiel *nt*; **~ furniture/scaffolding** Stahlrohrmöbel *pl*/-gerüst *nt*.

TUC *abbr of* **Trades Union Congress**.

tuck [tʌk] **1** *n* (a) (*Sew*) Saum *m*; (*ornamental*) Biese *f*. **to put a ~ in sth** einen Saum in etw (*acc*) nähen.
(b) (*Sch sl: food*) Süßigkeiten *pl*. **~ box** Schachtel *f* mit Süßigkeiten; **~ shop** Bonbonladen *m*.

2 *vt* (a) (*put*) stecken. **he ~ed his umbrella under his arm** er steckte *or* klemmte (*inf*) sich (*dat*) den Regenschirm unter den Arm; **the bird's head was ~ed under its wing** der Vogel hatte den Kopf unter den Flügel gesteckt; **he ~ed his coat round the shivering child** er legte seinen Mantel fest um das frierende Kind; **she sat with her feet ~ed under her** sie saß mit untergeschlagenen Beinen da.
(b) (*Sew*) Biesen steppen in (+*acc*). **a ~ed bodice** ein Oberteil *nt* mit Biesen.
3 *vi* **your bag will ~ under the seat** du kannst deine Tasche unter dem Sitz verstauen.

♦**tuck away** *vt sep* (a) (*hide*) wegstecken. **he ~ed it ~ in his**

pocket er steckte es in die Tasche; **~ it ~ out of sight** steck es weg, daß man es nicht sieht!; **the hut is ~ed ~ among the trees** die Hütte liegt versteckt zwischen den Bäumen.
(b) (*inf: eat*) **he can certainly ~ it ~!** er kann ganz schön was wegputzen (*inf*); **I can't think where he ~s it all ~** ich weiß nicht, wo er das alles läßt (*inf*).

♦**tuck in 1** *vi* (*inf*) zulangen, reinhauen (*inf*). **~ ~!** langt zu! haut rein! (*inf*); **to ~ ~ to sth** sich (*dat*) etw schmecken lassen.
2 *vt sep* (a) *flap etc* hineinstecken, reinstecken (*inf*); *sheet also* an den Seiten feststecken. **to ~ one's shirt ~(to) one's trousers, to ~ one's ~ shirt ~** das Hemd in die Hose stecken; **~ your tummy ~!** zieh den Bauch ein!
(b) **to ~ sb ~** jdn zudecken; **to ~ sb ~to bed** jdn ins Bett stecken.

♦**tuck up** *vt sep* (a) *skirt, hair* hochnehmen; *sleeve* hochkrempeln; *legs* unterschlagen. (b) **to ~ sb ~ (in bed)** jdn zudecken.

tucker[1] ['tʌkəʳ] *n* (*old: Fashion*) Schultertuch *nt*; *see* **bib**.

tucker[2] *vt* (*US inf*) fertigmachen (*inf*).

tucker[3] *n* (*esp Austral*) Proviant *m*. **~bag** Provianttasche *f*.

tuck-in ['tʌkɪn] *n* (*inf*) Essen *nt*. **to have a (good) ~** kräftig zulangen, ordentlich futtern (*inf*) *or* reinhauen (*inf*).

Tudor ['tjuːdəʳ] **1** *adj* Tudor-. **2** *n* Tudor *mf*.

Tue(s) *abbr of* **Tuesday** Di.

Tuesday ['tjuːzdɪ] *n* Dienstag *m*. **on ~** (am) Dienstag; **on ~s, on a ~** dienstags, an Dienstagen (*form*); **I met her on a ~** ich habe sie an einem Dienstag kennengelernt; **on ~ morning/evening** (am) Dienstag morgen/abend, am Dienstagmorgen/-abend; **on ~ mornings/evenings** dienstags *or* Dienstag morgens/abends; **I'll never forget that ~ evening** diesen Dienstagabend werde ich nie vergessen; **last/next/this ~** Dienstag letzter/nächster/dieser Woche, letzten/nächsten/diesen Dienstag; **a year (ago) last/next ~** letzten/nächsten Dienstag vor einem Jahr; **~'s newspaper** die Zeitung vom Dienstag; **our ~ meeting** (this week) unser Treffen am Dienstag; (*every week*) unser dienstägliches Treffen, unser Dienstagstreffen.

tuffet ['tʌfɪt] *n* (*old*) kleiner Hügel, Buckel *m*.

tuft [tʌft] *n* Büschel *nt*. **a ~ of hair/feathers** ein Haarbüschel *nt*/Federbusch *m*.

tufted ['tʌftɪd] *adj bird* Hauben-; *species* (*Orn*) mit Federbusch; (*Bot*) büschelförmig. **~ duck** Reiherente *f*.

tug [tʌg] **1** *vt* zerren, ziehen; *vessel* (ab)schleppen. **she ~ged his sleeve** sie zog an seinem Ärmel; **she ~ged a tuft of his hair out by the roots** sie zog *or* riß ihm ein Büschel Haare aus.
2 *vi* ziehen, zerren (*at* an +*dat*); *see* **heartstrings**.
3 *n* (a) (*pull*) **to give sth a ~** an etw (*dat*) ziehen; **I felt a ~ on my sleeve** ich spürte, wie mich jemand am Ärmel zog; **parting with it was quite a ~** es fiel mir *etc* sehr schwer, mich *etc* davon zu trennen; **~ of war** (*Sport, fig*) Tauziehen *nt*; **~ of love** Tauziehen um das Kind/die Kinder bei einer Ehescheidung.
(b) (*also* **~boat**) Schlepper, Schleppkahn *m*.

tuition [tjuːˈɪʃən] *n* Unterricht *m*. **extra ~** Nachhilfeunterricht.

tulip ['tjuːlɪp] *n* Tulpe *f*. **~ tree** Tulpenbaum *m*.

tulle [tjuːl] *n* Tüll *m*.

tumble ['tʌmbl] **1** *n* (a) (*fall*) Sturz *m*. **to have a ~** stürzen; **to have a ~ in the hay** (*euph*) sich lieben; **to take a ~** stürzen, straucheln; (*fig*) fallen; **his pride has taken a ~** sein Stolz ist verletzt worden.
(b) (*mess*) Durcheinander *nt*, Unordnung *f*. **in a ~** völlig durcheinander.
2 *vi* (a) (*fall*) straucheln, (hin)fallen; (*move quickly*) stürzen; (*fig: prices*) fallen. **he ~d off his bicycle** er stürzte vom Fahrrad; **the children ~d up the stairs** die Kinder stürzten die Treppe hinauf; **to ~ out of/into bed** aus dem Bett/ins Bett fallen; **to ~ over** sth über etw (*acc*) fallen *or* stolpern.
(b) (*inf: realize*) **to ~ to sth** etw kapieren (*inf*); **at last he ~d to it** endlich hat er's kapiert (*inf*) *or* ist der Groschen gefallen (*inf*).
(c) (*gymnast*) Bodenakrobatik machen.
3 *vt* (*make fall*) stoßen; (*make untidy*) *hair* zerzausen, durcheinanderbringen. **he ~d the clothes out of the washing-machine** er zerrte die Kleider aus der Waschmaschine.

♦**tumble about** *vi* durcheinanderpurzeln; (*children, kittens etc*) herumpurzeln. **the clothes ~d ~ in the drier** die Wäsche wurde im Trockenautomaten durcheinandergewirbelt.

♦**tumble down** *vi* (a) (*fall down*) (*person*) hinfallen, stürzen; (*object*) hinunter-/herunterfallen; (*building*) einstürzen. **to ~ ~ the stairs** die Treppe hinunter-/herunterfallen. (b) (*move quickly*) **they came tumbling ~ the stairs** sie kamen die Treppe heruntergestürzt.

♦**tumble in** *vi* (*come in*) hereinpurzeln.

♦**tumble out** *vi* (*go out*) heraus-/hinauspurzeln.

♦**tumble over** *vi* umfallen, umkippen.

tumble: ~down *adj* verfallen, baufällig; **~drier** *n* Trockenautomat, Heißlufttrockner *m*.

tumbler ['tʌmbləʳ] *n* (a) (*glass*) (Becher)glas *nt*, Tumbler *m*. (b) (*in lock*) Zuhaltung *f*. (c) (*acrobat*) Bodenakrobat *m*. (d) (*toy*) Stehaufmännchen *nt*. (e) (*tumble drier*) Trockenautomat *m*. (f) (*Orn*) Tümmler *m*.

tumbleweed ['tʌmblwiːd] *n* (*US*) Steppenläufer *m* *or* -hexe *f*.

tumbrel, tumbril ['tʌmbrəl] *n* (*Hist*) Karren *m*.

tumescence [tuːˈmesns] *n* (*form*) Schwellung *f*.

tumescent [tjuːˈmesnt] *adj* (*form*) anschwellend.

tumid ['tjuːmɪd] *adj* (*Med*) geschwollen; (*fig*) *style, speech* schwülstig; *style also* geschwollen.

tummy ['tʌmɪ] *n* (*inf*) Bauch *m*, Bäuchlein *nt* (*baby-talk*). **she is getting a bit of a ~** sie bekommt langsam einen Bauch; **(a) ~ ache** Bauchschmerzen *pl*, Bauchweh *nt*; **those green apples will give you (a) ~ ache** von diesen grünen Äpfeln kriegst du Bauchschmerzen *or* Bauchweh.

tumour, (*US*) **tumor** ['tjuːməʳ] *n* Geschwulst *f*, Tumor *m*. **a ~ on the brain, a brain ~** ein Gehirntumor *m*.

tumult ['tjuːmʌlt] n (a) (uproar) Tumult m. the ~ of battle das Schlachtgetümmel. (b) (emotional) his mind was in a ~ sein Inneres befand sich in Aufruhr; a ~ of rage/emotion/weeping ein Wut-/Gefühls-/Tränenausbruch m.

tumultuous [tjuːˈmʌltjʊəs] adj tumultartig, stürmisch; applause stürmisch. they gave him a ~ welcome sie begrüßten ihn stürmisch; a ~ sea stürmische See.

tumultuously [tjuːˈmʌltjʊəslɪ] adv stürmisch.

tumulus ['tjuːmjʊləs] n Tumulus, Grabhügel m.

tun [tʌn] n (cask) Faß nt.

tuna (fish) ['tjuːnə('fɪʃ)] n Thunfisch m.

tundra ['tʌndrə] n Tundra f.

tune [tjuːn] 1 n (a) (melody) Melodie f. sung to the ~ of … gesungen nach der Melodie (von) …; there's not much ~ to it das ist or klingt nicht sehr melodisch; give us a ~! spiel uns was vor!; to change one's ~ (fig) seine Meinung ändern; he changed his ~ as soon as he heard that troublemakers would be fired sein Verhalten änderte sich (schlagartig), als er hörte, daß Unruhestifter entlassen würden; to the ~ of £100 in Höhe von £ 100.
(b) (pitch) to sing in ~/out of ~ richtig/falsch singen; the piano is out of ~ das Klavier ist verstimmt; to go out of ~ (instrument) sich verstimmen; (singer) anfangen, falsch zu singen; the piano is not in ~ with the flute das Klavier und die Flöte sind nicht gleich gestimmt; to be in/out of ~ with sb/sth (fig) mit jdm/etw harmonieren/nicht harmonieren, mit jdm/etw in Einklang/nicht in Einklang stehen; he's a successful teacher because he's in ~ with the young er ist ein erfolgreicher Lehrer, weil er auf der gleichen Wellenlänge mit den Jugendlichen ist (inf); he felt out of ~ with his new environment er fühlte sich in seiner neuen Umgebung fehl am Platze.
(c) (Aut) the carburettor is out of ~ der Vergaser ist falsch eingestellt.
2 vt (a) (Mus) instrument stimmen.
(b) (Rad) einstellen. you are ~d to the BBC World Service Sie hören den or hier ist der BBC World Service.
(c) (Aut) engine, carburettor einstellen.
♦ **tune in** 1 vi (Rad) einschalten. to ~ ~ to Radio London Radio London einschalten or hören. 2 vt sep radio einschalten (to acc). you are ~d ~ to Radio 2 Sie hören or hier ist Radio 2.
♦ **tune up** 1 vi (Mus) (sein Instrument/die Instrumente) stimmen. 2 vt sep (Aut) engine tunen.

tuneful adj, **~ly** adv ['tjuːnfʊl, -fəlɪ] melodisch.

tunefulness ['tjuːnfʊlnɪs] n Melodik f. the ~ of her voice ihre melodische Stimme.

tuneless adj, **~ly** adv ['tjuːnlɪs, -lɪ] unmelodisch.

tuner ['tjuːnəʳ] n (a) (Mus) Stimmer m. (b) (Rad etc) (part of set) Empfangsteil nt; (separate set) Empfänger, Tuner m. **~-amp(lifier)** Steuergerät nt, Receiver m.

tune-up ['tjuːnʌp] n (Aut) the car needs/has had a ~ das Auto muß getunt werden/ist getunt worden.

tungsten ['tʌŋstən] n Wolfram nt. ~ **lamp/steel** Wolframlampe f/-stahl m.

tunic ['tjuːnɪk] n Kasack m, Hemdbluse f; (of uniform) Uniformrock m; (of school uniform) Kittel m; (in ancient Greece) Chiton m; (in ancient Rome) Tunika f.

tuning ['tjuːnɪŋ] n (a) (Mus) Stimmen nt. **~-fork** Stimmgabel f.
(b) (Rad) Einstellen nt. it takes a lot of ~ to find the right station man muß lange suchen, bis man den richtigen Sender gefunden hat; ~ **knob** Stationswahlknopf m.
(c) (Aut) Einstellen nt. all the engine needed was a little ~ der Motor mußte nur richtig eingestellt werden.

Tunisia [tjuːˈnɪzɪə] n Tunesien nt.

Tunisian [tjuːˈnɪzɪən] 1 n Tunesier(in f) m. 2 adj tunesisch.

tunnel ['tʌnl] 1 n Tunnel m; (under road, railway also) Unterführung f; (Min) Stollen m. ~ **vision** (Med) Gesichtsfeldeinengung f.
2 vi (into in +acc, through durch) einen Tunnel bauen; (rabbit) einen Bau graben; (mole) Gänge graben. they ~led under the walls of the jail sie gruben (sich dat) einen Tunnel unter den Mauern des Gefängnisses hindurch.
3 vt they ~led a road through the mountain sie bauten einen Straßentunnel durch den Berg; they ~led a passage under the prison wall sie gruben sich unter der Gefängnismauer durch; the hillside had been ~led by rabbits Kaninchen hatten ihre Baue in den Hang gegraben; to ~ one's way through sth sich durch etw hindurchgraben.

tunny (fish) ['tʌnɪ('fɪʃ)] n Thunfisch m.

tuppence ['tʌpəns] n zwei Pence. I don't care ~ das interessiert mich nicht für fünf Pfennig (inf), das ist mir doch so egal (inf).

tuppenny ['tʌpənɪ] adj für zwei Pence; stamp, piece etc Zweipence-. we took a ~ bus ride into the centre of town wir fuhren für zwei Pence mit dem Bus in die Innenstadt; ~ **bit** Zweipencestück nt.

tuppenny-ha'penny ['tʌpnɪ'heɪpnɪ] adj (Brit inf) lächerlich.

turban ['tɜːbən] n Turban m.

turbid ['tɜːbɪd] adj (a) liquid trübe, schmutzig. ~ **clouds of smoke** dicke Rauchwolken. (b) (fig: confused) verworren.

turbidity [tɜːˈbɪdɪtɪ] n see adj (a) Trübheit, Schmutzigkeit f. (b) Verworrenheit f.

turbine ['tɜːbaɪn] n Turbine f.

turbojet ['tɜːbəʊˈdʒet] n (engine) Turbotriebwerk nt; (aircraft) Düsenflugzeug nt, Turbojet m.

turboprop ['tɜːbəʊˈprɒp] n (engine) Propellerturbine, Turboprop f; (aircraft) Turbo-Prop-Flugzeug nt.

turbot ['tɜːbət] n Steinbutt m.

turbulence ['tɜːbjʊləns] n (of person, crowd) Ungestüm nt, Wildheit f; (of emotions) Aufgewühltheit f; (of career, period) Turbulenz f. **air** ~ Turbulenz f; **the** ~ **of the water** das stürmische Wasser.

turbulent ['tɜːbjʊlənt] adj stürmisch; person, crowd ungestüm,

wild; emotions also aufgewühlt; career, period also turbulent.

turd [tɜːd] n (vulg) (a) Kacke (sl), Scheiße (sl) f no pl. (b) (pej: person) Scheißkerl m (sl).

tureen [təˈriːn] n (Suppen)terrine f.

turf [tɜːf] 1 n, pl -s or turves (a) (no pl: lawn) Rasen m; (no pl: squares of grass) Soden pl; (square of grass) Sode f.
(b) (no pl: peat) Torf(soden pl) m; (square of peat) Torfsode f. to cut ~(s) Torf(soden) stechen.
(c) (Sport) the T~ die (Pferde)rennbahn; all his life he was a devotee of the T~ sein Leben galt dem Pferderennsport; ~ **accountant** Buchmacher m.
2 vt (a) he ~ed the garden er verlegte (Gras)soden im Garten.
(b) (inf) to ~ sb down the stairs/up to bed jdn die Treppe hinunterscheuchen (inf)/ins Bett scheuchen (inf); to ~ sth into the corner/up in the attic etw in die Ecke/auf den Dachboden werfen.
♦ **turf out** vt sep (inf) person rauswerfen, rausschmeißen (inf); plan umschmeißen (inf), verwerfen; suggestions abtun; (throw away) wegschmeißen (inf).
♦ **turf over** vt sep (a) garden mit (Gras)soden bedecken. (b) (inf: throw over) rüberwerfen (inf) (to sb jdm).

turgid ['tɜːdʒɪd] adj (swollen) (an)geschwollen; (fig) style schwülstig, überladen.

turgidity [tɜːˈdʒɪdɪtɪ] n see adj Schwellung f; Schwülstigkeit f. **the** ~ **of this writer's style** der schwülstige Stil dieses Schriftstellers.

Turk [tɜːk] n Türke m, Türkin f.

Turkey ['tɜːkɪ] n die Türkei.

turkey ['tɜːkɪ] n (a) Truthahn m/-henne f, Pute(r) m f (esp Cook). (b) to talk ~ (US inf) Tacheles reden (inf).

turkey: ~ **buzzard** n Truthangeier m; ~**cock** n Truthahn, Puter (esp Cook) m; he's a real little ~cock of a man er ist ein richtiger kleiner Fatzke (inf).

Turkish ['tɜːkɪʃ] 1 adj türkisch. ~ **bath** türkisches Bad; ~ **delight** Lokum nt; ~ **towel** Frotteehandtuch nt. 2 n (language) Türkisch nt.

turmeric ['tɜːmərɪk] n Kurkuma, Gelbwurz f.

turmoil ['tɜːmɔɪl] n Aufruhr m; (confusion) Durcheinander nt. he was glad to escape from the ~ of politics er war froh, daß er sich aus der Hektik der Politik zurückziehen konnte; everything is in a ~ alles ist in Aufruhr; her mind was in a ~ sie war völlig verwirrt; her mind was in a ~ of indecision sie wußte überhaupt nicht mehr, wie sie sich entscheiden sollte.

turn [tɜːn] 1 n (a) (movement) Drehung f. six ~s of the wheel sechs Umdrehungen des Rades; to give sth a ~ etw drehen; give the handle another ~ dreh den Griff noch einmal herum; done to a ~ (Cook) genau richtig.
(b) (change of direction) (in road) Kurve f; (Sport) Wende f. to make a ~ to the left nach links einbiegen; (driver, car also, road) nach links abbiegen; (road) eine Linkskurve machen; take the left-hand ~ biegen Sie links ab; to make a ~ to port (Naut) nach Backbord abdrehen; "no left ~" „Linksabbiegen verboten"; the Canadian swimmer made the better ~ der kanadische Schwimmer wendete besser; he gets his horse to make a very tight ~ er wendet sein Pferd sehr eng; watch out for that sudden ~ in the road paß auf, die Straße macht eine scharfe Kurve; the ~ of the tide der Gezeitenwechsel; the children were trapped on the island by the ~ of the tide die Kinder wurden durch das Einsetzen der Flut auf der Insel festgehalten; the government just seems to be sitting back waiting for the ~ of the tide (fig) die Regierung scheint einfach nur dazusitzen und auf einen Umschwung or eine Wende zu warten; the tide is on the ~ (lit) die Ebbe/Flut setzt ein. She ist im Stau (spec); (fig) es tritt eine Wende ein; the milk/meat is on the ~ die Milch/das Fleisch hat einen Stich; at the ~ of the century um die Jahrhundertwende; at the ~ of the 18th century an der or die Wende des 18. Jahrhunderts; the ~ of the year die Jahreswende, der Jahreswechsel; at every ~ (fig) auf Schritt und Tritt; things took a ~ for the worse/the better das Blatt wendete sich zum Guten/zum Schlechten; the patient took a ~ for the worse/the better das Befinden des Patienten wendete sich zum Schlechteren/zum Besseren; things took a new ~ die Dinge nahmen eine neue Wendung; I'm very upset by the ~ of events ich bin über den Verlauf der Dinge sehr beunruhigt; events took a tragic ~ die Dinge nahmen einen tragischen or verhängnisvollen Verlauf.
(c) (in game, queue, series) in ~ der Reihe nach; out of ~ außer der Reihe; it's your ~ du bist an der Reihe or dran; it's your ~ to do the washing-up du bist mit (dem) Abwaschen an der Reihe or dran; it's your ~ to serve (Tennis) du schlägst auf; now it's his ~ to be jealous jetzt ist er zur Abwechslung eifersüchtig; whose ~ is it? wer ist an der Reihe or dran?; it's my ~ next ich komme als nächste(r) an die Reihe or dran; wait your ~ warten Sie, bis Sie an der Reihe sind; to miss a ~ eine Runde aussetzen; your ~ will come du kommst auch noch mal dran; my secretary was speaking out of ~ es stand meiner Sekretärin nicht zu, sich darüber zu äußern; sorry, have I spoken out of ~? Entschuldigung, habe ich etwas Falsches gesagt?; and then Anne Boleyn too, in her ~, … und dann kam auch die Reihe an Anne Boleyn …; ~ and ~ about abwechselnd; the children will just have to take ~ and ~ about with the swing die Kinder werden eben abwechselnd schaukeln müssen; in ~, by ~s abwechselnd; she was confident then depressed by ~s sie war abwechselnd zuversichtlich und depressiv; to take ~s at doing sth, to take it in ~(s) to do sth etw abwechselnd tun; take it in ~s! wechselt euch ab!; to take ~s at the wheel sich am Steuer or beim Fahren abwechseln; to take a ~ at the wheel (für eine Weile) das Steuer übernehmen.
(d) (service) to do sb a good/bad ~ jdm einen guten/ schlechten Dienst erweisen; a boy scout has to do a good

~ every day ein Pfadfinder muß jeden Tag eine gute Tat tun; **one good ~ deserves another** (*Prov*) eine Hand wäscht die andere (*prov*), hilfst du mir, so helf ich dir.

(e) (*tendency, talent*) Hang *m*, Neigung *f*. **to have a mathematical ~ of mind** mathematisch begabt sein; **an optimistic/a strange ~ of mind** eine optimistische/seltsame Einstellung; **a melancholy ~ of mind** ein Hang zur Melancholie.

(f) (*Med inf*) he had one of his ~s last night er hatte letzte Nacht wieder einen Anfall; **you/it gave me quite a ~** du hast/es hat mir einen schönen Schrecken eingejagt.

(g) (*Theat*) Nummer *f*. **they got him to do a ~ at the party** sie brachten ihn dazu, auf der Party etwas zum besten zu geben; **isn't he a ~!** (*inf*) ist er nicht ein richtiger Komiker?

(h) (*purpose*) **it will serve my ~** das ist für meine Zwecke gerade richtig; **we'll throw these old carpets away once they've served their ~** wir werfen diese alten Teppiche weg, wenn sie ihren Zweck erfüllt *or* wenn sie ausgedient haben.

(i) (*walk, stroll*) **to take a ~ in the park** eine Runde durch den Park machen.

(j) ~ **of phrase** Ausdrucksweise *f*; **to have a good ~ of speed** (*car*) sehr schnell fahren; (*horse, athlete*) sehr schnell sein.

2 *vt* **(a)** (*revolve*) knob, key, screw, steering wheel drehen. **to ~ the key in the lock** den Schlüssel im Schloß herumdrehen; **what ~s the wheel?** wie wird das Rad angetrieben?; **he ~ed the wheel sharply** er riß das Steuer herum; **to ~ a somersault** einen Purzelbaum schlagen.

(b) he ~ed his head towards me er wandte mir den Kopf zu; **he ~ed his back to the wall** er kehrte den Rücken zur Wand; **success has ~ed his head** der Erfolg ist ihm zu Kopf gestiegen; **she seems to have ~ed his head** sie scheint ihm den Kopf verdreht zu haben; **she can still ~ a few heads** die Leute schauen sich immer noch nach ihr um; **to ~ sb's brain** jds Sinne *or* Geist verwirren; **the tragedy ~ed his brain** durch die Tragödie ist er völlig verstört; **as soon as his back is ~ed** sobald er den Rücken kehrt; **to ~ one's eyes towards sb** jdn anblicken; **the sight of all that food quite ~ed my stomach** beim Anblick des vielen Essens drehte sich mir regelrecht der Magen um; **without ~ing a hair** ohne mit der Wimper zu zucken; **he can ~ his hand to anything** er kann alles, er ist sehr geschickt; **she ~ed her hand to cooking** sie versuchte sich im Kochen.

(c) (~ *over*) mattress, collar, soil, hay wenden; record umdrehen; page umblättern.

(d) (*change position of,* ~ *round*) car, lorry wenden; chair, picture etc umdrehen.

(e) (*direct*) **to ~ one's thoughts/attention to sth** seine Gedanken/Aufmerksamkeit auf eine Sache (*dat*) zuwenden; **to ~ one's steps homeward** seine Schritte heimwärts lenken (*liter, hum*); **to ~ a gun on sb** ein Gewehr auf jdn richten; **the police ~ed the hoses on the demonstrators** die Polizei richtete die Wasserwerfer auf die Demonstranten.

(f) (*pass*) **he is** *or* **has ~ed forty** er hat die Vierzig überschritten; **it is** *or* **has ~ed 2 o'clock** es ist 2 Uhr vorbei.

(g) the car ~ed the corner das Auto bog um die Ecke; **to have ~ed the corner** (*fig*) über den Berg sein.

(h) (*transform, make become*) verwandeln (*in(to)* in +*acc*). **his courage ~ed defeat to victory** sein Mut verwandelte die Niederlage in einen Sieg; **the play was ~ed into a film** das Stück wurde verfilmt; **to ~ verse into prose** Lyrik in Prosa übertragen; **to ~ English expressions into German** aus englischen Ausdrücken deutsche machen; **the shock ~ed his hair grey overnight** durch den Schock bekam er über Nacht graue Haare; **that house ~s me green with envy** das Haus läßt mich vor Neid erblassen; **the smoke ~ed the walls black** der Rauch schwärzte die Wände; **to ~ the lights low** das Licht herunterdrehen; **this hot weather has ~ed the milk (sour)** bei dieser Hitze ist die Milch sauer geworden.

(i) (*deflect*) nothing will ~ him from his purpose nichts wird ihn von seinem Vorhaben abbringen.

(j) (*shape*) wood drechseln; metal, pot drehen. **a well-~ed sentence/leg** ein gutformulierter Satz/wohlgeformtes Bein.

(k) (*set*) **to ~ a boat adrift** ein Boot losmachen und treiben lassen; **to ~ sb loose** jdn loslassen *or* laufen lassen; **just ~ John loose in a library and he'll be quite happy** John brauchst du nur in eine Bibliothek zu setzen, dann ist er ganz zufrieden; **the children were ~ed loose on the moor** man ließ die Kinder in der Heide laufen; **to ~ a dog on sb** einen Hund auf jdn hetzen.

3 *vi* **(a)** (*revolve, move round: key, screw, wheel*) sich drehen. **the world ~s on its axis** die Erde dreht sich um ihre Achse; **he ~ed to me and smiled** er drehte sich mir zu und lächelte; **this tap won't ~** dieser Hahn läßt sich nicht drehen; **to ~ upside down** umkippen; **my head is ~ing** in meinem Kopf dreht sich alles; **his stomach ~ed at the sight** bei dem Anblick drehte sich ihm der Magen um; *see* tail, toss, turtle.

(b) (*change direction*) (*to one side*) (*person, car*) abbiegen; (*plane, boat*) abdrehen; (~ *around*) wenden; (*person: on the spot*) sich umdrehen; (*wind*) drehen. **to ~ and go back** umkehren; **until the tide ~s** bis zum Gezeitenwechsel, bis die Flut/Ebbe einsetzt; **to ~ (to the) left** links abbiegen; **left ~!** (*Mil*) linksum!; **our luck ~ed** das Blatt hat sich gewendet.

(c) (*go*) **to ~ to sb/sth** sich an jdn wenden/sich einer Sache (*dat*) zuwenden; **after her death, he ~ to his books for comfort** nach ihrem Tod suchte er Trost bei seinen Büchern; **this job would make anyone ~ to drink!** bei dieser Arbeit muß man ja zum Trinker werden!; **our thoughts ~ to those who ...** wir gedenken derer, die ...; **the conversation ~ed to the accident** das Gespräch kam auf den Unfall, man kam auf den Unfall zu sprechen; **I don't know which way** *or* **where to ~ for help/money** ich weiß nicht, an wen ich mich um Hilfe wenden kann/wen ich um Geld bitten kann; **I don't know which way to ~** ich weiß nicht, was ich machen soll.

(d) (*leaves*) sich (ver)färben; (*milk*) sauer werden; (*meat*) schlecht werden; (*weather*) umschlagen. **to ~ into sth** sich in etw (*acc*) verwandeln; (*develop into*) sich zu etw entwickeln; **their short holiday ~ed into a three-month visit** aus ihrem Kurzurlaub wurde ein Aufenthalt von drei Monaten; **the prince ~ed into a frog** der Prinz verwandelte sich in einen Frosch; **his admiration ~ed to scorn** seine Bewunderung verwandelte sich in Verachtung; **to ~ to stone** zu Stein werden.

(e) (*become*) werden. **to ~ traitor** zum Verräter werden; **XY, an actor ~ed director, ...** der Regisseur XY, ein ehemaliger Schauspieler, ...; **he began to ~ awkward** er wurde unangenehm *or* ungemütlich; **to ~ red** (*leaves etc*) sich rot färben; (*person: blush*) rot werden; (*traffic lights*) auf Rot umspringen; **his hair is ~ing grey** sein Haar wird grau; **he has** *or* **is just ~ed 18** er ist gerade 18 geworden.

♦**turn about 1** *vi* (*person*) sich umdrehen; (*car, boat, driver etc*) wenden. **we had to ~** ~ **and go home** wir mußten umkehren (und nach Hause gehen).
2 *vt sep* car wenden. **he ~ed himself ~** er wandte sich um.

♦**turn against 1** *vi* +*prep obj* sich wenden gegen. **2** *vt sep* +*prep obj* they ~ed him ~ his parents sie brachten ihn gegen seine Eltern auf; they ~ed his argument ~ him sie verwendeten sein Argument gegen ihn.

♦**turn around 1** *vt sep* **(a)** *see* turn about 2. **(b)** (*factory, docks*) ship etc abfertigen; (*develop into*) sich zu etw entwickeln. **2** *vi* +*prep obj* corner biegen um. **3** *vi see* turn about 1. the wheel ~s around on its axis das Rad dreht sich um seine Achse.

♦**turn aside 1** *vi* sich abwenden (*from* von). **2** *vt sep* abwenden.

♦**turn away 1** *vi* sich abwenden. **2** *vt sep* **(a)** (*move*) head, eyes, gun abwenden. **(b)** (*send away*) person wegschicken, abweisen; business zurückweisen, ablehnen.

♦**turn back 1** *vi* **(a)** (*traveller*) zurückgehen, umkehren; (*aeroplane*) umkehren; (*look back*) sich umdrehen. **we can't ~** ~ **now, there can be no ~ing ~ now** (*fig*) jetzt gibt es kein Zurück mehr.
(b) (*in book*) **to ~ ~ to page 100** auf Seite 100 zurückblättern.
2 *vt sep* **(a)** (*fold*) bedclothes zurück- *or* aufschlagen; corner umknicken; hem umschlagen.
(b) (*send back*) person zurückschicken. **bad weather ~ed the plane ~ to Heathrow** schlechtes Wetter zwang das Flugzeug zur Rückkehr nach Heathrow; **they were ~ed ~ at the frontier** sie wurden an der Grenze zurückgewiesen.
(c) clock zurückstellen; (*fig*) zurückdrehen. **to ~ the clock ~ fifty years** die Uhr um fünfzig Jahre zurückdrehen.

♦**turn down 1** *vt sep* **(a)** (*fold down*) bedclothes zurück- *or* aufschlagen; collar, brim herunterklappen; corner of a page umknicken.
(b) gas, heat herunterdrehen, kleiner stellen; volume, radio, television leiser stellen; lights herunterdrehen.
(c) (*refuse*) candidate, novel etc ablehnen; offer also zurückweisen; suitor abweisen.
(d) card verdeckt hin- *or* ablegen.
2 *vi* +*prep obj* he ~ed ~ a side street er bog in eine Seitenstraße ab.

♦**turn in 1** *vi* **(a)** her toes ~ ~ when she walks sie läuft nach innen, sie läuft über den großen Onkel (*inf*).
(b) (*drive in*) the car ~ed ~ at the top of the drive das Auto bog in die Einfahrt ein.
(c) (*inf: go to bed*) sich hinhauen (*inf*), in die Falle gehen (*inf*).
(d) **to ~ ~ on oneself** sich in sich (*acc*) selbst zurückziehen.
2 *vt sep* **(a)** she ~ed ~ her toes as she walked sie lief nach innen, sie lief über den großen Onkel (*inf*); **to ~ ~ the ends of sth** die Enden von etw umschlagen.
(b) (*inf: to police*) **to ~ sb ~** jdn anzeigen *or* verpfeifen (*inf*).
(c) (*inf: give back*) equipment zurückgeben *or* -bringen; weapons (*to police*) abgeben (*to* bei).
(d) (*exchange*) eintauschen (*for* gegen).
(e) (*Brit sl*) **to ~ it ~!** jetzt mach aber mal einen Punkt! (*inf*).

♦**turn into** *vti* +*prep obj see* turn 2 (h), 3 (d).

♦**turn off 1** *vi* abbiegen (*for* nach, prep obj von).
2 *vt sep* **(a)** light ausdrehen, ausmachen (*inf*); gas, radio also abdrehen; tap zudrehen; TV programme abschalten; water, electricity, engine, machine abstellen.
(b) (*sl*) **to ~ sb ~** (*disgust*) jdn anwidern; (*put off*) jdm die Lust verderben *or* nehmen; **when they mentioned the price that ~ed me right ~** als sie den Preis nannten, war für mich der Kuchen gegessen (*sl*); **this town really ~s me ~** diese Stadt stinkt mir (*sl*).

♦**turn on 1** *vi* (*Rad, TV*) we ~ed ~ at 8 o'clock wir haben um 8 Uhr eingeschaltet.
2 *vt sep* **(a)** gas, heat anstellen, anmachen (*inf*); radio, television, the news also einschalten; light einschalten, andrehen, anmachen (*inf*); tap, central heating aufdrehen; bath water einlaufen lassen; engine, machine anstellen. **to ~ ~ the charm** seinen (ganzen) Charme spielen lassen; **he can really ~ ~ the charm** er kann wirklich sehr charmant sein.
(b) (*sl: with drugs*) anturnen (*sl*).
(c) (*sl: appeal to: music, novel etc*) sth ~s sb ~ jd steht auf etw (*acc*) (*sl*), jd findet etw Spitze (*sl*), jd fährt auf etw (*acc*) voll ab (*sl*); whatever ~s you ~ wenn du das gut findest (*inf*); he/it doesn't ~ me ~ er/das läßt mich kalt (*also sexually*).
(d) (*sl: sexually*) scharf machen (*sl*), anmachen (*sl*). she really ~s me ~ auf sie kann ich voll abfahren (*sl*); you know how to ~ me ~ du kannst mich wirklich auf Touren bringen (*sl*); it ~s me ~ when ... ich werde ganz scharf, wenn ... (*inf*).
3 *vi* +*prep obj* **(a)** (~ *against*) sich wenden gegen; (*attack*) angreifen.
(b) (*depend on*) abhängen von, ankommen auf (+*acc*).

♦**turn out 1** *vi* **(a)** (*appear, attend*) erscheinen, kommen.
(b) (*firemen, police*) ausrücken; (*doctor*) einen Krankenbesuch machen.

(c) (*point*) his toes ~ ~ er läuft nach außen.

(d) the car ~ed ~ of the drive das Auto bog aus der Einfahrt.

(e) (*transpire*) sich herausstellen. he ~ed ~ to be the murderer himself es stellte sich heraus, daß er selbst der Mörder war.

(f) (*develop, progress*) sich entwickeln, sich machen (*inf*). how did it ~ ~? (*what happened*) was ist daraus geworden?; (*cake etc*) wie ist er *etc* geworden?; it all depends how things ~ ~ es kommt darauf an, wie sich die Dinge ergeben; as it ~ed ~ wie sich herausstellte; everything will ~ ~ all right es wird sich schon alles ergeben.

2 *vt sep* (a) *light* ausmachen; *gas also* abstellen.

(b) he ~s his toes ~ er läuft nach außen.

(c) (*produce*) produzieren; *novel etc* schreiben. the college ~s ~ good teachers das College bringt gute Lehrer hervor.

(d) (*expel*) vertreiben (*of aus*), hinauswerfen (*inf*) (*of aus*); *tenant* kündigen (+*dat*), auf die Straße setzen (*inf*). he was ~ed ~ of his job er verlor seinen Arbeitsplatz.

(e) (*Cook: tip out*) *cake* stürzen. he ~ed the photos ~ of the box er kippte die Fotos aus der Schachtel.

(f) (*empty*) *pockets* (aus)leeren.

(g) (*clean*) *room* gründlich saubermachen.

(h) *guard* antreten lassen.

(i) (*usu pass: dress*) well ~ed-~ gut gekleidet *or* ausstaffiert; *troops* tadellos, geschniegelt und gestriegelt (*inf*).

♦**turn over 1** *vi* (a) (*person*) sich umdrehen; (*car, plane etc*) sich überschlagen; (*boat*) umkippen, kentern; (*stomach*) sich umdrehen. he ~ed ~ on(to) his back/stomach er drehte sich auf den Rücken/Bauch.

(b) (*with pages*) please ~ ~ bitte wenden.

(c) (*Aut: engine*) laufen. with the engine ~ing ~ mit laufendem Motor.

2 *vt sep* (a) umdrehen; (*turn upside down*) umkippen; *page* umblättern; *soil* umgraben; *mattress, steak* wenden. he ~ed the car ~ er überschlug sich (mit dem Auto); the police ~ed the whole place ~ (*search*) die Polizei durchsuchte das ganze Haus *etc*; this doesn't make sense, I must have ~ed ~ two pages das ergibt keinen Sinn, ich muß eine Seite überschlagen haben; to ~ an idea ~ in one's mind eine Idee überdenken, sich (*dat*) eine Idee durch den Kopf gehen lassen; see leaf.

(b) (*hand over*) übergeben (*to dat*).

(c) (*Comm*) *goods* umsetzen. to ~ ~ £500 a week einen Umsatz von £ 500 in der Woche haben; how much do you ~ ~ per week? welchen Umsatz haben Sie pro Woche?

(d) (*Aut*) *engine* laufen lassen.

♦**turn round 1** *vi* (a) (*face other way*) sich umdrehen; (*go back*) umkehren. to ~ ~ and go back umkehren; to ~ ~ and go back to camp ins Lager zurückkehren.

(b) (*inf*) one day she'll just ~ ~ and leave you eines Tages wird sie dich ganz einfach verlassen; but you can't just ~ ~ and refuse aber du kannst dich doch nicht einfach weigern!; he just ~ed ~ and hit him er drehte sich einfach um und schlug ihn.

2 *vi* +*prep obj* we ~ed ~ the corner wir bogen um die Ecke; the earth ~s ~ the sun die Erde dreht sich um die Sonne.

3 *vt sep* (a) *head* drehen; *box* umdrehen. ~ the picture ~ the other way dreh das Bild andersherum.

(b) (*factory, docks etc*) *ship* abfertigen; *goods* fertigstellen.

♦**turn to 1** *vi* (*get busy*) sich an die Arbeit machen. **2** *vi* +*prep obj* (a) to ~ ~ sb/sth see turn 3 (c). (b) (*get busy*) after a short rest, they ~ed ~ their work again nach einer kurzen Pause machten sie sich wieder an die Arbeit.

♦**turn up 1** *vi* (a) (*arrive*) erscheinen, auftauchen (*inf*). I was afraid you wouldn't ~ ~ ich hatte Angst, du würdest nicht kommen; two years later he ~ed ~ in London zwei Jahre später tauchte er in London auf; the queen hasn't ~ed ~ yet (*Cards*) die Dame ist noch im Spiel.

(b) (*be found*) sich (an)finden, (wieder) auftauchen (*inf*); (*smaller things also*) zum Vorschein kommen.

(c) (*happen*) something is sure to ~ ~ irgend etwas tut sich *or* passiert schon; things have a habit of ~ing ~ irgendwie findet sich alles; it's amazing the way things ~ ~ es ist manchmal erstaunlich, wie sich die Dinge finden.

(d) (*point up*) his nose ~s ~ er hat eine Himmelfahrts- (*inf*) *or* Stupsnase; a ~ed-~ nose eine Himmelfahrts- (*inf*) *or* Stupsnase; to ~ ~ at the ends sich an den Enden hochbiegen.

2 *vt sep* (a) (*fold*) *collar* hochklappen; *sleeve* aufrollen, aufkrempeln (*inf*); *hem* umnähen. to ~ ~ one's nose at sth (*fig*) die Nase über etw (*acc*) rümpfen.

(b) *heat, gas* aufdrehen, höher drehen; *radio* lauter drehen; *volume* aufdrehen; *light* heller machen.

(c) (*fluid*) finden, entdecken. to ~ ~ some information Informationen auftreiben, an Informationen kommen.

(d) *soil* umpflügen.

(e) (*Brit sl*) ~ it ~! Mensch, hör auf damit! (*inf*).

turn-: ~about, ~around *n* Kehrtwendung *f*; ~coat *n* Abtrünnige(r), Überläufer *m*.

turner ['tɜːnə'] *n* (*of metal*) Dreher *m*; (*of wood*) Drechsler *m*.

turning ['tɜːnɪŋ] *n* (a) (*in road*) Abzweigung *f*. take the second ~ on the left nimm die zweite Abfahrt links; it's a long road that has no ~ (*prov*) nichts dauert ewig. (b) (*Tech*) (*of metal*) Drehen *nt*; (*of wood*) Drechseln *nt*.

turning: ~ circle *n* (*Aut*) Wendekreis *m*; ~ lathe *n* Drehbank *f*; ~ point *n* Wendepunkt *m*.

turnip ['tɜːnɪp] *n* Rübe *f*; (*swede*) Steckrübe *f*; (*hum inf: pocket watch*) Zwiebel *f* (*hum inf*).

turn-: ~key *n* (*old*) Kerkermeister (*old*), Schließer, Gefängniswärter *m*; ~-off *n* Abzweigung *f*; (*on motorway*) Abfahrt, Ausfahrt *f*; the Birmingham ~-off die Abzweigung nach Birmingham; die Abfahrt *or* Ausfahrt Birmingham.

turnout ['tɜːnaʊt] *n* (a) (*attendance*) Teilnahme, Beteiligung *f*.

in spite of the rain there was a good/big ~ for the match trotz des Regens war das Spiel gut besucht; there was a big ~ of friends to meet us at the station eine Menge Freunde waren gekommen, um uns am Bahnhof zu begrüßen.

(b) (*clean-out*) she gave the room a thorough ~ sie machte den Raum gründlich sauber.

(c) (*Comm: output*) Produktion *f*.

(d) (*dress*) Aufmachung *f*.

turnover ['tɜːnˌəʊvə'] *n* (*total business*) Umsatz *m*; (*Comm, Fin: of capital*) Umlauf *m*; (*Comm: of stock*) (Lager)umschlag *m*; (*of staff*) Personalwechsel *m*, Fluktuation *f*.

turn: ~pike *n* (*Brit Hist*) Mautschranke *f*; (*US*) gebührenpflichtige Autobahn *f*; ~-round *n* (*of ship*) Abfertigung *f*; (*of goods*) Fertigstellung *f*; ~-round time Abfertigungs-/ Fertigstellungszeit *f*; ~stile *n* Drehkreuz *nt*; ~table *n* Drehscheibe *f*; (*on record player*) Plattenteller *m*; ~table ladder Drehleiter *f*; ~-up *n* (a) (*Brit: on trousers*) Aufschlag *m*; (b) (*inf: event*) that was a ~-up for the book das war eine (echte) Überraschung, das war (vielleicht) ein Ding (*inf*).

turpentine ['tɜːpəntaɪn] *n* Terpentin(öl) *nt*. ~ substitute Terpentin(öl)ersatz *m*.

turpitude ['tɜːpɪtjuːd] *n* Verderbtheit *f*.

turps [tɜːps] *n sing* (*inf*) *abbr of* turpentine.

turquoise ['tɜːkwɔɪz] **1** *n* (a) (*gem*) Türkis *m*. (b) (*colour*) Türkis *nt*. **2** *adj* türkis(farben).

turret ['tʌrɪt] *n* (*Archit*) Mauer- *or* Eckturm *m*; (*on tank*) Turm *m*; (*on ship*) Gefechtsturm *m*. ~ gun Türmgeschütz *nt*.

turreted ['tʌrɪtɪd] *adj* a ~ castle ein Schloß mit Mauer- *or* Ecktürmen.

turtle ['tɜːtl] *n* (*Wasser*)schildkröte *f*; (*US also*) (Land)-schildkröte *f*. to turn ~ kentern; see mock ~ soup.

turtle: ~-dove *n* (*lit, fig inf*) Turteltaube *f*; ~-neck (pullover) *n* Schildkrötenkragenpullover *m*.

turves [tɜːvz] *pl of* turf.

Tuscan ['tʌskən] **1** *adj* toskanisch. **2** *n* (a) Toskaner(in *f*) *m*. (b) (*language*) Toskanisch *nt*.

Tuscany ['tʌskənɪ] *n* die Toskana.

tush [tʌʃ] *interj* (*dated*) pah, bah.

tusk [tʌsk] *n* (*of elephant*) Stoßzahn *m*; (*of walrus*) Eckzahn *m*; (*of boar*) Hauer *m*.

tusker ['tʌskə'] *n* Elefantenbulle *m*; (*boar*) Keiler *m*.

tussle ['tʌsl] **1** *n* (*lit, fig*) Gerangel *nt*. **2** *vi* sich rangeln (*with sb for sth* mit jdm um etw).

tussock ['tʌsək] *n* (Gras)büschel *nt*.

tut [tʌt] *interj, vti see* tut-tut.

tutelage ['tjuːtɪlɪdʒ] *n* (*form*) (a) (*teaching*) Führung, Anleitung *f*. the students made good progress under his able ~ bei diesem guten Unterricht machten die Schüler große Fortschritte. (b) (*guardianship*) Vormundschaft *f*.

tutelary ['tjuːtɪlərɪ] *adj* (*form*) (*of guardian*) vormundschaftlich. a ~ saint ein Schutzpatron *m*.

tutor ['tjuːtə'] **1** *n* (a) (*private teacher*) Privat- *or* Hauslehrer *m*. (b) (*Brit Univ*) Tutor *m*.

2 *vt* (a) (*as private teacher*) privat unterrichten; (*give extra lessons to*) Nachhilfe(unterricht) geben (+*dat*). to ~ sb in Latin jdm Privatunterricht/Nachhilfe in Latein geben. (b) (*liter: discipline*) *emotions* beherrschen.

tutorial [tjuːˈtɔːrɪəl] **1** *n* (*Brit Univ*) Kolloquium *nt*. **2** *adj* duties Tutoren-. the ~ system das Tutorensystem; he has found a ~ post with a wealthy family er hat bei einer reichen Familie eine Stelle als Haus- *or* Privatlehrer gefunden.

tutti-frutti ['tuːtɪ'fruːtɪ] *n* (*ice-cream*) Tuttifrutti *nt*.

tut-tut ['tʌt'tʌt] **1** *interj* (*in disapproval*) na, na, aber, aber. **2** *vi* she ~ted in disapproval na, na! *or* aber, aber!, sagte sie mißbilligend. **3** *vt* *idea* mißbilligen.

tutu ['tuːtuː] *n* (*Ballet*) Tutu, Ballettröckchen *nt*.

tu-whit tu-whoo [tuˈwɪttuˈwuː] *interj* (sch)uhu.

tux [tʌks] (*inf*), **tuxedo** [tʌkˈsiːdəʊ] *n* (*US*) Smoking *m*.

TV *n* (*inf*) *abbr of* television Fernsehen *nt*; (*set*) Fernseher *m* (*inf*). on ~ im Fernsehen; a ~ programme eine Fernsehsendung; a ~ personality ein Fernsehstar *m*; ~ dinner (*US*) Fertigmahlzeit *f*; see also television.

TVA *abbr of* Tennessee Valley Authority.

twaddle ['twɒdl] *n* (*inf*) Geschwätz *nt*, dummes Zeug (*inf*). to talk ~ dummes Zeug reden (*inf*).

twain [tweɪn] *n* (*old*) zwei. in ~ entzwei (*old*); and ne'er the ~ shall meet ... sie werden nie zueinanderfinden.

twang [twæŋ] **1** *n* (a) (*of wire, guitar string*) Doing *nt*; (*of rubber band, bowstring*) scharfer Ton.

(b) (*of voice*) Näseln *nt*, näselnder Tonfall. to speak with a ~ mit näselndem Tonfall *or* einem Näseln sprechen.

2 *vt* zupfen; *guitar, banjo also* klimpern auf (+*dat*).

3 *vi* (a) einen scharfen Ton von sich geben; (*rubber band*) pitschen (*inf*).

(b) to ~ on a guitar *etc* auf einer Gitarre *etc* herumklimpern.

twangy ['twæŋɪ] *adj* (+*er*) *voice* näselnd; *guitar etc* Klimper-.

'twas [twɒz] (*old*) *contr of* it was.

twat [twæt] *n* (*Brit vulg*) (a) (*vagina*) Fotze (*vulg*), Möse (*vulg*) *f*. (b) (*fool*) Saftarsch *m* (*sl*).

tweak [twiːk] **1** *vt* (a) kneifen. she ~ed back the curtain sie drehte den Vorhang etwas zur Seite; to ~ sb's ear jdn am Ohr ziehen; to ~ sth off/out etw abkneifen/auszupfen.

(b) (*sl*) *engine* hochfrisieren (*sl*).

2 *n*: to give sth a ~ an etw (*dat*) (herum)zupfen; to give sb's ear/nose a ~ jdn am Ohr/an der Nase ziehen.

twee [twiː] *adj* (+*er*) (*inf*) niedlich, putzig (*inf*); *clothes* niedlich; *description* verniedlichend; *expression* tantenhaft.

tweed [twiːd] **1** *n* (a) (*cloth*) Tweed *m*. (b) ~s *pl* (*clothes*) Tweedkleidung *f*, Tweedsachen *pl*; his old ~s sein alter Tweedanzug, seine alten Tweedsachen. **2** *adj* Tweed-.

Tweedledum [ˌtwiːdl'dʌm] n the twins were as alike as ~ and Tweedledee die Zwillinge glichen sich wie ein Ei dem anderen.

tweedy ['twiːdɪ] adj (+er) material Tweed-, tweedartig.

'tween [twiːn] (poet) adv, prep = **between**.

tweeny ['twiːnɪ] n (old) Hausmagd f.

tweet [twiːt] **1** n (of birds) Ziepen, Piepsen nt no pl. ~ ~ ziep, ziep, pieps, pieps. **2** vi ziepen, piepsen.

tweeter ['twiːtəʳ] n Hochtonlautsprecher m.

tweezers ['twiːzəz] npl (also pair of ~) Pinzette f.

twelfth [twelfθ] **1** adj zwölfte(r, s). a ~ part ein Zwölftel nt; ~ man (Cricket) zwölfter Mann; T~ Night Dreikönige; (evening) Dreikönigsabend m. **2** n (in series) Zwölfte(r, s); (fraction) Zwölftel nt; see also sixth.

twelve [twelv] **1** adj zwölf. ~ noon zwölf Uhr (mittags). **2** n Zwölf f; see also six.

twelve: ~-mile limit n Zwölfmeilenzone f; ~month n (old) zwölf Monate pl, ein Jahr; I haven't seen him in a ~month ich habe ihn ein Jahr lang or seit einem Jahr nicht mehr gesehen; ~-tone adj (Mus) Zwölfton-.

twentieth ['twentɪɪθ] **1** adj zwanzigste(r, s). a ~ part ein Zwanzigstel nt. **2** n (in series) Zwanzigste(r, s); (fraction) Zwanzigstel nt; see also sixth.

twenty ['twentɪ] **1** adj zwanzig. **2** n Zwanzig f; (banknote) Zwanziger m; see also six.

twentyfold ['twentɪfəʊld] adj, adv (old) zwanzigfach.

'twere [twɜːʳ] (old) contr of it were.

twerp [twɜːp] n (sl) Einfaltspinsel (sl), Hohlkopf (inf) m.

twice [twaɪs] adv zweimal. ~ as much/many doppelt or zweimal soviel/so viele; ~ as much bread doppelt soviel or zweimal soviel Brot, die doppelte Menge Brot; ~ as long as ... doppelt or zweimal so lange wie ...; at ~ the speed of sound, at a speed ~ that of sound mit doppelter Schallgeschwindigkeit; she is ~ your age sie ist doppelt so alt wie du; ~ 2 is 4 zweimal 2 ist 4; ~ weekly, ~ a week zweimal wöchentlich, zweimal in der or pro Woche; a ~-weekly newspaper eine Zeitung, die zweimal wöchentlich erscheint; he didn't need to be asked ~ da brauchte man ihn nicht zweimal zu fragen; he's ~ the man John is er steckt John in die Tasche (inf); he's ~ the man he was er ist ein ganz anderer Mensch geworden; I'd think ~ before trusting him with it ihm würde ich das nicht so ohne weiteres anvertrauen; see once 1 (a).

twiddle ['twɪdl] **1** vt herumdrehen an (+dat). she ~d the pencil in her fingers sie drehte den Bleistift zwischen den Fingern; to ~ one's thumbs (lit, fig) Däumchen drehen.

2 vi to ~ with a knob an einem Knopf herumdrehen.

3 n he gave the knob a ~ er drehte den Knopf herum.

twig¹ [twɪg] n (thin branch) Zweig m.

twig² [twɪg] (Brit inf) **1** vt (realize) mitkriegen (inf), mitbekommen. when she saw his face, she ~ged his secret als sie sein Gesicht sah, erriet sie sein Geheimnis (inf); he's ~ged it er hat's kapiert (inf). **2** vi schalten, es mitkriegen or -bekommen (all inf). to ~ to sth etw mitkriegen (inf) or mitbekommen (inf).

twilight ['twaɪlaɪt] n (time) Dämmerung f; (semi-darkness also) Dämmer- or Zwielicht nt. at ~ in der Dämmerung; ~ sleep (Med) Dämmerschlaf m; the ~ of the gods die Götterdämmerung; the ~ of western civilization der Herbst (liter) der westlichen Zivilisation; the ~ of his life, his ~ years sein Lebensabend.

twill [twɪl] n (Tex) Köper m.

'twill [twɪl] (old) contr of it will.

twin [twɪn] **1** n Zwilling m; (of vase, object) Gegenstück, Pendant nt. her ~ ihre Zwillingsschwester/ihr Zwillingsbruder m; where's the ~ of this sock? wo ist die andere Socke?

2 adj attr Zwillings-; (fig) genau gleiche(r, s).

3 vt town verschwistern. Oxford was ~ned with Bonn Oxford und Bonn wurden zu Partnerstädten.

twin: ~-bedded [ˌtwɪn'bedɪd] adj Zweibett-; ~ beds npl zwei (gleiche) Einzelbetten; ~ brother n Zwillingsbruder m; ~ carburettors npl Doppelvergaser m; ~-cylinder engine n Zweizylinder(motor) m.

twine [twaɪn] **1** n Schnur f, Bindfaden m. **2** vt winden. to ~ one's arms round sb seine Arme um jdn schlingen. **3** vi sich winden; (plants also) sich ranken. to ~ around sth sich um etw winden/ranken.

twin-engined [ˌtwɪn'endʒɪnd] adj zweimotorig.

twinge [twɪndʒ] n (of pain) Zucken nt, leichtes Stechen. a ~ of toothache/pain leicht stechende Zahnschmerzen/ein leichtes zuckender Schmerz; my back still gives me the occasional ~ ich spüre gelegentlich noch ein Stechen im Rücken; a ~ of rheumatism rheumatisches Reißen; a ~ of regret leichtes Bedauern; a ~ of conscience/remorse Gewissensbisse pl.

twining ['twaɪnɪŋ] adj plant rankend, Kletter-.

twinkle ['twɪŋkl] **1** vi (stars) funkeln, flimmern, glitzern; (eyes) blitzen, funkeln. her feet ~d across the stage sie bewegte sich leichtfüßig über die Bühne.

2 n (a) Funkeln, Flimmern, Glitzern nt. there was a ~/a mischievous ~ in her eyes man sah den Schalk in ihren Augen/ihr Augen blitzten übermütig or vor Übermut; no, he said with a ~ (in his eye) nein, sagte er augenzwinkernd.

(b) (instant) in a ~ sofort, im Handumdrehen.

twinkletoes ['twɪŋkl,təʊz] n here comes ~! (iro) da kommt ja unser Trampeltier! (inf).

twinkling ['twɪŋklɪŋ] n in the ~ of an eye im Nu, im Handumdrehen.

twin: ~ propellers npl Doppelschiffsschraube f; ~set n Twinset nt; ~ sister n Zwillingsschwester f; ~-tone horn n Zweiklanghorn nt; ~ town n Partnerstadt f; ~-tub (washing-machine) n Waschmaschine f mit getrennter Schleuder.

twirl [twɜːl] **1** vt (herum)wirbeln; skirt herumwirbeln; moustache zwirbeln. he ~ed his partner round the dance-floor er wirbelte seine Partnerin übers Parkett.

2 vi wirbeln. the skater ~ed round on the ice die Eiskunstläufer wirbelte über das Eis.

3 n Wirbel m; (in dance) Drehung f; (of moustache) hochstehende or Zwillingswirbelte Spitze; (in writing) Schnörkel m. to give a knob/one's moustache a ~ einen Knopf herumdrehen/seinen Schnurrbart zwirbeln; he gave his partner a ~ er wirbelte seine Partnerin herum.

twirp [twɜːp] n (sl) see **twerp.**

twist [twɪst] **1** n (a) (action) to give sth a ~ etw (herum)drehen; to give sb's arm a ~ jdm den Arm verdrehen or umdrehen; to give one's ankle a ~ sich (dat) den Fuß vertreten; with a quick ~ of the hand mit einer schnellen Handbewegung.

(b) (bend) Kurve, Biegung f; (fig: in story etc) Wendung f. the road is full of ~s and turns die Straße hat viele Biegungen und Windungen; his character has a peculiar ~ in it er hat irgendwie einen seltsamen Charakter.

(c) (coiled shape) salt in little ~s of paper in kleine Papierstückchen eingewickeltes Salz; ~s of thread Garnknäuel nt; a ~ of French bread ein französisches Weißbrot (in Zopfform).

(d) (type of yarn) Twist m, Stopfgarn nt.

(e) (Brit inf) to be/go round the ~ verrückt sein/werden; it's driving me round the ~! das macht mich wahnsinnig!, das bringt mich noch um den Verstand!

(f) (dance) Twist m. to do the ~ Twist tanzen, twisten.

(g) (on ball) Drall m; (esp Billiards) Effet m or nt. to give a ~ to or put a ~ on a ball einem Ball einen Drall geben.

2 vt (a) (wind, turn) drehen; (coil) wickeln (into/a +dat). to ~ threads etc together Fäden etc zusammendrehen or verflechten; to ~ pieces of string into a rope Bindfäden zu einem Seil drehen; to ~ flowers into a garland Blumen zu einer Girlande binden; she ~ed her hair into a knot sie drehte sich (dat) die Haare zu einem Knoten; to ~ the top off a jar/the cap off a tube of toothpaste den Deckel von einem Glas/den Verschluß von einer Zahnpastatube abdrehen; to ~ sth round sth etw um etw (acc) wickeln; see finger.

(b) (bend, distort) rod, key verbiegen; part of body verdrehen; (fig) meaning, words verdrehen, entstellen. to ~ sth out of shape etw verbiegen; to ~ sb's arm (lit) jdm den Arm verdrehen; I'll do it if you ~ my arm (fig) wenn ich mich schlagen lasse (hum); to ~ one's ankle sich (dat) den Fuß vertreten; his face was ~ed with pain sein Gesicht war verzerrt vor Schmerz or schmerzverzerrt.

(c) ball einen Drall geben (+dat). she somehow managed to ~ the red around the black sie hat es irgendwie geschafft, die rote an der schwarzen Kugel vorbeizumanövrieren.

3 vi (a) sich drehen; (smoke) sich kringeln or ringeln; (plant) sich winden or ranken; (road, river, person: wriggle) sich schlängeln or winden. the kite-strings have ~ed round the pole die Drachenschnüre haben sich um den Pfahl verwickelt; the rope ~ed and turned das Seil drehte sich hin und her.

(b) (dance) Twist tanzen, twisten.

(c) (Cards) aufnehmen und ablegen.

♦**twist about** or **around 1** vi sich (her)umdrehen; (road, river) (wind its way) sich dahinschlängeln; (be twisty) gewunden sein. he ~ed about in pain er wand or krümmte sich vor Schmerzen. **2** vt sep see **twist round.**

♦**twist off 1** vi the top ~s ~ der Deckel läßt sich abschrauben or ist abschraubbar. **2** vt sep abdrehen; lid abschrauben; flowerheads abknipsen.

♦**twist out 1** vi to ~ ~ of sb's grasp sich jds Griff (dat) entwinden. **2** vt sep herausdrehen.

♦**twist round 1** vi sich umdrehen; (road etc) eine Biegung machen. **2** vt sep head, chair herumdrehen. she ~ed her handkerchief ~ in her fingers sie drehte ihr Taschentuch zwischen den Fingern.

♦**twist up 1** vi (rope etc) sich verdrehen; (smoke) in Kringeln hochsteigen; (person: with pain etc) sich winden or krümmen. **2** vt sep (ropes, wires) verwickeln.

twisted ['twɪstɪd] adj (a) wires, rope (zusammen)gedreht; (bent) verbogen. **(b)** ankle verrenkt. **(c)** (fig) mind, logic verdreht. **(d)** (inf: dishonest) unredlich.

twister ['twɪstəʳ] n (a) (Brit pej: person) Gauner, Halunke m. **(b)** (Brit) (question) harte Nuß (inf); (problem) harter Brocken (inf). **(c)** (US inf: tornado) Wirbelsturm, Tornado m. **(d)** (dancer) Twisttänzer(in f) m.

twisty ['twɪstɪ] adj (+er) road kurvenreich, gewunden.

twit [twɪt] **1** vt to ~ sb (about sth) jdn (mit or wegen etw) aufziehen or hochnehmen.

2 n (Brit inf: person) Trottel m (inf).

twitch [twɪtʃ] **1** n (a) (tic) Zucken nt; (individual spasm) Zuckung f. to give a ~ zucken.

(b) (pull) Ruck m (of an +dat). to give sth a ~ an etw (dat) rucken.

2 vi (face, muscles) zucken. the cat's nose ~ed when I brought in the fish die Katze schnupperte, als ich den Fisch hereinbrachte.

3 vt (a) tail, ears zucken mit.

(b) (pull) zupfen. he ~ed the letter from her hands er schnappte ihr den Brief aus den Händen.

twitch-grass ['twɪtʃgrɑːs] n Quecke f.

twitter ['twɪtəʳ] **1** vi (lit, fig) zwitschern. **2** vt zwitschern. **3** n (a) (of birds) Zwitschern, Gezwitscher nt. **(b)** (inf) to be all of a ~, to be in a ~ ganz aufgeregt or aufgelöst sein.

twittery ['twɪtərɪ] adj attr zwitschernd.

twittish ['twɪtɪʃ] adj (a) (Brit inf: stupid) hirnlos (inf). **(b)** (teasing) remarks hänselnd.

'twixt [twɪkst] prep (old) = **betwixt.**

two [tuː] **1** adj zwei. to break/cut sth in ~ etw in zwei Teile brechen/schneiden; ~ by ~, in ~s zwei und zwei, zu zweit, zu zweien; in ~s and threes immer zwei oder drei (Leute) auf einmal; **the ~ of them** die beiden; **~ minds with but a single thought** (*prov*) zwei Seelen – ein Gedanke; **to put ~ and ~ together** (*fig*) seine Schlüsse ziehen, sich (*dat*) seinen Vers darauf machen; **to put ~ and ~ together and make five** einen Fehlschluß *or* falschen Schluß ziehen; **~'s company, three's a crowd** ein dritter stört nur; **~ can play at that game** (*inf*) den Spieß kann man auch umdrehen; *see also* **six**.

2 *n* Zwei *f*. **just the ~ of us/them** nur wir beide/die beiden.

two: **~-bit** *adj* (*US inf*) mies (*inf*); **~-by-four 1** *n* (*wood*) *ein Stück Holz mit den Ausmaßen zwei auf vier Inches*; **2** *adj* (*esp US inf*) (*small*) *apartment* Kasten-, Schachtel-; (*petty*) *life, job* nullachtfünfzehn (*inf*); **~-chamber system** *n* Zweikammersystem *nt*; **~-cylinder** *adj* Zweizylinder-; **~-dimensional** *adj* zweidimensional; **~-door** *adj* zweitürig; **~-edged** *adj* (a) (*lit*) zweischneidig, doppelschneidig; (b) (*fig*) zweideutig; *argument also* zweischneidig; **~-faced** *adj* (*lit*) doppelgesichtig; (*fig*) falsch; **~-fisted** *adj* (a) **a ~-fisted boxer** ein Boxer, der mit beiden Fäusten gleich gut boxen kann; (b) (*US sl*) knallhart; **~fold 1** *adj* zweifach, doppelt; **a ~fold increase** ein Anstieg um das Doppelte; **the advantages of this method are ~fold** diese Methode hat einen doppelten *or* zweifachen Vorteil; **2** *adv* **to increase ~fold** um das Doppelte steigern; **~-four time** *n* (*Mus*) Zweivierteltakt *m*; **~-handed** *adj* **a ~-handed sword** ein Zweihänder *m*; **a ~-handed saw** eine Säge mit zwei Griffen; **a ~-handed backhand** *eine Rückhand, bei der der Schläger mit beiden Händen gehalten wird*; **~-legged** *adj* zweibeinig; **a ~-legged animal** ein Zweibeiner *m*; **~-party system** *n* Zweiparteiensystem *nt*; **~-pence** *n see* **tuppence**; **~ pence** *or* **zwei Pence**; **~ pence piece/stamp** Zweipencestück *nt*/Zweipencemarke *f*; **~penny** ['tʌpənɪ] *adj see* **tuppenny**; **~-phase** *adj* (*Elec*) Zweiphasen-; **~-piece 1** *adj* zweiteilig; **2** *n* (*suit*) Zweiteiler *m*; (*swimming costume*) zweiteiliger Badeanzug; **~-pin plug** *n* Stecker *m* mit zwei Kontakten; **~-ply** *adj* *wool* zweifädig; *wood* aus zwei Lagen *or* Schichten bestehend; *tissue* zweilagig; **~-seater 1** *adj* zweisitzig; **2** *n* (*car, plane*) Zweisitzer *m*; **~some** *n* (a) (*people*) Paar, Pärchen *nt*; **to go out in a ~some** zu zweit *or* zu zweien ausgehen; (b) (*game*) **to have a ~some at golf/tennis** zu zweit Golf/Tennis spielen; **to play a ~some** zu zweit spielen; **~-star** *adj* *hotel etc* Zweisterne-; **~-star petrol** (*Brit*) Normalbenzin *nt*; **a ~-star general** (*US*) ein Zweisternegeneral *m*; **~step** *n* Twostep *m*; **~-storey** *adj* zweistöckig; **~-stroke 1** *adj* Zweitakt-; **2** *n* Zweitakter *m*; (*fuel*) Zweitaktgemisch *nt*.

twot [twɒt] *n* (*Brit vulg*) *see* **twat**.

two: **~-time** *vt* (*inf*) *boyfriend, accomplice* betrügen; **the crooks realized that he was ~-timing them** die Ganoven merkten, daß er ein doppeltes Spiel spielte *or* trieb; **~-timer** *n* (*inf*) falscher Hund (*inf*); **~-timing** *adj* (*inf*) falsch; **~-tone** *adj* (*in colour*) zweifarbig; (*in sound*) Zweiklang-.

'twould [twʊd] (*old*) *contr of* **it would**.

two: **~-up ~-down** *n* (*Brit inf*) kleines Reihenhäuschen; **~-way** *adj* **~-way** (**radio**) Funksprechgerät *nt*; **~-way communications** (*Telec*) Sprechverkehr *m* in beide Richtungen; **~-way fabric** von beiden Seiten zu tragender Stoff; **~-way street** Straße *f* mit Gegenverkehr *or* mit Verkehr in beiden Richtungen; **~-way switch/adaptor** Wechselschalter *m*/Doppelstecker *m*; **~-way traffic** Gegenverkehr *m*, Verkehr *m* in beiden Richtungen; **~-wheeler** (**bike**) *n* Zweirad, Fahrrad *nt*.

tycoon [taɪˈkuːn] *n* Magnat, Gigant *m*. **business ~/oil ~** Industrie-/Ölmagnat *m*.

tyke [taɪk] *n* (a) (*dog*) Köter *m*. (b) (*inf: child*) Lausbub *m*.

tympani *npl see* **timpani**.

tympanic [tɪmˈpænɪk] *adj* (*Anat*) Mittelohr-. **~ membrane** Trommelfell, Tympanum (*spec*) *nt*.

tympanist ['tɪmpənɪst] *n* Pauker *m*.

tympanum ['tɪmpənəm] *n* (*Anat*) (*membrane*) Trommelfell, Tympanum (*spec*) *nt*; (*middle ear*) Mittelohr *nt*; (*Archit*) Tympanon *nt*.

typal ['taɪpl] *adj* artspezifisch.

type¹ [taɪp] **1** *n* (a) (*kind*) Art *f*; (*of produce, plant also*) Sorte *f*; (*esp of people; character*) Typ, Typus *m*. **different ~s of cows/roses** verschiedene Arten von Rindern/Rosensorten *or* -arten *pl*; **what ~ of car is it?** was für ein Auto(typ) ist das?; **the very latest ~ of hi-fi** das allerneuste Hi-Fi-Gerät; **she has her own particular ~ of charm** sie hat ihren ganz besonderen Charme; **he has an English ~ of face** dem Gesicht nach könnte er Engländer sein; **to be English in ~** vom Typ her englisch sein; **gruyere-~** verschiedene Art Schweizer Käse; **most of the characters are recognizable ~s** die meisten Charaktere lassen sich einem bestimmten Typ zuordnen; **they're totally different ~s of person** sie sind vom Typ her völlig verschieden, sie sind völlig verschiedene Typen; **a man of this ~** ein Mann dieser Art *or* dieses Schlages, diese Art *or* Sorte (von) Mann; **I object to that ~ of behaviour** ich protestiere gegen ein solches Benehmen; **it's not my ~ of film** diese Art Film gefällt mir

nicht; **he's not my ~** er ist nicht meinTyp; **she's my ~ of girl** sie ist mein Typ; **he's not the ~ to hit a lady** er ist nicht der Typ *or* Mensch, der eine Frau schlägt.

(b) (*inf: man*) Typ *m*. **a strange ~** ein seltsamer Mensch, ein komischer Typ (*inf*), eine Type (*inf*).

2 *vt* bestimmen.

type² **1** *n* (*Typ*) Type *f*. **small ~** kleine Buchstaben, Gemeine (*spec*) *pl*; **to set ~** setzen; **in ~** (*typed*) maschinegeschrieben, getippt (*inf*); (*set*) gesetzt, gedruckt; **to set sth up in ~** etw setzen; **in italic ~** kursiv, in Schrägbuchstaben; **printed in italic ~** kursiv gedruckt.

2 *vt* tippen, (mit der Maschine) schreiben. **a badly ~d letter** ein schlecht geschriebener *or* getippter Brief.

3 *vi* maschineschreiben, tippen (*inf*).

♦**type out** *vt sep* *copy, letter* schreiben, tippen (*inf*); *error* ausixen.

♦**type up** *vt sep* auf der Maschine zusammenschreiben.

type: **~-cast** *vt* (*Theat*) (auf eine bestimmte Rolle) festlegen; **to be ~-cast as a villain** auf die Rolle des Schurken festgelegt werden; **~face** *n* Schrift *f*; **~script** *n* mit Maschine geschriebenes Manuskript, Typoskript *nt* (*geh*); **to be in ~script** mit Maschine geschrieben sein; **~setter** *n* (*person*) Schriftsetzer(in *f*) *m*; (*machine*) Setzmaschine *f*; **~ size** *n* Schriftgröße *f*.

typewrite ['taɪpraɪt] **1** *vi* maschineschreiben, tippen (*inf*). **2** *vt* (mit der Maschine) schreiben, tippen (*inf*).

typewriter ['taɪpˌraɪtə'] *n* Schreibmaschine *f*. **~ bell** Klingel *f* an der Schreibmaschine; (*sound*) Klingelzeichen *nt*; **~ ribbon** Farbband *nt*.

typewriting ['taɪpˌraɪtɪŋ] *n see* **typing**.

typewritten ['taɪpˌrɪtn] *adj* maschinegeschrieben, getippt.

typhoid ['taɪfɔɪd] *n* (*also* **~ fever**) Typhus *m*. **~ injection** Impfung gegen Typhus, Typhusimpfung *f*.

typhoon [taɪˈfuːn] *n* Taifun *m*.

typhus ['taɪfəs] *n* Fleckfieber *nt*, Flecktyphus *m*.

typical ['tɪpɪkl] *adj* typisch (*of* für). **a ~ English town** eine typisch englische Stadt; **that's ~ of him** das ist typisch für ihn; **isn't that ~!** ist das nicht wieder mal typisch!

typically ['tɪpɪklɪ] *adv see adj*. **~, he did nothing but complain about the food** bezeichnenderweise hat er sich ständig über das Essen beschwert; **~, he insisted on getting there early** er wollte natürlich unbedingt früh hingehen, typisch.

typify ['tɪpɪfaɪ] *vt* bezeichnend sein für. **he typifies the reserved Englishman** er verkörpert (genau) den Typ des zurückhaltenden Engländers.

typing ['taɪpɪŋ] **1** *n* Maschineschreiben, Tippen (*inf*) *nt*. **the noise of her ~ drove me mad** ihr Tippen *or* der Lärm ihrer Schreibmaschine machte mich wahnsinnig; **his ~ isn't very good** er kann nicht besonders gut maschineschreiben.

2 *attr* Schreibmaschinen-. **~ error** Tippfehler *m*; **~ pool** Schreibzentrale *f*; **~ speed** Schreibgeschwindigkeit *f*.

typist ['taɪpɪst] *n* (*professional*) Schreibkraft *f*, Schreibfräulein *nt* (*dated*), Stenotypist(in *f*) *m*, Tippse *f* (*pej inf*). **he couldn't find a ~ for his thesis** er konnte niemanden finden, der ihm seine Doktorarbeit tippte.

typographer [taɪˈpɒɡrəfə'] *n* Typograph *m*.

typographic(al) [ˌtaɪpəˈɡræfɪk(əl)] *adj* typographisch. **~ error** Druckfehler *m*.

typography [taɪˈpɒɡrəfɪ] *n* Typographie *f*; (*subject also*) Buchdruckerkunst *f*.

typological [ˌtaɪpəˈlɒdʒɪkəl] *adj* typologisch.

typology [taɪˈpɒlədʒɪ] *n* Typologie *f*.

tyrannic(al) *adj*, **tyrannically** *adv* [tɪˈrænɪk(əl), tɪˈrænɪkəlɪ] tyrannisch.

tyrannize ['tɪrənaɪz] **1** *vt* (*lit, fig*) tyrannisieren. **2** *vi* eine Tyrannenherrschaft ausüben. **to ~ over sb** (*lit, fig*) jdn tyrannisieren.

tyrannosaurus [tɪˌrænəˈsɔːrəs] *n* Tyrannosaurus *m*.

tyrannous ['tɪrənəs] *adj* tyrannisch.

tyranny ['tɪrənɪ] *n* (*lit, fig*) Tyrannei, Tyrannenherrschaft *f*. **he ruled by ~** er führte eine Tyrannenherrschaft.

tyrant ['taɪərənt] *n* (*lit, fig*) Tyrann *m*.

tyre, (*US*) **tire** [taɪə'] *n* Reifen *m*. **to have a burst ~** einen geplatzten Reifen haben.

tyre: **~ gauge** *n* Reifendruckmesser *m*; **~ lever** *n* Montiereisen *nt*; **~ pressure** *n* Reifendruck *m*.

tyro ['taɪərəʊ] (*US*) *n* Anfänger(in *f*) *m*. **a ~ skier** *etc* ein Anfänger beim *or* im Skilaufen *etc*.

Tyrol [tɪˈrəʊl] *n* **the ~** Tirol *nt*.

Tyrolean ['tɪrəliən], **Tyrolese** [tɪrəˈliːz] **1** *adj* Tiroler. **~ hat** Tirolerhut *m*. **2** *n* Tiroler(in *f*) *m*.

Tyrrhenian Sea [tɪˈriːnɪənˈsiː] *n* Tyrrhenisches Meer.

tzar *n see* **tsar**.

tzarina *n see* **tsarina**.

tzarist *adj, n see* **tsarist**.

tzetze (fly) *n see* **tsetse (fly)**.

u

U, u [ju:] **1** n (a) U, u nt. (b) (Brit Film) jugendfreier Film. **2** adj (Brit: upper class) charakteristisch für die Gewohnheiten, Sprechweise etc der Oberschicht, vornehm.

UAR abbr of **United Arab Republic.**

U-bend ['juːbend] n (in pipe) U-Bogen m; (in road) Haarnadelkurve f.

ubiquitous [juːˈbɪkwɪtəs] adj allgegenwärtig. **sandstone is ~ in this district** Sandstein ist in dieser Gegend überall zu finden.

ubiquity [juːˈbɪkwɪtɪ] n Allgegenwart f; (prevalence) weite Verbreitung.

U-boat ['juːbəʊt] n U-Boot nt.

UCCA ['ʌkə] (Brit) abbr of **Universities Central Council on Admissions.**

UDC (Brit) abbr of **Urban District Council.**

udder ['ʌdər] n Euter nt.

UDI abbr of **Unilateral Declaration of Independence.**

UDR abbr of **Ulster Defence Regiment.**

U-film ['juːfɪlm] n (Brit) jugendfreier Film.

UFO ['juːfəʊ] abbr of **unidentified flying object** Ufo, UFO nt.

Uganda [juːˈgændə] n Uganda nt.

Ugandan [jʊˈgændən] **1** adj ugandisch. **2** n Ugander(in f) m.

ugh [ɜːh] interj i, igitt.

ugli (fruit) ['ʌglɪ(fruːt)] n Kreuzung f aus Grapefruit, Apfelsine und Mandarine.

uglify ['ʌglɪfaɪ] vt häßlich machen, verunstalten.

ugliness ['ʌglɪnɪs] n Häßlichkeit f; (of news) Unerfreulichkeit f; (of wound) übler Zustand; (of situation) Ekelhaftigkeit f; (of crime) Gemeinheit f; (of vice) Häßlichkeit, Garstigkeit f.

ugly ['ʌglɪ] adj (+er) (a) (not pretty) häßlich. **as ~ as sin** häßlich wie die Sünde or Nacht; **~ duckling** (fig) häßliches Entlein.
(b) (unpleasant, nasty) übel; news, wound also schlimm; rumour, scenes, crime, clouds also häßlich; mood, situation, scenes also ekelhaft; crime also gemein; vice also häßlich, garstig; sky bedrohlich. **an ~ customer** ein übler Kunde; **to cut up or turn ~** (inf) gemein or fies werden (inf).

UHF abbr of **ultra-high frequency** Dezimeterwellen pl, UHF.

UK abbr of **United Kingdom** Vereinigtes Königreich.

ukase ['juːkɑːz] n (Hist) Ukas m; (fig) Anordnung f.

uke [juːk] n (inf) see **ukulele.**

Ukraine [juːˈkreɪn] n the ~ die Ukraine.

Ukrainian [juːˈkreɪnɪən] **1** adj ukrainisch. **2** n (a) Ukrainer(in f) m. (b) (language) Ukrainisch nt.

ukulele, ukelele [ˌjuːkəˈleɪlɪ] n Ukulele f.

ulcer ['ʌlsər] n (Med) Geschwür nt; (stomach ~) Magengeschwür nt; (fig) Übel nt.

ulcerate ['ʌlsəreɪt] **1** vt stomach ein Geschwür verursachen in (+dat); skin Geschwüre verursachen auf (+dat); wound eitern lassen. **2** vi (stomach) ein Geschwür bilden or bekommen; (skin) geschwürig werden; (wound) eitern.

ulcerated ['ʌlsəreɪtɪd] adj geschwürig; wound vereitert. **an ~ stomach** ein Geschwür nt im Magen, ein Magengeschwür nt.

ulceration [ˌʌlsəˈreɪʃən] n (process) Geschwürbildung f; (of wound) Vereiterung f; (state) Geschwüre pl; Vereiterung f.

ulcerous ['ʌlsərəs] adj geschwürig; wound vereitert; (causing ulcers) geschwürbildend. **this ~ growth of nationalism** (fig) diese krebsartige Ausbreitung des Nationalismus.

ullage ['ʌlɪdʒ] n Leckage f, Flüssigkeitsschwund m.

ulna ['ʌlnə] n, pl -e ['ʌlniː] or -s (Anat) Elle f.

Ulster ['ʌlstər] n Ulster nt. **U~man/woman** Mann m/Frau f aus Ulster, Einwohner(in f) m von Ulster.

ulster ['ʌlstər] n (dated: coat) Ulster m.

ult [ʌlt] abbr of **ultimo.**

ulterior [ʌlˈtɪərɪər] adj (a) ~ **motive** Hintergedanke m; **I have no ~ motive/s** in doing that ich tue das ganz ohne Hintergedanken. (b) (rare: lying beyond) jenseitig.

ultima [ˌʌltɪˈmeɪtə] pl of **ultimatum.**

ultimate ['ʌltɪmɪt] **1** adj (a) (final) letzte(r, s); destiny, solution, decision endgültig; result endgültig, End-; outcome, aim End-; control oberste(r, s); authority höchste(r, s); beneficiary eigentlich. **he came to the ~ conclusion that ...** er kam schließlich zur Einsicht, daß ...; **the day of his ~ appointment** der Tag, an dem er schließlich ernannt wurde; **what is your ~ ambition in life?** was streben Sie letzten Endes or letztlich im Leben an?; although they had no ~ hope of escape obwohl letztlich or im Endeffekt keine Hoffnung auf Flucht bestand.
(b) (that cannot be improved on) vollendet, perfekt, in höchster Vollendung. **we have produced the ~ sports car** wir haben den Sportwagen in höchster Vollendung or den Supersportwagen gebaut; **the ~ insult** der Gipfel der Beleidigung; **the ~ deterrent** (Mil) das endgültige Abschreckungsmittel; (fig) die äußerste Abschreckungsmaßnahme; the ~ **weapon** (Mil) die Superwaffe; (fig) das letzte und äußerste Mittel; **death is the ~ sacrifice** der Tod ist das allergrößte Opfer.
(c) (basic) principle grundlegend, Grund-; constituents Grund-, unteilbar; cause eigentlich; explanation grundsätzlich; truth letzte(r, s).
(d) (furthest) entfernteste(r, s); boundary of universe äußerste(r, s); ancestors früheste(r, s). **the ~ origins of man** die frühesten Ursprünge des Menschen; **the ~ frontiers of knowledge** die äußersten Grenzen des Wissens.
2 n Nonplusultra nt. **that is the ~ in comfort** das ist Superkomfort or das Höchste an Komfort.

ultimately ['ʌltɪmɪtlɪ] adv (in the end) letztlich, letzten Endes; (eventually) schließlich; (fundamentally) im Grunde genommen, letztlich. **it's ~ your decision** im Grunde genommen or letztlich müssen Sie das entscheiden; **~ we are all descended from Adam** letztlich or letzten Endes stammen wir alle von Adam ab.

ultimatum [ˌʌltɪˈmeɪtəm] n, pl -s or **ultimata** (Mil, fig) Ultimatum nt. **to deliver an ~ to sb** jdm ein Ultimatum stellen.

ultimo ['ʌltɪməʊ] adv (Comm) des letzten or vorigen Monats.

ultra- ['ʌltrə-] pref ultra-.

ultra: ~**fashionable** adj ultramodern, supermodisch; ~**-high frequency 1** n Dezimeterwellen pl; **2** adj Dezimeterwellen-; ~**marine 1** n Ultramarin nt; **2** adj ultramarin(blau); ~**modern** adj ultra- or hypermodern; ~**montane** adj (Eccl) ultramontan; ~**short wave** n Ultrakurzwelle f; ~**violet** adj ultraviolett; ~**violet treatment** Ultraviolettbestrahlung f.

ululate ['juːljʊleɪt] vi (liter) (mourning women) (weh)klagen (liter); (dog etc) heulen.

ululation [ˌjuːljʊˈleɪʃən] n see vi (liter) (Weh)klagen nt (liter); Heulen nt.

Ulysses [juːˈlɪsiːz] n Odysseus, Ulixes (rare), Ulysses (rare) m.

um [əm] interj äh; (in decision, answering) hm.

umbel ['ʌmbəl] n Dolde f.

umber ['ʌmbər] **1** n (earth) Umbraerde f; (pigment: also raw ~) Umbra f, Umber m. **burnt ~** gebrannte Umbra. **2** adj umbrabraun.

umbilical [ˌʌmbɪˈlaɪkəl] **1** adj Nabel-. **2** n (also ~ cord) (a) (Anat) Nabelschnur f. (b) (Space) Kabelschlauch m; (to astronaut also) Nabelschnur f.

umbilicus [ˌʌmbɪˈlaɪkəs] n (spec) Nabel m.

umbra ['ʌmbrə] n, pl -e ['ʌmbriː] or -s (Astron) (shadow) Kernschatten m; (in sunspot) Umbra f.

umbrage ['ʌmbrɪdʒ] n **to take ~ at sth** an etw (dat) Anstoß nehmen; **he took ~** er nahm daran Anstoß.

umbrella [ʌmˈbrelə] n (Regen)schirm m; (sun ~) (Sonnen)schirm m; (Mil: air ~) (for ground troops) Abschirmung f, Luftschirm m; (for plane) Jagdschutz m. **collapsible or telescopic ~** Taschen- or Faltschirm, Knirps ® m; **under the ~ of** (fig) unter der Kontrolle von; **to bring sth under one ~** etw zusammenfassen.

umbrella: ~ **organization** n Dachorganisation f; ~ **stand** n Schirmständer m.

umlaut ['ʊmlaʊt] n (sign) Umlautpunkte pl; (sound change) Umlaut m. **a ~ ä** [ɛː].

umpire ['ʌmpaɪər] **1** n Schiedsrichter(in f) m; (fig) Unparteiische(r) mf. **to act as ~** (lit) als Schiedsrichter fungieren, Schiedsrichter sein; (fig) schlichten.
2 vt (Sport) als Schiedsrichter fungieren bei, Schiedsrichter sein bei, schiedsrichtern bei; (fig) schlichten.
3 vi (in bei) Schiedsrichter sein, schiedsrichtern.

umpteen ['ʌmpˈtiːn] adj (inf) zig (inf). **I've told you ~ times** ich habe dir zigmal or x-mal gesagt (inf).

umpteenth ['ʌmpˈtiːnθ] adj (inf) x-te(r, s). **for the ~ time** zum x-ten Mal.

UN abbr of **United Nations** UNO f, UN pl. ~ **troops** UNO-Truppen pl.

'un [ən] pron (inf) **he's a good ~** er ist 'n feiner Kerl; **a big ~** 'n großer; **the little ~s** die Kleinen pl.

un- [ʌn-] pref (before adj, adv) un-, nicht; (before n) Un-.

unabashed [ˌʌnəˈbæʃt] adj (not ashamed, embarrassed) dreist, unverfroren; (not overawed) unbeeindruckt.

unabated [ˌʌnəˈbeɪtɪd] adj unvermindert. **the rain/storm continued ~** der Regen/Sturm ließ nicht nach.

unable [ˌʌnˈeɪbl] adj pred **to be ~ to do sth** etw nicht tun können, außerstande sein, etw zu tun; **we're still ~ to cure cancer** wir sind immer noch außerstande or nicht imstande or nicht in der Lage, Krebs zu heilen.

unabridged [ˌʌnəˈbrɪdʒd] adj ungekürzt.

unacceptable [ˌʌnəkˈseptəbl] adj plans, terms unannehmbar; excuse, offer, behaviour nicht akzeptabel; standard, unemployment level, working conditions nicht tragbar, untragbar. **it's quite ~ that we should be expected to ...** es kann doch nicht von uns verlangt werden, daß ...; **it's quite ~ for young children to ...** es kann nicht zugelassen werden, daß kleine Kinder ...; **the ~ face of capitalism** die Kehrseite des Kapitalismus.

unacceptably [ˌʌnəkˈseptəblɪ] adv untragbar. **these fuels are ~ dangerous** diese Brennstoffe sind in nicht mehr tragbarem Maße gefährlich; **he suggested, quite ~, that ...** er schlug vor, was völlig unakzeptabel war, daß ...

unaccommodating [ˌʌnəˈkɒmədeɪtɪŋ] adj ungefällig; attitude unnachgiebig.

unaccompanied [ˌʌnəˈkʌmpənɪd] adj person, child, singing ohne Begleitung; instrument Solo-. ~ **luggage** aufgegebenes Reisegepäck; **the flute plays two bars ~** die Flöte spielt zwei Takte solo.

unaccountable [ˌʌnə'kaʊntəbl] adj unerklärlich; *phenomenon also* unerklärbar.

unaccountably [ˌʌnə'kaʊntəblɪ] adv unerklärlicherweise; *disappear* auf unerklärliche Weise. an ~ long time unerklärlich lange.

unaccounted for [ˌʌnə'kaʊntɪd'fɔːʳ] adj ungeklärt. £30 is still ~ es ist noch ungeklärt, wo die £ 30 geblieben sind; three of the passengers are still ~ drei Passagiere werden noch vermißt, der Verbleib von drei Passagieren ist noch nicht geklärt.

unaccustomed [ˌʌnə'kʌstəmd] adj (a) (*unusual*) ungewohnt. (b) (*of person: unused*) to be ~ to sth etw nicht gewohnt sein, an etw (*acc*) nicht gewöhnt sein; to be ~ to doing sth es nicht gewohnt sein *or* nicht daran gewöhnt sein, etw zu tun; ~ as I am to public speaking ... ich bin kein großer Redner, aber ...

unacknowledged [ˌʌnək'nɒlɪdʒd] adj *letter* unbeantwortet; *mistake* uneingestanden; *champion* verkannt. to leave a letter ~ den Empfang eines Briefes nicht bestätigen; to go ~ nicht anerkannt werden; the letter went ~ der Empfang des Briefes wurde nicht bestätigt.

unacquainted [ˌʌnə'kweɪntɪd] adj pred to be ~ with poverty die Armut nicht kennen; to be ~ with the facts mit den Tatsachen nicht vertraut sein; I'm not ~ with the facts die Tatsachen sind mir nicht gänzlich fremd; they're still ~ sie kennen sich noch immer nicht.

unadaptable [ˌʌnə'dæptəbl] adj nicht anpassungsfähig, nicht flexibel. to be ~ to sth sich an etw (*acc*) nicht anpassen können.

unadopted [ˌʌnə'dɒptɪd] adj (a) (*Brit*) ~ road öffentliche Straße, für deren Instandhaltung die Anlieger allein verantwortlich sind. (b) *child* nicht adoptiert. many children remain ~ viele Kinder werden nicht adoptiert.

unadorned [ˌʌnə'dɔːnd] adj schlicht; *woman's beauty* natürlich; *truth* ungeschminkt.

unadulterated [ˌʌnə'dʌltəreɪtɪd] adj (a) unverfälscht, rein; *wine* rein, ungepanscht; (*hum*) *whisky* unverdünnt. ~ by foreign influences durch fremde Einflüsse nicht verfälscht. (b) (*fig*) *nonsense* schier; *bliss* ungetrübt. this is ~ filth das ist der reinste Schmutz, das ist Schmutz in Reinkultur (*inf*).

unadventurous [ˌʌnəd'ventʃərəs] adj *time, life* wenig abenteuerlich, ereignislos; *tastes* hausbacken, bieder; *style, theatrical production, football* einfallslos; *person* wenig unternehmungslustig. where food is concerned he is very ~ in bezug aufs Essen ist er wenig experimentierfreudig.

unadventurously [ˌʌnəd'ventʃərəslɪ] adv *directed* einfallslos; *dressed, decorated* bieder or hausbacken. rather ~ they chose Tenerife again einfallslos or wenig abenteuerlich, wie sie sind, haben sie sich wieder für Teneriffa entschieden; to eat ~ in bezug aufs Essen nicht experimentierfreudig sein.

unadvisable [ˌʌnəd'vaɪzəbl] adj unratsam, nicht ratsam.

unaesthetic, (*US***) unesthetic** [ˌʌniːs'θetɪk] adj unästhetisch.

unaffected [ˌʌnə'fektɪd] adj (a) (*sincere*) ungekünstelt, natürlich, unaffektiert; *pleasure, gratitude* echt. (b) (*not damaged*) nicht angegriffen (*also Med*), nicht in Mitleidenschaft gezogen, nicht beeinträchtigt; (*not influenced*) unbeeinflußt, nicht beeinflußt; (*not involved*) nicht betroffen; (*unmoved*) ungerührt, unbewegt. she remained quite ~ by his tears sie blieb beim Anblick seiner Tränen völlig ungerührt; our plans/exports were ~ by the strike unsere Pläne wurden vom Streik nicht betroffen/unsere Exporte wurden durch den Streik nicht beeinträchtigt; he remained quite ~ by all the noise der Lärm berührte *or* störte ihn überhaupt nicht; no children are ~ by the violence they see die Brutalitäten, die Kinder sehen, gehen nicht spurlos an ihnen vorbei.

unaffectedly [ˌʌnə'fektɪdlɪ] adv (*sincerely*) ungeziert, natürlich; *say* unaffektiert. she was ~ pleased ihre Freude war echt.

unaffectedness [ˌʌnə'fektɪdnɪs] n (*sincerity*) Ungeziertheit, Natürlichkeit, Unaffektiertheit f; (*of joy etc*) Aufrichtigkeit f.

unafraid [ˌʌnə'freɪd] adj unerschrocken, furchtlos. to be ~ of sb/sth vor jdm/etw keine Angst haben.

unaided [ʌn'eɪdɪd] 1 adv ohne fremde Hilfe. to do sth ~ etw allein *or* ohne fremde Hilfe tun. 2 adj his own ~ work seine eigene Arbeit; by my own ~ efforts ganz ohne fremde Hilfe; ~ by sb/sth ohne jds Hilfe/ohne Zuhilfenahme von etw.

unaired [ʌn'εəd] adj *room, bed, clothes* ungelüftet.

unalike [ˌʌnə'laɪk] adj pred unähnlich, ungleich. the two children are so ~ die beiden Kinder sind so verschieden *or* sind sich so unähnlich.

unallocated [ʌn'æləkeɪtɪd] adj *funds* nicht zugewiesen *or* zugeteilt. ~ tickets Karten im freien Verkauf.

unalloyed [ˌʌnə'lɔɪd] adj usu attr *happiness* ungetrübt.

unalterable [ʌn'ɒltərəbl] adj *intention, decision* unabänderlich; *laws* unveränderlich.

unalterably [ʌn'ɒltərəblɪ] adv unveränderlich. to be ~ opposed to sth entschieden gegen etw sein.

unaltered [ʌn'ɒltəd] adj unverändert.

unambiguous adj, ~ly adv [ˌʌnæm'bɪgjʊəs, -lɪ] eindeutig, unzweideutig.

unambitious [ˌʌnæm'bɪʃəs] adj *person, plan* nicht ehrgeizig (genug); *theatrical production* anspruchslos.

unamenable [ˌʌnə'miːnəbl] adj unzugänglich (*to dat*). he is ~ to persuasion er läßt sich nicht überreden; ~ to medical treatment auf ärztliche Behandlung nicht ansprechend.

un-American [ˌʌnə'merɪkən] adj unamerikanisch. ~ activities unamerikanische Umtriebe pl.

unamiable [ʌn'eɪmɪəbl] adj unliebenswürdig.

unamused [ˌʌnə'mjuːzd] adj *laugh* gezwungen, unfroh. the dirty story left her ~ sie fand die schmutzige Geschichte überhaupt nicht lustig.

unanimity [ˌjuːnə'nɪmɪtɪ] n *see adj* Einmütigkeit f; Einstimmigkeit f.

unanimous [juː'nænɪməs] adj einmütig; *decision also*, (*Jur*) einstimmig. we were ~ in thinking ... wir waren einmütig der Ansicht ...; they were ~ in their condemnation of him sie haben ihn einmütig verdammt; by a ~ vote einstimmig.

unanimously [juː'nænɪməslɪ] adv einstimmig, einmütig; *vote* einstimmig.

unannounced [ˌʌnə'naʊnst] adj, adv unangemeldet.

unanswerable [ʌn'ɑːnsərəbl] adj *question* nicht zu beantworten pred, nicht zu beantwortend attr; *argument, case* zwingend, unwiderlegbar. that remark is ~ darauf läßt sich nichts erwidern.

unanswered [ʌn'ɑːnsəd] adj unbeantwortet.

unapologetic [ˌʌnəpɒlə'dʒetɪk] adj unverfroren, dreist. he was so ~ about it es schien ihn überhaupt nicht zu kümmern *or* ihm überhaupt nicht leid zu tun.

unappealable [ˌʌnə'piːləbl] adj (*Jur*) nicht berufungsfähig. the judgement is ~ gegen das Urteil kann keine Berufung eingelegt werden.

unappealing [ˌʌnə'piːlɪŋ] adj nicht ansprechend, nicht reizvoll; *person also* unansehnlich; *prospect, sight* nicht verlockend.

unappeased [ˌʌnə'piːzd] adj *appetite, lust* unbefriedigt; *hunger, thirst* ungestillt.

unappetizing [ʌn'æpɪtaɪzɪŋ] adj unappetitlich; *prospect, thought* wenig verlockend.

unappreciated [ˌʌnə'priːʃɪeɪtɪd] adj nicht geschätzt *or* gewürdigt. she felt she was ~ by him sie hatte den Eindruck, daß er sie nicht zu schätzen wußte; the ~ heroines of the war die ungewürdigten *or* unbeachteten Heldinnen des Krieges.

unappreciative [ˌʌnə'priːʃɪətɪv] adj undankbar; *audience* verständnislos. to be ~ of sth etw nicht zu würdigen wissen.

unapproachable [ˌʌnə'prəʊtʃəbl] adj *place* unzugänglich; *person also* unnahbar. ~ except by air nur aus der Luft zu erreichen.

unapt [ʌn'æpt] adj (*inappropriate*) unpassend, unangebracht.

unarguable [ʌn'ɑːgjʊəbl] adj *theory etc* nicht vertretbar.

unarguably [ʌn'ɑːgjʊəblɪ] adv unbestreitbar, zweifellos.

unargued [ʌn'ɑːgjuːd] adj (*without argumentation*) unbegründet; (*undisputed*) unangefochten, unbestritten. the point was left ~ dieser Punkt wurde nicht begründet; (*undiscussed*) dieser Punkt wurde nicht erörtert.

unarm [ʌn'ɑːm] vt see **disarm**.

unarmed [ʌn'ɑːmd] adj unbewaffnet. ~ combat Nahkampf m ohne Waffe.

unashamed [ˌʌnə'ʃeɪmd] adj schamlos. naked but ~ nackt aber ohne Scham; his ~ conservatism sein unverhohlener Konservatismus; he was quite ~ about it er schämte sich dessen überhaupt nicht, er war darüber kein bißchen beschämt.

unashamedly [ˌʌnə'ʃeɪmɪdlɪ] adv unverschämt; *say, admit* ohne Scham; *in favour of, partisan* ganz offen, unverhohlen. he's ~ proud of ... er zeigt unverhohlen *or* macht kein Hehl daraus, wie stolz er auf ... ist; they are ~ in love sie schämen sich ihrer Liebe nicht.

unasked [ʌn'ɑːskt] adj (*unrequested*) unaufgefordert, ungefragt, ungebeten; (*uninvited*) un(ein)geladen, ungebeten.

unasked-for [ʌn'ɑːsktfɔːʳ] adj ungewünscht, unwillkommen.

unaspirated [ʌn'æspɪreɪtɪd] adj unbehaucht.

unassailable [ˌʌnə'seɪləbl] adj *fortress* uneinnehmbar, unbezwingbar; *position, reputation* unantastbar, unanfechtbar; *conviction* unerschütterlich; *argument* unwiderlegbar, unanfechtbar, zwingend. he is quite ~ on that point in diesem Punkt kann er nicht widerlegt werden.

unassisted [ˌʌnə'sɪstɪd] adj, adv see **unaided**.

unassuming [ˌʌnə'sjuːmɪŋ] adj bescheiden.

unattached [ˌʌnə'tætʃt] adj (a) (*not fastened*) unbefestigt; (*Mil*) keinem Regiment/keiner Einheit etc zugeteilt; (*US*) athlete ohne Vereinszugehörigkeit. ~ vote Wechselwähler m. (b) (*emotionally*) ungebunden. she's worried about being still ~ sie macht sich Sorgen, weil sie immer noch keinen Partner gefunden hat *or* sich immer noch nicht gebunden hat; there aren't many ~ girls around die meisten Mädchen hier sind nicht mehr zu haben *or* sind nicht mehr frei.

unattainability ['ʌnəˌteɪnə'bɪlɪtɪ] n Unerreichbarkeit f.

unattainable [ˌʌnə'teɪnəbl] adj unerreichbar.

unattended [ˌʌnə'tendɪd] adj (a) (*not looked after*) *children* unbeaufsichtigt; *car-park, car, luggage* unbewacht; *wound, patient* unbehandelt, nicht behandelt; *shop* ohne Bedienung; *customer* nicht bedient; *business* unerledigt. to leave sb/sth ~ *children, car, luggage* jdn/etw unbeaufsichtigt/unbewacht lassen; *shop* etw unbeaufsichtigt lassen; to leave sb/sth ~ (to) *guests, wound* sich nicht um jdn/etw kümmern; *work* etw liegenlassen, etw nicht erledigen; *patient, wound* jdn/etw nicht behandeln; *customer* jdn nicht bedienen; to leave a car/dangerous tendencies ~ to ein Auto nicht reparieren lassen/gegen gefährliche Tendenzen nichts unternehmen; to be ~ go ~ to (*wound, injury*) nicht behandelt werden; (*car, fault*) nicht repariert werden; (*customer*) nicht bedient werden; (*work*) nicht erledigt sein/werden. (b) (*not escorted*) ohne Begleitung (*by gen*), unbegleitet.

unattractive [ˌʌnə'træktɪv] adj *sight, place* unschön, wenig reizvoll; *offer* unattraktiv, uninteressant, nicht verlockend; *trait, scar* unschön, abstoßend; *character* unsympathisch; *woman* unattraktiv. he's ~ to women Frauen finden ihn nicht attraktiv *or* anziehend.

unattractiveness [ˌʌnə'træktɪvnɪs] n Unschönheit f; (*of woman*) geringe Attraktivität. the ~ of the offer das unattraktive *or* nicht verlockende Angebot; the ~ of his character sein unsympathischer Charakter.

unauthenticated [ˌʌnɔː'θentɪkeɪtɪd] adj unverbürgt; *document* unbeglaubigt.

unauthorized [ʌn'ɔːθəraɪzd] adj unbefugt, unberechtigt. no entry for ~ persons Zutritt für Unbefugte verboten!

unavailable [ˌʌnə'veɪləbl] adj nicht erhältlich; *person* nicht zu erreichen pred; *library book* nicht verfügbar.

unavailing [ˌʌnə'veɪlɪŋ] *adj* vergeblich, umsonst *pred.*
unavailingly [ˌʌnə'veɪlɪŋlɪ] *adv* vergeblich.
unavenged [ˌʌnə'vendʒd] *adj* ungerächt.
unavoidable [ˌʌnə'vɔɪdəbl] *adj* unvermeidlich, unvermeidbar; *conclusion* zwangsläufig, unausweichlich.
unavoidably [ˌʌnə'vɔɪdəblɪ] *adv* notgedrungen. **to be ~ detained** verhindert sein.
unaware [ˌʌnə'wɛəʳ] *adj pred* **to be ~ of sth** sich (*dat*) einer Sache (*gen*) nicht bewußt sein; **I was ~ of his presence** ich hatte nicht bemerkt, daß er da war; **I was ~ that he was interested** es war mir nicht bewußt *or* ich war mir nicht bewußt, daß er (daran) interessiert war; **I was ~ that there was a meeting going on** ich wußte nicht, daß da gerade eine Besprechung stattfand; **I was ~ of the fact that you knew** es war mir nicht bewußt *or* ich wußte nicht, daß Sie Bescheid wußten; **not ~ of sth** sich (*dat*) einer Sache (*gen*) durchaus bewußt; **I was not ~ that ...** es war mir durchaus bewußt *or* klar, daß ...; **he's so ~** er weiß überhaupt nicht Bescheid.
unawares [ˌʌnə'wɛəz] *adv* (*by surprise*) unerwartet; (*accidentally*) unbeabsichtigt, versehentlich; (*without knowing*) unwissentlich. **to catch** *or* **take sb all ~** jdn überraschen.
unbalance [ʌn'bæləns] *vt* (*physically, mentally*) aus dem Gleichgewicht bringen; *painting* das Gleichgewicht (+*gen*) stören. **to ~ sb's mind** jdn um den Verstand bringen.
unbalanced [ʌn'bælənst] *adj* (a) *painting* unausgewogen; *diet also, report, view of life* einseitig; *ship etc* nicht im Gleichgewicht. **the structure of the committee was ~** der Ausschuß war sehr einseitig *or* unausgewogen besetzt.
    (b) (*also mentally ~*) (*deranged, mad*) irre, verrückt; (*slightly crazy*) nicht ganz normal. **is he a bit ~?** ist er nicht ganz normal *or* nicht ganz richtig im Kopf? (*inf*).
    (c) *account* nicht saldiert *or* ausgeglichen.
unbandage [ʌn'bændɪdʒ] *vt* den Verband abnehmen von.
unbar [ʌn'bɑːʳ] *vt* aufsperren.
unbearable [ʌn'bɛərəbl] *adj* unerträglich.
unbearably [ʌn'bɛərəblɪ] *adv see adj.* **almost ~ beautiful** überwältigend *or* hinreißend schön, fast zu schön.
unbeatable [ʌn'biːtəbl] *adj* unschlagbar; *army also* unbesiegbar; *record also* nicht zu überbieten *pred,* nicht zu überbietend *attr; offer, price also* unübertrefflich.
unbeaten [ʌn'biːtn] *adj* ungeschlagen; *army also* unbesiegt; *record* ungebrochen, nicht überboten.
unbecoming [ˌʌnbɪ'kʌmɪŋ] *adj* (a) *behaviour, language etc* unschicklich, unziemlich (*geh*). **conduct ~ to a gentleman** ein Benehmen, das sich für einen Herrn nicht schickt; **it was ~ of him to ...** es war kein schöner Zug von ihm, daß er ...
    (b) (*unflattering*) *clothes* unvorteilhaft; *facial hair* unschön.
unbeknown(st) [ˌʌnbɪ'nəʊn(st)] *adv* ohne daß es jemand wußte. **~ to me/his father** ohne mein Wissen/ohne Wissen seines Vaters.
unbelief [ˌʌnbɪ'liːf] *n* Ungläubigkeit *f.* **a look of ~** ein ungläubiger Blick; **in ~** ungläubig.
unbelievable [ˌʌnbɪ'liːvəbl] *adj* unglaublich; (*inf*) (*bad*) unglaublich; (*good*) sagenhaft (*inf*).
unbelievably [ˌʌnbɪ'liːvəblɪ] *adv* unglaublich; *good, pretty etc also* sagenhaft (*inf*).
unbeliever [ˌʌnbɪ'liːvəʳ] *n* Ungläubige(r) *mf.*
unbelieving *adj,* **~ly** *adv* [ˌʌnbɪ'liːvɪŋ, -lɪ] ungläubig.
unbend [ʌn'bend] *pret, ptp* **unbent 1** *vt* (*straighten*) *metal etc* geradebiegen; *arms* strecken. **~ your body** richten Sie sich auf; (*lying down*) legen Sie sich ausgestreckt hin.
    2 *vi* (*person: relax*) aus sich herausgehen; (*straighten body*) sich aufrichten; sich gerade hinlegen.
unbending [ʌn'bendɪŋ] *adj person, attitude* unnachgiebig; *determination* unbeugsam.
unbent [ʌn'bent] *pret, ptp of* **unbend.**
unbias(s)ed [ʌn'baɪəst] *adj* unvoreingenommen; *opinion, report also* unparteiisch.
unbidden [ʌn'bɪdn] *adj* (*form*) ungebeten; (*not ordered also*) unaufgefordert; (*uninvited also*) ungeladen. **to do sth ~** etw unaufgefordert tun.
unbind [ʌn'baɪnd] *pret, ptp* **unbound** *vt* (*free*) *prisoner* losbinden, befreien; (*untie*) *hair* lösen; (*unbandage*) den Verband ablösen von.
unbleached [ʌn'bliːtʃt] *adj* ungebleicht.
unblemished [ʌn'blemɪʃt] *adj* (*lit, fig*) makellos; *reputation also* unbescholten; *skin also* tadellos. **their relationship was ~ by quarrels** kein Streit hatte je ihre Beziehung getrübt.
unblinking [ʌn'blɪŋkɪŋ] *adj* look unverwandt; *eyes* starr.
unblock [ʌn'blɒk] *vt* frei machen; *sink, pipe* die Verstopfung in (+*dat*) beseitigen; *chimney* ausputzen.
unblushing [ʌn'blʌʃɪŋ] *adj* schamlos; *liar also* unverschämt. **he's quite ~ about it** er schämt sich kein bißchen.
unblushingly [ʌn'blʌʃɪŋlɪ] *adv* ohne sich zu schämen, frech.
unbolt [ʌn'bəʊlt] *vt* aufriegeln. **he left the door ~ed** er verriegelte die Tür nicht.
unborn [ʌn'bɔːn] *adj* ungeboren. **generations yet ~** kommende Generationen, zukünftige Geschlechter (*geh*).
unbosom [ʌn'bʊzəm] *vt feelings* offenbaren, enthüllen (*to sb* jdm). **to ~ oneself to sb** jdm sein Herz ausschütten.
unbound [ʌn'baʊnd] **1** *pret, ptp of* **unbind. 2** *adj* (a) (*not tied*) *hair* gelöst, nicht zusammengehalten *or* zusammengebunden; *prisoner* losgekettet, von den Fesseln befreit. **Prometheus ~** der befreite Prometheus. **(b)** *book* ungebunden.
unbounded [ʌn'baʊndɪd] *adj* grenzenlos; (*fig also*) unermeßlich, unendlich.
unbowed [ʌn'baʊd] *adj* (*fig*) ungebrochen; *pride* ungebeugt. **with head ~** mit hocherhobenem Kopf; **he was ~ by misfortune** sein Unglück hatte ihn nicht gebrochen *or* gebeugt; **the army was defeated but ~** das Heer war besiegt, sein Mut aber ungebrochen.

unbreakable [ʌn'breɪkəbl] *adj glass, toy* unzerbrechlich; *record* nicht zu brechen *pred; rule* unumstößlich, feststehend *attr; promise, silence* unverbrüchlich. **an ~ habit** eine Angewohnheit, die man nicht loswerden *or* ablegen kann.
unbribable [ʌn'braɪbəbl] *adj* unbestechlich.
unbridled [ʌn'braɪdld] *adj lust, passion* ungezügelt, zügellos; *anger* hemmungslos; *tongue* lose; *capitalism* ungehemmt.
un-British [ʌn'brɪtɪʃ] *adj* unbritisch, unenglisch.
unbroken [ʌn'brəʊkən] *adj* (a) (*intact*) unbeschädigt; *crockery also* nicht zerbrochen, unzerbrochen; *seal* nicht erbrochen; *heart, promise* nicht gebrochen. **there wasn't an ~ cup** keine Tasse war ganz *or* unbeschädigt *or* unzerbrochen.
    (b) (*continuous*) ununterbrochen; *silence also* ungebrochen; (*Mil*) *ranks* geschlossen, nicht durchbrochen; *line of descent* direkt. **an ~ night's sleep** eine ungestörte Nacht.
    (c) (*unbeaten*) *record* ungebrochen, unüberboten.
    (d) *horse* nicht zugeritten; *pride* ungebeugt. **his spirit remained ~** er war ungebrochen.
    (e) *voice* nicht gebrochen. **boys with ~ voices** Jungen vor dem Stimmbruch.
unbrotherly [ʌn'brʌðəlɪ] *adj* unbrüderlich.
unbuckle [ʌn'bʌkl] *vt* aufschnallen.
unburden [ʌn'bɜːdn] *vt* (*liter: unload*) abladen; (*fig*) *conscience, heart* erleichtern. **to ~ oneself/one's heart/one's soul to sb** jdm sein Herz ausschütten; **to ~ oneself of sth** (*lit liter*) etw abladen, sich von etw befreien; (*fig*) sich (*dat*) etw von der Seele reden; *of anxiety, guilt* sich von etw befreien *or* losmachen; *of sins* etw offenbaren *or* gestehen; **to ~ one's troubles to sb** seine Sorgen bei jdm abladen.
unbusinesslike [ʌn'bɪznɪslaɪk] *adj* unsystematisch. **it's very ~ to keep all your correspondence in cardboard boxes** es ist äußerst unordentlich, die ganze Korrespondenz in Kartons aufzubewahren; **the firm handled the transaction in such an ~ way** die Firma hat die Transaktion so ungeschäftsmäßig abgewickelt; **in spite of his ~ appearance ...** obwohl er gar nicht wie ein Geschäftsmann aussieht ...
unbutton [ʌn'bʌtn] *vt* aufknöpfen.
uncalled-for [ʌn'kɔːldfɔːʳ] *adj* (*unjustified*) *criticism* ungerechtfertigt; (*unnecessary*) unnötig; (*rude*) *remark* ungebührlich, deplaciert. **that was quite ~** das war nun wirklich nicht nötig *or* nett.
uncannily [ʌn'kænɪlɪ] *adv* unheimlich. **his guesses are ~ accurate** es ist unheimlich *or* nicht ganz geheuer, wie genau er alles errät.
uncanny [ʌn'kænɪ] *adj* unheimlich. **it's quite ~** das ist geradezu unheimlich.
uncap [ʌn'kæp] *vt bottle* aufmachen, öffnen.
uncared-for [ʌn'kɛədfɔːʳ] *adj garden, hands* ungepflegt; *child* vernachlässigt, verwahrlost.
uncaring [ʌn'kɛərɪŋ] *adj* gleichgültig, teilnahmslos; *parents* lieblos. **the state as an impersonal and ~ machine** der Staat als unpersönliche und gefühllose Maschine.
uncarpeted [ʌn'kɑːpɪtɪd] *adj* ohne Teppich, nicht ausgelegt.
uncatalogued [ʌn'kætələgd] *adj* nicht katalogisiert.
unceasing *adj,* **~ly** *adv* [ʌn'siːsɪŋ, -lɪ] unaufhörlich.
uncensored [ʌn'sensəd] *adj film, version* unzensiert; (*unblamed*) *remark* ungetadelt, ungerügt.
unceremonious [ˌʌnserɪ'məʊnɪəs] *adj* (a) (*abrupt, rude*) *dismissal* brüsk, barsch; *reply* unverbrämt, unverblümt; *behaviour* ungehobelt, ruppig; *exit, departure* überstürzt; *haste* unfein, unfeierlich. **the rather ~ treatment we got so kurz, wie wir abgefertigt wurden; he responded with an ~ punch on the nose** als Antwort hat er ihm eine eins kurzerhand *or* ohne viel Federlesens einen Schlag auf die Nase versetzt.
    (b) (*informal, simple*) zwanglos, formlos. **he greeted me with an ~ "hi"** er begrüßte mich mit einem formlosen *or* saloppen *or* lässigen „hallo".
unceremoniously [ˌʌnserɪ'məʊnɪəslɪ] *adv* (a) (*abruptly, rudely*) ohne Umschweife, ohne viel Federlesen(s), kurzerhand. **(b)** zwanglos, formlos.
uncertain [ʌn'sɜːtn] *adj* (a) (*unsure, unsteady*) unsicher; *light* undeutlich, schwach. **to be ~** whether sich (*dat*) nicht sicher sein, ob; **to be ~ of** *or* about sth sich (*dat*) einer Sache (*gen*) nicht sicher sein.
    (b) (*unknown*) *date, result* ungewiß; *origins* unbestimmt. **he's still ~ of the contract** er ist noch im ungewissen über den Vertrag; **a woman of ~ age** (*hum*) eine Frau von unbestimmtem Alter.
    (c) (*unreliable*) *weather, prices* unbeständig; *temper* unberechenbar; *judgement* unverläßlich, unzuverlässig.
    (d) (*unclear*) vage. **in no ~ terms** klar und deutlich, unzweideutig.
uncertainly [ʌn'sɜːtnlɪ] *adv say* unbestimmt; *look, move* unsicher.
uncertainty [ʌn'sɜːtntɪ] *n* (*state*) Ungewißheit *f;* (*indefiniteness*) Unbestimmtheit *f;* (*doubt*) Zweifel *m,* Unsicherheit *f.* **~ principle** (*Phys*) Unbestimmtheits- *or* Ungenauigkeits- *or* Unschärferelation *f;* **in order to remove any ~** um alle eventuellen Unklarheiten zu beseitigen; **there is still some ~ as to whether ...** es besteht noch Ungewißheit, ob ...
unchain [ʌn'tʃeɪn] *vt dog, prisoner* losketten, losbinden; *door* die Sicherheitskette (+*gen*) lösen; (*fig liter: free*) befreien, erlösen; *heart* freigeben.
unchallengeable [ʌn'tʃælɪndʒəbl] *adj* unerschütterlich, unanfechtbar; *proof also* unwiderlegbar.
unchallenged [ʌn'tʃælɪndʒd] *adj* unbestritten, unangefochten; (*Jur*) *juryman* nicht abgelehnt; *evidence* nicht angefochten, unangefochten. **to go ~** (*Mil*) ohne Anruf passieren; **we passed the sentry ~** die Wache ließ uns ohne Anruf passieren; **the record was** *or* **went ~ for several years** der Rekord wurde jahrelang nicht überboten; **I cannot let that remark go ~** diese Bemerkung kann ich nicht unwidersprochen hinnehmen.

unchanged [ʌnˈtʃeɪndʒd] *adj* unverändert.

unchanging [ʌnˈtʃeɪndʒɪŋ] *adj* unveränderlich.

unchaperoned [ʌnˈʃæpərəʊnd] *adj* unbegleitet.

uncharacteristic [ˌʌnkærəktəˈrɪstɪk] *adj* uncharakteristisch, untypisch (*of* für). **such rudeness is ~ of him** es ist gar nicht seine Art, so unhöflich zu sein; **with ~ enthusiasm** mit an ihm völlig ungewohnter *or* für ihn völlig untypischer Begeisterung.

uncharitable [ʌnˈtʃærɪtəbl] *adj* hartherzig; *remark* unfreundlich, nicht nett, lieblos; *view* unbarmherzig, herzlos; *criticism* schonungslos, unbarmherzig. **it was most ~ of you to ...** es war wirklich nicht nett, daß Sie ...; **some of the examiners were very ~ in their decision** einige Prüfer waren in ihrer Beurteilung sehr hart *or* unbarmherzig.

uncharted [ʌnˈtʃɑːtɪd] *adj* (*not explored*) unerforscht, unergründet; (*not on map*) nicht verzeichnet *or* eingezeichnet.

unchaste [ʌnˈtʃeɪst] *adj* unzüchtig; *thoughts, actions* unkeusch; *life, wife* untugendhaft.

unchecked [ʌnˈtʃekt] *adj* (a) (*unrestrained*) ungehemmt, unkontrolliert; *advance* ungehindert; *anger* hemmungslos, ungezügelt. **to go ~** (*abuse*) geduldet werden; (*advance*) nicht gehindert werden; (*inflation*) nicht eingedämmt *or* aufgehalten werden; **if the epidemic goes ~** wenn der Epidemie nicht Einhalt geboten wird. **(b)** (*not verified*) ungeprüft, nicht überprüft.

unchivalrous [ʌnˈʃɪvəlrəs] *adj* unritterlich; *remark* ungalant.

unchristian [ʌnˈkrɪstjən] *adj* unchristlich. **at an ~ hour** (*inf*) zu unchristlicher Zeit (*inf*) *or* Stunde (*inf*).

uncial [ˈʌnsɪəl] **1** *adj* Unzial-. **2** *n* (*letter*) Unzialbuchstabe *m*; (*script*) Unziale, Unzialschrift *f*; (*manuscript*) Schriftstück *or* Dokument *nt* in Unzialschrift.

uncircumcised [ʌnˈsɜːkəmsaɪzd] *adj* unbeschnitten.

uncivil [ʌnˈsɪvɪl] *adj* unhöflich.

uncivilized [ʌnˈsɪvɪlaɪzd] *adj* *country, tribe, behaviour* unzivilisiert; (*inf*) *habit* barbarisch.

unclad [ʌnˈklæd] *adj* (*euph, hum*) bar jeglicher Kleidung.

unclaimed [ʌnˈkleɪmd] *adj* *prize* nicht abgeholt; *property also* herrenlos; *right* nicht geltend gemacht; *social security etc* nicht beansprucht.

unclasp [ʌnˈklɑːsp] *vt* *necklace* lösen; *cloak* öffnen, aufhaken; *hands* voneinander lösen. **he ~ed her hand** er löste ihre Hand.

unclassified [ʌnˈklæsɪfaɪd] *adj* (a) (*not arranged*) nicht klassifiziert *or* eingeordnet. **(b)** (*not secret*) nicht geheim. **(c)** (*Brit*) **~ road** schlecht ausgebaute Landstraße.

uncle [ˈʌŋkl] *n* Onkel *m*. **U~ Sam** Uncle *or* Onkel Sam; **to say** *or* **cry ~** (*US*) aufgeben; *see* **Dutch**.

unclean [ʌnˈkliːn] *adj* unsauber (*also Bibl*); (*Rel*) *animal* unrein; *thoughts* unkeusch; (*fig: contaminated*) schmutzig.

unclear [ʌnˈklɪəʳ] *adj* unklar; *essay etc* undurchsichtig. **to be ~ about sth** sich (*dat*) über etw (*acc*) im unklaren *or* nicht im klaren sein; **his motives are ~ to me** mir sind seine Motive nicht klar.

unclimbable [ʌnˈklaɪməbl] *adj* unbesteigbar.

unclog [ʌnˈklɒg] *vt* *pipe, drain* die Verstopfung in (+*dat*) beseitigen; *wheel* befreien.

unclothed [ʌnˈkləʊðd] *adj* unbekleidet.

unclouded [ʌnˈklaʊdɪd] *adj* *sky* unbewölkt; (*fig*) *happiness, vision, mind* ungetrübt; *mind* klar.

unclubbable [ʌnˈklʌbəbl] *adj* ohne Gruppenzugehörigkeitsgefühl.

uncluttered [ʌnˈklʌtəd] *adj* schlicht, einfach; *desk, room* nicht überfüllt *or* überladen. **a mind ~ by excess information** ein von überflüssigem Wissen freier *or* unbelasteter Kopf.

uncoil [ʌnˈkɔɪl] **1** *vt* abwickeln. **2** *vir* (*snake*) sich langsam strecken; (*person*) sich ausstrecken; (*wire etc*) sich abwickeln, sich abspulen. **to ~ oneself from a car/bar stool** sich aus einem Auto herauswinden *or* herausschlängeln/von einem Barhocker heruntergleiten.

uncollected [ˌʌnkəˈlektɪd] *adj* *tax* nicht eingezogen *or* vereinnahmt; *fare* nicht kassiert, unkassiert.

uncoloured, (*US*) **uncolored** [ʌnˈkʌləd] *adj* (*colourless*) farblos; (*white*) weiß; (*fig: unprejudiced*) nicht gefärbt; *judgement* unparteiisch. **his judgement was ~ by ...** sein Urteil war nicht durch ... gefärbt.

uncombed [ʌnˈkəʊmd] *adj* ungekämmt.

uncomfortable [ʌnˈkʌmfətəbl] *adj* (a) unbequem; *chair, position also* ungemütlich. **I feel ~ sitting like this** es ist unbequem, so zu sitzen; **I feel ~ on this bed** ich finde das Bett nicht bequem; **if the room is too hot it'll make you feel ~** wenn das Zimmer zu heiß ist, fühlt man sich nicht wohl; **I feel ~ in this jacket** in dieser Jacke fühle ich mich nicht wohl; **it feels ~** es ist unbequem. **(b)** (*uneasy*) *feeling* unangenehm, ungut; *silence* (*awkward*) peinlich; (*nerve-racking*) beklemmend. **to feel ~** sich unbehaglich *or* sich nicht wohl fühlen; **I felt ~ about it** ich hatte ein ungutes Gefühl dabei, mir war nicht wohl dabei; **he was ~ in that job** er fühlte sich in dieser Stelle nicht wohl; **they make me feel ~** in ihrer Gegenwart fühle ich mich unbehaglich. **(c)** (*unpleasant*) *time, position* unerfreulich. **we could make things ~ for you** (*euph*) wir können ungemütlich werden.

uncomfortably [ʌnˈkʌmfətəblɪ] *adv* (a) unbequem. **(b)** (*uneasily*) unbehaglich, unruhig. **(c)** (*unpleasantly*) unangenehm. **I became ~ aware of having insulted him** es wurde mir peinlich bewußt, daß ich ihn beleidigt hatte.

uncommitted [ˌʌnkəˈmɪtɪd] *adj* nicht engagiert; *party, country* neutral. **we want to remain ~ till we get a full report** wir wollen uns nicht festlegen, bevor wir nicht einen ausführlichen Bericht haben; **~ to** nicht festgelegt auf (+*acc*).

uncommon [ʌnˈkɒmən] *adj* (a) (*unusual*) ungewöhnlich. **it is not ~ for her to be late** es ist nichts Ungewöhnliches, daß sie zu spät kommt; **a not ~ occurrence** eine häufige Erscheinung. **(b)** (*outstanding*) außergewöhnlich.

uncommonly [ʌnˈkɒmənlɪ] *adv* (a) (*unusually*) ungewöhnlich. **(b)** (*exceptionally*) außergewöhnlich. **that's ~ civil of you** (*dated*) das ist äußerst freundlich von Ihnen; **he was ~ rude to her** (*dated*) er war ausnehmend *or* äußerst unhöflich zu ihr.

uncommunicative [ˌʌnkəˈmjuːnɪkətɪv] *adj* (*by nature*) verschlossen, wortkarg; (*temporarily*) schweigsam.

uncompetitive [ˌʌnkəmˈpetɪtɪv] *adj* *industry* nicht wettbewerbsfähig, wettbewerbsunfähig; *price* nicht marktgerecht.

uncomplaining [ˌʌnkəmˈpleɪnɪŋ] *adj* duldsam. **with ~ patience** klaglos.

uncomplainingly [ˌʌnkəmˈpleɪnɪŋlɪ] *adv* geduldig, klaglos.

uncompleted [ˌʌnkəmˈpliːtɪd] *adj* unbeendet, unvollendet.

uncomplicated [ʌnˈkɒmplɪkeɪtɪd] *adj* unkompliziert. **his life was ~ by emotional problems** sein Leben wurde nicht durch emotionale Probleme kompliziert *or* erschwert.

uncomplimentary [ˌʌnkɒmplɪˈmentərɪ] *adj* unschmeichelhaft. **to be ~ about sb/sth** sich nicht sehr schmeichelhaft über jdn/etw äußern.

uncomprehending *adj*, **~ly** *adv* [ˌʌnkɒmprɪˈhendɪŋ, -lɪ] verständnislos.

uncompromising [ʌnˈkɒmprəmaɪzɪŋ] *adj* kompromißlos; *dedication, honesty* rückhaltlos; *commitment* hundertprozentig.

uncompromisingly [ʌnˈkɒmprəmaɪzɪŋlɪ] *adv* unerbittlich; *frank* rückhaltlos, völlig; *committed* hundertprozentig. **he is ~ opposed to ...** er ist ein kompromißloser Gegner (+*gen*) ...

unconcealed [ˌʌnkənˈsiːld] *adj* *joy, delight etc* offen, unverhüllt; *hatred, distaste etc also* unverhohlen.

unconcern [ˌʌnkənˈsɜːn] *n* (*lack of worry*) Unbesorgtheit, Unbekümmertheit *f*; (*indifference*) Gleichgültigkeit *f*.

unconcerned [ˌʌnkənˈsɜːnd] *adj* (a) (*unworried*) unbekümmert; (*indifferent*) gleichgültig. **to be ~ about sth** sich nicht um etw kümmern; **how could he be so ~ about her safety/the problem?** wie konnte ihm ihre Sicherheit/das Problem so egal *or* gleichgültig sein?; **I was not ~ about your safety** ich habe mir Sorgen um deine Sicherheit gemacht. **(b)** (*not involved*) unbeteiligt (*in an* +*dat*).

unconcernedly [ˌʌnkənˈsɜːnɪdlɪ] *adv* unbekümmert; (*indifferently*) gleichgültig.

unconditional [ˌʌnkənˈdɪʃənl] *adj* vorbehaltlos; **~ surrender** bedingungslose Kapitulation.

unconditionally [ˌʌnkənˈdɪʃnəlɪ] *adv* *offer, agree* vorbehaltlos; *surrender* bedingungslos.

unconditioned [ˌʌnkənˈdɪʃənd] *adj* (*Psych*) nicht konditioniert.

unconfirmed [ˌʌnkənˈfɜːmd] *adj* unbestätigt.

uncongenial [ˌʌnkənˈdʒiːnɪəl] *adj* *person* unliebenswürdig, nicht einnehmend; *work, surroundings* unerfreulich. **he finds this place ~** dieser Ort entspricht ihm *or* seinem Wesen nicht.

unconnected [ˌʌnkəˈnektɪd] *adj* (a) (*unrelated*) nicht miteinander in Beziehung stehend *attr*. **the two events are ~** es besteht keine Beziehung zwischen den beiden Ereignissen; **his illness is ~ with that accident** es besteht keine Beziehung zwischen seiner Krankheit und diesem Unfall. **(b)** (*incoherent*) zusammenhanglos, unzusammenhängend.

unconquerable [ʌnˈkɒŋkərəbl] *adj* *army* unbesiegbar; *peak* unbezwinglich, unerreichbar; *spirit* unbezwinglich, unbezwingbar; *courage* unbezähmbar.

unconquered [ʌnˈkɒŋkəd] *adj* *army* unbesiegt; *mountain* unbezwungen; *courage, spirit* ungebrochen. **large parts of Britain remained ~** weite Teile Großbritanniens wurden nicht erobert.

unconscionable [ʌnˈkɒnʃənəbl] *adj* unerhört. **an ~ time** eine unerhört lange Zeit, unerhört lange.

unconscious [ʌnˈkɒnʃəs] **1** *adj* (a) (*Med*) bewußtlos. **the blow knocked him ~** durch den Schlag wurde er bewußtlos. **(b)** *pred* (*unaware*) **to be ~ of sth** sich (*dat*) einer Sache (*gen*) nicht bewußt sein; **I was ~ of the fact that ...** ich *or* es war mir nicht bewußt, daß ... **(c)** (*unintentional*) *insult, allusion etc* unbewußt, unbeabsichtigt; *blunder* ungewollt, unbeabsichtigt; *humour* unfreiwillig. **she was the ~ cause for his unhappiness** ohne es zu wissen, wurde sie zur Ursache seines Unglücks; **he was the ~ tool of ...** er wurde unwissentlich zum Werkzeug (+*gen*) ... **(d)** (*Psych*) unbewußt. **the ~ mind** das Unbewußte. **2** *n* (*Psych*) **the ~** das Unbewußte; **he probed his ~** er erforschte das Unbewußte in sich (*dat*).

unconsciously [ʌnˈkɒnʃəslɪ] *adv* unbewußt. **an ~ funny remark** eine ungewollt *or* unbeabsichtigt lustige Bemerkung.

unconsciousness [ʌnˈkɒnʃəsnɪs] *n* (a) (*Med*) Bewußtlosigkeit *f*. **(b)** (*unawareness*) mangelndes Bewußtsein. **his ~ of the real situation** seine Unkenntnis der tatsächlichen Lage. **(c)** (*of insult etc*) Ungewolltheit *f*; (*of humour*) Unfreiwilligkeit *f*.

unconsecrated [ʌnˈkɒnsɪkreɪtɪd] *adj* (*Rel*) ungeweiht.

unconsidered [ˌʌnkənˈsɪdəd] *adj* *fact etc* unberücksichtigt; (*rash*) *action etc* unbedacht, unüberlegt.

unconstitutional [ˌʌnkɒnstɪˈtjuːʃənl] *adj* nicht verfassungsgemäß, verfassungswidrig.

unconstitutionally [ˌʌnkɒnstɪˈtjuːʃnəlɪ] *adv* verfassungswidrig.

unconstructive [ˌʌnkənˈstrʌktɪv] *adj* nicht konstruktiv. **this is one of the most ~ suggestions I've ever heard** einen so wenig konstruktiven Vorschlag habe ich noch nie gehört.

unconsummated [ʌnˈkɒnsjʊmeɪtɪd] *adj* unvollzogen.

uncontaminated [ˌʌnkənˈtæmɪneɪtɪd] *adj* nicht verseucht; *people* (*by disease*) nicht angesteckt; (*fig*) unverdorben.

uncontested [ˌʌnkənˈtestɪd] *adj* unbestritten; *election, seat* ohne Gegenkandidat. **the election/seat/district was ~ by the Liberals** die Liberalen stellten in der Wahl/für das Mandat/in dem Wahlkreis keinen Kandidaten auf; **the championship went**

~ **for many years** der Meisterschaftstitel wurde jahrelang nicht angefochten; **the chairmanship was** ~ **in** der Wahl für den Vorsitz gab es keinen Gegenkandidaten.

uncontrollable [ˌʌnkən'trəʊləbl] *adj* unkontrollierbar; *child* nicht zu bändigend *attr*, nicht zu bändigen *pred; horse, dog* nicht unter Kontrolle zu bringen *pred; desire, urge* unbezwinglich, unwiderstehlich; *(physical)* unkontrollierbar; *twitch* unkontrolliert; *laughter, mirth* unbezähmbar. **the epidemic is now** ~ die Epidemie ist nicht mehr unter Kontrolle zu bekommen; **to become** ~ außer Kontrolle geraten; **to have an** ~ **temper** unbeherrscht sein.

uncontrollably [ˌʌnkən'trəʊləblɪ] *adv* unkontrollierbar; *weep* hemmungslos; *laugh* unkontrolliert.

uncontrolled [ˌʌnkən'trəʊld] *adj* ungehindert; *dogs, children* unbeaufsichtigt; *laughter* unkontrolliert; *weeping* hemmungslos, haltlos. **if inflation is allowed to go** ~ wenn die Inflation nicht unter Kontrolle gebracht wird.

uncontroversial [ˌʌnkɒntrə'vɜ:ʃəl] *adv* unverfänglich.

unconventional *adj*, ~ **ly** *adv* [ˌʌnkən'venʃənl, -əlɪ] unkonventionell.

unconversant [ˌʌnkən'vɜ:snt] *adj* **to be** ~ **with sth** mit etw nicht vertraut sein.

unconvinced [ˌʌnkən'vɪnst] *adj* nicht überzeugt *(of* von); *look* wenig überzeugt. **his arguments leave me** ~ seine Argumente überzeugen mich nicht; **he remained** ~ **of the necessity for this** er konnte von der Notwendigkeit nicht überzeugt werden; **I remain** ~ ich bin noch immer nicht überzeugt.

unconvincing [ˌʌnkən'vɪnsɪŋ] *adj* nicht überzeugend. **rather** ~ wenig überzeugend.

unconvincingly [ˌʌnkən'vɪnsɪŋlɪ] *adv* wenig überzeugend.

uncooked [ʌn'kʊkt] *adj* ungekocht, roh.

uncooperative [ˌʌnkəʊ'ɒpərətɪv] *adj attitude* stur, wenig entgegenkommend; *witness, colleague* wenig hilfreich, nicht hilfsbereit. **the government office remained** ~ das Regierungsamt war auch weiterhin nicht zur Kooperation bereit; **if the prisoner is still** ~ wenn sich der Gefangene weiterhin weigert, mit uns zusammenzuarbeiten; **why are you being so** ~? warum helfen Sie denn nicht mit?; **you're being rather** ~ Sie sind nicht sehr hilfreich; **an** ~ **partner** ein Partner, der nicht mitmacht; **they didn't exactly go on strike, they just became** ~ sie haben nicht gerade gestreikt, sie haben nur auf stur geschaltet.

uncooperatively [ˌʌnkəʊ'ɒpərətɪvlɪ] *adv* wenig entgegenkommend; *say* wenig hilfreich.

uncoordinated [ˌʌnkəʊ'ɔ:dɪneɪtɪd] *adj* unkoordiniert.

uncork [ʌn'kɔ:k] *vt bottle* entkorken.

uncorroborated [ˌʌnkə'rɒbəreɪtɪd] *adj* unbestätigt; *evidence* nicht bekräftigt.

uncorrupted [ˌʌnkə'rʌptɪd] *adj* unverdorben, nicht korrumpiert; *person also* rechtschaffen.

uncountable [ʌn'kaʊntəbl] *adj (Gram)* unzählbar.

uncounted [ʌn'kaʊntɪd] *adj (innumerable)* unzählig.

uncouple [ʌn'kʌpl] *vt train, trailer* abkuppeln, abkoppeln.

uncouth [ʌn'ku:θ] *adj person* ungehobelt, ordinär; *behaviour* unflätig, ungehobelt; *manners* ungeschliffen, ungehobelt; *expression, word* unflätig, unfein. **it's very** ~ **to eat with your hands** es ist sehr unfein, mit den Fingern zu essen.

uncover [ʌn'kʌvəʳ] **1** *vt* **(a)** *(remove cover from)* aufdecken; *head* entblößen *(liter)*. **the men ~ed their heads** die Männer nahmen ihren Hüte ab. **(b)** *scandal* enthüllen, aufdecken; *plot* aufdecken; *ancient ruins* zum Vorschein bringen. **2** *vi (form: remove hat)* den Kopfbedeckung abnehmen.

uncritical [ʌn'krɪtɪkəl] *adj* unkritisch *(of, about* in bezug auf +*acc*).

uncross [ʌn'krɒs] *vt* **he ~ed his legs** er nahm das Bein vom Knie.

uncrossed [ʌn'krɒst] *adj legs* nicht übereinandergeschlagen *or* gekreuzt; *(Brit) cheque* nicht gekreuzt, Bar-.

uncrowded [ʌn'kraʊdɪd] *adj* ziemlich leer.

uncrowned [ʌn'kraʊnd] *adj (lit, fig)* ungekrönt.

uncrushable [ʌn'krʌʃəbl] *adj dress* knitterfrei; *carton* Hart-.

unction ['ʌŋkʃən] *n* **(a)** *(Rel: anointing)* Salbung, Ölung *f*. **extreme** ~ Letzte Ölung. **(b)** *(insincere fervour)* hohles *or* unechtes Pathos.

unctuous *adj*, ~ **ly** *adv* ['ʌŋktjʊəs, -lɪ] salbungsvoll.

unctuousness ['ʌŋktjʊəsnɪs] *n* salbungsvolle Art; *(of speech)* falsches Pathos. **the** ~ **of his voice/manner** seine salbungsvolle Stimme/Art.

uncultivated [ʌn'kʌltɪveɪtɪd] *adj land* unkultiviert, unbebaut; *person, behaviour* unkultiviert; *mind* nicht ausgebildet. **a potential but as yet** ~ **talent** ein potentielles aber noch brachliegendes Talent.

uncultured [ʌn'kʌltʃəd] *adj person, mind* ungebildet; *behaviour* unkultiviert, unzivilisiert.

uncurl [ʌn'kɜ:l] **1** *vt* auseinanderrollen. **to** ~ **oneself** sich strecken; **she ~ed herself from the chair** sie löste sich aus ihrer zusammengerollten Stellung im Sessel. **2** *vi* glatt werden; *(cat, snake)* sich langsam strecken; *(person)* sich ausstrecken.

uncut [ʌn'kʌt] *adj* **(a)** ungeschnitten; *ham, untrimmed pages* nicht aufgeschnitten; *diamond* ungeschliffen, Roh-; *stone, rock* unbehauen; *lawn* nicht gemäht. **an** ~ **rug** ein Schlingenteppich. **(b)** *film, play, novel* ungekürzt.

undamaged [ʌn'dæmɪdʒd] *adj* unbeschädigt; *(fig) reputation* makellos.

undated [ʌn'deɪtɪd] *adj* undatiert.

undaunted [ʌn'dɔ:ntɪd] *adj (not discouraged)* nicht entmutigt, unverzagt; *(fearless)* unerschrocken; *courage* unerschütterlich. **in spite of these failures he carried on** ~ trotz dieser Mißerfolge machte er unverzagt weiter; ~ **by these threats** ... nicht eingeschüchtert von diesen Drohungen ...

undeceive [ˌʌndɪ'si:v] *vt* aufklären.

undecided [ˌʌndɪ'saɪdɪd] *adj* **(a)** *person* unentschlossen. **he is** ~ **as to whether he should go or not** er ist (sich) noch unschlüssig, ob er gehen soll oder nicht; **to be** ~ **about sth** sich *(dat)* über etw *(acc)* im unklaren sein.

(b) *question* unentschieden. **what are we going to do?** — **I don't know, it's** ~ was sollen wir tun? — ich weiß nicht, das steht noch nicht fest *or* ist noch nicht entschieden.

undecipherable [ˌʌndɪ'saɪfərəbl] *adj handwriting* unleserlich, schwer zu entziffernd *attr; code, signs* nicht entzifferbar.

undeclared [ˌʌndɪ'kleəd] *adj love* heimlich, unerklärt; *war* unerklärt; *interest* uneingestanden; *(Customs) goods* nicht deklariert. **could he leave her with his love** ~? konnte er von ihr gehen, ohne ihr seine Liebe erklärt *or* gestanden zu haben?

undefeated [ˌʌndɪ'fi:tɪd] *adj army, team* unbesiegt; *spirit* ungebrochen.

undefendable [ˌʌndɪ'fendəbl] *adj (Mil) coast, frontier* schwer zu verteidigend *attr*, schwer zu verteidigen *pred*.

undefended [ˌʌndɪ'fendɪd] *adj town, goal* unverteidigt. **the case was** ~ in dem Fall wurde auf Verteidigung verzichtet.

undefiled [ˌʌndɪ'faɪld] *adj* unbefleckt.

undefined [ˌʌndɪ'faɪnd] *adj* undefiniert, nicht definiert; *(vague)* undefinierbar.

undemanding [ˌʌndɪ'mɑ:ndɪŋ] *adj* anspruchslos, keine Anforderungen *or* Ansprüche stellend *attr; task* wenig fordernd, keine großen Anforderungen stellend *attr*. **this job is so** ~ dieser Job fordert mich überhaupt nicht.

undemocratic *adj*, ~ **ally** *adv* [ˌʌndemə'krætɪk, -əlɪ] undemokratisch.

undemonstrative [ˌʌndɪ'mɒnstrətɪv] *adj* reserviert, zurückhaltend. **a fairly** ~ **race** ein Volk, das seine Gefühle wenig zeigt.

undeniable [ˌʌndɪ'naɪəbl] *adj* unbestreitbar, unleugbar. **it is** ~ **that ...** es läßt sich nicht bestreiten *or* leugnen, daß ...

undeniably [ˌʌndɪ'naɪəblɪ] *adv* zweifelsohne, zweifellos; *successful, proud* unbestreitbar.

undenominational [ˌʌndɪnɒmɪ'neɪʃənl] *adj* interkonfessionell. ~ **school** Simultan- *or* Gemeinschaftsschule *f*.

undependable [ˌʌndɪ'pendəbl] *adj* unzuverlässig.

under ['ʌndəʳ] **1** *prep* **(a)** *(beneath)* *(place)* unter (+*dat*); *(direction)* unter (+*acc*). ~ **it** darunter; **to come out from** ~ **the bed** unter dem Bett hervorkommen; **it's** ~ **there** es ist da drunter *(inf)*; ~ **barley** mit Gerste bebaut.

(b) *(less than)* unter (+*dat*); *(of price etc also)* weniger als. **it took** ~ **an hour** es dauerte weniger als eine Stunde; **there were** ~ **50 of them** es waren weniger als *or* unter 50.

(c) *(subordinate to,* ~ *influence of etc)* unter (+*dat*). **he had 50 men** ~ **him** er hatte 50 Männer unter sich; **who were you** ~? *(Univ)* bei wem haben Sie studiert?; *(Mil)* unter wem haben Sie gedient?; **he was born** ~ **Virgo** *(Astrol)* er wurde im Zeichen der Jungfrau geboren; **he died** ~ **the anaesthetic** er starb in der Narkose; **you're** ~ **a misapprehension** Sie befinden sich im Irrtum; ~ **construction** im Bau; **the matter** ~ **discussion** der Diskussionsgegenstand; **to be** ~ **treatment** *(Med)* in Behandlung sein; **to be** ~ **the doctor** in (ärztlicher) Behandlung sein; **which doctor are you** ~? bei welchem Arzt sind Sie?; **it's classified** ~ **history** es ist unter „Geschichte" eingeordnet; **you'll find him** ~ **"garages"** Sie finden ihn unter „Werkstätten"; ~ **sentence of death** zum Tode verurteilt; ~ **penalty of death** unter Androhung der Todesstrafe; ~ **an assumed name** unter falschem Namen; **the house is** ~ **threat of demolition** das Haus ist vom Abbruch bedroht.

(d) *(according to)* nach, gemäß, laut *(all +dat)*. ~ **his will** in seinem Testament; ~ **the terms of the contract** nach *or* gemäß den *or* laut Vertragsbedingungen.

2 *adv* **(a)** *(beneath)* unten; *(unconscious)* bewußtlos. **he came to the fence and crawled** ~ er kam zum Zaun und kroch darunter durch; **to go** ~ untergehen; **to get out from** ~ *(fig inf)* wieder Licht sehen *(inf)*.

(b) *(less)* darunter.

under- *pref* **(a)** *(in rank)* Unter-, Hilfs-. **for the ~-twelves/ -eighteens/-forties** für Kinder unter zwölf/Jugendliche unter achtzehn/Leute unter vierzig. **(b)** *(insufficiently)* zuwenig, ungenügend.

under: ~ **achieve** *vi* hinter den Erwartungen zurückbleiben; ~ **achievement** *n* schwache *or* enttäuschende Leistungen *pl*; ~ **achiever** *n* Johnny **is an** ~ **achiever** Johnnys Leistungen bleiben hinter den Erwartungen zurück; ~ **act** *vti* betont zurückhaltend spielen; *(pej)* schwach spielen; ~ **age** *adj attr* minderjährig; ~ **age drinking** Alkoholgenuß *m* Minderjähriger; *see also* **age;** ~ **arm 1** *adj* hair, perspiration Unterarm-; *seam* Ärmel-; **(b)** *throw* von unten; ~ **arm serve** *(Tennis)* Aufschlag *m* von unten; **2** *adv* throw von unten; **to serve** ~ **arm** *(Tennis)* von unten aufschlagen; ~ **belly** *n (Zool, fig: of plane)* Bauch *m*; **the soft** ~ **belly of Europe/democracy** die Achillesferse Europas/der Demokratie; ~ **bid** *pret, ptp* ~ **bid** *vt (Comm, Bridge)* unterbieten; ~ **brush** *n see* ~ **growth;** ~ **buy** *pret, ptp* ~ **bought** *vi* zuwenig kaufen; ~ **carriage** *n (Aviat)* Fahrwerk, Fahrgestell *nt;* ~ **charge 1** *vi* zuwenig berechnen; **2** *vt* zuwenig berechnen *(sb* jdm); **he** ~ **charged me by 10p** er berechnete mir 10 Pence zuwenig; ~ **clothes** *npl;* ~ **clothing** *n* Unterwäsche *f;* ~ **coat** *n (paint)* Grundierfarbe *f; (coat)* Grundierung *f; (US Aut)* Unterbodenschutz *m;* ~ **cook** *vt* nicht durchgaren; *(accidentally also)* nicht lange genug kochen; ~ **cover** *adj agent* Geheim-; *deal also* geheim; **he did** ~ **cover work for the police** er arbeitete insgeheim für die Polizei; ~ **current** *n (lit, fig)* Unterströmung *f; (in speech, attitude)* Unterton *m;* ~ **cut** *pret, ptp* ~ **cut** *vt competitor (im Preis)* unterbieten; ~ **developed** *adj* unterentwickelt; *resources* ungenutzt; ~ **dog** *n (in society)* Schwächere(r), Benachteiligte(r) *m; (in game also)* sicherer Verlierer; ~ **done** *adj* nicht gar; *(deliberately)* steak nicht durchgebraten;

~**dressed** *adj* to be ~**dressed** (*too lightly*) zu leicht angezogen sein; (*not formally enough*) zu einfach angezogen sein; ~**employed** *adj* nicht ausgelastet; *person also* unterbeschäftigt; *plant, equipment also* nicht voll (aus)genutzt; ~**employment** *n* Unterbeschäftigung *f*; (*of person, plant also*) mangelnde Auslastung; (*of abilities, plant also*) mangelnde Ausnutzung; ~**estimate** 1 *vt cost, person* unterschätzen; 2 *n* Unterschätzung *f*; ~**estimation** *n* Unterschätzung *f*; ~**expose** *vt* (*Phot*) unterbelichten; ~**exposed** *adj* (*Phot*) unterbelichtet; ~**exposure** *n* (*Phot*) Unterbelichtung *f*; (*fig*) Mangel *m* an Publizität; ~**fed** *adj* unterernährt; ~**feed** *pret, ptp* ~**fed** *vt* zuwenig zu essen geben (+*dat*); *animals* zuwenig füttern ~**felt** *n* Filzunterlage *f*; ~**floor heating** *n* Fußbodenheizung *f*; ~**foot** *adv* am Boden; it is wet ~**foot** der Boden ist naß; to trample sb/sth ~**foot** (*lit, fig*) auf jdm/etw herumtrampeln; to have the children ~**foot** all day die Kinder den ganzen Tag um die Beine haben; ~**garment** *n* Unterkleid *nt*; ~**garments** Unterkleidung *f*; ~**go** *pret* ~**went**, *ptp* ~**gone** *vt suffering* durchmachen, mitmachen; *change also* erleben; *test, treatment*, (*Med*) *operation* sich unterziehen (+*dat*); (*machine*) *test* unterzogen werden (+*dat*); to ~**go experiences** Erlebnisse haben; to ~**go repairs** in Reparatur sein; she has ~**gone** a lot sie hat viel durch- or mitgemacht; ~**grad** (*inf*), ~**graduate** 1 *n* Student(in *f*) *m*; 2 *attr* Studenten-; ~**graduate student** Student(in *f*) *m*; ~**graduate courses** Kurse *pl* für nichtgraduierte Studenten.

underground ['ʌndəgraʊnd] 1 *adj* ~ *explosion, lake, cave, passage* unterirdisch; (*Min*) Untertage-. ~ **cable** Erdkabel *nt*; ~ **railway** *or* (*US*) **railroad** Untergrundbahn *f*. (**b**) (*fig*) *press, movement* Untergrund-. 2 *adv* (**a**) unterirdisch; (*Min*) unter Tage. 3 m ~ 3 m unter der Erde. (**b**) (*fig*) to go ~ untertauchen. 3 *n* (**a**) (*Brit Rail*) U-Bahn, Untergrundbahn *f*. (**b**) (*movement*) Untergrundbewegung *f*; (*sub-culture*) Underground *m*.

under: ~**growth** *n* Gestrüpp, Gebüsch *nt*; (*under trees*) Unterholz *nt*; ~**hand** 1 *adj* (**a**) (*sly*) hinterhältig; (**b**) (*Sport*) *see* ~**arm**; 2 *adv* (*Sport*) *see* ~**arm**; ~**hung** *adj jaw* vorgeschoben; ~**insured** *adj* unterversichert; ~**lay** *n* Unterlage *f*; ~**lie** *pret* ~**lay**, *ptp* ~**lain** *vt* (*lit*) liegen unter (+*dat*); (*fig: be basis for or cause of*) zugrunde liegen (+*dat*); ~**line** *vt* (*lit, fig*) unterstreichen.

underling ['ʌndəlɪŋ] *n* (*pej*) Untergebene(r) *mf*; Befehlsempfänger(in *f*) *m* (*pej*).

under: ~**lining** *n* Unterstreichung *f*; with red ~**lining** rot unterstrichen; why all this ~**lining**? warum ist so viel unterstrichen?; ~**lying** *adj* (**a**) *soil, rocks* tieferliegend; (**b**) *cause* eigentlich; (*deeper also*) tiefer; *problem* zugrundeliegend; *honesty, strength* grundlegend; the ~**lying cause of all this** was all dem zugrunde liegt; a certain ~**lying sense** of tragedy eine gewisse unterschwellige Tragik; ~**manned** *adj* unterbemannt; ~**manning** *n* Personalmangel *m*, Personalknappheit *f*; (*deliberate*) Unterbesetzung *f*; (*Mil, of police force etc*) Unterbemannung *f*; ~**mentioned** *adj* untengenannt, untenerwähnt; ~**mine** *vt* (**a**) (*tunnel under*) unterhöhlen; (*Mil*) unterminieren; (*weaken*) schwächen; (*sea*) *cliffs* unterspülen, unterhöhlen; (**b**) (*fig: weaken*) *authority, confidence* unterminieren, untergraben; *health* angreifen; ~**most** *adj* unterst.

underneath [ʌndə'niːθ] 1 *prep* (*place*) unter (+*dat*); (*direction*) unter (+*acc*). ~ it darunter; it came from ~ the table es kam unter dem Tisch hervor; from ~ the trees it seems ... unter den Bäumen scheint es ... 2 *adv* darunter. the ones ~ die darunter. 3 *n* Unterseite *f*.

under: ~**nourished** *adj* unterernährt; ~**nourishment** *n* Unterernährung *f*; ~**paid** 1 *pret, ptp of* ~**pay**; 2 *adj* unterbezahlt; ~**pants** *npl* Unterhose(n *pl*) *f*; a pair of ~**pants** eine Unterhose, ein Paar Unterhosen; ~**pass** *n* Unterführung *f*; ~**pay** *pret, ptp* ~**paid** *vt* unterbezahlen; ~**payment** *n* zu geringe Bezahlung, Unterbezahlung *f*; because of ~**payment of tax** ... weil zuwenig Steuer gezahlt wurde ...; there was an ~**payment of 50p** in your salary Sie bekamen 50 Pence zuwenig Gehalt ausbezahlt; ~**pin** *vt* (*Archit*) *wall, building* untermauern; (*fig*) *argument, claim* untermauern; *economy etc* stützen; ~**pinning** *n* (*Archit*) Untermauerung *f*; ~**play** *vt* (**a**) (*Cards*) *hand* nicht voll ausspielen; to ~**play one's hand** (*fig*) nicht alle Trümpfe ausspielen; (**b**) (*Theat*) *role* zurückhaltend spielen; (**c**) (*keep low key*) *role etc* sich zurückhalten in (+*dat*); ~**populated** *adj* unterbevölkert; ~**price** *vt* zu billig *or* unter Preis anbieten; to be ~**priced** zu billig gehandelt werden; at £10 it is ~**priced** mit £ 10 ist es zu billig; ~**privileged** *adj* unterprivilegiert; the ~**privileged** die Unterprivilegierten *pl*; ~**produce** *vi* zuwenig produzieren; ~**production** *n* Unterproduktion *f*; ~**proof** *adj spirits* unterprozentig; ~**qualified** *adj* unterqualifiziert; ~**rate** *vt* (~**estimate**) *danger, chance, opponent, person* unterschätzen; (~**value**) *qualities* unterbewerten; ~**represented** *adj* unterrepräsentiert; ~**ripe** *adj fruit* unreif; *slightly* ~**ripe** (noch) nicht ganz reif; ~**score** *vt see* ~**line**; ~**sea** *adj diving, exploration, equipment* Unterwasser-; ~**seal** (*Brit Aut*) 1 *n* Unterbodenschutz *m*; 2 *vt* mit Unterbodenschutz versehen; is it ~**sealed**? hat es Unterbodenschutz?; I must have my car ~**sealed** ich muß Unterbodenschutz machen lassen; ~**secretary** *n* (**a**) (*also* **Parliamentary U~secretary**) (Parlamentarischer) Staatssekretär; (**b**) **Permanent U~secretary** Ständiger Unterstaatssekretär; ~**sell** *pret, ptp* ~**sold** *vt* (**a**) (*sell at lower price*) *competitor* unterbieten; *goods* unter Preis verkaufen, verschleudern; (**b**) (*not publicize*) nicht gut verkaufen; (*as advertising technique*) nicht anpreisen; he tends to ~**sell** himself/his ideas er kann sich/seine Ideen normalerweise nicht verkaufen; ~**sexed** *adj* to be ~**sexed** einen unterentwickelten Geschlechtstrieb haben (*form*), nicht viel für Sex übrig haben; he's not exactly ~**sexed**

er ist der reinste Lustmolch (*inf*); ~**shirt** *n* (*US*) Unterhemd *nt*; ~**shoot** *pret, ptp* ~**shot** 1 *vi* (*Aviat, missile*) zu früh landen; 2 *vt* to ~**shoot** the runway vor der Landebahn aufsetzen; to ~**shoot** the target das Ziel nicht erreichen; ~**shorts** *npl* (*US*) Unterhose(n *pl*) *f*; ~**side** *n* Unterseite *f*; ~**signed** *adj* (*form*) unterzeichnet; we the ~**signed** wir, die Unterzeichneten; ~**sized** *adj* klein; (*less than proper size*) zu klein; (*pej*) *person also* zu kurz geraten (hum); ~**skirt** *n* Unterrock *m*; ~**sold** *pret, ptp of* ~**sell**; ~**spend** *pret, ptp* ~**spent** *vi* zu wenig ausgeben; ~**staffed** *adj office* unterbesetzt; we are very ~**staffed** at the moment wir haben momentan zu wenig Leute.

understand [ʌndə'stænd] *pret, ptp* **understood** 1 *vt* (**a**) *language, painting, statement, speaker* verstehen; *action, event, person, difficulty also* begreifen. I don't ~ Russian ich verstehe *or* kann kein Russisch; that's what I can't ~ das kann ich eben nicht verstehen *or* begreifen; I can't ~ his agreeing to do it ich kann nicht verstehen *or* es ist mir unbegreiflich, warum er sich dazu bereit erklärt hat; but ~ this! aber eins sollte klar sein; what do you ~ by "pragmatism"? was verstehen Sie unter „Pragmatismus"?

(**b**) (*comprehend sympathetically*) *children, people, animals, doubts, fears* verstehen. to ~ **one another** sich verstehen.

(**c**) (*believe*) I ~ that you are going to Australia ich höre, Sie gehen nach Australien; I ~ that you've already met her Sie haben sich, soviel ich weiß, schon kennengelernt; I understood that he was abroad ich dachte, er sei im Ausland; am I/are we to ~ that ...? soll das etwa heißen, daß ...?; did I ~ him to say that ...? habe ich richtig verstanden, daß er sagte, ...?; but I understood her to say that she agreed aber soweit ich sie verstanden habe, hat sie zugestimmt; I understood we were to have been consulted! ich dachte, wir sollten dazu befragt werden; to give sb to ~ that ... jdm zu verstehen geben, daß ...; it is understood that he has gone abroad es heißt *or* es wird angenommen, daß er ins Ausland gegangen ist; I understood from his speech that ... ich schloß aus *or* entnahm seiner Rede (*dat*), daß ...; what do you ~ from his remarks? wie verstehen Sie seine Bemerkungen?

(**d**) (*Gram: supply*) *word* sich (*dat*) denken, (im stillen) ergänzen; *see also* understood.

2 *vi* (**a**) verstehen. ~? verstanden?; you don't ~! du verstehst mich nicht!; but you don't ~, I must have the money now aber verstehen Sie doch, ich brauche das Geld jetzt!; I quite ~ ich verstehe schon.

(**b**) so I ~ es scheint so; he was, I ~, a widower wie ich hörte, war er Witwer.

understandable [ʌndə'stændəbl] *adj* (**a**) (*intelligible*) verständlich. (**b**) (*reasonable, natural*) verständlich, begreiflich.

understandably [ʌndə'stændəblɪ] *adv* verständlicherweise, begreiflicherweise.

understanding [ʌndə'stændɪŋ] 1 *adj* verständnisvoll. he asked me to be ~ er bat mich, Verständnis zu haben, er bat mich um Verständnis.

2 *n* (**a**) (*intelligence*) Auffassungsgabe *f*; (*knowledge*) Kenntnisse *pl*; (*comprehension, sympathy*) Verständnis *nt*. I bow to your superior ~ ich beuge mich deinem überlegenen Wissen; her ~ of children ihr Verständnis *nt* für Kinder; because of his complete lack of ~ for the problems da ihm jedes Verständnis für die Probleme fehlte; my ~ of the situation is that ... ich verstehe die Situation so, daß ...; his behaviour is beyond human ~ sein Verhalten ist absolut unbegreiflich; she's a woman of great ~ sie ist eine sehr verständnisvolle Frau; it was my ~ that ... ich nahm an *or* war der Meinung, daß ...; he has a good ~ of the problem er kennt sich mit dem Problem gut aus; to promote international ~ um die internationale Verständigung zu fördern.

(**b**) (*agreement*) Abmachung, Vereinbarung, Übereinkunft *f*. to come to *or* reach an ~ with sb eine Abmachung *or* Vereinbarung mit jdm treffen; Susie and I have an ~ Susie und ich haben unsere Abmachung; a degree of ~ eine gewisse Übereinstimmung, ein gewisses Einvernehmen.

(**c**) (*assumption*) Voraussetzung *f*. on the ~ that ... unter der Voraussetzung, daß ...; on this ~ unter dieser Voraussetzung.

understandingly [ʌndə'stændɪŋlɪ] *adv* verständnisvoll.

understate [ʌndə'steɪt] *vt* untertreiben, herunterspielen. to ~ one's case untertreiben.

understatement ['ʌndəsteɪtmənt] *n* Untertreibung *f*, Understatement *nt*.

understeer ['ʌndəstɪər] (*Aut*) 1 *n* Untersteuerung *f*. 2 [ʌndə'stɪər] *vi* untersteuern.

understood [ʌndə'stʊd] 1 *pret, ptp of* understand.

2 *adj* (**a**) (*clear*) klar. to make oneself ~ sich verständlich machen; do I make myself ~? ist das klar?; I wish it to be ~ that ... ich möchte klarstellen, daß ...; ~? klar?; ~! gut!

(**b**) (*agreed*) ~ conditions stillschweigende Bedingungen *pl*; it was ~ between them that ... sie hatten eine stillschweigende Vereinbarung, daß ...; I thought that was ~! ich dachte, das sei klar.

(**c**) (*believed*) angenommen, geglaubt. he is ~ to have left es heißt, daß er gegangen ist; it is ~ that ... es heißt *or* man hört, daß ...; he let it be ~ that ... er gab zu verstehen, daß ...

(**d**) (*Gram: pred*) ausgelassen.

understudy ['ʌndəstʌdɪ] (*Theat*) 1 *n* zweite Besetzung; (*fig*) Stellvertreter(in *f*) *m*. 2 *vt* zweite Besetzung sein für.

undertake [ʌndə'teɪk] *pret* **undertook** [ʌndə'tʊk], *ptp* **undertaken** [ʌndə'teɪkn] *vt* (**a**) *job, duty, responsibility* übernehmen; *risk* eingehen, auf sich (*acc*) nehmen. he undertook to be our guide er übernahm es, unser Führer zu sein. (**b**) (*agree, promise*) sich verpflichten; (*guarantee*) garantieren.

undertaker [ʌndə'teɪkər] *n* (*esp Brit*) (Leichen)bestatter *m*; Bestattungs- *or* Beerdigungsinstitut *nt*.

undertaking [ʌndə'teɪkɪŋ] *n* (**a**) (*enterprise*) Unternehmen *nt*; (*Comm: project also*) Projekt *nt*.

(b) *(promise)* Zusicherung f, Wort nt. **I give you my solemn ~ that I will never do it again** ich verpflichte mich feierlich, es nie wieder zu tun; **I can give no such ~** das kann ich nicht versprechen.

(c) *(funeral business)* Bestattungsgewerbe nt.

under: **~-the-counter** adj, adv see **counter** Schleich-; **~tone** n **(a)** *(of voice)* in an **~tone** mit gedämpfter Stimme; **(b)** *(fig: of criticism, discontent)* Unterton m; **an ~tone of racialism** ein rassistischer Unterton; **~took** pret of **~take**; **~tow** n Unterströmung f; **there is a lot of ~tow** es gibt viele Unterströmungen; **~value** vt antique, artist unterbewerten, unterschätzen; *(price too low)* zu niedrig schätzen or veranschlagen; person zu wenig schätzen; **~water 1** adj diving, exploration Unterwasser-; **2** adv unter Wasser; **~wear** n Unterwäsche f; **men's ~wear** Herrenunterwäsche f; **~weight** adj untergewichtig; **to be (2 kg) ~weight** (2 kg) Untergewicht haben; **~went** pret of **~go**; **~world** n *(criminals, Myth)* Unterwelt f; **~write** pret **~wrote**, ptp **~written** vt *(finance)* company, loss, project tragen, garantieren; *(guarantee)* insurance policy garantieren, bürgen für; *(insure)* shipping versichern; *(St Ex)* shares zeichnen; *(fig: agree to)* policies etc billigen; **~writer** n *(Insur)* Versicherer, Versicherungsgeber m.

undeserved [ˌʌndɪˈzɜːvd] adj unverdient.

undeservedly [ˌʌndɪˈzɜːvɪdlɪ] adv unverdient(ermaßen).

undeserving [ˌʌndɪˈzɜːvɪŋ] adj person, cause unwürdig. **to be ~ of sth** *(form)* einer Sache *(gen)* unwürdig sein *(form)*.

undesirability [ˌʌndɪzaɪərˈbɪlɪtɪ] n see adj **(a)** Unerwünschtheit f. **because of the general ~ of the site** da der Bauplatz durchweg nur Nachteile hat. **(b)** Übelkeit f.

undesirable [ˌʌndɪˈzaɪərəbl] **1** adj **(a)** policy, effect unerwünscht. **~ alien** unerwünschter Ausländer, unerwünschte Ausländerin; **an ~ person to have as a manager** kein wünschenswerter Manager; **they consider her fiancé ~** sie glauben, daß ihr Verlobter keine wünschenswerte Partie ist; **it is ~ that ...** es wäre höchst unerwünscht, wenn ...

(b) influence, characters, area übel. **he's just generally ~** er ist ganz einfach ein übler Kerl.

2 n *(person)* unerfreuliches Element; *(foreigner)* unerwünschtes Element.

undetected [ˌʌndɪˈtektɪd] adj unentdeckt. **to go/remain ~** nicht entdeckt werden/unentdeckt bleiben.

undetermined [ˌʌndɪˈtɜːmɪnd] adj *(indefinite)* unbestimmt; *(unknown also)* ungewiß; *(unsure)* person unentschlossen, unschlüssig. **he is ~ about his plans** er ist noch unentschlossen or unschlüssig, was seine Pläne angeht.

undeterred [ˌʌndɪˈtɜːd] adj keineswegs entmutigt. **to carry on ~** unverzagt weitermachen; **the teams were ~ by the weather** das Wetter schreckte die Mannschaften nicht ab.

undeveloped [ˌʌndɪˈveləpt] adj unentwickelt; land, resources ungenutzt.

undeviating [ʌnˈdiːvɪeɪtɪŋ] adj *(straight)* line gerade; *(fig: unchanging)* route, path direkt; fairness, determination unbeirrbar; accuracy unfehlbar.

undiagnosed [ˌʌndaɪəgˈnəʊzd] adj disease unerkannt.

undid [ʌnˈdɪd] pret of **undo**.

undies [ˈʌndɪz] npl *(inf)* (Unter)wäsche f.

undifferentiated [ˌʌndɪfəˈrenʃɪeɪtɪd] adj undifferenziert.

undigested [ˌʌndaɪˈdʒestɪd] adj *(lit, fig)* unverdaut.

undignified [ʌnˈdɪgnɪfaɪd] adj person, behaviour würdelos; *(inelegant)* way of sitting etc unelegant. **he was never afraid of appearing ~** er hatte keine Angst, seine Würde zu verlieren.

undiluted [ˌʌndaɪˈluːtɪd] adj unverdünnt; *(fig)* truth, version unverfälscht; pleasure rein, voll.

undiminished [ˌʌndɪˈmɪnɪʃt] adj enthusiasm unvermindert; strength, courage also unbeeinträchtigt.

undiplomatic adj, **~ally** adv [ˌʌndɪpləˈmætɪk, -əlɪ] undiplomatisch.

undipped [ʌnˈdɪpt] adj *(Brit Aut)* **~ headlights** Fernlicht nt.

undiscerning [ˌʌndɪˈsɜːnɪŋ] adj reader, palate anspruchslos, unkritisch; critic unbedarft.

undischarged [ˌʌndɪsˈtʃɑːdʒd] adj **(a)** *(Fin)* debt unbezahlt, unbeglichen; bankrupt nicht entlastet. **(b)** cargo nicht abgeladen; gun nicht abgefeuert.

undisciplined [ʌnˈdɪsɪplɪnd] adj mind, person undiszipliniert; imagination zügellos; hair ungebändigt.

undisclosed [ˌʌndɪsˈkləʊzd] adj secret (bisher) unaufgedeckt; details etc also geheimgehalten. **an ~ sum** eine ungenannte or geheimgehaltene Summe.

undiscovered [ˌʌndɪsˈkʌvəd] adj unentdeckt.

undiscriminating [ˌʌndɪsˈkrɪmɪneɪtɪŋ] adj see **undiscerning**.

undisguised [ˌʌndɪsˈgaɪzd] adj ungetarnt; *(fig)* truth unverhüllt; dislike, affection unverhohlen.

undismayed [ˌʌndɪsˈmeɪd] adj ungerührt, unbeeindruckt.

undisposed [ˌʌndɪˈspəʊzd] adj: **~ of** *(Comm)* unverkauft.

undisputed [ˌʌndɪˈspjuːtɪd] adj unbestritten.

undistinguished [ˌʌndɪsˈtɪŋgwɪʃt] adj performance (mittel)mäßig; appearance durchschnittlich.

undisturbed [ˌʌndɪsˈtɜːbd] adj **(a)** *(untouched)* papers, dust unberührt; *(uninterrupted)* person, sleep, quiet etc ungestört. **(b)** *(unworried)* unbeirrt.

undivided [ˌʌndɪˈvaɪdɪd] adj country, *(fig)* opinion, attention ungeteilt; support voll; loyalty absolut. **we must stand firm and ~** wir müssen fest und einig sein.

undo [ʌnˈduː] pret **undid**, ptp **undone 1** vt **(a)** *(unfasten)* aufmachen; button, dress, zip, parcel also öffnen; shoelace, knot also lösen; knitting also aufziehen; sewing also auftrennen. **will you ~ me?** *(inf)* kannst du mir den Reißverschluß/die Knöpfe etc aufmachen?

(b) *(reverse)* mischief, wrong geschehen machen; work zunichte machen, ruinieren.

2 vi aufgehen.

undock [ʌnˈdɒk] *(Space)* **1** vt entkoppeln. **2** vi sich trennen.

undoing [ʌnˈduːɪŋ] n Ruin m, Verderben nt.

undomesticated [ˌʌndəˈmestɪkeɪtɪd] adj animal, pet nicht ans Haus gewöhnt; woman, husband nicht häuslich. **men aren't so ~ as they used to be** Männer sind heute häuslicher als früher.

undone [ʌnˈdʌn] **1** ptp of **undo**. **2** adj **(a)** *(unfastened)* offen. **to come ~** aufgehen. **(b)** *(neglected)* task unerledigt; work also ungetan. **we have left ~ what we ought to have done** *(Rel)* wir haben unser Tagwerk nicht getan. **(c)** *(obs: ruined)* **I am ~!** ich bin ruiniert.

undoubted [ʌnˈdaʊtɪd] adj unbestritten; success also unzweifelhaft.

undoubtedly [ʌnˈdaʊtɪdlɪ] adv zweifellos, ohne Zweifel.

undoubting [ʌnˈdaʊtɪŋ] adj unerschütterlich.

undramatic [ˌʌndrəˈmætɪk] adj undramatisch.

undreamed-of [ʌnˈdriːmdɒv], **undreamt-of** [ʌnˈdremtɒv] adj ungeahnt. **in their time this was ~** zu ihrer Zeit hätte man sich das nie träumen lassen.

undress [ʌnˈdres] **1** vt ausziehen. **to get ~ed** sich ausziehen. **2** vi sich ausziehen. **3** n: **in a state of ~** halb bekleidet.

undressed [ʌnˈdrest] adj **(a)** person *(still)* (noch) nicht angezogen; *(already)* (schon) ausgezogen. **I feel ~ without my watch** ohne Uhr komme ich mir nackt vor. **(b)** leather ungegerbt; wood unbehandelt, frisch; stone ungeschliffen; *(Cook)* salad nicht angemacht; wound unverbunden.

undrinkable [ʌnˈdrɪŋkəbl] adj ungenießbar.

undue [ʌnˈdjuː] adj *(excessive)* übertrieben, übermäßig; *(improper)* ungebührlich.

undulate [ˈʌndjʊleɪt] vi *(sea, corn)* wogen; *(path, river, snake)* sich schlängeln; *(hills)* sich in sanften Wellenlinien erstrecken; *(hair)* wallen. **she/her hips ~d as she walked** sie ging mit wiegenden Hüften.

undulating [ˈʌndjʊleɪtɪŋ] adj movement, line Wellen-; waves, sea wogend; hair wallend; countryside hügelig; hills sanft; hips wiegend. **the ~ movement of the waves** das Auf und Ab der Wellen.

undulation [ˌʌndjʊˈleɪʃən] n *(of waves, countryside)* Auf und Ab nt; *(of snake, single movement)* Windung f, schlängelnde Bewegung; *(curve)* Rundung f.

undulatory [ˈʌndjʊlətrɪ] adj movement Wellen-, wellenförmig.

unduly [ʌnˈdjuːlɪ] adv übermäßig, übertrieben; optimistic zu; punished unangemessen or übermäßig streng. **you're worrying ~** Sie machen sich *(dat)* unnötige Sorgen.

undutiful [ʌnˈdjuːtɪfʊl] adj pflichtvergessen; child ungehorsam.

undying [ʌnˈdaɪɪŋ] adj love unsterblich, ewig; fame also unvergänglich.

unearned [ʌnˈɜːnd] adj **(a)** increment unverdient. **~ income** Kapitaleinkommen nt, arbeitsloses Einkommen. **(b)** *(undeserved)* unverdient.

unearth [ʌnˈɜːθ] vt ausgraben; *(fig)* book etc aufstöbern; information, evidence zutage bringen, ausfindig machen.

unearthly [ʌnˈɜːθlɪ] adj *(eerie)* calm gespenstisch, unheimlich; scream schauerlich, unheimlich; beauty überirdisch. **at the ~ hour of 5 o'clock** *(inf)* zu nachtschlafender Stunde um 5 Uhr.

unease [ʌnˈiːz] n Unbehagen nt, Beklommenheit f.

uneasily [ʌnˈiːzɪlɪ] adv sit unbehaglich; smile, listen, speak etc also beklommen, unsicher; sleep unruhig. **to be ~ balanced/poised** sehr prekär sein/sehr wack(e)lig stehen.

uneasiness [ʌnˈiːzɪnɪs] n see adj Unruhe f; Unbehaglichkeit, Beklommenheit f; Unsicherheit f; Unsicherheit, Wack(e)ligkeit f *(inf)*; *(of person)* Beklommenheit f; Unruhe f. **a certain ~ of mind** ein gewisses Unbehagen; **the ~ of his conscience** sein schlechtes Gewissen.

uneasy [ʌnˈiːzɪ] adj *(uncomfortable)* sleep, night unruhig; conscience schlecht; *(worried)* laugh, look, *(awkward)* silence, atmosphere unbehaglich, beklommen; behaviour unsicher; peace, balance unsicher, prekär, wack(e)lig *(inf)*; *(worrying)* suspicion, feeling beunruhigend, beklemmend, unangenehm. **to be ~** *(person)* *(ill at ease)* beklommen sein; *(worried)* beunruhigt sein; **I am ~ about it** mir ist nicht wohl dabei; **to make sb ~** jdn beunruhigen, jdn unruhig machen; **I have an ~ feeling that ...** ich habe das ungute or unangenehme Gefühl, daß ...; **to become ~** unruhig werden; **to grow or become ~ about sth** sich über etw *(acc)* beunruhigen; **his conscience was ~** sein Gewissen plagte ihn, er hatte ein schlechtes Gewissen.

uneatable [ʌnˈiːtəbl] adj ungenießbar.

uneaten [ʌnˈiːtn] adj nicht gegessen. **he left the frogs' legs ~** er ließ die Froschschenkel auf dem Teller; **the ~ food** das übriggebliebene Essen.

uneconomic [ʌnˌiːkəˈnɒmɪk] adj unwirtschaftlich, unökonomisch.

uneconomical [ʌnˌiːkəˈnɒmɪkəl] adj unwirtschaftlich, unökonomisch; style of running unökonomisch; person verschwenderisch. **to be ~ with sth** verschwenderisch mit etw umgehen.

unedifying [ʌnˈedɪfaɪɪŋ] adj unerbaulich. **rather ~** nicht gerade erbaulich.

uneducated [ʌnˈedjʊkeɪtɪd] adj person ungebildet; speech, handwriting also unkultiviert; style also ungeschliffen.

unemotional [ˌʌnɪˈməʊʃənl] adj person, character nüchtern; *(without passion)* leidenschaftslos, kühl *(pej)*; reaction, description also unbewegt. **try and stay ~** versuchen Sie, nüchtern und sachlich zu bleiben.

unemotionally [ˌʌnɪˈməʊʃnəlɪ] adv unbewegt, kühl *(pej)*; say, describe also nüchtern.

unemployable [ˌʌnɪmˈplɔɪəbl] adj person als Arbeitskraft nicht brauchbar; *(because of illness)* arbeitsunfähig.

unemployed [ˌʌnɪmˈplɔɪd] adj person arbeitslos, erwerbslos; *(unused)* machinery ungenutzt; *(Fin)* capital tot, brachliegend. **the ~** pl die Arbeitslosen, die Erwerbslosen pl.

unemployment [ˌʌnɪmˈplɔɪmənt] **1** n Arbeitslosigkeit, Erwerbslosigkeit f. ~ **has risen this month** die Arbeitslosenziffer ist diesen Monat gestiegen. **2** attr ~ **benefit** (Brit) or **compensation** (US) Arbeitslosenunterstützung f; ~ **figures** Arbeitslosenziffer f; ~ **rate** Arbeitslosenquote f.

unending [ʌnˈendɪŋ] adj (everlasting) ewig, nie endend attr; stream nicht enden wollend attr, endlos; (incessant) endlos, unaufhörlich. **it seems** ~ es scheint nicht enden zu wollen.

unendurable [ˌʌnɪnˈdjʊərəbl] adj unerträglich.

unenforceable [ˌʌnɪnˈfɔːsɪbl] adj law nicht durchsetzbar; policy undurchführbar.

un-English [ʌnˈɪŋɡlɪʃ] adj behaviour, appearance unenglisch.

unenlightened [ˌʌnɪnˈlaɪtnd] adj (a) (uninformed) reader, listener uneingeweiht. **to leave sb** ~ jdn im Dunkeln lassen. **(b)** age, country, person rückständig; (prejudiced) intolerant.

unenterprising [ˌʌnˈentəpraɪzɪŋ] adj person, policy ohne Unternehmungsgeist, hausbacken (inf). **it was very** ~ **of them to turn it down** daß sie abgelehnt haben, beweist, wie wenig Unternehmungsgeist sie haben.

unenthusiastic [ˌʌnɪnθuːzɪˈæstɪk] adj kühl, wenig begeistert. **he was** ~ **about it** er war wenig begeistert davon; **don't be so** ~ zeige doch ein bißchen Begeisterung!

unenthusiastically [ˌʌnɪnθuːzɪˈæstɪkəlɪ] adv wenig begeistert, ohne Begeisterung.

unenviable [ʌnˈenvɪəbl] adj position, task wenig beneidenswert.

unequal [ʌnˈiːkwəl] adj ungleich; standard, quality unterschiedlich, ungleichförmig; work unausgeglichen; teams also nicht gleichwertig. ~ **in length** unterschiedlich or verschieden or ungleich lang; **to be** ~ **to a task** einer Aufgabe (dat) nicht gewachsen sein; **to be** ~ **to doing sth** unfähig or nicht fähig sein, etw zu tun.

unequalled, (US also) **unequaled** [ʌnˈiːkwəld] adj unübertroffen; skill, record, civilization also unerreicht; beauty also, stupidity, ignorance beispiellos, ohnegleichen (after noun). **to be** ~ **for beauty** von beispielloser Schönheit sein, von einer Schönheit ohnegleichen sein (geh); **he is** ~ **by any other player** kein anderer Spieler kommt ihm gleich.

unequally [ʌnˈiːkwəlɪ] adv ungleichmäßig.

unequivocal [ˌʌnɪˈkwɪvəkəl] adj unmißverständlich, eindeutig; answer also unzweideutig. **he was quite** ~ **about it** er sagte es ganz unmißverständlich or eindeutig or klar.

unequivocally [ˌʌnɪˈkwɪvəkəlɪ] adv see adj.

unerring [ʌnˈɜːrɪŋ] adj judgement, eye, accuracy unfehlbar; instinct untrüglich; aim, blow treffsicher.

unerringly [ʌnˈɜːrɪŋlɪ] adv see adj.

UNESCO [juːˈneskəʊ] abbr of **United Nations Educational, Scientific and Cultural Organization** UNESCO f.

unesthetic [ˌʌnesˈθetɪk] adj (US) see **unaesthetic**.

unethical [ʌnˈeθɪkəl] adj unmoralisch; (in more serious matters) unethisch. **it's** ~ **for a doctor to do that** es verstößt gegen das Berufsethos or die Berufsehre, wenn ein Arzt das macht.

uneven [ʌnˈiːvən] adj (a) (not level) surface uneben; (irregular) line ungerade; thickness ungleich; pulse, breathing unregelmäßig; voice unsicher, schwankend; colour, distribution ungleichmäßig; quality unterschiedlich; temper unausgeglichen. **the engine sounds** ~ der Motor läuft ungleichmäßig. **(b)** number ungerade.

unevenly [ʌnˈiːvənlɪ] adv see adj (a). **the teams were** ~ **matched** die Mannschaften waren sehr ungleich.

unevenness [ʌnˈiːvənnɪs] n see adj (a) Unebenheit f, Ungeradheit f; Ungleichheit f; Unregelmäßigkeit f; Unsicherheit f; Ungleichmäßigkeit f; Unterschiedlichkeit f; Unausgeglichenheit f.

uneventful [ˌʌnɪˈventfʊl] adj day, meeting ereignislos; career wenig bewegt; life also ruhig, eintönig (pej): **the** ~ **routine** das gleichförmige Einerlei.

uneventfully [ˌʌnɪˈventfəlɪ] adv ereignislos.

unexampled [ˌʌnɪɡˈzɑːmpld] adj beispiellos, unvergleichlich.

unexceptionable [ˌʌnɪkˈsepʃnəbl] adj einwandfrei; person solide.

unexceptional [ˌʌnɪkˈsepʃənl] adj durchschnittlich.

unexciting [ˌʌnɪkˈsaɪtɪŋ] adj time nicht besonders aufregend. **not** ~ nicht gerade eintönig; **how** ~! wie langweilig!

unexpected [ˌʌnɪkˈspektɪd] adj unerwartet; arrival, result, development also unvorhergesehen. **this is an** ~ **pleasure** (also iro) welch eine Überraschung!; **their success was not** ~ ihr Erfolg kam nicht unerwartet or überraschend; **the role of the** ~ **in this novel** der Überraschungseffekt in diesem Roman.

unexpectedly [ˌʌnɪkˈspektɪdlɪ] adv unerwartet; arrive, happen also plötzlich, unvorhergesehen. **but then,** ~ **aber dann, wie aus heiterem Himmel, ...**

unexplainable [ˌʌnɪkˈspleɪnəbl] adj unerklärlich.

unexplained [ˌʌnɪkˈspleɪnd] adj (not cleared up) phenomenon nicht geklärt, ungeklärt; mystery unaufgeklärt; lateness, absence unbegründet. **a few** ~ **technical terms** einige unerklärte Fachausdrücke; **there are some things that must go** ~ einige Dinge können nicht erklärt werden; **his actions remain** ~ für seine Handlungen gibt es immer noch keine Erklärung.

unexploded [ˌʌnɪkˈspləʊdɪd] adj nicht explodiert.

unexploited [ˌʌnɪkˈsplɔɪtɪd] adj resources ungenutzt; talent also brachliegend attr; minerals also unausgebeutet.

unexplored [ˌʌnɪkˈsplɔːd] adj mystery unerforscht; territory also unerschlossen.

unexposed [ˌʌnɪkˈspəʊzd] adj (a) (hidden) villain nicht entlarvt; crime unaufgedeckt. **(b)** (Phot) film unbelichtet.

unexpressed [ˌʌnɪkˈsprest] adj sorrow unausgesprochen; wish also ungeäußert.

unexpressive [ˌʌnɪkˈspresɪv] adj style, eyes ausdruckslos.

unexpurgated [ʌnˈekspɜːɡeɪtɪd] adj book ungekürzt.

unfading [ʌnˈfeɪdɪŋ] adj (fig) unvergänglich, nie verblassend.

unfailing [ʌnˈfeɪlɪŋ] adj zeal, interest, source unerschöpflich; optimism, humour also unbezwinglich; supply also endlos; remedy unfehlbar; friend treu.

unfailingly [ʌnˈfeɪlɪŋlɪ] adv immer, stets.

unfair [ʌnˈfeəʳ] adj unfair; decision, method, remark, criticism also ungerecht; (Comm) competition also unlauter. **to be** ~ **to sb** jdm gegenüber unfair sein.

unfairly [ʌnˈfeəlɪ] adv unfair; treat, criticize etc also ungerecht; accuse, punish zu Unrecht. **he was, I thought,** ~ **dismissed** er ist, meiner Meinung nach, unfairerweise or ungerechterweise or zu Unrecht entlassen worden.

unfairness [ʌnˈfeənɪs] n Ungerechtigkeit f.

unfaithful [ʌnˈfeɪθfʊl] adj (a) wife, husband, lover untreu; friend, servant treulos. **to be** ~ **to sb** jdm untreu sein. **(b)** (inaccurate) translation, description ungenau. **the translator is** ~ **to the poem** der Übersetzer verfälscht das Gedicht.

unfaithfulness [ʌnˈfeɪθfʊlnɪs] n see adj (a) Untreue f; Treulosigkeit f. **(b)** Ungenauigkeit f.

unfaltering [ʌnˈfɔːltərɪŋ] adj step, voice fest; courage unerschütterlich.

unfalteringly [ʌnˈfɔːltərɪŋlɪ] adv walk mit festen Schritten; say mit fester Stimme.

unfamiliar [ˌʌnfəˈmɪljəʳ] adj (a) (strange, unknown) experience, taste, sight ungewohnt; surroundings also, subject, person fremd, unbekannt. **it is** ~ **to me** es ist ungewohnt für mich; **es ist mir fremd** or unbekannt.
(b) (unacquainted) **to be** ~ **with sth** etw nicht kennen, mit etw nicht vertraut sein; **I am not** ~ **with Greek/that problem** Griechisch/das Problem ist mir nicht gänzlich unbekannt.

unfamiliarity [ˌʌnfəmɪlɪˈærɪtɪ] n see adj (a) Ungewohntheit f; Fremdheit; Unbekanntheit f.
(b) his ~ **with economics** sein Mangel an ökonomischem Wissen; **because of my** ~ **with ...** wegen meiner mangelnden Kenntnisse (+gen) ... or Vertrautheit mit ...

unfashionable [ʌnˈfæʃnəbl] adj unmodern; district wenig gefragt; hotel, habit, subject nicht in Mode. **science became** ~ Naturwissenschaft geriet aus der Mode.

unfashionably [ʌnˈfæʃnəblɪ] adv dressed unmodern; strict etc altmodisch.

unfasten [ʌnˈfɑːsn] **1** vt aufmachen; string, belt also losmachen; (detach) tag, dog, horse etc losbinden; hair, bonds lösen. **2** vi aufgehen. **how does this dress** ~? wie macht man das Kleid auf?

unfathomable [ʌnˈfæðəməbl] adj unergründlich.

unfathomed [ʌnˈfæðəmd] adj (lit, fig) unergründet.

unfavourable, (US) **unfavorable** [ʌnˈfeɪvərəbl] adj outlook, weather, moment, result ungünstig; conditions, circumstances also, wind widrig; impression also, opinion, reaction negativ; reply ablehnend, negativ; trade balance passiv. **conditions** ~ **to** or for trade ungünstige Handelsbedingungen pl.

unfavourably, (US) **unfavorably** [ʌnˈfeɪvərəblɪ] adv see adj ungünstig; negativ; ablehnend, negativ. **to look** ~ **on sth** einer Sache (dat) ablehnend gegenüberstehen; **to report** ~ **on sth/to speak** ~ **of sth** negativ or ablehnend or ungünstig beurteilen; **to be impressed by sth** einen negativen or keinen guten Eindruck von etw bekommen.

unfeeling [ʌnˈfiːlɪŋ] adj gefühllos; response, reply also herzlos; look ungerührt; (without sensation also) empfindungslos.

unfeelingly [ʌnˈfiːlɪŋlɪ] adv gefühllos, herzlos; look, listen ungerührt.

unfeigned [ʌnˈfeɪnd] adj aufrichtig, echt, ungeheuchelt.

unfeminine [ʌnˈfemɪnɪn] adj unweiblich.

unfettered [ʌnˈfetəd] adj (fig) frei, unbehindert (by von).

unfilial [ʌnˈfɪljəl] adj nicht pflichtbewußt; (impudent) ungehörig, respektlos.

unfilled [ʌnˈfɪld] adj ungefüllt; job often, unbesetzt; order book un(aus)gefüllt. ~ **vacancies** offene Stellen pl.

unfinished [ʌnˈfɪnɪʃt] adj (a) (incomplete) unfertig; work of art unvollendet; business unerledigt. **Schubert's U**~ Schuberts Unvollendete. **(b)** (Tech) unbearbeitet; cloth Natur-. ~ **product** Rohprodukt nt.

unfit [ʌnˈfɪt] **1** adj (a) (unsuitable) person, thing ungeeignet, untauglich; (incompetent) unfähig. ~ **to drive** fahruntüchtig, nicht in der Lage zu fahren; **he is** ~ **to be a lawyer/for teaching** er hat nicht das Zeug zum Juristen/Lehrer; **this is** ~ **for publication** das kann nicht veröffentlicht werden; ~ **to eat** ungenießbar; road ~ **for lorries** für Lastkraftwagen nicht geeignete Straße; **to plead** (Jur) nicht zurechnungsfähig.
(b) (Sport: injured) nicht fit; (in health also) schlecht in Form, unfit. ~ **(for military service)** untauglich; **to be** ~ **for work** arbeitsunfähig sein.
2 vt (rare) **to** ~ **sb for sth** jdn für etw ungeeignet machen.

unfitness [ʌnˈfɪtnɪs] n (a) (unsuitableness) mangelnde Eignung, Untauglichkeit f; (incompetence) Unfähigkeit f. **(b)** (unhealthiness) mangelnde Fitneß; (for military service) Untauglichkeit f.

unfitted [ʌnˈfɪtɪd] adj ungeeignet, untauglich (for, to für).

unfitting [ʌnˈfɪtɪŋ] adj language, behaviour unpassend, unschicklich, unziemlich. **how** ~ **that one so talented should ...** wie unfaßbar, daß ein so begabter Mensch ... sollte.

unfittingly [ʌnˈfɪtɪŋlɪ] adv behave unpassend, unschicklich, unziemlich; dressed unpassend.

unfix [ʌnˈfɪks] vt losmachen; bayonets abmachen. **it came** ~ed es hat sich gelöst.

unflagging [ʌnˈflægɪŋ] adj person, zeal, patience unermüdlich, unentwegt; enthusiasm unerschöpflich; devotion, interest unverändert stark. **he has an** ~ **devotion to the cause** er stellte sich unermüdlich in den Dienst der Sache.

unflaggingly [ʌnˈflægɪŋlɪ] adv work, serve unentwegt, unermüdlich.

unflappable [ʌnˈflæpəbl] adj (inf) unerschütterlich, nicht aus der Ruhe zu bringend *attr.* **to be** ~ die Ruhe selbst sein, die Ruhe weghaben (*inf*).

unflattering [ʌn'flætərɪŋ] *adj portrait, comments* wenig schmeichelhaft; *dress, hairstyle, light also* unvorteilhaft.

unfledged [ʌn'fledʒd] *adj bird* (noch) nicht flügge; (*fig*) unerfahren. **an** ~ **youth** ein Grünschnabel *m*.

unflinching [ʌn'flɪntʃɪŋ] *adj* unerschrocken; *determination* unbeirrbar. **with** ~ **courage** unverzagt.

unflinchingly [ʌn'flɪntʃɪŋlɪ] *adv* unerschrocken.

unflyable [ʌn'flaɪəbl] *adj plane* unfliegbar.

unfocus(s)ed [ʌn'fəʊkəst] *adj eyes* unkoordiniert.

unfold [ʌn'fəʊld] **1** *vt* **(a)** *paper, cloth* auseinanderfalten, entfalten; (*spread out*) *map also, wings* ausbreiten; *arms* lösen; *chair, table* aufklappen, auseinanderklappen.
   (b) (*fig*) *story* entwickeln (**to** vor + *dat*); *plans, ideas also* entfalten, darlegen (**to** *dat*); *secret* enthüllen, eröffnen.
   2 *vi* (*story, plot*) sich abwickeln; *truth* an den Tag kommen, sich herausstellen; (*view, personality, flower*) sich entfalten; (*countryside*) sich ausbreiten.

unforced [ʌn'fɔːst] *adj* ungezwungen, natürlich.

unforeseeable [ˌʌnfɔː'siːəbl] *adj* unvorhersehbar.

unforeseen [ˌʌnfɔː'siːn] *adj* unvorhergesehen, unerwartet.

unforgettable [ˌʌnfə'getəbl] *adj* unvergeßlich.

unforgivable [ˌʌnfə'gɪvəbl] *adj* unverzeihlich.

unforgivably [ˌʌnfə'gɪvəblɪ] *adv* unverzeihlich. **he said, quite** ~, **that** ... er sagte, und das war einfach unverzeihlich, daß ...

unforgiving [ˌʌnfə'gɪvɪŋ] *adj* unversöhnlich.

unformed [ʌn'fɔːmd] *adj* (*unshaped*) *clay, foetus* ungeformt; (*undeveloped*) *character, idea* unfertig.

unforthcoming [ˌʌnfɔː'θkʌmɪŋ] *adj person* nicht sehr mitteilsam; *reply* wenig aufschlußreich. **to be** ~ **about sth** sich nicht zu etw äußern wollen.

unfortunate [ʌn'fɔːtʃnɪt] **1** *adj* unglücklich; *person* glücklos; *day, event, error* unglückselig; *turn of phrase* ungeschickt; *time* ungünstig. **to be** ~ (*person*) Pech haben; **to be** ~ **in life/in love** kein Glück im Leben haben/Pech *or* kein Glück in der Liebe haben; **it is most** ~ **that** ... es ist höchst bedauerlich, daß ...; **how very** ~ **(for you)** welch ein Pech; **it was** ~ **that he hadn't been informed** ihm ist bedauerlicherweise nicht Bescheid gesagt worden; **the** ~ **Mr Brown** der arme *or* bedauernswerte Herr Brown.
   2 *n* Arme(r), Unglückliche(r) *mf*.

unfortunately [ʌn'fɔːtʃnɪtlɪ] *adv* leider; *chosen* unglücklich; *worded* ungeschickt.

unfounded [ʌn'faʊndɪd] *adj* unbegründet, nicht fundiert; *suspicion also* grundlos; *rumour also, allegations* aus der Luft gegriffen.

unframed [ʌn'freɪmd] *adj picture* ungerahmt.

unfreeze [ʌn'friːz] *pret* **unfroze**, *ptp* **unfrozen 1** *vt* **(a)** auftauen. **(b)** (*Fin*) *wages, prices* freigeben. **2** *vi* auftauen.

unfrequented [ˌʌnfrɪ'kwentɪd] *adj* einsam; (*without traffic*) *road* unbefahren. **the place is** ~ **except for** ... der Ort wird nur von ... besucht, außer ... kommt niemand dahin.

unfriendliness [ʌn'frendlɪnɪs] *n see adj* Unfreundlichkeit *f*; Feindseligkeit *f*; Unwirtlichkeit *f*.

unfriendly [ʌn'frendlɪ] *adj* unfreundlich (**to** *sb* zu jdn); (*hostile also*) *natives, country, act* feindselig; *territory* unwirtlich.

unfrock [ʌn'frɒk] *vt* laisieren (*spec*), in den Laienstand zurückversetzen.

unfroze [ʌn'frəʊz] *pret of* **unfreeze**.

unfrozen [ʌn'frəʊzn] **1** *ptp of* **unfreeze**. **2** *adj food* ungefroren.

unfruitful [ʌn'fruːtfʊl] *adj soil, woman, discussion* unfruchtbar; *attempt* fruchtlos.

unfulfilled [ˌʌnfʊl'fɪld] *adj* unerfüllt; *person* unausgefüllt. **their prophecies are** ~ ihre Prophezeiungen haben sich nicht erfüllt; **to have an** ~ **desire** schon immer den Wunsch gehabt haben.

unfunded [ʌn'fʌndɪd] *adj* (*Fin*) unfundiert.

unfunny [ʌn'fʌnɪ] *adj* (*inf*) (gar) nicht komisch. **distinctly** ~ alles andere als komisch.

unfurl [ʌn'fɜːl] **1** *vt flag* aufrollen; *sail* losmachen; (*peacock*) *tail* entfalten. **2** *vi* sich entfalten; (*flag, sails also*) sich aufrollen.

unfurnished [ʌn'fɜːnɪʃt] *adj* unmöbliert.

ungainly [ʌn'geɪnlɪ] *adj animal, movement* linkisch, staksig; *appearance* unelegant, unansehnlich, unschön; *posture* ungraziös, unschön.

ungenerous [ʌn'dʒenərəs] *adj* kleinlich.

ungentlemanly [ʌn'dʒentlmənlɪ] *adj* unfein; (*impolite*) unhöflich. **it is** ~ **to do so** das gehört sich nicht für einen Gentleman; **it is** ~ **not to do so** ein Gentleman sollte das tun.

un-get-at-able [ˌʌnget'ætəbl] *adj* (*inf*) unerreichbar. **he/the cottage is** ~ man kommt an ihn/das Haus einfach nicht ran (*inf*).

ungird [ʌn'gɜːd] *vt sword* ablegen; *loins* entgürten.

unglazed [ʌn'gleɪzd] *adj window* unverglast; *pottery* unglasiert; *photograph* nicht satiniert.

ungodliness [ʌn'gɒdlɪnɪs] *n* Gottlosigkeit *f*.

ungodly [ʌn'gɒdlɪ] **1** *adj* gottlos; (*inf*) *noise, hour* unchristlich (*inf*). **an** ~ **noise** ein Heidenlärm *m* (*inf*). **2** *n* **the** ~ *pl* die Gottlosen *pl*.

ungovernable [ʌn'gʌvənəbl] *adj* **(a)** *desire* unbezähmbar; *passion also* zügellos; *temper* unbeherrscht. **(b)** *country, people* unlenkbar, nicht zu regieren *pred*.

ungraceful [ʌn'greɪsfʊl] *adj* nicht anmutig; *movement* plump, ungelenk; (*of girl also*) *dancer* ungraziös; *behaviour* unfein.

ungracefully [ʌn'greɪsfəlɪ] *adv see adj*.

ungracious [ʌn'greɪʃəs] *adj* unhöflich; (*gruff*) *grunt, refusal* schroff; *answer* rüde.

ungraciously [ʌn'greɪʃəslɪ] *adv see adj*.

ungrammatical [ˌʌngrə'mætɪkəl] *adj* ungrammatisch, gram-

matikalisch falsch. **she does tend to be** ~ **at times** sie drückt sich manchmal grammatikalisch falsch aus.

ungrammatically [ˌʌngrə'mætɪkəlɪ] *adv see adj*.

ungrateful *adj*, ~**ly** *adv* [ʌn'greɪtfʊl, -fəlɪ] undankbar (**to** gegenüber).

ungrounded [ʌn'graʊndɪd] *adj* **(a)** (*unfounded*) unfundiert; *accusations also* aus der Luft gegriffen; *fears* grundlos, unbegründet. **(b)** (*US Elec*) ungeerdet, ohne Erdung.

ungrudging [ʌn'grʌdʒɪŋ] *adj help, support* bereitwillig; *admiration* neidlos; (*generous*) *person, contribution* großzügig; *praise, gratitude* von ganzem Herzen kommend *attr*. **he gave his** ~ **consent** er stimmte bereitwillig zu; **he was** ~ **in his praise** er hat mit dem Lob nicht gespart.

ungrudgingly [ʌn'grʌdʒɪŋlɪ] *adv help, support, consent* bereitwillig; *admire, praise* von ganzem Herzen; *give, contribute* großzügig.

unguarded [ʌn'gɑːdɪd] *adj* **(a)** (*defended*) unbewacht. **(b)** (*fig: careless*) unvorsichtig, unachtsam. **to have** ~ **conversations** sich sorglos unterhalten; **in an** ~ **moment he** ... als er einen Augenblick nicht aufpaßte *or* sich nicht vorsah, ... er ...

unguent ['ʌŋgwənt] *n* Salbe *f*, Unguentum *nt* (*spec*).

unguessable [ʌn'gesəbl] *adj* nicht erratbar.

ungulate ['ʌŋgjʊleɪt] **1** *n* Huftier *nt*, Ungulat *m* (*spec*). **2** *adj* Huftier-; *creatures* mit Hufen.

unhallowed [ʌn'hæləʊd] *adj ground* ungeweiht.

unhampered [ʌn'hæmpəd] *adj* ungehindert. ~ **by clothes/regulations** ohne hemmende Kleidung/ohne den Zwang von Bestimmungen.

unhand [ʌn'hænd] *vt* (*old, hum*) freigeben, loslassen.

unhandy [ʌn'hændɪ] *adj* unpraktisch.

unhappily [ʌn'hæpɪlɪ] *adv* (*unfortunately*) leider, unglücklicherweise; (*miserably*) unglücklich. **rather** ~ **expressed** ziemlich unglücklich ausgedrückt.

unhappiness [ʌn'hæpɪnɪs] *n* Traurigkeit *f*; (*discontent*) Unzufriedenheit *f* (*with* mit). **this is a source of much** ~ **to me** das macht mich ganz unglücklich.

unhappy [ʌn'hæpɪ] *adj* (+ *er*) **(a)** (*sad*) unglücklich; *look, voice also* traurig; *state of affairs* bedauerlich, traurig.
   (b) (*not pleased*) unzufrieden (*about* mit), nicht glücklich (*about* über + *acc*); (*uneasy*) unwohl. **if you feel** ~ **about it** wenn Sie darüber nicht glücklich sind; (*worried*) wenn Ihnen dabei nicht wohl ist; **I feel** ~ **about letting him go** ich lasse ihn nur ungern gehen.
   (c) (*unfortunate*) *coincidence, day, match, phrasing* unglücklich; *person* glücklos. **an** ~ **choice/colour scheme** keine gute Wahl/Farbzusammenstellung.

unharmed [ʌn'hɑːmd] *adj person* unverletzt; *thing* unbeschädigt; *reputation* ungeschädigt; *beauty* nicht beeinträchtigt. **to be** ~ **by sth** durch etw nicht gelitten haben.

unharness [ʌn'hɑːnɪs] *vt horse* abschirren; (*from carriage*) abspannen.

unhealthy [ʌn'helθɪ] *adj* **(a)** *person* nicht gesund; *climate, place, life complexion,* ungesund; (*inf*) *car* nicht in Ordnung. **(b)** *curiosity, interest* krankhaft; *influence, magazine* schädlich, schlecht. **it's an** ~ **relationship** das ist eine verderbliche Beziehung. **(c)** (*inf: dangerous*) ungesund (*inf*), gefährlich.

unheard [ʌn'hɜːd] *adj* ungehört; (*fig*) *voice* unbeachtet. **to condemn sb** ~ jdn verurteilen, ohne ihn angehört zu haben.

unheard-of [ʌn'hɜːdɒv] *adj* (*unknown*) gänzlich unbekannt; (*unprecedented*) einmalig, noch nicht dagewesen; (*outrageous*) unerhört.

unheeded [ʌn'hiːdɪd] *adj* unbeachtet. **to go** ~ keine Beachtung finden, auf taube Ohren stoßen.

unheedful [ʌn'hiːdfʊl] *adj* ~ **of the danger/her plight** ohne von der Gefahr/ihrer mißlichen Lage Notiz zu nehmen, ungeachtet der Gefahr (*gen*)/ihrer mißlichen Lage (*gen*) (*geh*).

unheeding [ʌn'hiːdɪŋ] *adj* (*not attending*) unbekümmert; (*not caring also*) gleichgültig, achtlos.

unhelpful [ʌn'helpfʊl] *adj person* nicht hilfreich; *advice, book* nutzlos, wenig hilfreich. **that was very** ~ **of you** das war wirklich keine Hilfe; **you are being very** ~ du bist aber wirklich keine Hilfe.

unhelpfully [ʌn'helpfəlɪ] *adv* wenig hilfreich.

unhesitating [ʌn'hezɪteɪtɪŋ] *adj* (*immediate*) *answer, offer* prompt, unverzüglich; *help also, generosity* bereitwillig; (*steady*) *steps, progress* stet; (*undoubting*) *answer* fest. **he was** ~ **in his support** er half, ohne zu zögern; **I was surprised by his** ~ **acceptance** of the plan ich war erstaunt, daß er dem Plan sofort und ohne zu zögern zugestimmt hat.

unhesitatingly [ʌn'hezɪteɪtɪŋlɪ] *adv* ohne Zögern, ohne zu zögern; (*undoubtingly also*) ohne zu zweifeln.

unhindered [ʌn'hɪndəd] *adj* (*by clothes, luggage etc*) unbehindert, nicht behindert; (*by regulations*) ungehindert, nicht gehindert; (*by distraction*) ungestört. ~ **by luggage** ohne hinderndes Gepäck; **to make** ~ **progress towards sth** ungehindert auf etw (*acc*) zusteuern.

unhinge [ʌn'hɪndʒ] *vt* **to** ~ **sb/sb's mind** jdn aus der Bahn werfen, jdn völlig verstören; **his mind was** ~**d** er hatte den Verstand verloren.

unhistorical [ˌʌnhɪs'tɒrɪkəl] *adj* (*inaccurate*) unhistorisch, ungeschichtlich; (*legendary*) legendär.

unhitch [ʌn'hɪtʃ] *vt horse* (*from post*) losbinden; (*from wagon*) ausspannen; *caravan, engine* abkoppeln.

unholy [ʌn'həʊlɪ] *adj* (+ *er*) (*Rel*) *place* ungeweiht; *spirits* böse; (*inf: reprehensible*) *delight* diebisch (*inf*); *alliance, combination* übel; (*inf: awful*) *mess* heillos; *noise, hour* unchristlich (*inf*).

unhook [ʌn'hʊk] **1** *vt latch, gate* loshaken; *dress* aufhaken; (*take from hook*) *picture* abhaken; (*free*) losmachen. **the dress came** ~**ed** das Kleid ging auf. **2** *vi* sich aufhaken lassen.

unhoped-for [ʌn'həʊptfɔːʳ] *adj* unverhofft.

unhorse [ʌn'hɔːs] vt rider abwerfen.

unhurried [ʌn'hʌrɪd] adj pace, person gelassen; steps, movement gemächlich; meal, journey, life gemütlich, geruhsam. **after a little ~ reflection I** ... nachdem ich mir das in Ruhe überlegt habe, ... ich ...

unhurriedly [ʌn'hʌrɪdlɪ] adv gemächlich, in aller Ruhe.

unhurt [ʌn'hɜːt] adj unverletzt.

unhygienic [ˌʌnhaɪ'dʒiːnɪk] adj unhygienisch.

uni- ['juːnɪ-] pref ein-. **~cameral** Einkammer-; **~cellular** einzellig.

UNICEF ['juːnɪsef] abbr of **United Nations International Children's Emergency Fund** UNICEF f, Weltkinderhilfswerk nt der UNO.

unicorn ['juːnɪˌkɔːn] n Einhorn nt.

unicycle ['juːnɪˌsaɪkl] n Einrad nt.

unidentifiable [ˌʌnaɪ'dentɪfaɪɪbl] adj unidentifizierbar.

unidentified [ˌʌnaɪ'dentɪfaɪd] adj unbekannt; body nicht identifiziert; belongings herrenlos. **~ flying object** unbekanntes Flugobjekt.

unidiomatic [ˌʌnɪdɪə'mætɪk] adj unidiomatisch.

unification [ˌjuːnɪfɪ'keɪʃən] n (of country) Einigung f; (of system) Vereinheitlichung f.

uniform ['juːnɪfɔːm] **1** adj (a) (unvarying) length, colour, tax einheitlich; treatment also gleich; temperature also, pace gleichmäßig, gleichbleibend attr; (lacking variation) life gleichförmig, eintönig (pej); thinking gleichartig, gleichförmig, uniform (pej); scenery einförmig, eintönig (pej). **these houses are so ~** die Häuser gleichen sich alle so.
(b) (Mil, Sch etc) Uniform-.
2 n Uniform f. **in/out of ~** in Uniform/in Zivil, ohne Uniform.

uniformed ['juːnɪfɔːmd] adj uniformiert; person also in Uniform.

uniformity [ˌjuːnɪ'fɔːmɪtɪ] n see adj (a) Einheitlichkeit f; Gleichheit f; Gleichmäßigkeit f; Gleichförmigkeit f, Eintönigkeit f (pej) f; Gleichartigkeit, Gleichförmigkeit, Uniformität f (pej) f; Einförmigkeit, Eintönigkeit f (pej) f.

uniformly ['juːnɪfɔːmlɪ] adv measure, paint, tax einheitlich; heat gleichmäßig; treat gleich; (pej) einförmig (pej); think uniform (pej).

unify ['juːnɪfaɪ] vt einigen, einen (geh); theories, systems vereinheitlichen.

unilateral [ˌjuːnɪ'lætərəl] adj (Jur) einseitig; (Pol also) unilateral. **~ declaration of independence** einseitige Unabhängigkeitserklärung.

unilaterally [ˌjuːnɪ'lætərəlɪ] adv einseitig.

unimaginable [ˌʌnɪ'mædʒɪnəbl] adj unvorstellbar.

unimaginative [ˌʌnɪ'mædʒɪnətɪv] adj phantasielos, einfallslos; remark, book geistlos, phantasielos.

unimaginatively [ˌʌnɪ'mædʒɪnətɪvlɪ] adv see adj.

unimpaired [ˌʌnɪm'pɛəd] adj quality, prestige unbeeinträchtigt; health unvermindert. **to be ~** nicht gelitten haben.

unimpassioned [ˌʌnɪm'pæʃənd] adj leidenschaftslos.

unimpeachable [ˌʌnɪm'piːtʃəbl] adj reputation, conduct untadelig; proof, honesty unanfechtbar; source absolut zuverlässig.

unimpeded [ˌʌnɪm'piːdɪd] adj ungehindert; (by distraction also) ungestört.

unimportant [ˌʌnɪm'pɔːtənt] adj unwichtig, unbedeutend; detail also unwesentlich.

unimposing [ˌʌnɪm'pəʊzɪŋ] adj unscheinbar; building also wenig imponierend or beeindruckend.

unimpressed [ˌʌnɪm'prest] adj unbeeindruckt, nicht beeindruckt. **I was ~ by his story** seine Geschichte hat mich überhaupt nicht beeindruckt; **I remain ~** das beeindruckt mich überhaupt nicht.

unimpressive [ˌʌnɪm'presɪv] adj wenig beeindruckend; person also unscheinbar; argument, performance also, speaker wenig überzeugend.

unimproved [ˌʌnɪm'pruːvd] adj (a) (noch) nicht besser, unverändert schlecht; method nicht verbessert. **to leave sth ~** etw nicht verbessern. (b) land unbebaut, nicht kultiviert; house nicht modernisiert.

uninfluenced [ʌn'ɪnfluːɪnst] adj unbeeinflußt.

uninfluential [ˌʌnɪnflu'enʃəl] adj ohne Einfluß.

uninformative [ˌʌnɪn'fɔːmɪtɪv] adj person wenig mitteilsam; document ohne Informationsgehalt.

uninformed [ˌʌnɪn'fɔːmd] adj (not knowing) nicht informiert or unterrichtet (about über + acc); (ignorant also) unwissend; criticism blindwütig. **to be ~ about sth** über etw (acc) nicht Bescheid wissen; **to keep sb ~** jdn im dunkeln lassen.

uninhabitable [ˌʌnɪn'hæbɪtəbl] adj unbewohnbar.

uninhabited [ˌʌnɪn'hæbɪtɪd] adj unbewohnt.

uninhibited [ˌʌnɪn'hɪbɪtɪd] adj person frei von Hemmungen, ohne Hemmungen; greed, laughter hemmungslos, ungezügelt. **to be ~** keine Hemmungen haben.

uninitiated [ˌʌnɪ'nɪʃɪeɪtɪd] adj nicht eingeweiht. **~ members of a tribe** nicht initiierte Mitglieder eines Stammes. **2** n the ~ pl Nichteingeweihte pl; **for the ~ that may seem strange** Nichteingeweihten mag das merkwürdig vorkommen.

uninjured [ʌn'ɪndʒəd] adj person unverletzt; soldier also nicht verwundet; reputation ungeschädigt, nicht beeinträchtigt.

uninspired [ˌʌnɪn'spaɪəd] adj person, teacher, performance phantasielos, ideenlos, einfallslos; lecture, book einfallslos; translation einfallslos, schwach. **to be ~ by a subject** von einem Thema nicht begeistert werden.

uninspiring [ˌʌnɪn'spaɪərɪŋ] adj trocken; suggestion, idea wenig gerade aufregend.

uninsured [ˌʌnɪn'ʃʊəd] adj nicht versichert.

unintelligent [ˌʌnɪn'telɪdʒənt] adj person, remark unintelligent, (etwas) dumm; approach, action unklug, ungeschickt. **not ~ eigentlich ganz intelligent.**

unintelligibility [ˌʌnɪnˌtelɪdʒɪ'bɪlɪtɪ] n Unverständlichkeit f.

unintelligible [ˌʌnɪn'telɪdʒɪbl] adj person nicht zu verstehen; speech, writing unverständlich. **this makes him almost ~** das macht es fast unmöglich, ihn zu verstehen.

unintelligibly [ˌʌnɪn'telɪdʒɪblɪ] adv unverständlich.

unintended [ˌʌnɪn'tendɪd], **unintentional** [ˌʌnɪn'tenʃənl] adj unbeabsichtigt, unabsichtlich; joke also unfreiwillig.

unintentionally [ˌʌnɪn'tenʃnəlɪ] adv unabsichtlich, unbeabsichtigt, ohne Absicht; funny unfreiwillig.

uninterested [ʌn'ɪntrɪstɪd] adj desinteressiert, interesselos. **to be ~ in sth an etw (dat)** nicht interessiert sein.

uninteresting [ʌn'ɪntrɪstɪŋ] adj uninteressant.

uninterrupted [ˌʌnɪntə'rʌptɪd] adj (continuous) line ununterbrochen, kontinuierlich; noise, rain also anhaltend; (undisturbed) rest ungestört.

uninterruptedly [ˌʌnɪntə'rʌptɪdlɪ] adv see adj.

uninvited [ˌʌnɪn'vaɪtɪd] adj guest ungeladen, ungebeten; criticism unerwünscht, ungebeten.

uninviting [ˌʌnɪn'vaɪtɪŋ] adj appearance, atmosphere nicht (gerade) einladend; prospect nicht (gerade) verlockend; smell, food, sight unappetitlich. **rather ~** wenig einladend/wenig verlockend/ziemlich unappetitlich.

union ['juːnjən] **1** n (a) Vereinigung, Verbindung f; (uniting also) Zusammenschluß m; (Pol also) Union f. the U~ (US) die Vereinigten Staaten; (in civil war) die Unionsstaaten pl; **state of the U~ message** (US) = Bericht m zur Lage der Nation; **~ of Soviet Socialist Republics** Union f der Sozialistischen Sowjetrepubliken.
(b) (trade ~) Gewerkschaft f.
(c) (association) Vereinigung f; (customs ~) Union f; (postal ~) Postverein m; (students' also) Studentenclub m (also building).
(d) (harmony) Eintracht, Harmonie f.
(e) (form: marriage) Verbindung f.
(f) (Tech) Verbindung f. **~ joint** Anschlußstück, Verbindungsstück nt.
(g) (Math) Vereinigung(smenge) f.
2 adj attr (trade ~) Gewerkschafts-. **~ bashing** Angriffe pl auf die or Herumhacken nt auf den Gewerkschaften; **~ card** Gewerkschaftsausweis m; **~ dues** Gewerkschaftsbeitrag m.

unionism ['juːnjənɪzəm] n (a) (trade ~) Gewerkschaftswesen nt. (b) (Pol) Einigungsbewegung f. U~ (Brit) Unionismus m, unionistische Bewegung.

unionist ['juːnjənɪst] **1** n (a) (trade ~) Gewerkschaftler(in f) m. (b) (Pol) Unionist(in f), Unionsanhänger(in f) m. **Ulster U~** Ulster Unionist m. **2** adj (a) (trade ~) gewerkschaftlich. (b) (Pol) Unions-. **U~ MP** (Ir) Unionistischer Abgeordneter.

unionization [ˌjuːnjənaɪ'zeɪʃən] n (gewerkschaftliche) Organisierung.

unionize ['juːnjənaɪz] **1** vt gewerkschaftlich organisieren. **2** vi sich gewerkschaftlich organisieren.

union: **U~ Jack** n Union Jack m; **~ shop** n gewerkschaftspflichtiger Betrieb; **~ suit** n (US) lange Hemdhose.

unique [juː'niːk] adj einzig attr; (outstanding) einzigartig, einmalig (inf); (Math) eindeutig. **you are not ~ in that** da bist du nicht der/die einzige; **such cases are, of course, not ~ to Britain** solche Fälle sind natürlich nicht nur auf Großbritannien beschränkt.

uniquely [juː'niːklɪ] adv (solely) einzig und allein, nur; (outstandingly) einmalig (inf), unübertrefflich. **~ suited** außergewöhnlich geeignet.

uniqueness [juː'niːknɪs] n Einmaligkeit, Einzigartigkeit f. **because of its ~, this vase** ... weil sie die einzige Vase dieser Art ist, ...

unisex ['juːnɪseks] adj Unisex-, unisex.

unison ['juːnɪzn] n (Mus) Gleichklang, Einklang m (also fig). in ~ unisono (form), einstimmig; ~ singing einstimmiger Gesang; **to be in ~ (with sth)** übereinstimmen (mit etw); **to act in ~ with sb** (fig) in Übereinstimmung mit jdm handeln.

unit ['juːnɪt] n (a) (entity, Mil) Einheit f; (set of equipment also) Anlage f. **camera/x-ray ~** Kameraeinheit/Röntgenanlage f.
(b) (section) Einheit f; (of furniture) Element nt; (of machine also) Element, Teil nt; (of organization also) Abteilung f. **generative ~** Aggregat nt; **compressor ~** Kompressor m; **power ~** Aggregat nt; (of a rocket) Triebwerk nt; **where did you get those ~s in your bedroom?** wo haben Sie die Anbauelemente in Ihrem Schlafzimmer her?; **the new research ~** die neue Forschungsabteilung or -gruppe; **the family as the basic ~** die Familie als Grundelement.
(c) (measure) Einheit f. **~ of account/length** Rechnungs-/Längeneinheit f; **monetary ~** Währungseinheit f.
(d) (Math) Einer m. **tens and ~s** Zehner und Einer pl.

Unitarian [ˌjuːnɪ'tɛərɪən] **1** adj unitarisch. **2** n Unitarier(in f) m.

Unitarianism [ˌjuːnɪ'tɛərɪənɪzəm] n Unitarismus m.

unitary ['juːnɪtərɪ] adj (a) (used as a unit) Einheits-. **~ weight** Gewichtseinheit f. (b) (unified) einheitlich.

unit cost n (Fin) Kosten pl pro (Rechnungs)einheit.

unite [juː'naɪt] **1** vt (join, also form: marry) vereinigen, verbinden; party, country (treaty etc) (ver)einigen, zusammenschließen; (emotions, ties, loyalties) (ver)einen. **the common interests which ~ us** die gemeinsamen Interessen, die uns verbinden.
2 vi sich zusammenschließen, sich vereinigen. **to ~ in doing sth** gemeinsam etw tun; **to ~ in prayer/opposition to sth** gemeinsam beten/gegen etw Opposition machen; **workers of the world, ~!** Proletarier aller Länder, vereinigt euch!

united [juː'naɪtɪd] adj verbunden; family, group, people, nation, front geschlossen; people, nation einig; efforts vereint. **~ we stand, divided we fall** (prov) Einigkeit macht stark (Prov); **to present a ~ front** eine geschlossene Front bieten.

United: **~ Arab Republic** n Vereinigte Arabische Republik;

~ **Kingdom** n Vereinigtes Königreich (Großbritannien und Nordirland); ~ **Nations (Organization)** n Vereinte Nationen pl; ~ **States (of America)** npl Vereinigte Staaten pl (von Amerika).

unit: ~ **furniture** n Anbaumöbel pl; ~ **price** n (a) (price per unit) Preis m pro Einheit; (b) (inclusive price) Pauschalpreis m; ~ **trust** n (Brit Fin) (company) Unit Trust m, Investmentgesellschaft f; (share) Unit-Trust-Papiere, Investment-Papiere pl.

unity ['juːnɪtɪ] n (a) (oneness, Liter) Einheit f; (harmony) Einmütigkeit, Einigkeit f; (of a novel, painting etc) Einheitlichkeit, Geschlossenheit f. **national** ~ (nationale) Einheit; this ~ **of purpose** diese gemeinsamen Ziele; **to live in** ~ **with** in Eintracht leben mit; ~ **is strength** Einigkeit macht stark (Prov).
(b) (Math) Einheit f; (one) Eins f; (in set theory) neutrales Element.

Univ abbr of **University** Univ.
univalent [ˌjuːnɪˈveɪlənt] adj einwertig.
univalve ['juːnɪvælv] 1 n a Gastropod m. 2 adj einschalig.
universal [ˌjuːnɪˈvɜːsəl] 1 adj (a) phenomenon, applicability, remedy universal, universell; language, genius, remedy also Universal-; (prevailing everywhere also) custom, game allgemein or überall verbreitet; (applying to all also) truth, rule allgemein gültig; (general) approval, peace allgemein. ~ **education** Allgemeinbildung f; ~ **remedy** Allheilmittel nt; **to be a** ~ **favourite** überall beliebt sein; ~ **peace** Weltfrieden m; **to become** ~ allgemein verbreitet werden; **of** ~ **applicability** allgemein or universal anwendbar; (theory etc also) allgemeingültig.
(b) (Logic) universal, universell, allgemein.
2 n (Philos) Allgemeinbegriff m; (Logic: ~ proposition) Universalaussage f. **the** ~ das Allgemeine; **the various** ~**s of human society** die verschiedenen Grundelemente der menschlichen Gesellschaft.

universal: ~ **coupling** n see ~ **joint;** ~ **donor** n Universalspender m.
universality [ˌjuːnɪvɜːˈsælɪtɪ] n Universalität f; (of person also) Vielseitigkeit f; (prevalence also) allgemeine Verbreitung; (general applicability) Allgemeingültigkeit f.
universal: ~ **joint** n Universalgelenk nt; ~ **language** n Weltsprache f.
universally [ˌjuːnɪˈvɜːsəlɪ] adv allgemein. ~ **applicable** allgemeingültig.
universal: **U~ Postal Union** n Weltpostverein m; ~ **suffrage** n allgemeines Wahlrecht; ~ **time** n Weltzeit f.
universe ['juːnɪvɜːs] n (a) (cosmos) (Welt)all, Universum nt; (galaxy) Sternsystem nt; (world) Welt f. (b) (Logic) ~ **of discourse** Gesamtheit f aller Gegenstände der Abhandlung.
university [ˌjuːnɪˈvɜːsɪtɪ] 1 n Universität f. **the** ~ **of life** die Schule des Lebens; **what is his** ~? wo studiert er?; **to be at** ~/**to go to** ~ studieren; **to go to London** U~ in London studieren.
2 adj attr town, library, bookshop Universitäts-; qualifications, education also akademisch. ~ **man** Akademiker m; ~ **teacher** Hochschullehrer m.
unjust [ʌnˈdʒʌst] adj ungerecht (to gegen). **you're being** ~ **das ist ungerecht.**
unjustifiable [ʌnˈdʒʌstɪfaɪəbl] adj nicht zu rechtfertigen pred or rechtfertigend attr.
unjustifiably [ʌnˈdʒʌstɪfaɪəblɪ] adv expensive, severe, critical ungerechtfertigt; rude unnötig; criticize, dismiss, praise zu Unrecht. **he acted quite** ~ er hat ungerechtfertigt or ohne Rechtfertigung gehandelt.
unjustified [ʌnˈdʒʌstɪfaɪd] adj ungerechtfertigt. **to be** ~ **in thinking that** ... zu Unrecht denken, daß ...
unjustly [ʌnˈdʒʌstlɪ] adv zu Unrecht; judge, treat ungerecht.
unjustness [ʌnˈdʒʌstnɪs] n Ungerechtigkeit f.
unkempt [ʌnˈkempt] adj hair ungekämmt; appearance, garden etc ungepflegt, vernachlässigt.
unkind [ʌnˈkaɪnd] adj (+er) person, remark, action (not nice) unfreundlich, nicht nett; (cruel) lieblos, gemein; remark also spitz; (harsh) climate, country, substance, action schlecht (to für). **don't be (so)** ~! das ist aber gar nicht nett (von dir)!; **he was so** ~ **as to suggest** er hat die wenig schmeichelhafte Vermutung geäußert; **to be** ~ **to animals** nicht gut zu Tieren sein; ~ **to the skin** nicht hautfreundlich; **fate has been** ~ **to him** das Schicksal hat ihn unfreundlich behandelt; **it would be** ~ **not to tell him the truth** es wäre gemein, ihm nicht die Wahrheit zu sagen.
unkindly [ʌnˈkaɪndlɪ] adv unfreundlich, nicht nett; (cruelly) lieblos, gemein. **how** ~ **fate had treated her** wie grausam das Schicksal ihr mitgespielt hatte; **don't take it** ~ **if** ... nimm es nicht übel, wenn ...; **to take** ~ **to sth** etw übelnehmen.
unkindness [ʌnˈkaɪndnɪs] n Unfreundlichkeit f; (cruelty) Lieblosigkeit, Gemeinheit f. **to do sb an** ~ jdm Unrecht tun; **the** ~ **of the weather/terrain** das schlechte Wetter/das schwierige Gelände.
unknot [ʌnˈnɒt] vt aufknoten, entknoten.
unknowable [ʌnˈnəʊəbl] 1 adj truths unbegreiflich, unfaßbar; person verschlossen. 2 n **the U~** das Unfaßbare.
unknowing [ʌnˈnəʊɪŋ] adj agent, cause unwissentlich, ohne es zu wissen. **he was the** ~ **cause of** ... er war unwissentlich or ohne es zu wissen die Ursache für ...; **an** ~ **accomplice** unwissentlich (ein) Komplize.
unknowingly [ʌnˈnəʊɪŋlɪ] adv unwissentlich, ohne es zu wissen.
unknown [ʌnˈnəʊn] 1 adj unbekannt. ~ **quantity** unbekannte Größe; (Math) Unbekannte f; **the** ~ **soldier** or **warrior der Unbekannte Soldat;** ~ **territory** (lit, fig) Neuland nt; **to be** ~ **to sb** (feeling, territory) jdm fremd sein; **it's** ~ **for him to get up for breakfast** man ist es von ihm gar nicht gewohnt, daß er zum Frühstück aufsteht; **his intentions are** ~ **to me** seine Absichten sind mir unbekannt; **this substance is** ~ **to science** diese Sub-

stanz ist der Wissenschaft nicht bekannt; see **person.**
2 n (person) Unbekannte(r) mf; (factor, Math) Unbekannte f; (territory) unerforschte(s) Gebiet, Neuland nt. **the** ~ **das Unbekannte; a voyage into the** ~ (lit, fig) eine Fahrt ins Ungewisse.
3 adv ~ **to me** etc ohne daß ich etc es wußte.
unlace [ʌnˈleɪs] vt aufbinden, aufschnüren.
unladylike [ʌnˈleɪdɪlaɪk] adj undamenhaft, nicht damenhaft.
unlamented [ˌʌnləˈmentɪd] adj death, loss unbeklagt, unbeweint. **he died** ~ niemand trauerte um ihn.
unlatch [ʌnˈlætʃ] vt entriegeln.
unlawful [ʌnˈlɔːfʊl] adj gesetzwidrig; means, assembly ungesetzlich, illegal; wedding ungültig.
unlawfully [ʌnˈlɔːfəlɪ] adv gesetzwidrig, illegal; married ungültig.
unlearn [ʌnˈlɜːn] vt sich (dat) abgewöhnen; habit also ablegen.
unleash [ʌnˈliːʃ] vt dog von der Leine lassen; (fig) (cause) anger, war entfesseln, auslösen. **he** ~**ed his fury on his wife** er ließ seine Frau seinen Zorn spüren; **to** ~ **a war upon the whole world** die ganze Welt in einen Krieg stürzen.
unleavened [ʌnˈlevnd] adj bread ungesäuert.
unless [ənˈles] conj es sei denn; (at beginning of sentence) wenn ... nicht, sofern ... nicht. **don't do it** ~ **I tell you to** mach das nicht, es sei denn, ich sage es dir; ~ **I tell you to, don't do it** sofern or wenn ich es dir nicht sage, mach das nicht; ~ **I am mistaken** ... wenn or falls ich mich nicht irre ...; ~ **otherwise stated** sofern nicht anders angezeigt or angegeben; ~ **there is an interruption** vorausgesetzt, alles läuft ohne Unterbrechung.
unlettered [ʌnˈletəd] adj ungebildet; (illiterate) analphabetisch attr.
unliberated [ʌnˈlɪbəreɪtɪd] adj women unemanzipiert, nicht emanzipiert; masses, countries nicht befreit.
unlicensed [ʌnˈlaɪsənst] adj (having no licence) car, dog, TV nicht angemeldet; premises ohne Lizenz or (Schank)konzession; (unauthorized) unbefugt, unberechtigt. **people with** ~ **TV/radio sets** Schwarzseher pl/Schwarzhörer pl (inf).
unlike [ʌnˈlaɪk] 1 adj unähnlich, nicht ähnlich; poles ungleich, gegensätzlich.
2 prep (a) im Gegensatz zu (dat), anders als.
(b) (uncharacteristic of) **to be quite** ~ **sb** jdm (gar) nicht ähnlich sehen; (behaviour also) überhaupt nicht zu jdm passen; **how** ~ **him not to have told us** das sieht ihm gar nicht ähnlich, daß er uns nichts gesagt hat.
(c) (not resembling) **this photograph is quite** ~ **her** dieses Photo sieht ihr gar nicht ähnlich; **this house is** ~ **their former one** dieses Haus ist ganz anders als ihr früheres.
unlikelihood [ʌnˈlaɪklɪhʊd], **unlikeliness** [ʌnˈlaɪklɪnɪs] n Unwahrscheinlichkeit f. **despite the** ~ **of success** obwohl der Erfolg unwahrscheinlich war.
unlikely [ʌnˈlaɪklɪ] adj (+er) happening, outcome unwahrscheinlich; explanation also unglaubwürdig; (odd also) clothes merkwürdig, komisch. **it is (most)** ~/**not** ~ **that** ... es ist (höchst) unwahrscheinlich/es kann durchaus sein, daß ...; **she is** ~ **to come** sie kommt höchstwahrscheinlich nicht; **it looks an** ~ **place for mushrooms** es sieht mir nicht nach der geeigneten Stelle für Pilze aus; **he's an** ~ **choice/he's** ~ **to be chosen** seine Wahl ist sehr unwahrscheinlich, es ist unwahrscheinlich, daß er gewählt wird; **in the** ~ **event that it does happen** im unwahrscheinlichen Fall, daß das geschieht.
unlimited [ʌnˈlɪmɪtɪd] adj wealth, time unbegrenzt; power also schrankenlos; patience unendlich. ~ **company** (Fin) Gesellschaft f mit unbeschränkter Haftung.
unlined [ʌnˈlaɪnd] adj paper unliniert; face faltenlos; (without lining) dress ungefüttert.
unlisted [ʌnˈlɪstɪd] adj phone number, company, items nicht verzeichnet; name nicht aufgeführt.
unlit [ˌʌnˈlɪt] adj road unbeleuchtet; lamp nicht angezündet.
unload [ʌnˈləʊd] 1 vt ship, gun entladen; car also, boot, luggage ausladen; truck, luggage abladen; cargo löschen. (b) (inf: get rid of) (Fin) shares abstoßen; furniture, children, problems abladen (on/to bei); job, problem abwälzen (on/to auf +acc). 2 vi (ship) löschen; (truck) abladen.
unlock [ʌnˈlɒk] vt door etc aufschließen; (fig) heart, secret offenbaren. **the door is** ~**ed** die Tür ist nicht abgeschlossen; **to leave a door** ~**ed** eine Tür nicht abschließen.
unlooked-for [ʌnˈlʊktfɔːʳ] adj unerwartet, unvorhergesehen; (welcome also) unverhofft.
unloose [ʌnˈluːs] vt (a) (also ~n) knot, grasp, hair lösen; rope, chains also losmachen. (b) prisoner losbinden; dog also losmachen, loslassen.
unlovable [ʌnˈlʌvəbl] adj wenig liebenswert or liebenswürdig, unsympathisch.
unloved [ʌnˈlʌvd] adj ungeliebt.
unlovely [ʌnˈlʌvlɪ] adj sight unschön; person (in appearance) abstoßend; (in character) garstig, unliebenswert.
unloving [ʌnˈlʌvɪŋ] adj person, home lieblos, kalt.
unluckily [ʌnˈlʌkɪlɪ] adv zum Pech, zum Unglück. ~ **for him** zu seinem Pech; **the day started** ~ der Tag hat schlecht angefangen.
unlucky [ʌnˈlʌkɪ] adj (+er) (a) person unglückselig. ~ **wretch** Unglücksrabe, Pechvogel m; **he's always** ~ er ist vom Pech verfolgt; **to be** ~ Pech haben; (not succeed) keinen Erfolg haben; ~ **in love** unglücklich verliebt; **it was** ~ **for her that she was seen** Pech für sie, daß man sie gesehen hat; **how** ~ **for you!** was für ein Pech!, das ist wirklich dumm (für dich)!; **he was** ~ **enough to meet her/to have to work with her** er hatte das Pech, sie zu treffen/mit ihr arbeiten zu müssen.
(b) object, action, place unglückselig; coincidence, event also, choice unglücklich; day also Unglücks-; moment also ungünstig, schlecht gewählt. **to be** ~ Unglück or Pech bringen; **London has been an** ~ **place for me** London hat mir nur Pech gebracht; **broken mirrors are** ~ zerbrochene Spiegel bringen

Unglück; **it's not through any fault of yours, it's just** ~ **es ist nicht dein Fehler, es ist nur Pech.**

unmade [ʌn'meɪd] adj bed ungemacht.

unmade-up [ˌʌnmeɪd'ʌp] adj face ungeschminkt, ohne Make-up; road ungeteert.

unman [ʌn'mæn] vt schwach werden lassen; (make lose courage) entmutigen, verzagen lassen.

unmanageable [ʌn'mænɪdʒəbl] adj (unwieldy) vehicle, boat schwer zu handhaben or manövrieren; parcel, size unhandlich; (uncontrollable) animal, person, hair, child widerspenstig, nicht zu bändigen; situation unkontrollierbar. **she finds the stairs** ~ sie kann die Treppe nicht schaffen (inf) or bewältigen.

unmanly [ʌn'mænlɪ] adj tears, behaviour unmännlich; (cowardly) feige; (effeminate) weibisch.

unmanned [ʌn'mænd] adj (not requiring crew) level crossing, space flight unbemannt; (lacking crew) telephone exchange, lighthouse unbesetzt, nicht besetzt.

unmannerly [ʌn'mænəlɪ] adj ungesittet; child also ungezogen; behaviour ungehörig; (at table also) unmanierlich. **it is** ~ **to ... es gehört sich nicht, zu ...**

unmarked [ʌn'mɑːkt] adj (a) (unstained) ohne Flecken or Spuren, fleckenlos; (without marking) face ungezeichnet (also fig); banknotes also unmarkiert; linen nicht gezeichnet; boxes, crates, suitcases etc ohne Namen or Adresse; police car nicht gekennzeichnet. **luckily the carpet was** ~ **by the wine** glücklicherweise blieben keine Weinspuren auf dem Teppich zurück; **to leave sb** ~ spurlos an jdm vorübergehen. (b) (Sport) player ungedeckt. (c) (Sch) papers unkorrigiert. (d) (unnoticed) unbemerkt. (e) (Ling) unmarkiert.

unmarketable [ʌn'mɑːkɪtəbl] adj unverkäuflich, schlecht or nicht zu verkaufen.

unmarriageable [ʌn'mærɪdʒəbl] adj nicht zu verheiraten pred, nicht unter die Haube zu kriegen pred (inf).

unmarried [ʌn'mærɪd] adj unverheiratet. ~ **mother** ledige Mutter.

unmask [ʌn'mɑːsk] 1 vt (lit) demaskieren; (fig) entlarven. 2 vi die Maske abnehmen, sich demaskieren.

unmasking [ʌn'mɑːskɪŋ] n (fig) Entlarvung f.

unmatched [ʌn'mætʃt] adj unübertrefflich, einmalig, unübertroffen (for in bezug auf +acc). **the scenery is** ~ **anywhere in the world** die Landschaft sucht (in der Welt) ihresgleichen; **to be** ~ **for beauty/chivalry** alle anderen an Schönheit/Ritterlichkeit übertreffen.

unmechanical [ˌʌnmɪ'kænɪkəl] adj person technisch unbegabt.

unmentionable [ʌn'menʃnəbl] 1 adj tabu pred; word also unaussprechlich. **to be** ~ tabu sein; **to be an** ~ **topic** (als Thema) tabu sein. 2 n: **the** ~s (hum inf) die Unaussprechlichen pl (hum inf).

unmerciful adj, ~ly adv [ʌn'mɜːsɪfʊl, -fəlɪ] unbarmherzig, erbarmungslos.

unmerited [ʌn'merɪtɪd] adj unverdient.

unmetalled [ʌn'metld] adj (Brit) ungeteert.

unmethodical [ˌʌnmɪ'θɒdɪkəl] adj unmethodisch.

unmindful [ʌn'maɪndfʊl] adj **to be** ~ **of sth** nicht auf etw (acc) achten, etw nicht beachten; **I was not** ~ **of your needs** ich stand Ihren Bedürfnissen nicht gleichgültig gegenüber.

unmistak(e)able [ˌʌnmɪ'steɪkəbl] adj unverkennbar; (visually) nicht zu verwechseln. **he is** ~ **in his green suit** in seinem grünen Anzug ist er nicht zu verwechseln or verkennen.

unmistak(e)ably [ˌʌnmɪ'steɪkəblɪ] adv zweifelsohne (geh), unverkennbar.

unmitigated [ʌn'mɪtɪgeɪtɪd] adj (not lessened) wrath, severity ungemildert; (inf: complete) disaster vollkommen, total; rubbish komplett (inf); liar, rogue also Erz- (inf).

unmixed [ʌn'mɪkst] adj blood unvermischt; pleasure ungetrübt, rein.

unmolested [ˌʌnmə'lestɪd] adj (unattacked) unbelästigt; (undisturbed) in Frieden, in Ruhe.

unmoor [ʌn'mʊəʳ] vti losmachen.

unmotivated [ʌn'məʊtɪveɪtɪd] adj unmotiviert; attack also grundlos, sinnlos.

unmounted [ʌn'maʊntɪd] adj rider unberitten; (thrown from horse) abgeworfen; gem ungefaßt; gun nicht fest montiert; picture (not on mount) nicht aufgezogen; (not in album) lose.

unmourned [ʌn'mɔːnd] adj unbeweint; death also unbeklagt. **an** ~ **tyrant** ein Tyrann, dem niemand nachtrauert or nachweint; **they went largely** ~ kaum einer trauerte ihnen nach.

unmoved [ʌn'muːvd] adj person ungerührt. **they were** ~ **by his playing** sein Spiel(en) ergriff sie nicht; **it leaves me** ~ das (be)rührt mich nicht; **he remained** ~ **by her pleas** ihr Flehen ließ ihn kalt, ihr Flehen rührte or erweichte ihn nicht.

unmusical [ʌn'mjuːzɪkəl] adj person unmusikalisch; sound unmelodisch.

unnam(e)able [ʌn'neɪməbl] adj unsagbar.

unnamed [ʌn'neɪmd] adj (nameless) namenlos; (anonymous) ungenannt.

unnatural [ʌn'nætʃrəl] adj unnatürlich; (abnormal also) relationship, crime nicht normal pred, widernatürlich, wider die Natur pred. **it is** ~ **for him to be so rude** normalerweise ist er nicht so grob, es ist ungewöhnlich, daß er so grob ist; **it's not** ~ **to be upset** es ist nur natürlich, da bestürzt zu sein.

unnaturally [ʌn'nætʃrəlɪ] adv unnatürlich; (extraordinarily also) loud, anxious ungewöhnlich. **not** ~, **we were worried** es war nur normal or natürlich, daß wir uns Sorgen machten.

unnavigable [ʌn'nævɪgəbl] adj nicht schiffbar, nicht befahrbar.

unnecessarily [ʌn'nesɪsərɪlɪ] adv unnötigerweise; strict, serious unnötig, übertrieben.

unnecessary [ʌn'nesɪsərɪ] adj unnötig; (not requisite) nicht

notwendig or nötig; (superfluous also) überflüssig. **no, you needn't bother thanks, that's quite** ~ nein, machen Sie sich keine Umstände, das ist wirklich nicht nötig; **it was quite** ~ **to be so rude** es war wirklich nicht nötig, so grob zu werden; **really, that was quite** ~ **of you!** also, das war wirklich überflüssig!

unneighbourly [ʌn'neɪbəlɪ] adj behaviour nicht gutnachbarlich. **it's** ~ **to do that** als guter Nachbar tut man so etwas nicht.

unnerve [ʌn'nɜːv] vt entnerven; (gradually) zermürben; (discourage) speaker entmutigen. ~**d by their reaction** durch ihre Reaktion aus der Ruhe gebracht.

unnerving [ʌn'nɜːvɪŋ] adj experience entnervend; silence also zermürbend; (discouraging also) entmutigend.

unnoticed [ʌn'nəʊtɪst] adj unbemerkt. **to go** or **pass** ~ unbemerkt bleiben.

unnumbered [ʌn'nʌmbəd] adj (a) (countless) unzählig, zahllos. (b) (not numbered) nicht numeriert; house also ohne Nummer.

UNO abbr of **United Nations Organization** UNO f.

unobjectionable [ˌʌnəb'dʒekʃnəbl] adj einwandfrei. **as a person he is** ~ **enough** man kann nichts gegen ihn einwenden or sagen, er ist als Mensch soweit in Ordnung.

unobservant [ˌʌnəb'zɜːvənt] adj unaufmerksam. **to be** ~ ein schlechter Beobachter sein; **how** ~ **of me** wie unaufmerksam (von mir).

unobserved [ˌʌnəb'zɜːvd] adj (not seen) unbemerkt; (not celebrated) nicht (mehr) eingehalten or beachtet.

unobstructed [ˌʌnəb'strʌktɪd] adj view ungehindert; pipe frei, unverstopft; path, road frei, unversperrt.

unobtainable [ˌʌnəb'teɪnəbl] adj nicht erhältlich, nicht zu bekommen. **number** ~ (Telec) kein Anschluß unter dieser Nummer; **your number was** ~ deine Nummer war nicht zu bekommen.

unobtrusive adj, ~ly adv [ˌʌnəb'truːsɪv, -lɪ] unauffällig.

unoccupied [ʌn'ɒkjʊpaɪd] adj person unbeschäftigt; house leerstehend, unbewohnt; seat leer; (Mil) zone unbesetzt.

unofficial [ˌʌnə'fɪʃəl] adj inoffiziell; (unconfirmed also) information nicht amtlich. **to take** ~ **action** (Ind) inoffiziell streiken; **in an** ~ **capacity** inoffiziell.

unofficially [ˌʌnə'fɪʃəlɪ] adv inoffiziell.

unopened [ʌn'əʊpənd] adj ungeöffnet.

unopposed [ˌʌnə'pəʊzd] adj **they marched on** ~ sie marschierten weiter, ohne auf Widerstand zu treffen; ~ **by the committee** ohne Widerspruch or Beanstandung seitens des Ausschusses; **to be returned** ~ (Pol) ohne Gegenstimmen gewählt werden; **an** ~ **second reading** (Parl) eine zweite Lesung ohne Gegenstimmen.

unorganized [ʌn'ɔːgənaɪzd] adj unsystematisch; essay also konfus; person also unmethodisch; life ungeregelt; (Ind) nicht (gewerkschaftlich) organisiert. **he is so** ~ er hat überhaupt kein System.

unoriginal [ˌʌnə'rɪdʒɪnəl] adj wenig originell.

unorthodox [ʌn'ɔːθədɒks] adj unkonventionell, unorthodox.

unpack [ʌn'pæk] vti auspacken.

unpacking [ʌn'pækɪŋ] n Auspacken nt. **to do one's** ~ auspacken.

unpaid [ʌn'peɪd] adj unbezahlt.

unpalatable [ʌn'pælɪtəbl] adj food, drink ungenießbar; (fig) fact, truth, mixture unverdaulich, schwer zu verdauen. **he finds the truth** ~ die Wahrheit schmeckt ihm nicht.

unparalleled [ʌn'pærəleld] adj einmalig, beispiellos; (unprecedented also) noch nie dagewesen. **an** ~ **success** ein Erfolg ohnegleichen.

unpardonable [ʌn'pɑːdnəbl] adj unverzeihlich.

unparliamentary [ˌʌnpɑːlə'mentərɪ] adj behaviour, language nicht parlamentsfähig, der Würde des Parlamentes nicht entsprechend; procedure unparlamentarisch.

unpatented [ʌn'peɪtntɪd] adj nicht patentiert.

unpatriotic [ˌʌnpætrɪ'ɒtɪk] adj unpatriotisch.

unpaved [ʌn'peɪvd] adj road, courtyard nicht gepflastert.

unpeg [ʌn'peg] vt washing abnehmen; prices freigeben.

unperceptive [ˌʌnpə'septɪv] adj unaufmerksam.

unperfumed [ʌn'pɜːfjuːmd] adj nicht parfümiert.

unperson ['ʌnpɜːsən] n (Pol) Unperson f.

unperturbable [ˌʌnpə'tɜːbəbl] adj nicht aus der Ruhe zu bringen pred or bringend attr.

unperturbed [ˌʌnpə'tɜːbd] adj nicht beunruhigt (by von, durch), gelassen.

unphilosophical [ˌʌnfɪlə'sɒfɪkəl] adj unphilosophisch.

unpick [ʌn'pɪk] vt auftrennen.

unpin [ʌn'pɪn] vt dress, hair die Nadeln entfernen aus; notice abnehmen.

unplaced [ʌn'pleɪst] adj (Sport) nicht plaziert. **to be** ~ sich nicht plaziert haben.

unplanned [ʌn'plænd] adj ungeplant, nicht geplant.

unplayable [ʌn'pleɪəbl] adj unspielbar; pitch unbespielbar. **the ball was in an** ~ **position** der Ball war nicht spielbar.

unpleasant [ʌn'pleznt] adj unangenehm; person, smile, remark unliebenswürdig, unfreundlich; experience, situation also unerfreulich.

unpleasantly [ʌn'plezntlɪ] adv reply unliebenswürdig, unfreundlich; warm, smell unangenehm. **he was getting** ~ **close to the truth** es war unangenehm, wie nah er an der Wahrheit war.

unpleasantness [ʌn'plezntnɪs] n (a) (quality) see adj Unangenehmheit f; Unfreundlichkeit f; Unerfreulichkeit f. (b) (bad feeling, quarrel) Unstimmigkeit f.

unplug [ʌn'plʌg] vt radio, lamp den Stecker herausziehen von.

unplumbed [ʌn'plʌmd] adj unergründet.

unpolished [ʌn'pɒlɪʃt] adj (a) unpoliert; stone ungeschliffen. (b) (fig) person, manners ungeschliffen, ungehobelt; perfor-

mance unausgefeilt; *style, language* holprig, unausgefeilt.

unpolluted [ˌʌnpə'luːtɪd] *adj* sauber, unverschmutzt.

unpopular [ʌn'pɒpjʊləʳ] *adj person* unbeliebt (*with sb* bei jdm); *(for particular reason also)* unpopulär; *decision, move* unpopulär. **to make oneself ~** sich unbeliebt machen; **I'm ~ with him just now** zur Zeit bin ich bei ihm nicht gut angeschrieben (*inf*).

unpopularity [ʌnˌpɒpjʊ'lærɪtɪ] *n* Unbeliebtheit *f*; *(of decision, move)* Unpopularität *f*, geringe Popularität.

unpractical [ʌn'præktɪkəl] *adj* unpraktisch.

unpractised, *(US)* **unpracticed** [ʌn'præktɪst] *adj* ungeübt.

unprecedented [ʌn'presɪdəntɪd] *adj* noch nie dagewesen; *success also* beispiellos, ohnegleichen (*after n*); *profit, step* unerhört. **this event is ~** dieses Ereignis ist bisher einmalig; **an ~ success** ein beispielloser or noch nie dagewesener Erfolg, ein Erfolg ohnegleichen; **you realize it's quite ~ for a president to ...** es ist Ihnen wohl klar, daß es keinen Präzedenzfall dafür gibt, daß ein Präsident ...

unpredictable [ˌʌnprɪ'dɪktəbl] *adj* unvorhersehbar; *result* nicht vorherzusagen *pred or* vorherzusagend *attr*; *behaviour, person, weather* unberechenbar.

unprejudiced [ʌn'predʒʊdɪst] *adj (impartial)* objektiv, unparteiisch; *(not having prejudices)* vorurteilslos. **young children are ~** kleine Kinder haben keine Vorurteile.

unpremeditated [ˌʌnprɪ'medɪteɪtɪd] *adj* unüberlegt; *crime* nicht vorsätzlich.

unprepared [ˌʌnprɪ'peəd] *adj* **(a)** nicht vorbereitet; *person also* unvorbereitet. **to be ~ for sth** für etw nicht vorbereitet sein; *(be surprised)* auf etw *(acc)* nicht vorbereitet or gefaßt sein; **you've caught me ~** darauf bin ich nicht vorbereitet. **(b)** *(improvised)* unvorbereitet, nicht vorbereitet.

unprepossessing [ˌʌnpriːpə'zesɪŋ] *adj* wenig gewinnend, wenig einnehmend.

unpresentable [ˌʌnprɪ'zentəbl] *adj (in appearance)* nicht präsentabel; *clothes also* unansehnlich; *(socially)* nicht gesellschaftsfähig. **so ~** so wenig präsentabel; **most of his friends are completely ~** mit den meisten seiner Freunde kann man sich in der Öffentlichkeit nicht blicken lassen.

unpretentious [ˌʌnprɪ'tenʃəs] *adj* schlicht, bescheiden; *person, manner also* natürlich; *house, meal etc also* einfach; *style, book* einfach, nicht schwülstig.

unpretentiously [ˌʌnprɪ'tenʃəslɪ] *adv* schlicht, bescheiden, einfach; *speak* natürlich; *write* in einfachen Worten.

unpriced [ʌn'praɪst] *adj* ohne Preisschild, nicht ausgezeichnet.

unprincipled [ʌn'prɪnsɪpld] *adj* skrupellos; *person also* charakterlos.

unprintable [ʌn'prɪntəbl] *adj* nicht druckfähig. **his answer was ~** seine Antwort war nicht druckreif.

unproductive [ˌʌnprə'dʌktɪv] *adj* *capital* nicht gewinnbringend, keinen Gewinn bringend; *soil* unfruchtbar, ertragsarm; *discussion, meeting* unproduktiv, unergiebig.

unprofessional [ˌʌnprə'feʃənl] *adj conduct* berufswidrig; *(amateur) language* unprofessionell; *work* unfachmännisch, laienhaft, stümperhaft. **it's ~ to ...** es ziemt sich nicht, zu ...

unprofitable [ʌn'prɒfɪtəbl] *adj (financially)* keinen Profit bringend or abwerfend, wenig einträglich; *mine etc* unrentabel; *(fig)* nutzlos, sinnlos. **the company was ~** die Firma machte keinen Profit or warf keinen Profit ab; **we spent an ~ hour** wir haben eine Stunde verplempert; **it would be ~ to go on** es wäre sinnlos, noch weiterzumachen.

unpromising [ʌn'prɒmɪsɪŋ] *adj* nicht sehr vielversprechend; *start also* nicht sehr erfolgversprechend, wenig erfolgversprechend. **to look ~** nicht sehr hoffnungsvoll or gut aussehen; *(weather)* nichts Gutes versprechen.

unprompted [ʌn'prɒmptɪd] *adj* spontan. **~ by me** unaufgefordert; **his invitation was quite ~** seine Einladung kam ganz aus freien Stücken; **I'd rather he answered the questions ~** es wäre mir lieber, wenn er ohne Vorsagen antwortete.

unpronounceable [ˌʌnprə'naʊnsəbl] *adj* unaussprechlich. **that word is ~** das Wort ist nicht auszusprechen.

unpropitious [ˌʌnprə'pɪʃəs] *adj omen* schlecht, ungünstig; *moment* ungünstig, ungeeignet.

unprotected [ˌʌnprə'tektɪd] *adj* ohne Schutz, schutzlos; *machine* ungeschützt; *(by insurance)* ohne Versicherungsschutz; *(Mil) building etc* ungeschützt, ohne Deckung. **~ by** nicht geschützt durch.

unprovable [ʌn'pruːvəbl] *adj* nicht beweisbar.

unproved [ʌn'pruːvd] *adj* nicht bewiesen, unbewiesen. **he's still ~ as a minister** als Minister muß er sich erst noch bewähren; **his courage was ~** er mußte seinen Mut erst noch beweisen.

unprovided [ˌʌnprə'vaɪdɪd] *adj (not equipped)* **~ with** nicht ausgestattet mit, ohne.

unprovided-for [ˌʌnprə'vaɪdɪdfɔːʳ] *adj* **(a)** *(lacking)* unversorgt. **he died and left his children ~** er starb, ohne für seine Kinder gesorgt zu haben. **(b)** *(not anticipated)* **that eventuality was ~** auf dieses Ereignis war man nicht eingerichtet.

unprovoked [ˌʌnprə'vəʊkt] *adj* ohne Anlaß, grundlos.

unpublished [ʌn'pʌblɪʃt] *adj* unveröffentlicht.

unpunctual [ʌn'pʌŋktjʊəl] *adj* unpünktlich.

unpunctuality [ʌn'pʌŋktjʊ'ælɪtɪ] *n* Unpünktlichkeit *f*.

unpunished [ʌn'pʌnɪʃt] *adj* unbestraft. **to go ~** ohne Strafe bleiben; **if this goes ~ ...** wenn das nicht bestraft wird ...

unqualified [ʌn'kwɒlɪfaɪd] *adj* **(a)** unqualifiziert. **to be ~** nicht qualifiziert sein. **(b)** *(absolute) delight, praise, acceptance* uneingeschränkt; *denial* vollständig; *success* voll(ständig); *(inf) idiot, liar* ausgesprochen. **(c)** *(Gram)* nicht bestimmt.

unquenchable [ʌn'kwentʃəbl] *adj fire* unlöschbar; *thirst, desire* unstillbar.

unquestionable [ʌn'kwestʃənəbl] *adj authority* unbestritten, unangefochten; *evidence, fact* unbezweifelbar; *sincerity, hon-*

esty fraglos. **a man of ~ honesty** ein zweifellos or fraglos ehrlicher Mann; **one's parents' authority used to be ~** früher konnte man die Autorität seiner Eltern nicht in Frage stellen; **his honesty is ~** die Ehrlichkeit steht außer Frage.

unquestionably [ʌn'kwestʃənəblɪ] *adv* fraglos, zweifellos.

unquestioned [ʌn'kwestʃənd] *adj* unbestritten. **I can't let that statement pass ~** ich kann diese Behauptung nicht fraglos hinnehmen; **to be ~** *(honesty etc)* außer Frage stehen; *(social order etc)* nicht in Frage gestellt werden.

unquestioning [ʌn'kwestʃənɪŋ] *adj* bedingungslos; *belief, faith also* blind.

unquestioningly [ʌn'kwestʃənɪŋlɪ] *adv accept* blind, ohne zu fragen.

unquiet [ʌn'kwaɪət] *adj (liter)* unruhig; *(restless)* ruhelos.

unquote [ʌn'kwəʊt] *vi (imper only)* Ende des Zitats.

unravel [ʌn'rævl] **1** *vt knitting* au;ziehen; *(lit, fig: untangle)* entwirren; *mystery* lösen. **2** *vi (knitting)* sich aufziehen; *(fig)* sich entwirren, sich auflösen; *(mystery)* sich lösen.

unread [ʌn'red] *adj book* ungelesen; *person* wenig belesen.

unreadable [ʌn'riːdəbl] *adj writing* unleserlich; *book* schwer zu lesen *pred*, schwer lesbar.

unreadiness [ʌn'redɪnɪs] *n* Unvorbereitetheit *f*; *(of troops)* mangelnde Bereitschaft.

unready [ʌn'redɪ] *adj* (noch) nicht fertig. **~ to do sth** nicht bereit, etw zu tun; **he was ~ for what happened next** er war nicht auf das eingestellt or vorbereitet, was dann kam; **he is ~ for such responsibility** er ist noch nicht reif genug, solch eine Verantwortung zu übernehmen.

unreal [ʌn'rɪəl] *adj* unwirklich.

unrealistic [ˌʌnrɪə'lɪstɪk] *adj* unrealistisch.

unreality [ˌʌnrɪ'ælɪtɪ] *n* Unwirklichkeit *f*. **there is an air of ~ about it** es hat etwas Unwirkliches an sich; **the deserted castle gave me a sense of ~** das verlassene Schloß hatte für mich etwas Unwirkliches an sich; **extreme exhaustion gives a feeling of ~** extreme Erschöpfung läßt alles unwirklich erscheinen; **the ~ of the characters' emotions** die Unnatürlichkeit or Unechtheit der Gefühle der Personen.

unrealized [ʌn'rɪəlaɪzd] *adj* unverwirklicht; *(Fin) assets* unverwertet; *profit* nicht realisiert.

unreasonable [ʌn'riːznəbl] *adj demand, price etc* unzumutbar, übertrieben; *person* uneinsichtig; *(showing lack of sense)* unvernünftig. **to be ~ about sth** *(not be understanding)* kein Verständnis für etw zeigen; *(be overdemanding)* in bezug auf etw *(acc)* zuviel verlangen; **it is ~ to ...** es ist zuviel verlangt, zu ...; **it is ~ to expect children to keep quiet** man kann doch von Kindern nicht verlangen, ruhig zu sein; **that's not ~, is it?** das ist doch nicht zuviel verlangt, oder?; **you are being very ~!** das ist wirklich zuviel verlangt; **look, don't be ~, it is 100 miles** nun mach mal einen Punkt or nun sei mal vernünftig, es sind immerhin 100 Meilen; **an ~ length of time** übermäßig or übertrieben lange; **at this ~ hour** zu dieser unzumutbaren Zeit.

unreasonableness [ʌn'riːznəblnɪs] *n (of demands etc)* Unzumutbarkeit, Übermäßigkeit *f*; *(of person)* Uneinsichtigkeit *f*. **I hadn't reckoned with his ~** ich hatte nicht damit gerechnet, daß er so uneinsichtig sein würde; **I commented on his ~ in expecting 20%** ich bemerkte, daß 20% wohl zuviel verlangt wären.

unreasonably [ʌn'riːznəblɪ] *adv long, slow, high, strict* übermäßig, übertrieben. **he remained ~ stubborn** er blieb unnötig stur; **he argued, quite ~ I think, that we should have known** er sagte, meiner Meinung nach ungerechtfertigterweise, daß wir das hätten wissen müssen.

unreasoning [ʌn'riːznɪŋ] *adj person* kopflos, unvernünftig; *action, fear, hatred* blind, unsinnig.

unreceptive [ˌʌnrɪ'septɪv] *adj* unempfänglich (*to* für); *audience also* unaufgeschlossen.

unrecognizable [ˌʌn'rekəgnaɪzəbl] *adj* nicht wiederzuerkennen *pred or* wiederzuerkennend *attr*. **he was totally ~ in his disguise** er war in seiner Verkleidung nicht zu erkennen; **they've made the city centre ~** das Stadtzentrum ist nicht wiederzuerkennen.

unrecognized [ʌn'rekəgnaɪzd] *adj (not noticed) person, danger, value* unerkannt; *(not acknowledged) government, record* nicht anerkannt; *genius, talent* unwürdigt, unerkannt. **~ by the crowds** ohne von den Leuten erkannt zu werden; **his achievements went ~** seine Leistungen fanden keine Anerkennung or wurden nicht gewürdigt.

unrecorded [ˌʌnrɪ'kɔːdɪd] *adj* nicht aufgenommen; *(Rad, TV) programme* nicht aufgezeichnet; *(in documents)* nicht schriftlich erfaßt or festgehalten. **to be ~** nicht aufgenommen/aufgezeichnet worden sein; nicht festgehalten sein; **to go ~** nicht aufgenommen/festgehalten werden.

unredeemed [ˌʌnrɪ'diːmd] *adj* **(a)** *sinner* unerlöst. **a life/person of ~ wickedness** ein durch und durch schlechtes Leben/schlechter Mensch; **~ by** nicht ausgeglichen or wettgemacht durch. **(b)** *bill, (from pawn)* uneingelöst; *mortgage, debt* ungetilgt.

unreel [ʌn'riːl] **1** *vt* abspulen, abwickeln. **2** *vi* sich abspulen, sich abwickeln, abrollen.

unrefined [ˌʌnrɪ'faɪnd] *adj* **(a)** *petroleum, sugar, metal* nicht raffiniert. **(b)** *person* unkultiviert; *manners also* unfein.

unreflecting [ˌʌnrɪ'flektɪŋ] *adj person* gedankenlos, unbedacht; *act, haste* unbesonnen; *emotion* unreflektiert.

unregarded [ˌʌnrɪ'gɑːdɪd] *adj* unbeachtet, nicht beachtet. **to go ~** unbeachtet bleiben; **to be ~** nicht beachtet werden.

unregenerate [ˌʌnrɪ'dʒenərɪt] *adj (unrepentant)* reu(e)los, nicht reuig; *(unreformed)* unbekehrbar; *(stubborn)* reactionary* hartnäckig; *(wicked) life* sündig.

unregistered [ʌn'redʒɪstəd] *adj birth* nicht gemeldet; *car* nicht angemeldet; *voter* nicht (im Wählerverzeichnis) eingetragen; *trademark* nicht gesetzlich geschützt; *letter* nicht eingeschrieben; *lawyer, doctor, taxi* nicht zugelassen.

unregretted [,ʌnrɪ'gretɪd] *adj absence, death* nicht bedauert; *person* nicht vermißt; *words* nicht bereut. **he died ~ niemand hat seinen Tod bedauert.**

unregulated [ʌn'regjʊleɪtɪd] *adj* unkontrolliert.

unrehearsed [,ʌnrɪ'hɜːst] *adj (Theat etc)* nicht geprobt; *cast* schlecht eingespielt; *(spontaneous) incident* spontan.

unrelated [,ʌnrɪ'leɪtɪd] *adj (unconnected)* ohne Beziehung *(to* zu); *(by family)* nicht verwandt. **~ to reality** wirklichkeitsfremd; **the two events are ~/are not ~** die beiden Ereignisse stehen in keinem Zusammenhang miteinander/sind nicht gänzlich ohne Zusammenhang.

unrelenting [,ʌnrɪ'lentɪŋ] *adj pressure* unablässig; *opposition* unerbittlich; *determination* hartnäckig; *pace, severity* unvermindert; *attack, struggle* unerbittlich, unvermindert; *rain* anhaltend *attr*, nicht nachlassend *attr*; *(not merciful) person, heat* unbarmherzig. **we must be ~ in our struggle** wir müssen unablässig weiterkämpfen; **they kept up an ~ attack** sie führten den Angriff mit unverminderter Stärke durch.

unreliability ['ʌnrɪ,laɪə'bɪlɪtɪ] *n* Unzuverlässigkeit *f.*

unreliable [,ʌnrɪ'laɪəbl] *adj* unzuverlässig.

unrelieved [,ʌnrɪ'liːvd] *adj pain* ungehindert, ungemindert; *gloom, anguish* ungemindert; *mediocrity* unverändert, gleichbleibend *attr*; *grey* einheitlich, durch nichts aufgelokkert; *sameness* eintönig, einförmig; *monotony, boredom* tödlich. **a life of ~ drudgery** ein Leben, das eine einzige Schinderei ist; **to be ~ by** nicht aufgelockert sein durch *or* von; **the atmosphere was one of ~ gloom** es herrschte eine ausgesprochen gedrückte *or* niedergeschlagene Stimmung.

unremarkable [,ʌnrɪ'mɑːkəbl] *adj* nicht sehr bemerkenswert, wenig bemerkenswert.

unremarked [,ʌnrɪ'mɑːkt] *adj* unbemerkt. **to go ~** unbemerkt bleiben.

unremitting [,ʌnrɪ'mɪtɪŋ] *adj efforts, toil* unaufhörlich, unablässig; *zeal* unermüdlich; *hatred* unversöhnlich.

unremittingly [,ʌnrɪ'mɪtɪŋlɪ] *adv* unaufhörlich, ohne Unterlaß; **strive** unermüdlich.

unremunerative [,ʌnrɪ'mjuːnərətɪv] *adj* nicht lohnend, nicht einträglich.

unrepealed [,ʌnrɪ'piːld] *adj* nicht aufgehoben.

unrepeatable [,ʌnrɪ'piːtəbl] *adj* **(a)** *words, views* nicht wiederholbar. **(b)** *offer* einmalig.

unrepentant [,ʌnrɪ'pentənt] *adj* nicht reuig, nicht reumütig, reu(e)los. **he is ~ about it** er bereut es nicht.

unreported [,ʌnrɪ'pɔːtɪd] *adj events* nicht berichtet. **to go ~** nicht berichtet werden.

unrepresentative [,ʌnreprɪ'zentətɪv] *adj (Pol) government* nicht frei gewählt; *(untypical)* nicht repräsentativ *(of* für). **the Party is ~ of the people** die Partei repräsentiert das Volk nicht.

unrepresented [,ʌnreprɪ'zentɪd] *adj* nicht vertreten.

unrequited [,ʌnrɪ'kwaɪtɪd] *adj love* unerwidert, unglücklich.

unreserved [,ʌnrɪ'zɜːvd] *adj* **(a)** *(frank) person* nicht reserviert, offen. **he's quite ~ about his feelings** er zeigt seine Gefühle ganz offen. **(b)** *(complete) approval* uneingeschränkt. **(c)** *(not booked)* nicht reserviert.

unreservedly [,ʌnrɪ'zɜːvɪdlɪ] *adv speak* freimütig, offen; *approve, believe, trust* uneingeschränkt, vollständig; *sob* rückhaltlos.

unresisting [,ʌnrɪ'zɪstɪŋ] *adj* widerstandslos, keinen Widerstand leistend *attr*. **I pushed open the ~ door,** ich stieß die Tür auf, die ohne weiteres nachgab.

unresolved [,ʌnrɪ'zɒlvd] *adj* **(a)** *difficulty, problem* ungelöst. **(b)** *(uncertain) person* unschlüssig. **he is still ~ as to what to do** er ist sich *(dat)* noch (darüber) unschlüssig, was er tun soll.

unresponsive [,ʌnrɪ'spɒnsɪv] *adj (physically)* nicht reagierend *attr*; *(emotionally, intellectually)* gleichgültig, unempfänglich. **to be ~** nicht reagieren *(to* auf *+acc)*; *(to advances, pleas, request also)* nicht empfänglich sein *(to* für); **an ~ audience** ein Publikum, das nicht mitgeht *or* nicht reagiert; **I suggested it but he was fairly ~** ich habe es vorgeschlagen, aber er ist nicht groß darauf eingegangen *or* er zeigte sich nicht sehr interessiert; **still heavily sedated and totally ~** unter starkem Drogeneinfluß und völlig teilnahmslos.

unrest [ʌn'rest] *n* Unruhen *pl*; *(discontent)* Unzufriedenheit *f*. **there was ~ among the workers** die Arbeiter waren unzufrieden.

unrested [ʌn'restɪd] *adj* unausgeruht.

unresting [ʌn'restɪŋ] *adj efforts* unermüdlich.

unrestrained [,ʌnrɪ'streɪnd] *adj* uneingeschränkt, unkontrolliert; *feelings* offen, ungehemmt; *joy, enthusiasm, atmosphere* ungezügelt; *language, behaviour* ausfallend, unbeherrscht.

unrestricted [,ʌnrɪ'strɪktɪd] *adj power, use, growth* unbeschränkt, uneingeschränkt; *access* ungehindert.

unrevealed [,ʌnrɪ'viːld] *adj facts* nicht veröffentlicht. **hitherto ~ secrets** bis jetzt ungelüftete Geheimnisse.

unrewarded [,ʌnrɪ'wɔːdɪd] *adj* unbelohnt. **to go ~** unbelohnt bleiben; *(not gain recognition)* keine Anerkennung finden; **his efforts were ~ by any success** seine Bemühungen waren nicht von Erfolg gekrönt.

unrewarding [,ʌnrɪ'wɔːdɪŋ] *adj work* undankbar; *(financially)* wenig einträglich. **further study of this book would be ~** es würde sich nicht lohnen, das Buch weiterzulesen.

unrhymed [ʌn'raɪmd] *adj* ungereimt.

unrhythmical [ʌn'rɪðmɪkəl] *adj tune, person* unrhythmisch.

unrig [ʌn'rɪg] *vt (Naut)* abtakeln.

unrighteous [ʌn'raɪtʃəs] *adj (Rel)* sündig. **the ~ pl** die Sünder *pl.*

unripe [ʌn'raɪp] *adj* unreif.

unrivalled, *(US also)* **unrivaled** [ʌn'raɪvəld] *adj* unerreicht, unübertroffen. **~ in *or* for quality** von unübertroffener Qualität.

unroadworthiness [ʌn'rəʊd,wɜːðɪnɪs] *n* mangelnde Verkehrssicherheit.

unroadworthy [ʌn'rəʊd,wɜːðɪ] *adj* nicht verkehrssicher.

unroll [ʌn'rəʊl] **1** *vt carpet, map* aufrollen; *(fig) story also* darlegen, schildern. **2** *vi (carpet etc)* sich aufrollen; *(fig) (plot)* sich abwickeln; *(landscape)* sich ausbreiten.

unromantic [,ʌnrə'mæntɪk] *adj* unromantisch.

unrope [ʌn'rəʊp] **1** *vt box* losbinden. **2** *vi (Mountaineering)* sich vom Seil losmachen.

unrounded [ʌn'raʊndɪd] *adj (Phon)* ungerundet.

unruffled [ʌn'rʌfld] *adj person* gelassen; *sea* ruhig, unbewegt; *hair* ordentlich, unzerzaust; *calm* unerschütterlich. **she was quite ~** sie blieb ruhig und gelassen, sie bewahrte die Ruhe.

unruled [ʌn'ruːld] *adj paper* unliniert.

unruliness [ʌn'ruːlɪnɪs] *n* Wildheit, Ungebärdigkeit *f.*

unruly [ʌn'ruːlɪ] *adj (+er) child, behaviour* wild, ungebärdig; *hair* widerspenstig, nicht zu bändigen *attr.*

unsaddle [ʌn'sædl] *vt horse* absatteln; *rider* abwerfen.

unsafe [ʌn'seɪf] *adj ladder, machine, car,* person nicht sicher; *(dangerous) journey, toy, wiring* gefährlich. **this is ~ to eat/drink** das ist nicht genießbar/trinkbar; **to feel ~** sich nicht sicher fühlen; **he looked ~ swaying about at the top of the ladder** er sah gefährlich aus, wie er oben auf der Leiter hin und her schaukelte.

unsaid [ʌn'sed] **1** *pret, ptp of* **unsay. 2** *adj* ungesagt, unausgesprochen. **to leave sth ~** etw unausgesprochen lassen; **it's best left ~** das bleibt besser ungesagt.

unsalaried [ʌn'sælərɪd] *adj* ehrenamtlich.

unsaleable [ʌn'seɪləbl] *adj* unverkäuflich. **to be ~** sich nicht verkaufen lassen; **bread becomes ~ after 2 days** Brot kann man nach 2 Tagen nicht mehr verkaufen.

unsalted [ʌn'sɔːltɪd] *adj* ungesalzen.

unsanitary [ʌn'sænɪtrɪ] *adj* unhygienisch.

unsatisfactoriness [,ʌnsætɪs'fæktərɪnɪs] *n (of service, hotel, work)* Unzulänglichkeit *f*. **the ~ of these results/such a solution** solch unbefriedigende Resultate *pl*/eine so unbefriedigende Lösung; **the teacher had to inform the parents of the ~ of their son's work** der Lehrer mußte die Eltern davon unterrichten, daß die Arbeit ihres Sohnes mangelhaft *or* ungenügend war; **because of his ~ he was not kept on** da er nicht den Erwartungen entsprach, behielt man ihn nicht; **the ~ of our profit margin** die nicht ausreichende Gewinnspanne.

unsatisfactory [,ʌnsætɪs'fæktərɪ] *adj* unbefriedigend; *result also* nicht zufriedenstellend; *profits, figures, percentage* nicht ausreichend; *service, hotel* unzulänglich, schlecht; *(Sch)* mangelhaft; ungenügend. **he was ~** er entsprach nicht den Erwartungen; **this is highly *or* most ~** das läßt sehr zu wünschen übrig.

unsatisfied [ʌn'sætɪsfaɪd] *adj person* nicht zufrieden, unzufrieden; *(not fulfilled)* unbefriedigt, nicht zufrieden; *(not convinced)* nicht überzeugt; *appetite, desire, need* unbefriedigt; *curiosity* unbefriedigt, ungestillt. **the meal left me ~** das Essen hat mich nicht gesättigt; **the book's ending left us ~** wir fanden den Schluß des Buches unbefriedigend; **a job that leaves him ~** eine Arbeit, die ihn nicht befriedigt.

unsatisfying [ʌn'sætɪsfaɪɪŋ] *adj* unbefriedigend; *meal* unzureichend, nicht sättigend.

unsaturated [ʌn'sætʃəreɪtɪd] *adj (Chem)* ungesättigt.

unsavoury, *(US)* **unsavory** [ʌn'seɪvərɪ] *adj* **(a)** *(tasteless) food* fade, geschmacklos.
(b) *(unpleasant) smell, sight* widerwärtig, widerlich, unappetitlich; *appearance (repulsive)* abstoßend, widerwärtig; *(dishonest, shady etc)* fragwürdig; *subject, details, rumours* unerfreulich, unersprießlich; *joke* unfein; *district* übel, fragwürdig; *characters* zwielichtig, übel; *reputation* zweifelhaft, schlecht.

unsay [ʌn'seɪ] *pret, ptp* **unsaid** *vt* ungesagt machen.

unscalable [ʌn'skeɪləbl] *adj* unbezwingbar.

unscaled [ʌn'skeɪld] *adj heights* unbezwungen.

unscarred [ʌn'skɑːd] *adj (fig)* nicht gezeichnet.

unscathed [ʌn'skeɪðd] *adj (lit)* unverletzt, unversehrt; *(by war etc)* unverwundet; *(fig)* unbeschadet; *relationship* heil. **to escape ~** *(fig)* ungeschoren davonkommen.

unscented [ʌn'sentɪd] *adj* ohne Duftstoffe, geruchlos.

unscheduled [ʌn'ʃedjuːld] *adj stop, flight etc* außerfahrplanmäßig; *meeting* außerplanmäßig.

unscholarly [ʌn'skɒləlɪ] *adj work, approach* unwissenschaftlich; *person* unakademisch; *(not learned)* ungelehrt. **he was an ~-looking figure** er sah gar nicht wie ein Gelehrter aus.

unschooled [ʌn'skuːld] *adj* ungebildet, ohne Schulbildung; *talent* unausgebildet. **to be ~ in** nichts wissen über *(+acc).*

unscientific [,ʌnsaɪən'tɪfɪk] *adj* unwissenschaftlich.

unscramble [ʌn'skræmbl] *vt* entwirren, auseinanderklauben *(inf)*; *(Telec) message* entschlüsseln.

unscratched [ʌn'skrætʃt] *adj* nicht zerkratzt; *record* ohne Kratzer; *(unhurt)* heil, ungeschoren.

unscreened [ʌn'skriːnd] *adj* **(a)** *film* nicht gezeigt, unaufgeführt. **many films remain ~** viele Filme werden nie gezeigt *or* bleiben unaufgeführt. **(b)** *(not protected) door, window* offen, nicht abgeschirmt. **(c)** *(not inspected) (by security)* nicht überprüft; *(for disease)* nicht untersucht.

unscrew [ʌn'skruː] **1** *vt (loosen)* losschrauben; *plate, lid also* abschrauben. **to come ~ed** sich lösen. **2** *vi* sich los- *or* abschrauben lassen; *(become loose)* sich lösen.

unscripted [ʌn'skrɪptɪd] *adj* improvisiert.

unscrupulous [ʌn'skruːpjʊləs] *adj person, behaviour* skrupellos, gewissenlos. **he is ~ about money** er ist skrupellos *or* gewissenlos, wenn es um Geld geht.

unscrupulously [ʌn'skruːpjʊləslɪ] *adv see adj.*

unscrupulousness [ʌn'skruːpjʊləsnɪs] *n* Skrupellosigkeit, Gewissenlosigkeit *f.*

unseal [ʌn'siːl] vt öffnen; (remove wax seal also) entsiegeln.
unsealed [ʌn'siːld] adj see vt offen, unverschlossen; unversiegelt.
unseasonable [ʌn'siːznəbl] adj nicht der Jahreszeit entsprechend attr. **the weather is** ~ das Wetter entspricht nicht der Jahreszeit.
unseasonably [ʌn'siːznəblɪ] adv (für die Jahreszeit) ungewöhnlich or außergewöhnlich.
unseasoned [ʌn'siːznd] adj timber nicht abgelagert; food ungewürzt; (fig: inexperienced) troops unerfahren, unerprobt.
unseat [ʌn'siːt] vt rider abwerfen; (from office) seines Amtes entheben.
unseaworthiness [ʌn'siːˌwɜːðɪnɪs] n Seeuntüchtigkeit f.
unseaworthy [ʌn'siːˌwɜːðɪ] adj seeuntüchtig, nicht seetüchtig.
unsecured [ˌʌnsɪ'kjʊəd] adj (Fin) loan, bond ohne Sicherheiten.
unseeded [ʌn'siːdɪd] adj unplaziert.
unseeing [ʌn'siːɪŋ] adj (lit, fig) blind; gaze leer. **to stare at sb with** ~ **eyes** jdn mit leerem Blick anstarren.
unseemliness [ʌn'siːmlɪnɪs] n Unschicklichkeit, Ungebührlichkeit f.
unseemly [ʌn'siːmlɪ] adj unschicklich, ungebührlich.
unseen [ʌn'siːn] **1** adj ungesehen; (invisible) unsichtbar; (unobserved) escape unbemerkt. ~ **translation** (esp Brit Sch, Univ) unvorbereitete Herübersetzung. **2** n (esp Brit) unvorbereitete Herübersetzung.
unselfconscious adj, ~**ly** adv [ˌʌnself'kɒnʃəs, -lɪ] unbefangen.
unselfconsciousness [ˌʌnself'kɒnʃəsnɪs] n Unbefangenheit f.
unselfish adj, ~**ly** adv [ʌn'selfɪʃ, -lɪ] uneigennützig, selbstlos.
unselfishness [ʌn'selfɪʃnɪs] n Uneigennützigkeit, Selbstlosigkeit f.
unsentimental [ˌʌnsentɪ'mentl] adj unsentimental.
unserviceable [ʌn'sɜːvɪsəbl] adj unbrauchbar.
unsettle [ʌn'setl] vt (a) durcheinanderbringen; (throw off balance, confuse) aus dem Gleichgewicht bringen; (agitate, upset) aufregen; (disturb emotionally) verstören; animal, (news) beunruhigen; (defeat, failure, criticism) verunsichern; faith erschüttern. (b) foundations erschüttern.
unsettled [ʌn'setld] adj (a) (unpaid) unbezahlt, unbeglichen; (undecided) question ungeklärt, offen; future unbestimmt, ungewiß, in der Schwebe. **to be in an** ~ **state of mind** mit sich selbst nicht eins sein; **he was** ~ **in his mind about what to do** er war sich (dat) nicht schlüssig, was er tun sollte.
(b) (changeable) weather, (Fin) market unbeständig, veränderlich; (Pol) conditions also unsicher; life, character unstet, unruhig. **to be** ~ durcheinander sein; (thrown off balance) aus dem Gleis geworfen sein; (emotionally disturbed) verstört sein; **to feel** ~ sich nicht wohl fühlen.
(c) (unpopulated) territory unbesiedelt.
unsettling [ʌn'setlɪŋ] adj change, pace of life, travelling aufreibend; time also aufregend; defeat, knowledge verunsichernd; news beunruhigend. **to have an** ~ **influence on sb** jdn durcheinanderbringen, jdn aus dem Gleichgewicht bringen; **to have an** ~ **effect on sb** jdn aus dem Gleis werfen; (defeat, failure also) jdn verunsichern; on children also jdn verstören.
unsexy [ʌn'seksɪ] adj (inf) nicht sexy (inf).
unshackle [ʌn'ʃækl] vt prisoner befreien; (fig also) von seinen Fesseln befreien.
unshaded [ʌn'ʃeɪdɪd] adj (from sun) schattenlos; eyes etc ungeschützt; part of drawing nicht schattiert. ~ **lamp** or **bulb** nackte Birne.
unshakeable [ʌn'ʃeɪkəbl] adj unerschütterlich.
unshaken [ʌn'ʃeɪkən] adj unerschüttert. **he was** ~ **by the accident** der Unfall erschütterte ihn nicht; **his nerve was** ~ er behielt seine Kaltblütigkeit.
unshaven [ʌn'ʃeɪvn] adj unrasiert; (bearded) bärtig.
unsheathe [ʌn'ʃiːð] vt sword (aus der Scheide) ziehen.
unshed [ʌn'ʃed] adj tears ungeweint, unvergossen.
unship [ʌn'ʃɪp] vt cargo löschen, ausladen, entladen; tiller, oars abnehmen; mast abbauen.
unshockable [ʌn'ʃɒkəbl] adj durch nichts zu schockieren.
unshod [ʌn'ʃɒd] adj horse unbeschlagen; person barfuß, ohne Schuhe. **with** ~ **feet** barfuß, mit nackten Füßen.
unshrinkable [ʌn'ʃrɪŋkəbl] adj fabric nicht einlaufend.
unshrinking [ʌn'ʃrɪŋkɪŋ] adj unverzagt, furchtlos, fest.
unsightliness [ʌn'saɪtlɪnɪs] n see adj Unansehnlichkeit f; Häßlichkeit f.
unsightly [ʌn'saɪtlɪ] adj unansehnlich; (stronger) häßlich.
unsigned [ʌn'saɪnd] adj painting unsigniert; letter nicht unterzeichnet, nicht unterschrieben.
unsinkable [ʌn'sɪŋkəbl] adj unsinkbar; battleship unversenkbar.
unsisterly [ʌn'sɪstəlɪ] adj nicht schwesterlich. **a rather** ~ **remark** eine gar nicht schwesterliche Bemerkung.
unskilful, (US also) **unskillful** [ʌn'skɪlfʊl] adj (inexpert) ungeschickt; (clumsy also) unbeholfen.
unskilfully, (US also) **unskillfully** [ʌn'skɪlfəlɪ] adv see adj.
unskilfulness, (US also) **unskillfulness** [ʌn'skɪlfʊlnɪs] n see adj Ungeschicklichkeit f, Mangel m an Geschick, Unbeholfenheit f.
unskilled [ʌn'skɪld] adj (a) work, worker ungelernt. **the** ~ **pl** die ungelernten Arbeiter, die Hilfskräfte pl; **many people remained** ~ viele Menschen erlernten keinen Beruf. (b) (inexperienced) ungeübt, unerfahren.
unskilful etc (US also) see **unskillful** etc.
unslept-in [ʌn'sleptɪn] adj unberührt.
unsnubbable [ʌn'snʌbəbl] adj (inf) dickfellig (inf).
unsociability [ʌnˌsəʊʃə'bɪlɪtɪ] n Ungeselligkeit f.
unsociable [ʌn'səʊʃəbl] adj ungesellig.
unsocial [ʌn'səʊʃəl] adj **to work** ~ **hours** außerhalb der nor-

malen Arbeitszeiten arbeiten; **at this** ~ **hour** zu so nachtschlafender Zeit.
unsold [ʌn'səʊld] adj unverkauft.
unsoldierly [ʌn'səʊldʒəlɪ] adj unsoldatisch.
unsolicited [ˌʌnsə'lɪsɪtɪd] adj unerbeten; manuscript nicht angefordert, unangefordert.
unsolved [ʌn'sɒlvd] adj crossword etc ungelöst; mystery also, crime unaufgeklärt.
unsophisticated [ˌʌnsə'fɪstɪkeɪtɪd] adj (simple) person einfach; style also natürlich, simpel (pej); film, machine also unkompliziert; technique also simpel; (naïve) naiv, simpel; (undiscriminating) unkritisch. **the** ~ **pl** das einfache Volk.
unsought [ʌn'sɔːt] adj unaufgefordert; (unwanted) unerwünscht. **his help was** ~ seine Hilfe kam unaufgefordert.
unsound [ʌn'saʊnd] adj (a) heart, teeth krank; health angegriffen; timber morsch; construction, design unsolide; foundations, finances unsicher, schwach. **the ship was quite** ~ das Schiff war überhaupt nicht seetüchtig.
(b) argument nicht stichhaltig, anfechtbar; advice unvernünftig; judgement unzuverlässig; doctrine unvertretbar; policy, move unklug. **of** ~ **mind** (Jur) unzurechnungsfähig; politically ~ person politisch unzuverlässig; policy politisch unklug; ~ **banking procedures** heikle Bankgeschäfte pl; **the company is** ~ die Firma steht auf schwachen Füßen; **our financial position is** ~ unsere Finanzlage ist heikel; **I'm** ~ **on French grammar** ich bin unsicher in französischer Grammatik; **the book is** ~ **on some points** das Buch weist an einigen Stellen Schwächen auf; **his views on this are** ~ seine Ansichten sind nicht vertretbar.
unsoundness [ʌn'saʊndnɪs] n see adj (a) Krankheit f; Angegriffenheit f; Morschheit f; unsolide Bauweise; Unsicherheit, Schwäche f.
(b) geringe Stichhaltigkeit, Anfechtbarkeit f; Unvernünftigkeit f; Unzuverlässigkeit f; Unvertretbarkeit f; mangelnde Klugheit. ~ **of mind** (Jur) Unzurechnungsfähigkeit f; political ~ politische Unzuverlässigkeit; politische Unklugheit.
unsparing [ʌn'speərɪŋ] adj (a) (lavish) großzügig, verschwenderisch, nicht kleinlich. **to be** ~ **with sth** mit etw nicht geizen; **to be** ~ **in one's efforts** keine Kosten und Mühen scheuen. (b) (unmerciful) criticism schonungslos.
unsparingly [ʌn'speərɪŋlɪ] adv see adj (a) großzügig, verschwenderisch. **to work** ~ **for sth** unermüdlich für etw arbeiten; **he gave his time** ~ er opferte unendlich viel Zeit. (b) schonungslos.
unspeakable [ʌn'spiːkəbl] adj unbeschreiblich. **their** ~ **trade** ihr abscheuliches Geschäft.
unspeakably [ʌn'spiːkəblɪ] adv unbeschreiblich, unsagbar.
unspecified [ʌn'spesɪfaɪd] adj time, amount nicht spezifiziert or genannt, nicht genau angegeben.
unspectacular [ˌʌnspek'tækjʊləʳ] adj wenig eindrucksvoll; career wenig aufsehenerregend. **the team won by an** ~ **2-1** die Mannschaft gewann wenig eindrucksvoll mit 2:1.
unspent [ʌn'spent] adj money nicht ausgegeben; energy nicht verbraucht. **I got back with 50p** ~ ich kam mit 50 Pence in der Tasche zurück.
unspoiled [ʌn'spɔɪld], **unspoilt** [ʌn'spɔɪlt] adj person, fruit unverdorben; goods unbeschädigt; child nicht verwöhnt.
unspoken [ʌn'spəʊkən] adj words, thought unausgesprochen; agreement, consent stillschweigend.
unsporting [ʌn'spɔːtɪŋ], **unsportsmanlike** [ʌn'spɔːtsmənlaɪk] adj conduct, person unsportlich, unfair.
unsprung [ʌn'sprʌŋ] adj seat ungefedert; trap offen, nicht zugeschnappt.
unstable [ʌn'steɪbl] adj structure nicht or wenig stabil; foundations also, area unsicher; weather unbeständig; economy unsicher, schwankend; (Chem, Phys) instabil; (mentally) labil.
unstamped [ʌn'stæmpt] adj letter unfrankiert; document, passport ungestempelt.
unstatesmanlike [ʌn'steɪtsmənlaɪk] adj unstaatsmännisch.
unsteadily [ʌn'stedɪlɪ] adv see adj.
unsteadiness [ʌn'stedɪnɪs] n see adj Unsicherheit f; Wack(e)ligkeit f; Flackern nt; Schwanken nt; Unregelmäßigkeit f.
unsteady [ʌn'stedɪ] **1** adj hand unsicher; ladder wack(e)lig; flame unruhig, flackernd; voice, enonomy schwankend; growth unregelmäßig. **to be** ~ **on one's feet** unsicher or wackelig auf den Beinen sein; **the £ is still** ~ das Pfund schwankt noch.
2 vt durcheinanderbringen; (stronger) aus dem Gleichgewicht bringen.
unstick [ʌn'stɪk] pret, ptp **unstuck** vt lösen, losmachen; see also **unstuck**.
unstinted [ʌn'stɪntɪd] adj praise uneingeschränkt, vorbehaltlos; generosity, devotion, efforts unbegrenzt.
unstinting [ʌn'stɪntɪŋ] adj person großzügig; kindness, generosity uneingeschränkt, unbegrenzt; support uneingeschränkt, vorbehaltlos. **to be** ~ **in one's efforts/praise** keine Kosten und Mühen scheuen/uneingeschränkt or vorbehaltlos loben; **to be** ~ **of one's time** unendlich viel Zeit opfern.
unstintingly [ʌn'stɪntɪŋlɪ] adv großzügig; generous unendlich; work, labour unermüdlich; donate, contribute time or money verschwenderisch; praise uneingeschränkt, vorbehaltlos.
unstitch [ʌn'stɪtʃ] vt seam auftrennen; zip heraustrennen. **to come** ~**ed** aufgehen.
unstop [ʌn'stɒp] vt sink, drain freimachen; bottle öffnen, aufmachen.
unstoppable [ʌn'stɒpəbl] adj nicht aufzuhalten.
unstrap [ʌn'stræp] vt case etc aufschnallen. **to** ~ **sth (from sth)** etw (von etw) los- or abschnallen.
unstreamed [ʌn'striːmd] adj (Brit Sch) nicht in Leistungsgruppen eingeteilt.
unstressed [ʌn'strest] adj (Phon) unbetont.

unstring [ʌn'strɪŋ] pret, ptp **unstrung** vt violin die Saiten abnehmen or entfernen von; beads abfädeln.

unstructured [ʌn'strʌktʃəd] adj unstrukturiert, nicht strukturiert. **the child did better in an ~ situation** das Kind kam in einer unstrukturierten Umgebung besser zurecht.

unstrung [ʌn'strʌŋ] **1** pret, ptp of **unstring**. **2** adj (a) person demoralisiert, entnervt; nerves zerrüttet. **(b)** violin unbesaitet.

unstuck [ʌn'stʌk] **1** pret, ptp of **unstick**.

2 adj **to come ~** (stamp, notice) sich lösen; (inf) (plan) danebengehen (inf), schiefgehen (inf); (speaker, actor) steckenbleiben; (in exam) ins Schwimmen geraten; **the pay policy seems to have come ~** die Lohnpolitik scheint langsam aus dem Gleis zu kommen; **where they came ~ was ...** sie sind daran gescheitert, daß ...

unstudied [ʌn'stʌdɪd] adj grace etc ungekünstelt, natürlich.

unsubdued [ˌʌnsəb'dju:d] adj unbezwungen, unbesiegt. **the child was quite ~** das Kind war ganz unbeeindruckt.

unsubsidized [ʌn'sʌbsɪdaɪzd] adj unsubventioniert.

unsubstantial [ˌʌnsəb'stænʃəl] adj (flimsy) structure leicht, dürftig; (immaterial) ghost körperlos, wesenlos; meal leicht; evidence, proof nicht überzeugend, nicht schlagkräftig; claim ungerechtfertigt. **the boat seemed almost ~ in the mist** das Boot erschien im Dunst schemenhaft.

unsubstantiated [ˌʌnsəb'stænʃieitid] adj accusation, testimony, rumour unbegründet. **his claim was ~ by any evidence** seine Behauptung wurde durch keinerlei Indizien erhärtet.

unsubtle [ʌn'sʌtl] adj plump. **how ~ can you get!** plumper geht's nicht!

unsuccessful [ˌʌnsək'sesfʊl] adj negotiations, venture, visit, meeting, person etc erfolglos, ergebnislos; writer, painter erfolglos, ohne Erfolg; candidate abgewiesen; attempt vergeblich; marriage, outcome unglücklich. **to be ~ in doing sth** keinen Erfolg damit haben, etw zu tun; **I tried to persuade him but was ~** ich habe versucht, ihn zu überreden, hatte aber keinen Erfolg; **he is ~ in everything** he does nichts gelingt ihm; **I applied for three jobs but was ~** ich habe mich ohne Erfolg or erfolglos für drei Stellen beworben; **he was ~ in his exam** er hat kein Glück in seinem Examen gehabt; **he is ~ with women** er hat kein Glück or keinen Erfolg bei Frauen.

unsuccessfully [ˌʌnsək'sesfəlɪ] adv erfolglos; try vergeblich; apply ohne Erfolg, vergebens. **I tried ~ to grow tomatoes** ich habe ohne Erfolg versucht, Tomaten zu ziehen.

unsuitability [ˌʌnsu:tə'bɪlɪtɪ] n see adj Unangebrachtheit f; Ungeeignetsein nt. **his ~ for the job** seine mangelnde Eignung für die Stelle; **I commented on the ~ of his clothes/language** ich machte eine Bemerkung über seine unpassende Kleidung/seine unangebrachte Ausdrucksweise; **their ~ as partners** is clear es ist klar, daß sie keine geeigneten Partner füreinander sind.

unsuitable [ʌn'su:təbl] adj unpassend; language, attitude also unangebracht; moment, clothes, colour also ungeeignet. **it would be ~ at this moment to ...** es wäre im Augenblick unangebracht, ...; **this film is ~ for children** dieser Film ist für Kinder ungeeignet or nicht geeignet; **he's ~ for the post** er ist für die Stelle nicht geeignet; **she is ~ for him** sie ist nicht die Richtige für ihn; **we're ~ for each other** wir passen nicht zusammen; **she married a very ~ person** sie hat jemanden geheiratet, der gar nicht zu ihr paßt.

unsuitably [ʌn'su:təblɪ] adv dressed (for weather conditions) unzweckmäßig; (for occasion) unpassend; designed schlecht, ungeeignet. **they are ~ matched** sie passen nicht zusammen.

unsuited [ʌn'su:tɪd] adj **to be ~ for or to sth** für etw ungeeignet or untauglich sein; **to be ~ to do sth** sich nicht dazu eignen or nicht dazu taugen, etw zu tun; **to be ~ to sb** für jdm passen; **they are ~ (to each other)** sie passen nicht zusammen.

unsullied [ʌn'sʌlɪd] adj virtue, honour etc makellos, unbefleckt (liter); snow unberührt.

unsung [ʌn'sʌŋ] adj heroes, deeds unbesungen.

unsupported [ˌʌnsə'pɔ:tɪd] adj roof, person ungestützt, ohne Stütze; troops ohne Unterstützung; mother alleinstehend; family ohne Unterhalt; claim, theory ohne Beweise, nicht auf Fakten gestützt; statement unbestätigt, durch nichts gestützt. **if such families were ~ by the State** wenn solche Familien nicht vom Staat unterstützt würden; **should the bank leave us financially ~** sollte die Bank uns finanziell nicht absichern or nicht unter die Arme greifen; **the candidate/motion was ~** der Kandidat/Antrag fand keine Unterstützung.

unsure [ʌn'ʃʊə] adj person unsicher; (unreliable) method also unzuverlässig. **to be ~ of oneself** unsicher sein; **to be ~ (of sth)** sich (dat) (einer Sache gen) nicht sicher sein; **I'm ~ of him** ich bin mir bei ihm nicht sicher; **I am ~ of my welcome** ich bin nicht sicher, ob ich willkommen bin.

unsurpassable [ˌʌnsə'pɑ:səbl] adj unübertrefflich.

unsurpassed [ˌʌnsə'pɑ:st] adj unübertroffen. **to be ~ by anybody** von niemandem übertroffen werden.

unsuspected [ˌʌnsə'spektɪd] adj presence nicht vermutet, unvermutet; consequences unerwartet, ungeahnt; oilfields, coal deposits, causes unvermutet; wealth ungeahnt. **to be ~** (person) nicht unter Verdacht stehen.

unsuspecting adj, **~ly** adv [ˌʌnsə'spektɪŋ, -lɪ] ahnungslos, nichtsahnend.

unsuspicious [ˌʌnsə'spɪʃəs] adj (feeling no suspicion) arglos; (causing no suspicion) unverdächtig, harmlos.

unsweetened [ˌʌn'swi:tnd] adj ungesüßt.

unswerving [ʌn'swɜ:vɪŋ] adj resolve, loyalty unerschütterlich, unbeirrbar. **the road followed its ~ course across the desert** die Straße führte schnurgerade durch die Wüste.

unswervingly [ʌn'swɜ:vɪŋlɪ] adv **to be ~ loyal to sb** jdm unerschütterlich or unbeirrbar treu sein; **to hold ~ to one's course** unbeirrbar seinen Weg gehen.

unsymmetrical [ˌʌnsɪ'metrɪkəl] adj unsymmetrisch.

unsympathetic [ˌʌnsɪmpə'θetɪk] adj **(a)** (unfeeling) gefühllos, wenig mitfühlend; reaction, attitude, response ablehnend, abweisend. **I am not ~ to your request** ich stehe Ihrer Bitte nicht ablehnend gegenüber. **(b)** (unlikeable) unsympathisch.

unsympathetically [ˌʌnsɪmpə'θetɪkəlɪ] adv ohne Mitgefühl; say also gefühllos, hart.

unsystematic adj, **~ally** adv [ˌʌnsɪstɪ'mætɪk, -əlɪ] planlos, unsystematisch, ohne System.

untainted [ʌn'teɪntɪd] adj einwandfrei, tadellos; food also, person, mind unverdorben; reputation also makellos.

untalented [ʌn'tæləntɪd] adj unbegabt, untalentiert.

untam(e)able [ʌn'teɪməbl] adj animal unzähmbar; (fig) unbezähmbar, nicht zu bändigen pred.

untamed [ʌn'teɪmd] adj animal ungezähmt; jungle wild; person, pride ungebändigt; temper ungezügelt.

untangle [ʌn'tæŋgl] vt (lit, fig) entwirren.

untanned [ʌn'tænd] adj hide ungegerbt.

untapped [ʌn'tæpt] adj barrel unangezapft; resources also, source of wealth, talent ungenutzt.

untarnished [ʌn'tɑ:nɪʃt] adj makellos; silver also nicht angelaufen; (fig) name also einwandfrei, unbefleckt (liter).

untasted [ʌn'teɪstɪd] adj (lit, fig) ungekostet; food also unberührt. **the pleasures he had left ~** die Freuden, die er nicht gekostet hatte.

untaught [ʌn'tɔ:t] adj (not trained) person nicht ausgebildet; ability angeboren; behaviour natürlich. **basic skills which go ~ in our schools** Grundfähigkeiten, die in unseren Schulen nicht vermittelt werden.

untaxed [ʌn'tækst] adj goods, income steuerfrei, unbesteuert; car unversteuert.

unteachable [ʌn'ti:tʃəbl] adj person unbelehrbar; subject nicht lehrbar. **it is ~ at this level** auf diesem Niveau kann man es nicht lehren.

untempered [ʌn'tempəd] adj steel ungehärtet, unvergütet; rage unbändig. **justice ~ by mercy** Gerechtigkeit, die durch keinerlei Gnade gemildert wird/wurde.

untenable [ʌn'tenəbl] adj (lit, fig) unhaltbar.

untenanted [ʌn'tenəntɪd] adj house unbewohnt, leer.

untended [ʌn'tendɪd] adj patient unbehütet, unbewacht; garden vernachlässigt, ungepflegt.

untested [ʌn'testɪd] adj person unerprobt; theory, product also ungetestet, ungeprüft. **~ players** Spieler, die sich noch nicht bewährt haben.

unthinkable [ʌn'θɪŋkəbl] adj undenkbar, unvorstellbar; (Philos) undenkbar; (too horrible) unvorstellbar.

unthinking [ʌn'θɪŋkɪŋ] adj (thoughtless, unintentional) unbedacht, gedankenlos; (uncritical) bedenkenlos, blind.

unthinkingly [ʌn'θɪŋkɪŋlɪ] adv see adj.

unthought-of [ʌn'θɔ:tɒv] adj (inconceivable) undenkbar, unvorstellbar. **these hitherto ~ objections** diese Einwände, auf die bis dahin niemand gekommen war.

unthought-out [ˌʌnθɔ:t'aʊt] adj nicht (gut) durchdacht, unausgegoren (inf).

unthread [ʌn'θred] vt needle ausfädeln; pearls abfädeln.

untidily [ʌn'taɪdɪlɪ] adv see adj.

untidiness [ʌn'taɪdɪnɪs] n (of room) Unordnung, Unaufgeräumtheit f; (of person, dress) Unordentlichkeit f. **the ~ of the kitchen** die Unordnung in der Küche.

untidy [ʌn'taɪdɪ] adj (+er) unordentlich.

untie [ʌn'taɪ] vt knot lösen; string, tie, shoelaces also aufbinden; parcel aufknoten; person, animal, hands losbinden.

until [ən'tɪl] **1** prep **(a)** bis. **from morning ~ night** von morgens bis abends, vom Morgen bis zum Abend; **~ now** bis jetzt; **~ then** bis dahin.

(b) not ~ (in future) nicht vor (+dat); (in past) erst; **I didn't leave him ~ the following day** ich habe ihn erst am folgenden Tag verlassen, ich bin bis zum nächsten Tag bei ihm geblieben; **the work was not begun ~ 1970** die Arbeiten wurden erst 1970 begonnen; **I had heard nothing of it ~ five minutes ago** bis vor fünf Minuten wußte ich (noch) nichts davon, ich habe erst vor fünf Minuten davon gehört.

2 conj **(a)** bis. **wait ~ I come** warten Sie, bis ich komme.

(b) not ~ (in future) nicht bevor, erst wenn; (in past) nicht bis, erst als; **he won't come ~ you invite him** er kommt erst, wenn Sie ihn einladen; **they did nothing ~ we came** bis wir kamen, taten sie nichts; **don't start ~ I come** fangen Sie nicht an, bevor ich da bin; **fangen** Sie erst an, wenn ich da bin; **they didn't start ~ we came** sie fingen erst an, als wir da waren, sie fingen nicht an, bevor wir da waren.

untimeliness [ʌn'taɪmlɪnɪs] n (of death) Vorzeitigkeit f; (of end also) Verfrühtheit f. **because of the ~ of his arrival/this development** weil er/diese Entwicklung zur falschen Zeit kam.

untimely [ʌn'taɪmlɪ] adj (premature) death vorzeitig; end also verfrüht; (inopportune) moment unpassend, ungelegen; development, occurrence unpassend, ungelegen, zur falschen Zeit; shower, remark zur falschen Zeit. **his arrival was most ~** seine Ankunft kam sehr ungelegen.

untiring [ʌn'taɪərɪŋ] adj work, effort unermüdlich. **to be ~ in one's efforts** unermüdliche Anstrengungen machen.

untiringly [ʌn'taɪərɪŋlɪ] adv unermüdlich.

unto ['ʌntʊ] prep (old, liter) see to.

untold ['ʌntəʊld] adj story nicht erzählt, nicht berichtet; secret ungelüftet; wealth unermeßlich; agony, delights unsäglich; stars etc ungezählt, unzählig, zahllos. **this story is better left ~** über diese Geschichte schweigt man besser; **he died with his secret still ~** er nahm sein Geheimnis mit ins Grab; **~ thousands** unzählig viele.

untouchable [ʌn'tʌtʃəbl] **1** adj unberührbar. **2** n Unberührbare(r) mf.

untouched [ʌn'tʌtʃt] adj **(a)** (unhandled, unused) unberührt,

unangetastet; *bottle, box of sweets etc also* nicht angebrochen; (*unmentioned*) nicht erwähnt. ~ by human hand nicht von Menschenhand berührt; he left his meal ~ er ließ sein Essen unberührt stehen.
(b) (*unharmed*) heil, unversehrt; (*unaffected*) unberührt; (*unmoved*) ungerührt, unbewegt, unbeeindruckt. he was ~ by her tears ihre Tränen ließen ihn kalt.
(c) (*unequalled*) unerreicht. ~ for quality in der Qualität unerreicht; he is ~ by anyone niemand kommt ihm gleich.

untoward [,ʌntə'wɔːd] *adj* (*unfortunate*) *event* unglücklich, bedauerlich; (*unseemly*) unpassend, ungehörig. nothing ~ had happened es war kein Unheil geschehen.

untrained [ʌn'treɪnd] *adj person, teacher* unausgebildet; *voice* ungeschult; *animal* undressiert. to the ~ ear/eye dem ungeschulten Ohr/Auge.

untrammelled, (*US also*) **untrammeled** [ʌn'træməld] *adj* unbeschränkt. to be ~ by sth nicht von etw beschränkt werden.

untranslatable [,ʌntrænz'leɪtəbl] *adj* unübersetzbar.

untravelled, (*US*) **untraveled** [ʌn'trævld] *adj road* unbefahren; *person* nicht weitgereist, nicht weit herumgekommen.

untreated [ʌn'triːtɪd] *adj* unbehandelt.

untried [ʌn'traɪd] *adj* **(a)** (*not tested*) *person* unerprobt; *product, method also* ungetestet; (*not attempted*) unversucht.
(b) (*Jur*) *case* nicht verhandelt; *person* nicht vor Gericht gestellt. the case is still ~ der Fall ist noch nicht verhandelt worden; the case/the offender can remain ~ for months die Verhandlung kann monatelang verzögert werden/der Rechtsbrecher wird zuweilen erst nach Monaten vor Gericht gestellt.

untrodden [ʌn'trɒdn] *adj path* verlassen; *snow* unberührt. ~ paths (*fig*) neue Wege *pl*.

untroubled [ʌn'trʌbld] *adj period, ghost* friedlich, ruhig; *person also* ungestört; *smile also* unbeschwert. to be ~ by the news eine Nachricht gleichmütig hinnehmen; the children seemed ~ by the heat die Hitze schien den Kindern nichts anzuhaben *or* auszumachen; they were ~ by thoughts of the future der Gedanke an die Zukunft belastete sie nicht.

untrue [ʌn'truː] *adj* **(a)** (*false*) unwahr, falsch; (*Tech*) *reading, instrument* inkorrekt, ungenau. **(b)** (*unfaithful*) *person* untreu. to be ~ to sb jdm untreu sein.

untrustworthy [ʌn'trʌst,wɜːðɪ] *adj* (*not reliable*) *source, book, person* unzuverlässig; (*not worthy of confidence*) *person* nicht vertrauenswürdig.

untruth [ʌn'truːθ] *n* Unwahrheit *f*.

untruthful [ʌn'truːθʊl] *adj statement* unwahr; *person* unaufrichtig. you're being ~ da bist du unaufrichtig.

untruthfully [ʌn'truːθʊlɪ] *adv* fälschlich. he said, quite ~, that ... er sagte, und das war wirklich unaufrichtig, daß ...

untruthfulness [ʌn'truːθʊlnɪs] *n see adj* Unwahrheit *f*; Unaufrichtigkeit *f*.

untuneful [ʌn'tjuːnfʊl] *adj* unmelodisch.

unturned [ʌn'tɜːnd] *adj see* stone.

untutored [ʌn'tjuːtəd] *adj taste, person* ungeschult.

untypical [ʌn'tɪpɪkl] *adj* untypisch (*of* für).

unusable [ʌn'juːzəbl] *adj* unbrauchbar.

unused[1] [ʌn'juːzd] *adj* (*new*) unbenutzt, ungebraucht; (*not made use of*) ungenutzt; (*no longer used*) nicht mehr benutzt *or* gebraucht. but his suggestion went ~ aber von seinem Vorschlag wurde kein Gebrauch gemacht.

unused[2] [ʌn'juːst] *adj* to be ~ to sth nicht an etw (*acc*) gewöhnt sein, etw (*acc*) nicht gewohnt sein; to be ~ to doing sth nicht daran gewöhnt sein *or* es nicht gewohnt sein, etw zu tun.

unusual [ʌn'juːʒʊəl] *adj* (*uncommon*) ungewöhnlich; (*exceptional*) außergewöhnlich. it's ~ for him to be late er kommt normalerweise nicht zu spät; that's not ~ for him das wundert mich überhaupt nicht; how ~! das kommt selten vor; (*iro*) welch' Wunder!; that's ~ for him das ist sonst nicht seine Art; how do you like my new hat? – well, it's ~ wie gefällt Ihnen mein neuer Hut? – na, es ist mal was anderes.

unusually [ʌn'juːʒʊlɪ] *adv see adj.* most ~, he was late ganz gegen jede Gewohnheit kam er zu spät.

unutterable [ʌn'ʌtərəbl] *adj joy, longing, sadness* unsäglich, unbeschreiblich; (*inf also*) riesig, Riesen-. an act of ~ folly (*inf*) eine Riesendummheit (*inf*).

unutterably [ʌn'ʌtərəblɪ] *adv* unsäglich, unbeschreiblich. ~ stupid (*inf*) unsagbar blöd (*inf*).

unvaried [ʌn'veərɪd] *adj* unverändert; (*pej*) eintönig.

unvarnished [ʌn'vɑːnɪʃt] *adj wood* ungefirnißt, unlackiert; (*fig*) *truth* ungeschminkt.

unvarying [ʌn'veərɪɪŋ] *adj* gleichbleibend, unveränderlich.

unveil [ʌn'veɪl] **1** *vt statue, painting, plan* enthüllen; (*Comm*) *car* vorstellen; *face* entschleiern. women mustn't go ~ed Frauen dürfen nicht unverschleiert gehen. **2** *vi* sich entschleiern, den Schleier fallenlassen.

unveiling [ʌn'veɪlɪŋ] *n* (*lit, fig*) Enthüllung *f*. ~ ceremony Enthüllung *f*.

unventilated [ʌn'ventɪleɪtɪd] *adj* ungelüftet, nicht ventiliert.

unverifiable [ʌn'verɪfaɪəbl] *adj* nicht beweisbar, unverifizierbar (*geh*).

unverified [ʌn'verɪfaɪd] *adj* unbewiesen.

unversed [ʌn'vɜːst] *adj*: ~ in nicht vertraut mit, unbewandert in (+*dat*).

unvisited [ʌn'vɪzɪtɪd] *adj* nicht besucht. we left Heidelberg with the castle ~ wir verließen Heidelberg, ohne das Schloß besucht zu haben.

unvoiced [ʌn'vɔɪst] *adj* **(a)** unausgesprochen. **(b)** (*Phon*) stimmlos.

unwanted [ʌn'wɒntɪd] *adj furniture, clothing* unerwünscht. sometimes you make me feel ~ manchmal komme ich mir (bei dir) richtig unerwünscht vor.

unwarily [ʌn'weərɪlɪ] *adv see adj.*

unwariness [ʌn'weərɪnɪs] *n* Unvorsichtigkeit, Unbesonnenheit, Unachtsamkeit *f*.

unwarlike [ʌn'wɔːlaɪk] *adj* friedliebend, friedlich.

unwarrantable [ʌn'wɒrəntəbl] *adj* nicht zu rechtfertigen *pred or* rechtfertigend *attr*.

unwarranted [ʌn'wɒrəntɪd] *adj* ungerechtfertigt.

unwary [ʌn'weərɪ] *adj* unvorsichtig, unbesonnen, unachtsam.

unwashed [ʌn'wɒʃt] *adj* ungewaschen; *dishes* ungespült. the great ~ *pl* (*hum*) der Pöbel.

unwavering [ʌn'weɪvərɪŋ] *adj faith, resolve* unerschütterlich; *gaze* fest, unbewegt; *course* beharrlich.

unwaveringly [ʌn'weɪvərɪŋlɪ] *adv see adj.*

unweaned [ʌn'wiːnd] *adj baby* (noch) nicht entwöhnt.

unwearable [ʌn'weərəbl] *adj* it's ~ das kann man nicht tragen.

unwearied [ʌn'wɪərɪd], **unwearying** [ʌn'wɪərɪɪŋ] *adj* unermüdlich.

unwelcome [ʌn'welkəm] *adj visitor* unwillkommen; *news, memories* unerfreulich, unangenehm. the money was not ~ das Geld war höchst willkommen.

unwelcoming [ʌn'welkəmɪŋ] *adj manner* abweisend, unfreundlich; *host also* ungastlich.

unwell [ʌn'wel] *adj pred* unwohl, nicht wohl. to be *or* feel ~ (a little) ~ sich nicht (recht) wohl fühlen; I am afraid he's rather ~ today es geht ihm heute leider gar nicht gut.

unwholesome [ʌn'həʊlsəm] *adj* ungesund; *influence* ungut, verderblich; *appearance, place* schmierig; *food* minderwertig; *jokes* schmutzig. they are rather ~ company for her sie sind nicht gerade ein guter Umgang für sie.

unwholesomeness [ʌn'həʊlsəmnɪs] *n see adj* Ungesundheit *f*; Verderblichkeit *f*; Schmierigkeit *f*; Minderwertigkeit *f*; Schmutzigkeit *f*.

unwieldy [ʌn'wiːldɪ] *adj tool* unhandlich; *object also* sperrig; (*clumsy*) *body* schwerfällig, unbeholfen.

unwilling [ʌn'wɪlɪŋ] *adj helper, admiration, pupil* widerwillig; *accomplice* unfreiwillig. you can't force an ~ horse ein Pferd, das nicht will, kann man nicht zwingen; to be ~ to do sth nicht bereit *or* gewillt *or* willens (*geh*) sein, etw zu tun; to be ~ for sth to do sth nicht wollen, daß jd etw tut.

unwillingly [ʌn'wɪlɪŋlɪ] *adv* widerwillig.

unwillingness [ʌn'wɪlɪŋnɪs] *n see adj* Widerwilligkeit *f*; Unfreiwilligkeit *f*. their ~ to compromise ihre mangelnde Kompromißbereitschaft.

unwind [ʌn'waɪnd] *pret, ptp* **unwound** **1** *vt thread, film, tape* abwickeln; (*untangle*) entwirren. **2** *vi* **(a)** sich abwickeln; (*fig: story, plot*) sich entwickeln, sich entfalten. **(b)** (*inf: relax*) abschalten (*inf*), sich entspannen.

unwise [ʌn'waɪz] *adj* unklug. they were ~ enough to believe him sie waren so töricht, ihm das zu glauben.

unwisely [ʌn'waɪzlɪ] *adv see adj.* rather ~ the Government agreed die Regierung hat unklugerweise zugestimmt.

unwished-for [ʌn'wɪʃtfɔːʳ] *adj* unerwünscht.

unwitting [ʌn'wɪtɪŋ] *adj accomplice* unbewußt, unwissentlich; *action also* unabsichtlich; *victim* ahnungslos. he was the ~ cause of the argument er war unbewußt die Ursache des Streits, er war, ohne es zu wissen, die Ursache des Streits.

unwittingly [ʌn'wɪtɪŋlɪ] *adv* I agreed, all ~, to take part ich erklärte mich völlig ahnungslos dazu bereit mitzumachen; all ~, he provoked the tragedy ganz unbewußt verursachte er die Tragödie.

unwomanly [ʌn'wʊmənlɪ] *adj* unweiblich.

unwonted [ʌn'wəʊntɪd] *adj* ungewohnt. at this ~ hour! zu dieser unchristlichen Zeit!

unwontedly [ʌn'wəʊntɪdlɪ] *adv* ungewohnt.

unworkable [ʌn'wɜːkəbl] *adj scheme, idea* undurchführbar; (*Min*) *mine* nicht abbaubar.

unworkmanlike [ʌn'wɜːkmənlaɪk] *adj job* unfachmännisch.

unworldliness [ʌn'wɜːldlɪnɪs] *n see adj* Weltabgewandtheit *f*; Weltfremdheit *f*.

unworldly [ʌn'wɜːldlɪ] *adj life* weltabgewandt; (*naïve*) weltfremd.

unworn [ʌn'wɔːn] *adj* (*new*) ungetragen.

unworried [ʌn'wʌrɪd] *adj* unbekümmert, sorglos. he was quite ~ by my criticism meine Kritik (be)kümmerte ihn überhaupt nicht.

unworthily [ʌn'wɜːðɪlɪ] *adv behave* unwürdig. he said, rather ~, that ... er sagte, und das war eigentlich unter seiner Würde, daß ...

unworthiness [ʌn'wɜːðɪnɪs] *n* Unwürdigkeit *f*.

unworthy [ʌn'wɜːðɪ] *adj person* nicht wert (*of gen*); *conduct also* nicht würdig, unwürdig (*of gen*). to be ~ to do sth (es) nicht wert sein, etw zu tun; to be ~ of an honour einer Ehre (*gen*) nicht wert sein (*geh*); this is ~ of you das ist unter deiner Würde; it is ~ of our attention das verdient unsere Aufmerksamkeit nicht, das ist unserer Aufmerksamkeit (*gen*) nicht wert; it was ~ of you not to accept their kind offer es war nicht anständig von dir, ihren freundlichen Vorschlag nicht anzunehmen; it would be ~ of me not to mention also ... es wäre nicht recht, wenn ich nicht auch ... erwähnen würde.

unwound [ʌn'waʊnd] *pret, ptp of* unwind.

unwounded [ʌn'wuːndɪd] *adj* nicht verwundet, unverwundet.

unwrap [ʌn'ræp] *vt* auspacken, auswickeln.

unwritten [ʌn'rɪtn] *adj story, book, constitution* ungeschrieben; *agreement* stillschweigend. ~ law (*Jur, fig*) ungeschriebenes Gesetz.

unyielding [ʌn'jiːldɪŋ] *adj substance* unnachgiebig; (*fig*) *person, demand also, resistance* hart.

unyoke [ʌn'jəʊk] *vt* ausspannen. he ~d his oxen from the plough er spannte die Ochsen aus.

unzip [ʌn'zɪp] **1** *vt* zip aufmachen; *dress, case* den Reißverschluß aufmachen an (+*dat*). would you please ~ me? kannst du bitte mir den Reißverschluß aufmachen?

2 vi (zip) aufgehen, sich öffnen. **this dress won't ~ der Reißverschluß an dem Kleid geht nicht auf** or **läßt sich nicht öffnen; my dress must have ~ped der Reißverschluß an meinem Kleid muß aufgegangen sein.**

up [ʌp] **1** adv **(a)** (in high or higher position) oben; (to higher position) nach oben. ~ there dort oben, droben (liter, S Ger); ~ **here on the roof** hier oben auf dem Dach; **on your way ~ (to see us/them)** auf dem Weg (zu uns/ihnen) herauf/hinauf; **he climbed all the way ~ (to us/them)** er ist den ganzen Weg (zu uns/ihnen) herauf-/hinaufgeklettert or hochgeklettert; **to throw sth ~** etw hochwerfen; **to stop halfway ~** auf halber Höhe anhalten; (in standing up) auf halbem Weg einhalten; **we were 6,000 m ~ when ...** wir waren 6.000 m hoch, als ...; **5 floors ~ 5 Stockwerke hoch; 3 floors ~ from me** 3 Stockwerke über mir; **they were ~ above** sie waren hoch oben; **I looked ~ above** ich schaute nach oben; **this side ~** oben!, (diese Seite) oben!; **a little further ~** ein bißchen weiter oben; **to go a little further ~** ein bißchen höher (hinauf)gehen; **hang the picture a bit higher ~** häng das Bild ein bißchen höher; **from ~ on the hill** vom Berg oben; **~ on top (of the cupboard)** ganz oben (auf dem Schrank); **~ in the mountains/sky** oben or droben (liter, S Ger) in den Bergen/am Himmel, in den Bergen/am Himmel oben or droben (liter, S Ger); **the temperature was ~ in the thirties** die Temperatur war in den dreißig; **the sun/moon is ~** die Sonne/der Mond ist aufgegangen; **the tide is ~** es ist Flut, die Flut ist da; **the wind is ~** der Wind hat aufgefrischt; **with his collar ~** mit hochgeschlagenem Kragen; **the road is ~** die Straße ist aufgegraben; **to be ~ among** or **with the leaders** vorn bei den Führenden sein; **to move ~ into the lead** nach vorn an die Spitze kommen; **Red Rum with Joe Smith ~** Red Rum unter Joe Smith; **a truck with a load of bricks ~** (inf) ein Lastwagen mit einer Ladung Ziegelsteinen (drauf); **~ and away the balloon sailed** der Ballon stieg auf und segelte davon; **then ~ jumps Richard and says ...** und dann springt Richard auf und sagt ...; **the needle was ~ on 95** die Nadel stand auf 95; **come on, ~,** that's my chair! komm, auf mit dir, das ist mein Stuhl!; **~! he shouted to his horse** spring! schrie er seinem Pferd zu; **~ with the Liberals!** hoch die Liberalen; **~ with Spurs!** Spurs hoch!

(b) (installed, built) **to be ~** (building) stehen; (tent also) aufgeschlagen sein; (scaffolding) aufgestellt sein; (notice) hängen, angeschlagen sein; (picture) hängen, aufgehängt sein; (shutters) zu sein; (shelves, wallpaper, curtains, pictures) hängen; **they're putting ~ a new cinema** sie bauen ein neues Kino; **stick the notice ~ here** häng den Anschlag hier hin.

(c) (not in bed) auf. **~ (with you)!** auf mit dir!, raus aus dem Bett (inf); **to get ~** aufstehen; **to be ~ and about** auf sein; (after illness also) auf den Beinen sein; **she was ~ all night with him** (looking after) sie war seinetwegen die ganze Nacht auf.

(d) (geographically) (north of speaker) oben; (of students) am Studienort. **~ in Inverness** in Inverness oben, oben in Inverness; **we are going ~ to Aberdeen** wir fahren nach Aberdeen (hinauf); **to be/go ~ north** im Norden sein/in den Norden fahren; **~ from the country** vom Lande; **on my way ~ to York/London** auf dem Weg nach York/London; **we're ~ for the day** wir sind (nur) für heute hier; **to go ~ to Cambridge** (zum Studium) nach Cambridge gehen; **he was ~ at Oxford in 1972** er hat 1972 in Oxford studiert; **the students are only ~ for half the year** die Studenten sind nur die Hälfte des Jahres am Studienort; **he was ~ at Susie's place** er war bei Susie zu Hause.

(e) (in price, value) gestiegen (on gegenüber). **potatoes are ~ again** die Kartoffelpreise sind wieder gestiegen; **my shares are ~ 10p** meine Aktien sind um 10 Pence gestiegen; **then ~ go prices again** und wieder steigen die Preise.

(f) (in score) **to be 3 goals ~** mit 3 Toren führen or vorn liegen (on gegenüber); **the score was 9 ~** (US) es stand 9 beide; **I'll play you 100 ~** ich spiele auf 100 (mit dir); **we were £100 ~ on the deal** wir haben bei dem Geschäft £ 100 gemacht; **to be one ~ on sb** jdm um einen Schritt voraus sein.

(g) (upwards) **from £2 ~** von £ 2 (an) aufwärts, ab £ 2; **from the age of 13 ~** ab (dem Alter von) 13 Jahren, von 13 Jahren aufwärts; **~ to £10** bis zu £ 10.

(h) (inf: wrong) **what's ~?** was ist los?; **what's ~ with him?** was ist mit dem los?, was ist los mit ihm?; **there's something ~** (wrong) da stimmt irgend etwas nicht; (happening) da ist irgend etwas im Gange; **there's something ~ with it** irgendetwas stimmt damit nicht or hier nicht.

(i) (knowledgeable) firm, beschlagen (in, on in +dat). **he's well ~ in** or in **foreign affairs** in Auslandsfragen kennt er sich aus or ist er firm; **how are you ~ on French history?** wie gut kennst du dich in französischer Geschichte aus?

(j) (finished) **time's ~** deine Zeit ist um or zu Ende; **our holiday is nearly ~** unser Urlaub ist fast zu Ende or vorüber; **to eat/use sth ~** etw aufessen/aufbrauchen; **it's all ~ with him** (inf) es ist aus mit ihm (inf), es ist mit ihm zu Ende.

(k) **to be ~ for sale/discussion** zu verkaufen sein/zur Diskussion stehen; **to be ~ for election** (candidate) zur Wahl aufgestellt sein; (candidates) zur Wahl stehen; **the matter is ~ before the committee** die Sache ist vor dem Ausschuß; **the boys were ~ before the headmaster** die Jungen sind vor dem Direktor zitiert worden; **to be ~ for trial** vor Gericht stehen; **to be ~ before the Court/before Judge X** (case) verhandelt werden/vor Richter X verhandelt werden; (person) vor Gericht/Richter X stehen.

(l) (as far as) bis. **~ to now/here** bis jetzt/hier; **to count ~ to 100** bis 100 zählen; **it holds ~ to 8** es faßt bis zu 8; **I'm ~ to here in work** ich stecke bis hier in Arbeit; **what page are you ~ to?** auf welcher Seite bist du?, bis zu welcher Seite bist du gekommen?

(m) **~ to** (inf: doing) **what's he ~ to?** (actually doing) was macht er da?; (planning etc) was hat er vor?; (suspiciously) was führt er im Schilde?; **what have you been ~ to?** was hast du

angestellt?; **what are you ~ to with that?** was hast du damit vor?; **he's ~ to no good** er führt nichts Gutes im Schilde; **I'm sure he's ~ to something** ich bin sicher, er hat etwas vor or(sth suspicious) führt irgend etwas im Schilde; (child) ich bin sicher, er stellt irgend etwas an; **hey you! what do you think you're ~ to!** he Sie, was machen Sie eigentlich da!; **what does he think he's ~ to?** was soll das eigentlich?, was hat er eigentlich vor?

(n) **~ to** (equal to) **I don't feel ~ to it** ich fühle mich dem nicht gewachsen; (not well enough) ich fühle mich nicht wohl genug dazu; **he's not/it isn't ~ to much** mit ihm/damit ist nicht viel los (inf); **is he ~ to advanced work/the heavier weights?** schafft er anspruchsvollere Arbeit/schwerere Gewichte?; **it isn't ~ to his usual standard** das ist nicht sein sonstiges Niveau; **we're going up Ben Nevis — are you sure you're ~ to it?** wir wollen Ben Nevis besteigen — glaubst du, daß du das schaffst? or (experienced enough) glaubst du, daß du dem gewachsen bist?

(o) **~ to** (depending on) **it's ~ to us to help him** wir sollten ihm helfen; **if it was ~ to me** wenn es nach mir ginge; **your success is ~ to you now** Ihr Erfolg hängt jetzt nur noch von Ihnen (selbst) ab, es liegt jetzt ganz an Ihnen, ob Sie Erfolg haben; **it's ~ to you whether you go or not** es liegt an or bei dir or es bleibt dir überlassen, ob du gehst oder nicht; **I'd like to accept, but it isn't ~ to me** ich würde gerne annehmen, aber ich habe da nicht zu bestimmen or das hängt nicht von mir ab; **shall I take it? — that's entirely ~ to you** soll ich es nehmen? — das müssen Sie selbst wissen; **what colour shall I choose? — ~ to you** welche Farbe soll ich nehmen? — das ist deine Entscheidung; **no, it's not ~ to me, it's your choice as well** nein, es ist nicht allein meine Entscheidung, du mußt mit aussuchen.

(p) **~ to** (duty of) **it's ~ to the government to put this right** es ist Sache der Regierung, das richtigzustellen; **it's not ~ to the government** das ist keine or nicht Sache der Regierung.

(q) **~ and down** auf und ab; **to walk ~ and down** auf und ab gehen; **to bounce ~ and down** hochfedern, auf und ab hüpfen; **he's been ~ and down all evening** (from seat) er hat den ganzen Abend keine Minute stillgesessen; (on stairs) er ist den ganzen Abend die Treppe rauf und runter gerannt; **she's still a bit ~ and down** es geht ihr immer noch mal besser, mal schlechter.

(r) **it was ~ against the wall** es war an die Wand gelehnt; **put it ~ against the wall** lehne es an die Wand; **to be ~ against a difficulty/an opponent** einem Problem/Gegner gegenüberstehen, es mit einem Problem/Gegner zu tun haben; **I fully realize what I'm ~ against** mir ist völlig klar, womit ich es hier zu tun habe; **they were really ~ against it** sie hatten wirklich schwer zu schaffen.

2 prep oben auf (+dat); (with movement) hinauf (+acc). **further ~ the page** weiter oben auf der Seite; **to live/go ~ the hill** am Berg wohnen/den Berg hinaufgehen; **they live further ~ the hill/street** sie wohnen weiter oben am Berg/weiter die Straße entlang; **he lives ~ a gloomy passage** seine Wohnung liegt an einem düsteren Flur; **~ the road from me** (von mir) die Straße entlang; **he went off ~ the road** er ging (weg) die Straße hinauf; **he hid it ~ the chimney** er versteckte es (oben) im Kamin; **what? you have to put it ~ your nose!** was? in die Nase soll man sich das tun?; **the water goes ~ this pipe** das Wasser geht durch dieses Rohr; **~ one's sleeve/a tube** (position) im Ärmel/in einer Röhre; (motion) in den Ärmel/in eine Röhre; **as I travel ~ and down the country** wenn ich so durchs Land reise; **I've been ~ and down the stairs all night** ich bin in der Nacht immer die Treppe rauf und runter gerannt; **he was ~ the pub** (inf) er war in der Kneipe (inf); **let's go ~ the pub/~ Johnny's place** (inf) gehen wir doch zur Kneipe/zu Johnny (inf); **to go/march etc ~ to sb** auf jdn zugehen/-marschieren etc.

3 n **(a)** **~s and downs** gute und schlechte Zeiten pl; (of life) Höhen und Tiefen pl; **after many ~s and downs** nach vielen Höhen und Tiefen; **they have their ~s and downs** bei ihnen gibt es auch gute und schlechte Zeiten.

(b) **to be on the ~ and ~** (inf: improving) auf dem aufsteigenden Ast sein (inf); (sl: honest, straight) (person) keine krummen Touren machen (sl); (offer) sauber sein (sl); **he/his career is on the ~ and ~** (inf) mit ihm/seiner Karriere geht es aufwärts.

4 adj (going up) escalator nach oben; (Rail) train, line zur nächsten größeren Stadt. **platform 14 is the ~ platform** auf Bahnsteig 14 fahren die Züge nach London etc.

5 vt (inf) price, offer hinaufsetzen; production ankurbeln; bet erhöhen (to auf +acc).

6 vi (inf) **she ~ped and hit him** sie knallte ihm ganz plötzlich eine (inf); **he ~ped and ran** er rannte ganz plötzlich davon.

up-and-coming [ˈʌpənˈkʌmɪŋ] adj aufstrebend.

up-and-under [ˈʌpənˈʌndəʳ] n (Rugby) hohe Selbstvorlage.

upbeat [ˈʌpbiːt] **1** n (Mus) Auftakt m. **2** adj (inf) (cheerful) fröhlich; (optimistic) optimistisch.

up-bow [ˈʌpbəʊ] n Aufstrich m.

upbraid [ʌpˈbreɪd] vt rügen. **to ~ sb for doing sth** jdn dafür rügen, daß er etw getan hat.

upbringing [ˈʌpbrɪŋɪŋ] n Erziehung f; (manners also) Kinderstube f. **to have a good ~** eine gute Kinderstube haben; **he hasn't got any ~** er hat keine Kinderstube; **where's your ~?** wo ist deine gute Kinderstube?

up-country [ˈʌpˈkʌntrɪ] **1** adv landeinwärts. **2** adj person im Landesinnern.

up-current [ˈʌpkʌrənt] n (Aviat) Aufwind m, Aufströmung f.

update [ʌpˈdeɪt] vt auf den neuesten Stand bringen.

up-draught, (US) **up-draft** [ˈʌpdrɑːft] n Zug m; (Aviat) Aufwind m, Aufströmung f.

up-end [ʌpˈend] vt box, sofa hochkant stellen; person, animal umdrehen.

upgrade [ˈʌpˌgreɪd] **1** n **(a)** (US) Steigung f. **(b)** (fig) **to be on the ~** sich auf dem aufsteigenden Ast befinden (inf). **2** [ʌpˈgreɪd] vt *employee* befördern; *job* anheben; *product* verbessern.

upheaval [ʌp'hiːvəl] *n* (*Geol*) Aufwölbung, Erhebung *f*; (*fig*) Aufruhr *m*. **emotional** ~ Aufruhr *m* der Gefühle; **social/political** ~s soziale/politische Umwälzungen *pl*.

upheld [ʌp'held] *pret, ptp of* **uphold**.

uphill ['ʌp'hɪl] **1** *adv* bergauf. **to go** ~ bergauf gehen, steigen; (*road also*) bergauf führen; (*car*) Berge/den Berg hinauffahren. **2** *adj* *road* bergauf (führend); (*fig*) *work, struggle* mühsam, mühselig. **it's** ~ **all the way** (*lit*) es geht die ganze Strecke bergauf; (*fig*) es ist ein harter Kampf.

uphold [ʌp'həʊld] *pret, ptp* **upheld** *vt* (*sustain*) *tradition, honour* wahren; *the law* hüten; (*support*) *person, decision, objection* (unter)stützen; (*Jur*) *verdict* bestätigen.

upholder [ʌp'həʊldəʳ] *n* Wahrer *m*; (*supporter*) Verteidiger *m*.

upholster [ʌp'həʊlstəʳ] *vt chair etc* polstern; (*cover*) beziehen. ~ed Polster-; **well**-~ed (*hum inf*) gut gepolstert (*hum inf*).

upholsterer [ʌp'həʊlstərəʳ] *n* Polsterer *m*.

upholstery [ʌp'həʊlstərɪ] *n* (*padding and springs*) Polsterung *f*; (*cover*) Bezug *m*; (*trade*) Polsterei *f*; (*skill*) das Polstern.

upkeep ['ʌpkiːp] *n* (*running*) Unterhalt *m*; (*cost*) Unterhaltskosten *pl*; (*maintenance*) Instandhaltung *f*; Instandhaltungskosten *pl*.

upland ['ʌplənd] **1** *n* (*usu pl*) Hochland *nt no pl*. **2** *adj* Hochland-.

uplift ['ʌplɪft] **1** *n* (**a**) (*exaltation*) Erhebung *f*; (*moral inspiration*) Erbauung *f*. **his sermons were full of** ~ seine Predigten waren voll erbaulicher Worte; **to give sb spiritual** ~ jdn erbauen. (**b**) ~ **bra** Stützbüstenhalter *m*. **2** [ʌp'lɪft] *vt* (**a**) *spirit, voice* erheben. **to feel** ~ed sich erbaut fühlen. (**b**) (*Scot: collect*) abholen.

up-market ['ʌp'mɑːkɪt] **1** *adj* anspruchsvoll. **2** *adv* **sell** an anspruchsvollere Kunden.

upmost ['ʌpməʊst] *adj, adv see* **uppermost**.

upon [ə'pɒn] *prep see* **on**.

upper ['ʌpəʳ] **1** *adj* (**a**) obere(r, s); *lip, arm, jaw, deck* Ober-. **temperatures in the** ~ **thirties** Temperaturen hoch in den dreißig; **the** ~ **reaches of the Thames** der Oberlauf der Themse; **U**~ **Egypt/the** ~ **Loire** Oberägypten *nt*/die obere Loire; **U**~ **Rhine** Hochrhein *m*; ~ **storey** (*of house*) oberes Stockwerk; **he's a bit lacking in the** ~ **storey** (*inf*) er ist ein bißchen schwach im Oberstübchen; ~ **circle** (*Brit*) zweiter Rang.

(**b**) (*in importance, rank*) höhere(r, s), obere(r, s). **the** ~ **ranks of the Civil Service** das gehobene Beamtentum; **in the** ~ **income bracket** in der oberen Einkommensklasse; ~ **school** Oberschule *f*; **U**~ **House** (*Parl*) Oberhaus *nt*; *see* **hand 1** (**k**).

2 *n* (**a**) ~s *pl* (*of shoe*) Obermaterial *nt*; **to be on one's** ~s **auf den Hund gekommen sein**. (**b**) (*sl: drug*) Aufputschmittel *nt*.

upper-: ~ **case** *n* (*Typ*) (*also* ~**-case letter**) Großbuchstabe, Versal (*spec*) *m*; **to set sth in** ~ **case** etw in Versalien setzen; an ~**-case T** ein Versal-T; ~ **class** *n* obere Klasse, Oberschicht *f*; **the** ~ **classes** die Oberschicht; ~**-class** *adj accent, district, person* vornehm, fein; *sport, expression, attitude* der Oberschicht; **to be** ~**-class** (*person*) zur Oberschicht gehören; ~**classman** *n* (*US*) Mitglied nt einer High School oder eines College; ~ **crust** *n* (*inf*) obere Zehntausend *pl* (*inf*); ~**-crust** *adj* (*inf*) (schrecklich) vornehm (*inf*); ~**-cut** *n* Aufwärtshaken, Uppercut *m*; ~**most 1** *adj* oberste(r, s); (*fig*) *ambition* größte(r, s), Höchste(r, s); **safety should be** ~**most in your minds** Sicherheit sollte für Sie an erster Stelle stehen; **it's quite obvious what is** ~**most in your mind** es ist ziemlich klar, wo deine Prioritäten liegen; **2** *adv face/the blue side* ~**most** mit dem Gesicht/der blauen Seite nach oben.

uppish ['ʌpɪʃ], **uppity** ['ʌpɪtɪ] *adj* (*inf: arrogant*) hochnäsig (*inf*), hochmütig; *woman also* schnippisch. **to get** ~ **with sb** jdm gegenüber frech *or* anmaßend werden; **jdm frech kommen; there's no need to be** ~ **about it** deshalb braucht man doch nicht gleich frech zu werden.

upraised [ʌp'reɪzd] *adj* erhoben.

upright ['ʌpraɪt] **1** *adj* (**a**) (*erect*) aufrecht; (*vertical*) *post* senkrecht. ~ **piano** Klavier *nt*; ~ **chair** Stuhl *m*. (**b**) (*fig: honest*) *person, character* aufrecht, rechtschaffen. **2** *adv* (*erect*) aufrecht, gerade; (*vertical*) senkrecht. **to hold oneself** ~ sich gerade halten. **3** *n* (**a**) (*post*) Pfosten *m*. (**b**) (*piano*) Klavier *nt*.

uprightly ['ʌp‚raɪtlɪ] *adv* aufrecht, rechtschaffen.

uprightness ['ʌp‚raɪtnɪs] *n* Rechtschaffenheit *f*.

uprising ['ʌpraɪzɪŋ] *n* Aufstand *m*, Erhebung *f*.

upriver ['ʌp'rɪvəʳ] *adv* **2 miles** ~ **from Fen Ditton** 2 Meilen flußaufwärts von Fen Ditton.

uproar ['ʌprɔːʳ] *n* Aufruhr, Tumult *m*. **he tried to make himself heard above the** ~ er versuchte, sich über den Lärm *or* Spektakel (*inf*) hinweg verständlich zu machen; **at this there was** ~, **this caused an** ~ das verursachte einen (wahren) Aufruhr *or* Tumult; **the whole place was in** ~ der ganze Saal/das ganze Haus *etc* war in Aufruhr.

uproarious [ʌp'rɔːrɪəs] *adj meeting* tumultartig; *crowd* lärmend; *laughter* brüllend; *success, welcome* überwältigend, spektakulär; (*very funny*) *joke* wahnsinnig komisch, zum Schreien *pred*. **in** ~ **spirits** in überschäumender Stimmung.

uproariously [ʌp'rɔːrɪəslɪ] *adv* lärmend; *laugh* brüllend. ~ **funny** wahnsinnig komisch, zum Schreien *or* Brüllen.

uproot [ʌp'ruːt] *vt plant* entwurzeln; (*fig: eradicate*) *evil* ausmerzen. **to be** ~**ed by the war** durch den Krieg entwurzelt; **to** ~ **sb from his familiar surroundings** jdn aus seiner gewohnten Umgebung herausreißen; **he** ~**ed his whole family and moved to New York** er riß seine Familie aus ihrer gewohnten Umgebung und zog nach New York.

upsadaisy ['ʌpsə‚deɪzɪ] *interj* hoppla.

upset [ʌp'set] (*vb: pret, ptp* ~) **1** *vt* (**a**) (*knock over*) umstoßen, umwerfen; *boat* umkippen, zum Kentern bringen; (*spill also*) umleeren. **she** ~ **the milk all over the best carpet** sie stieß die

Milch um, und alles lief auf den guten Teppich.

(**b**) (*make sad: news, death*) bestürzen, erschüttern, mitnehmen (*inf*); (*question, insolence etc*) aus der Fassung bringen; (*divorce, experience, accident etc*) mitnehmen (*inf*); (*distress, excite*) *patient, parent etc* aufregen; (*offend: unkind behaviour, words etc*) verletzen, weh tun (+*dat*); (*annoy*) ärgern. **you shouldn't have said/done that, now you've** ~ **her** das hätten Sie nicht sagen/tun sollen, jetzt regt sie sich auf *or* (*is offended*) jetzt ist sie beleidigt; **don't** ~ **yourself** regen Sie sich nicht auf; **there's no point in** ~**ting yourself** es hat doch keinen Zweck, das so tragisch zu nehmen; **I don't know what's** ~ **him** ich weiß nicht, was er hat.

(**c**) (*disorganize*) *calculations, balance etc* durcheinanderbringen; *plan, timetable also* umwerfen. **the whole office was** ~ **by the changes** die Veränderungen haben das ganze Büro durcheinandergebracht; **that's** ~ **my theory** das hat meine Theorie umgestoßen.

(**d**) (*make ill*) **the rich food** ~ **his stomach** das schwere Essen ist ihm auf den Magen geschlagen, das schwere Essen ist ihm nicht bekommen; **onions** ~ **me** von Zwiebeln bekomme ich Magenbeschwerden; **to** ~ **one's stomach** (*dat*) den Magen verderben.

2 *vi* umkippen.

3 *adj* (**a**) (*about divorce, accident, rebuff, dismissal etc*) mitgenommen (*inf*); (*about death, bad news etc*) bestürzt (*about* über +*acc*); (*sad*) betrübt, geknickt (*inf*) (*about* über +*acc*); (*distressed, worried*) aufgeregt (*about* wegen); *baby, child* durcheinander *pred*; (*annoyed*) ärgerlich, aufgebracht (*about* über +*acc*); (*hurt*) gekränkt, verletzt (*about* über +*acc*). **she was pretty** ~ **about it** das ist ihr ziemlich nahegegangen, das hat sie ziemlich mitgenommen (*inf*); (*distressed, worried*) sie hat sich deswegen ziemlich aufgeregt; (*annoyed*) das hat sie ziemlich geärgert; (*hurt*) das hat sie ziemlich gekränkt *or* verletzt; **she was** ~ **about the news/that** he'd left her es hat sie ziemlich mitgenommen (*inf*), als sie das hörte/daß er sie verlassen hat; **don't look so** ~, **they'll come back** guck doch nicht so traurig, sie kommen ja zurück; **would you be** ~ **if I decided not to go after all?** wärst du traurig *or* würdest du's tragisch nehmen, wenn ich doch nicht ginge?; **I'd be very** ~ **if ...** ich wäre sehr traurig *or* betrübt wenn ...; **how** ~ **was he by the news?** hat ihn die Nachricht sehr mitgenommen? (*inf*); **the house has been burgled so of course I'm** ~ bei mir ist eingebrochen worden, und natürlich rege ich mich auf; **to get** ~ sich aufregen (*about* über +*acc*); (*hurt*) gekränkt *or* verletzt werden; **don't get** ~ **about it, you'll find another** nimm das noch nicht so tragisch, du findest bestimmt einen anderen; **she'd be** ~ **if I used a word like that** sie wäre entsetzt, wenn ich so etwas sagen würde; **she's** ~ **because she wasn't invited** sie ist gekränkt *or* eingeschnappt (*inf*), weil sie nicht eingeladen wurde.

(**b**) ['ʌpset] *stomach* verstimmt, verdorben *attr*. **to have an** ~ **stomach** (*dat*) den Magen verdorben haben, eine Magenverstimmung haben.

4 ['ʌpset] *n* (**a**) (*disturbance*) Störung *f*; (*emotional*) Aufregung *f*; (*inf: quarrel*) Verstimmung *f*, Ärger *m*; (*unexpected defeat etc*) unliebsame *or* böse Überraschung. **I don't want to cause any** ~s **in your work** ich möchte bei Ihrer Arbeit kein Durcheinander verursachen; **children don't like** ~s **in their routine** Kinder mögen es nicht, wenn man ihre Routine durcheinanderbringt; **it was an** ~ **to our plans/for us** es hat unsere Pläne durcheinandergebracht/war eine böse Überraschung für uns; **he's had a bit of an** ~ er ist etwas mitgenommen (*inf*) *or* geknickt (*inf*).

(**b**) (*of stomach*) Magenverstimmung *f*, verdorbener Magen.

upset price *n* (*Comm*) Mindestpreis *m*.

upsetting [ʌp'setɪŋ] *adj* (*saddening*) traurig; (*stronger*) bestürzend; (*disturbing*) *changes* störend; *situation* unangenehm, schwierig; (*offending*) beleidigend, verletzend; (*annoying*) ärgerlich. **that must have been very** ~ **for you** das war bestimmt nicht einfach für Sie; (*annoying*) das muß sehr ärgerlich für Sie gewesen sein; **she found this experience/his language most** ~ diese Erfahrung hat sie sehr mitgenommen (*inf*), diese Erfahrung ist ihr sehr nahegegangen/sie hat sich sehr über seine Ausdrucksweise erregt; **I find these constant changes** ~ diese ständigen Veränderungen werfen mich aus dem Gleis *or* machen mir zu schaffen (*inf*); **the divorce/the change was very** ~ **for the child** das Kind hat unter der Scheidung/dem Wechsel sehr gelitten; **he mustn't have any more** ~ **experiences** es darf nichts mehr passieren, was ihn aufregt; **it's** ~ **to my routine** das bringt meine Routine durcheinander.

upshot ['ʌpʃɒt] *n* (*result*) Ergebnis *nt*. **the** ~ **of it all was that ...** es lief darauf hinaus, daß ...; **what was the** ~ **of your meeting?** was kam bei Ihrem Treffen heraus?; **in the** ~ letztes Endes.

upside down ['ʌpsaɪd'daʊn] **1** *adv* verkehrt herum. **the monkey was hanging** ~ der Affe hing verkehrt herum *or* mit dem Kopf nach unten; **to turn sth** ~ (*lit*) etw umdrehen; (*fig*) etw auf den Kopf stellen (*inf*).

2 *adj* **an** ~ **position** verkehrt herum; **to be** ~ (*picture*) verkehrt herum hängen, auf dem Kopf stehen; (*world*) kopfstehen.

upstage [ʌp'steɪdʒ] **1** *adv* (*Theat*) im Hintergrund der Bühne; (*with movement*) in den Hintergrund der Bühne. **2** *adj* blasiert, hochnäsig (*with* gegenüber). **3** *vt* **to** ~ **sb** (*Theat*) jdn zwingen, dem Publikum den Rücken zuzukehren; (*fig*) jdn ausstechen, jdm die Schau stehlen (*inf*).

upstairs [ʌp'steəz] **1** *adv* oben; (*with movement*) nach oben. **to kick sb** ~ (*fig*) jdn wegloben; **may I go** ~? (*euph*) kann ich mal aufs Örtchen?; **he hasn't got much** ~ (*inf*) er ist ein bißchen schwach im Oberstübchen (*inf*). **2** *adj* ~ **window** im oberen Stock(werk); *room also* obere(r, s). **3** *n* oberes Stockwerk.

upstanding [ʌp'stændɪŋ] *adj* (**a**) (*strong*) kräftig; (*honourable*) rechtschaffen. (**b**) (*Jur, form*) **to be** ~ stehen; **gentlemen,**

please be ~ for the toast (meine Herren,) bitte erheben Sie sich zum Toast; the court will be ~ bitte erheben Sie sich.

upstart ['ʌpstɑːt] **1** *n* Emporkömmling *m*. **2** *adj behaviour* eines Emporkömmlings. these ~ courtiers diese höfischen Emporkömmlinge, diese Emporkömmlinge *pl* bei Hof; an ~ publisher ein Emporkömmling *m* (unter den Verlegern).

upstate ['ʌpsteɪt] (*US*) **1** *adj* im Norden (des Bundesstaates). to live in ~ New York im Norden des Staates New York wohnen. **2** *adv* im Norden (des Bundesstaates); (*with movement*) in den Norden (des Bundesstaates).

upstream ['ʌpstriːm] *adv* flußaufwärts. **3 kms** ~ **from Henley** 3 km oberhalb Henley.

upstretched [ʌp'stretʃt] *adj* hands ausgestreckt; neck gereckt.

upstroke ['ʌpstrəʊk] *n* (*of pen*) Aufstrich *m*; (*of piston*) aufgehender Hub, Aufwärtsgang *m*.

upsurge ['ʌpsɜːdʒ] *n* Zunahme, Eskalation (*pej*) *f*. she felt an ~ of affection/hatred/revulsion sie fühlte Zuneigung/Haß/Ekel in sich (*dat*) aufwallen.

upswept [ʌp'swept] *adj* hair hoch- *or* zurückgebürstet. ~ into a chignon zu einem Knoten hochgesteckt.

upswing ['ʌpswɪŋ] *n* (*lit, fig*) Aufschwung *m*; (*Sport*) Ausholen *nt no pl*.

upsy-daisy ['ʌpsə,deɪzɪ] *see* upsadaisy.

uptake ['ʌpteɪk] *n* (*inf*): to be quick/slow on the ~ schnell verstehen/schwer *or* langsam von Begriff sein (*inf*).

upthrust ['ʌpθrʌst] *n* (*upward movement*) Aufwärtsdruck *m*; (*Geol*) Hebung *f*.

uptight ['ʌp'taɪt] *adj* (*sl*) (*nervous*) nervös (*inf*); (*angry*) sauer (*sl*); voice gepreßt; expression verkrampft, verkniffen. to get ~ (about sth) sich (wegen etw) aufregen; (auf etw *acc*) verklemmt reagieren (*inf*); (wegen etw) sauer werden (*sl*); he's pretty ~ about these things der sieht so was ziemlich eng (*sl*); no need to get ~ about it! nun mach dir mal keinen! (*sl*).

up-to-date ['ʌptə'deɪt] *adj* auf dem neusten Stand; fashion also, book, news aktuell; person, method, technique also up to date pred (*inf*). her clothes are always ~ sie ist immer nach der neusten Mode gekleidet; to keep ~ with the fashions/news mit der Mode/den Nachrichten auf dem laufenden bleiben; to keep sb/sth/oneself ~ jdn/etw/sich auf dem laufenden halten; would you bring me ~ on developments? würden Sie mich über den neusten Stand der Dinge informieren?

up-to-the-minute ['ʌptəðə'mɪnɪt] *adj* news, reports allerneuste(r, s), allerletzte(r, s); style also hochmodern. her clothes are ~ ihre Kleider sind immer der allerletzte Schrei.

uptown ['ʌptaʊn] (*US*) **1** *adj* (*in Northern part of town*) im Norden (der Stadt); (*in residential area*) im Villenviertel. **2** *adv* im Norden der Stadt; im Villenviertel; (*with movement*) in den Norden der Stadt; ins Villenviertel. **3** *n* Villenviertel *nt*.

upturn ['ʌptɜːn] **1** *vt* umdrehen. **2** ['ʌptɜːn] *n* (*fig: improvement*) Aufschwung *m*.

upturned [ʌp'tɜːnd] *adj* box etc umgedreht; face nach oben gewandt. ~ nose Stupsnase, Himmelfahrtsnase (*inf*) *f*.

upward ['ʌpwəd] **1** *adj* Aufwärts-, nach oben; glance nach oben. ~ movement Aufwärtsbewegung *f*; ~ steigung *f*; ~ mobility (*Sociol*) soziale Aufstiegsmöglichkeiten *pl*.

2 *adv* (*also* ~s) (a) move aufwärts, nach oben. to look ~ hochsehen, nach oben sehen; face ~ mit dem Gesicht nach oben.

(b) (*with numbers*) prices from 50p ~ Preise von 50 Pence an, Preise ab 50 Pence; from childhood ~ von Kind auf *or* an, von Kindheit an; and ~ und darüber; ~ of 3000 über 3000.

upwind ['ʌpwɪnd] *adj, adv* to be/stand ~ of sb gegen den Wind zu jdm sein/stehen.

Ural ['jʊərəl] *n* the ~ (*river*) der Ural; the ~ Mountains, the ~s das Uralgebirge, der Ural.

uranium [jʊə'reɪnɪəm] *n* Uran *nt*.

Uranus [jʊə'reɪnəs] *n* (*Astron*) Uranus *m*.

urban ['ɜːbən] *adj* städtisch; life also in der Stadt. ~ renewal Stadterneuerung *f*; ~ guerilla Stadtguerilla *m*; ~ warfare Stadtguerilla *f*.

urbane [ɜː'beɪn] *adj* person, manner, style weltmännisch, gewandt, urban (*geh*); (*civil*) höflich; manner, words verbindlich.

urbanely [ɜː'beɪnlɪ] *adv see adj*.

urbanity [ɜː'bænɪtɪ] *n see adj* weltmännische Art, Gewandtheit, Urbanität (*geh*) *f*; Höflichkeit *f*; Verbindlichkeit *f*.

urbanization [,ɜːbənaɪ'zeɪʃən] *n* Urbanisierung, Verstädterung (*pej*) *f*.

urbanize ['ɜːbənaɪz] *vt* urbanisieren, verstädtern (*pej*).

urchin ['ɜːtʃɪn] *n* Gassenkind *nt*; (*mischievous*) Range *f*; see sea ~.

Urdu ['ʊədu:] *n* Urdu *nt*.

urea ['jʊərɪə] *n* Harnstoff *m*, Urea (*spec*) *f*.

ureter [jʊə'riːtə'] *n* Harnleiter, Ureter (*spec*) *m*.

urethra [jʊə'riːθrə] *n* Harnröhre, Urethra (*spec*) *f*.

urge [ɜːdʒ] **1** *n* (*need*) Verlangen, Bedürfnis *nt*; (*drive*) Drang *m no pl*; (*physical, sexual*) Trieb *m*. to feel an ~ to do sth das Bedürfnis verspüren, etw zu tun; to feel the ~ to win unbedingt gewinnen wollen; I resisted the ~ (to contradict him) ich habe mich beherrscht (und ihm nicht widersprochen); an ~ to steal it came over me der Drang, es zu stehlen, überkam mich; creative ~s Schaffensdrang *m*, Kreativität *f*; come and stay with us if you get the ~ (*inf*) komm uns besuchen, wenn du Lust hast.

2 *vt* (a) (*try to persuade*) sb eindringlich bitten. to ~ sb to do sth (*plead with*) jdn eindringlich bitten, etw zu tun; (*earnestly recommend*) darauf dringen, daß jd etw tut; to ~ sb to accept/join in/come along jdn drängen, anzunehmen/mitzumachen/mitzukommen; he needed no urging er ließ sich nicht lange bitten; do it now! he ~d tun Sie's jetzt!, drängte er.

(b) to ~ sb onward jdn vorwärts- *or* weitertreiben.

(c) (*advocate*) measure etc, caution, acceptance drängen auf (+*acc*). to ~ that sth should be done darauf drängen, daß etw getan wird; to ~ the need for sth (on sb) (jdm gegenüber) die Notwendigkeit einer Sache (*gen*) nachdrücklich betonen; to ~ sth upon sb jdm etw eindringlich nahelegen.

(d) (*press*) claim betonen; argument vorbringen, anführen.

♦**urge on** *vt sep* (*lit*) horse, person, troops antreiben, vorwärtstreiben; (*fig*) team, workers antreiben (to zu); team anfeuern. to ~ sb ~ to do sth jdn (dazu) antreiben, etw zu tun.

urgency ['ɜːdʒənsɪ] *n* Dringlichkeit *f*; (*of tone of voice, pleas also*) Eindringlichkeit *f*. a matter of ~ dringend; to treat sth as a matter of ~ etw als dringend behandeln; there's no ~ es eilt nicht, das hat keine Eile; there was a note of ~ in his voice es klang sehr dringend; the ~ of our needs die dringende Notwendigkeit; his statement lacked ~ seinen Worten fehlte der Nachdruck; the ~ of his step seine eiligen Schritte; the sense of ~ in the music das Drängen in der Musik.

urgent ['ɜːdʒənt] *adj* (a) dringend; letter, parcel Eil-. is it ~? (*important*) ist es dringend?; (*needing speed*) eilt es?; it is ~ that the matter should be settled die Angelegenheit muß dringend bereinigt werden; to be in ~ need of medical attention dringend ärztliche Hilfe benötigen.

(b) (*insistent*) tone, plea dringend, dringlich; (*hurrying*) steps eilig. he was very ~ about the need for swift action er betonte nachdrücklich, wie notwendig schnelles Handeln sei.

urgently ['ɜːdʒəntlɪ] *adv* required dringend; requested also dringlich; talk eindringlich. he is ~ in need of help er braucht dringend Hilfe.

uric ['jʊərɪk] *adj* Harn-, Urin-. ~ acid Harnsäure *f*.

urinal ['jʊərɪnl] *n* (*room*) Pissoir *nt*; (*vessel*) Urinal *nt*; (*for patient*) Urinflasche *f*.

urinary ['jʊərɪnərɪ] *adj* Harn-, Urin-; tract, organs Harn-.

urinate ['jʊərɪneɪt] *vi* Wasser lassen, urinieren (*geh*), harnen (*spec*).

urine ['jʊərɪn] *n* Urin, Harn *m*.

urn [ɜːn] *n* (a) Urne *f*. (b) (*also* tea ~, coffee ~) Tee-/Kaffeemaschine *f*.

urogenital [,jʊərəʊ'dʒenɪtl] *adj* urogenital.

urologist [jʊə'rɒlədʒɪst] *n* Urologe *m*, Urologin *f*.

urology [jʊə'rɒlədʒɪ] *n* Urologie *f*.

Ursa Major ['ɜːsə'meɪdʒə'] *n* Großer Bär *or* Wagen.

Ursa Minor ['ɜːsə'maɪnə'] *n* Kleiner Bär *or* Wagen.

Uruguay ['jʊərəgwaɪ] *n* Uruguay *nt*.

Uruguayan [,jʊərə'gwaɪən] **1** *n* (*person*) Uruguayer(in *f*) *m*. **2** *adj* uruguayisch.

US *abbr of* **United States** US *pl*.

us [ʌs] *pers pron* (a) (*dir and indir obj*) uns. give it (to) ~ gib es uns; who, ~? wer, wir?; younger than ~ jünger als wir; it's ~ wir sind's; he is one of ~ er gehört zu uns, er ist einer von uns; this table shows ~ the tides auf dieser Tafel sieht man die Gezeiten; ~ and them wir und die.

(b) (*inf*) (*me*) (*dir obj*) mich; (*indir obj*) mir; (*pl subj*) wir. give ~ a look laß mal sehen; ~ English wir Engländer; as for ~ English was uns Engländer betrifft.

USA *abbr of* **United States of America** USA *pl*; **United States Army.**

usable ['juːzəbl] *adj* verwendbar; suggestion, ideas brauchbar. to be no longer ~ nicht mehr zu gebrauchen sein.

USAF *abbr of* **United States Air Force.**

usage ['juːzɪdʒ] *n* (a) (*treatment, handling*) Behandlung *f*. it's had some rough ~ es ist ziemlich unsanft behandelt worden.

(b) (*custom, practice*) Brauch *m*, Sitte *f*, Usus *m* (*geh*). it's common ~ es ist allgemein üblich *or* Sitte *or* Brauch; the ~s of society die gesellschaftlichen Gepflogenheiten.

(c) (*Ling: use, way of using*) Gebrauch *m no pl*, Anwendung *f*. words in common ~ allgemein gebräuchliche Wörter *pl*; it's common in Northern ~ es ist im Norden allgemein gebräuchlich; it's not an acceptable ~ so darf das nicht gebraucht werden; the finer points of ~ die Feinheiten des Sprachgebrauchs.

use¹ [juːz] **1** *vt* (a) benutzen, benützen (*S Ger*); (*utilize*) dictionary, means, tools, object, materials also, sb's suggestion, idea verwenden; word, literary style gebrauchen, verwenden, benutzen; swear words gebrauchen, benutzen; brains, intelligence also gebrauchen; method, system, technique, therapy, force, trickery anwenden; one's abilities, powers of persuasion, one's strength aufwenden, anwenden; tact, care walten lassen; drugs einnehmen. ~ only in emergencies nur im Notfall gebrauchen *or* benutzen; what's this ~d for? wofür wird das benutzt *or* gebraucht?; to ~ sth for sth etw zu etw verwenden; he ~d it as a spoon er hat es als Löffel benutzt *or* verwendet; he ~d a lot of money/time to get it finished er hat viel Geld/Zeit darauf verwendet, es fertigzubekommen; the police ~d truncheons die Polizei setzte Schlagstöcke ein, die Polizei benutzte *or* gebrauchte Schlagstöcke; what did you ~ the money for? wofür haben Sie das Geld benutzt *or* verwendet *or* gebraucht?; the money is to be ~d to set up a trust das Geld soll dazu verwendet werden, eine Stiftung einzurichten; what sort of toothpaste/petrol do you ~? welche Zahnpasta benutzen *or* verwenden Sie/welches Benzin verwenden Sie?, mit welchem Benzin fahren Sie?; what sort of fuel does this rocket ~? welcher Treibstoff wird für diese Rakete verwendet?; ointment to be ~d sparingly Salbe nur sparsam verwenden *or* anwenden; why don't you ~ a hammer? warum nehmen Sie nicht einen Hammer dazu?, warum benutzen *or* verwenden Sie nicht einen Hammer dazu?; to ~ sb's name jds Namen verwenden *or* benutzen; (*as reference*) jds Namen angeben, sich auf jdn berufen; we can ~ the extra staff to do this dafür können wir das übrige Personal einsetzen *or* verwenden; I'll have to ~ some of your men ich brauche ein paar Ihrer Leute.

(b) (*make use of, exploit*) *information, one's training, talents, resources, chances, opportunity* (aus)nutzen, (aus)nützen (*S Ger*); *advantage* nutzen; *waste products* nutzen, verwerten. **not ~d to capacity** nicht voll genutzt; **you can ~ the leftovers to make a soup** Sie können die Reste zu einer Suppe verwerten; **you should ~ your free time for something creative** Sie sollten Ihre Freizeit für etwas Schöpferisches nutzen *or* gebrauchen; **don't just bank the money, ~ it** lassen Sie das Geld nicht einfach in der Bank, nutzen Sie es.

(c) (*inf*) **I could ~ a ...** ich könnte einen/eine/ein ... (ge)brauchen; **I could ~ a drink** ich könnte etwas zu trinken (ge)brauchen *or* vertragen (*inf*); **it could ~ a bit of paint** das könnte ein bißchen Farbe vertragen.

(d) (~ *up, consume*) verbrauchen. **this car ~s too much petrol** dieses Auto verbraucht zuviel Benzin; **have you ~d all the ink?** haben Sie die Tinte aufgebraucht (*inf*) *or* die ganze Tinte verbraucht?

(e) (*obs, liter: treat*) behandeln; (*cruelly, ill etc also*) mitspielen (+*dat*). **she was ill ~d** ihr ist übel mitgespielt worden; **how has the world been using you?** (*not obs, liter*) wie geht's, wie steht's?

(f) (*pej: exploit*) ausnutzen. **I feel (I've just been) ~d** ich habe das Gefühl, man hat mich ausgenutzt; (*sexually*) ich komme mir mißbraucht vor.

2 [ju:s] *n* **(a)** (*employment*) Verwendung *f*; (*of materials, tools, means, dictionary also*) Benutzung *f*; (*operation: of machines etc*) Benutzung *f*; (*working with: of dictionary, calculator etc*) Gebrauch *m*; (*of word, style also, of swearwords, arms, intelligence*) Gebrauch *m*; (*of method, system, technique, therapy, force, one's strength, powers of persuasion*) Anwendung *f*; (*of personnel, truncheons etc*) Verwendung *f*, Einsatz *m*; (*of drugs*) Einnahme *f*. **once you've mastered the ~ of this calculator** wenn Sie den Gebrauch *or* die Benutzung des Rechners einmal beherrschen; **the ~ of a calculator to solve ...** die Verwendung eines Rechners, um ... zu lösen; **directions for ~** Gebrauchsanweisung *f*; **for the ~ of** für; **for ~ in case of emergency** für Notfälle; **for external ~** äußerlich anzuwenden, zur äußerlichen Anwendung; **it's for ~ not ornament** es ist ein Gebrauchsgegenstand, und nicht zur Zierde; **ready for ~** gebrauchsfertig; (*machine*) einsatzbereit; **to improve with ~** sich mit der Zeit bessern; **worn with ~** abgenutzt; **to make ~ of sth** von etw Gebrauch machen, etw benutzen; **can you make ~ of that?** können Sie das brauchen?; **in ~/out of ~** in *or* im/außer Gebrauch; (*machines also*) in/außer Betrieb; **to be in daily ~/no longer in ~** täglich/nicht mehr benutzt *or* verwendet *or* gebraucht werden; **to come into ~** in Gebrauch kommen; **to go *or* fall out of ~** nicht mehr benutzt *or* verwendet *or* gebraucht werden.

(b) (*exploitation, making ~ of*) Nutzung *f*; (*of waste products, left-overs etc*) Verwertung *f*. **to make ~ of sth** etw nutzen; **to put sth to ~/good ~** etw benutzen/etw ausnutzen *or* gut nutzen; **to make good/bad ~ of sth** etw gut/schlecht nutzen.

(c) (*way of using*) Verwendung *f*. **to learn the ~ of sth** lernen, wie etw verwendet *or* benutzt *or* gebraucht wird; **it has many ~s** es ist vielseitig verwendbar; **to find a ~ for sth** für etw Verwendung finden; **to have no ~ for** (*lit, fig*) nicht gebrauchen können, keine Verwendung haben für; **to have no further ~ for sth** keine Verwendung mehr haben für etw, etw nicht mehr brauchen.

(d) (*usefulness*) Nutzen *m*. **to be of ~ to sb/for doing sth** für jdn von Nutzen sein *or* nützlich sein/nützlich sein, um etw zu tun; **this is no ~ any more** das taugt nichts mehr, das ist zu nichts mehr zu gebrauchen; **does it have a ~ in our society?** ist es für unsere Gesellschaft von Nutzen?; **is this (of) any ~ to you?** können Sie das brauchen?, können Sie damit was anfangen?; **he/that has his/its ~s** er/das ist ganz nützlich; **you're no ~ to me** if **you can't spell** du nützt mir nichts, wenn du keine Rechtschreibung kannst; **he's no ~ as a goalkeeper** er taugt nicht als Torhüter, er ist als Torhüter nicht zu gebrauchen; **can I be of any ~?** kann ich irgendwie behilflich sein?; **a lot of ~ that will be to you!** (*inf*) da hast du aber was davon (*inf*); **this is no ~, we must start work** so hat das keinen Zweck *or* Sinn, wir müssen etwas tun; **it's no ~ you** *or* **your protesting** es hat keinen Sinn *or* Zweck *or* es nützt nichts, wenn *or* daß du protestierst; **what's the ~ of telling him?** was nützt es, wenn man es ihm sagt?; **what's the ~ in trying/going?** wozu überhaupt versuchen/gehen?; **it's no ~** es hat keinen Zweck; **ah, what's the ~!** ach, was soll's!

(e) (*right*) Nutznießung *f* (*Jur*). **to have the ~ of the gardens/a car/money** die Gartenanlagen/einen Wagen benutzen können/über einen Wagen/Geld verfügen (können); **to give sb the ~ of sth** jdm etw benutzen lassen; (*of car also, of money*) jdm etw zur Verfügung stellen; **to have lost the ~ of one's arm** seinen Arm nicht mehr gebrauchen *or* benutzen können; **to have the full ~ of one's faculties** im Vollbesitz seiner (geistigen und körperlichen) Kräfte sein; **have you lost the ~ of your legs?** (*hum*) hast du das Gehen verlernt?

(f) (*custom*) Brauch, Usus (*geh*) *m*.

(g) (*Eccl*) Brauch *m*. **in the Roman ~** nach römisch-katholischem Brauch.

♦**use up** *vt sep food, objects, one's strength* verbrauchen; (*finish also*) aufbrauchen; *scraps, leftovers etc* verwerten. **the butter is all ~d** die Butter ist alle (*inf*) *or* aufgebraucht; **I feel completely ~d** ich fühle mich völlig ausgelaugt; **all his energy was ~d** all seine Energie war verbraucht.

use² [ju:s] *v aux as in* **I didn't ~ to like it** *see* **used².**

used¹ [ju:zd] *adj* (*second-hand*) *clothes, car etc* gebraucht; (*soiled*) *towel etc* benutzt; *stamp* gestempelt.

used² [ju:st] *v aux only in past* **I ~ to swim every day** ich bin früher täglich geschwommen, ich pflegte täglich zu schwimmen (*geh*); **I ~ not to smoke, I didn't ~ to smoke** ich habe früher nicht geraucht, ich pflegte nicht zu rauchen (*geh*); **what ~ he to do** *or* **what did he use to do on Sundays?** was hat er früher *or* sonst sonntags getan?; **he ~ to play golf, didn't he?** er hat doch früher *or* mal Golf gespielt, nicht wahr?; **I didn't know you smoked** — **I ~ not to** ich habe nicht gewußt, daß Sie rauchen — habe ich früher auch nicht; **I don't now but I ~ to** früher schon, jetzt nicht mehr!; **he ~ to be a good singer** er war einmal ein guter Sänger; **there ~ to be a field here** hier war (früher) einmal ein Feld; **things aren't what they ~ to be** es ist alles nicht mehr (so) wie früher; **life is more hectic than it ~ to be** das Leben ist hektischer als früher.

used³ [ju:st] *adj* **to be ~ to sth** an etw (*acc*) gewöhnt sein, etw gewohnt sein; **to be ~ to doing sth** daran gewöhnt sein *or* es gewohnt sein, etw zu tun; **I'm not ~ to it** ich bin das nicht gewohnt; **to get ~ to sth/doing sth** sich an etw (*acc*) gewöhnen/sich daran gewöhnen, etw zu tun; **you might as well get ~ to it!** (*inf*) daran wirst du dich gewöhnen müssen!

useful ['ju:sfʊl] *adj* **(a)** (*helpful*) *person, citizen, contribution, addition also* wertvoll; *contribution, hint also* brauchbar; (*handy*) *tool, person, language also* praktisch; *size* zweckmäßig; *discussion* fruchtbar; *life, employment* nutzbringend. **it is ~ for him to be able to ...** das ist günstig *or* praktisch, daß er ... kann; **to make oneself ~** sich nützlich machen; **he likes to feel ~** er hat gern das Gefühl, nützlich zu sein; **he wants to be ~ to others** er möchte anderen nützen; **thank you, you've been very ~** vielen Dank, Sie haben mir/uns etc sehr geholfen; **is that ~ information?** nützt diese Information etwas?; **to come in ~** sich als nützlich erweisen; **we spent a ~ week in London** wir waren eine Woche in London, was sehr nützlich war; **that's ~!** (*iro*) das nützt uns was!; **he's a ~ man to know** es ist sehr nützlich, ihn zu kennen; **that advice was most ~ to me** der Rat hat mir sehr genützt; **that's a ~ thing to know** es gut, das zu wissen; **I'm sure he'll be ~ to you** ich bin sicher, daß er für Sie nützlich sein wird *or* Ihnen nützlich sein kann; **it has a ~ life of 10 years** es hat eine Nutzdauer von 10 Jahren.

(b) (*inf: capable*) *player* brauchbar, fähig; (*creditable*) *score* wertvoll. **he's quite ~ with a gun/his fists** er kann ziemlich gut mit der Pistole/seinen Fäusten umgehen.

usefully ['ju:sfəli] *adv* *employed, spend time* nutzbringend. **you could ~ come along** es wäre von Nutzen, wenn Sie kämen; **is there anything I can ~ do?** kann ich mich irgendwie nützlich machen?; **this book can ~ be given to first year students** dieses Buch ist für Erstsemester nützlich.

usefulness ['ju:sfʊlnɪs] *n see adj* Nützlichkeit *f*; Wert *m*; Brauchbarkeit *f*; Zweckmäßigkeit *f*; Fruchtbarkeit *f*; Nutzen *m*; *see* **outlive.**

useless ['ju:slɪs] *adj* **(a)** (*unusable*) unbrauchbar; *advice, suggestion also* unbrauchbar, unnütz; *person also* zu nichts nütze; *remedy also* unwirksam, wirkungslos. **it's ~ without a handle** ohne Griff nützt es nichts *or* ist es unbrauchbar; **he's full of ~ information** er steckt voller nutzloser Informationen; **he's ~ as a goalkeeper** er ist als Torwart nicht zu gebrauchen, er taugt nichts als Torwart; **you're just ~!** du bist auch zu nichts zu gebrauchen; **I'm ~ at languages** Sprachen kann ich überhaupt nicht.

(b) (*pointless*) zwecklos, sinnlos.

uselessly ['ju:slɪsli] *adv* nutzlos.

uselessness ['ju:slɪsnɪs] *n see adj* **(a)** Nutzlosigkeit *f*; Unbrauchbarkeit *f*; Unwirksamkeit *f*. **(b)** Zwecklosigkeit, Sinnlosigkeit *f*.

user ['ju:zə'] *n* Benutzer(in *f*) *m*. **he's a ~ of heroin** er nimmt Heroin.

U-shaped ['ju:ʃeɪpt] *adj* U-förmig.

usher ['ʌʃə'] **1** *n* (*Theat, at wedding etc*) Platzanweiser *m*; (*Jur*) Gerichtsdiener *m*.

2 *vt* **to ~ sb into a room/to his seat** jdn in ein Zimmer/zu seinem Sitz bringen *or* geleiten (*geh*); **the drunk was discreetly ~ed out (of the hall)** der Betrunkene wurde unauffällig (aus dem Saal) hinauskomplimentiert.

♦**usher in** *vt sep people* hinein-/hereinführen *or* -bringen *or* -geleiten (*geh*). **to ~ a new era** ein neues Zeitalter einleiten.

usherette [ʌʃə'ret] *n* Platzanweiserin *f*.

USM *abbr of* **United States Mail; United States Marines; United States Mint.**

USN *abbr of* **United States Navy.**

USNG *abbr of* **United States National Guard.**

USNR *abbr of* **United States Naval Reserve.**

USS *abbr of* **United States Ship; United States Senate.**

USSR *abbr of* **Union of Soviet Socialist Republics UdSSR** *f*.

usual ['ju:ʒʊəl] **1** *adj* (*customary*) üblich; (*normal also*) gewöhnlich, normal. **beer is his ~ drink** er trinkt gewöhnlich *or* normalerweise Bier; **7 is his ~ time to get up** gewöhnlich *or* normalerweise steht er um 7 auf; **when shall I come?** — **oh, the ~ time** wann soll ich kommen? — oh, wie üblich *or* immer *or* zur üblichen Zeit; **as is ~ on these occasions** wie (es) bei derartigen Gelegenheiten üblich (ist); **as is ~ with second-hand cars** wie gewöhnlich bei Gebrauchtwagen; **it's the ~ thing nowadays** das ist heute so üblich; **small families are the ~ thing nowadays** kleine Familien sind heutzutage die Norm; **with his ~ tact** (*iro*) taktvoll wie immer, mit dem ihm eigenen Takt; **it's ~ to ask first** normalerweise fragt man erst; **as ~, as per ~** (*inf*) wie üblich, wie gewöhnlich; **business as ~** normaler Betrieb; (*in shop*) Verkauf geht weiter; **later/less/more than ~** später/weniger/mehr als sonst; **it's not ~ for him to be late** er kommt gewöhnlich *or* normalerweise nicht zu spät; **it's hardly ~** es ist eigentlich nicht üblich.

2 *n* (*inf*) der/die/das Übliche. **the ~ please!** (*drink*) dasselbe wie immer, bitte!; **a pint of the ~** eine Halbe wie immer; **what's his ~?** (*drink*) was trinkt er gewöhnlich?; **what sort of mood was he in?** — **the ~** wie war er gelaunt? — wie üblich.

usually ['ju:ʒʊəli] *adv* gewöhnlich, normalerweise. **more than**

~ **careful/drunk** noch vorsichtiger/betrunkener als sonst; **do you go to Spain/work overtime?** — ~ fahren Sie nach Spanien/ machen Sie Überstunden? — normalerweise *or* meist(ens); **is he** ~ **so rude?** ist er sonst auch so unhöflich?; **he's** ~ **early, but ...** er kommt sonst *or* meist *or* normalerweise früh, aber ...; **I can** ~ **manage two hours in the evening** ich schaffe meist(ens) *or* normalerweise zwei Stunden pro Abend; **I can** ~ **manage two hours but this time I didn't** normalerweise schaffe ich *or* sonst schaffe ich immer zwei Stunden, aber diesmal nicht.

usufruct ['juːzjufrʌkt] *n (Jur)* Nutznießung *f*.

usufructuary [ˌjuːzjuˈfrʌktjuərɪ] *n (Jur)* Nutznießer(in *f*) *m*.

usurer ['juːʒərəᵃ] *n* Wucherer *m*.

usurious [juːˈzjʊərɪəs] *adj* wucherisch; *interest also* Wucher-; *person* Wucher treibend *attr*.

usurp [juːˈzɜːp] *vt* sich *(dat)* widerrechtlich aneignen, usurpieren *(geh)*; *power, title, inheritance also* an sich *(acc)* reißen; *throne* sich bemächtigen (+ *gen*) *(geh)*; *role* sich *(dat)* anmaßen; *person* verdrängen. **he's** ~ **his father/his father's throne** er hat seinen Vater verdrängt/er hat seinem Vater den Thron geraubt; **she has** ~**ed his wife's place** sie hat seine Frau von ihrem Platz verdrängt.

usurpation [ˌjuːzɜːˈpeɪʃən] *n* Usurpation *f (geh)*; *(of power also)* widerrechtliche Übernahme; *(of title, inheritance)* widerrechtliche Aneignung. ~ **of the throne** Thronraub *m*, Usurpation *f* des Thrones *(geh)*.

usurper [juːˈzɜːpəᵃ] *n* unrechtmäßiger Machthaber, Usurpator *m (geh)*; *(fig)* Eindringling *m*. **the** ~ **of the throne/his father's throne** der Thronräuber/der unrechtmäßige Nachfolger seines Vaters auf dem Thron.

usury ['juːʒʊrɪ] *n* Wucher *m*. **to practise** ~ Wucher treiben; **32% interest is** ~ 32% Zinsen sind *or* ist Wucher, 32%, das sind ja Wucherzinsen.

utensil [juːˈtensl] *n* Gerät, Utensil *nt*.

uterine ['juːtəraɪn] *adj (Anat)* uterin. ~ **brother** Halbbruder *m* mütterlicherseits.

uterus ['juːtərəs] *n* Gebärmutter *f*, Uterus *(spec) m*.

utilitarian [ˌjuːtɪlɪˈtɛərɪən] **1** *adj* auf Nützlichkeit ausgerichtet; *qualities* nützlich, praktisch; *(Philos)* utilitaristisch. **2** *n (Philos)* Utilitarist, Utilitarier *m*.

utilitarianism [ˌjuːtɪlɪˈtɛərɪənɪzəm] *n (Philos)* Utilitarismus *m*.

utility [juːˈtɪlɪtɪ] **1** *n* **(a)** *(usefulness)* Nützlichkeit *f*, Nutzen *m*.
(b) public ~ *(company)* Versorgungsbetrieb *m*; *(service)* Leistung *f* der Versorgungsbetriebe; **the utilities** versorgungswirtschaftliche Einrichtungen *pl*.
2 *adj goods, vehicle* Gebrauchs-. ~ **man** *(US)* Mädchen *nt* für alles *(inf)*; ~ **room** Allzweckraum *m*; ~ **furniture** im 2. Weltkrieg in Großbritannien hergestellte Möbel, die einfach, aber zweckmäßig waren.

utilization [ˌjuːtɪlaɪˈzeɪʃən] *n see vt* Verwendung *f*; Benutzung *f*; Nutzung *f*; Verwertung *f*.

utilize ['juːtɪlaɪz] *vt* verwenden; *situation, time* (be)nutzen; *(take advantage of)* opportunity, talent nutzen; *(to make sth*

new) waste paper, old wool etc verwerten.

utmost ['ʌtməust] **1** *adj* **(a)** *(greatest)* ease, danger größte(r, s), höchste(r, s); *caution also* äußerste(r, s); *candour* größte(r, s), äußerste(r, s). **they used their** ~ **skill** Sie taten ihr Äußerstes; **with the** ~ **speed/care** so schnell/sorgfältig wie nur möglich; **matters of the** ~ **importance** Angelegenheiten von äußerster Wichtigkeit; **it is of the** ~ **importance that ...** es ist äußerst wichtig, daß ...
(b) *(furthest)* äußerste(r, s).
2 *n* to do/try one's ~ sein möglichstes *or* Bestes tun; **that is the** ~ **I can do** mehr kann ich wirklich nicht tun; **that is the** ~ **that can be said of her/it** das ist das Höchste, was man über sie/dazu sagen kann; **to the** ~ **of one's ability** so gut man nur kann; **he tried my patience to the** ~ er strapazierte meine Geduld aufs äußerste; **he exerts himself to the** ~ er strapaziert sich bis zum äußersten; **one should enjoy life/oneself to the** ~ man sollte das Leben in vollen Zügen genießen/sich amüsieren, so gut man nur kann; **I can give you £50 at the** ~ ich kann Ihnen allerhöchstens £ 50 geben.

Utopia [juːˈtəupɪə] *n* Utopia *nt*.

Utopian [juːˈtəupɪən] **1** *adj* utopisch, utopistisch *(pej)*. **2** *n* Utopist(in *f*) *m*.

Utopianism [juːˈtəupɪənɪzəm] *n* Utopismus *m*.

utricle ['juːtrɪkl] *n (Bot)* Fangbläschen *nt*, Schlauch, Utrikel *(spec) m*; *(Anat)* Utriculus *m (spec)*.

utter¹ ['ʌtəᵃ] *adj* total, vollkommen; *rogue, drunkard* unverbesserlich, Erz-. **what** ~ **nonsense!** so ein totaler Blödsinn!

utter² *vt* **(a)** von sich *(dat)* geben; *word* sagen; *word of complaint* äußern; *cry, sigh, threat* ausstoßen; *libel* verbreiten. **(b)** *(form)* forged money in Umlauf bringen; *cheque* ausstellen.

utterance ['ʌtərəns] *n* **(a)** *(sth said)* Äußerung *f*. **the child's first** ~**s** die ersten Worte des Kindes; **his last** ~ seine letzten Worte; **his recent** ~**s in the Press** seine jüngsten Presseäußerungen.
(b) *(act of speaking)* Sprechen *nt*. **upon her dying father's** ~ **of her name** als ihr sterbender Vater ihren Namen nannte; **to give** ~ **to a feeling** einem Gefühl Ausdruck geben *or* verleihen *(geh)*, ein Gefühl zum Ausdruck bringen.

utterly ['ʌtəlɪ] *adv* total, völlig; *depraved also, despise* zutiefst. ~ **beautiful** ausgesprochen schön.

uttermost ['ʌtəməust] *n, adj see* utmost.

U-turn ['juːtɜːn] *n (lit, fig)* Wende *f*. **no** ~**s** Wenden verboten!; **the government has done a** ~ in pensions die Rentenpolitik der Regierung hat sich um 180 Grad gedreht.

uvula ['juːvjələ] *n* Zäpfchen *nt*, Uvula *f (spec)*.

uvular ['juːvjələᵃ] **1** *adj* uvular. **the** ~ **R** das Zäpfchen-R. **2** *n* Zäpfchenlaut, Uvular *m*.

uxorious [ʌkˈsɔːrɪəs] *adj husband* treuergeben *attr*, treu ergeben *pred*. **his** ~ **behaviour** seine liebevolle Art *or* seine Ergebenheit seiner Frau gegenüber.

uxoriousness [ʌkˈsɔːrɪəsnɪs] *n* Ergebenheit *f* seiner Frau gegenüber.

V

V, v [viː] *n* V, v *nt*.

V, v *abbr of* **verse(s)** V; **volt(s)** V; **vide** v; **versus**.

VA *(US) abbr of* **Veterans (of Vietnam) Administration**.

Va *abbr of* **Virginia**.

vac [væk] *n (Univ inf)* Semesterferien *pl*.

vacancy ['veɪkənsɪ] *n* **(a)** *(emptiness)* Leere *f*; *(of look also)* Ausdruckslosigkeit *f*; *(of post)* Unbesetztsein, Freisein *nt*.
(b) *(in boarding house)* (freies) Zimmer. **have you any vacancies for August?** haben Sie im August noch Zimmer frei?; **"no vacancies"** „belegt".
(c) *(job)* offene *or* freie Stelle; *(at university)* Vakanz *f*, unbesetzte Stelle. **we have a** ~ **for a keen young man** wir haben eine offene Stelle für einen strebsamen jungen Mann; **we have a** ~ **in our personnel department** in unserer Personalabteilung ist eine Stelle zu vergeben; **to fill a** ~ eine Stelle besetzen; **we are looking for somebody to fill a** ~ **in our personnel department** wir suchen einen Mitarbeiter für unsere Personalabteilung; **vacancies** Stellenangebote, offene Stellen.

vacant ['veɪkənt] *adj* **(a)** *post* frei, offen; *(Univ)* unbesetzt, vakant; *WC, seat, hotel room* frei; *chair* unbesetzt; *house, room* unbewohnt, leerstehend; *lot* unbebaut, frei. **the house has been** ~ **for two months** das Haus steht seit zwei Monaten leer; **with** ~ **possession** *(Jur)* bezugsfertig; **to become** *or* **fall** ~ frei werden.
(b) *(empty)* days unausgefüllt, lang. **the** ~ **future stretched before him** die Zukunft lag leer vor ihm.
(c) *mind, stare* leer.

vacantly ['veɪkəntlɪ] *adv* *(stupidly)* blöde; *(dreamily)* abwesend. **he gazed** ~ **at me** er sah mich mit leerem Blick an.

vacate [vəˈkeɪt] *vt seat* frei machen; *post* aufgeben; *presidency etc* niederlegen; *house, room* räumen. **this post is going to be** ~**d** diese Stelle wird frei.

vacation [vəˈkeɪʃən] **1** *n* **(a)** *(Univ)* Semesterferien *pl*; *(Jur)* Gerichtsferien *pl*; *see* **long** ~.
(b) *(US)* Ferien *pl*, Urlaub *m*. **on** ~ im *or* auf Urlaub; **to take a** ~ Urlaub machen; **where are you going for your** ~? wohin fahren Sie in Urlaub?, wo machen Sie Urlaub?; **to go on** ~ auf Urlaub *or* in die Ferien gehen.
(c) *see* **vacate** Aufgabe *f*; Niederlegung *f*; Räumung *f*.
2 *vi (US)* Urlaub *or* Ferien machen.

vacation course *n* Ferienkurs *m*.

vacationer [veɪˈkeɪʃənəᵃ], **vacationist** [veɪˈkeɪʃənɪst] *n (US)* Urlauber(in *f*) *m*.

vacation trip *n* (Ferien)reise *f*.

vaccinate ['væksɪneɪt] *vt* impfen.

vaccination [ˌvæksɪˈneɪʃən] *n* (Schutz)impfung *f*. **have you had your** ~ **yet?** sind Sie schon geimpft?, haben Sie sich schon impfen lassen?

vaccine ['væksiːn] *n* Impfstoff *m*, Vakzine *f (spec)*.

vacillate ['væsɪleɪt] *vi (lit, fig)* schwanken. **she** ~**d so long about accepting** sie schwankte lange, ob sie annehmen sollte oder nicht.

vacillating ['væsɪleɪtɪŋ] *adj (fig)* schwankend, unschlüssig, unentschlossen.

vacillation [ˌvæsɪˈleɪʃən] *n* Schwanken *nt*; *(fig also)* Unentschlossenheit, Unschlüssigkeit *f*.

vacua ['vækjuə] *pl of* **vacuum**.

vacuity [væˈkjuːɪtɪ] *n (liter)* *(lack of intelligence)* Geistlosigkeit f; (*emptiness*) Leere f. **vacuities** (*inane remarks*) Plattheiten, Platitüden pl.

vacuous ['vækjʊəs] adj *eyes, face, stare* ausdruckslos, leer; *remarks* nichtssagend.

vacuum ['vækjʊəm] n, pl **-s** or **vacua** (*form*) 1 n (*Phys, fig*) (luft)leerer Raum, Vakuum nt. **cultural** ~ kulturelles Vakuum. 2 vt carpet saugen.

vacuum: ~ **bottle** n (*US*) *see* ~ **flask**; ~ **brake** n Unterdruckbremse f; ~ **cleaner** n Staubsauger m; ~ **flask** n Thermosflasche f; ~**-packed** adj vakuumverpackt; ~ **pump** n Vakuumor Aussaugepumpe f; ~ **tube** n Vakuumröhre f.

vade mecum ['vɑːdɪ'meɪkəm] n (*liter*) Vademekum nt (*liter*).

vagabond ['vægəbɒnd] 1 n Vagabund, Landstreicher(in f) m. 2 adj vagabundenhaft; *life* unstet, Vagabunden-; *person* vagabundierend, umherziehend; *thoughts* (ab)schweifend.

vagary ['veigəri] n usu pl Laune f; (*strange idea*) verrückter Einfall. **the vagaries of life** die Wechselfälle des Lebens.

vagina [və'dʒaɪnə] n Scheide, Vagina f.

vaginal [və'dʒaɪnl] adj vaginal, Scheiden-.

vagrancy ['veigrənsi] n Landstreichertum nt, Land-/Stadtstreicherei f (*also Jur*).

vagrant ['veigrənt] 1 n Land-/Stadtstreicher(in f) m. 2 adj *person* umherziehend; *life* unstet, nomadenhaft.

vague [veig] adj(+er) (a) (*not clear*) vage, unbestimmt; *outline, shape* verschwommen; *photograph* unscharf, verschwommen; *report, question* vage, ungenau; *murmur* dumpf, undeutlich. I haven't the ~st idea ich habe nicht die leiseste Ahnung; there's a ~ resemblance es besteht eine entfernte Ähnlichkeit; I had a ~ idea she would come ich hatte so eine (dunkle) Ahnung, daß sie kommen würde; I am still very ~ on this theory die Theorie ist mir noch nicht sehr klar; I am very ~ on Dutch politics von holländischer Politik habe ich nicht viel Ahnung; he was ~ about the time of his arrival er äußerte sich nur vage or unbestimmt über seine Ankunftszeit.

(b) (*absent-minded*) geistesabwesend, zerstreut. do you really understand, you look rather ~? verstehst du das wirklich, du siehst so verwirrt aus?; to have a ~ look in one's eyes einen verständnislosen/abwesenden Gesichtsausdruck haben.

vaguely ['veigli] adv vage; *remember also* dunkel; *speak also* unbestimmt; *understand* ungefähr, in etwa. to look ~ at sb jdn verständnislos ansehen; they're ~ similar sie haben eine entfernte Ähnlichkeit; it's only ~ like yours es ist nur ungefähr wie deines; it's ~ blue es ist bläulich; there's something ~ sinister about it es hat so etwas Düsteres an sich.

vagueness ['veignis] n (a) (*of outline, shape*) Verschwommenheit f; (*of report, question*) Vagheit, Ungenauigkeit f. the ~ of the resemblance die entfernte Ähnlichkeit; his ~ on Dutch politics seine lückenhafte or wenig fundierte Kenntnis der holländischen Politik.

(b) (*absent-mindedness*) Geistesabwesenheit, Zerstreutheit f. the ~ of her look ihr verwirrter or verständnisloser/abwesender Blick.

vain [vein] adj (a) (+er) (*about looks*) eitel; (*about qualities also*) eingebildet. he's very ~ about his musical abilities er bildet sich (dat) auf sein musikalisches Können viel ein; he is ~ about his appearance er ist eitel.

(b) (*useless, empty*) eitel (*liter*); *attempt also* vergeblich; *pleasures, promises, words also* leer; *hope also* töricht. he had ~ hopes of getting the job er machte sich vergeblich Hoffnung auf den Posten; in ~ umsonst, vergeblich, vergebens (*geh*). it was all in ~ das war alles umsonst etc.

(c) to take God's name in ~ den Namen Gottes mißbrauchen, Gott lästern; was someone taking my name in ~? (*hum*) hat da wieder jemand von mir geredet?

(d) (*liter: worthless*) *display, ceremony* eitel (*liter*).

vainglorious [vein'glɔːrɪəs] adj (*old*) *person* dünkelhaft; *talk* prahlerisch, ruhmredig (*old liter*); *spectacle* pompös, bombastisch.

vainglory [vein'glɔːrɪ] n (*old*) Prahlerei, Selbstverherrlichung f; (*characteristic*) Dünkel m; (*of appearance*) Pomp m, falscher Glanz.

vainly ['veinli] adv (a) (*to no effect*) vergeblich, vergebens. (b) (*conceitedly*) (*about looks*) eitel; (*about qualities also*) eingebildet.

valance ['væləns] n (*round bed frame*) Volant m; (*on window*) Querbehang m, Schabracke f; (*wooden*) Blende f.

vale [veil] n (*liter*) Tal nt. **this** ~ **of tears** dies Jammertal.

valediction [,vælɪ'dɪkʃən] n (a) (*form*) (*act*) Abschied(nehmen nt) m; (*words*) Abschiedsworte pl; (*speech*) Abschiedsrede f. (b) (*US Sch*) Abschieds- or Entlassungsrede f.

valedictorian [,vælɪdɪk'tɔːrɪən] n (*US Sch*) Abschiedsredner(in f) m (*bei der Schulentlassungsfeier*).

valedictory [,vælɪ'dɪktərɪ] 1 adj (*form*) Abschieds-. 2 n (*US Sch*) *see* **valediction** (b).

valence ['veiləns], **valency** ['veilənsi] n (*Chem*) Wertigkeit, Valenz f; (*Ling*) Valenz f.

valency bond n kovalente Bindung.

valentine ['væləntain] n (a) (*person*) Freund(in f) m, dem/der man am Valentinstag einen Gruß schickt. St V~'s Day Valentinstag m. (b) ~ (*card*) Valentinskarte f.

valerian [və'lɪərɪən] n Baldrian m.

valet ['vælei] n Kammerdiener m. ~ **service** Reinigungsdienst m.

valetudinarian ['vælɪ,tjuːdɪ'nɛərɪən] 1 n kränkelnde Person; (*health fiend*) Gesundheitsapostel (*inf*), Gesundheitsfanatiker(in f) m. 2 adj (*sickly*) kränklich, kränkelnd; *person* sehr um seine Gesundheit besorgt; *habits, attitude* gesundheitsbewußt.

Valhalla [væl'hælə] n Walhall nt, Walhalla nt or f.

valiant ['væliənt] adj (a) (*liter*) *soldier, deed* tapfer, kühn (*geh*).

(b) he made a ~ effort to save him er unternahm einen kühnen Versuch, ihn zu retten; she made a ~ effort to smile sie versuchte tapfer zu lächeln; never mind, it was a ~ try machen Sie sich nichts draus, es war ein löblicher Versuch.

valiantly ['væliəntli] adv (a) (*liter*) mutig, tapfer. (b) he ~ said he would help out er sagte großzügig seine Hilfe zu.

valid ['vælɪd] adj (a) *ticket, passport* gültig; (*Jur*) *document, marriage* (rechts)gültig; *contract* bindend, rechtsgültig; *claim* berechtigt, begründet.

(b) *argument, reasoning* stichhaltig; *excuse, reason* triftig, einleuchtend; *objection* berechtigt, begründet. this argument isn't ~ (*in itself*) dieses Argument ist nicht stichhaltig; (*not relevant*) dieses Argument ist nicht zulässig or gilt nicht; is it ~ to assume this? ist es zulässig, das anzunehmen?; that's a very ~ point das ist ein sehr wertvoller Hinweis.

validate ['vælɪdeit] vt *document* (*check validity*) für gültig erklären; (*with stamp, sign*) (rechts)gültig machen; *claim* bestätigen; *theory* bestätigen, beweisen; (*Jur*) Rechtskraft verleihen (+*dat*).

validation [,vælɪ'deiʃən] n (*of document*) Gültigkeitserklärung f; (*of claim*) Bestätigung f; (*of theory*) Beweis, Nachweis m.

validity [və'lɪdɪtɪ] n (*Jur etc: of document*) (Rechts)gültigkeit f; (*of ticket etc*) Gültigkeit f; (*of claim*) Berechtigung f. (b) (*of argument*) Stichhaltigkeit f; (*of excuse etc*) Triftigkeit f. the ~ of your objection Ihr berechtigter or begründeter Einwand; we discussed the ~ of merging these two cinematic styles wir diskutierten, ob es zulässig ist, diese beiden Filmstile zu mischen.

valise [və'liːz] n Reisetasche f.

Valkyrie ['vælkɪrɪ] n Walküre f.

valley ['vælɪ] n Tal nt; (*big and flat*) Niederung f. to go up/down the ~ talaufwärts/talabwärts gehen/fließen etc; the Upper Rhine ~ die Oberrheinische Tiefebene.

valor n (*US*) see **valour**.

valorous ['vælərəs] adj (*liter*) heldenmütig (*liter*), tapfer.

valour, (*US*) **valor** ['vælər] n (*liter*) Heldenmut m (*liter*), Tapferkeit f.

valuable ['væljʊəbl] 1 adj (a) *jewel* wertvoll; *time, oxygen* kostbar. (b) (*useful*) wertvoll; *help, advice also* nützlich. 2 n ~s pl Wertsachen, Wertgegenstände pl.

valuation [,væljʊ'eiʃən] n (*act*) Schätzung f; (*fig: of person's character*) Einschätzung f; (*value decided upon*) Schätzwert m, Schätzung f; (*fig*) Beurteilung f. what's your ~ of him? wie schätzen Sie ihn ein?; to have a ~ of a picture done ein Bild schätzen lassen; to make a correct ~ of sth etw genau abschätzen; we shouldn't take him at his own ~ wir sollten seine Selbsteinschätzung nicht einfach übernehmen.

value ['væljuː] 1 n (a) Wert m; (*usefulness*) Nutzen m. to be of ~ Wert/Nutzen haben, wertvoll/nützlich sein; her education has been of no ~ to her ihre Ausbildung hat ihr nichts genützt; to put a ~ on sth etw schätzen or bewerten; (*on leisure etc*) einen Sache (*dat*) (hohen) Wert beimessen; to put too high a ~ on sth etw zu hoch schätzen or bewerten; (*on leisure etc*) etw überbewerten; he attaches no/great ~ to it er legt keinen/großen Wert darauf, ihm liegt nicht/sehr viel daran; they don't appreciate her real ~ sie kennen ihren wahren Wert nicht; of little ~ nicht sehr wertvoll/nützlich; of no ~ wertlos/nutzlos; of great ~ sehr wertvoll.

(b) (*in money*) Wert m. what's the ~ of your house? wieviel ist Ihr Haus wert?; what is its second-hand ~? wieviel ist es gebraucht wert?; to gain/lose (in) ~ im Wert steigen/fallen; increase in/loss of ~ Wertzuwachs m/Wertminderung f, Wertverlust m; it's good ~ es ist preisgünstig; in our shop you get ~ for money in unserem Geschäft bekommen Sie etwas für Ihr Geld (*inf*); this TV I bought ten years ago was good ~ dieser Fernseher, den ich vor zehn Jahren gekauft habe, ist sein Geld wert; lazy employees don't give you ~ for money faule Angestellte sind ihr Geld nicht wert; goods to the ~ of £100 Waren im Wert von £ 100; they put a ~ of £50 on it sie haben es auf £ 50 geschätzt.

(c) ~s pl (*moral standards*) (sittliche) Werte pl, Wertwelt f; he has no sense of ~s er hat keine sittlichen Maßstäbe.

(d) (*Math*) (Zahlen)wert m; (*Mus*) (Zeit- or Noten)wert m, Dauer f; (*Phon*) (Laut)wert m; (*of colour*) Farbwert m. what exactly is the ~ of this word in the poem? welchen Ausdrucksor Stellenwert hat dieses Wort innerhalb des Gedichtes?

2 vt (a) *house, jewels* (ab)schätzen. the property was ~ed at £10,000 das Grundstück wurde auf £ 10 000 geschätzt.

(b) *friendship, person* (wert)schätzen, (hoch)achten; *opinion, advice* schätzen; *comforts, liberty, independence* schätzen, Wert legen auf (+*acc*). I ~ it (highly) ich weiß es zu schätzen; if you ~ my opinion ... wenn Sie Wert auf meine Meinung legen ...; wenn Sie meiner Meinung irgendwelchen Wert beimessen ...; if you ~ your life, you'll stay away bleiben Sie weg, wenn Ihnen Ihr Leben lieb ist.

value-added tax n (*Brit*) Mehrwertsteuer f.

valued ['væljuːd] adj *friend* (hoch)geschätzt, lieb. he is a ~ colleague er ist als Kollege hochgeschätzt.

value: ~ **judgement** n Werturteil nt; ~**less** adj wertlos; (*useless also*) nutzlos, unnütz; *judgement* wertfrei.

valuer ['væljʊər] n Schätzer m.

valve [vælv] n (*Anat*) Klappe f; (*Tech, on musical instrument*) Ventil nt; (*in pipe system*) Absperrhahn m; (*Rad, TV*) Röhre f. **inlet/outlet** ~ (*Aut*) Einlaß-/Auslaßventil nt.

valvular ['vælvjʊlər] adj (*Tech*) Ventil-; (*shaped like valve*) ventilartig; (*Med*) Klappen-. ~ **inflammation** (*Med*) Herzklappenentzündung f.

vamoose [və'muːs] vi (*US sl*) abhauen (*inf*), abzischen (*sl*).

vamp[1] [væmp] 1 n (*woman*) Vamp m. 2 vt she's been ~ing him all the time sie hat die ganze Zeit ihre Reize bei ihm spielen lassen. 3 vi den Vamp spielen.

vamp[2] 1 n (a) (*of shoe: upper*) Oberleder nt. (b) (*Mus*)

Improvisation *f*, improvisierte Einleitung/Begleitung. **2** *vt* **(a)** (*repair*) flicken. **(b)** (*Mus*) *accompaniment* improvisieren, sich (*dat*) einfallen lassen. **3** *vi* (*Mus*) improvisieren, aus dem Stegreif spielen.
♦**vamp up** *vt sep* aufpolieren (*inf*), aufmotzen (*sl*).
vampire ['væmpaɪəʳ] *n* (*lit*) Vampir, Blutsauger (*old*) *m*; (*fig*) Vampir *m*. ~ **bat** Vampir, Blutsauger (*old*) *m*.
van¹ [væn] *n* **(a)** (*Brit Aut*) Liefer- *or* Kastenwagen, Transporter *m*. **(b)** (*Rail*) Waggon, Wagen *m*. **(c)** (*inf: caravan*) (Wohn)-wagen *m*. gipsy's ~ Zigeunerwagen *m*.
van² *n abbr of* **vanguard** (*lit, fig*) Vorhut *f*; (*fig also*) Spitze, Führung *f*. **he was in the** ~ **of** legal reform er stand an der Spitze der Rechtsreformer.
van³ *n abbr of* **advantage** (*Tennis inf*) Vorteil *m*. ~ **in/out** Vorteil auf (*inf*)/rück (*inf*).
vanadium [və'neɪdɪəm] *n* Vanadin, Vanadium *nt*.
vandal ['vændəl] *n* (*fig*) Rowdy, Demolierer (*inf*) *m*; (*Hist*) Vandale *m*. it was damaged by ~s es ist mutwillig beschädigt worden.
vandalism ['vændəlɪzəm] *n* Vandalismus *m*, blinde Zerstörungswut; (*Jur*) mutwillige Beschädigung (fremden Eigentums). **destroyed by acts of** ~ mutwillig zerstört/beschädigt; **these acts of** ~ dieser Vandalismus, diese mutwilligen Beschädigungen.
vandalize ['vændəlaɪz] *vt painting* mutwillig zerstören/beschädigen; *building* verwüsten; (*wreck*) demolieren.
vane [veɪn] *n* (*also* weather ~) Wetterfahne *f*, Wetterhahn *m*; (*of windmill*) Flügel *m*; (*of propeller*) Flügel *m*, Blatt *nt*; (*of turbine*) (Leit)schaufel *f*.
vanguard ['vængɑːd] *n* (*Mil, Naut*) Vorhut *f*; (*fig also*) Spitze, Führung *f*. **in the** ~ **of** progress an der Spitze des Fortschritts.
vanilla [və'nɪlə] **1** *n* Vanille *f*. **2** *adj* ice-cream, flavour Vanille-.
vanish ['vænɪʃ] *vi* verschwinden, entschwinden (*liter*); (*traces also*) sich verlieren; (*fears*) sich legen; (*hopes*) schwinden; (*become extinct*) untergehen. **I've got to** ~ (*inf*) ich muß weg (*inf*) *or* abzwitschern (*inf*); *see* thin (d).
vanishing ['vænɪʃɪŋ]: ~ **act** *n see* ~ **trick**; ~ **cream** *n* (Haut)pflegecreme, Tages-/Nachtcreme *f*; ~ **point** *n* (*Math*) Fluchtpunkt *m*; (*fig*) Nullpunkt *m*; ~ **trick** *n* he did a ~ **trick** with it er hat es weggezaubert; every time he's needed he does his ~ **trick** (*inf*) jedesmal, wenn man ihn braucht, verdrückt er sich (*inf*).
vanity ['vænɪtɪ] *n* **(a)** (*concerning looks*) Eitelkeit *f*; (*concerning own value*) Einbildung, Eingebildetheit *f*. **he said without any** ~ **that ...** er sagte ohne jede Eitelkeit, daß ...; ~ **made him think he was bound to succeed** er war so eingebildet *or* von sich eingenommen, daß er einen Mißerfolg für ausgeschlossen hielt.
(b) *worthlessness: of life, pleasures*) Nichtigkeit, Hohlheit *f*; (*of words*) Hohlheit *f*; (*of efforts*) Vergeblichkeit *f*. **the** ~ **of all** his hopes/promises all seine törichten Hoffnungen/leeren Versprechungen; all is ~ alles ist eitel (*liter*) *or* vergebens.
(c) (*US*) Frisiertisch *m*.
vanity case *n* Schmink- *or* Kosmetikkoffer *m*.
vanquish ['væŋkwɪʃ] *vt* (*liter*) enemy, fears bezwingen (*geh*).
vantage ['vɑːntɪdʒ] *n* (*rare*) Vorteil *m*; (*Tennis*) Vorteil *m*.
vantage: ~ **ground** *n* (*Mil*) günstige (Ausgangs)stellung; ~ **point** *n* (*Mil*) (günstiger) Aussichtspunkt; **our window is a good** ~ **point for watching the procession** von unserem Fenster aus hat man einen guten Blick auf die Prozession; **from our modern** ~ **point** aus heutiger Sicht.
vapid ['væpɪd] *adj* (*liter*) conversation, remark nichtssagend, geistlos; *smile* (*insincere*) leer; (*bored*) matt; *style* kraftlos; *beer, taste* schal.
vapidity [væ'pɪdɪtɪ] *n* (*liter*) (*of conversation, remark*) Geistlosigkeit *f*; (*of smile*) Ausdruckslosigkeit *f*; Mattheit *f*; (*of style*) Kraftlosigkeit *f no pl*; (*of taste*) Schalheit *f*.
vapor *etc* (*US*) *see* **vapour** etc.
vaporization [ˌveɪpəraɪ'zeɪʃən] *n* (*by boiling etc*) Verdampfung *f*; (*natural*) Verdunstung *f*.
vaporize ['veɪpəraɪz] **1** *vt* (*by boiling etc*) verdampfen; (*naturally*) verdunsten lassen. **2** *vi see* **vt** verdampfen; verdunsten.
vaporizer ['veɪpəraɪzəʳ] *n* Verdampfer, Verdampfapparat *m*; (*for perfume*) Zerstäuber *m*.
vaporous ['veɪpərəs] *adj* **(a)** (*like vapour*) dampf-/gasförmig; (*full of vapour*) dunstig; (*of vapour*) Dunst-. ~ **mists rising from the swamp** Dünste, die aus dem Sumpf aufsteigen; ~ **gases round the planet** nebelartige Gase um den Planeten.
(b) (*liter: fanciful*) nebulös, verblasen (*geh*).
vapour, (*US*) **vapor** ['veɪpəʳ] *n* Dunst *m*; (*Phys also*) Gas *nt*; (*steamy*) Dampf *m*. **the** ~**s** (*Med old*) Schwermut *f*; ~ **trail** Kondensstreifen *m*; **thick** ~**s around the planet** eine dichte Dunsthülle um den Planeten.
vapouring, (*US*) **vaporing** ['veɪpərɪŋ] *n* (*liter*) (*boastful*) Prahlerei *f*; (*empty*) Geschwafel *nt*.
variability [ˌvɛərɪə'bɪlɪtɪ] *n see* **adj** **(a)** Veränderlichkeit *f*; Variabilität *f*; Unbeständigkeit, Wechselhaftigkeit *f*; (*of costs*) Schwankung(en *pl*), Unbeständigkeit *f*; (*of work*) unterschiedliche Qualität. **(b)** Regulierbarkeit *f*.
variable ['vɛərɪəbl] **1** *adj* **(a)** (*likely to vary*) (*Math*) veränderlich, variabel; (*Biol*) variabel; *weather, mood* unbeständig, wechselhaft. ~ **winds** wechselnde Winde *pl*; **certain costs will always remain** ~ bestimmte Kosten werden immer schwanken *or* variabel bleiben; **his work is very** ~ er arbeitet sehr unterschiedlich.
(b) *speed* regulierbar; *salary level* flexibel; **the height of the seat is** ~ die Höhe des Sitzes kann reguliert werden.
2 *n* (*Chem, Math, Phys*) Veränderliche, Variable *f*; (*fig*) veränderliche Größe, Variable *f*.
variance ['vɛərɪəns] *n* to be at ~ with sb anderer Meinung sein als jd (*about* hinsichtlich +*gen*); he is constantly at ~ with his parents er hat ständig Meinungsverschiedenheiten mit

seinen Eltern; this is at ~ with what he said earlier dies stimmt nicht mit dem überein, was er vorher gesagt hat.
(b) (*difference*) Unterschied *m*. a slight ~ **of opinion** eine unterschiedliche Auffassung; the predictable ~ **between the two sets of figures** die vorhersehbare Abweichung der beiden Zahlenreihen (voneinander).
variant ['vɛərɪənt] **1** *n* Variante *f*. a spelling ~ eine Schreibvariante. **2** *adj* **(a)** (*alternative*) andere(r, s). there are two ~ **spellings** es gibt zwei verschiedene Schreibweisen. **(b)** (*liter: diverse*) verschieden, unterschiedlich.
variation [ˌvɛərɪ'eɪʃən] *n* **(a)** (*varying*) Veränderung *f*; (*Sci*) Variation *f*; (*Met*) Schwankung *f*, Wechsel *m*; (*of temperature*) Unterschiede *pl*, Schwankung(en *pl*) *f*; (*of prices*) Schwankung *f*. an unexpected ~ **in conditions** eine unerwartete Veränderung der Bedingungen; there's been a lot of ~ **in the standard** recently in letzter Zeit war das Niveau sehr unterschiedlich; the result showed a wide ~ **in the range of comprehension** das Ergebnis zeigte ein sehr unterschiedliches Verständnis; these figures are subject to seasonal ~ diese Zahlen sind saisonbedingten Schwankungen unterworfen; ~ **in opinions/views** unterschiedliche Auffassungen/Ansichten.
(b) (*Mus*) Variation *f*. ~**s on a theme** Thema mit Variationen; Variationen zu einem *or* über ein Thema.
(c) (*different form*) Variation, Variante *f*; (*Biol*) Variante *f*. this is a ~ **on** that das ist eine Variation *or* Abänderung dessen *or* davon; a new ~ **in the design** eine neue Variation des Musters; regional ~**s in pronunciation** regionale Aussprachevarianten *pl*; several ~**s on a basic idea** mehrere Variationsmöglichkeiten einer Grundidee.
varicoloured, (*US*) **varicolored** ['vɛərɪ'kʌləd] *adj* mehrfarbig.
varicose ['værɪkəʊs] *adj*: ~ **veins** Krampfadern *pl*.
varied ['vɛərɪd] *adj* unterschiedlich; career, life bewegt; selection reichhaltig. a ~ **group of people** eine gemischte Gruppe; a ~ **collection of records** eine vielseitige *or* sehr gemischte Plattensammlung.
variegated ['vɛərɪɡeɪtɪd] *adj* buntscheckig; (*Bot*) geflammt, panaschiert.
variegation [ˌvɛərɪ'ɡeɪʃən] *n* Buntscheckigkeit *f*; (*Bot*) Panaschierung *f*.
variety [və'raɪətɪ] *n* **(a)** (*diversity*) Abwechslung *f*. to give *or* add ~ to sth Abwechslung in etw (*acc*) bringen; a job with a lot of ~ eine sehr abwechslungsreiche Arbeit; ~ is the spice of life (*prov*) öfter mal was Neues (*inf*), variatio delectat (*geh*).
(b) (*assortment*) Vielfalt *f*; (*Comm*) Auswahl *f* (*of* an + *dat*). that's quite a ~ for one company das ist ein ziemlich breites Spektrum für eine (einzige) Firma; an amazing ~ **of different moods** erstaunlich unterschiedliche Stimmungen *pl*; in a great ~ **of ways** auf die verschiedensten Arten *pl*; in a ~ **of colours** in den verschiedensten Farben *pl*; for a ~ **of reasons** aus verschiedenen *or* mehreren Gründen *pl*; for a great ~ **of reasons** aus vielen verschiedenen Gründen *pl*; a large ~ **of birds** eine Vielfalt an Vogelarten, viele verschiedene Vogelarten; you meet a great ~ **of people at this hotel** in diesem Hotel können Sie die verschiedensten Leute treffen.
(c) (*Biol, Bot*: *species*) Art, Varietät (*spec*) *f*.
(d) (*type*) Art *f*; (*of cigarette, potato*) Sorte *f*; (*of car, chair*) Modell *nt*. a new ~ **of** tulip/potato eine neue Tulpen-/Kartoffelsorte.
(e) (*esp Brit Theat*) Varieté *nt*.
variety: ~ **act** *n* Variaténummer *f*; ~ **artist** *n* Variétékünstler(in *f*) *m*; ~ **show** *n* (*Theat*) Varietévorführung *f*; (*TV*) Fernsehshow *f*; (*Rad, TV*) Unterhaltungssendung *f*; ~ **theatre** *n* Varietétheater *nt*.
variform ['vɛərɪfɔːm] *adj* vielgestaltig.
variola [və'raɪələ] *n* (*Med*) Pocken *pl*.
various ['vɛərɪəs] *adj* **(a)** (*different*) verschieden. **(b)** (*several*) mehrere, verschiedene.
variously ['vɛərɪəslɪ] *adv* **(a)** unterschiedlich. the news was ~ reported in the papers die Nachricht wurde in den Zeitungen unterschiedlich wiedergegeben. **(b)** verschiedentlich. he has been ~ described as a rogue and a charmer er wurde verschiedentlich ein Schlitzohr und Charmeur genannt.
varlet ['vɑːlɪt] *n* (*obs*) (*page*) Knappe *m*; (*rascal*) Schurke *m*.
varmint ['vɑːmɪnt] *n* (*dial, esp US*) Schurke, Halunke *m*. **(b)** (*animal*) Schädling *m*.
varnish ['vɑːnɪʃ] **1** *n* (*lit*) Lack *m*; (*on pottery*) Glasur *f*; (*fig*) Politur *f*. **2** *vt* lackieren; *painting* firnissen; *pottery* glasieren; (*fig*) truth, facts beschönigen.
varsity ['vɑːsɪtɪ] *n* (*Univ inf*) Uni *f* (*inf*); (*US also* ~ **team**) Schul-/Uniauswahl *f*.
vary ['vɛərɪ] **1** *vi* **(a)** (*diverge, differ*) sich unterscheiden, abweichen (*from* von). they ~ in price from the others sie unterscheiden sich im Preis von den anderen; opinions ~ on this point in diesem Punkt gehen die Meinungen auseinander; witnesses ~ about the time die Zeugen machen unterschiedliche Zeitangaben.
(b) (*be different*) unterschiedlich sein. the price varies from shop to shop der Preis ist von Geschäft zu Geschäft verschieden; his work varies seine Arbeit ist sehr unterschiedlich; it varies es ist unterschiedlich, das ist verschieden.
(c) (*change, fluctuate*) sich (ver)ändern; (*pressure, prices*) schwanken. prices that ~ with the season saisonbedingte Preise *pl*; to ~ with the weather sich nach dem Wetter richten.
2 *vt* (*alter*) verändern, abwandeln; (*give variety*) abwechslungsreich(er) gestalten, variieren. they never ~ their diet sie essen sehr eintönig; try to ~ your approach to the problem Sie sollten das Problem mal von einer anderen Seite angehen.
varying ['vɛərɪɪŋ] *adj* (*changing*) veränderlich; (*different*) unterschiedlich. our different results were due to ~ conditions

unsere verschiedenen Resultate beruhten auf unterschiedlichen Voraussetzungen; the ~ **weather conditions here** die veränderlichen Wetterverhältnisse hier; **with ~ degrees of success** mit unterschiedlichem Erfolg *m.*

vascular ['væskjuləʳ] *adj* vaskulär.

vase [vɑːz, *(US)* veɪz] *n* Vase *f.*

vasectomy [væ'sektəmɪ] *n* Vasektomie *f* (*spec*), Sterilisation *f* (*des Mannes*).

vaseline ® ['væsɪliːn] *n* Vaseline *f.*

vassal ['væsəl] **1** *n* (*lit, fig*) Vasall *m.* **2** *adj* vasallisch, Vasallen-. ~ **state** Vasallenstaat *m.*

vassalage ['væsəlɪdʒ] *n* (*Hist*) (*condition*) Vasallentum *nt*, Vasallität *f*; (*services due*) Vasallen- *or* Lehenspflicht *f*; (*land*) Lehen *nt*; (*fig*) Unterworfenheit *f* (*geh*) (to unter +*acc*).

vast [vɑːst] *adj* (+*er*) gewaltig, riesig; *area also* weit, ausgedehnt; *bulk also* riesengroß; *sums of money, success also* Riesen-; *difference also* riesengroß; *knowledge* enorm; *majority* überwältigend; *wealth, powers also* unermeßlich. a ~ **expanse** eine weite Ebene; **the ~ expanse of the ocean** die unermeßliche Weite des Ozeans; **to a ~ extent** in sehr hohem Maße.

vastly ['vɑːstlɪ] *adv* erheblich, wesentlich, bedeutend; *grateful* überaus, äußerst. **I was ~ amused at his remark** ich habe mich über seine Bemerkung köstlich amüsiert; **it is ~ different** da besteht ein erheblicher *or* wesentlicher Unterschied; ~ **rich** steinreich; **he is ~ superior to her** er ist ihr haushoch überlegen.

vastness ['vɑːstnɪs] *n* (*of size*) riesiges *or* gewaltiges Ausmaß, riesige Größe; (*of distance*) ungeheures Ausmaß; (*of ocean, plane, area*) riesige Weite; (*of sums of money*) ungeheure Höhe; (*of success*) Ausmaß *nt*; (*of difference*) Größe *f*; (*of knowledge, wealth*) gewaltiger Umfang.

vat [væt] *n* Faß *nt*; (*without lid*) Bottich *m.*

VAT ['viːeɪ'tiː, væt] (*Brit*) *abbr of* **value-added tax** Mehrwertsteuer *f*, MwSt.

vatic ['vætɪk] *adj* (*liter*) prophetisch.

Vatican ['vætɪkən] *n* Vatikan *m.* **the ~ Council** das Vatikanische Konzil; ~ **City** Vatikanstadt *f*; ~ **roulette** (*hum inf*) Knaus-Ogino(-Methode) *f.*

vaudeville ['vəʊdəvɪl] *n* (*US*) Varieté *nt.*

vaudeville: ~ **show** *n* Varieté(vorführung *f*) *nt*; ~ **singer** *n* Varietésänger(in *f*) *m.*

vault¹ [vɔːlt] *n* (a) (*cellar*) (Keller)gewölbe *nt*; (*tomb*) Gruft *f*; (*in bank*) Tresor(raum) *m.* **in the ~s** im Gewölbe *etc.* (b) (*Archit*) Gewölbe *nt.* **the ~ of heaven** (*liter*) das Himmelsgewölbe (*liter*).

vault² **1** *n* (*scissors*) Schersprung *m*; (*legs behind*) Flanke *f*; (*legs through arms*) Hocke *f*; (*legs apart*) Grätsche *f*; *see* **pole** ~.
2 *vi* springen; einen Schersprung/eine Flanke/eine Hocke/eine Grätsche machen. **to ~ into the saddle** sich in den Sattel schwingen.
3 *vt* springen über (+*acc*), überspringen; einen Schersprung/eine Flanke/eine Hocke/eine Grätsche machen über (+*acc*).

vaulted ['vɔːltɪd] *adj* (*Archit*) gewölbt.

vaulting ['vɔːltɪŋ] *n* (*Archit*) Wölbung *f.*

vaulting horse *n* (*in gym*) Pferd *nt.*

vaunt [vɔːnt] **1** *vt* rühmen, preisen (*geh*). **much-~ed** vielgepriesen; **Cologne ~s a splendid cathedral** Köln kann sich eines herrlichen Doms rühmen. **2** *n* Loblied *nt*, Lobgesang *m.*

VC *abbr of* **Victoria Cross** (*Mil*) Viktoriakreuz *nt* (*höchste britische Tapferkeitsauszeichnung*).

VD *abbr of* **venereal disease** Geschlechtskrankheit *f.* ~ **clinic** Klinik *f* für Geschlechtskrankheiten, ≈ Hautklinik *f.*

VDU *abbr of* **visual display unit** Sichtgerät.

veal [viːl] *n* Kalbfleisch *nt.* ~ **cutlet** Kalbsschnitzel *nt.*

vector ['vektəʳ] *n* (*Math, Aviat*) Vektor *m*; (*Biol*) Träger *m.*

vector *in cpds* (*Math*) Vektor(en)-.

vectorial [vek'tɔːrɪəl] *adj* vektoriell.

Veda ['veɪdə] *n* Weda *m.*

V-E Day *n* Tag *m* des Sieges in Europa im 2. Weltkrieg.

veep [viːp] *n* (*US sl*) ≈ **vice-president**.

veer [vɪəʳ] **1** *vi* (*wind*) (sich) drehen (*im Uhrzeigersinn*) (to nach); (*ship*) abdrehen; (*car*) ausscheren; (*load*) scharf abbiegen, abknicken. **the ship ~ed round** das Schiff drehte ab; **to ~ off course** vom Kurs abkommen; **it ~s from one extreme to the other** es schwankt zwischen zwei Extremen; **he ~s from one extreme to the other** er fällt von einem Extrem ins andere; **he ~ed round to my point of view** er ist auf meine Richtung umgeschwenkt; **he ~ed off or away from his subject** er kam (völlig) vom Thema ab; **~ing swallows** umherschwirrende Schwalben *pl*; **the road ~ed to the left** die Straße machte eine scharfe Linkskurve; **the car ~ed off the road** das Auto kam von der Straße ab; **the driver was forced to ~ sharply** der Fahrer mußte plötzlich das Steuer herumreißen; **the drunken driver was ~ing all over the road** der betrunkene Fahrer fuhr im Zickzack die Straße entlang; **the car skidded and ~ed right round** der Rennwagen kam ins Schleudern und drehte sich um die eigene Achse.
2 *n* (*of wind*) Drehung *f*; (*of ship, fig: in policy*) Kurswechsel *m*; (*of car*) Ausscheren *nt*; (*of road*) Knick *m.* **with a sudden ~ the car left the road** das Auto scherte plötzlich aus und kam von der Straße ab; **the driver corrected the ~ just in time** der Fahrer konnte das Auto gerade noch rechtzeitig abfangen; **a ~ to the left politically** ein politischer Ruck nach links.
♦ **veer** (a)**round** *vt sep car* herumreißen; (*by 180°*) wenden. **he ~ed the ship ~ to avoid the rocks** er schwenkte ab, um den Felsen auszuweichen.

vegetable ['vedʒtəbl] *n* (a) Gemüse *nt.* **with fresh ~s** mit frischem Gemüse; (*on menu*) mit frischen Gemüsen; **what ~s do you grow in your garden?** welche Gemüsesorten hast du in

deinem Garten?; **cabbage is a ~** Kohl ist eine Gemüsepflanze.
(b) (*generic term: plant*) Pflanze *f.*
(c) **he's just a ~** er vegetiert nur dahin *or* vor sich hin; **she's become a ~** sie ist zum körperlichen und geistigen Krüppel geworden, sie vegetiert nur noch dahin.

vegetable: ~ **dish** *n* (*to eat*) Gemüsegericht *nt*; (*bowl*) Gemüseschüssel *f*; ~ **garden** *n* Gemüsegarten *m*; ~ **kingdom** *n* Pflanzenreich *nt*; ~ **knife** *n* kleines Küchenmesser; ~ **marrow** *n* Gartenkürbis *m*; ~ **matter** *n* pflanzliche Stoffe *pl*; ~ **oil** *n* pflanzliches Öl; (*Cook*) Pflanzenöl *nt*; ~ **salad** *n* Gemüsesalat *m*; ~ **soup** *n* Gemüsesuppe *f.*

vegetarian [,vedʒɪ'tɛərɪən] **1** *n* Vegetarier(in *f*) *m.* **2** *adj* vegetarisch.

vegetarianism [,vedʒɪ'tɛərɪənɪzəm] *n* Vegetarismus *m.*

vegetate ['vedʒɪteɪt] *vi* (a) wachsen. (b) (*fig*) dahinvegetieren.

vegetation [,vedʒɪ'teɪʃən] *n* (a) Vegetation *f.* **could we live on the ~ here?** könnten wir uns von dem ernähren, was hier wächst?
(b) (*wasting away*) (*of sick people*) Dahinvegetieren *nt*; (*of mind*) Verödung, Verarmung *f.* **the patients just lie there in a state of ~** die Patienten dämmern nur noch vor sich hin *or* vegetieren nur noch dahin.

vegetative ['vedʒɪtətɪv] *adj* (*Bot*) vegetativ.

vehemence ['viːɪməns] *n* Vehemenz *f* (*geh*); (*of actions, feelings also*) Heftigkeit *f*; (*of love, hatred also*) Leidenschaftlichkeit *f*; (*of protests also*) Schärfe, Heftigkeit *f.*

vehement ['viːɪmənt] *adj* vehement (*geh*); *feelings, speech also* leidenschaftlich; *attack also* heftig, scharf; *desire, dislike, opposition also* heftig, stark.

vehemently ['viːɪməntlɪ] *adv* vehement (*geh*), heftig; *love, hate also* leidenschaftlich; *protest also* heftig, mit aller Schärfe.

vehicle ['viːɪkl] *n* Fahrzeug *nt*; (*Pharm*) Vehikel *nt*, Trägersubstanz *f*; (*Art*) Lösungsmittel *nt*; (*fig: medium*) Mittel, Vehikel (*geh*) *nt.* **this paper is a ~ of** right-wing opinions diese Zeitung ist ein Sprachrohr *nt* der Rechten; **language is the ~ of thought** die Sprache ist das Medium des Denkens.

vehicular [vɪ'hɪkjʊləʳ] *adj* Fahrzeug-. ~ **traffic** Fahrzeugverkehr *m.*

veil [veɪl] **1** *n* Schleier *m.* **to take the ~** den Schleier nehmen, ins Kloster gehen; **the valley lay in a ~ of mist** über dem Tal lag ein Nebelschleier; **to draw** *or* **throw a ~ over sth** den Schleier des Vergessens über etw (*acc*) breiten; **under a ~ of secrecy** unter dem Mantel der Verschwiegenheit; **the ~ of secrecy over all their activities** der Schleier des Geheimnisses, der all ihre Aktivitäten umgibt.
2 *vt* (a) verschleiern.
(b) (*fig*) *facts* verschleiern; *truth also* verheimlichen; *feelings* verbergen. **the clouds ~ed the moon** die Wolken verhüllten *or* verdeckten den Mond; **the town was ~ed by mist** die Stadt lag in Nebel gehüllt.

veiled [veɪld] *adj reference* versteckt; *face* verschleiert.

veiling ['veɪlɪŋ] *n* Schleier *m*; (*fig*) (*of facts*) Verschleierung *f*; (*of truth also*) Verheimlichung *f.*

vein [veɪn] *n* (a) (*Anat, Bot, Min*) Ader *f.* ~**s and arteries** Venen und Arterien *pl*; **there is a ~ of truth in what he says** es ist eine Spur von Wahrheit in dem, was er sagt; **an artistic ~** eine künstlerische Ader; **there's a ~ of spitefulness in his character** er hat einen gehässigen Zug in seinem Charakter; **the ~ of humour which runs through the book** ein humorvoller Zug, der durch das ganze Buch geht.
(b) (*fig: mood*) Stimmung, Laune *f.* **in a humorous ~** in lustiger Stimmung; **to be in the ~ for sth** zu etw aufgelegt sein; **in the same ~** in derselben Art.

veined [veɪnd] *adj* geädert; *hand* mit hervortretenden Adern.

velar ['viːləʳ] **1** *adj* velar. **2** *n* Velar(laut) *m.*

veld, veldt [velt] *n* (*in South Africa*) Steppe *f.*

vellum ['veləm] *n* Pergament *nt.*

vellum: ~ **binding** *n* Pergamenteinband *m*; ~ **paper** *n* Pergamentpapier *nt.*

velocipede [və'lɒsɪpiːd] *n* (*form*) Fahrrad, Veloziped (*old*) *nt.*

velocity [və'lɒsɪtɪ] *n* Geschwindigkeit *f.*

velour(s) [və'lʊəʳ] *n* Velours *m.*

velvet ['velvɪt] **1** *n* Samt *m.* **like ~** wie Samt, samtig. **2** *adj dress, jacket* Samt-; *skin, feel* samtweich, samten (*geh*). **the ~ touch of his hand** seine sanften Hände.

velveteen ['velvɪtiːn] *n* Veloursamt *m.*

velvety ['velvɪtɪ] *adj* samtig.

Ven *abbr of* **Venerable**.

venal ['viːnl] *adj* (*liter*) *person* käuflich, feil (*liter*); *practices* korrupt. **out of ~ interests** aus eigennützigen Motiven.

venality [viː'nælɪtɪ] *n* (*liter*) *see adj* Käuflichkeit *f*; Korruption *f*; eigennützige Motive *pl.*

vend [vend] *vt* verkaufen.

vendetta [ven'detə] *n* Fehde *f*; (*in family*) Blutrache *f*; (*of gangsters*) Vendetta *f.* **to carry on a ~ against sb** sich mit jdm bekriegen, mit jdm in Fehde liegen/an jdm Blutrache üben.

vending machine ['vendɪŋmə'ʃiːn] *n* (Verkäufer)automat *m.*

vendor ['vendɔːʳ] *n* (*esp Jur*) Verkäufer *m.* **newspaper ~** Zeitungsverkäufer *m*; **street ~** Straßenhändler *m.*

veneer [və'nɪəʳ] **1** *n* (*lit*) Furnier *nt*; (*fig*) Politur *f.* **it's just a ~** es ist nur Politur *or* schöner Schein; **the way he behaved presented a ~ of refinement** nach außen hin machte er einen kultivierten Eindruck; **the cities with their thin ~ of civilization** die Städte mit ihrem dünnen Lack *or* Putz der Zivilisation.
2 *vt wood* furnieren.

venerable ['venərəbl] *adj* ehrwürdig.

venerate ['venəreɪt] *vt* verehren, hochachten; *sb's memory* ehren. **his memory was highly ~d** sein Andenken wurde sehr in Ehren gehalten.

veneration [,venə'reɪʃən] *n* Bewunderung, Verehrung *f* (*of für*); (*of idols*) Verehrung *f*; (*of traditions*) Ehrfurcht *f* (*of vor*

+*dat*). **to hold sb/sb's memory in** ~ jdn hochachten *or* verehren/jds Andenken in Ehren halten.

venereal [vɪ'nɪərɪəl] *adj* venerisch. ~ **disease** Geschlechtskrankheit *f*, venerische Krankheit (*spec*).

Venetian [vɪ'ni:ʃən] **1** *adj* venezianisch. ~ **blind** Jalousie *f*; ~ **glass** venezianisches Glas. **2** *n* Venezianer(in *f*) *m*.

Venezuela [ˌvene'zweɪlə] *n* Venezuela *nt*.

Venezuelan [ˌvene'zweɪlən] **1** *adj* venezolanisch. **2** *n* Venezolaner(in *f*) *m*.

vengeance ['vendʒəns] *n* **(a)** Vergeltung, Rache *f*. **to take** ~ **(up)on sb** Vergeltung an jdm üben.
   (b) (*inf*) **with a** ~ gewaltig (*inf*); **then the brass section comes in with a** ~ dann kommt der kraftvolle *or* gewaltige Einsatz der Bläser; **to work with a** ~ hart *or* mächtig (*inf*) arbeiten.

vengeful ['vendʒfʊl] *adj* rachsüchtig.

venial ['vi:nɪəl] *adj* verzeihlich, entschuldbar. ~ **sin** läßliche Sünde.

veniality [ˌvi:nɪ'ælɪt] *n* Entschuldbarkeit *f*; (*of sin*) Läßlichkeit *f*.

Venice ['venɪs] *n* Venedig *nt*.

venison ['venɪsən] *n* Reh(fleisch) *nt*.

venom ['venəm] *n* (*lit*) Gift *nt*; (*fig*) Bosheit, Gehässigkeit *f*. **he spoke with real** ~ **in his voice** er sprach mit haßerfüllter Stimme; **a theatre review full of** ~ ein giftiger Verriß eines Stückes; **she spat her** ~ **at him** sie giftete ihn wütend an; **his pen, dipped in** ~ seine giftige Feder.

venomous ['venəməs] *adj* (*lit*, *fig*) giftig; *snake* Gift-; *tone also* gehässig; *tongue also* scharf, böse; *sarcasm* beißend.

venomously ['venəməslɪ] *adv* boshaft; *look*, *say* giftig.

venous ['vi:nəs] *adj* (*form*) (*Anat*) venös; (*Bot*) geädert.

vent [vent] **1** *n* (*for gas, liquid*) Öffnung *f*; (*in chimney*) Abzug *m*; (*in barrel*) Spundloch *nt*; (*in coat*) Schlitz *m*; (*for feelings*) Ventil *m*. **jacket with a single/double** ~ Jacke mit Rückenschlitz *m*/Seitenschlitzen *pl*; **inlet/outlet** ~ Belüftungs-/Entlüftungsöffnung *f*; **to give** ~ **to sth** (*fig*) einer Sache (*dat*) Ausdruck verleihen; **to give** ~ **to one's feelings** seinen Gefühlen freien Lauf lassen; **to give** ~ **to one's anger** seinem Ärger Luft machen.
   2 *vt feelings*, *anger* abreagieren (*on* an +*dat*).

ventilate ['ventɪleɪt] *vt* **(a)** (*control air flow*) belüften; (*let fresh air in*) lüften. **(b)** *blood* Sauerstoff zuführen (+*dat*), mit Sauerstoff versorgen. **(c)** (*fig*) *grievance* vorbringen. **(d)** (*fig*) *question*, *issue* erörtern; *opinion*, *view* äußern.

ventilation [ˌventɪ'leɪʃən] *n* **(a)** (*control of air flow*) Belüftung, Ventilation *f*; (*letting fresh air in*) Lüften *nt*. ~ **shaft** Luftschacht *m*; **there's very poor** ~ **in here** die Belüftung dieses Raumes ist schlecht.
   (b) (*of blood*) Sauerstoffzufuhr *f*.
   (c) (*of grievance*) Vorbringen *nt*.
   (d) (*of question, issue*) Erörterung *f*; (*of opinion, view*) Äußerung *f*.

ventilator ['ventɪleɪtəʳ] *n* Ventilator *m*.

ventral ['ventrəl] *adj* (*form*) ventral (*form*), Bauch-.

ventricle ['ventrɪkəl] *n* Kammer *f*, Ventrikel *m* (*form*).

ventriloquism [ven'trɪləkwɪzəm] *n* Bauchredekunst *f*, Bauchreden *nt*.

ventriloquist [ven'trɪləkwɪst] *n* Bauchredner(in *f*) *m*.

venture ['ventʃəʳ] **1** *n* Unternehmung *f*, Unternehmen, Unterfangen *nt*. **mountain-climbing is his latest** ~ seit neuestem hat er sich aufs Bergsteigen verlegt; **one of the government's more controversial** ~**s** eines der umstritteneren Projekte der Regierung; **a new** ~ **in publishing** ein neuer verlegerischer Versuch, ein neues verlegerisches Experiment; **this was a disastrous** ~ **for the company** dieses Projekt *or* dieser Versuch war für die Firma ein Fiasko; **his first** ~ **at novel-writing** sein erster Versuch, Romane zu schreiben; **our greatest** ~ **in the field of space exploration** unser bedeutendstes Projekt auf dem Gebiet der Raumforschung; **he made a lot of money out of his** ~**s in the world of finance** er verdiente bei seinen Spekulationen in der Finanzwelt viel Geld; **his purchase of stocks was his first** ~ **into the world of finance** mit dem Erwerb von Aktien wagte er sich zum erstenmal in die Finanzwelt; **his early** ~**s into crime were successful** seine frühen kriminellen Abenteuer waren erfolgreich; **rowing the Atlantic alone was quite a** ~ allein über den Atlantik zu rudern, war ein ziemlich gewagtes Abenteuer; **the astronauts on their** ~ **into the unknown** die Astronauten auf ihrer abenteuerlichen Reise ins Unbekannte.
   2 *vt* **(a)** *life*, *reputation* aufs Spiel setzen; *money also* riskieren (*on* bei). **nothing** ~**d nothing gained** (*Prov*) wer wagt, gewinnt (*Prov*).
   (b) *guess*, *explanation*, *statement* wagen; *opinion* zu äußern wagen. **if I may** ~ **an opinion** wenn ich mir erlauben darf, meine Meinung zu sagen; **in his latest article he** ~**s an explanation of the phenomenon** in seinem letzten Artikel versucht er, eine Erklärung des Phänomens zu geben; **I** ~ **to add that ...** ich wage sogar zu behaupten, daß ...
   3 *vi* sich wagen. **no other traveller had dared to** ~ **so far** noch kein anderer Reisender hatte sich so weit vorgewagt; **to** ~ **out of doors** sich vor die Tür wagen; **they lost money when they** ~**d into book publishing** sie verloren Geld bei ihrem Versuch, Bücher zu verlegen; **the company** ~**d into a new field** die Firma wagte sich in ein neues Gebiet vor.

♦**venture forth** (*liter*) *or* **out** *vi* sich hinauswagen. **the soldiers** ~**d** ~ **to find the enemy** die Soldaten wagten sich vor, um den Feind ausfindig zu machen; **the astronauts** ~**d** ~ **into the unknown** die Astronauten wagten sich ins Unbekannte; **we** ~**d** ~ **on this intellectual enterprise** wir wagten uns an dieses intellektuelle Unterfangen heran.

♦**venture on** *vi* +*prep obj* sich wagen an (+*acc*). **Drake** ~**d** ~ **a**

voyage of exploration round the world Drake wagte sich auf eine Entdeckungsreise um die Welt; **they** ~**d** ~ **a programme of reform** sie wagten sich an ein Reformprogramm heran; **the Prime Minister** ~**d** ~ **a statement of the position der** Premier hatte den Mut, eine Erklärung zur Lage abzugeben; **when we first** ~**d** ~ **this voyage of scientific discovery** als wir uns zum ersten Mal auf wissenschaftliches Neuland wagten.

venturesome ['ventʃəsəm] *adj* person, *action* abenteuerlich.

venue ['venju:] *n* (*meeting place*) Treffpunkt *m*; (*Sport*) Austragungsort *m*; (*Jur*) Verhandlungsort *m*.

Venus ['vi:nəs] *n* Venus *f*. ~**'s-flytrap** Venusfliegenfalle *f*.

Venusian [və'nju:ʃən] **1** *n* Bewohner(in *f*) *m* der Venus. **2** *adj* Venus-.

veracious [və'reɪʃəs] *adj* person ehrlich, aufrichtig; *report* wahrheitsgemäß.

veracity [və'ræsɪtɪ] *n* (*of person*) Ehrlichkeit, Aufrichtigkeit *f*; (*of report, evidence*) Wahrheit, Richtigkeit *f*.

veranda(h) [və'rændə] *n* Veranda *f*.

verb [vɜ:b] *n* Verb, Zeitwort, Verbum *nt*.

verbal ['vɜ:bəl] *adj* **(a)** (*spoken*) *statement*, *confession* mündlich; *agreement also* verbal. **(b)** (*of words*) *error*, *skills*, *distinction* sprachlich. ~ **memory** Wortgedächtnis *nt*. **(c)** (*literal*) *translation* wörtlich. **(d)** (*Gram*) verbal. ~ **noun** Verbalsubstantiv *nt*.

verbalize ['vɜ:bəlaɪz] *vt* **(a)** (*put into words*) ausdrücken, in Worte fassen. **(b)** (*Gram*) verbal ausdrücken.

verbally ['vɜ:bəlɪ] *adv* **(a)** (*spoken*) mündlich, verbal. **(b)** (*as a verb*) verbal.

verbatim [vɜ:'beɪtɪm] **1** *adj* wörtlich. **2** *adv* wortwörtlich.

verbena [vɜ:'bi:nə] *n* Eisenkraut *nt*.

verbiage ['vɜ:bɪɪdʒ] *n* Wortwust *m*, Wortfülle *f*, Blabla *nt* (*inf*). **you won't impress the examiners with a lot of** ~ mit Geschwafel *nt or* Blabla (*inf*) ist kannst du die Prüfer nicht beeindrucken; **there's too much** ~ **in this report** dieser Bericht ist zu umständlich geschrieben.

verbose [vɜ:'bəus] *adj* wortreich, langatmig, weitschweifig.

verbosely [vɜ:'bəuslɪ] *adv* langatmig.

verbosity [vɜ:'bɒsɪtɪ] *n* Langatmigkeit *f*. **it sounds impressive but it's sheer** ~ es klingt beeindruckend, ist aber nichts als Geschwafel.

verdant ['vɜ:dənt] *adj* (*liter*) grün.

verdict ['vɜ:dɪkt] *n* **(a)** (*Jur*) Urteil *nt*. ~ **of guilty/not guilty** Schuldspruch *m*/Freispruch *m*; **what's the** ~? wie lautet das Urteil?; *see* **bring in**, **return**.
   (b) (*of doctor*) Urteil *nt*; (*of press, critic etc also*) Verdikt *nt* (*geh*); (*of electors*) Entscheidung *f*, Votum *nt*. **what's your** ~ **on this wine?** wie beurteilst du diesen Wein?; **to give one's** ~ **about** *or* **on sth** sein Urteil über etw (*acc*) abgeben.

verdigris ['vɜ:dɪgri:s] *n* Grünspan *m*.

verdure ['vɜ:djuəʳ] *n* (*liter*) (*colour*) sattes Grün; (*vegetation*) reiche Flora (*geh*).

verge [vɜ:dʒ] *n* (*lit, fig*) Rand *m*. **"keep off the** ~**"** „Bankette *or* Seitenstreifen nicht befahrbar"; **to be on the** ~ **of ruin/war** am Rande des Ruins/eines Krieges stehen; **to be on the** ~ **of a nervous breakdown** am Rande eines Nervenzusammenbruchs sein; **to be on the** ~ **of a discovery** kurz vor einer Entdeckung stehen; **to be on the** ~ **of tears** den Tränen nahe sein; **to be on the** ~ **of doing sth** im Begriff sein, etw zu tun; **I was on the** ~ **of giving away the secret** (*accidentally*) ich hätte das Geheimnis um ein Haar verraten.

♦**verge on** *vi* +*prep obj* (*ideas, actions*) grenzen an (*acc*). **he's verging** ~ **bankruptcy** er steht kurz vor dem Bankrott; **she is verging** ~ **fifty** sie geht auf die Fünfzig zu; **she was verging** ~ **madness** sie stand am Rande des Wahnsinns.

verger ['vɜ:dʒəʳ] *n* (*Eccl*) Küster *m*.

Vergil ['vɜ:dʒɪl] *n* Virgil, Vergil *m*.

veridical [və'rɪdɪkl] *adj* (*form*) wahrheitsgetreu, wahrheitsgemäß.

verifiable ['verɪfaɪəbl] *adj* nachweisbar, nachprüfbar, verifizierbar (*geh*).

verification [ˌverɪfɪ'keɪʃən] *n* (*check*) Überprüfung *f*; (*confirmation*) Bestätigung, Verifikation (*geh*) *f*; (*proof*) Nachweis *m*. **this completes the** ~ **of the truth of the complaint** damit ist die Berechtigung der Beschwerde endgültig nachgewiesen; **these claims are open to empirical** ~ diese Behauptungen lassen sich empirisch nachweisen.

verify ['verɪfaɪ] *vt* (*check up*) (über)prüfen; (*confirm*) bestätigen, beglaubigen; *theory* beweisen, verifizieren (*geh*). **(b)** *suspicions*, *theory* bestätigen.

verily ['verɪlɪ] *adv* (*obs*) wahrlich (*obs*), fürwahr (*obs*). ~ **I say unto you** wahrlich, ich sage euch.

verisimilitude [ˌverɪsɪ'mɪlɪtju:d] *n* (*form*) Wahrhaftigkeit (*liter*), Echtheit *f*; (*of theory*) Plausibilität, Evidenz (*liter*) *f*.

veritable ['verɪtəbl] *adj* *genius* wahr. **a** ~ **disaster/miracle** die reinste Katastrophe/das reinste Wunder.

veritably ['verɪtəblɪ] *adv* in der Tat, fürwahr (*obs*).

verity ['verɪtɪ] *n* (*liter*) Wahrheit *f*.

vermicelli [ˌvɜ:mɪ'selɪ] *n* Fadennudeln, Suppennudeln *pl*.

vermicide ['vɜ:mɪsaɪd] *n* Wurmmittel, Vermizid (*spec*) *nt*.

vermifuge ['vɜ:mɪfju:dʒ] *n* Wurmmittel, Vermifugum (*spec*) *nt*.

vermilion [və'mɪljən] **1** *n* Zinnoberrot *nt*. **2** *adj* zinnoberrot.

vermin ['vɜ:mɪn] *n, no pl* **(a)** (*animal*) Schädling *m*. **(b)** (*insects*) Ungeziefer *nt*. **(c)** (*pej: people*) Pack, Ungeziefer *nt*.

verminous ['vɜ:mɪnəs] *adj* *people*, *clothes* voller Ungeziefer.

vermouth ['vɜ:məθ] *n* Wermut *m*.

vernacular [və'nækjʊləʳ] **1** *n* **(a)** (*dialect*) Mundart *f*; (*not Latin, not official language*) Landessprache *f*. **this word has now come into the** ~ dieses Wort ist jetzt in die Alltagssprache eingegangen.
   (b) (*jargon*) Fachsprache *f or* -jargon *m*.

(c) (*hum: strong language*) deftige Sprache. **please excuse the ~** entschuldigen Sie bitte, daß ich mich so drastisch ausdrücke.

2 *adj* **~ newspaper** Zeitung *f* in der regionalen Landessprache; **~ poet** Mundartdichter *m*.

vernal ['vɜːnl] *adj* **equinox**, (*liter*) **flowers** Frühlings-.

veronica [və'rɒnɪkə] *n* (*Bot*) Ehrenpreis *m or nt*, Veronika *f*.

versatile ['vɜːsətaɪl] *adj* vielseitig. **he has a very ~ mind** er ist geistig sehr flexibel.

versatility [ˌvɜːsə'tɪlɪtɪ] *n see adj* Vielseitigkeit *f*; Flexibilität *f*.

verse [vɜːs] *n* (a) (*stanza*) Strophe *f*. **a ~ from "The Tempest"** ein Vers *m* aus dem „Sturm". (b) *no pl* (*poetry*) Poesie, Dichtung *f*. **in ~** in Versform; **~ drama** Versdrama *nt*. (c) (*of Bible, Koran*) Vers *m*.

versed [vɜːst] *adj* (*also* **well ~**) bewandert, beschlagen (*in* in +*dat*). **he's well ~ in the art of self-defence** er beherrscht die Kunst der Selbstverteidigung; **I'm not very well ~ in ...** ich verstehe nicht viel *or* habe wenig Ahnung von ...

versification [ˌvɜːsɪfɪ'keɪʃən] *n* (*act*) Versbildung *f*; (*style*) Versform *f*; (*rules*) Verskunst *f*.

versifier ['vɜːsɪfaɪəʳ] *n* (*pej*) Verseschmied, Dichterling *m*.

versify ['vɜːsɪfaɪ] **1** *vt* in Versform bringen. **2** *vi* Verse schmieden (*pej*), dichten.

version ['vɜːʃən] *n* (a) (*account: of event, of facts*) Version, Darstellung *f*. (b) (*variant*) Version *f*; (*of text also*) Fassung *f*; (*of car*) Modell *nt*, Typ *m*. (c) (*translation*) Übersetzung *f*.

verso ['vɜːsəu] *n* Rückseite *f*; (*of book also*) Verso *nt* (*spec*); (*of coin also*) Revers *m* (*spec*).

versus ['vɜːsəs] *prep* gegen (+*acc*).

vertebra ['vɜːtɪbrə] *n, pl* **-e** ['vɜːtɪbriː] Rückenwirbel *m*.

vertebral ['vɜːtɪbrəl] *adj* (*form*) Wirbel-. **~ column** Wirbelsäule *f*.

vertebrate ['vɜːtɪbrət] **1** *n* Wirbeltier *nt*. **the ~s** die Wirbeltiere *or* Vertebraten (*spec*). **2** *adj* Wirbel-.

vertex ['vɜːteks] *n, pl* **vertices** Scheitel(punkt) *m*.

vertical ['vɜːtɪkəl] **1** *adj* **line** senkrecht, vertikal. **~ cliffs** senkrecht abfallende Klippen; **~ take-off aircraft** Senkrechtstarter *m*. **2** *n* (*line*) Vertikale, Senkrechte *f*. **to be off the ~** or out of the **~** nicht im Lot stehen.

vertically ['vɜːtɪkəlɪ] *adv* senkrecht, vertikal. **stand it ~ or it'll fall over** stell es aufrecht hin, sonst fällt es um.

vertices ['vɜːtɪsiːz] *pl of* **vertex**.

vertiginous [vɜː'tɪdʒɪnəs] *adj* (*liter*) **heights** schwindelerregend, schwindelnd (*geh*).

vertigo ['vɜːtɪɡəu] *n* Schwindel *m*; (*Med*) Gleichgewichtsstörung *f*. **he suffers from ~** ihm wird leicht schwindlig; (*Med*) er leidet an Gleichgewichtsstörungen *pl*.

verve [vɜːv] *n* Schwung *m*; (*of person, team also*) Elan *m*; (*of play, performance also*) Ausdruckskraft, Verve (*geh*) *f*.

very ['verɪ] **1** *adv* **a** (*extremely*) sehr. **it's ~ well written** es ist sehr gut geschrieben; **that's not ~ funny** das ist überhaupt nicht lustig; **it's ~ possible** es ist durchaus *or* (sehr) gut möglich; **~ probably** höchstwahrscheinlich; **he is so ~ lazy** er ist *so* faul; **how ~ odd** wie eigenartig; **V~ Important Person** prominente Persönlichkeit; **~ little** sehr wenig; **~ little milk** ganz *or* sehr wenig Milch.

(b) (*absolutely*) aller-. **~ best quality** allerbeste Qualität; **~ last/first** allerletzte(r, s)/allererste(r, s); **she is the ~ cleverest in the class** sie ist die Klassenbeste; **at the ~ latest** allerspätestens; **this is the ~ last time** I'll warn you ich warne dich jetzt zum allerletzten Mal; **to do one's ~ best** sein Äußerstes tun; **this is the ~ best** das ist das Allerbeste; **this is the ~ most** I can offer das ist mir mein äußerstes Angebot; **at the ~ most/ least** allerhöchstens/allerwenigstens; **to be in the ~ best of** health sich bester Gesundheit erfreuen; **they are the ~ best of** friends sie sind die dicksten Freunde.

(c) **~ much** sehr; **thank you ~ much** vielen Dank; **I liked it ~** much es hat mir sehr gut gefallen; **~ much bigger** sehr viel größer; **~ much respected** sehr angesehen; **he is ~ much the** more intelligent er ist bei weitem der Intelligentere; **he doesn't** work **~ much** er arbeitet nicht sehr viel; **~ much so sehr** (sogar).

(d) (*for emphasis*) **he fell ill and died the ~ same day** er wurde krank und starb noch am selben Tag; **he died the ~ same** day as Kennedy er starb genau am selben Tag wie Kennedy; **the ~ same** hat genau der gleiche Hut; **we met again the ~ next** day wir trafen uns am nächsten *or* folgenden Tag schon wieder; **the ~ next day** he walked under a bus schon einen Tag später kam er unter einen Bus; **what he predicted happened the ~** next week was er vorhersagte, trat in der Woche darauf tatsächlich ein; **my ~ own car** mein eigenes Auto; **a house of** your **~ own** ein eigenes Häuschen.

(e) **~ well**, if that's what you want nun gut, wenn du das willst; **~ good**, sir geht in Ordnung, mein Herr, sehr wohl, mein Herr (*dated*); **if you want that, ~ well, but ...** wenn du das willst, in Ordnung *or* bitte, aber ...

2 *adj* (a) (*precise, exact*) genau. **that ~ day/moment** genau an diesem Tag/in diesem Augenblick; **in the ~ centre of the picture** genau in der Mitte des Bildes; **this laboratory is the ~** heart of our factory dieses Labor ist der Kern unseres Werkes; **at the ~ heart of the organization** direkt im Zentrum der Organisation; **a man in the ~ prime of life** ein Mann im besten Alter; **on the ~ spot where ...** genau an der Stelle, wo ...; **those were his ~ words** genau das waren seine Worte; **you are the ~** person I want to speak to mit *Ihnen* wollte ich sprechen; **the ~** thing/man I need genau das, was ich brauche/genau der Mann, den ich brauche; **the ~ thing!** genau das richtige!; **to catch sb in** the **~ act** jdn auf frischer Tat ertappen.

(b) (*extreme*) äußerste(r, s). **in the ~ beginning** ganz am Anfang; **at the ~ end** ganz am Ende; **at the ~ back/front** ganz hinten/vorn(e); **go to the ~ end of the road** gehen Sie die Straße

ganz entlang *or* durch; **to the ~ end of his life** bis an sein Lebensende; **in the ~ depths of the sea/forest** in den Tiefen des Meeres/im tiefsten Wald.

(c) (*mere*) **the ~ thought of it** allein schon der Gedanke daran, der bloße Gedanke daran; **the ~ idea!** nein, so etwas!

Very ® ['vɪərɪ] *adj* (*Mil*) **~ light** Leuchtkugel *f*.

very high frequency *n* Ultrakurzwelle *f*.

vesicle ['vesɪkl] *n* Bläschen *nt*; (*Med also*) Vesicula *f* (*form*).

vespers ['vespəz] *npl* Vesper *f*.

vessel ['vesl] *n* (a) (*Naut*) Schiff *nt*. (b) (*form: receptacle*) Gefäß *nt*. **drinking ~** Trinkgefäß *nt*. (c) (*Anat, Bot*) Gefäß *nt*.

vest¹ [vest] *n* (a) (*Brit*) Unterhemd *nt*. (b) (*US*) Weste *f*. **~-pocket** *adj* (*US*) Taschen-, im Westentaschenformat.

vest² *vt* (*form*) **to ~ sb with sth, to ~ sth in sb** jdm etw verleihen; **the rights ~ed in the Crown** die der Krone zustehenden Rechte; **Congress is ~ed with the power to declare war** der Kongreß verfügt über das Recht, den Krieg zu erklären; **the authority ~ed in me** die mir verliehene Macht; **he has ~ed interests in the oil business** er ist (finanziell) am Ölgeschäft beteiligt; **the ~ed interests in the oil business** (*people*) die am Ölgeschäft Beteiligten *pl*; **he has a ~ed interest in the play** (*fig*) er hat ein persönliches Interesse an dem Stück.

vestal ['vestl] *adj* vestalisch. **~ virgin** Vestalin *f*, vestalische Jungfrau. **2** *n* Vestalin *f*.

vestibule ['vestɪbjuːl] *n* (a) (*of house*) Vorhalle *f*, Vestibül *nt* (*dated*); (*of hotel*) Halle *f*, Foyer *nt*; (*of church*) Vorhalle *f*. (b) (*Anat*) Vorhof *m*, Vestibulum *nt* (*spec*).

vestige ['vestɪdʒ] *n* (a) Spur *f*. **the ~ of a moustache** der Anflug eines Schnurrbarts; **there is not a ~ of truth** in what he says es ist kein Körnchen Wahrheit an dem, was er sagt.

(b) (*Anat*) Rudiment *nt*.

vestigial [ve'stɪdʒɪəl] *adj* spurenhaft; **moustache**, **growth** spärlich; (*Anat*) rudimentär. **the ~ remains of the old city walls** die Spuren *or* die rudimentären Reste der alten Stadtmauer; **the ~** remains of his ambitions/of their love affair die kümmerlichen Überreste seiner Ambitionen/ihrer Liebschaft.

vestment ['vestmənt] *n* (a) (*of priest*) Ornat *m*, Gewand *nt*. (b) (*ceremonial robe*) Robe *f*, Ornat *m*.

vestry ['vestrɪ] *n* Sakristei *f*.

Vesuvius [vɪ'suːvɪəs] *n* der Vesuv.

vet [vet] **1** *n abbr of* **veterinary surgeon, veterinarian** Tierarzt *m*/-ärztin *f*. **2** *vt* überprüfen.

vetch [vetʃ] *n* Wicke *f*.

veteran ['vetərən] *n* (*Mil, fig*) Veteran(in *f*) *m*. **a ~ teacher/** golfer ein (alt)erfahrener Lehrer/Golfspieler; **a ~ actor** ein Veteran der Schauspielkunst, ein altgedienter Schauspieler; **she's a ~ campaigner for women's rights** sie ist eine Veteranin der Frauenbewegung; **~ car** Oldtimer *m*, Schnauferl *nt* (*inf*).

veterinarian [ˌvetərɪ'neərɪən] *n* (*US*) Tierarzt *m*/-ärztin *f*.

veterinary ['vetərɪnərɪ] *adj* **medicine**, **science** Veterinär-; **training** tierärztlich. **~ surgeon** Tierarzt *m*/-ärztin *f*.

veto ['viːtəu] **1** *n, pl* **-es** Veto *nt*. **power of ~** Vetorecht *nt*; **to have a ~** das Vetorecht haben; **to use one's ~** von seinem Vetorecht Gebrauch machen. **2** *vt* sein Veto einlegen gegen. **if they** ~ **it** wenn sie ihr Veto einlegen.

vex [veks] *vt* (a) (*annoy*) ärgern, irritieren; **animals** quälen. **to be ~ed with sb** mit jdm böse sein, auf jdn ärgerlich sein; **to be ~ed about sth** sich über etw (*acc*) ärgern; **to be/get ~ed** ärgerlich *or* wütend sein/werden; **a problem which has been ~ing me** ein Problem, das mich quält *or* mir keine Ruhe läßt.

(b) (*afflict*) plagen, bedrücken.

vexation [vek'seɪʃən] *n* (a) (*state*) Ärger *m*; (*act*) Verärgerung *f*, Ärgern *nt*; (*of animal*) Quälen *nt*, Quälerei *f*. (b) (*affliction*) Bedrückung *f*; (*cause*) Plage *f*. (c) (*thing*) Ärgernis *nt*. **the little** ~s of life die kleinen Sorgen und Nöte des Lebens.

vexatious [vek'seɪʃəs] *adj* (a) ärgerlich; **regulations**, **headache** lästig; **child** unausstehlich. (b) (*Jur*) schikanös.

vexed [vekst] *adj* (a) (*annoyed*) verärgert. (b) **question** vieldiskutiert, schwierig.

vexing ['veksɪŋ] *adj* ärgerlich, irritierend; **problem** verzwickt.

vg *abbr of* **very good**.

VHF *abbr of* **very high frequency** UKW.

via ['vaɪə] *prep* über (+*acc*); (*with town names also*) via. **they got in ~ the window** sie kamen durchs Fenster herein.

viability [ˌvaɪə'bɪlɪtɪ] *n* (a) (*of life forms*) Lebensfähigkeit *f*.

(b) (*of plan, project*) Durchführbarkeit, Realisierbarkeit *f*; (*of firm*) Rentabilität *f*. **the ~ of the EEC** die Lebens- *or* Existenzfähigkeit der EWG.

viable ['vaɪəbl] *adj* (a) **plant**, **foetus** lebensfähig.

(b) **company** rentabel; **economy** lebensfähig; **suggestion** brauchbar; **scheme**, **plan** durchführbar, realisierbar. **the company is not economically ~** die Firma ist unrentabel; **is this newly created state ~?** ist dieser neuentstandene Staat lebens- *or* existenzfähig?

viaduct ['vaɪədʌkt] *n* Viadukt *m*.

vial ['vaɪəl] *n* Fläschchen, Gefäß *nt*.

viands ['vaɪəndz] *npl* (*form*) Lebensmittel *pl*; (*for journey*) Proviant *m*.

vibes [vaɪbz] *npl* (a) Vibraphon *nt*. (b) (*sl*) *see* **vibration (b)**.

vibrancy ['vaɪbrənsɪ] *n see adj* Dynamik *f*; voller Klang, Sonorität *f*.

vibrant ['vaɪbrənt] *adj* **personality etc** dynamisch; **voice** volltönend, sonor. **the ~ life of the city** das pulsierende Leben der Großstadt.

vibraphone ['vaɪbrəfəun] *n* Vibraphon *nt*.

vibrate [vaɪ'breɪt] **1** *vi* (*lit, fig*) zittern, beben (*with* vor +*dat*); (*machine*, **string**, **air**) vibrieren; (*notes*) schwingen. **the blade cuts more easily by being made to ~** das Schneideblatt schneidet dadurch besser, daß es vibriert; **the steel mill ~d with the thump of the hammers** das Hüttenwerk bebte im Rhythmus der Hammerschläge; **the painting ~s with life** das

Bild bebt *or* sprüht vor Leben; **the city centre ~s with activity** im Stadtzentrum pulsiert das Leben; **the town was vibrating with excitement** Aufregung hatte die Stadt ergriffen.

2 *vt* zum Vibrieren bringen; *string* zum Schwingen bringen. **they study the way the machine ~s the body** sie untersuchen, wie die Maschine den Körper erschüttert.

vibration [vaɪˈbreɪʃən] *n* **(a)** *(of string, sound waves)* Schwingung *f*; *(of machine)* Vibrieren *nt*; *(of voice, ground)* Beben *nt*. **the medium felt mysterious ~s** das Medium fühlte geheimnisvolle Schwingungen; **the ~s the body undergoes when one flies** die Erschütterung, der der Körper beim Fliegen ausgesetzt ist.

(b) *(sl: usu pl)* **what sort of ~s do you get from him?** wie wirkt er auf dich?; **I get good ~s from this music** diese Musik bringt mich auf Touren; **this town is giving me bad ~s** diese Stadt macht mich ganz fertig (*inf*).

vibrato [vɪˈbrɑːtəʊ] **1** *n* Vibrato *nt*. **2** *adv* vibrato.

vibrator [vaɪˈbreɪtə^r] *n* Vibrator *m*.

vibratory [ˈvaɪbrətərɪ] *adj* vibrierend, Vibrations-.

vicar [ˈvɪkə^r] *n* Pfarrer *m*. **good evening, ~** guten Abend, Herr Pfarrer; **~ apostolic** Apostolischer Vikar; **~ general** Generalvikar *m*.

vicarage [ˈvɪkərɪdʒ] *n* Pfarrhaus *nt*.

vicarious [vɪˈkeərɪəs] *adj* **(a)** *pleasure, enjoyment* indirekt, mittelbar, nachempfunden; *experience* ersatzweise; Ersatz-. **~ sexual thrill** Ersatzbefriedigung *f*; **the ~ thrill he gets out of watching ski-jumping** der Nervenkitzel, den er hat, wenn er beim Skispringen zusieht; **he can't walk himself but he gets enormous ~ pleasure from watching athletics** er kann nicht gehen, aber das Zuschauen bei sportlichen Wettkämpfen vermittelt ihm einen großen Genuß.

(b) *authority, suffering* stellvertretend.

vicariously [vɪˈkeərɪəslɪ] *adv* indirekt, mittelbar. **I can appreciate the island's beauty ~ through your writing** Ihre Beschreibung vermittelt mir die Schönheit der Insel *or* läßt mich die Schönheit der Insel nachempfinden.

vicariousness [vɪˈkeərɪəsnɪs] *n* Indirektheit, Mittelbarkeit *f*. **the necessary ~ of this pleasure** diese zwangsläufig indirekte *or* nachempfundene *or* mittelbare Freude; **the appreciation of art always involves a degree of ~** Kunstgenuß setzt immer eine bestimmte Fähigkeit des Nachempfindens voraus.

vice[1] [vaɪs] *n* Laster *nt*; *(of horse)* Unart, Untugend *f*, Mucken *pl* (*inf*). **his main ~ is laziness** sein größter Fehler ist die Faulheit; **you don't smoke or drink, don't you have any ~s?** (*hum*) Sie rauchen nicht, Sie trinken nicht, haben Sie denn gar kein Laster? (*hum*); **a life of ~** ein Lasterleben *nt*; **~ squad** Sittenpolizei *f*, Sittendezernat *nt*, Sitte *f* (*sl*).

vice[2], *(US)* **vise** *n* Schraubstock *m*. **to have/hold sth in a ~-like grip** etw fest umklammern; *(between legs, under arm)* etw fest einklemmen.

vice- *pref* **~-admiral** *n* Vizeadmiral *m*; **~-chairman** *n* stellvertretender Vorsitzender; **~-chairmanship** *n* stellvertretender Vorsitz; **~-chancellor** *n* (*Univ*) ≈ Rektor *m*; **~-consul** *n* Vizekonsul *m*; **~-presidency** *n* Vizepräsidentschaft *f*; **~-president** *n* Vizepräsident *m*; **~-regent** *n* Vizeregent *m*, stellvertretender Regent; **~-roy** *n* Vizekönig *m*.

vice versa [ˈvaɪsɪˈvɜːsə] *adv* umgekehrt.

vicinity [vɪˈsɪnɪtɪ] *n* **(a)** Umgebung *f*. **in the ~** in der Nähe (*of* von, *gen*); **in the immediate ~** in unmittelbarer Umgebung; **in the ~ of £500** um die £ 500 (herum). **(b)** *(closeness)* Nähe *f*.

vicious [ˈvɪʃəs] *adj* **(a)** gemein, boshaft; *remark also* gehässig; *look* boshaft, böse. **to have a ~ tongue** eine böse *or* spitze Zunge haben.

(b) *habit* lasterhaft.

(c) *animal* bösartig; *dog* bissig; *blow, kick* brutal; *criminal* brutal, abgefeimt; *murder* grauenhaft, brutal. **that animal can be ~** das Tier kann heimtückisch sein.

(d) (*inf*: *strong, nasty*) *headache* fies (*inf*), gemein (*inf*).

(e) **~ circle** Teufelskreis, Circulus vitiosus (*geh*) *m*.

viciously [ˈvɪʃəslɪ] *adv see adj* **(a, c)** gemein, boshaft; gehässig; böse. **(b)** bösartig; brutal; auf grauenhafte Art, brutal. **the dog attacked him ~** der Hund fiel wütend über ihn her.

viciousness [ˈvɪʃəsnɪs] *n see adj* **(a)** Gemeinheit, Boshaftigkeit *f*; Gehässigkeit *f*; Boshaftigkeit *f*. **(c)** Bösartigkeit *f*; Bissigkeit *f*; Brutalität *f*; Grauenhaftigkeit *f*.

vicissitude [vɪˈsɪsɪtjuːd] *n usu pl* Wandel *m*. **the ~s of life** die Launen des Schicksals, die Wechselfälle des Lebens; **the ~s of war/business** die Wirren des Krieges/das Auf und Ab im Geschäftsleben.

victim [ˈvɪktɪm] *n* Opfer *nt*. **he was the ~ of a practical joke** ihm wurde ein Streich gespielt; **to be the ~ of sb's sarcasm** eine Zielscheibe für jds Sarkasmus sein; **the hawk flew off with its ~ in its claws** der Falke flog mit seiner Beute in den Klauen davon; **to fall (a) ~ to sth** einer Sache (*dat*) zum Opfer fallen; **I fell ~ to the flu** mich hatte die Grippe erwischt (*inf*); **she fell a ~ to the climate** das Klima wurde für sie unerträglich; **to fall ~ to sb's charms** jds Charme (*dat*) erliegen; **the whole of the region fell ~ to the drought** die ganze Gegend wurde ein Opfer der Dürre.

victimization [ˌvɪktɪmaɪˈzeɪʃən] *n see vt* ungerechte Behandlung; Schikanierung.

victimize [ˈvɪktɪmaɪz] *vt* ungerecht behandeln; *(pick on)* schikanieren. **she feels ~d** sie fühlt sich ungerecht behandelt; **this ~s the public** darunter hat die Öffentlichkeit zu leiden.

victor [ˈvɪktə^r] *n* Sieger *m*.

Victoria Cross [vɪkˈtɔːrɪəˈkrɒs] *n* (*Brit*) Viktoriakreuz *nt* (*höchste britische Tapferkeitsauszeichnung*).

Victoria Falls [vɪkˈtɔːrɪəˈfɔːlz] *npl* Viktoriafälle *f*.

Victorian [vɪkˈtɔːrɪən] **1** *n* Viktorianer(in *f*) *m*. **2** *adj* viktorianisch; (*fig*) (sitten)streng.

Victoriana [vɪkˌtɔːrɪˈɑːnə] *n* viktorianische Antiquitäten *pl*.

victorious [vɪkˈtɔːrɪəs] *adj army* siegreich; *smile* triumphierend, siegesbewußt. **to be ~ over sb/sth** jdn/etw besiegen; **to be ~ in the struggle against ...** siegen *or* den Sieg davontragen im Kampf gegen ...

victoriously [vɪkˈtɔːrɪəslɪ] *adv* siegreich, als Sieger.

victory [ˈvɪktərɪ] *n* Sieg *m*. **to gain** *or* **win a ~ over sb/sth** einen Sieg über jdn/etw erringen, jdn/etw besiegen; **his final ~ over his fear** die endgültige Überwindung seiner Angst.

victual [ˈvɪtl] (*form*) **1** *vt army, troop* verpflegen, verproviantieren. **2** *vi* sich verpflegen *or* verproviantieren.

victualler [ˈvɪtlə^r] *n see* **licensed**.

victuals [ˈvɪtlz] *npl* Lebensmittel *pl*; (*for journey*) Proviant *m*, Verpflegung *f*.

vide [ˈvaɪdɪ] *imper* (*form, Jur*) siehe, vide (*liter*).

videlicet [vɪˈdiːlɪset] *adv* (*abbr* viz) nämlich.

video [ˈvɪdɪəʊ] *n* (*US*) Fernsehen *nt*. **on ~** im Fernsehen.

video: ~phone *n* Fernsehtelefon *nt*; **~-recording** *n* Fernsehaufnahme *f*; **~tape** **1** *n* Magnetbild- *or* Videoband *nt*; **2** *vt* aufzeichnen.

vie [vaɪ] *vi* wetteifern; (*Comm*) konkurrieren. **to ~ with sb for sth mit** jdm um etw wetteifern; **they are vying for the championship** sie kämpfen um die Meisterschaft; **they ~d successfully with their competitors** es gelang ihnen, ihre Konkurrenten auszustechen.

Vienna [vɪˈenə] **1** *n* Wien *nt*. **2** *adj* Wiener.

Viennese [ˌvɪəˈniːz] **1** *adj* wienerisch. **2** *n* Wiener(in *f*) *m*.

Vietnam [ˌvjetˈnæm] *n* Vietnam *nt*.

Vietnamese [ˌvjetnəˈmiːz] **1** *adj* vietnamesisch. **2** *n* **(a)** Vietnamese *m*, Vietnamesin *f*. **(b)** (*language*) Vietnamesisch *nt*.

view [vjuː] **1** *n* **(a)** (*range of vision*) Sicht *f*. **in full ~ of thousands of people** vor den Augen von Tausenden von Menschen; **the magician placed the box in full ~ of the audience** der Zauberer stellte die Kiste so auf, daß das ganze Publikum sie sehen konnte; **the ship came into ~** das Schiff kam in Sicht; **I came into ~ of the lake** der See kam in Sicht *or* lag vor mir; **to keep sth in ~** etw im Auge behalten; **the cameraman had a job keeping the plane in ~** der Kameramann fand es schwierig, das Flugzeug zu verfolgen; **to go out of ~** außer Sicht kommen, verschwinden; **the house is within ~ of the sea** vom Haus aus ist das Meer zu sehen; **the house is exposed to ~ from passing trains** das Haus kann von vorbeifahrenden Zügen aus eingesehen werden; **hidden from ~** verborgen, versteckt; **the horses were hidden from ~ behind the trees** die Pferde waren von den Bäumen verdeckt; **she keeps the old china hidden from ~** sie bewahrt das alte Porzellan im Verborgenen auf; **the house is hidden from ~ from the main road** das Haus ist von der Hauptstraße aus nicht zu sehen; **on ~** (*for purchasing*) zur Ansicht; (*of exhibits*) ausgestellt; **the house will be on ~ tomorrow** das Haus kann morgen besichtigt werden.

(b) (*prospect, sight*) Aussicht *f*. **there is a splendid ~ from here/from the top** von hier/von der Spitze hat man einen herrlichen Blick *or* eine wunderschöne Aussicht; **a ~ over ...** ein Blick über (+*acc*); **a good ~ of the sea** ein schöner Blick auf das Meer; **a room with a ~** ein Zimmer mit schöner Aussicht; **I only got a side ~ of his head** ich habe seinen Kopf nur im Profil gesehen; **a trip down the Thames to see the ~s** eine Fahrt die Themse hinunter, um die Sehenswürdigkeiten zu bewundern.

(c) (*photograph etc*) Ansicht *f*. **I want to take a ~ of the forest** ich möchte eine Aufnahme vom Wald machen.

(d) (*opinion*) Ansicht, Meinung *f*. **in my ~** meiner Ansicht *or* Meinung nach; **to have** *or* **hold ~s on sth** Ansichten über etw (*acc*) haben; **what are his ~s on this problem?** was meint er zu diesem Problem?; **do you have any special ~s on the matter?** haben Sie eine besondere Meinung zu dieser Sache?; **I have no ~s on that** ich habe keine Meinung dazu; **to take the ~ that ...** die Ansicht vertreten, daß ...; **to take a dim** (*inf*) *or* **poor ~ of sb's conduct** jds Verhalten mißbilligen; **see point**.

(e) (*mental survey*) **an idealistic ~ of the world** eine idealistische Welt(an)sicht; **a general** *or* **overall ~ of a problem** ein allgemeiner *or* umfassender Überblick über ein Problem; **a clear ~ of the facts** eine klare Übersicht über die Fakten; **in ~ of** wegen (+*gen*), angesichts (+*gen*); **at first ~** auf den ersten Blick; **we must not lose from ~ the fact that ...** wir dürfen die Tatsache nicht aus dem Auge verlieren, daß ...; **I'll keep it in ~** ich werde es im Auge behalten.

(f) (*intention, plan*) Absicht *f*. **to have sth in ~** etw beabsichtigen; **with a ~ to doing sth** mit der Absicht, etw zu tun; **with this in ~** im Hinblick darauf; **he has the holidays in ~ when he says ...** er denkt an die Ferien, wenn er sagt ...

2 *vt* **(a)** (*see*) betrachten.

(b) (*examine*) *house* besichtigen.

(c) (*consider*) *problem etc* sehen. **he ~s the prospect with dismay** er sieht dieser Sache mit Schrecken entgegen.

3 *vi* (*watch television*) fernsehen.

viewer [ˈvjuːə^r] *n* **(a)** (*TV*) Zuschauer(in *f*) *m*. **(b)** (*for slides*) Dia- *or* Bildbetrachter *m*, Gucki (*inf*) *m*.

view-finder [ˈvjuːˌfaɪndə^r] *n* Sucher *m*.

viewing [ˈvjuːɪŋ] *n* **(a)** (*of house, at auction etc*) Besichtigung *f*. **~ time** Besichtigungszeiten *pl*.

(b) (*TV*) Fernsehen *nt*. **9 o'clock is peak ~ time** neun Uhr ist (die) Haupteinschaltzeit; **this programme will be given another ~ next week** dieses Programm wird nächste Woche wiederholt; **I don't do much ~** ich sehe nicht viel fern.

viewpoint [ˈvjuːpɔɪnt] *n* Standpunkt *m*. **from the ~ of economic growth** unter dem Gesichtspunkt des Wirtschaftswachstums; **to see sth from sb's ~** von jds Sicht (*dat*) sehen.

vigil [ˈvɪdʒɪl] *n* **(a)** (Nacht)wache *f*. **to keep ~ over sb** bei jdm wachen; **the dog kept ~ over his injured master** der Hund hielt bei seinem verletzten Herrn Wache; **her long ~s at his bedside** ihr langes Wachen an seinem Krankenbett.

(b) (*Rel*) Vigil, Nachtwache *f*.

vigilance ['vɪdʒɪləns] n Wachsamkeit f. no move escaped their ~ keine Bewegung entging ihrem wachsamen Auge; ~ committee Bürgerwehr f, Selbstschutzkomitee nt.

vigilant ['vɪdʒɪlənt] adj wachsam. the customs officers are ever ~ for drug traffickers die Zollbeamten haben stets ein wachsames Auge auf Drogenhändler.

vigilante [ˌvɪdʒɪ'læntɪ] 1 n Mitglied nt einer Selbstschutzorganisation. the ~s die Bürgerwehr, der Selbstschutz. 2 adj attr Bürgerwehr-, Selbstschutz-.

vigilantly ['vɪdʒɪləntlɪ] adv aufmerksam; patrol wachsam.

vignette [vɪ'njet] n Vignette f; (character sketch) Skizze f, kurze und prägnante Darstellung.

vigor n (US) see vigour.

vigorous ['vɪgərəs] adj kräftig; prose, tune kraftvoll; protest, denial, measures, exercises energisch; walk forsch, flott; nod eifrig, heftig; match, player dynamisch; speech feurig; debater leidenschaftlich.

vigorously ['vɪgərəslɪ] adv see adj

vigour, (US) **vigor** ['vɪgəʳ] n Kraft, Energie f; (of protest, denial) Heftigkeit f; (of exercises) Energie f; (of player) Dynamik f; (of speech, debater) Leidenschaftlichkeit f; (of prose) Ausdruckskraft f. **bodily/sexual/youthful** ~ körperliche/sexuelle/jugendliche Spannkraft; **to speak with** ~ mit Nachdruck sprechen; **to grow with** ~ prächtig gedeihen; **the debate was conducted with** ~ die Debatte verlief sehr lebhaft; **all the** ~ **has gone out of the undertaking** das Unternehmen hat jeglichen Schwung verloren.

Viking ['vaɪkɪŋ] 1 n Wikinger m. 2 adj ship Wikinger-.

vile [vaɪl] adj abscheulich; mood, smell, habit also übel; thoughts also niedrig, gemein; language also unflätig; weather, food also scheußlich, widerlich. that was a ~ thing to say es war eine Gemeinheit, so etwas zu sagen; he was ~ to his wife er benahm sich scheußlich gegenüber seiner Frau.

vilely ['vaɪllɪ] adv abscheulich, scheußlich.

vileness ['vaɪlnɪs] n Abscheulichkeit f; (of thoughts) Niederträchtigkeit f; (of smell) Widerwärtigkeit f; (of language also) Unflätigkeit f; (of weather) Scheußlichkeit f. the ~ of his mood seine Übellaunigkeit.

vilification [ˌvɪlɪfɪ'keɪʃən] n Diffamierung f, Verleumdung f.

vilify ['vɪlɪfaɪ] vt diffamieren, verleumden.

villa ['vɪlə] n Villa f.

village ['vɪlɪdʒ] n Dorf nt.

village in cpds Dorf-; ~ green n Dorfwiese f or -anger m; ~ idiot n Dorftrottel m (inf).

villager ['vɪlɪdʒəʳ] n Dörfler(in f), Dorfbewohner(in f) (also Admin) m.

villain ['vɪlən] n (a) (scoundrel) Schurke m; (sl: criminal) Verbrecher, Ganove (inf) m. (b) (in drama, novel) Bösewicht m. (c) (inf: rascal) Bengel m. he's the ~ of the piece er ist der Übeltäter.

villainous ['vɪlənəs] adj (a) böse; deed niederträchtig, gemein. a ~ face ein Verbrechergesicht nt. (b) (inf: bad) scheußlich.

villainously ['vɪlənəslɪ] adv smile hämisch. he ~ murdered his brothers in seiner Niedertracht ermordete er seine Brüder; he ~ stole the jewels wie ein Verbrecher stahl er den Schmuck.

villainy ['vɪlənɪ] n Gemeinheit, Niederträchtigkeit f.

villein ['vɪlɪn] n (Hist) Leibeigene(r) mf.

vim [vɪm] n (inf) Schwung m. he writes with great ~ er schreibt sehr schwungvoll; **full of** ~ **and vigour** voller Schwung und Elan.

vinaigrette [ˌvɪnɪ'gret] n Vinaigrette f (Cook); (for salad) Salatsoße f.

vindicate ['vɪndɪkeɪt] vt (a) opinion, action rechtfertigen. (b) (clear from suspicion etc) rehabilitieren.

vindication [ˌvɪndɪ'keɪʃən] n (a) Rechtfertigung f. in ~ of zur Rechtfertigung (+gen). (b) Rehabilitation f.

vindictive [vɪn'dɪktɪv] adj speech, person rachsüchtig; mood nachtragend, unversöhnlich. he is not a ~ person er ist nicht nachtragend; these measures are likely to make the unions feel ~ diese Maßnahmen könnten bei den Gewerkschaften auf Unwillen or Ressentiments stoßen; I hope you won't feel ~ because of my rather harsh criticism ich hoffe, Sie tragen mir meine etwas harte Kritik nicht nach or Sie nehmen mir meine etwas harte Kritik nicht übel; corporal punishment can make pupils feel ~ towards the teacher die Prügelstrafe kann die Schüler gegen den Lehrer aufbringen; insecure people often feel ~ unsichere Menschen sind oft voller Ressentiments.

vindictively [vɪn'dɪktɪvlɪ] adv see adj.

vindictiveness [vɪn'dɪktɪvnɪs] n Rachsucht f; (of mood) Unversöhnlichkeit f. the ~ of his speech seine rachsüchtige Rede.

vine [vaɪn] n (a) (grapevine) Rebe, Weinrebe f. (b) (similar plant) Rebengewächs nt. ~ dresser Winzer(in f) m.

vinegar ['vɪnɪgəʳ] n Essig m.

vinegary ['vɪnɪgərɪ] adj (lit, fig) säuerlich; taste also Essig-.

vine: ~ grower n Weinbauer m; ~-growing district n Weingegend f, (Wein)anbaugebiet nt; ~ harvest n Weinlese, Weinernte f; ~ leaf n Rebenblatt nt; ~yard ['vɪnjəd] n Weinberg m.

vintage ['vɪntɪdʒ] 1 n (a) (given year) (of wine, fig) Jahrgang m; (of car) Baujahr nt.
(b) (wine of particular year) the 1972 ~ der Jahrgang 1972, der 72er.
(c) (harvesting, season) Weinlese, Weinernte f.
2 adj attr (old) uralt; (high quality) glänzend, hervorragend. this typewriter is a ~ model diese Schreibmaschine hat Museumswert; a ~ performance from Humphrey Bogart eine einmalige künstlerische Leistung Humphrey Bogarts.

vintage: ~ car n Vorkriegsmodell, Vintage-Car nt; ~ port n Vintage-Port m, schwerer Port eines besonderen Jahrgangs; ~ wine n edler Wein; ~ year n: a ~ year for wine ein besonders

gutes Weinjahr; a ~ year for burgundy ein besonders gutes Jahr für Burgunder; it was a ~ year for plays in diesem Jahr wurden viele hervorragende Stücke aufgeführt.

vintner ['vɪntnəʳ] n Weinhändler m.

vinyl ['vaɪnɪl] n Vinyl nt.

viol ['vaɪəl] n Viola f.

viola¹ [vɪ'əʊlə] n (Mus) Bratsche f.

viola² ['vaɪəʊlə] n (Bot) Veilchen nt

viola da gamba [vɪ'əʊldə'gæmbə] n Gambe f.

violate ['vaɪəleɪt] vt (a) treaty, promise brechen; (partially) verletzen; law, rule, moral code verletzen, verstoßen gegen; rights verletzen; truth vergewaltigen.
(b) (disturb) holy place entweihen, schänden; peacefulness stören. to ~ sb's privacy in jds Privatsphäre eindringen; it's violating a person's privacy to ... es ist ein Eingriff in jemandes Privatsphäre, wenn man ...; the shriek of the jets now ~s that once peaceful spot durch das Heulen der Düsenflugzeuge ist die Idylle dieses Fleckchens zerstört worden; the new buildings ~ the landscape die Neubauten verunstalten or verschandeln die Landschaft.
(c) (rape) vergewaltigen, schänden.

violation [ˌvaɪə'leɪʃən] n (a) (of law) Übertretung (of gen), Verletzung f (of gen), Verstoß m (of gegen); (of rule) Verstoß m (of gegen); (of rights) Verletzung f; (of truth) Vergewaltigung f. a ~ of a treaty ein Vertragsbruch m; (partial) eine Vertragsverletzung; traffic ~ Verkehrsvergehen nt; he did this in ~ of the conditions agreed er verstieß damit gegen die Vereinbarungen.
(b) (of holy place) Entweihung, Schändung f; (of peacefulness) Störung f; (of privacy) Eingriff m (of in +acc). that building is a ~ of the old city dieses Gebäude ist eine Verunstaltung or Verschandelung der Altstadt.
(c) (rape) Vergewaltigung, Schändung f.

violator ['vaɪəleɪtəʳ] n (of treaty) Vertragsbrüchige(r) mf; (of laws) Gesetzesübertreter m; (of holy place) Schänder, Entehrer m; (of woman) Schänder m. the ~ of these rules ... wer gegen diese Regeln verstößt, ...

violence ['vaɪələns] n (a) (forcefulness, strength) Heftigkeit f; (of protest also) Schärfe f; (of speech also) Leidenschaftlichkeit f. the ~ of the contrast der krasse Gegensatz; the ~ of his temper sein jähzorniges Temperament, seine Jähzornigkeit.
(b) (brutality) Gewalt f; (of people) Gewalttätigkeit f; (of actions) Brutalität f. the ~ of his nature seine gewalttätige Art; crime of ~ Gewaltverbrechen nt; act of ~ Gewalttat f; robbery with ~ Raubüberfall m; an increase in ~ eine Zunahme der Gewalttätigkeit; to use ~ against sb Gewalt gegen jdn anwenden; was there any ~? kam es zu Gewalttätigkeiten?; outbreak of ~ Ausbruch von Gewalttätigkeiten.
(c) (fig) to do ~ to sth etw entstellen; it does ~ to common sense das vergewaltigt den gesunden Menschenverstand.

violent ['vaɪələnt] adj person, nature, action brutal, gewalttätig; blush heftig, tief; wind, storm heftig, stark, gewaltig; feeling, affair, speech leidenschaftlich; dislike, attack, blow heftig; death gewaltsam; (severe) contrast kraß; pain heftig, stark; colour grell. to have a ~ temper jähzornig sein; to be in a ~ temper toben; the beginning of the second movement is rather ~ der zweite Satz beginnt sehr leidenschaftlich; don't be so ~, open it gently sei nicht so stürmisch, öffne es vorsichtig; to get ~ gewalttätig werden; by ~ means (open sth) mit Gewalt(anwendung); (persuade) unter Gewaltanwendung.

violently ['vaɪələntlɪ] adv kick, beat, attack brutal; blush tief, heftig; speak heftig, leidenschaftlich; fall in love unsterblich. the two colours clash ~ die beiden Farben bilden einen krassen Gegensatz; they have quite ~ opposed temperaments sie haben völlig unvereinbare Temperamente; he expresses himself rather ~ er drückt sich sehr kraß aus.

violet ['vaɪəlɪt] 1 n (Bot) Veilchen nt; (colour) Violett nt. 2 adj violett.

violin [ˌvaɪə'lɪn] n Geige, Violine f; (player) Geiger(in f), Geigenspieler(in f) m. ~ case Geigenkasten m; ~ concerto Violinkonzert nt; ~ sonata Violinsonate f.

violinist [ˌvaɪə'lɪnɪst] n Geiger(in f), Violinist(in f) m.

violoncello [ˌvaɪələn'tʃeləʊ] n (form) Violoncello nt.

VIP n prominente Persönlichkeit, VIP m. he got/we gave him ~ treatment er wurde/wir haben ihn als Ehrengast behandelt; ~ lounge VIP-Halle f.

viper ['vaɪpəʳ] n (Zool) Viper f; (fig) Schlange f.

viperish ['vaɪpərɪʃ] adj (fig) giftig.

virago [vɪ'rɑːgəʊ] n Xanthippe f.

viral ['vaɪərəl] adj Virus-.

Virgil ['vɜːdʒɪl] n Vergil(ius), Virgil m.

virgin ['vɜːdʒɪn] 1 n Jungfrau f. the (Blessed) V~ (Rel) die (heilige) Jungfrau Maria; he's still a ~ er ist noch unschuldig.
2 adj daughter jungfräulich, unberührt; (fig) forest, land unberührt; freshness rein; snow jungfräulich, unberührt. ~ birth unbefleckte Empfängnis; (Biol) Jungfernzeugung f; the V~ Isles die Jungferninseln pl.

virginal ['vɜːdʒɪnl] 1 adj jungfräulich. 2 npl (Mus) Tafelklavier nt.

Virginia [və'dʒɪnjə] n (state) Virginia nt; (tobacco) Virginia m. ~ creeper wilder Wein, Jungfernrebe f; ~ tobacco Virginiatabak m; he smokes ~s er raucht Virginiazigaretten.

Virginian [və'dʒɪnjən] 1 n Einwohner(in f) m von Virginia, Virginier(in f) m. 2 adj Virginia-.

virginity [vɜː'dʒɪnɪtɪ] n Unschuld f; (of girls also) Jungfräulichkeit f.

Virgo ['vɜːgəʊ] n (Astrol) 1 n Jungfrau f. 2 adj ~ characteristics Eigenschaften der Jungfrau(menschen).

virile ['vɪraɪl] adj männlich; (fig) ausdrucksvoll, kraftvoll.

virility [vɪ'rɪlɪtɪ] n (lit) Männlichkeit f; (sexual power) Potenz f; (fig) Ausdruckskraft f. **political** ~ politische Potenz.

virologist [‚vaɪə'rɒlədʒɪst] n Virologe m, Virologin f, Virusforscher(in f) m.

virology [‚vaɪə'rɒlədʒɪ] n Virologie f, Virusforschung f.

virtual ['vɜːtjʊəl] adj attr (a) he is the ~ leader er ist quasi der Führer or der eigentliche Führer, praktisch ist er der Führer; it was a ~ admission of guilt es war so gut wie or praktisch ein Schuldgeständnis nt; it was a ~ disaster es war geradezu eine Katastrophe; it was a ~ failure es war praktisch ein Mißerfolg; this reply is a ~ insult diese Antwort ist geradezu eine Beleidigung.
(b) (Phys) virtuell.

virtually ['vɜːtjʊəlɪ] adv praktisch; blind, lost also fast, nahezu, mehr oder weniger. yes, ~ ja, fast, ja so gut wie; he is ~ the boss er ist praktisch or quasi der Chef; it was ~ a disaster das war geradezu or direkt eine Katastrophe; to be ~ certain sich (dat) so gut wie sicher sein.

virtue ['vɜːtjuː] n (a) (moral quality) Tugend f. to make a ~ of necessity aus der Not eine Tugend machen; a life of ~ ein tugendhaftes Leben.
(b) (chastity) Keuschheit, Tugendhaftigkeit f. a woman of easy ~ (euph) ein leichtes Mädchen.
(c) (advantage, point) Vorteil m. what's the ~ of that? welchen Vorteil hat das, wozu ist das gut?; there is no ~ in doing that es scheint nicht sehr zweckmäßig, das zu tun.
(d) (healing power) Heilkraft f. in or by ~ of aufgrund (+gen); in or by ~ of the authority/power etc vested in me kraft meiner Autorität/Macht etc (form).

virtuosity [‚vɜːtjʊ'ɒsɪtɪ] n Virtuosität f.

virtuoso [‚vɜːtjʊ'əʊzəʊ] 1 n (esp Mus) Virtuose m. 2 adj performance meisterhaft, virtuos.

virtuous adj, **~ly** adv ['vɜːtjʊəs, -lɪ] tugendhaft, tugendsam.

virulence ['vɪrʊləns] n (a) (Med) Heftigkeit, Bösartigkeit f; (of poison) Stärke f. (b) (fig) Schärfe, Virulenz (geh) f.

virulent ['vɪrʊlənt] adj (a) (Med) bösartig; poison stark, tödlich. (b) (fig) geharnischt, scharf, virulent (geh).

virulently ['vɪrʊləntlɪ] adv (fig) scharf.

virus ['vaɪərəs] n (a) (Med) Virus, Erreger m. polio ~ Polioerreger m; ~ disease Viruskrankheit f. (b) (fig) Geschwür nt.

visa ['viːzə] n, (US) **visé** 1 n Visum nt; (stamp also) Sichtvermerk m. entrance/exit ~ Einreise-/Ausreisevisum nt. 2 vt ein Visum ausstellen (+dat). to get a passport ~ed einen Sichtvermerk in den Paß bekommen.

visage ['vɪzɪdʒ] n (liter) Antlitz nt (liter).

vis-a-vis ['viːzəviː] 1 prep in Anbetracht (+gen). 2 adv gegenüber.

viscera ['vɪsərə] npl innere Organe pl; (in abdomen) Eingeweide pl.

visceral ['vɪsərəl] adj viszeral (spec); (of intestines also) Eingeweide-.

viscid ['vɪsɪd] adj (form) zähflüssig; (Bot) klebrig.

viscose ['vɪskəʊs] n Viskose f.

viscosity [vɪs'kɒsɪtɪ] n Zähflüssigkeit f; (Phys) Viskosität f.

viscount ['vaɪkaʊnt] n Viscount m.

viscountcy ['vaɪkaʊntsɪ], **viscounty** n Rang m des Viscounts.

viscountess ['vaɪkaʊntɪs] n Viscountess f.

viscounty ['vaɪkaʊntɪ] n see viscountcy.

viscous ['vɪskəs] adj (form) zähflüssig; (Phys) viskos.

vise [vaɪs] n (US) see vice².

visé ['viːzeɪ] (US) see visa.

visibility [‚vɪzɪ'bɪlɪtɪ] n (a) Sichtbarkeit f. (b) (Met) Sichtweite f. poor/good ~ schlechte/gute Sicht; low ~ geringe Sichtweite; ~ is down to only 100 metres die Sichtweite beträgt nur 100 Meter.

visible ['vɪzəbl] adj (a) sichtbar. ~ to the naked eye mit dem bloßen Auge zu erkennen; it wasn't ~ in the fog es war im Nebel nicht zu erkennen; the Englishman prefers his emotions not to be ~ der Engländer zeigt nicht gern seine Gefühle.
(b) (obvious) sichtlich. with no ~ means of support (Jur) ohne bekannte Einkommensquellen pl.

visibly ['vɪzəblɪ] adv sichtbar, sichtlich; deteriorate, decay zusehends.

Visigoth ['vɪzɪgɒθ] n Westgote m.

vision ['vɪʒən] n (a) (power of sight) Sehvermögen nt. within/outside the range of ~ in/außer Sichtweite; see field.
(b) (foresight) Weitblick m.
(c) (in dream, trance) Vision f, Gesicht nt (liter). it came to me in a ~ ich hatte eine Vision.
(d) (image) Vorstellung f. Orwell's ~ of the future Orwells Zukunftsvision f.
(e) to have ~s of wealth von Reichtum träumen, sich (dat) Reichtum vorgaukeln; I had ~s of having to walk all the way home (inf) ich sah mich im Geiste schon den ganzen Weg nach Hause laufen.

visionary ['vɪʒənərɪ] 1 adj (impractical) unrealistisch; (of visions) vorhersehend, visionär (geh); (unreal) eingebildet. 2 n Visionär, Seher (geh) m; (pej) Phantast m.

visit ['vɪzɪt] 1 n (a) Besuch m; (of doctor) Hausbesuch m; (of inspector) Kontrolle f. to pay sb/sth a ~ jdm/einer Sache einen Besuch abstatten (form), jdn/etw besuchen; to pay a ~ (euph) mal verschwinden (müssen); to have a ~ from sb von jdm besucht werden; give us a ~ some time besuchen Sie uns (doch) mal; he went on a two-day ~ to Paris er fuhr für zwei Tage nach Paris; I'm going on a ~ to Glasgow next week ich fahre nächste Woche (zu einem Besuch) nach Glasgow; we're expecting a ~ from the police any day wir rechnen jeden Tag mit dem Besuch der Polizei.
(b) (stay) Aufenthalt, Besuch m. to be on a ~ to London zu einem Besuch in London sein; to be on a private/official ~ inoffiziell/offiziell da sein.
2 vt (a) person, the sick, museum besuchen. you never ~ us these days Sie kommen uns ja gar nicht mehr besuchen.

(b) (go and stay) besuchen, aufsuchen (geh).
(c) (inspect) inspizieren, besichtigen, besuchen. to ~ the scene of the crime (Jur) den Tatort besichtigen.
(d) (Bibl) sins heimsuchen (upon an +dat, über +acc).
3 vi (a) einen Besuch machen. come and ~ some time komm mich mal besuchen; I'm only ~ing here ich bin nur auf Besuch hier. (b) (US inf: chat) schwatzen, ein Schwätzchen halten.
♦ **visit with** vi +prep obj (US) schwatzen mit.

visitation [‚vɪzɪ'teɪʃən] n (a) (form: visit) (by official) Besichtigung f, Besuch m; (by ghost) Erscheinung f. after another ~ from the mother-in-law (hum) nachdem uns die Schwiegermutter wieder einmal heimgesucht hatte.
(b) (Rel) the V~ Mariä Heimsuchung f.
(c) (Rel: affliction) Heimsuchung f. a ~ for their sins die Strafe für ihre Sünden; the ~ of the sins of the fathers on succeeding generations die Bestrafung der folgenden Generationen für die Sünden ihrer Väter.

visiting ['vɪzɪtɪŋ] n Besuche pl.

visiting: ~ **card** n (Brit) Visitenkarte f; ~ **hours** npl Besuchszeiten pl; ~ **professor** n Gastprofessor m; the ~ **team** die Gäste pl; ~ **terms** npl: I'm not on ~ terms with him ich kenne ihn nicht so gut, daß ich ihn besuchen gehen würde.

visitor ['vɪzɪtə'] n Besucher(in f) m; (in hotel) Gast m. to have ~s or a ~ Besuch haben; the great tit is a rare ~ in these parts die Kohlmeise hält sich selten in diesen Breiten auf; ~s' book Gästebuch nt.

visor ['vaɪzə'] n (on helmet) Visier nt; (on cap) Schirm m; (Aut) Blende f. sun ~ Schild, Schirm m; (Aut) Sonnenblende f.

vista ['vɪstə] n (a) (view) Aussicht f, Blick m. (b) (of past) Bild nt; (of future) Aussicht (of auf +acc), Perspektive (of von) f.

visual ['vɪzjʊəl] adj field, nerve Seh-; memory, impression visuell. ~ **aids** Anschauungsmaterial nt; ~ **display unit** Sichtgerät nt.

visualize ['vɪzjʊəlaɪz] vt (a) (see in mind) sich (dat) vorstellen.
(b) (foresee) erwarten. we do not ~ many changes wir rechnen nicht mit großen Veränderungen; he ~s some changes (intends) er hat einige Veränderungen im Auge; that's not how I'd ~d things so hatte ich mir das nicht vorgestellt.

visually ['vɪzjʊəlɪ] adv visuell. ~, the film is good entertainment von der Aufmachung her ist der Film sehr unterhaltend; I remember things ~ ich habe ein visuelles Gedächtnis.

vital ['vaɪtl] adj (a) (of life) vital, Lebens-; (necessary for life) lebenswichtig. ~ **force** Lebenskraft f; ~ **organs** lebenswichtige Organe pl; ~ **parts** wichtige Teile pl; ~ **statistics** Bevölkerungsstatistik f; (inf: of woman) Maße pl.
(b) (essential) unerläßlich. of ~ **importance** von größter Wichtigkeit; this is ~ das ist unbedingt notwendig; your support is ~ to us wir brauchen unbedingt ihre Unterstützung; is it ~ for you to go? müssen Sie denn unbedingt gehen?; it's ~ that this is finished by Tuesday das muß bis Dienstag unbedingt fertig sein; how ~ is this? wie wichtig ist das?
(c) (critical) error schwerwiegend; problem Kern-. at the ~ moment im kritischen or entscheidenden Moment.
(d) (lively) person vital; artistic style also lebendig.
2 n the ~s die lebenswichtigen Organe pl; (hum: genitals) die edlen Teile pl.

vitality [vaɪ'tælɪtɪ] n (energy) Energie f, Leben nt, Vitalität f; (of prose, language) Lebendigkeit, Vitalität f; (of companies, new state) Dynamik f; (durability) Beständigkeit f.

vitalize ['vaɪtəlaɪz] vt beleben.

vitally ['vaɪtəlɪ] adv important äußerst, ungeheuer. he writes freshly and ~ er schreibt einen frischen und lebendigen or kraftvollen Stil.

vitamin ['vɪtəmɪn] n Vitamin nt. ~ A Vitamin A; with added ~s mit Vitaminen angereichert.

vitamin: ~ **deficiency** n Vitaminmangel m; ~**-deficiency disease** n Vitaminmangelkrankheit f; ~ **pills** npl Vitamintabletten pl.

vitiate ['vɪʃɪeɪt] vt (a) (spoil) air, blood verunreinigen. (b) (Jur etc: invalidate) ungültig machen; thesis widerlegen.

viticulture ['vɪtɪkʌltʃə'] n Weinbau m.

vitreous ['vɪtrɪəs] adj Glas-. ~ **china** Porzellanemail nt; ~ **enamel** Glasemail nt.

vitrifaction [‚vɪtrɪ'fækʃən], **vitrification** [‚vɪtrɪfɪ'keɪʃən] n Verglasung, Frittung f.

vitrify ['vɪtrɪfaɪ] 1 vt zu Glas schmelzen, verglasen. 2 vi verglasen, fritten.

vitriol ['vɪtrɪəl] n (Chem) (salt) Sulfat, Vitriol nt; (acid) Schwefelsäure f; (fig) Bissigkeit, Bosheit f. the bitter ~ of his jealousy die ihn zerfressende Eifersucht.

vitriolic [‚vɪtrɪ'ɒlɪk] adj Vitriol-; (fig) remark beißend, haßerfüllt; criticism ätzend, beißend; attack, speech haßerfüllt.

vituperate [vɪ'tjuːpəreɪt] vi schmähen (geh) (against acc), verunglimpfen (against acc).

vituperation [vɪ‚tjuːpə'reɪʃən] n (form) Schmähungen pl (geh).

vituperative [vɪ'tjuːpərətɪv] adj (form) speech Schmäh-; language, criticism schmähend.

viva n see viva voce 2.

vivacious [vɪ'veɪʃəs] adj lebhaft; character, person also temperamentvoll; colour, clothes also leuchtend bunt; smile, laugh munter, aufgeweckt.

vivaciously [vɪ'veɪʃəslɪ] adv see adj.

vivaciousness [vɪ'veɪʃəsnɪs] n Lebhaftigkeit f; (of smile, laugh) Munterkeit, Aufgewecktheit f.

vivacity [vɪ'væsɪtɪ] n Lebhaftigkeit f; (of style) Lebendigkeit f; (of smile, laugh) Munterkeit, Aufgewecktheit f.

vivarium [vɪ'veərɪəm] n Vivarium nt.

viva voce [‚vaɪvə'vəʊsɪ] 1 adj, adv mündlich. 2 n mündliche Prüfung.

vivid ['vɪvɪd] adj (a) light hell; colour kräftig, leuchtend, lebhaft. the ~ feathers of the bird das bunte or auffallende

Gefieder des Vogels; a ~ **blue dress** ein leuchtendblaues Kleid; a ~ **tie** eine auffällige Krawatte.

(b) (*lively*) *imagination, recollection* lebhaft; *description, metaphor, image* lebendig, anschaulich; *emotions* stark. **the memory of that day is still quite ~** der Tag ist mir noch in lebhafter Erinnerung.

vividly ['vividli] *adv* **(a)** *coloured* lebhaft; *shine* hell, leuchtend. **the red stands out ~ against its background** das Rot hebt sich stark vom Hintergrund ab; **a ~ coloured bird** ein buntgefiederter *or* auffällig gefiederter Vogel.

(b) *remember* lebhaft; *describe* anschaulich, lebendig.

vividness ['vividnis] *n* **(a)** (*of colour*) Lebhaftigkeit *f*; (*of light*) Helligkeit *f*. **(b)** (*of style*) Lebendigkeit *f*; (*of description, metaphor, image also*) Anschaulichkeit *f*; (*of imagination, memory*) Lebhaftigkeit *f*.

vivify ['vivifai] *vt* beleben.

viviparous [vi'vipərəs] *adj* (*Zool*) lebendgebärend.

vivisect [,vivi'sekt] *vt* vivisezieren.

vivisection [,vivi'sekʃən] *n* Vivisektion *f*.

vivisectionist [,vivi'sekʃənist] *n jd, der Eingriffe am lebenden Tier vornimmt/befürwortet.*

vixen ['viksn] *n* (*Zool*) Füchsin *f*; (*fig*) zänkisches Weib, Drachen *m* (*inf*).

viz [viz] *adv* nämlich.

vizier [vi'ziə⁺] *n* Wesir *m*.

V-J Day *n* Tag *m* des Sieges gegen Japan im 2. Weltkrieg.

V: **~-neck** *n* spitzer *or* V-Ausschnitt *m*; **~-necked** *adj* spitz ausgeschnitten.

vocabulary [vəu'kæbjuləri] *n* Wortschatz *m*, Vokabular *nt* (*geh*); (*in textbook*) Wörterverzeichnis *f*. **he has a limited ~** er hat einen beschränkten Wortschatz; **the ~ of the legal profession** das Vokabular der Juristen; **~ book** Vokabelheft *nt*; (*printed*) Vokabelbuch *nt*; **~ test** (*Sch*) Vokabelarbeit *f*.

vocal ['vəukəl] **1** *adj* **(a)** Stimm-. **~ cords** Stimmbänder *pl*; **~ music** Vokalmusik *f*; **~ group** Gesangsgruppe *f*.

(b) *communication* mündlich.

(c) (*voicing one's opinions*) *group, person* lautstark. **to be/become ~** sich zu Wort melden.

2 *n* (*of pop song*) (gesungener) Schlager; (*in jazz*) Vocal *nt*. **who's doing the ~s for your group now?** wen habt ihr denn jetzt als Sänger?

vocalic [vəu'kælik] *adj* vokalisch.

vocalist ['vəukəlist] *n* Sänger(in *f*) *m*.

vocalize ['vəukəlaiz] *vt* **(a)** *thoughts* aussprechen, Ausdruck verleihen (+*dat*). **(b)** (*Phon*) *consonant* vokalisieren.

vocally ['vəukəli] *adv* mündlich. **the tune has now been done ~ by** ... die Melodie wurde jetzt auch gesungen von ...

vocation [vəu'keiʃən] *n* **(a)** (*Rel etc*) Berufung *f*; (*form: profession*) Beruf *m*. **to have a ~ for teaching** zum Lehrer berufen sein. **(b)** (*aptitude*) Begabung *f*, Talent *nt*.

vocational [vəu'keiʃənl] *adj* Berufs-. **~ guidance** Berufsberatung *f*; **~ school** (*US*) = Berufsschule *f*; **~ training** Berufsausbildung *f*.

vocative ['vɒkətiv] *n* Anredeform *f*, Vokativ *m*. **~ case** Anredefall *m*, Vokativ *m*.

vociferate [vəu'sifəreit] *vti* schreien. **he ~d his grievances** er machte seinem Unmut Luft.

vociferation [vəu,sifə'reiʃən] *n* Geschrei *nt*. **their ~ of their discontent** ihr lautstarker Protest.

vociferous [vəu'sifərəs] *adj* *class, audience* laut; *demands, protest* lautstark.

vociferously [vəu'sifərəsli] *adv* lautstark.

vodka ['vɒdkə] *n* Wodka *m*.

vogue [vəug] *n* Mode *f*. **the ~ for jeans** die Jeansmode; **wigs are the ~ or are in ~ this year** Perücken sind in diesem Jahr (in) Mode; **to come into ~** (*dresses*) in Mode kommen, modern werden; (*writers*) populär werden, in Mode kommen; **to go out of ~** (*dresses*) aus der Mode kommen, unmodern werden; (*writers*) aus der Mode kommen; **to have a great ~** mit sehr beliebt sein unter (+*dat*), große Mode sein unter (+*dat*).

vogue: **~ expression,** **~ word** *n* Modewort *nt*.

voice [vɔis] **1** *n* **(a)** (*faculty of speech, Mus, fig*) Stimme *f*. **to lose one's ~** die Stimme verlieren; **I've lost my ~** ich habe keine Stimme mehr; **she hasn't got much of a ~** sie hat keine besonders gute Stimme; **to be in (good)/poor ~** disponiert/schlecht disponiert sein; **in a deep ~** mit tiefer Stimme; **to like the sound of one's own ~** sich gern(e) reden hören; **his ~ has broken** er hat den Stimmbruch hinter sich; **tenor/bass ~** Tenor *m*/Baß *m*; **a piece for ~ and piano** ein Gesangsstück *nt* mit Klavierbegleitung; **with one ~** einstimmig; **to give ~ to sth** etw aussprechen, einer Sache (*dat*) Ausdruck verleihen; *see* exercise.

(b) (*fig: say*) **have a/no ~ in the matter** wir haben in dieser Angelegenheit ein/kein Mitspracherecht *nt*.

(c) (*Gram*) Aktionsart *f*, Genus (verbi) *nt*. **the active/passive ~** das Aktiv/Passiv.

(d) (*Phon*) Stimmhaftigkeit *f*. **plus ~** stimmhaft.

2 *vt* **(a)** (*express*) *feelings, opinion* zum Ausdruck bringen.

(b) (*Phon*) stimmhaft aussprechen. **~d** stimmhaft.

voice box *n* Kehlkopf *m*.

-voiced [-vɔist] *adj suf* mit ... Stimme.

voice: **~less** *adj* **(a)** stumm; **(b)** (*having no say*) ohne Mitspracherecht *nt*; **(c)** (*Phon*) *consonant* stimmlos; **~-over** *n* Filmkommentar *m*; **~ part** *n* **the ~ parts** (*Mus*) die Singstimmen *pl*; **~ production** *n* Stimmbildung *f*; **~ projection** *n* Stimmresonanz *f*; **~ range** *n* Stimmumfang *m*.

void [vɔid] **1** *n* (*lit, fig*) Leere *f*. **the dead astronaut floated off into the ~** der tote Astronaut schwebte in das All.

2 *adj* **(a)** (*empty*) leer. **~ of any sense of decency** bar jeglichen Gefühls (*geh*) *or* ohne jegliches Gefühl für Anstand; **~ of hope** bar jeder Hoffnung (*geh*), ohne Hoffnung.

(b) (*Jur*) ungültig, nichtig.

(c) (*useless*) nichtig (*geh*). **you've made all my efforts totally ~** du hast all meine Bemühungen völlig zunichte gemacht.

3 *vt* **(a)** (*Jur*) ungültig machen, aufheben.

(b) (*form: empty*) *bowels* entleeren.

voile [vɔil] *n* Voile, Schleierstoff *m*.

vol *abbr of* **volume** Bd.; (*Measure*) **volume** V(ol).

volatile ['vɒlətail] *adj* **(a)** (*Chem*) flüchtig. **~ oils** ätherische Öle *pl*. **(b)** *person* (*in moods*) impulsiv; (*in interests*) sprunghaft; *political situation* brisant; (*St Ex*) unbeständig.

volatility [,vɒlə'tiliti] *n see adj* **(a)** Flüchtigkeit *f*. **(b)** Impulsivität *f*; Sprunghaftigkeit *f*; Brisanz *f*.

volatilize [vɒ'lætəlaiz] **1** *vt* verflüchtigen. **2** *vi* sich verflüchtigen.

vol-au-vent ['vɒləuvɑ̃] *n* (Königin)pastetchen *nt*.

volcanic [vɒl'kænik] *adj* (*lit*) *dust* vulkanisch; *region, eruption* Vulkan-; (*fig*) heftig.

volcano [vɒl'keinəu] *n* Vulkan *m*.

vole [vəul] *n* Wühlmaus *f*; (*common ~*) Feldmaus *f*.

Volga ['vɒlgə] *n* Wolga *f*.

volition [vɒ'liʃən] *n* Wille *m*. **the power of ~** Willenskraft, Willensstärke *f*; **simply by the exercise of your ~** mit dem Willen allein; **of one's own ~** aus freiem Willen.

volitional [və'liʃənl] *adj* Willens-, willentlich.

volley ['vɒli] **1** *n* **(a)** (*of shots*) Salve *f*; (*of arrows, stones*) Hagel *m*; (*fig: of insults*) Flut *f*, Hagel *m*; (*of applause*) Sturm *m*.

(b) (*Tennis*) Volley, Flugball *m*.

2 *vt* **to ~ a ball** (*Tennis*) einen Ball im Volley spielen, einen Volley spielen *or* schlagen.

3 *vi* **(a)** (*Mil*) eine Salve abfeuern; (*guns, shots*) (in einer Salve) abgefeuert werden.

(b) einen Volley schlagen.

volleyball ['vɒli,bɔːl] *n* Volleyball *m*.

Vols *abbr of* **Volumes** Bde.

volt [vəult] *n* Volt *nt*. **~ meter** Voltmeter *nt*.

voltage ['vəultidʒ] *n* Spannung *f*. **what ~ is this cable?** wieviel Volt hat dieses Kabel?

voltaic [vɒl'teiik] *adj* voltaisch, galvanisch. **~ cell** galvanisches Element.

volte-face ['vɒlt'fɑːs] *n* (*fig*) Kehrtwendung *f*. **to do a ~** sich um 180 Grad drehen.

volubility [,vɒlju'biliti] *n* Redseligkeit *f*.

voluble ['vɒljubl] *adj* *speaker* redegewandt, redselig (*pej*); *protest* wortreich.

volubly ['vɒljubli] *adv* wortreich. **to speak ~** sehr redselig sein.

volume ['vɒljuːm] *n* **(a)** Band *m*. **in six ~s** in sechs Bänden; **a six-~ dictionary** ein sechsbändiges Wörterbuch; **to write ~s** ganze Bände *pl* schreiben; **that speaks ~s** (*fig*) das spricht Bände (*for* für); **it speaks ~s for him** das spricht sehr für ihn.

(b) (*space occupied by sth*) Volumen *nt*, Rauminhalt *m*.

(c) (*size, amount*) Umfang *m*, Ausmaß *nt* (*of* an +*dat*). **a large ~ of sales/business** ein großer Umsatz; **the ~ of traffic** das Verkehrsaufkommen; **trade has increased in ~** das Handelsvolumen hat sich vergrößert.

(d) (*large amount*) **~s of smoke** Rauchschwaden *pl*; **~s of white silk** Massen *pl* von weißer Seide; **we've ~s of work to get through** wir haben noch Berge von Arbeit.

(e) (*sound*) Lautstärke *f*. **is the ~ right up?** ist das volle Lautstärke?; **turn the ~ up/down** (*Rad, TV*) stell (das Gerät) lauter/ leiser; **~ control** (*Rad, TV*) Lautstärkenregler *m*.

volumetric [,vɒlju'metrik] *adj* volumetrisch.

voluminous [və'luːminəs] *adj* voluminös (*geh*); *figure also* üppig; *writings* umfangreich; *dress* wallend.

voluntarily ['vɒləntərili] *adv* freiwillig, von sich aus.

voluntary ['vɒləntəri] **1** *adj* **(a)** *confession* freiwillig.

(b) (*unpaid*) *help, service, work* freiwillig. **~ worker** freiwilliger Helfer, freiwillige Helferin; (*overseas*) Entwicklungshelfer(in *f*) *m*.

(c) (*supported by charity*) **a ~ organization for social work** ein freiwilliger Wohlfahrtsverband.

(d) (*having will*) *movements* willkürlich, willentlich; *crime* vorsätzlich. **man is a ~ agent** der Mensch handelt aus freiem Willen.

(e) (*Physiol*) **~ muscles** willkürliche Muskeln *pl*.

2 *n* (*Eccl, Mus*) Solo *nt*.

volunteer [,vɒlən'tiə⁺] **1** *n* (*also Mil*) Freiwillige(r) *mf*. **~ army** Freiwilligenheer *nt*; **any ~s?** wer meldet sich freiwillig?

2 *vt help, services* anbieten; *suggestion* machen; *information* geben, herausrücken mit (*inf*). **we didn't ask you to ~ any advice** wir haben Sie nicht um Rat gebeten; **he ~ed his brother** (*hum*) er hat seinen Bruder (als Freiwilligen) gemeldet.

3 *vi* **(a)** etw freiwillig tun. **to ~ for sth** sich freiwillig für etw zur Verfügung stellen; **to ~ to do sth** sich anbieten, etw zu tun; **who will ~ to clean the windows?** wer meldet sich freiwillig zum Fensterputzen?

(b) (*Mil*) sich freiwillig melden (*for* zu, *for places* nach).

voluptuary [və'lʌptjuəri] *n* Lüstling *m*.

voluptuous [və'lʌptjuəs] *adj* *mouth, woman, movement* sinnlich; *curves* üppig; *body* verlockend; *life* ausschweifend; *kiss* hingebungsvoll.

voluptuously [və'lʌptjuəsli] *adv* *move* aufreizend, sinnlich; *kiss* hingebungsvoll; *live* ausschweifend.

voluptuousness [və'lʌptjuəsnis] *n see adj* Sinnlichkeit *f*; Üppigkeit *f*; verlockende Formen *pl*; Hingabe *f*. **the ~ of his life** sein ausschweifendes Leben, sein Leben der Wollust.

volute [və'luːt] *n* (*Archit*) Volute *f*.

voluted [və'luːtid] *adj* (*Archit*) mit Voluten (versehen).

vomit ['vɒmit] **1** *n* Erbrochene(s) *nt*; (*act*) Erbrechen *nt*. **have a good ~** erbrechen Sie sich ruhig.

2 *vt* (*lit, fig*) spucken, speien (*geh*); *food* erbrechen.

3 *vi* sich erbrechen, sich übergeben.

♦**vomit out 1** vt sep (lit) erbrechen; (fig) smoke, flames speien. **2** vi (fig) **the flames were still ~ing ~ of the volcano** der Vulkan spie immer noch Feuer.
♦**vomit up** vt sep food (wieder) erbrechen.
voodoo ['vuːduː] n Voodoo, Wodu m.
voodooism ['vuːduːɪzəm] n Voodoo- or Wodukult m.
voracious [və'reɪʃəs] adj person gefräßig. **she is a ~ reader** sie verschlingt die Bücher geradezu; **to have a ~ appetite** einen Riesenappetit haben.
voraciously [və'reɪʃəslɪ] adv eat gierig. **to read ~** die Bücher nur so verschlingen.
voracity [vɒ'ræsɪtɪ] n Gefräßigkeit f; (fig) Gier f (for nach).
vortex ['vɔːteks] n, pl **-es** or **vortices** ['vɔːtɪsiːz] (lit) Wirbel, Strudel (also fig) m.
votary ['vəʊtərɪ] n (Rel) Geweihte(r) mf; (fig) Jünger m.
vote [vəʊt] **1** n (a) (expression of opinion) Stimme f; (act of voting) Abstimmung, Wahl f; (result) Abstimmungs- or Wahlergebnis nt. **to put sth to the ~** über etw (acc) abstimmen lassen; **to take a ~ on sth** über etw (acc) abstimmen; **elected by the ~ of the people** vom Volk gewählt; **the ~ for/against the change surprised him** daß für/gegen den Wechsel gestimmt wurde, erstaunte ihn; **the ~ was 150 to 95** das Abstimmungsergebnis war 150 zu 95; **we would like to offer a ~ of thanks to Mr Smith** wir möchten Mr Smith unseren aufrichtigen Dank aussprechen; see **censure, confidence**.
(b) (~ cast) Stimme f. **to give one's ~ to a party/person** einer Partei/jdm seine Stimme geben; **single-~ majority** Mehrheit f von einer Stimme; **a photo of the Prime Minister casting his ~** ein Photo des Premierministers bei der Stimmabgabe; **what's your ~?** (in panel game, competition) wie lautet Ihr Urteil?; **he won by 22 ~s** er gewann mit einer Mehrheit von 22 Stimmen; **10% of the voters invalidated their ~s** 10% der Wähler machten ihren Stimmzettel ungültig.
(c) (Pol: collective) **the Labour ~** die Labourstimmen pl.
(d) (franchise) Wahlrecht nt. **~s for women!** Wahlrecht für die Frauen!
(e) (money allotted) Bewilligung f.
2 vt (elect) wählen. **he was ~d chairman** er wurde zum Vorsitzenden gewählt; **to ~ Labour** Labour wählen.
(b) (inf: judge) wählen zu. **the group ~d her the best cook** die Gruppe wählte sie zur besten Köchin; **the panel ~d the record a miss** die Jury erklärte die Platte für einen Mißerfolg; **I ~ we go back** ich schlage vor, daß wir umkehren.
(c) (approve) bewilligen.
3 vi (cast one's ~) wählen. **to ~ for/against** für/gegen stimmen.
♦**vote down** vt sep proposal niederstimmen.
♦**vote in** vt sep law beschließen; person wählen.
♦**vote on** vi +prep obj abstimmen über (+ acc).
♦**vote out** vt sep abwählen; amendment ablehnen.
voter ['vəʊtər] n Wähler(in f) m.
voting ['vəʊtɪŋ] n Wahl f. **which way is the ~ going?** welchen Verlauf nimmt die Wahl?; **a system of ~** ein Wahlsystem nt; **to analyze the ~** das Wahlergebnis analysieren; **~ was high this year** die Wahlbeteiligung war dieses Jahr hoch.
voting: ~ booth n Wahlkabine f; **~ machine** n (US) Wahlmaschine f; **~ paper** n Stimmzettel m.
votive ['vəʊtɪv] adj Votiv-.
vouch [vaʊtʃ] vi **to ~ for sb/sth** sich für jdn/etw verbürgen; (legally) für jdn/etw bürgen; **to ~ for the truth of sth** sich für die Richtigkeit einer Sache verbürgen.
voucher ['vaʊtʃər] n (a) (for cash, petrol) Gutschein m; (for meals also) Bon m; (cigarette ~) Coupon m; see **luncheon ~**.
(b) (receipt) Beleg m; (for debt) Schuldschein m.
vouchsafe [vaʊtʃ'seɪf] vt (form) gewähren (sb jdm). **to ~ a reply** sich zu einer Antwort herablassen; **to ~ to do sth** die Güte haben or geruhen (geh), etw zu tun.
vow [vaʊ] **1** n Versprechen, Gelöbnis nt; (Rel) Gelübde nt. **lover's ~** Treueschwur m; **to make a ~ to do sth** geloben, etw zu tun; **to take one's ~s** sein Gelübde ablegen; **to be under a**

~ **to do sth** durch ein Versprechen verpflichtet sein, etw zu tun.
2 vt obedience geloben. **to ~ vengeance on sb** jdm Rache schwören; **he is ~ed to silence** er hat Schweigen gelobt.
vowel ['vaʊəl] n Vokal, Selbstlaut m. **~ system** Vokalismus m; **~ sound** Vokal(laut) m.
voyage ['vɔɪdʒ] **1** n (a) Reise, Fahrt, Seereise f; (Space also) Flug m. **to go on a ~** auf eine Reise etc gehen; **to make a ~** eine Reise etc machen; **the ~ out** die Hinreise/der Hinflug; **the ~ back** or **home** die Rück- or Heimreise/der Rückflug.
(b) (fig) **~ of discovery** Entdeckungsreise f.
2 vi eine Seereise machen; (spaceship) fliegen. **to ~ across an ocean** einen Ozean überqueren.
voyager ['vɔɪədʒər] n Passagier m; (Space) Raumfahrer m.
voyeur [vwaː'jɜːr] n Voyeur m.
voyeurism [vwaː'jɜːrɪzəm] n Voyeurismus m, Voyeurtum nt.
VP abbr of **vice-president**.
V: ~-shaped adj pfeil-förmig, V-förmig; **~-sign** n (victory) Victory-Zeichen nt; (rude) ≈ Götzgruß m; **he gave me the ~-sign** ≈ er zeigte mir den Vogel.
VSO abbr of **Voluntary Service Overseas** ≈ Deutscher Entwicklungsdienst (BRD).
Vulcan ['vʌlkən] n Vulcanus m.
vulcanite ['vʌlkənaɪt] n Hartgummi m, Ebonit nt.
vulcanization [ˌvʌlkənaɪ'zeɪʃən] n Vulkanisierung f.
vulcanize ['vʌlkənaɪz] vt vulkanisieren.
vulgar ['vʌlgər] adj (a) (pej: unrefined) ordinär, vulgär; clothes, joke ordinär; (tasteless) geschmacklos. **the ~ herd** der Pöbel (pej).
(b) (old: of the common people) gemein (old). **~ beliefs** volkstümliche Auffassungen pl; **~ Latin** Vulgärlatein nt; **in the ~ tongue** in der Sprache des Volkes.
(c) (Math) **~ fraction** gemeiner Bruch.
vulgarism ['vʌlgərɪzəm] n Gassenausdruck m, primitiver Ausdruck; (swearword) vulgärer Ausdruck.
vulgarity [vʌl'gærɪtɪ] n Vulgarität f, (of gesture, joke also) Anstößigkeit f; (of colour, tie etc) Geschmacklosigkeit f. **the ~ of his behaviour** sein ordinäres or pöbelhaftes Benehmen.
vulgarize ['vʌlgəraɪz] vt (a) (make coarse) vulgarisieren. (b) (popularize) popularisieren, allgemeinverständlich machen.
vulgarly ['vʌlgəlɪ] adv (a) (coarsely) vulgär; dressed geschmacklos. (b) (commonly) allgemein, gemeinhin. **~ known as snapdragons** allgemein or im Volksmund als Löwenmäulchen bekannt.
Vulgate ['vʌlgɪt] n Vulgata f.
vulnerability [ˌvʌlnərə'bɪlɪtɪ] n see adj Verwundbarkeit f; Verletzlichkeit f; Verletzbarkeit f; Ungeschütztheit f. **the ~ of the young fish to predators** die Wehrlosigkeit der jungen Fische gegen Raubtiere; **such is their ~ only 2% survive** sie sind so wehrlos, daß nur 2% überleben; **his emotional ~** seine Empfindsamkeit or Verletzbarkeit; **a feeling of ~ in discussions** ein Gefühl der Wehrlosigkeit in Diskussionen.
vulnerable ['vʌlnərəbl] adj verwundbar; (exposed) verletzlich; (fig) verletzbar; police, troops, fortress ungeschützt. **the skin is ~ to radiation** die Haut hat keinen Schutz gegen Radioaktivität; **the turtle on its back is completely ~** auf dem Rücken liegend ist die Schildkröte völlig wehrlos; **to be ~ to the cold** kälteanfällig sein; **to be ~ to temptation** für Versuchungen anfällig sein; **to be ~ to criticism** (exposed) der Kritik ausgesetzt sein; (sensitive) keine Kritik vertragen; **I felt extremely ~ in the discussion** ich kam mir in der Diskussion völlig wehrlos vor; **the one ~ spot in his armour** die einzige ungeschützte Stelle in seiner Rüstung; **a ~ point in our defences** ein schwacher or wunder Punkt in unserer Verteidigung; **economically ~** wirtschaftlich wehrlos.
vulpine ['vʌlpaɪn] adj schlau, listig.
vulture ['vʌltʃər] n (lit, fig) Geier m.
vulva ['vʌlvə] n (weibliche) Scham, Vulva f (geh).
vv abbr of **verses**.
V wings ['viːwɪŋz] npl pfeilförmige Tragflügel pl.
vying ['vaɪɪŋ] n (Konkurrenz)kampf m (for um).

W

W, w ['dʌbljuː] n W, w nt.
W abbr of **west** W.
w abbr of **watt(s)** W.
WAAF abbr of **Women's Auxiliary Air Force**.
Waaf [wæf] n (Brit) Mitglied nt der weiblichen Luftwaffe.
WAC (US) abbr of **Women's Army Corps**.
wack [wæk] n (Brit sl: as address) Kumpel m (inf).
wacky ['wækɪ] adj (+er) (inf) verrückt (inf).
wad [wɒd] **1** n (a) (compact mass) Knäuel m; (in gun, cartridge) Pfropfen m; (of cotton wool etc) Bausch m. **to use sth as a ~** etw zum Ausstopfen or als Polster benutzen.

(b) (of papers, banknotes) Bündel nt. **he's got ~s of money** (inf) er hat Geld wie Heu (inf).
2 vt (secure, stuff) stopfen; (squeeze) zusammenknüllen; (Sew) wattieren. **the glasses must be firmly ~ded down** die Gläser müssen bruchsicher verpackt sein or werden.
wadding ['wɒdɪŋ] n (for packing) Material nt zum Ausstopfen; (Sew) Wattierung f; (Med: on plaster) (Mull)tupfer m.
waddle ['wɒdl] **1** n Watscheln nt. **to walk with a ~** einen watschelnden Gang haben. **2** vi watscheln.
wade [weɪd] **1** vt durchwaten. **2** vi waten.
♦**wade in** vi (a) (lit) hineinwaten.

(b) (fig inf) (join in a fight, controversy) sich einmischen (inf); (tackle problem etc) sich voll reinstürzen or -werfen (inf), sich hineinknien (inf). **the new boss ~d = with a few staff changes** der neue Chef hat sich gleich mächtig ins Zeug gelegt (inf) und ein paar Umbesetzungen vorgenommen.

♦ **wade into** vi +prep obj (fig inf: attack) auf jdn losgehen/etw in Angriff nehmen.

♦ **wade through** vi +prep obj **(a)** (lit) waten durch. **(b)** (fig) sich durchkämpfen durch; (learning sth also) durchackern.

wader ['weɪdəʳ] n **(a)** (Orn) Watvogel m. **(b)** ~s pl (boots) Watstiefel pl.

wafer ['weɪfəʳ] n **(a)** (biscuit) Waffel f. **a vanilla ~** eine Vanilleeiswaffel. **(b)** (Eccl) Hostie f. **(c)** (silicon ~) Wafer m.

wafer-thin ['weɪfə'θɪn] adj hauchdünn.

waffle¹ ['wɒfl] n (Cook) Waffel f. **~ iron** Waffeleisen nt.

waffle² (Brit inf) **1** n Geschwafel nt (inf). **2** vi (also ~ on) schwafeln (inf). **I managed to ~ on somehow** irgendwie habe ich was (daher)geschwafelt (inf).

waft [wɑːft] **1** n Hauch m. **a ~ of smoke/cool air** eine dünne Rauchschwade/ein kühler Lufthauch. **2** vt tragen, wehen. **3** vi wehen. **a delicious smell ~ed up from the kitchen** ein köstlicher Geruch zog aus der Küche herauf.

wag¹ [wæg] **1** n **he admonished me with a ~ of his finger** tadelnd drohte er mir mit dem Finger; **with a ~ of its tail** mit einem Schwanzwedeln.

2 vt tail wedeln mit; (bird) wippen mit. **to ~ one's finger at sb** jdm mit dem Finger drohen.

3 vi (tail) wedeln; (of bird) wippen. **her tongue never stops ~ging** (inf) ihr Mundwerk steht keine Sekunde still (inf); **as soon as he left the tongues started ~ging** sobald er gegangen war, wurde über ihn geredet or fing das Gerede an; **to stop the tongues ~ging** um dem Gerede ein Ende zu machen; **her tongue would ~ from morning till night** ihr Mundwerk ging von morgens bis abends; **that'll set the tongues ~ging** dann geht das Gerede los.

wag² n (joker) Witzbold m (inf). **a bit of a ~** ein alter Witzbold.

wage¹ [weɪdʒ] n usu pl Lohn m.

wage² vt war, campaign führen. **to ~ war against sth** (fig) gegen etw einen Feldzug führen.

wage in cpds Lohn-; **~ demand** n Lohnforderung f; **~ earner** n Lohnempfänger m; **~ freeze** n Lohnstopp m; **~ increase** n Lohnerhöhung f; **~ packet** n Lohntüte f.

wager ['weɪdʒəʳ] **1** n Wette f (on auf +acc). **to lay or make a ~** eine Wette eingehen or abschließen.

2 vti wetten (on auf +acc); one's honour, life verpfänden. **I'll ~ you £2 my horse wins** ich wette mit Ihnen um £ 2, daß mein Pferd gewinnt; **he won't do it, I ~!** (dated) ich wette, daß er es nicht tut!

wages ['weɪdʒɪz] npl Lohn m. **the ~ of sin** die gerechte Strafe, der Sünde Lohn (old).

wage: **~ scale** n Lohnskala f; **~s clerk** n Lohnbuchhalter(in f) m; **~ worker** n (US) Lohnempfänger m.

waggish ['wægɪʃ] adj schalkhaft, schelmisch. **he has a ~ sense of humour** ihm sitzt der Schalk im Nacken.

waggishly ['wægɪʃlɪ] adv schalkhaft.

waggle ['wægl] **1** vt wackeln mit; tail wedeln mit; (bird) wippen mit. **he ~d his finger at me** disapprovingly er drohte mir mißbilligend mit dem Finger; **he ~d his loose tooth** er wackelte an dem lockeren Zahn.

2 vi wackeln; (tail) wedeln.

3 n **with a ~ of her hips** she left the stage mit den Hüften wackelnd ging sie von der Bühne; **with a ~ of its tail** mit einem Schwanzwedeln.

waggly ['wæglɪ] adj (loose) wackelig; hips wackelnd; tail wedelnd.

waggon n (Brit) see wagon.

Wagnerian [vɑːgˈnɪərɪən] **1** n Wagnerianer mf. **2** adj Wagner-; (like Wagner) wagner(i)sch.

wagon ['wægən] n **(a)** (horse-drawn) Fuhrwerk nt, Wagen m; (covered ~) Planwagen m; (US: delivery truck) Lieferwagen m; (child's toy cart) Leiterwagen m; (tea ~ etc) Wagen m; (US inf: police car) Streifenwagen, Peterwagen (N Ger inf) m; (US inf: for transporting prisoners) grüne Minna (inf); (Brit sl: car) Kutsche f (sl); (Brit sl: lorry) Laster m (inf).

(b) (Brit Rail) Waggon m.

(c) (inf) **I'm on the ~** ich trinke nichts; **to go on the ~** unter die Abstinenzler gehen (inf).

wagoner ['wægənəʳ] n Fuhrmann m.

wagon: **~load** n Wagenladung f; **books/prisoners arrived by the ~load** ganze Wagenladungen von Büchern/Gefangenen kamen an; **~ train** n Zug m von Planwagen.

wagtail ['wægteɪl] n (Orn) Bachstelze f.

waif [weɪf] n obdachloses or heimatloses Kind; (animal) herrenloses Tier. **the poor little ~ ...** das arme kleine Ding, hat kein Zuhause, ...; **~s and strays** obdachlose or heimatlose Kinder pl.

wail [weɪl] **1** n (of baby) Geschrei nt; (of mourner, music) Klagen nt; (of sirens, wind) Heulen nt; (inf: complaint) Gejammer nt (inf). **a great ~/a ~ of protest** went up es erhob sich lautes Wehklagen/Protestgeheul.

2 vi (baby, child, cat) schreien; (mourner, music) klagen; (sirens, wind) heulen; (inf: complain) jammern (over über +acc).

Wailing Wall ['weɪlɪŋ'wɔːl] n Klagemauer f.

wain [weɪn] n (old) Wagen m. **the W~** (Astron) der Große Wagen.

wainscot ['weɪnskət] n, no pl Täfelung f.

wainscot(t)ed ['weɪnskətɪd] adj holzgetäfelt, paneeliert.

wainscot(t)ing ['weɪnskətɪŋ] n Täfelung f.

waist [weɪst] n Taille f; (of violin) Mittelbügel m; (Naut) Mittelteil m. **stripped to the ~** mit nacktem or entblößtem Oberkörper; **too tight round the ~** zu eng in der Taille.

waist: **~band** n Rock-/Hosenbund m; **~coat** n (Brit) Weste f;

~-deep adj hüfthoch, bis zur Taille reichend; **the water was/corn stood ~-deep** das Wasser/Korn reichte bis zur Taille; **we stood ~-deep in ...** wir standen bis zur Hüfte im ...

waisted ['weɪstɪd] adj clothes tailliert.

-waisted [-'weɪstɪd] adj suf mit einer ... Taille.

waist: **~-high** adj hüfthoch, bis zur Taille reichend; **we picnicked in a field of ~-high grass** wir picknickten in einem Feld, wo uns das Gras bis zur Hüfte reichte; **~line** n Taille f.

wait [weɪt] **1** vi **(a)** warten (for auf +acc). **to ~ for sb to do sth** darauf warten, daß jd etw tut; **it was definitely worth ~ing for** es hat sich wirklich gelohnt, darauf zu warten; **that'll be worth ~ing for** (iro) da bin ich aber gespannt (inf); **well, what are you ~ing for?** worauf wartest du denn (noch)?; **~ for it, now he's going to get mad** wart's ab, gleich wird er wild (inf); **right, class — ~ for it — OK now you can go** das wär's — Moment mal — so, jetzt könnt ihr gehen (inf); **let him ~!, he can ~!** laß ihn warten, soll er warten!, der kann warten!; **can't it ~?** kann das nicht warten?, hat das nicht Zeit?; **this work will have to ~ till later** diese Arbeit muß bis später warten or liegenbleiben; **this work is still ~ing to be done** diese Arbeit muß noch gemacht or erledigt werden; **~ a minute or moment or second** (einen) Augenblick or Moment (mal); **(just) you ~!** warte nur ab!; (threatening) warte nur!; **Mummy, I can't ~** Mami, ich muß dringend mal!; **I can't ~** ich kann's kaum erwarten; (out of curiosity) ich bin gespannt; **I can't ~ to see his face** da bin ich (aber) auf sein Gesicht gespannt; **I can't ~ to try out my new boat** ich kann es kaum noch erwarten, bis ich mein neues Boot ausprobiere; **I can hardly ~** (usu iro) ich kann es kaum erwarten!; **"repairs while you ~"** "Sofortreparaturen", „Reparaturschnelldienst"; **~ and see!** warten Sie (es) ab!, abwarten und Tee trinken! (inf); **we'll have to ~ and see how ...** wir müssen abwarten, wie ...

(b) (~ at table) servieren; **she used to ~ at the ...** sie bediente früher im ...

2 vt **(a)** **to ~ one's turn** (ab)warten, bis man an der Reihe ist; **to ~ one's chance/opportunity** auf eine günstige Gelegenheit warten, eine günstige Gelegenheit abwarten; **don't ~ supper for me** warte mit dem Abendessen nicht auf mich.

(b) (US) **to ~ table** servieren, bedienen.

3 n **(a)** Wartezeit f. **did you have a long ~?** mußten Sie lange warten?

(b) **to lie in ~ for sb/sth** jdm/einer Sache auflauern.

(c) **~s** pl Sternsinger pl.

♦ **wait about** or **around** vi warten (for auf +acc).

♦ **wait behind** vi zurückbleiben. **to ~ ~ for sb** zurückbleiben und auf jdn warten.

♦ **wait in** vi zu Hause bleiben (for wegen).

♦ **wait on 1** vi (continue to wait) noch (weiter) warten. **2** vi +prep obj **(a)** (also ~ upon) (serve) bedienen. **(b)** (US) **to ~ ~ table** servieren, bei Tisch bedienen. **(c)** (wait for) warten auf (+acc).

♦ **wait out** vt sep das Ende (+gen) abwarten.

♦ **wait up** vi aufbleiben (for wegen, für).

waiter ['weɪtəʳ] n Kellner, Ober m. **~!** (Herr) Ober!

waiting ['weɪtɪŋ] n **(a)** Warten nt. **all this ~ (around)** dieses ewige Warten, diese ewige Warterei (inf); **no ~** Halteverbot nt. **(b)** (royal service) those in ~ at the court ... wer bei Hof dient ... **(c)** (by waiter etc) Servieren, Bedienen nt. **courses in ~** Servierkurse pl.

waiting: **~ game** n Wartespiel nt; **to play a ~ game** ein Wartespiel nt spielen; **the siege/negotiations developed into a ~ game** die Belagerung entwickelte sich/die Verhandlungen entwickelten sich zu einer Geduldsprobe; **~ list** n Warteliste f; **~ room** n Warteraum m; (at doctor's) Wartezimmer nt; (in railway station) Wartesaal m.

waitress ['weɪtrɪs] n Kellnerin, Serviererin f. **~!** Fräulein!

waive [weɪv] vt **(a)** (not insist on) rights, claim verzichten auf (+acc); principles, rules, age limit etc außer acht lassen. **(b)** (put aside, dismiss) question, objection abtun.

waiver ['weɪvəʳ] n (Jur) Verzicht m (of auf +acc); (document) Verzichterklärung f; (of law, contract, clause) Außerkraftsetzung f.

wake¹ [weɪk] n (Naut) Kielwasser nt. **in the ~ of** (fig) im Gefolge (+gen); **to follow in sb's ~** in jds Kielwasser segeln; **X follows in the ~ of Y** Y bringt X mit sich; **X brings Y in its ~** X bringt Y mit sich; **X leaves Y in its ~** X hinterläßt Y; **with ten children in her ~** (inf) mit zehn Kindern im Schlepptau (inf).

wake² n (esp Ir: over corpse) Totenwache f.

wake³ pret **woke**, ptp **woken** or **~d 1** vt (auf)wecken; (fig) wecken, erwecken (geh).

2 vi aufwachen, erwachen (geh). **he woke to find himself in prison** als er aufwachte or erwachte, fand er sich im Gefängnis wieder; **he woke to the sound of birds singing** als er aufwachte, sangen die Vögel; **he woke one day to find himself a rich man** als er eines Tages erwachte or aufwachte, war er ein reicher Mann; **they woke to their danger too late** (fig) sie haben die Gefahr zu spät erkannt.

♦ **wake up 1** vi (lit, fig) aufwachen. **he woke ~ to find a burglar in the room** als er aufwachte, war ein Einbrecher im Zimmer; **to ~ ~ to sth** (fig) sich (dat) einer Sache (gen) bewußt werden; **I wish he'd ~ ~ to what's happening** ich wünschte, ihm würde endlich bewußt or aufgehen or klar, was (hier) vor sich geht; **he woke ~ to a new life** ein neues Leben brach für ihn an.

2 vt sep (lit) aufwecken, (fig: rouse from sloth) wach- or aufrütteln. **to ~ sb ~ to sth** (fig) jdm etw klarmachen or bewußt machen or vor Augen führen; **to ~ one's ideas ~** sich zusammenreißen; **getting married woke him ~ a bit** die Ehe hat ihn etwas wachgerüttelt.

wakeful ['weɪkful] adj (sleepless) schlaflos; (alert) wachsam.

wakefulness ['weɪkfulnɪs] n see adj Schlaflosigkeit f; Wachsamkeit f.

waken ['weɪkən] **1** vt (auf)wecken. **2** vi (liter, Scot) erwachen (geh), aufwachen. **he ~ed to see ...** beim Erwachen sah er ...; **he ~ed to another dreary day** ein neuer, trostloser Tag brach für ihn an.

waker ['weɪkə'] n **to be an early ~** früh aufwachen.

waking ['weɪkɪŋ] adj **one's ~ hours** von früh bis spät; **thoughts of her filled all his ~ hours** der Gedanke an sie beschäftigte ihn von früh bis spät; **his ~ hours were spent ...** von früh bis spät beschäftigte er sich mit ...

Wales [weɪlz] n Wales nt. **Prince of ~** Prinz m von Wales.

walk [wɔːk] **1** n **(a)** (stroll) Spaziergang m; (hike) Wanderung f; (Sport) Gehen nt; (competition) Geher-Wettkampf m; (charity ~) Marsch m (für Wohltätigkeitszwecke). **a 20 mile ~ along the roads** ein 20-Meilen-Marsch die Straße entlang; **it's only 10 minutes' ~** es sind nur 10 Minuten zu Fuß or zu gehen; **it's a long/short ~ to the shops** etc zu den Läden etc ist es nicht weit zu Fuß or zu gehen or zu laufen (inf); **it's a long ~ but a short drive** das ist es weit, aber mit dem Auto ganz nah; **that's quite a ~** das ist eine ganz schöne Strecke or ganz schön weit zu Fuß or zu laufen (inf); **he thinks nothing of a 10 mile ~** 10 Meilen zu Fuß sind für ihn gar nichts; **to go for or have or take a ~** einen Spaziergang machen, spazierengehen; **to take sb/the dog for a ~** mit jdm/dem Hund spazierengehen or einen Spaziergang machen, den Hund aus- or spazierenführen.

(b) (gait) Gang m; (of horse also) Gangart f. **he went at a ~** er ging schnellen Schrittes (geh) or schnell; **the horse went at a ~** das Pferd ging im Schritt; **he slowed his horse to a ~** er brachte sein Pferd in den Schritt; **he ran for a bit, then slowed to a ~** er rannte ein Stück und ging dann normalen Schrittes weiter or verfiel dann in ein normales Schritttempo.

(c) (path in garden etc) (Park)weg m; (in hills etc) Weg m.

(d) (route) Weg m; (signposted etc) Wander-/Spazierweg m. **he knows some good ~s in the Lake District** er kennt ein paar gute Wandermöglichkeiten or Wanderungen im Lake District.

(e) **~ of life** Milieu nt; **people from all ~s of life** Leute aus allen Schichten und Berufen.

(f) (US: Baseball) Walk m, Freibase nt.

2 vt **(a)** (lead) person, horse (spazieren)führen; dog ausführen; (ride at a ~) im Schritt gehen lassen. **to ~ sb home/to the bus** jdn nach Hause/zum Bus bringen; **she ~ed her baby up to the table** das Kind lief, von der Mutter gehalten or mit Hilfe der Mutter, zum Tisch; **to ~ sb off his feet/legs** jdn total erschöpfen; **if we go hiking, I'll ~ you off your feet** wenn wir zusammen wandern gehen, dann wirst du (bald) nicht mehr mithalten können; **they ~ed me off my feet** ich konnte nicht mehr mitlaufen (inf), ich ging auf dem Zahnfleisch (sl).

(b) distance laufen, gehen. **I've ~ed this road many times** ich bin diese Straße oft gegangen.

(c) **to ~ the streets** (prostitute) auf den Strich gehen (inf); (in search of sth) durch die Straßen irren; (aimlessly) durch die Straßen streichen; **to ~ the boards** (Theat) auf den Brettern stehen; **he learned his trade by ~ing the boards before turning to films** er hat sein Handwerk auf den Brettern gelernt, bevor er zum Film ging; **to ~ the plank** mit verbundenen Augen über eine Schiffsplanke ins Wasser getrieben werden; **to ~ the wards** (Med) familieren.

(d) (US: Baseball) einen Walk or ein Freibase geben (+dat).

3 vi **(a)** gehen, laufen. **~ a little with me** gehen Sie ein Stück mit mir; **to ~ in one's sleep** schlaf- or nachtwandeln.

(b) (not ride) zu Fuß gehen, laufen (inf); (stroll) spazierengehen; (hike) wandern. **you can ~ there in 5 minutes** da ist man in or bis dahin sind es 5 Minuten zu Fuß; **to ~ home** nach Hause laufen (inf), zu Fuß nach Hause gehen; **we were out ~ing when the telegram arrived** wir waren gerade spazieren or auf einem Spaziergang, als das Telegramm kam.

(c) (ghost) umgehen, spuken.

(d) (inf: disappear) Beine bekommen (inf).

♦**walk about** or **around 1** vi herumlaufen (inf). **to ~ ~ sth** um etw herumlaufen (inf) or -gehen; (in room etc) in etw (dat) herumlaufen (inf) or -gehen. **2** vt sep (lead) person, horse auf und ab führen; (ride at a walk) im Schritt gehen lassen.

♦**walk away** vi weg- or davongehen. **he ~ed ~ from the crash unhurt** er ist bei dem Unfall ohne Verletzungen davongekommen; **to ~ ~ with a prize** etc einen Preis etc kassieren or einstecken (inf).

♦**walk in** vi herein-/hineinkommen; (casually) herein-/hineinspazieren (inf). **"please ~ ~"** „bitte eintreten".

♦**walk into** vi +prep obj room herein-/hineinkommen in (+acc); person annehmen; wall laufen gegen. **to ~ ~ sb** (meet unexpectedly) jdm in die Arme laufen, jdn zufällig treffen; **to ~ ~ a trap** in eine Falle gehen; **to ~ ~ a job** eine Stelle ohne Schwierigkeiten bekommen; **he just ~ed ~ the first job he applied for** er hat gleich die erste Stelle bekommen, um die er sich beworben hat; **to ~ right ~ sth** (lit) mit voller Wucht gegen etw rennen; **I didn't know I was going to ~ ~ an argument** ich wußte nicht, daß ich hier mitten in einen Streit hineingeraten würde; **you ~ed right ~ that one, didn't you?** da bist du aber ganz schön reingefallen (inf).

♦**walk off 1** vt sep pounds ablaufen (inf). **I'm going out to try and ~ ~ this headache/hangover** ich gehe jetzt an die Luft, um meine Kopfschmerzen/meinen Kater loszuwerden; **we ~ed ~ our lunch with a stroll in the park** nach dem Mittagessen haben wir einen Verdauungsspaziergang im Park gemacht. **2** vi weggehen. **he ~ed ~ in the opposite direction** er ging in die andere Richtung davon.

♦**walk off with** vi +prep obj (inf) **(a)** (take) (unintentionally) abziehen mit (inf); (intentionally) abhauen mit (inf). **don't ~ ~ ~ the idea that ...** (fig) gehen Sie nicht weg in dem Glauben, daß ... **(b)** (win easily) prize kassieren, einstecken (inf).

♦**walk on** vi **(a)** +prep obj grass etc betreten. **(b)** (continue walking) weitergehen. **she hesitated, then ~ed ~ by** sie zögerte

und ging dann weiter. **(c)** (Theat) auftreten; (in walk-on part) auf die Bühne gehen. **to ~ ~(to) the stage** auf die Bühne treten, auf der Bühne erscheinen.

♦**walk out 1** vi **(a)** (quit) gehen. **to ~ ~ of a meeting/room** eine Versammlung/einen Saal verlassen; **to ~ ~ on sb** jdn verlassen; (let down) jdn im Stich lassen; (abandon) girlfriend etc sitzenlassen (inf); **to ~ ~ on sth** aus etw aussteigen (inf). **(b)** (strike) streiken, in Streik treten. **(c)** **to ~ ~ with sb** (dated) mit jdm gehen. **2** vt sep (dated: court) gehen mit.

♦**walk over** vi +prep obj **(a)** (defeat) in die Tasche stecken (inf). **(b)** **to ~ all ~ sb** (inf) (dominate) jdn unterbuttern (inf); (treat harshly) jdn fertigmachen (inf); **she lets her husband ~ all ~ her** sie läßt sich von ihrem Mann herumschikanieren (inf) or völlig unterbuttern (inf).

♦**walk through** vi +prep obj **(a)** (inf: do easily) exam etc spielend schaffen (inf). **(b)** (Theat) part durchgehen.

♦**walk up** vi **(a)** (go up, ascend) hinaufgehen. **the lift is broken so you'll have to ~ ~** der Aufzug ist außer Betrieb, Sie müssen zu Fuß hinaufgehen. **(b)** (approach) zugehen (to auf +acc). **a man ~ed ~ (to me/her)** ein Mann kam auf mich zu/ging auf sie zu; **~ ~!**, **~ ~!** treten Sie näher!

walkable ['wɔːkəbl] adj **to be ~** sich zu Fuß machen lassen.

walk: **~about** n Rundgang, Walk-about m; **the Queen went (on a) ~about** die Königin machte einen Walk-about; **~away** n (US) see **~over**.

walker ['wɔːkə'] n **(a)** (stroller) Spaziergänger(in f) m; (hiker) Wanderer(in f) m; (Sport) Geher(in f) m. **to be a fast/slow ~** schnell/langsam gehen. **(b)** (for baby, invalid) Laufstuhl m.

walker-on ['wɔːkər'on] n Statist(in f) m.

walkie-talkie ['wɔːkɪ'tɔːkɪ] n Hand-Funksprechgerät, Walkie-Talkie nt.

walk-in ['wɔːkɪn] **1** adj a **~cupboard** ein begehbarer Einbau- or Wandschrank. **2** n (US) (cupboard) see adj; (victory) spielender Sieg.

walking ['wɔːkɪŋ] **1** n Gehen nt; (as recreation) Spazierengehen nt; (hiking) Wandern nt. **there's some good ~ in these hills** in diesen Bergen gibt es ein paar gute Wandermöglichkeiten; **we did a lot of ~ on holiday** in den Ferien sind wir viel gewandert or gelaufen.

2 adj attr encyclopaedia, miracle etc wandelnd; doll Lauf-. **at a ~ pace** im Schrittempo; **the ~ wounded** die Leichtverwundeten pl; **it's within ~ distance** dahin kann man laufen or zu Fuß gehen.

walking: **~ bass** n einfache, meist aus 2 Tönen bestehende Kontrabaßbegleitung; **~ holiday** n Wanderferien pl; **~ shoes** npl Wanderschuhe pl; **~ stick** n Spazierstock m; **~ tour** n Wanderung f.

walk: **~-on 1** adj **(a)** part, role Statisten-; **(b)** (in transport) Walk-on-; **2** n Statistenrolle f; **~out** n (from conference) Auszug m, demonstratives Verlassen des Saales; (strike) Streik m; **~over** n **1** (Sport) Walk-over m; (easy victory) spielender Sieg; (fig) Kinderspiel nt; **the government had a ~over in the debate** die Regierung hatte leichtes Spiel in der Debatte; **2** adj attr **~over victory** spielender Sieg; **~-up** n (US inf) (Wohnung/Büro etc in einem) Haus nt ohne Fahrstuhl or Lift; **~way** n Fußweg m; **a pedestrian ~way** ein Fuß(gänger)weg m.

wall [wɔːl] **1** n **(a)** (outside) Mauer f; (inside, of mountain) Wand f. **the Great W~ of China** die Chinesische Mauer; **the north ~ of the Eiger** die Eigernordwand; **a ~ of fire** eine Feuerwand; **a ~ of policemen/troops** eine Mauer von Polizisten/Soldaten; **~s have ears** die Wände haben Ohren; **to come up against a ~ of prejudice/silence** auf eine Mauer von Vorurteilen/des Schweigens stoßen; **to go up the ~** (inf) die Wände rauf- or hochgehen (inf); **he/his questions drive me up the ~** (inf) er/seine Fragerei bringt mich auf die Palme (inf); **this constant noise is driving me up the ~** (inf) bei diesem ständigen Lärm könnte ich die Wände rauf- or hochgehen (inf); **to go to the ~** (firm etc) kaputtgehen (inf); see **brick ~**, **back ~**.

(b) (Anat) Wand f. **abdominal ~** Bauchdecke f.

2 vt mit einer Mauer umgeben.

♦**wall about** vt sep (old, liter) ummauern. **a life so ~ed ~ with prejudice** ein so von Vorurteilen eingeengtes Leben.

♦**wall in** vt sep mit einer Mauer or von Mauern umgeben. **~ed ~ on all sides by bodyguards** auf allen Seiten von Leibwächtern abgeriegelt or eingeschlossen.

♦**wall off** vt sep (cut off) durch eine Mauer (ab)trennen; (separate into different parts) unterteilen. **the monks ~ed themselves ~ from the outside world** die Mönche riegelten sich hinter ihren Mauern von der Welt ab.

♦**wall round** vt sep ummauern.

♦**wall up** vt sep zumauern.

wallaby ['wɒləbɪ] n Wallaby nt.

wallah ['wɒlə] n (dated sl) Knabe (inf), Hengst (inf) m.

wall: **~ bars** npl Sprossenwand f; **~board** n (US) Sperrholz nt; **~ cabinet/cupboard** n Wandschrank m; **~ chart** n Wandkarte f; **~ clock** n Wanduhr f.

walled [wɔːld] adj von Mauern umgeben.

wallet ['wɒlɪt] n Brieftasche f.

wall: **~flower** n (Bot) Goldlack m; (fig inf) Mauerblümchen nt (inf); **~ hanging** n Wandbehang, Wandteppich m; **~ map** n Wandkarte f.

Walloon [wɒ'luːn] **1** n **(a)** Wallone m, Wallonin f. **(b)** (dialect) Wallonisch nt. **2** adj wallonisch.

wallop ['wɒləp] **1** n **(a)** (inf: blow) Schlag m. **he fell flat on his face with a ~** mit einem Plumps fiel er auf die Nase (inf); **to give sb/sth a ~** jdm/einer Sache einen Schlag versetzen. **(b)** **at a fair old ~** (dated inf) mit Karacho (inf). **(c)** (Brit sl: beer) Bier nt.

2 vt (inf) (hit) schlagen; (punish) verdreschen (inf), versohlen (inf); (defeat) in die Pfanne hauen (sl). **to ~ sb one/**

over the head jdm eins reinhauen (*inf*)/eins überziehen.

walloping [ˈwɒləpɪŋ] (*inf*) **1** *n* Prügel *pl* (*inf*), Abreibung *f* (*inf*); (*defeat*) Schlappe *f*. **to give sb a ~** jdm eine Tracht Prügel geben (*inf*); (*defeat*) jdn fertigmachen (*inf*); **to take a ~** (*defeat*) eine Schlappe erleiden.
    2 *adj* (*also ~ great*) riesig; *price* gesalzen (*inf*), saftig (*inf*); *loss, defeat* gewaltig (*inf*); *lie* faustdick (*inf*).

wallow [ˈwɒləʊ] **1** *n* (*act*) Bad *nt*; (*place*) Suhle *f*. **2** *vi* (a) (*lit*) (*animal*) sich wälzen, sich suhlen; (*boat*) rollen. (b) **to ~ in** *luxury/wealth/sensuality/self-pity etc* im Luxus/Reichtum/in Sinnenlust/Selbstmitleid *etc* schwelgen; **to ~ in money** (*inf*) im Geld schwimmen (*inf*).
    ♦ **wallow about** *or* **around** *vi* sich herumwälzen.

wall: **~ painting** *n* Wandmalerei *f*; **~paper 1** *n* Tapete *f*; **2** *vt* tapezieren; **~ socket** *n* Steckdose *f*; **W~ Street** *n* Wall Street *f*; **~-to-~** *adj* **~-to-~ carpeting** Teppichboden, Spannteppich, Ausleg(e)teppich *m*.

walnut [ˈwɔːlnʌt] *n* (*nut*) Walnuß *f*; (~ *tree*) (Wal)nußbaum *m*; (*wood*) Nußbaum(holz *nt*) *m*.

walrus [ˈwɔːlrəs] *n* Walroß *nt*. **~ moustache** Walroßbart *m*.

waltz [wɔːls] **1** *n* Walzer *m*.
    2 *vi* (a) *Walzer* tanzen. **would you care to ~?** möchten Sie einen Walzer tanzen?; **they ~ed** expertly sie tanzten ausgezeichnet Walzer; **they ~ed across the ballroom** sie walzten durch den Ballsaal; **as the couples ~ed by smiling ...** wie *or* als die Paare lächelnd vorbeiwalzten ...
    (b) (*inf: move, come etc*) walzen (*inf*). **he came ~ing up** er kam angetanzt (*inf*).
    3 *vt Walzer* tanzen mit. **he ~ed her out onto the balcony** er walzte mit ihr auf den Balkon hinaus.
    ♦ **waltz about** *or* **around** *vi* (*inf*) herumtanzen *or* -tänzeln.
    ♦ **waltz in** *vi* (*inf*) hereintanzen (*inf*). **to come ~ing ~** angetanzt kommen (*inf*).
    ♦ **waltz off** *vi* (*inf*) abtanzen (*inf*).
    ♦ **waltz off with** *vi* +*prep obj* (*inf*) *prizes* abziehen mit.

waltz: **~ music** *n* Walzermusik *f*; **~ time** *n* Walzertakt *m*.

wan [wɒn] *adj* bleich, *light, smile, look* matt.

wand [wɒnd] *n* (*magic ~*) Zauberstab *m*; (*of office*) Amtsstab *m*.

wander [ˈwɒndəʳ] **1** *n* Spaziergang *m*; (*through town, park also*) Bummel *m*. **I'm going for a ~ round the shops** ich mache einen Ladenbummel.
    2 *vt hills, world* durchstreifen (*geh*). **to ~ the streets** durch die Straßen wandern *or* (*looking for sb/sth also*) irren.
    3 *vi* (a) herumlaufen; (*more aimlessly*) umherwandern (*through, about, in* +*dat*); (*leisurely*) schlendern; (*to see the shops*) bummeln. **he ~ed past me in a dream** er ging wie im Traum an mir vorbei; **he ~ed over to speak to me** er kam zu mir herüber, um mit mir zu reden; **his hands ~ed over the keys** seine Hände wanderten über die Tasten; **the coach just ~ed through the lanes for a few hours** der Bus zuckelte ein paar Stunden durch die Straßchen; **the river ~ed through the valley** der Fluß zog sich durch das Tal; **I enjoy just ~ing around** ich bummele gerne einfach nur herum; **his speech ~ed on and on** seine Rede wollte gar nicht aufhören *or* kein Ende nehmen; **if his hands start ~ing ...** (*hum*) wenn er seine Finger nicht bei sich (*dat*) behalten kann ...
    (b) (*go off, stray*) **to ~ from the path** vom Wege *or* Pfad abkommen; **the cattle must not be allowed to ~** das Vieh darf nicht einfach so herumlaufen; **he ~ed too near the edge of the cliff** er geriet zu nahe an den Rand des Abhangs; **I accidentally ~ed into Squire Thomas' property** ich bin aus Versehen in das Gelände von Squire Thomas geraten; **the children had ~ed out onto the street** die Kinder waren auf die Straße gelaufen; **the needle tends to ~ a bit** der Zeiger schwankt ein bißchen.
    (c) (*fig: thoughts, eye*) schweifen, wandern. **to let one's mind ~** seine Gedanken schweifen lassen; **during the lecture his mind ~ed a bit** während der Vorlesung wanderten seine Gedanken umher *or* schweiften seine Gedanken ab; **the old man's mind is beginning to ~ a bit** der alte Mann wird ein wenig wirr; **for years he ~ed in false beliefs** jahrelang war er im falschen Glauben befangen; **to ~ from the straight and narrow/the true religion** vom Pfad der Tugend/vom rechten Glauben abirren *or* abkommen; **to ~ from *or* off a point/subject** von einem Punkt/vom Thema abschweifen *or* abkommen.
    ♦ **wander about** *vi* umherziehen, umherwandern.
    ♦ **wander back** *vi* (*cows, strays*) zurückkommen *or* -wandern. **shall we start ~ing ~ to the car?** (*inf*) wollen wir langsam *or* allmählich zum Auto zurückgehen?; **after two years she ~ed ~ to her husband** nach zwei Jahren fand *or* ging sie zu ihrem Mann zurück.
    ♦ **wander in** *vi* ankommen (*inf*), anspazieren (*inf*). **he ~ed ~ to see me this morning** (*inf*) er ist heute morgen bei mir vorbeigekommen.
    ♦ **wander off** *vi* (a) weggehen, davonziehen (*geh*). **to ~ ~ course** vom Kurs abkommen; **if you ~ ~** you'll get lost wenn du einfach weggehst, wirst du dich verlaufen; **he ~ed ~ into one of his fantasies** er geriet wieder ins Phantasieren; **he must have ~ed ~ somewhere** er muß (doch) irgendwohin verschwunden sein.
    (b) (*inf: leave*) allmählich *or* langsam gehen.

wanderer [ˈwɒndərəʳ] *n* Wandervogel *m*. **the Masai are ~s** die Massai sind ein Wandervolk *nt*; **that child is a real ~** das Kind treibt sich überall herum.

wandering [ˈwɒndərɪŋ] *adj tribesman, refugees* umherziehend; *minstrel* fahrend; *thoughts* (ab)schweifend; *path* gewunden. **the old man's ~** mit die wirren Gedanken des Alten; **to have ~ hands** (*inf*) seine Finger nicht bei sich (*dat*) behalten können; **the W~ Jew** der Ewige Jude.

wanderings [ˈwɒndərɪŋz] *npl* Streifzüge, Fahrten *pl*; (*mental*) wirre Gedanken *pl*; (*verbal*) wirres Gerede. **it's time he stopped his ~ and settled down** es wird Zeit, daß er mit dem

---

Herumzigeunern aufhört und seßhaft wird.

wanderlust [ˈwɒndəlʌst] *n* Fernweh *nt*.

wane [weɪn] **1** *n* **to be on the ~** (*fig*) im Schwinden sein. **2** *vi* (*moon*) abnehmen; (*fig*) (*influence, strength, life, power*) schwinden; (*reputation*) verblassen; (*daylight*) nachlassen.

wangle [ˈwæŋgl] (*inf*) **1** *n* Schiebung (*inf*), Mauschelei (*inf*) *f*. **it's a ~** das ist Schiebung; **I think we can arrange some sort of ~** ich glaube, wir können es so hinbiegen (*inf*) *or* hindrehen (*inf*).
    2 *vt job, ticket etc* organisieren (*inf*), verschaffen. **to ~ oneself/sb in** sich hineinlavieren *or* -mogeln (*inf*)/jdn reinschleusen (*inf*); **he'll ~ it for you** er wird das schon für dich drehen (*inf*) *or* deichseln (*inf*); **to ~ money/the truth etc out of sb** jdm Geld abluchsen (*inf*)/die Wahrheit *etc* aus jdm rauskriegen (*inf*); **we ~d an extra week's holiday** wir haben noch eine zusätzliche Woche Urlaub rausgeschlagen (*inf*).

wangler [ˈwæŋgləʳ] *n* (*inf*) Schlawiner *m* (*inf*).

wangling [ˈwæŋglɪŋ] *n* (*inf*) Schiebung *f* (*inf*). **there's a lot of ~ goes on** da gibt's ziemlich viel Schiebung *or* Mauschelei (*inf*).

wank [wæŋk] (*sl*) **1** *vi* (*also ~ off*) wichsen (*sl*). **2** *vt* **to ~ sb (off)** jdm einen abwichsen (*sl*) *or* runterholen (*sl*). **3** *n* **to have a ~** sich (*dat*) einen runterholen (*sl*).

wanly [ˈwɒnlɪ] *adv* matt.

wanness [ˈwɒnnɪs] *n* (*paleness*) Blässe *f*; (*of light*) Mattheit *f*.

want [wɒnt] **1** *n* (a) (*lack*) Mangel *m* (*of an* +*dat*). **~ of judgement** mangelndes Urteilsvermögen, Mangel an Urteilsvermögen; **for ~ of** aus Mangel an (+*dat*); **for ~ of anything better** mangels Besserem, in Ermangelung von etwas Besserem *or* eines Besseren; **I kept quiet for ~ of anything better to say** ich schwieg, da *or* weil ich nichts Besseres zu sagen hatte; **for ~ of something to do I joined a sports club** weil ich nichts zu tun hatte, bin ich einem Sportverein beigetreten; **though it wasn't for ~ of trying nicht**, daß er sich nicht bemüht hätte; **to feel the ~ of sth** etw vermissen.
    (b) (*poverty*) Not *f*. **to be/live in ~** Not leiden.
    (c) (*need*) Bedürfnis *nt*; (*wish*) Wunsch *m*. **my ~s are few** meine Ansprüche *or* Bedürfnisse sind gering, meine Ansprüche sind bescheiden; **the farm supplied all their ~s** der Bauernhof versorgte sie mit allem Nötigen *or* Notwendigen; **this factory supplies all our ~s** diese Fabrik liefert unseren gesamten Bedarf; **to be in ~ of sth** einer Sache (*gen*) bedürfen (*geh*), etw brauchen *or* benötigen; **to be in ~ of help/repair** Hilfe brauchen/reparaturbedürftig sein; **to attend to sb's ~s** sich um jdn kümmern; **it fills a long-felt ~** es wird einem lange empfundenen Bedürfnis gerecht; **his marriage fills a long-felt ~ in his life** er heiratete und schloß damit eine seit langem empfundene Lücke.
    2 *vt* (a) (*wish, desire*) wollen; (*more polite*) mögen. **to ~ to do sth** etw tun wollen; **I ~ you to come here** ich will *or* möchte, daß du herkommst; **I ~ it done now** ich will *or* möchte das sofort erledigt haben; **I was ~ing to leave the job next month** ich hätte gerne nächsten Monat mit der Arbeit aufgehört; **what does he ~ with me?** was will er von mir?; **darling, I ~ you** Liebling, ich will dich; **I ~ my mummy** ich will meine Mami, ich will zu meiner Mami; **you don't ~ much** (*iro*) sonst willst du nichts?; (*iro*) **I don't ~ strangers coming in** ich wünsche *or* möchte nicht, daß Fremde (hier) hereinkommen.
    (b) (*need, require*) brauchen. **you ~ to see a doctor/solicitor** Sie sollten zum Arzt/Rechtsanwalt gehen; **you ~ to be careful** (*inf*) du mußt aufpassen; **you ~ to stop doing that** (*inf*) du mußt damit aufhören; **he ~s to be more careful** (*inf*) er sollte etwas vorsichtiger sein; **that's the last thing I ~** (*inf*) alles, bloß das nicht (*inf*); **that's all we ~ed!** (*iro inf*) das hat uns gerade noch gefehlt!; **it only ~ed the police to turn up** ... das hätte gerade noch gefehlt, daß auch noch die Polizei anrückt ...; **does my hair ~ cutting?** muß mein Haar geschnitten werden?; **"~ed"** „gesucht"; **he's a ~ed man** er wird (polizeilich) gesucht; **to feel ~ed** das Gefühl haben, gebraucht zu werden; **you're ~ed on the phone** Sie werden am Telefon verlangt *or* gewünscht.
    (c) (*lack*) **he ~s talent/confidence etc** es mangelt (*geh*) *or* fehlt ihm an Talent/Selbstvertrauen *etc*; **all the soup ~s is a little salt** das einzige, was an der Suppe fehlt, ist etwas Salz.
    3 *vi* (a) (*wish, desire*) wollen; (*more polite*) mögen. **you can go if you ~ (to)** wenn du willst *or* möchtest, kannst du gehen; **I don't ~ to** ich will *or* möchte nicht; **do as you ~** tu, was du willst; **he said he'd do it, but does he really ~ to?** er sagte, er würde es machen, aber will er es wirklich?
    (b) **he does not ~ for friends** es fehlt *or* mangelt (*geh*) ihm nicht an Freunden; **they ~ for nothing** es fehlt *or* mangelt (*geh*) ihnen an nichts; **he doesn't ~ for a pound or two** er ist nicht gerade arm (*inf*), ihm fehlt es nicht an Kleingeld (*inf*).
    (c) (*liter: live in poverty*) darben (*liter*).
    ♦ **want in** *vi* (*inf*) reinwollen.
    ♦ **want out** *vi* (*inf*) rauswollen.

want ad *n* Kaufgesuch *nt*.

wanting [ˈwɒntɪŋ] *adj* (a) (*lacking, missing*) fehlend. **humour is ~ in the novel** diesem Roman fehlt es an Humor; **there are some parts ~** einige Teile fehlen; **it's a good novel, but there is something ~** der Roman ist gut, aber irgend etwas fehlt.
    (b) (*deficient, inadequate*) **he is ~ in confidence/enterprise etc** es fehlt *or* mangelt (*geh*) ihm an Selbstvertrauen/Unternehmungslust *etc*; **his courage/the new engine was found ~** sein Mut war nicht groß genug/der neue Motor hat sich als unzulänglich erwiesen; **he was (weighed in the balance and) found ~** (*liter*) er wurde (gewogen und) (für) zu leicht befunden; **he was not found ~** (*liter*) er hat sich bewährt.
    (c) (*inf: mentally deficient*) **he's a bit ~ (up top)** er ist ein bißchen unterbelichtet (*inf*).

wanton [ˈwɒntən] **1** *adj* (a) (*licentious*) *life* liederlich; *behaviour, woman also, pleasures* schamlos; *looks, thoughts* lüstern. **Cupid, that ~ boy** Amor, dieser kleine Lüstling.
    (b) (*wilful*) *cruelty* mutwillig; *disregard, negligence* sträf-

lich, völlig unverantwortlich; *waste* sträflich, kriminell (*inf*). **to spend money with** ~ **extravagance** Geld mit sträflichem Leichtsinn ausgeben; **decorated with** ~ **extravagance** üppig und verschwenderisch eingerichtet.
  (c) (*poet: capricious*) *persons* übermütig, mutwillig (*poet*).
  2 *n* (*old: immoral woman*) Dirne *f*.

wantonly [ˈwɒntənlɪ] *adv* **(a)** (*immorally*) liederlich, schamlos; *look* lüstern. **(b)** (*wilfully*) mutwillig; *neglect also, waste* sträflich. **she was** ~ **extravagant with her husband's money** sie gab das Geld ihres Mannes mit sträflichem Leichtsinn aus.

wantonness [ˈwɒntənnɪs] *n see adj* **(a)** Liederlichkeit *f*; Schamlosigkeit *f*; Lüsternheit *f*. **(b)** Mutwilligkeit *f*; Sträflichkeit *f*.

war [wɔː^r] **1** *n* Krieg *m*. **the art of** ~ die Kriegskunst; **this is** ~! (*fig*) das bedeutet Krieg!; **the** ~ **against poverty/disease** der Kampf gegen die Armut/Krankheit; ~ **of nerves** Nervenkrieg; ~ **of words** Wortkrieg; **to be at** ~ sich im Krieg(szustand) befinden; **to declare** ~ den Krieg erklären (*on dat*); (*fig also*) den Kampf ansagen (*on dat*); **to go to** ~ (*start*) (einen) Krieg anfangen (*against* mit); (*declare*) den Krieg erklären (*against dat*); (*person*) in den Krieg ziehen; **to make** *or* **wage** ~ Krieg führen (*on, against* gegen); **he/this car has been in the** ~**s a bit** er/dieses Auto sieht ziemlich ramponiert (*inf*) *or* mitgenommen aus; **I hear you've been in the** ~**s recently** (*inf*) ich höre, daß du zur Zeit ganz schön angeschlagen bist (*inf*).
  2 *vi* sich bekriegen; (*fig*) ringen (*geh*) (*for* um).

war baby *n* Kriegskind *nt*.

warble [ˈwɔːbl] **1** *n* Trällern *nt*. **2** *vti* trällern. **he** ~**d away as he lay in the bath** (*inf*) er trällerte fröhlich vor sich hin, während er in der Badewanne saß.

warbler [ˈwɔːblə^r] *n* (*Orn*) Grasmücke *f*; (*wood* ~) Waldsänger *m*.

war: ~ **bond** *n* Kriegsanleihe *f*; ~ **bride** *n* Kriegsbraut *f*; ~ **clouds** *npl* **the** ~ **clouds are gathering** Kriegsgefahr droht; ~ **correspondent** *n* Kriegsberichterstatter, Kriegskorrespondent *m*; ~ **crime** *n* Kriegsverbrechen *nt*; ~ **criminal** *n* Kriegsverbrecher *m*; ~ **cry** *n* Kriegsruf *m*; (*fig*) Schlachtruf *m*; **the** ~ **cries of the Red Indians** das Kriegsgeheul *or* Kriegsgeschrei der Indianer.

ward [wɔːd] *n* **(a)** (*part of hospital*) Station *f*; (*room*) (*small*) (Kranken)zimmer *nt*; (*large*) (Kranken)saal *m*.
  (b) (*Jur: person*) Mündel *nt*. ~ **of court** Mündel *nt* unter Amtsvormundschaft; **to make sb a** ~ **of court** jdn unter Amtsvormundschaft stellen.
  (c) (*Jur: state*) (**to be**) **in** ~ unter Vormundschaft (stehen).
  (d) (*Admin*) Stadtbezirk *m*; (*election* ~) Wahlbezirk *m*.
  (e) (*of key*) Einschnitt *m* (im Schlüsselbart); (*of lock*) Aussparung *f*, Angriff *m*.

♦ **ward off** *vt sep attack, blow, person* abwehren; *danger also* abwenden; *depression* nicht aufkommen lassen.

war dance *n* Kriegstanz *m*.

warden [ˈwɔːdn] *n* (*of youth hostel*) Herbergsvater *m*, Herbergsmutter *f*; (*game* ~) Jagdaufseher *m*; (*traffic* ~) ≈ Verkehrspolizist *m*, ≈ Politesse *f*; (*air-raid* ~) Luftschutzwart *m*; (*fire* ~) Feuerwart *m*; (*of castle, museum etc*) Aufseher *m*; (*head* ~) Kustos *m*; (*of port*) (Hafen)aufseher *m*; (*of mint*) Münzwardein *m*; (*Univ*) Heimleiter(in *f*) *m*; (*of Oxbridge college*) Rektor *m*; (*US: of prison*) Gefängnisdirektor *m*.

War Department *n* (*old US*) Kriegsministerium *nt* (*old*).

warder [ˈwɔːdə^r] *n* (*Brit*) Wärter, Aufseher *m*.

ward heeler *n* (*US Pol sl*) Handlanger *m* (*inf*).

wardress [ˈwɔːdrɪs] *n* (*Brit*) Wärterin, Aufseherin *f*.

wardrobe [ˈwɔːdrəʊb] *n* **(a)** (*cupboard*) (Kleider)schrank *m*.
  (b) (*clothes*) Garderobe *f*. (*Theat*) (*clothes*) Kostüme *pl*; (*room*) Kleiderkammer *f*, Kostümfundus *m*.

wardrobe: ~ **mistress** *n* (*Theat*) Gewandmeisterin *f*; ~ **trunk** *n* Kleiderkoffer *m*.

wardroom [ˈwɔːdruːm] *n* (*Naut*) Offiziersmesse *f*.

-ward(s) [-wəd(z)] *adv suf* -wärts. **town-/pub-** ~ in Richtung Stadt/Wirtshaus; **in a home-** ~ **direction** Richtung Heimat (*inf*).

wardship [ˈwɔːdʃɪp] *n* (*Jur*) Vormundschaft *f*.

ware [wɛə^r] *n* Delft/Derby ~ Delfter/Derby Porzellan *nt*.

-ware *n suf* -waren *pl*. **kitchen-** ~ Küchenutensilien *pl*.

war effort *n* Kriegsanstrengungen *pl*.

warehouse [ˈwɛəhaʊs] **1** *n* Lager(haus) *nt*. **2** *vt* einlagern.

warehouseman [ˈwɛəhaʊsmən] *n, pl* **-men** [-mən] Lagerarbeiter *m*.

wares [wɛəz] *npl* Waren *pl*. **to cry one's** ~ (*dated*) seine Waren anpreisen.

warfare [ˈwɔːfɛə^r] *n* Krieg *m*; (*techniques*) Kriegskunst *f*.

war: ~ **fever** *n* Kriegsbegeisterung *f*; ~ **game** *n* Kriegsspiel *nt*; ~ **grave** *n* Kriegsgrab *nt*; ~ **head** *n* Sprengkopf *m*; ~ **horse** *n* (*lit, fig*) Schlachtroß *nt*.

warily [ˈwɛərɪlɪ] *adv* vorsichtig; (*suspiciously*) mißtrauisch, argwöhnisch. **to tread** ~ (*lit, fig*) sich vorsehen.

wariness [ˈwɛərɪnɪs] *n* Vorsicht *f*; (*mistrust*) Mißtrauen *nt*, Argwohn *m*. **he has a reputation for** ~ er gilt als ein vorsichtiger Mann; **the** ~ **of his reply** die Zurückhaltung, mit der er antwortete; **she had a great** ~ **of strangers** sie hegte starkes Mißtrauen *or* großen Argwohn gegen Fremde; **there was** ~ **in his eyes/voice** in seinem Blick/seiner Stimme lag Mißtrauen.

warlike [ˈwɔːlaɪk] *adj* kriegerisch; *tone, speech* militant.

warlord [ˈwɔːlɔːd] *n* Kriegsherr *m*.

warm [wɔːm] **1** *adj* (+ *er*) **(a)** warm. **I am** *or* **feel** ~ mir ist warm; **come to the fire and get** ~ komm ans Feuer und wärm dich; **it's** ~ **work moving furniture about** beim Möbelumstellen wird einem ganz schön warm *or* kommt man ins Schwitzen; **to make things** ~ **for sb** es jdm ungemütlich machen (*inf*).
  (b) (*in games*) **am I** ~? ist es (hier) warm?; **you're getting** ~ es wird schon wärmer; **you're very** ~! heiß!
  (c) (*hearty, warm-hearted*) *person, welcome* herzlich, warm.

(d) (*heated*) *dispute, words* hitzig, heftig.
  2 *n* **we were glad to get into the** ~ wir waren froh, daß wir ins Warme kamen; **come and have a** ~ **at the fire** komm und wärm dich ein bißchen am Feuer; **to give sth a** ~ etw wärmen.
  3 *vt* wärmen. **it** ~**s my heart to ...** mir wird (es) ganz warm ums Herz, wenn ...; **his kind gesture** ~**ed my heart** bei seiner freundlichen Geste wurde mir ganz warm ums Herz.
  4 *vi* **the milk was** ~**ing on the stove** die Milch wurde auf dem Herd angewärmt; **my heart** ~**ed mir wurde** warm; **I/my heart** ~**ed to him** ich wurde mir sympathischer/ich habe mich für ihn erwärmt; **his voice** ~**ed as he spoke of his family** seine Stimme bekam einen warmen Ton, als er von seiner Familie sprach; **he spoke rather hesitantly at first but soon** ~**ed to his subject** anfangs sprach er noch sehr zögernd, doch dann fand er sich in sein Thema hinein; **to** ~ **to one's work** sich mit seiner Arbeit anfreunden, Gefallen an seiner Arbeit finden.

♦ **warm over** *vt sep* (*esp US*) aufwärmen.

♦ **warm up 1** *vi* (*lit, fig*) warm werden; (*party, game, speaker*) in Schwung kommen; (*Sport*) sich aufwärmen. **things are** ~**ing** ~ es kommt Schwung in die Sache; (*becoming dangerous*) es wird allmählich brenzlig *or* ungemütlich (*inf*).
  2 *vt sep engine* warm werden lassen, warmlaufen lassen; *food etc* aufwärmen; (*fig*) *party* in Schwung bringen; *audience* in Stimmung bringen.

warm-blooded [ˈwɔːmˈblʌdɪd] *adj* warmblütig; (*fig*) heißblütig. ~ **animal** Warmblüter *m*.

warmer [ˈwɔːmə^r] *n* foot-/bottle ~ Fuß-/Flaschenwärmer *m*.

warm front *n* (*Met*) Warm(luft)front *f*.

warm-hearted [ˈwɔːmˈhɑːtɪd] *adj person* warmherzig; *action, gesture* großzügig.

warm-heartedness [ˈwɔːmˈhɑːtɪdnɪs] *n* Warmherzigkeit, Herzlichkeit *f*; (*of action, gesture*) Großherzigkeit *f*.

warming pan [ˈwɔːmɪŋˌpæn] *n* Wärmepfanne *f*.

warmish [ˈwɔːmɪʃ] *adj* ein bißchen warm. ~ **weather** ziemlich warmes Wetter.

warmly [ˈwɔːmlɪ] *adv* warm; *welcome* herzlich; *recommend* wärmstens. **we** ~ **welcome it** wir begrüßen es sehr.

warmness [ˈwɔːmnɪs] *n see* **warmth**.

war: ~**monger** [ˈwɔːˌmʌŋgə^r] *n* Kriegshetzer *m*; ~**mongering** [ˈwɔːˌmʌŋgərɪŋ] **1** *adj* kriegshetzerisch; **2** *n* Kriegshetze *f*.

warmth [wɔːmθ] *n* **(a)** (*lit*) Wärme *f*. **there isn't much** ~ **in the winter sun** die Wintersonne hat nicht viel Wärme *or* Kraft. **(b)** (*fig*) (*friendliness of voice, welcome etc*) Wärme, Herzlichkeit *f*; (*heatedness*) Heftigkeit, Hitzigkeit *f*.

warm-up [ˈwɔːmʌp] *n* (*Sport*) Aufwärmen *nt*; (*Mus*) Einspielen *nt*. **the teams had a** ~ **before the game** die Mannschaften wärmten sich auf vor dem Spiel; **the audience was entertained with a** ~ **before the TV transmission began** das Publikum wurde vor der Fernsehübertragung in Stimmung gebracht.

warn [wɔːn] **1** *vt* **(a)** warnen (*of, about, against vor* +*dat*); (*police, judge etc*) verwarnen. **to** ~ **sb not to do sth** jdn davor warnen, etw zu tun; **be** ~**ed sei gewarnt!; I'm** ~**ing you** ich warne dich!; **you have been** ~**ed!** sag nicht, ich hätte dich nicht gewarnt *or* es hätte dich niemand gewarnt!; **she just won't be** ~**ed** sie hört auf keine Warnung(en).
  (b) (*inform*) **to** ~ **sb that ...** jdn darauf aufmerksam machen *or* darauf hinweisen, daß ...; **her expression** ~**ed me that she was not enjoying the conversation** ich merkte schon an ihrem Gesichtsausdruck, daß ihr die Unterhaltung nicht gefiel; **you might have** ~**ed us that you were coming** du hättest uns ruhig vorher wissen lassen können *or* Bescheid sagen können, daß du kommst; **I forgot to** ~ **them that we would be late** ich habe vergessen, ihnen Bescheid zu sagen, daß wir später kommen; **to** ~ **sb of an intended visit** jdm seinen Besuch ankündigen.
  2 *vi* warnen (*of vor* +*dat*).

♦ **warn off** *vt sep* warnen. **to** ~ **sb** ~ **doing sth** jdn (davor) warnen, etw zu tun; **he** ~**ed me** ~ **er hat mich davor gewarnt; I** ~**ed him** ~ **my property** ich habe ihn von meinem Grundstück verwiesen; **to** ~ **sb** ~ **a subject** jdn von einem Thema abraten; **he sat there shaking his head obviously trying to** ~ **me** ~ er saß da und schüttelte den Kopf, offensichtlich, um mich davon abzubringen; **he** ~**s everybody** ~ **who tries to get friendly with his girlfriend** er läßt nicht zu, daß sich jemand um seine Freundin bemüht.

warning [ˈwɔːnɪŋ] **1** *n* Warnung *f*; (*from police, judge etc*) Verwarnung *f*. **without** ~ unerwartet, ohne Vorwarnung; **they had no** ~ **of the enemy attack** der Feind griff sie ohne Vorwarnung an; **he had plenty of** ~ er ist oft *or* häufig genug gewarnt worden; (*early enough*) er wußte früh genug Bescheid; **to give sb a** ~ jdn warnen; (*police, judge etc*) jdm eine Verwarnung geben; **let this be a** ~ **to you/to all those who ...** lassen Sie sich (*dat*) das eine Warnung sein!, das soll Ihnen eine Warnung sein/allen denjenigen, die ..., soll das eine Warnung sein; **to take** ~ **from sth** sich (*dat*) etw eine Warnung sein lassen; **the bell gives** ~ *or* **is a** ~ **that ...** die Klingel zeigt an, daß ...; **they gave us no** ~ **of their arrival** sie kamen unangekündigt *or* ohne Vorankündigung; **please give me a few days'** ~ bitte sagen *or* geben Sie mir ein paar Tage vorher Bescheid; **to give sb due** ~ (*inform*) jdm rechtzeitig Bescheid sagen.
  2 *adj* Warn-; *look, tone* warnend. **a** ~ **sign** ein erstes Anzeichen; ein Warnzeichen *nt*/-schild *nt*.

warningly [ˈwɔːnɪŋlɪ] *adv* warnend.

War Office *n* (*old Brit*) Kriegsministerium *nt* (*old*).

warp [wɔːp] **1** *n* **(a)** (*in weaving*) Kette *f*.
  (b) (*in wood etc*) Welle *f*. **the** ~ **makes it impossible to use this wood** das Holz ist so verzogen *or* wellig, als daß man es noch verwenden könnte; **the damp has caused a severe** ~ durch die Feuchtigkeit hat sich das Holz *etc* stark verzogen.
  (c) (*towing cable*) Schleppleine *f*.
  (d) (*of mind*) hatred of his mother had given his mind an evil ~ der Haß, den er gegen seine Mutter hegte, hatte seinen

ganzen Charakter entstellt *or* verbogen; **the ~ in his personality** das Abartige in seinem Wesen.

2 *vt wood* wellig werden lassen, wellen; *character* verbiegen, entstellen; *judgement* verzerren; *(Aviat)* verwinden.

3 *vi (wood)* sich wellen, sich verziehen, sich werfen.

war: ~**paint** *n* (lit, fig inf) Kriegsbemalung *f*; ~**path** *n* Kriegspfad *m*; **on the ~path** auf dem Kriegspfad.

warped [wɔːpt] *adj* (a) *(lit)* verzogen, wellig. **(b)** *(fig) sense of humour* abartig; *character also* verbogen; *judgement* verzerrt.

warping ['wɔːpɪŋ] *n* Krümmung *f*.

war plane *n (US)* Kampfflugzeug *nt*.

warrant ['wɒrənt] **1** *n* **(a)** *(Comm)* Garantie *f*; *(Mil)* Patent *nt*; *(search* ~*)* Durchsuchungsbefehl *m*; *(death* ~*)* Hinrichtungsbefehl *m*. **a ~ of arrest** ein Haftbefehl *m*; **there is a ~ out for his arrest** gegen ihn ist Haftbefehl erlassen worden *(Jur)*, er wird steckbrieflich gesucht.
  (b) *(rare) (justification)* Berechtigung *f*; *(authority)* Befugnis, Ermächtigung *f*.
  2 *vt* **(a)** *(justify) action etc* rechtfertigen. **to ~ sb to do sth** jdn dazu berechtigen, etw zu tun.
  (b) *(merit)* verdienen.
  (c) *(dated inf: assure)* wetten. **I('ll) ~ (you)** ich wette.
  (d) *(guarantee)* gewährleisten. **these goods are ~ed for three months by the manufacturers** für diese Waren übernimmt der Hersteller eine Garantie von drei Monaten; **a pill ~ed to cure influenza** eine Pille, die garantiert Grippe heilt.

warrantee [,wɒrən'tiː] *n* Garantieinhaber *m*.

warrant officer *n Rang m zwischen Offizier und Unteroffizier.*

warrantor ['wɒrəntɔː] *n* Garantiegeber *m*.

warranty ['wɒrəntɪ] *n (Comm)* Garantie *f*. **it's still under ~** darauf ist noch Garantie.

warren ['wɒrən] *n (rabbit* ~*)* Kaninchenbau *m*; *(fig)* Labyrinth *nt*.

warring ['wɔːrɪŋ] *adj nations* kriegführend; *interests, ideologies* gegensätzlich; *factions* sich bekriegend.

warrior ['wɒrɪə] *n* Krieger *m*.

Warsaw ['wɔːsɔː] *n* Warschau *nt*. **~ Pact** Warschauer Vertrag *or* Pakt *(esp BRD)* *m*.

warship ['wɔːʃɪp] *n* Kriegsschiff *nt*.

wart [wɔːt] *n* Warze *f*. **~s and all** *(hum inf)* mit allen seinen/ihren *etc* Fehlern.

wart-hog ['wɔːthɒg] *n* Warzenschwein *nt*.

wartime ['wɔːtaɪm] **1** *n* Kriegszeit *f*. **in ~** in Kriegszeiten. **2** *adj* Kriegs-. **in ~ England** in England im Krieg *or* während des Krieges; **~ regulations/rationing** *etc* Vorschriften *pl*/Rationierungen *pl etc* in Kriegszeiten, Kriegsvorschriften *pl*/Kriegsrationierungen *pl*.

wartorn ['wɔːtɔːn] *adj* vom Krieg erschüttert.

war: ~**-weary** *adj* kriegsmüde; ~ **widow** *n* Kriegswitwe *f*.

wary ['wεərɪ] *adj (+er)* vorsichtig; *(looking and planning ahead)* umsichtig, klug, wachsam; *look* mißtrauisch, argwöhnisch. **to be ~ of sb/sth** sich vor jdm/einer Sache in acht nehmen, vor jdm/einer Sache auf der Hut sein; **to be ~ about doing sth** seine Zweifel *or* Bedenken haben, ob man etw tun soll; **he was ~ about picking up the fireworks** nur mit größter Vorsicht hob er die Feuerwerkskörper auf; **be ~ of talking to strangers** hüte dich davor, mit Fremden zu sprechen; **to keep a ~ eye on sb** ein wachsames Auge auf jdn haben.

war zone *n* Kriegsgebiet *nt*.

was [wɒz] *pret of* **be**.

wash [wɒʃ] **1** *n* **(a)** *(act of ~ing)* **sb/sth needs a ~** jd/etw muß gewaschen werden; **to give sb/sth a (good) ~** jdn/etw (gründlich) waschen; **to have a ~** sich waschen; **call that a ~!** das nennst du dich waschen!, das soll gewaschen sein! *(inf)*.
  (b) *(laundry)* Wäsche *f*. **to be at/in the ~** in der Wäsche sein; **it will all come out in the ~** *(lit)* in der ~ *(fig inf)* es wird schon alles rauskommen, es wird sich schon noch alles zeigen *(inf)*.
  (c) *(of ship)* Kielwasser *nt*; *(Aviat)* Luftstrudel *m*.
  (d) *(lapping) (gentle sound)* Geplätscher *nt*; *(of ocean)* sanftes Klatschen der Wellen. **the rocks were worn away by the ~ of the sea** die Felsen waren vom Meer ausgewaschen.
  (e) *(mouth~)* Mundwasser *nt*; *(liquid remains, also pej)* Spülwasser *nt*. **a coat of blue ~** ein Anstrich *m* von blauer Tünche.
  (f) *(in painting)* a drawing in ink and ~ eine kolorierte Federzeichnung; **a ~ of brown ink** eine leichte *or* schwache Tönung mit brauner Tünche.
  2 *vt* **(a)** waschen; *dishes* spülen, abwaschen; *floor* aufwaschen, aufwischen; *(parts of) sth* *(dat)* waschen. **to ~ one's hands** *(euph)* sich *(dat)* die Hände waschen *(euph)*; **to ~ one's hands of sb/sth** mit jdm/etw nichts mehr zu tun haben wollen; **I ~ my hands of it** ich wasche meine Hände in Unschuld; **to ~ sth clean** etw reinwaschen; **the sea ~ed it clean of oil** das Öl wurde vom Meer weggewaschen; **to ~ one's dirty linen in public** *(fig)* seine schmutzige Wäsche in *or* vor aller Öffentlichkeit waschen.
  (b) *(sea etc)* umspülen; *wall, cliffs etc* schlagen gegen.
  (c) *(river, sea: carry)* spülen. **the body was ~ed downstream** die Leiche wurde flußabwärts getrieben; **to ~ ashore** an Land spülen *or* schwemmen, anschwemmen.
  (d) **the water had ~ed a channel in the rocks** das Wasser hatte eine Rinne in die Felsen gefressen.
  (e) *(paint) walls* tünchen; *paper* kolorieren.
  3 *vi* **(a)** *(have a ~)* sich waschen.
  (b) *(do the laundry etc)* waschen; *(Brit:* ~ **up)** abwaschen.
  (c) **a material that ~es well/won't ~** ein Stoff, der sich gut wäscht/den man nicht waschen kann *or* der sich nicht waschen läßt; **that excuse won't ~** *(Brit fig inf)* diese Entschuldigung nimmt *or* kauft dir keiner ab! *(inf)*.
  (d) *(sea etc)* schlagen. **the sea ~ed over the promenade** das Meer überspülte die Strandpromenade.

♦**wash away** *vt sep* **(a)** (hin)wegspülen. **(b)** *(fig)* **to ~ ~ sb's sins** jdn von seinen Sünden reinwaschen.

♦**wash down** *vt sep* **(a)** *(clean) car, walls, deck* abwaschen. **(b)** *meal, food* hinunterspülen, runterspülen *(inf)*.

♦**wash off** **1** *vi (stain, dirt)* sich rauswaschen lassen. **most of the pattern has ~ed** ~ das Muster ist fast ganz verwaschen. **2** *vt sep* abwaschen. **~ that grease ~ your hands** wasch dir die Schmiere von den Händen (ab)!

♦**wash out** **1** *vi* sich (r)auswaschen lassen. **2** *vt sep* **(a)** *(clean)* auswaschen; *mouth* ausspülen. **(b)** *(stop, cancel) game etc* ins Wasser fallen lassen *(inf)*. **the game was ~ed** ~ das Spiel fiel buchstäblich ins Wasser *(inf)*.

♦**wash over** *vi* + *prep obj* all that criticism just seemed to ~ ~ **him** die ganze Kritik schien an ihm abzuprallen; **he lets everything just ~ ~ him** er läßt alles einfach ruhig über sich ergehen.

♦**wash up** **1** *vi* **(a)** *(Brit: clean dishes)* abwaschen, (ab)spülen. **(b)** *(US: have a wash)* sich waschen. **2** *vt sep* **(a)** *(Brit)* dishes abwaschen, (ab)spülen. **(b)** *(sea etc)* anschwemmen, anspülen. **(c)** *(inf: finished)* that's/we're all ~ed ~ *(fig inf)* das *or* der Film ist gelaufen *(inf)*.

washable ['wɒʃəbl] *adj* waschbar; *wallpaper* abwaschbar.

wash: ~**-and-wear** *adj clothing, fabric* bügelfrei; ~ **basin** *n* Waschbecken *nt*; ~ **board** *n* Waschbrett *nt*; ~ **bowl** *n* Waschschüssel *f*; *(in unit)* Waschbecken *nt*; ~ **cloth** *n (US)* Waschlappen *m*; ~**day** *n* Waschtag *m*.

washed-out ['wɒʃt'aʊt] *adj (inf)* erledigt *(inf)*, schlapp *(inf)*. **to feel ~** sich ausgelaugt fühlen *(inf)*; **to look ~** mitgenommen aussehen.

washer ['wɒʃə] *n* (a) *(Tech)* Dichtung(sring *m*) *f*. **(b)** *(clothes* ~*)* Waschmaschine *f*; *(dish~)* (Geschirr)spülmaschine *f*.

washerwoman ['wɒʃə,wʊmən] *n*, *pl* -**women** [-,wɪmɪn] Waschfrau, Wäscherin *f*. **to gossip like a ~** klatschen wie eine Waschweib.

wash: ~**-hand basin** *n* Handwaschbecken *nt*; ~ **house** *n* Waschhaus *nt*.

washing ['wɒʃɪŋ] *n* Waschen *nt*; *(clothes)* Wäsche *f*. **many small boys dislike ~** viele kleine Jungen waschen sich nicht gerne; **to do the ~** Wäsche waschen; **to take in ~** (für Kunden) waschen; **if we don't get a rise soon, I'll have to take in ~!** *(hum)* wenn wir nicht bald eine Gehaltserhöhung bekommen, muß ich noch putzen gehen *(inf)*.

washing: ~ **day** *n see* **washday**; ~ **machine** *n* Waschmaschine *f*; ~ **powder** *n* Waschpulver *nt*; ~ **soda** *n* Bleichsoda *nt*; ~**-up** *n (Brit)* Abwasch *m*; **to do the ~-up** spülen, den Abwasch machen; ~**-up basin** *or* **bowl** *n* Spülschüssel *f*; ~**-up cloth** *n* Spültuch *nt*, Spüllappen *m*; ~**-up liquid** *n* Spülmittel *nt*.

wash: ~ **leather** *n* Waschleder *nt*; ~**out** *n (inf)* Reinfall *m (inf)*; *(person)* Flasche *(inf)*, Niete *(inf)* *f*; ~ **rag** *n (US) see* ~ **cloth**; ~**room** *n* Waschraum *m*; ~ **stand** *n (a)* Waschbecken *nt*; **(b)** *(old)* Waschgestell *nt*; ~ **tub** *n* (Wasch)zuber *m*.

washy ['wɒʃɪ] *adj* wässerig; *see* **wishy-washy**.

wasn't ['wɒznt] *contr of* **was not**.

wasp [wɒsp] *n* Wespe *f*.

WASP [wɒsp] *(US) abbr of* **White Anglo-Saxon Protestant** weißer angelsächsischer Protestant.

waspish *adj*, ~**ly** *adv* ['wɒspɪʃ, -lɪ] giftig.

wasp-waist ['wɒspweɪst] *n* Wespentaille *f*.

wastage ['weɪstɪdʒ] *n* Schwund *m*; *(action)* Verschwendung *f*; *(amount also)* Materialverlust *m*; *(from container also)* Verlust *m*; *(unusable products etc also)* Abfall *m*. **a ~ rate of 10%** eine Verlustquote von 10%; *see* **natural** ~.

waste [weɪst] **1** *adj (superfluous)* überschüssig, überflüssig; *(left over)* ungenutzt; *land* brachliegend, ungenutzt. ~ **food** Abfall *m*; ~ **material/matter** Abfallstoffe *pl*; **to lay ~** verwüsten; **to lie ~** brachliegen.
  2 *n* **(a)** Verschwendung *f*; *(unusable materials)* Abfall *m*. **it's a ~ of time/money** es ist Zeit-/Geldverschwendung; **it's a ~ of your time and mine** das ist nur (eine) Zeitverschwendung für uns beide; **it's a ~ of effort** das ist verschwendete *or* vergeudete Mühe; **a ~ of opportunities** eine nicht wahrgenommene *or* genutzte Chance *or* Gelegenheit; **to go or run to ~** *(food)* umkommen; *(training, money, land)* ungenutzt sein/ bleiben, brachliegen; *(talent etc)* verkümmern.
  (b) *(~ material)* Abfallstoffe *pl*; *(in factory)* Schwund *m*; *(rubbish)* Abfall *m*. **cotton ~** Putzwolle *f*; **metal ~** Metallabfall.
  (c) *(land, expanse)* Wildnis *no pl*, Einöde *f*. **a ~ of snow, a snowy ~** eine Schneewüste.
  3 *vt* **(a)** *(use badly or wrongly)* verschwenden, vergeuden *(on* an +*acc*, für); *food* verschwenden; *life, time* vergeuden, vertun. **you're wasting your time** das ist reine Zeitverschwendung, damit vertust du nur deine Zeit; **don't ~ my time** stiehl mir nicht meine Zeit; **you didn't ~ much time getting here!** *(inf)* da bist du ja schon, du hast ja nicht gerade getrödelt! *(inf)*; **all our efforts were ~d** all unsere Bemühungen waren umsonst *or* vergeblich; **nothing is ~d** es wird nichts verschwendet; **your work won't be ~d** deine Arbeit ist nicht vergeblich *or* umsonst getan; **I ~d three litres of petrol coming here** ... und dafür habe ich drei Liter Benzin verfahren *or* verschwendet; **he didn't ~ any words in telling me** ... ohne viel(e) Worte zu machen *or* zu verlieren, sagte er mir ...; **to ~ oneself on sb** sich an jdn verschwenden; **I wouldn't ~ my breath talking to him** ich würde doch nicht für den meine Spucke vergeuden! *(inf)*; **don't ~ your efforts on him** vergeuden Sie keine Mühe mit ihm!; **Beethoven/your joke/she is ~d on him** Beethoven/dein Witz ist an den verschwendet *or* vergeudet/sie ist zu schade für ihn; **you're ~d in this job** Sie sind zu schade für diese Arbeit.
  (b) *(weaken)* auszehren; *strength* aufzehren.
  (c) *(lay waste)* verwüsten.
  4 *vi (food)* umkommen; *(skills)* verkümmern; *(body)* ver-

fallen; (*strength, assets*) schwinden. ~ **not, want not** (*Prov*) spare in der Zeit, so hast du in der Not (*Prov*).

♦**waste away** *vi* (*physically*) dahinschwinden (*geh*), immer weniger werden. **you're not exactly wasting** ~**!** (*iro*) du siehst doch aus wie das blühende Leben!

waste: ~**-basket,** ~**-bin** *n* Papierkorb *m*; ~ **disposal** *n* Müllbeseitigung *f*; ~ **disposal unit** *n* Müllschlucker *m*.

wasteful ['weistful] *adj* verschwenderisch; *method, process* aufwendig, unwirtschaftlich; *expenditure* unnütz. **leaving all the lights on is a** ~ **habit** es ist Verschwendung, überall Licht brennen zu lassen; **to be** ~ **with sth** verschwenderisch mit etw umgehen; **it is** ~ **of effort** es ist unnötiger Aufwand; **this project is** ~ **of the country's resources** dieses Projekt ist eine unnütze Vergeudung unserer Ressourcen.

wastefully ['weistfəli] *adv* verschwenderisch; *organized* unwirtschaftlich. **she's** ~ **extravagant with money** sie geht sehr verschwenderisch mit (dem) Geld um.

wastefulness ['weistfulnis] *n* (*of person*) verschwenderische Art; (*in method, organization, of process etc*) Unwirtschaftlichkeit, Aufwendigkeit *f*. **throwing it away is sheer** ~ es ist reine Verschwendung, das wegzuwerfen; **sb's** ~ **with sth/in doing sth** jds verschwenderische Art, mit etw umzugehen/etw zu machen; **the** ~ **of the government's expenditure in the field of defence** die Verschwendung, die die Regierung auf dem Gebiet der Verteidigung betreibt.

waste: ~**land** *n* Ödland *nt*; (*fig*) Einöde *f*; ~**paper** *n* Papierabfall *m*; (*fig*) Makulatur *f*; ~**paper basket** (*Brit*) *n* Papierkorb *m*; **they go straight into the** ~**paper basket** die wandern sofort in den Papierkorb; ~ **pipe** *n* Abflußrohr *nt*; ~ **product** *n* Abfallprodukt *nt*.

waster ['weistə^r] *n* (a) Verschwender(in *f*) *m*. **it's a real time-/money-**~ das ist wirklich Zeit-/Geldverschwendung; **she's a terrible** ~ **of electricity** sie verschwendet schrecklich viel Strom. (b) (*good-for-nothing*) Taugenichts *m*.

wasting ['weistiŋ] *adj attr* ~ **disease** Auszehrung *f*. **this is a** ~ **disease** das ist eine Krankheit, bei der der Körper allmählich verfällt.

wastrel ['weistrəl] *n* (*liter*) Prasser *m* (*liter*).

watch¹ [wɒtʃ] *n* (Armband)uhr *f*.

watch² 1 *n* (a) (*vigilance*) Wache *f*. **to be on the** ~ aufpassen; **to be on the** ~ **for sb/sth** nach jdm/etw Ausschau halten; **to keep** ~ Wache halten; **to keep a close** ~ **on sb/sth** jdn/etw scharf bewachen; **to keep a close** ~ **on the time** genau auf die Zeit achten; **to keep** ~ **over sb/sth** bei jdm/etw wachen *or* Wache halten; **to set a** ~ **on sb/sth** jdn/etw überwachen lassen.

(b) (*period of duty, Naut, people*) Wache *f*; (*people also*) Wachmannschaft *f*. **to be on** ~ Wache haben, auf Wacht sein (*geh*); **officer of the** ~ wachhabender Offizier; **in the still** ~**es of the night** (*old, liter*) in den stillen Stunden der Nacht.

(c) (*Hist: to protect public*) Wache *f*.

2 *vt* (a) (*guard*) aufpassen auf (+*acc*); (*police etc*) überwachen.

(b) (*observe*) beobachten; *match* zusehen *or* zuschauen bei; *film, play, programme on TV* sich (*dat*) ansehen. **to** ~ **TV** fernsehen; **to** ~ **sb doing sth** jdm zusehen *or* zuschauen *or* sich (*dat*) ansehen, wie jd etw macht; **I'll come and** ~ **you play** ich komme und sehe dir beim Spielen zu; **he just stood there and** ~**ed her drown** er stand einfach da und sah zu, wie sie ertrank; **I** ~**ed her coming down the street** ich habe sie beobachtet, wie *or* als sie die Straße entlang kam; **she has a habit of** ~**ing my mouth when I speak** sie hat die Angewohnheit, mir auf den Mund zu sehen *or* schauen, wenn ich rede; **let's go and** ~ **the tennis** sehen wir uns (das) Tennis ansehen; **are you** ~**ing the blackboard!** du guckst *or* siehst zur Tafel!; **don't** ~ **the camera** sehen Sie nicht zur Kamera!; ~ **this young actor, he'll be a star** beachten Sie diesen jungen Schauspieler, das wird mal ein Star; ~ **the road in front of you** paß auf die Straße auf!, guck *or* achte auf die Straße!; **to** ~ **a case/negotiations for sb** für jdn als Beobachter bei einem Prozeß/einer Verhandlung auftreten; **now** ~ **this closely** sehen *or* schauen Sie jetzt gut zu!, passen Sie mal genau auf!; ~ **this!** paß auf!; **I want everyone to** ~ **me** ich möchte, daß mir alle zusehen *or* -schauen!, alle mal hersehen *or* -schauen!; **just** ~ **me!** guck *or* schau mal, wie ich das mache!; **just you** ~ **me tell him!** na, jetzt kannst du mal sehen, wie ich dem Bescheid sage!; **just** ~ **me go and make a mess of it!** da siehst du mal, was für einen Mist ich mache (*inf*); **we are being** ~**ed** wir werden beobachtet; **I just can't stand being** ~**ed** ich kann es einfach nicht aussehen, wenn mir ständig einer zusieht; **a new talent to be** ~**ed** ein neues Talent, das man im Auge behalten muß; **a** ~**ed pot never boils** (*Prov*) wenn man daneben steht, kocht das Wasser nie.

(c) (*be careful of*) achtgeben *or* aufpassen auf (+*acc*); *expenses* achten auf (+*acc*); *time* achten auf (+*acc*), aufpassen auf (+*acc*). **(you'd better)** ~ **it!** (*inf*) paß (bloß) auf! (*inf*); ~ **yourself** sieh dich vor!; sei vorsichtig!; (*well-wishing*) mach's gut; ~ **your manners/language!** bitte benimm dich!/drück dich bitte etwas gepflegter aus!; ~ **him, he's crafty** sieh dich vor *or* paß auf, er ist raffiniert; ~ **where you put your feet** paß auf, wo du hintrittst; ~ **how you talk to him, he's touchy** sei vorsichtig, wenn du mit ihm sprichst, er ist sehr empfindlich; ~ **how you drive, the roads are icy** paß beim Fahren auf *or* fahr vorsichtig, die Straßen sind vereist!; ~ **how you go!** mach's gut!; (*on icy surface etc*) paß beim Laufen/Fahren auf!; *see* **step**.

(d) *chance* abpassen, abwarten. **to** ~ **one's chance/time** eine günstige Gelegenheit/einen günstigen Zeitpunkt abwarten.

3 *vi* (a) (*observe*) zusehen, zuschauen. **to** ~ **for sb/sth** nach jdm/etw Ausschau halten *or* ausschauen; **they** ~**ed for a signal from the soldiers** sie warteten auf ein Signal von den Soldaten; **to** ~ **for sth to happen** darauf warten, daß etw geschieht; **the doctor is** ~**ing for signs of recovery** der Arzt beobachtet den Patienten auf Anzeichen, die auf eine Besserung hinweisen; **to**

be ~**ing for signs of** ... nach Anzeichen von ... Ausschau halten; **you should** ~ **for symptoms of** ... du solltest auf ...-symptome achten.

(b) (*keep* ~) Wache halten; (*at sickbed also*) wachen. **there are policemen** ~**ing all round the house** das Haus wird rundherum von Polizisten bewacht.

♦**watch out** *vi* (a) (*look carefully*) Ausschau halten, ausschauen (*for sb/sth* nach jdm/etw).

(b) (*be careful*) aufpassen, achtgeben (*for auf* +*acc*). **there were hundreds of policemen** ~**ing** ~ **for trouble at the football match** bei dem Fußballspiel waren Hunderte von Polizisten, die aufpaßten, daß es nicht zu Zwischenfällen kam; ~ ~**!** Achtung!, Vorsicht!; **you'd better** ~ ~**!** (*threatening also*) paß bloß auf!, nimm dich in acht!, sieh dich ja vor!; ~ ~ **for him, he's a crafty negotiator** nimm dich vor ihm in acht, er ist ein schlauer Verhandlungspartner!

♦**watch over** *vi* +*prep obj* wachen über (+*acc*).

watchable ['wɒtʃəbl] *adj* sehenswert.

watch: ~**band** *n* (*US*) Uhrarmband *nt*; ~**case** *n* Uhrengehäuse *nt*; ~ **chain** *n* Uhrkette *f*; **W**~ **Committee** *n* (*Brit*) Aufsichtskommission *f*; ~**dog** *n* (*lit*) Wachhund *m*; (*fig*) Aufpasser (*inf*), Überwachungsbeauftragte(r) *m*; **government** ~**dog** Regierungsbeauftragter zur Überwachung von ...; ~**dog body** Überwachungsgremium *nt*.

watcher ['wɒtʃə^r] *n* Schaulustige(r) *mf*; (*observer*) Beobachter(in *f*) *m*. **the** ~**s by the dying man's bedside** die am Bett des Sterbenden Wachenden.

watchful ['wɒtʃful] *adj* wachsam. **to be** ~ **for/against** wachsam Ausschau halten nach/auf der Hut sein vor (+*dat*).

watchfully ['wɒtʃfəli] *adv* wachsam. **policemen sat** ~ **at the back of the hall** ganz hinten im Saal saßen Polizisten, die aufpaßten; **the opposition waited** ~ **for the Government's next move** die Opposition beobachtete aufmerksam, welchen Schritt die Regierung als nächstes unternehmen würde.

watchfulness ['wɒtʃfulnis] *n* Wachsamkeit *f*.

watch-glass ['wɒtʃglɑːs] *n* Uhrenglas *nt*.

watching brief ['wɒtʃiŋ briːf] *n* **to hold a** ~ eine Kontrollfunktion ausüben; **he holds a** ~ **for the Government over all aspects of industrial development** er ist der Regierungsbeauftragte zur Überwachung der gesamten industriellen Entwicklung.

watch: ~**maker** *n* Uhrmacher *m*; ~**man** *n* (*night-*~, *in bank, factory etc*) (Nacht)wächter *m*; ~**night service** *n* Jahresschlußmette *f*; ~**strap** *n* Uhrarmband *nt*; ~ **tower** *n* Wachturm *m*; ~**word** *n* (*password, motto*) Parole, Losung *f*.

water ['wɔːtə^r] 1 *n* (a) Wasser *nt*. **the field is under** ~ das Feld steht unter Wasser; **to make** ~ (*ship*) lecken.

(b) (*sea, of lake etc*) ~**s** Gewässer *pl*; **the** ~**s** (*Bibl, liter*) die Wasser *pl*; **the** ~**s of the Rhine** die Wasser des Rheins (*liter*); **by** ~ auf dem Wasserweg, zu Wasser (*geh*); **on land and** ~ zu Land und zu Wasser; **we spent an afternoon on the** ~ wir verbrachten einen Nachmittag auf dem Wasser.

(c) (*urine*) Wasser *nt*. **to make** *or* **pass** ~ Wasser lassen.

(d) (*at spa*) **the** ~**s** die Heilquelle; **to drink** *or* **take the** ~**s** eine Kur machen; (*drinking only*) eine Trinkkur machen.

(e) (*Med*) ~ **on the brain** Wasserkopf *m*; ~ **on the knee** Kniegelenkerguß *m*.

(f) (*toilet* ~) **rose** ~ *etc* Rosenwasser *nt etc*.

(g) **to stay above** ~ sich über Wasser halten; **to pour cold** ~ **on sb's idea** jdm etw miesmachen (*inf*); **to get (oneself) into deep** ~**(s)** ins Schwimmen kommen; **they got into deep** ~ **when they tried to meddle in politics** sie begaben sich aufs Glatteis, als sie versuchten, in der Politik mitzumischen; **of the first** ~ erster Güte; **a lot of** ~ **has flowed under the bridge since then** (*fig*) seitdem ist soviel Wasser den Berg *or* den Bach hinuntergeflossen; **to hold** ~ (*lit*) wasserdicht sein; **that excuse/argument etc won't hold** ~ (*inf*) diese Entschuldigung/ dieses Argument *etc* ist nicht hieb- und stichfest (*inf*); **to be in** *or* **get into hot** ~ (*fig inf*) in Schwierigkeiten *or* in (des) Teufels Küche (*inf*) sein/geraten (*over wegen* +*gen*); **he's in hot** ~ **with his father** (*inf*) er hat Ärger *or* Stunk (*sl*) mit seinem Vater; **to spend money like** ~ (*inf*) mit dem Geld nur so um sich werfen (*inf*).

2 *vt* (a) *garden, roads* sprengen; *lawn also* besprengen; *land, field* bewässern; *plant* (be)gießen.

(b) *horses, cattle* tränken.

(c) *wine* verwässern, verdünnen.

(d) **to** ~ **capital** (*Fin*) Aktienkapital verwässern.

3 *vi* (a) (*mouth*) wässern; (*eye*) tränen. **the smoke made his eyes** ~ **ihm** tränten die Augen vom Rauch; **my mouth** ~**ed** mir lief das Wasser im Mund zusammen; **to make sb's mouth** ~ jdm den Mund wässerig machen.

(b) (*animals*) trinken.

♦**water down** *vt sep* (*lit, fig*) verwässern; (*fig also*) abmildern, abschwächen; *liquids* (mit Wasser) verdünnen.

water: ~ **beetle** *n* Wasserkäfer *m*; ~ **bird** *n* Wasservogel *m*; ~ **biscuit** *n* = Kräcker *m*; ~ **blister** *n* Wasserblase *f*; ~ **boatman** *n* Rückenschwimmer *m*; ~**borne** *adj* **to be** ~**borne** (*ship*) auf dem *or* im Wasser sein; ~**borne trade** Handel *m* auf dem Seeweg *or* Wasserweg, Handelsschiffahrt *f*; ~**borne goods/troops** Güter/ Truppen, die auf dem Wasserweg *or* zu Wasser befördert werden; **a** ~**borne disease** eine Krankheit, die durch das Wasser übertragen wird; ~**-bottle** *n* Wasserflasche *f*; (*for troops, travellers etc*) Feldflasche *f*; ~**buck** *n* Wasserbock *m*; ~ **buffalo** *n* Wasserbüffel *m*; ~ **butt** *n* Regentonne *f*; ~ **cannon** *n* Wasserwerfer *m*; ~ **carrier** *n* Wasserträger(in *f*) *m*; **the W**~ **Carrier** (*Astrol*) der Wassermann; ~**-cart** *n* Wasserwagen *m*; (*for roads*) Sprengwagen *m*; ~ **closet** *n* (*abbr* **WC**) Wasserklosett *nt*; ~**-colour,** (*US*) ~**color** 1 *n* Wasserfarbe, Aquarellfarbe *f*; (*picture*) Aquarell *nt*; 2 *attr* Aquarell-; ~**colourist,** (*US*) ~**colorist** *n* Aquarellmaler(in *f*) *m*; ~**-cooled** *adj* wassergekühlt; ~ **cooler** *n* Thermoskanister *m*, isolierter

Trinkwasserbehälter/-kanister; ~**course** n (stream) Wasserlauf m; (bed) Flußbett nt; (artificial) Kanal m; ~**cress** n (Brunnen)kresse f; ~**cure** n Wasserkur f; ~ **diviner** n (Wünschel)rutengänger m; ~**fall** n Wasserfall m; ~**fowl** n Wasservogel m; pl Wassergeflügel nt; ~**front** 1 n Hafenviertel nt; we drove along the ~**front**/down to the ~**front** wir fuhren am Wasser entlang/hinunter zum Wasser; 2 attr am Wasser; a ~**front** restaurant/a restaurant am Wasser ein Restaurant direkt am Hafen or am Wasser/im Hafenviertel; they live on the Mississippi ~**front** sie wohnen direkt am Mississippi; ~-**gauge** n (in tank) Wasserstandsmesser or -anzeiger m; (in rivers, lakes etc also) Pegel m; ~ **heater** n Heißwassergerät nt; ~ **hole** n Wasserloch nt; ~-**ice** n Fruchteis nt.

wateriness ['wɔːtərɪnɪs] n (weakness) Wässerigkeit, Wäßrigkeit f; (of colour) Blässe f.

watering ['wɔːtərɪŋ] n (of land, field) Bewässern nt; (of garden) Sprengen nt; (of lawn also) Besprengen nt; (of plant) (Be)gießen nt.

watering: ~ **can** n Gießkanne f; ~ **place** n (spa) Kurort m; (seaside resort) Badeort m, Seebad nt; (for animals) Tränke, Wasserstelle f.

water: ~ **jacket** n Kühlmantel, Kühlwassermantel m; ~ **jump** n Wassergraben m; ~**less** adj trocken; a ~**less planet** ein Planet ohne Wasser; ~ **level** n Wasserstand m (in engine also); (measured level of river, reservoir etc also) Pegelstand m; (surface of water) Wasserspiegel m; ~**lily** n Seerose f; ~**line** n Wasserlinie f; ~**logged** adj the fields are ~**logged** die Felder stehen unter Wasser; the ship was completely ~**logged** das Schiff war voll Wasser gelaufen; to get ~**logged** sich voll Wasser saugen; (ship) voll Wasser laufen.

Waterloo [wɔːtə'luː] n to meet one's ~ (hum) Schiffbruch erleiden; (with that woman he has finally met his ~ bei dieser Frau hat er sein Waterloo erlebt (hum).

water: ~ **main** n Haupt(wasser)leitung f; (the actual pipe) Hauptwasserrohr nt; ~**man** n Fährmann m; ~**mark** n (a) (on wall) Wasserstandsmarke f; (b) (on paper) Wasserzeichen nt; ~**melon** n Wassermelone f; ~ **mill** n Wassermühle f; ~ **nymph** n (Wasser)nixe f; ~ **pipe** n Wasserrohr nt; (for smoking) Wasserpfeife f; ~**pistol** n Wasserpistole f; ~-**polo** n Wasserball nt; ~-**power** n Wasserkraft f; ~**proof** 1 adj clothes wasserundurchlässig; roof also, window (wasser)dicht; paint wasserfest; 2 n (esp Brit) Regenhaut f; 3 vt wasserundurchlässig machen; material also wasserdicht machen; clothes also imprägnieren; ~ **rat** n Wasserratte f; (US sl) Hafenstrolch m (inf); ~-**rate** n (Brit) Wassergeld nt; ~**repellent** adj wasserabstoßend; ~**shed** n (Geol) Wasserscheide f; (fig) Wendepunkt m; ~**side** 1 n Ufer nt; (at sea) Strand m; 2 attr am Wasser wachsend/lebend etc; ~**ski** 1 n Wasserski m; 2 vi wasserschilaufen, Wasserski laufen; ~-**skiing** n Wasserskilaufen nt; ~ **snake** n Wasserschlange f; (in lake) Seeschlange f; ~ **softener** n Wasserenthärter m; ~-**soluble** adj wasserlöslich; ~**spaniel** n Wasserspaniel m; ~ **spout** n (a) (Met) Wasserhose, Trombe f; (b) (pipe) Regenrinne f; ~ **supply** n Wasserversorgung f; ~**table** n Grundwasserspiegel m; ~ **tank** n Wassertank m; ~**tight** adj (lit) wasserdicht; (fig) agreement, argument, alibi, contract also hieb- und stichfest; ~-**tower** n Wasserturm m; ~ **vapour** or (US) **vapor** n Wasserdampf m; ~**way** n Wasserstraße f; (channel) Fahrrinne f; ~-**wheel** n (Mech) Wasserrad nt; (Agr) Wasserschöpfrad nt; ~-**wings** npl Schwimmflügel, Schwimmarme (inf) pl; ~**works** npl or sing Wasserwerk nt; to turn on the ~**works** (fig inf) zu heulen anfangen; to have trouble with one's ~**works** (fig inf) ständig laufen müssen (inf).

watery ['wɔːtərɪ] adj (weak) soup, beer etc wässerig, wäßrig; eye tränend; (pale) sky, sun blaß; colour wässerig, wäßrig. all the sailors went to a ~ **grave** alle Seeleute fanden ein feuchtes or nasses Grab or fanden ihr Grab in den Wellen.

watt [wɒt] n Watt nt.

wattage ['wɒtɪdʒ] n Wattleistung f. what ~ is that bulb? wieviel Watt hat diese Birne?

wattle ['wɒtl] n (a) (material) Flechtwerk nt. a ~ **fence** ein Zaun aus Flechtwerk. (b) (Bot) australische Akazie. (c) (Orn) Kehllappen m.

wave [weɪv] 1 n (a) (of water, Phys, Rad, in hair, fig) Welle f; (of water, hatred, enthusiasm also) Woge (liter) f. who rules the ~s? wer beherrscht die Meere?; a ~ of strikes/enthusiasm eine Streikwelle/ Welle der Begeisterung; during the first ~ of the attack beim ersten Ansturm or in der ersten Angriffswelle; the attacks/attackers came in ~s die Angriffe/Angreifer kamen in Wellen or wellenweise; from the 5th century onwards England was attacked by ~s of invaders vom 5. Jahrhundert an wurde England immer wieder von Eroberungswellen heimgesucht.
(b) (movement of hand) to give sb a ~ jdm (zu)winken; he gave us a ~ to show that he was ready er winkte uns (dat) zu, um zu zeigen, daß er bereit war; with a ~ he was gone er winkte kurz und verschwand; with a ~ of his hand mit einer Handbewegung.
2 vt (a) (in order to give a sign or greeting) winken mit (at, to sb jdm); (to ~ about) schwenken; (gesticulating, in a dangerous manner) herumfuchteln mit. to ~ one's hand to sb jdm winken; he ~d a greeting to the crowd er winkte grüßend der Menge zu; to ~ sb goodbye/to ~ goodbye to sb jdm zum Abschied winken; he ~d his hat (at the passing train) er schwenkte seinen Hut/er winkte dem vorbeifahrenden Zug mit seinem Hut (zu); don't just ~ your racket about fuchtele nicht so mit dem Schläger (in der Gegend) herum or durch die Luft!; he ~d the ticket under my nose er fuchtelte mir mit der Karte vor der Nase herum; she ~d her umbrella threateningly at him sie schwang drohend ihren Schirm in seine Richtung or nach ihm; he ~d his stick at the children who were stealing the apples er drohte den Kindern, die die Äpfel stahlen, mit dem Stock; he ~d his fist at the intruders er drohte den Eindringlingen mit der Faust.

(b) (to indicate sb should move) the traffic warden ~d the children across the road der Verkehrspolizist winkte die Kinder über die Straße; he ~d me over to his table er winkte mich zu sich an den Tisch; he ~d me over er winkte mich zu sich herüber.
(c) (hair) wellen.
3 vi (a) winken. to ~ at or to sb jdm winken; (greeting) jdm zuwinken; there's daddy, ~! da ist der Papi, wink mal!; don't just ~ at the ball, aim to hit it nicht nur in Richtung Ball fuchteln, du sollst ihn auch treffen!
(b) (flag) wehen; (branches) sich hin und her bewegen; (corn) wogen.
(c) (hair) sich wellen.

♦ **wave aside** vt sep (a) (lit) person auf die Seite or zur Seite winken. (b) (fig) person, objection, suggestions etc ab- or zurückweisen; help also ausschlagen.

♦ **wave away** vt sep abwinken (+dat).

♦ **wave down** vt sep anhalten, stoppen.

♦ **wave on** vt sep the policeman ~d us ~ der Polizist winkte uns weiter.

wave: ~**band** n (Rad) Wellenband nt; ~**length** n (Rad) Wellenlänge f; we're not on the same ~**length** (fig) wir haben nicht dieselbe Wellenlänge.

wavelet ['weɪvlɪt] n (poet) kleine Welle.

waver ['weɪvə'] vi (a) (quiver) (light, flame, eyes) flackern; (voice) zittern. I knew he was lying because of the way his eyes ~ed away from my face daran, daß er meinem Blick auswich, sah ich, daß er log.
(b) (weaken) (courage, self-assurance) wanken, ins Wanken geraten; (courage also) weichen; (support) nachlassen. he ~ed in his resolution sein Entschluß geriet ins Wanken; the old man's mind was beginning to ~ der alte Mann wurde langsam etwas wirr im Kopf.
(c) (hesitate) schwanken (between zwischen +dat). if he begins to ~ wenn er ins Schwanken or Wanken gerät; he's ~ing between accepting and ... er ist sich (dat) darüber unschlüssig, ob er annehmen soll oder ...

waverer ['weɪvərə'] n Zauderer m.

wavering ['weɪvərɪŋ] adj light, flame flackernd; shadow tanzend; courage, determination wankend; support (hesitating) wechselhaft; (decreasing) nachlassend.

wavy ['weɪvɪ] adj (+er) hair, surface wellig, gewellt; design Wellen-; (of uneven length) ungleich. ~ **line** Schlangenlinie f.

wax [wæks] 1 n Wachs nt; (ear ~) Ohrenschmalz nt; (sealing ~) Siegellack m. to be like ~ in sb's hands (wie) Wachs in jds Händen (dat) sein. 2 adj Wachs-. 3 vt floor, furniture wachsen; floor also bohnern; moustache wichsen.

wax² vi (a) (moon) zunehmen. to ~ **and wane** (lit) ab- und zunehmen; (fig) schwanken, kommen und gehen. (b) (liter: become) werden. to ~ **enthusiastic** in Begeisterung geraten.

waxed [wækst] adj paper Wachs-; floor, thread gewachst; moustache gewichst.

wax(ed) paper n Wachspapier nt.

waxen ['wæksən] adj (a) (old) wächsern. (b) (fig: pale) wachsbleich, wächsern.

waxing ['wæksɪŋ] 1 adj moon zunehmend; enthusiasm etc also wachsend. 2 n Zunehmen nt; Wachsen nt.

wax: ~ **work** n Wachsfigur f; ~ **works** n sing or pl Wachsfigurenkabinett nt.

waxy ['wæksɪ] adj (+er) wächsern.

way [weɪ] 1 n (a) (road) Weg m. across or over the ~ gegenüber, vis-à-vis; (motion) rüber; W~ of the Cross Kreuzweg m; to fall by the ~ (fig) auf der Strecke bleiben.
(b) (route) Weg m. the ~ to the station der Weg zum Bahnhof; by ~ of (via) über (+acc); which is the ~ to the town hall, please? wo geht es hier zum Rathaus, bitte?; ~ in/out (also on signs) Ein-/Ausgang m; please show me the ~ out bitte zeigen Sie mir, wo es hinausgeht (inf) or wie ich hinauskomme; can you find your own ~ out? finden Sie selbst hinaus?; on the ~ out/in beim Hinaus-/Hereingehen; to be on the ~ in (fig inf) im Kommen sein; to be on the ~ out (fig inf) am Verschwinden or Aussterben sein; there's no ~ out (fig) es gibt keinen Ausweg; ~ up/down Weg nach oben/unten; (climbing) Aufstieg/Abstieg m; ~ up/back Hinweg/Rückweg m; prices are on the ~ up/down again die Preise steigen/fallen; there's a little cafe on the ~ up to London es gibt da ein kleines Café auf dem Weg nach London; the shop is on the/your ~ der Laden liegt auf dem/deinem Weg; is it on the ~? (place) liegt das auf dem Weg?; (parcel etc) ist es unterwegs?; to stop on the ~ unterwegs anhalten; on the ~ (here) auf dem Weg (hierher); on the ~ to London auf dem Weg nach London; you pass it on your ~ home du kommst auf deinem Nachhauseweg or Heimweg daran vorbei; they're on their ~ now sie sind jetzt auf dem Weg or unterwegs; he's on the ~ to becoming an alcoholic er ist dabei or auf dem besten Weg, Alkoholiker zu werden; she's well on the ~ to being a first-rate singer sie ist auf dem besten Weg, eine erstklassige Sängerin zu werden; there's another baby on the ~ da ist wieder ein Kind unterwegs; I haven't finished it yet but it's on the ~ ich bin noch nicht damit fertig, aber es ist im Werden (inf); if it is out of your ~ wenn es ein Umweg für Sie ist; we had to go out of our ~ wir mußten einen Umweg machen; it took us out of our ~ es war ein Umweg für uns; to go out of one's ~ to do sth (fig) sich besonders anstrengen, um etw zu tun; please, don't go out of your ~ for us (fig) machen Sie sich (dat) bitte unsertwegen keine Umstände; to feel the/one's ~ sich weiter-/vorwärts-/entlangtasten; to find a ~ in hineinfinden, hineinkommen, eine Möglichkeit finden hineinzukommen; can you find your ~ out/home? finden Sie hinaus/nach Hause?; I know my ~ about town ich finde mich in der Stadt zurecht, ich kenne mich in der Stadt aus; she knows her ~ about (fig inf) sie kennt sich aus, sie weiß

Bescheid (*inf*); **to lose one's ~** sich verlaufen, sich verirren (*geh*); **to make one's ~ to somewhere** sich an einen Ort *or* irgendwohin bewegen *or* begeben; **can you make your own ~ to the theatre?** kannst du allein zum Theater kommen?; **to make one's ~ home** nach Hause gehen; (*start*) sich auf den Heimweg begeben; **to make/fight/push one's ~ through the crowd** sich einen Weg durch die Menge bahnen, sich durch die Menge (durch)drängen/-kämpfen/-schieben; **to make one's ~ in the world** seinen Weg machen, sich durchsetzen; **to go one's own ~** (*fig*) eigene Wege gehen; **they went their separate ~s** (*lit, fig*) ihre Wege trennten sich; **to pay one's ~** für sich selbst bezahlen; (*company, project, machine*) sich rentieren; **can the nation pay its ~?** kann das Volk *or* Land für sich selber aufkommen?; **the ~ of virtue** der Pfad der Tugend; **the ~ forward** der Weg vorwärts *or* in die Zukunft; **to go down the wrong ~** (*food, drink*) in die falsche Kehle kommen; **to prepare the ~** (*fig*) den Weg bereiten (*for sb/sth* jdm/einer Sache); **could you see your ~ to lending me a pound?** wäre es Ihnen wohl möglich, mir ein Pfund zu leihen?; **to get under ~** in Gang kommen, losgehen (*inf*); (*Naut*) Fahrt aufnehmen *or* machen; **to be (well) under ~** im Gang /in vollem Gang sein; (*Naut*) in (voller) Fahrt sein; (*with indication of place*) unterwegs sein; **to lose/gather ~** (*Naut*) Fahrt verlieren/aufnehmen.

(**c**) (*room for movement, path*) Weg *m.* **to bar** *or* **block the ~** den Weg ab- *or* versperren; **to leave the ~ open** (*fig*) die Möglichkeit offen lassen, einen Weg frei lassen (*for sth* für etw); **make ~!** mach Platz!, Platz machen, Platz da!; **to make ~ for sb/sth** (*lit, fig*) für jdn/etw Platz machen; (*fig also*) für jdn/etw den Platz räumen; **to be/get in sb's/the ~** (jdm) im Weg stehen *or* sein/in den Weg kommen; (*fig*) jdn stören/stören; **get out of the/my ~!** (*geh*) aus dem Weg!, weg da!; **to get sb out of the ~** (*get rid of*) jdn loswerden (*inf*); (*remove: lit, fig*) jdn aus dem Wege räumen; **to get sth out of the ~ work** etw hinter sich (*acc*) bringen; **difficulties, problems etc** etw loswerden (*inf*), etw aus dem Weg räumen, etw beseitigen; **to get sth out of the ~ of sb/sth** jdm etw aus dem Weg räumen/etw aus etw (weg)räumen; **they got the children out of the ~ of the firemen** sie sorgten dafür, daß die Kinder den Feuerwehrleuten nicht im Weg waren; **get those people out of the ~ of the trucks** sieh zu, daß die Leute den Lastwagen Platz machen *or* aus der Bahn gehen; **to keep out of sb's/the ~** (*not get in the ~*) jdm nicht in den Weg kommen, (jdm) aus dem Weg bleiben; (*avoid*) (jdm) aus dem Weg gehen; **keep out of the ~!** weg da!, zurück!; **keep out of my ~!** komm mir nicht mehr über den Weg!; **to keep sb/sth out of the ~ of sb** jdn/etw nicht in jds Nähe *or* Reichweite (*acc*) kommen lassen; **to put difficulties in sb's ~** jdm Hindernisse in den Weg stellen; **to stand in sb's ~** (*lit, fig*) jdm im Weg stehen *or* sein; **don't let me stand in your ~** (*fig*) ich will dir nicht im Weg stehen; **he lets nothing stand in his ~** (*fig*) er läßt sich durch nichts aufhalten *or* beirren; **now nothing stands in our ~** (*fig*) jetzt steht uns (*dat*) nichts mehr im Weg, jetzt haben wir freie Bahn; **to stand in the ~ of progress** den Fortschritt aufhalten *or* hemmen; **to want sb out of the ~** jdn aus dem Weg haben wollen; **to put sb in the ~ of (doing) sth** (*inf*) jdm zu etw verhelfen/dazu verhelfen, etw zu tun.

(**d**) (*direction*) Richtung *f.* **this ~, please** hier(her) *or* hier entlang, bitte; **he went that ~** er ging dorthin *or* in diese Richtung; **"this ~ for the lions"** „zu den Löwen"; **this ~ and that** hierhin und dorthin; **down our ~** (*inf*) bei uns (in der Nähe), in unserer Gegend *or* Ecke (*inf*); **it's out Windsor ~** es ist *or* liegt in Richtung Windsor; **which ~ are you going?** in welche Richtung *or* wohin gehen Sie?; **which ~** in welche/aus welcher Richtung; **look this ~** schau hierher!; **look both ~s** schau nach beiden Seiten; **she didn't know which ~ to look** (*fig*) sie wußte nicht, wo sie hinschauen *or* -sehen sollte; **to look the other ~** (*fig*) wegschauen *or* -sehen; **this one is better, there are no two ~s about it** (*inf*) dieses hier ist besser, da gibt es gar keinen Zweifel *or* das steht fest; **you're going to bed, there are no two ~s about it** (*inf*) du gehst ins Bett, da gibt es gar nichts *or* und damit basta (*inf*); **it does not matter (to me) one ~ or the other** es macht (mir) so oder so nichts aus, es ist mir gleich; **either ~, we're bound to lose** (so oder so,) wir verlieren auf jeden Fall *or* auf alle Fälle; **if the chance comes your ~** wenn Sie (dazu) die Gelegenheit haben; **if a good job comes my ~** wenn ein guter Job für mich auftaucht; **each ~, both ~s** (*Racing*) auf Sieg und Platz; **we'll split it three/ten ~s** wir werden es dritteln/in zehn Teile (auf)teilen *or* durch zehn teilen; **it's the wrong ~ up** es steht verkehrt herum *or* auf dem Kopf (*inf*); **"this ~ up"** „hier oben"; **it's the other ~ round** es ist (genau) umgekehrt; **put it the right ~ up/the other ~ round** stellen Sie es richtig (herum) hin/andersherum *or* andersrum (*inf*).

(**e**) (*distance*) Weg *m*, Strecke *f.* **it rained all the ~ there** és hat auf der ganzen Strecke *or* die ganze Fahrt (über) geregnet; **I'm behind you all the ~** (*fig*) ich stehe voll (und ganz) hinter Ihnen; **a little/long ~ away** *or* **off** nicht/sehr weit weg *or* entfernt, ein kleines/ganzes *or* gutes Stück weit weg *or* entfernt; **it's only a little ~ to the next stop** es ist nur ein kleines Stück bis zur nächsten Haltestelle; **that's a long ~ away** bis dahin ist es weit *or* (*time*) noch lange; **a long ~ out of town** weit von der Stadt weg; (*live also*) weit draußen, weit außerhalb; (*drive also*) weit raus (*inf*), weit nach draußen; **that's a long ~ back** das war schon vor einer ganzen Weile; **a long ~ back**, in 1902, when ... vor langer Zeit, im Jahre 1902, als ...; **he'll go a long ~** (*fig*) er wird es weit bringen; **to have (still) a long ~ to go** (noch) weit vom Ziel entfernt sein; (*with work*) (noch) bei weitem nicht fertig sein; (*with practice*) (noch) viel vor sich haben; **it should go some/a long ~ towards solving the problem** das sollte *or* müßte den Problem schon etwas/ein gutes Stück weiterhelfen; **will that go a little ~ towards helping?** hilft das schon ein Stückchen *or* ein kleines Stück weiter?; **a little (of sth) goes a long ~ (with me)** ein kleines bißchen (+ *nom*) reicht

(mir) sehr lange; **a little kindness goes a long ~** ein bißchen Freundlichkeit hilft viel; **better by a long ~** bei weitem *or* um vieles besser; **not by a long ~** bei weitem nicht.

(**f**) (*method, manners*) Weise *f.* **that's the ~** ja, (so geht das)!, ja, genau!; **do it this ~** machen Sie es so *or* auf diese Art und Weise; **do it the ~ I do it** machen Sie es so *or* auf dieselbe Art und Weise wie ich (es mache); **that's not the right ~ to do it** so geht das nicht, so kann man das nicht machen; **do it any ~ you like** machen Sie es, wie Sie wollen; **what's the best ~ to do it?** wie macht man das am besten?; **we have ~s of making you talk** wir haben gewisse Mittel, um Sie zum Reden zu bringen; **I don't like the ~ he's looking at you** ich mag nicht, wie er dich ansieht, ich mag die Art nicht, wie er dich ansieht; **do you understand the ~ things are developing?** verstehst du, wie sich die Dinge entwickeln?; **you could tell by the ~ he was dressed** das merkte man schon an seiner Kleidung; **the ~ she walks/talks** (so) wie sie geht/spricht; **it's terrible the ~ she swears/drinks** *etc* es ist schrecklich, wie sie flucht/trinkt *etc*; **it's just the ~ you said it** du hast es nur so komisch gesagt; **it's not what you do, it's the ~ you do it** es kommt nicht darauf an, was man macht, sondern wie man es macht; **it was all the ~ you said it would be** es war alles so, wie du (es) gesagt hattest; **do you remember the ~ it was/we were?** erinnerst du dich noch (daran), wie es war/wie wir damals waren?; **it's not the ~ we do things here** so *or* auf die Art machen wir das hier nicht; **to show sb the ~ to do sth** jdm zeigen, wie *or* auf welche Art und Weise etw gemacht wird; **show me the ~** zeig mir, wie (ich es machen soll); **there's only one ~ to do it properly** es gibt nur eine richtige Methode, man kann das nur so *or* nur auf eine Art und Weise machen; **there is only one ~ to speak to him** man kann mit ihm nur auf (die) eine Art und Weise reden; **the French ~ of doing it** (die Art,) wie man es in Frankreich macht; **the Smith ~** wie es Smith macht/gemacht hat; **to do sth the hard ~** etw auf die schwierigste *or* komplizierteste Art (und Weise) machen; **why do it the hard ~?** warum es sich (*dat*) schwer machen?; **to learn the hard ~** aus dem eigenen Schaden lernen; **we'll find a ~** wir werden (schon) einen Weg finden; **love will find a ~** die Liebe überwindet jedes Hindernis *or* alle Schwierigkeiten; **I'd rather do it my ~** ich möchte es lieber auf meine (eigene) Art machen; **that's his ~ of saying thank-you** das ist seine Art, sich zu bedanken; **that's no ~ to speak to your mother** in einem solchen Ton *or* so spricht man nicht mit seiner Mutter; **~s and means** Mittel und Wege; **Committee of W~s and Means** Steuerausschuß *m*; **~ of life** Lebensstil *m*; (*of nation*) Lebensart *f*; **~ of thinking** Denk(ungs)art *f*; **to my ~ of thinking** meiner Meinung *or* Auffassung *or* Anschauung nach; **an old/a funny ~ of talking** eine altertümliche Sprechweise/eine komische Art, sich auszudrücken; **the Eastern ~ of looking at things** die östliche Lebensanschauung; **there are many ~s of solving the problem** es gibt viele Wege, das Problem zu lösen; **ha, that's one ~ of solving it!** ja, so kann man das auch machen!; **that's the ~ the money goes** so geht das Geld weg; **it was this ~** ... es war so *or* folgendermaßen ...; **that's the ~ it goes!** so ist das eben, so ist das nun mal!; **the ~ things are** so, wie es ist *or* wie die Dinge liegen; **leave everything the ~ it is** laß alles so, wie es ist; **to go on in the same old ~** wie vorher *or* auf die alte Tour (*inf*) weitermachen; **in one ~ or another** so oder so, irgendwie, auf irgendeine Art und Weise; **in a general ~** this is true ganz allgemein ist das richtig; **he had his ~ with her** er hat sie genommen; **to get** *or* **have one's (own) ~** seinen Willen durchsetzen *or* bekommen; **our team had it all their own ~ in the second half** in der zweiten Halbzeit ging für unsere Mannschaft alles nach Wunsch; **have it your own ~!** wie du willst!; **you can't have it both ~s** du kannst nicht beides haben, beides (zugleich) geht nicht (*inf*); **he wants it both ~s** er will das eine haben und das andere nicht lassen; **what a ~ to speak!** so spricht man doch nicht!; **what a ~ to live/die!** so möchte ich nicht leben/sterben.

(**g**) (*custom, habit*) Art *f.* **the ~s of the Spaniards** die spanische Lebensweise; **the ~s of Providence/God** die Wege der Vorsehung/Gottes; **the ~ of the world** der Lauf der Welt *or* der Dinge; **that is our ~ with traitors** so machen wir das mit Verrätern; **it is not/only his ~ to ...** es ist nicht/eben seine Art, zu ...; **he has a ~ with him** er hat so eine (gewisse) Art; **he has a ~ with children** er versteht es, mit Kindern umzugehen, er hat eine geschickte Art (im Umgang) mit Kindern; **he has his little ~s** er hat so seine Eigenheiten *or* Marotten (*inf*); **to get out of/into the ~ of sth** sich (*dat*) etw ab-/angewöhnen.

(**h**) (*respect*) Hinsicht *f.* **in a ~** in gewisser Hinsicht *or* Weise; **in no ~** in keiner Weise; **no ~!** nichts drin! (*inf*), ausgeschlossen!, is' nich' (*sl*); **there's no ~ I'm going to agree/you'll persuade him** auf keinen Fall werde ich zustimmen/ werden Sie ihn überreden können; **what have you got in the ~ of drink/food?** was haben Sie an Getränken *or* zu trinken/an Lebensmitteln *or* zu essen?; **in every possible ~** auf jede mögliche *or* denkbare Art, auf jedwede Art (*geh*); **to be better in every possible ~** in jeder Hinsicht besser sein; **in many/some ~s** in vieler/gewisser Hinsicht; **in a big ~** (*not petty*) im großen Stil; (*on a large scale*) in großen; **in the ~ of business** durch *or* über das Geschäft, geschäftlich; **in a small ~** in kleinem Ausmaß *or* im Kleinen; **he's not a plumber in the ordinary ~** er ist kein Klempner im üblichen Sinn; **in the ordinary ~ we** ... normalerweise *or* üblicherweise ... wir ....

(**i**) (*state*) Zustand *m.* **he's in a bad ~** er ist in schlechter Verfassung; **things are in a bad ~** die Dinge stehen schlecht; **he's in a fair ~ to succeed** (*inf*) er ist auf dem besten Wege, es zu schaffen.

(**j**) (*with by*) **by the ~** übrigens; **all this is by the ~** (*irrelevant*) das ist alles Nebensache *or* zweitrangig; (*extra*) das nur nebenher *or* nebenbei; **by ~ of an answer/excuse** als Antwort/Entschuldigung; **by ~ of illustration** zur Illustration;

he's by ~ of being a painter (*inf*) er ist so'n Maler (*inf*).

(k) ~s *pl* (*Naut: slip*~) Helling, Ablaufbahn *f*.

2 *adv* (*inf*) ~ back/over/up weit zurück/drüben/oben; ~ **back when** vor langer Zeit, als; **since** ~ **back** seit Urzeiten; **since** ~ **back in 1893** ... schon seit (dem Jahre) 1893 ...; **that was** ~ **back** das ist schon lange her, das war schon vor langer Zeit; **he was** ~ **out with his guess** er hatte weit daneben- *or* vorbeigeraten, er hatte weit gefehlt *or* er lag weit daneben (*inf*) mit seiner Annahme; **his guess was** ~ **out** seine Annahme war weit gefehlt; **you're** ~ **out if you think** ... da liegst du aber schief (*inf*) *or* da hast du dich aber gewaltig geirrt, wenn du glaubst, ...

way: ~**bill** *n* Frachtbrief *m*; ~**farer** ['weɪ‚fɛərə^r] *n* (*liter*) Wanderer, Wandersmann (*liter*) *m*; ~**faring** *adj* (*liter*) wandernd, reisend; ~**faring man** Wandervogel, Zugvogel *m*; ~**lay** *pret*, *ptp* ~**laid** *vt* (*ambush*) überfallen; (*inf*) abfangen; **I was** ~**laid by the manager der Manager hat mich abgefangen; ~-out *adj* (*sl*) irr(e) (*inf*), extrem (*sl*); ~**side 1** *n* (*of path, track*) Wegrand *m*; (*of road*) Straßenrand *m*; **by the** ~**side am Weg(es)-/ Straßenrand; to fall by the** ~**side auf der Strecke bleiben; 2 *adj* café, inn am Weg/an der Straße gelegen; ~**side flowers** Blumen, die am Weg-/Straßenrand blühen; ~ **station** *n* (*US*) Zwischenstation *f*, Kleinbahnhof *m*; ~ **train** *n* (*US*) Personenzug *m*; ~**ward** ['weɪwəd] *adj* (*self-willed*) *child, horse, disposition* eigenwillig, eigensinnig; (*capricious*) *fancy, request, passion* abwegig; (*liter*) *stream, breeze* unberechenbar, launisch (*liter*); *their* ~**ward son** ihr ungeratener Sohn; ~**wardness** *n see adj* Eigenwilligkeit *f*, Eigensinn *m*; Abwegigkeit *f*; Unberechenbarkeit, Launenhaftigkeit (*liter*) *f*.

WC *abbr of* **water closet** WC *nt*.

w/e *abbr of* (a) **weekend.** (b) **week ending.**

we [wiː] *pron* wir. **the Royal** ~ der Pluralis maiestatis, der Majestätsplural; **the editorial** ~ der Autorenplural; (*in narrative*) das Wir des Erzählers; **how are** ~ **this morning?** (*inf*) wie geht es uns (denn) heute morgen? (*inf*).

weak [wiːk] *adj* (+*er*) (*all senses*) schwach; *character* labil; *tea, solution etc* dünn; *stomach* empfindlich. **he was** ~ **from hunger** ihm war schwach vor Hunger; **to go/feel** ~ **at the knees** (*after illness*) sich wackelig fühlen, wackelig *or* schwach auf den Beinen sein (*inf*); (*with fear, excitement etc*) weiche Knie haben/bekommen; **the** ~**er sex** das schwache Geschlecht; **he must be a bit** ~ **in the head** (*inf*) er ist wohl nicht ganz bei Trost (*inf*); **her maths is** ~ sie ist schwach in Mathematik.

weaken ['wiːkən] **1** *vt* (*lit, fig*) schwächen; *influence also, control, suspicion etc* verringern; *argument also* entkräften; *walls, foundations* angreifen; *hold* lockern. **he** ~**ed his grip on my arm** er hielt meinen Arm nicht mehr ganz so fest.

2 *vi* (*lit, fig*) schwächer werden, nachlassen; (*person*) schwach *or* weich werden; (*foundations*) nachgeben; (*defence, strength also*) erlahmen. **his grip on my arm** ~**ed** er hielt meinen Arm nicht mehr ganz so fest.

weak-kneed ['wiːk'niːd] *adj* (*after illness*) wackelig auf den Beinen, (*with fear, excitement*) mit weichen Knien; (*fig inf*) schwach, feige.

weakling ['wiːklɪŋ] *n* Schwächling *m*; (*of litter etc*) Schwächste(s) *nt*.

weakly ['wiːklɪ] **1** *adj* (*dated*) schwächlich. **2** *adv* schwach. **he gave in** ~/**he** ~ **gave in to their demands** schwach wie er war, gab er gleich nach/ging er gleich auf ihre Forderungen ein.

weak-minded ['wiːk'maɪndɪd] *adj* **(a)** (*feeble-minded*) schwachsinnig. **(b)** (*weak-willed*) willensschwach.

weakness ['wiːknɪs] *n* (*all senses*) Schwäche *f*; (*weak point*) schwacher Punkt. **the opposition criticised the** ~ **of the country's defences** die Opposition kritisierte, wie schwach die Verteidigung des Landes sei; **to have a** ~ **for sth** für etw eine Schwäche *or* Vorliebe haben.

weak-willed ['wiːk'wɪld] *adj* willensschwach.

weal[1] [wiːl] *n* (*liter*) Wohl *nt*. **the common** *or* **general/public** ~ das Wohl der Allgemeinheit, das Allgemeinwohl, das allgemeine/öffentliche Wohl; ~ **and woe** Wohl und Wehe *nt*.

weal[2] *n* (*welt*) Striemen *m*.

wealth [welθ] *n* (**a**) Reichtum *m*; (*private fortune also*) Vermögen *nt*. ~ **tax** Vermögenssteuer *f*. **(b)** (*fig: abundance*) Fülle *f*.

wealth-creating ['welθkrɪˈeɪtɪŋ] *adj* vermögensbildend.

wealthily ['welθɪlɪ] *adv* wohlhabend.

wealthiness ['welθɪnɪs] *n* Wohlhabenheit *f*.

wealthy ['welθɪ] *adj* (+*er*) wohlhabend, reich; *appearance* wohlhabend; (*having a private fortune also*) vermögend. **the** ~ *pl* die Reichen *pl*.

wean [wiːn] *vt* *baby* entwöhnen. **to** ~ **sb from sb/sth** jdn einer Person (*gen*)/einer Sache (*gen*) entwöhnen (*geh*).

weaning ['wiːnɪŋ] *n* (*of baby*) Entwöhnung *f*.

weapon ['wepən] *n* (*lit, fig*) Waffe *f*.

weaponry ['wepənrɪ] *n* Waffen *pl*.

wear [wɛə^r] (*vb: pret* **wore**, *ptp* **worn**) **1** *n* (**a**) (*use*) **I've had a lot of/I haven't had much** ~ **out of** *or* **from this jacket** (*worn it often/not often*) ich habe diese Jacke viel/wenig getragen; (*it wore well/badly*) ich habe diese Jacke lange/nur kurz getragen; **I've had very good** ~ **from these trousers/this carpet** diese Hosen haben sich sehr gut getragen/dieser Teppich hat sehr lange gehalten; **he got four years'** ~ **out of these trousers/that carpet** diese Hose/dieser Teppich hat vier Jahre lang gehalten; **there isn't much** ~/**there is still a lot of** ~ **left in this coat/carpet** dieser Mantel/Teppich hält noch/nicht mehr lange; **this coat will stand any amount of hard** ~ dieser Mantel ist sehr strapazierfähig; **for hard/long** ~ **nothing beats real leather** nichts ist strapazierfähiger/haltbarer als echtes Leder; **for casual/evening/everyday** ~ für die Freizeit/den Abend/ jeden Tag.

(b) (*clothing*) Kleidung *f*.

(c) (*damage through use*) Abnutzung *f*, Verschleiß *m*. ~ **and tear** Abnutzung *f*, Verschleiß *m*; **fair** ~ **and tear** normale

Abnutzungs- *or* Verschleißerscheinungen; **she couldn't stand the** ~ **and tear on her nerves** sie konnte die nervliche Belastung nicht ertragen; **to show signs of** ~ (*lit*) anfangen, alt auszusehen; (*fig*) angegriffen aussehen; **to look the worse for** ~ (*lit*) (*clothes, curtains, carpets etc*) verschlissen aussehen; (*shoes, clothes*) abgetragen aussehen; (*furniture etc*) abgenutzt aussehen; (*fig*) verbraucht aussehen; **I felt a bit the worse for** ~ ich fühlte mich etwas angeknackst (*inf*) *or* angegriffen.

2 *vt* **(a)** *clothing, jewellery, spectacles, beard etc* tragen. **what shall I** ~? was soll ich anziehen?; **I haven't a thing to** ~! ich habe nichts zum Anziehen *or* nichts anzuziehen; **I haven't worn that for ages** das habe ich schon seit Ewigkeiten nicht mehr angezogen *or* angehabt (*inf*) *or* getragen; **to** ~ **white/rags** *etc* Weiß/Lumpen *etc* tragen, in Weiß/Lumpen *etc* gehen; **he wore an air of triumph/a serious look** (on his face) er trug eine triumphierende/ernste Miene zur Schau; **she always** ~**s a smile** sie trägt stets ein Lächeln auf den Lippen; **he wore a big smile** er strahlte über das ganze Gesicht.

(b) (*reduce to a worn condition*) abnutzen; *clothes* abtragen; *sleeve, knee etc* durchwetzen; *velvet etc* blankwetzen; *leather articles* abwetzen; *steps* austreten; *tyres* abfahren; *engine* kaputtmachen. **to** ~ **holes in sth** etw durchwetzen; (*in shoes*) etw durchlaufen; **the carpet has been worn threadbare** der Teppich ist abgewetzt *or* ganz abgelaufen; **to** ~ **smooth** (*by handling*) abgreifen; (*by walking*) austreten; *pattern* angreifen; *sharp edges* glattmachen; **centuries of storms had worn the inscription smooth** die Inschrift war durch die Stürme im Laufe der Jahrhunderte verwittert; **the sea/the weather had worn the rocks smooth** die See hatte die Felsen glattgewaschen/die Felsen waren verwittert; **the rough edges of the table had been worn smooth by years of use** die rauhen Tischkanten hatten sich durch jahrelangen Gebrauch abgeschliffen; **to have been worn smooth** (*by weather*) verwittert sein; (*by sea*) glattgewaschen sein; (*pattern*) abgegriffen sein; **to** ~ **a path to sb's door** (*fig*) jdm das Haus *or* die Türe einlaufen *or* einrennen (*inf*); **you'll** ~ **a track in the carpet** (*hum*) du machst noch mal eine richtige Bahn *or* einen Trampelpfad (*inf*) in den Teppich; *see also* **worn.**

(c) (*inf: accept, tolerate*) schlucken (*inf*).

3 *vi* **(a)** (*last*) halten; (*dress, shoes etc also*) sich tragen. **she has worn well** (*inf*) sie hat sich gut gehalten (*inf*); **the theory has worn well** die Theorie hat sich bewährt.

(b) (*become worn*) kaputtgehen; (*engine, material also*) sich abnutzen, verbraucht sein; (*tyres also*) abgefahren sein. **the cloth has worn into holes** das Tuch ist ganz zerlumpt *or* zerlöchert; **to** ~ **smooth** (*by water*) glattgewaschen sein; (*by weather*) verwittern; (*pattern*) abgegriffen sein; **the sharp edges will** ~ **smooth in time/with use** die scharfen Kanten werden sich mit der Zeit/im Gebrauch abschleifen; **to** ~ **thin** (*lit*) dünn werden, durchgehen (*inf*); **my patience is** ~**ing thin** meine Geduld ist langsam erschöpft *or* geht langsam zu Ende; **that excuse is** ~**ing thin** diese Ausrede ist (doch) schon etwas alt; *see* **shadow.**

(c) (*proceed gradually*) **the party etc is** ~**ing to its end/towards its close** die Party etc geht dem Ende zu.

♦ **wear away 1** *vt sep* (*erode*) *steps* austreten; *rock* abschleifen, abtragen; (*from underneath*) aushöhlen; *pattern, inscription* tilgen (*geh*), verwischen; (*fig*) *determination* untergraben; *sb's patience* zehren an (+*dat*). **his illness wore him** ~ die Krankheit zehrte an ihm; **he wore his life** ~ **in a boring job** er vergeudete seine Tage in einem langweiligen Beruf.

2 *vi* (*disappear*) (*rocks, rough edges etc*) sich abschleifen; (*inscription*) verwittern; *pattern* verwischen; (*fig: patience, determination*) schwinden.

♦ **wear down 1** *vt sep* **(a)** (*reduce by friction*) abnutzen; *heel* ablaufen, abtreten; *tyre tread* abfahren; *lipstick* verbrauchen; *pencil* verschreiben.

(b) (*fig*) *opposition, strength etc* zermürben; *person also* (*make more amenable*) mürbe *or* weich machen (*inf*); (*tire out, depress*) fix und fertig machen (*inf*).

2 *vi* sich abnutzen; (*heels*) sich ablaufen *or* abtreten; (*tyre tread*) sich abfahren; (*lipstick etc*) sich verbrauchen; (*pencil*) sich verschreiben.

♦ **wear off** *vi* **(a)** (*diminish*) nachlassen, sich verlieren. **don't worry, it'll** ~ keine Sorge, das gibt sich; *see* **novelty.** **(b)** (*disappear*) (*paint*) abgehen; (*plating, gilt*) sich abwetzen.

♦ **wear on** *vi* sich hinziehen, sich (da)hinschleppen; (*year*) voranschreiten. **as the evening/year etc wore** ~ im Laufe des Abends/Jahres *etc*.

♦ **wear out 1** *vt sep* **(a)** kaputtmachen; *carpet also* abtreten; *clothes, shoes* kaputttragen; *record, machinery* abnutzen.

(b) (*fig: exhaust*) (*physically*) erschöpfen, erledigen (*inf*); (*mentally*) fertigmachen (*inf*). **to be worn** ~ erschöpft *or* erledigt sein; (*mentally*) am Ende sein (*inf*); **to** ~ **oneself** ~ sich überanstrengen, sich kaputtmachen (*inf*); **to** ~ **himself** ~ **in the service of his country** er hat sich im Dienst für das Vaterland aufgerieben.

2 *vi* kaputtgehen; (*clothes, curtains, carpets also*) verschleißen. **his patience has worn** ~/**is rapidly** ~**ing** ~ seine Geduld ist erschöpft *or* am Ende/erschöpft sich zusehends.

♦ **wear through 1** *vt sep* durchwetzen; *elbows, trousers also* durchscheuern; *soles of shoes* durchlaufen. **2** *vi* sich durchwetzen; (*elbows, trousers also*) sich durchscheuern; (*soles of shoes*) sich durchlaufen. **his sweater has worn** ~ **at the elbows** sein Pullover ist an den Ellenbogen durchgewetzt.

wearable ['wɛərəbl] *adj* (*not worn out etc*) tragbar. **this young designer's clothes are supremely** ~ die Kleider dieses jungen Modeschöpfers tragen sich ganz ausgezeichnet.

wearer ['wɛərə^r] *n* Träger(in *f*) *m*. ~ **of spectacles** Brillenträger(in *f*) *m*.

wearily ['wɪərɪlɪ] adv see adj.

weariness ['wɪərɪnɪs] n see adj (a) Müdigkeit f; Lustlosigkeit f; Mattigkeit f. he felt a great ~ of life er empfand großen Lebensüberdruß or große Lebensmüdigkeit.

wearing ['wɛərɪŋ] adj (a) ~ apparel (form) (Be)kleidung f. (b) (exhausting) anstrengend; (boring) ermüdend.

wearisome ['wɪərɪsəm] adj ermüdend; climb etc beschwerlich; (bothersome) questions lästig; (tedious) discussion langweilig.

weary ['wɪərɪ] 1 adj (+er) (a) (tired, dispirited) müde; (fed up) lustlos; smile, groan matt. to feel or be ~ müde sein; to be/grow ~ of sth etw leid sein/werden, einer Sache (gen) überdrüssig or müde sein/werden (geh).
  (b) (tiring) wait, routine etc ermüdend. for three ~ hours drei endlose Stunden (lang); five ~ miles fünf lange or beschwerliche Meilen.
  2 vt ermüden.
  3 vi to ~ of sth einer Sache (gen) müde or überdrüssig werden (geh); she wearied of being alone sie wurde es leid or müde (geh) or überdrüssig (geh), allein zu sein.

weasel ['wiːzl] 1 n (a) Wiesel nt. (b) (US inf: person) Heimtücker m. 2 vi (esp US inf: be evasive) schwafeln (inf).
♦ **weasel out** vi (wriggle out) sich rauslavieren (inf) (of aus).

weaselly ['wiːzəlɪ] adj (inf) appearance Fuchs-; (shifty) character aalglatt.

weather ['wɛðər] 1 n Wetter nt; (in ~ reports) Wetterlage f; (climate) Witterung f. in cold/wet/this ~ bei kaltem/nassem/diesem Wetter; what's the ~ like? wie ist das Wetter?; lovely ~ for ducks! bei dem Wetter schwimmt man ja fast weg!; in all ~s bei jedem Wetter, bei jeder Witterung (geh); to be or feel under the ~ (inf) angeschlagen sein (inf); to make heavy ~ of sth (inf) sich mit etw fürchterlich anstellen (inf); to keep a or one's ~ eye open (inf) Ausschau halten (for nach).
  2 vt (a) (storms, winds etc) angreifen; skin gerben. the rock had been ~ed der Fels war verwittert.
  (b) (expose to ~) wood ablagern.
  (c) (survive: also ~ out) crisis, awkward situation überstehen. to ~ (out) the storm abwettern.
  3 vi (rock etc) verwittern; (skin) vom Wetter gegerbt sein/werden; (paint etc) verblassen; (resist exposure to ~) wetterfest sein; (become seasoned: wood) ablagern.

weather in cpds Wetter-; ~-beaten adj face vom Wetter gegerbt; house verwittert; skin wettergegerbt; ~-boarding n, ~-boards npl Schindeln pl; ~-bound adj boat auf Grund der schlechten Wetterverhältnisse manövrierunfähig; ~ bureau n Wetteramt nt; ~ chart n Wetterkarte f; ~-cock n Wetterhahn m.

weathered ['wɛðəd] adj verwittert; skin wettergegerbt.

weather forecast n Wettervorhersage f.

weathering ['wɛðərɪŋ] n (Geol) Verwitterung f.

weather: ~-man n Mann m vom Wetteramt; ~-proof 1 adj wetterfest; 2 vt wetterfest machen; ~ report n Wetterbericht m; ~ ship n Wetterschiff nt; ~ station n Wetterwarte f; ~ vane n Wetterfahne f; ~-wise adv wettermäßig.

weave [wiːv] (vb: pret wove, ptp woven) 1 n (patterns of threads) Webart f; (loosely/tightly etc woven fabric) Gewebe nt. material in a fancy/tight ~ ein Stoff in einer raffinierten/festen Webart; you need a tighter ~ for a skirt für einen Rock braucht man ein festeres Gewebe.
  2 vt (a) thread, cloth etc weben (into zu); cane, flowers, garland flechten (into zu); web spinnen. he wove the threads together er verwob die Fäden miteinander.
  (b) (fig) plot, story ersinnen, erfinden; (add into story etc) details, episode einflechten (into in +acc). he wove a romantic tale round his experiences abroad er spann seine Erlebnisse im Ausland zu einer romantischen Geschichte aus.
  (c) pret also ~d (wind) to ~ one's way through the traffic/to the front sich durch den Verkehr fädeln or schlängeln/nach vorne (durch)schlängeln; the drunk ~d his way down the street der Betrunkene torkelte die Straße hinunter.
  3 vi (a) (lit) weben.
  (b) pret also ~d (twist and turn) sich schlängeln; (drunk) torkeln. to ~ in and out among or through the traffic sich durch den Verkehr schlängeln or fädeln.
  (c) (inf) to get weaving sich ranhalten (inf); to get weaving on sth sich hinter etw (acc) klemmen (inf).

weaver ['wiːvər] n Weber(in f) m.

weaver bird n Webervogel m.

weaving ['wiːvɪŋ] n Weberei f; (as craft) Webkunst f.

web [web] n (a) (lit, fig) Netz nt; (of lies also) Gespinst, Gewebe nt. a ~ of snow-covered branches ein Geflecht nt von schneebedeckten Ästen; a ~ of little streets ein Gewirr nt von kleinen Gassen. (b) (of duck etc) Schwimmhaut f.

webbed [webd] adj (a) foot, toes Schwimm-; animal mit Schwimmfüßen. (b) seats gurtbespannt.

webbing ['webɪŋ] n Gurte pl; (material) Gurtband nt.

web: ~-footed, ~-toed adj schwimmfüßig, mit Schwimmfüßen; ~-offset n Rollenrotations-Offsetdruck m.

Wed abbr of **Wednesday** Mittw.

wed [wed] (old) pret, ptp ~ or ~ded 1 vi sich vermählen (form), trauen.
  2 vt (a) (bride, bridegroom) ehelichen (form), sich vermählen mit (form); (priest) vermählen (form), trauen.
  (b) (fig: combine) paaren. his ability ~ded to her money should make the business a success mit seinen Fähigkeiten und ihrem Geld müßte das Geschäft eigentlich ein Erfolg werden.
  (c) (fig) to be ~ded to sth (devoted) mit etw verheiratet sein; he's ~ded to the view that ... er ist felsenfest der Ansicht, daß ...

we'd [wiːd] contr of **we would; we had**.

wedded ['wedɪd] adj bliss, life Ehe-; see **lawful**.

wedding ['wedɪŋ] n (a) (ceremony) Trauung f; (ceremony and festivities) Hochzeit, Vermählung (form) f; (silver, golden ~ etc) Hochzeit f. to have a registry office/church ~ sich standesamtlich/kirchlich trauen lassen, standesamtlich/kirchlich heiraten; when's the ~? wann ist die Hochzeit, wann wird geheiratet?; to have a quiet ~ in aller Stille heiraten; to go to a ~ zu einer or auf eine Hochzeit gehen.
  (b) (fig) Verbindung f.

wedding in cpds Hochzeits-; ~ anniversary n Hochzeitstag m; ~ breakfast n Hochzeitsessen nt; ~ cake n Hochzeitskuchen m; ~ day n Hochzeitstag m; ~ dress n Brautkleid, Hochzeitskleid nt; ~ march n Hochzeitsmarsch m; ~ night n Hochzeitsnacht f; ~ present n Hochzeitsgeschenk nt; ~ ring n Trauring, Ehering m.

wedge [wedʒ] 1 n (a) (of wood etc, fig) Keil m. rubber ~ Gummibolzen m; it's the thin end of the ~ so fängt's immer an.
  (b) (triangular shape) (of cake etc) Stück nt; (of cheese) Ecke f. a ~ of land ein keilförmiges Stück Land; the seats were arranged in a ~ die Sitzreihen waren keilförmig angeordnet.
  (c) (shoe) Schuh m mit Keilabsatz; (also ~ heel) Keilabsatz m.
  2 vt (a) (fix with a ~) verkeilen, (mit einem Keil) festklemmen. to ~ a door/window open/shut eine Tür/ein Fenster festklemmen or verkeilen; try wedging the cracks with newspaper versuchen Sie, die Spalten mit Zeitungspapier zuzustopfen.
  (b) (fig: pack tightly) to ~ oneself/sth sich/etw zwängen (in in +acc); to be ~d between two things/people zwischen zwei Dingen/Personen eingekeilt or eingezwängt sein; the fat man sat ~d in his chair der dicke Mann saß in seinen Stuhl gezwängt; we were all ~d together in the back of the car wir saßen alle zusammengepfercht or eingezwängt im Fond des Wagens.
♦ **wedge in** vt sep (lit) post festkeilen. to be ~d in (car, house, person etc) eingekeilt or eingezwängt sein; if you park there, you'll ~ me/my car ~ wenn du da parkst, keilst du mich ein/wird mein Auto eingekeilt; he ~d himself ~ between them er zwängte sich zwischen sie.

wedge-shaped ['wedʒʃeɪpt] adj keilförmig.

Wedgwood ® ['wedʒwʊd] n Wedgwood nt. ~ blue/green Wedgwoodblau/-grün.

wedlock ['wedlɒk] n (form) Ehe f. to be born out of/in ~ unehelich/ehelich geboren sein.

Wednesday ['wenzdɪ] n Mittwoch m; see also **Tuesday**.

wee¹ [wiː] adj (+er) (inf) winzig; (Scot) klein. a ~ bit ein kleines bißchen; ~ (small) hours frühe Morgenstunden.

wee² (inf) 1 n to have or do/need a ~ Pipi machen/machen müssen (inf). 2 vi Pipi machen (inf).

weed [wiːd] 1 n (a) Unkraut nt no pl. (b) (dated inf: tobacco) Kraut nt (inf). (c) (sl: marijuana) Gras nt (sl). (d) (inf: person) Schwächling, Kümmerling (inf) m. 2 vt (a) also vi (lit) jäten.
  (b) (fig) see **weed out** (b).
♦ **weed out** vt sep (a) plant ausreißen; flower-bed Unkraut jäten in (+dat). (b) (fig) aussondern; poor candidates, lazy pupils also aussieben.
♦ **weed through** vt sep durchsortieren.

weeding ['wiːdɪŋ] n Unkrautjäten nt. to do some ~ Unkraut jäten.

weed-killer ['wiːdkɪlər] n Unkrautvernichter m, Unkraut-bekämpfungsmittel nt.

weeds [wiːdz] npl (mourning clothes) Trauerkleider pl.

weedy ['wiːdɪ] adj (+er) (a) ground unkrautbewachsen, voll(er) Unkraut. (b) (inf) person (in appearance) schmächtig; (in character) blutarm.

week [wiːk] n Woche f. it'll be ready in a ~ in einer Woche or in acht Tagen ist es fertig; ~ in, ~ out Woche für Woche; twice/£15 a ~ zweimal/£ 15 in der Woche or pro Woche or die Woche (inf); a ~ today, today or this day ~ (dial) heute in einer Woche or in acht Tagen; tomorrow/Tuesday ~, a ~ tomorrow/on Tuesday morgen/Dienstag in einer Woche or in acht Tagen; for ~s wochenlang; to knock sb into the middle of next ~ (inf) jdn windelweich schlagen (inf); a ~'s/a two ~ holiday ein einwöchiger/zweiwöchiger Urlaub; two ~s' holiday zwei Wochen Ferien; that is a ~'s work das ist eine Woche Arbeit.

week: ~-day 1 n Wochentag m; 2 attr Wochentags-, Werktags-; ~-end 1 n Wochenende nt; to go/be away for the ~-end übers or am Wochenende verreisen/nicht da sein; to take a long ~-end ein langes Wochenende machen; 2 attr Wochenend-; ~-end case Wochenendköfferchen nt; 3 vi he ~-ends/~-ended in the country er verbringt seine Wochenenden/verbrachte das Wochenende auf dem Land; ~-ender [,wiːk'endər] n (person) Wochenendler(in f) m; (ticket) Wochenendrückfahrkarte f.

weekly ['wiːklɪ] 1 adj Wochen-; visit allwöchentlich. the ~ shopping expedition der (all)wöchentliche Großeinkauf. 2 adv wöchentlich. 3 n Wochenzeitschrift f.

weeny ['wiːnɪ] adj (+er) (inf) klitzeklein (inf), winzig.

weenybopper ['wiːnɪ,bɒpər] n popbesessenes Kind; Pipi-mädchen nt (pej inf).

weep [wiːp] (vb: pret, ptp wept) 1 vi (a) weinen (over über +acc). to ~ for sb/sth (because sb/sth is missed) um jdn/etw weinen; (out of sympathy) für jdn/etw weinen; he wept for his lost youth er weinte seiner verlorenen Jugend nach; the child was ~ing for his mother das Kind weinte nach seiner Mutter; to ~ with or for joy/rage vor or aus Freude/Wut weinen; I wept to hear the news ich weinte or mir kamen die Tränen, als ich die Nachricht hörte.
  (b) (wound, cut etc) tränen, nässen.
  2 vt tears weinen. to ~ oneself to sleep sich in den Schlaf weinen.
  3 n to have a good/little ~ tüchtig/ein bißchen weinen; after a ~ she felt better nachdem sie geweint hatte, fühlte sie sich besser.

weepie n (inf) see **weepy** 2.

weeping ['wiːpɪŋ] 1 n Weinen nt. 2 adj weinend; wound tränend.

weeping willow n Trauerweide f.

weepy ['wi:pɪ] (inf) **1** adj (+er) person weinerlich; film rührselig. that was a very ~ film (inf) der Film hat schwer auf die Tränendrüsen gedrückt (inf). **2** n Schmachtfetzen m (inf).

weevil ['wi:vl] n Rüsselkäfer m.

wee-wee ['wi:wi:] n, vi (baby-talk) see wee².

weft [weft] n Einschlagfaden, Schußfaden m.

weigh [weɪ] **1** vt **(a)** goods, person, oneself etc wiegen. could you ~ these bananas/this piece for me? könnten Sie mir diese Bananen/dieses Stück abwiegen or auswiegen?
  (b) (fig) words, problem, merits etc abwägen. to ~ **sth in one's mind** etw erwägen; to ~ **A against B** A gegen B abwägen, A und B gegeneinander abwägen.
  (c) (Naut) to ~ **anchor** den Anker lichten.
  2 vi **(a)** wiegen. to ~ **heavy/light** (scales) zu viel/zu wenig anzeigen; (inf: material) schwer/leicht wiegen.
  (b) (fig: be a burden) lasten (on auf +dat).
  (c) (fig: be important) gelten. to ~ **with sb** Gewicht bei jdm haben, jdm etwas gelten; his age ~ed against him in die Waagschale geworfen.

◆**weigh down** vt sep **(a)** (bear down with weight) niederbeugen. the heavy snow ~ed the branches ~ die schwere Schneelast drückte or bog die Zweige nieder; a branch ~ed ~ with fruit ein Ast, der sich unter der Last des Obstes biegt; she was ~ed ~ with parcels/a heavy suitcase sie war mit Paketen überladen/der schwere Koffer zog sie fast zu Boden.
  (b) (fig) niederdrücken. to be ~ed ~ with sorrows von Sorgen niedergedrückt werden, mit Sorgen beladen sein.

◆**weigh in 1** vi **(a)** (Sport) sich (vor dem Kampf/Rennen) wiegen lassen. he ~ed ~ at 70 kilos er brachte 70 Kilo auf die Waage. **(b)** (at airport) das Gepäck (ab)wiegen lassen. **(c)** (fig inf: join in) zu Hilfe kommen (with mit); (interfere) sich einschalten. **2** vt sep luggage wiegen lassen.

◆**weigh out** vt sep abwiegen.

◆**weigh up** vt sep pros and cons, alternatives, situation abwägen; person einschätzen.

weigh: ~bridge n Brückenwaage f; ~-in n (Sport) Wiegen nt. **weighing machine** ['weɪɪŋməˈʃiːn] n (for people) Personenwaage f; (coin-operated) Münzwaage f, Wiegeautomat m; (for goods) Waage f.

weight [weɪt] **1** n **(a)** (heaviness, Phys) Gewicht nt; (Sport, esp Boxing) Gewichtsklasse f, Gewicht nt (inf); (of cloth) Schwere f; (of blow) Wucht, Heftigkeit f. **3 kilos in** ~ 3 Kilo Gewicht, ein Gewicht von 3 Kilo; the grocer gave me short or light ~ der Kaufmann hat mir/ schlecht or knapp gewogen; **100g of flour and the same** ~ **of sugar** 100 g Mehl und die gleiche Menge Zucker; a suit in a heavier ~ for winter ein Anzug in einer schwereren Qualität für den Winter; a blow without much ~ behind it ein Schlag mit wenig or ohne viel Wucht or Kraft dahinter; **to feel/test the** ~ **of sth** sehen/probieren, wie schwer etw ist; the ~ **of the snow made the branches break** die Zweige brachen unter der Schneelast; **to gain or put on/lose** ~ zunehmen/abnehmen; he carries his ~ **well** man sieht ihm sein Gewicht nicht an; I hope the chair takes my ~ ich hoffe, der Stuhl hält mein Gewicht aus; he's worth his ~ **in gold** er ist Gold(es) wert.
  (b) (metal, unit of ~, heavy object) Gewicht nt; (for weighting down also) Beschwerer m. ~s and measures Maße und Gewichte (+pl vb); will he manage to lift the 20kg ~? wird er die 20 Kilo heben können?; the doctor warned him not to lift heavy ~s der Arzt warnte ihn davor, schwere Lasten zu heben; she's quite a ~ sie ist ganz schön schwer.
  (c) (fig: load, burden) Last f. the ~ **of evidence** die Beweislast; they won by ~ **of numbers** sie gewannen durch die zahlenmäßige Überlegenheit; that's a ~ **off my mind** mir fällt ein Stein vom Herzen.
  (d) (fig: importance) Bedeutung f, Gewicht nt. he/his opinion carries no ~ seine Stimme/Meinung hat kein Gewicht or fällt nicht ins Gewicht; those arguments carry ~ **with the minister/carry great** ~ diesen Argumenten mißt der Minister Gewicht bei/wird großes Gewicht beigemessen; to give due ~ **to an argument** einem Argument das entsprechende Gewicht geben or beimessen; to add ~ **to sth** einer Sache (dat) zusätzliches Gewicht geben or verleihen; to pull one's ~ seinen Teil dazutun, seinen Beitrag leisten; to put one's full ~ **behind sb/sth** sich mit seinem ganzen Gewicht or mit dem ganzen Gewicht seiner Persönlichkeit für jdn/etw einsetzen; to throw or chuck (inf) one's ~ **about** seinen Einfluß geltend machen.
  2 vt **(a)** (make heavier, put ~s on) beschweren.
  (b) (fig: bias) results verfälschen. to ~ **sth in favour of/against sb** etw zugunsten einer Person/gegen jdn beeinflussen; to ~ **sth in favour of/against sth** etw zugunsten einer Sache/gegen etw beeinflussen; to be ~ed in favour of sb/sth so angelegt sein, daß es zugunsten einer Person/Sache ist; to be ~ed against sb/sth jdn/etw benachteiligen.

◆**weight down** vt sep person (with parcels etc) überladen; corpse beschweren; (fig) belasten, niederdrücken.

weightily ['weɪtɪlɪ] adv gewichtig.

weightiness ['weɪtɪnɪs] n (lit) Gewicht nt; (fig) Gewichtigkeit f; (of responsibility also) Schwere f.

weighting ['weɪtɪŋ] n (Brit: supplement) Zulage f.

weight: ~less adj schwerelos; ~lessness n Schwerelosigkeit f; ~lifter n Gewichtheber m; ~lifting n Gewichtheben nt.

weighty ['weɪtɪ] adj (+er) **(a)** (lit) schwer. **(b)** (fig) gewichtig; (influential) argument also schwerwiegend; (burdensome) responsibility also schwerwiegend, schwer.

weir [wɪə^r] n **(a)** (barrier) Wehr nt. **(b)** (fish trap) Fischreuse f.

weird [wɪəd] adj (+er) (uncanny) unheimlich; (inf: odd) seltsam.

weirdie ['wɪədɪ] n (sl) verrückter Typ (inf).

weirdly ['wɪədlɪ] adv see adj.

weirdness ['wɪədnɪs] n (inf: oddness) Seltsamkeit f.

weirdo ['wɪədəʊ] n (sl) verrückter Typ (inf).

welch vi see welsh.

welcome ['welkəm] **1** n Willkommen nt. to give sb a hearty or warm ~ jdm einen herzlichen Empfang bereiten; to meet with a cold/warm ~ kühl/herzlich empfangen werden, einen kühlen/herzlichen Empfang bekommen; to bid sb ~ (form) jdm ein Willkommen entbieten (geh); what sort of a ~ will this product get from the public? wie wird das Produkt von der Öffentlichkeit aufgenommen werden?
  2 adj **(a)** (received with pleasure, pleasing) willkommen; visitor also gerngesehen attr; news also angenehm. the money is very ~ just now das Geld kommt gerade jetzt sehr gelegen; to make sb ~ jdn sehr freundlich aufnehmen or empfangen; to make sb feel ~ jdm das Gefühl geben, ein willkommener or gerngesehener Gast zu sein; you will always be ~ here Sie sind uns (dat) jederzeit willkommen; I didn't feel very ~ there ich habe mich dort nicht sehr wohl gefühlt.
  (b) you're ~! nichts zu danken!, keine Ursache!, bitte sehr!, aber gerne!, (iro) von mir aus gerne!, wenn's Ihnen Spaß macht!; you're ~ to use my room Sie können gerne mein Zimmer benutzen; you're ~ to try (lit, iro) Sie können es gerne versuchen; you're ~ to it! (lit, iro) von mir aus herzlich gerne!
  3 vt (lit, fig) begrüßen, willkommen heißen (geh). to ~ **sb to one's house** jdn bei sich zu Hause or in seinem Haus begrüßen or willkommen heißen (geh); they ~d him home with a big party sie veranstalteten zu seiner Heimkehr ein großes Fest.
  4 interj ~ **home/to Scotland/on board!** herzlich willkommen!, willkommen daheim/in Schottland/an Bord!

welcome-home ['welkəm'həʊm] adj attr party Begrüßungs-, Willkommens-.

welcoming ['welkəmɪŋ] adj zur Begrüßung; smile, gesture einladend. a ~ **cup of tea was on the table for her** eine Tasse Tee stand zu ihrer Begrüßung auf dem Tisch; a ~ **fire blazed in the hearth when he arrived** ein warmes Feuer begrüßte ihn bei seiner Ankunft; the crowds raised a ~ **cheer for him** die Menge jubelte ihm zur Begrüßung zu.

weld [weld] **1** vt **(a)** (Tech) schweißen. to ~ **parts together** Teile zusammenschweißen or verschweißen; to ~ **sth on etw** anschweißen (to an +acc); ~ed joint Schweißnaht f.
  (b) (fig: also ~ **together**) zusammenschmieden (into zu).
  2 vi sich schweißen lassen.
  3 n Schweißnaht, Schweißstelle f.

welder ['weldə^r] n (person) Schweißer(in f) m; (machine) Schweißapparat m, Schweißgerät nt.

welding ['weldɪŋ] n Schweißen nt. ~ **torch** Schweißbrenner m.

welfare ['welfeə^r] n **(a)** (well-being) Wohl, Wohlergehen nt. **(b)** (~ **work, social security**) Fürsorge, Wohlfahrt (dated) f. **child/social** ~ Kinderfürsorge f/soziale Fürsorge.

welfare: ~ **state** n Wohlfahrtsstaat m; ~ **work** n Fürsorgearbeit, Wohlfahrtsarbeit (dated) f; ~ **worker** n Fürsorger(in f) m.

well¹ [wel] **1** n **(a)** (water ~) Brunnen m; (oil ~) Ölquelle f; (drilled) Bohrloch nt; (fig: source) Quelle f. to drive or sink a ~ einen Brunnen bohren or anlegen or graben; ein Bohrloch anlegen or vorantreiben.
  (b) (shaft) (for lift) Schacht m; (for stairs) Treppenschacht m; (down centre of staircase) Treppenhaus nt.
  (c) (of theatre) Parkett nt; (of auditorium) ebenerdiger Teil des Zuschauer-/Konferenz-/Versammlungsraums; (Brit: of court) Teil des Gerichtssaals, in dem die Rechtsanwälte und Protokollschreiber sitzen.
  (d) (ink~) Tintenfaß nt.
  2 vi quellen.

◆**well up** vi (water, liquid) emporsteigen, emporquellen; (fig) aufsteigen; (noise) anschwellen. tears ~ed ~ in her eyes Tränen stiegen or schossen ihr in die Augen.

well² comp **better**, superl **best 1** adv **(a)** (in a good or satisfactory manner) gut. the child speaks ~ (is ~ spoken) das Kind spricht ordentlich Deutsch/Englisch or gutes Deutsch/Englisch; it is ~ painted (portrait) es ist gut gemalt; (house, fence) es ist sauber or ordentlich angestrichen; he did it as ~ as he could/I could have done er machte es so gut er konnte/ ebenso gut, wie ich es hätte machen können; he's doing ~ at school/in maths er ist gut or er kommt gut voran in der Schule/ in Mathematik; he did ~ in the maths exam er hat in der Mathematikprüfung gut abgeschnitten; for an eight-year-old he did very ~ für einen Achtjährigen hat er seine Sache sehr gut gemacht; his business is doing ~ sein Geschäft geht gut; mother and child are/the patient is doing ~ Mutter und Kind/dem Patienten geht es gut, Mutter und Kind sind/der Patient ist wohlauf; he did quite ~ at improving sales er war recht erfolgreich in der Erhöhung des Absatzes; if you do ~ you'll be promoted wenn Sie sich bewähren, werden Sie befördert; you did ~ to help du tatest gut daran zu helfen, es war gut, daß du geholfen hast; ~ done! gut gemacht!, bravo!, sehr gut!; ~ played! gut gespielt!; to do oneself ~ (inf) es sich (dat) gut gehen lassen; to do ~ by sb (inf) jdm gegenüber or zu jdm großzügig sein; everything went ~/quite ~ es ging alles gut or glatt (inf)/recht gut or ganz gut or ganz ordentlich.
  (b) (favourably, fortunately) gut. to speak/think ~ of sb über jdn Gutes sagen/Positives denken, von jdm positiv sprechen/ denken; to be ~ spoken of in certain circles/by one's colleagues einen guten Ruf in gewissen Kreisen haben/bei seinen Kollegen in gutem Ruf stehen; to stand ~ with sb bei jdm angesehen sein; to be ~ in with sb (inf) auf gutem Fuß mit jdm stehen; to marry ~ eine gute Partie machen; to do ~ out of sth von etw ganz schön or ordentlich profitieren, bei etw gut wegkommen (inf); you would do ~ to arrive early Sie täten gut daran, früh zu kommen; you might as ~ go du könntest eigentlich geradesogut or ebensogut (auch) gehen; are you coming? — I might as ~ kommst du? — ach, könnte ich eigentlich (auch) (inf) or ach, warum nicht.

(c) (*thoroughly, considerably, to a great degree*) gut, gründlich. **shake the bottle** ~ schütteln Sie die Flasche kräftig; (*on medicine*) Flasche kräftig *or* gut schütteln; **he loved her too ~ to leave her** (*liter*) er liebte sie zu sehr, als daß er sie verlassen hätte; **we were ~ beaten** wir sind gründlich geschlagen worden; **he could ~ afford it** er konnte es sich (*dat*) sehr wohl leisten; **I'm ~ content with my lot** ich bin wohl zufrieden mit meinem Schicksal; **all *or* only too ~ nur** (all)zu gut; ~ **and truly** (*ganz*) gründlich; *married, settled in* ganz richtig; (*iro also*) fest; *westernized, conditioned* durch und durch; **he was ~ away** (*inf*) er war in Fahrt *or* Schwung (*inf*); (*drunk*) er hatte einen sitzen (*inf*); **he sat ~ forward in his seat** er saß weit vorne auf seinem Sitz; **it's ~ worth the trouble** das hat sich wohl *or* sehr gelohnt; ~ **out of sight** ein gutes Stück *or* weit außer Sichtweite; ~ **within ...** durchaus in (+*dat*); ~ **past midnight** lange *or* ein gutes Stück (*inf*) nach Mitternacht; **he's ~ over fifty** er ist einiges *or* weit über fünfzig; ~ **over a thousand** weit mehr als *or* weit über tausend.

(d) (*probably, reasonably*) ohne weiteres, gut, wohl. **I may ~ be late** es kann leicht *or* wohl or ohne weiteres sein, daß ich spät komme; **it may ~ be that ...** es ist gut *or* wohl *or* ohne weiteres möglich, daß ...; **you may ~ be right** Sie mögen wohl recht haben; **she cried, as ~ she might** sie weinte, und das (auch) mit Grund *or* wozu sie auch allen Grund hatte; **you may ~ ask!** (*iro*) das kann man wohl fragen; **I couldn't very ~ stay** ich konnte wohl nicht mehr gut bleiben.

(e) (*in addition*) as ~ auch; **if he comes as ~** wenn er auch kommt; **x as ~ as y** x sowohl als auch y, x und auch y; **she sings as ~ as** dances sie singt und tanzt auch noch.

2 *adj* (a) (*in good health*) gesund. **get ~ soon!** gute Besserung; **are you ~?** geht es Ihnen gut?; **I'm very ~, thanks** danke, es geht mir sehr gut; **he's not a ~ man** er ist gar nicht gesund; **she's not been ~ lately** ihr ging es in letzter Zeit (gesundheitlich) gar nicht gut; **I don't feel at all ~** ich fühle mich gar nicht gut *or* wohl.

(b) (*satisfactory, desirable, advantageous*) gut. **all is not ~ with him/in the world** mit ihm/mit *or* in der Welt steht es nicht zum besten; **that's all very ~, but ...** das ist ja alles schön und gut, aber ...; **if that's the case, (all) ~ and good** wenn das der Fall ist, dann soll es mir recht sein; **it's all very ~ for you to suggest ...** Sie können leicht vorschlagen ...; **it's all very ~ for you, you don't have to ...** Sie können leicht reden, *Sie* können leicht reden, Sie müssen ja nicht ...; **it was ~ for him that no-one found out** es war sein Glück, daß es niemand entdeckt hat; **it would be as ~ to ask first** es wäre wohl besser *or* gescheiter (*inf*), sich erst mal zu erkundigen; **it's just as ~ he came** es ist (nur *or* schon) gut, daß er gekommen ist; **you're ~ out of that** seien Sie froh, daß Sie damit nichts/nichts mehr zu tun haben; **all's ~ that ends ~** Ende gut, alles gut.

3 *interj* also; (*expectantly also*) na; (*doubtfully*) na ja. ~ ~ ~!, ~ **I never (did)!** also, so was!, na so was!; ~ **now also;** ~, **it was like this also,** es war so *or* folgendermaßen; ~ **there you are, that proves it!** na bitte *or* also bitte, das beweist es doch; ~, **as I was saying** also, wie (bereits) gesagt; ~ **then also** (gut); (*in question*) na?, nun?, also?; **very ~ then!** na gut, also gut!; (*indignantly*) also bitte (sehr); ~, **that's a relief!** na (also), das ist ja eine Erleichterung!

4 *n* Gute(s) *nt*. **to wish sb ~** (*in general*) jdm alles Gute wünschen; (*in an attempt, iro*) jdm Glück wünschen (in bei); (*be well-disposed to*) jdm gewogen sein; **I wish him ~, but ...** ich wünsche ihm nichts Böses, aber ...

we'll [wiːl] *contr of* we shall; we will.

well *in cpds* gut; ~**-adjusted** *adj* (*Psych*) gut angepaßt; ~**-advised** *adj plan, move* klug; **to be ~-advised to ...** wohl *or* gut beraten sein *or* gut daran tun, zu ...; ~**-aimed** *adj shot, blow, sarcasm* gut- *or* wohlgezielt *attr*; ~**-appointed** *adj* gut ausgestattet; ~**-argued** *adj* wohl- *or* gutbegründet *attr*; ~**-balanced** *adj* (a) *person, mind* ausgeglichen; (b) *scheme, budget, diet* (gut) ausgewogen; ~**-behaved** *adj child* artig, wohlerzogen; *animal* guterzogen *attr*; ~**-being** *n* Wohl, Wohlergehen *nt*; **to have a sense of ~-being** (ein Gefühl der) Behaglichkeit *or* Wohligkeit empfinden; ~**-born** *adj* aus vornehmer Familie, aus vornehmem Haus; ~**-bred** *adj* (a) (*polite*) *person* wohlerzogen; *manners* vornehm, gepflegt; *accent* distinguiert; (b) (*of good stock*) *animal* aus guter Zucht; (*iro*) *person* aus gutem Stall; ~**-built** *adj house* gut *or* solide gebaut; *person* stämmig, kräftig; ~**-chosen** *adj remarks, words* gut *or* glücklich gewählt; **in a few ~-chosen words** in wenigen wohlgesetzten Worten; ~**-connected** *adj* mit Beziehungen zu *or* in höheren Kreisen; **to be ~-connected** Beziehungen zu *or* in höheren Kreisen haben; ~**-deserved** *adj* wohlverdient; ~**-developed** *adj arm, muscle* gutentwickelt *attr*; *sense* (gut) ausgeprägt; ~**-disposed** *adj* **to be ~-disposed towards sb/sth** jdm/einer Sache gewogen sein *or* freundlich gesonnen sein; ~**-done** *adj steak* durchgebraten, durch *inv*; ~**-dressed** *adj* gut angezogen *or* gekleidet; ~**-earned** *adj* wohlverdient; ~**-educated** *adj person* gebildet; *voice* (gut) ausgebildet; ~**-equipped** *adj office, studio* gut ausgestattet; *expedition, army* gut ausgerüstet; ~**-established** *adj practice, custom* fest; *tradition* alt; ~**-favoured** *adj* (*old*) *girl, family* ansehnlich (*old*); ~**-fed** *adj* wohl- *or* gutgenährt *attr*; ~**-founded** *adj* wohlbegründet *attr*; ~**-groomed** *adj* gepflegt; ~**-grown** *adj animal, child* groß (gewachsen); ~**-head** *n* (a) (*of spring etc*) Quelle *f*; (*fig*) Ursprung *m*; (b) (*head of oilwell*) Bohrturm *m*; ~**-heeled** *adj* (*inf*) betucht; ~**-hung** *adj meat* abgehangen; *man* mit imposanter Männlichkeit, gut ausgestattet; ~**-informed** *adj* gutinformiert *attr*; *sources also* wohlunterrichtet *attr*; **to be ~-informed about sb/sth** über jdn/etw gut informiert *or* gut unterrichtet sein.

wellington (boot) [ˈwelɪŋtən(ˈbuːt)] *n* (*Brit*) Gummistiefel *m*.

well: ~**-intentioned** *adj see* ~**-meaning;** ~**-kept** *adj garden, hair etc* gepflegt; *secret* streng gehütet, gutgewahrt *attr*; ~**-knit** *adj*

body drahtig, straff; (*fig*) gut durchdacht *or* aufgebaut; ~**-known** *adj place, singer* bekannt; *fact also* wohl- *or* altbekannt; **it's ~-known that ...** es ist allgemein bekannt, daß ...; ~**-loved** *adj* vielgeliebt; ~**-mannered** *adj* mit guten Manieren; **to be ~-mannered** gute Manieren haben; ~**-matched** *adj teams, opponents* gleich stark; **they're a ~-matched pair** sie passen gut zusammen; ~**-meaning** *adj* wohlmeinend *attr*; ~**-meant** *adj action, lie* gutgemeint *attr*; ~**-nigh** *adv* (*form*) nahezu, beinahe, nachgerade (*old*); **this is ~-nigh impossible** das ist nahezu *or* beinahe unmöglich; ~**-off** 1 *adj* (a) (*affluent*) reich, begütert, gut d(a)ran (*inf*); (b) *pred* (*fortunate*) gut daran; **you don't know when you're ~-off** (*inf*) du weißt (ja) nicht, wann es dir gut geht; **2** *n* **the ~-off** *pl* die Begüterten *pl*; ~**-oiled** *adj* (*inf: drunk*) beduselt (*inf*); ~**-preserved** *adj* guterhalten *attr*; *person also* wohlerhalten *attr*; ~**-read** *adj* belesen; ~**-spent** *adj time* gut genützt *or* verbracht; *money* sinnvoll *or* vernünftig ausgegeben *or* verwendet; ~**-spoken** *adj* mit gutem Deutsch/Englisch *etc*; **to be ~-spoken** gutes Deutsch/ Englisch *etc* sprechen; ~**-stacked** *adj* (*sl*) *woman* mit Holz vor der Hütte (*inf*); **to be ~-stacked** Holz vor der Hütte haben (*inf*); ~**-stocked** *adj* gutbestückt *attr*; (*Comm also*) mit gutem Sortiment; *larder, shelves also* gutgefüllt *attr*, reichlich gefüllt; *library also* reichhaltig, umfangreich; ~**-thought-of** *adj* angesehen; ~**-timed** *adj* (*zeitlich*) gut abgepaßt, zeitlich günstig; **that was a ~-timed interruption** die Unterbrechung kam im richtigen Augenblick; ~**-to-do 1** *adj* wohlhabend, reich; *district* Reichen-, Vornehmen-; **2** *n* **the ~-to-do** *pl* die Begüterten *pl*; ~ **water** *n* Brunnenwasser *nt*; ~**-wisher** *n cards from* ~-wishers Briefe von Leuten, die ihm/ihr *etc* alles Gute wünschen; **our cause has many ~-wishers** unsere Sache hat viele Sympathisanten; **"from a ~-wisher"** „jemand, der es gut mit Ihnen meint"; ~**-worn** *adj garment* abgetragen; *carpet etc* abgelaufen; *book* abgenützt, abgegriffen; *path* ausgetreten; *saying, subject etc* abgedroschen.

welly [ˈwelɪ] *n* (*inf*) Gummistiefel *m*.

Welsh [welʃ] **1** *adj* walisisch. **2** *n* (a) (*language*) Walisisch *nt*. (b) **the ~** *pl* die Waliser *pl*.

welsh, welch [welʃ] *vi* (*sl*) sich drücken (*on sth* vor etw *dat*) (*inf*); (*bookmaker* etc: *avoid payment*) die Gewinne nicht ausbezahlen (*on sb* jdm); (*by disappearing*) mit dem Geld durchgehen (*inf*). **to ~ on sb** jdn (auf)sitzen lassen (*inf*).

Welsh: ~ **dresser** *n* Anrichte *f* mit Tellerbord; ~**man** *n* Waliser *m*; ~ **rabbit** *or* **rarebit** *n* überbackene Käseschnitte; ~**woman** *n* Waliserin *f*.

welt [welt] *n* (a) (*of shoe*) Rahmen *m*; (*of pullover*) Bündchen *nt*. (b) (*weal*) Striemen *m*.

welted [ˈweltɪd] *adj shoe* randgenäht.

welter [ˈweltər] (*liter*) **1** *n* Unzahl *f*; (*of blood, cheers*) Meer *nt*; (*of emotions*) Sturm, Tumult *m*; (*of verbiage*) Flut *f*.
2 *vi* (*in mud, blood etc*) sich wälzen. **to ~ in sin** in einem Sündenpfuhl leben; **to ~ in sorrow** sich (rückhaltlos) seinem Schmerz hingeben.

welterweight [ˈweltəweɪt] *n* Weltergewicht *nt*.

wench [wentʃ] **1** *n* (*old*) Maid *f* (*old*); (*serving* ~) Magd *f*; (*hum*) Frauenzimmer *nt*. **2** *vi* sich mit Mädchen herumtreiben.

wend [wend] *vt* **to ~ one's way home/to the pub** *etc* sich auf den Heimweg/zur Wirtschaft *etc* begeben.

Wendy house [ˈwendɪˌhaus] *n* Spielhaus *nt*.

went [went] *pret of* go.

wept [wept] *pret, ptp of* weep.

were [wɜː] *2nd pers sing, 1st, 2nd, 3rd pers pl pret of* be.

we're [wɪər] *contr of* we are.

weren't [wɜːnt] *contr of* were not.

werewolf [ˈwɪəwulf] *n* Werwolf *m*.

wert [wɜːt] (*old*) *2nd pers sing pret of* be.

Wesleyan [ˈwezlɪən] **1** *adj* wesleyanisch. **2** *n* Wesleyaner(in *f*) *m*.

west [west] **1** *n* (a) Westen *m*. **in/to the ~** im Westen/nach *or* gen (*liter*) Westen; **to the ~ of** westlich von, im Westen von; **he comes from the ~ (of Ireland)** er kommt aus dem Westen (von Irland); **the wind is blowing from the ~** der Wind kommt von West(en) *or* aus (dem) Westen.
(b) (*western world*) **the ~** *or* **W~** der Westen.
2 *adj* West-, westlich.
3 *adv* (a) nach Westen, westwärts. **it faces ~** es geht nach Westen; ~ **of** westlich von.
(b) **to go ~** (*fig inf*) flöten gehen (*sl*); (*to die*) vor die Hunde gehen (*sl*).

west *in cpds* West-; **W~ Berlin** *n* West-Berlin *nt*; ~**-bound** *adj traffic, carriageway* in Richtung Westen; **to be ~-bound nach** Westen unterwegs sein, westwärts reisen *or* fahren; ~**-by-north/south** *n* West über Nord/Süd *no art*.

westerly [ˈwestəlɪ] **1** *adj* westlich. **2** *n* (*wind*) Westwind, West (*poet*) *m*.

western [ˈwestən] **1** *adj* (*all senses*) westlich. **on the W~ front** an der Westfront; **W~ Europe** Westeuropa *nt*. **2** *n* Western *m*.

westerner [ˈwestənər] *n* (a) (*Pol*) Abendländer(in *f*) *m*. (b) (*US*) Weststaatler *m*.

westernization [ˌwestənaɪˈzeɪʃən] *n* (*westernizing*) Einführung *f* der westlichen Kultur *or* Zivilisation; (*western character*) westliche Zivilisation *f*; (*pej*) Verwestlichung *f*.

westernize [ˈwestənaɪz] *vt* die westliche Zivilisation/Kultur einführen in (+*dat*); (*pej*) verwestlichen.

westernized [ˈwestənaɪzd] *adj person, culture* vom Westen beeinflußt, westlich ausgerichtet; (*pej*) verwestlicht.

westernmost [ˈwestənməust] *adj* westlichste(r, s), am weitesten westlich (gelegen).

west: **W~ Germany** *n* Westdeutschland *nt*, Bundesrepublik *f* (Deutschland); **W~ Indian 1** *adj* westindisch; **2** *n* Westindier(in *f*) *m*; **W~ Indies** *npl* Westindische Inseln *pl*; ~**-north-~** *n* Westnordwest *no art*.

Westphalia [west'feɪlɪə] n Westfalen nt.
Westphalian [west'feɪlɪən] **1** adj westfälisch. **2** n Westfale m, Westfälin f.
west: ~-**south**-~ n Westsüdwest no art; ~**ward(s)** ['westwəd(z)], ~**wardly** [-wədlɪ] **1** adj westlich; in a ~**wardly direction** nach Westen, (in) Richtung Westen; **2** adv westwärts, nach Westen.
wet [wet] (vb: pret, ptp ~ or ~**ted**) **1** adj (+er) **(a)** naß. **to be** ~ (paint, varnish, ink) naß or feucht sein; **to be** ~ **through** durch und durch naß sein, völlig durchnäßt sein; ~ **with tears** tränenfeucht; **her eyes were** ~ **with tears** sie hatte feuchte Augen, sie hatte Tränen in den Augen; **"~ paint"** „Vorsicht, frisch gestrichen"; **to get one's feet** ~ nasse Füße bekommen, sich (dat) nasse Füße holen (inf); **to be** ~ **behind the ears** (inf) noch feucht or noch nicht trocken hinter den Ohren sein (inf).
(b) (rainy) naß, feucht; climate, country feucht. **the** ~ **season** die Regenzeit; **in** ~ **weather** bei nassem Wetter, bei Regenwetter; **it's been** ~ **all week** es war die ganze Woche (über) regnerisch.
(c) (allowing alcohol) state, city wo kein Alkoholverbot besteht, nicht prohibitionistisch. **the area is still not** ~ in dieser Gegend ist immer noch kein Alkoholausschank (erlaubt).
(d) (Brit inf: weak, spiritless) weichlich, lasch. **don't be so** ~! sei nicht so ein or kein solcher Waschlappen! (inf).
2 n **(a)** (moisture) Feuchtigkeit f.
(b) (rain) Nässe f. **it's out in the** ~ es ist draußen im Nassen.
(c) (inf: ~ season) Regenzeit f.
(d) (US inf: anti-prohibitionist) Antiprohibitionist(in f) m.
(e) (Brit sl: person) Waschlappen m (inf).
3 vt naß machen; lips, washing befeuchten. **to** ~ **the baby's head** (inf) den Sohn/die Tochter begießen (inf); **to** ~ **one's whistle** (inf) sich (dat) die Kehle anfeuchten (inf); **to** ~ **the bed/one's pants/oneself** das Bett/seine Hosen/sich naß machen, ins Bett/in die Hose(n) machen; **I nearly** ~ **myself** (inf) ich habe mir fast in die Hose gemacht (inf).
wet: ~-**and-dry** n Schmirgelpapier nt; **2** vt (naß)schmirgeln; ~**blanket** n (inf) Miesmacher(in f) (inf), Spielverderber(in f) m; ~ **cell** n Naßelement nt; ~ **dock** n Dock, Flutbecken nt; ~ **dream** n feuchter Traum, kalter Bauer (sl).
wether ['weðəʳ] n Hammel, Schöps (dial) m.
wet-look ['wetlʊk] adj Hochglanz-.
wetly ['wetlɪ] adv **(a)** naß. **(b)** (Brit inf) weich, lasch.
wetness ['wetnɪs] n **(a)** Nässe f; (of weather also, climate, paint, ink) Feuchtigkeit f. **(b)** (Brit inf) Weichlichkeit f.
wet: ~-**nurse** n Amme f; ~**suit** n Neoprenanzug, Taucheranzug m.
wetting ['wetɪŋ] **1** n unfreiwillige Dusche (inf); (falling into water) unfreiwilliges Bad. **to get a** ~ klatschnaß werden, eine Dusche abbekommen (inf); ein unfreiwilliges Bad nehmen; **to give sb a** ~ jdm eine Dusche/ein Bad verabreichen (inf).
2 adj (Chem) ~ **agent** Netzmittel nt.
we've [wiːv] contr of **we have**.
whack [wæk] **1** n **(a)** (blow) (knallender) Schlag. **to give sb/sth a** ~ jdm einen Schlag versetzen/auf etw (acc) schlagen.
(b) (inf: attempt) Versuch m. **to have a** ~ **at sth/at doing sth** etw probieren or versuchen, sich an etw (dat) versuchen; **I'll have a** ~ **at it** ich will mich mal (d)ranwagen.
(c) (inf: share) (An)teil m.
2 vt **(a)** (hit) schlagen, hauen (inf).
(b) (inf: defeat) (haushoch) schlagen.
(c) (inf: exhaust) erschlagen (inf).
whacked [wækt] adj (inf: exhausted) kaputt (inf).
whacking ['wækɪŋ] **1** adj (Brit inf) lie, defeat, meal Mords- (inf). **a** ~ **great spider/a** ~ **big book** ein Mordstrumm nt (inf) von einer Spinne/von (einem) Buch.
2 n **(a)** (beating) Keile f (inf). **to give sb a** ~ jdm Keile or eine Tracht Prügel verpassen (inf).
(b) (inf: defeat) **we got a real** ~ **from their team** die Mannschaft hat uns richtig in die Pfanne gehauen (inf).
whacko ['wækəʊ] interj (dated) trefflich (dated), tipp-topp, Ia.
whacky adj (+er) (inf) see **wacky**.
whale [weɪl] **1** n **(a)** Wal m. **(b)** (inf: exceedingly great, good etc) **a** ~ **of** ein Riesen-, ein(e) riesige(r, s); **a** ~ **of a difference** ein himmelweiter Unterschied; **to have a** ~ **of a time** sich prima amüsieren.
whale: ~**bone** n Fischbein nt; ~ **fishing** n Wal(fisch)fang m; ~ **oil** n Walöl nt, Tran m.
whaler ['weɪləʳ] n (person, ship) Walfänger m.
whaling ['weɪlɪŋ] n Wal(fisch)fang m. **to go** ~ auf Walfang gehen; ~ **ship** Walfänger m, Walfangboot, Walfangschiff nt; ~ **station** Walfangstation f.
wham [wæm], **whang** [wæŋ] **1** interj wumm. **2** n (blow) Schlag m; (bang, thump) Knall m. **3** vt (hit) schlagen; (bang, thump) knallen. **4** vi knallen. **to** ~ **into sth auf etw (acc) krachen (inf).
wharf [wɔːf] n, pl -s or **wharves** [wɔːvz] Kai m.
what [wɒt] **1** pron **(a)** (interrog) was. ~ **is this called?** wie heißt das?, wie nennt man das?; ~'s **the weather like?** wie ist das Wetter?; ~ **do 4 and 3 make?** wieviel ist or macht 4 und or plus 3?; **you need (a)** ~? was brauchen Sie?; ~ **is now?**, ~ **do you want now?** was ist denn?; ~'s **that (you/he etc said)?** was hast du/hat er da gerade gesagt?, wie or was war das noch mal (inf)?; ~'s **that to you?** was geht dich das an?; ~ **for?** wozu?, wofür?; ~'s **that tool for?** wofür ist das Werkzeug?; ~ **are you looking at me like that for?** warum or was (inf) siehst du mich denn so an?; ~ **did you do that for?** warum hast du denn das gemacht?; ~ **about ...?** wie wär's mit ...?; **well,** ~ **about it? are we going?** na, wie ist's, gehen wir?; **you know that pub?** — ~ **about it?** kennst du die Wirtschaft? — was ist damit?; ~ **of** or **about it?** na und? (inf); ~ **if ...?** was ist, wenn ...?; **so** ~? (inf) ja or na und?; ~ **does it matter?** was macht das schon?; ~-**d'you(- ma)-call-him/-her/-it** (inf), ~'s-**his/-her/-its name** (inf) wie heißt er/sie/es gleich or schnell.

(b) (rel) was. **he knows** ~ **it is to suffer** er weiß, was leiden heißt or ist; **that is not** ~ **I asked for** danach habe ich nicht gefragt; **that's exactly** ~ **I want/said** genau das möchte ich/habe ich gesagt; **do you know** ~ **you are looking for?** weißt du, wonach du suchst?; **come** ~ **may** komme was wolle; ~ **I'd like is a cup of tea** was ich jetzt gerne hätte, (das) wäre ein Tee; ~ **with x and y ...** und dazu mit x und y, da ...; ~ **with one thing and the other** und wie es sich dann so ergab/ergibt, wie das so ist or geht; **and** ~'s **more** und außerdem, und noch dazu; **he knows** ~'s ~ (inf) er kennt sich aus, der weiß Bescheid (inf); **(I'll) tell you** ~ (inf) weißt du was?; **and** ~ **not** (inf), **and** ~ **have you** (inf) und was sonst noch (alles), und was weiß ich; **to give sb** ~ **for** (inf) es jdm ordentlich geben (inf).
(c) (with vb +prep see also there) ~ **did he agree/object to?** wozu hat er zugestimmt/wogegen or gegen was hat er Einwände erhoben?; **he agreed/objected to** ~ **we suggested** er stimmte unseren Vorschlägen zu/lehnte unsere Vorschläge ab, er lehnte ab, was wir vorschlugen; **he didn't know** ~ **he was agreeing/objecting to** er wußte nicht, wozu er zustimmte/was er ablehnte; **she fell in with** ~ **everyone else wanted/he had said** sie schloß sich den Wünschen der Allgemeinheit an/sie schloß sich dem, was er gesagt hatte, an; **he didn't go into** ~ **he meant** er erläuterte nicht im einzelnen, was er meinte.
2 adj **(a)** (interrog) welche(r, s), was für (ein/eine) (inf). ~ **age is he?** wie alt ist er?; ~ **good would that be?** (inf) was sollte das gut sein?; ~ **book do you want?** was für ein Buch wollen Sie?; ~ **time is it?** wieviel Uhr ist es?, wie spät ist es?
(b) (rel) der/die/das. ~ **little I had** das wenige, das ich hatte; **buy** ~ **food you like** kauf das Essen, das du willst.
(c) (in set constructions) ~ **sort of** was für ein/eine; ~ **else** was noch, ~ **more** was mehr.
(d) (in interj: also iro) was für (ein/eine). ~ **a man!** was für ein or welch ein (geh) Mann!; ~ **luck!** welch(es) Glück, was für ein Glück, so ein Glück; ~ **a fool I've been/I am!** ich Idiot!; ~ **terrible weather** was für ein scheußliches Wetter.
3 interj was; (dated: isn't it/he etc also) wie.
whate'er [wɒt'ɛəʳ] pron, adj (poet) see **whatever**.
whatever [wɒt'evəʳ] **1** pron **(a)** was (auch) (immer); (no matter what) egal was, ganz gleich was. ~ **you like** was (immer) du (auch) möchtest; **shall we go home now?** — ~ **you like** gehen wir jetzt nach Hause? — ganz wie du willst; ~ **it's called** egal wie es heißt, soll es heißen, wie es will; ... **or** ~ **they're called** ... oder wie sie sonst heißen; **or** ~ oder sonst (so) etwas.
(b) (interrog) was ... wohl; (impatiently) was zum Kuckuck (inf). ~ **does he want?** was will er wohl? was er wohl will?; (impatiently) was, zum Kuckuck, will er denn?; ~ **do you mean?** was meinst du denn bloß?
2 adj **(a)** egal welche(r, s), welche(r, s) (auch) (immer). ~ **book you choose** welches Buch Sie auch wählen; ~ **else you do** was immer du or egal was du auch sonst machst; **for** ~ **reasons** aus welchen Gründen auch immer.
(b) (with neg) überhaupt, absolut. **nothing/no man** ~ überhaupt or absolut gar nichts/niemand überhaupt; **it's of no use** ~ es hat überhaupt or absolut keinen Zweck.
(c) (interrog) ~ **good can come of it?** was kann daraus nur Gutes werden?; ~ **reason can he have?** was für einen Grund kann er nur or bloß or wohl haben?; ~ **else will he do?** was wird er nur or bloß or wohl noch alles machen?
whatnot ['wɒtnɒt] n (inf) adj see **what 1 (b)**. **(b)** (thingum-myjig) Dingsbums (inf), Dingsda (inf) nt.
what's [wɒts] contr of **what is; what has**.
whatsit ['wɒtsɪt] n (inf) Dingsbums (inf), Dingsda (inf), Dingens (dial inf) nt.
whatsoe'er [ˌwɒtsəʊ'ɛəʳ] (poet), **whatsoever** [ˌwɒtsəʊ'evəʳ] pron, adj see **whatever 1 (a), 2 (a, b)**.
wheat [wiːt] **1** n Weizen m. **to separate the** ~ **from the chaff** die Spreu vom Weizen trennen. **2** attr ~**germ** Weizenkeim m.
wheaten ['wiːtn] adj Weizen-.
wheedle ['wiːdl] vt **to** ~ **sb into doing sth** jdn überreden or herumkriegen (inf), etw zu tun; **to** ~ **sth out of sb** jdm etw abschmeicheln.
wheedling ['wiːdlɪŋ] **1** adj tone, voice schmeichelnd, schmeichlerisch. **2** n Schmeicheln nt.
wheel [wiːl] **1** n **(a)** Rad nt; (steering ~) Lenkrad nt; (Naut) Steuer(rad) nt; (roulette ~) Drehscheibe f; (paddle ~) Schaufelrad nt; (potter's ~) (Töpfer)scheibe f. **at the** ~ (lit) am Steuer; (fig also) am Ruder; ~ **of fortune** Glücksrad nt; **the** ~**s of progress** der Fortschritt; (in history) die Weiterentwicklung; **the** ~**s of government/justice** die Mühlen der Regierung/der Gerechtigkeit; ~**s within** ~**s** gewisse Verbindungen or Beziehungen.
(b) (Mil) Schwenkung f. **a** ~ **to the right, a right** ~ eine Schwenkung nach rechts, eine Rechtsschwenkung.
2 vt **(a)** (push) bicycle, pram, child schieben; (pull) ziehen; (invalid) wheelchair fahren. **the cripple** ~**ed himself into the room/along the Krüppel** fuhr mit seinem Rollstuhl ins Zimmer/ fuhr in seinem Rollstuhl.
(b) (cause to turn) drehen.
3 vi (turn) drehen; (birds, planes) kreisen; (Mil) schwenken. **to** ~ **left** nach links schwenken; **left** ~! links schwenkt!
♦**wheel in** vt sep **(a)** trolley, invalid hereinrollen. **(b)** (inf: bring into room) vorführen (inf).
♦**wheel round** vi sich (rasch) umdrehen; (troops) (ab)schwenken.
wheel: ~**barrow** n Schubkarre f, Schubkarren m; ~**barrow race** n Schubkarrenrennen nt; ~**base** n Rad(ab)stand m; ~**chair** n Rollstuhl m; **he spent six months in a** ~**chair** er saß sechs Monate im Rollstuhl.
wheeled [wiːld] adj traffic, transport auf Rädern; vehicle mit Rädern.
-wheeled adj suf -räd(e)rig.

wheeler-dealer ['wiːlə'diːlə'] n (inf) Schlitzohr nt (inf), gerissener Kerl; (in finance also) Geschäftemacher m.

wheelhouse ['wiːlhaus] n Ruderhaus nt.

wheeling and dealing ['wiːlɪŋən'diːlɪŋ] n Machenschaften pl, Gemauschel nt (inf); (in business) Geschäftemacherei f.

wheelwright ['wiːlraɪt] n Wagenbauer, Stellmacher m.

wheeze [wiːz] 1 n (a) (of person) pfeifender Atem no pl; (of machine) Fauchen nt no pl.
(b) (dated inf) Jokus (dated), Scherz m. to think up a ~ sich (dat) etwas einfallen lassen.
2 vt keuchen. to ~ out a tune eine Melodie herauspressen.
3 vi pfeifend atmen; (machines, asthmatic) keuchen. if he smokes too much he starts to ~ wenn er zu stark raucht, fängt sein Atem an zu pfeifen or bekommt er einen pfeifenden Atem.

wheezily ['wiːzɪlɪ] adv pfeifend, keuchend.

wheeziness ['wiːzɪnɪs] n Keuchen nt; (of breath) Pfeifen nt.

wheezy ['wiːzɪ] adj (+er) old man mit pfeifendem Atem; breath pfeifend; voice, cough keuchend; car keuchend, schnaufend.

whelk [welk] n Wellhornschnecke f.

whelp [welp] 1 n Welpe m; (pej: boy) Lauser (inf), Lausbub (inf) m. 2 vi werfen, jungen.

when [wen] 1 adv (a) (at what time) wann. since ~ have you been here? seit wann sind Sie hier?; ... since ~ he has been here ... und seitdem ist er hier; say ~! (inf) sag' or schrei (inf) halt!
(b) (rel) on the day ~ an dem or als or da (liter) or wo (inf); at the time ~ zu der Zeit, zu der or als or da (liter) or wo (inf); he wrote last week, up till ~ I had heard nothing from him er schrieb letzte Woche, und bis dahin hatte ich nichts von ihm gehört; in 1960, up till ~ he ... im Jahre 1960, bis zu welchem Zeitpunkt er ...; during the time ~ he was in Germany während der Zeit, als or wo or die (inf) er in Deutschland war.
2 conj (a) wenn; (with past reference) als. you can go ~ I have finished du kannst gehen, sobald or wenn ich fertig bin; he did it ~ young er tat es in seiner Jugend.
(b) (+gerund) beim; (at or during which time) wobei. ~ operating the machine beim Benutzen or bei Benutzung der Maschine; be careful ~ crossing the road seien Sie vorsichtig beim Überqueren der Straße vorsichtig, seien Sie vorsichtig, wenn Sie über die Straße gehen; the Prime Minister is coming here in May, ~ he will ... der Premier kommt im Mai hierher und wird dann ...
(c) (although, whereas) wo ... doch. why do you do it that way ~ it would be much easier like this? warum machst du es denn auf die Art, wo es doch so viel einfacher wäre?

whence [wens] adv (a) (old, form) woher, von wannen (old, liter). (b) (form) ~ I conclude ... woraus ich schließe, ...

whenever [wen'evə'] adv (a) (each time) jedesmal wenn.
(b) (at whatever time) wann (auch) immer, ganz egal or gleich or einerlei wann; (as soon as) sobald. I'll visit you ~ you like ich werde dich besuchen, wann immer du willst; ~ you like! wann du willst!; we'll leave ~ he's ready wir brechen auf, sobald er fertig ist.
(c) (emph) ~ can he have done it? wann kann er das nur or wohl getan haben?; ~ do I have the time for such things? wann habe ich schon or je Zeit für sowas?; tomorrow, or ~ (inf) morgen, oder wann auch immer or sonst irgendwann.

where [weə'] 1 adv wo. ~ (to) wohin, wo ... hin; ~ (from) woher, wo ... her; ~ are you going (to)? wohin gehst du, wo gehst du hin?; ~ to, sir? wohin (wollen Sie) bitte?; ~ are you from? woher kommen Sie, wo kommen Sie her?; from ~ I'm sitting I can see the church von meinem Platz aus kann ich die Kirche sehen; ~ should we be if ...? was wäre nur, wenn ...?; this is ~ it's at (sl) (das ist) extrem (sl); he doesn't know ~ it's at (sl) der weiß nicht, was läuft (sl).
2 conj wo; (in the place where) da, wo ..., an der Stelle, wo ... go ~ you like geh, wohin du willst, geh hin, wo du willst; the bag is ~ you left it die Tasche ist an der Stelle or da, wo du sie liegengelassen hast; this is ~ we got out hier sind wir ausgestiegen; that's ~ Nelson fell/I used to live/we differ hier or an dieser Stelle fiel Nelson/hier or da habe ich (früher) gewohnt/in diesem Punkt haben wir unterschiedliche Ansichten; we carried on from ~ we left off wir haben da weitergemacht, wo wir vorher aufgehört haben; I've read up to ~ the king ... ich habe bis dahin or bis an die Stelle gelesen, wo der König ...; this is ~ we got to soweit or bis hierhin or bis dahin sind wir gekommen; we succeeded ~ we expected to fail wir hatten da Erfolg, wo wir ihn nicht erwartet hatten; you can trust him ~ money is concerned in Geldsachen können Sie ihm trauen, Sie können ihm trauen, wo es ums Geld geht; that's ~ da; that's ~ his strong point is da liegt seine Stärke.

whereabouts [,weərə'bauts] 1 adv wo, in welcher Gegend. I wonder ~ Martin put it ich frage mich, wohin Martin es wohl gelegt hat.
2 [weərə'bauts] n sing or pl Verbleib m; (of people also) Aufenthaltsort m.

whereas [weər'æz] conj (a) (whilst) während; (while on the other hand) wohingegen. (b) (esp Jur: considering that) da, in Anbetracht der Tatsache, daß ...

whereat [weər'æt] adv (old) wobei.

whereby [weə'baɪ] adv (form) the sign ~ you will recognize him das Zeichen, an dem or woran Sie ihn erkennen; the rule ~ it is not allowed die Vorschrift, laut derer or wonach es verboten ist; a plan ~ the country can be saved ein Plan, durch den or wodurch das Land gerettet werden kann.

where'er [weər'eə'] conj, adv (poet) contr of wherever.

wherefore ['weəfɔː'] 1 adv (obs) warum, weswegen. 2 conj (obs) weswegen. 3 n see why 3.

wherein [weər'ɪn] adv (form) worin.

whereof [weər'ɒv] adv (obs) (about which) worüber; (out of which) woraus; (Jur) dessen. in witness ~ ... zu Urkund or Zeugnis dessen ... (old).

whereon [weər'ɒn] adv (obs) worauf; (whereupon) woraufhin.

wheresoever [,weəsəu'evə'] adv (obs), **wheresoe'er** [,weəsəu'eə'] adv (obs, poet) see **wherever**.

wherever [weər'evə'] 1 conj (a) (no matter where) egal or einerlei wo, wo (auch) immer. ~ it came from egal or einerlei or ganz gleich, woher es kommt, woher es auch kommt.
(b) (anywhere, in or to whatever place) wohin. we'll go ~ you like wir gehen, wohin Sie wollen; he comes from Bishopbriggs, ~ that is er kommt aus Bishopbriggs, wo immer das auch sein mag (geh) or fragen Sie mich nicht, wo das ist.
(c) (everywhere) überall wo. ~ you see this sign überall, wo Sie dieses Zeichen sehen.
2 adv wo nur, wo bloß. ~ have I seen that before? wo habe ich das nur or bloß schon gesehen?; ~ did you get that hat! wo haben Sie nur or bloß diesen Hut her?; in London or Liverpool or ~ in London oder Liverpool oder sonstwo.

wherewith [weə'wɪθ] adv (obs) womit, mit dem/der.

wherewithal ['weəwɪðɔːl] n nötiges Kleingeld; (implements) Utensilien pl.

wherry ['werɪ] n (light rowing boat) Ruderkahn m; (Brit: barge) (Fluß)kahn m; (US: scull) Einer m, Skiff nt.

whet [wet] vt knife, scythe wetzen; axe schleifen, schärfen; appetite, curiosity anregen.

whether ['weðə'] conj ob; (no matter whether) egal or ganz gleich or einerlei, ob. I am not certain ~ they're coming or not or ~ or not they're coming ich bin nicht sicher, ob sie kommen oder nicht; ~ they come or not, we'll go ahead egal or ganz gleich or einerlei, ob sie kommen oder nicht (kommen), wir fangen (schon mal) an; he's not sure ~ to go or stay er weiß nicht, ob er gehen oder bleiben soll.

whetstone ['wetstəun] n Wetzstein m.

whew [hwuː] interj puh, uff.

whey [weɪ] n Molke f.

whey-faced ['weɪ'feɪst] adj (liter) bleichgesichtig (geh).

which [wɪtʃ] 1 adj (a) (interrog) welche(r, s). ~ one? welche(r, s)?; (of people also) wer?
(b) (rel) welche(r, s). ... by ~ time I was asleep ... und zu dieser Zeit schlief ich (bereits); look at it ~ way you will ... man kann es betrachten or sehen, wie man will ...; ~ he said, ~ remark made me very angry ...sagte er, was mich sehr ärgerte.
2 pron (a) (interrog) welche(r, s); (of people also) wer. ~ of the children/books welches Kind/Buch; ~ is ~? (of people) wer ist wer?, welche(r) ist welche(r)?; (of things) welche(r, s) ist welche(r, s)?, welche(r, s) ist der/die/das eine und welche(r, s) der/die/das andere?; ~ is for ~? was ist wofür?
(b) (rel) (with n antecedent) der/die/das, welche(r, s) (geh); (with clause antecedent) was. the bear ~ I saw der Bär, den ich sah; at ~ he remarked ... woraufhin er bemerkte, ...; it rained hard, ~ upset her es regnete stark, was sie aufregte; ~ reminds me ... dabei fällt mir ein, ...; from ~ we deduce that ... woraus wir ableiten, daß ...; after ~ we went to bed worauf or wonach wir zu Bett gingen; on the day before/after ~ he left her an dem Tag, bevor er sie verließ/nachdem er sie verlassen hatte; the shelf on ~ I put it das Brett, auf das or worauf ich es gelegt habe.

whichever [wɪtʃ'evə'] 1 adj welche(r, s) auch immer; (no matter which) ganz gleich or egal or einerlei welche(r, s). 2 pron welche(r, s) auch immer. ~ (of you) has the most money wer immer (von euch) das meiste Geld hat.

whichsoever [,wɪtʃsəu'evə'] adj, pron (form) see **whichever**.

whiff [wɪf] n (a) (puff) Zug m; (wisp) kleine Fahne, Wolke f; (smell) Hauch m; (pleasant) Duft, Hauch m; (fig: trace) Spur f; (of spring) Hauch m, Ahnung f. to catch a ~ of sth den Geruch von etw wahrnehmen; to go out for a ~ of air hinausgehen, um (etwas) Luft zu schnappen.
(b) (small cigar) kleiner Zigarillo.

whiffy ['wɪfɪ] adj (+er) (inf) to be ~ streng riechen; it's a bit ~ here hier müffelt es etwas (inf).

whig [wɪg] (Brit Hist) 1 n frühere Bezeichnung für Mitglied der liberalen Partei, Whig m. 2 adj attr Whig-.

while [waɪl] 1 n (a) Weile f, Weilchen nt (inf). for a ~ (für) eine Weile, eine Zeitlang; (a short moment) (für) einen Augenblick or Moment; a good or long ~ eine ganze or lange Weile, eine ganze Zeitlang; for/after quite a ~ ziemlich or recht lange, (für) eine geraume/nach einer geraumen Weile (geh); a little or short ~ ein Weilchen (inf), kurze Zeit; it'll be ready in a short ~ es wird bald fertig sein; a little/long ~ ago vor kurzem/vor einer ganzen Weile, vor längerer or langer Zeit; some ~ ago vor einiger Zeit; all the ~ die ganze Zeit (über); between ~s (inf) zwischendurch, in der Zwischenzeit.
(b) the ~ (liter) derweil, unterdessen.
(c) to be worth (one's) ~ to ... sich (für jdn) lohnen, zu ...; we'll make it worth your ~ es soll ihr Schaden nicht sein.
2 conj (a) während; (as long as) solange. she fell asleep ~ reading sie schlief beim Lesen ein; he became famous ~ still young er wurde berühmt, als er noch jung war; you must not drink ~ on duty Sie dürfen im Dienst nicht trinken.
(b) (although) ~ one must admit there are difficulties ... man muß zwar zugeben, daß es Schwierigkeiten gibt, trotzdem ...; ~ the text is not absolutely perfect, nevertheless ... obwohl (zwar) der Text nicht einwandfrei ist, ... trotzdem; it is difficult to be fair ~ at the same time being honest es ist schwierig, fair und gleichzeitig auch gerecht zu sein.
(c) (whereas) während.

♦ **while away** vt sep time sich (dat) vertreiben.

whilst [waɪlst] conj see **while 2**.

whim [wɪm] n Laune f. a passing ~ eine vorübergehende Laune, ein vorübergehender Spleen; her every ~ jede ihrer Launen; as the ~ takes me ganz nach Lust und Laune.

whimper ['wɪmpə'] 1 n (of dog) Winseln nt no pl; (of person) Wimmern nt no pl. a ~ of pain ein schmerzliches Wimmern;

without a ~ ohne einen (Klage)laut. **2** *vti* (*dog*) winseln; (*person*) wimmern.

whimsical ['wɪmzɪkəl] *adj* wunderlich; *look, remark* neckisch; *idea, tale* schnurrig; *decision* seltsam, spinnig (*inf*); *notion* grillenhaft; *ornament* verrückt. **to be in a ~ mood** in einer neckischen Laune sein; **a ~ joke** ein verrücktes Witzchen.

whimsicality [ˌwɪmzɪˈkælɪtɪ] *n* Wunderlichkeit *f*; (*of behaviour*) Launenhaftigkeit, Grillenhaftigkeit *f*; (*of decision*) Seltsamkeit *f*; (*of mood, tale also*) Grillenhaftigkeit *f*; (*of architecture*) Verrücktheit *f*, Manierismus *m*.

whimsically ['wɪmzɪkəlɪ] *adv look, say* neckisch.

whimsy ['wɪmzɪ] *n* **(a)** (*caprice, fancy*) Spleen *m*, Grille *f* (*dated*). **(b)** *see* **whimsicality**.

whin [wɪn] *n* (*esp Brit*) Ginster *m*.

whine [waɪn] **1** *n* (*of dog*) Jaulen, Heulen *nt no pl*; (*complaining cry*) Jammern, Gejammer *nt no pl*; (*of child*) Quengelei *f no pl*; (*of siren, jet engine*) Heulen *nt no pl*; (*of bullet*) Pfeifen *nt no pl*.

2 *vi* (*dog*) jaulen; (*person: speak, complain*) jammern, klagen; (*child*) quengeln; (*siren, jet engine*) heulen; (*bullet*) pfeifen. **the dog was whining to be let in** der Hund jaulte, um hereingelassen zu werden; **don't come whining to me about it** du brauchst nicht anzukommen und mir was vorzujammern.

whiner ['waɪnə^r] *n* (*complainer*) Jammerer, Jammerknochen (*inf*) *m*.

whining ['waɪnɪŋ] *n* (*of dog*) Gejaule *nt*; (*of complaining*) Gejammer *nt*.

whinny ['wɪnɪ] **1** *n* Wiehern, Gewieher *nt no pl*. **2** *vi* wiehern.

whip [wɪp] **1** *n* **(a)** Peitsche *f*; (*riding ~*) Reitgerte *f*.

(b) (*Parl*) (*person*) Einpeitscher, Geschäftsführer *m*; (*call*) Anordnung *f* des Einpeitschers. **three-line ~** Fraktionszwang *m*; **they have put a three-line ~ on the vote** bei der Abstimmung besteht Fraktionszwang; **chief ~** Haupt-Einpeitscher *m*.

(c) (*Cook*) Creme, Speise *f*.

2 *vt* **(a)** (*with whip*) *people* auspeitschen; *horse* peitschen; (*with stick etc*) schlagen. **the conductor ~ped the orchestra into a frenzy** der Dirigent brachte das Orchester in Ekstase; **to ~ sb/sth into shape** (*fig*) jdn/etw zurechtschleifen.

(b) (*Cook*) *cream, eggs* schlagen.

(c) (*bind*) *seam* umnähen; *stick, rope* umwickeln.

(d) (*inf: defeat*) vernichtend schlagen.

(e) (*fig: move quickly*) **he ~ped the book off the desk** er schnappte sich (*dat*) das Buch vom Schreibtisch; **he ~ped his hand out of the way** er zog blitzschnell seine Hand weg; **the thief ~ped the jewel into his pocket** der Dieb ließ den Edelstein schnell in seiner Tasche verschwinden; **to ~ sb into hospital** jdn in Windeseile ins Krankenhaus bringen; (*doctor*) jdn schnell ins Krankenhaus einweisen.

(f) (*inf: steal*) mitgehen lassen (*inf*).

3 *vi* **(a)** *branches* ~ped against the window Äste schlugen gegen das Fenster.

(b) (*move quickly*) (*person*) schnell (mal) laufen. **the car ~ped past** das Auto brauste *or* sauste *or* fegte (*inf*) vorbei.

♦ **whip away** *vt sep* wegreißen, wegziehen (*from sb* jdm).

♦ **whip back** *vi* **(a)** (*spring, plank*) zurückschnellen, zurückfedern. **(b)** (*inf: go back quickly*) schnell (mal) zurücklaufen.

♦ **whip off** *vt sep* *clothes* herunterreißen, vom Leib reißen; *tablecloth* wegziehen. **the wind ~ped my hat ~** der Wind riß mir den Hut vom Kopf; **a car ~ped him ~ to the airport** ein Auto brachte ihn in Windeseile zum Flugplatz.

♦ **whip on** *vt sep* **(a)** (*urge on*) *horse* anpeitschen, antreiben; (*fig*) antreiben. **(b)** (*put on quickly*) *clothes* sich (*dat*) überwerfen; *lid* schnell drauftun.

♦ **whip out 1** *vt sep* *gun, pencil, camera etc* zücken. **he ~ped a gun/pencil** *etc* ~ **of** his pocket er zog rasch eine Pistole/einen Bleistift *etc* aus der Tasche; **they ~ped ~ his tonsils** (*inf*) sie haben ihm schnell die Mandeln entfernt.

2 *vi* (*inf: go out quickly*) schnell (mal) rausgehen (*inf*). **he's just ~ped ~ for a drink** er ist schnell mal *or* nur schnell einen trinken gegangen.

♦ **whip round** *vi* **(a)** (*inf: move quickly*) **I'll just ~ ~ to the shops/to the butcher** ich werd' schnell mal einkaufen gehen/zum Metzger (rüber)laufen; **he ~ped ~ when he heard** ... er fuhr herum, als er hörte ...; **the car ~ped ~ the corner** das Auto brauste *or* sauste *or* fegte (*inf*) um die Ecke.

(b) (*inf: collect money*) zusammenlegen, den Hut herumgehen lassen.

♦ **whip up** *vt sep* **(a)** (*pick up*) schnappen.

(b) (*set in motion*) *horses* antreiben; (*Cook*) *cream* schlagen; *mixture* verrühren; *eggs* verquirlen; (*inf: prepare quickly*) *meal* hinzaubern; (*fig: stir up*) *interest, feeling* anheizen, entfachen; *support* finden, auftreiben (*inf*); *audience, crowd* mitreißen. **I'll just ~ ~ something to eat** ich mach' nur schnell was zu essen; **the sea, ~ped ~ by the wind** das Meer, vom Wind aufgepeitscht.

whip: ~**cord** *n* (*rope*) Peitschenschnur *f*; (*fabric*) Whipcord *m*; ~ **hand** *n* **to have the ~ hand** (**over sb**) (über jdn) die Oberhand haben; ~**lash** *n* (Peitschen)riemen *m*; (*Med: also* ~**lash injury**) Peitschenhiebverletzung *f*.

whipped cream ['wɪptˈkriːm] *n* Schlagsahne *f*, Schlagrahm *m*.

whipper-in [ˌwɪpərˈɪn] *n* Piqueur, Pikör, Parforcejäger *m*.

whippersnapper ['wɪpəˌsnæpə^r] *n* (*dated*) junger Spund.

whippet ['wɪpɪt] *n* Whippet *m*.

whipping ['wɪpɪŋ] *n* (*beating*) Tracht *f* Prügel; (*inf: defeat*) Niederlage *f*; (*fig: in debate etc*) Pleite *f*. **to give sb a ~** (*lit*) jdm eine Tracht Prügel versetzen; (*with whip*) jdn auspeitschen; (*fig inf*) jdn in die Pfanne hauen (*inf*); **our team/the government got a ~** unsere Mannschaft wurde in die Pfanne gehauen (*inf*)/die Regierung erlebte eine Pleite (*inf*).

whipping: ~ **boy** *n* Prügelknabe *m*; **to use sb as a ~ boy** jdn zum Prügelknaben machen; ~ **cream** *n* Schlagsahne *f*, Schlagrahm *m*; ~ **top** *n* Kreisel *m*.

whippoorwill ['wɪpˌpʊəˌwɪl] *n* schreiender Ziegenmelker.

whippy ['wɪpɪ] *adj cane, fishing rod* biegsam, elastisch, federnd.

whip-round ['wɪpraʊnd] *n* (*esp Brit inf*) **to have a ~** den Hut herumgehen lassen.

whir [wɜː^r] *n, vi see* **whirr**.

whirl [wɜːl] **1** *n* (*spin*) Wirbeln *nt no pl*; (*of dust, water etc, also fig*) Wirbel *m*; (*of cream etc*) Tupfer *m*. **to give sb/sth a ~** (*lit*) jdn/etw herumwirbeln; (*fig inf: try out*) jdn/etw ausprobieren; **he disappeared in a ~ of dust** er verschwand in einer Staubwolke; **the busy ~ of her social life** der Trubel ihres gesellschaftlichen Lebens; **a ~ of pleasure** Jubel, Trubel, Heiterkeit *no art* (+ *sing vb*); **my head is in a ~** mir schwirrt der Kopf.

2 *vt* **(a)** (*make turn*) wirbeln. **to ~ sb/sth round** jdn/etw herumwirbeln; **he ~ed his hat round his head** er schwenkte seinen Hut; **he ~ed the water about with his stick** er rührte mit seinem Stock im Wasser herum.

(b) (*transport*) eilends wegbringen; (*person*) mit sich nehmen, entführen (*inf*). **the train/the plane/he ~ed us off** der Zug brauste mit uns davon/das Flugzeug/er entführte uns.

3 *vi* (*spin*) wirbeln; (*water*) strudeln. **to ~ round** herumwirbeln; (*water*) strudeln; (*person: turn round quickly*) herumfahren; **my head is ~ing** mir schwirrt der Kopf; **after a few drinks the room starting ~ing** nach ein paar Gläsern fing der Raum an, sich zu drehen; **they/the countryside ~ed past us** sie wirbelten/die Landschaft flog an uns vorbei.

whirligig ['wɜːlɪɡɪɡ] *n* (*top*) Kreisel *m*; (*roundabout*) Karussell, Ringelspiel *nt*; (*fig*) ewiges) Wechselspiel *nt*.

whirlpool ['wɜːlpuːl] *n* Strudel *m*; (*in health club*) ≈ Kneippbecken *nt*.

whirlwind ['wɜːlwɪnd] *n* Wirbelwind *m*; (*fig*) Trubel, Wirbel *m*. **like a ~** wie der Wirbelwind; **to reap the ~** (*prov*) Sturm ernten; **he did some very stupid things, and now he's reaping the ~** er hat einige sehr große Dummheiten gemacht, und jetzt muß er dafür büßen; **a ~ romance** eine stürmische Romanze.

whirlybird ['wɜːlɪˌbɜːd] *n* (*esp US inf*) Hubschrauber *m*.

whirr, whir [wɜː^r] **1** *n* (*of wings*) Schwirren *nt*; (*of wheels, camera, machine*) (*quiet*) Surren *nt*; (*louder*) Brummen, Dröhnen *nt*. **2** *vi see* **n** schwirren; surren; brummen, dröhnen.

whisk [wɪsk] **1** *n* **(a)** (*fly* ~) Wedel *m*; (*Cook*) Schneebesen *m*; (*electric*) Rührbesen, Rührstab *m*, Rührgerät *nt*. **give the eggs a good ~** schlagen Sie die Eier gut durch.

(b) (*movement*) Wischen *nt*; (*of skirts*) Schwingen *nt*. **with a ~ of his hand/its tail** mit einer schnellen Handbewegung/mit einem Schwanzschlag.

2 *vt* **(a)** (*Cook*) schlagen; *eggs* verquirlen. **to ~ the eggs into the mixture** die Eier unter die Masse einrühren.

(b) the horse ~ed its tail das Pferd schlug mit dem Schwanz.

3 *vi* (*move quickly*) fegen (*inf*), stieben.

♦ **whisk away** *vt sep* **(a)** *fly, wasp etc* wegscheuchen.

(b) (*take away suddenly*) **the magician ~ed ~ the tablecloth** der Zauberer zog das Tischtuch schnell weg; **her mother ~ed the bottle ~ from her** just in time ihre Mutter schnappte (*inf*) *or* zog ihr die Flasche gerade noch rechtzeitig weg; **he ~ed her ~ to the Bahamas** er entführte sie auf die Bahamas; **a big black car turned up and ~ed him ~** ein großes schwarzes Auto erschien und sauste *or* brauste mit ihm davon; **the kidnappers ~ed him ~** die Entführer fuhren schnell *or* sausten *or* brausten mit ihm davon.

♦ **whisk off** *vt sep see* **whisk away (b)**.

♦ **whisk up** *vt sep* *eggs, mixture etc* schaumig schlagen.

whisker ['wɪskə^r] *n* Schnurrhaar *nt*; (*of people*) Barthaar *nt*. ~**s** (*moustache*) Schnurrbart *m*; (*side* ~**s**) Backenbart *m*; (*Zool*) Schnurrbart *m*; **to win/miss sth by a ~** etw fast gewinnen/etw um Haaresbreite verpassen.

whiskered ['wɪskəd] *adj* schnurrbärtig.

whiskery ['wɪskərɪ] *adj* behaart, haarig.

whisky, (*US, Ir*) **whiskey** ['wɪskɪ] *n* Whisky *m*. ~ **and soda** Whisky (mit) Soda *m*; **two whiskies, please** zwei Whisky, bitte.

whisper ['wɪspə^r] **1** *n* **(a)** Geflüster, Flüstern *nt no pl*; (*of wind, leaves*) Wispern *nt no pl*; (*mysterious*) Raunen *nt no pl*. **to speak/say sth in a ~** im Flüsterton sprechen/etw im Flüsterton sagen; **they were talking in ~s** sie sprachen flüsternd *or* im Flüsterton.

(b) (*rumour*) Gerücht *nt*. **there are ~s (going round) that** ... es geht das Gerücht *or* es gehen Gerüchte um, daß ...; **have you heard any ~s about who might be promoted?** haben Sie irgendwelche Andeutungen gehört *or* etwas läuten hören (*inf*), wer befördert werden soll?

2 *vt* **(a)** flüstern, wispern. **to ~ sth to sb** jdm etw zuflüstern *or* zuwispern; (*secretively*) jdm etw zuraunen; **to ~ a word in(to) sb's ear** (*fig*) jdm einen leisen Tip geben, jdm etw andeuten.

(b) (*rumour*) **it's (being) ~ed that** ... es geht das Gerücht *or* es gehen Gerüchte um, daß ...; **man munkelt** *or* es wird gemunkelt, daß ...; **they ~ed it round in the neighbourhood** in der Nachbarschaft flüsterten *or* tuschelten sie darüber.

3 *vi* flüstern, wispern (*also fig*); (*poet: wind*) säuseln; (*secretively*) raunen; (*schoolchildren*) tuscheln. **to ~ to sb** jdm zuflüstern/zuwispern/zuraunen; mit jdm tuscheln; **just ~ to me** sag's mir flüsternd; **stop ~ing!** hör/hört auf zu flüstern!; (*schoolchildren*) hört auf zu tuscheln, laßt das Getuschel!

whispering ['wɪspərɪŋ] *n see vi* Flüstern, Geflüster, Wispern *nt no pl*; Säuseln *nt no pl*; Raunen *nt no pl*; Tuscheln, Getuschel *nt no pl*; (*fig*) Gerede, Gemunkel, Getuschel *nt no pl*.

whispering: ~ **campaign** *n* Verleumdungskampagne *f*; ~ **gallery** *n* Flüstergewölbe *nt or* -galerie *f*.

whist [wɪst] *n* Whist *nt*. ~ **drive** Whistrunde *f* mit wechselnden Parteien.

whistle ['wɪsl] **1** *n* **(a)** (*sound*) Pfiff *m*; (*of wind*) Pfeifen *nt*; (*of kettle*) Pfeifton *m*. **the ~ of the escaping steam** das Pfeifen des ausströmenden Dampfes; **to give a ~** einen Pfiff ausstoßen.

(b) (*instrument*) Pfeife *f*. to blow a/one's ~ pfeifen; *see* wet.

2 *vt* pfeifen. to ~ (to) sb to stop jdn durch einen Pfiff stoppen; to ~ sb back/over *etc* jdn zurück-/herüberpfeifen *etc*.

3 *vi* pfeifen. the boys ~d at her die Jungen pfiffen ihr nach; the crowd ~d at the referee die Menge pfiff den Schiedsrichter aus; he ~d for a taxi ein Taxi heran, er pfiff nach einem Taxi; the referee ~d for a foul der Schiedsrichter pfiff ein Foul; the referee ~d for play to stop der Schiedsrichter pfiff das Spiel ab; he can ~ for it (*inf*) da kann er lange warten *or* warten, bis er schwarz wird (*inf*).

whistle-stop ['wɪsl,stɒp] (*US*) **1** *n* **(a)** (*small town*) Kleinstadt *f*, Nest, Kaff *nt*. **(b)** (*stop*) kurzer Aufenthalt an einem kleinen Ort; (*fig*) Stippvisite *f*. ~ **tour** (*US Pol*) Wahlreise *f*; (*fig*) Reise *f* mit Kurzaufenthalten an allen Orten. **2** *vi* auf die Dörfer gehen.

whistling kettle ['wɪslɪŋ'ketl] *n* Pfeifkessel *m*.

whit [wɪt] *n* not a ~ keine *or* nicht eine Spur; (*of humour*) kein *or* nicht ein Funke(n); (*of truth, common sense*) kein *or* nicht ein Gramm *or* Körnchen; **every** ~ **as good** genauso gut, (um) keinen Deut schlechter.

white [waɪt] **1** *adj* weiß; *skin, racially also* hell; (*with fear, anger, exhaustion etc also*) blaß, kreidebleich. **to go** *or* **turn** ~ (*thing*) weiß werden; (*person also*) bleich *or* blaß werden.

2 *n* (*colour*) Weiß *nt*; (*person*) Weiße(r) *mf*; (*of egg*) Eiweiß, Klar (*Aus*) *nt*; (*of eye*) Weiße(s) *nt*. **shoot when you see the** ~**s of their eyes** schießt, wenn ihr das Weiße im Auge des Feinds erkennen könnt; ~**s** (*household*) Weißwäsche *f*; (*Sport*) weiße Kleidung; **the tennis players were wearing** ~**s** die Tennisspieler trugen Weiß *or* spielten in Weiß; **I've forgotten my** ~**s** ich habe mein Zeug vergessen.

white: ~ **ant** *n* Termite *f*, weiße Ameise; ~**bait** *n, pl* -**bait** Breitling *m*; ~**beam** *n* Mehlbeere *f*; ~ **book** *n* (*US Pol*) Weißbuch *nt*; ~**cap** *n* Welle *f* mit Schaumkronen; **a** ~ **Christmas** *n* weiße Weihnacht(en); ~ **coal** *n* weiße Kohle; ~ **coffee** *n* (*Brit*) Kaffee *m* mit Milch, Milchkaffee *m*; ~**-collar** *adj* ~**-collar worker** Schreibtischarbeiter *m*; ~**-collar job** Angestelltenstelle *f*, Schreibtisch- *or* Büroposten *m*; ~**-collar crime** White-collar-crime *nt*, Weiße-Kragen-Kriminalität *f*; ~ **corpuscle** *n* weißes Blutkörperchen.

whited sepulchre ['waɪtɪd'seplkə'] *n* (*liter*) Pharisäer *m*.

white: ~ **dwarf** *n* (*Astron*) weißer Zwerg(stern); ~ **elephant** *n* nutzloser Gegenstand; (*waste of money*) Fehlinvestition *f*; ~ **elephant stall** *n* Stand *m* mit allerlei Krimskrams; ~ **ensign** *n* Fahne *f* der Royal Navy; ~ **feather** *n* weiße Feder (*Zeichen der Feigheit*); **to show the** ~ **feather** den Schwanz einziehen; ~ **fish** *n* Weißfisch *m*; ~ **flag** *n* (*Mil, fig*) weiße Fahne; **W**~ **Friar** *n* Karmeliter *m*; ~ **gold** *n* Weißgold *nt*; ~**-haired** *adj* **(a)** weißhaarig; (*blonde*) weißblond, semmelblond; **(b)** (*US inf: favourite*) Lieblings-; **the boss's** ~**-haired boy** der Liebling *or* das Goldkind des Chefs; **W**~**hall** *n* (*British government*) Whitehall *no art*; **if W**~**hall decides** ... wenn London beschließt ...; ~**-headed** *adj* (*as* ~**-haired**); **(b)** gull, eagle weißköpfig; ~ **heat** *n* Weißglut *f*; (*fig*) Hitze *f*; (*with enthusiasm*) Feuereifer *m*; **to work at** ~ **heat** (*under pressure*) fieberhaft arbeiten; **in the** ~ **heat of his rage/passion** in seiner besinnungslosen Wut/Leidenschaft; **his rage reached** ~ **heat** seine Wut erreichte den Siedepunkt; ~ **hope** *n* große *or* einzige Hoffnung; ~ **horse** *n* **(a)** Schimmel *m*; **(b)** (*wave*) Welle *f* mit einer Schaumkrone; **now there are** ~ **horses** jetzt haben die Wellen Reiter; ~**-hot** *adj* weißglühend; (*fig*) brennend, glühend; **the W**~ **House** *n* das Weiße Haus; ~ **lead** *n* Bleiweiß *nt*; ~ **lie** *n* kleine Unwahrheit, Notlüge *f*; **we all tell a** ~ **lie from time to time** wir alle sagen nicht immer ganz die Wahrheit; ~ **light** *n* weißes Licht; ~**-lipped** *adj* mit bleichen Lippen, angstbleich; ~ **magic** *n* weiße Magie; ~ **man** *n* Weiße(r) *m*; **the** ~ **man's burden** die Bürde des weißen Mannes; ~ **meat** *n* helles Fleisch.

whiten ['waɪtn] **1** *vt* weiß machen. **2** *vi* weiß werden.

whiteness ['waɪtnɪs] *n* Weiße *f*; (*of skin*) Helligkeit *f*; (*due to illness etc*) Blässe *f*. **the dazzling** ~ **of ...** die strahlende Weiß des/der ...

whitening ['waɪtnɪŋ] *n* (*of colour*) weiße Farbe, Schlämmkreide *f*.

white: ~ **noise** *n* weißes Rauschen; ~**-out** *n* starkes Schneegestöber; **in** ~**-out conditions** bei starkem Schneegestöber; ~ **paper** *n* (*Pol*) Weißbuch *nt*; **W**~ **Russia** *n* Weißrußland *nt*; **W**~ **Russian** *n* Weißrusse *m*, Weißrussin *f*; ~ **sale** *n* weiße Woche, Ausverkauf *m* von Haus- und Tischwäsche; ~ **sauce** *n* Mehlsoße *f*, helle Soße; ~ **slave** *n* weiße Sklavin; ~ **slave trade** *n* Mädchenhandel *m*; ~ **spirit** *n* Terpentinersatz *m*; ~ **supremacy** *n* Vorherrschaft *f* der weißen Rasse; ~**thorn** *n* Weißdorn *m*; ~**throat** *n* Grasmücke *f*; ~ **tie** *n* (*tie*) weiße Fliege; (*evening dress*) Frack *m*; ~ **tie occasion/dinner** eine Veranstaltung/ein Essen mit Frackzwang; **is the dinner** ~ **tie?** besteht bei dem Essen Frackzwang?; ~ **trash** *n* (*US inf*) weißes Pack; ~**wall** **1** *n* (*tyre*) Weißwandreifen *m*; ~**wash** **1** *n* Tünche *f*; (*fig*) Schönfärberei *f*; **2** *vt* **walls** tünchen; (*fig*) schönfärben, beschönigen; *person* reinwaschen; **there's no point trying to** ~**wash him, he's a liar and that's that** da hilft keine Schönfärberei, er ist und bleibt ein Lügner; ~ **wedding** *n* Hochzeit *f* in Weiß; ~ **whale** *n* Weißwal, Beluga *m*; ~ **wine** *n* Weißwein *m*; ~ **woman** *n* Weiße *f*; ~**wood** *adj* ~**wood furniture** Möbel *pl* aus hellem Weichholz.

whitey ['waɪtɪ] *n* (*pej inf*) Weiße(r) *mf*.

whither ['wɪðə'] *adv* **(a)** (*old*) wohin. **(b)** (*journalese*) ~ **America/socialism?** Amerika/Sozialismus, wohin? *or* was nun?

whiting¹ ['waɪtɪŋ] *n, no pl* see **whitening**.

whiting² *n, pl* -, Weißling, Weißfisch *m*.

whitish ['waɪtɪʃ] *adj colour* weißlich.

whitlow ['wɪtləʊ] *n* Nagelbettentzündung *f*, Umlauf *m*.

Whit Monday [,wɪt'mʌndɪ] *n* Pfingstmontag *m*.

Whitsun ['wɪtsən] **1** *n* Pfingsten *nt*; (*Eccl also*) Pfingstfest *nt*. **2** *attr* Pfingst-.

Whit Sunday [,wɪt'sʌndɪ] *n* Pfingstsonntag *m*.

Whitsuntide ['wɪtsəntaɪd] *n* Pfingstzeit *f*. **around** ~ um Pfingsten (herum).

whittle ['wɪtl] **1** *vt* schnitzen. **2** *vi* **to** ~ (**away**) **at sth** an etw (*dat*) (herum)schnippeln *or* -schnitzen *or* -schneiden.

♦ **whittle away** *vt sep* **(a)** bark *etc* wegschneiden, wegschnitzen.

(b) (*gradually reduce*) allmählich abbauen, nach und nach abbauen; rights, power *etc also* allmählich *or* nach und nach beschneiden *or* stutzen. **the benefit/pay rise has been** ~**d** ~ **by inflation** der Gewinn/die Gehaltserhöhung ist durch die Inflation langsam zunichte gemacht worden.

♦ **whittle down** *vt sep* **(a)** piece of wood herunterschneiden. **to** ~ ~ **to size** zurechtschneiden, zurechtstutzen.

(b) (*reduce*) kürzen, reduzieren, stutzen; gap, difference verringern. **to** ~ **sth** ~ **to sth** etw auf etw (*acc*) reduzieren; **the play/novel has been** ~**d** ~ **to 1½ hours/20,000 words** das Stück/der Roman ist auf 1½ Stunden/20 000 Worte gekürzt *or* gestutzt worden; **to** ~ **sb** ~ **to size** (*fig*) jdn zurechtstutzen.

whiz(z) [wɪz] **1** *n* **(a)** (*of arrow*) Schwirren, Sausen *nt*. **(b)** (*US inf*) Kanone *f* (*inf*). **2** *vi* (*arrow*) schwirren, sausen.

whi(z)z-kid ['wɪz'kɪd] *n* (*inf*) **(a)** (*in career*) Senkrechtstarter *m*. **financial/publishing** ~ Finanz-/Verlagsgenie *nt or* -größe *f*; **a** ~ **like him will soon find a solution** ein solcher Intelligenzbolzen wird bald auf eine Lösung kommen (*inf*).

WHO *abbr of* **World Health Organization** WGO, Weltgesundheitsorganisation *f*.

who [huː] *pron* **(a)** (*interrog*) wer; (*acc*) wen; (*dat*) wem. **and** ~ **should it be but May?** und wer war's? natürlich May!; ~ **do you think you are?** was glaubst du *or* bildest du dir ein, wer du bist?, für wen hältst du dich eigentlich?; **"W**~**'s W**~**"** „Wer ist Wer"; **you'll soon find out** ~**'s** ~ **in the office** Sie werden bald im Büro alle kennenlernen; ~ **are you looking for?** wen suchen Sie?; ~ **did you stay with?** bei wem haben Sie gewohnt?

(b) (*rel*) der/die/das, welche(r, s). **any man** ~ ... jeder (Mensch), der ...; **he** ~ **wishes/those** ~ **wish to go** ... wer gehen will ...; (*for pl also*) diejenigen, die gehen wollen ...; **deny it** ~ **may** (*form*) das mag bestreiten *or* bestreite das, wer will.

whoa [wəʊ] *interj* brr.

who'd [huːd] *contr of* **who had; who would**.

whodun(n)it [huː'dʌnɪt] *n* (*inf*) Krimi *m* (*bei dem der Täter bis zum Schluß unbekannt ist*).

whoever [huː'evə'] *pron* wer (auch immer); (*acc*) wen (auch immer); (*dat*) wem (auch immer); (*no matter who*) einerlei *or* ganz gleich *or* egal (*inf*) wer/wen/wem. ~ **told you that?** wer hat dir das denn (bloß) gesagt?

whole [həʊl] **1** *adj* (*entire, unbroken, undivided*) ganz; truth voll; (*Bibl: well*) heil. **but the** ~ **purpose was to** ... aber der ganze Sinn der Sache *or* aber der Zweck der Übung (*inf*) war, daß ...; **three** ~ **weeks** drei volle *or* ganze Wochen; **the** ~ **lot** das Ganze; (*of people*) alle, der ganze Verein (*inf*); **a** ~ **lot of people** eine ganze Menge Leute; **a** ~ **lot better** (*inf*) ein ganzes Stück besser (*inf*), sehr viel besser; **she is a** ~ **lot of woman** (*esp US inf*) sie ist eine richtige *or* echte Frau; **out of** ~ **cloth** (*US*) von Anfang bis Ende erdichtet; **to our surprise he came back** ~ zu unserer Überraschung kam er heil zurück; **not a cup was left** ~ nicht eine Tasse blieb ganz *or* heil; **she swallowed it** ~ sie schluckte es ganz *or* unzerkaut (hinunter); **a pig roasted** ~ ein ganzes Schwein im *or* am Stück gebraten.

2 *n* Ganze(s) *nt*. **the** ~ **of the month/his savings/London** der ganze *or* gesamte Monat/seine gesamten *or* sämtlichen Ersparnisse/ganz London; **nearly the** ~ **of our production** fast unsere gesamte Produktion; **as a** ~ als Ganzes; **these people, as a** ~, **are** ... diese Leute sind in ihrer Gesamtheit ...; **on the** ~ im großen und ganzen, im ganzen gesehen, alles in allem.

whole: ~**-hearted** *adj* völlig, uneingeschränkt; ~**hearted congratulations/thanks to X X** (*dat*) gratulieren/danken wir von ganzem Herzen; **to be** ~**hearted in one's cooperation** sich rückhaltlos miteinsetzen; ~**heartedly** *adv* voll und ganz; ~**heartedness** *n* Rückhaltlosigkeit *f*; ~ **hog** *n* **to go the** ~ **hog** (*inf*) aufs Ganze gehen; ~**meal** **1** *adj* Vollkorn-; **2** *n* feiner Vollkornschrot; ~ **milk** *n* Vollmilch *f*; ~ **note** *n* (*esp US Mus*) ganze Note; ~ **number** *n* ganze Zahl.

wholesale ['həʊlseɪl] **1** *n* Großhandel *m*.

2 *adj attr* **(a)** (*Comm*) Großhandels-. ~ **dealer** Großhändler, Grossist *m*; ~ **business/trade** Großhandel *m*.

(b) (*fig: widespread*) umfassend, massiv; slaughter, redundancies Massen-; (*indiscriminate*) wild, generell. **the terrorists have a policy of** ~ **slaughter** die Terroristen betreiben eine Politik des wilden Darauflostötens; **the** ~ **slaughter of the infected animals** die Abschlachtung aller infizierten Tiere.

3 *adv* **(a)** im Großhandel.

(b) (*fig*) in Bausch und Bogen; (*in great numbers*) massenweise, massenhaft; (*without modification*) (so) ohne weiteres.

4 *vt* goods einen Großhandel betreiben mit, Großhändler *or* Grossist sein für.

5 *vi* (*item*) einen Großhandelspreis haben (*at* von).

wholesaler ['həʊlseɪlə'] *n* Großhändler, Grossist *m*.

wholesome ['həʊlsəm] *adj* gesund.

wholesomeness ['həʊlsəmnɪs] *n* Bekömmlichkeit *f*; (*of appearance*) Gesundheit *f*. **the** ~ **of the air** die gesunde Luft.

whole-wheat ['həʊlwiːt] *n* Voll(korn)weizen *m*.

who'll [huːl] *contr of* **who will; who shall**.

wholly ['həʊlɪ] *adv* völlig, gänzlich. **the project was** ~ **successful** das Projekt war gänzlich erfolgreich *or* ein völliger Erfolg; **this is** ~ **but** ~ ... das ist völlig und ganz *or* von Grund auf ...

whom [huːm] *pron* **(a)** (*interrog*) (*acc*) wen; (*dat*) wem. **(b)** (*rel*) (*acc*) den/die/das; (*dat*) dem/der/dem. ..., **all of** ~ **were drunk** ..., die alle betrunken waren; **none/all of** ~ von denen keine(r, s)/alle.

whom(so)ever [,huːm(səʊ)'evəʳ] pron (form) wen/wem auch immer; (no matter who) ganz gleich or egal wen/wem.

whoop [huːp] 1 n Ruf, Schrei m; (war cry also) Geschrei, Geheul nt no pl. **with a ~ of** joy unter Freudengeschrei.
2 vt **to ~ it up** (inf) auf die Pauke hauen (inf).
3 vi rufen, schreien; (with whooping cough) pfeifen; (with joy) jauchzen.

whoopee ['wʊpiː] 1 n **to make ~** (dated inf) Rabatz machen (dated inf). 2 [wʊ'piː] interj hurra, juchhe(i).

whooping cough ['huːpɪŋ,kɒf] n Keuchhusten m.

whoops [wʊps] interj hoppla, huch, hups.

whoosh [wuːʃ] 1 n (of water) Rauschen nt; (of air) Zischen nt. 2 vi rauschen; zischen. **a train ~ed past** ein Zug schoß or brauste vorbei.

whop [wɒp] vt (sl) schlagen. **Pierre always ~s me at tennis** Pierre macht mich beim Tennis immer fertig (inf); **he ~ped me on the chin** er hat mir eine ans Kinn gegeben (inf).

whopper ['wɒpəʳ] n (sl) (sth big) Brocken, Trümmer m (inf), Trumm m (inf); (lie) faustdicke Lüge.

whopping ['wɒpɪŋ] adj (sl) Mords- (inf), Riesen-. **a ~ big fish** ein mordsgroßer Fisch (inf), ein (gewaltiges) Trumm von einem Fisch (inf).

whore [hɔːʳ] 1 n Hure f. 2 vi (also **to go whoring**) (herum)huren (sl).

whore: ~**house** n Bordell, Freudenhaus nt; ~**monger** n (old) Hurenbock m.

whorl [wɜːl] n Kringel m; (of shell) (Spiral)windung f; (Bot) Quirl, Wirtel m; (of fingerprint) Wirbel m.

whortleberry ['wɜːtlbərɪ] n Heidelbeere, Blaubeere (dial) f.

who's [huːz] contr of who has; who is.

whose [huːz] poss pron (a) (interrog) wessen. **~ is this?** wem gehört das?; **~ car did you go in?** in wessen Auto sind Sie gefahren? (b) (rel) dessen; (after f and pl) deren.

whosoever [,huːsəʊ'evəʳ] pron (old) see **whoever**.

why [waɪ] 1 adv warum, weshalb; (asking for the purpose) wozu; (how come that ...) wieso. **~ not ask him?** warum fragst du/fragen wir etc ihn nicht?; **~ wait?** warum or wozu (soll(t)en wir/sie) (noch) warten?; **~ do it this way?** warum denn so?; **that's ~** darum, deshalb, deswegen; **that's exactly ~ ...** genau deshalb or deswegen ...
2 interj **~, of course, that's right!** ja doch or aber sicher, das stimmt so!; **are you sure? — ~ yes (of course/I think so)** sind Sie sicher?; — (aber) ja doch; **~ that's easy!** na, das ist doch einfach!; **take the bus! ~, it's only a short walk** den Bus nehmen! - ach was, das ist doch nur ein Katzensprung; **~, if he isn't Charles!** na so was, das ist doch (der) Charles!; **who did it? ~ it's obvious** wer das war? na or also, das ist doch klar; **if he hits the ball so hard, ~ it's no wonder his racket breaks** wenn er den Ball so fest schlägt, (na) also dann ist es kein Wunder, wenn sein Schläger kaputtgeht.
3 n: **the ~s and (the) wherefores** das Warum und Weshalb.

WI abbr of (a) Women's Institute. (b) West Indies.

wick [wɪk] n Docht m. **to get on sb's ~** (inf) jdm auf den Wecker gehen (inf) or fallen (inf).

wicked ['wɪkɪd] adj (a) (evil) person etc böse; (immoral) schlecht, gottlos; (indulging in vices) lasterhaft. **that was a ~ thing to do** das war aber gemein or böse or niederträchtig (von dir/ihm etc); **it's ~ to tease animals/tell lies/swear** Tiere zu quälen ist gemein/Lügen/Fluchen ist häßlich.
(b) (vicious) böse; weapon gemein (inf), niederträchtig, heimtückisch; satire boshaft; blow, frost, wind, weather also gemein (inf). **he/the dog has a ~ temper** er ist unbeherrscht or aufbrausend or jähzornig/der Hund ist bösartig.
(c) (mischievous) smile, look, grin frech, boshaft. **you ~ girl, you** du schlimmes Mädchen or du freches Stück (inf), (du)!; **I've just had a ~ idea** mir fällt (gerade) was Tolles (inf) or (practical joke) ein guter Streich ein.
(d) (inf: scandalous) price etc hanebüchen (inf), unverschämt. **it's a ~ shame** es ist jammerschade; **it's ~ what they charge** es ist hanebüchen (inf) or unverschämt or nicht mehr feierlich (inf), was die verlangen.

wickedly ['wɪkɪdlɪ] adv see adj (a) böse; schlecht, gottlos; lasterhaft. (b) cold gemein. **a ~ accurate satire** eine scharf treffende Satire. (c) frech. (d) (inf) expensive unverschämt.

wickedness ['wɪkɪdnɪs] n (a) (of person) Schlechtigkeit f; (immorality) Verderbtheit f; (indulgence in vices) Lasterhaftigkeit f. (b) see adj (b) Bösartigkeit f; Boshaftigkeit f; Gemeinheit f. **the ~ of his temper** seine aufbrausende or unbeherrschte Art. (c) (mischievousness) Boshaftigkeit, Bosheit f. (d) (inf: of prices etc) Unverschämtheit f.

wicker ['wɪkəʳ] 1 n Korbgeflecht nt. 2 adj attr Korb-.

wicker: ~ **basket** n (Weiden)korb m; ~ **fence** n Weidenzaun m; ~**work** n (activity) Korbflechten nt; (material) Korbgeflecht nt; (articles) Korbwaren pl.

wicket ['wɪkɪt] n (a) Gatter nt; (for selling tickets) Fenster nt. (b) (Cricket) (stumps: also ~s) Mal, Pfostentor nt; (pitch) Spielbahn f. **to take a ~** einen Schlagmann ausworfen; **three ~s fell before lunch** es gab drei Malwürfe vor der Mittagspause; **we won by four ~s** wir gewannen und hatten vier Schlagmänner noch nicht in Einsatz gehabt; **to keep ~** Torwächter sein or machen; see **sticky**. (c) (US: croquet hoop) Tor nt.

wicket-keeper ['wɪkɪt,kiːpəʳ] n (Cricket) Torwächter m.

widdle ['wɪdl] (inf) 1 vi pinkeln (inf). 2 n **to go for a ~** (hum) pinkeln gehen (inf).

wide [waɪd] 1 adj (a) road, smile, feet, gap breit; skirt, trousers, plain weit; eyes groß. **it is three metres ~** es ist drei Meter breit; (material) es liegt drei Meter breit; (room) es ist drei Meter in der Breite; **the big ~ world** die (große) weite Welt.
(b) (considerable, comprehensive) difference, variety groß; experience, choice reich, umfangreich; public, knowledge,

range breit; interests vielfältig, breitgefächert attr; coverage of report umfassend; network weitverzweigt attr; circulation weit, groß; question weitreichend. **~ reading is the best education** viel zu lesen ist die beste Art der Erziehung or Bildung; **his ~ reading** seine große Belesenheit.
(c) (missing the target) daneben pred, gefehlt. **you're a bit ~ there** da liegst du etwas daneben; **~ of the truth** nicht ganz wahrheitsgetreu; **a ~ ball** (Cricket) ein Ball, der nicht in Reichweite des Schlagmanns abspringt.
2 adv (a) (extending far) weit. **they are set ~ apart** sie liegen weit auseinander; see **far**.
(b) (fully) weit. **open ~!** bitte weit öffnen; **the general/writer left himself ~ open to attack** der General/Verfasser hat sich (überhaupt) nicht gegen Angriffe abgesichert; **the law is ~ open to criticism/abuse** das Gesetz bietet viele Ansatzpunkte für Kritik/öffnet dem Mißbrauch Tür und Tor; **the game is still ~ open** der Spielausgang ist noch völlig offen; **to be ~ awake** hellwach sein; (alert) wach sein.
(c) (far from the target) daneben. **to go ~ of** sth über etw (acc) hinausgehen, an etw (dat) vorbeigehen.

-wide [-waɪd] adj suf über or für den/die/das gesamte(n), in dem/der gesamte(n); (country- etc) -weit. **a company-~ pay increase** eine Gehaltserhöhung für die ganze Firma.

wide: ~**-angle** (lens) n (Phot) Weitwinkel(objektiv nt) m; ~**-awake** adj (fully awake) hellwach; (alert) wach; **you can't fool her, she's much too ~-awake** du kannst ihr nichts vormachen, dazu paßt sie viel zu genau auf or dazu ist sie viel zu wach or helle (inf); **he has to be ~-awake to all their dodges** er muß genau aufpassen, daß ihm keiner ihrer Tricks entgeht; ~**-awake** hat n Schlapphut m; ~**-band** adj (Rad) Breitband-; ~ **boy** n (Brit inf) Fuchs (inf), Gauner m; ~**-eyed** adj mit großen Augen; **she gazed at him with ~-eyed innocence** sie starrte ihn mit großen, unschuldigen Kinderaugen an; **in ~-eyed amazement** mit großen, erstaunten Augen.

widely ['waɪdlɪ] adv weit; (by or to many people) weit und breit, überall, allgemein; differing völlig. **his remarks were ~ publicized** seine Bemerkungen fanden weite Verbreitung; **the opinion is ~ held** ... es herrscht in weiten Kreisen die Ansicht ...; **it is not ~ understood why** ... es wird nicht überall or von allen verstanden, warum ...; **he became ~ known as** ... er wurde überall or in weiten Kreisen bekannt als ...; **a ~ read student** ein sehr belesener Student.

widen ['waɪdn] 1 vt road verbreitern; passage erweitern; knowledge, interests etc erweitern. 2 vi breiter werden; (interests etc) sich ausweiten.

♦ **widen out** vi (a) (river, valley etc) sich erweitern (into zu). (b) (interests etc) sich ausweiten.

wideness ['waɪdnɪs] n (a) (of road, gap) Breite f; (of skirt) Weite f. (b) (of knowledge, coverage, interests) Breite f; (of variety, choice) Reichtum m.

wide: ~**-open** adj (a) (fully open) door, window ganz or weit or sperrangelweit (inf) offen; beak weit aufgerissen or aufgesperrt; **the ~-open spaces** die Weite (b) (not decided) match etc völlig offen; (c) (US inf) **wo liberale Gesetze bezüglich Prostitution, Glücksspiele etc herrschen**; ~**-ranging** adj weitreichend; ~**-screen** adj Breit(lein)wand-; ~**-spread** adj weitverbreitet attr; **to become ~-spread** weite Verbreitung erlangen.

widgeon ['wɪdʒən] n Pfeifente f.

widow ['wɪdəʊ] 1 n (a) Witwe f. **to be left a ~** als Witwe zurückbleiben; ~**'s mite** (fig) Schärflein nt (der armen Witwe); ~**'s peak** spitzer Haaransatz; ~**'s pension** Witwenrente f; **golf ~** (hum) Golfwitwe f; see **grass ~**.
(b) (Typ) Hurenkind nt.
2 vt zur Witwe/zum Witwer machen. **she was twice ~ed** sie ist zweimal verwitwet.

widowed ['wɪdəʊd] adj verwitwet.

widower ['wɪdəʊəʳ] n Witwer m.

widowhood ['wɪdəʊhʊd] n (of woman) (period) Witwenschaft f; (state also) Witwentum nt; (rare: of man) Witwerschaft f.

width [wɪdθ] n (a) Breite f; (of trouser legs, skirts etc) Weite f; (of interests also) Vielfalt f. **the ~ of his reading** seine umfassende Belesenheit; **six centimetres in ~** sechs Zentimeter breit; **what is the ~ of the material?** wie breit liegt dieser Stoff? (b) (of material) Breite f. **three ~s of cloth** drei mal die Breite.

widthways ['wɪdθweɪz], **widthwise** ['wɪdθwaɪz] adv der Breite nach.

wield [wiːld] vt pen, sword führen; axe schwingen; power, influence ausüben, haben. ~**ing his sword above his head** das Schwert über seinem Haupte schwingend; **to ~ power over sth** über etw (acc) Macht ausüben.

wife [waɪf] n, pl **wives** Frau, Gattin (form), Gemahlin (liter, form) f. **the ~** (inf) die Frau; **a woman whom he would never make his ~** eine Person, die er niemals zu seiner Frau machen würde; **businessmen who take their wives with them on their trips** Geschäftsleute, die ihre (Ehe)frauen or Damen mit auf Geschäftsreise nehmen; **to take a ~** (old) sich (dat) eine Frau or ein Weib (old) nehmen; **to take sb to ~** (old) jdn zum Weibe nehmen (old).

wifely ['waɪflɪ] adj ~ **duties** Pflichten pl als Ehefrau; ~ **devotion** Hingabe f einer Ehefrau.

wife-swapping ['waɪf,swɒpɪŋ] n Partnertausch m. ~ **party** Party f mit Partnertausch.

wig [wɪg] n Perücke f.

wigeon n see **widgeon**.

wigging ['wɪgɪŋ] n (dated Brit inf) Standpauke, Gardinenpredigt f. **to give sb a ~** jdm eine Standpauke or Gardinenpredigt halten, jdm die Leviten lesen (dated).

wiggle ['wɪgl] 1 n Wackeln nt no pl. **give it a ~ and it might come free** wackeln Sie mal daran, dann geht es vielleicht raus; **to get**

a ~ **on** (*inf*) Dampf dahintermachen (*inf*). **2** *vt* wackeln mit; *eyebrows* zucken mit. **she** ~**d her way through the crowd** sie lavierte sich durch die Menge. **3** *vi* wackeln; (*eyebrows*) zucken.

wiggly ['wɪglɪ] *adj* wackelnd; *line* Schlangen-; (*drawn*) Wellen-; *amateur film etc* wackelig, verwackelt.

wight [waɪt] *n* (*old*) Wicht *m*.

wigmaker ['wɪgmeɪkəʳ] *n* Perückenmacher(in *f*) *m*.

wigwam ['wɪgwæm] *n* Wigwam *m*.

wilco ['wɪlkəʊ] *interj* (*Mil etc*) wird gemacht, zu Befehl.

wild [waɪld] **1** *adj* **(a)** (*not domesticated, not civilized*) wild; *people* unzivilisiert; *garden, wood* verwildert; *flowers* wildwachsend *attr*; (*in meadows*) Wiesen-; (*in fields*) Feld-. **the** W~ **West** der Wilde Westen; ~ **silk** Wildseide *f*; ~ **animals** Tiere *pl* in freier Wildbahn; **the** ~ **animals of Northern Europe** Tiere *pl* Nordeuropas, die Tierwelt Nordeuropas; **a seal is a** ~ **animal** der Seehund ist kein Haustier *or* lebt in freier Wildbahn; **the plant in its** ~ **state** die Pflanze im Naturzustand.
  (b) (*stormy*) *weather, wind* rauh, stürmisch; *sea also* wild.
  (c) (*excited, frantic, unruly, riotous*) wild (*with vor* +*dat*); (*disordered*) *hair also* wirr, unordentlich; *children also, joy, desire* unbändig. **the** ~ **disorder of the room** das wilde Durcheinander im Zimmer.
  (d) (*inf: angry*) wütend (*with, at* mit, auf +*acc*), rasend. **it drives** *or* **makes me** ~ das macht mich ganz wild *or* rasend; **to get** ~ wild werden (*inf*).
  (e) (*inf: very keen*) **to be** ~ **on** *or* **about sb/sth** auf jdn/etw wild *or* scharf (*inf*) *or* versessen sein; **to be** ~ **to do sth** (*esp US*) wild *or* scharf (*inf*) *or* versessen darauf sein, etw zu tun.
  (f) (*rash, extravagant*) verrückt; *talk, scheme also* unausgegoren, *promise* unüberlegt; *exaggeration* maßlos, wild; *allegation* wild; *fluctuations* stark; *expectations, imagination, fancies* kühn. **never in my** ~**est dreams** auch in meinen kühnsten Träumen nicht.
  (g) (*wide of the mark, erratic*) *throw, shot* Fehl-; *spelling* unsicher. **it was just/he had a** ~ **guess** es war/er hatte nur so (wild) drauflosgeraten.
  (h) (*Cards*) beliebig verwendbar.
  (i) (*sl: fantastic, great*) *attr* toll, Klasse-, Spitzen-; *pred* toll, klasse, Spitze (*all inf*).

2 *adv* **(a)** (*in the natural state*) *grow* wild; *run* frei. **to let one's imagination run** ~ seiner Phantasie (*dat*) freien Lauf lassen; **the roses/the children have run** ~ die Rosen/die Kinder sind verwildert, die Rosen sind ins Kraut gewachsen; **he lets his kids run** ~ (*pej*) er läßt seine Kinder auf der Straße aufwachsen; **in the country the kids can run** ~ auf dem Land kann man die Kinder einfach laufen *or* herumspringen lassen.
  (b) (*without aim*) *shoot* ins Blaue, drauflos; (*off the mark*) *go, throw* daneben.

3 *n* Wildnis *f*. **in the** ~ in der Wildnis, in freier Wildbahn; **the call of the** ~ der Ruf der Wildnis; **the** ~**s** die Wildnis; **out in the** ~**s** (*hum: not in the city*) auf dem platten Lande (*inf*), jwd (*inf*). **out in the** ~**s of Berkshire** im hintersten Berkshire.

wildcat ['waɪldkæt] **1** *n* **(a)** (*Zool, inf: woman*) Wildkatze *f*.
  (b) (*US inf*) (*Comm: risky venture*) gewagte *or* riskante Sache; (*trial oil well*) Probe- *or* Versuchsbohrung *f*.
  2 *adj attr* (*trial*) Versuchs-, Probe-; (*risky*) riskant, gewagt; (*unofficial*) *company etc* Schwindel-. ~ **strike** wilder Streik.

wildebeest ['wɪldɪbiːst] *n* Gnu *nt*.

wilderness ['wɪldənɪs] *n* Wildnis *f*; (*fig*) Wüste *f*. **a voice crying in the** ~ die Stimme eines Rufenden in der Wüste; **a** ~ **of ruins/roofs** ein Gewirr von Ruinen/Dächern; **a** ~ **of waters** eine Wasserwüste.

wild: ~-**eyed** *adj person* wild dreinblickend *attr*; *look* wild; ~**fire** *n* **to spread like** ~**fire** sich wie ein Lauffeuer ausbreiten; ~**fowl** *n, no pl* Wildgeflügel *nt*; ~-**goose chase** *n* fruchtloses Unterfangen, Wolpertingerjagd *f* (*S Ger*); **to send sb out on a** ~-**goose chase** jdn für nichts und wieder nichts losschicken; ~**life** *n* **(a)** die Tierwelt; ~**life sanctuary** Wildschutzgebiet, Wildreservat *nt*; **(b)** (*sl hum: girls*) Weiber *pl* (*inf*).

wildly ['waɪldlɪ] *adv* **(a)** (*violently*) wild, heftig.
  (b) (*in disorder*) wirr. **his hair fell** ~ **over his forehead** sein Haar fiel ihm wirr in die Stirn.
  (c) (*without aim*) wild. **to hit out/shoot** ~ wild um sich schlagen/drauflosschießen.
  (d) (*extravagantly*) *guess* drauflos, ins Blaue hinein; *talk* unausgegoren; *happy* rasend; *exaggerated* stark, maßlos; *wrong, different* total, völlig.
  (e) (*excitedly, distractedly*) wild, aufgeregt.
  (f) (*riotously*) wild.

wildness ['waɪldnɪs] *n* **(a)** (*rough, uncivilized state*) Wildheit *f*.
  (b) (*of storm etc*) Wildheit, Stärke, Heftigkeit *f*. **the** ~ **of the weather** das rauhe *or* stürmische Wetter.
  (c) (*frenzy, unruliness*) Wildheit *f*.
  (d) (*extravagance*) *see adj* (*f*) Unüberlegtheit *f*; Maßlosigkeit *f*; Stärke *f*; Kühnheit *f*.
  (e) (*lack of aim*) Unkontrolliertheit *f*; (*erratic nature: of spelling*) Unsicherheit *f*.

wild oat *n* Windhafer *m*; *see* **oat**.

wile [waɪl] *n usu pl* List *f*, Schliche *pl*. **she used all her** ~**s** sie ließ ihren ganzen *or* all ihren Charme spielen.

wilful, (*US*) **willful** ['wɪlfʊl] *adj* **(a)** (*self-willed*) eigensinnig, eigenwillig. **(b)** (*deliberate*) *neglect, damage, waste* mutwillig; *murder* vorsätzlich; *disobedience* wissentlich.

wilfully, (*US*) **willfully** ['wɪlfəlɪ] *adv see adj*.

wilfulness, (*US*) **willfulness** ['wɪlfʊlnɪs] *n see adj* **(a)** Eigensinn *m*, Eigenwilligkeit *f*. **(b)** Mutwilligkeit *f*; Vorsätzlichkeit *f*.

wiliness ['waɪlɪnɪs] *n* Listigkeit, Schläue, Hinterlist (*pej*) *f*.

will¹ [wɪl] *pret* **would 1** *modal aux vb* **(a)** (*fut*) werden. **I'm sure that he** ~ **come** ich bin sicher, daß er kommt; **you** ~ **come to see us,** won't you Sie kommen uns doch besuchen, ja?; **I'll be**

right there komme sofort!, bin gleich da!; **I** ~ **have finished by Tuesday** bis Dienstag bin ich fertig; **you won't lose it,** ~ **you?** du wirst es doch nicht verlieren, oder?; **you won't insist on that,** ~ **you?** — **oh yes, I** ~ Sie bestehen doch nicht darauf, oder? — o doch!, o ja!, doch, doch!
  (b) (*emphatic, expressing determination, compulsion etc*) **I** ~ **not have it!** das dulde ich nicht, das kommt mir nicht in Frage (*inf*); ~ **you be quiet!** willst du jetzt wohl ruhig sein!, bist du *or* sei jetzt endlich ruhig!; **you** ~ **not talk to me like that!** so lasse ich nicht mit mir reden!; **he says he** ~ **go and I say he won't** er sagt, er geht, und ich sage, er geht nicht.
  (c) (*expressing willingness, consent etc*) wollen. **he won't sign** er unterschreibt nicht, er will nicht unterschreiben; **if she won't say yes** wenn sie nicht ja sagt; **he wouldn't help me** er wollte *or* mochte mir nicht helfen; **wait a moment,** ~ **you?** warten Sie einen Moment, ja bitte?; (*impatiently*) jetzt warte doch mal einen Moment!; ~ **she, won't she** ob sie wohl ...?
  (d) (*in questions*) ~ **you have some more tea?** möchten Sie noch Tee?; ~ **you accept these conditions?** akzeptieren Sie diese Bedingungen?; **won't you take a seat?** wollen *or* möchten Sie nicht sitzen?; **won't you please come home?** komm doch bitte nach Hause!; **there isn't any tea,** ~ **coffee do?** es ist kein Tee da, darf *or* kann es auch Kaffee sein?, tut es Kaffee auch? (*inf*).
  (e) (*insistence*) well, **if he** ~ **drive so fast** also, wenn er (eben) unbedingt so schnell fahren muß *or* fährt; **well, if you won't take advice** wenn du (eben) keinen Rat annimmst, na bitte; **he** ~ **interrupt all the time** er muß ständig dazwischenreden.
  (f) (*assumption*) **he'll be there by now** jetzt ist er schon da *or* dürfte er schon da sein; **was that the door-bell? that** ~ **be for you** hat's geklingelt? — das ist bestimmt für dich *or* das wird *or* dürfte für dich sein; **this** ~ **be the bus** das wird *or* dürfte unser Bus sein; **this** ~ **be the one you want** das dürfte (es) wohl sein, was sie wünschen.
  (g) (*tendency*) **the solution** ~ **turn red if ...** die Lösung färbt sich rot, wenn ...; **sometimes he** ~ **sit in his room for hours** manchmal sitzt er *or* stundenlang in seinem Zimmer; **accidents** ~ **happen** Unfälle passieren nun (ein)mal.
  (h) (*capability*) ~ **the engine start now?** springt der Motor jetzt an?; **the car won't start** das Auto springt nicht an *or* will nicht anspringen; **the door won't open** die Tür läßt sich nicht öffnen *or* geht nicht auf (*inf*); **the cut won't heal** die Schnittwunde will nicht (ver)heilen; **the car** ~ **do up to 120 mph** das Auto fährt bis zu 120 mph *or* kann bis zu 120 mph fahren.

2 *vi* wollen. **say what you** ~ du kannst sagen *or* sag, was du willst; **as you** ~! wie du willst!; **it is, if you** ~, **a kind of mystery** das ist, wenn du so willst, eine Art Rätsel.

will² **1** *n* **(a)** Wille *m*. **to have a** ~ **of one's own** einen eigenen Willen haben; (*hum*) so seine Mucken haben (*inf*); **the** ~ **to win/live** der Wille *or* das Bestreben, zu gewinnen/zu leben, der Siegeswille/Lebenswille; (**to go**) **against one's/sb's** ~ gegen seinen/jds Willen (handeln); **if that's your** ~ wenn das dein Wunsch ist; **at** ~ nach Belieben *or* Lust und Laune; **fire at** ~! ohne Befehl schießen; **of one's own free** ~ aus freien Stücken *or* freiem Willen; **with the best** ~ **in the world** beim *or* mit (dem) (aller)besten Willen; **where there is a** ~ **there is a way** (*Prov*) wo ein Wille ist, ist auch ein Weg (*Prov*); **to do sb's** ~ (*dated*) jdm seinen Willen tun; **to have one's** ~ (*dated*) seinen Kopf durchsetzen; **Thy** ~ **be done** Dein Wille geschehe; **to work with a** ~ mit (Feuer)eifer arbeiten; *see* **goodwill, ill** 1 (b).
  (b) (*testament*) Letzter Wille, Testament *nt*. **the last** ~ **and testament of ...** der Letzte Wille *or* das Testament des/der ...; **to make one's** ~ sein Testament machen.

2 *vt* **(a)** (*old: ordain*) wollen, bestimmen, verfügen (*geh*). **God has so** ~**ed** Gott hat es so gewollt *or* gefügt *or* bestimmt.
  (b) (*urge by willpower*) (durch Willenskraft) erzwingen. **to** ~ **sb to do sth** jdn durch die eigene Willensanstrengung dazu bringen, daß er etw tut; **he** ~**ed himself to stay awake/to get better** er hat sich (dazu) gezwungen, wach zu bleiben/er hat seine Genesung durch seine Willenskraft erzwungen; **he** ~**ed the ball into the net** er hat den Ball ins Netz hypnotisiert (*inf*).
  (c) (*by testament*) (testamentarisch) vermachen, vererben (*sth to sb* jdm etw).

3 *vi* wollen. **if God** ~**s** so Gott will.

willful *etc* (*US*) *see* **wilful** *etc*.

William ['wɪljəm] *n* Wilhelm *m*.

willies ['wɪlɪz] *npl* (*inf*) **to get the** ~ Zustände kriegen (*inf*); **it/he gives me the** ~ da/bei dem wird mir ganz anders (*inf*).

willing ['wɪlɪŋ] *adj* **(a)** (*prepared*) **to be** ~ **to do sth** bereit *or* gewillt (*geh*) *or* willens (*liter, old*) sein, etw zu tun; **God** ~ so Gott will; **he was** ~ **for me to take it** es war ihm recht, daß ich es nahm; **he was not** ~ **for us to go/for this to be done** er war nicht gewillt, uns gehen zu lassen/das geschehen zu lassen.
  (b) (*ready to help, cheerfully ready*) *workers, helpers, assistance* bereitwillig. **prepared to lend a** ~ **hand** gerne dazu bereit zu helfen.

willingly ['wɪlɪŋlɪ] *adv* bereitwillig, gerne. **will you help?** — **yes,** ~ wollen Sie helfen? — (ja,) gerne.

willingness ['wɪlɪŋnɪs] *n see adj* **(a)** Bereitschaft *f*. **(b)** Bereitwilligkeit *f*.

will-o'-the-wisp ['wɪləðə'wɪsp] *n* Irrlicht *nt*; (*fig*) Trugbild *nt*.

willow ['wɪləʊ] *n* (*also* ~ **tree**) Weide *f*, Weidenbaum *m*; (*wood*) Weidenholz *nt*; (*twigs*) Weidenruten *or* -gerten *pl*.

willowherb ['wɪləʊhɜːb] *n* Weidenröschen *nt*.

willow pattern 1 *n* chinesisches Weidenmotiv (*auf Porzellan*).
  2 *adj attr* mit chinesischem Weidenmotiv.

willowy ['wɪləʊɪ] *adj* gertenschlank.

willpower ['wɪlpaʊəʳ] *n* Willenskraft *f*.

willy-nilly ['wɪlɪ'nɪlɪ] *adv* wohl oder übel, nolens volens.

wilt¹ [wɪlt] (*old*) *2nd pers sing of* **will¹**.

wilt² **1** *vi* **(a)** (*flowers*) welken, verwelken, welk werden. **(b)**

(person) matt werden; (after physical exercise) schlapp werden; (enthusiasm, energy) abflauen. 2 vt ausdörren.

Wilts [wɪlts] abbr of **Wiltshire**.

wily ['waɪlɪ] adj (+er) listig, raffiniert, schlau, hinterlistig (pej).

wimple ['wɪmpl] n Rise f (spec), Schleier m; (worn by nuns) (Nonnen)schleier m.

win [wɪn] (vb: pret, ptp **won**) 1 n Sieg m. **to back a horse for a ~** auf den Sieg eines Pferdes setzen; **to have a ~** (money) einen Gewinn machen; (victory) einen Sieg erzielen; **to play for a ~** auf Sieg spielen.

2 vt (a) race, prize, battle, election, money, bet, sympathy, support, friends, glory gewinnen; reputation erwerben; scholarship, contract bekommen; victory erringen. **to ~ sb's heart/love/hand** jds Herz/Liebe/Hand gewinnen; **he tried to ~ her** er versuchte, sie für sich zu gewinnen; **it won him the first prize** es brachte ihm den ersten Preis ein; **to ~ sth from or off (inf) sb** jdm etw abgewinnen.

(b) (obtain, extract) gewinnen. **the oil won from the North Sea** das aus der Nordsee gewonnene Öl; **land won from the sea** dem Meer abgewonnenes Land.

(c) (liter: reach with effort) shore, summit erreichen.

3 vi (a) gewinnen, siegen. **if ~ning becomes too important** wenn das Siegen or das Gewinnen zu wichtig wird; **OK, you ~, I was wrong** okay, du hast gewonnen, ich habe mich geirrt.

(b) (liter) **to ~ free** sich freikämpfen, sich befreien.

♦ **win back** vt sep zurück- or wiedergewinnen.

♦ **win out** vi letztlich siegen (over sb über jdn), sich durchsetzen (over sb jdm gegenüber).

♦ **win over** or **round** vt sep für sich gewinnen. **it is hard to ~ him ~** es ist schwer, ihn für uns or für unsere Seite zu gewinnen; **his speech won ~ all the government's critics** mit seiner Rede hat er alle Kritiker der Regierung für sich gewonnen; **to ~ sb ~ to Catholicism/one's own way of thinking** jdn zum Katholizismus/zur eigenen Denkungsart bekehren; **to ~ sb ~ to a plan** jdn für einen Plan gewinnen.

♦ **win through** vi (patient) durchkommen. **to ~ ~ to a place** sich zu einem Ort durch- or vorkämpfen; **we'll ~ ~ in the end** wir werden es schon schaffen (inf).

wince [wɪns] 1 n (Zusammen)zucken nt. ouch, **he said with a ~** autsch, sagte er und zuckte zusammen; **to give a ~ (of pain)** (vor Schmerz) zusammenzucken. 2 vi zusammenzucken. **without wincing he faced his torturers** er stand seinen Peinigern gegenüber, ohne eine Miene zu verziehen.

winceyette [,wɪnsɪ'et] n Flanellette nt.

winch [wɪntʃ] 1 n Winde, Winsch f. 2 vt winschen.

♦ **winch up** vt sep hochwinschen.

Winchester (rifle) ['wɪntʃestə('raɪfl)] n Winchesterbüchse f.

wind¹ [wɪnd] 1 n (a) Wind m. **the ~ is from the east** der Wind kommt aus dem or von Osten; **before the ~** (Naut) vor dem Wind; **into the ~** (Naut) in den Wind; **to sail close to the ~** (fig) sich hart an der Grenze des Erlaubten bewegen; (Naut) hart am Wind segeln; **(to run) like the ~** (rennen) wie der Wind; **a ~ of change** (fig) ein frischer(er) Wind; **there's something in the ~** (irgend) etwas bahnt sich an or liegt in der Luft; **to get/have the ~ up** (inf) (nervous) Angst or Schiß (sl) kriegen/haben; **to put the ~ up sb** (inf) jdm Angst machen, jdn ins Bockshorn jagen; **to raise the ~** (dated Brit inf) das nötige Kleingeld auftreiben (inf); **to see which way the ~ blows** (fig) sehen, woher der Wind weht; **to take the ~ out of sb's sails** (fig) jdm den Wind aus den Segeln nehmen; **he's full of ~** (fig) er ist ein Schaumschläger (inf), er macht viel Wind (inf).

(b) (scent) **to get ~ of sth** (lit, fig) von etw Wind bekommen.

(c) (compass point) **to the four ~s** in alle (vier) Winde; **to cast or fling or throw caution etc to the ~s** Bedenken etc in den Wind schlagen.

(d) (from bowel, stomach) Wind m, Blähung f. **to break ~** einen Wind streichen lassen; **to bring up ~** aufstoßen; (baby also) ein Bäuerchen machen; **to have a touch of ~** leichte Blähungen haben.

(e) (breath) Atem m, Luft f (inf). **to be short of ~** außer Atem sein; **to get one's ~ back** wieder Luft bekommen or zu Atem kommen; **to get one's second ~** den toten Punkt überwunden haben; **he's losing his ~** ihm geht der Atem aus; **sound in ~ and limb** kerngesund.

2 vt (a) (knock breathless) den Atem nehmen (+dat). **he was ~ed by the ball** der Ball nahm ihm den Atem.

(b) (scent) wittern.

(c) horses verschnaufen lassen.

wind² [waɪnd] (vb: pret, ptp wound) 1 vt (a) (twist, wrap) wool, bandage wickeln; turban etc winden; (one time around) winden; (on to a reel) spulen.

(b) (turn, ~ up) handle kurbeln, drehen; clock, watch, clockwork toy aufziehen.

(c) (proceed by twisting) **to ~ one's way** sich schlängeln.

2 vi (a) (river etc) sich winden or schlängeln.

(b) (handle, watch) **which way does it ~?** wierum zieht man es auf/(handle) dreht or kurbelt man es?; **it won't ~** er/es läßt sich nicht aufziehen/(handle) drehen or kurbeln.

3 n (a) **I'll give the clock a ~** ich werde die Uhr aufziehen; **give it one more ~** zieh es noch eine Umdrehung weiter auf; (handle) kurbele or drehe es noch einmal weiter.

(b) (bend) Kehre, Windung f.

♦ **wind around** 1 vt sep +prep obj wickeln um. **~ it once/twice ~ the post** winde or lege or wickele es einmal/zweimal um den Pfosten; **to ~ one's arms ~ sb** seine Arme um jdn schlingen or winden (geh); **to ~ itself ~** sich um etw schlingen. 2 vi (road) sich winden, +prep obj (road) sich schlängeln durch; (procession) sich winden durch.

♦ **wind back** vt sep film zurückspulen.

♦ **wind down** 1 vt sep (a) car windows etc herunterdrehen or -kurbeln. (b) operations reduzieren; production zurück-

schrauben. 2 vi (a) (lose speed: clock) ablaufen. (b) (path etc) sich hinunterwinden or -schlängeln.

♦ **wind forward** vt sep film weiterspulen.

♦ **wind in** vt sep fish einziehen or -holen; rope also aufspulen.

♦ **wind on** vt sep film weiterspulen.

♦ **wind out** vt sep cable abwickeln, ab- or runterspulen.

♦ **wind round** vti sep see **wind around**.

♦ **wind up 1** vt sep (a) bucket herauf- or hochholen; car window hinaufkurbeln or -drehen.

(b) clock, mechanism aufziehen. **to be wound ~ about sth** (fig) über etw (acc) or wegen einer Sache (gen) erregt sein; **to be wound ~ to a state of ...** sich in einen Zustand des/der ... steigern.

(c) (close, end) meeting, debate, speech beschließen, zu Ende bringen. **he wound ~ the arguments for the government** er faßte die Argumente der Regierung(sseite) zusammen.

(d) company auflösen; service, series auslaufen lassen. **to ~ one's affairs** seine Angelegenheiten abwickeln.

2 vi (a) (inf: end up) enden. **to ~ ~ in hospital/Munich** im Krankenhaus/in München landen; **to ~ ~ for the government** die abschließende Rede für die Regierung halten; **to ~ ~ doing sth/broke/with nothing** am Ende etw tun/pleite sein/ohne etwas da stehen; **he'll ~ ~ as director** er wird es noch bis zum Direktor bringen; **we sang a song to ~ ~** abschließend or zum Schluß sangen wir noch ein Lied.

(b) (proceed by twisting) sich hinaufwinden; (road also) sich hinaufschlängeln.

wind ['wɪnd-]: **~bag** n (inf) Schwätzer, Schaumschläger m; **~blown** adj hair, tree windzerzaust; **~break** n Windschutz m; **~breaker** ® n (US) see **~cheater; ~burn** n Rötung f der Haut auf Grund von Wind; **~cheater** n (Brit) Windjacke or -bluse f; **~cone** n (Aviat) Wind- or Luftsack m.

winded ['wɪndɪd] adj atemlos, außer Atem.

winder ['waɪndə²] n (of watch) Krone f, (Aufzieh)rädchen nt; (of alarm clock, toy etc) Aufziehschraube f.

wind ['wɪnd-]: **~fall** n Fallobst nt; (fig) unerwartetes Geschenk, unverhoffter Glücksfall; **~ gauge** n Wind(stärke)messer m.

windiness ['wɪndɪnɪs] n Wind m. **because of the ~ of the area** wegen des starken Windes in dieser Gegend.

winding ['waɪndɪŋ] 1 adj river gewunden; road also kurvenreich. 2 n (a) (of road, river) Windung, Kehre f; (fig) Verwicklung f. (b) (Elec) (coil) Wicklung f; (simple twist) Windung f.

winding: **~ sheet** n (old) Leichentuch nt; **~ staircase** n Wendeltreppe f; **~-up** n (of project) Abschluß m; (of company, society) Auflösung f; **~-up sale** n Räumungsverkauf m.

wind ['wɪnd-]: **~ instrument** n Blasinstrument nt; **~jammer** n Windjammer m.

windlass ['wɪndləs] n (winch) Winde f; (Naut) Ankerwinde f.

wind ['wɪnd-]: **~less** adj windfrei, ohne Wind, windstill; **~machine** n Windmaschine f; **~mill** n Windmühle f; (Brit: toy) Windrädchen nt; **to tilt at or fight ~mills** (fig) gegen Windmühlen(flügel) kämpfen.

window ['wɪndəʊ] n Fenster nt; (shop ~) (Schau)fenster nt; (of booking office, bank) Schalter m. **a ~ on the world** (fig) ein Fenster zur Welt.

window: **~ box** n Blumenkasten m; **~-cleaner** n Fensterputzer m; **~ display** n Auslage(n pl), Schaufensterdekoration f; **~-dresser** n (Schaufenster)dekorateur(in f) m; **~-dressing** n Auslagen- or Schaufensterdekoration f; (fig) Mache, Schau (inf), Augen(aus)wischerei (pej) f; **that's just ~-dressing** das ist alles nur Mache or alles, um nach Außen hin zu wirken; **~ envelope** n Briefumschlag m mit Fenster; **~ ledge** n see **~sill; ~pane** n Fensterscheibe f; **~ seat** n (in house) Fensterbank f or -sitz m; (Rail etc) Fensterplatz m; **~ shade** n (esp US) Springrollo nt; **~-shopper** n jd, der einen Schaufensterbummel macht; **~-shopping** n Schaufensterbummel m; **to go ~-shopping** einen Schaufensterbummel machen; **~sill** n Fensterbank f or -brett nt; (outside also) Fenstersims m.

wind ['wɪnd-]: **~pipe** n Luftröhre f; **~proof** adj luftdicht, windundurchlässig; **~screen, (US) ~shield** n Windschutzscheibe f; **~screen or (US) ~shield wiper** n Scheibenwischer m; **~ section** n (Mus) Bläser pl; **~ sleeve, ~sock** n Luft- or Windsack m; **~swept** adj plains über den/die/das der Wind fegt; person, hair (vom Wind) zerzaust; **~-tunnel** n Windkanal m.

windup ['waɪndʌp] n (US) see **winding-up**.

windward ['wɪndwəd] 1 adj Wind-, dem Wind zugekehrt; direction zum Wind. 2 n Windseite f. **to steer to ~ of an island** auf die Windseite einer Insel zusteuern.

windy ['wɪndɪ] adj (+er) day, weather, place windig. (b) (inf: verbose) speech, style langatmig. **a ~ speaker** ein Schwätzer m. (c) (esp Brit inf: frightened) **to be/get ~** Angst or Schiß (sl) haben/bekommen.

wine [waɪn] 1 n Wein m. **~ and cheese party** Einladung, bei der Wein und Käse gereicht wird; **to put new ~ in old bottles** jungen Wein in alte Schläuche füllen.

2 vt **to ~ and dine sb** jdn zu einem guten Abendessen einladen; **the businessmen were ~d and dined in every city they visited** die Geschäftsleute wurden in jeder Stadt, die sie besuchten, ausgezeichnet bewirtet; **he ~d and dined her for months** er hat sie monatelang zum Abendessen ausgeführt.

wine: **~ bottle** n Weinflasche f; **~ bucket** n Sektkühler m; **~ cellar** n Weinkeller m; **~-cooler** n Weinkühler m; **~ glass** n Weinglas nt; **~-grower** n Winzer, Weinbauer or -gärtner m; **~-growing 1** adj district Wein(an)bau-; **2** n Wein(an)bau m; **~ list** n Weinkarte f; **~-making** n nichtprofessionelle Herstellung von (Beeren)wein; **~ merchant** n Weinhändler m; **~press** n Weinpresse, Kelter f.

winery ['waɪnərɪ] n (US) (Wein)kellerei f.

wine: **~skin** n Weinschlauch m; **~-taster** n Weinverkoster or -prüfer m; **~-tasting** n Weinprobe f; **~ waiter** n Weinkellner, Getränkekellner m.

wing [wɪŋ] **1** *n* **(a)** (*of bird, plane, building, Mil, Pol, Sport*) Flügel *m*; (*of bird also*) Schwinge *f* (*poet*), Fittich *m* (*liter*); (*of chair*) Backe *f*; (*Brit Aut*) Kotflügel *m*. **on the ~** im Flug(e); **to take sb under one's ~** (*fig*) jdn unter seine Fittiche nehmen; **to spread one's ~s** (*fig: children*) flügge werden; **to take ~s** (*lit*) davonfliegen; (*project etc*) Auftrieb bekommen; **on the ~s of fantasy** (*liter*) auf den Flügeln *or* Schwingen der Phantasie; **on the ~s of song** (*liter*) auf (den) Gesanges Flügeln (*liter*); **fear/hope lent ~s to his feet** (*liter*) (die) Angst hat ihm Beine gemacht/Hoffnung beflügelte seinen Schritt (*liter*); **do you expect me to grow or sprout ~s?** (*inf*) du glaubst wohl, ich kann fliegen? (*inf*); **to play on the ~** (*Sport*) auf dem Flügel spielen.
(b) (*Aviat: section of air-force*) Geschwader *nt*. **~s pl** (*pilot's badge*) Pilotenabzeichen *nt*; **to get one's ~s** (*fig*) sich (*dat*) seine Sporen verdienen.
(c) **~s pl** (*Theat*) Kulisse *f*; **to wait in the ~s** (*lit, fig*) in den Kulissen warten.
2 *vt* **(a)** **to ~ one's way** fliegen.
(b) (*fig liter: give ~s to*) beflügeln.
(c) (*graze*) *person, bird* (mit einem Schuß) streifen. **you only ~ed it** das war nur ein Streifschuß, du hast es nur gestreift.
3 *vi* fliegen.

wing: ~ assembly *n* Tragwerk *nt*; **~-beat** *n* Flügelschlag *m*; **~ case** *n* Deckflügel, Flügeldecken *pl*; **~ chair** *n* Ohren- *or* Backensessel *m*; **~ collar** *n* Eckenkragen *m*; **~-commander** *n* (*Brit*) Oberstleutnant *m* (der Luftwaffe).
wingding ['wɪŋˌdɪŋ] *n* (*US sl*) tolle Party (*inf*).
winged [wɪŋd] *adj* **(a)** (*Zool, Bot*) mit Flügeln. **the W~ Victory** die Nike von Samothrake; **the W~ Horse** (der) Pegasus. **(b)** (*liter*) *sentiments, words* geflügelt. **on ~ feet** mit beflügeltem Schritt (*liter*), auf schnellem Fuß.
-winged *adj suf* **mit ... Flügeln;** *bird also* **-flügelig.**
winger ['wɪŋər] *n* (*Sport*) Flügelspieler(in *f*), Flügelmann *m*.
wing: ~ feather *n* Flügelfeder *f*; **~-forward** *n* (*Rugby*) Flügelstürmer *m* (*im Rugby*); **~less** *adj* flügellos; **~ nut** *n* Flügelmutter *f*; **~span** *n* Flügelspannweite *f*; **~spread** *n* Spannweite *f*; **~-three-quarter** *n* (*Rugby*) Dreiviertelspieler *m* auf dem Flügel (*im Rugby*); **~tip** *n* Flügelspitze *f*.
wink [wɪŋk] **1** *n* **(a)** (*with eye*) Zwinkern, Blinzeln *nt*. **to give sb a ~** jdm zuzwinkern *or* zublinzeln; **to tip sb the ~** (*inf*) jdm einen Wink geben; *see* **nod**.
(b) (*instant*) **I didn't get a ~ of sleep** *or* **I didn't sleep a ~** ich habe kein Auge zugetan.
2 *vt eye* blinzeln, zwinkern mit (+*dat*). **he ~d a mischievous eye at me** *or* blinzelte *or* zwinkerte mir pfiffig zu.
3 *vi* **(a)** (*meaningfully*) zwinkern, blinzeln; (*light, star etc*) blinken, funkeln. **to ~ at sb** jdm zuzwinkern *or* zublinzeln; **to ~ at sth** (*inf*) etw geflissentlich übersehen, einfach wegsehen *or* **-schauen**; **it's as easy as ~(ing)** (*dated inf*) das ist ein Kinderspiel; **~ing lights** (*Aut*) Blinklichter, Blinker *pl*.
winker ['wɪŋkər] *n* (*Brit Aut inf*) Blinker *m*.
winkle ['wɪŋkl] *n* Strandschnecke *f*.
♦ **winkle out** *vt sep* (*inf*) **to ~ sth/sb** etw herausklauben *or* (*behind sth*) hervorklauben (*inf*)/jdn loseisen (*inf*); **to ~ sth ~ of sb** etw aus jdm herauskriegen (*inf*).
winkle-pickers ['wɪŋklˌpɪkəz] *npl* (*inf*) spitze Schuhe *pl*.
winnable ['wɪnəbl] *adj* zu gewinnen.
winner ['wɪnər] *n* (*in race, competition*) Sieger(in *f*) *m*; (*of bet, pools etc*) Gewinner(in *f*) *m*; (*card*) Gewinnkarte *f*; (*Tennis etc: shot*) Schlag, der sitzt, Treffer *m*; (*inf: sth successful*) Renner (*inf*), (Verkaufs)schlager, (Publikums)erfolg *m*. **to be onto a ~** (*inf*) das große Los gezogen haben (*inf*).
winning ['wɪnɪŋ] **1** *adj* **(a)** (*successful*) *person, entry* der/die gewinnt; *horse, team* siegreich; *goal* Sieges-; *point, stroke* (das Spiel) entscheidend. **the ~ time** die beste Zeit; **~ post** Zielpfosten *m or* -stange *f*; **~ score** Spielergebnis *nt*. **(b)** (*charming*) *smile, ways* gewinnend, einnehmend. **2** *n* **~s** *pl* Gewinn *m*.
winningly ['wɪnɪŋlɪ] *adv smile* gewinnend, einnehmend.
winnow ['wɪnəʊ] *vt corn* worfeln, von der Spreu reinigen; (*fig liter*) sichten. **to ~ the chaff from the wheat** die Spreu vom Weizen trennen *or* scheiden (*also fig liter*).
winnower ['wɪnəʊər], **winnowing machine** ['wɪnəʊɪŋməˌʃiːn] *n* Worfschaufel, Worfelmaschine *f*.
wino ['waɪnəʊ] *n* (*sl*) Penner (*sl*), Saufbruder (*inf*) *m*.
winsome ['wɪnsəm] *adj child, lass* reizend, sympathisch; *ways, smile* gewinnend, einnehmend.
winter ['wɪntər] **1** *n* (*lit, fig*) Winter *m*.
2 *adj attr* Winter-. **~ quarters** Winterquartier *nt*; **~ solstice** Wintersonnenwende *f*; **~ sports** Wintersport *m*; **~time** Winter *m*; (*for clocks*) Winterzeit *f*.
3 *vi* überwintern, den Winter verbringen.
4 *vt cattle* durch den Winter bringen.
wintergreen ['wɪntəˌgriːn] *n* (*plant*) Teebeere *f*; (*flavouring*) Wintergrünöl *n*.
winterize ['wɪntəraɪz] *vt* (*US*) winterfest machen.
wint(e)ry ['wɪnt(ə)rɪ] *adj* winterlich; (*fig*) *look* eisig; *smile* frostig, kühl.
wintriness ['wɪntrɪnɪs] *n* Winterlichkeit *f*.
wipe [waɪp] **1** *n* Wischen *nt*. **to give sth a ~** etw abwischen.
2 *vt* wischen; *floor* aufwischen; *window* überwischen; *hands, feet* abwischen, abputzen (*rare*). **to ~ sb/sth dry/clean** jdn/etw abtrocknen *or* trockenreiben/jdn/etw sauberwischen *or* säubern; **to ~ sth with/on a cloth** etw mit/an einem Tuch abwischen; **to ~ one's brow/eyes/nose** sich (*dat*) über die Stirn/Augen wischen *or* fahren, sich (*dat*) den Stirn abwischen/Augen wischen/Nase putzen; **to ~ one's feet** sich (*dat*) die Füße *or* Schuhe abstreifen *or* -wischen *or* -treten; **to ~ the tears from one's eyes** sich die Tränen aus den Augen wischen; **to ~ oneself** *or* **one's bottom** sich (*dat*) den Hintern *or* sich abputzen; **to ~ the floor with sb** (*fig sl*) jdn fertigmachen (*inf*).
♦ **wipe away** *vt sep* (*lit, fig*) wegwischen; *tears also* abwischen.

♦ **wipe down** *vt sep* abwaschen; (*with dry cloth*) abreiben; *window* überwischen.
♦ **wipe off 1** *vt sep mark* weg- *or* abwischen; (*from blackboard also*) ab- *or* auslöschen. **~ that smile ~ your face** (*inf*) hör auf zu grinsen (*inf*); **I'll soon ~ that smile ~ his face** (*inf*) dem wird bald das Lachen vergehen; **to be ~d ~ the map** *or* **the face of the earth** von der Landkarte *or* Erdoberfläche verschwinden *or* gefegt werden. **2** *vi* sich weg- *or* abwischen lassen.
♦ **wipe out** *vt sep* **(a)** (*clean*) *bath, bowl* auswischen. **(b)** (*erase*) *memory, part of brain, sth on blackboard* (aus)löschen; *guilt feelings* verschwinden lassen. **(c)** (*cancel*) *debt* bereinigen; *gain, benefit* zunichte machen. **(d)** (*destroy*) *disease, village, race* ausrotten; *enemy, battalion* aufreiben.
♦ **wipe up 1** *vt sep liquid* aufwischen, aufputzen (*Sw*); *dishes* abtrocknen. **2** *vi* abtrocknen.
wipe: ~-down *n* Abreibung *f*; **~-over** *n* **to give sth a ~-over** etw über- *or* abwischen.
wiper ['waɪpər] *n* (Scheiben)wischer *m*.
wiping-up ['waɪpɪŋˌʌp] *n* **to do the ~** abtrocknen.
wire [waɪər] **1** *n* **(a)** Draht *m*; (*for electricity supply*) Leitung *f*; (*insulated flex, for home appliance etc*) Schnur *f*; (*for television*) Fernsehanschluß *m or* -kabel *nt*; (*in circus: high ~*) (Hoch)seil *nt*. **to get in under the ~** (*US*) etwas gerade (eben) noch rechtzeitig *or* mit Hängen und Würgen (*inf*) schaffen; **to pull ~s** (*inf*) seinen Einfluß geltend machen, seine Beziehungen spielen lassen; **he's pulling your ~** (*Brit inf*) er nimmt dich auf den Arm (*inf*).
(b) (*Telec*) telegraphieren, kabeln (*old*).
2 *vt* **(a)** (*put in wiring*) *house* die (elektrischen) Leitungen verlegen in (+*dat*); (*connect to electricity*) (an das Stromnetz) anschließen. **it's all ~d (up) for television** Fernsehanschluß *or* die Verkabelung für das Fernsehen ist vorhanden.
(b) (*Telec*) telgraphieren, kabeln (*old*).
(c) (*fix on ~*) *beads* auf Draht auffädeln; (*fix with ~*) mit Draht zusammen- *or* verbinden. **to ~ the parts together** die Teile mit Draht zusammen- *or* verbinden.
3 *vi* telegraphieren, drahten, kabeln (*old*).
♦ **wire up** *vt sep fights, battery, speakers* anschließen; *house* elektrische Leitungen *or* den Strom verlegen. **we ~d the room ~ as a recording studio** wir haben den Raum als Aufnahmestudio eingerichtet.
wire: ~-cutters *npl* Drahtschere *f*; **~-haired** *adj terrier* drahthaarig, Drahthaar-.
wireless ['waɪəlɪs] (*esp Brit dated*) **1** *n* **(a)** (*also ~ set*) Radio, Rundfunkgerät *nt*, Radioapparat *m*.
(b) (*radio*) Rundfunk *m*; (*also ~ telegraphy*) drahtlose Telegraphie; (*also ~ telephony*) drahtlose Übertragung, drahtloses Telephon. **to send a message by ~** eine Botschaft über Funk schicken *or* senden.
2 *vti* funken; *base etc* anfunken.
wireless operator *n* (*on ship, plane*) Funker *m*.
wire: ~ netting *n* Maschendraht *m*; **~photo** *n* (*method*) Bildtelegraphie *f*; (*picture*) Bildtelegramm *nt*; **~-puller** *n* (*inf*) Drahtzieher *m*; **~-pulling** *n* (*inf*) Drahtzieherei, Drahtzieherei *f*; **~ rope** *n* Drahtseil *nt*; **~ service** *n* (*US*) Nachrichtendienst *m*, Nachrichtenagentur *f*; **~-tap** **1** *n* (*device*) Abhörgerät *nt*, Wanze *f*; (*activity*) Abhören *nt*; **2** *vt phone* abhören, anzapfen; *building* abhören in (+*dat*); **~-tapper** *n* Abhörer *m*; **~-tapping** *n* Abhören *nt*, Anzapfen *nt* von Leitungen; **~ wheel** *n* Rad *nt* mit Sportfelgen; **~ wool** *n* Stahlwolle *f*; **~worm** *n* Drahtwurm *m*.
wiring ['waɪərɪŋ] *n* elektrische Leitungen, Stromkabel *pl*.
wiring diagram *n* Schaltplan *m or* -schema *nt*.
wiry ['waɪərɪ] *adj* (+*er*) drahtig; *hair also* borstig.
wisdom ['wɪzdəm] *n* Weisheit *f*; (*prudence*) Einsicht *f*. **to show great ~** große Klugheit *or* Einsicht zeigen; **to doubt the ~ of sth** bezweifeln, ob etw klug *or* sinnvoll ist.
wisdom tooth *n* Weisheitszahn *m*.
wise[1] [waɪz] *adj* (+*er*) weise; (*prudent, sensible*) *move, step etc* klug, gescheit, vernünftig; (*inf: smart*) klug, schlau. **a ~ choice** eine kluge *or* gute Wahl; **the Three W~ Men** die drei Weisen; **to be ~ in the ways of the world** Lebenserfahrung haben, das Leben kennen; **to be ~ after the event** hinterher den Schlauen spielen *or* gut reden haben; **I'm none the ~r** (*inf*) ich bin nicht klüger als zuvor *or* vorher; **nobody will be any the ~r** (*inf*) niemand wird etwas (davon) merken *or* das spitzkriegen (*inf*); **you'd be ~ to ...** du tätest gut daran, ...; **you'd better get ~** (*US inf*) nimm endlich Vernunft an; **to get ~ to sb/sth** (*inf*) etw spitzkriegen (*inf*), dahinterkommen, wie jd/etw ist; **to be ~ to sb/sth** (*inf*) jdn/etw kennen; **he fooled her twice, then she got ~ to him** zweimal hat er sie hereingelegt, dann ist sie ihm auf die Schliche gekommen; **to put sb ~ to sb/sth** (*inf*) jdn über jdn/etw aufklären (*inf*).
♦ **wise up** (*esp US inf*) **1** *vi* **if he doesn't ~ ~ soon to what's going on/the need for ...** wenn er nicht bald dahinterkommt *or* ihm nicht bald ein Licht aufgeht (*inf*), was da gespielt wird/ wenn er nicht bald hinter die Notwendigkeit zu ... kommt ...; **he's never going to ~ ~** der lernt's nie!, der wird auch nie klüger; **~ ~, man!** Mann, wach auf *or* nimm Vernunft an!
2 *vt sep* aufklären (*inf*) (*to* über +*acc*).
wise[2] *n, no pl* (*old*) Weise *f*. **in this ~** auf diese Weise, so; **in no ~** in keiner Weise, keineswegs.
-wise *adv suf* -mäßig, in puncto.
wise: ~acre *n* Besserwisser, Neunmalkluger *m*; **~crack** (*esp US*) **1** *n* Witzelei *f*; (*pej*) Stichelei *f*; **to make a ~crack (about sb/sth)** witzeln (über jdn/etw); **2** *vi* witzeln; **~ guy** *n* (*esp US inf*) Klugschwätzer (*inf*), Klugscheißer (*sl*) *m*.
wisely ['waɪzlɪ] *adv smile* (*sensibly*) klugerweise. **he nodded his head ~** er nickte weise mit dem Kopf.
wish [wɪʃ] **1** *n* **(a)** Wunsch *m* (*for* nach). **your ~ is my command** dein Wunsch ist *or* sei mir Befehl; **I have no great ~ to see him** ich habe kein Bedürfnis *or* keine große Lust, ihn zu sehen;

to make a ~ sich (*dat*) etwas wünschen; **you can make three ~es** du hast drei Wünsche; **the ~ is father to the thought** (*prov*) der Wunsch ist Vater des Gedankens (*prov*); **well, you got your ~** jetzt hast du ja, was du wolltest; **you shall have your ~** dein Wunsch soll (dir) erfüllt werden *or* soll in Erfüllung gehen.

(b) ~es *pl* (*in greetings*) **with best** ~es mit den besten Wünschen *or* Grüßen, alles Gute; **please give him my good** ~es bitte grüßen Sie ihn (vielmals) von mir, bitte richten Sie ihm meine besten Wünsche aus; **he sends his best** ~es er läßt (vielmals) grüßen; **a message of good** ~es eine Gruß- *or* Glückwunschbotschaft; **best** ~es **for a speedy recovery** viele gute Wünsche *or* alles Gute für eine baldige Genesung.

2 *vt* **(a)** (*want*) wünschen. **I do not** ~ **it** ich möchte *or* wünsche (*form*) es nicht; **he** ~es **to be alone/to see you immediately** er möchte allein sein/dich sofort sehen; **I** ~ **you to be present** ich wünsche, daß Sie anwesend sind; **what do you** ~ **me to do?** was soll ich (bitte) tun?; **do you** ~ **more coffee, sir?** (*Scot, form*) hätten Sie gern *or* wünschen Sie noch Kaffee?

(b) (*desire, hope, desire sth unlikely*) wünschen, wollen. **I** ~ **the play would begin** ich wünschte *or* wollte, das Stück finge an; **I do** ~ **you'd let me help** ich wünschte *or* wollte, du ließest mich helfen; **I** ~ **you'd be quiet** ich wünschte *or* wollte, du wärest ruhig; **how he** ~ed **that his wife was** *or* **were there** wie sehr er sich (*dat*) wünschte, daß seine Frau hier wäre; ~ **you were here** ich wünschte *or* wollte, du wärest hier.

(c) (*entertain* ~es *towards sb*) wünschen. **to** ~ **sb well/ill** jdm Glück *or* alles Gute/Schlechtes *or* Böses wünschen; **I don't** ~ **her any harm** ich wünsche ihr nichts Böses; **to** ~ **sb good luck/happiness** jdm viel Glück *or* alles Gute/Glück (und Zufriedenheit) wünschen.

(d) (*bid, express* ~) wünschen. **to** ~ **sb a pleasant journey/good morning/a happy Christmas/goodbye** jdm eine gute Reise/guten Morgen/frohe Weihnachten wünschen/auf Wiedersehen sagen.

(e) to ~ **a wish** sich (*dat*) etwas wünschen; **he** ~ed **himself anywhere but there** er wünschte sich nur möglichst weit weg; **if I could** ~ **myself into the castle** wenn ich mich nur in das Schloß wünschen könnte.

3 *vi* (*make a wish*) sich (*dat*) etwas wünschen. ~ing **won't solve the problem** der Wunsch allein wird das Problem nicht lösen; **to** ~ **upon a star** (*liter*) sich (*dat*) bei einer Sternschnuppe etwas wünschen.

♦ **wish away** *vt sep* difficulty weg- *or* fortwünschen (*inf*).

♦ **wish for** *vi* + *prep obj* **to** ~ sich (*dat*) etw wünschen; **what more could you** ~ ~? etwas Besseres kann man sich doch gar nicht wünschen, was kann sich der Mensch noch mehr wünschen? (*inf*); **it was everything we had** ~ed ~ es war genauso, wie wir es uns gewünscht hatten; **she had everything she could** ~ ~ sie hatte alles, was man sich nur wünschen kann.

♦ **wish on** *or* **upon** *vt sep* + *prep obj* (*inf: foist*) **to** ~ **sb/sth** ~ **sb** jdn jdm/jdm etw aufhängen (*inf*); **I would not** ~ **that/that job** ~ **my worst enemy!** das/diese Arbeit würde ich meinem ärgsten Feind nicht wünschen.

wishbone ['wɪʃbəʊn] *n* Gabelbein *nt*.

wishful ['wɪʃful] *adj* **that's just** ~ **thinking** das ist nur Wunschdenken *or* ein frommer Wunsch.

wish-fulfilment ['wɪʃfulfɪlmənt] *n* Wunscherfüllung *f*.

wishing well ['wɪʃɪŋwel] *n* Wunschbrunnen *m*.

wishy-washiness ['wɪʃɪˌwɒʃɪnɪs] *n see adj* Labberigkeit, Wäßrigkeit *f*; saft- und kraftlose Art, Farblosigkeit, Laschheit *f*; Verwaschenheit *f*; Schwachheit *f*. **the** ~ **of this report** das allgemeine Geschwätz (*inf*) in diesem Bericht.

wishy-washy ['wɪʃɪˌwɒʃɪ] *adj* coffee, soup labberig, wäßrig; person, character saft- und kraftlos, farblos, lasch; colour verwaschen; argument schwach (*inf*); report, story ungenau, wachsweich, mischiwaschi (*inf*).

wisp [wɪsp] *n* **(a)** (*of straw, hair etc*) kleines Büschel; (*of cloud*) Fetzen *m*; (*of smoke*) Fahne *f*, Wölkchen *nt*. **(b)** (*person*) elfenhaftes *or* zartes *or* zerbrechliches Geschöpf. **(c)** (*trace*) zarte Spur *or* Andeutung; (*fragment*) Hauch *m*.

wispy ['wɪspɪ] *adj* (+ *er*) grass dürr, fein; girl zerbrechlich, zart. ~ **clouds** Wolkenfetzen *pl*; ~ **hair** dünne Haarbüschel.

wisteria [wɪs'tɪərɪə] *n* Glyzinie, Wistarie *f*.

wistful ['wɪstful] *adj* smile, thoughts, mood, eyes wehmütig; song also schwermütig.

wistfully ['wɪstfəlɪ] *adv see adj*.

wistfulness ['wɪstfulnɪs] *n see adj* Wehmut *f*; Schwermut *f*.

wit[1] [wɪt] *vi* (*old Jur*): **to** ~ nämlich, und zwar.

wit[2] *n* **(a)** (*understanding*) Verstand *m*. **beyond the** ~ **of man** jenseits des *or* jedes menschlichen Verständnisses *or* Horizonts, über den menschlichen Verstand *or* Horizont hinaus; **a battle of** ~s ein geistiges Kräftemessen; **to be at one's** ~s' **end** am Ende seiner Weisheit sein, mit seinem Latein am Ende sein (*hum inf*); **I was at my** ~s' **end for a solution** ich wußte mir keinen Rat *or* Ausweg mehr *or* mir reicht nicht mehr, wie ich eine Lösung finden könnte; **to drive sb out of his** ~s jdn um seinen Verstand bringen; **to lose one's** ~s den *or* seinen Verstand verlieren; **to collect one's** ~s seine fünf Sinne (wieder) zusammennehmen; **to frighten** *or* **scare sb out of his** ~s jdn zu Tode erschrecken; **to be frightened** *or* **scared out of one's** ~s zu Tode erschreckt sein; **to have** *or* **keep one's** ~s **about one** seine (fünf) Sinne zusammen- *or* beisammenhalten *or* -haben, einen klaren Kopf haben; **he hadn't the** ~ **to see that ...** er hatte nicht genug Köpfchen *or* Grips (*inf*), um zu sehen *or* erkennen, daß ...; **to sharpen one's** ~s seinen Verstand schärfen; **to use one's** ~s seinen Verstand gebrauchen, sein Köpfchen (*inf*) *or* seinen Grips (*inf*) anstrengen; **to live by one's** ~s sich schlau *or* klug durchs Leben schlagen.

(b) (*humour, wittiness*) Geist, Witz *m*. **full of** ~ geistreich; **to have a ready** *or* **pretty** ~ (*old*) schlagfertig sein; **there's a lot of** ~ **in the book** es ist sehr viel Geistreiches in dem Buch.

(c) (*person*) geistreicher Kopf.

witch [wɪtʃ] *n* (*lit, fig*) Hexe *f*. ~es' **sabbath** Hexensabbat *m*.

witch: ~**craft** *n* Hexerei, Zauberei *f*; **a book on** ~**craft** ein Buch über (die) Hexenkunst; ~ **doctor** *n* Medizinmann *m*.

witch elm *n* Bergulme *f*.

witchery ['wɪtʃərɪ] *n* (*witchcraft*) Hexerei *f*; (*fascination*) Zauber *m*.

witch hazel *n* (*Bot*) Zaubernuß *f*; (*Med*) Hamamelis *f*.

witch-hunt ['wɪtʃˌhʌnt] *n* (*lit, fig*) Hexenjagd *f*.

witching ['wɪtʃɪŋ] *adj*: **the** ~ **hour** die Geisterstunde.

with [wɪð, wɪθ] *prep* **(a)** mit. **are you pleased** ~ **it?** bist du damit zufrieden?; **bring a book** ~ **you** bring ein Buch mit; ~ **no ...** ohne ...; ~ **the Victory, it's the biggest ship of its class** neben der Victory ist es das größte Schiff in seiner Klasse; **to walk** ~ **a stick am** *or* **mit einem Stock gehen; put it** ~ **the rest** leg es zu den anderen; **the wind was** ~ **us** wir hatten den Wind im Rücken, wir fuhren *etc* mit dem Wind; **how are things** ~ **you?** wie geht's?, wie steht's? (*inf*); **see** with **it**.

(b) (*at house of, in company of etc*) bei. **I'll be** ~ **you in a moment** einen Augenblick, bitte, ich bin gleich da; **10 years** ~ **the company** 10 Jahre bei *or* in der Firma; **the problem is still** ~ **us** wir haben immer noch das alte Problem.

(c) (*on person, in bag etc*) bei. **I haven't got my cheque book** ~ **me** ich habe mein Scheckbuch nicht bei mir.

(d) (*cause*) vor (+ *dat*). **to shiver** ~ **cold** vor Kälte zittern; **the hills are white** ~ **snow** die Berge sind weiß vom Schnee; **to be ill** ~ **measles** die Masern haben, an (den) Masern erkrankt sein.

(e) (*in the case of*) bei, mit. **it's always the same** ~ **you** es ist (doch) immer dasselbe *or* dieselbe Geschichte mit dir; **the trouble** ~ **him is that he ...** die Schwierigkeit bei *or* mit ihm ist (die), daß er ...; **it's a habit** ~ **him** das ist bei ihm Gewohnheit; ~ **God, all things are possible** bei *or* für Gott ist kein Ding unmöglich; **it's a holiday** ~ **us** bei *or* für uns ist das ein Feiertag.

(f) (*when sb/sth is*) wo. **you can't go** ~ **your mother ill in bed** wo deine Mutter krank im Bett liegt, kannst du nicht gehen; **I cannot concentrate** ~ **all this noise going on** bei diesem Lärm kann ich mich nicht konzentrieren; **to quit** ~ **the job unfinished** von der halbfertigen Arbeit weglaufen; ~ **the window open** bei offenem Fenster.

(g) (*in proportion*) mit. **it varies** ~ **the temperature** es verändert sich je nach Temperatur; **wine improves** ~ **age** Wein wird mit zunehmendem Alter immer besser; **it gets bigger** ~ **the heat** in der Wärme wird es immer größer.

(h) (*in spite of*) trotz, bei. ~ **all his faults** bei allen seinen Fehlern, trotz aller seiner Fehler; ~ **the best will in the world** beim allerbesten Willen.

(i) (*expressing agreement, on side of*) **I'm** ~ **you there** (*inf*) stimme ich dir zu; **is he** ~ **us or against us?** ist er für oder gegen uns?

(j) (*inf: expressing comprehension*) **are you** ~ **me?** kapierst du? (*inf*), hast du's? (*inf*), kommst du mit? (*inf*); **I'm not** ~ **you** da komm ich nicht mit (*inf*); **are you still** ~ **me?** kommst du (da) noch mit? (*inf*), **ist das noch klar?**

withdraw [wɪθ'drɔː] *pret* **withdrew**, *ptp* **withdrawn 1** *vt* object, motion, charge zurückziehen; troops, team also abziehen; ambassador zurückrufen *or* -beordern; coins, stamps einziehen, aus dem Verkehr ziehen; (*from bank*) money abheben; words, comment zurücknehmen, widerrufen; privileges entziehen. **the workers withdrew their labour** die Arbeiter haben ihre Arbeit niedergelegt; **she withdrew her hand from his** sie entzog ihm ihre Hand; **we must** ~ **our team** wir werden/können unsere Mannschaft nicht antreten lassen.

2 *vi* sich zurückziehen; (*Sport also*) zurücktreten (*from* von), nicht antreten (*from* von/bei); (*move away*) zurücktreten *or* -gehen. **to** ~ **in favour of sb else** zu Gunsten eines anderen zurücktreten; **to** ~ **into oneself** sich in sich (*acc*) selber zurückziehen; **you can't** ~ **now** (*from agreement*) du kannst jetzt nicht zurücktreten *or* abspringen (*inf*).

withdrawal [wɪθ'drɔːəl] *n* (*of objects*) Zurückziehen *nt*; (*of ambassador*) Abziehen *nt*; (*of coins, stamps*) Einziehen *nt*; (*of money*) Abheben *nt*; (*of words*) Zurücknehmen *nt*, Zurücknahme *f*; (*of charge*) Zurückziehen *nt*; (*of troops*) Rückzug *m*; (*withdrawing*) Abziehen *nt*; (*in sport*) Abzug *m*; (*from drugs*) Entzug *m*. **to make a** ~ **from the bank** von einer Bank etwas *or* Geld abheben.

withdrawal: ~ **slip** *n* Rückzahlungsschein *m*; ~ **symptoms** *npl* Entzugserscheinungen *pl*.

withdrawn [wɪθ'drɔːn] **1** *ptp of* **withdraw. 2** *adj* person verschlossen; manner also reserviert, zurückhaltend; life zurückgezogen.

withdrew [wɪθ'druː] *pret of* **withdraw.**

withe [wɪθ] *n* (*old*) (dünne) Weidenrute.

wither ['wɪðər] *vi* *vt* plants *etc* verdorren, austrocknen; (*fig*) zum Schwinden bringen. **to** ~ **sb with a look** jdn mit einem Blick vernichten. **2** *vi* (*a*) verdorren, ausdorren; (*limb*) verkümmern. **(b)** (*fig*) welken; (*religion*) dahinschwinden.

♦ **wither away** *vi see* wither 2.

♦ **wither up** *vi see* wither 2 (a).

withered ['wɪðəd] *adj* plant, grass verdorrt, vertrocknet; skin verhutzelt, hutzelig; limb verkümmert. **a** ~**-looking old man** ein verschrumpfter *or* hutzeliger Alter.

withering ['wɪðərɪŋ] *adj* heat ausdörrend; criticism, look, tone vernichtend.

witheringly ['wɪðərɪŋlɪ] *adv* say, look vernichtend.

withers ['wɪðəz] *npl* Widerrist *m*.

withhold [wɪθ'həʊld] *pret, ptp* **withheld** [wɪθ'held] *vt* vorenthalten; truth also verschweigen; (*refuse*) consent, help verweigern, versagen (*geh*). **the citizens threatened to** ~ **their rates** die Bürger drohten, die Zahlung der Abgaben zu verweigern; **to** ~ **sth from sb** jdm etw vorenthalten/verweigern; ~**ing tax** (*US*) (vom Arbeitgeber) einbehaltene Steuer.

within [wɪð'ɪn] **1** *prep* innerhalb (+*gen*); (*temporal also*) binnen (+*gen*), innert (+*gen*) (*Aus, S Ger*). **a voice ~ me said ...** eine Stimme in meinem Inneren *or* in mir sagte ...; **we were/came ~ 100 metres of the summit** wir waren auf den letzten 100 Metern vor dem Gipfel/wir kamen bis auf 100 Meter an den Gipfel heran; **~ his power in seiner Macht; to keep ~** sich im Rahmen des Gesetzes bewegen; **to live ~ one's income** im Rahmen seiner finanziellen Möglichkeiten leben.

2 *adv* (*old, liter*) innen. **from ~** von drinnen; (*on the inside*) von innen; **let us go ~** wollen wir hineingehen; **but he's rotten ~** aber innerlich ist er verderbt.

with it [wɪð'ɪt] *adj* (*inf*) (a) (*attr* with-it) (*up-to-date, trendy*) up to date. (b) *pred* (*awake, alert*) **to be ~** da sein (*inf*).

without [wɪð'aʊt] **1** *prep* ohne. **~ a tie/passport** ohne Krawatte/(einen) Paß; **~ a friend in the world** ohne einen einzigen Freund; **~ speaking** ohne zu sprechen, wortlos; **~ my noticing it** ohne daß ich es bemerke/bemerkte; **times ~ number** unzählige Male *pl*.

2 *adv* (*old, liter*) außen. **from ~** von draußen; (*on the outside*) von außen.

3 *adj pred* ohne. **to be ~** etw nicht haben, einer Sache (*gen*) entbehren (*form*); **those who are ~** (*needy*) die Bedürftigen *pl*.

withstand [wɪθ'stænd] *pret, ptp* withstood *vt* cold standhalten (+*dat*); *enemy, climate, attack, temptation also* trotzen (+*dat*); *persuasion etc* widerstehen (+*dat*).

withy [wɪðɪ] *n* (*willow*) Korbweide *f*; (*twig*) Weide(nrute) *f*.

witless [wɪtlɪs] *adj* (*mentally defective*) schwachsinnig; (*stupid, silly*) dumm, blöd(e) (*inf*); (*lacking wit*) prose geistlos.

witlessly [wɪtlɪslɪ] *adv see adj*.

witlessness [wɪtlɪsnɪs] *n see adj* Schwachsinn *m*; Dummheit, Blödheit (*inf*) *f*; Geistlosigkeit *f*.

witness [wɪtnɪs] **1** *n* (a) (*person: Jur, fig*) Zeuge *m*, Zeugin *f*. **~ for the defence/prosecution** Zeuge/Zeugin der Verteidigung/Anklage; **as God is my ~** Gott sei *or* ist mein Zeuge; **to call sb as a ~** jdn als Zeugen vorladen; **I was then ~ to a scene** ... ich wurde Zeuge einer Szene ...

(b) (*evidence*) Zeugnis *nt*. **to give ~ for/against sb** Zeugnis ablegen für/gegen jdn, aussagen für/gegen jdn; **in ~ whereof** (*form*) zu Urkund *or* zum Zeugnis dessen; **to bear ~ to sth** (*lit, fig*) Zeugnis über etw (*acc*) ablegen; (*actions, events also*) von etw zeugen.

2 *vt* (a) (*see*) accident Zeuge sein bei *or* (+*gen*); scenes also (mit)erleben, mitansehen; *changes* erleben. **the year 1945 ~ed great changes** das Jahr 1945 sah einen großen Wandel.

(b) (*testify*) bezeugen. **to call sb to ~ that ...** jdn zum Zeugen dafür rufen, daß ...

(c) (*consider as evidence*) denken an (+*acc*), denken Sie nur daran *or* nehmen Sie zum Beispiel; **~ what happened ...** denken Sie nur daran *or* nehmen Sie zum Beispiel, was geschah, als ...; **~ the case of X** denken Sie nur an den Fall X, nehmen Sie nur den Fall X zum Beispiel.

(d) (*attest by signature*) signature, will bestätigen.

3 *vi* (*testify*) bestätigen, bezeugen. **to ~ to sth** etw bestätigen *or* bezeugen; **to ~ against sb** gegen jdn aussagen.

witness: ~ box *or* (*US*) **stand** *n* Zeugenbank *f*, Zeugenstand *m*. **-witted** [-'wɪtɪd] *adj suf* dull-~ geistig träge; **quick-~** geistig rege.

wittiness [wɪtɪnɪs] *n* Witzigkeit *f*.

wittingly [wɪtɪŋlɪ] *adv* bewußt, absichtlich, wissentlich (*form*).

witty [wɪtɪ] *adj* (+*er*) witzig, geistreich.

wives [waɪvz] *pl of* wife.

wizard [wɪzəd] **1** *n* (a) Zauberer, Hexenmeister *m*. (b) (*inf*) Genie *nt*, Leuchte *f* (*inf*). **a financial ~** ein Finanzgenie *nt*; **a ~ with the ball** ein Zauberer am *or* mit dem Ball; **a ~ at maths** ein Mathegenie *nt* (*inf*). **2** *adj* (*dated Brit inf*) famos, prima (*inf*).

wizardry [wɪzədrɪ] *n* (*magic*) Hexerei, Zauberei *f*; (*great skill*) Zauberkünste *pl*. **his ~ with the ball** seine Zauberkunststücke *pl* mit dem Ball.

wizened [wɪznd] *adj* verhutzelt, verschrumpelt.

wk *abbr of* week Wo.

wkly *abbr of* weekly wö.

Wm *abbr of* William.

WNW *abbr of* west-north-west WNW.

w/o *abbr of* without o.

woad [wəʊd] *n* (*dye*) Waid *m*; (*plant*) (Färber)waid *m*.

wobble [wɒbl] **1** *n* Wackeln *nt*. **the chair has a ~** der Stuhl wackelt; **there is a dangerous ~ in the front wheel** das Vorderrad hat einen gefährlichen Schlag *or* eiert gefährlich.

2 *vi* wackeln; (*tightrope walker, dancer also, cyclist*) schwanken; (*voice, hand, compass needle*) zittern; (*wheel*) eiern (*inf*), einen Schlag haben; (*chin, jelly etc*) schwabbeln. **the child ~d about on his new bicycle** das Kind wackelte auf seinem neuen Fahrrad durch die Gegend; **he was wobbling like a jelly** (*nervous*) er zitterte wie Espenlaub; (*fat*) an ihm wabbelte alles.

3 *vt* rütteln an (+*dat*), ruckeln an (+*dat*), wackeln an (+*dat*).

wobbly [wɒblɪ] *adj* (+*er*) wackelig; voice, notes also, hand zitterig, zitternd; *jelly* (sch)wabbelig; *wheel* eiernd. **to be ~** (*inf: after illness*) wackelig auf den Beinen sein (*inf*); **to feel ~** sich schwach fühlen, wackelig auf den Beinen sein (*inf*).

wodge [wɒdʒ] *n* (*Brit inf*) (*of cake, plaster etc*) Brocken *m*; (*ball of paper*) Knäuel *nt or m*; (*of cotton wool*) Bausch *m*; (*of documents, papers*) Stoß *m*.

woe [wəʊ] *n* (a) (*liter, hum: sorrow*) Jammer *m*. **~ is me!** Weh mir!; **~ betide him who ...!** wehe dem, der ...!; **a tale of ~** eine Geschichte des Jammers. (b) (*esp pl: trouble, affliction*) Kummer *m*. **to tell sb one's ~s** jdm sein Leid klagen; **to pour out one's ~s** sich (*dat*) seinen Kummer von der Seele reden.

woebegone [wəʊbɪˌgɒn] *adj* kläglich, jämmerlich; *expression also* jammervoll; *voice* (weh)klagend, jammernd.

woeful [wəʊfʊl] *adj* (*sad*) traurig; (*deplorable*) neglect also, ignorance bedauerlich, beklagenswert.

woefully [wəʊfəlɪ] *adv* kläglich, jämmerlich; (*very*) bedauerlich. **he is ~ ignorant of ...** es ist bestürzend, wie wenig er über ... weiß; **he discovered they were ~ ignorant of ...** er stellte zu seiner Bestürzung fest, wie wenig sie über ... wußten; **the house is ~ lacking in modern conveniences** es ist bestürzend, wie wenig moderne Einrichtungen das Haus hat.

wog [wɒg] *n* (*Brit pej sl*) Kaffer *m* (*sl*); (*Arab*) Kameltreiber *m* (*sl*).

woke [wəʊk] *pret of* wake.

woken [wəʊkn] *ptp of* wake.

wolf [wʊlf] **1** *n, pl* wolves (a) Wolf *m*. (b) (*fig inf: womanizer*) Don Juan *m*. (c) (*phrases*) **a ~ in sheep's clothing** ein Wolf im Schafspelz; **to cry ~** blinden Alarm schlagen; **to keep the ~ from the door** sich über Wasser halten; **to throw sb to the wolves** jdn den Wölfen zum Fraß vorwerfen; *see* lone.

2 *vt* (*also ~ down*) food hinunterschlingen.

wolf: ~-cub *n* (*lit*) Wolfsjunge(s) *nt*; (*Brit: boy scout*) Wölfling *m*; **~hound** *n* Wolfshund *m*.

wolfish [wʊlfɪʃ] *adj* appetite wie ein Wolf; *hunger* Wolfs-.

wolfishly [wʊlfɪʃlɪ] *adv* gierig.

wolf-pack [wʊlfpæk] *n* Rudel *nt* Wölfe; (*of submarines*) Geschwader *nt*.

wolfram [wʊlfrəm] *n* Wolfram *nt*.

wolfsbane [wʊlfsbeɪn] *n* (*Bot*) Eisenhut *m*.

wolf-whistle [wʊlf,wɪsl] (*inf*) **1** *n* bewundernder Pfiff. **they gave her a ~** sie pfiffen ihr nach. **2** *vi* nachpfeifen.

wolverine [wʊlvəriːn] *n* Vielfraß *m*.

wolves [wʊlvz] *pl of* wolf.

woman [wʊmən] **1** *n, pl* women Frau *f*, Frauenzimmer (*pej hum*) *nt*; (*domestic help*) (Haushalts)hilfe *f*; (*inf: girlfriend*) Mädchen *nt*; (*mistress*) Geliebte *f*, Weib *nt* (*pej*). **a ~'s work is never done** Frauenhände ruhen nie; **man that is made of ~** (*Rel*) der Mensch, vom Weib geboren; **how like a ~!** typisch Frau!; **cleaning ~** Putzfrau, Reinmachefrau *f*; **~ is a mysterious creature** Frauen sind geheimnisvolle Wesen; **where's my supper, ~!** Weib, wo ist das Essen!; **the little ~** (*inf: wife*) die *or* meine Frau; **to run after women** den Frauen nachrennen; **women's rights** Frauenrechte *pl*, die Rechte *pl* der Frau; **women's page** Frauenseite *f*; **that's ~'s work** das ist Frauenarbeit; **women's talk** Gespräche *pl* von Frau zu Frau; **women's lib** (*inf*) Frauenrechtsbewegung *f*; **women's libber** (*inf*) Frauenrechtlerin, Emanze (*sl*) *f*; *see* old ~.

2 *adj attr* ~ **doctor** Ärztin *f*; ~ **lawyer** Anwältin *f*; ~ **teacher** Lehrerin *f*; ~ **driver** Frau *f* am Steuer.

woman: ~-hater *n* Frauenhasser *m*; **~hood** *n* (*women in general*) alle Frauen, die Frauen *pl*; **you should be proud of your ~hood** du solltest stolz darauf sein, daß du eine Frau bist; **to reach ~hood** (zur) Frau werden; **the sufferings of ~hood** die Leiden einer Frau.

womanish [wʊmənɪʃ] *adj* (*womanly*) *woman* fraulich; (*pej: effeminate*) *man* weibisch.

womanize [wʊmənaɪz] *vi* hinter den Frauen her sein. **this womanizing will have to stop** die Frauengeschichten müssen aufhören; **young men out for an evening's womanizing** junge Männer, die ausziehen, um sich mit Mädchen zu amüsieren.

womanizer [wʊmənaɪzə] *n* Schürzenjäger *m*.

womankind [wʊmənˌkaɪnd] *n* das weibliche Geschlecht.

womanliness [wʊmənlɪnɪs] *n* Weiblichkeit *f*.

womanly [wʊmənlɪ] *adj* figure, person fraulich; qualities, virtues weiblich.

womb [wuːm] *n* (*Mutter*)schoß, Mutterleib *m*, Gebärmutter *f* (*Med*); (*fig*) Schoß *m*. **the foetus in the ~** der Embryo im Mutterleib; **he's still living with his parents, he does not want to leave the ~** er lebt noch bei seinen Eltern, er möchte den Schoß der Familie nicht verlassen; **it's just a craving to return to the ~** das ist nur die Sehnsucht nach der Geborgenheit des Mutterschoßes.

wombat [wɒmbæt] *n* Wombat *m*.

women [wɪmɪn] *pl of* woman.

womenfolk [wɪmɪnfəʊk] *npl* Frauen *pl*.

won [wʌn] *pret, ptp of* win.

wonder [wʌndə] **1** *n* (a) (*feeling*) Staunen *nt*, Verwunderung *f*. **in ~** voller Staunen; **to be lost in ~** von Staunen erfüllt sein; **the birth of a baby never loses its ~** eine Geburt bleibt immer etwas Wunderbares; **it fills one with a sense of ~** es erfüllt einen mit Erstaunen; **he has never lost that almost childlike sense of ~** er hat nie dieses kindliche Staunen verlernt.

(b) (*object or cause*) Wunder *nt*. **the ~ of electricity** das Wunder der Elektrizität; **the seven ~s of the world** die sieben Weltwunder; **the ~ of it was that ...** das Erstaunliche *or* Verblüffende daran war, daß ...; **it is a ~ ...** es ist ein Wunder, daß ...; **it is no** *or* **little** *or* **small ~** (es ist) kein Wunder, es ist nicht zu verwundern; **no ~** (he refused)! kein Wunder(, daß er abgelehnt hat)!; **to do** *or* **work ~s** wahre Wunder vollbringen, Wunder wirken; **~s will never cease!** es geschehen noch Zeichen und Wunder!; *see* nine.

2 *vt* **I ~ what he'll do now** ich bin gespannt (*inf*), was er jetzt tun wird; **I ~ first said that/why he did it** ich möchte (zu gern) wissen *or* ich wüßte (zu) gern, wer das zuerst aufgebracht hat/warum er das getan hat; **I ~ why!** (*iro*) ich frag mich warum?; **I was ~ing if you'd like to buy a copy** möchten Sie nicht vielleicht ein Exemplar kaufen?; **I was ~ing if you'd like to come too** möchten Sie nicht vielleicht auch kommen?; **I was ~ing when you'd realize that** ich habe mich (schon) gefragt, wann du das merkst; **I was ~ing if you could ...** könnten Sie nicht vielleicht ...

3 *vi* (a) (*ask oneself, speculate*) **it set me ~ing** es gab mir zu denken; **why do you ask?** — oh, **I was just ~ing** warum fragst du? — ach, nur so; **what will happen next, I ~?** ich frage mich *or* ich bin gespannt, was als nächstes kommt; **what's going to happen next?** — **I ~!** was kommt als nächstes? — das

frage ich mich auch!; **I was** ~**ing about that** ich habe mir darüber schon Gedanken gemacht, ich habe mich das auch schon gefragt; **I've been** ~**ing about him** ich habe mir auch schon über ihn Gedanken gemacht; **I've been** ~**ing about him as a possibility** ich hatte ihn auch schon als eine Möglichkeit ins Auge gefaßt; **I expect that will be the end of the matter — I** ~! ich denke, damit ist die Angelegenheit erledigt — da habe ich meine Zweifel or da bin ich gespannt; **I'm** ~**ing about going to the cinema** ich habe daran gedacht, vielleicht ins Kino zu gehen; **John, I've been** ~**ing, is there really any point?** John, ich frage mich, obs es wirklich (einen) Zweck hat; **could you possibly help me, I** ~ könnten Sie mir vielleicht helfen; **does he realize who we are, I** ~ ich frage mich, ob er weiß, wer wir sind.
 (b) (be surprised) sich wundern. **I** ~ **(that) he didn't tell me** es wundert mich, daß er es mir nicht gesagt hat; **to** ~ **at sth** sich über etw (acc) wundern, über etw (acc) erstaunt sein; **that's hardly to be** ~**ed at** das ist kaum verwunderlich; **she'll be married by now, I shouldn't** ~ es würde mich nicht wundern, wenn sie inzwischen verheiratet wäre.
wonder in cpds Wunder-; ~ **boy** n Wunderknabe m; ~ **drug** n Wunderheilmittel nt.
wonderful ['wʌndəfʊl] adj wunderbar.
wonderfully ['wʌndəfəlɪ] adv see adj. **he looks** ~ **well** er sieht wunderbar aus.
wondering ['wʌndərɪŋ] adj (astonished) tone, look verwundert, erstaunt; (doubtful) fragend.
wonderingly ['wʌndərɪŋlɪ] adv see adj.
wonderland ['wʌndəˌlænd] n (fairyland) Wunderland nt; (wonderful place) Paradies nt. **the** ~ **of the Alps** die Wunderwelt der Alpen.
wonderment ['wʌndəmənt] n see **wonder 1 (a)**.
wonder-worker ['wʌndəˌwɜːkəʳ] n Wundertäter m.
wondrous ['wʌndrəs] (old, liter) **1** adj wunderbar; ways also wundersam. **2** adv wise, fair wunderbar.
wondrously ['wʌndrəslɪ] adv (old, liter) wunderbar. ~ **beautiful** wunderschön.
wonky ['wɒŋkɪ] adj (+er) (Brit inf) chair, table, marriage, grammar wackelig; machine nicht (ganz) in Ordnung. **he's feeling rather** ~ still er fühlt sich noch ziemlich wackelig auf den Beinen or angeschlagen; **your hat's a bit/your collar's all** ~ dein Hut/dein Kragen sitzt ganz schief; **your arithmetic must be** ~ in deiner Berechnung muß der Wurm drin sein (inf).
won't [wəʊnt] contr of **will not**.
wont [wəʊnt] **1** adj gewohnt. **to be** ~ **to do sth** gewöhnlich etw tun, etw zu tun pflegen. **2** n (An)gewohnheit f. **as is/was his** ~ wie er zu tun pflegt/pflegte.
wonted ['wəʊntɪd] adj (liter) gewohnt.
woo [wuː] vt **(a)** (dated: court) woman den Hof machen (+dat), umwerben; (fig) person umwerben. **(b)** (fig) stardom, sleep etc suchen; audience etc für sich zu gewinnen versuchen.
♦**woo away** vt sep employee, executive abwerben.
wood [wʊd] **1** n **(a)** (material) Holz nt. **touch** ~! dreimal auf Holz geklopft!
 (b) (small forest) Wald m. ~**s** Wald m; **we're not out of the** ~ **yet** (fig) wir sind noch nicht über den Berg or aus dem Schneider (inf); **he can't see the** ~ **for the trees** (prov) er sieht den Wald vor (lauter) Bäumen nicht (prov).
 (c) (sth made of ~) (cask) Holzfaß nt; (Bowls) Kugel f; (Golf) Holz nt. **whisky matured in the** ~ im Holzfaß gereifter Whisky; **beer from the** ~ Bier vom Faß; **that was off the** ~ (Tennis) das war Holz, das war vom Rahmen.
 (d) (Mus) **the** ~**s** pl die Holzblasinstrumente, die Holzbläser pl.
 2 adj attr **(a)** (made of ~) Holz-.
 (b) (living etc in a ~) Wald-.
wood: ~ **alcohol** n Holzgeist m; ~ **anemone** n Buschwindröschen nt.
woodbine ['wʊdbaɪn] n (honeysuckle) Geißblatt nt; (US: Virginia creeper) wilder Wein, Jungfernrebe f.
wood: ~ **block** n (Art) Holzschnitt m; ~ **carver** n (Holz)schnitzer(in f) m; ~ **carving** n (Holz)schnitzerei f; ~**chuck** n Waldmurmeltier nt; ~**cock** n, no pl Waldschnepfe f; ~**craft** n (a) (skill at living in forest) Waldläufertum nt; **(b)** (skill at woodwork) Geschick nt im Arbeiten mit Holz; ~**cut** n Holzschnitt m; ~**cutter** n (a) Holzfäller m; (of logs) Holzhacker m; (b) (Art) Holzschnitzer m; ~**cutting** n (a) Holzfällen nt; (of logs) Holzhacken nt; (b) (Art) Holzschnitzen nt; (item) Holzplastik, Holzschnitzerei f.
wooded ['wʊdɪd] adj bewaldet; countryside also Wald-.
wooden ['wʊdn] adj **(a)** Holz-. **the** ~ **horse** das hölzerne Pferd; ~ **leg** Holzbein nt; ~ **spoon** (lit) Holzlöffel m, hölzerner Löffel; (fig) Trostpreis m. **(b)** (fig) expression, smile, manner hölzern; personality steif.
wooden-headed ['wʊdn'hedɪd] adj dumm.
woodenly ['wʊdnlɪ] adv (fig) smile, act, bow gekünstelt, steif; stand wie ein Klotz.
wood: ~**-free** adj paper holzfrei; ~**land** n Waldland nt, Waldung f; ~**lark** n Heidelerche f; ~**louse** n Bohrassel f; ~**man** n see **woodsman**; ~ **nymph** n Waldnymphe f; ~**pecker** n Specht m; ~**pigeon** n Ringeltaube f; ~**pile** n Holzhaufen m; see **nigger**; ~**pulp** n Holzschliff m; ~**shed** n Holzschuppen m.
woodsman ['wʊdzmən] n, pl **-men** [-mən] Waldläufer m.
wood sorrel n Waldsauerklee m.
woodsy ['wʊdzɪ] adj (+er) (US inf) waldig. ~ **smell** Waldgeruch m, Geruch m von Wald.
wood-turning ['wʊdˌtɜːnɪŋ] n Drechslerei f.
wood: ~**wind** n Holzblasinstrument nt; **the** ~**wind(s), the** ~**wind section** die Holzbläser pl; ~**work** n (a) (craft) Tischlerei f; **the boys do** ~**work on Tuesday afternoons** Dienstags nachmittags beschäftigen sich die Jungen mit Tischlern; **a nice piece of** ~**work** eine schöne Tischlerarbeit; (b) (wooden parts) Holz-

teile pl; ~**worm** n Holzwurm m; **it's got** ~**worm** da ist der Holzwurm drin.
woody ['wʊdɪ] adj (+er) **(a)** (wooded) waldig, bewaldet. **(b)** (like wood in texture) tissue holzig.
wooer ['wuːəʳ] n (dated) Werber m; (fig) Buhler m (of sth um etw). **a** ~ **of the unions** ein Buhler um die Gunst der Gewerkschaften.
woof¹ [wʊf] n (Tex) Schuß m.
woof² **1** n (of dog) Wuff nt. **2** vi kläffen. ~, ~! wau, wau!, wuff, wuff!
woofer ['wʊfəʳ] n Tieftöner m.
wool [wʊl] **1** n **(a)** Wolle f; (cloth also) Wollstoff m. **all** ~, **pure** ~ reine Wolle; **to pull the** ~ **over sb's eyes** (inf) jdm Sand in die Augen streuen (inf). **(b)** (glass ~, wire ~) Wolle f. **2** adj Woll-; (made of wool also) aus Wolle.
woolen etc (US) see **woollen** etc.
wool: ~**-gathering** n Träumen nt; **to be** ~**-gathering** vor sich (acc) hinträumen; ~**-grower** n Schafzüchter m (für Wolle).
woollen, (US) **woolen** ['wʊlən] **1** adj Woll-; (made of wool also) wollen, aus Wolle. **2** n ~**s** pl (garments) Wollsachen, Strick-sachen pl; (fabrics, blankets) Wollwaren pl.
woolliness, (US) **wooliness** ['wʊlɪnɪs] n Wolligkeit f; (softness also) Flauschigkeit f; (fig: of outline) Verschwommenheit f; (pej: of mind, idea) Verworrenheit, Wirrheit f.
woolly, (US) **wooly** ['wʊlɪ] **1** adj (+er) wollig; (soft also) flau-schig; (fig) outline verschwommen; (pej) mind, thinking, idea verworren, wirr. **2** n (inf: sweater etc) Pulli m (inf). **winter woollies** (esp Brit: sweaters etc) dicke Wollsachen (inf); (esp US: underwear) Wollene pl (inf).
woolsack ['wʊlsæk] n (seat) Wollsack m (Sitz des Lordkanzlers im britischen Oberhaus); (office) Amt nt des Lordkanzlers.
wooziness ['wuːzɪnɪs] n (inf) Benommenheit f.
woozy ['wuːzɪ] adj (+er) (inf) benommen, duselig (inf).
wop [wɒp] n (pej sl) Spaghettifresser (pej sl) m.
Worcs abbr of **Worcestershire**.
word [wɜːd] **1** n **(a)** (unit of language) Wort nt. ~**s** Wörter pl; (meaningful sequence) Worte pl; ~ **order/formation/division** Wortstellung f/Wortbildung f/Silbentrennung f; **foreign** ~**s** Fremdwörter pl; ~ **for** ~ Wort für Wort; (exactly also) wortwörtlich; **cold isn't the** ~ **for it** kalt ist gar kein Ausdruck (dafür); ~**s cannot describe it** so etwas kann man mit Worten gar nicht beschreiben; **beyond** ~**s** unbeschreiblich; **too funny for** ~**s** unbeschreiblich komisch; **to put one's thoughts into** ~**s** seine Gedanken in Worte fassen or kleiden; **"irresponsible" would be a better** ~ **for it** „unverantwortlich" wäre wohl das treffendere Wort dafür; ~**s fail me** mir fehlen die Worte; **in a** ~ mit einem Wort, kurz gesagt; **in so many** ~**s** direkt, ausdrück-lich; **in other** ~**s** mit anderen Worten, anders gesagt or ausge-drückt; **the last** ~ (fig) der letzte Schrei (in an +dat); **he had the last** ~ er hatte das letzte Wort; **that's not the** ~ **I would have chosen** ich hätte es nicht so ausgedrückt; **in the** ~**s of Goethe** mit Goethe gesprochen, um mit Goethe zu sprechen.
 (b) (remark) Wort nt. ~**s** Worte pl; **a** ~ **of advice** ein Rat(schlag) m; **a** ~ **of encouragement/warning** eine Ermunterung/Warnung; **fine** ~**s** schöne Worte pl; **a man of few** ~**s** ein Mann, der nicht viele Worte macht; **I can't get a** ~ **out of him** ich kann kein Wort aus ihm herausbekommen; **by** ~ **of mouth** durch mündliche Überlieferung; **to say a few** ~**s** ein paar Worte sprechen; **to take sb at his** ~ jdn beim Wort nehmen; **to have a** ~ **with sb (about sth)** mit jdm (über etw) sprechen; (reprimand, discipline) jdn ins Gebet nehmen; **John, could I have a** ~? John, kann ich dich mal sprechen?; (could I have) **a** ~ **in your ear?** kann ich Sie bitte unter vier Augen or allein sprechen?; **you took the** ~**s out of my mouth** du hast mir das Wort aus dem Mund genommen; **I wish you wouldn't put** ~**s into my mouth** ich wünschte, Sie würden mir nicht das Wort im Munde herumdrehen; **to put in** or **say a (good)** ~ **for sb** für jdn ein gutes Wort einlegen; **nobody had a good** ~ **to say for him** niemand wußte etwas Gutes über ihn zu sagen; **without a** ~ ohne ein Wort; **don't say** or **breathe a** ~ **about it** sag aber bitte keinen Ton or kein Sterbenswörtchen (inf) davon; **remember, not a** ~ **to anyone** vergiß nicht, kein Sterbenswörtchen (inf).
 (c) ~**s** pl (quarrel) **to have** ~**s with sb** mit jdm eine Auseinandersetzung haben.
 (d) ~**s** pl (text, lyrics) Text m.
 (e) no pl (message, news) Nachricht f. ~ **came/went round that ...** es kam die Nachricht/es ging die Nachricht um, daß ...; **to leave** ~ **(with sb/for sb) that ...** (bei jdm/für jdn) (die Nachricht) hinterlassen, daß ...; **is there any** ~ **from John yet?** schon von John gehört?, schon Nachrichten von John?; **there's been no** ~ **from the advance party for three days** seit drei Tagen haben wir nicht(s) mehr vom Vorschubtrupp gehört or keine Nach-richt mehr vom Vorschubtrupp gehabt; **to send** ~ Nachricht geben; **to send** ~ **to sb** jdn benachrichtigen; **to send sb** ~ **of sth** jdn von etw benachrichtigen; **to spread the** ~ **around** (inf) es allen sagen (inf); **what's the** ~ **on Charlie?** (inf) was gibt's Neues über Charlie?
 (f) (promise, assurance) Wort nt. ~ **of honour** Ehrenwort nt; **a man of his** ~ ein Mann, der zu seinem Wort steht; **to be as good as one's** ~, **to keep one's** ~ sein Wort halten; **I give you my** ~ ich gebe dir mein (Ehren)wort; **to go back on one's** ~ sein Wort nicht halten; **to break one's** ~ sein Wort brechen; **I have his** ~ **for it** ich habe sein Wort; **take my** ~ **for it** verläß dich drauf, das kannst du mir glauben; **you don't have to take my** ~ **for it** du kannst das ruhig nachprüfen; **it's his** ~ **against mine** Aussage steht gegen Aussage; **upon my** ~! (old), **my** ~! meine Güte!
 (g) (order) Wort nt; (also ~ **of command**) Kommando nt, Befehl m. **to give the** ~ **(to do sth)** (Mil) das Kommando geben(, etw zu tun); **just say the** ~ sag nur ein Wort; **his** ~ **is law here** sein Wort ist hier Gesetz.

(h) (*Rel*) Wort *nt*. the W~ of God das Wort Gottes; **to preach the W~** das Wort Gottes *or* das Evangelium verkünden.

(i) (*Computers*) Wort *nt* (*pl*: Wörter).

2 *vt* (in Worten) ausdrücken, formulieren, in Worte fassen (*geh*); *letter* formulieren; *speech* abfassen.

word: ~ **association** *n* Wortassoziation *f*; ~**blind** *adj* wortblind; ~ **class** *n* Wortklasse *f*; ~ **game** *n* Buchstabenspiel *nt*.

wordily ['wɜːdɪlɪ] *adv* see *adj*.

wordiness ['wɜːdɪnɪs] *n* Wortreichtum *m*, Langatmigkeit *f* (*pej*).

wording ['wɜːdɪŋ] *n* Formulierung *f*.

word: ~**less** *adj* wortlos; *grief* stumm; ~ **list** *n* Wortliste *f*; ~ **order** *n* Satzstellung, Wortstellung *f*; ~**perfect** *adj* sicher im Text; **to be ~-perfect** den Text perfekt beherrschen, den Text bis aufs Wort beherrschen; ~ **picture** *n* Bild *nt* (in Worten); **to paint a vivid ~ picture of** sth etw in lebhaften Farben beschreiben; ~**play** *n* Wortspiel *nt*; ~ **processing** *n* Textverarbeitung *f*; ~ **processor** *n* (*machine*) Textverarbeitungs)system *nt*, Textverarbeitungsanlage *f*; ~ **square** *n* magisches Quadrat.

wordy ['wɜːdɪ] *adj* (+*er*) wortreich, langatmig (*pej*).

wore [wɔːʳ] *pret of* **wear**.

work [wɜːk] **1** *n* (a) (*toil, labour, task*) Arbeit *f*. **have you got any ~ for me?** haben Sie was für mich zu tun?; (*employment*) haben Sie Arbeit für mich?; **he doesn't like ~** er arbeitet nicht gern; **that's a good piece of ~** das ist gute Arbeit; **is this all your own ~?** haben Sie das alles selbst gemacht?; **closed for ~** on the roof wegen (Reparatur)arbeiten am Dach geschlossen; **when ~ begins on the new bridge** wenn die Arbeiten an der neuen Brücke anfangen; **to be at ~** (on sth) (an etw *dat*) arbeiten; **there are forces at ~ which ...** es sind Kräfte am Werk, die ...; **it's the ~ of the devil** das ist Teufelswerk *or* ein Machwerk des Teufels; **to do a good day's ~** ein schönes Stück Arbeit leisten; **we've a lot of ~ to do** before this choir can give a concert wir haben noch viel zu tun, ehe dieser Chor ein Konzert geben kann; **you need to do some more ~** on your accent/your baton-change Sie müssen noch an Ihrem Akzent/am Stabwechsel arbeiten; **I've been trying to get some ~** done ich habe versucht zu arbeiten; **to put a lot of ~ into** sth eine Menge Arbeit in etw (*acc*) stecken; **it's in the ~s** (*inf*) es ist in der Mache (*inf*); **to get on with one's ~** sich (wieder) an die Arbeit machen; **to make short** *or* **quick ~ of** sb/sth mit jdm/etw kurzen Prozeß machen; **to make ~ for sb** jdm Arbeit machen; **time/the medicine had done its ~** die Zeit/Arznei hatte ihr Werk vollbracht/ihre Wirkung getan; **the ~ of a moment** eine Angelegenheit von Sekunden; **it was hard ~** for the old car to get up the hill das alte Auto hatte am Anstieg schwer zu schaffen.

(b) (*employment, job*) Arbeit *f*. **to be (out) at ~** arbeiten sein; **to go out to ~** arbeiten gehen; **to be out of/in ~** arbeitslos sein/eine Stelle haben; **he travels to ~ by car** er fährt mit dem Auto zur Arbeit; **do you live close to your ~?** hast du es weit zur Arbeit?; **how long does it take you to get to ~?** wie lange brauchst du, um zu deiner Arbeitsstelle zu kommen?; **at ~** an der Arbeitsstelle, am Arbeitsplatz; **what is your ~?** was tun Sie (beruflich)?; **to put** *or* **throw** sb **out of ~** jdn auf die Straße setzen (*inf*); **to put out of ~** arbeitslos machen, um den Arbeitsplatz bringen; **to be off ~** (am Arbeitsplatz) fehlen.

(c) (*product*) Arbeit *f*; (*Art, Liter*) Werk *nt*. **~ of art/reference** Kunstwerk *nt*/Nachschlagewerk *nt*; **a ~ of literature** ein literarisches Werk; **a fine piece of ~** eine schöne Arbeit; **good ~s** gute Werke *pl*; **a chance for artists to show their ~** eine Gelegenheit für Künstler, ihre Arbeiten *or* Werke zu zeigen.

(d) **~s** *pl* (*Mil*) Befestigungen *pl*; **road ~s** Baustelle *f*.

(e) **~s** *pl* (*Mech*) Getriebe, Innere(s) *nt*; (*of watch, clock*) Uhrwerk *nt*.

(f) **~s** *sing or pl* (*factory*) Betrieb *m*, Fabrik *f*; **gas ~s/steel ~s** Gas-/Stahlwerk *nt*; **~s gate** Fabrik- *or* Werkstor *nt*; **~s council** *or* **committee/outing** Betriebsrat *m*/Betriebsausflug *m*.

(g) (*inf*) **the ~s** alles Drum und Dran; **to give** sb **the ~s** (*treat harshly*) jdn gehörig in die Mangel nehmen (*inf*); (*treat generously*) jdn nach allen Regeln der Kunst nach Strich und Faden verwöhnen (*inf*); **to get the ~s** (*be treated harshly*) gehörig in die Mangel genommen werden (*inf*); (*be treated generously*) nach allen Regeln der Kunst *or* nach Strich und Faden verwöhnt werden (*inf*); **we had gorgeous food, wine, brandy, the ~s** es gab tolles Essen, Wein, Kognak, alle Schikanen (*inf*); **he was giving his opponent the ~s** er machte seinen Gegner nach allen Regeln der Kunst fertig (*inf*).

2 *vi* (a) arbeiten (*at an* +*dat*). **to ~ towards/for** sth auf etw hin/für etw arbeiten; **to ~ for better conditions** etc sich für bessere Bedingungen etc einsetzen; **to ~ among the poor** mitten unter den Armen arbeiten; **to ~ against a reform** gegen eine Reform kämpfen; **these factors which ~ against us** diese Faktoren, die sich uns entgegenstellen.

(b) (*function, operate*) funktionieren; (*marriage, plan also*) klappen (*inf*); (*medicine, spell*) wirken; (*be successful*) klappen (*inf*). **it won't ~** das klappt nicht; **"not ~ing"** (*lift etc*) „außer Betrieb"; **to get** sth **~ing** in Gang bringen; **it's by** *or* **on electricity** es läuft auf Strom; **it ~s both ways** es trifft auch andersherum zu; **but this arrangement will have to ~ both ways** aber diese Abmachung muß für beide Seiten gelten.

(c) (*yeast*) arbeiten, treiben.

(d) (*mouth, face*) zucken; (*jaws*) mahlen.

(e) (*move gradually*) **to ~ loose/along** sich lockern/sich entlangarbeiten; **to ~ round** (*wind, object*) sich langsam drehen (*to* nach); **he ~ed round to asking her** er hat sich aufgerafft, sie zu fragen.

3 *vt* (a) (*make ~*) *staff, employees, students* arbeiten lassen, herannehmen (*inf*), schinden (*pej*). **to ~ oneself hard/to death** sich nicht schonen/sich zu Tode arbeiten; **he ~s himself too hard** er übernimmt sich.

(b) (*operate*) *machine* bedienen; *lever, brake* betätigen. **to ~ sth by electricity/hand** etw elektrisch/mit Hand betreiben; **can we ~ that trick again?** können wir den Trick noch einmal anbringen *or* anwenden?

(c) (*bring about*) *change, cure* bewirken, herbeiführen. **to ~ mischief** Unheil anrichten; **to ~ mischief between friends** Zwietracht zwischen Freunden säen; **to ~ it (so that ...)** (*inf*) es so deichseln, daß ...) (*inf*); **to ~ one's passage** seine Überfahrt abarbeiten; **you don't have to ~ your notice** Sie brauchen Ihre Kündigungsfrist nicht einzuhalten; **he has managed to ~ his promotion** er hat es geschafft, seine Beförderung durchzukriegen; **surely you can ~ a better deal than that** du kannst doch sicherlich einen besseren Abschluß herausschlagen; *see* ~ **up**.

(d) (*Sew*) arbeiten; *design* etc sticken.

(e) (*shape*) *wood, metal* bearbeiten; *dough, clay also* kneten, durcharbeiten. **he ~ed the clay into a human shape** er formte den Ton zu einer menschlichen Gestalt; ~ **the flour in gradually/the ingredients together** mischen Sie das Mehl allmählich unter/die Zutaten (zusammen).

(f) (*exploit*) *mine* ausbeuten, abbauen; *land* bearbeiten; *smallholding* bewirtschaften; (*salesman*) *area* bereisen.

(g) (*move gradually*) **to ~ one's hands free** seine Hände freibekommen; **to ~ sth loose** etw losbekommen; **to ~ one's way through a book/Greek grammar** sich durch ein Buch/die griechische Grammatik arbeiten *or* kämpfen; **to ~ one's way to the top/up from nothing/through college** sich nach oben arbeiten *or* kämpfen/sich von ganz unten hocharbeiten/sein Studium selbst *or* durch eigene Arbeit finanzieren; **he ~ed his way across the rock-face/through the tunnel** er überquerte die Felswand/kroch durch den Tunnel; **to ~ oneself into a better job/**sb's **confidence** sich hocharbeiten/sich in jds Vertrauen (*acc*) einschleichen.

♦ **work away** *vi* vor sich hinarbeiten.

♦ **work down** *vi* (*stockings*) (herunter)rutschen (*inf*).

♦ **work in 1** *vt sep* (a) (*rub in*) einarbeiten; *lotion also* einmassieren. **it had ~ed its way right ~** es war (tief) eingedrungen.

(b) (*insert*) *bolt* etc (vorsichtig) einführen.

(c) (*in book, speech*) *reference* einbauen, einarbeiten; *jokes* einbauen. **to ~ sth ~to** sth etw in etw (*acc*) einbauen.

(d) (*in schedule* etc) einschieben. **to ~ sb ~to a plan** jdn in einen Plan miteinbeziehen.

2 *vi* (a) (*fit in*) passen. **that'll ~ ~ quite well** das paßt ganz gut; **that doesn't ~ ~ with our plans for ...** das paßt nicht in unsere Pläne für ...

(b) (*Ind*) den Arbeitsplatz besetzen.

♦ **work off 1** *vi* sich losmachen *or* lockern. **2** *vt sep* *debts, fat* abarbeiten; *energy* loswerden; *feelings* auslassen, abreagieren (*on an* +*dat*).

♦ **work on 1** *vi* weiterarbeiten.

2 *vt sep* *lid, washer* darauf bringen. **she ~ed her boots ~** sie zwängte sich in ihre Stiefel.

3 *vi* +*prep obj* (a) *car, book, subject, accent* arbeiten an (+*dat*). **who's ~ing ~ this case?** wer bearbeitet diesen Fall?

(b) *evidence* ausgehen von; *principle* (*person*) ausgehen von; (*machine*) arbeiten nach. **there are not many clues to ~ ~** es gibt nicht viele Hinweise, auf die man zurückgreifen könnte; **I'm ~ing ~ this one hunch** ich habe alles an diesem einen Verdacht aufgehängt; **if we ~ ~ the assumption that ...** wenn wir von der Annahme ausgehen, daß ...

(c) **we haven't solved it yet but we're still ~ing ~** it wir haben es noch nicht gelöst, aber wir sind dabei; **if we ~ ~ him** a little longer we might persuade him wenn wir ihn noch ein Weilchen bearbeiten, können wir ihn vielleicht überreden; **obviously the other side have been ~ing ~** him ihn hat offensichtlich die Gegenseite in der Mache gehabt (*inf*); **just keep ~ing ~ his basic greed** appellieren Sie nur weiter an seine Habgier.

♦ **work out 1** *vi* (a) (*allow solution: puzzle, sum* etc) aufgehen.

(b) (*amount to*) **that ~s ~ at £105** das gibt *or* macht £ 105; **it ~s ~ more expensive in the end** am Ende kommt *or* ist es teurer; **how much does that ~ ~ at?** was macht das?

(c) (*succeed*) *plan, marriage, idea* funktionieren, klappen (*inf*). **things didn't ~ ~ at all well for him** es ist ihm alles schiefgegangen; **how's your new job ~ing ~?** was macht die neue Arbeit?; **I hope it all ~s ~ for you** ich hoffe, daß alles klappt (*inf*) *or* daß dir alles gelingt; **things didn't ~ ~ that way** es kam ganz anders.

(d) (*in gym etc*) trainieren.

2 *vt sep* (a) (*solve, calculate*) herausbringen; *code also* brechen; *mathematical problem also* lösen; *problem* fertig werden mit (+*dat*); *sum also* ausrechnen. **you can ~ that ~ for yourself** das kannst du dir (doch) selbst denken; **surely he can manage to ~ things ~ for himself** (*in life*) er kann doch bestimmt allein zurechtkommen; **things will always ~ themselves ~** Probleme lösen sich stets von selbst.

(b) (*devise*) *scheme* (sich *dat*) ausdenken; (*in detail*) ausarbeiten.

(c) (*understand*) *person* schlau werden aus (+*dat*). **can you ~ ~ where we are on the map?** kannst du herausfinden *or* -bringen, wo wir auf der Karte sind?; **I can't ~ ~ why it went wrong** ich kann nicht verstehen, wieso es nicht geklappt hat.

(d) (*complete*) *prison sentence* absitzen. **to ~ ~ one's notice** seine Kündigungsfrist einhalten.

(e) (*exhaust*) *mine* ausbeuten, erschöpfen; *minerals* abbauen. **to ~ sth ~ of one's system** (*fig*) etw überwinden, mit etw fertigwerden.

(f) (*remove*) *nail, tooth* etc (allmählich) herausbringen.

♦ **work over** *vt sep* (*inf*) jdn zusammenschlagen (*inf*).

♦ **work through 1** *vi* +*prep obj* (a) (*blade* etc) sich arbeiten durch; (*water*) sickern durch. (b) (*read through*) sich (durch)arbeiten *or* (durch)ackern durch. **2** *vt* +*prep obj* he ~ed the rope ~ the crack er führte das Seil durch die Spalte. **3** vi (*come through: benefit, pay rise etc*) durchsickern.

♦**work up 1** vt sep **(a)** (*develop*) *business* zu etwas bringen, entwickeln; *enthusiasm* (*in oneself*) aufbringen; *appetite* sich (*dat*) holen. **to ~ one's way ~ (through the ranks/from the shop floor)** von der Pike auf dienen.

(b) *lecture, theme, notes* ausarbeiten.

(c) (*stimulate*) *audience* aufstacheln. **to ~ ~ feeling against sb** gegen jdn Stimmung machen; **to feel/get ~ed** ~ aufgeregt sein/sich aufregen; **to ~ oneself** ~ sich erhitzen; *see* **frenzy.**

2 vi (*skirt etc*) sich hochschieben.

♦**work up to** vi +prep obj *question, proposal etc* zusteuern auf (+*acc*). **I know what you're ~ing ~** ~ ich weiß, worauf Sie herauswollen; **the music ~s ~ ~ a tremendous climax** die Musik steigert sich zu einem gewaltigen Höhepunkt.

workable ['wɜːkəbl] adj *mine* abbaufähig; *land* bebaubar; *clay* formbar; *plan* durchführbar.

workaday ['wɜːkədeɪ] adj Alltags-.

workaholic [ˌwɜːkə'hɒlɪk] n (*inf*) Arbeitswütige(r), Arbeitssüchtige(r) mf.

work: ~bag n Näh- or Handarbeitsbeutel m; **~basket** n Näh- or Handarbeitskorb m; **~bench** n Werkbank f; **~book** n Arbeitsheft nt; **~ camp** n Arbeitslager nt; **~day** n (*esp US*) Arbeitstag m; (*day of week*) Werktag m.

worker ['wɜːkə'] n **1** (a) Arbeiter(in f) m. **~s' education** Arbeiterbildung f; **~ priest** Arbeiterpriester m; *see* **fast**[1] **1 (a).**

(b) (*also* **~ ant/bee**) Arbeiterin f.

work: ~ force n Arbeiterschaft f; **~horse** n (*lit, fig*) Arbeitspferd nt; **~house** n (*Brit Hist*) Armenhaus nt; **~-in** n Work-in nt.

working ['wɜːkɪŋ] **1** adj (a) (*engaged in work*) *population* arbeitend, berufstätig; (*Comm*) *partner* aktiv. **~ man** Arbeiter m; **I'm a ~ man, I need my rest** ich arbeite den ganzen Tag, ich brauch meine Ruhe; **~ wives** berufstätige Ehefrauen pl.

(b) (*spent in or used for* ~) *day, week, conditions, clothes* Arbeits-. **~ capital** Betriebskapital nt; **~ lunch** Arbeitsessen nt; **~ party** (*Arbeits*)ausschuß m.

(c) (*provisional*) *hypothesis, drawing, model* Arbeits-; (*sufficient*) *majority* arbeitsfähig, Arbeits-. **in ~ order** in betriebsfähigem Zustand; **~ knowledge** Grundkenntnisse pl.

2 n (a) (*work*) Arbeiten nt, Arbeit f. **~ so hard tired him out** er war erschöpft von der harten Arbeit.

(b) **~s** pl (*way sth works*) Arbeitsweise, Funktionsweise f; **~s of fate/the mind** Wege pl des Schicksals/Gedankengänge pl; **to understand the ~(s) of this machine/system** um zu verstehen, wie die Maschine/das politische System funktioniert.

(c) **~s** pl (*Min*) Schächte, Gänge pl; (*of quarry*) Grube f.

working class n (*also* **~ ~es**) Arbeiterklasse f.

working-class ['wɜːkɪŋklɑːs] adj der Arbeiterklasse, Arbeiter- ; (*pej*) ordinär, proletenhaft. **to be ~** zur Arbeiterklasse gehören.

working-over ['wɜːkɪŋ'əʊvə'] n (*inf*) Abreibung f (*inf*).

work: ~ load n Arbeit(slast) f; **~man** n Handwerker(in f) m; **~manlike** ['wɜːkmən'laɪk] adj *attitude*, *job* fachmännisch; *product* fachmännisch gearbeitet; **~manship** ['wɜːkmənʃɪp] n Arbeit(squalität) f; **~out** n (*Sport*) Training nt; **to have a ~out** (*boxer*) Sparring machen; **~ permit** n Arbeitserlaubnis f; **~piece** n Arbeit f; **~room** n Arbeitszimmer nt; **~shop** n Werkstatt f; *a music* **~shop** ein Musikkurs, ein Musik-Workshop m; **~shy** adj arbeitsscheu; **~ study** n REFA- or Arbeitsstudie f; **~table** n Arbeitstisch m; **~to-rule** n Dienst m nach Vorschrift; **~ week** n (*esp US*) Arbeitswoche f.

world [wɜːld] n (a) Welt f. **in the ~** auf der Welt; **all over the ~** auf der ganzen Welt; **he jets/sails etc all over the ~** er jettet/ segelt *etc* in der Weltgeschichte herum; **it's the same the whole ~ over or all the ~ over** es ist (doch) überall das Gleiche; **to go/sail round the ~** eine Weltreise machen/rund um die Welt segeln; **to feel or be on top of the ~** munter und fidel sein; **it's a small ~** die Welt ist klein; **it's not the end of the ~!** (*inf*) deshalb or davon geht die Welt nicht unter! (*inf*); **to live in a ~ of one's own** in seiner eigenen (kleinen) Welt leben; **money/love makes the ~ go round** es dreht sich alles um das Geld/die Liebe, Geld regiert die Welt.

(b) **the New/Old/Third W~** die Neue/Alte/Dritte Welt; **the business/literary ~** die Geschäftswelt/die literarische Welt; **the animal/vegetable ~** die Tier-/Pflanzenwelt; **in the Roman ~** zur Zeit der Römer.

(c) (*society*) Welt f. **man/woman of the ~** Mann m/Frau f von Welt; **to come or go down in the ~** herunterkommen; **to go up or rise in the ~** es (in der Welt) zu etwas bringen; **to set the ~ on fire** die Welt erschüttern; **he had the ~ at his feet** die ganze Welt lag ihm zu Füßen; **to lead the ~ in sth** in etw (*dat*) in der Welt führend sein; **how goes the ~ with you?** wie geht's, wie steht's?; **all the ~ knows ...** alle Welt or jeder weiß ...; **all the ~ and his wife were there** Gott und die Welt waren da (*inf*); **in the eyes of the ~** vor der Welt.

(d) (*this life*) Welt f. **to come into the ~** zur or auf die Welt kommen; **~ without end** (*Eccl*) von Ewigkeit zu Ewigkeit; **to renounce the ~** (*Rel*) der Welt (*dat*) entsagen; **to have the best of both ~s** das eine tun und das andere nicht lassen; **out of this ~** (*sl*) phantastisch; **he is not long for this ~** er steht schon mit einem Fuß im Jenseits; **to bring sb/sth into the ~** jdn zur Welt bringen/etw in die Welt setzen; **to go to a better ~** in eine bessere Welt eingehen; **to be alone in the ~** allein auf der Welt sein.

(e) (*emph*) Welt f. **not for all (the ~)** nicht um alles in der Welt; **nothing in the ~** nichts auf der Welt; **what/who in the ~** was/wer in aller Welt; **it did him a ~ of good** es hat ihm (unwahrscheinlich) gut getan; **a ~ of difference** ein himmelweiter Unterschied; **there was a ~ of meaning in his look** sein Blick sprach Bände; **they're ~s apart** sie sind total verschieden; **for all the ~ like ...** beinahe wie ...; **he looked for all the ~ as if nothing had happened** er sah aus, als wäre überhaupt nichts geschehen; **to be all the ~ to sb** jdm alles bedeuten; **to think the ~ of sb/sth** große Stücke auf jdn halten/etw über alles stellen.

world in cpds Welt-; **W~ Bank** n Weltbank f; **~-beater** n (*inf*) **to be a ~-beater** unschlagbar sein; **~ champion** n (*Brit*) Weltmeister(in f) m; **~ championship** n (*Brit*) Weltmeisterschaft f; **W~ Court** n Weltgerichtshof m; **W~ Cup** n Fußballweltmeisterschaft f; (*cup*) Weltpokal m; **~ Fair** n Weltausstellung f; **~-famous** adj weltberühmt; **~ language** n Weltsprache f.

worldliness ['wɜːldlɪnɪs] n Weltlichkeit f; (*of person*) weltliche Gesinnung.

worldly ['wɜːldlɪ] adj (+er) weltlich; *person* weltlich gesinnt. **~-wise** weltklug; **~ wisdom** Weltklugheit f.

world: ~ picture n see **~ view; ~ power** n Weltmacht f; **~ record** n Weltrekord m; **~ record holder** n Weltrekordinhaber(in f) m; **~'s champion** n (*US*) Weltmeister(in f) m; **W~'s Fair** n (*US*) Weltausstellung f; **~-shattering** adj welterschütternd, weltbewegend; **~'s record** n (*US*) Weltrekord m; **~ view** n Weltbild nt; **~ war** n Weltkrieg m; **~-weariness** n Lebensmüdigkeit f; **~-weary** adj lebensmüde; **~-wide** adj, adv weltweit.

worm [wɜːm] **1** n (a) (*lit, fig inf*) Wurm m; (*wood* ~) Holzwurm m. **~s** (*Med*) Würmer pl; **even a ~ will turn** (*prov*) es geschehen noch Zeichen und Wunder; **to get a ~'s eye view of sth** etw aus der Froschperspektive sehen.

(b) (*screw*) Schnecke f; (*thread*) Schneckengewinde nt.

2 vt **(a)** zwängen. **to ~ one's way or oneself along/through/into sth** sich an etw (*dat*) entlangdrücken/durch etw (*acc*) durchschlängeln or -zwängen/in etw (*acc*) hineinzwängen; **to ~ one's way forward** (*creep*) sich nach vorne schleichen; **to ~ one's way into a position/into sb's confidence/into a group** sich in eine Stellung/jds Vertrauen/eine Gruppe einschleichen; **to ~ one's way out of a difficulty** sich aus einer schwierigen Lage herauswinden.

(b) (*extract*) **to ~ sth out of sb** jdm etw entlocken; **you have to ~ everything out of him** ihm muß man die Würmer aus der Nase ziehen.

(c) *dog* eine Wurmkur machen mit (+*dat*).

worm: ~-cast n vom Regenwurm aufgeworfenes Erdhäufchen f; **~-eaten** adj *wood* wurmstichig; *cloth* von Würmern zerfressen; (*fig inf*) wurmzerfressen; **~ gear** n Schneckengetriebe nt; **~hole** n Wurmloch nt; **~ powder** n Wurmmittel nt; **~ wheel** n Schneckenrad nt; **~wood** n Wermut m; (*fig*) Wermutstropfen m.

wormy ['wɜːmɪ] adj *apple* wurmig; *wood* wurmstichig; *dog* von Würmern befallen; *soil* wurmreich.

worn [wɔːn] **1** ptp of **wear. 2** adj (a) (**~-out**) *coat* abgetragen; *book* zerlesen; *carpet* abgetreten; *tyre* abgefahren. **(b)** (*weary*) *smile* müde; *person* angegriffen. **to look ~** (with care/worry) besorgt aussehen.

worn-out adj attr, **worn out** [ˈwɔːnˌaʊt] adj pred (a) *coat* abgetragen; *carpet* abgetreten; *phrase* abgedroschen. **(b)** (*exhausted*) *person* erschöpft, ausgelaugt (*inf*); *horse* ausgemergelt.

worried ['wʌrɪd] adj besorgt (*about, by* wegen); (*anxious also*) beunruhigt. **to be ~ sick** krank vor Sorge(n) sein (*inf*).

worriedly ['wʌrɪdlɪ] adv besorgt; (*anxiously also*) beunruhigt.

worrier ['wʌrɪə'] n Pessimist, Schwarzseher m.

worrisome ['wʌrɪsəm] adj beunruhigend, besorgniserregend; (*annoying*) lästig.

worry ['wʌrɪ] **1** n Sorge f. **the ~ of bringing up a family** die Sorgen, die eine Familie mit sich bringt; **it's a great ~ to us** all wir machen uns alle große Sorgen darüber; **I know it's a ~ for you** ich weiß, es macht dir Sorgen; **what's your ~?** was drückt dich?; **that's the least of my worries** das macht mir noch am wenigsten Sorgen; **~ beads** Betperlen pl.

2 vt **(a)** (*cause concern*) beunruhigen, Sorgen machen (+*dat*). **it worries me** es macht mir Sorgen; **you ~ me** sometimes manchmal machst du mir wirklich Sorgen; **it's no use just ~ing, do something** es hat keinen Zweck, sich nur den Kopf zu zerbrechen, tu endlich was; **to ~ oneself sick or silly/to death** (*about or over sth*) (*inf*) sich krank machen/sich umbringen vor Sorge (um or wegen etw) (*inf*).

(b) (*bother*) stören. **to ~ sb with sth** jdn mit etw stören; **don't ~ me with trivialities** komm mir nicht mit Kleinigkeiten; **to ~ sb for sth/to do sth** jdn um etw plagen/jdn plagen, etw zu tun; **is this man ~ing you, madam?** belästigt Sie dieser Mann?

(c) (*dog etc*) *sheep* nachstellen (+*dat*); (*bite*) reißen; *bone* (herum)nagen an (+*dat*).

3 vi sich sorgen, sich (*dat*) Sorgen or Gedanken machen (*about, over* um, wegen). **he worries a lot** er macht sich immer soviel Sorgen; **don't ~!**, **not to ~!** keine Angst or Sorge!; **don't ~, I'll do it** laß mal, das mach ich schon; **he said not to ~** er sagte, wir sollten uns keine Sorgen machen; **don't ~ about letting me know** es macht nichts, wenn du mich nicht benachrichtigen kannst; **don't you ~ about that, I'll do it** mach dir darum keine Sorgen, das mach ich; **you should ~!** (*inf*) du hast (vielleicht) Sorgen!

worrying ['wʌrɪɪŋ] **1** adj *problem* beunruhigend, besorgniserregend. **it's very ~** es macht mir große Sorge; **I know it's a ~ for you** ich weiß, es macht dir Sorgen; **it is a ~ time for us** wir haben zur Zeit viel Sorgen.

2 n ~ **won't help** sich nur Sorgen machen, nützt nichts.

worse [wɜːs] **1** adj, comp of **bad** schlechter; (*morally, with bad consequences*) schlimmer, ärger. **it gets ~ and ~** es wird immer schlimmer; **the patient is ~ than he was yesterday** dem Patienten geht es schlechter als gestern; **and to make matters ~** und zu allem Übel; **his "corrections" only made it ~** er hat alles nur verschlimmbessert; **it could have been ~** es hätte schlimmer kommen können; **it's no ~ than I'd expected** es ist nicht ärger *or* schlimmer, als ich erwartet hatte; ~ **luck!** (so ein) Pech!; **the patient gets** *or* **grows** ~ der Zustand des Patienten verschlechtert sich *or* wird schlechter; **it will be the** ~ **for you** das wird für dich unangenehme Folgen haben; so much the ~ **for him** um so schlimmer; **to be the** ~ **for drink** betrunken sein; **he's none the** ~ **for it** er hat sich nichts dabei getan, es ist ihm nichts dabei passiert; **you'll be none the** ~ **for some work** etwas Arbeit wird dir nicht schaden; **I don't think any the** ~ **of you for it** ich halte deswegen aber nicht weniger von dir; ~ **things happen at sea** (*inf*) es könnte schlimmer sein.

2 *adv, comp of* **badly** schlechter. **it hurts** ~ es tut mehr weh; **to be** ~ **off than ...** schlechter dran sein (*inf*) *or* in einer schlechteren Lage sein als ...; **I could do a lot** ~ **than accept their offer** es wäre bestimmt kein Fehler, wenn ich das Angebot annähme.

3 *n* Schlechteres *nt*; (*morally, with regard to consequences*) Schlimmeres *nt*. **there is** ~ **to come** es kommt noch schlimmer; **it's changed for the** ~ es hat sich zum Schlechteren gewendet.

worsen ['wɜːsn] **1** *vt* verschlechtern, schlechter machen. **2** *vi* sich verschlechtern, schlechter werden.

worship ['wɜːʃɪp] **1** *n* **(a)** (*of God, person etc*) Verehrung *f*. **public** ~ Gottesdienst *m*; **place of** ~ Andachtsstätte *f*; (*non-Christian*) Kultstätte *f*.

(b) (*Brit: in titles*) **Your W~** (*to judge*) Euer Ehren/Gnaden; (*to mayor*) (verehrter *or* sehr geehrter) Herr Bürgermeister; **His W~ the Mayor of ...** der verehrte Bürgermeister von ...; **if your W~ wishes** wenn Euer Ehren *or* Gnaden wünschen.

2 *vt* anbeten. **he** ~**ped the ground she trod on** er betete den Boden unter ihren Füßen an.

3 *vi* (*Rel*) den Gottesdienst abhalten; (*RC*) die Messe feiern. **the church where we used to** ~ die Kirche, die wir besuchten.

worshipful ['wɜːʃɪpfʊl] *adj* **(a)** look, gaze verehrend. **(b)** (*Brit: in titles*) sehr verehrt *or* geehrt.

worshipper ['wɜːʃɪpə'] *n* Kirchgänger(in *f*) *m*. ~ **of Baal** Baalsverehrer *m*; ~ **of the sun** Sonnenanbeter(in *f*) *m*; **he was a lifelong** ~ **at this church** er ist sein Leben lang hier zur Kirche gegangen; **a** ~ **of wealth** jemand, der das Geld anbetet.

worst [wɜːst] **1** *adj, superl of* **bad** schlechteste(r, s); (*morally, with regard to consequences*) schlimmste(r, s). **the** ~ **possible time** die ungünstigste Zeit.

2 *adv, superl of* **badly** am schlechtesten.

3 *n* **the** ~ **is over** das Schlimmste *or* Ärgste ist vorbei; **in the** ~ **of the winter/storm** im ärgsten Winter/Sturm; **when the crisis/storm was at its** ~ als die Krise/der Sturm ihren/seinen Höhepunkt erreicht hatte; **at (the)** ~ schlimmstenfalls; **you've never seen him at his** ~ er kann noch (viel) schlimmer (sein); **the** ~ **of it is ...** das Schlimmste daran ist, ...; **if the** ~ **comes to the** ~ wenn alle Stricke reißen (*inf*); **do your** ~! (*liter*) mach zu!; **to get the** ~ **of it** den kürzeren ziehen.

4 *vt* enemy, opponent besiegen, schlagen.

worsted ['wʊstɪd] **1** *n* (*yarn*) Kammgarn *nt*; (*cloth also*) Kammgarnstoff *m*. **2** *adj* Kammgarn-.

worth [wɜːθ] **1** *adj* **(a)** wert. **it's** ~ **£5** es ist £ 5 wert; **it's not** ~ **£5** es ist keine £ 5 wert; **what's this** ~? was *or* wieviel ist das wert?; **it can't be** ~ **that!** soviel kann es unmöglich wert sein; **it's** ~ **a great deal to me** es ist mir viel wert; (*sentimentally*) es bedeutet mir sehr viel; **what's it** ~ **to me to do that?** (*in money*) was springt für mich dabei heraus? (*inf*); (*in advantages*) was bringt es mir, wenn ich das tue?; **will you do this for me?** — **what's it** ~ **to you?** tust du das für mich? — was ist es dir wert?; **he was** ~ **a million** *or* **besaß eine Million**; **he's** ~ **all his brothers put together** er ist soviel wert wie all seine Brüder zusammen; **for all one is** ~ so sehr man nur kann; **to sing/try for all one is** ~ aus voller Kehle *or* vollem Halse singen/alles in seinen Kräften Stehende versuchen; **for what it's** ~, **I personally don't think ...** wenn mich einer fragt, ich persönlich glaube nicht, daß ...; **I'll tell you this for what it's** ~ ich sage dir das, ich weiß nicht, ob was dran ist; **that's my opinion for what it's** ~ das ist meine bescheidene Meinung; **it's more than my life/job is** ~ **to tell you** ich sage es dir nicht, dazu ist mir mein Leben zu lieb/dazu liegt mir zu viel an meiner Stelle.

(b) (*deserving, meriting*) wert. **to be** ~ **it** sich lohnen; **to be** ~ **sth** etw wert sein; **it's not** ~ **it** es lohnt sich nicht; **it's not** ~ **the trouble** es ist der Mühe nicht wert; **the book is** ~ **reading** das Buch ist lesenswert; **life isn't** ~ **living** das Leben ist nicht lebenswert; **is there anything** ~ **seeing in this town?** gibt es in dieser Stadt etwas Sehenswertes?; **it's a film** ~ **seeing** es lohnt sich, diesen Film anzusehen; **hardly** ~ **mentioning** kaum der Rede wert; **an experience** ~ **having** eine lohnenswerte Erfahrung; **is that book** ~ **having?** ist das Buch es wert (*inf*), lohnt es sich, dieses Buch anzuschaffen?; **it't not** ~ **having** es ist nichts; **if a thing's** ~ **doing, it's** ~ **doing well** wenn schon, denn schon; *see* salt **1** (a), while **1** (c).

2 *n* Wert *m*. **£10's** ~ **of books** Bücher im Werte von £ 10 *or* für £ 10; **a man of great** ~ ein wertvoller Mensch; **to show one's true** ~ zeigen, was man wirklich wert ist, seinen wahren Wert zeigen; **to increase in** ~ im Wert steigen; **what's the current** ~ **of this?** wieviel ist das momentan wert?; *see* money.

worthily ['wɜːðɪlɪ] *adv* löblich, lobenswert.

worthiness ['wɜːðɪnɪs] *n* (*of charity, cause etc*) Wert *m*; (*of person*) Ehrenhaftigkeit *f*.

worthless ['wɜːθlɪs] *adj* wertlos; *person also* nichtsnutzig.

worthlessness ['wɜːθlɪsnɪs] *n* see *adj* Wertlosigkeit *f*; Nichtsnutzigkeit *f*.

worthwhile ['wɜːθ'waɪl] *adj* lohnend *attr*. **to be** ~ sich lohnen; (*worth the trouble also*) der Mühe (*gen*) wert sein; **it's a thoroughly** ~ **film/book** es lohnt sich wirklich, den Film zu sehen/das Buch zu lesen; **it's hardly** ~ (*asking him*) es lohnt sich wohl kaum(, ihn zu fragen); *see also* while **1** (c).

worthy ['wɜːðɪ] **1** *adj* (+*er*) **(a)** ehrenwert, achtbar; *opponent* würdig; *motive, cause* löblich, lobenswert. **my** ~ **friend/opponent** mein werter Freund/Widersacher.

(b) *pred* wert, würdig. ~ **of** remark/mention bemerkenswert/erwähnenswert; **to be** ~ **of sb/sth** jds/einer Sache würdig sein (*geh*); **any journalist** ~ **of the name** jeder Journalist, der diesen Namen verdient; **this makes him** ~ **of (our) respect** dafür verdient er unseren Respekt; **he is** ~ **to be ranked among ...** er ist es wert, ... gezählt zu werden.

2 *n* (*hum*) **the local worthies** die Ortsgrößen *pl* (*hum*).

would [wʊd] *pret of* **will**[1] *modal aux vb* **(a)** (*conditional*) **if you asked him he** ~ **do it** wenn du ihn fragtest, würde er es tun; **if you had asked him he** ~ **have done it** wenn du ihn gefragt hättest, hätte er es getan; **I thought you** ~ **want to know** ich dachte, du wüßtest es gerne *or* du würdest es gerne wissen; **who** ~ **have thought it?** wer hätte das gedacht?; **you** ~ **think ...** man sollte meinen ...

(b) (*in indirect speech*) **she said she** ~ **come** sie sagte, sie würde kommen *or* sie käme; **I said I** ~, **so I will** ich habe gesagt, ich würde es tun, und ich werde es auch tun.

(c) (*emph*) **you** ~ **be the one to get hit** typisch, daß ausgerechnet du getroffen worden bist; **you** ~ **be the one to forget** typisch, daß du das vergessen hast, das sieht dir ähnlich, daß du es vergessen hast; **I** ~**n't know** keine Ahnung; **you** ~**!** das sieht dir ähnlich!; **he** ~ **have to come right now** ausgerechnet jetzt muß er kommen; **you** ~ **think of that/say that**, ~**n't you!** von dir kann man ja nichts anderes erwarten; **it** ~ **have to rain** es muß auch ausgerechnet regnen!

(d) (*insistence*) **I warned him, but he** ~ **do it** ich habe ihn gewarnt, aber er mußte es ja unbedingt *or* um jeden Preis tun; **he** ~**n't listen/behave** er wollte partout nicht zuhören/sich partout nicht benehmen; **he** ~**n't be told** er wollte sich (*dat*) einfach nichts sagen lassen.

(e) (*conjecture*) **it** ~ **seem so** es sieht wohl so aus; **it** ~ **have been about 8 o'clock** es war (wohl) so ungefähr 8 Uhr; **what** ~ **this be?** was ist das wohl?; **you** ~**n't have a cigarette,** ~ **you?** Sie hätten nicht zufällig eine Zigarette?

(f) (*wish*) **möchten. what** ~ **you have me do?** was soll ich tun?; **try as he** ~ so sehr er es auch versuchte; **the place where I** ~ **be** (*old, liter*) **der Ort, an dem ich sein möchte;** ~ **(that) it were not so!** (*old, liter*) wenn das doch nur nicht wahr wäre!; ~ **to God** *or* **heaven he would come** gebe Gott, daß er kommt; ~ **to God** *or* **heaven he hadn't come** ich wünsche zu Gott, er wäre nicht gekommen.

(g) (*in questions*) ~ **he come?** würde er vielleicht kommen?; ~ **he have come?** wäre er gekommen?; ~ **you mind closing the window?** würden Sie bitte das Fenster schließen?; ~ **you care for some tea?** hätten Sie gerne etwas Tee?

(h) (*habit*) **he** ~ **paint it each year** er strich es jedes Jahr, er pflegte es jedes Jahr zu streichen (*geh*); **50 years ago the streets** ~ **be empty on a Sunday** vor 50 Jahren waren sonntags die Straßen immer leer.

would-be ['wʊdbiː] *adj attr* ~ **poet/politician** jemand, der gerne (ein) Dichter/(ein) Politiker würde; (*pej*) Möchtegern-Dichter(in *f*) *m*/-Politiker(in *f*) *m*; **with** ~ **kindness** in wohlgemeinter Absicht.

wouldn't ['wʊdnt] *contr of* **would not**.

wound[1] [wuːnd] **1** *n* (*lit*) Wunde *f*; (*fig also*) Kränkung *f*. **my old war** ~ meine alte Kriegsverletzung; **the** ~ **to his pride** sein verletzter Stolz; *see* kiss.

2 *vt* (*lit*) verwunden, verletzen; (*fig*) verletzen. **the** ~**ed** *pl* die Verwundeten *pl*; ~**ed pride/vanity** verletzter Stolz/gekränkte Eitelkeit.

wound[2] [waʊnd] *pret, ptp of* **wind**[2].

wounding ['wuːndɪŋ] *adj* remark, tone verletzend.

wove [wəʊv] *pret of* **weave**.

woven ['wəʊvən] *ptp of* **weave**.

wow[1] [waʊ] **1** *interj* hui (*inf*), Mann (*inf*), Mensch (*inf*). **2** *n* (*sl*) **it's a** ~ das ist Spitze (*inf*) *or* 'ne Wucht (*inf*).

wow[2] *n* (*on recording*) Jaulen *nt*.

wpm *abbr of* **words per minute** WpM, wpm.

WRAC [ræk] (*Brit*) *abbr of* **Women's Royal Army Corps**.

wrack[1] [ræk] *n* (*Bot*) Tang *m*.

wrack[2] *n, vt* see **rack**[1], **rack**[2].

WRAF [ræf] (*Brit*) *abbr of* **Women's Royal Air Force**.

wraith [reɪθ] *n* Gespenst *nt*, Geist *m*.

wraithlike ['reɪθlaɪk] *adj* durchgeistigt, ätherisch.

wrangle ['ræŋgl] **1** *n* Gerangel, Hin und Her *no pl nt*. **2** *vi* streiten, rangeln (*about* um); (*in bargaining*) feilschen.

wrangler ['ræŋglə'] *n* (*US: cowboy*) Cowboy *m*; (*Univ*) Mathematikstudent in Cambridge, der mit Auszeichnung bestanden hat.

wrap [ræp] **1** *n* **(a)** (*garment*) Umhangtuch *nt*; (*for child*) Wickeltuch *nt*; (*stole*) Stola *f*; (*cape*) Cape *nt*; (*coat*) Mantel *m*.

(b) **under** ~**s** (*lit*) verhüllt; (*car, weapon*) getarnt; (*fig*) geheim; **they took the** ~**s off the new project** sie haben, was das neue Projekt betrifft, die Katze aus dem Sack gelassen (*inf*).

2 *vt* **(a)** einwickeln; *parcel, present also* verpacken, einpacken, einschlagen; *person* (*for warmth*) einpacken (*inf*). **shall I** ~ **it for you?** soll ich es Ihnen einpacken *or* einwickeln?; ~ **the joint in foil** den Braten in Folie einschlagen; ~**ped cakes/bread** abgepackte Teilchen/abgepacktes Brot; **to** ~ **sth round sth** etw um etw wickeln; **he** ~**ped the car round a lamppost** (*inf*) er hat das Auto um eine Laterne gewickelt (*inf*); **to** ~ **one's arms round sb** jdn in die Arme schließen.

(b) (*fig: envelop*) **to be** ~**ped in sth** in etw gehüllt sein; **she lay** ~**ped in his arms** sie lag in seinen Armen; **the project is so** ~**ped in secrecy** das Projekt ist so vom Schleier des Geheimnisses umhüllt.

♦ **wrap up 1** *vt sep* **(a)** (*lit, fig*) einpacken, einwickeln, verpacken. **an expensive deal cunningly** ~**ped** ~ **as a bargain** ein teurer Kauf, der geschickt als Sonderangebot getarnt ist/war.

(b) (*inf: finalize*) deal, arrangement festmachen, unter Dach und Fach bringen.

(c) to be ~ped ~ in sb/sth in jdm/etw aufgehen.
2 vi (a) (dress warmly) sich warm einpacken (inf).
(b) (sl: be quiet) den Mund halten (inf).
wrap: ~(a)round, ~over adj attr Wickel-.
wrapper ['ræpə'] n (a) Verpackung f; (of sweets) Papier(chen) nt; (of cigar) Deckblatt nt; (of book) (Schutz)umschlag m; (postal) Streifband nt. (b) (garment) leichter Morgenmantel. (c) (person: in factory etc) Packer(in f) m.
wrapping ['ræpɪŋ] n Verpackung f (round gen, von). ~ paper Packpapier nt; (decorative) Geschenkpapier nt.
wrath [rɒθ] n Zorn m; (liter: of storm) Wut f.
wrathful adj, ~ly adv ['rɒθful, -fəlɪ] wutentbrannt, zornentbrannt.
wreak [ri:k] vt destruction anrichten; chaos also stiften; (liter) vengeance üben (on an +dat); (liter) punishment auferlegen (on dat); (liter) anger auslassen (on an +dat); see havoc.
wreath [ri:θ] n, pl -s [ri:ðz] Kranz m; (of smoke etc) Kringel m.
wreathe [ri:ð] **1** vt (encircle) (um)winden; (clouds, mist) umhüllen; (entwine) flechten. the ivy ~d itself round the pillar das Efeu rankte sich um die Säule; a garland ~d the victor's head ein Kranz (um)krönte das Haupt des Siegers; his face was ~d in smiles er strahlte über das ganze Gesicht.
2 vi the smoke ~d upwards der Rauch stieg in Kringeln auf; to ~ round sth (ivy etc) sich um etw ranken; (snake) sich um etw schlängeln or ringeln; (smoke) sich um etw kringeln or kräuseln; (mist) um etw wallen.
wreck [rek] **1** n (a) (Naut) Schiffbruch m; (~ed ship, car, train) Wrack nt. lost in the ~ beim Schiffbruch verloren.
(b) (fig) (old bicycle, furniture etc) Trümmerhaufen m; (person) Wrack nt; (of hopes, life, marriage etc) Trümmer, Ruinen pl. I'm a ~, I feel a ~ ich bin ein (völliges) Wrack; (exhausted) ich bin vollkommen fertig or erledigt; (in appearance) ich sehe verheerend or unmöglich aus; see nervous ~.
2 vt (a) ship, train, plane zum Wrack machen, einen Totalschaden verursachen an (+dat); car kaputtfahren (inf), zu Schrott fahren (inf); machine, mechanism zerstören, kaputtmachen (inf); furniture, house zerstören; (person) zertrümmern, kurz und klein schlagen (inf). to be ~ed (Naut) Schiffbruch erleiden; ~ed ship/car wrackes or havariertes Schiff/zu Schrott gefahrenes Auto.
(b) (fig) hopes, plans, chances zunichte machen; marriage zerrütten; career, health, sb's life zerstören, ruinieren; person kaputtmachen (inf); party, holiday verderben.
wreckage ['rekɪdʒ] n (lit, fig: remains) Trümmer pl; (of ship also) Wrackteile pl; (washed ashore) Strandgut nt; (of house, town also) Ruinen pl. the ship narrowly escaped ~ on the reef das Schiff entging am Riff nur knapp einem Schiffbruch.
wrecker ['rekə'] n (a) (shipwrecker) Strandräuber (der Schiffe durch Lichtsignale zum Stranden bringt).
(b) (Naut: salvager) Bergungsarbeiter m; (vessel) Bergungsschiff nt.
(c) (US: breaker, salvager) Schrotthändler m; (for buildings) Abbrucharbeiter m.
(d) (US: breakdown van) Abschleppwagen m.
wrecking ['rekɪŋ] n: ~ bar n (US) Brechstange f; ~ service n (US Aut) Abschleppdienst m.
wren [ren] n Zaunkönig m.
Wren [ren] n (Brit) weibliches Mitglied der britischen Marine.
wrench [rentʃ] **1** n (a) (tug) Ruck m; (Med) Verrenkung f. to give sth a ~ einer Sache (dat) einen Ruck geben; he gave his arm/shoulder a nasty ~ er hat sich (dat) den Arm/die Schulter schlimm verrenkt.
(b) (tool) Schraubenschlüssel m.
(c) (fig) to be a ~ weh tun; the ~ of parting der Trennungsschmerz.
2 vt to ~ sth winden. to ~ sth (away) from sb jdm etw entwinden; to ~ a door open eine Tür aufzwingen; to ~ a door off its hinges eine Tür aus den Angeln reißen; he ~ed the steering wheel round er riß das Lenkrad herum; to ~ sb's arm out of its socket jdm den Arm ausrenken.
(b) (Med) to ~ one's ankle/shoulder sich (dat) den Fuß/die Schulter verrenken.
(c) (fig) reißen. to ~ sb/sth off his/her/its course or axis jdn/etw aus der Bahn werfen; if you could ~ yourself away from the TV wenn du dich vom Fernseher losreißen könntest.
wrest [rest] vt to ~ sth from sb/sth jdm/einer Sache etw abringen; (leadership, title) jdm etw entreißen; to ~ sth from sb's grasp jdm etw entreißen; to ~ sb/oneself free jdn/sich losreißen.
wrestle ['resl] **1** n Ringkampf m. to have a ~ with sb mit jdm ringen.
2 vt ringen mit; (Sport also) einen Ringkampf bestreiten gegen. he ~d the thief to the ground er brachte or zwang den Dieb zu Boden.
3 vi (a) (lit) ringen (for sth um etw).
(b) (fig: with problem, conscience etc) ringen, kämpfen (with mit). the pilot ~d with the controls der Pilot kämpfte mit den Instrumenten.
wrestler ['reslə'] n Ringkämpfer m; (modern) Ringer(in f) m.
wrestling ['reslɪŋ] n Ringen nt. ~ as a discipline Ringen or der Ringkampf als Disziplin.
wrestling in cpds Ringer-; ~ match n Ringkampf m.
wretch [retʃ] n (a) (miserable) armer Teufel or Schlucker (inf).
(b) (contemptible) Wicht, Schuft m; (nuisance) Blödmann m (inf); (child) Schlingel m.
wretched ['retʃɪd] adj (a) elend; conditions, life, clothing etc also erbärmlich; (ill also) miserabel (inf); (unhappy, depressed) (tod)unglücklich. I feel ~ (ill) mir geht es miserabel (inf), ich fühle mich elend; I feel ~ about having to say no es tut mir in der Seele weh, daß ich nein sagen muß.
(b) (very bad) housing conditions, weather, novel, player

erbärmlich, miserabel (inf); (inf: damned) verflixt, elend, Mist- (all inf). what a ~ thing to do! so etwas Schäbiges!; what ~ luck! was für ein verflixtes or elendes Pech (inf).
wretchedly ['retʃɪdlɪ] adv (a) (in misery) erbärmlich; weep, apologize, look kläglich; (very badly also) miserabel (inf). (b) (inf: extremely) verflixt (inf), verdammt (inf).
wretchedness ['retʃɪdnɪs] n Erbärmlichkeit f; (of person: misery) Elend nt. the ~ of his health seine miserable (inf) or elende Gesundheit.
wrick [rɪk] **1** vt to ~ one's neck/shoulder sich (dat) den Hals/die Schulter ausrenken. **2** n to have/get a ~ in one's neck sich (dat) den Hals ausgerenkt haben/sich (dat) den Hals ausrenken.
wriggle ['rɪgl] **1** n Schlängeln nt no pl; (of child, fish) Zappeln nt no pl. she gave her toes a ~ sie wackelte mit den Zehen; to move with a series of ~s sich vorwärtsschlängeln; with a final ~ he emerged from the tunnel er wand sich noch durch das letzte Stück und kam aus dem Tunnel; with a sensuous ~ she ... sie räkelte sich sinnlich und ...; to give a ~ see 3 vi.
2 vt toes, ears wackeln mit. to ~ one's way through sth sich durch etw (hin)durchwinden or -schlängeln.
3 vi (also ~ about or around) (worm, snake, eel) sich schlängeln; (fish) sich winden, zappeln; (person) (restlessly, excitedly) zappeln; (in embarrassment) sich winden. to ~ along/down sich vorwärts schlängeln/sich nach unten schlängeln; the fish ~d off the hook der Fisch wand sich vom Haken; she managed to ~ free es gelang ihr, sich loszuwinden; he ~d through the hole in the hedge er wand or schlängelte sich durch das Loch in der Hecke; do stop wriggling about hör endlich mit der Zappelei auf.
♦**wriggle out** vi (lit) sich herauswinden (of aus); (fig also) sich herausmanövrieren (of aus). he's ~d (his way) ~ of it er hat sich gedrückt.
wriggly ['rɪglɪ] adj (+er) sich windend attr, sich krümmend attr; fish, child zappelnd attr.
wring [rɪŋ] (vb: pret, ptp wrung) **1** vt (a) (also ~ out) clothes, wet rag etc auswringen, auswinden. to ~ water out of clothes (nasse) Kleider auswringen or auswinden; do not ~ (on washing instructions) nicht wringen.
(b) hands (in distress) ringen. to ~ a duck's neck einer Ente (dat) den Hals umdrehen; I could have wrung his neck ich hätte ihm den Hals or Kragen (inf) umdrehen können; he wrung my hand er schüttelte mir (kräftig) die Hand; to ~ sb's heart jdm in der Seele weh tun.
(c) (extract) to ~ sth out of or from sb etw aus jdm herausquetschen, jdm etw abringen.
2 n to give clothes a ~ Kleider auswringen or auswinden.
wringer ['rɪŋə'] n (Wäsche)mangel f.
wringing ['rɪŋɪŋ] adj (also ~ wet) tropfnaß; person also patschnaß (inf).
wrinkle ['rɪŋkl] **1** n (in clothes, paper) Knitter m; (on face, skin) Runzel, Falte f; (in stocking) Falte f.
2 vt fabric, paper, surface, sheet verknittern, verkrumpeln (inf); skin runzlig or faltig machen. to ~ one's nose/brow die Nase rümpfen/die Stirne runzeln.
3 vi (sheet, material) (ver)knittern; (stockings) Falten schlagen; (skin etc) runzlig or faltig werden, Runzeln or Falten bekommen.
wrinkled ['rɪŋkld] adj sheet, skirt, paper zerknittert; stockings Ziehharmonika- (inf); skin runzlig, faltig; nose gerümpft; brow gerunzelt; apple, old lady schrumpelig, verschrumpelt.
wrinkly ['rɪŋklɪ] adj (+er) schrumpelig; fabric zerknittert.
wrist [rɪst] n Handgelenk nt. to slash one's ~s sich (dat) die Pulsadern aufschneiden.
wristband ['rɪst,bænd] n Armband nt; (on dress, shirt) Ärmelbündchen nt; (Sport) Schweißband nt.
wristlet ['rɪstlɪt] n Armband nt.
wrist: ~ lock n Polizeigriff m; to put a ~ lock on sb jdn im Polizeigriff halten; ~watch n Armbanduhr f.
writ [rɪt] n (a) (Jur) Verfügung f, ~ of attachment Haft- or Verhaftungsbefehl m; ~ of execution Vollstreckungsbefehl m; to issue a ~ eine Verfügung herausgeben; to issue a ~ against sb jdn vorladen (for wegen). (b) Holy W~ (old, form) Heilige Schrift.
write [raɪt] pret wrote or (obs) writ [rɪt], ptp written or (obs) writ [rɪt] **1** vt schreiben; cheque also, copy ausstellen; notes sich (dat) aufschreiben, sich (dat) machen; application form ausfüllen. he wrote me a letter er schrieb mir einen Brief; he wrote himself a note to remind him er machte sich (dat) eine Notiz, um sich zu erinnern; he wrote five sheets of paper er schrieb fünf Seiten voll; print your name, don't ~ it schreiben Sie Ihren Namen in Druckschrift, nicht in Schreibschrift; how is that written? wie schreibt man das?; it is written that ... (old) es steht geschrieben, daß ...; writ(ten) large (fig) verdeutlicht; (on a larger scale) im Großen; it was written all over his face es stand ihm im or auf dem Gesicht geschrieben; he had "policeman" written all over him man sah ihm den Polizisten schon von weitem an; see shorthand.
2 vi schreiben. as I ~ ... während ich dies schreibe, ...; to ~ to sb jdm schreiben; we ~ to each other wir schreiben uns; I wrote to him to come ich habe ihm geschrieben, er solle kommen or daß er kommen solle; that's nothing to ~ home about (inf) das ist nichts Weltbewegendes; I'll ~ for it at once ich bestelle es sofort, ich fordere es gleich an; he always wanted to ~ er wollte immer (ein) Schriftsteller werden.
♦**write away** vi schreiben. to ~ ~ for sth etw anfordern; he wrote ~ asking for further information er forderte weitere Information an, er schrieb um weitere Information.
♦**write back** vi zurückschreiben, antworten. he wrote ~ saying ... er schrieb zurück, um mir zu sagen, ...
♦**write down** vt sep (make a note of) aufschreiben; (record, put in writing) niederschreiben.

◆**write in 1** vt sep (a) word, correction etc hineinschreiben, einfügen (prep obj in +acc).
(b) (US Pol) to ~ sb ~ seine Stimme für jdn abgeben, der nicht in der Liste aufgeführt ist.
(c) (build in) condition, provision aufnehmen. is there anything written ~ about that? steht was dazu drin?
2 vi schreiben (to an +acc). someone has written ~ (to us) requesting this record jemand hat uns (dat) geschrieben und uns um diese Platte gebeten; to ~ ~ for sth etw anfordern, um etw schreiben.

◆**write off 1** vi see write away. **2** vt sep (a) (write quickly) (schnell) hinschreiben; essay, poem herunterschreiben. (b) debt, losses, (fig: regard as failure) abschreiben. (c) car etc (driver) zu Schrott fahren; (insurance company) als Totalschaden abschreiben.

◆**write out** vt sep (a) (in full) notes ausarbeiten; name etc ausschreiben. (b) cheque, prescription ausstellen. (c) actor, character einen Abgang schaffen. he's been written ~ ihm wurde ein Abgang aus der Serie geschaffen.

◆**write up** vt sep notes ausarbeiten; report, diary schreiben; event schreiben über (+acc); (review) play, film eine Kritik schreiben über (+acc). the play was well written ~ das Stück bekam gute Kritiken/eine gute Kritik.

write: ~-in n (US) Stimmabgabe f für einen nicht in der Liste aufgeführten Kandidaten; ~-off n (a) (car etc) Totalschaden m; (b) (Comm) Abschreibung f.
writer ['raɪtəʳ] n Schreiber(in f) m; (of scenario, report etc also) Autor(in f) m; (of TV commercials, subtitles) Texter(in f) m; (of music) Komponist(in f) m; (as profession) Schriftsteller(in f) m. the (present) ~ der Schreiber (dieser Zeilen/dieses Artikels etc); he's a very poor ~ er schreibt sehr schlecht; (correspondent) er ist kein großer Briefschreiber; ~'s cramp Schreibkrampf m.
write-up ['raɪtʌp] n Pressebericht m; (of play, film) Kritik f.
writhe [raɪð] vi sich krümmen, sich winden (with, in vor +dat). to ~ in ecstasy sich vor Lust wälzen; to make sb ~ (painfully) jdn vor Schmerzen zusammenzucken lassen; (with disgust) jdm kalte Schauer über den Rücken jagen, jdn erschauern lassen; (with embarrassment) jdn in peinliche Verlegenheit bringen.
writing ['raɪtɪŋ] n Schrift f; (act, profession) Schreiben nt; (inscription) Inschrift f. at the time of ~ als dies geschrieben wurde; (in present) während ich dies schreibe; in ~ schriftlich; evidence/permission in ~ schriftliche Beweise/ Genehmigung; to commit sth to ~ etw schriftlich festhalten; this is a nice piece of ~ das ist gut geschrieben; his ~s seine Werke or Schriften; in sb's own ~ (not typewritten) handgeschrieben; (not written by sb else) in jds eigener (Hand)schrift (dat); he earns a bit from his ~ er verdient sich ein bißchen (Geld) mit Schreiben; the ~ is on the wall for them ihre Stunde hat geschlagen; he had seen the ~ on the wall er hat die Zeichen erkannt.
writing in cpds Schreib-; ~ case n Schreibmappe f; ~ desk n Schreibtisch m, Schreibpult nt; ~ pad n Schreib- or Notizblock m; ~ paper n Schreibpapier nt.
written ['rɪtn] **1** ptp of write. **2** adj examination, statement, evidence schriftlich; language Schrift-; word geschrieben.
WRNS [renz] (Brit) abbr of Women's Royal Naval Service.
wrong [rɒŋ] **1** adj (a) falsch; (when choice is given also) verkehrt. to be ~ nicht stimmen; (person) unrecht haben; (answer also) falsch or verkehrt sein; (watch) falsch gehen; it's all ~ das ist völlig verkehrt or falsch; (not true) das stimmt alles nicht; it's all ~ that I should have to … das ist doch nicht richtig, daß ich … muß; I was ~ about him ich habe mich in ihm getäuscht or geirrt; you were ~ in thinking he did it du hast unrecht gehabt, als du dachtest, er sei es gewesen; how ~ can you get! falscher geht's (wohl) nicht!; I took a ~ turning ich habe eine verkehrte or falsche Abzweigung genommen; he went in the ~ direction er ging in die verkehrte or falsche Richtung; this is the ~ train for Bournemouth dies ist der falsche Zug, wenn Sie nach Bournemouth wollen; to say/do the ~ thing das Falsche sagen/tun; the ~ side of the fabric die Abseite or die linke Seite des Stoffes; you live in the ~ part of town du wohnst nicht im richtigen Stadtteil; he's got the ~ kind of friends er hat die falschen Freunde; you've come to the ~ man or person/place da sind Sie an den Falschen/an die Falsche/an die falsche Adresse geraten; brown is definitely the ~ colour to be wearing this season Braun ist diese Saison absolut nicht modern; I feel all ~ here ich fühle mich hier völlig fehl am Platz; it's the ~ time for jokes es ist nicht die richtige Zeit für Witze; it's the ~ time and the ~ place for that das ist weder die Zeit noch der Ort dafür; the ~ use of drugs die falsche or verkehrte Anwendung von Arzneimitteln; (misuse) Drogenmißbrauch m; to do sth the ~ way etw falsch or verkehrt machen; see number, side.

(b) (morally) schlecht, unrecht; (unfair) ungerecht, unfair. it's ~ to steal es ist unrecht zu stehlen, Stehlen ist Unrecht; that was very ~ of you das war absolut nicht richtig von dir; you were ~ to do that es war nicht richtig or recht von dir, das zu tun; it's ~ of you to laugh Sie sollten nicht lachen; it's ~ that he should have to ask es ist unrecht or falsch, daß er überhaupt fragen muß; what's ~ with a drink now and again? was ist schon (Schlimmes) dabei, wenn man ab und zu einen trinkt?; what's ~ with working on Sundays? was ist denn schon dabei, wenn man sonntags arbeitet?; I don't see anything ~ in or with that ich kann nichts Falsches daran finden, ich finde nichts daran auszusetzen.

(c) pred (amiss) something is ~ (irgend) etwas stimmt nicht or ist nicht in Ordnung; (suspiciously) irgend etwas stimmt da nicht or ist da faul (inf); is anything or something ~? ist was? (inf); there's nothing ~ (es ist) alles in Ordnung; what's ~? was ist los?; what's ~ with you? was fehlt Ihnen?; there's nothing medically ~ with her medizinisch (gesehen) fehlt ihr nichts; I hope there's nothing ~ at home ich hoffe, daß zu Hause alles in Ordnung ist; something's ~ with my watch mit meiner Uhr stimmt (et)was nicht or ist etwas nicht in Ordnung; to be ~ in the head (inf) nicht ganz richtig (im Oberstübchen) sein (inf).
2 adv falsch. you do him ~ du tust ihm unrecht; you did ~ to do it es war falsch or unrecht or nicht richtig von dir, das zu tun; to get sth ~ sich mit etw vertun; he got the answer ~ er hat die falsche Antwort gegeben; (Math) er hat sich verrechnet; I think you got things a bit ~ ich glaube, Sie sehen die Sache or das nicht ganz richtig; to get one's sums ~ sich verrechnen; you've got him ~ (misunderstood) Sie haben ihn falsch verstanden; (he's not like that) Sie haben sich in ihm getäuscht; to go ~ (on route) falsch gehen/fahren; (in calculation) einen Fehler machen; (morally) auf Abwege geraten; (plan etc) schiefgehen; (affair etc) schieflaufen; my washing-machine has gone ~ meine Waschmaschine ist nicht in Ordnung; I hope the television doesn't go ~ hoffentlich bleibt der Fernseher in Ordnung; you can't go ~ du kannst gar nichts verkehrt machen; you can't go ~ if you buy him a bottle of whisky mit einer Flasche Whisky liegst du immer richtig.
3 n Unrecht nt no pl. (social) ~s (soziale) Ungerechtigkeiten pl; to be in the ~ im Unrecht sein; to put sb in the ~ jdn ins Unrecht setzen; to labour under a sense of ~ ein altes Unrecht nicht vergessen können; two ~s don't make a right Unrecht und Unrecht ergibt noch kein Recht; to do sb ~/a great ~ jdm Unrecht/(ein) großes Unrecht (an)tun; he can do no ~ er macht natürlich immer alles richtig; all the little ~s he'd done her all die kleinen Kränkungen, die er ihr zugefügt hat.
4 vt to ~ sb jdm unrecht tun; to be ~ed ungerecht behandelt werden.
wrongdoer ['rɒŋˌdu:əʳ] n Missetäter(in f), Übeltäter(in f) m.
wrongdoing ['rɒŋˌdu:ɪŋ] n Missetaten pl; (single act) Missetat, Übeltat f.
wrong-foot [ˌrɒŋ'fʊt] vt (Sport) auf dem falschen Fuß erwischen.
wrongful ['rɒŋfʊl] adj ungerechtfertigt.
wrongfully ['rɒŋfəlɪ] adv zu Unrecht.
wrong-headed ['rɒŋ'hedɪd] adj querköpfig, verbohrt (about sth in etw acc or dat).
wrong-headedly ['rɒŋ'hedɪdlɪ] adv see adj.
wrong-headedness ['rɒŋ'hedɪdnɪs] n Verbohrtheit f.
wrongly ['rɒŋlɪ] adv (a) (unjustly, improperly) unrecht; punished, accused zu Unrecht. (b) (incorrectly) falsch, verkehrt; maintain zu Unrecht; believe fälschlicherweise.
wrongness ['rɒŋnɪs] n (incorrectness) Unrichtigkeit f; (unfairness) Ungerechtigkeit f. the ~ of your behaviour dein falsches Benehmen.
wrote [rəʊt] pret of write.
wrought [rɔːt] **1** vt (a) (obs, liter) pret, ptp of work.
(b) great changes have been ~ große Veränderungen wurden errungen or herbeigeführt; the accident ~ havoc with his plans der Unfall durchkreuzte alle seine Pläne; the storm ~ great destruction der Sturm richtete große Verheerungen an.
2 adj iron Schmiede-; silver getrieben, gehämmert.
wrought: ~-iron adj schmiedeeisern attr, aus Schmiedeeisen; ~-iron gate schmiedeeisernes Tor; ~-up adj to be ~-up aufgelöst sein, außer sich (dat) sein.
wrung [rʌŋ] pret, ptp of wring.
WRVS (Brit) abbr of Women's Royal Voluntary Service.
wry [raɪ] adj (ironical) ironisch; joke, sense of humour etc trocken. to make or pull a ~ face das Gesicht verziehen.
wryly ['raɪlɪ] adv ironisch.
WSW abbr of west-south-west WSW.
wt abbr of weight Gew.
WX abbr of women's extra-large size.
wych-elm ['wɪtʃ'elm] n see witch elm.
wych-hazel ['wɪtʃˌheɪzl] n see witch hazel.

X

X, x [eks] *n* (a) X, x *nt.* (b) (*Math, fig: number*) x. **Mr** ∼ Herr X; ∼ **pounds x** Pfund; ∼ **marks the spot** die Stelle ist mit einem Kreuzchen gekennzeichnet. (c) ∼**-certificate film** für Jugendliche nicht geeigneter Film, für Jugendliche ab 18 Jahren freigegebener Film.
xenophobe ['zenəfəʊb] *n* Fremdenhasser *m.*
xenophobia [ˌzenə'fəʊbɪə] *n* Fremdenfeindlichkeit *f*, Fremdenhaß *m*, Xenophobie (*liter*) *f.*
xenophobic [ˌzenə'fəʊbɪk] *adj* fremdenfeindlich, xenophob (*liter*).
Xerox ® ['zɪərɒks] 1 *n* (*copy*) Xerokopie *f*; (*process*) Xeroxverfahren *nt.* 2 *vt* xerokopieren, xeroxen (*inf*).
Xmas ['eksməs, 'krɪsməs] *n* = **Christmas** Weihnachten *nt.*

X-ray ['eks'reɪ] 1 *n* Röntgenstrahl *m*; (*also* ∼ **photograph**) Röntgenaufnahme *f* or *-*bild *nt.* **to take an** ∼ **of sth** etw röntgen, eine Röntgenaufnahme von etw machen; **to have an** ∼ geröntgt werden; **she's gone in for an** ∼ sie ist zum Röntgen gegangen.
2 *vt person, heart* röntgen, durchleuchten (*dated*); *envelope* durchleuchten.
X-ray *in cpds* Röntgen-; ∼ **examination** *n* Röntgenuntersuchung *f*, röntgenologische Untersuchung; ∼ **eyes** *npl* (*fig*) Röntgenaugen *pl.*
xylograph ['zaɪləgrɑːf] *n* Holzschnitt *m.*
xylography [zaɪ'lɒgrəfɪ] *n* Holzschneidekunst, Xylographie *f.*
xylophone ['zaɪləfəʊn] *n* Xylophon *nt.*

Y

Y, y [waɪ] *n* Y, y *nt.*
yacht [jɒt] 1 *n* Jacht, Yacht *f.* ∼ **club** Jacht- *or* Segelklub *m*; ∼ **race** (Segel)regatta *f.* 2 *vi* segeln. **to go** ∼**ing** segeln gehen; (*on cruise*) eine Segeltour *or* einen Törn machen.
yachting ['jɒtɪŋ] *n* Segeln *nt.*
yachting: ∼ **cap** *n* Seglermütze *f*; ∼ **circles** *npl* Seglerkreise *pl*; ∼ **cruise** *n* (Segel)kreuzfahrt, Segelreise *f*; ∼ **holiday** *n* Segelurlaub *m*; ∼ **jacket** *n* Segeljacke *f.*
yachtsman ['jɒtsmən] *n, pl* **-men** [-mən] Segler *m.*
yachtsmanship ['jɒtsmənʃɪp] *n* Segelkunst *f.*
yackety-yak ['jækɪtɪ'jæk] (*inf*) 1 *vi* schnattern (*inf*), quasseln (*inf*). **listen to those two,** ∼ hör dir mal die beiden Schnattergänse an (*inf*); **it was** ∼ **all evening** den ganzen Abend nichts als Gequatsche (*inf*) *or* Geschnatter (*inf*). 2 *n* Blabla (*pej inf*), Gequassel (*pej inf*).
yah [jɑː] *interj* (*expressing disgust*) uh, igittigitt; (*expressing derision*) ätsch, hähä.
yahoo [jɑːˈhuː] *n* Schwein *nt* (*inf*).
yak¹ [jæk] *n* (*Zool*) Jak, Yak, Grunzochse *m.*
yak² *vi* (*inf*) schnattern (*inf*), quasseln (*inf*).
Yale lock ® ['jeɪl,lɒk] *n* Sicherheitsschloß *nt.*
yam [jæm] *n* (a) (*plant*) Yamswurzel *f.* (b) (*US: sweet potato*) Süßkartoffel, Batate *f.*
yammer ['jæməʳ] *vi* (*inf: moan*) jammern.
yank [jæŋk] 1 *n* Ruck *m.* **give it a good** ∼ zieh mal kräftig dran. 2 *vt* **to** ∼ **sth** mit einem Ruck an etw (*dat*) ziehen, einer Sache (*dat*) einen Ruck geben; **he** ∼**ed the rope free** er riß das Seil los.
◆**yank off** *vt sep* abreißen.
◆**yank out** *vt sep* ausreißen; *tooth* ziehen.
Yank [jæŋk] 1 *n* Ami (*inf*) *m.* 2 *adj attr* Ami- (*inf*).
Yankee ['jæŋkɪ] (*inf*) 1 *n* Yankee (*inf*) *m*; (*Hist auch*) Nordstaatler *m.* 2 *adj attr* Yankee- (*inf*).
yap [jæp] 1 *vi* (*dog*) kläffen; (*talk noisily*) quatschen (*inf*), labern (*inf*). **it's been** ∼, ∼, ∼ **all day** von morgen bis abends nur Gequatsche (*inf*). 2 *n* (*of dog*) Kläffen, Gekläff *nt*; (*inf: of person*) Gequatsche (*inf*), Gelaber (*inf*) *nt.* **she spoke in a high-pitched** ∼ sie schnatterte mit schriller Stimme (*inf*).
yapping ['jæpɪŋ] 1 *adj dog* kläffend; (*inf*) *women* quatschend (*inf*). 2 *n see* **yap** 2.
yard¹ [jɑːd] *n* (a) (*Measure*) Yard *nt* (0.91 m). **he can't see a** ∼ **in front of him** er kann keinen Meter weit sehen; **to buy cloth by the** ∼ ≈ Stoff meterweise *or* im Meter kaufen; **he pulled out** ∼**s of handkerchief** (*inf*) er zog ein riesiges Taschentuch hervor (*inf*); **words a** ∼ **long** (*inf*) Bandwurmwörter *pl* (*inf*); **to have a face a** ∼ **long** (*inf*) ein Gesicht wie drei Tage Regenwetter machen (*inf*); **calculations by the** ∼ (*fig*) endlose Zahlenkolonnen *pl*; **he wrote poetry by the** ∼ er produzierte Gedichte am Fließband *or* am laufenden Meter.
(b) (*Naut*) Rah *f.*
yard² *n* (a) (*of farm, hospital, prison, school, house etc*) Hof *m.* **back** ∼ Hinterhof *m*; **in the** ∼ auf dem Hof.
(b) (*worksite*) Werksgelände *nt*; (*for storage*) Lagerplatz *m.* **builder's** ∼ Bauhof *m*; **shipbuilding** ∼ Werft *f*; **timber** ∼ Holzlager(platz) *nt*; **naval** (**dock**)∼, (*US*) **navy** ∼ Marinewerft *f*; **railway** ∼ Rangierbahnhof, Verschiebebahnhof *m*; **goods** ∼, (*US*) **freight** ∼ Güterbahnhof *m.*

(c) **the Y**∼, **Scotland Y**∼ Scotland Yard *m.*
(d) (*US: garden*) Garten *m.*
yardage ['jɑːdɪdʒ] *n* Anzahl *f* von Yards, ≈ Meterzahl *f.*
yard: ∼**-arm** *n* (*Naut*) Nock *f*; **to hang sb from the** ∼**-arm** jdn am Mast aufknüpfen; ∼**stick** *n* (a) (*measuring rod*) Elle *f*; (b) (*fig*) Maßstab *m.*
yarn [jɑːn] 1 *n* (a) (*Tex*) Garn *nt.* (b) (*tale*) Seemannsgarn *nt.* **to spin a** ∼ Seemannsgarn spinnen; **to spin sb a** ∼ **about sth** jdm eine Lügengeschichte über etw (*acc*) erzählen. 2 *vi* Seemannsgarn spinnen, Geschichten erzählen.
yarrow ['jærəʊ] *n* (*Bot*) (gemeine) Schafgarbe.
yashmak ['jæʃmæk] *n* Schleier *m* (*von Moslemfrauen*).
yaw [jɔː] 1 *vi* (*Naut*) gieren, vom Kurs abkommen; (*Aviat, Space*) (*off course*) vom Kurs abkommen *or* abweichen; (*about axis*) gieren. **it** ∼**ed 20 degrees to port** es gierte um 20 Grad nach Backbord. 2 *n see vi* Kursabweichung, Gierung *f*, Gieren *nt*; Kursabweichung *f*; Gieren *nt.*
yawl [jɔːl] *n* (*Naut*) (*rowing boat*) Beiboot *nt*; (*sailing boat*) (Segel)jolle *f.*
yawn [jɔːn] 1 *vi* (a) (*person*) gähnen. **to** ∼ **with boredom** vor Langeweile gähnen.
(b) (*chasm etc*) gähnen.
2 *vt* gähnen. **to** ∼ **one's head off** fürchterlich gähnen (*inf*).
3 *n* (a) Gähnen *nt.* **I could tell by your** ∼**s ... an deinem Gähnen konnte ich sehen ...; to give a** ∼ gähnen.
(b) (*inf: bore*) **the film was a** ∼ **from start to finish** der Film war von Anfang bis Ende zum Gähnen (langweilig); **what a** ∼! wie langweilig!; **life is just one big** ∼ das Leben ist vielleicht langweilig.
yawning ['jɔːnɪŋ] 1 *adj chasm etc* gähnend. 2 *n* Gähnen *nt.*
yaws [jɔːz] *n* Frambösie *f.*
yd *abbr of* **yard(s).**
ye [jiː] (*obs*) 1 *pers pron* (*nominative*) Ihr (*obs*); (*objective*) Euch (*obs*). ∼ **gods!** (*not obs*) allmächtiger Gott! 2 *def art* = **the.**
yea [jeɪ] 1 *adv* (*obs*) (a) (*yes*) ja. (b) (*indeed*) fürwahr (*old*). 2 *n* **the** ∼**s and the nays** die Jastimmen und die Neinstimmen.
yeah [jeə] *adv* (*inf*) ja.
year [jɪəʳ] *n* (a) Jahr *nt.* **last** ∼ letztes Jahr; **this** ∼ dieses Jahr; **every other** ∼ jedes zweite Jahr; **three times a** ∼ dreimal pro *or* im Jahr; **in the** ∼ **1969** im Jahr(e) 1969; **in the** ∼ **of Our Lord 1974** (*form*) im Jahr(e) des Herrn 1974 (*geh*); ∼ **after** ∼ Jahr für Jahr; ∼ **by** ∼, **from** ∼ **to** ∼ von Jahr zu Jahr; **listed** ∼ **by** ∼ Jahr für Jahr aufgeführt; ∼ **in,** ∼ **out** jahrein, jahraus; **all (the)** ∼ **round** das ganze Jahr über *or* hindurch; **as** ∼**s go by** mit den Jahren; ∼**s** (**and** ∼**s**) **ago** vor (langen) Jahren; **to pay by the** ∼ jährlich zahlen; **a** ∼ **last January** (im) Januar vor einem Jahr; **it'll be a** ∼ **in** *or* **next January** (*duration*) es wird nächsten Januar ein Jahr her sein; **a** ∼ **from now** nächstes Jahr um diese Zeit; **a hundred-**∼**-old tree** ein hundert Jahre alter Baum, ein hundertjähriger Baum; **he is six** ∼**s old** er ist sechs Jahre (alt); **he is in his fortieth** ∼ er steht (*geh*) *or* ist im vierzigsten Lebensjahr; **it costs £10 a** ∼ es kostet £ 10 pro *or* im Jahr; **he gets £13,000 a** ∼ er bekommt £ 13.000 jährlich *or* pro Jahr *or* im Jahr; **that new hairdo has taken** ∼**s off you** diese neue Frisur macht dich um Jahre jünger; **it's taken** ∼**s off my life** es hat mich Jahre meines

Lebens gekostet; **it has put ~s on me** es hat mich (um) Jahre älter gemacht.

(b) (*Univ, Sch, of coin, stamp, wine*) Jahrgang *m*. **he is bottom in his ~** (*Univ, Sch*) er ist der Schlechteste seines Jahrgangs *or* in seinem Jahrgang; **first-~ student** Student(in *f*) *m* im ersten Jahr; (*first term student*) = Student(in *f*) *m* im ersten Semester, Erstsemester *nt*; **she was in my ~ at school** sie war im selben Schuljahrgang wie ich.

(c) from his earliest ~s von frühester Kindheit an, seit seiner frühesten Kindheit; **he looks old for his ~s** er sieht älter aus als er ist; **young for his ~s** jung für sein Alter; **well advanced or well on in ~s** im vorgerückten Alter; **to get on in ~s** in die Jahre kommen; **difference in ~s** Altersunterschied *m*.

yearbook ['jɪəbʊk] *n* Jahrbuch *nt*.

yearling ['jɪəlɪŋ] **1** *n* (*animal*) Jährling *m*; (*racehorse also*) Einjährige(r) *mf*. **2** *adj* einjährig.

year-long ['jɪə'lɒŋ] *adj* einjährig. **a ~ struggle** ein Kampf, der ein Jahr dauert/dauerte; **a three-year long fight** ein dreijähriger Kampf.

yearly ['jɪəlɪ] **1** *adj* jährlich. **2** *adv* jährlich, einmal im Jahr. **twice ~** zweimal jährlich *or* im Jahr.

yearn [jɜːn] *vi* sich sehnen (*after, for* nach). **to ~ to do sth** sich danach sehnen, etw zu tun; **to ~ for home** sich nach Hause sehnen; **to ~ for sb** sich nach jdm sehnen, nach jdm verlangen.

yearning ['jɜːnɪŋ] **1** *n* Sehnsucht *f*, Verlangen *nt* (*to do* etw zu tun, *for* nach). **a look full of ~** ein sehnsuchtsvoller Blick; **a ~ for the past** die Sehnsucht nach der Vergangenheit. **2** *adj desire* sehnsüchtig; *look also* sehnsuchtsvoll, verlangend.

yearningly ['jɜːnɪŋlɪ] *adv* sehnsuchtsvoll, voller Sehnsucht; *gaze also* sehnsüchtig.

year-round ['jɪə'raʊnd] *adj* das ganze Jahr über *or* hindurch.

yeast [jiːst] *n, no pl* Hefe *f*.

yeasty ['jiːstɪ] *adj taste* hefig. **the beer's very ~** das Bier schmeckt stark nach Hefe.

yell [jel] **1** *n* Schrei *m*. **to let out** *or* **give a ~** einen Schrei ausstoßen, schreien; **could you give me a ~ when we get there?** könnten Sie mir Bescheid sagen *or* mich rufen, wenn wir da sind?; **college ~** (*US*) Schlachtruf *m* eines College.

2 *vi* (*also ~ out*) schreien, brüllen (*with vor* +*dat*). **he ~ed at her** er schrie *or* brüllte sie an; **just ~ if you need help** ruf, wenn du Hilfe brauchst; **to ~ with laughter** vor Lachen brüllen.

3 *vt* (*also ~ out*) schreien, brüllen. **he ~ed abuse at the teacher** er beschimpfte den Lehrer wüst; **the sergeant ~ed out my name** der Feldwebel brüllte meinen Namen; **she ~ed up the stairs that dinner was ready** sie rief die Treppe hinauf, daß das Essen fertig sei.

yellow ['jeləʊ] **1** *adj* (+*er*) **(a)** gelb. **~ hair** strohblondes *or* gelbblondes Haar; **to go** *or* **turn** *or* **become ~** gelb werden; (*paper*) vergilben; **~ fever** Gelbfieber *nt*; **~ flag, ~ jack** (*Naut*) gelbe Flagge, Quarantäneflagge *f*; **~ ochre** ockergelb; **~ pages** Branchenverzeichnis *nt*; **the ~ peril** die gelbe Gefahr; **~ press** Sensationspresse *f*; **Y~ River** gelber Fluß; **Y~ Sea** gelbes Meer.

(b) (*sl: cowardly*) feige.

2 *n* (*colour*) Gelb *nt*; (*of egg*) Eigelb *nt*; (*sl: cowardice*) Feigheit *f*. **a streak of ~** ein feiger Zug.

3 *vt* gelb färben. **the sunlight had ~ed the pages** die Sonne hatte die Seiten vergilben lassen; **paper ~ed with age** vor Alter vergilbtes Papier.

4 *vi* gelb werden, sich gelb färben; (*corn also*) reifen; (*pages*) vergilben. **the leaves were ~ing** die Blätter färbten sich gelb.

yellow: **~-belly** *n* (*sl*) Angsthase (*inf*), Waschlappen (*inf*) *m*; **~hammer** *n* (*Orn*) Goldammer *f*.

yellowish ['jeləʊɪʃ] *adj* gelblich.

yellowness ['jeləʊnɪs] *n, no pl* **(a)** Gelb *nt*; (*of skin*) gelbliche Färbung. **(b)** (*sl: cowardice*) Feigheit *f*.

yellowy ['jeləʊɪ] *adj* gelblich.

yelp [jelp] **1** *n* (*of animal*) Jaulen *nt no pl*; (*of person*) Aufschrei *m*. **to give a ~** (*auf*)jaulen; (*person*) aufschreien. **2** *vi* (*animal*) (*auf*)jaulen; (*person*) aufschreien.

yelping ['jelpɪŋ] *n see vi* Jaulen *nt*; Aufschreien *nt*.

yen¹ [jen] *n* (*Fin*) Yen *m*.

yen² *n* (*inf*) Lust *f* (*for auf* +*acc*). **I've always had a ~ to go to Pasadena** es hat mich schon immer nach Pasadena gezogen; **I had a sudden ~ to do that/for oysters** ich hatte plötzlich Lust, das zu machen/auf Austern.

yeoman ['jəʊmən] *n, pl* **-men** [-mən] **(a)** (*Hist: small landowner*) Freibauer *m*. **~ farmer** (*Hist*) Freibauer *m*. **(b) Y~ of the Guard** königlicher Leibgardist; **to do ~ service** treue Dienste leisten (*for sb* jdm).

yeomanry ['jəʊmənrɪ] *n* **(a)** (*Hist*) Freibauernschaft *f*, Freibauernstand *m*. **(b)** (*Mil*) freiwillige Kavallerietruppe.

yep [jep] *adv* (*inf*) ja. **is he sure?** — **~!** ist er sicher? — klar!

yes [jes] **1** *adv* ja; (*answering neg question*) doch. **to say ~** ja sagen; **to say ~ to a demand** einer Forderung (*dat*) nachkommen; **he said ~ to all my questions** er hat alle meine Fragen bejaht *or* mit Ja beantwortet; **if they say ~ to an increase** wenn sie eine Lohnerhöhung bewilligen; **I'd say ~ to 35%, no to 32%** ich würde 35% akzeptieren, 32% nicht; **she'll say ~ to anything** sie kann nicht nein sagen; **~ sir!** (*Mil*) jawohl, Herr General/Leutnant *etc*; (*general*) jawohl, mein Herr!; **waiter!** — **~ sir?** Herr Ober! — ja, bitte?; **~ indeed** o ja, allerdings; **I didn't say that** — **oh yes, you did** das habe ich nicht gesagt — o doch *or* o ja, das hast du; **~ and no** ja und nein, jein (*inf*); **~ ~, I know!** jaja, ich weiß doch.

2 *n Ja nt*. **he just answered with ~es and noes** er hat einfach mit Ja oder Nein geantwortet.

yes man ['jesmæn] *n, pl* **~ men** [-men] Jasager *m*.

yesterday ['jestədeɪ] **1** *n* Gestern *nt*. **the fashions of ~** die Mode von gestern; **all our ~s** unsere ganze Vergangenheit.

2 *adv* (*lit, fig*) gestern. **~ morning/afternoon/evening** gestern

morgen/nachmittag/abend; **he was at home all (day) ~** er war gestern den ganzen Tag zu Hause; **the day before ~** vorgestern; **a week ago ~** gestern vor einer Woche; **see born**.

yesteryear ['jestə'jɪə] *n* (*poet*) vergangene Jahre *pl*.

yet [jet] **1** *adv* **(a)** (*still*) noch; (*thus far*) bis jetzt, bisher. **they haven't ~ returned** *or* **returned ~** sie sind noch nicht zurückgekommen; **this is his best book ~** das ist bis jetzt sein bestes Buch, das ist sein bisher bestes Buch; **as ~** (*with present tenses*) bis jetzt, bisher; (*with past*) bis dahin; **no, not ~** nein, noch nicht; **I've hardly begun ~** ich habe noch gar nicht richtig angefangen; **not just ~** jetzt noch nicht; **don't come in (just) ~** komm (jetzt) noch nicht herein.

(b) (*with interrog: so far, already*) schon. **has he arrived ~?** ist er schon angekommen?, ist er schon da?; **I wonder if he's come ~** ich frage mich, ob er schon gekommen ist; **do you have to go just ~?** müssen Sie jetzt schon gehen?

(c) (*with affirmative: still, remaining*) noch. **they have a few days ~** sie haben noch ein paar Tage; **a ~ to be decided question** eine noch unentschiedene Frage, eine Frage, die noch entschieden werden muß; **I've ~ to learn how to do it** ich muß erst noch lernen, wie man es macht; **and they are doubtless waiting ~** und sie warten zweifellos noch immer.

(d) (*with comp: still, even*) noch. **this is ~ more difficult** dies ist (sogar) noch schwieriger; **he wants ~ more money** er will noch mehr Geld.

(e) (*in addition*) (and) **~ again** und wieder, und noch einmal; **and ~ again** they rode off und sie ritten wieder weg; **another arrived and ~ another** es kam noch einer und noch einer.

(f) (*with future and conditional: before all is over*) noch. **he may come ~** *or* **~ come** er kann noch kommen; **he could come ~** er könnte noch kommen; **I may ~ go to Italy** ich fahre vielleicht noch nach Italien; **I'll do it ~** ich schaffe es schon noch.

(g) (*liter*) nor **~** noch; **they didn't come nor ~ write** sie sind weder gekommen, noch haben sie geschrieben.

2 *conj* doch, dennoch, trotzdem. **and ~** und doch *or* trotzdem *or* dennoch; **it's strange ~ true** es ist seltsam, aber wahr.

yeti ['jetɪ] *n* Yeti, Schneemensch *m*.

yew [juː] *n* (*also ~ tree*) Eibe *f*; (*wood*) Eibe(nholz *nt*) *f*.

Y-fronts ® ['waɪfrʌnts] *npl* (Herren)unterhose *f*.

YHA *abbr of* **Youth Hostels Association** = DJH.

Yid [jɪd] *n* (*pej*) Jud *m* (*pej*).

Yiddish ['jɪdɪʃ] **1** *adj* jiddisch. **2** *n* (*language*) Jiddisch *nt*.

yield [jiːld] **1** *vt* **(a)** (*land*) fruit, crop hervorbringen; (*tree*) fruit tragen; (*mine, oil-well*) bringen; (*shares, money*) interest, profit (ein)bringen, abwerfen; result (hervor)bringen. **the information ~ed by the poll** die Information, die die Meinungsumfrage ergeben hat; **this would ~ an excellent opportunity for ...** dies würde eine ausgezeichnete Gelegenheit ergeben, um ...; **this ~ed a weekly increase of 20%** das brachte eine wöchentliche Steigerung von 20%.

(b) (*surrender, concede*) aufgeben. **to ~ sth to sb** etw an jdn abtreten; **to ~ ground to the enemy** vor dem Feind zurückweichen; **to ~ the floor to sb** (*fig*) jdm das Feld überlassen; **to ~ a point to sb** jdm einen Punkt zukommen lassen; (*in competition*) einen Punkt an jdn abgeben; **to ~ concessions** Zugeständnisse machen; **to ~ right of way to sb** (*Mot*) jdm die Vorfahrt gewähren *or* lassen.

2 *vi* **(a)** (*tree, land*) tragen; (*mine, oil-well*) Ertrag bringen; (*shares, money*) sich verzinsen, Zinsen *or* Profit einbringen *or* abwerfen. **land that ~s well/poorly** Land, das ertragreich ist/das wenig Erträge bringt.

(b) (*surrender, give way*) they **~ed to us** (*Mil*) sie haben sich uns (*dat*) ergeben; (*general*) sie haben nachgegeben; **at last she ~ed to him/to his charm** schließlich erlag sie ihm/seinem Charme doch; **to ~ to force/superior forces/superior numbers** (*Mil*) der Gewalt/Überzahl/Überzahl weichen *or* nachgeben; **to ~ to reason** sich der Vernunft beugen; **to ~ to sb's entreaties/threats/argument** jds Bitten (*dat*) nachgeben/ sich jds Drohungen/Argument (*dat*) beugen; **he ~ed to her requests** er gab ihren Bitten nach; **the disease ~ed to treatment** die Krankheit sprach auf die Behandlung an; **to ~ to temptation** der Versuchung erliegen; **to ~ to one's emotions** seinen Gefühlen nachgeben; **they begged him but he would not ~** sie baten ihn, aber er gab nicht nach; **I'll have to ~ to you on that point** in diesem Punkt muß ich Ihnen recht geben.

(c) (*give way: branch, beam, rope, floor, ground*) nachgeben. **to ~ under pressure** unter Druck nachgeben; (*fig*) einem Druck weichen.

(d) (*Mot*) **to ~ to oncoming traffic** den Gegenverkehr vorbeilassen; "**~**" (*US, Ir*) „Vorfahrt gewähren!"

3 *n* (*of land, field, earth, tree*) Ertrag *m*; (*of work also*) Ergebnis *nt*; (*of mine, well*) Ausbeute *f*; (*of industry: amount of goods*) Produktion *f*; (*profit*) Gewinne, Erträge *pl*; (*Fin: of shares, business*) Ertrag, Gewinn *m*. **~ of tax** Steueraufkommen *nt*.

♦**yield up** *vt sep* rights, privileges abtreten, verzichten auf (+*acc*). **to ~ sth to sb** etw an jdn abtreten; **he ~ed ~ his life** to the cause er gab sein Leben für diese Sache; **he ~ed himself ~ to his fate** er ergab sich in sein Schicksal.

yielding ['jiːldɪŋ] *adj* person nachgiebig; surface, material nachgebend. **the ground is ~** der Boden gibt nach.

yippee [jɪ'piː] *interj* juchhu, hurra.

YMCA *abbr of* **Young Men's Christian Association** CVJM.

yobbish ['jɒbɪʃ] *adj* (*Brit inf*) Halbstarken-, Rowdy-.

yob(bo) ['jɒb(əʊ)] *n* (*Brit inf*) Halbstarke(r), Rowdy *m*.

yodel ['jəʊdl] **1** *vti* jodeln. **2** *n* Jodler *m*.

yodelling ['jəʊdlɪŋ] *n* Jodeln *nt*.

yoga ['jəʊgə] *n* Joga, Yoga *m*.

yoghourt, yog(h)urt ['jɒgət] *n* Joghurt *m or nt*.

yogi ['jəʊgɪ] *n* Jogi, Yogi *m*.

yo-heave-ho ['jəʊ'hiːv'həʊ] *interj* hau-ruck.

yoke [jəʊk] **1** *n* **(a)** *(for oxen)* Joch *nt*; *(for carrying pails)* (Trag)-joch *nt*, Schultertrage *f*.
 (b) *pl* - *(pair of oxen)* Joch, Gespann *nt*.
 (c) *(fig: oppression)* Joch *nt*. **to throw off the ~** das Joch abschütteln.
 (d) *(on dress, blouse)* Passe *f*; *(on pullover also)* Joch *nt*.
 2 *vt* **(a)** *(also ~ up) oxen* (ins Joch) einspannen. **to ~ oxen to the plough** Ochsen vor den Pflug spannen.
 (b) *pieces of machinery* zusammenschließen. **to ~ sth to sth** etw an etw *(acc)* anschließen.
 (c) *(fig: join together)* zusammenschließen, vereinen.
yokel [ˈjəʊkəl] *n (pej)* Bauerntölpel, Bauerntrampel *m*.
yolk [jəʊk] *n (of egg)* Eigelb *nt*.
yon [jɒn] *adv, adj (poet, dial) see* **yonder**.
yonder [ˈjɒndəʳ] *(poet, dial)* **1** *adv (over)* ~ dort drüben. **2** *adj* **from ~** house von dem Haus (dort) drüben.
yoo-hoo [ˈjuːˈhuː] *interj* huhu, hallo.
yore [jɔːʳ] *n (obs, liter)* **in days of ~** in alten Zeiten; **men of ~** die Menschen in alten Zeiten; **in the world of ~** in alten *or* längst vergangenen Zeiten; **in the Britain of ~** im Großbritannien längst vergangener Zeiten; **..., whose ancestors of ~ ...**, dessen Ahnen ehedem *or* einstmals.
Yorkshire pudding [ˈjɔːkʃəˈpʊdɪŋ] *n* Yorkshire Pudding *m (Beilage zu Rindsbraten)*.
you [juː] *pron* **(a)** *(German familiar form, can also be written with a capital in letters)* *(sing)* *(nom)* du; *(acc)* dich; *(dat)* dir; *(pl)* *(nom)* ihr; *(acc, dat)* euch; *(German polite form: sing, pl) (nom, acc)* Sie; *(dat)* Ihnen. **all of ~** *(pl)* ihr alle/Sie alle; **I want all of ~** *(sing)* ich will dich ganz; **if I were ~** wenn ich du/Sie wäre, an deiner/eurer/Ihrer Stelle; **~ Germans** ihr Deutschen; **silly old ~** du Dussel *(inf)*, du Dumm(er)chen *(inf)*; **~ darling du** bist ein Schatz *or* Engel; **is that ~?** bist du's/seid ihr's/sind Sie's?; **it's ~** du bist es/ihr seid's/Sie sind's; **what's the matter — it's ~ or ~ are** was ist los? — es liegt an dir/euch/Ihnen; **there's a fine house for ~!** das ist mal ein schönes Haus!; **now there's a woman for ~!** das ist mal eine (tolle) Frau; **now there's a typical Irishman for ~!** das ist mal ein typischer Ire; **now ~ say something** sag du/sagt ihr/sagen Sie (auch) mal was; **just ~ dare!** trau dich bloß!, untersteh dich!; **sit ~ down** *(hum)* setz dich/setzt euch/setzen Sie sich; **that hat just isn't ~** *(inf)* der Hut paßt einfach nicht zu dir/zu Ihnen.
 (b) *(indef) (nom)* man; *(acc)* einen; *(dat)* einem. **~ never know, ~ never can tell** man kann nie wissen, man weiß nie; **it's not good for ~** es ist nicht gut.
you-all [ˈjuːɔːl] *pron (US inf)* ihr.
you'd [juːd] *contr of* **you would; you had**.
you'd've [ˈjuːdəv] *contr of* **you would have**.
you'll [juːl] *contr of* **you will; you shall**.
young [jʌŋ] **1** *adj (+er)* jung; *wine, grass also* neu. **the ~ moon** der Mond im ersten Viertel; **~ people** junge Leute *pl*; **a ~ people's magazine** eine Jugendzeitschrift; **~ people's fashions** Jugendmoden *pl*; **~ lady/man** junge Dame/junger Mann; **they have a ~ family** sie haben kleine Kinder; **he is ~ at heart** er ist innerlich jung geblieben; **you are only ~ once** man ist *or* du bist nur einmal jung; **you ~ rascal *or* monkey!** *(inf)* du kleiner Schlingel!; **~ Mr Brown** der junge Herr Brown; **Pitt the Y~er** Pitt der Jüngere; **the night is ~** die Nacht ist (noch) jung; **Y~ America** die Jugend in Amerika, die amerikanische Jugend; **he's a very ~ forty** er ist ein jugendlicher *or* junggebliebener Vierziger.
 2 *npl* **(a)** *(people)* **the ~** die Jugend, die jungen Leute; **~ and old** jung und alt; **books for the ~** Jugendbücher *pl*.
 (b) *(animals)* Junge *pl*. **with ~** trächtig.
youngish [ˈjʌŋɪʃ] *adj* ziemlich jung.
youngster [ˈjʌŋstəʳ] *n (boy)* Junge *m*; *(child)* Kind *nt*. **he's just a ~** er ist eben noch jung *or* ein Kind.
your [jʊəʳ] *poss adj (German familiar form, can also be written with a capital in letters)* *(sing)* dein/deine/dein; *(pl)* euer/eure/euer; *(German polite form: sing, pl)* Ihr/Ihre/Ihr. **~ mother and father** deine/Ihre Mutter und dein/Ihr Vater; **one of ~ friends** einer deiner/Ihrer Freunde, einer von deinen/Ihren Freunden; *see* **majesty, worship** *etc*.
 (b) *(indef)* sein. **you give him ~ form and he gives you back ~ passport** Sie geben ihm Ihr *or* dies Formular, und dann bekommen Sie Ihren Paß zurück; **the climate here is bad for ~ health** das Klima hier ist ungesund *or* ist nicht gut für die Gesundheit; **up here you need ~ warm clothing** hier oben braucht man warme Kleidung.

 (c) *(typical)* der/die/das. **~ typical American** der typische Amerikaner; **~ average Englishman** der durchschnittliche Engländer.
you're [jʊəʳ] *contr of* **you are**.
yours [jʊəz] *poss pron (pers) (German familiar form, can also be written with a capital in letters)* *(sing)* deiner/deine/deins; *(pl)* eurer/eure/euers; *(German polite form: sing, pl)* Ihrer/Ihre/Ihr(e)s. **this is my book and that is ~** dies ist mein Buch und das (ist) deins/Ihres; **the idea was ~** es war deine/Ihre Idee, die Idee stammt von dir/Ihnen; **she is a cousin of ~** sie ist deine Kusine, sie ist eine Kusine von dir; **that is no business of ~** das geht dich/Sie nichts an; **that dog of ~!** dein/Ihr blöder Hund!; **you and ~** du und deine Familie, du und die Deinen *(geh)*/Sie und Ihre Familie, Sie und die Ihren *(geh)*; **~** *(in letter-writing)* Ihr/Ihre; **~ faithfully, ~ truly** *(on letter)* mit freundlichem Gruß, mit freundlichen Grüßen, hochachtungsvoll *(form)*; **in reply to ~ of the 15th May** *(Comm form)* in Antwort auf Ihr Schreiben vom 15. Mai; **what's ~?** *(to drink)* was möchtest du/was möchten Sie?, was trinkst du/was trinken Sie?; **~ truly** *(inf: I, me)* meine Wenigkeit; **guess who had to do all the dirty work? ~ truly** und wer mußte die Dreckarbeit machen? ich natürlich; **and then ~ truly got up and said ...** und dann stand ich höchstpersönlich auf und sagte ...; **up ~!** *(vulg)* du kannst mich mal *(sl)*; *see* **affectionately, ever (g)**.
yourself [jəˈself] *pron, pl* **yourselves** **(a)** *(reflexive) (German familiar form, can also be written with a capital in letters)* *(sing)* *(acc)* dich; *(dat)* dir; *(pl)* euch; *(German polite form: sing, pl)* sich. **have you hurt ~?** hast du/haben Sie sich weh getan?; **you never speak about ~** du redest nie über dich (selbst)/Sie reden nie über sich (selbst).
 (b) *(emph)* **selbst. you ~ told me, you told me ~** du hast/Sie haben mir selbst gesagt; **you are not quite ~ today** du bist heute gar nicht du selbst, du bist/Sie sind heute irgendwie verändert *or* anders; **how's ~?** *(inf)* und wie geht's dir/Ihnen?; **you will see for ~** du wirst/Sie werden selbst sehen; **did you do it by ~?** hast du/haben Sie das allein gemacht?
youth [juːθ] *n* **(a)** *no pl* Jugend *f*. **in (the days of) my ~** in meiner Jugend(zeit); **the town of my ~** die Stadt *or* Stätte *(hum)* meiner Jugend; **the disappointments of my ~** die Enttäuschungen meiner Jugend(zeit); **he radiates ~** er vermittelt den Eindruck von Jugendlichkeit; **in early ~** in früher Jugend; **she has kept her ~** sie ist jung geblieben.
 (b) *pl* **-s** [juːðz] *(young man)* junger Mann, Jugendliche(r) *m*. **when he was a ~** als er ein junger Mann war; **pimply ~** pickliger Jüngling.
 (c) **~** *pl (young men and women)* Jugend *f*; **she likes working with (the) ~** sie arbeitet gerne mit Jugendlichen; **the ~ of the country** die Jugend des Landes; **the ~ of today** die Jugend von heute; **the Hitler Y~ Movement** die Hitlerjugend; **~ club** Jugendklub *m*; **~ hostel** Jugendherberge *f*.
youthful [ˈjuːθfʊl] *adj* jugendlich. **a ~ mistake** eine Jugendsünde.
youthfulness [ˈjuːθfʊlnɪs] *n* Jugendlichkeit *f*. **the ~ of the Prime Minister** die Jugendlichkeit des Premierministers.
you've [juːv] *contr of* **you have**.
yowl [jaʊl] **1** *n (of person)* Heulen *nt no pl*; *(of dog)* Jaulen *nt no pl*; *(of cat)* klägliches Miauen *no pl*. **2** *vi (person)* heulen; *(dog)* jaulen; *(cat)* kläglich miauen.
yo-yo [ˈjəʊjəʊ] *n* Jo-Jo, Yo-Yo *nt*. **I've been going up- and down-stairs like a ~ all morning** ich bin den ganzen Morgen wie irre die Treppe rauf- und runtergerannt *(inf)*.
yr *abbr of* **(a) year(s). (b) your**.
yrs *abbr of* **(a) years. (b) yours**.
Y-shaped [ˈwaɪʃeɪpt] *adj* Y-förmig.
yucca [ˈjʌkə] *n* Yucca, Palmlilie *f*.
Yugoslav [ˈjuːgəʊˈslɑːv] **1** *adj* jugoslawisch. **2** *n* Jugoslawe *m*, Jugoslawin *f*.
Yugoslavia [ˈjuːgəʊˈslɑːvɪə] *n* Jugoslawien *nt*.
Yugoslavian [ˈjuːgəʊˈslɑːvɪən] *adj* jugoslawisch.
yuk [jʌk] *interj* bäh.
yukky [ˈjʌkɪ] *adj (+er) (sl)* eklig, widerlich, fies *(inf)*.
Yule [juːl] *n (old)* Weihnachten, Julfest *nt*. **~ log** Julblock *m*; **~tide** Weihnachtszeit, Julzeit *f*.
yummy [ˈjʌmɪ] **1** *adj (+er) (sl) food* lecker; *man* toll. **2** *interj* **~!, ~ ~!** lecker!, jamjam! *(inf)*.
yum yum [ˈjʌmˈjʌm] *interj* lecker, jamjam *(inf)*.
YWCA *abbr of* **Young Women's Christian Association** CVJF.

Z

Z, z [(*Brit*) zed, (*US*) zi:] *n* Z, z *nt*.
Zaire [zɑːˈiːɔʳ] *n* Zaïre, Zaire *nt*.
Zambesi, Zambezi [zæmˈbiːzɪ] *n* Sambesi *m*.
Zambia [ˈzæmbɪə] *n* Sambia *nt*.
zany [ˈzeɪnɪ] **1** *adj* (+*er*) (*crazy, funny*) *joke, sense of humour* verrückt; *person also* irrsinnig komisch. **2** *n* (*Theat Hist*) Narr, Hanswurst *m*.
Zanzibar [ˈzænzɪbɑːʳ] *n* Sansibar *nt*.
zap [zæp] (*inf*) **1** *n* (*energy, pep*) Schwung, Pep (*inf*) *m*. **2** *interj* zack. **3** *vt* (*hit*) to ~ **sb** (**one**) jdm eine pfeffern (*inf*) *or* kleben (*inf*).
♦**zap up** *vt sep* (*sl*) aufmotzen (*sl*).
zeal [ziːl] *n, no pl* Eifer *m*. to work with great ~ mit Feuereifer arbeiten; **he is full of** ~ **for the cause** er ist mit Feuereifer bei der Sache.
zealot [ˈzelət] *n* Fanatiker(in *f*) *m*; (*religious also*) (Glaubens)-eiferer(in *f*) *m*. Z~ (*Hist*) Zelot *m*.
zealotry [ˈzelətrɪ] *n* Fanatismus *m*, blinder Eifer.
zealous [ˈzeləs] *adj student, worker* eifrig, emsig. ~ **for sth** eifrig um etw bemüht; **to be** ~ **to begin/help** erpicht darauf sein, anzufangen/zu helfen; ~ **for the cause** für die Sache begeistert; ~ **for liberty** freiheitsdurstig; ~ **for a change** auf einen Wechsel erpicht.
zealously [ˈzeləslɪ] *adv see adj*.
zebra [ˈzebrə] *n* Zebra *nt*. ~ **crossing** (*Brit*) Zebrastreifen *m*.
Zen [zen] *n* Zen *nt*. ~ **Buddhism** Zen-Buddhismus *m*.
zenith [ˈzenɪθ] *n* (*Astron, fig*) Zenit *m*.
zephyr [ˈzefəʳ] *n* (*poet*) Zephir (*poet*), Zephyr (*poet*) *m*.
zeppelin [ˈzeplɪn] *n* Zeppelin *m*.
zero [ˈzɪərəʊ] **1** *n*, *pl* -(*e*)**s** (**a**) (*figure*) Null *f*; (*point on scale*) Nullpunkt *m*; (*Roulette*) Zero *f*. **15 degrees below** ~ 15 Grad unter Null; **the needle is at** *or* **on** ~ der Zeiger steht auf Null; **his chances were put at** ~ man meinte, seine Aussichten seien gleich Null.
  (**b**) (*fig: nonentity*) Null *f* (*inf*).
  2 *adj* **at** ~ **altitude** (*Aviat*) im Tiefflug; ~ **altitude flying** Tiefflug *m*; ~ **degrees** null Grad; ~ **gravity** Schwerelosigkeit *f*; **at** ~ **gravity** unter Schwerelosigkeit; ~ **hour** (*Mil, fig*) die Stunde X; ~-**rated** (*for VAT*) ohne Mehrwertsteuer; **he's getting absolutely** ~ **satisfaction from it** (*inf*) das bringt ihm überhaupt nichts (*inf*); **she showed** ~ **interest in him** (*inf*) sie zeigte sich nicht im geringsten an ihm interessiert.
♦**zero in** *vi* (*Mil*) sich einschießen (*on* auf +*acc*). **to** ~ ~ **on sb/sth** (*fig*) *gang leader, force of problem* jdn/etw einkreisen; *difficulty, topic* sich (*dat*) etw herausgreifen; *opportunity* sich auf etw (*acc*) stürzen; **we're beginning to** ~ ~ **on the final selection** langsam kommen wir der endgültigen Auswahl näher.
zest [zest] *n* (**a**) (*enthusiasm*) Begeisterung *f*. ~ **for life** Lebensfreude *f*; **he hasn't got much** ~ er hat keinen Schwung; **he's lost his old** ~ er der alte Schwung ist hin (*inf*); **he doesn't show much** ~ er scheint nicht sehr begeistert zu sein.
  (**b**) (*in style, of food etc*) Pfiff (*inf*), Schwung *m*. **a story full of** ~ eine Geschichte mit Schwung; **add** ~ **to your meals with ...!** geben Sie Ihren Gerichten Pfiff mit ...! (*inf*).
  (**c**) (*lemon etc peel*) Zitronen-/Orangenschale *f*.
zestful *adj*, ~**ly** *adv* [ˈzestfʊl, -fəlɪ] schwungvoll.
zeugma [ˈzjuːgmə] *n* Zeugma *nt*.
Zeus [zjuːs] *n* (*Myth*) Zeus *m*.
ziggurat [ˈzɪgəræt] *n* Zikkur(r)at *f*.
zigzag [ˈzɪgzæg] **1** *n* Zickzack *m or nt*. **the river cuts a** ~ **through the rocks** der Fluß bahnt sich im Zickzack einen Weg durch die Felsen; **we had to make a long** ~ **across the ice** wir mußten uns lange im Zickzack über das Eis bewegen; **a pattern of straight lines and** ~**s** ein Muster aus Geraden und Zickzacklinien.
  2 *adj course, line* Zickzack-; *road, path* zickzackförmig. **to steer a** ~ **course** (*Naut*) Zickzack(kurs) fahren.
  3 *adv* zickzackförmig, im Zickzack.
  4 *vi* im Zickzack laufen/fahren *etc*; (*Naut*) Zickzack(kurs) fahren.
Zimbabwe [zɪmˈbɑːbwɪ] *n* Zimbabwe, Simbabwe *nt*.
zinc [zɪŋk] *n* Zink *nt*. ~ **ointment** Zinksalbe *f*; ~ **oxide** Zinkoxid *nt*.
zing [zɪŋ] (*inf*) **1** *n* (**a**) (*noise of bullet etc*) Pfeifen, Zischen *nt*.
  (**b**) (*zest*) Pfiff *m* (*inf*). **2** *vi* (*bullets*) pfeifen, zischen.
zinnia [ˈzɪnɪə] *n* Zinnie *f*.
Zion [ˈzaɪən] *n* Zion *nt*.
Zionism [ˈzaɪənɪzəm] *n* Zionismus *m*.
Zionist [ˈzaɪənɪst] **1** *adj* zionistisch. **2** *n* Zionist(in *f*) *m*.
ZIP [zɪp] (*US*) *abbr* of **Zone Improvement Plan**. ~ **code** PLZ, Postleitzahl *f*.
zip [zɪp] **1** *n* (**a**) (*fastener*) Reißverschluß *m*.

(**b**) (*sound of bullet*) Pfeifen, Zischen *nt*.
  (**c**) (*inf: energy*) Schwung *m*. **we need a bit more** ~ **in these translations** wir müssen etwas mehr Schwung in diese Übersetzungen kriegen (*inf*).
  2 *vt* **to** ~ **a dress/bag** den Reißverschluß eines Kleides/einer Tasche zumachen *or* zuziehen.
  3 *vi* (*inf: car, person*) flitzen (*inf*); (*person also*) wetzen (*inf*). **to** ~ **past/along** *etc* vorbei-/daherflitzen *etc* (*inf*); **he** ~**ped through his work in no time** er hatte die Arbeit in Null Komma nichts erledigt (*inf*).
♦**zip on 1** *vt sep* **he** ~**ped** ~ **his special gloves** er zog die Reißverschlüsse seiner Spezialhandschuhe zu. **2** *vi* **the hood** ~**s** ~**to the jacket** die Kapuze wird mit einem Reißverschluß an der Jacke befestigt.
♦**zip up 1** *vt sep to* **to** ~ ~ **a dress** den Reißverschluß eines Kleides zumachen; **will you** ~ **me** ~ **please?** kannst du mir bitte den Reißverschluß zumachen? **2** *vi* **the dress** ~**s** ~ das Kleid hat einen Reißverschluß; **it** ~**s** ~ **at the back** der Reißverschluß ist hinten.
zip: ~ **fastener** *n* Reißverschluß *m*; ~ **gun** *n* (*US*) selbstgebastelte Pistole.
zipper [ˈzɪpəʳ] *n* Reißverschluß *m*.
zippy [ˈzɪpɪ] *adj* (+*er*) (*inf*) *car* flott; *person also* flink.
zircon [ˈzɜːkən] *n* Zirkon *m*.
zither [ˈzɪðəʳ] *n* Zither *f*.
zodiac [ˈzəʊdɪæk] *n* Tierkreis *m*. signs of the ~ Tierkreiszeichen *pl*.
zombie [ˈzɒmbɪ] *n* (**a**) (*lit: revived corpse*) Zombi *m*. (**b**) (*fig*) Idiot (*inf*), Schwachkopf (*inf*) *m*. **like a** ~/**like** ~**s** wie im Tran; **that new hairstyle makes her look a complete** ~ mit der neuen Frisur sieht sie total bescheuert *or* bekloppt aus (*sl*).
zonal [ˈzəʊnl] *adj* Zonen-, zonal.
zone [zəʊn] **1** *n* (**a**) (*Geog*) Zone *f*.
  (**b**) (*area*) Zone *f*; (*fig also*) Gebiet *nt*. **no-parking** ~ Parkverbot *nt*; **time** ~ Zeitzone *f*; **the English-speaking** ~ der englische Sprachraum; ~**s of the body** Körperzonen *pl*.
  (**c**) (*US: postal* ~) Post(zustell)bezirk *m*.
  2 *vt* (**a**) *town, area* in Zonen aufteilen.
  (**b**) **to** ~ **a district for industry** einen Bezirk zur Industriezone ernennen.
zoning [ˈzəʊnɪŋ] *n* (**a**) Zoneneinteilung *f*. (**b**) **the** ~ **of this area as ...** die Erklärung dieses Gebietes zum ...
zonked [zɒŋkt] *adj* (*sl*) (*drunk, high*) total ausgeflippt (*sl*); (*tired*) total geschafft (*sl*).
zoo [zuː] *n* Zoo, Tiergarten *m*. ~ **keeper** Tierpfleger(in *f*), Wärter(in *f*) *m*.
zoological [ˌzuːəˈlɒdʒɪkəl] *adj* zoologisch. ~ **gardens** zoologischer Garten.
zoologist [zʊˈɒlədʒɪst] *n* Zoologe *m*, Zoologin *f*.
zoology [zʊˈɒlədʒɪ] *n* Zoologie *f*.
zoom [zuːm] **1** *n* (**a**) (*sound of engine*) Surren *nt*.
  (**b**) (*Aviat: upward flight*) Steilanstieg *m*.
  (**c**) (*Phot: also* ~ **lens**) Zoom(objektiv) *nt*.
  2 *vi* (**a**) (*engine*) surren.
  (**b**) (*inf*) sausen. **the car** ~**ed past us** der Wagen sauste an uns vorbei (*inf*); **we were** ~**ing along at 90** wir sausten mit 90 daher (*inf*); **he** ~**ed through his work** er hat die Arbeit in Null Komma nichts erledigt (*inf*); **he** ~**ed through it so quickly he can't have read it properly** er war in Null Komma nichts damit fertig, er kann das unmöglich gründlich gelesen haben.
  (**c**) (*Aviat: plane, rocket*) steil (auf)steigen. **the rocket** ~**ed up into the sky** die Rakete schoß in den Himmel; **prices have** ~**ed up to a new high** die Preise sind erneut in die Höhe geschnellt.
  3 *vt plane* steil hochziehen *or* hochreißen; *engine* auf Hochtouren laufen lassen.
♦**zoom in** *vi* (*Phot*) zoomen (*sl*), nah herangehen; (*inf: come or go in*) herein-/hineinsausen (*inf*). **to** ~ ~ **on sth** (*Phot*) etw heranholen; ~ ~! (*Phot*) näherfahren!; **he** ~**ed** ~ **on the main point** (*inf*) er kam ohne (viel) Umschweife gleich zum Hauptthema.
♦**zoom out** *vi* (*Phot*) aufziehen; (*inf: go or come out*) hinaus-/heraussausen (*inf*).
zoomorphic [ˌzəʊəʊˈmɔːfɪk] *adj* zoomorph.
zoot suit [ˈzuːtsuːt] *n* (*US*) Anzug *m* mit wattierten Schultern und eng zulaufender Hose.
Zoroaster [ˌzɒrəʊˈæstəʳ] *n* Zoroaster, Zarathustra *m*.
Zoroastrian [ˌzɒrəʊˈæstrɪən] *adj* zoroastrisch.
zucchini [zuːˈkiːnɪ] *n* (*US*) Zucchini *pl*.
Zulu [ˈzuːluː] **1** *adj* Zulu-, der Zulus. **2** *n* (**a**) Zulu *m*, Zulufrau *f*. ~**land** Zululand (*old*), Kwazulu *nt*. (**b**) (*language*) Zulu *nt*.
zwieback [ˈzwiːbæk] *n* (*US*) Zwieback *m*.
zygote [ˈzaɪgəʊt] *n* (*Biol*) Zygote *f*.

GERMAN VERBS

Conjugation of regular verbs

1. Present tense
1.1 The present tense is formed by adding
-e, -st, -t, -en, -t, -en
to the stem of the verb.
1.2 Verbs ending in *-s, -ß, -z, -tz* form the second person singular by adding *-t*
heißen – du heißt
except in literary usage when the ending *-est* may be added
preisen – du preisest (*liter*)
2. The preterite, or past tense, is formed by adding
-te, -test, -te, -ten, -tet, -ten
to the stem of the verb.
3. The past participle is formed by adding the prefix *ge-* and the ending *-t* to the stem of the verb.
4. The present participle is formed by adding *-d* to the infinitive.

5. Verbs whose stem ends in *-ss* change to *-ß* in the following cases:
5.1 Before the present tense endings for the non-literary 2nd person singular and for the 3rd person singular and the 2nd person plural
küssen – du küßt *but* **du küssest** (*liter*)
er/sie/es/küßt
ihr küßt
5.2 In the informal singular imperative
küssen – küß!
5.3 In the preterite
küssen – küßte
5.4 In the past participle
küssen – geküßt

GERMAN IRREGULAR VERBS

1 The forms of compound verbs (beginning with the prefixes *auf-, ab-, be-, er-, zer-* etc) are the same as for the simplex verb.
2 The past participle of modal auxiliary verbs (dürfen, müssen *etc*) is replaced by the infinitive form when following another infinitive form, eg ich habe gehen dürfen; non-modal use: ich habe gedurft.
3 The formation of the present subjunctive is regular, requiring the following endings to be added to the verb stem:

ich seh-e	wir seh-en	ich sei	wir sei-en
du seh-est	ihr seh-et	du seist, du seiest (*liter*)	ihr sei-et
er seh-e	sie seh-en	er sei	sie sei-en

Infinitive	Present Indicative 2nd pers sing; 3rd pers sing	Imperfect Indicative	Imperfect Subjunctive	Imperative sing; pl	Past Participle
backen	bäckst, backst; bäckt, backt	backte, buk (*old*)	backte, büke (*old*)	back(e); backt	gebacken
befehlen	befiehlst; befiehlt	befahl	beföhle, befähle	befiehl; befehlt	befohlen
befleißen (*old*)	befleißt; befleißt	befliß	beflisse	befleiß(e); befleißt	beflissen
beginnen	beginnst; beginnt	begann	begänne; begönne (*rare*)	beginn(e); beginnt	begonnen
beißen	beißt; beißt	biß	bisse	beiß(e); beißt	gebissen
bergen	birgst; birgt	barg	bärge	birg; bergt	geborgen
bersten	birst; birst	barst	bärste	birst; berstet	geborsten
bewegen (*veranlassen*)	bewegst; bewegt	bewog	bewöge	beweg(e); bewegt	bewogen
biegen	biegst; biegt	bog	böge	bieg(e); biegt	gebogen
bieten	bietest; bietet	bot	böte	biet(e); bietet	geboten
binden	bindest; bindet	band	bände	bind(e); bindet	gebunden
bitten	bittest; bittet	bat	bäte	bitt(e); bittet	gebeten
blasen	bläst; bläst	blies	bliese	blas(e); blast	geblasen
bleiben	bleibst; bleibt	blieb	bliebe	bleib(e); bleibt	geblieben
bleichen (*vi, old*)	bleichst; bleicht	blich (*old*)	bliche	bleich(e); bleicht	geblichen
braten	brätst; brät	briet	briete	brat(e); bratet	gebraten
brechen	brichst; bricht	brach	bräche	brich; brecht	gebrochen
brennen	brennst; brennt	brannte	brennte (*rare*)	brenn(e); brennt	gebrannt
bringen	bringst; bringt	brachte	brächte	bring(e); bringt	gebracht
denken	denkst; denkt	dachte	dächte	denk(e); denkt	gedacht
dingen	dingst; dingt	dang	dingte	ding; dingt	gedungen
dreschen	drischst; drischt	drosch, drasch (*old*)	drösche, dräsche (*old*)	drisch; drescht	gedroschen
dringen	dringst; dringt	drang	dränge	dring(e); dringt	gedrungen
dünken	dünkt, deucht (*old*)	dünkte, deuchte (*old*)	dünkte, deuchte (*old*)		gedünkt, gedeucht (*old*)
dürfen	1st darf; 2nd darfst; 3rd darf	durfte	dürfte		gedurft; (*after infin*) dürfen

Infinitive	Present Indicative 2nd pers sing; 3rd pers sing	Imperfect Indicative	Imperfect Subjunctive	Imperative sing; pl	Past Participle
empfangen	empfängst; empfängt	empfing	empfinge	empfang(e); empfangt	empfangen
empfehlen	empfiehlst; empfiehlt	empfahl	empföhle, empfähle (rare)	empfiehl; empfehlt	empfohlen
empfinden	empfindest; empfindet	empfand	empfände	empfind(e); empfindet	empfunden
essen	ißt; ißt	aß	äße	iß; eßt	gegessen
fahren	fährst; fährt	fuhr	führe	fahr(e); fahrt	gefahren
fallen	fällst; fällt	fiel	fiele	fall(e); fallt	gefallen
fangen	fängst; fängt	fing	finge	fang(e); fangt	gefangen
fechten	fichtst, fichst (inf); ficht	focht	föchte	ficht; fechtet	gefochten
finden	findest; findet	fand	fände	find(e); findet	gefunden
flechten	flichtst, flichst (inf); flicht	flocht	flöchte	flicht; flechtet	geflochten
fliegen	fliegst; fliegt	flog	flöge	flieg(e); fliegt	geflogen
fliehen	fliehst; flieht	floh	flöhe	flieh(e); flieht	geflohen
fließen	fließt; fließt	floß	flösse	fließ(e); fließt	geflossen
fressen	frißt; frißt	fraß	fräße	friß; freßt	gefressen
frieren	frierst; friert	fror	fröre	frier(e); friert	gefroren
gären	gärst; gärt	gor, gärte (esp fig)	göre, gärte (esp fig)	gär(e); gärt	gegoren, gegärt (esp fig)
gebären	gebierst; gebiert	gebar	gebäre	gebier; gebärt	geboren
geben	gibst; gibt	gab	gäbe	gib; gebt	gegeben
gedeihen	gedeihst; gedeiht	gedieh	gediehe	gedeih(e); gedeiht	gediehen
gehen	gehst; geht	ging	ginge	geh(e); geht	gegangen
gelingen	gelingt	gelang	gelänge	geling(e) (rare); gelingt (rare)	gelungen
gelten	giltst; gilt	galt	gölte, gälte	gilt (rare); geltet (rare)	gegolten
genesen	genest; genest	genas	genäse	genese; genest	genesen
genießen	genießt; genießt	genoß	genösse	genieß(e); genießt	genossen
geschehen	geschieht	geschah	geschähe	geschieh; gescheht	geschehen
gewinnen	gewinnst; gewinnt	gewann	gewönne, gewänne	gewinn(e); gewinnt	gewonnen
gießen	gießt; gießt	goß	gösse	gieß(e); gießt	gegossen
gleichen	gleichst; gleicht	glich	gliche	gleich(e); gleicht	geglichen
gleiten	gleitest; gleitet	glitt	glitte	gleit(e); gleitet	geglitten
glimmen	glimmst; glimmt	glomm, glimmte (rare)	glömme, glimmte (rare)	glimm(e); glimmt	geglommen, geglimmt (rare)
graben	gräbst; gräbt	grub	grübe	grab(e); grabt	gegraben
greifen	greifst; greift	griff	griffe	greif(e); greift	gegriffen
haben	hast; hat	hatte	hätte	hab(e); habt	gehabt
halten	hältst; hält	hielt	hielte	halt(e); haltet	gehalten
hängen	hängst; hängt	hing	hinge	häng(e); hängt	gehangen
hauen	haust; haut	haute, hieb	haute, hiebe	hau(e); haut	gehauen, gehaut (dial)
heben	hebst; hebt	hob, hub (old)	höbe, hübe (old)	heb(e); hebt	gehoben
heißen	heißt; heißt	hieß	hieße	heiß(e); heißt	geheißen
helfen	hilfst; hilft	half	hülfe, hälfe (rare)	hilf; helft	geholfen
kennen	kennst; kennt	kannte	kennte	kenn(e); kennt	gekannt
kiesen	kiest; kiest	kor, kieste	köre, kieste	kies(e); kiest	gekoren
klieben	kliebst; kliebt	kliebte, klob	kliebte, klöbe	klieb(e); kliebt	geklobt, gekloben
klimmen	klimmst; klimmt	klomm, klimmte	klömme, klimmte	klimm(e); klimmt	geklimmt, geklommen
klingen	klingst; klingt	klang	klänge	kling(e); klingt	geklungen
kneifen	kneifst; kneift	kniff	kniffe	kneif(e); kneift	gekniffen
kommen	kommst; kommt	kam	käme	komm(e); kommt	gekommen
können	1st kann; 2nd kannst; 3rd kann	konnte	könnte		gekonnt; (after infin) können
kreischen	kreischst; kreischt	kreischte, krisch (old, hum)	kreischte, krische (old, hum)	kreisch(e); kreischt	gekreischt, gekrischen (old, hum)
kriechen	kriechst, kreuchst (obs, poet); kriecht, kreucht (obs, poet)	kroch	kröche	kriech(e); kriecht	gekrochen
küren	kürst; kürt	kürte, kor (rare)	kürte, köre (rare)	kür(e); kürt	gekürt, gekoren (rare)
laden[1]	lädst; lädt	lud	lüde	lad(e); ladet	geladen
laden[2]	lädst, ladest (dated, dial); lädt, ladet (dated, dial),	lud	lüde	lad(e); ladet	geladen
lassen	läßt; läßt	ließ	ließe	laß; laßt	gelassen; (after infin) lassen
laufen	läufst; läuft	lief	liefe	lauf(e); lauft	gelaufen
leiden	leidest; leidet	litt	litte	leid(e); leidet	gelitten
leihen	leihst; leiht	lieh	liehe	leih(e); leiht	geliehen
lesen	liest; liest	las	läse	lies; lest	gelesen
liegen	liegst; liegt	lag	läge	lieg(e); liegt	gelegen
löschen	lischst; lischt	losch	lösche	lisch; löscht	geloschen
lügen	lügst; lügt	log	löge	lüg(e); lügt	gelogen
mahlen	mahlst; mahlt	mahlte	mahlte	mahl(e); mahlt	gemahlen
meiden	meidest; meidet	mied	miede	meid(e); meidet	gemieden
melken	melkst, milkst; melkt, milkt	molk, melkte (old)	mölke	melk(e), milk; melkt	gemolken, gemelkt (rare)
messen	mißt; mißt	maß	mäße	miß; meßt	gemessen
mißlingen	mißlingt	mißlang	mißlänge		mißlungen

Infinitive	Present Indicative 2nd pers sing; 3rd pers sing	Imperfect Indicative	Imperfect Subjunctive	Imperative sing; pl	Past Participle
mögen	1st mag; 2nd magst; 3rd mag	mochte	möchte		gemocht; (after infin) mögen
müssen	1st muß; 2nd mußt; 3rd muß	mußte	müßte		gemußt; (after infin) müssen
nehmen	nimmst; nimmt	nahm	nähme	nimm; nehmt	genommen
nennen	nennst; nennt	nannte	nennte (rare)	nenn(e); nennt	genannt
pfeifen	pfeifst; pfeift	pfiff	pfiffe	pfeif(e); pfeift	gepfiffen
pflegen	pflegst; pflegt	pflegte, pflog (old)	pflegte, pflöge (old)	pfleg(e); pflegt	gepflegt, gepflogen (old)
preisen	preist; preist	pries	priese	preis(e); preis(e)t	gepriesen
quellen	quillst; quillt	quoll	quölle	quill (rare); quellt	gequollen
raten	rätst; rät	riet	riete	rat(e); ratet	geraten
reiben	reibst; reibt	rieb	riebe	reib(e); reibt	gerieben
reißen	reißt; reißt	riß	risse	reiß(e); reißt	gerissen
reiten	reitest; reitet	ritt	ritte	reit(e); reitet	geritten
rennen	rennst; rennt	rannte	rennte (rare)	renn(e); rennt	gerannt
riechen	riechst; riecht	roch	röche	riech(e); riecht	gerochen
ringen	ringst; ringt	rang	ränge	ring(e); ringt	gerungen
rinnen	rinnst; rinnt	rann	ränne, rönne (rare)	rinn(e); rinnt	geronnen
rufen	rufst; ruft	rief	riefe	ruf(e); ruft	gerufen
saufen	säufst; säuft	soff	söffe	sauf(e); sauft	gesoffen
saugen	saugst; saugt	sog, saugte	söge, saugte	saug(e); saugt	gesogen, gesaugt
schaffen	schaffst; schafft	schuf	schüfe	schaff(e); schafft	geschaffen
schallen	schallst; schallt	schallte, scholl (rare)	schallte, schölle (rare)	schall(e); schallt	geschallt
scheiden	scheidest; scheidet	schied	schiede	scheide; scheidet	geschieden
scheinen	scheinst; scheint	schien	schiene	schein(e); scheint	geschienen
scheißen	scheißt; scheißt	schiß	schisse	scheiß(e); scheißt	geschissen
schelten	schiltst; schilt	schalt	schölte	schilt; scheltet	gescholten
scheren	scherst; schert	schor, scherte (rare)	schöre	scher(e); schert	geschoren, geschert (rare)
schieben	schiebst; schiebt	schob	schöbe	schieb(e); schiebt	geschoben
schießen	schießt; schießt	schoß	schösse	schieß(e); schießt	geschossen
schinden	schindest; schindet	schindete, schund (rare)	schünde	schind(e); schindet	geschunden
schlafen	schläfst; schläft	schlief	schliefe	schlaf(e); schlaft	geschlafen
schlagen	schlägst; schlägt	schlug	schlüge	schlag(e); schlagt	geschlagen
schleichen	schleichst; schleicht	schlich	schliche	schleich(e); schleicht	geschlichen
schleifen	schleifst; schleift	schliff	schliffe	schleif(e); schleift	geschliffen
schleißen	schleißt; schleißt	schliß; (vt auch) schleißte	schlisse; schleißte	schleiß(e); schleißt	geschlissen; (vt auch) geschleißt
schließen	schließt; schließt	schloß	schlösse	schließ(e); schließt	geschlossen
schlingen	schlingst; schlingt	schlang	schlänge	schling(e); schlingt	geschlungen
schmeißen	schmeißt; schmeißt	schmiß	schmisse	schmeiß(e); schmeißt	geschmissen
schmelzen	schmilzt; schmilzt	schmolz	schmölze	schmilz; schmelzt	geschmolzen
schnauben	schnaubst; schnaubt	schnaubte, schnob (old)	schnaubte, schnöbe (old)	schnaub(e); schnaubt	geschnaubt, geschnoben (old)
schneiden	schneid(e)st; schneidet	schnitt	schnitte	schneid(e); schneidet	geschnitten
schrecken	schrickst; schrickt	schreckte, schrak	schreckte, schräke	schrick; schreckt	geschreckt, geschrocken (old)
schreiben	schreibst; schreibt	schrieb	schriebe	schreib(e); schreibt	geschrieben
schreien	schreist; schreit	schrie	schrie	schrei(e); schreit	geschrie(e)n
schreiten	schreitest; schreitet	schritt	schritte	schreit(e); schreitet	geschritten
schweigen	schweigst; schweigt	schwieg	schwiege	schweig(e); schweigt	geschwiegen
schwellen	schwillst; schwillt	schwoll	schwölle	schwill; schwellt	geschwollen
schwimmen	schwimmst; schwimmt	schwamm	schwömme, schwämme (rare)	schwimm(e); schwimmt	geschwommen
schwinden	schwindest; schwindet	schwand	schwände	schwind(e); schwindet	geschwunden
schwingen	schwingst; schwingt	schwang	schwänge	schwing(e); schwingt	geschwungen
schwören	schwörst; schwört	schwor	schwüre, schwöre (rare)	schwör(e); schwört	geschworen
sehen	siehst; sieht	sah	sähe	sieh(e); seht	gesehen; (after infin) sehen
sein	1st bin; 2nd bist; 3rd ist; pl 1st sind; 2nd seid; 3rd sind	war	wäre	sei; seid	gewesen
senden	sendest; sendet	sandte, sendete	sendete	send(e); sendet	gesandt, gesendet
sieden	siedest; siedet	siedete, sott	siedete, sötte	sied(e); siedet	gesiedet, gesotten
singen	singst; singt	sang	sänge	sing(e); singt	gesungen
sinken	sinkst; sinkt	sank	sänke	sink(e); sinkt	gesunken
sinnen	sinnst; sinnt	sann	sänne	sinn(e); sinnt	gesonnen
sitzen	sitzt; sitzt	saß	säße	sitz(e); sitzt	gesessen
sollen	1st soll; 2nd sollst; 3rd soll	sollte	sollte		gesollt; (after infin) sollen
spalten	spaltest; spaltet	spaltete	spalte	spalt(e); spaltet	gespalten, gespaltet
speien	speist; speit	spie	spiee	spei(e); speit	gespie(e)n
spinnen	spinnst; spinnt	spann	spönne, spänne	spinn(e); spinnt	gesponnen
spleißen	spleißt; spleißt	spliß	splisse	spleiß(e); spleißt	gesplissen
sprechen	sprichst; spricht	sprach	spräche	sprich; sprecht	gesprochen

Infinitive	Present Indicative 2nd pers sing; 3rd pers sing	Imperfect Indicative	Imperfect Subjunctive	Imperative sing; pl	Past Participle
sprießen	sprießt; sprießt	sproß, sprießte	sprösse	sprieß(e); sprießt	gesprossen, gesprießt
springen	springst; springt	sprang	spränge	spring(e); springt	gesprungen
stechen	stichst; sticht	stach	stäche	stich; stecht	gestochen
stecken (*vi*)	steckst; steckt	steckte, stak	steckte, stäke (*rare*)	steck(e); steckt	gesteckt
stehen	stehst; steht	stand	stünde, stände	steh; steht	gestanden
stehlen	stiehlst; stiehlt	stahl	stähle, stöhle (*obs*)	stiehl; stehlt	gestohlen
steigen	steigst; steigt	stieg	stiege	steig; steigt	gestiegen
sterben	stirbst; stirbt	starb	stürbe	stirb; sterbt	gestorben
stieben	stiebst; stiebt	stob, stiebte	stöbe, stiebte	stieb(e); stiebt	gestoben, gestiebt
stinken	stinkst; stinkt	stank	stänke	stink(e); stinkt	gestunken
stoßen	stößt; stößt	stieß	stieße	stoß(e); stoßt	gestoßen
streichen	streichst; streicht	strich	striche	streich(e); streicht	gestrichen
streiten	streitest; streitet	stritt	stritte	streit(e); streitet	gestritten
tragen	trägst; trägt	trug	trüge	trag(e); tragt	getragen
treffen	triffst; trifft	traf	träfe	triff; trefft	getroffen
treiben	treibst; treibt	trieb	triebe	treib; treibt	getrieben
treten	trittst; tritt	trat	träte	tritt; tretet	getreten
triefen	triefst; trieft	triefte, troff (*geh*)	triefte, tröffe (*geh*)	trief(e); trieft	getrieft, getroffen (*rare*)
trinken	trinkst; trinkt	trank	tränke	trink; trinkt	getrunken
trügen	trügst; trügt	trog	tröge	trüg(e); trügt	getrogen
tun	*1st* tue; *2nd* tust; *3rd* tut	tat	täte	tu(e); tut	getan
verderben	verdirbst; verdirbt	verdarb	verdürbe	verdirb; verderbt	verdorben
verdrießen	verdrießt; verdrießt	verdroß	verdrösse	verdrieß(e); verdrießt	verdrossen
vergessen	vergißt; vergißt	vergaß	vergäße	vergiß; vergeßt	vergessen
verlieren	verlierst; verliert	verlor	verlöre	verlier(e); verliert	verloren
verzeihen	verzeihst; verzeiht	verzieh	verziehe	verzeih(e); verzeiht	verziehen
wachsen	wächst; wächst	wuchs	wüchse	wachs(e); wachst	gewachsen
wägen	wägst; wägt	wog, wägte (*rare*)	wöge, wägte (*rare*)	wäg(e); wägt	gewogen, gewägt (*rare*)
waschen	wäschst; wäscht	wusch	wüsche	wasch(e); wascht	gewaschen
weben	webst; webt	webte, wob (*liter, fig*)	webte, wöbe (*liter, fig*)	web(e); webt	gewebt, gewoben (*liter, fig*)
weichen	weichst; weicht	wich	wiche	weich(e); weicht	gewichen
weisen	weist; weist	wies	wiese	weis(e); weist	gewiesen
wenden	wendest; wendet	wendete, wandte (*geh*)	wendete	wend(e); wendet	gewendet, gewandt
werben	wirbst; wirbt	warb	würbe	wirb; werbt	geworben
werden	wirst; wird	wurde, ward (*old, liter*)	würde	werde; werdet	geworden; (*after ptp*) worden
werfen	wirfst; wirft	warf	würfe	wirf; werft	geworfen
wiegen	wiegst; wiegt	wog	wöge	wieg(e); wiegt	gewogen
winden	windest; windet	wand	wände	wind(e); windet	gewunden
winken	winkst; winkt	winkte	winkte	wink(e); winkt	gewinkt, gewunken (*dial*)
wissen	*1st* weiß; *2nd* weißt; *3rd* weiß	wußte	wüßte	wisse (*liter*); wisset (*liter*)	gewußt
wollen	*1st* will; *2nd* willst; *3rd* will	wollte	wollte	wolle (*liter*); wollt	gewollt; (*after infin*) wollen
wringen	wringst; wringt	wrang	wränge	wring(e); wringt	gewrungen
zeihen	zeihst; zeiht	zieh	ziehe	zeih(e); zeiht	geziehen
ziehen	ziehst; zieht	zog	zöge	zieh(e); zieht	gezogen
zwingen	zwingst; zwingt	zwang	zwänge	zwing(e); zwingt	gezwungen

ENGLISCHE VERBEN
Konjugation der regelmäßigen Verben im Englischen
1. Bildung des Präteritums und des 2. Partizips
1.1 In den meisten Fällen wird -ed an die Infinitivform angehängt.

> remain *pret, ptp* remained

1.2 Verben mit Konsonant +y im Auslaut werden zu -ied.

> try *pret, ptp* tried

1.3 Verben mit stummem -e oder mit -ee, -ye, -oe, -ge im Auslaut verlieren das zweite -e.

> abate *pret, ptp* abated
> agree *pret, ptp* agreed
> dye *pret, ptp* dyed
> hoe *pret, ptp* hoed
> singe *pret, ptp* singed

1.4 Verben, die auf Konsonant nach einfachem, betontem Vokal enden, verdoppeln diesen Endkonsonanten.

> bar *pret, ptp* barred
> permit *pret, ptp* permitted

Nach Doppelvokal wird der Konsonant im Auslaut nicht verdoppelt

> dread *pret, ptp* dreaded

ebensowenig nach unbetontem Vokal

> visit, *pret, ptp* visited

mit Ausnahme von auslautendem -l und -p im britischen Englisch.

> level *pret, ptp* levelled *or (US)* leveled
> worship *pret, ptp* worshipped *or (US)* worshiped

Verben mit Vokal +c im Auslaut werden zu -cked.

> panic *pret, ptp* panicked

2. Bildung des 1. Partizips
2.1 Die meisten Verben bilden das 1. Partizip durch Anhängen von -ing.
2.2 Für Verben, die auf Vokal + Konsonant enden, gelten die gleichen Regeln wie für die Bildung des Präteritums; siehe 1.4.
2.3 Verben, die auf -ie enden, werden zu -ying.

> die *prp* dying

2.4 Verben mit stummem -e im Auslaut verlieren diesen Vokal

> like *prp* liking

außer wenn sie in der Kombination -ye, -oe auftreten.

> dye *prp* dyeing
> hoe *prp* hoeing

UNREGELMÄSSIGE ENGLISCHE VERBEN

Infinitiv	Präteritum	Partizip Perfekt	Infinitiv	Präteritum	Partizip Perfekt
abide	abode, abided	abode, abided	light	lit, lighted	lit, lighted
arise	arose	arisen	lose	lost	lost
awake	awoke	awaked	make	made	made
be	was *sing*, were *pl*	been	may	might	–
bear	bore	borne	mean	meant	meant
beat	beat	beaten	meet	met	met
become	became	become	mow	mowed	mown, mowed
beget	begot, begat *(obs)*	begotten	pay	paid	paid
begin	began	begun	put	put	put
bend	bent	bent	quit	quit, quitted	quit, quitted
beseech	besought	besought	read [ri:d]	read [red]	read [red]
bet	bet, betted	bet, betted	rend	rent	rent
bid	bade, bid	bid, bidden	rid	rid	rid
bind	bound	bound	ride	rode	ridden
bite	bit	bitten	ring²	rang	rung
bleed	bled	bled	rise	rose	risen
blow	blew	blown	run	ran	run
break	broke	broken	saw	sawed	sawed, sawn
breed	bred	bred	say	said	said
bring	brought	brought	see	saw	seen
build	built	built	seek	sought	sought
burn	burned, burnt	burned, burnt	sell	sold	sold
burst	burst	burst	send	sent	sent
buy	bought	bought	set	set	set
can	could	–	sew	sewed	sewed, sewn
cast	cast	cast	shake	shook	shaken
catch	caught	caught	shave	shaved	shaved, shaven
chide	chid	chidden, chid	stave	stove, staved	stove, staved
choose	chose	chosen	steal	stole	stolen
cleave¹	clove, cleft	cloven, cleft	shear	sheared	sheared, shorn
(cut)			shed	shed	shed
cleave²	cleaved, clave	cleaved	shine	shone	shone
(adhere)			shoe	shod	shod
cling	clung	clung	shoot	shot	shot
come	came	come	show	showed	shown, showed
cost	cost,	cost,	shrink	shrank	shrunk
	(Comm) costed	*(Comm)* costed	shut	shut	shut
creep	crept	crept	sing	sang	sung
cut	cut	cut	sink	sank	sunk
deal	dealt	dealt	sit	sat	sat
dig	dug	dug	slay	slew	slain
do	did	done	sleep	slept	slept
draw	drew	drawn	slide	slid	slid
dream	dreamed, dreamt	dreamed, dreamt	sling	slung	slung
drink	drank	drunk	slink	slunk	slunk
drive	drove	driven	slit	slit	slit
dwell	dwelt	dwelt	smell	smelled, smelt	smelled, smelt
eat	ate	eaten	smite	smote	smitten
fall	fell	fallen	sow	sowed	sowed, sown
feed	fed	fed	speak	spoke	spoken
feel	felt	felt	speed	speeded, sped	speeded, sped
fight	fought	fought	spell	spelled, spelt	spelled, spelt
find	found	found	spend	spent	spent
flee	fled	fled	spill	spilled, spilt	spilled, spilt
fling	flung	flung	spin	spun, span *(old)*	spun
fly	flew	flown	spit	spat	spat
forbid	forbad(e)	forbidden	split	split	split
forget	forgot	forgotten	spoil	spoiled, spoilt	spoiled, spoilt
forsake	forsook	forsaken	spread	spread	spread
freeze	froze	frozen	spring	sprang	sprung
get	got	got, *(US)* gotten	stand	stood	stood
gild	gilded	gilded, gilt	stick	stuck	stuck
gird	girded, girt	girded, girt	sting	stung	stung
give	gave	given	stink	stank	stunk
go	went	gone	strew	strewed	strewed, strewn
grind	ground	ground	stride	strode	stridden
grow	grew	grown	strike	struck	struck
hang	hung, *(Jur)*	hung, *(Jur)* hanged	string	strung	strung
	hanged		strive	strove	striven
have	had	had	swear	swore	sworn
hear	heard	heard	sweep	swept	swept
heave	heaved, *(Naut)*	heaved, *(Naut)*	swell	swelled	swollen
	hove	hove	swim	swam	swum
hew	hewed	hewed, hewn	swing	swung	swung
hide	hid	hidden	take	took	taken
hit	hit	hit	teach	taught	taught
hold	held	held	tear	tore	torn
hurt	hurt	hurt	tell	told	told
keep	kept	kept	think	thought	thought
kneel	knelt	knelt	thrive	throve, thrived	thriven, thrived
know	knew	known	throw	threw	thrown
lade	laded	laden	thrust	thrust	thrust
lay	laid	laid	tread	trod	trodden
lead	led	led	wake	woke, waked	woken, waked
lean	leaned, leant	leaned, leant	wear	wore	worn
leap	leaped, leapt	leaped, leapt	weave	wove	woven
learn	learned, learnt	learned, learnt	weep	wept	wept
leave	left	left	win	won	won
lend	lent	lent	wind	wound	wound
let	let	let	wring	wrung	wrung
lie	lay	lain	write	wrote	written

1 Metric System — Metrisches System

Measures formed with the following prefixes are mostly omitted.
Nicht erfaßt sind in der Regel Maße mit folgenden Vorsilben:

deca-	10 times	10mal	Deka-
hecto-	100 times	100mal	Hekto-
kilo-	1000 times	1000mal	Kilo-
deci-	one tenth	ein Zehntel	Dezi-
centi-	one hundredth	ein Hundertstel	Zenti-
mil(l)i-	one thousandth	ein Tausendstel	Milli-

Linear measures — Längenmaße

1 millimetre (Millimeter)	=	0.03937 inch
1 centimetre (Zentimeter)	=	0.3937 inch
1 metre (Meter)	=	39.37 inches
	=	1.094 yards
1 kilometre (Kilometer)	=	0.6214 mile (⅝ mile)

Square measures — Flächenmaße

1 square centimetre (Quadratzentimeter)	=	0.155 square inch
1 square metre (Quadratmeter)	=	10.764 square feet
	=	1.196 square yards
1 square kilometre (Quadratkilometer)	=	0.3861 square mile
	=	247.1 acres
1 are (Ar)=100 square metres	=	119.6 square yards
1 hectare (Hektar)=100 ares	=	2.471 acres

Cubic measures — Raummaße

1 cubic centimetre (Kubikzentimeter)	=	0.061 cubic inch
1 cubic metre (Kubikmeter)	=	35.315 cubic feet
	=	1.308 cubic yards

Measures of capacity — Hohlmaße

1 litre (Liter)=1000 cubic centimetres	=	1.76 pints
	=	0.22 gallon

Weights — Gewichte

1 gramme (Gramm)	=	15.4 grains
1 kilogramme (Kilogramm)	=	2.2046 pounds
1 quintal (Quintal)=100 kilogrammes	=	220.46 pounds
1 metric ton (Tonne)=1000 kilogrammes	=	0.9842 ton

2 British system — Britisches System

Linear measures — Flächenmaße

1 inch (Zoll)	=	2,54 Zentimeter
1 foot (Fuß)=12 inches	=	30,48 Zentimeter
1 yard (Yard)=3 feet	=	91,44 Zentimeter
1 furlong = 220 yards	=	201,17 Meter
1 mile (Meile)=1760 yards	=	1,609 Kilometer

Surveyors' measures — Feldmaße

1 link=7.92 inches	=	20,12 Zentimeter
1 rod (or pole, perch)=25 links	=	5,029 Meter
1 chain=22 yards=4 rods	=	20,12 Meter

Square measures — Flächenmaße

1 square inch (Quadratzoll)	=	6,45 cm²
1 square foot (Quadratfuß)=144 square inches	=	929,03 cm²
1 square yard (Quadratyard)=9 square feet	=	0,836 m²
1 square rod=30.25 square yards	=	25,29 m²
1 acre=4840 square yards	=	40,47 Ar
1 square mile (Quadratmeile)=640 acres	=	2,59 km²

Cubic measures — Raummaße

1 cubic inch (Kubikzoll)	=	16,387 cm³
1 cubic foot (Kubikfuß)=1728 cubic inches	=	0,028 m³
1 cubic yard (Kubikyard)=27 cubic feet	=	0,765 m³
1 register ton (Registertonne)=100 cubic feet	=	2,832 m³

Measures of capacity — Hohlmaße

(a) Liquid — Flüssigkeitsmaße

1 gill	=	0,142 Liter
1 pint (Pinte)=4 gills	=	0,57 Liter
1 quart=2 pints	=	1,136 Liter
1 gallon (Gallone)=4 quarts	=	4,546 Liter

(b) Dry — Trockenmaße

1 peck=2 gallons	=	9,087 Liter
1 bushel=4 pecks	=	36,36 Liter
1 quarter=8 bushels	=	290,94 Liter

Weights — Avoirdupois system — Handelsgewichte

1 grain (Gran)	=	0,0648 Gramm
1 drachm *or* dram=27.34 grains	=	1,77 Gramm
1 ounce (Unze)=16 drachms	=	28,35 Gramm
1 pound (britisches Pfund)=16 ounces	=	453,6 Gramm
		0,453 Kilogramm
1 stone=14 pounds	=	6,348 Kilogramm
1 quarter=28 pounds	=	12,7 Kilogramm
1 hundredweight=112 pounds	=	50,8 Kilogramm
1 ton (Tonne)=2240 pounds=20 hundred-weight	=	1,016 Kilogramm

3 US Measures — Amerikanische Maße

In the US, the same system as that which applies in Great Britain is used for the most part; the main differences are mentioned below.

In den Vereinigten Staaten gilt großenteils dasselbe System wie in Großbritannien; die Hauptunterschiede sind im folgenden aufgeführt:

Measures of Capacity — Hohlmaße

(a) Liquid — Flüssigkeitsmaße

1 US liquid gill	=	0,118 Liter
1 US liquid pint=4 gills	=	0,473 Liter
1 US liquid quart=2 pints	=	0,946 Liter
1 US gallon=4 quarts	=	3,785 Liter

(b) Dry — Trockenmaße

1 US dry pint	=	0,550 Liter
1 US dry quart=2 dry pints	=	1,1 Liter
1 US peck=8 dry quarts	=	8,81 Liter
1 US bushel=4 pecks	=	35,24 Liter

Weights — Gewichte

1 hundredweight (*or* short hundredweight)=100 pounds	=	45,36 Kilogramm
1 ton (*or* short ton)=2000 pounds=20 short hundredweights	=	907,18 Kilogramm

TEMPERATURE CONVERSION — TEMPERATURUMRECHNUNG

Fahrenheit – Centigrade (Celsius)

Subtract 32 and multiply by 5/9
32 abziehen und mit 5/9 multiplizieren

°F	°C
0	17.8
32	0
50	10
70	21.1
90	32.2
98.4 ≈	37
212	100

Centigrade (Celsius) – Fahrenheit

Multiply by 9/5 and add 32
Mit 9/5 multiplizieren und 32 addieren

°C	°F
-10	14
0	32
10	50
20	68
30	86
37 ≈	98.4
100	212

German	Abbr	English
Abkürzung	abbr	abbreviation
Akkusativ	acc	accusative
Adjektiv	adj	adjective
Verwaltung	Admin	administration
Adverb	adv	adverb
Landwirtschaft	Agr	agriculture
Anatomie	Anat	anatomy
Archäologie	Archeol	archaeology
Architektur	Archit	architecture
Artikel	art	article
Kunst	Art	art
Astrologie	Astrol	astrology
Astronomie	Astron	astronomy
attributiv	attr	attributive
österreichisch	Aus	Austrian
australisch	Austral	Australian
Kraftfahrzeuge	Aut	automobiles
Hilfsverb	aux	auxiliary
Luftfahrt	Aviat	aviation
Kindersprache	baby-talk	
biblisch	Bibl	biblical
Biologie	Biol	biology
Botanik	Bot	botany
Bundesrepublik Deutschland	BRD	Federal Republic of Germany
britisch	Brit	British
Hoch- und Tiefbau	Build	building
Kartenspiel	Cards	
Chemie	Chem	chemistry
Schach	Chess	
Handel	Comm	commerce
Komparativ	comp	comparative
Konjunktion	conj	conjunction
Zusammenziehung	contr	contraction
Kochen und Backen	Cook	cooking
Kompositum, zusammen-gesetzes Wort	cpd	compound
Dativ	dat	dative
veraltend, altmodisch	dated	
Deutsche Demokratische Republik	DDR	German Democratic Republic
dekliniert	decl	declined
bestimmt	def	definite
demonstrativ, hinweisend	dem	demonstrative
Dialekt	dial	dialect
diminutiv, verkleinernd	dim	diminutive
Akkusativobjekt	dir obj	direct object
kirchlich	Eccl	ecclesiastical
Volkswirtschaft	Econ	economics
Elektrizität	Elec	electricity
betont, emphatisch	emph	emphatic
besonders	esp	especially
et cetera, und so weiter	etc	et cetera
etwas	etw	
Euphemismus, Hüllwort	euph	euphemism
Femininum	f	feminine
Mode	Fashion	
figurativ, übertragen	fig	figurative
Finanzen	Fin	finance
Angeln/Fischerei	Fishing	
Forstwesen	Forest	forestry
förmlich	form	formal
Fußball	Ftbl	football
gehoben	geh	elevated
Genitiv	gen	genitive
Geographie	Geog	geography
Geologie	Geol	geology
Grammatik	Gram	grammar
Heraldik	Her	heraldry
Geschichte	Hist	history
Gartenbau	Hort	horticulture
scherzhaft	hum	humorous
Jagd	Hunt	hunting
Imperativ, Befehlsform	imper	imperative
unpersönlich	impers	impersonal
Industrie	Ind	industry
unbestimmt	indef	indefinite
Dativobjekt	indir obj	indirect object
umgangssprachlich	inf	informal
Infinitiv	infin	infinitive
untrennbar	insep	inseparable
Versicherungswesen	Insur	insurance
Interjektion, Ausruf	interj	interjection
interrogativ, fragend	interrog	interrogative
unveränderlich	inv	invariable
irisch	Ir	Irish
ironisch	iro	ironic
unregelmäßig	irreg	irregular
jemand, jemandes, jemandem, jemanden	jd, jds, jdm, jdn	
Rechtswesen	Jur	law
Sprachwissenschaft	Ling	linguistics
wörtlich	lit	literal
literarisch	liter	literary
Literatur	Liter	pertaining to literature
Maskulinum	m	masculine
Mathematik	Math	mathematics
Maß	Measure	